D1130564

IN
LIBRARY
ONLY

BENEZIT

DICTIONARY OF ARTISTS

PUBLISHER'S GUARANTEE

Whilst a great deal of care has gone into the production of this book, it may contain a printing or manufacturing defect. In the event of such a defect, the book will be exchanged free of charge.

Simply return the book to the place of purchase or write to us at the following address, stating the precise nature of the defect. Your complaint will be dealt with immediately.

Éditions Gründ - 60 Rue Mazarine - 75006 Paris - France

www.grund.fr

ISBN 2 7000 3070 2 (complete set)
ISBN 2 7000 3075 3 (vol. 5)
dépôt légal mars 2006

BENEZIT

DICTIONARY OF ARTISTS

VOLUME 5
DYCK - GÉMIGNANI

GRÜND
2006

NOTES ON THE AUCTION RECORDS SECTION

Never intended to be an exhaustive directory of sales, these listings provide an invaluable record of the movement in prices of an artist's work. Prices are given in the currency of the country of sale (see abbreviations below) as recorded on the date of sale.

The below tables give an indication of the current value of past sales:
- purchasing power of the US Dollar since 1913
- purchasing power of the British Pound since 1901
- purchasing power of the French Franc/Euro since 1901

CURRENCY ABBREVIATIONS (ISO 4217)

ARS Argentinian Nuevo Peso
ATS Austrian Schilling
AUD Australian Dollar
BEF Belgian Franc
BRL Brazilian Real
CAD Canadian Dollar
CHF Swiss Franc
CZK Czech Koruna
DEM German Mark
DKK Danish Krone
EGP Egyptian Pound
ESP Spanish Peseta
EUR Euro
FIM Finnish Markka
FRF French Franc
GBP British Pound
Gns Guineas
GRD Greek Drachma
HKD Hong Kong Dollar
HUF Hungarian Forint
IEP Irish Punt
ILS Israeli Shekel
ITL Italian Lira
JPY Japanese Yen
MXN Mexican New Peso
NLG Dutch Guilder
NOK Norwegian Krone
NZD New Zealand Dollar
PLN Polish New Zloty
PTE Portuguese Escudo
SEK Swedish Krona
SGD Singapore Dollar
TWD Taiwan Dollar
USD United States Dollar
UYU Uruguayan New Peso
ZAR South African Rand

PURCHASING POWER OF THE US DOLLAR SINCE 1913

1 USD in	in USD in 2002
2002	1.000
2001	1.016
2000	1.045
1999	1.079
1998	1.104
1997	1.121
1996	1.147
1995	1.180
1994	1.214
1993	1.245
1992	1.282
1991	1.320
1990	1.378
1989	1.451
1988	1.522
1987	1.583
1986	1.642
1985	1.669
1984	1.728
1983	1.804
1982	1.862
1981	1.975
1980	2.185
1979	2.482
1978	2.755
1977	2.966
1976	3.160
1975	3.344
1974	3.649
1973	4.049
1972	4.300
1971	4.435
1970	4.629
1969	4.903
1968	5.167
1967	5.383
1966	5.540
1965	5.694
1964	5.791
1963	5.872
1962	5.942
1961	6.007
1960	6.067
1959	6.164
1958	6.218
1957	6.383
1956	6.615
1955	6.712
1954	6.685
1953	6.718
1952	6.772
1951	6.917
1950	7.466
1949	7.541
1948	7.466
1947	8.047
1946	9.200
1945	9.986
1944	10.216
1943	10.394
1942	11.029
1941	12.209
1940	12.817
1939	12.941
1938	12.757
1937	12.520
1936	12.973
1935	13.095
1934	13.424
1933	13.871
1932	13.160
1931	11.804
1930	10.766
1929	10.491
1928	10.491
1927	10.351
1926	10.156
1925	10.254
1924	10.513
1923	10.534
1922	10.723
1921	10.045
1920	8.973
1919	10.394
1918	11.933
1917	14.016
1916	16.460
1915	17.703
1914	17.881
1913	18.124

source: US Bureau of Labor Statistics

PURCHASING POWER OF THE BRITISH POUND SINCE 1901

1 GBP in	in GBP in 2003
2003	1.0000
2002	1.0289
2001	1.0461
2000	1.0646
1999	1.0961
1998	1.1130
1997	1.1511
1996	1.1873
1995	1.2159
1994	1.2580
1993	1.2884
1992	1.3089
1991	1.3579
1990	1.4376
1989	1.5736
1988	1.6960
1987	1.7791
1986	1.8533
1985	1.9164
1984	2.0330
1983	2.1343
1982	2.2322
1981	2.4244
1980	2.7122
1979	3.2000
1978	3.6286
1977	3.9297
1976	4.5525
1975	5.3056
1974	6.5917
1973	7.6492
1972	8.3454
1971	8.9400
1970	9.7839
1969	10.4105
1968	10.9693
1967	11.4799
1966	11.7825
1965	12.2466
1964	12.8172
1963	13.2444
1962	13.4943
1961	14.0787
1960	14.5662
1959	14.7160
1958	14.7769
1957	15.2495
1956	15.7881
1955	16.5940
1954	17.3172
1953	17.6593
1952	18.1985
1951	19.8667
1950	21.6727
1949	22.3500
1948	22.9968
1947	24.7474
1946	26.4889
1945	27.2977
1944	28.0471
1943	28.8387
1942	29.8000
1941	31.9286
1940	35.4059
1939	41.3410
1938	42.5714
1937	43.0843
1936	44.7000
1935	44.9811
1934	45.2658
1933	45.2658
1932	44.1481
1931	43.0843
1930	41.3410
1929	40.1798
1928	39.7333
1927	39.7333
1926	38.6595
1925	38.4516
1924	38.4516
1923	38.2460
1922	35.9397
1921	30.9610
1920	28.2688
1919	32.6575
1918	35.9397
1917	43.8773
1916	55.0154
1915	65.0182
1914	72.9796
1913	72.9796
1912	72.2424
1911	74.5000
1910	74.5000
1909	75.2842
1908	76.0851
1907	76.0851
1906	76.9032
1905	76.9032
1904	76.9032
1903	76.9032
1902	77.7391
1901	77.7391

source: British Office for National Statistics

PURCHASING POWER OF THE FRENCH FRANC SINCE 1901 (EURO SINCE 2002)

1 EUR in	in EUR in 2004
2004	1.000
2003	1.021
2002	1.042

1 FRF in	in EUR in 2004
2001	0.16199
2000	0.16468
1999	0.16747
1998	0.16830
1997	0.16947
1996	0.17156
1995	0.17494
1994	0.17796
1993	0.18093
1992	0.18469
1991	0.18907
1990	0.19513
1989	0.20170
1988	0.20899
1987	0.21461
1986	0.22136
1985	0.22724
1984	0.24049
1983	0.25830
1982	0.28315
1981	0.31661
1980	0.35906
1979	0.40772

1 FRF in	in EUR in 2004
1978	0.45158
1977	0.49252
1976	0.53866
1975	0.59046
1974	0.65993
1973	0.75053
1972	0.81968
1971	0.87012
1970	0.91952
1969	0.96747
1968	1.02990
1967	1.07638
1966	1.10572
1965	1.13551
1964	1.16382
1963	1.20384
1962	1.26156
1961	1.32228
1960	1.36597
1959	0.01415
1958	0.01503
1957	0.01729
1956	0.01781
1955	0.01856
1954	0.01874
1953	0.01882
1952	0.01850

1 FRF in	in EUR in 2004
1951	0.02070
1950	0.02406
1949	0.02647
1948	0.02996
1947	0.04755
1946	0.07093
1945	0.10826
1944	0.16078
1943	0.19643
1942	0.24388
1941	0.29331
1940	0.34453
1939	0.40570
1938	0.43410
1937	0.49330
1936	0.62015
1935	0.66785
1934	0.61141
1933	0.58663
1932	0.56377
1931	0.51679
1930	0.49330
1929	0.49897
1928	0.52939
1927	0.52939
1926	0.54950
1925	0.72351

1 FRF in	in EUR in 2004
1924	0.77519
1923	0.88593
1922	0.96468
1921	0.94370
1920	0.81906
1919	1.14238
1918	1.40033
1917	1.80877
1916	2.17052
1915	2.41169
1914	2.89403
1913	2.89403
1912	2.89403
1911	2.89403
1910	3.33926
1909	3.33926
1908	3.33926
1907	3.33926
1906	3.61753
1905	3.33926
1904	3.33926
1903	3.33926
1902	3.33926
1901	3.33926

source: INSEE

GENERAL ABBREVIATIONS

AG	Art Gallery
AI	Art Institute
AM	Art Museum
BNF	Bibliothèque nationale de France
CAPC	Centre d'Arts Plastiques Contemporains
FAM	Fine Art Museum
FMAC	Fonds municipal d'Art contemporain
FNAC	Fonds national d'Art contemporain
FRAC	Fonds régional d'Art contemporain
GA	Gallery of Art
Gal.	Galerie, Gallery, Galleria, Galeria
GMA	Gallery of Modern Art
ICA	Institute of Contemporary Art
MA	Museum of Art
MAA	Museum of Art and Archaeology
MAC	Musée d'Art Contemporain, Museo de Arte Contempóraneo, Museu de Arte Contemporânea
MAH	Musée d'Art et d'Histoire
MAM	Musée d'Art Moderne, Museo de Arte Moderno, Museo d'Arte Moderna
Mamco	Musée d'Art moderne et contemporain
MBA	Musée des Beaux-Arts, Museo de Bellas Artes, Museo di Belli Arti
MCA	Museum of Contemporary Art
MDA	Musée des Arts Décoratifs
MFA	Museum of Fine Art
MMA	Museum of Modern Art
MoCA	Museum of Contemporary Art
MoMA	Museum of Modern Art
Mus.	Musée, Museum, Muséum, Museo, Museu, Museet
Muz.	Muzeum, Muzeul, Muzej
NG	National Gallery
NGA	National Gallery of Art

DYCK, Anton van, or Antoon or Anthony (Sir)
Flemish School, 17th century.
Born 22 March 1599, in Antwerp; died 9 December 1641, in Blackfriars, London.
Painter, engraver. History painting, portraits.

Anton van Dyck was 11 when his father Franchois van Dyck, a wealthy cloth and silk merchant, found him an apprenticeship with van Bâlen, with whom he stayed for two years before entering Ruben's studio. Rubens had just returned from Italy, and, struck by van Dyck's aptitude, wasted no time in training him in his new style. Rubens considered him to be the best of his pupils and van Dyck collaborated on many of his master's great religious works. His reputation was made so quickly that in early 1618, at the age of 19, he was registered as a master of the Guild of St Luke, and at the same time set up an independent workshop in Antwerp with Jan Brueghel the Younger, although he continued to work in Ruben's studio. For three years he continued to work either alone or with Rubens, until in 1620 he travelled to England, where he stayed briefly at the invitation of the Earl of Arundel, painting portraits and working for James I. Encouraged perhaps by the Earl, van Dyck travelled to Italy in November 1621, staying in Genoa, Rome and Venice where he copied works by Michelangelo, Leonardo da Vinci, Raphael, Veronese and Giorgione. The biggest single influence on van Dyck, however, was the work of Titian, which he particularly sought out and studied. His reputation earned him several commissions from Prince Emmanuel Albert of Savoy, Viceroy of Sicily, who summoned him to Palermo in 1624. He was received at court and produced works resonant of Titian, although he left Palermo hurriedly at the outbreak of plague and returned to Genoa, painting portraits of the Genoese aristocracy and continuing to study Titian's technique until his return to Antwerp in September 1627. Van Dyck returned with a well-established reputation, and this period saw a prodigious output of portraits as well as numerous history and religious paintings and some of his best etchings.

Van Dyck's work and reputation came to the attention of Charles I of England who must have offered considerable incentives to entice van Dyck to London early in 1632. Charles gave him a generous salary, a house in a privileged area, appointed him 'Principalle Paynter in ordinary to their Majesties' and, in 1632, knighted him as a mark of honour, so that he eclipsed Mytens as court painter. Van Dyck lived ostentatiously, but he earned well, his studio operating a kind of production line of portraits with van Dyck concentrating on the heads and touching up. His portraits of the English royal family (full-length and equestrian) are amongst his most successful and most famous, and his wide-ranging portraits of the English aristocracy largely creates our contemporary image of Charles' court. Among his other achievements was the decoration of the Banqueting Hall in Whitehall for Charles I. During his time in England, van Dyck made frequent trips to the Continent, particularly to Antwerp and Brussels, where he continued to carry out commissions, beginning the cycle of paintings for the town hall in Brussels. On Ruben's death in 1640, he was appointed dean of the academy of St Luke and may have considered settling permanently in Antwerp. However, he was already troubled by illness by this time, and was also drained by his battle to win the competition to decorate the Grande Galerie of the Louvre, which he lost to Poussin. Returning to London in 1641, he died, probably of tuberculosis, going into decline just a few days after the birth of his daughter. He left a large estate.

His first works, prior to his trip to Italy in 1621, reveal the influence of Rubens, as depicted in van Dyck's *St Martin* in the church of Saventhem (1621), or in his mythological paintings, such as *Drunken Silenus, Jupiter and Antiope*, or *Studies of Four Negro Heads* (1617). In Genoa he most notably painted the lovely *Portrait of Maria de' Medici*, which is one of his best works, as well as numerous family portraits, such as those of De Wael, Durazzo and Grimaldi. In Rome in 1623 he painted the *Portrait of Cardinal Bentivoglio*. Upon his return to Antwerp in 1627, he concentrated his attentions on portraits of members of high society, whom he painted in rigorous poses and extremely sober compositions. Van Dyck was able to convey the personality of the figures he painted while at the same time suggesting something of the melancholy or Romanesque. He harmonises bright colours, delicate greys and golden tones and his subdued shadows make colours all the more vibrant. He sometimes preferred to sacrifice accessories in the interests of emphasising hands and faces. In England in 1635 he painted one of the most beautiful portraits of *Charles I* (Louvre), who appears with all his royal self-assurance, having no need for sumptuous clothing, painted in a bold composition in which the horse, servants and landscape occupy a good part of the painting but do not distract attention from the sovereign's personality.

Van Dyck helped to create a link between Flemish and Italian painting through his study of works seen in Rome, Genoa and Venice, particularly by Titian and Veronese. He remained uninfluenced by Caravaggio. Above all, van Dyck played a decisive role in the establishment of a future school of English painting in the 18th century, influencing Gainsborough, Reynolds and Lawrence. The vast majority of van Dyck's output was portraiture, though he may have wished for more commissions for religious and history painting. In portraiture, his development of the Grand Manner portrait from Titian's model proved his legacy of the longest standing, influencing artists down to Singer Sargent. Van Dyck's imaginative handling of portraiture covered a vast social range, from princes and princesses to prelates, bankers, jewellers and merchants, young and old, posing them in a vast array of positions, placing them against personalised decors and flanking them with fashionable props and status symbols. A perfect example of this is the *Portrait of Elena Grimaldi Cattanco*, where a black servant carries a red parasol and the fabrics, costumes, armour and jewellery are all emphasised, contributing to an expression of the psychology of a figure from a society built on a cult of personal display.

Van Dyck's paintings rarely leave the museums and collections where they are kept. Nevertheless, certain events, such as the commemoration of his birth in 1999, give rise to special exhibitions. The work of van Dyck has been regularly represented in joint exhibitions on different themes, including the following: *Le portrait dans l'art Flamand: de Memling à Van Dyck* (*The Portrait in Flemish Art: From Memling to Van Dyck*) at the Orangerie des Tuileries in Paris (1952); *Van Dyck and his Age* at the Tel Aviv Museum of Art in Tel Aviv (1995); *Van Dyck und sein Kreis: Zeichnungen und Druckgraphik aus dem Kupferstichkabinett des Herzog-Anton-Ulrich-Museums* (*Van Dyck and his Circle: Drawings and Printed Graphics from the Collection of Copper Engravings at the Duke Anton Ulrich Museum*) (1999); and *Van Dyck: Landscapes, Sources of Inspiration* at the Rubenshuis Museum in Antwerp (1999). Notable among the individual, retrospective exhibitions are the following: *Van Dyke* at the Royal Academy of Art in London (1900); *Antoon van Dyck et son iconographie: eaux-fortes, gravures et dessins de la Fondation Custodia, collection Frits Lugt* (*Anton van Dyck and his Iconography: Etchings, Engravings and Drawings of the Fondation Custodia, Frits Lugt Collection*) at the Netherlands Institute in Paris (1981); *Van Dyck in England* at the National Portrait Gallery in London (1982); *Van Dyck Paintings* at the National Gallery of Art in Washington (1990); *The Drawings of Anthony van Dyck* at the Pierpont Morgan Library in New York (1991); Plantin-Moretus Museum in Antwerp (1991);

Van Dyck a Genova: Grande Pittura e Collezionismo at the Palazzo Ducale in Geneva (1997); *Anton van Dyck 1599-1641* at the Royal Museum of Fine Arts in Antwerp (1999), an exhibition that then moved to the Royal Academy of Arts in London; and *Anton van Dyck in Print* at the Plantin-Moretus Museum in Antwerp (1999), an exhibition that then moved to the Rijksmuseum in Amsterdam.

BIBLIOGRAPHY:

Guiffrey, Jules, *Sir Anthony Van Dyck. His life and Works*, A. Quantin, 1882. Gevaert, Fierens, *'Van Dyck'* in *Great Artists Series*, H. Laurens, Paris, 1904. Hollstein, Friedrich Wilhelm Heinrich, *'Dutch and Flemish Etchings, Engravings and Woodcuts, circa 1450-1700'* in vol 2-16, Menno Hertzberger, Amsterdam, 1949-1974. Magurn, Ruth, *The Letters of Peter Paul Rubens*, Cambridge (MA), 1955. Van Puyvelde, Leo, *'Van Dyck'* in *Flemish Painters of the 17th Century Series*, Elsevier, Brussels, 1959. Jaffé, Michael, *Van Dyck's Antwerp Sketchbook*, London, 1962 (2 volumes). Vey, H., *Die Zeichnungen Anto Van Dycks*, Verlag Arcade, Brussels, 1962. Strong, Roy C., *Van Dyck: Charles I on Horseback*, London, 1972. Hook, J., *The Baroque Age in England*, London, 1976. Martin, John Rupert/Feigenbaum, Gail, *Van Dyck as a Religious Artist*, The Art Museum, Princeton University, 1979. Gaunt, W., *Court Paintings in England from Tudor to Victorian Times*, London, 1980. Larsen, Erik, *L'opera completa di Van Dyck*, catalogue raisonné, Rizzoli, Milan, 1980. McNarin, Alain, *The Young Van Dyck*, National Gallery of Canada, Ottawa, 1980. *Van Dyck in England*, exhibition catalogue, National Portrait Gallery, London, 1982. Brown, Christopher, *Van Dyck*, monograph, Oxford, 1982. Millar, Oliver, *Van Dyck in England*, National Portrait Gallery, London, 1982-1983. Howarth, David, *Lord Arundel and his Circle*, New Haven, 1985. Filipczak, Z. Z., *Picturing Art in Antwerp*, Princeton, 1987. Smuts, R. Malcolm, *Court Culture and the Origins of Royalist Tradition in Early Stuart England*, Philadelphia, 1987. Larsen, Erik, *'The Paintings of Anthony Van Dyck'* in *2 volumes*, Luca Verlag, Freren, 1988. *Van Dyck paintings*, exhibition catalogue, National Gallery of Art, Washington, 1990. Brown, Christopher, *Van Dyck drawings*, Thames and Hudson, London, 1991. Pauw, Carl de, et al., *Van Dyck's Antwerp*, Antwerp, 1991. Wheelock, Arthur Kingsland, et al., *Van Dyck: peintures*, Fonds Mercator, Anvers, Albin Michel, Paris, 1991. Mauquoy-Henrickx, Marie, *L'Iconographie d'Antoine Van Dyck: catalogue raisonné*, Bibliothèque Royale Albert Ier, Brussels, 1991 (2nd revised, extended edition). Jaffé, Michael, *'Review of the 1991 National Gallery and Morgan Library Exhibitions'* in *The Burlington Magazine 133*, February 1991 and October 1991. Cifari, Arabella/Moretti, Franco, *'New Light on the Abbé Scaglia and Van Dyck'* in *The Burlington Magazine 134*, August 1992. Barnes, S.J./Wheelock, A.K. (ed.), *'Van Dyck 350'* in *Studies in the History of Art 46*, Washington, 1994. Moir, Alfredlfred, *Anthony van Dyck*, Thames and Hudson, London, 1994. White, C., *'Anthony van Dyck, Thomas Howard, The Earl of Arundel'* in *Getty Museum Studies on Art*, Malibu, 1995. Gritsai, N., *Anthony van Dyck*, Bournemouth and St Petersburg, 1996. Hedley, Jo, *Van Dyck at the Wallace Collection*, Wallace Collection, London, 1999. Lawson, James, *Van Dyck, Paintings and Drawings*, Prestel, New York, 1999. Depauw, Carl/Luijten, Ger, *Anthony van Dyck as a printmaker*, exhibition catalogue, Antwerpen Open, Antwerp, 1999 (exhibition at the Plantin-Moretus Museum, Antwerp). Royalton-Kisch, Martin, *The Light of Nature. Landscape Drawings and Watercolours by Van Dyck and his Contemporaries*, British Museum, London, 1999. Brown, Christopher (ed.), *Van Dyck*, exhibition catalogue, Royal Academy of Arts, London, 1999. Stewart, J. Douglas, *'Reflections on eroticisme, love and the antique in Van Dyck's art'* in *Apollo* n° 462 p. 26, periodical, London, August 2000. Vlieghe, Hans, *Van Dyck 1599 - 1999: conjectures and refutations*, Brepols, Turnhout, 2001. Barnes, Susan J., et al., *Van Dyck: a complete catalogue of the paintings*, catalogue raisonné, Yale University Press, New Haven, 2003.

MUSEUMS AND GALLERIES:

AIX: *Portrait of Van Diepenbeeck and Rickaert* - AMIENS: *Man's Head* (two works); *Assumption of the Virgin* - AMSTERDAM: *Repentant Mary Magdalene; François (?) van der Borght; Johanne Baptista Franck; Nicolaes van der Borcht; Prince William II and his Wife, Princess Mary Stuart; Petrus Paulus Rubens; Caspar Gevaerts; Salvator Mundi* - ANTWERP (Koninklijk Mus. voor Schone Kunsten): *Christ on the Cross; Jan Malderus, Fifth Bishop of Antwerp; Deposition of Christ; Christ Entombed; Portrait of César Alexandre Seaglia; Christ on the Cross; Portrait of a Priest; Portrait of the Artist Marten Pepyn* - BALTIMORE (MA): *Rinaldo and Armida* (1629) - BAYONNE: *Raising of the Cross* (sketch); *Head of St John; Head of a Young Man; Portrait of van Baelen; Henrietta of France and her Two Children; Portrait of Isabella Clara Eugenia of Austria* - BERGAMO (Accademia Carrara): *Roman Charity; Portrait of a Child; Portrait of the Family of Philip Herbert, Fourth Earl of Pembroke* (rough sketch) - BERLIN (Gemäldegal.): *Christ Ridicule; Lamentation of Christ; Portrait of Ph. Fr. de Carignan, Prince of Savoy; Nymph Bathing; Portrait of a Nobleman from Genoa; Portrait of Marchioness Geronina Spinola; Apostle's Head; The Two Johns* - BÉZIERS: *Portrait of a Man* - BRUSSELS: *Jean Vincent Imperial, Duke of S Angelo; Alexandre Dellafaille; Drunken Silenus; Martyrdom of St Peter; St Anthony of Padua; St Francis of Assisi; Crucifixion; Portrait of a Man; Rinaldo and Armida* - BUDAPEST: *Self-portrait; Venus Crying over the Death of Adonis; Portrait of a Couple; The Trinity; St Eligius; Portrait of Archduke Ferdinand* (after Rubens) - CAEN: *Jesus Wearing a Crown of Thorns* - CHANTILLY: *Portrait of Gaston d'Orléans, Duke of*

Orléans; Portrait of Count Henri de Berghe; Portrait of Princess Marie de Barbançon, Duchess of Arenberg; Portrait of William of Neuburg - CHERBOURG: *Meleager and Atalanta* - COURTRAI (Notre Dame): *Raising of the Cross* - DARMSTADT: *Portrait of a Young Woman* - DOUAI: *Lamentation of Christ; Reception of St Placid and St Maur by St Benedict; Portrait of a Man* - DRESDEN: *Three Eldest Daughters of Charles I of England; Christ Approaching the Serpent; Portrait of a General; Portrait of a Man in Black; Portrait of a Lady in Black; Portrait of a Lady and Child; Portrait of a Gentleman; Portrait of a Lady; St Hieronymus; Portrait of St Bartholomew; Portrait of St Matthew; Portrait of St Simeon; Portrait of St Peter; Portrait of St Paul; Portrait of an Old Gentleman; Portrait of a Lady; Portrait of a Young Man; Portrait of a Gentleman in Black; Portrait of a Man with a Blond Beard; Portrait of a Man with a Blond Moustache; Portrait of Thomas Parr at 150 Years Old; Drunken Silenus Walking* - DUBLIN: *Portrait of Frédéric Marselar; Study for a Painting of St Sebastian* - EDINBURGH (Nat. Gal. of Scotland): *An Italian Noble* (oil on canvas); *The Lomellini Family: Nicolo and Gio. Francesco Lomellini with Barbara Spinola Lomellini and the children Vittoria and Agostino* (c. 1623-1627, oil on canvas, group portrait); *St Sebastian Bound for Martyrdom* (c. 1621-1623, oil on canvas) - EDINBURGH (Nat. Gal. of Scotland, Print Room): *Studies of Heads* (drawing) - FLORENCE (Palazzo Pitti): *Portrait of Cardinal Guido Bentivoglio; Head of the Virgin; Portrait of Charles I of England and Henrietta Maria of France; Rest on the Flight to Egypt* - FLORENCE (Uffizi): *Portrait of a Lady; Portrait of Princess Margaret of Lorraine; Virgin and Child Jesus; Portrait of a Man; Portrait of Jecunde Monfort; Portrait of Charles I; Jean de Montfort* - FRANKFURT AM MAIN: *The Cross; Portrait of Mme Brignole-Sale and her Daughter; Portrait of Pauline Brignole-Sale; Portrait of the Prince of Orange; Portrait of Father and Son; Portrait of the Marquis and Poet Antoine Jules Brignole-Sale* - GENEVA: *Maternal Ecstacy; Georges de la Rive; Christ on the Cross* - GENOA: *Portraits of Genoese Families; Christ* - GHENT (Church of St Michiels): *Calvary* - GLASGOW: *Rest on the Flight to Egypt; Portrait of an Old Man* - GRENOBLE: *Repentant Mary Magdalene* - HAMBURG: *Portrait of Holmalius* - HANOVER: *Study of a Head; Cavalryman; Cavalryman; Christ and the Paralytic* - KASSEL: *Portrait of Isabelle d'Assche (?); Portraits of a Man Aged between 50 and 55, and his Wife* (a pair); *Portraits of the Brothers Lucas and Cornelius de Wael; Sebastian Leerse with his Wife and Child; Portrait of a Man and a Woman; Portrait of the Painter F. Snyders and his Wife; Portrait of Justus van Meerstraeten; Portrait of the Landscape Artist Jan Wildens; Child Jesus; Portrait of a Woman Aged between 45 and 48; Portrait of an Italian Gentleman* - LA FÈRE: *Miracle of the Plague Sufferer; Repentant Mary Magdalene* - LE PUY-EN-VELAY: *Christ Weeping* - LILLE: *Jesus on the Cross; Miracle of St Anthony of Padua in Toulouse; Portrait of a Woman; Portrait of Maria de' Medici; Adoration of the Shepherds* - LONDON (Dulwich Picture Gal.): *Samson and Delilah* (c. 1618-1620, oil on canvas); *Emmanuel Philibert of Savoy, Prince of Oneglia* (1624, oil on canvas, portrait); *The Madonna and Child* (before 1632, oil on canvas); *Venetia Stanley, Lady Digby, on her Death-bed* (1633, oil on canvas); *George, Lord Digby, later Earl of Bristol* (c. 1638-1639, oil on canvas, portrait); *Sunset Landscape with a Shepherd and his Flock* (oil on canvas, attributed) - LONDON (National Portrait Gal.): *Venetia, Lady Digby* (c. 1633-1634, oil on canvas); *Lord George Stuart* (c. 1638, oil on canvas); *Sir Kenelm Digby* (c. 1640, oil on canvas) - LONDON (NG): *The Emperor Theodosius is forbidden by Saint Ambrose to enter Milan Cathedral* (c. 1619-1620, oil on canvas, loose copy after Rubens); *Portrait of Cornelis van der Geest* (c. 1620, oil/wood); *Portrait of François Langlois* (1630-1635, oil on canvas); *Carlo and Ubaldo see Rinaldo conquered by Love for Armida* (1634-1635, oil/wood); *Equestrian Portrait of Charles I* (c. 1637-1638, oil on canvas) - LONDON (Tate Collection): three portraits (c. 1633-1638, oil on canvas) - LONDON (Victoria and Albert Mus.): *Man Wearing Armour* - LONDON (Wallace Collection): *Portrait of a Lady, called Isabella van Waerbeke, Wife of Paul de Vos* (1628-1632, oil on canvas); *Marie de Raet, Wife of Philippe Le Roy* (1631, oil on canvas); *Paris* (c. 1632, oil on canvas); *Philippe Le Roy* (1630, oil on canvas) - LOS ANGELES (Getty Mus.): *Thomas Howard, Second Earl of Arundel* (c. 1620-1621, oil on canvas); *Portrait of Agostino Pallavicini* (c. 1621, oil on canvas) - LYONS: *Study of Two Heads* - MADRID (Prado): *St Jerome Repenting; Crown of Thorns; Portrait of the Painter David Ryckaert; Portrait of the Infante; Cardinal D. Fernando of Austria; Portrait of the Countess of Oxford; Portrait of Henry of Nassau, Prince of Orange; Portrait of the Princess of Orange; Equestrian Portrait of Charles I of England; Portrait of a Mature Woman; Portrait of Henry, Count of Berg; Portrait of a Musician; Portrait of an Unknown Person; Portrait of Van Dyck and the Count of Bristol; Portrait of Henri Liberti; Old Man's Head; Virgin of Anguish; Portrait of a Monk; Arrest of Christ; Diana and Endymion Asleep; St Francis of Assisi as a Slave; Portrait of Polexena, First Marchioness of Leganes* - MAINZ: *Head of a Dying Man; Repentant Mary Magdalene* - MECHELEN (Sint-Rombouts Kathedraal): *Crucifixion* - MELBOURNE: *Portrait of Francis Frank; Portrait of the Artist; Portrait of Jucodus Momper* - METZ: *Portrait of Rykaert* - MILAN (Pinacoteca di Brera): *Portrait of Amelia de Solms; Madonna with Jesus and St Anthony of Padua* - MONTAUBAN: *Portrait of a Monk* - MONTREAL (Learmont): *Deposition* - MOSCOW (Rumiantsev Mus.): *Portrait of Lady Philadelphia Wharton; Portrait of a Nun; Philogyny; Child Christ and St John the Baptist; Portraits of Men* - MUNICH: *General Tilly; Count Albrecht of Wallenstein, Duke of Friedland; King Gustav Adolph of Sweden; Princess Margaret of Lorraine; Prince Franz Thomas of Carignan; Bust Portrait of the Antwerp Painter of Battles and Landscapes, P. Sivayers; Portrait of the Artist's Wife, Maria Ruthwen; Portrait of Heinrick Liberti of Groningen; Portrait of the Engraver Karl Malery of Antwerp; Portrait of the Painter Jan de Wael and his Wife; Portrait of the Wife of Jan de Wael; Portrait of the Sculptor Colyn de Nole; Portrait of a Man in Black; Portrait of Geneviève d'Urphé; Portrait of Duke Carl Alexandre of Croi; Study of a Child's Head; Martyrdom of St Sebastian; Portrait of the Merchant Sebastian Leerse in Antwerp; St Sebastian Tied to the Tree; Christ on the Cross; Virgin and Child; Lamentation of Christ* (two works); *Battle near Martin d'Église; Portrait of the Artist; Portrait of a Young Man; Portrait of the Young Marquis of Mirabella; Portrait of D. Filippo Spinola; Portrait of Duke Wolfgang Wilhelm of Neuburg* (two works); *Study of an Apostle; Portrait of the Battle Painter Palamedes Palamedesz.; Portrait of the Painter Jan Brueghel with Red Hair; Landscape Artist Lucas van Uden; Count John of Nassau; Abbé César; Alexandre Scaglio* - MUNICH (Alte Pinakothek): *Susanna Bathing; Rest on the Flight to Egypt* - NANCY: *Virgin and Child; Portrait of the Painter Anthony van Opstal; Portrait of Count John of Nassau and his Family* - NAPLES: *Jesus on the Cross* - NEW HAVEN (Yale Center for British Art): *Mountjoy Blount, 1st Earl of Newport* (c. 1637-1638, oil on canvas, portrait) - NEW YORK (Frick Collection): *Frans Snyders* (c. 1632-1641, oil on canvas) - NICE: *St Dominic* - NOTTINGHAM (Castle Mus. and AG): *Portrait of Charles I* - OPORTO: *Portrait of a Man* - PALERMO (Oratorio della Compagnia del Rosario di San Domenico of the Rosary): *Madonna of the Rosary* - PARIS (Louvre): *Virgin and Child Jesus; Virgin with Donors; Lamentation of Christ; St Sebastian; Venus and Vulcan; Rinaldo and Armida; Portrait of Charles I, King of England; Portrait of the Children of Charles I; Portrait of Charles Louis, Duke of Bavaria, and his Brother Robert, later Duke of Cumberland; Portrait of Isabella Clara Eugenia of Austria, Infanta of Spain, Sovereign of The Netherlands; Equestrian Portrait of François de Moncade, Marquis of Aytona; Bust Portrait of François de Moncade;*

Portrait of a Man and a Child; Portrait of a Lady and her Daughter; Portrait of the Duke of Richmond (three male portraits); *Head of an Old Man; Bust of St Joseph; Martyrdom of St Sebastian; Portrait of a Woman; Portrait of Van Dyck* - PERPIGNAN: *Virgin with Four Donors* - ROME (Gal. Colonna): *Charles Colonna; Portrait of Lucretia Tomacelli* - ROME (Mus. e Gal. Borghese): *Jesus Christ Crucified* - ROME (Palazzo Doria Pamphili): *Portrait of an Elderly Lady* - ROTTERDAM (Mus. Boijmans Van Beuningen): *Portrait of Charles I of England with his Wife Henrietta and their Two Children* - SAVENTHEM: *St Martin Sharing his Cloak* - ST PETERSBURG: *Holy Communion; Christ on the Cross; Christ Descended from the Cross; Incredulity of St Thomas; St Sebastian; Portrait of a Man; Portrait of a Woman; Charles I, King of England; Henrietta Maria of France; William II of Nassau; William Lound, Archbishop of Canterbury; Antoine de Trieste, Bishop of Ghent; Henry Danoers, Count of Danby; Lord Philip Wharton; Sir Thomas Wharton; Elisabeth Philadelphia Wharton; Lady Jane Goodwin; Thomas Chaloner; Lord Rowland Wandesford; Jan van den Wouver; Adriaen Stevens, Almoner of the Town of Antwerp; Portrait of the Wife of Adriaen Stevens; Portrait of the Painter Jan 'Velvet' Brueghel; Portrait of the Architect Inigo Jonès; Family Portrait; Portrait of a Young Man; Bust Portrait of an Old Man; Portrait of Marc-Antoine Lumagne; Portrait of Evenard; Portrait of Lazarus Markijzus; Two Ladies; Portrait of a Lady* - ST PETERSBURG (Hermitage): *Holy Family* - STOCKHOLM: *St Hieronymus; Portrait of Prince William of Hessen-Kassel* - STRASBOURG: *Portrait of a Lady Dressed in Black; Study of a Head* - TERMONDE (Church of Notre Dame): *Adoration of the Shepherds; Christ on the Cross Surrounded by Saints* - THE HAGUE: *Portrait of Sir Sheffield; Portrait of Anna Wake, Wife of Sir Sheffield; Portrait of Qurintyn Simons; Portraits of Peter Stevens and his Wife* - TOULOUSE: *Christ with Angels; Miracle of the Mule; Achilles Recognised by Ulysses* - TROYES: *Portrait of François Snyders* - TURIN: *Portraits of the Children of Charles I, King of England* - VADUZ: *Portrait of Gaspard de Crayer; Portrait of Jean Vermeulen* - VALENCIENNES: *Martyrdom of St James; Portrait of Jacques le Roy, Seigneur of Horbaix; Head of St Matthew; Portrait of Madame de Cantecroix* - VENICE: *Christ Crucified; Portrait of a Child* - VENICE (Gal. Reale): *Head of a Sleeping Child* - VERSAILLES: *Thomas of Savoy, Prince of Carignan* - VIENNA: *Portrait of Countess Amelia Solms, Princess of Orange; Portrait of an Elderly Woman; Study of a Woman's Head; Portrait of Queen Mary of England; Portrait of Prince Rhodokani; Portrait of a Young Captain; Venus with Vulcan; St Francis; Portrait of a Man; Portrait of Prince Karl Ludwig of the Palatinate; St Germain Joseph; St Rosalie Receiving a Crown from Jesus; Portrait of a Young Man; Ecce Homo; Portrait of Archduchess Isabella Clara; Portrait of Marquis Francesco de Moncada; Holy Family; Portrait of the Spanish Consulate; Jean de Montfort; Portrait of Carolus Sribani; Portrait of a Man; Portrait of a Woman; Portrait of the Painter; Cupid with Bow and Arrows; Mary and the Child Jesus; Portrait of the Painter Paul de Vos* - VIENNA (Czernin'sche Gemäldegal.): *Neptune; Ecce Homo; Portrait of a Man in an Armchair (Generally Identified as the Painter of Animals, Paul de Vos); Portrait of a Man; Portrait of a Young Man; Cupid* - VIENNA (Kunsthistorisches Mus.): *Samson and Delilah; Portrait of Prince Ruprecht of the Palatinate* - WASHINGTON DC (Georgetown University): *Portrait of Jean-Baptiste Janssens van Bisthoven* (c. 1630, oil on canvas) - WASHINGTON DC (NGA): *Filippo Cattaneo, Son of Marchesa Elena Grimaldi* (1623, oil on canvas); *Clelia Cattaneo, Daughter of Marchesa Elena Grimaldi* (1623, oil on canvas); *A Genoese Noblewoman and Her Son* (c. 1626, oil on canvas); other paintings, numerous prints - WINDSOR CASTLE: *Charles I in Three Poses; Portraits of the Children of Charles I* - YPRES: *Male Portrait; Female Portrait.*

AUCTION RECORDS:

AMSTERDAM, 13 May 1705, *Portrait of an Old Man*, FRF 35. AMSTERDAM, 17 May 1710, *A Sketch*, FRF 325. PARIS, 1792, *King Charles I of England and his Family*, FRF 26,250; *Portrait of Snyders*, FRF 10,000. PARIS, 1800, *Painting on Panel*, FRF 150,000. PARIS, 1810, *Jesus with the Paralysed Man*, FRF 82,500. LONDON, 1810, *St Sebastian Surrounded by Soldiers*, FRF 22,305. ANTWERP, 1822, *Portrait of Le Roy*, FRF 11,440; *Portrait of the Wife of Le Roy*, FRF 13,200. PARIS, 1872, *The Young Composer*, FRF 37,800. LONDON, 1886, *Equestrian Portrait of Charles I*, FRF 375,000; *Portrait of Mary, Duchess of Richmond*, FRF 39,190. GHENT, 1887, *Virgin and Child*, FRF 220. PARIS, 1891, *Portrait of the Count of Aligre*, FRF 69,000. NEW YORK, 1895, *The Marquis of Spinola and his Granddaughter*, FRF 250,000. ANTWERP, 1898, *Portrait of Martin Pepyn*, FRF 60,000. PARIS, 1898, *Mystic Marriage of St Catherine*, FRF 13,500. LONDON, 1898, *Portrait of a Young Boy in Purple Hose and Green Breeches*, FRF 42,000. BRUSSELS, 1899, *Portrait of Ambrose Doria*, BEF 40,000. NEW YORK, 1899, *Lord Arundel*, FRF 44,000. LONDON, 1900, *Portrait of Bartholomeo Guisdimani, One of Van Dyck's Masters*, FRF 606,250. LONDON, 3 July 1908, *Portrait of Cardinal Domenico Rivarole*, GBP 819; *Portrait of the Countess of Northumberland*, GBP 210. LONDON, 12 Dec 1908, *Portrait of a Gentleman*, GBP 50. LONDON, 30 April 1909, *Portrait of Mutio Vitelleschi, Leader of the Jesuits* (held in Art Treasures in Great Britain) GBP 99. LONDON, 2 July 1909, *Portrait of a Jesuit Priest*, GBP 189. LONDON, 16 July 1909, *Charity* (grisaille) GBP 65. PARIS, April 1910, *Portrait of Wolfgang, Duke of Neuburg*, FRF 12,500. LONDON, 6 May 1910, *Portrait of Catherine Hastings*, GBP 357; *Portrait of Queen Henrietta Maria*, GBP 367; *Portrait of a Lady in Black and Silver Dress*, GBP 367; *Portrait of Cardinal Domenico Rivarole*, GBP 945; *Portrait of Dorothy Devereux*, GBP 157. PARIS, 25 Nov 1918, *Two Heads of Children*, FRF 111,000. LONDON, 26 May 1922, *Elizabeth, Countess de Southampton*, GBP 6,510. LONDON, 4-7 May 1923, *Adoration of the Shepherds*, GBP 178. LONDON, 6 July 1923, *Portrait of De Witte*, GBP 2,100; *Portrait of the Wife of De Witte*, GBP 892; *Princess Mary, Daughter of Charles I*, GBP 1,050. LONDON, 13 July 1923, *Portrait of the Artist*, GBP 5,985; *Henri Liberti of Groningen*, GBP 2,100. PARIS, 2 June 1924, *Martrydom of St Sebastian* (sketch) FRF 30,000; *Portrait of Ferdinand Boisschot, Baron of Saventhem*, FRF 86,000. LONDON, 4 July 1924, *Virgin, Child and St Catherine*, GBP 3,150. LONDON, 1 May 1925, *George Stuart, Lord Aubigny*, GBP 840. LONDON, 7 May 1926, *Genevieve d'Urfe, Duchess of Croy*, GBP 609. PARIS, 27 and 28 May 1926, *Portrait of Jan van den Wouver*, FRF 185,000; *Portrait of the Engraver Jean-Baptiste Barbé*, FRF 50,000; *Portrait of Paul de Halmale*, FRF 47,000; *Head of a Young Man* (study) FRF 41,000; *Head and Hands of a Young Man*, FRF 37,000. LONDON, 12 May 1927, *Head of a Woman*, GBP 2,100. LONDON, 17 and 18 May 1928, *Marchioness Catherine Durazzo*, GBP 1,575; *Count Brandolini*, GBP 1,312. PARIS, 21 and 22 May 1928, *Heads of Children*, FRF 255,000. LONDON, 8 June 1928, *Jupiter and Antiope*, GBP 787. LONDON, 25 June 1928, *St Francis in Prayer*, GBP 472. PARIS, 28 Nov 1928, *Study of a Man Standing in Semi-profile in the Costume of the Brandenburgs* (drawing) FRF 4,000. PARIS, 19 Dec 1928, *Two-thirds Portrait of a Young Woman with a Necklace*, FRF 4,000. LONDON, 3 May 1929, *Portrait of Jacques Le Roy*, GBP 17,850. LONDON, 21 June 1929, *Portrait of Charles II as a Child*, GBP 4,830. LONDON, 1 Aug 1929, *Anne-Marie de Camudio*, GBP 99. LONDON, 27 June 1930, *Portrait of Queen Henrietta Maria*, GBP 997. LONDON, 25 July 1930, *Child Jesus on a Globe*, GBP 189. NEW YORK, 22 Jan 1931, *St Paul*, USD 1,500; *St Philip*, USD 900; *St John the Evangelist*, USD 13,000. NEW YORK, 4 and 5 Feb 1931, *Portrait of a Burgomaster*, USD 1,650. NEW YORK, 22 April 1932, *Portrait of Three of the Children of Charles I*, USD 3,600. LONDON, 27-30 May 1932, *Prince Ru-*

pert, GBP 231. PARIS, 11 Dec 1934, *Christ on the Cross,* FRF 46,000. NEW YORK, 3 Dec 1936, *Edward Sutton,* USD 2,900. COLOGNE, 4 May 1937, *Portrait of a Man,* DEM 8,000. LONDON, 1 July 1938, *Portrait of a Woman,* GBP 2,100; *William Feilding,* GBP 1,995; *Mary, Duchess of Richmond,* GBP 1,552. NEW YORK, 20 April 1939, *Wolfgang, Prince of Pfalz-Neuburg,* USD 1,600. NEW YORK, 4 Jan 1945, *Portrait Presumed to be of Constantin Huygens,* USD 13,000. NEW YORK, 21 Feb 1945, *Ferdinand Boisschot,* USD 3,500; *Donna Polyxera Spinola, Marchioness of Leganes,* USD 10,000. LONDON, 1 June 1945, *Inspiration of St Jerome,* GBP 2,145. NEW YORK, 25 Oct 1945, *Count Wolfgang Wilhelm von Pfalz-Neuburg,* USD 3,000. LONDON, 12 July 1946, *Portrait of a Gentleman,* GBP 4,189. PARIS, 25 May 1949, *Portrait of the Engraver Paul Pontius,* FRF 3,900,000. PARIS, 9 Dec 1952, *Heads of Children,* FRF 3,950,000. LONDON, 28 Nov 1956, *Heads of Two Negroes,* GBP 7,800. NEW YORK, 13 March 1957, *Portrait of Cardinal Guido Bentivoglio,* USD 5,000. LONDON, 26 June 1957, *St Jerome Repenting,* GBP 2,500. LONDON, 27 June 1958, *St Judas Thaddeus,* GBP 5,775. LONDON, 26 Nov 1958, *Portrait of a Man,* GBP 7,000. LONDON, 8 July 1959, *Virgin, Child and St Anne,* GBP 3,400. GENEVA, 13 June 1960, *Ecstasy of St Francis* (pen and bistre wash) CHF 1,000. LONDON, 15 July 1960, *Portrait of a Woman,* GBP 6,300. LONDON, 7 Dec 1960, *St Rosalie Interceding on Behalf of the City of Palermo,* GBP 5,000. LONDON, 14 June 1961, *Portrait of a Gentleman,* GBP 19,000. PARIS, 20 June 1961, *Portrait of Clarissimus Erycius Puteanus* (chalk, wash and gouache) FRF 4,100. NEW YORK, 15 Nov 1961, *Portrait of a Genoese Officer,* USD 27,000. LONDON, 3 July 1963, *Portrait of Lucy, Countess of Carlisle,* GBP 14,000. LONDON, 12 June 1968, *Virgin, Child and St Anne,* GBP 21,000. LONDON, 26 March 1969, *Portrait of a Man with a Beard,* GBP 8,600. LONDON, 25 June 1971, *Heads of Four Negroes,* Gns 400,000. LONDON, 6 Dec 1972, *Two Studies of the Head of a Man* (oil on mounted paper on canvas) GBP 17,000. LONDON, 11 July 1973, *Marchioness Lomellini-Donazzo,* GBP 180,000. LONDON, 2 July 1976, *Virgin and Child* (c. 1627-1632, oil on panel, 60 3/4 x 42 1/2 ins / 154.5 x 108 cm) GBP 200,000. NEW YORK, 16 June 1977, *Portrait of Don Paolo Gordano Orsini, Duke of Bracciano* (oil on canvas, 74 1/4 x 53 1/4 ins / 188.5 x 135 cm) USD 27,000. BERN, 9 June 1978, *Frans Francken* (c. 1635, etching) CHF 7,000. NEW YORK, 16 Feb 1979, *Pieter Brueghel the Younger* (etching, 9 1/2 x 6 ins / 24.4 x 15.5 cm) USD 12,000. LONDON, 3 May 1979, *Study of a Kneeling Man* (double-sided drawing in black chalk, 8 1/2 x 6 3/4 ins / 21.7 x 17 cm) GBP 2,000. LONDON, 9 April 1981, *Studies of the Holy Family and the Head of a Monk (recto); Virgin and Child with Two Saints and a Cottage (verso)* (pen and brown ink/paper, 7 1/2 x 5 1/2 ins / 19.3 x 14 cm) GBP 13,000. BERN, 24 June 1983, *Lucas Vorstermans* (c. 1640, etching) CHF 1,500. LONDON, 3 July 1984, *Wooded Landscape with a House on the Right* (watercolour, pen and brown ink, 7 1/2 x 14 1/4 ins / 18.9 x 36.3 cm) GBP 240,000. LONDON, 3 July 1984, *Portrait of Hendrick van Balen* (black chalk, 9 1/2 x 7 3/4 ins / 24.3 x 19.7 cm) GBP 540,000. LONDON, 23 Nov 1984, *Portrait of Anne Carr, Countess of Bedford, Holding a Rose* (oil on canvas, 39 3/4 x 32 1/2 ins / 101 x 82.5 cm) GBP 150,000. LONDON, 9 July 1986, *Portrait of Dorothy, Lady Dacre* (oil on canvas, 51 1/4 x 40 1/2 ins / 130 x 103 cm) GBP 145,000. NEW YORK, 17 Nov 1986, *St Jerome, St George, St Catherine of Alexandria, and Holy Monks* (brush, brown ink and grey wash, 11 1/2 x 9 1/2 ins / 29.5 x 24 cm) USD 130,000. NEW YORK, 20 Nov 1986, *Jan de Wael* (before 1632, etching and burin, 10 x 7 ins / 25.3 x 18 cm) USD 32,000. LONDON, 6 July 1987, *Mystic Marriage of St Catherine* (black chalk, pen and brown ink, brown and grey wash, 7 1/4 x 11 ins / 18.2 x 27.9 cm) GBP 220,000. STOCKHOLM, 29 April 1988, *Portrait of Queen Henrietta Maria* (oil on canvas, 48 1/2 x 35 1/2 ins / 123 x 90 cm) SEK 16,000. STOCKHOLM, 15 Nov 1988, *Portrait of a Man Dressed in Dark Colours* (oil, 30 3/4 x 22 ins / 78 x 55 cm) SEK 10,000. NEW YORK, 31 May 1989, *Portrait of Nicholas Rockox Aged 76 Dressed in Black with a White Ruff* (1636, oil on panel, diam. 6 ins / 15.2 cm) USD 231,000. NEW YORK, 2 June 1989, *Portrait of a Horseman* (1634, oil on panel, 28 3/4 x 22 ins / 73 x 55 cm) USD 374,000. LONDON, 17 Nov 1989, *Full-length Portrait of Mary, Princess Royal, in a Silver Embroidered Pink Dress with Ribbands and Lace Collar* (oil on canvas, 61 x 42 ins / 155 x 106.5 cm) GBP 880,000. NEW YORK, 1 June 1990, *St James the Greater* (oil on paper/canvas, 33 1/4 x 24 3/4 ins / 84.5 x 63 cm) USD 176,000. LONDON, 6 July 1990, *St Jerome Penitent* (oil on canvas, 51 3/4 x 70 1/4 ins / 131.5 x 178.5 cm) GBP 110,000. LONDON, 14 Nov 1990, *Portrait of Thomas Wentworth, First Count of Strafford, Standing Holding his Armour* (oil on canvas, 40 x 33 ins / 101.5 x 84 cm) GBP 19,800. LONDON, 2 July 1991, *Paris* (black and white chalk/light brown paper, 15 3/4 x 10 ins / 40 x 25.5 cm) GBP 9,900. LONDON, 9 Nov 1994, *Portrait of George Hay, Count of Kinnoul, in Armour* (oil on canvas, 85 3/4 x 52 ins / 218 x 132 cm) GBP 82,900. LONDON, 3 April 1996, *Bust Portrait of Elizabeth Stuart, Countess of Arundel, Dressed in a White Satin Dress with a Fur Stole on her Right Shoulder* (oil on canvas, 29 1/4 x 23 1/4 ins / 74.5 x 59 cm) GBP 177,500. NEW YORK, 30 Jan 1997, *Vanitas: Two Very Young Boys Blowing Bubbles* (oil on paper/panel, 25 1/4 x 20 3/4 ins / 64.1 x 52.7 cm) USD 41,400. LONDON, 9 April 1997, *Portrait of Sir Arthur Hopton* (c. 1637-1638, oil on canvas, oval, 23 1/4 x 18 3/4 ins / 59 x 47.5 cm) GBP 95,000. LONDON, 3-4 Dec 1997, *Full-length Portrait of Prince Charles Louis, Elector Palatine* (oil on canvas, 86 x 49 ins / 218.5 x 124.5 cm) GBP 771,500. NEW YORK, 29 Jan 1998, *Venus and Adonis* (oil on canvas, 68 1/4 x 68 1/4 ins / 173.5 x 173.5 cm) USD 992,500. NEW YORK, 28 Jan 1999, *Studies of Two Hands. Forearm and Legs of Man* (black and white chalk, double-sided, 9 x 9 ins / 22 x 23 cm) USD 8,500. LONDON, 8 July 1999, *Portrait of Nobleman, possibly Emanuel Frockas Pereira y Pimentel, Standing* (oil on canvas, 87 x 50 ins / 220 x 128 cm) GBP 390,000. NEW YORK, 11 May 2000, *Paulus Pontius* (etching, 9 x 6 ins / 23 x 16 cm) USD 5,000. LONDON, 13 Dec 2000, *Bridled Grey Stallion, with Saddle Cloth and Partially Plaited Mane* (oil on canvas, 52 x 42 ins / 132 x 107 cm) GBP 700,000. LONDON, 10 July 2001, *Portrait of Lady Mary Villiers, Wearing Bronze Gown and Holding a Rose* (oil on canvas, 42 x 33 ins / 106 x 84 cm) GBP 390,000. NEW YORK, 3 Oct 2001, *Portrait of Charles, Lord Strange, Later 8th Earl of Derby* (oil on canvas, 28 x 22 ins / 70 x 57 cm) USD 550,000. NEW YORK, 24 Jan 2002, *Bust of the Apostle Thomas* (oil on canvas, 24 x 19 ins / 62 x 49 cm) USD 1,900,000. NEW YORK, 24 Jan 2002, *Bust of the Apostle Peter* (oil on canvas, 24 x 19 ins / 62 x 49 cm) USD 2,850,000. NEW YORK, 24 Jan 2003, *Portrait of Anne Carr, Countess of Bedford* (oil on canvas, 40 x 32 ins / 101 x 82 cm) USD 280,000. NEW YORK, 24 Jan 2003, *Portrait of Mary Hill, Lady Killigrew, Wearing a Russet Dress before a Landscape* (oil on canvas, 42 x 33 ins / 107 x 83 cm) USD 600,000.

DYCK, Ary van I

Dutch, 18th century.

Sculptor.

Ary van Dyck I was elected a member of the Guild of St Luke in Leiden in 1696.

DYCK, Ary van II

Dutch, 18th century.

Sculptor.

The son of Ary van Dyck I, Ary van Dyck II became a member of the Guild of St Luke in Leiden in 1730 after the death of his father.

DYCK, César van

Flemish School, 16th century.

Active in Antwerp.
Painter. Historical subjects, portraits.

César van Dyck was a pupil of Adam van Noort in 1598. According to Siret, he is one and the same as Siger van Dyck.

DYCK, Christophe van
Dutch, 17th century.
Engraver. Seals.

Christophe van Dyck was an engraver who used the chasing-chisel for the elzevir typeface. He was held in high regard as a master of this distinctive form of lettering.

DYCK, Cornelis van den, or Dycke
Flemish School, 15th century.
Painter.

A pupil of his father Joannis in Antwerp, Cornelis van den Dyck became a burgher of Mechelen on 5 August 1496.

DYCK, Daniel van den
Flemish, 17th century.
Born c. 1610, in Antwerp; died 1670, in Mantua.
Painter, engraver. History painting.
Flemish School.

Daniel van den Dyck was the pupil of Pieter Verhaeght in 1631 and a master in Antwerp in 1634. He married the painter Lucretia Regnier and was inspector of the gallery of the Duke of Mantua in 1658.

AUCTION RECORDS:
PARIS, 1875, *Bacchanalia* (drawing) FRF 28.

DYCK, Edmonde Djakéli (Mme)
French (?), 20th century.
Active in Paris.
Painter. Genre scenes.

In 1943 Mme Edmonde Djakéli Dycke exhibited *Man with a Pipe* at the Salon des Indépendants.

DYCK, Floris or Floreus van, or Dyk or Dijk
Dutch, 17th century.
Born 1575, in Haarlem; died November 1651, in Haarlem.
Painter. Still-lifes (including fruit).
Haarlem School.

In 1610 Floris van Dyck belonged to the guild of Haarlem. He went to Italy and returned in 1637. Some biographers claim that he lived for a prolonged period in Italy with his friend Jos. Arpinas. When they fell ill the Pope sent them his own doctor, whom they thanked with a picture on their recovery. Van Dyck then returned to his native town where he died (in 1648 according to some sources).

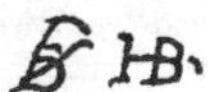

MUSEUMS AND GALLERIES:
AMSTERDAM: *Fruit and Plants.*

AUCTION RECORDS:
LONDON, 20 March 1964, *Still-life with Fruit,* Gns 750. AMSTERDAM, 9 June 1977, *Still-life with Fruit and Cheese* (oil on panel, 17 3/4 x 33 ins / 45 x 84 cm) NLG 250,000. PARIS, 25 March 1994, *Still-life with Cheese, Fruit, Ewer and Wine Glass Arranged on an Embroidered Tablecloth* (oil on panel, 31 3/4 x 48 3/4 ins / 80.5 x 124 cm) FRF 3,500,000. LONDON, 6 Dec 1995, *Still-life with Table Arranged with Fruit in China Dishes, Cheese in Pewter Plates, a Ewer, a Glass, Knife and other Small Fruit Scattered over a Covered Table* (oil on oak panel, 29 1/4 x 45 ins / 74.5 x 114 cm) GBP 320,500. LONDON, 9 July 1998, *Still-life of Grapes and Cheese on Pewter Plates* (oil on panel, 17 x 28 ins / 43 x 71 cm) GBP 200,000. LONDON, 14 Dec 2000, *Still-life of Pears, Apples and Other Fruit on a White Porcelain Bowl all on Table, Red Damask Cloth* (oil on panel, 20 x 30 ins / 50 x 77 cm) GBP 75,000.

DYCK, Hendrik van
Dutch, 17th century.
Sculptor.

Hendrik van Dyck studied under Jan van der Heyde and qualified as a master in The Hague in 1672. He is easily confused with a Hendrik van Dick, a sculptor active in Haarlem in 1743.

DYCK, Henri J. van
Belgian, 19th - 20th century.
Born 1849, in Bruges.
Painter. Genre scenes, portraits.

Henri J. van Dyck was a student at the academies of Roubaix and Antwerp.

MUSEUMS AND GALLERIES:
ANTWERP.

DYCK, Hermann
German, 19th century.
Born 4 October 1812, in Würzburg; died 25 March 1874, in Munich.
Painter, caricaturist. Landscapes, architectural views.

MUSEUMS AND GALLERIES:
DUBLIN: *Last of the Brothers* - HAMBURG: *Antichamber of a Courtroom* - STUTTGART: *Old Gate in German Town.*

DYCK, J. A.
Flemish, 17th century.
Painter.
Flemish School.

MUSEUMS AND GALLERIES:
KARLSRUHE: *The Throne of Venus.*

DYCK, J. van
Dutch, 19th century.
Painter, engraver (etching).

In 1850 J. van Dyck painted *Peter and John at the Tomb of Christ* which was singled out for distinction by the Netherlands Institute for Art and Science.

DYCK, Jacobus van
Flemish School, 16th century.
Miniaturist.
Antwerp School.

Jacobus van Dyck became a master of the guild in 1595.

DYCK, Jan van, or Noyen
Dutch, 16th century.
Active in Utrecht.
Sculptor.
Antwerp School.

Jan van Dyck was admitted into the guild in Antwerp in 1545.

DYCK, Jan van
Flemish, 17th century.
Miniaturist.
Flemish School.

Jan van Dyck qualified as a master in Antwerp in 1689.

DYCK, Jan van
Dutch, 17th century.
Painter.

A *Fortune-teller* painted before 1692 is attributed to Jan van Dyck.

DYCK, Jan van, or Dyk
Dutch, 18th century.
Painter, engraver, writer.

DYCK, Joséphine van
Belgian, 19th century.
Active c. 1843.
Painter. Genre scenes.

DYCK, Justina van
Flemish, 17th century.
Born 1 December 1641, in England; died before 6 July 1690.
Painter.
Flemish School.
Justina van Dyck was the daughter of Anton van Dyck. Her aunt Suzanne van Dyck, a beguine, attempted to entice her as early as 1645 to Antwerp. In 1654 her uncle Waltmann van Dyck also tried to inveigle her, but to no avail, because she had already married Sir John Stepney de Frendergast at the age of 12. After going to Antwerp she returned to England where she received an annual income of 200 livres, albeit irregularly paid, from King Charles II. She was to return again to Antwerp in 1665 after the death of her aunt Suzanne to whom she had given one of her paintings, *Calvary*, in 1660.

DYCK, Loys van
Flemish, 17th century.
Active in Antwerp.
Sculptor (wood).
Flemish School.
Loys van Dyck became a master in 1627.

DYCK, P. R. van
Dutch, 18th century.
Draughtsman.
J. van de Schley engraved the façade of a hospice after one of P. R. van Dyck's drawings.

DYCK, Pauline van
Belgian, 19th century.
Active c. 1843.
Painter. Genre scenes.

DYCK, Philip van. See **DYK**

DYCK, Philip Van
18th century.
Sculptor.
He was recognised as master in Antwerp in 1755.

DYCK, Pieter Emanuelszoon van
Dutch, 17th century.
Active in Amsterdam.
Sculptor.
Pieter Emanuelszoon van Dyck was commissioned by van Uffelen of Amsterdam to execute a stone pulpit and a staircase. He shared this work with the sculptor Pieter Keijser of Amsterdam.

DYCK, Pieter Pieterszoon van
Dutch, 17th century.
Engraver.
Pieter Pieterszoon van Dyck is documented to have led a debauched life. In 1677 he engraved 20 plates showing ribald subjects.

DYCK, Pieter van
Dutch, 18th century.
Born c. 1675.
Active in Leiden.
Painter.
Pieter van Dyck was a member of the guild in Leiden.

DYCK, Willem Cornelis van. See **DYK Willem Cornelis van**

DYCKE, Antoni van
Flemish School, 16th century.
Painter.
Antwerp School.
Antoni van Dycke was a pupil of Jan van Cleve. He was admitted to the guild as a master painter in Antwerp in 1556.

DYCKE, Yvon Van. See **VANDYCKE Yvon**

DYCKERHOFF, Jakob Friedrich
German, 18th - 19th century.
Born 12 December 1774, in Mannheim; died 12 October 1845, in Mannheim.
Painter (gouache), watercolourist, draughtsman.
Allegorical subjects, still-lifes, landscapes, animals.
Jakob Dyckerhoff trained at the Berlin academy and was the friend of W. von Kobell. He exhibited the gouache *Remains of the Temple of the Sibyl in Tivoli* at the Salon of the Berlin academy in 1797. His design *Saxon Troops Crossing the Rhine* was painted in watercolours by W. von Kobell. He was also an engineer and architect.
AUCTION RECORDS:
HEIDELBERG, 12 Oct 1991, *Allegory of a Scene from Greek Mythology* (Indian ink and watercolour, 18 x 24 1/2 ins / 46 x 62.5 cm) DEM 4,800.

DYCKMANS, Anthony
Dutch, 17th century.
Painter.
The son of Sacharias Dyckmans, Anthony Dyckmans became a member of the guild of The Hague in 1665 and dean in 1696. He probably also carried out paintings in the Nieuwe Kerk.

DYCKMANS, Bruno
Belgian, 20th century.
Born 1920, in Lier (Antwerp).
Painter.
Dyckmans trained at Berchem and Antwerp art academies.

DYCKMANS, Gerard Jacobszoon
Dutch, 17th century.
Active in The Hague.
Painter.

DYCKMANS, Jacob
Dutch, 17th century.
Active in Amsterdam.
Painter.
Jacob Dyckmans is known to have carried out a pen and ink drawing, *Bandit Attack*, after Callot.

DYCKMANS, Josephus Laurentius, or Dijkmans, called The Belgian Gérard Dou
Dutch, 19th century.
Born 9 August 1811, in Lier; died 8 January 1888, in Antwerp.
Painter. Genre scenes, figures.
The pupil of Thielman and Wappers, Josephus Laurentius Dyckmans was a professor at the academy in Antwerp between 1841 and 1854. He became a member of the academy in Antwerp in 1853. From 1846 to 1869 he exhibited at Antwerp and the Royal Academy, London.

In his work he paid great attention to the accurate rendering of details. His style is reminiscent of Meissonier but he opted for a brighter palette.

J Dyckmans 1852

MUSEUMS AND GALLERIES:
ANTWERP: *Ancient Façade; Ceremony in Antwerp; Blind Person.*
AUCTION RECORDS:
PARIS, 1872, *The Blind Man*, FRF 25,000. LONDON, 1875, *The Virgin at the Foot of the Cross*, FRF 13,125. PARIS, 1886, *Old*

Woman Praying, FRF 4,200. PARIS, 1899, *Opportunity makes the Thief,* FRF 6,950. LONDON, 25 Jan 1908, *Old Woman in Church,* GBP 15. LONDON, 21 July 1922, *Singers of Love Songs* (drawing) GBP 15. LONDON, 30 July 1924, *Blind Beggar,* GBP 42. LONDON, 8 Feb 1930, *Thrilling Recital,* GBP 15. LONDON, 15 May 1931, *Host* (drawing) GBP 5. LONDON, 18 March 1932, *Lace-maker,* GBP 89. PARIS, 25 May 1932, *Sleeping Acrobat,* FRF 620. LONDON, 22 June 1934, *Industry,* GBP 9. ANTWERP, 3-6 Oct 1938, *Waiting,* BEF 6,400. VIENNA, 5 Dec 1984, *Young Woman doing Needlework* (1849, oil on panel, 19 3/4 x 15 ins / 50 x 38 cm) ATS 450,000. AMSTERDAM, 11 Sept 1990, *Interior with Old Woman Pouring Milk into a Saucer for the Cat* (oil on panel, 7 1/4 x 6 3/4 ins / 18.5 x 17 cm) NLG 4,600. LONDON, 19 March 1993, *Lace-maker* (1844, oil on panel, 19 x 15 ins / 48 x 37.2 cm) GBP 6,670. AMSTERDAM, 7 Nov 1995, *Two Women in an Interior* (oil on canvas, 17 1/4 x 15 ins / 44 x 38 cm) NLG 5,900. LONDON, 21 Nov 1997, *Grandmother's Tales* (1841, oil on panel, 26 x 20 1/2 ins / 66 x 52 cm) GBP 14,950; *New Shawl* (1847, oil on panel, 35 x 28 3/4 ins / 89 x 73 cm) GBP 31,050. LONDON, 21 Oct 1999, *Peaceful Interlude* (1849, oil on panel, 19 x 15 ins / 49 x 38 cm) GBP 38,000. LONDON, 5 April 2001, *Fast Asleep* (oil on board, 13 x 11 ins / 34 x 29 cm) GBP 7,800. AMSTERDAM, 24 April 2001, *Girl Doing Needlework* (oil on panel, 8 x 7 ins / 20 x 18 cm) NLG 10,000. LONDON, 20 June 2002, *The New Shawl* (1847, oil on panel, 36 x 29 ins / 91 x 74 cm) GBP 32,000.

DYCKMANS, Sacharias

Dutch, 17th century.
Active in The Hague.
Painter.

Sacharias Dyckmans was a member of the Guild of St Luke.

DYE, Charlie

American, 20th century.
Born 1906, in Canon City (Colorado); died 1972.
Painter, illustrator. Local scenes, landscapes.

Charlie Dye worked as a cowboy in the American West, as the handwritten note on the back of one of his paintings, *Open Range Branding,* attests: 'This scene is typical of the activities of my youth'. He later turned to art, inspired by the paintings of Charlie Russell.

AUCTION RECORDS:

NEW YORK, 28 May 1987, *Night Stage* (oil on canvas, 24 x 30 ins / 61 x 76.2 cm) USD 12,000. NEW YORK, 26 May 1988, *Cutting Out Mexican Cows* (oil/synthetic resin, 30 x 39 3/4 ins / 76 x 101.2 cm) USD 18,700. NEW YORK, 25 Sept 1991, *Brush Popping* (oil/synthetic resin, 18 x 24 ins / 45.7 x 61 cm) USD 19,800. NEW YORK, 24 Sept 1992, *Open Range Branding* (oil on canvas, 24 x 36 ins / 61 x 91.4 cm) USD 27,500. HAYDEN, 31 July 1999, *Cheyenne Pony Raid* (oil on board, 18 x 24 ins / 46 x 61 cm) USD 37,500. SAN FRANCISCO, 14 June 2000, *The Long Road to Town* (oil on masonite, 24 x 49 ins / 61 x 124 cm) USD 25,000. SAN FRANCISCO, 14 June 2000, *Cheyenne Sundown* (oil on masonite, 30 x 48 ins / 76 x 122 cm) USD 42,500. HAYDEN, 27 July 2002, *Pancho Villa at Zacatecas* (oil on board, 30 x 48 ins / 76 x 122 cm) USD 30,000. SANTA FE, 9 Nov 2002, *Navajo Trading Post* (oil on canvas, 24 x 36 ins / 61 x 91 cm) USD 30,000. HAYDEN, 26 July 2003, *Now or Never* (oil on board, 20 x 30 ins / 51 x 76 cm) USD 17,000. SANTA FE, 1 Nov 2003, *Study for 'Trailing Them North'* (graphite, 23 x 48 ins / 58 x 122 cm) USD 3,250. SANTA FE, 15 May 2004, *Robes for Trade* (oil on board, 24 x 36 ins / 61 x 91 cm) USD 30,000. SANTA FE, 15 May 2004, *Villa at Zacatecas* (oil on board, 29 x 47 ins / 74 x 119 cm) USD 35,000.

DYE, Clarkson

American, 19th - 20th century.
Born 1869; died 1955.
Painter. Landscapes.

Clarkson Dye is referred to by Florence Levy, author of a number of books on the history of the New York art scene.

AUCTION RECORDS:

NEW YORK, 1-2 April 1902, *A Street in Winter,* USD 45. LOS ANGELES-SAN FRANCISCO, 7 Feb 1990, *St Anthony of Padua Mission* (oil on canvas, 25 x 30 ins / 63.5 x 76 cm) USD 3,300. LOS ANGELES-SAN FRANCISCO, 12 July 1990, *Palm Desert Sunset* (oil on panel, 16 1/4 x 24 ins / 41 x 61 cm) USD 3,025. LOS ANGELES-SAN FRANCISCO, 10 Oct 1990, *Desert Palms* (oil on card, 23 x 33 1/2 ins / 58.5 x 85 cm) USD 3,025. LOS ANGELES, 24 Oct 2000, *The Golden Gate, San Francisco Harbour* (oil on canvas, 18 x 24 ins / 46 x 61 cm) USD 20,000. CONNECTICUT, 5 Dec 2000, *Museum of Natural History, Balboe Park, San Diego, CA* (oil on board, 17 x 20 ins / 43 x 51 cm) USD 1,500. LOS ANGELES, 7 Nov 2001, *Chinatown Billboard* (oil on canvas, 18 x 24 ins / 46 x 61 cm) USD 6,000. SAN FRANCISCO, 10 Dec 2003, *Two Women Gathering Flowers Outside of the Santa Barbara Mission* (oil on canvas, 20 x 30 ins / 51 x 76 cm) USD 5,500.

DYE, David

British, 20th century.
Born 1945, in Ryde (Isle of Wight).
Photographer, film producer.

David Dye studied at St Martin's College in London from 1967 to 1971. His participation in group exhibitions includes *Beyond Painting and Sculpture* in 1974 at the Arts Council in London and the ninth Paris Biennale in 1975. He has shown his work in solo exhibitions since 1972. He works with photography, exploring its relationship with text, and also makes films.

MUSEUMS AND GALLERIES:

LONDON (Arts Council Collection, Hayward Gal.).

DYENEN. See **DEYNUM**

DYENS, Georges

French, 20th century.
Born 1932, in Tunis.
Since 1966 active in Quebec.
Sculptor, installation artist.

Georges Dyens was taught by Janniot and Henri Georges Adam in Paris at the École des Beaux-Arts where he gained his diploma. He won the Prix de Rome in 1961, the Susse prize at the Paris Biennale, and the German Critic prize. In 1970 and later he received several study and research grants at public and private institutions in North America. In 1966 he settled in Quebec and taught sculpture at the art college in Montreal and drawing at Quebec University and in Montreal.

Some of his pre-1980s work, abstract and formless, had echoes of Expressionism. In 1981 he became interested in holography, working with lasers to produce three-dimensional coloured images. This is popular in the USA, in Canada thanks to Dyens, in Great Britain and in Germany, but is not much known in France.

It was Dyens who introduced monumental holography with the creation of an *Arch,* a 'holo-sculpture', on the bank of the St Lawrence River near Montreal. His creations *Big Bang I* and *II* are composed of holography, sculpture and electronic music.

In Paris in the 1960s his work appeared in numerous collective exhibitions, at the Salons de la Jeune Sculpture (Young Sculpture), Comparaisons, Réalités Nouvelles (New Realities), de Mai and at the Biennale. He represented France at international shows, including the *Salon de la Sculpture Internationale* in Paris, the New Delhi Biennale, the *Mostra Internazionale di Scultura* in Milan and others. During the 1980s he exhibited lost-wax sculpture at the University of Quebec gallery in Montreal, and took part in the 1990 exhibition *Images du Futur* (*Images of the Future*) in Montreal, and at Rheims in 1991 he displayed his holographic installation *Big Bang II* as part of the exhibition *Les Artistes et la Lumière* (*Artists and Light*).

Bibliography:

Fisher, Hervé, *Holographie, art majeur*, Paris, 1991. *'Georges Dyens'* in *Art Press special edition, 'Nouvelles Technologies un Art sans Modèle?'*, periodical, Paris, 1992.

Museums and Galleries:

Montreal (MAC) - New York (Mus. of Holography) - Paris (MAM).

DYER, Abraham

German, 18th century.
Active in Bamberg (Bavaria).
Painter.

DYER, Charles Gifford

American, 19th - 20th century.
Born 1840, in Chicago; died 27 January 1912, in Munich.
Painter, draughtsman. Genre scenes, landscapes, architectural views, ruins, church interiors, interiors.

Charles Dyer began his career in the Navy and the diplomatic corps (he was consul in Bristol and then Beirut). He left the diplomatic corps to devote himself to painting under the guidance of L. Jacquesson de la Chavreuse in Paris. In 1871 he travelled to Munich where he studied at the Academy and was a pupil of his fellow countryman David Neal; from 1872 he made a series of study trips to Italy, Syria and Greece. He featured in American exhibitions from 1873; a painting by him of an interior view of St Mark's was bought by Pierpont Morgan. He sent a genre painting, *L'Étudiant (The Student)* to the exhibition held by the Royal Academy in London in 1880. After a long trip to the Far East, he returned to Munich in 1910, where he executed a series of 30 large paintings representing the remains of the most important monuments of ancient Greek civilisation.

During the course of his travels he produced numerous sketches, particularly of ancient monuments. His architectural paintings in Venice, executed in oil, met with great success among his fellow countrymen.

Museums and Galleries:

Chicago: *17th Century Interior.*

Auction records:

New York, 25-26 March 1931, *The Grand Canal in Venice* (1889) USD 150. Milwaukee, 2 Nov 1980, *Interior of St Mark's* (oil on canvas, 32 x 42 1/2 ins / 81.3 x 108 cm) USD 1,150. Moulins, 25 Nov 1983, *Orientalist Scene* (oil on canvas) FRF 34,700.

DYER, G. E. O.

British, 19th century.
Painter, miniaturist. Portraits.

G.E.O. Dyer showed a series of portrait miniatures at the Royal Academy in London in 1821, 1822, 1826 and 1847. He showed three portrait miniatures at the Royal Academy in 1835.

DYER, Hezekiah Anthony

American, 20th century.
Born 28 October 1872, in Providence (Rhode Island); died 1943.
Painter. Landscapes.

Hezekiah Anthony studied in Providence before taking study leave in Europe, notably Holland, France and Italy. He was president of the art club in Providence, his home town.

Auction records:

New York, 31 May 1985, *English Cottage* (watercolour, 30 x 22 ins / 76 x 55.6 cm) USD 2,600.

DYER, John

British, 18th century.
Born c. 1700, in Aberglasney (Camarthen); died 24 July 1758.
Painter, poet.

John Dyer studied painting in London with the portrait painter J. Richardson. After travelling on foot all over Wales to get views of landscapes and ruins, he went to Italy to complete his study of painting. He brought back landscapes of the countryside around Rome and Florence, which were reproduced by various engravers. His *Portrait of the Bishop of Worcester, John Hough* was engraved by J. Faber the Younger. He was also admired by his contemporaries for his poetry: he published a series of poems in London in 1840 called *The Ruins of Rome*.

DYER, R. H.

British, 19th century.
Active in London.
Engraver.

R.H. Dyer engraved illustrations and portraits in stipple pointillism. He contributed to the illustration of the work of T.K.Hervey, *Illustrations of Modern Sculpture*, and engraved a portrait of the London antiquarian J. Miller after a miniature by Charles Bestland.

DYF, Marcel, pseudonym of Dreyfus Marcel

French, 20th century.
Born 7 October 1899, in Paris; died 15 September 1985, in Bois d'Arcy (Yvelines).
Painter. Figures, portraits, landscapes, urban landscapes, still-lifes, seascapes, flowers.

Marcel Dyf abandoned engineering to become a painter. He spent some months studying in a Paris studio, then explored Provence and settled first in Arles and later in Paris. He then divided his time between the Paris area and Cannes.

Dyf's art derived from classical tradition and from moderate Post-Impressionism. His landscapes, which form the greater part of his output, are often painted in shades of ochre and in horizontal planes, with additional matter worked in. He produced many in the Île-de-France, in Provence where he lived, in Brittany and Normandy, in Venice, Morocco and Israel. He also painted portraits and figures, in the 1950s often of gypsy women, and frequently of his wife Claudine. He produced decorative work in the town halls of Stes-Maries de la Mer (Camargue) and St-Martin-de-Crau (Arles), and painted frescoes in the Musée Arlaten in Arles in 1936.

In Paris he exhibited at the Salon des Artistes Français, the Salon d'Automne and the Tuileries. He also had solo shows in Paris, three of them at the Galerie Petrides, and from 1956 in London at the Frost and Reed Gallery. In 1995 the General Council of Bouches-du-Rhône put on a retrospective exhibition of his early work, and in 1999 an exhibition at L'Espace Dyf in Bois-d'Arcy commemorated the hundredth anniversary of his birth.

Bibliography:

Marcel Dyf centenary exhibition, exhibition catalogue, Frost & Reed, London, 1999.

Museums and Galleries:

Geneva (Petit Palais): *Gipsy Scene* - Nice (Mus. de la Ville): *The Place Masséna at the Liberation* - Pittsburgh (Carnegie MA): *Flowers.*

Auction records:

Paris, 30 April 1945, *Harlequin and Dancing Girl*, FRF 1,500. Zurich, 12 Nov 1976, *Bouquet of Roses* (oil on canvas, 36 1/4 x 28 3/4 ins / 92 x 73 cm) CHF 2,200. London, 7 Dec 1979, *Summer Flowers* (oil on canvas, 18 x 15 ins / 46 x 38 cm) GBP 1,600. Versailles, 2 March 1980, *Claudine's Dinner* (oil on canvas, 28 3/4 x 23 1/2 ins / 73 x 60 cm) FRF 17,000. London, 24

Oct 1984, *Two Spanish Dancers* (pastel, 20¾ x 14¼ ins / 53 x 36 cm) GBP 1,700. Lyons, 22 Oct 1985, *Landscape* (oil on canvas, 18¼ x 21¾ ins / 46.3 x 55.5 cm) GBP 48,000. London, 3 July 1987, *Woman Playing a Mandolin in front of a Mirror* (oil on canvas, 28¾ x 23¾ ins / 73 x 60.5 cm) GBP 11,000. Paris, 21 and 22 Dec 1987, *Fishing Village* (oil on canvas, 20¾ x 29¼ ins / 53 x 74 cm) FRF 12,000. London, 24 Feb 1988, *Seascape, Boats in the Roads* (oil on canvas, 18 x 21¾ ins / 46 x 55.5 cm) GBP 4,950. Versailles, 20 March 1988, *Young Woman Half Clothed* (oil on canvas, 18 x 15 ins / 46 x 38 cm) FRF 27,000. Paris, 21 April 1988, *The Letter* (oil on canvas, 28¾ x 23½ ins / 73 x 60 cm) FRF 30,000; *Meal on the Grass* (oil on canvas, 18 x 22 ins / 46 x 55 cm) FRF 23,000. Calais, 28 April 1988, *Gypsy Camp* (oil on canvas, 18 x 22 ins / 46 x 55 cm) FRF 9,000. Paris, 29 April 1988, *Jardin du Luxembourg* (oil on canvas, 18 x 22 ins / 46 x 55 cm) FRF 28,000. Los Angeles, 9 June 1988, *Sailing Vessels in Calm Weather* (oil on canvas, 18 x 22 ins / 46 x 55 cm) USD 4,400. L'Isle-Adam, 11 June 1988, *Fantasia* (oil on canvas, 22 x 18 ins / 55 x 46 cm) FRF 32,000; *Sea Coast in Normandy* (oil on canvas, 22 x 18 ins / 55 x 46 cm) FRF 35,500. Paris, 26 June 1988, *Entrance to the Souk* (oil on canvas, 18 x 22 ins / 46 x 55 cm) FRF 35,000. L'Isle-Adam, 25 Sept 1988, *Figures on a Beach* (oil on canvas, 22 x 18 ins / 55 x 46 cm) FRF 40,000. London, 21 Oct 1988, *Young Woman with Bouquet* (oil on canvas, 23½ x 28¾ ins / 59.7 x 73 cm) GBP 7,700. Calais, 13 Nov 1988, *Chapel in the Alyscamps, Arles* (oil on canvas, 21¼ x 28¾ ins / 54 x 73 cm) FRF 17,000. Paris, 14 Dec 1988, *The Jetty* (oil on canvas, 15 x 18 ins / 38 x 46 cm) FRF 6,500. Paris, 16 Dec 1988, *Young Woman in Profile* (oil on canvas, 22 x 18 ins / 55 x 46 cm) FRF 36,000. London, 21 Feb 1989, *Bouquet of Flowers* (oil on canvas, 21 x 17¾ ins / 53.3 x 45.1 cm) GBP 13,200. New York, 3 May 1989, *St-Tropez Harbour* (oil on canvas, 21½ x 25½ ins / 54.5 x 65 cm) USD 66,600. Paris, 18 May 1989, *Dark-Haired Girl with Ribbon* (oil on canvas, 16¼ x 13 ins / 41 x 33 cm) FRF 32,000. London, 20 Oct 1989, *Wheat Field* (oil on canvas, 29¼ x 24 ins / 74 x 61 cm) GBP 18,700. Le Touquet, 12 Nov 1989, *Bathers on the Beach* (oil on panel, 15 x 18½ ins / 38 x 47 cm) FRF 22,000. Paris, 27 Nov 1989, *Gypsies* (oil on canvas, 18 x 22 ins / 46 x 55 cm) FRF 18,000. Paris, 20 Feb 1990, *Vase of Dahlias* (oil on canvas, 24 x 20 ins / 61 x 51 cm) FRF 35,000. New York, 21 Feb 1990, *Girl in a Hat* (oil on canvas, 21½ x 18 ins / 54.6 x 45.5 cm) USD 11,550. Calais, 4 March 1990, *Young Woman and her Memories* (1943, oil on canvas, 15 x 18 ins / 38 x 46 cm) FRF 49,000. Neuilly, 27 March 1990, *Seated Nude* (oil on canvas, 41¼ x 21¼ ins / 105 x 54 cm) FRF 69,000. New York, 7 May 1991, *Bouquet of Flowers* (oil on canvas, 21¾ x 18¾ ins / 55.2 x 47.6 cm) USD 10,450. Neuilly, 11 June 1991, *Flower Market* (oil on canvas, 23½ x 28¾ ins / 60 x 73 cm) FRF 105,000. London, 16 Oct 1991, *Vase of Flowers* (oil on canvas, 21½ x 26 ins / 54.4 x 65.2 cm) GBP 4,950. Paris, 13 Dec 1991, *Landscape* (oil on panel, 7 x 9 ins / 18 x 22 cm) FRF 6,000. London, 24 March 1992, *Farm with Poplars* (oil on canvas, 18 x 21¾ ins / 45.8 x 55.3 cm) GBP 3,300. Paris, 26 May 1992, *Country Church* (1931, oil on canvas, 22 x 18 ins / 55 x 46 cm) FRF 5,000. New York, 12 June 1992, *Landscape in Spring* (oil on canvas, 28¾ x 36 ins / 73 x 91.4 cm) USD 5,500. New York, 10 Nov 1992, *Nude Dressing* (oil on canvas, 21½ x 18 ins / 54.6 x 46 cm) USD 4,180. Edinburgh, 13 May 1993, *Straw Stacks* (oil on canvas, 23¾ x 28¾ ins / 60.3 x 73 cm) GBP 5,500. London, 13 Oct 1993, *Autumn in Provence* (oil on canvas, 18 x 22 ins / 46 x 55 cm) GBP 6,325. Paris, 13 April 1994, *Washerwomen in North Africa* (oil on canvas, 28¼ x 23½ ins / 72 x 60 cm) FRF 60,000. New York, 9 May 1994, *Girl Dressing* (oil on canvas, 22 x 18½ ins / 56 x 47 cm) USD 4,600. London, 14 March 1995, *Peasant Women in the Country* (oil on canvas, 23¾ x 28¾ ins / 60.2 x 73 cm) GBP 5,980. Calais, 24 March 1996, *Vase of Wild Flowers* (oil on canvas, 22 x 18 ins / 55 x 46 cm) FRF 48,000. New York, 30 April 1996, *Jacqueline Dressing* (1960, oil on canvas, 21½ x 18 ins / 54.5 x 46 cm) USD 4,025. Calais, 7 July 1996, *Window Open onto the Roads* (oil on canvas, 35 x 46 ins / 89 x 116 cm) FRF 52,000. New York, 10 Oct 1996, *Fields and Stacks of Wheat* (oil on canvas, 23¾ x 28¾ ins / 60.3 x 73.3 cm) USD 9,200. London, 23 Oct 1996, *Harbour* (oil on canvas, 18½ x 22 ins / 47 x 55 cm) GBP 3,450. New York, 12 Nov 1996, *Portrait of Claudine* (c. 1970, oil on canvas, 21½ x 18 ins / 54.6 x 46 cm) USD 2,760. Calais, 15 Dec 1996, *The Tuileries Gardens and the Place du Carrousel at the Louvre* (oil on canvas, 21¼ x 25½ ins / 54 x 65 cm) FRF 28,800. Calais, 23 March 1997, *Vase of Flowers* (oil on canvas, 18 x 15 ins / 46 x 38 cm) FRF 25,000. Paris, 23 June 1997, *Bouquet of Flowers* (oil on canvas, 28¼ x 23½ ins / 72 x 60 cm) FRF 30,000. Jersey, 29 Sept 1999, *The Poppy Field* (oil on canvas, 23 x 28 ins / 59 x 72 cm) GBP 9,000. Jersey, 29 Sept 1999, *View of St Armel, Brittany* (oil on canvas, 15 x 18 ins / 38 x 46 cm) GBP 11,000. London, 25 Oct 2000, *Harvesters in the Wheat* (1963, oil on canvas, 24 x 29 ins / 61 x 73 cm) GBP 21,000. Calais, 5 Nov 2000, *Paris, the Seine Seen from Port Alexandre III* (oil on canvas, 51 x 64 ins / 130 x 162 cm) FRF 235,000. Jersey, 28 March 2001, *Provence Landscape* (oil on canvas, 23 x 28 ins / 58 x 72 cm) GBP 16,500. Jersey, 28 March 2001, *River at the Île de France* (oil on canvas, 23 x 28 ins / 58 x 71 cm) GBP 16,500. Paris, 8 Feb 2002, *Still-life with Flowers* (oil on canvas, 29 x 24 ins / 73 x 60 cm) EUR 17,500. London, 22 Oct 2002, *Poppy Field* (oil on canvas, 24 x 29 ins / 60 x 73 cm) GBP 11,000. London, 11 Sept 2003, *Claudine as Ballerina* (oil on canvas, 28 x 23 ins / 72 x 58 cm) GBP 12,000. Detroit, 19 Sept 2003, *Landscape* (oil on canvas, 24 x 29 ins / 61 x 74 cm) USD 18,000. Birmingham, 18 May 2004, *Dancer in the Mirror* (oil on canvas, 23 x 28 ins / 58 x 71 cm) GBP 8,000. Philadelphia, 27 June 2004, *Fruit, Flowers and Burgundy in front of Shutters* (oil on canvas, 24 x 29 ins / 60 x 73 cm) USD 18,000.

DYFVERMAN, Karl Johan

Swedish, 19th century.

Born 18 February 1844, in Morlanda; died 10 January 1892, in Stockholm.

Sculptor.

Karl Dyfverman studied at the academy in Stockholm. His work was mainly decorative. He produced the bronze doors for Lund Cathedral.

DYG, Hans

Swiss, 16th century.

Born in Zurich.

Painter.

Several of Dyg's paintings survive in the church of St Peter in Basel. The same city also has many of his wall paintings, including a large *Last Judgement* in the town hall.

DYK. See **also DYCK**

DYK, Philip van, or Dyck, Dijk, called le Petit van Dyk

Flemish, 18th century.

Born 10 January 1680, in Amsterdam; died 3 February 1753, in The Hague.

Painter. History painting, genre scenes, portraits. Flemish School.

Philip van Dyk was a pupil of Arnold Boonen. He lived in Amsterdam until 1708, Middelburg in 1718 and subsequently in The Hague. He was painter to the court of the landgrave Wilhelm VIII of Hessen-Kassel, to whom he had sold collections of paintings. Between 1725 and 1736 he was in Kassel, where he taught Louis de Moni.

Museums and Galleries:
Amsterdam: *Adriaen Parduyn, Commandant of Vlissingen; Caspar Adriaen Parduyn; Marie van Atten, his Wife; Adriaen Caspar Parduyn; Abraham Boudaen; Justina Johanna Ramskrammer, his Wife; The Same with her Daughter* - Berlin: *Lute Player; Woman Giving a Child a Drawing Lesson* - Brussels: *Young Woman at her Toilette* - Gotha: *Venus and Amor* - Kassel: *Family of the Landgrave Karl of Hessen; The Landgrave Wilhelm VIII; The Penitent Magdalene* - Paris (Louvre): *Sarah Leading Hagar to Abraham; Abraham Banishing Hagar* - Stockholm: *Prince Wilhelm, Son of Charles VI of Hessen-Kassel; Portrait of a Man* - The Hague: *Judith; Lute Player; Young Lady at her Toilette; Man Sharpening a Quill* - Toulon: *Portrait of the Artist* - Troyes: *Portrait of a Woman.*
Auction records:
Paris, 1857, *The Servant in Love,* FRF 2,100. Paris, 1868, *Susanna and the Elders,* FRF 855. Paris, 1873, *The Servant in Love,* FRF 2,460; *The Chaste Susanna,* FRF 3,050. Paris, 27 Oct 1919, *Portrait of a Man in a Blue Overcoat,* FRF 390. Paris, 11 Dec 1919, *Portrait of a Man,* FRF 1,410. Paris, 30 May 1924, *Portrait of a Prelate* (attributed) FRF 125. Paris, 6 March 1929, *Portrait of a Woman,* FRF 2,500. Paris, 26 Feb 1931, *Portrait of a Woman in a Yellow Dress and Red Coat Lined with Ermine,* FRF 1,200. London, 5 March 1937, *Sportsman,* GBP 42. Paris, 12 May 1937, *Fortune-teller,* FRF 3,500. London, 3 Nov 1937, *Figures on Balcony,* GBP 26. London, 22 Dec 1937, *Gypsy Fortune-teller,* GBP 30. London, 18 Dec 1942, *Shepherds and Shepherdesses,* GBP 25. New York, 20 Jan 1945, *A Woman,* USD 270. London, 30 Nov 1973, *Portrait of a Gentleman* (1743) Gns 1,600. London, 8 July 1977, *Couple making Music on a Balcony* (oil on panel, 14¼ x 12 ins / 36.2 x 30.7 cm) GBP 24,000. London, 24 July 1981, *Portrait of a Naval Officer* (1732, oil on panel, 19½ x 15 ins / 49.5 x 38.2 cm) GBP 750. London, 17 Dec 1982, *Portrait of a Young Gentleman* (oil on canvas, 32 x 26½ ins / 81.2 x 67.3 cm) GBP 5,000. New York, 6 June 1984, *Susanna and the Elders* (1721, oil on panel, 22½ x 18½ ins / 57.2 x 47 cm) USD 10,000. London, 11 Dec 1987, *Elegant Young Couple making Music with a Child Holding a Bird Cage* (oil on panel, 14¾ x 12½ ins / 37.5 x 31.8 cm) GBP 26,000. Amsterdam, 14 Nov 1988, *Portrait of a Gentleman using a Pair of Compasses, with a Dog and Parrot by him and a Window Looking out to Sea in the Background* (1743, oil on canvas, 33 x 25 ins / 84 x 63.5 cm) NLG 14,950. New York, 13 Oct 1989, *Portrait of a Gentleman using a Pair of Compasses, with a Dog and Parrot by him and a Window Looking out to Sea in the Background* (1743, oil on canvas, 33 x 25 ins / 84 x 63.5 cm) USD 8,250. London, 10 April 1992, *Group Portrait of Jan Albert Sighterman with his Son Albert, a Servant and a Dog* (oil on canvas, 58½ x 46 ins / 148.5 x 117 cm) GBP 12,100. London, 9 Dec 1992, *Lady Seated in a Landscape near an Urn of Flowers* (oil on panel, 14¾ x 11½ ins / 37.5 x 29.5 cm) GBP 4,400. New York, 15 Jan 1993, *Portrait of a Gentleman* (1722, oil on canvas, 32 x 27 ins / 81.3 x 68.6 cm) USD 4,025. New York, 11 Jan 1996, *Portrait of a Lady* (1726, oil on canvas, oval, 19¾ x 16½ ins / 50.2 x 41.9 cm) USD 3,450. Paris, 16 May 1997, *Susanna and the Elders* (oil on oak panel, 18¼ x 16¼ ins / 46.5 x 41 cm) FRF 40,000.

DYK, Philip van, the Younger
Dutch, 18th century.
Painter. Seascapes.

DYK, Philip van de Linden van
Dutch, 18th century.
Born in The Hague; died after 1776.
Painter. Portraits.
The pupil of his uncle Philip van Dyke, Philip van de Linden van Dyk studied in The Hague in 1719 and went to England.
Museums and Galleries:
Utrecht: *Portrait of Jean de Haart.*

DYK, Willem Cornelis van, or Dijk
Dutch, 19th century.
Born 1825; died 1881, in Amsterdam.
Painter, engraver. Portraits, genre scenes.
Drawings, sketches and etchings by Willem Cornelis van Dyk are extant, including *Child with Hoop* (1856), *Seamen's Alehouse,* and a *Portrait of the Painter Pieter Lyonet* (1842).
Museums and Galleries:
Utrecht: *Portrait of the Painter Jan de Haart.*
Auction records:
London, 21 May 1982, *Rest* (1853, oil on panel, 12½ x 11 ins / 31.7 x 28 cm) GBP 550. Amsterdam, 24 April 1991, *Mother and Daughter on a Farm* (1857, oil on canvas, 25¼ x 21 ins / 64 x 53.5 cm) NLG 3,910.

DYKAS, Thomas
Polish, 19th century.
Born 1850, in Gumniska (Galicia).
Sculptor.
Thomas Dykas studied at the fine arts school in Cracow, and was then a student of K. von Zumbusch in Vienna. He settled in Cracow after studying and travelling in Germany, Italy and France. The plans he produced for a monument in Mickiewitz won him two first prizes in 1881 and 1885. He then moved to Lemberg (now Lviv, Ukraine), where he sculpted many monuments for tombs, and a series of marble statues for the Roman-Catholic cathedral and for the Armenian church. He also produced several monuments of Mickiewicz for Przemysl, Tarnopol and Zloczów in Galicia.

DYKE, Peter van
Flemish School, 16th century.
Painter.
Antwerp School.
Peter van Dyke became a master painter in 1497.

DYKE, Pieter van or Vandyke
Dutch, 18th century.
Active in England.
Painter.

It is conceivable that Pieter van Dyke was the son of Philip van de Linden van Dyke. It was probably Joshua Reynolds who attracted him to London. He was a portrait painter between 1762 and 1772 and was taught by Allan Ramsay. He made his first appearance at the Society of Artists with a *Portrait of a Woman* and a *Diana*. From 1764 to 1772 he exhibited a series of portraits at the Free Society of Artists and around 1795 he settled in Bristol where he painted the portraits of the young poets *Southey* and *Coleridge* for the bookseller and publisher, Joseph Cottle.
MUSEUMS AND GALLERIES:
LONDON (National Portrait Gal.): *Robert Southey* (1795, oil on canvas); *Samuel Taylor Coleridge* (1795, oil on canvas).

DYKE, R. H.
British, 19th century.
Active in London.
Painter.
R.H. Dyke exhibited landscapes and seascapes at the Suffolk Street Gallery and the British Institution in London between 1856 and 1867.

DYKE, Richard William
Irish, 18th century.
Painter.
Richard Dyke was a pupil at the academy in Dublin in 1787 and set up, first in Belfast, then in Dublin, as a painter of portraits and miniatures. One of his portraits in pastel was the *Reverend Hugh O'Donnel*

DYKER, Bernardus
German, 15th century.
Active in Bremen.
Calligrapher, miniaturist.

DYKHOFF, J. (Jonker)
Dutch, 19th century.
Active in Amsterdam during the first half of the 19th century.
Painter. Landscapes.
J. Dykhoff was a pupil of J. Hulswit.

DYKMAN-LEMONNIER, Jeanne (Mme)
French, 19th - 20th century.
Born 20 May 1872, in Paris.
Painter.
Jeanne Dykman-Lemonnier joined the Société des Artistes Français in 1895.

DYKMANS. See **DYCKMANS**

DYKSTRA, B.
Dutch, 18th century.
Active in Leeuwarden.
Sculptor.
B. Dykstra worked on the Leeuwarden town hall in 1715.

DYL, Dirk van
Dutch, 18th - 19th century.
Born 1742, in Amsterdam; died 1814, in Amsterdam.
Painter. Scenes with figures.
Like his master G. van der Myn, Dirk van Dyl was a collector. He painted carriages.
AUCTION RECORDS:
PARIS, 1850, *The Herb Market, Antwerp*, FRF 6,510.

DYL, Hans
German, 16th century.
Active in Nuremberg.
Sculptor.

DYL, Yan Bernard
French, 20th century.
Painter.
Yan Bernard Dyl exhibited at the Salon des Tuileries in Paris in 1938 and 1939.

AUCTION RECORDS:
PARIS, 16 Oct 1981, *Meditation* (1939, oil on canvas, 51 1/4 x 32 ins / 130 x 81 cm) FRF 5,200. PARIS, 26 Jan 1983, *Rhythmic Painting* (1938, oil on panel, 42 1/2 x 30 1/4 ins / 108 x 77 cm) FRF 8,000. VERSAILLES, 8 March 1987, *Meditation* (1939, oil on canvas, 50 3/4 x 31 1/2 ins / 129 x 80 cm) FRF 15,100.

DYLCZYNSKI, Cyprian
Polish, 19th century.
Born 1836, in Warsaw.
Painter.
Cyprian Dylczynski studied at the art academy in Warsaw, and continued his artistic training in Dresden, Munich, where he studied under W. von Kaulbach, and Paris. He initially devoted himself to historical painting, and later specialised in genre scenes.

DYLER, Johann
French, 17th century.
Active in Strasbourg c. 1618.
Painter.

DYLEV, Peter Aleksandrovich
Russian, 19th century.
Born 1842; died 1886.
Sculptor.
Dylev was a student at the St Petersburg academy, where in 1868 he exhibited *Prometheus Enchained*, which won him a gold medal, and in 1870 the low relief in plaster *Alexander the Great and his Doctor Philip* and in 1871, a statue of *Peter the Great*.

DYMINSKI, Jan
Polish, 17th century.
Active in Niedzwiedz.
Painter.

DYNEN. See **DEYNUM and DUYNEN**

DYNGA, Georg
Austrian, 18th century.
Miniaturist, illustrator.
Georg Dynga worked in Lipov, Moravia, where he was well known as a pastor. He wrote and illustrated a Slovak hymn book (1740) which is now owned by the church of Kuzelan near Lipov.

DYNO. See **TINO da Camaino**

DYNYS, Chiara
Italian, 20th - 21st century.
Born 1958, in Mantua.
Installation artist.
Chiara Dynys shows her work in Rome and in 1990 presented an installation at the Museum of the Imagination in Domodossola. She considers and works on the limits of painting and its possible relations with space in general and places in particular.

DYONNET, Edmund
Canadian, 19th - 20th century.
Born 25 June 1859, in Crest (Drôme); died 1954.
Painter. Portraits.
Edmund Dyonnet was a pupil in Italy of P.C. Gilardi and Andrea Gastuldi. He exhibited in Rome in 1890, in Buffalo, New York, in 1901, where he gained a silver medal and at the St Louis International Exhibition in 1904; he also took part in exhibitions at the Royal Academy of Arts in Montreal; he also featured in exhibitions in Toronto and Quebec. Appointed a member of the Royal College of Art in 1893, he became secretary of the Royal Canadian Academy of Arts in 1910.
AUCTION RECORDS:
MONTREAL, 26 Nov 1986, *Portrait of Dr. Boulet* (oil on panel, 13 x 10 1/4 ins / 33 x 26 cm) CAD 1,300.

DYPRÉ, Abraham
French, 16th century.
Active in Alençon.
Painter.
Abraham Dypré was the son of Guillaume Dupré. In 1564, he painted a *Madonna* for the high altar in the church of Notre-Dame in Alençon.

DYPRÉ, Guillaume I, or Dipré
French, 16th century.
Active in Alençon.
Painter, glass painter.

DYPRÉ, Guillaume II
French, 16th century.
Active in Alençon.
Glass painter.
Guillaume Dypré II was the son of Guillaume Dypré I.

DYRDON, Henryk
Polish, 19th century.
Born 1860; died 1894, in Cracow.
Painter.
Henryk Dyrdon studied under Jan Matejko in Cracow, and, like his teacher, produced many works for the church of St Mary. He was also a painter of genre scenes.

DYRICK. See **DIRCK**

DYS, Gheert
Flemish School, 16th century.
Painter.
Antwerp School.
Gheert Dys was admitted to the guild as a master painter in Antwerp in 1528.

DYSAART. See **DIEUSSORT François**

DYSHLENKO, Yuri
Russian, 20th century.
Born 1936, in Novosibirsk; died 30 January 1995, in Richmond Hills (New York).
Active in the USA from 1989.
Collage artist.
Yuri Dyshlenko graduated from the polytechnic institute in Leningrad (now St Petersburg) in 1958 and the theatre institute there in 1962. His works consist of juxtapositions of disparate elements, cut-up papers and photographs producing unusual effects of association. He first exhibited in 1988 at the Phyllis Kind Gallery in New York.

MUSEUMS AND GALLERIES:
RUTGERS (Zimmerli Art Mus.).

AUCTION RECORDS:
MOSCOW, 7 July 1988, *Nasty Provocation: Scandalous Details* (1988, acrylic/canvas, 58½ x 38½ ins / 148.5 x 97.5 cm) GBP 2,200.

DYSSELHOF, Gerrit Willem. See **DIJSSELHOF**

DYXHOORN, Pieter Aarnout
Dutch, 19th century.
Born 1810, in Rotterdam; died 14 September 1839, in Groningen.
Painter. Seascapes.
Pieter Aarnout Dyxhoorn was the pupil of Martinus Schouman and Schotel. His paintings were sometimes embellished by Willem Hendrik Schmidt.

AUCTION RECORDS:
LONDON, 19 Jan 1923, *Danger in the Wind*, GBP 10. NEW YORK, 30 Oct 1980, *Sailing Boats in Surging Sea* (oil on canvas, 16½ x 22 ins / 42 x 56 cm) USD 1,750. VLAAMSE KAAI, 30 May 2000, *Seascape* (oil on panel, 15 x 21 ins / 38 x 54 cm) BEF 200,000. COLOGNE, 17 Nov 2001, *Fishing Boat on Choppy Sea* (oil on panel, 11 x 13 ins / 28 x 34 cm) DEM 5,500.

DYZERIN, Paul
Flemish School, 15th century.
Active in Bruges c. 1450.
Painter.

DZAMA, Marcel
Canadian, 20th - 21st century.
Born 1974, in Winnipeg.
Active in New York.
Draughtsman, painter. Figures, animals.
Marcel Dzama has a degree in Fine Arts from the University of Manitoba, Winnipeg, Canada (1994-1997). He held his first solo exhibition in the year of his graduation at the Richard Heller gallery, and for such a young artist has an impressive history of solo exhibitions in Canada, the USA, Brazil, Germany, Sweden and Italy. He has also participated in a number of group exhibitions worldwide.

Dzama's drawings are noted for their unusual if not outright strange compositions, often featuring naked human figures and animals. The figures are clothed in comic-book hero/heroine like costumes, in metal hoods, masks, leather boots and nothing else or dressed as animals. In one drawing (*Untitled*, 2000), the costumed figures are shown seated at a table, raising their glasses to a bear who is smoking. While some drawings are merely bizarre in their choice of composition, others combine sexually explicit scenes with the bizarre. In terms of style and execution, the figures and animals resemble comic book figures, neatly and clearly drawn. The backgrounds are sparse if not absent - the compositions are minimalist and simple. The focus is on the figures and the action alone, and his use of colour is equally sparing.

Recent solo exhibitions include: 2003, *Marcel Dzama*, Richard Heller Gallery, Santa Monica, California; *Marcel Dzama*, David Zwirner, New York, New York; *Marcel Dzama*, Rizziero Arte, Pescara, Italy; *Marcel Dzama: More Famous Drawings*, Art Gallery of Windsor, Ontario, Canada; *Daily Apocalypse: One Drawing by Two Artists*, Perugi Artecontemporanea, Padua, Italy; 2004, *Marcel Dzama*, Christophe Daviet-Thery Livres et Editions d'Artistes, Paris, France; *The Albatross Note*, Galleri Magnus Karlsson, Stockholm, Sweden; *The Last Winter*, Timothy Taylor Gallery, London, England; *Marcel Dzama*, Sies und Höke, Düsseldorf, Germany; *Marcel Dzama*, Olga Korper, Toronto, Canada; *Marcel Dzama*, Susan Inglett Gallery, New York; *Bears in My Room: Works on Paper by Marcel Dzama*, Second Street Gallery, Charlottesville, Virginia.

BIBLIOGRAPHY:
'*Dzamizations: The Drawings of Marcel Dzama*' in *Bordercrossings*, July 1998. *More Famous Drawings*, exhibition catalogue, Plug in Editions, Canada, 1999. Bartorelli, Guido, *The Royal Art Lodge*, exhibition catalogue, Perugi Artecontemporanea, Padua, 2001. Sommerman, Eileen, '*Looking at Dzama*' in *Canadian Art*, Summer 2001. *Expect: Art*, exhibition catalogue, The What to Expect Foundation, New York, 2002.

AUCTION RECORDS:
NEW YORK, 12 Nov 2002, *Untitled* (ink, watercolour and root beer, set of six, 13 x 10 ins / 32 x 25 cm) USD 3,200. NEW YORK, 14 Nov 2003, *Untitled* (pen, ink and watercolour, set of eight, 122 x 10 ins / 311 x 25 cm) USD 3,800. LOS ANGELES, 2 May 2004, *Untitled* (mixed media on wood, 11 x 14 ins / 28 x 36 cm) USD 2,250.

DZAMONJA, Dusan
Macedonian, 20th century.

Born 31 January 1928, in Strumica, Yugoslavia (now Macedonia).
Sculptor.

Dusan Dzamonja studied at the school of fine arts in Zagreb from 1945 to 1951. He won the Rembrandt Prize in 1977 and moved to Brussels in 1987. After a period that might be described as figurative (in that Dzamonja drew his inspiration from the human body), he stood back from any obvious desire to represent the bodily form from 1959 onwards, as witnessed in his *Fiancées* series. Torsos are sculpted in wood and mutilated by iron and fire; studded with nails and subjected to more or less radical combustion; the artist decorates them with glass studs in the guise of funerary jewellery. His works emerge as witnesses to acts of sorcery, in which the earlier influences of Pevsner and particularly Chadwick can be seen. The style of his later works remains faithful to a certain Abstraction, although on the face of it his sculptures are very simple, often relating to volumes that look as if they have been kneaded by a sensual hand or inspired by the world of plants.

He has taken part in many group exhibitions showcasing the world of young Yugoslav sculptors since 1954, especially in the capital and in Zagreb. His work has also gone on show overseas, including at the following: the Venice Biennale (1954, 1960); the Antwerp-Middelheim Biennale (1959, 1961); the 2nd Biennale de Paris (1961); and countless other exhibitions in Brussels, Paris and Ghent, among other places. His solo exhibitions include one in Belgium in 1992, and one in Regent's Park in London in 2004.

DZBANSKI, Constantin
Polish, 19th century.
Born 1823, in Lomna (Galicia).
Painter.

Costantin Dzbanski studied under J. Maszkowski in Lemberg (now Lviv, Ukraine), and then at the Akademie der Bildenden Künste in Vienna. He was a founder of the Society of Friends of the Arts in Lemberg in 1855. His works include genre scenes, such as *Shepherds Around a Campfire*, compositions such as *Cimon and Pero* and small watercolour portraits including a self-portrait, a *Portrait of a Child* (1859) and a *Group of Five Officers* (1858).

DZENIS, Burkards
Latvian, 20th century.
Born 1870, near Riga.
Sculptor. Busts, monuments.

Burkards Dzenis studied at the Stieglitz school of fine art in St Petersburg. In 1905 he received a grant and travelled. He created many public monuments and was director of the State Museum in Riga. He showed busts in 1939 at the exhibition of Latvian art in Paris.

DZHOGIN, Pavel Pavlovich
Russian, 19th century.
Born 1834, in Starodub (Bryanskaya); died February 1885, in St Petersburg.
Painter, draughtsman.

After having finished his studies in Chernigov, Dzhogin studied at the St Petersburg academy of fine arts, before becoming one of its members. He painted landscapes of the surrounding areas of Leningrad, Novogrod and Chernigov.

MUSEUMS AND GALLERIES:
MOSCOW (State Tretyakov Gal.).

DZIEKONSKI, Bogdan Jozef
Polish, 19th century.
Born 1815; died 1885.
Painter, engraver, writer.

Bogdan Jozef Dziekonski's only known works are several engravings made from drawings, including a *Madonna of Czestochowa* and a *Dembowski's Pilgrimage to Podgórze*.

DZIELINSKA, Sophia
Polish, 20th century.
Born in Gorzow.
Sculptor.

Sophia Dzielinska exhibited busts at the Salon d'Automne in Paris in 1935.

DZIERZWIC, Dominik
Polish, 17th century.
Active in Cracow.
Painter.

DZIERZYNSKI, Andreas
Polish, 20th century.
Born 3 December 1936, in Warsaw.
Active in England and in Italy.
Painter, draughtsman. Landscapes.

Andreas Dzierzynski studied history of art at the University of Warsaw from 1953 to 1957 and was a pupil of Kazimir Michalowski, professor of archaeology. He settled in London in 1957 and the following year he tackled painting, receiving encouragement from the Polish sculptor Irene Kunicka. In 1970, he decided to live for part of the year in Italy, near San Gimignano in Tuscany.

While his prime source of inspiration was, of course, the Polish countryside, he had no trouble in diversifying the way he looked at things and in learning from new fashions. Inquisitive and eager to see, he travelled the world producing and exhibiting landscapes of Italy, Poland, Ireland, the Netherlands, England, the Holy Land, Mexico, Iran, India and Brazil.

After his trip to the West Indies in 1973-74, Dzierzynski changed his painting technique: he replaced the knife with the brush, obtaining a lightness of execution apparent in his Brazilian landscapes, which had eluded him previously when he had used a thick impasto. His landscapes have always been thumbnail sketches, not overloaded with details, with a good contrast of colours from which the fresh form seems to open out.

Dzierzynski first exhibited in 1959 in a private house with other young artists; he showed landscapes of France and Italy. But his first important show was held shortly afterwards at the Charles Peguy Centre in London, where he exhibited with the sculptor Elena Gaputyte. From 1962 onwards, he also regularly exhibited solo: Upper Grosvenor Gallery, London (1964, 1965, 1966 and 1967); Charles Peguy Centre, London (1966); Galleria Vaccarino, Florence (1970); Studius gallery, Rio de Janeiro (1975).

DZIEWONSKI, Jozef
Polish, 19th century.
Born 1827, in Swiatniki, near Cracow; died after 1900, in Jaroslaw.
Painter, engraver, lithographer.

Jozef Dziewonski studied under F. Lobeski and N. Strzegocki in Lemberg (now Lviv, Ukraine), and completed his training at the Akademie der Bildenden Künste in Vienna. He took part in the *Retrospective Exhibition* in Lemberg in 1894 with a pen drawing entitled *Uprising in Cracow in 1848*, an oil painting *Landscape in the Roznov Region*, and a self-portrait in charcoal.

DZIGUSKI, Alexander, called Alex
Slav, 20th century.
Born 1911.
Active in the USA.
Painter. Seascapes.

AUCTION RECORDS:
LOS ANGELES, 16 March 1981, *Sea at Dusk* (oil on canvas, 24 1/4 x 36 ins / 61.5 x 91.5 cm) USD 1,200. LOS ANGELES, 29 June 1982, *Seaside* (oil on canvas, 24 x 36 ins / 61 x 91.5 cm) USD 1,400. NEW YORK, 4 March 1987, *Coastal Landscape* (oil

on canvas, 24 x 36 ins / 61 x 91.5 cm) USD 1,300. NEW YORK, 18 Dec 1991, *Seascape* (oil on canvas, 24 x 36 ins / 61 x 91.4 cm) USD 1,320.

DZIUBANIUK, Ela
Polish, 20th century.
Born in Lviv (now in Ukraine).
Painter. Genre scenes.

Ela Dziubaniuk exhibited at the Salon des Indépendants in Paris from 1932.

DZIWAK, Petr, also known as Wunderlich
Polish, 16th century.
Born in Cracow.
Painter.

DZMERCOVIC, Bozidar
Macedonian, 20th century.
Born 1930, in Mogila.
Engraver.

Bozidar Dzmercovic studied at the school of art in Belgrade with Celebonovic. His abstract engravings, with an informal tendency, gave way to important research on the subject. He began exhibiting in Belgrade in 1965 and took part in the Ljubliana Biennale (1965 and 1967) and the Cracow Biennale (1966).

DZUBAS, Friedel
German, 20th century.
Born 1915, in Berlin.
Active in the USA from 1940.
Painter.

Dzubas is said by some biographical sources to have trained at the art academy in Berlin from 1931 to 1934. However, according to another source he was self-taught, working as an apprentice painter and decorator for a Berlin-based company from 1933 to 1936 while studying painting by himself in galleries. In the 1930s he showed his opposition to the rise of Nazism by joining a communist youth organisation. In 1939 he managed to leave Germany, heading first for London and then, in 1940, for New York. Later that year he moved to Chicago, where he became a designer in the publishing business. Meanwhile, he continued to harbour an interest in the development of modern painting and the writings of Clement Greenberg. In 1954 he returned to New York where he met Greenberg, who introduced him to Jackson Pollock and other abstract Expressionist artists. He also got in contact with Katherine Dreier and the Société Anonyme, designing the first catalogue for the collection in 1950. In 1952 he shared his New York studio with Helen Frankenthaler. He spent some time in Europe in the 1960s.

His early style was heavily influenced by the paintings of Klee. Later, in the 1960s, Dzubas became an abstract Expressionist. He was a member, along with Sam Francis and Helen Frankenthaler, of the Color-Field Painting group of painters who rejected the pictorial Expressionism of De Kooning and championed the 'all-over' style of Pollock. Their chief principles were the rejection of the illusion of depth, the affirmation of the 2-dimensionality of the surface to be painted, the elimination of visible brushwork, and the liberation of the colour palette. Amid this intense artistic atmosphere, he said of the painters who imitated De Kooning: 'It is just the idle chit-chat of the self-satisfied, and you find all the ingredients of what is fashionable, the trailing brushwork, the modest and reasonable tones, apparent nonchalance and dressed-up violence'.

Dzubas has taken part in numerous collective exhibitions including *60 Americans 1960* in 1961. There have been solo exhibitions of his works: at the Tibo de Nagy Gallery in New York in 1952; at the Galerie French & Co in New York in 1958 and 1959, organised by Clement Greenberg; and a retrospective at the Museum of Fine Arts in Houston in 1974.

BIBLIOGRAPHY:
Atkins, Robert, *A Guide to Contemporary Ideas, Movements, and Buzzwords*, Abbeville Press, New York, 1990.

MUSEUMS AND GALLERIES:
BUFFALO (Albright-Knox AG) - SYRACUSE, NY (Everson MA): *Condor* (1968, acrylic).

AUCTION RECORDS:
LONDON, 5 Dec 1974, *Satori I* (1963) GBP 640. NEW YORK, 30 Nov 1980, *Angel's Wing* (1977, acrylic/canvas, 62 x 153 ins / 157.5 x 388.5 cm) USD 14,000. NEW YORK, 9 Nov 1983, *Untitled* (1965, oil on canvas, 84 x 69 ins / 213.4 x 175.3 cm) USD 13,000. LONDON, 18 June 1985, *Night Flight* (acrylic/canvas, 72 x 72 ins / 183 x 183 cm) USD 9,000. NEW YORK, 5 May 1987, *Untitled* (1966, acrylic/canvas, 28 x 167 ins / 71.2 x 424.2 cm) USD 16,500. LONDON, 13 April 1988, *Grey Abbey* (1968, oil on canvas, 95 x 72 ins / 241.3 x 183 cm) USD 3,080. NEW YORK, 4 May 1988, *Henge* (1965, oil on canvas, 69 x 84 ins / 175.2 x 213.2 cm) USD 8,800. NEW YORK, 8 Oct 1988, *1965* (oil on canvas, 46 x 92 ins / 117 x 233.7 cm) USD 7,700. NEW YORK, 10 Nov 1988, *Mesita Run* (1976, acrylic/canvas, 40 x 40 ins / 101.8 x 101.8 cm) USD 10,450. LONDON, 6 April 1989, *Nuptial* (1978, acrylic/canvas, 40 x 40 ins / 101.6 x 101.6 cm) GBP 1,870. NEW YORK, 3 May 1989, *Other Desert* (1974, acrylic/canvas, 72 x 72 ins / 183 x 183 cm) USD 19,800. NEW YORK, 5 Oct 1989, *Untitled* (1980, acrylic/canvas, 72 x 72 ins / 183 x 183 cm) USD 30,250. NEW YORK, 23 Feb 1990, *Bantu, 1973* (acrylic/canvas, 61 1/4 x 103 1/4 ins / 155.5 x 262.2 cm) USD 33,000. NEW YORK, 8 May 1990, *After Grey* (1974, acrylic/canvas, 61 x 103 ins / 154.9 x 261.9 cm) USD 33,000. NEW YORK, 7 May 1991, *Scherazade* (1988, acrylic/canvas, 28 1/2 x 42 1/2 ins / 72.4 x 108 cm) USD 4,180. NEW YORK, 12 June 1991, *Saints' Passion* (1976, acrylic/canvas, 40 x 40 ins / 101.6 x 101.6 cm) USD 6,600. NEW YORK, 3 Oct 1991, *Entrance* (1974, acrylic/canvas, 72 x 106 ins / 183 x 269.3 cm) USD 27,500. NEW YORK, 13 Nov 1991, *Voyage of the Vikings* (1975, acrylic/canvas, 57 x 131 ins / 145 x 333 cm) USD 14,300. NEW YORK, 25-26 Feb 1992, *Cold Hedge* (1973, oil on canvas, 39 x 39 ins / 99.1 x 99.1 cm) USD 16,500. NEW YORK, 7 May 1992, *Blood of Christ* (1972, acrylic/canvas, 72 x 72 ins / 182.9 x 182.9 cm) USD 26,400. NEW YORK, 5 May 1993, *Hesperus* (acrylic/canvas, 62 x 116 ins / 157.5 x 294.6 cm) USD 16,100. NEW YORK, 11 Nov 1993, *Falling Shadow* (1979, acrylic/canvas, 72 x 72 ins / 182.9 x 182.9 cm) USD 17,250. NEW YORK, 22 Feb 1996, *Construction* (1981, treated/canvas, 46 3/4 ins / 119 cm, 1 1/2 x 107 3/4 ins/4 x 274 cm, 1 1/4 ins/3 cm) USD 23,000. NEW YORK, 10 Oct 1996, *Northern* (1963, oil on canvas, 35 x 35 ins / 88.9 x 88.9 cm) USD 5,175. NEW YORK, 19 Feb 1997, *Hidden Course* (1983, acrylic/canvas, 72 x 72 1/4 ins / 182.9 x 183.5 cm) USD 12,650.

DZUBENKO, Mikhail
Finnish, 20th century.
Born in Vyborg.
Painter. Interiors, landscapes, flowers.

Michel Dzubenko exhibited at the Salon d'Automne in Paris in 1930 and 1931.

DZWENK, Stanislaw
Polish, 16th century.
Active in Cracow.
Painter.

DZWONOWSKI, Zacharias
Polish, 17th century.
Active in Cracow.
Painter.

In Cracow in 1636, Zacharias Dzwonowski produced eight oil paintings of scenes from the life of St Augustine for the convent of St Catherine in Kazimierz.

E.
16th century.
Monogram of a painter, engraver.

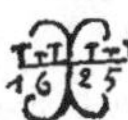

E.
German, 16th century.
Active c. 1546.
Monogram of an engraver (burin).
One of this artist's works is an engraving of *A Lord and Lady Kneeling before Christ.*

E., Josep Antonio
Spanish (?), 18th century.
Painter. Historical subjects, figure compositions.
Josep Antonio E. appears to be known only by the initial of his surname and his two forenames; this is how the artist signed the painting sold on 19-20 May 1992 in New York. This group piece shows signs of semi-amateurism, or an almost naive simplicity.
AUCTION RECORDS:
NEW YORK, 19-20 May 1992, *Devotion of Don Felipe Antonio del Valle* (1741, oil on canvas, 87 1/2 x 126 1/2 ins / 222.3 x 321.3 cm) USD 68,750.

E. A.
Monogram of a painter.

E. A.
German, 16th century.
Active in the 16th century.
Monogram of an engraver (wood).
This artist executed an engraving of a *Woman Holding an Escutcheon.*

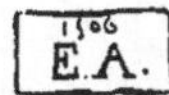

E. B.
German.
Monogram of an engraver (burin).
Worked in Germany. There is an engraving by this artist, whose work is reminiscent of Sadeler, entitled *Rest of the Flight into Egypt.*

E. C.
Italian, 16th century.
Monogram of an engraver (burin).
This engraver was active around 1516. He produced three models of knife sheaths.

E. D. C. F.
French, 18th century.
Active in Paris.
Monogram of an engraver.
Brulliot mentions a *Renaut and Armide* by E.D.C.F. after N. Cochin.

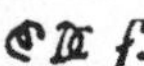

E. H. S.
Monogram of an engraver.

E. L. L. A.
Flemish School, 16th century.
Mark of an engraver.
This Augustinian monk was active in Liège around 1577.

E. R. K.
German.
Monogram of an engraver.
He is known for a matching copy of Albrecht Dürer's *Education of the Virgin.*

E. S.
German, 15th century.
Monogram of an engraver.

An extremely rare engraving dated 1467, the *Virgin Praying*, is attributed to this artist.

E. S., MASTER OF THE INITIALS, also called
Master of 1466
Swiss, 15th century.
Born 1420
c. 1467-1468.
Engraver (burin), draughtsman, goldsmith.

Skilled in composition, this artist brought new life to traditional themes such as the Annunciation, the Visitation and the Nativity. He was equally successful with religious and profane subjects. A chronological list of his works is given in Volume 2 of Lehr's catalogue. He seems to have been born somewhere near Lake Constance and is thought to have been the inventor of the technique of engraving on copper. More than 500 prints are known to have been by him, their technique suggesting that his original training may have been as a goldsmith. The line is elegant, and the subjects, both sacred and profane, are very varied. His influence spread all over Germany, the Netherlands, Italy, France and Spain. No paintings have survived that might be his work. It was thought at one time that one of his pupils had been Schongauer. His influence as an engraver was great both in Germany and the Netherlands. The *Hans Memling* exhibition, held in the Groeningemuseum in Bruges in 1994, showed some of his works in the section devoted to Memling's precursors.

BIBLIOGRAPHY:
Bevers, Holm, *Meister E. S.: ein oberrheinischer Kupferstecher der Spaetgotik*, exhibition catalogue, Staatliche Graphische Sammlung, Munich, 1987.

MUSEUMS AND GALLERIES:
DRESDEN (Prints Collection): *The Man of Sorrows between Four Angels* (c. 1460, engraving) - WASHINGTON DC (NGA): *The Madonna and Child in a Garden* (c. 1465-1467, engraving in white on laid paper prepared with black ink).

AUCTION RECORDS:
BERN, 8 June 1977, *St John the Evangelist* (engraving/copper) CHF 32,000.

E. T. B.
German, 16th century.
Active between 1541 and 1564.
Monogram of an engraver (burin).

This artist's works include: *Maximilian II, Emperor of Germany*; *Sigismund das Liber Baro in Herberstain*; *Abbot Paul of Temeswar*; *Ubermann*; and the *Coats of Arms of the Bishop of Passau*.

E. V. H.
German, 16th century.
Active in the mid-16th century.
Monogram of an engraver.

A small engraving entitled *Superbia* is attributed to this artist.

E. V. H.
Dutch (?), 17th century.
Monogram of a painter. Landscapes.

MUSEUMS AND GALLERIES:
BUCHAREST (Muz. National de Arta al României): landscape.

E. V. T.
French, 16th century.
Monogram of an engraver (etching).
Fontainebleau School.

This artist was active in the first half of the 16th century, and belonged to the Fontainebleau School. He is known for two series of portraits of illustrious men (12 in all).

EADIE, Agnes S.
British, 20th century.
Born in London.
Miniaturist.

Agnes S. Eadie exhibited at the Salon des Artistes Français in 1934.

EADIE, Robert
British, 19th - 20th century.
Born 1877; died 1954.
Painter, watercolourist. Urban landscapes, landscapes.

AUCTION RECORDS:
GLASGOW, 1 Oct 1981, *View of Largs* (oil on panel, 28 x 36 ins / 71 x 91.5 cm) GBP 340. EDINBURGH, 30 Aug 1988, *Crossing a Bridge* (oil on canvas, 28¼ x 36 ins / 72 x 91.5 cm) GBP 1,760. PERTH, 28 Aug 1989, *Prince's Street from the Royal Scottish Academy* (watercolour on black chalk/paper, 14½ x 22 ins / 37 x 55 cm) GBP 4,070. GLASGOW, 11 Dec 1996, *View of Largs* (oil on canvas, 28 x 36¼ ins / 71 x 92 cm) GBP 747. GLASGOW, 25 Aug 1997, *Girl Sleeping* (pencil and watercolour heightened with white, 11 x 15 ins / 27.8 x 38.3 cm) GBP 1,150. BILLINGSHURST, 23 Oct 2000, *Clyde Street, Glasgow* (oil on canvas, 40 x 50 ins / 101 x 127 cm) GBP 4,000. EDINBURGH, 24 Aug 2001, *Crail Harbour* (oil on canvas, 28 x 36 ins / 71 x 91 cm) GBP 1,100. LONDON, 5 Sept 2001, *Picking Flowers* (watercolour, 14 x 10 ins / 36 x 26 cm) GBP 1,200. LONDON, 14 April 2003, *Evening, West George Street* (1919, watercolour, 17 x 13 ins / 42 x 32 cm) GBP 1,650. LONDON, 27 Aug 2003, *Perth High Street, Looking from John Street* (1840, oil on board, 14 x 24 ins / 35 x 61 cm) GBP 2,800.

EADIE, William
British, 19th - 20th century.
Painter. Genre scenes.

William Eadie exhibited frequently in London, notably at the Royal Academy from 1871.

EADIE-REID, James
British, 19th - 20th century.
Born in the second half of the 19th century, in Dundee, Scotland.
Painter, draughtsman.

James Eadie-Reid exhibited in Paris at the Salon de la Société Nationale in 1913.

EADWIN
British, 12th century.
Active c. 1150.
Miniaturist.

A monk, this artist collaborated in the decoration of a psalter at Christ Church Cathedral, Canterbury.

EAGLE, Edward
Irish, 19th - 20th century.
Born c. 1850; died 28 March 1910, in Dublin.
Painter, engraver (etching). Landscapes.

Edward Eagle submitted a number of paintings to the Dublin Academy exhibitions.

EAGLES, Edmund

British, 19th century.

Painter. Mythological subjects, portraits, genre scenes. Edmund Eagles exhibited frequently at the Royal Academy and at Suffolk Street in London, between 1851 and 1877. Among his works are *Childhood of Bacchus* (1851); *La Ciocara* (1858); *Evelyn* (1873); and *Gee! Gee!* (1875).

AUCTION RECORDS:

LONDON, 13 Dec 1984, *Little Girl Playing Cards* (1870, oil on canvas, 17 1/4 x 19 ins / 44 x 48 cm) GBP 6,800. LONDON, 15 June 1988, *The Disguise* (1869, oil on canvas, 19 x 14 3/4 ins / 48 x 37.5 cm) GBP 1,980.

EAGLES, John (Revd.)

British, 18th - 19th century.

Born 1783, in Bristol; died 1855, in Bristol.

Watercolourist, critic.

John Eagles was the son of the renowned classical scholar, Thomas Eagles. He was educated at Winchester College and then at Wadham College, Oxford from 1809 to 1818. Although noted for his watercolours - works such as *The Enchanted Forest* illustrated Eagles' ability to describe with sensitivity a given landscape or scene - he found a greater degree of success as a writer and critic. Aside from his sonnets and essays, Eagles made a name for himself as a regular contributor to the *Blackwood's Magazine*, often submitting original artwork and reviewing the work of Sir John Everett Millais, J.M.W. Turner and John Ruskin. It was the vicious verbal attack of Turner's 1836 painting *Juliet and Her Nurse* that brought Eagles the most notoriety, a move which caused Ruskin to take up the defence of Turner in his *Modern Painters* series.

BIBLIOGRAPHY:

Eagles, John, *The Sketcher*, W. Blackwood, Edinburgh, 1856.

MUSEUMS AND GALLERIES:

CAMBRIDGE (Fitzwilliam Museum): *Boats in a Dry Creek or Sketch of a Landscape with Trees* (watercolour and pencil); *Harbour Scene by Moonlight* (watercolour and pencil) - MANCHESTER (Whitworth Art Gallery): *The Enchanted Forest* (chalk and watercolour).

EAKINS, Thomas Cowperthwaite

American, 19th - 20th century.

Born 25 July 1844, in Philadelphia; died 25 June 1916, in Philadelphia.

Painter, sculptor. Nudes, portraits, genre scenes, sporting subjects.

Thomas Eakins' father was a writing master. Between 1861and 1866 he enrolled on a drawing course at the Pennsylvania Academy of Fine Art and at the same time followed a course in anatomy at the medical faculty. At Jefferson Medical College he attended and participated in dissections and produced studies of nudes. In 1866 he went to Paris, enrolled at the École des Beaux-Arts and spent over three years working in Jean-Léon Gérôme's studio. His meticulous attention to detail and taste for drawing gave him an advantage at the School, an institution that was still dominated by the art of Ingres. After a trip to Spain, where he was impressed by Ribera and Velázquez, he returned to Philadelphia in 1870. In 1877 he was appointed professor of drawing at the Pennsylvania Academy of Art. In 1886 a dispute about his decision to use a male nude model in a mixed class led to his forced resignation. He became an isolated painter painting subjects acceptable to the larger public but where the introduction of nudes was unavoidable. An example is *Crucifixion* (1880), in which he gives free rein to his passion for painting the human body. Other examples are *William Rush Carving His Allegorical Figure of the Schuylkill River.*

Eakins' knowledge of anatomy enabled him to paint with confidence and honesty, as shown by the *Gross Clinic* (1875) in which Dr Gross appears in the half-light of the amphitheatre, explaining to his pupils an operation that he was performing on a quite garishly lit patient. This painting shocked his contemporaries with its cold realism. The depiction of reality and actuality were always Eakins' main preoccupations and also the focus of controversy.

He also painted portraits in a sombre style, with a few highlighted points, in a style somewhat reminiscent of Rembrandt, whom he admired. He paid particular attention to representing the character and psychology of the individual, more than detailing the clothes or accessories that surrounded him. This desire to penetrate the human person, his being, recurs in later portraits, including the *Thinker* (1900), who is none other than his brother-in-law, Kenton. But it is above all in outdoor painting that Eakins gave of his best. In 1871 he painted *Max Schmitt in a Single Scull*, a seemingly simple painting, yet very carefully composed on the basis of a tight geometric plan. He combined a theoretical study of perspective with the observation of real models. And this combination does not detract from the accent of truth that emerges from most of his paintings, in particular the hunting scenes, such as that of *Will Schuster and a Black Man Going to Shoot the Rail* (1876). This extremely sombre work arranged in tiers of three horizontal strips indicating water, hedge and sky, the number of figures limited to two, conceals a strict composition and a complete study of gestures that are scarcely drawn, giving a sense of spontaneity that suits a hunting scene. Eakins also played with simple, contrasting colours, for example, the red of the hunter's shirt and the white of that worn by the oarsman. However, the best of Eakins' art is to be found in his outdoor paintings and, on this subject, one can imagine him having been influenced by the French outdoor school more than by Impressionism. He took pleasure in capturing the moment, be it in *Pool* (1882), where he depicts his friends swimming and diving, or *Fairman Roger's Team of Horses* (1879), for which he had wax studies of the horses produced (as Degas used to do). He was also the author of sporting scenes.

A painter of reality, who wanted to reflect the image of life of the moment, he can be regarded as the forerunner of the 'Ash-Can School', which came into being in Philadelphia and was to carry the American Realist tradition right into the mid-20th century.

His retrospective exhibitions include: 1945, Carnegie Institute, Pittsburgh; 2002, *Thomas Eakins: American Realist*, touring exhibition, Philadelphia Museum of Art, Musée d'Orsay, Paris, Metropolitan Museum of Art, New York.

BIBLIOGRAPHY:

Goodrich, Lloyd, *Thomas Eakins: His Life and Work*, Whitney Museum of American Art, New York, 1933. Domit, Moussa M., *The sculpture of Thomas Eakins*, exhibition catalogue, Corcoran Gall. of Art, Washington DC, 1969. Johns, Elizabeth, *Thomas Eakins, the heroism of modern life*, exhibition catalogue, Princeton University Press, Princeton, 1983. Wilmerding, John, *Thomas Eakins*, Smithsonian Institution Press, Washington DC, 1993. Danly, Susan/Leibold, Cheryl, et al., *Eakins and the photograph: works by Thomas Eakins and his circle in the collection of the Pennsylvania Academy of the Fine Arts*, catalogue raisonné, Smithsonian Institution Press, Washington DC, 1994. Cooper, Helen A., *Thomas Eakins: The Rowing Pictures*, Yale University Press, New Haven, 1996. Berger, Martin A., *Man made: Thomas Eakins and the construction of Gilded Age manhood*, University of California Press, Berkeley, 2000. Sewell, Darrel, et al., *Thomas Eakins*, exhibition catalogue, Philadelphia Museum of Art, Yale University Press, New Haven, 2001.

MUSEUMS AND GALLERIES:

FORT WORTH (Amon Carter Mus.): *Swimming* (1885, oil on canvas) - GLEN FALLS (Hyde Collection): *Henry O'Tanner* (1902, oil on canvas) - NEW YORK (Metropolitan Mus. of Art):

The Champion Single Sculls (Max Schmitt in a Single Scull) (1871); *The Thinker: Portrait of Louis N. Kenton* (1900) - NORTHAMPTON, MA (MA, Smith College): *Mrs Edith Mahon* (1904) - PHILADELPHIA (Jefferson Medical College): *The Gross Clinic* - PHILADELPHIA (MA): *Fairman Roger's Team of Horses; Crucifixion; William Rush Carving his Allegorical Figure of the Schuylkill River* - PHILADELPHIA (Pennsylvania Academy of the Fine Arts Gal.) - WORCESTER, MA (AM): *Study of the Head of Samuel David Gross* (1875, oil on canvas, study for the 'Gross Clinic').

AUCTION RECORDS:

NEW YORK, 24 Oct 1946, *Mrs Richard Day,* USD 600. NEW YORK, 23-25 Jan 1947, *Maybelle* (1898) USD 2,000. NEW YORK, 22 Jan 1966, *Youth Playing Pipes* (bronze, low relief) USD 2,500. NEW YORK, 10 Dec 1970, *Cowboys in a Landscape,* USD 210,000. NEW YORK, 7 April 1971, *The Spinner* (c. 1878) USD 120,000. NEW YORK, 23 May 1974, *Portrait of Florence Einstein* (1905) USD 36,000. NEW YORK, 21 April 1978, *Archbishop William Henry Elder* (1903, oil on canvas, 66 1/4 x 45 1/2 ins / 168.5 x 115.5 cm) USD 265,000. NEW YORK, 20 April 1979, *Portrait of Florence Einstein* (1905, oil on canvas, 24 x 20 ins / 61 x 50.8 cm) USD 50,000. NEW YORK, 23 April 1981, *Study of a Young Girl with a Cat, Kathrin* (pencil/mounted paper/card, 14 x 11 ins / 35.6 x 28 cm) USD 8,500. NEW YORK, 2-3 June 1983, *Portrait of Dr William Thompson* (c. 1907, oil on canvas, 67 3/4 x 48 1/4 ins / 172 x 122.4 cm) USD 280,000; *Spinning* (1881, watercolour, 16 x 11 ins / 39.8 x 27 cm) USD 500,000. NEW YORK, 29 May 1986, *Portait of Dr Gilbert Lafayette Parker* (oil on canvas, 24 x 20 ins / 61 x 50.8 cm) USD 125,000. NEW YORK, 17 Nov 1986, *Nude Lying Stretched Out* (c. 1863-1866, charcoal/pink paper, 18 3/4 x 24 ins / 47.6 x 61 cm) USD 52,500. NEW YORK, 28 May 1987, *The Artist-Student Portrait of James Wright* (1890, oil on canvas, 42 1/2 x 32 ins / 107.7 x 81.3 cm) USD 2,200,000. NEW YORK, 24 May 1989, *Portrait of Professor William D. Marks* (oil on canvas, 76 x 54 ins / 193 x 137.1 cm) USD 165,000. NEW YORK, 23 May 1990, *John Biglin Training in a Single Scull* (1873, watercolour/paper, 17 x 24 ins / 42.9 x 61 cm) USD 3,520,000. NEW YORK, 24 May 1990, *Portrait of a Woman* (oil on canvas, 24 1/4 x 20 ins / 61.5 x 50.8 cm) USD 19,800. NEW YORK, 29 Nov 1990, *Meadows at Gloucester, New Jersey* (oil on panel, study, 10 1/4 x 14 ins / 26 x 35.5 cm) USD 33,000. NEW YORK, 1 Dec 1994, *Young Girl Reflecting* (oil on canvas, 7 x 5 ins / 17.8 x 12.7 cm) GBP 34,500. NEW YORK, 25 May 1995, *Portrait of the Artist Charles Linford* (oil on canvas, 48 x 37 ins / 121.9 x 94 cm) USD 90,500. NEW YORK, 5 June 1997, *Netting* (1882, watercolour/paper, 11 1/4 x 16 3/4 ins / 28.7 x 42.5 cm) USD 1,542,500.

EAMES, Charles

American, 20th century.
Born 1907, in St Louis (Missouri); died 21 August 1978.
Designer, architect, graphic designer.

Charles Eames was made famous by a lounge chair designed in 1955. Apart from his work as designer of international repute, Eames experimented with sculpture. His works include *Machine for Doing Nothing* (1955) which was run on solar energy and discussed by Frank Popper in his *Origins and Development of Kinetic Art* (1968).

EAMES, Dickon

American, 20th century.
Born 1945, in New York.
Active in France.
Sculptor.

Dickon Eames has lived and worked in France since 1972. His sculptures, which have an average size of 28 to 32 inches (70-80 cm) high, consist of metal rods fixed together with screws and bolts, forming fragments of curved lines. This type of art takes on some of the aesthetic principles of constructivism: the line indicates the power and rhythm of the object, while its volume is rejected. The curvilinear structures, which have nothing finite about them apart from their material, sweep through the space and arouse curiosity. Grey, the dominant colour, evokes neutrality, experimentation and temporariness. The constructions create tension between movement and balance, with spheres moving through space, suspended pulleys and helicoids. If, as they say, every work of art has an internal structure, the works of Dickon Eames are closely connected with theirs.

After holding several collective and solo exhibitions outside France, Eames has been regularly exhibiting in Paris at the Galerie Jean-Claude Riedel since 1983.

EANES, Gil, or Eannes

Flemish School, 15th century.
Active in Portugal during the 15th century.
Sculptor.

Gil Eanes worked in 1465 at the convent of Our Lady of Victory in Batalha, and then at the convent of Miraflore. Here, in 1496, with Diego de la Cruz, he made the high altar.

EANES, Gonçalo

Portuguese, 15th century.
Died 1455.
Miniaturist.

Eanes was active at the royal court of Portugal.

EANES, Vasco

Portuguese, 15th century.
Miniaturist.

EARDLEY, Joan Kathleen Harding

British, 20th century.
Born May 1921, in Warnham (Sussex); died 19 August 1963.
Painter (including gouache), pastellist, watercolourist, draughtswoman (including charcoal/ink). Figures, portraits, scenes with figures, genre scenes, fishing scenes, interiors with figures, landscapes, urban landscapes, seascapes.

Joan Kathleen Harding Eardley studied in London and at the Glasgow School of Art from 1940 to 1943. In 1948 she became a member of the Society of Scottish Artists. She travelled in France and Italy before working in Glasgow and then moved to the small fishing village of Catterline. In 1955 she became an associate of the Royal Scottish Academy and in 1963, the year of her death, she was made a full academy member.

She painted everday figures in a robust, Expressionist style and demonstrated a particular fondness for painting street children, working-class interiors, vast landscapes in generously applied pigment and wild seascapes at the mercy of the waves and wind.

Eardley took part in many group exhibitions of contemporary Scottish and English painting, notably at the Glasgow School of Fine Arts (1949), in Aberdeen (1950), London (1955, 1963), and Edinburgh (1959, 1961).

BIBLIOGRAPHY:

Joan Eardley, retrospective exhibition catalogue, Glasgow, Edinburgh, 1964. Buchanan, William, *Joan Eardley,* Edinburgh University Press, Edinburgh, 1976. Oliver, Cordelia, *Joan Eardley, RSA,* Mainstream, Edinburgh, 1988 (with photographs by Audrey Walker and Oscar Marzaroli).

AUCTION RECORDS:

GLASGOW, 8 April 1982, *Glasgow Children* (gouache, 4 x 4 3/4 ins / 10 x 12 cm) GBP 360. SCOTLAND, 30 Aug 1983, *Sleeping Child* (coloured chalk, 10 x 11 1/2 ins / 25.5 x 29 cm) GBP 600; *Stove* (oil on canvas, 35 x 16 1/4 ins / 89 x 41 cm) GBP 3,000. LONDON, 26 Sept 1984, *Shop Interior: Jeannie* (gouache and Indian ink, 15 x 10 ins / 38 x 25.5 cm) GBP 1,650. PERTH, 26 Aug 1986, *Summer Fields III* (gouache, 13 x 16 ins / 33 x 40.5 cm) GBP 1,200. SOUTH QUEENSFERRY, 29 April 1987, *Children*

Playing, Back Street, Glasgow (1956, oil on canvas, 36 x 64 ins / 91.5 x 162.5 cm) GBP 43,000. LONDON, 13 May 1987, *Young Boy with a Cat* (charcoal and coloured chalk, 20 x 14 1/4 ins / 51 x 36 cm) GBP 2,400. LONDON, 29 July 1988, *Head of an Urchin* (oil on card, 10 x 8 1/4 ins / 25.7 x 20.7 cm) GBP 825. EDINBURGH, 30 Aug 1988, *Salmon Nets II* (oil and collage/card, 25 1/2 x 48 1/4 ins / 64.5 x 122.5 cm) GBP 9,350. EDINBURGH, 22 Nov 1988, *Little Backward Boy* (pastel/paper, 10 1/2 x 8 1/2 ins / 26.7 x 21.5 cm) GBP 5,500; *Sea No. 4* (oil and collage/card, 44 x 46 1/2 ins / 111.7 x 118 cm) GBP 9,000. PERTH, 28 Aug 1989, *Urchin with Blue Jumper* (pastel, 19 3/4 x 14 1/2 ins / 50 x 37 cm) GBP 14,300. EDINBURGH, 22 Nov 1989, *Lady with Red Wallpaper* (oil on canvas, 35 1/2 x 35 3/4 ins / 90.3 x 90.8 cm) GBP 14,300. GLASGOW, 6 Feb 1990, *Urchin with a Cat* (charcoal and coloured chalk, 20 x 14 1/4 ins / 51 x 36 cm) GBP 4,620. EDINBURGH, 26 April 1990, *Sea No. 4* (oil and collage/card, 44 x 46 1/2 ins / 111.7 x 118 cm) GBP 7,700. PERTH, 27 Aug 1990, *Child's Caress* (coloured chalk, 11 x 9 ins / 27 x 23 cm) GBP 4,950. GLASGOW, 22 Nov 1990, *The Two Samson Children* (pastel and watercolour, 4 3/4 x 3 3/4 ins / 12 x 9.5 cm) GBP 1,650. GLASGOW, 5 Feb 1991, *Children in a Working-class District of Glasgow* (oil on canvas, 28 1/4 x 54 ins / 72 x 137 cm) GBP 55,000. PERTH, 26 Aug 1991, *Portrait of Angus Neil* (oil on canvas, 30 x 25 1/2 ins / 76 x 65 cm) GBP 11,000. EDINBURGH, 19 Nov 1992, *Cow Parsley at Catterline* (oil on card, 33 3/4 x 44 1/2 ins / 85.7 x 113 cm) GBP 7,700. EDINBURGH, 23 March 1993, *Glasgow Tenement* (oil on canvas, 29 1/2 x 26 1/2 ins / 75 x 67 cm) GBP 11,500. EDINBURGH, 13 May 1993, *Urchin in Red Pullover, Seated* (pastel/glazed paper, 11 ins / 27 cm, 1 1/4 x 8 3/4 ins/3 x 22.5 cm) GBP 3,300. GLASGOW, 1 Feb 1994, *Gypsy Encampment* (watercolour and gouache, 6 1/2 x 9 1/2 ins / 16.5 x 24 cm) GBP 2,415. PERTH, 30 Aug 1994, *Cottage* (oil on canvas, 9 3/4 x 14 ins / 25 x 35.5 cm) GBP 4,830. GLASGOW, 14 Feb 1995, *Child in Blue* (oil on card, 10 1/2 x 8 ins / 26.5 x 20.5 cm) GBP 1,380. PERTH, 29 Aug 1995, *Snow I* (oil on canvas, 24 x 27 1/4 ins / 61 x 69 cm) GBP 7,820. EDINBURGH, 23 May 1996, *Street Market in France* (oil on canvas, 24 x 30 ins / 61 x 76.2 cm) GBP 17,250. PERTH, 26 Aug 1996, *Catterline Bay* (oil on card, 11 1/2 x 48 ins / 29 x 122 cm) GBP 6,325. GLASGOW, 11 Dec 1996, *Glasgow Boy* (oil on canvas, 18 x 12 ins / 45.5 x 30.5 cm) GBP 11,500. GLASGOW, 20 Feb 1997, *Little Girl in a Push Chair: Study for 'Glasgow Harbour Children'* (pastel/buff-coloured paper, 11 1/2 x 6 1/4 ins / 29.2 x 15.8 cm) GBP 4,830. LONDON, 28 Oct 1999, *The Stove. Cottages in a Landscape* (oil on canvas, double-sided, 36 x 18 ins / 91 x 46 cm) GBP 10,000. LONDON, 26 Oct 2000, *Shipbuilders' Street* (c. 1951, oil on canvas, 36 x 13 ins / 91 x 34 cm) GBP 23,000. EDINBURGH, 8 Dec 2000, *Andrew with Comic* (oil on canvas, 36 x 30 ins / 92 x 77 cm) GBP 82,000. LONDON, 1 Nov 2001, *Children and Chalked Wall, Glasgow* (1958, oil on board, 9 x 11 ins / 23 x 27 cm) GBP 23,000. LONDON, 1 Nov 2001, *Between Fields of Barley, Catterline* (1960, oil on board, 48 x 54 ins / 122 x 137 cm) GBP 28,000. LONDON, 31 Oct 2002, *Beehives, Storm Approaching* (oil on board, 39 x 39 ins / 98 x 98 cm) GBP 32,000. EDINBURGH, 5 Dec 2002, *February Sunset* (oil on canvas, 20 x 20 ins / 51 x 51 cm) GBP 24,000. LONDON, 14 April 2003, *Fishing Nets* (1963, oil on board, 19 x 20 ins / 49 x 52 cm) GBP 12,000. EDINBURGH, 21 Aug 2003, *Pat Samson in a Red Jersey* (pastel, 7 x 7 ins / 17 x 17 cm) GBP 14,000. LONDON, 28 Oct 2004, *Boy in Blue Jersey* (1953, oil on canvas, 18 x 14 ins / 45 x 35 cm) GBP 23,000. LONDON, 28 Oct 2004, *Old Woman with Dog* (oil on canvas, 36 x 24 ins / 91 x 61 cm) GBP 26,000.

EARHART, John Franklin

American, 19th century.
Born 12 March 1853, in Ohio.
Active in Fernbank.
Painter. Landscapes.

John Franklin Earhart was a member of the Cincinnati Art Club, and exhibited there in 1903. He won the $100 Landscape Prize awarded by the Cincinnati Art Club.

EARL, George

British, 19th - 20th century.
Born 1824; died 1908.
Painter. Hunting scenes, sporting subjects, animals, landscapes, landscapes with figures.

George Earl exhibited frequently in London, notably at the Royal Academy from 1856. He may have been related to the landscape artist G. Earl who exhibited at the Royal Academy in 1840.

AUCTION RECORDS:

LONDON, 1 Feb 1908, *Leaving Pasture*, GBP 9; *On the Falkerk Tryst Road*, GBP 16. LONDON, 3 April 1909, *Scottish Terrier and Rat*, GBP 4. LONDON, 4 June 1909, *Stags* (two hunting paintings) GBP 33. LONDON, 9 Feb 1923, *Favourite Lap Dog* (sold with another painting, by Callow) GBP 5. LONDON, 11 Feb 1938, *Day's Bag*, GBP 17. LONDON, 20 June 1972, *Portrait of a Gentleman on Horseback* (1872) GBP 280. LONDON, 16 March 1973, *Hunting Scene*, Gns 1,100. NEW YORK, 14 May 1976, *Field Trial* (oil on canvas, 33 x 54 ins / 84 x 137 cm) USD 25,000. LONDON, 7 Oct 1981, *Thoroughbred in a Landscape* (1869, oil on canvas, 25 1/4 x 35 1/4 ins / 64 x 89.5 cm) GBP 1,600. NEW YORK, 8 June 1984, *Mare and Foal in a Landscape* (oil on canvas, 17 1/4 x 20 ins / 43.8 x 51.1 cm) USD 2,000. LONDON, 12 June 1985, *On the Moors* (1871, oil on canvas, 51 1/4 x 39 1/4 ins / 130 x 100 cm) GBP 8,800. LONDON, 23 Sept 1988, *Return from the Hunt* (1870, oil on canvas, 28 1/4 x 40 1/4 ins / 72 x 102 cm) GBP 2,860. LONDON, 22 June 1990, *Looking North: King's Cross Station* (1893, oil on canvas, 48 1/2 x 84 ins / 122.9 x 213.4 cm) GBP 264,000; *Looking South: Perth Station* (1895, oil on canvas, 48 1/2 x 84 ins / 122.9 x 213.4 cm) GBP 308,000. LONDON, 13 March 1992, *Briton, a Mastiff in the Outbuildings of a Property* (1873, oil on canvas, 40 x 54 ins / 101.6 x 137.2 cm) GBP 4,400. NEW YORK, 5 June 1992, *Queeny, a Young Pug Dog* (oil on panel, diam. 11 ins / 27.9 cm) USD 11,000. PERTH, 31 Aug 1993, *Pointers on the Trail of a Grouse* (1880, oil on canvas, 26 x 36 ins / 66 x 91.5 cm) GBP 9,430. LUDLOW, 29 Sept 1994, *Young Spaniel* (oil on panel, diam. 13 ins / 33 cm) GBP 7,590. MONACO, 7 Oct 1995, *Young Girl and her Dog* (oil on canvas, 47 1/4 x 70 3/4 ins / 120 x 180 cm) FRF 300,000. LONDON, 6 Nov 1995, *In the Brambles* (oil on card, diam. 13 1/2 ins / 34 cm) GBP 7,130. LONDON, 17 Oct 1996, *Frank, a Retriever* (oil on canvas, 19 1/2 x 26 1/2 ins / 49.5 x 67.3 cm) GBP 1,265.

EARL, Justin

British, 20th - 21st century.
Born 1959, in Oxford.
Painter. Figure compositions.

Justin Earl graduated from Winchester School of Art. He worked in the USA from 1980 to 1981 and in 1982 studied at Virginia Commonwealth University in Richmond. Earl has lived and worked in London since 1982. Earl shows groups of figures - for example, gathered around a table - and gives emphasis to their very existence. The clothes these figures wear are often printed with colourful, bright, varied motifs which give shape to the lines of their bodies. Several stories are contained in a single scene, forcing the viewer to interpret and identify the relationships between those involved, to question the representation of a world which at first glance is familiar but which gradually and inevitably creates an impression of existential unease. Some of his figures appear to be vacant, some discretely cheerful while others appear to hide. The men have a grey or dark green appearance, their heads enlarged or ridiculously angular; sometimes the body of a figure is entirely concealed by that of an animal wearing clothes and a hat, sitting among the guests. No one appears to be surprised by this presence. This perhaps represents some deviation of human identity, a mimicry whispered in the representation of certain faces, a kind of symbol of the randomness and unpredictability of life. The women are smart and colourful and have such presence that they appear to be the instigators of this strange gathering. Their large mouths, drawn features and furrowed brows contribute to this subtly disordered atmosphere. Earl exhibits regularly in London and also New York and exhibited at the Galerie Jean-Claude Riedel in Paris in 1988 and 1990.

BIBLIOGRAPHY:

Hillier, Bevis, *'Remembering the Future: Justin Earl'* in *Modern Painters,* Vol 3, No. 2, Summer 1990.

EARL, Maud

British, 19th - 20th century.
Born 1864; died 1943.
Painter, draughtswoman. Animals.

Maud Earl studied under her father George Earl. The 1908 edition of *The Sportsman's Year* contains 12 colour drawings by Maud Earl. She also painted the favourite pet dogs of Queen Victoria and Edward VII. She exhibited at the Royal Academy in London from 1884 to 1908 and then at the Paris Salon and various other English and American exhibitions.

AUCTION RECORDS:

LONDON, 23 March 1928, *Far North, End of the Expedition,* GBP 1. LONDON, 14 Feb 1936, *Three Pekinese* (1911) GBP 1. LONDON, 14 Nov 1969, *Three Pekinese Dogs,* Gns 380. LONDON, 26 April 1974, *Ace of Hearts,* Gns 1,400. LONDON, 29 June 1976, *Setters in a Landscape* (oil on canvas, 17 1/4 x 29 ins / 44 x 73.5 cm) GBP 750. LONDON, 19 April 1978, *Arab Horsemen* (four canvases, 43 1/2 x 18 1/2 ins / 110.5 x 47 cm) GBP 1,500. LONDON, 19 April 1979, *Arab Horsemen* (four canvases, 43 1/2 x 18 1/2 ins / 110.5 x 47 cm) GBP 1,500. LONDON, 20 Oct 1981, *Spaniels and Labrador at the Edge of a Wood* (1892, oil on canvas, 18 x 26 ins / 46 x 66 cm) GBP 3,400. NEW YORK, 8 June 1984, *Irish Setter in a Landscape* (oil on canvas, 34 3/4 x 41 3/4 ins / 88.3 x 106 cm) USD 5,000. LONDON, 28 Nov 1986, *Spaniel in a Landscape* (1910, oil on canvas, 18 1/4 x 24 1/2 ins / 46.5 x 62.3 cm) GBP 6,000. NEW YORK, 24 Oct 1989, *Flight of Small Blue Herons* (oil on card, 35 1/4 x 59 1/2 ins / 89.5 x 151.1 cm) USD 15,400. LONDON, 3 Nov 1989, *Michael, a Gold Cocker Spaniel* (1920, oil on canvas, 30 x 25 ins / 76.5 x 63.5 cm) GBP 5,280. LONDON, 14 Feb 1990, *Luska, a Siberian Sled Dog in a Snowy Landscape* (oil on canvas, 30 1/2 x 40 1/4 ins / 77.5 x 102.2 cm) GBP 15,400. LONDON, 15 Jan 1991, *Two Greyhounds, One Brindle and the Other White, in a Landscape* (oil on canvas, 40 1/2 x 51 ins / 102.8 x 129.5 cm) GBP 14,850. NEW YORK, 16 Oct 1991, *Spaniel Retrieving a Pheasant; Labrador Retrieving a Duck* (1924, oils on card, a pair, 40 x 26 1/2 ins / 100.7 x 67.3 cm) USD 13,200. NEW YORK, 5 June 1992, *Terrier; Spaniel* (1890, oils on canvas, a pair, each 16 x 16 ins / 40.6 x 40.6 cm) USD 15,400. NEW YORK, 13 Oct 1993, *Cockatoos* (1936, oil on card, 48 x 36 ins / 121.9 x 91.4 cm) USD 3,450. LONDON, 5 Nov 1993, *Beauty and the Beasts* (oil on canvas, 18 x 24 ins / 45.7 x 61 cm) GBP 10,350. NEW YORK, 15 Feb 1994, *A Black and Tan Basset Hound* (1890, oil on canvas, 24 x 22 ins / 61 x 55.9 cm) USD 12,650. GLASGOW, 14 Feb 1995, *Setters on the Moors* (oil on canvas, 20 x 30 ins / 50.5 x 76 cm) GBP 7,475. LONDON, 29 March 1996, *Tan and Black Pekinese with Lotus Flowers on a Shore* (1916, oil/gold silk background/card, 26 x 23 1/2 ins / 66 x 59.7 cm) GBP 9,775. NEW YORK, 11 April 1997, *Hounds* (oil on canvas, 18 x 30 ins / 45.7 x 76.2 cm) USD 9,200; *Bostwick Pond Ducks* (oils on panel, triptych, 48 1/2 x 30 1/2 ins / 123.2 x 77.5 cm and 48 1/2 x 32 1/2 ins/123.2 x 82.5 cm) USD 13,800. LONDON, 18 Dec 1997, *Dogs at Point in a Landscape,* GBP 2,070. BILLINGSHURST, 26 Jan 1999, *The Terrier's Tea* (oil on canvas, 17 x 23 ins / 44 x 59 cm) GBP 4,500. LONDON, 10 Nov 1999, *Frandley Stephanie, the Champion St Bernard* (oil on canvas, 48 x 60 ins / 121 x 152 cm) GBP 5,000. LONDON, 15 June 2000, *Three Pekingese with Macaw* (oil and gold on silk on fold screen, 71 x 72 ins / 180 x 183 cm) GBP 13,000. LONDON, 28 Nov 2000, *Best o' Spirits* (oil on canvas, 34 x 44 ins / 87 x 113 cm) GBP 15,000. NEW YORK, 6 June 2001, *On the Moor, Two Pointers* (1904, oil on canvas, 29 x 40 ins / 73 x 102 cm) USD 10,000. KNOWLE, 3 Oct 2001, *Dinette, a Champion French Bulldog* (oil on canvas, 20 x 24 ins / 50 x 61 cm) GBP 6,900. NEW YORK, 18 April 2002, *Parrot and Pekinese* (1914, oil on silk on canvas, ? x ? ins /? x ? cm) USD 8,500. LEWES, 2 Dec 2002, *Two Dachshunds* (oil on canvas, 28 x 36 ins / 71 x 91 cm) GBP 6,600. BOSTON, 7 March 2003, *Toy Spaniels, King Charles and Rudy, The Pillow is the Best* (oil on canvas, 18 x 24 ins / 46 x 61 cm) USD 26,000. NEW YORK, 5 Dec 2003, *What We Have We'll Hold, Portrait of Dimboola the Champion Bulldog* (1896, oil on canvas, 30 x 40 ins / 77 x 102 cm) USD 55,000. NEW YORK, 18 May 2004, *Two Sealyham Dogs* (1895, oil on canvas, 26 x 22 ins / 66 x 56 cm) USD 18,000. NEW YORK, 3 June 2004, *German Shepherd and Parrot* (1917, oil on canvas, 47 x 57 ins / 119 x 145 cm) USD 30,000.

EARL, Ralph. See **EARLE Ralph**

EARL, Thomas

British, 19th century.
Born 1815; died 1885.
Painter. Animals.

Thomas Earl exhibited very frequently in London, between 1836 and 1885, at the Royal Academy, the British Institution and, chiefly, at the Suffolk Street Gallery.

AUCTION RECORDS:

LONDON, 28 April 1924, *Spaniel* (sold with 'An Imminent Battle' by Fannie Moody) GBP 21. LONDON, 20 Jan 1981, *Kittens Playing* (oil on canvas, 18 x 24 ins / 46 x 61 cm) GBP 360. LONDON, 5 Oct 1984, *A Terrier* (oil on canvas, diam. 13 3/4 ins / 34.9 cm) GBP 1,700. LONDON, 22 Feb 1985, *Terrier with a Rabbit* (1859, oil on canvas, 21 1/2 x 18 ins / 54.5 x 45.7 cm) GBP 1,900. NEW YORK, 9 June 1988, *I Hear a Voice* (oil on canvas, 28 x 36 ins / 71.1 x 91.5 cm) USD 3,300. LONDON, 14 Feb 1990, *Head of a Terrier* (oil on canvas, diam. 12 1/2 ins / 31.7 cm) GBP 1,100. LONDON, 1 Nov 1990, *Reward* (1854, oil on canvas, 26 x 26 ins / 66 x 66 cm) GBP 4,950. LONDON, 15 Jan 1991, *Head of a Terrier in the Highlands* (oil on card/panel, 10 x 7 1/4 ins / 25.3 x 18.1 cm) GBP 935. NEW YORK, 9 Feb 1999, *Winning Look* (1864, oil on board, 17 x 13 ins / 43 x 33 cm) USD 19,000. NEW YORK, 15 Feb 2000, *Waiting for Dinner* (oil on canvas, 18 x 12 ins / 45 x 30 cm) USD 6,000. DORCHESTER, 29 June 2000, *Terrier with a Rabbit* (1879, oil on board, 15 x 17 ins / 38 x 43 cm) GBP 1,500. BUENOS AIRES, 3 July 2002, *Head of a Dog* (1870, oil on canvas) USD 6,175. LONDON, 28 Aug 2002, *Skye Terrier* (1868, oil on canvas, 22 x 26 ins / 55 x 66 cm) GBP 4,500. NEW YORK, 11 Feb 2003, *English Setter* (1870, oil on canvas on board, 16 x 16 ins / 41 x 41 cm) USD 9,500. LONDON, 12 June 2003, *Pet Goldfish* (oil on paper on canvas, 11 x 15 ins / 28 x 38 cm) GBP 1,700.

EARL, Thomas Percy
British, 20th century.
Born 1874; died 1947.
Painter (gouache), watercolourist. Sporting subjects, animals.
Thomas Percy Earl was active from 1900 to 1930. He specialised in equestrian scenes.
AUCTION RECORDS:
LONDON, 30 May 1985, *Racehorse and Jockey* (gouache, 13 1/2 x 20 ins / 34 x 50.5 cm) GBP 850. LONDON, 12 June 1986, *Ascetic Silver with the Hon. Aubrey Hastings up in a Landscape* (1906, oil on canvas, 23 1/2 x 30 ins / 59.6 x 76.2 cm) GBP 4,500. LONDON, 30 Jan 1991, *Horses at the Weigh-in with their Jockeys* (1900, gouache, 15 x 22 ins / 38 x 56 cm) GBP 1,980. NEW YORK, 7 June 1991, *Enfield Mounted by his Jockey* (1934, oil on canvas, 18 x 24 ins / 45.7 x 61 cm) USD 7,150. NEW YORK, 5 June 1992, *Jason, a Bay, in a Landscape* (1913, oil on canvas, 27 1/4 x 34 1/4 ins / 69.2 x 87 cm) USD 7,975. LONDON, 13 Nov 1996, *Precipitation Mounted by his Jockey* (oil on canvas, 25 x 30 ins / 63.5 x 76 cm) GBP 4,370. LONDON, 28 May 1999, *Insurance* (oil on canvas, 25 x 30 ins / 63 x 76 cm) GBP 5,500. LONDON, 22 June 1999, *Precipitation with Jockey R. Beasley Up* (1939, oil on canvas, 25 x 30 ins / 63 x 76 cm) GBP 3,600. NEW YORK, 15 Feb 2000, *Binks, Favourite Pup* (1943, oil on canvas, 14 x 10 ins / 35 x 25 cm) USD 2,400. NEW YORK, 7 June 2001, *Hock, Bay Hunter in a Landscape* (1915, oil on canvas, 28 x 34 ins / 70 x 86 cm) USD 15,000. LONDON, 11 June 2002, *Portrait of Frank Greswold Williams* (1907, oil on canvas, 30 x 41 ins / 77 x 103 cm) GBP 16,000. NEW YORK, 28 Oct 2004, *Walter Jeffords Sr on his Favourite Grey Field Mare* (1919, oil on canvas, 19 x 17 ins / 49 x 44 cm) USD 40,000. NEW YORK, 28 Oct 2004, *Man-o-War* (1920, oil on canvas, 30 x 25 ins / 77 x 64 cm) USD 55,000.

EARL, William Robert
British, 19th century.
Active in London.
Painter. Landscapes.
William Earl exhibited frequently in London, notably at the Royal Academy, the British Institution and at the Suffolk Street Gallery.
AUCTION RECORDS:
LONDON, 16 May 1929, *Wood with Lake and Children* (1820) GBP 16. LEOMINSTER, 6 Feb 2002, *Chertsey Preserve, River Thames, View of the Eeltrap Weir* (1836, oil on canvas, 27 x 37 ins / 69 x 94 cm) GBP 3,600.

EARLE, Augustus
British, 19th century.
Born 1793, in London; died 1838, in London.
Painter, watercolourist, draughtsman. Portraits, landscapes, seascapes.
Augustus Earle was the son of the painter Ralph Earle. He was nicknamed 'the wandering painter' because of his love of travelling, and from his travels he developed a love of nature. An intimate friend of Lesli and Morse, Earle worked with them at the Royal Academy in 1813, but they lost contact with each other once he began his travels. He visited all the Mediterranean coasts, Africa, the USA and the Cape of Good Hope. He was shipwrecked on Tristan da Cunha, where he lived for six months in a hut with the local inhabitants until a boat finally came to take him away. After visiting Van Diemen's Land (now Tasmania), New South Wales and New Zealand, he returned to Sydney, then went to the Caroline Islands and stopped at Madras, where he earned money as a portrait painter. Unhappy with his situation, he travelled to Pondicherry, where he embarked for France and finally returned home.

He published a series of views of New South Wales, an account of his nine-month stay in New Zealand in 1832 and a journal of his stay on Tristan da Cunha. He sent pictures to the Royal Academy between 1806 and 1815 and in 1837 and 1839, including *The Judgment of Midas, Life on the Ocean* and *A Travellers' Camp in Australia*.
AUCTION RECORDS:
LONDON, 4 May 1926, *Views of New South Wales and New Zealand* (drawing, series of 60) GBP 1,800. LONDON, 22 June 1967, *Portrait of Aranghi Tooker, New Zealand,* GBP 700. LONDON, 10 June 1986, *Panorama of Mauritius with Boats in the Bay of Port-Louis* (watercolour and pencil/three joined sheets, 9 1/2 x 43 1/4 ins / 24.2 x 109.8 cm) GBP 8,000. LONDON, 28 Sept 2001, *View of Part of the Ruins of Lepida, Barbary* (watercolour, 9 x 21 ins / 23 x 53 cm) GBP 2,500.

EARLE, Charles
British, 19th century.
Born 1832; died 8 April 1893, in London.
Painter (gouache), watercolourist, draughtsman. Landscapes with figures, urban landscapes.
Charles Earle was a member of the Royal Institute of Painters in Watercolours and exhibited in London, particularly at the Royal Academy and the Suffolk Street Gallery, from 1857. He also visited France.
AUCTION RECORDS:
LONDON, 29 Jan 1910, *Early Spring at Eccles. Bourn Glenn* (watercolour) GBP 3. LONDON, 5 March 1910, *The Windmill* (watercolour) GBP 8; *Scene in a Village* (watercolour) GBP 10. LONDON, 7 March 1910, *On the City Walls at Avignon* (watercolour) GBP 9. LONDON, 17 June 1910, *A Farm near the South Downs* (watercolour) GBP 5. LONDON, 15 May 1984, *The Rectory Garden* (watercolour heightened with white, 20 x 13 3/4 ins / 50.8 x 35 cm) GBP 1,300. LONDON, 10 Oct 1985, *Marketplace in Venice* (watercolour heightened with gouache, 21 1/4 x 15 1/2 ins / 54 x 39.5 cm) GBP 850. EDINBURGH, 22 Nov 1988, *Fruit Market at Venice* (watercolour and gouache, 13 1/2 x 23 ins / 34.3 x 58.4 cm) GBP 800. LONDON, 25 Jan 1989, *Fruit Market at Venice* (watercolour and gouache, 13 1/2 x 23 ins / 34 x 58.5 cm) GBP 2,200. LONDON, 14 June 1991, *Evening Walk in the Manor Park* (pencil and watercolour heightened with white, 22 x 13 1/2 ins / 56 x 34.3 cm) GBP 1,980. LONDON, 7 Oct 1992, *Flower Market in Brussels* (watercolour, 12 1/2 x 19 ins / 32 x 48.5 cm) GBP 1,650. LONDON, 9 June 1994, *Whitby* (watercolour and gouache, 11 x 19 1/4 ins / 27 x 49 cm) GBP 977. LONDON, 7 June 1996, *Fountain, Villa Borghese, Rome* (pencil and watercolour, 19 1/4 x 29 1/2 ins / 48.8 x 74.9 cm) GBP 1,265. DORCHESTER, 26 Oct 2000, *Midsummer Flowers* (watercolour, 10 x 21 ins / 25 x 53 cm) GBP 1,200. DORCHESTER, 26 Oct 2000, *City of Norwich from Mousehold Common* (watercolour and gouache, 13 x 22 ins / 33 x 56 cm) GBP 1,400. LONDON, 14 March 2001, *Summer Evening* (watercolour and gouache, 30 x 19 ins / 75 x 47 cm) GBP 1,500. NORFOLK, 24 Nov 2001, *City of Norwich from Mousehold* (watercolour, 13 x 21 ins / 33 x 54 cm) GBP 1,600. LONDON, 4 Nov 2003, *View from the Palatine Hill, Rome* (watercolour, 15 x 21 ins / 37 x 54 cm) GBP 1,400.

EARLE, Cornelia
American, 19th - 20th century.
Born 25 November 1863, in Houtsville (Alabama).
Painter, teacher.
Cornelia Earle was a pupil of G.L. Noyes and was awarded first prize by the Columbia Art Association in 1922.

EARLE, Elinor
American, 19th - 20th century.
Born in Philadelphia.
Painter.
Elinor Earle studied in Paris, and won the Grand Prix at the Museum of Fine Art in Philadelphia, and the Mary Smith prize in 1902. She ceased painting at the age of 40, and only a few of her pieces are extant, mostly in the homes of relatives.

EARLE, Eyvind
American, 20th century.
Born April 26 1916, in New York; died July 20, 2000.
Painter.

A restless traveller, Earle is best remembered for his serigraphs and the five murals he designed for Disneyland. He preferred solo exhibitions, from the first one he held in Ascain, France, in 1929. After moving to Carmel, California in 1988, he exhibited regularly at Gallery 21.

BIBLIOGRAPHY:

Earle, Eyvind, *Horizon Bound on a Bicycle. The Autobiography of Eyvind Earle*, autobiography, Eyvind Earle Publishing, Carmel (CA), 1991. Earle, Eyvind, *Complete Graphics of Eyvind Earle and Selected Poems and Writings, 1991-2000*, album, Eyvind Earle Publishing, Carmel (CA), 1998.

AUCTION RECORDS:

LOS ANGELES, 17 March 1981, *Big Sur Country* (1973, oil on canvas, 20 x 18 ins / 50.8 x 45.7 cm) USD 1,900. NEW YORK, 7 May 1996, *Big Sur* (1972, oil/synthetic resin, 28 x 22 ins / 71.2 x 55.9 cm) USD 8,050.

EARLE, J. H.
British, 19th century.
Painter. History painting.

J. H. Earle sent several canvases to the British Insititution and to the Suffolk Street Gallery from 1842 and 1845, one of which was *Scene from Lalla Rookh* in 1845.

EARLE, James
American, 18th century.
Born 1751, in Leicester (Massachusetts); died 1796, in Charleston, of yellow fever.
Painter. Portraits.

James Earle was probably the brother of Ralph Earle and exhibited at the Royal Academy in London between 1787 and 1796.

AUCTION RECORDS:

NEW YORK, 22 Sept 1993, *Frances Hortin and her Sister* (oils on canvas, a pair, each 24 x 20 1/4 ins / 61.2 x 51.5 cm) USD 9,200.

EARLE, Kate
British, 19th century.
Active in London.
Painter. Genre scenes.

Kate Earle exhibited in London on several occasions between 1887 and 1893.

EARLE, Lawrence Carmichael
American, 19th - 20th century.
Born 1845, in New York; died 1921.
Painter, watercolourist. Genre scenes, landscapes, still-lifes.

Lawrence Earle studied in Munich, Florence and Rome. An associate of the National Academy, he was also a member of the Watercolours Society and an honorary member of the Art Institute of Chicago.

AUCTION RECORDS:

NEW YORK, 3 April 1903, *Spring*, USD 200. NEW YORK, 10 March 1906, *The Fisherman*, USD 170. PORTLAND, 17 July 1982, *Woman in Landscape* (watercolour, 16 x 12 ins / 40.5 x 30.5 cm) USD 900. NEW YORK, 27 Jan 1984, *Floral Still-life* (1876, oil on canvas, 12 x 10 ins / 30.5 x 25.4 cm) USD 2,000. NEW YORK, 10 March 1993, *Marsh* (1908, oil on canvas, 35 1/2 x 49 ins / 90.2 x 124.5 cm) USD 6,900. NEW YORK, 21 May 1996, *At the Doorway* (1883, watercolour/paper, 28 x 19 1/2 ins / 71 x 49.5 cm) USD 1,610.

EARLE, Olive
British, 20th century.
Born 27 December 1888, in London.
Painter. Seascapes.

EARLE, Ralph, or Earl
American, 18th century.
Born 11 May 1751, in Worcester (Massachusetts); died 1801, in Bolton (Connecticut).
Painter. History painting, figures, portraits, landscapes, landscapes with figures.

Ralph Earle was a self-taught painter who started life as a shoe repairer and ended it as a judge of the Supreme Court of Connecticut. One of his most remarkable portraits, *Roger Sherman*, was painted between 1775 and 1777. In 1778 he went to England and lived in Norwich and London, becoming a pupil of Benjamin West and exhibiting at the Royal Academy in 1783, 1784 and 1785. He married and had several children, but this did not prevent him leaving his family and returning alone to America in 1786. He painted *Niagara Falls* and portraits of George III, Dr Dwitg and the president of Yale University.

Earle painted both portraits and landscapes, sometimes combining the two genres, as in *Mrs William Moseley and her Son Charles*, in which the figures stand against a background of views of Connecticut that are as interesting as the portraits themselves. He treated his sitters with an archaising simplicity, uniting, for example, the colours of Sherman's clothes with those used in the background. Earle was one of the few artists of the late 18th century to show any interest in the American landscape. It is thought that his four *Scenes of the Battle of Lexington*, painted in 1775, were the first American historical paintings.

In 1989 Earle was represented in the exhibition *200 Ans de Peinture Américaine. Collection du Wadsworth Atheneum* (*200 Years of American Painting. The Wadsworth Atheneum Collection*) at the Galeries Lafayette in Paris.

BIBLIOGRAPHY:

Connecticut Portraits by Ralph Earl, 1751-1801, exhibition catalogue, Gall. of Fine Arts, Yale University Press, New Haven, 1935. Sawitsky, William, *Ralph Earl, 1751-1801: catalogue*, L. F. White Co., New York, 1945. Kornhauser, Elizabeth Mankin/Bushman, Richard L./Kornhauser, Stephen H./Ribeiro, Aileen, *Ralph Earl: the Face of the Young Republic*, Yale University Press, New Haven, Wadsworth Atheneum, Hartford, 1991.

MUSEUMS AND GALLERIES:

HARTFORD (Wadsworth Atheneum): *Oliver Ellsworth and Abigail Wolcott Ellsworth* (*Double Portrait of Oliver Ellsworth and Abigail Wolcott Ellsworth*) (1792, oil on canvas) - NEW YORK (Metropolitan Mus. of Art): *Lady Williams and her Child* (1783) - WORCESTER, MA (AM): *Looking East from Denny Hill* (1800, oil on canvas).

AUCTION RECORDS:

LONDON, 8 Nov 1928, *Mr James Madison, Fourth President of the United States, with his Wife and Three Children*, GBP 78. NEW YORK, 12 Nov 1931, *General Gabriel Christie*, USD 525. NEW YORK, 16 April 1936, *Young Girl with a Bird*, USD 525. LONDON, 23 April 1941, *General Andrew Jackson, President of the United States, in Uniform*, GBP 52. LONDON, 6 March 1942, *Portrait of a Notable with his Wife and Family*, GBP 31. LONDON, 6 Nov 1959, *Portrait of Colonel George Onslow*, GBP 630. NEW YORK, 3 Feb 1978, *Portrait of Mr Loganbank* (oil on canvas, 36 1/2 x 30 1/4 ins / 92.7 x 76.8 cm) USD 2,100. NEW YORK, 30 Jan 1980, *Portrait of Dr Seth Bird* (1798, oil on canvas, 30 x 24 ins / 76.2 x 61 cm) USD 4,000. NEW YORK, 26 Oct 1985, *Nathaniel Ruggles; Martha Ruggles, Massachusetts* (oils on canvas, a pair, 45 1/4 x 36 1/4 ins / 115 x 92 cm) USD 40,000. NEW YORK, 25 May 1995, *Portrait of a Child* (oil on canvas, 25 3/4 x 21 ins / 65.4 x 53.3 cm) USD 129,000. NEW YORK, 23 May 1996, *Portrait of John Phelps* (1792, oil on canvas, 77 x 49 ins / 195.6 x 124.5 cm) USD 233,500.

EARLE, Thomas
British, 19th century.
Born 1810, in Hull; died 1876, in London.
Sculptor. Statues, busts, groups.
Thomas Earle was a pupil at the Royal Academy. He began in 1834 and exhibited up to 1873. Among his works shown were: *Hercules Delivering Hesione from the Sea Monster* (1840, gold medal); *Ophelia* (1848); *Queen Victoria* (1864); *Statue of Edward I* for Hull city; *Miranda* (1865).

EARLE, Winthrop
American, 19th century.
Born 1870, in Yonkers; died 2 March 1902, in New York.
Sculptor.
Winthrop Earle first studied sculpture in New York with St-Gaudens, then worked in Paris with Rodin and at the Académie Colarossi. On his return to America he became a member of the Art Students League.

EARLES, Chester
British, 19th century.
Active in London.
Painter. Portraits.
Chester Earles exhibited frequently in London between 1842 and 1863.

EARLEY, James Parrington
American, 19th century.
Born 27 September 1856, in Birmingham, England; died 1906.
Active in Washington.
Painter.
After studying at the Royal Academy in London, James Parrington Earley went to the USA, where he took American citizenship in 1882. He won medals at a number of exhibitions.

EARLOM, Richard
British, 18th - 19th century.
Born 1743, in London; died 1822, in London.
Engraver.
Richard Earlom was a pupil of Cipriani, and was, it is said, the first to use the point in mezzotint engraving. His first work in 1777 was the engraving of 200 plates after the drawings of the *Liber Veritatis* (*Book of Truth*) of Claude Lorraine, which were for the most part in the possession of the Crown. Earlom is chiefly known for his groupings of flowers after Huysum and Van Os, and he also did etchings. He sometimes signed himself *Poirche (Henry)*.

He exhibited a *Faun dancing* in 1762 and *Pyrrhus before Glaucus* after Bemjamin West in 1767, both at the Free Society of Artists. Among his main works were *Susannah and the Elders*, after Rembrandt (Bodemuseum, Berlin); *The Holy Family*, after Guercino; *The Water Mill*, after Hobbema; *King George III and his Family*, after J. Zoffany; *Portrait of Lord Heathfield*, after Reynolds; *Portrait of Lady Hamilton*, after Romney; *Tobias and the Angel*, after Salvator Rosa; *The Last Supper*, after B. West; *Portrait of G.C.Berkely*, after Thomas Gainsborough.

MUSEUMS AND GALLERIES:
LONDON (Houghton Hall): *Still-life with Fruit and Flowers* (after J. Van Huysum) - ST PETERSBURG (Hermitage): *David and Absalom*.
AUCTION RECORDS:
LONDON, 13 Sept 1982, *Tulips* (colour mezzotint, after Reinagle, 18 3/4 x 14 ins / 47.5 x 35.5 cm) GBP 650. YORK, 12 Nov 1991, *Bird Song* (aquatint, 16 1/2 x 22 1/2 ins / 42 x 57 cm) GBP 990. PARIS, 25 March 1994, *Still-life with Flowers; Still-life with Fruit* (1778, engraving, a pair, each 20 x 15 1/4 ins / 50.5 x 39 cm) FRF 18,000. LONDON, 13 Nov 1997, *Smithy* (1773, mezzotint, 2 x 2 1/4 ins / 4.80 x 5.90 cm) GBP 5,520. HAMBURG, 27 May 1999, *Flower Piece. Fruit Piece* (1778, 1781, colour stencils, a pair, 20 x 15 ins / 50 x 39 cm) DEM 10,000. MUNICH, 6 June 2000, *Flower Piece. Fruit Piece* (mezzotint etching, 20 x 15 ins / 50 x 39 cm) DEM 9,600. LONDON, 7 June 2000, *Colonel Mordaunt's Cock Match* (hand-coloured mezzotint, 19 x 26 ins / 49 x 66 cm) GBP 2,600. HAMBURG, 7 June 2001, *Iron Forge* (etching, 19 x 23 ins / 48 x 59 cm) DEM 5,000. LONDON, 6 July 2001, *Flower Piece. Fruit Piece* (1778, 1781, mezzotint, a pair, 22 x 17 ins / 55 x 42 cm) GBP 5,000. PARIS, 13 Nov 2002, *Book of Truth* (etching) EUR 6,000.

EARLOM, William
British, 18th century.
Born 1772, in England; died 1789.
Painter.
William Earlom, was the son of Richard Earlom, and showed great promise of high artistic ability. He died at the age of 17.

EARNSHAW, M.
British, 19th century.
Born in the second half of the 19th century, in England.
Active in London.
Painter, pastellist.
M. Earnshaw specialised in compositions of flora and fauna. He also did landscapes.
AUCTION RECORDS:
LONDON, 30 June 1922, *Spring, Song Thrush with a Flower* (pastel) GBP 2; *Summer, Plover and Frogs; Winter, Crows in the Snow* (two pastels) GBP 4.

EARP, Frederick
British, 19th - 20th century.
Born 1828; died 1914.
Painter, watercolourist.
MUSEUMS AND GALLERIES:
BRIGHTON (Brighton & Hove Museums): *Manor House, Hangleton* (1850, watercolour).

EARP, G. van
Dutch, 19th century.
Painter. Architectural views.
While G. van Earp appears to be Dutch, he lived primarily in England. He exhibited from 1871 to 1884 in Suffolk Street.
MUSEUMS AND GALLERIES:
NOTTINGHAM: (watercolour).
AUCTION RECORDS:
LONDON, 24 Feb 1908, *View of Venice and Cathedral Entrance* (drawing) GBP 2. LONDON, 1 June 1909, *The Conversion of Saul*, GBP 3.

EARP, Henry
British, 19th century.
Painter. Horse racing scenes, animals.
Henry Earp worked at Brighton, and exhibited in London from 1871 to 1884.
AUCTION RECORDS:
LONDON, 8 Nov 1928, *Jockey on Horseback and Trainer Standing near a Pony*, GBP 6. SCARBOROUGH, 15 March 1999, *Cattle Watering. Horses in a Wooded Landscape* (watercolour, a pair, 29 x 21 ins / 74 x 53 cm) GBP 1,700. HASLEMERE, 24 Nov 1999, *Cattle Watering, Cottages and Mill. Figures and Horses on a Country Track* (watercolour heightened with white, a pair, 9 x 7 ins / 23 x 18 cm) GBP 1,050. BURY ST EDMUNDS, 29 June 2000, *On the Way to Market* (oil on canvas, 8 x 12 ins / 20 x 30 cm) GBP 2,300. BATH, 27 Nov 2000, *Drovers* (watercolour, 20 x 29 ins / 51 x 74 cm) GBP 1,150. LONDON, 4 Sept 2001, *Cattle at a Waterhole* (oil

on canvas, 12 x 16 ins / 30 x 40 cm) GBP 1,150. LONDON, 4 Sept 2001, *Horses on a Country Road* (oil on canvas, 16 x 12 ins / 40 x 30 cm) GBP 1,600. BISHOPS STORTFORD, 6 Feb 2002, *Figures and Animals on a Wooded Lane* (oil on canvas, 30 x 24 ins / 75 x 62 cm) GBP 3,000. NEWBURY, 18 Sept 2002, *Beside the Cottage Door. First Riding Lesson* (oil on canvas, a pair, 8 x 10 ins / 20 x 25 cm) GBP 2,400. LEYBURN, 19 Nov 2003, *Landscape and Cattle* (oil on board, 12 x 16 ins / 30 x 40 cm) GBP 1,100. LEYBURN, 19 Nov 2003, *River Landscape with Cattle, Sheep and Figures nearby* (1887, oil on canvas, 36 x 50 ins / 91 x 127 cm) GBP 2,600. NOTTINGHAM, 22 April 2004, *Hauling Timber in Calke Park, Derbyshire* (pencil and watercolour heightened with white, 19 x 29 ins / 49 x 74 cm) GBP 9,000. LONDON, 27 May 2004, *Homeward Bound* (oil on canvas, 30 x 25 ins / 76 x 63 cm) GBP 1,500.

EARP, Henry (Senior)
British, 19th - 20th century.
Born 1831; died 1914.
Painter, watercolourist. Landscapes.

MUSEUMS AND GALLERIES:
SYDNEY: *Landscape.*

AUCTION RECORDS:
LONDON, 3 April 1909, *Sunset*, GBP 1. LONDON, 28 July 1909, *The Thames at Richmond; On the Arun*, GBP 5; *Evening near Chichester; Landscape with Animals*, GBP 3. LONDON, 13 June 1910, *Wells Cathedral*, GBP 1. LONDON, 25 July 1983, *Wooden Cart on a Forest Path; Wooded Landscape* (oils on canvas, a pair, 33 x 26 ins / 84 x 66 cm) GBP 920. LONDON, 12 March 1985, *Worcester Cathedral from the River Severn* (oil on panel, 9 3/4 x 11 3/4 ins / 25 x 30 cm) GBP 900. LONDON, 25 Jan 1989, *Cattle Drinking* (watercolour, 7 x 16 1/2 ins / 17.5 x 42 cm) GBP 550. LONDON, 25-26 April 1990, *Salisbury Cathedral; Environs of Ballater in Scotland* (watercolours, a pair, each 10 x 13 ins / 25.5 x 33 cm) GBP 1,650. LONDON, 1 Nov 1990, *Harvest Scene with a Cart on a Wooded Path* (watercolour heightened with white, 22 x 16 ins / 55.9 x 40.7 cm) GBP 935. LONDON, 19 Dec 1991, *Cattle Grazing near a Wood with a Castle in the Background* (watercolour, 10 x 14 3/4 ins / 25.7 x 37.7 cm) GBP 715.

EASLING, J. C.
British, 19th century.
Engraver.

J.C. Easling was a pupil of Turner, with whom he often collaborated. He engraved portraits of Dr J. Andrews, General Sir Thomas Picton and the actor Daniel Terry. He exhibited from 1825 to 1833 at the Society of British Artists in London.

EAST, Alfred (Sir)
British, 19th - 20th century.
Born 1849, in Kettering; died 1913, in London.
Painter (including gouache), watercolourist, engraver, draughtsman. Genre scenes, landscapes, landscapes with figures.

Alfred East originally intended to work in commerce and did not begin studying art until 1872 in Glasgow. He then went to Paris where he studied under Robert-Fleury and William Bouguereau. He later returned to Glasgow and eventually moved to London. He was a member of the Royal Institution and the Royal Society and became an associate member of the Royal Academy in 1899.

East was closely connected with the London art scene and played an important role in the artistic groups to which he belonged. He is considered a representative of late 19th-century English landscape painting and was also an engraver of note.

He was awarded a gold medal in Paris in 1889 at the Exposition Universelle. He also regularly took part in Royal Academy exhibitions.

ALFRED EAST

MUSEUMS AND GALLERIES:
BIRMINGHAM (Mus. and AG): *Hayle, from Lelant, Cornwall* (oil); *Reedy Mere and Sunlit Hills* (oil); *Village Scene, Japan* (1889, watercolour and pencil) - LEEDS (City AG): *River Scene, Algeciras* (drawing); *The Golden Valley* (oil on canvas); *Afternoon on the River Somme* (oil on canvas) - LONDON (Victoria and Albert Mus.): *Lake Bieva, Japan* - SYDNEY: *Cambourne Valley, Berkshire; View of the Clyde at Helensburgh.*

AUCTION RECORDS:
LONDON, 15 June 1908, *Lambourne Valley*, GBP 10. LONDON, 10 June 1909, *Shepherds*, GBP 67. LONDON, 6 Dec 1909, *Fryiyama; Rocky River*, GBP 8; *Setting Sun; Hayle from Lulant Pool*, GBP 6. LONDON, 18 Nov 1921, *Moonlight* (drawing) GBP 42. LONDON, 27 Jan 1922, *Ferry* (drawing); *Harem Guard* (drawing, collection) GBP 19. LONDON, 17 March 1922, *Last Rays of the Sun* (1885) GBP 31; *Château de Nemours* (drawing) GBP 35. LONDON, 21 April 1922, *Silent Lake* (drawing) GBP 15. LONDON, 9 June 1922, *Spring*, GBP 33. LONDON, 20 July 1922, *Country Road at Sunset*, GBP 9; *Oriental Scene* (drawing) GBP 6. LONDON, 25-26 July 1922, *Sacred Mountain* (1887) GBP 6. LONDON, 27 Nov 1922, *Aix-les-Bains Town Hall* (drawing) GBP 19. LONDON, 8 Dec 1922, *On the Edge of the Cotswolds*, GBP 5. LONDON, 28 May 1923, *Near Cromer* (drawing) GBP 16. LONDON, 15 Feb 1924, *Forest Scene in Kent*, GBP 12. LONDON, 28 April 1924, *Lake Shore*, GBP 5. LONDON, 16 May 1924, *Angler*, GBP 18. LONDON, 30 May 1924, *Citadel in Cairo*, GBP 168. LONDON, 19 Dec 1924, *Near Mont Blanc* (drawing) GBP 13. LONDON, 27 Feb 1925, *On the Banks of the Tagus, Toledo* (drawing) GBP 4. LONDON, 20 March 1925, *Grey Day in Picardy*, GBP 56. LONDON, 20 April 1925, *Dawn*, GBP 15. LONDON, 18 May 1925, *Corner of Normandy* (drawing) GBP 10. LONDON, 8 June 1925, *Early Morning*, GBP 27. LONDON, 8 March 1926, *O'Burns Country* (drawing) GBP 4. LONDON, 31 March 1926, *In Sicily* (drawing) GBP 18; *Silent Lake* (drawing) GBP 5; *Spring on the Coast* (drawing) GBP 5. LONDON, 18 June 1926, *All Saints Church, Northampton* (drawing) GBP 7. LONDON, 16 July 1926, *Japanese Village*, GBP 14; *First Days of Summer*, GBP 33; *Nightfall*, GBP 14. LONDON, 26 July 1926, *The Somme*, GBP 18. LONDON, 10 Dec 1926, *Moon over a Castle*, GBP 22. LONDON, 28 March 1927, *View of Nikko, Japan* (drawing) GBP 15. LONDON, 1 April 1927, *In the Cornfields* (drawing) GBP 5. LONDON, 22 April 1927, *Angler*, GBP 9; *Grey Day in Picardy*, GBP 27. LONDON, 27 Nov 1927, *Angler* (drawing) GBP 10. LONDON, 12 March 1928, *Lake* (drawing) GBP 5; *Tansor in the Valley of the Nene*, GBP 10. LONDON, 13 Oct 1930, *Village Gossips*, GBP 5. LONDON, 28 Nov 1930, *Joyful Spring*, GBP 9. LONDON, 13 July 1931, *Market Square, Segovia* (watercolour) GBP 2. LONDON, 26 Nov 1931, *Joyful Spring*, GBP 21. NEW YORK, 17-18 May 1934, *Clearing*, USD 90. LONDON, 11 June 1934, *Peasant Woman* (drawing) GBP 5. LONDON, 2 Nov 1934, *On the Edge of the Moor* (sold with 'Mykonos of Delos' by W. B. Richmont and 'Café in Algiers' by Leighton) GBP 16. LONDON, 30 Nov 1934, *Picardy Landscape*, GBP 10. LONDON, 21-24 Feb 1936, *Landing* (drawing) GBP 13. LONDON, 8-18 July 1940, *Road Scene* (drawing) GBP 7. GLASGOW, 3 March 1943, *Farm Scene: Horses Drinking*, GBP 24. GLASGOW, 3 March 1944, *In Marshland*, GBP 25. NEW YORK, 31 May 1945, *Dance in the Woods*, USD 210. LONDON, 21 March 1972, *Landscape*, GBP 270. LONDON, 16 July 1973, *St Ives, Cornwall*, GBP 550. LONDON, 11 June 1976, *Sunset* (oil on canvas, 40 x 50 ins / 101.5 x 127 cm) GBP 480. LONDON, 10 May 1978, *Summer Landscape, Norfolk* (oil on

canvas, 19 1/4 x 29 1/4 ins / 49 x 74.5 cm) GBP 1,000. SYDNEY, 10 Sept 1979, *Blackthorn* (1885, oil on canvas, 30 1/4 x 25 1/4 ins / 77 x 64 cm) AUD 2,000. LONDON, 8 May 1981, *Fishermen in a Wooded River Landscape* (oil on canvas, 26 x 47 1/2 ins / 66 x 120.6 cm) GBP 3,000. LONDON, 25 May 1983, *Fruit Market, Venice* (oil on canvas, 42 1/4 x 59 3/4 ins / 107 x 152 cm) GBP 2,500. LONDON, 18 April 1984, *New Neighbourhood* (watercolour/pencil outlines, 21 1/2 x 39 ins / 54.4 x 99 cm) GBP 420. LONDON, 13 Nov 1985, *Wooded Landscape with Pond* (watercolour, 28 x 36 ins / 71 x 91.5 cm) GBP 4,800. LONDON, 12 Nov 1986, *In the Orchard* (oil on canvas, 40 x 59 3/4 ins / 101.5 x 152 cm) GBP 9,500. LONDON, 4 March 1987, *Kyoto* (watercolour heightened with gouache, 14 x 20 ins / 35.5 x 51 cm) GBP 1,900. LONDON, 29 July 1988, *Shepherds under a Tree* (1899, oil on panel, 9 1/4 x 6 1/2 ins / 23.8 x 16.2 cm) GBP 1,375. LONDON, 2 March 1989, *Tintern* (oil on canvas, 58 1/2 x 47 1/4 ins / 148.7 x 120 cm) GBP 13,200. LONDON, 21 Sept 1989, *In Picardy* (oil on canvas, 15 3/4 x 21 1/2 ins / 40.1 x 54.6 cm) GBP 1,375. LONDON, 8 March 1990, *Golden Landscape* (oil on canvas, 29 1/4 x 39 ins / 74 x 99.1 cm) GBP 7,150. LONDON, 7 June 1990, *Street in North Africa* (oil on panel, 15 x 20 ins / 38 x 50.5 cm) GBP 2,090. LONDON, 26 Sept 1990, *Spring Morning* (1881, oil on canvas, 27 1/4 x 42 1/4 ins / 69 x 107 cm) GBP 11,550. NEW YORK, 21 May 1991, *Market Place, Cairo* (oil on canvas, 27 1/2 x 40 ins / 69.8 x 101.4 cm) USD 6,050. LONDON, 5 June 1991, *Heavy Shower Passing over Streatley* (1885, watercolour, 23 x 35 3/4 ins / 57.5 x 91 cm) GBP 2,420. LONDON, 18 Dec 1991, *Shepherd and Flock by a River* (oil on canvas, 36 x 52 ins / 91.5 x 132 cm) GBP 704. LONDON, 13 March 1992, *Road in Marsh Valley* (oil on canvas, 17 x 22 3/4 ins / 43.2 x 57.8 cm) GBP 2,090. NEW YORK, 29 Oct 1992, *View of Kettering* (oil on canvas/synthetic resin, 9 1/2 x 1 1/4 ins / 24 x 3 cm) USD 1,760. MONTREAL, 23-24 Nov 1993, *Capel Curig* (oil on panel, 7 x 9 3/4 ins / 17.8 x 24.8 cm) CAD 800. LONDON, 4 Nov 1994, *Walkton, Kettering* (oil on canvas, 22 x 15 ins / 55.9 x 38.1 cm) GBP 1,840. NEW YORK, 19 Jan 1995, *Rowing by the Edge of a Wood* (oil on canvas, 18 x 24 ins / 45.7 x 61 cm) USD 2,185. LONDON, 6 Nov 1996, *Spring in Japan* (oil on panel, 9 1/2 x 6 1/2 ins / 24 x 16.5 cm) GBP 4,025. NEW YORK, 26 Feb 1997, *Pastoral Scene* (oil on canvas, 48 x 60 ins / 122 x 152.5 cm) USD 7,475. LONDON, 5 Nov 1997, *Village in Gloucestershire* (oil on canvas, 40 x 31 1/2 ins / 101.5 x 80 cm) GBP 3,220.

EAST, Benoît
Canadian, 20th century.
Born in Quebec.
Painter.

EAST, J. B.
British, 19th century.
Miniaturist.

J.B. East exhibited at the Royal Academy in London from 1818 to 1830.

EAST, Mabel
British, 20th century.
Born in Malvern.
Painter.

Mabel East exhibited in Paris at the Salon des Artistes Français in 1932.

EASTLAKE, Caroline H.
British, 19th century.
Active in Plymouth.
Painter. Flowers.

Caroline Eastlake exhibited from 1868 to 1873 in London and Plymouth.

MUSEUMS AND GALLERIES:
LONDON (Victoria and Albert Mus.): *Child's Bouquet.*

EASTLAKE, Charles H.
British, 20th century.
Born at the end of the 19th century, in London.
Active from 1889 to c. 1930.
Painter. Genre scenes, landscapes.

Charles H. Eastlake studied in Antwerp and Paris. He showed his work at various exhibitions in England, notably at the Royal Academy and the Royal Institute.

EASTLAKE, Charles Lock (Sir)
British, 19th century.
Born 17 November 1793, in Plymouth; died 24 December 1865, in Pisa, Italy.
Painter, pastellist, draughtsman. Religious subjects, portraits, landscapes, architectural views.

Charles Eastlake was the son of George Eastlake, Judge Advocate at Plymouth. He was one of the first pupils of Prout, whom he accompanied in excursions around the countryside. At 14 he was sent to Charterhouse School, but in 1808 he left there to work with Haydon. In 1814 he visited Paris and in 1815, finding himself back in Plymouth, he took advantage of the arrival of Napoleon at Plymouth on board the *Bellérophon (Bellerophon)*, to make a study of the Emperor. He painted a portrait of Napoleon standing on the ship's bridge, surrounded by his officers. This work caused a sensation and sold at such a high price that the young artist was able to visit Italy in 1817 and Greece in 1819. In Greece he was given the task of drawing Greek architectural ruins, aided by Brockedon. After a stay of about a year, he went back to England because of the death of his father. He returned to Italy and stayed there 14 years.

In 1827, he was nominated an associate of the Royal Academy with *Isidas Appearing in Battle, Naked, Armed with a Sword and Taken for a God.* Elected as an academician in 1830, he returned to England. Appointed President of the Academy in 1850 and curator of the National Gallery in 1843, he became director in 1855. He exhibited from 1813 at the British Instititution and at the Royal Academy from 1823. He wrote several works on art. A number of his works show the costumes and customs of Greece and Italy.

MUSEUMS AND GALLERIES:
LONDON (Royal Academy of Arts): *Hagar and Ishmael* (1830, oil/panel, competition piece) - LONDON (Tate Collection): *The Colosseum from the Esquiline* (1822, oil on canvas); *The Colosseum from the Campo Vaccino* (1822, oil on canvas); *Lord Byron's 'Dream'* (1827, oil on canvas, exhibited in 1829); *Haidée, a Greek Girl* (1827, oil on canvas, exhibited in 1831); *Mrs Charles H. Bellenden Ker* (1835, oil on canvas, portrait in italian peasant woman); *Christ Lamenting over Jerusalem* (1846, oil on canvas); *The Escape of Francesco Novello di Carrara, with his Wife, from the Duke of Milan* (exhibited in 1850, oil on canvas) - LONDON (Victoria and Albert Mus.): *Roman Peasant Woman; The Trajan Forum, Rome* (1821, oil on canvas); *Italian Peasant Woman and Her Children* - MANCHESTER: *Christ Blessing the Little Children.*

AUCTION RECORDS:
LONDON, 1 May 1908, *Sleeping Peasant Woman,* GBP 1. LONDON, 4 Dec 1909, *View of the Surroundings of Rome,* GBP 13. LONDON, 19 Jan 1923, *Christ Weeping over Jerusalem,* GBP 22. LONDON, 26 Jan 1923, *Portrait of the Rear Admiral Sir Thomas Byam Martin, in Uniform* (pastel); *Portrait of Henry Byam Martin, in Officer Cadet's Uniform* (pastel, collection) GBP 25; *Portrait of Rear Admiral Sir Thomas Byam Martin in Uniform* (1816, drawing) GBP 21. LONDON, 28 May 1923, *Legend of Ivanhoe* (1820) GBP 12. LONDON, 10 Dec 1923, *Scene of the Holy Year, Pilgrims Arriving in Rome,* GBP 50. LONDON, 24 June 1927, *Greeks in Flight* (1883) GBP 8. LONDON, 30 Nov 1928, *Two Views of the Colosseum,* GBP 17. LONDON, 16 Dec 1929, *King John Signing the Magna Carta, 15th June 1215,* GBP 13. LONDON, 13 Oct 1967, *Spring, Summer* (two pendants) Gns 260. LONDON, 18 June 1969, *Temple of Theseus at Athens,* GBP 750. LONDON, 13 Oct 1978, *A Girl of Albano* GBP 1,500. EDINBURGH, 30

April 1986, *Panorama of Rome* (oil on canvas, 20 1/2 x 65 3/4 ins / 52.1 x 167.3 cm) GBP 4,500. LONDON, 10 April 1991, *Landscape around Naples* (oil on paper/canvas, 9 x 13 1/2 ins / 23 x 34.5 cm) GBP 1,320. LONDON, 9 Nov 1994, *Napoleon on Board the Bellerophon* (oil on canvas, 23 1/2 x 16 1/4 ins / 59.5 x 41 cm) GBP 13,225. LONDON, 13 Oct 1999, *Temple of Erechtheus, Athens* (oil on canvas, 25 x 35 ins / 64 x 88 cm) GBP 46,000. KNOWLE, 10 Jan 2001, *Study of a Young Shepherdess Surrounded by Eight Putti* (1848, pencil on white oil ground on linen, 31 x 40 ins / 80 x 102 cm) GBP 4,700. MILAN, 5 June 2001, *Hagar and Ishmael* (1843, oil on canvas, 30 x 38 ins / 75 x 96 cm) ITL 8,000,000. WELLINGTON, 8 May 2002, *Portrait of Napoleon* (ink) NZD 3,400. LONDON, 20 Feb 2003, *Salutation to the Aged Friar* (oil on canvas, 37 x 44 ins / 94 x 113 cm) GBP 12,000. MUNICH, 28 March 2003, *Pilgrim Procession on a Hilltop outside Rome* (1848, oil on canvas, 42 x 65 ins / 107 x 164 cm) EUR 8,000.

EASTLAKE, Mary A.

Maiden name: Bell
British, 19th century.
Born 19th century, in Canada.
Painter. Landscapes.

Mary Eastlake was the wife of Charles H. Eastlake and exhibited at the Salon in Paris, at the Royal Academy in London, and in America. She was mentioned, around 1905-1906, in Boston.

MUSEUMS AND GALLERIES:
OTTAWA - SHERBROOKE - WELLINGTON.

EASTMAN, Frank Samuel

British, 19th - 20th century.
Born 27 April 1878, in Anerley (London).
Painter, designer.

Frank Samuel Eastman studied at the Croydon School of Art near London and in 1889 at the Royal Academy. In 1902 he was awarded a prize for mural decoration. He exhibited regularly at the Royal Academy.

EASTMAN, Maud (Mrs)

British, 20th century.
Active in London.
Miniaturist.

EASTMAN, Ruth

American, 20th century.
Born in the USA.
Illustrator.

Ruth Eastman was a member of the New York Society of Illustrators and the Artists' Guild of the Authors' League of America in New York.

EASTMAN, Seth

American, 19th century.
Born 1808, in Brunswick (Maine); died 1875.
Painter, watercolourist, draughtsman. Figures, landscapes, topographical views.

Seth Eastman studied at West Point Military Academy from 1824 to 1828 and it was there that he learned topographical drawing. He served five years in the field and returned to West Point, studying with Robert W. Weir in 1833 and becoming assistant lecturer. In 1842, posted to Minnesota and then Texas, he began to specialise in painting the Native American tribes, and in 1867 Congress commissioned him to paint scenes of indigenous life to be exhibited in the Capitol in Washington DC. Mainly a painter of oil and watercolour landscapes, he was often associated with the Hudson River School.

MUSEUMS AND GALLERIES:
FORT WORTH (Amon Carter Mus.): *Ballplay of the Dakota on St Peter's River in Winter* (1848, oil on canvas).

AUCTION RECORDS:
NEW YORK, 5-6 Feb 1932, *Fort Snelling, Minnesota*, USD 165; *View of Mendota from Fort Snelling*, USD 65; *Fort Snelling, Minnesota*, USD 60. NEW YORK, 11-12 Feb 1944, *Fort Snelling*, USD 475. NEW YORK, 9 Jan 1991, *Cave on Lake Superior; Keokuk on the Mississippi* (watercolour/paper/card and pencil/paper, 5 1/4 x 7 1/4 ins / 13.3 x 18.1 cm and 6 3/4 x 10 1/4 ins/17.2 x 25.8 cm) USD 9,900. NEW YORK, 3 Dec 1992, *View of Texas to the North of San Antonio* (1849, watercolour and ink/paper, 5 x 7 3/4 ins / 12.7 x 19.7 cm) USD 5,500. NEW YORK, 22 May 2001, *Sun Worship, Dakota Dancers* (1852, watercolour, 6 x 11 ins / 15 x 29 cm) USD 120,000. NEW YORK, 4 March 2003, *Inscription Rock at Esopus Landing on the Hudson River* (watercolour, 6 x 9 ins / 15 x 23 cm) USD 2,000. SOUTH DEERFIELD, 9 May 2003, *Sioux Chief* (gouache and watercolour, 13 x 10 ins / 33 x 25 cm) USD 2,000. FAIRFIELD, 8 Jan 2004, *Sioux Chief* (gouache and watercolour, oval, 14 x 11 ins / 36 x 28 cm) USD 2,250. NEW YORK, 11 March 2004, *Indian Encampment* (watercolour on paper on linen, 17 x 28 ins / 42 x 70 cm) USD 13,000.

EASTMAN, William J.

American, 20th century.
Born 14 November 1888; died 1950.
Painter.

William Eastman was winner of the Penton Medal at Cleveland Museum of Art in 1919. A member of the Cleveland Society of Artists and Cleveland Art Association. He was also a writing master.

EASTON, A.

British, 19th century.
Active in London.
Engraver.

A. Easton may be the artist who signed a portrait of Sir Rowland Hill, a stipple engraving after W. Lodder, in 1814.

EASTON, Linwood

American, 20th century.
Born 17 May 1892, in Portland (Oregon).
Engraver.

Linwood Easton was a pupil of A.E. Moore and A. Bower and a member of the Salmagundi Club and the Portland Society of Artists. He practised etching.

EASTON, Reginald

British, 19th century.
Born 1807; died 1893.
Active in London.
Miniaturist. Portraits.

Reginald Easton exhibited at the Royal Academy in London between 1835 and 1887.

MUSEUMS AND GALLERIES:
LONDON (National Portrait Gal.): *King William IV* (c. 1838-1839, watercolour); *George James Guthrie* (watercolour and bodycolour/ivory, miniature).

EASTROM, Marika d'

Swedish, 20th century.
Born in Sweden.
Active in Paris in 1930.
Painter. Interiors, still-lifes.

EASTWOOD, Francis Hurst

British, 19th century.
Born 1855, in Huddersfield; died 1902.
Painter. Landscapes.

Francis Eastwood exhibited frequently in London between 1875 and 1893.

AUCTION RECORDS:
LONDON, 24 Oct 1978, *A Fine Step* (oil on canvas, 33 3/4 x 51 1/4 ins / 86 x 130 cm) GBP 1,400. LEYBURN, 22 Nov 2001, *Woman Cutting Cotton with a Sickle* (oil on canvas, 30 x 24 ins / 76 x 62 cm) GBP 1,300.

EASTWOOD, Raymond James
American, 20th century.
Born 25 May 1898, in Bridgeport Connecticut, USA.
Painter.

Raymond James Eastwood studied under F.V. du Mond, W.S. Kendall and E.C. Taylor. He was a member of the Art Students' League of New York and was also a teacher.

EATON, Charles Harry
American, 19th century.
Born 13 December 1850, in Akron (Ohio); died 4 August 1901, in Leonia (New Jersey).
Painter, illustrator. Landscapes, waterscapes.

Charles Harry Eaton painted initially as an amateur, but when his father died bankrupt he turned to art for a living. He went to New York, where he became an associate of the National Academy of Design and a member of the American Watercolor Society, of which he was secretary for 14 years. He was awarded a silver medal and a gold medal in Boston and also exhibited successfully in Philadelphia and Buffalo.

MUSEUMS AND GALLERIES:
DETROIT: *Lily Pond.*

AUCTION RECORDS:
NEW YORK, 13 Jan 1902, *By a Pond,* USD 150. NEW YORK, 24-26 Feb 1904, *Wet October Day,* USD 480. NEW YORK, 15 and 16 Feb 1906, *River Shaiwassee,* USD 300. NEW YORK, 14 Dec 1933, *River,* USD 70. NEW YORK, 4 March 1937, *Where the Water Lilies Grow: Man in a Boat Crossing a Pond,* USD 90. NEW YORK, 27 Jan 1984, *Landscape with Cattle* (oil on canvas, 18 x 24 ins / 45.7 x 61 cm) USD 1,800. NEW YORK, 17 Dec 1990, *Landscape with Cows* (oil on canvas, 16 1/2 x 24 ins / 42 x 61 cm) USD 3,080. NEW YORK, 25 Sept 1992, *Autumn Landscape* (1887, oil on card/card, 15 1/2 x 22 ins / 39.4 x 55.9 cm) USD 2,090. NEW YORK, 15 Nov 1993, *Along the River* (oil on canvas, 27 x 36 ins / 68.5 x 91.5 cm) USD 633. MILFORD, 21 Oct 1999, *River Landscape with Distant Town* (oil on canvas, 16 x 24 ins / 41 x 61 cm) USD 7,500. BOSTON, 7 Sept 2001, *Autumn Landscape* (oil on canvas, 18 x 24 ins / 46 x 61 cm) USD 2,200. OAKLAND, 20 Sept 2003, *Marshlands* (1887, oil on board) USD 12,000.

EATON, Charles Warren
American, 19th - 20th century.
Born 22 February 1857, in Albany; died 1937.
Painter. Genre scenes, landscapes.

Charles Eaton was a pupil at the National Academy of Design and the Art Students' League in New York. He gained an honourable mention at the International Exhibition of 1900 and a medal for third place at the Paris Salon in 1906. He also received a large number of awards at the main American exhibitions. He also exhibited in London on different occasions, notably at the Royal Academy on Suffolk Street.

MUSEUMS AND GALLERIES:
CINCINNATI: *Dunes Near Knokke, Belgium* - WASHINGTON DC (NGA): *Landscape* (c. 1910, monotype/woven paper).

AUCTION RECORDS:
NEW YORK, 7 Feb 1901, *Valley at Sunset,* USD 375. NEW YORK, 20 Feb 1903, *Moonrise,* USD 105. NEW YORK, 14 and 15 April 1904, *Old Windmills,* USD 210. NEW YORK, 8 Jan 1930, *Elms and Sunset,* USD 100. NEW YORK, 29 Oct 1931, *Sunset* (1896) USD 30; *Landscape,* USD 75. NEW YORK, 16 March 1934, *Woodland Landscape,* USD 50; *New England Landscape,* USD 25; *Winter Afternoon,* USD 60. NEW YORK, 24 Oct 1946, *Large Pine Trees,* USD 150. NEW YORK, 16 Jan 1982, *October Tints* (pastel, 23 1/4 x 19 3/4 ins / 59 x 50.4 cm) USD 650. NEW YORK, 28 Jan 1982, *Autumn Landscape* (1882, oil on canvas, 16 1/2 x 22 1/2 ins / 42 x 57 cm) USD 1,700. NEW YORK, 23 June 1983, *Melting Snow* (oil on canvas, 30 x 28 ins / 76.2 x 71.1 cm) USD 6,500. NEW YORK, 28 Sept 1983, *Woodland Landscape at Sunset* (pastel, 30 x 20 1/4 ins / 76.2 x 51.2 cm) USD 800. NEW YORK, 4 Dec 1987, *Melting Snow* (oil on canvas, 30 x 28 1/4 ins / 76.5 x 71.5 cm) USD 13,000. NEW YORK, 26 Sept 1990, *Winter Landscape with a Stream* (oil on canvas, 30 x 36 ins / 76.2 x 91.4 cm) USD 5,500. NEW YORK, 27 Sept 1990, *Snow-Covered Mountains* (pastel/canvas, 30 x 28 1/4 ins / 76 x 71.5 cm) USD 4,950. NEW YORK, 15 May 1991, *Pine Trees at Dusk* (1904, oil on canvas, 30 1/4 x 36 1/4 ins / 76.8 x 92.1 cm) USD 2,640. NEW YORK, 21 May 1991, *Setting Sun* (oil on canvas, 24 x 20 ins / 61 x 50.8 cm) USD 6,050. NEW YORK, 15 April 1992, *Landscape with a Church* (oil on canvas, 16 x 22 ins / 40.6 x 55.9 cm) USD 1,210. NEW YORK, 12 Sept 1994, *Woodland Landscape at Dawn* (oil on canvas, 24 x 20 ins / 61 x 50.8 cm) GBP 1,725. NEW YORK, 9 March 1996, *Start of Spring* (oil on canvas, 24 x 36 ins / 61 x 91.4 cm) USD 16,100.

EATON, Dorothy
American, 20th century.
Born 5 May 1893, in East Orange (New Jersey).
Painter. Scenes with figures.

Dorothy Eaton was a pupil of Kenneth Hayes Miller and a member of the Art Students' League in New York.

AUCTION RECORDS:
NEW YORK, 4 March 1987, *Street Scene, New York* (oil on canvas, 20 x 30 ins / 50.8 x 76.2 cm) USD 1,400. NEW YORK, 3 Feb 1999, *Harvest Still-life* (1942-1943, oil on canvas, 33 x 45 ins / 84 x 114 cm) USD 2,400.

EATON, Elisabeth K.
American, 19th - 20th century.
Born in Boston.
Painter.

EATON, Ellen (Miss)
British, 19th century.
Born in Chelsea, London.
Painter. Landscapes.

Ellen Eaton exhibited regularly at the Royal Academy in London between 1817 and 1822.

EATON, Hugh McDougal
American, 19th century.
Born 25 January 1865, in Brooklyn; died 1924.
Active in New York.
Painter.

Hugh McDougal Eaton was a pupil of J.B. Whittaker, Kenyon, Cox and H. Siddons Mowbray. He produced many book illustrations.

EATON, J. B.
British, 19th century.
Active in London.
Painter. Genre scenes.

J. B. Eaton exhibited nine times at the Royal Academy, from 1810 to 1821.

EATON, Joseph O.
American, 19th century.
Born 1829; died 1875, in Yonkers.
Painter. Portraits.

Joseph O. Eaton was a portrait painter who worked in oils and watercolour. Among the works he exhibited were *View of the Hudson, Lady Godiva* and *Self-portrait.*

EATON, Louise Herreshoff
American, 20th century.
Born in Providence (Rhode Island).
Painter.

Louise Herreshoff was a pupil of Mary C. Wheeler, Laurens and Collin in Paris, where she exhibited at the Salon des Artistes Français, most notably in 1900. She was a member of Providence Water Club, the North Shore Art Association and the Gloucester Society of Artists.

EATON, Margaret Fernie
British, 19th - 20th century.

Born 22 April 1871, in Leamington.
Active in the USA.
Painter, illustrator.

Margaret Fernie Eaton studied under J.B. Whitaker in Brooklyn and at the Art Students' League of New York under Cox and Mowbray. She was a member of the New York Watercolor Club and the Art Students' League of New York. She also worked as a craft artist.

EATON, Maria
British, 20th century.
Born in Macclesfield.
Engraver.

Maria Eaton exhibited in Paris at the Salon des Artistes Français from 1928.

EATON, William Sylvester
American, 19th century.
Born 12 December 1861, in Waltham (Massachusetts).
Painter, engraver (etching).

William Sylvester Eaton was a member of the Society of Independent Artists, the Salmagundi Club and the Pen and Brush Club in New York.

EATON, Wyatt
Canadian, 19th century.
Born 6 May 1849, in Phillipsburg; died 1896, in Brooklyn.
Painter, pastellist, watercolourist. Nudes, portraits, genre scenes, landscapes.

Wyatt Eaton studied at the National Academy, then became a pupil of J. O. Eaton in New York and, from 1872, of Gérôme in Paris. He also studied in England. In 1884 he exhibited at the Salon de Paris.

MUSEUMS AND GALLERIES:
MONTREAL: *Harvest; Self-portrait* (two canvases).

AUCTION RECORDS:
NEW YORK, 25 Sept 1980, *Reclining Nude* (pastel, watercolour, charcoal and pencil, 13 3/4 x 17 3/4 ins / 35 x 45 cm) USD 900. NEW YORK, 28 Jan 1982, *Autumn Landscape* (1882, oil on canvas, 16 1/2 x 22 1/2 ins / 42 x 57 cm) USD 1,700. TORONTO, 3 June 1986, *Ariadne* (1891, oil on canvas, 16 x 20 ins / 40.6 x 50.8 cm) CAD 1,500.

EAUBONNE, d'
French, 17th century.
Active during the second half of the 17th century.
Illuminator.

D'Eaubonne, a monk at the monastery at St Ouen, spent much of his life decorating a large gradual (now in Rouen) which he finished in 1682. The initials are particularly fine.

EAUBONNE, Louis Lucien d'
French, 19th century.
Born 1834, in Boulogne-Billancourt; died 1894, in Paris.
Painter. Landscapes.

A pupil of Corot, Louis Lucien d'Eaubonne exhibited at the Salon from 1868 to 1879. He also painted on earthenware.

MUSEUMS AND GALLERIES:
AUXERRE: *Autumn* (after Poussin).

EAUBONNE, Lucien d'
French, 19th - 20th century.
Painter. Religious subjects, portraits.

From 1894 to 1900 Lucien d'Eaubonne sent religious paintings and portraits to the Salon, exhibiting thereafter at the Salon des Indépendants. He settled in Chaville.

EBAU, Rudolf Hellebaut
Belgian, 20th - 21st century.
Born 1954, in Ghent.
Painter.

Ebau attended the Koninklijke Academie voor Schone Kunsten in Ghent. He also learned how to restore paintings. He lived in Italy for three years. Since 1973, he has exhibited in various Belgian towns and also in Holland, Germany and France.

EBBE, Axel
Swedish, 19th century.
Born 1868, in Hököpinge (Skåne); died 1941.
Sculptor. Statues.

Ebbe featured at the Salon des Artistes Français, gaining an honourable mention in 1893.

AUCTION RECORDS:
LONDON, 17 May 1991, *The Young Girl on the Rock* (1920, marble, h. 31 ins / 78.5 cm) GBP 5,720.

EBBEHRAT. See **EBERHART**

EBBELAER, Jan, or Hebbelaer
Dutch, 17th century.
Sculptor.

The pupil of van Tongeren at The Hague in 1679, Jan Ebbelaer had a predilection for mythological subjects. His works include *Bacchus, Abduction of Proserpine, Apollo and Daphne* and *Nymph on a Dolphin.*

EBBESEN, T.
Danish, 17th century.
Sculptor (wood).

The pulpit in the church of Svenstrup is by Ebbesen, and dates from 1688.

EBBESEN, Torben
Danish, 20th century.
Born 1945.
Sculptor of assemblages, mixed media.

Ebbesen lives and works in Copenhagen. He produces very varied objects, both in their overall appearance and in the materials he uses. He combines disparate items, such as iron with plastic and loudspeakers; flower or sulphur on porcelain; iron and magnets, and so on. Three-dimensional consistency is clearly not his intention, nor does he seek consistency of ideas. Deliberately alluding to the artists and engineers of the Renaissance, he moves spontaneously from one idea to the next, according to the circumstances which provoke their sudden appearance.

Since 1982, he has participated in many group exhibitions there and in other Danish cities, also in Sweden, Finland, Norway and Iceland; he exhibited at the 1990 Venice Biennale; in 1991, at *Questions de Sens* (*Questions of Meaning*), at the Centre d'Art Ivry-sur-Seine and at the Centre d'Art Contemporain in Corbeil-Essonnes. Since 1982, he has held solo shows in towns and cities including Copenhagen, Aarhus and Randers.

BIBLIOGRAPHY:
Töjner, Poul Erik, *Questions de sens - Huit artistes danois*, group exhibition catalogue, Centre d'Art contemporain, Corbeil-Essonnes, centre d'Art d'Ivry, Ivry-sur-Seine, 1991.

MUSEUMS AND GALLERIES:
AARHUS (Kunstmus.) - COPENHAGEN (Statens Mus. for Kunst) - SORØ (Vestsjællands Kunstmuseum).

AUCTION RECORDS:
COPENHAGEN, 14 June 1994, *Untitled* (1987, bronze, h. 37 3/4 ins / 96 cm) DKK 18,000. COPENHAGEN, 6 Dec 1994, *Impromptu No. 2* (1976, paint and collage, 27 1/2 x 19 3/4 ins / 70 x 50 cm) DKK 5,000. COPENHAGEN, 6 Oct 1999, *Plate and Broken China with Photos on Tiles* (1987-1988, collage, 47 x 29 ins / 120 x 74 cm) DKK 14,500. COPENHAGEN, 7 Oct 2003, *Brain Landscape* (1986, oil on panel, 43 x 67 ins / 110 x 170 cm) DKK 15,000.

EBBINGHAUS, Karl
German, 20th century.
Born 1872, in Hamburg.
Sculptor, decorative designer. Busts, statues.

Ebbinghaus worked in Munich, and exhibited busts and miniature works in silver in Munich in 1901 and 1905. He took part in other exhibitions including in Dresden in 1904 and in Weimar in 1906. He exhibited again in Munich in 1908, this time showing plastic garden ornaments: *The Four Seasons* and *Imagination*, as well as some monumental statues. In 1910 he exhibited a statue on a plinth in Brussels: *Woman on Horseback with Horn of Plenty*, and he also exhibited in Berlin in 1912. He was heavily influenced by Hildebrand and Volkman.

EBBIUS, N.
Dutch, 17th century.
Born c. 1597; died 1656.
Painter. Portraits.

EBEL, Fritz Carl Werner
German, 19th century.
Born 21 April 1835, in Lauterbach; died 20 December 1895, in Düsseldorf.
Painter. Landscapes with figures, landscapes.

In 1855 Fritz Ebel trained under the painter A. Lucas in Darmstadt. In 1857 he moved to the art school in Karlsruhe and trained under the supervision of J.-W. Schirmer. He settled in Düsseldorf in 1861.

MUSEUMS AND GALLERIES:
BREMEN: *Forest Landscape*.
AUCTION RECORDS:
COLOGNE, 17 Oct 1969, *Woodland Landscape*, DEM 3,800. COLOGNE, 27 May 1971, *Hessian Landscape*, DEM 16,000. LUCERNE, 30 June 1973, *Woodland Landscape* (1891) CHF 15,000. NEW YORK, 7 Oct 1977, *Woodcutter* (1868, oil on canvas, 32 3/4 x 32 ins / 83 x 81 cm) USD 3,750. NEW YORK, 28 May 1980, *Mountain Landscape* (1864, oil on canvas, 14 x 19 ins / 35.5 x 48.5 cm) USD 1,400. LONDON, 26 March 1982, *Herd in Woodland Landscape* (oil on canvas, 32 x 46 1/2 ins / 81 x 118 cm) GBP 2,000. LONDON, 23 Feb 1983, *Woodland Landscape with Figures* (1860, oil on canvas, 16 x 21 ins / 40.5 x 52.5 cm) GBP 2,200. LONDON, 20 March 1985, *Children in a Clearing* (1868, oil on canvas, 54 3/4 x 45 1/2 ins / 139 x 115.5 cm) GBP 3,500. AMSTERDAM, 2 Nov 1992, *Figures in an Oxcart in a Wood* (oil on canvas, 30 1/4 x 52 ins / 77 x 132 cm) NLG 34,500. MUNICH, 6 Dec 1994, *Herdsmen with Cows in Woodland and River Landscape* (1879, oil on canvas, 26 3/4 x 18 1/4 ins / 68 x 46.5 cm) DEM 10,925. LONDON, 11 Oct 1995, *Woodland Landscape with Herd of Cows and Herdsman* (1875, oil on canvas, 34 1/4 x 54 1/2 ins / 87 x 138.7 cm) GBP 7,475. COLOGNE, 20 May 2000, *Wooded Landscape with Stream and Farmhouse* (oil on canvas, 26 x 39 ins / 66 x 98 cm) DEM 11,500. MALMÖ, 18 Nov 2000, *Wooded Landscape with Girl* (1885, oil on canvas, 29 x 42 ins / 74 x 107 cm) SEK 48,000. BERN, 9 May 2001, *Wooded Lakeside with Cows Grazing* (1891, oil on canvas, 43 x 67 ins / 110 x 171 cm) CHF 11,000. KEMPTEN, 8 Nov 2001, *Children Playing by Woodland Stream* (oil on canvas, 26 x 20 ins / 65 x 52 cm) DEM 10,000. LUCERNE, 15 May 2002, *Landscape with Trees and Figures* (1872, oil on canvas, 27 x 43 ins / 68 x 110 cm) CHF 17,000. NEW YORK, 4 Sept 2002, *Forest Clearing with Figures* (1867, oil on canvas, 39 x 33 ins / 99 x 85 cm) USD 3,800. COLOGNE, 17 May 2003, *Wooded Mountain Landscape* (oil on canvas, 37 x 30 ins / 93 x 77 cm) EUR 4,200. HAMBURG, 21 June 2003, *Hessen Landscape with Herder and Cows* (1890, oil on canvas, 42 x 63 ins / 107 x 160 cm) EUR 9,000. HAMBURG, 14 Feb 2004, *Extensive Wooded Landscape with Pond* (1879, oil on canvas, 13 x 19 ins / 33 x 47 cm) EUR 3,100.

EBEL, Henry or Heinrich
German, 19th - 20th century.
Born 1849, in Gimmeldingen (Rhineland Palatinate); died 1931.
Painter. Genre scenes, landscapes. Murals.

Ebel trained at the school of decorative arts in Munich. His genre scenes with their sombre tones and muted atmosphere contrast with the very precise draughtsmanship of his small landscapes. From 1870 onwards he decorated various churches in Alsace, specialising in decorative compositions. He exhibited at various official shows in Paris, notably the Salon d'Automne, of which he became a member in 1928. An exhibition of his works was held in Strasbourg in 1912.

MUSEUMS AND GALLERIES:
STRASBOURG: *Bedroom*.

EBEL, Hermann
German, 18th century.
Born 1713, in Rüsselheim; died 1 October 1781, in Frankfurt am Main.
Painter.

Hermann Ebel trained for nine years under J. C. Fiedler, then Georg des Marées with whom he travelled and some of whose works he completed. He was also a painter of miniatures.

EBEL, René
French, 20th century.
Born 26 May 1889, in Paris.
Potter. Designs for mosaics.

René Ebel began exhibiting in Paris at the Salon d'Automne in 1925, and in the same year showed at the International Exhibition of Decorative Art. He was a member of the French exhibitions committee and of the Société des Arts Appliqués aux Métiers (Society of Art Applied to Trades).

EBELEN, Aelbrecht, or Ebelyn
Flemish School, 16th century.
Painter.

Active in Antwerp and Middelburg, Ebelen may be the same person as the painter Aelbrecht Ebeling who was admitted to the guild in The Hague in 1602.

EBELING, Aelbrecht
Flemish, 17th century.
Painter.
Flemish School.

Aelbrecht Ebeling was a member of the Guild of St Luke in The Hague in 1602.

EBELMANN, Johann Jacob
German, 17th century.
Active in Germany c. 1600.
Draughtsman.

EBELYN. See **EBELEN**

EBEN, Franz Ephraïm
German, 18th century.
Born 1727.
Active in Berlin.
Sculptor.

Franz Ephraïm Eben and his son Johann Ephraïm worked in stone, clay and especially wood. They were particularly well known for their coloured frames and clocks.

EBEN, Johann Ephraïm
German, 18th century.
Born 1748; died 1 October 1805.
Sculptor.
Johann Ephraïm Eben was the son of Franz Ephraïm Eben, with whom he worked in Berlin.

EBEN, Johann Georg
Russian, 18th century.
Died 1710, of the plague.
Active in Riga.
Engraver, goldsmith.
His work as an engraver is of little importance. Works to be cited are: *A Series of Six Pieces, Diverse Ornaments, Friezes* and others.

EBEN, Johann Michael
German, 18th century.
Born May 1716, in Biebrich; died 1761.
Engraver (burin).
Johann Eben engraved panels for booksellers and portraits.

EBENBERGER, Friedrich
Austrian, 17th century.
Born c. 1620; died c. 1690.
Active in Vienna.
Painter.
Friedrich Ebenberger is probably the painter Ebenberger who worked on the paintings for the chancel in the parish church of Hietzing between 1660 and 1670, and on the paintings in a convent chapel in Klosterneuburg in 1681.

EBENHECHT, Georg Franz, or Ebenhoch
German, 18th century.
Died 21 February 1757.
Active in Leipzig and Potsdam.
Sculptor (including ivory). Religious subjects. Ornaments.
Georg Ebenhecht worked initially in Leipzig, then in Potsdam near Berlin, where he became an honorary member of the academy in 1751. He worked jointly with F. G. Adams on the decoration of the Sans-Souci park, which houses a marble vase, two sphinx playing with cupids and four mythological groups, which he carved with several Italian sculptors from Adams' studio. He also worked at the palace, especially on the sculptures and paintings of the marble Salle. Several statues and decorations at the Opera House in Berlin are attributed to him. His masterpiece is considered to be the statues of the twelve apostles for the catholic church in Berlin. The municipal library in Leipzig owns several of his ivory sculptures.

EBENHOCH, Wilhelm
German, 18th century.
Born 18th century, in Kastl (Bavaria).
Painter.
The old Benedictine cloister in Kastl owns a *Handing over the Keys to St Peter*, signed *Wilhelm Ebenhoch*.

EBENHOFFER, Anton
Austrian, 18th century.
Born c. 1721, in Swabia; died 11 July 1786.
Painter.
Anton Ebenhoffer trained at the Vienna academy and also worked at the house of the painter Kessler.

EBER, Joseph
German, 18th century.
Engraver.
Joseph Eber sculpted a *General View of Koblenz* after J. Eipelt in 1770.

EBER, Sandor
Hungarian, 20th century.
Born 6 June 1878, in Rackeresztur.
Painter, fresco artist. Religious subjects, allegorical subjects, portraits.
A student of B. Szekely in Budapest from 1896 to 1900, Sandor Eber painted a large fresco in 1904 of an *Allegory of an Education in Art* for the masters school in Baja. In 1909, he obtained a prize that enabled him to study in Rome. On his return from Italy, he painted the fresco *The Disciples of Emmaus* for the Cistercian church in Baja and *Jesus and St Margaret* in 1911 for the church in Lanycsok. He also painted several portraits.

EBERBACH, Alice Kinsey
American, 20th century.
Born 16 June 1872, in Philadelphia.
Painter.
Alice Eberbach worked in her native city with Robert Henri and W. M. Chase, she pursued her studies in Paris with Girardot, Courtois and Bouguereau. She was a member of the Plastic Club.

EBERBACH, Walther
German, 19th century.
Born 1 January 1866, in Besigheim (Württemberg).
Sculptor, metal worker.
Walther Eberbach was trained in Swabian Gmünd and Stuttgart, then in Cologne, London, Berlin and Frankfurt. He set himself up as a metal worker in Strasbourg where he was a teacher, and then in Heilbronn. He produced the Budde funeral monument in Essen.

EBERENZ, J.
Czech, 19th century.
Active c. 1804.
Miniaturist.
The museum in Liberec, in the Czech Republic, owns a work by J. Eberenz: a reproduction of a marble bust of a man, painted on parchment. He also painted sepia portraits.

EBERHARD
Austrian, 13th - 14th century.
Active in Klosterneuburg (Lower Austria) between 1291 and 1331.
Glass painter.

EBERHARD
German, 15th century.
Active in Ulm c. 1402.
Sculptor (wood), cabinet maker.

EBERHARD
German, 19th century.
Active in Cologne at the beginning of the 19th century.
Lithographer.
Eberhard produced five illustrated panels for *Contributions to the History of the City of Cologne*. It is known that there are two satirical cartoons after Michelangelo by him, and *Milking* after Zimmermann.

EBERHARD, Cogell Pehr. See **COGELL Pierre**

EBERHARD, Franz
German, 18th - 19th century.
Born 29 November 1767, in Hindelang (Allgäu); died 1836, in Munich, of cholera.
Painter, sculptor. History painting.
Franz Eberhard was the oldest brother of Konrad Eberhard, with whom he worked.

EBERHARD, Georg Adam
Czech, 17th century.
Active in Eger.
Painter.
Georg Adam Eberhard's works include an *Adoration of the Magi* (1668), in the parish church of Svojsin, near Stribro, as well as a painting for the high-altar of the church at Seeberg

castle, and some well-executed *Portraits of the Lobkowitz Family* at Roudnice castle.

EBERHARD, Heinrich
German, 20th century.
Born 24 February 1884, in Ellwangen.
Painter. Religious subjects, figures, landscapes, urban landscapes.

Eberhard was a pupil of Pötzelberger, Landenberger and Hölzel in Stuttgart. His works include landscapes painted at Brenz castle in 1910, two *Crucifixions* dating from 1912 and 1914, and a *Holy Family* from 1903. His paintings tend to be large in size.

AUCTION RECORDS:
NEW YORK, 10 Oct 1990, *Soldiers* (1912, oil on card, 13 1/2 x 17 1/4 ins / 34.4 x 43.9 cm) USD 4,400. MUNICH, 26 May 1992, *Bridge* (1914, oil on paper, 9 1/2 x 11 3/4 ins / 24 x 30 cm) DEM 4,600. MUNICH, 1-2 Dec 1992, *Urban Landscape* (1923, oil on paper, 21 1/4 x 25 3/4 ins / 54 x 65.5 cm) DEM 8,280. MUNICH, 29 May 2001, *Kneeling Figure before People* (1910, oil on board, 9 x 11 ins / 23 x 29 cm) DEM 5,000.

EBERHARD, Heinrich Wilhelm
German, 19th century.
Engraver.

Heinrich Eberhard worked in Darmstadt, where he also practised the profession of architect. He preferred engraving to etching.

EBERHARD, Johann Paul
German, 18th century.
Born 25 January 1723, in Allona; died 1795.
Engraver, architect.

Johann Eberhard was a teacher of architecture in Göttingen and engraved a few panels of the town's surrounding area.

EBERHARD, Johann Richard
German, 18th - 19th century.
Born 1739, in Hindelang (Allgäu); died 1813, in Hindelang (Allgäu).
Cabinet maker, sculptor.

Johann Eberhard trained simultaneously at the Vienna academy and under the sculptor Franz Sattler, at whose house he worked. He settled in Hindelang in 1767. Tabernacles in the churches of Hindelang and Scheidegg and four busts of the church fathers in the parish church of Immenstadt are attributed to him, as well as numerous other works for churches in the region, produced with the help of his sons Franz and Konrad.

EBERHARD, Konrad
German, 18th - 19th century.
Born 25 November 1768, in Hindelang (Allgäu); died 12 March 1859, in Munich.
Painter, draughtsman, sculptor. Religious subjects, mythological subjects. Funerary monuments, groups, statues, busts.

Konrad Eberhard was trained first of all by his father Johann Richard Eberhard, then in 1796 by the court sculptor Roman Boos in Munich. He went to Rome in 1806, where he continued his studies. In 1816 he became a teacher of sculpture at the Munich academy. His notable works include the triptych *Triumph of Christianity*, *Judgement of Paris* (1819), *Descent from the Cross* (fresco), and *Adam and Eve* (1809).

MUSEUMS AND GALLERIES:
MUNICH (Glyptothek): *Muse and Cupid* - MUNICH (Institute of the Blind): *Four Statues of Saints* - MUNICH (Porte de L'isar): *St Michael and St George* - MUNICH (Schloss Nymphemburg): *Faun and Bacchus; Leda and the Swan; Diana and Apollo; Endymion* - MUNICH (Theatinerkirche): *Funeral Monument of Princess Caroline* - REGENSBURG (Cathedral): *Funeral Monuments of Bishops Saeler and Wittmann* - REGENSBURG (Walhalla): *Bust of P. Vischer; Bust of Höwart; Bust of Wohlgemuh.*

AUCTION RECORDS:
MUNICH, 1-2 Dec 1992, *Sketch for Ilias Fries* (1823, graphite, 11 x 13 3/4 ins / 28 x 35 cm) DEM 1,955.

EBERHARD, Robert Georges
Swiss, 20th century.
Born 18 June 1884, in Geneva.
Sculptor.

Eberhard was a pupil of MacNeil, Mercié, Carlié, Peter and Rodin. He was a member of the Salon des Artistes Français and of the New Haven Paint and Clay Club. In the USA, he was head of the sculpture department at Yale University. Among his notable works are plaques commemorating World War I. He took part in the Salon des Artistes Français, receiving an honourable mention in 1909.

EBERHARDT, Jacob
German, 19th century.
Born 1820; died 1889, in Nuremberg.
Active in Munich.
Painter. History painting, genre scenes.

Jacob Eberhardt exhibited at the Munich Royal Academy between 1848 and 1858. Notable works by him include *Sophie de Brabant and her Son* and *Return to the Fatherland.*

EBERHARDT, Johann
German, 18th century.
Born in Kastl, near Mainz.
Active at the beginning of the 18th century.
Sculptor.

EBERHARDT, Sebastien
Swiss, 17th century.
Active in Meersburg on Lake Constance.
Painter.

Sebastien Eberhardt produced a portrait of Archbishop Franz Johann of Constance, engraved by J. Sadeler. He worked for some time as a painter at the court in Würzburg. His painting depicting scenes from the history of the monastery of St Gall was destroyed by the French in 1799.

EBERHARDT, Wilhelm
German, 20th century.
Born 6 April 1875, in Hamburg.
Painter. Murals.

Eberhardt trained under M. Seliger at the Berlin school of industrial art and design. He collaborated with R. Bohland on the paintings for the exterior of the German pavilion at the Exposition Universelle of 1900 in Paris, and with H. Vozel on the murals for Hamburg town hall.

EBERHART, or Ebbehrat
German.
Active in St Emmeran, Regensburg.
Painter.

EBERHART
Swiss, 10th century.
Miniaturist.

A miniature in an old religious book in the Library of St Gall, is attributed to this prior. It depicts a monk offering a book to St Gall and St Gregory.

EBERHART
German, 10th - 11th century.
Miniaturist.

This artist was a deacon, and is mentioned in a Salzburg obituary list as having been a scribe and miniaturist of some note.

EBERHART, Serafin
Austrian, 19th century.
Born 6 December 1844, in Vendels (Inn Valley).
Active in Innsbruck.
Sculptor.

Serafin Eberhart trained at the Vienna academy in painting and sculpture, then under J. Ritter von Gasser. He exhibited a plaster group in Innsbruck, *Jesus Bids Farewell to Mary*, in 1875. After a year-long trip to Rome and Florence, he returned and settled in Innsbruck where he carved several funeral monuments for distinguished persons in the town. Notable works in the cemetery of Innsbruck include the following subjects: *Adoration of the Cross by Two Angels Carrying the Instruments of the Passion* (the Bandeson family); *Head of Christ in Relief* (the Peterlongo family); *Mater Dolorosa* (the Hauser and Rauch families); *Monument of Councillor J. von Ficker*; *Madonna in Affliction* (the Nebel family); and *Assumption* (the Köllensberger family). He also produced a great number of wood carvings for Austrian churches: *Immaculate Conception* for Hötting; *Mary and Bernadette* for the grotto of Lourdes in the church of St-Martin in Altenstadt; and *Christ Crucified between Mary and St John* for the high altar of the church of St-Nicholas in Innsbruck. The two large stone statues *Mary with the Infant Jesus* and *St Joseph* in the cloister of Bindenburg are also known to be by him.

EBERHARTH, Augusta
German, 19th century.
Born 19 November 1856, in Munich.
Painter. Still-lifes.

Augusta Eberharth trained under F. Diehl in Munich. She then settled in Vienna.

EBERL, François Maurice Augustin
Czech, 20th century.
Born 25 June 1887, in Prague; died October 1962.
Active from 1910, then naturalised in France.
Painter, draughtsman, watercolourist. Figure compositions, nudes, portraits.

After many trips punctuated by stays in Amsterdam, François Eberl finally settled in Paris in 1911. From 1927 to 1931 he was one of the artists in an important gallery in the Faubourg St Honoré. He joined the Resistance during the war.

Eberl painted figure compositions, nudes and portraits. He was particularly involved in representing the life of the poor, in keeping with a certain pictorial Realism, and the Paris nightclubs.

Eberl took part in many collective exhibitions as he was a member of the Salon d'Automne and the Salon des Artistes Indépendants. Special exhibitions in Paris marked his creative career: he had a major show in 1929 in the gallery in the Faubourg St Honoré and, some time later, an important exhibition of drawings and watercolours in Rue de Seine. After the war, he exhibited in 1946 in Rue de la Boétie and in 1954 in the Faubourg St Honoré. His work can be found in several European museums. He was made a Chevalier of the Légion d'Honneur.

F Eberl.

BIBLIOGRAPHY:
Cathelin, J./Chaudun, J.-Cl. de, *Eberl (1887-1962)*, Riss, Paris, 1973. Nieszawer, Nadine/Boyé, Marie/Lanzmann, Claude (preface), *Peintres juifs de l'école de Paris 1905-1939*, Denoël, Paris, 2001.

AUCTION RECORDS:
PARIS, 20 April 1926, *Flowers at the Window*, FRF 650. PARIS, 27 Dec 1926, *Woman's Head*, FRF 2,000. PARIS, 26 Nov 1927, *Woman's Head*, FRF 1,350. PARIS, 27 Feb 1928, *Female Bust*, FRF 2,500. PARIS, 4 July 1928, *Nude* (bust) FRF 1,080. PARIS, 2 March 1929, *Prostitute*, FRF 7,000. PARIS, 27 Feb 1930, *Portrait of a Woman* (watercolour) FRF 460. PARIS, 24 March 1930, *Bust of a Nude Girl*, FRF 600. PARIS, 12 April 1930, *At the Dance*, FRF 3,500. PARIS, 23 April 1931, *Model*, FRF 2,400. PARIS, 19 March 1932, *Lolita*, FRF 1,300. PARIS, 29 April 1933, *Absinthe*, FRF 1,800. PARIS, 20 June 1935, *Bust of Woman Sitting, Resting on Her Right Elbow*, FRF 280. PARIS, 21 March 1938, *Woman Sitting, Three-Quarter View*, FRF 240. PARIS, 23 March 1938, *Dancer*, FRF 270. PARIS, 28 June 1939, *Head of Woman with Green Necklace*, FRF 150. PARIS, 12 March 1941, *Bust of Bare-Breasted Woman*, FRF 300. PARIS, 30 Nov 1942, *Portrait of a Woman*, FRF 3,000. PARIS, 15 Jan 1943, *Bust of Nude Woman*, FRF 2,000. PARIS, 2 June 1943, *Bust of a Woman*, FRF 1,600. PARIS, 5 June 1944, *Woman's Head*, FRF 500. PARIS, July 1946, *Dance*, FRF 2,700. PARIS, July 1947, *Recumbent Nude*, FRF 11,500; *Two Girls*, FRF 6,000. PARIS, 1954, *Young Woman with Necklace*, FRF 27,000. PARIS, 30 March 1971, *Recumbent Nude* (oil on canvas, 18 x 26½ ins / 46 x 67 cm) FRF 1,600. PARIS, 31 May 1972, *Flowers in a Vase* (oil on canvas, 16¼ x 13 ins / 41 x 33 cm) FRF 500. PARIS, 13 March 1974, *At the Café Concert*, FRF 2,000. VERSAILLES, 24 Oct 1976, *Vase of Flowers* (oil on canvas, 23½ x 32 ins / 60 x 81 cm) FRF 3,800. PARIS, 11 Dec 1981, *Inn in Provence* (oil on canvas) FRF 3,000. HONFLEUR, 17 July 1983, *Genre Scene with Accordion Player* (oil on canvas, 28¾ x 23½ ins / 73 x 60 cm) FRF 8,500. PARIS, 26 Oct 1987, *Recumbent Nude* (oil on canvas, 35½ x 44½ ins / 90 x 113 cm) FRF 10,000. VERSAILLES, 24 Sept 1989, *Recumbent Nude* (oil on canvas, 14¼ x 24¼ ins / 36.5 x 61.5 cm) FRF 8,500. PARIS, 23 March 1990, *Nude Outstretched* (oil on canvas, 15 x 23½ ins / 38 x 60 cm) FRF 31,000. NEUILLY, 3 Feb 1991, *Recumbent Nude* (oil on canvas, 17¼ x 30 ins / 44 x 76 cm) FRF 12,000. PARIS, 26 May 1992, *Beach* (1954, oil on canvas, 28¾ x 39¼ ins / 73 x 100 cm) FRF 23,000. PARIS, 24 March 1996, *Bunch of Roses* (oil on canvas, 18 x 15 ins / 46 x 38 cm) FRF 7,600.

EBERL, Georg Anton
German, 18th century.
Born in Friesberg (Bavaria).
Active in Vienna from 1715 to 1730.
Sculptor.

Georg Eberl worked in particular at the home of Lorenzo Mattieli.

EBERL, Sebastian
Austrian, 18th century.
Born 1711, in Neumarkt, near Salzburg; died February 1770, in Grosskestendorf.
Sculptor.

Sebastian Eberl obtained the right of citizenship in Neumarkt in 1744. Altar sculptures for the churches in Neumarkt and Grosskestendorf are attributed to him.

EBERLE
Austrian, 18th century.
Active in Tyrol.
Painters.

A *Sibyl* after Domenichino dated 1793 bears the signature *Eberle*. It could be that of several painters of this name who were living in Tyrol around the same period.

EBERLE, Adam
German, 19th century.
Born 27 March 1804, in Aachen; died 18 April 1832, in Rome.
Painter. History painting.

Adam Eberle trained under Cornelius at the Düsseldorf academy and followed him to Munich in 1825. He met him again in Rome in 1830. Notable works by Eberle include

Burial of Christ, Maximilian of Bavaria being Invested with the Rank of Elector, Jesus and his First Disciples and *Peter and Paul on the Way to Rome.*

EBERLE, Adolf
German, 19th - 20th century.
Born 11 January 1843, in Munich; died 24 January 1914, in Munich.
Painter. Figures, genre scenes, hunting scenes, interiors with figures, landscapes with figures, animals.

Eberle was the son of the animal painter Robert Eberle; he trained at Munich art academy and was a pupil of K. von Piloty. He exhibited in Vienna, Dresden and Munich, winning a medal in Vienna in 1873.

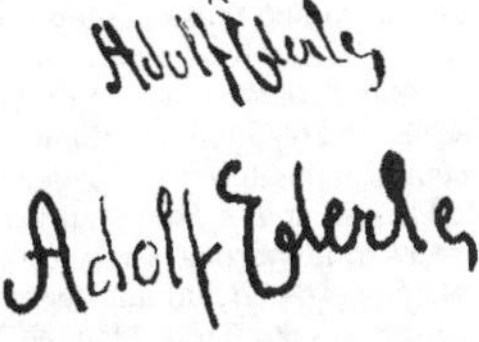

MUSEUMS AND GALLERIES:
HAMBURG: *The Capture* - MUNICH: *Hunting Supplies.*

AUCTION RECORDS:
NEW YORK, 3 Feb 1904, *Pastoral Scene,* USD 150; *Temptation,* USD 100. NEW YORK, 25 Nov 1908, *Fishing Scene,* USD 77. NEW YORK, 29 Jan 1943, *Poachers* (1886) USD 340. NEW YORK, 18-20 Nov 1943, *Child and Sheep,* USD 825. COLOGNE, 17 Oct 1969, *Stable,* DEM 9,500. COLOGNE, 27 May 1971, *The Favourite Basset,* DEM 2,600. COLOGNE, 27 June 1974, *Flock of Sheep in a Landscape* (1857) DEM 6,000. COLOGNE, 14 June 1976, *Two Dogs in an Interior* (oil on panel, 23 x 26 3/4 ins / 58.5 x 68 cm) DEM 20,000. ZURICH, 26 May 1978, *The Hunter's Visit* (oil on panel, 23 x 27 1/2 ins / 58.5 x 70 cm) CHF 27,000. NEW YORK, 12 Oct 1979, *Puppies* (oil on panel, 22 1/4 x 20 ins / 56.5 x 51 cm) USD 18,000. NEW YORK, 29 May 1981, *Stable Companions* (oil on panel, 23 1/2 x 29 3/4 ins / 59.7 x 75.5 cm) USD 32,000. LONDON, 20 June 1984, *Lunchtime* (oil on canvas, 23 1/2 x 28 ins / 60 x 71 cm) GBP 14,000. LONDON, 29 Nov 1985, *Lamb* (oil on panel, 24 x 30 3/4 ins / 61 x 78 cm) GBP 10,000. STOCKHOLM, 15 Nov 1989, *Peasant Woman and her two Children in the Kitchen Feeding a Bitch and her Pups* (oil on canvas, 23 1/2 x 29 1/4 ins / 60 x 74 cm) SEK 125,000. NEW YORK, 20 Feb 1992, *In the Hunting Lodge* (oil on panel, 16 x 19 ins / 40.6 x 48.3 cm) USD 29,700. NEW YORK, 27 May 1992, *Newborn Lamb* (oil on canvas, 19 x 23 1/4 ins / 48.3 x 59 cm) USD 41,800. NEW YORK, 26 May 1993, *New Puppies* (oil on panel, 16 3/4 x 20 1/2 ins / 42.5 x 52.1 cm) USD 40,250. MUNICH, 7 Dec 1993, *Fox Cub* (oil on panel, 13 1/2 x 18 1/4 ins / 34.5 x 46.5 cm) DEM 32,200. MUNICH, 6 Dec 1994, *Peasant Woman and her Children in a Barn with a Litter of Young Puppies* (oil on panel, 29 1/4 x 23 1/2 ins / 74 x 60 cm) DEM 69,000. LONDON, 21 Nov 1997, *Preparing to go Hunting* (oil on panel, 22 x 27 ins / 56 x 68.5 cm) GBP 15,525.

EBERLE, Jakob
Bohemian School, 18th century.
Born 21 April 1720, in Mastov; died c. 1770, in Mastov.
Sculptor.
Bohemian School.

Jakob Eberle studied under Simon Thaler in Prague, and also trained in Rome, which earned him the nickname 'il Romano' (the Roman) on his return to Prague. His work featured in an exhibition entitled *Lumière et ténèbres, art et civilisation du Baroque en Bohême* (*Light and Darkness. Baroque Art and Civilisation in Bohemia*), Palais des Beaux-Arts, Lille (2002). He produced wooden and stone sculptures.

BIBLIOGRAPHY:
Cirglová, Katerina, '*Jakub Eberle: sochar ceského pozdního baroka*' in *Umení*, Institute of the History of Art of the Academy of Sciences of the Czech Republic, Prague, 1999 (text in Czech and German). Vlnas, Vit (ed.), *Lumière et ténèbres, art et civilisation du Baroque en Bohême*, exhibition catalogue, Palais des Beaux-Arts, Lille, Réunion des musées nationaux, Paris, 2002.

EBERLE, Joseph
German, 19th century.
Born 13 February 1839, in Munich; died 7 June 1903, in Überlingen, on Lake Constance.
Sculptor.

Joseph Eberle trained under Von der Launitz in Frankfurt and Knabl at the Munich academy. He soon dedicated himself to religious art and settled in Überlingen. His works can be seen in several churches in Baden (Überlingen, Heiligenberg, Freiberg and Constance) and in Winterthur (Switzerland).

EBERLE, Robert
Swiss, 19th century.
Born 22 July 1815, in Meersburg, on Lake Constance; died 19 September 1860, in Eberling (Upper Bavaria).
Painter. Figures, landscapes with figures, animals.

Robert Eberle worked initially with J. J. Biedermann in Constance, then at the Munich academy where he received advice and encouragement from Cornelius. Later he became an honorary member of the academy of this city.

MUSEUMS AND GALLERIES:
BERN: *Grazing in the Bavarian Alps* - CONSTANCE (Städtische Wessenberg-Gal.) - LEIPZIG: *Sheep in Cowshed* - MUNICH: *Shepherd with his Flock.*

AUCTION RECORDS:
PARIS, 3 Feb 1919, *Shepherds and Sheep under an Oak Tree,* FRF 900. LONDON, 31 Jan 1929, *Tempest,* GBP 13. NEW YORK, 7 Oct 1977, *Flock of Sheep Attacked by an Eagle in High Mountain Landscape* (oil on canvas, 51 3/4 x 43 1/2 ins / 131.5 x 110.5 cm) USD 3,000. LONDON, 27 Nov 1981, *Shepherd and Flock of Sheep in Woodland Landscape* (oil on canvas, 18 x 22 ins / 45.6 x 56 cm) GBP 5,000. PARIS, 1 March 1983, *Cows Grazing* (oil on panel, 4 3/4 x 6 1/4 ins / 12 x 16 cm) FRF 5,500. MUNICH, 10 Dec 1991, *Swabian Shepherd with his Flock* (oil on canvas, 35 1/2 x 43 3/4 ins / 90 x 111 cm) DEM 32,200. MUNICH, 25 June 1992, *Swabian Shepherd with his Flock* (oil on canvas, 24 1/2 x 31 ins / 62 x 79 cm) DEM 28,250. VIENNA, 29-30 Oct 1996, *Herd of Cows on the Way to the Cowshed* (oil on canvas, 34 x 42 1/2 ins / 86.2 x 108 cm) ATS 184,000.

EBERLE, Syrius
German, 19th century.
Born 1844, in Pfronten (Allgäu); died 1903, in Bozen, South Tyrol (now Bolzano, Italy).
Sculptor.

Syrius Eberle was a teacher at the academy of fine arts in Munich and produced important works for Ludwig II of Bavaria.

ÉBERLÉ SAINT LÉGER, Abastenia
American, 20th century.
Born 1878; died 1942.
Sculptor. Genre scenes, mythological subjects. Statuettes.

Abastenia Éberlé Saint Léger made a trip to Italy in 1907 and supervised the execution of several sculptures in a foundry in Naples. In 1908 she won the prize for the 17th exhibition of the New York Female Art Club with her sculpture *Dancer,* inspired by artists such as Loïe Fuller and Isadora Duncan.

AUCTION RECORDS:
NEW YORK, 3 June 1983, *Water Carrier* (bronze, h. 11 ins / 27 cm) USD 1,200. NEW YORK, 14 March 1986, *On Avenue A* (1914, greenish-brown patinated bronze, h. 14 1/2 ins / 36.8 cm) USD 15,500. NEW YORK, 28 Sept 1989, *Indians Kneeling around a Buffalo* (bronze, tobacco box, h. 7 ins / 17.5 cm) USD 3,850. NEW YORK, 16 March 1990, *On Avenue A, Group of Two Young Girls* (greenish-brown-patinated bronze, h. 14 1/2 ins / 36.8 cm) USD 30,800. NEW YORK, 30 May 1990, *Child Crouching Blowing Bubbles* (black-patinated bronze, h. 5 1/4 ins / 13.3 cm) USD 3,080. NEW YORK, 14 March 1991, *Two Children Playing Hide and Seek* (brown-patinated bronze, a pair of book ends, h. 6 1/2 ins / 16.5 cm and 6 3/4 ins/17.2 cm) USD 3,850. NEW YORK, 10 March 1993, *Bacchanale* (1914, bronze, h. 19 ins / 48.3 cm) USD 9,200. NEW YORK, 3 Dec 1993, *Salome* (bronze, h. 23 1/2 ins / 59.5 cm) USD 52,900. NEW YORK, 30 Oct 1996, *Children* (bronze, a pair of book ends, h. 6 1/2 ins / 16.5 cm) USD 4,025. NEW YORK, 5 May 1999, *L'Isolée* (brown patinated bronze, h. 7 ins / 18 cm) USD 2,000. NEW YORK, 15 June 2000, *Omar Khayyam Bookends* (1913, brown patinated bronze, a pair, h. 6 ins / 16 cm) USD 3,200. NEW YORK, 5 Dec 2002, *Salome - The Dancer* (brown patinated bronze, h. 22 ins / 57 cm) USD 28,000. NEW YORK, 27 Sept 2004, *Hide and Seek* (brown patinated bronze, bookends, h. 7 ins / 17 cm) USD 4,500. NEW YORK, 27 Sept 2004, *Windy Doorstep* (brown patinated bronze, h. 14 ins / 35 cm) USD 65,000.

EBERLEIN, or Ebirlen, Ebirlyn
German, 14th century.
Active in Friesberg.
Painter.

EBERLEIN, Andreas
German, 18th century.
Active in Hall.
Painter.

The town hall in Hall has miniature portraits of municipal councillors by Andreas Eberlein.

EBERLEIN, Christian Eberhard
German, 18th century.
Born 1749, in Walfenbuttel; died 1804, in Göttingen (Lower Saxony).
Painter.

Christian Eberlein was the son of Christian Nicolaus Eberlein.

EBERLEIN, Christian Nicolaus
German, 18th century.
Born 1720, in Rudolstadt; died 1788, in Salzdahlum (Lower Saxony).
Painter. History painting.

Christian Eberlein worked in Göttingen, Walfenbuttel and Salzdahlum. In 1775 he was appointed museum inspector in Salzdalhum

EBERLEIN, Ernest
American, 20th century.
Died 28 January 1931, in Free Aires.
Painter. Landscapes.
Berkeley Heights Artists' Colony.

Ernest Eberlein was the driving force behind the artist's colony in Berkeley Heights. He is also thought to have been active in New York.

EBERLEIN, Georg
German, 19th century.
Born 13 April 1819, in Linden; died 1884, in Nuremberg.
Painter, engraver, lithographer. History painting, architectural views.

Georg Eberlein trained under K. A. Heideloff. He was a teacher of Gothic architecture at the school of arts and crafts in Nuremberg.

EBERLEIN, Gustav Heinrich
German, 19th - 20th century.
Born 14 July 1847, in Spiekershausen; died 5 February 1926, in Berlin.
Painter, sculptor.

Eberlein trained at Nuremberg art school, and under the sculptor Blaser. He spent several years in Italy before settling in Berlin. In 1887 he became an honorary member of the art academy in Berlin. His best-known works include *Men of Peace in 1870-1871* and *Tragedy*. He is also credited with a large number of monuments to German emperors and famous figures including those of Emperor Wilhelm I in Elberfeld, Altona, Gera, Geisslingen and Munich; of Friedrich III in Elberfeld; of Bismarck in Krefeld and Berlin; of Wagner in Berlin; and of Goethe in Rome.

He was represented at the Berlin art academy exhibition of 1887 with *Greek Flautist*, and in 1884 with *Venus Chastising Cupid*. He also showed numerous works at the Berlin exhibitions from 1881 onwards, including *Mercury and Psyche* (1881); *Cupid Drawing his Bow* (1888); *Injured Nymph* (1890); *Pygmalion and Galatea* (1896); *Original Sin*; *Abel*; *Cain*; *Adam and Eve at the End of their Lives*; *Eve Beside Abel's Body*; *Goethe Looking at Schiller's Skull* (1898); *Angels Moving the Stone from Christ's Tomb*; *The Ascension*; and *Faun giving a Nymph a Drink* (1900).

MUSEUMS AND GALLERIES:
BERLIN: *The Thorn Remover* - BERLIN (Eberlein Mus.) - HANN. MÜNDEN (Städtisches Mus.).

AUCTION RECORDS:
BERLIN, 24 Oct 1985, *Adam and Eve at the End of their Lives* (1898, bronze, h. 22 ins / 56 cm) DEM 6,000. STOCKHOLM, 5-6 Dec 1990, *Dancing Female Nude* (dark-patinated bronze, h. 16 ins / 40.5 cm) SEK 3,700.

EBERLEIN, Johann Christian
German, 18th - 19th century.
Born c. 1770, in Göttingen (Lower Saxony); died 1815, in Göttingen (Lower Saxony).
Active in Rome c. 1811.
Painter. Landscapes.

A notable work by Johann Eberlein is *View over the Aventin*. He exhibited at the royal academy in Berlin.

MUSEUMS AND GALLERIES:
MUNICH: *Historic Landscape*.

EBERLEIN, Johann Michael
German, 19th century.
Active in Nuremberg.
Engraver (including etching).

Johann Eberlein worked particularly for the Campe publishing company in Nuremberg.

EBERLIN
Austrian, 14th century.
Died 1357, in Vienna.
Painter.

EBERLIN, L.
German, 17th century.
Active probably in Nuremberg.
Painter.

J. C. Sartorius engraved a portrait of J. H. Beil, a merchant of Nuremberg, after one of L. Eberlin's paintings.

EBERLIN, Peter
German, 16th century.
Active in Heilbronn.
Painter.

Peter Eberlin painted escutcheons. He is known to have contributed to the decoration of the new town hall in Heilbronn in 1582.

EBERLING, Alfred Rudolfovich
Russian, 20th century.
Born 3 January 1872, in Zgierz.
Painter. Religious subjects, allegorical subjects, portraits, landscapes.

A pupil of Ilya Repin at the academy in St Petersburg, Alfred Eberling completed his studies in Munich with Lenbach and in Italy. He worked on several occasions for Nicolas II and for Ferdinand of Bulgaria and painted fourteen scenes of the *Life of Jesus* for the Russian church in Istanbul.

Eberling took part in many collective exhibitions. In one he showed a large allegorical picture, *Art Ancien and Art Nouveau*, now at the school of fine art in Kazan. He also featured each year in the spring exhibition in St Petersburg with large, allegorical compositions of portraits and landscapes.

MUSEUMS AND GALLERIES:
SAN FRANCISCO: *Artist's Dream; Italian Landscapes* - SARATOV: *Ukrainian Woman; Portrait of N. M. Galkin-Vraski.*

EBERMAYER, Paul
German, 17th century.
Active in Nuremberg.
Glass painter.

Paul Ebermayer also painted watercolours, especially of coat of arms.

EBERMAYR, Johann Erhard
German, 17th century.
Born 1659; died 1692, in Nuremberg.
Active in Nuremberg.
Painter. History painting.

Johann Ebermayr trained under Jean Murrer and worked in Venice. Most of his paintings can be found in Weissenfels.

EBERS, Emil
German, 19th century.
Born 14 December 1807, in Breslau (now Wroclaw, Poland); died 1884, in Beuthen (Silesia).
Painter, engraver. Genre scenes, seascapes.

Emil Ebers trained at the Düsseldorf academy from 1830 to 1837. After that he went on study trips to Holland and Normandy with R. Jordan and K. Ritter. He settled in Breslau, then Grolitz, and finally moved to Beuthen. He exhibited at the royal academy in Berlin and in Dresden from 1830 to 1883. Notable works of his include *Fear of the Storm, Shipwrecked on a Raft* and *Smugglers in a Tavern.*

Ebers

MUSEUMS AND GALLERIES:
BERLIN (Nationalgal.): *Smugglers* - WROCLAW: *Mutiny on Board.*

AUCTION RECORDS:
COLOGNE, 22 May 1986, *Sailors' Departure* (1843, oil on canvas, 8½ x 11½ ins / 21.5 x 29.5 cm) DEM 1,800.

EBERS, Hermann
German, 20th century.
Born 21 June 1881, in Leipzig.
Painter. Portraits, still-lifes, flowers.

Ebers was the son of the Egyptologist and writer Georg Ebers. He trained under Hackel, Herterich and Wilhelm von Zügel in Munich. His works appeared in numerous exhibitions in Munich, Leipzig and Bremen.

AUCTION RECORDS:
MUNICH, 5 Nov 1986, *Undergrowth* (1919, oil on canvas, 31½ x 23½ ins / 80 x 60 cm) DEM 2,500.

EBERSBACH, E.
German.
Engraver.

He engraved a *Joseph in Egypt* after F. Trevisani, as well as a view of the cloister of Einsiedeln.

EBERSBACH, H., or Eberspach
Swiss, 17th - 18th century.
Active probably in Einsiedeln.
Engraver.

According to Dr Carl Brun, H. Ebersbach, who is well known as a result of several views of Einsiedeln, may be the same person as Johann-Heinrich Ebersbach, mentioned from 1693 to 1711 as a printer of books at the monastery of Einsiedeln.

EBERSBACH, J. D.
Dutch, 19th century.
Active in Amsterdam.
Painter, lithographer.

J. D. Ebersbach is cited in *Art Prices Current.* One of his paintings, *Luther in his Erfurt Library*, was shown in Rostock and in 1857 in Szczecin.

AUCTION RECORDS:
LONDON, 27 April 1908, *Winter's Day*, GBP 1.

EBERSBACH, Johann Jacob
German, 18th century.
Born 1717, in Augsburg; died 1754.
Engraver (burin).

Johann Ebersbach engraved 30 panels for *Masculi Encomia Coelituum.*

EBERSBACH, Johann Mathias
German, 18th century.
Engraver.

A *Four Seasons* is known to be by Johann Ebersbach.

EBERSBERG, Carl Martin
German, 19th century.
Born 1824, in Biberach; died 1880, in Graz.
Painter. Genre scenes, figures.

A *Lady on Horseback* is attributed to Carl Ebersberg.

AUCTION RECORDS:
LUCERNE, 25 May 1982, *Amazon* (oil on canvas, 36 x 32 ins / 90.5 x 81 cm) CHF 5,400. VIENNA, 19 Jan 1983, *Officer on Horseback* (1862, oil on canvas, 14½ x 16¼ ins / 37 x 41 cm) ATS 28,000.

EBERSBERGER, Max
German, 19th century.
Born 22 February 1852, in Nuremberg.
Painter.

Max Ebersberger trained at the academy in Munich under Piloty. He was a painter of genre and still-lifes, and also decorated hotels and restaurants in Munich.

EBERSBERGER, Therese or Thea
German, 19th - 20th century.
Active in Munich.
Painter.

Ebersberger was the daughter of Max Ebersberger. She mainly painted miniatures.

EBERSOLD, Ludwig Rudolf
Swiss, 18th - 19th century.
Baptised 23 October 1773; died 24 January 1834, in Bern.
Active in Burgdorf.
Painter.

Ludwig Ebersold exhibited paintings and drawings (mostly copies) in Bern between 1804 and 1830. He worked for the postal services in this city.

EBERSOLE, Mabel Helen
American, 20th century.

Born 27 June 1885, in Keokuk (Iowa).
Painter.

Mabel Ebersole was a pupil of Buehr, Obertenfler, Norton and Anisfeld. In 1930 she won the portrait prize at the Delgado Museum in New Orleans.

EBERT, Anton

Czech, 19th century.
Born 29 June 1845, in Kladruby in the castle of the Windischgratz family; died 1896, in Vienna.
Painter. Portraits, genre scenes, landscapes.

Born in Bohemia, Anton Ebert trained first at the art academy in Prague and then in Vienna under Waldmüller. He initially painted genre scenes of peaceful family life with children and portraits. Later he painted landscapes, particularly of the surroundings of Vienna. He also executed the altarpiece of St Peter's church in Kladruby. He exhibited work at the royal academy in Vienna, and in other exhibitions between 1868 and 1888.

Museums and Galleries:

Dallas (Texas AG): *Unknown Portrait* - Mainz: *Portrait of Prince Windischgratz, Governor of Mainz* - Moscow (Rumiantsev Mus.): *Mother and Her Children* - Szczecin: *At the Fountain* - Vienna: *Self-portrait.*

Auction records:

London, 24 Feb 1908, *Woman from Genoa; Head Portrait of a Young Girl,* GBP 2. London, 13 Dec 1909, *Head Portrait of a Viennese Woman,* GBP 1. London, 21 July 1976, *Lacemaker* (1895, oil on canvas, 30 1/4 x 19 1/4 ins / 77 x 49 cm) GBP 300. London, 24 June 1981, *Medieval Celebration* (oil on canvas, 30 1/4 x 46 ins / 77 x 117 cm) GBP 2,400. Vienna, 14 Sept 1983, *Children in a Wood on a Mountainside* (1883, oil on panel, 22 3/4 x 16 1/4 ins / 58 x 41 cm) ATS 70,000. Vienna, 19 March 1986, *Birthday Cake* (oil on canvas, 31 1/2 x 25 1/4 ins / 80 x 64 cm) ATS 300,000. New York, 23 Feb 1989, *Gift of a Rose* (1887, oil on canvas, 43 1/2 x 31 ins / 110.5 x 79 cm) USD 7,700. Paris, 7 March 1989, *Bacchante* (1869, oil on panel, 22 1/4 x 17 ins / 56.5 x 43 cm) FRF 6,000. New York, 16 Feb 1995, *Portrait of a Young Woman* (oil on panel, 20 3/4 x 16 1/2 ins / 52.7 x 41.9 cm) USD 9,200. New York, 26 Feb 1997, *Lost in Thought* (oil on canvas, 39 1/2 x 29 ins / 100.3 x 73.7 cm) USD 3,680. Vienna, 20 May 1999, *Interior with Family Scene, Woman Feeding Young Child* (oil on panel, 15 x 12 ins / 39 x 30 cm) ATS 80,000. Aarhus, 28 June 1999, *Woman Writing Letter. Woman Reading Letter* (oil on panel, a pair, 8 x 7 ins / 21 x 17 cm) DKK 18,000. Vienna, 23 May 2000, *Grandmother's Recovery* (oil on canvas, 37 x 28 ins / 95 x 71 cm) ATS 250,000. Stockholm, 29 May 2001, *The Opera Singer Adelina Patti* (oil on canvas, 21 x 17 ins / 53 x 42 cm) SEK 30,000. Barcelona, 22 Jan 2002, *Motherhood* (oil on canvas, 39 x 28 ins / 98 x 71 cm) EUR 3,500. Aarhus, 26 Feb 2002, *Portrait of Lady* (oil on canvas, 21 x 17 ins / 53 x 42 cm) DKK 42,000. Munich, 19 Sept 2003, *Giving Alms after Church* (oil on panel, 25 x 20 ins / 64 x 50 cm) EUR 5,700. Vienna, 24 Nov 2003, *Surprise* (1872, oil on panel, 25 x 20 ins / 63 x 50 cm) EUR 9,000. Vienna, 27 May 2004, *Girl with Coral Necklace and Japanese Fan* (oil on panel, 13 x 10 ins / 34 x 26 cm) EUR 3,800. London, 6 July 2004, *Broken Pitcher* (oil on canvas, after Jean Baptiste Greuze, 41 x 30 ins / 105 x 76 cm) GBP 7,500.

EBERT, Carl

German, 19th century.
Born 13 March 1821, in Stuttgart; died 1 March 1885, in Munich.
Painter, illustrator. Landscapes, landscapes with figures.

Carl Ebert trained under Steinkopf at the art school in Stuttgart. He travelled to Italy, Holland and France, then settled in Munich in 1846. He exhibited in Munich, Vienna and Düsseldorf from 1858 to 1883. He became a member of the Amsterdam academy and was awarded a gold medal in 1872 and another in Munich in 1876. He handled subjects such as winter landscapes, wind-swept countrysides, forests, caves and storm scenes.

Museums and Galleries:

Stuttgart: *Valley in Upper Bavaria; Landscape with Children.*

Auction records:

Vienna, 14 March 1967, *Cottage in Chiemsee,* ATS 22,000. Vienna, 14 June 1977, *Bather in Undergrowth* (oil on canvas, 20 x 30 3/4 ins / 51 x 78 cm) ATS 320,000. Munich, 30 Nov 1978, *Alpine Landscape* (oil on panel, 4 1/2 x 7 1/4 ins / 11.5 x 18.5 cm) DEM 9,000. New York, 28 May 1981, *Harvest Scene* (1848, oil on canvas, 32 3/4 x 46 ins / 83 x 116 cm) USD 28,000. Munich, 20 Oct 1983, *Harvest Scene by Starnberg Lake* (oil on canvas, 33 x 46 ins / 84 x 117 cm) DEM 130,000. London, 20 June 1986, *Bathing in Undergrowth* (oil on canvas, 35 3/4 x 49 ins / 91 x 124.4 cm) GBP 28,000. New York, 1 March 1990, *Old Mill* (oil on canvas, 24 x 34 1/2 ins / 61 x 87.7 cm) USD 6,600. New York, 12 Oct 1994, *Shepherd in a Wood* (oil on panel, 14 1/2 x 12 3/4 ins / 36.8 x 32.7 cm) USD 4,025. Munich, 27 Feb 1999, *Forest Landscape with Bathing Children* (oil on canvas, 36 x 50 ins / 92 x 127 cm) DEM 17,500. Munich, 24 March 1999, *Hay Boat in a Mountain Lake, Castle Beyond* (1852, oil on canvas, 13 x 24 ins / 34 x 62 cm) DEM 35,000. Munich, 5 July 2000, *River Landscape* (oil on paper/canvas, 12 x 16 ins / 30 x 40 cm) DEM 7,000. Stuttgart, 22 Sept 2000, *Wooded Landscape with Boys Bathing* (oil on canvas, 36 x 50 ins / 92 x 127 cm) DEM 32,000. St Gall, 8 May 2001, *Wooded Landscape* (1874, oil on canvas, 15 x 22 ins / 37 x 57 cm) CHF 7,500. Zurich, 10 Dec 2001, *Children Bathing* (oil on canvas, 39 x 52 ins / 98 x 131 cm) CHF 21,000. Vienna, 16 May 2002, *Fortress Vranduk, Bosnia* (oil on canvas, 43 x 71 ins / 110 x 180 cm) EUR 32,000.

EBERT, Charles H.

American, 20th century.
Born 20 July 1873, in Milwaukee (Wisconsin); died 1959.
Painter.

Charles Ebert studied in the USA and was a pupil at the Cincinnati Art Academy and the Art Students' League in New York and, while in France, at the Académie Julian in Paris. He won a bronze medal at the Buenos Aires exhibition of 1910.

Auction records:

New York, 24 April 1981, *House on the Hill* (oil on canvas, 23 x 29 ins / 58.4 x 73.7 cm) USD 2,600. New York, 25 May 1989, *Giverny* (oil on canvas, 25 x 30 ins / 63.5 x 76 cm) USD 24,200. New York, 28 Sept 1989, *Village Pump* (oil on canvas, 25 x 30 ins / 63.5 x 76.2 cm) USD 8,800. New York, 14 Feb 1990, *In the Cove* (oil on panel, 11 3/4 x 16 ins / 30 x 40.5 cm) USD 4,400. New York, 21 May 1991, *Spring in Connecticut* (oil on canvas, 27 x 24 3/4 ins / 68.6 x 62.8 cm) USD 3,850. New York, 23 Sept 1992, *Ebert's Pond* (oil on canvas, 36 x 36 ins / 91.5 x 91.5 cm) USD 4,950. New York, 24 May 2000, *Monhegan Island, Maine* (oil on canvas, 25 x 30 ins / 63 x 77 cm) USD 35,000. New York, 4 Oct 2000, *Fishing Boats. Fishing Boats Entering Safe Harbour* (oil on panel, a pair, 8 x 10 ins / 20 x 25 cm) USD 7,500. Milford, 24 April 2003, *Monhegan Island, Maine* (oil on canvas, 20 x 25 ins / 51 x 64 cm) USD 22,000. Milford, 6 May 2004, *Monhegan Cove* (oil on plasterboard, 8 x 10 ins / 20 x 25 cm) USD 7,000. Portland, 6 Aug 2004, *Monhegan Harbour* (oil on canvasboard, 11 x 16 ins / 29 x 41 cm) USD 4,250.

EBERT, Chr.

German, 18th century.
Born 18th century, to a family originally from Hilburghausen.
Painter.

Chr. Ebert finished several paintings started by J. Heinrich Müller in the church in Mupperg.

EBERT, Emanuel
Swiss, 18th century.
Active in Basel.
Draughtsman, engraver (including wood).

Emanuel Ebert is known for a wood carving depicting a warrior from the Middle Ages. In panel form it was used for a long time as the frontispiece for the Basel calendar *Little War Book*. He also produced a view of the city of Basel and a family tree of the Burckhardt family.

EBERT, Johann Sigismund
German, 18th century.
Died 1727.
Active in Berlin.
Engineer, painter.

EBERT, Mary Robert
American, 20th century.
Born 8 February 1873, in Titusville (Pennsylvania); died 1956.
Painter. Landscapes.

Mary Ebert was also involved in decorative art.

Auction records:
New York, 14 Nov 1991, *Mohegan Island in Maine* (oil on canvas, 25 x 30 ins / 63.5 x 76.2 cm) USD 9,900.

EBERTS, Jean Henri
French, 18th century.
Active in Paris.
Draughtsman, engraver (burin).

Jean Henri Eberts engraved war subjects.

EBERZ, Josef
German, 20th century.
Born 1880, in Limburg; died 1942.
Painter.

Eberz was a pupil of Halm and Stuck in Hann Muenden before training in Karlsruhe and Düsseldorf, then in Stuttgart under Landenberger and Hölzel. He was a member of the November group. He is known principally for his brightly coloured mosaic-type compositions of the 1910s and 1920s. His works include *Christ and Mary Magdalene* (1911), *Pietà* (1912), and *The Way of the Cross* for St Mary's church in Kaiserslautern (1914).

Between 1910 and 1920 he exhibited at the Hans Goltz gallery in Munich and the Alfred Flechtheim gallery in Düsseldorf.

I.EBERZ.18

Auction records:
Munich, 11 Dec 1978, *Houses in Summer* (1920, gouache, 10¼ x 15 ins / 25.8 x 38.4 cm) DEM 2,300. Munich, 2 June 1980, *Tropical Garden* (oil on canvas, 23¾ x 20 ins / 60.5 x 50.5 cm) DEM 11,000. Munich, 30 June 1982, *Landscape with Fishing Boats* (1923, watercolour and gouache, 13½ x 19¾ ins / 34 x 50 cm) DEM 1,400. Cologne, 6 Dec 1983, *Bathers in the Wood* (1918, oil on canvas, 32¼ x 22½ ins / 82 x 57 cm) DEM 22,000. Munich, 14 June 1985, *View of a Park* (1918, watercolour and pencil, 19¼ x 15 ins / 49 x 38 cm) DEM 5,000. Cologne, 29 May 1987, *Wilderness* (1918, oil on panel, 13¼ x 10¼ ins / 33.6 x 26.2 cm) DEM 28,000. London, 9 Oct 1997, *Tropical Landscape* (1918, oil on canvas, 43¼ x 32 ins / 110 x 81 cm) GBP 29,900. Cologne, 29 May 1999, *Road in the Mountains* (oil on canvas, 28 x 23 ins / 70 x 58 cm) DEM 21,000. London, 6 Oct 1999, *San Francisco Cloister* (oil on canvas, 30 x 27 ins / 77 x 69 cm) GBP 7,500. Cologne, 11 Nov 2000, *Crucifixion* (oil on canvas, 35 x 41 ins / 90 x 105 cm) DEM 62,000. Berlin, 25 Nov 2000, *Street* (oil on canvas, 28 x 23 ins / 70 x 58 cm) DEM 37,000. Munich, 19 May 2001, *Woman at her Toilette* (1907, watercolour over pencil, 14 x 11 ins / 36 x 27 cm) DEM 3,200. Berlin, 1 Dec 2001, *The Wonder of Jesus' Heart* (oil/tempera on board, 19 x 17 ins / 47 x 42 cm) DEM 5,000. Munich, 17 May 2002, *Rocca in Evening* (1920, oil on canvas, 28 x 31 ins / 70 x 78 cm) EUR 14,000. Cologne, 4 Dec 2002, *Landscape with Fortress* (oil on canvas, 28 x 31 ins / 70 x 78 cm) EUR 9,000. Hamburg, 24 Oct 2003, *Cacti Field* (watercolour lithograph, 17 x 14 ins / 43 x 35 cm) EUR 3,000.

EBHARDT, Johann Christian
German, 18th century.
Born to a family originally from Rochlitz; died 1739, in Dresden.
Sculptor.

Between 1730 and 1731 Johann Ebhardt worked on the altar of the church in Leubnitz, near Dresden, with Johann-Bernhard Reinboth.

EBIHARA, Kinosuke
Japanese, 20th century.
Born 1904, in Kagoshima; died 19 September 1970, in Paris.
Painter.

Ebihara Kinosuke studied at the Kawabata School of Painting in Tokyo. In 1923 he went to Paris, where he studied with Fujita Tsuguji and exhibited at the 1925 and 1929 Salon d'Automne and the Salon des Indépendants. He returned to Japan in 1934. In 1935 he became a member of the Independent Art Association. He won the Bunka prize twice, in 1950 and 1954, and in 1960 received the Mainichi art prize. He founded an Art Institute in 1951. A large retrospective exhibition was organised in Tokyo in 1963.

EBIRLEN. See **EBERLEIN**

EBIRLYN. See **EBERLEIN**

EBLE, Bruno
French, 20th - 21st century.
Born 1964, in Romilly-sur-Seine (Aube).
Painter.

Bruno Eble was a student at the École des Beaux-Arts in Paris. His paintings, which are composed of alternate warm and cool colours, are arranged in polyptychs and set in lead frames. His titles are borrowed from mythology, for example, *Antigone (But Also the Lips of the Hot-blooded Courtesans)*.

Eble has exhibited at collective exhibitions: 1993, École des Beaux-Arts, Paris; 1994, Salon de Montrouge; 1995, SIAC (Salon International d'Art Contemporain), Strasbourg; 1996, *Peinture? Peintures! (Painting? Paintings!)*, at the Crédac in Ivry-sur-Seine and the Kunstihoone Gallery, Tallinn (Estonia). He had solo shows in 1995 in Strasbourg and in 1996 at the Institut Français in Freiburg.

Bibliography:
Peinture? Peintures!, group exhibition catalogue, Crédac centre d'Art contemporain, Ivry-sur-Seine, 1996.

EBLE, Théo
Swiss, 20th century.
Born 1899, in Basel; died 1974, in Basel.
Painter.
Neo-Constructivism.
Gruppe 33.

Eble trained at the Basel art school, and later under Karl Hofer at the Berlin art academy. On his return to Switzerland in 1933 he and Walter Bodmer founded Gruppe 33, which attracted avant-garde artists from the city of Basel. His *Construction* (1937), in the Basel Museum, is executed in the constructivist spirit of El Lissitsky. Another canvas at the same museum displays a much more formalist abstraction.

Museums and Galleries:
Basel: *Construction.*
Auction records:
Lucerne, 25 May 1991, *Turning Round and Round* (1965, oil on canvas, 39 x 39 ins / 99 x 99 cm) CHF 5,000. Zurich, 30 Nov 1995, *The Area Around Bruderholz near Basel* (1928, oil on canvas, 25 1/4 x 32 3/4 ins / 64 x 83 cm) CHF 6,900. Bern, 5 Nov 1999, *Girl in Carnival Costume* (oil on canvas, 44 x 31 ins / 111 x 80 cm) CHF 10,000. Zurich, 7 Dec 1999, *Kapriole* (mixed media on panel, 16 x 11 ins / 41 x 27 cm) CHF 3,200. Zurich, 11 June 2001, *Portrait of a Woman* (oil on canvas, 17 x 13 ins / 43 x 33 cm) CHF 3,000. Lucerne, 14 Nov 2001, *Rhine Landscape near Basel* (1922, oil on canvas, 22 x 27 ins / 57 x 68 cm) CHF 3,600. St Gall, 24 Oct 2003, *Memory* (tempera on canvas, 17 x 13 ins / 42 x 32 cm) CHF 2,800.

EBLING, Sonia
Brazilian, 20th century.
Born 1926, in Rio Grande do Sul.
Sculptor, painter.
Sonia Ebling studied at the fine arts college of Porto Allegre and then in Rio de Janeiro. She continued her training with Zadkine. Her sculptures are abstract and comprise assemblies of filiform structures.

EBNER, Franz Anton
Austrian, 18th century.
Born c. 1698; died 31 August 1756, in Salzburg.
Painter.
Franz Ebner was a court painter and lived most of his life in Salzburg, with the exception of a three-year stay in Rome from 1726 to 1729. Churches in Salzburg have most of his works.

EBNER, Georg Sebastian
German, 19th century.
Born 1776, in Nuremberg.
Painter. Flowers.

EBNER, Ludwig. See **DEAK EBNER Lajos**

EBNER, Ludwig
German, 19th century.
Active at the beginning of the 19th century.
Engraver (aquatint).
Ludwig Ebner illustrated a number of books. Notable works by him include *Neptune's Cave in Tivoli* after Gmelin, and a *Series of Costumes* after J. B. Seele.

EBNER, Richard
German, 20th century.
Died 12 February 1911, in Munich.
Active in Munich.
Painter. Genre scenes.
Ebner is known for *Memory* and *At the Market.* He exhibited in Stuttgart, Nuremberg and Munich between 1881 and 1889.

EBNER, Sil.
German, 18th century.
Active in Karlsruhe c. 1780.
Miniaturist.

EBNETH, Lajos d'
Hungarian, 20th century.
Born 1902, in Szilagysomlyo; died 1982, in Lima, Peru.
Active from 1923 in the Netherlands and from 1949 in Peru.
Painter.
Neo-Plasticism, Constructivism.
Lajos d'Ebneth studied at the academy of fine art in Budapest and at the Franz von Stuck higher academy in Munich in 1921. In 1923, he settled in The Hague. He was in contact at that time with Kurt Schwitters, Vilmos Huszar and the leaders of the De Stijl group. To start with his painting was in keeping with the Neo-Plasticism of this group which concentrated around Mondrian and Van Doesburg. Later influenced by the works of Moholy-Nagy, he moved towards Constructivism, which was less sectarian and exclusive than Neo-Plasticism. Lajos d'Ebneth was also interested in advertising graphics and photography and was active in the Bauhaus movement. He settled in Peru from 1949 onwards.
D'Ebneth exhibited in Berlin with Kurt Schwitters at Der Sturm gallery.
Bibliography:
Hahn, Otto, *Aspects historiques du constructivisme et de l'art concret,* exhibition catalogue, Musée d'Art moderne de la Ville de Paris, Paris, 1977. Passuth, Krisztina/Szabó, Júlia, *L'Art en Hongrie 1905-1930. Art et révolution,* exhibition catalogue, Musée d'Art et d'Industrie, Saint-Étienne, musée d'Art moderne de la ville de Paris, Paris, 1980.

EBOLITANO, Gioanluca Benedetto
Italian, 16th century.
Active in Naples.
Painter.

EBRARD
French.
Illuminator, copyist. Religious subjects.
He was a monk and transcriber at the abbey of St-Germain d'Auxerre; to him is attributed the book of Homilies, produced for the Emperor Charlemagne.

EBSTEIN, Joseph
French, 20th century.
Born 12 May 1881, in Batna, Algeria.
Sculptor.
Joseph Ebstein studied with Barrias and Coutan. In 1905 he became a member of the Société des Artistes Français in Paris, exhibited with them regularly and won an honourable mention in 1906. He was declared *hors concours,* and was made a Chevalier of the Légion d'Honneur in 1930.

EBSWORTH, Joseph Woodfall
British, 19th century.
Born 2 September 1824; died 7 June 1908.
Painter, draughtsman.
Joseph Ebsworth, the son of an Edinburgh musician, was a pupil of Charles Heath Wilson, Sir William Allan and David Scott in Edinburgh. In 1848 he went to Manchester where he joined the lithographic and letterpress printing firm Falkner Brothers as chief draughtsman. He later became a teacher at the School of Fine Arts in Glasgow. His main works were etchings and lithographs as illustrations for 17th-century works such as *Scottish Ballads.*
Museums and Galleries:
Edinburgh: *Four Views of Edinburgh* - Edinburgh (Scottish National Portrait Gallery): *Joseph Ebsworth, Musician* (1848, watercolour).

EBY, Charles
French, 18th century.
Active in Paris in 1781.
Painter, sculptor.

EBY, Kerr
American, 20th century.
Born 19 October 1889, in Tokyo (Japan); died 1946, in Norwalk (Connecticut).
Painter, engraver.
Kerr Eby was a member of the Associated National Academy of Design in New York and the Chicago Society of Etchers. He won the prize awarded by the latter organisation at the International Exhibition in 1931. He practised etching.
Auction records:
New York, 17 May 1982, *Study for the Great Black Cloud* (charcoal, 13 x 17 ins / 33 x 43.2 cm) USD 1,100. London, 25 April 1984, *September 13th 1918* (etching, 10 1/4 x 15 3/4 ins /

26.2 x 40.2 cm) GBP 1,000. SHAKER HEIGHTS, 9 Oct 1999, *September 13, 1918, St Mihiel* (etching and aquatint on sandpaper ground, 11 x 16 ins / 28 x 41 cm) USD 4,250. SHAKER HEIGHTS, 25 March 2000, *September 13, 1918, St Mihiel* (etching and aquatint on sandpaper ground, 11 x 16 ins / 28 x 41 cm) USD 3,750.

ECALLE, Georges Charles
French, 20th century.
Born 8 February 1875, in Paris.
Painter.

Georges Charles Ecalle studied with Dauphin. He joined the Salon des Artistes Français in Paris in 1923.

ECCARDT (Miss)
British, 18th century.
Painter. Landscapes.

Miss Eccardt was probably the granddaughter of Johann Aegidius Eccardt. She appeared in 1798 at the Royal Academy in London with an *Italian Landscape*.

ECCARDT. See also **ECKARD, ECKARDT, ECKHARD**

ECCARDT, Johann Aegidius or John Giles, or Eckhardt or Echardt
German, 18th century.
Born in Germany; died October 1779, in Chelsea.
Painter. Portraits.

As a young man Johann Eccardt went to England and trained under Van Loo around 1740. He travelled to Italy in the company of Sir Joshua Reynolds and then settled in London. He found protectors such as Walpole, who in 1745 commissioned him to do a painting of himself and his first wife. In 1746 the famous statesman dedicated a poem to Eccardt: *Beauties*. His collection of art works, which he sold in 1770, was famous for its quality.

Eccardt painted with extreme care and acquired a very fine reputation as a portrait painter.

MUSEUMS AND GALLERIES:

LONDON (National Portrait Gal.): *Conyers Middleton* (1746, oil on canvas); *Thomas Gray* (1747-1748, oil on canvas); *Horatio ('Horace') Walpole, 4th Earl of Orford* (1754, oil on canvas); other portraits.

AUCTION RECORDS:

NEW YORK, 3 March 1908, *Portrait of Lady Maria Walpole*, USD 130. LONDON, 25 July 1924, *Robert Booth in Brown Apparel; Matthew Booth in Brown and Red Apparel* (collection) GBP 9. LONDON, 7 Dec 1925, *Lady Jane Musgrave in Brown Apparel Embellished with Red Scarf Trimmed with Ermine* (1850) GBP 63. LONDON, 11 June 1926, *Man in Brown Apparel; Man in Brown Apparel with Red Jacket* (collection) GBP 32. LONDON, 5 April 1929, *Man in Blue Suit with Red Sash; Lady in Black with White Hat* (collection) GBP 22; *Portrait of Sir Charles Hanbury Williams in Brown Apparel with Red Belt; Portrait of Thomas Winnington* (collection) GBP 27. LONDON, 7 March 1930, *Portrait of Sir Robert Walpole with his First Wife, Catherine Shorter*, GBP 336. NEW YORK, 12 April 1935, *Lady Catherine Maria Walpole*, USD 750. NEW YORK, 23 Jan 1936, *Lady Catherine Maria Walpole*, USD 500. LONDON, 9 July 1986, *Portrait of Richard Bentley* (oil on canvas, 16½ x 12½ ins / 42 x 32 cm) GBP 5,200. LONDON, 14 July 1993, *Bust Portrait of James, 8th Count of Abercorn, Wearing Clothes in the Style of Van Dyck* (oil on canvas, 18 x 11½ ins / 45.5 x 29.5 cm) GBP 8,050. LONDON, 30 Nov 2000, *Portrait of Horace Walpole, Wearing Van Dyck Dress* (oil on canvas, 17 x 13 ins / 43 x 34 cm) GBP 26,000. LONDON, 3 Dec 2002, *Portrait of an Officer* (oil on canvas, oval, 30 x 25 ins / 76 x 64 cm) GBP 1,000.

ECCLESIA AND SYNAGOGA OF..., Master of the. See **MASTERS**

ECCLESTON, T.
British, 19th century.
Active in England.
Painter. Landscapes, seascapes.

T. Eccleston was mentioned by *Art Prices Current*

AUCTION RECORDS:

LONDON, 3 May 1909, *On the Coast of Norfolk; River Scene*, GBP 1.

ECCLINE
French, 18th century.
Painter.

Only one picture by Eccline is known, a saint, dated 1773, in the church of La Gonfrière, near Bernay (Eure).

ECCLISSI, Antonio. See **ECLISSI**

ECHARD, Auguste Daniel Charles
French, 19th century.
Born c. 1820, in St-Lucien, near Beauvais.
Painter. Church interiors. Murals.

From 1838 to 1844 Auguste Echard was a regular exhibitor at the Paris Salon. With his Flemish Realism and his way of filtering light through stained glass, he was a successor to Peeter Neefs and the other 17th-century Dutch painters of church interiors, the genre in which he specialised.

ÉCHARD, Charles. See **ESCHARD**

ÉCHARD, Charles Marcel
French, 20th century.
Born 10 January 1915, in Paris; died 2 July 1958.
Painter, watercolourist, draughtsman, engraver, lithographer, illustrator. Figures, nudes, landscapes, seascapes, still-lifes.

Charles Marcel Échard began his studies at the École des Beaux-Arts in Paris, but left early. He showed work in some group exhibitions, especially the Salon d'Automne, afterwards preferring solo exhibitions, also in Paris. In 1946 he was given a grant by the government, which bought several of his pieces.

Échard's best known oil paintings are of figures, nudes and seascapes. His line is strong, the whole well put together, like his colours which are laid on in firm almost unmodulated planes. He produced many drawings and watercolours, very direct, and lively spontaneous sketches, and illustrated a number of handsome publications, including *Au Seuil de la Mer* (*On the Threshold of the Sea*) by Jean de la Varende and *Colette, mon amie* by Francis Carco.

ECHARRI, Isabel
Spanish, 20th century.
Born 10 February 1929, in Vera de Bidasoa (Navarre).
Sculptor, engraver. Artists' books.

Isabel Echarri studied in Nancy from 1950 to 1954 and then in Paris until 1957. Her first exhibition was in Paris in 1956. She has taken part in many Salons including the Salon Comparaisons from 1963 to 1967 and the Salon de Mai. Her works have been exhibited worldwide: in 1972-1973 museums in Germany ran a touring exhibition of her work; in 2001 an exhibition accompanied by object-books created by the artist and by Fernando Arrabal *La Marelle* (*Hopscotch*) was held.

Echarri's work is unique and contains elements of both engraving and sculpture. Using liquid paper pulp she creates high relief embossings that are virtually paper sculptures. Always white, her works display a heightened sense of the use of material.

BIBLIOGRAPHY:

Ruiz Sastre, Elena, *Isabel Echarri*, exhibition catalogue, Museu d'art contemporani, Ibiza, 1999 (Text in Catalan).

ECHAUREN. See **MATTA Roberto**

ECHAURI, Vicente
Spanish, 19th century.
Born in the 19th century, in San Sebastián.
Painter. Landscapes.
Vicente Echauri first exhibited in 1881 at the exhibition of the fine arts society of Madrid.

ECHAURREN, Pablo
Italian, 20th century.
Born 1941, in Rome.
Painter, draughtsman.
Pablo Echaurren lives in Rome. His work explores the effects of crowding a multitude of images onto a single surface, a linear space-time connection drawn strictly from the picture-writing of certain primitive peoples. Henry Martin wrote of him that, 'Use of multiple images allows painting to accept its natural boundaries, while at the same time offering a sense of the complexity of events which is always noted with scornful simplicity'.

He has shown work in a number of collective exhibitions, including: 1970, 1973, Salon de la Jeune Peinture in Paris; 1974, *Contemporanea* in Rome; 1974, *Pittura e Musica*, Lugano, Switzerland; and the 9th Paris Biennale in 1975. Solo exhibitions have included: 1971, Berlin; 1972, Florence; 1973, Basel; 1974, Philadelphia, Milan, Zurich and Berlin.
BIBLIOGRAPHY:
IXe Biennale de Paris, exhibition catalogue, Idea Books, Musée d'Art Moderne de la Ville de Paris, Paris, 1975.

ECHAVE, Balthasar, also known as Baltasar de Echave Orio the Elder
Spanish, 16th - 17th century.
Born in Zumaya (Guipúzcoa).
Painter. Religious subjects.
Valencian School.
Echave belonged to the Valencia School. When he was very young, he emigrated to Mexico, where he became the pupil and then the husband of a renowned painter, Ibia, called La Sumaya, several of whose works are in Mexico cathedral. His own works include *Holy Sepulchre*, *St Anne and the Virgin*, *Meeting of Mary and Elizabeth* and *Adoration of the Magi*.
MUSEUMS AND GALLERIES:
MEXICO CITY (Mus. Nacional de San Carlo) - MEXICO CITY (Sacristy of the Church of Puebla): *Triumph of the Cross*; *Triumph of Mary*.

ECHAVE, Balthasar, also known as Baltasar de Echave Ibia, the Younger
Mexican, 17th century.
Painter.
Balthasar Echave was the son of Balthasar de Echave the Elder.
MUSEUMS AND GALLERIES:
MEXICO CITY (Mus. Nacional de San Carlos).

ECHAVE, Balthasar, also known as Baltasar de Echave el Mozo
Mexican, 17th century.
Born 1632, in Mexico City.
Painter. Religious subjects.
Balthasar de Echave el Mozo was the son of Baltasar de Echave Ibia the Younger. He trained at his father's studio but also learned about painting from the works of Zurbarán, Pereda, Cano and Murillo and from Flemish paintings sent out to Mexico, drawing elements from these that he incorporated into his own form of the Baroque.
MUSEUMS AND GALLERIES:
PUEBLA (Cathedral): *The Triumph of the Church.*

ECHAVE, José
Uruguayan, 20th century.
Born 1921, in Salto.
Painter, decorative designer. Murals.
José Echave was self-taught. He produced mural paintings and theatrical sets and was influenced by the Expressionist trend that characterised the development of painting in Latin America. He first exhibited in his native town of Salto. He later moved to Montevideo where he worked on a fresco with Portinari. His first solo exhibition took place in Salto around 1945; he also exhibited in Montevideo in 1954 and in Washington in 1956.

ECHEANDIA Y GAL, Julio
Spanish, 19th century.
Active in Spain.
Sculptor.
Julio Echeandia y Gal was awarded a bronze medal at the Exposition Universelle in Paris in 1900.

ECHEGARAY, Martín
Spanish, 20th century.
Born in Vigo (Galicia).
Painter.
Martín Echegaray exhibited in Paris at the Salon d'Automne from 1931 to 1934.

ECHENA, José
Spanish, 19th century.
Born 1 February 1845, in Fuenterrabia (Guipúzcoa); died 1909, in Rome.
Painter. Figures, portraits, genre scenes.
José Echena exhibited at the royal academy in Munich in 1883. He is known for his *To Whom the Victory?* After working in Madrid he lived in Rome and remained there until his death.
AUCTION RECORDS:
LONDON, 13 Dec 1909, *On the Way to Market*, GBP 13. LONDON, 2 Dec 1927, *Horseman; Troubador* (two panels) GBP 21. NEW YORK, 28 Oct 1982, *The Painter with His Easel at Biarritz* (oil on canvas, 22 x 41 1/2 ins / 55 x 105.5 cm) USD 18,000. LONDON, 9 Oct 1987, *The Harem Favourite in Danger* (oil on canvas, 25 1/2 x 41 ins / 65 x 104 cm) GBP 8,000. LONDON, 22 Nov 1989, *The Young Shell Collectors* (oil on panel, 13 1/2 x 9 ins / 34.5 x 23 cm) GBP 3,520. ROME, 29 May 1990, *Model Holding a Pose* (1881, watercolour, 13 1/2 x 8 1/2 ins / 34 x 21.5 cm) ITL 2,070,000. LONDON, 22 May 1992, *The Departure* (oil on panel, 5 x 9 ins / 12.6 x 23 cm) GBP 1,320. LONDON, 26 March 1997, *Harem Women on a Terrace Overlooking Cairo* (oil on canvas, 26 1/2 x 43 ins / 67 x 109 cm) GBP 109,300. LONDON, 18 June 1998, *Harem Resting at Sunset with Constantinople Beyond* (oil on canvas, 20 x 34 ins / 51 x 86 cm) GBP 55,000. LONDON, 9 Sept 1998, *Turkish Lady at Rest* (watercolour, 18 x 27 ins / 45 x 69 cm) GBP 2,200. LONDON, 21 June 2000, *Musical Interlude* (oil on panel, 15 x 9 ins / 37 x 23 cm) GBP 14,000.

ÉCHÉRAC, Auguste Arthur d'
French, 19th century.
Born 1832, in Guéret.
Sculptor, art writer.
From 1870 to 1881 Auguste Arthur d'Échérac sent busts and medallions to the Paris Salon. He is best known for his bronze bust of *Michel Möring*. He was also an author, writing works on art under the pseudonym G. Dargenty.

ECHERT, Florence
American, 20th century.
Born in Cincinnati.
Painter, decorative artist.
Florence Echert was a pupil of W.M. Chase and member of the Women's Art Club in Cincinnati.

ECHEVARRIA, Domingo de. See **CHAVARITO Dominique**

ECHEVARRIA Y ZURICALDAY, Juan José Pedro

Spanish, 20th century.

Born 14 April 1875, in Bilbao; died 8 July 1931, in Madrid.

Painter. Figures, portraits, landscapes, still-lifes, flowers.

Juan Echevarria y Zuricalday was the son of a family who ran an iron and steel business. He studied engineering in Cambridge, in Germany from 1897 and later in France and Belgium. He returned to Bilbao in 1900 to run the family factory and start new businesses but was devastated by the death of his mother in 1902. He underwent a deep emotional and existential crisis and abandoned his business interests to become a painter. He went to Paris with Francisco Iturrino and Paco Durrio and lived at 3 Rue Alfred Stevens. There he attended classes at the Académie Julian and became friends with Degas, Douanier Rousseau, Picasso, Vuillard, Canals and Zuloaga, among others. He had no financial worries as his father continued to fund him and was even able to help out his artist friends. Echevarria was a great traveller and went all over Europe while living alternately in Paris and Bilbao. In 1908 he moved into the building where Toulouse-Lautrec lived at 23 Rue de Caulaincourt and married Enriqueta Normand Böer in London. Around 1915 he left for Granada to paint landscapes. A year before his death in 1931 he was appointed director of the museum of modern art.

Echevarria was a painter of landscapes, flowers, portraits and still-lifes (bodegones). He took a traditional approach in both aesthetics and form. His work and personality are characterised by an unflinching and individual determination to continue painting without any reductive abstraction. His representations of gypsy men and women, the typical streets of Spanish towns and his portraits always reveal a calm and constant quest for truth and authenticity. Some of his figure compositions and village scenes display a realism associated with Courbet, while his brush technique, composition and use of colour often reveal the influence of Post-Impressionism. It is perhaps Echevarria's flower paintings, a genre about which he was passionate, that best reveal his very subtle art and sensibility; in these he immersed himself in a world where freedom blended with poetry and hallucination. His flowers, painted without any decorative affectation and free from excessive Mannerism, can be seen as metaphors of his real or idealised life. In contrast, his portraits mark a return to a harsher, deeper reality. He produced a series of portraits of intellectuals and from their faces, and above all from their eyes, emanate memories rather than dreams and feelings experienced rather than a longing for another age.

In 1908 he took part in his first collective exhibition in France at the Salon d'Automne in Paris; in 1913 a room was devoted to his work at the international exhibition of paintings of the Schools of Albe and Bilbao; he exhibited regularly at a number of regional and national exhibitions including the Iberian Artists Salon of 1925. Echevarria also held solo exhibitions, including one around 1915 at the Association of Basque Artists. Others include: the Spanish Society of Friends of the Arts attended by King Alfonso XIII and Queen Victoria Eugenia (1923); and Buenos Aires (1927). Since his death a number of retrospectives and exhibitions in his honour have been held: at the museum of modern art in Madrid and Bilbao (1949); at the fine arts circle and at the Théo gallery in Madrid (1961); in 1974 at a major event sponsored by the Banco de Bilbao.

BIBLIOGRAPHY:

Arnáiz, José Manuel/López Jiménez, Javier/Merchán Díaz, Manuel (ed.), *Cien años de pintura en Espana y Portugal (1830-1930)*, Antiqvaria, Madrid, 1988 (One Hundred Years of Painting in Spain and Portugal (1830-1930)).

MUSEUMS AND GALLERIES:

BILBAO (MBA): *Man from the Mountains*; *Vase and Tapestry*; *Pampliega Landscape*; *Flowers, Fan and Books*; *Gypsy from Granada*; *Band of Gypsies* - MADRID (Mus. Nacional Centro de Arte Reina Sofía): *Self-portrait*; *Montmartre*; *Vase with Daisies*; *Half-Caste Unclothed*; *Pampliega*; *Blue Flowers*; *Portrait of a Child*; *Still-life*; *Portrait of Unamuno*; *Portrait of the Sculptor Paco Durrio*; *Portrait of Azorín*; *Portrait of Iturrino*; *Avila*; *Gypsies*; *Portrait of Valle Inclán* - VITORIA (MBA de Alava): *Flowers, Books, Engravings and Green Pears*.

AUCTION RECORDS:

MADRID, 26 May 1987, *Granada Landscape* (oil on card, 18 x 15 ins / 46 x 38 cm) ESP 1,200,000.

ECHEVIN, Marius

French, 20th century.

Born 31 August 1899, in Toulon; died 1982, in Toulon.

Painter. Nudes, portraits, landscapes, still-lifes.

With qualifications from Oxford University and from the College of Preceptors, Marius Echevin, a pharmacist's son, considered a medical training, but opted for painting. He trained at the art college in Marseilles and the Académie de la Grande Chaumière in Paris, where he was taught by Antoine Bourdelle. He went home to Toulon, where he became a friend of José Mange. On 24 November 1943 his studio was destroyed in the bombardment of Toulon.

Othon Friesz invited him to contribute to the first Salon des Tuileries in Paris in 1923, and he continued to exhibit there regularly, also sending pieces to the Salon d'Automne. His work featured in the 2003 exhibition *José Mange* in Toulon art museum. In 1975 he had a solo exhibition in this museum.

BIBLIOGRAPHY:

José Mange, exhibition catalogue, Musée d'Art, Toulon, 2003.

ECHIVARD, Albert

French, 20th century.

Born 1886, in Le Mans; died 1939, in Solesmes.

Painter, glassmaker. Figure compositions.

Albert Echivard studied with Hucher. He sent *Child with Chrysanthemums* to the 1900 Paris Exposition Universelle, *The Eaglet* to the Salon des Artistes Français in 1910, and *Leda* in 1913. In 2001 his work was included in the exhibition *Les Peintres et la Sarthe* (*Painters and the Sarthe Region*) staged in Le Mans in the Queen Berengaria museum (19th-century artists) and Épau abbey (20th-century).

BIBLIOGRAPHY:

Arpentinier, Jean, *Sarthe, Terre d'Artistes*, Éd. de la Reinette, Le Mans, 2001.

ECHIZEN NO HOKKYO. See **JOKEI**

ECHTELER, Josef

German, 19th century.

Born 5 January 1853, in Legau; died 23 December 1908, in Mainz.

Sculptor. Mythological subjects, religious subjects, animals. Busts.

Josef Echteler was a cowherd during his childhood but entered into the services of a sculptor of religious imagery at the age of 12 and was irresistibly attracted by art. He initially trained at the school of fine arts in Stuttgart and then went to Munich where he trained under Widmann and Knabl. He sculpted busts, animals, and especially subjects drawn from mythology and the life of Christ. Echteler took part in the competition organised to find a design for the tomb of General Grant in New York. He sent a project but it was not accepted.

ECHTER, Eduard

German, 19th century.

Painter. Portraits.

Eduard Echter settled in Danzig and in 1842 sent a portrait of Emperor Franz I to the exhibition at the Berlin academy. He also lived in Riga and St Petersburg.

ECHTER, Franz Georg
Austrian, 17th century.
Active in Graz.
Sculptor.

Franz Echter did a statue of *St Roch* in 1688 for the church of St John and St Paul in Graz.

ECHTER, Matthias
Austrian, 17th century.
Born before 1642, in Weiz (Styria).
Painter, draughtsman, engraver.

Matthias Echter worked especially in Graz where he taught Mathias von Görz. He painted a *Birth of the Virgin* for the church of Gnas. He engraved *Hercules Overcoming Achelous* and a *Mercury and Argus* from his own drawings.

ECHTER, Michael
German, 19th century.
Born 5 March 1812, in Munich; died 4 February 1879, in Munich.
Painter. History painting, portraits, genre scenes.

Michael Echter trained at the Munich academy and worked with J. Schnorr on the production of paintings for the community hall in Munich. In 1846 he worked with Kaulbach on the decoration of the new Berlin museum. In 1862 he became an honorary member of the Munich academy and from 1868 onwards was a teacher at the school of arts and crafts in the same city. Notable works of his include *St Elizabeth*, portraits of Kepler, Merz and Steinheil, *Treaty of Pavia*, and *The Four Elements*.

ECHTER, Simon
Austrian, 17th century.
Died 6 September 1664, in Graz.
Active in Graz.
Painter.

Simon Echter was a painter of coats of arms and also contributed to the decoration of the church of St Gotthard in Graz.

ECHTERMEIER, Carl Friedrich
German, 19th - 20th century.
Born 27 October 1845, in Kassel; died 30 July 1910, in Brunswick.
Sculptor.

Echtermeier showed such a keen interest in sculpture that he obtained a grant from his home town at a very young age. He became a pupil, then a colleague, of Hanel in Dresden. From 1883 he taught modelling and embossing at Brunswick technical college. His best-known works are *Faun* and *Bacchante* (which were bought by the Berlin National Gallery), several huge groups for Brunswick's Hochschule für Bildende Künste and eight marble figures for the Kunstgalerie Kassel.

ECHTLER, Adolf
German, 19th century.
Born 5 January 1843, in Danzig (now Gdansk, Poland); died 1914.
Painter. Portraits, genre scenes.

Adolf Echtler studied art in Venice, Vienna and Munich, where he trained under the supervision of Wilhelm Diez. From 1877 to 1886 he stayed in Paris, then settled in Munich. He was awarded the 'petite médaille d'or' in Berlin in 1874. He exhibited at the royal academy in Berlin, Vienna, Munich and at the Salon de Paris from 1869 to 1889.

MUSEUMS AND GALLERIES:
ALTENBURG: *Visit of Condolence* - BAUTZEN: *Children Gathering Sunflowers; Sappho* - DRESDEN: *Downfall of a Family* - HAMBURG (Kunsthalle): *Orphans* - LEIPZIG: *Abandoned* - MUNICH (Pinakothek): *Fallen* - WÜRZBURG: *Ash Wednesday*.

AUCTION RECORDS:
NEW YORK, 17 Jan 1902, *Firsts Steps*, USD 340. NEW YORK, 20 March 1902, *Young Pipe Player*, USD 190. NEW YORK, 15-16 Feb 1906, *Repenting Sinner*, USD 260. NEW YORK, 18 Sept 1981, *Stroll* (oil on canvas, 12¼ x 21¼ ins / 31.1 x 54 cm) USD 950. LONDON, 22 June 1983, *At the Cobbler's* (1887, oil on panel, 16½ x 12¼ ins / 42 x 31 cm) GBP 4,000. NEW YORK, 21 May 1986, *Little Girl Knitting* (oil on canvas, 26 x 18¾ ins / 66 x 47.6 cm) USD 14,000. BILLINGSHURST, 18 May 1999, *Going to the Ball* (1871, oil on canvas, 33 x 27 ins / 84 x 69 cm) GBP 4,000. NEW YORK, 3 Nov 1999, *Feeding the Pigeons* (1884, oil on canvas, 29 x 23 ins / 73 x 58 cm) USD 40,000.

ECHTLER, Johann Peter
German, 18th - 19th century.
Born 21 August 1741, in Steingaden (Bavaria); died c. 1810, in Berlin.
Sculptor, stucco artist.

Johann Echtler trained under Zimmermann in Lemberg and became an artist who was greatly appreciated by his contempories and sought after for the decoration of churches, palaces and special hotels. Examples include his contribution to the works at the new palace in Potsdam. Yet it was particularly in Silesia where he practised his profession, including in Minister Schloendorff's palace in Seppau, the Hatzfeld palace in Breslau (now Wroclaw), and the episcopal residence. He specialised in the imitation of porphyry and marble.

ECK. See also **EGG**

ECK, Adam, or Egg
Hungarian, 17th century.
Born in Eger; died 1664, in Eger.
Sculptor (wood).

Adam Eck was the son of Erhard Eck, and the grandson of the wood sculptor Peter Eck. He produced mostly altarpieces, including altarpieces for the Franciscan chapel in Eger and for the chapel at Seeberg castle. The treasury of the parish church of Altötting in Bavaria has a low relief sculpted by him, depicting *St George and the Dragon*.

MUSEUMS AND GALLERIES:
BERLIN (Kunstgewerbemus.): *Passion of Christ* (four low reliefs).

ECK, Daniel
French, 19th century.
Born 20 December 1807; died 20 June 1846, in Hirtzbach, near Mulhouse.
Active in Mulhouse.
Painter.

The brother of Frédéric and Jacques Eck, Daniel Eck studied in Paris.

ECK, David
German, 16th century.
Active in Würzburg in 1557.
Painter.

ECK, Edmund
German, 18th century.
Active in Diessen (Bavaria).
Painter.

Edmund Eck produced several paintings after Bassano for the old Benedictine abbey of Andech. He may also have been know as Edmundus Egg.

ECK, Frédéric
French, 19th century.
Born 1810, in Mulhouse; died 1860, in Paris.
Active in Mulhouse.
Painter.
Like his brothers Daniel and Jacques Eck, Frédéric Eck worked in Mulhouse. He executed the portrait of Gaspard Baumgartner and his wife, and that of the painter Georges Zipelius.

ECK, Georg Mathaeus, or Egg
Hungarian, 17th century.
Active at the end of the 17th century.
Sculptor (wood).
Two limewood low reliefs by Georg Mathaeus Eck, depicting battle scenes from the Turkish wars, are in the town of Klosterneuburg. He also produced a low relief depicting the siege of Buda.

ECK, Isaac van
Dutch, 18th century.
Active in Amsterdam at the beginning of the 18th century.
Engraver.
Isaac van Eck was whipped and imprisoned for 15 years after having insulted the burgomaster of Haze in the street.

ECK, Jacques
French, 19th century.
Born 1812, in Mulhouse; died 1887.
Painter. Portraits.
MUSEUMS AND GALLERIES:
MULHOUSE: *Portrait of M. Pellerin; Portrait of M. E. Dollfus.*

ECK, Jan van
Italian, 17th century.
Born c. 1615; died 30 September 1641, in Rome.
Painter.

ECK, N. van
Flemish, 17th century.
Painter. Flowers, fruit.
Flemish School.
Weyermann maintains that N. van Eck was burgomaster of Brussels around 1690.

ECK, Peter
Hungarian, 16th century.
Active at the end of the 16th century.
Sculptor (wood).

ECK, Walter
German, 20th century.
Born c. 1895, in Würzburg.
Painter. Figures, landscapes.
Eck went on several working trips to Switzerland, Italy, Britain and the USA. He often used the monotype technique for his landscapes. He lived in Munich from 1950 onwards.

ECKARD
German, 13th century.
Died before 1303.
Active in Cologne.
Painter.

ECKARD
Czech, 18th century.
Born in the 18th century, to a family originally from Prague.
Painter. Portraits.

ECKARD. See also **ECKARDT, ECKART, ECKHARD, ECKHARDT**

ECKARD, Balthasar
German, 17th century.
Active in Sondheim.
Sculptor.
With his brother Heinrich, Balthasar Eckard sculpted baptism fonts decorated with low relief for the church in Sondheim in 1606.

ECKARD, Georg Ludwig, or Eckhardt
German, 18th century.
Born 5 January 1770, in Hamburg; died 4 June 1794, in Hamburg.
Painter. Portraits, landscapes.
Georg Eckard was the son of Johann Jacob Eckard, an objets d'art merchant. He became acquainted with painting at an early age. Three etchings are known to be by him: *Landscape with Peasants, a Peasant Woman and a Child, Hercules in the Augean Stables* and *Louise and Marie*. He also did some drawings in red chalk: *Entombment* after Rembrandt, *Soldiers* after Salvator Rosa, and *Interior of a Forge*.
MUSEUMS AND GALLERIES:
HAMBURG (Kunsthalle): *Portrait of the Author; Young Girl Asleep; Devil's Bridge near Hamburg* (drawing); *View of Blankenese* (drawing); *Landscape with Three Figures* (watercolour); *Canal with Small Boats* (watercolour).

ECKARD, Heinrich. See **ECKARD Balthasar**

ECKARD, Johann
German, 14th - 15th century.
Painter.
Cologne School.
The son of Tilman Eckardi, Johann Eckard was the first member of the council elected by the guild of painters in Cologne after the new democratic constitution of 1396. He was elected again in 1403, 1407 and 1413.

ECKARD, Mathias, or Eckart
German, 17th century.
Active in Schwallungen.
Sculptor.
Mathias Eckard sculpted baptism fonts for the church in Schwallungen in 1661. He is probably a descendant of Balthasar or Heinrich Eckard.

ECKARDI, Tilman
German, 14th century.
Active in Cologne.
Painter.

ECKARDSTEIN, Hans von (Baron)
German, 19th century.
Born 23 December 1859, in Prötzel, near Berlin.
Painter. Landscapes.
Hans von Eckardstein trained at the Berlin academy and under Eugène Bracht. He appeared several times in the exhibitions in Berlin and Munich. He specialised in painting Brandenburg landscapes but also sought sources of inspiration in Italy, America, Norway and the Orient.

ECKARDT. See also **ECKARD**

ECKARDT, Aloys
German, 19th century.
Born 1845, in Lichta (Thuringia); died 1906, in Munich.
Painter. Figures, genre scenes, interiors with figures.
Aloys Eckardt exhibited in Munich and at the royal academy in Berlin from 1883 to 1889. Known works by him include: *Amusing Story, At the Fishmonger's, Poultry Seller, Little City Dwellers and the Broken Sleigh*, and *Carpenter's Workshop*.
AUCTION RECORDS:
COPENHAGEN, 13 Nov 1985, *Interior Scene* (oil on canvas, 33 1/2 x 39 1/4 ins / 85 x 100 cm) DKK 16,000. PARIS, 5 Dec 1997, *Young Woman and Trophies* (oil on canvas, 32 x 39 1/4 ins / 81 x 100 cm) FRF 40,000.

ECKARDT, Andreas Clemens
German, 18th century.
Born 28 October 1769, in Gerlachsheim (Baden-Württemberg), Gemany; died 13 June 1808, in Aschaffenburg.
Sculptor.

ECKARDT, Christian Frederik Emil
Danish, 19th century.
Born 2 July 1832, in Copenhagen; died 1921.
Painter. Landscapes with figures, seascapes.

Eckardt attended the Kunstakademi in Copenhagen from 1846 to 1853, after which he embarked on a study tour of Germany and Italy to hone his skills as a seascape painter. In 1886, he returned to Copenhagen and worked as a retoucher of photographs. For his first showing at the Salon (1856) he exhibited his very first seascape, *View of Venice*. He participated in the Salon's exhibitions annually from 1859 onwards, submitting either pure seascapes, or coastal views and views of ports. He won the Neuhausen prize in 1863 and again in 1871, with *Fishermen Trying to Reach the Shore during a Storm* and *Fishermen Getting into a Yacht*.

MUSEUMS AND GALLERIES:
COPENHAGEN (Artists' Association).

AUCTION RECORDS:
COPENHAGEN, 30 July 1977, *Seascape* (1873, oil on canvas, 48 x 74 3/4 ins / 122 x 190 cm) DKK 12,500. LONDON, 14 Jan 1981, *The Port of Genoa* (1874, oil on canvas, 11 3/4 x 19 ins / 30 x 48 cm) GBP 400. LONDON, 28 Nov 1984, *Beach in the Bay of Naples, with Figures* (1856, oil on canvas, 16 x 24 1/2 ins / 40.5 x 62 cm) GBP 5,000. COPENHAGEN, 20 Aug 1986, *Seaside Scene* (1865, oil on canvas, 35 1/2 x 55 ins / 90 x 140 cm) DKK 90,000. STOCKHOLM, 19 April 1989, *Fishermen on the Coast* (oil on canvas, 15 x 24 1/2 ins / 38 x 62 cm) SEK 8,200. COPENHAGEN, 21 Feb 1990, *Russian Frigate in the Waters of a Fjord near the Coast* (oil on canvas, 26 3/4 x 39 3/4 ins / 68 x 101 cm) DKK 22,000. COPENHAGEN, 6 Dec 1990, *Seascape with Sailing Ships in Summer* (1868, oil on canvas, 17 x 26 3/4 ins / 43 x 68 cm) DKK 8,500. COPENHAGEN, 6 March 1991, *Seascape with Danish and Dutch Sailing Ships* (oil on canvas, 15 1/4 x 21 1/4 ins / 39 x 54 cm) DKK 9,500. COPENHAGEN, 5 May 1993, *Neapolitan Fishermen on the Shore* (1881, oil on canvas, 14 1/4 x 22 3/4 ins / 36 x 58 cm) DKK 13,000. LONDON, 11 Feb 1994, *Sailing Vessels off Copenhagen* (oil on canvas, 18 3/4 x 24 3/4 ins / 47.6 x 62.9 cm) GBP 4,025. LONDON, 22 Feb 1995, *Cattaro at Sunset* (oil on card, 7 3/4 x 11 ins / 20 x 28 cm) GBP 713. COPENHAGEN, 21 May 1997, *Seascape with Many Sailing Ships at Sea in a Stiff Breeze* (1862, 12 1/2 x 20 ins / 32 x 51 cm) DKK 19,000. COPENHAGEN, 10-12 Sept 1997, *Seascape* (1876, oil on canvas, 19 1/4 x 31 ins / 49 x 79 cm) DKK 13,000. COPENHAGEN, 23 Feb 1999, *Swedish Pilot Boat in Sundet* (oil on canvas, 34 x 57 ins / 87 x 145 cm) DKK 50,000. HAVNEN, 30 Oct 1999, *Lifeboat Arriving to Ship in Distress* (1873, oil on canvas, 47 x 75 ins / 120 x 190 cm) DKK 45,000. VENICE, 13 May 2000, *Road at Porto Ferraio* (1876, oil on canvas, 32 x 50 ins / 82 x 126 cm) ITL 22,000,000. COPENHAGEN, 3 Sept 2001, *Sailing Vessels in Sundet, Hveen in Background* (1870, oil on canvas, 30 x 43 ins / 75 x 110 cm) DKK 36,000. VEJLE, 13 Nov 2001, *Coastal Landscape with Washerwomen and View towards Town, Italy* (1874, oil on canvas, 18 x 28 ins / 46 x 71 cm) DKK 25,000. COPENHAGEN, 27 Aug 2002, *Seascape with Sailing Ship and Steamer at Entrance to Copenhagen Harbour* (1859, oil on canvas, 10 x 14 ins / 25 x 35 cm) DKK 25,000. COPENHAGEN, 2 Dec 2002, *Entrance to Korsor Harbour, Morning* (1870, oil on canvas, 30 x 39 ins / 75 x 100 cm) DKK 50,000. COPENHAGEN, 5 March 2003, *Morning in the Bay of Corfu* (1875, oil on canvas, 31 x 50 ins / 80 x 127 cm) DKK 70,000. HAVNEN, 24 May 2003, *Seascape with Many Ships* (1888, oil on canvas, 43 x 71 ins / 110 x 180 cm) DKK 30,000. NEW YORK, 10 Feb 2004, *Latvian Coastal Craft and Paddle Steamer in the Bay of Riga* (1877, oil on canvas, 24 x 38 ins / 60 x 97 cm) USD 6,500. COPENHAGEN, 2 March 2004, *Seascape with Frigates in Fresh Breeze* (1851, oil on canvas, 24 x 33 ins / 61 x 84 cm) DKK 34,000.

ECKARDT, Johann Aegidius. See **ECCARDT**

ECKARDT, Johann Christian, or Eckard
German, 18th - 19th century.
Born 1757, in Laufen; died after 1832, in Munich.
Active in Düsseldorf and Munich.
Engraver.

Johann Christian Eckardt engraved portraits and historical subjects.

AUCTION RECORDS:
PARIS, 23 Nov 1927, *Virgin and Child* (pencil, bistre and white) FRF 140.

ECKARDT, Johann Kaspar. See **ECKHARDT**

ECKARDT, Johann Paul
German, 18th century.
Active in Darmstadt.
Sculptor.

Johann Paul Eckardt contributed to the decoration of the palace of Dianaburg. He also produced a funeral monument of his friend, the court painter J. C. Fiedler. He is probably the brother of Johann Kaspar Eckard.

ECKARDT, Johann Tobias
German, 18th - 19th century.
Born 1744; died 1819.
Active in Darmstadt.
Sculptor.

Johann Tobias Eckardt was the son of the sculptor Johann Paul Eckardt. He trained for a long time in Vienna, Berlin and Mannheim, then settled in Darmstadt where he worked at the home of Chancellor von Moser and at court.

ECKARDT, Michael, or Eckert
German, 18th century.
Painter, decorative designer.

Michael Eckardt was probably the son of Sebastian Eckardt. The church of Stadtprozelten owns several paintings by him of the *Way of the Cross*. He also worked for the parish church in his native village of Walldürn, and a painting for the altar of St Anne (1778) and the *Ascension* for the high altar are attributed to him.

ECKARDT, Sebastian, or Eckert
German, 18th century.
Born 18th century, to a family originally from Walldürn.
Painter.

ECKART. See also **ECKARD**

ECKART, Christian
Canadian, 20th - 21st century.
Born 1959.
Painter.

The monochrome paintings of Christian Eckart are an investigation into the notion of the work of art (its execution, use and conservation) and the phenomenon of its transition to sacred object. He begins his analysis with the 'art object'. He reflects at length upon this type of presentation, attempting to renew the genre and 'restore' the idea. Freshly gilded frame mouldings are exhibited, enclosing nothing more than the open space on the back wall. Sometimes the frames are cut up and dismantled, and placed against a white Formica background, in search of balance. At other times, again defying the classic quadrilateral scheme, they make an opening within the first frame - a sort of *vedutà* that breaks the flatness of the idea of the stretched canvas. Although Eckart's major contemporary references are Barnett Newman's zips and Frank Stella's *Black Paintings*, he explains his viewpoint thus:

'There are two things: the frame and the surface. And the frame is the context. For me this is the means of describing and indicating what is outside the frame: the wall, the museum, etc. I am much more interested in what is outside the frame.'

His 1989 works are rectangular cases, whose red or blue monochrome frontal surfaces and bare, natural wood sides give them an imposing appearance.

Eckart has participated in a number of collective exhibitions, among them: 1986, *Abstract Paintings*, Nice; 1990, *Colour Alone*, Musée d'Art Contemporain, Lyons; and 2002, *Diskursive Malerei*, MUMOK (Museum Moderner Kunst Stiftung Ludwig), Vienna.

BIBLIOGRAPHY:

Schütz, H., *Christian Eckart*, exhibition catalogue, Gal. Tanit, Munich, 1987. Sterckx, Pierre, '*Christian Eckart et Allan Mc Collum: avatars actuels du monochrome*' in *Artstudio* n° 16, periodical, Gal. Templon, Paris, 1990.

MUSEUMS AND GALLERIES:

GRENOBLE (Mus. de Grenoble).

ECKART, Hermann Joseph

German, 18th century.
Died 20 May 1790.
Active in Hamburg.
Painter.

ECKART, Jost

Swiss, 17th century.
Died 22 August 1591.
Active in Lucerne from 1562 to 1575.
Painter.

After 1575 Jost Eckart gave up his artistic career and became a statesman. He painted on glass.

ECKEL, Basilius

German, 17th century.
Active in Nuremberg.
Painter. Topographical views.

ECKEL, Carl

Austrian, 19th century.
Born 19 April 1833, in Kumberg, near Weiz (Styria); died 1858, in Munich.
Painter. Genre scenes.

Carl Eckel trained under Tunner at the art academy in Graz. One of his paintings is housed in the landscape gallery in Graz.

ECKEL, Konrad

German, 15th century.
Active in Nuremberg.
Painter.

ECKELL, Ana

Argentinian, 20th - 21st century.
Born 1947.
Painter. Figure compositions.

Taking nature as her subject, Ana Eckell reconstructs it using forms, figures and colours. Her creative method concentrates on means of expression she considers more specifically poetic. Her painting is lively, colourful and sometimes rapidly executed and displays a combination of several planes and various perspectives. She took part in the Nouvelle Biennale in Paris in 1985. She has also held solo exhibitions in Argentina since 1978.

BIBLIOGRAPHY:

La Nouvelle Biennale de Paris, exhibition catalogue, Electa, Le Moniteur, Paris, 1985.

ECKENBRECHER, Karl Paul Themistocles von

German, 19th - 20th century.
Born 17 November 1842, in Athens; died 1921, in Berlin.
Painter (gouache), watercolourist. Battles, genre scenes, landscapes.
Orientalism.

Eckenbrecher was a pupil of Achenbach in Düsseldorf before settling in Berlin around 1866. He painted a great many landscapes in the course of his travels all over Europe, travelling solo or in the company of Prince Sayn-Wittgenstein. He sometimes collaborated with Marc Wolkhardt on battle scenes, and with A. Simmler on genre scenes.

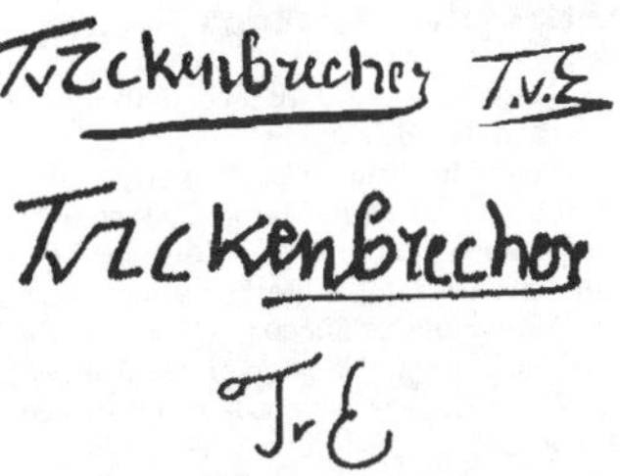

MUSEUMS AND GALLERIES:

BERLIN (Nationalgal.): *On Maerö Fjord* - BRUNSWICK: *Sawmill in the Forest* - NEUBRANDENBURG: *Waterfall in Norway* - SCHWERIN: *Victoria on Lake Naerö*.

AUCTION RECORDS:

COLOGNE, 11 March 1966, *Fjord in Norway*, DEM 4,000. LOS ANGELES, 22 May 1972, *Winter Landscape* (1867) USD 3,000. COLOGNE, 12 Nov 1976, *Norwegian Landscape* (oil on canvas, 16 x 20 ins / 40.5 x 51 cm) DEM 3,500. COLOGNE, 18 March 1977, *Still-life with Grapes* (1879, oil on card, 15 3/4 x 22 1/2 ins / 40 x 57 cm) DEM 2,700. NEW YORK, 13 Oct 1979, *View of a Fjord* (1913, oil on canvas, 21 1/2 x 12 1/2 ins / 54.5 x 32 cm) USD 1,500. LONDON, 10 June 1982, *View of a Living Room* (1887, watercolour, 9 1/4 x 12 1/4 ins / 23.5 x 31 cm) GBP 1,000. VIENNA, 16 Nov 1983, *In the Naeryfjord* (1902, oil on canvas, 31 1/2 x 45 ins / 80 x 114 cm) ATS 55,000. LONDON, 26 Nov 1986, *Summer's Day in Romsdal* (1894, oil on canvas, 44 x 74 1/2 ins / 112 x 189.5 cm) GBP 9,500. LONDON, 16 March 1989, *Lofor Stream in Valders, Norway* (1905, oil on canvas, 43 1/2 x 61 3/4 ins / 110.5 x 157 cm) GBP 7,700. COLOGNE, 15 June 1989, *View of a Norwegian Fjord* (1911, oil on card, 17 x 24 1/2 ins / 43 x 62 cm) DEM 1,400. COLOGNE, 20 Oct 1989, *Norwegian Fjord* (1898, oil on panel, 13 3/4 x 23 ins / 35 x 57.5 cm) DEM 4,400. LONDON, 30 March 1990, *Constantinople with the Dolmabahçe Palace* (1871, oil on canvas/card, 9 1/2 x 16 1/4 ins / 24 x 41 cm) GBP 3,300. BERN, 12 May 1990, *Rocky Norwegian Landscape* (1906, watercolour and gouache, 11 3/4 x 9 ins / 30 x 23 cm) CHF 1,800. COLOGNE, 29 June 1990, *Waterfall in Norway* (oil on canvas, 29 1/2 x 45 1/4 ins / 75 x 115 cm) DEM 5,000. NEW YORK, 24 Oct 1990, *The Naero Fjord* (oil on canvas, 24 x 36 ins / 61 x 91.5 cm) USD 7,150. LONDON, 28 Nov 1990, *The Permanent Snow on the Romsdal Massif* (1894, oil on canvas, 36 1/4 x 54 1/4 ins / 92 x 138 cm) GBP 7,700. LONDON, 17 June 1992, *Waterfalls in Norway* (1904, oil on canvas, 19 3/4 x 14 1/4 ins / 50 x 36 cm) GBP 1,210. LONDON, 16 June 1993, *The Oihonna in the Spitzberg Ice Field* (1905, oil on canvas, 14 3/4 x 22 ins / 37.5 x 55 cm) GBP 2,990. PARIS, 22 March 1994, *Besiktas Mosque and the Bosphorus* (1864, oil on canvas, 14 x 20 1/2 ins / 35.5 x 52 cm) FRF 80,000. NEW YORK, 20 July 1995, *In the Spitzberg Ice Field* (1905, oil on canvas, 12 3/4 x 18 1/2 ins / 32.4 x 47 cm) USD 2,070. LONDON, 15 March 1996, *View of Constantinople at Dawn with Besiktas Mosque in the Background* (1864, oil on canvas, 13 x 20 1/2 ins / 33.3 x 51.9 cm) GBP 13,800.

ECKENER, Alexander

German, 19th - 20th century.

Born 21 August 1870, in Flensburg.
Painter, engraver, lithographer. Interiors with figures, rustic scenes, landscapes.

Eckener was a pupil of Herterich, Wagner and Raab in Munich, then of Count Kalckreuth in Stuttgart, before becoming a teacher at Stuttgart art academy. Noted works include the oil paintings: *Harvest Time at Lake Constance; Storm over the Marsh; Gluksburg Castle; Misty Morning on the Neckar; Frisian Interior; In the Studio; Frisian Peasants; The Labourer's House; Foundry;* and lithographs of the Constance region.

ECKENFELDER, Friedrich
German, 19th - 20th century.
Born 6 March 1861, in Bern; died 1938.
Painter. Landscapes, animals.

Friedrich Eckenfelder trained particularly under Hölder in Rottweil and under Löfftz in Munich. He settled in Munich after having trained under Von Zügel, by whom he was strongly influenced. Notable works by him include: *Horses Ploughing* (1883), *Flock of Sheep* (1890), *Rest* (1896), *Horses at the Edge of a Wood* (1899), and *Horse Market* (1913). His main subject was horses, which he often placed in a well-studied landscape.

F. Eckenfelder

AUCTION RECORDS:
LONDON, 11 March 1938, *Winter Halt,* GBP 11. LONDON, 2 June 1939, *Horses Resting* (1887) GBP 11 6 d,. COLOGNE, 18 Nov 1965, *Mule Cart,* DEM 5,000. COLOGNE, 25 Oct 1968, *Undergrowth,* DEM 4,400. LONDON, 16 Oct 1974, *Returning from the Fields,* GBP 2,900. COLOGNE, 1 June 1978, *Draught Horses* (oil on panel, 10 1/2 x 13 3/4 ins / 26.5 x 35 cm) DEM 12,000. NEW YORK, 11 Feb 1981, *Cariole Crossing a River* (oil on canvas, 13 3/4 x 18 1/4 ins / 35 x 46.5 cm) USD 8,000. LONDON, 12 Oct 1984, *Hitched Up Cart at Door of the Cottage* (1887, oil on canvas, 14 1/2 x 20 ins / 37 x 51 cm) GBP 11,000. BERN, 8 May 1987, *Peasant and Draught Horses in a Field* (oil on canvas, 12 1/4 x 17 ins / 31 x 43 cm) CHF 12,000. NEW YORK, 25 Feb 1988, *Hitching up the Cart* (oil on canvas, 35 1/4 x 50 3/4 ins / 89.5 x 129.2 cm) USD 13,200. LONDON, 23 March 1988, *Stable* (oil on canvas, 14 1/4 x 20 3/4 ins / 36 x 53 cm) GBP 7,150. LONDON, 16 March 1994, *Sheep and Goats Grazing* (1886, oil on canvas, 22 1/2 x 35 3/4 ins / 57 x 91 cm) GBP 5,520.

ECKENTHALER. See also **ECKTHALER**

ECKENTHALER, Hans
French, 17th century.
Died 1634, in Bischheim.
Active in Strasbourg.
Engraver.

ECKEPUT, François
Flemish, 17th century.
Active in Ghent.
Painter.
Flemish School.

François Eckeput became a master in 1618.

ECKER, Franz Karl, or Eckher, Egger
German, 18th century.
Painter, miniaturist.

ECKER, Johann Anton
Austrian, 18th - 19th century.
Born 6 May 1755, in Graz; died 1820, in Vienna.
Miniaturist. Topographical views.

Johann Ecker was a surgeon, but he abandoned his patients to dedicate himself to painting and geography.

ECKERDT, Alexander
Slovak, 20th century.
Born 6 July 1932, in Košice.
Painter.

Alexander Eckerdt studied art in Bratislava where he exhibited. He featured in the *Fifty years of Czechoslovak Painting from the Collections of the Galleries, 1918-1958* exhibition, organised for the 50th anniversary of the Czechoslovak Republic with a painting *Old Peasant Woman in Traditional Costume.*

ECKERLER, Carl
German, 19th century.
Active in Germany.
Painter. Genre scenes.

Carl Eckerler is mentioned by Ms. Florence Levy.

AUCTION RECORDS:
NEW YORK, 2 Jan 1907, *'Who is it?',* USD 112.

ECKERLIN, Cajo
Portuguese, 19th century.
Active in Lisbon.
Engraver.

Cajo Eckerlin was the son of Carl August Eckerlin.

ECKERLIN, Carl August
German, 19th century.
Born 4 April 1773, in Werningerode, near Nordhausen; died 1843, in Milan.
Painter.

Carl Eckerlin lived in Rome, Marseilles, Reggio and Milan, where he was an interpreter for the Austrian government. He appeared in several exhibitions in Milan.

ECKERMANN, Karl
German, 19th century.
Born 1834, in Weimar; died 29 August 1891, in Göttingen (Lower Saxony).
Painter, engraver. Figures, landscapes, still-lifes.

Karl Eckermann trained under Preller and also studied in Brussels and Karlsruhe before settling in Hanover. A known engraving by him is *Sawmill in the Black Forest*

MUSEUMS AND GALLERIES:
WEIMAR (Schloss Ettersburg): series of still-lifes.

AUCTION RECORDS:
AMSTERDAM, 16 Nov 1988, *Shepherdess and her Flock in a Gullied Clearing* (1878, oil on canvas, 30 1/4 x 40 1/2 ins / 77 x 103 cm) NLG 3,450.

ECKERSBERG, Christoffer Wilhelm or Christian Wilhelm
Danish, 19th century.
Born 2 January 1783, in Sundeved (Slesvig); died 22 July 1853, in Copenhagen.
Painter, draughtsman. Religious subjects, mythological subjects, nudes, portraits, genre scenes, landscapes, seascapes, still-lifes.

Christoffer Wilhelm Eckersberg was a pupil of Abildgaard and Louis David. During the time he spent in David's studio in Paris, Eckersberg painted only nudes, but once in Rome he tried his hand at landscapes. In 1810, he took a trip to Germany, visiting the upper Rhineland, and from which he brought back a number of works, especially drawings. On his return to Copenhagen, he was made a professor at the academy of fine arts in 1818. A specialist in the rules of perspective, in 1833 he introduced the practice of drawing from live models in his course.Eckersberg was the father of Danish Neoclassical painting. His sober though by no means unfeeling style and a brush that sometimes seems to adopt a rather sharp manner do not detract from the merit of these outstanding works.

Eckersberg has featured in several joint exhibitions, including *Twee gouden eeuwen: schilderkunst uit Nederland en Denemarken (Two Golden Ages: masterpieces of Dutch and Danish painting)* at the Rijksmuseum in Amsterdam in

2001 and *Un Paese incantato. Italia dipinta da Thomas Jones a Corot* (*An Enchanted Country. Italy Depicted by Artists from Thomas Jones to Corot*) at the Centro Internazionale d'Arte e di Cultura at the Palazzo Tè in Mantua.

BIBLIOGRAPHY:

Christensen, L., *Graenselandets Maler, Christoffer Wilhelm Eckersberg*, Sonderborg, Copenhagen, 1962. Bramsen, H., *Om Christoffer Wilhelm Eckersberg og hans mariner*, Copenhagen, 1972. Winkel, Niels, *Naturstudiet i C. W. Eckersbergs marinemaleri*, Kunstakademiet, Copenhagen, 1976. Buck, A.M.N., *The Roman architectural landscapes of Christoffer Wilhelm Eckersberg*, Oregon, 1979. Fisher, E., et al., *Tegninger af Christoffer Wilhelm Eckersberg*, Copenhagen, 1983. Helsted, Dyveke, *C. W. Eckersberg i Rom 1813-1816*, Thorvaldsens museum, Copenhagen, 1983. Jönsson, Hanna, *C. W. Eckersberg og hans elever*, exhibition catalogue, Statens Museum for Kunst, Copenhagen, 1983. Lerber, E./Skedsmo, T. (ed.), *Fire danske klassikere: Nicolai Abildgaard, Jens Juel, Christoffer Wilhelm Eckersberg og Bertel Thorvaldsen*, exhibition catalogue, Nasjonalgalleriet, Oslo, 1992. Fisher, E./Dupont, E., *Christoffer Wilhelm Eckersberg, his mind and times*, Hellerup, 1993. Schulter-Wülwer, U., *Künstlerkolonie Ekensund*, Heide, 2000. Ottani Cavina, Anna (ed.), *Un Paese incantato. Italia dipinta da Thomas Jones a Corot*, exhibition catalogue, Electa, Milan, 2001.

MUSEUMS AND GALLERIES:

COPENHAGEN (Den Hirschsprungske Samling): *Portrait of Anna Maria Magnani; The Corvette 'Najaden' (Naiad) and Frigate 'Bellona'; Panoramas of Rome; Portrait of Mrs Schmidt* (1818); *Woman at a Mirror* (1841) - COPENHAGEN (Ny Carlsberg Glyptotek): *The Daughter of Cecrops; The Via Sacra with the Temple of Antoninus and Faustina* (oil on canvas) - COPENHAGEN (Rosenborg Slot): *King Frederick VI and His Family* - COPENHAGEN (Statens Mus. for Kunst): *View of Part of a Street in Paris* (1812); *View of Part of the Aventine Hill in Rome* (1814); *The Church of SS Giovanni e Paolo in Rome* (1814); *Molière's Tomb in Paris; Bertel Thorvaldsen; Cupid with a Butterfly; View of Part of the Garden of the Villa Borghese; Scene from 'The Inseparables' by Heiberg; A Hunt; A Brig under Sail; Thorvaldsen's Arrival in Copenhagen on 17th September 1838; Italian Woman; The Astronomer Christoffer Handstein; Landscape with Figures, Sjkoldncesholm; A Greek Storyteller among his Listeners; Woman Asleep; Eckersberg's Landlady in Paris with Her Daughter; View of Bonn on the Rhine* (1810); *Three Russian Warships; The Entrance to Copenhagen Harbour; Seven People Leaning against a Parapet; Two Shepherds; Moses and the Israelites at the Red Sea; View of the Tiber; A Construction in the Campagna Romana; View of the Garden of the Villa Borghese; The Church of S Agnese in Rome; The Monastery of S Maria in Aracœli; Several Portraits of the Merchant Mendel Nathanson and his Family; Portrait of the Elder Daughters of Mendel Levin Nathanson, Bella and Hanna* (1820); *Unfinished Portrait of Princess Wilhelmina; Portrait of A. A. Orsted; View from Ramberg to Flensburg; Russian Ship of the Line at Anchor in the Sund; Portrait of the Police Doctor Rost; Beneath the Cliff at Moen; A Danish Warship without Sail; Maritime Painting, Overcast Weather; The Corvette 'Galathea' in the North Sea; A Frigate with a Good Breeze; Vessels in Copenhagen Harbour; View of the Pont Royal in Paris; View of the Château of Meudon and its Surroundings; Two Russian Ships of the Line; A Danish Corvette Drops Anchor; A Russian Fleet in Harbour at Helsingborg; Portrait of the Artist by Himself; Portrait of Rebecca Hyssing; The Artist's Second Wife Julie, née Juel; Portrait of Suzanne Juel, the Artist's Third Wife; The Artist's Daughter Emilie; Halcyon on the Beach; The Interior of the Coliseum; Study of the Zoological Gardens; Study of a Model in David's Studio; Mrs Rosing the Actress; Morning after the Storm* (unfinished); *Fire near a Mill; The Garden of the Villa Albani; A Pergola; View of Ponterotto; View of Fontana Acetosa; Danish Landscapes; A Mother Teaching Her Daughter to Read; View of Kronborg Castle; View of the Angel's Gate* (oil on canvas); *In the Gardens of the Villa Albani* (oil on canvas) - COPENHAGEN (Thorvaldsens Mus.): *Woman Asleep in a Classical Robe* - OSLO: *Distribution of Alms at the Gate of a Monastery* - RIBE (Kunstmus.): *Roman Courtyard* (oil on canvas).

AUCTION RECORDS:

COPENHAGEN, 28-29 May 1963, *The Sailing Ship 'Najaden' (Naiad)*, DKK 37,000. COPENHAGEN, 15 June 1966, *Street Scene in Copenhagen* (watercolour and pen) DKK 7,100. COPENHAGEN, 10 Dec 1968, *Frederiksborg Church* (watercolour) DKK 8,000. COPENHAGEN, 19 March 1969, *St Peter's Square, Rome*, DKK 94,000. COPENHAGEN, 9 Feb 1971, *Young Woman at her Mirror* (1808) DKK 5,200. COPENHAGEN, 24 May 1973, *A Small Port* (1830) DKK 19,000. COPENHAGEN, 4 Sept 1974, *Seascape* (1825) DKK 44,000. COPENHAGEN, 10 Feb 1976, *Sailing Ship at Sea* (1832, oil on canvas, 15 x 22 ins / 38 x 56 cm) DKK 25,000. COPENHAGEN, 27 Sept 1977, *Sailing Ships at Sea* (1832, oil on canvas, 12 1/4 x 18 ins / 31 x 46 cm) DKK 30,000. COPENHAGEN, 27 March 1979, *Street Scene* (1809, watercolour and pen, 9 x 13 1/2 ins / 22 x 34 cm) DKK 26,000. COPENHAGEN, 27 March 1979, *Seamen and a Young Woman on the Quays* (1848, pen, 9 1/4 x 6 3/4 ins / 23.5 x 17 cm) DKK 8,500. LONDON, 27 Nov 1981, *Joseph and His Brothers* (1811, oil on canvas, 19 1/2 x 24 ins / 49.5 x 61 cm) GBP 3,000. COPENHAGEN, 13 June 1984, *Frigates with a Following Breeze* (1824, oil on canvas, diam. 17 1/4 ins / 44 cm) DKK 300,000. COPENHAGEN, 16 April 1986, *Danish Frigates* (1846, oil on canvas, 23 1/2 x 31 ins / 60 x 79 cm) DKK 650,000. COPENHAGEN, 29 Oct 1987, *View of the Port of Copenhagen* (pen and wash, 6 1/4 x 11 1/2 ins / 16 x 29 cm) DKK 27,000. LONDON, 24 June 1988, *Christ and the Woman Taken in Adultery* (1843, oil on canvas, 51 x 45 ins / 129.5 x 114 cm) GBP 16,500. LONDON, 16 March 1989, *Study of a Woman* (1812, oil on canvas, 32 x 25 1/2 ins / 81 x 65 cm) GBP 30,800. COPENHAGEN, 5 April 1989, *Portrait of Louise Lahde* (1827, oil on canvas, 12 1/2 x 9 1/2 ins / 32 x 24 cm) DKK 80,000. COPENHAGEN, 25 Oct 1989, *Monceau Park in Paris* (1811, ink and wash, 8 3/4 x 9 1/4 ins / 22.5 x 23.5 cm) DKK 80,000. LONDON, 27-28 March 1990, *People on the Towpath along the Rhine* (1810, oil on canvas, 18 x 23 ins / 46 x 58.5 cm) GBP 41,800. LONDON, 6 June 1990, *The Establishment of Absolute Monarchy in 1660* (oil on canvas/panel, 9 1/4 x 7 1/2 ins / 23.5 x 19 cm) GBP 2,090. COPENHAGEN, 1 May 1991, *Corvette in Dry Dock in a Naval Shipyard* (1851, oil on canvas, 15 1/4 x 14 1/4 ins / 39 x 36 cm) DKK 290,000. LONDON, 17 May 1991, *Women Through a Half-open Door* (1848, oil on canvas, 13 1/2 x 10 1/4 ins / 34.3 x 26.2 cm) GBP 4,950. COPENHAGEN, 6 May 1992, *Three Young Women Dragging a Man in a Garden* (1807, oil on canvas, 13 3/4 x 11 ins / 35 x 28 cm) DKK 22,000. COPENHAGEN, 18 Nov 1992, *The Foro Romano* (1814, oil on canvas, 12 1/2 x 16 1/4 ins / 32 x 41 cm) DKK 1,400,000. COPENHAGEN, 10 Feb 1993, *Ladies Walking near a Bridge in Frederiksborg Park* (oil on canvas, 12 1/2 x 10 1/4 ins / 32 x 26 cm) DKK 90,000. COPENHAGEN, 15 Nov 1993, *Portrait of Bertel Thorvaldsen* (1820, oil on canvas, 19 1/2 x 15 3/4 ins / 49.5 x 40 cm) DKK 460,000. COPENHAGEN, 2 Feb 1994, *The Port of Dragør* (1830, oil on canvas, 11 x 8 1/2 ins / 27 x 21.5 cm) DKK 220,000. COPENHAGEN, 7 Sept 1994, *The Eclipse of the Sun* (1851, ink and wash, 9 3/4 x 6 1/4 ins / 25 x 16 cm) DKK 31,000. COPENHAGEN, 8 Feb 1995, *Portrait of Queen Mary Sophia Frederica* (1819, oil on canvas, 17 3/4 x 14 1/2 ins / 45 x 37 cm) DKK 48,000. NEW YORK, 2 April 1996, *Neoclassical Male Nudes* (1824, pencil/paper, three drawings, 18 x 12 3/4 ins / 45.7 x 32.4 cm; 19 x 13 1/4 ins/48.3 x 33.7 cm; 17 1/2 x 12 1/2 ins/44.5 x 31.8 cm) USD 9,200. COPENHAGEN, 3-5 Dec 1997, *Cottage and Trees* (oil on canvas, 6 1/4 x 7 1/2 ins / 16 x 19 cm) DKK 30,000. COPENHAGEN, 23 Feb 1999, *Duke Adolf Turning Down Offer of the Danish Throne* (1819, oil on canvas, 18 x 15 ins / 46 x 39 cm) DKK 320,000. COPEN-

HAGEN, 23 Feb 1999, *English Frigate at Anchor, Drying Sails with Danish Pilot Boat* (1822, oil on canvas, 15 x 21 ins / 39 x 54 cm) DKK 1,500,000. COPENHAGEN, 13 Sept 2000, *Two Cadets* (1811-1813, pencil, 8 x 7 ins / 21 x 18 cm) DKK 14,000. COPENHAGEN, 5 March 2001, *Odysseus Creeping out of Polyphemus' Grotto* (oil on canvas, 32 x 25 ins / 81 x 64 cm) DKK 330,000. COPENHAGEN, 3 June 2002, *Model Study of a Young Man* (c. 1823, pencil, 20 x 10 ins / 51 x 26 cm) DKK 16,000. COPENHAGEN, 3 June 2002, *The Vessels Chr. VIII and Allars Get Underway at Hveen* (1850, oil on canvas, 22 x 13 ins / 57 x 34 cm) DKK 25,000. COPENHAGEN, 26 Feb 2003, *Frigates in Copenhagen Harbour* (pencil, 9 x 15 ins / 22 x 39 cm) DKK 14,000.

ECKERSBERG, Erling Carl Wilhelm

Danish, 19th century.
Born 15 September 1808, in Copenhagen; died 27 November 1889, in Copenhagen.
Engraver.

The son of Christoffer Wilhelm Eckersberg, Erling Eckersberg attended courses at the academy under the direction of O. O. Bagge, visited France and Italy and studied with Leroux and Müller in Paris, where he engraved, among other subjects, the work *Fishermen of Hornbæk*. After studying with Toschi and Parme, Eckersberg visited Rome, returning to Copenhagen in 1838. He exhibited from 1828 to 1840, and worked as an engraver at the national bank until 1871. When he retired, the banks directorate granted him a pension of 1,200 crowns annually.

ECKERSBERG, Johan Fredrik

Norwegian, 19th century.
Born 1822, in Drammen; died 1870, in Sandvika, near Christiania (now Oslo).
Painter, draughtsman. Landscapes.

Johan Eckersberg was a pupil of J.W. Schrimer in Düsseldorf from 1846 to 1848. He spent time in Madeira to improve his health, returning to Düsseldorf in 1854. Eckersberg went back to Norway the following year, settling in Christiania, where he ran a painting school until his death. His paintings are characterised by great accuracy in their draughtsmanship.

MUSEUMS AND GALLERIES:

OSLO: *Large Landscape Design* (drawing); *View of Part of Hvideseid; View of Part of Valle in Saterdalen; Alpine Location; Landscape* - STOCKHOLM: *Norwegian Mountains.*

AUCTION RECORDS:

LONDON, 18 June 1980, *Rural Scene* (1868, oil on canvas, 36 x 50 1/2 ins / 91.5 x 128.5 cm) GBP 5,200. LONDON, 19 Nov 1993, *Oslo Fjord* (1861, oil on canvas, 25 1/2 x 39 1/4 ins / 65 x 100 cm) GBP 8,280. OSLO, 26 April 1999, *Farmers by Lake in Mountain Landscape* (1848, oil on canvas, 26 x 33 ins / 65 x 85 cm) NOK 130,000. OSLO, 16 Dec 1999, *Landscape* (1859, oil on canvas, 20 x 28 ins / 50 x 71 cm) NOK 125,000. LONDON, 6 April 2000, *Madeira* (1852, oil on canvas, 26 x 31 ins / 66 x 80 cm) GBP 15,500. OSLO, 10 April 2000, *Landscape from Romsdalen* (1867, oil on canvas, 32 x 46 ins / 81 x 117 cm) NOK 2,370,000. NEW YORK, 13 March 2001, *Summer Landscape* (1849, oil on canvas, 21 x 36 ins / 54 x 91 cm) USD 7,000. OSLO, 22 May 2001, *Landscape View from Borgen towards Bygdoe* (1859, oil on canvas/panel, 9 x 11 ins / 23 x 28 cm) NOK 80,000. OSLO, 27 May 2002, *Mountain Landscape with a Parish* (1849, oil on canvas, 13 x 16 ins / 33 x 41 cm) NOK 60,000. OSLO, 2 Dec 2002, *Landscape with Two Figures* (1863, oil on panel, 11 x 17 ins / 28 x 42 cm) NOK 15,000. OSLO, 13 Oct 2003, *Coastal Landscape with Figures* (1868, oil on canvas, 26 x 37 ins / 66 x 94 cm) NOK 125,000. OSLO, 19 Nov 2003, *Mountain Landscape from Romsdalen* (1850, oil on canvas, 24 x 31 ins / 62 x 79 cm) NOK 160,000. OSLO, 25 May 2004, *Mountain Landscape with Figures under Romsdalshorn* (1860, oil on paper/canvas, 10 x 13 ins / 26 x 32 cm) NOK 165,000. TORONTO, 14 June 2004, *Artist Resting at a Waterfall* (1854, watercolour, 9 x 13 ins / 22 x 32 cm) CAD 2,500.

ECKERSSEN, Heinrich

Dutch, 16th - 17th century.
Born at the end of the 16th century, to a family originally from Middelburg (Zealand).
Painter.

Heinrich Eckerssen worked in Leipzig under Thomas Lichteinstein and, at the end of 1597, assisted him in decorating the great organ at the church of St Nicolas with paintings. Unfortunately, they were lost when alterations were made to the church.

ECKERT, Georg Maria

German, 19th century.
Born 17 September 1828, in Heidelberg; died 22 January 1903, in Karlsruhe.
Painter, watercolourist. Landscapes.

Georg Eckert trained at the Düsseldorf academy under Schirmer. He also studied in Munich, and visited Bavaria, Italy and Switzerland at the age of 50. He then settled in Heidelberg where he specialised in art photography. From 1877 onwards he painted watercolours of landscapes in the region of Baden.

AUCTION RECORDS:

HEIDELBERG, 9 Oct 1992, *Heidelberg Castle in the Evening* (oil on canvas, 19 3/4 x 27 1/2 ins / 50 x 70 cm) DEM 4,200. HEIDELBERG, 2 April 2004, *Ruins of Tower of Heidelberg Castle* (oil on canvas, 27 x 26 ins / 69 x 66 cm) EUR 2,500.

ECKERT, Heinrich Gottlieb

German, 18th - 19th century.
Died 1817.
Active in Berlin in 1751.
Painter, engraver (etching/aquatint).

Heinrich Eckert engraved portraits and mythological subjects.

ECKERT, Henri Ambros or Ambrose

German, 19th century.
Born 16 October 1807, in Würzburg; died 10 February 1840, in Munich.
Painter. Military subjects, battles, hunting scenes, landscapes with figures, seascapes, harbour views.

AUCTION RECORDS:

COLOGNE, 26 March 1982, *Fishing Village on English Coast* (1835, oil on canvas, 25 x 32 3/4 ins / 63.5 x 83.5 cm) DEM 15,000. MUNICH, 18 Sept 1985, *War Scene, Tyrol 1809* (1832, oil on canvas, 18 1/2 x 24 3/4 ins / 47 x 63 cm) DEM 8,000. HEIDELBERG, 14 Oct 1988, *Undulating Landscape on a Sunny Day* (1923, oil on canvas, 20 1/2 x 29 1/2 ins / 52 x 75 cm) DEM 1,900. NEW YORK, 17 Jan 1990, *Travellers Taking a Break* (oil on panel, 12 1/4 x 16 3/4 ins / 31.1 x 42.6 cm) USD 4,125. MUNICH, 7 Dec 1993, *Capture of Andreas Hofer* (1828, oil on panel, 14 3/4 x 18 ins / 37.5 x 46 cm) DEM 20,700. STUTTGART, 8 Dec 2000, *At the Blacksmith's* (1833, oil on panel, 13 x 17 ins / 32 x 43 cm) DEM 16,000.

ECKERT, Jakob

German, 19th century.
Born 25 November 1847, in Mainz; died 23 February 1882, in Munich.
Sculptor.

After having worked in the decorative section of a furniture factory in Vienna and Furth, Jakob Eckert went to the Munich academy. He then became Anton Hess's assistant at the school of arts and crafts in the same city. He created models for fountains and all sorts of domestic utility objects. He made a monumental eagle for Kissingen's mausoleum. His best creation was a small wax model for the bronze door of Cologne Cathedral, to which he added a life-sized low relief of *Joseph Sold by his Brothers*. This project gained him first prize in the competition, but the work never materialised because Eckert had not kept to the pre-defined 14th-century style, but instead had adopted for the Renaissance style.

ECKERT, Joachim
German, 18th century.
Active in Freiberg, Silesia.
Illuminator. Topographical views.

ECKERT, Michael. See **ECKARDT**

ECKFORD, Jessiejo
American, 20th century.
Born 21 November 1895, in Dallas (Texas).
Painter.
Jessiejo Eckford was a pupil of Félicie Waldo Howell. He was a member of, among other things, the American Federation of Arts and the Texas Society of Fine Arts.

ECKH. See **ECK** and **HECKE**

ECKHARD. See also **ECKARD**

ECKHARD, Conrad
German, 17th century.
Active at the end of the 17th century.
Painter.
J. C. Sartorius engraved portraits of the pastor Martin Limburger and Regine Magdalena Limburger after two of Conrad Eckhard's works.

ECKHARD, Louis
German, 18th century.
Born 1769, in Hamburg; died 1794, in Hamburg.
Painter, scholar.

ECKHARDT. See also **ECKARD**

ECKHARDT, Adolf
German, 19th century.
Born 1868, in Hamburg.
Painter, glass painter, engraver.
Adolf Eckhardt trained in Hamburg, Karlsruhe, Berlin and at the Académie Julian in Paris. He travelled to Italy. He specialised in decoration.

ECKHARDT, Anton I
Austrian, 18th century.
Born 1761.
Active in Vienna.
Sculptor.
Anton Eckhardt I was the son of Johann Kaspar Eckhardt.

ECKHARDT, Anton II
Austrian, 19th century.
Born 20 December 1783.
Active in Vienna.
Sculptor.
Anton Eckhardt II was the son of Lorenz Eckhardt and was trained at the Vienna academy from 1797 to 1806.

ECKHARDT, Carl Peter
German, 19th century.
Active in Hanau.
Painter. Genre scenes, portraits.
Carl Peter Eckhardt trained under Joseph Muxel. He also studied at the Munich academy and lived in Düssseldorf.

ECKHARDT, Friedrich
German, 18th century.
Died 7 May 1781.
Active in Berlin.
Painter, draughtsman. Portraits.
Friedrich Eckhardt was the son of Modestin Eckhardt and was appointed art teacher at the Berlin academy in 1762.

ECKHARDT, Friedrich
Austrian, 19th century.
Born c. 1818.
Active in Vienna.
Sculptor.
Friedrich Eckhardt attended the Vienna academy in 1834.

ECKHARDT, Gabriel
German, 17th century.
Active in Freiberg (Saxony).
Sculptor.
Gabriel Eckhardt produced baptism fonts for the church in Penig in 1609, which were decorated in low reliefs of Christ and John the Baptist.

ECKHARDT, Georg
German, 17th century.
Born c. 1590; died September 1637.
Sculptor.
Georg Eckhardt produced an altar for the church in Neuhausen near Freiberg in Saxony. It was destroyed by fire in 1863.

ECKHARDT, Gottfried
German, 19th century.
Born 9 March 1865.
Active in Düsseldorf.
Painter.
Gottfried Eckhardt trained in Düsseldorf, then went to Italy, Switzerland and Belgium. He specialised in portraits and religious and historical painting, but also produced some decorative paintings. The Basilica in Echternach houses an altar made by him.

ECKHARDT, J.
German, 18th century.
Painter.
A painting in grisaille, *Monks in a Vault*, bears the signature *J. Eckhardt*.

ECKHARDT, Jenny
Swiss, 19th century.
Born 4 February 1816, in La Chaux-de-Fonds (Neuchâtel); died 12 December 1850, in Cortaillod.
Painter.
Jenny Eckhardt trained in Düsseldorf under Karl Sohn, then became established as a portrait painter in Switzerland where she exhibited in 1840. Most of her works are in the Musée de la Chaux-de-Fonds.

ECKHARDT, Johann
Austrian, 19th century.
Born 1795.
Active in Vienna.
Sculptor.
Johann Eckhardt was the son of Anton Eckhardt I and trained at the Vienna academy.

ECKHARDT, Johann Kaspar, or Eckart or Eckardt
Austrian, 18th century.
Born 1712, in Hesse-Darmstadt; died 17 April 1778.
Sculptor.
Johann Kaspar Eckhardt settled in Vienna in 1740 and trained at the academy there. He was probably the brother of Johann Paul Eckardt.

ECKHARDT, John Giles. See **ECCARDT**

ECKHARDT, Lorenz, or Eckart or Eckardt
Austrian, 18th - 19th century.
Born 1757; died after 1822.
Active in Vienna.
Sculptor.

Lorenz Eckhardt was the son of Johann Kaspar Eckhardt and was trained at the Vienna academy.

ECKHARDT, Modestin
German, 18th century.
Born 1684, in Kempten (Allgäu); died 1768, in Berlin.
Painter, engraver (mezzotint).
Modestin Eckhardt engraved some portraits and panels for the Campe book.

ECKHARDT, Philipp
German, 18th century.
Born 16 October 1690, in Neuburg (Swabia); died 15 April 1765, in Ebersberg (Bavaria).
Sculptor (wood).
Philipp Eckhardt was a lay brother at the Jesuit college in Rottweil. Together with Michel Mayr he sculpted altars, confessionals and pulpit for the Jesuit church in Rottweil, Württemberg.

ECKHARDT, Rudolf Johann Christian
German, 19th century.
Born 2 February 1842, in Frankfurt am Main; died 9 December 1897, in Frankfurt am Main.
Sculptor.
Rudolf Eckhardt trained under Zwerger and Blaser. He worked in Berlin on the monuments of Frederick William III and Frederick Willliam IV for the city of Cologne, and Frederick William IV for Sans-Souci. He worked in Frankfurt for several public monuments (including the stock market, opera house and fountains).

ECKHARDT, Uriel
German, 17th century.
Born 1582; died 12 May 1612.
Sculptor.
Uriel Eckhardt settled in Freiberg in Saxony and carved the tomb of Caspar von Schönberg and his wife in the church in Sayda.

ECKHARDT VON ECKHARDSBURG, Victor
German, 19th century.
Born 28 August 1864, in Rastatt.
Painter, engraver (etching).
Victor Eckhardt von Eckhardsburg trained at the academies in Prague, Vienna, Munich and Karlsruhe. He appeared in several different German and Austrian exhibitions. He specialised in military painting and painting of horses. He also painted landscapes of Herzegovina.

ECKHER. See **ECKER**

ECKL, Vilma
Austrian, 20th century.
Born 1892, in Lorch; died 1954, in Linz.
Draughtswoman, pastellist, engraver. Landscapes, local scenes.
Eckl tended to favour pastels for her scenes from rural life and landscapes, enabling her to tackle these subjects in a more impressionist style than that of Steinhart and Kubin, from whom she drew her inspiration.

ECKLER, Johann
Austrian, 18th century.
Active in Rome in 1781 and 1796.
Painter, engraver.

ECKMAN, Anthoine
French, 17th century.
Active in Paris c. 1675.
Engraver (wood).
Antoine Eckman was the brother of Jean Eckman and son of Édouard Eckman.

ECKMAN, Edouard, or Ecqman, Egman
Flemish, 17th century.
Born c. 1600, in Mechelen.
Engraver (wood).
Flemish School.
Edouard Eckman worked with Lodewyk Businck, Abraham Bosse and Callot, and lived in Paris.

E E

ECKMAN, Jean
French, 17th century.
Born 1641, in Paris; died 16 July 1677, in Paris.
Miniaturist.
The son of Édouard Eckman, Jean Eckman became a member of the academy on 3 August 1675 on the strength of his miniature painting of *Parnassus*, which was subsequently offered by the academy to the son of Colbert, the Marquis of Seignelay.
AUCTION RECORDS:
PARIS, 6 May 1955, *Arrival of the King at the Château of Vincennes* (gouache) FRF 140,000.

ECKMANN, Helmut
German, 19th century.
Died 17 March 1904.
Active in Hamburg.
Painter.
Helmut Eckmann was the brother of Otto Eckmann and worked as a decorator and illustrator of periodicals.

ECKMANN, Otto
German, 19th century.
Born 19 November 1865, in Hamburg; died 11 June 1902, in Badenweiler.
Painter, decorative artist, illustrator, engraver, designer, ceramicist, textile designer. Portraits, landscapes, flowers. Designs for stained glass, designs for tapestries, ex-libris plates, advertising posters, fabrics, ceramics, metal objects, ironware, lamps, furniture, typefaces, jewellery, wallpaper.
Symbolism, Jugendstil, Japonism.
Otto Eckmann trained at the Kunstgewerbeschule (School of Industrial Art and Design) in Hamburg, the Kunstgewerbeschule in Nuremberg and the Akademie der Bildenden Künste in Munich in 1885. With his naturalist, and later Symbolist, works he soon found success, but abandoned painting in 1894, having sold all his works at auction, to devote himself to a career in the applied arts. He became one of the most acclaimed creators in this field. He was taught engraving and the Japonist aesthetic by Justus Brinkmann, the then director of the Museum für Kunst und Gewerbe in Hamburg. In 1897 he began teaching ornamental painting at the Kunstgewerbeschule in Berlin.

He first exhibited in Munich in 1890, and participated in the first Munich Secession exhibition in 1893. In 1894, he co-founded the Freie Vereinigung (Free Association) in Munich, which came out of the Secession, along with Lovis Corinth, Max Slevogt and Wilhelm Trübner.

Eckmann was one of the most important Jugendstil artists. The key to his modernity lay in his ability to fuse the abstraction of sinewy lines and contrasting colours with naturalism. He did so by always basing his work on an interpretation of nature and natural forms such as flowers, leaves, buds and stems. He and Obrist were the most successful artists at understanding the organic aspect of nature. In the graphic arts field, Eckmann was soon acclaimed for his colour woodcuts, some of which were reproduced in the *Pan* art review (published in Berlin). He also produced engravings and vignettes for the Munich magazine *Die Jugend* (founded in 1896), and he provided illustrations for many books by Sudermann and Hauptmann. Another of his achievements in the graphic arts was creating the Eckmann font for the newspaper *Die Woche* (The Week). On the advice of Friedrich Deneken, a founding member of the Kunstgewerbeschule in Scherrebek in 1896, he then began to produce designs which were woven at the school. One of his designs even became an emblematic image of European Art Nouveau - *Five Swans* (1896-1897). This image, which was almost a motif, was presented at the Exposition Universelle of 1900, and would be reproduced countless times in magazines around the world. Eckmann also supplied other designs for commercial weaving factories in Krefeld (Deuss & Oetker and Kneusel & Co.). In 1897 Grand Duke Ernst Ludwig von Hessen commissioned him to decorate and design items of furniture for his office in the Darmstadt Palace. Eckmann was naturally part of the renaissance in decorative art in Munich, which was put on show at the seventh Internationale Kunstausstellung (International Art Exhibition) at the Glaspalast, Munich, in 1897. There, the contribution of the Secessionist designers was evident, with works by artists like Richard Riemerschmid, Hermann Obrist, August Endell and Bernhard Pankok. Eckmann also proved to be a key designer of metal objects, with his candlesticks, lamps, vases and kettles, which were manufactured by the firm Josef Zimmermann & Co.

BIBLIOGRAPHY:

Otto Eckmann. Ein Hauptmeister des Jugendstils, exhibition catalogue, Kaiser-Wilhelm-Museum, Krefeld, 1977. Cho, Nam-Si, *Otto Eckmann (1865 - 1902): sein Beitrag zum Jugendstil durch die Rezeption des Japonismus*, dissertation, Universität, Hamburg, 1988. Depas, Rosalind, *'Medievalism, and the art of the book in Germany in the Jugendstil period: Melckmanchior Loechter, Heinrich Vogeler and otto Eckmann'* in *Studies in Medievalism*, vol 3, No. 4, Spring, 1991. Savigny, Brigitte von, *Otto Eckmann (1865-1902): Graphiker und Kunsthandwerker*, dissertation, Albert-Ludwig Universität, Freiburg im Breisgau, 1993. Ottomeyer, Hans (ed.)/Brandlhuber, Margot, *Wege in die Moderne. Jugendstil in München 1896 bis 1914*, Klinkhardt & Biermann, Munich, Berlin, 1997. Thummler, Sabine, *'Sources of Jugendstil in Germany: facets of the renewal of nature'* in *Apollo*, vol. 151, No. 459, May, periodical, 2000. *Scherrebek - Wandbehänge des Jugendstils*, exhibition catalogue, Museum Künstlerkolonie, Mathildenhöhe Darmstadt, 2003.

MUSEUMS AND GALLERIES:

BERLIN (Staatliche Mus. Preussischer Kulturbesitz, Kunstbibliothek): *Iris* (1895, engraving on wood) - COPENHAGEN (Danish Mus. of Decorative Art): *Five Swans* (1897, weaving) - DARMSTADT (Städtische Kunstmuseum Kunstsammlungen): candelstick in the shape of a flower - HAMBURG (Kunsthalle) - HAMBURG (Mus. für Kunst und Gewerbe): *Five Swans* (1896-1897, woven rug); *Gulls in Flight* (1896, woven rug); *Narcissi* (1896-1897, metal candlestick); *bowl* (porcelain) - KARLSRUHE (Badisches Landesmus.): *Swans* (1897, woven rug) - KREFELD (Kaiser Wilhelm Mus.): *Sky with Moon over the Water* (1896-1897, coloured woodcut) - LONDON (Victoria and Albert Mus.): *Iris* (coloured engraving, publication Pan, 1895) - OFFENBACH (Klingspor-Museum) - SCHLESWIG (Schleswig-Holdsteinisches Landesmuseum): *Five Swans* (1896-1897, woven rug).

ECKSTEIN

German, 18th century.
Sculptor.

Eckstein produced the enormous statues of the four evangelists for the church of Ludwigslust.

ECKSTEIN, Anton

Austrian, 18th century.
Born 1685, in Prague; died 12 August 1729, in Vienna.
Painter.

Anton Eckstein was the brother of Wenzel Eckstein and probably Franz Gregor Eckstein.

ECKSTEIN, Carl Alphons

Dutch, 19th century.
Born 16 September 1840.
Lithographer.

Carl Alphons Eckstein was director of the topographical institute at the war office in The Hague.

ECKSTEIN, Franz Gregor Ignaz

Czech, 17th - 18th century.
Born at the end of the 17th century, in Zidowice near Zatec; died after 1736, in Lemberg (now Lviv, Ukraine).
Painter.

Franz Eckstein was born in Bohemia. He studied in Rome and settled in Brno where he was a member, in 1700, of the newly founded Accademia di San Luca. Early in his career, he produced a series of frescoes in Moravia and Austrian Silesia. He also executed a ceiling fresco with scenes from the life of St Peter in the Jesuit church in Lemberg, and several other frescoes for the high altar and the chapels. The best known of the oil paintings is an *Assumption* on a side panel of the high altar in the Jesuit church in Brno.

ECKSTEIN, Friedrich

German, 19th century.
Born 1787, in Berlin; died 1832, in America.
Sculptor.

Friedrich Eckstein was probably the son of Johannes Eckstein I and did the bust of General Jackson in Cincinnati in 1820.

ECKSTEIN, Georges Paul

British, 18th - 19th century.
Sculptor.

Georges Eckstein was probably the son and pupil of Johan I. Eckstein. He worked in London, where he exhibited at the Royal Academy from 1777 to 1802.

ECKSTEIN, Johann

German, 17th century.
Active in Nuremberg at the end of the 17th century.
Engraver.

ECKSTEIN, Johann Georg

German, 18th century.
Active in Nuremberg and Berlin.
Painter, modeller.

ECKSTEIN, Johannes I or John

German, 18th century.
Born in Strelitz (Mecklemburg); died c. 1798 or 1802, in London.
Painter, sculptor, lithographer.

Johannes Eckstein I worked initially in Potsdam, then went to England where he spent most of his life.

MUSEUMS AND GALLERIES:

BERLIN: low relief - BIRMINGHAM (Mus. and AG): *John Freeth and his Circle (Birmingham Men of the Last century)* - LONDON (National Portrait Gal.): *Sir William Sidney Smith* (1801-1802, oil on canvas).

ECKSTEIN, Johannes II or John

German, 18th century.
Active in Potsdam.
Modeller, painter, engraver.

Johannes Eckstein II exhibited an equestrian statue of Frederick II as a Roman emperor at the Berlin academy in 1786, clay sculptures in 1788, and a painting of *The Family of Darius before Alexander the Great* in 1791. He then settled in America under the name of John Eckstein and in 1806 participated in a project for a statue of Washington. In 1809 he engraved illustrations for poems by Freneau.

AUCTION RECORDS:

NEW YORK, 16 April 1936, *Richard Webster*, USD 300.

ECKSTEIN, John
British, 18th - 19th century.
Sculptor.
John Eckstein exhibited 19 times at the Royal Academy in London from 1762 to 1802.

ECKSTEIN, Karl Gustaf
Swedish, 18th - 19th century.
Born 1766, in Stockholm; died 1838, in Stockholm.
Painter, engraver.
Eckstein was a pupil of Masreliez and a member of the Stockholm academy. Notable works by him include *David Anointed by the King* and *Cupid Brought to Virtue by Happiness*, as well as several views of Stockholm.

ECKSTEIN, Sebastian
Polish, 18th century.
Active in Poland.
Painter.
Sebastian Eckstein was commissioned by Blasius Krasinski to produce frescoes for the parish church of Krasne, north of Warsaw. He might be identified with 'Frater Ekstein' who taught painting to the young A. Radwanski in a Piarist monastery in Cracow, and who painted the fresco of the high altar and the vault in the same monastery.

ECKSTEIN, Wenzel
Austrian, 18th century.
Born 1695, in Prague; died 26 January 1731, in Vienna.
Painter.
Wenzel Eckstein was the brother of Anton Eckstein.

ECKSTEIN, Wilhelm
German, 19th century.
Born 28 October 1863, in Auerbach.
Painter.
Wilhelm Eckstein trained at the academies in Düsseldorf and Berlin and exhibited a *Holy Night* in Berlin in 1896.

ECKSTEYN, Georg David, or Eckstein
German, 18th century.
Active in Nuremberg c. 1721.
Engraver.
Georg Ecksteyn engraved portraits.

ECKSTRÖM, Carl Emanuel
Danish, 19th century.
Born 1776, in Sweden; died 4 December 1826, in Copenhagen.
Painter. Portraits.
Eckström was a student at the Kunstakademi in Copenhagen from 1798 to 1806. He exhibited several paintings (chiefly portraits) at Charlottenborg castle between 1807 and 1817.

ECKTHALER, Hartmann, or Eckenthaler
German, 17th century.
Died after 1654.
Active in Frankfurt am Main.
Engraver, printer.

ECLISSI, Antonio, or Ecclissi
Italian, 17th century.
Active in Rome.
Painter.
Eclissi worked for the pope and for Cardinal Francesco Barberini, for whom he made watercolour copies of medieval Christian frescoes and mosaics.

ECO, Umberto
Italian, 20th century.
Born 1932, in Alessandria (Piedmont).
Mixed media, writer.
Kinetic Art.
Umberto Eco worked with Bruno Munari. He defines the meaning behind his works thus: 'the movement of forms, colours and planes is the means of obtaining a changing ensemble'. Although his research activities as a creative artist began with kinetic art, today he is much better known for lecturing at the University of Bologna, for his research into semiology, his theories on medieval art and literature, and for being a successful writer. His books include *The Name of the Rose*.

BIBLIOGRAPHY:
Popper, Frank, *Naissance de l'art cinétique*, Gauthier-Villars, Paris, 1967.

ÉCOLE, Pierre Henri
French, 20th century.
Born in Argenteuil.
Painter. Figures, landscapes.
Pierre Henri École exhibited in Paris at the Société Nationale des Beaux-Arts from 1935 onwards.

ECONOMOS, Gérard
French, 20th century.
Born 17 December 1935, in Paris.
Painter, illustrator.
Gérard Economos trained as an architect and town-planner. In 1955, he met Jean Cocteau, of great importance in his development. He often paints in public, almost in the spirit of 'performance painting'. Similarly he has developed his concept of 'Music to Watch', 'a concept of artistic and pictorial creation on a very large canvas, done directly and in public with a symphony orchestra'. He has 'composed' on canvas with music by Iannis Xenakis, Berlioz (the *Symphonie Fantastique* in Paris, Guadalajara and Taipei) and with improvisations by Jean Guillou. He has illustrated various authors: Kipling, Laxness, Sinclair Lewis, Jean Giono and Jean-Paul Sartre. Jean Cocteau, Michel del Castillo and Yann Queffelec have written about his work.

Economos' art derives from lyrical abstraction, from action painting. He uses symbols to celebrate the forces of the universe, the sea, space and nature, often in muted tones of blue heightened with touches of white. Sometimes a moment of figurative realism is glimpsed among these raging and formless hues.

In 1955 the Musée Galliera in Paris put on a retrospective exhibition of his work, as did the Musée Luxembourg in Paris in 1981.

BIBLIOGRAPHY:
Schlumberger, Jean-Claude, et al., *Le Chant du Cosmos. Gérard Économos et Jean Guillou*, 1999 (pamphlet published on the occasion of the Rhine-Palatinate Cultural Summer, text in German and French).

ECONOMOS, Michael
Greek, 20th century.
Born 1937, in Athens.
Painter.
Kinetic Art.
Michael Economos worked in the USA. He featured at an exhibition in 1970 at the Hudson Museum in New York entitled *Light, Motion and Sound Show*, which suggests that he worked in a genre similar to kinetics employing movement and light in art. In 1974, however, he exhibited Hyperrealist pictures, in which he described with meticulous care close-ups of grass scattered with tiny pieces of rubbish.

ECONOMOU, Michel, or Economon
Greek, 20th century.
Born 1888, in Piraeus; died 1933, in Athens.
Also active in France.
Painter. Landscapes.
Michel Economou was a pupil of Constantin Volonakis at the school of fine art in Athens. He also attended the École

des Beaux-Arts in Paris, where he stayed and worked until 1926, enjoying friendly relationships with Juan Gris and Fujita. Economou was committed to a Post-Impressionist technique. The luminous atmosphere and poetic nature of his landscapes are noteworthy. He featured in many collective exhibitions in Athens, London and Paris where he exhibited at the Salon de la Société Nationale des Beaux-Arts (1913).

Museums and Galleries:
Athens (Dimotiki Pinakothíki) - Athens (Ethnikí Pinakothíki) - Rhodes (Dimothiki Pinakothík).

ECOUIS, Roger d'
French, 16th century.
Active in Caen.
Painter, sculptor.

Roger d'Ecouis is known to have painted coats of arms.

ECPHANTUS I
7th - 6th century BC.
Born on Melos.
Painter, sculptor.
Ancient Greek.

Ecphantus was born on the island of Melos, and left his inscription on a marble column that was taken from there to Venice in 1755. Today it is in Berlin. Nothing definite is known about his abilities as a painter.

ECPHANTUS II, OF CORINTH
7th century BC.
Painter.
Ancient Greek.

Ecphantus, according to Pliny, was the first to think of using crushed brick in painting.

ECQMAN. See **ECKMAN**

ECREMENT, Odon Louis
French, 19th - 20th century.
Born in the second half of the 19th century, in Paris.
Painter. Landscapes.

From 1906 Odon Louis Ecrement exhibited in Paris at the Salon des Indépendants.

EDADES, Victorio C.
Filipino, 20th century.
Born 1895, in Dagupan.
Painter. Genre scenes, landscapes. Murals.

Victorio Edades trained at the Grande Chaumière studio in Paris. He then left the Philippines for the USA, where he remained for nine years, particularly in Alaska and on the west coast. He continued his art studies and was awarded a diploma in architecture from the American School of Fine Arts. In 1928 he returned to his native country for his first solo exhibition, since which time he exhibited regularly, and in 1935 he painted a mural for the Capitol Theater in Manila. For thirty-three years he was director of the college of architecture and fine arts at the University of Santo Tomas, Manila. He received frequent commissions and in 1976 was declared a 'national artist'.

Edades was very influenced by Cézanne, Gauguin and Matisse. Together with the mural painter Carlos V. Francisco and the surrealist Ocampo, he is considered one of the founders of modern art in the Philippines.

Museums and Galleries:
Manila (NM).

EDARD, Albertine
French, 19th century.
Born in La Chapelle-St-Denis.
Painter. Portraits.

A pupil of Maxime Lalanne, Albertine Edard exhibited a drawing at the 1863 Salon.

EDDELBÜTTEL, Richard
German, 19th century.
Born 18 November 1856, in Harburg.
Painter, illustrator.

Richard Eddelbüttel appeared at the exhibition at the Berlin academy in 1884 and 1888 with still-lifes, from 1899 onwards at the exhibition of art with illustrative drawings, and in Munich in 1911 with two landscapes.

EDDELER
German, 14th century.
Active in Brunswick.
Illuminator.

EDDELIEN, Matthias Heinrich Elias
Danish, 19th century.
Born 22 January 1803, in Greifswald; died 24 December 1852, in Copenhagen.
Painter. Religious subjects, mythological subjects, genre scenes.

At 16, Eddelien was sent to Copenhagen by his father, who had worked there as a carpenter. While studying with the painter Hambro, he also attended classes at the Kunstakademi from 1821. In 1838, he won a travel scholarship and left for Rome, where he painted a large altarpiece entitled (*Christ Blessing The Little Children*) for the church of Kronborg, and on his return repeated the subject for the church at Maarum. He exhibited between 1826 and 1844, before dying of an attack of apoplexy.

His works are notable for their pure draughtsmanship and clear coloration.

Museums and Galleries:
Copenhagen (Statens Mus. for Kunst): *Young Faun*; four paintings.

Auction records:
Copenhagen, 6 Dec 1990, *Scene from the Odyssey: Ulysses with Nausicaa* (oil on canvas, 59 x 51 1/4 ins / 150 x 130 cm) DKK 68,000.

EDDINGTON, William Clarke
British, 19th century.
Active in Worcester.
Painter, watercolourist. Landscapes.

William Eddington exhibited between 1861 and 1885 in London at the Royal Academy, at the Suffolk Street Gallery and at the Royal Institute.

Museums and Galleries:
London (Victoria and Albert Mus.): *Around Dinas, in Wales* - Reading: *Harvest.*

Auction records:
London, 27 Jan 1922, *In the Hopfields* (1864) GBP 18.

EDDIS, Eden Upton
British, 19th century.
Born 1812; died 1901, in Shalford.
Painter, watercolourist, draughtsman.

Eden Eddis was a pupil of Sass and of the schools of the Royal Academy. Initially a landscape artist, he later launched himself into portrait painting and achieved great success in this area. He was a very popular artist, although he withdrew to settle at Shalford (near Guildford) towards the end of his life because he had become deaf. Among the portraits of famous men that he had painted are those of Sydney Smith, Theodore Hook and Macaulay. He produced several remarkable portraits of children in both oil and pencil.

Museums and Galleries:
Dublin: *Portrait of Lord Heytesbury.*

Auction records:
London, 26 Jan 1923, *Ayah and her Child,* GBP 12. London, 26 Feb 1926, *G.M.Dallas, Vice-President of the United States, in a Black Suit,* GBP 73. London, 12 Dec 1930, *Charles Philip, 4th Count of Hardwick in Black Suit and Red Waistcoat,* GBP

21; *Portrait of the Honourable Eliot Yorke, Aged, in a Black Suit, with a Knitted Red and Green Coat,* GBP 27. LONDON, 11 July 1972, *Portrait of a Little Girl in a Blue Dress,* GBP 210. LONDON, 15 May 1979, *Alone in the Prairie* (oil on canvas, 55 1/2 x 33 1/2 ins / 141 x 85 cm) GBP 5,500. LONDON, 18 Jan 1984, *Study after Nature* (oil on canvas, 30 x 25 ins / 76 x 63.5 cm) GBP 600. LONDON, 11 July 1985, *Children of John Peter Fearon* (c. 1841, watercolour and pencil, 13 1/4 x 14 1/4 ins / 33.5 x 36 cm) GBP 840. EAST DENNIS (MASSACHUSETTS), 31 July 1987, *Portrait of Helen and Eden Powell* (oil on canvas, 30 x 25 ins / 76.2 x 63.8 cm) GBP 2,000. NEW YORK, 21 May 1991, *The Little Vegetable Seller* (oil on canvas, 64 x 40 ins / 162.5 x 101.5 cm) USD 5,500. LONDON, 4 June 1997, *Study of Albury Heath* (oil on canvas, 56 x 44 ins / 142 x 112 cm) GBP 9,775. BURY ST EDMUNDS, 22 Sept 1999, *Little Fortune Teller* (oil on panel, 12 x 9 ins / 30 x 24 cm) GBP 1,650. LONDON, 30 Nov 2001, *Portrait of a Girl Adorned with Berries* (1881, oil on canvas, 24 x 20 ins / 61 x 51 cm) GBP 7,500. TORONTO, 18 Nov 2002, *Roy the Terrier in a Wood* (oil on canvas, 24 x 20 ins / 61 x 51 cm) CAD 4,600.

EDDROP, Th.
French, 18th century.
Painter. Genre scenes, landscapes.

MUSEUMS AND GALLERIES:
ST-OMER: *Philosophical Landscape; Landscape; Seascape.*

EDDY, Don
American, 20th century.
Born 1944, in Long Beach (California).
Painter.

Don Eddy studied at the University of California in Santa Barbara, then at the University of Hawaii in Honolulu. He moved to New York in 1972.

Hyperrealism appeared in the USA during the late 1960s, in California and New York. It was a reaction against the avant-garde movements of Conceptual Art, Land Art and Arte Povera, which abandoned painting and its conventional media. It marked a return to a more traditional technique and to a figurative representation, but a direct and efficient one, insofar as Hyperrealism aims to reproduce reality as faithfully as possible, with a sense of precision close to photography. This pictorial movement has specifically American roots, with the Ash Can School at the turn of the 20th century, the Precisionists of the 1920s and the American Scene painters such as Edward Hopper.

Hyperrealism became extremely popular straight away, being much more easily accessible than abstract painting. Eddy was one of the artists to emerge from this movement. He specialises in representing the bodywork of cars - like his contemporaries, though each of them in different fields, and for both aesthetic and commercial reasons. Working with the aid of colour photographs, like most of the Hyperrealist artists, Eddy gives his paintings a raw, even cold, tonality. What interests him specifically are the chrome, reflective surfaces of these cars - the objects of the American myth - with their gleaming colours and polished aesthetic. Endowed with astonishing technical skill, his compositions constantly veer between illusionism and trompe-l'œil.

Once again, it is reflection and all the mechanisms of optical distortion that he emphasises in his series of paintings: in *Showroom Windows,* the reality of the shopfronts is captured with the maximum realism possible, as is the reality reflected in the glass. This game of mirrors, and the creation of a new pictorial and mental space, seems to be the most interesting aspect of his painting, since it is very much an exaggerated form of realism. Although these illusionist processes are not new (one might think of the Dutch primitive painters), they powerfully prove that the magic of representing what is real is always astonishing, and its mystery far from exhausted.

A large section of the 1971 Paris Biennale was devoted to Eddy's work. Many successful exhibitions brought him to public attention, both in the USA and in Europe, including Documenta in Kassel in 1972. In 2002 his work appeared in the exhibition *Les Années 70: l'art en cause* (*The 1970s: Art in Question*) at the Capc-Musée d'Art Contemporain, Bordeaux; then again in 2003 in *Hyperréalismes USA 1965-75* at the Musée d'Art Moderne et Contemporain, Strasbourg.

BIBLIOGRAPHY:
Don Eddy, hyperréaliste américain, exhibition catalogue, André François Petit, Paris, 1973. Fréruchet, Maurice, et al., *Les Années soixante-dix: l'art en cause,* exhibition catalogue, Capc musée d'Art contemporain, Bordeaux, 2002. Kuspit, Donald, *Don Eddy: the art of paradox,* Hudson Hills Press, New York, 2002. Lebensztejn, Jean-Claude, et al., *Hyperréalismes USA 1965-75,* group exhibition catalogue, Musée d'Art moderne et contemporain, Strasbourg, Hazan, Paris, 2003.

MUSEUMS AND GALLERIES:
ST-ÉTIENNE: *Untitled* (1971).

AUCTION RECORDS:
LOS ANGELES, 10 June 1976, *12:45 Waiting V* (1969, acrylic/canvas, 54 x 44 ins / 137 x 112 cm) USD 4,750. LONDON, 1 July 1982, *Bumper Section XXIII: Chevrolet* (1970, oil on canvas, 48 x 33 3/4 ins / 122 x 86 cm) GBP 3,000. NEW YORK, 2 Nov 1984, *BMW Showroom Window I* (1971, acrylic/canvas, 66 x 66 ins / 167.5 x 167.5 cm) USD 24,000. NEW YORK, 4 Nov 1987, *Untitled (Volkswagen)* (1971, acrylic/canvas, 48 x 66 ins / 122 x 167.8 cm) USD 30,000. NEW YORK, 9 Nov 1989, *'G II'* (1979, acrylic/canvas, 44 x 40 ins / 111.8 x 101.6 cm) USD 60,500. NEW YORK, 18 Nov 1992, *Private Parking IV* (1971, acrylic/canvas, 48 x 66 ins / 121.9 x 167.6 cm) USD 14,300. NEW YORK, 14 June 1995, *Pontiac Showroom Window II* (1972, acrylic/canvas, 47 3/4 x 47 1/2 ins / 121.3 x 120.7 cm) USD 7,475. PARIS, 20 June 1997, *Untitled* (1971, oil on canvas, 65 3/4 x 20 ins / 167 x 50.5 cm) FRF 38,000. LOKEREN, 11 Oct 1997, *Bumper Section IX: Isla Vista* (1970, oil on canvas, 47 3/4 x 66 1/4 ins / 121.5 x 168 cm) BEF 250,000. NEW YORK, 13 Nov 2001, *Autumn Light* (1986, acrylic on canvas, 50 x 60 ins / 127 x 152 cm) USD 6,500.

EDDY, Henry Stephens
American, 20th century.
Born 31 December 1878, in Rahway (New Jersey); died 1944.
Painter.

Henry Eddy was a pupil of Alphonse Mucha and George Elmer Browne. He was a member of the Salmagundi Club.

AUCTION RECORDS:
NEW YORK, 30 Sept 1997, *Gloucester* (oil on canvas, 20 x 24 ins / 50.8 x 61 cm) USD 3,162. WEST CHESTER, 21 May 2002, *Harbour View of Nantucket* (oil on canvas) USD 1,900.

EDDY, Isaac
British, 19th century.
Engraver.

Isaac Eddy engraved illustrations for the Bible for Merifield and Cochran at Windsor.

EDDY, James
American, 19th century.
Active in New York and Boston.
Engraver (stippling).

EDDY, Marvin Hannibal
American, 19th - 20th century.
Born in Louisville (Kentucky).
Painter.

Marvin Eddy was a pupil of Clarence Boyd and Hewett Green.

EDE, Basil
British, 20th century.

Born 1931.
Painter (gouache), watercolourist. Birds.

BASIL EDE

AUCTION RECORDS:
PERTH, 26 Aug 1991, *Water Hen* (watercolour and gouache, 7 x 9³/₄ ins / 18 x 25 cm) GBP 1,100. LONDON, 25 Feb 1992, *Goldfinch* (watercolour and gouache/grey paper, 9 x 11¹/₂ ins / 22.8 x 29 cm) GBP 880. LONDON, 16 March 1993, *Long-tailed Tits* (watercolour and gouache, 10 x 13 ins / 25.7 x 33 cm) GBP 1,725. PERTH, 31 Aug 1993, *Swallows Feeding their Young in a Nest* (watercolour and gouache, 13¹/₂ x 17¹/₄ ins / 34 x 44 cm) GBP 2,070. LONDON, 22 Nov 1995, *Snowy Owl* (1968, watercolour, 25 x 20 ins / 63.5 x 51 cm) GBP 1,380. LONDON, 14 May 1996, *Hoopoes Perching on the Branch of a Silver Birch* (watercolour heightened with white on grey paper, 15³/₄ x 12¹/₄ ins / 40 x 31.2 cm) GBP 2,530. LONDON, 30 Sept 1997, *Pair of Purple Gallinules* (1996, oil on canvas, 24 x 36 ins / 61 x 91.5 cm) GBP 3,910. BILLINGSHURST, 23 Feb 1999, *Tawny Owl on Ivy Covered Branch* (1968, watercolour heightened with gouache, 25 x 20 ins / 64 x 52 cm) GBP 2,400. LONDON, 18 Nov 1999, *Blackbird* (pencil, watercolour and gouache, 17 x 13 ins / 42 x 34 cm) GBP 1,500. LONDON, 17 May 2000, *Mandarin Ducks* (watercolour heightened with white, 10 x 14 ins / 26 x 36 cm) GBP 1,100. LONDON, 16 Nov 2000, *Eurasian Green Woodpecker* (watercolour and gouache, 13 x 9 ins / 33 x 24 cm) GBP 1,300. NEW YORK, 3 April 2003, *Snowy Egret with Palmetto, Charleston, South Carolina* (1979, watercolour and gouache, 25 x 19 ins / 63 x 48 cm) USD 9,000. LONDON, 20 May 2003, *House Martins* (1976, watercolour and gouache, 11 x 7 ins / 29 x 19 cm) GBP 1,200. MONTANA, 19 March 2004, *Black-billed Magpies* (watercolour, 25 x 20 ins / 64 x 51 cm) USD 2,000.

EDE, Frederick Charles Vipont
American, 19th century.
Born 22 February 1865, in Nottawa (Michigan); died 1907.
Painter. Figures, landscapes with figures, landscapes.
Frederick Charles Vipont Ede initially studied in America and then went to Paris, where he became a pupil of Tony Robert-Fleury and Bouguereau. Among his main works are *Landscape* (1891) for which he won a first prize in Montreal, and *Marlote*. He took part in the Universal Exhibition of Chicago in 1893 and won a medal of honour at the Museum of Fine Arts in Boston.
AUCTION RECORDS:
NEW YORK, 1900-1903, *Along the Loing*, USD 240; *Meadow*, USD 275; *Stone Bridge*, USD 230. NEW YORK, 1904, *Landscape*, USD 180. NEW YORK, 1906, *Shepherd and his Flock*, USD 270. NEW YORK, 8 Feb 1907, *Bonnières*, USD 400. NEW YORK, 1908, *River Le Ru*, USD 200. LONDON, 18 Jan 1908, *Mill Stream*, GBP 6. LONDON, 10 Jan 1909, *Spring*, GBP 9. NEW YORK, 12-13 and 14 April 1909, *Cow Drinking*, USD 310; *Old Farm*, USD 380; *Farm by a River*, USD 325; *Old Bridge*, USD 315. PARIS, 16 Dec 1925, *Sheep Grazing*, FRF 405. PARIS, 22 Jan 1927, *River in Autumn with Man Drawing Water*, FRF 650; *Washhouse in Ferrières*, FRF 450. PARIS, 25 March 1927, *Eddies*, FRF 300. PARIS, 16 Nov 1928, *La Cagne, near Windmills in Autumn*, FRF 450. LONDON, 30 June 1972, *Little Boy Fishing*, GBP 220. NEW YORK, 12 May 1978, *At Marlote, Seine et Marne* (oil on canvas, 32¹/₂ x 56¹/₂ ins / 82.5 x 143.5 cm) USD 1,600. NEW YORK, 18 Sept 1980, *Pastoral Scene* (oil on canvas, 23³/₄ x 28³/₄ ins / 60.3 x 73 cm) USD 1,100. PARIS, 8 June 1984, *Washerwoman* (oil on canvas, 21¹/₄ x 28³/₄ ins / 54 x 73 cm) FRF 9,000. LONDON, 19 March 1986, *Small Hut by River Lunain* (1925, oil on canvas, 23¹/₂ x 28³/₄ ins / 60 x 73 cm) GBP 3,200. AMSTERDAM, 16 Nov 1988, *Farms by a Stream in Autumn* (oil on canvas, 22 x 27¹/₄ ins / 56 x 69 cm) NLG 3,795. PARIS, 8 Nov 1989, *Cows and Hens* (oil on canvas, 23¹/₂ x 28³/₄ ins / 60 x 73 cm) FRF 12,500. MONTREAL, 19 Nov 1991, *Lady with a Parasol* (1888, watercolour, 10³/₄ x 16 ins / 27.2 x 40.6 cm) CAD 700. NEW YORK, 10 June 1992, *House by a Snowy Stream* (oil on canvas, 24 x 29¹/₂ ins / 61 x 75 cm) USD 3,080. NEW YORK, 25 Sept 1992, *Bend in the River* (oil on canvas, 23¹/₂ x 32 ins / 59.7 x 81.3 cm) USD 3,850. NEW YORK, 31 March 1993, *Summer Landscape with a Stream* (oil on canvas, 15 x 18 ins / 38.1 x 45.7 cm) USD 3,565. PARIS, 5 Nov 1993, *Shepherdess and her Flock near a Bridge* (1905, oil on canvas, 77¹/₂ x 51¹/₂ ins / 197 x 131 cm) FRF 10,000. NEW YORK, 28 Sept 1995, *Bucolic Landscapes* (1892, oils on canvas, a pair, 18³/₄ x 25¹/₄ ins / 47.9 x 64.1 cm and 15 x 21³/₄ ins/37.8 x 55.2 cm) USD 1,840. PARIS, 17 Oct 1997, *Landscape with River* (oil on canvas, 19 x 23¹/₂ ins / 48 x 60 cm) FRF 10,000. FONTAINEBLEAU, 3 Dec 2000, *Trout River* (oil on canvas, 21 x 29 ins / 54 x 73 cm) FRF 17,000. MONTREAL, 26 June 2002, *Shepherd and Sheep* (1892, oil on canvas, 19 x 25 ins / 48 x 63 cm) CAD 2,800. BETHESDA, 20 Sept 2003, *Riverside in Moret-sur-Long* (1928, oil on canvas, 22 x 26 ins / 56 x 66 cm) USD 2,800. WASHINGTON, 24 April 2004, *Ducks by a Stream* (oil on board, 13 x 17 ins / 32 x 44 cm) USD 3,000. LONDON, 16 June 2004, *By the Lumain* (1885, oil on canvas, 24 x 29 ins / 60 x 73 cm) GBP 5,500.

EDE, Pieter Danielszoon van
Dutch, 17th century.
Born c. 1635.
Active in Amsterdam.
Painter.

EDEIKIN, Ephraim
Latvian, 20th century.
Born in Riga.
Sculptor. Busts.
A member of the Salon des Artistes Français, Ephraim Edeikin exhibited a *Bust of President Aristide Briand* in 1929 in Paris. It is believed that he lived in France

EDEL, Alfredo
Italian, 19th - 20th century.
Born 1859, in Codogno; died 16 December 1912, in Boulogne-sur-Mer, France.
Active in France.
Painter, watercolourist, sculptor. Stage costumes, figurines.
Edel made figurines and theatre costumes. He worked for Coquelin, Sarah Bernhardt, the Comédie Française and Barnum in Paris, as well as the Olympia Theatre in London and La Scala in Milan.
AUCTION RECORDS:
PARIS, 14 Dec 1990, *Sketches of Opera Costumes for the Religious Drama by Jules Massenet Entitled 'Mary Magdalene'* (1902, collection of 15 watercolours) FRF 15,000.

EDEL, Edmund
German, 19th century.
Born 10 September 1863, in Stolp.
Painter, illustrator, draughtsman, writer.
Edmund Edel trained at the royal academy in Munich and at the Académie Julian in Paris. He worked in Berlin and specialised as a painter and illustrator for humorous reviews. He acquired quite a reputation as a painter of posters.

EDEL, Florence
American, 20th century.
Miniaturist.
Florence Edel spent some time in France and was the pupil of William Bouguereau and Gabriel Ferrier. She made her debut in Paris, exhibiting at the 1914 Salon des Artistes Français.

EDEL, Johann Samuel
German, 17th century.

Active in Augsburg and Munich.
Engraver.
Johann Edel engraved scenes from the bible and illustrations for pious works.

EDEL, Michel
German, 16th century.
Active in Murnau in Bavaria.
Sculptor (wood).

EDELE, Benedikt
Moravian School, 19th century.
Died 1867, in Brno.
Sculptor.
Benedikt Edele studied under J. E. Ruhl in Kassel. Most of his works are in Moravia, where he settled in 1821. His works include a *St Mary Magdalene and St Peter* (wood sculptures), *Magdalene and Christ* (1842), *The Last Supper* (a high relief in Kunín), and *Two Angels* (wooden sculptures, in Racetice). He also worked for churches in Kaigern, Brüsan and Lysice.

EDELFELT, Albert Gustaf Aristide
Finnish, 19th - 20th century.
Born 21 July 1854, in Helsinki; died 1905, in Borgaen.
Painter, watercolourist, pastellist, draughtsman.
Religious subjects, figures, portraits, genre scenes, landscapes, still-lifes.
Edelfelt trained at the art association and then at the university of Helsinki, before studying history of art at Antwerp art academy. In 1874 he took up a place at the École des Beaux-Arts in Paris, where he was taught by Gérôme and participated in numerous exhibitions. Tsar Alexander III of Russia commissioned him to paint portraits of his children. On his return to Finland in 1889, he became leader of the protest movement opposing the amendments to the Finnish constitution and, as a member of parliament, was a staunch defender of his country's freedom. Decorated with the Légion d'Honneur in 1887, Edelfelt was promoted to Officer in 1889 and Commander in 1901.

He took up open-air painting and was a noted pastellist and watercolourist. Intensely proud of his Finnish roots, Edelfelt depicted historical and realist scenes showing his country's fight for independence and its Scandinavian heritage, all of them executed with great technical expertise. In 1883 in Haiko, influenced by Manet and Christian Krogh, he painted one of his major works, *At Sea*. He, along with Akseli Gallen-Kallela, was one of the most important Finnish artists of the 19th century.

Edelfelt took part in the Salon de Paris from 1877 onwards, winning a third-place medal in 1880, a second-place medal in 1882 and a grand prize in 1889. He exhibited at the Royal Academy in London from 1891. His works have been shown in recent exhibitions including at the Valtion Taidemuseo (Finnish National Gallery) in Helsinki in 1997 and in the travelling exhibition, *The Unknown Horizon, Art in Finland 1870-1920* at the Ateneum art gallery in Helsinki and at the Musée des Beaux-Arts in Strasbourg and the Musée des Beaux-Arts in Lille, 1999-2000.

EDELFET

BIBLIOGRAPHY:
Hintze, Bertel, '*Albert Edelfelt*', *3 vol.*, Söderström, Helsinki, 1944. Kaipainen, Marja, *Albert Edelfelt: kuihtumaton ruusutarha*, Watti-kustannus, Helsinki, 1983. Kämäräinen, Eija, *Albert Edelfelt: kultainen häkki*, Söderström, Helsinki, 1992 (with a summary in English). Lukkarinen, Ville, *Albert Edelfelt ja Runebergin Vänrikki Stoolin tarinat: pois mielist'ei se päivä jää*, exhibition catalogue, Valtion taidemuseo, Helsinki, 1997. *L'Horizon inconnu, l'art en Finlande 1870-1920*, travelling exhibition catalogue, Ateneum, Helsinki, Musées des Beaux-Arts, Lille, Strasbourg, 1999 (text in French and English). Anttila, Elina, *Albert Edelfelt et la nouvelle peinture*, Taidehistorian seura, Helsinki, 2001 (text in French and Finnish).

MUSEUMS AND GALLERIES:
COPENHAGEN (Statens Mus. for Kunst): *Summer Evening in Finland* (1885) - GÖTEBORG (Konstmus.): *At Sea* (1883) - HELSINKI: *Duke Karl at the Deathbed of Klas Flemming; Woman with a Basket; The Jardin du Luxembourg; Dalin's Spring Song; Seaside Serenade* (watercolour); *Women in Front of Ruo-Kolak Church; Jesus Christ and Mary Magdalene; Lady Reading; Lady Dressed in Black; Young Girl Reading* (watercolour); *Young Lady in Profile* (watercolour); *Portrait of the Painter Aug. Notila; Portrait of the Minister C.-G. Estlander; At the Last Reading; Portrait of Miss Elsa Lindberg; Portrait of the Singer Aino Ackté* - LUXEMBOURG: *December Day in Finland; Religious Service by the Sea* - MULHOUSE: *Mid-Lent* - NICE: *Funeral Procession for a Child in Finland; Religious Service* - PARIS (Mus. d'Orsay): *December Day in Finland; Religious Service by the Sea; Portrait of Louis Pasteur* (1885, oil on canvas) - ST PETERSBURG (Gosudarstvennyj Russkij Muz.): *Laundress* - STOCKHOLM: *Portrait of Victor Rydberg, Swedish Writer, Aged 63; Jesus Christ Washing the Apostles' Feet.*

AUCTION RECORDS:
PARIS, 26-27 March 1896, *Midnight Sun*, FRF 200. NEW YORK, 23-24 Jan 1901, *Sunlight Effect*, USD 230. PARIS, 25 Jan 1926, *Portrait of a Young Girl in Profile*, FRF 2,750. PARIS, 20 April 1932, *Profile of a Young Woman*, FRF 1,320. LONDON, 18 May 1938, *General in Russian Uniform*, GBP 30. STOCKHOLM, 31 March 1971, *Portrait of a Young Woman*, SEK 28,000. PARIS, 27 June 1977, *L'Arlésienne* (*Woman from Arles*) (wash, 13 3/4 x 9 ins / 35 x 22 cm) FRF 2,700. NEW YORK, 26 Jan 1979, *The Declaration* (oil on canvas, 19 3/4 x 28 3/4 ins / 50 x 73 cm) FRF 103,000. COPENHAGEN, 24 April 1979, *Seated Female Saint* (1898, gouache and pastel, 17 3/4 x 14 1/4 ins / 45 x 36.5 cm) DKK 21,000. LUCERNE, 2 June 1981, *Wooded Riverscape with Figures* (oil on canvas, 33 1/2 x 43 1/4 ins / 85 x 110 cm) CHF 11,500. STOCKHOLM, 24 April 1984, *Two Young Girls* (Indian ink, 7 x 6 1/4 ins / 18 x 16 cm) SEK 11,000. STOCKHOLM, 30 Oct 1984, *Young Woman Sitting Down* (watercolour and pencil, 9 x 9 3/4 ins / 23 x 25 cm) SEK 21,000. STOCKHOLM, 4 Nov 1986, *Portrait of an Elegant Woman* (1892, pastel, 50 x 39 1/4 ins / 127 x 100 cm) SEK 160,000. LONDON, 25 March 1987, *The Laundry* (pencil heightened with white gouache, 8 1/2 x 11 1/4 ins / 21.5 x 28.5 cm) GBP 3,000. STOCKHOLM, 19 Oct 1987, *Goodbye* (oil on canvas, 22 x 17 3/4 ins / 56 x 45 cm) SEK 1,900,000. LONDON, 23 March 1988, *View of a Glaciated Valley* (pastel, 18 1/2 x 23 ins / 47 x 57.5 cm) GBP 3,300. LONDON, 24 March 1988, *Horserider* (1892, watercolour heightened with white, 20 3/4 x 13 ins / 53 x 33 cm) GBP 20,900. LONDON, 16 March 1989, *Summer's Evening in the Port of Borga* (1889, oil on canvas, 29 1/2 x 22 ins / 75 x 55 cm) GBP 121,000. LONDON, 21 Nov 1989, *Portrait of Mrs Vallery-Radot* (1888, oil on canvas, 17 3/4 x 12 1/4 ins / 45 x 31 cm) GBP 77,000. LONDON, 27-28 March 1990, *Woman and Child in a Sunlit Room* (1889, oil on canvas, 17 1/4 x 23 1/4 ins / 44 x 59 cm) GBP 170,500. STOCKHOLM, 16 May 1990, *Little Girl Reading* (oil on canvas, 16 1/4 x 13 ins / 41 x 33 cm) SEK 30,000. STOCKHOLM, 14 Nov 1990, *The Pilot* (oil on canvas, 26 x 21 1/4 ins / 66 x 54 cm) SEK 350,000. PARIS, 18 Dec 1991, *Young Woman with a Jabot* (1880, oil/panel, 18 x 15 ins / 46 x 37.8 cm) FRF 125,000. NEW YORK, 22-23 July 1993, *Gentleman Helping a Lady Across the Ford* (1881, watercolour/card, 23 x 16 ins / 58.4 x 40.6 cm) USD 2,415. NEW YORK, 1 Nov 1995, *Going to the Christening* (1880, oil on canvas, 29 x 39 1/2 ins / 73.7 x 100.3 cm) USD 409,500.

EDELINCK, Gaspar François, the Younger
Flemish, 17th - 18th century.
Born c. 1652, in Antwerp; died 21 May 1722, in Paris.

Engraver.
Flemish School.
Gaspar François Edelinck the Younger was the younger brother of Gérard Edelinck and lived in Paris, where he married on 3 August 1684.

EDELINCK, Gérard, or Edelink
Flemish, 17th century.
Born 20 October 1640, in Antwerp; died 2 April 1707, in Paris.
Active in France.
Engraver.
Flemish School.
Although Flemish by birth, Gérard Edelinck could easily be ascribed to the École Française (French School). From 1652 onwards he was the pupil of Gaspard Huberti and Cornelius Galle in Antwerp, later becoming a master in the same town in 1663, but it was above all in France that he made a name for himself. Summoned to Paris by Jean-Baptiste Colbert in 1665, he worked under the guidance of François de Poilly and Robert Nanteuil. He was then elected engraver to Louis XIV, who provided him with a pension and accommodated him in the Gobelins tapestry works. In 1672 he married Madeleine Reguesson and it is interesting to note that the wedding witnesses of the husband and wife were Charles Le Brun, Philippe de Champaigne and Gérard's two brothers, Jan and Gaspar. In 1677 he became a member of the Académie Royale on the strength of his *Portrait of Philippe de Champaigne*, engraved after a self-portrait.

Gérard Edelinck made a significant contribution to the art of engraving. It was he who first substituted diamond-shaped dimensions for square dimensions and who infused engravings with colour. He treated the works he reproduced with a little more realism, but preserved the softness of the art of Nanteuil. His output totals over 300 pieces.

G. Ed. x.

EDELINCK, Jan
Flemish School, 17th century.
Born c. 1643, in Antwerp; died 14 May 1680, in Paris.
Engraver, art dealer.
Jan Edelinck was the brother of Gérard Edelinck and a pupil of Gaspard Huberti in Antwerp. He went to Paris around 1665, where he was 'graveur ordinaire du Roi' (engraver in ordinary to the king) and married Anna Sauvage on 12 October 1673.

EDELINCK, Loduwyck
Flemish School, 16th century.
Painter.
Antwerp School.
A pupil of Claes Scuelens in 1510, Loduwyck Edelinck was admitted to the guild as a master painter in 1515.

EDELINCK, Michel Gérard or Gérard (son)
French, 18th century.
Born 1 December 1679, in Paris; died 25 May 1728, in Rochefort-sur-Mer.
Painter, draughtsman.
The son of Gérard Edelinck, Michel Gérard Edelinck should not be confused with his brother, another son of this famous engraver. He obtained a position at Rochefort in 1715 and on 21 January 1721 was appointed a professor of drawing at the École des Gardes de la Marine.
MUSEUMS AND GALLERIES:
LA ROCHELLE: *View of La Rochelle in 1725.*

EDELINCK, Nicolas Étienne
French, 18th century.
Born 1681, in Paris; died 11 May 1767, in Paris.
Engraver.
Son of Gérard Edelinck, Nicolas Edelinck spent part of his career in Venice. He was 'engraver to the king'.

EDELINE, Emile
Belgian, 19th century.
Born 19th century, in Antwerp.
Painter.
Having studied under L. Cogniet and Hébert, Emile Edeline sent a portrait of a man to the Salon de Paris in 1870.

EDELINE, Guillaume
Belgian, 20th century.
Born 1902, in Namur; died 1987, in Chairière.
Painter, watercolourist, draughtsman. Portraits, landscapes, still-lifes.
Edeline trained at Brussels art academy and became a member of Luxembourg art academy. He specialised in views of the Meuse and its tributary, the Semois, and also produced paintings recalling his stays in the South of France.
BIBLIOGRAPHY:
Edeline, F./Duquène, Cl./Brucher, R./Chariot, C., *Guillaume Edeline, peintre de la Semois*, Ars Libris, Brussels, 2001.
MUSEUMS AND GALLERIES:
BOUILLON - IXELLES - LIÈGE - NAMUR - VIRTON.

ÉDELINE, Odette
French, 20th century.
Born in Elbeuf (Seine-Maritime).
Painter. Portraits.
In 1933, Odette Édeline began exhibiting in Paris at the Société Nationale des Beaux-Arts. She was best known for her portraits of children.

EDELMANN, Charles Auguste
French, 20th century.
Born 16 August 1879, in Soultz-sous-Forêts, near Wissembourg (Haut-Rhin); died 1950, in Paris.
Painter, watercolourist, draughtsman, illustrator. Nudes, scenes with figures, genre scenes, landscapes, still-lifes.
Charles Auguste Edelmann studied at the École des Beaux-Arts in Paris with Jean Léon Gérôme and Ferdinand Humbert. In Paris he exhibited at the Salon des Artistes Français, to which he belonged, and at the Union des Artistes Alsaciens. He had solo shows in Strasbourg and Mulhouse.

Edelmann painted various subjects, often street scenes. His landscapes came later - Alsace, Brittany in the Île de Bréat, the Landes and Corrèze, the countryside near Paris and L'Isle-d'Adam. Then he painted domestic interiors, often including nudes. He illustrated a number of books, among them *Valentine Pacquault* by Gaston Chérau, *Boubouroche* by Georges Courteline, *Nuits de Princes* (*Princes' Nights*) by Joseph Kessel, *Un Coeur Vierge* (*An Untouched Heart*) by Eugène Montfort, *Les nuits chaudes du Cap Français* (*Warm Nights at Cap Français*) by Hugues Rebell, *Éloge de la Danse* (*In Praise of Dance*) by Gustave Welter, novels by Balzac and others. He could produce a swift and accurate sketch, knowing just how to evoke the gesture, attitude or detail that reveals character.
AUCTION RECORDS:
PARIS, 2 March 1929, *American Bar* (watercolour) FRF 950; *Still-life with Apples*, FRF 1,500. PARIS, 27 June 1929, *Seated Nude*, FRF 300. PARIS, 8 Dec 1944, *In a Garden*, FRF 5,000. PARIS, 20 Dec 1944, *Still-life*, FRF 4,200. ZURICH, 3 May 1965, *River Landscape*, CHF 3,800. LONDON, 19 June 1968, *Landscape by a Stream*, GBP 300. VIENNA, 2 Dec 1969, *River Landscape*, ATS 30,000. PARIS, 8 March 1989, *Pierrot, Harlequin and Columbine in a Park* (39 1/4 x 31 1/2 ins / 100 x 80 cm) FRF 15,000. CALAIS, 20 Oct 1991, *Still-life with Flower Vase and Books* (oil on panel, 23 1/2 x 36 1/4 ins / 60 x 92 cm) FRF 13,000. CALAIS, 5 July 1992, *Vase of Flowers* (oil on canvas, 23 1/2 x 19 3/4 ins / 60 x 50 cm) FRF 7,000. PARIS, 18 June 2004, *Young*

Woman in Front of a Shop (oil on canvas, 16 x 13 ins / 41 x 33 cm) EUR 3,000.

EDELMANN, Heinz
German, 20th century.
Born 1934.
Poster artist, illustrator, graphic designer. Advertising art.

Edelmann, like all graphic designers in the advertising field, draws inspiration from a multitude of sources, depending on the economic objectives of the project in question. He does not hesitate to borrow or quote from artists of the modern era, in particular the Surrealists, incorporating these references into his works in a humorous manner. In 1994 the Atria World Trade Center in Grenoble presented a major exhibition of his works.

ÉDELMANN, Jean
French, 20th century.
Born 2 May 1916, in Pantin.
Painter.

Jean Édelmann trained as a scientist and studied at the École Polytechnique. However, he began to exhibit in Paris in 1953 as a member of the Société du Salon d'Automne, and at the Salon Comparaisons. He also had solo exhibitions including, in Paris, at the Galerie d'Art International in 1986, 1987 and 1989; jointly at the same gallery from 1960 to 1990 showing paintings and drawings; and at the Paris Art Centre in 1991 and 1993.

Édelmann's early painting seemed based on Cubist sources, but soon developed its own radical abstraction. This Abstract style may have come from an external influence, something half recognised but not identified, linking Édelmann's progression to that of Estève, for example. His creations are very individual; on very pale backgrounds, at the far edge of white, are placed jagged forms sharply delineated, painted in flat tints, soft tones or darkly intense, even pure black, and on these are drawn clear-cut markings, so precise and exact as to make them seem identifiable. The painting is done with a light touch, as with watercolours, and although the drawing is as precise as a blue-print it is not in the least like geometric abstract work.

Jean Edelmann

AUCTION RECORDS:
PARIS, 7 Oct 1991, *Delay at Austerlitz Station* (acrylic/canvas, 45 x 63 3/4 ins / 114 x 162 cm) FRF 9,000.

EDELMANN, Joos
German, 15th century.
Active in Ulm.
Painter.

EDELMANN, Yrjö
Swedish, 20th century.
Born 1941.
Painter. Landscapes, still-lifes.

Edelmann has held solo shows, including: 2001, *Le Froissé des Choses* (*The Crumpling of Things*), alongside Christian Renonciat, at the Galerie Alain Blondel, Paris. Even though he handles various subjects, *trompe l'œil*, which he applies to still-lifes, is the technique he prefers.

AUCTION RECORDS:
STOCKHOLM, 17 Nov 1981, *Mr Nobody* (lithograph, 19 x 24 ins / 48 x 61 cm) SEK 3,200. STOCKHOLM, 14 April 1984, *Girl in Green Jeans with Tree* (1976, oil on canvas, 29 1/2 x 25 1/2 ins / 75 x 65 cm) SEK 15,500. STOCKHOLM, 27 May 1986, *Composition* (1984, oil on canvas, 31 1/2 x 31 1/2 ins / 80 x 80 cm) SEK 36,000. STOCKHOLM, 6 June 1988, *Homage to James Havard* (oil on canvas, 35 1/2 x 31 1/2 ins / 90 x 80 cm) SEK 16,500. STOCKHOLM, 5-6 Dec 1990, *Rough Landscape* (1979, oil on canvas, 39 1/4 x 39 1/4 ins / 100 x 100 cm) SEK 24,000. STOCKHOLM, 10-12 May 1993, *Various Papers* (1989, oil on canvas, 61 x 62 1/2 ins / 154 x 159 cm) SEK 28,000; *Packet* (1989, oil on canvas, 51 1/4 x 43 1/4 ins / 130 x 110 cm) SEK 28,000. STOCKHOLM, 30 Nov 1993, *Packet with Blue Ribbon* (1989, oil on canvas, 55 x 47 1/4 ins / 140 x 120 cm) SEK 38,000. STOCKHOLM, 17 May 1999, *Wrapping Paper* (1996, oil on canvas, 31 x 20 ins / 79 x 51 cm) SEK 43,000. STOCKHOLM, 22 Nov 1999, *Creased Paper* (1985, oil on canvas, 24 x 24 ins / 60 x 60 cm) SEK 29,000. STOCKHOLM, 15 May 2000, *Trompe l'Oeil with Paper* (1981, oil on canvas, 47 x 47 ins / 120 x 120 cm) SEK 37,000. STOCKHOLM, 23 May 2000, *Composition with Paper* (1989, oil on canvas, 61 x 58 ins / 155 x 148 cm) SEK 51,000. HELSINKI, 22 March 2001, *Packed Snow Landscape* (oil on canvas, 27 x 24 ins / 69 x 60 cm) FIM 28,000. STOCKHOLM, 12 Nov 2001, *Untitled* (1984, oil on canvas, 39 x 33 ins / 100 x 85 cm) SEK 20,000. STOCKHOLM, 23 April 2002, *Woman* (1977, oil on canvas, 43 x 41 ins / 109 x 103 cm) SEK 37,000. STOCKHOLM, 17 June 2002, *House and Tree* (1978, oil on canvas, 39 x 39 ins / 100 x 100 cm) SEK 19,000. STOCKHOLM, 4 Nov 2003, *A Child Disappears* (1966, mixed media on paper, 19 x 15 ins / 49 x 37 cm) SEK 19,500. HELSINKI, 13 Dec 2003, *All Together* (1983, oil on canvas, 47 x 55 ins / 120 x 140 cm) EUR 13,000. STOCKHOLM, 27 April 2004, *Night Object* (1981, oil on canvas, 39 x 33 ins / 100 x 85 cm) SEK 40,000. STOCKHOLM, 2 Nov 2004, *Car in Cardboard* (1979, oil on canvas, 40 x 38 ins / 102 x 96 cm) SEK 33,000.

EDELWEHR, Joh. Konrad
German, 17th century.
Active in Saxony.
Sculptor.

The pulpit of the church in Bertsdorf near Zittau is attributed to Edelwehr. He produced it with the help of the carpenter Christian Bürger.

EDEMA, Gérard van
Dutch, 17th century.
Born c. 1652, in Amsterdam; died c. 1700, in Richmond.
Painter. Scenes with figures, landscapes, landscapes with figures, waterscapes.

Gérard van Edema was the pupil of A. van Everdingen. In 1670 he went to London where he worked for the Duke of St Albans, the Count of Exeter and Sir Richard Edgcombe, in whose house he lived for a prolonged period with Jan Wyck, who often embellished his landscapes. He also stayed in Norway and Newfoundland. He painted landscapes with waterfalls and horror scenes.

BIBLIOGRAPHY:
Ogden, H./Ogden, M., *English Taste in Landscape in the Seventeenth century*, University of Michigan Press, Ann Arbor, 1955. Maccubbin, R./Hamilton-Phillips, M., eds, *The Age of William III and Mary II: Power, Politics and Patronage, 1688-1702, pp. 244-258*, exhibition catalogue, Grolier Club (New York)/Folger Shakespeare Library (Washington DC), New York, Washington DC, 1988-1989.

MUSEUMS AND GALLERIES:
LONDON (Royal Collection): *Landscape with Figures* (four paintings).

AUCTION RECORDS:
GLASGOW, 2 Nov 1933, *Landscape with Figures*, GBP 11; *Landscape with Figures and Ruined Castle*, GBP 15. LONDON, 24 July 1941, *Landscape with River, Figures, Boats and Houses* (1680) GBP 16. LONDON, 5 Dec 1941, *Fishermen and their Cottage* (1680) GBP 10. VIENNA, 16 March 1971, *River Landscape*, ATS 75,000. VIENNA, 16 March 1976, *Precipitous Landscape with Figures* (oil on canvas, 16 x 21 3/4 ins / 40.5 x 55.5 cm) ATS 60,000. LONDON, 13 April 1983, *River Landscape with Bridge* (oil on canvas, 36 1/2 x 54 1/4 ins / 93 x 138 cm) GBP 2,300. LONDON, 13 Feb 1985, *River Landscape with*

Figures (oil on canvas, 46 x 70¾ ins / 117 x 180 cm) GBP 6,800. LONDON, 5 July 1989, *Landscape with Figures and River on Rocky Bed* (oil on canvas, 45¾ x 35¾ ins / 116.5 x 91 cm) GBP 3,520. LONDON, 23 March 1990, *Landscape on a Rocky Coast during a Storm* (oil on canvas, 42 x 66 ins / 106.4 x 167.8 cm) GBP 16,500. LONDON, 14 April 1999, *Winter Landscape with Skaters on Frozen River* (oil on canvas/board, 24 x 30 ins / 62 x 75 cm) GBP 7,000. NEW YORK, 14 Oct 1999, *Extensive Mountainous Landscape with Figures in Foreground* (oil on canvas, 44 x 45 ins / 113 x 115 cm) USD 32,500.

EDEN, pseudonym of Borel, Raymond C.
American, 20th century.
From 1956 active in France.
Painter. Figure compositions.
Eden's family, originally from Talence (Gironde), emigrated to South America and then to the USA after the fall of Napoleon III and the cholera epidemic in Bordeaux. In 1949 he was an art student at Colombia University. In New York he learned the technique of egg painting and met the Brazilian painter Emiliano Di Cavalcanti, who took him off to Rio de Janeiro and São Paulo. At that time he was exhibiting in São Paulo, notably at the Museum of Modern Art. He then met Diego Rivera in Mexico and studied the characteristics of monumental painting with him. He also collaborated with the Mexican film director, Herbert Kline. He was less active during the Korean war. After settling in the town of Neuilly-sur-Seine in France, he pursued painting activities alongside work as a journalist and film director. He showed his work in international solo exhibitions. In France, he exhibited in Paris at the Galerie Vendôme, in 1990 and 1997, and in Bordeaux in 1992.

He followed the Realist style of painting, which was robust, with simplified forms and volumes and accentuated colours or contrasts. His figures captured in their everyday interior environment or in landscapes, are shaped by distinct lighting. The circumstance of the moment in which they find themselves is sufficient to define the affective climate, the faces remain impermeable, whether they are setting out on a hunt in snow-covered mountains or spy the reflection in a mirror of a woman undressing.

EDEN, Denis William
British, 19th - 20th century.
Born 20 July 1878, in Liverpool; died 1949.
Painter, illustrator. History painting, portraits.
Denis William Eden was the son of the landscape painter William Eden. He received guidance from the Pre-Raphaelite Frederick George Stephens and studied at St John's Wood Art School and the Royal Academy in London. He showed his work at Royal Academy exhibitions from 1900.

Eden did not become a landscape painter like his father but was attracted to the more ambitious subjects of Stephens and the Pre-Raphaelites. He also addressed Symbolist subjects such as marital fidelity, illustrating Boccaccio's *Griselda*, perhaps using Chaucer's translation. He produced an historical composition for the Parliament buildings in London entitled *Henry VII Granting the Charter to Jean Cabot and his Three Sons*.

MUSEUMS AND GALLERIES:
LIVERPOOL: *Griselda with the Sheaf of Corn*.

AUCTION RECORDS:
LONDON, 30 June 1922, *Dish* (1904) GBP 3. LONDON, 13 Feb 1991, *Pilgrim* (oil on canvas, 22 x 20 ins / 56 x 51 cm) GBP 1,760.

EDEN, Emily
British, 19th century.
Born 1797; died 1869.
Draughtswoman, writer.
Emily Eden made drawings, lithographed in 1844 by L.C. Dickinson, for the *Portraits of the Hindu Princes and People*.

EDEN, William
British, 19th century.
Born in Durham; died 1915, in London.
Active from 1866 to 1898.
Painter. Landscapes.
William Eden was the father of Denis William Eden. He exhibited from 1866 in London at the Royal Academy, at the Suffolk Street gallery and at the New Water-Colour Society.

MUSEUMS AND GALLERIES:
NORWICH (Castle Mus. and AG): *Trout Stream* (watercolour); *Oatfield, Evening* (watercolour); *Tanyard* (watercolour).

EDEN, William (Sir)
British, 19th century.
Born 4 March 1849.
Painter, watercolourist, draughtsman. Landscapes.
Sir William Eden appeared in numerous exhibitions in London and Paris. Among his works are *The Villa d'Este*, *Bognor*, *Cadogan Square*. His landscapes were strongly influenced by Whistler, who began proceedings against him in 1895.

AUCTION RECORDS:
LONDON, 26 Nov 1923, *Ter Taylor Cauz* (drawing) GBP 10.

EDENBERGER, J. N.
Dutch, 18th century.
Born 18th century, in Baden-Durlach.
Miniaturist.
In 1773 J. N. Edenberger was a member of the guild in The Hague, where he returned after an interlude in England.

EDER, Andreas
German, 18th century.
Born in Wasserburg (Bavaria); died 1715, in Vienna.
Painter.

EDER, Bartholomaus
Austrian, 18th century.
Born c. 1711, in Tyrol; died 1778.
Sculptor.
Bartholomaus Eder worked particularly in Bohemia, Budin and Libochowitz on churches and bridges.

EDER, Christian
Austrian, 18th century.
Born c. 1740, in Vienna.
Painter (porcelain).

EDER, Georg
Austrian, 18th century.
Active in Vienna.
Engraver.

EDER, Gyula
Slovak, 20th century.
Born 25 December 1875, in Košce.
Painter, draughtsman, humorist. Historical subjects, allegorical subjects.
Gyula Eder was a pupil of Wilhelm von Diez and of Gabriel von Hackl at the academy of fine art in Munich and of Gyula Benczur in Budapest.

In Budapest he worked for cartoon journals. He also painted historical, allegorical and mythological themes.

MUSEUMS AND GALLERIES:
BUDAPEST: *Bellerophon*, *Salome*.

AUCTION RECORDS:
LONDON, 9 Oct 1997, *Pan Trapping a Nymph* (oil on canvas, 21¼ x 17 ins / 53.7 x 43 cm) GBP 437. LUCERNE, 2 May 2001, *Putti Playing Music* (1925, oil on canvas, 24 x 31 ins / 60 x 80 cm) CHF 4,310.

EDER, Hans
Romanian, 20th century.
Born 19 April 1883, in Kronstadt (now Brasov).
Painter. Religious subjects, portraits.
A pupil of Hugo von Habermann at the academy of fine art in Munich, while staying in Paris Hans Eder discovered Impressionism and the paintings of Goya in the Louvre and travelled to Bruges. He opened a workshop in Munich, then finally settled in Kronstadt in Romania. Mainly a portrait painter, he is known for *Schuller, the Architect.* He also painted religious compositions including: *Crucifixion; The Adulterous Woman.* He featured in collective exhibitions in Munich and Budapest.

EDER, Johann
Austrian, 18th century.
Born 18th century, in Vienna.
Modeller.

EDER, Johann Friedrich
Austrian, 17th century.
Active in Vienna.
Painter.

EDER, Johann Georg
Austrian, 18th century.
Born 18th century, in Vienna.
Painter.

EDER, Josef
Austrian, 19th century.
Born 1824, in Vienna.
Miniaturist, draughtsman. Architectural views.
Josef Eder trained at the Vienna academy. A notable work by him is a miniature in ivory of the opera singer Fornani, signed *Vienna Gioseppe Eder.*

EDER, Joseph
Austrian, 18th century.
Born 1760, in Vienna.
Engraver.

EDER, Joseph
German, 18th century.
Active in Velburg (Bavaria) at the end of the 18th century.
Painter.
Paintings at the old Benedictine church in Herrenchiemse bear the signature *Joseph Eder* and are dated 1795. He also worked in Muttenhofen and Riedenburg in the catholic church of the Sacred Heart of Jesus.

EDER, Joseph
Austrian, 18th century.
Born c. 1750.
Engraver.
Joseph Eder went to the Vienna academy on 13 April 1763.

EDER, Kaspar
German, 18th - 19th century.
Born 1744, in Bamberg; died 7 June 1817, in Bamberg.
Draughtsman.
Kaspar Eder drew portraits, miniatures and landscapes. The Bamberg Museum owns a 19th-century pen drawing depicting *Christ* on the cross, and bearing the signature: *Joh. Caspar E.*

EDER, Maria
Austrian, 19th century.
Active in Innsbruck and Vienna.
Painter.
Maria Eder painted miniatures, portraits and small religious paintings.

EDER, Martin
Austrian.
Born in Mais, near Meran, South Tyrol (now Merano, Italy).
Sculptor.
He worked in Mais, Vienna and Salzburg, for churches and religious establishments.

EDER, Mathias
Austrian, 18th - 19th century.
Born at the end of the 18th century, in Ybbs; died after 1810.
Sculptor.

EDER, Michael
German, 18th century.
Born 1766, in Augsburg.
Painter. Landscapes.
Michael Eder trained under Michael Persalter in Augsburg.

EDER, Otto
Austrian, 20th century.
Born 1924, in Seeboden (Carinthia); died 1982.
Sculptor.
Eder was a pupil of Fritz Wotruba in Vienna, then of Walter Ritter in Graz. His sculptures are figurative, but the lines and forms are highly stylised, simplified, stretched and lengthened upwards in the style of totems. His first solo exhibition took place in Vienna in 1960. He later exhibited on his own or with others in Rome, Florence and Zagreb.
AUCTION RECORDS:
VIENNA, 10 Dec 1985, *Figure* (patinated stone, h. 28 1/4 ins / 72 cm) ATS 10,000.

EDER, Peter
Austrian, 18th century.
Active in Vienna.
Painter (porcelain).
Peter Eder was the son of Christian Eder.

EDER, Stephan
Austrian, 18th century.
Active in Vienna.
Painter.
Stephan Eder was the son of Andreas Eder.

EDER Y GATTENS, Federico Maria
Spanish, 19th century.
Born in Seville.
Painter. Genre scenes, figures, landscapes.
Federico Maria Eder y Gattens exhibited in Seville, Madrid and Bayonne between 1858 and 1880.
MUSEUMS AND GALLERIES:
MADRID (Prado): a canvas.
AUCTION RECORDS:
LONDON, 14 March 1969, *The Matadors,* Gns 500. NEW YORK, 28 May 1982, *Crossing the River* (1867, oil on canvas, 39 1/2 x 62 1/4 ins / 100.3 x 158.1 cm) USD 2,000. LONDON, 15 June 1994, *Peasant Family with an Ox Cart* (oil on panel, 13 x 10 ins / 33 x 25.5 cm) GBP 4,025. CANTERBURY, 15 Oct 2002, *Spanish Country Landscape* (1883, oil on canvas, 20 x 27 ins / 51 x 69 cm) GBP 4,200.

EDERER, Carl
Austrian, 20th century.
Born 23 April 1875, in Vienna.
Painter, watercolourist, lithographer.
Ederer trained at the Akademie der Bildenden Künste in Vienna, and in 1911 took up a teaching post at the art academy in Düsseldorf, where he settled. He practised a wide range of techniques including drawing, pastels, watercolours and lithography, and his works cover all genres from religious painting to animals.

EDESIA, Andreino da. See **ANDREINO DA EDESIA**

EDGAR, G. H.
German, 16th century.
Painter.
The church of St Peter in Hamburg houses a wall painting by Edgar, dating from 1553, that depicts the *Sack of the Temple of Jerusalem by Heliodorus*.

EDGAR, James H.
British, 19th century.
Painter. Portraits, genre scenes.
James Edgar exhibited between 1860 and 1864 in London at the British Institution and at the Suffolk Street Gallery, and worked in Liverpool.
MUSEUMS AND GALLERIES:
VICTORIA: *Portrait of Thomas Weston Milne*.
AUCTION RECORDS:
LONDON, 9 Dec 1980, *Light and Shade* (1863, oil on canvas, 36 x 30 ins / 91.5 x 76 cm) GBP 840. LONDON, 17 Dec 1986, *Hallowe'en* (1864, oil on canvas, 32 x 48 ins / 81 x 122 cm) GBP 6,200.

EDGARD-FRANÇOIS
Haitian, 20th century.
Born 1926, in Haiti.
Painter. Landscapes with figures.
Edgard-François exhibited a *View of Port-au-Prince* with artists from the young Haitian School at the open exhibition organised in 1946 by the United Nations Organisation at the Musée d'Art Moderne in Paris.

EDGARTH, C. B.
French, 19th century.
Born in Strasbourg.
Painter. Genre scenes, landscapes.
A pupil of M. Schutzemberger, C. B. Edgarth made his Salon début in 1880.

EDGECOMBE, T. L.
British, 19th century.
Active in England.
Painter. Landscapes.
T. L. Edgecombe was mentioned by *Art Prices Current*.
AUCTION RECORDS:
LONDON, 27 May 1909, *Scene in a Village* (1846) GBP 2.

EDGEL, Fanny
British, 20th century.
Born in the Indies.
Miniaturist.

EDGÜ, Ferit
Turkish, 20th century.
Born 1936, in Istanbul.
Also active in France.
Painter.
Ferit Edgü studied at Istanbul's school of fine art before moving to Paris in 1958. He held his first exhibition in 1962, and is a writer as well as an artist.

EDHOLM, Charlton Lawrence
American, 20th century.
Born 21 March 1879, in Omaha; died 1940.
Painter.
Charlton Edholm was a pupil of Ludwig Herterich at the Academy of Fine Arts in Munich. He was also a writer. He was a member of the Hudson Valley Art Association.

EDINGER, Burchard
German, 19th century.
Active in Hamburg.
Lithographer.
Burchard Edinger's best works include: *Pilgrims at Door of Cloister* after Pollak; *St Madeleine* after Maes; *Burgomaster Bartels*; *Jenny Lind*; *Altona, View of Bridge*; and *Swirls of Snow* after Hermann Kaufmann.

EDINGER, Johann Gottlob
German, 19th century.
Died before 1850, in Ravensburg.
Miniaturist.
Johann Edinger was an art teacher and master ironsmith.

EDINGTON, A.
British, 19th century.
Engraver.
There is only one known aquatint by A. Edington, *Panorama of Brighton*, after a drawing by the architect H. Wildes.

ÉDION, Henri
Austrian, 20th century.
Born 1905, in Vienna; died 1987, in London.
Active in England.
Painter.
Édion was from a French family, and trained in Austria, where he learned to paint portraits in the medieval style. He then travelled the world, from Vienna to Milan to Paris, Montreal, New York and Melbourne before finally settling in London. He participated in collective exhibitions in Montreal between 1958 and 1962; in London in 1962, and in particular in several British cities in 1981. There have also been solo exhibitions of his works: in 1958 in New York and Montreal; in 1961 in New York; in 1962 in London; and a posthumous exhibition at the Crane Kalman Gallery in London in 1993.
BIBLIOGRAPHY:
Henri Edion. Wien 1905 - London 1987, exhibition catalogue, Crane Kalman Gall., London, 1993.

EDKINS, Michel
British, 18th century.
Active in Bristol.
Glass painter.
MUSEUMS AND GALLERIES:
LONDON (British Mus.): white vase (enamelled glass).

EDLE VON PAEPKE. See **EICKEN Elisabeth von**

EDLER, Anton
German, 19th century.
Active in Munich.
Painter, lithographer.
Anton Edler's notable works include *Presentation of a Gold Cup to Maximilian Joseph I* and *Roman Landscape*.

EDLERSHAW, John
Australian, 20th century.
Born in Sydney.
Painter, watercolourist.

EDLEWER, Johann
German, 17th century.
Sculptor.
Johann Edlewer carved the pulpit of the church in Grupenhague, Pomerania, and an altar in wood in Mützenow.

EDLIBACH, Gerold
Swiss, 15th - 16th century.
Born 1454, in Zurich; died 28 August 1530.
Draughtsman.
Gerold Edlibach illustrated a *Passion* (*Passion*), completed in 1498, a *Légende de saint Georges* (*Legend of St George*) (1474) and a 'Chronicle of Zurich'. He also produced views of castles around Zurich to illustrate a book of coats of arms now in the library in Donaueschingen. He was also a statesman.

EDLICH, Stephan
20th century.
Born 1944.
Painter (mixed media).

AUCTION RECORDS:
NEW YORK, 8 Nov 1979, *Untitled* (1975, collage/canvas and paper/canvas, 59 1/2 x 39 1/4 ins / 151 x 100 cm) USD 4,000. NEW YORK, 13 May 1981, *Chord suite n° 177 A* (1977, acrylic, polymer, jute, charcoal, card/canvas, 24 1/4 x 18 ins / 61.5 x 45.5 cm) USD 2,500. NEW YORK, 9 Nov 1983, *Untitled 'THE'* (1977, collage with acrylic, paper, jute, charcoal and coloured chalks/canvas, 83 3/4 x 60 ins / 213 x 152.5 cm) USD 8,000. NEW YORK, 23 Feb 1985, *Untitled '5, Fugue VII'* (1980, collage with acrylic, paper, charcoal and string/canvas, 54 x 36 ins / 137 x 91.5 cm) USD 4,000. NEW YORK, 9 May 1989, *Untitled* (1980, acrylic, chalk and paper collage/canvas, 86 1/2 x 106 1/2 ins / 219.6 x 270.4 cm) USD 3,850. NEW YORK, 21 Feb 1990, *untitled- "J" Bach* (1977, acrylic, paper, jute, charcoal and pastel/canvas, 84 x 61 ins / 213.6 x 155.1 cm) USD 4,400. NEW YORK, 7 May 1990, *Orer. 32 Cafe Santos...* (1975, oil, wrapping paper, string and paper collage/canvas, 59 3/4 x 40 ins / 152 x 101.6 cm) USD 3,080. NEW YORK, 7 Nov 2000, *Before an Open Window* (1981, acrylic on paper, 54x36 ins / 137x91 cm) USD 1,500. LOS ANGELES, 5 Dec 2000, *Dolce* (acrylic, printed paper, charcoal and jute collaged canvas, 78x54 ins / 198x137 cm) USD 5,000. MIAMI, 16 Jan 2001, *Untitled JS* (1977, charcoal, acrylic, polymer, jute and paper on cotton canvas, 68x84 ins / 173x213 cm) USD 1,100. MORRIS PLAINS, 21 Sept 2001, *Untitled* (oil, wood, string and paper, 35x53 ins / 89x135 cm) USD 750. NEW YORK, 26 Sept 2002, *Seascape with Fish Form* (1984, acrylic, gouache, jute and wood collage on linen, 80x40 ins / 203x102 cm) USD 1,500. ELGIN, 22 Feb 2003, *Untitled* (c. 1978, mixed media, 24x18 ins / 61x46 cm) GBP 295. CHICAGO, 1 June 2003, *Untitled* (mixed media and collage, 24x18 ins / 61x46 cm) USD 1,400. PETERBOROUGH, 10 April 2004, *84 Transports Jean Chatel* (mixed media, 54x36 ins / 137x91 cm) USD 2,600.

EDLINGER, Carl Franz

German, 19th century.
Born 1785, in Dresden; died 1823, in Dresden.
Painter, miniaturist. Historical subjects, portraits.

EDLINGER, Josef or Johann Georg, or Etlinger

German, 18th - 19th century.
Born 1741, in Graz; died 1819, in Munich.
Painter. Portraits.

Josef Edlinger trained under Desmarées and became a court painter in Munich. His works showed the influence of Rembrandt. Several of his portraits were engraved by Friedrich John. The collection of these engravings appeared in 1821. He was nicknamed the 'Anton Graff of Munich'.

MUSEUMS AND GALLERIES:
AUGSBURG: *Portrait of the Artist as a Young Man* - BERLIN: *Portrait of Count Freysing* - DARMSTADT: *French Soldiers* - GRAZ: *Portrait of a Man* - MUNICH: *Portrait of Count Rumford; Portrait of the Artist; Portrait of Barbara Welser, the Artist's Wife; Bookseller Strobel and his Family* - NUREMBERG: *At the Munich Orphanage; Portrait with the Thorn Puller.*

AUCTION RECORDS:
MUNICH, 17 Oct 1984, *Portrait of Joseph von Utzschneider* (oil on canvas, 22 x 16 1/2 ins / 55 x 42 cm) DEM 8,000. VIENNA, 13 Feb 1985, *Portrait of a Painter with his Palette* (oil on canvas, 30 1/4 x 24 ins / 77 x 61 cm) ATS 18,000. MUNICH, 7 Dec 1993, *Portrait of a Young Man* (pencil/paper, oval 20 x 7 1/4 ins / 51 x 18.5 cm) DEM 1,610.

EDLINGER, Joseph

Austrian, 18th century.
Born c. 1700, in Salzburg; died 26 January 1745, in Salzburg.
Painter.

EDLINGER, Moritz Johann

German, 19th century.
Born 1823, in Dresden; died 1847.
Painter, engraver. Portraits.

Moritz Edlinger was the son of Carl Franz Edlinger.

EDLINGER, Xaver

German, 19th century.
Painter. Portraits.

Xaver Edlinger sent a series of portraits of members of the Rechberg family to the 1881 exhibition in Stuttgart.

EDME, François

French, 17th century.
Active in Auxerre.
Sculptor.

With François Lambert, François Edme executed the high altar of the church of Irancy in 1663.

EDMIER, Keith

American, 20th - 21st century.
Born 6 September 1967, in Chicago.
Active in New York.
Sculptor.

Keith Edmier graduated from the California Institute of the Arts with a Bachelor's degree in Fine Arts in 1986. He is known for his eye-catching sculptures that have resonances of popular culture and contemporary history. The connection between contemporary history and personal experience is a recurring theme in Edmier's art.

The Tate Collection in London has two of his sculptures, both connected thematically. One is *Beverley Edmier 1967*, a sculpture of his mother aged 22 and pregnant with Edmier who can be seen through her transparent skin. She is dressed in a pink Chanel suit similar to that worn by Jackie Kennedy when President Kennedy was assassinated. The second sculpture, *A Dozen Roses* (1998) features a cast of a bunch of red roses exactly like the bunch Jackie Kennedy had with her in the car at the time of the assassination.

The influence of Edmier's previous career creating prosthetic special effects for the horror-film industry is evident in his eerie, Triffid-like sculptures entitled *Victoria Regia (First Night Bloom)* (1998) and *Victoria Regia (Second Night Bloom)* (1998). These are casts of a species of giant water lily that bears male and female blossoms on alternate nights.

For a recent project Edmier chose to experiment with sculptures cast from naturally occurring molten volcanic lava. For this project he worked with the University of Florida's Graphicstudio to discover a method to melt and cast basalt lava in a foundry. For his exhibition *Cycas Orogeny* in Novemeber 2004, Edmier used lava to create casts of two cycads and a life-sized male seahorse from the species hippocampus abdomalis where the creatures grow up to a foot long. Like the giant lilies, the cycads are plants with distinct and primitive sexual characteristics, and seahorses are unusual too because it is the males who carry baby embryos to term.

Other recent solo exhibitions by Edmier include: 1998: at The Douglas Hyde Gallery, Trinity College, Dublin; Metro Pictures, New York; Sadie Coles HQ, London; and Friedrich Petzel Gallery, Basel Statements. 2000: at Neugerriemschneider, Berlin. 2003, Keith Edmier and Farrah Fawcett, And Warhol Museum, Pittsburgh; Keith Edmier, Contemporary Art Museum, University of South Florida.

BIBLIOGRAPHY:
Keith Edmier, exhibition catalogue, University of South Florida Contemporary Art Museum, Tampa (FL), 1997 (Essays by M. Miller, J. Dillinger, N. Wakefield and K. Bousman). *Gothic: Transmutations of Horror in Late Twentieth century Art*, exhibition catalogue, Institute of Contemporary Arts, Boston, 1997.

MUSEUMS AND GALLERIES:
LONDON (Tate Collection): *Beverley Edmier 1967* (1998, sculpture); *A Dozen Roses* (1998, sculpture) - SAN FRANCISCO

(MoMA) - TAMPA (University of South Florida Contemporary AM).

EDMISTON, Alice R.
American, 20th century.
Born in Monroe.
Painter.
Alice Edmiston was winner of the Omaha Society of Fine Arts prize in 1923 ($100).

EDMOND, Adrienne
French, 20th century.
Miniaturist, painter. Portraits.
Adrienne Edmond began exhibiting at the Salon des Artistes Français in 1944.

EDMOND-GROS
French, 19th century.
Born 16 November 1864, in Aubagnes.
Lithographer.
From 1896 Edmond-Gros exhibited in Paris at the Salon des Artistes Français.

EDMONDS, E. M.
British, 19th century.
Active in Kendal.
Landscape artist.
E. M. Edmonds exhibited in London between 1872 and 1893.

EDMONDS, Edith
British, 20th century.
Born in Wigan.
Painter. Landscapes.
Edith Edmonds exhibited at the Salon des Artistes Français in 1938.

EDMONDS, G.
British, 19th century.
Active in London.
Painter. Landscapes.
G. Edmonds exhibited in London from 1825 to 1836.

EDMONDS, John Francis William
American, 19th century.
Born 1806, in Hudson (New York); died 1863.
Painter (including gouache), draughtsman. Scenes with figures, genre scenes, landscapes, landscapes with figures.
For most of his life John Francis William Edmonds worked as a bank clerk and devoted his mornings and evenings to painting. He first entered a work at the Academy of New York in 1836. He went to Europe in 1840 and became especially interested in the paintings of the Flemish and Dutch artists. From 1837 to 1844 he exhibited landscapes and views of Italy.

MUSEUMS AND GALLERIES:
MONTGOMERY (MFA, Blount Collection): *Time to Go* (1857, oil on canvas).

AUCTION RECORDS:
NEW YORK, 17 Feb 1944, *Stratford-upon-Avon,* USD 425. NEW YORK, 21 April 1978, *Country Scene* (c. 1856, oil on card, 9 1/4 x 13 1/4 ins / 23.5 x 33.6 cm) USD 7,000. NEW YORK, 23 April 1981, *Landscape with a Cabin and Figures* (c. 1850, oil on canvas, 15 3/4 x 21 1/2 ins / 40 x 54.3 cm) USD 7,000. NEW YORK, 28 Sept 1983, *Just in Time* (drawing with wash, gouache and pencil, 11 1/4 x 15 1/2 ins / 28.5 x 39.5 cm) USD 600. NEW YORK, 7 Dec 1984, *'Devotion'* (1857, oil on canvas, 20 1/4 x 24 ins / 51.5 x 60.9 cm) USD 45,000. NEW YORK, 24 April 1985, *Landscape with a Cabin and Figures* (c. 1850, oil on canvas, 15 3/4 x 21 ins / 40 x 53.5 cm) USD 14,000. NEW YORK, 1 Dec 1989, *Facing the Enemy* (oil on canvas, 19 x 16 ins / 48.2 x 40.6 cm) USD 17,600. NEW YORK, 3 Dec 1993, *Punished* (1850, oil on canvas, 25 x 30 ins / 63.5 x 76.3 cm) USD 57,500. NEW YORK, 25 April 1999, *Sparking* (oil on canvas, 22 x 30 ins / 56 x 76 cm) USD 3,000. NEW YORK, 18 May 2004, *Sammy the Tailor* (1836, oil on canvas, 10 x 12 ins / 25 x 30 cm) USD 65,000.

EDMONDS-ALT, Jean-Paul
Belgian, 20th century.
Born 1928, in Etterbeek (Brussels).
Sculptor.
Edmonds-Alt studied under O. Jespers at the Cambre, and later became a teacher there as well as at the art academy in Atermael-Boitsfort. He went on a working trip to central Africa. He produced several public monuments.

EDMONDSON, William
American, 19th - 20th century.
Born 1882, in Nashville (Tennessee); died 7 February 1951, in Nashville (Tennessee).
Sculptor. Religious subjects, figures, animals.
William Edmondson was the son of former slaves who were emancipated following the Civil War, and grew up illiterate. He worked at various jobs, in particular, for the Nashville, Chattanooga, and St Louis Railroads until 1907, and for the Nashville Women's Hospital until the Crash of 1929. Following a dream in which God commanded him to take up sculpture, Edmondson started to carve, using stone from demolished buildings and making his own chisels out of railwaymen's tools. He carved garden sculpture, as well as tombstones for Nashville's two African-American cemeteries. A neighbour, Sidney Hirsch, who was a member of a literary circle at Vanderbilt University, discovered him. The fashion photographer Louise Dahl-Wolfe photographed him at work, surrounded by his sculptures, and brought him to the attention of Alfred Barr, the director of the Museum of Modern Art, New York.

As a member of a fundamentalist church, the United Primitive Baptist Church, Edmondson mainly drew his inspiration from religious scenes, carving angels and Biblical figures and animals. He also carved figures from his own surroundings, depicting eminent people such as Eleanor Roosevelt, and animals. He would set up his work in his yard, following an African-American belief that this would ensure the spiritual protection of those who lived in the house. His *'critters'*, as he called them, fall somewhere between primitive and folk art. His sculptures are joyful, rounded and filled with spirituality, much like Romanesque art. Like other self-taught African-American artists of his time, Edmondson sought above all to express a culture anchored in a syncretistic religion, and to celebrate the familiar world that had always been around him. He worked exclusively in limestone.

After his death, Edmondson's work was included in various thematic exhibitions, such as: 1976, *Two centuries of Black American Art,* Los Angeles County Museum of Art, Los Angeles; 1982, *Black Folk in America, 1930-1980,* Corcoran Gallery of Art, Washington, DC; 1998, *African-American Art: 20th century Masterworks, V,* Michael Rosenfeld Gallery, New York. He also had a number of solo exhibitions: 1937, Museum of Modern Art, New York, which was his debut; 1941, Nashville Art Gallery, Nashville; 1951, Nashville Artist Guild, Nashville. Posthumous retrospectives were held of his work: in 1964, Cheekwood Museum of Art, Cheekwood, Tennessee; 1975, Montclair Art Museum, Montclair, New Jersey; 1981, Tennessee State Museum, Nashville; 2000, *The Art of William Edmondson,* Cheekwood Museum of Art, Museum of American Folk Art, New York, and the High Museum of Art, Atlanta.

BIBLIOGRAPHY:
Fuller, Edmund L., *Visions in Stone: The Sculpture of William Edmondson,* University of Pittsburgh Press, Pittsburgh, 1973. *William Edmondson,* exhibition catalogue, Tennessee State Museum, Nashville, 1981. *The Art of William Edmond-*

son, exhibition catalogue, Cheekwood Museum of Art, University Press of Mississippi, Cheekwood, 2000. Thompson, Robert Farris, et al., *William Edmondson*, University Press of Mississippi, 2000.
Museums and Galleries:
Cheekwood (MA): *Bess and Joe* - Milwaukee (AM) - Newark (Mus.): *Angel* (1932-1938) - Portland (MA) - San Francisco (MoMA): *Untitled* (1934-1941, limestone) - Trenton (New Jersey State Mus.) - Washington DC (Smithsonian American AM): *Crucifixion* (c. 1932-1937, limestone); *Rabbit* (c. 1940, carved limestone).
Auction records:
New York, 19 Oct 1985, *Mother and Child* (c. 1934-1939, limestone, h. 15 ins / 38 cm) USD 9,000.

EDMONDSON, William J.
American, 19th century.
Born 1868, in Norwalk (Ohio); died 1966.
Painter.

William J. Edmondson was a pupil at the Academy of Fine Arts in Philadelphia, and at the Académie Julian in Paris, where he was taught first by Jules Lefebvre and then by Aman-Jean. He was a member of the Pennsylvania Academy of Fine Arts and the Cleveland Society of Artists. He won the Toppan second prize at the Pennsylvania Academy of Fine Arts.
Museums and Galleries:
Cleveland (MA): *The Blue Feather* (1917); *California Coast* (1925-1926).

EDMONSTON, Samuel
British, 19th century.
Born 1825, in Edinburgh.
Painter, watercolourist. Genre scenes, landscapes, seascapes.

Samuel Edmonston was a pupil of Sir William Allan and Thomas Duncan at the Royal Scottish Academy. He exhibited at the Royal Academy in London and the Royal Scottish Academy.
Auction records:
Scotland, 1 Sept 1981, *Coldingham Shore, Berwickshire* (oil on canvas, 24 1/2 x 35 1/2 ins / 62 x 90 cm) GBP 1,900. Chester, 3 March 1984, *Fisherman's Return* (oil on card, 16 1/4 x 14 1/4 ins / 41 x 36 cm) GBP 1,400. Auchterarder, 1 Sept 1987, *Fishermen on the Shore* (oil on panel, 25 x 38 ins / 63.5 x 96.5 cm) GBP 2,200. South Queensferry, 1 May 1990, *Return of the Boats* (1863, oil on panel, 25 x 38 ins / 63.5 x 96.5 cm) GBP 3,740. Perth, 26 Aug 1991, *Charms of Music* (1862, oil on canvas, 26 3/4 x 23 ins / 68 x 58.5 cm) GBP 8,580. Glasgow, 1 Feb 1994, *Asking the Time* (oil on panel, 17 1/4 x 14 1/4 ins / 44 x 36.5 cm) GBP 1,495. Glasgow, 21 Aug 1996, *Young Gypsy Woman* (oil on canvas, 24 x 20 ins / 61 x 50.8 cm) GBP 1,380. Edinburgh, 14 Sept 2001, *Portrait of a Young Girl with a Kitten and Two Dogs* (1879, oil on canvas, 43 x 33 ins / 110 x 85 cm) GBP 1,800. Edinburgh, 20 Oct 2001, *View of St Andrews from the Pier* (oil on canvas, 16 x 24 ins / 41 x 62 cm) GBP 1,000. London, 22 Nov 2001, *Portrait of a Girl Seated in a Blue Dress, Holding a Kitten and Two Terriers at her Side* (1879, oil on canvas, 44 x 33 ins / 112 x 85 cm) GBP 2,300.

EDMONSTONE, Robert
British, 19th century.
Born 1795, in Kelso, Scotland; died 1834, in Kelso.
Painter. Portraits, genre scenes.

Robert Edmonstone studied at the Royal Academy in London. He exhibited for the first time in 1818. He travelled on the continent and lived for a time in Rome, where he fell ill. On his return to England, he painted portraits in London from 1824 to 1831. He went to Italy for a second time before coming back to England, where he died.

Among the works he exhibited are *Italian Children Playing Cards*; *The Faithful Kissing St Peter's Chains*; *Maternal Solicitude*; *The Children of Sir E. Cust*; and *The White Mouse* (his last work).
Auction records:
Edinburgh, 30 Aug 1988, *The Soldier's Goodbye* (1830, oil on canvas, 30 x 37 1/2 ins / 76.5 x 95 cm) GBP 1,650. London, 3 June 1992, *The Soldier's Goodbye* (1830, oil on canvas, 30 x 37 1/2 ins / 76 x 95 cm) GBP 1,870.

EDMUNDS, Nellie. See **HEPBURN-EDMUNDS**

EDO, or Aedo
Spanish, 17th century.
Active in Granada c. 1600.
Painter.

EDO
Dutch, 17th century.
Active in Jever.
Painter.

Edo embellished the town hall in 1619.

EDON, Anne
French, 20th century.
Born in Ham (Somme).
Painter. Genre scenes.

Anne Edon showed work in Paris at the Salon des Artistes Français from 1928.

EDORH, Sokey
Togolese, 20th - 21st century.
Born 5 July 1955, in Lomé.
Painter (mixed media).

After studying philosophy at the University of Benin, in 1989 Edorh went to Bordeaux, where he obtained a place at the school of fine arts. In 1993, he studied engraving with Penck at the Kunstakademie in Düsseldorf.

He has taken part in group exhibitions in Togo, Ivory Coast and Senegal, and in France and Germany, including in 2000 Togolese week at the Assemblée Nationale, Paris; in 2000 and 2001 the Salon Grands et Jeunes d'Aujourd'hui, Paris and Luxemburg; also in 2001 *Artistes Togolais d'aujourd'hui. L'École de Lomé* (*Contemporary Togolese Artists: The Lomé School*), at the Espace St-Jean, Melun; in 2003 *Rencontre autour de trois artistes africains* (*Meeting around Three African Artists*), at the Musée de l'Aventure Industrielle, Apt. He has also shown his work in solo exhibitions, including those at the French cultural centre in Lomé in 1997; at the Zaka Gallery in Ouagadougou and the Xenios Gallery in Frankfurt in 1999; and at the Galerie Ambre Congo in Brussels in 2000.

His paintings, which are produced on unstretched canvases, are filled with snakes, birds and stylised figures.
Bibliography:
Persin, Patrick-Gilles, *L'École de Lomé. Artistes togolais d'aujourd'hui*, exhibition catalogue, Association Grands et Jeunes d'Aujourd'hui, Paris, 2001.

ÉDOU-CHEVRIER, Cornélie
French, 20th century.
Born in Chalon-sur-Saône.
Painter. Landscapes, still-lifes.

Cornélie Édou-Chevrier studied with Louis Biloul. In 1931 she began exhibiting in Paris at the Salon des Artistes Français.

EDOUARD, Albert Jules
French, 19th century.
Born 12 April 1845, in Caen.
Painter. Historical and genre scenes.

Albert Jules Edouard studied under Cornu, Gérôme, L. Cogniet and E. Delaunay. He exhibited at the Paris Salon from 1868, receiving a third-class medal in 1882, a second-class medal in 1885, and a bronze medal in 1889 as well as a mention for outstanding merit. His best-known works include

Don Juan Thrown on the Shore, *Meditation* and *Dante and Virgil on the Frozen Lake*.

MUSEUMS AND GALLERIES:

CHÂLONS-EN-CHAMPAGNE: *Caligula and the Gallic Cobbler*.

AUCTION RECORDS:

PARIS, 11 Feb 1919, *Orange Seller in Spain*, FRF 111. SAN FRANCISCO, 24 June 1981, *Art and Beauty* (oil on canvas, 53¼ x 33¼ ins / 135 x 84.5 cm) USD 2,600. PARIS, 23 June 1986, *Apotheosis of Alphonse de Lamartine* (oil on canvas, 33¾ x 27½ ins / 86 x 70 cm) FRF 15,000. PARIS, 17 Nov 1997, *Music on the Terrace* (oil on canvas, 22 x 18¼ ins / 56 x 46.5 cm) FRF 8,500.

EDOUARD, Jean, or Odoard, Odard
French, 16th century.
Active in Lyons.
Painter.

Jean Edouard worked on the decorations for the town of Lyons on the occasion of the entry of Cardinal Hippolyte d'Este, archbishop of Lyons. He is described in documents as 'carver of images'.

ÉDOUARD, Philippe. See **HODART**

EDOUARD, Pierre
French, 20th - 21st century.
Born 1959, in Paris.
Painter, draughtsman, sculptor. Figures, portraits, interior scenes.

Pierre Edouard produces work in a style reminiscent of Rembrandt and Seurat, and with complete disregard for modern trends. He works mainly with the chiaroscuro technique, making shapes appear, like mists, striving to come into being. In 1980, was awarded the Prix de Dessin by the Salon de Montrouge.

Edouard showed his works in solo exhibitions, including: 1983, Brussels; 1989, *L'Homme à Terre* (*Man on Earth*) and *Portraits*, Paris; and 2001, Galerie Claude Bernard, Paris.

BIBLIOGRAPHY:

Bonafoux, Pascal, *Pierre Edouard*, exhibition catalogue, Gal. Claude Bernard, Paris, 1989. Tasset, J.-M., '*Pierre Edouard: le style des cimes*' in *Le Figaro*, periodical, Paris, April 1989.

EDOUARD, Richard, or Edwards
French, 17th century.
Active in Tours.
Sculptor.

In 1613, Richard Edouard undertook to execute two statues for the candlemakers' guild, one of St Louis and one of St Genevieve, for the chapel of St Francis in the church of the Cordeliers (Franciscan Friars).

EDOUARD-FOURNIER, Paul Joseph Albert
French, 19th century.
Born 19th century, in Paris.
Engraver.

EDOUARD-MAHÉ. See **MAHÉ Edouard**

EDOUART, A.
British, 19th century.
Active in London.
Painter. Animals.

A. Edouart exhibited at the Royal Academy in London in 1815 and 1816.

EDOUART, Augustin Amant Constant Fidèle
French, 19th century.
Born 1789, in Dunkirk; died 1861, in Guisnes, near Calais.
Silhouettist.

Having settled in London in 1813, Augustin Edouart first painted animals before becoming silhouettist to the French royal family. He is probably the same person as the A. Edouart who exhibited at the Royal Academy in 1815 and 1816. He travelled in Scotland, Ireland and America and was one of the most skilful silhouettists of his time.

MUSEUMS AND GALLERIES:

DUBLIN (NG of Ireland) - EDINBURGH (Scottish National Portrait Gallery): *Sir Robert Ker Porter and Members of his Family* (1829, paper cut-out, series of four silhouettes); large collection of silhouettes - LONDON (Victoria and Albert Mus.).

AUCTION RECORDS:

LONDON, 20 May 1927, *Room with Six Ladies and Gentlemen* (1838, drawing) GBP 25. NEW ORLEANS, 4 Dec 1998, *Portrait of the Mapes Family of New York* (1839, silhouette, a pair, miniature, 11 x 19 ins / 28 x 48 cm) USD 2,000. LONDON, 19 April 1999, *Silhouette Interior Scene with Figures, Harp and Dog* (1830, card, miniature, 11 ins / 28 cm) GBP 2,900. LONDON, 8 Sept 1999, *Silhouette of Boy, Probably Master Thomas Fleming* (1831, cut-out card lithograph, miniature, 10 ins / 25 cm) GBP 1,100. NEW ORLEANS, 3 June 2000, *Family portrait, Cut Silhouette* (sepia wash, miniature, 11 x 14 ins / 28 x 36 cm) USD 3,750. CLEVELAND, 14 Sept 2000, *Silhouettes of Sgt Elmer Hackett and Polly Hackett* (1840, cut-outs/ink, 12 x 10 ins / 30 x 25 cm) USD 4,200. NEW ORLEANS, 3 Feb 2001, *Colonel Hustler, Royal Engineers* (1833, oil/silhouette/paper, 10 x 6 ins / 25 x 15 cm) USD 1,900. LONDON, 6 March 2001, *William and Eliza Boyd Seated in a Drawing Room with Various Animals* (1839, cut out/monochrome watercolour, miniature, 11 ins / 29 cm) GBP 5,400. LONDON, 25 June 2002, *Sir Walter Scott. Seated, Writing at his Desk* (1830, cut out card, miniature, 10 ins / 25 cm) GBP 1,900. PORTSMOUTH, 2 Nov 2002, *Silhouettes of Eight Figures in a Classical Drawing Room* (1840, oil on canvas, 23 x 29 ins / 58 x 74 cm) USD 22,000.

EDRIDGE, Henry
British, 18th - 19th century.
Born 1769, in Paddington; died 1821, in London.
Painter, miniaturist, watercolourist, draughtsman. Portraits.

Henry Edridge may have been a pupil of Pether, the mezzotint engraver and landscape artist, but he excelled above all at miniatures, which he did in Indian ink and watercolour. Elected an associate of the Royal Academy in 1820, he exhibited there from 1782. In 1783 he sent portraits of, among others, *King George III* and *Queen Charlotte*. His last exhibition entry occurs in 1821.

MUSEUMS AND GALLERIES:

DUBLIN: *The Beach at Brighton*; *View near Redleaf, Kent* - EDINBURGH (Nat. Gal. of Scotland, Print Room): *Coast Scene with Figures* (pencil and watercolour) - LONDON (Tate Collection): *Farm Buildings* (c. 1810-1815, pencil and watercolour/paper) - LONDON (Victoria and Albert Mus.): *Chenies House, Buckinghamshire*; *Row of Trees and Horses*; *Meule, Ashford, Kent*; *Farm, Buckinghamshire*; *Environs of Bromley, Kent*; *Seashore, Brighton*; *Sir Edward Paget*; *Bromley, Kent*; *Pont-Neuf, Paris*; *Pont-Neuf, Paris*; *Landscape, Cottage and Figures*; *Landscape with Soldiers*; *Portrait of a Man and Two Children*; *Portrait of a Young Woman*; *Cottage at Bookham, Surrey*; *Landscape*; *Landscape*; *Marketplace at Rouen*; *Rue de la Grosse-Horloge at Rouen*; *Pigs near a Farm*; *Portrait of Thomas Hearne* - MANCHESTER: *King's Langley, Hertfordshire*; *Farms in Surrey*; *Shore at Hastings*; *Near Harrow*; *Church at Wormley, Kent*; *Lane in Surrey with Farm and Cattle*.

AUCTION RECORDS:

LONDON, 13 April 1908, *On the Thames*, GBP 3. LONDON, 7 Dec 1908, *Princess Sophia*, GBP 27. LONDON, 12 Dec 1908, *Portrait of Sir William Ballard* (heightened pencil) GBP 10. LONDON, 11 Dec 1909, *Portrait of George, Count of Sheffield, and of his Baby Sister*, GBP 118. LONDON, 28 Feb 1910, *Portrait of Sir William Ballard* (heightened pencil) GBP 3. LONDON, 23 May 1910, *Walton Bridge, on the Thames*, GBP 12. AMSTERDAM, 22 June 1910, *Portrait of a Woman*, NLG 470. PARIS, 26 and 27 May

1919, *Bust of a Woman* (pencil drawing lightly heightened with watercolour) FRF 1,000. PARIS, 21 April 1921, *Portraits of Thomas Winfield and of Ursula, Wife of J. Winfield* (two sketches in lead pencil) FRF 1,300. LONDON, 27 June 1924, *Woman in a White Muslin Dress Seated in a Garden* (drawing) GBP 21; *Woman in Black, Seated near a Desk, a Castle in the Distance* (1804, drawing) GBP 21. LONDON, 28 July 1924, *Hunters at Rest* (drawing) GBP 14. LONDON, 5 June 1925, *Man in a Robe Standing on a Terrace* (drawing) GBP 7. LONDON, 3 Nov 1926, *Admiral Duncan* (drawing) GBP 23. LONDON, 22 Nov 1926, *Princess Mary in a White Muslin Dress Standing on a Terrace* (1802, drawing) GBP 16. LONDON, 4 July 1927, *Woman Seated near a Window, doing Lacework* (pencil and colour) GBP 6. LONDON, 18 July 1927, *View of the North Terrace of Windsor Castle* (drawing) GBP 5. PARIS, 23 Jan 1928, *Portraits of Little Girl and Little Boy with their Dog* (drawing in watercolour) FRF 7,700. LONDON, 22 Feb 1928, *John, First Count of Sheffield; Anne Countess of Sheffield* (1798, two drawings in black and white) GBP 10; *Lady Amelia Pelham* (1795; *Thomas, Count of Chichester* (drawing) GBP 11; *Three Little Portraits*, GBP 26. LONDON, 4 April 1935, *Turner in front of his Easel, holding a Palette and a Brush* (pencil) GBP 100. LONDON, 26 April 1935, *Hills in Bromley, Kent; Lane in Surrey* (two drawings) GBP 10; *Church in Wormley* (drawing) GBP 6. LONDON, 7 Feb 1936, *Portrait of Mary Moser* (pencil and sepia) GBP 6. LONDON, 25 May 1939, *Windmill in Bushey*, GBP 7. LONDON, 25 April 1940, *Mrs Bridgman Simpson* (1811, drawing) GBP 5. LONDON, 3 July 1940, *William Pitt* (1801) GBP 15. LONDON, 14 Nov 1940, *Queen Charlotte* (1804; *Princess Mary; Princess Sophia* (1803; *Princess Eizabeth; Princess Amelia* (1802; *Portrait of a Woman, Standing on a Terrace* (six drawings) GBP 40. LONDON, 13 March 1942, *Dean of Magdalen College, Oxford* (pencil and watercolour) GBP 4. LONDON, 31 July 1945, *Young Man Standing on a Terrace* (pencil) GBP 15. LONDON, 20 March 1979, *Portrait of Lady Sophia Cust as a Little Girl* (1817, watercolour and pencil heightened with white, 13¾ x 10 ins / 35 x 25.3 cm) GBP 750. LONDON, 19 June 1979, *Portrait of a Young Aristocrat* (1796, pencil and wash, 10¾ x 7¾ ins / 27.3 x 20 cm) GBP 550. LONDON, 27 Nov 1981, *Portrait of Barrington Pope Blanchard, of Osborne House, Isle of Wight* (1811, pencil and wash with touches of watercolour/paper, 16¾ x 11½ ins / 42.5 x 29.5 cm) GBP 1,600. LONDON, 14 June 1983, *Portrait of Miss Morice* (1797, pencil and brown wash, 9 x 6 ins / 22 x 15.2 cm) GBP 1,200; *Naval Officer holding a Telescope* (watercolour and pencil heightened with white, 16¼ x 11 ins / 41 x 28 cm) GBP 700. LONDON, 10 July 1986, *Portrait of Two Fishermen with their Servant* (watercolour and pencil, 19½ x 23½ ins / 49.5 x 60 cm) GBP 3,800. NEW YORK, 11 Jan 1989, *Portrait of Colonel Drinkwater-Bethune in Uniform, Seated Holding a Book and Gibraltar in the Distance* (pencil and wash, 10 x 7¼ ins / 25.1 x 18.6 cm) USD 1,650. YORK, 12 Nov 1991, *Portrait of a Gentleman* (1796, pencil, 10¼ x 6½ ins / 26 x 16.5 cm) GBP 990. LONDON, 13 July 1993, *Portrait of Mrs Scott and her Daughter Patience* (1795, pencil and wash, 9½ x 6½ ins / 24.1 x 16.5 cm) GBP 1,495. PARIS, 25 Nov 1997, *Woman Seated on a Divan* (1816, lead pencil, pen and black ink, watercolour, 13¾ x 10¼ ins / 35 x 26 cm) FRF 8,000. LONDON, 9 Nov 1999, *Mrs Janes Braddyll in a White Dress* (oval miniature, h. 3 ins / 7 cm) GBP 8,700. LONDON, 24 Nov 1999, *Elizabeth Francis with Blue Bandeau in her Powdered Hair, in a Blue Coat* (oval miniature, h. 3 ins / 7 cm) GBP 1,300. LONDON, 22 March 2000, *William, 7th Earl of Northesk. Mrs Ricketts with her Granddaughter, aged 8* (1796, 1797, grey wash and pencil, a pair, 10 x 7 ins / 25 x 17 cm) GBP 2,400. LONDON, 15 June 2000, *Portrait of a Girl in a Landscape, in a White Dress* (watercolour over pencil, 13 x 8 ins / 33 x 21 cm) GBP 1,800. LONDON, 21 March 2001, *Portrait of Two Girls, said to be Anne and Louisa, Daughters of the 2nd Earl of Lucan* (watercolour over pencil, 13 x 9 ins / 33 x 23 cm) GBP 1,600. LONDON, 30 Oct 2001, *Portrait of a Gentleman in a Blue-Green Coat* (oval miniature, h. 4 ins / 9 cm) GBP 4,000. MILAN, 12 Nov 2003, *Gentleman* (oval miniature, h. 2 ins / 6 cm) EUR 3,800. TAUNTON, 27 Nov 2003, *Full-length Portrait of Cavalry Officer Standing on a Terrace* (1808, pencil and watercolour, a pair, 17 x 12 ins / 43 x 30 cm) GBP 4,400. DETROIT, 12 March 2004, *Portrait of a Man* (c. 1780, oval miniature, 2 x 2 ins / 5 x 5 cm) USD 8,000. LONDON, 22 April 2004, *Marmaduke Sealy* (oval miniature, h. 3 ins / 8 cm) GBP 1,800.

EDROP, Arthur Norman

British, 20th century.
Born 15 May 1884, in Birmingham.
Active in the USA.
Painter, illustrator, graphic designer.

Arthur Norman Edrop moved to the USA where he studied under Whittaker (John Barnard?) in Boston. He collaborated on many magazines and worked in advertising.

EDSON, Allan Aaron

Canadian, 19th century.
Died 1888.
Painter. Genre scenes, landscapes with figures, landscapes.

Allan Aaron Edson was a member of the Royal Canadian Academy. He exhibited in Paris in 1883 at the Société des Artistes Français, and in London in 1886 at the Royal Academy and Suffolk Street.

MUSEUMS AND GALLERIES:

MONTREAL: *Home, Sweet Home* - MONTREAL (Learmont Collection): *Landscape with Trees.*

AUCTION RECORDS:

LONDON, 15 June 1973, *Wooded Landscape*, Gns 850. TORONTO, 30 Oct 1978, *Duck Pond on Mount Royal, Montreal* (1880, oil on canvas, 15¾ x 25½ ins / 40 x 65 cm) CAD 1,750. TORONTO, 1 June 1982, *Lake of Isles, Terrebone* (1883, watercolour, 9½ x 13½ ins / 24.4 x 34.4 cm) CAD 3,000. TORONTO, 14 May 1984, *Deer beside a Mountain Stream* (1872, watercolour, 21¼ x 35 ins / 53.8 x 88.8 cm) CAD 2,600. TORONTO, 28 May 1985, *Low Tide, Restigouche, near Campbelton* (watercolour, 10 x 16¾ ins / 25.6 x 42.5 cm) CAD 2,000. MONTREAL, 1 May 1989, *December Day* (1884, oil on canvas, 29¼ x 22¾ ins / 74 x 58 cm) CAD 8,500. MONTREAL, 5 Nov 1990, *Pathway through the Forest* (1885, watercolour, 27¼ x 19¾ ins / 69 x 50 cm) CAD 3,300. MONTREAL, 23-24 Nov 1993, *View of a Church beyond the Trees* (oil on canvas, 24 x 15¾ ins / 61 x 40 cm) CAD 1,000. MONTREAL, 7 Dec 1999, *Cattle Watering in an Eastern Township's River* (oil on canvas, 16 x 22 ins / 41 x 56 cm) CAD 2,500. MONTREAL, 7 Dec 1999, *Preparing the Campsite at Sunset* (1876, oil on canvas, 17 x 28 ins / 42 x 72 cm) CAD 3,600. TORONTO, 26 Nov 2001, *Old Willows at Cernay* (1883, oil on canvas, 18 x 28 ins / 46 x 72 cm) CAD 2,800. TORONTO, 4 Dec 2001, *Preparing the Campsite at Sunset* (1876, oil on canvas, 16 x 28 ins / 41 x 71 cm) CAD 7,000. CALGARY, 10 June 2002, *Fast Flowing Stream* (watercolour, 22 x 17 ins / 57 x 42 cm) CAD 3,000. TORONTO, 3 Dec 2002, *Girl with a Wheelbarrow* (oil on canvas on board, 17 x 12 ins / 42 x 30 cm) CAD 5,500. TORONTO, 3 June 2003, *Children Fishing by a Quiet Pool* (oil on canvas, 19 x 33 ins / 47 x 85 cm) CAD 15,000. TORONTO, 2 Dec 2003, *Forest Scene with Farmhouse* (oil on canvas, 24 x 18 ins / 60 x 45 cm) CAD 4,500.

EDSTROM, David

Swedish, 19th - 20th century.
Born 27 March 1873, in Småland.
Sculptor. Busts.

Edstrom travelled in America before training at Stockholm art academy. He then spent time in Paris, Italy and London, participating in collective exhibitions in London, Florence and Paris.

MUSEUMS AND GALLERIES:

GÖTEBORG: *Caliban* - STOCKHOLM: *Head of a Man* - STOCKHOLM (Thielska Gal.): *The Hunchback.*

EDUARD PORTUGALOIS.
See **PORTUGALOIS Eduard**

EDUARDO, Jorge
Brazilian, 20th century.
Born 1936, in Rio de Janeiro.
Painter (mixed media). Scenes with figures, landscapes, urban landscapes, seascapes.

Jorge Eduardo began studying architecture in 1956 at the university of Rio de Janeiro and received his degree in 1960. He was also a self-taught artist and continued to paint. It was not until 1981, after working in advertising and marketing, that he decided to devote himself exclusively to painting. As frames for his compositions, Eduardo uses old window frames retrieved from houses in Rio de Janeiro that are being demolished. The views he paints are therefore shown in the spaces originally intended for the window glazing. These condition our field of vision and are ideally suited to the constraints of perspective.

Eduardo has exhibited his work in solo exhibitions including: in 1972, 1974 and 1975 at the Oca Gallery in Rio de Janeiro; in 1973 at the Ponto de Arte Gallery; in 1982 at the Homero Massena Gallery in Vitoria; in 1983 at the Ect Gallery in Brasilia; in 1986 at the 1900-2000 Gallery in Paris where the exhibition was prefaced by Pierre Restany.

AUCTION RECORDS:
NEW YORK, 18 Nov 1987, *Lapa* (1986, oil on panel, 30 1/2 x 35 3/4 ins / 77.5 x 91 cm) USD 5,000. NEW YORK, 21 Nov 1989, *Villa Adriana in Venice* (1988, oil/synthetic resin, 63 3/4 x 26 1/2 ins / 162 x 67 cm) USD 11,000. NEW YORK, 20-21 Nov 1990, *Boa Viagen Island* (1989, oil/synthetic resin, 23 1/4 x 40 1/4 ins / 59 x 102.5 cm) USD 8,800. NEW YORK, 21 Nov 1995, *Rio, Five o'Clock in the Morning* (1986, oil on panel and wooden construction, 42 1/4 x 48 ins / 107 x 122 cm) USD 10,925.

EDUARDS, Boris Vasilievich
Ukrainian, 19th century.
Born 1861, in Odessa, of English origin according to Edwards.
Sculptor.

Eduards studied at the St Petersburg academy of fine arts, where he made his debut at its Exhibition of 1888 with *Bust of Pasteur* and *The Mother of the Musicain Anton Rubinstein*.

MUSEUMS AND GALLERIES:
ST PETERSBURG (Gosudarstvennyj Russkij Muz.): *The Glory of God in Heaven*.

EDUIN, Marie Élisabeth
French, 18th century.
Active in Paris in 1748.
Sculptor.

EDVI-ILLES, Aladar
Hungarian, 19th - 20th century.
Born 25 May 1870, in Budapest.
Painter, watercolourist. Landscapes with figures.

Aladar Edvi-Illes first showed watercolours in Budapest, then exhibited in Munich, Dresden, Berlin, Paris and Amsterdam. He painted rural landscapes (*Landscape at Kiskunsag, Ladmoc on the Bodrog*) and cattle in the field (*Cow and Her Calf*).

MUSEUMS AND GALLERIES:
BUDAPEST: *March*; *Back from the Harvest*.

AUCTION RECORDS:
LONDON, 20 June 1984, *Little Girl and Her Goat* (oil on card, 9 1/2 x 14 1/4 ins / 24 x 36 cm) GBP 1,000.

EDVI-ILLES, Emma
Hungarian, 20th century.
Born in Budapest.
Active in Venezuela, then in the USA.
Painter.

Emma Edvi-Illes studied at the academy of fine art in Budapest. She married the portrait painter George Edvi-Illes in 1948. They emigrated first to Austria and later settled in Caracas. She subsequently lived in Atlanta (Georgia). Emma Edvi-Illes painted very diverse compositions, from a bunch of flowers to Symbolist landscape or geometrical abstraction, with an often heavy technique and a naive imagination. In 1992 she exhibited a selection of her works in Caracas.

EDVI-ILLES, Georges
Hungarian, 20th century.
Born in Budapest.
Active in Venezuela.
Painter.

Georges Edvi-Illes was probably the son of Aladar Edvi-Illes. Married to Emma Edvi-Illes, they initially emigrated to Austria, then finally to Caracas where they established the Illes School of Design.

EDWARD
British, 13th century.
Painter.

A painter in the court of Henry III and Abbot of Westminster, Edward did work for the Royal Chapel at Windsor, the Tower of London and Westminster Abbey.

EDWARD, Albert S.
British, 19th century.
Born 1852, in Dundee.
Active in London.
Landscape artist.

Albert Edward exhibited in 1873 and in 1876 in London at the Royal Academy, and also at Suffolk Street.

MUSEUMS AND GALLERIES:
MELBOURNE (Nat. Gal. of Victoria): *View of Dordrecht*.

EDWARD, Berthe
French, 19th century.
Born in Paris.
Painter.

A pupil of M. Delobbe, Berthe Edward sent several paintings to the Salon from 1880 to 1882. Her best-known works are *Women Spinning* and *Christmas Roses*.

EDWARD, George. See **GEORGE-EDWARD**

EDWARDES, Clara
British, 20th century.
Born in London.
Active in the 1920s.
Sculptor.

Clara Edwardes exhibited in Paris at the Salon des Artistes Français from 1924.

EDWARDES, May de Montravel
British, 20th century.
Born 1887, in London.
Miniaturist.

May de Montravel Edwardes exhibited in Paris at the Salon des Artistes Français from 1926.

EDWARDS, Boris. See **EDUARDS Boris**

EDWARDS, C. A.
British, 18th century.
Painter. Flowers.

C. A. Edwards exhibited at the Royal Academy in London from 1792 to 1797.

EDWARDS, E.
British, 19th century.
Sculptor. Statues, busts.

E. Edwards exhibited in London in 1825 a *Portrait of a Woman*; in 1826 *David and Goliath* and a *Psyche*. He worked in Islington.

EDWARDS, Edward
British, 18th - 19th century.
Born 1738, in London; died 1806.
Painter, engraver, illustrator. History painting.
Edward Edwards was the son of a chair maker and was employed by John Boydell to make drawings after the old masters for publications. He was also employed by an antiquarian for the same purpose. He studied at the Gallery of the Duke of Richmond and at the Academy of St Martin's Lane. For Boydell's *Shakespeare*, he painted a scene from *Two Gentlemen of Verona*. He also did arabesques and 52 published engravings. In 1778 he was given the position of teacher of perspective.

He exhibited between 1766 and 1806, at the society of incorporated artists, the society of free artists, the British Institution and the Royal Academy from 1771. He was elected an associate of the Royal Academy in 1773. He published a treatise on perspective and a volume *Anecdotes on Painters*.
MUSEUMS AND GALLERIES:
LONDON (Victoria and Albert Mus.): *David Garrick; Castle Eden, Durham* - NOTTINGHAM: drawing in sepia.
AUCTION RECORDS:
LONDON, 23 Feb 1934, *Portrait of Edmond Boyle, Count of Cork*, GBP 8. LONDON, 18 June 1947, *Consecration, Westminster Abbey, under the Patronage and in the Presence of George IV in 1784*, GBP 65.

EDWARDS, Edward B.
American, 19th - 20th century.
Born 8 February 1873, in Columbia (Pennsylvania).
Painter, draughtsman, illustrator.
Edward Edwards studied in Paris and Munich. He was a member of the Salmagundi Club.

EDWARDS, Edwin
British, 19th century.
Born 1823, in Framlingham; died 1879, in London.
Painter, watercolourist, engraver. Landscapes.
Edwin Edwards was intended for the bar and only began painting watercolours after visiting the Tyrol. After meeting the painter Legros in 1861, he decided to take up engraving. He had several exhibits at the Royal Academy and the Dudley Gallery.
MUSEUMS AND GALLERIES:
MELBOURNE: *Southwold, Suffolk.*
AUCTION RECORDS:
LONDON, 30 March 1908, *London Bridge*, GBP 2.

EDWARDS, G.
British, 19th century.
Active in London.
Painter.
G. Edwards exhibited landscapes in London between 1811 and 1818.

EDWARDS, G. H.
British, 19th century.
Active in London.
Painter.
G.H. Edwards exhibited landscapes and views of ancient abbeys from 1837 to 1847.

EDWARDS, George
British, 18th century.
Born 1694, in Stratford (Essex); died 1773, in Plaistow.
Painter, watercolourist. Natural history (animals).
George Edwards visited Holland, Norway, Belgium and France from 1716 to 1731. In 1733 he was named librarian of the College of Physics. From 1747 to 1751, he published a *Natural History of Rare Birds and Animals*.
AUCTION RECORDS:
LONDON, 26 June 1980, *Jay on a Branch* (watercolour, 10 1/2 x 8 3/4 ins / 26.5 x 22.5 cm) GBP 600. LONDON, 22 April 1982, *Norwegian Hunter* (watercolour, 11 1/4 x 9 1/4 ins / 28.5 x 23.5 cm) GBP 200. NEW YORK, 21 Jan 1983, *Bird in a Landscape* (watercolour, 13 1/2 x 18 ins / 34.3 x 45.7 cm) USD 2,100.

EDWARDS, George Henry
British, 19th century.
Active in London.
Painter. Genre scenes.
George Henry Edwards exhibited in London from 1883 to 1893. Among his works were: *The Garden of Sleep; Phyllis; The Bather.*

EDWARDS, George Wharton
American, 19th - 20th century.
Born 14 March 1859 or 1869, in Fair Haven (Connecticut); died 18 January 1950, in Greenwich (Connecticut).
Painter, watercolourist, draughtsman, illustrator.
George Edwards studied in Antwerp and Paris before settling in New York. He participated in group exhibitions in Boston, winning bronze and silver medals, and also appeared in exhibitions of the American Watercolor Society. He was also a writer.

He executed a mural in the West Point Cadets School: *Hendrik Hudson*. He created posters for the magazine *The century* and a number of book plates. He illustrated numerous works, including those he had written: *Belgium Old and New* 1889, *Alsace-Lorraine* 1908, *Brittany and Bretons* 1910, *Holland Today* 1912, *The Forest of Ardennes*, etc., as well as books by Nathaniel Hawthorne: *Tanglewood Tales for Girls and Boys* and other literary works published by Macmillan.
BIBLIOGRAPHY:
Osterwalder, Marcus (ed.), *Dictionnaire des illustrateurs 1800-1914*, Ides et Calendes, Neuchâtel, 1989.
AUCTION RECORDS:
NEW YORK, 24 June 1988, *Old Bridge and Wash-houses on the Seine in Paris* (oil on canvas, 23 1/2 x 19 3/4 ins / 60 x 50 cm) USD 3,850. NEW YORK, 30 Sept 1988, *Tea-time* (1904, watercolour and gouache/paper, 17 x 23 1/4 ins / 43.1 x 58.8 cm) USD 3,300. NEW YORK, 28 Sept 1989, *The Flemish Lace-Maker* (gouache, pastel and pencil/paper/card, 17 1/4 x 12 3/4 ins / 43.8 x 32.5 cm) USD 9,900. NEW YORK, 28 May 1992, *Île de la Cité in Paris* (oil and charcoal/canvas, 25 x 19 ins / 63.8 x 48.3 cm) USD 12,100. NEW YORK, 26 May 1993, *Gardens of the Alcazar in Seville (Spain)* (oil on canvas, 24 x 19 3/4 ins / 61 x 50 cm) USD 5,750. LOS ANGELES, 9 Dec 1999, *Towers of St Basil, Moscow* (oil on canvas, 37 x 26 ins / 93 x 67 cm) USD 3,500.

EDWARDS, J. C.
British, 19th century.
Painter, engraver, illustrator.
J.C. Edwards presented the painting *Little Girl* to the Royal Academy in London in 1821, then became known in London as an illustrator and engraver. He illustrated the works of Shakespeare.

EDWARDS, James
British, 19th century.
Painter. Landscapes.
James Edwards exhibited in Nottingham in 1868.
MUSEUMS AND GALLERIES:
LONDON (Victoria and Albert Mus.): *Robber's Mill* (watercolour).

EDWARDS, John
British, 18th - 19th century.
Painter. Flowers.
John Edwards was a member of the Society of Artists in Brentford and took part in exhibitions from 1763 to 1812. He also exhibited at the Royal Academy in London during the same period.

EDWARDS, John Kelt
British, 19th century.

Born in Blaenau Festiniog.
Painter, illustrator.

John Kelt Edwards illustrated the works of several Welsh writers and painted portraits of British statesmen such as David Lloyd George, Sir S.T. Evans, W. Vaughan Morgan and the Lord Mayor of London.

EDWARDS, Joseph

British, 19th century.
Born 1814, in Merthyr Tydfil, Wales.
Active in London.
Sculptor.

Joseph Edwards exhibited at the Royal Academy in London from 1838 to 1878.

EDWARDS, Kate F. Lairnoy

American, 20th century.
Born in Marshallville (Georgia).
Painter. Portraits.

Kate Edwards was a pupil at the Art Institute of Chicago. She also studied in Paris under Lucien Simon. She won first prize in the South-Eastern Fair exhibition in Atlanta in 1916.

EDWARDS, Les

British, 20th - 21st century.
Born 1949, in London.
Painter, illustrator.

From 1968 to 1973, Les Edwards studied at the Hornsey School of Art. He illustrates the covers of science fiction books.

AUCTION RECORDS:

PARIS, 14 Oct 1989, *Tomb World* (oil on card, 16 3/4 x 26 ins / 42.5 x 66 cm) FRF 30,000.

EDWARDS, Lionel Dalhousie Robertson

British, 20th century.
Born 9 November 1878, in Clifton, Oxfordshire; died 13 April 1966, in Salisbury, Wiltshire.
Painter (gouache), watercolourist, draughtsman.
Hunting scenes (hunting with hounds), landscapes with figures, animals, sporting scenes.

Lionel Edwards studied at the School of Animal Painting in South Kensington in London under Arthur Stockdale Cope and Frank Calderon. He is best known as an equestrian artist and for his hunting scenes (he was a keen hunter himself). In 1910 he worked for *The Graphic* and reported the Lisbon Revolution. During World War I he served in the Army Remount Service. During the 1920s he worked as an illustrator for a number of well-known magazines such as *Punch, Country Life, Printer's Pie* and *Tatler*. He ultimately settled in the country, making a living painting sporting pictures, and is known for his portraits of racehorses and hunters. He is considered one of the most important sporting artists of the early 20th century. In addition to his painting and contributions to magazine illustration he illustrated an impressive number of books on horses such as *The Aga Khan's Horses* (1938). He was a member of the London Sketch Club and was elected to the Royal Institute of Painters in Watercolour in 1927. In 1959 he was commissioned to paint the annual inspection of the Household Cavalry Mounted Regiment.

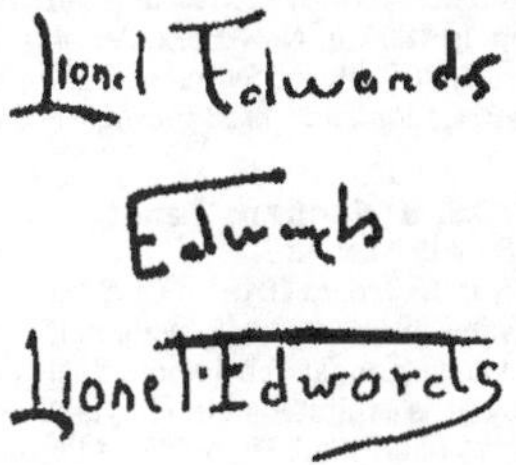

BIBLIOGRAPHY:

Edwards, Lionel, *Reminiscences of a Sporting Artist*, London, 1947. Watson, J.N.P., *Lionel Edwards: Master of the Sporting Scene*, Sportsman's Press, London, 1986. Watson, J.N.P., '*Chase and Turf in All Their Glory: Lionel Edwards 1878-1966*' in *Country Life*, no. 4647, 11 September 1986.

MUSEUMS AND GALLERIES:

BATH (Art Gallery).

AUCTION RECORDS:

LONDON, 30 Jan 1946, *Norfolk Greyhounds* (drawing) GBP 24; *Pack of Norfolk Greyhounds* (drawing) GBP 52. LONDON, 25 April 1969, *Rider* (gouache) Gns 240. LONDON, 12 Nov 1976, *Horses Training* (watercolour and pencil, 16 1/4 x 21 3/4 ins / 41 x 55.5 cm) GBP 320; *Lord Midmay on 'Cromwell'* (1947, oil on canvas, 15 x 20 1/4 ins / 38 x 51.5 cm) GBP 1,700. LONDON, 4 March 1977, *Hunting Scenes* (one dated 1961, two canvases, 20 x 24 ins / 51 x 61 cm) GBP 2,500. LONDON, 16 May 1979, *Jumping the Obstacle* (watercolour and pencil heightened with gouache, 9 3/4 x 13 1/2 ins / 25 x 34.5 cm) GBP 2,000. LONDON, 22 Oct 1981, *Hunting Scene, Dartmoor* (1921, watercolour, 13 1/2 x 19 1/2 ins / 34.5 x 49.5 cm) GBP 2,400. NEW YORK, 8 June 1984, *Huntsman with Pack* (1957, oil on canvas, 20 x 24 ins / 50.8 x 61 cm) USD 6,000; *The Meynell Hunt Away from Bentley Carr, Staffordshire* (1937, watercolour heightened with white, 18 x 29 ins / 45.7 x 73.7 cm) USD 9,500. NEW YORK, 7 June 1985, *Motcombe Vale, the South and West Wilts* (1932, watercolour and gouache, 20 1/4 x 30 ins / 51.4 x 75.9 cm) USD 10,000. LONDON, 13 May 1987, *The Starting Gate, Newmarket* (1933, oil on canvas, 20 x 30 ins / 51 x 76 cm) GBP 44,000. LONDON, 12 June 1987, *The New Forest Foxhounds* (1912, watercolour, gouache and pencil, 20 x 31 ins / 50.8 x 79 cm) GBP 22,000. LONDON, 29 April 1988, *Untitled* (charcoal and watercolour, 15 1/2 x 10 ins / 39.6 x 25.4 cm) GBP 6,600. NEW YORK, 9 June 1988, *The Motcombe Vale* (1932, watercolour and gouache/paper, 20 x 29 1/2 ins / 51.1 x 74.8 cm) USD 11,000. LONDON, 2 March 1989, *Good Morning!* (watercolour and gouache, 13 1/4 x 19 1/4 ins / 33.7 x 48.7 cm) GBP 16,500. LONDON, 8 March 1990, *Morning of the Hunt* (watercolour and gouache, 14 1/2 x 13 3/4 ins / 36.9 x 35 cm) GBP 22,000. LONDON, 8 Nov 1990, *Hunting in Ashford Valley* (1949, watercolour and gouache, 14 1/2 x 20 1/2 ins / 37 x 52 cm) GBP 6,050. LONDON, 25 Jan 1991, *October Evening in Glen Garry* (pencil, watercolour and gouache, 13 x 21 ins / 33 x 53.5 cm) GBP 1,100. LONDON, 2 May 1991, *The Cotswold Foxhounds at Snowhill* (1905, pencil, watercolour and gouache, 7 x 13 1/4 ins / 18 x 33.5 cm) GBP 2,750. NEW YORK, 4 June 1993, *Transporting Cavalry Horses by Boat* (1915, watercolour and gouache/paper, 17 1/2 x 12 1/2 ins / 44.5 x 31.8 cm) USD 7,475. NEW YORK, 15 Feb 1994, *Colonel Wyndham's Hounds Finding the Fox* (1930, watercolour and gouache/paper, a pair, each 13 1/2 x 9 3/4 ins / 34.3 x 24.8 cm) USD 13,800. NEW YORK, 9 June 1995, *The 1960 Grand National* (1960, oil on canvas, 20 x 28 ins / 50.8 x 71.1 cm) USD 23,000. LONDON, 13 Nov 1996, *Cheltenham Gold Cup, 1964* (watercolour, 16 x 21 ins / 40.5 x 53.5 cm) GBP 9,200. LONDON, 10 July 1997, *Fifteen Miles from Marble Arch* (1935, oil on canvas, 19 1/4 x 29 1/4 ins / 49 x 74.3 cm) GBP 5,980. LONDON, 26 Nov 1999, *After Forty Minutes, The Fernie* (oil on canvas, 20 x 30 ins / 51 x 76 cm) GBP 25,000. NEW YORK, 1 Dec 1999, *Crawley and Horsham Hunt* (1934, watercolour and gouache over pencil, 19 x 28 ins / 48 x 71 cm) USD 55,000. HATFIELD, 7 June 2000, *Before Race* (watercolour and gouache, 14 x 21 ins / 36 x 53 cm) USD 12,500. NEW YORK, 6 Dec 2000, *Meet of the Quorn* (1928, watercolour and gouache, 15 x 22 ins / 38 x 56 cm) USD 65,000. LEICESTER, 26 July 2001, *Quorn from Ellas Gorse* (1952, oil on canvas, 20 x 30 ins / 51 x 76 cm) GBP 75,500. LONDON, 5 Dec 2001, *Whaddon Chase, Hunt from Oving, Buckinghamshire* (1926, pencil, watercolour and gouache, 19 x 29 ins / 47 x 74 cm) GBP 36,000. LE-

ICESTER, 25 April 2002, *Quorn Running into Hoby Vale with Hoby Clump in the Rear* (1934, oil on canvas, 20 x 30 ins / 51 x 76 cm) GBP 60,000. LONDON, 27 Nov 2002, *Duke of Rutland's Hounds* (1924, watercolour and gouache, 13 x 20 ins / 33 x 50 cm) GBP 14,000. LONDON, 3 June 2003, *Off to the Meet* (oil on canvas, 20 x 24 ins / 51 x 61 cm) GBP 11,000. NEW YORK, 5 Dec 2003, *Ditch, Newmarket* (1932, watercolour and gouache heightened with white on paper on card, 14 x 20 ins / 36 x 51 cm) USD 28,000. LONDON, 21 May 2004, *Prairie Waltz. Bucking Bronco* (1903, watercolour and gouache, a pair, 13 x 9 ins / 32 x 22 cm) GBP 13,000. LONDON, 25 Nov 2004, *Polo at Cowdray Park* (oil on canvas, 20 x 30 ins / 51 x 77 cm) GBP 12,000.

EDWARDS, Maïsic, or Mia
Australian, 20th century.
Born in the second half of the 19th century, in Sydney.
Painter, pastellist. Genre scenes.

Maïsic Edwards exhibited in Paris at the Salon des Artistes Français in 1914.

AUCTION RECORDS:

LONDON, 15 May 1979, *A Fine Story* (oil on canvas, 37 x 27 1/4 ins / 94 x 69 cm) GBP 1,000.

EDWARDS, Mary Ellen, Mrs John Freer, later Mrs John C. Staples
British, 19th - 20th century.
Born 6 November 1839, in Kingston-upon-Thames.
Painter, illustrator. Genre scenes.

Mary Ellen Edwards exhibited in several exhibitions in London from 1862 to 1908. She worked mainly as a book and newspaper illustrator.

AUCTION RECORDS:

LONDON, 21 March 1990, *The Reply* (oil on canvas, 28 x 36 ins / 71 x 91.5 cm) GBP 5,500. LONDON, 5 Nov 1997, *Spring* (oil on canvas, 30 1/4 x 20 ins / 77 x 51 cm) GBP 6,210.

EDWARDS, Melvin (Mel)
American, 20th century.
Born 4 May 1937, in Houston.
Sculptor, print artist, monotype artist.
Minimal Art.

Mel Edwards studied at the University of Southern California, the University of California, Los Angeles, and the Chouinard Art Institute, Los Angeles. He began teaching at Rutgers University, near New Brunswick (New Jersey), in 1972.

At his exhibition in 1970 in a small gallery at the Whitney Museum, Mel Edwards displayed *Lynch Fragments*, metal sculptures made out of debris from the Watts race riots. These sculptures were the building blocks of a sculptural language that he developed from minimalist theory in order to bring out African-American history. The chains, barbed wire, hammers and shovels all take part in this wish to give his work 'brutal connotations', to symbolise the cruelty of racism and slavery while overcoming it in the beauty of the materials and the power of artistic expression. He has also executed monuments such as *Homage to My Father and the Spirit* (1969) for the Herbert F. Johnson Museum, Cornell University, Ithaca, New York, and *Education is an Open Book* (1988) for the Rutgers University Livingston College Student Center.

He has taken part in various group exhibitions, such as 1971, *Artist as Advocate*, MoMA, New York; 1977, *Drawn and Matched*, Museum of Modern Art, New York; 1984, *Since the Harlem Renaissance*, Center Gallery, Bucknell University, Lewisburg, Pennsylvania; 1985, *Traditions and Conflict: Images of a Turbulent Decade 1963-1973*, Studio Museum in Harlem, New York; 1988, *Sculpture: Inside, Outside*, Walker Art Center, Minneapolis, Minnesota; 2000, *Narratives of African Art and Identity*, High Museum of Art, Atlanta. He has also had a number of solo exhibitions, including 1965, Museum of Art, Santa Barbara, California; 1970, Whitney Museum of American Art, New York; 1978, Studio Museum in Harlem, New York; 1980, American Culture Center, Nairobi; 1981, New Jersey State Museum, Trenton, New Jersey; 1984, UNESCO, Paris; 1985, *Drawings, Monoprints and Maquettes*, Jersey City Museum, Jersey City, New Jersey; 1990, 1993, 1996, CDS Gallery, New York; 1993, *A Thirty Year Retrospective. Melvin Edwards*, Neuberger Museum of Art, State University of New York, Purchase, New York; 2000, *Melvin Edwards: The Prints of a Sculptor*, Jersey City Museum, Jersey City.

BIBLIOGRAPHY:

Fine, Elsa Honig, *Afro-American Art, A Search for Identity*, Holt, Rinehart and Winston, New York, 1973. *Melvin Edwards, sculptor*, exhibition catalogue, Studio Museum in Harlem, New York, 1978. Bass, Ruth, *'Melvin Edwards'* in *Art News*, periodical, New York, September 1990. Johnson, Ken, *'Melvin Edwards'* in *Art in America* n° 78, periodical, New York, September 1990. Gedeon, Lucinda H. (ed), *Melvin Edwards Sculpture: A Thirty-Year Retrospective 1963-1993*, exhibition catalogue, University of Washington Press, 1993. Powell, Richard J., *Black Art and Culture in the 20th century*, Thames and Hudson, London, 1997. *Narratives of African Art and Identity*, group exhibition catalogue, High Museum of Art, Atlanta, 2000.

MUSEUMS AND GALLERIES:

CARACAS (Museo de Artes Visuales Alejandro Otero) - HARTFORD (Wadsworth Atheneum) - ITHACA (Herbert F Johnson Mus. of Art, Cornell University) - LONG BEACH (MA) - LOS ANGELES (California African American Mus.) - LOS ANGELES (County MA) - NEW YORK (Brooklyn Mus.) - NEW YORK (Metropolitan Mus. of Art) - NEW YORK (MoMA) - NEW YORK (Studio Mus. in Harlem) - NEWARK (Mus.): *Resolved* (1986, sculpture) - PURCHASE (Neuberger Mus. of Art) - SPRINGFIELD, MA (MFA) - TRENTON (New Jersey State Mus.) - WASHINGTON DC (Library of Congress): *For the Brave Young Students in Soweto* (1984, engraving).

EDWARDS, Morton. See **EDWARDS-MARTON**

EDWARDS, R.
British, 18th century.
Engraver.

R. Edwards is mentioned by *Art Prices Current*.

EDWARDS, Richard. See **EDOUARD**

EDWARDS, Robert
American, 20th century.
Born 4 October 1879, in Buffalo (New York State); died 1948, in New York.
Painter, illustrator.

Robert Edwards became a member of the Society of Illustrators in 1910. He illustrated: *Eve's Second Husband, Songbook*.

EDWARDS, Samuel Arlent
British, 19th century.
Born 12 July 1861, in Somerset.
Engraver.

Samuel Edwards was a pupil at a school in South Kensington and exhibited in 1887 at the Royal Academy in London, before settling, in 1890, in New York. Among his works are *The Firstborn* after G. Hilyard Swinstead, *Eton Seen from the Thames* after R. Gallon and *Christ Curing the Sick* after Gabriel Max.

EDWARDS, Sydenham Teast
British, 18th - 19th century.
Born 1768, in Usk; died 1819, in Chelsea.
Painter, watercolourist, draughtsman, illustrator.
Natural history (animals/birds/botanical subjects).

Sydenham Edwards exhibited at the Royal Academy in London between 1792 and 1813. He published *Cynographia Bri-*

tannica in 1800 and *The New British Flora* in 1812. He founded the botanic register in 1815. He also did drawings for *Botanic Magazine* and *Sportsman's Magazine*. At the end of his life he retired to Brompton.
MUSEUMS AND GALLERIES:
LONDON (Victoria and Albert Mus.): *Nepalese Snipe; Woodcock*.
AUCTION RECORDS:
PARIS, 30 June 1932, *Shepherds and Animals* (watercolour, a pair) FRF 280. MILWAUKEE, 2 Nov 1980, *Great Titmouse* (1794, watercolour, 7³/4 x 11 ins / 19.5 x 27 cm) USD 500. LONDON, 18 Nov 1987, *Feathered Creatures in a Landscape* (1811, oil on canvas, 29¹/4 x 24¹/4 ins / 74.5 x 61.5 cm) GBP 6,500. GODALMING, 20 Oct 2004, *Bramling. Blue Tit. Chaffinches. Linnets* (oil on panel, four, 9 x 7 ins / 24 x 19 cm) GBP 3,000.

EDWARDS, Thomas
American, 19th century.
Lithographer.

EDWARDS, W. H.
British, 18th - 19th century.
Active in London.
Painter. Fruit.
W.H. Edwards exhibited in London at the Royal Academy and the Suffolk Street gallery from 1793 to 1850.

EDWARDS, W. H. (Mrs)
British, 19th century.
Active in London.
Painter.
Mrs W.H. Edwards exhibited in London in 1847 at the Royal Academy and at Suffolk Street. She was probably the wife of the fruit painter W.H. Edwards.

EDWARDS, W. Joseph
British, 19th century.
Active in London.
Engraver.

EDWARDS, William Camden
British, 19th century.
Born 1777, in Monmouthshire; died 1855, in Bungay (Suffolk).
Engraver.
William Camden Edwards worked for the publishing house Edition Ch. Brightly, and for archaeological publications. He also engraved numerous portraits, including those of *Hogarth* and *Reynolds*. There are also reproductions of *H. Fuseli* after Thomas Lawrence, *D. Sayers* after Opie and *Milton and his daughters* after G. Romney.

EDWARDS, William Croxford
British, 19th century.
Painter, watercolourist. Seascapes.
William Croxford Edwards exhibited in London, notably at the Royal Academy, from 1871 to 1892, and at Suffolk Street. He was active in Brentford and painted landscapes in Cornwall.
AUCTION RECORDS:
LONDON, 13 Dec 1909, *Tugboat and Fishing Boat at Yarmouth* (watercolour) GBP 2. LONDON, 1 March 1984, *The Beach at Scheveningen* (watercolour heightened with white, 20³/4 x 36¹/4 ins / 53 x 92 cm) GBP 900. LONDON, 16 July 1993, *Grading the Fish; Near the Harbour* (oil on canvas, a pair, each 7 x 9 ins / 18 x 23 cm) GBP 2,300.

EDWARDS-HOROWITZ, Fernande.
See **HOROWITZ-EDWARDS**

EDWARDS-MARTON, or Morton
British, 19th century.
Active in London.
Sculptor.
Edwards-Marton exhibited at the Royal Academy in London from 1864 to 1870.

EDWARMAY, Louis
French, 19th century.
Born 19th century, in Paris.
Painter, lithographer.
Having trained under Léon Cogniet, Louis Edwarmay exhibited at the Salon from 1839 to 1875. His best-known paintings are *Giotto in Cimabue's Studio, Pan and the Nymphs* and *A Mother's Dream*.

EDWELT, Bernice
British, 19th century.
Painter, miniaturist.
MUSEUMS AND GALLERIES:
SYDNEY: *Study*.

EDWIN, David
American, 18th - 19th century.
Born 1776, in Bath, England; died 1841, in Philadelphia.
Engraver.
A son of the actor John Edwin, David Edwin was apprenticed to an engraver. He ran away, took ship and reached America in 1797. There, he attached himself to Edward Savage, the portraitist, and soon became known as one himself. He worked for 20 years before his sight failed him and he was reduced to all sorts of expedients to make ends meet.
MUSEUMS AND GALLERIES:
NEW HAVEN (Knights of Columbus Mus.): *Landing of Christopher Columbus on the Morning of October 12th, 1492* (engraving).

EDWIN, Henry
British, 19th century.
Active at the end of the 19th century.
Silhouettist.
Henry Edwin made portraits of famous men of his time such as Salisbury, Tennyson and Gladstone.

EDWIN, Salomon
Romanian, 20th century.
Born 3 February 1935, in Cona-Mures.
Active in Israel from 1961.
Painter, draughtsman. Scenes with figures, animals.
Salomon Edwin was a pupil of the Ion Andreescu Institute of fine arts in Cluj, from which he graduated in 1957. That same year he entered the competition to decorate the Auschwitz Memorial in Jerusalem. His plan was selected for the permanent exhibition at this memorial and he became a member of the association of painters and sculptors of Israel. In 1965 he spent some time in Paris, taking art history classes at the Sorbonne.

Edwin began by painting portraits. After a short journey through Abstraction, he went back to representation. He had a traditional pictorial style dominated and characterised by a technique of small strokes and chiaroscuro. He painted groups of ill-defined objects, often evoking ruins of some kind, symbolic of all the chaos reigning in the world, amongst which lie crushed, broken, suffocated animals, themselves symbols of life constantly under threat. These are not strictly speaking still-lifes and he was not a painter of wildlife. His undefined objects and animals replace the world of humans and of death at large.

Edwin took part in collective exhibitions in Romania, Israel, the USA, the former USSR and the Philippines and held several solo shows from 1963, particularly in Israel (Jerusalem, Holon, Jaffa, Tel-Aviv) and in Montreal in 1972. He was involved in teaching in various higher education institutions. In 1965 he was awarded the Max Nordau prize and in 1983 a prize of Tel-Aviv Museum of as part of an exhibition on the Bible.

Bibliography:

Jianou, Ionel, *Romanian Artists and the West,* American Romanian Academy of Arts and Sciences, Los Angeles, 1986.

EDY, John William

Danish, 19th century.

Painter, engraver. Landscapes.

Edy painted views of Denmark, Norway and Switzerland, mainly in the form of aquatints.

Auction records:

London, 1-8 May 1924, *Adelphi; Somerset House; Waterloo Bridge* (drawings, sold with a watercolour by an unnamed artist) GBP 36. London, 27 Oct 1982, *Boydell's Picturesque Scenery of Norway* (80 aquatints) GBP 2,700.

ÉDY-LEGRAND, pseudonym of Legrand, Édouard Léon Louis

French, 20th century.

Born 24 July 1892, in Bordeaux; died September 1970, in Bonnieux (Vaucluse).

Painter, watercolourist, draughtsman (including ink), engraver, illustrator. Figure compositions, figures, scenes with figures, local scenes, interiors with figures, animals. Murals.

Orientalism.

Édy-Legrand created large decorative compositions for some of the big Paris stores and the great French liners of the period. He also contributed to the revival of book illustration, producing among others: *Siegfried et le Limousin* by Jean Giraudoux, *Poèmes en Prose* by Pierre Mac-Orlan, *L'Île Rose* by Charles Vildrac and Dante's *Inferno,* altogether some 150 books from Rabelais to Anatole France, François Mauriac, André Malraux and Albert Camus.

Édy-Legrand had much success in the 1930s and 1940s. In 1985 the Galerie Antinea in Paris mounted an exhibition of his work.

Auction records:

New York, 26 May 1983, *Four Algerians* (1924, watercolour and ink, 9¾ x 11½ ins / 25 x 29 cm) USD 1,000. Paris, 21 Jan 1987, *Party in the Country* (oil on canvas, 32 x 39¼ ins / 81 x 100 cm) FRF 18,500. Paris, 19 March 1990, *Seated Young Woman* (oil on canvas, 18 x 15 ins / 46 x 38 cm) FRF 10,500. Paris, 27 April 1990, *Encampment in Morocco* (oil on card, 19¾ x 25½ ins / 50 x 65 cm) FRF 20,000. Paris, 22 June 1990, *Family Scene in Morocco* (oil on paper, 25½ x 39 ins / 65 x 99 cm) FRF 18,000. Paris, 14 Nov 1990, *Chanteuses chirates dans les jardins du Caïd Telouet* (oil on canvas, 39¼ x 51¼ ins / 100 x 130 cm) FRF 25,000. Paris, 19 Nov 1991, *Interior in Goulmina* (oil on paper, 18¾ x 21¼ ins / 47.5 x 53.7 cm) FRF 17,500. Paris, 13 April 1992, *Horsemen in Camp* (oil and gouache/card, 25½ x 39¼ ins / 65 x 100 cm) FRF 34,000. Paris, 7 Dec 1992, *Siesta* (gouache, 13 x 17¼ ins / 33 x 43.5 cm) FRF 10,000. Paris, 5 April 1993, *Two Girls* (1945, oil on panel, 41 x 29½ ins / 104 x 75 cm) FRF 62,000. Paris, 18 June 1993, *Young Woman Reclining* (oil on canvas, 19¾ x 25½ ins / 50 x 65 cm) FRF 23,000. Paris, 13 March 1995, *Le Cheval rose* (oil on panel, 39¼ x 51¼ ins / 100 x 130 cm) FRF 60,000. Paris, 17 Nov 1997, *Street Scene in Fez* (1939, mixed media, 24¾ x 38½ ins / 63 x 98 cm) FRF 26,000. Paris, 26 March 1998, *Camp in Goulmina* (oil/c, 25½ x 39¼ ins / 65 x 100 cm) FRF 34,000. Paris, 17 Dec 2001, *Bunch of Flowers* (oil on canvas, 30 x 26 ins / 75 x 65 cm) FRF 13,000.

EDZARD, Dietz

German, 20th century.

Born 1893, in Bremen; died 1963.

Painter, engraver. Figures, portraits, nudes, scenes with figures, interiors, landscapes with figures, landscapes, still-lifes, flowers.

Edzard was a pupil of Max Beckmann. He travelled in Germany, the Netherlands and France, and settled in Provence for a time. In 1929 he took part in the Exposition des Peintres-Graveurs Contemporains at the Musée du Jeu de Paume in Paris. He specialised in the female figure, painting several female portraits including young Parisian women, young girls, elegant ladies, actresses and dancers. He also painted numerous still-lifes, often with flowers.

Bibliography:

Meuhram, G., *D. Edzard,* Bittner, New York, 1948. Gauthier, Maximilien, *D. Edzard,* Les Gémeaux, Paris, 1952. Roger-Marx, Claude, *D. Edzard - Tableaux de 1917 à 1963,* Quatre Chemins, Paris, 1971.

Auction records:

London, 13 Feb 1936, *Two Dancers,* GBP 54. New York, 16 March 1944, *Maria Lani* (1928) USD 175. Paris, 21 Feb 1951, *Vase of Flowers,* FRF 70,000. Paris, 16 June 1953, *The Fair,* FRF 290,000. New York, 19 March 1958, *Flowers and Mandolin,* USD 2,200. London, 1 July 1959, *Young Girl in a Café,* GBP 520. Paris, 29 Nov 1962, *Fortune-Teller,* FRF 6,500. London, 1 July 1964, *Young Girl,* GBP 830. New York, 11 Feb 1965, *Dancer,* USD 3,100. New York, 28 March 1969, *Two Young Girls by a River,* USD 5,000. Los Angeles, 26 Feb 1974, *Place de la Madeleine,* USD 6,500. Los Angeles, 10 June 1976, *Woman with a White Feather Boa* (oil on canvas, 32 x 23¾ ins / 81.3 x 60.3 cm) USD 3,000. New York, 28 Oct 1977, *The Duo* (oil on canvas, 27 x 20½ ins / 68.5 x 52 cm) USD 2,250. Los Angeles, 6 Nov 1978, *Ballerina with a Bouquet* (oil on canvas, 25½ x 32 ins / 65 x 81.2 cm) USD 3,500. London, 1 Dec 1981, *Elegant Woman on the Beach* (oil on canvas, 19¾ x 24 ins / 50 x 61 cm) GBP 6,000. New York, 10 Oct 1984, *Singer in a White Dress* (oil on canvas, 36¾ x 23 ins / 93.3 x 58.5 cm) USD 6,000. Paris, 11 June 1987, *Entrance to the Dance* (1937, oil on canvas, 36¼ x 23½ ins / 92 x 60 cm) FRF 80,000. New York, 13 May 1988, *On Stage* (1934, oil on canvas, 24 x 19¾ ins / 61 x 50.2 cm) USD 3,080. Versailles, 15 May 1988, *Young Woman in a Basque* (1929, oil on canvas, 24 x 18 ins / 61 x 46 cm) FRF 6,800. London, 19 Oct 1988, *At the Opera* (1934, oil on canvas, 24¼ x 19¾ ins / 61.4 x 50.2 cm) GBP 3,520. London, 21 Feb 1989, *Portrait of Suzanne Eisendieck* (oil on canvas, 16¼ x 13 ins / 41 x 33 cm) GBP 3,300. New York, 9 May 1989, *Caprice* (oil on canvas, 28¾ x 20 ins / 73 x 50.8 cm) USD 18,700. Paris, 18 June 1989, *Elegant Woman in a Hat* (oil on canvas, 26 x 19¾ ins / 66 x 50 cm) FRF 30,000. Paris, 21 Nov 1989, *Entrance to the Dance* (oil on canvas, 36¼ x 23½ ins / 92 x 60 cm) FRF 75,000. Paris, 24 Jan 1990, *Two Apremont Roses for Mme Kerbley* (1933, oil on canvas, 11 x 9 ins / 27 x 22 cm) FRF 9,000. Montreal, 30 April 1990, *Pink Rose in Front of a Sheet of Music* (oil on panel, 13 x 5½ ins / 33 x 14 cm) CAD 2,750. New York, 10 Oct 1990, *The Ballerinas' Dressing Room* (1945, oil on canvas/card, 26¼ x 39¼ ins / 66.7 x 99.7 cm) USD 7,700. New York, 7 May 1991, *Waiting* (1946, oil on canvas, 32 x 23½ ins / 81.2 x 59.7 cm) USD 4,400. Montreal, 4 June 1991, *Little Girl with Roses* (oil on canvas, 24 x 19¾ ins / 61 x 50.2 cm) CAD 8,000. Amsterdam, 2-3 Nov 1992, *Still-life with Flowers* (oil on card, 11 x 8¼ ins / 27 x 21 cm) NLG 4,600. New York, 29 Sept 1993, *Woman and Child* (oil on canvas, 23½ x 29 ins / 59.7 x 73.7 cm) USD 6,325. London, 23-24 March 1994, *Reclining Nude* (oil on canvas, 27½ x 36¼ ins / 70 x 92 cm) GBP 4,370. New York, 3 June 1994, *The Races at Longchamp* (oil on canvas, 32 x 40 ins / 81.3 x 101.6 cm) USD 31,050. New York, 30 April 1996, *On the Balcony* (oil on canvas, 28¾ x 23½ ins / 73 x 60 cm) USD 7,475. New York, 10 Oct 1996, *Elegant Woman at the Port* (oil on canvas, 25¾ x 32 ins / 65.4 x 81 cm) USD 10,925. London, 23 Oct 1996, *Circus Scene* (1941, oil on canvas, 25½ x 19¾ ins / 65 x 50 cm) GBP 4,600.

NEW YORK, 12 Nov 1996, *Celebration Bouquet* (oil on canvas, 25 1/2 x 21 1/2 ins / 65 x 54.6 cm) USD 6,900. OAKLAND, 25 April 1999, *Portrait of a Lady* (oil on canvas, 33 x 43 ins / 84 x 109 cm) USD 6,500. TORONTO, 1 June 1999, *Landing Stage in Venice* (1959, oil on canvas, 25 x 31 ins / 63 x 79 cm) CAD 12,000. BREMEN, 1 April 2000, *Two Women at the Edge of the Water* (oil on canvas, 32 x 26 ins / 81 x 65 cm) DEM 22,000. MONTREAL, 18 Sept 2000, *Carnaval in Venice* (oil on canvas, 25 x 31 ins / 63 x 79 cm) CAD 12,000. NEW YORK, 23 May 2001, *Woman on Balcony* (oil on canvas, 30 x 24 ins / 75 x 60 cm) USD 12,000. NEW YORK, 5 Dec 2001, *Singer in White Swiss Dots* (oil on canvas, 36 x 24 ins / 91 x 61 cm) USD 14,000. LONDON, 9 April 2002, *Elegant Woman with Dog* (oil on canvas, 22 x 18 ins / 56 x 45 cm) GBP 28,000. NEW YORK, 18 April 2002, *Floral Bouquet with Venice in the Distance* (oil on canvas, 26 x 32 ins / 65 x 81 cm) USD 16,000. PARIS, 12 March 2003, *Renée et Gerard Albouy, le salon du modiste* (oil on canvas, 39 x 31 ins / 100 x 80 cm) EUR 11,800. NEW YORK, 25 Sept 2003, *Dancers and Clown* (oil on canvas, 26 x 32 ins / 65 x 81 cm) USD 10,000. NEW YORK, 12 Feb 2004, *Place de la Concorde* (oil on canvas, 32 x 25 ins / 81 x 64 cm) USD 19,000. LONDON, 24 March 2004, *Angelica at the Theatre* (oil on canvas, 24 x 29 ins / 60 x 73 cm) GBP 9,000.

EDZGVERADZE, Giya
Georgian, 20th - 21st century.
Born 1953, in Tbilisi.
Painter, draughtsman.

Giya Edzgveradze graduated from the academy of arts in Georgia in 1980. In 1986 he became a member of the Union of Soviet Artists. His paintings and drawings seek to graphically challenge the subjective (the traces left on the unconscious mind by events) and the exterior (the space inhabited by reality), and occasionally feature highly schematised objects.

AUCTION RECORDS:
MOSCOW, 7 July 1988, *Jacob's Dream* (1987, oil on canvas, 78 3/4 x 63 ins / 200 x 160 cm) GBP 5,500.

EEBECKEN. See **EGGEBECK**

EECHAULT, Constant
Flemish, 19th century.
Active c. 1843.
Painter. Landscapes.
Flemish School.

AUCTION RECORDS:
LOKEREN, 8 Oct 1988, *At the Inn* (1861, oil on panel, 14 3/4 x 18 ins / 37.5 x 46 cm) BEF 190,000.

EECHAUT, Eugène
Belgian, 20th century.
Born 1928, in Raismes, France.
Painter, draughtsman, watercolourist.

Eechaut trained at the Académie St-Gilles in Brussels.

MUSEUMS AND GALLERIES:
BRUSSELS (Bibliothèque royale Albert Ier, Prints Collection): drawings - LEXHY: watercolours.

EECHAUTE, Aegidius van den
Flemish, 18th century.
Born 1736, in Astene; died 22 July 1791, in Ghent.
Painter.
Flemish School.

In 1763 Aegidius van den Eechaute became a member of the guild of painters.

EECHAUTE, Gillis Joanne
Flemish, 18th century.
Active in Ghent.
Painter.
Flemish School.

EECHOUTE, Jacop van den, or Eechaute
Flemish School, 15th century.
Died 1498.
Active in Ghent.
Sculptor.

Jacop van den Eechoute specialised in carving organ cases, and worked at several churches in Flanders.

EECHOUTE, Karryn van den
Flemish School, 15th century.
Active in Ghent at the end of the 15th century.
Sculptor.

Karryn van den Eechoute worked with Jacop van den Eechoute, whose illegitimate son he was.

EECK. See also **HECKE**

EECK, André François van
French, 18th century.
Active in Paris c. 1700.
Painter.

EECK, Nicolas van
French, 18th century.
Born December 1700, in Paris.
Painter.

Nicolas van Eeck was the son of André van Eeck.

EECKELE, Aelbrecht van, or Heeckele
Flemish School, 16th century.
Died after 1568.
Painter.
Bruges School.

The son of Jan van Eeckele, Aelbrecht van Eeckele was a master of the Bruges guild in 1548.

EECKELE, Jan van, or Eecke, Heckele
Flemish School, 16th century.
Died 1561.
Painter. Religious subjects.
Bruges School.

A master in Bruges in 1534, Jan van Eeckele remained there until his death. Works by him can be found both in the cathedral of St Salvator in Bruges, which houses a *Mater Dolorosa*, and in the church of the Black (Augustinian) Sisters, where a wing of a tripych shows *St Nicholas of Tolentino* on one side, and *Roger de Jonghe, Augustinian Monk* on the other.

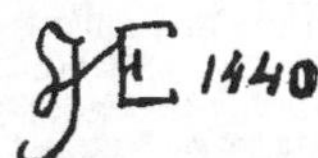

MUSEUMS AND GALLERIES:
TOURNAI: *Legend of St Bernard*.

EECKEREN, Joseph van
Belgian, 20th century.
Born 1895, in Antwerp.
Painter, draughtsman. Landscapes.

Van Eeckeren started drawing as a child, and was a self-taught artist.

EECKHOUDT, Jean van den
Belgian, 20th century.
Born 15 July 1875, in Brussels; died 28 September 1946, in Bourgeois-Rixensart.
Also active in France.
Painter. Figures, portraits, landscapes, still-lifes, flowers.

Van den Eeckhoudt was the grandson of François Verheyden and the nephew and son-in-law of Isidore Verheyden. He trained under the latter and at the studio of Ernest Blanc-Garin, where he formed a friendship with Henri Evenepoel. He was the father of the painter Zoum Walter. He was good friends with Théo Van Rysselberghe, who in 1926 asked him to complete a commission for a group of decorative paintings. In 1935 he painted the portrait of *Catherine Gide, Daughter of Mme van Rysselberghe*. From 1904 onwards his time was divided between Belgium and Menton. Then, during World War I, after a trip to Venice and Tuscany in 1914, he settled in Roquebrune where he met numerous artists and writers including Matisse and André Gide. It was not until 1937 that he returned to Belgium for good.

In his early works dating from about 1892 - portraits of people close to him, seascapes and landscapes with figures - Van den Eeckhoudt appeared to be torn between the Realism of the 19th century and Impressionism. He soon adopted the light colours and massed brushstrokes of the latter, and was influenced especially by the luminosity of his father-in-law's paintings. Around 1909 he moved on to synthetic drawing, using flowing outlines and the vibrant colours of the Fauvist palette and founding what came to be known as 'Brabançon Fauvism'. Later, evolving in the same way as the Fauves themselves, he moved on to a bold, post-Cézanne-style recreation of space and volume in structured and rather severe landscapes and solidly modelled still-lifes. When he finally returned to Belgium, the scenery and light, which were quite different from those he experienced in Roquebrune, influenced the psychological feel of his works, although the solidity of their construction remained unchanged. Van den Eeckhoudt's work also includes numerous portraits of his nearest and dearest, his wife, his daughter Zoum, his friends, some group portraits and some commissioned portraits.

He exhibited at the Salon Triennal in Ghent as early as 1892. In 1895 he took part in the Salon de la Libre Esthétique, in 1919 he participated in a group exhibition in Brussels, and in 1922 he exhibited at the Galerie Druet in Paris. In 1934 a solo exhibition of nearly 150 works was held in Brussels. The same year several of his works were shown in the Belgian Pavilion at the Venice Biennale. In 1938 he staged an exhibition in Luxembourg with his daughter Zoum and a friend. An exhibition of his complete works, which he himself had organised, took place in 1946, soon after his death.

BIBLIOGRAPHY:

Lambotte, Paul, *Jean Van den Eeckhoudt*, Brussels, 1934. Gide, André, et al., *Jean Van den Eeckhoudt*, Éd. de la Connaissance, Brussels, 1948.

MUSEUMS AND GALLERIES:

ANTWERP: *Self-portrait in Grey* - BRUSSELS: *In the Garden* (1906); *Lemons* (1913); *Mexican Hat* (1922); *Lady in a Black Hat* (1926); *Olive Grove in Gorbio* (1932); *Portrait of Paul Lambotte* (1933); *Portrait of the Sculptor Louis-Henri Devillez* (1938); *Place d'Ohain* (1939); *Still-life with a Bag of Flour* (1942); *Still-life with a Grey Curtain* (1943); *Portrait of the Painter and his Wife* (1946) - GHENT: *Self-portrait*; *Corner of the Studio*; *Accessories*; *The Artist's Wife*; *Seated Figure* - INDIANAPOLIS (MA): *Under the Orange Trees or The Terrace at Les Pâquerettes* - IXELLES: *Under the Orange Trees*; *Portrait of a Young Girl*; *Interior* - LIÈGE: *Portrait of François Walter*; *Seated Figure* - LUXEMBOURG: *Interior with Armchair* - MONS (MBA): *Portrait of the Painter Marguerite Putsage* - STAVELOT: *March* - UZÈS: *Portrait of the Painter Simon Bussy*; *Portrait of Janie Bussy*.

AUCTION RECORDS:

LONDON, 31 Oct 1973, *Flowers in a Vase* (1915) GBP 220. ANTWERP, 19 Oct 1976, *House in a Pine Forest* (oil on canvas, 37¾ x 31 ins / 96 x 79 cm) BEF 110,000. ANTWERP, 17 Oct 1978, *Drève* (oil on canvas, 27½ x 33 ins / 70 x 84 cm) BEF 55,000. ANTWERP, 29 April 1981, *Standing Nude* (1931, 46 x 28¾ ins / 116 x 73 cm) BEF 30,000. ANTWERP, 3 April 1984, *Nude* (1931, oil on canvas, 46 x 28¾ ins / 116 x 73 cm) BEF 50,000. LOKEREN, 22 Feb 1986, *Midi Landscape* (oil on canvas, 34¼ x 35¾ ins / 87 x 91 cm) BEF 130,000. LOKEREN, 5 March 1988, *Landscape with Olive Trees* (oil on canvas, 27¼ x 33 ins / 69.5 x 84 cm) BEF 270,000. LOKEREN, 8 Oct 1988, *Vase of Flowers* (1944, oil on canvas, 29¾ x 22 ins / 75.5 x 56 cm) BEF 140,000. AMSTERDAM, 12 Dec 1991, *Portrait of a Young Boy with a Rose* (1909, pastel/paper, 48½ x 30¾ ins / 123 x 78 cm) NLG 8,050. LOKEREN, 21 March 1992, *Still-life with a Jug* (oil on paper/panel, 27¼ x 20 ins / 69 x 51 cm) BEF 240,000. LOKEREN, 10 Oct 1992, *Blonde Woman with a Black Hat* (oil on canvas, 19¼ x 16¼ ins / 49 x 41.5 cm) BEF 140,000. LOKEREN, 12 March 1994, *Blonde Woman with a Black Hat* (oil on canvas, 19¼ x 16¼ ins / 49 x 41.5 cm) BEF 140,000.

EECKHOUT, Albert van der, or Eeckholt

Dutch, 17th century.
Born 1610, in Groningen; died 1666.
Painter, draughtsman. Portraits, hunting scenes, landscapes, natural history (botanical subjects/animals), still-lifes.

Little can be ascertained about the life of Albert van der Eeckhout. It is known that he worked for Johan Maurits, future Prince of Nassau-Siegen, whom he joined on an expedition to Brazil in 1636 (Prince Maurits was governor of the Dutch colony of Brazil). Eeckhout remained in Brazil until 1644. Some of the paintings he carried out there were presented to King Frederik III of Denmark by Johan Maurits in 1654. From 1653 he worked in Dresden at the court of Johann Georg II, the Prince-Elector.

He mainly painted the native inhabitants of Brazil and still-lifes of Brazilian fruits. His paintings executed in Brazil (1636-1644) are among the oldest known in that country. Among these, especially noteworthy are the full-length figures and still-lifes. It is only recently that the paintings have been definitively attributed to Eeckhout (the sketches and drawings are still shrouded in uncertainty). It is known that in 1679 Johan Maurits presented Eeckhout's paintings to Louis XIV. These served as models for tapestries at the Gobelins tapestry works and are known as *Tapestries of the Indies*, carried out in 1689-1690.

In 2002 the Nationalmuseet in Copenhagen mounted an exhibition of all Eeckhout's works which are held there. In the same year a travelling exhibition in Brazil, *Albert Eckhout volta ao Brasil 1644-2002* (*Albert Eeckhout Returns to Brazil 1644-2002*) was mounted at the Instituto Ricardo Brennand in Recife, then in Brasilia, and then at the Pinacoteca do Estado in São Paulo. This exhibition, co-organised by the Nationalmuseet in Copenhagen and a Brazilian board, was ground-breaking in that it was also the first time that such a collection of paintings by Eeckhout had been shown in Brazil, the locality of their execution.

BIBLIOGRAPHY:

Berlowicz, Barbara/Berete, Due, et al., '*Albert Eckhout volta ao Brasil 1644-2002 (Albert Eckhout returns to Brazil)*' in *catalogue d'exposition*, Nationalmuseet, Copenhagen, 2002. Buvelot, Quentin, '*Albert Eckhout. Exhibitions Reviews*' in *The Burlington Magazine* vol. CXLV n° 1198, periodical, London, January 2003.

MUSEUMS AND GALLERIES:

COPENHAGEN (Ethnographic Mus.): *Brazilian Men and Women* (several other paintings) - CRACOW (Biblioteka Jagiellonski): *Theatrum rerum naturalium Brasilae* (*The Theatre of the Nature of Brazil*) (sketchbooks).

AUCTION RECORDS:

LONDON, 17 Nov 1982, *Oportunia Vulgaris* (oil on canvas, 43 x 37½ ins / 109 x 95 cm) GBP 17,000. NEW YORK, 12 Jan 1996, *Still-life of a Cactus* (oil on canvas, 42½ x 36¾ ins / 108 x 93.4 cm) USD 332,500.

EECKHOUT, Anthonie van den

Flemish, 17th century.
Born 1656, in Brussels or Bruges; died 1695, in Lisbon.

Painter. Flowers, fruit.
Flemish School.
Anthonie van den Eeckhout worked for an extended period in Italy with his son-in-law L. Deyster, returning there after a long stay in Bruges. He then went to Lisbon, where he married and was shot by a rival.

EECKHOUT, Gerbrand van den

Dutch, 17th century.
Born 19 August 1621, in Amsterdam; died 1674; buried 29 September in Amsterdam.
Painter, engraver. Religious subjects, portraits, genre scenes.
Amsterdam School.
Gerbrand van den Eeckhout was a friend of Rembrandt, and was his pupil from 1635 to 1640. He was also on intimate terms with Rogman. His father Jan Pietersz. van der Eeckhout, a goldsmith in Amsterdam, was probably very wealthy and it is alleged that it was only by paying a fortune that Gerbrand succeeded in being accepted into Rembrandt's studio. He began with a portrait of his father which was highly commended by his master. Shortly thereafter he turned to historical painting, echoing his master in his choice of subjects, particularly the Old and New Testaments.

To a greater extent than any other of Rembrandt's pupils, Gerbrand evolved under the traditional influence of his master, reworking forms in his own way. His mastery of draughtsmanship is evident in his smallest sketches. Through his pencil strokes, forms took on a lively flexibility. Such power of execution allowed him to deal with significant historical subjects before which other Dutch painters sometimes flinched.

His works, which were not well known in France, received critical attention in the Netherlands and Germany. Gerbrand tried his hand at etching with *Young Man, Three-quarter Profile* and *Portrait of Corneille Tromp*. He also drew designs for gold plate, a few of which are signed with his translated name *G. du Chesne*.

G. V. Eeckhout. fe. A° 1655.

MUSEUMS AND GALLERIES:

AMSTERDAM: *Christ and the Woman Taken in Adultery; Huntsmen Resting with Two Dogs; The Guest Turned Out because he is not in Wedding Attire; Swimmers near a Rock* - AMSTERDAM (Six Collection): *The Adulterous Woman before Christ* - AUGSBURG: *The Circumcision of Christ* - AVIGNON: *Calvary* - BAMBERG: *Meleager and Atlanta* - BAYEUX: *Portrait of Rembrandt* - BERLIN: *The Presentation of Christ at the Temple; Mercury Kills Argus; The Resurrection of the Daughter of Jairus* - BORDEAUX: *Young Man Playing Flute* - BREMEN: *Ruth and Boaz; Samson and Delilah* - BRUNSWICK: *Solomon Sacrificing to the Idols; Tobias and the Angel; Sophonisba and the Poison Cup; Mother and Child* - BUDAPEST: *Vertumnus and Pomona* - CHERBOURG: *Armenian Jew* - COLOGNE: *Esther and Haman before Ahasuerus* - COPENHAGEN (Moltke Collection): *St Jerome; Hermit* - COPENHAGEN (Statens Mus. for Kunst): *Lady with her Music Master* - DARMSTADT: *Lady in Black; Man in Black* - DRESDEN: *Presentation of Christ at the Temple; Jacob's Dream* - DUBLIN: *Portrait of Lady; Sketch of a Woman Running; Christ Teaching in the Temple; A Rabbi* - FRANKFURT AM MAIN: *Portrait of Isaac Commelin* - FRANKFURT AM MAIN (Städel): *The Historian Olfert Dapper* - GRENOBLE: *Jan de Witt* - KASSEL: *Abraham Receiving the Three Angels* - LEIPZIG: *Dutch Woman Cleaning her Dog; Abraham's Servant Asks for Rebecca* - LILLE: *The Continence of Scipio; Portrait of a Young Man; The Denier of Caesar* - LONDON (Lesser Gal.): *Isaac Blessing Jacob* - LONDON (NG): *Four Officers of the Amsterdam Coopers' and Wine-rackers' Guild* (1657, oil on canvas); *Rebekah and Eliezer at the Well* (1661, oil on canvas) - LONDON (Stafford House): *Three Soldiers at the Table* - LYONS: *Portrait of Young Man* - MILAN (Pinacoteca di Brera): *Biblical Scene* - MOSCOW (Rumiantsev Mus.): *Judah and Tamar; The Expulsion of Hagar; Head of an Old Man; Laban Dismissing Jacob; Adoration of the Magi; Biblical Scene* - MUNICH: *Christ among the Teachers; Abraham Dismissing Hagar; Isaac Blessing Jacob in the Presence of Rebecca* - OBERSCHLEISSHEIM: *Abigail before King David* - OLDENBURG: *Satyr and Peasant* - PARIS (Louvre): *Anna and Elcana Sacrifice their Son to the Lord; The Infant Samuel brought by Hanna to Eli* - PRAGUE: *Eleazar and Rebecca at the Well* - ROME (Gal. Nazionale): *Christ at Emmaus* - ROTTERDAM: *Ruth and Boaz* - ST PETERSBURG (Hermitage): *Sacrifice of King Jeroboam; Two Officers; A Scholar; Four Children in a Park; The Family of Darius before Alexander; Jacob and Rachel Learn of the Death of Joseph* - STOCKHOLM: *The Satyr and the Peasant; Sacrifice of Abraham; The Angel and Gideon* - STOCKHOLM (Kungliga Husgerådskammaren): *Portrait of a Woman* - THE HAGUE (Koninklijke Bibliotheek): *Adoration of the Magi; Flight into Egypt* - VIENNA: *Jacob's Dream* - VIENNA (Czernin): *Judah and Tamar; Arrest of Tamar* - VIENNA (Liechtenstein Mus.): *King at his Meal, Biblical Scene* - VIENNA (Stummer Collection): *Young Woman at her Toilette* - WARSAW: *An Angel Appears to Jacob*.

AUCTION RECORDS:

PARIS, 7 Feb 1898, *Returning from the Market*, FRF 50. PARIS, 22-24 April 1901, *Portrait of a Man*, FRF 850; *The Farm*, FRF 1,950. AMSTERDAM, 22 June 1910, *Little Boy Lying Down*, NLG 1,025. PARIS, 8-10 June 1920, *Adoration of the Magi* (Indian ink) FRF 950. PARIS, 18 Dec 1920, *Portrait of a Man Wearing a Cap*, FRF 1,750. PARIS, 28 Feb 1921, *Eliezar and Rebecca*, FRF 5,700. PARIS, 23 March 1921, *Portrait of a Rabbi*, FRF 420. LONDON, 25 Nov 1921, *Messenger of the Queen of Sheba before Solomon*, GBP 7. LONDON, 24 Feb 1922, *Hagar Dismissed*, GBP 7. LONDON, 8-9 March 1922, *Crowning of the Victor*, GBP 21. LONDON, 26 June 1922, *The Calling of St Matthew*, GBP 8. LONDON, 28 July 1922, *Mercury and Argus*, GBP 23. LONDON, 15 Dec 1922, *Rembrandt's Picture Framer*, GBP 10. LONDON, 23 Feb 1923, *Joseph and the Wife of Potiphar*, GBP 73. PARIS, 4 Feb 1924, *Portrait of a Man in a Brown Coat*, FRF 990. LONDON, 27 April 1925, *Isaac Blessing Jacob*, GBP 8. LONDON, 26 June 1925, *Sacrifice of Isaac*, GBP 18. LONDON, 4 Dec 1925, *Eliezar Leading Rebecca to Abraham*, GBP 336. LONDON, 8 Feb 1926, *The Angel Appears to Abraham*, GBP 16. LONDON, 19 May 1926, *Philosopher*, GBP 54. LONDON, 25 Oct 1928, *Esther before Ahasuerus*, GBP 5. LONDON, 5 Dec 1928, *Angels and Tobias Finding Fish*, GBP 16. LONDON, 7 June 1929, *Portrait of a Man Wearing Black with a White Collar* (1664) GBP 99. PARIS, 26 May 1933, *The Guards*, FRF 1,350. PARIS, 11 July 1941, *Christ in the Garden of Gethsemane*, FRF 7,000. PARIS, 4 Dec 1941, *Christ in Gethsemane*, FRF 5,000. LONDON, 5 Dec 1941, *Parable of the Loaves and Fishes; The Sermon on the Mount* (two panels) GBP 42. LONDON, 2 Oct 1942, *Christ before Pontius Pilate*, GBP 52. LONDON, 13 July 1945, *St Peter and St Paul* (1667) GBP 378. LONDON, 26 June 1946, *The Young Philosopher*, GBP 110. LONDON, 29 Nov 1946, *Adoration of the Magi*, GBP 399. LONDON, 31 Jan 1947, *Head of an Elderly Woman*, GBP 47. PARIS, 18 Nov 1953, *Ruth and Boaz*, FRF 150,000. NEW YORK, 12 Oct 1963, *Portrait of a Monk*, USD 1,200. LONDON, 17 July 1964, *Jacob*, Gns 850. AMSTERDAM, 3 Nov 1965, *Portrait of a Rabbi*, NLG 8,000. LUCERNE, 7 Dec 1965, *Biblical Scene* (watercolour) CHF 5,000. AMSTERDAM, 12 May 1971, *Joseph Recounting his Dreams*, NLG 8,000. VIENNA, 21 March 1972, *Tavern Scene* (1673) ATS 150,000. LONDON, 9 May 1973, *Family Group*, GBP 2,200. COLOGNE, 22 Nov 1973, *The Musical Hour*, DEM 23,000. COPENHAGEN, 9 Nov 1977, *The Huntress Diana* (oil on panel, 25 1/2 x 19 3/4 ins / 65 x 50 cm) DKK 16,300. AMSTERDAM, 17 Nov 1980, *Rebecca Arriving in the House of Isaac* (pen/paper, 6 1/2 x 9 1/2 ins / 16.2 x 24.3 cm) NLG 30,000. NEW YORK, 18 Jan 1984, *Oriental Horseman* (pen and brown ink, 6 1/4 x 5 1/4 ins / 16 x 13.6 cm) USD 7,250. MONTE CARLO, 15 June 1986, *Isaac and Rebecca at the Well of King Lahau* (1665, oil on canvas, 50 3/4 x 67 1/4 ins / 129 x 171 cm) FRF 1,700,000. PARIS, 18 Nov 1987, *Mercury and Argus* (1672, oil on canvas, 16 1/4 x 12 1/2 ins / 41.5 x 32 cm) FRF 80,000. NEW YORK, 2 June 1989, *Ruth and Boaz* (1672, oil on canvas, 58 1/4 x 66 ins / 148 x 167.5 cm) USD 88,000. LONDON, 24 May 1991, *The Six Children of Altetus Tolling and Aleid Jansson Posing for a Pastoral* (1667, oil on canvas, 56 1/4 x 67 ins / 142.8 x 170 cm) GBP 82,500. LONDON, 2 July 1991, *The Circumcision* (ink and wash, 3 3/4 x 6 ins / 9.5 x 14.4 cm) GBP 4,950. LONDON, 1 April 1992, *Ruth and Boaz* (1663, oil on panel, 13 3/4 x 14 1/4 ins / 34.8 x 36.3 cm) GBP 6,050. LONDON, 15 April 1992, *Soldiers Playing Backgammon in an Interior* (1651, oil on canvas, 17 1/4 x 15 ins / 43.8 x 37.8 cm) GBP 340,000. AMSTERDAM, 15 Nov 1994, *Young Man Seated near a Barrel with a Pitcher in his Hand* (ink and wash/paper, 9 1/2 x 6 1/2 ins / 23.9 x 16.5 cm) NLG 5,750. NEW YORK, 11 Jan 1995, *Young Boy Wearing a Hat, Seated, with Elbows Resting on the Back of his Chair and his Chin in the Hollow of his Hand* (ink and wash/buff-coloured paper, 5 1/2 x 4 1/2 ins / 14 x 11.5 cm) USD 365,500. PARIS, 4 Dec 1995, *Baptism of the Eunuch* (oil on panel, 23 1/4 x 32 1/4 ins / 59 x 82 cm) FRF 100,000. BRUSSELS, 22 Feb 1999, *Raising of Lazarus* (1669, oil on canvas, 47 x 80 ins / 120 x 203 cm) BEF 210,000. AMSTERDAM, 10 Nov 1999, *Bearded Figure Wearing Turban and Fur Coat* (pen, brown ink and brown wash, 10 x 7 ins / 25 x 18 cm) NLG 55,000. LONDON, 7 July 2000, *Elegant Company Playing Cards in an Interior with Painting of Venus and Cupid* (1652, oil on canvas, 20 x 24 ins / 51 x 61 cm) GBP 150,000. AMSTERDAM, 8 Nov 2000, *Potiphar's Wife Falsely Accuses Joseph* (pen, brown ink wash, red chalk, 9 x 8 ins / 23 x 20 cm) NLG 44,000. NEW YORK, 25 Jan 2001, *Tobit and Anna* (1652, oil on canvas, 19 x 15 ins / 48 x 39 cm) USD 30,000. LONDON, 26 April 2001, *An Interior with Soldiers Playing Backgammon around a Table* (oil on canvas, 17 x 20 ins / 42 x 50 cm) GBP 14,000. LONDON, 10 July 2002, *Jadah and Hira the Adullamite* (1671, oil on canvas, 24 x 28 ins / 61 x 72 cm) GBP 120,000. LONDON, 10 July 2002, *Guardroom Scene with Two Soldiers Playing* (1653, oil on canvas, 20 x 26 ins / 52 x 65 cm) GBP 280,000. PARIS, 27 March 2003, *Circumcision* (pen and ink wash, 4 x 6 ins / 9 x 14 cm) EUR 6,000. VENICE, 3 May 2003, *Deposition* (oil on board, 10 x 8 ins / 26 x 20 cm) EUR 3,000. NEW YORK, 22 Jan 2004, *Volumnia Pleading with her Son to Spare Rome* (1674, oil on canvas, 81 x 67 ins / 207 x 170 cm) USD 50,000.

EECKHOUT, Jakob Joseph

Flemish, 19th century.

Born 6 February 1793, in Antwerp; died 25 December 1861, in Paris.

Painter, lithographer. History painting, portraits, genre scenes.

Flemish School.

Jakob Joseph Eeckhout was a jeweller and only turned to painting at the age of 28. He became director of the academy in The Hague in 1839. He settled in Paris. The museum in Montpellier holds a painting under the name of Eukhout which could well be by Jakob Joseph Eeckhout.

MUSEUMS AND GALLERIES:

AMSTERDAM: *Marriage of Jaqueline von Bayern to Jean IV, Duke of Brabant* - ANTWERP: *Portrait of the Artist* - BAYEUX: *Portrait of Luthereau* - DOUAI: *Farmer Surprised by Storm* - MONTPELLIER (?) - YPRES: *Jacques-Albert Senove.*

AUCTION RECORDS:

LONDON, 23-24 March 1922, *The Raising of Lazarus* (drawing) GBP 3. PARIS, 28-29 Nov 1923, *Reading Lesson*, FRF 1,080. LONDON, 25 Oct 1928, *Hassele and Vischer, Members of the Alvas Board, Leaving Prison in 1577*, GBP 21. LONDON, 16 Dec 1935, *Woman at Spinning Wheel; Reading the News* (series) GBP 15. LONDON, 13 Nov 1936, *Basket Workers*, GBP 6. LONDON, 10 May 1937, *Adoration of the Magi*, GBP 30. PARIS, 11 Jan 1943, *Young Sculptor Working in Lamp Light*, FRF 4,500. PARIS, 4 Dec 1944, *Reading from the Bible*, FRF 20,000. AMSTERDAM, 15 Nov 1976, *Merry Company on a Terrace* (oil on panel, 8 3/4 x 12 3/4 ins / 22.5 x 32.5 cm) NLG 13,000. ZURICH, 26 May 1978, *The Blind Violinist* (oil on canvas, 21 3/4 x 27 1/2 ins / 55.5 x 70 cm) CHF 26,000. LONDON, 2 April 1980, *Charity* (oil on panel, 15 x 11 ins / 38 x 28 cm) GBP 320. LONDON, 11 May 1984, *Young Woman and her Dogs in an Interior* (oil on panel, 28 1/2 x 23 1/4 ins / 72.5 x 59 cm) GBP 3,000. BRUSSELS, 18 May 1987, *Tavern Scene* (oil on panel, 28 x 39 1/4 ins / 71 x 100 cm) BEF 320,000. AMSTERDAM, 5-6 Nov 1991, *Soldier Returning* (oil on panel, 10 x 13 1/2 ins / 25.5 x 34.5 cm) NLG 1,495. PARIS, 16 Dec 1991, *Portrait of Mr Chesnaye as a Huntsman* (1845, oil on canvas, 57 1/2 x 49 1/4 ins / 146 x 125 cm) FRF 66,000. NEW YORK, 5 June 1992, *Portrait of Mr Chesnaye* (1845, oil on canvas, 57 1/2 x 49 1/4 ins / 146.1 x 125.1 cm) USD 15,950. AMSTERDAM, 2 Nov 1992, *Young Woman Arranging a Bouquet of Flowers in a Vase with a Parrot Nearby* (oil on panel, 11 3/4 x 9 ins / 30 x 23 cm) NLG 5,750. NEW YORK, 24 May 1995, *Children Playing Fancy Dress* (1824, oil on panel, 21 1/2 x 24 3/4 ins / 54.6 x 62.9 cm) USD 40,250. PARIS, 28 June 1999, *Huntsman Having Lunch. Romantic Rendez-vous. Blind Man's Buff* (oil on canvas, after Carl van Loo and others, set of four, 32 x 39 ins / 82 x 99 cm) FRF 140,000. BRUSSELS, 19 March 2001, *Small Fisherman Meeting an Elegant Man and his Daughter* (oil on panel, 40 x 31 ins / 101 x 79 cm) BEF 380,000. DUBLIN, 5 Sept 2001, *Cherry Party* (oil on canvas, 26 x 22 ins / 65 x 56 cm) IEP 3,000. LONDON, 14 Nov 2002, *Rescued from the Sea* (1859, oil on panel, 31 x 28 ins / 79 x 70 cm) GBP 3,800. LOKEREN, 17 May 2003, *Parting* (1836, oil on canvas, 33 x 26 ins / 84 x 67 cm) EUR 3,300.

EECKHOUT, Victor

Flemish, 19th century.

Born 1821, in Antwerp; died 1879, in Antwerp.

Painter, watercolourist, engraver. Genre scenes, local scenes, figures.

Flemish School.

The pupil of his father Jakob Joseph Eeckhout, Victor Eeckhout exhibited a number of times in Brussels and Paris. His preferred medium was etched engraving.

AUCTION RECORDS:

COLOGNE, 12 Nov 1976, *Painter and Model* (1859, oil on canvas, 34 1/2 x 27 3/4 ins / 87.5 x 70.5 cm) DEM 3,500. LONDON, 2 Nov 1979, *Arabian Procession* (oil on canvas, 10 x 14 ins / 25.4 x 35.6 cm) GBP 1,700. LONDON, 21 Oct 1983, *Arabs at the Wells* (oil on panel, 10 x 7 1/2 ins / 25.5 x 19 cm) GBP 1,400. LONDON, 8 Feb 1985, *Street Scene, Fez* (oil on panel, 11 1/4 x 15 1/2 ins / 28.5 x 39.4 cm) GBP 2,800. BERN, 26 Oct 1988, *Moroccan Huntsman in Winter Landscape* (oil on canvas, 19 1/2 x 14 1/2 ins / 49.5 x 37 cm) CHF 2,000. NEW YORK, 14 Oct 1993, *Moroccan Soldier* (1878, watercolour/card, 13 3/4 x 9 1/2 ins / 34.9 x 24.2 cm) USD 863. LONDON, 1 Nov 2001, *Religious Procession, Tangiers* (oil on board, 13 x 16 ins / 32 x 40 cm) GBP 1,800. VANCOUVER, 11 June 2002, *Letter* (oil on panel, 29 x 20 ins / 74 x 51 cm) CAD 4,300. PARIS, 24 March 2003, *Moroccan*

Man from Tangiers (watercolour and gouache, 8 x 6 ins / 21 x 15 cm) EUR 1,800.

EECKMAN, Eustachius
Flemish, 17th - 18th century.
Born 14 October 1668, in Ghent; died 16 April 1761, in St-Pieters, near Ghent.
Sculptor.
Flemish School.

Eustachius Eeckman qualified as a master in 1694.

EEDEN, Nicolas van den
Belgian, 19th - 20th century.
Born 30 September 1856, in Ghent; died 1918.
Painter, lithographer. Figures, portraits, scenes with figures, genre scenes, church interiors.

Eeden lived in Brussels and Namur, where he became director of the art academy. He started out as a lithographer, later turning to painting. He exhibited at the Paris Salon several times.

MUSEUMS AND GALLERIES:
BRUSSELS: *Rogier on his Deathbed* - GHENT: *Vespers at Ste-Gudule* - LOUVAIN: *Auction in the Market* - MONS (MBA): *At Prayer* - NAMUR: *Lady with Camellias* - TERMONDE: *At Church*.

EEDT, Henrich van der
Flemish, 17th century.
Active in Antwerp.
Painter.
Flemish School.

Henrich van der Eedt was a pupil of Adam van Noort and became a master in 1610.

EEDT, Nicolaus van der, or Heedt
Flemish, 17th century.
Active in Antwerp.
Painter.
Flemish School.

Nicolaus van der Eedt became a master in 1651.

EEGBERG, H. H.
Danish, 18th century.
Painter.

Between 1747 and 1750, Eegberg received payment from the king for 33 paintings.

EEGHEM, Henri van, or Eghem
Dutch, 16th century.
Active in Mechelen.
Sculptor.

In 1550, Henri van Eeghem was paid 400 florins for his work on the tomb of Margaret of Austria, which he undertook with with M. Smets.

EEGHEM, J. van
Dutch, 19th century.
Active in Amsterdam.
Painter, art dealer, collector. Landscapes.

EEGHEM, Lievin van, or Eghem
Flemish, 17th century.
Born before 1605; died 14 February 1638.
Active in Mechelen.
Sculptor, painter.
Flemish School.

Lievin van Eeghem was a member of the Guild of St Luke.

EEKMAN, Nicolas Mathieu
Belgian, 20th century.
Born 1889, in Brussels; died 1973, in Paris.
Also active in France.
Painter, watercolourist, engraver, lithographer. Figure compositions, nudes, portraits.

Eekman trained in architecture at the Académie de Bruxelles, but gave it up in favour of painting. During World War I he lived in the Netherlands, where he worked on various techniques, specialising in wood engraving. He later moved to Paris where he took part in group exhibitions.

His works were firmly figurative. Early on he was influenced by Surrealism, moving towards Expressionism from 1960 onwards. His style is very distinctive due to the fact that he takes subjects painted by Pieter Brueghel and Hieronymus Bosch and gives them a subtler treatment using blackish-brown tones, perhaps with more detail.

Eekman

MUSEUMS AND GALLERIES:
MOSCOW (Central Army Mus.) - PARIS (BNF, Prints Collection) - PARIS (Mus. de la Ville) - ROTTERDAM (Mus. Boijmans Van Beuningen).

AUCTION RECORDS:
VERSAILLES, 11 June 1965, *Young Woman and Old Woman*, FRF 3,800. ANTWERP, 22 Oct 1974, *Herring Eaters* (1961) BEF 32,000. VERSAILLES, 27 Nov 1977, *Hanged Man* (1943, oil on canvas, 28¾ x 36¼ ins / 73 x 92 cm) FRF 10,000. ANTWERP, 26 Oct 1982, *Nude between two Masks* (watercolour, 15¼ x 11 ins / 39 x 27 cm) BEF 28,000. BRUSSELS, 15 Dec 1983, *The Bird Charmers* (1950, oil on panel, 19¾ x 25¼ ins / 50 x 64 cm) BEF 140,000. ÉPINAL, 16 Dec 1984, *Barrel Organ* (1929, pencil, 32 x 21¼ ins / 81 x 54 cm) FRF 7,800. LOKEREN, 1 June 1985, *Grace* (watercolour, 15 x 17¾ ins / 38 x 45 cm) BEF 46,000. BRUSSELS, 17 Dec 1987, *Old Fishermen Sitting on the Quay* (1953, oil on card, 19¼ x 28¼ ins / 49 x 72 cm) BEF 200,000. PARIS, 12 April 1991, *The Ferryman* (lead pencil/paper/canvas, 38¼ x 44 ins / 97 x 112 cm) FRF 18,000. PARIS, 14 Feb 1992, *Fantastic Fishing in Saint Jean-de-Luz* (oil on canvas, 13 x 16¼ ins / 33 x 41 cm) FRF 13,000. PARIS, 3 July 1992, *Two Nudes with Fruit* (oil/hardboard, 24 x 19¾ ins / 61 x 50 cm) FRF 25,000. LOKEREN, 10 Oct 1992, *The Goodbye* (watercolour and pen, 17¾ x 12 ins / 45 x 30.5 cm) BEF 44,000. AMSTERDAM, 9 Dec 1993, *Composition with Figures on a Staircase* (black chalk and pencil/paper/card, 29¼ x 21½ ins / 74 x 54.7 cm) NLG 2,875. LOKEREN, 12 March 1994, *Barrel Organ* (1929, black chalk, 31½ x 20½ ins / 80 x 52 cm) BEF 65,000. AMSTERDAM, 1 June 1994, *Woman and Flower* (oil on card, 18 x 15 ins / 45.5 x 38 cm) NLG 4,600. LOKEREN, 20 May 1995, *In the Cart* (pastel and ink, 15½ x 22 ins / 39.5 x 56 cm) BEF 60,000. PARIS, 22 Nov 1995, *Waiting* (oil/synthetic resin, 13 x 16¼ ins / 33 x 41 cm) FRF 5,000. AMSTERDAM, 6 Dec 1995, *Mandolin Player in the Port* (1941, oil on canvas, 25½ x 32 ins / 65 x 81.5 cm) NLG 6,900. AMSTERDAM, 10 Dec 1996, *Self-portrait* (1930, oil on canvas, 25½ x 21¼ ins / 65 x 54 cm) NLG 4,382.

EELKEMA, Eelke Jelles
Dutch, 19th century.
Born 8 July 1788, in Leeuwarden; died 27 November 1839, in Leeuwarden.
Painter, watercolourist. Landscapes, still-lifes (fruit/game).

Eelke Jelles Eelkema was brought up in a deaf-mute institution in Groningen. He worked with G. de San. After spending two years in Paris and visiting Switzerland, he went to Haarlem in 1819 and lived in the house of the gardener M. van Eeden. He went to England in 1823 and became blind in 1837.

MUSEUMS AND GALLERIES:
AMSTERDAM: three canvases - HAARLEM (Teylers Mus.): watercolour.

AUCTION RECORDS:
AMSTERDAM, 15 Nov 1976, *Still-life with Fruit* (oil on panel, 28 1/4 x 22 3/4 ins / 72 x 58 cm) NLG 7,200. AMSTERDAM, 30 Oct 1991, *Still-life with Peaches and Grapes on an Entablature* (oil on panel, 11 1/2 x 13 3/4 ins / 29.5 x 35 cm) NLG 3,450. AMSTERDAM, 22 April 1992, *Still-life with Partridge Hanging on a Rope and Other Dead Birds on an Entablature* (oil on panel, 15 1/4 x 12 1/2 ins / 39 x 31.5 cm) NLG 1,725. LONDON, 18 Sept 2003, *Summer Flowers in a Vase on a Ledge. Fruit on a Marble Ledge* (oil on canvas, 22 x 18 ins / 57 x 46 cm) GBP 15,000.

EEM, Aert or Arnoldus van der
Dutch, 17th century.
Active in Utrecht.
Painter.
In 1611 Aert Eem was one of the founders of the new Lucas guild, and in 1627 he became director of Hiob hospital.

EEM, Cornelis van der
Dutch, 17th century.
Active in Utrecht.
Painter.

EEMANN. See **EHEMANN**

EEMANS, Marc or Marcel
Belgian, 20th century.
Born 1907, in Termonde.
Painter.
Constructivism.
Belgian Surrealist Group.
Eemans trained at the Académie de Molenbeek St-Jean and the Académie de Bruxelles. In 1922 he met Servanckx and joined the first Belgian Constructivist group. He was also a poet and an art historian who wrote several works on modern art in Belgium.

His first abstract paintings date from 1922. In around 1926 he abandoned the abstract approach, regarding this period as an aesthetic mistake. He then moved towards a type of 'different Surrealism' and became a member of the first Belgian Surrealist group. The works from his abstract period have a spiritual dimension which can also be found in his Surrealist paintings. The works from this later period are hard to categorise, but their style can maybe best be described as magical realism. The mystical aura is reminiscent of the English Pre-Raphaelites, the German Romantics and the fin-de-siècle Symbolists.

MUSEUMS AND GALLERIES:
BRUSSELS (Bibliothèque royale Albert Ier, Prints Collection) - GHENT (Stedelijk Mus. voor Actuele Kunst).

AUCTION RECORDS:
PARIS, 29 Nov 1972, *Aux Frontières de l'Oiseau* (*At the Frontiers of Birds*) (1928) FRF 16,000. PARIS, 26 Nov 1973, *Tragic Friend*, FRF 14,000. ANTWERP, 20 Oct 1976, *Nude* (collage, 13 x 10 1/4 ins / 33 x 26 cm) BEF 7,500. BRUSSELS, 21 May 1981, *Interrogation* (1928, oil on canvas, 18 x 22 ins / 46 x 55 cm) BEF 20,000. ANTWERP, 3 April 1984, *Archer* (1928, oil on canvas, 28 3/4 x 23 1/2 ins / 73 x 60 cm) BEF 42,000. LOKEREN, 21 March 1992, *The Attitude of Appearances* (1928, oil on canvas, 51 1/4 x 38 1/4 ins / 130 x 97 cm) BEF 260,000.

EEMONT, Adriaen van
Dutch, 17th century.
Born c. 1627, in Dordrecht; died 1662, in Dordrecht.
Painter.
Adriaen van Eemont painted landscapes and birds, and seems to have enjoyed a certain reputation.

AUCTION RECORDS:
LONDON, 30 Oct 1997, *The Tomb of the Planti on the Anio, near Rome, with Peasants on a Bridge* (oil on panel, 18 1/2 x 26 ins / 46.7 x 65.9 cm) GBP 12,650.

EEMONT, Maria
Maiden name: Cauer
Dutch, 17th century.
Died 1667, in Middelburg.
Painter. Landscapes.
Maria Eemont was the wife of Adriaen van Eemont.

EEMST, Michiel van
Dutch, 17th century.
Died 17th century, in Haarlem.
Potter.
Michiel van Eemst settled in Delft where he became a member of the painters' guild in 1675.

EEMSTEDE, Thierry de, or Heemstede, called Thierry de Haarlem
Dutch, 16th century.
Died 3 April 1542.
Miniaturist.
Thierry de Eemstede became a Carthusian monk in Louvain on 17 January 1505. He was also a calligrapher.

EEPOEL, Diane
Belgian, 20th - 21st century.
Born 1949.
Painter, screen printer. Murals.
Eepoel attended the École Nationale Supérieure des Arts in La Cambre and the Académie in Watermael-Boitsfort. She has produced many murals in Belgium and Brazil.

EERELMAN, Otto
Dutch, 19th century.
Born 23 March 1839, in Groningen; died 1926.
Active in The Hague and Arnhem.
Painter (gouache), watercolourist, draughtsman.
History painting, genre scenes, animals.
Otto Eerelman was a pupil of J. H. Egenberger.

MUSEUMS AND GALLERIES:
AMSTERDAM: *Entry of Queen Wilhelmina in Amsterdam in 1898*.

AUCTION RECORDS:
AMSTERDAM, 17-18 Dec 1946, *Morning Promenade*, NLG 1,350. AMSTERDAM, 28 Nov 1967, *Figures in an Interior*, NLG 18,300. AMSTERDAM, 12 May 1972, *Queen Wilhelmina*, NLG 8,000. NEW YORK, 9 Oct 1974, *Village Celebration*, USD 6,000. NEW YORK, 14 May 1976, *Danish Mastiff with Young* (oil on canvas, 35 1/2 x 51 1/4 ins / 90 x 130 cm) USD 9,500. NEW YORK, 12 May 1978, *Cavalier and Young Peasant Woman* (1880, oil on panel, 22 1/4 x 16 ins / 56.5 x 40.5 cm) USD 4,750. AMSTERDAM, 1 Oct 1981, *Horse Market* (watercolour, 15 1/4 x 27 ins / 39 x 68.5 cm) NLG 13,000. NEW YORK, 26 Oct 1983, *Saddled Horse* (oil on canvas, 18 x 27 1/2 ins / 46 x 70 cm) USD 10,750. AMSTERDAM, 19 Nov 1985, *Puppies* (oil on canvas, 18 x 23 1/2 ins / 46 x 60 cm) NLG 9,000. LONDON, 19 June 1986, *Horseguards, Whitehall* (watercolour and gouache, 29 x 21 ins / 73.5 x 53.2 cm) GBP 2,600. AMSTERDAM, 3 May 1988, *Borzoi Dog in an Interior* (oil on panel, 8 1/4 x 12 1/4 ins / 21 x 31 cm) NLG 6,325. AMSTERDAM, 16 Nov 1988, *A Bloodhound* (watercolour and gouache/paper, 25 1/2 x 17 ins / 65 x 43 cm) NLG 4,600. NEW YORK, 25 Oct 1989, *Afternoon at the Beach* (watercolour and gouache, 18 1/2 x 29 ins / 47 x 73.6 cm) USD 20,900. AMSTERDAM, 10 April 1990, *The Delayed Companion* (ink and watercolour heightened with white/paper, 13 3/4 x 19 3/4 ins / 35 x 50 cm) NLG 11,500. AMSTERDAM, 30 Oct 1990, *Elegant Young Woman in an Ornately Decorated Harnessed Sleigh before the Snow-clad Steps of a House* (oil on canvas, 23 1/2 x 35 1/2 ins / 60 x 90 cm) NLG 51,750. AMSTERDAM, 24 April 1991, *Rustic Wedding Festivities* (oil on canvas, 37 1/2 x 55 1/4 ins / 95.5 x 140.5 cm) NLG 172,500. AMSTERDAM, 30 Oct 1991, *Pleasures of Winter: Richly Dressed Citizens Watching Skaters* (oil on canvas, 35 x 59 1/4 ins / 88 x 150.5 cm) NLG

80,500. AMSTERDAM, 2-3 Nov 1992, *St Bernard Puppies* (oil on canvas, 17 1/4 x 23 ins / 43.5 x 58.5 cm) NLG 23,000. AMSTERDAM, 19 Oct 1993, *Horse Racing* (oil on canvas, 20 3/4 x 32 ins / 53 x 81 cm) NLG 25,300. AMSTERDAM, 8 Nov 1994, *Amazon* (oil on panel, 9 3/4 x 8 1/4 ins / 25 x 21 cm) NLG 7,130. NEW YORK, 9 June 1995, *Study of Grey and Bay Horses* (oil on canvas/synthetic resin, 29 x 36 ins / 73.7 x 91.4 cm) USD 3,737. LONDON, 18 Dec 1997, *St Bernard Puppies* (oil on canvas, 12 1/2 x 16 ins / 31.8 x 40.6 cm) GBP 13,225. AMSTERDAM, 27 April 1999, *Fascinating Encounter* (oil on canvas, 35 x 51 ins / 90 x 130 cm) NLG 260,000. LOKEREN, 9 Oct 1999, *In the Winter Garden* (watercolour, 20 x 14 ins / 52 x 35 cm) BEF 260,000. AMSTERDAM, 18 April 2000, *Parade for the Commander in Chief of the Royal Netherlands Horse Artillery during a Field Exercise* (1912, oil on canvas, 28 x 39 ins / 70 x 100 cm) NLG 80,000. AMSTERDAM, 24 Oct 2000, *Jacoba van Beieren with her Horse* (oil on canvas, 45 x 38 ins / 115 x 96 cm) NLG 90,000. AMSTERDAM, 24 April 2001, *Little Intruders* (pencil and watercolour heightened with white, 14 x 21 ins / 35 x 54 cm) NLG 38,000. LONDON, 19 Nov 2001, *Preparing the Sleigh* (oil on canvas, 23 x 35 ins / 58 x 88 cm) GBP 15,000. AMSTERDAM, 23 April 2002, *Circus Girl Grooming the Horses* (oil on panel, 17 x 26 ins / 43 x 66 cm) EUR 42,000. AMSTERDAM, 24 April 2002, *Riding Tour on a Sunny Afternoon* (oil on canvas, 18 x 14 ins / 45 x 35 cm) EUR 35,000. AMSTERDAM, 29 April 2003, *Courteous Greeting* (oil on canvas, 24 x 35 ins / 60 x 90 cm) EUR 34,000. AMSTERDAM, 28 Oct 2003, *Two Pointers - Hans and Spot on the Heath* (oil on canvas, 24 x 35 ins / 60 x 90 cm) EUR 16,000. AMSTERDAM, 20 April 2004, *St Bernard Puppy* (oil on canvas, 11 x 14 ins / 27 x 35 cm) EUR 22,000. AMSTERDAM, 21 April 2004, *Duitse dwerg pinchers* (oil on canvas, 11 x 18 ins / 29 x 45 cm) EUR 8,000.

EERENBROECK, Gommaer van, or Nerenbroeck
Flemish School, 16th century.
Died c. 1554.
Active in Antwerp.
Painter.

EERENBROECK, Jan van
Flemish School, 16th century.
Painter.
Antwerp School.

Jan van Eerenbroeck became a master painter in 1505.

EERNSTMAN, Tjeerd
Dutch, 19th century.
Born 1801, in Leeuwarden.
Painter. Genre scenes, portraits.

Tjeerd Eernstman was a pupil of W. B. van der Kooi.

EERTVELT, Andries van, or Aertveld, Arteveldt, Artvelt, Ertvelt
Dutch, 17th century.
Born 1590, in Antwerp; died 1652.
Painter. Battles, figures, seascapes.

Andries van Eertvelt went to Italy and spent some time in Genoa. In 1632 van Dyck painted his portrait, now in the gallery in Augsburg. His seascapes reveal a visual acuity which makes him stand out in Dutch marine painting of the period. Few of his works are extant.

MUSEUMS AND GALLERIES:

BERGUES: *Battle of Lepanto* - GRAZ: *Canal in Holland* - VALENCIENNES: *Seascape* - VIENNA (Österreichische Gal. Belvedere): *Seascape*.

AUCTION RECORDS:

LONDON, 21 May 1976, *French Frigates Bombing Town* (oil on canvas, 27 3/4 x 44 ins / 70.5 x 112 cm) GBP 1,300. LONDON, 28 Oct 1977, *Young Physicist in Laboratory* (oil on canvas, 35 1/2 x 44 ins / 90 x 112 cm) GBP 6,500. LONDON, 26 May 1978, *Sea Battle* (oil on canvas, 58 x 81 ins / 147.5 x 206 cm) GBP 3,000. NEW YORK, 30 May 1979, *Boats in High Sea* (oil on panel, 18 x 31 1/2 ins / 46 x 80 cm) USD 8,500. AMSTERDAM, 14 Nov 1983, *Seaside with Round Tower with Figures; Seaside Scene* (gouache, a pair, 7 1/2 x 9 1/4 ins / 19.2 x 23.5 cm) NLG 14,000. LONDON, 19 Feb 1986, *Boats off Mountainous Coast* (1630, oil on panel, 7 1/4 x 14 1/4 ins / 18.7 x 36.5 cm) GBP 10,000. PARIS, 26 June 1989, *Dutch Fleet at Anchor in Northern Port; The Battle of Lepanto in 1591* (oil on canvas, two pendants, 46 3/4 x 88 ins / 119 x 223.5 cm) FRF 2,600,000. NEW YORK, 10 Jan 1990, *Sea Battle between Dutch Fleet and Barbary Pirates* (oil on canvas, 28 3/4 x 39 ins / 73 x 99.1 cm) USD 44,000. AMSTERDAM, 12 June. 1990, *Dutch Three-masted Ships in Storm* (oil on panel, 7 3/4 x 14 1/4 ins / 19.8 x 36.4 cm) NLG 48,300. PARIS, 27 June 1991, *Sea Battle* (oil on panel, 19 3/4 x 32 ins / 50 x 81.5 cm) FRF 50,000. AMSTERDAM, 7 May 1992, *Frigate in Levantine Port with Sailors Unloading Cargo and Sea Battle in Background* (oil on panel, 9 1/2 x 24 ins / 24 x 60.8 cm) NLG 4,600. MONACO, 2 Dec 1994, *Sea Battle* (oil on panel, 17 1/4 x 26 3/4 ins / 43.5 x 68 cm) FRF 149,850. LONDON, 7 Dec 1994, *Navigating in Wild Sea* (oil on panel, 23 1/2 x 46 ins / 59.5 x 116 cm) GBP 17,250. NEW YORK, 12 Jan 1995, *Fleet of the Dutch East India Company Returning to Amsterdam* (oil/copper, 17 x 26 1/2 ins / 43.2 x 67.3 cm) USD 189,500. LONDON, 5 April 1995, *Dutch Vessels in Raging Sea* (oil on panel, 24 1/2 x 42 1/4 ins / 62.5 x 107 cm) GBP 12,650. PARIS, 20 June 1997, *Seascape in Storm* (oak panel, 17 1/2 x 24 1/2 ins / 44.5 x 62 cm) FRF 160,000. PARIS, 19 March 1999, *Turkish Vessels in Harbour* (oil on panel, 28 x 41 ins / 72 x 103 cm) FRF 57,000. VIENNA, 24 March 1999, *Three-master and Other Ships on Southern Coast* (oil on canvas, 40 x 62 ins / 101 x 157 cm) ATS 140,000. PARIS, 18 Dec 2000, *Seascape with Ships near the Shore* (oil on panel, 28 x 41 ins / 72 x 104 cm) FRF 70,000. AMSTERDAM, 14 May 2002, *Coastal Landscape with Frigates and Soldiers in a Breeze* (oil on canvas, 36 x 53 ins / 91 x 134 cm) EUR 19,000. LONDON, 9 July 2002, *Naval Engagement between Spanish and Dutch Ships* (oil on panel, 18 x 24 ins / 45 x 61 cm) GBP 4,500.

EF ZAMBO, Istvan
Hungarian, 20th - 21st century.
Born 1950, in Salgotarjanvier.
Painter. Landscapes.
Art'Eria Group.

Istvan Ef Zambo studied art at the Layota Studio. He is one of the best-known members of the Szentendre movement's Art'Eria Gallery. He also exhibits in the gallery of the Young Artists' Studio and has shown his work outside Hungary in Hamburg (1983) and Uppsala (1988). His painting technique is close to Naive and he uses it as a vehicle for his concerns, which are closely linked to the tragic events of his times.

AUCTION RECORDS:

PARIS, 14 Oct 1991, *Red Landscape* (1991, oil on paper, 23 1/2 x 47 1/4 ins / 60 x 120 cm) FRF 8,000. BUDAPEST, 12 Oct 2001, *Head with a Bone* (acrylic on board, 39 x 28 ins / 100 x 70 cm) HUF 750,000.

EFFEL, Jean, pseudonym of Lejeune, François
French, 20th century.
Born 12 February 1908, in Paris; died 11 October 1982, in Paris.
Draughtsman, humorist, illustrator.

Jean Effel began as a caricaturist of politicians. In the 1950s he worked on the *Figaro Littéraire*. Without abandoning politics, keeping 'Marianne' commenting on daily events, he enjoyed teasing the academies. Then with cheerful scepticism he brought God Himself, bearded and friendly, on stage, frequently chatting with Adam and Eve in *The Creation of the World*. After the beginning of the 1939-1945 war he never made caricatures of any politician but De Gaulle, whom he called *L'Unique*, 'the Only One'. He published some 17,000 sketches and 180 books.

EFFENBERG, Hans
German, 16th century.
Painter.
Breslau School.

Hans Effenberg became a master painter in 1507.

EFFENBERGER, Hermann
German, 19th - 20th century.
Born 14 September 1842, in Lauban (now Luban, Poland); died 1911, in Rome.
Painter. Religious subjects, figures, portraits.

Effenberger trained at the Dresden art academy and under Schnorr and Andreae. He continued his studies at the Antwerp art academy, and travelled in Germany and Italy. He worked mainly in Leipzig and Rome. He is known for *Shepherd Praying, Portrait of Emperor Friedrich III, Young Neapolitan Girl,* and *The Birth of Christ.*

EFFINGER, Léon J.
French, 20th century.
Painter. Landscapes with figures, still-lifes, flowers.

AUCTION RECORDS:
PARIS, 23 Dec 1942, *Short Arm of the Seine at Villennes,* FRF 20,000. PARIS, 23 June 1943, *The Bridge,* FRF 35,100. PARIS, 10 Nov 1943, *Vase of Flowers,* FRF 8,000. PARIS, 6 Dec 1943, *Outing in a Boat,* FRF 4,000. PARIS, 29 June 1945, *Cup of Tea,* FRF 74,500.

EFFINGER VON WILDEGG, Ludwig Rudolf
Swiss, 19th century.
Born 25 February 1803, in Bern; died 29 May 1872, probably in Bern.
Painter, draughtsman.

Ludwig Effinger von Wildegg spent time in Paris, Italy, England and Vienna. In the latter city he made frequent visits to the studios of Ranftl and Ammerling. He painted genre and historical subjects and exhibited between 1840 and 1850. He was the founder and director of the Bern Canton Artistic Union in 1854.

EFFLATOUN, Inji
Egyptian, 20th century.
Born 1925, in Cairo; died 1989.
Painter. Figure compositions, figures, genre scenes, landscapes, flowers.

Inji Efflatoun was self-taught. She painted typically Egyptian landscapes, and was known above all for her paintings of the Egyptian people. These she depicted in a somewhat elliptical style, simplifying details of attitude or facial expression in order to give greater emphasis to the general lines describing the movements of bodies enveloped in long tunics. Her settings and backgrounds are highly ornamented with items associated with the traditional decorative features of fabrics and interiors. Her works *Fellah, Woman at Karbradé* and *Our Daily Bread* clearly indicate her interest in subjects and topics pertaining to daily Egyptian life.

In 1959 she won first prize for *Egyptian Landscape,* and in 1965 was awarded a scholarship from her country's Ministry of Culture.

She began showing at collective exhibitions in 1941 and her works have featured in the following international events: the Venice Biennale (1952 and 1958); São Paulo Biennale (1953); Biennale de la Méditerranée (1960 and 1965); Salon des Indépendants in Paris in 1966; Rome and Paris exhibitions (1967); *Visage de l'art contemporain égyptien* (*Aspects of Contemporary Egyptian Art*) held in 1971 at the Musée Galliera. She also had a number of solo exhibitions including Cairo (1952); and Dresden, Berlin, Warsaw and Moscow (1970).

BIBLIOGRAPHY:
Badr El-Din Abou Ghazy, *Visages de l'Art contemporain égyptien,* group exhibition catalogue, Musée Galliera, Paris, 1971.

MUSEUMS AND GALLERIES:
ALEXANDRIA (MMA) - CAIRO (Egyptian MMA) - DRESDEN (Gemäldegal. Neue Meister) - MOSCOW (Mus. of Eastern Art) - WARSAW (Muz. Narodowe).

EFIM
Russian, 18th century.
Engraver.

One engraving signed *Efim* is known: *Mellowing the Hard-hearted.*

EFIMENKO, Viktor Romanovich
Russian, 20th - 21st century.
Born 1952, in Donetsk.
Painter, draughtsman. Figures, genre scenes.

Viktor Efimenko comes from a family of painters. He studied at the N. Samokich school of fine arts in Simferopol, where he worked under the direction of P. Stolerenko. He was appointed Painter Emeritus of the USSR. Employing a somewhat old-fashioned technique, he paints mild scenes of everyday life.

MUSEUMS AND GALLERIES:
KIEV (National Museum of Fine Arts) - MOSCOW (Ministry of Culture).

AUCTION RECORDS:
PARIS, 12 Dec 1992, *Table with Samovar* (oil on canvas, 22 x 23 1/2 ins / 55 x 60 cm) FRF 8,000. PARIS, 20 March 1993, *Irises* (oil on canvas, 27 1/4 x 31 ins / 69 x 79 cm) FRF 7,200. PARIS, 18 Oct 1993, *Summer's Day* (oil on canvas, 25 1/2 x 21 1/4 ins / 65 x 54 cm) FRF 10,500. PARIS, 29 Nov 1993, *Woman in the Blue Hat* (oil on canvas, 23 1/2 x 28 3/4 ins / 60 x 73 cm) FRF 17,000. PARIS, 1 June 1994, *Young Girl with Bouquet* (oil on canvas, 32 x 23 1/2 ins / 81 x 60 cm) FRF 10,000. PARIS, 1 Dec 1994, *White Sunshade* (oil on canvas, 36 1/4 x 28 3/4 ins / 92 x 73 cm) FRF 21,000. PARIS, 7 June 1995, *Young Girl with Mirror* (oil on canvas, 32 x 25 1/2 ins / 81 x 65 cm) FRF 17,000. HASLEMERE, 8 Dec 2002, *Figures in a Rowing Boat with Lilies* (oil on canvas, 29 x 24 ins / 73 x 60 cm) GBP 1,500. HASLEMERE, 8 Dec 2002, *Sunny Day* (oil on canvas, 26 x 21 ins / 65 x 54 cm) GBP 1,500.

EFIMOV
Russian, 19th century.
Lithographer.

Many drawings for Aleksandr Orlovsky have been engraved by Efimov.

EFIMOV, Anton
Russian, 17th century.
Icon painter.

In 1688, Anton Efimov worked at the Cloister of Savino-Storoyev. He may be the same artist as A. Evfimov.

EFIMOV, Dmitri Egorovich
Russian, 19th century.
Born 7 November 1811, in Nikolayev; died 24 May 1864, in Sednev.
Engraver, architect.

Dmitri Egorovich Efimov trained at the academy of art in St Petersburg and worked in Egypt, Greece and Italy.

EFIMOV, F.
Russian, 19th century.
Active in Moscow in 1854.
Lithographer.

EFIMOV, Gavrilo
Russian, 19th century.
Active in St Petersburg in 1859.
Painter.

Gavrilo Efimov worked for the academy painting mainly portraits.

EFIMOV, Ivan
Russian, 20th century.
Born 1878; died 1959.
Sculptor.

Ivan Efimov was represented by a *Cockerel* symbolising 'Morning' at the exhibition *L'Art Russe, des Scythes à nos jours* (*Russian Art from the Scythians to Today*) held in 1967-1968 at the Galeries Nationales du Grand Palais in Paris.

MUSEUMS AND GALLERIES:
MOSCOW (State Tretyakov Gal.): *Cockerel*.

EFIMOV, Nikolai Efimovich
Russian, 19th century.
Born 5 May 1799; died 23 September 1851.
Engraver, architect.

Nokolai Efimov trained at the academy of art in St Petersburg. He is known for two engravings of the *Parthenon* and one of the *Russian Embassy in Beijing*.

EFIMOV, Nikolai Efimovich
Russian, 19th century.
Born 1838, in Ryazan.
Painter. Portraits.

Nikolai Efimovich Efimov trained at the academy of art in St Petersburg where he learned first engraving and then painting.

MUSEUMS AND GALLERIES:
MOSCOW (State Tretyakov Gal.): *Palm Sunday; Kirghiz hunting* - MOSCOW (Tsvetkov Gallery): *Head of Old Woman*.

EFIMOV, Petr
Russian, 17th century.
Active in Moscow in 1680.
Icon painter.

EFIMOV, Stepan
Russian, 18th century.
Active in Moscow.
Engraver.

Stepan Efimov is known for: *Noah, St John Damascene, Portrait of a Woman* and *St John Chrysostom*.

EFRAT, Benni
Israeli, 20th century.
Born 1936.
Performance artist, installation artist. Multimedia.

Educated on a kibbutz, he expresses himself through performances, such as *Ararat Express*, given in Lyons in spring 1987, as well as through exhibitions, notably that of the same year at the Museum of Israeli Art Ramat Gan.

All his performances and installations involve and project a sinister future for the world and humanity. He brings his work into being by means of metaphor. For example, in his Lyons performance, horse-drawn trailers, each carrying two television sets broadcasting film showing the migration of humans and animals and the onrush of waves and clouds, convey the panic which threatens to overcome the world's population.

AUCTION RECORDS:
TEL AVIV, 19 June 1990, *Composition* (1966, oil on canvas, 21 1/4 x 23 1/2 ins / 54 x 60 cm) USD 1,320. TEL AVIV, 6 April 2002, *Collage III* (1991, acrylic and paper collage on canvas, 56x40 ins / 142x102 cm) USD 2,000. NEW YORK, 18 March 2004, *Broadcast* (1976, steel and painted aluminium, h. 9 ins / 22 cm) USD 3,250.

EFREMOV, Fedor
Russian, 17th century.
Icon painter.

Fedor Efremov was mainly active in the Trinity Sergiyev Monastery near Kiev. He also worked in Moscow for the Tsar.

EFREMOV, Igor
Russian, 20th - 21st century.
Born 1946.
Painter. Figure compositions, still-lifes.

Igor Efremov studied at the Mukhina Institute in Leningrad (now St Petersburg). He took regular part in many national and international exhibitions and became a member of the Union of Soviet Artists. His paintings incorporate elements of the everyday set against Abstract backgrounds.

AUCTION RECORDS:
PARIS, 8 Dec 1990, *Still-life after Claez* (oil on canvas, 27 1/2 x 39 1/4 ins / 70 x 100 cm) FRF 5,200.

EFREMOV, Kim. See **IEFREMOV**

EFTIMIADI, Froso
Greek, 20th century.
Born 1916, in Athens.
Sculptor, ceramicist.

Froso Eftimiadi studied sculpture and ceramics in Vienna and received advice from Marcel Gimond in Paris. From 1955 onwards he abandoned terracotta and worked with metal. He produced major decorative pieces for the public gardens in Athens. He exhibited in Buenos Aires (1947), Athens (1954 and 1961) and in London (1955).

BIBLIOGRAPHY:
Provelenghios, A., *Froso Eftimiadi: sculpture 1955-1960*, Athens, 1960. Jianou, Ionel, *Froso Eftimiadi*, Arted, Paris, 1977.

AUCTION RECORDS:
NEW YORK, 27 Feb 1992, *Bird* (1960, copper, 48 x 45 1/4 x 14 ins / 121.9 x 114.9 x 35.5 cm) USD 2,090.

EGAIRAM. See **MARIAGE Louis François**

EGAN, Beatrice
British, 20th century.
Born in London.
Painter. Genre scenes.

Beatrice Egan trained in England, where she studied with G. Elmes-Browne. She also exhibited in Paris at the Salon des Artistes Français with genre scenes: *Washerwomen; In the Moonlight* and rustic scenes.

EGAN, C.
British, 19th century.
Active in London.
Painter. Waterscapes, landscapes.

C. Egan exhibited at the Royal Academy in London from 1807 to 1813.

EGAN, Éloïse
American, 20th century.
Born 1874, in Ithaca (New York); died 1967, in New York.
Painter. Seascapes, flowers.

Éloïse Egan exhibited in Paris at the Salon des Artistes Français and the Salon d'Automne from 1931.

AUCTION RECORDS:
NEW YORK, 15 May 1991, *Picnic in Summer* (oil on canvas, 22 3/4 x 27 3/4 ins / 57.8 x 70.5 cm) USD 1,650. NEW YORK, 4 May 1993, *Slave Quarters in Charleston, South Carolina* (oil on canvas, 25 1/4 x 30 ins / 64 x 76.3 cm) USD 920. MILFORD, 11 May 2000, *After School, Charleston, South Carolina* (oil on canvas, 32 x 40 ins / 81 x 102 cm) USD 1,900.

EGAN, J.
Irish, 19th century.
Painter, draughtsman. Landscapes.

J. Egan's works were wood engravings. There are certain similarities between this artist and James Egan.

EGAN, James
Irish, 19th century.
Born 1799, in Roscommon; died 1842, in London.
Engraver.

James Egan was employed by S.W. Reynolds. His last work, the best he produced, was *English Hospitality in the Old Days*, after Cattermole. He specialised in mezzotint engraving.

EGAN, Pierce
British, 19th century.
Born 9 December 1814, in London; died 6 July 1880, in London.
Engraver (burin).

Pierce Egan was the son of the writer and journalist Pierce Egan (1772-1849) and illustrated his father's work *The Pilgrims of the Thames in search of the National*. He also illustrated his own writings, including *Wat Tyler, Robin Hood* and *William de Clousdelie*, and the frontispiece and the wood engravings for his novel in two volumes *Paul Jones*. Among his other etchings is a portrait of *Miss Davenport at the age of 10*.

EGAN, William O'Mulligan
Irish, 16th century.
Sculptor.

Egan sculpted the funerary monument of Oliver Plunkett and his wife at Clonabraney between 1581 and 1595.

EGAÑA, Miguel
Spanish, 20th century.
Sculptor of assemblages, mixed media.
Copy Art.

Egaña's assemblages typically have a metaphorical meaning: a lamp emits rays of sunlight with sunglasses; a showerhead sucks in the stitches of a jumper. At Thiers he showed his own take on Ovid's *Golden Age*: a beehive spilling out a sheet of steel nuts welded together like the cells of a honeycomb (an reference to the local metal industry). Egaña's other work carries a broader critical message: a piece also exhibited in Thiers (a place famous for its knives) is a road sign showing a stag pierced with two knives whose handles are made of antler.

Miguel Egaña has held solo exhibitions of his work including: Galerie de Paris (1989); *Le Creux de l'Enfer (The Depths of Hell)* at the Centre d'Art Contemporain in Thiers (1990); *L'art (c'est) secondaire (Secondary Art -Art is Secondary)*, Fondation Mamco et musée d'Art moderne et contemporain, Geneva (2003); double exhibition *Froissages (Creasings)*, Galerie Satellite and *Pas un jour sans une ligne (Not a day without a Line)* at the Galerie Lamarre in Paris (2003).

BIBLIOGRAPHY:
Carrayrou, Stéphane, '*Miguel Egaña*' in *Art Press*, periodical, Paris, January 1990. Richard, Anne, '*Miguel Egaña*' in *Opus international* n° 119, periodical, Paris, May-June 1990.

EGAS
Spanish, 13th century.
Miniaturist.

The archives of the Torre do Tombo in Lisbon hold a *Commentary on the Apocalypse* which is dated 1221 and signed by this artist.

EGAS (El Maestro)
Flemish School, 15th - 16th century.
Sculptor.

Egas worked with his brother Anequin at Toledo Cathedral between 1466 and 1507.

EGAS, Anequin de, also known as Jan van den Eycken
Flemish School, 15th century.
Born in Brussels; died c. 1494, in Toledo.
Sculptor, architect.

In a number of documents this sculptor is referred to as 'egas cueman'. He first worked in his native land, but moved to Toledo some time after 1458, where he was appointed chief architect of the cathedral. He made several pieces of sculpture for it, and was also responsible for a number of tombs.

EGAS, Camilo, or Camillo Egaz
Ecuadorean, 20th century.
Born 1899, in Quito; died 1962.
Painter. Figures, local scenes.

Camilo Egas is believed to have spent time in Paris and in 1925 exhibited at the Salon des Artistes Indépendants and the Salon d'Automne, showing paintings inspired by Ecuador. At this period most Latin American countries were fascinated by the scale - in dimensional but also in aesthetic and sociological terms - of the sudden appearance of muralism in Mexico, in the wake of Diego Rivera. Most of these countries took up this trend and although at times it seemed like an inescapable fashion, the movement was founded on genuine conviction. Although Victor Mideros was the first of Ecuador's mural artists, Egas is considered to be the finest exponent of Ecuadorian muralism. Egas himself does not regard himself as influenced primarily by the founding father of social Latin American muralism, Diego Rivera, but by the younger artist José Clemente Orozco, who was also Mexican. With the younger Eduardo Kingman, Egas worked on the decoration of the Ecuador pavilion for the New York Exhibition of 1939.

BIBLIOGRAPHY:
Historia del Arte Ecuatoriano, Quito, 1977 (vol 4). *Camilo Egas*, exhibition catalogue, Mus Camilo Egas Banco Cent, Quito, 1978. Monteforte, M., *Los signos del hombre*, Quito, 1985. Pérez, M. Trinidad, *The Indian in the 1920s Painting of the Ecuadorean Painter Camilo Egas*, dissertation, University of Texas, Austin, 1987. Pérez, T., '*La apropriacíon do lo indígena popular en el arte ecuatoriano del primer de siglo: Camilo Egas (1915-1923)*' in *Artes académicas y populares del Ecuador*, Quito, 1995 (ed. A. Kennedy).

AUCTION RECORDS:
PARIS, 27 Dec 1926, *Mexicans*, FRF 450; *Mexicans*, FRF 400; *Mexican Woman*, FRF 320. NEW YORK, 28 Nov 1984, *The Spanish Civil War* (oil on canvas, 20 x 16 ins / 50.8 x 40.6 cm) USD 800.

EGAS, Diego de
Spanish, 16th century.
Sculptor.

Diego de Egas was working on Toledo cathedral in 1531.

EGAS, Pedro de
Spanish, 16th century.
Active c. 1533.
Painter. Historical painting.

Pedro de Egas was probably the brother of Diego de Egas. He worked on Toledo cathedral.

EGASSE, Jean Denis Fulgence
French, 19th century.
Born 9 October 1815, in Paris; died 25 April 1868, in Paris.
Painter.

On 5 October 1829, Jean Egasse joined the École des Beaux-Arts where he studied under Guérin. From 1833 to 1850 he exhibited mainly portraits at the Salon.

EGBERT
German, 10th century.
Miniaturist.

Active from 978 to 993, Egbert was bishop of Trier and an art patron. Several manuscripts of this period bear his name, but we cannot say with certainty that he actually worked on them.

EGBERT, Henry
American, 19th century.
Born 1826; died 12 March 1900, in Brooklyn.
Draughtsman.
Henry Egbert was mainly employed by the company Harpers and Bros., where there is evidence of his working in 1844, when he published *Egbert's Drawing Books.* He also collaborated on the newspaper *It's the Day's Doings.*

EGBERTS, Peter
German, 16th century.
Active in Emden.
Painter.

EGBERTSZON, Claes
Dutch, 16th century.
Active in Utrecht.
Sculptor (wood).

EGE, Eberhard
German, 19th - 20th century.
Born 17 August 1868, in Stuttgart.
Painter.
Ege trained under E. Charlemont at the Académie Julian in Paris, copying old masters, especially Titian. He completed his artistic training during his travels in the Netherlands, Germany and Italy. He was mainly a landscape painter, but also painted portraits. In 1905 he organised a collective exhibition of his portraits in Stuttgart and Dresden. His works include *Homeric Shore, The Spring Tower* and *Portraits of King Wilhelm and Queen Olga of Württemberg.*

EGE, Franz Sales
German, 16th century.
Active in Waldsee (Württemberg) c. 1580.
Draughtsman.
This artist was also a canon.

EGEA Y LECAROZ, Pablo
Spanish, 19th century.
Born in the 19th century, in Estopinana.
Painter. Genre scenes.
Pablo Egea y Lecaroz took part in the Madrid exhibition of 1876.

EGEA Y MARIN, Juan
Spanish, 19th century.
Born c. 1860, in Murcia.
Painter.
Juan Egea y Marin exhibited a number of times at the Madrid exhibition.

EGEA Y MARIN, Lopez
Spanish, 19th century.
Portrait painter.

EGEDIUS, Halfdan Johnsen
Norwegian, 19th century.
Born 5 May 1877, in Drammen; died 2 February 1899, in Christiania (now Oslo).
Painter, illustrator. Figures, portraits, landscapes.
Symbolism.
Egedius' artistic leanings became evident at a very young age; he attended a painting school from the age of eight. From 1887 to 1890 he was a pupil at the school of arts and crafts in Christiania, and journeyed from there to Copenhagen to study with Kristian Zahrtmann. His death at only 22 was a cruel blow to the new Norwegian art.

Egedius painted summer landscapes in eastern Norway and did book illustrations. Captivated by the ideas of the Symbolists in the 1890s, which he discovered during the summer he spent in Vågå in 1894, he painted landscapes charged with emotion. The autumn exhibition at the academy in Christiania in 1893 confirmed his position as a leading figure of the Neo-Romantic movement, and he continued to exhibit in Christiania from 1894 to 1898.

In 2001, Egedius' work featured in the exhibition *Da Dahl a Munch. Romanticismo, realismo e simbolismo nella pittura di paesaggio norvegese* (*From Dahl to Munch: Romanticism, Realism and Symbolism in Norwegian Landscape Painting*) at the Palazzo dei Diamanti in Ferrara.

H Egedius

BIBLIOGRAPHY:
Parmann, Oistein, *Halfdan Egedius: liv og verk,* Dreyer, Oslo, 1979. Solheim, Steinar, *Halfdan Egedius: den unge dode,* S. Solheim, Oslo, 1997. Lange, Marit (ed.), *Da Dahl a Munch. Romanticismo, realismo e simbolismo nella pittura di paesaggio norvegese,* exhibition catalogue, Palazzo dei Diamanti, Ferrara Arte editore, Ferrara, 2001.
MUSEUMS AND GALLERIES:
OSLO (Nasjonalgal.): *Storm Threatening in the Telemark Region* (1896, oil on canvas).

EGELE
Swiss, 18th century.
Painter.
Egele lived for a time in Presburg, Hungary, and painted portraits and frescoes there.

EGELGRESSER, Heinrich
German, 17th century.
Sculptor (including wood).
Heinrich Egelgresser was the son of the Nuremberg sculptor Konrad Osner, and was probably summoned to Russia with him by Peter the Great in 1697.

EGELI, Bjorn P.
Norwegian, 20th century.
Born 15 November 1900, in Christiania (now Oslo); died 1984.
Active and naturalised in the USA.
Painter, illustrator.
Egeli was a pupil of Richard Summer Meryman and Eugen Weisz.

EGELL, Augustin
German, 18th century.
Born 1731, in Mannheim; died 1785, in Munich.
Painter, architect.
A pen design, *Ceiling Project,* and an etching, *Virgin and Child,* are known to be by Augustin Egell.

EGELL, Heinrich
German, 18th century.
Born 1759, in Mannheim; died 19th century, in Munich.
Painter.
Heinrich Egell was the son of Augustin Egell and trained under his father and at the school of fine arts in Munich. He became a court painter in 1787 and produced historical paintings and portraits.

EGELL, Paul
German, 18th century.
Born 9 April 1691, in Mannheim; died 10 January 1752, in Mannheim.
Sculptor.
Paul Egell trained under Balthasar Permoser in Dresden or Vienna around 1717. His main works are: decorations in the Rococo style for the gardens and palace of the 'Grand Elector' (German prince in the Holy Roman Empire who was entitled to elect the Emperor) in Schwetzingen; a funeral monument in Durlach; the *Trinity* low relief on the façade of the chapel at the castle in Mannheim; and sculptures in the

libraries in the reading room. The cathedral in Hildesheim has a head of Christ which was carved by him housed in the Knights' Room.
AUCTION RECORDS:
PARIS, 8 Dec 1924, *Vase in Park* (pen and wash) FRF 200.

EGELL, Peter
Dutch, 17th century.
Active in Regensburg, Germany in 1698.
Painter.

EGEN, Gert van
Dutch, 16th century.
Born in the Netherlands.
Sculptor.
Egen went to Denmark in 1591, where he carved an alabaster bust of Christian IV. From 1594 onwards, he worked on the monument to King Frederick II in the chapel of Roskilde Cathedral. In 1600, he made an alabaster medallion of the king, but thereafter his name disappears from the official records. It is not known whether he returned home or died in Denmark.

EGEN, Peter
German, 18th century.
Active in Cologne.
Painter.
Peter Egen was accepted into the Corporation in 1721. He was paid in 1735 for decorative paintings.

EGENBERGER, Johannes Henderikus
Dutch, 19th century.
Born 22 April 1822, in Arnhem; died 1897, in Utrecht.
Painter. History painting.
Johannes Henderikus Egenberger's paintings are in Haarlem. Noteworthy is his *Kenau Hasselaar on the Ramparts of Haarlem*, which he executed in collaboration with Wijnveld. This painting is now to be found in the museum in Haarlem.

EGENMULLER, Hans
Swiss, 16th century.
Born to a family originally from Schaffhausen.
Active in Einsiedeln.
Sculptor.
Egenmuller collaborated with Augustin Hengkel on the choir at Einsiedeln from 1514 to 1516.

EGENOLFF, Christian, or Eginolphe or Egnolpt
German, 16th century.
Born 1503.
Active in Frankfurt.
Engraver (wood), printer.

EGENSVILLER. See **EGGENSCHWYLER**

EGER, Christoph
German, 16th century.
Born 1544, in Kreglingen.
Sculptor.
Christoph Eger worked in 1569 at the castle of Heiligenberg near Constance, and collaborated with others on the funerary monument of Count Albrecht of Hohenlohe in the collegiate church in Stuttgart. In 1591, he made the funerary monument of Duke Ludwig of Wurtemberg in Tübingen.

EGER, Georg Adam
German, 18th century.
Born 1727, in Württemberg; died 1808.
Painter.
Georg Eger was a painter at the court of the landgrave Ludwig VIII of Hesse, for whom he generally painted hunting scenes. A few works by him are housed at Kranichstein Castle, including *Self-portrait* and *Portrait of Chamberlain Czepricki*. There are some miniature portraits by him at the town hall in Hall in Württemberg.
AUCTION RECORDS:
LONDON, 27 June 1939, *Hunting Stag in Kranichstein: Ludwig VII*, GBP 18; *Hunting Stag near Dianaburg*, GBP 14.

EGER, Hans Jakob
German, 17th century.
Painter.
Hans Eger was a burgess of Frankfurt am Main in 1637 but settled in Mainz in 1664, where he did paintings of the council chamber.

EGEREN. See **NÈGRE**

EGERHÁZI, János
Hungarian, 17th century.
Painter.
János Egerházi's works include ceiling paintings at the palaces of Prince Gabriel Bethlen in Alvine and Alba Julia.

EGERI. See **AEGERI**

EGERMANN, Friedrich
Czech, 19th century.
Born 5 March 1777, in Sluknov; died 1 January 1864, in Nový Bor.
Glass painter.
Friedrich Egermann played an important role in the development and refinement of the art of stained glass painting in Bohemia. The Austrian museum in Vienna and the art and craft school in Liberec in Bohemia own sketches of his works.

EGERMANS
Flemish, 18th century.
Active in Utrecht at the beginning of the 18th century.
Painter.
Flemish School.
Egermans is known to have executed portraits of the Marez family.

EGERSDÖRFER, Andreas
German, 19th century.
Born 28 September 1866, in Nuremberg.
Painter. Landscapes.
Andreas Egersdörfer originally trained at the school of arts and crafts in Munich and at the academy in this city. He then became an art teacher in Frankfurt am Main. He appeared in a great many exhibitions, notably at the International Exhibition of Art in Berlin in 1890 and 1892; at the Salon de Paris in 1891; at the International Exhibition of Art in Berlin in 1891 and 1896; and at the 'Crystal Palace' in Munich. His oil paintings mostly depict the mountainous regions of Germany, mainly Franconia. He also painted seascapes of the Netherlands and views of old Frankfurt. A great many of his paintings belong to private collections.
MUSEUMS AND GALLERIES:
FRANKFURT AM MAIN (Städel): *Meadows*.

EGERSDÖRFER, Konrad
German, 19th - 20th century.
Born 21 January 1868, in Nuremberg.
Painter, illustrator. Genre scenes.
Egersdörfer was a pupil of Wilhelm von Diez at the art academy in Munich. Primarily a book illustrator, his paintings also tackled narrative subjects, as in *The Visit* and *Operetta*. He took part in the Berlin exhibitions of 1901, 1903 and 1911, and in the Ice Palace exhibitions in Munich in 1907 and 1911. He was a member of the Society of German Illustrators.

EGERTON, Daniel Thomas
British, 19th century.
Born 1797, in England; died 1842.
Painter, watercolourist. Landscapes.

Daniel Egerton was a member of the Society of British Artists and exhibited in London between 1824 and 1829 and between 1838 and 1840. An inveterate traveller, Egerton was one of the first and, no doubt, one of the most important artists to settle in Mexico from 1830, where he undertook a series of landscape works. Given the many drawings and lithographs showing realistic views of places in Mexico, he must have had a particular predilection for Mexican landscapes (as he had for the Niagara Falls). He was murdered on a road in Mexico.

He was represented at the exhibition *Expedition Kunst, Die Entdeckung der Natur von C.D. Friedrich bis Humboldt* (*Expedition Art. The Discovery of Nature from C.D. Friedrich to Humboldt*), at the Kunsthalle in Hamburg in 2002, which showed the links between nature and landscape art.

Bibliography:

Egerton, Daniel Thomas/Kiek, Martin (présentation), *Egerton en México, 1830-1842 reproducción de la edición del autor con sus textos originales y otras obras aisladas*, Cartón y Papel de México, Mexico, 1976. *Expedition Kunst. Die Entdeckung der Natur von C. D. Friedrich bis Humboldt*, exhibition catalogue, Hamburger Kunsthalle, Hamburg, 2002.

Auction records:

London, 17 May 1974, *Mexican Travellers*, Gns 1,900. New York, 5 May 1981, *View of Xochimilco* (1833, oil on canvas, 16 x 20 ins / 40.5 x 50.8 cm) USD 40,000. New York, 29 May 1984, *Hacienda of Santa Clara in the Valley of Cuantla de Amilpas, Mexico* (1838, oil on paper mounted/canvas, 15 3/4 x 20 ins / 40.3 x 50.5 cm) USD 15,000. New York, 22 May 1986, *Vista del Ixtacihuatl* (oil on canvas, 9 x 14 1/4 ins / 23 x 36 cm) USD 19,000. New York, 21 Nov 1988, *Ravine in the Desert* (1838, oil on canvas, 13 1/2 x 17 3/4 ins / 34.3 x 45.4 cm) USD 26,400. New York, 23 Nov 1992, *Mount Iztaccihuatl since Chalco* (oil on card, 13 x 16 1/4 ins / 33 x 41 cm) USD 165,000. New York, 19 May 1993, *The Road from San Joachin to Tlanapantla near Meciso* (1833, oil on canvas, 15 3/4 x 20 3/4 ins / 40.3 x 52.9 cm) USD 57,500. New York, 23-24 Nov 1993, *Near the Hacienda of Olivar with the Jacubaya* (watercolour/paper/paper, 10 1/4 x 13 1/2 ins / 26 x 34 cm) USD 24,150. London, 15 Nov 2001, *Hot Waters, Mexico* (1839, oil on canvas, 29 x 39 ins / 74 x 100 cm) GBP 122,000. New York, 16 Nov 2004, *British Embassy in Mexico* (gouache, watercolour and pencil on board, 5 x 11 ins / 12 x 28 cm) USD 13,000. New York, 16 Nov 2004, *Views of Towns* (1840, colour print, four, 15 x 22 ins / 38 x 55 cm) USD 13,000.

EGERTON, Jane Sophia

British, 19th century.

Active in London.

Miniaturist. Portraits.

Jane Egerton exhibited in London from 1844 to 1857.

EGERTON, M.

British, 19th century.

Active c. 1825.

Draughtsman.

M. Egerton did several humorous drawings, etched by George Hunt and other artists, including *Here, There and Over the Water, Aerial Nothings* and *Collindo Furioso, or Matters to Tatters*.

EGERTON, Margaret

British, 20th century.

Born 1938, in London.

Painter.

Margaret Egerton exhibited in Paris at the Salon des Artistes Français.

EGERTON, Shân

British, 20th - 21st century.

Born 12 June 1948, in London.

Painter. Landscapes, scenes with figures, still-lifes, portraits.

Shân Egerton trained from 1966 to 1970 at the Byam Shaw School of Art in London under Diana Armfield and Bernard Dunstan. Her work is based on her extensive travels round the world, especially on the Indian subcontinent, and also on the scenery surrounding her home on the Welsh/English borders. Her first solo show was held in 1980 in London, and she has exhibited regularly since then, notably in 1993 and 1995 at the Christopher Wood Gallery in London, and in 2000 and 2005 at the Hay-on-Wye Literary Festival.

EGG. See also ECK

EGG, Augustus Leopold

British, 19th century.

Born 2 May 1816, in London; died 26 March 1863, in Algiers.

Painter, illustrator. Figures, portraits, genre scenes.

Augustus Egg, the son of a Piccadilly gunsmith, did not take up painting until about 1834, the year he entered the Sass School of Art. In 1836 he was admitted as a student to the Royal Academy. He was made associate in 1848 and member in 1860. His first important work was *The Victim*, inspired by *Lame Devil* by Le Sage, which was shown at the academy of arts at Liverpool. From 1836 he sent pictures to London, to the Society of British Artists, the British Institute and the Royal Academy, which he was related and member in 1860. Among his most notable exhibits at the Royal Academy were seven scenes taken from Shakespeare. Delicate in health, he often spent time in countries with temperate climates such as Italy, the south of France and, later, Algeria.

His best works include *Young Spaniard* (1838), *Scene from Henry IV* (1839), *Queen Elizabeth* (1848) and *Travelling Companions* (1862). There is a collection of his letters in the National Art Library at the Victoria and Albert Museum.

Bibliography:

MacLeod, Catharine / Marciari Alexander, Julia / Sharpe, Kevin / Dethloff, Diana / Wynne, Sonya, *Painted Ladies. Women at the Court of Charles II*, exhibition catalogue, National Portrait Gallery, London, 2001.

Museums and Galleries:

Leicester: *Scene from Two Gentlemen of Verona* - London (National Portrait Gal.): *Unknown woman, formerly known as Florence Nightingale* (after 1840, oil/panel) - London (Royal Academy of Arts): *The Night before Naseby* (1859, oil on canvas, competition piece) - London (Tate Collection): *Beatrix Knighting Esmond* (1857, oil on canvas); *Scene from 'The Devil upon Two Sticks'* (1844, oil on canvas, exhibited in 1844); *Past and Present* (1858, oil on canvas, trilogy) - London (Victoria and Albert Mus.): *Young Lady*; *Head of Young Lady* - Preston: *Young Lady*; *The Opera Cloak* - Sheffield: *Scene from the Lame Devil*.

Auction records:

New York, 10-11 April 1902, *Cromwell* USD 500. London, 29 April 1908, *Head of Charles Dickens* (drawing) GBP 12. London, 24 June 1908, *Scene from the Taming of the Shrew*, GBP 11; *First Meeting of Peter the Great and Catherine the Great* (study for the large painting) GBP 18. London, 6 March 1909, *The Past and the Present* (study of trees) GBP 18. London, 2 April 1910, *Subject taken from Walter Scott*, GBP 3. London, 24 June 1910, *If you Please, Monsieur*, GBP 27. London, 7 July 1922, *The Honouring of Esmond*, GBP 9. London, 19 July 1922, *The Night before Naseby*, GBP 6. London, 11 Dec 1922, *Scene from 'The Monastery'*, GBP 51. London, 20 June 1924, *LIfe and Death of Buckingham* (both) GBP 10; *The Proposition*, GBP 11. London, 25 Nov 1924, *Henrietta Maria Afflicted, helped by Cardinal de Retz*, GBP 26. London, 24 June 1927, *Toast to the King*; *Chamber of Death* (both) GBP 25. London, 19 Dec 1930, *Scene from The Taming of the Shrew*, GBP 5. London, 7 Dec 1945, *At the Opera*, GBP 52.

LONDON, 26 April 1946, *Queen Elizabeth Discovering that she is no Longer Young*, GBP 110; *The Letter*, GBP 52. LONDON, 4 June 1947, *At the Opera*, GBP 32. LONDON, 20 March 1963, *Ninetta wearing a Mask*, GBP 300. LONDON, 10 June 1966, *Buckingham's Happy Life; The Death of Buckingham* (two pendants) Gns 850. LONDON, 19 Oct 1971, *Pensive Young Man*, GBP 420. LONDON, 14 July 1972, *Young Lady with Flowers*, Gns 900. LONDON, 14 May 1976, *Katharina and Petruchio* (1860, oil on canvas, 15 1/2 x 26 1/2 ins / 39.5 x 67.3 cm) GBP 1,600. LONDON, 6 Dec 1977, *Life and Death of Buckingham* (two canvases, 29 1/2 x 36 ins / 75 x 91.5 cm) GBP 6,000. LONDON, 27 June 1978, *Thou art not False but Thou art Fickle* (oil on card, 13 1/2 x 11 1/4 ins / 34.5 x 28.5 cm) GBP 2,000. LONDON, 10 Nov 1981, *Thou art not False but Thou art Fickle* (oil on card, 13 1/2 x 11 1/4 ins / 34.5 x 28.5 cm) GBP 500. LONDON, 14 Feb 1986, *The Gaming House* (1846, oil on panel, 9 1/2 x 12 1/2 ins / 24.1 x 31.7 cm) GBP 850. LONDON, 10 April 1991, *The Victim, Scene Taken from the Lame Devil* (1842, oil on canvas, 24 x 29 3/4 ins / 61 x 75.5 cm) GBP 8,250. LONDON, 14 June 1991, *Art Gallery, Knowle* (oil on canvas, 10 x 12 1/4 ins / 25.5 x 31 cm) GBP 1,650. PARIS, 18 Nov 1994, *Portrait of a Young Lady Standing* (oil on paper, 10 1/4 x 7 1/4 ins / 26 x 18.6 cm) FRF 5,000. LONDON, 6 Nov 1995, *Portrait of a Woman in a Wide-Brimmed Hat* (oil on panel, 10 3/4 x 9 1/4 ins / 27.5 x 23.5 cm) GBP 1,495. NEW YORK, 18-19 July 1996, *The Prisoner* (1855, oil on canvas, 18 x 14 ins / 45.7 x 35.6 cm) USD 6,325. LEWES, 30 May 2000, *Teasing Riddle* (oil on canvas, 24 x 20 ins / 61 x 51 cm) GBP 2,500. LONDON, 26 Nov 2002, *Queen Elizabeth Discovers She Is No Longer Young* (oil on canvas, 48 x 72 ins / 122 x 183 cm) GBP 32,000. LONDON, 20 Feb 2003, *Night on the Thames. Woman and Child* (oil on board, double-sided, 7 x 9 ins / 17 x 22 cm) GBP 7,000. LONDON, 20 Feb 2003, *Contemplation* (oil on board, 14 x 11 ins / 35 x 28 cm) GBP 10,000.

EGG, Edmundus
German, 18th century.
Painter.

Edmundus Egg painted the work *Assumption* in the church of the St Mary Pilgrimage in Vilgertshofen in Upper Bavaria. He is probably the same person as Edmund Eck.

EGG, Franz
Austrian, 19th century.
Born 20 February 1861, in Fernpass, near Nassereith (Upper Inn Valley).
Sculptor (including wood).

Franz Egg trained at the school of sculpture in Imst. He also trained in different studios in Germany and at the Munich academy. He settled in Innsbruck in 1888. His very great number of works include: the allegorical statues of the staircase of the Hofburg (Imperial Palace) in Innsbruck; the coat of arms of Archduke Eugene on the communion railings of the court chapel; an altar of Mary for the Ursulines; statues of angels on the pulpit of the church of the Sacred Heart; statues in the parish church of Attinghausen (Switzerland); ornamentation of an altar in the parish church of Bozen (now Bolzano, Italy); and a high altar in Wörgl (Lower Inn Valley). A large number of carved wooden sculptures by him can still be found in Bohemia, Hungary and Saxony. He was also the sculptor of the Chamber of Grand-Duke Ferdinand d'Este.

EGGEBECK, Maria Eva
Maiden name: Briekmann
German, 18th century.
Born in Geneva; died June 1714, in Hamburg.
Painter. Portraits.

Maria Eggebeck specialised in the painting of miniatures, and was the wife of the surgeon Erasmus Eggebeck.

EGGEBECK, Maria F., or Egbeck or Ecbeck
German, 18th century.
Painter. Portraits.

Maria F. Eggebeck is perhaps the same as Maria Eva Eggebeck. The largest part of the task of organising the collection of portraits of the municipal councillors of Hamburg was assigned to her and B. Denner.

MUSEUMS AND GALLERIES:
HAMBURG (Mus. für Hamburgische Geschichte): *Portrait of Mayor Andersen.*

EGGEBRECHT, Carl Friedrich
German, 18th century.
Born 1713, in Dresden; died 1773, in Meissen.
Painter (porcelain).

Meissen porcelain at this time, painted in blue and bearing the letter E. next to the crossed swords, was very likely produced by Carl Eggebrecht.

EGGEBRECHT, Carl Friedrich
German, 18th century.
Born 1752, in Meissen (Saxony-Anhalt).
Active in Leipzig.
Sculptor, draughtsman. Landscapes. Statues, funerary monuments.

EGGEL, Emma
German, 19th century.
Born 1848, in Michelbach; died 1890, in Michelbach.
Painter. History painting.

Emma Eggel studied for ten years at the art school in Stuttgart. The Stuttgart museum houses *Wotan's Hunt* by her.

EGGELHOFF, Johann Friedrich
German, 18th century.
Born 1680, in Augsburg; died 1731, in Frankfurt am Main.
Active in Frankfurt from 1712.
Engraver.

Johann Eggelhoff's engravings include the portrait of *Peter the Great* after Kupetzky, and *Auguste II of Poland.*

EGGELING, Andreas Carl August
Danish, 19th century.
Born 17 September 1862, in Torby (Lolland); died 20 June 1893, in Copenhagen.
Sculptor, decorative artist.

Eggeling was admitted to the academy of fine arts as a wood carver, and studied there from 1884 to 1888. He produced a number of decorative works, and was also known as a sculptor in wood. However, an incurable illness prevented the development of a talent of great promise, and he died in hospital aged 30.

EGGELING, Herman
American, 20th century.
Born 17 August 1884, in New York; died 14 January 1932, in the Bronx (New York).
Painter, illustrator. Landscapes.

Herman Eggeling was a pupil of Frederick Bridgman and John Sloan. Apart from his landscape paintings, he illustrated the *Encyclopaedia of Food* by Artemas Ward.

EGGELING, Viking
Swedish, 20th century.
Born 12 October 1880, in Lund; died 19 May 1925, in Berlin.
Painter, film maker.
Dadaism.

Eggeling studied in Switzerland and in Milan between 1900 and 1908. In 1911 he moved to Paris, where he became friendly with Modigliani. In 1915 he got to know Jean Arp and Kisling, then in Switzerland he met Tristan Tzara. In 1916 in Zurich, Tzara introduced him to Hans Richter, who had come to Switzerland after being wounded in World War I, and who would become his closest friend. In 1917 Eggeling joined the Zurich Dada group - there were many different Dada groups each with a different focus depending on their historico-geographic situation: the movement in Switzerland, which was virtually unaffected by the war, was interested in plastic and literary reflections and activities. Although he remained a secondary figure within the group, he contributed to its publications.

Eggeling's paintings were essentially Post-Cubist with a markedly abstract approach similar to that of Jean Arp. However, very early on he began experimenting with the development of a form - specifically an abstract geometric form - in space and hence especially in time, particularly the moment of looking. This quest demonstrates his awareness of Futurist objectives. In 1919-1920, while visiting Hans Richter's parents at Klein-Koelzig castle, he produced two scrolls of abstract figures entitled *Horizontal Vertical Mass* and *Diagonal Symphony*. Meanwhile he was developing an interest in the ideograms of Chinese writing, and his figures were influenced by this. These scrolls, which unrolled horizontally like makemonos from left to right, were 50 centimetres (20 inches) tall and up to 7 metres (280 inches) long. They consisted of sequential images, each in turn displaying a slight change from the previous one in the manner of cartoons. Hans Richter's *Rhythm 21* was in the same vein.

In addition to their painting, Eggeling and Richter were concerned with moving on from the graphic presentation of movement to its cinematographic expression. Frank Popper, in *Origins and Development of Kinetic Art*, states that Eggeling 'was the first to use cinema to express the rhythmic movement of pure forms, finding in the different phases of external life a fundamental identity: movement'. In 1921, in Berlin, while Richter was working on his *Rhythm 21* based on the same principles, Eggeling, with the help of his wife, produced what he called an 'absolute film' based on the second scroll and also entitled *Diagonal Symphony*. It had its first public screening in 1923 in Berlin.

BIBLIOGRAPHY:

Seuphor, Michel, *L'Art abstrait, ses origines, ses premiers maîtres*, Maeght, Paris, 1949. *Viking Eggeling*, exhibition catalogue, Nationalmuseum, Stockholm, 1950. Dorival, Bernard/Hoog, Michel, *Dada*, group exhibition catalogue, Musée national d'Art moderne, Paris, 1966-1967.

AUCTION RECORDS:

PARIS, 3 June 1992, *Landscape* (1916, oil on canvas, 32 1/4 x 22 ins / 82 x 55 cm) FRF 160,000.

EGGEMEYER, Maude Kaufman

American, 20th century.
Born 1877, in New Castle (Indiana); died 1934.
Painter.

Maude Eggemeyer was a pupil at the Cincinnati Art Academy and also a member of several art associations. She won several prizes between 1924 and 1928.

EGGEN, Tietsia

Dutch, 20th - 21st century.
Born 1954.
Painter.

Eggen attended the art academy in Maastricht. She exhibits in many Dutch towns.

EGGENA, Gustav

German, 19th century.
Born 30 August 1850, in Marburg.
Painter, draughtsman. Portraits, genre scenes.

Gustav Eggena settled in Munich around 1873. A notable work of his is *Knight and Friar*.

MUSEUMS AND GALLERIES:

BAUTZEN: *Letter of Indulgence* - KASSEL: *View over Ammer Lake* - MANNHEIM: *Study of Head of a Woman.*

AUCTION RECORDS:

LONDON, 30 Nov 1977, *Abduction* (1881, oil on canvas, 20 3/4 x 31 ins / 53 x 78.5 cm) GBP 600. LONDON, 30 Jan 1981, *Gallop* (oil on panel, 14 3/4 x 11 1/4 ins / 37.5 x 28.5 cm) GBP 500. COLOGNE, 15 Oct 1988, *Welcome: Young Girl Offering a Drink to a Knight* (oil on canvas, 11 3/4 x 15 3/4 ins / 30 x 40 cm) DEM 1,300. MUNICH, 23 June 1999, *Monk with Donkey on Road in Landscape* (oil on canvas, 24 x 37 ins / 60 x 94 cm) DEM 3,000.

EGGENFELDER, Johann Ernst

German, 18th century.
Active in Glogau (now Glogów Malopolski).
Painter.

Johann Eggenfelder belonged to the Corporation of Painters and Sculptors, where he was mentioned until 1737.

EGGENHOFER, Nick

American, 20th century.
Born 1897, in Bavaria, Germany; died 1985.
Painter (gouache), draughtsman. Local scenes.

Nick Eggenhoffer concentrated mainly on heightened gouache and coloured pencils. He painted traditional scenes from life in the American West.

AUCTION RECORDS:

NEW YORK, 30 April 1980, *Buffalo Hunt* (pen and wash/paper, 12 x 17 ins / 30.5 x 43.2 cm) USD 2,900. NEW YORK, 17 April 1982, *The Bank Robber* (pen and traces of pastel, 10 3/4 x 14 ins / 27.3 x 35.5 cm) USD 1,200. NEW YORK, 7 Dec 1984, *Learning the Land* (watercolour and gouache/paper, 14 3/4 x 11 ins / 37.7 x 27.8 cm) USD 800. NEW YORK, 31 May 1985, *The Scouting Party* (gouache, 15 1/4 x 15 1/4 ins / 38.6 x 38.5 cm) USD 4,600. NEW YORK, 16 March 1990, *Herdsmen* (gouache and pencil/card, 15 1/4 x 20 ins / 39 x 51 cm) USD 9,350. NEW YORK, 26 Sept 1990, *Horse Relay Post* (oil on card, 16 x 20 ins / 40.6 x 50.8 cm) USD 8,800. NEW YORK, 27 Sept 1990, *Attack on a Convoy of Trappers* (gouache and pencil/card, 15 1/4 x 19 1/2 ins / 38.5 x 49.5 cm) USD 4,400. NEW YORK, 14 March 1991, *Santa Fe Waggons Fording the Cimarron* (gouache and pencil/paper, 15 1/4 x 20 ins / 38.5 x 50.8 cm) USD 3,520. NEW YORK, 15 May 1991, *White Man's Weapons* (1968, gouache/card, 16 x 26 ins / 40.6 x 66 cm) USD 6,050. NEW YORK, 15 April 1992, *Indian Warrior on his Horse* (watercolour and gouache/card, 18 1/2 x 14 3/4 ins / 47 x 37.5 cm) USD 2,200. NEW YORK, 27 May 1992, *Custer's Last Stand* (tempera/card, 22 x 30 1/4 ins / 55.9 x 76.8 cm) USD 28,600. NEW YORK, 11 March 1993, *The Stage Coach* (1981, gouache and ink, 9 1/4 x 15 1/4 ins / 23.6 x 38.5 cm) USD 2,530. NEW YORK, 31 March 1994, *Rebels of the Rio Grande; Diligence* (ink and pencil, two drawings, 14 3/4 x 20 ins / 37.5 x 50.8 cm and 9 1/4 x 14 ins/23.5 x 35.6 cm) USD 1,725. NEW YORK, 11 March 1999, *Meeting of the Tribes* (watercolour and gouache on board, 15 x 26 ins / 39 x 67 cm) USD 9,500. LOS ANGELES, 29 April 1999, *On the Move* (oil on board, 21 x 30 ins / 53 x 76 cm) USD 29,000. HAYDEN, 29 July 2000, *On to Town* (gouache, 9 x 18 ins / 23 x 46 cm) USD 6,500. BOSTON, 22 Sept 2000, *Stagecoach* (watercolour and gouache on paperboard, 11 x 14 ins / 28 x 35 cm) USD 3,500. NEW YORK, 24 May 2001, *Watchers - Dakota Indians* (oil on board, 15 x 20 ins / 37 x 50 cm) USD 16,000. HAYDEN, 28 July 2001, *Goin' West* (gouache, 18 x 28 ins / 46 x 71 cm) USD 8,000. CHEYENNE, 15 March 2002, *Oregan Trail* (gouache, 15 x 30 ins / 38 x 76 cm) USD 9,000. HAYDEN, 27 July 2002, *Buffalo Hunt* (gouache, 20 x 30 ins / 51 x 76 cm) USD 14,000. MONTANA, 1 March 2003, *Guarding the Government Wagon Train* (mixed media on paper, 20 x 30 ins / 51 x 76 cm) USD 8,000. HAYDEN, 26 July 2003, *Out for Coups* (gouache, 18 x 14 ins / 46 x 36 cm) USD 14,000. MONTANA, 19 March 2004, *Cowboy on Horse* (watercolour, 8 x 7 ins / 20 x 18 cm) USD 5,000. HAYDEN, 24 July 2004, *Plains Scout* (gouache, 11 x 10 ins / 28 x 25 cm) USD 5,000.

EGGENSCHWILER, Franz
Swiss, 20th century.
Born 1930, in Solothurn.
Sculptor (mixed media).
Conceptual Art.

Eggenschwiler initially studied painting on glass before completing his training, between 1951 and 1953, at the art school in Bern, where he lives. He took part in several collective exhibitions in Bern, before participating in the Salon de Mai in Paris in 1969. In 1970 he exhibited with Joseph Beuys and several others at the Kunstmuseum in Lucerne, and he was invited to take part in the Documenta V exhibition in Kassel in 1972.

His work started attracting attention from 1969 onwards, when Arte povera and conceptual expression were causing a stir in international avant-garde circles. Eggenschwiler's work falls into three areas: 'Found objects', some of which are presented without modification, while others are enhanced in such a way as to make them express meaning; 'Sausage paraphrases', in which he creates volume using all sorts of materials, giving them the shape and appearance of sausages; and 'UFOs' (unidentified flying objects) which use American photographs that are claimed to show unexplained celestial phenomena.

Eggenschwiler's works generally have a humorous dimension (for example, his *Movable Boundary* of 1968-1969) and often have erotic connotations (as with those works that paraphrase the shape of a woman's breast, and the almost anonymous *Volume* in cement dating from 1969, which is reminiscent of Roman phallic representations).

BIBLIOGRAPHY:
Kneubühler, Theo, *Kunst: 28 Schweizer*, exhibition catalogue, Gal. Raeber, Lucerne, 1972.

MUSEUMS AND GALLERIES:
LAUSANNE (Cantonal MFA): *The Tree of Europe with Blade of Grass* (1988).

AUCTION RECORDS:
LUCERNE, 8 June 1996, *Reliquary for a Phalanx* (1972, object in iron, wood, Plexiglas and stone, 13 1/2 x 5 x 4 1/4 ins / 34.5 x 12.5 x 11 cm) CHF 2,700. ZURICH, 21 March 2000, *Broken Cement* (cement/iron bars, 30 x 29x6 ins / 76 x 74x14 cm) CHF 3,000. BERN, 19 June 2003, *Untitled* (stone/bronze/wood/iron, 11 x 15x11 ins / 28 x 38x28 cm) CHF 6,000.

EGGENSCHWYLER, Urs
Swiss, 19th century.
Born 24 January 1849, in Subingen.
Sculptor, painter.

Urs Eggenschwyler made frequent visits to the canton school in Solothurn and practised drawing under Taverna. He later studied sculpture under Pflüger, under Spiess in Aüssersihl, and under the teacher Max Widmann at the Munich academy. After having spent a few years in the employment of King Ludwig II of Bavaria, Eggenschwyler went to Zurich and provided several statues for the corporations in the city between 1884 and 1886, as well as a marble lion for the St Gall museum. He specialised in the portrayal of animals, and in order to improve his skill in this genre he acquired a small zoo and made frequent visits to the owners of circuses and zoos to study the habits of exotic animals. He visited Vienna and Berlin, among other places, and provided statues of lions for several Swiss cities between 1898 and 1902, including those for the Bern Bundeshaus (Houses of Parliament) and for the Stauffach bridge. He also produced a number of paintings of animals.

EGGENSCHWYLER, Urs Pankraz
Swiss, 18th - 19th century.
Born 23 February 1756, in Matzendorf; died 11 October 1821, in Solothurn.
Sculptor.

During his apprenticeship as a carter, Urs Pankraz Eggenschwyler displayed his liking for sculpture and was commissioned to produce figures for coaches. He spent time in Paris where he continued to develop his artistic aptitude. He exhibited in 1802 at the academy and as a result of winning a first prize he spent seven years in Rome. During the reign of Napoleon I he sculpted a statue of *Cupid* for the Palace of Fontainebleau and finished the large statue of *Napoleon*. The fall of the latter led him to return to his own country. He joined the brotherhood of St Luke in Solothurn in 1815. Notable works by him include: *Cleobis and Biton* in a room of the town hall in Solothurn; the coats of arms of the town on the façade of this building; a *Charity* on the portal of the old orphanage; busts of Nikolaus von Flüe, Ulrich, Byst and Kosciuszko; and his last work, *Christ on the Cross*, in the parish church in Deitingen.

EGGENSPERGER, Karl Adolf
German, 19th century.
Active in Potsdam.
Painter.

Karl Eggensperger was trained at the Berlin academy where he exhibited in 1818, 1824 and 1830 with portraits, a *Madonna*, and a *Nymph*, among other works.

EGGER. See also **ECKER**

EGGER, Balthasar
Austrian, 17th century.
Born in Winkler (Carinthia); died 15 September 1688, in Munich.
Painter.

Balthasar Egger was trained by the painter Josef Camerlainder in Lienz and settled in Munich in 1657. However, he was not accepted into the Corporation of this city until 1667. He acquired the right of burgess in 1668. In 1682 he worked on the installation of the church of the Theatines.

EGGER, Eduard
Swiss, 20th century.
Born 15 March 1882.
Painter.

Egger was originally from Kerns, and studied at the Gymnase and under Robert Elminger in Sarnen. He was also taught by Karl Georg Kaiser in Stans. He visited Lucerne and Italy, where he continued his studies.

EGGER, Ernst
Swiss, 20th century.
Born 13 March 1874, in Solothurn.
Painter. Landscapes.

Egger trained in Florence and was a pupil of Matisse in Paris. At the Munich exhibition of 1909 he exhibited a painting entitled *Lago Maggiore, Morning*.

EGGER, Franz, or Öcker
Austrian, 18th century.
Born 1757; died 1781, in Vienna.
Sculptor.

Franz Egger was the son of Konrad Egger.

EGGER, Hanna
Swiss, 20th century.
Born 3 May 1881, in Bern.
Painter, engraver.

Egger trained at the École des Arts Industriels in Geneva, and was a pupil of Angelo Janck and the school of Wilhelm von Debschitz in Munich. She also attended the Académie Ranson in Paris. She had works shown - mostly etchings and wood engravings - at collective exhibitions in Switzerland.

EGGER, Ida
French, 19th century.
Painter (gouache), watercolourist. Flowers.
Ida Egger exhibited at the Paris Salon from 1834 to 1838.
AUCTION RECORDS:
MONTE CARLO, 8 Dec 1984, *Two Roses* (gouache, 9 3/4 x 7 1/2 ins / 25 x 19.3 cm) FRF 8,000.

EGGER, Jakob
Swiss, 17th century.
Painter.
Jakob Egger worked on the high altar of the collegiate church of St Gall in 1644.

EGGER, Jakob
Swiss, 18th - 19th century.
Born c. 1770, in Gossau (St Gall); died 1842, in Vienna.
Engraver, miniaturist.
Jakob Egger trained in Zurich under Diogg and entered the Vienna academy in 1797. Notable works by him include a series of heads drawn from the *Massacre of the Innocents* by Raphael, *Book of Drawings* after the drawings of Füger and Cauzig, and *Portrait of Prince Karl von Schwarzenberg* after J. Merz.

EGGER, Jean
Austrian, 20th century.
Born 1897, in Hüttenberg (Carinthia); died 1934.
Painter. Portraits, landscapes.
Egger spent time in Sicily and later in Paris, where he exhibited at the Salon of the Société Nationale des Beaux-Arts and the Salon des Tuileries between 1925 and 1930.
AUCTION RECORDS:
VIENNA, 22 Sept 1971, *The Earth,* ATS 40,000. VIENNA, 7 June 1972, *Portrait of Cardinal Merio,* ATS 25,000. VIENNA, 21 March 1973, *Landscape,* ATS 50,000. VIENNA, 22 Sept 1978, *Country Church* (oil on canvas, 32 1/4 x 26 ins / 82 x 66 cm) ATS 40,000. VIENNA, 12 Nov 1985, *Waterfall* (oil on panel, 15 x 14 1/2 ins / 38 x 37 cm) ATS 60,000. PARIS, 6 Oct 1993, *Portrait of a Young Woman* (oil on canvas, 33 3/4 x 23 1/4 ins / 86 x 59 cm) FRF 45,000. VIENNA, 1 Dec 1999, *Trees* (oil on canvas, 26 x 21 ins / 65 x 54 cm) ATS 1,000,000. PARIS, 15 Dec 2000, *Female Face on Pink Ground* (1929, oil on canvas, 18 x 15 ins / 46 x 38 cm) FRF 120,000. PARIS, 15 Dec 2000, *Woman's Head* (oil on canvas, 18 x 15 ins / 46 x 38 cm) FRF 165,000. VIENNA, 26 Nov 2003, *St Martin am Silberberg, Karnten* (oil on canvas, 32 x 26 ins / 81 x 65 cm) EUR 75,000. VIENNA, 12 Oct 2004, *Portrait of a Girl* (oil on canvas, 16 x 13 ins / 41 x 33 cm) EUR 50,000.

EGGER, Konrad Wenzel, or Öcker
Austrian, 18th century.
Born 1708; died 1785, in Vienna.
Sculptor.
Konrad Egger trained at the academy of fine arts in Vienna in 1743 and was appointed a member in 1757. He was the son of Simon Egger.

EGGER, Nicolaus
Austrian, 17th century.
Active in Linz.
Sculptor.

EGGER, Simon, or Öcker
Austrian, 18th century.
Born 1680, in Terling (Tyrol); died 29 April 1753.
Sculptor.

EGGER, Wilhelm
Swiss, 18th - 19th century.
Born in Staad.
Draughtsman.
Wilhelm Egger received lessons from the painter F. G. A. Schöners in Yverdon. Egger devoted himself to teaching, visited Italy, and specialised in lead pencil portraits done in profile

EGGER-LIENZ, Albin, pseudonym of Trojer, Igenuin Albuin
Austrian, 19th - 20th century.
Born 29 January 1868, in Striebach, near Lienz (Tyrol); died 4 November 1926, in Zwölfmalgreien or Santa-Justinia, near Bolzano (South Tyrol).
Painter, watercolourist, draughtsman. Historical subjects, religious subjects, figure compositions, rustic scenes, figures, still-lifes, flowers. Church decoration.
Egger-Lienz trained under Gabriel von Hackl and Wilhelm von Lindenschmit the Younger at the Munich art academy between 1884 and 1893. He worked in Linz, then lived in Vienna from 1899 until 1911, when the emperor opposed his appointment as a teacher. He taught at the art academy in Weimar from 1912-1913, and enlisted as a volunteer in 1915 in World War I. After the war he returned to his homeland for good. He exhibited regularly at the Berlin, Vienna and Munich exhibitions.

In around 1905 Egger-Lienz began to be influenced by Hodler, then around 1910 shifted towards a more distinctly Expressionist style. He adopted a simplified, efficient approach to drawing, henceforth painting with large brushstrokes cycles of pictures representing the lives of simple Tyrolean folk. He regarded these peasants as symbolising the different stages of life. His early works depicted their lives and struggles in an anecdotal style in the tradition of 19th-century genre painting in Munich and reminiscent of Franz von Defregger's works, and he returned to this style later on.

The 1914-1918 war inspired him to paint a cycle of paintings demonstrating the horror and catastrophic nature of war. His *Heroes* and *Unknown Soldiers* of 1916, and *Missa Eroica* of 1918 combine a decorative execution very much in the mural style with a brutally painful subject. In 1918, his composition *Final* depicted an appalling heap of bodies. In 1925, in Linz, he produced murals for the war memorial chapel: *Storm, Sacrifice of the Dead,* and *Resurrection,* which remained banned until 1950. He painted historical compositions (*After the Signing of the Tyrolean Peace Accord*) and religious works (*The Holy Family*). After 1922, he mainly concentrated on scenes from the lives of the Tyroleans: the triptych entitled *The Earth, Grace, Young Man Lifting a Beam, The Peasant's Return, The Request, Lunch,* and *The Sower and the Devil,* all of which demonstrate a true-to-life but solidly structured and comprehensive technique.

Egger Lienz

BIBLIOGRAPHY:
Sotriffer, Kristian, *Albin Egger-Lienz, 1868 bis 1926,* monograph, Rosenheimer, Rosenheim, 1983.
MUSEUMS AND GALLERIES:
INNSBRUCK: *Resurrection* (1924) - LIENZ (Schloss Bruck): *First Days of Spring; Life* (1915) - MANNHEIM: *Pilgrims* - VIENNA (Heeresgeschichtliches Mus.): *The Unknown Soldiers* (1916); *Missa Eroica* (1908) - VIENNA (Österreichische Gal. Belvedere): *Good Friday; The Dance of Death of 1809* (1906-1908); *Grace* (1928); *The Cross; After the Signing of the Tyrolean Peace Accord.*
AUCTION RECORDS:
VIENNA, 4 Dec 1962, *The Request,* ATS 75,000. VIENNA, 18 March 1964, *To the Unknown Soldier,* ATS 110,000. VIENNA, 2 Dec 1969, *Andras Hofer,* ATS 100,000. VIENNA, 17 March 1971, *The Peasant's Return,* ATS 150,000. VIENNA, 28 May 1974, *The Hail Mary said after the Battle,* ATS 70,000. VIENNA, 17 March 1978, *Three Reapers* (watercolour/card, 32 1/2 x

49 3/4 ins / 82.5 x 126.5 cm) ATS 650,000. VIENNA, 18 March 1981, *Mountains* (1910-1911, charcoal, black chalk and pastel/grey paper, 30 1/4 x 25 1/4 ins / 76.9 x 64.3 cm) ATS 75,000. VIENNA, 31 March 1984, *Weberei* (1924, oil/tempera, 20 3/4 x 39 1/4 ins / 53 x 100 cm) ATS 250,000. VIENNA, 11 Sept 1984, *Sketch of a Thatched Cottage* (pencil, 7 x 10 1/2 ins / 17.8 x 26.9 cm) ATS 16,000. MUNICH, 5 Dec 1985, *Vase of Flowers* (oil on card, 27 3/4 x 38 3/4 ins / 70.7 x 98.5 cm) DEM 110,000. MUNICH, 13 May 1987, *Reaper* (watercolour/mounted paper/card, 20 x 25 1/2 ins / 51 x 65 cm) DEM 53,000. LONDON, 10 Feb 1988, *Study for a Pietà* (pencil, 12 1/2 x 8 3/4 ins / 32 x 22.5 cm) GBP 825. LONDON, 29 Nov 1988, *The Leader* (oil on canvas, 24 1/2 x 22 1/4 ins / 62.3 x 56.8 cm) GBP 41,800. ROME, 30 Oct 1990, *May Roses* (oil on panel, 19 1/4 x 22 1/2 ins / 49 x 57 cm) ITL 60,000,000; *Lunch, second version* (1910, oil on panel, 22 x 31 1/2 ins / 55 x 80 cm) ITL 225,000,000. MUNICH, 10 Dec 1992, *Still-life with Vegetables* (1890, oil on canvas, 32 x 43 1/2 ins / 81 x 110.5 cm) DEM 90,400. MUNICH, 27 June 1995, *Study of a Peasant for Christmas Eve* (pencil/paper, 15 1/2 x 10 1/4 ins / 39.5 x 26 cm) DEM 8,625; *Reaper* (oil on canvas, 28 x 24 1/2 ins / 71 x 62.5 cm) DEM 193,700. MUNICH, 2 Dec 1997, *Study for Christmas Eve* (1903, oil on canvas, 14 1/4 x 11 1/2 ins / 36 x 29 cm) DEM 21,600. VIENNA, 27 May 1999, *Two Cutters* (c. 1920-1923, watercolour, 26 x 39 ins / 65 x 99 cm) ATS 1,230,000. VIENNA, 11 Oct 1999, *Two Peasants Harvesting Corn* (watercolour, 26 x 39 ins / 65 x 99 cm) ATS 11,150,000. VIENNA, 25 May 2000, *Man Drinking from Spring* (black chalk/pencil/ink/pen, four, 20 x 31 ins / 51 x 79 cm) ATS 50,000. LONDON, 18 Oct 2000, *Die Quelle* (oil on board, 22 x 31 ins / 55 x 78 cm) GBP 55,000. VIENNA, 25 Sept 2001, *Head Study for 'Life'* (19 x 16 ins / 48 x 41 cm) ATS 350,000. VIENNA, 27 Nov 2001, *The Patrol Resting* (watercolour on paper/board exec.1915, 15 x 20 ins / 39 x 51 cm) ATS 130,000. VIENNA, 13 May 2002, *Midday Meal* (oil on canvas, 35 x 55 ins / 90 x 140 cm) EUR 290,000. LONDON, 9 Oct 2002, *Bergmaher - Mountain Mower* (1907, oil on canvas, 21 x 17 ins / 53 x 43 cm) GBP 130,000. VIENNA, 27 May 2003, *Farmhouse in St Martin, Passeier* (oil on canvas, 19 x 32 ins / 49 x 82 cm) EUR 60,000. VIENNA, 26 Nov 2003, *Man Sharpening Scythe* (watercolour on paper/board, 20 x 24 ins / 51 x 62 cm) EUR 60,000. VIENNA, 28 April 2004, *Sketch for Corpus Christi Procession* (1906, oil on board, 7 x 11 ins / 17 x 28 cm) EUR 9,000. VIENNA, 28 April 2004, *Man Stoking Flames Watched by Women* (pastel, 18 x 27 ins / 46 x 69 cm) EUR 13,000.

EGGERDES, Hans, or Eggers
German, 16th century.
Painter.
Lübeck School.
Hans Eggerdes was working in Lübeck between 1561 and 1573.

EGGERDES, Heinrich
German, 16th century.
Active in Brunswick.
Painter.

EGGERDES, Joachim
German, 16th century.
Active in Lübeck in 1533.
Sculptor (wood).

EGGERS, Bartholomaus
Swiss, 17th century.
Born in Rheineck.
Sculptor. Statues.
Bartholomaus Eggers trained under Schlüter. In 1686 he produced a marble statue of Charles of Hesse in Rome. He is probably the same person as Bartholomeus Eggers.

EGGERS, Bartholomeus
Dutch, 17th century.
Died before 1692, in Amsterdam.
Sculptor. Monuments, groups, statues.
Batholomeus Eggers was perhaps German in origin. Resident in Amsterdam, he initially studied under Quellinus. From 1662 onwards he worked for the Prince-Elector of Brandenburg. In 1665 he was in The Hague, in 1667 in Amsterdam and in 1669 and 1687 in Berlin. One of his major works is *Pallas and Four Dolphins.*

MUSEUMS AND GALLERIES:
AMSTERDAM: *Portrait of Jan Munter* - AMSTERDAM (South façade of the exchange): *Mercury* - POTSDAM (Schloss Sanssouci): *Rape of Proserpina* - POTSDAM (The Royal Palace): *Brandenburg Princes* (11 marble statues); *Caesar; Constantine; Charlemagne; Rudolf of Hapsburg;* six marble low reliefs - THE HAGUE (Church of St James): *Tomb of Admiral Wassenaer van Obdam.*

EGGERS, Hans. See **EGGERDES**

EGGERS, Hans
German, 17th century.
Active in Hamburg.
Glass painter.

EGGERS, Jakob
Dutch, 17th century.
Active in Amsterdam.
Sculptor.
Jakob Eggers was the brother of Bartholomeus Eggers and worked with him in Amsterdam in 1674.

EGGERS, Johann Carl
German, 19th century.
Born 1787, in Neustrelitz; died 1863, in Neustrelitz.
Painter. History painting, religious subjects, portraits.
Johann Eggers trained in art under Matthai in Dresden. He then went to Rome where he linked up with Cornelius, Overbeck and Philipp Jeit. He worked with Cornelius on frescoes for the hall of the new museum in Berlin. He also worked in Rome at the Chiaramonti Museum of the Vatican and at Caffarelli Palace, and for the princes of Mecklenburg in Germany.

MUSEUMS AND GALLERIES:
BERLIN (Schloss Bellevue): *Kneeling Cupid* - FLORENCE (Acad. of S Marco): *Archangel St Michael of Perugino* (copy) - LEIPZIG: *St Catherine of Alexandria; Portrait of Italian Woman; Portrait of Mariane Rehberg.*

AUCTION RECORDS:
COPENHAGEN, 3 April 1981, *Seaside* (1885, oil on canvas, 33 1/2 x 49 1/4 ins / 85 x 125 cm) DKK 5,500. LUCERNE, 3 June 1987, *Visit* (1853, oil on panel, 24 1/4 x 20 3/4 ins / 61.5 x 53 cm) CHF 3,400. STOCKHOLM, 15 Nov 1989, *Small Boat at Dusk* (oil on canvas, 26 x 37 ins / 66 x 94 cm) SEK 16,500.

EGGERT, Daniel
German, 18th century.
Born c. 1732, in Danzig (now Gdansk, Poland); died after 1768.
Sculptor.
Daniel Eggert worked in several countries - Russia, Sweden, Denmark, Holland, France and England. He produced a marble group in London, *Sacrifice of Iphigenia.*

EGGERT, Frans Xaver
German, 19th century.
Born 1802, in Höchstädt; died 1876, in Munich.
Glass painter.
Frans Eggert practised decorative painting in Augsburg and Munich, then dedicated his life to painting on glass, acquiring a sound reputation. He worked on the stained glass windows of a great many churches in Cologne, Munich, Basel, Constance, Regensburg and Baden-Baden.

EGGERT, Fridolin
Swiss, 17th - 18th century.
Active in Switzerland.
Painter.
Fridolin Eggert, a monk from the Benedictine order, seems to have painted for his order and the churches in Rabius, Disenti, Laax, Truns, Ruis and Neukirch. His first known painting dates from 1682 and was produced for the altar in the parish church of Rabius. His notable paintings include those in the church of the Benedictines near Truns and, in particular, *Triumphant Procession of the Mother of God* dating from 1687. His last preserved painting dates from 1705.

EGGERT, Sigmund
German, 19th century.
Born 13 February 1839, in Munich; died 25 August 1896, in Walchstadt.
Painter, illustrator. Genre scenes.
Sigmund Eggert was the son of Frans Xaver Eggert. He did the illustrations for *Summerhouse* and *Over Land and Sea* between 1880 and 1886. Notable works by him include *Art in the Countryside* and *Peasant and Fox*.
AUCTION RECORDS:
LONDON, 16 Oct 1974, *Botanist*, GBP 400. NEW YORK, 11 Feb 1981, *Gingerbread Heart* (oil on canvas, 26 1/2 x 30 3/4 ins / 67 x 78 cm) USD 8,500. NEW YORK, 26 May 1983, *Grandfather Telling a Story to His Grandchildren* (1872, oil on canvas, 23 x 29 ins / 58.5 x 73.5 cm) USD 10,500. CHESTER, 19 April 1985, *Packed Up* (oil on panel, 11 x 8 1/4 ins / 27 x 21 cm) GBP 1,700. NEW YORK, 26 May 1993, *Pretty Inn Servant* (oil on canvas/card, 33 x 27 ins / 83.8 x 68.6 cm) USD 6,900. NEW YORK, 24 May 1995, *Unexpected Visitor* (oil on canvas/synthetic resin, 28 1/4 x 37 1/4 ins / 71.8 x 94.6 cm) USD 8,050. LONDON, 22 June 1999, *Reading Lesson* (1874, oil on canvas, 24 x 19 ins / 61 x 49 cm) GBP 2,600. BREMEN, 29 June 2001, *Confidential Conversation with Lawyers* (1879, oil on panel, 12 x 10 ins / 31 x 25 cm) DEM 5,500.

EGGERT, Wilhelm
German, 20th century.
Born 10 November 1886, in Remscheid.
Painter. Figure compositions, nudes, portraits.
Eggert trained at the art academy in Karlsruhe. He stayed in Paris for a short time before becoming a pupil of Hugo von Habermann at Munich art academy. He worked in Switzerland and Italy, as well as Cologne, where he exhibited frequently and was a member of the artists' association. He was a prolific portrait painter, and in particular painted several self-portraits. He also painted seascapes and other subjects, as, for example, in his large painting, *Factory Interior*.

EGGIMANN, Hans
Swiss, 19th - 20th century.
Born 29 September 1872, in Bern.
Draughtsman, engraver, illustrator.
Eggimann studied painting, architecture and music in Dresden from 1891 to 1895. Between 1898 and 1901 he continued his artistic education at the École des Beaux-Arts in Paris. After a trip to Italy he settled in Bern. He produced a large number of drawings, ex-libris, etchings and book illustrations, most of them depicting satirical and philosophical subjects. From 1909 onwards he took part in Swiss and international collective exhibitions.
MUSEUMS AND GALLERIES:
BASEL - ZURICH.

EGGINK, Johann Leberecht
Latvian, 19th century.
Born 1787, in Curlandia; died 1867, in Mitau (now Jelgava).
Painter. History painting.
Eggink was a pupil of the Munich and Vienna academies of art. In 1817 he went to Italy and then to St Petersburg, becoming a member of its academy. In 1837 he became professor at the Mitau School of Drawing. Works by him to be cited are: *The Battle of the Neva*, *View of Eboli, near Paestum*, several altarpieces and altar tables and numerous portraits. The Hermitage Gallery in St Petersburg has seventeen of these miniature copies of the Italian Masters.
MUSEUMS AND GALLERIES:
JELGAVA: *Aleksandr Newsky's Victory over the Swedish in 1240*; *Aleksandr Newsky Entering Pleskau in 1242*; *Ulysses and Nausicaa*; *Woman from Rome in front of her Mirror*; *Portrait of J.F. von der Recke*; *Portrait of F. von Osten-Sacken* - ST PETERSBURG (Academy of Fine Art): *Portrait of the Fabulist Krylov* - ST PETERSBURG (Gosudarstvennyj Russkij Muz.): *The Baptism of Vladimir I in 988* - ST PETERSBURG (Hermitage): *The Entombment* (in the style of Raphael).

EGGINTON, Frank J., or Eggington
Irish, 20th century.
Born 1908; died 1990.
Watercolourist. Landscapes, landscapes with figures.
Frank J. Egginton painted typical Irish landscapes.
BIBLIOGRAPHY:
Waters, Grant M., *Dictionary of British Artists, working 1900-1950*, Eastbourne Fine Art, Eastbourne, 1975.
AUCTION RECORDS:
LONDON, 3 Nov 1982, *Connemara Ponies near Recess* (watercolour, 20 3/4 x 29 1/2 ins / 53 x 75 cm) GBP 300. LONDON, 30 March 1983, *Corraun Achill, Co. Mayo* (watercolour, 20 1/2 x 29 1/4 ins / 52 x 74 cm) GBP 400. BELFAST, 30 May 1990, *Port of Killary near Leenane in Galway County* (watercolour, 21 x 29 3/4 ins / 53.3 x 75.6 cm) GBP 2,200. LONDON, 8 Feb 1991, *Returning Home in a Gig on an Irish Road* (watercolour, 20 1/2 x 29 1/2 ins / 52.1 x 75 cm) GBP 1,320. DUBLIN, 26 May 1993, *Early Morning in Ballyconneely* (1972, watercolour, 28 1/2 x 29 1/2 ins / 72.7 x 75 cm) IEP 1,980. MONTREAL, 23-24 Nov 1993, *Ring of Kerry* (watercolour, 21 x 29 ins / 53.3 x 73.6 cm) CAD 2,200. LONDON, 2 June 1995, *Lake in Galway County* (watercolour, 20 3/4 x 30 ins / 53 x 76 cm) GBP 1,495. DUBLIN, 31 March 1999, *Pony and Trap in Connemara Landscape* (1973, watercolour, 21 x 30 ins / 53 x 76 cm) IEP 6,500. LONDON, 19 April 1999, *The Maamturk Mountains, Connemara* (watercolour, 21 x 29 ins / 53 x 74 cm) GBP 7,000. DUBLIN, 31 May 2000, *Road to Carna, Connemara* (watercolour, 21 x 29 ins / 53 x 74 cm) IEP 4,000. LONDON, 17 May 2001, *Sheephaven and Melmore Head, from Horn Head, Co. Donegal* (pencil and watercolour, 20 x 29 ins / 52 x 74 cm) GBP 6,000. LONDON, 17 May 2002, *Autumn Colours, Ards, Co Donegal* (1988, watercolour, 20 x 28 ins / 51 x 70 cm) GBP 3,200. LONDON, 15 May 2003, *Ducks on a Wet Road, Co Down* (pencil and watercolour, 15 x 20 ins / 37 x 52 cm) GBP 3,500. DUBLIN, 27 April 2004, *Waterville Lake, County Kerry. Meenish Island, Connemara* (watercolour, 15 x 21 ins / 38 x 53 cm) EUR 5,000. BELFAST, 6 Oct 2004, *Connemara Cottage* (1973, oil on canvas, 36 x 48 ins / 91 x 122 cm) GBP 7,000.

EGGINTON, Wycliffe
British, 19th - 20th century.
Born 1875; died 1951.
Draughtsman, watercolourist. Landscapes with figures.
Wycliffe Egginton mainly produced landscapes of moorland in Dartmoor in Devon, sheep grazing and sometimes horses and ponies. Influenced to some extent by the Post-Impressionism of the period, he was careful to convey the effects of the time of day, the seasons and the weather in works such as *Morning*, *Peaceful Evening*, *October Morning*, *Cloudy Weather* and *Stormy Day*. He exhibited in Paris at the Salon des Artistes Français in the 1920s.

AUCTION RECORDS:
LONDON, 23 July 1926, *Moorland Scene, Hampsted* (drawing) GBP 8. LONDON, 31 March 1943, *Harbour Scene* (watercolour) GBP 11. LONDON, 26 Nov 1943, *Domestic Scene with Sheep* (drawing) GBP 19. LONDON, 10 May 1946, *Morning at Loch Moro* (drawing) GBP 24; *Peaceful Evening, Arisaig* (drawing) GBP 16; *Evening, Windsor Pond* (1925; *Loch Macraig, near Aberfeldy* (1924, two drawings, collection) GBP 37. LONDON, 27 Feb 1985, *On the Teign Marshes* (watercolour, 9¾ x 13¾ ins / 25 x 35 cm) GBP 500. LONDON, 26 Sept 1990, *Return of the Livestock* (watercolour, 23½ x 35½ ins / 60 x 90 cm) GBP 1,540. DUBLIN, 26 May 1993, *Sheep on the Way to Pasture* (watercolour, 6¾ x 9¼ ins / 17.2 x 23.5 cm) IEP 715. ST ASAPH, 2 June 1994, *Crossroads* (watercolour, 14 x 20¾ ins / 35.5 x 53 cm) GBP 1,897. LONDON, 9 May 1996, *Wind in the Meadow* (watercolour, 21 x 29 ins / 53.3 x 73.7 cm) GBP 1,380. LONDON, 21 May 1999, *Drinking Pool. Highland River. Cattle Grazing* (watercolour, three, 10 x 14 ins / 25 x 35 cm) GBP 2,800. DUBLIN, 8 Dec 1999, *Cloud-swept Moor* (oil on canvas, 15 x 21 ins / 38 x 53 cm) IEP 3,000. DUBLIN, 31 May 2000, *Farmyard Scene* (watercolour, 9 x 13 ins / 23 x 33 cm) IEP 2,000. DUBLIN, 28 March 2001, *Moorland River Landscape* (watercolour, 21 x 30 ins / 54 x 76 cm) IEP 2,600. LEEDS, 23 July 2002, *Road Across the Common* (oil on canvas, 30 x 50 ins / 76 x 127 cm) GBP 4,600. DUBLIN, 10 Dec 2003, *Asking the Way. Marshes* (watercolour, a pair, 11 x 14 ins / 27 x 36 cm) EUR 1,900. EDINBURGH, 17 Sept 2004, *Haldon Hill* (oil on board, 30 x 47 ins / 75 x 120 cm) GBP 2,300. EDINBURGH, 17 Sept 2004, *Coastal Scene with Fisherman at Sunset* (watercolour, 30 x 48 ins / 75 x 122 cm) GBP 2,600.

EGGLESTON, Allegra
American, 19th - 20th century.
Born in Stillwater.
Painter.
Allegra Eggleston was a pupil of Charles Lesar and Wyatt Eaton.

EGGLESTON, Benjamin Osro
American, 19th - 20th century.
Born 22 January 1867, in Belvedere; died 1937.
Painter. Figures, landscapes.
He was a pupil of Douglas Volk. He settled in Brooklyn, where he was a member of several art clubs.
AUCTION RECORDS:
NEW YORK, 28-30 Jan 1903, *Children in Bygone Times*, USD 300. NEW YORK, 3 April 1903, *The Stream*, USD 130; *Autumn Leaves*, USD 250. NEW YORK, 30 Jan 1976, *The Hunter* (oil on canvas, 42¼ x 36 ins / 107 x 91.5 cm) USD 700. NEW YORK, 23 Sept 1981, *Market Scene, Paris* (1896, oil on canvas, 17½ x 15 ins / 44.5 x 38.1 cm) USD 4,800. NEW YORK, 15 June 1984, *Peasant in a Field* (1888, oil on canvas, 10 x 12¼ ins / 25.3 x 31 cm) USD 2,000. NEW YORK, 5 Dec 1985, *A June Morning* (1888, oil on canvas, 10 x 12 ins / 25.4 x 30.5 cm) USD 3,500. NEW YORK, 24 Jan 1989, *Brooklyn Bridge* (oil on canvas, 47¼ x 37½ ins / 120 x 95 cm) USD 7,700. NEW YORK, 26 May 1999, *November Day* (oil on canvas, 14 x 18 ins / 36 x 46 cm) USD 3,250. NEW YORK, 29 Sept 1999, *Wood Nymph. Echoes* (one oil on board, one oil on panel, a pair, 10 x 9 ins / 25 x 23 cm) USD 4,250. NEW YORK, 5 Dec 2000, *Woodcutters* (oil on canvas) USD 3,250. NEW YORK, 22 May 2001, *Afternoon Idle* (oil on canvas, 28 x 50 ins / 72 x 127 cm) USD 20,000. NEW YORK, 5 Dec 2001, *November Day* (acrylic on canvas, 14 x 18 ins / 36 x 46 cm) USD 1,500. NEW ORLEANS, 5 April 2003, *Autumn Pastoral Landscape* (1915, oil on canvas, 16 x 24 ins / 41 x 61 cm) USD 4,500. MILFORD, 23 Oct 2003, *Landscape* (1915, oil on canvas, 16 x 24 ins / 41 x 61 cm) USD 3,000. BOSTON, 5 March 2004, *On the Beach* (oil on board, 10 x 13 ins / 25 x 33 cm) USD 9,500.

EGGLESTON, Edward M.
American, 20th century.
Born 1887, in Ohio.
Painter, illustrator.
Edward Eggleston was a member of several art associations, including the Society of Illustrators.

EGGLI, Daniel, or Egli
Swiss, 16th century.
Born to a family originally from Sursee.
Glass painter.
Eggli is thought to have made some armorial windows for Melchior Entli in Beromünster.

EGGLI, Hans Jakob, or Egli
Swiss, 17th century.
Active in Aarau.
Glass painter.
Hans Eggli was accepted as a burgess of Bern on 20 July 1629.

EGGLI, Jakob
Swiss, 19th century.
Born 17 February 1812, in Dachsen; died in Rheinau.
Painter (gouache), lithographer. Landscapes.
Jakob Eggli specialised in painting landscapes in gouache. He travelled to southern Germany and lived in Dachsen in the castles of Laufen and Wyden near Andelfingen.

EGHEM. See **EEGHEM**

EGIDIO DEGLI SCALZI
Italian, 13th century.
Died 1283, in Perugia.
Miniaturist.
This artist was a Dominican monk.

EGIDIO DI DOMENICO
Italian, 14th century.
Active in Bologna at the end of the 14th century.
Sculptor.
Egidio di Domenico worked with Berto di Antonio, Francesco di Guardo and Berto di Giacomo at the Loggia del Carrobio.

EGIDIO DI ONOFRIO. See **ONOFRIO DI GILIO**

EGIDIO FIAMMINGO. See **VLIETE Gillis van den**

EGIDIO TEUTONICO
Italian, 15th century.
Active in Perugia.
Illuminator.
An *Officium Passionis Jesu Christi* of 1474 has the signature *Egidius Reuto fecit*.

EGIDIUCCI, Cruciano
Italian, 17th century.
Active at the beginning of the 17th century.
Sculptor, mosaicist.
The ciborium of S Maria Maggiore in Bettona, and the baptismal fonts decorated with mosaics at S Lorenzo in Spello, are by Egiducci.

EGIDIUS. See also **EGIDIO** and **AEGIDIUS**

EGIDIUS, Halfdan. See **EGEDIUS**

EGIDIUS DE DES, or Dézsi Egyed
Hungarian, 15th century.
Painter.
Egidius de Des produced the mural paintings of the church at Feketegyármat (now Lermata Neagra, near Arad, in Romania) in 1467.

EGIDY, Constantin
Engraver.

Mentioned by Nagler as having engraved two plates representing altars.

EGIDY, Emmy von
German, 19th - 20th century.
Born 1872, in Pirna.
Sculptor. Statuettes, busts.

Egidy primarily produced statuettes in coloured plaster, but also executed busts and portraits. She was represented at the great exhibition in Dresden in 1904.

EGINTON, E. A.
British, 19th century.
Active in Worcester.
Draughtsman, engraver (etching).

A series of etchings *Our Village* bearing E.A. Eginton's signature appeared at Worcester in 1842. He was probably the son of the architect Harvey Eginton.

EGINTON, Francis
British, 18th - 19th century.
Born 1737; died 1805, in Handsworth.
Glass painter.

Francis Eginton was a pupil at Handsworth, near Birmingham and contributed greatly to the development of the art of glass painting from 1784 to 1805. His best works include a *Resurrection* in the churches of Salisbury and Lichfield and *The Conversion of St Paul* in St Pauls in Birmingham. His stained-glass windows can be found in St Asaph Cathedral, Fonthill Abbey and Magdalen College, Oxford.

EGINTON, Francis
British, 19th century.
Born 1775, in Birmingham; died 20 October 1823, in Meertown House, near Newport (Shropshire).
Engraver.

Francis Eginton was the son and pupil of John Eginton. He engraved stippling illustrations in the style of his own designs for a *New Guide to Bath*. Other notable works by him are two watercolours for *Soho Manufactory* by Matthew Boulton, illustrations for the *Historical and Topographical Account of Leominster* by J. Price, illustrations for the *A Poetic Survey Round Birmingham* by James Bisset and illustrations for the *History and Antiquities of Staffordshire* by Stebbing Shaw.

MUSEUMS AND GALLERIES:
BIRMINGHAM (Mus. and AG): *View of Soho Manufactory, Handsworth* (1800, engraving).

EGINTON, John
British, 18th century.
Active in England c. 1790.
Engraver (stippling).

Le Blanc mentions the following work by John Eginton: *Hebe Pours a Drink for the Eagle of Jupiter*, in the style of W. Hamilton.

EGINTON, William Raphael
British, 19th century.
Died 17 September 1834, in Perdeswell Cottage, near Worcester.
Glass painter.

William Raphael Eginton was the son of the glass painter Francis Eginton. He was very prolific and worked in Birmingham and elsewhere.

EGIS, Boris Issakovich
Ukrainian, 19th - 20th century.
Born 1869, in Odessa; died 1946.
Painter. Portraits, genre scenes.

Boris Issakovich Egis trained in Odessa between 1889 and 1892, then at the Académie Colarossi and the Académie Julian in Paris. He painted women's portraits and genre scenes like *Love Letter*. He featured at the exhibition of the academy in St Petersburg in 1907.

EGLAUER, Johann Andreas, or Iglauer
Austrian, 17th - 18th century.
Born 1647, in Vienna; died 21 May 1726, in Vienna.
Sculptor.

Johann Eglauer trained under the sculptor J. Keller and married the latter's daughter in 1691.

EGLAUER, Johann Georg
Austrian, 17th century.
Born 17th century, in Vienna.
Painter.

Johann Georg Eglauer was the brother of the sculptor Johann Andreas Eglauer. After a stay of three years in Italy, he worked at the monastery of Krema.

ÉGLÉE. See **ADORNE DE TSCHARNER Louise**

EGLÈNE-SURIEUX, Blanche
French, 20th century.
Born in Lyons.
Painter. Landscapes, seascapes.

Blanche Eglène-Surieux began exhibiting at the Salon des Artistes Français in 1935.

EGLETON, William Henry
British, 19th century.
Active in London.
Engraver.

William Henry Egleton engraved plates for the *Illustrations of Landscapes for Sir Walter Scott, the Author of the Waverley Novels*, illustrations for the *Book on Beauty* by J. Heath and the illustrations for the *Portraits of the Female Aristocracy* by Finden.

EGLEY, William, or Egly
British, 19th century.
Born 1798, in Doncaster; died 1870, in London.
Miniaturist.

Although in employment, William Egley also found time to paint. He showed a special aptitude for painting from a very early age. In 1824 he sent his *Portrait of the Actor Yale* to the Royal Academy. From then on, he devoted himself to portraits. Two years before his death he executed a *Portrait of the Sculptor Foeey*. He achieved his greatest success through his paintings of children. He exhibited several times at the Royal Academy, and sent several miniatures to the Suffolk Street Gallery and the British Institution.

EGLEY, William Maw
British, 19th century.
Born 1826; died 1916.
Painter. History painting, genre scenes.

Willliam Maw Egley was the son of William Egley. He very ably portrayed English humour in his paintings, and exhibited in London at the Royal Academy and Suffolk Street Gallery from 1843 to 1898.

MUSEUMS AND GALLERIES:
BATH (Holburne Mus. of Art): *Military Aspirations or 'Music Hath Charms'* (1861, oil on canvas) - LONDON (Victoria and Albert Mus.): after the novel by Dickens, *Florence Dombey; Monsieur de Pourceaugnac; Scene from The Imaginary Invalid* (two versions); *Scene from Tartuffe; Scene from Doctor in Spite of Himself.*

AUCTION RECORDS:
LONDON, 30 Nov 1907, *Dance*, GBP 4. LONDON, 2 April 1910, *Cardinal Richelieu Dancing before Anne of Austria*, GBP 21. LONDON, 10 Dec 1926, *Scene from The School for Scandal, Act IV, Scene I* (1882) GBP 21. LONDON, 12 April 1934, *Dance*, GBP 5. LONDON, 6 June 1935, *New Acquisition* (1889) GBP 6. LONDON, 12 Feb 1969, *Young Girl Leaning against a Tree*,

GBP 2,300. LONDON, 5 Oct 1973, *Pyramus and Thisbe* (1861) Gns 2,000. LONDON, 27 June 1978, *Pyramus and Thisbe* (1861, oil on canvas, 17 1/2 x 13 3/4 ins / 44.5 x 35 cm) GBP 5,500. LONDON, 24 March 1981, *Miranda's First Sight of Ferdinand* (1863, oil on canvas, 25 x 16 ins / 63.5 x 40.5 cm) GBP 1,350. LONDON, 17 June 1987, *Return Home* (1866, oil on canvas, 30 x 49 1/4 ins / 76 x 125 cm) GBP 5,000. LONDON, 4 Nov 1994, *Letter* (1863, oil on canvas, 10 x 8 ins / 25.4 x 20.3 cm) GBP 5,175. LONDON, 6 Nov 1995, *Forget-Me-Not* (1872, oil on canvas, 11 1/2 x 9 1/2 ins / 29 x 24 cm) GBP 2,185. LONDON, 17 April 1996, *Slave Market* (oil on canvas, 27 1/2 x 35 3/4 ins / 70 x 91 cm) GBP 2,760. LONDON, 12 March 1997, *Connoisseur* (oil on canvas, 39 x 29 3/4 ins / 99 x 75.5 cm) GBP 6,900. BURY ST EDMUNDS, 6 Oct 2001, *Study of a Seated Girl Looking at a Locket with Her Father* (1875, oil on canvas, 30 x 24 ins / 76 x 61 cm) GBP 4,200. LONDON, 11 June 2002, *Catherine of Aragon* (oil on canvas, 36 x 48 ins / 91 x 122 cm) GBP 17,000. LONDON, 17 Sept 2002, *Repose* (1883, oil on canvas, 18 x 26 ins / 45 x 65 cm) GBP 2,000. TORONTO, 4 May 2004, *Preparing for Christmas* (1868, oil on canvas, 24 x 19 ins / 62 x 47 cm) CAD 30,000. STOCKHOLM, 26 May 2004, *The Taming of the Shrew, Act 4 scene 3* (1856, oil on canvas, 37 x 29 ins / 93 x 74 cm) SEK 66,000.

EGLI. See also **EGGLI**

EGLI, David

Swiss, 18th - 19th century.

Active in Wald (Zurich).

Painter, draughtsman. History painting, portraits.

David Egli trained under Joh. Pfenninger.

MUSEUMS AND GALLERIES:

ZURICH: *Portrait of Woman in Village Costume.*

EGLI, Gotthilf

Swiss, 20th century.

Born 1896, in Witikon; died 1954, in Zurich.

Painter. Landscapes, still-lifes.

EGLI-SCHÄTTI, Johannes

Swiss, 19th century.

Born 30 May 1828, in Zurich; died 26 March 1870, in Zurich.

Draughtsman, lithographer.

Johannes Egli-Schätti trained at the Munich academy and operated a lithography studio in Zurich. Notable works of his include an *Album of Views of Zurich*, a frontispiece with eight portraits of founders of the Artistic Union of Zurich, and the *Book of the Coats of Arms of the City and of former Zurich Nobility*.

EGLIN, Anton

Swiss, 19th century.

Active in Lucerne.

Lithographer.

Anton Eglin was the brother of Carl Martin Eglin.

EGLIN, Bernhard

Swiss, 19th century.

Born 15 August 1798, in Lucerne; died 5 September 1875.

Draughtsman, lithographer. Genre scenes, animals.

Bernhard Eglin trained in the studio of the lithographer Engelmann in Mulhouse. After having joined forces with his brother Carl Martin in a lithography studio, which was the first of its kind in Lucerne, he set up his own business in 1826. His notable works include lithographic views and genre panels, such as *Reprimand* and *Dogs of the St-Bernard Hospice*.

EGLIN, Carl Martin

Swiss, 19th century.

Born 16 June 1787, in Lucerne; died 14 or 18 October 1850, in Lucerne.

Painter, engraver, lithographer.

According to Wegler, Carl Eglin worked as a portrait and still-life painter in Munich before joining forces with his brother in Lucerne. In 1832 Eglin restored the *Dance of Death* by Von Wyl in Lucerne and copied frescoes by Holbein on the façade of Dullick House in Lucerne.

EGLIN, Philip

British, 20th - 21st century.

Born 1959, in Gibraltar.

Sculptor (ceramics). Figures.

Philip Eglin trained at the Staffordshire Polytechnic and the Royal College of Art in London. He is particularly known for his figures of 'long-limbed' nudes, often compared to the slender ladies painted by the 16th-century German painter Lucas Cranach. Eglin is clearly conscious of this influence and connection; one of his pieces (a decorated/painted 'bucket') is called *Oliver's 'Cranach Nudes'* (2003).

He uses a technique of folding and modelling sheets of clay that he has decorated with the emblems and 'waste' of modern life. Thus, one of his Madonnas will have a headdress decorated with the 'M' of McDonald's or the label of discarded plastic bottles or pieces of packaging. This combination of 'recycled' materials and symbols of the modern everyday with a representation and symbol of the ancient and sacred is a hallmark of Eglin's work. He deliberately combines such elements to arrive, in the artist's words, at 'a balance between the high and the lowbrow, the reverent and the irreverent, the raw and the subtle, the sophisticated and the crude'. Eglin also created a series of Madonnas inspired by and based on northern European medieval woodcarvings housed at the Victoria and Albert Museum in London.

Eglin won the Jerwood Prize for Applied Arts (ceramics) in 1996, and his work is held at the Stedelijk Museum in Amsterdam, the National Museums of Scotland in Edinburgh, the Victoria and Albert Museum in London and the Fitzwilliam Museum in Cambridge.

BIBLIOGRAPHY:

Philip Eglin, exhibition brochure, Scottish Gallery, Edinburgh, 1997. Harrod, Tanya, *Philip Eglin*, exhibition brochure, Barret Marsden Gallery, London, June 2001.

MUSEUMS AND GALLERIES:

AMSTERDAM (Stedelijk Mus.) - CAMBRIDGE (Fitzwilliam Museum): *Popular Madonna* (2002, porcelain); *Madonna col Bambino* (1992, earthenware) - EDINBURGH (National Museums of Scotland) - LONDON (Victoria and Albert Mus.).

EGLING, Georg

German, 17th century.

Died 25 October 1632.

Painter.

Georg Egling trained under Georg Hauer in Breslau. After having presented a *Crucifixion*, he was accepted as a master painter in 1624.

EGLINGTON, James T.

British, 19th century.

Active in Liverpool.

Painter. History painting, genre scenes.

James T. Eglington exhibited at the Royal Academy, the British Institution and Suffolk Street Gallery between 1847 and 1859.

MUSEUMS AND GALLERIES:

LIVERPOOL: *Richard III Entering London.*

AUCTION RECORDS:

LONDON, 2 July 1941, *Riding Liberties of Liverpool* (1834) GBP 10.

EGLINGTON, Samuel
British, 19th century.
Active in Liverpool.
Painter. Landscapes.
Samuel Eglington exhibited in London, notably at the Royal Academy and the British Institution, from 1833 to 1855.
MUSEUMS AND GALLERIES:
LIVERPOOL: *Old Haymarket.*
AUCTION RECORDS:
LONDON, 12 June 1908, *Emigrants,* FRF 26. LONDON, 22 Feb 1972, *Children's Games,* GBP 460.

EGLITE, Laima
Latvian, 20th century.
Painter.
Laima Eglite attended the Rozental school in Riga from 1958 to 1965 and continued her studies at the Latvian academy of fine art from 1966 to 1974. She was a member of the Union of Artists and participated in national and international exhibitions in Riga, Finland, the USA and Germany.
MUSEUMS AND GALLERIES:
MOSCOW (Ministry of Culture) - RIGA (Valsts makslas muz.).
AUCTION RECORDS:
PARIS, 11 July 1990, *Portrait in Black and White* (1990, oil on panel, 53 1/2 x 46 ins / 136 x 116 cm) FRF 4,800.

EGLOFF, Anton
Swiss, 20th century.
Born 1933, in Wettingen.
Sculptor of assemblages, mixed media.
Egloff lives and works in Lucerne. He trained at the schools of applied arts in Zurich and Lucerne, before enrolling at the national art academy in Düsseldorf.
Up until 1968, his sculptures were based on variations on the cube. However, since then, he has abandoned all formal coherence in favour of complete freedom of imagination and diversity of form. Whether the idea precedes the execution or whether the qualities of the material give rise to the idea, his works are above all vehicles for ideas, though generally consisting of meticulous concrete embodiments, juxtaposing heterogeneous elements.
Egloff has participated in group exhibitions, notably *Art of Today* at the Musée Suermondt in Aachen in 1970. He has also held solo exhibitions of his works at the Raeber gallery in Lucerne since 1968.
BIBLIOGRAPHY:
Kneubühler, Theo, *Kunst: 28 Schweizer,* exhibition catalogue, Gal. Raeber, Lucerne, 1972.

EGLOFFSTEIN, Julie von (Countess)
German, 19th century.
Born 1792, in Hildesheim; died 1869, in Marienroda.
Painter. Portraits, genre scenes.
Notable works by Julie von Egloffstein include: *Portrait of Goethe, Charles-Auguste, Grand-Duke of Saxony-Weimar, at his Desk, Neapolitan Fisherman, Portrait of the Grand-Duchess of Saxony-Weimar, Hagar and Ishmael* and *Young Girl Braiding her Hair.*
MUSEUMS AND GALLERIES:
HANOVER (Kestner-Mus.): *Portrait of Kestner* - WEIMAR: *Portrait of Goethe.*

EGMAN. See **ECKMAN**

EGMONT, d' (Mlle)
French, 17th century.
Miniaturist.
Two works by Mlle d'Egmont, *Marriage of St Catherine* and *Christ at the House of Martha and Mary* were in the collection of the kings of France in 1709.

EGMONT, Harmen
Dutch, 17th century.
Active in Amsterdam in 1684.
Sculptor.

EGMONT, Jan van
French, 18th century.
Born in the 18th century, in Amsterdam.
Painter.
Jan van Egmont entered the guild in Leiden in 1763.

EGMONT, Justus van, or Justus Verus ab Egmont
Flemish, 17th century.
Born 22 September 1601, in Leiden; died 8 January 1674, in Antwerp.
Painter. History painting, allegorical subjects, portraits. Flemish School.
Justus van Egmont was a pupil of Kaspar van den Hoecke in 1615. After a period in Italy in 1618 he studied under Rubens, who sent him in his place to Mechelen to paint a *Last Supper* for the cathedral. Egmont continued to assist Rubens in a number of his works until 1628. Afterwards he became a master and went to France with his family. He was painter to Louis III and Louis XIV and was one of the founders of the Académie Royale de Peinture et de Sculpture in 1648. He returned to Brussels in 1649 and to Antwerp not later than 1653. He worked on tapestry designs for Marshal Daumont in 1658, the history of Caesar Augustus in 1659, and the history of Antony and Cleopatra in 1661. He executed a large painting of the family tree of the counts of Egmont, wishing to be ranked alongside them even though he was a carpenter's son. His collection of paintings by his contemporaries was stunning. In 1673 he exhibited the *Portrait of Mme Perceval* in Paris.
While assisting Vouet, in the same vein as he had formerly supported Rubens, he came into conflict with the Académie de St-Luc, which claimed the right to prohibit artists who were not members of the guild from painting and sculpting. His few extant works evince a Flemish flavour in their lively tints and crispness of touch.
MUSEUMS AND GALLERIES:
AUGSBURG: *Portrait of Archduchess Anne of Austria, Queen of Spain* - CHANTILLY (Mus. Condé): *Portrait of the Grand Condé; Same Subject; Portrait of François de la Mothe-Houdancourt; Portrait* - MECHELEN (Sint-Rombouts Kathedraal): *Last Supper, under the Name of Rubens* - OBERSCHLEISSHEIM: *Maria de Medici* - POMMERSFELDEN: *Portrait of Man and Woman in Red* - RHEIMS: *Love and Hope* - VIENNA: *The Child Philippe II; Archduke Léopold-Guillaume in Armour.*
AUCTION RECORDS:
LONDON, 26 Sept 1980, *Portrait of Charlotte, Countess of Derby* (oil on canvas, 43 1/4 x 36 1/4 ins / 109.6 x 92 cm) GBP 450. LONDON, 19 May 1989, *Portrait of Philippe, Duke of Anjou as a Child* (oil on grisaille panel, 15 1/2 x 11 1/2 ins / 39.3 x 29.3 cm) GBP 6,050. LONDON, 9 Dec 1992, *Portrait of a Woman Holding Jasmine Flowers* (oil on canvas, 51 1/4 x 38 1/2 ins / 130 x 98 cm) GBP 10,450. LONDON, 4 July 1994, *Allegorical Scene* (black chalk and ink, 13 3/4 x 19 ins / 35.1 x 48.5 cm) GBP 3,450. LONDON, 4 July 1994, *Allegorical Scene* (black chalk and brown ink heightened with white, 13 3/4 x 19 ins / 35.1 x 48.5 cm) GBP 3,450. LUCERNE, 19 May 1999, *Portrait of Young Girl in Puritan Dress* (oil on canvas, 18 x 15 ins / 46 x 38 cm) CHF 4,800. VIENNA, 30 March 2000, *Portrait of Young Lady as Diana* (oil on canvas, 53 x 36 ins / 135 x 91 cm) ATS 220,000. NEW YORK, 26 May 2000, *Portrait of Archduke Leopold Wilhelm of Austria* (oil on canvas, 17 x 13 ins / 43 x 34 cm) USD 18,000. MADRID, 27 March 2001, *Portrait of Luis II de Borbon, the Great Earl* (oil on canvas, 46 x 55 ins / 116 x 139 cm) ESP 12,000,000.

EGMONT, Konstantyn van
Flemish, 17th century.

Baptised 19 September 1624 in Antwerp; died 31 January 1679, in Paris.
Painter.
Flemish School.

Konstantyn van Egmont was the natural son of Justus van Egmont. He married Marie-Antoinette des Brières on 29 November 1656 in Paris, and was 'Peintre ordinaire du Roy et Gentilhomme de la chambre Royale' (painter in ordinary to the king and gentleman of the royal chamber).

EGMONT, Pieter Cornelisz. van
Flemish, 17th century.
Born c. 1615; died c. 1664.
Active in Leiden.
Painter. Portraits, genre scenes, interiors.
Flemish School.

Pieter Cornelisz. van Egmont entered the painters' guild on 12 December 1661. Extant are his *Two Hermits*, *Portrait with Cradle*, and *Portrait with Spinning Wheel*.

AUCTION RECORDS:
LONDON, 18 Oct 1989, *Old Man Seated at a Table in his Study* (oil on panel, 11 1/2 x 10 ins / 29.5 x 24.5 cm) GBP 9,350. AMSTERDAM, 22 May 1990, *Woman in a Kitchen* (oil on panel, 8 1/4 x 7 1/4 ins / 21 x 18.5 cm) NLG 32,200.

EGMONT, Théodore Juste d'
French, 17th century.
Born 1639, in Paris; died 25 April 1672, in Paris.
Painter.

Théodore Juste d'Egmont was Painter in Ordinary to the king and Steward of the Chambers of the duke of Orléans.

MUSEUMS AND GALLERIES:
CHARTRES: *Portrait of Madame de Normainville*.

EGMONT, Willem van
Flemish, 18th century.
Active in Amsterdam and Leiden.
Painter.
Flemish School.

Willem van Egmont entered the guild in 1743.

EGNER, Hans Michel
French, 16th century.
Active in Strasbourg.
Sculptor (including wood).

This artist is presumably the same person as the sculptor Hans Michel Egner who, to celebrate becoming a burgher of the city of Basel, sculpted a stone statue of *Munatius Plancus*. This was then painted by J. Nussbaum and placed in the town hall.

EGNER, Marie
Austrian, 19th - 20th century.
Born 25 August 1850, in Radkersburg (Styria); died 1940.
Painter (gouache). Still-lifes, flowers, landscapes.

Egner trained at Graz and Düsseldorf art academies, and was a pupil of K. Schindler in Vienna. She was an open air painter who drew inspiration from the Barbizon school. She took part in numerous exhibitions, firstly in Vienna in 1882, where she showed *Village Street in Lombardy*; and later in London at the Royal Academy, Paris, Munich and Düsseldorf. Some of her works were included in the 1994 exhibition *Chefs-d'Oeuvre du Belvédère de Vienne* (*Masterpieces from the Belvedere in Vienna*) at the Musée Marmottan in Paris.

MUSEUMS AND GALLERIES:
GRAZ: *Ducks on the Pond* - VIENNA (Österreichische Gal. Belvedere).

AUCTION RECORDS:
VIENNA, 13 March 1971, *Flowers*, ATS 35,000. VIENNA, 6 June 1972, *Flowers*, ATS 32,000. VIENNA, 4 Dec 1973, *Flowering Meadow*, ATS 50,000. VIENNA, 13 Jan 1976, *Still-life* (oil on canvas, 21 3/4 x 26 3/4 ins / 55.5 x 68 cm) ATS 28,000. VIENNA, 14 March 1978, *Bouquet of Wild Flowers* (mixed media, 24 1/2 x 18 1/2 ins / 62 x 47 cm) ATS 32,000. VIENNA, 20 May 1981, *Alpine Landscape* (watercolour, 12 1/2 x 11 1/4 ins / 32 x 28.5 cm) ATS 20,000. VIENNA, 23 March 1983, *From Hofgastein* (c. 1915, gouache, 11 x 15 ins / 28 x 38 cm) ATS 32,000. VIENNA, 14 Sept 1983, *Autumn Morning* (oil on canvas, 27 1/4 x 20 1/2 ins / 69 x 52 cm) ATS 110,000. VIENNA, 15 Oct 1987, *Orchard* (watercolour heightened with white, 23 1/2 x 17 3/4 ins / 60 x 45 cm) ATS 50,000. VIENNA, 9 Dec 1987, *Bella Vista* (oil on canvas, 37 3/4 x 26 3/4 ins / 96 x 68 cm) ATS 250,000. LONDON, 22 Nov 1989, *Barbary Figs in the Corner of the Terrace* (oil on canvas, 11 3/4 x 15 3/4 ins / 30 x 40 cm) GBP 6,600. MUNICH, 23 June 1997, *Orchids* (oil on canvas, 21 3/4 x 22 ins / 55.5 x 56 cm) DEM 21,600.

EGNOLT, Thomas
Austrian, 15th century.
Painter.

Thomas Egnolt is thought to be the painter of some frescoes, dated 1440, in the basilica of St Peter in Altenburg.

EGO, Ernest
French, 19th - 20th century.
Born in the second half of the 19th century, in Douai.
Painter.

Ernest Ego was a pupil of the elder Chigot. One of his canvases was shown at the Salon des Artistes Français in 1919.

EGO, Nelly
French, 20th century.
Painter.

Nelly Ego was a member of the Société du Salon des Artistes Français in Paris, where she was awarded an honourable mention and in 1941 won the Zwiller prize.

EGOGNI, Ambrogio. See **BORGOGNONE Ambrogio**

EGORKIN, Vasili, or Yegorkin
Russian, 20th century.
Born 1936.
Painter. Landscapes, flowers.

Vasili Egorkin studied at the Repin Institute in Leningrad (now St Petersburg) and was a member of the USSR Artists Union. He painted uncontroversial subjects using a thick impasto.

MUSEUMS AND GALLERIES:
KIEV (Museum of Russian Art) - MOSCOW (Central Museum of the Revolution) - MOSCOW (Ministry of Culture) - ST PETERSBURG (Academy).

AUCTION RECORDS:
PARIS, 4 March 1991, *Ferapontov Monastery* (oil on canvas, 33 x 23 1/2 ins / 84 x 60 cm) FRF 4,100.

EGORNOFF. See **EGOROV**

EGOROFF. See **EGOROV**

EGOROV, Aleksei Egorovich
Russian, 19th century.
Born c. 1776, in the Kalmyles Steppes; died 22 (10) September 1851, in St Petersburg.
Painter, engraver, draughtsman. Religious subjects, history painting, portraits.

Taken prisoner by the Cossacks at the age of six, Egorov was brought up in an educational institute in Moscow, then studied at the St Petersburg academy of fine arts, where he was a pupil of Akimov and Ugryumov. He won a scholarship in 1803 and went to live in Rome, where he met Camuccini and Canova.

He had a great influence on Russian art, as he taught several generations of painters, including Bassin, Savailov, Bryullov and Shamshin. His works can be found in a number of churches, in St Petersburg, at Peterhof, Pushkin and Moscow. He also produced a great number of drawings and etchings.

MUSEUMS AND GALLERIES:

GORKI: *St Peter and St Paul* - KRASNOYARSK: *Portrait of Aleksandr Niewsky* - MOSCOW (Rumiantsev Mus.): *The Holy Family; The Madonna and Child; The Virgin; The Entombment; The Descending of the Holy Spirit; Christ Appears Before Mary Magdalene* - MOSCOW (State Tretyakov Gal.): *Virgin; Susanna; The Entombment; Taking Away of the Cross; The Evangelists; Michael the Archangel Striking Down the Devil; St George and the Dragon; Joseph's Reconciliation with his Brothers; The Holy Spirit Descending to the Apostles; The Annunciation; The Ascension of Jesus Christ; 'Appease my Sorrow'; Allegorical Paintings of the Flourishing State of Science and the Arts; Allegorical Painting of Peace; Allegorical Painting about Poltava; Allegorical Painting of the Flooding of St Petersburg in 1824; Pope Silvester Bringing an Ox back to Life; Portrait of the Artist; Portrait of Princess E. Golitsyn, 'The Nocturnal Princess'; Portrait of Sukhanov, Pupil of the Painter; The Agony of Christ* (design); *Preaching to the Shepherds; Joseph and the Wife of Potiphar; Self-portrait* - ST PETERSBURG (Academy): *St Jerome; St Elizabeth and St John the Baptist* - ST PETERSBURG (Gosudarstvennyj Russkij Muz.): *Portrait of Buyalkaia; St Simon and the Infant Jesus; Holy Family; The Agony of Christ; Portrait of AR Tomilov.*

EGOROV, Andrei Simonoviev, or Semenovich or Simionovitch, or Egoroff, Egornoff, Egornov
Russian, 19th - 20th century.
Born 1858, 1860 or 1861, in Moscow; died 1920 or 1924.
Painter (gouache), watercolourist. Still-lifes, landscapes.

Andrei Simonoviev Egorov studied at the academy of St Petersburg and worked under the direction of Akimoff.

MUSEUMS AND GALLERIES:

MOSCOW (State Tretyakov Gal.): *Winter in France* - ST PETERSBURG (Gosudarstvennyj Russkij Muz.): *Before the Rain; Pyrenees* (watercolour); *Morning in the Forest* (watercolour); *Autumn Evening* (watercolour); *Haymaking* (watercolour).

AUCTION RECORDS:

LONDON, 6 Oct 1988, *View of Riga on the Baltic Sea* (oil on panel, 9 1/2 x 12 3/4 ins / 24 x 32.5 cm) GBP 660. LONDON, 5 Oct 1989, *Halt in the Forest* (1896, oil on canvas, 31 1/4 x 24 1/4 ins / 79.5 x 61.4 cm) GBP 4,400. PARIS, 18 March 1991, *Still-life with Cornflowers* (1911, watercolour and gouache, 9 x 11 1/2 ins / 23 x 29 cm) FRF 5,300.

EGOROV, Iévdokime Alexéiévitch
Russian, 19th century.
Born 1832, in St Petersburg; died 1891, in Paris.
Painter (porcelain), engraver (etching).

The son of Aleksei Egorov, Edovkim Alekseevich Egorov made etchings inspired by the history of Russia, especially Ancient Russia. He is known for a set of 27 etching plates, mostly of scenes from peasant life and subjects wearing historical costume.

MUSEUMS AND GALLERIES:

LONDON (British Mus.): collection of 68 etchings (etching).

EGOROV, Mikhail
Russian, 19th century.
Painter.

EGOROV, Petr Ivanovich
Russian, 19th century.
Painter. History painting, portraits.

Petr Ivanovich Egorov trained at the academy of art in St Petersburg where he won various medals. He took part in the 1855 academy exhibition where he showed *Beggar*, in that of 1857, where he showed several watercolour portraits and in that of 1861.

EGOROV, Pronika Prokopi
Russian, 17th century.
Icon painter.

EGOROV, Vladimir Ivanovich
Russian, 19th century.
Painter.

Vladimir Ivanovich Egorov trained at the academy of art in St Petersburg. He took part in the 1861 academy exhibition, where he showed *Self-portrait* which earned him his painter's diploma.

EGRET
French, 17th century.
Painter. History painting.

Egret was a pupil of Ch. Parrocel.

EGRET, Mathieu
French, 16th century.
Active in Cambrai.
Sculptor.

In 1536, Mathieu Egret worked at the château of Escaudoeuvres near Cambrai.

EGRET, Pieter, or Hegret
Flemish, 17th century.
Born 22 September 1637.
Active in Mechelen.
Painter.
Flemish School.

Pieter Egret was taught by Jean van Rintel around 1655 and became a master in 1663.

EGRET, Theodorus, or Hegret
Flemish, 17th - 18th century.
Baptised 12 January 1640; died 29 July 1722, in Mechelen.
Painter. Landscapes.
Flemish School.

Theodorus Egret was a pupil of Cornélis Beerings in 1652 and the master of Egde Baudouin in 1665. He decorated churches in Mechelen and the priory in Hanswyk (two landscapes in which the sky was added by J. M. Coxie).

EGRY, Jozsef
Hungarian, 20th century.
Born 15 March 1883, in Ujlak; died 16 June 1951, in Babacsnytomaj.
Painter (gouache), pastellist, draughtsman, illustrator. Landscapes with figures, waterscapes.
European School group.

Jozsef Egry initially studied at the school of fine art in Budapest, then Munich and Vienna in 1904 and at the Académie Julian in Paris in 1905. He continued his studies in Brussels before returning to his native country. In Budapest he worked in the workshop of Karoly Ferenczy and Paul von Szinyei-Merse from 1906 to 1908. From 1918 until he died, Egry lived on the banks of Lake Balaton. The atmosphere of this landscape influenced his work. His oil, gouache and pastel paintings are characterised by a highly individual style, but one which does not break with the Post-Impressionist tradition firmly established among Hungarian painters of the time. Egry painted the lake and the vineyards along the surrounding hills, the work of the winegrowers, the fishermen in their boats and the work in the fields. But the true theme of his works lay in the sun and water, where the reflections transformed the characters and the landscape. A tightly constructed composition supports this play of light. Egry's work, proclaiming the harmony of man with nature, was recognised very early on. He exhibited first in 1903 in Budapest showing *Greasy Spoon - Study*. His first solo exhibition was also held in Budapest in 1909. He featured in collective exhibitions in Hungary and abroad. He was awarded the Kossuth Prize in 1948. Egry was also a cartoonist and collaborated as an illustrator on various satirical reviews.

BIBLIOGRAPHY:

Németh, Lajos, *Moderne ungarische Kunst*, Corvina Kiadó, Budapest, 1969.

AUCTION RECORDS:

AMSTERDAM, 27-28 May 1993, *Nudes on the Veranda* (oil on canvas, 19 3/4 x 24 ins / 50 x 61 cm) NLG 4,140. BUDAPEST, 1 Nov 2000, *Storm at Lake Balaton* (oil on canvas, 17 x 25 ins / 44 x 64 cm) HUF 4,000,000. BUDAPEST, 1 Dec 2000, *Riverside* (oil on canvas, 19 x 28 ins / 48 x 70 cm) HUF 2,000,000. BUDAPEST, 12 Oct 2001, *Homewards on the Hills* (1914, oil on card, 20 x 28 ins / 50 x 71 cm) HUF 2,600,000. BUDAPEST, 7 Dec 2001, *In the Field* (oil on card, 20 x 26 ins / 50 x 65 cm) HUF 650,000. BUDAPEST, 6 Dec 2002, *Rainbow over the Lake Balaton* (oil on card, 19 x 23 ins / 48 x 58 cm) HUF 6,000,000. BUDAPEST, 6 Dec 2002, *Evening Lights* (oil on canvas, 35 x 28 ins / 90 x 70 cm) HUF 7,500,000. BUDAPEST, 11 April 2003, *Evening Lights on Bank of the River Danube* (pastel, 19 x 26 ins / 48 x 66 cm) HUF 9,500,000. BUDAPEST, 11 April 2003, *Lake Balaton in Sunlight* (1943, oil and pastel on canvas, 28 x 39 ins / 70 x 99 cm) HUF 11,000,000. BUDAPEST, 14 April 2004, *Figure* (1941, watercolour and pastel, 28 x 39 ins / 70 x 100 cm) HUF 4,400,000. BUDAPEST, 2 June 2004, *Outing* (1910, oil on card, 27 x 20 ins / 68 x 50 cm) HUF 1,500,000.

EGSTEIN. See **ECKSTEIN**

EGUCHI, Shu

Japanese, 20th century.
Born 1932, in Kyoto.
Sculptor.

Shu Eguchi studied at the Tokyo School of Fine Arts. In 1965, he took part in the exhibition *New Japanese Painting and Sculpture* at the Museum of Modern Art, New York. In 1969, his work appeared in the exhibition *Contemporary World Art* at the Museum of Modern Art in Tokyo. In 1972, he received the Kobe Modern Sculpture Prize.

EGUCHI, Sogen

Japanese, 20th century.
Born 1919.
Painter, calligrapher.

Sogen Eguchi was educated in the basics of traditional calligraphy. From 1949 to 1951, he exhibited his work at the Japanese Calligraphy Institute, where calligraphy is regarded as a means of artistic expression, and took part in many exhibitions of Japanese abstract calligraphy in Tokyo, Osaka and other venues, as well as the Museum of Modern Art in New York in 1954, Paris in 1955, the Stedelijk Museum in Amsterdam, in Basel, and in the Musée Cernuschi in Paris in 1956. He was a member of the *Bokuzin-Kai School* and collaborated on the abstract calligraphy reviews *Bokubi* and *Bokuzin*.

BIBLIOGRAPHY:

Seuphor, Michel, '*La Calligraphie japonaise*' in *Art d'aujourd'hui*, periodical, Boulogne-sur-Seine, December 1954.

EGUILAZ, Rosa

Spanish, 19th century.
Painter. Portraits, genre scenes.

Rosa Eguilaz was a pupil of José Parada y Santin.

EGUSQUIZA BARRENA, Rogelio de

Spanish, 19th - 20th century.
Born 1845, in Santander; died 1913.
Painter. History painting, genre scenes.

Rogelio de Eguquiza Barrena studied under Francisco Mendoza before attending the Ècole des Beaux Arts in Paris. He exhibited in Madrid and Paris and from 1883 to 1887 in Berlin, Munich and Hamburg. He was awarded a silver medal at the Exposition Universelle of 1900. The Seville fine arts museum held a retrospective of his work in 1995. He is known for his painting *The Engaged Couple*.

BIBLIOGRAPHY:

Beruete y Moret, Aureliano de, *Rogelio de Egusquiza, pintor y grabador*, Blass y Cia., Madrid, 1918 (Rogelio de Egusquiza, Painter and Engraver). Barón Thaidigsmann, Javier/Bedia Casanueva, Diego, *Rogelio de Egusquiza (1845-1915)*, exhibition catalogue, Museo de Bellas Artes, Fundación Marcelino Botín, Santander, 1995.

MUSEUMS AND GALLERIES:

ARRAS: decorative panel - NEW YORK (Hispanic Society of America): *Reclining Woman with Mirror* (1873).

AUCTION RECORDS:

LONDON, 25 Jan 1908, *Ready for the Ball*, GBP 10. LONDON, 3 April 1909, *The Ball*, GBP 36. LONDON, 22 April 1932, *Unexpected Visitors*, GBP 6. NEW YORK, 18 Oct 1944, *In her Boudoir*, USD 230. NEW YORK, 14 May 1969, *View of Venice*, USD 625. LONDON, 24 Nov 1976, *Spanish Beauties* (two canvases, 30 1/4 x 24 ins / 77 x 61 cm) GBP 2,600. NEW YORK, 11 Feb 1981, *Family Concert* (oil on canvas, 24 1/4 x 34 ins / 61.5 x 86.5 cm) USD 30,000. NEW YORK, 25 Feb 1983, *The Love Letter* (oil on canvas, 18 x 15 ins / 45.7 x 38.2 cm) USD 7,000. LONDON, 9 Oct 1987, *Reverie* (1883, oil on panel, 36 x 26 ins / 91.5 x 66 cm) GBP 10,000. NEW YORK, 24 May 1988, *The Private Concert* (1878, oil on canvas, 24 1/4 x 34 ins / 61.5 x 86.5 cm) USD 104,500. MONACO, 17 June 1988, *Young Woman with Flowers* (oil on canvas, 39 x 27 1/4 ins / 99 x 69.5 cm) FRF 72,150. LONDON, 17 Feb 1989, *Spanish Beauty* (oil on canvas, 31 1/2 x 25 3/4 ins / 80 x 65.4 cm) GBP 7,700. NEW YORK, 22 May 1991, *Unexpected Visitors* (oil on panel, 25 1/2 x 21 1/2 ins / 64.8 x 54.6 cm) USD 35,750. PARIS, 14 June 1991, *The Singer Elsa de Lohengren in Barcelona in 1908* (oil on canvas, 39 1/4 x 32 ins / 100 x 81 cm) FRF 75,000. NEW YORK, 12 Oct 1994, *The Confidence* (oil on panel, 14 x 10 3/4 ins / 35.6 x 27.3 cm) USD 11,500.

EGVILLE, James T. Hervé d'

British, 19th century.
Died 1880.
Painter, watercolourist, draughtsman. Landscapes.

James T. Egville exhibited a *Church Interior* in Milan in 1828. Later on, he went to London, and from 1837 to 1880, a great many of his landscapes appeared in the exhibitions held by the New Water-Colour Society. He also exhibited at the Royal Academy and the British Institution until 1840.

AUCTION RECORDS:

LONDON, 7 March 1924, *On the Lagoons at Murano* (1873; *On Giudecca* (two drawings) GBP 12. LONDON, 30 July 1924, *View of Venice* (1848) GBP 9. LONDON, 15 June 1945, *Fishing Boats with the Public Gardens of Venice in the Distance* (drawing) GBP 52. LONDON, 23 June 1981, *Village in Italy* (1879, watercolour, 22 x 35 1/2 ins / 55 x 90 cm) GBP 300.

EGWEILER, Heinrich

German, 14th century.
Active in Nuremberg at the end of the 14th century.
Painter.

Heinrich Egweiler may be the same person as Heinrich von Eichstätt, who appears in documents between the years 1363 and 1370. He was also probably the father of Sebald Egweiler.

EGWEILER, Hermann

German, 14th - 15th century.
Active c. 1392-1408.
Painter.

EGWEILER, Sebald von Eichstätt

German, 14th - 15th century.
Active in Nuremberg.
Painter.

Egweiler's name appears in documents dated 1397, 1400 and 1408.

EGYED. See **EGIDIUS DE DES**

ÉHANNO, Jean-Marc

French, 20th century.

Born 7 November 1942, in Lorient.

Painter, pastellist, draughtsman.

Jean-Marc Éhanno spent his youth in Brittany, where he trained as a designer. Alongside this activity, he took up painting, starting with an austere figurative style. After leaving Nantes, he spent four years in the south-west before settling near Paris, where he studied for and obtained a degree in Fine Arts. In 1976, he was awarded a state bursary for artistic creation. He signs his works with a sloping capital *É*.

After a figurative period, in which precise drawing played a large part, Éhanno moved on to Geometric Abstraction, with black and white monochrome pastels. Without abandoning this abstraction, he applied it to his depiction of nature, with a fusion of observed landscape and an interior scheme, where, at its best, a certain level of poetic inwardness was attained. The square, a 'cosmic symbol', was omnipresent. A preoccupation with light, always present in his work, intensified over time. Toward the late 1980s, at the time of his first exhibitions at the Galerie Galarté, he began to devote himself exclusively to soft pastel and Conté crayon: *From the Line to the Gesture*, then *Cubes and Curves*.

Éhanno's landscapes are drawn with sensitivity, but evoke a highly rigorous architecture. Starting from the view of a cube, the composition develops in counterpoint: triangles of light, grey rectangles, and an occasional break in the picture, which has some kind of symbolic significance. A few severely straight, horizontal or oblique lines define planes covered in pointillist coloration, which overlay and interpenetrate each other as though transparent. Space is expressed in terms of light. This may be the vacant space of the atmosphere, at the mercy of sudden changes in the weather and where light mists or heavy cloud can veil or obscure the sun. Or it may be the limitless spaces stretching toward the horizon, an extensive seascape beyond the gleaming shores. Sequences of paintings in light colours contrast with others in dark tones, such as night landscapes with evocative titles: *Small Brown Light, Square of Night at Sea*. Many of these works come in a small, square format; the images are precisely outlined and there is a restrained lyricism about them, an effect that is enhanced by the use of pastels.

Éhanno first exhibited between 1964 and 1968. Since 1969, he has taken part in numerous collective exhibitions, including: 1971, with the Archipel group (Louis Ferrand, Jorj Morin), Musée des Beaux-Arts and at the Galerie Michel Columb, Nantes; 1971-1977, *Rencontre d'Octobre* (*October Meeting*), Musée de Nantes; 1974-1976, Musée d'Ingres, Montauban, and *Rencontre d'Art en Quercy* (*Meeting with Art in Quercy*); from 1975, Salon des Réalités Nouvelles, Paris (of which he became a committee member in 1985); 1976, Biennale at Villeneuve-sur-Lot; 1981, *Petits Formats* (*Small Formats*), Galerie Darial, Paris; 1983, *Autour de Véra Pagava et Janikowsky* (*Around Véra Pagava and Janikowsky*), Galerie Darial, Paris; from 1986, Galerie Galarté, Paris; 1987, 2nd International Contemporary Art Fair, London, and *Panorama of the French School*, Tel Aviv; 1987 and 1988, Stockholm Art Fair; 1988 and 1990, St-Quentin International Pastel Biennale, where he was an award-winner in 1988; 1992, *Renouveau et Modernité du Pastel* (*Revival and Modernity in Pastel*), Pierrefonds Festival, Musée de Libourne, and *Sélection du Salon des Réalités Nouvelles*; 1993, Salon de Mars, Paris; and 1994, St-Quentin, Fourth Biennale Internationale du Pastel.

Solo exhibitions include: 1973 and 1979, Galerie Michel Columb, Nantes; 1976, Galerie 'La Galerie', Paris; 1982, Galerie Darial, Paris; 1987, 1989 and 1992 Galerie Galarté, Paris; 1990, Galerie J, Strasbourg; and 1996, Galerie Alix Lemarchand, Paris.

BIBLIOGRAPHY:

Lanoë, Julien (preface), *J.- M. Éhanno. Pastels*, exhibition catalogue, Paris, 1973. *Pastels monochromes noir et blanc*, Amis de l'Archipel, Nantes, 1973. Ragon, Michel/Pleynet, Marcellin, *L'Art abstrait 1970-1987*, Maeght, Paris, 1987. Raynal, Henri, '*J.- M. Éhanno*', coll. *Dossiers d'Art contemporain*, Éd. Porte du Sud, Bussy-le-Repos, 1990.

MUSEUMS AND GALLERIES:

NANTES (MBA): three works - PARIS (FNAC): three works.

ÉHANNO, Maurice

French, 20th century.

Born 7 July 1924, in Toulinda-Baden (Morbihan).

Painter. Landscapes, seascapes.

Maurice Éhanno began painting in 1944. He had trained as a sculptor in wood and granite, but was self-taught as a painter. He painted landscapes in the Morbihan and inland Brittany as well as seascapes and North African scenes. He used a rich palette of strong dark colours laid thickly on.

Éhanno's work was shown in collective exhibitions in Vannes, and in Paris at the Salon des Artistes Indépendants in 1963 and later.

MUSEUMS AND GALLERIES:

PONT-AVEN: *Landscape in St-Nolff, Recollection of Verkade* (1982).

EHBISCH, Johan Frederik

Danish, 17th - 18th century.

Born 1668, in Copenhagen; died 6 May 1748, in Copenhagen.

Sculptor.

Johan Ehbisch is thought to have been the son of Hans Ehbisch, a gardener to Queen Sophia Amalia, but there is no indication of where and by what means he studied. From 1705, he was the royal sculptor with a stipend of 200 rdl (640 crowns) a year, paid from the king's private fund. He is first mentioned in 1705, when he cast a *Hercules* in lead for the garden at Rosenborg.

EHBISCH, Johann Friedrich

German, 18th century.

Born c. 1765, in Breslau (now Wroclaw, Poland).

Sculptor.

Johann Ehbisch worked in Dresden around 1790 on the decoration of the church of the Cross, and acquired the right of burgess there in 1792.

ÉHEHALT, Henri

French, 20th century.

Born 13 September 1879, in Strasbourg.

Sculptor, medallist. Monuments.

Henri Éhehalt trained under Ludwig Schmid-Reutte and Hermann Volz at the art college in Karlsruhe. He made many medals, and sculpted fountains and funerary monuments in the districts of Bruchsal, Philippsbourg, Karlsdorf and Ottenheim.

EHEMANN, A., or Ehmann

German, 18th century.

Active in Augsburg.

Engraver.

A. Ehemann illustrated a work by Kistler which apeared in 1733 and engraved the frontispiece of a work by Benno Wurm which appeared in 1751. There is a copy of the map of the town of Weissenau in the Stuttgart library. It was engraved by Ehemann after a design by A. Gosner.

EHEMANN, Hans

German, 16th century.

Painter.

Nuremberg School.

On 6 November 1512, Hans Ehmann became a burgher of the city of Nuremberg.

EHEMANN, Peter
German, 16th century.
Active in Nuremberg.
Sculptor.
Peter Ehemann is thought to have carved the small alabaster statue of *Cleopatra*, dated 1532, that bears his initials.

EHEMANT, Friedrich Joseph or Fritz
German, 19th century.
Born 1804, in Frankfurt am Main; died January 1842, in Munich.
Landscape painter.
Friedrich Ehemant trained at the Düsseldorf academy in the studio of J.W. Schirmer. He exhibited at the royal academy in Berlin in 1834. Notable works by him include *Four Views of Frankfurt am Main*.

EHENBERG, Anna Beata. See **KLEEN**

EHESCHEUH, Veit, or Eschay, Oechey or Oeschey
German, 16th century.
Born to a family originally from Augsburg; died 1603, in Munich.
Sculptor (marble, wood).
After a period of study in Italy, Ehescheuh moved to Munich in 1603 while still a young man.

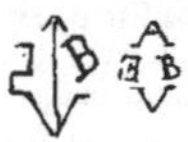

EHINGER, Elias, or Ellmiger
German.
Active in Augsburg.
Engraver.
Mentioned by Nagler.

EHINGER, Gabriel, or Ellmiger
German, 17th - 18th century.
Born 1652, in Augsburg; died 1736.
Painter, engraver.

EHINGER, Johann Michael
French, 17th century.
Active in Strasbourg.
Sculptor.
Johann Michael Ehinger worked at Nordlingen on the church of St-Georges and later at the court of Saxe-Meiningen.

EHINGER, Zacharias
German, 17th century.
Active in Augsburg.
Painter.

EHLE, Michael
American, 20th - 21st century.
Born 1953, in Salina (California).
Engraver.
Symbolism.
Michael Ehle lives and works in Seattle. His engravings are clearly symbolist, and even esoteric, and feature figures and animals in an often conflicting relationship. In 1995 he was one of the artists from the USA invited to show his work at the exhibition Jeune Gravure Contemporaine (Young Contemporary Engraving).

EHLERS, Carl
German, 19th century.
Born 25 June 1854, in Altona.
Painter.
Carl Ehlers studied at the academies in Weimar and Dresden. He lived a long time in Munich and worked in Hamburg, where he produced paintings of the old city.

EHLERS, Karl
German, 20th century.
Born 1904, in Hollenbek (Schleswig-Holstein).
Sculptor.
Ehlers trained at the Essen art school from 1921 to 1922, and then at the Düsseldorf art academy until 1928, when he went on a trip to Istanbul.

In the 1930s, his sculptures were figurative, displaying an expressionistic elongation and stylisation of forms. He produced numerous busts and wooden heads in this style, probably influenced by African art, in around 1935. He later shifted towards a more abstract approach, still with some references to reality. In the 1950s he produced large totems with exposed gaps, inspired by primitive art. His sculptures grew more and more austere, becoming almost linear by 1955. From 1960 onwards, his works now entirely abstract, he continued to work on totemic shapes in the form of either rounded humps or diamond points.

Ehlers started exhibiting in 1930 in Düsseldorf, and subsequently exhibited very regularly in Germany. He also participated in international collective exhibitions including in Chicago in 1932 and 1934, and in Antwerp-Middelheim from 1953 to 1961.

EHLINGER, Maurice
French, 20th century.
Born 25 September 1896, in Champagney (Haute-Saône); died 1981.
Painter. Nudes, portraits.
Maurice Ehlinger studied with François Flameng and Jules Adler. He exhibited regularly at the Salon des Artistes Français in Paris, winning an honourable mention in 1928 and a second-class medal in 1929. In 2002 his work was included in the exhibition *En Passant par... La Lorraine Vue par ses Peintres* (*Passing through... the Lorraine Seen by its Painters*) at the Musée Pierre Noël, St-Dié-des-Vosges.

AUCTION RECORDS:
BERN, 21 Oct 1983, *Portrait of a Girl Seen from in Front* (oil on canvas, 24 x 19 3/4 ins / 61 x 50 cm) CHF 2,400. PARIS, 4 Dec 1985, *Reclining Nude* (oil on canvas, 28 3/4 x 36 1/4 ins / 73 x 92 cm) FRF 22,000. PARIS, 22 Feb 1988, *Weariness* (oil on canvas, 18 x 22 ins / 46 x 55 cm) FRF 11,500. PARIS, 16 Oct 1988, *Nude in a Mirror* (oil on canvas, 25 1/4 x 32 ins / 64 x 81 cm) FRF 7,000. PARIS, 18 June 1989, *Fair-Haired Nude on a Pink Sofa* (oil on canvas, 21 1/4 x 28 3/4 ins / 54 x 73 cm) FRF 9,000. ST-DIÉ, 23 July 1989, *Reclining Nude at a Mirror* (oil on canvas, 21 1/4 x 32 ins / 54 x 81 cm) FRF 20,000. STRASBOURG, 29 Nov 1989, *Model Awaking* (oil on canvas, 21 1/4 x 25 1/2 ins / 54 x 65 cm) FRF 11,500. PARIS, 24 Jan 1990, *Nude before a Glass* (oil on canvas, 22 x 18 ins / 55 x 46 cm) FRF 10,500. VERSAILLES, 22 April 1990, *Girl in a Necklet of Flowers* (oil on canvas, 25 1/2 x 21 1/4 ins / 65 x 54 cm) FRF 14,000. SCEAUX, 13 Dec 1992, *Nude with White Cloth* (oil on canvas, 22 x 25 3/4 ins / 55 x 65.5 cm) FRF 13,000. PARIS, 13 Feb 1995, *Woman with a Basket of Cherries* (oil on canvas, 28 3/4 x 23 1/2 ins / 73 x 60 cm) FRF 4,000. PARIS, 6 May 1999, *Ariane Ackerman* (1930, oil on canvas, 77 x 45 ins / 195 x 114 cm) FRF 19,000. PARIS, 6 May 1999, *Reeds* (1967, oil on canvas, 77 x 67 ins / 195 x 169 cm) FRF 22,000. SWITZERLAND, 30 Nov 2001, *Nude Man Seen from Behind in a Bedroom* (oil on canvas, 21 x 29 ins / 54 x 73 cm) CHF 2,400. PARIS, 28 March 2003, *Young Woman by the Sea* (oil on canvas, 26 x 21 ins / 65 x 54 cm) EUR 1,500. LONDON, 22 Oct 2003, *Big Bouquet of Flowers* (oil on canvas, 29 x 24 ins / 73 x 60 cm) GBP 1,100. BESANCON, 3 April 2004,

Nude Young Girl Stretched Out (oil on canvas, 32 x 39 ins / 81 x 100 cm) EUR 5,000. CALAIS, 30 May 2004, *Nap in the Sun* (oil on canvas, 24 x 29 ins / 60 x 73 cm) EUR 5,000.

EHMANN. See **EHEMANN**

EHMCKE, Fritz Hellmut, or Ehmke
German, 20th century.
Born 16 October 1878, in Hohensalza; died 3 February 1965, in Seefeld/Obb.
Architect, typographer, illustrator, engraver, writer. Designs (book-binding).
Jugendstil.

Fritz Hellmut Ehmcke trained in lithography in Berlin between 1893 and 1897 and became a professional lithographer. He joined the applied arts teaching institution at the Kunstgewerbemuseum in Berlin. He taught at the Kunstgewerbeschule in Düsseldorf, and at the Staatschule für Angewandte Kunst in Munich. In 1907 he was one of the founders of the Deutscher Werkbund, an association set up by architects, designers and industrialists which proposed using simple, solid forms both for architecture and consumer goods. Between 1920 and 1921 he became director of the graphic arts department at the School of Industrial Art and Design in Zurich.

Ehmcke worked with Friedrich Wilhelm Kleukens, and together they set up the Steglitzer Werkstatt (Steglitz art print workshop) in 1900 in Berlin. In 1914, he opened the Rupprecht-Presse publishing house. He was particularly active in the field of book art and typography, such as inventing print characters, and he became one of the representatives of the modern style. His sense of aesthetics caused him to separate the text from the ornamentation. He published several writings on book art, including *Drei Jahrzehnte Deutscher Buchkunst 1890-1920* (Berlin, Euphorion, 1921) and *Amtliche Graphik* (Munich, 1918).

BIBLIOGRAPHY:
Lechner, Herbert, *F. H. Ehmcke zum 100. Geburtstag*, exhibition catalogue, Staatsbibliothek, Munich, 1978. Severing, H.M., *Der Bildhauer Benno Elkan*, Hist. Ver. Dortmund, Dortmund, 1980. Assel, Jutta, *F. H. Ehmcke und seine Neusser Schüler H. Cossmann, E. Malzburg, J. Urbach*, Clemens-Sels-Museum, Neuss, 1984. Mirknik, Ivan, '*Benno Elkan's portrait of Milka Ternina*' in *Medal*, No. 23, Autumn, periodical, 1993. *Die Rupprecht-Presse zu München*, Antiquariat Heribert Tenschert, Rotthalmünster, 2001.

EHMIG, Georg
German, 20th century.
Born 1892, in Altona.
Painter. Portraits, landscapes.

EHMSEN, Heinrich
Austrian, 20th century.
Born 1886; died 1964.
Painter, watercolourist. Scenes with figures.

AUCTION RECORDS:
LONDON, 25 March 1986, *Cactus* (1936, oil on canvas, 30 3/4 x 23 3/4 ins / 78 x 60.5 cm) GBP 6,200. MUNICH, 8 June 1988, *Beach Hut* (watercolour, 18 3/4 x 13 1/4 ins / 47.7 x 33.4 cm) DEM 11,550. MUNICH, 7 June 1989, *In the Beach Hut* (1953, watercolour and pencil, 19 1/4 x 15 1/4 ins / 49 x 39 cm) DEM 3,300. LONDON, 22 Feb 1995, *Farm Labourers* (oil on canvas, 31 1/2 x 39 ins / 80 x 99 cm) GBP 2,300. LONDON, 18 Oct 2000, *Bathing Hut* (watercolour/pencil, 19 x 13 ins / 48 x 33 cm) GBP 5,500. STUTTGART, 30 Nov 2000, *In the East* (1931, oil on canvas, 39 x 31 ins / 100 x 80 cm) DEM 6,000. BERLIN, 8 June 2002, *Pond in Town* (1910, oil on canvas, 24 x 18 ins / 60 x 45 cm) EUR 5,100.

EHNINGER, John Whetten
American, 19th century.
Born 1827, in New York; died 1889.
Painter, engraver, draughtsman, illustrator. Genre scenes, landscapes.

John Whetten Ehninger went to Paris in 1847 and became a pupil of Couture. He travelled in Europe, returned to America and became a member of the National Academy in 1860. In England he did many drawings and engraved illustrations.

AUCTION RECORDS:
LONDON, 23 April 1937, *Dixie*; *J. Massa* (1863, collection) GBP 5. NEW YORK, 22 Oct 1982, *Flute and Drum* (1867, oil on canvas, 14 1/4 x 12 ins / 36.5 x 30.5 cm) USD 13,000. NEW YORK, 22 May 1996, *Flute and Drum* (1867, oil on canvas, 14 x 12 ins / 35.5 x 30.5 cm) USD 18,400. BERN, 7 May 2003, *Rendez-vous* (1884, oil on canvas, 24 x 31 ins / 62 x 78 cm) CHF 4,000. NEW YORK, 16 Nov 2003, *Catch of the Day* (oil on panel, 5 x 8 ins / 13 x 20 cm) USD 2,300. PARIS, 24 June 2004, *Portrait of a Rider in a Landscape* (1863, oil on canvas, 25 x 30 ins / 63 x 76 cm) EUR 2,500.

EHNLE, Adrianus-Johannes
Dutch, 19th century.
Born 5 February 1819, in The Hague; died 1863, in Haarlem.
Painter. Portraits, genre scenes.

Adrianus-Johannes Ehnle was a pupil of C. Kruseman and keeper of the engravings in the Teyler museum in Haarlem.

MUSEUMS AND GALLERIES:
HAMBURG: *Entry of a Young Boy into Haarlem Orphanage*.

EHO, monk's name: Eho Tokutei
Japanese, 15th century.
Active c. 1470.
Painter.

Eho Tokutei was a suiboku (ink painting) artist of the Muromachi period. He and specialised in figures.

EHRBAR-REICHLE, Johannes
Swiss, 19th century.
Born 16 June 1863, in Herisau (Appenzell).
Draughtsman.

Johannes Ehrbar-Reichle spent a great deal of time in Cannes and Nice, and also lived in Zurzach. He settled in Zurich in 1897.

EHRÉ, Jürgen
German, 20th century.
Born 23 July 1941, in Kassel.
Also active in France.
Painter, engraver. Animals.

Initially, Ehré studied design and scenography. Then, from 1963 to 1967, he attended the École des Beaux-Arts in Paris, where he settled. His painting is based on an analysis of the animal world, primarily monkeys; this consists in Ehré confronting the animal with measuring devices in a scenic, pictorial atmosphere reminiscent of the work of Serbian painter and architect Vladimir Velickovic.

He has participated in many group exhibitions, including: 1969, Biennale de Paris; since 1970, regularly at the Salon de Mai and the Biennale de l'Estampe (engravers' Biennale), also in Paris. He has held solo shows, including: 1969, Zurich and Paris; 1972, Brussels; 1975, Paris again.

EHREN, Julius von
German, 19th century.
Born 23 August 1864, in Altona.
Painter, engraver. Genre scenes, animals.

Julius von Ehren trained in Weimar and worked in Hamburg, Copenhagen and Paris. His work appeared frequently in exhibitions in Hamburg and other German cities, such as Berlin, Munich, Dresden, Düsseldorf and Weimar.

MUSEUMS AND GALLERIES:
HAMBURG: *On the Way to School*; *Peasants' Bedroom*; *Ferry in Finkenwärder*; *Ducks*; *Reeds*.

AUCTION RECORDS:
LONDON, 2 Dec 1986, *Smithy* (1897, oil on canvas, 26 x 32 1/4 ins / 66 x 82 cm) GBP 7,000.

EHRENBERG, Carl Ferdinand von
German, 19th century.
Born 27 July 1806, in Halle; died 9 April 1841, in Zurich.
Painter. Figures, architectural views.
Carl von Ehrenberg was an architect and exhibited architectural views and a painting of a family in sepia in Zurich in 1832 and 1835.

EHRENBERG, Carl Gottfried Ferdinand
German, 19th century.
Born 6 November 1840, in Dannau, near Oldenburg.
Painter. History painting.
Carl Ehrenberg trained at the Dresden academy, then settled in this city. He exhibited at the Royal Academy from 1876 onwards. Notable works by him include: *Morning, Evening, Fight of the Valkyries*, the allegory *Water, Air and Light*, and *Portrait of Princess Feodora of Schleswig-Holstein*.

EHRENBERG, Paul
German, 20th century.
Born 8 August 1876, in Dresden.
Painter. Figures, landscapes.
Ehrenberg trained at Dresden and Munich art academies. He lived in Munich, where he exhibited from 1906 onwards. He painted landscapes, particularly in France (*Evening on the Shore, In the Port of Honfleur*) as well as figures (*Young Peasant Woman, Painting Students, Woman from Dachau*).
MUSEUMS AND GALLERIES:
CHEMNITZ: *Woman from Dachau; After the Rain*.

EHRENBERG, Peter Schubert von
German, 17th century.
Born 1668, in Antwerp.
Painter.
Peter Ehrenberg was the son of Wilhelm Schubert von Ehrenberg. He worked in Germany as a draughtsman and portrait painter.

EHRENBERG, Wilhelm von, or Wilhelm Schubert von, or Hardenberg or Herdenberg
Dutch, 17th century.
Baptised 12 May 1630 in Antwerp; died c. 1676, in Antwerp.
Painter. Architectural views, church interiors.
Some biographers claim that Wilhelm von Ehrenberg was born in Germany in 1637. He was a master in Antwerp in 1663 and married Maria Seys, the daughter of the painter, on 5 August. His paintings were embellished by H. van Minderhout, Gonzales Coques, K. E. Biset, and Jeroom Janssens, among others.

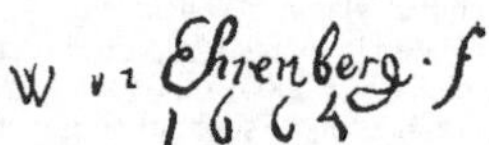

MUSEUMS AND GALLERIES:
ANTWERP: *Caricine before the King of Ethiopia* (figures by H. van Minderhout) - BERGUES (Town Hall): *Sexton of St-Jacques Church in Antwerp* - BRUSSELS: *William Tell Shooting the Apple on the Head of his Son* (figures by C. B. Biset) - OSLO: *Architectural Painting* - THE HAGUE: *Architecture of the Studio Painting by G. Coques* - VIENNA: *Interior of Church*.
AUCTION RECORDS:
LONDON, 7 May 1926, *Interior of the Church of St Peter's in Rome, View of the High Altar with the Cardinal and Numerous Other Figures* (1665, in collaboration with Biset) GBP 68. LONDON, 9 July 1926, *Interior of the Church of the Jesuits, Antwerp*, GBP 21. LONDON, 14 June 1935, *Interior of the Church in Antwerp with Figures* (1666) GBP 14. PARIS, 11 Dec 1946, *Interior of the Church of the Jesuits in Antwerp with Paintings by Rubens*, FRF 42,500. LONDON, 6 April 1977, *Numerous Figures near a Palace* (oil on canvas, 25 3/4 x 37 1/2 ins / 65.5 x 95 cm) GBP 3,200. LONDON, 27 Feb 1981, *Landscape with Figures* (oil on canvas, 32 3/4 x 54 1/4 ins / 83.5 x 138 cm) GBP 1,200. LONDON, 25 Oct 1985, *Interior of Church* (oil on canvas, 24 x 20 ins / 61 x 50.8 cm) GBP 2,200. NEW YORK, 5 April 1990, *Elegant Figures before a Wrought-iron Gate Enclosing the Choir of a Gothic Church* (oil on canvas, 20 x 24 ins / 51 x 61 cm) USD 9,900. LONDON, 18 Oct 1995, *The Liberation of St Peter* (1663, oil on canvas, 24 1/2 x 34 3/4 ins / 62.3 x 88.3 cm) GBP 4,140. PARIS, 16 June 2000, *Virgin and Child with St John the Baptist Surrounded by Angels* (oil on panel, 26 x 56 ins / 65 x 143 cm) FRF 70,000. LONDON, 23 April 2004, *Interior of St Charles Borromeo, Antwerp, with Elegant Company* (oil on panel, 16 x 19 ins / 41 x 47 cm) GBP 2,500.

EHRENCRON, Jacob Heinrich
Danish, 19th century.
Born 7 August 1809, in Augustenborg; died 4 May 1876, in Copenhagen.
Painter, decorative artist. Figures.
Ehrencron was admitted to the Kunstakademi in Copenhagen in 1826, initially studying portraiture but later abandoning it for decorative painting. He carried out a number of theatrical commissions, some of them at the royal theatre under the direction of C.F. Christiansen, and some for other theatres, until 1859, when he was appointed painter to the casino.
AUCTION RECORDS:
LONDON, 20 June 1980, *Girl Dancing* (oil on canvas, 20 x 16 1/4 ins / 50.7 x 41.3 cm) GBP 650.

EHRENFRIED, Theophilus
German, 16th century.
Sculptor.
Between 1514 and 1525, Ehrenfried worked with two other sculptors on a series of low reliefs showing biblical scenes for the gallery of the church in Annaberg.

EHRENHALT, Amaranth-Roslyn
American, 20th century.
Born in New Jersey.
Since 1965 active in France.
Painter. Designs for tapestries.
Amaranth-Roslyn Ehrenhalt was a pupil at the Philadelphia Museum School of Art, where she later taught. She held a bursary at the Pennsylvania Academy of the Fine Arts. She travelled and exhibited in France, Spain, North Africa, Italy, Belgium Holland, Germany, England, Turkey, Greece and the USA. Since 1961 she has held exhibitions with Glenn Robles in Rhodes, Istanbul, at the Downey Museum of Art (California) and the University at Albany (New York) and in 1969 at Châtillon and Bagneux. In Paris she regularly appeared at the Salon des Réalités Nouvelles. She also exhibited alone in Majorca, New York, Paris and Ostend. A creator of designs for tapestries, she appeared at the Paris Salon d'Automne in the *Magic of Tapestry* section, as well as at the École des Beaux-Arts in Paris and the Musée d'Aubusson in *Architextures: 40 ans de la tapisserie française* (*Architextures: 40 Years of French Tapestry*). She was invited to the Juan-les-Pins Tapestry Biennale. In 1990 the town of Bagneux commissioned a 1,615 square feet (150 square metre) mural from her.

Sonia Delaunay was interested in her work. She practised abstract painting, frequently connected with the informal and with chromatic matterism. However, she is also able to organise a surface, composition and formal elements for decorative purposes.

MUSEUMS AND GALLERIES:
PARIS (BNF) - PARIS (Mobilier National) - WASHINGTON DC (Hirshhorn Mus. and Sculpture Garden).
AUCTION RECORDS:
PARIS, 21 Sept 1989, *Composition* (oil on canvas, 28 3/4 x 23 1/2 ins / 73 x 60 cm) FRF 6,000. PARIS, 28 Nov 1989, *November* (1988, oil on canvas, 24 x 28 3/4 ins / 61 x 73 cm) FRF 6,000. PARIS, 5 March 1990, *What's Your Name?* (1988, oil on canvas, 31 1/2 x 25 1/2 ins / 80 x 65 cm) FRF 6,000. PARIS, 19 Jan 1992, *Script* (acrylic/paper, 19 x 15 ins / 48 x 38 cm) FRF 5,000.

EHRENORT, Pierre
Italian, 17th century.
Active in Rome.
Sculptor (ivory).
Ehrenort worked for Pope Alexander VII.

EHRENPREUSS, Carl Didrik (Count)
Swedish, 18th century.
Born 18 January 1692, in Örebro; died 21 September 1760, in Stockholm.
Miniaturist.
Ehrenpreuss was a privy councillor and art patron.

EHRENREICH, Adam Sándor
Slovak, 19th century.
Born 1784, in Pozsony (now Bratislava); died after 1840.
Active in Vienna.
Engraver (burin).
Sándor Ehrenreich engraved some plates for the Belvedere Gallery in Vienna, and portraits, mostly using a stippling technique. These include: *Justus Hausknecht, Johann Wachter* and *Henriette, Princess of Nassau*. He also published a series of portraits of famous Hungarian men entitled: *Icones Principum, Procerum ac praeter hos illustrium Virorum, Matronarumque veteris et praesentis aevi, quibus, Hungaria* and *Transylvania Clarent*.

EHRENREICH, Johann Benjamin
Austrian, 18th century.
Born 1739, in Ludwigsburg; died 1806, in Hamburg.
Painter, engraver (etching).
Johann Ehrenreich engraved genre subjects and portraits.

EHRENREITER, Jakob
Austrian, 18th - 19th century.
Born 1772, in Vienna.
Painter (porcelain).
Jakob Ehrenreiter worked at the Royal Porcelain Factory in Vienna from 1798 onwards.

EHRENSTETTER
Swiss, 18th century.
Active in St Gall.
Painter.
Ehrenstetter is believed to have worked on the decoration of the cathedral of St Gall.

EHRENSTRAHL, Anna Maria Klocker von
Swedish, 17th - 18th century.
Born 1666, in Stockholm; died 22 December 1729, in Stockholm.
Painter.
Anna Maria was the daughter of David von Ehrenstrahl and also his pupil. In 1688, she married the vice-president of the royal court, Johan Wattrang. She mainly produced copies of her father's works, but also painted portraits and religious or allegorical works.
MUSEUMS AND GALLERIES:
DROTTNINGHOLM (Slott): *Charles XI as Apollo, Conqueror of Python the Dragon* - STOCKHOLM: *Kneeling Man; Portrait of a Young Woman.*

EHRENSTRAHL, David Klocker von
German, 17th century.
Born 23 September 1629, in Hamburg; died 23 October 1698, in Stockholm.
Painter. History painting, allegorical subjects, portraits.
David von Ehrenstrahl trained under Juriaen Jacobsz. in 1648 in Amsterdam. He went to Rome and worked there with Pietro da Cortona. In 1651 he went to Sweden and returned there in 1654 after a trip to Germany and Italy. He was appointed a court painter in 1661. He produced a great many portraits of the royal family and worked for the palaces and Swedish churches.
MUSEUMS AND GALLERIES:
DROTTNINGHOLM (Castle): *Truth Revealed in Time, Wisdom and Justice; King Charles XI on Horseback* - HELSINKI (Ateneumin Taidemus.): *Portrait of Charles XII on Horseback; Portrait of Minister Count Bengt Oxenstierna; Portrait of Charles XI; Charles XI and his Family; Interior of Cottage in Nagu; Morannel and Cihanna; Nude; Portrait of Queen Ulrika Eleonora, Mother* - HELSINKI (Sinebrychoffin taidemus.): *Charles XII as a Child; Portrait of Count Johan Gabriel Stenbock; Portrait of Mrs or Miss Jennings; Portrait of Count J. J. Hastler* - LUND (Students House): *Consecration of Charles X Gustave* - LUND (Universitets Konstsamling): *Portrait of Admiral Gustaf Otto Stenbock* - MARIEFRED (Gripsholms Slott): *Faith, Hope and Charity; Charles XI and his Family; Master Fontenier and his Sons* - NARKES BOO: *Portrait of Abraham Brahe* - STOCKHOLM: *Portrait of Beata de la Gardie; Three of Charles XI's Children, Little Charles XII Sitting on Lion; Self-portrait; Allegory of the Fine Arts, Female Figures; Negro with Parrots and Monkeys; Portrait of Negotiator in 1652* - TIDO: *Portrait of K. G. Oxenstierna* - UPPSALA (Universitet Konstsamling): *Portrait of Anna von Königsmark; Portrait of Marshal Lorens von der Linde; Portrait of Marshal Erik Dahlberg; Portrait of Charles XI.*
AUCTION RECORDS:
STOCKHOLM, 11-12 April 1935, *Flora*, SEK 810. NEW YORK, 17 March 1945, *Duke Frederick IV of Schleswig-Holstein-Gottorp*, USD 310. PARIS, 8 Nov 1950, *Still-life with Monkey and Exotic Birds*, FRF 82,000. STOCKHOLM, 22 April 1986, *Royal Family of Karl XI* (oil on canvas, 25 1/4 x 26 3/4 ins / 64 x 68 cm) SEK 106,000. STOCKHOLM, 19 April 1989, *Eternal Truths* (oil on canvas, 85 x 70 3/4 ins / 216 x 180 cm) SEK 17,500. STOCKHOLM, 15 Nov 1989, *Equestrian Portrait of Karl XI* (oil, 65 x 61 ins / 165 x 154 cm) SEK 77,000. STOCKHOLM, 16 May 1990, *Allegory with Woman holding an Olive Branch and Cupid next to her with his Quiver* (oil on canvas, 41 1/4 x 47 1/4 ins / 105 x 120 cm) SEK 11,000. STOCKHOLM, 19 May 1992, *Allegory of Europe with the Features of a Young Woman Holding the Symbols of Power* (oil on canvas, 32 x 25 1/4 ins / 81 x 64 cm) SEK 35,000. STOCKHOLM, 10-12 May 1993, *Portrait of Queen Ulrika Eleonora Seated and Dressed in a Brown Dress and a Blue Draped Stole* (oil on canvas, 57 x 47 1/4 ins / 145 x 120 cm) SEK 28,000. STOCKHOLM, 18 May 1999, *Portrait of Countess Kristina Katarina de la Gerdie* (1683, oil on canvas, 42 x 33 ins / 107 x 84 cm) SEK 31,000. STOCKHOLM, 26 May 1999, *Vanis Labor* (1689, oil on canvas, 52 x 44 ins / 131 x 111 cm) SEK 200,000. STOCKHOLM, 16 May 2000, *Diana with Gundog in Landscape* (1669, oil on canvas, 57 x 48 ins / 146 x 122 cm) SEK 270,000. STOCKHOLM, 29 May 2000, *Portrait of Johan Gabriel Stenbock at the Age of 38* (1678, oil on canvas, 50 x 46 ins / 128 x 117 cm) SEK 130,000. STOCKHOLM, 29 May 2001, *Portrait of Maria Aurora von Konigsmarck* (oil on canvas, 33 x 26 ins / 83 x 66 cm) SEK 52,000. STOCKHOLM, 4 Dec 2001, *Councillor Lars Wallenstedt* (oil on canvas, 57 x 46 ins / 144 x 117 cm) SEK 33,000. NEW YORK, 7 June 2002, *Perseus and Andromeda* (oil on canvas, 69 x 55 ins / 175 x 140 cm) USD 10,000.

EHRENSVARD, Carl August (Count)
Swedish, 18th century.

Born 5 May 1745; died 21 May 1800, in Örebro.
Draughtsman, illustrator, caricaturist.
Ehrensvard was both an admiral and a philosopher, and was appointed an honorary member of the Stockholm academy in 1783. He illustrated his own work, *Italian Journey*, with drawings of art, people, customs and manners. He also drew a large number of caricatures.

EHRENTRAUT, Julius
German, 19th - 20th century.
Born 3 April 1841, in Frankfurt an der Oder; died 1923, in Berlin.
Painter. Portraits, genre scenes.
Ehrentraut trained at the art academy in Berlin and under J. Schrader. He also studied art in the Netherlands and Paris, where he was influenced by Meissonnier. In 1888, having returned to Berlin, he was given a teaching post at the academy. His best known works include: *Resting, Waiting, Serious Question, Mandolin Player with Two Peasants*, and *The Sick Madman*.
Museums and Galleries:
Stuttgart: *Musical Entertainment* - Wroclaw: *Lute Player*.
Auction records:
New York, 1-2 April 1902, *The Halberdier's Greeting*, USD 200. Paris, 26 May 1954, *Tyrolean Drinker*, FRF 30,000. Stuttgart, 29 Sept 1977, *Happy Guests* (oil on panel, 13 3/4 x 11 ins / 35 x 27 cm) DEM 11,800. Bern, 30 April 1980, *Shepherd Lighting his Pipe* (oil on panel, 8 1/4 x 6 ins / 21 x 15 cm) CHF 3,200. London, 5 May 1989, *On the Shore* (oil on canvas, 18 1/4 x 14 ins / 46.5 x 35.3 cm) GBP 6,820. Cologne, 23 March 1990, *Portrait of Gustavus Adolphus (bust)* (1875, oil on canvas, 10 1/4 x 8 1/4 ins / 26 x 21 cm) DEM 1,500. London, 28 Oct 1992, *A Plot* (oil on panel, 11 3/4 x 9 ins / 30 x 23 cm) GBP 2,310.

EHRENZELLER, Daniel
Swiss, 18th - 19th century.
Born 1765, in St Gall; died 1836.
Painter.
Daniel Ehrenzeller abandoned an artistic career to accept a post as secretary to the government. He received lessons from Freudweiler in Zurich and also trained under Daniel Hartmann in St Gall, as well as in Düsseldorf and Frankfurt.

EHRENZELLER, Daniel
Swiss, 19th century.
Born 18 December 1788, in St Gall; died 28 November 1849, in St Gall.
Painter, engraver.
Daniel Ehrenzeller trained under Kuster in Winterthur and at the art school in Lyons. He was one of the founders of the Artistic Union of St Gall and was employed as an art teacher at the school for young girls and as a teacher at the grammar school in this city. He joined forces for a time with Gsell's lithographic studio in Dornbirn (Vorarlberg). He was appointed archivist for the Artistic Union of St Gall in 1828. It houses watercolours, drawings and collections of sketches by him.

EHRER, Johann P.
German, 18th century.
Active in Munich.
Painter. Landscapes.
Johann Ehrer is mentioned by Nagler.

EHRET, Georg Dyonis or Dyonisius
German, 18th century.
Born 1710, in Erfurt; died 1770, in Chelsea, London.
Painter (including gouache), watercolourist, engraver, draughtsman. Botanical subjects.
Georg Ehret was the son of a gardener in Heidelberg and was destined for the same career. His sketches attracted the attention of the margrave and were published in botanical reviews in Nuremberg. He settled in England after 1740, illustrated the treatises of famous botanists of the time and painted a botanical collection for the Duchess of Portland. He was elected a member of the Royal Society in 1757 and a member of the imperial academy of Germany in 1758.
Museums and Galleries:
London (Natural History Mus.): numerous drawings and watercolours - Pittsburgh (Hunt Institute For Botanical Documentation, Carnegie Mellon University): more than 200 plates, including numerous gouaches.
Auction records:
London, 27 March 1946, *Tulips and Other Flowers* (1749, gouache) GBP 30. London, 10 March 1965, *Magnolia Grandiflora* (watercolour heightened with white) GBP 400. London, 8 June 1976, *Flower* (1764, watercolour and gouache, 9 x 6 1/4 ins / 23 x 15.7 cm) GBP 950. London, 20 June 1978, *Branch of Magnollia in Flower* (watercolour/parchment mounted on board, 31 x 22 1/4 ins / 79 x 56.5 cm) GBP 6,500. London, 7 July 1981, *Amaryllis Formosissima* (gouache, 18 3/4 x 14 1/2 ins / 47.5 x 36.8 cm) GBP 1,300. New York, 1 March 1984, *Branches of Dogwood in Flower* (1761, watercolour/parchment, 17 1/2 x 13 ins / 44.5 x 33 cm) USD 5,000. New York, 12 Jan 1988, *Branch of Red Double Camellia* (1742, watercolour and gouache, 21 x 14 1/2 ins / 53.3 x 36.8 cm) USD 6,600. Le Touquet, 19 May 1991, *Still-life with Fruit* (gouache, a pair, each 12 1/2 x 17 3/4 ins / 32 x 45 cm) FRF 35,000. London, 9 April 1992, *Large-flowered Magnolia* (watercolour with highlights/vellum, 21 x 14 1/2 ins / 52.5 x 37 cm) GBP 16,500. New York, 10 Jan 1996, *Figs and Cherries* (1747, gouache/vellum, 17 x 12 1/4 ins / 42.3 x 31.1 cm) USD 9,200. London, 2 July 1996, *White Water Lily* (1763, pencil, watercolour and gouache/vellum, 10 x 6 3/4 ins / 25.4 x 17.4 cm) GBP 1,265.

EHRHARD. See **ERHARD**

EHRHARDT. See also **ERHARDT**

EHRHARDT, Frieda
German, 19th century.
Born 1867 (?); died September 1904, in Munich.
Painter. Portraits, still-lifes (fruit).
Museums and Galleries:
Munich: *Head of a Young Girl*.
Auction records:
Amsterdam, 5 June 1990, *Composition of Fruit in Glass Plate and Roses in Crystal Vase* (oil on canvas, 29 1/4 x 39 1/2 ins / 74 x 100.5 cm) NLG 6,325.

EHRHARDT, Johann Christoph
German, 18th century.
Active in Volkstedt near Rudolstadt in 1782.
Painter (porcelain).

EHRHARDT, Johannes
Danish, 17th century.
Painter.
Ehrhardt is mentioned several times in the accounts of Christian IV for the years 1607-1608, as a painter resident at Helsingør. It appears that most of his works were copies or decorative works.

EHRHARDT, Karl Ludwig Adolf
German, 19th century.
Born 21 November 1813, in Berlin; died 19 November 1899, in Wolfenbüttel.
Painter. History painting.
Karl Ehrhardt trained at the Berlin academy and at the Düsseldorf academy with Schadow from 1832. In 1838 he went to Dresden and worked on Bendeman's paintings for the palace in Dresden. In 1846 he was appointed a teacher of the academy and in 1880 became a member of this institute. His work consists of religious paintings, such as *Daughter of Jephtha, Resurrection, Ascension*; genre paintings, such as

Young Girl in Forest; historical paintings and frescoes, including *Reconciliation of Ludwig of Bavaria and Frederick of Austria*; portraits, including that of *Ludwig Richter*; and a great many illustrations for the poetic works of Dante, Tasso, Lessing, Heine and Uhland, such as *Dante's Dream, Lorelei*, and *Emilia Galotti*.

MUSEUMS AND GALLERIES:

DRESDEN: *Portrait of Frederick Auguste II; Portrait of Ludwig Richter* - LEIPZIG: *Martin Luther; Portrait of Ludwig Richter* - ZURICH: *Separation of Rinaldo and Armida*.

EHRHARDT, Paul W.

German, 19th - 20th century.
Born 21 June 1872, in Weimar.
Painter. Genre scenes, flowers.

Ehrhardt trained at the Weimar and Munich art academies. He painted genre paintings and private scenes: *Birthday Visit, Two Friends*, and *Corner of the Studio*. He exhibited from 1906 onwards, notably in Munich and at the great art exhibition in Berlin.

EHRICH, Bruno

German, 19th century.
Born 23 May 1861, in Ratibor (now Racibórz, Poland); died 6 December 1947, in Kempen.
Active in Düsseldorf.
Painter.

Ehrich was a pupil of E. von Gebhardt and A. Schill at the Düsseldorf academy. He devoted himself to religious art, working with Wilhelm Doeringer on the Kreuzkirche and the Gnadenkirche in Berlin, the church at Wittenberg castle (mosaic and stained glass), Schleswig St Peter's cathedral (mosaic) and the Lieberfrauenkirche in Trier. His frescoes and paintings grace a number of churches in Wiesbaden, Essen, Dessau, Aachen and Düsseldorf.

EHRICH, H.

German, 19th century.
Active in Hamburg.
Painter, lithographer.

One picture is known by this artist, the *Family of Migrants*, painted before 1852.

EHRICHT, Ferdinand I, or Erich

Austrian, 18th century.
Born 1758, in Vienna; died 31 January 1804, in Vienna.
Painter, miniaturist.

EHRICHT, Ferdinand II, or Erich

Austrian, 19th century.
Born 1785, in Vienna.
Miniaturist.

The son of Ferdinand Ehricht, this artist entered the academy in Vienna in 1801 and showed miniatures copied from old masters such as Rubens and Titian at exhibitions mounted in the city in 1822, 1824 and 1825.

EHRINGHAUSEN, Wilhelm

German, 19th century.
Born 28 March 1868, in Münster.
Painter, draughtsman.

Ehringhausen was a pupil of Huber-Feldkirch and Knirr in Munich. Initially a landscape painter, he later devoted himself to drawing concentrating on reproductions. His bookplates were held in particularly high esteem.

EHRISMANN, Joseph

French, 20th century.
Born 2 March 1880, in Mutzig.
Painter. Designs for stained glass.

Joseph Ehrismann lived in Strasbourg, where he studied at the art school. He worked for a number of churches in Alsace.

EHRKE, Eduard

German, 19th century.
Born 17 February 1837, in Ludwigslust.
Painter. Landscapes.

Having studied in Düsseldorf and Munich, Ehrke travelled to England in 1860 and settled in Bath in 1876.

MUSEUMS AND GALLERIES:

SCHWERIN (AG): landscape.

EHRL, Alexius

German, 19th - 20th century.
Born 1871; died 17 February 1913, in Nuremberg.
Sculptor. Busts.

Ehrl trained in Munich and stayed there afterwards, producing mainly busts. He is said to have worked with Professor Hautmann in Munich on the deathmask of Ludwig II von Wittelsbach, King of Bavaria, after Ludwig committed suicide by drowning himself in 1886. However, this is inconsistent with Ehrl's birth date of 1871. He later settled in Nuremberg, where he produced numerous portrait sculptures.

EHRLER

School of Alsace, 18th century.
Painter. Portraits.

EHRLER, Jean Henri

French, 19th century.
Active in Strasbourg.
Draughtsman.

Jean Henri Ehrler executed colour architectural drawings. He is best known for two views of the Château de Rohan in Strasbourg and a plan of the façade of Strasbourg theatre.

EHRLER, Luise. See **MAX-EHRLER Luise**

EHRLICH, Bianca

Maiden name: Alexander-Katz
German, 19th century.
Born 1852, in Ols (Silesia).
Sculptor.

Bianca Ehrlich stayed in Paris, Rome and Berlin, executing busts of figures such as the doctor Paul Ehrlich, Max Reger and a peasant woman from the Alps. She exhibited these in Paris at the Salon des Indépendants. Her *Baroque Fountain* is in the style of Bernini.

EHRLICH, Carl Gottlob

German, 18th century.
Born 1744, in Torgau (near Leipzig); died 1799, in Meissen.
Painter, engraver (burin).

Ehrlich was an engraver of *Landscapes*, many of which can be found in the museums of Dresden and Meissen.

EHRLICH, Georg

Austrian, 20th century.
Born 1897, in Vienna; died 1966, in Lucerne.
Active in England from 1939 and naturalised from 1947.
Sculptor.

Ehrlich attended the school of art and architecture in Vienna. He worked mainly in bronze, sculpting human figures in a highly classical style. In 1921 he travelled to Berlin, where he exhibited with the sculptor Ernst Barlach and the painter Oskar Kokoschka, both of them Expressionists. In 1939 he emigrated to London. In 1947 he travelled to New York, where he staged his first American exhibition, returning to London in 1949.

Ehrlich started exhibiting in 1919 in Vienna. He exhibited in Paris in 1926 and took part in the Venice Biennale in 1934 and 1936. He had his own exhibition at the Venice Biennale in 1958, and in 1997 a major retrospective of his works took place at the Albertine in Vienna. In 2001 he was represented at the exhibition *Verfemt. Vergessen. Wiederentdeckt.*

Schicksale expressiver Bildkunst im 20. Jahrhundert (*Condemned. Forgotten. Rediscovered. The Fate of Expressive Art in the 20th century*) at the Kulturgeschichtliches Museum in Osnabrück. The purpose of this exhibition was to rediscover a generation of German and Austrian artists who appeared in the 1920s and 1930s but, following the cultural and political repression of the Nazis, disappeared from the scene after the war.

BIBLIOGRAPHY:

Georg Ehrlich: bronzes, early drawings, lithographs and etchings, exhibition catalogue, O'Hana Gallery, London, 1972. *Georg Ehrlich: Plastiken und Zeichnungen*, exhibition catalogue, Galerie Wolfgang Ketterer, Munich, 1977. Hoerschelmann, Antonia, *Georg Ehrlich*, exhibition catalogue, Albertina, Vienna, 1997.

MUSEUMS AND GALLERIES:

LONDON (British Mus.) - NEW YORK (Metropolitan Mus. of Art) - OTTERLO (Kröller-Müller Mus.) - VIENNA (Albertina Mus.).

AUCTION RECORDS:

MUNICH, 29 Nov 1976, *Two Sisters* (patinated bronze, h. 31 ins / 78.5 cm) DEM 4,200. MUNICH, 27 Nov 1981, *Recumbent Child* (bronze, h. 2 1/2 ins / 6.5 cm) DEM 2,600. LONDON, 4 Nov 1983, *The Bronze Girl* (1958, bronze, h. 35 ins / 88 cm) GBP 1,500. VIENNA, 19 March 1985, *Goat and Kid* (bronze, 6 1/4 x 8 1/2 ins / 16 x 21.5 cm) ATS 14,000. LONDON, 8 Oct 1986, *Gustav Mahler's Kindertotenlieder* (1913, watercolour and pencil, 8 1/2 x 8 3/4 ins / 21.5 x 22.5 cm) GBP 2,800. LONDON, 2 Dec 1986, *Goat's Head* (c. 1949-1950, dark-green patinated bronze, h. 16 1/2 ins / 42 cm) GBP 500. LONDON, 13 Nov 1987, *Standing Child, Bronze* (black patina, h. 43 ins / 109 cm) GBP 1,900.

EHRLICH, Johann Christian
German, 18th century.
Born in Dessau, Saxony-Anhalt; died c. 1780.
Sculptor.

Ehrlich is known for two statues at the entrance to the castle at Wörlitz, and the low reliefs on the *Dietrich Monument* in Wörlitz park. There is also work by him in Dessau: a copy of the *Dying Gladiator* in the park, and the river personifications *Elbe* and *Mulde* and the statues of *Ceres* and *Fortuna* at the entrance to the Lustgarten (Pleasure Gardens).

EHRLICH, Moritz
German, 19th century.
Born 27 October 1862, in Berlin.
Painter.

Moritz Ehrlich studied at the academy in Berlin, where he exhibited genre paintings, portraits and landscapes.

EHRLICH, Simon Franziskus
German, 17th century.
Of Silesian origin.
Painter.

A reference to this artist in Mainz is dated 1669.

EHRMAN, Hyman M.
Russian, 20th century.
Born 1884, in Russia.
Active in the USA.
Painter, sculptor.

Hyman Ehrman began his art studies in Russia and continued them at the Pennsylvania Academy of Fine Arts in Philadelphia. He became a member of the American Artists Professional League.

EHRMANN, François Émile
French, 19th - 20th century.
Born 5 September 1833, in Strasbourg; died March 1910, in Paris.
Painter, watercolourist, potter. History painting, allegorical subjects, mythological subjects. Designs for tapestries.

François Émile Ehrmann entered the École des Beaux-Arts in 1857 to study architecture, but three years later transferred to the painting course run by Charles Gleyre. He began to exhibit as a historical painter at the Salon de Paris in 1863, and continued to send in canvases, large works on mythological subjects, until 1906. He won various medals from 1865 to 1868, and was appointed a Chevalier of the Légion d'Honneur in 1879.

Ehrmann's painting *The Muses* is in the Palais de la Chancellerie of the Légion d'Honneur. He enjoyed working in ceramics, and created a number of cartoons for tapestries, decorative panels and ceilings which Parisian art lovers commissioned from him for their homes. He designed these in a high-flown style, whereas his easel paintings are less heavy.

F.EHRMANN

F.EHRMANN

MUSEUMS AND GALLERIES:

LE HAVRE: *Defence of Strasbourg* - MONTPELLIER: *Allegorical Subject* - MULHOUSE: *The Fountain of Youth* - NEUCHÂTEL: *Allegorical Subject* - PARIS (Mus. d'Orsay): *Ariadne Deserted* (watercolour) - ROUBAIX: *The Manuscript* - STRASBOURG: *Oedipus and the Sphinx*.

AUCTION RECORDS:

PARIS, 26 April 1944, *History* (watercolour) FRF 450. PARIS, 3 May 1988, *Study of a Female Nude* (lead pencil/grey paper, 17 1/2 x 10 ins / 44.5 x 25.5 cm) FRF 2,000.

EHRMANN, Léonie
French, 19th century.
Born 19th century, in Metz.
Painter. Portraits.

Léonie Ehrmann was a pupil of Devilly, Chaplin and Barrias. She exhibited at the Paris Salon from 1877.

EHRMANN-LEBEL, Madeleine
French, 20th century.
Born in Paris.
Painter. Landscapes, flowers.

Madeleine Ehrmann-Lebel exhibited at the Salon de la Société Nationale from 1934 onwards.

EHRMANNS, Theodor von (Baron)
Austrian, 19th century.
Born 6 May 1846.
Painter, watercolourist. Landscapes.

Following his studies with Zimmermann at the academy in Vienna, Ehrmanns studied in Munich and Copenhagen and showed watercolours at various exhibitions in Austria, Germany and Venice. He contributed to the work *Austria-Hungary in Words and Images*.

AUCTION RECORDS:

VIENNA, 13 Jan 1976, *Landscape View of Pörtschach* (1876, oil on canvas, 20 3/4 x 37 1/2 ins / 53 x 95 cm) ATS 18,000. VIENNA, 29 Nov 1977, *View of Gmunden* (1872, oil on canvas, 28 3/4 x 39 1/4 ins / 73 x 100 cm) ATS 22,000. COLOGNE, 21 March 1981, *Shepherd with Flock* (1889, watercolour, 4 3/4 x 9 ins / 12 x 22 cm) DEM 1,000. VIENNA, 16 May 1984, *Alpine Landscape in Spring* (oil on canvas, 20 x 36 1/2 ins / 51 x 92.5 cm) ATS 50,000. VIENNA, 20 May 1999, *View of Hofgastein, Village in Extensive Hilly Landscape* (oil on canvas, 28 x 39 ins / 72 x 99 cm) ATS 50,000.

EHRMÜLLER, Peter
Austrian, 18th century.

Active in Salzburg.
Painter.
Ehrmüller worked in several churches in Salzburg, where he painted 14 pictures illustrating the Way of the Cross, a number of Old Testament scenes and a *Madonna*.

EIA, Ferdinando
Italian, 17th century.
Painter.
Artist at the court of Parma.

EIBISCH, Eugeniusz
Polish, 20th century.
Born 1896, in Lublin; died 1987, in Warsaw.
Also active in France.
Painter. Portraits, landscapes, still-lifes.
Eugeniusz Eibisch studied at the academy of fine art in Cracow from 1919 to 1921. He spent some time in Paris from 1922 to 1939 and was appointed to teach at the academy of fine art in Cracow, then in Warsaw. He featured in many collective exhibitions of Polish art, in Poland and abroad, notably at the Venice Biennale in 1962. He held solo exhibitions in Cracow (192), Paris (1924), and Marseilles (1937) and was awarded the National Prize of the Guggenheim Foundation in 1960 and several prizes in Poland.
BIBLIOGRAPHY:
Nieszawer, Nadine/Boyé, Marie/Lanzmann, Claude (preface), *Peintres juifs de l'école de Paris 1905-1939*, Denoël, Paris, 2001.

EIBL, Ludwig
Austrian, 19th - 20th century.
Born 14 December 1842, in Vienna; died 1918.
Painter. Still-lifes (including flowers/fruit). Murals.
Eibl trained in sculpture in Vienna and Paris before studying painting in Munich. His paintings, which were mainly still-lifes of fruit, vegetables and game, appeared in international exhibitions in Berlin from 1881 to 1899, and at the Künstlerhaus in Vienna. He was involved in decorating the ceiling of the hunting room at Herrenchiemsee castle.
MUSEUMS AND GALLERIES:
BERLIN (Nationalgal.): *Head of a Woman* (study) - MUNICH (North Cemetery): *Monument to the Dead*.
AUCTION RECORDS:
MUNICH, 13 May 1987, *Still-life with Flowers* (oil on canvas, 24 x 35 1/2 ins / 61 x 90 cm) DEM 15,000.

EIBNER, Friedrich
German, 19th century.
Born 25 February 1825, in Hilpolstein (Bavaria); died 18 November 1877, in Munich.
Painter. Landscapes with figures, architectural views.
Eibner travelled in Germany and France and accompanied Prince Mestschersky on his travels in Spain from 1860 to 1861. He lived in Munich. He is noted for works including *Burgos Cathedral* and *Landscapes and Architectural Views of Spain*.
AUCTION RECORDS:
LONDON, 1 Aug 1935, *View of a Town, with Figures*, GBP 7. COLOGNE, 20 Oct 1967, *Regensburg Cathedral*, DEM 3,000. LONDON, 17 July 1979, *Market Square* (watercolour, 14 1/2 x 11 1/4 ins / 36.6 x 28.4 cm) GBP 1,600. LONDON, 15 July 1980, *Seville* (watercolour and pencil, 17 1/2 x 12 3/4 ins / 44.2 x 32.6 cm) GBP 300. LONDON, 24 Nov 1983, *View of Munich* (1848, watercolour and pencil, 7 1/2 x 10 1/4 ins / 19 x 26 cm) GBP 6,500. MUNICH, 14 March 1985, *Market Scene in the Old City of Regensburg* (1849, oil on panel, 18 3/4 x 14 1/2 ins / 47.5 x 36.7 cm) DEM 21,000. LONDON, 20 June 1985, *Marienplatz, Munich* (1851, watercolour and pencil heightened with white and gold, 10 x 11 3/4 ins / 24.5 x 30 cm) GBP 7,000. AMSTERDAM, 24 April 1991, *Crowd in the Market Square in Munich* (1849, oil on canvas, 12 1/4 x 9 3/4 ins / 31 x 25 cm) NLG 103,500. MUNICH, 27 Feb 1999, *Straubing - View of Theresien Place Trinity Column* (oil on paper/board, 13 x 11 ins / 32 x 27 cm) DEM 13,000. JERSEY, 29 Sept 1999, *Moonlight, Venice* (oil on canvas, 23 x 31 ins / 59 x 78 cm) GBP 3,200. DÜSSELDORF, 31 Jan 2000, *Cathedral and Severikirche in Erfurt* (oil on canvas, 28 x 33 ins / 71 x 83 cm) DEM 55,000. STOCKHOLM, 4 Dec 2001, *Medieval Town Scene* (1851, oil on canvas, 21 x 18 ins / 54 x 45 cm) SEK 72,000. MUNICH, 20 Sept 2002, *Venice* (1869, oil on panel, 16 x 13 ins / 41 x 34 cm) EUR 10,000. LEYBURN, 21 Nov 2002, *Doge's Palace and La Santa Maria Della Salute, Venice by Moonlight* (oil on canvas, 23 x 31 ins / 59 x 78 cm) GBP 4,200.

EICH, Gustav
German, 19th century.
Active in Berlin.
Painter. Genre scenes.
A pupil of W. Wach, Eich exhibited at the Berlin academy from 1842 to 1856.

EICH, Johann Friedrich
German, 18th - 19th century.
Born 1748; died 1807, in Altona.
Painter.
A native of the Harz region, Eich's travels covered the whole of Europe on two separate occasions. He settled in Brunswick, where he painted the portraits of P.J.F. Weitsch and Dr. Brückmann, which were engraved by Chodowiecki, in addition to a portrait of the philosopher F.H. Jacobi, engraved by Geyser.

EICH, Robert
German, 19th century.
Painter. Architectural views.
Eich worked in Munich, Düsseldorf and Italy.
MUSEUMS AND GALLERIES:
MOSCOW (Rumiantsev Mus.): *Temple of Minerva*.

EICHE, Johann Georg
German, 18th century.
Born c. 1745; died 23 January 1799, in Brunswick.
Painter (porcelain).
Eiche worked initially at the Furstenberg porcelain factory and later for the same manufacturer in Brunswick, where he settled and was accorded the title of 'sole painter of figures'.

EICHEL
British, 18th century.
Active in London.
Painter.
Eichel exhibited landscapes at the Free Society in 1770 and 1771. Four of these have been preserved at the British Museum.
MUSEUMS AND GALLERIES:
LONDON (British Mus.): four landscapes.

EICHEL
Polish, 19th century.
Active c. 1850.
Miniaturist.
Eichel's only known work is a watercolour portrait of *Princess Catherine Galicyn, formerly Countess Soltokub* which featured in an exhibition of miniatures in Lemberg (now Lviv, Ukraine) in 1912.

EICHEL, Emmanuel
German, 18th century.
Born 1717; died 1782.
Active in Augsburg.
Engraver (burin).
Eichel was a pupil of Herz. He engraved a number of *Saints* and 51 plates for the *Life of Man*.

EICHELBERGER, Robert A.
American, 19th century.
Died probably in 1900.
Painter, engraver. Genre scenes, landscapes.

Robert A. Eichelberger exhibited *Wave* at the Exposition Universelle in Paris. Also among his works is *Breakers and Mist*.

AUCTION RECORDS:
NEW YORK, 12 May 1978, *Sentinel and Serving Girl* (1896, oil on canvas, 41¼ x 35½ ins / 105 x 90 cm) USD 2,500.

EICHELROTH, Mathias
German, 18th century.
Potter.

After beginning work at the Dorotheenthal earthenware factory near Arnstadt, Eichelroth became director of the earthenware works at Gera-Untermhaus in 1750.

EICHEN, Aleksandr Georg von, or Aleksandr Fedrovich
Russian, 19th century.
Born 8 April 1818; died 4 October 1846.
Painter.

Eichen was a pupil of Bruyllov at the St Petersburg academy of fine arts. Works that can be cited are: *St Jerome* and *Mercury Sending Argus to Sleep*.

EICHENBERGER, Jean-Pierre
Swiss, 20th century.
Died 25 August 2000.
Active in France.
Painter, sculptor. Murals.

Eichenberger graduated from the École des Beaux-Arts in Geneva. He founded the artistic centre in Piegon in the Drôme.

EICHENS, Friedrich Eduard
German, 19th century.
Born 1804, in Berlin; died 5 May 1877, in Berlin.
Painter, engraver, draughtsman. Religious subjects, portraits.

Eichens studied in Berlin, in Paris with Forster and Richomme, and then in Parma with Paolo Toschi. He became a member of the academy of fine arts in Berlin in 1832.

His engravings include *Dead Christ on the Knees of the Virgin* after Carracci, *Scenes from the Deliverance of Jerusalem*, the *Vision of Ezekiel* after Raphael, *St Mary Magdalene* after Domenichino, the *Adoration of the Magi* after Raphael, and numerous portraits.

AUCTION RECORDS:
NEW YORK, 26 Oct 1990, *Drawing room with the Family Artists* (1826, black and white chalk/paper, 21¼ x 28½ ins / 54 x 72.4 cm) USD 20,900.

EICHENS, Philipp Hermann
German, 19th century.
Born 13 September 1813, in Berlin; died 17 May 1886, in Paris.
Painter, lithographer, engraver. Genre scenes, portraits.

Philipp Hermann Eichens was the younger brother of the engraver Eduard Eichens. He studied at the academy in Berlin with Hensel. In 1835, he made a special study of lithography in Paris and also studied engraving in Berlin with Lüderitz. He settled in Paris in 1849, and was a member of the Berlin academy. His notable works include *View of Paris from the Artist's Studio, Fair-Haired and Brunette* after Dubufe, *Am I Beautiful?* after Weisz, *Christian Martyr* after Delaroche, *Pageboy* after Wittich, the *Mona Lisa* after da Vinci, *Virgin and Child* after Götting, and *The Talking Well* after Vély.

AUCTION RECORDS:
PARIS, 26 Feb 1943, *Public at the Salon of 1837* (watercolour) FRF 1,250.

EICHER, A.
Swiss, 19th century.
Born c. 1815.
Active in Switzerland.
Painter.

According to Dr Carl Brun, Eicher began his career as a 'vagabond' artist. He travelled around the countryside painting portraits of farmers, who gave him food and lodging in payment. Towards the end of his life, he became a master draughtsman at Muri. He also executed a number of oil paintings for Swiss village churches.

EICHFELD, Hermann
German, 19th - 20th century.
Born 27 February 1845, in Karlsruhe.
Painter. Landscapes.

Eichfeld, a graduate of the Stuttgart art academy and pupil of Wengheim in Munich, was appointed director of Mannheim art gallery in 1912. Noted works include *Summer Evening, Clouds and Trees, March Sun, Gloomy Day*, and *Clouds*.

EICHFELD, Sophie
German, 19th century.
Born 20 January 1856, in Augsburg.
Painter.

After studying at the school of arts and crafts in Munich, Sophie Eichfeld married the painter Hermann Eichfeld. She painted landscapes and still-lifes.

EICHHOLTZ, Jacob, or Eicholtz
American, 18th - 19th century.
Born 1776; died 1842.
Painter. Portraits.

AUCTION RECORDS:
NEW YORK, 18 Nov 1977, *Portrait of Mrs Belle Simon Cohen* (c. 1824, 30 x 25 ins / 76.2 x 63.5 cm) USD 2,800. NEW YORK, 17 Oct 1980, *Mr and Mrs Longenecker* (c. 1820, oils on canvas, a pair, 30 x 25 ins / 76.2 x 63.5 cm) USD 40,000. RALEIGH, 5 Nov 1985, *Portrait of a Woman in a Red Shawl; Portrait of a Woman in a Blue Shawl with Fur* (1823, oils on canvas, a pair, 30¼ x 25¼ ins / 77.1 x 64.2 cm) USD 8,000. NEW YORK, 24 Jan 1989, *Portrait of Captain Jacob da Costa* (oil on canvas, 23 x 17½ ins / 57.5 x 44.5 cm) USD 2,200. NEW YORK, 15 Nov 1993, *Portrait of Mrs John Bannister, née Sarah Work* (oil on canvas, 29 x 24¼ ins / 73.8 x 61.5 cm) USD 5,175. ST LOUIS, 24 Feb 2001, *Portraits of Rebecca and Henry Sleighmaker* (oil on canvas, a pair, 30 x 24 ins / 76 x 61 cm) USD 11,750. NEW YORK, 11 Oct 2001, *Portrait of Eliza Jacob* (c. 1825, oil on canvas, 29 x 24 ins / 74 x 61 cm) USD 3,000.

EICHHOLZER, Bernhard
Swiss, 17th century.
Born in Bremgarten; died 5 October 1635, in Solothurn.
Painter.

Eichholzer was received into the brotherhood of St Luke at Solothurn in 1603 and became a burgher of that town in 1630. He is also thought to have spent some time living abroad. He was probably the son of Jakob Eichholzer.

EICHHOLZER, Jakob
Swiss, 16th century.
Died c. 1602.
Active in Bremgarten (Aargau).
Painter.

EICHHOLZER, M.
Austrian, 19th century.
Active in Vienna.
Painter, lithographer.

Eichholzer studied at the academy in Vienna. His lithographic work includes drawings for plates after Michelangelo.

EICHHORN, Albert
German, 19th century.
Born 7 July 1811, in Freienwalde an der Oder; died 19 October 1851, in Potsdam.
Painter. Architectural views, landscapes.

A pupil of Eduard Biermann, Eichhorn travelled in Greece and Italy. He exhibited at the royal academy in Berlin.

AUCTION RECORDS:
COLOGNE, 8 May 1969, *View of the Acropolis,* DEM 3,000.

EICHHORN, Franz Joseph
German, 18th century.
Born c. 1712, in Düsseldorf; died 1785, in Neuwied (near Koblenz).
Painter.

Eichhorn worked as a portrait painter with Lippold in Frankfurt am Main, after which he spent some time working in Mainz and in Amsterdam. He then settled at Neuwied and painted historical pictures for the castle there. His portraits were engraved by J.J. Haid, A. Rheinhardt and Bernigeroth.

EICHHORN, Hans
German, 16th century.
Born in Nuremberg; died 1583, in Frankfurt.
Painter, engraver (wood).

Eichhorn worked for the elector Joachim II.

EICHHORN, Jacob
German, 19th century.
Died 3 November 1906, in Eisenach.
Active in Weimar.
Painter. Genre scenes, landscapes.

Jacob Eichhorn exhibited in Berlin and Munich in 1848 and 1886. He is noted for his *Fish* and *Dutch Fishing Villages.*

EICHHORN, Johann Paul
German, 18th century.
Born 18th century, in Schalkau (Thuringia).
Painter (porcelain).

Johann Eichhorn worked at the Rauenstein porcelain factory.

EICHHORN, Leo Bernhard
Austrian, 19th - 20th century.
Born 1872, in Lemberg (now Lviv, Ukraine).
Painter. Genre scenes.

Eichhorn trained under Casimir Pochwalski at the Akademie der Bildenden Künste in Vienna. He also exhibited at the Salon des Artistes Français in Paris, receiving an honourable mention in 1905.

AUCTION RECORDS:
VIENNA, 6 Nov 1984, *The Dejected* (1908, oil on canvas, 55 x 88 1/2 ins / 140 x 225 cm) ATS 32,000.

EICHHORN, Maria
German, 20th - 21st century.
Born 1962, in Bamberg.
Installation artist.

Eichhorn lives and works in Berlin, where she attended the art academy from 1984-1990. She has won several grants and prizes, including the George Maciunas prize in 1992. Her work broadens the ready-made concept, and her artistic language draws upon architecture. She has participated in various group exhibitions in Germany, including *Skulptur. Projekte in Münster 1997* (*Sculpture. Projects in Münster 1997*) in Berlin, Munich, and Münster in 1977, and abroad: Rome, Vienna, St Petersburg, Copenhagen and Paris (*Qui, quoi, où?* (*Who, What, Where?*) at the Musée d'Art Moderne de la Ville de Paris in 1992). She has held solo shows since 1986 in Berlin, Cologne and Stuttgart; in 1999 at the Portikus Museum in Frankfurt; and at the Sprengel Museum in Hanover; in 2002 at the Galerie Hauser & Wirth & Presenhuber, in Zurich; in 2004 at the Centre d'Art Santa Monica, Barcelona; and in 2005 at the Stiftung Kunsthalle in Bern.

BIBLIOGRAPHY:
Bader, Jorg, '*Maria Eichhorn*' in *Art Press* n° 276 p. 70, periodical, Paris, February 2002.

EICHHORST, Franz
German, 20th century.
Born 7 September 1885, in Berlin; died 1948.
Painter. History painting, portraits.

Eichhorst painted portraits, war scenes and especially scenes from peasant life in the Tyrol.

AUCTION RECORDS:
COLOGNE, 18 Nov 1982, *Weavers* (1919, oil on panel, 35 3/4 x 28 3/4 ins / 91 x 73 cm) DEM 7,500. LONDON, 31 March 1987, '*Seventh Heaven*' *Cabaret, Berlin* (1913, oil on canvas, 33 1/2 x 48 ins / 85 x 121 cm) GBP 15,000. FRANKFURT, 20 Nov 1999, *Young Peasant Woman in Interior* (oil on panel, 28 x 24 ins / 72 x 61 cm) DEM 6,000. COLOGNE, 6 April 2000, *Harvest* (oil on canvas, 20 x 26 ins / 52 x 65 cm) DEM 5,500. MUNICH, 13 May 2004, *Peasant Market* (oil on canvas/board, 20 x 24 ins / 52 x 62 cm) EUR 1,500.

EICHINGER, Erwin
Austrian, 20th century.
Born 1882; died 1950.
Painter. Genre scenes.

E. Eichinger

AUCTION RECORDS:
LONDON, 15 June 1979, *Clergymen in a Library* (oil on panel, 14 x 22 1/2 ins / 35.5 x 57 cm) GBP 1,000. LUCERNE, 6 Nov 1981, *Portrait of a Peasant (Bust)* (oil on panel, 6 1/4 x 4 ins / 16 x 10 cm) CHF 1,300. NEW YORK, 27 May 1983, *A Nice Glass* (oil on card, 10 1/4 x 8 ins / 26 x 20.3 cm) USD 950. MUNICH, 2 July 1986, *Young Dutch Woman with her Little Daughter Indoors* (oil on panel, 16 1/2 x 20 3/4 ins / 42 x 53 cm) DEM 6,000. NEW YORK, 23 Feb 1989, *The Sum of the Debt* (oil on panel, 16 x 18 1/2 ins / 40.6 x 47 cm) USD 11,000. CHESTER, 20 July 1989, *Architect* (oil on canvas, 17 x 12 3/4 ins / 43 x 32.5 cm) GBP 2,310. LONDON, 19 June 1991, *Returning from Hunting; Peaceful Moment* (oil on panel, a pair, each 7 3/4 x 6 ins / 20 x 15 cm) GBP 2,860. LONDON, 27 Oct 1993, *Old Man Tasting a Glass of Wine* (oil on panel, a pair, each 10 x 7 1/2 ins / 25.5 x 19 cm) GBP 1,265. MUNICH, 6 Dec 1994, *A Sculptor-Monk* (oil on panel, 15 1/2 x 12 ins / 39.5 x 30.5 cm) DEM 3,680. BERN, 5 May 1999, *Three Card Players in a Tavern* (oil on canvas, 20 x 24 ins / 50 x 60 cm) CHF 2,900. CLEVELAND, 30 Sept 1999, *The Scholarly Cardinal* (oil on panel, 10 x 12 ins / 25 x 30 cm) USD 3,150. TOESTORF, 26 Aug 2000, *Interior Scene with Man Reading. Interior Scene with Man Playing Chess* (oil on panel, a pair, 13 x 10 ins / 32 x 26 cm) DEM 10,800. BURY ST EDMUNDS, 28 Sept 2000, *Scholar Monk* (oil on panel, 10 x 12 ins / 25 x 30 cm) GBP 1,900. LONDON, 18 Jan 2001, *Good Vintage. Pinch of Snuff* (oil on board, a pair, 10 x 7 ins / 25 x 19 cm) GBP 2,400. LONDON, 23 May 2001, *Man with Pewter Tankard* (oil on board, 10 x 8 ins / 26 x 20 cm) GBP 1,200. BURY ST EDMUNDS, 4 March 2002, *Alpine Guide* (oil on board, a pair, 8 x 6 ins / 21 x 16 cm) GBP 1,500. LONDON, 17 July 2002, *Connoisseur* (oil on panel, 12 x 10 ins / 31 x 25 cm) GBP 2,600. LONDON, 24 Oct 2002, *Pondering the Next Move* (oil on canvas, 16 x 19 ins / 41 x 49 cm) GBP 1,700. LONDON, 18 March 2003, *Bibliophile* (oil on panel, 10 x 12 ins / 25 x 31 cm) GBP 3,200. PHILADELPHIA, 22 June 2003, *Card Game* (oil on canvas, 23 x 31 ins / 58 x 79 cm) USD 5,000. LONDON, 25 March 2004, *Lucky Throw* (oil on panel, 15 x 17 ins / 38 x 44 cm) GBP 4,000.

EICHINGER, Otto
Austrian, 20th century.
Born 1922.
Painter. Local figures, genre scenes.
AUCTION RECORDS:
VIENNA, 17 Feb 1981, *Monk with a Glass of Wine* (oil/hardboard, 10 1/2 x 7 3/4 ins / 26.5 x 20 cm) ATS 11,000. SAN FRANCISCO, 6 Nov 1985, *Rabbi* (oil on card, 11 x 7 3/4 ins / 27 x 20 cm) USD 1,000. AMSTERDAM, 23 April 1991, *Portrait of a Rabbi* (oil on panel, 11 x 7 3/4 ins / 27 x 20 cm) NLG 3,450. NEW YORK, 20 July 1994, *Rabbi* (oil on card, 10 1/2 x 7 3/4 ins / 26.7 x 20 cm) USD 1,380. NEW YORK, 20 July 1995, *Scholar with his Books* (oil on panel, 9 1/2 x 11 3/4 ins / 24.1 x 29.8 cm) USD 9,200. BILLINGSHURST, 18 May 1999, *Study of a Rabbi* (oil on panel, 10 x 7 ins / 26 x 19 cm) GBP 1,600. LONDON, 30 Nov 1999, *Card Players Wearing Traditional Costume* (oil on canvas, 24 x 31 ins / 60 x 78 cm) GBP 4,500. LONDON, 6 April 2000, *Learned Rabbi. Meditation* (oil on board, a pair, 11 x 8 ins / 27 x 20 cm) GBP 4,500. LONDON, 21 June 2000, *Rabbi* (oil on panel, 10 x 7 ins / 26 x 19 cm) GBP 2,600. SAN FRANCISCO, 16 May 2001, *Portrait of a Seated Rabbi* (oil on masonite, 11 x 8 ins / 27 x 20 cm) USD 2,000. LONDON, 26 March 2003, *Portrait of a Rabbi* (oil on board, 10 x 8 ins / 26 x 20 cm) GBP 1,800. NEW YORK, 18 March 2004, *Portrait of a Rabbi* (oil on panel, 7 x 10 ins / 19 x 26 cm) USD 3,000. CHICAGO, 11 Sept 2004, *Portrait of a Rabbi* (oil on board, 10 x 7 ins / 25 x 18 cm) USD 2,280.

EICHLER, Antonie
German, 19th century.
Active in Berlin.
Painter.
Antonie Eichler showed genre paintings and portraits at the Berlin academy exhibitions from 1860 to 1878, at the Society of Women Artists and at the Grosse Kunstausstellung in Berlin. She painted a retable for the Protestant church at Oberholzheim in Württemberg.

EICHLER, Balthasar Johann
German, 17th century.
Died 1672; buried on 19 January in Dresden.
Draughtsman.
The collection of copper engravings in Dresden includes a pen and ink drawing and a *View of Dresden* by this artist.

EICHLER, Carl Gottfried
German, 19th century.
Active in Munich from 1818 onwards.
Engraver.
This artist was probably the son of Mathias Gottfried Eichler. He engraved landscapes and portraits.

EICHLER, Ernst Ferdinand
German, 19th century.
Born 17 January 1850, in Werdau (near Leipzig); died 6 December 1895, in Zurickau.
Portrait artist, draughtsman.
Ernst Eichler was a pupil at the Dresden academy and worked in the studio of Julius Heibner. He settled in Rome, where he taught drawing at the archaeological institute there. His works include a *Portrait of the Artist*.

EICHLER, Gottfried, the Elder
German, 18th century.
Born 1677, in Lippstadt; died 1757, in Augsburg.
Painter. History painting, portraits.
Gottfried Eichler travelled extensively in Germany and visited Vienna and Rome, where he was a pupil of Carlo Maratta. He died a pauper. He produced a large number of portraits, well known thanks to the reproductions engraved by artists such as J.J. Haid, G.A. Wolfgang, J. Stenglin, C. Engelbrecht and others.
MUSEUMS AND GALLERIES:
AUGSBURG (Maximilianmus.): *Portrait of the Artist* - GENEVA (Mus. Ariana): *Portrait of General Jérôme d'Erlach*.

EICHLER, Gottfried, the Younger
German, 18th century.
Born 1715; died 1770.
Active in Augsburg.
Painter, engraver.
The son and pupil of Gottfried Eichler the Elder, this artist travelled for several years as his father had done, staying in Vienna and Nuremberg.

EICHLER, Hermann
Austrian, 19th century.
Born 1842, in Vienna; died 17 September 1901, in Vienna.
Painter. History painting, genre scenes.
Hermann Eichler was a pupil of Christian Ruben. He travelled in Italy and stayed in Rome for a time before settling in Vienna. He exhibited in Vienna and in Berlin from 1869 to 1879. His notable works include *Charles I of England, Idyll, Picnic in the Countryside* and *Faun and Nymph*.
MUSEUMS AND GALLERIES:
VIENNA (Akademie der Bildenden Künste): *Episode from the Peasant War in Germany*.
AUCTION RECORDS:
VIENNA, 23 June 1982, *View of Venice* (oil on canvas, 39 1/2 x 23 1/2 ins / 100.5 x 60 cm) ATS 12,000. LONDON, 23 Feb 1983, *Street Musicians near Rome* (oil on canvas, 98 3/4 x 39 1/4 ins / 251 x 100 cm) GBP 600. VIENNA, 19 June 1985, *Scene from the Thirty Years' War* (1882, oil on canvas, 26 1/2 x 49 1/2 ins / 67 x 126 cm) ATS 35,000.

EICHLER, Johann Conrad, also known as Wollust
German, 17th - 18th century.
Born 1668, in Peine, Brunswick; died 1 January 1748, in Wolfenbüttel, Brunswick.
Painter. Portraits, still-lifes (fruit).
Johann Eichler studied in Rome and later, after a stay in Nuremberg, was appointed court painter at Brunswick. He painted numerous portraits of Duke Rudolph of Brunswick and his wife Christiane Louise, as well as portraits of other members of the ruling family of Brunswick, including the dukes Ferdinand Albert II, Augustus William and Karl I. A number of still-lifes are also attributed to this artist.
MUSEUMS AND GALLERIES:
BLANKENBURG (Mus. Kleines Schloss) - BRUNSWICK (Herzog Anton Ulrich-Mus.): *Self-portrait* - HANOVER (Fürstenhaus Herrenhausen) - LUCKLUM (Castle).
AUCTION RECORDS:
AMSTERDAM, 2 Dec 1987, *Still-life with Fruit* (1739, oil on canvas, 26 1/2 x 31 1/2 ins / 67 x 80 cm) NLG 34,000. VIENNA, 6 Oct 1999, *Still-life with Peaches, Grapes, Pomegranates, Plums* (1739, oil on canvas, 26 x 31 ins / 67 x 80 cm) ATS 600,000. AHLDEN, 3 May 2002, *Ludwig Rudolf Herzog von Braunschweig-Wolfenbuttel* (oil on canvas, 59 x 48 ins / 151 x 123 cm) EUR 5,000.

EICHLER, Joseph Franz Maria
German, 18th century.
Born 1724, in Brunswick; died 1783.
Painter, pastellist.
This artist, who was the son and pupil of J. Conrad Eichler, travelled in Holland, England, France and Italy and later stayed in Brunswick and Hanover. He painted in oils and in pastel.
MUSEUMS AND GALLERIES:
ANSBACH (Residenz): two copies after Jan Fyt and M. Hondeköeter.

AUCTION RECORDS:
AMSTERDAM, 12 May 1992, *Portrait of a General* (1749, oil on canvas, 45 x 36 ins / 114.6 x 91.6 cm) NLG 5,060.

EICHLER, Joseph Ignaz or Giuseppe Ignazio
German, 18th century.
Born 25 January 1714, in Rome; died 16 May 1763, in Brunswick.
Modeller, sculptor (ivory). Low reliefs.
The museum in Brunswick has a low relief in white wax by this artist depicting *Hercules, Omphale and Cupid* as well as eight ivory sculptures.

EICHLER, Julian
German, 18th century.
Born 4 January 1712, in Rome.
Painter.
The son of Johann Conrad Eichler, this artist painted a portrait of Anna Sophie Overlach, wife of the court physician J.H. Burckhard, in addition to portraits of the archivist J.G. Burckhard and his wife.

EICHLER, Mathias Gottfried
German, 18th - 19th century.
Born 1748, in Erlangen; died after 1818, in Augsburg.
Engraver.
This artist was the son and pupil of Gottfried Eichler the Younger. His engravings include a *Portrait of Gessner*, after A. Graff, the illustrations for the *Heptameron of Marguerite of Navarre*, after Dunker, and *Views of Livorno, of the House of Horatius and Ancona*, after P. Hackert.

EICHLER, Otto Erich
German, 19th - 20th century.
Born 25 September 1871, in Königsberg (now Kaliningrad, Russia); died 19 June 1904, in Königsberg.
Painter, engraver (etching). Figures, landscapes, seascapes, animals.
Eichler trained under Max Schmidt and Emil Neide at the Königsberg art academy, then studied at the Berlin art academy, before becoming a pupil of Heinrich Zügel in Munich, where he settled. In 1895 he was awarded the silver medal by the Munich art academy for his painting *Knight on the Run*. He then returned to Prussia. Despite his premature death, he left a large number of studies, sketches and paintings. He also produced some etchings, including *Knight on the Look-Out* and *Stream by Moonlight*.

Early on, Eichler specialised in studies of animals. He also painted a number of figures and illustrated stories, such as *Mazeppa* and *The Tale of the Seven Swans*. On his return to Prussia he took up landscape painting, depicting the coast around Gross Kuhren (today Primorje, Russia) where he lived, as well as executing studies of horses and livestock. Noted works from this period include *Moonlit Night in Gross Dirckheim* and *The Zipfelberg at Sunset*. His subjects taken from the world of chivalry and his moonlit and sunset landscapes link him to the German Romantic tradition of landscape painting.

EICHLER, Reinhold Max
German, 19th - 20th century.
Born 4 March 1872, near Hubertusburg (Saxony); died 1947.
Painter, illustrator. Allegorical subjects, landscapes with figures, landscapes, interiors, figures, still-lifes (flowers/fruit).
Eichler enrolled at the Dresden art academy in 1889. In 1893 he went to Munich, where he became a pupil of the landscape painter Paul Hoecker. While in Munich he contributed to the magazine *Die Jugend*, and joined the group of illustrators there. He painted the occasional allegorical composition such as *Ceres* and a noted self-portrait, but was essentially a painter of landscapes, sometimes with figures. He was always sensitive to the effects of variations of light on the landscape, as in *Spring Storm*, *Autumn Melancholy*, and *In the Evening Sunlight*.
MUSEUMS AND GALLERIES:
BERLIN (Nationalgal.): *Blossoming*; *The Apple Store* - MUNICH (Brackl): *Ceres*; *The Seasons*.
AUCTION RECORDS:
HEIDELBERG, 3 May 1982, *Apple Tree in Blossom* (1897, oil on canvas, 31 1/2 x 27 1/4 ins / 80 x 69.5 cm) DEM 2,600. VIENNA, 17 March 1987, *Bathers* (oil on canvas, 57 1/2 x 51 1/4 ins / 146 x 130 cm) ATS 140,000. MUNICH, 17 May 2001, *Nude by Punt* (oil on canvas, 18 x 22 ins / 46 x 55 cm) DEM 4,500. MUNICH, 13 May 2004, *Still-life of Flowers* (oil on canvas, 24 x 20 ins / 62 x 51 cm) EUR 4,800.

EICHLER, Theodor Karl
German, 19th - 20th century.
Born 15 May 1868, in Oberspaar, near Meissen (Saxony).
Sculptor, modeller (porcelain). Genre scenes.
Eichler worked at the Meissen porcelain factory before attending the industrial art and design school and the art academy in Dresden. From 1899 onwards he showcased his works at fine arts and decorative arts exhibitions in Dresden, Berlin, Düsseldorf, Hanover and elsewhere.

He sculpted little genre subjects: *Little Girl with a Spinning Top, Young Boy with a Basket*. At Meissen porcelain factory he created groups of figures, especially groups of dancers, one of the factory's most sought-after subjects.

EICHLER, Wilhelm
German, 19th century.
Painter. Landscapes.
Wilhelm Eichler showed works at the Berlin academy exhibitions in 1828 and 1830.

EICHMANN, Heinrich
Swiss, 20th century.
Born 1915, in Flühli.
Painter.
Die Allianz Group.
Eichmann worked in Zurich and belonged to the group known as Die Allianz. From 1944 onwards he took part in group exhibitions in Zurich and in Paris where, in particular, he participated in the Salon des Réalités Nouvelles in 1950, presenting constructivist-inspired paintings.

EICHMANN, K.
German, 19th century.
Active in Berlin.
Painter. Landscapes.
Works by this artist were shown at the Berlin academy exhibitions in 1856 and 1860, and in 1860 he also showed *Thuringia by Moonlight* at the Artists' Association exhibition.

EICHNER, E.
German, 19th century.
Active in Rostock (Mecklenburg).
Painter.
A painting by this artist, *Christ among the Teachers*, can be found in the church of St Nicholas in Rostock. Eichner also helped decorate the Pinakotek in Munich.

EICHORN. See **EICHHORN**

EICHRODT, Helmut
German, 19th - 20th century.
Born 27 February 1872, in Bruchsal.
Painter, illustrator. Murals.
Eichrodt trained under Leopold de Kalckreuth and Hans Thoma at Karlsruhe art academy, and settled in Karlsruhe. He did a lot of work as an illustrator, and undertook murals in Karlsruhe (for the church of Christ), Pforzheim and

Freiburg, among other places. He also painted several still-lifes of flowers.

Eichrodt was above all a genre painter of figures (*Woman in Spanish Costume, Lute Player, Woman of Ill Repute, Waiting*), although he sometimes painted figures in a landscape (*In the Park*) and portraits (*Portrait of the Painter's Wife, Portraits of Children, Portrait of Grand Duke Friedrich II and the Grand Duchess*).

EICHRODT, Otto
German, 19th century.
Born 25 June 1867, in Freiburg.
Painter, draughtsman.

Eichrodt first studied at the academy in Karlsruhe, and later in Munich and Paris. His major works are his portraits, including those of the singer Buffard, Helmut Eichrodt, the critic Florian, and the emperor William II. In addition he painted still-lifes, interiors, such as those at the castle at Bruchsal, and Black Forest landscapes. He was also a musician and dramatist.

EICHSTAEDT, Rudolf
German, 19th - 20th century.
Born 20 April 1857, in Berlin; died 1924 or 1927, in Berlin.
Painter. Figures, portraits, genre scenes, interiors.

Eichstaedt was a pupil of Geselschaps. In 1887 he was awarded the top state scholarship for a working trip to Italy. He lived in Berlin.

MUSEUMS AND GALLERIES:
KALININGRAD: *Between Ligny and Belle-Alliance.*

AUCTION RECORDS:
LONDON, 30 Jan 1981, *The Young Servant* (oil on canvas, 37 1/4 x 25 3/4 ins / 94.6 x 65.4 cm) GBP 750. COLOGNE, 29 June 1984, *Rustic Interior* (oil on canvas, 33 1/2 x 24 1/2 ins / 85 x 62 cm) DEM 3,000. BERN, 26 Oct 1988, *Two Women in a Vegetable Garden* (oil on canvas, 29 1/4 x 37 1/2 ins / 74 x 95 cm) CHF 2,000.

EICHSTÄTT, Heinrich and Sebald von. See **EGWEILER**

EICHTHORN, Johann Friedrich Wilhelm
German, 18th century.
Painter (porcelain).

Eichthorn worked at the Gera porcelain works in Thuringia.

EICK, J. F.
Dutch, 19th century.
Active in Amsterdam c. 1820.
Painter. Portraits.

There exists by J. F. Eick a portrait of Alexander P. van der Capellen, engraved in 1791 by R. Vinkeles.

EICK, Martin de. See **MARINUS VAN ROEJMERSWAELEN**

EICKELBERG, Willem Hendrik
Dutch, 19th - 20th century.
Born 1845; died 1920 or 1929.
Painter. Genre scenes, landscapes, urban landscapes, seascapes.

Eickelberg specialised in highly animated seascapes and landscapes.

W. H. Eickelberg.

AUCTION RECORDS:
NEW YORK, 31 Oct 1980, *Fishermen on the Beach* (oil on canvas, 18 x 25 3/4 ins / 45.7 x 65.4 cm) USD 2,200. COLOGNE, 22 March 1985, *Beach Scene, Scheveningen* (oil on canvas, 18 1/4 x 26 ins / 46.5 x 66 cm) DEM 7,500. AMSTERDAM, 10 Feb 1988, *Mother and her Child on a Snowy Forest Path at Dusk* (oil on canvas, 15 3/4 x 18 1/2 ins / 40 x 47 cm) NLG 3,910. AMSTERDAM, 16 Nov 1988, *View of Oude Gracht in Utrecht with the Belfry* (oil on panel, 13 3/4 x 11 ins / 35 x 27 cm) NLG 6,325. AMSTERDAM, 28 Feb 1989, *Forest in Winter with Woodcutters on their Sledge* (oil on panel, 11 3/4 x 10 ins / 30 x 24.5 cm) NLG 6,325. AMSTERDAM, 2 May 1990, *Fishermen at Work around a Round Boat in Katwijk* (oil on panel, 13 3/4 x 9 3/4 ins / 35 x 25 cm) NLG 8,050. AMSTERDAM, 14-15 April 1992, *Fishermen at Work as the Fleet Returns to the French Coast* (oil on panel, 10 x 13 1/2 ins / 25.5 x 34.5 cm) NLG 8,280. LONDON, 16 June 1993, *Fishing in a River near a Mill* (oil on panel, 11 x 13 3/4 ins / 27 x 35 cm) GBP 2,185. AMSTERDAM, 19 Oct 1993, *Lovely Summer's Day* (oil on canvas, 17 1/4 x 26 ins / 44 x 66 cm) NLG 9,200. AMSTERDAM, 5 Nov 1996, *Winter Landscape* (oil on canvas, 26 1/4 x 37 3/4 ins / 66.5 x 96 cm) NLG 3,068.

EICKEN, Elisabeth von, later Edle von Paepke
German, 19th century.
Born 18 July 1862, in Mülheim; died 21 July 1940, in Michendorf (near Potsdam).
Painter. Landscapes.

Elisabeth von Eicken was a pupil of E. Yon in Paris and worked in Berlin-Grünewald. Her work appeared in exhibitions in Berlin, Munich, Düsseldorf and Paris from 1894 onwards. She painted views of Grünewald, the Baltic coast, Pomeranian villages and similar subjects.

MUSEUMS AND GALLERIES:
GDANSK: *Behind the Birches* - HANOVER: *Late Autumn* - NEUBRANDENBURG: *Cowshed Interior* - ROSTOCK: *Forest Landscape; Same subject.*

AUCTION RECORDS:
STOCKHOLM, 15 Nov 1988, *Undergrowth in a Birch Forest* (oil on canvas, 26 3/4 x 39 1/4 ins / 68 x 100 cm) SEK 13,000. BREMEN, 3 July 1999, *Young Birch Trees at Bodden* (oil on canvas, 15 x 11 ins / 38 x 29 cm) DEM 4,900. DRESDEN, 4 March 2000, *Birch Wood* (oil on canvas, 19 x 13 ins / 48 x 33 cm) DEM 4,000. HAMBURG, 8 Dec 2001, *Heath Landscape with Trees* (oil on canvas, 33 x 54 ins / 85 x 136 cm) DEM 5,800. HAMBURG, 9 Feb 2002, *Farm near Ahrenshoop with Ostsee in Background* (oil on canvas, 19 x 26 ins / 48 x 66 cm) EUR 5,500. HAMBURG, 15 June 2002, *Winter Scene with Farmhouse near Ahrenshoop* (oil on canvas, 26 x 40 ins / 67 x 102 cm) EUR 6,000. BREMEN, 18 June 2004, *Autumn Evening* (oil on canvas, 24 x 29 ins / 62 x 74 cm) EUR 2,100.

EICKHOF-REITZENSTEIN, Marie von
German, 19th - 20th century.
Born 1 January 1872, in Breslau (now Wroclaw, Poland).
Painter. Portraits, still-lifes.

Von Eickhof-Reitzenstein was a pupil of the portraitist Gustave Courtois in Paris. She took part in numerous collective exhibitions in Berlin, Munich and Paris.

EICKHOFF, Gerda
Danish, 20th century.
Born in Copenhagen.
Painter.

Eickhoff exhibited at the Salon des Indépendants in Paris in 1928 and 1929 and as a guest at the Salon des Tuileries.

EICKHOFF, Gottfried
Danish, 20th century.
Born 1902.
Sculptor. Figures, nudes.

Eickhoff specialised in the female figure.

AUCTION RECORDS:
COPENHAGEN, 13 Oct 1981, *Standing Nude* (1937, bronze, h. 38 1/2 ins / 98 cm) DKK 7,000. COPENHAGEN, 9 May 1984, *Young Girl Standing* (1935, bronze, h. 23 1/4 ins / 59 cm) DKK 9,000. COPENHAGEN, 24 April 1985, *Young Girl Standing* (1957, bronze, h. 45 ins / 114 cm) DKK 60,000. COPENHAGEN,

20 Oct 1993, *Woman Walking* (1934, bronze, h. 16½ ins / 42 cm) DKK 8,000. COPENHAGEN, 27 April 1995, *Young Girl Standing* (stone, h. 23½ ins / 60 cm) DKK 5,200.

EICKMANN, Heinrich
German, 19th - 20th century.
Born 13 June 1870, in Nienhausen, near Lübeck; died January 1911, in Berlin.
Painter, engraver. Religious subjects, local scenes, landscapes.

Eickmann trained at the art academies in Berlin and Munich. He specialised in religious subjects: *Annunciation, Christ Beneath the Cross*. He also took subjects from peasant life, as in *Happy Family*. His paintings were mostly landscapes. From 1897 onwards he took part in various collective exhibitions in Berlin, Munich and Düsseldorf.

EIDELIMAN, Albert
Romanian, 20th century.
Born 1915, in Bessarabia.
Active in France from 1929.
Painter. Scenes with figures.

While still a child, Albert Eideliman was a messenger in the fur trade. After being imprisoned in World War II he worked in the building trade and at the age of 48 he started studying at university. At 55, he obtained a master's degree in modern history. He retired and began working in arts and crafts (collages, tapestries and finally pictures based on wild straw). Eideliman painted typical scenes of daily life and traditional celebrations in Jewish communities and exhibited in Paris at the Salon International de l'Art Naif.

BIBLIOGRAPHY:

IVe Salon international de l'Art naïf, exhibition catalogue, Paris, 1989.

EIEBAKKE, August
Norwegian, 19th - 20th century.
Born 25 April 1867, in Askim; died 1938.
Painter. Religious subjects, portraits, interiors, landscapes. Religious furnishings.

Eiebakke attended the school of industrial art and design in Oslo before studying in Copenhagen. He visited the Netherlands, Belgium and Italy and stayed in Paris. He painted an altarpiece, *Christ Blessing the Disciples*, for the church in Arendal. He participated in collective exhibitions in Oslo, Copenhagen and Rome.

EIELSON, Jorge
Peruvian, 20th century.
Born 13 April 1924, in Lima.
Active in France.
Painter (mixed media).

Jorge Eielson was first known as a poet and was awarded the national poetry prize in Peru in 1945. He published poems in magazines and provided illustrations for these in 1946, before going on to produce his first artworks. Between 1948 and 1950 he was closely associated with the geometric abstraction of kinetic art, producing the *Mobiles* which he exhibited at several exhibitions in Europe. From 1949 onwards he took part in group exhibitions including: in Paris, the Salon des Réalités Nouvelles, the Salon Comparaisons and the Salon de Mai in 1967. In 1964 and 1966, he took part in the Venice Biennale and in 1971 in the Paris Biennale. For a time he stopped working in the fine arts and returned to writing, producing reviews, novels and drama.

In 1954 Eielson returned to the fine arts, producing relief pictures using sand, earth and cement. Around 1962 he began working with crumpled, torn and burnt fabric in the spirit of the New Realists, the Affichistes and also Alberto Burri. Around 1970 Eielson's began working with woven, knotted cords stretched over monochrome surfaces, analysing and perpetuating the *Quipus* of ancient Peruvian writing. He went on to explore the triangle in various forms but continuing to use tension systems. He also produced 'postal packages' - his artistic production often being situated at the juncture between painting and writing.

BIBLIOGRAPHY:

Ugarte Eléspuru, J. M., *Pintura y escultura en el Perú contemporáneo*, Lima, 1970. Lavalle, J.A. de/Lang, W., *Pintura contemporánea*, Lima, 1975-1976 (2 vols). Lauer, M., *'Artes visuales en el Perú: 1920-1980'* in *Arte moderno en América Latina*, Madrid, 1985 (ed. D. Bayón). Bernales Ballesteros, J. (ed.), *La escultura del Perú*, Lima, 1991. Tello Garust, J., *Pinturas y pintores del Perú*, Lima, 1992. Antrobus, P., *Peruvian Art of the Patria Nueva: 1919-1930*, dissertation, University of Essex, Colchester, 1997.

AUCTION RECORDS:

ROME, 18 May 1976, *Quipus 16 BL* (1966-1971, knotted white canvas, 51¼ x 37½ x 7¾ ins / 130 x 95.5 x 20 cm) ITL 550,000. PARIS, 19 Jan 1992, *Quipus* (1966-1971, oil on canvas and relief/panel, 46 x 28¾ ins / 116 x 73 cm) FRF 3,800. PRATO, 29 Nov 2002, *Never-ending Stairs* (1979, fabric and board, 31 x 30x5 ins / 80 x 75x13 cm) EUR 1,600. PRATO, 28 Nov 2003, *Quipus 33 T-1* (canvas on board, 47 x 47 ins / 120 x 120 cm) EUR 6,000. PRATO, 28 Nov 2003, *Quipus 30 T-1* (1971, canvas on board, 59 x 31x9 ins / 150 x 78x22 cm) EUR 12,000.

EIFFE, Johann Gottfried
German, 18th - 19th century.
Born 13 August 1773, in Hamburg; died 13 August 1818, in Haiti.
Painter.

In 1816, following visits to Copenhagen and Dresden, Eiffe travelled to Haiti where the king of northern Haiti, Henri Christophe, was looking for artists. Eiffe executed paintings and decorative works for the king, but when he asked to return home the king starved him to death. A number of Eiffe's pictures were shown at the Patriotic Exhibition mounted in Hamburg in 1815, among them *Outpost of the Civil Guard in Winter*, 1813-1814, and a *Forest Landscape*. His etchings include *Three Women with Children Feeding Swans from a Balcony, Child Asleep, with Ball and Wooden Horse, Three Cossacks at the Outposts, Cossack on Horseback* and *Hamburg Civil Guard*. The art gallery in Hamburg has a copy by Eiffe of the *Self-portrait of Philipp Otto Runge*.

EIFFE, Martin Johann Ludwig
German, 19th century.
Born 25 August 1842, in Hamburg; died 15 January 1893, in Rome.
Sculptor.

A bust of the poet M.F. Chemnitz is attributed to this artist.

EIFFEL, Albert
French, 19th - 20th century.
Born in the second half of the 19th century, in Levallois-Perret.
Painter. Seascapes.

Albert Eiffel was a pupil of Fernand Humbert. He first showed his work at the Salon des Artistes Français in 1911.

EIGA, real name: Takuma Arinobu, artist names: Yushin, Eiga
Japanese, 14th century.
Active 1350-1395.
Painter.

Eiga specialised in Buddhist painting and is one of the earliest representatives of Muromachi ink painting. The honorific title 'hogen' was bestowed on him.

He probably painted the *Portrait of Prince Shokotu* before 1351, a work that has since disappeared, whilst his *Portrait of Hitomaro,* dating from 1395, is preserved in the Tokiwayama archives of Kanagawa. His other known works are not dated and include *The Sakyamuni Triad,* the *Sixteen Arhats, Acala and Two Acolytes, Amida Raigo Triad Crossing the Mountains* and *Nirvana.* Characteristic of Eiga's style is the combination of traditional methods, Buddhist painting of the post-Heian period and the Song style introduced during the Kamakura period.

BIBLIOGRAPHY:

Sei-ichi, Taki, '*Takuma Eiga*' in *The Kokka* n° 465, periodical, London, Tokyo, 1929. Yoshi, Shirabatake, '*À propos du portrait de Hitomaro de Takuma Eiga*' in *The Kokka* n° 664, periodical, London, Tokyo, 1947. Masuto, Toyooka, *Le Nirvana de Eiga,* Aichi kenritsu geijutsudaigaku kiyo 1, 1971.

MUSEUMS AND GALLERIES:

KYOTO (National Mus.): *Sakyamuni Triad; Sixteen Arhats* - OSAKA (Fujita Mus. of Art): *Sixteen Arhats* - TOKYO (Idemitsu MA): *Amida Raigo Triad Crossing the Mountains* - WASHINGTON DC (Freer Gal. of Art): *Samantabhadra.*

EIGEL, Istvan

Hungarian, 20th century.

Born 1922.

Painter. Murals.

Istvan Eigel studied at the school of fine art in Budapest where he exhibited from 1957 to 1966; he also exhibited in Athens.

EIGENHEER, Hans

Swiss, 20th century.

Born 1937, in Lucerne.

Draughtsman, engraver. Scenes with figures.

Eigenheer trained at the Lucerne school of industrial art and design, and at various private academies and schools in Paris, Florence and Rome. He lived in Lucerne. His subjects are extremely diverse and his compositions, which look rather like pages of sketches, are complex. Fear and nightmares are a common source of material for his works, in which the themes of mutilation and confinement recur frequently. He took part in the Biennale des Jeunes Artistes in Paris in 1969.

BIBLIOGRAPHY:

Kneubühler, Theo, *Kunst: 28 Schweizer,* exhibition catalogue, Gal. Raeber, Lucerne, 1972.

EIGLER, Franz

Austrian, 18th century.

Active in Vienna c. 1760.

Miniaturist.

EIGNER, Andreas

German, 19th century.

Born 1801, in Dieteldorf; died 1870, in Augsburg.

Painter. Genre scenes.

Eigner invented a method of conserving old paintings.

EIGNER, F.

Bohemian School, 18th century.

Active in Prague.

Sculptor.

F. Eigner produced two altarpieces for the church of Our Lady in Kladruby, Bohemia.

EIGNER, Ignaz

Hungarian, 19th century.

Born 1854, in Budapest.

Painter, lithographer.

Eigner was a pupil at the academy in Vienna. Two lithographed portraits are attributed to him, one of the burgomaster Baron von Felder, the other of Josef Kanlich, director of the Opera.

EIGNER-PÜTTNER, Pauline

German, 19th - 20th century.

Born 5 March 1872, in Schwandorf.

Painter. Landscapes, still-lifes.

Eigner-Püttner studied art in Munich and was married to the painter Walther Püttner. While in Munich she contributed to the magazine *Die Jugend* (*Youth*). She took part in group exhibitions in Munich, Berlin, Bremen and Mannheim.

EIJBERG, André

Belgian, 20th century.

Born 1929, in Ixelles (Brussels).

Sculptor, draughtsman, watercolourist. Nudes, animals.

Eijberg was a student at the Institut Provincial des Arts et Métiers du Centre in La Louvière, where he trained in ceramics and earthenware. His mixed-technique drawings and watercolours express dynamism and rhythm. In sculpture, he works in marble, onyx, granite and bronze. His sculptures are figurative, though his female nudes and animals owe their elegant simplification of form to the influence of abstract art. He produced monumental public sculptures in bronze such as *Research* in 1973 for the Monsanto research centre in Louvain-la-Neuve, and *Elevation and Rhythm,* two totems for Avenue Hamoir in Brussels, in 1976.

In 1967 Eijberg won the Louis Schmidt first prize for sculpture, and in 1980 was awarded top prize in the competition for the Œuvre Nationale des Beaux-Arts in Brussels. His works have been displayed in solo exhibitions: from 1965 to 1968 at the Galerie d'Egmont in Brussels; from 1973 to 1984 at the Galerie Albert Ier in Brussels; in 1993 at the Espace d'Art du Paradou in Le Paradou; and in 1995, 1997, 1999 and 2001 at the Galerie ABC in Brussels.

BIBLIOGRAPHY:

Kneubühler, Theo, *Kunst: 28 Schweizer,* exhibition catalogue, Gal. Raeber, Lucerne, 1972. Eijberg, André/Gillemon, Danièle, *Sculptures Eijberg, 1998-2001,* exhibition catalogue, A. Eijberg, Gal. ABC, Brussels, 2001.

EIJUN

Japanese, 14th century.

Painter.

Eijun was the son of Tosa Mitsuaki. He painted a number of panels representing miracles of the Yuzu Nembutsu sect, which are preserved in the Seiryoji temple near Kyoto.

EIKAAS, Ludvig

Norwegian, 20th century.

Born 1920, in Jölster.

Painter. Still-lifes.

Eikaas lives in Oslo, having been a student at the city's art school. His paintings, which tend to be non-figurative, are often austere, sometimes displaying the influence of Paul Klee. Pierre Courthion wrote that his still-lifes were of real quality, being both robust and improvised.

MUSEUMS AND GALLERIES:

BROOKLYN, NY - COPENHAGEN - LUGANO - OSLO.

EIKAI, real name: Satake Eishi, artist names: Eikai, Aisetsu, Aisetsuro, Kyuseido, Shuson, Ten'ei, Tensui, Yohoshi

Japanese, 19th century.

Born 1803, in Aizu; died 1874.

Painter.

Eikai went to Edo to study with Tani Buncho (1763-1840) and Sakai Hoitsu (1761-1828). He was a landscape painter and received the rank of hokkyo.

EIKAN, Imao. See **KEINEN**

EIKELENBERG, Symon. See **EYKELENBERG**

EIKO, real name: Satake Kintaro, artist name: Eiko

Japanese, 19th century.

Born 1835; died 1909.
Painter.
Eiko was a landscape and figure painter, and a pupil of Oki Ichiga and Satake Eikai. He was a member of the Japan Art Association.

EIKYU, real name: Matsuoka Teruo, artist name: Eikyu
Japanese, 20th century.
Born 1881, in Hyogo Prefecture; died 1938.
Painter. Figures.
Eikyu studied with Hashimoto Gaho and Yamana Kangi and graduated from the Tokyo School of Fine Arts in 1904. He taught at the school from 1908 to 1935. He was a member of the Imperial Art Academy and president of the National Painting Society.

EIKYU, real name: Sugita Hideo
Japanese, 20th century.
Born 1911, in Miyazaki (Kyushu); died 1960.
Painter, print artist.
Eikyu studied at the Tokyo School of Fine Arts until 1926, when he became an art critic. He began to paint in about 1935. In 1937, he became a member of the Independent Art Association.

EIL, Julius
German, 19th century.
Active in Berlin.
Painter.
Eil was a pupil at the academy in Berlin and exhibited works there from 1830 to 1834, among them a *Portrait of a Woman* and a genre painting, *Old Woman Instructing a Young Boy*.

EILBRACHT, G. F.
Dutch, 19th century.
Died January 1854, in The Hague.
Lithographer.

EILERS, Conrad
German, 19th - 20th century.
Born 1845; died 1915.
Painter. Landscapes with figures, landscapes.
Eilers exhibited in Berlin and Munich, where he worked from 1886 onwards. His best known works are *Spring* and *Forest Near Allach*.
AUCTION RECORDS:
MUNICH, 13 Sept 1984, *Peasant on a Path on the Edge of a Wood* (oil on canvas, 33 1/2 x 24 1/2 ins / 85 x 62 cm) DEM 3,000.

EILERS, Emma
American, 19th - 20th century.
Born in Brooklyn (New York City).
Sculptor.
Emma Eilers was a pupil at the Art Students' League, of which she became a member. She was also taught by Professor W.M. Chase.

EILERS, Gustav
German, 19th - 20th century.
Born 28 July 1834, in Königsberg (now Kaliningrad, Russia); died 27 January 1911, in Berlin.
Engraver.
Ellers was a pupil of the engraver R. Trossin in Königsberg. He moved to Berlin in 1869 where he became a member of Berlin art academy and a teacher. He is known for his *Views of the Shores of the Baltic Sea*, *St Cecilia* copied after Rubens, *Portrait of Wilhelm II* and *Portrait of Adolf Menzel*. In 1876 he was awarded the second-class medal in Munich, and in 1878 he took the winning gold medal in Brussels. In 1887 he won the second-place gold medal in Berlin and the winning gold medal in Vienna.

EILERSEN, Eiler Rasmussen
Danish, 19th - 20th century.
Born 1 March 1827, in Goterby (Svaninge); died April 1912.
Painter. Landscapes with figures, landscapes.
Eilersen arrived in Copenhagen in 1847 to begin a course at the art academy there, but his studies were soon interrupted when he had to take part in the Danish-Prussian war of 1848-1850. He participated in exhibitions from 1849 onwards, and in 1858 obtained a scholarship from the academy for a two-year working trip during which he visited Paris, the Midi region of France, Switzerland and Belgium. Accepted as a member of the academy in 1871, he was made a Knight of Danebrog in 1876.

His works include *Summer Landscape*, *View of Frijsenborg Park* and *Spring Day in the Sund*.
MUSEUMS AND GALLERIES:
COPENHAGEN (Statens Mus. for Kunst): *View of Frijsenborg Park* (exhibited in 1864).
AUCTION RECORDS:
COPENHAGEN, 25 Feb 1987, *Figures on a Country Road* (1852, oil on canvas, 43 1/4 x 61 1/2 ins / 110 x 156 cm) DKK 33,000. LONDON, 5 May 1989, *Amalfi Seen from the Capuchin Convent* (1880, oil on canvas, 25 1/2 x 37 ins / 65 x 94 cm) GBP 4,400. LONDON, 17 May 1991, *Sorrento* (1876, oil on canvas, 17 1/4 x 25 1/2 ins / 44 x 65 cm) GBP 3,300. LONDON, 4 Oct 1991, *View of Capri from Sorrento* (1876, oil on canvas, 17 1/4 x 25 1/2 ins / 44 x 65 cm) GBP 2,200. LONDON, 22 May 1992, *Sorrento* (oil on canvas, 19 x 30 3/4 ins / 48 x 78 cm) GBP 2,750. LONDON, 25 Nov 1992, *Wooded River Scene* (1886, oil on canvas, 42 1/2 x 56 1/4 ins / 108 x 143 cm) GBP 3,520. NEW YORK, 15 Oct 1993, *Faaborg Landscape with a Town in the Background* (1869, oil on canvas, 7 1/2 x 11 ins / 19 x 28 cm) USD 1,035. COPENHAGEN, 8 Feb 1995, *Houses in a Mountainscape* (oil on canvas, 17 x 22 ins / 43 x 55 cm) DKK 4,000. LONDON, 17 Nov 1995, *The Colosseum with a View of the Forum* (1887, oil on canvas, 23 x 36 ins / 58.5 x 91.5 cm) GBP 8,280. LONDON, 15 March 1996, *Capri with Vesuvius in the Background* (oil on canvas, 22 1/4 x 29 1/2 ins / 56.5 x 75.2 cm) GBP 9,200.

EILLARTS, Joannes, also called Frisius
Dutch, 17th century.
Active in the Netherlands during the first half of the 17th century.
Draughtsman.

EILLARTS, Laurens
Italian, 17th century.
Active in Rome.
Engraver.
Son of Johannes Eillarts. He engraved a series of plates of Roman emperors.

EILON, Éliaku
Belgian, 20th century.
Born 1923, in Brussels.
Active in Israel.
Painter, draughtsman.
Eilon was a pupil of Marcel Janco at the Oranin kibbutz in Kiryat-Tivon (Haifa). He worked for the World Zionist Organization, and travelled all over the world, exhibiting wherever he happened to be at the time. His paintings are of plant-like forms treated in a plastic style in combinations of fresh, vibrant colours.

EILSHEMIUS, Louis Michel George
American, 19th - 20th century.
Born 1864, in Newark (New Jersey); died 1941 or 1942.
Painter, watercolourist, draughtsman. Figure compositions, landscapes, seascapes.
Louis Eilshemius came from a Dutch family. He joined the Art Students' League in New York in 1884 and then travelled to Paris in 1886, where he was a pupil of William Bouguereau at the Académie Julian. In 1908 he met the post-Ro-

mantic, pre-Expressionist painter Albert Pinkham Ryder, whose work impressed him greatly. Eilshemius came from a wealthy family, which left him financially independent. He undertook numerous trips around the world, particularly to Morocco and the Samoa Islands. He brought back numerous paintings and sketches from these trips, particularly from the Samoa Islands, to which he constantly referred. However, the landscapist of the early days evolved into a painter of dream fantasies that were rejected by the juries of institutional exhibitions and therefore unknown to the public. Eilshemius became isolated in his increasingly tragic dreams, though he had been part of art associations, notably the Modern Artists of America. In 1917 the Salon des Artistes Indépendants in Paris, which operated without a jury or awards, welcomed his paintings, which were commented on, most notably by Marcel Duchamp, who organised his first solo exhibition in 1920 at the brand new *Société Anonyme, Inc.* in New York. Despite this late recognition, Eilshemius decided at that point to give up painting. In 2001, a retrospective exhibition was dedicated to his work at the National Academy of Design in New York.

During his early period, at the end of the 19th century, when his numerous travels only brought out the landscapist in him, he practised a pure, traditional technique, which resembled that of Winslow Homer, with a few post-Impressionist touches added. From the early 20th century, and certainly under the influence of Albert Pinkham Ryder, his technique evolved into a powerful Expressionism, more especially as his subject-matter moved towards visionary fantasy. A characteristic and eloquent example of this is *Flying Dutchman.*, Here, the whole of nature, the stormy sea, the menacing reefs, the angry sky, all seem to cry out for the death of the vessel depicted fleeing from the storm. He subsequently added nude women to his landscapes and seascapes. His dreams, although still innocent, were then transformed into fantastic imaginations of tragic and horror scenes.

BIBLIOGRAPHY:

Harvey, Stephen, *Louis Eilshemius (1864-1941). An Independent Spirit,* exhibition catalogue, National Academy of Design, New York, 2001.

MUSEUMS AND GALLERIES:

NEW YORK (MoMA): *Afternoon Wind* (1899) - NEW YORK (Whitney Mus. of American Art): *Flying Dutchman* - WASHINGTON DC (Phillips Collection): *Fishermen's Bridge.*

AUCTION RECORDS:

NEW YORK, 23 April 1936, *Landscape,* USD 360. NEW YORK, 13 April 1944, *Landscape,* USD 425. NEW YORK, 28 March 1946, *Nymphs after Bathing* (1898) USD 600. NEW YORK, 9-10 April 1947, *Man in a Boat on Lake Geneva,* USD 325; *Moonlight,* USD 200. NEW YORK, 23 March 1961, *New York, East Coast,* USD 850. NEW YORK, 11 May 1967, *Beach Scene in Samoa,* USD 1,500. NEW YORK, 22 Oct 1969, *Woodland Landscape with River* (watercolour) USD 1,100. NEW YORK, 29 April 1976, *Railway Bridge* (oil on canvas remounted on board, 11 1/2 x 17 1/4 ins / 29.2 x 43.5 cm) USD 1,800. NEW YORK, 13 Oct 1976, *Nudes at the Waterfall* (1908, oil on card, 41 x 26 ins / 104 x 66 cm) USD 1,100. NEW YORK, 29 Jan 1981, *The Intruder* (1905, oil on canvas, 24 x 38 ins / 61 x 96.5 cm) USD 3,500. NEW YORK, 20 June 1985, *Central Park, New York* (1917, oil on card, 18 x 31 ins / 45.7 x 78.8 cm) USD 2,700. NEW YORK, 17 March 1988, *Woman with a Bunch of Yellow Flowers in a Landscape* (1908, oil/Hardboard, 15 x 22 ins / 38 x 55 cm) USD 2,750. NEW YORK, 24 June 1988, *Bathers in a Landscape* (oil on card, 8 3/4 x 8 3/4 ins / 22.5 x 22.5 cm) USD 1,100. NEW YORK, 24 Jan 1989, *Nude in a Landscape* (oil on paper/synthetic resin, 38 1/2 x 29 ins / 97.5 x 73.8 cm) USD 2,475. NEW YORK, 24 Jan 1990, *Fishermen in a Hut on the Shore* (1878, watercolour and pencil/paper, 9 1/2 x 12 3/4 ins / 24 x 32.4 cm) USD 770. NEW YORK, 14 Feb 1990, *The Sirens* (1909, oil on panel, 15 1/4 x 22 1/4 ins / 38.5 x 56.5 cm) USD 5,500. NEW YORK, 15 May 1991, *Small Boy Sitting on a Barrier* (oil on card, 18 3/4 x 14 1/2 ins / 47.6 x 36.8 cm) USD 3,300. NEW YORK, 25 Sept 1992, *Sunny Coastline* (oil/synthetic resin, 20 x 30 ins / 50.8 x 76.2 cm) USD 1,760. NEW YORK, 31 March 1993, *The Spring* (1901, oil/synthetic resin, 20 x 14 3/4 ins / 50.8 x 37.5 cm) USD 1,955. NEW YORK, 12 Sept 1994, *Street at the End of Broadway* (oil on card, 13 3/4 x 13 1/4 ins / 34.9 x 33.7 cm) USD 2,587. NEW YORK, 28 Sept 1995, *The Rescue* (oil on card, 25 1/2 x 34 1/2 ins / 64.8 x 87.9 cm) USD 2,760. NEW YORK, 30 Oct 1996, *Brightness after the Storm; The Three Graces; Boat at Sea* (1919, oil on card, oil/Masonite and oil on paper, three paintings, 15 x 21 ins / 38.1 x 53.3 cm; 17 x 12 1/2 ins/42.9 x 31.8 cm and 8 x 10 ins/20.3 x 25.4 cm) USD 3,450. NORTH BETHESDA, 29 Oct 1999, *Rescue from Fire* (oil on canvas, 25 x 33 ins / 64 x 84 cm) USD 2,300. DOWNINGTON, 1 Dec 2000, *Nudes Reclining in the Woods* (oil on canvas, 11 x 24 ins / 28 x 61 cm) USD 1,600. NEW YORK, 13 June 2001, *Cove* (watercolour, 8 x 15 ins / 21 x 38 cm) USD 1,500. NORTH BETHESDA, 9 Feb 2002, *Horsecart* (oil on board, 17 x 23 ins / 42 x 59 cm) USD 1,900. PHILADELPHIA, 20 Sept 2002, *Afternoon Bather* (1919, oil on board, 18 x 20 ins / 46 x 51 cm) USD 2,300.

EIMBECK, Johann Raphon von. See **RAPHON**

EIMER, Ernst

German, 20th century.
Born 14 July 1881, in Gross-Eichen (Hesse).
Painter, engraver, watercolourist.

Eimer trained under Friedrich Fehr and Wilhelm Trübner at the art academy in Karlsruhe. He exhibited in Munich, Berlin, Düsseldorf and Darmstadt from 1906 onwards. He was a member of the association of German artists.

EIMMART

Austrian, 19th century.
Active in Vienna c. 1850.
Engraver (etching).

This artist is noted for his *Portrait of Baroness Felicita Stubenberg.*

EIMMART, Christian, or Eimart

German, 17th century.
Born 22 July 1642, in Regensburg.
Painter.

The son of Georg Christoph the Elder, this artist travelled to Rome at a very early age and settled there. He painted religious and secular subjects.

EIMMART, Georg Christoph, the Elder

German, 17th century.
Born 1603, in Königsberg (now Kaliningrad, Russia); died 1658, in Regensburg.
Painter, engraver. History painting, portraits, landscapes, still-lifes.

EIMMART, Georg Christoph, the Younger

German, 17th century.
Born 1638, in Regensburg; died 1705, in Nuremberg.
Painter, engraver. Religious subjects, portraits.

The son and pupil of Eimmart the Elder, this artist was made a member of the Nuremberg academy, and later, as an astronomer, he became director of the Nuremberg observatory. He illustrated Christophe Weigel's *Bible* and the *Mundus Mirabilis* by Johann Zahn.

G. CE.

EIMMART, Maria Clara

German, 17th century.
Born 1676, in Regensburg; died 1707, in Altdorf.
Painter, engraver.

The daughter of Eimmart the Younger, this artist married an astronomer and collaborated on her father's artistic and scientific projects.

EIMMART, Matthaüs
German, 17th century.
Born 29 May 1640, in Regensburg.
Painter, engraver.

This artist was the son of Georg Christoph Eimmart (Eimmart the Elder). The town hall at Regensburg houses a large stone plaque engraved by him.

EINAR-WEGENER. See **WEGENER Einar**

EINBECK, Georges or Georg
German, 19th - 20th century.
Born 5 January 1871, in Golluschütz (West Prussia, now Poland); died 21 January 1951, in Lucerne.
Active in Switzerland and in France.
Painter (gouache), watercolourist. Figure compositions, figures, landscapes.

Einbeck came from a well-off, cultured family. During his childhood they moved to Berlin and then Dresden, where he attended school before embarking on a career in banking. After a few years he gave up his job to learn painting in Munich and Paris, studying especially in museums. In 1906 he gave up painting and went to North Africa for a long period, making frequent visits to Paris. He eventually settled in the South of France where, at the age of 42, he began to find his own means of expression.

World War I broke out while Einbeck was in Lucerne in 1914 and he stayed in Switzerland. In 1919, as his place of birth had become part of Poland, he opted for Polish citizenship. From 1920 onwards he habitually spent the winter months in Menton, returning to the Lac des Quatre Cantons in Switzerland in the spring. He applied for Swiss citizenship, which was only granted shortly after his death.

His work, which did not take on an original character until shortly before the War, is heavily influenced by French painting from that period in terms of both subject and technique. His drawing style is clean, simplified and synthetic, and the colouring is pure and bright. His flowing drawing style and saturated colours link him to Fauvism, whereas his subjects - his landscapes depicted the Mediterranean coast and Provence, and his figure paintings and group scenes portrayed Parisian women and typical figures observed on the streets of Paris - underline his affinity with French culture.

Einbeck took part in official exhibitions in Berlin, Dresden and Weimar. In Lucerne, where he had a wide circle of prominent contacts in the world of art and culture, he exhibited frequently at the town museum. After his death, the Raeber gallery in Lucerne undertook to raise awareness of his work by putting on exhibitions and publishing a monograph.

BIBLIOGRAPHY:
Georges Einbeck 1871-1951, Gal. Raeber, Lucerne, 1976.

AUCTION RECORDS:
LUCERNE, 18 Nov 1978, *Christ and the Woman of Samaria* (1921, tempera, 36 1/4 x 32 1/4 ins / 92 x 82 cm) CHF 2,400. LUCERNE, 19 May 1983, *View of Menton* (1926, oil/tempera, 23 1/2 x 19 3/4 ins / 60 x 50 cm) CHF 3,800. ZURICH, 22 May 1987, *The Sermon* (1933, gouache/paper, 13 1/4 x 19 3/4 ins / 33.6 x 50 cm) CHF 3,500. LUCERNE, 24 Nov 1990, *The Mistral* (1909, watercolour and tempera/paper, 13 1/2 x 10 1/4 ins / 34 x 26 cm) CHF 1,300. LUCERNE, 23 May 1992, *Head of a Woman* (1936, tempera/card, 9 1/2 x 7 ins / 24 x 18 cm) CHF 1,000.

EINBERGER, Andreas
German, 20th century.
Born 30 October 1878; died 1952.
Painter, fresco artist, watercolourist, sculptor. Figure compositions, local figures, portraits, mountainscapes. Murals.

Einberger was the son of peasants and lived in Kramsach near Schwaz (Tyrol). He was initially a wood sculptor, before studying painting with Gabriel von Hackl in Munich, later becoming a pupil of Alois Delug in Vienna. He then spent some time in Rome. In 1911 he was represented at the Innsbruck exhibition with *Portrait of a Woman in White*.

On his return to Schwaz from Rome he painted frescoes in the style of Michelangelo. He also painted oil portraits, as well as Tyrolean landscapes in oil and watercolours, such as *High Mountain Pasture, Sunny Autumn Day*.

EINBERGER, Josef
Austrian, 19th century.
Born 1847, in Brixlegg (near Innsbruck); died 1 December 1905.
Sculptor (including wood).

Einberger joined the studio of the sculptor Dominikus Trenkwalker in Innsbruck in 1871, completing a number of Trenkwalker's wood sculptures after the latter's death. He worked primarily on crucifixes and his major work is a *Way of the Cross* in the cemetery at Mariahilf near Innsbruck. Many of his works can be found in the Innsbruck region, in the upper reaches of the Inn river valley and in southern Tyrol.

EINHARDT
German, 16th century.
Active in Würzburg c. 1515.
Painter.

EINHART, Andreas
German, 16th century.
Sculptor.
Würzburg School.

Andreas Einhart was admitted as a member of the Guild of St Luke in Würzburg in 1514.

EINO, real name: Kano Yoshinobu, alternate name: Hakuju, popular name: Nuinosuke, artist names: Eino, Ichiyosai, Baigaku, Sojunken, Sansei, Kyoo, Sokenken, court title: Nuidonosuke
Japanese, 17th century.
Born 1634; died 1700.
Active in Kyoto.
Painter.

Eino was a painter of the Kyoto branch of the Kano school and the grandson of Kano Sanraku (1559-1635). He wrote a history of Japanese painting, the *Honcho-Gashi* (Lives of the Japanese Painters).

EINOUT, Johannes
Dutch, 16th century.
Active in Rotterdam c. 1525.
Painter.

EINSCHLAG, Eduard
German, 20th century.
Born 28 February 1879, in Leipzig.
Engraver, painter.

Einschlag trained under the engraver Peter Halm at Munich art academy. He also went to study in Paris. He engraved portraits and nudes in the style of the old masters and his French contemporaries.

MUSEUMS AND GALLERIES:
BERLIN - LEIPZIG - MUNICH.

AUCTION RECORDS:
MUNICH, 25 Nov 1981, *Still-life with Flowers* (1929, oil on canvas, 23 1/2 x 19 ins / 59.5 x 48.5 cm) DEM 2,600. NEW YORK, 21 Feb 1985, *Seated Nude in an Interior* (1916, pastel/mounted paper/card, 21 1/2 x 18 ins / 54.7 x 45.6 cm) USD 650.

EINSLE, Anton

Austrian, 19th century.

Born 30 January 1801, in Vienna; died 10 March 1871, in Vienna.

Painter. Religious subjects, portraits.

A pupil at the academy in his native city, Einsle became extremely well known as a result of the patronage by the court and the nobility. In particular he is noted for his *Portrait of Francis Joseph I*, painted in 1848, *Portrait of Ferdinand I, Archduchess Sophie, Emperor Francis I, Archduke Charles on his Deathbed, Archduchess Hermine, Abbess the Archduchess Marie-Caroline, Melanie Metternich, Count Chotek, Marshal Radetzky, Giacomo Meyerbeer, Hermit at Prayer, St Jerome, Woman Playing the Lute, Susanna and the Elders* and *Hebe and the Eagle*. Most of his works are in private collections.

Museums and Galleries:

Budapest: *Archduke Joseph; Archduchess Marie-Dorothée* - Budapest (Budavári Palata): *Archduke Joseph* - Budapest (Magyar Nemzeti Múz.): *Archduke Joseph, Elector Palatine of Hungary* - Budapest (Szépmuvészeti Múz.): *Bishop Pyrker* - Mainz: *Archduke Charles of Austria* - Trieste (Miramar Palace): *Francis Joseph I, aged 23; Marshal Radetzky; Marshal Jellacis* - Vienna: *Thérèse Grafenberg, Actress; Portrait of the Artist* - Vienna (Akademie der Bildenden Künste): *Sculptor Joseph Klieber* - Vienna (Hofburg): *Francis Joseph I, aged 20; Francis Joseph I on his Accession; Francis Joseph I in Marshal's Uniform; Francis Joseph I Wearing the Order of the Golden Fleece; Cupid Peeping from behind a Curtain.*

Auction records:

Vienna, 30 Nov 1976, *Portrait of a Young Woman* (oil on canvas, 39 1/4 x 30 3/4 ins / 100 x 78 cm) ATS 40,000. Cologne, 16 June 1977, *Lady of the Camellias* (oil on canvas, 20 x 15 1/4 ins / 51 x 39 cm) DEM 3,600. Monte Carlo, 15 June 1986, *Portrait of Archduke Stefan Victor of Austria* (1847, oil on canvas, 101 x 66 1/4 ins / 256.5 x 168 cm) FRF 70,000. Munich, 27 June 1995, *Countess Wanda Festetics von Tolna, née Countess Raczynska* (oil on canvas, 42 3/4 x 35 3/4 ins / 108.5 x 91 cm) DEM 57,500. Vienna, 29-30 Oct 1996, *Young Woman at her Mirror* (1841, oil on canvas, 37 3/4 x 50 ins / 96 x 127 cm) ATS 850,000. Vienna, 9 Feb 1999, *Madonna and Child* (1824, oil on canvas, 28 x 22 ins / 70 x 56 cm) ATS 45,000. Vienna, 9 April 2002, *Kaiser Franz I von Osterreich* (1841, oil on canvas, 26 x 20 ins / 65 x 50 cm) EUR 9,000. Vienna, 16 June 2003, *Portrait of Baron Drasche-Wartinberg* (oil on canvas/panel, 31 x 25 ins / 78 x 63 cm) EUR 2,200. Prague, 6 March 2004, *Sleeping Child* (1869, oil on canvas, 24 x 30 ins / 62 x 75 cm) CZK 110,000. New York, 8 Sept 2004, *Sleeping Beauty* (oil on paper, 8 x 8 ins / 20 x 20 cm) USD 3,800.

EINSLE, Joseph

German, 19th century.

Born 1794, in Göggingen; died after 1850, in Augsburg.

Miniaturist.

Einsle worked in Augsburg and Frankfurt. His works were exhibited in Mannheim, Rotterdam, Munich, Lemberg and Breslau between 1905 and 1913.

EINSLIE, S.

British, 18th - 19th century.

Active in London.

Miniaturist.

S. Einslie sent miniatures to the exhibitions at the Royal Academy from 1785 to 1808.

EINSPINNER, Josef

Austrian, 19th century.

Born 4 September 1861, in Mürzzuschlag.

Sculptor.

Having been a pupil of Hellmer and Zumbusch at the academy in Vienna, Einspinner worked in Vienna, where he executed the statue of *Emperor Francis Joseph I*, now at the Palace of Justice, and the statue of *Baron A von Dietrichstein*, now at the town hall in Graz, followed by a *Cain, Faun, Nymph* and numerous busts.

EINSTEIN, William

American, 20th century.

Born 1907, in St Louis (Missouri); died 1972, in Acheux-en-Vimeu, France.

Active in France.

Painter. Designs for stained glass.

William Einstein was a pupil at the St Louis School of Fine Arts. He went to France at the age of twenty, studying the Old Masters at the Louvre, while taking a course at the École du Louvre. At the same time, in 1927 he was receiving advice on his own painting from Léger and Ozenfant at the Académie Moderne and was sensitive to the influence of Soutine, Pascin and Friesz. Between 1929 and 1931 he met Mondrian, Duchamp, Arp, Delaunay, Pevsner, Freundlich, Hélion and Calder and in 1931 joined the *Abstraction-Creation* group, appearing in the first issue of its magazine. In 1931 he travelled to Russia with Hélion, meeting Gabo and Tatlin. With regard to his work at the time, he took a two-year course at the Institut d'Optique in Paris. He returned to New York in 1933, participating in the organisation of painting exhibitions, principally focusing on European avant-garde works, for Alfred Stieglitz's gallery *An American Place*. In 1936 he organised a John Marin exhibition at the Museum of Modern Art along with Georgia O'Keeffe. During his stay in New York from 1933 until 1938, he put on exhibitions of his own work, the first in 1937 at An American Place gallery. He returned to settle in Europe in 1938 having served in the American Army during the war. Shortly after the war, he worked as an art critic, acting as a correspondent for the New York Herald Tribune from 1946-1947. Between 1947 and 1955 he lived in Aix-en-Provence, organising exhibitions that were important to his own evolution as a painter: Humblot, Rebeyrolle, Balthus, Gruber, Rohner, etc. In 1953 he exhibited with the American Associated Artists in New York. In 1966 he settled in Picardy. Following his return to Paris, he appeared in the Salon d'Automne and the Salon des Artistes Indépendants in 1960 and exhibited alone in 1946 and 1954 at the Galerie Jeanne Castel, then in 1955 and 1958 at the Galerie Barbizon, in 1959 and 1960 at the Galerie René Drouin and in New York in 1953. In 1972 the Maison de la Culture d'Amiens organised an exhibition of his entire works.

Around 1930 in the context of the Abstraction-Creation group, he tended towards an abstract expression. From 1932 his conception of man and humanism led him towards figuration, something to which he remained attached, finding expressive, narrative expressions with the Venetians in the 18th century and Corinth and Kokoschka. However, the work involved in designing a series of stained glass windows for the historical church of St Vulfran d'Abbeville, undertaken and pursued from 1965, reflects once again, undoubtedly for reasons of spirituality, the relative abstraction of the Paris School.

Bibliography:

William Einstein, exhibition catalogue, Maison de la culture, Amiens, 1972.

Auction records:

Paris, 29 April 1997, *Concretion 1931 No. 1* (1931, oil on panel, 13 x 22 ins / 33 x 55 cm) FRF 39,000.

EINWAG, Johann Christoph

German, 17th century.

Died 1666, in Venice.

Active in Nuremberg.

Painter.

Einwag was a pupil of Daniel Preisler.

EIPELT, Joseph
German, 18th (?) century.
Painter (?), draughtsman (?).
A general view of Coblenz by this artist was engraved in 1770 by Joseph Eber.

EIRI, real name: Hosoda Eiri, artist names: Rekisentei, Meikyusai
Japanese, 18th century.
Active c. 1790.
Painter, print artist. Figure compositions.
Rekisentei Eiri designed ukiyo-e prints. He was a pupil of Hosoda Eishi but only retained his master's taste for delicate women. In a further departure from normal practice, something of a romantic feeling shows through in the prints in which he depicts lovers in Japanese erotic style.
AUCTION RECORDS:
NEW YORK, 16 Oct 1989, *Prince Genji Accompanied by a Procession of Young Women Carrying Presents Escorting the Imperial Palanquin Drawn by Oxen* (set of five oban tate-e woodblock prints, each 14 1/2 x 9 1/2 ins / 37 x 24 cm) USD 4,400.

EIRI, real name: Hosoda (?), artist names: Chokyusai, Shikyusai (?)
Japanese, 18th - 19th century.
Active c. 1795-1800.
Painter, print artist.
Chokyosai Eiri is not to be confused with Rekisentei Eiri, as established by Lane. He was a pupil of Hosoda Eishi. Only a few works by this artist are known to us: some very fine okubi-e (large-scale portraits) of beautiful women (*bijin-ga*), a set of three prints illustrating the costumes of women from Osaka, Kyoto and Edo, which is regarded as his finest work, and the series *Sangatsu Soka Bijin Awase* (a comparison of ladies from three cities). Also attributed to him is a portrait of Santo Kyoden on a background of black mica, and several paintings.
BIBLIOGRAPHY:
Hillier, *Japanese Prints and Drawings from the Vever Collection*, Rizzoli international, New York, 1976. Lane, Richard, *Images from the Floating World: the Japanese Print, including an illustrated dictionary of ukiyo-e*, Putnam, New York, 1978.
AUCTION RECORDS:
NEW YORK, 16 April 1988, *Elegant Ladies in the Costumes of the Three Capitals: Osaka, Kyoto, Edo* (complete set of three prints, 15 1/2 x 10 1/4 ins / 39.2 x 26.3 cm and 15 1/2 x 10 1/2 ins/39.3 x 26.5 cm and 15 1/4 x 10 ins/38.6 x 25.7 cm) USD 1,540,000.

EISAI, Shigekiyo
Japanese, 19th century.
Print artist. Scenes with figures, urban landscapes.
AUCTION RECORDS:
NEW YORK, 27 March 1991, *View of the Construction of Electric Lighting in a Ginza Street in Tokyo* (1883, Chuban print, triptych, 10 x 6 1/2 ins / 25.6 x 16.4 cm) USD 2,420.

EISCH, Erwin
German, 20th century.
Born 1927.
Painter (including glass), draughtsman.
Figuration Libre.
Eisch presents crudely executed human figures in postures of motion, using a number of techniques. His paintings on drinking glasses are on show at the Centre du Verre in the Musée des Arts Décoratifs. There was a double exhibition dedicated to him in Paris in 1988 sponsored by the Goethe Institut in co-operation with the Musée des Arts Décoratifs.
AUCTION RECORDS:
NEW YORK, 25-26 Feb 1994, *Untitled* (1971, blown glass, 23 x 9 x 4 1/2 ins / 58.4 x 22.9 x 11.4 cm) USD 2,300.

EISEL, Johann
Bohemian School, 18th century.
Active in Prague c. 1729.
Engraver.
Johann Eisel engraved some religious subjects.

EISELE, Hans
German, 19th century.
Born 2 July 1865, in Munich; died 16 July 1907, in Munich.
Painter. Portraits, landscapes.
After devoting himself initially to lithography, Eisele became a pupil at the Munich academy where he studied with John Herterich and Wilhelm Diez.

EISELE, Martin
Austrian, 16th century.
Active in Vienna in 1593.
Painter.

EISEMANN. See **EISENMANN** and **EISMANN**

EISEN
German, 18th century.
Active in Cologne in 1707.
Engraver.

EISEN, real name: Ikeda Yoshinobu, alternate name: Konsei, popular names: Zenjiro, Teisuke, artist names: Eisen, Keisai, Ippitsuan, Kokushunro, Hokugo, Mumeio, Kako
Japanese, 19th century.
Born 1790; died 1848.
Print artist.
Eisen began by studying the Kano and Tosa styles before becoming a pupil of Eizan. He specialised in depictions of beautiful women. Between 1837 and 1842 he also assisted Hiroshige (1797-1858) with his series *Kiso Kaido* (the 69 stages of the great east-west route through the central mountains). Eisen designed 24 of the 69 prints in this collection. Among them, *The Nojiri Falls* contrasts the torrent and the rocks drawn very prominently in the foreground and in the distance a landscape of blue or grey mountains with an imaginary Fuji lost in the mists. It could be said that the foreground is Hokusai and the background, just as the small figures suggest, is Hiroshige. These references for this particular instance place the work of Eisen within its scope.
BIBLIOGRAPHY:
Lane, R., *L'Estampe japonaise*, Somogy, Paris, 1962. Fahr-Becker, Gabriele (ed.), *Japanese Prints*, Taschen, Cologne, 1999.
AUCTION RECORDS:
LONDON, 16 May 1988, *View of Mount Asama from Urawa* (oban yeko-e print, number four of the series 'On the Kiso Highway') GBP 1,980; *Standing Courtesan Holding a Paper Scroll* (oban aizuri-e print) GBP 572. NEW YORK, 21 March 1989, *Tea House Servant Carrying a Soup Tureen on a tray, large scale* (oban tate-e woodblock print, 15 x 10 ins / 37.8 x 24.5 cm) USD 4,620. NEW YORK, 25 March 2003, *Urami Waterfall* (colour print, 14 x 10 ins / 36 x 25 cm) USD 5,500. NEW YORK, 25 March 2003, *Sumida River* (black and white border, print, 10 x 15 ins / 26 x 38 cm) USD 5,500. NEW YORK, 23 March 2004, *Beauty after Bath* (colour and ink, hanging scroll, 47 x 17 ins / 119 x 42 cm) USD 8,000.

EISEN. See also **EYSEN**

EISEN, Anton Friedrich
German, 19th century.
Active in Nuremberg.
Engraver.

This artist is mentioned in 1800 and 1806 and appears also to be known as Anton-Paul Eisen.

EISEN, Anton Paul
German, 19th century.
Born 1777, in Nuremberg.
Engraver (burin/stippling).

Eisen engraved *Historical Subjects* and *Landscapes*.

EISEN, Charles
French, 18th century.
Active in Lyons.
Painter.

In 1766 or 1767, Charles Eisen painted four low reliefs in the vestry of the chaplains' residence. Eisen, 'established at Lyons' (probably the same artist), exhibited in 1786 in the Salon des Arts: *Croesus Showing his Riches; The Sultan has One of His Wives Led*, two pictures where 'children' represent *The Rape of Europa* and *Venus on the Waters; Cupids at Play* (two pictures) and three supra portas in low relief.

In 1791 he decorated the hall of the Audience des Chanoines at Lyons. He is probably the same artist who entered the Académie de St-Luc in Paris in 1751.

EISEN, Charles Dominique Joseph
French, 18th century.
Born 17 August 1720, in Valenciennes; died 4 January 1778, in Brussels.
Painter, watercolourist, draughtsman (ink/wash/red chalk), engraver, illustrator. Mythological subjects, allegorical subjects, figures, portraits, genre scenes, interiors with figures, architectural interiors. Vignettes, frontispieces.

The son of François Eisen, Charles Dominique Joseph Eisen received his artistic education from his father. He found favour with Madame de Pompadour to whom he gave drawing lessons. He was so vivacious that she had no trouble in having him admitted to the court, where he quickly became painter and draughtsman to the king as well as professor at the Académie de St-Luc.

However, an unfortunate faux pas meant he had to leave France and take refuge in Brussels: one day Louix XV's favourite asked Eisen to draw an outfit for him - plain yet new - for she desired to give the king the pleasure of an original costume. Eisen delivered the drawing, but kept a copy and had an identical outfit made for himself. He appeared in Versailles in the costume in question on the day that the King was identically attired. Madame de Pompadour was exceedingly angry, and it was she who caused him to flee.

Eisen figured in Académie de St-Luc exhibitions from 1751 to 1774. He is best known for his drawings, especially the vignettes of the *Fables of La Fontaine* and his compositions on Ovid's *Metamorphoses*. His works are distinguished by their charm and variety.

Eisen. CG Eis f.

MUSEUMS AND GALLERIES:

ALENÇON - BORDEAUX: *Shepherd and Shepherdess; Bird Catcher; Village Dance; Rest in Village* - BOURG.

AUCTION RECORDS:

PARIS, 1767, *Two Palace Interiors with Figures*, FRF 131. PARIS, 1855, *Cup-and-ball*, FRF 490; *Concert in Drawing Room*, FRF 600. PARIS, 1855, *Interior Family Scene, Lamp Lit* (drawing with washes in Indian ink and in colour) FRF 106. PARIS, 1878, *Washing and Dressing*, FRF 1,000; *Conversation*, FRF 1,340. PARIS, 1880, *For the Fables of La Fontaine* (two drawings in lead pencil) FRF 1,679. PARIS, 1885, *Dice Players*, FRF 2,550; *Mothers of the Family*, FRF 2,200. PARIS, 30-31 Jan 1894, *Little Savoyards; Angling* (two childhood scenes, pendants) FRF 375. PARIS, 10-18 Feb 1898, *Rustic Pleasures* (drawing) FRF 3,050; *Autumn* (Indian ink) FRF 3,050; *Two Lamp Bases* (pen heightened with watercolour) FRF 1,105; *Convalesence* (graphite) FRF 290. PARIS, 1899, *Comely Charlatan*, FRF 1,900; *Handsome Inspector*, FRF 1,900; *Night*, FRF 1,710; *Choiseul Family*, FRF 8,000; *Night* (drawing) FRF 1,910. PARIS, 3-5 May 1900, *Children's Games*, FRF 880. PARIS, 28 May 1900, *In Praise of Folie (Illustration for the L'Éloge de la Folie)* (27 drawings) FRF 8,000; *Scenes Taken from Arnaud's Short Stories* (series of six drawings) FRF 2,060; *Series of Six Lamp Bases*, FRF 1,200. NEW YORK, 26-28 Feb 1902, *Harvesters*, USD 225; *Reverie*, USD 340. COLOGNE, 19-29 Oct 1905, *Portrait of Ch. Eisen*, FRF 625. PARIS, 4-6 April 1910, *Twelfth Night, the King Drinks*, FRF 2,500. LONDON, 10 June 1910, *Cupids* (supra porta) GBP 120; *Young Girl*, GBP 26. PARIS, 27 March 1919, *A Cupid* (red chalk) FRF 210. PARIS, 16 and 19 June 1919, *Frontispiece for a Book* (pen and wash) FRF 1,100; *Title of an Exercise Book of Romances* (wash) FRF 3,800. PARIS, 15 Feb 1923, *Cupids and Young Woman Holding a Perfume-brazier; Cupids and Peace Leaning on Cornucopia* (two pendants) FRF 7,600; *Musician Putti; Travelling Putti* (pendants) FRF 1,700; *Putti as Painters; Putti Gardeners* (two pendants) FRF 2,700. PARIS, 7-8 May 1923, *Concert of Lovers* (pencil) FRF 3,300; *Nymph and Shepherd; Europe* (graphite, pair) FRF 5,000. PARIS, 24 May 1923, *Bird Catchers*, FRF 1,020. PARIS, 2 June 1923, *Musical Putti* (graphite) FRF 75. PARIS, 7-8 Nov 1924, *Gay Conversation* (bistre wash, heightened) FRF 700. LONDON, 22 May 1925, *Moment of Triumph*, GBP 52. PARIS, 8 June 1925, *Cherries* (Indian ink wash) FRF 10,400. PARIS, 17-18 June 1925, *Venus and Vulcan* (pen and Indian ink wash) FRF 4,000. PARIS, 9 Dec 1926, *Robbed Gallant*, FRF 4,000. PARIS, 5 May 1927, *Putto as Doctor*, FRF 2,700. PARIS, 25 Jan 1929, *Meeting of Disguised Children in Park*, FRF 10,600. PARIS, 9 March 1929, *Small Putti as Carpenters* (drawing) FRF 150. PARIS, 13-15 May 1929, *Allegory on the Erection of a Statue to Louis XV* (drawing) FRF 1,650; *Vignettes for Illustrations* (three drawings) FRF 7,300; *Vignette for 'Angola'* (drawing) FRF 3,100. PARIS, 26 and 28 Dec 1933, *Abundance; Painting* (collection) FRF 5,100. PARIS, 1 Dec 1934, *Frontispiece* (pen drawing, with Indian ink wash and watercolour) FRF 400. PARIS, 12 Dec 1935, *Invention of the Lightning Conductor*, FRF 385. PARIS, 17 Dec 1935, *Lady of Charity* (watercolour on outlines in pen and ink) FRF 3,000; *Allegory on the Erection of a Statue to Louis XV* (pen drawing and Indian ink wash, lightly heightened with watercolour) FRF 1,000; *Vignettes for Illustrations* (three drawings in lead pencil on vellum) FRF 3,900. PARIS, 14 Dec 1936, *Rejected Gallant* (graphite) FRF 420. PARIS, 5 March 1937, *Lamp Base Decorated with Putti Personifying the Arts and Sciences* (pen drawing heightened with watercolour) FRF 900. PARIS, 12 May 1937, *Children's Scene*, FRF 1,750. LONDON, 22 July 1937, *Frontispiece with Motifs of Medallions and Palm Trees* (drawing) GBP 15. PARIS, 9 Dec 1938, *French* (series of four drawings in lead pencil) FRF 550. PARIS, 1 June 1940, *Music* (pen and Indian ink wash) FRF 685. PARIS, 13 Feb 1941, *Dice Game*, FRF 52,000. PARIS, 28 Nov 1941, *Fortune Teller; Cat's Meal; Cooks* (three drawings in pen and watercolour) FRF 3,500; *Allegory Pertaining to the Reign of Louis XV* (1754, pencil) FRF 6,400. PARIS, 16 Nov 1953, *Child Geometrician*, FRF 66,000. NEW YORK, 6 April 1960, *Dancing Dog*, USD 750. LONDON, 16 Oct 1963, *Garden with Statue of Cupid and Fountains* (watercolour) GBP 440. PARIS, 26 May 1981, *Reeling Girl; Harvester's Refreshment* (two pen drawings and grey wash over a sketch in graphite, 7 x 6 1/2 ins / 18 x 16.5 cm) FRF 4,500. PARIS, 30 March 1987, *Dance of the Bear; Dance of the Dog* (two oils on canvas, 18 x 14 3/4 ins / 46 x 37.5 cm) FRF 100,000. PARIS, 14 Dec 1989, *Alchemist Apprentices* (oil on canvas, 17 x 31 ins / 43 x 78.5 cm) FRF 20,000. MONACO, 22 June 1991, *Allegory of the Arts* (oil on canvas, 33 1/4 x 52 3/4 ins / 84.5 x 134 cm) FRF 88,800. LON-

DON, 7 July 1992, *Apollo, Pegasus and the Muses* (ink and wash, 7 x 8 1/2 ins / 18 x 21.6 cm) GBP 1,430. PARIS, 15 Dec 1993, *Musician Putti* (oil on oak panel, 26 1/2 x 20 ins / 67 x 51 cm) FRF 30,000. LONDON, 18 April 1994, *Amorous Temptation* (ink and watercolour, 14 3/4 x 11 ins / 37.6 x 27.1 cm) GBP 6,670. PARIS, 21 March 1995, *Scene from the Life of Don Quixote* (Indian ink and sepia, pen, 6 1/4 x 4 3/4 ins / 16 x 12 cm) FRF 4,500. PARIS, 17 July 1996, *Picking Cherries* (oil on panel, 13 1/4 x 10 1/2 ins / 33.5 x 26.5 cm) FRF 22,000. NEUILLY, 19 June 2000, *Allegory of the Four Seasons* (oil on canvas, four, 26 x 32 ins / 65 x 82 cm) FRF 305,000. PARIS, 2 Dec 2002, *Mythological Scenes* (oil on canvas, a pair, 19 x 33 ins / 47 x 84 cm) EUR 7,500. PARIS, 17 Dec 2003, *Perseus and Andromeda* (1750, graphite on vellum, 5 x 4 ins / 13 x 9 cm) EUR 2,600.

EISEN, Christophe Charles
French, 18th century.
Born 4 October 1744, in Paris.
Painter, draughtsman.

Christophe Eisen was the son of Charles Dominique Eisen. In 1777 he entered the Académie de St-Luc.

EISEN, François
Flemish, 18th century.
Born c. 1695, in Brussels; died after 1778, in Brussels.
Painter, watercolourist, engraver, draughtsman.
Religious subjects, allegorical subjects, mythological subjects, genre scenes, interiors with figures.
Flemish School.

François Eisen lived in Valenciennes and married Marie-Marguerite Gaine on 28 July 1716. He returned to Brussels in 1720, went to Paris in 1745 and was a member of the Académie de Rouen. His son was the famous painter and illustrator Charles Dominique Joseph Eisen.

MUSEUMS AND GALLERIES:
ABBEVILLE: *Young Woman at her Toilette* - DIJON: two grisailles with cupids - VALENCIENNES: *Vision of St Magdalene; Astronomer in his Study* - VIENNA (Liechtenstein Mus.): *Boy with Blond Curls, Dressed in Red; Old Man with Book; Old Woman with Golden Coin.*

AUCTION RECORDS:
PARIS, 10-14 and 18 Feb 1898, *Young Musicians,* FRF 520. PARIS, 3-5 May 1900, *Children's Games,* FRF 880. PARIS, 26 March 1902, *Prudence and Wisdom,* FRF 350. PARIS, 15 May 1902, *Children's Games,* FRF 730. PARIS, 29-30 Nov 1918, *Woman Darning; Shoemaker* (two canvases) FRF 4,110. PARIS, 30-31 May 1919, *Interior of a Seraglio,* FRF 1,000. PARIS, 12 June 1919, *Flora and Zephirus,* FRF 4,200. PARIS, 20 Oct 1920, *The Little Birdcatchers* (attributed) FRF 3,150. PARIS, 6-8 Dec 1920, *Monkey Fanciers,* FRF 4,500. PARIS, 18 Dec 1920, *Little Cupids in Undergrowth,* FRF 4,000. PARIS, 23-25 May 1921, *Children's Games* (two panels) FRF 5,500. PARIS, 4 June 1921, *Abundance; Painting* (two panels) FRF 10,000. PARIS, 16 Jan 1928, *Reading Lesson* (school of Eisen) FRF 3,100. PARIS, 7-8 June 1928, *Plan for Frontispiece* (pen and wash) FRF 110. PARIS, 28 Jan 1929, *Suffer the Little Children to Come unto Me,* FRF 3,750. PARIS, 22-23 Feb 1929, *Gardens of the Isle of Love* (watercolour) FRF 1,000; *Mill; Cottages* (two watercolours) FRF 1,700. LONDON, 10 March 1930, *Suffer the Little Children to Come unto Me,* GBP 9. PARIS, 11 March 1931, *Revived Bird; Pancakes* (series) FRF 7,200. LONDON, 27 April 1934, *Young Girl and Monkey* (1767) GBP 42. PARIS, 17 May 1934, *Children's Fancy Dress; Childish Mischievousness* (series) FRF 7,600. PARIS, 3-4 Dec 1934, *Woman Mending,* FRF 9,000; *Shoemaker,* FRF 59,000. PARIS, 7 Dec 1934, *Promenade* (pen drawing with wash of bistre and Indian ink) FRF 300. PARIS, 14 May 1936, *Revelling Cupid; The Dragons of Venus* (series) FRF 12,800. PARIS, 27 May 1936, *Hot Cockles; Colin-Maillard* (series) FRF 5,600. PARIS, 25 Nov 1936, *Woman Mending; Shoemaker* (pendants) FRF 9,200. PARIS, 18 March 1937, *Favourite Sultana,* FRF 5,100. LONDON, 19 Dec 1941, *Garden Scene in Torch Light, with Figures,* GBP 13. PARIS, 12 Dec 1953, *The Choiseul Family,* FRF 462,000. PARIS, 11 June 1958, *Sultan in Love,* FRF 280,000. NEW YORK, 18 Nov 1961, *Pastoral* (gouache) USD 500. LONDON, 26 June 1963, *Deceptive Lure; Bird Having Flown Off* (two pendants) GBP 1,600. PARIS, 9 Dec 1967, *Gallant Offer; Fortune-teller,* FRF 6,000. PARIS, 9 March 1972, *Marie Theresa of Austria; François III of Lorraine* (two pendants) FRF 25,000. PARIS, 15 March 1973, *Romantic Conversation,* FRF 22,000. NEW YORK, 7 April 1989, *Inn Scenes, Soldiers Drinking, Smoking and Playing Cards* (oils on canvas, a pair, each 12 3/4 x 17 1/4 ins / 32.5 x 44 cm) USD 13,200. NEW YORK, 9 Oct 1991, *Rustic Amusement in an Inn* (oil on panel, 14 1/2 x 20 3/4 ins / 36.9 x 52.7 cm) USD 3,850. PARIS, 15 Dec 1992, *Cupids* (oil on panel, 6 3/4 x 9 3/4 ins / 17.3 x 25 cm) FRF 4,500. PARIS, 16 June 1995, *Concert; Supper* (1762, oils on canvas, a pair, 13 x 10 ins / 33 x 24.5 cm) FRF 138,000. PARIS, 16 Dec 1996, *Diana and Endymion* (oil on panel, 12 1/2 x 12 1/2 ins / 31.5 x 31.5 cm) FRF 6,000. NEW YORK, 17 Oct 1997, *Elegant Interior with Ladies in Conversation; Elegant Interiors with figures Drinking Hot Chocolate around a Table* (1760, oils on canvas, a pair, each 12 1/4 x 15 1/2 ins / 31.4 x 39.4 cm) USD 15,525. PARIS, 27 Oct 2000, *Allegory of Winter* (oil on canvas, 15 x 10 ins / 38 x 26 cm) FRF 25,000. PARIS, 25 June 2002, *Fruit Seller. Vegetable Seller* (1769, oil on panel, a pair, 14 x 11 ins / 36 x 27 cm) EUR 22,000.

EISEN, Jacques Philippe
French, 18th century.
Born 3 November 1747, in Paris; died after 1778.
Active in Caen.
Painter, gilder.

Jacques Eisen was the son of Charles Eisen.

EISENBACH, Dorothy L.
American, 20th century.
Born in Lafayette (Indiana).
Painter.

Dorothy Eisenbach taught painting. She won a major prize at the Artists of Indiana exhibition in 1929.

EISENBACH, Johann Heinrich
German, 18th century.
Active in Frankfurt am Main.
Painter.

Eisenbach was probably the son of the painter Johann Remigius Eisenbach.

EISENBACH, Johann Remigius
German, 18th century.
Born in Kromberg (Taunus); died 13 April 1774.
Active in Frankfurt am Main.
Painter.

EISENBECK, H.
German, 19th century.
Miniaturist, painter. Genre scenes.

Two paintings by this artist, depicting merchants selling vegetables and game, are to be found in the historical museum in Frankfurt am Main.

EISENBERG
German, 18th century.
Painter.

Eisenberg decorated the church roof in Stalle, Prussia, with paintings depicting scenes from the gospels, the evangelists and angels.

EISENBERG, d' (Baron)
French, 18th century.
Draughtsman, writer.

Baron d'Eisenberg illustrated part of his own work on the art of equitation *Description of Modern Horsemanship*, as well as his *Against Horse-dealing*, with his own drawings.

EISENBERG, Johann
German, 17th century.
Sculptor (ivory).

A native of Gotha, Eisenberg is thought to have been a court painter and to have painted at the palace of Coburg. His works are to be found in Vienna and the state museum in Kassel.

EISENBERG, Nicolaus, or Ysenbergk
German, 15th century.
Born c. 1420, probably in Eisenberg (Saxony); died after 1482.
Painter.

Likely to have been a Franciscan monk himself, Eisenberg painted works at the Franciscan monastery of Zeitz, and for the church in Delitzsch near Leipzig where some fragments of his wall paintings remain. His main work, however, was decorating bells.

MUSEUMS AND GALLERIES:
LEIPZIG (Stadtgeschichtliches Mus.): *Christ on the Cross with the Virgin, Sts John, Paul and Elizabeth and an Ecclesiastic; Christ on the Cross with the Virgin, Sts John, Andrew and Barbara and Two Donors* (two paintings on wood with tempera).

EISENBERG, Sonja
American, 20th century.
Born 1930.
Painter.

Sonja Eisenberg works in a seemingly informal style. Her painting presents subtle chromatic variations in which the spots spread across a very finely grained paper, impregnating the texture and 'creating a body' with this support. This exploitation of the impregnation of colour by the support is also practised by the *Support-Surface* artists.

EISENBERGER, Nikolaus Friedrich
German, 18th century.
Born 20 October 1707; died 1771.
Painter, draughtsman, engraver (etching).

Eisenberger was a pupil of P. Decker and worked in Nuremberg. His notable works include 170 plates for the *Herbarium Blackwellianum* (*Blackwell Herbal*).

EISENBLATTER, Wilhelm
German, 19th century.
Born 5 November 1866, in Duisburg (near Essen).
Painter.

Eisenblatter was taught by Lechner at the Theatre Royal in Berlin and executed decorative paintings for the municipal theatre in Königsberg (now Kaliningrad). He was primarily a landscapist, producing pictures in watercolour and oils of the Königsberg countryside, Eastern Prussia and the Baltic Sea.

EISENDIECK, Suzanne
German, 20th century.
Born 1908, in Danzig (now Gdansk, Poland).
Painter. Figures, genre scenes, landscapes, flowers.

Eisendieck mainly painted young women, paying particular attention to their clothing and capturing them at their work as, for instance, a singer or milliner, or at leisure, on the beach or at a show. She exhibited at the Salon des Artistes Indépendants in Paris around 1930. Her many works frequently come up for sale in international public auctions, particularly in the USA, where she appears to have lived.

AUCTION RECORDS:
LONDON, 2 Aug 1940, *Milliner*, GBP 23. NEW YORK, 30 April 1943, *At the Milliner's*, USD 275. PARIS, 19 May 1954, *Tea on the Waterside*, FRF 58,000. NEW YORK, 6 May 1959, *Mother and Child*, USD 850. NEW YORK, 21 Nov 1963, *At the Opera*, USD 1,400. NEW YORK, 18 March 1972, *The Port of St-Aubin*, USD 1,400. LOS ANGELES, 11 Nov 1974, *The Theatre Box* (after Renoir) USD 2,000. NEW YORK, 27 Feb 1976, *14th July in St-Jean* (oil on canvas, 21 x 25¾ ins / 53.5 x 65.5 cm) USD 1,800. NEW YORK, 28 Oct 1977, *Place de la Concorde* (oil on canvas, 18½ x 24¼ ins / 47 x 61.5 cm) USD 2,000. LOS ANGELES, 6 Nov 1978, *Ballerinas about to go on Stage* (oil on canvas, 23½ x 36 ins / 60 x 91.5 cm) USD 3,700. NEW YORK, 19 Jan 1979, *The Arbours in Jumièges* (oil on canvas, 28½ x 39¼ ins / 72.4 x 99.7 cm) USD 3,500. LONDON, 3 July 1981, *Young Girl in Grey* (gouache, 19 x 13½ ins / 48.2 x 34.2 cm) GBP 650. NEW YORK, 14 Nov 1985, *Clearing in the Bois de Boulogne* (oil on canvas, 23½ x 28¾ ins / 60 x 73 cm) USD 4,000. VERSAILLES, 25 Oct 1987, *The Mouth of the Canche at Low Tide* (oil on canvas, 18 x 22 ins / 46 x 55 cm) FRF 14,500. MONTREAL, 25 April 1988, *Young Girl with a Parasol* (oil on panel, 11½ x 9 ins / 29 x 23 cm) CAD 1,900. VERSAILLES, 15 May 1988, *By the Pond* (oil on canvas, 15 x 18 ins / 38 x 46 cm) FRF 13,800. LOS ANGELES, 9 June 1988, *Singer* (oil on canvas, 29¼ x 24 ins / 74 x 61 cm) USD 4,675. MONTREAL, 17 Oct 1988, *Bouquet of Flowers in the Window* (oil on canvas, 9 x 13¾ ins / 23 x 35 cm) CAD 2,000. LONDON, 21 Oct 1988, *Roses in a Glass* (oil on canvas, 9¼ x 6½ ins / 23.8 x 16.2 cm) GBP 572. TORONTO, 30 Nov 1988, *Singer* (oil on canvas, 13¾ x 8¼ ins / 35 x 21 cm) CAD 1,650. LONDON, 22 Feb 1989, *Woman with an Umbrella* (oil on canvas, 21½ x 25½ ins / 54.5 x 65 cm) GBP 4,400. MONTREAL, 1 May 1989, *Young Girl Holding Flowers* (oil on canvas, 18 x 15 ins / 46 x 38 cm) CAD 3,500. MONTREAL, 30 Oct 1989, *Little Girl by the Lake* (oil on canvas, 22 x 18 ins / 56 x 46 cm) CAD 5,500. NEW YORK, 21 Feb 1990, *Dress Rehearsal* (oil on canvas, 29 x 24 ins / 73.7 x 61 cm) USD 5,775. MONTREAL, 30 April 1990, *Muleta* (oil on canvas, 10¼ x 18 ins / 26 x 46 cm) CAD 3,300. AMSTERDAM, 13 Dec 1990, *Couple in a Bar* (oil on canvas, 22 x 18 ins / 56 x 46 cm) NLG 10,925. NEW YORK, 13 Feb 1991, *Applause* (oil on canvas, 19¾ x 24 ins / 50 x 61 cm) USD 3,300. NEW YORK, 7 May 1991, *The First Bouquet* (oil on canvas, 18 x 15 ins / 45.7 x 38 cm) USD 2,200. NEW YORK, 5 Nov 1991, *The Ponds at Arques* (oil on canvas, 15 x 18 ins / 37.8 x 46 cm) USD 3,080. PARIS, 27 Jan 1992, *Roses in a Glass* (1908, oil on canvas, 9½ x 6¼ ins / 24 x 16 cm) FRF 6,000. NEW YORK, 27 Feb 1992, *Summer in Juvisy* (oil on canvas, 23¾ x 28¾ ins / 60.3 x 73 cm) USD 3,520. CALAIS, 5 April 1992, *Young Girl among the Flowers* (oil on paper, 8¼ x 5½ ins / 21 x 14 cm) FRF 8,000. LONDON, 15 Oct 1992, *Young Girl* (oil on canvas, 33¾ x 25¼ ins / 86 x 64 cm) GBP 2,200. AMSTERDAM, 27-28 May 1993, *Young Girl* (oil on canvas, 33¾ x 25¼ ins / 86 x 64 cm) NLG 10,580. NEW YORK, 14 June 1995, *Sunday at Sablettes Beach in Menton* (oil on canvas, 20½ x 26 ins / 52.1 x 66 cm) USD 3,737. NEW YORK, 30 April 1996, *View of Fécamp Harbour* (oil on canvas, 25½ x 32 ins / 65 x 81 cm) USD 5,175. LONDON, 23 Oct 1996, *Young Girl Seated* (oil on canvas, 24 x 19¾ ins / 61 x 50 cm) GBP 1,725. NEW YORK, 12 Nov 1996, *Curtain Call* (oil on canvas, 22 x 18 ins / 55 x 46 cm) USD 3,680. LONDON, 26 March 1999, *Elegant Figures* (oil on canvas, 22 x 29 ins / 55 x 74 cm) GBP 3,200. NEW YORK, 7 Dec 1999, *Sunday in the Country* (oil on canvas, 21 x 29 ins / 53 x 74 cm) USD 6,250. LONDON, 24 March 2000, *At the Theatre* (oil on canvas, 24 x 24 ins / 60 x 60 cm) GBP 1,100. OAK PARK, 22 Oct 2000, *Hill of Poppies* (oil on canvas, 18 x 21 ins / 46 x 53 cm) USD 4,000. SAN FRANCISCO, 16 May 2001, *Gathering Wildflowers* (oil on canvas, 18 x 22 ins / 46 x 56 cm) USD 3,750. LONDON, 28 June 2001, *Night at the Ballet* (oil on canvas, 24 x 29 ins / 61 x 74 cm) GBP 4,500. NEW YORK, 21 May 2002, *Woman on Green Bench* (oil on canvas, 26 x 21 ins / 66 x 53 cm) USD 3,500. TORONTO, 3 June 2002, *Woman and Child on the Riverbank* (oil on canvas, 18 x 22 ins / 46 x 56 cm) CAD 4,250. VIENNA, 24 April 2003, *On the Beach* (oil on canvas, 22 x 33

ins / 57 x 83 cm) EUR 3,400. PHILADELPHIA, 22 June 2003, *Patrica* (oil on canvas, 22 x 18 ins / 55 x 46 cm) USD 3,250. NEW YORK, 29 Sept 2004, *Ballet School* (c. 1960, oil on canvas, 24 x 64 ins / 61 x 162 cm) USD 6,000. NEW YORK, 29 Sept 2004, *Ballet Practice* (oil on canvas, 26 x 36 ins / 65 x 92 cm) USD 11,000.

EISENGRABER, Felix
German, 20th century.
Born 7 March 1874, in Leipzig.
Painter. Landscapes.

Eisengraber trained under Ludwig Nieper, director of the art academy in Leipzig, then under Paul Höcker and Ludwig Herterich at the Munich art academy. He is known for some of his landscapes, all of them displaying a special awareness of climatic variations, including *After the Rain, Inn Garden in Autumn, Autumn at the Chiemsee*, and *Midnight in the Snow*. He took part in exhibitions in Munich.

EISENHOUT, Anton, or Eisenhoit, or Iserenhodt
German, 16th century.
Born c. 1554, in Wartburg; died 1603, in Wartburg.
Goldsmith, medallist.

While working in Rome around the year 1580, Eisenhout made an *Ecce Homo* after Zuccaro and copied a fresco from an original in the church of S Maria della Consolazione. His engravings include a *Portrait of Gregory XIII*, a *Portrait of Duchess Hedwige of Marburg* and a *Portrait of Bishop Theodor von Fürstenberg*.

EISENHUT, Ferencz Franz
Serb, 19th century.
Born 26 January 1857, in Backa Palanka; died 2 June 1903, in Munich.
Painter, engraver. Genre scenes, local scenes.

Ferencz Eisenhut was a student at the art academy in Munich in Wilhem Diez's workshop. He visited the Caucasus mountains, Turkey, Africa, Italy and France, and eventually settled in Munich. He exhibited in Vienna and Munich from 1888 and at the Salon de Paris (1895), and at the Exposition Universelle, Paris (1900).

MUSEUMS AND GALLERIES:
BUCHAREST: *Tunisian Scene* - BUDAPEST (Budavári Palata): *Death of Gül Baba* - BUDAPEST (Pina.): *Fight for the Spoils* - BUDAPEST (Szépmuvészeti Múz.): *Dream; Cockfight in Cairo*.

AUCTION RECORDS:
LONDON, 13 Dec 1909, *At the Harem*, GBP 21. LONDON, 25 June 1982, *Slave Market* (1888, oil on canvas, 53 1/2 x 88 1/4 ins / 136 x 224 cm) GBP 30,000. LONDON, 24 June 1983, *Guards Playing with a Monkey* (1888, oil on canvas, 23 1/2 x 33 ins / 59.5 x 83.8 cm) GBP 17,000. LONDON, 19 March 1986, *Arab and Moors in an Alley* (1887, oil on canvas, 28 x 22 ins / 71 x 55 cm) GBP 15,000. NEW YORK, 24 Oct 1989, *Backgammon Game* (1886, oil on canvas, 29 1/2 x 21 3/4 ins / 74.9 x 55.3 cm) USD 33,000. LONDON, 16 June 1993, *Street Market in an Arab Town* (1885, oil on canvas, 22 3/4 x 16 1/2 ins / 58 x 42 cm) GBP 7,475. LONDON, 16 Nov 1994, *Suburbs in an Arab Town* (1891, oil on panel, 15 1/4 x 24 1/2 ins / 39 x 62 cm) GBP 11,500. NEW YORK, 16 Feb 1995, *Favourite of the Pasha* (oil on panel, 23 1/2 x 15 1/2 ins / 59.7 x 39.4 cm) USD 107,000. VIENNA, 30 Nov 2000, *Man Guarding the Prisoners* (oil on canvas, 25x35 ins / 64x88 cm) ATS 200,000. STUTTGART, 8 Dec 2000, *Interior Scene with Two Women on the Bed* (1892, oil on canvas, 8x11 ins / 21x27 cm) DEM 30,000. COLOGNE, 10 April 2003, *North African Bazaar* (1886, oil on canvas, 23x17 ins / 59x43 cm) EUR 6,000. ERLANGEN, 20 March 2004, *Standing Armed Albanian* (1902, oil on board, 20x13 ins / 50x34 cm) EUR 2,500.

EISENHUT, Lienhart. See **YSENHUT**

EISENHUT, Max Ernst
Swiss, 20th century.
Born 1899, in Herisau (Appenzell).
Painter. Landscapes.

Eisenhut was a pupil of Ernst Würtenberger.

EISENLOHR, Edward G.
American, 19th - 20th century.
Born 9 November 1872, in Cincinnati (Ohio); died 1961.
Painter, draughtsman, lithographer, art theorist.
Figures, landscapes, winter landscapes.

Edward Eisenlohr was a pupil of Gustav Schönleber at the Karlsruhe Academy of Fine Arts. He then became a teacher in America. He was also a lecturer, art theorist and writer of several works: *Study and Charm of Images, Art Trends and their Meaning, Landscape Painters*. He was a member of numerous art associations and an honourable member of the Dallas Art Association. He won several distinctions and in 1920 was awarded the Southern States Art League prize, then in 1931 first prize for landscapes from the Dallas Association.

MUSEUMS AND GALLERIES:
DALLAS (MA): *The Sentinel of Box Canyon* (1923, oil on canvas); *Winter Landscape* (oil on canvas/panel); *Abandoned Trail* (oil on canvas); *Spring Fields at Grand Prairie* (oil on canvas); *An Old Landmark* (oil on canvas); *After the Cutting* (oil on panel); *Stubblefield* (oil on canvas); *Corral at Fredericksburg, Nimitz Hotel* (oil on canvas); *Spring Thaw* (oil on canvas); *Autumn's Woods* (oil on card); drawings, lithographs - NEW ORLÉANS (Isaac Delgado Fine Arts Gal., Delgado Community College): *When the Cotton Fields are Brown* - SAN ANTONIO (Witte Memorial Mus.): *At the Start of the Year*.

EISENLOHR, Louise von, or von Stupka-Eisenlohr
German, 19th century.
Born c. 1860, in Mainz.
Painter.

This artist was a pupil of Zeleny in Brno and of Wilhelm Dürr in Munich. She was primarily a painter of still-lifes, several of which are housed in the museum in Brno, where she had settled. She also painted racehorses.

MUSEUMS AND GALLERIES:
BRNO (Muz. Mesta): Still-lifes.

EISENLOHR-CAMPOFIORITO, Hilda
Brazilian, 20th century.
Born in Rio de Janeiro.
Painter.

EISENMAN, Nicole
French, 20th - 21st century.
Born 1963, in Verdun.
Active in the USA.
Draughtswoman.

Nicole Eisenman lives and works in New York, where she also exhibits. She creates wash drawings that are reminiscent of ancient works of art. She dramatises the world of childhood - its cruelty, and the fantasies that adults have about its familiar and confusing universe. In 2003, she took part in the collective exhibition *Phantom der Lust. Visionen des Masochismus in der Kunst* (*Phantom of Desire. Visions of Masochism in Art*), dedicated to Sacher-Masoch, who gave his name to Masochism, at the Neue Galerie am Landesmuseum in Graz.

BIBLIOGRAPHY:
Clearwater, Bonnie, '*Arrêt sur enfance*' in *Art Press* n° 197, periodical, Paris, December 1994. Weibel, Peter (ed.), '*Phantom der Lust. Visionen des Masochismus in der Kunst*', *2 vol.*,

exhibition catalogue, Neue Galerie am Landesmuseum, Graz, Belleville Verlag, Munich, 2003.

EISENMANGER, Georg
German, 15th century.
Active in Munich.
Painter.

Between 1480 and 1482, Eisenmanger executed a number of works for the town of Innsbruck.

EISENMANN. See also **EISMANN**

EISENMANN, Andreas
German, 17th century.
Died 27 March 1701, in Nuremberg.
Active in Nuremberg.
Engraver (copper/steel).

EISENMANN, Georg, or Eisemann
German, 18th century.
Painter, engraver.

Georg Eisenmann probably worked in Nuremberg and produced numerous etchings, including four landscapes entitled *Hungarian on Horseback, representing the Four Seasons*; four other landscapes with ruins and figures; four landscapes after J.C. Dietzsch; and two *Views of the Fortress at Rothenberg*. Three of his landscape paintings can be found in the art gallery at Bamberg.

EISENMANN, Germaine Suzanne
French, 20th century.
Born 23 August 1894, in Paris.
Painter.

Germaine Suzanne Eisenmann studied with Fernand Humbert at the École des Beaux-Arts in Paris from 1912 to 1915. In 1921, on the Mont-St-Michel she met Suzanne Valadon, whose teaching and friendship she was always proud to have received. She exhibited regularly in Paris at the Salon d'Automne and at the Tuileries.

MUSEUMS AND GALLERIES:
GRENOBLE - LA ROCHELLE.

EISENMANN, Jakob Andreas
German, 18th century.
Active in Nuremberg.
Engraver (mezzotint).

EISENMANN, Wolf
German, 17th century.
Died 1616, in Würzburg.
Active in Nuremberg.
Painter.

Eisenmann worked on the high altar in Würzburg cathedral in 1611 and 1614.

EISENMENGER, August
Austrian, 19th century.
Born 11 February 1830, in Vienna; died 1907, in Vienna.
Painter. History painting.

Eisenmenger began studying art with Leopold Schulz. In 1845, he went to the Akademie in Vienna, where he won first prize, then became a pupil of Rahl and his collaborator. In 1872 Eisenmenger was appointed professor at the Akademie. He founded a private school of painting in Vienna, where he worked on a number of public monuments. The historical museum in Vienna has a *Portrait of Johann Strauss* by this artist in its collection.

EISENMEYER, Johann Paul
Austrian, 19th century.
Born c.1789.
Active in Vienna c. 1820.
Painter.

Eisenmeyer is noted for a portrait of *Charles Joseph Prince of Ligne*.

EISENPREIN, Hans
Austrian, 16th century.
Painter. Portraits.
Viennese School.

Hans Eisenprein became a burgher of Vienna in 1518.

EISENSCHER, Yaacov
Israeli, 20th century.
Born 1896; died 1980.
Painter (gouache). Scenes with figures, interiors with figures.

His compositions are put together strictly according to the thematic elements and according to the elements as a group in relation to the size of the work. The presiding spirit over this organisation of shapes and space is in keeping with the post-cubism of its time.

Eisenscher

AUCTION RECORDS:
TEL AVIV, 16 May 1982, *The Slave Market* (1888, oil on canvas, 53 1/2 x 88 1/4 ins / 136 x 224 cm) GBP 30,000. TEL AVIV, 16 May 1983, *Houses and a Figure* (oil on canvas, 28 x 28 1/4 ins / 71 x 71.5 cm) ILS 46,000. TEL AVIV, 17 June 1985, *Landscape* (oil on canvas, 15 x 18 ins / 38 x 46 cm) ILS 800,000. TEL AVIV, 2 Jan 1989, *Houses* (oil on card, 12 1/2 x 17 3/4 ins / 31.5 x 45 cm) USD 820. TEL AVIV, 3 Jan 1990, *The Artist's Studio* (oil on canvas, 18 x 24 1/4 ins / 46 x 61.5 cm) USD 1,650; *Interior* (gouache, 18 x 26 1/2 ins / 46 x 67.5 cm) USD 710. TEL AVIV, 19 June 1990, *Figures in a Café by the Sea* (1944, oil on card, 21 1/4 x 25 1/2 ins / 54 x 65 cm) USD 1,650. TEL AVIV, 1 Jan 1991, *Figures in a Shop Entrance* (oil on canvas, 23 3/4 x 28 3/4 ins / 60.5 x 73 cm) USD 3,520. TEL AVIV, 12 June 1991, *Parrots in a Cage* (oil on canvas, 29 1/4 x 39 1/4 ins / 74 x 100 cm) USD 5,280. TEL AVIV, 30 June 1994, *Theme Park* (oil on canvas, 28 1/4 x 35 3/4 ins / 72 x 91 cm) USD 4,140. TEL AVIV, 12 Jan 1997, *Two Sisters* (c. 1956, oil on canvas, 53 1/4 x 42 1/2 ins / 135 x 108 cm) USD 13,800; *Safed* (oil on canvas, 21 x 25 1/4 ins / 53.5 x 64 cm) USD 2,415. TEL AVIV, 5 Jan 1999, *Houses in a Landscape* (oil on canvas, 29x20 ins / 73x50 cm) USD 1,800. TEL AVIV, 4 July 1999, *Fishermen* (watercolour, 13x19 ins / 34x48 cm) USD 550. TEL AVIV, 29 June 2000, *Figures by the Sea of Galilee* (oil on canvas, 20x26 ins / 50x65 cm) USD 5,400. TEL AVIV, 29 June 2000, *Houses in a Landscape* (oil on canvas, 18x24 ins / 46x61 cm) USD 4,200. TEL AVIV, 15 Jan 2001, *Fishermen* (gouache, 13x19 ins / 32x48 cm) USD 800. TEL AVIV, 1 Dec 2003, *Red House* (1950s, oil on canvas/board, 14x10 ins / 35x25 cm) USD 1,200. TEL AVIV, 1 June 2004, *Painter and Model* (oil on canvas, 18x22 ins / 46x55 cm) USD 2,800. TEL AVIV, 1 Oct 2004, *Landscape at Jaffa* (oil on canvas, 18x24 ins / 46x61 cm) USD 2,550.

EISENSCHITZ, Willy
Austrian, 20th century.
Born 29 October 1889, in Vienna; died 8 July 1974, in Paris.
Active from 1911, then naturalised in France.
Painter, watercolourist, draughtsman (including charcoal), illustrator. Figures, interiors, landscapes, waterscapes, harbour views, architectural views, urban views, village views, still-lifes, flowers.

Eisenschitz studied first at the art academy in Vienna and then, between 1911 and 1914, trained under Georges Desvallières, Lucien Simon, and the painter and art historian René Ménard at the Académie de la Grande-Chaumière in Paris. He did not return to Austria, but married the French painter Claire Bertrand. During World War I he took refuge in Switzerland, where he stayed until 1920. On returning to France, he and Claire Bertrand went to live in Dieulefit in the department of Drôme, moving in 1927 to La Valette near Toulon. Their home became a meeting place for artists from the Toulon region. As he had Jewish roots, he spent the time of the German occupation of France during World War II in hiding.

After the war, Eisenschitz went travelling in search of subjects. He made frequent trips to Spain, and in 1959 he was captivated by the Sudan. He brought back notes and sketches from his travels which he later used in the studio. The last years of his life were divided between Toulon and Paris. He got to know Jean Giono, who later wrote a preface for an exhibition of his watercolours in London; he illustrated several books by Giono and Aldous Huxley. He painted landscapes of places where he had lived and places he visited. Landscapes from the Midi, the region around Dieulefit, the Drôme, and the Var area of Provence dominate his output. He also painted in Paris and Savoie, and carried out studio paintings based on his trips to Spain and the Sudan.

Eisenschitz was a member of the Société Nationale des Beaux-Arts and the Salon d'Automne in Paris and was also represented at the Salon des Tuileries. In 1964 he was involved in the Biennale des Peintres de Provence in Aix-en-Provence. In 1991 his work featured in the exhibition *Les Artistes réfugiés à Dieulefit pendant la Seconde Guerre mondiale* (*The Refugee Artists of Dieulefit during the World War II*) at the Musée de Valence, and in 2003 in the exhibition *José Mange* at the Musée d'Art in Toulon. He also organised solo exhibitions. The first in Paris in 1922 was followed by numerous others. The Musée de Toulon held a major retrospective of his entire works in 1957, and again in 1977 and 2001.

W. Eisenschitz

BIBLIOGRAPHY:

Les artistes réfugiés à Dieulefit pendant la Seconde Guerre mondiale, exhibition catalogue, Musée de Valence, Valence, 1991. Perreau, Jean, *Willy Eisenschitz*, catalogue raisonné, Schütz Kunst & Antiquitäten, Linz, 1999. Baum, Peter/Eisenschitz, Willy, *Willy Eisenschitz, 1889 - 1974*, exhibition catalogue, Neue Galerie, Linz, 1999. Nieszawer, Nadine/Boyé, Marie/Lanzmann, Claude (preface), *Peintres juifs de l'école de Paris 1905-1939*, Denoël, Paris, 2001.

MUSEUMS AND GALLERIES:

AIX-EN-PROVENCE (Mus. Granet) - BRISTOL: *Figure in a Garden* - LONDON (British Mus.): *Mountain Path; The Verdon; Boats on a Canal; Landscape* - LYONS (MBA): *Interior* - MARSEILLES (Mus. Cantini): *Olive Trees* - NARBONNE: *Ibiza Landscape* (watercolour) - PARIS (MNAM-CCI): *Spanish Scene; Landscape at Dieulefit.*

AUCTION RECORDS:

PARIS, 29 Oct 1926, *Village in the Drôme,* FRF 1,750. PARIS, 18 April 1929, *Landscape,* FRF 400. PARIS, 2 March 1939, *Snow in Courchevel* (watercolour) FRF 750. PARIS, 13 July 1942, *Midi Landscape,* FRF 1,900. ZURICH, 2 June 1983, *Bouquet of Flowers* (1928, oil on canvas, 18 x 22 ins / 46 x 55 cm) CHF 3,400. VIENNA, 9 Dec 1987, *Fraga, a Town in Spain* (1929, oil on canvas, 26 1/2 x 32 ins / 67 x 81 cm) ATS 90,000. PARIS, 20 March 1988, *Man Walking* (oil on canvas, 25 1/2 x 21 1/4 ins / 65 x 54 cm) FRF 10,000. PARIS, 10 April 1989, *Vase of Flowers* (oil on canvas, 22 x 21 1/4 ins / 56 x 54 cm) FRF 17,000. PARIS, 18 June 1989, *The Port* (pastel, 12 1/4 x 17 ins / 31 x 43 cm) FRF 4,200. PARIS, 22 Oct 1989, *Roofs of Provence* (1928, oil on canvas, 28 3/4 x 36 1/4 ins / 73 x 92 cm) FRF 73,000. VERSAILLES, 28 Jan 1990, *The Port* (charcoal and pastel, 14 1/4 x 17 1/4 ins / 36 x 43.5 cm) FRF 3,000. PARIS, 11 March 1990, *Nude at the Window* (oil on canvas, 38 1/2 x 31 ins / 98 x 78.5 cm) FRF 38,000. ST-DIÉ, 21 April 1991, *Village in the Country* (oil on canvas, 21 1/4 x 25 1/2 ins / 54 x 65 cm) FRF 15,000. NEW YORK, 7 May 1991, *Landscape* (oil on canvas, 25 3/4 x 31 1/2 ins / 65.4 x 80 cm) USD 6,050. NEUILLY, 20 Oct 1991, *Chapel in Provence* (watercolour, 14 1/2 x 20 ins / 37 x 51 cm) FRF 6,000. PARIS, 11 Dec 1991, *Le Grand Village* (1927, oil on canvas, 32 x 51 1/4 ins / 81 x 130 cm) FRF 39,000. PARIS, 5 Feb 1992, *Midi Landscape* (oil on canvas, 28 x 28 ins / 71 x 71 cm) FRF 14,000. NEW YORK, 10 Nov 1992, *Les Minimes, La Valette sur Var* (oil on canvas, 23 1/2 x 28 1/2 ins / 59.7 x 72.7 cm) USD 4,620. AMSTERDAM, 8 Dec 1993, *Terraced Landscape* (oil on canvas, 32 x 23 1/4 ins / 81 x 59 cm) NLG 3,450. NEUILLY, 12 Dec 1993, *Ibiza* (oil on canvas, 28 3/4 x 23 1/2 ins / 73 x 60 cm) FRF 18,000; *Still-life with a Vase of Flowers* (oil on panel, 22 x 22 ins / 55 x 55 cm) FRF 18,000. PARIS, 29 April 1994, *Mountainscape* (oil on panel, 22 x 15 ins / 55 x 38 cm) FRF 5,200. PARIS, 22 Nov 1994, *Autumn in Provence* (oil on canvas, 23 1/2 x 28 3/4 ins / 60 x 73 cm) FRF 8,000. SARLAT, 10 March 1996, *Siesta* (oil on canvas, 54 x 37 1/2 ins / 137 x 95 cm) FRF 38,000. PARIS, 29 Nov 1996, *Undulating Landscape* (oil on canvas, 26 3/4 x 23 1/4 ins / 68 x 59 cm) FRF 5, 500. PARIS, 4 April 1997, *Provence Landscape in the Rain* (watercolour, 13 1/2 x 21 1/4 ins / 34.5 x 54 cm) FRF 4,000. PARIS, 6 June 1997, *In Provence* (oil on canvas, 37 1/2 x 61 ins / 95 x 154 cm) FRF 25,000.

EISENSCHMIED, Johann

Austrian, 19th century.

Born in Knittelfeld (Styria); died 1858, in Knittelfeld.

Painter.

Eisenschmied was a pupil of the painter Lederwasch and painted numerous retables for Styrian churches.

EISENSTEIN, Avi

Israeli, 20th - 21st century.

Born 21 July 1946, in Haifa.

Painter, draughtsman.

A student at the Bezalel Academy in Jerusalem, from 1967 to 1971, he became a teacher there in 1973 in the graphics department, then became its head in 1988. He has taken part in group exhibitions, in Tel Aviv, at the Jerusalem Museum and elsewhere. He has also had some solo exhibitions, in Tel Aviv and in Paris in 1991.

He draws symbols and splashes, often in black.

EISENSTEIN, Rosa

Austrian, 19th century.

Born 2 October 1844, in Vienna; died 1889, in Africa.

Painter. Genre scenes, still-lifes.

A pupil of Mrs O. Wiesinger-Florian, the painter F. Schilcher, C. Probst and R. Huber, this artist exhibited in Berlin and Vienna from 1886 onwards.

EISENTRÄGER, Johann Heinrich

German, 18th century.

Born c. 1730, in Kassel; died 1788, in Kassel.

Painter (porcelain).

Eisenträger was initially a landscape painter at the Fürstenberg porcelain works, then became a figure painter. He worked at the porcelain factory in Kassel from 1769 onwards. The works by this artist in the museum in Kassel include a *Miniature Portrait of a Woman* on porcelain, a *View of Mulang at Wilhelmshöhe Bergpark* and the *Portraits of Landgraves Frederick II and Charles.*

EISENTRÄGER, Johann Karl

German, 18th century.

Active in Kassel.

Painter (porcelain).

This artist was probably the son of Johann Heinrich Eisenträger.

EISENZOPF, Michel

French, 20th century.

Born 1938, in Paris.

Painter, engraver. Scenes with figures.
Michel Eisenzopf studied in Paris at the École Estienne and the Beaux-Arts. He set up his studio in Neuville-en-Hez (Oise), and taught drawing and engraving at the Espace Matisse in Creil. He used various techniques, sometimes combining different ones in a single work, and engraved complex compositions full of scenery and figures, rather in the manner of Jacques Callot. In his sometimes caustic humour, his rich vein of good companionship, his fearless use of strong and even loud colours he resembles Jerome Bosch and his devilments, or Brueghel and his merry-making.

Eisenzopf showed work in various collective exhibitions including the Paris Salon des Artistes Français, of which he became a member, afterwards winning a gold medal and a medal of honour and also the prize awarded by the Friends of French Artists. Besides these he belonged to the Salon d'Automne and to the Salon de Point et Burin, and was connected with the Salon du Trait ('of the Line'). He exhibited in several groups in Paris, including in 1996 *4 Universes, 4 Engravers of Fantasy* at the Galerie Graphes, and in other cities across France. He showed collections of his engravings in solo exhibitions in galleries in Paris - Fondation Taylor, Breheret, Michèle Brouta, and in Lille, Rouen, Senlis, Soissons and elsewhere.

Bibliography:
'*Michel Eisenzopf, le magicien de la couleur*' in *Art et Métiers du Livre* n° 199, periodical, Paris, 1996.

EISER, Ferdinand

German, 17th century.
Active in Neuburg.
Painter.

From 1611 to 1615, Eiser worked for the collegiate church in Neuburg, probably with Terzano.

EISER, Johann Tobias

Bohemian School, 18th century.
Born 1767, in Prague; died in Vienna.
Painter.

Johann Eiser enrolled in the Akademie der Bildenden Künste in Vienna on 13 May 1783.

EISERMANN, Richard

German, 19th century.
Painter. Genre scenes, figures.

Eisermann worked in Munich and exhibited in Vienna in 1878. He is noted for works including *Returning from the Baptism*, *Favourite Flower*, *Tyrolean Woman* and *On the Balcony*.

Auction records:
London, 10 July 1908, *Sixteenth-century Woman*, GBP 17. London, 26 March 1981, *Sleeping Beauty* (1881, oil on canvas, 36 1/2 x 52 ins / 93 x 132 cm) GBP 3,600. London, 17 June 1994, *Sleeping Beauty* (1881, oil on canvas, 36 1/2 x 52 ins / 93 x 132 cm) GBP 7,130. Vienna, 30 Nov 2000, *At the Pawnshop* (oil on canvas, 30 x 31 ins / 75 x 78 cm) ATS 100,000. Budapest, 28 April 2004, *Children with Bucket of Spring Flowers* (pastel, 67 x 37 ins / 170 x 95 cm) HUF 2,200,000.

EISFELD, H.

German, 17th century.
Painter.

An *Ecce Homo* by this artist, dated 1699, can be found in the church at Rathebur near Anklam in Pomerania.

EISHI, real name: Fujiwara Hosoda Tokitomi Jibukyo, popular name: Yasaburo Kuzaemon (or Kyusaemon), artist names: Eishi, Chobunsai, Hosoi

Japanese, 18th - 19th century.
Born 1756, in Edo (now Tokyo); died 1829; in 1815 according to some sources.
Painter, print artist.

Eishi was a samurai descended from a military family, and a member of the personal entourage of the shogun. He gave up all his official duties to devote himself to his art. He was probably a disciple of Utamaro (1753-1806), his contemporary. A prolific painter, he was regarded as one of the outstanding artists of the last decade of the eighteenth century. As a print artist, he is known for his portrayals of beautiful women with slender waists and long faces, a certain expression of nobility and rather indistinct silhouettes against a background of a cold chromatic quality characteristic of the close of the century.

Bibliography:
Watanabe, Toshio, '*Eishi prints in Whistler's studio? 18th century Japanese prints in the West before 1870*' in *Burlington Magazine CXXVIII/1005*, December 1986. Fahr-Becker, Gabriele (ed.), *Japanese Prints*, Taschen, Cologne, 1999.

Auction records:
Paris, 28 and 29 March 1955, *Leaning on a Table Adorned with a Large Peony a Young Woman Observes the Flight of a Butterfly*, FRF 36,000. New York, 16 April 1988, *Beauty Observing through the Window a Tiger on the Opposite Bank of a River Bordered by Irises* (print, 15 1/4 x 10 ins / 38.8 x 25.5 cm) USD 5,500. London, 16 June 1988, *Moment of Relaxation for Three Courtesans in the Pleasure Quarters* (dai oban yoko-e woodblock print, 14 3/4 x 19 3/4 ins / 37.7 x 50.3 cm) GBP 22,000. New York, 21 March 1989, *Three Young Women on a Raft Catching Butterflies* (oban tate-e woodblock print, 15 1/4 x 9 1/2 ins / 38.7 x 24 cm) USD 3,300. New York, 16 Oct 1989, *The Courtesan Takahashi of Ogiya with her Kamuro* (oban tate-e woodblock print, from the series A Collection of Young Beauties, 14 1/2 x 9 1/2 ins / 36.9 x 24.4 cm) USD 3,300. London, 13 Nov 1989, *Three Ladies Under Verandah* (oban tate-e woodblock print, 15 x 10 ins / 38 x 25.7 cm) GBP 1,430. London, 22 March 1990, *Two Women and Boy Near Ferry where Peach Tree is in Blossom* (aiban tate-e print, 12 1/4 x 8 1/4 ins / 30.8 x 20.9 cm) GBP 1,320. London, 6 June 1990, *Two Women, One Standing Holding a Fan, the Other Seated* (oban tate-e woodblock print, 14 3/4 x 9 3/4 ins / 37.5 x 24.6 cm) GBP 2,090. Paris, 3 June 1992, *Meeting of Seven Young Women in a Boat Symbolising the Seven Gods of Happiness* (1793, print, triptych, each plate 15 x 10 ins / 38 x 25.5 cm) FRF 28,000. Paris, 16 Feb 1996, *The Oiran Someyama Accompanied by her Two Kamuros Hanano and Momiji* (oban tate-e colour print) FRF 12,500.

EISHIN. See **YASUNOBU** and **KANO Isen**

EISHO, real name: Hosoda Eisho, artist names: Chokosai, Shoeido

Japanese, 18th century.
Born 1780; died 1800.
Active c. 1790.
Painter, print artist.

Eisho's prints lack the refinement of those of his master, Eishi. By contrast his large format portraits of beautiful women have a more human character.

Bibliography:
Fahr-Becker, Gabriele (ed.), *Japanese Prints*, Taschen, Cologne, 1999.

Auction records:
London, 16 June 1988, *Woman Holding a Poem and a Fan in the Shade of a Parasol Carried by a Servant* (oban tate-e woodblock print, 15 x 9 3/4 ins / 38.3 x 24.6 cm) GBP 1,100. New York, 21 March 1989, *Portrait in Large Format of the Courtesan Shizuka Adjusting her Hairpins Before a Beauty Contest in the Pleasure Quarters* (oban tate-e woodblock print, 15 1/2 x 10 1/4 ins / 39.3 x 26 cm) USD 22,000. New York, 16 Oct 1989, *Okubi-e Portrait of the Courtesan Eizan de Takeya* (oban tate-e woodblock print, 15 x 10 1/4 ins / 38 x 25.8 cm) USD 9,350. London, 22 March 1990, *Woman*

Reading a Poem Followed by a Servant with an Umbrella and by a Child with a Lacquered Casket (oban tate-e woodblock print, 14 1/2 x 9 3/4 ins / 37.1 x 24.7 cm) GBP 990. NEW YORK, 27 March 1991, *Portrait of the Courtesan Shizuka Holding a Pipe and Pushing a Pin into her Hair* (oban tate-e woodblock print, 15 1/4 x 10 1/4 ins / 38.7 x 25.9 cm) USD 7,150.

EISHUN, real name: Tosa Eishun
Japanese, 15th century.
Born 1369; died 1418.
Active in the first half of the 15th century.
Painter.

Eishun is known for his work on the two woodblock picture scrolls *Yuzu-nembutsu-engi* (origin and development of the Yuzu sect), which were produced between 1414 and 1423. This historic work depicts the life of the monk Ryonin (1072-1132), who founded the *Yuzu Nembutsu* sect, according to whose teacings the virtues of an invocation addressed to Amida Buddha are beneficial to all, just like the miracles brought about by the prayer itself. There are versions of these scrolls pre-dating 1414. Many copies and printed versions have been made of the original, which dates back to 1314. The copy in the Seiryo-ji temple, which is after a xylographic version of 1390, was the work of Rokkaku Jakusai, Awataguchi Takamitsu, Fujiwara Yukihiro and Fujiwara Mitsukuni, as well as Eishun. The copy from 1414 conserved in the Seiryo-ji in Kyoto was lost in the 1923 earthquake.

BIBLIOGRAPHY:

'Rouleaux de Kobodaishi, du Yûnembutsu et du temple Kiho.ji' in *Shinshu.nihon.emakimono.zenshu (New complete collection of Japanese historical scrolls)* vol. 1, Kadokawashoten, 1980.

EISING, Ejnar
Danish, 20th century.
Born 1909, in Copenhagen.
Painter. Figure compositions. Murals, designs for stained glass.

Eising trained at the Kongelige Danske Kunstakademi in Copenhagen. He took part in exhibitions in Denmark, Sweden, Finland, France, Germany and Switzerland.

EISLER
Bohemian School, 18th century.
Active in Jablonne nad Orlici, Bohemia.
Painter. Portraits.

Possibly the same as J. Thomas Eyselt.

EISLER, Gaspar Gottlieb
German, 18th century.
Active in Nuremberg c. 1750.
Engraver, medallist.

This artist is noted for his engraved portrait of J. Adam Tresenreuter, a *Self-portrait* and a plate depicting an *Arab with Two Dromedaries*. Eisler was above all a fine illustrator.

EISLER, Georg
Austrian, 20th century.
Born 1928, in Vienna; died 1998, in Vienna.
Painter, pastellist, engraver. Figure compositions, figures, portraits, nudes, interiors, urban landscapes.

Eisler fled to Britain when World War II broke out in 1939; there, he studied painting at various institutions, notably the Manchester School of Art between 1944 and 1946. He also knew Oskar Kokoschka in 1944, who exerted what later proved to be a lasting influence on him. In 1946 he went to Vienna, where he attended courses run by the Expressionist Herbert Boeckl at the art academy until 1950. Soon after the war he formed an alliance with three artists who were firm believers in figurative representation: the sculptor and engraver Alfred Hrdlicka, the painter Fritz Martinz and the engraver Rudolf Schönwald, with whom he exhibited in 1969 under the collective name Figur. He settled in Vienna, becoming a member of the Secession in 1960 and its president in 1968. (By the 1960s the Secession really existed in name only, despite its earlier historical importance.) Eisler travelled in the Netherlands, Britain and France.

His early paintings were portraits or views of working-class suburbs and industrial estates. He then turned his attention to the human being. He excelled at drawing nudes, while his paintings depicted figures in indoor or outdoor settings or, for another series, in a jazz or dance setting. Up until 1957 Eisler's painting expressed a psychological approach characterised by intimist humanism. After that date his focus broadened from man as an individual to the man in a crowd or on public transport. At that time he started painting more ambitious compositions, inspired by past masters, from the 16th-century Venetians Tintoretto and Veronese to the French Romantics around Delacroix, to the Realists Courbet, Daumier and Hans von Marées, the Expressionists Soutine and Gerstl and - a constant figure of inspiration since his youth - Kokoschka. During this period, he combined the Classical tradition with a kind of Modernism using simple harmonies of mixed tones and vigorous brushstrokes.

Eisler's work has been displayed in collective themed exhibitions such as *Selbst und Andere. Das Bildnis in der Kunst nach 1960 (Self and Others: Portraiture since 1960)* which took place at the Rupertinum in Salzburg in 2003.

MUSEUMS AND GALLERIES:

LONDON (Victoria and Albert Mus.).

AUCTION RECORDS:

VIENNA, 18 Nov 1981, *The Vegetable Garden* (oil on canvas, 26 1/2 x 38 1/4 ins / 67 x 97 cm) ATS 11,000. PARIS, 18 May 1982, *Sleep* (watercolour wash, 11 x 7 ins / 28 x 18 cm) FRF 2,800. VIENNA, 15 Nov 1983, *Big Metro* (1968, oil on canvas, 59 x 51 1/4 ins / 150 x 130 cm) ATS 28,000. VIENNA, 18 March 1986, *Street Scene* (1969, oil on canvas, 17 3/4 x 25 1/2 ins / 45 x 65 cm) ATS 14,000. VIENNA, 25 June 1986, *Two Women* (1978, pastel, 18 x 24 1/2 ins / 46 x 62 cm) ATS 25,000. VIENNA, 20 April 1999, *Cafe Scala* (oil on canvas, 14 x 18 ins / 36 x 45 cm) ATS 30,000. VIENNA, 13 Oct 1999, *Neumarkt an der Raab* (oil on canvas, 24 x 31 ins / 60 x 80 cm) ATS 60,000. VIENNA, 11 April 2000, *Little Bus* (1967, oil on canvas, 9 x 13 ins / 24 x 33 cm) ATS 25,000. VIENNA, 11 April 2000, *Portrait of Ernst Fischer* (oil on canvas, 31 x 24 ins / 80 x 60 cm) ATS 50,000. SALZBURG, 12 June 2002, *Street with Runners* (oil on canvas, 51 x 59 ins / 130 x 150 cm) EUR 8,500. VIENNA, 24 Sept 2002, *Hommage to Erich Fried* (oil on canvas, 50 x 57 ins / 127 x 146 cm) EUR 12,000. VIENNA, 27 May 2003, *Paris, Metro station Tuilleries* (1986, oil on canvas, 14 x 18 ins / 36 x 45 cm) EUR 3,600. VIENNA, 27 May 2003, *Nude* (1965, oil on canvas, 31 x 23 ins / 78 x 58 cm) EUR 3,800. VIENNA, 28 April 2004, *Untitled* (1985, pastel/chalk, 19 x 24 ins / 48 x 61 cm) EUR 3,000.

EISLER, Jeremias, or Eissler
German, 17th century.
Born 15 June 1641; died 18 March 1702.
Active in Nuremberg.
Sculptor.

Eisler collaborated with his master, Georg Schweigger, on a *Fountain* for the large market square in Nuremberg, and completed the work after Schweigger's death.

EISLER, Maria, or Eissler
German, 17th century.
Active in Nuremberg c. 1694.
Miniaturist.

Maria Eisler painted portraits, birds and flowers. She was the wife of Jeremias Eisler.

EISLER, Stephan, or Eysler
German, 15th century.
Active in Nuremberg in 1490.
Painter.

EISMAN-SEMENOWSKY.
See **SEMENOWSKY Eisman**

EISMANN, Carlo, real name: Brisighella
Italian, 17th - 18th century.
Born c. 1630, in Venice; died after 1718.
Painter, art writer.

A relative of the painter Carlo Bononi, Carlo was a pupil of Lodovico Lana and Johann Anton Eismann, who later adopted him as his son. He lived in Ferrara, where he wrote an account of the city's art treasures, and in Verona. He specialised in landscapes, marines and battle scenes. Dresden Museum has four of his paintings, representing *Cavaliers in Combat*.

EISMANN, Johann Anton, or Eisemann or Leismann
German, 17th century.
Born 1604, in Salzburg; died 1698, in Venice.
Painter. Historical subjects, battles, landscapes with figures, landscapes, ruins, harbour scenes, seascapes, waterscapes.

Eismann was influenced by Salvator Rosa, his favourite master.

MUSEUMS AND GALLERIES:
AUGSBURG: *Landscape with Ruins* - BAMBERG: *Sea-port* - DRESDEN: *Ruins* (two works) - OBERSCHLEISSHEIM: *Ruin* - VIENNA: *Battle*.

AUCTION RECORDS:
MILAN, 27 April 1978, *Marine Landscape* (oil on canvas, 46 1/2 x 64 1/2 ins / 118 x 164 cm) ITL 3,600,000. ROME, 28 April 1981, *River Landscape with Figures* (two oils on canvas, 33 1/2 x 45 1/4 ins / 85 x 115 cm) ITL 15,000,000. LONDON, 4 April 1984, *Landscape with Waterfall* (oil on canvas, 43 1/4 x 79 1/2 ins / 110 x 202 cm) GBP 6,500. LONDON, 10 July 1987, *Cart with Peasants in a Landscape* (oil on canvas, 38 1/2 x 59 1/2 ins / 98 x 151 cm) GBP 7,000. ROME, 19 Nov 1990, *Creek with Tower, Travellers and Frigate Moored Offshore* (oil on canvas, 13 3/4 x 19 3/4 ins / 35 x 50 cm) ITL 11,500,000. LONDON, 11 Dec 1992, *Fighting between Turks and Christians* (oil on canvas, a pair, each 17 3/4 x 25 ins / 45.2 x 63.7 cm) GBP 9,900. NEW YORK, 16 June 1999, *Mediterranean Landscape with Workmen near Walled Village* (oil on canvas, 37 x 52 ins / 94 x 133 cm) USD 14,000. MILAN, 12 June 2001, *Landscape with Travellers. Landscape with Gentleman on Horseback* (oil on canvas, a pair, 12 x 17 ins / 31 x 44 cm) ITL 40,000,000. VENICE, 12 May 2002, *View of Harbour and Vessels Approaching. Landscape with Cattle Watering and Ruins* (oil on canvas, a pair, 27 x 45 ins / 69 x 114 cm) EUR 51,000. PARIS, 18 Dec 2002, *Capriccios with Peasants* (oil on panel, a pair, 11 x 13 ins / 29 x 33 cm) EUR 4,500. MILAN, 29 Oct 2003, *View of Harbour with Figures* (oil on canvas, 23 x 62 ins / 58 x 158 cm) EUR 12,000.

EISNER, Franz
Austrian, 19th century.
Active in Vienna.
Engraver.

This artist was a pupil at the Viennese academy's school of engraving and worked in Vienna. He was the brother of Joseph Eisner II.

EISNER, Joseph I, or Eissner
Austrian, 18th - 19th century.
Born 10 July 1756; died 20 April 1837.
Draughtsman.

This artist began studying at the school of engraving at the academy in Vienna in 1768; he is also mentioned at the school of architecture in 1772.

EISNER, Joseph II, or Eissner
Austrian, 19th century.
Born 15 October 1788, in Vienna; died 2 May 1861, in Vienna.
Engraver, draughtsman, illustrator.

Having studied at the academy in Vienna with Maurer, Schmutzer and Leybold, Joseph Eisner II became professor of drawing at the military academy in Wiener-Neustadt in 1822. He produced engravings after artists such as Raphael, Correggio and Giordano. He is noted for the *Dying Christ Praying for his Enemies*, after Füger; the *The Virgin at Prayer*, after Sassoferrato; the *Madonna della Seggiola*, after Raphael; the *Holy Family*, after Andrea del Sarto; the *Death of Caesar* and *Judgement of Paris*, after Füger; and *Prometheus in the Caucasus*, after Abel. His work also includes some small vignettes and the illustrations for Müller's *Natural History* after the drawings by Lumnitz.

EISNER, Rose
German, 20th century.
Born 12 April 1883, in Myslowitz (Upper Silesia).
Painter. Portraits, landscapes.

Eisner studied in Breslau (now Wroclaw, Poland) and Munich, and under Jean-Paul Laurens at the Académie Julian in Paris. She lived in Breslau for a time before moving to Berlin in 1912.

EISS, Alois
Austrian, 19th century.
Died 11 September 1874, in Vienna.
Painter. History painting.

Eiss painted a *Good Samaritan*, a *St Elizabeth* and a *St Martin* for the convent at Göttweig near Krems.

EISSELBURG, Peter. See **ISSELBURG**

EISSEMANN. See **EISENMANN** and **EISMANN**

EISSENHARDT, Johannes Kaspar
German, 19th century.
Born 8 November 1824, in Frankfurt am Main; died 11 October 1896, in Frankfurt am Main.
Painter, engraver, illustrator. Religious subjects, figures, portraits.
Kronberg Colony.

Eissenhardt studied at Frankfurt am Main at the Städel Institute with Schaeffer and worked at Kronberg. Notable early works include *Judgement of Solomon*, after Steinle; *Italy*, after Veit; and *Choir of Young Boys*. He worked on designs for banknotes in Darmstadt and in St Petersburg produced a series of engraved portraits of the tsarina Maria Feodorovna, Queen Olga of Greece and Pushkin. However, he only engraved reproductions. He is noted for various other works, including *Views of Frankfurt*, after C.G. Schütz the Elder and A. Burger; *Virgin with Angels Carrying Torches*, after Botticelli; and *Refectory*, after G. van Muyden. Eissenhardt engraved the illustrations for Duller's *Grand Duke Charles* after the drawings of Schwind, several vignettes for an illustrated volume of German poetry after J.B. Scholl and two portraits for *Art and Artists in Frankfurt* by Gwinner.

BIBLIOGRAPHY:
Wiederspahn, August, *Die Kronberger Malerkolonie*, Verlag Waldemar Kramer, Frankfurt am Main, c. 1971.

EISSFELDT, Hermann
German, 20th century.
Born 2 January 1875, in Schladen (Harz).
Painter. Portraits, genre scenes.

Eissfeldt trained at the Académie Julian in Paris, and under Heinrich Zügel and Karl von Marr at the Munich art academy. He painted some portraits, but mainly produced informal genre scenes such as *Fishermen Mending their Nets, Car Ride, Harvesting Potatoes* and *The Storybook*. After his studies, he exhibited frequently in Munich, starting in 1901. His first exhibit was a *Self-portrait*.

EISSL, Therese von
Maiden name: Oberndorfer
Austrian, 19th century.
Born 1792, in Wiener-Neustadt.
Painter.
Eissl lived in Vienna, Graz and Dresden, where she copied many famous paintings. She showed history paintings in several exhibitions in Graz from 1828 onwards.

EISSLER. See **EISLER**

EISSNER, Joseph. See **EISNER**

EISUI, real name: Hosoda Eisui, artist names: Ichirakutei, Ichirakusai
Japanese, 19th century.
Born c. 1790; died 1823.
Print artist.
Eisui was a pupil of Hosoda Eishi. He designed prints of the heads of courtesans which hint at the influence of Utamaro (1753-1806), although the stylisation makes it difficult to say that he was a portrait artist. These particular prints are nonetheless subjective and poetic.
BIBLIOGRAPHY:
Fahr-Becker, *Japanese Prints*, Taschen, Cologne, 1999.
AUCTION RECORDS:
NEW YORK, 16 Oct 1989, *Okubi-e Portrait of the Courtesan Komurasaki of Tamaya* (oban tate-e woodblock print, from the series Beauties Compared to the Five Seasons, 15 x 10 ins / 38.3 x 25.4 cm) USD 6,050.

EITAKU, real name: Kobayashi Tokusen, popular names: Hidejiro, Shujiro, artist names: Sensai, Eitaku, Issensai
Japanese, 19th century.
Born 1843; died 1890.
Painter.
Eitaku painted figures and historical subjects. At first he followed the lessons of the Kano school but later found his own style. He lived in Tokyo.

EITEL, Anton
German, 19th century.
Engraver.
Eitel was active in Düsseldorf around 1864. He engraved several plates after Fra Angelico, F. Overbeck and Holthausen. He is also noted for his *Immaculate Conception* after von Felsburg.

EITEL, Jacques, pseudonym of Eitelwein
French, 20th century.
Born 15 August 1926, in Paris.
Painter. Landscapes, seascapes.
Jacques Eitel trained in Paris at the École Boulle and then with Eugène Narbonne at the École des Beaux-Arts. He showed work at several of the annual Paris Salons - Jeune Peinture, on whose committee he sat, Automne, Artistes Français, Artistes Indépendants, Beaux-Arts, Comparaisons, Grands et Jeunes d'Aujourd'hui and the Salon de Mai, as well as collective exhibitions. He also had solo shows in Paris in 1957, 1959, 1962, 1986 and 1992, at Mulhouse, Nantes and elsewhere, in London 1959, 1972, 1979, many in New York from 1964, and in Chicago, Beverley Hills, Palm Beach and other cities. He painted landscapes full of rich plant life, and many seascapes, treating these in a spirit of synthesis of forms and with a light touch, as with watercolours.
AUCTION RECORDS:
PARIS, 6 Feb 1991, *Cotignac Village* (oil on canvas, 28 3/4 x 25 1/4 ins / 73 x 64 cm) FRF 4,000. PARIS, 20 May 1992, *Cotignac Village* (oil on canvas, 28 3/4 x 36 1/2 ins / 73 x 93 cm) FRF 7,000.

EITNER, Wilhelm Heinrich Ernst
German, 19th - 20th century.
Born 30 August 1867, in Hamburg; died 1955.
Painter, engraver. Portraits, genre scenes, landscapes.
Eitner was taught by Schönleber at the academy in Karlsruhe and Vriendt at the academy in Antwerp. His work was shown frequently in Germany, Paris and Rome.
MUSEUMS AND GALLERIES:
HAMBURG: *Spring: the Painter and Family; Valley of the Alster; Autumn in Billwärder; Portrait of Gustave Falke* - LÜBECK: *The Evening of Life*.
AUCTION RECORDS:
HAMBURG, 9 June 1983, *Autumn Landscape* (1926, oil on canvas, 31 1/2 x 39 1/4 ins / 80 x 100 cm) DEM 6,800. HAMBURG, 7 Dec 1985, *Seaside Scene* (oil on canvas, 27 3/4 x 31 1/2 ins / 70.5 x 80 cm) DEM 3,200. MUNICH, 26 Oct 1988, *Children on Seesaw* (oil on canvas, 35 1/2 x 27 1/2 ins / 90 x 70 cm) DEM 22,000. MUNICH, 7 June 1989, *Village Street* (oil on card, 20 x 27 1/4 ins / 50.5 x 69 cm) DEM 13,200.

EITOKU. See also **KANO Eitoku**

EITOKU, real name: Kano Kuninobu, childhood: Genjiro, artist name: Eitoku
Japanese, 16th century.
Born 1543, in Yamashiro Prefecture; died 1590.
Painter. Screens.
Kano School.
Eitoku was the incarnation of the Momoyama period (end of the 16th century), in the course of which warriors such as Nobunaga and Hideyoshi, ambitious men with new ideas, attempted to unify the country and assert their prestige by the sumptuousness of their dwellings, which they had decorated by Eitoku. This created a style that would soon become classical and would remain the official genre, albeit one tinged with academism, until the end of the Tokugawa shogunate (1868).

The son of Kano Shoei (1519-1592) and the grandson of Kano Motonobu (1476-1559), Eitoku was the official painter of the Ashikaga court. He embarked upon a brilliant career under the guidance of his grandfather. He quickly acquired a personal style, proof of which was to be seen from 1566 in the paintings he executed in collaboration with his father for the reception hall of the Juko-in, a sanctuary within the Daitoku-ji temple in Kyoto. The work comprises sixteen sliding doors centred on two large compositions, one of birds with a blossoming plum tree and the other of a crane beside a twisted pine. Motonobu's influence is still in evidence, but a more flowing touch breathes new dynamism into the work, as can be seen in another work of his youth, the pair of six-fold screens, the *Rakuchu-Rakugai zu byobu* representing views of the capital, Kyoto, and its surroundings. In 1567 and 1568, Eitoku and three of his disciples decorated the residence of the ministerial Konoe family, which shows that at the age of 24 he was already in charge of a workshop recognised by the court. But he largely owes his fame to the decoration of the Azuchi castle built by Nobunaga from 1576 on Lake Biwa, near Kyoto. Eitoku was to devote four years to decorating this astonishing building, which was unfortunately soon to disappear in a fire in 1582. The documents of the period attest to the unusual splendour of the whole edifice and the richness of the great polychrome compositions, accentuated with gold leaf, that adorned the rooms of the seven floors, each devoted to a single floral theme: plum blossom, peonies, red maples, all evoking the changing of the seasons. To carry out this commission, Eitoku created a new technique, the *dami-e*, which used the vivid, opaque colours of the Tosa school against a gold background. The paintings, with their thick, flowing outlines, were executed on white paper, then surrounded by rectangles of gilded paper cut out and stuck to the background. This golden space infused the polychrome painting with the most decorative effect and reflected the splendour of the period. Nothing now remains of the wall paintings of the Osaka castles built in 1583, or of the Juraku palace built in 1587 by Nobunaga's successor, Toyotomi Hideyoshi, which surpassed in splendour all the dwellings of former sovereigns.

Eitoku was assisted in his works by artists from his studio, among whom were numerous members of his family, including his younger brothers Soshu (1551-1601) and Nagonobu (1577-1654), his sons Mitsonobu (1565-1608) and Takanobu (1571-1618), and his favourite disciple and adopted son, Sanraku (1559-1635). The work was shared out room by room and he reserved the most important parts for himself.

Since he devoted himself almost exclusively to major projects, Eitoku had very little time for smaller works, only three of which survive as faint echoes of his lost masterpieces. Yet they, too, reflect the style of his mature years. Two of them are official pieces, the *Chinese Lion Screen*, in the possession of the Imperial Household Agency, and the *Cypress Screen* in the Tokyo National Museum. Although these works perhaps have a harsher quality than the works of his youth, the absence of detail proves the power of synthesis that he attained; the two lions, in white, green and brown, stand out against a gold background and seem to move in an abstract space, whilst against the gold background of the second screen a huge cypress spreads its remarkably symmetrical branches above a sheet of water of the deepest blue. The increasingly decorative emphasis tends to subordinate feeling to effect in a trend that would grow in the Kano studio.

BIBLIOGRAPHY:

Akiyama, Terukazu, *La Peinture japonaise*, Skira, Geneva, 1961. David, Madeleine, '*Kano Eitoku*' in *Encyclopædia Universalis* vol. V, Paris, 1969. Tazawa, Yutaka, *Biographical Dictionary of Japanese Art*, Kodansha International Ltd, Tokyo, 1981. Guth, Christine, *Japanese Art of the Edo Period*, Calmann and King, London, 1996.

MUSEUMS AND GALLERIES:

KYOTO (Daitoku-Ji Temple): *Plum Tree and Pine* (ink and colour on paper, sliding doors) - TOKYO (National Mus.): screen with hinoki*Hinoki byobu* (dated 1590); *Chinese Landscapes (cypress)* (ink on paper, a pair of hanging scrolls).

EIXARCH, Bartolomé de
Spanish, 14th century.
Painter.

Bartolomé de Eixarch worked on Valencia cathedral in 1395.

EIXARCH, Juan
Spanish, 14th century.
Painter.

Juan Eixarch painted frescoes in Valencia cathedral in 1393. He appears to be identical to, or a relative of, Bartolomé de Eixarch.

EIZAN, real name: Kikukawa Toshinobu, popular name: Mangoro, artist names: Chokyusai, Eizan
Japanese, 19th century.
Born 1787; died 1867.
Painter.

Eizan was the son of Omiya Kikukawa, who taught him the Kano style. Later he studied ukiyo-e painting with Totoya Hokkei and afterward worked in Edo with one of the great ukiyo-e print artists, Toyokuni. One of his disciples of Keisai Eisen.

BIBLIOGRAPHY:

Fahr-Becker, Gabriele (ed.), *Japanese Prints*, Taschen, Cologne, 1999.

AUCTION RECORDS:

PARIS, 14 Dec 1987, *Oiran Standing Undoing her Obi. Her kamuro is crouching by a hibachi* (oban tate-e woodblock print, from the series Twelve Hours of the Green Houses) FRF 3,600. LONDON, 9 Nov 1988, *The Courtesan Shinohara of Tsuruya Reading a Letter* (oban tate-e woodblock print, 14 x 9 1/4 ins / 35.8 x 23.3 cm) GBP 1,100. NEW YORK, 21 March 1989, *Geisha Climbing a Staircase with Box of Finery* (oban tate-e woodblock print, 15 1/2 x 10 1/4 ins / 39.1 x 26.3 cm) USD 4,180. LONDON, 22 March 1990, *The Courtesan Nagadayu of Okamotoya Accompanied by Two Kamuros* (oban tate-e woodblock print, 13 3/4 x 9 3/4 ins / 35.1 x 24.8 cm) GBP 418. NEW YORK, 15 June 1990, *Full-length Portrait of a Young Beauty with Umbrella* (oban tate-e woodblock print, 14 x 10 1/4 ins / 35.5 x 25.8 cm) USD 1,320. NEW YORK, 16 Oct 1990, *Prostitute Reading a Loveletter* (ink and colour on silk, hanging scroll, 12 x 21 1/4 ins / 30.3 x 53.9 cm) USD 18,700. NEW YORK, 26 March 1991, *Beauty* (ink and colour on silk, hanging scroll, 39 3/4 x 14 3/4 ins / 101 x 37.5 cm) USD 38,500. PARIS, 16 Feb 1996, *Tryptych Representing Young Women Walking in Apple Blossom Time* (oban tate-e colour print) FRF 4,800.

EIZIKMAN, Jean-Pierre
French, 20th century.
Born 19 April 1934, in Paris.
Active in Paris.
Painter. Figures.

Jean-Pierre Eizikman trained at the Bezalel art college in Jerusalem. His work has been shown in collectives including 1988, Salon des Artistes Français in Paris; and in 1993, *Painting Biennale SUD 92* at Issy-les-Moulineaux. His solo exhibitions have included 1987, Galerie Étienne de Causans in Paris; 1987, Galerie Berthet-Aïttouarès, Paris; and 1990, Galerie Margot Virgil, Paris. His dark action-painted canvases display vacant-eyed figures, sometimes half-human, half-animal, sometimes deformed, bathed in a strange light, outside time.

BIBLIOGRAPHY:

Jean Pierre Eizikman, exhibition leaflet, Gal. Margot Virgil, Paris, 1990.

AUCTION RECORDS:

PARIS, 23 March 1991, *Man with a Book* (oil/paper, 48 x 59 ins / 122 x 149.8 cm) FRF 38,000.

EJBISZ, Eugene
Polish, 20th century.
Born in Lublin.
Painter.

Eugene Ejbisz exhibited at the Salon d'Automne in Paris in 1925.

EJSMOND, Franz von
Polish, 19th century.
Born 1859, in Krogulowa (Radom).
Painter. Genre scenes, still-lifes.

Franz von Ejsmond studied under Wojciek Gerson in Warsaw. He completed his artistic training at the art academy in Munich. He exhibited work from 1880 in Cracow, Berlin and Vienna. On returning to Warsaw, he painted genre scenes which were later shown in Warsaw, Cracow and Lemberg (now Lviv, Ukraine). He painted scenes from the daily lives of Polish people.

AUCTION RECORDS:

LONDON, 20 March 1985, *Still-life with Flowers* (oil on canvas remounted on board, 38 1/2 x 26 3/4 ins / 98 x 68 cm) GBP 3,200. WARSAW, 14 March 1999, *Happiness - Interior with*

Parents and Sleeping Child (1887, oil on board, 7x9 ins / 17x23 cm) PLZ 44,000. LUCERNE, 8 Nov 2000, *After the Hailstorm* (1888, oil on panel, 13x17 ins / 32x42 cm) CHF 21,000. COPENHAGEN, 4 Dec 2002, *Model Picture* (oil on canvas, 28x20 ins / 70x50 cm) DKK 6,000.

EK, Sandor, or Aleks Keil, Alexandr Ivanovich Keil, A.K., Aks.
Hungarian, 20th century.
Born 1902, in Szentmihalyfa; died 1975, in Budapest. Also active in Germany.
Painter, engraver, poster artist. Scenes with figures. Socialist Realism.

Sandor Ek was a student in 1919 at the school of proletarian art in Budapest and got involved in Socialist Realism with the intention of exalting the proletarian class and the benefits of revolutionary Socialism. After the fall of Bela Kun's republic in 1919, he emigrated to Germany and, under the pseudonym Alex Keil, he produced posters and revolutionary engravings. He returned to Hungary in 1944 and resumed Realist figurative painting.

Ek featured in the collective exhibition *Traumfabrik Kommunismus - die Visuelle Kultur der Stalinzeit* (*Dream Factory Communism, the Visual Culture of the Stalin Period*), Schirn Kunsthalle, Frankfurt (2003).

BIBLIOGRAPHY:
Hollein, Max, et al., *Dream Factory Communism, the Visual Culture of the Stalin Period*, exhibition catalogue, Schirn Kunsthalle, Frankfurt, 2003 (text in English and German).

EKEARNY
British, 19th century.
Engraver.

Ekearny is mentioned by Nagler.

EKEGARDH, Hans
Swedish, 20th century.
Born 17 January 1881, in Kristianstad; died 14 May 1962, in Paris.
From 1902 active in France.
Painter. Figures, nudes, portraits, landscapes, urban landscapes, flowers.

From the outset, Hans Ekegardh showed an aptitude for both music and drawing. At the age of 15 he entered the Stockholm music academy, where he trained for 10 years to become a violinist. Between 1901 and 1906, when he was living in Paris, he continued his musical education and undertook tours, as well as beginning to paint. For guidance he turned to Henri Matisse, whose large colouristic expanses and bold chromatic splendours he admired. Maintaining good relations, Ekegardh salvaged the master's atelier at the Sacré Coeur convent in 1909. However, he did not become his pupil but attended the Académie de la Grande Chaumière instead.

On his arrival in France, Hans Ekegarth was particularly impressed by Rubens and Fragonard. He was also drawn to the Impressionists, especially Alfred Sisley and Auguste Renoir. He sought to convey the play of light through dashing brush stokes. He was passionate about Paris, and painted the Place de la Concorde and the Seine embankment at different times of the day. He also returned to another of his preferred themes - the Three Graces - year after year. Closely involved with all groups of living art, he was fascinated by Othon Friesz's application of colour and by André Derain's succinct classical statements. As his style of painting opened out, his nudes and portraits became more constructed and rigid. His palette attests to a research of harmony without violence. For Ekegardh, the nude was a chance to bring to the fore an idea of mysterious perfection not devoid of sensuality. He handled women with a depth of understanding that made it seem for the most part as though his models were not posing.

In 1909 he exhibited for the first time in the Salon d'Automne, where he became a member of the selection committee in 1929; he also had a show at the Salon des Indépendants. In 1910 he married Marguerite Lemaire, who painted under the name of Guy-Lemm, and he exhibited with her in the same salons, notably the Salon des Tuileries, from 1923. He showed his canvases in one-man shows in France, from 1913 in Paris, and also in Sweden - he exhibited in Stockholm in 1922 and 1930, Kristianstad in 1951, Ystad in 1952 and Malmö. The Musée Bernadotte in Pau dedicated a retrospective to him in 1968.

MUSEUMS AND GALLERIES:
BESANÇON (MBA et d'Archéologie): *Place de la Concorde* (1939); *Sleeping Woman* - KRISTIANSTAD: *Nymph* - MALMÖ: *Fontenay-le Château* (1915); *View of Longchamp* (1916); *View of Paris towards the Eiffel Tower* (1921) - NANTES (MBA): *Nude in Interior* - PARIS (Institut Tessin): *Portrait of the Artist; Portrait of Girl with Plait* (1924); *The Three Graces* (1924); *The Artist's Wife* (1924); *Portrait of an Elderly Man; Seated Woman in White; Place de la Concorde; The Artist's Studio, Rue Compans; Anemones* - PARIS (MAMVP): *Place de la Concorde* - PARIS (MNAM-CCI): *Seated Nude* - PARIS (Mus. Carnavalet): *Place de la Concorde* - PAU (MBA): *On the Banks of the Seine, Pont des Arts; Recumbent Nude* - STOCKHOLM (Moderna Mus.): *The Artist's Wife* (c. 1920); *The Seine Embankment, Pont des Arts and île de la Cité* (c. 1930) - TOURS (MBA): *Place de la Concorde; On the Embankment* - VÄSTERÅS: *Chalon-sur-Saône* - YSTAD: *Notre-Dame, Paris.*

AUCTION RECORDS:
PARIS, 16 March 1925, *Bruges*, FRF 105. PARIS, 27 April 1929, *Tub*, FRF 300. STOCKHOLM, 24 April 1947, *The Three Graces*, SEK 725. PARIS, 13 May 1981, *Woman in Landscape* (oil on card, 19 3/4 x 24 ins / 50 x 61 cm) FRF 2,350. PARIS, 6 April 1984, *Place de la Concorde* (hardboard, 19 3/4 x 25 1/2 ins / 50 x 65 cm) FRF 8,900. PARIS, 7 July 1987, *At the Racecourse* (oil on panel, 18 x 24 ins / 46 x 61 cm) FRF 4,000. PARIS, 10 Feb 1988, *Trees and Houses* (oil on panel, 11 x 13 3/4 ins / 27 x 35 cm) FRF 3,200. PARIS, 20 Feb 1989, *Woman on Sofa* (oil on canvas, 25 1/2 x 32 ins / 65 x 81 cm) FRF 14,200. VERSAILLES, 29 Oct 1989, *Reflection of Houses in Canal* (1946, Indian ink, 5 x 7 3/4 ins / 13 x 20 cm) FRF 36,000. BRUSSELS, 27 March 1990, *Village* (oil on panel, 12 1/2 x 15 3/4 ins / 32 x 40 cm) BEF 40,000. STOCKHOLM, 14 June 1990, *Still-life with Bouquet in Vase* (oil on panel, 23 1/2 x 19 1/4 ins / 60 x 49 cm) SEK 6,500. PARIS, 3 April 1992, *Panorama of Town Bordering on Forest* (oil on canvas, 21 x 25 1/2 ins / 53.5 x 64.5 cm) FRF 9,000. PARIS, 24 Jan 1996, *Sleep* (1936, oil on panel, 26 x 36 1/4 ins / 66 x 92 cm) FRF 13,800.

EKELAND, Arne
Norwegian, 20th century.
Born 1908, in Eidsvoll.
Painter. Figure compositions.
Socialist Realism.

Arne Ekeland studied under Axel Revold at the art academy in Oslo in 1928. He went on numerous study trips: in Germany, in 1932, he came under the influence of the Central European Expressionists; in 1935 he visited Italy and France, where he emulated the artists of the Italian Renaissance and the Surrealists; in 1947 he was in the USA; and in 1948 he visited Russia.

From 1930, his paintings contained an element of social and political protest in the spirit of the Neue Sachlichkeit (New Objectivity) of the German artists close to Georges Grosz and Otto Dix, but his style was also marked by a number of other influences such as primitive art, the German Expressionists, Surrealism and the Cubo-Expressionism of Picasso. From 1935 onwards he painted large compositions whose subject matter was arranged around symbolic allegories, which were sometimes highly enigmatic. In this period, which was arguably the most intense of his artistic output, he used two contrasting coloured registers: sometimes using dark tones mixed into almost muted monochrome harmony, and sometimes clashing, violent colours. In devastated landscapes or overwhelming cities, emaciated people struggle in scenes of rebellion, alluding to real or merely imaginary events. In contrast, other paintings of the same period express quiet and dreamy sensations. Following his long journey to Russia in 1948, he returned to figurative painting more in keeping with the precepts of Social Realism. Finally, after 1960, Ekeland returned to the Expressionist themes which characterise the most intensely personal and successful part of his output.

MUSEUMS AND GALLERIES:

BERGEN - GÖTEBORG - OSLO (Nasjonalgal.): *The Last Shots* (1940); *Outside Factory*; 17 paintings altogether and numerous drawings - STOCKHOLM.

AUCTION RECORDS:

LONDON, 25 March 1987, *Medviter* (1939, oil on canvas, 25 1/2 x 29 1/4 ins / 64.5 x 74.5 cm) GBP 5,500. OSLO, 6 Dec 1999, *Spring* (1948, oil on card, 24 x 20 ins / 61 x 50 cm) NOK 100,000. OSLO, 6 Dec 1999, *Mother-of-pearl Clouds II* (1940, oil on card, 24 x 20 ins / 61 x 50 cm) NOK 100,000. OSLO, 8 May 2000, *In the Temple* (oil on board, 20 x 24 ins / 50 x 61 cm) NOK 46,000. OSLO, 23 Oct 2000, *Women and Skeleton* (oil on board, 26 x 21 ins / 65 x 54 cm) NOK 160,000. OSLO, 7 June 2001, *Woman in Landscape* (oil on canvas, 35 x 30 ins / 89 x 75 cm) NOK 150,000. OSLO, 27 Nov 2001, *Hope* (1941, oil on panel, 26 x 21 ins / 65 x 54 cm) NOK 140,000. OSLO, 18 March 2002, *Imaginary Picture of Women, Jugs and a Tree* (oil on canvas, 39 x 53 ins / 100 x 135 cm) NOK 60,000. OSLO, 17 June 2002, *Fallen Warrior* (oil on canvas, 50 x 57 ins / 126 x 144 cm) NOK 120,000. OSLO, 17 March 2003, *From the Village* (1946, oil on canvas, 57 x 53 ins / 144 x 134 cm) NOK 600,000. OSLO, 19 Nov 2003, *Seated Nude* (1957, oil on canvas, 20 x 17 ins / 50 x 42 cm) NOK 36,000. OSLO, 29 Nov 2004, *The Queen* (1939, oil on panel, 28 x 20 ins / 70 x 50 cm) NOK 155,000. OSLO, 6 Dec 2004, *Star of Bethlehem* (oil on panel, 26 x 22 ins / 66 x 55 cm) NOK 90,000.

EKELS, Jan, the Elder

Dutch, 18th century.

Born 21 November 1724, in Amsterdam; died 22 November 1781, in Amsterdam.

Painter. Landscapes with figures, urban landscapes.

Jan Ekels was a pupil of Dirck Dalens the Younger. He was also an art restorer.

I. Ekels.f

MUSEUMS AND GALLERIES:

AMSTERDAM: *View of Amsterdam Dam* - AVIGNON: *View of Amsterdam* - BRUSSELS: *Townscape* - DOUAI: *View of Amsterdam.*

AUCTION RECORDS:

PARIS, 18 June 1937, *Houses next to the Canal,* FRF 585. PARIS, 20 March 1942, *View of Amsterdam,* FRF 27,000. PARIS, 28 May 1954, *View of Amsterdam Dam,* FRF 260,000. LONDON, 1 March 1972, *View of a Small Town,* GBP 850. AMSTERDAM, 26 April 1976, *View of Amsterdam* (1776, oil on canvas, 19 x 22 1/2 ins / 48 x 57 cm) NLG 68,000. LONDON, 24 April 1981, *View of a Town, perhaps Delft* (1753, oil on canvas, 15 x 19 ins / 38 x 48.2 cm) GBP 4,000. LONDON, 5 July 1991, *Street of a Dutch Town with an Itinerant Merchant Selling Fruit to a Servant* (oil on canvas, 21 1/2 x 17 3/4 ins / 54.6 x 45.4 cm) GBP 4,180. AMSTERDAM, 17 Nov 1994, *View of Ijsselstein with Town Hall* (oil on canvas, 15 x 19 1/4 ins / 38 x 48.8 cm) NLG 25,300. AMSTERDAM, 9 May 1995, *Amsterdam, Herengracht* (1764, oil on canvas, 17 x 21 1/4 ins / 43 x 54 cm) NLG 16,520. NEW YORK, 5 Oct 1995, *View of the Mint Tower in Amsterdam* (1764, oil on panel, 10 1/2 x 13 1/4 ins / 26.7 x 33.8 cm) USD 9,200. NEW YORK, 15 May 1996, *Figures Promenading along the Singel near Leidse Poort with Amsterdam in Background* (oil on canvas, 13 1/2 x 17 ins / 34.3 x 43.2 cm) USD 4,600. AMSTERDAM, 11 Nov 1997, *Amsterdam, Trippenhuis and St. Antonius* (oil on panel, 13 3/4 x 18 ins / 35 x 46 cm) NLG 22,420. AMSTERDAM, 16 April 2002, *Herengracht, Amsterdam* (1764, oil on canvas, 17 x 21 ins / 43 x 54 cm) EUR 14,000. AMSTERDAM, 16 April 2002, *Singel and the Munttoren, Amsterdam* (oil on panel, 15 x 18 ins / 37 x 46 cm) EUR 16,000.

EKELS, Jan, the Younger

Dutch, 18th century.

Born 2 June 1759, in Amsterdam; died 4 June 1793.

Painter. Genre scenes, landscapes.

Jan Ekels the Younger was the son and pupil of Jan Ekels the Elder. He worked in Paris, travelled on the Rhine in 1783 and then lived in Amsterdam.

I·Ekels·f
A^o 1784

MUSEUMS AND GALLERIES:

AMSTERDAM: *Writer Seen from Behind* - FRANKFURT AM MAIN (Städel): *Young Man Drawing; Peasant Lighting his Pipe.*

AUCTION RECORDS:

LONDON, 28 June 1929, *Town Hall; Binnenhof in The Hague* (series) GBP 24. LONDON, 14 Feb 1941, *Square in Dutch Town,* GBP 6. LONDON, 12 Feb 1942, *View of a Dutch Town, perhaps Haarlem,* GBP 13. LONDON, 8 March 1944, *Square in Haarlem with Figures,* GBP 36. LONDON, 20 Dec 1944, *View in Holland,* GBP 31. LONDON, 5 Dec 1969, *Young Woman Reading a Letter,* Gns 700. LONDON, 10 April 1970, *View of the Church of St Peter, Leiden,* Gns 1,300. AMSTERDAM, 26 April 1976, *View of Amsterdam* (oil on panel, 17 1/4 x 22 1/4 ins / 43.5 x 56.5 cm) NLG 58,000. NEW YORK, 16 June 1977, *Village Square with Numerous Figures* (oil on panel, 15 3/4 x 19 ins / 40 x 48.5 cm) USD 7,000. LONDON, 18 Oct 1989, *Pilgrim Monk Kneeling on the Steps of a Church* (oil on panel, 14 1/4 x 11 ins / 36.5 x 28 cm) GBP 1,430. AMSTERDAM, 16 Nov 1994, *Family Recital* (oil on canvas, 29 1/4 x 34 1/4 ins / 74.5 x 87 cm) NLG 4,140. AMSTERDAM, 8 Nov 1999, *View of the Prins Hendrikkade, Amsterdam* (1778, oil on canvas, 17 x 22 ins / 43 x 55 cm) NLG 8,000. LONDON, 14 Dec 2000, *Amsterdam, view of the Munt Tower and Doelenshuis on the Singel* (oil on panel, 16 x 20 ins / 40 x 51 cm) GBP 30,000. VIENNA, 1 Oct 2003, *Young Gentleman in Elegant Interior with Hunting Equipment* (oil on canvas, 19 x 17 ins / 47 x 42 cm) EUR 10,000.

EKELUND, Poul or Paul

Danish, 20th century.

Born 1920; died 1976.

Painter. Landscapes.

Ekelund painted mostly rustic landscapes, often at the height of summer or harvests. His repertoire also included a few figures.

AUCTION RECORDS:

COPENHAGEN, 28 April 1976, *Landscape* (1971, oil on canvas, 18 x 28 3/4 ins / 46 x 73 cm) DKK 4,500. COPENHAGEN, 8 April 1981, *Summer Landscape* (1963, oil on canvas, 21 1/4 x 28 3/4 ins / 54 x 73 cm) DKK 4,800. COPENHAGEN, 25 Feb 1987, *Landscape* (oil on canvas, 19 3/4 x 27 1/2 ins / 50 x 70 cm) DKK 13,000. COPENHAGEN, 4 May 1988, *Field of Golden Corn* (20 x 26 ins / 51 x 66 cm) DKK 5,000. GÖTEBORG, 18 Oct 1988, *Landscape* (oil on canvas, 23 1/2 x 19 ins / 60 x 48 cm) SEK 3,400. COPENHAGEN, 10 May 1989, *Model in Green* (oil on canvas, 26 x 22 ins / 66 x 56 cm) DKK 4,500. COPENHAGEN, 20 Sept 1989, *Rural Landscape* (oil on canvas, 20 3/4 x 25 1/2 ins / 53 x 65 cm) DKK 5,000. COPENHAGEN, 22 Nov 1989, *Fields* (oil on canvas, 19 3/4 x 26 1/2 ins / 50 x 67 cm) DKK 5,500. COPENHAGEN, 30 May 1990, *Landscape at Harvest Time* (oil on canvas, 24 3/4 x 29 1/2 ins / 63 x 75 cm) DKK 7,900. COPENHAGEN, 13-14 Feb 1991, *Harvest* (1963, oil on canvas, 24 3/4 x 29 1/2 ins / 63 x 75 cm) DKK 7,000. COPENHAGEN, 1 April 1992, *Rustic Landscape* (oil/synthetic resin, 9 3/4 x 17 3/4 ins / 25 x 45 cm) DKK 3,000. COPENHAGEN, 20 Oct 1993, *Summer Landscape* (oil on canvas, 23 1/2 x 27 1/2 ins / 60 x 70 cm) DKK 5,200. COPENHAGEN, 19 Oct 1994, *Sea with Ship* (1963, oil on canvas, 18 x 28 ins / 46 x 71 cm) DKK 5,500. COPENHAGEN, 26 April 1995, *Sailing Boat near Shore* (oil on canvas, 25 1/2 x 39 1/4 ins / 65 x 100 cm) DKK 10,000. COPENHAGEN, 16 April 1997, *Seated Child* (1955, oil on canvas, 26 1/2 x 22 1/2 ins / 67 x 57 cm) DKK 5,000. COPENHAGEN, 12-14 Nov 1997, *Landscape* (oil on canvas, 19 3/4 x 22 ins / 50 x 55 cm) DKK 5,000. VEJLE, 25 Sept 2000, *Landscape from Thy with Animals in Fields* (oil on canvas, 31 x 39 ins / 80 x 100 cm) DKK 15,000.

EKEMANN-ALESSON, Lorenz, or Echemann-Alleson

Swedish, 19th century.

Born 1791, in Sweden; died 1828, in Stuttgart.

Painter, lithographer.

After studying and practising his art in Vienna, Munich and Augsburg, Ekemann-Alesson was appointed to the post of professor and director of the newly inaugurated lithographic institute in Stuttgart. He executed pictures of animals and landscapes with animals, but his most frequent subjects were landscapes and views of architecture in the style of Adam, P. Hess and Wagenbauer. Ekemann-Alesson's best prints are *A Forest Scene* (after Waterloo) and *Landscape* (after Wynants).

EKENAES, Jahn

Norwegian, 19th - 20th century.

Born 28 September 1847, in Christiania (now Oslo); died 1920.

Painter, watercolourist, draughtsman. Figures, genre scenes, landscapes with figures.

Ekenaes is known to have been active in Norway, Copenhagen and Munich in 1892.

MUSEUMS AND GALLERIES:

MUNICH: *Trout Fishermen.*

AUCTION RECORDS:

LONDON, 9 Feb 1923, *Sailor's Head,* GBP 4. LONDON, 18 May 1925, *Raft* (1885; *Lake Scene with Fishermen* (collection) GBP 32. LONDON, 10 Jan 1968, *Children's Games,* GBP 390. NEW YORK, 14 May 1976, *Washing on a Frozen River* (1892, oil on canvas, 26 x 41 3/4 ins / 66 x 106 cm) USD 7,500. NEW YORK, 19 April 1977, *Seaside* (oil on canvas, 19 x 32 3/4 ins / 48.5 x 83 cm) USD 1,700. LONDON, 27 Nov 1980, *Fishermen on Raft* (1892, watercolour, 10 1/2 x 19 ins / 26.5 x 48 cm) GBP 1,050. COPENHAGEN, 23 March 1983, *Fishermen in Boat* (oil on canvas, 17 3/4 x 29 1/4 ins / 45 x 74 cm) DKK 33,000. LONDON, 7 Oct 1987, *Fishermen on Raft* (oil on canvas, 25 1/4 x 36 1/2 ins / 64 x 93 cm) GBP 6,200. LONDON, 23 March 1988, *River Fishermen on Raft* (1892, watercolour, 10 1/2 x 19 ins / 26.5 x 48.5 cm) GBP 2,200. NEW YORK, 23 May 1990, *Washing on a Winter's Day* (1892, oil on canvas, 26 x 41 3/4 ins / 66 x 106 cm) USD 22,000. LONDON, 28 Nov 1990, *Family of Fishermen Travelling by Boat* (1895, oil on canvas, 22 3/4 x 41 ins / 58 x 104 cm) GBP 17,600. LONDON, 17 June 1992, *Ready to Fish* (1887, oil on canvas, 11 x 7 ins / 27 x 18 cm) GBP 3,850. LONDON, 11 Feb 1994, *Family of Fishermen on Boat on Lake* (1909, oil on canvas, 23 1/4 x 42 ins / 59.1 x 106.8 cm) GBP 6,325. NEW YORK, 17 Jan 1996, *Good Catch* (1892, watercolour/paper/card, 10 1/2 x 19 1/2 ins / 26.7 x 49.5 cm) USD 2,300. LONDON, 31 Oct 1996, *Fishermen Resting* (oil on canvas, 10 3/4 x 9 ins / 27.5 x 22 cm) GBP 3,335. NEW YORK, 23 Oct 1997, *Catching a Fish in a River* (1892, oil on canvas, 53 x 98 ins / 134.6 x 248.9 cm) GBP 79,500.

EKGORST, Vasili Efimovich

Russian, 19th century.

Born 1831; died 1901.

Painter. Landscapes.

Ekgorst studied at the St Petersburg academy of fine arts, where he exhibited landscapes from 1867. His work was also shown in Philadelphia from 1876. Some of his landscapes are also reproduced in a signed album, published in St Petersburg in 1867.

MUSEUMS AND GALLERIES:

MOSCOW (State Tretyakov Gal.): *View of the Outskirts of St Petersburg.*

EKIERT, Jan or Jean

Polish, 20th century.

Born 10 December 1907, in Kombornia; died 1991.

Active in France.

Painter.

Jan Ekiert arrived in France in 1945 and attended the École des Beaux-Arts in Paris, in Eugène Narbonne's workshop, while attending André Lhote's private academy. His painting moved from structured representations in split planes according to Lhote's teaching, with references to religious symbols and myths, to a more bare canvas with scattered strokes in a sort of Abstract Impressionism. Jan Ekiert exhibited at the Salon d'Automne and the Salon de la Société Nationale des Beaux-Arts in Paris until 1957.

AUCTION RECORDS:

PARIS, 1 June 1988, *At Dusk* (c. 1960, oil on card, 15 x 18 ins / 38 x 46 cm) FRF 6,000; *Yellow Composition* (oil on canvas, 11 x 16 1/4 ins / 27 x 41 cm) FRF 2,000. PARIS, 16 Oct 1988, *Olive Trees* (1960, oil on canvas, 28 3/4 x 36 1/4 ins / 73 x 92 cm) FRF 5,500. PARIS, 24 March 1996, *Young Girl with Mandolin* (oil on canvas, 24 x 19 3/4 ins / 61 x 50 cm) FRF 5,000.

EKIESER

17th century.

Engraver (burin).

Was mentioned by Nagler. He worked on *The Art of Chivalry* and *Roman Architecture*, by Johann Jacobi.

EKIMOV, Andrei Petrovich

Russian, 18th - 19th century.

Born 1752; died c. 1830.

Engraver.

Andrei Petrovich Ekimov trained at the academy of art in St Petersburg. He was drawing instructor for the Cadet Corps. Among his known works are: *Portrait of Prince Friedrich von Anhalt, Portrait of Pavel Krinitsky, the priest, Peter the Great Receiving a Petition Attached to the Collar of his Dog Lisette* after I Akimov, *Blessing the Betrothed Peasants,* after I. Akimov, and *Old Woman in Turkish Costume* after Dietrich.

EKIMOV, Ivan Petrovich, or Yakimov, Ekikhmov

Russian, 18th century.

Born 1748; died 1807.

Painter. Religious subjects.

Ivan Petrovich Ekimov trained at the academy of art in St Petersburg.

MUSEUMS AND GALLERIES:

DOUAI: *Mother of God.*

EKIMOV, Minya

Russian, 17th century.

Active in Moscow.

Icon painter.

As a painter at the court of the Tsar, Minya Ekimov worked on the Cathedral of the Nativity of the Holy Virgin in the Monastery of Savino-Storoyev in 1650 and, in 1652, on the murals in the Cathedral of the Archangel in Moscow.

EKKEHARD

Swiss, 10th century.

Died 23 April 990, in Mainz.

Active in St Gall.

Monk, painter.

Ekkehard was the teacher of Duchess Hedwige of Swabia in Hohentwiel, and may have painted the decoration on the triumphal arch in the monastery church of St Gall.

EKMAN, Carl Anders

Finnish, 19th century.

Born 1833; died 1855, in Düsseldorf.

Painter.

Carl Anders was the nephew of Robert Wilhelm Ekman.

MUSEUMS AND GALLERIES:

HELSINKI: *Rustic Interior in Nauvo; Morannal and Oihonna* (first sketch).

EKMAN, Emil

Swedish, 20th century.

Born 1880; died 1951.

Painter. Seascapes.

Ekman was a painter of fishing fleets, who also enjoyed bringing out the play of light at dawn and dusk, rather than limiting himself to the standard, run-of-the-mill seascapes you can see in any provincial gallery on any day of the week.

AUCTION RECORDS:

GÖTEBORG, 5 April 1979, *Seascape* (oil on canvas, 32 1/4 x 51 1/4 ins / 82 x 130 cm) SEK 5,100. STOCKHOLM, 8 April 1981, *Seascape* (oil on canvas, 30 3/4 x 49 1/4 ins / 78 x 125 cm) SEK 9,800. STOCKHOLM, 20 April 1983, *Seascape* (oil on canvas, 32 x 52 1/4 ins / 81 x 133 cm) SEK 10,200. COPENHAGEN, 18 Nov 1987, *Fishing Boats on Beach* (oil on canvas, 32 x 51 1/4 ins / 81 x 130 cm) DKK 14,500. LONDON, 23 March 1988, *Fishermen on Lake at Twilight* (oil on canvas, 26 1/2 x 38 1/2 ins / 67 x 98 cm) GBP 5,500. STOCKHOLM, 15 Nov 1988, *Fishing Boat in Pelago in the Morning* (oil on canvas, 26 x 43 3/4 ins / 66 x 111 cm) SEK 19,000. STOCKHOLM, 19 April 1989, *Fishing Fleet at Sunrise* (oil on canvas, 26 1/2 x 35 ins / 67 x 89 cm) SEK 27,000. GÖTEBORG, 18 May 1989, *Seascape with Fishermen* (1931, oil on canvas, 27 1/2 x 36 1/4 ins / 70 x 92 cm) SEK 22,500. STOCKHOLM, 15 Nov 1989, *Seascape with Fleet of Fishing Boats at Sunrise* (1927, oil on canvas, 29 1/2 x 51 1/4 ins / 75 x 130 cm) SEK 23,000. STOCKHOLM, 16 May 1990, *Fishing off Skagen* (oil on canvas, 26 3/4 x 50 ins / 68 x 127 cm) SEK 36,000. STOCKHOLM, 14 Nov 1990, *Fishing Boats on Sunny Day* (1935, oil on canvas, 30 1/4 x 38 1/2 ins / 77 x 98 cm) SEK 16,000. STOCKHOLM, 29 May 1991, *Seascape with Ship in Flames and Lifeboat in Foreground* (1942, oil on canvas, 50 x 79 1/2 ins / 127 x 202 cm) SEK 7,000. VEJLE, 10 Nov 2003, *Fishing Boats in Morning Light off the Swedish Skerries* (1939, oil on canvas, 30 x 43 ins / 75 x 110 cm) DKK 16,500.

EKMAN, Nicolas

Dutch, 20th century.

Born 9 August 1889, in Brussels.

Painter, engraver, draughtsman. Figure compositions, figures.

Ekman exhibited in Paris, at the Salon des Artistes Indépendants. He specialised in wood and dry-point engravings. His finest engravings are *Dance of Death, the Lame, the Crowd, Separation.*

MUSEUMS AND GALLERIES:

AMSTERDAM - BERLIN - GLASGOW - MOSCOW - MUNICH - ROTTERDAM - THE HAGUE.

EKMAN, Robert Wilhelm

Finnish, 19th century.

Born 1808, in Uusikaupunki; died 1873, in Åbo (Turku).

Painter. Religious subjects, portraits, genre scenes, interior scenes, landscapes with figures.

After working with Sandberg at the academy in Stockholm, Robert Wilhelm Ekman travelled widely, particularly in Italy. In Paris, he studied with P. Delaroche. His paintings most frequently depict scenes of Scandinavian life.

MUSEUMS AND GALLERIES:

HELSINKI: *Villagers Resting; Beggar Family on the Road; Landscape with Village Children; The Morning Before the Exam; Greta Haapasaio Playing the Flute; Mary Magdalene at Christ's Tomb; Elk-Hunting Scene; Italian Inn; The Raising of Lazarus* - TURKU: *Woman Reading.*

AUCTION RECORDS:

LUCERNE, 2 June 1981, *Woman and Child in an Interior* (1843, oil on canvas, 17 3/4 x 13 1/2 ins / 45 x 34.5 cm) CHF 6,000. STOCKHOLM, 24 Nov 1999, *The Emigrants* (1837, oil on canvas, 29 x 36 ins / 74 x 92 cm) SEK 130,000. HELSINKI, 11 Dec 1999, *Interior Scene with Greta Haapasalo Playing Musical Instrument* (1869, oil on canvas, 32 x 45 ins / 82 x 114 cm) FIM 300,000. HELSINKI, 6 May 2000, *Woman Rocking Baby* (1839, oil on canvas, 22 x 18 ins / 55 x 46 cm) FIM 28,000. HELSINKI, 13 May 2000, *The Steamship Noden at Sea in Evening Glow* (1867, pastel, 12 x 19 ins / 30 x 47 cm) FIM 10,000. HELSINKI, 1 Dec 2001, *Resting in an Italian Grotto* (oil on panel, 6 x 6 ins / 15 x 16 cm) EUR 1,765. HELSINKI, 1 Dec 2002, *Girl with Basket of Berries* (1860, oil on canvas, 14 x 10 ins / 35 x 26 cm) EUR 3,200. HELSINKI, 1 Dec 2002, *Catching Crayfish* (oil on board, 20 x 16 ins / 50 x 40 cm) EUR 4,000. HELSINKI, 10 May 2003, *The Reproachful Mother* (1840, oil on canvas, 51 x 41 ins / 130 x 103 cm) EUR 8,000. HELSINKI, 13 Dec 2003, *Peasant Boy Smoking* (1868, oil on canvas, 22 x 18 ins / 56 x 46 cm) EUR 10,000.

EKSTEIN (frater). See **ECKSTEIN Sebastian**

EKSTROM, Marika d'

Swedish, 20th century.

Born in Niklasdam.

Painter.

Ekstrom exhibited at the Salon d'Automne, Paris.

EKSTRÖM, Per

Swedish, 19th - 20th century.

Born 1844, on the island of Öland; died 1935, on the island of Öland.

Painter. Landscapes.

Barbizon School.

Ekström's first exhibition took place around 1865. He was one of the Stockholm Bohemians, and it was in this guise that he figured in Auguste Strindberg's novel *The Red Room*, under the name of Stéllen. In 1875, he went to France, where he belonged to the 'Swedes of Paris' and the 'Swedes of Barbizon'. Thereafter, he spent five years in Normandy followed by a three-year sojourn in Paris, before returning to Sweden in 1889. He also lived and worked in Holland. His landscapes of France and Sweden show an awareness of their respective atmospheres. Sharing the Post-Romantic Realism of the Barbizon painters, he was, as an open-air painter, drawn to the Impressionists, with whom he shared both a concern to convey moments of the day and seasons and a preoccupation with the course of the sun, as is shown in *Glittering of the Sun on the Sea, the Sun Sets behind the Heath.*

P. Ekström

MUSEUMS AND GALLERIES:

GÖTEBORG: *Landscapes* - HELSINKI: *Summer Landscape; Autumn Landscape* - OSLO: *On the Banks of the Seine; Misty Morning* - STOCKHOLM: *The Sun Sets behind the Heath; Motif of Öland; In the Mountains; Glittering of the Sun on the Sea.*

AUCTION RECORDS:

STOCKHOLM, 7-9 Nov 1934, *Summer Landscape in France,* SEK 1,650. STOCKHOLM, 31 Jan 1947, *Polders in Holland,* SEK 2,600. STOCKHOLM, 3 April 1968, *Landscape,* SEK

6,600. STOCKHOLM, 8 Nov 1972, *Seaside*, SEK 9,800. GÖTEBORG, 8 Nov 1973, *Wooded Landscape*, SEK 11,600. GÖTEBORG, 24 March 1976, *Landscape with River* (1905, oil on canvas, 22 x 31 1/2 ins / 55 x 80 cm) SEK 16,000. STOCKHOLM, 20 April 1977, *Forest Interior* (1897, oil on canvas, 55 x 42 1/4 ins / 139.5 x 107.5 cm) SEK 20,000. GÖTEBORG, 5 April 1979, *Landscape with Cottage* (oil on canvas, 26 1/2 x 41 ins / 67 x 104 cm) SEK 14,000. STOCKHOLM, 8 April 1981, *Wooded River Landscape* (oil on canvas, 54 3/4 x 37 3/4 ins / 139 x 96 cm) SEK 17,500. STOCKHOLM, 30 Oct 1984, *Marshy Landscape* (1902, oil on canvas, 38 1/4 x 58 1/4 ins / 97 x 148 cm) SEK 37,000. STOCKHOLM, 4 Nov 1986, *Normandy Landscape in Summer* (1882, oil on canvas, 20 3/4 x 31 1/2 ins / 53 x 80 cm) SEK 36,000. LONDON, 24 March 1988, *Sunset in Öland* (oil on canvas, 31 3/4 x 43 1/2 ins / 80.7 x 110.3 cm) GBP 11,550. STOCKHOLM, 27 April 1988, *Reflections of the Sun on the Sea with Islets and Tree* (oil on canvas, 27 1/4 x 43 ins / 69 x 109 cm) SEK 91,000. STOCKHOLM, 15 Nov 1988, *Meadow by River Bank with Houses in Background* (oil, 19 1/4 x 31 ins / 49 x 79 cm) SEK 95,000. LONDON, 16 March 1989, *Stockholm Royal Palace and Parliament in Winter* (oil on canvas, 34 x 49 3/4 ins / 86.3 x 126.3 cm) GBP 14,300. STOCKHOLM, 19 April 1989, *Dutch Landscape with Farm at Edge of Canal in Twilight* (oil on canvas, 25 1/2 x 39 1/4 ins / 65 x 100 cm) SEK 83,000. STOCKHOLM, 15 Nov 1989, *Sunrise through the Trees* (oil, 39 1/4 x 28 1/4 ins / 100 x 72 cm) SEK 650,000. LONDON, 27-28 March 1990, *Marshes* (oil on canvas, 48 x 27 3/4 ins / 122 x 70.5 cm) GBP 22,000. STOCKHOLM, 16 May 1990, *Karlberg Canal in Stockholm* (oil on canvas, 36 1/4 x 28 ins / 92 x 71 cm) SEK 250,000. STOCKHOLM, 14 Nov 1990, *Wooded River Landscape in Summer* (oil on canvas, 39 1/4 x 28 1/4 ins / 100 x 72 cm) SEK 125,000. STOCKHOLM, 29 May 1991, *Sunrise through Poplars* (oil on canvas, 39 1/4 x 28 1/4 ins / 100 x 72 cm) SEK 350,000. STOCKHOLM, 30 Nov 1993, *Low Tide, Rocky Coast in Twilight* (oil on canvas, 32 x 46 ins / 81 x 117 cm) SEK 50,000.

EKSTUBE

Swedish.

Engraver.

Was referred to by Nagler as having engraved several portraits.

EKVALL, Emma, or Ekwall

Swedish, 19th - 20th century.

Born 18 January 1838, in Säby (Småland); died 1925.

Painter. Figures, portraits, genre scenes, interiors with figures, still-lifes.

The sister of Knut Ekvall, Emma Ekvall attended the academy in Stockholm and was the first woman to receive the royal medal from this academy. Her genre paintings show domestic scenes or children.

MUSEUMS AND GALLERIES:

STOCKHOLM (Kungliga Akademien): a portrait.

AUCTION RECORDS:

STOCKHOLM, 22 April 1981, *Still-life with Fruit* (oil on panel, 9 x 13 1/2 ins / 23 x 34 cm) SEK 5,000. STOCKHOLM, 14 Nov 1984, *Little Girl Seated in Interior* (oil on canvas, 13 3/4 x 11 ins / 35 x 27 cm) SEK 20,000. STOCKHOLM, 20 Oct 1987, *Girl in Kitchen* (oil on canvas, 19 3/4 x 11 3/4 ins / 50 x 30 cm) SEK 52,000.

EKVALL, Knut, or Ekwall

Swedish, 19th - 20th century.

Born 3 April 1843, in Säby; died 16 April 1912, in Jönköping.

Painter, draughtsman, illustrator. Genre scenes.

Ekvall attended the academy in Stockholm and then settled in Berlin, where he drew. Influenced by Knaus, he became deeply interested in genre painting. In 1889 he transferred to Rommanö in Sweden and from 1873 exhibited in Berlin. His key works are: *Before Taking a Bath, Final Agreement, April Snow, Old Couple, Welcome* and *Ten Minutes' Wait*.

MUSEUMS AND GALLERIES:

STOCKHOLM: *Mother and Child*.

AUCTION RECORDS:

COLOGNE, 18 March 1977, *Boat Outing* (1877, oil on canvas, 33 1/2 x 26 1/2 ins / 85 x 67 cm) DEM 4,400. GÖTEBORG, 8 Nov 1978, *Portrait of a Girl* (oil on canvas, 81 x 44 1/2 ins / 206 x 113 cm) SEK 9,700. NEW YORK, 28 May 1981, *Family Evening Party* (oil on panel, 28 x 23 ins / 71 x 58.5 cm) USD 19,000. NEW YORK, 19 Oct 1984, *Emigrants* (oil on canvas, 45 x 60 ins / 114.3 x 152.4 cm) USD 35,000. LONDON, 28 Nov 1986, *Happy Family* (oil on panel, 31 1/2 x 39 1/2 ins / 80 x 100.3 cm) GBP 12,000. STOCKHOLM, 20 Oct 1987, *Portrait of a Woman* (pastel, oval, 19 x 15 ins / 48 x 38 cm) SEK 10,000. STOCKHOLM, 15 Nov 1988, *Old Man Reading, with Elbows on Table and Little Girl by his Side* (oil, 10 1/4 x 7 ins / 26 x 17.5 cm) SEK 25,000. NEW YORK, 25 Oct 1989, *Reading Lesson* (oil on panel, 29 3/4 x 23 3/4 ins / 75.5 x 60.2 cm) USD 44,000. LONDON, 29 March 1990, *At Warsaw Station Restaurant* (1873, oil on canvas, 44 x 59 ins / 111.8 x 149.8 cm) GBP 33,000. STOCKHOLM, 19 May 1992, *Boat on Canal with Red Houses, near Uddevalla* (oil on panel, 18 x 24 1/2 ins / 46 x 62 cm) SEK 12,500.

EL ADAOUI, Said

Egyptian, 20th century.

Born 1938, in Alexandria; died c. 1970.

Painter.

After studying art at the University of Alexandria, Said El Adaoui was appointed a lecturer there. He showed at a number of different collective exhibitions, including the Alexandria Biennale, and also had several solo exhibitions of his works. His abstract creations are inspired by the local ornamental tradition in terms of their colours and designs.

MUSEUMS AND GALLERIES:

ALEXANDRIA (MFA) - CAIRO (Egyptian MMA).

EL ANATSUI

Ghanaian, 20th century.

Born 1944, in Anyako, Ghana.

Active in Nigeria.

Sculptor.

El Anatsui did a degree in education and took up a teaching post in sculpture at Nsukka University in Lagos in 1975. He works in wood in a 'violent' manner, sawing, burning and painting in an eclectic mix of different artistic traditions, including the Uli painting and Nok sculpture of Nigeria, which he treats in a modern way. His work is based on contemporary relationships with the sacred and the consequences of Africa's history.

He has exhibited at a number of international events and notably represented Africa at the Venice Biennale of 1990 where he received a commendation. In 1995 he was awarded the Kansai Telecastin Prize at the Sculpture Triennale in Osaka. His work was featured in the open-air exhibition *Les Champs de la Sculpture* (*Fields of Sculpture*) on the Avenue des Champs-Élysées in Paris. He has also shown his work in solo exhibitions, including at the following: the Goethe Institute in Lagos (1982); the National Museum in Lagos (1991); and the October Gallery in London (1995).

BIBLIOGRAPHY:

Picton, John, et al., *El Anatsui: A Sculpted History of Africa*, October Gallery, London, 1998.

EL BACHA, Amine

Lebanese, 20th century.

Born 1932, in Beirut.

Painter, draughtsman. Figure compositions, figures, landscapes, still-lifes.

He studied at ALBA (Lebanese academy of fine arts) from 1954 to 1957, and then in Paris, under Henri Goetz. He made trips to France, the Netherlands, Italy and Spain.

He has taken part in a number of group exhibitions, including the Paris Biennale in 1959 and that in Alexandria in 1962, the Salon des Réalités Nouvelles from 1966 to 1985, the annual salon at the Sursock Museum in Beirut, and many others. Since 1950 he has also had solo exhibitions in Beirut, Kuwait, Spain, Amman and Paris, and has won various awards.

His work includes a wide range of themes, such as compositions with figures: *The Fortune-teller* (1958), portraits: *Portrait of the Painter Jean Khalifé in a Café in Beirut* (1958), rural landscapes: *Landscape in Blue and Green* (1981), urban landscapes: *The al Jamal Hammam* (1970), interiors: *Interior of a House in Mazra'a, Beirut* (1984), and still-lifes: *Fruit in Four Sections* (1985). The execution of his paintings has changed over the years, those of the 1980s clearly demonstrating the facility he has achieved. Freshness, an apparent ease, a humorous and affectionate way of looking at things and an enjoyment of painting, give *Fruit in Four Segments* its charm.

BIBLIOGRAPHY:

Liban. Le Regard des peintres. 200 ans de peinture libanaise, group exhibition catalogue, Institut du Monde Arabe, Paris, 1989.

MUSEUMS AND GALLERIES:

BEIRUT (Sursock Mus.): paintings 1962-1985.

EL BAHR, Sarwat

Egyptian, 20th century.

Born 1944.

Painter.

Sarwat El Bahar's paintings feature a combination of abstract geometrical shapes and hints of external reality. He has shown at various collective art exhibitions in Egypt and at *Visage de l'art contemporain égyptien* (*Aspects of Contemporary Egyptian Art*), an exhibition held at the Musée Galliera in Paris in 1971.

BIBLIOGRAPHY:

Badr El-Din Abou Ghazy, *Visages de l'Art contemporain égyptien*, exhibition catalogue, Musée Galliera, Paris, 1971.

EL BAZ, Mohamed

20th century.

Installation artist. Multimedia.

He took part in the Johannesburg Biennale *Africus*, and exhibited in 1993 at the contemporary arts centre in Meymac and at the Villeneuve d'Ascq museum, and in 1994 at the Laage-Salomon gallery in Paris.

He combines photographs, video and assembled objects.

BIBLIOGRAPHY:

Pittolo, Véronique, *'Mohamed El Baz'* in *Beaux-Arts Magazine* n° 130, periodical, Paris, January 1995. *Never basta: Mohamed El Baz, Thierry Hauch*, Éd. Villa Saint-Clair, Sète, 1999.

MUSEUMS AND GALLERIES:

PARIS (FNAC).

EL BEKRI, Abdelmajid

Tunisian, 20th century.

Born 8 November 1942, in Gabes.

Painter, draughtsman.

Abdelmajid El Bekri studied art in a number of different countries, including France, Holland, Italy and Russia.

He remained faithful to the Islamic artistic tradition of organic architectural decoration but enriched it with his own imagination. His is an extremely refined art form, and combines tradition with invention and modernity.

From 1973 onwards he took part in several public exhibitions, including the Biennials of the Arab Union held at Damascus, Baghdad and Rabat; the Kuwait and Alexandria Biennials; the Triennial of Contemporary Art held in New Delhi in 1982. He has also had a number of solo exhibitions: Linz and Salzburg (1978); Vienna (1981); Tunis (1964, 1981, 1984 and 1986).

EL BELUTJI, Ibrahim. See **IBRAHIM EL BELUTJI**

EL CETOUHI, Abbas

Egyptian, 20th century.

Born 1940, in Cairo.

Painter. Figure compositions.

Abbas El Cetouhi graduated from the fine art school, where he subsequently worked as a tutor. He painted groups of people with intense expressions, sometimes within the context of contemporary dramatic events. He showed his work at several exhibitions, including *Visages de l'art contemporain égyptien* (*Aspects of Contemporary Egyptian Art*) at the Musée Galliera in Paris in 1971.

BIBLIOGRAPHY:

Badr El-Din Abou Ghazy, *Visages de l'Art contemporain égyptien*, exhibition catalogue, Musée Galliera, Paris, 1971.

EL DAWAKHLI, Abdel Hamid

Egyptian, 20th century.

Born 1940.

Painter, sculptor, ceramicist.

Abdel El Dawakhli studied at Cairo's higher academy of art, then qualified as an art teacher from the San Fernando academy in Madrid and as a master potter and ceramicist from Madrid's central school. He was appointed professor at the higher academy of art in Cairo and, from 1961 onwards, exhibited in a number of countries, including England, France and Spain. In 1965 he received first prize in the sculpture section of the Alexandria Biennale and, in 1967, he received first prize in the ceramics section of the International Biennale held in Ibiza.

BIBLIOGRAPHY:

Badr El-Din Abou Ghazy, *Visages de l'Art contemporain égyptien*, exhibition catalogue, Musée Galliera, Paris, 1971.

EL GAZZAR, Abdel Hadi

Egyptian, 20th century.

Born 1925; died 1966.

Painter, watercolourist.

After studying at the faculty of fine arts in Cairo, Abdel Hadi El Gazzar continued his artistic education in Italy. He was later appointed professor in the same faculty he had himself studied at. He often showed his works both in Egypt and abroad.

In his home country he was considered one of the first surrealist artists, and in his paintings one can detect the echo of automatic writing that the surrealists practiced. His oils and watercolours represent imaginary towns and fantastic worlds, spatial constructions and infernal machines.

BIBLIOGRAPHY:

Badr El-Din Abou Ghazy, *Visages de l'Art contemporain égyptien*, exhibition catalogue, Musée Galliera, Paris, 1971.

MUSEUMS AND GALLERIES:

ALEXANDRIA (MMA) - CAIRO (Egyptian MMA).

EL GLAOUI, Hassan

Moroccan, 20th century.

Born 1924, in Marrakech.

Painter (gouache). Figure compositions, figures, animals.

Hassan El Glaoui trained as a painter at the École des Beaux-Arts in Paris at the beginning of the 1950s under the guidance of Souverbi and Émilie Charmy. After fifteen years spent in France, he returned to Morocco in 1965.

Remaining faithful to figurative art, his work represents a continuation of the nationalist tradition in Morocco, depicting mainly cavalcades of military horses and their riders.

He showed at a number of solo exhibitions: Galerie Weil, Paris (1950); Wildenstein Gallery, New York (1952); Galerie de Paris and Ohana Gallery, London (1960); Hammer Gallery, New York (1967); Galerie Isy Brachot (1969); Galerie V (1975); and the Venice-Cadres Gallery in Casablanca (between 1976 and 1988).

BIBLIOGRAPHY:
M' Rabet, Khalil, *Peinture et identité - L'Expérience marocaine*, L'Harmattan, Rabat, apr. 1986.

MUSEUMS AND GALLERIES:
FEZ (Royal Palace Collection) - RABAT (Parliament Collection).

AUCTION RECORDS:
DOUAI, 29 March 1987, *Cavalrymen* (gouache, 25 1/4 x 19 ins / 64 x 48 cm) FRF 4,200. PARIS, 6 May 1988, *Fantasia* (gouache, 19 1/4 x 24 1/2 ins / 49 x 62 cm) FRF 3,600. PARIS, 19 Nov 1991, *Couple on Horseback* (gouache, 19 1/4 x 25 1/4 ins / 49 x 64 cm) FRF 3,500. PARIS, 12 March 1999, *Fantasia* (oil on hardboard, 30 x 42 ins / 75 x 107 cm) FRF 8,000. PARIS, 8 Nov 2000, *Horsemen* (oil on canvas) FRF 25,000. PARIS, 8 Feb 2001, *Arab Horsemen* (watercolour/gouache, 20 x 26 ins / 50 x 65 cm) FRF 10,000. PARIS, 25 Nov 2001, *Horsemen* (gouache/masonite/paper, 29 x 42 ins / 74 x 106 cm) FRF 10,000. RENNES, 3 March 2002, *Horses* (oil on hardboard/panel, 30 x 42 ins / 75 x 107 cm) EUR 850. PARIS, 15 Dec 2003, *Departure of the Pasha* (watercolour, 12 x 9 ins / 30 x 23 cm) EUR 650. PARIS, 15 Dec 2003, *Arab Horses* (mixed media/panel, 30 x 42 ins / 75 x 106 cm) EUR 11,000. LONDON, 15 Sept 2004, *Arab Horsemen* (gouache on board, 30 x 42 ins / 76 x 107 cm) GBP 2,000.

EL HANI, Nureddin
Tunisian, 20th - 21st century.
Born 5 October 1954, in Tunis.
Painter.

Nureddin El Hani finished his studies at the Tunis technology institute in 1977, and in 1980 he obtained a doctorate in aesthetics from the Sorbonne. He spent 1981-82 at the Cité des Arts in Paris.

His work uses acrylic paints in a style that is graphical, elliptical and often humorous, located somewhere between realism and abstraction.

He has taken part in public exhibitions in Tunisia, Morocco and France and has had a number of solo exhibitions, including Tunis (1979 and 1984) and Sousse (1983). In 1983, he also had a joint exhibition with the Moroccan painter Chaïbia in Tunis.

EL HUSSEINI BAYAZID, Joumana
Palestinian, 20th century.
Born 1932, in Jerusalem.
Active in Lebanon and in France.
Painter. Figure compositions.

Joumana El Husseini Bayazid arrived in Lebanon with her family in 1948 to study political science. She is a self-taught artist, having only attended a short course in Paris. She married very young and painted on the dining table surrounded by her children: at that time, she signed her works with her maiden name, *Joumana Bayazid*. After separating from her husband she moved to Paris, where she still lives and works. Her paintings are full of delicate coloured harmonies, humour and naive charm; they describe everyday events and adventures in the life of her characters, one example of which is Fatima, the daughter of the Prophet Mohammed.

Joumana el Husseini Bayazid has shown at several collective exhibitions including: annual Exhibition, Sursock Museum, Beirut (1960 to 1967), Alexandria Biennale (1969); Kuwait Biennale (1973); Baghdad Biennale (1974); Venice Biennale (1979). She has also shown at the itinerant exhibition organised by the Smithsonian Institute in Washington DC (1971 to 1973) and, since 1965, at exhibitions held in London, Tokyo, Geneva, Moscow, Madrid, Warsaw, Vienna. She has had solo exhibitions in Kuwait (1970), Bonn and Stuttgart (1971) and Beirut (1972).

BIBLIOGRAPHY:
Liban. Le Regard des peintres. 200 ans de peinture libanaise, exhibition catalogue, Institut du Monde Arabe, Paris, 1989.

EL KALMAK, Farrouk, or Farroug Beg, Farrukh Beg
Indian, 16th - 17th century.
Miniaturist.

Farrouk El Kalmak worked at the court of Emperor Akbar the Great in India. The *Akbarnama*, a manuscript record of Akbar the Great's reign Abu-al-fazl, a philosopher of the time (now in the Victoria and Albert Museum, London) has illustrations by him.

MUSEUMS AND GALLERIES:
LONDON (British Mus., Department of Prints and Drawings) - LONDON (Victoria and Albert Mus.): *Old Mullah* (c. 1615); *Akbar enters Surat* (c. 1590) - PARIS (Louvre).

EL KAMEL, Rafik
Tunisian, 20th century.
Born 4 June 1944, in Tunis.
Painter.

Rafik El Kamel studied at the school of fine art in Tunis from 1962 to 1967, and then spent the period 1968-1969 at the Cité des Arts in Paris, studying at the city's École des Arts Décoratifs under Despierre: in fact, he took his teacher's place for two years during the latter's absence, after having received his diploma in 1970. Subsequently he was appointed Professor at the school of fine arts in Tunis. He paints using acrylics on canvas and his compositions resemble abstract collages, as if he first created a collage and then reproduced it in the form of a painting. His assemblages display an elegant style and sober colouring, and often include numbers, arrows and crossed-out comments.

Rafik El Kamel has shown at numerous public exhibitions, starting with the 1966 annual exhibition held at the school of fine art in Tunis which was followed by the 1970 Salon du Mai in Paris. Subsequent exhibitions have included the group exhibition *Irtissem*, held in Tunis from 1974 to 1981, and the 1977 Biennale des Jeunes Artistes in Paris. In 1984 he won the Premier Prix awarded by the city of Tunis, together with the Premier Prix awarded at the Tunis annual exhibition of contemporary art.

MUSEUMS AND GALLERIES:
TUNIS.

EL LOKO. See **LOKO El**

EL MEKKI, Hatem
Tunisian, 20th century.
Born 1918, in Jakarta, Indonesia.
Also active in France.
Painter, illustrator, draughtsman. Cartoon films.

Hatem El Mekki was born in Indonesia but moved to Tunisia in 1924. He started to exhibit his works at the Salon Tunisien in 1934. In 1938 he won a grant to study art in Paris and, while he was there, he did some work for *Marianne*, a weekly publication. In 1939 he returned to Tunis, where he had his first solo exhibition. Later, in 1947, he went back to Paris, working as illustrator for *Combat, Carrefour* and *La Gazette des Lettres*. In 1951 he returned to Tunis for good and in 1958 he made two cartoon films about colonialism for German television. He has worked as a cartoonist for the newspaper *L'action* and has designed posters and a set of postage stamps.

His artistic style is deliberately synthetic, drawing on many materials and influences, including Jean Dubuffet. Hatem El Mekki creates simple figures whose expressiveness is achieved by deforming them. His apparently unpolished, minimalist style points to the false naivety of an artist who is a follower of the *Art Brut* school. He has had a number of solo exhibitions in various cities throughout the world, including Paris, Tunis, Cairo, Beijing and in Germany.

BIBLIOGRAPHY:

Goujon, J., *Hatim El Mekki ou la Tentation du péché*, Cérès Productions, Tunis, 1980. *Art contemporain tunisien*, exhibition catalogue, Théâtre du Rond-Point, Paris, 1986.

EL NAGDI, Omar

Egyptian, 20th century.
Born 1931.
Painter, engraver.

After studying at the faculty of applied arts in Cairo, Omar El Nagdi was appointed Professor in the same faculty. He also studied painting at the school of fine art in Cairo. Subsequently he continued his training at various art academies including Venice, Ravenna and the Ruskin Institute in LondonHis abstract paintings and engravings draw their inspiration from Arabic writing and Greek decorative architectural motifs. Their subdued nature does not detract from their elegance. Omar El Nagdi has shown his works at numerous national and international collective exhibitions, including the 1968 Venice Biennale and *Visages de l'Art contemporain égyptien* (*Aspects of Contemporary Egyptian Art*), an exhibition held in 1971 at the Musée Galliera in Paris. He has also shown work at solo exhibitions abroad and in particular in Paris.

BIBLIOGRAPHY:

Badr El-Din Abou Ghazy, *Visages de l'Art contemporain égyptien*, exhibition catalogue, Musée Galliera, Paris, 1971.

MUSEUMS AND GALLERIES:

ALEXANDRIA (MMA) - CAIRO (Egyptian MMA).

EL RAWWAS, Mohammad

Lebanese, 20th - 21st century.
Born 1951, in Beirut.
Painter, collage artist, engraver. Portraits.

He was a student at the institute of fine arts of the Lebanese University from 1971 to 1975, then studied at the Slade School of Fine Art, London, from 1979 to 1981. He lives in Beirut, where he is secretary of the association of Lebanese artists, painters and sculptors.

He took part in group exhibitions including that held at the Iraqi cultural Centre in London (1980), the *Contemporary Arab Graphics* exhibition at the Graffiti Gallery in London (1981, 1982, 1983), the International Engraving Biennale in Frederikstad, Norway (1982, 1984, 1986), Fourth International Engraving Fair at the San Francisco Museum of Arts (1983), the International Engraving Biennial, Bradford, England (1984 and 1985), the Kanagawa International Engraving Exhibition in Japan (1985), the Cabo Frio International Biennale in Brazil (1985 and 1986), and *Liban - Le Regard des peintres - 200 ans de peinture libanaise* (*Lebanon as Seen by Painters - 200 Years of Lebanese Painting*) at the Institut du Monde Arabe, Paris. He also had a solo exhibition at the Galerie Rencontre, Beirut, in 1979. He was given an honourable mention at the Iraqi Cultural Centre in London in 1980, and was awarded third prize at the first Exhibition of Contemporary Arabic Art in Tunisia and an honorary prize at the Cabo Frio Biennale.

A painter and engraver, he also produced a number of collages composed of newspaper cuttings relating to the history of Lebanon. Among his works are *Self-portrait with a Cat, A Letter, The Bride and the Storm, Relatively Unknown.*

BIBLIOGRAPHY:

Liban. Le Regard des peintres. 200 ans de peinture libanaise, exhibition catalogue, Institut du Monde Arabe, Paris, 1989.

EL RAZZAZ, Mustafa

Egyptian, 20th century.
Born 1942, in Cairo.
Painter. Scenes with figures.

In 1965 Mustafa El Razzaz graduated from Cairo's school of art. He won numerous prizes as a student and, eventually, became a tutor at the same institute.

His paintings are like surrealist collages translated onto canvas, in which the various elements are represented on different scales. They are composed of fragments of landscapes, of buildings and of Islamic symbols, of animals and figures, which together illustrate an idea as in *Land of Peace*, shown at the *Visages de l'Art contemporain égyptien* (*Aspects of Contemporary Egyptian Art*) exhibition held in 1971 at the Musée Galliera in Paris. The spirit of his compositions links them to the world of fantasy, but with a naively fresh tone.

El Razzaz has shown at various collective exhibitions in Egypt, in Latin America (1963), at the 1966 Venice Biennale, at the 1967 Montreal International Exhibition, and in Brussels and Paris (1968).

BIBLIOGRAPHY:

Badr El-Din Abou Ghazy, *Visages de l'Art contemporain égyptien*, exhibition catalogue, Musée Galliera, Paris, 1971.

MUSEUMS AND GALLERIES:

CAIRO (Egyptian MMA).

EL SAYED, Sabri

Egyptian, 20th century.
Born 1933, in Cairo.
Painter.

After graduating from the faculty of decorative arts in Cairo, Sabri was appointed professor at the same institute. He creates highly decorative compositions using the batik method: the abstract nature of their motifs gives the impression of an infinite flowering. Sabri has shown at various collective and solo exhibitions, receiving a number of prizes.

BIBLIOGRAPHY:

Badr El-Din Abou Ghazy, *Visages de l'Art contemporain égyptien*, exhibition catalogue, Musée Galliera, Paris, 1971.

MUSEUMS AND GALLERIES:

ALEXANDRIA (MMA) - CAIRO (Egyptian MMA).

EL SEGUEINI, Gamal

Egyptian, 20th century.
Born 1917, in Cairo.
Sculptor.

A graduate of the arts faculty of Cairo University, Gamal El Segueini continued his studies in Paris and then at the Accademia di Belle Arti in Rome. He was later appointed professor in Cairo.

His style is highly personal: while his sculptures are basically abstract, characterised by full, curvilinear volumes after Henry Moore, their details include certain discrete figurative features which seem give them an additional meaning, as in *Maternity* and *Our Earth*, shown at the *Visages de l'Art contemporain égyptien* (*Aspects of Contemporary Egyptian Art*) exhibition held in 1971 at the Musée Galliera, Paris. He has taken part in numerous collective and solo exhibitions in Egypt and abroad.

BIBLIOGRAPHY:

Badr El-Din Abou Ghazy, *Visages de l'Art contemporain égyptien*, exhibition catalogue, Musée Galliera, Paris, 1971.

MUSEUMS AND GALLERIES:

ALEXANDRIA (MFA) - CAIRO (Egyptian MMA).

EL SOUTOUHI, Mahmoud

Egyptian, 20th century.

Born 26 June 1940, in Kafr El Sheikh.
Painter.
Mahmoud El Soutouhi has shown his work in Egypt since 1962, and has also shown at collective exhibitions in Beirut (1969), Paris (1971) and Moscow (1972). His painting is highly influenced by the later works of Picasso.

EL TRANSITO, Master of. See **MASTERS**

EL WECHAHI, Abdul-Hadi
Egyptian, 20th century.
Born 1936, in Al Ma'sarah.
Sculptor.
A teacher at Alexandria's arts faculty, Abdul Hadi El Wechahi exhibited at the Cairo Salons from 1959 to 1966, the 1965 Paris Biennale, and also in Moscow. He has received numerous prizes in Egypt for his sculptures.

EL ZEIN, Danielle
French, 20th century.
Born 21 November 1941, in Avignon.
Painter, draughtswoman, watercolourist.
Danielle El Zein is the daughter of Michel Rodde. She studied graphic arts at the École des Métiers d'Art in Paris. She has exhibited at several collective shows, including the Salon d'Automne, where she became a member in 1981, the Salon d'Issy-les-Moulineaux in 1984 and the Salon de Bagneux in 1986. She won the watercolour prize in 1985 at the Salon de la Celle-St-Cloud.

EL-HAJJ, Fatima
Lebanese, 20th - 21st century.
Born 1953, in Al Wardaniyah.
Painter. Figure compositions, landscapes with figures.
She studied at the fine arts institute of the Lebanese University in 1974. From 1980 to 1983, she studied at the Leningrad (now St Petersburg) academy of fine arts, then went to the École des Arts Décoratifs in Paris. She became the wife of the painter Ali Chams, also born in Wardanieh. She has taken part in group exhibitions, in 1982 at the UNESCO building in Paris and in 1988 in London. In 1984, she was awarded the Picasso Prize by the Spanish Cultural Centre in Beirut, which earned her a solo exhibition there in 1985, the year in which she received the International Picasso Prize in Madrid.

Her paintings are very freely drawn, highly textured and colourful. Her drawing is a powerful but minimalist expression of the essential. The pigment, used in direct colours, as in Fauvism, varies from being simply rubbed on to being energetically impasted. *Solitary Song* (1987) sees a harsh green silhouette of a woman sitting on a beach, the yellowy orange body of a small child on her knees, around and behind the white sand squirted from the tube, a purple and red cabin, an ochre parasol with black stripes, on the horizon the deep blue line of the sea, and, above, the brushed white and blue sky and a bright purple cloud.

BIBLIOGRAPHY:
Liban. Le Regard des peintres. 200 ans de peinture libanaise, exhibition catalogue, Institut du Monde Arabe, Paris, 1989.

ELAGABALUS, or Heliogabalus
3rd century.
Born 204, in Syria; died 222, in Rome.
Painter.
Ancient Roman.
Elagabalus, Roman emperor AD 218-222, is thought to have painted a self-portrait dressed as a Syrian priest of the god Elagabalus, from whom he took his name.

ELAND, John Shenton
British, 19th - 20th century.
Born 4 March 1872, in Market Harborough.
Painter, watercolourist, lithographer, illustrator.
Portraits.
John Shenton Eland studied at the Royal Academy in London. He also studied in Paris. He painted portraits of well-known members of the English aristocracy of the time and produced illustrations for children's books. Eland exhibited in London at the Royal Academy from 1896.

ELAND, Leonardus Joseph
Dutch, 20th century.
Born 1884; died 1952.
Painter. Local figures, landscapes, landscapes with figures.
Eland painted typical aspects of Indonesia, where most of his career was spent.

AUCTION RECORDS:
AMSTERDAM, 10 Feb 1988, *Indonesian Woman Returning from Market* (oil on canvas, 11¾ x 15¾ ins / 30 x 40 cm) NLG 2,070. AMSTERDAM, 30 Aug 1988, *Indonesian Landscape with Travellers on Precipitous Path near Farms* (oil on canvas, 39¼ x 35½ ins / 100 x 90 cm) NLG 1,150. AMSTERDAM, 19 Sept 1989, *Tandjongbriok Harbour with Moored Ships* (oil on canvas, 15¼ x 23¼ ins / 39 x 59 cm) NLG 2,300. AMSTERDAM, 11 Sept 1990, *Sawmill Workers in Indonesia* (oil on canvas, 23¾ x 36 ins / 60.5 x 90.5 cm) NLG 2,990. AMSTERDAM, 18 Feb 1992, *View of Sawas in Indonesia* (oil on panel, 23¾ x 38¼ ins / 60.5 x 97 cm) NLG 4,025. AMSTERDAM, 11 April 1995, *The Steamer 'Op ten noort' of the Royal Maritime Company in Singapore Harbour* (oil on canvas, 29 x 42¾ ins / 73.5 x 108.5 cm) NLG 4,248. AMSTERDAM, 7 Nov 1995, *Mountainous Landscape with Numerous Travellers at Sawa (Sumatra)* (oil on canvas, 23½ x 31½ ins / 60 x 80 cm) NLG 6,136. SINGAPORE, 27 Sept 1997, *Planting Padi* (oil on canvas, 25¼ x 30 ins / 64.25 x 76.5 cm) SGD 5,750. SINGAPORE, 28 March 1999, *Volcano Landscape* (oil on canvas, 27 x 48 ins / 69 x 122 cm) SGD 5,000. SINGAPORE, 28 March 1999, *Sawah* (oil on canvas, 30 x 54 ins / 77 x 138 cm) SGD 7,000. SINGAPORE, 2 April 2000, *Sibajak, Sumatra* (oil on canvas, 32 x 40 ins / 81 x 101 cm) SGD 8,000. SINGAPORE, 6 Oct 2002, *Landscape* (oil on board, 18 x 14 ins / 45 x 35 cm) SGD 4,800. SINGAPORE, 12 Oct 2003, *River Landscape. Moonlit Village* (oil on canvas, two works, 24 x 31 ins / 60 x 80 cm) SGD 6,500. SINGAPORE, 12 Oct 2003, *Forest Landscape* (oil on canvas, 59 x 39 ins / 150 x 100 cm) SGD 8,000. AMSTERDAM, 16 March 2004, *Indonesian Landscape with Figures, Ox-carts in the distance* (oil on canvas, 36 x 24 ins / 91 x 60 cm) EUR 3,800. SINGAPORE, 4 April 2004, *View of a Lake* (oil on canvas, 32 x 40 ins / 81 x 101 cm) SGD 8,000.

ELANDT, Hendrik, or Eland
Dutch, 18th century.
Died 1705; buried 21 September in Amsterdam.
Active in Amsterdam.
Draughtsman, engraver.
Hendrik Elandt was related to Cornelis Elandts.

ELANDTS, Cornelis, or Elands or Elandt
Flemish, 17th century.
Died after 1666.
Active in The Hague from 1660.
Painter, draughtsman, engraver (etching). Urban landscapes, topographical views. Maps.
Flemish School.

MUSEUMS AND GALLERIES:
THE HAGUE: *View of Scheveningen in 1570* (copy of an older painting); *Plan of The Hague in 1570* (copy of an older painting).

ELANSBERGHE, Willem van
Dutch, 18th century.

Active in Leiden from 1703 to 1726.
Painter.

ELASIPPUS
5th century BC.
Active before 450 BC.
Painter.
Ancient Greek.

Elasippus, whose place of birth is unknown, was one of the first Greek painters to use wax in painting.

ELAUTER, Georges. See **SEMIGINOWSKI Jersy**

ELB, Carl
German, 19th century.
Born 6 April 1817, in Dresden; died 1881, in Dresden.
Painter. Genre scenes, portraits.

Elb studied at the academies in Dresden and Düsseldorf. He settled at Dresden, where he exhibited portraits almost every year. His genre paintings include *Young Winegrower from the Rhine Region* and *Young Girl Dressing*.

MUSEUMS AND GALLERIES:
DRESDEN: *Portrait of the Actor Emil Devrient*.

ELBANO, Méndez Osuna
Venezuelan, 20th century.
Born 1918, in Tovar (Merida).
Painter.

Mendez-Osuna Elbano studied at the school of fine arts in Caracas and in 1948 exhibited at the American-Venezuelan centre in Paris.

ELBAZ, André
Moroccan, 20th century.
Born 26 April 1934, in El Jadida.
Also active in France.
Painter, draughtsman, lithographer.

André Elbaz studied at Rabat's school of graphic art while at the same time training in the theatre. He began painting in 1955 and moved to Paris two years later. In 1960 he studied lithography at the École des Beaux-Arts and first showed in 1959 at the Salon d'Hiver. This was followed by other collective exhibitions, including the Salon de la Jeune Peinture (1960), the Salon des Surindépendants, the Salon de l'École Française, and at the Biennale des Jeunes Artistes (1961, 1963, 1965, 1967 and 1973). In 1961 he exhibited at Balliol College, Oxford University. Since 1959 he showed work in several international exhibitions, including *Six peintres marocains à Paris*, an exhibition held at the Galerie Nationale de Tunis.

After a long period of expressionist-inspired creations, depicting famous people or crowds milling about in indistinct spaces, André Elbaz began to be influenced by abstract art. He completed a number of series of drawings, accompanied by lithographs, such as *Sewers, Cartography, Wanderings, The Augurs, Return of the Bird, Trapeze Artists, Icares, Inventory, Confrontation* and *Forced Silence*.

ELBERTS, Hendrick
Dutch, 17th century.
Active in Amsterdam from 1660 to 1679.
Painter.

ELBERTS, Jan
Dutch, 16th century.
Active in Hoorn in 1532.
Painter.

ELBFAS, Jakob Henrik
Swedish, 17th century.
Born in Livonia (now Latvia); died 1664, in Stockholm.
Painter. Portraits.

Elbfas was a court painter in Stockholm and did portraits of many of the leading personalities of the day, such as King Gustavus Adolphus II, Maria Eleanor, and General Axel Oxenstierna.

ELBING, Christian
German, 18th century.
Active in Oels (now Olesnica, Poland) in 1789.
Painter.

ELBING, Hans Jacob
German, 17th century.
Active in Regensburg c. 1641.
Painter.

ELBING, Josef
German, 18th century.
Active in Landshut (Bavaria).
Painter.

MUSEUMS AND GALLERIES:
MUNICH (Bayerisches Nationalmus.): *Portrait of a Woman of the Bourgeoisie* (1760, signed and dated).

ELBO, José
Spanish, 19th century.
Born 26 March 1804, in Ubeda; died before 1846.
Painter, draughtsman.

José Elbo came from a family of moderate means; he learned only drawing and painting. Having come to Madrid as a young man he received the patronage of José Aparicio and Ceán Bermúdez and was awarded a grant to study in Rome by King Ferdinand VII. Elbo is known for his *Plaza de Toros in Madrid, Smuggler, Woman Bathing* and *Leda*. His work appeared in the famous *Liceo* exhibition which, in 1846, paid a somewhat belated homage to Goya, an artist much misunderstood until that time.

BIBLIOGRAPHY:
Laínez Alcalá, R., '*El pintor Elbo en el Museo Romántico*' in *Archivo Español de Arte*, vol xiv/1, 1940-41.

AUCTION RECORDS:
LONDON, 10 March 1965, *Picadors; Bulls Crossing a River* (two canvases) GBP 500. LONDON, 20 Oct 1998, *Horsemen; Horseman in Field* (oil on canvas, a pair, 26 x 34 ins / 66 x 86 cm) GBP 26,000. SAN FRANCISCO, 16 May 2001, *Figures Merrymaking Outside a Tavern* (1841, oil on canvas, 26 x 36 ins / 66 x 91 cm) USD 45,000. MADRID, 25 Sept 2001, *Dance Outside Inn* (1841, oil on canvas, 26 x 36 ins / 66 x 92 cm) ESP 6,500,000. MADRID, 12 March 2002, *Venta de la Trinidad* (1841, oil on canvas, 26 x 37 ins / 66 x 93 cm) EUR 27,500. MADRID, 27 May 2003, *Venta de la Trinidad* (1841, oil on canvas, 26 x 37 ins / 66 x 93 cm) EUR 20,000.

ELBON
British, 18th century.
Engraver.

ELBRUCHT, Jan van der, or Hans or Elburcht, also known as Jan van Elsborch or Cleen-Hansken (Little Jan)
Flemish School, 16th century.
Painter, draughtsman. Religious subjects, seascapes.
Antwerp School.

Jan van der Elbrucht was a member of the Antwerp Guild in 1535, master of Hameken der Kunderen in 1540 and master of Melsen Salebos in 1551. In the cathedral of Onze Lieve Vrouw in Antwerp he painted a *Miraculous Draught of Fishes* for the altar dedicated by the fishermen. He was received into the Antwerp Guild of St Luke in 1536.

AUCTION RECORDS:
PARIS, 1858, *Seascape* (pen drawing with colour wash) FRF 6. BRUSSELS, 10 March 1964, *Miraculous Draught of Fishes*, BEF 240,000.

ELBURG, Hansje van, or Elburgh or Elburch or Elburcht, called Hanskin
Flemish School, 16th century.

Born 1500, in Elburg; died 1571, in Antwerp.
Painter. Historical subjects.
Likely to be the same person as Jan Elbrucht, this artist collaborated with Frans Floris.

ELCANO
Italian, 18th century.
Active in Germany.
Engraver (metal).
In 1733, Elcano engraved a silver plaque with the arms of the Grand-Elector of Westphalia, to commemorate the laying of the foundation stone of the monastery of the Brothers of Mercy in Münster.

ELCAREATA, Bernardo
Spanish, 17th century.
Active in Santo Domingo.
Sculptor.
Bernardo Elcareata was a pupil of Pedro Arbulo Marguvete. He carved statues of *The Virgin, St Michael, St Peter and St Dominic* for the retable at San Pedro de Vergara.

ELCHANINOV, Martin
Russian, 17th century.
Icon painter.
In 1660, Martin Elchaninov worked on the murals in the Kremlin church of the Archangel.

ELD, George
British, 19th century.
Born 1791, in Coventry; died 22 May 1862, in Coventry.
Engraver (etching).
George Eld made several copies of ancient monuments in Coventry.

ELDEN, Toomas van
Dutch, 18th century.
Active in The Hague in 1720.
Painter.

ELDER, Arthur John
British, 19th - 20th century.
Born 28 March 1874, in London.
Painter, engraver, designer.
Arthur John Elder studied under Walter Sickert at the Royal Academy in London and under Theodore Roussel, Charles Huard, David Muirhead and James Pryde. He was a member of the Chelsea Art Club and the Junior Art Workers' Guild. In 1901 he was awarded a medal at the Crystal Palace Exhibition.

ELDER, Charles
British, 19th century.
Born 1821; died 1851, in London.
Painter. History painting.
Charles Elder exhibited at the Royal Academy from 1845 until his death in 1851. The works he sent to these exhibitions included: *Sappho* in 1845; *Death of Mark Antony* in 1847; *Celia and Rosalind* and *Ruth* in 1848, and *Jael* in 1850.

ELDER, William
British, 17th century.
A Scot who lived in London c. 1680.
Engraver.
William Elder was employed by a bookseller. He executed several portraits, including a self-portrait, and portraits of the physicist Sir Theodore de Mayerne, the astrologer George Parker, the theologian J. Pearson, the Archbishop of Canterbury W. Sancroft and Admiral Lord Edward Russel (among others).

ELDEROGLU, Abidin
Turkish, 20th century.
Born 1901, in Denizli.
Painter.
Abidin Elderoglu studied in Istanbul until 1926, when he left to live and work in Paris. There he studied under Albert Laurens and then, in 1930, under André Lhote. Subsequently he returned to his home country, settling in Ankara.

His painting is a combination of abstraction and calligraphy evoking the traditional Turkish decorative style, where signs and curvilinear, S-shaped strokes intermingle.

ELDH, Carl Johan
Swedish, 19th - 20th century.
Born 1873, in Film; died 1955.
Sculptor. Statues, busts, low reliefs, monuments.
Eldh was in Paris between 1898 and 1899. He was a pupil of Antoine Injaert, and also worked at the Calarossi Academy under the guidance of Auguste Rodin. While he was still in Paris, his work was shown at the Salon des Artistes Français on the strength of having been awarded a distinction at the 1900 Exposition Universelle and a third class medal in 1902. In 1929, he participated in the Exposition de l'Art Suédois at the Musée du Jeu de Paume. In 1956, he presented a *Bust of the King of Sweden* to the sculpture collection at the Musée Rodin. He was made a member of the art academy in Stockholm. Noteworthy are his *Bust of Auguste Strindberg* of 1903, *Eve* in bronze, *Daggkapa, Statue of a Woman* in marble, *Girl Reading; Resurrection* a low relief altarpiece, *Bust of Oscar II; Bust of Olof Rudbeck*. He was an official portraitist and handled his subjects with classical Realism. His repertoire also included allegorical subjects, including *Innocence*, in marble and *Evening*.

MUSEUMS AND GALLERIES:
COPENHAGEN (Ny Carlsberg Glyptotek): *Maternal Concerns* (marble) - GÖTEBORG: *Gunnar Wennerberg* (statuette) - STOCKHOLM: *Auguste Strindberg* (monumental bust); *Young Woman* (full-length statuette); *Youth* (bronze) - STOCKHOLM (Nordiska Mus.): *Low Relief* (granite) - UPPSALA (Universitet Konstsamling): *Mother* (bronze).

AUCTION RECORDS:
STOCKHOLM, 24 April 1980, *Standing Nude* (bronze, h. 34 1/4 ins / 87 cm) SEK 16,000. STOCKHOLM, 26 April 1982, *Innocence* (bronze, h. 17 3/4 ins / 45 cm) SEK 13,000. STOCKHOLM, 26 April 1983, *Dancer* (bronze, h. 74 3/4 ins / 190 cm) SEK 130,000. HONFLEUR, 9 April 1985, *Seated Nude* (1905, white marble, h. 55 ins / 140 cm) SEK 20,000. STOCKHOLM, 13 Nov 1986, *Girl Seated* (patinated bronze, h. 9 3/4 ins / 25 cm) SEK 26,000. STOCKHOLM, 21 Oct 1987, *Girl Seated* (patinated bronze, h. 9 3/4 ins / 25 cm) SEK 30,000. LONDON, 23 March 1988, *Bust of Auguste Strindberg* (plaster, h. 4 3/4 ins / 12 cm) GBP 715. STOCKHOLM, 6 June 1988, *Standing Woman* (bronze, h. 22 ins / 55 cm) SEK 15,500. STOCKHOLM, 15 Nov 1988, *Youth* (bronze, h. 4 1/4 ins / 11 cm) SEK 14,000. LONDON, 16 March 1989, *Innocence* (bronze, h. 34 1/4 ins / 87 cm) GBP 15,400. STOCKHOLM, 19 April 1989, *Couple of Nude Lovers* (bronze, h. 7 3/4 ins / 20 cm) SEK 22,000. STOCKHOLM, 5-6 Dec 1990, *In Lane* (1907, green-patinated bronze, h. 11 ins / 28 cm) SEK 25,000. STOCKHOLM, 30 May 1991, *Nymph* (green-patinated lost-wax bronze, h. 11 1/2 ins / 29.5 cm) SEK 16,000. STOCKHOLM, 18 May 1999, *Brita - Nude Girl Standing* (c. 1909, patinated bronze, h. 11 ins / 27 cm) SEK 19,000. GÖTEBORG, 2 June 1999, *Seated Girl* (1904, patinated bronze) SEK 24,000. STOCKHOLM, 28 Nov 2000, *Brita - Seated Girl* (carved pear wood, h. 13 ins / 34 cm) SEK 33,000. STOCKHOLM, 28 Nov 2000, *The Dance* (gold-patinated bronze, h. 11 ins / 28 cm) SEK 38,000. STOCKHOLM, 28 Nov 2001, *Youth - Nude Boy and Girl Holding Hands* (gold-patinated bronze, h. 16 ins / 41 cm) SEK 29,000. STOCKHOLM, 28 Nov 2001, *Innocence* (dark patinated bronze, h. 17 ins / 44 cm) SEK 33,000. STOCKHOLM, 28 May 2002, *Linnea* (brown patinated bronze, h. 13 ins / 33 cm) SEK 37,000. STOCKHOLM, 4 Dec 2002, *Small Girl Kneeling* (patinated bronze, h. 28 ins / 70 cm) SEK 30,000. STOCKHOLM, 4 June 2003, *Ariadne* (1899, dark patinated bronze, h. 10 ins / 25 cm) SEK

18,000. STOCKHOLM, 2 Dec 2003, *Young Girl* (1904, dark patinated bronze, h. 10 ins / 25 cm) SEK 30,000. STOCKHOLM, 25 May 2004, *Ariadne* (1899, bronze, h. 10 ins / 26 cm) SEK 24,000.

ELDNER, Valentin. See **ELNER**

ELDRED LEMUEL, D.
American, 19th - 20th century.
Born 1848; died 1921.
Painter, engraver. Landscapes, seascapes.

D. Eldred Lemuel exhibited in New York from 1889 to 1892. The works exhibited mainly featured seascapes.

AUCTION RECORDS:
CHICAGO, 4 June 1981, *New Hampshire Landscape* (1878, oil on canvas, 26 x 46 ins / 66 x 117 cm) USD 1,200. EAST DENNIS, 30 July 1987, *Sailing Ships at Sea* (oil on canvas, 16 x 26 ins / 40.5 x 66 cm) USD 3,700.

ELEAU, Léon
French, 18th century.
Born c. 1738; died 4 July 1794.
Active in Paris.
Sculptor.

ELÉAZAR, or Eléazard
French, 18th century.
Painter.

About 1760 Eléazar carried out an altar painting for the church of Bény-Bocage (Calvados).

ELECTUS (Brother), real name Zwinner
Bohemian School, 17th century.
Active in Prague.
Draughtsman.

Brother Electus produced drawings of holy sites in Palestine. They were engraved on copper by D. Wussin.

ELEFTHERIOU, Lily
Greek, 20th century.
Painter.

Lily Eleftheriou painted a series of faceless torn bodies from which emanates a violent feeling. She featured in collective exhibitions (Salon de Mai in Paris) and in solo shows including: Maison de la Grèce, Paris (1982).

ELEKFY, Jeno
Hungarian, 20th century.
Born 1895.
Painter, watercolourist, graphic designer.

Jeno Elekfy studied at the school of fine art in Budapest and then taught watercolours there, from 1940 to 1946 in particular. He exhibited his paintings in individual exhibitions in 1930 and 1955.

BIBLIOGRAPHY:
Hongrie 68, Pannonia, Budapest, 1968.

MUSEUMS AND GALLERIES:
BUDAPEST (Magyar Nemzeti Gal.): watercolours.

ELEMENTO, Nathalie
French, 20th - 21st century.
Born 1965, in St-Nazaire.
Installation artist.

Nathalie Elemento was a student at the École des Beaux-Arts in Paris before going on in 1991 to study fine arts at the Institut des Hautes Études en Arts Plastiques. In 1988, she abandoned painting in favour of sculpture. In 1989, and again in 1992, she was awarded a FIACRE bursary from the Ministry of Culture. In 1990, she spent a year in Great Britain on an Erasmus European exchange programme. In 1994, she was a resident at the Villa Medici in Rome. She lives and works in Paris.

Elemento's work, chiefly in wax and lead, consists of installations, structures, and puzzles, of which each piece, such as a door, a box or a projector, is sold separately. She is attempting in her work to create an autonomous place where 'the part has nothing to do with the whole', and where separation permits new creation.

Elemento has exhibited at collective shows, notably at the Salon de la Jeune Peinture in Paris and the Salon de Montrouge, at the FIAC (Foire Internationale d'Art Contemporain) in Paris, and, in 1997, at the Contemporary Art Biennale in Lyons. She has shown her works in solo exhibitions as follows: 1993, Galerie du Forum St-Eustache, Paris; 1994, Galerie Nationale du Jeu de Paume, Paris, Villa Medici, Rome, the Stockholm centre for contemporary art; 1995, Ho-Am Museum, Seoul, and Galerie Météo and Le Monde de l'Art, Paris; 1996, Galerie Nathalie Obadia, Paris, and Centre d'Art Contemporain, Vassivière; and 1999, *France, a New Generation*, Madrid.

BIBLIOGRAPHY:
Nathalie Elemento - Tu vois le tableau, exhibition catalogue, Gal. nationale du Jeu de Paume, Paris, 1994. Boulbès, Carole, '*Nathalie Elemento enfant de Saturne*' in *Art Press* n° 216, periodical, Paris, September 1996.

MUSEUMS AND GALLERIES:
PARIS (FNAC): *Au secours, ma Bosse* (1994).

ELEMOSINA. See first name

ELEN, Mia
French, 20th century.
Painter.

Mia Elen joined the Société du Salon d'Automne in Paris in 1919. He was a member of its judging panel in 1921.

ELEN, Philip West
British, 19th century.
Painter. Landscapes.

Philip West Elen is regarded as one of the most prolific English landscape painters. Between 1838 and 1872 he exhibited no less than 240 works, notably at the Royal Academy and the Suffolk Street Gallery in London.

AUCTION RECORDS:
LONDON, 29 March 1983, *On the Surrey Hills near Dorking* (1855, oil on canvas, 21 x 32 ins / 53.5 x 81 cm) GBP 550.

ELENA, Giuseppe
Italian, 19th century.
Born 1801; died 1867.
Painter, engraver. Portraits, landscapes.

Giuseppe Elena made a lithographed portrait of Canning in 1828. His other well-known works as a lithographer include *Scenes from the Crusades*; a series of plates of *Historical Costumes*; and *Popular Dress in Lombardy*. As a painter, he exhibited landscapes and a *Portrait of the Flute Virtuoso Picchi* at exhibitions held at the Accademia di Brera in Milan.

AUCTION RECORDS:
MILAN, 12 Dec 1985, *S Lorenzo Church in Milan* (1833, oil on canvas, 29 1/2 x 38 1/2 ins / 75 x 98 cm) ITL 44,000,000.

ELENETTI, Antonio
Italian, 18th century.
Born 1696, in Verona; died 14 June 1767, in Verona.
Painter.

A pupil of S. Brentana and a member of the academy at Verona, Elenetti produced religious paintings, some of which survive: *St Anthony* for the church of Ognissanti, now S Maria della Scala; a *Madonna with St Gaetano* in the sacristy of the church of St Nicholas; a *Madonna with Saints* for S Fermo Maggiore; the *Apostles* in the church of the same name, and an altarpiece showing *St Roch and St Sebastian*, in the church of S Paolo.

ELERS, Hans
German, 16th century.
Active in Lüneburg.
Sculptor (wood).

Between 1576 and 1580, Elers worked at the church of Our Lady at Lüneburg.

ELERS, J. G.
German, 18th century.
Engraver. Landscapes.
A jurist and engraver, Elers worked in Regensburg at the end of the 18th century. He engraved five landscapes after J.G. Kraer.

ELESKIEWICZ, Stanislas
Polish, 20th century.
Born 29 February 1900, in Warsaw; died 1963, in France.
Active in France from 1920.
Painter. Figures, landscapes, landscapes with figures.
Designs for stained glass, designs for mosaics.
Stanislas Eleskiewicz studied at the academy of fine art in Warsaw and at the school of fine art in Athens. He travelled to Persia, Greece and Italy. He was briefly acquainted with Modigliani in Paris.

He produced stained glass windows, mosaics and engraved glass and was known among the artists in Paris in the inter-war years for his lyrical strength. An Expressionist, he mixed the tragic, grotesque, nostalgic and poetic in the same atmosphere. He was somewhat forgotten after World War II.

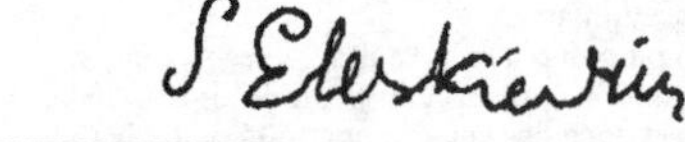

AUCTION RECORDS:
PARIS, 27 April 1932, *Village at Night*, FRF 87. PARIS, 29 June 1945, *On the Front: The Thinker; On the Reverse: Same Subject* (graphite, study) FRF 7,850. PARIS, 24 Feb 1947, *Vagrants*, FRF 4,200; *Elegant Woman*, FRF 1,000. PARIS, 30 April 1947, *Meeting*, FRF 2,100. PARIS, 18 June 1991, *Man Sitting at Table* (oil on card, 20 x 25 1/2 ins / 50.5 x 65 cm) FRF 3,800. PARIS, 10 Feb 1993, *Park Scene* (oil on card, 15 x 18 ins / 38 x 46 cm) FRF 4,800. PARIS, 6 Nov 1995, *Allegory* (oil on panel, 22 3/4 x 31 ins / 58 x 78.5 cm) FRF 10,000. PARIS, 30 May 2001, *Village Street* (oil on panel, 26 x 31 ins / 65 x 80 cm) FRF 33,000. WARSAW, 10 March 2002, *Man in Hat Sitting at Table* (oil on board, 15 x 18 ins / 38 x 46 cm) PLN 12,000. CALAIS, 9 Nov 2003, *Partie de Des* (oil on card/canvas, 18 x 22 ins / 46 x 55 cm) EUR 1,550.

ELESLEY, Arthur
British, 19th - 20th century.
Active in England.
Painter.
Arthur Elesley is mentioned by Florence Levy.
AUCTION RECORDS:
NEW YORK, 18-19 and 20 April 1906, *Old Friends*, USD 450.

ELEUSINIUS
1st century.
Active in Athens.
Sculptor.
Ancient Greek.
Eleusinius is known only from a signature on a fragment of a statue of a female figure, the remains of which were found at Olympia.

ELEUTER, Georges. See **SEMIGINOWSKI Jersy**

ELEUTHÈRE DU PRET
Flemish School, 15th century.
Illuminator.
Tournai School.
Eleuthère du Pret was a pupil of Jacques Daret in 1436 and a master in Tournai in 1438.

ELEUTHERIADE, Micaela or Michaela
Romanian, 20th century.
Born in Bucharest.
Painter.
Micaela Eleutheriade was praised by national critics for her qualities of discreet, simple and sincere intimism. She exhibited in Paris at the Salon d'Automne and the Salon des Artistes Indépendants.

ELEUTHERIADIS, Stephan
Romanian, 20th century.
Born 26 September 1922, in Mangalia.
Active in Brazil from 1951.
Painter.
Stephan Eleutheriadis graduated from the faculty of architecture in Bucharest in 1948. He taught himself to paint and received advice from his Romanian painter friends. He went through several periods and styles from Socialist Realism to more constructed representation, then an abstract period returning to landscapes of Mangalia, his home town, and finally to figure compositions. He had already taken part in a collective exhibition in Bucharest in 1947 but his painting really took off when he settled in Brazil, where he carried out brilliant work as a architect. His work featured in collective and in solo exhibitions, including: Rio de Janeiro (1956, 1962, 1965, 1969, 1979) and São Paulo in 1986.
BIBLIOGRAPHY:
Jianou, Ionel, *Romanian Artists and the West*, American Romanian Academy of Arts and Sciences, Los Angeles, 1986.

ELEUTHERUS, or Eloitheros
6th century BC.
Born in Athens; died at the end of the 6th or at the beginning of the 5th century BC.
Sculptor.
Ancient Greek.
Eleutherus is known only from a signature on the fragment of a base of a statue found in the ruins of the Acropolis.

ELEWRES, Jozef
Polish, 17th century.
Painter.
Jozef Elewres was a painter at the court of King John Sobieski III.

ELEWYT, François van
Flemish, 18th century.
Active in Mechelen.
Sculptor.
Flemish School.
In collaboration with M. van de Voord and Th. Verhagens, François van Elewyt carried out sculptures in churches in Mechelen, including the choir stalls of the church of St John.

ELEWYT, Jan van
Flemish, 18th century.
Died September 1744, in Mechelen.
Active in Mechelen in 1702.
Sculptor.
Flemish School.
Jan van Elewyt executed the high altar and two smaller altars in the church of the Cloister of Bethlehem in Mechelen.

ELEY, Mary
British, 19th century.
Active in London.
Painter. Genre scenes.
Mary Eley exhibited in London from 1874 to 1897, notably at the Royal Academy and Suffolk Street Gallery.
AUCTION RECORDS:
NEW YORK, 23 Jan 1903, *Children and Little Dogs*, USD 700.

ELEZADI, Miguel, or Lezalde, Lezaldi or Hizaldi
Spanish, 17th century.

Born in Elizondo (Navarre); died 3 February 1622, in Valladolid.
Sculptor.
Miguel Elezadi was the son of an associate of the Holy Office. In 1621 he married Damiana Fernández, daughter of his master Gregorio Fernández at the church of San Ildefonso. He died shortly thereafter, leaving his wife a widow at the age of fourteen years three months.

ELFEN (brothers)
German, 17th century.
Active in Hildesheim (near Hanover).
Sculptors (wood).
The Elfen brothers were lay brothers at the monastery of St Michael. They executed the high altar representing the Passion in the church of St Michael, a work that was later moved to the cathedral at Hildesheim. Subsequently they worked on a wing of the altar in the church of St Paul featuring scenes from the life of Mary, now in the Cumberland Gallery in the provincial museum in Hanover.

ELFEN, Alfred (Mme)
Belgian, 19th century.
Born 15 August 1833, in Antwerp.
Engraver (etching).

ELFEN, Fria
Austrian, 20th century.
Born 1934, in Vienna.
Collage artist.
Fria Elfen attended the art Akademie der Bildenden Künste in Vienna around 1958.

ELFERDING
Russian, 18th century.
Active in St Petersburg.
Painter.
Elferding worked on the decoration of the reception rooms of the Winter Palace, with the Italian artists Fontebasso Barozzi and Urbani.

ELFERT, Theodor
German, 19th century.
Born 1 May 1868, in Berlin.
Painter.
A pupil of Eugen Bracht at the Berlin academy, Elfert was represented in the Grosse Kunstausstellung in Berlin in 1891, where he showed a watercolour, *View of Heringsdorf.* After 1893, in addition to genre paintings, he exhibited landscapes depicting the countryside around Berlin and the coast. He also exhibited a history painting, *Moses and Aaron Demanding from Pharaoh the Exodus of the Jews from Egypt*. As a member of the association of German illustrators, Elfert's pen drawings appeared frequently at the Grosse Kunstausstellung in Berlin.

ELFERT, Willy
German, 19th - 20th century.
Born 20 June 1870, in Berlin.
Painter, illustrator. Landscapes.
Elfert attended the art school in Berlin between 1890 and 1894. In 1901, his Winter Morning was shown at an important Berlin exhibition, to which he continued to contribute landscapes from 1901 onwards. He was a member of the association of German illustrators.

ELFORD, William (Sir)
British, 18th - 19th century.
Born 1747, in Bickham (Devon); died 1837, in Totnes (Devon).
Painter, draughtsman. Landscapes.
Sir William Elford sent landscapes to the Royal Academy from 1784 onwards. Windsor Castle owns one of his landscapes. He was knighted in 1800.

MUSEUMS AND GALLERIES:
LONDON (British Mus.): *Ruins* (drawing, two drawings).

ELGERSMA, Michiel
Dutch, 18th century.
Born in Bolsward; died 1764, in Amsterdam.
Engraver.
Michiel Elgersma was a pupil of Bernard Picart and master of J. Greenvood. His engraved work includes *Arcadian Landscapes* after J. van Huysum, *Heroic Landscapes* after J. van Huysum, *Jeremias de Decker* perhaps after Rembrandt, *Old Woman Seated at a Table* and *Landscapes* after L. F. Dubourg.

ELGESTRON, Ossian
Swedish, 20th century.
Born 1883.
Painter. Genre scenes.
Elgestron studied at the art school in Stockholm. He continued his studies in Copenhagen and then trained further with Christian Krohg, in Paris. In 1929, his genre paintings *Viking Expeditions, The Flood* and *Lapp Legend* were shown at the Exposition d'Art Suédois at the Musée du Jeu de Paume in Paris

ELGGER, Franz von
Swiss, 19th century.
Born 1 August 1794 or 1795, in Rheinfelden; died 4 November 1858, in Lucerne.
Painter, draughtsman.
In addition to pursuing a busy military career, Elgger was a devotee of painting and drawing, exhibiting in 1842 and 1844. His legacy includes several portraits, notably those of *Dr Suidter* and *S. Hirzel*, and a military genre painting.

ELGHELO, Philippe
French, 17th century.
Painter.
Philippe Elghelo is mentioned in 1657 as being on the staff of the Royal Household.

ELGOOD, George Samuel
British, 19th - 20th century.
Born 26 February 1851, in Leicester; died 1943.
Painter. Genre scenes, landscapes.
George Samuel Elgood exhibited from 1872 at the Suffolk Street Gallery and regularly at the Fine Arts Society. He was a member of the Royal Institute.

George S. Elgood

MUSEUMS AND GALLERIES:
LEICESTER: *St Mary's Church; Leicester Castle* - SYDNEY: *Trellises; From the Terrace; Jew Orley Gardens.*
AUCTION RECORDS:
NEW YORK, 12-13 March 1903, *Old English House,* USD 225. LONDON, 24 May 1910, *Preston Cottage near Stratford-upon-Avon* (watercolour) GBP 9; *Chrysanthemums* (watercolour) GBP 5. LONDON, 3 April 1922, *Bolton Abbey* (1899, drawing) GBP 2. LONDON, 21 April 1922, *Giardino Eden Canal, Venice; Pergola* (1898, drawings, two) GBP 9. LONDON, 9 June 1922, *Michaelmas Daisies at Tangley Manor* (1897, drawing) GBP 4. LONDON, 1 March 1984, *Berkeley Castle Terrace, Gloucestershire* (1887, watercolour/pencil outlines, 12 x 19 3/4 ins / 30.5 x 50 cm) GBP 1,400. LONDON, 16 Oct 1986, *Garden Overlooking Florence Cathedral* (1901, watercolour heightened with gouache, 9 x 14 ins / 23 x 35.5 cm) GBP 3,100. LONDON, 25 Jan 1988, *Walk on the Terrace* (1887, watercolour, 16 1/2 x 13 1/2 ins / 42 x 34 cm) GBP 3,080. LONDON, 25 Jan 1989, *Pleasure Garden* (1911, watercolour, 10 x 7 1/4 ins / 25.5 x 18.5 cm) GBP 1,540. CHESTER, 20 July

1989, *Spring in Roundscliffe Garden* (1907, oil on canvas, 10 x 6 1/2 ins / 25.5 x 16.5 cm) GBP 2,420. LONDON, 31 Jan 1990, *Brymton d'Evercy House, Somerset* (watercolour, 18 1/2 x 14 1/4 ins / 47 x 36 cm) GBP 4,840. LONDON, 25-26 April 1990, *Statues of Flora and Pomona at Villa Aison, Nice* (1912, watercolour, 14 1/4 x 11 ins / 36 x 27 cm) GBP 3,630. LONDON, 1 Nov 1990, *Temple of Castor and Pollux, Girgenti* (watercolour, 9 3/4 x 14 ins / 24.8 x 35.6 cm) GBP 605. LONDON, 14 June 1991, *Compton Wynyates, Warwickshire* (1890, pencil and watercolour, 14 1/4 x 21 ins / 36.2 x 53.4 cm) GBP 12,100. LONDON, 25 March 1994, *Rose Avenue* (1891, pencil and watercolour, 9 x 14 ins / 22.8 x 35.3 cm) GBP 1,150. LONDON, 10 March 1995, *Mixed Flower Border, Penshurst* (1882, pencil and watercolour, 16 1/2 x 13 3/4 ins / 42 x 35 cm) GBP 2,070.

ELHAFEN, Ignaz, or Oelhafen, Helhafen, Eulhofer
Austrian, 17th century.
Born 1 August 1658, in Innsbruck; died 1 June 1715, in Düsseldorf.
Sculptor.

After a long stay in Rome, Elhafen settled in Vienna, then was summoned to Düsseldorf by the Elector John William. He was inspired mainly by ancient history in paintings such as *Battles* and the *Rape of the Sabine Women*, and by mythology, in paintings such as the *Judgement of Paris*. This artist also executed carvings in wood in the same vein as his carvings in ivory.

MUSEUMS AND GALLERIES:
BRUNSWICK (Herzog Anton Ulrich-Mus.): wood carvings - DRESDEN (Grünes Gewölbe): wood carvings - FRANKFURT AM MAIN: *Crucifixtion* - LONDON (Victoria and Albert Mus.): *Rape of the Sabine Women* - LONDON (Wallace Collection): *Pan and Nymph* - MUNICH (Bayerisches Nationalmus.): ivory carvings - VIENNA: ivory carvings - VIENNA (NM): wood carvings.

AUCTION RECORDS:
LONDON, 22 April 1982, *Jupiter, Antiope and Cupid* (ivory, 6 1/4 x 5 ins / 15.7 x 12.5 cm) GBP 15,000.

ELHARAR-LEMBERG, Sylvia, or Elharrar
Moroccan, 20th - 21st century.
Born 1950, in Casablanca.
Active in France.
Painter, sculptor, sculptor of assemblages, draughtswoman, illustrator.

Sylvia Elharar-Lemberg studied at the École des Beaux-Arts in Paris and at the art teachers training college in Tel Aviv. Her paintings and drawings create the effect of transparency and obliteration, often starting from the square design of a tetragram. She also creates assemblages, such as mysterious grills, iron rods placed alongside labels and photographic plates. Sylvia Elharar-Lemberg has shown at group exhibitions in France since 1974, including the 1981 Salon de la Jeune Peinture-Jeune Expression at Vincennes, the Salon de Montrouge (1983, 1984 and 1986), and the Salon de la Jeune Peinture (1991). She has also shown in Belgium, Italy, Israel and the USA. She has had a series of solo exhibitions since 1976, both in France and abroad, and in particular at the Galerie Lélia Mordoch, Paris (1991 and 1993).

BIBLIOGRAPHY:
'*Sylvia Elharar-Lemberg*' in *Salon de Montrouge*, exhibition catalogue, Montrouge, 1990. Sibony, Daniel, *Sylvia Elharar-Lemberg*, exhibition catalogue, Gal. Lélia Mordoch, Paris, 1991-92. Sibony, Daniel, '*Elharar-Lemberg*' in *Art Press* n° 166, periodical, Paris, February 1992.

AUCTION RECORDS:
PARIS, 17 June 1991, *Tetragram* (1989, acrylic and ink/paper/vellum d'Arches, 30 x 22 ins / 76 x 56 cm) FRF 5,000.

ELI, Adolf
German, 19th century.
Born 1821, in Brunswick; died 1889.
Painter (porcelain).

Adolf Eli, the brother of Christel Eli, was a court painter. A dinner service adorned with his paintings can be found at the royal palace in Brunswick.

ELI, Christel or Johann Heinrich Christian
German, 19th century.
Born 1800; died 1881.
Painter, painter (porcelain). Insects, still-lifes (flowers).

A court painter, Christel Eli was in charge of the decorative paintings at the Fürstenberg porcelain works and liked painting insects and flowers directly from nature. He also painted in oils, watercolour and gouache.

MUSEUMS AND GALLERIES:
BRUNSWICK.

AUCTION RECORDS:
LONDON, 24 June 1987, *Still-life with Flowers on an Entablature* (oil on canvas, 38 1/4 x 30 1/2 ins / 97 x 77.5 cm) GBP 13,000. SALISBURY, 18 March 2002, *Still-life of Roses with a Butterfly* (watercolour/gouache, a pair, 13 x 11 ins / 32 x 28 cm) GBP 3,200.

ELI, Philippe Joseph
French, 19th century.
Born in Arras.
Lithographer.

Philippe Joseph Eli was a pupil of Hersent. In 1869 he sent his portrait of *Mathieu Dombasle* to the Paris Salon.

ELIA. See also **GAGGINI**

ELIA. See also first name

ELIA, Beniamino d'
Italian, 19th century.
Born 1825, in Naples; died 1907, in Naples.
Painter.

Beniamino d'Elia studied at the Accademia in Naples with D. Morelli. In 1848 he presented a painting of *St Matthew with the Angel* at the exhibition of the national museum of Capodimonte in Naples, and showed two genre paintings in 1851. In 1855, he exhibited *Christians in the Catacombs* and painted a *Madonna of the Magnificat* for the Marquis of Capelli.

ELIA, Edoardo d'
Italian, 19th century.
Sculptor.

Edoardo d'Elia's works are indicative of a benevolent personality. He exhibited a marble bust of *Euterpe* in Milan in 1881 with great success. His other works include *Capricious Tranquillity*; *First Gust of Wind*; *Head of Garibaldi*; and *Alms*. These were exhibited in several cities in Italy, notably Turin, in 1880 and 1883.

ELIA, Edouard Pierre Joseph, or Elias
Belgian, 19th century.
Born in Brussels.
Painter.

Edouard Pierre Joseph Elia received a distinction at the Salon des Artists Français in 1882.

ELIA, L. G. T. d'
Italian, 20th century.
Born 1944, on Capri.
Painter. Figures.

L.G.T. d'Elia had no artistic training. He has travelled since the age of 16. His painting is markedly expressionist, and he makes rather morbid use of the human form.

ÉLIA, Michel
French, 20th century.
Born 11 November 1903, in Paris.
Sculptor.

Michel Élia exhibited regularly in Paris 1929-1941 at the Salon des Artistes Français, of which he became a member in 1932. He worked principally with marble in a classical style.

AUCTION RECORDS:

NEW YORK, 16 April 1969, *Meditation I* (marble) USD 1,700.

ÉLIACHEFF, Geneviève

French, 20th century.

Born 24 September 1910, in Bordeaux.

Painter. Local scenes, urban landscapes.

Geneviève Éliacheff travelled widely. She painted country scenes and towns placed in settings and atmospheres of the 1900s.

ELIAERTS, Jean François or Jan Frans

Belgian, 18th - 19th century.

Born 1 January 1761, in Deurne (Flanders); died 17 May 1848, in Antwerp.

Painter. Genre scenes, still-lifes (including flowers).

A French citizen, Jean François Eliaerts was a professor at the institution of the Legion of Honour. Between 1810 and 1848 he exhibited at the Salon de Paris. He had a predilection for fruit and flowers. A genre oil painting by him also exists, *The Watchful Cupid in a Rose Bush*. Eliaerts ranks among the imitators of Jan van Huysum.

J.F. Eliaerts.

MUSEUMS AND GALLERIES:

ANTWERP: *Flowers* - GHENT: *Still-life*.

AUCTION RECORDS:

PARIS, 22 May 1897, *Flowers and Fruit on Marble Ledge*, FRF 500. PARIS, 28 Feb 1919, *Bouquet of Flowers in a Terracotta Vase*, FRF 2,220. PARIS, 20 June 1961, *Fruit*, FRF 5,000. PARIS, 12 March 1976, *Flowers on an Entablature* (oil on canvas, 18 x 14½ ins / 46 x 37 cm) FRF 13,000. LUCERNE, 7 Nov 1982, *Still-life with Flowers* (oil on wood, 18 x 14 ins / 46 x 35.5 cm) CHF 8,800. ROUBAIX, 27 Feb 1983, *Vase of Flowers and Nest on an Entablature* (oil on panel, 17 x 13 ins / 43 x 33 cm) FRF 29,000. LONDON, 11 Dec 1987, *Flowers on an Entablature* (1790, oil on canvas, 25¼ x 20½ ins / 64 x 52 cm) GBP 20,000. ROME, 23 May 1989, *Fruit next to a Floral Composition in a Vase against a Landscape Background* (oil on canvas, 39 x 30¼ ins / 99 x 77 cm) ITL 13,500,000. AMSTERDAM, 10 Nov 1992, *Large Floral Composition with Roses, a Tulip, Peonies and an Imperial Crown in a Terracotta Vase on an Entablature* (oil on canvas, 16 x 13 ins / 40.5 x 32.8 cm) NLG 32,200. PARIS, 28 June 1993, *Bouquet of Flowers Placed on an Entablature* (oil on canvas, 34¼ x 26½ ins / 87 x 67.5 cm) FRF 125,000. ORLÉANS, 30 Sept 1993, *Composition of Irises, Hollyhocks, Roses and Various Flowers in a Basket on a Marble Entablature* (1826, oil on canvas, 32¾ x 27 ins / 83 x 68.5 cm) FRF 520,000. PARIS, 13 March 1995, *Flowers in a Vase Placed on an Entablature* (oil on canvas, 18 x 15 ins / 46 x 38 cm) FRF 74,000. NEW YORK, 4 Oct 1996, *Imperial Crown with Roses, Tulips, Poppies, Hyacinth and Other Flowers in a Terracotta Vase on a Stone Entablature* (1832, oil on canvas, 29¼ x 22 ins / 74 x 56 cm) USD 68,500. PARIS, 13 Dec 1996, *Vase of Flowers on an Entablature* (oil on panel, 13¾ x 11 ins / 35 x 28 cm) FRF 72,000. AMSTERDAM, 6 Nov 2001, *Still-life of Flowers* (gouache, 29 x 23 ins / 74 x 58 cm) NLG 15,000. NEW YORK, 2 Oct 2002, *Mixed Flowers in an Urn on a Ledge* (oil on canvas, 18 x 15 ins / 46 x 38 cm) USD 10,000. PARIS, 25 June 2004, *Still-life of Fruit. Still-life of Flowers* (1838, oil on canvas, a pair, 21 x 18 ins / 53 x 45 cm) EUR 45,000.

ELIAN, Catherine

Romanian, 20th century.

Born 1937, in Galati.

Active in France from 1965.

Painter. Murals, designs for stained glass.

Catherine Elian graduated from the Grigorescu Institute of fine arts in Bucharest in 1961. In her Romanian period, she was bound by the demands of Socialist Realism. On her arrival in France, she was tempted for a time by Surrealist expression. Subsequently she freed herself from the image in an abstract geometric period, then blossomed in lyrical abstraction, in which a symphony of colours tightly bound within a network of dark rings joyfully explode. She eventually settled in France in the Savoy region, where she executed commissions to decorate the area's buildings and exhibited locally. She took part in collective exhibitions in Romania, Italy and France (Salon des Surindépendants, Salon d'Automne and Salon des Artistes Indépendants) from 1956 onwards and received various awards, including a UNESCO grant in 1967 for the Cité des Arts in Paris.

BIBLIOGRAPHY:

Jianou, Ionel, *Romanian Artists and the West*, American Romanian Academy of Arts and Sciences, Los Angeles, 1986.

ELIAS

German, 14th century.

Active in Lübeck from 1305 to 1307.

Painter.

ELIAS, Alfred

British, 19th century.

Painter. Landscapes with figures, animals.

Alfred Elias exhibited in London, notably at the Royal Academy, from 1875. He was awarded a bronze medal at the Paris Exposition Universelle of 1889. He worked in Tunbridge Wells.

AUCTION RECORDS:

VIENNA, 13 Sept 1966, *Two Horses Drinking at a River*, ATS 25,000. LONDON, 16 May 1986, *Horses Grazing* (oil on canvas, 30 x 48 ins / 76 x 122 cm) GBP 1,100. VERSAILLES, 18 March 1990, *Ponies in the Fields* (oil on canvas, 32¼ x 46 ins / 82 x 117 cm) FRF 11,000. PARIS, 12 June 2002, *La Fleche in Her Stable* (1893, oil on canvas, 24 x 36 ins / 61 x 91 cm) EUR 2,100.

ELIAS, Annette

British, 19th century.

Active in London.

Painter, engraver. Landscapes, waterscapes.

From 1881 onwards, Annette Elias exhibited at the Royal Academy (from 1889 to 1904), Suffolk Street Gallery and Grosvenor Gallery. She was a member of the Society of Woman artists.

ELIAS, Edouard Pierre Joseph. See **ELIA**

ELIAS, Emily

British, 19th century.

Painter, draughtswoman. Portraits, genre scenes, landscapes, still-lifes.

Emily Elias exhibited in Paris in 1882, 1889 and 1890, and at the Royal Academy in London in 1884. She was the wife of Alfred Elias.

AUCTION RECORDS:

LONDON, 4 March 1980, *Reader* (oil on canvas, 44 x 31 ins / 112 x 79 cm) GBP 800. LONDON, 23 April 1986, *Portrait of a Girl in a White Dress* (oil on canvas, 50½ x 37½ ins / 128 x 95 cm) GBP 450.

ÉLIAS, Étienne, pseudonym of Michiels, Étienne

Belgian, 20th century.

Born 1932 or 1936, in Ostend.

Painter, draughtsman.

Pop Art.

Elias attended the art academy in Ghent. He won the Prix Deleu for graphic art in 1959, the Prix de la Jeune Peinture Belge in 1965, and other prizes in 1968 and 1969. His work was first shown in Ghent in 1960. Thereafter, he exhibited regularly in Belgium, as well as Amsterdam in 1968 and Sao Paulo in 1971. At the outset, his action painting connected him to the international Lyrical Abstraction movement. He later returned to figuration, swept along by the Pop Art movement of the 1960s.

MUSEUMS AND GALLERIES:
GRONINGEN - OSTEND - ROTTERDAM - UTRECHT.
AUCTION RECORDS:
ANTWERP, 6 April 1976, *Behind a Small Curtain* (1965, oil on canvas, 48 x 40 1/4 ins / 122 x 102 cm) BEF 36,000. ANTWERP, 25 Oct 1977, *A Man* (oil on canvas, 47 1/4 x 39 1/4 ins / 120 x 100 cm) BEF 40,000. ANTWERP, 27 April 1981, *Still-life* (oil on canvas, 31 1/2 x 39 1/4 ins / 80 x 100 cm) BEF 24,000. ANTWERP, 27 Oct 1987, *Notary's Family* (1967, oil on canvas, 59 x 55 ins / 150 x 140 cm) BEF 200,000. LOKEREN, 5 March 1988, *Picking Apples* (oil on canvas, 43 1/4 x 39 1/4 ins / 110 x 100 cm) BEF 110,000. LOKEREN, 21 March 1992, *Couple* (oil on canvas, 37 1/2 x 31 1/2 ins / 95 x 80 cm) BEF 36,000. LOKEREN, 10 Oct 1992, *Fishing* (1989, oil on canvas, 31 1/2 x 27 1/2 ins / 80 x 70 cm) BEF 33,000. LOKEREN, 15 May 1993, *Self-portrait and Portrait of Titian in the XXth century* (oil on canvas, a pair, each 27 1/2 x 22 ins / 70 x 55 cm) BEF 75,000. AMSTERDAM, 8 Dec 1994, *Despair* (oil on panel, 22 x 17 3/4 ins / 55 x 45 cm) NLG 4,600. AMSTERDAM, 31 May 1995, *Prophet* (1988, oil on canvas, 31 1/2 x 27 1/2 ins / 80 x 70 cm) NLG 3,540. LOKEREN, 7 Oct 1995, *Jet-foil* (oil on canvas, 59 x 47 1/4 ins / 150 x 120 cm) BEF 90,000. AMSTERDAM, 5 June 1996, *Conversation with Lucas* (oil on canvas, 31 1/2 x 27 1/2 ins / 80 x 70 cm) NLG 4,600. AMSTERDAM, 10 Dec 1996, *Red Mountain* (1980, oil on canvas, 27 1/2 x 22 ins / 70 x 55 cm) NLG 4,382. LOKEREN, 6 Dec 1997, *Mother and Daughter* (oil on canvas, 39 1/4 x 47 1/4 ins / 100 x 120 cm) BEF 50,000. AMSTERDAM, 10 June 1999, *De Ontmoeting* (1966, acrylic, 59 x 47 ins / 150 x 120 cm) NLG 9,000. ANTWERP, 19 Oct 1999, *Achter een gordijntje* (oil on canvas, 47 x 39 ins / 120 x 100 cm) BEF 75,000. AMSTERDAM, 12 June 2001, *Really Erotic Painting* (1968, oil on canvas, 47 x 47 ins / 120 x 120 cm) NLG 8,000. AMSTERDAM, 3 Dec 2002, *Portrait of a Hippie* (1970, oil on canvas, 22 x 18 ins / 55 x 45 cm) EUR 2,000. AMSTERDAM, 3 Dec 2002, *I Have Lost My Heart to Kemmelberg* (1967, oil on canvas, 39 x 31 ins / 100 x 80 cm) EUR 3,200. VLAAMSE KAAI, 21 Oct 2003, *Raveel in his Garden* (oil on canvas, 39 x 39 ins / 100 x 100 cm) EUR 3,000.

ELIAS, F.
German, 19th century.
Died 1846, in Stuttgart.
Active in Stuttgart.
Lithographer.

Elias produced lithographs to illustrate his own work, *Introduction to Figure Drawing*, under the direction of the painter F. Seubert, and to illustrate the work by F. Gross, *Ten of Jesus' Parables*, and *New Decorations*, by A. Rieman. He is also noted for a lithographed plate of the *Mistress of Titian*, after Titian.

ELIAS, H. J.
Dutch, 19th century.
Born c. 1865, in Amsterdam; died in Blaricum.
Active in Blaricum.
Painter. Landscapes.

H. J. Elias was a pupil of J. Portaels at the academy in Brussels. At the Exposition Universelle in Paris he showed an *Autumn Landscape*.

ELIAS, Isack, or Elyas
Dutch, 17th century.
Active at the beginning of the 17th century.
Painter. Genre scenes.

MUSEUMS AND GALLERIES:
AMSTERDAM: *Merry Gathering*.

ELIAS, Levin
Danish, 18th century.
Painter.

In 1759, Elias was awarded two silver medals by the Kunstakademi in Copenhagen. The city's museum contains a *Portrait of a Young Girl* by him dating from 1767.

ELIAS, Mathieu, or Elyas or Elie, Elye
French, 17th - 18th century.
Born 1658, in Peene, near Cassel; died 22 April 1741, in Dunkirk.
Painter, sculptor (?).

A pupil of Philippe de Corbehem, Mathieu Elias was director of the Académie de St-Luc in Paris. An 'Elye Matthieu' was active in Paris in 1684.

A large number of Elias's works are in Dunkirk, Menin and Ypres. In the mendicant church at Menin are *St Felix Raising a Dead Man*; in the Carmelite church at Ypres, *Moses Striking the Rock* and *Raising of Lazarus*. In the churches in Dunkirk are *Angel Appearing to the Sleeping Saint Joseph; Miracle of the Loaves and Fishes; Guardian Angel Leading a Child; St Louis Leaving for the Holy Land; Elijah's Offering*; at the church of St-Jean-Baptiste: *Town of Dunkirk Personified Implores the Holy Trinity; Distribution of Bread and Wine to Abraham's Servants; Tottla, King of the Visigoths, Visiting St Benedict; Children of Israel Gathering Manna; Feast of Balthazar; St Urinoc Distributing Bread*.

MUSEUMS AND GALLERIES:
BERGUES: *Self-portrait; St Peter; Judith and Holofernes* - DUNKIRK: *The Sacrifice of Abraham; View of Military Dock and Inner Harbour of Dunkirk in 1709* - PARIS (Louvre): *The Son of Sceva, Jewish Exorcists, Beaten by the Demon* - VIENNA (Albertina Mus.): two drawings.

ELIAS, Nicolaes or Claes. See **PICKENOY**

ELIAS, Ramon
Spanish, 19th century.
Sculptor.

Ramon Elias exhibited in Barcelona in 1870.

ÉLIAS BURGOS, Francisco
Spanish, 19th century.
Born in the 19th century, in Madrid.
Sculptor.

Francisco Élias Burgos was the son of the sculptor Elias Vallejo. He became a member of the Real Academia de San Fernando in 1840. He is known for a bust of his father and some low reliefs of *Priam at the Feet of Achilles, Death of Epaminondas* and a group piece *Murder of Abel*.

ELIAS VALLEJO, Francisco
Spanish, 19th century.
Born 1783, in Soto de Cameres; died 22 September 1858, in Madrid.
Sculptor.

Francisco Elias Vallejo studied at the Real Academia de San Fernando. In 1818 he became director of the department of sculpture at the academy. He is known for numerous busts of distinguished individuals at the Spanish court. He executed a *Hercules as a Child* for the fountain of Hercules in Aranjuez and numerous groups for public buildings in Madrid.

ELIAS Y BRACONS, Feliu
Spanish, 20th century.
Born 9 October 1878, in Barcelona; died 1948.
Painter, newspaper cartoonist, humorist. Figures, interiors.

Feliu Elias y Bracons studied at the school of fine arts in Barcelona before going to study in Paris. He took part in collective exhibitions including the international art exhibition in Barcelona in 1910 where he received a commendation, the Barcelona fine arts exhibitions of 1918, 1919 and 1921, the international exhibition of 1929 and the Spring exhibition of 1936. He was made a Chevalier of the Légion d'Honneur in France and a member of the St Luke art circle in Spain.

Elias y Bracons published drawings in weekly publications and magazines including in France, *Paris Journal, Paris Midi* and *L'Assiette au Beurre* and in Spain, *La Campana de Gracias and Mirador*. His humorous drawings are in a stylised, elliptical and effective style and display a Mannerism clearly marked by the Art Deco of the 1930s. Some of his paintings show the influence of the Nabis group and the Revue Blanche in their use of highly complex flat tints while others display a realism with a tendency towards the photographic that is closer to Otto Dix's Neue Sachlichkeit (New Objectivity).

Bibliography:

Arnáiz, José Manuel/López Jiménez, Javier/Merchán Díaz, Manuel (ed.), *Cien años de pintura en Espana y Portugal (1830-1930)*, Antiqvaria, Madrid, 1988 (One Hundred Years of Painting in Spain and Portugal (1830-1930)).

Museums and Galleries:

Barcelona (MAM del Mus. Nacional d'Art de Catalunya).

ELIASBERG, Paul

German, 20th century.
Born 1907, in Munich; died 1 October 1983, in Hamburg.
Also active in France.
Painter, engraver.

Eliasberg was born in Russia, but spent his childhood in Munich. At the age of 19, he went to Paris where he attended the Académie Ranson and was in contact with Roger Bissière, who taught there from 1925. He contributed to numerous group exhibitions, including the Salon des Surindépendants and the Salon de Mai. His first one-man show was also held in Paris in 1934. In 1962, the museum in Munich arranged an important exhibition of his entire output and from 1966 he taught at the art school in Frankfurt am Main. In his book *Engraving*, E. Rouir mentions Eliasberg, giving an outline of the essence of his work: 'he creates a moving monumental world through a clever game of more or less sustained vertical lines'; an example of this *Notre-Dame in the Mist*.

Auction records:

Munich, 5 June 1981, *Lovers' Beach* (1973, pen/paper, 14 1/2 x 19 ins / 37 x 48.5 cm) DEM 2,200. Heidelberg, 12-13 Oct 1985, *Fantastic Landscape* (1976, oil and black chalk/canvas, 23 1/2 x 15 3/4 ins / 60 x 40 cm) DEM 2,700; *St-Étienne-du-Mont* (c. 1975, watercolour and pen, 15 x 18 ins / 37.8 x 45.7 cm) DEM 1,900. Munich, 26 May 1992, *Leukadia* (1976, brown ink, 14 1/4 x 20 ins / 36 x 50.5 cm) DEM 2,645.

ELIASOPH, Paula

American, 20th century.
Born 26 October 1895, in New York; died 1983.
Painter, watercolourist, engraver, illustrator.

Paula Eliasoph was a pupil at the Pratt Institute and the American Students' League in New York. She became a member of the American Water Color Society and the American Students' League. She produced etchings.

ELIASSON, Olafur

Danish, 20th - 21st century.
Born 1967, in Copenhagen, to Icelandic parents.
Active in Germany.
Installation artist, environmental artist, photographer.

From 1989 to 1995 Olafur Eliasson attended the Kongelige Danske Kunstakademi in Copenhagen. He lives and works in Berlin. He designs and makes installations and environments with the help of very simple, ephemeral materials, and his works themselves are ephemeral. He manipulates light, heat, humidity, steam and ice to create artificial settings: a rainbow entitled *Beauty* (1993), an ice fountain, a waterfall and a geyser outside the Carnegie International in Pittsburgh entitled *Your Natural Denudation Inverted* (1999). In 2000 he exhibited an installation at the MOMA, New York comprising 50 glass and mirrored panels which tricked the spectators and increased their numbers. His experimental works, in or near museums, expose our system of perception of recreated natural phenomena. They update the nature-technology relationship in an ideological context, influenced by the ecological debate in developed countries. He also photographs natural phenomena including icebergs, grottos and views of Iceland.

He has participated in group exhibitions, including: 1996, Manifesta 1, Rotterdam; 1997, *Heaven*, PSI, New York; 1998, 24th São Paulo Biennale; 1998, *Nuit Blanche. La Jeune Scène Nordique* (*Sleepless Night. The Young Nordic Scene*) at the Musée d'Art Moderne de la Ville de Paris; 1999 and 2003, Venice Biennale; 2002-2003, *Moving Pictures*, an exhibition exploring the use of photography, film and video in art since the late 1960s, and at the Solomon R. Guggenheim Museum, New York.

He has held a great many solo shows, mainly in museums, including: 1995, Kunstverein, Hamburg; 1996, Kunstmuseet, Malmö; 1997, Kunsthalle, Basel; 1999, *Your Position Surrounded and your Surroundings Positioned*, Dundee Contemporary Art, Dundee; 1999, Kunstverein, Frankfurt; 2000, *Surrounding Surrounded*, Neue Galerie, Graz; 2000, *Your Intuitive Surroundings versus your Surrounded Intuition*, Art Institute of Chicago; 2001, *Project for Garden Hall*, Museum of Modern Art, New York; 2001, *Your Only Real Thing is Time*, Institute of Contemporary Arts, Boston; 2002, Lenbachhaus Kunstbau, Munich, and Musée d'Art Moderne de la Ville de Paris; 2002, *Projects' Show*, MOMA, New York; 2003, Lenbachhaus Kunstbau, Munich; 2003, Tate Modern, London.

Bibliography:

Weibel, Peter, *Olafur Eliasson. Surroundings surrounded. Essays on space and science*, exhibition catalogue, Neue Gal. am Landesmuseum, Graz, 2000. Medvedow Plaut, Jill/Lerup, Lars/Morgan, Jessica, *Your only real thing is time*, exhibition catalogue, Institute of Contemporary Art, Boston, 2001. Obrist, Hans-Ulrich/Friedman, Yona/Krogh Jensen, Marianne, et al., *Olafur Eliasson*, exhibition catalogue, Musée d'Art moderne de la Ville de Paris, Paris musées, Paris, 2002 (text in French and German). *Moving Pictures*, exhibition catalogue, Solomon R. Guggenheim Museum, New York, 2002.

Museums and Galleries:

New York (Solomon R. Guggenheim Mus.): *Glacier Series* (1999, photos).

Auction records:

London, 23 Oct 2001, *Untitled, n° 49* (colour print, 24 x 35 ins / 60 x 90 cm) GBP 2,500. New York, 13 Nov 2002, *Large Stone Series* (1998, c-print in six parts, 15 x 23 ins / 38 x 58 cm) USD 11,000. New York, 14 Nov 2002, *Untitled - Iceland Series* (1998, seven colour prints, 23 x 35 ins / 58 x 89 cm) USD 15,000. London, 22 Oct 2003, *Untitled, from the Iceland Series* (1995, c-print, 24 x 35 ins / 60 x 90 cm) GBP 9,000. New York, 14 Nov 2003, *3D Five-Fold Symmetry* (2000, cut paper adhesive, 13 x 15 x 15 ins / 34 x 38 x 38 cm) USD 4,000. London, 25 June 2004, *Untitled* (1997, c-print, 24 x 35 ins / 60 x 90 cm) GBP 6,500. Copenhagen, 5 Oct 2004, *Composition* (1993, oil on canvas, 39 x 57 ins / 100 x 145 cm) DKK 190,000.

ELIASZ, Wladyslaw

Polish, 19th century.
Sculptor.

Wladyslaw Eliasz exhibited religious sculptures and busts in Cracow from 1871 to 1885.

Museums and Galleries:
Cracow (Lubomirski): *Bust of Prince Lubomirski* - Rapperswil: eight busts of the Kings of Poland.

ELIASZ-RADZIKOWSKI, Walery
Polish, 19th century.
Born 13 September 1840, in Cracow; died 23 March 1905, in Cracow.
Painter, illuminator, writer.
Walery Eliasz-Radzikowski trained first at the art academy in Cracow under L. Luszczkiewicz, and then in Munich under H. Anshütz, M. von Schwind and Franz Adam. He travelled around Germany, then spent time in Paris, Florence and Venice, and settled in Cracow in 1868, where he painted a series of scenes from Polish history including: *The Defence of Cracow against the Swedes, Sobieski Entering Vienna following its Liberation, The Death of Zólkievski* and *Rebel Camp in June 1863*. In addition he painted landscapes and genre scenes. He was also a writer, and produced works on the history of civilisation which he illustrated himself, as well as a work entitled *Sketches from my Travels in the Tatra Mountains*
Museums and Galleries:
Rapperswil (Polenmus.): *The Mother of the Jagellons.*

ELICHE, Jean Baptiste
French, 19th - 20th century.
Born 21 February 1866, in Morières-les-Avignon.
Painter. Landscapes.
Jean Baptiste Eliche was a pupil of Jules Lefebvre and Tony Robert-Fleury. He did not exhibit at the Salon des Artistes Français until 1910.

ELICHINGER, Antoni
Swiss, 16th century.
Born to a family originally from Baden.
Active in Basel in 1519.
Painter.
Antoni Elichinger was assistant to Hans Dyg.

ELIE (Veuve)
French, 19th century.
Born in Paris.
Painter. Portraits.
A pupil of Greuze, Elie exhibited several times at the Paris Salon from 1814 to 1824.

ÉLIE, pseudonym of Vignes, Jacques
French, 20th century.
Born 1929.
Painter, pastellist.
In 1994 the Galerie Katia Granoff in Honfleur mounted an exhibition of pastels in oils by Élie (Jacques Vignes). His paintings gain substance from an inversion of reality; incorporated material provides their visual flavour.

ELIE, Joseph
French, 18th century.
Active in Paris from 1748.
Painter, sculptor.

ELIE, Louis
French, 20th century.
Born in Niort.
Painter. Genre scenes.
Louis Elie exhibited in Paris at the Salon des Indépendants from 1935 onwards.

ÉLIE DE BEAUMONT
French, 19th - 20th century.
Born 18 March 1871, in Montluçon.
Miniaturist.
Élie de Beaumont began to show her work in Paris at the Salon des Artistes Français in 1910.

ELIGIO DA CAPUA
Italian, 16th century.
Active in Montevergine (Campania) c. 1545.
Sculptor (ivory), goldsmith.
Eligio da Capua was a monk.

ÉLIM, Franck, pseudonym of Le Morinière, Élie de
French, 20th century.
Painter. Sporting subjects, animals.
Franck Élim was a member of the Société des Peintres et Sculpteurs de Chevaux (Society of Painters and Sculptors of Horses) and exhibited in the Section Artistique du Concours Hippique (Art Section of the Equestrian Competition). He specialised in painting the world of the horse, the races and people of that world, including portraits of famous horses. His best known works are the 1928 *Diana Prize*, and *Jockey Club Prize, The Finish*.

F Elim

Auction records:
Paris, 26 Nov 1981, *Maestro II, Portrait of a Horse* (1938, oil on canvas, 15 x 18 ins / 38 x 46 cm) FRF 2,800. New York, 24 Feb 1983, *The Finish* (1929, oil on canvas, 25 3/4 x 32 ins / 65.5 x 81 cm) USD 3,000. Paris, 16 June 1987, *Vittel, the Last Bend* (1921, oil on panel, 10 1/4 x 13 3/4 ins / 26 x 35 cm) FRF 4,000. Paris, 14 June 1988, *Racehorse and Jockey* (oil on canvas, 25 1/2 x 32 ins / 65 x 81 cm) FRF 9,000. Paris, 17 June 1988, *Deauville, the Queen Matilda Prize* (1920, oil on canvas, 15 x 21 1/2 ins / 38 x 54.5 cm) FRF 10,000. Versailles, 5 March 1989, *Belfonds in his Box* (oil on canvas, 25 1/2 x 32 ins / 65 x 81 cm) FRF 3,500. Versailles, 19 Nov 1989, *The Queen Matilda Prize, Deauville 1920* (oil on canvas, 15 x 22 ins / 38 x 55 cm) FRF 28,000. Paris, 10 Dec 1990, *The Queen Arrives at Ascot Racecourse* (1949, oil on panel, 19 x 23 1/2 ins / 48.5 x 60 cm) FRF 10,000. Paris, 22 May 1992, *Prince Riding at Longchamp* (1946, oil on canvas, 18 x 22 ins / 46 x 55 cm) FRF 6,000. London, 24-25 March 1993, *The Fourteenth of July* (oil on canvas, 21 1/4 x 25 1/2 ins / 54 x 65 cm) GBP 3,220. Paris, 18 June 1993, *The Pasha, Chantilly* (1941, oil on canvas, 28 3/4 x 37 ins / 73 x 94 cm) FRF 45,000. London, 11 Feb 1994, *Polo Match* (1914, watercolour and gouache/brown paper, 31 x 19 1/2 ins / 77.8 x 49.5 cm) GBP 2,530. Paris, 5 Feb 1998, *14 July Cavalcade* (oil on panel, 15 x 17 3/4 ins / 38 x 45 cm) FRF 14,000. Cannes, 15 Aug 2000, *Le Padok* (1945, oil on canvas, 22 x 25 ins / 56 x 64 cm) FRF 12,000. Lille, 9 Dec 2001, *Deauville Beach* (1930, oil on panel, a pair, 10 x 13 ins / 26 x 34 cm) FRF 48,000. Neuilly, 28 March 2003, *Portrait of Lannilis* (1927, oil on canvas, 26 x 32 ins / 65 x 81 cm) EUR 2,600. Melun, 15 June 2003, *Going Out of Trouville Port* (oil on panel, 9 x 11 ins / 22 x 27 cm) EUR 2,100. New York, 14 Jan 2004, *Before the Start* (oil on canvas, 11 x 16 ins / 27 x 41 cm) USD 2,600.

ELIN, Johan Christiaan
Dutch, 18th century.
Born 1733, in Berlin, to Dutch parents.
Active in Leiden.
Miniaturist, engraver (etching).
Johan Christiaan Elin received his early artistic instruction from J. Harper in Berlin and left for the Netherlands at the age of 16. He settled in Utrecht and later in Leiden. Extant is his etched engraving *Elderly Woman Threading a Needle under the Lamp*. The portrait of the Leiden physician *A. Balthazaar* was engraved by B. de Bakker after Elin. Three portraits on ivory of a man, after 17th-century portraits, have also come down to us.

ELINA, Erofei
Russian, 17th century.
Died 20 February 1696.
Painter.

Erofei Elina entered court service at the Kremlin in Moscow in 1679. He painted decorative and religious murals as well as canvases for various churches in the Kremlin and a number of rooms in the imperial palace.

ELINA, Odette
French, 20th century.
Painter. Portraits, flowers.

Odette Elina belonged to the Salon des Artistes Français and to the Union des Femmes Peintres et Sculpteurs (Union of Women Painters and Sculptors) in Paris.

ELINGA, Pieter. See **JANSSENS Pieter Elinga**

ELINK STERK, J. C.
Dutch, 19th century.
Active c. 1850.
Lithographer.

J. C. Elink Sterk worked in the manner of the 17th-century Netherlandish artists such as F. Bol, P. van Laar and G. Meton. He executed lithographies of about 20 portraits, mostly after his own drawings.

ELION, Jacques
Dutch, 19th century.
Born 20 May 1842, in Amsterdam; died 22 February 1893, in Amsterdam.
Draughtsman, engraver (including etching).

Jacques Elion was a pupil at the academy in Amsterdam. He produced sketches for decorative sculpture. He also engraved coins and medals.

ELIOT, Gabriel
French, 19th century.
Born in Paris.
Painter, pastellist. Genre scenes, still-lifes.

Having studied in the studio of Léger Chérelle, Gabriel Eliot sent pastels depicting genre scenes and still-lifes to the Salon from 1872 to 1880.

ELIOT, Jeanne
French, 19th century.
Born 22 March 1861, in Paris.
Painter.

Jeanne Eliot exhibited at the Salon of the Société des Artistes Français, becoming a member in 1892. She was the sister and pupil of Maurice Eliot.

AUCTION RECORDS:
PARIS, 23 April 1937, *Village Street in the Sun* (pastel) FRF 30.

ÉLIOT, Maurice
French, 19th - 20th century.
Born 1864, in Paris; died 1945, in Épinay, near Paris.
Painter, pastellist, draughtsman, engraver, illustrator. Genre scenes, landscapes.

At the age of 16 Maurice Éliot became a pupil of Émile Bin, who had a studio in Montmartre where Éliot met Signac and Henri Rivière. He entered the École des Beaux-Arts where he took courses by Adolphe Yvon and by Cabanel. In 1883 he was accepted as a teacher in city of Paris schools. Appointed in 1901 to the École Polytechnique, he taught pastel and drawing for almost 40 years. He was made a Chevalier of the Légion d'Honneur in 1908. Éliot was a painter of small everyday delights. He produced lithographs illustrating Michelet, Victor Hugo, Jean Richepin and Maupassant.

Éliot exhibited in Paris at the Société des Artistes Français. His many distinctions included a travel grant in 1888, which he used to explore southern Europe, and a second-class medal in 1937. In the same year he joined the administrative committee of the Society. He was a founder member of the Salon d'Automne, and in 1923 served on its judges' panel. From 1881 onwards he exhibited every year in Paris and in the provinces. In 1888 the museum in Brunoy (Essonne) put on a retrospective exhibition in his honour. In 2001 the Musée Robert Dubois-Corneau in Brunoy held the exhibition *Hero et Léandre: Charles Léandre (1862-1934), Maurice Éliot (1892-1945).*

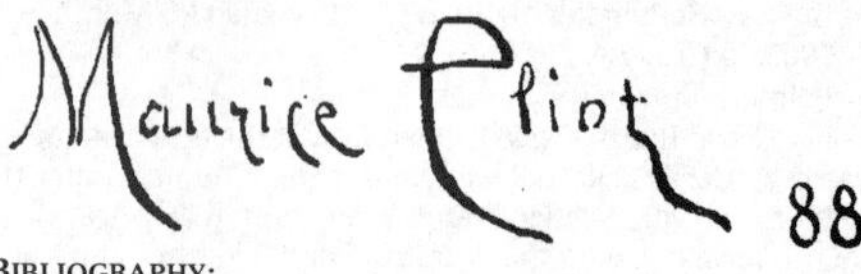

BIBLIOGRAPHY:
Maupassant, Guy de, *L'Héritage. Vingt et une compositions originales de Maurice Eliot, gravées à l'eau-forte par L. Ruet*, L. Carteret, Paris, 1907. *Maurice Eliot, 1862-1945*, exhibition catalogue, Brunoy, 1989.

MUSEUMS AND GALLERIES:
ABBEVILLE: *Interior* - AUXERRE: *Water Song* - BASEL: *Young Woman at Table* - BÉZIERS: *Twilight Hours* - LILLE: *A Country Girl is Buried* - MORLAIX (Mus. des Jacobins): *Baptismal Day* (c. 1890) - NÎMES: *Twilight Hours* - QUIMPER: *Harvesters* - RHEIMS: *Peasant Girl* (pastel) - SEDAN: *Prize Day* - SOISSONS: *In the Grass in Normandy* - ST-BRIEUC: *Reaper* - STRASBOURG: *Life in the Fields.*

AUCTION RECORDS:
PARIS, 9-10 May 1900, *Summer Thursday*, FRF 350; *Étretat*, FRF 460. PARIS, 22 Dec 1909, *Landscape in the Côte d'Azur* (pastel) FRF 47. PARIS, 27 Feb 1919, *Seated Woman* (pencil study) FRF 22. PARIS, 8 March 1919, *Study of a Standing Woman* (pastel) FRF 65. PARIS, 6 May 1929, *Landscapes* (two pastels) FRF 420; *Flowers* (pastel) FRF 7,500. PARIS, 23 April 1937, *Pastures in the Jura* (pastel) FRF 50. TOKYO, 15 Feb 1980, *Supper* (lithograph, 14 1/4 x 12 3/4 ins / 36.4 x 32.6 cm) JPY 150,000. LONDON, 5 Oct 1990, *At the Barrier* (1887, oil on canvas, 20 x 26 1/4 ins / 50.5 x 66.7 cm) GBP 3,080. NEW YORK, 17 Jan 1996, *Girls in a Park* (1901, oil on canvas, 29 x 23 1/2 ins / 73.7 x 60 cm) USD 2,300.

ELIOTT, Harry, pseudonym of Hermet, Charles Edmond
French, 20th century.
Born 14 June 1882, in Paris; died 25 May 1959, in Villez-sous-Bailleul (Eure).
Draughtsman, illustrator, lithographer.

Harry Elliott was a son of a printer and lithographer in Paris. He chose an English pseudonym because he liked the work of English illustrators. He illustrated magazines and books, and produced lithographs and prints made on zinc, showing hunting scenes, golf, billiards, interiors, seascapes and other subjects.

AUCTION RECORDS:
PARIS, 19 Dec 1988, *The Diligence; Beside the Fire* (two watercolours, each 9 1/2 x 7 ins / 24 x 18 cm) FRF 7,100.

ELIOTT-LOCKHART, Katharine Clare
British, 20th century.
Born 20th century, in Camberley.
Painter.

Katharine Clare Eliott-Lockhart studied under Fouqueray and exhibited at the Salon des Artistes Français in Paris.

ELISABETH, Maria E. Amalia
German, 19th century.
Born 5 May 1784; died 1 June 1849, in Paris.
Engraver.

The daughter of Duke William of the Palatinate and wife of Louis Alexandre Berthier, prince of Wagram, this artist engraved landscapes, including one after A. Waterloo which is signed *Elisabeth 1805*.

ELISABETH, Maria Josepha (Archduchess of Austria)
Austrian, 18th century.
Born 13 August 1743; died 23 September 1808.
Draughtswoman, engraver (etching).
This artist's legacy includes an etching of a *Landscape with Woman Carrying an Infant on her Back* and a miniature of the *Holy Family*, signed and dated 1789. She was made an honorary member of the Akademie in Vienna in 1789 and died an abbess at Innsbruck.

ELISABETH CHRISTINE OF PRUSSIA (Queen)
German, 18th century.
Born 8 November 1715; died 13 January 1797.
Engraver.
This artist is known for her *View of a Village with Two Peasants*, an etching after A. Bloemaert. She was the daughter of Ferdinand Albert, Duke of Brunswick.

ELISABETH OF BELGIUM (Queen)
Belgian, 20th century.
Born 1876, in Passenhofen; died 1965, in Laeken.
Painter, sculptor.
Queen Elisabeth of Belgium was self-taught. She was a member of the Académie Royale of Belgium.
Museums and Galleries:
Antwerp (Openluchtmus. Middelheim).

ELISAREV, Fedor
Russian, 17th century.
Icon painter.
Fedor Elisarev is mentioned in documents as an icon painter working for the Metropolitan of Rostov. In 1657 he painted two apartments in the Kremlin Palace and in 1660 the Tsar's apartment. In 1665 and 1666 he painted decorative murals in the palace and frescoes in one of the churches of the Saviour in the Kremlin.

ELISAREV, Ivan
Russian, 17th century.
Born to a family originally from Yaroslavl.
Icon painter.
Ivan Elisarev was summoned to the court of the Tsar in 1659, where he helped with the murals in the Cathedral of the Archangel. In 1666 he worked in one of the court churches and the monastery of Novodevich.

ELISEEV, Boris, Fedor and Parsen
Russian, 17th century.
Icon painters.
Fedor and Parsen Eliseev worked on the murals in the Cathedral of the Dormition in 1660.

ELISEUS, or Heliseus
Swiss, 16th century.
Active in Bern.
Painter.
Eliseus is recorded between 1512 and 1527 as painting several works for the town of Bern. He was the father of stained glass painter Mathys Walther.

ELIZABETH (Princess)
British, 18th - 19th century.
Born 1770, in London; died 1840, in Frankfurt.
Painter.
Princess Elizabeth was the third daughter of George III. She married Frederick William, the Grand Duke of Hessen-Homburg, in 1818. She maintained a strong attachment to the arts throughout her entire life. Her works released publicly included *Birth and Triumph of Cupid* (in 1796) and *Power and Progress of the Genius* (1806).

ELIZAERT. See **LISAERT**

ÉLIZAGA, pseudonym of Élissague, Hélène
French, 20th century.
Born 3 March 1896; died 25 September 1981, in St-Jean-de-Luz.
Painter, art restorer. Genre scenes, portraits, landscapes, flowers.
Élizaga was a violinist. In 1915 she was a pupil of Henry du Sorbier de la Tourrasse, whom she married. In 1922 she began attending the Julian and Grande Chaumière academies and the studio of Sacred Art run by Maurice Denis and Georges Desvallières in Paris. Between 1930 and 1947 she exhibited on her own and with others, principally in the Basque country. Most of her paintings were of Basque landscapes and scenes with figures. During her last 25 years she and her husband worked on the restoration of paintings.
Museums and Galleries:
Bayonne (Mus. Basque): *Pelota Players, the Arayet Brothers, French Champions; Three Chistera Players, a Mountain in the Background; Ahetze.*

ELK, Ger van, for Gerard Pieter van
Dutch, 20th century.
Born 1941, in Amsterdam.
Also active in the USA.
Environmental artist, assemblage artist, painter (mixed media).
Conceptual Art.
Van Elk attended the applied arts institute in Amsterdam from 1959 to 1961. He also studied history of art at the Immaculate Heart College in Los Angeles from 1961 to 1963, then at Groningen State University in 1965 and 1966. In 1972 he became a teacher at the Ateliers '63 in Haarlem (established in 1963 by several visual artists dissatisfied with formal art education. Since 1993 it has been based in Amsterdam and is known as 'De Ateliers'). He lives and works in Los Angeles and often travels to Italy, England, and France, where he stays in Sologne.

Since 1965, within the context of Conceptual Art and its international sphere of influence, Van Elk's work has conveyed an initial idea through the appropriate choice and assemblage of various materials. His work generally appeared in series. In an initial period, he chose and contrasted materials and situations according to their incompatibility in the form of installation-environments like a floor covered with a moquette below a stone column at the Amalfi Arsenal in 1968, or a curtain cutting across stairs, *Installation Dividing the Steps* in 1969. He then distanced himself from installations whose sole aim was to demonstrate a contradictory concept, often a very basic one. In the course of his later work, Van Elk focused on the one hand on the essence of painting (and the painter) compared with reality, and on the other hand on the three historically archetypal forms of painting, still contrasted with reality: still-life, landscape, portrait.

After 1970, he very often used photography, in a first series to reconstruct contemporary paintings, thus calling into question the reality of a painting, the reality of a photograph, and the reality of reality. He explored this question of the reality of perception through newspaper photographs or by putting a photograph on a support which could be put out of shape. In 1974, with the *Farewell* series, and in 1975 with the *Symmetrical Landscapes* series, he used painting to modify photographs or reproductions, with the same aim of highlighting the ambiguities of representation. In the *Symmetrical Landscapes*, in accordance with various processes, he doubled up the landscape, either by painting a landscape which had already been painted, or by painting a landscape inside another landscape. In the same way as the symmetrical doubling of an image, this distancing of a work, in perspective, is a strategy frequently used by Van Elk in his creative activity.

After 1980, still by means of painting on photographs, on flat surfaces and in traditional frameworks, he produced a number of series based on the interpretation of traditional painting: still-life with the *Flowers* series in 1982; with the 17th - century Dutch portrait series *Masters of the Western Style* in 1987; with the *Vanities* series in 1988. The flower painting series was produced by multicoloured marks and splashes in lacquered pictures projected on a photographic support, which is not easily identifiable; the resulting image had the exact appearance of the informal paintings of the 1950s. In the portrait series, it was often his own portrait which replaced figures in an image of photographic origin, sometimes assuming the role and identity of several figures at once; situations which can be either humorous or anxiety-ridden. These effects of symmetry, of doubling up the image, are common in the development of his periods and series; they are metaphorical in the ambiguous doubling of reality through its image; there is a permanent ambiguity at the heart of his general approach. For the most part, his use of photography consists of his taking photographs of objects and himself, which he then, after a fashion, retouches skilfully in paint; this makeover has the effect of denial by tampering with the alleged photographic accuracy.

Van Elk's attitude towards his work is not always obvious, all the more so as he creates and assembles his work according to chance encounters and discoveries. In *Portrait of Red, Yellow and Blue* of 1987 (now in the Musée de Grenoble), he has divided the canvas into two equal parts by means of an oblique; the top half is monochrome or blank; the bottom is composed of a photograph (of reality or a classical painting?), in which the only thing visible in the upper right acute angle is a small face in profile, the remainder of the surface being covered with a kind of informal composition of dark, neutral tones, with the exception of three halves of red, yellow and blue patches on the line separating the two halves. In this example, part of Van Elk's thought process can be deciphered: he questions, interprets and reverses codes of representation and the methods and materials used in this representation. It is based on a traditionally painted canvas, in which he already compares the blank part - which is the place itself, the space for the future painting - with the treated part; he compares in this treated part the image of reality - or painted or photographed reality - with the image of an informal painting, which itself is compared to what is in the end the final, true image of this multiple confrontation: the *Portrait of Red, Yellow and Blue* itself.

He has participated in group exhibitions, including: 1972, 1977, 1982, Documenta in Kassel; 1980, Venice Biennale, representing the Netherlands; 1994, *Art - Pays-Bas - XX Siècle - Du Concept à l'Image* (*Twentieth century Dutch Art: From Concept to Image*), at the ARC (contemporary art section) Musée d'Art Moderne de la Ville de Paris; 2002, *Les Années 70: l'Art en Cause* (*The 1970s: Art in Question*), at the Capc-Musée d'Art Contemporain, Bordeaux. In the 1970s, Van Elk exhibited on a regular basis, notably at the Galerie Art and Project in Amsterdam. In 1980, the Musée d'Art Moderne de la Ville de Paris and the Boymans van Beuningen Museum in Rotterdam held a restrospective exhibition of his work. He has held solo shows, including: since 1990, the Galerie Durand-Dessert Paris; 1996, the Centre d'Art Contemporain in Quimper and the Kröller Müller Museum in Otterlo; 2003, the Galerie Liliane & Michel Durand-Dessert, Paris.

BIBLIOGRAPHY:

Ger Van Elk, exhibition catalogue, ARC Musée d'Art moderne de la Ville de Paris, Paris, 1980. Blistène, Bernard, '*G.V.E. ou l'Envers est contre tout*' et '*Entretien avec Ger van Elk*'' in *Artistes* n° 8, periodical, Paris, March-April 1982. Donker Duyvis, Paul, *Ger van Elk: de la nature des genres*, Centre national d'Art contemporain, Grenoble, 1988. Lageira, Jacinto, '*Ger van Elk: un art contre nature*' in *Artstudio* n° 18, periodical, Gal. Templon, Paris, autumn 1990. '*Entretien avec Ger van Elk*' in *Lettres françaises*, periodical, Paris, September 1990. Cueff, Alain/Jansen, Bert, *Art - Pays-Bas - XXe siècle. Du concept à l'image*, exhibition catalogue, Musée d'Art moderne de la Ville de Paris, Paris, 1994. Fréruchet, Maurice, et al., *Les Années soixante-dix: l'art en cause*, exhibition catalogue, Capc Musée d'Art contemporain, Bordeaux, 2002. Lageira, Jacinto, *Ger Van Elk*, La lettre volée, Brussels, 2002.

MUSEUMS AND GALLERIES:

AMSTERDAM (Stedelijk Mus.): *Apparatus Scalas Dividens* (1969); *Sandwich under Pressure* (1990) - CLERMONT-FERRAND (FRAC Auvergne): *Sculpture of Historic Camping* (1990) - GRENOBLE (Mus. de Grenoble): *Portrait of Red, Yellow and Blue* (1987) - HAARLEM (Frans Halsmus.): *Roquebrune Sculpture* (1979) - NEW YORK (MoMA): *Farewell III* (1974) - ROTTERDAM (Mus. Boijmans Van Beuningen): *Regarding the Reality of G. Morandi* (1971); *Bouquet in the Style of Haarlem* (1982); *Masters of the Western Style* (1987).

AUCTION RECORDS:

NEW YORK, 5 May 1987, *Storm* (1975, gouache/colour photos/zinc plates, diptych, 94 x 42½ ins / 239 x 108 cm) USD 20,000. NEW YORK, 8 May 1990, *View of Lake Kinsel* (1986, polyurethane/photograph, 54 x 120 x 10¼ ins / 137.2 x 304.8 x 26.2 cm) USD 33,000. AMSTERDAM, 23 May 1991, *Sculpture between Two Noses* (1981, oil and photo collage/paper, 55 x 78¾ ins / 140 x 200 cm) NLG 25,300. NEW YORK, 8 Oct 1992, *Study for Honda Gothic* (1986, Cibachrome in a frame by the artist, 40¼ x 25¾ ins / 102.2 x 65.4 cm) USD 3,300. NEW YORK, 10 Nov 1993, *Return of Jkr. Six* (1986, oil/colour photograph/chipboard mounted by the artist, 84½ x 51½ x 3½ ins / 214.6 x 130.8 x 9 cm) USD 6,900. AMSTERDAM, 10 Dec 1996, *Dutch Corners III* (1978, enamel/colour photograph/aluminium construction, 39¼ x 116¼ x 13 ins / 99.7 x 295.5 x 33 cm) NLG 18,451. AMSTERDAM, 2-3 June 1997, *Seven Cubist Mouthpieces* (1979, acrylic, pencil and watercolour/paper, 29¼ x 61½ ins / 74 x 156 cm) NLG 8,260. AMSTERDAM, 11 June 2001, *Conversation Piece* (1977, coloured photograph, 12 x 24 ins / 31 x 60 cm) NLG 8,000. PARIS, 29 April 2003, *Study for 'Orange Blanche Bleu'* (1985, coloured crayon and paint on paper, 83 x 40 ins / 210 x 102 cm) EUR 4,000.

ELKAN, Benno

German, 20th century.
Born 2 December 1877, in Dortmund; died 10 January 1960, in London.
Active in England.
Sculptor, medallist, painter, draughtsman, writer.
Portraits. Busts, medallions, monuments.
Jugendstil.

Benno Elkan was the son of a tailor who had been given Jewish religious instruction. He initially began training for a career in business, but gave it up to study painting in Munich. He studied with Walter Thor and Johann Caspar Herterich, the director of the Akademie der Bildenden Künste, and later with Nicolas Gysis. Later, he worked with Friedrich Fehr at the Karlsruhe academy in 1901 and 1902. During this time he took up sculpture. He spent three years in Paris studying with Albert Bartholomé, who sculpted the monument to the dead in Père-Lachaise Cemetery. He then went to Rome. When he returned to Germany, he settled in Alsbach, near Frankfurt am Main. In 1933, when the Nazis came to power, he fled his country and went to England, settling in Oxford. After the war, a few exhibitions of his works were held in Dortmund and Frankfurt.

His sculptures include medal and bust portraits, for example: *Walter Rathenau* (bust); *Ludwig von Bar*; *Carl Einstein*; *Lotte Herbst*; *G.L. Meyer*; *Pascin*; *Edward VII* (medal, 1902); and *Gustav Mahler* (medal, 1911). He also produced numerous funeral monuments decorated with sculptures, often on allegorical themes, including sculptures in the Ostenfriedhof (Eastern Cemetery) in Dortmund for Christian and Jewish graves. These include: *Tears of Goodbye; Resurrection; Persephone* (bronze); *Nostalgia; Funeral March;* and *The Song that Fades*. He also sculpted other monuments: *Adieu* in Heidelberg; *Pyramid with Low Reliefs* in Cologne; a monument to the war dead in Frankfurt, which was removed by the Nazis, and then replaced after the war; and ornaments in Karlsruhe, Aachen, Cologne and Mainz. In England he was commissioned to make sculptures and a low relief plaque in homage to Rudyard Kipling (1939), which was placed on the Kipling Building in Windsor. He also executed some reliefs for Westminster Abbey and a low relief in the church of Buckfast Abbey. When he was exiled in England, he became preoccupied with his Jewish roots. He made several candlesticks. The British government commissioned him to make a *Menorah*, the symbol of the State of Israel. It measured 16 x 13 feet (5 x 4 metres), with twenty-nine historiated images. It was presented to Israel as a gift and erected at the entrance to the Knesset (the Israeli parliament). He worked on it for six years. Although he was mainly a sculptor, he also continued to paint and draw portraits.

BIBLIOGRAPHY:

Hofmann, Fritz, *Benno Elkan: ein jüdischer Künstler aus Dortmund*, Klartext-Verlag, Essen, 1997. Menzel-Severing, Hans, '*Benno Elkan: ein Bildhauer zwischen Tradition und Moderne*' in *Archiv für Frankfurts Geschichte und Kunst* n° 69 p. 79-97, Frankfurt, 2003.

MUSEUMS AND GALLERIES:

BREMEN (Kunsthalle): medal*Émile Combes*; medal*Mudding Richter* (c. 1905); medal*Hans Thoma* (1904) - COLOGNE (Kunsthalle): *medals* - DORSTEN (Jüdisches Mus. Westfalen) - HAMBURG (Mus. für Kunst und Gewerbe) - MANNHEIM: *Bust of Trübner*.

AUCTION RECORDS:

LONDON, 17 Oct 1980, *The Great Menorah* (bronze, h. 26 ins / 66 cm) GBP 1,700. LOS ANGELES, 9 June 1988, *Pipe Player* (bronze, h. 23 ins / 58.5 cm) USD 2,750. ZURICH, 18 Oct 1990, *Jeremiah* (1957, bronze) CHF 1,800.

ELKAN, David Levy

German, 19th century.

Born 1808, in Cologne; died 1865, in Cologne.

Painter, lithographer.

A pupil at the Düsseldorf academy, Elkan is noted for the *Reichstag of Emperor Maximilian I*, now in the museum in Cologne.

ELKAN, Ernst Joseph

German, 18th century.

Active in Berlin c. 1798.

Miniaturist.

ELKAN, Hugo Siegmund

German, 19th century.

Born 28 December 1868, in Frankfurt am Main; died 9 April 1904, in Frankfurt am Main.

Painter, engraver (etching).

Elkan studied at the schools of arts and crafts in Karlsruhe and Munich and was the pupil of P. Höcker at the Munich academy. He worked in Frankfurt and London, where he painted portraits. He is known for his book-plates and for a plate entitled *Reading*.

ELKEN, E.

British, 19th century.

Painter.

AUCTION RECORDS:

NEW YORK, 30 and 31 Oct 1929, *Ware Hare* USD 110.

ELL, Bernhard

German, 16th century.

Born to a family originally from Schweinfurth.

Sculptor.

Bernhard Ell made the Italianate funerary monument to Count Georg Ernst of Henneberg in the church at Schleusingen.

ELL, Elis., perhaps Elisabeth

German, 15th century.

Active in Nuremberg.

Painter, sculptor (wood).

Elis Ell is thought to have been the wife of the artist Martin.

ELLE, Edouard

Belgian, 19th - 20th century.

Born 1854, in Brussels; died July 1911, in Wépion.

Painter, watercolourist. Genre scenes, seascapes.

Elle was an honorary member of the Société Nationale des Beaux-Arts, and his work was shown in the salons of this institution. In 1910 and 1911, he exhibited at the Salon de la Société des Beaux-Arts in 1910 and 1911.

AUCTION RECORDS:

LOKEREN, 20 May 1995, *Sailing Boats near a Beach* (watercolour, 17 1/4 x 25 1/4 ins / 44 x 64 cm) BEF 44,000.

ELLE, Ferdinand, or Helle, called Ferdinand

Flemish, 17th century.

Born c. 1580, probably in Mechelen; died between 1637 and 1640, in Paris.

Painter.

Flemish School.

Ferdinand Elle went to Paris at a young age and was 'painter in ordinary' to Louis XIII and possibly the master of Nicolas Poussin. In 1609 he carried out a large painting of provosts, merchants, aldermen, procurators and clerks for 400 francs. He was not a member of the academy, as it was not founded until 1648. Despite the fact that he enjoyed considerable success at the time, none of his works has survived, although a *Portrait of Henri de Lorraine, Marquis of Mouy*, now in the museum in Rheims, is attributed to him. Since he was above all known by his first name Ferdinand, his sons Louis and Pierre Elle added this first name to their family name.

MUSEUMS AND GALLERIES:

RHEIMS: *Portrait of Henri de Lorraine, Marquis of Mouy* (attributed).

ELLE, Louis, the Elder, called Ferdinand

French, 17th century.

Born 1612, in Paris; died 12 December 1689, in Paris.

Painter, engraver. Portraits.

Louis Elle was the son of Ferdinand Elle. One of the 12 founders of the Académie de St-Luc in 1648, he was appointed a professor in 1657 but on 10 October 1681 excluded because he was a Protestant. He was reinstated on 26 January 1686. In 1673 Elle exhibited a few portraits in the Salon.

In his portrait painting Elle continued the archaic Flemish tradition of Pourbus, sometimes borrowing from Van Dyke. He conforms exactly to the image of 17th-century portraiture, not characterised by any one particular feature.

Elle.

MUSEUMS AND GALLERIES:

BORDEAUX: *Portrait of a Woman* - PARIS (Louvre): *Portrait of Thomas Regnaudin* - RHEIMS: *St Luke; Presumed Portrait of François d'Épinay*.

AUCTION RECORDS:

PARIS, 13 May 1904, *Portrait of Marie de Rabutin-Chantal, Marquise de Sévigné*, FRF 3,200; *Portrait of Mme de Sévigné*,

FRF 2,700. PARIS, 12 March 1923, *Portrait of a Princess*, FRF 320. PARIS, 8 June 1925, *Portrait of a Young Woman* (school of Louis Elle) FRF 510. PARIS, 25 Feb 1942, *Portrait of Mlle de Lude*, FRF 8,500. LONDON, 2 Nov 2000, *Portrait of Philippe D'Orleans, Duc de Chartres, Wearing a Long Wig and Attired in Embroidered Coat* (oil on canvas, 52 x 39 ins / 131 x 98 cm) GBP 25,000. PARIS, 18 Dec 2000, *Portrait of the Grande Mademoiselle before a Garden* (oil on canvas, 43 x 35 ins / 108 x 90 cm) FRF 250,000.

ELLE, Louis, the Younger, or Ferdinand
French, 17th - 18th century.
Born 1648, in Paris; died 5 September 1717, in Rennes.
Painter. Religious subjects, portraits.

Louis Elle the Younger was the son of Louis Elle the Elder. On 28 June 1681 he became a member of the Académie de St-Luc on the strength of *Miniature Portrait of Samuel Bernard* and in that same year he was excluded with his father for being a Protestant. He was only reinstated after his renunciation on 30 March 1686.

MUSEUMS AND GALLERIES:
LONDON: *Portrait of Thomas Burnet* - PARIS (ENSBA): *Portrait of Regnaudin* - PARIS (Louvre): *Portrait of Samuel Bernard* - RENNES: *Presentation of the Virgin at the Temple* - RENNES (Church of Notre-Dame): *Son of Sceva, Possessed by the Demon*.

AUCTION RECORDS:
PARIS, 13 May 1904, *Presumed Portrait of the Marquise de Sablé*, FRF 3,600. PARIS, 17 June 1985, *Half-length Portrait of a Noblewoman* (oil on canvas, oval, 28 3/4 x 22 3/4 ins / 73 x 58 cm) FRF 12,000.

ELLE, Pierre, called Ferdinand
French, 17th century.
Born 1609, in Paris; died 4 September 1665, in Rheims.
Painter. Portraits.

Pierre Elle was the pupil of his father, Ferdinand Elle.

ELLE, Pieter van
Flemish School, 15th century.
Painter.

According to Siret, Pieter van Elle was involved in preparations for the banquet in Lille in 1453.

ELLEBRANS, Joachim
Flemish School, 16th century.
Active in Ghent in 1526.
Painter.

ELLEBY, William A.
British, 19th century.
Active in Ashbourne.
Painter. Landscapes.

William A. Elleby exhibited frequently at the Royal Academy from 1888 onwards.

ELLENBARCH, Joachim
German, 16th century.
Active in Lüneburg.
Sculptor (wood).

Joachim Ellenbarch worked with Hans Elers.

ELLENDORF, Hans
Swiss, 15th century.
Born to a family originally from Zofingen.
Active in Füssen in 1488.
Painter.

ELLENRIEDER, Maria or Anna Maria
Swiss, 19th century.
Born 20 March 1791, in Constance; died 5 June 1863, in Constance.
Painter, engraver, draughtsman. Religious subjects, portraits.

This artist painted in Zurich between 1816 and 1822. She studied with the miniaturist J. Einsle and later at the Munich academy, and also spent four years studying in Rome. In 1829 she was appointed court painter at the court of the Grand Duchess of Baden. She was awarded a gold medal at Karlsruhe in 1827.

MUSEUMS AND GALLERIES:
CONSTANCE: *Madonna between Two Angels; Head of Christ; Young Boy at Prayer; Girl before a Prayerbook; Abduction of Lydia; Two Angels; Portrait of Baron von Wessenberg; Virgin, Infant Jesus and St Nicholas; Altarpiece* (draft); *Studies; Watercolours* - CONSTANCE (Rosgartenmus.): *Portrait of the Artist; The Artist's Parents; Portrait of the Grand Duchess Louise* - DONAUESCHINGEN (Fürstlich Fürstenbergisches Sammlungen): *Virgin with Child* - HANOVER: *Portrait of the Artist* - KARLSRUHE: *Portrait of the Artist; Virgin of the Bower; Peter and Tabitha* - ZURICH (Kunsthaus): *Caspar Fries* - ZURICH (Society of Art Collection): studies and sketches.

AUCTION RECORDS:
PARIS, 13-14 April 1942, *Portrait of a Girl*, FRF 1,700. ZURICH, 18 Nov 1981, *Portrait of a Young Girl* (black and coloured chalk/pencil outlines/paper, 14 3/4 x 11 1/2 ins / 37.5 x 29.5 cm) CHF 3,300. AMSTERDAM, 10 April 1990, *Contemplation* (1847, pencil and ink/paper, 5 x 3 1/2 ins / 12.4 x 8.8 cm) NLG 2,530. MUNICH, 1-2 Dec 1992, *Wir Huldigen dem heiligen und Ehrwürdigen* (1836, oil on canvas, 12 1/4 x 14 1/4 ins / 31 x 36 cm) DEM 9,200. MUNICH, 7 Dec 1993, *St Cecilia* (black chalk/paper, 18 3/4 x 14 1/4 ins / 47.5 x 36 cm) DEM 1,495. HEIDELBERG, 3 April 1998, *Virgin with Lily* (oil on panel, 26 x 18 ins / 67 x 45 cm) DEM 12,000. MUNICH, 27 Feb 1999, *St Rosa of Lima with Rose Garland on Head* (oil on panel, 20 x 15 ins / 50 x 38 cm) DEM 8,000. BERLIN, 4 June 1999, *Clouds Passing over Wheat Fields* (oil on canvas, 27 x 35 ins / 69 x 90 cm) DEM 26,000. MUNICH, 26 Sept 2001, *Two Angels Praying* (1850, oil on canvas, 36 x 29 ins / 92 x 74 cm) DEM 10,000. STAUFEN, 23 May 2003, *St John the Baptist as a Child in Landscape* (1830, oil on canvas, 42 x 23 ins / 106 x 59 cm) EUR 4,000.

ELLENRIEDER, Rudolph
German, 19th century.
Born 1781, in Ulm.
Engraver (burin/wood).

Ellenrieder is noted for views and genre subjects.

ELLÉOUËT, Aube, or Breton-Elléouët
French, 20th century.
Born 20 December 1935, in Paris.
Collage artist.

Aube Elléouët was the daughter of André Breton and Jacqueline Lamba. She lived in the USA from 1940 to 1946, with a year, 1944, in Mexico. From 1946 until her father's death in 1966 she lived in Paris; then in 1966 settled in Saché. In 1972 she produced her first collages. Her method of making collages was inspired by those of Max Ernst. Starting with a collection of all sorts of documents, cut to pieces and reassembled, she would produce baffling scenes, situations and creatures, all the more confusing because the original documents were quite unrelated, so that the elements of the final collage were on different scales, some in colour, some in black and white. Michel Leiris wrote, 'The charm of Aube Elléouët's collages lies in the fact that they do not look like collages at all, so natural do the juxtapositions of the varied elements appear'.

Elléouët began to exhibit in solo and collective shows in 1974, including several Surrealist exhibitions in Germany, England and France 1977-1981; 1984, *International Exhibi-*

tion of Women's Posters in Los Angeles; 1987, *Autour d'André Breton (Around André Breton)*, Galerie Artcurial, Paris; 1989, Surrealist exhibitions in Milan, Frankfurt and Canada; 1991, *Autour d'André Breton (Around Andrè Breton)* at St-Cirq-Lapopie (Lot); 2000, *Le Mouvement Phases de 1952 à l'horizon 2001 (The Phases Movement from 1952 to the New Millennium)* at the Kiosque Cultural Centre in Mayenne and the Noirot Centre in Arras.

Elléouët's solo exhibitions included 1974, the Salle Jean Vilar in Tours; 1977, 1978, Galerie Le Triskèle, Paris; 1991, Villeneuve-Loubet; 1993, Azay-le-Rideau; 1994, Centre Culturel Ernest Renan in Tréguier; 1995, Fougères; 1997, Azay-le-Rideau and St-Malo; 1998, St-Pierre-des-Corps and 2000, Galerie 1900-2000 in Paris.

BIBLIOGRAPHY:

Aube Elléouët, Collages, exhibition catalogue, Galerie 1900-2000, Paris, 2000.

AUCTION RECORDS:

PARIS, 20 May 1994, *Du côté de chez Swann (Swann's Way)* (1978, collage, 13 3/4 x 10 1/4 ins / 35 x 26 cm) FRF 6,000.

ELLER, pseudonym of Roudier, Lucien
French, 20th century.
Born 2 January 1894, in Marseilles.
Painter, draughtsman, watercolourist. Figures, scenes with figures, interiors with figures, nudes.

Eller illustrated *Marseille sur le vif (Marseilles Taken from Life)*. He showed work at the Salon des Humoristes.

AUCTION RECORDS:

PARIS, 19 Dec 1944, *Don Quixote*, FRF 3,000; *Dancer in a Yellow Dress*, FRF 3,100; *Dancing*, FRF 2,500. PARIS, 3 June 1987, *Vision in the Harem* (watercolour, 11 1/2 x 16 1/2 ins / 29 x 42 cm) FRF 4,000. PARIS, 5 July 1989, *Young Woman Nude on a Sofa* (painting/canvas, 9 x 12 1/2 ins / 23 x 32 cm) FRF 3,700. PARIS, 8 Nov 1989, *Two Friends in a Café* (oil on canvas, 18 x 22 ins / 46 x 55 cm) FRF 8,000. PARIS, 1 Oct 2003, *Characters from the Films of Pagnol* (oil on canvas, 37 x 29 ins / 93 x 73 cm) EUR 3,500.

ELLERBROCK
German, 17th century.
Painter.

Siret refers to this artist. Several painters of the same name lived in Hamburg in the 17th and 18th centuries.

ELLERBROCK, Hinrich
German, 17th century.
Born before 1600; died 1651.
Active in Hamburg.
Painter.

Ellerbrock received the accolade of master in 1620. He is noted for a wash drawing depicting a crippled beggar, dated 1608.

ELLERBY, Thomas
British, 19th century.
Active in London.
Painter. Genre scenes, figures.

Thomas Ellerby exhibited in London, notably at the Royal Academy and Suffolk Street Gallery, from 1821 to 1857.

ELLERHUSEN, Florence Cooney
Canadian, 20th century.
Born in Canada.
Active in the USA.
Painter.

Florence Ellerhusen studied in the USA, where she settled. She was a member of the Allied Artists of America and the National Association of Women Painters and Sculptors. She was also a teacher.

ELLERHUSEN, Ulric Henry
German, 20th century.
Born 7 April 1879, in Germany.
Active in the USA.
Sculptor.

Ellerhusen went to the USA at the age of 15 and later became a member of the Art Institute of Chicago. He was also taught by Karl Bitter. A member of a number of art associations, he was awarded first prize for the medal of the St Louis Art League, as well as a medal of honour for sculpture from the Architectural League of New York in 1929. His best-known works are: *Monument for Peace - Table of Communion* of St Gregory the Great in New York, and *The March of Religion*, which is on the south pediment of the chapel of the University of Chicago.

ELLEROHT, Andreas
German, 18th century.
Active in Lübeck.
Sculptor.

In 1725, Elleroht worked on the woodcarvings for the organ in the church of St Peter.

ELLEROHT, Herman Andreas
German, 18th century.
Active in Lübeck.
Sculptor (wood).

Undoubtedly the same person as Andreas, he worked on the woodcarvings for the stalls in the church of St Mary.

ELLERT, Nikolai Lyudvigovich
Russian, 19th century.
Born 1845; died 1901.
Active in Moscow.
Painter, theatre designer.

Ellert was initially a painter of stage sets for the Imperial Opera in Moscow; it was not until 1880 that he went to study at the academy there and devoted himself to landscape and animal painting.

MUSEUMS AND GALLERIES:

MOSCOW (State Tretyakov Gal.): *Herd of Horses*; *Before the Storm*; *Evening* (sepia).

ELLERTON, Frances
British, 20th century.
Born in York.
Painter. Genre scenes.

In 1934, Frances Ellerton exhibited at the Salon de la Société Nationale, showing *Redhead* and *Olivia*.

ELLERTSON, Homer E.
American, 20th century.
Born 23 December 1892, in River Falls (Wisconsin); died 1935.
Painter, illustrator.

Homer Ellertson was a member of the Scandinavian-American Society of Artists.

MUSEUMS AND GALLERIES:

WASHINGTON DC (Phillips Collection): *The Encore*; *The Ebro*.

ELLICOTT, Henry Jackson A.
American, 19th century.
Born 1848, near Ellicott (Maryland); died 11 February 1901, in Washington DC.
Sculptor.

Henry Jackson A. Ellicott began his studies in Washington and completed them in New York. Generally considered to be among his best works are the equestrian statue of *General Hancock* in Washington DC, and that of *General McClellan* in Philadelphia.

ELLIEUL, Christian d'
19th century.
Painter (?), draughtsman (?).

Is known only through a lithograph, dated 1823, made from his *Portrait of Leo XII*, by an unknown artist. He was mentioned as an engraver by Nagler.

ELLIGER, Antoni
Dutch, 18th century.
Born 1701, in Amsterdam; died 1781; buried 5 June in Ede op de Veluwe.
Painter. History painting, portraits.

Antoni Elliger was a pupil of his father Ottmar II and lived in Amsterdam. In 1724 he married Cristina Houbraken. Around 1766 he lived in Haarlem and taught Juriaan Andrienssen and Jan Gérard Waldorp.

AUCTION RECORDS:
COLOGNE, 25 Aug 1862, *Inebriated Peasant Asleep,* FRF 34.

ELLIGER, Christiana Maria, wife of Sam
Dutch, 18th century.
Born 1732, in Amsterdam.
Painter.

Christiana Maria Elliger was the daughter of Antoni Elliger.

ELLIGER, Ottmar or Ottomars, the Elder
Swedish, 17th century.
Born 18 September 1633, in Göteborg or Copenhagen; died 1679; buried 31 December in Berlin.
Painter. Genre scenes, figures, insects, still-lifes (flowers/fruit).

Elliger was a pupil of Daniel Seghers in Antwerp. Around 1660 he was resident in Amsterdam, marrying Teuntje van Walscappel there on 12 March. By 1666 he was living in Hamburg, and by 1670 in Berlin, where he was court painter at the court of Elector Frederick William, with an allowance of 400 thalers.

Ottmar. Elliger.
Fecit Ano 1677

MUSEUMS AND GALLERIES:
AMSTERDAM: *Flowers and Grapes* - BASEL: *Hamadryad* - BERLIN (Gemäldegal.): *Princess Dorothea of Holstein, Second Wife of the Great Elector, Surrounded by a Garland of Flowers;* six still-lifes - DRESDEN: *Flowers and Fruit; Flowers and Fruit with a Blue Ribbon* - FRANKFURT AM MAIN (Städel): *Butterflies and Other Insects on a Marble Table* - HAMBURG: *Flowers; Young Woman in a Garden; Portrait of the Theologian J. Hellwig* - HAMBURG (Kunsthalle): *St George* (after Raphael) - SCHWERIN: *Two Garlands of Fruit* - SIBIU: *Breakfast* - STOCKHOLM (Ekman Collection): *Five Women in a Bath* - STOCKHOLM (Stuart Collection): *Fruit.*

AUCTION RECORDS:
AMSTERDAM, 17 April 1708, *The Flowering of Art,* FRF 125. PARIS, 1888, *Still-life,* FRF 250. PARIS, 5 June 1921, *Fruit, Ears of Barley; Dragonflies and Butterflies,* FRF 530. LONDON, 24 March 1922, *Lobster with Fruit, Wineglasses and Other Objects on a Marble Table* (1665) GBP 63. PARIS, 24 June 1929, *Flying Cupids Bearing Flowers* (drawing) FRF 430. PARIS, 23 Feb 1951, *Flowers and Lizards* (two pictures) FRF 143,000. LUCERNE, 29 Nov 1968, *Still-life,* CHF 18,000. STOCKHOLM, 26-28 March 1969, *Still-life with Flowers,* SEK 51,000. LONDON, 2 Dec 1977, *Still-life with Flowers* (oil on canvas, 18 1/2 x 12 ins / 47 x 30.5 cm) GBP 7,500. LONDON, 13 Dec 1985, *Still-life with Fruit, Wineglass and Nautilus Shell* (1667, oil on panel, 26 x 21 1/4 ins / 66 x 54 cm) GBP 65,000. LONDON, 15 Dec 1989, *Salome Offering the Head of St John the Baptist to Herod* (1660, oil on panel, 18 1/2 x 24 1/2 ins / 47 x 62.3 cm) GBP 7,700. AMSTERDAM, 13 Nov 1995, *Irises, Tulips, Anemones, Roses, Forget-me-nots, Buttercups, Guelder Roses and Other Flowers in a Glass Vase with Butterflies and an Orange on an Entablature* (oil on canvas, 29 x 23 3/4 ins / 73.4 x 60.3 cm) NLG 69,000. LUCERNE, 19 May 1999, *Romer in a Niche Surrounded by Garland of Fruit* (oil on canvas, 27 x 35 ins / 69 x 88 cm) CHF 22,000.

ELLIGER, Ottmar, the Younger
German, 17th - 18th century.
Born 19 February 1666, in Hamburg; died 19 February 1735, in St Petersburg.
Painter. Religious subjects, mythological subjects, allegorical subjects, still-lifes (flowers/fruit).

Elliger's father, Ottmar the Elder, was his first master; he then worked with Michiel de Musscher in Amsterdam in 1679 and with Gérard de Lairesse in 1686. He worked in Mainz in 1716 or 1717 for the prince elector on the paintings of *Alexander on his Deathbed* and the *Marriage of Peleus and Thetis.*

Elliger O.

MUSEUMS AND GALLERIES:
BORDEAUX: *Allegory* - GÖTTINGEN (Kunstsammlung, Georg-August-Universität): *Dead Christ with Angels* (after Van Dyck) - HAMBURG: *Death of Sophonisba; Cleopatra's Banquet* - KASSEL: *Cleopatra's Banquet; Dance of Salome* - PUSHKIN: *Dido on the Funeral Pyre* - VIENNA: *Woman at a Window.*

AUCTION RECORDS:
AMSTERDAM, 17 April 1708, *Allegory on the Town Hall,* FRF 145. PARIS, 1755, *Mark Antony and Cleopatra; Death of Cleopatra* (two pendants) FRF 225. PARIS, 1875, *Subjects from the Life of Jesus Christ* (twelve pen and Indian ink drawings) FRF 15. PARIS, 28 Feb 1919, *Antique Banquet,* FRF 160. PARIS, 24 May 1923, *Young Woman with Black Pageboy* (unclear whether attributable to Ottmar the Younger or Ottmar the Elder) FRF 500. COLOGNE, 17 Nov 1966, *Vulcan Surprising Venus and Mars,* DEM 26,000. LONDON, 29 March 1968, *Peach Tree in an Urn,* Gns 380. NEW YORK, 8 Jan 1981, *Still-life with Flowers and Fruit* (oil on canvas, 25 1/2 x 30 3/4 ins / 65 x 78 cm) USD 10,000. PARIS, 16 March 1990, *Elijah and the Chariot of Fire* (Indian ink heightened with white on pencil sketch, 5 1/2 x 8 ins / 14 x 20.5 cm) FRF 4,000. NEW YORK, 12 Jan 1995, *Aeneas and his Son Ascanius Visiting Dido* (oil on canvas, 24 1/2 x 20 1/4 ins / 62.2 x 51.4 cm) USD 29,900. PARIS, 12 Dec 1995, *Achilles Discovered among the Daughters of Lycomedes; Salome Dancing before Herod* (oil on canvas, a pair, each 22 x 26 3/4 ins / 55 x 68 cm) FRF 120,000. PARIS, 16 Dec 1997, *Death of Cleopatra* (oil on canvas, 22 3/4 x 31 1/4 ins / 58 x 79.5 cm) FRF 18,000. VIENNA, 30 March 2000, *The Feast of Plato* (oil on canvas, 14 x 26 ins / 35 x 65 cm) ATS 110,000. LONDON, 31 Oct 2001, *Banquet of Cleopatra* (oil on canvas, 24 x 28 ins / 60 x 72 cm) GBP 5,800. HEIDELBERG, 20 April 2002, *Cleopatra's Banquet* (oil on canvas, 23 x 27 ins / 58 x 68 cm) EUR 8,000. NEW YORK, 7 June 2002, *Banquet of Cleopatra* (oil on canvas, 24 x 28 ins / 60 x 72 cm) USD 6,000. PARIS, 24 June 2004, *Allegory of Autumn* (oil on canvas, 19 x 16 ins / 49 x 41 cm) EUR 9,000.

ELLING, Jacobus
Dutch, 18th century.
Active in Middelburg.
Painter.

Jacobus Elling entered the Academy of St Luke in 1764.

ELLINGER (Abbot of Tegernsee), or Werner, Werinher, Wernher
German, 11th century.
Died 1056.
Illuminator, copyist.

At first an ordinary monk in the monastery of Tegernsee, Ellinger became abbot and encouraged his monks to cultivate the art of calligraphy and illumination. Known to be by him are miniatures in the four gospels, and a painting showing Jesus Christ offering his hand to the Pope that is in a manuscript dated 1017. A Gospel written by him is held

by the national library in Munich; he decorated a *Life of the Virgin* in the library of Berlin; he is also thought to be the painter of the animals that decorate a copy of Pliny's *Natural History*.
MUSEUMS AND GALLERIES:
BERLIN (Deutsches Staatsbibliothek) - MUNICH (Bayerische Staatsbibliothek).

ELLINGER (Dr)
Polish, 19th century.
Active in Vienna.
Painter, watercolourist. Portraits.
Ellinger produced a watercolour portrait of *M.T. Nartowski* which featured in an exhibition of miniatures in Lemberg (now Lviv, Ukraine) in 1912.

ELLINGER, Gaspar
Hungarian, 17th century.
Died 1621 or 1622, in Kassa (now Košice, Slovakia).
Painter.
Gaspar Ellinger was made a citizen of Kassa in 1616.

ELLINKHUYSEN, M. J.
18th century.
Active in 1783.
Engraver (glass).
MUSEUMS AND GALLERIES:
ROTTERDAM (Mus. Boijmans Van Beuningen): *Equestrian Portrait of Prince Peter Petrovitch of Russia*.

ELLIOT. See also **ELLIOTT**

ELLIOT, Bert
American, 19th - 20th century.
Died 1931, in New York.
Painter.
Bert Elliot spent his youth in Japan. He was a member of the *No Jury Group of Artists* in Chicago.
MUSEUMS AND GALLERIES:
CHICAGO (AI).

ELLIOT, Edward
British, 19th - 20th century.
Born 1850; died 1916.
Active in Wymondham.
Painter. Figure compositions, landscapes.
Edward Elliot exhibited frequently in London from 1879, notably at the Royal Academy and the Suffolk Street Gallery.
AUCTION RECORDS:
LONDON, 4 Nov 1994, *Herring Market at Lowestoft* (1901, oil on canvas, 41 x 72 1/4 ins / 104.1 x 183.5 cm) GBP 5,175.

ELLIOT, Rebecca
British, 19th century.
Active in London.
Painter, watercolourist. Genre scenes, flowers.
Rebecca Elliot exhibited flower paintings at the Suffolk Street Gallery in 1878.
AUCTION RECORDS:
LONDON, 13 Dec 1909, *Oscar and Sandy* (watercolour) GBP 2.

ELLIOT, Ric
Australian, 20th century.
Born 1933.
Painter. Landscapes.
AUCTION RECORDS:
SYDNEY, 28 June 1981, *Mosman Bay* (oil on card, 12 1/2 x 19 3/4 ins / 32 x 50 cm) AUD 700. SYDNEY, 20 March 1989, *Island Village* (oil on card, 17 3/4 x 33 3/4 ins / 45 x 86 cm) AUD 1,100. SYDNEY, 26 March 1990, *Start of the Drought at Cowra* (oil on card, 17 3/4 x 23 1/2 ins / 45 x 60 cm) AUD 1,500. SYDNEY, 2 July 1990, *Fortified Farm at Windsor* (oil on card, 11 3/4 x 17 1/4 ins / 30 x 44 cm) AUD 900. SYDNEY, 2 Dec 1991, *On the Luminous Ridge* (oil on card, 11 3/4 x 15 3/4 ins / 30 x 40 cm) AUD 950. SYDNEY, 6 March 2002, *Country Town* (oil on board, 18 x 15 ins / 45 x 37 cm) AUD 3,800. SYDNEY, 27 Aug 2002, *Afternoon on the Street* (oil on board, 13 x 18 ins / 33 x 46 cm) AUD 3,000.

ELLIOT, Robert James (Captain)
British, 19th century.
Died 30 April 1849, in Pentonville (London).
Painter. Seascapes.
Prout and Stanfields published numerous drawings in the style of works produced by Robert Eliot during his long journeys between 1784 and 1789. Elliot also sent several works to the Royal Academy between 1784 and 1789, including *View of the City of Quebec* in 1786 and *Fire in Kensington (Jamaica)* in 1788.

ELLIOT, William, or Elliott
British, 18th century.
Born 1727, in London; died 1766, in London.
Painter, engraver, reproductions engraver.
Landscapes.
William Elliot engraved several landscapes. The best are in the style of the paintings of the Smith brothers of Chichester.

ELLIOTT, Aileen Mary Edith
British, 20th century.
Born 1896, in Southampton.
Watercolourist.
Aileen Mary Edith Elliott worked with E. T. Jones and exhibited watercolours in Paris at the Salon des Artistes Français from 1930.

ELLIOTT, Charles Loring
American, 19th century.
Born 12 October 1812, in Auburn (New York State); died 25 August 1868, in Albany.
Painter. Portraits.
Initially Charles Loring Elliott worked as a clerk in Syracuse, where he spent all his leisure time drawing and painting, and then went to New York in 1824 and became a pupil of Trumbull. He lived for 10 years on the west coast before finally settling in New York. He sent a *Portrait of Fletcher Harper* to the Exposition de Paris in 1867. It is said that he painted more than 700 portraits of notable people and only one landscape, *Lake Skaneateles*. He painted portraits of the poet Fitz-Halleck Greene, James Fenimore Cooper, Watthew Vassar, the painters Cluirch and Durand, and Governor Morgan, as well as works of a quite different genre, such as *Don Quixote* and *Falstaff*. His portraits are remarkable likenesses.
MUSEUMS AND GALLERIES:
SYRACUSE (Everson MA): *Self-portrait* (1834, oil on canvas); *Portrait of Samuel Larned* (oil on canvas).
AUCTION RECORDS:
NEW YORK, 23 March 1979, *Portrait of a Man* (oil on canvas, 25 x 20 3/4 ins / 63.5 x 53 cm) USD 1,700. NEW YORK, 8 Sept 2004, *Portrait of H.W. Hewitt* (oil on canvas, 30 x 25 ins / 76 x 63 cm) USD 2,000.

ELLIOTT, Edith
British, 20th century.
Born in Kippax (West Yorkshire).
Watercolourist.

ELLIOTT, Elizabeth Shippen. See **GREEN**

ELLIOTT, Hannah
American, 20th century.
Born 29 September 1876, in Atlanta; died 1956.
Miniaturist, illustrator.
Hannah Elliot studied in the USA and Europe. In 1921 she won third prize in the miniature category in Charleston. She was also a teacher.

ELLIOTT, James, or Elliot
British, 19th century.
Painter. Genre scenes, landscapes.

James Elliott appeared at the Royal Academy and Suffolk Street Gallery in London from 1848 to 1873.

AUCTION RECORDS:
LONDON, 6 Feb 1985, *Return from the Fields* (oil on canvas, 11 1/4 x 10 ins / 28.5 x 25.5 cm) GBP 1,300. NEWBURY, 18 Sept 2002, *Pilchard Boats. Lobster Fishing. Herring Fishing* (1874, pencil and watercolour, three, 12 x 20 ins / 30 x 52 cm) GBP 1,300.

ELLIOTT, James, or Elliot
British, 19th century.
Painter. Landscapes.

James Elliott worked in Manchester and appeared in exhibitions in London, notably at the Royal Academy, from 1882 to 1897, with landscapes of Wales.

ELLIOTT, John
American, 19th - 20th century.
Born 22 April 1858, in England; died 1925.
Painter, watercolourist, draughtsman. Allegorical subjects, figures, portraits. Murals.

John Elliott studied at the British Museum in London and the Académie Julian in Paris, where he was a pupil of Carolus-Duran, before working with José Villegas in Rome. He visited Egypt and Greece and finally settled in America.

Notable among his portraits are those of King Humbert I of Italy, Lord Alva, Lord Winchester, Lord Cromer, General Wanchope and the Duke of Cambridge.

MUSEUMS AND GALLERIES:
BOSTON (Old State House): *Portrait of Mrs Julia Ward Howe* - BOSTON (Public Library): *The Triumph of Time* (wall painting, ceiling) - CHICAGO (Palmer House): *The Grape Harvest* (wall and ceiling painting) - NEW YORK (Metropolitan Mus. of Art) - WASHINGTON DC (Smithsonian American AM): *Diana of the Tides* (1908, oil on canvas).

AUCTION RECORDS:
LONDON, 6 Feb 1980, *Cook's Sailing Boat The Resolution in the Pacific* (watercolour and pen, 10 x 16 ins / 24.5 x 40.5 cm) GBP 2,200. NEW YORK, 14 March 1996, *Putti Wine Harvesters* (oil on canvas, 35 x 82 3/4 ins / 88.9 x 210.2 cm) USD 13,800.

ELLIOTT, Robinson, or Elliot
British, 19th century.
Born 1814; died 1894.
Painter. Genre scenes, landscapes with figures.

MUSEUMS AND GALLERIES:
SUNDERLAND: *At School.*

AUCTION RECORDS:
AMSTERDAM, 30 Oct 1991, *Wooded Landscape with a Child Playing on the Rocky Shore of a River and with a Peasant and His Cow* (1884, oil on canvas, 20 x 30 ins / 50.5 x 76 cm) NLG 1,840. CLWYD, 25 April 2000, *Fisherman's Wife and Child Looking Out to Sea* (oil on canvas, 17 x 13 ins / 43 x 33 cm) GBP 1,400. LONDON, 20 Feb 2003, *Soldier's Child* (1880, oil on board, 9 x 7 ins / 22 x 17 cm) GBP 8,500.

ELLIOTT, Ronnie, or Elliot
American, 20th century.
Born 1916, in New York.
Painter.

Ronnie Elliott held solo exhibitions in Paris in 1948 and 1952, then in the USA in New York. He was initially influenced by the Impressionism of Cézanne, then in 1937 by the Surrealists. He evolved towards the abstract style of Kandinsky and Mondrian and from 1945 his work was strictly abstract, resembling Monet's Luminism of the 1870s.

ELLIOTT, William (Captain), or Elliot
British, 18th century.
Died 21 July 1792, in Leeds.
Painter. Military subjects, seascapes.

William Elliott was active from 1784 to 1791. He chiefly painted detailed episodes from historical maritime battles, and also views of harbours, particularly Portsmouth harbour in wartime.

MUSEUMS AND GALLERIES:
LONDON (Royal Collection): *A Naval Review* (1790); *View of Part of the British Fleet at Spithead* (179?); *View of Part of the British Fleet at Portsmouth* - OPORTO: *Battle between Two Ships.*

AUCTION RECORDS:
LONDON, 13 Dec 1972, *Boats off the Coast of Portsmouth* (two pendants) GBP 8,000. LONDON, 4 April 1973, *Warships in Portsmouth Harbour,* GBP 2,600. LONDON, 14 July 1976, *Warships in Portsmouth Harbour* (oil on canvas, 26 x 44 ins / 66 x 112 cm) GBP 2,400. LONDON, 14 July 1976, *Fishing Boats in Portsmouth Harbour* (oil on canvas, 26 x 44 ins / 66 x 112 cm) GBP 2,400. LONDON, 2 Dec 1977, *View of the Port of Portsmouth* (oil on canvas, 33 1/2 x 54 1/2 ins / 85 x 138.5 cm) GBP 1,700. LONDON, 11 April 1980, *English Warships at Sea* (oil on canvas, 16 3/4 x 26 3/4 ins / 42.5 x 68 cm) GBP 3,500. LONDON, 27 June 1980, *Naval Battle of the Saints, 12 April 1782* (oil on canvas, 60 1/2 x 103 3/4 ins / 153.6 x 263.6 cm) GBP 4,800. LONDON, 16 Nov 1983, *Boats and Fleet off the Coast of Portsmouth* (oil on canvas, a pair, 22 3/4 x 35 1/4 ins / 58 x 89.5 cm) GBP 10,500. LONDON, 15 July 1987, *Lord Howe's Flagship The Queen Charlotte after the Battle of the Glorious First of June 1794* (1794, oil on canvas, 49 1/2 x 59 3/4 ins / 126 x 152 cm) GBP 7,500. LONDON, 11 July 1990, *Royal Fleet Covering the Retreat of the Frigates 'Druid' and 'Eurydice' off the Coast of Guernsey* (oil on canvas, a pair, each 23 x 34 3/4 ins / 58.5 x 88.5 cm) GBP 33,000. LONDON, 12 July 1990, *Battle of the Saints: the 'City of Paris' Lowering Its Colours before the 'Barfleur' of the Royal Fleet in the West Indies in 1782* (oil on canvas, 36 1/2 x 54 1/2 ins / 92.7 x 138.5 cm) GBP 15,400. NEW YORK, 7 June 1991, *Warship in the Harbour of Portsmouth* (oil on canvas, 34 1/2 x 55 1/2 ins / 87.9 x 141 cm) USD 33,000. LONDON, 18 Nov 1992, *War Vessel and Other English Ships in the Port of Portsmouth* (oil on canvas, 33 1/2 x 54 1/4 ins / 85 x 138 cm) GBP 18,150. LONDON, 11 May 1994, *The Vessel Boyne in Flames and Other Small Craft off the Coasts at Spithead* (oil on canvas, 23 1/4 x 35 ins / 59 x 89 cm) GBP 6,900. LONDON, 13 July 1994, *Portsmouth Harbour* (1794, oil on canvas, 23 1/4 x 35 ins / 59 x 89 cm) GBP 9,775. LONDON, 6 Nov 1995, *Vice Admiral Sir Allen Gardner on His Ship Firing a Broadside* (oil on canvas). LONDON, 3 April 1996, *Cannons of Southsea Castle with the 98-Cannon Ship 'Queen' in the Forefront and the Channel Fleet in Spithead in the Distance, 1795* (1795, oil on canvas, 23 1/4 x 35 ins / 59 x 89 cm) USD 23,000. NEW YORK, 11 April 1997, *Admiral Sir Samuel Hood on the 'Barfleur'. 98 Cannons* (1790, oil on canvas, 36 1/2 x 54 ins / 92.7 x 137.2 cm) USD 33,350. LONDON, 16 Jan 2002, *Large Scale Anglo-French Naval Engagement* (oil on canvas, 60 x 103 ins / 152 x 262 cm) GBP 18,000.

ELLIS, Alice Blanche
British, 19th century.
Painter.

Alice Blanche Ellis appeared at the Suffolk Street Gallery and the Royal Academy between 1876 and 1883.

ELLIS, Arthur
British, 19th - 20th century.
Born 1856, in Holloway; died 1918.
Painter. Genre scenes, landscapes.

Arthur Ellis exhibited eight times at the Royal Academy in London from 1874 to 1892.

AUCTION RECORDS:
LONDON, 26 Sept 1984, *Harvest Scene* (oil on canvas, 36 1/4 x 54 1/4 ins / 92 x 137.8 cm) GBP 1,100. LONDON, 2 June 1989, *Pensive Young Woman* (oil on canvas, 24 x 20 ins / 61 x 51 cm) GBP 1,320.

ELLIS, C. Wynn
British, 19th - 20th century.
Painter. Portraits, genre scenes.

From 1882 to 1908, C. Wynn Ellis exhibited in London at the Royal Academy and the New Water-Colour Society. He also took part in many other London exhibitions.

ELLIS, Clifford
British, 20th century.
Born 1907, in Bognor Regis (Sussex); died 1985.
Painter, designer, printmaker. Buildings, animals, natural subjects. Mosaics, murals, book jackets and posters.

Clifford Ellis came from an artistic family: his grandfather was an artist, while his uncle Ralph Ellis had studied at the Slade School of Art and worked as a designer. As a child, he enjoyed drawing animals at London Zoo. He first attended St Martin's School of Art in London for one year, then studied illustration at the Regent Street Polytechnic School of Art from 1924 to 1927, and did a postgraduate teacher-training course in 1928 at the London Day Training College. His teacher, Marion Richardson, known for her innovative approach in teaching art to children, was a great influence on him and introduced him to the artist and writer Roger Fry. In 1929 he obtained a diploma in Art History from London University.

Ellis taught at the Regent Street Polytechnic School from 1928 to 1936. In 1936 he moved to Bath Technical College (later Bath Academy of Art), and in 1938 he was appointed director of its School of Art until 1972. There he pioneered an innovative syllabus in 1946 by creating a foundation course, a first-year study of materials and techniques, as a preliminary to the diploma in Art and Design. He also introduced a broad range of other subjects such as music and literature. He declined the offer of a chair in fine art at Newcastle in 1946, preferring to remain at the Bath Academy. In 1962, the Research Centre in Art Education was established at the Bath Academy, with Ellis as one of the senior advisers.

Collaborating with his wife, the artist Rosemary Collinson, Ellis created many designs for book jackets, posters, decorative tiles, ceramic statuettes and mosaics. In the 1930s they made poster designs for the London Passenger Transport Board, BP Ltd and the Post Office. For Shell Mex, they designed the Shell 'Professions' series of advertising posters, such as *Antiquaries Prefer Shell* and *Anglers Prefer Shell*. Book jackets include a number for the Collins *New Naturalist* series. Clifford and Rosemary Ellis also created mosaics for walls and floors of bathrooms and for swimming pools, their work being shown in the British Art in Industry exhibition and the British Art in Relation to Home exhibition. They designed the entrance hall floor for the British Pavilion at the 1937 Paris International Exhibition. Ellis also did work for the Pilgrim Trust *Recording Britain* project during World War II, such as his watercolour *VE Day, Bath, 8 May 1945*. His works have been exhibited in *Landscape in Britain 1850-1950*, Hayward Gallery, London (1983); *Art Deco Underground*, London Transport Museum (1988); and at the Michael Parkin Gallery, London (1989).

BIBLIOGRAPHY:
Pope, Derek (ed.), *A Celebration of the Bath Academy of Art at Corsham*, Illustrated book, Rose and Unicorn House, Corsham, 1997.

MUSEUMS AND GALLERIES:
BRISTOL (City Mus. & AG): *Lansdown Place Bath, Bombed Interior 1942* (1942, pen and ink, wash) - DARTINGTON (College of Arts): *Pigs and Ducks* (1948, gouache) - LONDON (Imperial War Mus.): *VE Day, Bath, 8 May 1945* (1945, watercolour) - LONDON (Transport Mus.): *Third Test Match, the Oval* (1939, lithographic poster); *River* (1933, lithographic poster); *Wood* (1933, lithographic poster) - LONDON (UK Government Art Collection): *Here Lived Edmund Burke* (1942, watercolour).

ELLIS, Clyde Garfield
American, 20th century.
Born 25 December 1879, in Humboldt (Kansas); died 1970, in Los Angeles.
Painter.

Clyde Ellis was a decorative artist and teacher. He won first prize at the Oklahoma State Fair.

ELLIS, Edith Kate
British, 20th century.
Born in Staffordshire.
Painter.

Edith Kate Ellis exhibited in Paris at the Salon des Artistes Français from 1929.

ELLIS, Edmond Lewis
American, 19th - 20th century.
Born 30 October 1872, in Omaha (Nebraska).
Painter, engraver, decorative designer.

Edmond Ellis was also an architect. He decorated the interiors of public buildings, notably the Protestant episcopal church of Fordham, and private houses. He produced etchings.

ELLIS, Edwin John
British, 19th century.
Born 1841, in Nottingham; died 19 April 1895.
Painter, draughtsman. Landscapes, seascapes.

Edwin Ellis was employed as a designer in a lace factory. Around the age of 20, he switched to studying art. After having benefited from lessons from Henry Dawson, he went to France. In 1893, he exhibited 84 of his paintings at Nottingham Art Museum, including *In Midsummer*. He was known particularly for his seascapes.

E. ELLIS

MUSEUMS AND GALLERIES:
BLACKBURN: *Welsh Coast* - GLASGOW: *On the Coast of England* - LEICESTER: *Captain's Birthday* - LONDON (Victoria and Albert Mus.): *Tynemouth, Northumberland Coastline* - MANCHESTER: *Harbour at the Foot of the Hill* - MELBOURNE: *Summer Morning, North Wales* - NOTTINGHAM: *After Three Days of Storms* - SHEFFIELD: *Far from the Shore*.

AUCTION RECORDS:
LONDON, 28 April 1999, *Off the Fishing Grounds* (oil on canvas, 28 x 58 ins / 72 x 147 cm) GBP 3,800. BILLINGSHURST, 19 Oct 1999, *Deganwy, North Wales* (oil on canvas, 28 x 48 ins / 71 x 122 cm) GBP 3,400. LONDON, 7 Sept 2000, *Mussel Gatherers* (oil on canvas, 18 x 32 ins / 46 x 81 cm) GBP 1,400. LEYBURN, 22 Nov 2001, *Breezy Day* (oil on canvas, 26 x 51 ins / 67 x 129 cm) GBP 2,100. LONDON, 5 Sept 2002, *Unloading the Catch* (oil on canvas, 24 x 42 ins / 61 x 107 cm) GBP 1,900. LEYBURN, 21 Nov 2002, *Harvest Scene with Figures in the Foreground and View of Robin Hood's Bay* (oil on canvas, 18 x 25 ins / 46 x 64 cm) GBP 1,800. BATH, 17 Feb 2003, *Seascape with Figures on the Shore* (oil on canvas, 42 x 83 ins / 107 x 212 cm) GBP 1,300. LONDON, 29 May 2003, *Sketching the Coast* (oil on canvas, 160 x 84 ins / 407 x 213 cm) GBP 1,910.

LONDON, 23 Nov 2004, *On the Conway* (oil on canvas, 18 x 33 ins / 46 x 84 cm) GBP 3,000.

ELLIS, Edwin M.
American, 19th century.
Engraver.
Edwin M. Ellis, who was living in Philadelphia in 1844, engraved mainly portraits and landscapes.

ELLIS, Elizabeth
British, 18th century.
Draughtswoman, engraver (etching).
Elizabeth Ellis was the wife or sister of the etcher William Ellis, with whom she worked. Her signature can be seen on the etchings of the *Solitary Traveller*, in the style of James Pie. Their joint signature appears on *Peasants Dancing*, in the style of Nik Berchem; 32 aquatint plates in the style of J. Gardnors; *Views of the Rhine*; and a portrait of Elizabeth of York, the wife of Henry VII of England.

ELLIS, Eveline Corbould. See **CORBOULD-ELLIS**

ELLIS, Fremont F.
American, 20th century.
Born 2 October 1897, in Virginia City (Montana); died 1985.
Painter, engraver.
Fremont Ellis was a pupil at the Art Students League in New York, he was a member of the California Art Club and the Santa Fe Art Club. He was also a teacher. He produced etchings.

AUCTION RECORDS:
SAN FRANCISCO, 3 Oct 1981, *The Waggon in front of the Mill* (oil on canvas, 22 x 30 ins / 56 x 76 cm) USD 5,000. NEW YORK, 23 Jan 1984, *Indian Woman with her Child* (hardboard, 25 x 30 ins / 63.5 x 76.2 cm) USD 3,500. NEW YORK, 30 May 1990, *The Blue Door* (oil on canvas, 25 x 20 ins / 63.5 x 50.8 cm) USD 3,630. NEW YORK, 27 Sept 1990, *Poplars and Fir Trees* (1926, oil on canvas, 30 x 40 ins / 76.5 x 101.5 cm) USD 8,800. NEW YORK, 14 Nov 1991, *Lakes and Beavers in Spring* (1963, oil on canvas, 30 x 25 1/4 ins / 76.5 x 64 cm) USD 4,620. NEW YORK, 22 Sept 1993, *San Sebastian Ranch in Santa Fe* (oil on canvas, 30 x 40 ins / 76.4 x 101.8 cm) USD 14,950. NEW YORK, 23 May 1996, *New Mexico Landscape* (oil on canvas, 28 x 36 ins / 71.1 x 91.4 cm) USD 9,200. NEW YORK, 27 Sept 1996, *Village Indian, Red River Canyon, near Taos, New Mexico* (oil on canvas, 30 x 40 ins / 76.2 x 101.6 cm) USD 46,000. ST LOUIS, 5 Dec 1999, *Autumn Scene of a Log Cabin in a Birch Forest* (oil on canvas, 20 x 28 ins / 51 x 71 cm) USD 15,000. LOS ANGELES, 9 Dec 1999, *Poplars of San Juan* (oil on canvas, 24 x 30 ins / 61 x 76 cm) USD 17,000. LOS ANGELES, 24 Oct 2000, *On the Pankey Pasture* (oil on canvasboard, 22 x 30 ins / 56 x 76 cm) USD 50,000. LOS ANGELES, 24 Oct 2000, *Navajo Country* (oil on canvas, 28 x 36 ins / 71 x 92 cm) USD 70,000. LOS ANGELES, 2 May 2001, *Cool Waters* (oil on canvas, 29 x 36 ins / 74 x 91 cm) USD 24,000. LOS ANGELES, 2 May 2001, *Apache Canyon* (oil on board, 22 x 30 ins / 56 x 76 cm) USD 32,000. SANTA FE, 9 Nov 2002, *El Rancho de San Sebastian - Mora Valley* (oil on canvas, 16 x 20 ins / 41 x 51 cm) USD 16,500. SANTA FE, 9 Nov 2002, *Santa Fe Canyon* (oil on canvas, 22 x 30 ins / 56 x 76 cm) USD 31,000. LOS ANGELES, 18 June 2003, *El Cabellero* (oil on canvasboard, 30 x 22 ins / 76 x 56 cm) USD 38,000. SANTA FE, 1 Nov 2003, *El Vaquero (Cowboy)* (oil on board, 24 x 20 ins / 61 x 51 cm) USD 26,000. LOS ANGELES, 28 April 2004, *Summer Cottonwoods on the Pecos* (oil on canvasboard, 22 x 30 ins / 55 x 76 cm) USD 16,000. SANTA FE, 23 Oct 2004, *Spring* (oil on canvas, 24 x 30 ins / 61 x 76 cm) USD 18,000.

ELLIS, George B.
American, 19th century.
Engraver (burin).
George B. Ellis is referred to by Nagler.

ELLIS, Harriet
American, 20th century.
Born 4 April 1886, in Springfield (Massachusetts).
Painter, draughtsman.
Harriet Ellis was a pupil of Hawthorne, Mabel Welch, Johonnot, A Jones, Cecilia Beaux and the Pratt Institute in Brooklyn. She was a member of the N. A. Women Painters and Sculptors, Springfield Artists League and Springfield Art Club

ELLIS, Harvey
American, 19th century.
Born 17 October 1852, in Rochester; died 2 January 1904, in Syracuse (New York).
Painter, sculptor, architect, designer. Landscapes.
New York Water Color Club.
Harvey Ellis attended West Point Military Academy from 1871 to 1872, but was dishonourably dismissed. He then travelled to Europe to view fine architecture, and from 1875 to 1876 studied at the National Academy of Design under Edwin White. Ellis worked as an architectural draughtsman with Arthur Gilman and later established his own practice in Rochester, New York with his brother Charles Ellis (1879-1885), designing commercial premises and fashionable residences. He later worked for architectural firms in Minnesota and Missouri until 1893 when he returned to Rochester and began to concentrate on painting. A number of furniture designs in Gustav Stickley's workshop have been attributed to Ellis, but his authorship is not certain. Ellis was president of the Rochester Society of Arts and Crafts.

He was well known for his design for the monument, *General Ulysses Grant* (1822-1825), winning first prize in a competition sponsored by *American Architect and Building News*, a journal which later published perspectives of a number of his architectural projects. Ellis' architectural designs were characteristically romantic versions of contemporary styles. As a painter, Ellis initially designed illusionistic posters, but after 1893 his work exhibited two-dimensional organisation in an avant-garde style. He did illustrations as designer for *Craftsman* magazine from 1903 to 1904. Many of his architectural drawings are held at the University of Minnesota, while other papers are held at the University of Rochester. His works have been exhibited at Rochester Art Club. Other exhibitions include: *A Rediscovery - Harvey Ellis, Artist, Architect*, Memorial Art Gallery, University of Rochester, (1972-1973); *Genius in the Shadows: The Furniture Designs of Harvey Ellis*, Jordan-Volpe Gallery, New York (1981); and *American Drawings and Watercolors, 1800-1945: Selections from the Permanent Collection*, Memorial Art Gallery, University of Rochester, (1987-1988).

BIBLIOGRAPHY:
Bragdon, C., '*Harvey Ellis: A Portrait Sketch*' in *Architectural Review*, vol 15, 1908. Kennedy, R., '*Long, Dark Corridors: Harvey Ellis*' in *Prairie School Review*, vol 5, nos 1-2, Journal article, 1968. *A Rediscovery - Harvey Ellis, Artist, Architect*, exhibition catalogue, Memorial Art Gallery, University of Rochester, Rochester (NY), 1972. *Genius in the Shadows: The Furniture Designs of Harvey Ellis*, Exhibition catalogue, Jordan-Volpe Gallery, New York, 1981. Michaels, Eileen Manning, *Reconfiguring Harvey Ellis*, exhibition catalogue, Illustrated book, Beaver's Pond Press, Edina (MN), 2004.

MUSEUMS AND GALLERIES:
ROCHESTER, NY (Memorial Art Gallery, University of Rochester): *Burning Brush* (1896, watercolour); *Charlotte-Coburg Ferry* (1897, ink and watercolour); *Farm at Twilight* (1900, ink, watercolour, charcoal); *Little Harbour* (1898, wa-

tercolour); *Evening* (1900, pastel); *Mending Nets* (1894, watercolour).

ELLIS, John
Irish, 19th century.
Born in Dublin; died after 1812, in Dublin.
Painter, draughtsman. Landscapes, seascapes. Stage sets.

John Ellis attended the Dublin Fine Art School in 1766. Shortly afterwards he exhibited an oil seascape, a wash drawing and a landscape design there. He also painted decorations and stage sets. Having opened a museum in his own house in Dublin, he exhibited his painting of *Alexandria* there. He had further exhibitions of a seascape and pencil drawings at the Society of Artists in Dublin in 1809 and 1812.

ELLIS, Joseph Bailey
American, 20th century.
Born 24 May 1890, in North Scituate (Massachusetts).
Sculptor.

Joseph Ellis was a pupil of A.H. Munsell, Bela Pratt, Peter and of d'Injalbert in Paris. He was a member of the Copley S. Boston Architectural Club, the Pittsburgh Art Association and the Salmagundi Club.

ELLIS, Joseph F.
British, 19th century.
Born c. 1783; died 1848, in Richmond (Surrey).
Painter. Landscapes, seascapes.

Joseph F. Ellis went to London in 1818. He exhibited only a few paintings at the Royal Academy and the British Institution. He made skilled copies of the works of Canaletto, which were so accurate that some of them were taken for the original works.

AUCTION RECORDS:
LONDON, 24 Nov 1922, *Brussels Town Hall; View of Rouen* (collection) GBP 10. LONDON, 19 July 1972, *The Royal Exchange, London* GBP 1,500. LOS ANGELES, 23 June 1980, *The Royal Yacht 'Royal Sovereign'* (oil on canvas, 29 x 41 ins / 73.5 x 104 cm) USD 3,000. LONDON, 27 July 1984, *Canal Scene, Amsterdam* (oil on canvas, 28 1/4 x 36 1/4 ins / 71.7 x 92.1 cm) GBP 3,800. LONDON, 17 July 1992, *San Marco Basin During Venice Carnival* (oil on canvas, 34 x 43 1/2 ins / 86.4 x 110.8 cm) GBP 8,250. LONDON, 16 July 1993, *Port of Antwerp* (oil on canvas, 25 1/4 x 30 ins / 64 x 76.5 cm) GBP 4,600. LONDON, 26 Jan 2000, *British Man-o'-war and Other Shipping* (watercolour over pencil heightened with white, 19 x 24 ins / 49 x 61 cm) GBP 1,100. LONDON, 8 June 2000, *Amsterdam* (oil on canvas, 28 x 36 ins / 71 x 91 cm) GBP 6,000.

ELLIS, Marian
British, 20th century.
Born in England.
Engraver.

Marian Ellis first exhibited in 1925.

ELLIS, Paul-H.
British, 19th century.
Painter, watercolourist. Local scenes, landscapes.

Paul-H. Ellis worked in Handsworth and exhibited at Suffolk Street Gallery, the Royal Academy and elsewhere in London from 1883 to 1891.

AUCTION RECORDS:
LONDON, 19 Jan 1968, *View of Jerusalem*, Gns 280. LONDON, 13 Sept 1977, *View of the Acropolis, Athens* (oil on canvas, 29 1/2 x 39 1/4 ins / 75 x 100 cm) GBP 1,300. LONDON, 24 March 1981, *Lane Scene, Arborfield, Berkshire* (oil on canvas, 20 x 30 ins / 51 x 76 cm) GBP 1,450. LONDON, 7 Oct 1983, *Arabs and Camels in the Desert* (oil on canvas, 22 x 32 ins / 55.9 x 81.2 cm) GBP 950. NEW YORK, 17 Jan 1996, *Looking Towards Jerusalem; At the Market* (1900, watercolour, a pair, each 19 x 25 1/2 ins / 48.3 x 64.8 cm) USD 4,887. LONDON, 2 Oct 2002, *View of the Acropolis* (oil on canvas, 30 x 40 ins / 76 x 101 cm) GBP 26,000. GODALMING, 26 Nov 2003, *Peasants and Wagon on a Track in a Mountainous Landscape* (oil on canvas, 24 x 36 ins / 62 x 91 cm) GBP 1,050.

ELLIS, Ralph
British, 20th century.
Born in Arundel.
Painter. Genre scenes.

AUCTION RECORDS:
LONDON, 3 Feb 1982, *El Rio* (oil on canvas, 27 x 35 ins / 68.5 x 89 cm) GBP 20.

ELLIS, S.
Canadian, 19th century.
Active in Toronto.
Painter, draughtsman. Portraits.

Around 1850, S. Ellis did drawings for medal portraits of generals Winfield Scott and Zacchary Taylor, presidents Fillmore, Pierce, Buchanan and Lincoln, and of Cornelius Vanderbilt.

ELLIS, Stephen
American, 20th - 21st century.
Born 1951, in High Point (California).
Painter.

Stephen Ellis lives and works in New York. Representative of the new generation of American abstract painters, he examines one of the sources of abstraction: the diagrammatic image. This synthetic image is intersected by cinematographic, architectural and musical evocations (jazz in particular), and served by colours that reflect its content. The image can be perceived behind a grid system and its texture, which is often fuzzy, evokes a horizontal movement or a rhythm.

Ellis participates in collective exhibitions: 1991, *Conceptual Abstraction* at the Sidney Janis Gallery, New York; 1991, *New Generations: New York* at the Carnegie Mellon University and Art Gallery, Pittsburgh; 1996, *Nuevas Abstracciones (New Abstractions)* at the Centro d'Arte Contemporaneo Reina Sofia, Madrid; and 1997, *Abstraction/Abstractions. Géométries provisoires (Abstraction/Abstractions - Provisional Geometry)* at the Musée d'Art Moderne, St-Étienne. He also shows his works in solo exhibitions: 1986 and 1987 at the Galerie Allfred Kren, Cologne; 1993 and 1996 at the Galerie Nathalie Obadia, Paris; and 1996 at the Andre Emmerich Gallery, New York.

BIBLIOGRAPHY:
Damianovic, Maia, '*La Peinture au risque du dilemme*' in *Art Press* n° 211, periodical, Paris, March 1996. Ceysson, Bernard/Chassey, Éric de/Morineau, Camille, *Abstraction/Abstractions. Géométries provisoires*, exhibition catalogue, Musée d'Art moderne, St-Étienne, 1997.

AUCTION RECORDS:
NEW YORK, 24 Feb 1993, *Three Panels* (1990, oil and alkyd resin/canvas, 54 x 144 ins / 137.2 x 366 cm) USD 4,400. LONDON, 26 Oct 2000, *Untitled* (1990, oil, acrylic and ink on linen, 108 x 117 ins / 275 x 297 cm) GBP 2,500. NEW YORK, 7 Nov 2000, *Untitled* (1989, oil on canvas, 48 x 36 ins / 122 x 91 cm) USD 2,600.

ELLIS, Tristam, or Tristram James Ellis
British, 19th - 20th century.
Born 1844, in Great Malvern; died 1922.
Painter, watercolourist, draughtsman. Seascapes, landscapes.

Tristam Ellis was an associate of the Royal Society of Painter-Etchers and exhibited frequently in London from 1868 to 1893.

AUCTION RECORDS:
LONDON, 11 Dec 1922, *Golden Horn, Constantinople*, GBP 4. LONDON, 8 Nov 1984, *View of Santorini, Greece* (1903, water-

colour/pencil outlines, 9 1/2 x 20 1/2 ins / 24 x 52 cm) GBP 1,000. London, 19 June 1986, *Boats off the Golden Horn, Constantinople* (watercolour and pencil, 21 x 39 ins / 53.3 x 99.1 cm) GBP 4,500. London, 14 Nov 1988, *Panorama of the Kremlin in Moscow Seen from the River* (1899, watercolour, 13 1/2 x 28 ins / 34 x 71 cm) GBP 1,760. London, 29 Oct 1991, *Cintra, Portugal* (pencil and watercolour, 14 x 20 3/4 ins / 35.7 x 52.8 cm) GBP 880. London, 12 June 1992, *Jerusalem* (1905, pencil and watercolour, 13 1/2 x 28 ins / 34.3 x 70.2 cm) GBP 3,850. New York, 14 Oct 1993, *Port of Tangiers* (1894, watercolour/paper, 9 1/2 x 20 3/4 ins / 24.2 x 52.7 cm) USD 2,530. London, 11 May 1994, *Spitzberg Landscape* (1894, watercolour, 13 3/4 x 28 ins / 35 x 71 cm) GBP 1,127. London, 14 June 1996, *Vessels on the Golden Horn at Constantinople* (1887, pencil and watercolour/paper, 12 3/4 x 20 ins / 32.4 x 51 cm) GBP 6,325. London, 22 Nov 1996, *Constantinople* (1889, pencil and watercolour/paper, 9 x 20 1/4 ins / 22.6 x 51.7 cm) GBP 1,840.

ELLIS, William

British, 18th - 19th century.
Born 1747, in London; died 1810.
Engraver (including etching). Battles, landscapes, architectural views.

William Ellis trained under William Woollett. He executed several plates, working together with his former teacher. He produced several engravings, most of them landscapes, in the style of the drawings of Paul Sandby and Thomas Hearne. He published four etchings of the *Battles of the Nile* in 1800, in the style of William Anderson.

Museums and Galleries:

London (Victoria and Albert Mus.): *Blythburgh Priory, Suffolk.*

ELLIS, William

British, 19th century.
Born 1824; died July 1882, in Sheffield.
Sculptor.

William Ellis trained under Alfred Stevens in London, and was a member of the Sheffield Society of Artists. The hospital in Sheffield housed a marble bust by him of the poet James Montgomery.

ELLIS, William H.

American, 19th century.
Active in Philadelphia.
Engraver.

William H. Ellis engraved mainly landscapes.

ELLISSITZKY. See **LISSITZKY El**

ELLIUR, Geoffroy

French, 19th century.
Born 19th century, in Angers.
Painter.

A pupil of Princeteau, Geoffroy Elliur sent some watercolours to the Salon from 1880 to 1882.

ELLIVAL, Charles Édouard Xavier

French, 19th century.
Born 19th century, in Boulogne-Billancourt.
Painter.

Charles Ellival was a pupil of Troyon, Jacque and Mols. He is best known for his *Lady Waiting for her Carriage* (1878 Salon), *Careless Child* (1879 Salon), and the fantasy painting *Morning* (1880 Salon).

Auction records:

Paris, 17 Nov 1922, *Corner of a Studio,* FRF 190.

ELLMER, Peter

German, 19th century.
Born 1785, in Haimhausen (Bavaria); died 1873, in Freising.
Painter, draughtsman, lithographer, decorative designer. Historical subjects, figures.

Ellmer is known for a series of lithographs after the historical frescoes in the royal gardens in Munich and for four lithographs depicting musicians in grotesque poses.

ELLMIGER. See **EHINGER Elias** and **Gabriel**

ELLMINGER, Ignaz

Austrian, 19th century.
Born 14 June 1843, in Währing near Vienna; died 2 February 1894, in Vienna.
Painter. Genre scenes.

Ellminger was a pupil at the academy in Vienna, where he became established; he exhibited in Vienna from 1880 onwards. He is noted for his *Fair at Langenois, In March* and *Return from the Pastures*.

Auction records:

Vienna, 14 March 1967, *Village Street,* ATS 28,000. Vienna, 16 March 1976, *Flock of Sheep* (1868, oil on canvas, 15 1/4 x 31 1/2 ins / 39 x 80 cm) ATS 25,000. Vienna, 19 April 1977, *Oxen Yoked on the Road to the Village* (oil on panel, 10 1/4 x 15 1/2 ins / 26 x 39.5 cm) ATS 18,000. Liverpool, 3 July 1980, *Children in a Cart* (oil on canvas, 20 x 35 1/2 ins / 50.8 x 90 cm) GBP 550. London, 24 June 1987, *Departure for the Pastures* (oil on canvas, 19 3/4 x 32 ins / 50 x 81 cm) GBP 4,000. London, 4 Oct 1989, *Outside the Tavern* (1889, oil on panel, 14 1/2 x 22 3/4 ins / 37 x 58 cm) GBP 4,400. Vienna, 19 Oct 1999, *Sunday in Wine Region* (1882, oil on canvas, 32 x 48 ins / 81 x 121 cm) ATS 300,000. Vienna, 17 Sept 2001, *Busy Village Track* (oil on canvas, 9 x 16 ins / 24 x 40 cm) ATS 22,000. Vienna, 29 Oct 2002, *Peasants Resting* (oil on panel, a pair, 12 x 25 ins / 31 x 63 cm) EUR 3,500. Vienna, 28 Nov 2002, *Preparation for Corpus Christi* (oil on canvas, 35 x 51 ins / 88 x 130 cm) EUR 20,000. London, 5 June 2003, *Shoeing the Horses* (oil on panel, 14 x 18 ins / 35 x 45 cm) GBP 1,300. Salzburg, 20 Nov 2003, *Market on the Main Square of Krems* (1889, oil on panel, 15 x 23 ins / 37 x 58 cm) EUR 3,000. Munich, 25 June 2004, *Cart Transporting Wine by Stream* (oil on canvas, 22 x 27 ins / 55 x 69 cm) EUR 3,000.

ELLSON, John

British, 19th century.
Active in London.
Painter. Animals.

John Ellson exhibited at the British Institution and Suffolk Street Gallery from 1833 to 1852.

ELLSWORTH, David

American, 20th - 21st century.
Born 25 June 1944, in Iowa City.
Active in Quakertown (Pennsylvania).
Woodturner.

David Ellsworth has both a Bachelor's and a Master's degrees in Fine Arts, specialising in sculpture, from the University of Colorado (1970-1973). Before turning to the fine arts, he studied architecture and was a folksinger and guitarist.

He is noted for his thin-walled bowls, pots and vessels, of a kind one would normally expect to find in other materials such as glass or clay rather than wood. He has also created more abstract non-functional pieces, extending his repertoire, using painted surfaces and other techniques. Examples are the series *Man and the Forest Architecture, 1983-1984* or the *Solstice Series, 1989-1991*.

He runs a school of woodturning from his base near Quakertown in Pennsylvania. He makes his own tools, which he also markets, and uses wood from his private forests, often preferring to work with green rather than dried wood, since he considers green wood to be easier and more fun to work with.

Ellsworth is an established and famous master craftsman, and has received a number of awards such as the Lifetime Achievement Award, Collectors of Wood Art (2002).

He also has an impressive history of solo exhibitions, including: at the Del Mano Gallery, Los Angeles, 1997 and 2000; the Belles Artes Gallery, New York, 1991 and 1989; the Cooper-Lynn Gallery, New York, 1985, and several at the American Craft Museum in the 1980s and 1990s. He is a lifetime member of the American Association of Woodturners, and was its President from 1986-1991. His work is included in the collection at the White House.

Bibliography:
LeCoff, Albert, *A Gallery of Turned Objects*, Brigham Young University Press, Provo (UT), 1981. Smith, Paul J., *American Craft Today: Poetry of the Physical*, Grove Press, New York, 1986. Nish, Dale L., *Master Woodturners*, Artisan Press, Provo (UT), 1986.

Museums and Galleries:
Allentown (AM) - Atlanta (High Mus. of Art) - Boston (MFA) - Denver, CO (Art Museum) - Honolulu (Contemporary Mus.) - Little Rock (Arkansas Center for the Arts) - Los Angeles (County MA) - New York (American Craft Mus.) - New York (Metropolitan Mus. of Art) - Philadelphia (Musuem of Art) - San Francisco (FAM).

ELLUIN, Blaise. See ELWIN

ELLUIN, François Rolland

French, 18th - 19th century.
Born 5 May 1745, in Abbeville; died c. 1810, in Abbeville.
Engraver. Vignettes.

François Elluin was a pupil and relative of J.-F. Beauvarlet, with whom he lived. He made engravings after Boucher, Le Tellier, Greuze, Dugourc and Charlier. His most important work is the vignettes he executed for the literature of the period.

ELLYS, John

British, 18th century.
Born 1701; died 1757, in London.
Painter. Portraits.

John Ellys trained under Thornhill and Schmutz. He was the successor of Van der Banck. In 1755, he was on a committee responsible for founding an Academy.

Auction records:
London, 19 Nov 1986, *Portrait of Charles, the First Lord Whitworth, with His Nephew* (oil on canvas, 46¼ x 63 ins / 117.5 x 160 cm) GBP 3,000. London, 15 Nov 1989, *Portrait of Mrs Hester Booth, the Dancer, in a Harlequin Costume* (oil on canvas, 48 x 35 ins / 122 x 89 cm) GBP 72,600.

ELMAN

Belgian, 20th century.
Born 1938, in Alost.
Installation artist.

Elman's one-man shows included an exhibition at the Veranneman Foundation at Kruishoutem in 1979. He was preoccupied with space, form and colour.

ELMEN, Ludwig

German, 19th century.
Active in Augsburg c. 1800.
Engraver.

The only known work by this artist is an aquatint entitled *Cossacks*, 'drawn from nature and engraved by Ludwig Elmen in Augsburg'.

ELMER, Edwin Romanzo

American, 19th - 20th century.
Born 1850, in Ashfield (Massachusetts); died 1923, in Ashfield.
Painter, draughtsman. Figure compositions, portraits, still-lifes (flowers).

Edwin Elmer worked with agricultural machinery. As was the tradition at the time in the USA, people commissioned him to paint their portraits, but photography was gaining ground and portrait commissions became more and more rare. He felt the need to consolidate his trade, which had until then been purely instinctive, and followed a one-year course run by the National Academy of Design in New York.

He painted figure scenes in meticulous detail, which made him one of the representatives of the subsequent American Primitive School.

Bibliography:
Bihalji-Merin, Oto, *Les Peintres naïfs*, Delpire, Paris, 1960.

Auction records:
New York, 28 Sept 1989, *White Magnolias in a Glass Jug* (oil on canvas, 17¼ x 15¼ ins / 43.5 x 39 cm) USD 7,700.

ELMER, Pierre

French, 20th century.
Born 30 May 1881, in Bourbon-Lancy (Saône-et-Loire).
Painter. Landscapes.

Pierre Elmer was invited to participate in the Salon des Tuileries in Paris from 1924.

ELMER, Stephen

British, 18th century.
Born 1714 or 1717; died 1796, in Farnham (Surrey).
Painter. Landscapes, still-lifes, animals, birds.

Stephen Elmer was elected an associate of the Royal Academy in London in 1772, the same year he sent in his first painting. His works can be distinguished by their very delicate technique. A considerable number of his works were destroyed by the fire in Gerrard Street, Soho.

Museums and Galleries:
London (Victoria and Albert Mus.): *Still-life*.

Auction records:
New York, 24 March 1905, *The Poet Gray's Cat*, USD 140. London, 27 July 1923, *Dead Game*, GBP 3. London, 20 Nov 1968, *Pheasants in a Wooded Landscape*, GBP 550. London, 23 March 1977, *Partridge in Landscape* (oil on canvas, 27½ x 35½ ins / 70 x 90 cm) GBP 1,200. London, 27 June 1980, *Partridge in a Landscape* (oil on canvas, 21 x 29½ ins / 53.3 x 74.9 cm) GBP 1,100. Stockholm, 20 April 1983, *Bird of Prey Attacking a Partridge* (oil on canvas, 26½ x 22½ ins / 67.5 x 57 cm) USD 6,000. New York, 6 June 1985, *Hare Sitting in a Landscape* (oil on canvas, 27½ x 35¼ ins / 70 x 89.5 cm) USD 27,000. New York, 9 June 1988, *Lapwings with their Young* (oil on panel, 21¼ x 19 ins / 54 x 48 cm) USD 8,800. Glasgow, 6 Feb 1990, *Grouse* (oil on canvas, 7¾ x 9¾ ins / 20 x 25 cm) GBP 660. London, 16 May 1990, *Woodcock* (oil on canvas, 36½ x 40¼ ins / 93 x 102.2 cm) GBP 2,420. Stockholm, 14 Nov 1990, *Cat Playing with Game Feathers* (oil on canvas, 23½ x 26½ ins / 60 x 67 cm) SEK 35,000. London, 12 April 1991, *Clutch of Partridge in an Extensive Landscape* (oil on canvas, 11¼ x 18 ins / 28.5 x 46 cm) GBP 4,620. Stockholm, 29 May 1991, *Still-life with Dead Birds* (oil on canvas, 30 x 25¼ ins / 76 x 64 cm) SEK 14,000. London, 25 Feb 1992, *Black Grouse in a Rocky Landscape* (oil on canvas, 24¼ x 29½ ins / 61.7 x 74.9 cm) GBP 4,400. London, 7 Oct 1992, *Hunting Scene in a Landscape* (oil on canvas, 43 x 55 ins / 109 x 140 cm) GBP 2,860. London, 10 Nov 1993, *Grouse in a Landscape* (oil on canvas, 28¾ x 35½ ins / 73 x 90 cm) GBP 4,025. New York, 11 April 1997, *Bird of Prey with Its Quarry* (oil on canvas, 27½ x 23½ ins / 69.8 x 59.7 cm) USD 9,200. London, 21 March 2001, *Covey of Partridges* (oil on canvas, 27 x 35 ins / 69 x 89 cm) GBP 4,000. London, 21 March 2001, *Still-life with Fish, Rod and Basket* (oil on canvas, 43 x 54 ins / 109 x 136 cm) GBP 6,000. Stockholm, 3 Dec 2002, *Still-life with Fish* (oil on canvas, 18 x 20 ins / 46 x 52 cm) SEK 18,000. London, 22 May 2003, *Fox with Dead Cockerel in a Landscape* (oil on

canvas, 28 x 36 ins / 71 x 91 cm) GBP 5,500. LONDON, 21 Jan 2004, *Spaniel Guarding Game* (oil on canvas, 40 x 50 ins / 101 x 127 cm) GBP 3,000. BATH, 26 July 2004, *Flock of Partridge with Lake and Swallows* (oil on canvas, 15 x 18 ins / 37 x 45 cm) GBP 3,700.

ELMER, William

British, 18th century.

Painter. Still-lifes (fruit).

William Elmer studied with his father Stephen Elmer and worked notably in Dublin and elsewhere in Ireland. He exhibited at the Royal Academy and the Society of Artists from 1778 to 1799. Like his father, whom he probably assisted, he was very successful at painting still-lifes.

AUCTION RECORDS:

LONDON, 9 Feb 1990, *Still-life with Melon, Apples and Grapes* (oil on card, 7 x 18 ins / 17.5 x 45.5 cm) GBP 2,420.

ELMERICH, Charles Édouard

French, 19th century.

Born 1813, in Besançon; died 1889, in Paris.

Painter, sculptor, engraver, draughtsman. Allegorical subjects, scenes with figures, genre scenes, landscapes, urban landscapes.

A pupil of Horace Vernet, Charles Édouard Elmerich first worked as a draughtsman for a weapons manufacturer in Klingenthal, Germany. He subsequently settled in Paris and took lessons at the Académie Suisse. He took up sculpture in 1849. In 1837 he exhibited at the Paris Salon and continued to feature there until 1882. He was appointed an executive member of the Commission des Monuments Historiques, in charge of the restoration of Notre-Dame cathedral under Viollet-le-Duc.

The subjects Elmerich chose for his paintings were mainly extremely Romantic; concerts, impressions of night. His best-known works include *Religious Concert; Prisoner; Grape Harvest in Alsace; Chactas and Atala after the Storm*; and *Lesueur with the Monks*. His best-known sculptures include *William Tell and his Son; She Fears Even the Sound of Breathing Could Wake Him*; a group of marble figures; *Young Girl Carrying Fruit*; and a group of bronze figures. Elmerich was also an engraver, working primarily for *Le Magasin Pittoresque*.

MUSEUMS AND GALLERIES:

BESANÇON: *Mother and Child* - DOUAI: *Family of Exiles* - SAINTES: *After the Battle*.

AUCTION RECORDS:

PARIS, 16 Oct 1985, *Children's Games* (1865, oil on panel, 14 1/2 x 18 1/2 ins / 37 x 47 cm) FRF 6,400. LONDON, 26 Feb 1988, *Travelling Circus* (oil on canvas, 32 1/4 x 23 1/2 ins / 82 x 59.7 cm) GBP 2,750. PARIS, 9 Dec 1988, *Grape Harvest in Alsace* (oil on canvas, 6 x 7 ins / 15 x 18 cm) FRF 8,000.

ELMES, James

British, 19th century.

Born 1782, in London; died 2 April 1862, in Greenwich.

Painter, architect.

James Elmes trained under G. Gibson and at the Royal Academy, where he was awarded a medal in 1805. He sent architectural designs and paintings, such as the *Death of Pliny the Elder*, to the Royal Academy Exhibition from 1801 to 1842. Elmes produced the drawings illustrating the work of Aikin on St Paul's in London. He was renowned for his essays on fine art and compiled the *Annals of the Fine Arts*, which was the first English art review, *Art and Artists*, and a *Biographical Dictionary of the Fine Arts*.

ELMES, William

British, 18th century.

Active in London.

Painter, engraver.

Notable works by William Elmes are the painting *Tour of Waterford Harbour* (exhibited at the Royal Academy in 1797) and two copper engravings featuring caricatures of Napoleon after his own drawings, entitled *Blücher's Discipline* and *John Bull Carrying Bony's Nose to the Grindstone*. He is probably also the engraver by the name of Elmes who contributed an aquatint plate entitled *Persian Cyclamen* to R.J. Thornton's work *Temple of Flora*.

ELMIGER, Franz Jakob

Swiss, 20th century.

Born 1882, in Ermensee; died 1934.

Painter. Local scenes.

Elmiger's picture, *Harnessing White Horses*, was shown at the Munich exhibition in 1905. Two further paintings by him are also still extant: *Cow in the Fields* and *Evening, Ox Ploughing*.

AUCTION RECORDS:

BERN, 6 May 1981, *Woman with Shawl* (1903, oil on canvas, 13 1/2 x 11 ins / 34 x 28 cm) CHF 1,300. LUCERNE, 7 Nov 1985, *Snowy Village* (oil on canvas, 24 x 33 1/4 ins / 61 x 84.5 cm) CHF 6,000. LUCERNE, 20 Nov 2002, *Two Cows in a Meadow* (oil on canvas, 24 x 31 ins / 60 x 80 cm) CHF 3,000. LUCERNE, 15 Nov 2003, *Barn in a Field* (oil on panel, 18 x 25 ins / 46 x 63 cm) CHF 3,600. LUCERNE, 15 Nov 2003, *Autumn Meadow* (oil on canvas, 39 x 53 ins / 98 x 135 cm) CHF 6,500. LUCERNE, 22 May 2004, *Chestnut Tree outside a House* (oil on canvas/board, 14 x 19 ins / 36 x 48 cm) CHF 3,000.

ELMIGER, Robert

Swiss, 19th - 20th century.

Born 10 December 1868, in Ermensee (Lucerne).

Watercolourist, draughtsman. Architectural views.

Elmiger attended the École des Arts Industriels in Lucerne. He became a drawing master both at the École Cantonale in Sarnen and, from 1900, at the École des Arts Industriels in Lucerne. He also exhibited watercolours at the Société Tournus.

ELMO, Serafino

Italian, 18th century.

Of Neapolitan origin.

Active in Lecce (Puglia).

Painter.

A pupil of Paolo de Matteis.

ELMORE, Alfred W.

British, 19th century.

Born 18 June 1815, in Clonakilty (County Cork); died 24 January 1881, in Kensington (London).

Painter. History painting, genre scenes.

The son of a retired sergeant, Alfred W. Elmore moved to London with his parents around the age of 12, and from then on started to draw at the British Museum in the style of the statues of antiquity. He attended the Royal Academy Schools in 1832 and exhibited his first painting there two years later. He visited Paris, Munich, Venice, Bologna and Florence, then settled in Rome for two years. Upon his return to England in 1844, he exhibited *Rienzi in the Forum*. His painting *Origin of the Struggle between the Guelphs and the Ghibellines in Florence* resulted in his election as an associate of the Royal Academy in 1846. He became a member in 1857.

Elmore excelled in painting historical subjects. His masterpiece in this genre is his representation of the *Tuileries, 20 June 1792*, which was exhibited at the Royal Academy in 1860 and quickly achieved success. The museum in Vizille (France) houses a signed reduced version of this painting, but all trace of the original has been lost. His main works include: *Martyrdom of St Thomas à Becket* (1840), *King Robert of Naples on His Deathbed* (1848), *Marie-Antoinette at the Temple* (1861) and *After the Expulsion* (1873).

Museums and Galleries:
Edinburgh (Nat. Gal. of Scotland, Print Room): *The Sonnet* (watercolour) - Preston: *Entreaty* - Rochdale (Art Gallery): *Charles V at the Monastery of Yuste* - Sydney: *Lenore* - Vizille (Mus. de la Révolution Française): *Tuileries, 20 June 1792* (c. 1860, oil on canvas).
Auction records:
London, 23 April 1875, *Katherine and Petrucchio* FRF 13,125. London, 28 May 1883, *Charles Quint at St-Just*, FRF 35,465. London, 3 April 1898, *Christopher Colombus in Porto Santo*, FRF 4,850. London, 2 Dec 1907, *Ruth* GBP 5; *Contemplation* GBP 2. London, 11 April 1908, *Getting Ready*, GBP 9. London, 1 May 1908, *Grinding the Mill* GBP 13. London, 25 April 1910, *Charles V at the Monastery of St-Just*, GBP 36. London, 11 and 14 Nov 1921, *Romeo and Juliet*, GBP 28. London, 9 June 1922, *Scene from the Life of Dante* (1858) GBP 18. London, 20 July 1979, *Lenore* (1871, oil on canvas, 42¼ x 64 ins / 107 x 162.6 cm) GBP 1,200. London, 23 June 1981, *Loving Thoughts* (oil on canvas, 14 x 17 ins / 35.5 x 43 cm) GBP 2,600. London, 1 June 1984, *Eastern Bath* (oil on canvas, 43½ x 23¼ ins / 110.5 x 59 cm) GBP 7,500. London, 30 Sept 1987, *Peace 1651* (1861, oil on canvas, 41 x 25½ ins / 104 x 65 cm) GBP 5,500. New York, 21 May 1991, *Return Home* (oil on canvas, 24 x 29 ins / 61 x 73.6 cm) USD 6,050. London, 12 Nov 1992, *Kabyle Orange Seller in a Street in Algiers* (1869, oil on canvas, 22 x 17 ins / 56 x 43 cm) GBP 5,500. London, 13 Nov 1992, *Lucretia Borgia* (1863, oil on canvas, 35 x 23 ins / 88.9 x 58.4 cm) GBP 17,600. London, 5 Nov 1993, *Marriage Proposal* (1860, oil on canvas, 36 x 30 ins / 91.5 x 76.2 cm) GBP 13,800. London, 6 Nov 1995, *Lenora* (1871, oil on canvas, 42¼ x 64 ins / 107 x 162.5 cm) GBP 8,625. Stockholm, 25 Oct 1999, *Seated Woman* (1870, oil on panel, 15 x 10 ins / 38 x 26 cm) SEK 15,000. Toronto, 2 Dec 1999, *Colombus at Porto Santo* (oil on canvas, 17 x 24 ins / 44 x 60 cm) CAD 6,000. London, 9 Nov 2000, *Alice Bridgenorth and Julian Peveril* (oil on canvas, 35 x 28 ins / 90 x 71 cm) GBP 3,800. London, 5 Sept 2002, *Mary Queen of Scots and Chrispher Norton at Bolton Castle* (oil on canvas on board, 48 x 71 ins / 121 x 180 cm) GBP 6,500. London, 7 Nov 2002, *Final Hour* (1870, oil on canvas, 48 x 39 ins / 122 x 99 cm) GBP 2,500. London, 1 Oct 2003, *Religious Debate* (1850-1852, oil on canvas, 12 x 18 ins / 30 x 45 cm) GBP 1,500. Knowle, 14 Sept 2004, *Two Women Shall Be Grinding at the Mill* (1868, oil on canvas, 14 x 18 ins / 36 x 46 cm) GBP 1,100.

ELMORE, Elisabeth

American, 20th century.
Born 7 August 1874, in Clinton (Wisconsin); died 1933, in Jersey City.
Painter, engraver. Portraits, seascapes.

Elisabeth Elmore was a pupil of W. M. Chase, C. Miclatz, G. de Forest Brush. This artist also studied portraiture in Italy. She was a member of numerous art associations. She won first prize in the portrait section in 1919 and first prize for an etching in 1919 from the Catherine Lorillard Wolje Club.

ELMORE, Richard

British, 19th century.
Painter. Genre scenes, landscapes.

Richard Elmore exhibited at the Royal Academy and Suffolk Street Gallery between 1852 and 1885.
Museums and Galleries:
Cardiff: *Twickenham*.
Auction records:
London, 12 June 1985, *Windsor Castle* (1883, oil on canvas, 19¾ x 29½ ins / 50 x 75 cm) GBP 1,250. Amsterdam, 9 Nov 1993, *Clown* (1876, oil on canvas, 22 x 30 ins / 56 x 76 cm) NLG 2,760. Melbourne, 24 Nov 2003, *Harvesters* (1872, oil on canvas, 35 x 51 ins / 88 x 129 cm) AUD 9,500.

ELMOVIST, Hugo

Swedish, 19th century.
Born 1862, in Karlshamn; died 1930.
Sculptor. Statues, busts.

Elmovist was a student at the academy in Stockholm and won the Rome prize, which enabled him to travel in Italy and France. Notable works by this artist include *The Arrival of Spring, Old Age, Cain* (bronze), *Urchin, Eve* (bronze) and *A Child Naturalist*.
Museums and Galleries:
Stockholm: *Gryning, the Artist's Daughter; Dawn* (marble) - Stockholm (Nordiska Mus.): *Ragnar Lodbrock the Viking*.
Auction records:
Stockholm, 27 Oct 1981, *Young Girl Sitting* (bronze, h. 9¼ ins / 23.5 cm) SEK 4,000. Stockholm, 13 Nov 1986, *Seated Nude* (green patinated bronze, h. 9¼ ins / 23.5 cm) SEK 7,000.

ELMQUIST-WICHMANN, Erna

German, 20th century.
Born 23 July 1869, in Hamburg.
Painter, watercolourist, pastellist. Portraits, still-lifes.

Elmquist-Wichmann was the daughter of Professor E. H. Wichmann and married Hogo Elmquist, whom she met in Paris. Her portraits, still-lifes, watercolours and pastels were shown at a number of exhibitions in Italy, France, Germany and Sweden.

ELMSTETER, Jakob

German, 16th century.
Active in Nuremberg in 1514.
Painter.

ELNER, Christoph

German, 16th century.
Died 1597.
Painter.
Breslau School.

Christoph Elner became a master painter in 1571. He was the son of the painter Ernst Elner.

ELNER, Ernst

German, 16th century.
Baptised 26 September 1578.
Active in Breslau (now Wroclaw).
Painter.

Ernst Elner was the son and pupil of Christoph Elner.

ELNER, Ernst

German, 16th century.
Died 1561.
Active in Breslau (Now Wroclaw).
Painter.
Breslau School.

Ernst Elner became a master painter in 1537. In 1538, he became a burgher of the town.

ELNER, Valentin, or Eldner

German, 16th century.
Painter.

Valentin Elner became a master painter in 1510 and was a master of the Freiberg Guild in 1518. A supporter of Luther, he knew Lucas Cranach and may have been his pupil. None of his works have been identified.

ELO

Danish, 19th century.
Born during the second half of the 19th century, in Copenhagen.
Sculptor.

Elo exhibited at the Salon of the national society in 1913.

ELOFF, Paul

British, 19th century.
Born in the second half of the 19th century, in Pretoria, South Africa.
Sculptor.

Paul Eloff exhibited for the first time at the Salon des Artistes Français in 1912.

ELOLA Y CAJAL, Julian
Spanish, 19th century.
Born in the 19th century, in Saragossa.
Painter.
Julian Elola y Cajal was mainly a scenery decorator.

ELORDUY, Pedro de
Spanish, 17th century.
Sculptor.
Pedro de Elorduy worked after Joanes de Azaldegui for the parish church of Renteria in the Basque Country.

ELORRIAGA, Ramon
Spanish, 19th century.
Born between 1825 and 1830, in Bilbao.
Painter. History painting.
Ramon Elorriaga exhibited his *Death of Abel* in Madrid in 1858. He subsequently took part in exhibitions in Barcelona and Madrid.

ELORY, Paul Hippolyte
French, 19th century.
Born 25 June 1818, in Dôle (Jura); died in Paris.
Painter. Portraits.
Paul Hippolyte Elory was a pupil of Delaroche.
MUSEUMS AND GALLERIES:
DÔLE: *Portrait of a Man* (two).

ELOSEGUI, Ruben
Argentinian, 20th century.
Born 1925, in La Plata.
Sculptor.
Ruben Elosegui joined the school of sculpture at the fine arts academy of La Plata. He carved abstract, expressionist pieces.

ELOUIS, Jean Pierre Henri
French, 18th - 19th century.
Born 20 January 1755, in Caen; died 23 December 1840, in Caen.
Painter.
Jean Pierre Elouis trained with Bernard Restout and exhibited a few portraits in the Salon in 1810 and 1819. He was curator of the museum at Caen. He also exhibited in London, where he lived from 1785 to 1787.
MUSEUMS AND GALLERIES:
CAEN: *Portrait of Old Man; Portrait of his Wife.*
AUCTION RECORDS:
PARIS, 11 Dec 1996, *Portrait of the Baron de Cheux Dressed as a Captain* (1824, oil on canvas, 29 x 23 1/2 ins / 73.5 x 60 cm) FRF 20,500.

ELOUT, Franchoys, or Eloutsz or Eloudt or Elaudts
Dutch, 17th century.
Born 5 October 1597; died 1661 or 1641.
Active in Haarlem.
Painter. Still-lifes.
Shown at the exhibition of 1894 in Utrecht was Franchoys Elout's *Still-life* representing two glasses, two lemons and dates, dated 1628 and signed with the artist's initials.
AUCTION RECORDS:
NEW YORK, 21 Jan 1982, *Still-life with Lemons and Olives on a Pewter Plate* (oil on panel, 11 1/2 x 17 ins / 29 x 43 cm) USD 30,000. PARIS, 20 Nov 1985, *Still-life with a Glass of Wine, Precious-metal Plate and Bunches of Grapes* (oil on wood, 18 1/2 x 32 ins / 47 x 81.5 cm) FRF 160,000. MONACO, 17 June 1989, *Still-life with Olives, Oysters and Wine Glass* (oil on panel, 15 1/4 x 23 1/2 ins / 39 x 59.5 cm) FRF 244,200. PARIS, 8 Dec 1989, *Still-life with a Ham, Precious-metal Plate and Wine Glass* (18 1/2 x 31 1/2 ins / 47 x 80.3 cm) FRF 90,000. LONDON, 21 April 1993, *Still-life with a Ham on a Dish with Glasses and Fruit on a Covered Table* (oil on panel, 20 1/4 x 33 ins / 51.6 x 83.7 cm) GBP 9,775. LONDON, 16 Dec 1999, *Still-life of Box of Draughts, Clay Brazier of Burning Coals* (oil on canvas, 25 x 31 ins / 63 x 80 cm) GBP 40,000. VIENNA, 2 Oct 2002, *Still-life with Oysters, Lemon on Pewter Plate, Olives, Bread* (oil on panel, 12 x 21 ins / 30 x 53 cm) EUR 26,000.

ELOY, Maryse
French, 20th century.
Born 16 December 1930, in Rouen.
Painter.
Maryse Eloy attended the Brianchon studio at the École des Beaux-Arts in Paris 1949-1955, and also studied at the Académie André Lhote in 1950 and 1951. She exhibited in Paris at the Salon Comparaisons, at the Grands et Jeunes d'Aujourd'hui, and from 1970 at the Salon des Réalités Nouvelles (New Realities). At first her painting was close to formless abstraction, then it developed into more geometric shapes in which the repetition of identical lines and the play of colours brought a degree of movement.

ELOY DE JESUS PEREIRA, Mario
Portuguese, 20th century.
Born 15 March 1900, in Lisbon; died 10 September 1951, in Lisbon.
Painter.
Mario Eloy de Jesus Pereira was a self-taught and started off as an actor. He later turned to painting and continued his training at the school of fine arts in Lisbon in 1923. In 1928 he worked for the press union in Lisbon. During the 1930s he entered an institution and died there in 1951.

Eloy exhibited in March 1924 at the Portuguese Illustration Salon and later in Paris and Berlin (1931) remaining residing in the latter town for some time. His paintings have been exhibited in many exhibitions both in Portugal and abroad including the Venice Biennale and the São Paulo Biennale (in 1950 and 1953) and also at an exhibition of Portuguese painting in 1955. A major retrospective of his work was held in 1958.

Eloy's work is characterised by Expressionism reminiscent of Hoffer, and by formalism and colour. He is known primarily for his self-portraits. Eloy played an important and influential role in contemporary Portuguese art.
BIBLIOGRAPHY:
Arnáiz, José Manuel/López Jiménez, Javier/Merchán Díaz, Manuel (ed.), *Cien años de pintura en Espana y Portugal (1830-1930)*, Antiqvaria, Madrid, 1988 (One Hundred Years of Painting in Spain and Portugal (1830-1930)).
MUSEUMS AND GALLERIES:
LISBON (Mus. do Chiado): *Self-portrait and Poet.*

ELPHINSTONE, Archibald H.
British, 19th - 20th century.
Active in London.
Painter. Seascapes, landscapes.
Archibald H. Elphinstone studied at the Slade School of Art in London. He showed his work at various London exhibitions, including the Royal Academy from 1894 and the Society of British Artists from 1905.

ELSACKERE, Claes van
Flemish School, 15th century.
Active in Antwerp.
Painter.
Claes van Elsackere became a master in 1486.

ELSAESSER, Christian
German, 19th century.
Born 29 October 1861, in Bauschlott, near Pforzheim; died 14 June 1922.
Sculptor.
Elsaesser studied at the academy in Karlsruhe with H Volz and at the Académie Julian in Paris. He is noted for works such as the *Bust of L Eichrodt; Six Large Decorative Reliefs*

Depicting the History of Mannheim; Memorial to the Conductor Langer in Mannheim; Lost Son; a bronze, *Audifax,* and a *Bust of Albert Geiger, Poet.*

ELSASSER
German, 17th century.
Active at Möckmühl (Württemberg).
Painter.

Elsaesser painted a *Fidelity Personified* for the town hall in Weinberg.

ELSASSER, Friedrich August
German, 19th century.
Born 24 July 1810, in Berlin; died 1 September 1845, in Rome.
Painter. Landscapes, architectural views.

A pupil at the Berlin academy with Hummel and Blechen, Elsasser continued his studies in Italy in 1832 and became a member of the Berlin academy in 1841.

MUSEUMS AND GALLERIES:
BERLIN (Nationalgal.): *Cloister of a Convent in Berlin* - COPENHAGEN (Ny Carlsberg Glyptotek): *St Peter's at Easter; Palatine Chapel at Palermo* - COPENHAGEN (Thorvaldsens Mus.): *Theatre in Taormina* - GDANSK: *View of Rome.*

AUCTION RECORDS:
BERLIN, 15 Feb 1898, *Grey Cloister in Berlin,* FRF 568; *Italian Landscape,* FRF 562; *Grey Cloister near Subbiaco,* FRF 419; *Landscape* (studies) FRF 256; *Palermo,* FRF 525. ZURICH, 21 Nov 1986, *Interior of St Peter's in Rome* (oil on paper remounted/canvas, 10½ x 8 ins / 26.5 x 20.5 cm) CHF 1,800. NEW YORK, 13 Oct 1993, *Clearing in Tropical Vegetation in a Mountainous Landscape* (oil on canvas, 47¼ x 68¾ ins / 120 x 174.6 cm) USD 4,025. LUCERNE, 13 Oct 1999, *Young Family in Jungle* (oil on canvas, 47 x 69 ins / 120 x 174 cm) CHF 5,500. MUNICH, 26 Sept 2001, *Mass at the High Altar in St Peter's, Rome* (oil on canvas, 29 x 25 ins / 74 x 63 cm) DEM 9,000. ROME, 4 Dec 2001, *Taormina* (1845, oil on canvas, 48 x 77 ins / 121 x 195 cm) ITL 33,000,000.

ELSASSER, Joachim Friedrich
German, 18th century.
Active in Meissen.
Engraver, modeller.

ELSASSER, Julius Albert
German, 19th century.
Born 1814, in Berlin; died 25 December 1859, in Rome.
Painter. Landscapes.

The younger brother of Friedrich-August Elsasser, this artist was a pupil at the Berlin academy and spent most of his life in Italy. He is noted for works including *Italian Landscape, Appian Way* and *Ruins of the Forum by Moonlight*

ELSASSER, Sigmund
Austrian, 16th century.
Died 1587, in Innsbruck.
Painter.

Sigmund Elsasser was court painter to Archduke Ferdinand.

ELSBORCH, Jan Van. See **ELBRUCHT Jan Van der**

ELSDORF, Michel
Belgian, 20th - 21st century.
Born 1952, in Liège.
Sculptor.

Elsdorf attended the Académie des Beaux-Arts in Liège.

MUSEUMS AND GALLERIES:
LIÈGE (Drawings and Prints Collection).

ELSE, Peeter van
Flemish School, 16th century.
Active in Antwerp.
Painter.

Peeter van Else was a pupil of Jeronimus Scuelens in 1513. He was also known as Peerken van Winckele.

ELSELAIRE, Vautier van
Flemish School, 15th century.
Active in Ypres.
Painter.

According to Siret, Elselaire was involved with preparations for a banquet held in Bruges in 1468.

ELSEN, Alfred
Belgian, 19th - 20th century.
Born 16 November 1850, in Antwerp; died 1914, in Antwerp.
Painter, engraver. Landscapes.

Elsen was taught by Lamorinière, Dugardin and Beaufaux. It was in his capacity as an etcher that he came into public view. He enjoyed his first success at the Salon des Artistes Français with a painting entitled *Autumn,* which attracted a good deal of attention. He went on to exhibit in Ghent, Brussels, London, Antwerp and Liège and showed his engravings at the Salon des Artistes Français in Paris.

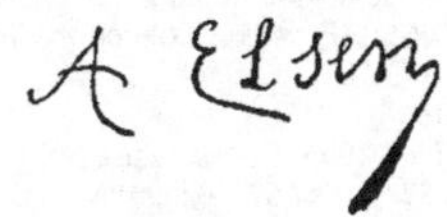

MUSEUMS AND GALLERIES:
ANTWERP: *Sun; Forest Interior* - LIÈGE.

AUCTION RECORDS:
LOKEREN, 8 Oct 1994, *Approaching Storm* (oil on canvas, 49¼ x 37½ ins / 125 x 95 cm) BEF 120,000. LOKEREN, 9 Dec 1995, *Approaching Storm* (oil on canvas, 49¼ x 37½ ins / 125 x 95 cm) BEF 140,000.

ELSEN, Barthélemy van
Flemish, 17th century.
Baptised 28 September 1622; died after 1676.
Miniaturist, sculptor.
Flemish School.

Barthélemy van Elsen was the son of Gauthier van Elsen.

ELSEN, Gauthier van
Flemish, 17th century.
Died 3 September 1664, in Mechelen.
Painter.
Flemish School.

ELSEN, Theodore van
French, 20th century.
Born 1896, in Java (Indonesia).
Active in Paris in the 20th century.
Painter, engraver, draughtsman, illustrator.

Theodore van Elsen exhibited at the Salon des Humoristes.

ELSENER, Jeanne
French, 20th century.
Born in Paris.
Miniaturist, pastellist.

Jeanne Elsener studied with R. Colin and Comtois. She was a member of the Société des Artistes Français in Paris and of the Salon d'Hiver (Winter Salon). She won a silver medal in 1938.

ELSEVIER, Arnout
Flemish, 17th century.
Born 1580, c. 1575 in Douai according to some sources; died after 1646.
Painter. Landscapes.
Delft School, Flemish School.

Arnout Elsevier married in Leiden on 9 February 1607 and remarried on 22 October 1626. In 1643 he lived in Rotterdam, entering the guild in Dordrecht in 1646.

ELSEVIER, Johannes
Dutch, 17th century.
Died 1687.
Active in Delft.
Painter.

Johannes Elsevier was the son of Louwys Elsvier. He became a member of the Guild of St Luke in Delft on 20 December 1675.

ELSEVIER, Louwys Aernouts
Dutch, 17th century.
Born 1617, in Leiden; died 1675, in Delft.
Painter. Landscapes with figures.

In 1635 Louwys Aernouts Elsevier was a member of the guild in Delft. He was perhaps the descendant of Arnout Elsevier.

L'Elsevier. 1647

MUSEUMS AND GALLERIES:
DESSAU (Anhaltische Gemäldegal.): *Landscape with Duck Hunting* - STOCKHOLM (Fraenkel Collection): *Landscape with Mallards.*

AUCTION RECORDS:
AMSTERDAM, 14 Nov 1995, *Ducks near a Snare by a River* (oil on panel, 22 1/2 x 32 1/4 ins / 57 x 82 cm) NLG 21,240. LONDON, 23 April 2004, *Allegory of Art, Putti Disporting with a Portrait of the Artist* (oil on canvas, grisaille, 34 x 48 ins / 86 x 122 cm) GBP 2,500.

ELSHEIMER, Adam, also called Adamo Tedesco
German, 16th - 17th century.
Born 1574 or 1578, in Frankfurt am Main; died December 1610 or 1620, in Rome.
Painter, engraver. Historical subjects, religious subjects, allegorical subjects, landscapes.

Adam Elsheimer was the son of a stone mason, who apprenticed him to the painter Philip Uffenbach. Adam left Germany for Italy while still a very young man. After a stay in Venice, he settled in Rome in 1600, where he earned the title of Germany's Roman painter. He knew a number of Dutch artists, including Peter Latsman and Jacob Pinas, with whom Rembrandt was to study. He also met Henrich Goudt, an aristocratic art-lover and amateur. Very taken by Elsheimer's work, Goudt encouraged him and even copied some of his works as engravings. Elsheimer was a member of the Accademia di San Luca. Of the students he taught, the most important was perhaps Jakob-Ernst Thomann von Hagelstein. While not achieving the delicacy and dexterity of his master, he was able to imitate his style sufficiently well to confuse even knowledgeable collectors. Of Elsheimer's more original followers, to whom he taught at least the basics of their art, the most important are David Teniers the Elder and Pieter J. van Laar.

Although living in Rome, Elsheimer remained faithful to the art of his homeland, continuing to paint works where seriousness and the expression of character were given greater weight than the elegance and frivolity in vogue at that time. It was only relatively late in his career that he began to introduce a greater element of elegance. His oil paintings have all the detail of miniatures. He delights in the use of light and shade, and his skies have a veiled brilliance. He seeks after extreme effects, particularly in his use of light sources. His *Flight into Egypt*, for example, contains in a single canvas the light of the full moon, the pale gleam of the Milky Way and the last stars, the glare of a fire lit by the shepherds, the flame of the torch held up by Joseph and, last but not least, the effect of the moon reflected in the water. He rarely sketched from nature, but his well-developed memory was able to retain every detail of landscapes observed and studied for many hours at a time. He also made etchings and produced some landscapes of great delicacy - now very rare. Elsheimer's works, although recognised as being of a high quality, did not meet with the same appreciation later as they had had in his own time. Nevertheless, the light touch and rigorous composition of his luminous landscapes had some influence on Claude Lorraine, another artist who spent the greater part of his life in Italy. Elsheimer was better known in Italy, both in his own day and later, perhaps for the very reason that his work, produced with such painstaking carefulness, contrasted so strikingly with the ease and facility of works by Italian artists.

Æ.Æ.

BIBLIOGRAPHY:
Drost, Willi, *Adam Elsheimer und sein Kreis*, Akademische Verlagsges Athenaion, Potsdam, 1935. Andrews, Keith, *Adam Elsheimer: Paintings, Drawings and Prints*, Harper Collins, 1982.

MUSEUMS AND GALLERIES:
BASEL: *Allegory* - BERGAMO (Accademia Carrara, Pinacoteca d'Arte Antica): *St Jerome; Landscape* - BERLIN (Bodemus.): *Landscape with St John the Baptist; Mercury and Argus; Death of Argus; St Christopher; Small Altarpiece with Scene from the Life of the Virgin; Nymph Bathing; St Martin and the Beggar; Forest Landscape* - BORDEAUX: *St Jerome in the Wilderness* - BRUNSWICK: *Aurora* - CAMBRIDGE (Fitzwilliam Mus.): *Venus and Cupid* (1600-1605, oil/copper) - DRESDEN: *Judith; Philemon and Baucis* - DUNKIRK: *Finding of Moses* - FLORENCE (Uffizi): *Landscape with Mercury and Nymphs; Five Small Saints; Landscape; Five Small Figures of Apostles and other Saints; Landscape with Shepherd; Portrait of the Artist* - FORT WORTH (Kimbell AM): *The Flight into Egypt* (c. 1605, oil/silver-plated copper) - FRANKFURT AM MAIN: *Sacrifice; Education of Bacchus; St Paul at Lystra* - FRANKFURT AM MAIN (Städel): *Drawings* - KASSEL: *Landscape with Mercury and Argus; Meeting of Moses and Aaron* - LA FÈRE: *Good Samaritan* - LEIPZIG: *Good Samaritan* - LONDON (NG): *The Baptism of Christ* (c. 1599, oil/copper); *St Paul on Malta* (c. 1600, oil/copper); *St Lawrence prepared for Martyrdom* (c. 1600-1601, oil/copper) - MADRID (Prado): *Ceres Searching for her Daughter* - MONTPELLIER: *St Lawrence* - MOSCOW (Rumiantsev Mus.): *Tobias and the Angel* - MUNICH: *Search for Happiness; Rich Woman Snatched from a Procession by Hermes; Troy Burning; St John the Baptist Preaching; Matyrdom of St Lawrence; Landscape with Cattle* - MUNICH (Alte Pinakothek): *Flight into Egypt* - NANCY: *Good Samaritan* - NANTES (MBA): *Flight into Egypt* - NAPLES: *Rape of Ganymede; Ariadne Abandoned; Theseus and Ariadne; Myth of Icarus* - NUREMBERG: *Meeting of Moses and Jethro* - PARIS (Louvre): *Flight into Egypt; Good Samaritan* - SEMUR-EN-AUXOIS: *St Mary Magdalene in the Wilderness* - ST PETERSBURG (Hermitage): *Forest; Paul the Apostle on the Island of Malta* - STOCKHOLM: *Shepherds* - VENICE (Gal. dell'Accademia): *The Denial* - VENICE (Gal. Nazionale): *The Denial* - VIENNA (Czernin): *Donkey Driver; Landscape; Nativity* - WEIMAR: *Beheading of St John the Baptist.*

AUCTION RECORDS:
PARIS, 6-9 March 1872, *Good Samaritan,* FRF 1,400. PARIS, 10-12 May 1900, *Group of People,* FRF 360. LONDON, 27 May 1908, *Classical Landscape* (drawing) GBP 21. LONDON, 25 Nov 1921, *Crucified Christ,* GBP 15. LONDON, 31 May 1922, *Lazarus,* GBP 4. LONDON, 25 and 26 July 1922, *Flight into Egypt,* GBP 5. PARIS, 22-24 Feb 1923, *Halt by a Lake,* FRF 280. LONDON, 6 April 1923, *Martyrdom of St Sebastian,* GBP 12. PARIS, 16 May 1923, *Philemon and Baucis* (drawing) FRF 65. LONDON, 25 June 1923, *Dives and Lazarus,* GBP

7. PARIS, 4 Feb 1924, *Last Judgement* (School of Adam Elsheimer) FRF 550. PARIS, 9 Feb 1924, *Landscape with Figures* (sepia) FRF 130. PARIS, 25 Feb 1924, *Landscape with Figures* (pen) FRF 380. PARIS, 12 March 1927, *Wooded Landscape with Figures* (attributed) FRF 2,000. PARIS, 17 and 18 March 1927, *Part of Solomon's Temple* (pen and wash) FRF 340. PARIS, 25 Nov 1927, *Landscape with Figures Taken from the Story of Tobias* (attributed) FRF 2,020. PARIS, 4 April 1928, *Tobias and the Angel*, FRF 1,750. PARIS, 8 Feb 1934, *Adoration of the Shepherds* (attributed) FRF 2,200. PARIS, 14 April 1937, *Childhood of Bacchus* (School of Adam Elsheimer) FRF 1,510. PARIS, 8 Dec 1938, *Page from a Sketchbook* (pen with traces of wash) FRF 4,000. PARIS, 28 Oct 1942, *Birth of the Virgin* (attributed) FRF 4,000. LONDON, 27 June 1958, *St Peter Delivered from Prison*, GBP 1,470. COLOGNE, 8 Nov 1961, *Tobias and the Angel*, DEM 3,800. LONDON, 28 Nov 1962, *Mountainous Landscape*, GBP 1,600. LONDON, 25 June 1971, *Finding of the True Cross*, Gns 36,000. LONDON, 30 Nov 1973, *Tobias and the Archangel Raphael*, Gns 15,000. MUNICH, 25 Nov 1976, *Tobias and the Angel* (etching) DEM 1,900. LONDON, 25 March 1977, *Tobias and the Archangel Raphael* (oil/copper, 4 1/2 x 7in/11.4 x 17.8cm) GBP 15,000. LONDON, 21 June 1978, *Jacob's Dream* (c. 1598-1600, oil/ copper, 7 1/2 x 10 1/4in/19 x 26cm) GBP 33,000. LONDON, 10 April 1981, *St Helen Questioning the Jew* (oil on card, 6 x 6 1/4in/15 x 15.8cm) GBP 110,000. BERN, 22 June 1984, *Tobias and the Fish* (etching) CHF 4,800. NEW YORK, 13 Jan 1994, *Flight into Egypt* (oil/silver-plated copper, 3 3/4 x 3in/9.8 x 7.6cm) USD 365,500.

ELSHEIMER, Johann

German, 17th century.
Born 1593, in Frankfurt am Main; died before 1636.
Painter. History painting.

Johann was the brother of Adam Elsheimer. The town hall in Frankfurt has a *Death of Virginia* painted by this artist in 1632.

ELSHIN, Yacov Aleksandrovich

Russian, 20th century.
Born 30 December 1891, in St Petersburg; died 1976.
Active then naturalised in the USA.
Painter, illustrator. Architectural views, ruins. Stage sets.

Yacov Elshin was a pupil of Zenin, Russanov, Andriev and Dmitriev and is known for his reminiscences of ancient ruins as well as for compositions for the *Russian Miniature Theatre* and his ballet of the *Danse Macabre* at the Metropolitan Theatre in Seattle. He was a member of artist groups in Seattle.

ELSHOECHT, Jean

Flemish, 18th century.
Born 18th century, in Brussels.
Active in Lille from 1762.
Sculptor, painter. Scenes with figures.
Flemish School.

MUSEUMS AND GALLERIES:
DUNKIRK: *Children Playing with a Nanny Goat* (painting).

ELSHOECHT, Jean Jacques Marie Carl Vital

French, 19th century.
Born 10 May 1797, in Dunkirk; died 27 February 1856, in Paris.
Sculptor.

The son of Jean-Louis Elshoecht, Jean Elshoecht first studied in his father's studio. After moving to Paris he studied under Bosio and made his Salon début in 1824. His most noteworthy works are in Paris and include *Two Angels* on the high altar and *Seraphs of the Pulpit* for the church of Notre-Dame-de-Lorette; a *Triton* and a *Nereid* for the fountains in the Place de la Concorde; *Merchant Navy* for one of the Louvre pediments; *Spirit of Asia*, a group for the new Louvre; the busts of *Horace* and *Quintilian* for the Collège de France; a bust of *Alfieri Sostegno* for the Italian embassy; a marble bust of *Abbé Suger* and a bust of *Claude Gelée* at the French ministry of the interior; a marble bust of the lecturer *Laromiguière* for the faculty of arts; a bust of *Mirabeau* for Ste-Geneviève library; and a marble statue of *Queen Matilda* for the Luxembourg palace garden. He also produced *The Good Pastor* and *The Four Evangelists* for Tourcoing church; *History and Justice* for the façade of Laon town hall; *Immaculate Conception* for the church of St-Ouen in Rouen; a bust of *Louis-Philippe* in Dunkirk; and a marble bust of the French architect *Soufflot* and of *Rondelet* for the city of Lyons.

MUSEUMS AND GALLERIES:
AMIENS: *Marble Bust of Napoleon I* - DIEPPE: *Napoleon I; Charlotte Corday; Andrieux* - DOUAI: *Lieutenant General Delcambre* (plaster) - DUNKIRK: *Bust of Rear Admiral L'Hermite; Amor and Psyche; Thoré; Model of Fountain; Fratello Mio; Prisalia Helvetia; Paul Geruzez Andrieux; Notre-Dame-des-Anges; Statue of Jean Bart*; plaster medallion; *Grawez; Sarah; Claude Lorraine* - LYONS: *Soufflot* (marble); *Rondelet* - MARSEILLES: *Espercieux* - SEMUR: *Napoleon I* - VERSAILLES: *Boulay; Charles, Duke of Berry; Henry of Lorraine, Duke of Mainz.*

ELSHOECHT, Jean Louis

French, 18th - 19th century.
Born 24 March 1760, in Bergues; died 18 July 1841, in Dunkirk.
Painter, sculptor.

Jean Louis Elshoecht was the son of Jean Elshoecht, father of Jean Jacques Elshoecht and pupil of Bosio. He was responsible for the altarpieces of the churches of St-Eloi and St-Jean-Baptiste in Dunkirk.

MUSEUMS AND GALLERIES:
DUNKIRK: *Bust* (self-portrait); three portraits - ST-OMER: *Portrait of M. Pohier.*

ELSHOLTZ, Ludwig

German, 19th century.
Born 2 June 1805, in Berlin; died 3 February 1850, in Berlin.
Painter. Battles, genre scenes.

A pupil at the Berlin academy, later of Franz Krüger, Elsholtz lived in Berlin. He is noted for his *Barber* and *Battle of Leipzig*. He exhibited at the royal academy from 1828 to 1844.

MUSEUMS AND GALLERIES:
BERLIN (Nationalgal.): *Start of Battle.*

AUCTION RECORDS:
NEW YORK, 29 May 1981, *Peacetime* (1844, oil on canvas, 12 x 15 3/4 ins / 30.5 x 40 cm) USD 3,500. LONDON, 18 Feb 1983, *Greeting the Cavalry* (1840, oil on canvas, 18 1/2 x 23 1/2 ins / 47 x 59.7 cm) GBP 2,600. NURNBERG, 14 Sept 2000, *Maids Resting* (1847, oil on canvas, 16 x 23 ins / 41 x 58 cm) DEM 3,500.

ELSINGA, Johannes. See **ELZINGA**

ELSKAMP, Max

Belgian, 19th - 20th century.
Born 1862, in Antwerp; died 1931, in Antwerp.
Engraver, illustrator.

Elskamp was an artist's son and a friend of Henri van de Velde, some of whose works he illustrated with engravings, notably: *The Alphabet of Notre-Dame the Virgin - Illuminations*, 1898.

BIBLIOGRAPHY:
Osterwalder, Marcus (ed.), *Dictionnaire des illustrateurs 1800-1914*, Ides et Calendes, Neuchâtel, 1989.

ELSLANDT, Peeter
Flemish School, 16th - 17th century.
Painter.
Antwerp School.

A pupil of Adam van Noort, Peeter Elslandt became a master painter in 1607.

ELSLEY, Arthur John
British, 19th - 20th century.
Born 1861; died 1952.
Active in St John's Wood (London).
Painter. Figures, genre scenes, animals.

Arthur John Elsley exhibited at the Royal Academy in London from 1878. His painting *First Love Letter* received great critical acclaim at the 1908 Exhibition.

AUCTION RECORDS:
LONDON, 9 Dec 1907, *Molly,* GBP 3. NEW YORK, 8-10 Jan 1908, *Old Friends,* USD 300. NEW YORK, 25-26 March 1909, *Old Friends,* USD 265. LONDON, 10 July 1922, *Swing* (1892) GBP 30. LONDON, 12 March 1923, *Sympathy,* GBP 30. NEW YORK, 13 Oct 1978, *Children Picking Apples* (1919, oil on canvas, 37 1/2 x 27 ins / 95.3 x 68.5 cm) USD 15,000. LOS ANGELES, 12 March 1979, *Two Children on a Donkey on the Beach* (1896, oil on canvas, 30 1/2 x 42 ins / 77.5 x 106.7 cm) USD 7,500. LONDON, 20 Oct 1981, *Surprised* (1899, oil on canvas, 48 x 35 3/4 ins / 122 x 91 cm) GBP 3,700. LONDON, 15 March 1983, *Springtime* (1911, oil on canvas, 37 x 47 1/4 ins / 94 x 120 cm) GBP 13,500. LONDON, 18 Dec 1985, *Never Mind!* (1907, oil on canvas, 46 x 34 1/4 ins / 117 x 87 cm) GBP 26,500. LONDON, 23 Sept 1988, *Meeting in a Park* (1907, oil on canvas, 42 1/4 x 56 ins / 107 x 142 cm) GBP 68,200. NEW YORK, 23 May 1990, *Blue Ribbon* (1909, oil on canvas, 34 3/4 x 24 3/4 ins / 88.3 x 62.8 cm) USD 104,500. LONDON, 25 Oct 1991, *Piggy-back Ride on Big Brother* (1900, oil on canvas, 36 x 28 ins / 91.4 x 71.2 cm) GBP 22,000. NEW YORK, 19 Feb 1992, *Goodnight* (1911, oil on canvas, 39 x 28 1/2 ins / 99.3 x 72.3 cm) USD 176,000. NEW YORK, 30 Oct 1992, *Summer Joy* (1915, oil on canvas, 31 1/4 x 43 ins / 79.5 x 109.2 cm) USD 77,000. LONDON, 13 Nov 1992, *Caught in the Act* (1894, oil on canvas, 32 x 24 ins / 81.3 x 61 cm) GBP 17,600. LONDON, 8-9 June 1993, *Into your Kennel!* (1895, oil on canvas, 34 1/2 x 24 1/2 ins / 87.5 x 62 cm) GBP 34,500. NEW YORK, 12 Oct 1994, *An Ill-suited Pair* (1915, oil on canvas, 43 x 31 ins / 109.2 x 78.7 cm) USD 107,000. LONDON, 6 Nov 1995, *There's No Room for You!* (oil on canvas, 28 1/4 x 44 ins / 72 x 112 cm) GBP 82,900. LONDON, 27 March 1996, *Pack Chasing a Fox through a Classroom* (1898, oil on canvas, 40 1/4 x 35 ins / 102 x 89 cm) GBP 41,100. NEW YORK, 12 April 1996, *Cup of Tea* (oil on canvas, 38 1/4 x 26 3/4 ins / 97.2 x 67.9 cm) USD 156,500. NEW YORK, 24 Oct 1996, *Leave, Sir!* (1891, oil on canvas, 28 1/2 x 24 1/4 ins / 72.4 x 61.6 cm) USD 85,000. LONDON, 8 Nov 1996, *Recreation* (1894, oil on canvas, 40 x 29 ins / 101.6 x 73.7 cm) GBP 23,000. LONDON, 12 March 1997, *I'se Biggest!* (1892, oil on canvas, 32 1/2 x 24 1/2 ins / 82.5 x 62.5 cm) GBP 91,100. NEW YORK, 2 Nov 1999, *I'se Biggest!* (1892, oil on canvas, 32 x 24 ins / 81 x 61 cm) USD 610,000. LONDON, 11 Nov 1999, *Punch and Judy Show* (1912, oil on canvas, 44 x 67 ins / 112 x 169 cm) GBP 650,000. NEW YORK, 18 Oct 2000, *Golden Hours* (1908, oil on canvas, 44 x 61 ins / 112 x 155 cm) USD 750,000. LONDON, 30 Nov 2000, *Full Inside* (1899, oil on canvas, 36 x 28 ins / 91 x 71 cm) GBP 260,000. NEW YORK, 1 May 2001, *One, Two, Three, Go* (1906, oil on canvas, 39 x 30 ins / 100 x 75 cm) USD 430,000. NEW YORK, 2 May 2001, *Private and Confidential* (1906, oil on canvas, 35 x 26 ins / 89 x 65 cm) USD 220,000. NEW YORK, 29 Oct 2002, *Snapdragon* (1894, oil on canvas, 28 x 37 ins / 70 x 93 cm) USD 220,000. NEW YORK, 30 Oct 2002, *Picking Apples* (1919, oil on canvas, 38 x 27 ins / 96 x 68 cm) USD 200,000. LONDON, 11 June 2003, *Punch and Judy Show* (1912, oil on canvas, 44 x 67 ins / 112 x 169 cm) GBP 360,000. NEW YORK, 29 Oct 2003, *Hide and Seek* (1908, oil on canvas, 36 x 29 ins / 92 x 73 cm) USD 280,000. NEW YORK, 22 April 2004, *This Little Pig Went to Market* (c. 1911, oil on canvas, 37 x 27 ins / 95 x 69 cm) USD 150,000. LONDON, 16 June 2004, *Baby's Turn* (1905, oil on canvas, 43 x 56 ins / 109 x 142 cm) GBP 135,000.

ELSMER
Flemish School, 16th century.
Sculptor.
Antwerp School.

The son of Wouter van der Elsmer, Elsmer became a master sculptor in 1559.

ELSMER, Wouter van der, or Elsmetere
Flemish School, 16th century.
Born to a family originally from Diest; died after 1586.
Sculptor.
Antwerp School.

Wouter van der Elsmer entered the Antwerp Guild in 1533 and was its dean in 1563.

ELSOB, William. See **MARSHALL William Elsob**

ELSONN, Mikhail Ivanovich
Russian, 19th century.
Born 1816, in St Petersburg; died 1857.
Painter.

Elsson was a pupil of Vorokiev at the St Petersburg academy of fine arts. He painted mainly portraits

ELSSNER, Jacob, or Elzner, Eisner
German, 16th century.
Died 1517, in Nuremberg.
Illuminator.
Nuremberg School.

Jacob Elssner was a heraldic painter of great renown. It was said that none could equal his skill in rendering the appearance of gold and jewels in paint. Two choir books and a missal, dated 1573, believed to be decorated by him can be found in the sacristy of the church of St Lawrence in Nuremberg, He is also known to have painted minutely detailed portraits.

MUSEUMS AND GALLERIES:
BERLIN: *Portrait of a Woman* - DRESDEN: *Man with Three Arrows* - MUNICH: *Portrait of Konrad Imhof* - NUREMBERG: *Portrait of Jorg Ketzler*; *Portrait of a Young Man.*

ELST. See also **HELST** and **VERELST**

ELST, Hieronymus van der
German, 16th century.
Active in 1595.
Painter.

Nothing is known about this artist except that he was the author of a pen drawing of *Bacchus and Ceres* that was in the Klinkosch sale of 1889.

ELST, Johannes van
Dutch, 20th century.
Born 1883; died 1952.
Painter. Genre scenes, scenes with figures.

AUCTION RECORDS:
MONTREAL, 23-24 Nov 1993, *Fish Market in Holland* (oil on canvas, 16 x 24 ins / 40.6 x 61 cm) CAD 2,900.

ELST, Ludovicus van der
Flemish, 17th century.
Died c. 1690.
Active in Antwerp.
Painter.
Flemish School.
Ludovicus van der Elst was a member of the Antwerp guild around 1673. He may be the same person as Lodewyck van der Helst.

ELSTER, Gottfried Rudolf
German, 19th century.
Born 5 April 1820, in Helmstedt (Lower Saxony); died 11 March 1872, in Berlin.
Painter. History painting.
A pupil at the Berlin academy, Elster also worked in Düsseldorf with Sohn and in Munich with Kaulbach. He painted *Scenes from German Legends* for the palace at Schwerin and a *Moses* and *Jeremiah* for the chapel of the palace in Berlin.

ELSTER, Gottlieb
German, 19th century.
Born 8 October 1867, in Greene (Lower Saxony).
Sculptor.
Elster was a pupil at the academy in Munich in 1888-1889. His notable works include the statues of *Kleist*, Frederick II and Queen Louise, and numerous memorials and monuments to the dead.
MUSEUMS AND GALLERIES:
BERLIN (Nationalgal.): *Bust of a Woman, or Ave Maria* - BRUNSWICK: *Eros; Joy; The Hero*.

ELSTER, Johann Christian
German, 19th century.
Born 16 April 1792, in Hedwigsburg, near Wolfenbüttel; died 9 May 1854, in Helmstadt near Würzburg.
Draughtsman.
This artist is responsible for a series of portraits, including those of the chancellor Münsinger and of Julius and Henry Julius, dukes of Brunswick. He was primarily a theologian.

ELSTER, Toni
German, 19th century.
Born 1862, in Bremen.
Painter, engraver.
In the course of her training as an artist, Elster made many visits to Munich and travelled to study in Scotland. In 1900, she exhibited three etchings at the Glaspalast in Munich and showed oil paintings, forest landscapes and views of seaports there, as well as at exhibitions in Berlin and Düsseldorf, almost every year thereafter.

ELSTERMANN VON
German, 19th century.
Active in Breslau (now Wroclaw, Poland) c. 1835.
Miniaturist.

ELSTRACKE, Renold or Reginold, or Elstrack
British, 16th - 17th century.
Born 1571, in London; died after 1625.
Engraver.
Elstracke's portraits are sought after more for their rarity and historical exactitude than for their artistic worth. He often worked for bookshops, and made a number of engraved portraits of the English monarchs from the Norman Conquest onwards, described in Hollands's *Baziologia*.

ELSTRAETEN, Peeter van der
Flemish, 17th century.
Active in Antwerp, in 1660.
Painter.
Flemish School.
Peeter van der Elstraeten was the pupil of Jan van den Hecke (or van Eck).

ELSTRATE
Flemish, 17th century.
Active in Antwerp.
Painter.
Flemish School.
Frans van den Steen engraved a *Virgin and Child* after one of Elstrate's paintings. He is perhaps identical with Peeter van der Elstraeten.

ELSTRÖM, Harry
Belgian, 20th century.
Born 1906, in Berlin.
Sculptor, medallist.
Elström attended the Académie des Beaux-Arts in Brussels, the Akademie in Dresden and the British Academy in Rome. He taught at the University of Louvain.
MUSEUMS AND GALLERIES:
ANTWERP - BRUSSELS - GHENT - KOEKELBERG (Basilica) - PARIS - THE HAGUE.
AUCTION RECORDS:
LOKEREN, 16 Feb 1980, *Two Horses* (bronze, h. 14 1/2 ins / 37 cm) BEF 45,000.

ELTEN. See **KRUSEMAN Van Elten**

ELTON, Samuel Averill
British, 19th century.
Born 20 August 1827, in Newnham; died 15 June 1886, in London.
Painter. Landscapes.
Samuel Averill Elton was a teacher at Darlington School of Art. He exhibited at the Royal Academy and Suffolk Street Gallery from 1860 to 1864.
MUSEUMS AND GALLERIES:
LONDON (Victoria and Albert Mus.): *View of the River Tees; Old Mill on the Eden, Westmoreland*.

ELTZ, Johann Friedrich von
German, 17th century.
Born 1632; died 1686, in Mainz.
Engraver (mezzotint).
Eltz was one of the first artists to have produced engravings using the mezzotint method. He is noted for portraits and several plates after Albrecht Dürer.

ELTZE, Erich
Luxembourg, 19th century.
Born 18 July 1865, in Luxembourg; died 27 November 1943, in Berlin.
Painter.
Eltze was a pupil at the Berlin academy and showed his work at the Grosse Kunstausstellung in there, the Glaspalast in Munich and in Düsseldorf. He mostly painted lamplit interiors, for instance his *Workers, The Wait, Reading* and *Teatime*.

ELTZNER, Adolph
German, 19th century.
Active in Hamburg c. 1850.
Draughtsman.
In 1849, Eltzner produced the drawing for a wood engraving, *Bird's-eye View of Hamburg*.

ELUER, Erneszt
Romanian, 16th century.
Painter.
Erneszt Eluer was famous within his lifetime for his painting of *Adam and Eve in Paradise*.

ELVE-MEROVITCH, Jeanne
French, 20th century.
Born in Paris.
Painter, watercolourist. Genre scenes.

Jeanne Elve-Merovitch belonged to the Union des Femmes Peintres et Sculpteurs (Union of Women Painters and Sculptors).

ELVEN, J. P.
British, 18th century.
Active in London at the end of the 18th century.
Painter.

J.P. Elven appeared at the Royal Academy from 1788 to 1791.

ELVEN, J. P.
British, 19th century.
Active in London at the beginning of the 19th century.
Engraver.

This J.P. Elven may be the same as the painter of the same name. There is a *Portrait of Hugh Clark* by him dating from 1820.

ELVEN, Tetar Van. See **TETAR Van Elven**

ELVERY, J.
British, 18th century.
Active in London.
Painter. Portraits.

J. Elvery exhibited at the Free Society in 1762.

ELVIRE-JAN. See **JAN Elvire**

ELWELL, D. Jerome
American, 19th - 20th century.
Born 1857, in Gloucester; died 1912, in Naples.
Painter, illustrator. Landscapes.

AUCTION RECORDS:
NEW YORK, 9 Jan 1902, *Essex River*, USD 120. NEW YORK, 23 June 1983, *Carthage* (1879, oil on paper, 12 1/2 x 9 1/2 ins / 31.8 x 24.1 cm) USD 1,500. SAN FRANCISCO, 27 Feb 1986, *Carthage* (1879, oil on paper, 12 1/2 x 9 1/2 ins / 32 x 24 cm) USD 2,000.

ELWELL, Frank Edwin
American, 19th - 20th century.
Born 15 June 1858, in Concord; died 1922.
Sculptor, art critic.

After working with D. C. French in New York, Frank Edwin Elwell completed his studies at the École des Beaux-Arts in Paris, and with Falguière. He won medals at many exhibitions. He carved the first statue by an American artist to be erected in Europe. Elwell sought to revive interest in Egyptian sculpture, and, as curator of ancient and modern sculpture at the Metropolitan Museum of Art in New York, he gave lectures and published art books.

MUSEUMS AND GALLERIES:
CHICAGO (AI): *Diana and a Lion* - NEW YORK (Metropolitan Mus. of Art): *Aqua Viva*.

AUCTION RECORDS:
NEW YORK, 26 Sept 1996, *The Young Cleopatra* (marble, relief, 13 1/2 x 21 3/4 ins / 34.3 x 55.2 cm) USD 9,775.

ELWELL, Frederick William
British, 19th - 20th century.
Born 29 June 1870, in Beverley (Yorkshire); died 3 January 1958, in Beverley.
Painter. Portraits, genre scenes, landscapes, still-lifes.

Frederick William Elwell was an artist famed for his naturalistic depictions of Victorian life. He trained initially at Lincoln School of Art under the tutelage of Alfred Webster, before moving on to schools in Antwerp and Paris. Elwell's decision to enrol at the Académie Julien in Paris in 1892 had a profound effect upon both his style and subject matter. Through various encounters with artists such as Degas, Toulouse-Lautrec and Gauguin, Elwell became increasingly attracted to the techniques of French Impressionism. Subsequently, compositions such as *The First Born* of 1913 illustrated the artist's newly acquired concern with the qualities of light and colour, and indicated a shift in subject matter away from formal landscape and portraiture, to scenes of everyday domestic life.

After the success of Paris, Elwell moved back to England - first to London before settling in Beverley in Yorkshire in 1896. Such was his popularity with patrons and the buying public that he began to exhibit regularly at the Royal Academy and formed close friendships with artists such as Alfred Munnings and Reginald Brundit. The documentary nature of works such as *The Old Inn Kitchen* of 1922 served as an antidote to the sentimentality and morality of much Victorian work of the time. Elwell's profile and influence soared so much that he was made an associate of the Royal Academy in 1931 and established an independent studio in London's fashionable Holland Park in 1935.

MUSEUMS AND GALLERIES:
BOURNEMOUTH (Russell-Coates Art Gallery and Museum): *Inventory and Valuation for Probate* (1947, oil on canvas) - BURY (AG and Mus.): *The Fish Stall* (oil on canvas) - HULL (Ferens Art Gal.): *The First Born* (1813, oil on canvas); *The Landlord* (1935, oil on canvas); *The Wedding Dress* (1911, oil on canvas); *The Last Purchase or The New Purchase* (1921, oil on canvas); *The Housekeeper's Room* (oil on panel); *In a Bar* (1943, oil on canvas) - LONDON (Royal Academy of Arts): *The Royal Academy Selection and Hanging Committee 1938* (1938, oil on canvas) - LONDON (Tate Collection): *The 'Beverley Arms' Kitchen* (1919, oil on canvas) - PRESTON (Harris Mus. and Art Gal.): *Girl with a Cigarette* (1942, oil on panel); *The Curiosity Shop* (1929, oil on canvas) - SHEFFIELD (Sheffield Galleries and Museums Trust): *The New Frock* (1919, oil on canvas).

AUCTION RECORDS:
LONDON, 10 Nov 1981, *Refuge in my Studio* (1915, oil on canvas, 51 1/2 x 64 ins / 131 x 162.5 cm) GBP 7,200. LONDON, 2 March 1984, *Polisher's Shop* (oil on canvas, 39 1/2 x 29 1/2 ins / 100.3 x 75 cm) GBP 3,500. LONDON, 22 July 1986, *Art Lover* (oil on canvas, 25 x 30 ins / 63.5 x 76 cm) GBP 1,300. LONDON, 6 Nov 1996, *New Acquisition* (1921, oil on canvas, 40 1/4 x 50 ins / 102 x 127 cm) GBP 56,500. STOCKHOLM, 26 May 1999, *Beautiful Morning* (1915, oil on canvas, 36 x 30 ins / 92 x 77 cm) SEK 290,000. LONDON, 10 Nov 1999, *Beautiful Morning* (1915, oil on canvas, 36 x 30 ins / 91 x 77 cm) GBP 38,000. DRIFFIELD, 4 Aug 2000, *The Little Visitor at the Beverley Arms Hotel in 1913, Baby and Mrs Florence Hall Née Thompson* (oil on canvas, 30 x 23 ins / 76 x 58 cm) GBP 7,400. DRIFFIELD, 3 Aug 2001, *Maids with Pigeons at the Window of the Bar House* (oil on hardboard, 19 x 15 ins / 48 x 38 cm) GBP 5,600. DRIFFIELD, 29 Nov 2002, *Maids Feeding the Pigeons* (oil on board, 18 x 14 ins / 46 x 36 cm) GBP 7,200. DRIFFIELD, 1 Aug 2003, *View of Lake Garda from the Hotel Garden Riva* (oil on board, 11 x 26 ins / 28 x 66 cm) GBP 1,300. LONDON, 27 May 2004, *Breakfast Time* (oil on canvas, 45 x 32 ins / 114 x 81 cm) GBP 8,000.

ELWELL, James
British, 19th century.
Active in Beverley (Yorkshire).
Sculptor (wood).

James Elwell was the father of Frederick W. Elwell. He was also a mayor.

ELWELL, John H.
American, 20th century.
Born 10 March 1878, in Marblehead (Massachusetts).
Engraver, draughtsman.

John Elwell was a pupil of V.L. George, R. Carpenter and the Evening Art School in Boston. He was a member of the Boston Art Club. He produced etchings.

ELWELL, Robert Farrington
American, 19th - 20th century.
Born 1874; died 1962.
Sculptor, painter. Local scenes.

Robert Elwell often devoted himself to typical subjects of the American West.

AUCTION RECORDS:

NEW YORK, 29 April 1976, *Hunter in a Landscape* (oil on canvas, 29 3/4 x 15 ins / 75.5 x 38 cm) USD 1,000. LONDON, 22 Oct 1976, *The Sunfisher* (bronze, h. 18 ins / 45.7 cm) GBP 1,100. LOS ANGELES, 23 June 1981, *Indian Chief on Horseback* (oil on canvas, 38 x 30 ins / 96.5 x 76 cm) USD 1,600. LONDON, 21 March 1985, *Indian in his Canoe* (brown-patinated bronze, h. 19 1/2 ins / 49.5 cm) GBP 500. NEW YORK, 3 Dec 1996, *Cowboy on a Wild Horse* (1911, bronze, h. 18 ins / 45.7 cm) USD 2,530. NEW YORK, 1 Dec 1999, *Out Shooting* (oil on canvas, 38 x 26 ins / 97 x 66 cm) USD 7,500. CONNECTICUT, 5 Dec 2000, *War Cry* (oil on canvas, 24 x 16 ins / 61 x 41 cm) USD 2,100. SAN FRANCISCO, 30 Sept 2001, *Bucking Bronco* (brown patinated bronze, h. 49 ins / 124 cm) USD 3,500. HAYDEN, 27 July 2002, *Link that Closed the Gap between East and West* (oil on canvas, 30 x 40 ins / 76 x 102 cm) USD 11,000. SANTA FE, 9 Nov 2002, *Going Home* (oil on canvas, 24 x 36 ins / 61 x 91 cm) USD 5,000. NEW YORK, 21 May 2003, *Roping a Bear* (oil on canvas laid on masonite, 22 x 34 ins / 56 x 86 cm) USD 2,500. HAYDEN, 26 July 2003, *Trail Drive* (oil on board, 22 x 15 ins / 56 x 38 cm) USD 10,000. PETERBOROUGH, 3 Jan 2004, *Southwestern Scene of Cowboys around the Chuck Wagon with a Cattle Herd* (oil on canvas, 29 x 40 ins / 74 x 102 cm) USD 4,250.

ELWELL, William S.
American, 19th century.
Born 1810; died 12 September 1881, in Springfield.
Painter.

William S. Elwell painted mainly portraits.

ELWES, Cecilia Noel
British, 19th - 20th century.
Born 1874, in Dumdum, near Calcutta; died 1952.
Watercolourist.

Cecilia Noel Elwes exhibited at the Salon des Artistes Français from 1935.

ELWES, Simon
British, 20th century.
Born 1902, in Rugby; died 1975.
Painter. Portraits, flowers.

Simon Elwes is known for his portraits of aristocrats, including those of the *Comtesse de Choiseul* and *The Honorable Miss Taffy Rodd* which he exhibited in 1928 and 1934 respectively. He was elected a member of the Royal Academy in 1967.

AUCTION RECORDS:

NEW YORK, 5 June 1978, *Vase of Flowers* (1960, oil on canvas, 39 1/2 x 29 1/4 ins / 100.4 x 74.3 cm) USD 1,300. LONDON, 14 Oct 2004, *Portrait of David Randolph Moray Stuart, 2nd Viscount Stuart of Findhorn, Aged 7* (oil on canvas, 32 x 26 ins / 81 x 65 cm) GBP 2,800.

ELWIN, Blaise, or Elluin
French, 18th century.
Born in Abbeville.
Engraver (burin).

Blaise Elwinwas a pupil of Jacques Firmin Beauvarlet and engraved genre subjects.

ELWIN, Emma
British, 19th century.
Active in Düsseldorf and London at the end of the 19th century.
Painter.

Emma Elwin exhibited genre scenes in Düsseldorf from 1873 to 1877, and at the Royal Academy in London in 1879.

ELWOOD, J.
British, 18th - 19th century.
Draughtsman, caricaturist.

ELWYN, John
British, 20th century.
Born 1916, in Newcastle; died 1997.
Painter. Genre scenes.

John Elwyn studied at the Royal College of Art and exhibited at the Royal Academy, the New English Art Club and the Royal College of Art. Inspired by the Romantics, he was one of the few painters to work in the Welsh style.

MUSEUMS AND GALLERIES:

GLASGOW.

AUCTION RECORDS:

LONDON, 25 Jan 1991, *Wool Dyeing* (oil on canvas, 20 x 30 ins / 51 x 76 cm) GBP 880. LONDON, 14 July 1999, *Cattle on the Path* (1954, oil on canvas, 20 x 24 ins / 51 x 61 cm) GBP 1,500. LONDON, 14 July 1999, *Figures on a Country Lane in Wales* (1952, oil on canvas, 20 x 24 ins / 51 x 61 cm) GBP 1,900. CARDIFF, 26 Sept 2001, *Autumn's Leafy Luxury* (oil on canvas, 28 x 35 ins / 70 x 90 cm) GBP 1,800. CARDIFF, 26 Sept 2001, *Spanish Hill Farm with Cows* (1954, oil on canvas, 18 x 24 ins / 46 x 61 cm) GBP 2,600. LONDON, 4 July 2002, *Glamorgan* (ink, gouache and watercolour, 13 x 17 ins / 32 x 42 cm) GBP 1,800. WALES, 29 April 2003, *Deserted Farm* (watercolour, 19 x 26 ins / 48 x 66 cm) GBP 2,000. OXFORD, 25 Feb 2004, *In Mid Cardiganshire* (oil on board, 4 x 5 ins / 9 x 13 cm) GBP 1,450. BATH, 21 June 2004, *Mid Wales Farm* (gouache, 14 x 18 ins / 35 x 45 cm) GBP 1,600.

ELYAKOV, Ivan
Russian, 18th century.
Born 1725.
Engraver.

Ivan Elyakov trained under C.A. Wortmann and Ivan Sokolov. He is known, among other works, for four illustrations which he drew and engraved for a Russian edition of *Cornelius Nepos*, a *View of the Neva* after a drawing by Makhaev, a *View of the Stock Exchange*, and a *View of the Gostiny Dvor, St Petersburg*. He is probably the same artist as the engraver Emukov.

ELYAS. See **ELIAS**

ELZEN, Staf van
Belgian, 20th century.
Born 1915, in Deurne.
Painter.

After attending the Académie and the Institut Supérieur des Beaux-Arts in Antwerp, Van Elzen became a director at the Académie in Kontich.

ELZER, Hendrik Jakob
Dutch, 19th century.
Born 1808, in Amsterdam; died 1866.
Painter. Seascapes.

Hendrik Jakob Elzer was a pupil of H.-S. Ten Cate.

AUCTION RECORDS:

AMSTERDAM, 5-6 Nov 1991, *Sailing in the Estuary* (oil on panel, 9 3/4 x 12 3/4 ins / 25 x 32.5 cm) NLG 6,440.

ELZEVIER. See **ELSEVIER**

ELZEVIR, Ludwig
Dutch, 17th century.
Active in the Netherlands.
Painter, engraver, draughtsman. Religious subjects.

Ludwig Elzevir primarily engraved in mezzotint. He may be the same person as Louwys Aernouts Elsevier.

ELZINGA, Johan or Johannes, or Elsinga
Dutch, 20th century.
Born 1893; died 1969.
Painter. Landscapes with figures, seascapes.

AUCTION RECORDS:

AMSTERDAM, 28 Feb 1989, *Frieland in Winter during Skating Race* (1956, oil on card, 9 1/2 x 13 1/2 ins / 24 x 34 cm) NLG

3,220. AMSTERDAM, 14-15 April 1992, *Walking in the Park of St-Cloud* (1931, oil on canvas/card, 8 3/4 x 12 1/2 ins / 22.5 x 32 cm) NLG 1,840. AMSTERDAM, 14 Sept 1993, *Fishing Boats Full Sail Outside* (1948, oil on canvas, 12 x 16 ins / 30.5 x 40.5 cm) NLG 1,610. AMSTERDAM, 9 Nov 1993, *On a Lake of the Frisians* (1934, oil on canvas, 11 3/4 x 15 3/4 ins / 30 x 40 cm) NLG 1,840. AMSTERDAM, 14 June 1994, *Veere* (1935, oil on paper/card, 9 3/4 x 12 1/2 ins / 25 x 32 cm) NLG 3,220. AMSTERDAM, 16 April 1996, *Market Day* (1946, oil on canvas, 24 3/4 x 19 3/4 ins / 63 x 50 cm) NLG 3,304. AMSTERDAM, 19-20 Feb 1997, *Horses* (1946, oil on card, 9 1/4 x 12 1/2 ins / 23.5 x 32 cm) NLG 2,998. AMSTERDAM, 22 Oct 2001, *Ship-building Yard at Grouw* (1933, oil on canvas, 15 x 19 ins / 39 x 49 cm) NLG 4,200.

ELZINGRE, Édouard
Swiss, 20th century.
Born in Neuchâtel.
Painter, draughtsman. Figure compositions, landscapes.

Elzingre exhibited circus scenes in Paris.

AUCTION RECORDS:
GENEVA, 14 Oct 1982, *Clump of Trees in Autumn* (oil on canvas, 25 1/2 x 21 1/4 ins / 65 x 54 cm) CHF 650.

ELZNER, Jacob. See **ELSSNER**

EM, Do Quang. See **DO QUANG EM**

EMALYANOV, Ilya
Russian, 17th century.
Icon painter.

Between 1660 and 1670, Ilya Emalyanov helped with the murals in various Moscow palaces and churches.

EMANUEL, Frank Lewis
British, 19th - 20th century.
Born 15 September 1865, in London; died 7 May 1948, in London.
Painter, watercolourist, draughtsman, engraver, illustrator. Interiors with figures, village views, topographical views.

Frank Lewis Emanuel first studied at the Slade School in London under Legros then under Bouguereau at the Académie Julian in Paris. Between 1918 and 1930 he taught engraving at the Central School of Art in London. He travelled in Europe, South Africa and Ceylon (now Sri Lanka).

He published articles on art and topographical drawings in the *Architectural Review* and the *Manchester Guardian*. He also produced *Illustrations of Montmartre*. His work includes *Small Village in Normandy, Dorset Village* and *Italy in England*.

He exhibited from 1881 at the Royal Academy in London and from 1886 at the Paris Salons. In 1912 he held an exhibition of watercolours.

MUSEUMS AND GALLERIES:
LONDON (Tate Collection): *Kensington Interior* (1912, oil on canvas).

AUCTION RECORDS:
LONDON, 3 Feb 1982, *Basement Lunch Time* (1912, oil on canvas, 25 x 31 ins / 63.5 x 79 cm) GBP 1,050. LONDON, 12 June 1986, *View of Concarneau* (oil on card, 12 1/4 x 15 1/2 ins / 31 x 39.5 cm) GBP 800. TRIESTE, 3 Dec 2003, *Fuques Old Port* (oil on canvas, 35 x 43 ins / 90 x 110 cm) EUR 3,100.

EMANUELI, Giovanni
Italian, 19th century.
Born 1816, in Brescia; died 18 December 1894, in Milan.
Sculptor.

Emanueli studied at the Accademia di Brera in Milan, and at the age of 14 he sculpted a *Bust of Emperor Francis I of Austria*. He also sculpted busts of *Napoleon I* and *Radetzky*.

He exhibited in Vienna, Munich and Paris. Among his best known works are the *Funeral Monument to Bishop Ferrari* in Brescia Cathedral; two statues for Milan Cathedral; and the statues on the high altar in the church of S Carlo in Brescia.

EMAUS, Gerhardus de Micault
Dutch, 19th century.
Born 27 February 1789, in Dordrecht; died 25 November 1863, in Gouda.
Draughtsman, engraver, painter.

Gerhardus de Micault Emaus was a pupil of Bagelaer and Janson. He was an engraver in stained glass.

EMBDE, August von der
German, 19th century.
Born 2 December 1780, in Kassel; died 10 August 1862, in Kassel.
Painter. Portraits, genre scenes.

Having begun his studies at the academy in Kassel, he completed them in Dresden, Düsseldorf, Munich and Vienna.

MUSEUMS AND GALLERIES:
BRUNSWICK: *Children by the Stream* - GOTHA (Schloss Friedenstein): *Princess Wilhelmine Caroline of Hessen* - KASSEL: *Self-portrait by the Artist* - NANTES (Mus. Dobrée): *Portrait of Louise Brentano* (sepia).

AUCTION RECORDS:
COLOGNE, 5 May 1966, *Spring*, DEM 4,600. VIENNA, 5 Sept 1982, *Vespers* (1862, oil on canvas, 16 1/4 x 19 ins / 41 x 48 cm) ATS 10,000. VIENNA, 20 May 1987, *Young Peasant Woman in a Landscape* (1834, oil on canvas, 38 1/2 x 30 3/4 ins / 98 x 78 cm) ATS 130,000. MUNICH, 6 Dec 1994, *Young Girl at a Window* (1845, oil on canvas, 19 1/4 x 15 3/4 ins / 49 x 40 cm) DEM 18,400. LUCERNE, 8 Nov 2000, *Two Girls Under Apple Bough in Blossom* (1845, oil on canvas, 26 x 19 ins / 65 x 49 cm) CHF 20,000.

EMBDE, Caroline von der, or Klauhold
German, 19th century.
Born 31 January 1812, in Kassel.
Painter. Genre scenes.

This artist, the daughter and pupil of August von der Embde, lived in Bremen and exhibited in Munich, Dresden and Cologne from 1854 to 1860.

EMBDE, Ernestine Emilie von der
German, 19th century.
Born 10 December 1816, in Kassel; died 14 May 1904, in Kassel.
Painter. Portraits, genre scenes.

The daughter and pupil of August von der Embde, this artist lived in Kassel and exhibited in Cologne and Dresden from 1861 to 1872.

EMBDEN, J. Ger. Van
Dutch.
Painter. Portraits.

This painter is mentioned by Siret.

EMBHARDT, Endris
German, 15th - 16th century.
Active in Crailsheim.
Sculptor.

Endris Embhardt may be the same person as Andreas Einhart.

EMBIL, Miguel
Cuban, 19th century.
Born 19th century, in Havana.
Sculptor.

Miguel Embil exhibited at the Salon des Artistes Français and was awarded a commendation in 1898. He also received a silver medal at the Exposition Universelle of 1900 in Paris.

EMBLEMA, Salvatore
Italian, 20th century.
Born 1929, in Terzigno.

Painter (mixed media).

AUCTION RECORDS:

MILAN, 10 March 1986, *Untitled* (1982, oil on canvas, 32 1/4 x 27 1/2 ins / 82 x 70 cm) ITL 2,100,000. ROME, 15 Nov 1988, *Untitled* (1965, mixed media/canvas, 70 3/4 x 78 3/4 ins / 180 x 200 cm) ITL 2,400,000. ROME, 17 April 1989, *Untitled* (1969, oil on canvas, 78 3/4 x 70 3/4 ins / 200 x 180 cm) ITL 2,000,000. ROME, 3 Dec 1991, *Abstract Flowers* (1985, oil on canvas, 59 x 59 ins / 150 x 150 cm) ITL 2,000,000.

EMBRECHTS, Jan
Flemish, 17th century.
Died c. 1677.
Active in Antwerp.
Sculptor.
Flemish School.

EMBRECHTS, Marten
Flemish School, 16th century.
Painter.
Antwerp School.

Marten Embrechts was admitted into the guild as a master in 1579.

EMBREE, Margaret Train
American, 20th century.
Born in New York.
Painter. Portraits.

Margaret Embree exhibited at the Salon de la Société Nationale from 1925. She is noted for her portraits of children.

EMBRY, Georges
French, 19th century.
Born during the second half of the 19th century, in Paris.
Sculptor.

Georges Embry received an honourable mention at the Salon des Artistes Français in 1897.

EMDEN, Harry
German, 19th century.
Active in Düsseldorf and Berlin, during the second half of the 19th century.
Painter.

This genre painter was a frequent exhibitor at various salons in Berlin.

EMDEN, Hermann
German, 19th century.
Born c. 1811, in Frankfurt am Main.
Active in Frankfurt am Main.
Engraver, lithographer.

A pupil at the Städel Institute, this artist is known mainly for his numerous views of Frankfurt.

EME, André
French, 20th century.
Born 18 September 1931, in Paris.
Active in Cannes.
Painter.

In 1968 André Eme showed work in Paris at the Salon des Surindépendants and the Salon des Indépendants. His solo shows include 2000, at the Galerie Faits & Gestes in Cannes; 2000, 2001, at the Galerie République, Cannes. His abstract painting evokes the coloured cells of a cosmic universe as they grow larger, caught at the moment they mutate. 'I paint a good many abstract works based on astrophysics, mathematics, the cosmos. This is metaphysical painting.'

EMEDEN, Nathan
Nigerian, 20th century.
Sculptor. Masks.

Nathan Emeden creates masks worn for Ekpeye ceremonies in Nigeria. For his brightly coloured creations he uses a variety of materials including wood, wool and feathers. Along with more traditional motifs, he includes elements deriving from foreign cultures. He works in collaboration with Chief Mark Unya.

BIBLIOGRAPHY:

Martin, Jean-Hubert/Mark, Francis/Magnin, André/Marcadé, Bernard, *Les Magiciens de la terre*, exhibition catalogue, Éd. du Centre Georges-Pompidou, Paris, 1989.

EMEFOWICZ, Auguste
Polish, 20th century.
Born in Lviv (now in Ukraine).
Painter. Genre scenes.

Auguste Emefowicz exhibited in Paris at the Société Nationale des Beaux-Arts in 1928. He was probably related to Maximilien Feuerring-Emefowicz.

EMELE, Wilhelm
German, 19th century.
Born 20 May 1830, in Buchen (near Hamburg); died 11 October 1905, in Freiburg.
Painter. Battles.

Emele was a pupil of Feodor Dietz in Munich, completing his studies in Antwerp and Paris. He became established in Munich in 1860 then moved to Vienna, finally settling in Berlin in 1887. He was awarded a medal in Vienna in 1878. He exhibited in Munich, Vienna, Dresden and at the royal academy in Berlin from 1873 to 1889.

He is noted for his *Wounded Officer, Outside Dijon, Fighting on the Neckar Bridge in Heidelberg, Battle of Belfort, Leonora* and *Inspection by the Officer of the Day.*

MUSEUMS AND GALLERIES:

DONAUESCHINGEN: *Battle of Stockach* - KARLSRUHE: Battle scenes - LÜBECK: *Battle Scene* - MUNICH (Neue Pinakothek): *Swedish Cavaliers Leaving Rotenburg.*

AUCTION RECORDS:

LONDON, 19 June 1981, *Huntsman and Horses outside a Hunting Lodge* (1861, oil on canvas, 18 x 26 3/4 ins / 46 x 68 cm) GBP 6,000. NEW YORK, 10 June 1983, *Awaiting the Departure* (1861, oil on canvas, 18 x 26 3/4 ins / 45.7 x 68 cm) USD 13,000. STUTTGART, 19 March 1999, *Troups of Captured Town Moved Past Gustav Adolf* (oil on canvas, 24 x 38 ins / 60 x 96 cm) DEM 5,500. AMSTERDAM, 18 Feb 2003, *Military Parade in North Italy with a Hussar Leading a Grey Horse* (1868, oil on canvas, 22 x 27 ins / 56 x 69 cm) EUR 8,000.

EMELIUS. See **EMMEL Johann Sigmund**

EMELRAAD. See **IMMENRAET**

EMELYAN MOSKVITIN, called the Muscovite
Russian, 17th century.
Active c. 1600.
Icon painter.

Several of the works by Emelyan Moskvitin survive: an icon in the Postnikov collection and, until 1914, four icons, each containing three figures of saints, in the Rogozhskoe Cemetery in Moscow. A painting, *Three Men on the Stove*, probably by him, was formerly in the Stroganov Collection.

EMELYANOV, Dmitri
Russian, 17th century.
Active in Kostroma.
Icon painter.

In 1665, together with other painters, Dmitri Emelyanov worked on four icons: *The Saviour and Saints at Prayer, Mother of God with the Apostle Peter and the Archangel Michael, St John the Baptist, the Apostle Paul and the Archangel Gabriel*, and *Guardian Angel.*

EMELYANOV, Fedor
Russian, 17th century.
Born to a family originally from Pskov.
Icon painter.

EMELYANOV, Mikhail
Russian, 17th century.
Active in Moscow.
Icon painter.

EMELYANOV, Nadeya
Russian, 17th century.
Active in Moscow.
Icon painter.

EMENS, Homer F.
American, 19th - 20th century.
Painter.
Homer Emens lived in New York and was a member of the Society of American Artists.

EMEREE, Bula Iyone
American, 20th century.
Born 7 August 1899, in Wichita (Kansas).
Painter.
Bula Emeree was a pupil of F.B.A. Linton and J. Arpa. He was the holder of three Blue Ribbons at the Kendall Country Fair in Boeme (Texas) in 1926 and 1927. He was also a teacher. His works include: *On the San Antonio River - Blue Bonnets*

EMERIC, pseudonym of Emeric Vagh-Weinmann
Hungarian, 20th century.
Born 25 December 1919, in Budapest.
Active from 1924, then naturalised in France.
Painter. Landscapes, still-lifes, flowers.
Emeric was born into a family of painters. He arrived in France at the age of five and quickly took up painting. From the outset he chose subjects familiar to him such as landscapes and bunches of flowers and executed a number of views of Provence using broad, vigorous, coloured strokes. His main preoccupation was not structure: he engaged in showing the transience of the landscape. He lived in Paris in 1945 and regularly exhibited there from 1948 at the Salon des Artistes Français and the Salon Comparaisons. In 1959 he went to New York was inspired to execute several views of that city. He exhibited in the South of France, the USA (New York regularly) and Japan. Emeric settled in Provence in 1971 at La Colle-sur-Loup.

EMERIC

AUCTION RECORDS:
VERSAILLES, 4 April 1976, *Still-life with Fruit and a Vase of Flowers* (oil on canvas, 36 1/4 x 25 1/2 ins / 92 x 65 cm) FRF 3,500. VERSAILLES, 17 May 1981, *Maisonnettes in the Trees* (1953, oil on canvas, 32 x 25 1/2 ins / 81 x 65 cm) FRF 2,000. VERSAILLES, 18 Nov 1984, *Bridge on the River Close to the Chateau* (oil on panel, 23 1/2 x 32 3/4 ins / 59.5 x 83.5 cm) FRF 4,500. PARIS, 22 Jan 1990, *Toulouse Landscape* (oil on panel, 14 x 18 ins / 35.5 x 46 cm) FRF 4,600. PARIS, 8 April 1993, *Conflans* (1960, oil on canvas, 28 3/4 x 36 1/4 ins / 73 x 92 cm) FRF 6,500. BORDEAUX, 29 April 1993, *Cargo in Manhattan* (oil on canvas, 23 1/2 x 32 ins / 60 x 81 cm) FRF 27,000.

EMERIC, Auguste
French, 19th century.
Painter, watercolourist. Landscapes, seascapes.
Auguste Emeric exhibited views of the Côte d'Azur at the Salon from 1833 to 1844.

EMERIC, Honorine
Maiden name: Bouvret
French, 19th century.
Born 1814, in Melun.
Painter (gouache), watercolourist. Portraits, flowers, still-lifes (flowers/fruit). Miniatures.
Honorine Emeric exhibited at the Paris Salon from 1843 to 1880. She also worked on porcelain, almost always depicting flowers or fruit. She is best known for her *Portrait of a Young Girl*, a miniature on vellum.
AUCTION RECORDS:
PARIS, 24 March 1947, *Portrait of a Young Girl with a Circlet of Violets* (1869, watercolour on vellum) FRF 710. LONDON, 16 June 1978, *Basket of Fruit on an Entablature* (oil on canvas, 16 1/2 x 20 1/2 ins / 42 x 52 cm) GBP 1,600.

EMERIC, Jules Théodore
French, 19th century.
Born in Paris.
Painter. Fruit.
Jules Théodore Emeric studied in Aix-en-Provence under the Clérians, father and son, and Grobon. In 1865 he sent his *Oranges and Grapes* to the Salon, followed in 1867 by his *Peaches and Grapes in a Granite Bowl.*
AUCTION RECORDS:
PARIS, 22 June 1942, *Honesty,* FRF 3,500.

ÉMERIC-TAMAGNON, Auguste Jean Joseph.
See **TAMAGNON Jean Joseph Auguste Émeric de**

EMERICH, Erwin
French, 20th century.
Born 1 February 1876, in Strasbourg.
Painter. Portraits.
MUSEUMS AND GALLERIES:
CONSTANCE: *Count Ferdinand von Zeppelin* - STRASBOURG: *Portrait of Schraut.*

EMERICH, Johann
Czech, 16th century.
Died 11 February 1606, in Goeritz, Germany.
Painter, sculptor.

EMERICI, János
Hungarian, 16th century.
Active in 1521 in Bartfa (now Bardejov, Slovakia).
Painter.

EMERICQ, Henri
French, 17th century.
Active in Paris.
Sculptor.
Henri Emerico was accepted into the Académie Royale in 1681 for a statue of *St Andrew* in terracotta.

EMERIT-DOVGANIUK, Ecaterina (Mme)
Romanian, 20th century.
Born in Cetatea Alba.
Painter.
Ecaterina Emerit-Dovganiuk was a pupil of Selmy. She exhibited *Evening Party* and a still-life at the Salon des Artistes Français (1932-1933) in Paris.

EMERSON, Arthur Welster
American, 20th century.
Born 5 December 1885, in Honolulu (Hawaii).
Painter, engraver, illustrator.
Arthur Emerson was a pupil of J.C. Johansen and the Art Students League in New York. He produced etchings.

EMERSON, Edith
American, 20th century.
Born 1888, in Oxford (Ohio); died 1965.
Painter.

Edith Emerson was a pupil at the Art Institute of Chicago and the Pennsylvania Academy of the Fine Arts under Cecilia Beaux and Violet Dakley. This artist illustrated *Asia in the century*; she gave numerous lectures on art.

EMERSON, Robert Jackson
British, 19th - 20th century.
Born 1878; died 1944.
Sculptor. Portraits.
Robert Jackson Emerson studied at the Leicester School of Art. A low relief he created received a gold medal in a national competition. He later exhibited at the Royal Academy in London.
MUSEUMS AND GALLERIES:
LEICESTER (New Walk Mus. and AG): *Portrait of a Young Boy* (bronze low relief).
AUCTION RECORDS:
LONDON, 2 Oct 1985, *Autumn* (1905, brown-patinated bronze, h. 19 1/2 ins / 49.5 cm) GBP 500.

EMERSON, Sybill Davis
American, 20th century.
Born 4 April 1892, in Worcester (Massachusetts); died 1980.
Painter, decorative designer. Local scenes.
Sybille Emerson was known for her *Crowning of Spring*, exhibited in Paris in 1928. She won first prize for drawing at the San Francisco Art Association in 1924. She specialised in family or popular scenes: *The Woman Driver, The Concierge's Little Girl*.

EMERSON, William
British, 19th century.
Painter. Figures.
William Emerson exhibited 28 times at the Royal Academy in London from 1817 to 1843.

EMERSON, William (Sir)
British, 19th - 20th century.
Born 1843.
Active in London.
Painter, architect. Architectural views, architectural interiors, landscapes.
William Emerson exhibited numerous landscapes at the Royal Academy in London between 1870 and 1911. Many of these show Indian monuments and landscapes.

EMERSON, William C.
American, 19th - 20th century.
Born 1865.
Active in Chicago.
Painter.
William Emerson was self-taught. He won the Englewood Club prize.

EMERT, Friedrich
German, 18th century.
Active in Graz.
Painter.
Emert painted a portrait in 1759 of the nun *Micheline Plassing in Ecstasy* and in 1769 a portrait of the same nun on her deathbed.

EMERT, Maximilian
German, 18th century.
Active in Munich.
Engraver.
Maximilian Emert was appointed court engraver in 1762.

EMERTON, James H.
American, 19th - 20th century.
Born 1847; died 1930, in Boston.
Illustrator.
James Emerton was a member of the Copley Society. From 1894 he illustrated zoological works.

EMERY
French, 17th century.
Painter.
Emery was professional master for painters in Lyons in 1697.

EMERY, Augustin
French, 16th century.
Sculptor.
Emery was commissioned by the confraternity of St Roch to carry out various pieces of work in the church of St Peter at Épernon near Chartres in 1542.

EMERY, Betsy Eugénie
Maiden name: Veillon
Swiss, 19th century.
Born 1838, in Aigle.
Lithographer.
From 1878 onwards, Betsy Emery was head of drawing at the girls' high school in Lausanne.

EMERY, Charles
French, 17th century.
Sculptor.
Charles Emery worked on the dome of the church of the Invalides in 1691.

EMERY, Édouard
French, 18th century.
Active in Paris in 1751.
Painter, sculptor.

EMERY, Georges
French, 19th century.
Born in Paris.
Painter.
Georges Emery exhibited at the Salon des Artistes Français, obtaining an honourable mention in 1897.

EMERY, John
British, 19th century.
Born 22 December 1777, in Sunderland (Durham); died 25 July 1822, in London.
Painter, actor.
John Emery exhibited landscapes, portraits and seascapes at the Royal Academy from 1801 to 1817.

EMERY, Martin
French, 18th century.
Active in Paris in 1737.
Painter, sculptor.

ÉMERY-MOENS, Juliette
Belgian, 20th century.
Born c. 1900; died 3 October 1990, in Ukkel.
Painter. Figures, landscapes.
Emery-Moens was mainly a painter of young girls' faces, Mediterranean landscapes and intimate domestic scenes.

EMES, Johann
German, 17th century.
Active in Kitzingen (near Würzburg).
Sculptor.
Johann Emes executed two altars for the church at Dimbach between 1685 and 1689.

EMES, John
British, 18th - 19th century.
Born 1762, in Mackworth (Derbyshire); died 22 March 1808.

Painter, watercolourist, engraver. Landscapes.
John Emes engraved *Destruction of the Spanish Batteries in front of Gibraltar*, in the style of Jefferey. He exhibited at the Royal Academy in 1790 and 1791.
MUSEUMS AND GALLERIES:
LONDON (Victoria and Albert Mus.): *Greenwich Park* (watercolour) - MANCHESTER: *View of Cumberland*.
AUCTION RECORDS:
LONDON, 16 Feb 1922, *Wynnstay Park* (watercolour) GBP 10.
LONDON, 11 Nov 1982, *Iver Church, Middlesex* (watercolour, 81/4 x 121/2 ins / 21 x 32 cm) GBP 450.

EMES, Julius
German, 17th century.
Active in Franconia.
Sculptor.
Julius Emes worked on the churches at Aschach and Münnerstadt from 1611 to 1615.

EMFOS, Bartolomé
Flemish School, 14th century.
Born c. 1280, in Bruges; died in Barcelona.
Active in Spain.
Painter.
Bartolomé Emfos was working in Barcelona between 1309 and 1331.

EMFOS, Bartolomeu
Spanish, 14th century.
Born to a family originally from Flanders (Spanish Netherlands).
Painter.
Emfos worked in Barcelona, like his father, Bartolomé Emfos.

EMI, Kinuko
Japanese, 20th century.
Born 1923, in the Hyogo region.
Painter.
Kinuko Emi studied at Western Painting Institute from 1945 to 1949. Then she became a member of the Bijutsu Kyokai salon, and made many trips to Europe and America between 1953 and 1955. She took part in the International Exhibition of the Carnegie Foundation in Pittsburgh in 1958, and at the 1962 Venice Biennale.

EMIG, Georg
German, 20th century.
Born 1892, in Altona (Hamburg).
Painter. Portraits, landscapes.

ÉMILE, pseudonym of Émile Clément
French, 20th century.
Born 27 September 1943, in Orange (Vaucluse).
Painter.
Émile paints in the naive style. His landscapes are very spontaneous in appearance.

EMILI, Giovanni
Italian, 16th century.
Born at the end of the 15th century, in Modena.
Painter.
Emili was the pupil of F. Francia.

EMILI, Giovanni
Italian, 18th century.
Born c. 1770, in Florence.
Engraver. Religious subjects.
Pupil of R. Morghen, Emili made a copy of Raphael's *Holy Family*. He is probably identifiable as the sculptor Giovanni Emily.

EMILIAN, Céline
French, 20th century.
Born in the second half of the 19th century, in Paris.
Sculptor. Busts.
Céline Emilian was a pupil of Bourdelle. She exhibited in Paris at the Salon des Artistes Français from 1930, and is best known for her busts of her teacher Bourdelle, of the composer Vincent d'Indy and the pianist Cortot.
MUSEUMS AND GALLERIES:
LONDON (Tate Collection): *Angela* (1930, sculpture).

EMILIANI, Troilo
Italian, 16th century.
Active in L'Aquila (Abruzzi).
Painter.
Emiliani assisted Giovanni da Udine in the decoration of the Lodges of the Vatican. He also produced a *Transfiguration* for the brotherhood of St Sixtus in L'Aquila.

EMILIE, princess of Hohenlohe-Ingelfingen.
See **HOHENLOHE-INGELFINGEN**

EMILUS
6th century BC.
Active in 550 BC.
Sculptor.
Ancient Greek.
Emilus, a pupil of Dipoenus and Scyllis, worked in gold and ivory. For the temple of Hera at Olympia he made a group representing the *Hours* seated on thrones.

EMILY, Giovanni
Spanish, 19th century.
Engraver.
Giovanni Emily worked in Spain. He made a line engraving of a portrait after Seff Casabona. He is probably the same as the engraver Giovanni Emili.

EMIN, Tracey
British, 20th - 21st century.
Born 3 July 1963, in London.
Sculptor, painter, draughtswoman, video installation artist.
Tracey Emin studied at the Maidstone College of Art (1983-1986) and studied for an MA in Painting at the Royal College of Art in London (1987-1989) where her work was greatly influenced by Munch and Schiele. From 1995 to 1998 she ran her personal gallery in London, the Tracey Emin Museum. She is a professor of confessional art at the European Graduate School in Switzerland, where she runs a summer workshop with Jochen Poetter.

Emin destroyed the paintings she produced at the Royal College in what she refers to as 'emotional suicide' following an abortion. Currently among the most famous of Young British Artists, she is known internationally for her autobiographical art; her multimedia work draws largely on, expresses and relates to her own personal experiences and life history. Her most famous installations include *Everyone I Have Ever Slept With* (1963-1995), which consisted of an embroidered tent in the shape of an igloo, emblazoned with the names of all the people she had shared a bed with since birth. In 1998 the centre piece of her Turner Prize display featured *My Bed*, Emin's unmade bed surrounded by the debris of her personal life. Both the confessional and autobiographical nature of her work and her behaviour have provoked labels such as 'enfant terrible' and 'Janeycam of the art world' (Will Self).

Her first exhibition with fellow artist Sarah Lucas, *The Shop* in Bethnal Green in London, featured art objects by both artists being sold as bric-a-brac. She held her first solo exhibition at the White Cube Gallery in London in 1994. She has exhibited widely all over the world, particularly in America, Germany and Japan.
BIBLIOGRAPHY:
I Need Art Like I Need God, exhibition catalogue, S. London A.G., London, 1997. Button, V., *The Turner Prize*, exhibition

catalogue, Tate Gallery, London, 1999. *The British Art Show 5*, exhibition catalogue, Hayward Gallery, London, 2000. Grosenick, Uta, *Women Artists in the 20th and 21st century*, Taschen, Cologne, 2001. Lucie-Smith, Edward, *Art Tomorrow*, Editions Terrail, Paris and London, 2002.

MUSEUMS AND GALLERIES:

HAMBURG (Kunsthalle) - LONDON (British Mus.) - LONDON (Saatchi Gal.): *My Bed* (1998, installation) - LONDON (Tate Collection) - LOS ANGELES (California Plaza, Mus. of Contemporary Art) - OXFORD (TI Group PLC): *Be Faithful To Your Dreams* (1998, neon).

AUCTION RECORDS:

LONDON, 30 June 2000, *And it Feels Alright* (1997, monoprint and pencil, 17 x 20 ins / 43 x 50 cm) GBP 2,800. LONDON, 8 Feb 2001, *Exorcism of the Last Painting I Ever Made* (1996, installation with many objects) GBP 95,000. LONDON, 23 Oct 2001, *It's Not Me that's Crying it's my Soul* (1996, sculpture, 6 x 87 ins / 14 x 220 cm) GBP 14,000. LONDON, 8 Feb 2002, *Sobasex* (neon on Plexiglas, 20 x 202x4 ins / 51 x 514x9 cm) GBP 9,000. LONDON, 28 June 2002, *Be Faithful to your Dreams* (2000, neon on plexiglas, 13 x 59 ins / 32 x 150 cm) GBP 10,000. LONDON, 6 Feb 2003, *Fantastic to Feel Beautiful Again* (neon on plexiglas, 42 x 50x4 ins / 107 x 127x10 cm) GBP 9,000. LONDON, 6 Feb 2003, *Kiss Me, Kiss Me, Cover by Body in Love* (neon on plexiglas, 48 x 54x2 ins / 122 x 137x6 cm) GBP 16,000. LONDON, 23 June 2004, *My Coffin* (casket, mattress and ink on four sheets, 17 x 72x23 ins / 42 x 183x59 cm) GBP 70,000. LONDON, 25 June 2004, *Legal Sex Anal?. Anal Sex Legal?* (1998, pink neons and dimmer switches, two, 13 x 62x4 ins / 34 x 158x10 cm) GBP 25,000.

EMINGER, Helene

Bohemian School, 19th century.
Born 1858, in Prague.
Painter.

Helena Emiger studied under K. Javureck in Prague, Dürr in Munich, and at the Académie Colarossi in Paris. She painted mostly pastel portraits.

ÉMIOT, Paul Pierre

French, 20th century.
Born 1887, in Marseilles.
Painter. Landscapes, seascapes.

Paul Pierre Émiot became a member of the Salon des Artistes Français in Paris in 1931.

AUCTION RECORDS:

PARIS, July 1945, *Old Houses*, FRF 800; *Moored Vessel*, FRF 600. PARIS, July 1946, *Red Sail*, FRF 15,800. PARIS, 21 Feb 1986, *Mediterranean Landscapes* (1927, two oils on canvas) FRF 12,000. PARIS, 24 Feb 1988, *Cap Brun at Sunset* (24 x 19 3/4 ins / 61 x 50 cm) FRF 2,500. PARIS, 19 March 1990, *Creeks near Cassis* (oil on canvas, 28 3/4 x 36 1/4 ins / 73 x 92 cm) FRF 10,500. PARIS, 31 Jan 1997, *Red Sails* (oil on canvas, 28 3/4 x 39 1/4 ins / 73 x 100 cm) FRF 7,000. DETROIT, 12 Feb 1999, *Red Rocks in Brittany* (oil on canvas, 18 x 24 ins / 46 x 61 cm) USD 1,900. SYDNEY, 7 April 2003, *Untitled, Coast in the Evening* (oil on canvas, 35 x 52 ins / 90 x 131 cm) AUD 4,000.

EMIR SHAHI, or Ak Melik

Persian School, 14th - 15th century.
Born at the end of the 14th century, in Sebzevar; died 1453.
Calligrapher, illuminator, miniaturist.

EMLER, Bonaventura

Austrian, 19th century.
Born 19 October 1831, in Vienna; died 20 April 1862, in Rome or Vienna.
Painter. Battles.

This artist, who worked at the academy in Vienna, is best known for his illustrations for Dante's *Divine Comedy*.

EMMANUEL (Father Emmanuel Tzana)

Greek, 17th century.
Born probably in Rethymno in Crete; died on Corfu.
Painter.

We know little about the life of this artist, identified by Siret. The signature on the painting in the National Gallery in London *St Cosmo and St Damian Receiving the Divine Blessing* tells us that the artist was a Priest in Tzana. He may be the same Emmanuel, spoken of by Lanzi, who lived in Venice in the 17th century and was a painter in 1660. A priest in Venice, he painted mainly religious subjects in the Italian Byzantine style, of which he is most representative. His works can be seen in the churches of Venice and Corfu.

EMMANUEL, C. J.

French, 20th century.
Born in Turin, Italy.
Painter. Genre scenes.

The *Lady in Black* by Emmanuel was exhibited at the Salon des Artistes Français in 1929.

EMMANUEL, Gratiant

French, 20th century.
Born in Le Dorat (Haute-Vienne).
Painter, watercolourist. Landscapes.

Emmanuel Gratiant exhibited in Paris at the Salon des Artistes Français in 1938.

EMMANUEL LE CALLIGRAPHE, the Calligrapher

French, 20th century.
Born 1908, in Guingamp; died 1965, in Guingamp.
Painter.

Emmanuel 'the Calligrapher', self-taught, did not start painting until 1958. The Surrealists were interested in his graphic productions, for which he employed automatic techniques.

EMMANUELLO DA COMO (Fra)

Italian, 17th century.
Born 1586, in Como, according to Orlandi; died 1662, in Rome.
Fresco artist.

A member of the Franciscan Order, Emmanuelo left his home region for Messina, where he lived and studied painting under Silla. The latter's advice and dedication did much to improve his early style, characterised by a *Last Supper* featuring all the flaws and decadence of the late Milanese School. By contrast, his *Pietà, with Saints* in the church at Messina is purer, nobler and simpler. He is also noted for his frescoes in the library of the Irish convent of St Isidore, in Rome.

EMMANUELLO TEDESCO D'AUGUSTA, pseudonym of E. Amberger

Italian, 16th century.
Painter.

Emmanuello Tedesco d'Augusta was the pupil of Titian, and worked for some years in his studio. He may have been the son of Christoph Amberger.

EMMANUILOVA, Vasca

Bulgarian, 20th century.
Born in Bulgaria.
Sculptor.

Vasca Emmanuilova was a pupil of I. Lazarov and also influenced by Marco Marcov. She lived for a year in Paris.

EMMEL

German, 17th - 18th century.
Died at the end of 17th century, in Lübeck, at the beginning of the 18th century according to some sources.
Painter.

This artist was the only son of Johann Sigmund Emmel.

EMMEL, Johann Sigmund, or Immel or Emelius
German, 17th century.
Born c. 1623; died after 1682.
Active in Danzig (now Gdansk, Poland).
Painter.

The artist's portraits of the famous citizens of Danzig were engraved by Johann Bensheimer.

EMMENEGGER, Hans
Swiss, 19th - 20th century.
Born 19 August 1866, in Küssnacht, near Zurich; died 1940, in Lucerne.
Also active in France.
Painter, engraver. Landscapes, still-lifes.

Emmenegger began his long artistic training at the École des Arts Industriels in Lucerne. In 1884 he went to Paris, where he attended the Académie Julian, receiving the guidance of Gustave Boulanger and Jules Lefebvre. Later, he was taught by Gérome and then attended Karl Raupp's course at the preparatory school of the Akademie in Munich. In about 1895-1896 he learnt engraving in Munich, where he worked in Bernhard Buttersack's studio. On his return to Paris he studied under Benjamin-Constant and Lucien Doucet. He visited Algiers before settling in Emmenbrücke. He exhibited in Switzerland and also regularly at the Salon d'Automne of which he was elected a member in 1919; in 1920 he was also nominated a member of the selection committee there. First and foremost a landscapist, he was deeply interested in the nuances of the sky and of cloud formations.

AUCTION RECORDS:
LUCERNE, 3 June 1987, *Bavarian Landscape* (1896, oil on canvas, 25 1/2 x 32 ins / 65 x 81 cm) CHF 2,000. LUCERNE, 30 Sept 1988, *Clouds in Sunny Sky* (oil on canvas, 15 3/4 x 19 1/2 ins / 40 x 49.5 cm) CHF 2,900. LUCERNE, 3 Dec 1988, *Big Cloud* (1903, oil on canvas, 22 x 29 ins / 55 x 73.5 cm) CHF 4,600. LUCERNE, 24 Nov 1990, *Still-life* (1911, oil on canvas, 9 1/2 x 14 1/2 ins / 24 x 37 cm) CHF 5,000. LUCERNE, 23 May 1992, *Bird's Flight* (1918, oil on canvas, 9 3/4 x 13 ins / 25 x 33 cm) CHF 2,800. LUCERNE, 21 Nov 1992, *Tower in Autumn Landscape* (1898, oil on canvas, 20 x 26 1/2 ins / 51 x 67.5 cm) CHF 1,700. LUCERNE, 26 Nov 1994, *Still-life with Apples* (oil on canvas, 10 1/4 x 14 1/4 ins / 26 x 36 cm) CHF 6,000. LUCERNE, 27 May 2000, *Still-life with Apples* (oil on canvas, 10 x 15 ins / 25 x 39 cm) CHF 9,500. LUCERNE, 27 May 2000, *Still-life of Flowers* (oil on canvas, 26 x 18 ins / 65 x 46 cm) CHF 9,500. LUCERNE, 2 May 2001, *Edge of Wood at Sunset* (1891, oil on canvas, 9 x 13 ins / 24 x 33 cm) CHF 3,000. LUCERNE, 17 Nov 2001, *Two Apples* (oil on canvas, 8 x 11 ins / 21 x 29 cm) CHF 9,500. LUCERNE, 25 May 2002, *Blackbird Flying* (1926, oil on canvas/board, 12 x 15 ins / 30 x 38 cm) CHF 6,500. LUCERNE, 1 June 2002, *Plant with Yellow Flowers* (oil on canvas, 16 x 11 ins / 40 x 28 cm) CHF 7,500. LUCERNE, 15 Nov 2003, *Still-life with Two Vases of Flowers* (1911, oil on canvas, 24 x 20 ins / 61 x 50 cm) CHF 9,500. LUCERNE, 22 May 2004, *Landscape in Late Summer* (oil on canvas, 17 x 24 ins / 43 x 62 cm) CHF 7,000.

EMMER, Suzanne
French, 20th century.
Born c. 1880; died c. 1965.
Painter. Landscapes.

The sculptor Marcel Bodart was Suzanne Emmer's son-in-law.

EMMERECHTS, Jacobus Josephus
Flemish, 18th century.
Active in Antwerp.
Painter.
Flemish School.

Jacobus Josephus Emmerechts became a master in 1755 and dean of the Guild of St Luke in 1760.

EMMERIK, D.
Dutch, 17th century.
Painter.

The only work known by D. Emmerik is a portrait of the *Preacher G. H. Petri* engraved after one of Emmerik's paintings.

EMMERIK, Govert van
Dutch, 19th century.
Born 1808, in Dordrecht; died 24 November 1882, in Hamburg.
Painter. Seascapes.

Govert van Emmerik studied under Hofmann and Schotel in Utrecht.

AUCTION RECORDS:
AMSTERDAM, 19 Oct 1976, *Boats in Surging Sea* (oil on canvas, 27 1/4 x 35 ins / 69.5 x 88 cm) NLG 6,200. AMSTERDAM, 31 Oct 1977, *Street in the Snow* (oil on canvas, 22 x 28 1/4 ins / 56 x 71.5 cm) NLG 7,200. ZURICH, 15 May 1981, *Port Scene in Moonlight* (oil on panel, 13 1/2 x 17 ins / 34 x 43 cm) CHF 2,400. AMSTERDAM, 15 May 1984, *Surging Sea* (oil on canvas, 22 1/4 x 28 1/4 ins / 56.5 x 72 cm) NLG 4,200. PARIS, 3 July 1987, *Long-distance Dutch Vessel with Boat and Yacht off the Coast, with Paddle Steamer in Background* (oil on canvas, 22 x 28 ins / 56 x 71 cm) FRF 35,000. AMSTERDAM, 3 May 1988, *Steamboat Entering Port with Fishing Boat in Bad Weather* (1849, oil on canvas, 22 3/4 x 28 3/4 ins / 58 x 73 cm) NLG 6,900. AMSTERDAM, 2 May 1990, *Boat and Sailing Boats nearing a Three-masted Ship under a Cloudy Sky* (oil on canvas, 22 3/4 x 29 ins / 58 x 73.5 cm) NLG 8,625. AMSTERDAM, 5 June 1990, *Merchant Vessel and Boat nearing a Two-masted Ship in Rough Sea* (oil on canvas, 23 x 29 ins / 57.5 x 73.5 cm) NLG 3,220. AMSTERDAM, 24 April 1991, *Rescue* (1851, oil on canvas, 26 x 34 1/4 ins / 66 x 87 cm) NLG 5,175. AMSTERDAM, 28 Oct 1992, *Sailors in Lifeboats Steering towards a Two-Masted Ship in Distress* (1844, oil on canvas, 35 x 45 1/4 ins / 89 x 115 cm) NLG 2,760. AMSTERDAM, 21 April 1993, *Sailing Ships off the Coast with a Village in the Distance* (oil on panel, 9 1/4 x 11 3/4 ins / 23.5 x 30 cm) NLG 8,050. AMSTERDAM, 19 April 1994, *Sailing in the Tempest* (1855, oil on canvas, 22 1/2 x 28 3/4 ins / 57 x 73 cm) NLG 12,650. LONDON, 22 Feb 1995, *Sailing in a Dutch Estuary* (1849, oil on card, 22 x 28 1/4 ins / 56 x 72 cm) GBP 3,105. AMSTERDAM, 5 Nov 1996, *View of the Gouvernementshuis with Different Boats in the Foreground, Curaçao* (1856, 28 x 35 1/2 ins / 71 x 90 cm) NLG 4,956. NEW YORK, 5 Oct 1999, *Ships on Stormy Sea* (1879, oil on canvas, 31 x 42 ins / 79 x 106 cm) USD 2,400. ROTTERDAM, 2 Nov 1999, *Boats in Estuary* (oil on canvas, 21 x 27 ins / 53 x 68 cm) NLG 7,600. COLOGNE, 29 June 2000, *River with Boats in the Evening* (oil on canvas, 30 x 38 ins / 77 x 96 cm) DEM 7,500. COPENHAGEN, 6 Sept 2000, *Sailing Vessels off Harbour Entrance, Stranded Vessel in Foreground* (oil on canvas, 26 x 37 ins / 66 x 95 cm) DKK 24,000. THE HAGUE, 7 Nov 2001, *Sailing Ships in Front of Harbour House* (oil on canvas, 25 x 37 ins / 63 x 93 cm) NLG 6,500. WASHINGTON, 8 Dec 2001, *Ships on a Stormy Sea off a Coast* (1850, oil on canvas, 22 x 29 ins / 57 x 73 cm) USD 3,600. LONDON, 26 March 2002, *Dutch Fishing Vessels in a Calm beside a Harbour* (oil on canvas, 30 x 38 ins / 76 x 96 cm) GBP 3,000. AMSTERDAM, 24 April 2002, *Shipping by Harbour Entrance. Dutch Sailing Vessels Attacking an English Fleet* (1843, oil on canvas, a pair, 20 x 26 ins / 50 x 66 cm) EUR 10,000. AMSTERDAM, 29 Sept 2003, *Shipping in Calm at Sunset* (oil on board, 7 x 9 ins / 19 x 24 cm) EUR 1,700. AMSTERDAM, 3 Feb 2004, *Shipping on a Choppy Sea by a Coast* (1856, oil on canvas, 23 x 29 ins / 58 x 74 cm) EUR 3,200. COLOGNE, 1 April 2004, *Fishing Boat and Cutter in Stormy Sea* (oil on canvas, 28 x 37 ins / 71 x 95 cm) EUR 4,000.

EMMERSON, Henry Hetherington
British, 19th century.
Born 1831; died 28 August 1895.

Painter. Genre scenes.

Henry Hetherington Emmerson worked in Chester. He exhibited at the Royal Academy between 1851 and 1893.

MUSEUMS AND GALLERIES:

YORK: *Critics.*

AUCTION RECORDS:

LOS ANGELES, 21 Sept 1976, *Little Red Riding Hood* (oil on canvas, 30 x 20 3/4 ins / 76 x 53 cm) USD 650. LONDON, 9 June 1981, *Young Fisherwoman* (oil on canvas, 66 1/4 x 35 3/4 ins / 168 x 91 cm) GBP 340. MADRID, 21 Oct 1986, *Three Generations* (1881, oil on canvas, 48 x 72 ins / 122 x 182 cm) ESP 1,300,000. LONDON, 23 Sept 1988, *Young Girl with Poppies and a Pug* (1883, oil on panel, 24 x 9 1/4 ins / 61 x 23.5 cm) GBP 5,500. LONDON, 27 Sept 1989, *My Pretty Lady* (oil on canvas, 41 1/4 x 29 1/4 ins / 105 x 74 cm) GBP 1,430. LONDON, 8 June 2000, *Parley of an Emissary and Napoleon. Requisition of a Farmhouse* (oil on canvas, a pair, 24 x 36 ins / 61 x 91 cm) GBP 5,000. NEWCASTLE, 12 June 2001, *Waiting for the Boats* (1870, oil on canvas, 44 x 34 ins / 111 x 86 cm) GBP 3,000. STOCKHOLM, 28 May 2002, *Feeding the Calves* (oil on canvas, 37 x 28 ins / 93 x 72 cm) SEK 29,000. LONDON, 20 May 2003, *Maid of Derwent* (oil on canvas, 17 x 20 ins / 42 x 50 cm) GBP 27,000. LONDON, 29 May 2003, *Calf Yard* (oil on canvas, 36 x 29 ins / 92 x 73 cm) GBP 6,000. LONDON, 13 Jan 2004, *First Bathe* (oil on board, 20 x 10 ins / 50 x 25 cm) GBP 4,000. NEWCASTLE, 28 Sept 2004, *The Picnic: Three Children Resting on an Old Stone Wall* (1861, oil on canvas, 17 x 13 ins / 44 x 34 cm) GBP 3,900.

EMMES, Thomas

American, 18th century.

Engraver.

Thomas Emmes engraved the portrait of Increase Mather that is the frontispiece of the latter's book, *Holy Hope*, which was published in Boston in 1701.

EMMET, Ellen G.

American, 20th century.

Born 4 March 1876, in San Francisco; died 1941.

Painter. Portraits.

Ellen Emmet won a silver medal at the St Louis Exhibition in 1904.

MUSEUMS AND GALLERIES:

NEW YORK (Metropolitan Mus. of Art): *Two Portraits.*

AUCTION RECORDS:

BOSTON, 2 May 1980, *Portrait of Eleanor Peabody* (oil on canvas, 34 x 27 ins / 86.4 x 68.6 cm) USD 2,800.

EMMETT, Lydia Field

American, 19th - 20th century.

Born 1866, in New Rochelle; died 1952.

Painter, pastellist, illustrator. Portraits.

Lydia Emmett was a pupil of W.M. Chase, Mowbray, Cox and Reid in New York and of W. Bouguereau, R. Collin, T.-R. Fleury and MacMonnies in Paris. She was a member of the New York Associate National Academy of Design in 1909. She won a bronze medal at the Atlanta Exhibition in 1895 and a silver medal at the St Louis Exhibition in 1904.

AUCTION RECORDS:

PORTLAND, 28 Sept 1985, *Portrait of a Child* (pastel, 20 1/2 x 17 1/2 ins / 52 x 44.5 cm) USD 3,500. NEW YORK, 28 May 1987, *Portrait of Miss Ginnie and Polly* (oil on canvas, 50 x 40 ins / 127 x 101.6 cm) USD 16,500. NEW YORK, 24 June 1988, *Two Sisters* (1897, pastel/canvas, 22 x 23 1/2 ins / 55 x 60 cm) USD 5,500. LONDON, 1 Nov 1990, *Portrait of a Young Boy Sitting in an Armchair* (oil on canvas, 62 x 42 ins / 157.5 x 106.5 cm) GBP 11,000. NEW YORK, 30 Sept 1997, *Madame Mary very Disobedient* (1891, gouache, black ink and grisaille/card, 7 1/4 x 10 1/2 ins / 18.4 x 26.7 cm) USD 2,300. NEW YORK, 5 May 1999, *Flowers along White Picket Fence* (1893, oil on canvas, 20 x 20 ins / 51 x 51 cm) USD 14,000. NEW YORK, 29 Sept 1999, *Portrait of Nora Iselin* (oil on canvas, 65 x 43 ins / 165 x 109 cm) USD 26,000. SAN FRANCISCO, 9 June 2002, *Portrait of Katherine MacKay at Age 12* (oil on canvas, 64 x 45 ins / 163 x 114 cm) USD 9,500.

EMMETT, Philipp

British, 16th - 17th century.

Active in London at the end of the 16th or the beginning of the 17th century.

Sculptor.

Philipp Emmett was the royal sculptor.

EMMETT, Rosina. See **SHERWOOD**

EMMETT, William I

British, 17th century.

Active in London.

Sculptor.

William Emmett I was the nephew of Philip Emmett. He preceded Grinling Gibbons in his post as Sculptor to the Crown.

EMMETT, William II

British, 18th century.

Active c. 1710.

Engraver, architect.

Notable works by William Emmett II include a large *Interior View of St Paul's Cathedral* and two external views of the same cathedral. These were executed in a clear, precise style.

EMMINGER, Eberhard

German, 19th century.

Born 16 October 1808, in Biberach; died 27 November 1885, in Biberach.

Painter, lithographer. Figures, landscapes, urban landscapes.

At the age of 16, after working for the painter J.B. Pflug in Biberach, Emminger published an album of 12 plates entitled *Album of Lake Constance*. He studied lithography with Lorenz Ekeman Allesson. His *Precious Stone*, a large plate after Steinkopf, earned him a bursary which allowed him to travel in Italy; he also visited Vienna and Styria. He brought back many more drawings of Roman views from a second trip to Italy. Other notable works include *Napoleon's Campaign in Russia*, consisting of 100 plates, the original drawings for which were produced by Faber du Faur, another work on Palestine with a large view of Jerusalem for Steinkopf and two plates, *Sunday Morning* and the *Little Shepherd*, by Uhland, after J. Moztet.

EMMINGER, Konstantin

German, 19th century.

Born after 1808, in Biberach.

Active in Biberach.

Painter. Landscapes.

Konstantin was the brother of Eberhard Emminger, whom he predeceased.

EMMONS, Chansonetta Stanley (Mrs)

American, 19th century.

Born 30 December 1858, in Kingfield (Minnesota); died 1937.

Miniaturist, decorative artist, photographer.

BIBLIOGRAPHY:

Peladeau, Marius B. Chansonetta, *The Life and Photographs of Chansonetta Stanley Emmons, 1858-1937*, Maine Antique Digest, Waldoboro, 1977. *Recollected Images*, exhibition catalogue, Portland Museum of Art, Portland, 2000.

MUSEUMS AND GALLERIES:

DORCHESTER (Atheneum).

EMMONS, Dorothy Stanley

American, 20th century.

Born 14 June 1891, in Roxbury (Massachusetts); died 1960.

Painter, engraver (etching).

Dorothy Emmons produced etchings.

AUCTION RECORDS:
EAST DENNIS, 31 July 1987, *Later afternoon, Rockport* (oil on canvas, 24 x 24 ins / 61 x 61 cm) USD 2,400.

EMMS, John
British, 19th - 20th century.
Born 21 April 1843, in Blowfield; died 1 November 1912, in Lyndhurst.
Painter, engraver. Genre scenes, hunting scenes, animals.

John Emms exhibited frequently in London from 1866 to 1889, particularly at the Royal Academy and the Suffolk Street Gallery.

AUCTION RECORDS:
LONDON, 27 April 1908, *Duodrop and Skilful,* GBP 5. LONDON, 21 March 1910, *Ready for the Hunt,* GBP 19; *The Kill,* GBP 19. PARIS, 27 Sept 1946, *Two Greyhound Bitches and a Rabbit,* FRF 5,100. LONDON, 22 Nov 1968, *The Horse Speculation,* Gns 420. LONDON, 13 June 1969, *Return to Earth,* Gns 650. LONDON, 7 May 1971, *Dogs Dreaming of the Hunt,* Gns 1,200. LONDON, 28 Nov 1972, *Group of Spaniels,* GBP 1,300. SCOTLAND, 31 Aug 1973, *Spaniels,* GBP 1,000. NEW YORK, 12 Jan 1974, *Farm Scene,* USD 1,900. LONDON, 2 Feb 1979, *Young Gamekeeper* (oil on canvas, 35¼ x 27¼ ins / 89.5 x 69.2 cm) GBP 1,300. LONDON, 10 Dec 1981, *Foxhound and Two Terriers* (oil on canvas, 21 x 18 ins / 53.5 x 45.8 cm) GBP 2,200. NEW YORK, 8 June 1984, *Gone to Water* (1899, oil on canvas, 36 x 60 ins / 91.4 x 152.4 cm) USD 6,000. NEW YORK, 6 June 1986, *Hunting Dogs near a Bridge* (1881, oil on canvas, 51 x 36 ins / 129.5 x 91.4 cm) USD 38,000. NEW YORK, 4 June 1987, *After the Hunt* (1907, oil on canvas, 40 x 61 ins / 101.5 x 155 cm) USD 67,500. LONDON, 25 March 1988, *Gamekeeper* (1897, oil on canvas, 29 x 59 ins / 73.6 x 150 cm) GBP 13,000. LONDON, 3 June 1988, *Ferret and its Prey* (oil on canvas, 12 x 16 ins / 30.5 x 40.4 cm) GBP 550. LONDON, 23 Sept 1988, *Horse with a Side Saddle and a Spaniel* (1880, oil on canvas, 20¾ x 28¼ ins / 53 x 71.5 cm) GBP 3,740. PERTH, 28 Aug 1989, *Landowner in the Hunting Season* (1895, oil on canvas, 37 x 31 ins / 94 x 79 cm) GBP 8,250. LONDON, 27 Sept 1989, *Crossing a Hedge* (oil on canvas, 28 x 45 ins / 71 x 114 cm) GBP 14,850. LONDON, 13 Dec 1989, *Pack with Riders at a Gallop* (oil on canvas, 30¼ x 45¼ ins / 77 x 115 cm) GBP 9,350. LONDON, 14 Feb 1990, *Clumber Spaniels at the End of the Day* (oil on canvas, 36 x 24 ins / 91.4 x 60.9 cm) GBP 22,825. LONDON, 15 Jan 1991, *Rough-coated Collie* (oil on canvas, 17 x 27¼ ins / 43.2 x 68.9 cm) GBP 1,100; *Hounds in their Kennels after the Hunt* (oil on canvas, 40 x 50 ins / 101.5 x 127 cm) GBP 28,600. LONDON, 5 June 1991, *Waiting for the Mistress* (1889, oil on canvas, 20½ x 27½ ins / 52 x 70 cm) GBP 2,530. NEW YORK, 7 June 1991, *Waiting for the Master* (1897, oil on canvas, 28 x 36 ins / 71.1 x 91.4 cm) USD 27,500. LONDON, 16 July 1991, *Shot and his Companions, Three Red and White Irish Setters* (1876, oil on canvas, 15 x 22 ins / 38.1 x 55.9 cm) GBP 4,180. NEW YORK, 5 June 1992, *Lairg, a Rough-coated Terrier* (oil on canvas, 16 x 20 ins / 40.6 x 50.8 cm) USD 5,500. MONTREAL, 1 Dec 1992, *Fitz* (1895, oil on canvas, 20 x 27 ins / 50.8 x 68.5 cm) CAD 3,800. NEW YORK, 4 June 1993, *Two Collies Looking out over a Plain* (oil on canvas, 23½ x 20¼ ins / 59.7 x 51.4 cm) USD 4,025. LONDON, 11 June 1993, *Distant Relations* (1895, oil on canvas, 28 x 44¼ ins / 71.1 x 112.1 cm) GBP 18,400. LONDON, 25 March 1994, *Waiting for the Mistress* (1881, oil on canvas, 20½ x 28 ins / 52.3 x 71.4 cm) GBP 5,290. NEW YORK, 3 June 1994, *In the Company of Friends* (1896, oil on canvas, 43¾ x 57¼ ins / 111.1 x 145.4 cm) USD 10,350. NEW YORK, 9 June 1995, *Waiting for the Master* (1897, oil on canvas, 28 x 36 ins / 71.1 x 91.4 cm) USD 23,000. PERTH, 29 Aug 1995, *The Joys of Outdoor Life* (oils on canvas, set of three scenes, 12¼ x 25½ ins / 31 x 65 cm) GBP 9,775. LONDON, 27 March 1996, *Dogs Watching the Arrival of a Terrier* (1882, oil on canvas, 50 x 37 ins / 127 x 94 cm) GBP 63,100. LONDON, 5 Sept 1996, *Geese in a Farmyard* (oil on canvas, 10 x 12 ins / 25.5 x 30.5 cm) GBP 1,955; *Ponies by a River* (1894, oil on canvas, 16 x 21¼ ins / 40.7 x 54 cm) GBP 2,760. NEW YORK, 11 April 1997, *Arab Maid, a Bay Hunter with Two Hounds, Prompter and Bashful* (1905, oil on canvas, 18 x 24 ins / 45.7 x 61 cm) USD 11,500; *Zulu* (1895, oil on canvas, 12 x 14 ins / 30.5 x 35.6 cm) USD 6,325; *New Forest Pack* (1896, oil on canvas, 30 x 43 ins / 76.2 x 109.2 cm) USD 55,200. LONDON, 18 Dec 1997, *On the Scent* (oil on panel, 16 x 24 ins / 40.6 x 61 cm) GBP 8,280. NEW YORK, 10 Feb 1998, *Pack Resting* (oil on panel, 14 x 9½ ins / 35.5 x 24 cm) USD 6,900.

EMMY, Ludwig
Austrian, 20th century.
Born in Feldkirch.
Painter. Genre scenes.

Emmy was taught by V. Lehar and worked in Lichtenstein. In 1934, he exhibited his *Window in Winter* at the Salon des Artistes Français.

EMOND, Marie
French, 18th century.
Active in Paris in 1770.
Painter.

EMOND, Martin
Swedish, 20th century.
Born 1895; died 1965.
Painter. Genre scenes, landscapes, architectural views.

AUCTION RECORDS:
MALMÖ, 2 May 1977, *Church of Verona* (oil on canvas, 22½ x 29½ ins / 57 x 75 cm) SEK 5,500. STOCKHOLM, 16 Nov 1985, *Fishmongers* (1942, oil on panel, 35 x 47¼ ins / 89 x 120 cm) SEK 7,600. STOCKHOLM, 6 June 1988, *Flowering Fruit Tree* (oil, 29¼ x 42½ ins / 74 x 108 cm) SEK 7,000. GÖTEBORG, 18 May 1989, *The Church of Sireköpinge* (oil on canvas, 17¾ x 23½ ins / 45 x 60 cm) SEK 7,700. STOCKHOLM, 6 Dec 1989, *Winter in Town* (oil on panel, 23½ x 35½ ins / 60 x 90 cm) SEK 12,000. LANDSKRONA, 1 May 2004, *Circus Altenburg is Coming to Town* (oil on canvas, 24 x 35 ins / 61 x 90 cm) SEK 17,000. LANDSKRONA, 1 May 2004, *Waitresses* (oil on canvas, 43 x 59 ins / 110 x 150 cm) SEK 17,000.

EMOND, Pierre
Canadian, 18th century.
Born 1738, in Quebec; died 1808.
Sculptor.

An artisan as well as a sculptor, Pierre Edmond transformed one of the rooms of the Seminary of Quebec into a chapel and very probably carved the *Immaculate Conception* and *St Joseph* there.

EMONGENDRE, François
French, 17th century.
Active in Rome.
Painter.

François Emongendre executed a copy of *Assembly of the Gods* by Raphael.

EMONT, Adriaen van. See **EEMONT**

EMORY, Hopper
American, 20th century.
Born 8 May 1881, in Baltimore (Maryland).
Painter, illustrator.

Hopper Emory produced etchings and was a member of the Baltimore Charcoal.

EMOSAKU, or Vemonsaku, real name: Yamada Emosaku
Japanese, 17th century.
Born in Nagasaki.
Painter. Religious subjects.

Yamada Emosaku was active at the beginning of the 17th century. He was a painter in the service of Lord Matsukura and probably studied western painting with a European missionary in Nagasaki. He was arrested by the shogunate after the famous Shimabara Uprising in 1637-1638, and subsequently lived in Edo (now Tokyo) until his death. He is probably one of the first Japanese painters to have approached Christian subjects in his work, and is said to have painted the battle flag of the uprising.

EMPAIN, Joseph Jules
Belgian, 20th century.
Born in Ath.
Painter.

EMPERAIRE, Achille
French, 19th century.
Born 1829, in Aix-en-Provence; died 1898.
Painter, draughtsman. Nudes.

A pupil of Thomas Couture in Paris, Achille Emperaire was also one of Cézanne's favourite models while at the same time pursuing a career as a painter in his own right.

A declared admirer of Titian, he was unable to embrace later techniques. His life drawings reveal the voluptuous forms that are so admired in Renoir and Maillol. He did not always succeed in imposing a style of his own and as a result remained practically unknown.

BIBLIOGRAPHY:
Rewald, John, *Studies in Impressionnism*, Thames & Hudson, New York, 1985. Rewald, John, *Cézanne: a Biography*, Abrams, New York, 1986.

MUSEUMS AND GALLERIES:
AIX-EN-PROVENCE (Mus. Granet): *Landscape with Bridge* (charcoal/paper); *Standing Nude (Bather)* (charcoal/paper).

AUCTION RECORDS:
NEW YORK, 9 May 1994, *Female Nude Seated* (red chalk/paper, 6 1/4 x 4 3/4 ins / 15.9 x 12.1 cm) USD 3,105.

EMPGIN, Christian
German, 14th century.
Active in Cologne from 1353 to 1380.
Painter.

EMPHINGER, Franz
Austrian, 19th century.
Active in Graz from 1860 to 1870.
Painter, lithographer.

Emphinger engraved a large number of landscapes and portraits.

EMPI, Maurice
French, 20th century.
Born 31 January 1933, in St-Étienne.
Pastellist, painter (gouache). Still-lifes, landscapes with figures, seascapes.

Maurice Empi studied under Gen Paul. He painted various subjects, including scenes by night, and in cafés, but the bulk of his work was always connected with horses. In 1995 Galerie 26 in Paris put on a solo exhibition of his paintings.

Maurice Empi

AUCTION RECORDS:
PARIS, 15 Oct 1987, *Racing Finish* (oil on canvas, 18 x 22 ins / 46 x 55 cm) FRF 5,200. VERSAILLES, 17 April 1988, *Paris, Notre Dame and the Seine* (soft pastel, 13 3/4 x 12 3/4 ins / 35 x 32.5 cm) FRF 2,600. PARIS, 8 June 1988, *The Black Vase* (oil on canvas, 24 x 18 ins / 61 x 46 cm) FRF 6,000. CALAIS, 3 July 1988, *The Great Prize* (oil on canvas, 15 x 18 1/2 ins / 38 x 47 cm) FRF 8,800. VERSAILLES, 25 Sept 1988, *Still-life with Violin* (gouache, 19 x 24 3/4s / 48.5 x 63 cm) FRF 2,800. PARIS, 18 Nov 1988, *Harbour* (oil on canvas, 17 3/4 x 22 ins / 45 x 55 cm) FRF 5,500. LA VARENNE-ST-HILAIRE, 21 May 1989, *The Paddock* (gouache, 19 x 24 3/4 ins / 48 x 63 cm) FRF 8,000. LE TOUQUET, 12 Nov 1989, *The Paddock* (1961, oil on canvas, 18 x 25 1/2 ins / 46 x 65 cm) FRF 13,000. PARIS, 24 Jan 1990, *Paddock* (gouache, 18 1/2 x 24 1/2 ins / 47 x 62 cm) FRF 6,000. RHEIMS, 26 April 1992, *The Place Clichy in Paris* (gouache, 19 1/4 x 25 1/4 ins / 49 x 64 cm) FRF 6,000. NEW YORK, 23 Feb 1994, *At the Races* (gouache/paper, 19 3/4 x 25 3/4 ins / 50 x 65.5 cm) USD 1,610. PARIS, 10 April 1996, *Racecourse* (oil on canvas, 29 x 39 1/4 ins / 73.5 x 100 cm) FRF 7,300.

EMPIS, Catherine Edmée (Mme)
Maiden name: Davesiès de Pontès
French, 19th century.
Born 1796, in Paris; died 23 January 1879, in Bellevue.
Painter.

According to some sources, Catherine Edmée Empis lived from 1707 to 1774. She was taught by Watelet and first exhibited at the Salon in 1831, when she was awarded a second-class medal. She continued to send works until 1875. She sent views, landscapes and some historical paintings, the best known of the latter being *Marie de' Medici Walking by the Ponds in the Forest of Compiègne during her Captivity in 1631*.

MUSEUMS AND GALLERIES:
COMPIÈGNE (Mus. national du Château): *Forest*; *View of Tréport* - ORLÉANS: *Road from Clermont to Royat*.

AUCTION RECORDS:
PARIS, 21 Feb 1924, *View from the Normandy Coast*, FRF 90.

EMPOLI, d'. See first name

EMPOLI, Jacopo Chimenti da.
See **CHIMENTI Jacopo**

EMPORIO, Benedetto
Greek, 16th century.
Active in Venice c. 1550.
Painter.

The iconostatis of St George of the Greeks in Venice is composed of several paintings by this artist, including a *Last Supper*.

EMPTAGE, Arthur
American, 20th century.
Born in New York.
Painter.

Arthur Emptage was an exhibitor at the Salon de la Société Nationale in 1933.

EMRICH, C.
German, 18th century.
Enameller.

MUSEUMS AND GALLERIES:
MUNICH (Mus.): *Portraits of the Duke of Marlborough and his Wife* (1701, two miniatures).

EMRICH, Harvey
American, 20th century.
Born 9 October 1884, in Indianapolis (Indiana); died 1972.
Painter.

EMSIO, Giovanni Demostene, or Eneci
Dutch, 16th - 17th century.
Active in Rome from 1589 to 1601.
Painter.

Giovanni Demostene Emsio was a member of the academy of St Luke in 1594. He is known to have painted a *Crucifixion* for a doctor in St-Paul-de-Varax (Ain), France, in 1589.

EMSLIE, Alfred Edward

British, 19th - 20th century.
Born 1848; died 1918.
Painter, watercolourist. Portraits, genre scenes. Orientalism.

Alfred Edward Emslie was an associate of the Royal Society of Painters in Watercolours. He worked in London and exhibited from 1867 at the Royal Academy, the Suffolk Street Gallery, the Royal Society of Painters and Watercolours, the New Water-Colour Society and the Grosvenor Gallery. He was awarded a bronze medal at the Paris Exposition Universelle of 1889. Exhibited works include *Mother and Son, Arrival of the Boats, Compulsory Education,* and *Japan and its Inhabitants.*

MUSEUMS AND GALLERIES:
LONDON (Guildhall AG): *Alderman William Lawrence, Sheriff 1849* (c. 1849, oil on canvas); *A Beethoven Sonata* (oil on canvas) - MANCHESTER: *Portrait of Henry Dunckley* - SALFORD (Museum and AG): *Passing to Eternity.*

AUCTION RECORDS:
LONDON, 23 April 1910, *Mother and Child* (watercolour) GBP 5. LONDON, 20 Nov 1973, *Sailors Repairing Damage,* GBP 1,500. TOKYO, 15 Feb 1980, *Two Sisters* (1890, oil on canvas, 30 3/4 x 43 1/4 ins / 78.1 x 109.8 cm) JPY 800,000. LONDON, 4 Nov 1983, *Portrait of a Young Girl* (oil on canvas, 16 x 11 3/4 ins / 40.5 x 30 cm) GBP 850. NEW YORK, 20 May 1986, *Chums* (1890, oil on canvas, 46 x 54 ins / 116.8 x 137.2 cm) USD 3,400. LONDON, 26 Sept 1990, *Puppet Theatre* (oil on canvas, 22 x 30 ins / 56 x 76 cm) GBP 1,980. LONDON, 12 May 1993, *Dairymaid* (1882, oil on canvas, 15 x 21 1/2 ins / 38 x 54.5 cm) GBP 1,840. LONDON, 6 Nov 1995, *Little Goose Girl* (1881, oil on canvas, 18 x 12 ins / 46 x 30.5 cm) GBP 8,625.

EMSLIE, John

British, 19th century.
Born 12 July 1813; died 8 June 1875.
Active in London.
Engraver.

John Emslie trained under Th. Harwood. He engraved geographic maps and illustrations for books.

EMSLIE, John Philipp

British, 19th - 20th century.
Born 21 May 1839; died 24 September 1913.
Active in London.
Painter, engraver. Genre scenes.

John Philipp Emslie was the son of John Emslie and exhibited from 1869 in London at the Royal Academy, the Suffolk Street Gallery and the Grosvenor Gallery.

MUSEUMS AND GALLERIES:
LONDON (Victoria and Albert Mus.): *Sir Paul Pindar Tavern* (drawing).

EMSLIE, Rosalie M.

British, 19th - 20th century.
Painter. Figures, portraits, genre scenes, landscapes with figures.

Rosalie M. Emslie worked in London and exhibited at the Royal Academy, the New Water-Colour Society and the Salon de la Société Nationale from 1888 to 1912, showing genre scenes and portraits. She married Alfred Edward Emslie. She also often painted miniatures.

AUCTION RECORDS:
MUNICH, 22 May 1978, *Young Girl in a Landscape* (oil on canvas, 15 3/4 x 11 1/2 ins / 40 x 29.5 cm) GBP 160. LONDON, 20 Sept 2004, *Self-portrait as a Coster Girl* (1917, oil on canvas, 44 x 30 ins / 112 x 76 cm) GBP 2,200.

EMSLIE, W.R.

British, 19th century.
Active in London.
Engraver.

W.R. Emslie was the brother of John Philipps Emslie, whom he worked with on the illustration of the magazine *The Architect.*

EMSTER, Tyman Van der, called Botterkull

Dutch.
Painter.

EMTHUSEN, Pieter Van

Dutch.
Born to a family originally from Nijmegen.
Sculptor.

Worked in Hanover and Herrenhausen.

EMY, Henry

French, 19th century.
Active in Paris.
Draughtsman, lithographer.

Henry Emy illustrated many works, including *Tales of Boccaccio; The Great City: New Painting of Paris; The French Painted by Themselves; Paris Summer; Theatrical Extravaganzas;* and *Fashionable Things.*

EMY, Joséphine

French, 19th century.
Painter.

Joséphine Emy exhibited some portraits at the Paris Salon in 1847 and 1848.

EN-I

Japanese, 13th century.
Active at the end of the 13th century.
Painter.

En-I had the honorary title *hogen.* His name and title appear on the back of the *Ippen Shonin Hiriji-e* (the illustrated biography of Ippen), the work he dedicated to him. Ippen (1239-1289) was the monk who founded the Jishu branch of Pure Land Buddhism and travelled across Japan to spread the faith and preach salvation in the name of Amida Buddha. Shortly after his death, Seikai, his favourite disciple, wrote his life story and En-I, in collaboration with his studio, illustrated it in 48 scenes mounted on 12 scrolls.

The *Ippen Shonin Hiriji-e* is classified as a national treasure and is of prime importance in the history of Japanese painting. Contrary to custom at the time, the work was carefully produced on silk, not on paper. It depicts the monk's travels in detail, and judging from the great concordance between the landscapes and buildings with those that still exist, it seems likely that the painter himself accompanied Ippen and drew these scenes from life, using them later in his final work. The scrolls, which were produced in 1299, ten years after the monk's death, are true to the yamato-e style of the period, but are already influenced by Chinese painting of the Song dynasty (960-1279), particularly in their clearly-divided backgrounds and foregrounds, the avoidance of vast spaces and the use of perspective. Not only does En-I evoke the different aspects of the Japanese countryside, but he also paints a comprehensive picture of the way of life at the time: the nobility, warriors, traders, farmers, beggars and vagabonds are all captured in such rich detail that this group of paintings becomes a true reflection of Japanese society of the time. After ten years of restoration work, the complete collection of scrolls was exhibited at the Kyoto National Museum in 2002.

It is unlikely that the monk from the Onjo-ji temple, who was a contemporary of En-I and had the same name, was the same person.

BIBLIOGRAPHY:
'*Nihon emakimono zenshû (Collection complète des rouleaux historiés du Japon)*' in vol. 10, Kakokawashoten, 1960.
MUSEUMS AND GALLERIES:
KYOTO (Kankiko-Ji Temple) - KYOTO (National Mus.): scrolls 7 to 12*Ippen Hijiri-e* - NARA (National Mus.): scrolls 1 to 6*Ippen Hijiri-e* - TOKYO (National Mus.).

ENARD, Fernand
French, 20th century.
Born in Croissy-Beaubourg (Seine-et-Marne).
Painter. Landscapes.
Fernand Enard exhibited in Paris at the Salon des Artistes Français in 1938.

ENARD, Raymond
French, 20th century.
Born in Létricourt (Meurthe-et-Moselle).
Painter.
Raymond Enard was a pupil of Paul Renouard and Louis Roger. He exhibited at the Salon des Artistes Français in Paris, showing views of churches and landscapes in Savoy.

ENARD, René
French, 20th century.
Born 1926, in Le Mans.
Painter.
Neo-Plasticism.
René Enard arrived in Paris in 1944. He studied at the École des Beaux-Arts, then worked in the studios of André Lhote and Fernand Léger. From 1950 onwards he was much influenced by Herbin. He exhibited in Paris at the Salon des Réalités Nouvelles (New Realities) from 1952 to 1957, and had a solo exhibition in Paris in 1952.

ENAUD, Zoé
French, 19th century.
Born in Paris.
Sculptor.
A pupil of M. A. Charpentier, Zoé Enaud exhibited a medallion in 1880 and a low relief in 1882.

ENAULT, Alix Louise (Mme)
French, 20th century.
Born in Paris; died 1913, in Paris.
Painter. Genre scenes.
Alix Louise Enault studied with A. Tissier and F. Willems. She first exhibited at the Salon of 1876 with *The Bride's Invocation*. She was a member of the Salon des Artistes Français from 1885, received an honourable mention in 1887, and won a bronze medal at the Exposition Universelle of 1889.

Alix Enault

AUCTION RECORDS:
PARIS, 1883, *The Study*, FRF 330; *Dreaming*, FRF 460; *First Prayer*, FRF 810; *Flower of the Earth*, FRF 1,300; *Visiting the Convalescent*, FRF 610; *Heartache*, FRF 780. PARIS, 1884, *At the Fountain*, FRF 115; *Garland*, FRF 260. PARIS, 1891, *Morning*, FRF 52.

ENAULT, François
French, 20th century.
Born in Varenguebec (Manche); died 24 November 1918, in Paris.
Painter. Figure compositions.
François Enault exhibited at the Salon d'Automne, where in 1919, just after his death, his *Harvest at Épinay-sur-Orge* was shown.

AUCTION RECORDS:
PARIS, 27 Feb 1996, *Returning to the Farm* (oil on canvas, 18 x 23 1/2 ins / 46 x 60 cm) FRF 4,100.

ENAULT, Gilles
French, 18th century.
Active in Caen.
Painter.
Gilles Enault worked between 1724 and 1735 for the church of St-Gilles at Caen and probably also at Vire in 1691.

ENAULT, Napoléon
French, 19th century.
Painter.
A pupil of L. Cogniet, Napoléon Enault exhibited two portraits at the Paris Salon in 1865.

ENCHAURREN. See **MATTA Roberto**

ENCINAS, Alejo de
Spanish, 16th century.
Active in Valladolid in 1532.
Painter.
Valladolid School.
Encinas was a well-regarded painter. He painted an important altarpiece, commissioned by Alonzo de Argüello. It seems that he also worked for Toledo cathedral in 1564.

ENCKE, Erdmann
German, 19th century.
Born 1843, in Berlin; died 1896, in Neubabelsberg.
Sculptor.
Encke was a pupil of A. Wolff and a student at the Berlin academy; his technique places him firmly within the school of the German sculptor Christian Rauch. Among other works he is noted for a *Statue of Frederick the Great* at the Arsenal in Berlin and the *Statue of the Grand Elector* at the town hall in Berlin. Encke also executed the sarcophagus of William I and the Empress Augusta at the mausoleum at Charlottenburg, together with numerous monuments to Goethe, Luther and Lessing.
MUSEUMS AND GALLERIES:
BERLIN (Nationalgal.): *Princess Elisabeth Teaching her Son Joachim*.

ENCKE, Fedor
German, 19th century.
Born 13 November 1851, in Berlin.
Painter. Portraits, genre scenes.
The brother of Erdmann Encke, Fedor Encke was taught by Karl Gussow and completed his studies in Rome and Paris, subsequently settling in Berlin. He received an honourable mention at the academy in Berlin in 1887 and exhibited in Berlin and Dresden from 1887 onwards. He is noted for his *Dolce Far Niente*, *Portrait of Robert Hausmann*, *In the Roman Ghetto* and *Portrait of Fritz Werner*.
MUSEUMS AND GALLERIES:
NEW YORK (Brooklyn Mus.): *Portrait of General J.-B. Woodword*.
AUCTION RECORDS:
NEW YORK, 23 Feb 1989, *Two Sisters* (1877, oil on canvas, 57 3/4 x 34 ins / 146.8 x 86.6 cm) USD 10,450. MUNICH, 29 Nov 1989, *Portrait of Martha Liebermann* (1888, oil on canvas, 50 1/2 x 35 ins / 128 x 89 cm) DEM 5,500.

ENCKELL, Knut Magnus
Finnish, 20th century.
Born 9 November 1870, in Hamina; died 26 November 1925, in Stockholm.
Painter. Figure compositions, landscapes, portraits.
Designs for stained glass.
Symbolism.
Septem Group.

Enckell received a silver medal at the 1900 Exposition Universelle. His work was shown at the exhibition *Les Mondes intérieurs. Le Symbolisme finlandais* (*Inner Worlds: Finnish Symbolism*) at the Musée Ixelles in Brussels. His painting sometimes borders on monumental art. His style is simple, his draughtsmanship fine and his handling of colours is remarkable. He produced the following pictures: *Gethsemane*, 1921), *The Resurrection of the Dead*, 1907 in the cathedral in Tampere and *Diana and Endymion*, 1921. He also made the stained glass in the church of Björneborg.

BIBLIOGRAPHY:

Puokka, Jaakko, *Magnus Enckell: ihminen ja taiteilija*, dissertation, Otava, Helsinki, 1949. Suominen, Tapio, *Magnus Enckell: 1870 - 1925*, exhibition catalogue, Taidemuseo, Tampere, 1988. *Magnus Enckell 1870 - 1925*, Helsingin kaupungin taidemuseo, Helsinki, 2000 (text in Finnish, Swedish and English).

MUSEUMS AND GALLERIES:

HELSINKI: *Annunciation* (after Leonardo da Vinci); *Expulsion from Paradise* (after Masaccio); *Concert*; *Imagination* - ST PETERSBURG: *Sailor Steering in the Sea*.

AUCTION RECORDS:

PARIS, 22 June 1945, *Portrait of Suzanne Desprès* (1915) FRF 1,000. HELSINKI, 3 Dec 2000, *Music Hall in Paris* (oil on board, Oil Painting, 13 x 12 ins / 34 x 31 cm) FIM 70,000. HELSINKI, 3 Dec 2000, *Landscape with Bridge* (1911, mixed media, 9 x 13 ins / 24 x 32 cm) FIM 34,000. HELSINKI, 3 Dec 2000, *Music Hall in Paris* (oil on board, 13 x 12 ins / 34 x 31 cm) FIM 70,000. HELSINKI, 12 May 2001, *Autumn Day* (1907, oil on canvas, 13 x 10 ins / 32 x 25 cm) FIM 17,000. HELSINKI, 13 Sept 2001, *White Roses* (oil on canvas, 17 x 20 ins / 44 x 50 cm) FIM 28,000. HELSINKI, 27 April 2002, *Boats* (1911, oil on card, 15 x 21 ins / 38 x 53 cm) EUR 6,200. HELSINKI, 12 Sept 2002, *Girl by Rosebush* (oil on canvas, 22 x 18 ins / 55 x 45 cm) EUR 3,800. HELSINKI, 26 Oct 2003, *By the Mirror* (1916, watercolour, 17 x 13 ins / 43 x 32 cm) EUR 1,650. HELSINKI, 8 May 2004, *Man on Veranda* (1919, oil on card, 19 x 18 ins / 47 x 46 cm) EUR 1,600. HELSINKI, 8 May 2004, *Still-life with Vase* (1915, oil on canvas, 26 x 22 ins / 66 x 55 cm) EUR 7,500.

ENCKELL, M.
French, 20th century.
Painter.

M. Enckell was a member of the Salon d'Automne, Paris, in 1919 and a member of the jury in 1920.

END, Christof
German, 17th century.
Painter. Plants.

ENDARA CROW, Gonzalo
Ecuadorean, 20th century.
Born 1936, in Quito; died 14 April 1996, in Quito.
Painter, sculptor. Scenes with figures.

Endara Crow studied in the faculty of arts of the Universidad Central in Quito and went on to teach in the Escuela de Bellas Artes de Loja. From 1977 onwards, he decided to forego his teaching career and devote himself to painting and sculpture. His naive style paintings draw on scenes of everyday life but often contain fantastical elements. A vigorous use of colour characterises his sculptures and murals. His work is renowned internationally.

BIBLIOGRAPHY:

Rodríguez Castelo, H., '*Gonzalo Endara Crow*' in *Revista Diners*, 1983. *Gonzalo Endara Crow*, exhibition catalogue, La Manzana Verde, Quito, 1984. Suárez, C., *Endara Crow*, Quito, 1986. Rodríguez Castelo, H., et al., *Gonzalo Endara Crow*, Quito, 1990.

AUCTION RECORDS:

NEW YORK, 19 Nov 1987, *Town with the Smell of Everything* (1987, oil on canvas, 31 1/2 x 47 1/2 ins / 80 x 120.6 cm) USD 13,000. NEW YORK, 17 May 1988, *Here, They Will Always Live* (1987, acrylic/canvas, 47 1/4 x 31 1/2 ins / 120 x 80 cm) USD 14,300. NEW YORK, 21 Nov 1988, *This is How They Appeared* (acrylic/canvas, 39 1/4 x 55 ins / 100 x 140 cm) USD 13,200; *They Will Be Known for This Reason* (1987, acrylic/canvas, 31 1/2 x 47 1/4 ins / 80 x 120 cm) USD 9,900. NEW YORK, 20 Nov 1989, *Untitled* (1988, acrylic/canvas, 31 1/2 x 35 1/2 ins / 80 x 90 cm) USD 11,000. NEW YORK, 21 Nov 1989, *Celebration in the Andes* (1988, acrylic/canvas, 31 1/2 x 35 1/2 ins / 80 x 90 cm) USD 13,200. NEW YORK, 2 May 1990, *In Truth They Are from There* (1988, acrylic/canvas, 31 1/2 x 47 1/4 ins / 80 x 120 cm) USD 18,700. NEW YORK, 20-21 Nov 1990, *Untitled* (1987, acrylic/canvas, 31 1/2 x 35 1/2 ins / 80 x 90 cm) USD 24,200. NEW YORK, 20 Nov 1991, *With the Splendour of Dawn* (1987, acrylic/canvas, 31 1/2 x 35 1/2 ins / 80.3 x 90.2 cm) USD 18,700. NEW YORK, 18-19 May 1992, *Untitled* (1988, acrylic/canvas, 31 1/2 x 47 1/4 ins / 80 x 120 cm) USD 14,300. NEW YORK, 21 Nov 1995, *He Went Out in the Night* (1994, acrylic/canvas, 27 1/4 x 38 3/4 ins / 69.2 x 98.7 cm) USD 5,175.

ENDE. See also **ENDEN** and **EYNDE**

ENDE, Andreas, or Endte
Austrian, 18th century.
Born in Troppau (now Opava, Czech Republic); died 28 July 1737, in Vienna.
Active in Vienna.
Sculptor.

ENDE, Anton I, or Endte
Austrian, 18th century.
Died 1715, in Bruck.
Active in Vienna.
Sculptor.

ENDE, Anton II, or Endte
Austrian, 18th century.
Active in Vienna.
Sculptor.

This artist was the son of Ferdinand Ende and enrolled at the academy in Vienna in 1737.

ENDE, Anton III, or Endte
Austrian, 18th century.
Born 1731; died 7 February 1782.
Active in Vienna.
Sculptor.

This artist was the second son of Franz Ende.

ENDE, Carl Theodor, or am Ende
German, 18th century.
Born 1752; died 11 July 1788.
Active in Buzlau.
Sculptor.

ENDE, Edgar
German, 20th century.
Born 1901, in Altona (Hamburg); died 1965, in Munich.
Draughtsman, painter (gouache). Figure compositions.

Edgar Ende attended the Akademie in Hamburg and from 1921 had his first show in Berlin. Under the Nazi regime, his work was declared Entartete Kunst (degenerate art) and he was prohibited from painting and exhibiting. A retrospective exhibition of his work was in circulation in the museums or institutions of Munich, Hamburg, Mannheim and Wuppertal. Although he worked as a solo artist, he belongs to the Surrealist movement. Marcel Brion said of him that 'penetrated by a dreamy melancholy poetry, he describes a world of devastation after great catastrophes'. His aggregates of anguished crushed human beings bring to mind the shipwrecked of *Raft of the Medusa*.

E ENDE

BIBLIOGRAPHY:
Edgar Ende, exhibition catalogue, Weitbrecht, Stuttgart, 1988.
AUCTION RECORDS:
MUNICH, 28 May 1973, *Fear of the Mountains*, DEM 4,500. MUNICH, 26 Nov 1979, *Three Travellers* (1933, oil on canvas, 27 1/2 x 35 1/2 ins / 70 x 90 cm) DEM 4,000. MUNICH, 27 Nov 1980, *Composition* (1951, gouache, 19 1/2 x 25 1/2 ins / 49.5 x 65 cm) DEM 3,000. HAMBURG, 4 Dec 1986, *Couple and Dog in Landscape* (1925, oil on canvas, 16 1/4 x 21 1/4 ins / 41 x 54 cm) DEM 10,000. MUNICH, 3 June 1987, *Die Rosse des Helios* (1964, gouache, 20 x 25 1/4 ins / 51 x 64 cm) DEM 4,800. MUNICH, 26 Oct 1988, *Day of the Resurrection* (1931, oil on canvas, 28 x 35 3/4 ins / 71 x 91 cm) DEM 24,200. LONDON, 28 June 1989, *Eruption* (1933, oil on canvas, 27 3/4 x 35 3/4 ins / 70.5 x 91 cm) GBP 14,300. STUTTGART, 24 April 1999, *The Mark* (1947, oil on panel, 28 x 36 ins / 71 x 91 cm) DEM 12,000. COLOGNE, 7 Dec 2002, *Vanishing* (1932, oil on canvas, 30 x 39 ins / 75 x 100 cm) EUR 9,000. PARIS, 27 April 2004, *Escape* (1933, oil on canvas, 28 x 36 ins / 71 x 91 cm) EUR 16,000.

ENDE, Felix von (Baron)
German, 19th century.
Born 4 April 1856, in Breslau (now Wroclaw, Poland).
Painter. Genre scenes, landscapes.

A pupil at the academies of Düsseldorf and Munich, Ende settled in Munich and exhibited in Berlin, Munich and Dresden from 1886 onwards.

He is noted for *Spring Morning*; *Reverie*; *Before Mass*; *Autumn*; and *In the Cloister*.

AUCTION RECORDS:
LONDON, 15 June 1979, *The Lover* (oil on canvas, 26 x 39 ins / 66 x 99.1 cm) GBP 2,000. LONDON, 26 Nov 1980, *Courtly Meeting* (oil on canvas, 26 x 39 ins / 66 x 99 cm) GBP 4,600. MUNICH, 29 Sept 1999, *Young Woman in Salon Reading* (1883, oil on canvas, 13 x 17 ins / 33 x 44 cm) DEM 3,500. NEW YORK, 2 May 2000, *The Pursuit* (oil on canvas, 30 x 39 ins / 75 x 100 cm) USD 26,000. WARSAW, 4 June 2000, *Two Young Ladies Reading* (1883, oil on panel, 13 x 17 ins / 33 x 44 cm) PLN 9,000. AMSTERDAM, 24 April 2001, *Autumn Elegance* (oil on canvas, 38 x 22 ins / 97 x 56 cm) NLG 90,000.

ENDE, Ferdinand, or Endte
Austrian, 18th century.
Born 1681; died 20 November 1731.
Active in Vienna.
Sculptor.

ENDE, Franz, or Endte
Austrian, 18th century.
Born 1701, in Balwitz (Silesia); died 29 October 1768, in Vienna.
Active in Vienna.
Sculptor.

ENDE, Hans or Hans am
German, 19th - 20th century.
Born 31 December 1864, in Trier; died 19 July 1918.
Painter, engraver. Landscapes.
Worpswede Artists' Colony.

Hans Ende attended the Akademie in Munich in 1884 and learnt engraving with Raab. In 1886, he painted under the guidance of Ferdinand Keller in Karlsruhe, returning to Munich in 1887 and settling in Worpswede with Mackensen and Modersohn in 1895. A volunteer in the army during World War I, he was wounded on the Arras front and died at Stethin hospital. His output has been shown in group exhibitions, including, in 1991, *Les Artistes de Worpswede (1889-1935)* (*Worpswede Artists 1889-1935*) (1889-1935), the departmental museum of the Prieuré (St-Germain-en-Laye); 1999, *Paula Modersohn-Becker et ses amis de Worpswede. Dessins et œuvres graphiques 1895-1906* (*Paula Modersohn-Becker and her Worpswede Friends. Drawings and Graphic Works 1895-1906*), Musée des Beaux-Arts, Nancy; 2003 *Rilke. Worpswede. Eine Austellung als Phantasie über ein Buch* (*Rilke. Worpswede. An Exhibition as Fantasy over a Book*), an exhibition which took as a starting point the book by the poet Rainer Maria Rilke on a number of painters active in Worpswede (1903), Kunsthalle, Bremen. Ende's landscapes are heavy and bold.

BIBLIOGRAPHY:
Weltge-Wortmann, Sigrid, *Die ersten Maler in Worpswede*, Lilienthal, Worpswede, 1997. Erling, Katharina, *Paula Modersohn-Becker et ses amis de Worpswede. Dessins et œuvres graphiques 1895-1906*, group exhibition catalogue, Musée des Beaux-Arts, Nancy, 1999 (text in German, insert in French). *Rilke. Worpswede*, exhibition catalogue, Kunsthalle, Bremen, 2003.
MUSEUMS AND GALLERIES:
BREMEN: *Birch Forest* - BRUNSWICK: *March* - CHEMNITZ: *Landscape* - MANNHEIM: *Month of May* - MUNICH: *Autumn Morning* - WEIMAR: *First Snow*.
AUCTION RECORDS:
BREMEN, 3 June 1978, *Autumn Landscape* (oil on canvas, 24 x 35 ins / 61 x 89 cm) DEM 18,000. BREMEN, 28 March 1981, *Landscape with Cloudy Sky* (oil on canvas, 27 1/4 x 35 1/2 ins / 69.5 x 90 cm) DEM 44,000. COLOGNE, 7 Dec 1984, *Stormy Landscape* (oil on card, 17 3/4 x 24 3/4 ins / 45 x 63 cm) DEM 17,000. BREMEN, 20 April 1985, *Landscape and Birches* (oil on card, 19 x 14 1/4 ins / 48 x 36 cm) DEM 24,000.

ENDE, Jan van den
Dutch, 18th century.
Painter, draughtsman. Portraits, landscapes, harbour scenes.

Jan van den Ende attended the Van de Teycken-Const academy. In 1791 he executed a portrait in oils of Madame Alewijn.

ENDE, Johann, or Endte
Austrian, 18th century.
Born 1730; died 5 September 1797.
Active in Vienna.
Sculptor.

The son of Franz Ende, this artist entered the Viennese academy in 1749.

ENDE, Johann Georg
German, 17th century.
Active in Berlin c. 1690.
Painter.

ENDE, Johann Georg, or Endte
Austrian, 18th century.
Born c. 1680.
Active in Vienna.
Sculptor.

ENDE, Johann Georg
Austrian, 18th century.
Active in Neustadt in 1707.
Sculptor (wood).

This artist is probably the same person as the sculptor Johann Georg Ende who was born around 1680.

ENDE, Joseph, or Endte
Austrian, 18th century.
Born c. 1755; died 14 June 1799.
Active in Vienna.
Sculptor.

ENDE, Simon, or Endte
Austrian, 18th century.
Born 1745; died 19 July 1790.
Active in Vienna.
Sculptor.

Ende was the youngest son of Franz Ende.

ENDECE, Giovanni Antonio
Italian, 16th century.
Active in Naples in 1531.
Painter.
Endece worked on a church in Naples with Giovanni Paolo de Lupo.

ENDELL, August
German, 20th century.
Born 12 April 1871, in Berlin; died 15 April 1925, in Breslau (now Wroclaw, Poland).
Draughtsman, architect, decorative artist, designer, illustrator, author. Furniture, jewellery, lamps, art objects.
Jugendstil.
Deutscher Werkbund.
In Munich, August Endell studied philosophy, art history, aesthetics and psychology, notably a course run by Theodor Lipp on the psychological effect of the perception of lines and forms. There, in 1896, he met Hermann Obrist, who encouraged him to take up art. He lived in Munich between 1892 and 1901, and then returned to Berlin. In 1904, he opened the Schule für Formkunst, Kunstgewerbe und Architektur there, which closed in 1914. Then, in 1918, he became director of the Akademie für Kunst und Kunstgewerbe in Breslau (Wroclaw). He wrote some important texts on art: *Um die Schönheit* (*On Beauty*) in 1896, the first work to earn him respect in the art world and as a critic; *Formschönheit und Dekorative Kunst* (*Beauty of Form and Decorative Art*), in 1898; *Originalität und Tradition* (*Originality and Tradition*), in 1901; and *Die Schönheit der Grossstadt* (*The Beauty of the City*), in 1906. He also wrote poetry. He was friends with many poets, critics and authors, including Stefan George, Lou Andreas-Salomé and Rainer Maria Rilke.

August Endell was a key figure in the Munich Jugendstil. He proposed an abstract aesthetic, which stemmed from the ideas of Otto Eckmann, and this was highly influential. His decorative motifs were an interpretation of organic structures. Nevertheless, in Berlin his formal language evolved towards a more functional approach. He worked on the magazines *Pan*, which was published in Berlin, and *Dekorative Kunst* (*Decorative Art*). At the seventh Internationale Kunstausstellung (International Art Exhibition) at the Glaspalast in 1897, the Munich designers garnered the most success, with August Endell among them, alongside Otto Eckmann, Richard Riemerschmid, Hermann Obrist and Bernhard Pankok. The same year, August Endell, Obrist, Bernhard Pankok and Bruno Paul established the Vereinigte Werkstätten für Kunst im Handwerk (United Workshops for Art in Handicraft) in Munich. These applied arts workshops, which passed on commissions to artists then sold and exhibited their creations, enabled the Munich Jugendstil to develop quickly. At the the Vereinigte Werkstätten, Obrist and Endell designed furniture with natural, graceful forms. They also worked on cheap furniture designs for the Dresdener Werkstätten für Handwerkskunst (Dresden workshops), a major centre for applied arts in the artistic heartland that Dresden and the surrounding region became at the turn of the century. In 1907, Endell was one of the co-founders of the Deutscher Werkbund, an association set up by architects, designers and industrialists, which proposed using simple, solid forms both for architecture and consumer goods.

He was also part of the pioneering generation of German architects and designers, along with Peter Behrens, Bruno Paul, Hermann Muthesius and Heinrich Tessenow, among others, who, after Jugendstil, made their ideals a concrete reality, particularly in Berlin between 1900 and 1930. Although he was a self-taught architect he designed several buildings, tower blocks, such as the Hackesche Höfe and houses in Berlin. From 1896 to 1897, he designed the Hof-Atelier Elivra on the request of Anita Augspurg and Sophia Goudstikker, two feminist photographers who wanted to open their own studio. The façade was made up of swirling, asymmetric abstract motifs, which are now Jugendstil icons. All that remains of the studio are photos, because in 1937 the Nazis destroyed the façade, considering it to be immoral. Endell co-signed certain pieces of furniture, the lamp in particular, and other items with Obrist. His other works which can be classed as Jugendstil include: the Buntes Theater in Berlin (1901) for the writer and theatre director Ernst von Wolzogen; the Kindersanatorium in Wyk on the island of Föhr (1898); the Neumannsche concert hall and ballroom in Berlin (1905-1906), which was partially destroyed; the Steinplatz house in Berlin (1906-1907), also partially destroyed; the Pension Müller in Berlin (1908); the Nelson house in Berlin (1910); and the Oskar Kühl house in Berlin (1910).

BIBLIOGRAPHY:
Weiss, P., '*Wassily Kandinsky: the formative Munich years (1896-1916) from Jugendstil to abstraction*', *Dissertation Abstracts, section Q*, vol 34, No. 10, 1973-1974. Sembach Klaus-Jürgen/Haeseler, Gottfried von, *August Endell: der Architekt des Photoateliers Elvira, 1871-1925*, Museum Villa Stuck, Munich, 1977. Buddensieg, T., '*The Early Years of August Endell. Letters to Kurt Breysig from Munich*' in *Art Journal*, vol 42, No. 1, periodical, New York, 1983. Bader-Griessmeyer, Gabriele, *Münchner Jugendstil-Textilien*, Tuduv-Verlag, Munich, 1985. Endell, August, '*Die Scheier der Nacht: The Veils of Night*' in *Daidalos*, No. 27, 15, March, periodical, 1988. Ottomeyer, Hans (ed.)/Brandlhuber, Margot, *Wege in die Moderne. Jugendstil in München 1896 bis 1914*, Klinkhardt & Biermann, Munich, Berlin, 1997.

MUSEUMS AND GALLERIES:
HAMBURG (Mus. für Kunst und Gewerbe): *Rug* (c. 1910) - MUNICH (Bayerische Staatsbibliothek): *Um die Schönheit* (*On Beauty*) (illustrated book) - MUNICH (Stadtmus.): *Chair* (1899); *Table* (1899); *Bookcase* (1899); *Bookshelf* (1899); *Chest* (1899, including the collection of furniture designed for the poet Henry von Heiseler).

ENDELL, Fritz August Gottfried
German, 20th century.
Born 2 November 1873, in Stettin (now Szczecin, Poland); died 8 February 1955, in Bayerischzell.
Painter, engraver (wood), illustrator. Ex-libris plates.
Jugendstil.
Fritz August Gottfried Endell was the son of the architect Karl Friedrich Endell (1843-1891) and the brother of August Endell, who was also an architect. He went to Munich in 1895, where he made drawings under the guidance of different artists, including Lenbach. In 1898, he entered the Académie Colarossi and the Académie Julian in Paris, where he learned to make woodcuts. From 1902 to 1907, he studied in Stuttgart, as a pupil of the school of fine arts with Max Weber, and then with Leopold von Kalckreuth and Adolf Hölzel. Between 1914 and 1920, he lived in America, where he worked as a teacher and studied the art of the North American Indians.

He illustrated books such as *By Land and by Sea*, and several others for the publishers Grote in Berlin and Voigtlander in Leipzig. He is also known for a *Book for Children* and a series of engravings entitled *Death and Consolation*. He was also a writer, and published *Weltkriegshetze der U.S.A. Presse in Schlagzeilen und Zerrbildern* (*USA World War Propaganda. Press in Headlines and Caricatures*) in 1942, accompanied by 45 caricatures, which was considered a work of Nazi propaganda; and *Antike Spiegel* (*Antique Mirror*) in 1952.

With his 'scroll' style, he played an important role in Jugendstil, paradoxically preparing the way for the Bauhaus. He also made woodcuts and etchings.

Bibliography:

Wichmann, Siegfried, *Jugensdtil Floral Funktional in Deutschland und Osterreich und den einflussgebieten*, Schuler Verlagsgesellschaft, Herrsching, 1984.

ENDEN. See also **ENDE** and **EYNDEN**

ENDEN, Josua van den

Dutch, 17th century.
Born c. 1584; died after 1634, probably in Amsterdam.
Engraver.

ENDEN, Martinus van den I, or Eyden

Flemish, 17th century.
Active in Antwerp.
Engraver, printer.
Flemish School.

Martinus van den Enden I was a member of the guild in Antwerp in 1630.

M. V. E.

ENDEN, Martinus van den II, or Eyden

Flemish, 17th century.
Died c. 1674.
Active in Antwerp.
Engraver, printer.
Flemish School.

The son of Martinus van den Enden I, Martinus van den Enden II executed a full-length portrait of King Charles II of Spain. He is also known to have produced 15 *Scenes from the Life of St Ignatius Loyola*, which are signed by him.

ENDER, Axel Hjalmar

Norwegian, 19th century.
Born 14 September 1853, in Asker, near Christiania (now Oslo); died 10 September 1920.
Painter, sculptor. Religious subjects, genre scenes, landscapes with figures. Statues.

Ender was a student at the school of fine arts in Christiania, and also attended Johan Fredrik Eckersberg's school of painting. He later studied at the academy in Stockholm, with royal subvention, and finally in Munich. He exhibited at the artists' association in Christiania from 1872 to 1889. Ender drew inspiration from national subjects for his genre paintings; his work also extended to religious paintings, including an altarpiece for a church at Molde.

Museums and Galleries:

Oslo (Arts Mus.): a statuette - Oslo (Bergen Gal.): a painting - Oslo (Tordenskjöld Square): *P. W. Tordenskjöld* (statue).

Auction records:

London, 19 Jan 1923, *The Stolen Kiss*, GBP 10. London, 22 Nov 1978, *The Love Letter* (oil on canvas, 16 x 13 1/2 ins / 40.5 x 34 cm) GBP 1,400. Copenhagen, 2 Nov 1982, *Young Farm Girl in a Field* (oil on canvas, 25 1/2 x 18 ins / 65 x 46 cm) DKK 30,000. Bremen, 22 Oct 1983, *Rustic Scene in a Norwegian Mountain Landscape* (oil on canvas, 17 1/2 x 26 1/2 ins / 44.5 x 67 cm) DEM 11,200. London, 7 Feb 1986, *A Sled Outing* (oil on canvas, 26 x 17 3/4 ins / 66 x 45 cm) GBP 6,000. London, 24 March 1988, *Haymaking* (oil on canvas, 33 1/2 x 22 3/4 ins / 85 x 58 cm) GBP 7,700; *Hunting Party* (oil on canvas, 28 3/4 x 20 3/4 ins / 73 x 53 cm) GBP 11,550. Stockholm, 29 April 1988, *View from the Geiranger* (oil on canvas, 13 3/4 x 20 1/2 ins / 35 x 52 cm) SEK 15,500. New York, 23 Feb 1989, *The Sled* (oil on panel, 11 1/4 x 9 ins / 28.8 x 22.7 cm) USD 24,200. London, 16 March 1989, *At the Top of the Mountain* (1911, oil on canvas, 50 x 37 ins / 127 x 94 cm) GBP 10,450. London, 17 May 1991, *Hunting Party* (1911, oil on canvas, 28 3/4 x 20 3/4 ins / 73 x 53 cm) GBP 3,080. London, 22 May 1992, *Walk in the Fjords* (oil on canvas/panel, 23 3/4 x 15 3/4 ins / 60.4 x 40 cm) GBP 2,640. London, 17 June 1992, *Skiing in Norway* (oil on canvas, 21 1/4 x 33 3/4 ins / 54 x 86 cm) GBP 8,250. Stockholm, 10-12 May 1993, *Winter Landscape with Skiers and a Lake Surrounded by Mountains in the Background* (oil on canvas, 19 3/4 x 25 1/2 ins / 50 x 65 cm) SEK 51,000. London, 15 Nov 1995, *Sleds on the Snow in Norway* (oil on canvas, 21 1/4 x 30 3/4 ins / 54 x 78 cm) GBP 9,200. Oslo, 25 Oct 1999, *Sleigh Ride* (oil on canvas, 20 x 29 ins / 50 x 73 cm) NOK 180,000. Oslo, 22 Nov 1999, *Sleigh Ride from the Farmyard* (oil on canvas, 45 x 66 ins / 114 x 167 cm) NOK 175,000. Oslo, 10 April 2000, *Sleigh Ride in Spring* (1890, oil on canvas, 25 x 19 ins / 63 x 48 cm) NOK 250,000. Oslo, 4 Dec 2000, *Sleigh Ride* (oil on canvas, 22 x 32 ins / 55 x 81 cm) NOK 270,000. Oslo, 7 May 2001, *Girl on Skates* (oil on canvas, 16 x 12 ins / 40 x 30 cm) NOK 140,000. Oslo, 22 May 2001, *Winter Landscape with Skiers* (oil on canvas, 24 x 35 ins / 60 x 90 cm) NOK 155,000. Oslo, 27 May 2002, *A Meeting - Two Ladies in Horse Carriage Talking to a Gentleman* (oil on canvas, 29 x 42 ins / 73 x 107 cm) NOK 145,000. Oslo, 2 Dec 2002, *Meeting on Country Road, Two Ladies in Horse-Carriage and Man* (oil on canvas, 23 x 33 ins / 58 x 84 cm) NOK 125,000. Uppsala, 7 Dec 2003, *Winter Landscape with Figures Tobogganing* (1915, oil on canvas, 24 x 35 ins / 60 x 90 cm) SEK 200,000. Oslo, 8 Dec 2003, *Sleigh Ride on Frozen Lake, Possibly Mjosa* (oil on canvas, 26 x 35 ins / 65 x 90 cm) NOK 310,000.

ENDER, Boris Vladimirovich

Russian, 20th century.
Born 1893; died 1960.
Painter, collage artist.

Boris Ender studied in Mikhail Vasilievich Matyushin's Free Art Studio (SVOMAS) and was a member of the group Zorved (See-Know), to which three other members of his family (Mariya, Xenia and Yuri) also belonged. From 1923 to 1926 he carried out research at the INKhUK (Institute of Artistic Culture, Moscow) set up after the October Revolution and led by the avant-garde artists of the time, Constructivists and Expressionists. He worked with Matyushin on the study of colour and developed the theory of the 'superior vision', which they planned to analyse in a collective work of several volumes and which was finally written up by Matyushin (*The Rules and Variability of Colour Combinations, a Manual*).

Members of the Ender family, Boris and Xenia, particularly distinguished themselves by applying their thoughts to colour in collages reminiscent of Matisse's work in his later years.

Auction records:

Munich, 27 Nov 1980, *Still-life (Odessa)* (1927, watercolour, 9 x 11 1/4 ins / 22 x 28.5 cm) DEM 4,400.

ENDER, Caspar

German, 17th century.
Died June 1615.
Active in Görlitz (Saxony).
Painter.

ENDER, Eduard

Austrian, 19th century.
Born 3 March 1822, in Rome; died 28 December 1883, in London.
Painter, watercolourist, draughtsman. Historical subjects, figures, portraits, genre scenes, interiors, still-lifes.

Ender was a pupil at the fine arts academy in Vienna, then studied under his father, the professor Johann Ender. After finishing his studies in Paris he returned to Vienna, where he became president of the circle of artists there. He worked in Vienna, Paris and London.

Edouard Ender

Museums and Galleries:

Tours: *Still-life* - Vienna: *Interior*; *Portrait of the Artist*.

AUCTION RECORDS:
VIENNA, 19 Sept 1972, *Courtly Conversation*, ATS 55,000. NEW YORK, 11 Feb 1981, *The Favourite* (1851, oil on panel, 15 1/2 x 12 1/4 ins / 39.5 x 31 cm) USD 7,000. VIENNA, 12 Sept 1984, *The Actress Julie Rettig in a Lace Gown* (1844, watercolour and pencil, 9 1/2 x 7 ins / 24 x 18 cm) ATS 14,000. NEW YORK, 22 May 1985, *The Pasha's Favourite* (1851, oil on panel, 15 1/2 x 12 1/4 ins / 39.5 x 31 cm) USD 14,000. LONDON, 15 Feb 1991, *The Inheritance* (1851, oil on panel, 21 3/4 x 17 1/2 ins / 55.3 x 44.4 cm) GBP 3,850. LONDON, 9 Oct 1996, *Portrait of a Woman, Seated* (1853, oil on canvas, oval, 56 1/4 x 43 3/4 ins / 142.9 x 111.4 cm) GBP 19,550. PARIS, 21 June 2001, *In the Tavern* (oil on panel, 12 x 15 ins / 31 x 38 cm) FRF 12,500.

ENDER, Johann Nepomuk

Austrian, 19th century.
Born 4 November 1793, in Vienna; died 16 March 1854, in Vienna.
Painter, watercolourist. Religious subjects, portraits.

The twin brother of Thomas Ender, Johann was appointed professor at the Akademie in Vienna in 1829.

He is known primarily for his oil paintings and watercolours.

MUSEUMS AND GALLERIES:
BUDAPEST: *Hungarian Civilisation* - FORCHTENSTEIN (Fürstlich Esterhazy'sche Sammlungen): *Marcus Aurelius on his Deathbed* - VIENNA (Akademie der Bildenden Künste): *Portrait of Prince Metternich* - VIENNA (Dobersberg): *Portrait of Countess Wallmoden; Portrait of Archduke Charles and his Family* - VIENNA (Gal.): *Madonna with the Infant Jesus.*

AUCTION RECORDS:
VIENNA, 28 May 1963, *Portrait of Charlotte-Johanne, Duchess Kinsky*, ATS 20,000. VIENNA, 20 Sept 1977, *Empress Maria Ludovika, née Princess of Modena* (oil on panel, 9 1/2 x 7 1/4 ins / 24 x 18.5 cm) ATS 45,000. LONDON, 30 March 1982, *Portrait of Herr Tain* (1822, watercolour and pencil, 7 1/2 x 6 ins / 19 x 15.4 cm) GBP 3,800. VIENNA, 23 Feb 1989, *Portrait of Duchess Auersperg* (oil on panel, 20 3/4 x 16 1/2 ins / 52.9 x 41.9 cm) ATS 341,000. AMSTERDAM, 19 Oct 1993, *Portrait of an Elegant Young Woman Dressed in a White Silk Gown and a Hat with Blue Ribbons* (oil/ivory, 5 3/4 x 4 ins / 14.5 x 10 cm) NLG 2,530. LONDON, 11 April 1995, *Two Sisters* (1846, oil on canvas, 47 1/2 x 35 1/2 ins / 120.5 x 90 cm) GBP 4,025. VIENNA, 19 Nov 1999, *Portrait of a Balkan Prince with Persian Collar* (1833, watercolour, 4 x 3 ins / 11 x 8 cm) ATS 80,000. LONDON, 22 Nov 1999, *Young Lady in Yellow Dress, Tall Black Hat with White Feathers* (miniature, 4 x 3 ins / 11 x 8 cm) GBP 22,000. DÜSSELDORF, 31 Jan 2000, *Vanity and Modesty* (1848, oil on canvas, 48 x 37 ins / 123 x 95 cm) DEM 52,000. VIENNA, 2 Oct 2001, *Portrait of Young Woman in White Dress* (watercolour, miniature, oval, 5 x 4 ins / 12 x 9 cm) ATS 55,000. VIENNA, 28 March 2003, *Portrait of Young Woman in White Dress* (watercolour, 9 x 6 ins / 22 x 16 cm) EUR 2,400. VIENNA, 28 March 2003, *Portrait of Woman Wearing Hat* (watercolour, 9 x 7 ins / 24 x 19 cm) EUR 2,600.

ENDER, Mariya Vlaridimovna

Russian, 20th century.
Born 1897; died 1943.
Painter.

Mariya Ender studied in Mikhail Vasilievich Matyushin's Free Art Studio (SVOMAS) and worked with the group Zorved (See-Know), to which three other members of her family (Yuri, Xenia and Boris) also belonged. From 1923 to 1926 she carried out research at the INKhUK (Institute of Artistic Culture, Moscow), set up after the October Revolution and led by the avant-garde artists of the time, Constructivists and Expressionists.

She worked with Matyushin on the study of colour and developed the theory of the 'superior vision', which they planned to analyse in a collective work of several volumes and which was finally written up by Matyushin (*The Rules and Variability of Colour Combinations, a Manual*).

ENDER, Thomas

Austrian, 19th century.
Born 4 November 1793, in Vienna; died 28 September 1875, in Vienna.
Painter, watercolourist, engraver, draughtsman. Landscapes.

Thomas Ender was the twin brother of Johann-Nepomuk Ender. From the age of 12 he worked at the academy in Vienna, where he won the major prize for painting in 1816. He became a member of the academy in 1836 and was subsequently appointed professor of landscape painting there. In 1817, thanks to the assistance of Archduke John and of Prince Metternich, he was able to accompany an Austrian scientific expedition to Brazil, which gave him the opportunity to amass a large number of studies. He brought back 700 drawings from this expedition.Works by Ender were featured in *Expedition Kunst. Die Entdeckung der Natur von C.D. Friedrich bis Humboldt* (*Expedition Art. The Discovery of Nature from C.D. Friedrich to Humboldt*), an exhibition at the art gallery in Hamburg in 2002 which explored the links between the natural sciences and landscape art.

BIBLIOGRAPHY:
Koschatzky, Walter, *Thomas Ender (1793-1875)*, Leykam, Graz, 1982. Wagner, Robert, *Thomas Ender in Brasilien 1817-1818: Aquarelle und Zeichnungen aus dem Kupferstichkabinett*, exhibition catalogue, Kupferstichkabinett der Akademie der bildenden Künste, Vienna, 1994. *Expedition Kunst. Die Entdeckung der Natur von C.D. Friedrich bis Humboldt*, exhibition catalogue, Hamburger Kunsthalle, Hamburg, 2002.

MUSEUMS AND GALLERIES:
BERLIN (Nationalgal.): *Italian Chapel in the Woods* - VIENNA: watercolours, drawings - VIENNA (Akademie der Bildenden Künste): *View of Rio de Janeiro* - VIENNA (Kunstverein): *View of Amalfi* - VIENNA (Persenberg): *View of the Castle at Persenberg.*

AUCTION RECORDS:
PARIS, 1823, *View of the Castle at Guttenstein* (gouache) FRF 35; *View of the Castle at Stüxenstein* (pen and coloured brush) FRF 12; *View of Misenbach* (gouache) FRF 27; *View of Guttenstein* (drawing in gouache) FRF 35. PARIS, 8 Dec 1924, *Italian Landscape with Ruins* (gouache) FRF 160. PARIS, 25 Nov 1946, *Landscape* (watercolour) FRF 900. LUCERNE, 7 Dec 1963, *View of Nussdorf, near Vienna*, CHF 3,600. VIENNA, 12 March 1974, *Mail-coach in a Tyrolean Landscape*, ATS 70,000. VIENNA, 3 Dec 1974, *Tyrolean Landscape* (watercolour) ATS 38,000. VIENNA, 15 March 1977, *View of a Village* (watercolour, 7 x 10 1/4 ins / 18 x 26 cm) ATS 50,000. VIENNA, 14 March 1978, *View of Grossglockner* (oil on canvas, 16 x 22 ins / 40.5 x 56 cm) ATS 250,000. VIENNA, 19 Sept 1978, *Alpine Landscape* (watercolour, 13 1/2 x 19 3/4 ins / 34 x 50 cm) ATS 25,000. MUNICH, 30 May 1979, *View of a Tyrolean Town* (watercolour, 10 1/2 x 18 3/4 ins / 26.5 x 47.5 cm) DEM 4,600. VIENNA, 17 March 1980, *View of a Mountain Village* (watercolour, 11 x 16 3/4 ins / 28 x 42.5 cm) ATS 55,000. NEW YORK, 23 Feb 1983, *Hallstadt, near Ischl, Austria* (1831, watercolour and pencil, 13 x 8 1/2 ins / 33 x 21.6 cm) USD 3,400. VIENNA, 21 March 1985, *Goats in a Mountain Landscape* (watercolour, 10 x 14 1/2 ins / 25.5 x 37 cm) ATS 38,000. VIENNA, 20 May 1987, *Bad Gastein* (1838, oil on canvas, 30 3/4 x 22 3/4 ins / 78 x 58 cm) ATS 320,000. VIENNA, 15 Oct 1987, *View of Pallanza on the Shores of Lake Maggiore* (watercolour, 14 1/2 x 22 1/4 ins / 37 x 56.8 cm) ATS 60,000. LONDON, 26 Feb 1988, *Unloading Boats on the Neapolitan Coast with Vesuvius in the Background* (oil on canvas, 15 1/4 x 22 ins / 39 x 55 cm) GBP 4,400. PARIS, 3 April 1988, *View of the Marcellina; View of the Papal Palace of Castelgondolfo* (two watercolours, 6 1/4 x 8 3/4 ins / 16 x 22.5 cm and 8 x 10 ins/20.2 x 25.5 cm) FRF 8,500. VIENNA,

23 Feb 1989, *Ponte della Maddalena, near Lucca* (watercolour/paper, 4 1/4 x 7 ins / 11 x 17.5 cm) ATS 60,500. PARIS, 7 March 1989, *Amalfi, Viewed from a Grotto* (watercolour, 11 1/2 x 14 1/2 ins / 29 x 37 cm) FRF 50,000. LONDON, 19 June 1991, *Figures in the Uffizi Gallery in Florence* (watercolour, 6 1/2 x 9 ins / 16.5 x 23 cm) GBP 2,200. MUNICH, 10 Dec 1992, *Lauterbrunnen Valley with the Jungfrau in the Background* (pencil and watercolour/paper, 13 x 19 ins / 33.1 x 48.4 cm) DEM 7,910. NEW YORK, 20 Jan 1993, *View of Mellau* (watercolour/paper, 21 1/2 x 13 3/4 ins / 54.6 x 34.9 cm) USD 8,338. MUNICH, 22 June 1993, *Resting Place near a Chapel on a Rocky Path Leading to a Village* (oil on canvas, 31 x 26 ins / 79 x 66 cm) DEM 17,250. MUNICH, 7 Dec 1993, *Florence Viewed from San Miniato* (watercolour and ink/paper, 8 1/2 x 13 3/4 ins / 21.5 x 35 cm) DEM 14,950. LONDON, 16 Nov 1994, *View of a Fortress in Eastern Europe; Panoramic View in the Tyrol* (watercolour, a pair, each 37 1/2 x 6 ins / 95 x 15 cm) GBP 3,450. MUNICH, 25 June 1996, *View of the Ruins at Rauhenstein* (watercolour/paper, 8 1/4 x 12 1/2 ins / 21 x 32 cm) DEM 9,600; *Panoramic View of Vienna* (watercolour/paper, 8 x 12 1/2 ins / 20.5 x 32 cm) DEM 19,200. VIENNA, 29-30 Oct 1996, *Sorrento* (oil on canvas, 29 1/2 x 41 3/4 ins / 75 x 106 cm) ATS 993,000. MUNICH, 23 June 1997, *View of the Residence of His Imperial Highness Johann at Wildbad Gastein* (watercolour and Indian ink/paper, 7 1/2 x 11 1/2 ins / 19 x 29 cm) DEM 33,600. MUNICH, 2 Dec 1997, *Painter at Work in a Mountain Landscape* (watercolour/paper, 6 x 8 1/2 ins / 15 x 21.5 cm) DEM 26,400. VIENNA, 29 April 1999, *Lower Sulzbach Glacier with Mountain Venediger* (watercolour, 13 x 19 ins / 33 x 47 cm) ATS 150,000. VIENNA, 27 May 1999, *Villa Hugel in Grinzing* (watercolour, 7 x 10 ins / 18 x 25 cm) ATS 180,000. DÜSSELDORF, 31 Jan 2000, *Vothau Castle, Owned by Duke Daun, in Mahren* (oil on canvas, two, 20 x 25 ins / 52 x 63 cm) DEM 42,000. VIENNA, 23 May 2000, *Landscape with Castle* (oil on panel, 7 x 9 ins / 17 x 24 cm) ATS 120,000. BERN, 9 May 2001, *Lower Salzbach Glacier with View of the Gross Venediger* (watercolour, 10 x 14 ins / 25 x 35 cm) CHF 22,000. VIENNA, 29 Nov 2001, *Dolomites from Bozen* (oil on canvas, 26 x 35 ins / 66 x 90 cm) ATS 250,000. VIENNA, 25 Nov 2002, *Prater Landscape* (watercolour, 7 x 12 ins / 19 x 30 cm) EUR 13,000. VIENNA, 28 Nov 2002, *Sorrento Grotto with View of Capp Mahea* (oil on panel, 20 x 24 ins / 50 x 60 cm) EUR 70,000. VIENNA, 28 Oct 2003, *Riva on Lake Garda* (oil on canvas, 16 x 20 ins / 40 x 50 cm) EUR 15,000. VIENNA, 28 Nov 2003, *Nassfeld* (watercolour, 9 x 13 ins / 24 x 34 cm) EUR 13,000. VIENNA, 26 March 2004, *Pfitzgrundl in Zemthale, Tyrol* (watercolour, 12 x 9 ins / 30 x 24 cm) EUR 9,000. VIENNA, 12 Oct 2004, *Amalfi* (watercolour, 13 x 20 ins / 33 x 50 cm) EUR 10,000.

ENDER, Xenia Vladimirovna or Ksenia

Russian, 20th century.
Born 1895, in St Petersburg; died 1955, in Leningrad (now St Petersburg).
Painter.

Xenia Vladimirovna Ender studied at the Svamag academy in Petrograd (now St Petersburg) in 1922 then she joined Mikhail Vasilievich Matyushin's Free Art Studio (SVOMAS) and worked with the group Zorved (See-Know), to which three other members of the her family (Mariya, Xenia and Boris) also belonged. From 1923 to 1926 she carried out research at the INKhUK (Institute of Artistic Culture, Moscow), set up after the October Revolution and led by the avant-garde artists of the time, Constructivists and Expressionists,

She worked with Matyushin on the study of colour and developed the theory of the 'superior vision', which they planned to analyse in a collective work of several volumes and which was finally written up by Matyushin (*The Rules and Variability of Colour Combinations, a Manual*).

Her artistic activity was recognised by the official authorities although linked to a trend deriving from Cubism and more particularly from Delaunay's Orphism.

Xenia Ender took part in 1923 in the exhibition *Painters of Petrograd of All Trends*, then became a member of the Leningrad section (this was and still is the same city: St Petersburg, Petrograd then Leningrad) and featured in the Soviet selection at the 14th Venice Biennale (1924). She was represented at the collective exhibition *Aux origines de l'abstraction (1800-1914)* (*The Origins of Abstraction (1800-1914)*), Musée d'Orsay, Paris (2003). Like her brother Boris Xenia Ender produced collages in which she translated her thoughts into colour in a way that suggests Matisse's work later.

BIBLIOGRAPHY:

Lemoine, Serge/Rousseau, Pascal, et al., *Aux origines de l'abstraction (1800-1914)*, exhibition catalogue, Musée d'Orsay, Paris, 2003.

AUCTION RECORDS:

MOSCOW, 7 July 1988, *Untitled* (watercolour/paper, 9 x 12 ins / 22 x 30.5 cm) GBP 4,950. LONDON, 6 April 1989, *Composition* (collage, 9 3/4 x 14 ins / 25 x 35.4 cm) GBP 11,000. LONDON, 23 May 1990, *Composition* (oil on paper, 21 x 18 3/4 ins / 53.5 x 47.5 cm) GBP 16,500.

ENDER, Yuri Vladimirovich

Russian, 20th century.
Born 1898; died 1963.
Painter.

Yuri Ender studied in Mikhail Vasilievich Matyushin's Free Art Studio (SVOMAS) and worked with the group Zorved (See-Know), to which three other members of his family (Mariya, Xenia and Boris) also belonged. From 1923 to 1926 he carried out research at the INKhUK (Institute of Artistic Culture, Moscow), set up after the October Revolution and led by the avant-garde artists of the time, Constructivists and Expressionists,

He worked with Matyushin on the study of colour and developed the theory of the 'superior vision', which they planned to analyse in a collective work of several volumes and which was finally written up by Matyushin (*The Rules and Variability of Colour Combinations, a Manual*).

ENDERBY, Samuel G.

British, 19th - 20th century.
Painter.

Samuel G. Enderby worked in London and exhibited at the Royal Academy from 1886 to 1908, showing portraits and genre scenes.

ENDERLE, Anton

German, 18th century.
Active in Günzburg (Bavaria).
Painter. History painting.

Anton Enderle is noted for the paintings on the ceiling of the church of Our Lady in Günzburg, frescoes in the parish church of Tapfheim (Bavaria), the fresco in the church of the Pilgrimage in Mindelaltheim and the paintings in the parish church of Waldkirch.

ENDERLE, Johann Baptist

German, 18th century.
Born 15 June 1725, in Söflingen near Ulm; died 1798, in Donauwörth (Swabia).
Painter, draughtsman. Religious subjects. Murals.

Johann Baptist Enderle, the cousin of Anton Enderle, is noted for altar pictures painted on canvas, in particular those at Welden and in the church of the Capuchin order in Donauwörth. He was a prolific artist, whose ceiling paintings and murals in numerous churches in Swabia show the influence of Tiepolo.

MUSEUMS AND GALLERIES:
HERBERTSHOFEN (Church) - HOHENSTADT (Altertumverein Mus.): fourteen drawings - HOHENSTADT (Church): *Way of the Cross* - KETTERSCHWANG (Church) - KIRCHDORF (Church) - MAINZ (Church of St Ignatius): *Scenes from the Life of St Ignatius* - OBERNDORF (Augustinian Church): *Birth of Christ; Crucifixion; Prophets; Apostles; Saints* - SCHEPPACH (Church of the Pilgrimage of All Saints) - SCHWABMÜHLHAUSEN (Church).
AUCTION RECORDS:
LONDON, 11 Dec 1992, *Baptism of Christ* (oil on canvas, 16 x 10 ins / 39.7 x 25.5 cm) GBP 2,420.

ENDERLEIN, Ewald Max Karl
German, 20th century.
Born 9 May 1872, in Leipzig.
Painter, lithographer, illustrator.
Enderlein attended the academy at Dresden and from 1904 his work was shown at various exhibitions in Dresden, Düsseldorf and Leipzig. He illustrated a picture book *Giants and Dwarfs* for the publishers Schreiber-Esslingen.
MUSEUMS AND GALLERIES:
DRESDEN: *Landscape* - DRESDEN (Kunstgenossenschaft): *Meadow*.

ENDERLEIN, Jacob
German, 17th century.
Born to a family originally from Isny (Swabia).
Engraver.
Enderlein's name appears as an inscription on engraved drawings depicting views of monuments in the book *Roma Regina Mundi*.

ENDERLEIN, Peter
Bavarian School, 17th century.
Active in 1650 in Nuremberg.
Sculptor.

ENDERLIN, Joseph Louis or Louis Joseph
French, 19th - 20th century.
Born 1851, in Aesch, near Basel, to French parents.
Sculptor. Statues.
Joseph Louis Enderlin was a pupil of Jouffroy and Roubaud the Younger. He exhibited at the Paris Salon in 1878, 1879 and in 1880, when he showed his plaster statue of a *Billiard Player*. He was awarded a third-class medal in 1880, followed by a second-class medal in 1888 and a gold medal in 1889 at the Exposition Universelle. He was made a Chevalier of the Légion d'Honneur in 1902.
MUSEUMS AND GALLERIES:
AMIENS: *Jeanne* (terracotta) - LYONS: *Bust of Meissonier* (plaster) - LYONS (Préfecture): *Bust of Meissonier* (marble) - MULHOUSE: *Bust of Engel-Dollfus* (plaster) - PARIS (Hôtel de Ville): *Music* (high-relief) - PARIS (Mus. des Arts et Métiers): *Bust of Engel-Dollfus* (marble) - RHEIMS: *Billiard Players* (marble) - TROYES: *Odile* (terracotta).
AUCTION RECORDS:
LONDON, 13 April 1983, *Stone Thrower* (plaster, h. with base 74 ins / 188 cm) GBP 600.

ENDERS, Caspar, or Anders
German, 17th - 18th century.
Active in Breslau (now Wroclaw, Poland), between 1690 and 1735.
Painter.

ENDERS, Frank or Franz
American, 19th - 20th century.
Born in Milwaukee.
Painter. Mythological subjects.
Franz Enders was a pupil in Munich of the teachers A. Gable and W. Linden Schmidt. He settled in Milwaukee.
AUCTION RECORDS:
DETROIT, 17 May 1981, *Eros and Psyche* (oil on canvas, after Bouguereau) USD 1,300.

ENDERS, Jean-Joseph
French, 19th - 20th century.
Born 22 August 1862, in Besançon; died 1930, in Paris.
Painter. Portraits, genre scenes, landscapes, still-lifes.
Jean-Joseph Enders was a pupil of Édouard Baille and Fernand Cormon at the École des Beaux-Arts, Paris. He exhibited at the Salon des Artistes Français, Paris, of which he was a member from 1891. He received an honourable mention in 1890, won third-class medals in 1893 and 1898, and was awarded the silver medal at the Exposition Universelle of 1900. He surrounded his figures with soft-focus effects and painted intimate scenes in subdued light.
MUSEUMS AND GALLERIES:
BESANÇON (Hospital): *Guardian Angel* - GRAY: *At Dawn; The Church of Beuré; St Francis*.
AUCTION RECORDS:
PARIS, 24 March 1924, *The Seine near Paris*, FRF 65. PARIS, 3 Feb 1928, *Bonjour Mimi*, FRF 410; *Corner of the Champs-de-Mars Park in Autumn*, FRF 210. PARIS, 4 Nov 1943, *Riverside*, FRF 60. VERSAILLES, 25 April 1982, *Red-headed Woman* (oil on canvas, 25 1/2 x 18 ins / 65 x 46 cm) FRF 3,200. NEW YORK, 23-24 May 1996, *Still-life with Vases and Mirrors* (oil on canvas/panel, 38 x 51 ins / 96.5 x 129.5 cm) USD 6,325.

ENDERS, Nicolaus
Dutch, 18th century.
Painter.
Nicolaus Enders was a member of the guild in Haarlem in 1748.

ENDFELDER, Johann
Austrian, 19th century.
Born 1791, in Schwaz (Tyrol); died 1864.
Painter.
Endfelder was the pupil of the Benedictine friar Eberhard von Zobel at the monastery of Vriecht, near Schwaz. One of his frescoes, *Resurrection of Christ and Sin Vanquished*, can be found in the church at Thaur, near Hall; others can be found in the parish churches at Alpach, Oberau, Santens and Tux.

ENDHOVEN, Willem van
Flemish School, 16th century.
Sculptor.
Antwerp School.
Willem van Endhoven became a master sculptor in 1517.

ENDINE, Francesco
Italian, 15th century.
Active in Brescia in 1465.
Painter.

ENDINE, Giorgio
Italian, 15th century.
Active in Brescia in 1465.
Painter.

ENDLER, Friedrich Gottfried
German, 18th - 19th century.
Born 1763, in Lüben; died after 1830, in Breslau (now Wroclaw, Poland).
Engraver (burin).
Nagler refers to this artist, who engraved views and portraits.

ENDLICH, Philippus
Dutch, 18th century.
Born 1700, in Amsterdam.
Draughtsman, engraver.
Philippus Endlich was taught by Bernard Picart. His output includes some portraits.

ENDLINGER, Johann
German, 18th century.
Born 1733, in Brno; died 3 February 1789, in Vienna.
Painter, engraver (etching).

Initially a pupil of Daniel Gran in Brno, then of Joseph Rotter at the academy in Vienna, Endlinger subsequently worked for the painter Bachmayer in Vienna and spent many years in Rome. He painted in oils and drew historical subjects in red chalk; he is also noted for etchings such as *Mary with the Infant Jesus in her Arms and the Young St John; Adoration of the Shepherds; Mary with her Dead Son at the Foot of the Cross, Supported by an Angel; Jupiter and Leda;* and *Child with a Cat.*

AUCTION RECORDS:
PARIS, 1823, *Virgin Suckling the Infant Jesus* (pen drawing with bistre wash) FRF 2.

ENDNER, Gustave Georg
German, 18th - 19th century.
Born 1754, in Nuremberg; died 1824, in Gohlis, near Leipzig.
Engraver (burin).

Endner engraved *Portraits* and *Views.*

ENDO, Toshikatsu
Japanese, 20th - 21st century.
Born 1950.
Sculptor.
Arte Povera.

Endo Toshikatsu works in wood, coal tar, earth, fire and water. He has taken part in numerous group exhibitions since 1974, mainly in Japan. Other exhibitions were: 1986, Documenta VIII, Kassel; 1987, New York; 1988 and 1990, Venice Biennale; 1990, Gutharc Ballin Gallery. He has also had numerous solo exhibitions in Tokyo and Osaka, as well as 1990, Paris and Oslo; 1992, Dublin and London.

In Documenta VIII, he exhibited *Epitath,* a sculpture formed from pieces of wood similar to large beams collected together and superimposed alternately in groups of six, forming a parallele piped rectangle 95 x 95 x 70 inches (185 x 185 x 150cm). The wood has the appearance of having been sculpted by fire and covered with tar. The lines and texture of the material from which these beams were taken are visible on the long sides and at the extremities, where part of the age rings could still be seen.

At the 1990 Venice Biennale, he exhibited a sort of tumulus, with a wood and earth base, sculpted with fire and tar and eroded by exposure to the air. The surface was also carefully worked. These works exuded an impression of sobriety that invited the viewer to silence. The physical presence of the object, the elemental nature of the materials employed and the living empiricism of these open-air experiences were reminiscent of the spirit of certain arte povera exhibitions.

BIBLIOGRAPHY:
Lutfy, Carol, '*Gaining Face: Japanese artists emerge*' in *ARTnews,* vol. 89, no. 3, March 1990.

AUCTION RECORDS:
LONDON, 23 June 1997, *To Circle* (1991, pencil and charcoal/paper, 74 1/2 x 54 1/4 ins / 189 x 138 cm) GBP 4,000.

ENDOEUS, or Endoios
6th century BC.
Athenian, active in 516 BC.
Sculptor.
Ancient Greek.

Endoeus made a seated Athena that was placed on the Acropolis in Athens, and a group of Graces and Hours in white marble in Erythrae in Ionia. For the same town he also made an enormous wooden statue of Athena Polias, and another of the same goddess in Alea in Arcadia. Augustus took this statue and set it up in Rome. The name Endoeus was found on a marble base discovered on Mount Hymettus, carved in Attic letters of a very ancient style.

ENDOFSKY
German, 18th century.
Born 18th century, in Königsberg (now Kaliningrad, Russia).
Sculptor (wood).

ENDOGOUROFF. See **ENDOGUROV**

ENDOGUROV, Ivan Ivanovich
Russian, 19th century.
Born 1861, in Kronstadt (now Brasov, Romania); died 1898.
Painter. Figures, landscapes.

This artist won a silver award at the Exposition Universelle of 1889. Among his works can be cited: *The Thaw, Autumn in the Crimea, Winter on Corsica, Winter Twilight, After the Storm.*

MUSEUMS AND GALLERIES:
MOSCOW (State Tretyakov Gal.): *By the Sea* - ST PETERSBURG (Gosudarstvennyj Russkij Muz.): *The Yalta Harbour; The Beginning of Spring; Moonlight in Ajaccio.*

AUCTION RECORDS:
NEW YORK, 24 May 1984, *Young Boy beside a Pond* (oil on card, 8 1/2 x 6 ins / 21.5 x 15.2 cm) USD 1,000.

ENDOGUROV, Sergei Ivanovich
Russian, 19th century.
Born 1864, in Russia; died 1894.
Painter. Landscapes.

MUSEUMS AND GALLERIES:
MOSCOW (Chekhov Mus.): *Meerbusen* - MOSCOW (State Tretyakov Gal.): *View of the Sea of Norway* (watercolour) - ST PETERSBURG (Gosudarstvennyj Russkij Muz.): *The Banks of a Stream* (watercolour); *On the Duna; The Pond; Forests.*

ENDORFFER, Hans
Austrian, 15th century.
Active in Salzburg in 1478.
Painter.

ENDOUT, Francon of. See **FRANCON DE KEMPE**

ENDRES
Bavarian School, 15th century.
Active in Ansbach from 1468 to 1499.
Painter.

ENDRES
German, 18th century.
Active in Obermünster.
Sculptor (wood).

In 1778, Endres executed a pulpit for the church at Geisling, near Regensburg.

ENDRES. See also **ANDRES**

ENDRES, Bernhard
German, 19th century.
Born 1805, in Owingen (Baden-Württemberg); died 8 December 1874, in Munich.
Painter. History painting, genre scenes.

Bernhard Endres was a pupil of Marie Ellenrieder in Constance and went to study at the Munich academy in 1826. He exhibited in Munich between 1829 and 1858. He is noted for *Mary with the Infant Jesus; St Cecilia;* and the *Portrait of Julius II,* after Raphael.

MUSEUMS AND GALLERIES:
DONAUESCHINGEN: *St Catherine.*

ENDRES, Ch. E.
French, 19th - 20th century.
Active in Paris.
Painter.

Ch. E. Endres exhibited at the Salon of the Société des Artistes Français, becoming a member in 1903.

ENDRES, Jakob
German, 17th century.
Active in Munich in 1671.
Painter.

ENDRES, Johann
German, 18th century.
Born in Neumarkt (Palatinate).
Active in Neumarkt c. 1750.
Painter.

Frescoes by this artist can be found on the ceilings of the churches of St Anne in Neumarkt and St Viet in Grossolfalterbach.

ENDRÈS, Louis-Joseph
American, 20th century.
Born 1896, in Cincinnati (Ohio); died 1989.
From 1926 to 1962 active in Morocco.
Painter. Portraits, figures, genre scenes.
Orientalism.

Louis-Joseph Endrès was American by birth but made numerous trips, notably to the Maghreb, between 1926 and 1930 and settled in Rabat in 1931. He left Morocco in 1962 for Rome, then Lausanne in 1963.

A member of the Société Coloniale des Artistes Français and the Société des Peintres Orientalistes Français, he took part in the French-African art exhibition in Paris in 1935. His works were also shown in solo exhibitions in Morocco, Algeria, Europe, New York and Cincinnati.

An Orientalist painter, he presented scenes from everyday life in North Africa.

L Endres

AUCTION RECORDS:

PARIS, 22 June 1990, *Fountain, Marrakesh* (oil on canvas, 24 3/4 x 25 1/4 ins / 63 x 64 cm) FRF 8,200. PARIS, 11 Dec 1991, *The Blue Man* (oil on canvas, 33 3/4 x 30 ins / 86 x 76 cm) FRF 9,200; *Morning in the Oudaias* (oil on canvas, 30 x 33 3/4 ins / 76 x 86 cm) FRF 10,000. PARIS, 22 June 1992, *Zobeida* (oil on canvas, 25 1/4 x 19 ins / 64 x 48 cm) FRF 7,800; *Pastoral* (1946, oil on canvas, 39 1/4 x 59 ins / 100 x 150 cm) FRF 31,000. PARIS, 7 Dec 1992, *Pilgrim for Moulay Brahim* (oil on canvas, 33 3/4 x 30 ins / 86 x 76 cm) FRF 7,500. PARIS, 5 April 1993, *Odalisque with Green Turkish Slippers* (oil on panel, 35 1/2 x 51 1/4 ins / 90 x 130 cm) FRF 20,000. PARIS, 21 June 1993, *The Good Companions* (oil on canvas, 30 x 33 ins / 76 x 84 cm) FRF 8,200; *Blue Man with Bellows* (oil on canvas, 33 x 30 ins / 84 x 76 cm) FRF 6,000. PARIS, 12 May 2000, *The Water Seller* (oil on gouache, 13 x 9 ins / 32 x 24 cm) FRF 18,000. PARIS, 5 April 2001, *Copperware Souk* (oil on canvas, 41 x 41 ins / 104 x 104 cm) FRF 38,000. PARIS, 5 April 2001, *Chellah in the Sun* (oil on canvas, 41 x 41 ins / 104 x 104 cm) FRF 85,000.

ENDREY, Sander
Hungarian, 20th century.
Born 1869, in Nagyvárad (now Oradea, Romania).
Painter.

Sander Endrey initially studied with Szamossy and worked in Budapest where he did his first portrait of the poet Vajda. Having studied in Paris with Jean Paul Laurens and Benjamin-Constant, he settled in Budapest where he painted many portraits, including those of Cardinal L. Schlauch, the Orientalist Vambery and the politician K. Tisza. He exhibited several times at the Ice Palace in Munich.

ENDRISS, Friedrich Meyer, or Endrisz.
German, 16th century.
Born in the middle of the 16th century, in Buchau (Württemberg).
Painter. Portraits.

In 1600, Endriss painted the portrait of Countess Friedrich zu Fürstenberg.

ENDTE. See **ENDE**

ENDTER, Jakob
German, 18th century.
Died 17 August 1714, in Nuremberg.
Active in Nuremberg.
Painter.

This artist was primarily a portrait painter.

ENEA. See also **PISANELLO, STEENVOORDEN Jacob Van** and **VICO Enea**

ENEA, Giuseppe
Italian, 19th century.
Born 1863, in Palermo.
Painter, pastellist. Allegorical subjects.

Enea's masters were Cavallaro and Covoni. His paintings decorate the foyer and rotunda of the Massimo theatre in Palermo.

MUSEUMS AND GALLERIES:

ROME (Gal. Nazionale): *Flemish low relief* (pastel) - TRIESTE (Civico Mus. Revoltella): *Music* (pastel).

AUCTION RECORDS:

LONDON, 22 Nov 1990, *Cherubs in Arcadia* (1901, pastel, 35 x 90 ins / 89 x 228.9 cm) GBP 3,080.

ENECI, Giovanni Demostene. See **EMSIO**

ÉNÉLINA, Madeleine
French, 20th century.
Born in Paris.
Painter. Landscapes.

Madeleine Énélina was a pupil of J. Lévy and A. Guillemet, and exhibited at the Salon des Artistes Français.

ENESCO, Andrée
Romanian, 20th century.
Born in Paris.
Painter. Genre scenes, portraits.

Andrée Enesco exhibited at the Salon des Artistes Français in Paris in 1921.

ENFANTIN
French, 18th century.
Miniaturist.

Enfantin was a pupil of Bertin, and probably the father of Augustin Enfantin. At the Exposition de la Jeunesse (Youth Exhibition) he exhibited miniature portraits in 1787, 1788 and 1789.

AUCTION RECORDS:

PARIS, 27 April 1910, *Portrait of a Man* (miniature) FRF 325. PARIS, 27-29 May 1929, *Portrait of a Man Dressed in Black* (miniature) FRF 1,900. PARIS, 8 April 1954, *Woman in a Black Dress, Transparent Shawl on her Shoulders* (miniature, oval) FRF 30,000.

ENFANTIN, Augustin
French, 19th century.
Born 29 August 1793, in Belleville; died 16 October 1827, in Naples.
Painter, engraver.

Augustin Enfantin sent some views and studies drawn from life to the Paris Salon in the year of his death.

MUSEUMS AND GALLERIES:

BOURGES: *View of the Port of Velletri* - CHERBOURG: *View of the Madonna di Puzzano at Castellamare in the Kingdom of Naples* - LE PUY-EN-VELAY: *Trees in the Forest of Fontainebleau* (studies) - MONTPELLIER: watercolours - PARIS (Mus.

Carnavalet): *Church of St-Pierre of Montmartre* - ROUEN: *Landscape; Man Bringing Down an Animal.*
AUCTION RECORDS:
PARIS, 13 May 1927, *Undergrowth in the Forest of Fontainebleau,* FRF 1,050.

ENFANTIN, Barthélemy Prosper, called le Père Enfantin
French, 19th century.
Born 8 February 1796, in Paris; died 31 August 1864, in Paris.
Painter, draughtsman. Architectural views.
Barthélemy Prosper Enfantin was perhaps the brother of Augustin Enfantin.
MUSEUMS AND GALLERIES:
NARBONNE: three sepia drawings.

ENFERMA-GOUTIL, Germaine Antoinette Nicole d'
French, 20th century.
Born 16 May 1890, in Paris.
Painter.
Germaine Enferma-Goutil was a pupil of Humbert and Mademoiselle Minier. She exhibited regularly at the Salon des Artistes Français, Paris, of which she was a member and where she received an honourable mention in 1922.

ENFIELD, Henry
British, 19th century.
Born 1849, in London.
Painter. Landscapes.
Henry Enfield worked in Nottingham. He exhibited nine times at the Royal Academy from 1872 to 1893, and often in Berlin, Düsseldorf and Munich.
MUSEUMS AND GALLERIES:
GDANSK: *The Maas in Winter* - NOTTINGHAM: *Naero Fjord.*
AUCTION RECORDS:
LOS ANGELES, 23 June 1980, *Seaside* (oil on canvas, 29 x 46 ins / 73.7 x 117 cm) USD 1,200. STOCKHOLM, 29 Nov 1999, *Hardangerfjord* (oil on canvas, 19 x 33 ins / 48 x 83 cm) SEK 14,000. CHICAGO, 13 March 2004, *Ship* (oil on canvas, 28 x 46 ins / 71 x 117 cm) USD 2,600. LONDON, 18 March 2004, *Naero Fjord* (oil on canvas, 28 x 46 ins / 72 x 117 cm) GBP 1,600.

ENGALIÈRE, Marius
French, 19th century.
Born 9 August 1824, in Marseilles; died 16 March 1857, in Paris.
Painter.
A pupil of Auguste Aubert, Marius Engalière travelled widely, working in Marseilles on development projects for the Pharo district, then moving to Toulouse and visiting Andalusia, where he painted many landscapes. From 1853 to 1857 he exhibited views, chiefly of Spain, at the Salon.

Engalière was one of the principal artists of what is known as the 19th-century Marseilles School.

MUSEUMS AND GALLERIES:
AIX-EN-PROVENCE (Mus. Granet): *Washerwoman at the Bank of the Stream* (oil/wood) - CARCASSONNE: *Street in Murcia; Street in Malaga* - MARSEILLES: *View of Grenada* - NARBONNE: *Environs of Elche* - TOULOUSE: *View of Monaco.*
AUCTION RECORDS:
PARIS, 6 May 1981, *Festival in Spain* (oil on canvas, 35 3/4 x 57 1/4 ins / 91 x 145.5 cm) FRF 17,000. PARIS, 23 Nov 1990, *View of Grenada with a Carriage Full of Travellers in the Foreground* (oil on canvas, 26 1/2 x 41 1/4 ins / 67 x 105 cm) FRF 28,000. PARIS, 16 Dec 1992, *View of Grenada with a Carriage Full of Travellers in the Foreground* (oil on canvas, 26 1/2 x 42 1/4 ins / 67 x 107 cm) FRF 27,000. PARIS, 30 March 1998, *View of the Pont Royal and the Town of Toulouse* (1856, watercolour and gouache, 13 x 24 1/4 ins / 33 x 61.5 cm) FRF 18,000. PARIS, 22 June 2004, *Convent in Spain* (oil on canvas on cardboard, 9 x 15 ins / 24 x 38 cm) EUR 2,100.

ENGAMMARE, Édouard
French, 20th century.
Born in the second half of the 19th century, in Dieppe.
Painter. Seascapes.
Édouard Engammare exhibited at the Salon des Artistes Indépendants from 1921 to 1931.

ENGBERG, Gabriel Karl
Finnish, 19th - 20th century.
Born 24 March 1872, in Tampere.
Landscape artist.
Engberg was awarded a distinction at the 1900 Exposition Universelle.
MUSEUMS AND GALLERIES:
HELSINKI: *Mediterranean Landscape.*

ENGE, August
German, 19th century.
Born 1797, in Königsberg (now Kaliningrad, Russia).
Painter, lithographer.
Enge was a pupil at the academy in Vienna. His works include a *St Cecilia* and a gouache entitled *Young Woman Seated on a Sofa,* dated 1834.

ENGEBRECHTSZ. See **ENGELBERTSZ**

ENGEL, Adolf Karel Maximilian
Flemish, 19th century.
Born 24 December 1801, in Courtrai; died 24 August 1833; committed suicide.
Painter. Landscapes.
Flemish School.
Adolf Karel Maximilian Engel was the pupil of P. J. de Noter in Ghent.
MUSEUMS AND GALLERIES:
AMSTERDAM: *Landscape with Livestock.*

ENGEL, André
Swiss, 20th century.
Born 4 May 1880, in Basel.
Active in France.
Painter, watercolourist. Landscapes.
In Basel, André Engel studied in Karlsruhe under Hans Sandreuter and Professor M. Läuger and in Paris under Luc-Olivier Merson and P. Vignal. After travelling to Italy, Japan and India, he exhibited landscapes, for the most part in watercolours, in Paris at the Societé Nationale des Beaux-Arts, of which he was a member from 1933. He was of Alsatian stock, and the Société des Artistes Alsatiens in Strasbourg organised an exhibition of his works in 1921.
AUCTION RECORDS:
PARIS, 24 May 1944, *Environs of Bénodet* (1910, watercolour) FRF 300.

ENGEL, Andrée Irène
French, 20th century.
Born 22 April 1906, in St-Civran (Indre).
Engraver (wood).
Andrée Irène Engel exhibited at the Salon des Artistes Français in 1928.

ENGEL, Arlette
French, 20th century.
Born 1940.
Engraver.
Arlette Engel was represented in the exhibition *Gravures contemporains en relief* (*Contemporary Relief Engravings*) held at the Musée du Dessin et de l'Estampe Originale, Gravelines, in 1987. The white is not an empty space: the bare, uninked sheets, embossed by the artist, have a real presence.

ENGEL, Erich Otto
German, 19th - 20th century.
Born 29 September 1866, in Alt-Mahlisch, near Frankfurt an der Oder; died possibly in 1949.
Painter. Figures, landscapes, animals.
The output of Eric Otto Engel can be compared to that of Otto Heinrich Engel. Predominantly a painter of animals, he settled in Dachau and from 1899 exhibited in Berlin and Munich.
MUSEUMS AND GALLERIES:
AACHEN: *Ducks.*
AUCTION RECORDS:
COLOGNE, 20 March 1981, *Young Peasant Woman* (pastel, 18 3/4 x 14 1/2 ins / 47.5 x 37 cm) DEM 3,300. NEW YORK, 15 Oct 1993, *Shady Courtyard* (oil on canvas, 24 x 29 ins / 61 x 73.7 cm) USD 2,990.

ENGEL, Frederik
Dutch, 19th - 20th century.
Born 1872; died 1958.
Painter. Landscapes with figures, animals.
AUCTION RECORDS:
LONDON, 26 April 1979, *Herd Grazing* (oil on canvas, 12 x 17 1/2 ins / 30.5 x 44.4 cm) GBP 800. AMSTERDAM, 21 April 1993, *Yearling Colts near Meadow Enclosure* (oil on canvas, 20 x 27 1/2 ins / 50.5 x 70 cm) NLG 4,025. AMSTERDAM, 14 Sept 1993, *Cows in a Meadow* (1915, oil on canvas, 13 3/4 x 20 ins / 35 x 50.5 cm) NLG 2,070. EDINBURGH, 9 June 1994, *Cattle in a Dutch Landscape* (oil on canvas, 13 x 18 ins / 33 x 45.7 cm) GBP 1,092. AMSTERDAM, 9 Nov 1994, *Cows in a Meadow* (1916, oil on canvas, 19 1/4 x 29 1/4 ins / 49 x 74 cm) NLG 3,680.

ENGEL, Fritz or Friedrich
German, 20th century.
Born 7 September 1877, in Eisenach (Thuringia).
Sculptor. Busts.
Engel studied under Kugel at the Akademie in Dresden and under Brausewetter in Berlin. He created a portrait of Princess Helene von Waldeck-Pymont. Part of his career was spent in Zurich, where he sculpted busts of Gottfried Keller and C.F. Mayer after photographs.

ENGEL, Harry
American, 20th century.
Born 1901, in Romania; died 1970.
Painter.
Harry Engel was a pupil of Maurice Denis in Paris. He won the Edward Hines prize for a still-life at the Hoosier Salon of 1931.

ENGEL, J.
British, 19th century.
Sculptor.
J. Engel exhibited eight times at the Royal Academy, from 1840 to 1847.

ENGEL, Johann Carl
German, 18th century.
Born at the beginning of 18th century, in Zittau (Saxony); died in Hamburg.
Painter, medallist. Landscapes.
He was primarily a landscape painter.

ENGEL, Johann Carl Ludwig
German, 19th century.
Born 1778, in Berlin; died 1840, in Helsinki.
Painter, watercolourist. Urban landscapes, landscapes.
Engel worked in Reval (now Tallinn, Estonia), St Petersburg and Helsinki.
MUSEUMS AND GALLERIES:
HELSINKI (Ateneumin Taidemus.): *View of Helsinki* (watercolour).

ENGEL, Johann Friedrich, later John Fred
German, 19th - 20th century.
Born 1844, in Bernkastel; died 1921.
Painter. Genre scenes, figures.
John Engel was a pupil of the painter François at the Munich Academy before leaving for America. He exhibited in Munich and Dresden from 1879 until 1884. He is noted for: *Our Grandmother, Congratulations, The Wedding, Morning on the Lake, Forest Walk.*
AUCTION RECORDS:
NEW YORK, 10 Oct 1973, *Mother Reading a Story to her Children,* USD 2,100. NEW YORK, 13 Oct 1976, *The Toast* (1879, oil on panel, 6 x 4 1/2 ins / 15 x 11.5 cm) USD 550. LONDON, 26 Nov 1982, *The Fisherman's Daughter* (oil on canvas, 28 x 21 1/2 ins / 71.1 x 54.5 cm) GBP 1,000. VIENNA, 20 March 1985, *Pusteblume* (oil on panel, 12 1/2 x 9 1/2 ins / 32 x 24 cm) ATS 60,000. NEW YORK, 19 July 1990, *Young Bavarian* (oil on panel, 10 x 7 ins / 25.4 x 17.8 cm) USD 2,090.

ENGEL, Johanna
German, 19th - 20th century.
Born at the end of the 19th century, in Leipzig.
Painter. Portraits, genre scenes.
A pupil of Gölz in Berlin, Engel exhibited portraits as well as genre scenes in Berlin, Munich, Paris and Prague.
AUCTION RECORDS:
LONDON, 5 Oct 1990, *The Seasons* (1910, oil on canvas, set of three panels, 82 3/4 x 41 1/2 ins / 210.2 x 105.4 cm) GBP 3,080.

ENGEL, Johannes
French, 20th century.
Born 15 January 1876, in Rüsdorf.
Painter. Religious subjects. Designs for mosaics.
After studying at the École des Arts et Métiers, Strasbourg, Johannes Engel joined the Munich academy of painting and worked under Otto Seitz and M. Feurstein. He then went to Rome and devoted himself to religious painting. There are paintings by him in several churches of Lorraine, including those of Metz, Stieringen-Wendel, and Mandern; and in Strasbourg one of his mosaics is placed above the main entrance of the St Joseph Orphanage.
MUSEUMS AND GALLERIES:
METZ: *Face of a Young Girl; Landscape.*

ENGEL, Johannes I
Dutch, 17th century.
Born c. 1619; died 1678.
Active in Amsterdam.
Painter.

ENGEL, Johannes II
Dutch, 17th century.
Born c. 1661.
Active in Amsterdam.
Painter.
Johannes van Engel II was possibly the son of the painter Johannes van Engel I.

ENGEL, José Louis, or Engel-Garry
French, 20th century.
Born 13 August 1873, in Joinville-le-Pont.
Painter.
José Louis Engel was a pupil of Roll. He exhibited first at the Salon des Indépendants, Paris, in 1890, and later at the Salon

des Artistes Français and the Société Nationale des Beaux-Arts, where he showed portraits, landscapes, seascapes and genre paintings. Among his works are: *The Anarchist, Normandy, Ruins at Night, Players, Little Beggars, Nocturnes, Louisette.*
Museums and Galleries:
Laeken: *Prayer* (triptych).

ENGEL, Jozsef
Hungarian, 19th century.
Born 1815, in Sátoraljaújhely; died 1891, in Budapest.
Sculptor. Historical figures. Busts.
Jozsef Engel sculpted the statue of István Széchenyi in Budapest. He was awarded a bronze medal at the 1889 Exposition Universelle in Paris. He exhibited at the Royal Academy in London in 1888.
Museums and Galleries:
Budapest: *Bust of King Matthias; Bust of Maria Theresa.*

ENGEL, Karl, pseudonym of Engel von den Rabenau
German, 19th century.
Born 1817, in Londorf; died 31 March 1870, in Rodelheim (Frankfurt am Main).
Painter, watercolourist, draughtsman. Figures, genre scenes, interiors, landscapes, architectural views.
Karl Engel studied with Hildebrand at the academy in Düsseldorf and at the Munich academy. He settled in Frankfurt initially and moved to Rodelheim in 1842, where he shared a house with the sculptor J.-B. Scholl.
Museums and Galleries:
Darmstadt: *Sculptor's Studio* - Frankfurt am Main (Städel): *Peasants of Hessen in their Sunday Best.*
Auction records:
London, 5 June 1968, *Winter Landscape with Skaters,* GBP 360. Munich, 6 Dec 1994, *View of the Church of St Leonard in Frankfurt am Main* (ink and watercolour/paper, 7 1/2 x 9 3/4 ins / 19 x 25 cm) DEM 10,350.

ENGEL, Otto Heinrich
German, 19th - 20th century.
Born 27 December 1866, in Erbach; died perhaps in 1949.
Painter, engraver. Figures, landscapes, seascapes, waterscapes.
Otto Heinrich Engel's output has definite similarities with that of Erich Otto Engel. From 1886 to 1890 he studied under Otto Brausewetter and Paul Meyerheim at the art academy in Berlin. In 1890 and 1891 he was active in Karlsruhe and from 1891 to 1892 he was a pupil of Paul Hoecker at the academy in Munich. He went to Italy to study, subsequently settling in Berlin.

Museums and Galleries:
Berlin: *Little Girl from Friesland; Dunes* - Kaliningrad: *Radiance of the Sea; Lights at Sea.*
Auction records:
New York, 4 May 1979, *Water's Edge at Twilight* (1893, oil on canvas, 59 x 74 1/2 ins / 150 x 189 cm) USD 3,100. Hamburg, 5 May 1999, *Neighbours Chatting, Lagmai near Ekensund* (1893, oil on linen/board, 13 x 17 ins / 33 x 43 cm) DEM 25,000. Hamburg, 8 May 1999, *Hay Harvest at Keitum* (oil on board, 19 x 26 ins / 47 x 65 cm) DEM 18,000. Toestorf, 26 Aug 2000, *Landscape with Trees and Fisherman* (oil on canvas, 28 x 38 ins / 72 x 97 cm) DEM 17,000. Cologne, 30 Nov 2000, *Tree-lined Village Street in Summer* (oil on canvas, 24 x 33 ins / 62 x 83 cm) DEM 16,000. Munich, 27 June 2001, *Midday Rest* (oil on canvas, 22 x 23 ins / 55 x 59 cm) DEM 23,000. Toestorf, 4 May 2002, *Sunlit Flat Land* (1922, oil on canvas, 42 x 60 ins / 106 x 152 cm) EUR 13,400. Bremen, 28 June 2003, *Flensburg Landscape* (oil on canvas/board, 14 x 24 ins / 36 x 61 cm) EUR 5,500. Bremen, 26 Sept 2003, *Friesian Interior* (oil on panel, 18 x 21 ins / 45 x 53 cm) EUR 9,500.

ENGEL, Richard Drun
American, 20th century.
Born 25 December 1889, in Washington DC; died 1961, in Baltimore.
Painter.
Richard Engel studied in Paris. He was also a writer. Member of the Society of Washington Artists.

ENGEL, Sam
Dutch, 17th - 18th century.
Draughtsman.
A number of drawings in pencil by Sam Engel are preserved: *The Flight into Egypt; Man, Woman and Child;* and *The Hermit in his Cave.*

ENGEL, Werner
Swiss, 20th century.
Born 1880, in Thun (Bern); died 1941.
Painter, engraver. Waterscapes, village views.
Werner Engel produced etchings. The museum at Bern conserves his picture of the banks of the Aar at Thun.
Museums and Galleries:
Solothurn: several works.
Auction records:
Lucerne, 30 Sept 1988, *View of Village on Lago Maggiore* (1932, watercolour/paper, 10 1/2 x 7 1/2 ins / 26.5 x 19 cm) CHF 480. Zofingen, 1 Dec 2000, *Trees* (1910, oil on canvas, 28 x 22 ins / 72 x 56 cm) CHF 2,800.

ENGEL, Willem
Dutch, 15th century.
Active in Leiden 1464.
Painter.
In 1464, Willem Engel painted a *Portrait of Charles the Rash.*

ENGEL DE SALM, Henri
French, 20th century.
Born 12 July 1913, in Fontenay-aux-Roses.
Painter.
Henri Engel de Salm was in Paris a member of the Salon des Indépendants and the Salon des Artistes Français. He was a pupil of Othon Friesz and was influenced by both him and Dunoyer de Segonzac.

ENGEL-GARRY, José Louis. See **ENGEL José Louis**

ENGEL-PAK, Ernest, or Engel-Rozier
Belgian, 20th century.
Born 1885, in Spa (Liège); died 1965, in Valabre-les-Gardanne, France.
Also active in France.
Painter, lithographer.
Abstraction-Création group.
Engel-Pak was self-taught. He had an eventful youth, spending time abroad in France, Germany and Holland where he worked in a variety of fields. He also painted under the name Engel-Rozier in around 1920. In 1924, he settled in Paris where he first exhibited in 1926. He was in contact with Torres-Garcia, whom he met in 1928 and was also a friend of Jean Hélion and Marcel Duchamp. In 1934, he settled in Provence. After the war, his work featured in group exhibitions of abstract artists, notably in the Salon des Réalités Nouvelles between 1947 and 1956. He had a number of one-man exhibitions in Spain, France, Holland and Belgium and a retrospective exhibition of his work was mounted in Aix-en-Provence in 1966. From 1954, he was conservator of the Château of the Roi René in Tarascon. He illustrated a collection *Objects of Words and Images* by Paul Éluard (1947) with lithographs in colour. When he took up permanent resi-

dence in Paris his works become Expressionist in spirit, and he then he went in for a premature Surrealism, until 1932. In 1928 Torres-Garcia pointed him towards a non-figuration tinged with Surrealism. From 1932 he was a precocious exponent of Tachisme and joined Abstraction-Création. Michel Seuphor describes his painting as 'biomorphic blots of lively colours standing out against a monochrome background'.

ENGEL-PAK

MUSEUMS AND GALLERIES:
BRUSSELS (MAM) - BRUSSELS (Mus. royaux des Beaux-Arts de Belgique): *Mélanie; Illusionary Crowd; Original Flower* - LIÈGE (Mus. de l'Art wallon).
AUCTION RECORDS:
AUBAGNE, 3 June 1984, *Composition* (oil on panel, 39 1/4 x 27 1/2 ins / 100 x 70 cm) FRF 6,800. DOUAI, 23 Feb 1989, *Composition* (1930, oil on panel, 25 1/2 x 18 ins / 64.5 x 45.5 cm) FRF 7,000. DOUAI, 23 April 1989, *Forms* (gouache and watercolour, 14 3/4 x 22 ins / 37.5 x 55 cm) FRF 6,500. DOUAI, 2 July 1989, *Composition* (charcoal, 8 1/4 x 10 1/4 ins / 21 x 26 cm) FRF 4,000. DOUAI, 3 Dec 1989, *Composition* (1961, oil on paper, 9 1/2 x 14 1/4 ins / 24 x 36 cm) FRF 8,500. DOUAI, 1 April 1990, *Composition* (1956, oil/hardboard, 15 3/4 x 10 ins / 40 x 24.5 cm) FRF 6,500. PARIS, 6 Oct 1990, *Composition* (1937, oil on card, 21 1/4 x 15 1/4 ins / 54 x 39 cm) FRF 15,000. CALAIS, 20 Oct 1991, *Young Women at Edge of Path* (1926, oil on panel, 13 x 9 ins / 33 x 22 cm) FRF 4,000. PARIS, 5 Feb 1992, *Composition* (mixed media/paper/canvas, 19 1/2 x 23 1/2 ins / 49.5 x 60 cm) FRF 6,500.

ENGEL-PRASOLO
Russian, 18th century.
Active at the beginning of the 18th century.
Sculptor (wood).
Called to St Petersburg by Peter the Great, this artist worked here during the first years of the 18th century. The Hermitage Museum has several drawings by him.

ENGEL-ROZIER, Ernest. See **ENGEL-PAK**

ENGELANDTS, Samuel
Flemish School, 16th century.
Painter.
Antwerp School.
Samuel Engelandts became a master painter in 1581.

ENGELBACH, Florence
British, 19th - 20th century.
Born 9 June 1872, in Jerez de la Frontera (Andalusia), Spain; died 27 February 1951, in London.
Painter. Portraits, landscapes, flowers.
Florence Engelbach's parents were English and she studied at the Slade School in London and then in Paris. In 1901 she began exhibiting at the Royal Academy under her maiden name of Neumengen. The following year she married C.F.R. Engelbach. After a break of 20 years she returned to painting in 1930 and again exhibited at the Royal Academy and at Salons in Paris. Originally a portrait painter, Engelbach later specialised in flower paintings and sometimes landscapes.
MUSEUMS AND GALLERIES:
LONDON (Tate Collection): *Roses* (c. 1934-1938, oil on canvas).

ENGELBACH, Georg
German, 19th century.
Born 28 February 1817, in Biedenkopf (Hesse).
Painter, draughtsman, lithographer, engraver of reproductions.
Engelbach is noted for his *Portrait of William I, Emperor of Germany; Portrait of Richard Wagner*; and engravings such as *The Geographer C. Riller*, after C Begas, and *The Theologian Dr A. Twesten*, after Schramm.

ENGELBACH, Jacques
French, 20th century.
Born in Le Havre.
Painter.
Jacques Engelbach exhibited in Paris at the Salon d'Automne and at the Salon des Artistes Indépendants from 1923.

ENGELBERCH, Franz
Polish, 18th century.
Active in Warsaw in 1754.
Painter.

ENGELBERS
Flemish School, 12th century.
Active in Liège.
Miniaturist, monk.

ENGELBERT, Gaspard Antoni
Flemish, 17th century.
Active in Antwerp, at the end of the 17th century.
Illuminator.
Flemish School.
Gaspard Antoni Engelbert was perhaps the son of Ignatius Engelbert.

ENGELBERT, Guillielmus
Flemish, 17th century.
Active in Antwerp, at the end of the 17th century.
Illuminator.
Flemish School.

ENGELBERT, Ignatius, or Engelberts
Flemish, 17th century.
Active in Antwerp.
Illuminator.
Flemish School.

ENGELBERT, Jan
Dutch.
Painter. Landscapes.
Mentioned by Siret.

ENGELBERTS, Albert Carel Fredrich
Dutch, 19th century.
Born 1830, in Gendringen; died 16 May 1854, in Cleef.
Painter. Landscapes.
Albert Carel Fredrich Engelberts was the son of Engelbert Michael Engelberts and was taught by B.-C. Koekkoek, J.-B. Klombeeck and Willem Roelofs.

ENGELBERTS, Engelbert Michael
Dutch, 18th - 19th century.
Born 17 December 1773, in Hoorn; died 7 December 1843, in Gendringen.
Active in Amsterdam.
Painter, art dealer. Landscapes.
Engelbert Michael Engelberts was the son of Engelbertus Matthias Engelberts. He painted townscapes and winter landscapes.

ENGELBERTS, Engelbertus Matthias
Dutch, 18th century.
Born 3 December 1731, in Noordlaren; died 26 March 1807, in Hoorn.
Draughtsman, engraver.

ENGELBERTS, Jacob Meynoud
Dutch, 19th century.
Born 3 July 1798.
Painter.
Jacob Meynoud Engelberts was the son of Engelbert Michael Engelberts. He went to the East Indies and returned with drawings and paintings.

ENGELBERTS, Willem Jodocus Mattheus
Dutch, 19th century.
Born 21 January 1809, in Amsterdam; died 9 May 1887, in Aalst.
Painter, engraver. Genre scenes.

Willem Jodocus Mattheus Engelberts was the son of Engelbert Michael Engelberts and a pupil of F. de Brakelaer in Antwerp. He was the curator of the museum in Amsterdam between 1850 and 1875.

MUSEUMS AND GALLERIES:
AMSTERDAM.

AUCTION RECORDS:
LONDON, 17 May 1923, *Fishermen's Cottage in Holland* (1878) GBP 2. AMSTERDAM, 19 Sept 1989, *Two Little Girls Offering an Apple to an Elderly Lady* (1854, oil on panel, 11 1/2 x 9 ins / 29 x 22 cm) NLG 1,840.

ENGELBERTSZ., Cornelis, or Engelbrechtsen, Engebrechtsz., also called Enghelbrecht the Elder
Dutch, 15th - 16th century.
Born probably in 1468, in Leiden; died probably in 1533, in Leiden.
Painter. Historical subjects, religious subjects.
Leiden School.

In 1499, Cornelis Engelbertsz. was a member of the town guard. Among his pupils were Lucas van Leiden and Aartgen van Leiden. His sons were Pieter Cornelisz., Cornelis Cornelisz. and Lucas Cornelisz. de Kok. A Cornelis de Hollandere, recorded as being a member of the Antwerp Guild, seems not to have been C. Engelbertsz. Some biographers have thought, wrongly, that he was not the master of Lucas van Leiden but the pupil.

Through Colin de Coter, he was introduced to the paintings of Rogier van der Weyden, although he inclined more towards a more Italianate art that was more decorative and luminous.

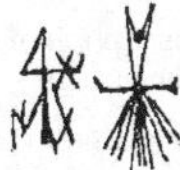

MUSEUMS AND GALLERIES:
AACHEN (Suermondt-Ludwig Mus.): *St John the Baptist and St Mary Magdalene; Deposition* - AMSTERDAM: *Christ on the Cross with the Virgin and Sts; Christ Preaching in the House of Lazarus; Christ Bidding Farewell to His Mother; Calvary* (triptych) - ANTWERP: *St Leonard Freeing the Prisoners (recto) and St George (verso); Procession with the Body of St Hubert (recto) and St Hubert (verso)* (two wings); *Christ Nailed to the Cross* - BERLIN (Bodemus.): *Crowning with Thorns; The Calling of St Matthew* - BRUSSELS: *Portrait of Dirk Ottens and His Wife* - BUDAPEST: *Sts Cecilia and Valerius* (medallion); *Mystic Lamb; Adoration of the Magi* (egg tempera painting, signed by Van Mander); *Portrait of a Couple* - DRESDEN: *Temptation of St Anthony* (medallion) - GHENT: *Deposition* - LEIDEN: *Crucifixion; Sacrifice of Abraham and the Brazen Serpent (recto of wings); Ecco Homo and the Mocking of Christ (verso of wings)* (triptych); *Deposition; St Cecilia, Mary Magdelene and Female Donor, James the Younger, St Gregory and Male Donor (recto and verso of wings)* (triptych surrounded by six small grisailles) - MUNICH (Alte Pinakothek): *Deposition; Constantine and St Helena* - NUREMBERG: *Portrait of a Man* - PARIS (Louvre): *Martyrdom of St John the Evangelist* - SCHWERIN: *Resurrection; The Three Marys at the Tomb and Christ Appearing to Mary Magdelene as a Gardener (recto of wings); St Anne, the Virgin and St John the Baptist (verso of wings)* (triptych with grisailles) - STOCKHOLM: *Christ on the Cross* - UTRECHT (Mus. Catharijneconvent): *Christ Bleeding Appears to the Virgin; Crucifixion; Resurrection and Christ Carrying the Cross (wings)* (triptych) - VIENNA: *Story of Naaman the Syrian Captain.*

AUCTION RECORDS:
PARIS, 19 Sept 1892, *Abraham and Melchisedek,* FRF 1,600. PARIS, 21 April 1910, *Christ on the Cross,* FRF 2,280. PARIS, 15 March 1924, *The Law of Moses; Family in a Park* (pair of paintings. School of C. Engelbertsz) FRF 9,000. PARIS, 6 Feb 1942, *Calvary* (School of C. Engelbertsz) FRF 92,000. PARIS, 19 March 1947, *Calvary* (pen heightened with white gouache, attributed) FRF 41,000. LONDON, 28 Nov 1962, *Virgin, Child and St Anne,* GBP 9,500. LONDON, 9 April 1965, *Adoration of the Kings,* Gns 1,600. LONDON, 12 June 1968, *Adoration of the Magi (central panel); St Ursula (righthand panel); St Bartholomew (lefthand panel); Sts Peter and Paul (verso of the side panels)* (triptych) GBP 5,000. LONDON, 12 Dec 1973, *Deposition,* GBP 34,000. AMSTERDAM, 9 June 1976, *Nativity* (oil on panel, 12 3/4 x 9in/32.5 x 23cm) NLG 36,000. AMSTERDAM, 23 April 1979, *Lower Reaches of the Escaut River* (oil on canvas, 23 1/2 x 27 1/2in/60 x 70cm) BEF 10,000. LILLE, 14 March 1981, *Church Prelate; Golgotha; St Michael* (triptych, 37 x 9in/94 x 23cm) FRF 260,000. NEW YORK, 7 Nov 1984, *Virgin, Child and Other Figures* (oil on panel, 9 3/4 x 8 3/4in/25 x 22.5cm) USD 9,500. AMSTERDAM, 17 Nov 1993, *Christ on the Cross with the Virgin, Mary Magdalene and Sts John, Peter, Augustine, Lawrence, Barbara, Cecilia and Catherine* (oil on panel, 8 x 11 1/4in/20.5 x 28.5cm) NLG 87,400. NEW YORK, 15 Oct 1998, *Crucifixion with SS Peter, Gregory, Lawrence, the Madonna* (oil on panel, 8 x 11 ins / 20 x 29 cm) USD 24,000.

ENGELBERTSZ., Lucas Cornelisz. Engelbertsz. de Kok, or Engelbrechtsen, Enghelbrecht, also called Kunst
Dutch, 16th century.
Born 1493 or 1495, in Leiden; died probably in 1552.
Painter. Historical subjects, portraits.
Leiden School.

The son of Cornelis Engelbertsz. the Elder, Lucas was his father's pupil. The story goes that he became a cook in order to support his family when he could not earn enough through his painting. He went to England, where he was welcomed by Henry VIII. He may also have worked in Ferrara and stayed several times in Bruges. He is sometime confused with Luca Cornelis or Luca d'Olanda who, under the direction of Hercule II, worked at the Gobelin tapestry factory. Engravings signed with the initials *L.K.* have in the past been attributed to him, but they may be the work of Ludwig Krug of Nuremberg.

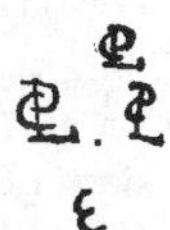

AUCTION RECORDS:
LONDON, 20 April 1923, *Margaret of Austria,* GBP 126.

ENGELBERTSZ., Pieter Cornelisz., or Enghelbrecht, also known as Kunst
Dutch, 16th century.
Born 1490, in Leiden.
Painter, draughtsman. Historical subjects. Designs for stained glass.
Leiden School.

The eldest son of Cornelis the Elder, Pieter Cornelisz. Engelbertsz. was a friend of Lucas van Leiden. He painted the arms of Leiden. In 1523, the head of the monastery of Marienpoel bought a small stained glass window from him.

MUSEUMS AND GALLERIES:
PARIS (Louvre): one stained glass window.

AUCTION RECORDS:
AMSTERDAM, 18 April 1977, *St Augustine in a Landscape* (1532, pen) NLG 11,000. LONDON, 8 Dec 1981, *Beheading of St John the Baptist* (pen and black ink, 11 3/4 x 8 1/4in/29.8 x 21.2cm) GBP 3,000. AMSTERDAM, 25 April 1983, *Allegory of Geometry* (pen and black ink on outlines in black chalk, 9 1/2 x 6 1/2in/23.9 x 16.8cm) NLG 3,800. MONTE CARLO, 8 Dec 1984, *Pilgrim Led Astray by the Devil Entering an Inn* (1530, oil on panel, 22 x 17 1/4in/56 x 43.5cm) FRF 140,000. LONDON, 2 July 1991, *Seven Acts of Mercy; Ransoming of Prisoners* (1532, black chalk and ink, 9 x 7in/22.8 x 16.9cm) GBP 30,800.

ENGELBERTUS
German, 13th century.
Active in Frankfurt am Main from 1220 to 1230.
Sculptor.
This sculptor worked on the tympanum of the north porch of the church of St Leonard.

ENGELBERTUS
German, 13th century.
Active in Cologne in 1220.
Painter.

ENGELBRECHT, Christian, or Enghelbrecht
German, 17th - 18th century.
Born 1672, in Augsburg; died 1735, in Augsburg.
Engraver.
This artist, the brother of Martin Engelbrecht, produced plates for the *History of Architecture* by J. Hernahrd (1721), illustrated part of *Ovid's Metamorphoses* after the drawings by Sandart and engraved numerous portraits.

ENGELBRECHT, Ignaz
Austrian, 18th century.
Active in Vienna c. 1793.
Sculptor.

ENGELBRECHT, Johann
Austrian, 18th century.
Active in Vienna.
Sculptor.

ENGELBRECHT, Josef
Austrian, 18th century.
Active in Vienna in 1768.
Sculptor.
This artist was the son of Johann Engelbrecht.

ENGELBRECHT, Karl
German, 19th century.
Born 19th century, in Stettin (now Szczecin, Poland).
Painter. Genre scenes.
This artist worked in Rome from 1857 to 1863. He exhibited at the Berlin academy's Salon in 1874.

ENGELBRECHT, Martin, or Enghelbrecht
German, 18th century.
Born 1684, in Augsburg; died 1756, in Augsburg.
Engraver.
Martin, like his brother Christian Engelbrecht, illustrated numerous works including the *War of the Spanish Succession* and P. Decker's *Princely Architects*. He also engraved 92 *Views of Venice*.

ENGELBRECHT, Paul Friedrich
German, 18th century.
Born 1719; died 1776.
Active in Augsburg.
Painter.
The son of Friedrich Engelbrecht, this artist was a member of the Augsburg academy in 1770.

ENGELBRECHTEN, Alma von
German, 19th century.
Born 25 April 1857, in Hamelin, near Hanover.
Painter.
The pupil of Jakobides and Roth in Munich, and of Bouguereau and Lasar in Paris, this artist became established in Hildesheim. She was primarily a portrait artist, but also painted genre scenes and landscapes.

ENGELEN, Antoine François Louis van
Belgian, 19th - 20th century.
Born 1856, in Lier (Antwerp); died 1940, in Antwerp.
Painter. History painting, portraits, landscapes, urban landscapes, genre scenes.
Engelen studied under Verlat at the academy in Lierre and also attended the Koninklijke Academie voor Schone Kunsten in Antwerp. An enthusiastic traveller, he was a member of the Als Ik Kan (As I Can) group and founder member of De XIII (The XIII) group in 1891.

Louis van Engelen
XX 1890.

MUSEUMS AND GALLERIES:
ANTWERP: *Belgian Emigrants; View of the Town of Antwerp.*
AUCTION RECORDS:
AATSLEAARD, 13 Oct 1987, *Cleydael Castle* (1889, oil on canvas, 26 3/4 x 35 ins / 68 x 88 cm) BEF 180,000. LOKEREN, 23 May 1992, *Southern Landscape* (oil on panel, 10 x 14 1/4 ins / 25.5 x 36.5 cm) BEF 36,000. LONDON, 17 Nov 1993, *Victory of Julius Caesar over the Flemish* (oil on canvas, 45 x 57 ins / 114 x 145 cm) GBP 4,830.

ENGELEN, Cornelis van
Flemish, 17th century.
Active in Antwerp.
Painter.
Flemish School.
Cornelis van Engelen was a pupil of Adriaen van Utrecht in 1641 and became a master in 1646.

ENGELEN, Peter van
Flemish, 17th - 18th century.
Baptised 13 March 1664; died 21 July 1711.
Active in Antwerp.
Painter, picture dealer. Scenes with figures, village scenes.
Flemish School.
Peter van Engelen was the son of Cornelis van Engelen and a pupil of his uncle Kasper de Witte. On 9 November 1687 he married Franciska Bruynel, with whom he had nine children.
MUSEUMS AND GALLERIES:
ANTWERP: *Fish Market; Village Fair* - MAINZ: *Fair.*

ENGELEN, Piet van
Belgian, 19th - 20th century.
Born 12 May 1863, in Lier (Antwerp); died 1924, in Antwerp.
Painter. Genre scenes, portraits, interiors, animals.
Engelen studied under Prosper Drion at the art academy in Liège and Charles Verlat at the academy in Antwerp. In 1886, he joined the Als ik Kan (As I Can) group, becoming, in 1897, professor at the academy in Antwerp. In 1894 he collaborated with Robert Mols on a diorama dedicated to what was then Belgian Congo.

Piet van Engelen 1902

MUSEUMS AND GALLERIES:
ANTWERP: *Cock-fight* - LIÈGE: *Poultry.*

AUCTION RECORDS:
BRUSSELS, 25 Feb 1981, *Ducks* (oil on canvas, 18½ x 22 ins / 47 x 56 cm) BEF 17,000. LONDON, 21 March 1984, *Partridge in Forest Interior* (oil on canvas, 29¼ x 36¾ ins / 74 x 93.5 cm) GBP 1,500. NEW YORK, 4 June 1987, *Spaniel in Landscape* (1898, oil on canvas, 62 x 79 ins / 157.5 x 200.5 cm) USD 8,000. AMSTERDAM, 20 April 1993, *Dog Bringing back Pheasant* (oil on canvas, 32¾ x 26 ins / 83.5 x 66 cm) NLG 3,450. LOKEREN, 4 Dec 1993, *Ducks near Pond* (oil on canvas, 32¾ x 41¾ ins / 83 x 106 cm) BEF 240,000. LOKEREN, 11 March 1995, *Hen and Cock* (oil on canvas, 26½ x 21¼ ins / 67 x 54 cm) BEF 44,000. ANTWERP, 11 Oct 1999, *Vase of Flowers with Grapes* (oil on canvas, 44 x 35 ins / 113 x 89 cm) BEF 70,000. ANTWERP, 29 Feb 2000, *Pheasant and Two Hunting Dogs* (oil on canvas, 53 x 39 ins / 134 x 100 cm) BEF 110,000. ANTWERP, 23 May 2000, *Proud Cock* (1894, oil on canvas, 29 x 68 ins / 73 x 173 cm) BEF 260,000. ANTWERP, 14 May 2001, *A Bird in Hand is Worth Two in the Bush* (oil on canvas, 43 x 28 ins / 109 x 70 cm) BEF 180,000. OSLO, 30 May 2002, *Ducks and Hunting Dogs* (1902, oil on canvas, 53 x 38 ins / 134 x 97 cm) NOK 55,000. BRUSSELS, 10 June 2002, *Three Donkeys at Shore of the North Sea* (oil on canvas, 22 x 30 ins / 55 x 75 cm) EUR 11,500. LYSAKER, 2 Feb 2004, *Donkeys on Beach* (oil on canvas, 43 x 59 ins / 109 x 149 cm) NOK 15,000. LOKEREN, 13 March 2004, *Donkeys on the Beach of Blankenberghe* (oil on canvas, 43 x 59 ins / 109 x 149 cm) EUR 12,000. BRUSSELS, 8 Nov 2004, *Hunting Dog and Pheasant* (oil on canvas, 33 x 27 ins / 85 x 68 cm) EUR 2,400.

ENGELEN, René
Belgian, 20th century.
Born 1897, in Antwerp; died 1971, in Antwerp.
Painter. Seascapes, landscapes.

Engelen attended the Koninklijke Academie voor Schone Kunsten in Anterp and was a founder member of the Antwerpse haven-en Scheldeschilders group. His works were purchased by the Province of Antwerp.

MUSEUMS AND GALLERIES:
ANTWERP.

AUCTION RECORDS:
LOKEREN, 9 Oct 1993, *Sunflowers* (oil on canvas, 23½ x 19¾ ins / 60 x 50 cm) BEF 60,000. LOKEREN, 12 March 1994, *Antwerp* (oil on canvas, 47¼ x 55 ins / 120 x 140 cm) BEF 48,000.

ENGELFRID, Hans
German, 17th century.
Active in Rottweil in 1628.
Sculptor.

ENGELHARD
German, 15th century.
Painter, sculptor.

This artist worked at the monastery of Reichenbach (Rheinland-Pfalz).

ENGELHARD. See also **ENGELHARDT, ENGELHART** and **ENGLHART**

ENGELHARD, Andreas
German, 17th century.
Active from 1657 to 1698 in Nuremberg.
Engraver (wood), modeller.

ENGELHARD, Christoph
German, 17th century.
Active in Cologne.
Painter.

ENGELHARD, F.
French, 19th century.
Active in Alsace.
Draughtsman, lithographer.

In 1839 F. Engelhard illustrated J. Rothmüller's work *Vues Pittoresques de l'Alsace* (*Picturesque Views of Alsace*).

ENGELHARD, Friedrich Wilhelm
German, 19th century.
Born 9 September 1813, in Grünhagen; died 22 June 1902, in Hanover.
Painter, sculptor (ivory).

A pupil of Thorvaldsen and Bissen in Copenhagen and of Schwanthaler in Munich, this artist worked in Paris, London, Munich, Rome, Hamburg and Hanover.

MUSEUMS AND GALLERIES:
BREMEN: *Lorelei*.

ENGELHARD, Gottlob
German, 19th century.
Born 18 December 1812, in Kassel; died 13 April 1876, in Münster.
Painter, architect.

The son of an architect, Engelhard was a pupil at the academy in Kassel; he then travelled to Italy, returning with studies for landscapes.

ENGELHARD, Hans
German, 15th century.
Painter.

Hans Engelhard was active in Nuremberg in 1469.

ENGELHARD, Hans
German, 16th century.
Active in Nuremberg in 1535.
Illuminator.

ENGELHARD, Hans
German, 16th century.
Died 1595, in Nuremberg.
Illuminator.

Possibly the same person as the previous entry.

ENGELHARD, Hans Baptista
German, 17th century.
Active in Nuremberg from 1643 to 1690.
Engraver (wood), modeller.

ENGELHARD, Johann
German, 17th century.
Died 29 January 1665.
Active in Nuremberg.
Engraver (wood), modeller.

ENGELHARD, Johann Anton Friedrich
Swiss, 19th century.
Born 13 May 1821, in Murten (near Bern); died 3 March 1870, in Murten.
Painter, draughtsman, illustrator.

Engelhard painted portraits and supplied illustrations for a book written by his father. He worked in Bern, Biel and Fribourg.

ENGELHARD, Josef
German, 19th century.
Born 23 June 1859, in Aschaffenburg (Hesse).
Sculptor.

After studying at Nuremberg, Munich and Berlin, Engelhard became established in Munich, where he exhibited from 1890 to 1896.

Engelhard

ENGELHARD, Karl
German, 18th century.
Born to a family originally from Speyer (near Mannheim).
Active in Rome in 1776.
Painter.

ENGELHARD, Roland
German, 19th century.
Born 18 April 1868, in Hanover.
Sculptor.
The son of Friedrich Wilhelm Engelhard, Roland Engelhard studied at the academy in Berlin with Otto Lessing and at the school of arts and crafts in Vienna. He settled in Hanover and executed numerous busts and memorials. In 1896 and 1901, he showed relief portraits at the Grosse Kunstausstellung in Berlin.

ENGELHARD, Veit Jakob
German, 17th century.
Born 1643; died 20 May 1668.
Active in Nuremberg.
Modeller, engraver (wood).

ENGELHARD, Wilhelm
German, 17th century.
Born 1645, in Nuremberg; died 1667, in Nuremberg.
Modeller, engraver (wood).

ENGELHARDT. See also **ENGELHARD**

ENGELHARDT, Anton
German, 18th century.
Born c. 1737; died 30 May 1807.
Active in Glatz (now Klodzko, Poland).
Painter.

ENGELHARDT, Daniel Friedrich
German, 19th century.
Born in Augsburg; died 1828, in Augsburg.
Painter, miniaturist, art writer. Landscapes.
Engelhardt initially studied as a miniaturist with C. Hoyer; he then studied landscape painting with Hofman in Cologne and was a pupil of Mannskirch. His paintings include the *Ollon Pass, Capo di Lago (Capo di Lago), Lake Brienz* and several views of the Vosges mountains.

ENGELHARDT, Georg Hermann
German, 19th century.
Born 3 June 1855, in Berlin.
Painter. Landscapes.
The son of Georg Engelhardt, this artist settled in Berlin in 1884, and after making his debut in 1878 exhibited regularly in Berlin, Dresden and Düsseldorf.
AUCTION RECORDS:
NEW YORK, 13 Oct 1978, *Alpine Landscape* (oil on canvas, 27 1/2 x 38 ins / 70 x 96.5 cm) USD 3,250. MUNICH, 26 June 1985, *House Beneath the Trees* (oil on canvas, 20 3/4 x 16 3/4 ins / 53 x 42.5 cm) DEM 2,800. DOWNINGTON, 21 Sept 2002, *Lake Brienz* (oil on canvas, 27 x 38 ins / 69 x 97 cm) USD 1,900.

ENGELHARDT, Georg or Georges
German, 19th century.
Born 1823, in Mülhausen (Thuringia); died 21 August 1883, in Charlottenburg.
Painter, watercolourist. Landscapes.
A pupil of Eduard Biermann in Berlin, Georg Engelhardt lived in Charlottenburg and Berlin. He exhibited mainly in Dresden and Berlin from 1857 to 1883. He is noted for his *Landscape in the Harz* and *Winter Afternoon*.
MUSEUMS AND GALLERIES:
BERLIN: 54 watercolours and pen drawings - SCHWERIN: *Mountain Stream* - SZCZECIN: *Ilse Falls; Wooded Landscape.*
AUCTION RECORDS:
COLOGNE, 25 June 1976, *Alpine Landscape* (oil on canvas, 26 1/2 x 38 1/4 ins / 67 x 97 cm) DEM 5,000. NEW YORK, 13 May 1978, *Alpine Landscape* (oil on canvas, 27 1/2 x 38 ins / 70 x 96.5 cm) USD 5,000. NEW YORK, 11 Feb 1981, *Alpine Lake* (oil on canvas, 27 1/2 x 39 ins / 70 x 99 cm) USD 3,000. NEW YORK, 24 Feb 1983, *Alpine Landscape* (oil on canvas remounted on hardboard, 27 1/4 x 39 1/4 ins / 69 x 100 cm) USD 1,400. AMSTERDAM, 5-6 Nov 1991, *Mountain Landscape with Travellers* (oil on canvas, 24 1/2 x 37 1/2 ins / 62 x 95 cm) NLG 5,750. NEW YORK, 28 May 1992, *Mountain Torrent* (oil on canvas, 27 x 38 1/2 ins / 68.6 x 97.8 cm) USD 6,600. LONDON, 19 April 1999, *Gentleman in Black Coat and White Frilled Shirt* (miniature, h. 4 ins / 9 cm) GBP 1,250. HELSINKI, 11 Dec 1999, *Mountain Brook* (oil on canvas, 28 x 37 ins / 70 x 95 cm) FIM 19,000. COLOGNE, 30 Nov 2000, *In the Alps* (oil on canvas, 27 x 38 ins / 69 x 96 cm) DEM 5,000. VIENNA, 28 May 2001, *Vent in the Otztal* (1877, oil on canvas, 27 x 38 ins / 68 x 97 cm) ATS 60,000. BREMEN, 29 June 2001, *Hallstadter See* (oil on canvas, 27 x 38 ins / 69 x 96 cm) DEM 3,600.

ENGELHARDT, Hans Jacob
French, 17th century.
Active in Strasbourg in 1620.
Painter.
In 1620, Hans Jacob Engelhardt painted the *Evangelists* and *Angels* in the upper part of the rood screen in the church of St-Pierre.

ENGELHARDT, Hermann
German, 20th century.
Born 28 June 1874, in Berlin.
Sculptor, decorative designer. Groups, statues.
Engelhardt attended the Akademie in Berlin, settling in this city after spending time in both Rome and Florence. From 1906, his work featured in exhibitions in Munich and Berlin as well as in exhibitions mounted by the association of artists of Darmstadt. To the 1910 show he contributed *Love*, an ensemble of wooden sculptures. Numerous monuments, churches, firms and houses are decorated with his sculpture. His key figural sculptures are *David* and *Slave*.
MUSEUMS AND GALLERIES:
BERLIN (Banque de Darmstadt) - SLUPSK (Chamber of Commerce) - TANGERMÜNDE (Rathaus) - WROCLAW (Railway headquarters).

ENGELHARDT, Hermann von (Baron)
German, 19th century.
Born 1 March 1853, in Wurken (Livonia).
Painter. Genre scenes.
This artist began studying in Düsseldorf and continued in Munich with Löfftz, Wagner and Lindenschmidt. He exhibited genre paintings at the Glaspalast in Munich in 1888, including *Nostalgia; Forgotten; The Sisters;* and *Consolation.*
MUSEUMS AND GALLERIES:
MUNICH (Knorr Gal.): *At the Studio; Café-concert* (pastel) - RIGA: *Nun at Prayer.*

ENGELHARDT, Maja Lisa
Austrian, 20th century.
Painter, pastellist. Genre scenes.
Engelhardt was awarded a bronze medal at the 1900 Exposition Universelle in Paris.

ENGELHART
German, 16th century.
Active in Landshut.
Painter. Portraits.
Engelhart painted a portrait of Duke William V of Bavaria.

ENGELHART. See also **ENGELHARD**

ENGELHART, Andreas
German, 18th century.
Active in Schneeberg (Saxony) c. 1700.
Painter.
Engelhart painted portraits of the Prince Electors Johann-Georg I, II and IV and Frederick Augustus I, and a picture of *Christ, Conqueror of Death and Satan* for the tomb of the burgomaster P. Blumberg.

ENGELHART, Catherine Caroline Cathinka,
later Mrs Amyot
Danish, 19th century.
Born 6 February 1845, in Copenhagen.
Painter (gouache), watercolourist. Portraits, genre scenes.

A pupil of Carl Bögh in 1865 and 1866, Catherine Engelhart went to Brussels and then Düsseldorf in 1867, where she worked for seven years under the direction of Vautier and Sohn. She exhibited genre paintings and portraits in Düsseldorf and Copenhagen, and several of her works were sold abroad. In 1875 she moved to Christiania (now Oslo) and then to Stockholm, where she completed two *Portraits of Charles XIV*, intended for King Oscar II. On 16 May 1878 she married an English doctor, Thomas Amyot, and from 1882 lived with her husband and exhibited at the Royal Academy in London. She also wrote and drew for German weekly magazines.

Amyot

MUSEUMS AND GALLERIES:
COPENHAGEN (Artists' Association): *No Roses without Thorns* (1874).

AUCTION RECORDS:
LONDON, 14 March 1980, *An Imp* (oil on canvas, 36 x 27 ins / 91.4 x 68.6 cm) GBP 280. NEW YORK, 23 May 1985, *Sunday in Tivoli Gardens* (1913, watercolour and gouache, 19 1/4 x 24 1/2 ins / 49 x 62.3 cm) USD 9,000. NEW YORK, 24 May 1995, *Evening in Paris* (oil on panel, 18 x 13 ins / 45.7 x 33 cm) USD 20,700. TOESTORF, 11 Nov 2000, *Young Girl with Cat* (1881, oil on canvas, 37 x 29 ins / 93 x 73 cm) DEM 15,000. BILLINGSHURST, 9 Jan 2001, *Artist in her Studio* (1894, oil on canvas, 31 x 22 ins / 79 x 55 cm) GBP 1,700.

ENGELHART, Hans Heinrich
Swiss, 16th - 17th century.
Born 1557, in Zurich; died 1612, in Zurich.
Glass painter.
Zurich School.

Among the works produced by this artist are the coats of arms of the Grebel family of Zurich and a window made of a single piece of glass depicting *Christ on the Cross with Virgin and St John*.

ENGELHART, Johann
Polish, 17th century.
Born 1585; died 1640, in Vilna (now Vilnius, Lithuania).
Engraver.

Johann Engelhart produced an engraved portrait of Andreas Bobola.

ENGELHART, Johann Andreas
German, 19th century.
Born 1801, in Nuremberg; died 1858, in Nuremberg.
Painter.

Engelhart was a pupil at the school of fine arts in Nuremberg, where he exhibited, in 1830, *Portrait, Card Players in an Inn* and *Young Boys with Easter Eggs*; in 1833, *Young Boy in Macedonian Dress*; and, in 1840, *Artist's Studio*. Other notable works include *For the New Year*, 1825, and *Scenes from Reynard the Fox* (*Reinecke*). He also produced a number of etchings, including the plate *The Will*. The municipal museum in Nuremberg has three series of oil paintings by this artist, each with a particular theme: the *Poems of Grübel in Pictures, Tender Woman* from the poem by Grübel, and the *Fall of Phaeton*, from the poem by Weikert.

ENGELHART, Josef, or Engelhardt, Englehardt
Austrian, 19th century.
Born 19 August 1864, in Vienna; died 19 December 1941.
Painter (including mixed media), watercolourist, sculptor, draughtsman. Portraits, genre scenes, landscapes.

This artist was a pupil at the Munich academy in the studio of Löfftz and subsequently lived in Vienna. He exhibited in Munich and Berlin from 1888 onwards and was awarded a bronze medal at the 1900 Exposition Universelle in Paris. He is noted for his *Portraits of Women; Pilgrim; In the Sunshine; Wind; Portrait of L. Speidl* and *Portrait of Burgomaster Lueger on his Deathbed*.

BIBLIOGRAPHY:
Josef Engelhart, 1864-Wien-1941: Ölbilder, Aquarelle & Zeichnungen, Kunstgewerbe, exhibition catalogue, Gallery Christian M. Nebehay, Vienna, 1979.

MUSEUMS AND GALLERIES:
VIENNA: *The Ball; At the Singer's; View from my Window*.

AUCTION RECORDS:
NEW YORK, 4-5 March 1909, *In the Mountains of Bavaria*, USD 265. VIENNA, 9 May 1980, *Last News* (1892, mixed media, 23 x 28 1/4 ins / 57.5 x 72 cm) ATS 25,000. VIENNA, 12 Nov 1985, *Head of a Woman* (c. 1902, white marble, h. 12 1/2 ins / 32 cm) ATS 50,000. VIENNA, 24 June 1986, *Dr Seipel* (1925, charcoal heightened with white, 18 x 23 3/4 ins / 46 x 60.5 cm) ATS 20,000. VIENNA, 19 May 1987, *Portrait of a Woman* (1935, oil on panel, 40 1/4 x 28 3/4 ins / 102 x 73 cm) ATS 30,000. ENGHIEN-LES-BAINS, 25 Oct 1987, *Man, Seated* (wax crayon and watercolour, 9 x 17 3/4 ins / 22 x 45 cm) FRF 35,000. LONDON, 19 Nov 1993, *Idle Moments* (oil on canvas, 32 1/4 x 116 ins / 81.8 x 294.6 cm) GBP 5,750.

ENGELHART, Josef
German, 20th century.
Born 2 September 1880, in Munich; died 14 August 1910, in Wittenberg (Saxony-Anhalt).
Painter, engraver, lithographer. Portraits, landscapes.

After travelling to Italy, Engelhart attended the Akademie in Munich and worked as a draughtsman in Berlin, Leipzig and Altona. At the same time, he carried out a few paintings including a portrait of himself with his wife, as well as landscapes, etchings, lithographs and preparatory drawings for book plates.

AUCTION RECORDS:
VIENNA, 18 March 1981, *Woman with a Cigarette* (charcoal and red chalk heightened with white/greenish paper, 23 1/2 x 16 1/4 ins / 60 x 41.5 cm) ATS 15,000. LONDON, 8 Oct 1986, *Head of Woman* (c. 1902, white marble, h. 12 1/2 ins / 32 cm) GBP 3,500. VIENNA, 20 April 1999, *Pulcher Choir* (mixed media, 12 x 12 ins / 30 x 30 cm) ATS 28,000. VIENNA, 15 June 1999, *Die Seilerstatte* (oil on panel, 18 x 15 ins / 46 x 37 cm) ATS 120,000. VIENNA, 30 May 2001, *The Red Hat* (1903, oil on panel, 47 x 39 ins / 120 x 99 cm) ATS 180,000. VIENNA, 27 Sept 2001, *Salamander* (dark patinated bronze, w. 13 ins / 33 cm) ATS 47,000. LONDON, 18 June 2003, *Salome* (charcoal and watercolour, 22 x 8 ins / 56 x 21 cm) GBP 1,000.

ENGELHART, Sebastian
German, 18th century.
Died c. 1750.
Active in Munich.
Painter. History painting, portraits.

MUSEUMS AND GALLERIES:
FRANKFURT AM MAIN (Historisches Mus.): *Christ on the Cross* - MUNICH (NM): *Portrait of the Emperor Joseph I; Portrait of the Emperor Charles VI and his Wife*.

ENGELHORN, Caspar
German, 18th century.
Died 11 June 1721.
Painter.

Engelhorn is documented at the Dorotheenthal earthenware factory, near Arnstadt.

ENGELHORN, Robert
German, 19th century.
Born 28 December 1856, in Mannheim.
Painter. Portraits, genre scenes, landscapes.
Robert Engelhorn studied at the Karlsruhe academy with Hildebrandt, then in Paris with Lefèvre. After living for a time in Munich, he settled in Baden-Baden where he founded the Free Association of Artists of Baden and the art exhibitions in the city.

ENGELINUS, Natalis de
Austrian, 16th century.
Active in Graz in 1557.
Painter.

ENGELKE, Karl Martin
German, 19th century.
Born 22 June 1852, in Tilsit (now Sovetsk).
Sculptor.
Having studied in Dresden in the studio of J. Schilling, and later in Vienna, Engelke settled in Dresden. He executed numerous works there, including the low reliefs *Entombment, Resurrection of Christ* and *Death and Entry into Heaven of a Christian Woman* for the Dresden-Löbtau cemetery. He is noted for his allegorical sculptures entitled *Poetry, Religion and History; Faith, Hope and Charity; Three Graces* and *Three Fates*. dH
MUSEUMS AND GALLERIES:
LÜBECK: *Bust of the Composer Carl Grammann* (marble) - PRAGUE (Rudolfinum Gal.): *Statue of Phidias*.

ENGELLENDER
German, 16th century.
Active in Munich in 1587.
Painter.

ENGELLOHNER, Lorenz Joseph, or Englaner, Englatner
Austrian, 18th century.
Born c. 1710, in Vienna.
Painter.
Engellohner was a pupil at the Akademie in Vienna in 1736.

ENGELMAN, Adriaan
Dutch, 20th century.
Born 1937, in Rotterdam.
Sculptor.
Engelman participated in the Antwerp Biennale in 1971.

ENGELMAN, Martin
Dutch, 20th century.
Born 1924.
From 1948 active in France.
Painter.
Martin Engelman took part in a number of group exhibitions including, most notably, the Salon de Mai in 1961, 1967 and 1968 and the Salon Comparaisons in 1962, 1963 and 1964. He was invited to the Documenta at Kassel and the Prix Marzotto in 1964. His key one-man shows were held in Paris in 1960, at the Minneapolis Institute of Arts and in Arnhem in 1963, in Amsterdam and at the Institut Néelandais in Paris in 1964. His painting shows the influence of the CoBrA group. His Expressionism is, however, sometimes characterised by a less intense pictorial technique than that of the CoBrA painters, drawing rather on the meticulousness of the Surrealists. He was not impervious to the narrative possibilities of the Pop Art movement of the 1960s.
MUSEUMS AND GALLERIES:
AMSTERDAM (Stedelijk Mus.) - HAARLEM (Frans Halsmus.) - NEW YORK (MoMA) - ROTTERDAM (Mus. Boijmans Van Beuningen) - THE HAGUE (Ministry of Fine Arts).
AUCTION RECORDS:
PARIS, 26 Jan 1990, *Conversation* (1960, mixed media, 19 1/4 x 25 1/4 ins / 49 x 64 cm) FRF 11,000. ROME, 9 Dec 1991, *No Smoking* (1969, oil on canvas, 45 1/4 x 37 1/2 ins / 115 x 95 cm) ITL 1,955,000.

ENGELMANN, Burkhard
Polish, 20th century.
Born 1944, in Poland.
Active in France from 1965.
Painter.
Burkhard Engelmann grew up in the former East Germany, but eventually settled in Paris in 1965. His paintings are strongly influenced by the work of Brauner. He painted a number of somewhat monstrous beings with multiple eyes and limbs. He exhibited in Paris from 1968 onwards, as well as in Amsterdam and London.

ENGELMANN, Daniel
German, 19th century.
Born c. 1800, probably in Berlin; died 1870.
Painter, draughtsman, glass painter.
Engelmann executed the frescoes at the royal palace in Munich, which were designed by Kaulbach, and those at the old Pinakotek museum, which were designed by Zimmermann. He exhibited at the Berlin academy from 1844 to 1862, showing sketches for stained glass windows for the cathedrals in Basel and Aachen. He made a lithographed reproduction of the fresco on the ceiling of the Protestant church in Munich.
MUSEUMS AND GALLERIES:
SCHWERIN: *Madonna in a Landscape*.

ENGELMANN, Eduard Wilhelm
German, 19th century.
Born 7 February 1825, in Leipzig; died 2 April 1853, in Leipzig.
Engraver (wood).
The pupil of J. Allanson and W.A. Nicholls, Engelmann mostly engraved works by Ludwig Richter.

ENGELMANN, Ernst Julius
German, 19th century.
Born 1820, in Gossnitz; died 1902, in Munich.
Active in Munich.
Painter. Landscapes.
Ernst Engelmann exhibited in Bremen in 1880. He is noted for his *Mill in the Tyrol; Evening in Munich*; and *Leustetten Castle*.

ENGELMANN, Franz
Austrian, 18th century.
Born 1771; died 22 April 1808.
Active in Vienna.
Engraver.
Franz Engelmann was the son of Wenzel Engelmann.

ENGELMANN, Godefroy I
French, 19th century.
Born 17 August 1788, in Mulhouse; died 25 April 1839, in Mulhouse.
Lithographer, miniaturist.
A pioneer of lithography in France, Godefroy Engelmann I made many refinements to the technique, improving inks, crayons and various processes. He invented the frame for registration (patented in 1837). He was awarded a second-class medal at the Salon. He was a pupil of Regnault and produced a lithography handbook.
BIBLIOGRAPHY:
'Les Engelmann: une lignée de grands lithographes français' in *Art et Métiers du Livre* n° 210, periodical, Paris, 1998.

ENGELMANN, Godefroy II
French, 19th century.
Born 1814; died 1897.
Lithographer.
Together with his father Godefroy Engelmann I, Godefroy Engelmann II invented chromo-lithography.

BIBLIOGRAPHY:
'*Les Engelmann: une lignée de grands lithographes français*' in *Art et Métiers du Livre* n° 210, periodical, Paris, 1998.

ENGELMANN, Hans
German, 17th century.
Born to a family originally from Lobau (Saxony); died 1620.
Painter.
Hans Engelmann worked on the church of Sts Peter and Paul in Görlitz.

ENGELMANN, Johann
Austrian, 18th century.
Born 1767; died 31 August 1805.
Active in Vienna.
Engraver.

ENGELMANN, Johann Wenzel or Wenzel
Austrian, 18th century.
Born 1713, in Langenau, near Leipa; died 15 November 1762, in Vienna.
Engraver.
This artist, who studied at the academy in Vienna, was the father of the engraver Wenzel Engelmann.

ENGELMANN, Joseph
Austrian, 18th century.
Born c. 1708.
Engraver.
This artist was connected with the university in Vienna.

ENGELMANN, Richard
German, 19th - 20th century.
Born 5 December 1868, in Bayreuth.
Sculptor.
Engelmann studied in Munich, Florence and Paris, later settling in Berlin.
MUSEUMS AND GALLERIES:
WEIMAR: *Recumbent Woman.*

ENGELMANN, Wenzel
Austrian, 18th century.
Born 1748, in Vienna; died 9 February 1803, in Vienna.
Engraver.
This artist was the son of the engraver Johann Wenzel Engelmann.

ENGELMULLER, Ferdinand
Czech, 19th - 20th century.
Born 22 December 1867, in Prague; died 1924.
Painter, engraver, pastellist. Landscapes.
Ferdinand Engelmuller studied at the academy in Prague with Marak and then in Munich and Rome. He exhibited landscapes in oil and pastel in Vienna, Prague, Munich, Berlin and Hamburg and received the gold medal at the Paris 1900 Exposition Universelle. He published fifty reproductions of his pictures in black and white in 1904 under the title *Tones and Tales* and in 1905 he published *Songs of the Evening*, eight pictures in pastel on V. Halek's poetry. His watercolours include *Impressions of the Homeland* and *Abroad: Impressions.*
MUSEUMS AND GALLERIES:
PRAGUE (Národní Gal.) - VIENNA (Österreichische Gal. Belvedere): *Landscapes of Bohemia* (16 sketches for the cycle of this name).
AUCTION RECORDS:
PARIS, 9 Dec 1986, *View of Prague* (oil on canvas, 35 1/2 x 66 1/4 ins / 90 x 168 cm) FRF 23,500. PRAGUE, 12 Oct 2002, *Summer Landscape with a Deciduous Tree* (oil on canvas, 17 x 14 ins / 42 x 35 cm) CZK 50,000. PRAGUE, 30 Nov 2002, *Landscape under Rip Mountain* (1904, oil on canvas, 46 x 59 ins / 116 x 150 cm) CZK 95,000. PRAGUE, 22 May 2004, *Forest Interior* (oil on canvas, 36 x 27 ins / 91 x 69 cm) CZK 80,000.

ENGELRAAM, Laurens, or Engelraeve
Dutch, 17th century.
Active in The Hague.
Engraver (including glass).
Laurens Engelraam was one of the founders of the Pictura confraternity in 1656. A certain Louweris Ingenraem was a 'fynschilder' (an artist who carries out detailed, fine work on any surface, especially in small format) in the guild in Middelburg in 1655.

ENGELRAMS. See **INGELRAMS**

ENGELS, A. Gabriel
German, 17th century.
Painter.
The only known work by this artist, who was probably the son of Gabriel Engels, is a *Portrait of A. Hutel*, dated 1662.

ENGELS, Alexander
German, 19th century.
Died 25 July 1857, in Cologne.
Active in Cologne.
Engraver, draughtsman.
Engels executed a portrait of Pope Pius IX. Other known works include a view of Cologne, which he engraved from his own drawing, and a portrait of the archbishop of Cologne, engraved by William Engels.

ENGELS, André, pseudonym: Guels
Dutch and French, 20th century.
Born 22 September 1940, in Anderlecht.
Painter (gouache), draughtsman. Religious subjects, landscapes.
André Engels trained at the Académie Royale des Beaux-Arts, Brussels, between 1958 and 1962.

Initially, between 1960 and 1970, he painted abstracts that show a balanced sensibility in both their forms and colour. He signed himself *Guels*, but in about 1970, he changed direction and began to use his real name again. He painted figurative landscapes, in which he protested against the pollution of the natural world, and then moved towards countryside scenes and fantastic visions, which were almost naive in treatment. He also painted large canvases inspired by the Bible, in particular the apocalyptic vision of St John and the idea of the Garden of Eden.

He took part in group exhibitions in 1964, 1966, 1968 and 1970 at the Salon d'Automne, Etterbeek; in 1983, 1984, 1985 and 1986 at the Salon d'Automne, Paris; and in 1985, 1986 and 1987 at the Galerie Katia Granoff, Honfleur. His solo exhibitions have included 1965, 1967 and 1973, Galerie l'Escalier, Brussels; 1975, Galerie Anne Colin, Paris; 1976, Galerie Lorelei, Brussels; 1980, Galerie Entremonde, Paris; 1982, 1984, 1985, 1986, 1987, Galerie Katia Granoff, Paris and Cannes.
BIBLIOGRAPHY:
Dubois, Jacques, '*André Angels. Un voyage au monde des merveilles*' in *L'Amateur d'art*, periodical, Paris, November 1988.
AUCTION RECORDS:
LOKEREN, 10 Oct 1992, *Ivory Towers* (1976, oil on canvas, 36 x 28 3/4 ins / 91.5 x 73 cm) BEF 26,000.

ENGELS, Bartholomeus
Dutch, 17th - 18th century.
Died after 1702.
Painter. Landscapes with figures.
Bartholomeus Engels was a member of the guild in Haarlem in 1656. His works include *A Blacksmith in a Grotto in Italy.*
AUCTION RECORDS:
LONDON, 17 Dec 1981, *Italian Landscape with Figures* (oil on panel, 20 1/4 x 31 ins / 51.3 x 78.6 cm) GBP 2,800.

ENGELS, F.
Flemish, 18th century.

Active in Mechelen.
Painter. Landscapes.
Flemish School.

ENGELS, Gabriel
German, 17th century.
Born 24 August 1592, in Hamburg; died 30 August 1654, in Hamburg.
Painter.

This artist travelled in England, France and Italy. His final work, dated 1630, the *Temple of Solomon* and a representation of the parable of the Pharisee and the Publican was hung in St Catherine's church in Hamburg. Other works in Hamburg by this artist have disappeared. Certain documents suggest that he worked at Gottorp for Frederick III and Christian Albert, dukes of Silesia.

ENGELS, Jan Baptiste
Flemish, 18th century.
Active in Mechelen in 1750.
Painter. History painting.
Flemish School.

ENGELS, Joseph François, or Ingels
Flemish, 18th - 19th century.
Born 9 March 1757, in Ghent; died 13 December 1842, in Ghent.
Sculptor.
Flemish School.

Joseph François Engels was a pupil of Charles van Poucke. He executed a bust of St Maurice for the church in Nevele in 1808.

ENGELS, M.
Dutch, 17th century.
Active in 1652.
Painter.

ENGELS, Michel
Luxembourg, 19th century.
Born 1851, in Luxembourg; died 1901, in Luxembourg.
Painter, watercolourist. Religious subjects, historical subjects, allegorical subjects, landscapes, urban landscapes, ruins.

Engels was the pupil of Jean-Baptiste Fresez and studied in Munich. He was professor of drawing at the Athénée in Luxembourg and in 1893 co-founded the Cercle Artistique, of which he was president from 1899 to his death. His style is described as meticulous.

BIBLIOGRAPHY:
Cent cinquante ans d'Art luxembourgeois, exhibition catalogue, Musée national d'Histoire et d'Art du Luxembourg, Luxembourg, 1989.

MUSEUMS AND GALLERIES:
LUXEMBOURG (Mus. national d'histoire et d'art): *Allegory of Feierwon* (watercolour); *Ruins of the Castle at Bourscheid* (1886, watercolour); *City of Luxembourg* (1898).

ENGELS, Peter
German, 17th century.
Born 21 September 1631, in Hamburg; died 1692, in Moscow.
Painter.

The son of Gabriel Engels, Peter Engels worked in Copenhagen, Italy and Moscow. He painted a series of biblical scenes for the Kremlin.

ENGELS, Pieter
Dutch, 20th century.
Born 1938, in Rosmalen.
Painter, sculptor.
Pop Art.

Pieter Engels attended the Kononklijk Academy and the Rijks Academy in Amsterdam. He participated in numerous exhibitions, the more significant being the Exposition Internationale in Montreal in 1967, the Biennale in Paris in the same year and Documenta in Kassel in 1968. He made an active contribution to Pop Art in the 1960s, presenting assemblages of objects, often made up of clothing, rather than paintings as such. Evident in Engel's work is a clear aseptic sense, the use of laminated smooth surfaces and chromium. He describes and at the same time appropriates (an essential term for these painters of the 1960s) an exterior contemporary world, magnifying it while denouncing showiness of style. Engels has been seen mainly in terms of objective art; in effect, it is the object which constitutes the subject matter and motive.

AUCTION RECORDS:
AMSTERDAM, 5 June 1984, *Prototype 63* (aluminium, 78 3/4 x 39 1/4 ins / 200 x 100 cm) NLG 6,200. AMSTERDAM, 22 May 1990, *Badly Constructed Canvas* (copper plaque and plastic objects on canvas in a wooden frame, 45 1/4 x 82 3/4 ins / 115 x 210 cm) NLG 4,140. AMSTERDAM, 19 May 1992, *Paramarche Shoes (Shoes for Walking Backwards)* (white box containing two shoes on cow hoofs next to a brush, 13 3/4 x 19 3/4 x 19 3/4 ins / 35 x 50 x 50 cm) NLG 2,530.

ENGELS, Rémi
Flemish, 18th century.
Active in Mechelen.
Painter.
Flemish School.

In 1736 Rémi Engels executed a statue of the Virgin for the main entrance of the old palace.

ENGELS, Robert
German, 19th - 20th century.
Born 9 March 1866, in Solingen (Ruhr); died 1926.
Painter, illustrator.

Engels attended the academy in Düsseldorf, and after a stay in Paris and London he also attended the Fehr art school in Vienna. He worked for some time in Düsseldorf, later taking up permanent residence in Munich, where he taught at the arts and crafts school in 1910 and contributed to the journal *Jeunesse* (*Youth*). His best-known illustrations include *Tristan and Isolda*, those of the *Ballads of Baron von Munchhausen*, the landscape drawings for the *Poems of Annette von Droste* and colour drawings for fairy-tale books, such as *Rübezahl* for the publisher J. Scholz in Mainz. In his capacity as a painter, he contributed a *Girl Knitting* in 1894 to the Düsseldorf exhibition, and to other exhibitions in Germany he presented *Family Painting* (1906) and *Summer Day* (1907). He was also a glass-painter and executed paintings on glass for the marriage hall of the Rathaus of Remscheid and the church of St John in Wroclaw: *Wedding at Cana* and *Raising of Lazarus*.

AUCTION RECORDS:
NEW YORK, 1 March 1984, *Woman Going to Market* (1907, oil on canvas, 39 3/4 x 35 1/2 ins / 101 x 90.1 cm) USD 2,000. MUNICH, 1 June 1987, *St Michael i. Eppan* (c. 1905, oil on canvas) DEM 1,800.

ENGELS, Wilhelm
German, 19th century.
Active from 1824 to 1840.
Engraver.

Having begun his career in Bonn, Engels then moved to Cologne. He engraved a *Portrait of Clement Augustus*, archbishop of Cologne, from the drawing by Alexander Engels, a *View of Düren* after W. Hollar and a portrait of the archbishop *Ferdinand Augustus* from his own drawing.

ENGELSBERG, Leon
Israeli, 20th century.
Born 1908.
Painter, watercolourist. Landscapes.

With a feverishly applied, heavy paste, he paints landscapes of Israel, according to a vision reminiscent of that of Soutine.
Auction records:
Tel Aviv, 4 May 1980, *Jerusalem* (oil on canvas, 28 3/4 x 32 ins / 73 x 81 cm) ILS 105,000. Tel Aviv, 15 May 1982, *Landscape* (oil on canvas, 25 1/4 x 28 1/4 ins / 64 x 72 cm) ILS 35,000. Tel Aviv, 1 June 1987, *Landscape* (oil on canvas, 25 1/2 x 36 3/4 ins / 64.5 x 93.5 cm) USD 4,260. Tel Aviv, 3 Jan 1990, *Landscape* (watercolour, 19 1/4 x 27 1/4 ins / 49 x 69 cm) USD 3,300. Tel Aviv, 1 Jan 1991, *Hills of Judaea* (oil on canvas, 21 3/4 x 30 ins / 55.5 x 76 cm) USD 8,800. Tel Aviv, 12 June 1991, *The Outskirts of Jerusalem* (oil on canvas, 23 3/4 x 38 1/2 ins / 60.5 x 98 cm) USD 7,700. Tel Aviv, 6 Jan 1992, *Cypress on the Outskirts of Jerusalem* (oil on canvas, 19 1/4 x 14 3/4 ins / 49 x 37.5 cm) USD 2,860. Tel Aviv, 14 Jan 1996, *View of the Old Town from an Interior* (oil on canvas, 16 3/4 x 20 1/4 ins / 42.5 x 51.5 cm) USD 9,200. Tel Aviv, 5 Jan 1999, *Jerusalem* (1980s, oil on canvas, 28x21 ins / 70x54 cm) USD 4,400. Tel Aviv, 4 July 1999, *Landscape* (watercolour, 17x11 ins / 43x28 cm) USD 1,100. Tel Aviv, 16 Jan 2000, *Jerusalem, Olive Trees in Wadi* (oil on canvas, 22x30 ins / 55x76 cm) USD 8,500. Tel Aviv, 29 April 2000, *Jerusalem, Yermin Moshe* (oil on canvas, 28x33 ins / 72x85 cm) USD 8,000. Tel Aviv, 12 June 2001, *Jerusalem Landscape* (oil on canvas, 37x28 ins / 93x71 cm) USD 9,500. Tel Aviv, 12 June 2001, *Jerusalem* (watercolour, 13x19 ins / 33x48 cm) USD 1,600.

ENGELSBERGER-DRIOLI, Trude
Austrian, 20th century.
Born 1920, in Salzburg.
Painter.
Engelsberger-Drioli attended the Akademie der Bildenden Künste in Vienna until 1939. His art was figurative and soft, sometimes bordering on affectation. He lived and exhibited in Salzburg.

ENGELSCHALK, Caspar
German, 17th century.
Active in Munich in 1665.
Painter.
Engelschalk was a member of the guild in Munich.

ENGELSCHALL, Georg Heinrich
German, 18th century.
Died 1714, in Nuremberg.
Painter.
Engelschall's portrait of J.C. Baumann was engraved by J. von Montalegre.

ENGELSCHALL, Joseph Friedrich
German, 18th century.
Born 16 December 1739, in Marburg (Hesse); died 18 March 1797, in Marburg.
Painter.
A professor of drawing and philosophy at the university in Marburg, Engelschall painted portraits in pastel and landscapes in watercolour. Geyser, Westermayr and J.L. Stahl engraved a series of his views of Hessen and other subjects.

ENGELSMAN, Jan Maertensz.
Dutch, 17th century.
Died April 1654, in Alkmaar.
Glass painter.
Jan Maertensz. Engelsman was the master of Josef Oosterfries. For the church of St Lawrence in Alkmaar he executed a *Siege of the Town by the Spanish in 1573*.

ENGELSTED, Malthe Odin
Danish, 19th - 20th century.
Born 8 August 1852, in Nivågård; died 1930.
Painter. Religious subjects, genre scenes.
Engelsted went with his parents to Copenhagen, where he completed a theology degree in 1870 before attending the art academy. He first exhibited at the Salon in 1879, and in 1881 and 1883 he took brief trips abroad. For his painting *Scene from Children's Life* he was awarded the Neuhausen prize in 1883. Winning a scholarship from the academy in 1887-1888, he spent some time in Italy and Greece. His output drew considerable attention. In addition to his subtle and lively genre paintings, in 1884 he began to paint religious pictures which imparted a firm sentiment. He handled a number of subjects in this way, inspired particularly by the Old Testament.
Museums and Galleries:
Stockholm: *Abraham on the Mountain.*
Auction records:
Copenhagen, 16 Sept 1987, *Orpheus* (1914, oil on canvas, 78 3/4 x 98 ins / 200 x 248 cm) DKK 50,000. London, 23 March 1988, *Wild Roses* (1897, 16 1/2 x 33 3/4 ins / 42 x 86 cm) GBP 4,400. London, 16 Feb 1990, *Game of Bridge* (1891, oil on canvas, 22 1/4 x 30 1/4 ins / 56.2 x 76.8 cm) GBP 4,400. London, 27-28 March 1990, *Young Boy Raking Straw* (oil on canvas, 36 1/2 x 26 3/4 ins / 93 x 68 cm) GBP 6,820.

ENGELSÜSS, Martin
French, 15th century.
Active in Strasbourg in 1454.
Painter.

ENGELSZ, Cornelis. See **VERSPRONCK**

ENGELUND, Svend
Danish, 20th century.
Painter. Landscapes.
Essentially a painter of rural landscapes, Engelund was fascinated by vast expanses of fields in the distance, which he observed throughout the seasons.
Auction records:
Copenhagen, 28 April 1976, *Markfelter* (1954, oil on canvas, 26 1/2 x 52 3/4 ins / 67 x 134 cm) DKK 15,700. Copenhagen, 8 March 1977, *Winter Landscape* (oil on canvas, 25 1/4 x 37 1/2 ins / 64 x 95 cm) DKK 14,400. Copenhagen, 8 April 1981, *Landscape* (1945, oil on canvas, 29 1/4 x 39 1/4 ins / 74 x 100 cm) DKK 9,000. Copenhagen, 9 May 1984, *Landscape* (1942, oil on canvas, 23 1/2 x 29 1/4 ins / 60 x 74 cm) DKK 9,000. Copenhagen, 26 Feb 1986, *Window and Landscape* (1978, oil on canvas, 39 1/4 x 39 1/4 ins / 100 x 100 cm) DKK 29,000. Copenhagen, 2 March 1988, *Fields and Farm Buildings* (19 1/4 x 23 1/2 ins / 49 x 60 cm) DKK 20,000. Copenhagen, 4 May 1988, *Fields* (9 3/4 x 14 1/4 ins / 25 x 36 cm) DKK 7,500. Copenhagen, 10 May 1989, *Winter Landscape* (1985, oil on canvas, 15 3/4 x 23 1/2 ins / 40 x 60 cm) DKK 14,000. Copenhagen, 21-22 March 1990, *Rural Landscape with Farm* (1942, oil on canvas, 29 1/2 x 37 3/4 ins / 75 x 96 cm) DKK 18,000. Copenhagen, 9 May 1990, *Fields* (1961, oil on canvas, 35 x 51 1/4 ins / 89 x 130 cm) DKK 48,000. Copenhagen, 30 May 1991, *Signs of Spring* (1962, oil on canvas, 28 3/4 x 39 1/4 ins / 73 x 100 cm) DKK 16,000. Copenhagen, 4 March 1992, *View of Fields in the Distance* (1967, oil/synthetic resin, 11 x 13 1/2 ins / 27 x 34 cm) DKK 7,000. Copenhagen, 1 April 1992, *Layout of Fields* (1974, oil on canvas, 28 3/4 x 46 ins / 73 x 116 cm) DKK 18,000. Copenhagen, 21 April 1993, *Boundaries of Fields* (1968, oil on canvas, 35 1/2 x 47 1/4 ins / 90 x 120 cm) DKK 20,000. Copenhagen, 17 April 1996, *Rustic Landscape* (1960, oil/synthetic resin, 15 1/4 x 18 1/2 ins / 39 x 47 cm) DKK 12,000. Copenhagen, 29 Jan 1997, *Fields in Winter* (1950, oil on canvas, 22 1/2 x 31 1/2 ins / 57 x 80 cm) DKK 16,500; *Rustic Landscape with Farmyard* (1942, oil on canvas, 28 x 35 1/2 ins / 71 x 90 cm) DKK 13,500. Aarhus, 6 March 1999, *Landscape* (1979, oil on canvas, 15 x 24 ins / 38 x 60 cm) DKK 15,500. Vejle, 11 Aug 1999, *Composition with Figures* (1964, oil on canvas, three works, 18 x 87 ins / 46 x 222 cm) DKK 30,000. Vejle, 15 March 2000, *Landscape with Houses* (1951, oil on canvas, 18 x 27 ins / 45 x 68 cm) DKK 18,500. Vejle, 7 Aug 2000, *Landscape with Figures and Houses* (oil on canvas, 15 x 22 ins / 37 x 57 cm) DKK 18,000. Copenhagen, 27 April

2001, *Landscape* (1959, oil on canvas, 26 x 45 ins / 65 x 115 cm) DKK 27,000. COPENHAGEN, 2 Oct 2001, *Landscape with Thunder Clouds* (oil on canvas, 30 x 39 ins / 75 x 100 cm) DKK 25,000. COPENHAGEN, 1 Oct 2002, *Landscape* (oil on canvas, 24 x 32 ins / 60 x 81 cm) DKK 27,000. COPENHAGEN, 23 Oct 2002, *Field Landscape* (oil on card, 10 x 15 ins / 25 x 37 cm) DKK 19,000. COPENHAGEN, 26 Feb 2003, *Fields at Vraa, Evening* (oil on masonite, 11 x 16 ins / 28 x 40 cm) DKK 16,000. COPENHAGEN, 1 April 2003, *Fields in Green and Black* (1962, oil on canvas, 35 x 52 ins / 90 x 132 cm) DKK 42,000. VEJLE, 12 Jan 2004, *View across Landscape* (1957, oil on canvas, 39 x 47 ins / 98 x 120 cm) DKK 40,000. COPENHAGEN, 29 March 2004, *View of Randers River in Winter* (oil on canvas, 22 x 37 ins / 55 x 94 cm) DKK 32,000.

ENGER, Erling
Norwegian, 20th century.
Born 1899, in Faberg near Lillehammer.
Painter. Landscapes.

Enger completed his forestry studies before turning to painting at 30. Taught by Revold, he travelled extensively - to Germany in 1933, to Paris in 1937 and to central and southern Europe in 1947. At the outset, he came under the influence of German Expressionism which, from 1940, he modified with his individual humour. He was primarily a landscapist known for his gift in handling colour.

MUSEUMS AND GALLERIES:
BERGSEN - COPENHAGEN - GÖTEBORG - OSLO - REYKJAVIK (Listasafn Islands).

ENGERLEN, Paul Sebastian
German, 18th century.
Born to a family originally from Augsburg.
Sculptor.

Engerlen worked in Munich around 1770.

ENGERT, Erasmus von (Ritter)
Austrian, 19th century.
Born 1796, in Vienna; died 14 April 1871, in Vienna.
Painter, art restorer. History painting, portraits, genre scenes.

Having worked at the academy in Vienna from 1809 to 1823, Engert spent some time in Italy. On returning to Austria he devoted himself primarily to the restoration of pictures, but also executed several portraits and history paintings in addition to some excellent copies of works by the great masters. He was professor of drawing at the engineering academy in Vienna and then from 1840 worked as a conservator and restorer at the Belvedere imperial art gallery, of which he became director in 1857.

His works, occasionally tinged with sentimentality, show evidence of a shift towards greater realism, a trend running counter to Romanticism.

MUSEUMS AND GALLERIES:
BERLIN (Staatliche Mus.): *Garden in the Viennese Suburbs* (1828) - VIENNA (Österreichische Gal. Belvedere): *Lamplit Interior; Ave Maria* (1829).

ENGERT, Johann Georg
German, 18th century.
Active in Hamburg-Altona.
Sculptor.

Engert executed the woodcarvings for the church of the Trinity in Altona around 1745 and for the church of St Michael in Hamburg. He was married to E.M. Maschmann, a painter who helped him colour or gild his sculptures.

ENGERTH, Eduard von (Ritter)
German, 19th century.
Born 13 May 1818, in Pless; died 28 July 1897, in Semmering.
Painter. Religious subjects, portraits, architectural views.

A pupil at the fine arts academy in Vienna in the studio of Kupelwieser and Führich, Engerth subsequently travelled in France, England and Italy. In 1854 he became director of the Prague academy and in 1865 was appointed professor at the fine arts academy in Vienna. He became president of a circle of artists in Vienna in 1867, and director of the imperial art gallery in 1871.

MUSEUMS AND GALLERIES:
VIENNA: *Son of Manfred Captured by the Duke of Anjou's Cavalry; Twelve Cartoons for the Staircase of the Imperial Salon at the Viennese Opera; Seven Cartoons for the Imperial Salon at the Opera; Ten Cartoons for the Murals in the Imperial Salon; Christ Entering Jerusalem; Angel Waking St Joseph before the Flight into Egypt; St John of Nepomuk; Job; St Anne and the Virgin Mary; Count Rudolph of Habsburg Hunting.*

AUCTION RECORDS:
VIENNA, 29-30 Oct 1996, *Young Master and his Dog* (1849, oil on canvas, 31 1/4 x 25 ins / 79.2 x 63.2 cm) ATS 253,000.

ENGERTH, Karl or Joseph
German, 19th century.
Born in Germany; died 1830 or 1831, in Lemberg (now Lviv, Ukraine).
Painter, decorative designer. Genre scenes, portraits, landscapes.

A painter at the court of the duke of Anhalt-Köthen, Engerth was in Lemberg in 1823. A picture bearing the signature Karl Engerth, *Camp of Thieves at Night*, was exhibited in Lemberg in 1837 and is attributed to this artist, who was also a theatre decorator.

ENGERTH, Wilhelm
Hungarian, 19th century.
Born c. 1818; died 1 January 1884, in Budapest.
Draughtsman, lithographer.

Wilhelm Engerth taught draughtsmanship at Budapest Polytechnic, and produced the design for the decorative page of the album dedicated to Emperor Franz-Joseph by Hungarian artists in 1857. He produced lithographs entitled *Hussar Camp, Queen Mary and her Mother at the Tomb of Louis I*, from a work by Liezen Mayer, and *Harvest*, from a work by K. Marko.

ENGESMET, A. van
Dutch, 19th century.
Active c. 1815.
Engraver (etching), copyist. Figures, genre scenes.

A. van Engesmet's works include *Taste, Woman at the Cross, Peasant Smoking*, and *Head of an Old Man.*

ENGGELGRAEFF, Françoys
Flemish, 17th century.
Active in Antwerp.
Painter.
Flemish School.

Françoys Enggelgraeff became a master in 1602.

ENGHEBERT, Jacobus
Dutch, 15th century.
Active in Haarlem.
Painter.

According to Siret, Jacobus Enghebert was the pupil of Philippot Truffin.

ENGHELRAMS. See **INGELRAMS**

ENGHELS, J.
British, 17th century.
Engraver. Portraits.

There is a well-known portrait by Enghels of Countess Barbara Villiers, in the style of Peter Levy, dated 1667, which appeared in 2001 at *Painted Ladies. Women at the Court of Charles II* at the National Portrait Gallery in London.

Bibliography:
MacLeod, Catharine/Marciari Alexander, Julia/Sharpe, Kevin/Dethloff, Diana/Wynne, Sonya, *Painted Ladies. Women at the Court of Charles II*, exhibition catalogue, National Portrait Gall., London, 2001.

Museums and Galleries:
London (British Mus.): *Barbara Villiers, Countess of Castlemaine, as the Magdalene* (1667, drawing, after Peter Lely).

ENGHERAN, Jan
Flemish School, 15th century.
Painter.
Jan Engheran was involved in preparing the Bruges banquet of 1467. He is mentioned in Siret.

ENGISCH, J. H.
German, 18th century.
Active in Dill, near Simmern, in 1714.
Painter.

ENGL, Hugo
Austrian, 19th century.
Born 17 November 1852, in Lienz; died 25 November 1926, in Silz.
Painter, illustrator. Portraits, genre scenes.
Engl worked in Munich and exhibited in Vienna, Bremen and Munich from 1877 onwards. He is noted for his *Return from the Hunt*.

Auction records:
Munich, 17 Oct 1984, *At the Dairymaid's* (oil on panel, 25 3/4 x 35 3/4 ins / 65.5 x 91 cm) DEM 36,000. Hamburg, 5 June 1985, *Portrait of an Old Man* (1877, oil on canvas, 11 1/4 x 8 1/4 ins / 28.5 x 21 cm) DEM 3,000. Amsterdam, 14 Sept 1993, *Confessions of the Servant Girl* (oil on canvas/card, 18 1/2 x 13 ins / 47 x 33 cm) NLG 5,520. Munich, 24 March 1999, *Grandfather and Grandchild in a Workshop* (1880, oil on panel, 13 x 9 ins / 34 x 23 cm) DEM 11,000. Munich, 26 March 2003, *Sleeping Hunter Disturbed by Small Boy* (oil on canvas, 15 x 20 ins / 37 x 51 cm) EUR 6,500.

ENGL, J. G.
German, 18th century.
Active at the end of the 18th century.
Miniaturist.

ENGL, Josef B.
German, 19th century.
Born 1867; died 25 August 1907, in Munich.
Sculptor, draughtsman.
Engl helped illustrate Grimmelshausen's *Simplizius Simplicissimus* in Munich. Other known works by the artist include his drawings of views of the city.

ENGLAND, Florence
British, 20th century.
Born in Newquay.
Watercolourist.

ENGLANDER, Louis
French, 20th century.
Born in Paris.
Painter.
Louis Englander exhibited in Paris at the Salon des Indépendants in 1927.

ENGLANER. See **ENGELLOHNER Lorenz Joseph**

ENGLATNER. See **ENGELLOHNER Lorenz Joseph**

ENGLE, Harry Leon
American, 20th century.
Born 1870, in Richmond (Indiana); died 1968.
Painter. Landscapes.
Harry Engle was a pupil at the Art Institute of Chicago. He won the Palette and Chisel Club prize in 1917, a gold medal in 1923 and the still-life prize at the Hoosier Salon in 1931. Engle notably painted: *Old Lyme Road* and *Laurels*.

Auction records:
Los Angeles, 6 Nov 1978, *Landscape* (1915, oil on canvas, 24 x 27 ins / 61 x 68.5 cm) USD 1,600. Cincinnati, 23 May 2004, *Heralds of Summer at Yorkville, Illinois* (1922, oil on canvas, 20 x 24 ins / 51 x 61 cm) USD 2,200.

ENGLEBERT, Pierre
French, 16th century.
Painter.
Fontainebleau School.
Pierre Englebert worked at Fontainebleau in 1570.

ENGLEBERT, Serge
Belgian, 20th - 21st century.
Born 1951, in Fraipont.
Draughtsman, engraver. Animals, birds, insects, fish.
Englebert attended the Académie Royale in Liège, where he became a professor. He was a sensitive draughtsman of different animal species, including: birds, insects and fish.

Museums and Galleries:
Liège (Drawings and Prints Collection).

ENGLEFIELD, Arthur
British, 19th century.
Born 1855, in Clapham, London.
Painter. Portraits, genre scenes.
Arthur Englefield trained at the Royal College of Art in London, and left with a medal. He appeared at the Royal Academy from 1892 to 1904.

ENGLEFIELD, Henry Charles (Sir)
British, 18th - 19th century.
Born 1752; died 21 March 1822, in London.
Painter, archaeologist.
Sir Henry Charles Englefield exhibited landscapes at the Royal Academy in 1787, 1788 and 1789.

ENGLEHEART, Francis
British, 19th century.
Born 1775, in London; died 1849, in London.
Engraver.
Francis Engleheart was the brother of the miniaturist George Engleheart. He trained as an apprentice under Joseph Collyer and as an assistant to James Heath. He engraved several drawings by Smirke for *Don Quixote* and several plates for other publications. He also executed *Only Daughter* in the style of Sir David Wilkies, *Castle* in the style of Cook, *Cupid and the Nymphs* in the style of W. Hilton, and *The Holy Family* in the style of Fra Bartolommeo.

ENGLEHEART, George
British, 18th - 19th century.
Born 1752, in Kew; died 1839, in Blackheath.
Painter, miniaturist, draughtsman. Portraits.
George Engleheart was the brother of Francis Engleheart. He started out by working in the studio of George Barret, whom he left shortly afterwards to become a pupil of Sir Joshua Reynolds. He produced miniature copies of many of the works by Reynolds. Engleheart was extremely prolific: between 1775 and 1813 he produced more than one thousand portraits of notable individuals of his era. A great number of these were exhibited at the Royal Academy. In 1813, having acquired a fortune, he left Hertford Street in Mayfair and settled in his country house in Bedfont. Later he retired to his son's house in Blackheath. Most of his works belong to private collections.

Engleheart left a book containing the names of every person whose portrait he painted. His miniatures are held in very high esteem.

Museums and Galleries:
London (Wallace Collection): *Portrait of a Young Woman.*
Auction records:
London, 27-28 June 1922, *Sir Henry Bate-Dudley Standing in a Landscape under a Tree* (black chalk and wash) GBP 15. London, 30 Nov - 1 Dec 1923, *Female Portrait* (miniature, attributed) FRF 2,320. London, 3 Dec 1925, *Portrait of a Young Woman* (miniature on box) FRF 1,500. London, 27 and 28 May 1927, *Portrait of an English Officer* (miniature) FRF 1,300; *Portrait of a Young Woman* (miniature) FRF 5,000. London, 12 June 1929, *Man in a Brown Outfit* (miniature) FRF 1,000. London, 22 March 1945, *Woman in a White Dress with a Blue Sash* (attributed) FRF 6,500; *Woman in a White Dress* (miniature, attributed) FRF 6,500. London, 7 Oct 1992, *Portrait of Elizabeth, Lady Fraser* (oil on panel, 16 1/4 x 12 3/4 ins / 41 x 32.5 cm) GBP 770. London, 21 June 1999, *Boy in a Blue Coat. Gentleman in a Blue Coat* (oval miniature, double-sided, h. 2 ins / 4 cm) GBP 6,500. London, 9 Nov 1999, *Colonel Otto William Offeney in Red Uniform* (1807, oval miniature, h. 4 ins / 9 cm) GBP 7,000. London, 2 Feb 2000, *Gentleman in a Brown Coat with White Waistcoat* (oval miniature, h. 2 ins / 5 cm) GBP 5,000. London, 21 Nov 2000, *Miss Delsel in a White Dress* (oval miniature, h. 2 ins / 6 cm) GBP 9,500. London, 3 July 2001, *Anne Papillon in a White Dress* (oval miniature, h. 2 ins / 5 cm) GBP 14,000. London, 30 Oct 2001, *Portrait of Mrs Mills, the Actress* (oval miniature, h. 2 ins / 5 cm) GBP 10,000. London, 10 April 2002, *Elizabeth Shergold* (oval miniature, h. 3 ins / 7 cm) GBP 7,500. London, 10 Dec 2002, *Young Lady in a Low Cut White Dress* (1807, miniature, 4 x 3 ins / 9 x 7 cm) GBP 38,000. London, 22 May 2003, *Gentleman in a High Collared Viridian Green Coat* (miniature, h. 2 ins / 6 cm) GBP 14,500. London, 9 Dec 2003, *John Weir* (oval miniature, h. 3 ins / 8 cm) GBP 9,500. London, 22 April 2004, *Portrait of Mr and Mrs Flint* (1802, oval miniatures, a pair, h. 3 ins / 8 cm) GBP 9,800. London, 22 April 2004, *Child in a Large Black Hat with Rosette and Feathers* (oval miniature, h. 2 ins / 6 cm) GBP 26,000.

ENGLEHEART, Henry
British, 19th century.
Born 1801, in London; died 1885.
Painter, watercolourist.
Henry Engleheart was a skilful artist who painted a great number of architectural designs in the style of foreign cathedrals. His works are very delicately painted and can be compared with the works of the most skilful engravers. He was the son of George Engleheart.

ENGLEHEART, John Cox Dillman
British, 19th century.
Born 1783; died 1862, in Tunbridge Wells.
Painter, miniaturist.
John Cox Dillman Engleheart was the nephew and pupil of George Engleheart, and a very popular artist. Some of his portraits are very beautiful. He exhibited very frequently at the Royal Academy and elsewhere. At the age of 44, the state of his health forced him to spend several years in Italy. After returning to England produced only a small amount of work.

ENGLEHEART, Jonathan
British, 19th century.
Active in London.
Engraver.
Only two small engravings are known to be by Jonathan Engleheart, who was a son and pupil of Francis Engleheart. These engravings are in the style of Abraham Cooper and are entitled *Stag* and *St Bernard.*

ENGLEHEART, Thomas
British, 18th century.
Born 1745; died 1786.
Draughtsman, sculptor.
Thomas Engleheart was the brother of Francis Engleheart, the engraver. Working with Flaxman, he executed pencil drawings for Joshua Wedgewood, which were outstanding for their fine detail. He is known for his works in wax, which he exhibited several times at the Royal Academy. His two nephews, Timothy and Jonathan, were engravers.

ENGLEHEART, Timothy Stansfeld
British, 19th century.
Born 1803, in London; died 1879, in London.
Engraver.
Timothy Stansfeld Engleheart was the son of Francis Engleheart. He engraved several plates for different publications.

ENGLEHERD, Melchior
British, 16th century.
Active in London in 1549.
Painter.

ENGLER
French, 19th century.
Died 1878.
Painter.
Museums and Galleries:
Clamecy: *Farm Interior* (two).

ENGLER, Friedrich Georg
German, 19th century.
Born 30 July 1877, in Loschwitz, near Dresden; died 24 February 1905.
Painter.
Engler entered the Dresden academy in 1898 and studied with L. Pohle and G. Kuehl. His only known works are his *Self-portrait* and the portrait of a fellow student.

ENGLER, P. J.
German, 18th century.
Engraver.
The museum in Frankfurt am Main has a single work by this artist.

ENGLER, Simon
German, 17th century.
Active in Breslau (now Wroclaw, Poland) in 1638.
Painter.

ENGLEY, Alice D.. See **BEEK**

ENGLHART. See also **ENGELHARD**

ENGLHART, Caspar
German, 17th century.
Died before 1675.
Active in Munich.
Painter.
Englhart was a master in the Munich artists' corporation in c. 1650.

ENGLHART, Johann Narziss
German, 17th century.
Died 1694.
Painter.
The son and pupil of Caspar Englhart, this artist was accepted as a master in the Munich artists' corporation in 1675.

ENGLISCH, Pangratz
French, 16th century.
Active in Strasbourg.
Painter.

ENGLISH, Frank F.
American, 19th - 20th century.
Born 1854; died 1922.
Painter (gouache), watercolourist, draughtsman.
Scenes with figures, local figures, landscapes.

Auction records:
New York, 24 Sept 1981, *By the Lock* (watercolour, 19 1/2 x 28 1/2 ins / 49.5 x 72.4 cm) USD 750. Portland, 22 Sept 1984, *Woodcutter on Snowy Path* (watercolour, 14 1/2 x 11 1/2 ins / 37 x 29.2 cm) USD 1,800. New York, 15 March 1986, *The Country Ploughman* (watercolour heightened with gouache, 15 1/4 x 22 3/4 ins / 39 x 58 cm) USD 750. New York, 22 Sept 1987, *Farm Scene* (oil on canvas, 24 1/4 x 36 1/4 ins / 61.5 x 92 cm) USD 6,300. New York, 24 Jan 1989, *Team of Horses on a Road alongside a Stream* (watercolour and gouache, 18 x 27 3/4 ins / 44.8 x 70.4 cm) USD 1,430. New York, 16 March 1990, *Sunset* (watercolour and Indian ink/card, 24 x 40 ins / 61 x 101.5 cm) USD 3,300. New York, 21 May 1991, *Dawn* (watercolour/paper/card, 30 x 19 3/4 ins / 76.2 x 50.2 cm) USD 1,870. New York, 10 June 1992, *A Stop on the Way* (watercolour/paper/card, 21 x 30 1/4 ins / 53.3 x 77.1 cm) USD 1,870. New York, 2 Dec 1992, *Returning Home* (watercolour/paper, 15 1/2 x 31 1/4 ins / 39.1 x 79.6 cm) USD 3,850. New York, 28 Nov 1995, *Autumn on the Farm* (watercolour and pencil/paper, 11 x 23 1/4 ins / 27 x 59 cm) USD 1,150.

ENGLISH, Harold
American, 20th century.
Born in Omaha (Nebraska).
Painter. Nudes, landscapes.

Harold English was an exhibitor in Paris at the Salon des Artistes Indépendants between 1925 and 1931.

Auction records:
Paris, 29 Oct 1926, *Traghetto*, FRF 2,600.

ENGLISH, J. J.
American, 19th - 20th century.
Active in Philadelphia.
Painter.

J.J. English was a gold medal winner for painting in 1902.

ENGLISH, Joe
Belgian, 20th century.
Born 1882, in Bruges; died 1918, in Vinkem.
Painter, engraver, illustrator.

Joe English attended the royal art academy in Bruges as well as the J. Devriendt academy, receiving the Prix de Rome and the Prix Godecharle (1907). He illustrated A. Rodenbach's *Gudrun* and was a supporter of Flemish nationalism.

Museums and Galleries:
Diksmuide (Yser Tower).

ENGLISH, Josias
British, 17th - 18th century.
Born c. 1630; died 1718, in Mortlake.
Engraver.

Notable works by Josias English are a half-length portrait of a man engraved in the style of Fleyn; an etching of *Christ and the Disciples at Emmaus* in the style of Titian; and several others from 1654 on the subject of *Gods and Demi-Gods*.

ENGLISH, Mabel (Mrs)
Maiden name: Bacon Plimpton
American, 19th century.
Born 18 February 1861, in Hartford (Connecticut); died 1944.
Painter.

Mabel English was a pupil of W. M. Chase, D. W. Tryon, Bruce Crane and Charles N. Flagg in New York.

ENGLISH, Michael
British, 20th - 21st century.
Born 1941, in Bicester, 1942 according to some sources.
Painter, print-maker, poster artist.

Michael English studied at the Ealing Art School and became well known in the 1960s for his psychedelic posters. From 1966 he worked in partnership with Nigel Waymouth, the owner of the boutique 'Granny Takes a Trip'. The duo were known as Hapshash and the Coloured Coat and created a series of posters published by Osiris Visions, known as the *Osiris 100 Series*. A prolific poster artist, English also produced carrier bags and T-shirts with slogans for the Carnaby Street boutique 'Gear', and in his partnership with Nigel Waymouth designed many record album covers, and posters for music venues and events, for the London clubs 'UFO' and 'Middle Earth', and for the Savile Theatre. Aubrey Beardsley and American painter Tom Wesselmann are cited as influences on English's poster art.

Bibliography:
Slattery, J., *3-D Eye: The Posters, Prints and Paintings of Michael English, 1966-1979*, Pedigree Books, New York, 1980.

Museums and Galleries:
London (Victoria and Albert Mus.): *Love Festival* (1967, coloured screen print, poster).

ENGLUND, Lars
Swedish, 20th century.
Born 1933, in Stockholm.
Sculptor, painter.

Englund studied in Stockholm in 1950 and 1951 with W. Rjerke-Petersen, then in Paris with Fernand Léger, in 1952. In 1971 his work featured at a group exhibition with that of eight young Swedish artists. A painter of abstract geometric forms, he was one of the exponents of the Constructivist movement in his collective perspectives of architectural integration.

Museums and Galleries:
Stockholm.

Auction records:
Stockholm, 5-6 Dec 1990, *Mobile* (lacquered metal sheet, h. 22 3/4 ins / 58 cm) SEK 16,000. Stockholm, 30 May 1991, *Mobile* (blackened steel, h. 32 1/4 ins / 82 cm, w. 19 3/4 ins/50 cm) SEK 18,500. Stockholm, 19 May 1992, *Supended Mobile* (1987, blackened steel, h. 28 3/4 ins / 73 cm, w. 19 3/4 ins/50 cm) SEK 12,500. Stockholm, 27 April 1999, *Plaited Work* (1989, black cut steel, h. 24 ins / 62 cm) SEK 16,000. Stockholm, 26 Oct 1999, *Plaited Work* (1988, black steel, h. 21 ins / 53 cm) SEK 18,500. Stockholm, 13 March 2000, *Untitled Plaited Mobile* (1985, black steel, h. 30 ins / 77 cm) SEK 17,000. Stockholm, 27 Nov 2000, *Plaited Work* (1987, black steel, h. 29 ins / 73 cm) SEK 20,000. Stockholm, 24 April 2001, *Pars Pro Toto* (1975, felt collage, 67 x 41 ins / 169 x 104 cm) SEK 50,000. Stockholm, 6 Nov 2001, *Untitled* (1964, wall object, 28 x 28 ins / 71 x 71 cm) SEK 24,000. Stockholm, 23 April 2002, *Untitled* (1959, oil on canvas, 20 x 20 ins / 50 x 50 cm) SEK 30,000. Stockholm, 7 May 2003, *Untitled* (mixed media and black plastic, 12 x 19 ins / 30 x 49 cm) SEK 17,000. Stockholm, 27 April 2004, *Mirror for the Galleries* (1991, tempera, shaped panel, 75 x 67 ins / 190 x 170 cm) SEK 65,000. Stockholm, 3 Nov 2004, *Communication III* (1963, oil and varnish on plastic film, 8 x 17 ins / 20 x 42 cm) SEK 42,000.

ENGMAN, Harald
Swedish, 20th century.
Born 1903; died 1968.
Painter. Figures, scenes with figures.

HARALD ENGMAN

Auction records:
Copenhagen, 22 Jan 1980, *Danish Festival* (1940, oil on canvas, 39 1/4 x 59 1/2 ins / 100 x 151 cm) DKK 20,000. Copenhagen, 14 May 1985, *Difficult Times* (1940, oil on canvas, 19 3/4 x 13 1/2 ins / 50 x 34 cm) DKK 10,000. London, 28 March 1990, *Harlem Nightclub* (1930, oil on canvas, 59 3/4 x 78 3/4 ins / 152 x 200 cm) GBP 10,450. Copenhagen, 16 May 1994, *Big Roundabout* (1938, oil on canvas, 37 3/4 x 45 1/4 ins / 96 x 115 cm) DKK 70,000. Copenhagen, 17 May 1995, *Son* (1943, oil on canvas, 13 3/4 x 11 1/2 ins / 35 x 29 cm) DKK 11,000. Copen-

HAGEN, 20 Feb 2002, *Raining Gold - Mystery from Heaven* (oil on canvas, 59 x 51 ins / 150 x 130 cm) DKK 220,000. COPENHAGEN, 23 April 2002, *The King's Town - 9 April 1940 - 5 May 1945* (oil on canvas, 39 x 52 ins / 100 x 131 cm) DKK 230,000. COPENHAGEN, 26 Feb 2003, *People's Friend* (1939, oil on canvas, 26 x 20 ins / 65 x 50 cm) DKK 36,000. COPENHAGEN, 26 Nov 2003, *Mother Denmark* (1941, oil on masonite, 15 x 12 ins / 37 x 30 cm) DKK 44,000. COPENHAGEN, 5 Oct 2004, *Mother Denmark* (1941, oil on masonite, 15 x 12 ins / 38 x 30 cm) DKK 24,000. COPENHAGEN, 5 Oct 2004, *Water from the Trenches* (1940, oil on canvas, 29 x 24 ins / 73 x 60 cm) DKK 45,000.

ENGMAN, Klas
Swedish, 20th century.
Born in Hornefors.
Painter.

After an initial exhibition at Umea (Sweden), Engman had shows at the Musée de Tessin, Paris and in Stockholm, Helsinki and throughout Scandinavia. In 1973-1974, he received a national award from the Belgian state for his painting.

MUSEUMS AND GALLERIES:
STOCKHOLM (Nationalmus.).

ENGONOPOULOS, Nicos or Nikos
Greek, 20th century.
Born 1910, in Athens; died 1985.
Painter, illustrator, decorative painter, poet.
Mythological subjects, genre scenes, urban landscapes.
Stage sets, stage costumes, icons.

Nico Engonopoulos spent his childhood in Istanbul, then known as Constantinople. After an aimless stay in Paris, he studied at the school of fine art in Athens from 1932 to 1938. He was generally influenced by the Surrealists. He taught in Athens: history of art at the polytechnic in 1943, and painting in the architecture section of the national technical university from 1967. He painted several stage sets, created costumes, was also involved in book illustration and decorated the Orthodox Church in New York with icons executed in Byzantine style and technique. His paintings used the inexhaustible fund of mythology, the history of ancient Greece, popular scenes and folklore.

Engonopoulos exhibited his first Surrealist-inspired paintings in Athens in 1939 and took part in the main exhibitions of contemporary Greek art; the Greek pavilion at the 1956 Venice Biennale was entirely devoted to him. He also published several collections of Surrealist poems.

AUCTION RECORDS:
LONDON, 26 March 1997, *Venice* (1958, oil on canvas, 21 1/4 x 17 1/4 ins / 54 x 44 cm) GBP 21,850.

ENGORANS LE BEHENGNON
Flemish School, 13th century.
Active in Liège.
Sculptor.

This sculptor worked in 1279 on Liège Cathedral.

ENGRAMELLE, Marie Dominique Joseph
French, 18th century.
Born 24 March 1727, in Neudonchel; died 1780 or 1781, in Paris.
Painter, draughtsman, engraver, musician.

Marie Dominique Joseph Engramelle belonged to the Community of the Petits-Augustins of Queen Marguerite. He was also an engineer. He exhibited in the Salon de la Correspondence in 1779.

ENGRAND, Félicie
French, 20th century.
Born 1889, in Marseilles.
Painter. Landscapes, flowers.

Félicie Engrand was a member of the Paris Salon des Artistes Français, where she first exhibited her work.

ENGRAND, Georges
French, 19th century.
Born 5 October 1852, in Aire.
Sculptor. Groups, busts.

In 1878 Georges Engrand sent *Arion*, a group of plaster figures, to the Salon. He was awarded a third-class medal in 1898, having gained a bronze medal at the 1889 Exposition Universelle. He became a member of the Société des Artistes Français in 1890. His best-known works are his bronze bust of *Hayem*, *Idyll*, *Sorrow*, *The Wave* and *Arion*.

MUSEUMS AND GALLERIES:
ARRAS: *Adam de la Halle* (plaster) - CONSTANTINE (Théâtre): *Moorish Dance* - ORANGE (Théâtre): *Molière* (marble).

ENGRANT, Louis Anne
French, 18th century.
Active in Paris in 1773.
Sculptor.

Louis Anne Engrant was a relative of Louis Antoine Engrant.

ENGRANT, Louis Antoine
French, 18th century.
Born c. 1720; died 1793, in Paris.
Sculptor.

ENGRANT, Pierre
French, 18th century.
Active in Paris in 1784.
Painter, sculptor.

ENGST, Johann
18th century.
Active c. 1740.
Engraver.

ENGSTFELD, Albert
German, 20th century.
Born 25 August 1876, in Düsseldorf.
Painter. Church interiors, landscapes, still-lifes.

Engsteld attended the academy in Düsseldorf and studied with P. Jansen and A. Kampf. His career was spent in Bruges, though he exhibited regularly in his home town as well as in Berlin, Munich and Dresden. He is primarily known for his church interiors.

MUSEUMS AND GALLERIES:
SAVANNAH: *Interior of the Church of St-Anne in Sluis, Holland*.

ENGSTLER, Peter
German, 18th century.
Active in Aub c. 1750.
Painter.

The church of the Assumption in Aub, near Ochsenfurt in Bavaria, contains a ceiling fresco signed by this artist, as well as medallions at the corners of this ceiling which are dated 1752 and which depict prophets, the childhood of Christ and scenes from the life of Mary.

ENGSTRÖM, Albert
Swedish, 19th - 20th century.
Born 1869; died 1940.
Humorist artist.

After his studies at the University of Uppsala, Albert Engström was taught by Karl Larsson, the renowned caricaturist, whose career goes back to the beginning of Swedish caricature in 1885. At the time, Grieg was 42 years of age, Ibsen 57 and Larsson 32. The brilliance of these men, albeit in different spheres, did not fail to influence Albert Engström. He was 16 at the time, and he later described his schoolboy farces, which to his way of thinking were also a sort of caricature.

From the age of 25, Engström's satirical verve found an outlet in the entertaining journal *Sundags Visse* from 1894 to

1896. In 1897, at the age of 28, he founded a journal *Le Strix*, which could be called his journal, since he was virtually the only contributor. From the outset, he enjoyed a considerable success with both the educated classes and ordinary people. He combined the two qualities of the present-day caricaturist - the subtle perspicacity required to appreciate the absurd behaviour and defects of his contemporaries and the courage to fustigate them. In addition, he seems to have appreciated superb draughtsmanship, a trait he shared with another caricaturist, his Russian-born French contemporary Caran d'Ache.

He relied heavily on contrasts between black and white, and often drew pictures in only a few subtle strokes. His preferred subjects were alcoholism and drunkenness, which he depicted in a truculent, moralizing and detached manner as in *Castigat ridenda mores complet* and *To the Two of Us*. However no one was safe from his attentions, and he also caricatured old women, magistrates, priests, nobles and commoners. As one of his compatriots wrote, Albert Engström drew the whole of Sweden.

AUCTION RECORDS:

GÖTEBORG, 3 Nov 1982, *Woman Reading* (1890, oil on canvas, 17 3/4 x 11 3/4 ins / 45 x 30 cm) SEK 9,500. STOCKHOLM, 20 Feb 1989, *Geography Lesson* (Indian ink, 7 1/2 x 11 ins / 19 x 27 cm) SEK 3,700. STOCKHOLM, 14 Nov 1990, *Skeppar Mattson Seated before a Table of Sailing Ship* (pastel, 22 1/2 x 27 1/2 ins / 57 x 70 cm) SEK 25,000. STOCKHOLM, 26 May 1999, *Large Mill Wheel* (oil on canvas, 29 x 39 ins / 74 x 100 cm) SEK 42,000. STOCKHOLM, 28 Feb 2000, *The Dean* (oil on canvas, 45 x 51 ins / 115 x 130 cm) SEK 35,000. STOCKHOLM, 29 May 2000, *Landscape* (1900, watercolour, 9 x 10 ins / 22 x 26 cm) SEK 22,000. STOCKHOLM, 3 Feb 2003, *Archipelago, Early Spring* (oil on canvas, 29 x 39 ins / 73 x 98 cm) SEK 15,000. UPPSALA, 5 Dec 2004, *Patron* (mixed media, 11 x 9 ins / 28 x 23 cm) SEK 15,000.

ENGSTRÖM, Leander Tord, or Leander-Engström Tord
Swedish, 20th century.
Born 1886, in Ytterhogdal (Norrland); died 1927.
Painter. Local scenes, landscapes.
Unga Group.

Leander Tord Engström attended the school of the association of Stockholm artists from 1907 to 1908. Thereafter, he worked in the studio of Pierre Matisse in Paris. Paul Gaugin and Vincent van Gogh were his artistic reference points. He went to Sweden but returned to Paris in 1912, discovering Paul Cézanne. Between 1920 and 1922, he was in Italy. His painting shows the influence of French and Italian work, while also paying homage to Swedish nature, featuring Lapland, the Lofoten islands and Norrland. His best-known works are *The Duck Hunter*, 1918, and *The Shipwreck*.

AUCTION RECORDS:

GÖTEBORG, 26 March 1974, *Nude before Mirror*, SEK 9,500. GÖTEBORG, 24 March 1976, *View of Fjord* (oil on canvas, 31 1/2 x 43 1/4 ins / 80 x 110 cm) SEK 14,000. MALMÖ, 2 May 1977, *Summer Landscape* (1909, oil on canvas, 28 1/4 x 23 1/2 ins / 72 x 60 cm) SEK 12,200. STOCKHOLM, 22 April 1981, *Interior* (oil on panel, 37 3/4 x 25 1/2 ins / 96 x 65 cm) SEK 18,000. STOCKHOLM, 22 April 1981, *Landscape* (1913, oil on panel, 32 1/4 x 47 1/4 ins / 82 x 120 cm) SEK 7,200. STOCKHOLM, 26-27 April 1983, *View of Viareggio* (1922, oil on canvas, 36 1/4 x 41 1/4 ins / 92 x 105 cm) SEK 98,000; *Reindeer in Landscape* (gouache, 23 1/2 x 28 ins / 60 x 71 cm) SEK 41,000. STOCKHOLM, 27 May 1986, *Landscape* (oil on canvas, 23 1/4 x 19 ins / 59 x 48 cm) SEK 92,000. STOCKHOLM, 5-6 Dec 1990, *House on Cliff* (oil on canvas, 31 1/2 x 25 1/4 ins / 80 x 64 cm) SEK 65,000. STOCKHOLM, 5 Sept 1992, *Child and Grandmother* (oil on panel, 17 3/4 x 12 1/2 ins / 45 x 32 cm) SEK 40,000. STOCKHOLM, 30 Nov 1993, *Female Nude* (1927, oil on panel, 9 x 4 3/4 ins / 22 x 12 cm) SEK 12,000. STOCKHOLM, 27 April 1999, *View of Stockholm* (c. 1917, oil on canvas, 24 x 29 ins / 60 x 74 cm) SEK 940,000. STOCKHOLM, 26 Oct 1999, *Palace Chapel in Jönköping* (1913, oil on panel, 22 x 17 ins / 56 x 44 cm) SEK 200,000. STOCKHOLM, 7 Nov 2000, *Ballerinas* (watercolour, a pair, 19 x 19 ins / 49 x 47 cm) SEK 18,000. STOCKHOLM, 11 Nov 2000, *Two Girls from Norrland* (1913, 29 x 15 ins / 74 x 38 cm) SEK 240,000. STOCKHOLM, 2 May 2001, *Lapland Landscape* (watercolour on paper/canvas, 20 x 26 ins / 50 x 66 cm) SEK 200,000. STOCKHOLM, 21 May 2001, *Wall in Tuscany* (1921, oil on panel, 20 x 28 ins / 50 x 70 cm) SEK 150,000. STOCKHOLM, 5 Nov 2002, *Woman Embroidering* (1918, oil on canvas, 33 x 27 ins / 83 x 68 cm) SEK 470,000. STOCKHOLM, 6 Nov 2002, *Still-life with Roses* (oil on canvas, 20 x 15 ins / 50 x 37 cm) SEK 145,000. STOCKHOLM, 28 April 2003, *Ode to Norrland I-III or Anthem to the Wilderness* (1921, gouache heightened with tempera, triptych, 26 x 30 ins / 65 x 77 cm) SEK 760,000. STOCKHOLM, 4 Nov 2003, *From the Deer Park, Stockholm* (1914, oil on canvas, 28 x 21 ins / 72 x 54 cm) SEK 850,000. STOCKHOLM, 26 April 2004, *Landscape from the Arno by Compiobbi* (1922, oil on canvas, 20 x 28 ins / 52 x 72 cm) SEK 1,375,000. STOCKHOLM, 27 April 2004, *Landscape from Nuolja Hill, Abisko* (1917, oil on panel, 28 x 24 ins / 72 x 62 cm) SEK 280,000.

ENGSTRÖM, Wage
Swedish, 20th century.
Born 1923, in Arkolma.
Painter.

Engström attended the academy in Stockholm from 1947 to 1949 and had shows in Stockholm in 1953 and 1955, and in Paris in 1955.

ENGSTROM, Wilhelm Oscar
German, 19th century.
Born 1830; died 25 January 1877, in Düsseldorf.
Painter. Animals.

MUSEUMS AND GALLERIES:

STOCKHOLM: *The Greeting*.

ENGUERRAND
French, 20th century.
Born 1926.
Painter, sculptor.

Enguerrand trained in a number of technical and scientific fields before turning to art. He exhibited from 1987, including in Paris and Geneva. In about 1948, he made some drawings influenced by Surrealism, then discovered the work of Calder and began to create mobiles. His sculptures are usually made of pieces of metal, weighted so that they swing and rotate at the touch of a hand and eventually come to rest.

ENGUIMEUTZ
French, 13th century.
Born to a family originally from the Languedoc.
Active in Montpellier.
Sculptor, architect.

This artist was a member of the ArchitectsGuild from 1250 to 1265.

ENHOLTZ, Walter
Swiss, 20th century.
Born 17 April 1875, in Kreuzlingen.
Painter, watercolourist. Landscapes.

Enholtz attended the art school in Geneva and worked from 1897 to 1901 in various German towns. He lived in Basel for some time and from 1907 onwards he exhibited landscapes in watercolour and oil.

MUSEUMS AND GALLERIES:

BASEL (Artists' Association) - ZURICH (Kunsthaus).

ENHORNING, Karl
Swedish, 18th - 19th century.

Born 30 September 1745, in Bälinge; died 11 January 1821, in Stockholm.

Sculptor, medallist. Portraits, figures. Busts.

Museums and Galleries:

Stockholm: *Head Portrait of Physician Karl Fr. v. Schulzenheim; Bust of Baron Sam. Gust. Hermelin, Royal Mines Inspector.*

ENHUBER, Karl von

German, 19th century.

Born 16 December 1811, in Hof (Bavaria); died 6 July 1867, in Munich.

Painter. Figures, genre scenes, interior scenes.

Enhuber entered the Munich academy in 1832 and became an honorary member in 1858. He exhibited in Munich in 1835.

Museums and Galleries:

Berlin: *Guards at the Castle in Munich* - Darmstadt: *Day of Judgement at Starnberg* - Leipzig: *Six Pictures of German Working-Class Life* - Munich: *Carver of Images; Grandfather and Grandson; Cobbler's Workshop* - Oberschleissheim: *Narrations of Riès* - Strasbourg: *Tired Workman.*

Auction records:

Paris, 24 May 1944, *Improvised Entertainment,* FRF 1,500. Cologne, 15 June 1973, *Two Young Boys in a Garden,* DEM 18,000. New York, 30 Oct 1980, *Children by the Grapevine* (1858, oil on panel, 16¾ x 12 ins / 42.5 x 30.5 cm) USD 14,000. Munich, 24 Nov 1983, *Keen Swimmer* (1857, oil on canvas, 19¼ x 17 ins / 49 x 43 cm) DEM 25,000. Lucerne, 3 June 1987, *Woman Knitting in an Interior* (oil on canvas, 10 x 8½ ins / 24.5 x 21.5 cm) CHF 18,000. Stockholm, 15 Nov 1989, *Old Man Sorting Mushrooms outside a Mountain Refuge* (oil on canvas, 19 x 15¾ ins / 48 x 40 cm) SEK 26,000. Munich, 27 Feb 1999, *Artist and his Student in Studio* (1847, oil on canvas/board, 16 x 13 ins / 41 x 33 cm) DEM 14,000. Munich, 27 Feb 1999, *Satisfied - Old Farmer's Wife Seated in Front of Spindle* (1855, oil on canvas, 7 x 7 ins / 19 x 18 cm) DEM 15,000. Munich, 8 Nov 2000, *Interior Scene with Two Farmers* (1858, oil on canvas, 11 x 11 ins / 29 x 27 cm) DEM 7,000. Munich, 6 Dec 2000, *Peasant Worker Asleep in Tavern* (1859, oil on panel, 8 x 7 ins / 20 x 17 cm) DEM 7,000. Hamburg, 23 June 2001, *The Love Letter* (oil on panel, 12 x 9 ins / 30 x 23 cm) DEM 6,600. Vienna, 29 Nov 2001, *Peasant Woman Reading* (oil on canvas, 11 x 11 ins / 27 x 28 cm) ATS 90,000. Vienna, 29 Sept 2004, *Homesickness* (1863, oil on canvas, 17 x 19 ins / 42 x 49 cm) EUR 7,500.

ENICHIBO. See JONIN

ENIODAS, Armand Clément Philippe

Belgian, 20th century.

Born in Ostend.

Painter.

Eniodas exhibited at the Salon des Artistes in Paris.

ENJOLRAS, Delphin

French, 19th - 20th century.

Born 13 May 1857, in Coucouron (Ardèche); died 1945.

Painter (gouache), watercolourist, pastellist. Figures, nudes, genre scenes, interiors with figures.

Delphin Enjolras was a pupil of the watercolourist Gaston Gérard at the Écoles des Dessins de la Ville de Paris. From 1901, he exhibited at the Salon des Artistes Français, of which he was a member. He was very prolific, especially in watercolours and pastels, and made a speciality of painting young women, often while dressing or at their daily tasks.

Museums and Galleries:

Avignon: *Provincial Woman* - Le Puy-en-Velay: *Castle Keep of Polignac.*

Auction records:

Paris, 18 Jan 1924, *Young Woman Reading her Cards,* FRF 270. Paris, 27 June 1924, *Mirror* (pastel) FRF 260. Paris, 8 April 1932, *Returning from the Ball* (pastel) FRF 550. Paris, 14 May 1943, *Woman Powdering her Face,* FRF 3,500. Paris, 10 Nov 1976, *Surprise* (oil on canvas, 28¾ x 21¼ ins / 73 x 54 cm) FRF 4,700. London, 20 April 1978, *Young Woman in her Boudoir* (oil on canvas, 20¾ x 14 ins / 53 x 35.5 cm) GBP 1,100. London, 14 Feb 1979, *Model Resting* (oil on canvas, 20¾ x 28½ ins / 53 x 72.5 cm) GBP 1,350. Barbizon, 1 Nov 1981, *Young Woman in her Négligé Doing her Hair* (pastel, 21¼ x 14½ ins / 54 x 37 cm) FRF 33,500. Enghien-les-Bains, 24 March 1984, *Young Girls near a Pond* (pastel, 35¾ x 25¼ ins / 91 x 64 cm) FRF 40,000. London, 20 June 1984, *Young Woman Doing her Hair* (oil on canvas, 28¼ x 20¾ ins / 71.5 x 53 cm) GBP 3,200. Angers, 7 Dec 1985, *Young Woman Dreaming* (pastel, 28¾ x 22 ins / 73 x 55 cm) FRF 81,000. London, 25 March 1987, *Nude Reclining on a Bearskin* (oil on canvas, 23½ x 36 ins / 60 x 91.5 cm) GBP 17,000. Paris, 15 June 1987, *Scent of the Rose* (pastel, 20½ x 28¼ ins / 52 x 72 cm) FRF 100,000. Neuilly, 25 Nov 1987, *Young Woman Doing her Hair* (pastel, 21¼ x 14½ ins / 54 x 37 cm) FRF 35,200. St-Dié, 14 Feb 1988, *Danaë* (1857, oil on canvas, 15 x 22 ins / 38 x 56 cm) FRF 44,500. Neuilly, 9 March 1988, *Young Woman in her Room* (pastel, 22½ x 15 ins / 57 x 38 cm) FRF 36,000. London, 23 March 1988, *Nude Seated on a Bed* (pastel, 45 x 45¼ ins / 114 x 115 cm) GBP 8,800. Paris, 6 May 1988, *Ballerina* (oil on canvas, 22 x 15 ins / 55 x 38 cm) FRF 40,000. La Varenne-St-Hilaire, 23 Oct 1988, *Young Woman Doing her Hair* (pastel, 28 x 20½ ins / 71 x 52 cm) FRF 63,500. Calais, 13 Nov 1988, *Young Woman Dressing* (pastel, 28¼ x 21¼ ins / 72 x 54 cm) FRF 60,000. Paris, 23 Jan 1989, *Young Woman Writing a Letter* (pastel, 29½ x 23¼ ins / 75 x 59 cm) FRF 90,000. London, 5 May 1989, *Spring Beauty* (pastel, 28¾ x 21¼ ins / 73 x 54 cm) GBP 4,400. Paris, 18 June 1989, *Woman with a Cake* (gouache, 20½ x 28 ins / 52 x 71 cm) FRF 14,000. Paris, 22 Oct 1989, *Reading under the Lamp* (pastel, 28¾ x 21¼ ins / 73 x 54 cm) FRF 95,000. Paris, 8 Nov 1989, *The Letter* (pastel, 28¼ x 20½ ins / 72 x 52 cm) FRF 65,000. Versailles, 19 Nov 1989, *Elegant Lady in a Yellow Dress* (pastel/canvas, 28¾ x 23½ ins / 73 x 60 cm) FRF 54,000. Paris, 23 Nov 1989, *Woman in her Boudoir* (oil on canvas, 28¾ x 21¼ ins / 73 x 54 cm) FRF 75,000. London, 24 Nov 1989, *Late Return* (oil on canvas, 29 x 21½ ins / 73.5 x 54.5 cm) GBP 5,500. Calais, 10 Dec 1989, *Evening on the Terrace* (oil on canvas, 18 x 22 ins / 46 x 55 cm) FRF 120,000. Paris, 4 May 1990, *Oriental Beauty* (pastel, 25½ x 21½ ins / 65 x 54.5 cm) FRF 60,000. Versailles, 7 June 1990, *Young Women Sitting on a Terrace by the Sea* (oil on canvas, 23¾ x 28¾ ins / 60.5 x 73 cm) FRF 100,000. Monaco, 15 June 1990, *Woman Reading* (pastel, 21¼ x 14½ ins / 54 x 37 cm) FRF 33,300. New York, 19 July 1990, *Evening in the Garden* (oil/synthetic resin, 29 x 21½ ins / 73.7 x 54.9 cm) USD 2,860. Rheims, 21 April 1991, *Reclining Nude Smelling a Rose* (pastel, 21¼ x 28¾ ins / 54 x 73 cm) FRF 48,000. New York, 21 May 1991, *Tea at Sunset* (oil on canvas, 24 x 28¾ ins / 61 x 73 cm) USD 11,000. Paris, 18 Dec 1991, *Knick-knacks* (pastel, 20¼ x 14¼ ins / 51.5 x 36.5 cm) FRF 10,000. Lokeren, 23 May 1992, *Young Woman* (pastel, 17¼ x 14¼ ins / 44 x 36 cm) BEF 75,000. Paris, 9 July 1992, *Woman Reclining* (pastel, 23 x 28 ins / 58.5 x 71 cm) FRF 33,000. London, 12 Feb 1993, *The Letter* (pastel/paper, 28¾ x 21¼ ins / 73 x 54 cm) GBP 4,950. New York, 26 May 1993, *The Boudoir* (oil on canvas, 28¾ x 21¼ ins / 73 x 54 cm) USD 16,100. Paris, 23 June 1993, *In Front of the Mantelpiece* (oil on canvas, diam. 23¼ ins / 59 cm) FRF 45,000. New York, 13 Oct 1993, *The Boudoir* (pastel/paper, 24½ x 35½ ins / 62.2 x 90.2 cm)

USD 23,000. LONDON, 27 Oct 1993, *Young Girl with a Branch of Mimosa* (pastel, 28 x 201/2 ins / 71 x 52 cm) GBP 2,645. RHEIMS, 6 Feb 1994, *On the Terrace by the Lake* (oil on canvas, 233/4 x 29 ins / 60.5 x 73.5 cm) FRF 84,000. LONDON, 17 June 1994, *By the Fire* (oil on canvas, diam. 233/4 ins / 60.3 cm) GBP 7,130. CALAIS, 3 July 1994, *Nude Surrounded by Flowers* (pastel/canvas, 23 1/2 x 283/4 ins / 60 x 73 cm) FRF 21,000. NEW YORK, 16 Feb 1995, *Young Woman in a Room* (pastel/paper, 28 x 203/4 ins / 71.1 x 52.7 cm) USD 11,500. MÂCON, 11 June 1995, *Evening on the Terrace* (oil on canvas, 283/4 x 24 ins / 73 x 61 cm) FRF 68,500. CHAUMONT, 17 Sept 1995, *Woman with a Rose* (pastel/paper/canvas, 211/4 x 283/4 ins / 54 x 73 cm) FRF 20,000. LONDON, 17 Nov 1995, *The Shoe* (oil on canvas, 263/4 x 19 ins / 68 x 48.5 cm) GBP 8,280. LONDON, 12 June 1996, *Nude with Roses* (oil on canvas, 231/2 x 36 ins / 60 x 91.5 cm) GBP 13,800. CALAIS, 7 July 1996, *Seated Nude* (oil on panel, 9 x 61/4 ins / 22 x 16 cm) FRF 18,000. PARIS, 30 Oct 1996, *Young Woman Crouching* (pastel heightened with gouache, 141/4 x 11 ins / 36 x 27 cm) FRF 40,000. LONDON, 20 Nov 1996, *Nude by a Bathing Pool Scattered with Roses* (oil on canvas, 203/4 x 281/4 ins / 53 x 72 cm) GBP 14,375. CALAIS, 15 Dec 1996, *Young Woman with a Bunch of Roses* (pastel, 281/4 x 231/4 ins / 72 x 59 cm) FRF 25,000. NEW YORK, 23 May 1997, *Dinner by the Lake* (oil on canvas, 231/2 x 281/2 ins / 59.7 x 72.4 cm) USD 23,000. PARIS, 18 June 1997, *Young Woman in a Négligé by a Lamp* (pastel, 211/4 x 141/4 ins / 54 x 36.5 cm) FRF 32,000. NEW YORK, 23 Oct 1997, *Reading by a Lamp* (oil on canvas, 283/4 x 211/4 ins / 73 x 54 cm) USD 24,150. LONDON, 21 Nov 1997, *In the Boudoir* (oil on canvas, 283/4 x 211/2 ins / 73 x 54.6 cm) GBP 6,325. CHAUMONT, 29 Nov 1997, *Woman by a Hearth* (oil on canvas, 22 x 15 ins / 55 x 38 cm) FRF 12,500. NEW YORK, 18 March 1998, *Woman Arranging a Bouquet of Flowers* (oil on canvas, 25 1/2 x 191/4 ins / 64.8 x 49.2 cm) USD 35,650.

ENJU, also known as Kobori Masakazu, Sakusuke, Go Soho, Kohoan
Japanese, 17th century.
Born 1579, in Koborimura (Omi); died 12 March 1647, in Fujimi, near Kyoto.
Painter, calligrapher, poet, architect. Landscapes.

Enju was a pupil of Taniju. He founded the Enju School, which was named after him.

ENKA CHOSO. See **NANKO**

ENKAI, also known as Jojobo
Japanese, 11th century.
Active during the first half of the 11th century.
Sculptor.

Enkai was a Buddhist monk from Mount Shigi near Nara. He was one of the first sculptors to use the *yosegi* (joined-wood) style of carving, whereby monumental sculptures were made from several different blocks of wood that had been carved separately and then put together. Until that time, these large wooden figures had been carved using the ichiboku technique, meaning out of a single block of wood. Enkai's famous seated statue of *Prince Shotoku Taishi* (572-622), the principal statue in the painting pavilion of Horyu-ji in Nara, is made in the joined-wood manner. An inscription inside it allows us to ascribe this work to him. The childlike features and the modelling of his face and hands display a great realism, undoubtedly due to this new method.

MUSEUMS AND GALLERIES:
NARA (Temple of Horyu-Ji): *Seated statue of Prince Shotoku* (dated 1069).

ENKINGER, Michael
German, 16th century.
Active in Danzig (now Gdansk, Poland).
Sculptor, engineer.

ENKU
Japanese, 17th century.
Born c. 1628, in Gifu Prefecture; died 1695, in Miroku-ji temple, Gifu Prefecture.
Monk-sculptor.

Little is known about the birthplace and life of Enku, a Tendai Buddhist monk, except that he travelled the country widely, sculpting on popular demand, and that his works are in fact a form of devotion. The immense amount of work he produced (he vowed to produce 120,000 pieces) stands apart from traditional Buddhist sculpture of the time. His prolific output was fired by a deep faith; he worked with great speed using a billhook and knife, taking into account the veins in the wood in order to respect its true nature. His works exude an undeniable serenity. They are to be found in numerous temples, most particularly in the regions of Mino and Hida (Gifu province) where he often stayed, but also on the northern island of Hokkaido, where he was to be found between 1665 and 1669, and many other provinces. But they are often difficult to locate, as they are not signed.

BIBLIOGRAPHY:
Dotzenko, Grisha, *Enku: Master Carver*, Kodansha, 1978. Tanahashi, Kazuaki, *Enku: Sculpture Buddhas*, Random House, 1982. Tanahashi, K., *Enku*, Shambhala Publications, 1991. Guth, Christine, *Japanese Art of the Edo Period*, Calmann and King, London, 1996. *Enku: Timeless Images*, Exhibitions International, 2000.

ENKYO, real name: Nakamura Jusuke, original name: Jusuke Shigesuke, artist names: Enkyo, Kabukido Enkyo
Japanese, 18th century.
Born 1749; died 1803.
Painter.

Enkyo was the artist name of Nakamura Jusuke, a writer of *kabuki* plays. Seven half-length drawings of actors from plays performed in 1794 are ascribed to him, works which are obviously highly influenced by Sharaku (who worked in c.1794) but which reveal a talent for analytical portraits and strong line drawing.

BIBLIOGRAPHY:
Fahr-Becker, Gabriele (ed.), *Japanese Prints*, Taschen, Cologne, 1999.

ENNDERSCHIN, Wilhelm, or Andschiz
Austrian, 17th century.
Active in Krems.
Painter.

ENNEKING, John Joseph
American, 19th - 20th century.
Born 4 October 1841; died 1916.
Painter, pastellist. Portraits, landscapes, still-lifes.

John Enneking travelled to Paris, where he was a pupil of Bonnat and Daubigny between 1872 and 1874, then of Lear in Munich. Prior to these travels he had worked in Cincinnati and Boston. He later returned to Boston, where he exhibited at the Boston Art Club. He won medals in numerous exhibitions. He also worked in Minster, Ohio.

MUSEUMS AND GALLERIES:
WORCESTER, MA (AM): *Evening Landscape* (1881, watercolour); *Late Autumn in New England* (1887); *Sunset*; *Ships at Harbor* (drawing).

AUCTION RECORDS:
NEW YORK, 9 Jan 1902, *Boats in Venice*, USD 45. BOSTON, 1903, *Afterglow*, USD 1,050; *November*, USD 400; *November Evening*, USD 1,500. BOSTON, 21-22 Jan 1909, *Landscape at Dusk*, USD 100. HYANNIS, 7 Aug 1973, *Autumn Landscape*, USD 1,200. NEW YORK, 12 May 1974, *Village Church*, USD 1,600. NEW YORK, 20 April 1979, *Autumn Landscape* (oil on canvas, 201/4 x 241/4 ins / 51.5 x 61.6 cm) USD 2,800. NEW YORK, 7 April 1982, *Peaches and Raspberries* (1865, pastel, 10 x 81/4 ins / 25.5 x 20.7 cm) USD 900. NEW YORK, 27 Jan 1983,

Still-life with Peaches and Grapes (pastel, 16¹/4 x 12¹/4 ins / 41.3 x 31.1 cm) USD 800. PORTLAND, 7 April 1984, *Portrait of Grace, the Artist's Daughter* (oil on canvas, 22 x 30 ins / 56 x 76.2 cm) USD 22,000. NEW YORK, 4 Dec 1987, *Fishing Pier* (1886, oil on canvas, 18¹/4 x 24¹/4 ins / 46.2 x 61.3 cm) USD 42,000. NEW YORK, 26 May 1988, *Sunset in Autumn* (oil on canvas, 60¹/4 x 68 ins / 153 x 172.7 cm) USD 39,600. NEW YORK, 30 Sept 1988, *The Old Red Mill* (oil on card, 10 x 14 ins / 25.5 x 35.5 cm) USD 8,800. NEW YORK, 1 Dec 1988, *Spring* (1888, oil on canvas, 22 x 30 ins / 55.9 x 76.2 cm) USD 16,500. NEW YORK, 25 May 1989, *Autumn Landscape* (1897, oil on canvas, 30 x 21³/4 ins / 76.2 x 55.2 cm) USD 19,800. NEW YORK, 1 Dec 1989, *Summer on a Lake* (1888, oil on canvas, 18 x 24 ins / 45.7 x 61 cm) USD 33,000. NEW YORK, 31 May 1990, *Setting Sun* (1877, oil on panel, 11 x 9 ins / 27.9 x 22.8 cm) USD 3,300. NEW YORK, 30 Nov 1990, *Evening Light* (1891, oil on canvas, 42¹/4 x 62¹/2 ins / 107 x 159 cm) USD 33,000. NEW YORK, 17 Dec 1990, *Sailing Boats in Venice* (oil on canvas, 14¹/2 x 22 ins / 36.9 x 55.9 cm) USD 5,775. NEW YORK, 26 Sept 1991, *Flowering Trees in Spring* (1905, oil on canvas, 18 x 24 ins / 45.7 x 61 cm) USD 11,000. NEW YORK, 6 Dec 1991, *Pears* (oil on canvas, 12 x 18 ins / 30.5 x 45.8 cm) USD 35,200. NEW YORK, 28 May 1992, *Summer Afternoon* (1895, oil on canvas, 22 x 34 ins / 55.8 x 86.4 cm) USD 30,800. NEW YORK, 4 Dec 1992, *Garden Flowers* (1897, oil on canvas, 30¹/4 x 22¹/4 ins / 76.6 x 56.2 cm) USD 66,000. NEW YORK, 1 Dec 1994, *Gravelly Path* (oil on canvas, 25 x 30 ins / 63.5 x 76.2 cm) USD 47,150. NEW YORK, 25 May 1995, *Flower Meadows* (1897, oil on canvas, 22 x 30 ins / 55.9 x 76.2 cm) USD 35,650. NEW YORK, 22 May 1996, *Forest at Sunset* (oil on canvas, 39 x 50 ins / 99.1 x 127 cm) USD 10,925. NEW YORK, 25 March 1997, *Winter Landscape; Pastoral Study* (1899, oil on panel and oil on canvas, a pair, 10 x 14¹/4 ins / 25.4 x 35.9 cm and 16 x 14¹/4 ins/40.6 x 35.9 cm) USD 3,162. NEW YORK, 3 Dec 1997, *Pulling out a Splinter* (1894, oil on canvas, 33¹/2 x 45¹/4 ins / 85.1 x 114.9 cm) USD 40,250.

ENNEKING, Joseph Eliot
American, 20th century.
Born 1881, in Hyde Park (Massachusetts); died 1942.
Painter.

Joseph Enneking was a member of the Boston Art Club, the Salmagundi Club and the Connecticut Academy of Fine Arts.

AUCTION RECORDS:
NEW YORK, 14 Feb 1990, *Port* (oil on card, 10 x 12 ins / 25.5 x 30.5 cm) USD 3,300. BOLTON, 1 July 1999, *Old Apple Orchard* (1914, oil on canvasboard, 11 x 14 ins / 28 x 36 cm) USD 1,600. BOSTON, 12 Nov 1999, *Rockport* (oil on canvasboard, 10 x 12 ins / 25 x 30 cm) USD 1,700. NEW YORK, 23 May 2000, *Hollyhocks Garden, Mystic, Connecticut* (oil on canvas, 25 x 30 ins / 63 x 76 cm) USD 20,000. BOSTON, 10 Nov 2000, *View with Country Stream and Bridge* (oil on canvas, 24 x 20 ins / 61 x 51 cm) USD 1,800. BOLTON, 12 July 2001, *Bathers in a Cove* (1909, oil on canvasboard, 10 x 14 ins / 25 x 36 cm) USD 4,000. BOSTON, 16 Nov 2001, *Tree-lined Street, Springtime* (oil on canvas, 20 x 24 ins / 51 x 61 cm) USD 3,750. BOSTON, 22 March 2002, *Breezy Day* (oil on canvas) USD 3,500. NEW YORK, 10 Dec 2002, *Hollyhocks Garden, Mystic, Connecticut* (oil on canvas, 25 x 30 ins / 64 x 76 cm) USD 13,000. BOSTON, 2 Feb 2003, *Old Apple Orchard* (1914, oil on board, 11 x 14 ins / 28 x 36 cm) USD 2,200.

ENNELARD, Henri
Flemish School, 14th century.
Painter.

Henri Ennelard worked at the castle at Hesdin between 1300 and 1306.

ENNEMOND THE PAINTER. See **EVRARD Ennemond**

ENNEVIÈRES, Cécile d'
French, 20th century.
Born in Comines.
Sculptor.

Cécile d'Ennevières was a pupil of E.-J. de Bremaeker. She exhibited at the Salon des Artistes Français from 1929.

ENNICH, Johann Georg
German, 17th century.
Active in Nuremberg in 1697.
Illuminator.

ENNION, Eric Arnold Roberts
British, 20th century.
Born 1900; died 1981.
Watercolourist. Birds.

AUCTION RECORDS:
LONDON, 25 Feb 1992, *Red Partridges on the Moors* (watercolour heightened with white/grey paper, 10³/4 x 13¹/2 ins / 27.3 x 34.2 cm) GBP 1,815. LONDON, 16 March 1993, *Ducks* (watercolour heightened with white/grey paper, 10³/4 x 13³/4 ins / 27.3 x 35.2 cm) GBP 483. LONDON, 22 Nov 1995, *Heron and Black Coots* (1936, watercolour, 13¹/4 x 19 ins / 33.5 x 48.5 cm) GBP 1,495. PENZANCE, 13 June 2002, *Wading Birds Amongst Foliage* (mixed media on paper, 19 x 24 ins / 48 x 61 cm) GBP 1,300. LONDON, 4 July 2002, *Birds* (watercolour and gouache, twelve in one frame, 20 x 26 ins / 52 x 67 cm) GBP 2,600.

ENNIS, Jacob
Irish, 18th century.
Born c. 1728; died 1771, in County Wicklow.
Painter. History painting, portraits.

Having trained under Robert West in Dublin, Jacob Ennis went to Italy. Upon returning to Ireland he became a teacher at Dublin Art School, and died as a result of falling off a horse.

ENO, Henry C.
American, 19th century.
Active in New York c. 1885.
Engraver (etching).

Henry C. Eno is known mainly for ex-libris and landscapes.

ENOCH, François
French, 17th century.
Active in Paris in 1678.
Painter.

ENOCK, Arthur Henry
British, 19th century.
Born 1828 or 1829, in Glamorgan; died 1917.
Painter, watercolourist. Landscapes.

Arthur Henry Enock worked in Birmingham and exhibited in London at the Royal Society of Painters in Watercolours from 1882.

AUCTION RECORDS:
LONDON, 27 April 1908, *In Clywd Valley* (watercolour) GBP 3. NOTTINGHAM, 17 Dec 1981, *Harvest Scene* (1877, oil on canvas, 11¹/2 x 11¹/2 ins / 29.5 x 29.5 cm) GBP 360. LONDON, 15 Dec 1983, *HMS Entreprise in Dartmouth Harbour* (watercolour, 15³/4 x 23¹/2 ins / 40 x 59.5 cm) GBP 1,100. LONDON, 30 Jan 1991, *Totnes on the Dart at Dusk* (watercolour, 20 x 29¹/2 ins / 51 x 75 cm) GBP 1,430. LONDON, 13 Nov 1992, *Surrounding Areas of Teignmouth* (watercolour, 28³/4 x 19¹/2 ins / 73.3 x 49.5 cm) GBP 1,430. LOUGHTON, 2 Nov 2000, *Twilight, Dartmouth* (watercolour, 13 x 23 ins / 33 x 58 cm) GBP 1,000. BATH, 22 July 2002, *Dartmouth, Extensive View across the Estuary to the Open Sea* (1895, watercolour, 13 x 20 ins / 34 x 52 cm) GBP 1,800. ASHBURTON, 13 Nov 2003, *Twilight at Totnes* (watercolour, 13 x 20 ins / 33 x 51 cm) GBP 2,100.

ENOKIDO, Maki
Japanese, 20th century.
Born 1938, in Tokyo.
Print artist.
Enokido Maki graduated in 1960 from the fine arts section of the Bunka-Gakuin School in Tokyo. He has taken part in several international print exhibitions, including the exhibition of contemporary Japanese prints in Geneva in 1966; the fifth Tokyo International Print Biennale in 1966; the Vancouver International Print Exhibition in 1967; and the third Japan Art Festival Association exhibition in 1968.

ENOTRIO, Pugliese
Argentinian, 20th century.
Born 1920, in Buenos Aires; died 1989, in Rome.
Active in Italy.
Painter. Landscapes.
Pugliese Enotrio worked mainly in Calabria.
AUCTION RECORDS:
ROME, 29 March 1976, *Boats* (oil on panel, 19 3/4 x 27 1/2 ins / 50 x 70 cm) ITL 480,000. ROME, 12 June 1986, *Ischia* (oil on canvas, 33 1/2 x 25 1/2 ins / 85 x 65 cm) ITL 1,300,000. ROME, 15 Nov 1988, *View of a Village* (oil on panel, 19 3/4 x 23 1/2 ins / 50 x 60 cm) ITL 1,300,000. ROME, 10 April 1990, *Ulivo at Rosarno* (oil on panel, 27 1/2 x 23 1/2 ins / 70 x 60 cm) ITL 2,000,000. ROME, 30 Oct 1990, *Calabrian Landscape* (oil on panel, 23 1/2 x 19 3/4 ins / 60 x 50 cm) ITL 1,700,000. ROME, 25 March 1993, *Calabrian Landscape* (oil on canvas, 19 3/4 x 27 1/2 ins / 50 x 70 cm) ITL 1,700,000. ROME, 30 Nov 1993, *Calabrian Landscape* (oil on card, 20 x 27 1/2 ins / 51 x 70 cm) ITL 2,530,000. ROME, 19 April 1994, *House in Ischia* (oil on panel, 23 1/2 x 27 1/2 ins / 60 x 70 cm) ITL 2,530,000. ROME, 28 March 1995, *Calabrian Landscape* (1971, oil on panel, 19 3/4 x 27 1/2 ins / 50 x 70 cm) ITL 2,760,000. ROME, 15 June 1999, *Italian Landscape* (1963, oil on canvas, 55 x 102 ins / 140 x 260 cm) ITL 6,200,000. ROME, 25 Nov 1999, *Rooftops* (oil on panel, 24 x 31 ins / 60 x 80 cm) ITL 3,200,000. ROME, 21 Nov 2002, *Landscape in Calabria* (1964, oil on canvas, 31 x 39 ins / 80 x 100 cm) EUR 1,900. ROME, 22 April 2004, *Landscape on the Tirreno* (oil on canvas, 24 x 35 ins / 60 x 90 cm) EUR 1,500. MILAN, 10 June 2004, *Railway* (oil on board, 28 x 39 ins / 70 x 100 cm) EUR 4,600.

ENRICH
Spanish, 15th century.
Painter.
Enrich worked in the court of Charles III of Navarre in Tafalla, around 1400.

ENRICH, Juan, or Henrich
Spanish, 18th century.
Born 1743 or 1744, in Barcelona; died c. 1795 or 1796, in Barcelona.
Sculptor.
Juan Enrich studied in Barcelona and Rome and on 1 December 1782 was made an honorary member of the Real Academia de San Fernando for a terracotta low relief. In Barcelona he produced a large number of statues, historical low reliefs, busts and funerary monuments. Various churches in Barcelona and the surrounding area have statues of saints by Enrich; one example is the statues of the apostles on the façade of the Monserrat monastery.

ENRICO
Italian, 13th century.
Miniaturist.
This artist was active in Pisa in 1238 and may be identical with Enrico da Pisa.

ENRICO
Italian, 15th century.
Painter.
Enrico was active in Venice in 1444. He may be one and the same person as the painter Henrico de Alemania, who was released from prison in Venice in 1462.

ENRICO. See also first name

ENRICO, Antonio d'. See **TANZIO DA VARALLO**

ENRICO, Giovanni d'
Italian, 17th century.
Born in Valsesia; died 1644, in Montrigone, near Borgosesia (Piedmont).
Sculptor, architect.
The churches in Varallo and Alagna (Valsesia) contain sculptural groups by Giovanni d'Enrico, who also worked on the Calvary at Crea (Monteferrato). He was the brother of Melchiorre d'Enrico and Tanzio da Varallo.

ENRICO, Melchiorre d'
Italian, 16th - 17th century.
Painter, fresco artist. Religious subjects.
Melchiorre d'Enrico was the brother of Giovanni d'Enrico and Tanzio da Varallo. He was active in Valsesia (Piedmont) at the end of the 16th century. He painted frescoes for the façade of the church of Riva Valdobbia, and *Christ in the Desert*, *Christ on the Mount of Olives* and *Arrest of Jesus* for Sacro Monte de Varallo.

ENRICO DA CERNUSCO
Italian, 15th century.
Sculptor.
Enrico da Cernusco worked on Milan cathedral from 1483 to 1492.

ENRICO DA MILANO, or Arichus Jacobini
Italian, 15th century.
Active in Brescia between 1438 and 1459.
Painter.
Enrico da Milano was the son of Jacobino de Papazzoni.

ENRICO DA PISA
Italian, 13th century.
Miniaturist.
This artist was a Franciscan monk.

ENRICO DE SPEDEDO
Italian, 15th century.
Painter.
Enrico de Spededo worked for Pope Martin V.

ENRICO DI TEDICE
Italian, 13th century.
Painter.
This artist was active in Pisa, where he painted for the church of S Martino a *Crucifix* with scenes of the Passion.

ENRICO FIAMMINGO. See **ARRIGO FIAMMINGO**

ENRICO MALINIS. See **ARRIGO FIAMMINGO**

ENRIGHT, Maginel
Maiden name: Wright
American, 19th - 20th century.
Born 19 June 1877, in Weymouth (Massachusetts); died 1966.
Painter.
Maginel Enright was the wife of Walter J. Enright. She studied in her home town.

ENRIGHT, Walter J.
American, 20th century.
Born 3 July 1879, in Chicago.
Painter.
Walter Enright studied at art schools in Chicago.

ENRILE Y FLÓREZ DE GUTIÉRREZ, Emilia
Spanish, 19th century.
Active in Cádiz.
Painter.

Emilia Enrile y Flórez de Gutiérrez studied at the Cádiz academy. She painted a number of portraits, genre pieces and religious subjects. Her works include *Andalusian Fiesta* and *Virgin of Sorrows*.

ENRIQUE
Spanish, 13th century.
Died 1284.
Sculptor (wood/ivory).

This artist was the son or grandson of King Alfonso X of Castille, and created in wood and ivory a statuette of the Virgin that is still in the possession of the convent of the Holy Clares in Allariz (Galicia).

ENRIQUE
Spanish, 15th century.
Died shortly before 1492, in Toledo.
Active in Toledo.
Glass painter.

Enrique is perhaps identical with 'maestro Henrique' (Master Henry) who made the stained glass windows for the cathedrals of Seville and Toledo.

ENRIQUE, or Anrique
Spanish, 16th century.
Born c. 1539, in Flanders.
Active in Spain.
Painter.

Enrique was a citizen of Valladolid in 1567.

ENRIQUE. See also **ANRIQUE, ENRICH** and **HENRI**

ENRIQUE, Barros Fernández
Spanish, 20th century.
Born in Bilbao.
Sculptor.

Barros Fernández Enrique studied in Paris under J. Boucher. In 1929 he exhibited *First Love* at the Salon des Artistes Français in Paris.

ENRIQUE, Juan
Spanish, 16th century.
Active in Seville in 1534.
Painter.

Juan Enrique may have carried out the decoration of the grand organ of Seville Cathedral in 1537. He may be identical with Juan Anriquez.

ENRÍQUEZ, Carlos
Cuban, 20th century.
Born 1901, in Santa Clara; died 1957.
Painter. Scenes with figures.

Carlos Enríquez studied at the central college in Cuba in 1920 before being sent to the USA by his family to study engineering. He abandoned this career and enrolled at the Fine Arts Academy of Pennsylvania but left the academy early to return to Cuba. In 1930, he went to Europe, remaining there for four years, mainly in Spain where he studied the painting of El Greco, Zurbarán, Velázquez and Goya. From 1937 his painting became steeped in the tropical atmosphere of Cuba. Whether painting the typical sugar cane cutters of Haiti or horses stampeding out of hell, Enríquez expressed himself through a strange blend of naivety and the fantastical. Between 1923 and 1925, he exhibited regularly with the association of painters and sculptors in Havana, and in 1992 his work appeared in the *Lam and his Contemporaries* exhibition at the Studio Museum in Harlem. He also showed his work in solo exhibitions in the 1930s in Madrid and Oviedo, in 1934 at the Liceo in Havana. The latter exhibition caused a scandal and was closed to the public.

BIBLIOGRAPHY:
Juan, A. de, '*Carlos Enríquez en Cuba*' in *Pintura cubana: Temas y variaciones*, Havana, Mexico City, 1978, 1980. *Carlos Enríquez*, exhibition catalogue, Museo Nacional de Bellas Artes, Havana, 1979. *Carlos Enríquez*, exhibition catalogue, Cuban Museum of Arts and Culture, Miami, 1986. Martínez, J., *Cuban Art and National Identity: The Vanguardian Painters, 1925-50*, Gainesville, 1994.

MUSEUMS AND GALLERIES:
NEW YORK (MoMA) - SAN FRANCISCO (MA).

AUCTION RECORDS:
NEW YORK, 9 July 1980, *Dancers* (1948, watercolour, gouache and Indian ink, 17¾ x 12¾ ins / 45 x 32.7 cm) USD 850. NEW YORK, 30 May 1984, *Untitled* (c. 1948, ink/mounted paper/card, 8¾ x 12¾ ins / 22.2 x 32.7 cm) USD 1,500. NEW YORK, 28 Nov 1984, *Eva* (oil on canvas remounted on board, 49 x 35 ins / 124.5 x 89 cm) USD 16,000. NEW YORK, 29 Nov 1984, *Rider* (gouache, 19¾ x 15 ins / 50 x 38 cm) USD 4,000. NEW YORK, 21 May 1986, *Wild Horses* (1955, watercolour and pen, 16 x 19½ ins / 39.7 x 49.8 cm) USD 1,800; *Two Prostitutes* (1944, oil on canvas, 26½ x 22¼ ins / 67 x 56.5 cm) USD 5,000. NEW YORK, 21 Nov 1988, *Sugar Cane Cutters* (oil on canvas, 30 x 23¾ ins / 76 x 60.5 cm) USD 4,400. PARIS, 21 June 1989, *Horse's Head* (oil on canvas, 17¼ x 15½ ins / 43.5 x 39.5 cm) FRF 27,000. NEW YORK, 2 May 1990, *Mahogany in the Garden* (1946, oil on canvas, 20 x 16¼ ins / 51 x 41 cm) USD 6,050. NEW YORK, 15 May 1991, *Horses* (oil on canvas, 31 x 25 ins / 79 x 63.5 cm) USD 9,900. NEW YORK, 19-20 May 1992, *Male Nude* (1949, oil on canvas, 24 x 20 ins / 61 x 50.8 cm) USD 18,700. NEW YORK, 25 Nov 1992, *Horses* (1955, watercolour, gouache and ink/paper, 15½ x 19¾ ins / 39.5 x 50 cm) USD 3,300. NEW YORK, 18 May 1993, *Little Girl with a Fish* (1947, oil on canvas, 25 x 18¼ ins / 63.5 x 46.3 cm) USD 11,500. NEW YORK, 18 May 1994, *Odile* (1945, oil on canvas, 31¼ x 25 ins / 79.1 x 63.5 cm) USD 25,300. NEW YORK, 14-15 May 1996, *The Abduction* (1937, oil on canvas, 42¼ x 36½ ins / 107 x 93 cm) USD 107,000. NEW YORK, 28 May 1997, *Female Nudes* (ink wash/paper, a pair, each 9¼ x 7½ ins / 23.8 x 19 cm) USD 5,175. MIAMI, 27 Feb 1999, *Strength and Desire* (oil on canvas, 24 x 18 ins / 61 x 46 cm) USD 12,000. NEW YORK, 2 June 1999, *Female Nude* (oil on panel, 18 x 13 ins / 46 x 32 cm) USD 12,000. NEW YORK, 20 Nov 2000, *Two Women* (1955, oil on canvas, 20 x 16 ins / 50 x 41 cm) USD 12,000. NEW YORK, 21 Nov 2000, *Guajiro on Horseback with a Colt* (1954, oil on canvas, 33 x 24 ins / 84 x 61 cm) USD 48,000. NEW YORK, 28 May 2002, *Two horses* (1956, gouache, watercolour and ink, 15 x 11 ins / 39 x 29 cm) USD 9,000. NEW YORK, 18 Nov 2003, *Woman* (c. 1945, oil on panel, 24 x 18 ins / 61 x 46 cm) USD 35,000. TORONTO, 14 June 2004, *Tilin García on Horseback* (1946, oil on canvas, 20 x 16 ins / 51 x 40 cm) CAD 17,000. TORONTO, 14 June 2004, *Horses in a Landscape* (1953, oil on canvas, 24 x 29 ins / 60 x 73 cm) CAD 25,000.

ENRÍQUEZ, César
Venezuelan, 20th century.
Born 1918, in Puerto Cabello.
Painter.

César Enríquez studied at the school of fine arts in Caracas and taught the children's class at the school.

ENRÍQUEZ, Flamenco
Spanish, 16th century.
Active in Valladolid.
Painter.

Valladolid School.
Enríquez Flamenco often worked with Juan de Juni, who held him in high esteem and invited him to stay for a prolonged period in his house. Enríquez died there at the age of 20.

ENRÍQUEZ, Francisco
Spanish, 18th century.
Active in Granada c. 1700.
Painter.
Francisco Enríquez worked for the monastery of San Bernardo.

ENRÍQUEZ, Nicolas
Mexican, 18th century.
Born possibly in Guadalajara; died after 1780.
Painter. Religious subjects.
Nicolas Enríquez was active in Mexico City from 1730 to 1768 and has also been identified in Guadalajara. In 1768 he painted eight scenes of the Passion in Mexico City.
MUSEUMS AND GALLERIES:
GUADALAJARA (Mus. Natural History) - GUADALAJARA (Museo de las Artes de la Universidad) - WROCLAW: *Virgin* (1770).
AUCTION RECORDS:
PARIS, 30 Nov 1981, *Adoration of the Magi* (1744, oil on card, 41 1/4 x 33 ins / 105 x 84 cm) FRF 9,200. NEW YORK, 17 May 1994, *Virgin of Guadalupe* (1777, oil on canvas, 32 1/4 x 23 3/4 ins / 82.2 x 60.3 cm) USD 101,500. NEW YORK, 18 May 1995, *Immaculate Conception* (1746, oil on canvas, 23 1/2 x 16 1/4 ins / 59.7 x 41 cm) USD 11,500. NEW YORK, 2 June 1999, *Virgin of Guadalupe* (1774, oil on copper, 28 x 20 ins / 72 x 52 cm) USD 18,000. COLUMBIA, 25 Sept 1999, *Grief of the Virgin Mary* (1766, oil on copper, 36 x 25 ins / 91 x 64 cm) USD 15,000. MADRID, 19 Dec 2000, *Virgin of Guadalupe* (1770, oil on canvas, 41 x 30 ins / 103 x 77 cm) ESP 2,750,000.

ENRÍQUEZ, Rafael
Spanish, 19th century.
Born in the Philippines.
Painter. Genre scenes.
AUCTION RECORDS:
PARIS, 19 June 1989, *Spanish Scene* (1884, oil on canvas, 21 1/4 x 17 1/4 ins / 54 x 44 cm) FRF 24,000.

ENRÍQUEZ Y FERRER, Francisco
Spanish, 19th century.
Born 30 July 1811, in Granada.
Painter, architect.
Francisco Enríquez y Ferrer was the son of Francisco Enríquez y García. He worked mainly as an architect.

ENRÍQUEZ Y FERRER, María Carmen
Spanish, 19th century.
Born in the 19th century, in Granada.
Painter. Genre scenes, portraits.
María Carmen Enríquez y Ferrer was the daughter of Francisco Enríquez y García.

ENRÍQUEZ Y FERRER, Soledad
Spanish, 19th century.
Painter. Portraits, genre scenes, landscapes.
Soledad Enríquez y Ferrer was the daughter and pupil of Francisco Enríquez y García. She exhibited in Granada and Madrid from 1835.
MUSEUMS AND GALLERIES:
MADRID (Prado): several paintings.
AUCTION RECORDS:
PARIS, 4 Jan 1897, *Performing Dog*, FRF 155; *Acrobat*, FRF 160.

ENRÍQUEZ Y GARCÍA, Francisco
Spanish, 19th century.
Portrait painter.
Francisco Enríquez y García was director of the fine arts academy in Granada.

ENROTH, Erik
Finnish, 20th century.
Born 1917, in Tampere.
Painter, fresco artist.
Erik Enroth initially painted industrial subjects observed in his hometown, the most important industrial centre in Finland. These included work sites, stadiums and railway tracks. From his stays in Spain, he brought back subjects inspired by bull-fighting. Thereafter, he went to the USA, where he was commissioned to carry out a number of frescoes. In 1950, he was awarded the state prize. His forms and colour are violent and his drawing, in which blue, red and black prevail, is full of contrasts.

ENS, Caspar
Danish, 17th century.
Active c. 1680.
Engraver, print publisher.
Caspar Ens is mentioned by Nagler. He engraved plates for the *Chronicle of Frederick II*.

ENS, Giovanni
Italian, 18th century.
Painter.
Ens painted the frescoes of the *Birth and Death of St Nicholas of Tolentino* at S Marco in Milan, as well as representations of *Saints Andrea and Charles Borromeo* in the council chamber of the Palazzo della Ragione.

ENS, Johann Karl
German, 18th century.
Active in Limbach (Bavaria) in 1791.
Painter (porcelain).

ENS, Karl
German, 19th century.
Born 14 April 1802, in Lauscha (Thuringia); died 12 November 1865, in Lauscha.
Painter (porcelain), lithographer, draughtsman.
The lithographs of this artist, like his oil paintings, depict scenes from the lives of huntsmen, colliers and shepherds in the forests of Thuringia. He was the director of the Ens and Greiner porcelain works at Lauscha.

ENS, L.
German, 19th century.
Active in Hamburg.
Lithographer.
Ens engraved portraits and genre scenes, working mainly for Charles Fuchs.

ENSCHEDÉ, Adriana Maria
Dutch, 19th century.
Born 29 September 1864, in Haarlem.
Painter. Flowers.

ENSCHEDÉ, Catharina Jacoba Abrahamina
Dutch, 19th century.
Born 7 June 1828, in Haarlem; died 24 October 1883, in Bloemendaal.
Painter.
The Gemeentemuseum (municipal museum) in Haarlem possesses a *Portrait of Aletta Hanemans* by Catharina Jacoba Abrahamina Enschedé.

ENSCHEDÉ, Christina Gérarda
Dutch, 19th century.
Born 10 December 1791, in Haarlem; died 6 March 1873, in Haarlem.
Painter, watercolourist, draughtswoman. Still-lifes (including flowers/fruit).

C Enschedé
1829

Museums and Galleries:
Haarlem: *Fruit* - Haarlem (Teylers Mus.): *Flowers* (two watercolours).
Auction records:
Amsterdam, 9 Nov 1993, *Still-life of Flowers and Fruit on a Marble Entablature* (1832, oil on canvas, 14¼ x 12¼ ins / 36.5 x 31 cm) NLG 12,650.

ENSCHEDE, Jan
Dutch, 18th century.
Sculptor.
Jan Enschede was a member of the Guild of St Luke in Haarlem in 1729.

ENSCHEDÉ, Sandrina Christina Elisabeth.
See **TROYEN**

ENSFELDER, Eugène
French, 19th century.
Born 7 October 1836, in Strasbourg; died 11 May 1876, in Strasbourg.
Painter, draughtsman.
In 1869 and 1870 Eugène Ensfelder exhibited pen-and-ink drawings, including his *Sermon*, at the Paris Salon.
Museums and Galleries:
Mulhouse: two drawings.

ENSING, Jan
Dutch, 19th century.
Active in Groningen c. 1850.
Lithographer.
Eight portraits by Jan Ensing are extant.

ENSLEN, G. Christian
French, 18th century.
Active in Strasbourg.
Painter.
G. Christian Enslen was the brother of Johann Carl Enslen, whom he accompanied on his journeys in hot-air balloons. In 1784 he drew a *View of Strasbourg* with the launching of a hot-air balloon. A portrait of his wife by him was shown at the Exposition Alsacienne of portraits at Strasbourg in 1910.

ENSLEN, Johann Karl
German, 18th - 19th century.
Born 1759, in Stuttgart; died 1848, in Dresden.
Painter. Landscapes.
A physicist, Enslen was one of the inventors of the panorama in Germany.
Museums and Galleries:
Dresden: *Panorama of Dresden New Town and of the Castle Tower*.

ENSLEN, Karl Georg
Austrian, 19th century.
Born 20 September 1792, in Vienna; died 17 April 1866, in Lille.
Painter, engraver. Landscapes.
This artist was the son of Johann Karl Enslen. After studying at the Berlin academy, he travelled in Italy, Sweden, Norway and Denmark. He produced numerous lithographs, and his expert knowledge of drawing and perspective are evident in his panoramic views.
Museums and Galleries:
Berlin - Dresden - Gdansk - Leipzig: *View of the Augustusplatz in Leipzig in 1851* - Lille: *Bay of Naples* (watercolour) - Lübeck - Munich - Naples - Pompeii - Rome - Stockholm.
Auction records:
Copenhagen, 7 Nov 1984, *San Giorgio Maggiore, Venice* (1855, gouache, 6¼ x 9¾ ins / 16 x 25 cm) DKK 22,000.

ENSOM, William
British, 19th century.
Born 1796; died 1832, in Wandsworth, near London.
Engraver.
William Ensom executed several plates for different Annals. The best of these are of George IV and Lady Wallscourt, in the style of Sir Thomas Lawrence, which were made for the *The Bijou*. Other notable works include: *Christ Blessing the Bread*, in the style of Carlo Ducci; *St John in the Desert*, in the style of Carlo Cignani; *Christ Appearing to Mary Magdalene*, in the style of Titian; and *Marchioness of Salisbury*, also in the style of Sir Thomas Lawrence.

ENSOR, James Sidney
Belgian, 19th - 20th century.
Born 13 April 1860, in Ostend, to a Flemish mother (Maria Catharina Haegheman) and a British father; died 19 November 1949, in Ostend.
Painter, watercolourist, pastellist, engraver. Figure compositions, figures, portraits, landscapes, still-lifes.
Groupe des Vingt (XX).
James Sidney Ensor's parents kept a somewhat unusual souvenir shop, 'Souvenirs d'Ostende', where sea-shell boxes, vases from the Far East, model ships in bottles, masks and carnival accessories were sold. He started to draw and paint at a young age, and his parents did not oppose his vocation. From 1873 to 1875 he was a pupil at Notre-Dame secondary school in Ostend and studied with two local painters, Dubar and Michel van Cuyck. In 1877, at 17, he left his hometown - for what was to be the only significant absence in his life - to study for three years at the Académie Royale des Beaux-Arts in Brussels, where he was a fellow student of Ferdinand Khnopff, whom he was to criticise in the future. He followed the guidance of the director Jan Portaels, but drew above all on the styles of Hals, Rembrandt, Goya, Turner, Daumier and Manet. He established a few important relationships in Brussels, notably with Ernest Rousseau, a physics professor and rector at the University of Brussels and his wife Mariette, as well as their son Pierre and their niece Blanche. It was the Rousseau family who introduced him to the intellectual milieu of Brussels.

In 1879, on his return to Ostend, Ensor set up his studio in a garret high above his parents' shop, where he was to produce almost all his work. From Ostend, he maintained his Brussels friendships, which kept him up to date with artistic and intellectual activities. In 1881 Félicien Rops, a major Belgian artist, introduced him to the Belgian avant-garde group La Chrysalide, in whose gallery he had his first exhibition. The following year, two of his paintings were accepted by the Salon de Paris. In this same year, 1882, he became a member of the Brussels art society Essor, taking part in the group's Salon as well as in the Salon of the Artistic and Literary Circle, while his much-criticized *Woman Eating Oysters* was rejected by the Antwerp Salon and refused again the next year, this time by the Essor group.

In 1883 17 painters, including Ensor, and three sculptors withdrew from Essor to establish the Les Vingt group with Octave Maus. The first exhibition of the new group took place in Brussels in 1884, and the group invited numerous foreign artists to attend every year. The annual events of the group were virtually Ensor's only opportunity to show his paintings and even in that milieu he met with incomprehension from some members. This was the period in which he was radically modifying his style. In 1884 the Salon de Bruxelles refused his entire contribution and, even worse, in 1888 and 1890 Les Vingt, of which he was one of the co-founders, separated his paintings from its annual exhibition. It was also during this same period of change in his painting that he began in 1886 to execute etchings and drypoints. Henceforth, his engraved work largely echoed his paintings.

Only a few intellectuals were interested in his painting. These included Eugène Demolder, Émile Verhaeren and Mauruce Maeterlinck. In 1891 he had dealings with La Libre Esthétique, but despite both the appreciation which the group afforded him and a first positive review published by

Demolder he put his studio and its contents up for sale in 1892 out of exasperation and severe discouragement. He failed to find a buyer.

In 1894, at the time of his one-man show, organized by Demolder in a Brussels gallery, the Musée des Beaux-Arts bought Ensor's *Lamp Boy*, a sombre painting from 1880. At the same time, the Musée de Liège refused the *Woman Eating Oysters*, the earliest clear canvas of 1882, which had already had a chequered career. From 1895, somewhat disillusioned, Ensor only painted periodically, abandoning his fantasies, daydreams and diabolical art, and even losing his predilection for painting the sea, which had always inspired him and which held higher symbolic meanings for him: 'The miraculous sea of Ostend, sea of opals and pearls, virgin sea which I love. Alas! The spongy slime of painting dares to soil your divine facets and stain your dresses woven with iris and spangled with white satin.'

In December 1898, the Parisian periodical *La Plume* commemorated an extensive exhibition presented by the same journal in Paris the year before, including tributes by Camille Lemonnier, Edmond Picard, Émile Verhaeren, Maurice Maeterlinck and others. 1899 saw all Ensor's work exhibited in the Palais des Beaux-Arts in Brussels and in 1900 he discovered negro art at an exhibition at the Palais de Tervueren. In this respect he was ahead of André Derain and Pablo Picasso. He was unsettled by the style and did not appreciate such masks: 'I condemn unremittingly the unwelcome mask from the underworld of Africa, Asia and Oceanea,' he is quoted as saying. These masks could not, however, leave him indifferent; even if their magic destination distinguished them from the derisory masks of his own kermesses, what they both had in common was the human face. In 1901 he joined the foundation of the Libre Académie de Belgique. In 1908 Émile Verhaeren wrote a monograph on him.

He continued to paint, albeit very slowly, until 1933, repeating his old themes, with slight variations, somewhat enthusiastically. He also continued engraving. But most often he preferred to sit in front of his harmonium and compose, for he was a talented musician. In 1911 he wrote the libretto, composed the music and drew or made lithographs for the costumes and set of a ballet for puppets *La Gamme d'amour*, which was to be shown at Brussels in 1920. He publicly criticized, with derisive sarcasm, the honours which were conferred on him too late. Not even his old fellow student from the Académie des Beaux-Arts in Brussels Ferdinand Khnopff was spared; for example, Ensor described him as 'an obstinate painter in grissaille, crammed with splenetic banalities. Retardaire, old-fashioned Mona Lisa-ist, M Khnopff remains above all the uncontested enigmatic poet beneath unfathomable mysteries'.

At the same time as Ensor's artistic verve waned, his reputation grew. He was 'discovered', as it were, especially by the collectors Emma Lambotte and François Franck, the Belgian minister of state, who did much to make his work known. Whereas in 1900 his work appeared at the Exposition Universelle in Paris almost anonymously and without glory, receiving a derisory third-class bronze medal, over the following decades more and more studies were dedicated to him.

His development was comparable to that of Edvard Munch, another important forerunner of modern Expressionism, in that he was at his most prolific before 1900 although his career continued for many years after that date. At his most productive, he elicited a pitifully meagre response. It was only later that he was understood, and when the time came for honours it was too late because bitterness had replaced his pleasure in painting. His isolated lifestyle hardly facilitated the promotion of his work. Although he lived until his death with Augusta Boogaerts, whom he nicknamed 'the siren', they never married. After his three years at the Académie des Beaux-Arts in Brussels, Ensor only left Ostend for occasional brief trips to Holland, London and Paris. He lived for a long time in the Ensor family house, having conserved the estate after the business had ceased on the death of his parents, and the fact that he lived among the sentimental objects of the shop for so long meant that he did not detach himself from his childhood memories, as is evident in his work.

With regard to his early drawings and paintings, numerous influences or associations have been evoked, including Turner, Manet, Daumier, Degas and Renoir. However, he had already found his individual direction, as witnessed in *Woman with Turned-up Nose* or the *Portrait of the Painter at his Easel*. From the 'sombre period ' of about 1879, most of his paintings still belonged to 19th-century Verism or, more particularly, to the Flemish Realist-Expressionist vein, as in *Lamps* or *The Lamp Boy* of 1880 and *The Colourist* or *The Rower* of 1883, while others reveal Parisian influences: *Middle-class Drawing-room* of 1881. *Woman Eating Oysters* of 1882 is considered to be his first clear painting, in which the fusion of the two former and contemporary styles is handled. The light is still subdued in this work but colour shimmers in its brilliance, piercing the shade, as in his *Portrait of the Painter in a Flowered Hat*.

It was at this time precisely that Ensor moved from an Intimist painting tradition, still traditionally Flemish in its soft lighting, to his new clear and coloured style. This was also the time when he came up against the incomprehension of his parents, of whom he was to write 'the old Realists spat on everything'. In the sombre paintings of his youth he handled traditional themes such as portraits, interiors, landscapes and still-lifes. From 1883 he dealt with diverse themes in a completely different spirit and moreover, there is evidence of the phasmagorical imagination which was to dominate his output and single him out.

Henceforth, Ensor practised a sort of Post-Impressionist Expressionism. He adopted the use of lively colours at their maximum intensity from Impressionism, juxtaposing them so as to obtain an optical mix. However, he deviated from the original intention of Impressionist technique, which was to capture light for its own sake and negate the reality of objects, so that they moved ceaselessly according to their lighting, becoming purely aesthetic and detached from all moral or psychological consideration. Instead, Ensor used the technique to produce significant images of everything which unsettled his own sensibility, his personal thoughts and obsessions.

From this period on, his work was mainly made up of landscapes of either the town itself and the harbour of Ostend or, more often, seascapes. He also produced still-lifes of fish, like the famous *Ray* of 1892, or speckled shells, masks painted in different colours and other choice objects from the curios of the family shop. These striking images have, perhaps, led to the critical neglect of his other work, which included fantastic scenes, carnivals and discussions between skeletons on stage, in which his own portrait sometimes figured.

In painting landscapes and still-lifes it should be noted that Ensor employed a very light, almost blinding technique with iridescent tones, whereas when he painted fantastic scenes the colours were mostly intense, aggressive and clashing, though still placed against a very light background. One might simplify by saying that landscapes, seascapes and still-lifes made up the bulk of his output and that the masks and skeletons typify a more sarcastic sideline. (His few self-portraits do not fall into either category.) His carnival scenes include corteges, grimacing or comic masks, meetings between demons assuming human airs or humans disguised as devils, as in the *Tribulations of St Antony* of 1887, and dealings between skeletons, such as his *Skeletons Trying to*

Warm Themselves of 1889. In general, critical commentaries deduce an ironic, even disillusioned analysis of the human comedy and a sense that nothing of this comedy counts in the face of death.

Ensor's most famous painting, the *Entry of Christ into Brussels in 1889* (now in the Paul Getty Museum in Los Angeles), was preceded in 1885-1886 by six charcoal sketches, *Christ's Haloes or the Sensitivities of Light*, of which the final painting was the development of the third halo, *Lively and Radiant Entry into Jerusalem*. In this work, an enormous canvas over 12 feet (3.5 metres) wide, painted in 1888, it is evident that he wished to show what would happen if Christ came back to the men of the modern world. He seems to imply that he knows exactly where he, James Ensor, would be - as the painter who was so often ignored by the multitude, he is identified with Christ, ignored by the crowd and denied by his disciples. Christ advances, a weak, almost naked, figure mounted on a poor ass, dwarfed by the carnival crowd, whose gross stupidity is represented by the fact that all the faces have been replaced by masks with fixed grotesque or comic expressions. They greet him in total confusion, with the slogan 'Vive Jésus Roi de Bruxelles,' (Long live Jesus, King of Brussels) at the same time as 'Vive La Sociale' (Long Live the Social State). The blues, reds and greens amplify the jerky tumult of the bystanders, even if the chrome-yellow used for the copper of the fanfares is now green and faded. It is kermesse, madness, and one understands that if one of them suddenly cried 'Kill him!' the same mob, alienated and manipulated, would put Christ to death, recrucify him with the same enthusiasm. In this demonic celebration of human stupidity, in its parades of monsters 'where all the hard races vomited by the sea are swarming', Ensor must be counted as having inherited the Flemish atmosphere of Pieter Brueghel and Hieronymous Bosche, in the Flemish tradition of the Kermesse.

Despite this apparent pessimism, Ensor's vision is not desperate - there is also enormous laughter in his kermesses. In numerous cases, by representing himself under the masks, he makes himself the accomplice of death, with which it is better to be on first name terms, inevitable as it is. The mask is not necessarily linked to caricature: 'for me the mask signifies purity of tones, overshrill expression, sumptuous decoration, large unexpected gestures, disordered movements, exquisite turbulence'.

In his output of engravings, which includes 138 numbers plus two series of lithographs - 31 for the *Scenes from the Life of Christ* of 1921 and 22 for the *Gamme d'amour* of 1929 - one finds the same themes depicted in his paintings, as in *Cathedral, Fantastic Ball, Kermess at the Mill, Death Pursuing the People, King Plague, Murderer, Battle of the Golden Spurs, Skeletons Fighting for the Body of a Hanged Man, Ray, Dead Cock, Intrigue* and of course *The Entry of Christ into Brussels*, which he engraved some 10 years after having painted the canvas, adding to the original banderoles those of the *Belges insensibles*, the *Vivisectors*, the *Butchers of Jerusalem* and even an advertising poster for *Colman's Mustard* - this to mark the return of the Son of God to earth at the end of the 19th century. As well as his engravings and lithographs, he also accumulated spontaneous sketches, preparatory drawings and watercolours.

In the two years before he painted the *Entry of Christ into Brussels* he had already carried out one third of his engraved output, and was at the height of his accomplishment. He had made a new and significant contribution to the history of painting but no one was yet aware of it: when he had begun to find his personal expression in 1883, Van Gogh had not yet painted *The Potato Eaters* and Gaugin had only just handed in his resignation to the bank. When general incomprehension got the better of Ensor's will, he continued to paint his old themes with occasional flashes of inspiration, as in *Rebel Angels Struck down by Lightning, Intrigue* and *Sketetons Fighting over the Body of a Hanged Man*. However, he continued his engraved work, again taking subjects from old paintings, and often handling the theme of Christ. It was also during these long years that Ensor hand-coloured certain prints of his engravings.

Like Edvard Munch and Van Gogh between 1885 and 1895, he becomes more comprehensible in the 20th-century context of Expressionism. Paul Klee admired his engravings and Emil Nolde visited him in 1911; the painters of Laethem-St-Martin, around Constant Permeke and Gustave de Smet, considered him their precursor, and the Dutch artists Jan Toorop and Jan Sluyters were impressed by him. Pierre Alechinsky, who painted a *Homage to James Ensor* in 1956, was strongly indebted to his *Entry of Christ into Brussels* of 1888. Surviving over half a century, Ensor had the bitter joke of reading several obituaries announcing his death in 1943, before he actually died. Perhaps this is fitting, as his work groaned with macabre humour, such as a draped skeleton disguised as a cardinal: 'Towards the land of derision and palpitating anxieties I have led a boat adorned with flames of inked adjectives full sail.'

In 1926, Ensor's works were shown at the Belgian Pavilion at the Venice Biennale. In 1929, on the occasion of the inauguration of the Palais des Beaux-Arts in Brussels, an exhibition was devoted exclusively to his works, and in 1930 King Albert I made him a Baron. In 1932 his work was shown at the Jeu de Paume and in 1939 a major exhibition was organised by the Gazette des Beaux-Arts in Paris. An exhibition, 'The Works of Ensor', was held at the National Gallery, London in 1946, and then, posthumously, at the Musée d'Art Moderne in Paris in 1954 and the Palace des Beaux-Arts in Brussels in 1958. To consecrate his international importance, the exhibition *The Sources of the XXth century: The Arts in Europe from 1884 to 1914*, organized by the Council of Europe at the Musée National d'Art Moderne in Paris, in 1960-1961, included several of his large paintings. In 1983 the museums of Zurich and Antwerp dedicated a retrospective exhibition to Ensor and in 1990 another important exhibition was organized in Paris - the whole of his work was shown at the Petit Palace.

His major one-man shows and retrospective exhibitions are: 1955, Musée national d'Art Moderne, Paris; 1960, Marlborough Fine Art, London; 1983, *James Ensor: Meisteliche Handzeichnungen 1880 bis 1888* (*James Ensor: Masterly Sketches from 1880 to 1888*), Kunsthaus, Zurich; *James Ensor: The Prints*, Musée du Dessin et de l'Estampe Originale, Gravelines; 1990, Musée du Petit Palais, Paris; 1993 *James Ensor: Etchings*, Kunsthalle, Bremen; 1995, *James Ensor: The Engravings. Mira Jacob Collection*, Ancienne Douane, Strasbourg; 1996, *James Ensor: The Baths in Ostend*, Galeries Vénitiennes d'Ostend; 1997, *James Ensor: Theatre of Masks*, Barbican Art Gallery, London; 1999, *James Ensor* Musées Royaux des Beaux-Arts, Brussels.

BIBLIOGRAPHY:

Demolder, E., *James Ensor*, Brussels, 1892. Mont, Pol de, *'De schilder en etser James Ensor'* in *De Vlaamsche School*, Antwerp, 1895. Demolder, E., *James Ensor*, Paris, 1898. Pica, V., *James Ensor*, Bergamo, 1902. Verhaeren, E., *James Ensor*, Van Oest, Brussels, 1908. Garvensburg, Herbert von, *James Ensor, Maler, Radierer, Komponist*, L. Hey, Hanover, 1913. Ensor, James, *Les écrits de...*, Éd. Sélection, Brussels, 1921 (with 36 sketches by the author). Le Roy, G., *James Ensor*, Van Oest, Brussels, 1922. Croquez, Albert, *James Ensor, catalogue de l'œuvre gravé*, catalogue raisonné, Éd. Pierre Cailler, Brussels, 1951. France, Hubert de, *James Ensor. Essai de bibliographie commentée*, Commission belge de bibliographie, Brussels, 1960. *Ensor dans les collections privées*, Gal. Isy Brachot, Brussels, 1965. Van Gindertael, R., *Ensor*, New York Graphic Society, New York, 1975. Farmer, J., *Ensor*, George Braziller, New York, 1976. Lesko, D., *James Ensor's 'The Entry of Christ into Brussels in 1889*, Garland Publishing, New York, 1985. Tricot, Xavier, *James Ensor dans les collections privées*, exhibition catalogue, Gal. Isy Brachot, Paris, 1986. *James Ensor: Radierungen*, exhibition catalogue, Kunsthalle, Bremen, 1993. Palmer, M., *From Ensor to Margritte: Belgian Art 1880-1940*, Editions Racine, Brussels, 1995. *L'Œuvre gravé d'Ensor*, exhibition catalogue, Kunstmuseum, Basel, Musées de la ville, Strasbourg, 1996. Brown, Carol (ed.), *James Ensor 1860-1949*, exhibition catalogue, Barbican Art Gall., London, 1997. Brown, C. (ed.), *James Ensor (1860-1949): Theatre Masks*, Lund Humphries, London, 1997. Ensor, James/Weyergans, François (preface), *James Ensor. Vive l'art vivant*, Séguier, Paris, 1997 (collection of texts by James Ensor). Hostyn, Norbert, *Ensor: la collection du musée des Beaux-Arts, Ostende*, Ludion, Gand, Flammarion, Paris, 1999. Ollinger-Zinque, Gisèle (ed.), *James Ensor*, exhibition catalogue, Musées royaux des Beaux-Arts de Belgique, Brussels, 1999. Becks-Malorney, U., *Ensor*, monograph, Taschen America, Los Angeles, 2000. Hostyn, Norbert, *James Ensor*, Ludion, Ghent, 2001. de Zegher, C. (ed.), *Between Street and Mirror: The Drawings of James Ensor*, University of Minnesota Press, Minneapolis, 2001.

MUSEUMS AND GALLERIES:

AMSTERDAM (Stedelijk Mus.): *Carnival in Flanders* (1888) - ANTWERP (Koninklijk Mus. voor Schone Kunsten): *Woman with Turned-up Nose* (1879); *Woman with a Fan* (1880); *The Painter Willy Finch* (1882); *Bourgeois Salon* (1881); *Afternoon at Ostend* (1881); *Woman Eating Oysters* (1882); *Rower* (1883); *Extensive View of Ostend* (1884); *Destruction of the Rebel Angels* (1889); *Surprise of the Mask Wouse* (1889); *Intrigue* (1890); *Music in the Rue de Flandre, Ostend* (1891); *Skeletons Fighting over a Hanged Man* (1891); *Battle at Waterloo* (1891); *Man of Sorrows* (1891); *Flowers and Vegetables* (1896); *Skeleton Painter* (1896-1897) - BRUSSELS (MAM): *Lamp Maker* (1880); *Chinese Vases and Fans* (1880); *The Artist's Father* (1881); *Russian Music* (1881); *Woman in Blue* (1881); *Scandalised Masks* (1883); *Calvary* (1886); *Carnival on the Beach* (1887); *Skeletons Fighting over a Herring* (1891); *Singular Masks* (1892); *Ray* (1892) - BRUSSELS (Université Libre): *Bad Doctors* (1892) - FLORENCE (Uffizi): *Self-portrait* (1879) - FORT WORTH (Kimbell AM): *Skeletons Warming Themselves* (1889) - GHENT (Mus. voor Schone Kunsten): *Figures* (1880); *Lively and Radiant, Christ's Entry into Jerusalem* (1885-1886, charcoal); *Old Woman with Masks* (1889) - KOMAKI (Menard AM): *Ensor with Masks* (1899) - LIÈGE (Mus. of Modern and Contemporary Art): *Masks and Death* (1897) - LOS ANGELES (Getty Mus.): *L'Entrée du Christ à Bruxelles en 1889* (*Christ's Entry into Brussels in 1889*) (1888, oil on canvas) - MAASTRICHT (Bonnefantenmus.): *Masks* - MUNICH (Neue Pinakothek): *Still-life in the Studio* (1889) - NEW YORK (MoMA): *Tribulations of St Antony* (1887) - OSTEND (Ensor-Museum): *Portrait of the Painter in a Flowered Hat* (1883); *Christ Calming the Storm* (1891); *Drunkards*; *Tramps Warming Themselves*; *Meats* - OSTEND (Mus. voor Schone Kunsten): *The Artist's Mother in Death* (1915) - OTTAWA (NG. of Canada): *Skeletons in the Studio* (1900) - OTTERLO (Kröller-Müller Mus.): *Still-life with Blue Jug* (1890); *Pierrot in Despair* (1890); *Fight* (1896); *Hop Frog's Revenge* (1896); *Flowers* (1909); *Still-life with Cabbage* (1921) - PARIS (Mus. d'Orsay): *Woman in Distress* (1882) - TEL AVIV (MA): *Artist and Model on the Beach* (1895) - TOURNAI (MBA): *Still-life with Duck* (1880) - ZURICH (Kunsthaus): *Fans and Cloth* (1885); *Great Judge (Masks)* (1898, trust); *Beach at Ostend* (1920); *Carnival in Flanders* (c. 1920).

AUCTION RECORDS:

PARIS, 16 June 1955, *Flowers in a Vase*, FRF 455,000. PARIS, 19 March 1958, *Republican Masks*, FRF 750,000. BRUSSELS, 10 June 1960, *Rainy Weather* (oil on card) BEF 34,000. STUTTGART, 3-4 May 1962, *Infamous Vivisectors, with Self-portrait*, DEM 32,000. LONDON, 24 April 1963, *La Gamme d'amour*, GBP 3,000. MILAN, 25 Nov 1965, *Souvenirs, with Self-portrait*, ITL 7,500,000. ANTWERP, 22 April 1969, *Landscape*, BEF 440,000. NEW YORK, 28 Oct 1970, *Vase of Flowers and Figurines*, USD 105,000. PARIS, 29 May 1972, *Penitent Old Soldiers* (1893) FRF 250,000. ANTWERP, 10 Oct 1972, *Players*, BEF 2,500,000. ANTWERP, 2 April 1974, *Plate, Mask and Shells* (pastel) BEF 500,000. ZURICH, 8 Nov 1974, *Garden of Love*, CHF 340,000. ANTWERP, 9 April 1976, *Main Dock* (1888, etching) BEF 85,000. NEW YORK, 20 Oct 1976, *Masks' Wedding* (1910, oil on canvas, 20 x 24 ins / 50.5 x 61 cm) USD 35,000. BREDA, 27 April 1977, *Cathedral* (1886, etching) NLG 5,400. MUNICH, 23 May 1977, *Monsieur de Phocas* (1915, pastel, 19 x 24 1/2 ins / 48 x 62 cm) DEM 46,000. ANTWERP, 18 April 1978, *Model in the Dunes* (1882, oil on canvas, 14 1/4 x 17 3/4 ins / 36 x 45 cm) BEF 950,000. LONDON, 28 June 1978, *Fan Decorated with Clowns and Pierrots* (watercolour/silk, diam. 20 3/4 ins / 53 cm) GBP 600. ANTWERP, 19 Oct 1978, *Cathedral* (etching) BEF 95,000. BRUSSELS, 13 June 1979, *L'assassinat* (1888, etching) BEF 40,000. LONDON, 5 July 1979, *The Artist and the Seven Deadly Sins* (1924, colouring pencil, 7 1/2 x 4 1/2 ins / 19 x 11.5 cm) GBP 2,000. LONDON, 30 June 1981, *Still-life with Kettle and Fan* (1888, lead pencil and graphite/paper, 8 3/4 x 7 1/2 ins / 22.5 x 19 cm) GBP 10,000. LONDON, 24 March 1983, *Landscape* (c. 1910, pastel/silk, 13 x 18 1/2 ins / 33 x 47 cm) GBP 4,000. ZURICH, 6 June 1984, *Figures in the Mountains* (1878, charcoal, heightened with white, 20 1/4 x 15 1/4 ins / 51.5 x 39 cm) CHF 34,000. NEW YORK, 8 Nov 1984, *Entry of Christ into Brussels* (1898, etching, 9 3/4 x 14 ins / 24.7 x 35.7 cm) USD 4,000. LONDON, 3 Dec 1984, *Masks Watching a Negro Juggler* (oil on canvas, 45 1/4 x 37 3/4 ins / 115 x 96 cm) GBP 70,000. LONDON, 24 June 1985, *Walkürenritt* (c. 1888, gouache and pencil, 8 x 11 1/4 ins / 20.3 x 28.5 cm) GBP 25,000. LONDON, 2 Dec 1986, *Old Woman and Masks* (pencil, 7 x 4 3/4 ins / 17.5 x 12 cm) GBP 5,500. NEW YORK, 11 May 1987, *Pierrot's Despair* (1892, oil on canvas, 57 x 76 1/2 ins / 144.5 x 194.5 cm) USD 480,000. LONDON, 1 July 1987, *Christ Crucified* (1900, pastel/mounted paper/panel, 33 3/4 x 25 1/2 ins / 86 x 65 cm) GBP 24,000. LOKEREN, 5 March 1988, *Poplars* (etching/Japanese paper, 6 x 2 x 9 1/4 ins / 15 x 5 x 23.3 cm) BEF 60,000. PARIS, 20 May 1988, *Fantastic Ball* (1889, etching) FRF 4,500. LOKEREN, 28 May 1988, *Hare and Crow* (1883, oil on canvas, 31 1/2 x 39 1/4 ins / 80 x 100 cm) BEF 6,500,000. LOKEREN, 8 Oct 1988, *Plague Here, Plague There, Plague Everywhere* (1904, etching, 7 1/2 x 11 1/2 ins / 19.2 x 29.1 cm) BEF 150,000. PARIS, 20 Nov 1988, *Street Scene* (charcoal, double-sided, 7 1/4 x 9 1/4 ins / 18.5 x 23.5 cm) FRF 50,000. PARIS, 9 April 1989, *Drunkard* (charcoal drawing, 28 1/4 x 22 3/4 ins / 72 x 58 cm) FRF 400,000. NEW YORK, 9 May 1989, *Infamous Vivisectors* (1927, oil on canvas, 24 x 31 ins / 61 x 78.7 cm) USD 264,000. AMSTERDAM, 24 May 1989, *Making a Face* (1889, pencil/paper, 8 1/4 x 6 3/4 ins / 21 x 17 cm) NLG 41,400. LONDON, 19 Oct 1989, *Seascape* (oil on canvas, 21 1/4 x 32 ins / 54 x 81 cm) GBP 29,700; *Rotondités* (oil on canvas, 20 x 24 ins /

50.8 x 60.9 cm) GBP 77,000. AMSTERDAM, 13 Dec 1989, *Self-portrait* (1937, oil on card, 7 1/4 x 6 3/4 ins / 18.5 x 17 cm) NLG 36,800. NEW YORK, 26 Feb 1990, *Still-life with Fruit* (oil on panel, 8 1/4 x 11 ins / 21 x 27 cm) USD 60,500. BRUSSELS, 7 Oct 1991, *Variation on an Adoration of the Shepherds* (etching in colour) BEF 130,000. LONDON, 3 Dec 1991, *Rayons de palette* (oil on canvas, 23 3/4 x 19 3/4 ins / 60.3 x 50.2 cm) GBP 51,700. AMSTERDAM, 12 Dec 1991, *Man with Scarf* (1881, charcoal/paper, 29 1/4 x 22 ins / 74 x 56 cm) NLG 31,050. LOKEREN, 21 March 1992, *View of a Town* (coloured etching, 8 1/4 x 5 3/4 ins / 20.8 x 14.7 cm) BEF 180,000. LONDON, 29 June 1992, *Baths at Ostend* (1890, oil, lead pencil and colour/panel, 14 3/4 x 18 ins / 37.5 x 45.5 cm) GBP 126,500. MILAN, 9 Nov 1992, *Music at Ostend* (1890, etching, 5 x 3 ins / 11.8 x 7.8 cm) ITL 2,000,000. LONDON, 24-25 March 1993, *Corner of Table* (charcoal, pencil and Indian ink, 9 x 13 3/4 ins / 22 x 35 cm) GBP 20,125. NEW YORK, 13 May 1993, *Shell and Tanagra* (coloured chalks and pencil/paper/card, 18 1/2 x 25 ins / 47 x 63.5 cm) USD 13,800. LOKEREN, 15 May 1993, *Landscape* (oil on canvas, 12 x 16 1/2 ins / 30.5 x 42 cm) BEF 700,000. PARIS, 11 June 1993, *Main Dock at Ostend* (1888, etching, 7 x 9 1/4 ins / 17.9 x 23.8 cm) FRF 9,000. LONDON, 21 June 1993, *Woman Eating Oysters* (1882, oil on canvas, 56 x 42 1/2 ins / 142 x 108 cm) GBP 276,500. LONDON, 30 Nov 1993, *Sleeping Woman* (black chalk/paper, 8 3/4 x 6 3/4 ins / 22.5 x 17 cm) GBP 5,750. PARIS, 3 Dec 1993, *Kermess at the Mill* (1889, etching in black heightened with colouring pencil, 5 1/4 x 6 3/4 ins / 13.5 x 17.4 cm) FRF 15,500. LOKEREN, 12 March 1994, *Cathedral* (1898, etching, 10 x 7 1/2 ins / 24.5 x 18.9 cm) BEF 190,000. AMSTERDAM, 31 May 1994, *Still-life with White and Pink Roses in a Chinese Vase and other Chinoiseries on a Table covered with a Cloth* (oil on canvas, 19 3/4 x 15 3/4 ins / 50 x 40 cm) NLG 138,000. PARIS, 3 June 1994, *Entry of Christ into Brussels* (1898, etching and dry-point, 9 3/4 x 13 3/4 ins / 24.7 x 35.2 cm) FRF 49,000. LOKEREN, 8 Oct 1994, *Self-portrait; Various studies* (coloured chalk, 7 3/4 x 9 1/2 ins / 20 x 24 cm) BEF 1,400,000. NEW YORK, 14 June 1995, *Masks and Points* (colouring pencil/paper, 8 1/4 x 6 3/4 ins / 21 x 17.1 cm) USD 6,900. LONDON, 25 Oct 1995, *Breakwater* (oil on canvas, 12 3/4 x 16 ins / 32.5 x 40.5 cm) GBP 26,450. LOKEREN, 9 Dec 1995, *Old Clock* (1941, oil on panel, 8 1/2 x 6 1/4 ins / 21.7 x 16 cm) BEF 550,000. LOKEREN, 9 March 1996, *Garden of Love* (1888, hand-coloured etching/Japanese paper, 4 1/2 x 3 1/4 ins / 11.7 x 8 cm) BEF 180,000. LONDON, 20 March 1996, *Shells and Marine Plants* (1932, oil on canvas, 20 x 24 ins / 50.5 x 61 cm) GBP 51,000. LOKEREN, 18 May 1996, *Huntsman* (1888, etching, 5 x 6 1/4 ins / 11.8 x 15.8 cm) BEF 400,000. LONDON, 3 Dec 1996, *Lady on the Breakwater* (1880, oil on canvas, 12 1/2 x 9 1/2 ins / 32 x 24 cm) GBP 31,050. AMSTERDAM, 4 Dec 1996, *Gilles and the Wild One* (1891, oil and pencil/panel, 4 3/4 x 6 1/4 ins / 12 x 16 cm) GBP 33,350. LOKEREN, 7 Dec 1996, *Shells and Chinoiseries* (oil on panel, 10 1/2 x 14 1/4 ins / 26.5 x 36.5 cm) BEF 1,200,000. AMSTERDAM, 10 Dec 1996, *Drum Major* (c. 1925-1929, oil on canvas, 20 1/4 x 28 1/4 ins / 51.5 x 72 cm) NLG 438,246. AMSTERDAM, 17-18 Dec 1996, *Annunciation* (c. 1912, oil on canvas, 24 x 28 ins / 61 x 71.1 cm) NLG 147,500. PARIS, 13 May 1997, *Les Braconnier* (1882, oil on canvas, 45 1/4 x 65 ins / 115 x 165 cm) FRF 1,600,000. AMSTERDAM, 2-3 June 1997, *Japonaiserie* (1876, oil on card, 10 1/4 x 12 3/4 ins / 26 x 32.5 cm) NLG 165,200. LONDON, 23 June 1997, *Still-life with Lobster and Crab* (1890, oil on canvas, 24 x 29 1/4 ins / 61 x 74.5 cm) GBP 210,500. AMSTERDAM, 12 Oct 1999, *Devils Bothering a Believer* (c. 1940, oil on canvas/board, 15 x 18 ins / 38 x 45 cm) NLG 200,000. AMSTERDAM, 25 Oct 1999, *Fish and Sea Shells* (1895, oil on canvas, 33 x 39 ins / 85 x 100 cm) NLG 420,000. AMSTERDAM, 10 Oct 2000, *Figure Study of Standing Man* (oil on canvas, 39 x 31 ins / 100 x 80 cm) NLG 70,000. AMSTERDAM, 10 Oct 2000, *Miraculous Fishing* (oil on canvas, 38 x 44 ins / 96 x 113 cm) NLG 250,000. LONDON, 6 Feb 2001, *Composition, Revival of Four Works* (1900, watercolour, brush and ink on card, 14 x 19 ins / 35 x 48 cm) GBP 26,000. LONDON, 27 June 2001, *The Virgin and Society Woman* (c. 1933, oil on canvas, 26 x 33 ins / 66 x 85 cm) GBP 85,000. NEW YORK, 9 May 2002, *Souvenirs* (1926, oil on canvas, 28 x 24 ins / 70 x 60 cm) USD 150,000. LONDON, 26 June 2002, *Drunks* (1910, oil on canvas, 33 x 41 ins / 84 x 104 cm) GBP 100,000. LONDON, 4 Feb 2003, *Masks Watching a Turtle* (oil on canvas/panel, 9 x 15 ins / 22 x 37 cm) GBP 100,000. LOKEREN, 13 Dec 2003, *Hare and Crow* (oil on canvas, 28 x 35 ins / 72 x 88 cm) EUR 130,000. LONDON, 2 Feb 2004, *Good Judges* (1891, oil on panel, 15 x 18 ins / 38 x 46 cm) GBP 650,000. LONDON, 22 June 2004, *Glass of Red Wine, Strawberries and Cherries* (1892, oil on panel, 7 x 9 ins / 18 x 24 cm) GBP 220,000.

ENSTAD, Ola

Norwegian, 20th century.

Born 1942, in Oslo.

Installation artist.

Ola Enstad has participated in group exhibitions, notably in 1985 at the Nouvelle Biennale de Paris. She has held solo shows in Norway: 1973 and 1983 at the Kunstnerforbondet Gallery, Oslo; 1976, Tromsø; 1978, Stavanger; 1988, Oslo. The work she exhibited at the Nouvelle Biennale de Paris in 1985 was inspired by the state of tension in East-West relations, and more particularly by the position of Norway in this political climate.

As the world of profundities interests Enstad, her research at that time confronted 'the culture of the frogman'. One of the installations shown, *Body of the Frogmen*, consisted of about 20 frogmen in polyester, all 25 cm (9 in) tall, lined up standing at ease, with webbed hands and feet, wearing wetsuits and masks. This produces an unsettling effect, the play of light and shade carving spaces of immateriality around the anonymous-looking men. However the group is not displayed without a certain humour: 'I produce the tall and small frogman, singing in chorus and communing during times of good and bad fortune. He is tortured under Pontius Pilate, he is dried, laid in the coffin and buried...You wonder how it will end... I don't expect the bubbles to come back up to the surface' (Ola Enstad).

BIBLIOGRAPHY:

Nouvelle Biennale de Paris, 1985, exhibition catalogue, Electa, Le Moniteur, Paris, 1985.

ENTLICHER, Adalbert

German, 18th century.

Born 27 December 1761, in Senftenberg; died 25 April 1806, in Bezdiekow, near Politz.

Painter.

Entlicher was primarily a painter of religious pictures and portraits. He entered the Benedictine monastery in Brewnow in 1795.

ENTOCHUS

1th century.

Sculptor.

Ancient Roman.

Entochus is said by Pliny to have made the statues of Jupiter and Oceanus that decorated the houses of Asinius Pollio.

ENTRALA Y LAMOY, José

Spanish, 19th century.

Born in the 19th century, in Manila (Philippines).

Painter. Landscapes.

José Entrala y Lamoy studied in Madrid under Carlos de Haes. He exhibited a number of landscapes in Madrid in 1880 including *Dutch Landscape* and *Asturian Coast*.

ENTRAYGUES, Charles Bertrand d'

French, 19th - 20th century.

Born 14 July 1851, in Brives.

Painter. Genre scenes, landscapes.

A pupil of Pils, Charles Bertrand d'Entraygues made his début at the Paris Salon in 1876 with *L'Embarras du choix* and was given an honourable mention in 1899. He became a member of the Société des Artistes Français in 1904.
AUCTION RECORDS:
PARIS, 9 March 1897, *Man's Best Friend*, FRF 46; *Invasion*, FRF 42. PARIS, 14 April 1923, *Little Washerwoman*, FRF 105; *Children Playing in a Street*, FRF 135. PARIS, 18 Jan 1924, *Teatime*, FRF 330; *Enfants Jouant à la Procession* FRF 200. LONDON, 4 April 1930, *Picnic* (1887) GBP 5. LONDON, 17 June 1932, *Broken Drum* (1883) GBP 14. LONDON, 21 Dec 1933, *Broken Drum* (1883) GBP 13. PARIS, 10 Oct 1946, *Child Playing*, FRF 4,200. NEW YORK, 14 May 1976, *House of Cards; Paper Cone* (oil on canvas, a pair, 17¾ x 12¼ ins / 45 x 31 cm) USD 2,100. NEW YORK, 18 Sept 1981, *Peasant Family in an Interior* (1883, oil on canvas, 35 x 42 ins / 89 x 106.8 cm) USD 850. NEW YORK, 27 Feb 1986, *La Nichée* (1887, oil on canvas, 13 x 16¼ ins / 33 x 41 cm) USD 6,000. NEW YORK, 28 Feb 1990, *Children's Table* (1882, oil on canvas, 38¾ x 52¼ ins / 98.5 x 132.7 cm) USD 77,000. LONDON, 20 March 1992, *Artillery Battle* (oil on canvas, 15 x 22 ins / 38.1 x 55.9 cm) GBP 8,250. LONDON, 25 Nov 1992, *New Toy* (1883, oil on canvas, 12 x 15¼ ins / 30.5 x 39 cm) GBP 5,500. LONDON, 27 Oct 1993, *Family Gathering* (1886, oil on canvas, 8¼ x 10¾ ins / 21 x 27.5 cm) GBP 2,070. PARIS, 6 March 1996, *Chimney Sweep, Kitchen Boy and Street Urchins on the Fortifications* (oil on canvas, 27¼ x 36¼ ins / 69 x 92 cm) FRF 43,500. NEW YORK, 12 Feb 1998, *Mischievious Choristers* (oil on canvas, 27¾ x 39½ ins / 70.5 x 100.3 cm) USD 13,800.

ENTRES, Guido
German, 19th century.
Born 4 October 1846, in Munich; died 2 June 1909.
Sculptor.
The son and pupil of Joseph Otto Entres, Guido Entres studied at the Munich academy. He executed small sculptures and the statue of the astronomer J. von Lamont in the cemetery in Munich-Bogenhausen. He also supervised the restoration of the church of St James in Munich.

ENTRES, Joseph Otto
German, 19th century.
Born 13 March 1804, in Fürth; died 14 May 1870, in Munich.
Sculptor.
At the age of 15, Entres was already producing sculptures in wood and stone. In 1820, he entered the Munich academy as the pupil of K. Eberhard. His notable works include the monumental *Christ, Godefroy de Bouillon on Horseback within Sight of Jerusalem*, memorials and wooden sculptures in the medieval style for churches, for instance the *Last Supper* in the cathedral in Munich and a statuette of the Madonna above the crypt in the chapter, and the double doors of the main portal of the church of St Peter. In his Munich studio, numerous assistants worked under his direction on altars, crucifixes and statues of saints. He amassed a remarkable collection of medieval sculptures.

ENTRESQUE, d'. See first name

ENTRINGER, Gallienus
Swiss, 16th century.
Active in Freiburg im Brisgau in 1565.
Painter.

ENTRINGER, Hans Ulrich
French, 16th century.
Active in Strasbourg in 1530.
Painter.

ENTZ, Marian W.
American, 19th - 20th century.
Born in New York.
Painter, miniaturist.
Marian Entz settled in New York. She studied with H. Siddons Mowbray, Lucia F. Fuller and Theodora Troyer.

ENTZINGER, Johann
German, 17th century.
Active in Baden at the end of the 17th century.
Engraver.
Entzinger was also a gunsmith.

ENU, Henri
French, 20th century.
Born 1944 (1949 according to some sources).
Mixed media.
In 1968, Henri Enu gave up painting at the easel. He started to reflect on the history of art, shapes and materials, with special reference to the use of the newspaper as an object, seen from the point of view of its texture and its different stages of production. He collaborated with the ART+ Agency. He has had several solo exhibitions since 1975, notably in Paris, Milan and Rio de Janeiro.
BIBLIOGRAPHY:
Parapluie une résistance culturelle 1968-1978, Éd. Alternatives et parallèles, Paris, 1978. *Cantini 84*, exhibition catalogue, Musée Cantini, Marseilles, 1984.
MUSEUMS AND GALLERIES:
MARSEILLES (Mus. Cantini): *Manifesto 1979*.

ENUM, Johan I, or von Enem
Danish, 16th century.
Died before 1594.
Active in Flensburg.
Painter.

ENUM, Johan II, or von Enem
Danish, 16th century.
Born 17th century, in Flensburg.
Painter.
Johan II was the son of Johan I Enum. In 1607, he painted a portrait of burgomaster Peter Jensen Schiffer and his wife for the church at Nyborg. That same year he painted two more portraits, of Mads Lerke and Sidsel Knudsdatter.
MUSEUMS AND GALLERIES:
COPENHAGEN (Statens Mus. for Kunst): *Miniature*.

ENZELBERGER. See **ENZISBERGER Martin**

ENZENBERG
Austrian, 19th century.
Born 31 May 1818, in Vienna.
Miniaturist.
Enzenberg showed a *Portrait of a Young Man* at the exhibition of miniatures in Vienna in 1905.

ENZENSBERGER, Johann Baptist
German, 18th century.
Born 1733, in Sonthofen (Upper Bavaria); died 1773, in Augsburg.
Painter, engraver (burin).
Enzensberger was an engraver of genre and religious subjects.

ENZINAS. See **ENCINAS Alejo de**

ENZING-MÜLLER, Johann Michael
German, 19th century.
Born 1804, in Nuremberg; died 1855, in America.
Engraver (burin).
While still in Germany, where he was a pupil of P. Walther and A. Reindel, this artist engraved religious subjects. In America he was primarily an engraver of portraits.

ENZINGER, Anton
Austrian, 18th century.
Born c. 1683; died 14 May 1768.
Active in Salzburg.
Painter. Hunting scenes.

Enzinger painted small hunting pictures in the Dutch style.
MUSEUMS AND GALLERIES:
INNSBRUCK (Tiroler Landesmus. Ferdinandeum) - MUNICH (NM) - SALZBURG.

ENZINGER, Hans
Austrian, 20th century.
Born 1889; died 1972.
Painter (mixed media), watercolourist. Scenes with figures, urban landscapes.
Hans Enzinger painted numerous views of Vienna.
AUCTION RECORDS:
VIENNA, 19 June 1979, *View of Vienna* (watercolour, 15 x 22 ins / 38 x 55 cm) ATS 32,000. VIENNA, 13 June 1980, *Huntsmen at Rest* (mixed media, 3 1/4 x 3 1/4 ins / 8 x 8 cm) ATS 22,000. VIENNA, 18 Nov 1981, *Vienna Station* (watercolour, 11 1/2 x 18 1/4 ins / 29 x 46.5 cm) ATS 12,000. VIENNA, 16 March 1982, *View of Vienna* (1918, watercolour, 19 3/4 x 26 1/2 ins / 50 x 67 cm) ATS 10,000. VIENNA, 13 Sept 1983, *Carriole in Farmyard* (mixed media/panel, 3 1/2 x 4 ins / 9 x 10 cm) ATS 22,000. VIENNA, 10 Sept 1985, *Market Day* (1939, oil on panel, 5 x 6 3/4 ins / 12.5 x 17 cm) ATS 35,000. VIENNA, 10 Dec 1985, *Sledging* (gouache, 3 1/2 x 4 ins / 8.7 x 10 cm) ATS 25,000. VIENNA, 15 June 1999, *Horse Sledge in Salzburg Winter Landscape* (oil on panel, 5 x 5 ins / 12 x 12 cm) ATS 22,000. VIENNA, 19 Nov 1999, *Hof Town Square with Radetzky Monument* (1913, watercolour, 11 x 16 ins / 29 x 40 cm) ATS 28,000.

ENZINGER, Johann
Bohemian School, 18th century.
Active in Prague.
Sculptor.

ENZISBERGER, Martin, or Enzelberger
Austrian, 15th - 16th century.
Painter.
In 1493, Martin Enzisberger worked for Duke Sigismond at the court of Innsbruck.

ENZO. See **HEINTZ Johann** and **HEINZ Joseph, the Younger**

EONNET DE CHAUDENAY, Lucile
French, 20th century.
Born in Rambouillet.
Painter.
Lucile Eonnet de Chaudenay was a pupil of R. Pougheon and exhibited at the Salon des Artistes Français from 1934.

EOTTES, Hans. See **EWOUTSZ**

EPAGATHUS
1th century.
Born at the beginning of the 1st century BC, in Athens.
Sculptor.
Ancient Greek.
Epagathus, the son of Aristodemus, left his signature on a pedestal that once supported the statue of a certain Tiberius Claudius Novius.

EPAGATUS
6th century BC.
Sculptor.
Ancient Greek.
Epagatus' name, carved in archaic letters, was found on the rocks of the island of Thera in the Cyclades.

EPAPHRAS. See **APHRODISIUS II**

EPARS, Axelle
Swiss, 20th century.
Born 27 June 1916, in Geneva.
Sculptor.
After studying at the Académie Julian, Axelle Epars was a pupil of Kokoschka in Sion. She then attended the Art Students League (ASL) and exhibited at the Salon d'Automne in Paris in 1960. Her sculptures are abstract and consist of combinations of simple shapes, yet they possess a lyrical quality.
AUCTION RECORDS:
PARIS, 11 Feb 1987, *Profiles* (brown-patinated bronze, h. 23 1/2 ins / 60 cm) FRF 9,000.

EPEIUS
13th century BC.
Active c. 1270 BC.
Sculptor, architect.
Ancient Greek.
The mythical Epeius, son of Panopeus, is said by Pausanias to have made the famous Trojan Horse, and a Hermes for the temple of Apollo Lycius in Argos.

EPHORUS OF EPHESUS
4th century BC.
Painter.
Ancient Greek.
Ephorus was the master of Apelles and Pamphilus.

EPHREM, or Ephraim
12th century.
Painter. Religious subjects.
According to a Greek inscription in the choir of the Church of the Nativity, Jerusalem, this painter carried out the magnificent mosaics for the Emperor Mauel Komnenos in 1169. Preserved in the choir are his paintings *The Entry into Jerusalem*, *Doubting Thomas* and *The Ascension*.

EPHRUSSI DE BAUER, Gisela
French, 20th century.
Painter.
Gisela Ephrussi de Bauer exhibited at the Salon des Tuileries.

EPICHARMUS
1th century.
Active in Solesap.
Sculptor.
Ancient Greek.
Epicharmus' name and that of his son, Epicharmus of Rhodes, were discovered on a base probably supporting a statue of a priest and found in 1841 at Rhodes.

EPICKMAN, Refik, or Refik Epikman
Turkish, 20th century.
Born 1901, in Istanbul.
Painter. Genre scenes.
Refik Epickman was one of the founders of the Association of Independent Painters and Sculptors. In 1946 he showed a work entitled *The Bar* at the exhibition organised by the United Nations at the Musée d'Art Moderne in Paris. A figurative painter, he represents reality using his own particular stylistic rules.

EPICRATES
2th century BC.
Sculptor.
Ancient Greek.
Epicrates' signature appears on the base of a statue found in the sanctuary of the Muses at Cnidus, a town in Asia Minor. Close to the base was found a fragment of sculptured drapery, probably from the statue in question.

EPICTETUS I
6th century BC.
Vase painter.
Ancient Greek.
Epictetus' signature is found both as a painter and as a potter. In the period around 525-520 BC, vase painters moved from painting black figures on a red background to red figures on a black background. Naturally, this change did not take place overnight and some artists continued to paint in

the older style while other, more innovative, artists developed a new style. Epictetus sometimes used the two techniques on the same vase, one on the interior and one on the exterior. Unlike his contemporary Cleophrades (also known as Epictetus II), however, he was not able to take advantage of all the implications of the new red-figure style. He produced little more than a negative version of black-figure painting: the white incisions indicating detail within the black figures are replaced by black lines that retain the stiffness of the incisions.

Epictetus' work did not gain in freedom, as it should have done with the adoption of the red-figure technique. He continues to use reddish-purple and white highlights. Despite a certain stiffness, however, it has an impressive sobriety and sureness of line. He decorated in particular the interiors of cups and the centres of plates, to which his simple and well-balanced compositions are particularly well suited. Most often he would depict a single figure, as for example the *Archer in Oriental Costume* (British Museum) and the *Ephebe Riding a Cockerel* (Castle Ashby). One of the most outstanding representatives of the so-called 'Severe Style', he painted subjects from the Dionysus cycle, warriors and ephebes (youths).

BIBLIOGRAPHY:

Arias, Paolo Enrico/Hirmer, Max, *Le Vase grec*, Flammarion, Paris, 1962. Boardman, John, *Athenian Red Figure Vases: The Archaic Period*, Thames and Hudson, London, 1975. Keuls, Eva, *'The Social Position of Attic Vase Painters and the Birth of Caricature'* in *Proceedings of the 3rd Symposium on Ancient Greek and Related Pottery, Copenhagen, August 31-September 4 1987, Nationalmuseet, Ny Carlsberg Glypotek, Thorvaldsens Museum*, Copenhagen, 1988.

MUSEUMS AND GALLERIES:

LONDON (British Mus.): *Archer in Oriental Costume*.

EPICTETUS II. See CLEOPHRADES PAINTER

EPIECES

5th century BC.

Sculptor.

Ancient Greek.

Epieces participated in the decoration of the temple of Athena Polias on the Acropolis in Athens.

EPIFANOV, Ivan

Russian, 17th century.

Active in Moscow in the late 17th century.

Icon painter.

Ivan Epifanov worked at the Moscow state press. In 1689 he painted five icons that were preserved in the Synod Press.

EPIGONUS

3th century BC.

Active in Pergamum at the end of the 3rd century BC.

Sculptor.

Ancient Greek.

Epigonus was one of the founders of the extraordinary blossoming of art that took place in Pergamum at the period when Attalus I sought to immortalise his victories over the Gauls and other neighbouring peoples. Sculpture was seen by the dynasty as an important propaganda weapon, and Epigonus was able to produce pieces that answered the requirements of the time, particularly in his realism. The portrait of *Philetaerus* can reasonably be said to be true to life, in that the features are rough and brutal (although that is not in itself a proof).

The *Dying Gaul* (Capitoline Museum, Rome), part of the group known as the Gauls, shows the sculptor attempting to render with extreme realism the agony of defeat. Another piece seeks rather to arouse a sense of pity, something that was to become a central preoccupation of Pergamene art. It represents a Gaul who, having saved his wife from the hands of the enemy by killing her, now turns his sword on himself (Ludovisi Collection, Palazzo Altemps, Rome). Epigonus succeeds skilfully in presenting figures that take possession of the space around them with great realism.

EPINAT, Fleury

French, 18th - 19th century.

Born 22 August 1764, in Montbrizon; died 7 June 1830, in Pierre-Scize.

Painter. History painting, landscapes.

Having accompanied his master David to Rome, Fleury Epinat spent 15 years in Italy. On his return to France in 1800 he abandoned history painting, which had been his strong point, to devote himself to historic landscape painting. To the 1822 Salon he sent *Destruction of the Town of Herculaneum by the Lava of Vesuvius*.

Under the patronage of the wealthy art enthusiast Lord Ailesbury, Epinat travelled through England and Scotland. He began his famous picture of *Lady of the Lake* with the sites described by Walter Scott in mind.

MUSEUMS AND GALLERIES:

LYONS: *Cool Morning; The St-Jean District; Old Exchange Bridge* (watercolour) - MONTPELLIER: *Two Views of Florence* (sepia).

AUCTION RECORDS:

LONDON, 26 Nov 1973, *View of Lyons* (watercolour and pen) Gns 500.

ÉPINAY, Marie d'

French, 19th - 20th century.

Born 19th century, in Rome.

Painter, pastellist, illustrator. Portraits, genre scenes, flowers.

Marie d'Épinay was a pupil of Prosper d'Épinay and exhibited several times at the Salon de Paris. She also painted and drew book illustrations. Among her paintings are *Anxiety* (1908), *Good Advice* (1909), *Azaleas* (pastel), *Self-portrait* (1910), and portraits of the *Comtesse de Bourbon-Chalus* and her sister, *Madame de la Villesboisnet*.

AUCTION RECORDS:

NEW YORK, 29 May 1981, *Masked Ball* (oil on panel, 18 x 13 ins / 45.7 x 33 cm) USD 1,000.

ÉPINAY, Prosper Charles Adrien d'

French, 19th - 20th century.

Born 13 July 1836, in Port Louis (Mauritius); died 23 September 1914.

Sculptor, draughtsman, caricaturist. Statues, busts.

The son of the politician Adrien d'Épinay, Prosper d'Épinay studied under the sculptor Jean-Pierre Dantan in Paris and Amici in Rome. He is best known for his busts of the empress, the statue of his father in Mauritius, *Golden Girdle*, *St John in the Desert* (bronze), *Sarah Bernhardt*, *Henri Regnault* and *Fortuny*. He exhibited at the Salon des Humoristes in 1909. Épinay also executed many caricature portraits.

MUSEUMS AND GALLERIES:

COPENHAGEN (Ny Carlsberg Glyptotek): *Arria* (terracotta) - NEW YORK (Metropolitan Mus. of Art): *Sappho* (marble) - ST PETERSBURG (Anitchkoff): *The Awakening* (marble).

AUCTION RECORDS:

PARIS, 10 May 1900, *Golden Girdle* (sculpture) FRF 2,400. PARIS, 10 Dec 1980, *Young Hannibal* (bronze, h. 51 1/4 ins / 130 cm) FRF 115,000. PARIS, 9 Dec 1987, *Bust Representing a Young Girl as Flora* (1865, white marble, h. 29 1/2 ins / 75 cm) FRF 7,500. PARIS, 14 June 1993, *Young Woman Doing her Hair* (1876, marble, h. 44 ins / 112 cm) FRF 210,000. NEW YORK, 26 May 1994, *Head of Medusa* (terracotta, h. 16 1/4 ins / 41.3 cm) USD 24,150. NEW YORK, 19 Jan 1995, *Portrait* (bronze relief, diam. 15 1/2 ins / 39.4 cm) USD 3,450.

EPINETTE, Marie
French, 19th century.
Born in Rouen.
Painter, pastellist. Portraits.

Marie Epinette was a pupil of Mademoiselle Keller and Mademoiselle A. Dubos. She made her Salon début in 1875. She also painted on earthenware.

AUCTION RECORDS:
PARIS, 27 Feb 1984, *Portrait of Marie Bachkirtseff* (pastel, 26½ x 17¾ ins / 67 x 45 cm) FRF 7,200.

EPISCOPIO, Bernardino
Italian, 16th century.
Active at the beginning of the 16th century in Castel Durante.
Painter (majolica).

EPISCOPIO, Giuseppe
Italian, 16th century.
Painter.

Giuseppe Episcopio was a pupil of Raphael.

EPISCOPIO, Giustino, called de Salvolini or Lavolini
Italian, 16th century.
Died 1609, in Castel Durante.
Active in Castel Durante.
Painter. History painting.

The son of Bernardino Episcopio and pupil of Luzio Dolce, Giustino Episcopio worked for some time in Rome. His works include an altarpiece in the church of S Clara in Castel Durante and the painting of the high altar, *The Three Magi* in the church of S Francesco. He was also an exponent of majolica decoration.

J. Episcopio.

EPISCOPIUS, Johannes, real name: Jan de Bisschop
Dutch, 17th century.
Born c. 1628, in Amsterdam; died 6 November 1671; in 1686 in The Hague according to some sources.
Draughtsman, engraver (etching), copyist. Religious subjects, genre scenes, rustic scenes, scenes with figures, figures, landscapes, seascapes, urban landscapes, urban views, ruins, animals.

Johannes Episcopius was a lawyer by profession. It is conceivable that after his law studies in Leiden he spent a period in Italy, as is borne out by the large number of Italian pictures cited in old auction catalogues. He seems to have been on intimate terms with C. Huygen the Elder. His drawings comprise both reproductions of Italian and Netherlandish landscapes and also copies of classical and contemporary works.

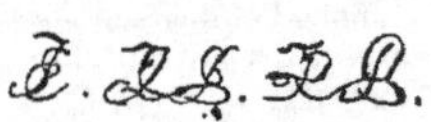

MUSEUMS AND GALLERIES:
AMSTERDAM (Rijksprentenkabinet) - BERLIN (Kupferstichkabinet) - HAARLEM (Prints Collection) - LONDON (British Mus., Department of Prints and Drawings) - VIENNA (Albertina Mus.).

AUCTION RECORDS:
PARIS, 1773, *The Raising of Lazarus* (drawing, after Zucchero) FRF 168; *Two Children Playing* (drawing, after Van Dyck) FRF 39. PARIS, 1847, *Charles II de Scheveningen Leaving* (drawing) FRF 1,186.50. PARIS, 1858, *View over the Town and Valkenof, in Breda* (drawing) FRF 18; *St Christopher Crossing the River* (drawing with bistre wash) FRF 130. PARIS, 7 Dec 1858, *Raising of Lazarus* (bistre drawing) FRF 19; *Palace of Cardinal Grimaldi* (bistre drawing) FRF 10. PARIS, 21-22 Feb 1919, *The Power of Love* (sepia) FRF 40. PARIS, 26 Feb 1923, *The Hollow Track; Market* (two pens and sepia) FRF 355. PARIS, 10 June 1925, *Time Tempers the Wings of Love* (sepia) FRF 210. PARIS, 18 Nov 1926, *Ruins of a Temple of Vesta in Italy* (pen and bistre wash) FRF 60. AMSTERDAM, 29 Oct 1979, *View of Catwyck* (pen and wash, 3¾ x 5¾ ins / 9.7 x 14.8 cm) NLG 8,200. LONDON, 9 Dec 1980, *Village Fête* (pen, wash and black chalk, 13½ x 20½ ins / 34.3 x 52.1 cm) GBP 650. AMSTERDAM, 22 Nov 1982, *Seaside Scene* (pen and wash, 3¾ x 6 ins / 9.7 x 15.3 cm) NLG 19,000. AMSTERDAM, 30 Nov 1987, *Studies of Horses* (pen, wash and red chalk, 3½ x 4¼ ins / 8.7 x 11.1 cm) NLG 7,500. NEW YORK, 11 Jan 1989, *Stranded Boats Laden with Casks* (ink, 4 x 6 ins / 9.3 x 15.1 cm) USD 3,300. PARIS, 28 Sept 1989, *The Washing of the Feet* (oil on canvas, 15¼ x 23¾ ins / 39 x 60.4 cm) FRF 75,000. LONDON, 2 July 1991, *Roman Horseman on a Rearing Horse* (black chalk and ink, 7¼ x 7½ ins / 18.6 x 19.2 cm) GBP 4,620. AMSTERDAM, 25 Nov 1991, *The Aurelian Wall and the Pyramid of Cestius in Rome* (red and black chalk with brown wash, 3¾ x 6 ins / 9.5 x 15.4 cm) NLG 5,750. AMSTERDAM, 25 Nov 1992, *Anchored Boats Laden with Casks* (ink and wash, 35¾ x 59½ ins / 91 x 151 cm) NLG 6,325. AMSTERDAM, 17 Nov 1993, *The Temple of Vesta in Rome* (ink, 4¾ x 8¼ ins / 12 x 20.7 cm) NLG 34,500. NEW YORK, 10 Jan 1995, *Fife and Drum Players* (ink and wash, 12 x 7 ins / 30.5 x 17.6 cm) USD 10,925. LONDON, 3 July 1995, *View of Rome towards the Giardini Farnese with the Arco di Tito on the Left* (4 x 6¼ ins / 9.3 x 15.6 cm) GBP 3,220. AMSTERDAM, 15 Nov 1995, *View of Houses in Deyl with a Peasant Leading his Cows through the Village* (1650, ink and wash, 3½ x 6¼ ins / 9 x 15.7 cm) NLG 51,920. LONDON, 16-17 April 1997, *Christ Washing the Disciples' Feet* (pen, brown ink and wash on black chalk, 10¾ x 12½ ins / 27.4 x 31.5 cm) GBP 575.

EPISTEMON
6th century BC.
Sculptor.
Ancient Greek.

Epistemon son of Hippostratus is attested by an incomplete signature, missing its first two letters, reconstructed from a statue base found near Cape Sunium.

EPKO
Dutch, 20th century.
Born 1918.
From 1950 active in France.
Painter.

Epko participated in the Salon d'Automne, Salon des Indépendants and Salon d'Art Libre in Paris. He had one-man shows in Paris, New York and Japan. He received the Paquement prize in 1959 and the Othon Friesz prize in 1960.

EPLER, Heinrich Karl
German, 19th century.
Born 5 August 1846, in Königsberg (now Kaliningrad, Russia); died 30 April 1905, in Dresden.
Sculptor.

Epler was a pupil in the studio of J. Schilling in Dresden, where he was awarded a silver medal for the bust of a man and a *Ulysses*. He settled permanently in Dresden where he decorated a number of public monuments, including the theatre royal, the palace of state and the academy building. One of the most important works by this artist is the group *Two Mothers*, a scene from the Flood which was bought by the city of Dresden. Epler is noted for his memorials, including that of General von Goeben in the cemetery at Coblenz and a *Victory Weaving a Crown of Laurels*, plaster copies of which are to be found in the municipal museums of Coburg and Dresden. He also executed genre statuettes in marble, including *Woman Gleaning, Child at Play* and a sculpture in bronze, *Bowls Players*.

EPOSIUS. See **JOHANNES**

EPP, Konrad
German, 17th century.
Active in Nuremberg in 1629.
Painter, illuminator.

EPP, Peter
German, 19th century.
Died after 1813.
Active in Heidelberg and Mannheim.
Painter.

Epp was a painter of miniatures; he also copied a large number of works by the masters.

EPP, Rudolf
German, 19th - 20th century.
Born June 1834, in Eberbach; died 8 August 1910, in Munich.
Painter. Figures, portraits, genre scenes.

Rudolf Epp attended the art school in Karlsruhe and was taught by the history painter Descoudres. In 1865 he transferred to Munich.

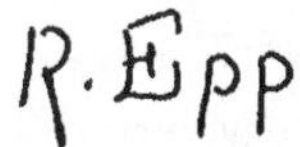

MUSEUMS AND GALLERIES:
BREMEN: *Maternal Faith* - COLOGNE: *Woman from the Black Forest* - GRAZ: *Sleeping Child.*

AUCTION RECORDS:
NEW YORK, 28 March 1901, *Sunday Morning,* USD 475. NEW YORK, 1905, *Young Italian Woman,* USD 110. NEW YORK, 22 March 1907, *Breakfast,* USD 165. NEW YORK, 4-5 March 1909, *Grandmother's Birthday,* USD 205. NEW YORK, 13-14 Feb 1930, *Playmates,* USD 50. BERLIN, 25 March 1965, *Young Tyrolean Woman Knitting,* DEM 3,000. MUNICH, 16-18 March 1966, *Painter and Young Peasant Woman,* DEM 6,300. NEW YORK, 2 April 1976, *Portrait of Young Girl* (oil on canvas, 19 1/4 x 15 1/4 ins / 49 x 38.5 cm) USD 2,800. NEW YORK, 28 April 1977, *Grandmother and Grandchildren* (1877, oil on canvas, 45 x 36 ins / 114 x 91.5 cm) USD 13,000. MUNICH, 21 Sept 1978, *Flirting with the Waiting-maid* (oil/panel, 17 1/4 x 12 1/2 ins / 44 x 32 cm) DEM 4,000. NEW YORK, 30 June 1981, *Woman at her Toilette* (oil on panel, 19 x 13 3/4 ins / 48 x 35 cm) USD 2,900. COLOGNE, 24 June 1983, *Portrait of Young Tyrolean Woman* (oil on card, 13 1/2 x 10 1/4 ins / 34.5 x 26 cm) DEM 13,000. NEW YORK, 19 Oct 1984, *Baby's Breakfast* (oil on canvas, 31 1/2 x 24 1/4 ins / 80 x 61.5 cm) USD 7,750. NEW YORK, 29 Oct 1986, *Pleasant Conversation* (1887, oil on canvas, 32 1/2 x 42 1/4 ins / 82.5 x 107.4 cm) USD 27,000. NEW YORK, 25 May 1988, *Woman and Guitar* (oil on canvas, 8 3/4 x 6 3/4 ins / 22.2 x 17.1 cm) USD 6,050. LONDON, 24 June 1988, *Sleeping Baby* (oil on canvas, 14 1/4 x 16 1/4 ins / 35.9 x 41.3 cm) GBP 6,820. NEW YORK, 23 Feb 1989, *Young Woman with Mantilla* (oil on panel, 11 x 8 1/2 ins / 27 x 21.3 cm) USD 6,050. NEW YORK, 24 May 1989, *Feeding the Youngest One* (oil on canvas, 31 x 25 1/2 ins / 78.7 x 64.8 cm) USD 30,800. NEW YORK, 17 Jan 1990, *Tyrolean Couple* (oil on panel, 5 x 3 3/4 ins / 13 x 9.7 cm) USD 3,850. NEW YORK, 23 Oct 1990, *Portrait of Young Peasant Woman* (oil on panel, 11 1/2 x 8 3/4 ins / 29.2 x 22.2 cm) USD 12,650. NEW YORK, 28 Feb 1991, *Handful of Grass for the Lamb* (oil on canvas, 38 x 26 1/4 ins / 96.5 x 66.7 cm) USD 16,500. NEW YORK, 22 May 1991, *Intruder* (1897, oil on canvas, 32 x 24 ins / 81.3 x 61 cm) USD 26,400. NEW YORK, 28 May 1992, *Feeding the Chickens* (oil on canvas, 33 3/4 x 26 1/2 ins / 85.7 x 67.3 cm) USD 16,500. NEW YORK, 13 Oct 1993, *Hop Harvest* (1870, oil on canvas/card, 36 x 48 ins / 91.4 x 121.9 cm) USD 63,000. NEW YORK, 12 Oct 1994, *Butterfly* (1877, oil on canvas/card, 33 x 23 3/4 ins / 83.8 x 60.3 cm) USD 34,500. LONDON, 17 March 1995, *Bowl of Milk* (oil on canvas, 18 1/4 x 14 3/4 ins / 46.3 x 37.7 cm) GBP 10,350. MUNICH, 27 June 1995, *Portrait of Small Girl* (oil on canvas, 16 1/4 x 12 1/2 ins / 41 x 32 cm) DEM 8,625. NEW YORK, 23-24 May 1996, *Young Drakes* (oil on canvas, 43 x 33 ins / 109.2 x 83.8 cm) USD 32,200.

EPP, William Harold
Canadian, 20th century.
Born 1930, in Glenbush (Saskatchewan).
Sculptor.

William Epp studied at the University of Saskatchewan with Elie Bornstein. He quickly fell under the influence of Rodin, then of Giacometti and Moore, before purifying his forms until only the primary elements remained - cylinder bodies, for example - which he assembled in monumental sculptures.

EPPAN
German, 18th century.
Sculptor.

Eppan worked on the New Palace at Potsdam in 1775.

EPPELE, Gérard
French, 20th century.
Born 1929, in Cherbourg.
Painter.

Gérard Eppele exhibited from 1960 in Vence, and later in Paris, Switzerland, and Sweden. His paintings are characterised by a tangled draughtsmanship that is expressive both of irony and mockery.

AUCTION RECORDS:
PARIS, 4 July 1991, *Frightened Face* (1971, oil on paper/canvas, 40 1/4 x 29 1/2 ins / 102 x 75 cm) FRF 8,500. PARIS, 17 Jan 1994, *Coloured Photograph* (1971, oil on canvas, 51 1/4 x 32 ins / 130 x 81 cm) FRF 6,500.

EPPELIN, Karl
German, 19th century.
Born 1816, in Staffelstein (Bavaria); died 1885, in Wiesbaden.
Painter.

MUSEUMS AND GALLERIES:
WIESBADEN: *Portrait of Bodenstedt.*

EPPENHOFF, Lorenz
Dutch, 17th century.
Active in Berlin c. 1685.
Miniaturist, enameller. Portraits.

Lorenz Eppenhoff executed portraits for the prince-elector and the princess.

EPPENS, Hans
Swiss, 20th century.
Born in Basel.
Painter.

From 1928 Hans Eppens exhibited at the Salon d'Automne in Paris. Some of his religious paintings were also shown at the Kunsthalle in Basel.

EPPENSTEINER, John Joseph
American, 20th century.
Born 14 February 1893, in St Louis (Missouri).
Painter, illustrator.

John Eppensteiner was a pupil at the St Louis School of Fine Arts. He gained numerous prizes: first prize for a landscape in 1923, first prize for modern painting from the St Louis Artists' Guild in 1928, first prize for a landscape in 1930.

EPPER, Ignaz
Swiss, 20th century.
Born 1892, in St Gall; died 1969, in Ascona.

Painter, watercolourist, draughtsman. Local figures, portraits, scenes with figures, landscapes, urban landscapes, still-lifes.

AUCTION RECORDS:

BERN, 6 May 1976, *St Sebastian (recto); City (verso)* (oil on canvas, 39 1/4 x 27 1/2 ins / 100 x 70 cm) CHF 3,800. ZURICH, 30 May 1979, *Portrait of a Man* (oil on canvas, 25 1/2 x 19 1/2 ins / 65 x 49.5 cm) CHF 4,800. ZURICH, 17 May 1980, *Landscape at Twilight* (coloured chalks/paper, 11 1/4 x 13 ins / 28.6 x 33.1 cm) CHF 1,700. BERN, 20 June 1984, *Nocturnal Scene, Three Men and Horse in Moonlight* (c. 1923, charcoal, 15 1/4 x 21 ins / 38.5 x 53.5 cm) CHF 3,300. ZURICH, 9 Nov 1984, *Toreadors* (1931, oil on canvas, 20 1/4 x 24 ins / 51.5 x 61 cm) CHF 5,000. BERN, 23 Oct 1985, *Brothel Scene* (1917-1918, charcoal, 14 1/4 x 19 ins / 36.5 x 48 cm) CHF 5,500. ZURICH, 6 June 1986, *Still-life* (oil on canvas, 23 1/2 x 28 ins / 60 x 71 cm) CHF 9,500. ZURICH, 12 June 1987, *View of Locarno* (watercolour, 12 1/4 x 17 ins / 30.8 x 43.4 cm) CHF 1,500. LUCERNE, 30 Sept 1988, *Near Ascona* (1937, watercolour and Indian ink, 9 x 14 1/4 ins / 22 x 36 cm) CHF 1,250. BERN, 26 Oct 1988, *Paris Street Scene with Gas Lamp* (coloured chalk, 11 1/2 x 14 1/2 ins / 29 x 37 cm) CHF 3,900. ZURICH, 18 Oct 1990, *Harbour* (colouring pencil, 11 x 12 3/4 ins / 27.7 x 32.5 cm) CHF 2,200. LUCERNE, 25 May 1991, *Maneges and Fun Fair* (charcoal/paper, 10 1/4 x 7 1/2 ins / 26 x 19 cm) CHF 3,650. ZURICH, 13 Oct 1993, *Station* (1920, charcoal, 11 1/2 x 14 1/2 ins / 29 x 37 cm) CHF 3,600. ZURICH, 24 Nov 1993, *Boulevard* (1924, soft chalk/paper, 19 3/4 x 16 1/2 ins / 50 x 42 cm) CHF 4,600. ZURICH, 30 Nov 1995, *Fun Fair* (charcoal/paper, 9 3/4 x 7 1/2 ins / 25 x 19 cm) CHF 4,600. ZURICH, 26 March 1996, *Tunnel* (oil on canvas, 17 3/4 x 14 ins / 45 x 35.3 cm) CHF 64,000. ZURICH, 14 April 1997, *Self-portrait* (charcoal/paper, 19 1/2 x 19 3/4 ins / 49.5 x 50 cm) CHF 8,625. ZURICH, 8 Dec 1999, *Meeting of the River Sihl and Schanzen Canal* (colour chalk, 11 x 13 ins / 28 x 33 cm) CHF 5,000. ZURICH, 8 Dec 1999, *Couple in Cafe* (charcoal, 20 x 15 ins / 50 x 39 cm) CHF 6,000. BERN, 22 June 2000, *Waiting Room* (c. 1920, charcoal) CHF 3,900. BERN, 22 June 2000, *Breast Feeding Mother* (c. 1918, charcoal, 18 x 16 ins / 45 x 40 cm) CHF 13,500. ZURICH, 19 June 2001, *Self-portrait* (charcoal, 12 x 13 ins / 30 x 32 cm) CHF 9,000. LUCERNE, 24 Nov 2001, *Family at Table* (1920, charcoal, 21 x 17 ins / 54 x 44 cm) CHF 7,500. ZURICH, 25 Nov 2002, *River* (oil on canvas, 20 x 17 ins / 52 x 44 cm) CHF 17,000. ZURICH, 26 Nov 2002, *Industrial Landscape with Train Track.* (c. 1919, oil on canvas, double-sided, 24 x 20 ins / 61 x 50 cm) CHF 48,000. ZURICH, 23 June 2003, *Interior with Woman* (charcoal, 34 x 19 ins / 86 x 47 cm) CHF 11,000. LUCERNE, 15 Nov 2003, *Nine Figures in Boat - Lifeboat* (pastel and chalk, 22 x 15 ins / 57 x 38 cm) CHF 9,500. ZURICH, 26 May 2004, *Barque with Three Men* (charcoal, three works, 10 x 8 ins / 25 x 21 cm) CHF 6,500. ZURICH, 26 May 2004, *Self-portrait* (charcoal, 15 x 11 ins / 39 x 28 cm) CHF 9,500.

EPPI, Giambono

Italian, 15th century.
Active in Borgo San Donnino (now Fidenza) near Parma in 1490.
Painter.

Giambono Eppi was the father of Giovanni Eppi.

EPPI, Giovanni, called Giannotto

Italian, 16th century.
Active in Borgo San Donnino (now Fidenza) near Parma in 1519.
Painter.

Giovanni Eppi was the son of Giambono Eppi and the father of Pier Angelo Eppi.

EPPI, Giovanni Battista

Italian, 16th century.
Born 1552; died after 1608.
Active in Borgo San Donnino (now Fidenza) near Parma.
Painter.

Giovanni Battista Eppi was the son of Angelo Eppi and executed armorial bearings for the commune in 1618.

EPPI, Pier Angelo

Italian, 16th century.
Born 1513; died 1583, in Borgo San Donnino (now Fidenza) near Parma.
Painter.

Pier Angelo Eppi was the son of Giovanni Eppi.

EPPINGHOFEN, Arthur von

Belgian, 19th - 20th century.
Born 25 September 1852, in Laeken; died 9 November 1940, in Etterbeek.
Active in Germany.
Painter. Animals.

Arthur von Eppinghofen was the first cousin of Henri Suykens.

MUSEUMS AND GALLERIES:

GOTHA (Schloss Friedenstein): *Wild Boar in Winter.*

EPPLE

German, 19th century.
Painter.

Epple exhibited in Karlsruhe from 1823 to 1839.

EPPLE, Emil

German, 20th century.
Born 6 March 1877, in Stuttgart.
Sculptor. Mythological subjects.

Emil Epple studied under A. Donndorf at the academy in Stuttgart and under W. Ruemann at the academy in Munich. He stayed in Berlin, London and Rome, exhibiting in 1900 at the Glaspalast in Munich. Amongst his numerous works are: *Orpheus* (bronze); *Bust of R. Guthmann*; *Roman Lady* (bronze head); *Bacchus at Rest, Diana Sleeping, Anadyomene Kneeling on a Tortoise* (white and green marble); *Prometheus Seated* (bronze); *Diana with Stag* (bronze).

AUCTION RECORDS:

NEW YORK, 24 Oct 1990, *Orpheus* (golden-brown-patinated bronze, h. 27 1/4 ins / 69.2 cm) USD 2,750. MUNICH, 5 July 2000, *Orpheus* (brown patinated bronze, h. 27 ins / 69 cm) DEM 4,600. AMSTERDAM, 16 May 2001, *Apollo Holding a Lyre* (green brown patinated bronze, h. 28 ins / 70 cm) NLG 3,600.

EPPLE, Wilhelm

German, 18th century.
Painter. Religious subjects.

Epple was active at the end of the 18th century. The church in Marienberg, near Altötting, has two altarpieces by this artist.

EPPS, E.

British, 19th century.
Born 1842, in London.
Painter. Genre scenes, landscapes.

E. Epps trained under Alma Tadema. He exhibited at the Suffolk Street Gallery in London from 1874 to 1880.

MUSEUMS AND GALLERIES:

THE HAGUE (Mus. Mesdag): *Townsendhouse Hall.*

EPPS, Jessie Katharine

British, 19th - 20th century.
Born in the second half of the 19th century, in London.
Miniaturist.

Jessie Katharine Epps exhibited at the Salon des Artistes Français in Paris in 1914.

EPPS, Nellie. See **GOSSE**

EPRÉMESNIL, Jacques Louis Raoul

French, 19th century.
Born in Paris.
Painter, watercolourist. Flowers.

A pupil of M. Lambotte, Jacques Eprémesnil made his Salon début in 1879.

EPRON
French, 20th century.
Born 26 May 1876, in Rochefort-sur-Mer.
Watercolourist.

Epron first exhibited in Paris at the Salon des Artistes Français in 1908.

EPSENROD, Dietrich, or Ipsenrod
German, 15th century.
Painter, glassmaker.
Hamburg School.

Dietrich Epsenrod worked for the town of Hamburg from 1463 to 1470.

EPSTEIN, Elisabeth. See **EPSTEIN-HEFTER**

EPSTEIN, Hans
German, 16th century.
Active in Frankfurt am Main in 1536.
Painter.

EPSTEIN, Henri
Polish, 20th century.
Born 20 June 1892, in Lódz; sent to Auschwitz in 1944.
Active in France.
Painter (gouache), watercolourist, pastellist, illustrator.
Portraits, landscapes, mountainscapes, harbour scenes, urban landscapes, still-lifes (flowers/fruit).

After studying in Munich, Henri Epstein went to Paris in 1911 or 1912. He took classes at a free academy in Montparnasse and lived in the artists' colony of La Ruche where he associated with Modigliani, Soutine and Kremegne. He was in Paris during the German occupation and was arrested in February 1944, then deported in June.

He painted landscapes and still-lifes and also produced a few portraits. He illustrated *Vagabondages* (*Wanderings*) by Gustave Coquiot and *Les Rois du maquis* (*Kings of the Maquis*) by P Bernardi.

Epstein exhibited at the Salon des Artistes Indépendants, the Salon d'Automne and the Salon des Tuileries in Paris and was represented at the exhibition *Verfemt. Vergessen. Wiederendeckt. Schicksale expressiver Bildkunst im 20. Jahrhundert* (*Condemned. Forgotten. Rediscovered. The Fate of Expressive Art in the 20th century*), held at the Kulturgeschichtes Museum, Osnabrück in 2001, the intent of which was to rediscover a generation of German or Austrian artists of the 1920s and 30s who had been repressed by the Nazis and fallen into oblivion after the war.

H. Epstein

BIBLIOGRAPHY:

Nieszawer, Nadine/Boyé, Marie/Lanzmann, Claude (preface), *Peintres juifs de l'école de Paris 1905-1939*, Denoël, Paris, 2001.

AUCTION RECORDS:

PARIS, 29 Dec 1927, *Landscape*, FRF 225. PARIS, 29 June 1928, *Bunches of Flowers and Fruit*, FRF 280. PARIS, 21 Nov 1928, *The Brothel*, FRF 170. PARIS, 3 May 1930, *Dancing* (watercolour) FRF 30. PARIS, 7 July 1932, *Flowers and Fruit*, FRF 45. PARIS, 10 Nov 1933, *Mountain VIllage in the Auvergne*, FRF 180; *Girls and Sailors* (watercolour) FRF 110. PARIS, 12 April 1935, *Village in Brittany Near the Sea*, FRF 40. PARIS, 2 Dec 1938, *Fishing Boats*, FRF 30. PARIS, 30 June 1941, *Landscape*, FRF 330. PARIS, 22 July 1942, *Village*, FRF 1,100. PARIS, 24 Feb 1947, *Meudon*, FRF 1,500. PARIS, 4 April 1974, *Bathers on the Beach*, FRF 14,000. VERSAILLES, 24 Oct 1976, *Village* (oil on canvas, 22 x 18 ins / 56 x 46 cm) FRF 10,000. BERN, 27 April 1978, *Landscape in Provence* (oil on canvas, 19 3/4 x 24 1/2 ins / 50 x 62 cm) CHF 3,500. VERSAILLES, 8 Nov 1981, *Village in the Basque Country* (1931, oil on canvas, 28 3/4 x 39 1/2 ins / 73 x 100.5 cm) FRF 9,600. GENEVA, 25 Nov 1983, *Seaside Village* (watercolour and pencil, 15 1/4 x 22 1/2 ins / 39 x 57 cm) CHF 1,400. VERSAILLES, 18 March 1984, *Houses in the Trees* (oil on canvas, 14 3/4 x 18 ins / 37.5 x 45.5 cm) FRF 6,800. PARIS, 11 Dec 1985, *Landscape* (oil on canvas, 21 1/4 x 25 1/2 ins / 54 x 65 cm) FRF 20,000. LONDON, 12 June 1987, *Study of Kathleen* (watercolour and pencil, 17 3/4 x 23 ins / 45 x 58.5 cm) GBP 1,900. PARIS, 30 Nov 1987, *Breton Landscape* (oil on canvas, 20 x 25 1/2 ins / 51 x 65 cm) FRF 8,100. PARIS, 20 March 1988, *Landscape with Red Roofs* (oil, 19 3/4 x 25 1/2 ins / 50 x 65 cm) FRF 19,000; *Water Mill* (1934, oil on canvas, 17 3/4 x 20 3/4 ins / 45 x 53 cm) FRF 13,000; *Harbour at Low Tide* (1930, oil on canvas, 19 3/4 x 25 1/2 ins / 50 x 65 cm) FRF 22,500. PARIS, 21 April 1988, *Girls in a Bar* (watercolour and gouache, 19 x 19 3/4 ins / 48 x 50 cm) FRF 3,200. PARIS, 29 April 1988, *Harbour* (watercolour, 15 3/4 x 19 3/4 ins / 40 x 50 cm) FRF 5,600. PARIS, 4 May 1988, *Country Party* (oil on canvas, 23 1/2 x 28 3/4 ins / 60 x 73 cm) FRF 15,600. TEL AVIV, 26 May 1988, *Two Women Near a River* (1931, oil on canvas, 21 1/4 x 25 1/2 ins / 54 x 65 cm) USD 4, 950. PARIS, 1 June 1988, *Small Harbour* (watercolour and pen, 15 1/4 x 19 3/4 ins / 39 x 50 cm) FRF 2,800. PARIS, 20 June 1988, *Off Fishing* (oil on canvas, 20 3/4 x 25 1/2 ins / 53 x 65 cm) FRF 12,000. PARIS, 23 June 1988, *Country Scene* (oil on canvas, 25 1/2 x 32 ins / 65 x 81 cm) FRF 7,600. VERSAILLES, 6 Nov 1988, *Harbour in Brittany* (watercolour, 15 1/4 x 19 ins / 38.5 x 48.5 cm) FRF 3,900. PARIS, 16 Dec 1988, *Cowman* (oil on canvas, 23 1/2 x 32 ins / 60 x 81 cm) FRF 6,500. PARIS, 12 Feb 1989, *Harbour* (watercolour, 15 3/4 x 19 3/4 ins / 40 x 50 cm) FRF 12,000. LONDON, 24 May 1989, *Fishermen's Village* (oil on canvas, 18 1/4 x 24 ins / 46.5 x 61 cm) GBP 5,720. TEL AVIV, 30 May 1989, *Village Street* (1934, oil on canvas, 15 x 24 1/4 ins / 38 x 61.5 cm) USD 8,800. PARIS, 22 June 1989, *Landscape with Trees* (watercolour, 15 x 17 3/4 ins / 38 x 45 cm) FRF 4,200. PARIS, 8 April 1990, *Young Sailor* (oil on canvas, 32 x 21 1/4 ins / 81 x 54 cm) FRF 50,000. PARIS, 11 May 1990, *Sunflowers* (oil on canvas, 25 1/2 x 21 1/4 ins / 65 x 54 cm) FRF 22,000. TEL AVIV, 31 May 1990, *Walk in the Park* (oil on canvas, 18 x 25 1/2 ins / 46 x 65 cm) USD 9,350. TEL AVIV, 19 June 1990, *Lake, Boats and Figures* (gouache, 18 x 23 1/4 ins / 45.5 x 59 cm) USD 1,430. NEW YORK, 10 Oct 1990, *Man with a Hat* (oil on canvas, 24 x 18 1/4 ins / 61 x 46.1 cm) USD 3,630. VERSAILLES, 21 Oct 1990, *Barges Moored Near a Bridge* (oil on canvas, 19 3/4 x 25 1/2 ins / 50 x 65 cm) FRF 23,000. PARIS, 25 March 1991, *Landscape* (oil on canvas, 25 1/2 x 32 ins / 65 x 81 cm) FRF 25,000. PARIS, 17 April 1991, *Village* (1917, oil on canvas, 18 x 24 ins / 46 x 61 cm) FRF 36,000. NEUILLY, 23 Feb 1992, *Tuna Boats* (watercolour, 14 1/2 x 18 ins / 37 x 46 cm) FRF 6,800. PARIS, 17 May 1992, *Beach Scene* (oil on canvas, 21 1/4 x 28 3/4 ins / 54 x 73 cm) FRF 16,000. LE TOUQUET, 8 June 1992, *Breton Harbour* (1930, oil on canvas, 22 x 25 1/2 ins / 55 x 65 cm) FRF 18,000. NEW YORK, 12 June 1992, *Area Around La Drouette* (oil on canvas, 18 1/4 x 24 ins / 46.4 x 61 cm) USD 1,980. TEL AVIV, 20 Oct 1992, *Vase of Flowers* (oil on canvas, 25 1/2 x 21 1/4 ins / 65 x 54 cm) USD 6,050. NEW YORK, 10 Nov 1992, *Still-life* (1930, oil on canvas, 24 x 28 3/4 ins / 61 x 73 cm) USD 1,870. NEW YORK, 23 Feb 1994, *Portrait of a Woman* (oil on canvas, 25 3/4 x 19 3/4 ins / 65.5 x 50 cm) USD 1,380. PARIS, 27 March 1994, *Pastoral Scene* (oil on canvas, 51 1/4 x 63 3/4 ins / 130 x 162 cm) FRF 53,000. PARIS, 26 March 1995, *Area Around the Village* (oil on canvas, 21 1/2 x 25 1/2 ins / 54.5 x 65 cm) FRF 12,000. PARIS, 15 May 1996, *River's Edge* (oil on canvas, 19 3/4 x 24 ins / 50 x 61 cm) FRF 12,000. CALAIS, 15 Dec 1996, *Garden* (1912, oil on canvas, 18 x 24 ins / 46 x 61 cm) FRF 15,000. PARIS, 20 Jan 1997, *Fishing Boats Returning to Concarneau* (oil on canvas, 38 1/4 x 51 1/4 ins / 97 x 130 cm) FRF 41,000. PARIS, 16 March 1997, *Paris, Quai d'Anjou and Ile St Louis* (oil on canvas, 21 1/4 x 25 1/2 ins / 54 x 65 cm) FRF 23,000. PARIS, 25 June 1997, *Landscape on the River* (oil on canvas, 18 x 22 ins / 46 x 55 cm) FRF 14,500. PARIS, 17 Oct 1997, *River at the Botttom of the Village* (oil on canvas, 19 3/4 x 28 3/4 ins / 50 x 73 cm) FRF 16,000. CALAIS, 23 May 1999, *Path near to Rivulet* (oil on canvas, 24 x 29 ins / 60 x 73 cm) FRF 29,000. PARIS, 25 Oct 1999, *View of Provence* (oil on canvas, 21 x 26 ins / 54 x 65 cm) FRF 34,000. PARIS, 16 Nov 2000, *Route through the Trees* (oil on canvas, 28 x 21 ins / 72 x 54 cm) FRF 57,000. PARIS, 8 Dec 2000, *Three Women Seated at a Table* (oil on canvas, 20 x 26 ins / 51 x 66 cm) FRF 40,000. CALAIS, 10 June 2001, *Little Path near Village* (oil on canvas, 21 x 29 ins / 54 x 73 cm) FRF 48,000. LONDON, 13 Nov 2001, *Still-life of a Pineapple beside a Vase of Flowers on a Table* (oil on canvas, 18 x 24 ins / 46 x 61 cm) GBP 4,600. PARIS, 27 June 2002, *Fishing Village* (oil on canvas, 20 x 26 ins / 50 x 65 cm) EUR 11,000. PARIS, 30 Oct 2002, *Dress-makers* (1923, oil on canvas, 28 x 35 ins / 72 x 90 cm) EUR 10,000. PARIS, 17 June 2003, *Village* (oil on canvas, 29 x 21 ins / 73 x 54 cm) EUR 14,000. WARSAW, 19 Oct 2003, *Still-life with Flowers and Pineapples* (c. 1930, oil on canvas, 18 x 24 ins / 46 x 61 cm) PLN 40,000. PARIS, 15 June 2004, *Landscape with Large Trees* (oil on canvas, 21 x 26 ins / 54 x 65 cm) EUR 6,000. PARIS, 15 June 2004, *Two Woman and Bird* (oil on canvas, 24 x 20 ins / 61 x 50 cm) EUR 6,200.

EPSTEIN, Jacob (Sir)
American, 19th - 20th century.
Born 1880, in New York, to Russian-Polish parents; died 19 August 1959, in London.
Active in Britain from 1905, naturalised 1907.
Sculptor (including bronze/marble), painter (including gouache), watercolourist, draughtsman. Religious subjects, portraits, animals. Statues, monuments.
Vorticism.
London Group.

Jacob Epstein first studied at the Arts Sudenets League in New York and then in 1902 moved to Paris and enrolled at the École Nationale des Beaux-Arts. In Paris he met Rodin, and, by visiting the Louvre, became strongly attracted to non-European sculpture. In 1905 he settled in London. Epstein promoted a new approach to sculpture, following the 'direct' sculptural process in which no model or detailed maquette is used but which concentrates on respecting and bringing to life the material employed, preserving its texture and colour while bringing forth from the material, for example a block of stone, the physical power of the form. This 'truth to materials' would have a direct impact on younger generation of British sculptors, notably Henry Moore and Barbara Hepworth.

In 1907 he received his first major commission to create a series of sculptures for the headquarters of the British Medical Association in The Strand, London (now Zimbabwe House). The 18 statues he made were considered scandalous. Epstein offended public taste, because the statues were stark, expressive and naked and had nothing of the classical decorum expected of public works. In 1911 he was commissioned to create the tomb of Oscar Wilde for the Père Lachaise cemetery in Paris. Again the work was controversial, for again it was frankly naked, and the style was drawn directly from Assyrian sculptures in the British Museum. While in Paris he met Picasso, Brancusi and Modigliani and became interested in their approach and creative methods which, in rejecting classical forms and looking for inspiration in both the nature of materials and non-Western traditions, while broadly similar to his own.

Back in London he was a founder member of the London Group (1913) and took part in the activities of the Vorticist movement, led by the painter and writer Wyndham Lewis and the American poet Ezra Pound. Epstein, with Pound, Wyndham Lewis, Christopher Nevinson, William Roberts, Edward Wadsworth and the sculptor Gaudier-Brzeska, founded the Rebel Art Centre group. The Modernist aims of Vorticism, the manifesto of which was published in 1915 in the magazine *Blast*, had something in common with the 'machine aesthetic' of the Italian Futurists. Epstein's *Rock Drill* (1913, Tate Britain), in which a semi-abstract human figure is fused with a real rock drill, is among the works he produced at this period. His first (and controversial) solo exhibition was held at the Twenty-One Gallery in London (Dec 1913-Jan 1914).

He soon distanced himself from the Vorticist movement, and after World War I, which had confirmed his fears about the 'machine age', he largely lost interest in contemporary artistic movements. In both his large sculptures and his 'direct' sculptures he retained the Expressionist power of the African sculptures with which he had become familiar during his time in Paris. His later works are an expression of the 'vitalism' that he had, from his earliest years, found in the works of the American poet Walt Whitman. He became successful both as a creator of monumental works (carved in stone or cast) and intimate portraits modelled in clay. Among the former are: *Rima* (1925), a memorial in Hyde Park, London; *Night and Day*, commissioned for the headquarters of the Underground Railway Company at St James's Park Station, London (1928); *The Visitation*, a monumental bronze sculpture (1926); *Genesis* (1931); *Ecce Homo* (1935); *Adam* (1935); *Lucifer*, a monumental bronze (1945); *Lazarus* (1949); *Christ in Majesty*, a bronze sculpture for Llandaff Cathedral (1957); *Madonna and Child*, a monumental bronze for Cavendish Square in London; *The Trade Union Congress War Memorial* at the Trade Union Congress Building in London (1958); and *St Michael*, a monumental bronze for the new Coventry Cathedral. He also sculpted many portraits of well-known figures of the time, including *Einstein*, *Bernard Shaw*, *Joseph Conrad*, *Somerset Maugham*, *Pandhit Nehru* and the singer *Paul Robson*.

He was made doctor *honoris causa* of the universities of Aberdeen and Oxford and was knighted in 1954. His work entitled *Let There Be Sculpture* (London, 1940) is an autobiography in which he gives his views on art and the life of the artist.

Epstein

BIBLIOGRAPHY:
Powel, L.B., *Jacob Epstein*, Chapman and Hall, London, 1937. Epstein, Jacob, *Epstein, An Autobiography*, Arno, 1955. Buckle, R., *Jacob Epstein, Sculptor*, The World Publishing Company, Cleveland, 1963. Cork, R. (ed), *Jacob Epstein: The Rock Drill Period*, exhibition catalogue, Anthony d'Offay Gall., London, 1973. Cork, R., *Vorticism and Abstract Art in the First Machine Age*, 2 vols, London, 1975-1976. Haskell, A. (ed.), *Epstein Centenary, 1980*, exhibition catalogue, Ben Uri Aart Gallery, London, 1980. Silber, E., *The Sculpture of Epstein*, Phaidon, Oxford, 1986. Silber, Evelyn (ed.), *Jacob Epstein: Sculpture and Drawings*, Henry Moore Sculpture Trust, 1987. Friedman, T./Silber, E. (ed.), *JJacob Epstein: Sculpture and Drawings*, exhibition catalogue, City Art Gallery Leeds, and Whitechapel Art Gallery, London, 1987. Gardiner, S., *Epstein: Artist Against the Establishment*, London, 1992. Cork, Richard, *Jacob Epstein*, Tate Publishing, 1999. Rose, June, *Daemons and Angels*, Constable, London, 2002.

MUSEUMS AND GALLERIES:
CHICAGO (AI): *Meum* - JOHANNESBURG (AG): *Portrait of Mrs Evoy* (marble) - LEEDS (City AG): *Mother and Child* (c. 1910, stone, sculpture) - LONDON (Contemporary Art Society): *Bust of Mrs Lamb* (bronze) - LONDON (Imperial War Mus.): *Admiral Fischer* - LONDON (National Portrait Gal.): *Sir Jacob Epstein* (c. 1912, bronze, head); *Joseph Conrad* (1924, bronze,

bust); *George Bernard Shaw* (1934, bronze, bust); other busts - LONDON (Tate Collection): *Nan* (1909, bronze, bust); *The Visitation* (1926, bronze, life-size figure); *Torso in Metal from 'The Rock Drill'* (1913-1914, bronze); *Female Figure in Flenite* (1913, serpentine); *Doves* (1914-1915, marble); *Portrait of Iris Beerbohm Tree* (1915, bronze, bust); *Albert Einstein* (1933, bronze, head); *Jacob and the Angel* (1940-1941, alabaster, group); *Somerset Maugham* (1951, bronze, bust); other sculptures; three still-lifes with flowers (c. 1933, c. 1936, watercolour and gouache on paper).

AUCTION RECORDS:

NEW YORK, 13 May 1961, *Nude Model* (pencil) USD 375. NEW YORK, 11 Dec 1963, *Head of Sir Winston Churchill* (ten copies printed) USD 21,000. LONDON, 30 Oct 1970, *Albert Einstein* (green-patinated bronze) Gns 6,800. LONDON, 14 March 1973, *Roses* (watercolour) GBP 600. LONDON, 19 June 1974, *Albert Einstein* (green-patinated bronze) GBP 3,800. LONDON, 17 March 1976, *Roses* (watercolour, 22 x 17 ins / 56 x 43 cm) GBP 320. LONDON, 30 April 1976, *Head of Smuts* (bronze, h. 20 ins / 51 cm) GBP 2,000. LONDON, 16 March 1977, *Eve Dervich* (1919, bronze, h. 18 ins / 46 cm) GBP 850. NEW YORK, 16 March 1978, *Self-portrait with Beard* (1918, bronze, h. 11 1/2 ins / 29 cm) USD 1,500. LONDON, 2 March 1979, *Dr Chaïm Weizmann* (1933, bronze, h. 18 1/2 ins / 47 cm) GBP 8,000. LONDON, 11 Nov 1981, *Peonies* (gouache, 17 x 22 1/4 ins / 43 x 56.5 cm) GBP 920. LONDON, 4 March 1983, *Sunflowers* (gouache, 22 x 17 ins / 56 x 43 cm) GBP 1,200. LONDON, 21 Sept 1983, *Little Girl and Kitten* (pencil, 22 1/2 x 17 1/4 ins / 57 x 44 cm) GBP 1,200. LONDON, 9 Nov 1984, *Portrait of Sir Winston Churchill* (1946, bronze, h. 11 3/4 ins / 30 cm) GBP 8,000. LONDON, 7 June 1985, *Reclining Nude* (watercolour and pencil, 22 1/4 x 16 3/4 ins / 56.6 x 42.5 cm) GBP 1,500. LONDON, 13 Nov 1985, *Pola Nerenska* (1937, bronze, h. 19 ins / 48 cm) GBP 2,000. LONDON, 13 June 1986, *Winston Churchill* (1945, bronze with brown and green patina, h. 12 ins / 30.5 cm) GBP 13,000. LONDON, 14 Oct 1987, *First Portrait of Kathleen* (1921, bronze, h. 18 ins / 46 cm) GBP 9,000. NEW YORK, 18 Feb 1988, *Sheila* (bronze, h. 14 ins / 35.5 cm) USD 5,720. LONDON, 3 and 4 March 1988, *Fifth Portrait of Leda* (bronze with gold patina, h. 9 3/4 ins / 24.6 cm) GBP 4,620; *Betty Peters* (watercolour and pencil, 22 x 16 3/4 ins / 55 x 42.5 cm) GBP 3,520. NEW YORK, 13 May 1988, *Self-portrait with Beard* (brown-patinated bronze, h. 15 ins / 38 cm) USD 3,850. LONDON, 9 June 1988, *Anthony* (bronze, h. 11 1/4 ins / 28.8 cm) GBP 3,300. NEW YORK, 9 May 1989, *Baby with Outstretched Arms* (1949, bronze, h. 9 1/2 ins / 24 cm) USD 8,580. LONDON, 9 June 1989, *Fifth Portrait of Leda Pouting* (bronze, h. 9 1/2 ins / 24.2 cm) GBP 10,450. LONDON, 10 Nov 1989, *Summer Flowers* (gouache, 17 x 22 ins / 43.3 x 55.9 cm) GBP 6,600. NEW YORK, 21 Feb 1990, *Portrait of Judith* (1951, bronze with gold patina, h. 9 ins / 22.9 cm) USD 6,600. LONDON, 9 March 1990, *Dahlias* (1926, gouache, 23 3/4 x 17 1/4 ins / 60.5 x 43.9 cm) GBP 7,150. LONDON, 24 May 1990, *Maquette for Madonna and Child* (lead wire and bronze, h. 13 3/4 ins / 35 cm) GBP 18,700. LONDON, 8 June 1990, *Portrait of Albert Epstein* (bronze, h. 17 ins / 43 cm) GBP 12,100. LONDON, 20 Sept 1990, *Roses and Summer Flowers* (gouache, 22 x 16 3/4 ins / 56 x 42.5 cm) GBP 4,620. NEW YORK, 10 Oct 1990, *The Artist's Left Hand* (bronze, h. 7 1/2 ins / 19.1 cm) USD 5,225. LONDON, 9 Nov 1990, *Baby Asleep* (lost-wax bronze with black patina, h. 5 1/2 ins / 14 cm) GBP 6,600. NEW YORK, 13 Feb 1991, *Judith Lade* (gold-patinated bronze, h. 7 1/2 ins / 19 cm) USD 4,400. LONDON, 8 March 1991, *Helena* (1919, green-patinated bronze, h. 23 1/2 ins / 60 cm) GBP 19,800. LUCERNE, 25 May 1991, *Two Heads* (pencil, 13 1/2 x 11 ins / 34 x 28 cm) CHF 1,700. LONDON, 7 June 1991, *Second Portrait of Deirdre with Blouse* (brown-patinated bronze, h. 22 ins / 56 cm) GBP 11,000. TEL AVIV, 26 Sept 1991, *Betty Peters, Reclining Nude* (bronze, l. 23 1/2 ins / 60 cm) USD 12,100. NEW YORK, 5 Nov 1991, *Head of a Little Girl* (green-patinated bronze, h. 9 ins / 22.9 cm) USD 4,400. LONDON, 14 May 1992, *Buttercups* (1936, gouache, 17 1/2 x 22 1/2 ins / 44.5 x 57 cm) GBP 4,400. LONDON, 11 June 1992, *Second Portrait of George Bernard Shaw* (black-patinated bronze, 17 x 10 ins / 43 x 24.5 cm) GBP 15,400. NEW YORK, 8 Oct 1992, *Second Portrait of Lilian Shelley* (brown-patinated bronze, h. 28 ins / 71 cm) USD 7,700. LONDON, 6 Nov 1992, *Dahlias* (gouache, 17 1/2 x 22 ins / 44.5 x 56 cm) GBP 4,070. NEW YORK, 10 Nov 1992, *Reclining Nude* (watercolour and pencil/paper, 17 1/2 x 22 1/2 ins / 44.4 x 57.2 cm) USD 2,860. LONDON, 26 March 1993, *Baby Asleep* (bronze, h. 6 1/4 ins / 16 cm) GBP 6,325. TEL AVIV, 14 April 1993, *Moses and the Israelites* (watercolour, 22 1/2 x 17 1/4 ins / 57 x 44 cm) USD 4,600. NEW YORK, 2 Nov 1993, *The Angel of the Annunciation* (bronze, h. 62 1/4 ins / 158 cm) USD 9,775. TEL AVIV, 25 Sept 1994, *Bust of Chaïm Weizmann* (1933, bronze, h. 18 1/4 ins / 46.3 cm) USD 9,200. NEW YORK, 14 June 1995, *Sunita* (bronze, h. 23 1/2 ins / 59.7 cm) USD 5,175. TEL AVIV, 14 April 1996, *Roses in a Vase* (watercolour/paper/card, 22 3/4 x 17 3/4 ins / 58 x 45 cm) USD 5,750. TEL AVIV, 7 Oct 1996, *Portrait of Jackie* (bronze, h. 13 3/4 ins / 35 cm) USD 4,025. NEW YORK, 10 Oct 1996, *Tabitha* (brown-patinated bronze, h. 6 1/2 ins / 16.5 cm) USD 3,450. PARIS, 20 Nov 1997, *Bunch of Dahlias* (oil on canvas, 21 1/4 x 15 ins / 54 x 38 cm) FRF 15,500. LONDON, 4 June 1999, *Ralph Vaughan Williams, OM* (1949, green patinated bronze, h. 15 ins / 39 cm) GBP 13,000. LONDON, 5 Nov 1999, *Seventh Portrait of Kathleen, Half-length in Shawl* (green patinated bronze, h. 29 ins / 74 cm) GBP 18,000. LONDON, 5 April 2000, *Portrait Head of Augustus John* (dark brown patinated bronze, h. 14 ins / 35 cm) GBP 13,000. LONDON, 22 Nov 2000, *Studies for Rock Drill* (pencil and watercolour, 19 x 11 ins / 47 x 27 cm) GBP 12,000. LONDON, 17 July 2001, *Sir Winston Churchill* (green patinated bronze, h. 12 ins / 30 cm) GBP 20,000. LONDON, 23 Nov 2001, *Second Portrait of Deirdre, in a Slip* (1941-1942, brown patinated bronze, h. 22 ins / 55 cm) GBP 11,000. LONDON, 3 Dec 2002, *Maquette for Night* (green-brown patinated bronze, h. 14 ins / 36 cm) GBP 10,500. LONDON, 4 Dec 2002, *Picanniny* (pale green patinated bronze, h. 9 ins / 22 cm) GBP 8,500. LONDON, 26 Feb 2003, *Piccaninny* (pale green patinated bronze, h. 11 ins / 29 cm) GBP 7,500. LONDON, 25 March 2003, *Jacob Kramer* (brown patinated bronze, h. 25 ins / 64 cm) GBP 10,000. LONDON, 16 March 2004, *Portrait of Rabindranath Tagore* (green patinated bronze, h. 20 ins / 50 cm) GBP 7,800. LONDON, 19 Nov 2004, *Second Portrait of George Bernard Shaw* (1934, brown patinated bronze, h. 19 ins / 47 cm) GBP 23,000.

EPSTEIN, Jehudo

Polish, 20th century.

Born July 1870, in Slonz (Minsk), now in Belarus, to Jewish Polish parents; died 16 November 1945.

Active from c. 1920 in Austria, from 1935 in South Africa.

Painter.

Jehudo Epstein studied at the design school in Vilnius and then in Vienna at the imperial academy of fine art, where he became a teacher in 1923. He obtained a travel grant to Italy from the Michael Beersch Foundation for his picture *Saul and David*. He won the Rome Prize twice and during World War I he was one of the Austrian army's official artists. He settled in South Africa in 1935.

Epstein painted popular scenes in Italy, particularly in Venice, as well as Italian portraits and landscapes. His works include *Burials in the Lagoon; Song of the Lagoon; Wrong Path; Preparations for a Celebration*.

AUCTION RECORDS:

VIENNA, 17 Sept 1974, *Resting in the Fields*, ATS 70,000. VIENNA, 2 Nov 1976, *David Playing the Harp for King Saul* (c. 1896, oil on canvas, 49 1/2 x 92 1/2 ins / 126 x 235 cm) ATS 38,000. LONDON, 22 Nov 1978, *Leaving the Synagogue* (oil on canvas, 27 3/4 x 22 ins / 70.5 x 56 cm) GBP 2,000. NEW YORK,

17 Feb 1982, *The Ghetto's Old Beggar* (watercolour and pencil, 11 3/4 x 7 3/4 ins / 30 x 19.8 cm) USD 650. VIENNA, 4 Dec 1984, *View of Austerlitz in the Evening* (oil on canvas, 13 3/4 x 25 1/4 ins / 35 x 64 cm) ATS 32,000. LONDON, 29 Oct 1987, *Johannesburg from the Goldmines* (1938, oil on canvas, 24 1/2 x 40 1/4 ins / 62.2 x 102.2 cm) GBP 3,000. PARIS, 14 April 1991, *Canal in Venice at Night* (1912, oil on panel, 25 1/4 x 30 1/4 ins / 64 x 77 cm) FRF 10,000. LONDON, 17 May 1991, *Recital* (1922, oil on canvas, 29 1/2 x 43 ins / 75 x 109 cm) GBP 3,300. LONDON, 19 June 1992, *Game of Chess* (1892, oil on canvas, 21 x 22 1/4 ins / 53.5 x 56.5 cm) GBP 20,350. TEL AVIV, 8 April 1999, *Drinkers* (oil on canvas, 39 x 48 ins / 99 x 122 cm) USD 11,000. VIENNA, 3 Nov 1999, *Reclining Female Nude* (oil on canvas, 16 x 35 ins / 40 x 88 cm) ATS 60,000. VIENNA, 30 May 2001, *After Church* (1899, oil on canvas/board, 12 x 16 ins / 31 x 41 cm) ATS 30,000. VIENNA, 19 Dec 2003, *Bridge* (oil on canvas, 24 x 37 ins / 61 x 94 cm) EUR 1,800. VIENNA, 19 Dec 2003, *Railway Station in Rome* (1901, oil on canvas, 44 x 59 ins / 111 x 150 cm) EUR 2,800.

EPSTEIN, John
British, 20th century.
Born 1937, in Sutton (Surrey).
Painter.
Minimal Art.

John Epstein studied at the Central School of Arts and Crafts from 1957 to 1960. His painting is exclusively monochrome and he often works on trapezoid canvases. Epstein belongs to the movement that explores the painted surface in its own right known as Art Concret or more often as Minimal Art.

EPSTEIN-HEFTER, Élisabeth
Swiss, 20th century.
Born 1879, in Gitomir, Russia; died 1956, in Geneva.
Painter. Landscapes, still-lifes, flowers.

Élisabeth Epstein-Hefter was one of the few contributors to the first exhibition of the Der Blaue Reiter group which took place in Munich in December 1911.

AUCTION RECORDS:
MUNICH, 27 Nov 1981, *Still-life with Flowers* (1939, oil on canvas, 16 1/4 x 13 ins / 41 x 33 cm) DEM 4,800. BERN, 12 May 1990, *Landscape* (1918, oil on panel, 14 1/4 x 17 ins / 36 x 43 cm) CHF 950. ZURICH, 3 April 1996, *Cubic Composition* (1919, oil on canvas, 14 3/4 x 13 ins / 37.7 x 33.1 cm) CHF 1,700. MUNICH, 8 May 1999, *Still-life with Tea Pot on Table* (1943, oil on board, 22 x 18 ins / 55 x 46 cm) DEM 3,500. MUNICH, 8 May 1999, *Forest Landscape* (1929, oil on board, 19 x 15 ins / 48 x 38 cm) DEM 7,000. STAUFEN, 23 May 2003, *Portrait of Woman with Bare Shoulders* (oil on canvas/board, 13 x 11 ins / 33 x 27 cm) EUR 1,500.

EPURE, Serban
Romanian, 20th century.
Born 18 February 1940, in Bucharest.
Active in the USA.
Painter, decorative designer. Designs for mosaics.
Cyber Art.

Serban Epure studied at the polytechnic in Bucharest, in the electronics and telecommunications section, from 1956 to 1961. A self-taught painter, he left his job as an electronics engineer to devote himself exclusively to painting. One of the problems Epure dealt with was the inclusion of technical invention in artistic design. Using a computer, Epure introduced into his designs shapes that develop cybernetic principles linked to a metaphysical meaning: 'My artistic ideal,' he stated, 'is to express the purity of light, the unceasing aspiration of matter towards purification and illumination.' Epure took part in many group exhibitions in Romania, France (Biennale des Jeunes, Paris in 1971 and 1973; Sygma Festival, Bordeaux in 1973), the USA, Great Britain, Italy, West Germany, Israel and Lebanon. He held his first solo exhibition in 1967 in Bucharest, followed by several in the USA. He created a 650 square feet (60 square metre) monumental mosaic in Romania (*Turnu-Magurele*) and costumes for avant-garde ballets.

BIBLIOGRAPHY:
Jianou, Ionel/Carp, Gabriela/Covrig, Ana Maria/Scantéyé, Lionel, *Romanian Artists and the West*, American Romanian Academy of Arts and Sciences, Los Angeles, 1986.

EPZENAET, Hans, or Epsenaet or Epsenroet
German, 16th century.
Active in Lüneburg.
Painter.

Hans Epzenaet was commissioned by the town of Lüneburg to decorate a room in the town hall.

EQUENNEZ, Antoine Joseph
Flemish, 18th century.
Active in Tournai in 1759.
Painter. History painting, portraits.
Flemish School.

AUCTION RECORDS:
LONDON, 8 April 1987, *Prince Charles of Lorraine Presiding over the Festivities on the Occasion of his Silver Jubilee* (1769, oil on canvas, 45 1/4 x 67 1/4 ins / 115 x 170.5 cm) GBP 16,000.

EQUENNEZ, Denis Joseph
Flemish, 18th century.
Active in Tournai.
Painter.
Flemish School.

Denis Joseph Equennez was the brother of Jean Baptiste Joseph Equennez. They both qualified as masters on 10 October 1787.

EQUENNEZ, Hippolyte François Joseph
Flemish, 18th - 19th century.
Born 1772; died 1854.
Active in Tournai.
Painter. Animals.
Flemish School.

Hippolyte François Joseph Equennez is cited by Siret. He painted animals and still-lifes. The museum in Tournai possesses several of his works.

EQUENNEZ, Jacques Joseph
Flemish, 18th century.
Active in Tournai, in 1770.
Painter.
Flemish School.

EQUENNEZ, Jean Baptiste Joseph
Flemish, 18th century.
Active in Tournai, in 1787.
Painter.
Flemish School.

Jean Baptiste Joseph Equennez was the brother of Denis Joseph Equennez. They both qualified as masters on 10 October 1787.

EQUENNEZ, Michel Joseph
Flemish, 18th century.
Active in Tournai, in 1734.
Painter.
Flemish School.

EQUER, Didier
French, 20th - 21st century.
Born 8 January 1946, in Paris.
Painter, designer.

Didier Équer studied at the École Nationale des Beaux-Arts between 1963 and 1967. Alongside his painting work, he has also designed sets for theatre and television. His works have been on show in several collective exhibitions, including in Paris at the Salon des Indépendants, the Salon de la Peinture à l'Eau, and the Salon des Artistes Français. He also had solo exhibitions in Paris in 1985 and 1986.

EQUIPO CRÓNICA, group
Spanish, 20th century.
Painters (including gouache), sculptors. Figure compositions.

Equipo Crónica was founded around 1964-1965 in Valencia and was originally composed of Rafael Solbes (born in Valencia in 1940, died 1981) and Manolo Valdés (born in Valencia in 1942) - both former students of the Valencia school of fine art - and Juan Toledo (born in Valencia in 1940). They exhibited some group pieces in 1965 at the 16th Salon de la Jeune Peinture in Paris. Juan Toledo left in 1966, but the group continued with the two other members up to 1981, the year of Rafael Solbes' death. Equipo Crónica is interesting in that the name it chose almost totally concealed the identity of its members and nothing about its work suggested that it was in fact a group endeavour.Equipo Crónica produces pastiches of works by famous Spanish artists such as Velázquez, Goya and Picasso and international artists such as Mondrian, Léger and Lichtenstein (1967-1970) including *Recuperation, Guernica* and *Autopsy of a Studio.* Some works focus on culture and repression (1971-1972) like *Police and Culture* and *Black Series*; some develop thoughts on painting (1973-1976) like *The Poster, Studios and Painters, Subversion of Signs* and *The Wall.* The final series (1978-1981) of the group were *Urban Landscapes* and *Chronicle of Transition and Travels.* Equipo Crónica originated from the group Crónica de la Realidad, a Valencian branch of the group Estampa Popular. These groups, and Equipo Crónica in particular, challenged consumer society on a global level and anticipated the new role of art in society, seeing artistic production not only in terms of its market value but also as a 'cultural object'. By seeking to redefine the framework of artistic action, Equipo Crónica issued a social and political challenge in a country still under the sway of traditionalist values, still marked by the history of its glorious past (both political and artistic) but withdrawn and forcibly tied to a powerful paternalistic ideal.

Equipo Crónica strived to restore culture's vocation as force of opposition by removing the sacred aura surrounding its substance and attributes, which for too long had been in the service of the dominant, conservative ideology, and to give back to representation its dynamic and libertarian function. In the art world of that time, the avant-garde was dominated by informal abstraction, now on its way out, having become conformist and over-individualised. Equipo Crónica countered this force but also drew on some of its formal characteristics and surpassed them. The group knew how to manipulate and hijack images with irony and originality by cutting and pasting, and transposing. The group's work combines the imagery of political propaganda posters, historical masterpieces of art, the day-to-day life of genre scenes and cartoon strip characters. They inserted Franco into Picasso's *Guernica* and soldiers into Velázquez's *Las Meniñas* (*Maids of Honour*), which they relocated to a modern living room. In the *Banquet*, an interpretation of Zurbarán's painting *St Hugo of Grenoble in the Carthusian Refectory*, it is politicians instead of monks that are about to eat.

Equipo Crónica was particularly interested in the dialectical movement of creation within the history of art. In the painting *Painter and Landscape*, a transposition of Peter Bruegel's *Parable of the Blind*, one of the figures 'looking at' the sky becomes a painter with palette and easel. In 1972 the group produced sculptures in the same vein, a series of which symbolising 'the painter' was exhibited at the Musée d'Art Moderne in Paris in 1974. All the statues, representing a painter and his palette, were executed in the style of the masters, from the Renaissance to Mondrian, Braque and Pop Art. In formal terms, the additions, removals, reworkings and pastiches the group practised always obeyed an organised scheme: the forms become more geometrical and modern than the traditional ones; space is filled by lines, strokes and figures are repeated and swept into the middle and foreground; colours are flattened or even cold.

Because of its discursive and condemnatory approach, Equipo Crónica is often associated with 'narrative representation'. The group was represented at the exhibitions organised by Gérald Gassiot-Talabot (notably *Everyday Mythologies*) which, for a time, brought cohesion to their painting. Pop Art, the other important movement already with a strong presence in Britain and the USA, was more concerned with the relationship with the object. Stylistically, Equipo Crónica came very close to Pop Art at times but without ever being assimilated into it.

With historical and sociological hindsight, the work of these three, and later two, artists can also be interpreted, like Pop Art, as a serious critique of the nature of representation in its creation of images based on other images (or quotations). It emerged in parallel with the contemporary and more radical conceptual art trend emerging by at the same period in New York. These movements developed in different registers but it is sometimes possible to identify similarities, however relative, in certain works by Equipo Crónica which contain linguistic signs and typically conceptual elements. For Rafael Solbes and Manolo Valdés their work was an ironic, figurative and iconographic critique with the meaning in the forefront and the structure carrying it in the background.

The group took part in many joint exhibitions including: Salon de la Jeune Peinture in Paris (1965); *Le Monde en Question* (*The World in Question*) exhibition in France (1967); *Art Vivant* (*Living Art*) exhibition at the Fondation Maeght in St-Paul-de-Vence (1968); *Homage to Joan Miró* in Barcelona (1971); Salon de Mai in Paris (1971); *Contemporary Spanish Painting* in Rotterdam and the 8th Paris Biennale (1973); Venice Biennale (1976); *Mythologies Quotidiennes* (*Everyday Mythologies*) at the Musée d'Art Moderne in Paris (1977); *Le Siècle de Picasso* (*Picasso's century*) at the Musée d'Art Moderne in Paris (1988). The group was also present in other exhibitions of social and political nature such as: *Art and Politics* in Germany (Karlsruhe, Frankfurt, Basel); *Spain, the Artistic Avant-Garde and Social Reality 1936-1976* in Italy and Spain.

The group has also exhibited solo on several occasions: Valencia (1968); Cologne (1971); Juana Mordo gallery in Madrid (1972 and 1976); Stadler gallery in Paris (1973); Musée d'Art Moderne in Paris (1974), an exhibition which later went on tour; Karl Flinker gallery in Paris (1977); Maeght gallery in Barcelona (1978).

EQUIPO CRÓNICA

BIBLIOGRAPHY:
Gassiot-Talabot, Gérald/Bonet, Juan Manuel, '*De la narration de combat à l'ironie sur l'art*' in *Chroniques de l'Art Vivant*, periodical, Maeght, Paris, February 1971 (From the Narration of Struggle to Irony on Art). *Équipo Cronica*, Ed. Gustavo Gili, Barcelona, 1972. *Équipo Cronica*, exhibition catalogue, Maison de la culture, Saint-Étienne, Maison de la Culture, Rennes, Musée de Pau, Pau, 1974-1975. *La Trame*, exhibition catalogue, Gal. Karl Flinker, Paris, 1977 (The Web). '*Écritures dans la peinture*', vol. I, Centre national des Arts plastiques, Villa Arson-Centre national des Arts plastiques, Nice, 1984 (Writings in Painting). *Equipo Cronica*, exhibition catalogue, Instituto Valenciano de Arte Moderno (IVAM), Barcelona, Centro Julio Gonzáles, Valencia, 1989.

R.T.B., *Groupes, mouvements, tendances de l'art contemporain depuis 1945,* École nationale supérieure des beaux-arts, Paris, 1990 (Groups, Movements and Trends in Contemporary Art since 1945). Marín Viadel, Ricardo, *Equipo Crónica: pintura, cultura y sociedad,* Institució Alfons el Magnànim, Valencia, 2002.

MUSEUMS AND GALLERIES:

ALICANTE (Mus. de La Asegurada) - BARCELONA (Fundació La Caixa) - BILBAO (MBA) - GRENOBLE (Mus. de Grenoble) - HAMBURG (Kunsthalle) - MADRID (Fundación Juan March) - MADRID (Mus. Nacional Centro de Arte Reina Sofía) - MARSEILLES (Mus. Cantini): *Black Mark on a Black Background* (1972) - PARIS (FNAC) - PARIS (MNAM-CCI): *Homage to Mayakovski* (1976) - SANTIAGO (Mus. de la Solidaridad Salvador Allende) - STOCKHOLM (Moderna Mus.) - VALENCIA (IVAM Centre Julio González) - VITORIA (MBA de Alava).

AUCTION RECORDS:

PARIS, 24 March 1988, *Wood Sculpture Numbered 1/12* (h. 12 1/2 ins / 32 cm) FRF 11,000. MADRID, 25 April 1991, *Expressionism in the Street* (1971, acrylic/canvas, 78 3/4 x 78 3/4 ins / 200 x 200 cm) ESP 8,400,000. PARIS, 16 April 1992, *Rupture No. 1* (1974, acrylic/canvas/panel, from the series 'Sur le langage D 11', 64 1/4 x 49 1/2 ins / 163 x 126 cm) FRF 115,000. PARIS, 23 Oct 1992, *Self-portrait* (1979, oil on canvas, 43 1/4 x 36 1/2 ins / 110 x 93 cm) FRF 100,000. LONDON, 23 Oct 1997, *The Staircase* (1978, gouache, pastel and pencil/paper, 41 3/4 x 30 3/4 ins / 106 x 78.2 cm) GBP 11,500. PARIS, 18 Dec 1997, *Las Meniñas* (*The Maids of Honour*) (1969, sculpture, acrylic/resin, 20 1/2 x 29 1/4 x 11 3/4 ins / 52 x 74 x 30 cm) FRF 70,000. MADRID, 18 Feb 1999, *Rembrandt* (1981, gouache, pencil and lacquer, 44 x 30 ins / 112 x 77 cm) ESP 1,500,000. PARIS, 12 April 1999, *Le mas des delices* (1973, acrylic on canvas, 55 x 55 ins / 140 x 140 cm) FRF 300,000. MADRID, 8 May 2000, *The Palette as Mirror of the Soul* (1973, acrylic on board, 31 x 43 ins / 80 x 110 cm) ESP 3,500,000. MADRID, 10 July 2000, *Untitled* (gouache on card, 39 x 28 ins / 100 x 70 cm) ESP 3,100,000. MADRID, 15 Feb 2001, *The Palette as Mirror of the Soul* (1973, acrylic on card, 31 x 43 ins / 80 x 110 cm) ESP 2,950,000. MADRID, 19 Nov 2001, *Window with Figure* (oil on canvas, 67 x 53 ins / 170 x 135 cm) ESP 5,000,000. MILAN, 4 June 2002, *Menina* (sculpture, 35 x 36x16 ins / 88 x 91x41 cm) EUR 2,800. MADRID, 16 Dec 2003, *Spears and Flags* (serigraph, cardboard and plexiglass, 16 x 13x16 ins / 40 x 34x40 cm) EUR 4,500. MADRID, 26 Jan 2004, *Spectator* (painted card, 50 x 16x30 ins / 127 x 41x75 cm) EUR 5,000. MADRID, 6 Oct 2004, *Sorolla as an Excuse* (1974, acrylic and pencil on canvas, triptych, 48 x 113 ins / 121 x 288 cm) EUR 95,000.

EQUIPO REALIDAD, group

Spanish, 20th century.

Painters.

Citationism.

The Equipo Realidad group was founded in Valencia in 1966. It was formed by Jorge Ballester, born in Valencia in 1941 and Juan Cardells, born in Valencia in 1948. Equipo Realidad originated from the Valencian branch of the group Estampa Popular and, following an approach similar to that of Equipo Crónica, produced series of works. In the series entitled 'Portrait of the portrait of the portrait of a...' the group creates a pastiche of some of the major works of Spanish and international art including Goya and Leonardo da Vinci. Equipo Realidad's work is socially and politically anti-establishment in a country of traditionalist values and combines the imagery of great historical works of art with everyday life, as in *Feat of War.*

The group has taken part in numerous collective and solo exhibitions, including: Latin-American engraving exhibition in Havana and *Le Monde en Question* (*The World in Question*) exhibition in Paris (1967); *Homage to Juan Miró* in Seville (1971); *Contemporary Art of Valencia* at the museum of contemporary art in Seville, a touring exhibition of Spanish painting and the Valencia Biennale (1972); Punto gallery in Valencia (1973, 1974 and 1977). It received first prize at the Ibiza international Biennale in the Balearic Islands in 1972.

BIBLIOGRAPHY:

Catálogo nacional de arte contemporáneo 1990-1991, Ibérico 2Mil, Barcelona, 1990-1991 (National Catalogue of Contemporary Art 1990-1991).

MUSEUMS AND GALLERIES:

IBIZA (MAC) - MADRID (Mus. Nacional Centro de Arte Reina Sofía) - MONTEVIDEO (Mus. Nacional de Artes Visuales) - ROTTERDAM (Mus. Boijmans Van Beuningen) - SEVILLE (Centro Andaluz de Arte Contemporáneo) - VALENCIA (MBA) - VILLAFAMÉS (Mus. Popular de Arte Contemporáneo).

ERACLIDE-VREME, Xenia

Romanian, 20th century.

Born 4 September 1930, in Timisoara.

Engraver, graphic artist.

Xenia Eraclide-Vreme studied at the Ion Andreescu Institute of Plastic Art in Cluj-Napoca, graduating in 1957. She has travelled widely on study trips, to Yugoslavia, Hungary, the USSR, Switzerland and Italy. She has taken part in numerous group exhibitions in Romania, Russia, Austria, Yugoslavia and Japan, and had her first solo exhibition in Timisoara in 1967. In 1970, she showed a series of prints in Switzerland together with her husband, Leon Vreme, and the Romanian sculptor Victor Gaga. Since then she has exhibited widely in group and solo exhibitions both in Romania and around the world. She is a member of the Romanian Union of Plastic Artists. She settled in Timisoara.

MUSEUMS AND GALLERIES:

CONSTANTA - TIMISOARA.

ERACLIUS

Italian, 10th - 11th century.

Active in Rome.

Painter. History painting.

Siret says that Eraclius is the author of a treatise in prose and verse on painting and sculpture entitled *De Artibus Romanorum* (On the Arts of the Romans).

ERAN, Lise

French, 20th century.

Painter, designer.

Édouard Joseph mentions the enamels on copper which Lise Eran exhibited at the Salon d'Automne, of which she was a member. She was also a member of the Société Nationale and exhibited at the Salon des Tuileries in 1939.

ERARD

French, 18th century.

Painter. Allegorical subjects.

A painting by Erard shows the flight of the first hot-air balloon.

ERARD, Charles, the Elder, or Errard

French, 16th - 17th century.

Born 1570; died c. 1635.

Active in Bressuire.

Painter, engraver, architect. Religious subjects, portraits.

As royal painter, Charles Erard worked for Marie de' Medici and was involved in decorating the Palais de Luxembourg in Paris in 1621. He was the father of Erard de Bressuire. In 1615, Louis XIII appointed him chief architect for the fortifications of the towns and strongholds of Brittany. He painted an equestrian portrait of Louis XIII for the Accounting Chamber in Nantes in 1622. Nantes Cathedral has one of his works, *Christ Giving the Keys to St Peter.* He also painted a *Portrait of the Duke of Montbazon.*

ERARD, Charles, or Errard, called Erard de Bressuire
French, 17th century.
Born 1606, in Nantes; died 25 May 1689, in Rome.
Painter, draughtsman, engraver, decorative designer, architect and writer. Historical subjects, mythological subjects. Wall decorations, designs for tapestries, medallions.

Charles Erard was his father's pupil, and at the age of 18 followed him to Rome where he undertook his serious studies. On his return to Paris the king awarded him a bursary to go to Rome and complete his education, where they arrived on 18 October 1627. Errard drew monuments, statues and ornaments, studying both architecture and painting. Guillet de St-Georges remarked, 'he was capable of carrying out six more times drawings alone as compared to other artists, yet his works still reveal remarkable exactitude'. His stay in Rome lasted 16 years. He sent copies of the major antique masterpieces to Paris, including low reliefs, Trajan's Column and the colossal Alexander of Piazza Monte-Cavallo in Rome. Poussin spoke highly of him.

On 20 February 1643 the king gave Erard by letters patent the title of painter or architect in ordinary, with accommodation at the Louvre and an income of 1200 francs per year. M. des Noyers received him in his Château de Dangu where he painted a gallery and cartoons for tapestries. His fame and influence escalated and he was sought out by the court and private individuals. He decorated the Louvre, the apartments of Cardinal Jules Mazarin and those of Anne of Austria, and embellished the chateaux of Versailles and St-Germain, among others. Noël Coypel, still young, successfully transformed his compositions into painting. Erard was one of the first members of the Académie de Peinture, founded in 1648.

It was Erard who proposed to Colbert the creation of the Académie de France in Rome, a plan which had been on the drawing board for some time. Colbert accepted and Erard set off as first director in March 1666 with 12 pupils. He returned to France in 1675 with Marguerite Catherine Goy, daughter of Charles Goy, painter in ordinary to the king. He left at the end of 1675 to take up the directorship of the Académie, a position he retained until 11 September 1683.

He inspired confidence in Colbert who consulted him about purchasing antique marble. In 1671, a medal was struck in his honour (a copy is in the Musée des Medailles de la Monnaie de Paris). He collaborated with M. de Chambray on the translation of Palladio, on the *Comparison of Antique and Modern Architecture* and the translation of Leonardo da Vinci's *Treatise on Painting* (1666). A collection of his antique vases is extant.

MUSEUMS AND GALLERIES:
RENNES: *Prudence and Truth* - ROME (Accademia di Francia, Villa Medici): plaster bust - ROME (Church of S Luigi Dei Francesi): one medallion of 1671.

AUCTION RECORDS:
NEW YORK, 12 Jan 1995, *Minerva Seated on the Edge of a Cartouche Bearing the Attributes of the Arts, Having Been Crowned by a Putto* (black chalk and ink heightened with white/brown paper, 9 1/2 x 7 1/2 ins / 24.3 x 19.2 cm) USD 4,370.

ERARD, Jacques
French, 16th century.
Born to a family originally from Bressuire.
Sculptor, stonemason.

Probably a relative of Charles Erard, Jacques was a master sculptor, working in Niort and, in 1594, at Fontenay.

ERARD, Paul, or Errard
French, 17th century.
Born 1609; died 2 April 1679.
Painter, engraver.

To Paul Erard, son of Charles Erard, is attributed an etching of a dog in a mountain landscape.

ÉRARD DE LA CHAUX DES BREULEUX, Pacifique
Swiss, 18th century.
Draughtsman, architect.

This artist was a monk in the Premonstrant order. He drew the plans for the church at abbey of Bellelay (diocese of Basel).

ERARTS, Arthur
Belgian, 20th century.
Born 8 September 1879, in Hasselt (Limburg); died 15 January 1939, in Hasselt.
Painter. Landscapes.

Orphaned at the age of 11, Arthur Erarts began painting in the following year. At the age of 18 he entered the school of the painter Crespin, later attending the academy in Brussels. After his studies he returned to Hasselt. He had numerous one-man shows in Brussels, Liège, Antwerp, Bruges, Ghent, Hasselt and Maastricht. Throughout his life he retained a predilection for nature, particularly in his native Campine which was his main source of inspiration. His most notable pictures are: *Marchland in Bockryck*; *End of the Day*; *Beeches in Autumn*.

MUSEUMS AND GALLERIES:
HASSELT (Town Hall).

ERASMA, Daniele
Italian, 15th century.
Died before 1457.
Probably active in Udine.
Painter.

ERASME-THEAULT
French, 19th century.
Painter. Portraits.

A pupil of Ducq, Erasme-Theault sent portraits to the Paris Salon in 1808, 1810 and 1812.

ERASMUS, or Erazym
Bohemian School, 14th century.
Active in Prague.
Painter.

ERASMUS
German, 15th century.
Active in Brunswick.
Painter.

ERASMUS
Italian, 15th century.
Active in Brunico, Bolzano.
Painter.

ERASMUS
German, 15th century.
Active in Passau.
Painter.

ERASMUS
Romanian, 16th century.
Born 1531; died 1601.
Active in Kronstadt (now Brasov).
Sculptor (wood).

ERASMUS, or Erazm
Polish, 17th century.
Born to a family originally from Lezajsk.
Painter.

Erasmus painted an altarpiece depicting the Annunciation for the Bernardine church in Lezajsk. The work dates from before 1642.

ERASMUS, Desiderius, or Desiderius Erasmus
Dutch, 15th - 16th century.
Born 28 October 1466, in Rotterdam; died 12 July 1536, in Basel.
Theologian, painter.
Erasmus, humanist and brilliant scholar, was the illegitimate son of the daughter of a doctor from Gudda. His father, Gerard, left Gouda to escape family problems taking refuge in Rome, where he took holy orders. At the age of nine, the boy Erasmus began his studies in Deventer. Orphaned at 17, he became a canon at the monastery of Stein near Gudda. It was at this time that he began to paint. There was once in Delft a crucifix that bore the following inscription in his own hand: *Do not despise this painting; Erasmus painted it while on his retreat at Stein.* He was subsequently able to obtain a dispensation to be released from his vows from Pope Julius II. He chose to spend his life as an independent scholar, and lived chiefly in Paris, England, Louvain and Basel. One of his most well known books, *In Praise of Folly*, written in 1509 but not published until 1511, was dedicated to Sir Thomas More. He also became a friend of Holbein the Elder in England and in 1515, Holbein drew the marginal figures for *In Praise of Folly*, one of which shows a student at a table, drinking, with his arm around his mistress. Under this drawing Erasmus wrote, as a joke, *Holbein*. Holbein was later to do three portraits of Erasmus, the last in 1530.

ERASMUS, Georg Cristoph
German, 18th century.
Died 1701; buried 13 October.
Active in Nuremberg.
Painter.

ERASMUS, Johann Georg
German, 17th - 18th century.
Born 19 September 1659, in Nuremberg; died 24 March 1710, in Nuremberg.
Draughtsman, engraver.
The municipal library in Nuremberg has a number of colour drawings dated 1677 by this artist, who was also a mathematician. L.C. Glotsch engraved a *Triumphal Arch in Honour of Joseph I* from his drawings, while Erasmus himself produced an etching depicting the *Bromig Fountain* in the Maximiliansplatz in Nuremberg.

ERASMUS, Nel
South African, 20th century.
Born 1928, in Bethal, Transvaal, of Dutch origin.
Active in Transvaal.
Painter.
Nel Erasmus studied fine arts at the University of Witwatersrand before working in a variety of occupations. In 1953 she visited London and then Paris where she studied at the École Nationale des Beaux-Arts and the Académie Ranson. She took part in several group exhibitions, notably the Salon des Réalités Nouvelles in Paris.

ERASO, Manuel
Spanish, 19th century.
Born in Saragossa; died in Burgos (Castilla y León).
Painter. History painting.
Manuel Eraso was director of the Burgos school of fine arts.
MUSEUMS AND GALLERIES:
MADRID (Real Academia de Bellas Artes de San Fernando): *Joseph in Prison*; *Echo and Narcissus* (two copies after B. Luti).

ERASO Y PRADOS, Modesto
Spanish, 19th century.
Born in the 19th century, in Granada.
Painter. Historical painting.
Modesto Eraso y Prados was a pupil of Enrique Nieto.

ERASSI, Mikhail Spiridonovich
Russian, 19th century.
Born 1823, in Russia; died 1898, in Berlin.
Painter. Landscapes.
MUSEUMS AND GALLERIES:
MOSCOW (Rumiantsev Mus.): *Lake of Lucerne*; *Landscape*; two works - MOSCOW (State Tretyakov Gal.): *Reichenbach, Switzerland*; *Seascape*; two works - ST PETERSBURG (Gosudarstvennyj Russkij Muz.): *View of Lac Leman near Chambéry*; *View of the Outskirts of Viborg in Finland*; *Switzerland*; *Winter Landscape*; *Portrait of Bobylev*.

ERAT-OUDET, Marie Augustine Clémentine (Mme)
French, 19th century.
Born in Paris.
Painter, miniaturist.
A pupil of Delacroix, Marie Erat-Oudet exhibited a study in 1850 and a miniature in 1877, both at the Paris Salon.

ERATON
1th (?) century BC.
Sculptor.
Ancient Roman.
Eraton's signature was found on a fragment of a statue once at the Villa Albani. Active at the time of the Roman Empire, he may be the same person as A. Sextius Eraton, a Greek sculptor known for a statue of a woman found at Olympia. This Eraton worked in the 1st century AD, probably at the time of the Flavian emperors.

ERAZM. See **ERASMUS**

ERB, Franz Josef
German, 18th century.
Active in Ravensburg (Württemberg).
Sculptor (wood).
Erb is responsible for the altars of several Württemberg churches.

ERB, Léo
German, 20th century.
Born 21 January 1928, in St Ingbert (Saarland).
Active in France.
Painter.
Kinetic Art.
Léo Erb studied in Kaiserlautern and at the school for decorative arts in Saarbrücken and lived in Mennecy near Paris. He was one of the co-founders of the New Sarrois Group, with whom he exhibited. He also exhibited with Group Zero. In 1968 he participated in the exhibition *Contemporary Plastic Art* in Kaiserlautern. His work also featured in various exhibitions of kinetic art. After a period in which he was more taken up with abstract action painting, since 1967 his attention has been turned to kinetic art. He is fascinated by the joy induced by the movement of forms in space and is also concerned with observing, experimenting with and revealing the effect of movement on pure colours.

ERBA, Carlo
Italian, 20th century.
Born 1884, in Milan; died 1917, in Ortigara.
Painter, watercolourist, pastellist, draughtsman.
Figures, nudes, portraits, still-lifes, flowers.
AUCTION RECORDS:
ROME, 1 March 1983, *La Signora con la Mantella* (1913-1914, pastel, 10 3/4 x 8 1/4 ins / 27.5 x 21 cm) ITL 2,000,000. ROME, 5 May 1983, *Fisherman* (1914, pencil, 10 1/2 x 14 1/4 ins / 26.5 x 36.5 cm) ITL 1,600,000. ROME, 3 Dec 1985, *Futurist Portrait* (1913-1914, pencil, 12 3/4 x 9 1/4 ins / 32.5 x 23.5 cm) ITL 3,500,000. ROME, 18 March 1986, *Little Girl in Red* (c. 1915, watercolour, 11 x 4 3/4 ins / 27 x 12 cm) ITL 950,000. ROME, 20 May 1986, *Little Girl with Flowers* (1914-1915, oil on canvas, 29 1/2 x 17 3/4 ins / 75 x 45 cm) ITL 26,000,000. ROME, 7 April

1988, *Seated Model* (pencil /paper) ITL 3,200,000; *Still-life with Vase of Flowers* (oil on canvas, 20 x 18 1/2 ins / 51 x 47 cm) ITL 13,000,000. MONACO, 21 April 1990, *View of a River at Dawn* (oil on canvas, 23 1/4 x 35 ins / 59 x 89 cm) FRF 72,150. ROME, 9 April 1991, *Study of a Nude* (1913, pencil/paper, 12 x 9 1/4 ins / 30.6 x 23.8 cm) ITL 3,600,000. ROME, 13 May 1991, *Nocturne* (1908, charcoal/paper, 9 x 10 ins / 22 x 25.5 cm) ITL 8,625,000. MILAN, 17 May 1999, *Tree Reflected in the Water* (1908-1909, oil on canvas, 14 x 11 ins / 35 x 27 cm) ITL 14,000,000. MILAN, 17 May 1999, *Le trottole del sobborgo, che vanno* (c. 1914, oil on canvas, 21 x 37 ins / 53 x 94 cm) ITL 125,000,000. MILAN, 29 May 2001, *Poplar Grove* (1909-1910, oil on canvas, 16 x 17 ins / 40 x 44 cm) ITL 30,000,000.

ERBA, Jacopo
Italian, 17th century.
Died 1632.
Active in Cremona.
Painter.

ERBASAN
Spanish, 16th century.
Active in Valencia.
Painter.

Erbasan executed a series of 10 signed paintings representing *Scenes from the Life of Christ.*

ERBAUGH, Ralph Waldo
American, 20th century.
Born 29 June 1885, in Miami (Florida).
Painter.

Ralph Erbaugh was a member of the Society of Independent Artists.

ERBE, Carl
German, 17th century.
Painter.

Erbe was the official painter of the diocese of Breslau.

ERBE, Julius
German, 19th century.
Active in Berlin.
Painter. Landscapes.

This artist exhibited from 1866 to 1870 at the Berlin academy and at the exhibitions mounted by the artists of Berlin and Vienna. He exhibited in Breslau in 1873.

AUCTION RECORDS:
NEW YORK, 1-3 May 1930, *Decorative Landscape,* USD 70.

ERBE, Robert
German, 19th century.
Born 28 March 1844, in Gera (Saxony); died 1903, in Oberlössnitz near Dresden.
Painter, watercolourist, draughtsman. Animals, farmyard scenes.

Erbe worked in Oberlössnitz, near Dresden. He is noted for his *Fox in Difficulties, Young Chickens* and *Family of Chickens in the Wild.*

MUSEUMS AND GALLERIES:
BERLIN (Nationalgal.): several watercolours and pencil drawings.

AUCTION RECORDS:
MUNICH, 25 Nov 1976, *Farmyard* (1890, watercolour, 8 1/2 x 10 ins / 21.5 x 25.5 cm) DEM 1,500. HAMBURG, 10 June 1982, *Farmyard* (watercolour, 11 1/2 x 10 ins / 29 x 25.5 cm) DEM 1,200.

ERBEN, Roman
Czech, 20th century.
Born 1940, in the Czech Republic.
Painter.

Roman Erben lived in Prague where he was part of the international Surrealist movement. He exhibited there, as well as in Rome and Paris.

ERBEN, Ulrich
German, 20th century.
Born 1940, in Düsseldorf.
Painter, collage artist.
Minimal Art.

Ulrich Erben attended the academy in Hamburg and then studied further in Italy, at Urbino and Venice where he took courses in fresco and other painting. He subsequently returned to Germany, notably Munich and Berlin, taking up a professorship at the academy in Düsseldorf in 1980. He exhibited in Amsterdam, Frankfurt, Düsseldorf, Turin, the Kunsthalle in Kiel in 1981 and the Kunsthalle in Mannheim in 1984. At the outset he focused on the representation of landscapes and cities. Later he turned his attention to pictorial matter and from 1968 his work acquired a new abstraction, both minimal and concrete, as a result of Kasimir Malevich's famous *White Square on Black Ground.* From 1977 Erben explored the same theme in collages, using different textures. The *Exteriors* series, in which the painter plays on the effects of the brush and on the points of triangular figures, dates from 1978. Recently, that is since 1983, he has been more preoccupied with colours.

ERBIL, Devrim
Turkish, 20th century.
Born 1937, in Usak.
Painter.

After having studied at Istanbul's school of fine art, Devrim Erbil set up the Mavi Grup (Blue Group) in 1963. He has showed at the Paris and Venice Biennials, as well as in Istanbul and Ankara.

ERBISMEHL, Johann Georg
German, 18th century.
Active in Nuremberg.
Painter, draughtsman.

ERBSLÖH, Adolf
German, 20th century.
Born 27 May 1881, in New York; died 1947, in Irschenhausen.
Painter. Nudes, landscapes.
Die Neue Künstlervereinigung München (New Artists' Association of Munich).

Returning from the USA with his family, Adolf Erbslöh settled in Barmen in 1888. He attended the academy at Karlsruhe, where he was taught by Schurth and Schmidt-Reutte. When he was subsequently established in Munich in 1904, he studied under Professor L. Herterich. In 1909 he was one of the co-founders of the Die Neue Künstlervereinigung (New Artists' Association) of Munich with Wassily Kandinsky, who became its president. In pictorial terms he was at this time particularly close to Alexei von Jawlensky. He then followed Kandinsky in the group of Der Blaue Reiter. He was called up from 1916 to 1918 and subsequently travelled to the USA in 1926. A remarkable collector, he possessed a *St Severin* by Robert Delaunay which was presented at the first exhibition of Der Blaue Reiter. A major retrospective exhibition was held at the museum in Wuppertal in 1967.

It was not the intention of either the New Association or Der Blaue Reiter to represent a defined aesthetic, as it were, but rather to group together the collection of research of the time. Erbslöh must be counted among the artists of the German Expressionist movement, to which Kandinsky also belonged before moving towards total abstraction. His best-known works include: *The Violet Veil; Nude Lying in Forest;* as well as the paintings which represented him at the show *French Fauvism and the Beginnings of German Expressionism* in Paris and Munich in 1966: *Nude with Order of the Garter* (1909), a construction; *Tennis* (1910); *Landscape of Upper Bavaria, near Brannenburg* (1911); *Sunset on Brannenburg*

(1911). While these paintings hold a place in the history of German Expressionism, they are also Fauvist in conception.

A. Erbslöh. 16

Museums and Galleries:
Bremen (Kunsthalle): *Elevated Railway* (1912) - Elberfeld (Verein Mus.): *Mountain Landscape* - Karlsruhe (Staatliche Kunsthalle): *Mountains of Upper Bavaria, near Bannenburg* - Munich (Bayerische Staatsgemaldesammlungen): *Nude with Order of the Garter.*
Auction records:
Cologne, 4 Dec 1981, *Women Bathing in Park* (1930, oil on panel, 27 1/2 x 31 1/2 ins / 70 x 80 cm) DEM 10,000. Munich, 29 June 1983, *The Old Mill at Positano* (1923, pencil, 11 3/4 x 10 ins / 30 x 25.5 cm) DEM 1,500; *Two Women Bathing* (1930, oil on cardboard, 27 1/2 x 31 1/2 ins / 70 x 80 cm) DEM 9,500. Munich, 14 June 1985, *Dressmaking School* (1907, oil on canvas, 26 3/4 x 19 3/4 ins / 68 x 50 cm) DEM 21,000. Cologne, 27 March 1987, *View of Park* (oil on card, 18 x 15 ins / 46 x 38 cm) DEM 22,000. Munich, 26 Oct 1988, *Bridge* (oil on canvas, 16 x 20 ins / 40.5 x 51 cm) DEM 37,400. Cologne, 20 Oct 1989, *Seated Female Nude* (oil on paper, 12 1/2 x 8 1/4 ins / 32 x 21 cm) DEM 3,800. Berlin, 24 Nov 2000, *Sleeping Woman, Nude* (oil on canvas, 27 x 36 ins / 68 x 91 cm) DEM 100,000. Berlin, 24 Nov 2000, *Mountains, Brannenberg* (oil on canvas, 37 x 52 ins / 93 x 133 cm) DEM 380,000. Munich, 4 July 2001, *Portrait of Young Woman* (oil on board, 16 x 12 ins / 40 x 31 cm) DEM 60,000. Berlin, 30 Nov 2001, *Bathing Women* (1913, oil on canvas, 68 x 76 ins / 173 x 193 cm) DEM 235,000. Munich, 25 May 2004, *Portrait of Anna Hirzel-Langenhan* (oil on canvas, 21 x 17 ins / 54 x 42 cm) EUR 4,500. Berlin, 11 June 2004, *Naked Female Figures under Trees* (oil on canvas, triptych, 11 x 22 ins / 27 x 57 cm) EUR 15,000.

ERBSMEHL, Joh. Gottlieb
German, 18th century.
Born 1708; died 1741.
Painter (porcelain).

Erbsmehl entered the Meissen porcelain works in 1722 as a painter of figures and landscapes and remained there until his death.

ERCEVILLE, Hélène d'
Polish, 19th century.
Born during the second half of the 19th century, in Poland.
Painter.

In 1921, Hélène d'Erceville submitted two Italian landscapes to the *Exposition des artistes polonais* (*Exhibition of Polish Artists*) organised by the Salon de la Société Nationale in Paris.

ERCEVILLE, Wenceslas d' (Count)
Polish, 20th century.
Born 27 October 1888, at the Pasynki Castle, Podolia; died 1966.
Active in France.
Painter.

Wenceslas d'Erceville studied at the academy of fine art in Cracow and travelled to Italy, France, Belgium and the Netherlands. He worked in Paris. M.E. Lacombe said of him: 'With Cubism as a starting point, he achieved a very pure, but extremely vivacious figurative expression, characterised by a real passion for light and matter (objects, flowers, faces)'.

D'Erceville featured at collective exhibitions including: Salon des Tuileries, Paris, of which he was one of the founders; Salon des Artistes Indépendants, of which he was a member; *Exposition des Artistes Polonais* (*Exhibition of Polish Artists*) organised by the Société des Beaux-Arts, Paris, with a self-portrait (1921); International Exhibition of the Decorative Arts, Paris, where he was a member of the jury and officially represented Poland (1925); Salon du Nu and the Salon du Portrait, Galerie Bernheim, Paris. He also mounted many solo exhibitions from 1912 including: Paris (1926 and 1964) Amsterdam (1927 and 1931) Warsaw and Poznan. He was made officer of Polonia Restituta.
Museums and Galleries:
Le Havre (Mus. Malraux).

ERCHELLES
Bohemian School, 19th century.
Active in Prague c. 1837.
Painter, draughtsman. Portraits.

ERCHOV, Yuri
Russian, 20th century.
Born 1927, in Leningrad (now St Petersburg).
Painter. Figure compositions, landscapes.

Yuri Erchov attended the school of fine art in Leningrad. His paintings, heavily Realist to begin with, evolved and the descriptive gave way to a more personal vision giving priority to relationships between shape and colour. Erchov exhibited regularly from 1960 onwards and was a member of the association of Leningrad painters.
Museums and Galleries:
Moscow (State Tretyakov Gal.).
Auction records:
Paris, 29 Nov 1990, *At the Market* (1953, oil on canvas, 28 3/4 x 41 1/4 ins / 73 x 105 cm) FRF 7,500.

ERCK, Jakob
Swiss (?), 16th century.
Active in Bern c. 1523-1527.
Glassmaker.

Jakob Erck is thought to have made some stained glass windows for Vechingen. Brun believes he is the same person as a certain Hans Jakob Erck who lived at this period and was provost in Biberstein in 1530 and in Landshut in 1538.

ERCKHOUT, Jacob Joseph
Flemish, 19th century.
Born 1793, in Antwerp; died 1861, in Paris.
Goldsmith, sculptor, painter. Genre scenes.
Flemish School.

In some biographies Jacob Joseph Erckhout is referred to as Jakob Joseph Eeckout.

ERCOLANETTI, Ercolano di Francesco
Italian, 17th century.
Born 1615; died 3 June 1687, in Perugia.
Painter. Landscapes.

Ercolanetti painted four landscapes after Orsini for the church of S Gregorio in Perugia.
Museums and Galleries:
Perugia (Pinacoteca): *Landscape.*

ERCOLANI, Giovanni
Italian, 17th century.
Active in Rome.
Painter.

ERCOLANI, Vincenzo, or Hercolani
Italian, 17th century.
Active in Fano at the beginning of the 17th century.
Painter.

ERCOLANO DI GABRIELE
Italian, 16th century.
Active in Perugia.
Sculptor (wood).

ERCOLANO DI MAESTRO BENEDETTO DA MUGNANO
Italian.
Miniaturist, illuminator.
Worked on the choirbook for Perugia Cathedral.

ERCOLANO DI MAESTRO PIETRO DA MUGNANO
Italian, 15th century.
Painter.
Perugian School.
Ercolano di maestro Pietro da Mugnano was treasurer of the guild of Perugia and should be considered alongside Pietro da Mugnano, whose brother he may have been.

ERCOLE, or Ercülle
Italian, 15th century.
Painter.
In 1479, Ercole painted the armorial bearings of the commune of Fano.

ERCOLE
Italian, 15th century.
Miniaturist.

ERCOLE
Italian, 16th century.
Active in Parma.
Sculptor (wood).
Ercole may be identical with the painter of the same name who painted the town armorial bearings for the hall windows of the council of Parma.

ERCOLE, d'. See also first name

ERCOLE, Giovanni Battista
Italian, 19th century.
Born in Piacenza; died 5 December 1811, in Piacenza.
Painter, architect.

ERCOLE DA BOLOGNA, called Herculin Bolonais
Italian, 15th century.
Active in Bologna c. 1450.
Painter. History painting.
Ercole da Bologna also worked in Rome, where he produced frescoes.

ERCOLE DA FERMO. See **SIDERIO DA FERMO**

ERCOLE DA FERRARA. See **ROBERTI Ercole Grandi d'Antonio de**

ERCOLE DI CENTO. See **AVIATI**

ERCOLE DI SEGON
Italian, 15th century.
Active in Modena.
Painter.

ERCOLE DI TOMASO. See **RICCIO Ercole**

ERCOLESE
Italian, 16th century.
Painter, gilder.

ERCOLI, Alcide Carlo
Italian, 19th century.
Portrait artist.
Ercoli exhibited at the Royal Academy in London on 11 occasions between 1857 and 1866.

ERCOLINO. See **GRAZIANI Ercole I, the Elder**

ERCOLINO BOLOGNESE. See **MARIA Ercole de**

ERCOLINO DEL GESSI. See **RUGGIERI Ercole**

ERCUMENT-KALMIK
Turkish, 20th century.
Born 1908, in Istanbul.
Painter. Figures, portraits. Murals.
This artist remained outside the two main artistic groups in Turkey, Group D and the Independents. In 1946, the artist showed the work *Portrait of a Young Girl on a Sunny Balcony* at the Exposition Internationale d'Art Moderne organised by the United Nations at the Musée d'Art Moderne, Paris.

ERDEI, Viktor
Hungarian, 20th century.
Born 16 October 1879, in Budapest.
Draughtsman.
Viktor Erdei studied in Nagybanya. He is known to have produced a series of lithographs entitled *Eros immaterialis*. He exhibited a series of charcoal drawings in Budapest in 1899 and in 1907 he put on a collective exhibition of his works.

ERDELL, Paulus
German, 18th century.
Painter.
Erdell was a master in the Munich guild in 1781.

ERDENBORCH, Michael van, or Arenborgh
Flemish, 17th century.
Sculptor.
Flemish School.
Michael van Erdenborch became a master in Antwerp in 1645.

ERDENBORG, Jakob van
Dutch, 17th century.
Active c. 1640-1650.
Painter, draughtsman.
Jakob van Erdenborg painted historical paintings and landscapes with mythological figures.

ERDMANN, Axel
Swedish, 20th century.
Born 2 July 1873, in Stockholm; died 1954.
Painter, draughtsman. Urban landscapes.
Erdmann attended the school of the association of artists in Stockholm and contributed to the exhibition of this group between 1897 and 1910. He took up a post as director at the school of drawing and painting in Göteborg. His paintings are inspired by subjects and impressions of Stockholm.
MUSEUMS AND GALLERIES:
STOCKHOLM: several works.
AUCTION RECORDS:
STOCKHOLM, 15 Nov 1988, *Fish Market in Stockholm* (1902, oil, 16 1/2 x 14 1/4 ins / 42 x 36 cm) SEK 31,000. STOCKHOLM, 14 June 1990, *Torghandel on Kornhamnstorg on Summer Morning seen from Stockholm* (oil on panel, 12 1/4 x 19 1/4 ins / 31 x 49 cm) SEK 9,200. BERLIN, 24 Nov 2000, *Sleeping Female Nude* (oil on canvas, 27 x 36 ins / 68 x 91 cm) DEM 100,000. BERLIN, 24 Nov 2000, *Mountains, Brannenberg* (oil on canvas, 37 x 52 ins / 93 x 133 cm) DEM 380,000. MUNICH, 4 July 2001, *Portrait of a Young Woman* (oil on board, 16 x 12 ins / 40 x 31 cm) DEM 60,000. BERLIN, 30 Nov 2001, *Bathing Women* (oil on canvas, 68 x 76 ins / 173 x 193 cm) DEM 235,000. MUNICH, 25 May 2004, *Portrait of Anna Hirzel-Langenhan* (oil on canvas, 21 x 17 ins / 54 x 42 cm) EUR 4,500. BERLIN, 11 June 2004, *Triptych with Naked Female Figures under Trees* (oil on canvas, 11 x 22 ins / 27 x 57 cm) EUR 15,000.

ERDMANN, Heinrich Eduard Moritz
German, 19th century.
Born 15 April 1845, in Arneburg (Brandenburg).
Painter, engraver. Landscapes.
Erdmann studied at the Berlin academy and was a pupil of Hermann Eschke. He travelled in Germany, Italy, Asia Minor

and Spain. He is noted for works including *Moonlight, Villa Adriana near Tivoli, Biblical Landscape with Mary at the Tomb* and a number of etchings, views of Italy and landscapes.
MUSEUMS AND GALLERIES:
HALLE: *Edge of the Forest.*
AUCTION RECORDS:
NEW YORK, 27 May 1982, *Summer Landscape* (oil on canvas, 19¾ x 27 ins / 50 x 68.5 cm) USD 3,600. HANOVER, 22 Sept 1984, *Old Mill in a Mountainous Landscape* (oil on canvas, 14 x 18¾ ins / 35.5 x 47.5 cm) DEM 3,500. ROME, 9 June 1992, *View of Capri* (oil on canvas, 15¼ x 22 ins / 39 x 55 cm) ITL 8,500,000. MUNICH, 18 Oct 2002, *Haycart Passing Village Church* (oil on board, 15 x 11 ins / 38 x 27 cm) EUR 2,000. UPPSALA, 7 Dec 2003, *Alpine Landscape with Farm* (oil on canvas, 35 x 49 ins / 90 x 125 cm) SEK 20,000.

ERDMANN, Jakob
Danish, 18th century.
Painter.

ERDMANN, Johann Fr.
German, 18th century.
Died 15 July 1777.
Active in Dorotheenthal, near Arnstadt.
Potter.

ERDMANN, Ludwig
German, 19th century.
Born 1820, in Bödecke, near Paderborn; died c. 1888.
Painter. Genre scenes, portraits.
Erdmann was a pupil at the academy in Düsseldorf. He is noted for his work entitled *The Satisfied Artist.*

ERDMANN, Otto
German, 19th century.
Born 7 December 1834, in Leipzig; died 9 December 1905, in Düsseldorf.
Painter. Genre scenes, figures.
Erdmann was a pupil at the Leipzig academy and continued his studies in Dresden and Munich. He became established in Düsseldorf in 1858.
MUSEUMS AND GALLERIES:
COLOGNE: *Game of Chess; Portrait of a Woman; Artist at the Court* - DÜSSELDORF: *An Attractive Fiction* - LEIPZIG: *Game of Blind Man's Buff.*
AUCTION RECORDS:
NEW YORK, 10 Feb 1903, *Is it for Me?,* USD 150. NEW YORK, 14 June 1973, *Chess Players,* USD 2,500. LONDON, 16 Oct 1974, *Young Gentleman,* GBP 1,300. LONDON, 10 Feb 1978, *Reading the Will* (1886, oil on canvas, 38½ x 49½ ins / 97.7 x 125.7 cm) GBP 6,000. NEW YORK, 28 May 1981, *Love Letter* (1873, oil on canvas, 36¼ x 28¾ ins / 92 x 73 cm) USD 6,000. ZURICH, 9 Nov 1984, *Cello Concert* (oil on canvas, 40¼ x 30 ins / 102 x 76 cm) CHF 12,000. LONDON, 27 Nov 1985, *Recital* (1881, oil on canvas, 47¼ x 59 ins / 120 x 150 cm) GBP 9,500. COLOGNE, 15 Oct 1988, *Show-girl and Valet Serving Dinner in 18th century Dress* (oil on panel, 27¼ x 19 ins / 69 x 48 cm) DEM 2,000. NEW YORK, 27 May 1992, *The Apologies* (1869, oil on canvas, 24½ x 20¼ ins / 62.2 x 51.4 cm) USD 5,280. NEW YORK, 28 May 1992, *The Bridegroom's Health* (1883, oil on canvas, 36¼ x 47½ ins / 92.1 x 120.7 cm) USD 20,900. NEW YORK, 12 Feb 1997, *Reading the Will* (1886, oil on canvas, 39½ x 50 ins / 100.3 x 127 cm) USD 40,250. LONDON, 3 June 2003, *Recitation* (oil on canvas, 35 x 43 ins / 89 x 110 cm) GBP 15,000. NEW YORK, 7 Oct 2003, *Unexpected Letter* (1870, oil on canvas, 28 x 20 ins / 70 x 52 cm) USD 2,250. MUNICH, 26 March 2004, *Elegant Rococo Scene in Salon* (oil on panel, 10 x 7 ins / 25 x 18 cm) EUR 3,300.

ERDMANN, Richard Frederich
American, 20th century.
Born 12 February 1894, in Chillicothe (Ohio); died 1965.
Painter.

ERDMANNSDORFER, A.
German, 19th century.
Active in Munich.
Miniaturist.
Two portraits by this artist were on show at the exhibition mounted by the antiquarians' society in Mannheim in 1909, namely that of *King Maximilian II of Bavaria* and *Queen Maria of Bavaria.*

ERDOSSY, Bela
Hungarian, 20th century.
Born 6 April 1871, in Ekel; died 1928.
Painter, engraver, draughtsman.
Bela Erdossy taught drawing at the academy in Budapest. He mainly worked in watercolours. One of his *Landscapes* was awarded the design prize in Budapest in 1912. A picture *Entrance to an Old Park* is in a private collection.

ERDT, Hans Rudi
German, 20th century.
Born 1883, in Benediktbeuren; died 1918.
Painter.
Hans Erdt studied in Munich. In Berlin before 1914 he was a major exponent of 'Sachplakat' (poster-object), characterised by a simplified style of drawing and images.
AUCTION RECORDS:
NEW YORK, 13 March 1982, *Cigarettes Problem* (lithograph, 25½ x 19¼ ins / 65 x 49 cm) SEK 1,150.

ERDTELT, Alois
German, 19th - 20th century.
Born 5 November 1851, in Herzogswalde (Silesia); died 18 January 1911, in Munich.
Painter. Figures, portraits, genre scenes.
Erdtelt studied under Steffecks in Berlin and in Wilhelm Diez's studio at the academy in Munich. He took up permanent residence in Munich. He obtained a third class medal at Antwerp in 1885 and a gold medal in Berlin in 1886 before receiving the silver medal at the 1900 Exposition Universelle in Paris. From 1881 he exhibited at the Königliche Akademie in Berlin and in Dresden.
MUSEUMS AND GALLERIES:
KALININGRAD: *Portrait of Girl* - MUNICH: *Head of a Small Girl; Portrait of the Artist.*
AUCTION RECORDS:
LUCERNE, 21-27 Nov 1961, *Mother and Child,* CHF 4,900. MUNICH, 15 Sept 1983, *Portrait of the Artist's Uncle* (1879, oil on canvas, 19¼ x 16 ins / 49 x 40.5 cm) DEM 2,800. VIENNA, 19 June 1985, *Little Girl in Lace Coiffe* (1899, oil on panel, 9½ x 7 ins / 24 x 18 cm) ATS 100,000. LONDON, 12 Feb 1986, *Young Gardener* (oil on panel, 16 x 12¼ ins / 40.5 x 31 cm) GBP 6,000. MUNICH, 10 Dec 1991, *Portrait of Woman* (oil on canvas, 18½ x 14¾ ins / 47 x 37.5 cm) DEM 6,325.

ERDTMAN, Élias
Swedish, 19th - 20th century.
Born 22 October 1862, in Linköping; died 1945.
Painter. Landscapes, seascapes.
Erdtmann exhibited in Paris at the 1900 Exhibition Universelle, where he obtained a distinction.
AUCTION RECORDS:
STOCKHOLM, 11 April 1984, *Summer Landscape* (oil on canvas, 29½ x 46 ins / 75 x 117 cm) SEK 8,300. STOCKHOLM, 17 April 1985, *Summer Landscape* (1886, oil on canvas, 15¼ x 9 ins / 39 x 23 cm) SEK 7,000. STOCKHOLM, 15 Nov 1988, *Mountain Landscape in the North* (oil, 10¼ x 15 ins / 26 x 38 cm) SEK 11,000. STOCKHOLM, 22 May 1989, *View of Kalmarsund, Summer, from Öland* (oil on canvas, 28¾ x 23½ ins / 73 x 60 cm) SEK 10,000. STOCKHOLM, 14 Nov 1990, *Sunlit Seascape* (oil on canvas, 20½ x 44 ins / 52 x 112 cm) SEK 15,000. STOCKHOLM, 29 May 1991, *Delivery of Boats to Lakeside* (oil on canvas, 34¼ x 44½ ins / 87 x 113 cm) SEK 9,200. STOCK-

HOLM, 19 May 1992, *Red House in Flowering Thicket in Summer* (oil on panel, 13 x 17 1/4 ins / 33 x 44 cm) SEK 8,700. STOCKHOLM, 22 Feb 1999, *Farm in the Outer Skerries* (oil on canvas, 20 x 60 ins / 51 x 152 cm) SEK 15,000. STOCKHOLM, 27 May 1999, *Cowslips, Grez* (1886, oil on canvas, 15 x 9 ins / 39 x 23 cm) SEK 25,000. STOCKHOLM, 16 May 2000, *Fishermen in the Skerries* (oil on canvas, 31 x 50 ins / 78 x 126 cm) SEK 18,000. COLOGNE, 13 Dec 2003, *Untitled* (1969, wood, 21 x 21x10 ins / 54 x 54x25 cm) EUR 3,500.

EREDI, Benedetto
Italian, 18th - 19th century.
Born 1750, in Ravenna; died 1812.
Engraver.

Eredi collaborated with G.-B. Cecchi on nine plates of the monument to Dante, with the poet's portrait. From his own drawings, Eredi engraved portraits of the Genoese painter *Luca Cambiaso*, and of *Federigo Zucchero*. He also reproduced Raphael's *Transfiguration* and Luca Giordano's *Death of Lucretia Borgia*.

EREIN, Philippe van
Flemish School, 14th century.
Sculptor.

Between 1384 and 1390, Erein was working in Dijon with J. de Marville on the tomb of Philip the Bold.

EREMEEV, Klime, also known as Retkin
Russian, 17th century.
Born to a family originally from Galich.
Icon painter.

EREMENKO, Vladislav
Russian, 20th century.
Born 1941, in the Krasnodar region.
Active in Orenburg from 1979.
Painter. Figure compositions, figures, landscapes with figures.

Vladislav Eremenko graduated from the faculty of graphic art at the Krasnodar Educational Institute in 1964. He then trained for three years in Moscow. He became a member of the Union of Soviet Artists in 1975. He chooses his subjects from the spectacles of everyday life and depicts them using a technique of planes and volumes translated into light and shadow by means of colour, not unlike the technique initiated by Cézanne during his *Bathers* period.

AUCTION RECORDS:
PARIS, 25 Nov 1991, *Homage to Chagall* (oil on canvas, 39 1/4 x 35 1/2 ins / 100 x 90 cm) FRF 16,000. PARIS, 11 Dec 1991, *Caviar Production* (oil on panel, 19 1/4 x 17 3/4 ins / 49 x 45 cm) FRF 3,500. PARIS, 16 Feb 1992, *Shepherd on Horseback* (oil on canvas, 43 1/4 x 46 3/4 ins / 110 x 119 cm) FRF 9,000.

EREMITA, Il. See **SWANEVELT Herman Van**

EREMITI, Jacopo
Italian, 17th century.
Painter. History painting, landscapes.

ERETRIA PAINTER
5th century BC.
Active 430 to 420 BC.
Painter.
Ancient Greek.

The Eretria Painter gets his name from a vase of unusual form - an onos or epinetron - found in Eretria and now in the Athens Museum. One side has a head in relief, while the other has painted scenes of *Alcestis* and *Thetis Captured by Peleus*. The artist has a clear preference for small forms that allows him to develop his talent as a miniaturist. Despite the scale, he is able to render the psychological mood of a situation. His graceful style makes much use of rich draperies, transparent fabrics and elaborate hairstyles.

EREVANTZI, David, pseudonym of David Babaian
Armenian, 20th century.
Born 1940, in Yerevan.
Active in France from 1971.
Painter, sculptor, draughtsman.

David Erevantzi was an apprentice goldsmith, silversmith and ceramist in his native town. In his student years he tried to renew the ancient goldsmith's art, traditional in Armenia, at the same time as he was practising ceramics, painting and drawing. His work as a sculptor consisted of monumental stone sculptures, ceramic compositions for decorative purposes, small reliefs and medals. He drew his inspiration from nature, the history of his native country and the art of the early Middle Ages in Romania, arriving at a kind of dreamlike figurativism. He participated successfully in pan-Soviet and East Bloc exhibitions after 1965 and received many public commissions in Yerevan. He subsequently exhibited works in other European countries and Japan and settled in France in 1971.

MUSEUMS AND GALLERIES:
MOSCOW - SOFIA - YEREVAN (MMA).

ERF, Nelly van der
Dutch, 20th century.
Active in Brazil.
Painter. Military subjects.

During World War II, Nelly van der Erf served in the armed forces in Italy and Egypt. She painted warships, *Monte Cassino, Monte Castello* and *Monteze* among others, which sometimes bore the name *V. Zagloba*. Her more recent works are signed in her own name.

ERFMANN, Ferdinand Georges
Dutch, 20th century.
Born 1901, in Rotterdam; died 1968.
Painter. Genre scenes, figures, landscapes.

Erfmann attended the Rijksakademie in Amsterdam. During a sojourn in Indonesia he painted landscapes in an Impressionist style, whereas he is renowned in Holland as a Magical-Realist painter.

BIBLIOGRAPHY:
Tegenbosch, Lambert, *Ferdinand Erfmann*, Gal. Mokum, Amsterdam, 1973.

AUCTION RECORDS:
AMSTERDAM, 11 May 1982, *Acrobat Passing Round the Hat* (oil on canvas, 23 3/4 x 20 ins / 60.5 x 50.5 cm) NLG 4,200. AMSTERDAM, 15 March 1983, *In the Fitting-room* (1943, oil on canvas, 37 x 25 1/2 ins / 94 x 64.5 cm) NLG 7,800. AMSTERDAM, 19 April 1984, *Women at Window* (1940, oil on canvas, 20 x 15 3/4 ins / 51 x 40 cm) NLG 4,200. AMSTERDAM, 18 March 1985, *Acrobats* (1959, oil on canvas, 23 1/4 x 31 ins / 59 x 79 cm) NLG 4,800. AMSTERDAM, 19 May 1992, *Theatre Box* (1956, oil on canvas, 15 3/4 x 20 ins / 40 x 51 cm) NLG 7,475. AMSTERDAM, 21 May 1992, *Acrobats at Ground Level* (1950, oil on canvas, 27 1/2 x 19 3/4 ins / 70 x 50 cm) NLG 8,625. AMSTERDAM, 10 Dec 1992, *Composition I* (1933, oil on canvas, 23 3/4 x 19 1/4 ins / 60.5 x 49 cm) NLG 5,750. AMSTERDAM, 27-28 May 1993, *Oasis* (1940, oil on panel, 9 1/4 x 13 1/4 ins / 23.5 x 33.5 cm) NLG 1,035. AMSTERDAM, 8 Dec 1994, *Popular Celebration* (oil on canvas, 23 1/2 x 15 3/4 ins / 60 x 40 cm) NLG 13,225. AMSTERDAM, 3 Dec 2001, *Italian Woman* (1953, oil on canvas, 31 x 16 ins / 80 x 40 cm) NLG 19,000. AMSTERDAM, 3 June 2003, *De Glabrio's* (1964, oil on canvas, 28 x 16 ins / 70 x 40 cm) EUR 20,000. AMSTERDAM, 25 Nov 2003, *Floorshow at the New Karseboom* (1967, oil on canvas, 24 x 16 ins / 61 x 40 cm) EUR 25,000. AMSTERDAM, 8 June 2004, *Sunbathing at the Beach* (oil on canvas, 20 x 28 ins / 50 x 71 cm) EUR 3,800. AMSTERDAM, 28 June 2004, *Woman from Crystal Palace* (1938, ink and watercolour, four works, 6 x 5 ins / 16 x 12 cm) EUR 6,700.

ERGGELET, Alfred von (Baron)
Austrian, 19th century.

Died May 1871, in Naples.
Painter. Landscapes, animals.

This artist exhibited several pictures of dogs at the society of artists' show in Vienna in 1865. He is also known for his *View of the Shore after the Tempest*.

ERGO, Engelbert
Flemish, 17th century.
Painter. Religious subjects.
Flemish School.

Engelbert Ergo became a master in Antwerp.

AUCTION RECORDS:
NEW YORK, 9 June 1983, *Noah Gathers Together the Animals* (oil on canvas, 35 x 50 ins / 89 x 127 cm) USD 13,000.

ERGO, Jacob
Flemish, 17th century.
Painter.
Flemish School.

Jacob Ergo was possibly the son of Engelbert Ergo. He became a master in Antwerp.

ERGO, Jacques
French, 17th century.
Sculptor.

Jacques Ergo is mentioned as 'Marbrier du Roy' (marble mason to the king) in Paris from 1692 to 1698.

ERGO, Ronald
Belgian, 20th century.
Born 1936, in Watervliet.
Painter, draughtsman.

A self-taught artist, Ronald Ergo travelled extensively through Israel, Egypt, Spain and Italy. His repertoire comprises timeless themes such as love, women and death.

MUSEUMS AND GALLERIES:
ANTWERP (Municipal Archives) - BRUSSELS (Bibliothèque royale Albert Ier, Prints Collection) - CAIRO.

ERGOTHING, Michel
French, 17th century.
Painter.

The paintings of the ancient altar of the church of Kaisersberg in Alsace representing the *Annunciation* and *Legend of the Holy Cross* were done by Michel Ergothing.

ERGOTIMUS
6th century BC.
Active during the first half of the 6th century BC.
Potter.
Ancient Greek.

Ergotimus is known principally for having made, with the painter Clitias, the famous *François Vase* (Archaeological Museum, Florence).

ERHARD
Austrian, 15th century.
Active in Vienna in 1454.
Painter.

Erhard is perhaps the same person as Erhart, a painter in Wiener Neustadt.

ERHARD
German, 15th century.
Born to a family originally from Isny (Wurtemberg).
Painter.

Erhard is mentioned as being a burgher of Ravensburg in 1400.

ERHARD
German, 16th century.
Active in Augsburg at the beginning of the 16th century.
Painter.

ERHARD, real name: Erhard Schieble
German, 19th century.
Born 1821, in Forchhelm; died 1880, in Paris.
Active in France as a naturalised citizen from 1870.
Engraver. Topographical views.

Erhard collaborated on a number of geographical publications.

ERHARD. See also **ERHARDT** and **ERHART**

ERHARD, Andreas
Swiss, 18th century.
Born in Bern (?); died 1725, in Madiswil.
Draughtsman, painter.

Erhard worked for the numismatist C. Patin, for whom he designed medals. He was a priest in Bern and also lived in Büren and Seeberg.

ERHARD, Johann Christoph
German, 19th century.
Born 21 February 1795, in Nuremberg; died 20 January 1822, in Rome.
Painter, engraver, draughtsman. Genre scenes, landscapes.

Erhard was a pupil at the school of drawing in Nuremberg in the studios of Zwinger and the engraver A. Gabler. In 2001 he was represented in the exhibition *Un Paese incantato. Italia dipinta da Thomas Jones a Corot* (*An Enchanted Country. Italy Depicted by Artists from Thomas Jones to Corot*) at the international centre for art and culture at the Palazzo Té in Mantua.

BIBLIOGRAPHY:
Cary, Frances/Griffiths, Antony, *German Printmaking in the Age of Goethe*, British Museum Publications, London, 1995. Apell, Aloys, *Johann Christoph Erhard: Das Druckgraphische Werk*, H. W. Fichter, Frankfurt am Main, Berlin, 1996. Schoch, Rainer, *Johann Christoph Erhard (1795-1822). Der Zeichner*, exhibition catalogue, Germanisches Nationalmuseum, Nürnberg, 1996. Ottani Cavina, Anna (ed.), *Un Paese incantato. Italia dipinta da Thomas Jones a Corot*, exhibition catalogue, Electa, Milan, 2001.

MUSEUMS AND GALLERIES:
BERLIN (Nationalgal.) - DRESDEN (Prints Collection) - DÜSSELDORF (Kunstmus.): *Ponte Salario* (watercolour) - HAMBURG (Kunsthalle): *View of the Roman Countryside beyond Porta Pia* (pencil, watercolour) - NUREMBERG (Germanisches Nationalmus.) - NUREMBERG (Municipal Collection): *Baggage Escorted by Cossacks.*

AUCTION RECORDS:
MUNICH, 27 Nov 1980, *Portraits, including a Portrait of Erhard; Landscapes* (1811-1817, etchings, series of 39) DEM 9,500. COLOGNE, 16 Nov 2002, *Tower of the Former Pillenreuth Monastery near Nuremberg* (1812, pen/wash, 6 x 7 ins / 16 x 18 cm) EUR 3,000. COLOGNE, 16 Nov 2002, *Erhard's Travelling Companions Klein and Welker* (Indian ink/brush/wash over pencil, 10 x 8 ins / 25 x 20 cm) EUR 3,800. MUNICH, 5 May 2003, *Rome, near Torre Quinto on the Tiber* (1820, pencil, 7 x 9 ins / 18 x 23 cm) EUR 5,000.

ERHARD, Johann Wolfgang
German, 17th century.
Born to a family originally from Schwandorf (Palatinate).
Painter.

ERHARD, Tobias
Swiss, 16th - 17th century.
Born 22 February 1569, in Winterthur (Zurich); died 6 December 1611, in Winterthur, of the plague.
Glass painter.
Zurich School.

Four stained glass windows in the Vincent collection in Constance, signed *T.E.* and *E.* and dated between 1607 and 1610, are attributed to this artist.

ERHARD-STEINBACH. See **STEINBACH Erhard**

ERHARDT
Austrian, 16th century.
Active in Salzburg.
Painter.

ERHARDT. See also **ERARD**

ERHARDT, Christian, or Erhard or Erhart
German, 18th century.
Born 20 November 1731, in Augsburg; died c. 10 October 1805, in Augsburg.
Active in Augsburg.
Painter.

Erhardt was a pupil of J.G. Bergmüller and was primarily a fresco painter. His works in Augsburg include the fresco in the conference hall at the municipal library and those on the ceiling in St Peter's; he is also noted for the ceiling paintings and high altar of the parish church in Kottingwörth. This artist was also a draughtsman and worked for the publisher J.J. Haid; he drew the sketches for the work *Der Mensch in seinen verschiedenen Lagen und Ständen* (*Man in his Different Situations and Conditions*).

ERHARDT, Christoff
German, 17th century.
Born 17th century, to a family originally from Reinsdorf (Saxony).
Painter.

ERHARDT, Georg Friedrich
German, 19th century.
Born 1825, in Winterbach; died 20 September 1881, in Stuttgart.
Painter.

Erhardt was a pupil at the Munich academy from 1848 to 1849. In 1876, he became court painter in Württemberg. He is noted for his *Italian Woman* and *Portrait of King Frederick*.

AUCTION RECORDS:
NEW YORK, 16 July 1992, *Portrait of a Young Officer* (oil on canvas, 19 x 132 1/4 ins / 48.3 x 335.6 cm) USD 990.

ERHARDT, Karl Friedrich Eduard
German, 19th century.
Born 1799, in Graudenz, Poland; died 1832, in Merseburg.
Painter. History painting.

A pupil at the academies of Dresden and Berlin, Erhardt was sent by the state to Italy, later settling in Merseburg. He is noted for his *Group of Children, Venus and Cupid, Child with Squirrel, Hebe* and *Moses Drawing Water from a Rock*.

ERHARDT, Wilhelm, or Erhart
Czech, 19th century.
Born 8 May 1815, in Litomerice; died 12 August 1890.
Painter. Landscapes.

Wilhelm Erhardt studied at the Akademie der Bildenden Künste in Vienna with Emler and Mössmer. Most of his works are of Alpine landscapes.

AUCTION RECORDS:
VERSAILLES, 9 Dec 1990, *Mediterraneam Bay* (oil on canvas, 29 1/4 x 39 1/4 ins / 74 x 100 cm) FRF 8,000. LONDON, 16 April 2003, *On the River at Dusk* (oil on canvas, 17x27 ins / 42x69 cm) GBP 500. COLOGNE, 20 Nov 2003, *Panorama* (1879, oil on canvas, 22x8 ins / 57x21 cm) EUR 1,500. VIENNA, 24 Feb 2004, *Salzkammergut Landscape* (1879, oil on canvas, 23x35 ins / 59x90 cm) EUR 2,800.

ERHARDY, Josef
American, 20th century.
Born 21 May 1928, in Welch (Virginia).
From 1952 active in France.
Sculptor. Figures, nudes. Monuments.

Josef Erhardy studied in Washington, Florence and Rome. He exhibited in France from 1962 and appeared in the Salon de Mai in Paris from 1967 to 1969. He also participated in the Salon de la Jeune Sculpture. He executed a monumental sculpture in Cergy-Pontoise: *Returning from the Market*.

AUCTION RECORDS:
PARIS, 31 Jan 1993, *Rest* (1975, bronze, 7 1/2 x 11 x 7 ins / 19 x 28 x 18 cm) FRF 10,000. PARIS, 22 Nov 1995, *Couple* (two bronze sculptures, h. 8 1/2 ins / 21.5 cm, w. 8 ins/20.5 cm) FRF 13,000. PARIS, 8 April 1998, *Siesta* (1987, brown-patinated bronze, 7 3/4 x 5 x 14 1/4 ins / 20 x 12.5 x 36 cm) FRF 12,000.

ERHART
German, 14th century.
Active in Nuremberg between 1360 and 1380.
Painter.

ERHART
Austrian, 15th century.
Active in Wiener-Neustadt.
Painter.

ERHART
German, 15th century.
Painter.

Erhart was in Nuremberg early in 1460 and in Basel in 1474.

ERHART
German, 16th century.
Born 16th century, to a family originally from Ochsenfurt.
Painter.

In 1516, Erhart was involved in painting coats of arms for the church at Frickenhausen (Franconia).

ERHART. See also **ERHARD**

ERHART, Bernhard
German, 16th century.
Active in Ulm.
Sculptor.

Bernhard Erhart worked on some of the 13 statues designed by his father Michael Erhart to stand on the Mount of Olives in Ulm.

ERHART, Gregor
German, 16th century.
Born in Ulm; died before 1540.
Sculptor.
Swabian School.

Gregor Erhart was probably the son or brother of Michael Erhart. Between 1502 and 1504, he worked with Holbein the Elder and Adolf Dauher on the high altar of the monastery church at Kaisheim. He also worked at the church of St Maurice in Augsburg, and in 1509 assisted in the carving of the stone monument to Emperor Maximilian for the church of St Ulrich. A large number of other pieces of work in Augsburg and other towns are also attributed to him. A wooden statue of St Mary Magdalene in the Louvre and known as *La Belle Allemande* (*The Beautiful German Girl*) is thought to be his work. The work of the Erharts stands at the turning point between the late Gothic and the early Renaissance periods.

ERHART, Michael
German, 15th - 16th century.
Sculptor (including wood).

Michael Erhart is mentioned in documents from Ulm as working on the cathedral there. He also worked at the church of St Ulrich in Augsburg and in Halle. In collaboration with Holbein the Elder, he made an altar for the monastery of Weingarten (1493).

ERHART, Michel
French, 17th century.
Active in Strasbourg.
Painter.

ERHART, Paulus
German, 16th century.
Sculptor (wood).
School of Augsburg.

Paulus Erhart became a member of the guild in Augsburg in 1550 under the name of Mair, his mother's name. Gregor Erhart was probably his father or step-father.

ERHETMAYGER, Johann, or Erletmayger
Bohemian School, 18th century.
Active in Prague.
Painter.

ERI
Japanese, 9th - 10th century.
Born 852 or 856; died 20 January or 24 December 935.
Painter, sculptor (wood).

Eri was the abbot of the Toji temple in Kyoto. He was initially bursar to the novices in 915. In August 928, he became assistant 'master of the law'; in December, second in superior; in 932, 'master of the law'; and in December, senior assistant to the monks.

According to the register of nominations of the superiors of the Toji temple, the *Toji.choshabunin*, Eri was an 'excellent sculptor of wood and painter'. He is thought to have taken part in much of the decoration work, both painted and sculpted, inside the Toji, Todai-ji and Daigo-ji temples. However, most of these attributions seem dubious. The two pieces of work unquestionably carried out by him concern the restoration of the statues of the *Niten* of Todai-ji by imperial order in 907, and that of the pagoda of the Toji temple in 920. He produced the portraits of 12 patriarchs of the Shingon sect in Gomado. It is also likely that he was responsible for a portrait of the goddess Emma-O at Toji, but this must date from a later period.

ERIBERTUS
Italian, 9th century.
Painter.

This artist's name is mentioned in the archives of Verona.

ERIC, W. Dominique Adolphe
Belgian, 20th century.
Born in Ukkel.
Painter. Figures, figure compositions. Stage sets.

Eric, who exhibited at the Salon des Artistes Indépendants, predominantly painted stage sets.

ERICELLO, Francesco di Agostino
Italian, 17th century.
Of Milanese origin.
Painter.

Ericello worked for Crescenzio Crescenzi, and subsequently for the Cesarini.

ERICH. See also **EHRICHT**

ERICH, August
German, 17th century.
Born to a family originally from Saxony.
Painter.

Erich worked in Kassel under the electors Maurice and William V. A number of his works were engraved by van Heyden, including *Family of Landgrave Maurice*; *Elisabeth of Hessen*; *Mérian: the Funeral Cortège of Maurice of Hessen* and the *Portrait of Duke Johann Albrecht von Mecklenburg*. A *Family Portrait* by this artist was shown at the fine arts exhibition in Gotha in 1908.

ERICH, Franz Heinrich
Flemish, 17th century.
Active in Antwerp.
Painter.
Flemish School.

Franz Heinrich Erich married the widow of the engraver Ph. J. Mayer in Vienna on 4 May 1699.

ERICHSEN, Helle Vibeke
Danish, 20th century.
Born 1940, in Copenhagen.
Painter. Figure compositions, figures.

Helle Erichsen attended the Kunstakademi in Copenhagen and first exhibited in 1962. Thereafter she exhibited in Bulgaria, Denmark, Finland and France (1991, Galerie Galise Petersen) as well as in Hungary, Norway and Sweden. She went in for Expressionist compositions in which her admiration of German artists like Otto Dix is evident. She portrayed haggard-looking figures in ochre, red and blue tones.

Museums and Galleries:
Copenhagen (København Kulturfond) - Copenhagen (Statens Kunstfond).

ERICHSEN, Johan Tuscher
Danish, 18th century.
Born in Viborg; died probably in 1728, in Meelby.
Engraver.

A student of theology, Johan Erichsen also developed skills in engraving. He was employed making prints for the work *Jacobæi Museum Regium*.

ERICHSEN, Nelly (Miss)
British, 19th century.
Painter. Genre scenes, figures.

Nelly Erichsen worked in Tooting and exhibited 11 times at the Royal Academy, from 1882 to 1893.

Auction records:
London, 19 May 1982, *Return Home* (oil on canvas, 48 x 72 ins / 122 x 183 cm) GBP 6,200. London, 13 Nov 1985, *Milkmaid* (oil on canvas, 39 x 48¾ ins / 99 x 124 cm) GBP 1,500.

ERICHSEN, Thorvald, or Ericksen
Norwegian, 19th - 20th century.
Born 18 July 1868, in Trondheim; died 1939, in Oslo.
Painter. Figures, interiors, landscapes, flowers.

Thorvald Erichsen attended the art academy and the school of arts and crafts in Oslo and at the same time the K. Bergslien school of painting in Oslo, continuing his training under Chr. Zahrtmann in Copenhagen. He undertook several expeditions to Italy, and also Paris where he entered the studio of Fernand Cormon. He exhibited in Oslo, Copenhagen, Göteborg and Cologne. In 2001 his *Forest Interior* (1900) was presented at the exhibition *Da Dahl a Munch. Romanticismo, realismo e simbolismo nella pittura di paesaggio norvegese* (*From Dahl to Munch: Romanticism, Realism and Symbolism in Norwegian Landscape Painting*) at the Palazzo dei Diamanti in Ferrara.

Deeply influenced by Paul Cézanne, he was mainly a painter of landscapes and figures, whose work was also influenced by Claude Monet. Like Monet, he painted series of canvases on the same theme in different lighting. However, unlike Monet, he does not spread out the contours of the objects represented under the effect of light, which infuses his paintings with a certain realism.

Bibliography:
Rolfsen, Alf, *Thorvald Erichsen*, Glydendal, Oslo, 1931. Boym, Per Bj., *Thorvald Erichsen pa Lillehammer*, exhibition catalogue, Nasjonalgalleriet, Oslo, Lillehammer bys Malerisammling, Lillehammer, 1990. Lange, Marit (ed.), *Da Dahl a Munch. Romanticismo, realismo e simbolismo nella pittura di paesaggio norvegese*, exhibition catalogue, Palazzo dei Diamanti, Ferrara Arte editore, Ferrara, 2001.

Museums and Galleries:
Oslo (Nasjonalgal.): *Forest Interior* (1900, oil on canvas).

Auction records:
Copenhagen, 25 Nov 1981, *Terracina* (1902, oil on canvas, 16¼ x 17 ins / 41 x 43 cm) DKK 16,000. London, 27-28 March

1990, *Flowers on Table* (1927, oil on canvas, 23 1/2 x 29 ins / 60 x 73.5 cm) GBP 34,100. LONDON, 29 March 1990, *Wooded Lake Landscape* (oil on canvas, 24 x 29 ins / 61 x 73.6 cm) GBP 44,000. NEW YORK, 23 Oct 1990, *Landscape at Stoa* (1919, oil on canvas, 25 1/4 x 31 1/2 ins / 64.1 x 80 cm) USD 19,800. LONDON, 17 May 1991, *Wooded Lake Landscape* (1910, oil on canvas, 36 x 39 3/4 ins / 90.5 x 101 cm) GBP 22,000. LONDON, 19 June 1991, *Village in Autumn* (1939, oil on canvas, 23 1/2 x 28 1/4 ins / 60 x 72 cm) GBP 15,400. LONDON, 22 May 1992, *Wooded Lake Landscape* (oil on canvas, 23 3/4 x 28 3/4 ins / 60.4 x 73 cm) GBP 17,600. OSLO, 22 March 1999, *From a Young Girl's Room* (1900, oil on canvas, 39 x 32 ins / 100 x 81 cm) NOK 390,000. OSLO, 31 May 1999, *The Stroll, Blue* (1913, oil on canvas, 35 x 40 ins / 90 x 101 cm) NOK 360,000. OSLO, 27 Jan 2000, *Landscape from Kjelsoy* (1916, oil on canvas, 26 x 32 ins / 65 x 81 cm) NOK 35,000. OSLO, 5 June 2000, *Flowers on Table* (oil on canvas, 35 x 39 ins / 90 x 100 cm) NOK 73,000. OSLO, 7 June 2001, *Lennart in the Wood* (1915, oil on panel, 15 x 12 ins / 37 x 31 cm) NOK 100,000. OSLO, 7 June 2001, *Grey Day, Skaane* (1916, oil on canvas, 26 x 29 ins / 65 x 73 cm) NOK 230,000. OSLO, 21 Nov 2002, *Landscape from Holmsbu* (1931, oil on canvas, 29 x 36 ins / 73 x 92 cm) NOK 270,000. OSLO, 2 Dec 2002, *The Church in Lillehammer* (oil on canvas, 29 x 24 ins / 73 x 60 cm) NOK 100,000. OSLO, 13 Oct 2003, *The Church and the Bank at Lillehammer* (1933, oil on canvas, 24 x 29 ins / 60 x 73 cm) NOK 300,000. OSLO, 8 Dec 2003, *From Oia* (oil on canvas, 24 x 29 ins / 60 x 73 cm) NOK 40,000. OSLO, 29 Nov 2004, *Summer Landscape, Holmsbu* (1916, oil on canvas, 36 x 39 ins / 91 x 100 cm) NOK 620,000. OSLO, 6 Dec 2004, *Dog Days - Landscape* (1930, oil on canvas, 24 x 29 ins / 61 x 73 cm) NOK 88,000.

ERICHSEN, Virgilius, or Eriksen
Danish, 18th century.
Born 2 September 1722, in Nuremberg; died 23 May 1782, in Nuremberg.
Painter, pastellist. History painting, portraits.

A pupil of J.S. Wahl, in 1755 Virgilius Erichsen painted two portraits of the king on enamel. In St Petersburg, Russia, where he was appointed court painter to Catherine II, he executed several portraits of the empress. On his return to Copenhagen in 1772, he was named court painter there also, with an annual salary of 960 crowns. In 1778, he was given the title of state counsellor. Two portraits of the dowager queen and crown prince, which he exhibited in 1778, attracted a great deal of attention. He also executed historical paintings, but it was principally to his portraits that he owed his success.

MUSEUMS AND GALLERIES:
BERLIN (Royal Palace): *Portrait of Catherine II on Her Throne* - COPENHAGEN (Amalienborg Slot): *Catherine II on Her Throne* (replica) - COPENHAGEN (Rosenborg Slot) - COPENHAGEN (Statens Mus. for Kunst): *Portrait of the Dowager Queen Juliane Marie* - FREDENSBORG: *Portrait of Catherine II on Her Throne* (replica) - GATCHINA (Gatchina Palace): *Paul I Petrovich as a Child Dressed as an Officer; Count Grigorij on Horseback; Count Alexei Orloff on Horseback* - HILLERØD (Frederiksborg Slot): *Portrait of Spengler; Portrait of Catherine II on Her Throne* (replica) - MOSCOW (Rumiantsev Mus.): *Volga Peasant Family* (pastel) - PUSHKIN: *Portrait of Tsarina Elizabeth Petrovna* - ST PETERSBURG (Winter Palace): *Catherine II, Profile in a Mirror; Catherine II in a Fur Cloak.*

AUCTION RECORDS:
COPENHAGEN, 19 March 1969, *Catherine II of Russia,* DKK 22,000. LONDON, 12 Dec 1984, *Portrait of Countess Mette Pauline Schack, née Rosenorn* (oil on canvas, 28 x 22 ins / 71 x 56 cm) GBP 8,000. COPENHAGEN, 18 Nov 1987, *Portrait of Crown Prince Frederick* (oil on canvas, oval, 25 1/4 x 20 ins / 64 x 51 cm) DKK 38,000. PARIS, 31 March 1998, *Portrait of a Russian Lady in a Blue Dress* (oil on canvas, attributed, 28 x 23 1/2 ins / 71 x 60 cm) FRF 26,000. LONDON, 29 April 1999, *Empress Catherine II Alexeevna* (oil on canvas, 31 x 26 ins / 80 x 65 cm) GBP 5,000. COPENHAGEN, 27 Nov 2001, *Portrait of Frederick V* (oil on canvas, 31 x 24 ins / 79 x 61 cm) DKK 400,000.

ERICKSON, Carl, called Eric
Swedish, 20th century.
Died 1958.
Draughtsman, illustrator.

Carl Erickson, who signed himself *Eric,* contributed to fashion magazines such as *Vogue* and *Harper's Bazaar* in the 1940s and 1950s.

AUCTION RECORDS:
LONDON, 25 Oct 1995, *Portrait of Boris Kochno* (1947, lead pencil/paper, 22 3/4 x 17 1/4 ins / 58 x 44 cm) GBP 1,380.

ERICSON, Anna Maria. See **GARDELL-ERICSON**

ERICSON, David
Swedish, 20th century.
Born 15 April 1870, in Motala; died 1946.
Active in the USA.
Painter, illustrator.

Ericson began his studies at the Art Students League (ASL) in New York with Chase and Mowbray. He trained further with Whistler and later in Paris with Colin. On a number of occasions he stayed in Étampes (France). His first exhibition in France was held in Paris at the Salon des Artistes Français in 1900. He settled in the USA, in New York and then in Duluth, Minnesota. He taught at the Fine Arts Academy in Buffalo and received medals in various exhibitions.

AUCTION RECORDS:
NEW YORK, 21 Sept 1984, *The Val de Grâce, Paris* (1925, oil on canvas, 25 3/4 x 20 ins / 65.4 x 50.5 cm) USD 700. NEW YORK, 15 Feb 1994, *Carnival in Venice* (oil on canvas, 32 x 32 ins / 81.3 x 81.3 cm) USD 7,475. NEW YORK, 21 May 1996, *The Tidal Mill in Ploumanach in Brittany in the Moonlight* (1925, oil on canvas, 23 1/2 x 23 1/2 ins / 60 x 60 cm) USD 2,530.

ERICSON, Johan Erik
Swedish, 19th - 20th century.
Born 17 October 1849, in Karlskrona; died 1925.
Painter, watercolourist. Landscapes with figures, landscapes, seascapes.

Johan Ericson studied in Stockholm and Paris and settled in Göteborg. He painted landscapes - both in oils and watercolours - of northern France and the Swedish coast and exhibited in Paris and the Salon des Artistes Français, as well as in Berlin and Munich.

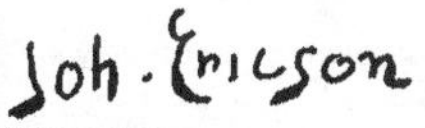

MUSEUMS AND GALLERIES:
STOCKHOLM (Nationalmus.) - VISBY (Gotlands Konstmus.).

AUCTION RECORDS:
PARIS, 20 Dec 1946, *Odalisque in Harem,* FRF 27,000. PARIS, 31 Jan 1947, *Marine,* FRF 6,100. COLOGNE, 12 Nov 1976, *Landscape of Normandy* (1879, oil on canvas, 17 1/4 x 28 1/4 ins / 43.5 x 72 cm) DEM 5,000. GÖTEBORG, 9 Nov 1977, *Road* (1889, oil on canvas, 24 3/4 x 30 1/4 ins / 63 x 77 cm) SEK 16,500. GÖTEBORG, 5 April 1978, *Spring Landscape* (1919, oil on canvas, 23 1/2 x 36 1/2 ins / 60 x 93 cm) SEK 12,000. STOCKHOLM, 26 April 1982, *Orchard in Flower* (1882, oil on canvas, 26 x 40 1/2 ins / 66 x 103 cm) SEK 36,000. STOCKHOLM, 24 April 1984, *Seaside, Marstrand* (1886, oil on canvas, 27 1/4 x 38 1/2 ins / 69 x 98 cm) SEK 57,000. STOCKHOLM, 4 Nov 1986, *Seated Man and his Dog in Field* (1878, oil on canvas, 11 x 18 1/2 ins / 28 x 47 cm) SEK 85,000. STOCKHOLM, 20 Oct 1987, *Summer Landscape* (1911, oil on canvas, 33 x 50 3/4 ins / 84 x 129 cm)

SEK 58,000. London, 23 March 1988, *Promenade, Upper Meudon* (oil on panel, 21 1/2 x 17 1/2 ins / 54.7 x 44.7 cm) GBP 7,920. Göteborg, 18 May 1989, *Rocky Coast with Figures and Sailing Boat Offshore* (oil on canvas, 21 1/4 x 32 1/4 ins / 54 x 82 cm) SEK 67,000. Stockholm, 16 May 1990, *Sunset on Sea* (oil on panel, 12 1/4 x 15 1/4 ins / 31 x 39 cm) SEK 19,500. Stockholm, 14 Nov 1990, *Sailing Boat on Sea near Marstrand* (oil on canvas, 23 1/2 x 31 1/2 ins / 60 x 80 cm) SEK 30,000. Stockholm, 28 Oct 1991, *Landscape of the Western Coast* (1917, oil on canvas, 14 1/2 x 22 1/2 ins / 37 x 57 cm) SEK 10,500. Stockholm, 5 Sept 1992, *Fishermen's Village* (1917, oil on canvas, 25 1/2 x 39 1/4 ins / 65 x 100 cm) SEK 27,000.

ERICSON, Leif
Swedish, 20th century.
Born 1927, in Göteborg.
Painter. Murals.
Group 54.

Leif Ericson attended the art school in Göteborg, studying under Ende Nemes between 1950 and 1955. He went on study excursions to Europe and participated in group exhibitions in Lübeck and Bochum in 1955, Amsterdam in 1956, Edinburgh in 1956 and Milan in 1959. He numbered among those West Swedish artists who made up Group 54. His work with this group featured in the exhibition *Aspects de la jeune peinture suédoise* (*Aspects of Young Swedish Painting*) in Paris. He also put on one-man exhibitions, notably in Göteborg in 1960. In 1961 he painted a mural in the stadium of Ullevi (Göteborg).

Museums and Galleries:
Stockholm (Nationalmus.).

ERICSON, Natalia
Russian, 20th century.
Born in Russia.
Painter. Landscapes.

Natalia Ericson exhibited in Paris at the Salon des Indépendants from 1937 onwards.

ERICSON, Suzanne
American, 20th century.
Born in Savannah (Georgia).
Active in France.
Painter.

Suzanne Ericson lived and studied in Paris and exhibited genre scenes inspired by maritime life in Britanny at the Paris Salon de la Société Nationale des Beaux-Arts and the Salon d'Automne.

ERICSON-MOLARD, Ida
Swedish, 19th century.
Born 13 February 1853, in Stockholm.
Sculptor.

This artist was a student at the academy in Stockholm before he settled in Paris.

ERICSSON, Henry
Finnish, 20th century.
Born 6 February 1898, in Mikkeli; died 16 October 1933, in Porvoo.
Painter, decorative artist. Seascapes, architectural views.

In 1925 Henry Ericsson decorated the Salle de Finlande at the Exposition Internationale des Arts Décoratifs in 1925 in Paris. He also contributed to the Salon d'Automne. He was connected with the Finnish architect Alvar Aalto. Several of his paintings attracted the attention of Ed Joseph.

Museums and Galleries:
Turku (Cathedral): *Frigate*; *Church of Christ*.

ERICSSON, Johan Edward
Swedish, 19th century.
Born 1836, in Göteborg; died 1871, in Stockholm.
Sculptor, medallist. Portraits, scenes with figures. Medallions, groups.

Museums and Galleries:
Göteborg: *Portrait of Sven Renström* (medallion) - Stockholm: *Playing Cligne-Musette*; *Young Mother Playing with Her Children* (plaster group).

ERIGONUS
3th century BC.
Painter.
Ancient Roman.

Erigonus, active in 236 BC, is said by Pliny to have started out by grinding colours for Nealces.

ERIK XIV (King of Sweden)
Swedish, 16th century.
Born 1533; died 1577.
Painter.

Siret mentions a miniature at Uppsala University and two portraits in Stockholm Museum traditionally attributed to the king.

ERIKE
German, 14th century.
Active c. 1350.
Sculptor.

Erike carved a portal in Worms.

ERIKSEN, Edward
Danish, 20th century.
Born 10 March 1870, in Copenhagen.
Sculptor.

Eriksen attended the art school in Copenhagen. He received a gold medal for his sculpture *Meditation*. He was also awarded a travelling scholarship and spent some time in Italy. His most famous work is *The Little Mermaid*, a sculpture in bronze on the Langelinie Promenade in Copenhagen.

ERIKSEN, Lars Martin
Norwegian, 19th - 20th century.
Born 18 October 1869, in Christiania (now Oslo).
Painter. Landscapes.

Lars Eriksen attended the Christiania school of arts and crafts and studied with Kristian Zahrtmann in Copenhagen. He travelled to Berlin, Dresden and Munich and later to Holland and Paris. His work featured in the exhibition at Christiania (Oslo) from 1889 and at the Norwegian exhibition in Stockholm in 1904. His repertoire consists mainly of Norwegian landscapes.

Museums and Galleries:
Oslo (Kongelige Slott) - Trondheim (Kunstmus.).

ERIKSEN, Thorvald and Virgilius.
See **ERICHSEN**

ERIKSON, Gosta
Swedish, 20th century.
Born 1908.
Painter, sculptor.

Gosta Erikson lived and worked in Stockholm. His work featured in several exhibitions including: *Stockholm Today, Colour and Form* in Brunswick. He also exhibited in Paris at the Salon des Réalités Nouvelles between 1952 and 1955, in Hamburg, Frankfurt, Biarritz and New York. His abstract compositions were often made up of rhythmic or angular elements, and concentric curves.

ERIKSON, Hans
Swedish, 16th century.
Born to a family originally from Strengnäs.
Painter.

The paintings decorating the chamber of the Grand Duke Charles on the lower floor of the castle of Gripsholm on Lake Malar are attributed to Hans Erikson.

ERIKSSON, Aja
Swedish, 20th century.
Sculptor.
In 1976 Aja Eriksson participated in the exhibition *Street Art* in Borlänge, which grouped together contemporary Swedish sculptors. She used textiles in her works.

ERIKSSON, Christian
Swedish, 19th - 20th century.
Born 1858, in Arvika; died 1935.
Sculptor, draughtsman.
Christian Eriksson studied under Falguière in Paris and obtained a third medal in 1888 and two gold medals in 1889 and 1900 at the Exposition Universelle. A talented sculptor, he executed a number of decorations in Sweden. For the theatre in Stockholm he carried out two sandstone reliefs: *The Procession of Dionysus* and *La Commedia dell'Arte*. His work was shown on several occasions in Paris, Munich and Venice.
MUSEUMS AND GALLERIES:
BÉZIERS: *Sorceress* (terracotta) - CHICAGO: *Linnaea* (low relief, plaster) - COPENHAGEN (Statens Mus. for Kunst): *Young Breton Woman* (faience); *Game* (bronze) - GÖTEBORG: *Blind Man's Buff* (vase, bronze); *Young Laplander* (sculpted wood) - HELSINKI: *Thuuri* (statuette) - SALTSJÖBADEN: *Youth Dancing* (bronze); *Skaters* (bronze) - STOCKHOLM (Kungliga Dramatiska teatern): *Jenny Lind* (marble) - STOCKHOLM (Nationalmus.): *Miracle* (vase, bronze); *Linnaea* (low relief, marble); *Young Breton Woman* (bronze); *Thuuri* (bronze).
AUCTION RECORDS:
STOCKHOLM, 26 April 1982, *Young Girl* (bronze, h. 6 3/4 ins / 17 cm) SEK 3,800. STOCKHOLM, 9 Nov 1984, *Seated Laplander* (1909, bronze, h. 8 1/4 ins / 21 cm) SEK 18,000. STOCKHOLM, 16 April 1986, *Seated Laplander* (1909, patinated bronze, h. 7 3/4 ins / 20 cm) SEK 23,000. STOCKHOLM, 10 Dec 1986, *Seaside* (watercolour and pencil, 11 x 39 1/4 ins / 28 x 100 cm) SEK 20,000. STOCKHOLM, 21 Oct 1987, *Diana* (patinated bronze, h. 14 1/2 ins / 37 cm) SEK 46,000. STOCKHOLM, 19 April 1989, *Elof* (1901, bronze, h. 7 3/4 ins / 20 cm) SEK 11,000. STOCKHOLM, 14 June 1990, *Elof, Standing Nude Boy* (1901, brown-patinated bronze, h. 7 3/4 ins / 20 cm) SEK 8,500. STOCKHOLM, 10-12 May 1993, *Smithy* (bronze, h. 8 1/4 ins / 21 cm) SEK 13,000.

ERIKSSON, Liss
Swedish, 20th century.
Born 1919, in Stockholm.
Sculptor.
The son of the sculptor Christian Eriksson, Liss Eriksson attended the art school in Stockholm from 1939 to 1941. His sculpture is Expressionist and sometimes abstract, but without losing sight of the living organism. A great tenderness, warmth, resolution and inner force inform his sculptures of individuals. He sculpted monumental pieces in stone, bronze and wood.
MUSEUMS AND GALLERIES:
OSLO - STOCKHOLM.
AUCTION RECORDS:
STOCKHOLM, 26 Nov 1982, *Girl Seated* (bronze, h. 11 1/2 ins / 29.5 cm) SEK 4,400. STOCKHOLM, 18 Nov 1984, *Standing Nude* (1955, patinated bronze, h. 13 ins / 33 cm) SEK 10,700. STOCKHOLM, 6 Dec 1989, *Reclining Model* (brown-patinated bronze, h. 3 3/4 ins / 9.5 cm) SEK 4,000. STOCKHOLM, 5-6 Dec 1990, *Ciss III - Head* (brown-patinated lost-wax bronze, h. 14 1/4 ins / 36 cm) SEK 12,000. STOCKHOLM, 27 Nov 2000, *Lovers* (dark patinated bronze, h. 12 ins / 30 cm) SEK 20,000. STOCKHOLM, 2 May 2001, *Boxer Squatting Down* (dark patinated bronze, h. 17 ins / 42 cm) SEK 20,000. STOCKHOLM, 5 Nov 2002, *Balancing* (dark gold patinated bronze, h. 17 ins / 44 cm) SEK 22,000. STOCKHOLM, 4 Nov 2003, *Mother and Child* (1956, brown patinated bronze, h. 16 ins / 40 cm) SEK 19,500. STOCKHOLM, 27 April 2004, *Lovers* (patinated bronze, h. 22 ins / 55 cm) SEK 30,000. STOCKHOLM, 3 Nov 2004, *The Mirror* (patinated bronze, h. 16 ins / 40 cm) SEK 35,000.

ERILLUS
5th century BC.
Active during the second half of the 5th century BC.
Painter, sculptor (?).
Ancient Greek.
Erillus, a painter of the Archaic Period, may be the same as a sculptor of the same name and period.

ERIMONDO (Fra)
Italian, 11th century.
Active in Civitella Casanova.
Miniaturist.

ERISMANN, Friedrich Johann
Swiss, 20th century.
Born 22 October 1911, in Gerzensee.
Painter. Portraits, landscapes, flowers.
Erismann studied in 1936-1937 in Bern, then from 1937 in Frankfurt am Main as well as in Paris. He practised painting with the palette knife and spatula. Until 1950 he painted above all Swiss landscapes, including numerous motifs of mountains in the Alps, but he was also commissioned to paint pictures of flowers. In 1951 he created coastal landscapes, seascapes and townscapes. During 1952-1954 during his annual stays in Paris he painted views of the Seine. In 1956 he continued his studies in Munich.
BIBLIOGRAPHY:
'Friecrich Johann Erismann' in *Künstler Lexikon der Schweiz XX. Jahrhundert*, Huber, Frauenfeld, 1958-1967.

ERISMANN, Vincenz
Swiss, 16th century.
Active in Zofingen.
Glass painter.
Vincenz Erismann is mentioned in 1577 as having made stained glass windows for Olten.

ERISTOV-KAZAK, Mariya (Princess)
Russian, 19th - 20th century.
Born in St Petersburg.
Active in France.
Painter, pastellist. Portraits, landscapes.
Mariya Eristov-Kazan was a student of the Hungarian Mihaly von Zichy, a renowned historical painter at the Court of the Tsars; she followed him as far as Paris where she settled for the rest of her life. Between two trips to the Far East and Italy, she produced portraits of Slav society, generally in pastel, including: *Portrait of Countess Apraxin; Portrait of Constantinesco; Portrait of Princess Voronzov* and *Portrait of Prince George of Serbia*. A long-standing friend of the comedian Paul Mounet, she painted a portrait of André de Lorde, her son-in-law, which she bequeathed to the Théâtre Français in Paris. *Under the Far East Sun, Venice, Lake Maggiore* and *Lake Como* are some of her works mentioned. She exhibited regularly from 1894 onwards at the Salon des Beaux-Arts in Paris of which she was a member.
AUCTION RECORDS:
NEW YORK, 22-23 July 1993, *Portrait of the American Painter, Frank Holman* (oil on canvas, 87 1/2 x 51 ins / 222.3 x 129.5 cm) USD 5,750.

ERITZIANE, Jean
French, 20th century.
Born in the second half of the 19th century, in Smyrna, Turkey.
Painter, pastellist.
Jean Eritziane was a pupil of Bonnet. He joined the 2nd Foreign Regiment as a volunteer in 1914 and was twice wounded. He was represented in the Exposition des Artistes

Mobilisés (exhibition of artists on active service) in 1919, and is known for his portrait of Felia Livinne.

ERIXSON, Sven Leonard
Swedish, 20th century.
Born 1899, in Tumba or Botkyrka, near Stockholm; died 1970, in Saltsjöbaden, near Stockholm.
Painter, decorative designer. Murals, designs for tapestries.
Färg och Form (Colour and Form) group.

Erixson set out as a house painter. Between 1922 and 1923 he attended the Konstakademi in Stockholm. On completion of his studies, he worked until 1928 as an assistant to the decorator Filip Maanson. He then travelled in Europe, notably Italy and France. His discovery of the Expressionists - Oskar Kokoschka, Emil Nolde and Chaim Soutine - and southern landscapes was pivotal in his development. On his return to Sweden, he joined the Nine Young Men group which rejected orthodox notions of painting. In 1930 he frequented the group Färg och Form (Colour and Form). In 1940 he executed mural decorations, in particular a fresco for the Stockholm forest cemetery and another large fresco, *Liv-Död-Liv* (*Life-Death-Life*). Between 1938 and 1940 he painted a further fresco for the chapel at Skogskyrkogårdens Crematorium in Stockholm. In 1935 he created a large tapestry for the Konserthus (concert hall) in Göteborg: *Melodies in the Market Place*. He also carried out stage sets for authors such as Lorca, Shakespeare and the opera *Aniara* by Blomdahl. He was professor at the Konstakademi in Stockholm from 1943 to 1953. His work featured in numerous exhibitions of Swedish art: in Brussels in 1935, Paris in 1939 and at the Biennale di Venezia in 1950. He contributed to an exhibition in Stockholm in 1961. His output is very varied - the life of women in towns, desert landscapes of the North, lively harbours of the southern coast and scenes of family life.

AUCTION RECORDS:
STOCKHOLM, 3 April 1968, *Yellow House*, SEK 7,000. STOCKHOLM, 19 April 1972, *Seaside* (Cannes) SEK 14,000. GÖTEBORG, 26 March 1974, *Summer Landscape*, SEK 11,200. GÖTEBORG, 31 March 1977, *Alchemist* (oil on canvas, 11 x 15 ins / 27 x 38 cm) SEK 10,000. COPENHAGEN, 17 May 1978, *View of Stockholm* (oil on canvas, 39 1/4 x 32 ins / 100 x 81 cm) DKK 35,000. GÖTEBORG, 8 May 1980, *Composition* (1954, gouache, 17 3/4 x 24 3/4 ins / 45 x 63 cm) SEK 4,400. STOCKHOLM, 23 April 1983, *Park in Venice* (1930, gouache, 12 1/2 x 16 ins / 32 x 40.5 cm) SEK 8,200. STOCKHOLM, 29 Nov 1983, *View of Park* (1928, oil on canvas, 23 1/4 x 24 3/4 ins / 59 x 63 cm) SEK 75,000. STOCKHOLM, 27 May 1986, *Seaside Park, Pesaro* (1924, watercolour, 17 x 22 ins / 43 x 56 cm) SEK 18,000. STOCKHOLM, 9 Dec 1986, *Summer Night*, SEK 51,000. STOCKHOLM, 6 June 1988, *Wooded Landscape with Figures* (oil, 14 1/2 x 17 3/4 ins / 37 x 45 cm) SEK 25,000. STOCKHOLM, 22 May 1989, *Children on Wooded Path in Red Sunlight in Evening* (oil on panel, 22 x 18 ins / 55 x 46 cm) SEK 100,000. STOCKHOLM, 6 Dec 1989, *Northern Landscape with Dwelling* (oil on canvas, 22 1/2 x 27 1/4 ins / 57 x 69 cm) SEK 100,000. STOCKHOLM, 14 June 1990, *Playing Field in Landscape* (1950, oil on panel, 13 x 18 1/2 ins / 33 x 47 cm) SEK 29,000. STOCKHOLM, 5-6 Dec 1990, *Landscape with Path Running between the Houses* (oil on canvas, 28 3/4 x 36 1/4 ins / 73 x 92 cm) SEK 44,000. STOCKHOLM, 21 May 1992, *The Funicular of Katarina in Stockholm* (oil on canvas, 39 1/4 x 32 ins / 100 x 81 cm) SEK 190,000. STOCKHOLM, 30 Nov 1993, *View of Forsmobron* (1937, oil on canvas, 24 3/4 x 31 1/2 ins / 63 x 80 cm) SEK 34,000. STOCKHOLM, 17 May 1999, *Figures at Katarina Churchyard* (1931, oil on canvas, 26 x 32 ins / 65 x 81 cm) SEK 105,000. STOCKHOLM, 26 Oct 1999, *Melodies by the River, Krangede* (1936, oil on canvas, 50 x 72 ins / 127 x 184 cm) SEK 325,000. STOCKHOLM, 15 May 2000, *Summer Celebration in the Harbour* (1961, oil on canvas, 37 x 45 ins / 94 x 114 cm) SEK 175,000. STOCKHOLM, 7 Nov 2000, *The Gardener* (1942, oil on canvas, 23 x 21 ins / 59 x 54 cm) SEK 98,000. STOCKHOLM, 2 May 2001, *The Artist's House* (1942, oil on panel, triptych, 98 x 142 ins / 250 x 360 cm) SEK 450,000. STOCKHOLM, 27 Nov 2001, *The Artist* (oil on panel, 48 x 62 ins / 122 x 158 cm) SEK 135,000. STOCKHOLM, 23 April 2002, *The Dancing Pavilion* (1925, oil on panel, 21 x 26 ins / 54 x 67 cm) SEK 340,000. STOCKHOLM, 24 April 2002, *Bastugatan - Street Scene with Figures* (1938, oil on canvas, 46 x 35 ins / 116 x 89 cm) SEK 210,000. STOCKHOLM, 7 May 2003, *My Wife among Autumn Flowers* (1928, oil on canvas, 28 x 22 ins / 70 x 55 cm) SEK 165,000. STOCKHOLM, 7 May 2003, *From My Studio in Paris* (1931, oil on canvas, 39 x 31 ins / 100 x 80 cm) SEK 170,000. STOCKHOLM, 26 April 2004, *Winter in Stockholm* (1932, oil on canvas, 35 x 46 ins / 89 x 117 cm) SEK 270,000. STOCKHOLM, 3 Nov 2004, *The Gardener at Tattby* (1942, oil on canvas, 23 x 21 ins / 58 x 54 cm) SEK 195,000.

ERKE, Jakob Ludolf
Russian, 19th century.
Born 1796, in Tartu; died 2 November 1845, in St Petersburg.
Engraver.

ERKELENS, Anthonie, or Abraham Erkeles
Dutch, 17th century.
Active in The Hague c. 1665.
Painter, draughtsman. Landscapes.

MUSEUMS AND GALLERIES:
AMSTERDAM (Fodor Mus.): several drawings.

ERKELENS, Pieter van
Dutch, 18th century.
Active in Middelburg c. 1767 and in Brussels.
Painter.

Pieter van Erkelens painted landscapes and seascapes.

ERKELES, Abraham. See **ERKELENS Anthonie**

ERKENBERT
German, 12th century.
Active in Bosan.
Miniaturist.

This monk illustrated a manuscript of St Augustine's *The City of God*.

ERL, Max
Austrian, 19th century.
Born 1845, in Vienna.
Painter.

A son of the opera singer Josef Erl, Max Erl studied under Wurzinger at the academy of art in Vienna. Erl painted a portrait of his father which is still known today.

ERLACH, Anna Elisabetha von
Swiss, 19th century.
Born 17 January 1856, in Bern; died 17 November 1906, in Bern.
Painter. Genre scenes, portraits.

This artist began her studies at the school of drawing in Basel, completing them in Karlsruhe, Berlin, Düsseldorf, Paris (with Carolus Duran and Henner) and Italy from 1876 onwards. She exhibited in Paris and at the Turnus in Switzerland. The museum in Bern contains the following works: *Study of a Black Man, Study of a Monk, Two Girls in an Armchair, Child with Pitcher, Head of a Young Girl in the Shade,* and *Still-life with Tomatoes, Melons and Pitcher*.

ERLACH, Gertrud von
Swiss, 19th - 20th century.
Born 29 December 1861, in La-Tour-de-Peil (Vaud).
Painter.

Gertrud von Erlach was the sister and pupil of Anna Elisabetha von Erlach. At the outset a painter and amateur draughtswoman, she then turned professional, from 1908 onwards regularly showing pastels and oil paintings in Swiss exhibitions.

ERLACH VON HINDELBANK, Ada von
Swiss, 19th - 20th century.
Born 29 September 1853, in Zurich; died 11 October 1907, in Strasbourg.
Painter. Portraits, genre scenes.

The pupil of Professor Karl Gussow in Berlin and Henner and Carolus-Duran in Paris, Ada von Erlach von Hindelbank exhibited in Bern, Geneva, Turnus and Paris from 1888. Around 1903 she lived in Strasbourg.

MUSEUMS AND GALLERIES:
BERN: *Study after School.*

ERLACH VON HINDELBANK, Sophie Maria von
Maiden name: von May
Swiss, 19th - 20th century.
Born 5 October 1829, in Bern; died 31 December 1911, in Strasbourg.
Painter, watercolourist.

Sophie von Erlach studied with F. Dietler in her birthplace, visited Berlin and the museum there and for some time worked in the service of Princess Louise of Prussia (Grand Duchess of Baden). She exhibited in Zurich and around 1902 lived in Vienna.

ERLACHER, Andreas
German, 18th century.
Active in Passau in 1732.
Sculptor.

ERLACHER, Sebastian
German, 17th century.
Born 1609, in Tegernsee; died 18 August 1649.
Sculptor.

This Bavarian artist became established in Graz in 1632.

ERLAND
Russian, 17th century.
Active in St Petersburg.
Painter, sculptor (?).

It seems to have been the same artist who produced paintings in 1753 for the Peterhof Palace and in 1767, sculptures for the Palace at Oranienbaum.

ERLANGER, Philipp Jakob
German, 20th century.
Born 3 March 1870, in Frankfurt am Main.
Painter, sculptor.

After attending the Städelsches Kunstinstitut with Hassel-Horst, Philipp Erlanger studied in Munich and Karlsruhe with Weisshaupt and Zügel. He settled in Breslau (now Wroclaw, Poland) in 1899 and undertook study excursions to Paris and Italy. He exhibited his works in Berlin, Düsseldorf and Munich.

AUCTION RECORDS:
NEW YORK, 1 March 1980, *Two Carthorses* (bronze, h. 13 1/2 ins / 34.3 cm) USD 750.

ERLANGER, Rodolphe François d'
French, 20th century.
Born 7 June 1872, in Boulogne-sur-Seine; died c. 1932.
Painter. Portraits, local scenes.
Orientalism.

Rodolphe François d'Erlanger was the son of the banker Baron d'Erlanger and studied at the Académie Julian with Jules Lefebrve and Tony Robert-Fleury. In his frequent visits to North Africa he got to know the Muslim peoples of Tunis, Algeria and Egypt well, and this led to his becoming a painter of oriental subjects. He first exhibited in Paris at the Salon des Artistes Français with *Old Philosopher.*

Among d'Erlanger's best-known oriental works are *Portrait of Omar Baccouche, Young Arab in Hunting Dress, Two Friends, Young Abyssinian Chief, The Favourite,* and among his other works are portraits of the *Baronne Rodolphe d'Erlanger,* the musicians *Galeotti* and *Lucien Delafond,* the *Marquise de Rochegude* and the *Parish Priest of Pessis-Piquet.*

MUSEUMS AND GALLERIES:
PARIS (Mus. du Petit Palais).

AUCTION RECORDS:
PARIS, 22 June 1992, *Sidi bou Said in Tunisia* (1913, oil on panel, a pair, each 4 3/4 x 7 ins / 12 x 18 cm) FRF 10,000. PARIS, 5 April 1993, *Women Water-Carriers and Children* (oil on canvas, 22 x 13 3/4 ins / 56 x 35 cm) FRF 28,000.

ERLANT
Russian, 18th century.
Active in St Petersburg.
Sculptor (wood).

ERLER, Franz Anton
German, 18th century.
Born to a family originally from Ottobeuren.
Painter.

Erler was a painter of religious subjects in Bavaria.

ERLER, Franz Chr.
Austrian, 19th - 20th century.
Born 5 October 1829, in Kitzbühel; died 6 January 1911, in Vienna.
Sculptor.

Franz Erler worked for the cathedral of St Stephen, the Arsenal and the Rathaus (town hall).

MUSEUMS AND GALLERIES:
GIESSHÜBEL (Parish Church) - KLOSTERNEUBURG (Stiftsmus.) - MAYERLING (Cloisters).

ERLER, Fritz, real name: Erich Erler-Samaden
German, 20th century.
Born 15 December 1868, in Frankenstein, Silesia, near Breslau (now Wroclaw, Poland); died 11 July 1940, in Munich.
Painter, graphic designer, draughtsman, illustrator, decorative designer. Posters, theatre sets, designs (art objects/jewellery/glassware/fabrics).
Die Scholle group. Utting-Holzhausen artists' colony.

Fritz Erler was educated at the Strehlen School, then began his artistic studies in Albrecht Bräuer's studio at the Kunstschule in Breslau. There he applied himself to life drawing. He completed his artistic education by travelling through France, Italy and northern Germany. In 1892, Erler went to Paris and entered the Académie Julian. He remained there until 1894, receiving guidance from Adolphe Bouguereau and Gabriel Ferrier. After a brief trip to Berlin, he returned to Breslau in 1894, and devoted his time to studying anatomy, perspective and *plein air* painting. He then settled in Munich in 1895, partially drawing inspiration from studying the works of the old masters in the Pinakothek.

While living in France, Erler travelled around the coasts of Normandy and Brittany, and brought back studies and landscapes which he would later use in his paintings, such as his major composition *Lotos,* a reminiscence from The Odyssey, which was exhibited on the Champ de Mars in 1893, and a landscape of *Morgat Bay.* Perhaps that same year, his marked tendencies towards decorative art were already becoming apparent, as evidenced by his *Prince and the Pirates* (1895), one of his last works in Paris. The series of portraits of the Rose family dates from the same period: *Skaters; Autumn Evening;* and *Dancer with Guitar.* Erler soon liberated himself entirely from all influences and demonstrated the temperament of a decorative painter with a very pure style. He is noted for the richness of his colours, the superb vigour of his composition and his artistic subtlety. Besides the paintings already mentioned, his most important works include: *Salas y Gomez* (1894); *Lullaby of the Siren* (1893); decorations in the Villa Neisser in Breslau, the Wiesbaden Casino and the Trabach restaurant in Berlin (a triptych representing an interpretation of the *Plague*, which was exhibited in Munich in 1899); *Young Hagen with the King's Children; Portrait of a Lady; Grey Day* (1902-1903); *Dancer; Solitude; Fencer; Strangers; Mother; St George; Solstice* (triptych); *Noah; The Modern Diana; Wave; Nature; Impression of Autumn; Fountain*; and *Studies of Peasants*. He also painted portraits of Richard Strauss, Gustav Mahler, Pablo de Sarasate, Gerhart Hauptmann, the prince of Hatzfeld, Professor Neisser, his brother Erich Erler-Samaden, and his wife and other ladies.

Erler played an important role in the creation of Jugendstil. In 1896, he was one of the founding members of the weekly magazine *Die Jugend*, which was published in Munich, and for which he created the frontispiece of the first edition. He was also a member of the Munich group Die Scholle (The Glebe), whose aims were to obtain free and group representations at the Glaspalast exhibitions in Munich. In the 1890s, Erler was extremely interested in the knightly fantasy world and imaginary universe of the fairytales of Hans Christian Andersen and the Brothers Grimm. He received a huge number of commissions for book illustrations (including *Ingwelde* by M. Schiling), ex-libris, posters and portraits. In 1898 the family of the doctor Albert Neisser commissioned him to design a music room for their new house in Wroclaw, with decoration and furniture in Jugendstil. This led to numerous commissions for compositions and murals in Germany. In a government building in Pankow; a set of decorative paintings for New Union carnival in Munich (1908); and frescoes for the meeting room at the Rückversicherung insurance company in Munich (1913). He also designed the stage sets for Faust and Hamlet for the Künstlertheater in Munich in 1908. Fritz Erler committed himself aesthetically and politically during World War I. He was an official war painter, and painted acts of heroism in the 1930s to illustrate the naturalist themes of National Socialism. He also painted a portrait of Adolf Hitler in 1939.

Erler

BIBLIOGRAPHY:

Hase, Ulrike von, *Schmuck in Deutschland und Österrreich. Symbolismus, Jugendstil, Neohistorismus*, Prestel, Munich, 1977. Bloom Hiesinger, Kathryn, *Art nouveau in Munich. Masters of Jugendstil*, exhibition catalogue, Museum of Art, Philadelphia, 1989. Schroeter, Christina, *Fritz Erler: Leben und Werk*, Christians, Hamburg, 1992. Ottomeyer, Hans (ed.)/Brandlhuber, Margot, *Wege in die Moderne. Jugendstil in München 1896 bis 1914*, Klinkhardt & Biermann, Munich, Berlin, 1997.

MUSEUMS AND GALLERIES:

LEIPZIG: *Solstice* (triptych) - LONDON (Victoria and Albert Mus.): *Die Jugend* (1901, coloured lithograph) - MUNICH (Bayerische Staatsbibliothek): *Die Jugend* (1898, cover) - SCHWEINFURT (Mus. Georg Schäfer).

AUCTION RECORDS:

MUNICH, 26 Nov 1976, *Flowers at Lakeside* (oil on canvas, 27 1/2 x 35 1/2 ins / 70 x 90 cm) DEM 2,600. MUNICH, 25 Nov 1981, *Morning* (c. 1905, colouring pencil/paper, 17 1/4 x 7 3/4 ins / 44 x 20 cm) DEM 9,500. LONDON, 28 Nov 1984, *Ophelia* (1893, oil on panel, 26 x 26 ins / 66 x 66 cm) GBP 5,200. MUNICH, 26 May 1992, *Male Nude* (blue chalk, 19 1/2 x 11 ins / 49.5 x 27 cm) DEM 2,070. MUNICH, 24 March 1999, *Nude Viking Woman Holding a Fish on the Seashore* (oil on canvas, 50 x 39 ins / 128 x 100 cm) DEM 18,000. MUNICH, 1 Dec 1999, *Portrait of Anna Erler in White Dress in Landscape* (1903, oil on canvas, 39 x 28 ins / 100 x 70 cm) DEM 18,000. MUNICH, 16 Nov 2000, *Men Working* (oil on canvas, 37 x 37 ins / 95 x 95 cm) DEM 7,000. MUNICH, 1 Dec 2001, *Lady with Mask* (c. 1909, wood, 74 x 62 ins / 187 x 158 cm) DEM 36,000. MUNICH, 14 Dec 2001, *Portrait Study* (oil on canvas, 19 x 12 ins / 48 x 31 cm) EUR 1,940. MUNICH, 18 Oct 2002, *Winter Walk* (oil on canvas, 16 x 21 ins / 40 x 54 cm) EUR 1,800. MUNICH, 18 Oct 2002, *Female Nude* (oil on panel, 46 x 41 ins / 118 x 103 cm) EUR 11,000. MUNICH, 14 May 2004, *Summer Solstice* (oil on canvas, 28 x 24 ins / 70 x 60 cm) EUR 4,050. MUNICH, 14 May 2004, *Springtime* (oil on canvas, 24 x 16 ins / 60 x 40 cm) EUR 6,400.

ERLER, Georg Oskar

German, 20th century.

Born 15 October 1871, in Dresden; died 1951, in Auring.

Painter, draughtsman, engraver (etching), lithographer. Historical portraits, genre scenes, rustic scenes, urban landscapes.

Georg Erler attended the school of arts and crafts in Dresden and the royal academy with Hugo Bürkner and G. Kuehl. For his etchings *Miners' Meditation in front of Ditch* and *Between the Hours of Work* he was awarded a gold medal and a two-year travelling scholarship for Rome. After spending some time in this city and in Paris and Munich, he settled definitively in Dresden. His key works include: *Louvre Embankment, Potato Harvest, Woman with Goat, Return, Gleaners* and the *Portrait of King George of Saxony*. Also noteworthy are a series of colour drawings and 20 lithographs of views of Dresden.

ERLER, Josef

Austrian, 19th century.

Born 9 February 1804, in Brixen, South Tyrol (now Bressanone, Italy); died 31 March 1844, in Innsbruck.

Painter.

Erler studied drawing in Brixen with Josef Tauber and spent 11 years at the academy in Vienna. He painted portraits, history paintings and landscapes. He is noted in particular for works in the church of Zinggen, near Brixen: a *Holy Trinity, Angels*, an *Assumption* and *Scenes from the Life of Mary*.

MUSEUMS AND GALLERIES:

BRESSANONE (Diocesan Mus.): *Studies of Heads* - INNSBRUCK (Tiroler Landesmus. Ferdinandeum): *Portrait of Ph. Jacob Fallmerayer; Self-portrait.*

ERLER, Margarethe

German, 19th - 20th century.

Active in Berlin.

Painter.

Margarethe Erler exhibited regularly in Berlin.

MUSEUMS AND GALLERIES:

KREFELD - MAGDEBURG - STUTTGART.

ERLER-SAMADEN, Erich

German, 19th - 20th century.

Born 16 December 1870, in Frankenstein; died 1946, in Icking, near Munich.

Painter, engraver. Figures, landscapes.

Symbolism.

The brother of Fritz Erler, Erich Erler-Samaden worked in Samaden and Breslau (now Wroclaw, Poland) where he was taught by A. Bräuer at the Kunsthochschule. He lived in the Swiss Alps. His works include *Peasants in Fancy Dress, Blue Door, Old Lady's Garden, Spring in Meadow* and *May Evening*. His output featured in the 2003 exhibition, *1914-1918. Mathurin Méheut un artiste combattant* (*1914-1918: Mathurin Méheut, an Artist in Combat*) in the museum in Arras where works executed from two sides of the front were shown. He was the subject of an exhibition in 2002: *Erich Er-*

ler - Ein Schollemaler at the Neues Stadtmuseum at Landsberg am Lech.

BIBLIOGRAPHY:

Erich Erler. Ein Schollemaler, exhibition catalogue, Neues Stadtmuseum, Landsberg am Lech, 2002.

MUSEUMS AND GALLERIES:

AACHEN (Suermondt-Ludwig Mus.): *Wild Land* - INGOLSTADT (Bayerisches Armeemus.): *Dorf unter feuer* (*Village under Fire*) (engraving) - LEIPZIG: *South* - MUNICH (Neue Pinakothek): *Promise of Spring* - WROCLAW: *Solitude*.

AUCTION RECORDS:

MUNICH, 25 Nov 1977, *Skier in High Mountain* (c. 1905, oil on canvas, 38 x 51 1/4 ins / 96.5 x 130 cm) DEM 3,800. ZURICH, 7 Nov 1981, *Mountainous Landscape* (oil on canvas, 37 1/2 x 37 1/2 ins / 95 x 95 cm) CHF 4,000. MUNICH, 26 Nov 1984, *Landscape of the Engadine* (oil on canvas, 27 1/2 x 31 1/2 ins / 70 x 80 cm) DEM 3,500. MUNICH, 5 June 1986, *Landscape of the Engadine in Spring* (oil on canvas, 48 x 47 1/4 ins / 122 x 120 cm) DEM 4,000. AMSTERDAM, 16 Nov 1988, *Mountain Lake* (oil on canvas, 27 3/4 x 31 1/2 ins / 70.5 x 80 cm) NLG 3,910. COLOGNE, 23 March 1990, *Beginning of Spring* (oil on canvas, 31 1/2 x 27 1/2 ins / 80 x 70 cm) DEM 5,500. MUNICH, 20 May 1999, *Hohenengadin Mountains* (oil on canvas, 28 x 32 ins / 70 x 81 cm) DEM 5,000. STUTTGART, 21 Sept 1999, *Spring in the Alps* (oil on canvas, 37 x 47 ins / 95 x 120 cm) DEM 10,000. COLOGNE, 6 April 2000, *Springtime in the Mountain* (oil on canvas, 37 x 37 ins / 95 x 95 cm) DEM 7,000. ZURICH, 29 May 2000, *Female Nude in Landscape* (oil on canvas, 39 x 39 ins / 100 x 100 cm) CHF 4,200. MUNICH, 19 May 2001, *Mountain Landscape* (oil on canvas, 38 x 38 ins / 96 x 96 cm) DEM 7,000. HAMBURG, 8 Dec 2001, *Nude with Dog in Autumnal Landscape* (oil on canvas, 47 x 43 ins / 120 x 108 cm) DEM 4,800. HAMBURG, 23 March 2002, *Moonlit Mountain Lake* (oil on canvas, 39 x 35 ins / 100 x 90 cm) EUR 2,700. HAMBURG, 7 Dec 2002, *Figures Harvesting in Landscape* (1913, oil on canvas, 36 x 37 ins / 92 x 95 cm) EUR 2,500. MUNICH, 13 Nov 2003, *Peasant Woman* (oil on canvas, 37 x 40 ins / 94 x 101 cm) EUR 3,800. MUNICH, 13 Nov 2003, *At the High Valley* (oil on canvas, 31 x 31 ins / 80 x 80 cm) EUR 8,000. MUNICH, 13 May 2004, *Mountain Church in the Snow* (oil on canvas, 24 x 20 ins / 60 x 50 cm) EUR 2,000. DÜSSELDORF, 25 Sept 2004, *Sunday in the Countryside* (oil on canvas, 38 x 38 ins / 96 x 96 cm) EUR 2,600.

ERLETMAYGER, Johann.
See **ERHETMAYGER**

ERLEWYN, Jan van
Flemish, 17th century.
Active in Antwerp, in 1650.
Painter.
Flemish School.

ERLIKH, Vladimir
Ukrainian, 20th century.
Born 1924, in Odessa.
Painter. Landscapes with figures.

Vladimir Erlikh studied at the school of fine art in Dnepropetrovsk from 1946 to 1950. He was a member of the union of Ukrainian painters in 1963.

AUCTION RECORDS:

PARIS, 13 March 1992, *On the Beach* (oil on canvas, 35 1/2 x 86 1/2 ins / 90 x 220 cm) FRF 9,000. PARIS, 17 June 1992, *In the Park* (oil on canvas, 15 x 25 1/2 ins / 38 x 65 cm) FRF 4,200.

ERLINGER, Georg
German, 16th century.
Born in Augsburg; died 1542, in Bamberg.
Painter, engraver (wood).
Bamberg School.

In 1516, Georg Erlinger was working in Augsburg. In 1519, he moved to Bamberg where he settled down. He was principally known as an astronomer.

ERLINGER, Johannes
German, 15th century.
Active in Augsburg.
Writer, miniaturist (?).

Johannes Erlinger is thought to have illustrated a number of chronicles.

ERLUIN
French, 9th century.
Active in Tours.
Miniaturist.

This artist illustrated religious books.

ERMA, Thomas
Estonian, 20th century.
Born 1939, in Tartu; died 1964, in Paris.
Active and naturalised in the USA, then active in France.
Painter.

Thomas Erma died at the age of twenty-five, before he had had time to establish himself fully. Nevertheless, his contribution to a certain kind of abstraction was far from negligible. Erma's painting was defined by a combination of dripping and collage. His paintings were actually reconstructed from painted fragments, in a style close to gestural lyric poetry, torn or cut into vertical strips, then assembled in a different order. This method of construction from an initial deconstruction was a way for Erma to repossess the spontaneous gesture, to assimilate and control it. Far from leaving his constructions to chance, Erma preferred a certain type of form dicatated by centrifugal forces which, leaving the centre of the canvas untouched, put the action on the periphery. In retrospect Erma's work heralds a certain form of analysis common after 1970, where deconstruction is a permanent. He exhibited in Paris (1959 and in 1962) and in London in 1963. He also participated in the Salon Comparaisons in Paris.

MUSEUMS AND GALLERIES:

NEW YORK (Solomon R. Guggenheim Mus.) - PARIS (MAM).

ERMANNO
Italian, 16th century.
Active in Rome in 1536.
Painter.

ERMANNO, Giovanni
Italian, 17th (?) century.
Painter. History painting.

Ermanno is mentioned by Siret.

ERMATINGER, Andreas
Swiss, 16th century.
Died between 1576 and 1580.
Active in Schaffhausen.
Glass painter.

Andreas Ermatinger was also a statesman.

ERMATINGER, Hans Ulrich
Swiss, 16th - 17th century.
Active in Schaffhausen between 1588 and 1614.
Glass painter.
Schaffhausen School.

According to Brun, Ermatinger was described in 1588 as being the youngest 'master' of his trade.

ERMELS, Georg Paul
German, 17th century.
Painter, engraver. Landscapes with figures.

A son and pupil of Johann Franciscus Ermels, Georg Ermels was active in Nuremberg in 1697.

AUCTION RECORDS:
LONDON, 17 April 1991, *Arcadian Landscapes with Figures and Classical Ruins* (oil on panel, a pair, each 14 x 14 1/4in/35.5 x 36cm) GBP 22,000.

ERMELS, J. H.
German, 18th century.
Engraver (etching).
J.H. Ermels made engravings after François Boucher.

ERMELS, Johann Franciscus
German, 17th century.
Born 1621 or 1641, near Cologne; died 3 December 1693, in Nuremberg.
Painter, engraver. Religious subjects, portraits, landscapes, still-lifes.
A pupil of Johann Hulsmann in Cologne and Jan Both in Holland, Johann Ermels lived in Nuremberg from 1660.

Ermels began his artistic career as an engraver, before turning to portrait painting. He did not, however, take up history and religious painting until 1660. In 1663, he worked with others on the *Resurrection* for the Muffel reredos painted for the church of St Sebald in Nuremberg. His landscapes are Classical in style, inspired both by Flemish and by Italian art. They often include ruins or country folk beneath a cloudy sky.

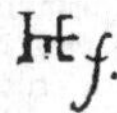

MUSEUMS AND GALLERIES:
FRANKFURT AM MAIN: *Two Landscapes; Still-life* - MILAN (Pinacoteca di Brera): *Wood* - MUNICH (Alte Pinakothek) - VIENNA: *Landscape with Mausoleum.*
AUCTION RECORDS:
NEW YORK, 24 March 1905, *Italian Landscape,* USD 150. NEW YORK, 12 Oct 1989, *Figures among Classical Ruins in a Mountain Landscape* (1688, oil on canvas, 17 3/4 x 23 1/4in/45 x 58.8cm) USD 9,900. LUCERNE, 20 Nov 2002, *Landscapes with Figures* (oil on panel, 7 x 9 ins / 17 x 23 cm) CHF 9,000. LONDON, 13 Dec 2002, *Coastal Landscape with Figures by Classical Ruins, Port Beyond* (1691, oil on canvas, 17 x 14 ins / 43 x 36 cm) GBP 7,500. LONDON, 10 Dec 2003, *Wooded Landscape with Travellers Resting amongst Classical Ruins, Cattle and Sheep Nearby* (oil on canvas, 25 x 26 ins / 63 x 67 cm) GBP 10,000.

ERMELTRAUT, Franz Anton
German, 18th century.
Born in Heidelberg.
Painter.
Franz Ermeltraut worked in Würzburg, where he decorated the frescoes of the Dominican church.

ERMELTRAUT, Johann Georg
German, 18th century.
Born 1697, in Salzungen.
Painter.
Johann Ermeltraut worked in Würzburg.

ERMENALDUS
French, 12th century.
Active in northern France c. 1100.
Miniaturist.
MUSEUMS AND GALLERIES:
AVRANCHES (Library): a miniature.

ERMENEV, Ivan
Russian, 18th century.
Born 1746; died 1790.
Painter.
His work appeared at the exhibition *L'Art Russe des Scythes à nos jours* (*Russian Art from the Scythians to Today*), at the Grand Palais in Paris, in 1967-1968,with a watercolour, now in the Russian Mueum in St Petersburg: *The Old Beggar and the Child.*

ERMENGEM, Frans
Belgian, 20th century.
Born 1893, in Wetteren.
Also active in Spain.
Painter, engraver, illustrator.
A pupil of J. Delvin in Ghent, Ermengem worked in Spain and on the Belgian coast. He illustrated texts by Charles Baudelaire and Charles van Lerberge.

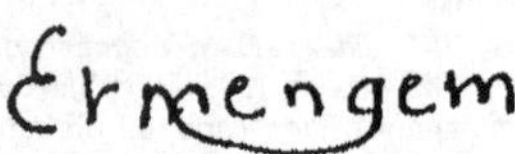

MUSEUMS AND GALLERIES:
TERMONDE.
AUCTION RECORDS:
BRUSSELS, 6 May 1986, *Seated Nude* (c. 1921, oil on canvas, 49 1/4 x 51 1/4 ins / 125 x 130 cm) BEF 55,000.

ERMER, C.
German, 19th century.
Active in Weimar in 1811.
Engraver (aquatint).
Ermer engraved *William Tell* after Kaatz.

ERMILOV, Foma
Russian, 17th century.
Born to a family originally from Kostroma.
Icon painter.
Foma Ermilov worked on murals and icons in churches of the Kremlin, in a church in Yaroslavl and in the Ipatiev Monastery in Kostroma.

ERMILOV, Vasili Dmitrievich
Russian, 20th century.
Born 1894, in Kharkov; died 1968, in Kharkov.
Painter, lithographer, poster artist.
Constructivism.
From 1905 to 1911 Vasili Ermolov studied decorative painting at the city school of design and painting and in private workshops in Kharkov; in 1912 he was admitted to the Institute of painting, sculpture and architecture in Moscow, then to the I. Mashkov and P. Konchalovsky workshop. In 1914, he received the title 'master of decorative painting'. In 1918 he got in contact with Kharkov's Futurist circles. In 1922 he taught at the technical institute of art in Kharkov.

Ermolov was one of the major representatives of the avant-garde movement in Ukraine. He was influenced from 1913 to 1916 by the principles of Neo-Primitivism (Larionov, Goncharova), Cubo-Futurism and Suprematism (Malevich). From 1917 onwards, he was one of the advocates of the Constructivist system (Pevsner, Gabo) and of one of its trends, Productivism (Tatlin), assigning to art the creation of objects of utilitarian value for the people and denouncing any deviationism towards 'pure' or autonomous art. In the course of the 1920s he practised mural agit-prop. From 1922 onwards, he taught art, town planning and typography in Kharkov.

Ermolov was not just a talented exponent of the guiding principles of Constructivism, he also knew how to innovate beyond the rules of this revolutionary movement. In his personal research, the colours and technique of the materials he chose, such as wood and metal, give his constructions an almost intimist aspect, and there lies his original contribution. He was also interested in architecture, graphic design, layout and posters and took part in collective exhibitions including: 16th and 17th exhibition of the Society of Artists, Kharkov (1913 and 1914), and in the first exhibition of the Association of Soviet Artists of the Ukraine-ARMOU (1927). Ermolov contributed to the USSR stand in Cologne in 1928.

BIBLIOGRAPHY:
Polichtchouk, V., *Vassili Ermilov*, Kharkov, 1931. Foguel, B., *Vassili Ermilov*, Moscow, 1975. Nakov, Andrei B., *Russian Constructivism: Laboratory Period*, Annely Juda Fine Art, London, 1975. Halturin, Aleksandr/Hulten, Pontus/Gunar, Karl (ed.), *Paris-Moscou*, group exhibition catalogue, Éd. du Centre Georges-Pompidou, Paris, 1979. Lodder, C., *Russian Constructivism*, Yale University Press, New Haven and London, 1983. Nakov, Andrei, *L'Avant-garde russe*, Hazan, Paris, 1984. Conio, Gérard (ed.), *Le Constructivisme russe: textes théoriques, manifestes, documents*, L'Âge d'Homme, Lausanne, 1987. *Vasily Dmitrievich Ermilov: Gouaches, Sculptures, Reliefs*, exhibition catalogue, Leonard Hutton Galleries, New York, 1990. *Russian Twentieth century and Avant-Garde Art*, auction catalogue, Sotheby's Publications, London, May 23, 1990.

AUCTION RECORDS:
LONDON, 29 March 1973, *Window* (oil, metal and sand) GBP 5,000. LONDON, 30 June 1983, *Abstract Composition* (c. 1922, mixed media/panel, 21 3/4 x 15 3/4 ins / 55.2 x 40 cm) GBP 3,000. LONDON, 26 March 1985, *Constructivist Composition* (1924, wood, metal and material/sandpaper, construction, 30 1/2 x 30 1/2 ins / 77.6 x 77.5 cm) GBP 80,000. LONDON, 2 April 1987, *Rest Room Project* (c. 1920-25, gouache, pencil and collage, 39 1/4 x 27 1/2 ins / 100 x 70 cm) GBP 23,500. LONDON, 1 Dec 1987, *Matchbox* (1922, wood, relief painting/panel, 18 1/4 x 14 3/4 ins / 46.4 x 37.5 cm) GBP 19,000. LONDON, 18 April 1988, *Flowers* (oil on panel, 20 1/2 x 16 1/2 ins / 52 x 42 cm) GBP 5,500. LONDON, 6 April 1989, *Construction* (1923, relief in painted wood, 17 3/4 x 13 1/2 ins / 45 x 34.5 cm) GBP 68,200; *Constructivist Composition* (1924, wood, metal and fabric on sandpaper, 30 1/2 x 30 1/2 ins / 77.5 x 77.5 cm) GBP 137,500.

ERMINGER, Christian
Austrian, 18th century.
Died 1787.
Active in Vienna.
Enameller.

ERMINGER, Christian August
German, 18th century.
Born in Dresden.
Painter (porcelain/enamel).
Christian August Erminger is probably the same person as the C. Ermer active in Weimar.

ERMINGER, Johann Adam
Austrian, 18th century.
Active in Vienna in 1752.
Painter.

ERMINGER, Josef
Austrian, 19th century.
Born 1776, in Vienna.
Painter.

ERMINI, Ludwig
Austrian, 19th century.
Active in Vienna.
Engraver, miniaturist.

ERMINI, Pietro
Italian, 19th century.
Active in Florence c. 1800.
Draughtsman, miniaturist.
Ermini is known for a *Portrait of Princess Grimaldi*, dated 1804, and a portrait of *Leopold II, Grand Duke of Tuscany*.

ERMISCH, Conrad
German, 19th century.
Born 1855, in Aschersleben; died 29 October 1886, in Dresden.
Painter. History painting, genre scenes.
After studying under Steinle at the Städel Institut in Frankfurt, Ermisch lived in Munich and Weimar, before settling in Dresden in 1877. He is best known for his *Dance of Death*.

ERMOLAEV, Boris Nikolaevich, or Ermolaiev
Russian, 20th century.
Born 1903, in St Petersburg; died 1982.
Painter, lithographer.
Socialist Realism.
Boris Ermolaev was represented at the 1967-1968 Exposition du Grand Palais in Paris *L'Art russe, des Scythes à nos jours* (*Russian Art from the Scythians to Today*) with a lithograph, *Towards the Father*, executed in an illustrative and moralising style. It is now in the Pushkin Museum in Moscow.

MUSEUMS AND GALLERIES:
MOSCOW (Pushkin MFA): *Towards the Father*.

ERMOLAO
Italian, 14th century.
Active in Venice in 1327.
Painter.

ERMOLIN, Fedor
Russian, 17th century.
Born to a family originally from Pskov.
Icon painter.

ERMOLIN, Ivan
Russian, 17th century.
Born to a family originally from Pskov.
Icon painter.

ERMOLIN, Nikita
Russian, 17th century.
Born to a family originally from Pskov.
Icon painter.

ERMOLIN, Semen
Russian, 17th century.
Born to a family originally from Pskov.
Icon painter.
As a painter at the court of the Tsar, Semen Ermolin and Semen Ushakov painted a *Crucifixion, Prophets and Angels* in one of the churches of Christ the Saviour in the Kremlin in 1677.

ERNAULT, Suzanne
French, 20th century.
Born in Pussay (Essonne).
Watercolourist.

ERNECKE, Hermann
German, 19th century.
Born c. 1817, in Berlin; died 12 June 1894.
Painter. Portraits.
Ernecke worked in Berlin. His best-known works are: *Portrait of a Boy, Portrait of the Artist* and *Portrait of Emperor Frederick III*.

ERNEST, Jeanne
French, 20th century.
Born in Paris.
Painter.
Jeanne Ernest was a pupil of Biloul and L. Simon and received an honourable mention in 1926.

ERNEST, John
American, 20th century.
Born 1922, in Philadelphia.
Active in England.
Painter, sculptor.
John Ernest studied in Pennsylvania until 1942, then lived in New York until 1946. He then spent three years living in Sweden before going to France and England in 1951. He studied sculpture at St Martin's School of Art until 1956.

There were numerous international exhibitions, notably that at the Stedelijk Museum in Amsterdam in 1962, entitled *Experiment in Constructie*.

He started out with an Expressionist tendency, before turning to abstraction. He was influenced by the writings of the artist Charles Biederman from 1952 until 1956. His abstract compositions are simple (horizontal and vertical) and made from uncomplicated yet machine-finished parts. The work of John Ernest has its references and continuations in the work of Piet Mondrian, Jean Gorin and Antony Hill.

ERNEST, Yvonne
French, 20th century.
Painter.

Yvonne Ernest was a pupil of Biloul and Humbert. She exhibited at the Salon des Artistes Français, where she received an honourable mention in 1926.

ERNEST T.
French, 20th century.
Painter, draughtsman. Artists' books.
Conceptual Art.

Ernest T. has been represented in collective exhibitions, including: 2003, *Une collection de 'chefs-d'oeuvre', emprunts, pastiches, copies, citations et interprétations* (*A Collection of 'Masterpieces', Borrowings, Pastiches, Copies, Quotations and Interpretations*), an exhibition dealing with the practice of appropriation in art, mainly from a European point of view, Fonds Régional d'Art Contemporain, Limoges; 2003, *Un tableau dans le décor. Peintures 1970-2000* (*A Painting in the Décor: Paintings 1970-2000*), an exhibition held to celebrate the 20th anniversary of the FRAC, Château des Ducs de Bretagne, Nantes. Solo exhibitions of his work were held at the Galerie Gabrielle Maubrie, Paris, in 1992, and the FRAC of Limoges in 2001.

The press release of the Limoges FRAC starts with the words, 'The artist who hides behind the pseudonym Ernest T. is a troublemaker'. His starting point is a caricature of the modernity of both artists and the public. He paints canvases, all much the same: checkerboards of blue, red and yellow squares. He attaches to them comments on the pointlessness of the work itself. He also enlarges humorous drawings that include a painting, which he replaces with his own stereotyped picture and a self-deprecating caption: 'I was Ernest T.'s favourite pupil,' says the woman who is showing the painting to an art lover. He also paints and draws after Rembrandt, Bruegel and Mondrian, thus challenging, like many artists, the work of art and its originality. He has written an artists' book, *La Vie d'artiste* (*The Artist's Life (1989-2001)*), published by the Centre National de l'Estampe et de l'Art, printed in Chatou.

Bibliography:
Jouannais, Jean-Yves, *'Ernest T.'* in *Art Press*, periodical, Paris, March 1992. Miloux, Yannick, *Ernest T., chronogical thematic empirical and systematic catalogue*, catalogue raisonné, Fonds régional d'Art contemporain du Limousin, Limoges, 2001.

Museums and Galleries:
Limoges (FRAC Limousin): *Exotic Landscape by the Douanier Rousseau* (1907/1990, oil on canvas); *Dash 3* (1989); *Group of Idiots, after Picabia* (1985, oil on canvas) - Marseilles (FRAC Provence-Alpes-Côte d'Azur): *Box No. 2* (1988) - Metz (FRAC Lorraine): *You Say Ernest T. is a Fraud?* - Paris (FNAC): *Bedroom for a Young Girl who is a Painter* (1990).

ERNESTI, Jordan
German, 18th century.
Painter.

Ernesti decorated the abbey at Gandersheim immediately after its reconstruction around 1730.

ERNESTINE CHARLOTTE ZU NASSAU-HADAMAR (Countess)
German, 17th century.
Born 13 November 1623, in Brussels; died 15 August 1668, in Mengerskirchen.
Painter.

The youngest daughter of Count Johann VIII zu Nassau-Siegen, Ernestine married Count Moritz Heinrich Fürst zu Nassau-Hadamar on 15 February 1650. She painted an important series of portraits at Raudnitz castle (Bohemia).

ERNESTO, or Ernestus
Flemish School, 11th century.
Active c. 1095.
Miniaturist.

A monk of the abbey of Stavelot (now in Belgium), this artist painted the Romanesque Bible held in the British Museum.

ERNESTO
Portuguese, 20th century.
Active in France.
Painter.

Ernesto exhibited in 1983 at the Salon des Indépendants in Paris and has exhibited his work in galleries in the USA, notably in San Francisco (1986 and 1987) and New York. He exhibited in Paris in 1987 and 1988 in two very fashionable night clubs, *Le Palace* and *Les Bains*. He has also exhibited in Singapore, Miami and Lisbon.

Ernesto's art is both figurative and Expressionist, sometimes verging on the very limits of abstraction. His ochre tones, the spirited line of his drawing and his figures, mostly female, express imaginary encounters or situations of expectation of moments of desire and carnal sensuality.

Auction records:
Paris, 13 April 1988, *Rendez-Vous* (acrylic/canvas, 57 1/2 x 45 ins / 146 x 114 cm) FRF 7,500; *Séchoir* (acrylic/canvas, 57 1/2 x 45 ins / 146 x 114 cm) FRF 8,000. Paris, 12 Feb 1989, *Bar in Haarlem* (acrylic/canvas, 57 1/2 x 45 ins / 146 x 114 cm) FRF 10,000. Paris, 27 June 1994, *La phrase, réverbère* (oil on canvas, 63 3/4 x 38 1/4 ins / 162 x 97 cm) FRF 30,000. Paris, 30 Nov 1995, *Tea with Cats* (oil on canvas, 63 3/4 x 51 1/4 ins / 162 x 130 cm) FRF 40,000.

ERNI, Hans
Swiss, 20th century.
Born 1909, in Lucerne.
From 1953 also active in France.
Painter, engraver, lithographer, ceramicist, sculptor, illustrator, decorative designer, writer. Murals, designs for mosaics.
Groups: Die Allianz, Abstraction-Creation.

The son of a mechanic, at the outset Hans Erni was a technical draughstman in an architect's studio. He attended the school of arts and crafts in Lucerne between 1927 and 1928, and the Académie Julian in Paris from 1928 to 1929. Between 1929 and 1930 he was at the Vereinigte Staatschule für Freie und Angewandte Kunst (school of applied arts) in Berlin. During his numerous stays in Paris he was in contact with Arp, Piet Mondrian, Constantin Brancusi, Alexander Calder, Wassily Kandinsky and Henry Moore among others. He was also strongly influenced by the work of Picasso and Braque. He joined the group Abstraction-Création (Abstraction-Creation) in 1934. He was also a founding member of the association Allianz in 1937. He continued to travel in Europe and from 1950 discovered Africa. Resident in Zurich, he also possessed a studio in Paris from 1953.

He contributed to numerous group exhibitions in Europe, including *Thesis Antithesis Synthesis* in the Kunstmuseum in Lucerne in 1935 and in the USA. After his first one-man show in Basel in 1935, several others were to follow including: a retrospective at Lucerne in 1944, Winterhur in 1945, Rotterdam in 1946, Geneva in 1948, Chicago in 1951, Olympique Museum in Lausanne in 1999. In 1992 he was awarded the Olympiart prize.

He was very productive, partly with mural compositions: *The Three Graces of Lucerne* for Lucerne train station (1935); *The Virgin Mary and Child* (1935), Hirchenplatz, Lucerne; *Abstract Composition* for the Triennale di Milano (1936); *Composition* for the Swiss National Exhibition (1939), in which he formulated his synthesis 'Abstraction-Realism'; *Creative Energy*, London (1946); *The Triumphs of Man*, Musée d'Ethnographie, Neuchâtel (1954); *Daedalus and Icarus* for the *Swissair* Company in 1957. He also executed woodcuts, numerous illustrations, political posters and advertisements: *Atomic Warfare, No* (1954), *National Peace Assembly* (1955). His talents also lay in the field of ceramics, and he produced sets and costumes for the open-air performance of Aeschylus' *Prometheus* in 1946 and a series of 31 pictures on Olympic sports for the Swiss national fair in 1983. He also wrote and gave lectures.

This artist, hovering between abstract and figurative, has been characterised by the Geneva critic Hélène Cingria as 'the master of Space'. His considerable output includes all genres and all techniques. A fully acknowledged Surrealist influence is detectable in some of his works. His tendency to break free from all great masters is compensated for by his extraordinary manual dexterity.

BIBLIOGRAPHY:

Rosner, Ch., *L'Œuvre graphique de H. Erni, intégration de l'art et des techniques*, Éd. Pierre Cailler, Geneva, 1957. Schneeberger, Pierre-Francis, *Hans Erni*, René Kister, Geneva, 1961. Rüegg, W., *Peintures en relief de H. Erni*, Éd. Pierre Cailler, Geneva, 1963. Cailler, Pierre, *'Catalogue raisonné de l'œuvre lithographié et gravé de Hans Erni'* in *2 vol*, Éd. Pierre Cailler, Geneva, 1969-1971. Rüegg, W., *Hans Erni: Das malerische Werk: Peintures: Paintings*, Huber, Bern, 1979 ((text in German, French and English)). Matheson, J., *Hans Erni: Das zeichnerische Werk und öffentliche Arbeiten: Dessins et commandes officielles: Drawings and Public Commisssions*, Huber, Bern, 1981 ((text in German, French and English)). Rigby, G., *Hans Erni at the Goldmark Gallery*, Goldmark Gallery, Leicester, 1988. Hofmaier, James/Couët, Madeleine de, *Erni Litograph: Werkverzeichnis der Litographien*, catalogue raisonné, ABC Verlag, Zurich, 1992 (text in German and French). Giroud, Jean-Charles, *Hans Erni. Catalogue raisonné des livres illustrés*, Gal. Patrick Cramer, Geneva, 1996 (text in German and French). Delamuraz, J.P., et al., *Hans Erni at Work*, Welwoche-ABS-Verlag, Zurich, 1996. Furger, Andres, *Ateliergespräche mit Hans Erni*, NZZ, Zurich, 1998. *Hans Erni: sport passion*, exhibition catalogue, Musée olympique, Lausanne, 1999. Obrist, Marco, *Hans Erni: Werke aus sieben*, exhibition catalogue, Verlag Hans Erni-Stiftung, Lucerne, 2000. Dérens, Jean/Leyris, Gérard, *L'Imagier humaniste et ses livres, Hans Erni*, exhibition catalogue, Bibliothèque historique de la Ville de Paris, Paris, 2001.

MUSEUMS AND GALLERIES:

NEUCHÂTEL (Mus. d'Ethnographie): *Man and Machine* (1954).

AUCTION RECORDS:

GENEVA, 18 Nov 1961, *Nude from Behind*, CHF 4,800. LUCERNE, 24 June 1966, *Cock* (tempera and gouache) CHF 2,500. NEW YORK, 18 Sept 1968, *Seated Nude* (tempera/canvas) USD 2,100. GENEVA, 8 Nov 1969, *Horses* (gouache) CHF 16,000. LUCERNE, 24 Nov 1972, *Artist in Studio* (tempera) CHF 8,500. GENEVA, 8 June 1974, *Couple* (gouache) CHF 5,000. BERN, 21 Oct 1976, *Two Friends* (tempera, Indian ink and charcoal, 39 3/4 x 34 1/2 ins / 101 x 87.5 cm) CHF 8,000. NEW YORK, 14-15 Dec 1976, *Wind* (1958, oil on canvas, 26 1/4 x 28 1/4 ins / 66.5 x 71.5 cm) USD 1,300. ZURICH, 23 Nov 1977, *Nude Couple* (1957, gouache and tempera, 15 1/2 x 15 1/4 ins / 39.5 x 38.5 cm) CHF 6,000. HAMBURG, 2 June 1978, *The Fabians* (1959, gouache, 13 1/4 x 15 1/4 ins / 33.6 x 39 cm) DEM 2,300. ZURICH, 22 Nov 1978, *Recumbent Couple* (1952, 25 1/4 x 32 3/4 ins / 64 x 83 cm) CHF 24,000. ZURICH, 30 May 1979, *Philosopher* (1960, tempera, 25 1/2 x 24 1/2 ins / 65 x 62 cm) CHF 22,000. ZURICH, 3 Nov 1979, *Mother and Child* (1962, oil and tempera/canvas, 38 1/2 x 32 1/4 ins / 98 x 82 cm) CHF 28,000. ZURICH, 30 Oct 1980, *Horses* (1956, pen and wash/paper, 19 x 26 1/2 ins / 48 x 67 cm) CHF 4,800. ZURICH, 27 Jan 1982, *Mother and Child* (lithograph, 37 1/2 x 28 1/4 ins / 95 x 72 cm) CHF 900. ZURICH, 18 May 1984, *Shepherd and Bull* (1963, ink, 24 1/4 x 35 ins / 61.5 x 89 cm) CHF 5,500. ZURICH, 7 June 1984, *Bull Lying Down* (1961, oil on card, 17 3/4 x 29 1/2 ins / 45 x 75 cm) CHF 16,000. ZURICH, 9 Nov 1984, *Philosopher* (1960, tempera/canvas, 25 1/2 x 24 1/2 ins / 65 x 62 cm) CHF 26,000. MUNICH, 29 Oct 1985, *Couple of Lovers* (1965, black and brown felt pens, 12 1/2 x 17 3/4 ins / 32 x 45 cm) DEM 5,800. ZURICH, 5 June 1986, *Couple of Lovers* (1956, tempera/canvas, 20 1/2 x 24 3/4 ins / 52 x 63 cm) CHF 32,000. ZURICH, 12 June 1987, *Three Figures* (1962, Indian ink drawing with gouache, 20 1/2 x 29 1/4 ins / 52 x 74 cm) CHF 6,000. NEW YORK, 7 Oct 1987, *Woman Swimming* (1959, oil on canvas, 22 x 40 1/2 ins / 56 x 102.9 cm) USD 15,000. LUCERNE, 30 Sept 1988, *Couple* (1959, watercolour, 14 3/4 x 11 1/4 ins / 37.5 x 28.5 cm) CHF 3,600. ROME, 17 April 1989, *Female Nude* (distemper/canvas, 50 3/4 ins / 129 cm, 2 x 18 1/4 ins/5 x 46.5 cm) ITL 20,000,000. PARIS, 23 Nov 1989, *Death and Peace* (oil on canvas, 72 x 72 3/4 ins / 182 x 185 cm) FRF 60,000. NEW YORK, 21 Feb 1990, *Shepherd Sleeping near Rock* (1948, oil on canvas, 18 1/2 x 24 1/4 ins / 46.8 x 61.6 cm) USD 14,300. ZURICH, 22 June 1990, *Couple* (1970, tempera, 14 1/2 x 11 ins / 37 x 28 cm) CHF 4,400. PARIS, 7 Dec 1990, *Cock* (Indian ink wash, 7 3/4 x 11 3/4 ins / 20 x 30 cm) FRF 4,500. LE TOUQUET, 19 May 1991, *Couple Playing* (1967, oil on canvas, 19 x 20 3/4 ins / 48 x 53 cm) FRF 78,000. LUCERNE, 25 May 1991, *Russian Ballet Dancer* (watercolour, 9 3/4 x 7 ins / 25 x 18 cm) CHF 1,300. ZURICH, 24 June 1993, *Horse* (mixed media/paper/cardboard, 20 x 15 1/4 ins / 50.5 x 38.5 cm) CHF 2,000; *Woman Stretched Out* (1958, oil on canvas, 11 3/4 x 24 3/4 ins / 30 x 63 cm) CHF 5,000. NEW YORK, 2 Nov 1993, *Farandole* (1953, ink, wash and coloured chalk/grey paper, 19 3/4 x 27 1/4 ins / 50.2 x 69.2 cm) USD 1,610. LUCERNE, 20 Nov 1993, *Bacchus* (1962, watercolour/Arches paper, 20 3/4 x 15 ins / 53 x 38 cm) CHF 3,000; *Girl Seated on White Cushions* (1973, tempera and ink/paper, 16 x 11 3/4 ins / 40.5 x 30 cm) CHF 6,500. CALAIS, 11 Dec 1994, *Everything Must Shine* (oil on canvas, 13 1/2 x 23 1/2 ins / 34 x 60 cm) FRF 27,000. ZURICH, 12 Nov 1996, *Girl with Three Horses* (1970, watercolour and Indian ink, 12 1/2 x 18 ins / 32 x 45.5 cm) CHF 2,600. ZURICH, 8 April 1997, *Couple* (1950, red chalk, 18 1/2 x 12 1/2 ins / 47 x 31.5 cm) CHF 1,500. ZURICH, 4 June 1997, *Mother and Child* (1967, tempera and oil on canvas, 38 1/4 x 26 ins / 97 x 66 cm) CHF 17,250. ZURICH, 19 March 1999, *Figure Reading* (1960, tempera, 26 x 24 ins / 65 x 62 cm) CHF 14,000. LUCERNE, 29 May 1999, *Still-life with Guitar - Castel Gandolfo* (1933, tempera on paper, 23 x 18 ins / 59 x 46 cm) CHF 24,000. CALAIS, 5 Nov 2000, *Dancer* (oil on canvas, 22 x 18 ins / 56 x 45 cm) FRF 43,000. CALAIS, 5 Nov 2000, *Bucking Horse* (oil on canvas, 22 x 19 ins / 55 x 48 cm) FRF 49,000. ZURICH, 2 May 2001, *Nude with Three Horses* (1968, mixed media, 20 x 28 ins / 50 x 71 cm) CHF 9,000. ST GALL, 21 Nov 2001, *Three White and Three Dark Horses* (1966, tempera on paper, 26 x 37 ins / 67 x 93 cm) CHF 8,500. LUCERNE, 20 Nov 2002, *Horse with Foal* (1971, tempera, 22 x 25 ins / 55 x 64 cm) CHF 7,500. LUCERNE, 20 Nov 2002, *Bull and Cow Lying Down* (1961, air brush and tempera on pavatex, 30 x 35 ins / 75 x 90 cm) CHF 8,500. BERN, 15 May 2003, *Horse and Bull* (1965, watercolour, 26 x 18 ins / 65 x 45 cm)

CHF 7,000. ZURICH, 9 Dec 2003, *More Cultivation or Hunger* (tempera on panel, 18 x 20 ins / 45 x 52 cm) CHF 20,000. BERN, 14 May 2004, *Peasant Woman Resting* (1963, oil on canvas, 19 x 36 ins / 47 x 92 cm) CHF 12,000. ZURICH, 8 June 2004, *Two Horses* (1972, fresco, tempera, scratching plaster on panel, 53 x 54 ins / 135 x 138 cm) CHF 10,000.

ERNI, Simone
Swiss, 20th - 21st century.
Born 1946.
Painter, draughtsman, engraver, lithographer. Nudes, local scenes, animals.

Erni is the daughter of the artists Hans Erni and Gertrude Erni-Bohnert. She was privileged to meet many composers and artists. From the time of her studies at the École Normale, she embarked on numerous trips across Europe. In addition, she attended the École des Beaux-Arts in Geneva, and went on a study trip to Venice. In 1980 she settled in Palm Springs (California) for a period of two years. When she returned to Switzerland, she settled in Lugano, then in her birthplace Lucerne, where she opened the Galerie 37 and continued her work as an artist. Her first solo shows date from the 1970s. She exhibits in towns including Lucerne, Bern and Monte Carlo.

ERNOTTE, Jacques
Belgian, 20th century.
Born 1897, in Brussels; died 1964.
Painter.

Ernotte exhibited at the Salon d'Automne in Paris in 1928.

ERNOU, François
French, 17th century.
Active in Angers.
Painter.

François Ernou painted a portrait of *Antoine Arnauld*.

ERNOU, Jean, the Elder
French, 17th century.
Died 23 April 1692.
Active in Angers.
Painter.

Jean Ernou the Elder painted a portrait of the bishop of Angers, *Henri Arnauld*.

ERNOU, Jean, the Younger
French, 17th century.
Born c. 1664, in Angers; died 19 April 1701.
Painter.

Jean Ernou was the son of Jean Ernou the Elder and brother of Pierre Ernou.

ERNOU, Pierre, called Le Chevalier Ernou
French, 17th century.
Born 23 March 1665, in Angers.
Painter.

Pierre Ernou came from Anjou, and was a painter of portraits and religious paintings. For some time between 1720 and 1739 he was in Lyons.

MUSEUMS AND GALLERIES:
ORLÉANS: *Portrait of Man*.

ERNOUL-DELF. See **DELF Ernoul**

ERNOULET
French, 15th century.
Active in Rouen.
Sculptor (wood).

Ernoulet worked under the direction of Philippot Viart on the choir stalls of Rouen Cathedral in 1460.

ERNST
German, 18th century.
Active in Oels (now Olesnica, Poland).
Painter.

ERNST, Adolphe Dionysius
German, 18th century.
Born 1748, in Dresden.
Engraver.

Adolphe Ernst made engravings after Boucher and Annibale Carracci.

ERNST, Alfred von
Swiss, 19th century.
Born 20 August 1799, in Bern; died 3 January 1850, in Bern.
Painter. Landscapes.

Alfred von Ernst, who was an officer, does not seem to have received any artistic training at all. From 1836, he exhibited in Zurich and Bern, painting as an amateur, principally in the manner of Bonstetten.

MUSEUMS AND GALLERIES:
BERN: *Rosenlaui Glacier*.

AUCTION RECORDS:
MILAN, 17 Dec 1992, *View of Pozzuoli* (1840, oil on canvas, 23 1/2 x 35 1/2in/60 x 90cm) ITL 18,000,000. KEMPTEN, 15 Jan 1999, *Swiss Mountain Landscape with Lakeside Fortress and Figures* (oil on canvas/panel, 37 x 50 ins / 95 x 126 cm) DEM 8,000.

ERNST, Amélie
Maiden name: Lévy
French, 19th century.
Born 1834, in Mutzig.
Painter, sculptor.

Amélie Ernst exhibited her paintings at the Salon of the Société des Artistes Français from 1887. She was also an actress.

MUSEUMS AND GALLERIES:
NICE: *M. Ernst; Violinist's Hand*.

ERNST, August
German, 18th century.
Active in Thuringia at the beginning of the 18th century.
Potter.

ERNST, Emil von
German, 19th century.
Active in Düsseldorf.
Landscape artist.

Emil von Ernst is best known for his *Mill near Bingen*.

ERNST, Hans
French, 15th century.
Active in Strasbourg c. 1466.
Painter.

ERNST, Helge
Danish, 20th century.
Born 1916; died 1990.
Painter. Still-lifes.

The work of Helge Ernst evinces a refined talent and subtle application of colour. Disciplined in her drawing, she worked in a late Post-Cubist style along the lines of the French painter, graphic artist and designer Jacques Villon.

AUCTION RECORDS:
COPENHAGEN, 6 May 1987, *Still-life* (1975, oil on canvas, 32 x 21 1/4 ins / 81 x 54 cm) DKK 22,000. COPENHAGEN, 30 Nov 1988, *Composition* (oil on canvas, 65 x 27 1/4 ins / 165 x 69 cm) DKK 5,000. COPENHAGEN, 10 May 1989, *Still-life* (oil on canvas, 22 x 33 ins / 56 x 84 cm) DKK 20,000. COPENHAGEN, 21-22 March 1990, *Oranges* (1975, oil on canvas, 15 x 22 ins / 38 x 55 cm) DKK 9,000. COPENHAGEN, 30 May 1990, *Christmas Image* (1968, oil on canvas, 39 1/4 x 25 1/2 ins / 100 x 65 cm) DKK 8,000. COPENHAGEN, 13-14 Feb 1991, *Still-life* (1985, oil on

canvas, 28 3/4 x 39 1/4 ins / 73 x 100 cm) DKK 33,000. COPENHAGEN, 4 Dec 1991, *Greek Head* (oil on canvas, 24 x 18 ins / 61 x 46 cm) DKK 18,000. COPENHAGEN, 4 March 1992, *Still-life* (1987, oil on canvas, 23 1/2 x 27 1/2 ins / 60 x 70 cm) DKK 17,000. COPENHAGEN, 2-3 Dec 1992, *Still-life in Yellow* (1988, oil on canvas, 23 1/2 x 32 ins / 60 x 81 cm) DKK 15,500. COPENHAGEN, 10 March 1993, *Greek Head* (1975, oil on canvas, 28 3/4 x 39 1/4 ins / 73 x 100 cm) DKK 18,000. COPENHAGEN, 1 Dec 1993, *Still-life and Vessels* (1988, oil on canvas, 39 1/4 x 32 ins / 100 x 81 cm) DKK 28,000. COPENHAGEN, 2 March 1994, *Studio* (1988, oil on canvas, 45 x 63 3/4 ins / 114 x 162 cm) DKK 23,000. COPENHAGEN, 8-9 March 1995, *Still-life* (1983, oil on canvas, 28 3/4 x 39 1/4 ins / 73 x 100 cm) DKK 17,000. COPENHAGEN, 12 March 1996, *Through the Window* (oil on canvas, 39 1/4 x 35 1/2 ins / 100 x 90 cm) DKK 18,000. COPENHAGEN, 24 Feb 1999, *Platanerne, Aix-en-Provence* (1987, oil on canvas, 35 x 39 ins / 90 x 100 cm) DKK 28,000. VEJLE, 17 March 1999, *Town Fragments - Paris* (1984, oil on canvas, 39 x 35 ins / 100 x 90 cm) DKK 24,000. VEJLE, 19 Jan 2000, *Contemporary Landscape* (collage and newspaper cutout, 35 x 57 ins / 89 x 146 cm) DKK 13,500. COPENHAGEN, 9 Feb 2000, *The Picture* (1952, oil on masonite, 36 x 22 ins / 91 x 56 cm) DKK 13,200. COPENHAGEN, 20 March 2002, *Still-life in Lamp Light* (oil on canvas, 36 x 24 ins / 92 x 60 cm) DKK 23,000. COPENHAGEN, 4 April 2002, *Still-life of Objects by Window* (1979, oil on canvas, 46 x 32 ins / 116 x 81 cm) DKK 27,000. COPENHAGEN, 26 Feb 2003, *Table in Summer* (oil on canvas, 26 x 32 ins / 65 x 81 cm) DKK 16,000. VEJLE, 10 Nov 2003, *Still-life* (1987-1988, oil on canvas, 29 x 35 ins / 73 x 90 cm) DKK 15,200. COPENHAGEN, 25 Feb 2004, *Studio* (1974, oil on canvas, 45 x 64 ins / 114 x 162 cm) DKK 23,000. VEJLE, 15 March 2004, *Still-life in Yellow* (1987, oil on canvas, 29 x 39 ins / 73 x 100 cm) DKK 25,500.

ERNST, J. G.
German, 18th century.
Painter.

J.G. Ernst is possibly the same person as Jordan Ernesti.

ERNST, Jakob
German, 16th - 17th century.
Born in Windsheim.
Sculptor.

Jakob Ernst settled in Nuremberg.

ERNST, Jimmy
German, 20th century.
Born 1920, in Brühl, near Cologne.
Active in the USA.
Painter.

The son of Max Ernst, Jimmy Ernst studied in Cologne and then at the school of applied arts in Altona. In 1938, after a period as a printer's apprentice, he emigrated to the USA, where he only began painting in 1940. From 1951 he taught at Brooklyn College and in 1961 he was awarded a scholarship by the Guggenheim Foundation, the same year in which he was sent on detached service to the Soviet Union by the State Department. He settled in Rowayton, Connecticut. His work featured in numerous group exhibitions, notably the Biennale di Venezia in 1956; in *Abstract Painting and Sculpture in America* at the Museum of Modern Art, New York (MOMA) in 1951; in *Younger American Painters* at the Solomon R. Guggenheim Museum, New York in 1954. He also had one-man shows - his first in 1941, then regularly from 1951 in New York. He uses a sure brushstroke in his paintings, which are abstract and geometric in composition.

MUSEUMS AND GALLERIES:

NEW YORK (Solomon R. Guggenheim Mus.): *Solitude* (1954).

AUCTION RECORDS:

NEW YORK, 24 Sept 1981, *Idea Sequence* (1963, watercolour, pen, gouache and pastel, 18 x 33 ins / 45.7 x 83.8 cm) USD 550. NEW YORK, 23 March 1984, *Nebula 1* (1954, brush, black ink and gouache, 21 1/4 x 14 3/4 ins / 54 x 37.3 cm) USD 950. NEW YORK, 7 Dec 1984, *Ancient Evidence* (1955, oil on canvas, 34 1/4 x 41 1/4 ins / 87 x 104.7 cm) USD 1,500. NEW YORK, 6 Dec 1985, *Southwestern Image* (1958, watercolour and gouache/paper, 22 1/4 x 30 1/2 ins / 56.5 x 77.5 cm) USD 1,900. NEW YORK, 4 Dec 1987, *Homage to Edgar Varèse* (1965, oil on canvas, 50 x 65 1/4 ins / 127 x 165.7 cm) USD 22,000. NEW YORK, 24 Jan 1990, *Abstract* (1951, watercolour, gouache and ink/paper, 19 3/4 x 14 3/4 ins / 50.1 x 37.7 cm) USD 1,430. NEW YORK, 14 Feb 1990, *Urban Icon* (1971, gouache/paper, 17 1/2 x 20 3/4 ins / 44.4 x 53 cm) USD 1,760. NEW YORK, 12 June 1991, *Quasars II* (1967, mixed media assemblage, 24 1/2 x 24 1/2 ins / 62.2 x 62.2 cm) USD 1,100. NEW YORK, 10 June 1992, *Breakfast* (1960, oil on canvas, 12 x 9 ins / 30.5 x 22.8 cm) USD 1,430. NEW YORK, 12 June 1992, *Thirty Days* (1965, ink/card, 30 x 40 ins / 76.2 x 101.6 cm) USD 3,850. NEW YORK, 2 Dec 1992, *Abstraction in Grey* (1951, gouache/paper, 23 x 17 ins / 58.4 x 43.2 cm) USD 2,860. NEW YORK, 15 Nov 1993, *S.R.O. no. 4* (1959, oil on panel, 3 3/4 x 6 ins / 9.5 x 15.1 cm) USD 978. NEW YORK, 24 Feb 1994, *Untitled* (1968, watercolour and gouache/paper, 18 x 21 1/2 ins / 45.7 x 54.6 cm) USD 3,450. NEW YORK, 10 Oct 1996, *Biomorphic Shapes* (1941, gouache/paper, 8 3/4 x 12 ins / 22.5 x 30.2 cm) USD 5,462.

ERNST, Joseph
Austrian, 18th century.
Born 1746, in Vienna; died 7 June 1796, in Vienna.
Painter.

ERNST, Joseph
Austrian, 19th century.
Born 1785, in Vienna.
Painter.

ERNST, Joseph Anton
German, 19th century.
Born 7 March 1816, in Schöllang (Bavaria); died 20 July 1893, in Schöllang (Bavaria).
Sculptor.

Joseph Anton Ernst worked with his brother, Michael, mainly in Passau.

ERNST, Julius
Swiss, 19th century.
Born 4 September 1830, in Winterthur; died 27 August 1861, in Munich.
Engraver (copper).

A pupil of Diethelm Stäbli at the Winterthur grammar school, then at the Munich academy of art, Julius Ernst exhibited at the Turnus in Zurich in 1853. He died at the start of a potentially brilliant career.

ERNST, Karl Mathias
German, 18th - 19th century.
Born 24 February 1758, in Mannheim; died 1830, in Mannheim.
Painter, draughtsman, engraver.

A pupil of F.A. Leydensdorff and of Verschaffelt, Karl Ernst made engravings after the old masters, including Rubens and Coypel. He went on to execute many portraits, such as *Duchess of Württemberg* and *General Pichegru.*

ERNST, Leopold
Austrian, 19th century.
Born 14 October 1808, in Vienna; died 17 October 1862, in Vienna.
Painter. Architectural views, church interiors, urban landscapes.

Leopold Ernst was a pupil at the Akademie der bildenden Künste in Vienna, where he continued to work, becoming a member in 1848.

MUSEUMS AND GALLERIES:

VIENNA: *Interior of an Old Italian Church.*

AUCTION RECORDS:
LUCERNE, 25 May 1982, *View of Venice* (oil on canvas, 12½ x 13in/32 x 33cm) CHF 750.

ERNST, Martha Christina von

Swiss, 18th - 19th century.
Born 1774, in Bern; died 5 June 1854, in Biel.
Painter (gouache), draughtswoman.

Martha von Ernst assisted the painter F.N. Kœnig at Unterseen, and exhibited in Bern in 1804. She is best known for her self-portrait.

ERNST, Martin

French, 15th century.
Active in Strasbourg.
Painter.

ERNST, Max

German, 20th century.
Born 2 April 1891, in Brühl, near Cologne; died 1 April 1976, in Paris.
From 1922 active in France, from 1941 to 1949 active and from 1948 naturalised in the USA, and from 1958 naturalised in France.
Painter, collage artist, engraver, illustrator, sculptor. Dadaism.
Groups: Das Junge Rheinland, Zentrale W/3, Cologne and Paris Dada groups, Paris Surrealist group.

Max Ernst's father taught at a school for deaf and dumb children in Brühl, near Cologne, and was also a keen amateur landscape painter. Max referred to his mother as possessing 'the sense of humour and fairy tales' - clearly a pastiche of Goethe's lines regarding his own mother from whom he received '...die frohe Natur und Lust zu fabulieren'. Like his father, Max began to draw at a very young age. Strangely affected by the death of his sister in 1897, his childhood was dominated by feelings of void and extinction. Mystical exaltation and hallucinations were brought on by childhood terror and fevers. In 1906 the death of his favourite cockatoo on the same night on which his sister Loni was born led to a confusion between birds and humans which was reflected in the symbols of his art, namely *Loplop, Bird Superior*, a surrogate self-image, as it were, a motif which was to be prevalent in his paintings.

He studied philosophy until 1911 and then psychiatry and history of art at Bonn University until 1912, and then abandoned academic study. In visits to the asylum he was fascinated and disturbed by the expressive power of mental patients. He began to paint with no professional training. His contradictory influences included Francisco Goya, Vincent van Gogh, Paul Gaugin, Henri Matisse and Wassily Kandinsky and he also read the German Romantics, Nietzsche, Max Stirner and Sigmund Freud.

It was in 1911 that he developed a friendship with August Macke, who introduced him to the Munich groups Die Brücke and the Der Blaue Reiter. During this period he did a few lino engravings adopting the energetic manner of the Die Brücke artists. He became a member of the group Das Junge Rheinland, led by Macke. In 1912 he saw the Cologne Sonderbund exhibition and in 1913 at August Macke's house he met Guillaume Apollinaire accompanied by Robert Delaunay. His first contact with Paris was also in this year.

During the war he served as an artillery engineer at the front, feeling 'the rage of the heart' in sacrificing 'his wonderful life'. The disillusionment engendered in him by war led him into militant Dadaism. He could not however totally break with painting and in 1916 he joined the group Der Sturm. After the war, in 1919, he returned to Cologne with Hans Arp and Johannes Theodor Baargelt, a banker's son who was attracted to extreme left-wing antics. He assumed the pseudonym Bargeld (Cash) and a Dada group in Cologne was founded under the name of Zentrale W/3, their activities having a decidedly political bent. Apart from an exhibition held around a public urinal as a 'ready-made', with a statue of Hindenburg stained in red paint and pierced with nails, there was the publication of an extremist journal *Der Ventilator*, then *Bulletin D*, then the first issue of the provocative Dada review *Die Schammade*. Ernst participated in the important Dada exhibition in Berlin in 1920 and a new sensational Dada exhibition *Dada Vorfrühling* (Dada Early Spring) in the Brauhaus Winter (a beer hall) in Cologne which was closed by the police.

He settled in Paris in 1922 after staying two summers in Tyrol with Tristan Tzara and Hans Arp. He lived in St-Brice, a suburb near Mormorency, in the same building as Paul Éluard, with whom he was friendly, since they were both scarred by the war. He participated in the activities of those artists who, grouped around the journal *Littérature*, were soon to make up the Surrealist group, which he depicted in a painting of 1922 *All Friends Together*, showing Raphael Sanzio, Fyodor Dostoyevsky and Giorgio di Chirico, accordingly inscribed, amongst other friends after the dissolution of Dada. In its use of imaginative imagery this composition is comparable to *The Island of the Dead* by Arnold Böcklin, who was often considered one of the precursors of Surrealism.

In 1924 Ernst travelled to the Far East. At this time André Breton's position was clear: he embraced the reality of psychic experience, having recourse also to the creative powers of chance and the unconscious, influenced as he had been by Freud's works when practising psychiatry early on. Max Ernst did not go as far as parapsychology, dubious spirituality and astrology, but adhered faithfully to the tenets of Dada. However, he participated in the first Surrealist exhibition in Paris in 1925. Without taking the form of Surrealism literally, he incorporated its spirit. He extended his activities, collaborating in 1926 with Joan Miró on the décor of *Romeo and Juliet*, a ballet in two tableaux for the Russian Ballet.

After participating in a large exhibition in Paris in 1938, he separated from the group and bought a house at St-Martin-d'Ardèche, near Pont St Esprit, 30 miles north of Avignon, which he decorated with murals and low reliefs, and where he lived with Léonora Carrington. In 1937-1939 he produced the stage sets for Alfred Jarry's *Ubu enchaîné*, written in 1899 and first presented at the Comédie des Champs-Élysées, Paris. When war was declared, he was interned as a German enemy in the camp at Les Milles in the south of France in 1939-1940. Thanks to a petition by Éluard he was released and managed to flee to the USA, where he was to stay until 1949, eventually becoming a USA citizen.

He arrived on 14 July 1941 in New York, where he met André Breton and Marcel Duchamp, with whom he founded the Surrealist publication *VVV*, contributing again to publications and Surrealist exhibitions. With Dorothea Tanning, a talented young woman painter who became his fourth wife in 1946, he retreated to Sedona in the mountains of Arizona. He returned to Europe in 1953, settling in 1955 in Huismes, in Touraine, near Chinon, then in Seillans in the Var, before taking up permanent residence in Paris. After winning a Grand Prix at the 27th Venice Biennale in 1954, he incurred the disapproval of André Breton, who this time excluded him from the Surrealist group for having accepted such recognition. He also won the Prix National des Arts in 1959.

It is notoriously difficult to reconstruct the chronology of the output of Max Ernst. At the outbreak of World War I, a period which can be considered one of his earliest influences, his first paintings on Rhineland themes of forests and Gothic architecture were influenced by the Expressionists of Die Brücke and Der Blaue Reiter. Cubist and Futurist influences also played their part. After the war, in 1919, he was considered by some to have been influenced by Pablo Picasso and Alexander Archipenko. His debt to De Chirico, whose works he discovered in the art periodical *Valori Plastici*, is evident in an album of eight lithographs plus title-page, called *Fiat Modes Pereat Ars*, in which mannequins revolved in empty spaces.

His next period consisted of Dada and his early collages. At the time of his early experiments with Dada, he collaborated with Arp, with whom he executed the *Fatagagas* (acronym for 'Fabrication de tableaux garantis gazométriques' - Fabrication of pictures guaranteed gazometric) collages which anticipated the process of automatic writing which the Surrealists were later to practice. His account of how the idea of the collage came to him is as follows: 'One rainy day in 1919 in a town on the Rhine, my excited gaze was provoked by the pages of a printed catalogue...Here I discovered the elements of a figuration so remote that its very absurdity provoked in me a sudden intensification of my faculties of sight... by simply painting or drawing, it suffices to add to the illustrations a colour, a line, a landscape foreign to the objects represented... These changes, no more than docile representations of *what is visible within me*, record a faithful and fixed image of my hallucination. They transform the banal pages of advertisement into dramas which reveal my most secret *desires*.'

From the outset his use of collage differed radically from Cubist practice. Whereas in the case of the Cubists collage corresponded exclusively to shape, for Ernst it was a means of expression, the search for new meanings where all circumstances could intervene at random. His collages are the result of two slightly different procedures: either Ernst completed drawings or paintings of a pre-existing image, catalogue engraving or other illustration or he freely juxtaposed dissected fragments from images taken from different sources - commercial catalogues, technical encyclopedias, illustrations by Jules Verne and photographs - to present startling and improbable combinations. These were the first collages from which he made two or three photographic reproductions - the photocollage - in which the traces of the operation of the preliminary collage could be erased. He sent them from Cologne to Paris and they were accepted by Breton and the group as a revelation. The collage commonly known as *L'Avionne meurtrière* of 1920 shows a flying machine composed of a woman's arms. It was from these collages that Ernst illustrated Éluard's *Répétitions* (*Repetitions*) in 1921 and the poems *Les Malheurs des Immortels* which he wrote in collaboration with Éluard in 1922. During his Dada period, Ernst also executed three-dimensional objects, made up of disparate elements brought together in a preposterous way.

The next period was characterised by his participation in Surrealism. From 1921 he painted in the same spirit as his collages, that is the 'hand-painted collages': *Oedipus Rex, Elephant of the Celebes, St Cecilia* and as far as *Pietà or Revolution by Night* of 1923, considered the first painting in the history of Surrealism and predating André Breton's Surrealist Manifesto by a year, at the same time marking for Ernst the last production of his Dada period: a man in a bowler hat and bourgeois attire carries an adolescent who seems to float in space and whose gaze is directed towards a silhouette on the wall of an old man wounded in the head. Shortly before 1924 he began painting in relief, mixing plaster and cork: *Pink Birds*. In 1924 in *Two Children are Threatened by a Nightingale* he introduced real elements, a push bell and a little gate. In 1925, still tirelessly experimenting with materials and techniques, he discovered frottage, a technique which consisted of rubbing with black-lead sheets of paper placed on all sorts of rough surfaces. He was initially fascinated by the grooves of floorboards, obtaining an impression of mysterious landscapes peopled with strange creatures and plants. He then made frottages from leaves of trees, grooves of chairs and frayed edges of sackcloth among other textures. But had he not as an adult discovered something which all children know? He himself stated, 'my work is both a reminder of childishness and the desire to create a pictorial universe of the tragic situation of man today'.

Examples of frottage appeared in *Histoire Naturelle* published in 1926 by Jeanne Bucher, the *Surrealist Dreams* and paintings where he used frottage on canvases to obtain a rugged texture, as in for example *Vision Induced by the Nocturnal Aspect of the Porte St-Denis* and the *Cities* series of 1927. In 1927 he also exhibited *Found Objects*- simple stones chosen for their graceful shape, exhibited so as to draw attention to the existence of a beautiful formation which is not due to artistic creation. At this time, as throughout his life, Ernst was taken up with several activities. This was also a moment of intense pictorial creation in which he developed most of the major themes of his personal symbolic vision, themes pivoting around an immobile universe: forests, vegetation and fossilised flowers, deserted cities, a dead sea under a sky of silent stars, and the dynamic subjects of wind, fire, love and the bird with which he was always preoccupied. With the series *The Interior of Sight* in 1929 he established a metaphorical relationship between the oval shape of the eye, egg and bird which was to be reiterated throughout his work, the bird symbolising the possibilities of liberty. Following the frottages he began the publication of his 'Romans-Collages' (collage-novels) *La Femme 100 Têtes* where *Loplop, Bird Superior* reigns, declared by Breton to be 'the picture book of the time, par excellence', then *Rêve d'une petite fille qui voulut entrer au Carmel* 1930, *Loplop Presents* 1932, *Une semaine de Bonté or les Sept Éléments capitaux* 1934, a novel in pictorial form without marginal commentaries. He cultivated the technique of collage, similar to the frottage, grattage and tracing methods, to obtain naive illustrations. By taking pictorial elements from other contexts like sentimental novels, adventure books and technical treatises, he created baffling juxtapositions and surprising effects, where monstrousness, anticlericalism and the erotic are diluted or intensified by humour.

A new period more or less coinciding with his distancing from the Surrealist group and institutional requirements was marked by the development of new subjects, notably in his rediscovered technique of painting. In 1933 he painted *La Foresta Inbalsamata* where he engraved man-birds and nymph-frogs on polished pebbles, hybrid creatures which were soon to people the mythical forests of his paintings. A stay in Switzerland in 1934-1935 with Alberto Giacometti provided the impetus for his first sculptural activity - *The German Beauty, Head-Bird*. The collage principle also formed the basis for his large symbolic figures: *Oedipus, Lunar Asparagus*. From 1934-1936 he moved away from the collage technique, returning to the traditional media of drawing and painting to deliberately allow the secrets of his expressive power to surface. As was the case throughout his career, his journey is hard to follow given that he substituted rational progression for inspiration to which he remained receptive. He had definitively resolved to accept unconditionally the irrationality of psychological intensity, thereby showing himself to be the most intransigent of the Surrealists. This accounts for the lack of a logical thread between his works, which to his way of thinking should be the outcome of experiments rather than studied creations.

Paintings from this period, considered one of his most prolific, include those around the subject of *The Nymph Echo, Garden Airplane Trap* of 1934-1935 - these were undoubtedly inspired by world events and his deep-seated fear of war as well as his terror of being inscribed on the Nazi blacklists, for he was still German - the *Hunger Feast* of 1935, again dedicated to André Breton, the *Entire Cities*, also known as *The Walls of China*, and again the *Jungles* series which exemplifies a continuation of the unexpected through his use of frottage, by applying 'decalcomania sans objet' invented by Oscar Domingues, consisting of creating images from pressed stains. Belonging to the American period are the works which make up the continuation of the *Jungles* series: 1940-1941: *The Triumph of Love, The Stolen Mirror*; *Europe After the Rain* from 1940-1942, inspired by the tragedy of war; *Napoleon in the Wilderness* of 1941; *Surrealism and Painting* from 1942; and from 1944: *The Eye of Silence, Rhenish Night*, as well as the *Decalmania* series which was not to be published until 1953.

Once established in Arizona with Dorothéa Tanning, he erected a group of large totemic figures in cement facing the desert and the monumental sculpture *Capricorn* of 1948. He also carried out a series of beings cast in bronze including *An Anxious Friend* and *The King Playing with the Queen*. In collaboration with Paul Éluard he illustrated the eight *Poèmes visibles: À l'intérieur de la vue* (*Visible Poems: Inside Sight*). With reference to painting since his use of frottages and other decalcomanias, Ernst saw himself as a 'spectator present at the birth of his own pictures'. Of the key paintings of this period - *Paintings for Young People, Vox Angelica* of 1943, *The Eye of Silence* of 1944, *Euclid* of 1945 and *Design in Nature* of 1947 - Frank Elgar claims that they 'took us back to time immemorial of fossils, floods, monstrous geneses' and Jacques Lassaigne described them as 'a strange chaos of forms which presents itself as a sort of shortcut of the cosmic evolution... plants which turn into insects, human eyes and muzzles of animals appearing on the surface of petrified silhouettes... One of the greatest successes of Surrealism in its exploration of unknown worlds stemming from dream and imagination'. In Arizona Ernst was exposed to landscapes of gigantic red rocks, tortured geological formations, in a sense prefiguring what he had created earlier in his pictures.

On his return from the USA a new and final phase began. Of all the techniques Max Ernst invented or experimented with, painting was only one means of expression among many. In his second French phase, still impregnated with the Dadaist or Surrealist spirit, he poured all his energies into sculptural works: *Are You Niniche?*, a sculpture made up of found objects, including two ox yokes; *The Genie of the Bastille* of 1960, a monument erected to a one-time glory effaced by its dedication; the *Sister Souls* of 1962. Once settled in the Touraine, he commissioned a stonemason to carry out a group of monumental sculptures, notably the *Corps enseignant pour une École de Tueurs* (*Teaching Profession for a School of Killers*) of 1967. The paintings of this later period radically broke away from the rest of his output, though it cannot be claimed that they were not in keeping with the principles of Surrealism. As Maurice Raynal puts it, he always counted on the 'chance to reveal disconcerting combinations in elements never associated and which contribute to systematic bewilderment as demanded by Surrealist doctrine', to which Raynal adds 'in his case infusing them with the personal form of his intentions and visions'. And indeed in these last works, self-conscious working out and concern for pictorial form prevail. It is no longer chance and imagination which control form, but the chances of the gesture which reveal the poetic idea, and the application of touches of white paint with the palette-knife on a blue background in which the title *Sign for a School of Herring* presents itself. To this ensemble belong *The Cry of the Gull* (1953), *Ophelia* (1953-55), *The Polish Rider* (1954), *The Twentieth century* (1955), *Cosmic Rays*, (1960-62), *The Sky Marries the Earth*, (1962). This continued intervention of chance and the self-conscious is often found in *action painting* or in the work of Henri Michaux in the period in question.

After 1960 Ernst again turned his attention to assemblages and collages, adding collected objects and painted elements in a seemingly abstracted way. Without ever accepting compromises, he followed his imagination from day to day. Rather than plotting out his path, he allowed it to unfold, finally gaining public recognition. Towards the end, as he neared inner harmony, his art became a more lyrical than intellectual experience and at the same time his former hallucinations gave way to lighter inventions where the new discovery of an interior peace prevailed.

Ernst participated in numerous group exhibitions. According to certain sources he contributed to exhibitions in Bonn and Cologne in 1913. Also in 1913 he took part with Expressionist painters in the first German autumn salon in Berlin - an exhibition presented by the journal *Der Sturm* and organised by Kandinsky, Macke and others in which works by Chagall, Delaunay, and Klee were included. In the same year he had shows at Bonn and Cologne with the young Rhineland Expressionists. In 1914 at the exhibition of the Werkbund (Creation Group) in Bonn, he was introduced to Hans Arp, with whom he was to remain in close contact and who acquainted him with the works of the French poet Rimbaud. In 1916 Der Sturm organised an exhibition of a few of his paintings. After the war, in 1920, he participated in the big 'Dada Austellung' (Dada Fair), also in Berlin. He contributed to the first Surrealist group exhibition in Paris in 1925 at the Galerie Pierre Loeb and in 1931 he took part in the show *Fantastic Art, Dada, Surrealism* at the Museum of Modern Art, New York (MOMA). In a different key signature his painting *La Belle Jardinière* (*The Fair Gardener*) of 1923 was exhibited by the Nazis in Munich in 1937 at the *Entartete Kunst* (*Degenerate Art*) exhibition. In 1938 he participated at the International Exhibition of Surrealism. On his arrival in New York, he again took part in Surrealist exhibitions.

Since his death Max Ernst has figured in numerous group or thematic exhibitions including in 1993 *Max Ernst, Dada and the Dawn of Surrealism*, Museum of Modern Art, New York (MOMA); 1997 *Arnold Böcklin, Giorgio de Chirico, Max Ernst, eine Reise ins Ungewisse* (*Arnold Böcklin, Giorgio de Chirico, Max Ernst: a Journey into the Unknown*), Kunsthaus, Zurich; 2002, *La Révolution Surréaliste*, Centre Georges-Pompidou, Paris.

His paintings and other works featured in numerous individual shows. In 1921 his collages were the subject of an exhibition organised by André Breton at the galerie *Au sans Pareil* in Paris. In 1931 he had his first exhibition in the USA, held at the Julien Ley Gallery, New York, and then exhibited 48 works in 1936. Although he was well received in New York, these exhibitions elicited a meagre response. In 1947, or according to other sources 1945, Paul Éluard organised a retrospective exhibition in his honour at the Galerie Denise René in Paris, where Ernst returned to live in 1949. In 1950 a retrospective exhibition organised at the Galerie René Drouin was a failure, but an extensive retrospective in 1951 mounted at the ruined castle of the archbishops of Cologne at Brühl, had considerable influence. In 1959 the Musée National d'Art Moderne in Paris dedicated an important retrospective to him, then the Museum of Modern Art, New York (MOMA) in 1961; the Tate Gallery in London and the Wallraf-Richartz Museum in Cologne in 1962; the Kunsthaus in Zurich in 1963; the Jewish Museum in New York in 1966; the Moderna Museet in Stockholm in 1969; the Stedelijk Museum in Amsterdam and the Wurttembergischer Kunstverein of Stuttgart in 1970; Paris again at the Musée de l'Orangerie in 1971 in celebration of his 80th birthday, this exhibition having done the rounds of numerous towns in Germany and France; and in 1975 in New York at the Guggenheim Museum, an exhibition then presented in Paris at the Grand-Palais.

Since his death the following exhibitions have been held: 1979, *Max Ernst*, Haus der Kunst, Munich; 1983, Fondation Maegt, St-Paul-de-Vence; 1986 Fondacíon Juan March, Madrid; 1988, *Max Ernst, Collagen: Inventar und Widerspruch* (*Max Ernst, Collages: Inventory and Contradiction*), itinerant exhibition, Kunsthalle Tübingen, then the Kunstmuseum in Bern and the Kunstsammlung Nordrhein-Westfalen in Düsseldorf; 1990, *Max Ernst, das Graphische Oeuvre* (*Max Ernst, the Graphic Works*), Sprengel Museum, Hanover; 1990 *Max Ernst, Druckgraphische Werke und illustriete Bücher* (*Max Ernst, Prints and Illustrated Books*), Museum Ludwig, Cologne; 1990-1991, Museum d'Art Moderne in Paris, itinerant exhibition for the commemoration of his 100th birthday also presented at the Tate Gallery, London, Stuttgart and Düsseldorf; 1999, *Max Ernst, die Retrospective* (*Max Ernst, Retrospective*), Nationalgalerie, Berlin; 2002, graphic works, Museum voor Schone Kunsten, Ghent.

Bibliography:

Bosquet, Alain, *Max Ernst, œuvre sculpté (1913-1961)*, Le Point Cardinal, Paris, 1961. Russell, J., *Max Ernst: Life and Work*, Thames and Hudson USA, New York, 1967. Schneede, U., *The Essential Max Ernst*, Thames and Hudson, London, 1972. Spies, Werner/Leppien, Helmut R., *Max Ernst. Œuvre-Katalog. Das Graphische Werk*, catalogue raisonné, Menil Foundation, Houston, Du Mont, Cologne, 1975. Spies, Werner/Metken, Günter/Metken, Sigrid, *Max Ernst, Œuvre-Katalog, werke 1906-1925*, catalogue raisonné, Menil Foundation, Houston, Du Mont, Cologne, 1975. Spies, Werner/Metken, Günter/Metken, Sigrid, *Max Ernst, Œuvre-Katalog, werke 1925-1929*, catalogue raisonné, Menil Foundation, Houston, Du Mont, Cologne, 1975. Spies, Werner/Metken, Günter/Metken, Sigrid, *Max Ernst, Œuvre-Katalog, werke 1929-1938*, catalogue raisonné, Menil Foundation, Houston, Du Mont, Cologne, 1975-1979. Hinton, G., '*Max Ernst: Les Hommes n'en sauront rien*' in *Burl. Mag. 117*, 1975. Spies, Werner/Trier, Eduard, et al., *Max Ernst*, exhibition catalogue, Prestel, Munich, 1979. Siegel, O., '*Max Ernst's 'One Night of Love'* ' in *A. Mag. 57*, 1983. Legge, E., *Conscious Sources of the Unconscious: Ernsts Use of Psychoanalytic Themes and Imagery, 1921-1924*, dissertation, University of London, 1985. Rainwater, Robert, et al., *Max Ernst, Beyond Surrealism: A Retrospective of the Artist's Books and Prints*, exhibition catalogue, The New York Public Library, New York, 1986. Gee, M., *Ernst: Pietà or Revolution by Night*, Tate Gallery, London, 1986. Legge, E., '*Max Ernst's 'Oedipus Rex' and the Implicit Sphinx*' in *A. Mag. 61*, 1986. Spies, Werner/Metken, Sigrid/Metken, Günter, *Max Ernst, Œuvre-Katalog, werke 1939-1953*, catalogue raisonné, Menil Foundation, Du Mont, Cologne, 1987. Legge, E., *Max Ernst: The Psychoanalytic Sources*, UMI Research Press, Ann Arbor, 1989. *Max Ernst, Druckgraphische Werke und illustrierte Bücher*, exhibition catalogue, Museum Ludwig, Cologne, 1990. Spies, Werner, et al., *Max Ernst*, exhibition catalogue, Musée national d'Art moderne, Paris, 1991. Spies, Werner/Maur, Karin von/Metken, Sigrid, *Max Ernst, a retrospective*, exhibition catalogue, Tate Gall., London, 1991. Camfield, W., *Max Ernst: Dada and the Dawn of Surrealism*, Prestel Publishing Ltd, Munich, 1993. Quinn, E., *Max Ernst*, Konemann UK Ltd, London, 1996. Faerna, J. (ed.), *Max Ernst*, Abrams, New York, 1997. Hopkins, D., *Marcel Duchamp and Max Ernst: The Bride Shared*, Clarendon Press, Oxford, 1998. Spies, Werner/Kaak, Joachim, et al., *Max Ernst, die Retrospektive*, Nationalgalerie, Berlin, 1999. Warlick, M., *Max Ernst and Alchemy: A Magician in Search of Myth*, University of Texas Press, Austin (TX), 2001.

Museums and Galleries:

Amsterdam (Stedelijk Mus.): *The Horde* (1927) - Basel (Kunstmus.): *Great Forest* (1927) - Bonn (Kunstmus.): *Fishbone Forest* (1926) - Chicago (MCA): *Loplop Introducing a Bird* (1929-1957, plaster, oil and wood) - Cologne (Mus. Ludwig): *All Friends Together* (1922) - Cologne (Wallraf-Richartz Mus.): *Grasshoppers Serenading the Moon* (1953) - Grenoble (Mus. de Grenoble): *The Forest* - Hartford (Wadsworth Atheneum): *Europe after the Rain* (1940-1942, oil on canvas) - Houston (MFA) - Houston (The Menil Collection): *River Love* (1925, frottage); *The 100 Headless Woman Opens Her Majestic Sleeve* (1929, collage); *Night and Day* (1941-1942); *L'Esprit de la Bastille* (bronze) - London (Tate Collection): *Celebes* (1921, oil on canvas); *Men Shall Know Nothing of This* (1923, oil on canvas); several other paintings and works on paper - Madrid (Mus. Thyssen-Bornemisza): *Solitary and Conjugal Trees* (1940) - Manchester (City AG): *City* (1937) - Marseilles (Mus. Cantini): *Monument with Birds* (1927); *Celebration at Seillans* (1964) - Montreal (MAC): *Young Woman in the Shape of a Flower* (1957, bronze) - New Haven (Société Anonyme Collection): '*Paris, Rêve*' (1924-1925) - New York (MoMA): *Everything Here is Still in Suspense* (1920, in collaboration with Arp); *The Hat Makes the Man* (1920); *Graminous Bicycle* (1921); *Woman, Old Man, Flower* (1923-1924); *Two Children are Threatened by a Nightingale* (1924); *Lunar Asparagus* (1935, sculpture, bronze); *The Nymph Echo* (1936); *Napoleon in the Wilderness* (1941) - New York (Solomon R. Guggenheim Mus.): *An Anxious Friend* (1944) - Paris (MNAM-CCI): *Ubu Imperator* (1923); *Shell Flowers* (1929); *Capricorn* (1945-1967, sculpture); *After the Sleep* (1958) - St Louis (GA, Washington University): *Eye of Silence* (1943-1944, oil on canvas) - Tel Aviv: *Bewildered Planet* (1942) - Venice (Collezione Peggy Guggenheim): *Garden Plane Trap* (1936) - Zurich (Kunsthaus): *The Entire City* (1935-1936).

Auction records:

Paris, 29 Dec 1944, *Two Figures*, FRF 1,800. Paris, 15 June 1945, *Compo-Abstraction* (1925) FRF 9,000. Paris, 28 Jan 1949, *Composition*, FRF 34,000. Paris, 21 June 1954, *Composition*, FRF 52,000. Paris, 11 Dec 1957, *Caged Bird* (chalk) FRF 260,000. Paris, 5 March 1958, *Blue Sky with Doves* (oil on canvas) FRF 380,000. Paris, 16 June 1959, *Composition* (oil on canvas) FRF 3,300,000. New York, 11 Nov 1959, *Sea Forms* (oil on canvas) USD 4,500. Stuttgart, 20 Nov 1959, *Glass* (frottage) DEM 3,400. London, 6 July 1960, *Fishbone-City* (oil on canvas) GBP 850. New York, 26 April 1961, *Surrealism and Painting* (pastel) USD 4,000. Stuttgart, 3-4 May 1962, *Birds and Ocean (recto); Arizona (verso)*, DEM 152,000. Bern, 10 May 1963, *Barbarians Marching towards the West* (gouache) CHF 15,500. London, 1 July 1964, *La Parisienne* (bronze) GBP 1,800. New York, 13 Oct 1965, *Turtle* (black-patinated bronze) USD 5,000. London, 3 Dec 1965, *Figures Including One Headless* (oil and sand/canvas) Gns 11,000. Geneva, 17 June 1966, *Shell-Flowers* (gouache) CHF 21,000. Milan, 27 April 1967, *Figures*, ITL 22,000,000. Geneva, 28 June 1968, *Composition with Horse*, CHF 117,000. New York, 16 April 1969, *Are you Niniche?* (patinated bronze) USD 8,000. New York, 26 Feb 1970, *Are you Niniche?* (patinated bronze) USD 9,000. London, 1 Dec 1971, *The Rule of the Game*, GBP 19,000. Paris, 1 Dec 1972, *The World is a Fable*, FRF 200,000. Paris, 8 April 1973, *Fall of the Angel* (1923) FRF 557,000. London, 4-5 Dec 1973, *Arizona, Frieze no. 2* (bronze relief) Gns 9,500; *Toreador*, GBP 90,000. Paris, 19 June 1974, *The World is a Fable*, FRF 400,000. Hamburg, 3 June 1976, *The Forest is a Board* (1925, frottage, 6 1/2 x 6 ins / 16.7 x 15.4 cm) DEM 12,000. Milan, 8 June 1976, *German*

Beauty, Paris (1934-1935, bronze, h. 22 3/4 ins / 58 cm) ITL 5,500,000. Bern, 9 June 1976, *Dancers* (lithograph) CHF 4,100. London, 29 Nov 1976, *Dream of Young Girl of a Lake* (1940, oil on canvas, 25 1/2 x 32 1/4 ins / 65 x 82 cm) GBP 88,000. Bern, 8 June 1977, *Dangerous Correspondences* (1947, dry-point, 70 prints made) CHF 8,200. London, 28 June 1977, *Head* (1951, mixed media/mounted paper/canvas, 12 3/4 x 10 ins / 32.5 x 25.5 cm) GBP 5,200. Bern, 7 June 1978, *Dancers* (1950, lithograph) CHF 4,200. New York, 1 Nov 1978, *Gypsy Rose Lee* (1943, oil on canvas, 17 3/4 x 23 1/2 ins / 45 x 59.6 cm) USD 110,000. Zurich, 23 Nov 1978, *The Queen, the Madman and the Horse* (1952, h. 4 3/4 ins / 12 cm) CHF 9,000. London, 5 Dec 1978, *Flowers* (c. 1927-1928, tempera/paper, 9 1/2 x 13 3/4 ins / 24 x 35 cm) GBP 10,000. Zurich, 30 May 1979, *Beatles* (1969, coloured photo enlargement on canvas, 44 1/2 x 30 3/4 ins / 113 x 78 cm) CHF 14,000. New York, 5 Nov 1979, *Evangeline* (1927, oil and plaster/canvas, 24 1/2 x 19 1/4 ins / 62 x 49 cm) USD 35,000. New York, 6 Nov 1979, *A Solicitous Friend* (1957, bronze, h. 26 1/4 ins / 66.5 cm) USD 60,000. New York, 6 Nov 1979, *Motherhood-Study for 'Surrealism and Painting'* (1942, oscillatory pen drawing, 24 3/4 x 19 1/4 ins / 63 x 49 cm) USD 36,000. New York, 5 Nov 1981, *Loplop Presents* (1930, pencil and frottage/paper, 12 1/4 x 9 ins / 31.1 x 22.7 cm) USD 11,500. London, 23 March 1983, *Pear* (1925, watercolour, pencil and frottage, 11 x 7 ins / 28 x 18 cm) GBP 18,000. London, 8 Dec 1983, *The Islands of the End of the World* (1955, etching and aquatint in black and green, 14 1/2 x 21 1/2 ins / 36.8 x 54.7 cm) GBP 1,200. London, 27 March 1984, *Monument to the Birds* (1927, oil on canvas, 63 3/4 x 51 1/4 ins / 162 x 130 cm) GBP 190,000. London, 5 Dec 1984, *False Positions* (1925, pencil and frottage, 17 1/4 x 11 ins / 43.5 x 27.5 cm) GBP 10,000. Cologne, 7 Dec 1984, *Janus Bird* (1974, bronze, h. 17 ins / 43 cm) DEM 22,000. New York, 14 May 1985, *Capricorn* (bronze, 98 1/2 x 82 x 60 1/4 ins / 250 x 208 x 153 cm) USD 875,000. London, 25 June 1986, *Loplop Introduces a Flower* (1931, watercolour, gouache, frottage and collage, 19 1/4 x 25 1/2 ins / 48.9 x 64.7 cm) GBP 29,000. London, 2 Dec 1986, *Vision Induced by the Nocturnal Aspect of the Porte St Denis* (1927, oil on canvas, 25 1/2 x 32 ins / 65 x 81 cm) GBP 240,000. Paris, 15 Dec 1986, *Portraits of Paul Éluard and Gala* (drawing and frottage in graphite, 10 x 6 3/4 ins / 24.5 x 17 cm) FRF 40,000. Paris, 7-8 Dec 1987, *Gulf Stream and Sun* (frottage, 10 x 16 1/2 ins / 25.5 x 42 cm) FRF 70,000. New York, 18 Feb 1988, *Egyptian* (gold medallion, 3 1/4 x 2 3/4 ins / 8.3 x 7 cm) USD 3,300; *Monsieur New Look* (silver statuette, h. 11 1/2 ins / 29.5 cm) USD 19,800. Paris, 19 March 1988, *The Dogs are Thirsty* (engraving/Japanese paper, 14 1/2 x 9 ins / 37 x 22 cm) FRF 4,000; *Prompt Tooth* (1969, coloured lithograph /Japanese paper) FRF 3,500. Paris, 22 March 1988, *Shell Flower* (1928, oil on canvas, 25 1/2 x 31 1/2 ins / 65 x 80 cm) FRF 930,000. New York, 12 May 1988, *Moon II* (oil on canvas, 25 3/4 x 31 1/2 ins / 65.7 x 80 cm) USD 297,000. Paris, 2 June 1988, *Leaf* (1963, oil collage and branches of plastic green leaves, 25 1/2 x 21 1/4 ins / 65 x 54 cm) FRF 347,000. Paris, 22 June 1988, *Petrified Forest* (1927, oil on canvas and scratching, 31 1/2 x 39 ins / 80 x 99 cm) FRF 4,000,000. London, 28 June 1988, *Chéri Bibi* (bronze, h. 13 1/4 ins / 33.5 cm) GBP 4,950. London, 29 June 1988, *Triangles* (1928, oil on canvas, 7 1/2 x 9 1/2 ins / 19 x 24 cm) GBP 42,900. New York, 6 Oct 1988, *Chéri Bibi* (bronze, h. 13 ins / 33 cm) USD 6,600. Paris, 28 Oct 1988, *Chéri Bibi* (black-patinated bronze, h. 13 1/4 ins / 33.5 cm) FRF 35,000; *Untitled* (frottage in paint and soft chalk/canvas, 13 1/2 x 11 1/4 ins / 34.5 x 28.5 cm) FRF 190,000. Paris, 20 Nov 1988, *Stark vergrösserter Gefrierschnitt...* (1920-1921, engraving heightened with major drawings and watercolours, 3 1/2 x 4 1/4 ins / 9 x 10.5 cm) FRF 500,000; *Boophile Plantation of Hyperborean from beyond the Seas* (1921, engraving heightened with major drawings and watercolours, 3 3/4 x 5 ins / 9.5 x 13 cm) FRF 540, 000; *Two Naked Girls* (1925, oil on canvas, 29 1/4 x 22 ins / 74 x 55 cm) FRF 5,400,000. Paris, 24 Nov 1988, *The Polish Rider* (1954, oil on canvas, 46 x 35 ins / 116 x 89 cm) FRF 46,000,000. Milan, 14 Dec 1988, *Gulf Stream* (1927, oil on panel, 13 x 16 1/4 ins / 33 x 41 cm) ITL 85,000,000. London, 3 April 1989, *Grey Forest* (oil on canvas, 31 1/2 x 39 1/4 ins / 80 x 100 cm) GBP 792,000. Paris, 9 April 1989, *Stylised Flowers* (1929, oil on canvas, 36 1/4 x 28 1/4 ins / 92 x 72 cm) FRF 4,800,000. New York, 3 May 1989, *Great Ignoramus* (mixed media with an original lithograph remounted on the central panel, screen with three wings, 73 1/4 x 65 1/4 ins / 186 x 166 cm) USD 155,400. New York, 11 May 1989, *Sleeper* (1955, oil on canvas, 18 1/4 x 21 3/4 ins / 46.3 x 55.2 cm) USD 258,500. Milan, 6 June 1989, *Green Halloween* (1959, oil on canvas, 25 1/4 x 22 ins / 64 x 55 cm) ITL 275,000,000. Paris, 12 June 1989, *Caged Moon* (mixed media, 20 3/4 x 17 1/4 ins / 53 x 44 cm) FRF 450,000. Paris, 21 June 1989, *Untitled* (c. 1935, oil on paper, 8 3/4 x 12 1/4 ins / 22.5 x 31 cm) FRF 935,000. Milan, 7 Nov 1989, *Sleeping Eskimo* (1948, oil on canvas, 28 x 24 ins / 71 x 61 cm) ITL 570,000,000. New York, 15 Nov 1989, *Discovery of Gold or Honey* (1946, oil on canvas, 14 x 20 ins / 35.6 x 51 cm) USD 297,000. Paris, 24 Nov 1989, *Les Mariés du vent* (1930, oil on canvas, 36 1/4 x 28 3/4 ins / 92 x 73 cm) FRF 5,400,000. London, 28 Nov 1989, *Crying Women Crossing River* (1927, oil on canvas, 32 x 23 1/2 ins / 81 x 60 cm) GBP 638,000. Paris, 13 Dec 1989, *Flowers and Seashells* (gouache, 9 x 12 1/4 ins / 23 x 31 cm) FRF 700,000. St-Germain-en-Laye, 4 Feb 1990, *Mobile Object Recommended for Family Use* (1970, wooden sculpture, h. 38 1/2 ins / 98 cm) FRF 165,000. New York, 26 Feb 1990, *Three Figures* (1952, golden-brown-patinated bronze, h. 4 3/4 ins / 12 cm, l. 10 ins/25.7 cm) USD 16,500. Paris, 27 March 1990, *Dust* (1965, canvas, 28 3/4 x 36 1/4 ins / 73 x 92 cm) FRF 1,500,000. Paris, 29 March 1990, *A Personality Always New Always Different* (1934, collage of cut-up illustrations, 3 3/4 x 11 3/4 ins / 9.5 x 30 cm) FRF 330,000. New York, 16 May 1990, *Desert Sun* (oil/synthetic resin, 7 ins / 18 cm, 1 1/2 x 33 1/2 ins/4 x 85 cm, 2 3/4 ins/7 cm) USD 77,000. Paris, 16 June 1990, *Great Ignoramus* (card cut into a circle and painted blue with a yellow card circle in the middle/black plywood, three-panelled screen) FRF 180,000. London, 17 Oct 1990, *Janus* (bronze, h. 17 1/4 ins / 43.5 cm) GBP 13,200. Douai, 11 Nov 1990, *Shelf of Found Object* (oil/Pavatex, 9 3/4 x 13 3/4 ins / 25 x 35 cm) FRF 446,000. New York, 13 Nov 1990, *Monument to the Birds* (1927, oil on canvas, 39 1/2 x 31 3/4 ins / 100.4 x 80.7 cm) USD 962,500. New York, 15 Nov 1990, *La Plus Belle* (1967, brown-patinated bronze, h. 72 ins / 182.8 cm) USD 308,000. Paris, 28 Nov 1990, *Nautilus, Seashell on Green Background* (c. 1928, oil on canvas, with frame 15 1/2 x 17 1/4 ins / 39.5 x 44 cm) FRF 1,030,000. Paris, 7 Dec 1990, *Untitled* (c. 1940, gouache and pencil/paper) FRF 82,000. New York, 8 May 1991, *Frog Pond* (1956, oil on canvas, 23 1/2 x 28 3/4 ins / 60 x 73 cm) USD 330,000. London, 24 June 1991, *Nuptial Flight* (1931, oil on canvas, 32 x 25 1/2 ins / 81 x 65 cm) GBP 231,000. London, 25 June 1991, *Forest and Sun* (1927, oil on canvas, 32 x 39 1/4 ins / 81 x 100 cm) GBP 528,000. Heidelberg, 12 Oct 1991, *Starfish* (1950, coloured lithograph/Arches, 16 3/4 x 10 1/2 ins / 42.6 x 26.7 cm) DEM 5,100. Paris, 17 Nov 1991, *The Horde* (1927, oil on canvas, 16 1/4 x 13 ins / 41.5 x 33 cm) FRF 2,100,000. London, 4 Dec 1991, *Two Assistants* (bronze, h. 40 cm/15 3/4 ins, diam. 40 cm/15 3/4 ins) GBP 30,800. Paris, 23 March 1992, *Great Ignoramus* (oil, wood, collage and lithograph, three-panelled screen, 72 x 64 1/2 ins / 183 x 164 cm) FRF 30,000. Lugano, 28 March 1992, *A Minute of Silence* (1964, oil and collage/panel, 16 1/4 x 13 ins / 41 x 33 cm) CHF 110,000. New York, 9 May 1992, *The King, the Queen and the Madman* (lost-wax bronze, l. 11 3/4 ins / 30 cm) USD 8,250. New York, 12 May 1992, *The Tuesday the Moon Puts on its Sunday Best* (1964, oil on canvas, 28 1/2 x 23 1/2 ins / 72.7 x 59.7 cm) USD 220,000. Lokeren, 23 May 1992, *The Animal Which Dances on My Friend's Head* (frottage, 8 1/4 x 5 1/2 ins / 21 x 14 cm) BEF 300,000. PARIS, 24 May 1992, *Tropical Landscape* (oil on paper, 6 x 2 1/4 ins / 15 x 6 cm) FRF 250,000. LONDON, 1 July 1992, *Flowers* (oil on canvas, in a frame by the artist, 11 x 9 ins / 27 x 22 cm) GBP 50,600. NEW YORK, 10 Nov 1992, *King Playing with the Queen* (bronze, h. 38 1/2 ins / 97.8 cm) USD 1,210,000. NEW YORK, 12 Nov 1992, *Tomorrow* (1959, oil and collage/panel, 13 x 9 1/4 ins / 33 x 23.8 cm) USD 99,000. PARIS, 24 Nov 1992, *Cypress Trees in Aix-en-Provence* (1939, oil on card, 15 3/4 x 12 ins / 40 x 30.5 cm) FRF 660,000. LONDON, 30 Nov 1992, *Ideal Postcard* (oil on canvas, 11 x 24 ins / 28 x 61 cm) GBP 66,000. LONDON, 1 Dec 1992, *The Forest and the Sun* (oil on paper/card, 9 1/2 x 12 1/2 ins / 24 x 32 cm) GBP 115,500. MUNICH, 1-2 Dec 1992, *Eternity* (1971, etching, 11 3/4 x 7 1/4 ins / 30 x 18.5 cm) DEM 2,415. MONACO, 6 Dec 1992, *Birds in the Forest* (gouache/paper/canvas, 11 3/4 x 8 3/4 ins / 30 x 22.3 cm) FRF 577,200. NEW YORK, 12 May 1993, *The Table Set* (brown-patinated bronze, 11 3/4 x 21 1/2 x 21 1/2 ins / 30 x 54.5 x 54.5 cm) USD 167,500. MILAN, 20 May 1993, *Figure* (pastel, 18 x 14 1/4 ins / 45.5 x 36 cm) ITL 22,000,000. PARIS, 21 June 1993, *Eddy* (oil on canvas, 26 x 22 ins / 66 x 55 cm) FRF 745,000. NEW YORK, 3 Nov 1993, *Landscape in Old Iron* (1921, gouache, ink and pencil/printed paper/canvas, 31 x 26 3/4 ins / 77.8 x 67.9 cm) USD 706,500. LONDON, 29 Nov 1993, *Shell-Flowers* (1929, oil on canvas, 44 1/2 x 35 ins / 113 x 89 cm) GBP 331,500. LOKEREN, 12 March 1994, *St Charlemagne* (lithograph triptych) BEF 60,000. PARIS, 20 May 1994, *Untitled* (engraving, 7 3/4 x 6 ins / 20 x 15 cm) FRF 10,200. PARIS, 1 June 1994, *Tortoise* (black marble original, 12 1/4 x 11 ins / 31 x 27 cm) FRF 110,000. LONDON, 29 June 1994, *My Friend Pierrot at Seillans* (1974, bronze, h. 20 ins / 51 cm) GBP 43,300. PARIS, 17 Nov 1994, *Flight* (1940, oil on canvas, 37 x 28 3/4 ins / 94 x 73 cm) FRF 1,380,000. ZURICH, 7 April 1995, *Mask with Round Eyes* (bronze, 30 x 13 ins / 76 x 33 cm) CHF 55,000. LOKEREN, 20 May 1995, *Fountain of Ambrosia, Tortoise* (black marble, h. 12 1/4 ins / 31 cm, w. 8 ins/20.5 cm) BEF 160,000. MILAN, 26 Oct 1995, *Geometry* (1966, collage and mixed media/plywood, 19 3/4 x 16 1/2 ins / 50 x 42 cm) ITL 46,000,000. NEW YORK, 8 Nov 1995, *Venus Seen from Earth* (1962, oil on canvas, 18 x 14 3/4 ins / 45.8 x 37.5 cm) USD 112,500. PARIS, 21 Nov 1995, *Bird Composition* (oil on panel, 16 1/4 x 11 ins / 41 x 27 cm) FRF 600,000. LONDON, 27 Nov 1995, *Forest, Sun, Birds* (1927, oil on canvas, 31 x 39 ins / 79 x 99 cm) GBP 463,500. PARIS, 13 Dec 1995, *Portrait of André Breton* (1926, lead pencil, 14 1/4 x 10 1/4 ins / 36 x 26 cm) FRF 100,000. PARIS, 8 March 1996, *My Friend Pierrot* (bronze, h. 19 3/4 ins / 50 cm) FRF 303,000. NEW YORK, 2 May 1996, *The Flight* (1940, oil on canvas, 37 x 28 3/4 ins / 94 x 73 cm) USD 453,500. PARIS, 7 June 1996, *Sign for Surprise of Chance* (1971, three coloured lithograph, 15 x 14 1/4 ins / 38 x 36.5 cm) FRF 4,700. LONDON, 24 June 1996, *Monument to the Birds* (1927, oil on canvas, 39 1/4 x 32 ins / 100 x 81 cm) GBP 364,500. NEW YORK, 10 Oct 1996, *King, Queen, Madman* (bronze, h. 5 1/2 ins / 14 cm and l. 11 3/4 ins/29.9 cm) USD 9,200. NEW YORK, 13 Nov 1996, *Cheri Bibi* (1973, black-patinated bronze, a pair, h. 13 ins / 33.3 cm) USD 13,800. LONDON, 3 Dec 1996, *False Poses, Histoire Naturelle* (1925, frottage and pencil/mounted paper/card, 19 x 10 1/2 ins / 48 x 26.5 cm) GBP 17,250. PARIS, 9 Dec 1996, *Figure* (c. 1955-1960, charcoal and oil on paper/canvas, 9 1/2 x 7 1/2 ins / 24.2 x 19 cm) FRF 142,000. LOKEREN, 8 March 1997, *Judith, Door Open on the Forest* (1961, oil on canvas/panel, 12 1/2 x 8 3/4 ins / 31.5 x 22.5 cm) BEF 500,000. NEW YORK, 14 May 1997, *Two Naked Girls* (1925, oil on canvas, 29 1/4 x 22 ins / 74 x 55 cm) USD 464,500. AMSTERDAM, 4 June 1997, *Janus* (1973-1975, bronze, h. 17 3/4 ins / 45 cm) NLG 71,498. PARIS, 18 June 1997, *Composition with Sun* (oil on panel, 5 1/2 x 3 3/4 ins / 14 x 9.5 cm) FRF 100,000. PARIS, 19 June 1997, *Big Oval Mask* (1959, chiselled 23 carat gold repoussé, sculpture, 11 x 7 1/4 ins / 28 x 18.5 cm) FRF 75,000. PARIS, 20 June 1997, *Rêve d'une petite fille qui voulut rentrer au Carmel* (1930, collage, 6 x 6 3/4 ins / 14.3 x 17.3 cm) FRF 125,000. LONDON, 24 June 1997, *Loplop Introduces a Fower - Anthropomorphic Figure and Shell-Flower* (c. 1930, oil and collage/canvas, 39 1/4 x 32 ins / 100 x 81 cm) GBP 309,500. LONDON, 22 Oct 1997, *Simplicity* (1925, frottage/paper, 8 x 6 1/4 ins / 20.6 x 16 cm) GBP 9,200. TEL AVIV, 23 Oct 1997, *Monsieur, Madame* (1960, silver/wooden boxes, h. 9 1/2 ins / 24 cm and 7 ins/18 cm) USD 33,350. NEW YORK, 6 and 7 March 1998, *Rhythms* (1950, coloured lithograph, 16 3/4 x 10 3/4 ins / 42.6 x 27.2 cm) USD 2,875. PARIS, 22 March 1998, *...Absolutely Limited to Them, Isolating from the Rest of the World* (frottage and pencil/paper, 9 1/2 x 7 1/2 ins / 24 x 19 cm) FRF 132,000. PARIS, 12 April 1999, *Dormeuse en coup de vent* (1950, oil on canvas, 35 x 46 ins / 89 x 116 cm) FRF 1,105,000. LONDON, 29 June 1999, *My Friend Pierrot* (1974, bronze, h. 20 ins / 51 cm) GBP 120,000. NEW YORK, 9 May 2000, *Landscape with Lac and Chimera* (oil on canvas, 20 x 26 ins / 51 x 66 cm) USD 950,000. NEW YORK, 8 Nov 2000, *Gypsy Rose Lee* (1943, oil on canvas, 18 x 24 ins / 45 x 60 cm) USD 1,300,000. LONDON, 6 Feb 2001, *Marriage of the Wind* (c. 1928, oil on canvas, 29 x 36 ins / 73 x 92 cm) GBP 700,000. NEW YORK, 6 Nov 2001, *La carmagnole de l'amour* (1926-1927, oil on canvas, 51 x 38 ins / 130 x 97 cm) USD 850,000. LONDON, 4 Feb 2002, *La Mariés du Vent* (1927, oil on canvas, 29 x 36 ins / 73 x 92 cm) GBP 500,000. NEW YORK, 5 Nov 2002, *The King Playing with the Queen* (1944, green and brown patinated bronze, h. 40 ins / 101 cm) USD 2,200,000. LONDON, 3 Feb 2003, *Convolvulus! Convolvulus* (1941, oil on canvas, 13 x 16 ins / 33 x 41 cm) GBP 660,000. LONDON, 3 Feb 2003, *Epiphany - Dream Landscape* (1940, oil on canvas, 21 x 26 ins / 54 x 65 cm) GBP 900,000. LONDON, 2 Feb 2004, *Escape* (1940, oil on canvas, 36 x 29 ins / 92 x 73 cm) GBP 880,000. COPENHAGEN, 29 March 2004, *Conversion of Fire in Landscape of the Antipodes* (1937, oil on canvas, 15 x 22 ins / 38 x 55 cm) DKK 6,200,000.

ERNST, Michael
German, 19th century.
Died 1850.
Active in Schöllang (Bavaria).
Sculptor.

Michael Ernst was the brother of Joseph Anton Ernst.

ERNST, Otto
Swiss, 20th century.
Born 25 November 1884, in Kölliken.
Painter, engraver.

Otto Ernst studied in Florence and Paris, where he was taught by Grasset at the Académie de la Grande Chaumière.

ERNST, Otto von
German, 19th century.
Born 10 July 1853, in Thorn.
Painter. Hunting scenes, landscapes.

Otto von Ernst worked in Düsseldorf. He is best known for his *Meeting for the Fox Hunt*.

AUCTION RECORDS:

COLOGNE, 18 March 1989, *Wooded Landscape near Langenfeld* (1881, oil on paper) DEM 1,100.

ERNST, Rudolf
Austrian, 19th - 20th century.
Born 14 February 1854, in Vienna; died 1932, in Paris.
Active and naturalised in France.
Painter (gouache), potter. Portraits, genre scenes, local scenes (harems).
Orientalism.

In 1869 Rudolf Ernst entered the academy in Vienna, where he studied under August Eisenmenger and Anselme Feuerbach. He then pursued his studies in Rome. In 1874 and 1875 he travelled throughout Italy, went to the USA, Spain and Morocco before taking up permanent residence in Paris in 1876. He exhibited in Vienna and Munich and from 1875 in

Paris. He received a bronze medal at the 1889 Exposition Universelle and a distinction in 1900. A number of his pictures were repeatedly shown at the annual events of the Société des Amis des Arts in Nantes. He was commissioned to execute the altarpiece of the church of the Favourites in Vienna. He received various prestigious commissions in Turkey and France including those of Sergeant MacMahon and the Duke of Castries.

Until 1884 his repertoire consisted mainly of portraits and genre scenes - charming children and musketeers - nearly always of small dimensions. From 1885, however, he limited himself to Orientalist paintings with Moroccan, Turkish or Hispano-Moorish décor. After travelling to Constantinople around 1890 he became fascinated by the decoration of faience tiles, a technique he had learnt from Léon Fargue, a Parisian ceramicist and glassmaker. Around 1900, he carried out several paintings of Hindu temples, such as *The Sacred Pond* and *The Underground Temple*. Ernst rivals his compatriot Ludwig Deutsch in his skilful rendering of details.

R.Ernst.

BIBLIOGRAPHY:

Thornton, L., *The Orientalists - Painter-Travellers, 1828-1908*, ACR Edition, 1983. Thornton, Lynne, *Les Orientalistes, peintres voyageurs, 1828-1908*, ACR Édition, Paris, 1993.

MUSEUMS AND GALLERIES:

MONTREAL: *At Study*.

AUCTION RECORDS:

LONDON, 30 Nov 1905, *Light from the Harem*, GBP 15. NEW YORK, 7 May 1909, *Rose Harvest*, USD 300. PARIS, 7 April 1921, *Mehemed's Tomb*, FRF 800. LONDON, 8 Dec 1922, *Copper Workers*, GBP 60. PARIS, 24-26 April 1929, *Carpet Seller*, FRF 2,300. NEW YORK, 8 Jan 1930, *Return from the Hunt*, USD 225. PARIS, 12-13 April 1943, *Harem Scene*, FRF 1,600. PARIS, 26 Feb 1947, *Oriental Scene, the Prostitute*, FRF 11,800. PARIS, 24 May 1976, *Rose Harvest* (oil on canvas, 28 1/4 x 36 1/4 ins / 72 x 92 cm) FRF 20,000. PARIS, 29 Nov 1976, *Moslem Women in Moorish Interior* (oil on panel, 36 1/4 x 28 3/4 ins / 92 x 73 cm) FRF 12,800. LONDON, 3 Nov 1977, *Servant's Greeting* (oil on panel, 28 x 35 1/2 ins / 71 x 90 cm) GBP 6,000. NEW YORK, 12 Oct 1978, *Tiger Hunt* (oil on panel, 32 x 39 1/2 ins / 81 x 100.3 cm) USD 26,000. LONDON, 2 Nov 1979, *Salome and the Tigers* (oil on panel, 27 3/4 x 35 3/4 ins / 70.5 x 90.8 cm) GBP 7,000. PARIS, 7 May 1980, *In Front of the Mosque* (gouache, 13 x 10 1/4 ins / 33 x 26 cm) FRF 15,500. BOLTON, 18 Nov 1982, *Narghile Smoker* (watercolour, 12 1/4 x 18 1/4 ins / 31 x 46.5 cm) USD 3,800. NEW YORK, 24 Feb 1983, *Itinerant Musicians at Sultan's Palace* (oil on panel, 36 1/2 x 28 1/4 ins / 93 x 72 cm) USD 63,000. LONDON, 29 Nov 1984, *Pensive Arab* (watercolour/pencil outlines, 21 1/4 x 15 ins / 54 x 38 cm) GBP 8,500. LONDON, 20 March 1985, *Woman Selling Fruit* (oil on panel, 39 1/4 x 29 1/4 ins / 100 x 74.5 cm) GBP 15,000. VICHY, 15 Nov 1987, *Reading the Letter* (watercolour) FRF 65,000. PARIS, 11 March 1988, *Arab Merchant in front of his Door* (oil on panel, 31 1/2 x 24 3/4 ins / 80 x 63 cm) FRF 365,000. PARIS, 17 June 1988, *Princess with Rose* (oil on panel, 20 3/4 x 25 1/2 ins / 53 x 65 cm) FRF 520,000. LA VARENNE-ST-HILAIRE, 23 Oct 1988, *In the Palace* (oil on panel, 17 1/2 x 14 3/4 ins / 44.5 x 37.5 cm) FRF 125,000. NEW YORK, 23 May 1989, *Turkish Baths* (oil on panel, 19 1/4 x 24 ins / 49 x 61 cm) USD 132,000. LONDON, 21 June 1989, *In the Mosque* (oil on panel, 13 1/2 x 10 ins / 34 x 25.5 cm) GBP 8,800. NEW YORK, 24 Oct 1989, *In the Alhambra* (1888, oil on panel, 24 1/4 x 19 1/4 ins / 61.3 x 49.2 cm) USD 93,500. PARIS, 8 Dec 1989, *The Toilette* (watercolour, 10 1/2 x 8 1/4 ins / 26.5 x 21 cm) FRF 62,000. LONDON, 30 March 1990, *Turkish Baths* (oil on canvas, 25 1/2 x 21 ins / 64.7 x 53.4 cm) GBP 35,200. PARIS, 6 April 1990, *Keeper of Seraglio* (watercolour and gouache, 20 1/2 x 12 1/2 ins / 52 x 32 cm) FRF 85,000. PARIS, 27 April 1990, *Rose Harvest* (oil on panel, 32 x 25 1/4 ins / 81 x 64 cm) FRF 350,000. PARIS, 22 June 1990, *Reading The Koran* (watercolour, 15 3/4 x 11 ins / 40 x 27 cm) FRF 52,000. LONDON, 5 Oct 1990, *Study of Tiger* (oil on panel, 11 x 14 1/4 ins / 27.9 x 36.2 cm) GBP 4,950. LONDON, 28 Nov 1990, *Keeper* (oil on panel, 19 3/4 x 24 1/4 ins / 50 x 61.5 cm) GBP 12,650. PARIS, 8 April 1991, *Healer* (watercolour, 19 1/4 x 12 3/4 ins / 49 x 32.5 cm) FRF 12,000. NEW YORK, 22 May 1991, *Evening Prayer* (oil on panel, 32 x 25 ins / 81.3 x 63.5 cm) USD 52,250. PARIS, 11 Dec 1991, *Portrait of Nubian* (oil on panel, 13 3/4 x 8 ins / 35 x 20.5 cm) FRF 11,500. NEW YORK, 28 May 1992, *Nubian Keeper* (oil on panel, 23 x 19 ins / 58.4 x 48.3 cm) USD 55,000. PARIS, 2 June 1992, *Musician and Heron* (oil on panel, 16 1/2 x 24 ins / 42 x 61 cm) FRF 86,000. LONDON, 19 June 1992, *Rose Harvest* (oil on panel, 28 1/4 x 36 ins / 71.7 x 91.5 cm) GBP 50,600. NEW YORK, 29 Oct 1992, *Beggar* (oil on panel, 17 3/4 x 14 1/2 ins / 45.1 x 36.8 cm) USD 19,800. NEW YORK, 30 Oct 1992, *Study of The Koran* (oil on panel, 16 1/4 x 9 3/4 ins / 41 x 24.8 cm) USD 24,200. PARIS, 7 Dec 1992, *The Favourite One* (oil on panel, 36 1/2 x 28 1/4 ins / 93 x 71.5 cm) FRF 410,000. PARIS, 21 June 1993, *Itinerant Musicians at Sultan's Palace* (pencil, bistre watercolour and gouache/card, 22 x 16 1/2 ins / 56 x 42 cm) FRF 45,000. NEW YORK, 13 Oct 1993, *Lighter of the Mosque Chandeliers* (1885, oil on panel, 24 x 19 1/4 ins / 61 x 48.9 cm) USD 34,500. PARIS, 8 Nov 1993, *Picking Roses* (oil on panel, 24 x 19 1/4 ins / 61 x 49 cm) FRF 510,000. LONDON, 19 Nov 1993, *Interior of Arab Palace* (oil on panel, 25 1/2 x 21 ins / 65 x 53.5 cm) GBP 78,500. NEW YORK, 16 Feb 1994, *After Prayer* (oil on panel, 32 x 25 ins / 81.3 x 63.5 cm) USD 96,000. PARIS, 22 March 1994, *Picking Roses* (charcoal, watercolour and gouache). COMPIÈGNE, 30 April 1994, *Interior of Mosque* (oil on panel, 16 1/4 x 12 1/2 ins / 41 x 32 cm) FRF 230,000. PARIS, 5 Dec 1994, *The Kief* (oil on panel, 15 x 18 ins / 38 x 46 cm) FRF 400,000. NEW YORK, 24 May 1995, *In the Harem* (oil on panel, 23 x 28 3/4 ins / 58.4 x 73 cm) USD 85,000. LONDON, 15 March 1996, *Narghile Smoker* (oil on panel, 21 3/4 x 18 ins / 55.2 x 45.7 cm) GBP 80,700. NEW YORK, 23-24 May 1996, *The Favourite One* (oil on panel, 24 x 19 1/2 ins / 61 x 49.5 cm) USD 109,750. LONDON, 20 Nov 1996, *Man in front of Entrance to Hindu Temple* (watercolour, 18 3/4 x 12 1/4 ins / 47.5 x 31 cm) GBP 6,900. NEW YORK, 9 Dec 1996, *Before the Hunt* (oil on panel, 28 1/4 x 36 1/4 ins / 71.5 x 92 cm) FRF 84,000; *Reading* (oil on canvas/panel, 8 1/2 x 10 1/2 ins / 21.5 x 26.5 cm) FRF 55,000. LONDON, 21 March 1997, *In the Garden of the Harem* (oil on panel, 22 x 17 3/4 ins / 55 x 45 cm) GBP 41,100. PARIS, 5 June 1997, *Nude with Flowers* (oil on panel, 17 1/2 x 9 ins / 44.5 x 23 cm) FRF 24,000. LONDON, 13 June 1997, *Turkish Bath* (oil on panel, 33 x 40 3/4 ins / 84.1 x 103.8 cm) GBP 103,800. PARIS, 17 Nov 1997, *Imam and the Column of Light* (oil on panel, 13 3/4 x 11 ins / 35 x 27 cm) FRF 95,000. NEW YORK, 18 March 1998, *Marriage Day* (oil on panel, 24 x 19 1/4 ins / 61 x 48.9 cm) USD 255,500.

ERNSTING, Daniel Albert

German, 18th - 19th century.
Born c. 1750; died 4 January 1820.
Active in Bremen.
Draughtsman, engraver.

Ernsting was a pupil of Kollenheger in Göttingen.

EROFEEV

Russian, 19th century.
Lithographer.

Erofeev is known for one plate, *Farm Interior*, after Chernyshev. He may be the same as one Nikolai Erofeev, who trained at the academy of art in St Petersburg in 1816-1817.

EROFEEV, Vasili

Russian, 20th century.
Born 1937, in Pokruskoie (Kursk).
Painter. Landscapes, portraits.

Vasili Erofeev studied at the school of art in Kursk; his painting complied completely, in style and technique, with the propagandist and academic directives of the authorities of the time. He was appointed People's Artist of the USSR and member of the Union of Artists of the USSR.
AUCTION RECORDS:
PARIS, 29 Nov 1990, *Woman in a Shawl* (oil on canvas/synthetic resin, 22 x 12$^{1}/_{4}$ ins / 55 x 31 cm) FRF 5,000.

EROL, Turan
Turkish, 20th century.
Born 20th century, in Turkey.
Painter, engraver.
After studying at the school of fine art in Istanbul, Turan Erol completed his artistic education by studying engraving under Friedlaender. He has shown on several occasions in Ankara and, in 1961, he won Turkey's national prize for painting. He paints abstract landscapes.

EROLI, Erulo
Italian, 19th century.
Born 31 August 1854; died 1916.
Painter. Historical scenes, genre scenes.
Eroli worked in Rome, and exhibited in Dresden and Munich in 1887 and 1889. His best known work is entitled *An Angel.*
AUCTION RECORDS:
ROME, 24 March 1992, *Musketeers in an Inn* (oil on panel, 5$^{1}/_{2}$ x 4$^{1}/_{4}$ ins / 14 x 10.5 cm) ITL 1,725,000. NEW YORK, 24 May 1995, *The Dream of Pilate's Wife, Claudia Procula* (oil on canvas, 79$^{1}/_{2}$ x 98$^{1}/_{2}$ ins / 201.9 x 250.2 cm) USD 79,500. NEW YORK, 29 Nov 1999, *Angel of Mercy* (1895, oil on canvas, 59 x 84 ins / 150 x 214 cm) USD 8,000. MILAN, 4 Dec 2000, *Blackberry Seller* (watercolour, 17 x 11 ins / 42 x 27 cm) ITL 3,200,000. NORTH BETHESDA, 14 Feb 2001, *Tea Party* (1907, watercolour on paperboard, 21 x 32 ins / 54 x 81 cm) USD 2,200.

ERÖS, Gabor
Hungarian, 19th century.
Died 30 January 1815.
Engraver.
Gabor Erös studied in Debrecen. He produced a work entitled *Anacreon.*

EROS OF ATHENS
2th century.
Sculptor.
Ancient Greek.
Eros' signature was found at Olympia.

EROSHEVSKY, Andrei
Russian, 18th century.
Active in St Petersburg.
Painter.
In 1744, Andrei Eroshevsky worked on the ceiling paintings of the Empress' formal apartments in the Winter Palace, in 1748 on the Summer Palace, in 1750 on the Anichkov Palace and in 1752 on the Hermitage at Tsarskoe-Selo. He also painted decorative paintings in the St Petersburg Opera.

EROSHEVSKY, Vasili
Russian, 18th century.
Painter.
From 1720 to 1739 Vasili Eroshevsky worked in the castles of St Petersburg and Peterhof. Among his works he is known for a *Conversion of Saul* in the Summer Palace and battlefield paintings. In 1736 he painted icons in the churches of St Simon and St Anne.

EROUKMANOFF, Marc. See **MARC-EROUKMANOFF**

ERPE, Johannes van
Flemish School, 15th century.
Active in Ghent.
Miniaturist.

ERPIKUM, pseudonym of Léon Vuilleminot
French, 19th century.
Born c. 1835, in Besançon.
Painter, lithographer. Nudes, portraits, genre scenes, landscapes.
A pupil of Hippolyte Flandrin, Erpikum exhibited at the Paris Salon from 1859 to 1880. His best-known works are *Hesitation, The Awakening, Andromeda,* and *Woman Sleeping.* He also executed a series of lithographs.
MUSEUMS AND GALLERIES:
PONTOISE: *Blond-haired Woman Reclining.*
AUCTION RECORDS:
PARIS, 4-6 April 1900, *Before the Bath,* FRF 520. PARIS, 20-21 April 1904, *Nymph by a Fountain,* FRF 105. PARIS, 15-16 June 1942, *Woman with Cupids,* FRF 2,000. PARIS, 12 May 1944, *Young Woman with a Blue Ribbon,* FRF 1,500. PARIS, 15 March 1976, *Woman Bathing* (oil on canvas, 13 x 9$^{1}/_{2}$ ins / 33 x 24 cm) FRF 1,400. PARIS, 2 April 1982, *Woman with a Blue Ribbon* (1905, oil on wood, 11 x 8$^{1}/_{2}$ ins / 27 x 21.7 cm) FRF 3,000. LONDON, 19 March 1986, *Nude Reclining in a Landscape* (1889, oil on canvas, 32 x 65$^{3}/_{4}$ ins / 81 x 167 cm) GBP 4,000. PARIS, 5 Feb 1998, *Young Woman in a Landscape* (oil on panel, 15 x 17$^{3}/_{4}$ ins / 38 x 45 cm) FRF 5,000. AHLDEN, 22 Sept 2000, *Bather in Park Landscape* (1871, oil on canvas, 15 x 12 ins / 39 x 31 cm) DEM 3,300.

ERRANI, Charles
French, 19th century.
Born 19th century, in Versailles.
Miniaturist.
From 1834 to 1838 Charles Errani sent miniatures to the Salon.
AUCTION RECORDS:
PARIS, 7 and 8 June 1927, *Portrait de Jeune Femme Brune* (miniature) FRF 420.

ERRANI, L.
19th century.
Active in Italy.
Engraver (burin).
He engraved plates for *Imp. e Reale Galleria Pitti.*

ERRANTE, Giuseppe
Italian, 18th - 19th century.
Born 19 March 1760, in Trapini; died 16 February 1821, in Rome.
Painter. Genre scenes, portraits.
Errante studied in Palermo and Rome, and was employed at the Palazzo Caserta in Naples. His political views forced him to move to Milan, and then to Rome in 1810. He excelled at portraits, but painted genre scenes as well.

ERRAR, Johann, or Errard
Flemish, 17th century.
Active in Liège c. 1670.
Engraver.
Flemish School.
Johann Errar engraved landscapes inspired by Waterloo.

ERRARD, Charles. See **ERARD**

ERRARD, Gérard Léonard, or Hérard
Flemish, 17th century.
Born 1630; died 8 November 1675.
Active in Liège, Paris and Versailles.
Sculptor, medallist.
Flemish School.
Gérard Léonard Errard worked in Paris with Varin. He was a member of the royal academy in 1670 and executed a number of sculptures for the Versailles gardens.

ERRARD, Jacques. See **ERARD**

ERRARD, Paul. See **ERARD**

ERRAZURIS, José Thomas
Chilean, 19th century.
Born in Santiago.
Painter. Genre scenes.
José Errazuris exhibited at the Salon des Artistes Français, receiving a commendation in 1888.
AUCTION RECORDS:
PARIS, 1 July 1981, *Child by the Sea* (oil on canvas, 25 1/2 x 26 1/2 ins / 65 x 67.5 cm) FRF 7,000.

ERREGOUTS. See **HERREGOUTS**

ERREIP-DESVALLIÈRES, Jean
French, 20th century.
Born in Paris.
Painter. Religious subjects, portraits.
Jean Erreip-Desvallières was a pupil of M. Desvallières. He exhibited in Paris from 1931 at the Salon d'Automne and obtained a travel scholarship from the Salon des Artistes Français in 1940.

ERRENS, Adolphe Pieter Herman Jacob van Weezel
Dutch, 19th century.
Born 8 July 1866, in The Hague.
Painter, engraver.
Adolphe van Weezel Errens studied in The Hague and exhibited in Holland, Belgium and Germany.

ERRI, Agnolo
Italian, 15th century.
Active in Modena in the second half of the 15th century.
Painter.
Agnolo Erri was the brother of Bartolommeo Erri. The museum at Padua has his *Virgin*.

ERRI, Annibale di Francesco di Giorgio
Italian, 16th century.
Active in Bologna c. 1500.
Painter.

ERRI, Bartolommeo
Italian, 15th century.
Painter. Religious subjects.
Bartolommeo Erri worked for Principe Borso d'Este and decorated the cathedral and church of S Domenico in Modena. He was the brother of Agnolo Erri.
MUSEUMS AND GALLERIES:
STRASBOURG: *Virgin*.
AUCTION RECORDS:
NEW YORK, 20 Jan 1983, *The Banquet of Herod* (tempera/panel, 11 3/4 x 20 ins / 30 x 51 cm) USD 45,000.

ERRI, Bartolommeo di Gemignano
Italian, 14th - 15th century.
Born in Modena.
Painter.
In 1410 Bartolommeo di Gemignano Erri was in Bologna. He was the father of Giorgio Erri.

ERRI, Benedetto
Italian, 15th century.
Active in Modena.
Painter.
Benedetto Erri was the father of Pellegrino Erri and worked for the oratory of the Ospedale della Morte in Modena.

ERRI, Camillo
Italian, 16th century.
Born c. 1557.
Painter.
Camillo Erri's *St John the Baptist Preaching*, signed and bearing the date 1577, is in the art gallery at Modena.

ERRI, Giorgio
Italian, 15th century.
Active in Modena c. 1400.
Painter.
Giorgio Erri was the son of Bartolommeo di Gemignano Erri.

ERRI, Ippolita
Italian, 17th century.
Died 1661, in Modena.
Painter.
Ippolita Erri was a nun.

ERRI, Pellegrino
Italian, 15th century.
Died 1497, in Modena.
Painter.
Pellegrino Erri was the son of Benedetto Erri.

ERRI, Pietro
Italian, 15th century.
Active in Modena.
Painter.
Pietro Erri worked with Benedetto Erri.

ERRICO, Antonio d'. See **TANZIO DA VARALLO**

ERRICO, Giovan Angelo de
Italian, 16th century.
Active in Naples in 1577.
Sculptor.
Giovan Angelo de Errico sculpted a tomb for the cathedral at Naples.

ERRÓ, pseudonym of Gudmundsson Gudmundur, first pseudonym: Ferro
Icelandic, 20th century.
Born 19 July 1932, in Olafsvik.
From 1958 also active in France and in the Balearic Islands.
Painter (mixed media), watercolourist, collage artist, engraver, draughtsman. Scenes with figures.
Nouvelle Figuration, Figuration Narrative.
'I was twelve years old when I began to paint, and I was all alone in the countryside', Erró relates. Guided by this creative passion, he attended the art academies in Rejkjavik and Oslo between 1949 and 1952. In 1951, he obtained an art teaching diploma. This period of apprenticeship introduced him to the art of fresco and engraving. From 1953, he embarked on a series of study trips to Spain, Germany and France, travelling to Italy in 1954. Between 1955 and 1958, he attended courses at the art academy in Florence and learnt mosaic techniques in Ravenna. His first exhibitions in Florence and Milan date from this period. In 1958, Erró settled in Paris, dividing his time between there and Iceland. In 1962, he organised a happening, *La Catastrophe*, with Jean-Jacques Lebel at the Raymond Cordier gallery in Paris. In the same year, he published his first *Mécanifest* (*Mecanifesto*) and made a film: *Mécamorphoses*. In 1963, he published his second *Mécanifest* and went to New York for a solo exhibition of his work. In 1964, he began work on the film *Grimaces*. In 1964, he travelled to Russia and again to New York. In 1966, he produced the film *Stars*. Between 1966 and 1971, he made several trips to New York and travelled to Russia twice, then to Cuba in 1967. He visited Thailand for the first time in 1972. He continued to travel all over the world. He painted his watercolours in Formentera, near Ibiza. In 1991, he donated over 2,000 works (paintings, drawings, engravings and collages) to his country.

Erró undertook a classification of his own works into periods. Up to the mid-1970s, the fifty or so listed include: *Carcasses* (1955-1957), *Trans-Aggressions* (1958-1959), *Masked Cloakroom Attendants* (1959-1962), *Meca-Make-Up* (1960),

Factories and *Engines* (1961-1962), *Sex-tremities* and *Mothers and Children* (1963-1964), *Disphysiognomies* (1965-1966), *Depictions* (1966), *Monsters* (1968) and *American Interiors* (1970). In 2003, he explored the imagery used in Disney and in Russian and Japanese cartoons. Although the formal content and connecting themes of his canvases have clearly changed over the years, Erró's technique has not fundamentally altered. He begins by making a preliminary model of the intended painting by assembling a large number of documents cut out from catalogues, periodical journals from all over the world, publicity fliers and cartoons, including political posters, reproductions of pictures, townscapes, famous or unknown figures and sketches of characters from science fiction. He positions the images according to their size, then proceeds to the superimpositions and structures his space. 'Collage is the most exciting and the freest part of my work: it is almost a form of automatic writing. It's there that I find formal solutions for filling space', he says. Once the composition has been completed, Erró redraws it in its entirety on the canvas and then paints it. These works are thus copies of collages, which allows him a certain freedom of interpretation and also gives some unity to the whole. Erró's universe is perfectly cosmopolitan. It presents a Maoist marching on St Mark's Square, or Kennedy giving a talk among some Chinese children, cosmonauts undressing before the women from Ingres' *Turkish Bath*, an aeroplane landing over a pair of naked Indian women, more recently some cartoon characters milling around and some more structured productions, in which perspective plays a major part, and which are composed of highly varied and coloured themes. This iconographic assemblage that redeploys image-based information from the media involves a decoding that requires the viewer's complete participation. The representations of figures, objects or landscapes, even before their pictorial use, are intrinsically significant both through their past histories or present lives and through their existence as known objects or facts, most often known worldwide via the media. Through this visual consecration, we associate these figures with the many collective or personal notions that surround them. Finally, seen in the new unity of Erró's canvas, they come to life again in the most deeply unsettling contrasts. In terms of form, the painter conducts an elimination of the medium of images (from newspapers, magazines, posters, photographs) but not of the image itself; he generally preserves their original appearance through the device of illusionism. Very often he colours them, always using strong and pure colours in flat tints. As Erró expressed it: 'I paint very quickly. I use the fast fresco technique that I learnt in Italy. The image has to be completed before the painting dries'. The appreciation of a painting by Erró involves a certain orientation. In search of self-assurance, our gaze scans this moving and challenging representation. More than a kaleidoscope of images, Erró's paintings also serve as a history of ideas in which all the following are mingled across time: science, religion, the old painting of the Middle Ages and that of industrial civilisation, the sacred, the profane, China, Italy, literature, comics, eroticism from many cultures in terms of the female image... Erró's painting forms part of the pictorial movement of the mid-1960s that sought to revive expressive forms, faced with an imperialist and reductionist abstraction. Thus, this new figuration or, to use Gassiot-Talabot's term, 'narrative figuration', unites artists of various sensibilities who revived figuration by introducing a temporal reality, in an indication, as Suzanne Pagé writes, of an urge to assess 'the entire human condition in its affective, ideological, cultural and social dimensions'. Although Erró denies any specific political meaning to his assemblages, it is impossible to overlook their proclamation of the right to know, explore and question. Erró has taken part in many collective exhibitions, since the 1961 exhibition at the Salon des Surindépendants in Paris, including: 1961, at the Salon de Mai in Paris, of which he later became a committee member; from 1963 to 1966, at the Salon Comparaisons in Paris; 1964, *Exposition Surréaliste de Paris* (*Surrealist Exhibition in Paris*); from 1965 to 1967, Salon de la Jeune Peinture, Paris; 1965, *Narrative Figuration in Contemporary Art*, an exhibition organised by G. Gassiot-Talabot; 1967, *The World in Question*; 1961, 1963, 1965, Biennale de Paris; 1954, Tokyo Biennale; 1964, São Paulo Biennale; 1985, with *Maggie and the Falklands, Beirut, Poland, Brezhnev of Russia, Petrol 1980* at the Nouvelle Biennale in Paris; 1986, the Venice Biennale; 1991, *Rencontres - Cinquante ans de Collages* (*Encounters - Fifty Years of Collage*), an exhibition organised by Françoise Monin at the Claudine Lustman gallery, Paris; 2000, *Great Anti-Fascist Collective Picture* at the museum of modern and contemporary art in Strasbourg; 2001, *Family Spirit*, Villa du Parc, Annemasse; 2003, Villa Arson, Nice; 2003, *Déchirures de l'histoire* (*Ruptures in History*), an examination of slavery and the Paris Commune at 'Le 19', the regional centre of contemporary art in Montbéliard.

A series of solo exhibitions has followed since 1955, both in France and elsewhere. In addition to those already mentioned, he had the following exhibitions: 1976, 1977, 1979, Beaubourg gallery, Paris; Gertrude Stein gallery, New York; 1981, Maeght gallery, Zurich; 1981, itinerant retrospective exhibition in several Scandinavian cities: Lund, Bergen, Helsinki and Copenhagen; 1985, *Landscapes 1959/1985*, Musée d'Art Moderne de la Ville de Paris; 1986, Abbaye de Montmajour; 1991, la Réunion; 1991, 1998, Montenay gallery, Paris; 1994, Palais des Congrès, Paris; 1999, retrospective, Galerie Nationale du Jeu de Paume, Paris; 2003, *Erró. Tribute to Walt Disney*, Louis Carré gallery, Paris.

Bibliography:

Brownstone, Gilbert, '*Erro*' in *coll. Bibli-Opus*, Georges Fall, Paris, 1972. Pierre, José, *Le Pop Art, dictionnaire de poche*, Hazan, Paris, 1975. Tilman, Pierre, *Erro*, Éd. Galilée, Paris, 1976. *Erro catalogue général*, Ed. Pre-Arte, Milan, 1976. Johanssen, M./Ásgeirson, B., '*Erró: Icelandic Artist*' in *Iceland Review, 3*, 1978. *Erro*, Christian Bourgois, Paris, 1979. Jouffroy, Alain, '*Célébration des collages d'Erro*' in *Erro-Collages-1957-1980*, exhibition catalogue, Gal. Le Dessin, Burrus-Montenay, Paris, 1981. Lebel, Jean-Jacques, *Erro 1974-1986 - Catalogue général*, Hazan, Paris, 1986. Bouisset, Maïten, '*Erro, pêcheur d'images*' in *Beaux-Arts*, periodical, Paris, 1991. Auge, Marc, *Erro, peintre mythique*, Le Lit du vent, Paris, 1994. Tronche, Anne, *Erró. Hommage à Walt Disney*, exhibition catalogue, Gal. Louis Carré, Paris, 2003 (text in French and English). *Déchirures de l'histoire*, exhibition catalogue, Le 19, Centre régional d'art contemporain, Montbéliard, 2003.

Museums and Galleries:

Antibes (Mus. Picasso) - Berlin (Nationalgal.) - Bern (Kunstmus.) - Châteauroux (Mus.-Hôtel Bertrand) - Geneva (Mamco) - Havana (Mus. Nacional, Palacio de Bellas Artes) - Humlebæk (Louisiana Mus. for Moderne Kunst) - Jerusalem (Israel Mus.) - Lille (Hôtel de Ville) - Marseilles (Mus. Cantini) - Montpellier (FRAC Languedoc-Roussillon) - Munich (Städtische Gal. im Lenbachhaus) - New York (MoMA) - Nîmes (Carré d'Art, MAC, donation Lintas) - Paris (BNF) - Paris (Cité des Sciences et de l'Industrie) - Paris (FNAC) - Paris (MAMVP) - Paris (MNAM-CCI) - Paris (Mus. d'Histoire Contemporaine) - Randers (Kunstmus.) - Reykjavik (Listasafn Islands): important collection of works - St-Paul-de-Vence (Fondation Maeght) - Stockholm (Moderna Mus.) - Tel Aviv (MA) - Tokyo (Hara MCA) - Utrecht (Centraal Mus.) - Washington DC (National Air and Space Mus.).

AUCTION RECORDS:
PARIS, 21 Dec 1981, *Freud* (1979, oil on canvas, 76 3/4 x 51 1/4 ins / 195 x 130 cm) FRF 11,500. PARIS, 5 Dec 1983, *The Experts* (1959, oil on canvas, 78 3/4 x 51 1/4 ins / 200 x 130 cm) FRF 32,000. PARIS, 4 Dec 1986, *Washington* (acrylic/canvas, 78 3/4 x 118 ins / 200 x 300 cm) FRF 57,000. PARIS, 8 Feb 1988, *This One for Fury* (oil on canvas, 39 1/2 x 25 1/2 ins / 100.5 x 65 cm) FRF 11,000. PARIS, 24 April 1988, *Tribute to Carnival, Léger Series* (1974, oil on canvas, 76 3/4 x 51 1/4 ins / 195 x 130 cm) FRF 40,000. PARIS, 1 June 1988, *In Assyria* (1978, collage, 11 x 11 ins / 27 x 28 cm) FRF 1,600; *Portrait* (1969, collage, 11 x 9 ins / 28 x 23 cm) FRF 1,300. PARIS, 17 June 1988, *Kokoschka and Grosz* (1968, acrylic/canvas, 40 1/4 x 25 1/4 ins / 102.5 x 64 cm) FRF 18,000. PARIS, 27 June 1988, *Picasso/Grosz, Ecce Homo Series* (oil on canvas, 25 1/4 x 40 1/4 ins / 64 x 102 cm) FRF 9,500; *Museum Visitors* (1959, acrylic/canvas, 63 x 78 3/4 ins / 160 x 200 cm) FRF 42,000. PARIS, 26 Oct 1988, *Van Gogh* (1986, oil on canvas, 13 x 18 1/4 ins / 33 x 46.5 cm) FRF 7,000. PARIS, 20 Nov 1988, *Who Needs You* (1972-1974, oil on canvas, 51 1/4 x 35 ins / 130 x 89 cm) FRF 35,000. PARIS, 12 Feb 1989, *Tall Nude* (1979, acrylic/canvas, 39 1/4 x 31 1/2 ins / 100 x 80 cm) FRF 67,000. PARIS, 6 April 1989, *Big Cats* (1966, oil on canvas, 78 3/4 x 39 1/4 ins / 200 x 100 cm) FRF 126,000. PARIS, 13 April 1989, *Gabrielle d'Estrées and the Cosmonauts* (1980, acrylic/canvas, 39 1/4 x 35 ins / 100 x 89 cm) FRF 60,000. BEIJING, 6 May 1989, *Handshake* (1974, collage and mixed media/paper, 8 1/4 x 8 3/4 ins / 21 x 22.2 cm) FRF 29,920. PARIS, 12 June 1989, *Composition with Engine, Skeleton and Mona Lisa* (1959, acrylic/canvas, 63 x 78 3/4 ins / 160 x 200 cm) FRF 70,000. PARIS, 29 Sept 1989, *Untitled* (1958, watercolour and ink, 19 1/4 x 13 3/4 ins / 49 x 35 cm) FRF 5,000. PARIS, 29 Sept 1989, *Untitled* (1958, watercolour and ink, 19 1/4 x 13 3/4 ins / 49 x 35 cm) FRF 5,000. PARIS, 9 Oct 1989, *Speed of Michelangelo* (acrylic/canvas, 63 3/4 x 51 1/4 ins / 162 x 130 cm) FRF 155,000. PARIS, 14 Oct 1989, *Rape of the Sabines* (oil and acrylic/canvas, 38 1/2 x 59 ins / 98 x 150 cm) FRF 131,000. PARIS, 8 Nov 1989, *Aeroplane, Big Cats and Naked Woman* (1968, collage, 11 3/4 x 24 1/2 ins / 30 x 62 cm) FRF 20, 000. PARIS, 13 Dec 1989, *Mythical Beasts* (1961, Indian ink and colouring pencil, 19 1/2 x 12 1/2 ins / 49.5 x 32 cm) FRF 23,500; *Welcome Johnny* (1977, oil on canvas, 40 1/4 x 26 ins / 102 x 66 cm) FRF 72,000. PARIS, 26 Jan 1990, *Place Denfert Rochereau* (1973, collage, 5 3/4 x 4 1/2 ins / 14.5 x 11.5 cm) FRF 9,000. PARIS, 15 Feb 1990, *Fall* (1975, acrylic/canvas, 76 3/4 x 51 1/4 ins / 195 x 130 cm) FRF 310,000. PARIS, 18 Feb 1990, *Across the Atlantic* (1970, acrylic/canvas, 76 3/4 x 59 ins / 195 x 150 cm) FRF 350,000. PARIS, 30 March 1990, *Chinese Paintings* (oil on canvas, 38 1/4 x 22 3/4 ins / 97 x 58 cm) FRF 110,000. PARIS, 3 May 1990, *Hôtel des Rognons* (1959, oil on canvas, 78 3/4 x 40 1/4 ins / 200 x 102 cm) FRF 125,000. PARIS, 30 May 1990, *It's Cutting Me* (1989, oil on canvas, 77 1/2 x 51 1/4 ins / 197 x 130 cm) FRF 200,000. PARIS, 29 Oct 1990, *All Power* (1974, oil on canvas, 76 3/4 x 51 1/4 ins / 195 x 130 cm) FRF 180,000. PARIS, 2 June 1991, *Taste for Kandinsky* (1963, acrylic/canvas, 33 3/4 x 29 1/2 ins / 86 x 75 cm) FRF 51,000. LOKEREN, 21 March 1992, *Every Ball Must Score* (oil on canvas, 78 3/4 x 63 ins / 200 x 160 cm) BEF 330,000. PARIS, 14 May 1992, *Tribute to Fernand Léger* (1990, acrylic/canvas, 76 3/4 x 51 1/4 ins / 195 x 130 cm) FRF 98,000. PARIS, 10 June 1993, *Dalai Lama* (1964, oil on canvas, 28 3/4 x 31 1/2 ins / 73 x 80 cm) FRF 22,000. MILAN, 15 March 1994, *Untitled* (1968, acrylic/canvas, 7 1/2 x 10 ins / 19 x 24.5 cm) ITL 1,150,000. PARIS, 21 March 1994, *Kafka, Portrait Series* (1975, acrylic/canvas, 63 3/4 x 38 1/4 ins / 162 x 97 cm) FRF 42,000. NEW YORK, 5 May 1994, *Kitchen Workers* (1974, oil on canvas, 36 x 38 1/2 ins / 91.4 x 97.8 cm) USD 6,900. PARIS, 29-30 June 1995, *Bicycle* (1975, acrylic/canvas, 64 x 38 1/4 ins / 162.5 x 97 cm) FRF 26,000. AMSTERDAM, 6 Dec 1995, *Cobra in Provo* (1966, oil on canvas, 50 x 39 1/4 ins / 127 x 100 cm) NLG 9,200. PARIS, 11 April 1996, *Tribute to Léger, Pinocchio Constructing His Wife* (1983, paint/canvas, 76 3/4 x 38 1/4 ins / 195 x 97 cm) FRF 35,000. PARIS, 3 June 1996, *Vietnam* (1969, oil on canvas, 38 1/4 x 23 1/2 ins / 97 x 60 cm) FRF 19,500. PARIS, 1 July 1996, *Space Series, Gravity* (1976, acrylic/canvas, 46 x 35 ins / 116 x 89 cm) FRF 18,000. PARIS, 16 Dec 1996, *Untitled* (1986, acrylic/canvas, 39 x 31 ins / 99 x 79 cm) FRF 19,000; *Reserve of 199 Personalities* (1961, oil on canvas, 19 3/4 x 39 1/4 ins / 50 x 100 cm) FRF 16,500. PARIS, 19 March 1997, *Untitled* (1986-1987, acrylic/canvas, 13 1/2 x 18 1/2 ins / 34 x 47 cm) FRF 9,500. PARIS, 28 April 1997, *Ethiopia* (1970, acrylic/canvas, 35 x 51 1/4 ins / 89 x 130 cm) FRF 21,500. PARIS, 26 May 1997, *Tribute to Van Gogh* (1985, acrylic/canvas, 13 x 18 ins / 33 x 46 cm) FRF 9,000. PARIS, 5 June 1997, *Suchard Series, Bangkok, Thailand* (1974, acrylic/canvas, 38 1/4 x 17 1/4 ins / 97 x 44 cm) FRF 12,500. PARIS, 19 Oct 1997, *Human Bloom-Slaughtered Animal* (1953, oil on canvas, 25 1/4 x 49 1/4 ins / 64 x 125 cm) FRF 16,000. PARIS, 23 Nov 1997, *Tarzan* (1980, acrylic/canvas, 50 1/4 x 26 1/4 ins / 127.5 x 66.5 cm) FRF 25,000. PARIS, 20 March 1998, *Desolate Journey* (oil on canvas, 32 x 39 1/4 ins / 81 x 100 cm) FRF 55,000. PARIS, 21 March 1999, *Alexandre Dumas* (1977, acrylic, from the 'Poets' series, 77 x 51 ins / 195 x 130 cm) FRF 65,000. PARIS, 29 Oct 1999, *Garibaldi* (1975, oil on canvas, from the portrait series, 65 x 51 ins / 165 x 130 cm) FRF 105,000. PARIS, 15 June 2000, *Turning Picasso* (1969, oil on canvas, from the 'Turning Paintings' series, 77 x 52 ins / 195 x 132 cm) FRF 115,000. PARIS, 27 Oct 2000, *The Appetite is a Crime* (oil on canvas, 79 x 118 ins / 200 x 300 cm) FRF 480,000. PARIS, 13 Oct 2001, *Detailscape-boxscape* (1985, acrylic, 79 x 118 ins / 200 x 300 cm) FRF 250,000. PARIS, 21 Nov 2001, *Expert* (1959, oil on canvas, 79 x 51 ins / 200 x 130 cm) FRF 70,000. PARIS, 4 Feb 2002, *Pillmaker* (1971, oil on canvas, 39 x 26 ins / 100 x 65 cm) EUR 14,500. PARIS, 4 Feb 2002, *Goethe* (1977, oil on canvas, 67 x 55 ins / 170 x 140 cm) EUR 14,500. PARIS, 11 Oct 2003, *The Painter's Paradise* (1962, oil on canvas, 39 x 26 ins / 100 x 65 cm) EUR 14,000. PARIS, 9 Dec 2003, *I Am Your New Host* (1995, oil on canvas, 77 x 38 ins / 195 x 97 cm) EUR 15,000. PARIS, 5 Oct 2004, *Childbirth without Pain* (1960, oil on canvas, 79 x 118 ins / 200 x 300 cm) EUR 31,000. PARIS, 5 Oct 2004, *Julien Levy* (1968, acrylic, 51 x 39 ins / 130 x 100 cm) EUR 57,000.

ERRO-RAUTA
Russian, 19th century.
Active in St Petersburg.
Painter.

This name is only a pseudonym.

ERSHOV, Stepan Semenovich
Russian, 19th century.
Active in St Petersburg.
Painter. Portraits.

Stepan Semenovich Ershov trained at the academy of art in St Petersburg, which appointed him member in 1850 for his portrait of the painter *M.N. Vorobev*, still in the academy's collection. Primarily a painter of churches and portraits, he is also known for two pictures of *Saints*, which he painted for the Black Sea Fleet, a portrait of *Tsar Alexander I*, which he painted for the St Petersburg Lyceum, and the portrait of the painter *A.I. Egorov* now in the Academy Museum.

MUSEUMS AND GALLERIES:
ST PETERSBURG (Academy): *Portrait of the Painter A.E. Egorov.*

ERSINGER, Michael
German, 16th century.
Active in Straubing in 1583.
Painter.

ERSKINE, Harrold Perry
American, 20th century.
Born 5 June 1879, in Racine (Wisconsin); died 1879, in Racine (Wisconsin).
Sculptor. Busts, monuments.

Harold Erskine studied at the École Nationale des Beaux-Arts in Paris and in the USA he was a pupil of Sherry E. Fry. Notable among this artist's works, apart from his busts, is the monument commemorating the war at the St Anthony Club in New York.

Museums and Galleries:
New York (American Mus. of Natural History).

ERTAN, Simona
Romanian, 20th century.
Born 27 November 1923, in Bucharest.
Active in Argentina from 1940 and in France from 1961; naturalised in 1981 in France.
Painter, engraver, ceramicist, collage artist. Figures, landscapes. Designs for stained glass.
Neo-Constructivism, Symbolism.

Simona Ertan took classes in drawing, painting and linoleum engraving in Bucharest from 1934 to 1940. At the end of 1940 she left with her family for Argentina and settled in Buenos Aires. There, while continuing to paint, she took classes in aesthetics and pottery. In 1950, her encounter with Picasso's *Guernica*, which was in the USA at that time, was one of the greatest shocks of her life. In 1952 she travelled in Europe, notably to Paris, where she made contact with abstract avant-garde painting. That same year she became a member of the Argentinian abstract group Arte Nuevo. She contributed to the *Ver y Estimar* review. Between 1955 and 1959, she practised pottery. She settled in Paris in 1961.

Ertan hesitated between Expressionism and Fauvism until 1950, when travelling in Europe started her on the path to abstract art. She said: 'I opted for the Constructivist movement; I left Geometric Abstraction, having begun to introduce narrative elements in 1967, and my world headed towards a certain figurative style which had its roots far back in the past'. This figurative style today is of an allegorical nature. The architectural objects and structures are pretexts for nostalgic reminiscences where the memories and requirements of the sacred are in control. The 1993 exhibition of paintings inspired by India added a highly ornamental, colourful, exotic and Matisse-like note to her register.

She exhibited her work in several collective exhibitions including: *Peintres et sculpteurs argentins en France* (*Argentinian Painters and Sculptors in France*), Maison de l'Amérique, Paris (1959); Salon de Mai, Barcelona (1960); *Structures*, Galerie Denise René, Paris (1961); Leverkusen and Céret (1962); *Group 62*, Munich (1963); *50 ans de collage de Picasso à nos jours* (*50 Years of Collage From Picasso to the Present Day*), St Étienne museum (1964); Salon des Réalités Nouvelles, Paris (from 1963 to 1967); Salon de l'Art Sacré, Paris from (1964 to 1966 and in 1982); Salon des Surindépendants, Paris (1965 and 1966); *Les Maîtres contemporains du vitrail* (*Contemporary Stained Glass Window Masters*), Palais de Chaillot, Paris (1969); Salon des Femmes-Peintres, Paris (1973); Salon Comparaisons, Paris (1982); *Ste-Thérèse d'Avila dans l'art contemporain* (*St Theresa of Avila in Contemporary Art*) (1983); Salon Grands et Jeunes d'Aujourd'hui, Paris (1983). She exhibited her works in solo exhibitions including: retrospective: of ten years of work, house in Argentina (1962, 1964 and 1970); Paris (1982); Essen (1964); Brussels and Madrid (1977); Galerie du Centre Culturel Arturo López, Neuilly and Fondation Vasarely, Aix-en-Provence (1988); Galerie Étienne de Causans, Paris (1993).

S. Ertan

Bibliography:
Jianou, Ionel, *Romanian Artists and the West*, American Romanian Academy of Arts and Sciences, Los Angeles, 1986.

Museums and Galleries:
Buenos Aires (ICA).

ERTÉ, pseudonym of Romain de Tirtov, or Tirtov
Russian, 20th century.
Born 1892, in St Petersburg; died 21 April 1990, in Paris.
Active from 1910 in France.
Painter (including gouache), sculptor, draughtsman, illustrator, stylist, decorative designer. Stage costumes and sets, designs for jewellery, furniture.
Art Deco.

The son of an admiral in the Imperial navy, Erté was a pupil of Ilya Repin in St Petersburg. He went to Paris at the age of eighteen, apparently attended the Académie Julian and was admitted to the Académie des Beaux-Arts in Jean-Paul Laurens' workshop. He began his career in 1913 with the couturier Paul Poiret. From that year onwards, he designed stage costumes for Mata-Hari, Mistinguett and Gaby Deslys and in 1914 he worked for the journals *Gazette du Bon Ton* and *Vogue*. He started his association with *Harper's Bazaar*, which lasted 22 years, in 1915. He became known in the USA and designed costumes for George White's *Scandals*. He was one of the stars of 1920s Art Deco movement, which he helped create, and his work extended to interior design, furniture, jewellery and book illustration. His arabesques, volutes and other unbridled curves contributed to the success of the Folies-Bergères shows from 1921 to 1929 and of those of the Casino in Paris and of the Bal Tabarin. In 1925, he went to work in Hollywood for Cecil B. de Mille and King Vidor. He designed film sets including those for *Ziegfield Folies* and theatre sets including those for Edmond Rostand's *The Distant Princess*. In 1947 he once again created the sets for *Les Mamelles de Tiresias* by Poulenc for the Opéra Comique in Paris.

Erté was inspired by the avant-garde styles of his time and was able to adapt them to decorative art in compositions, particularly fashion, in flat tints, line drawings, symmetrical effects or asymmetry and geometric motifs. He invented 'collective costumes', each individual costume of which becomes part of another group when those wearing them meet up, as well as 'costumes as objects'. The renewal of interest in 1920s art and fashion in around 1970 explains the renewed attention paid to Erté, so much so that Roland Barthes devoted a book to him. His sophistication, exoticism and invention was characteristic of the Belle Époque and the roaring 1920s and we are better able to understand from Erté's costume and sets just how brilliant and exciting this period was.

Erté worked in gouache and often exhibited at the Proscenium gallery, Rue de Seine, Paris, which devoted a solo show to him in 1971. The Cultural Centre in Boulogne-Billancourt exhibited his designs in 1986. A retrospective of his work took place in a gallery in Paris after his death.

ERTE

Bibliography:
Amaya, N., '*Costumes de théâtre par Erté*' in *Art et Industrie*, periodical, Paris, November 1926. Spencer, Charles, *Erté*, Studio Vista and C. N. Potter, London and New York, 1970. Erté, *Erté Fashions*, Academy Editions and St Martin's Press, London and New York, 1972. Erté, *Erté's Theatrical Costumes in Full Colour*, Dover Publications, New York, c. 1979. Erté, *Erté's Fashion Designs: 218 Illustrations From 'Harper's Bazar*, Dover Publications, New York, 1981. Marshall, Lee (ed.), *Erté Sculpture*, E. P. Dutton, New York, 1986. Lee, Marshall (ed.), *Erté at Ninety-Five: The Complete New Graphics*, Dutton, New York, c. 1987.

Museums and Galleries:
New York (Metropolitan Mus. of Art): large collection.

Auction records:
Paris, 18 June 1974, *Dresses for Paul Poiret* (40 drawing and watercolour) FRF 30,000. Munich, 29 Nov 1976, *Barometer* (gouache, decor, 7 x 10 ins / 17.5 x 24.5 cm) DEM 3,000. New York, 2 April 1981, *Temptation* (1918, pen and wash/paper, 12 x 8 1/4 ins / 30.2 x 21 cm) USD 1,800. London, 26 Oct 1983, *Film Set Design for the film 'Paris'* (1925, gouache and gold, 12 1/2 x 15 3/4 ins / 32 x 40 cm) GBP 3,400. Paris, 26 Nov 1984, *Rose with Diamond Pollen* (gouache, 13 x 9 1/2 ins / 33 x 24 cm) FRF 24,000. New York, 13 June 1985, *Victory* (1980, gilt and enamelled bronze, h. 19 ins / 48.3 cm) USD 13,000. New York, 19 March 1986, *Princess Eristov-Kazak, Portrait of Erté with Misha* (c. 1915, oil on canvas, 51 1/2 x 38 1/4 ins / 131 x 97 cm) USD 14,000. Paris, 4 Nov 1987, *Roof Garden at Manhattan Mary* (1927, gouache, 11 3/4 x 8 1/4 ins / 30 x 21 cm) FRF 66,000. Paris, 13 Dec 1987, *Flounced Dress and Plume* (gouache, 14 1/4 x 10 1/4 ins / 36 x 26 cm) FRF 13,000. Paris, 24 March 1988, *Lucky Doll, Horseshoe* (1926, gouache, 15 1/4 x 11 1/2 ins / 39 x 29 cm) FRF 26,000. Paris, 22 April 1988, *Gay Paris or Eve* (1972, watercolour heightened with gold, 14 1/4 x 11 ins / 36.5 x 27 cm) FRF 12,500. London, 18 May 1988, *Set Design Plan for 'Métal'* (Indian ink, 15 1/4 x 11 1/4 ins / 39 x 28.5 cm) GBP 1,760. Paris, 10 June 1988, *Hindu Tale* (1922, oil on paper, 11 3/4 x 18 3/4 ins / 30 x 47.5 cm) FRF 24,000. Paris, 22 June 1988, *Hindu Tale* (1922, gouache with gold highlights on a black background, 12 1/2 x 19 1/4 ins / 32 x 49 cm) FRF 25,000. London, 8 Sept 1988, *Harmony: Dress and Cloak Sketches for Harper's Bazaar* (gouache/paper, 11 1/2 x 9 1/4 ins / 29.2 x 23.5 cm) GBP 2,860. Paris, 14 Dec 1988, *Black Africa, Costume Design for Odette Pascaud* (gouache, 14 1/2 x 11 ins / 37 x 27 cm) FRF 9,000. Zurich, 25 Oct 1989, *Tigress* (gouache, 14 3/4 x 10 3/4 ins / 37.4 x 27.4 cm) CHF 4,600. Paris, 21 Nov 1989, *Dancer* (gouache, circular on a gold background, 14 1/4 x 9 3/4 ins / 36 x 25 cm) FRF 175,000. New York, 21 Feb 1990, *Tigress Woman* (1970, gouache/paper, 14 x 10 3/4 ins / 35.6 x 27.3 cm) USD 5,500. Sceaux, 11 March 1990, *Costume Design* (1922, watercolour, 11 3/4 x 15 3/4 ins / 30 x 40 cm) FRF 80,000. Amsterdam, 10 April 1990, *Costume Design* (gouache/paper, 13 x 10 ins / 33 x 24.5 cm) NLG 5,290. Sceaux, 10 June 1990, *Costume for Gaby Deslop* (1915, gouache, 15 3/4 x 11 3/4 ins / 40 x 30 cm) FRF 85,000. Paris, 13 Dec 1991, *Woman with Fan* (gouache, 12 1/4 x 9 ins / 31 x 22.7 cm) FRF 4,000. Paris, 13 May 1992, *Lucrecia Borgia* (gouache/paper, 15 x 11 ins / 38 x 28 cm) FRF 56,500. New York, 26 Feb 1993, *Cover Design for Harper's Bazaar* (1919, gouache/card, 15 3/4 x 11 1/2 ins / 40 x 29.2 cm) USD 35,650. London, 24-25 March 1993, *Costume Design for a Sultan in 'The Woman and the Devil'* (gouache and silver paint, 10 1/4 x 12 1/4 ins / 26.2 x 31 cm) GBP 4,370. New York, 29 Sept 1993, *Costume Design for Zizi Jeanmaire in ' Stormy Weather'* (1974, gouache and silver paint/paper, 14 3/4 x 11 ins / 37.5 x 27.9 cm) USD 2,645. Milan, 12 Oct 1993, *Wedding* (1986, bronze, 16 3/4 x 14 1/4 x 5 3/4 ins / 42.5 x 36 x 14.5 cm) ITL 11,500,000. Paris, 23 March 1994, *Chained Love* (1985, multicoloured-patinated bronze, h. 21 1/4 ins / 54 cm) FRF 9,000. Paris, 7 June 1995, *Summer Mannequin, Series 'Les fleurs du couturier'* (watercolour, 12 1/4 x 8 1/4 ins / 31 x 21 cm) FRF 5,200. New York, 14 June 1995, *Evening Gown, Henri Bendel* (watercolour and gouache/paper, 9 1/2 x 6 1/4 ins / 24.1 x 15.9 cm) USD 3,737. Milan, 23 May 1996, *Raining Stars* (tempera/paper, 14 3/4 x 10 1/4 ins / 37.5 x 26 cm) ITL 5,750,000. Paris, 7 June 1996, *Theatre Curtain Design* (gouache and Indian ink/card, 6 1/4 x 7 3/4 ins / 15.6 x 19.7 cm) FRF 4,500. New York, 10 Oct 1996, *Costume Design for the Folies Bergere* (gouache and silver paint/paper) USD 6,900. Paris, 17 Dec 1996, *Costume Design* (pen, Indian ink, watercolour with gold highlights, 12 1/2 x 8 1/2 ins / 32 x 21.5 cm) FRF 12,000. London, 19 Dec 1996, *On Waking Up to the Past, Persian book* (1927, gouache and ink with gold paint highlights/pencil, 10 x 16 ins / 25.5 x 40.7 cm) GBP 2,300. Paris, 9 Oct 1997, *Costume Design* (gouache, 14 1/4 x 10 ins / 36 x 25.5 cm) FRF 7,500. Houston, 15 May 1999, *Justice* (1984, bronze, h. 20 ins / 51 cm) USD 3,000. Los Angeles, 13 Dec 1999, *The Globe* (polychrome bronze, 23 x 9 ins / 58 x 24 cm) USD 3,000. Brussels, 14 Feb 2000, *Splendour* (colour patinated bronze, 14 x 13 ins / 36 x 32 cm) BEF 220,000. Los Angeles, 20 Nov 2000, *Three Graces* (polychrome bronze, 16 x 11x7 ins / 41 x 29x18 cm) USD 3,500. London, 21 Nov 2000, *Costume Design for Mme Ganna Wolska in 'Fidora'* (gouache heightened with gold and silver paint, 11 x 9 ins / 28 x 23 cm) GBP 6,000. Paris, 27 April 2001, *Woman of Melissinde* (1929, gouache, 15 x 11 ins / 38 x 27 cm) FRF 58,000. Paris, 18 Dec 2001, *Kiss Me Again, Decoration for Final Victor Herbert* (1928, gouache, 11 x 15 ins / 28 x 39 cm) FRF 46,000. Vernou en Sologne, 3 Feb 2002, *Window. Drawing-room. Clock. Grey Drawing-room. Smoking-room. Aquarium. Hair-dresser. Screen. Bedroom* (gouache, nine works, 6 x 8 ins / 16 x 21 cm) EUR 11,100. Milan, 4 Dec 2002, *Costumes* (Chinese ink and tempera on paper, two works, 15 x 11 ins / 37 x 27 cm) EUR 3,000. Houston, 2 Feb 2003, *Courtesan* (gouache on card, 8 x 12 ins / 20 x 30 cm) USD 4,500. London, 27 Feb 2003, *Cover of Harper's Bazaar Magazine, May 1928* (1928, gouache, 15 x 11 ins / 37 x 28 cm) GBP 4,200. London, 22 April 2004, *Fountain* (colour drypoint with aquatint, 21 x 9 ins / 53 x 22 cm) GBP 3,500. London, 26 May 2004, *Monkey. Its a Baby!. Motor Car* (gouache, eight works, 15 x 11 ins / 37 x 27 cm) GBP 9,500.

ERTEBOUT, Henri, or Hertebout
Flemish, 17th century.
Painter. Landscapes.
Flemish School.

Henri Ertebout was taught by David Teniers the Younger and is cited in a document dated 1771. Siret mentions him twice, under the letter E and the letter H.

ERTEL, Johann Georg
German, 18th century.
Born c. 1687, in Jauer (now Jawor, Poland); died 7 December 1747.
Sculptor.

ERTINGER, Franz
French, 17th - 18th century.
Born 1640, in Colmar or Weil (Swabia); died c. 1710, in Paris.
Draughtsman, engraver.

In 1667 Franz Ertinger was in Paris as engraver to the king. He also went to Rome and spent a long time in Antwerp. He produced the folios for the *Châteaux of the Nobles of Brabant; Tomb of the Count von Lalaing and his Wife; Tomb of Engebert I of Nassau, his Uncle Jean and Wife at Bréda*; four folios after Van der Meulen; and eight folios on the *Story of Achilles*, after Rubens' tapestries. He often engraved in the manner of Lafage.

ERTINGER, Franz Ferdinand
German, 17th century.
Born 18 August 1669, in Immenstadt.
Sculptor.

Museums and Galleries:
Munich (Bayerische Staatsbibliothek): *Rais Beschreibung (Travel Journal)*.

ERTINGER, Johann
Austrian, 18th century.
Active in Vienna in 1713.
Sculptor.

ERTINGER, Johann Daniel
German, 18th century.
Active in Nuremberg at the beginning of the 18th century.
Engraver.

ERTINGER, Joseph
Austrian, 18th century.
Born 1731, in Vienna; died 3 September 1788, in Vienna.
Sculptor.
Joseph Ertinger was the son of Wenzel Ertinger.

ERTINGER, Philipp Jacob
Austrian, 17th - 18th century.
Born 1670, in Kempten; died 12 November 1748, in Vienna.
Sculptor.

ERTINGER, Wenzel
Austrian, 18th century.
Active in Vienna during the first half of the 18th century.
Sculptor.

ERTL, Johann
Austrian, 19th century.
Born 10 February 1845, in Schwaz (Tyrol); died 26 June 1906, in Schwaz.
Painter.
Johann Ertl studied in Innsbruck, continuing to work primarily there and in his home town of Schwaz, particularly for religious buildings.

ERTL, Marie
Austrian, 19th century.
Born 6 September 1837, in Sternberg.
Painter. Genre scenes, landscapes, still-lifes.
Marie Ertl lived and exhibited in Vienna.
AUCTION RECORDS:
VIENNA, 29 Nov 1977, *A Sunday at Gauting* (oil on canvas, 18 x 24 3/4in/46 x 63cm) ATS 70,000. VIENNA, 29 Nov 2001, *Perchtoldsdorf* (oil on canvas, 13 x 15 ins / 32 x 39 cm) ATS 40,000.

ERTLE, Sebastian
German, 16th century.
Born c. 1570, in Überlingen (Baden).
Sculptor.
Ertle was a pupil of Hans Moringk and worked at Magdeburg. He was involved particularly with the decoration of the cathedral there.

ERTREYK, Edouard van
Dutch, 19th century.
Born in Oosterhout; died after 1847.
Painter. History painting, genre scenes.
Edouard van Ertreyk was a pupil of N. de Keyser in Antwerp and spent time in France and Italy.

ERTVELT, Andries van. See **EERTVELT**

ERTZ, Edward Frederick
American, 19th - 20th century.
Born 1 March 1862, in Chicago; died 1954.
Active in France and England.
Painter, watercolourist, engraver. Landscapes with figures.
Edward Ertz studied art in Paris under the guidance of Jules Lefebvre.

He participated in group exhibitions in the towns of French Provence and received awards. In Paris he participated in group exhibitions by the *Fifty* at the Galerie Georges Petit. He was a watercolour teacher at the Académie Delécluse. He later settled in Slapton, England, and became a member of the Society of British Artists in London.

He seems to have been mainly appreciated in engraving for his dry-point etching, aquatints, light varnishes and, in painting, for his rural views in landscapes with figures or livestock.

AUCTION RECORDS:
NEW YORK, 20 March 1987, *Summertime* (oil on canvas, 14 1/4 x 18 ins / 36 x 46 cm) USD 3,500. NEW YORK, 14 Feb 1990, *Sheep in Garden* (oil on canvas, 20 x 24 ins / 51 x 61 cm) USD 1,320. LONDON, 11 June 1993, *Boy in a Meadow* (1893, oil on card, 14 x 9 3/4 ins / 35.6 x 24.7 cm) GBP 1,092.

ERTZ, Ethel Margaret
Maiden name: Horsfall
British, 19th - 20th century.
Born 19 January 1871.
Painter, miniaturist, watercolourist. Portraits.
Ethel Margaret Ertz was the wife of the painter Edward Frederick Ertz.

ERUTTI
French, 20th - 21st century.
Born 1960, in Toulon.
Sculptor.
Erutti studied sculpture in Lyons, and finished with a degree in Fine Arts in 1985. Her works are concerned with nature. She presents large flat stones made of resin or polystyrene, standing up or on top of each other, and links them with ropes, cables, twisted and burnt wood, or glass containers. Her work explores the tension between the empty and the full, between the roughness of the stone and the transparency of the glass, between equilibrium and disequilibrium.

Erutti has been exhibiting in solo exhibitions since 1987, notably: since 1988-1989, regularly at the Galerie Dédal Art Contemporain, Annemasse, and at the Galerie Michel Guinle in Lyons; 1990, Galerie la Tête d'Obsidienne, la Seyne-sur-Mer; 1992, *Sculpture sur un Plateau*, Centre d'Art Contemporain, Lacoux; and 1995, L'Usine Éphémère, Maison des Arts, Thonon-les-Bains.
BIBLIOGRAPHY:
Mic, Bernard-Gilles, *Erutti*, exhibition catalogue, Maison des arts, Thonon-les-Bains, 1995.

ERVENE
British, 10th century.
Illuminator, calligrapher.
Attributed to this artist are not only the copying, but the painting of the initials and ornaments of the famous manuscript preserved in the British Museum under the title *Latin Gospels of King Canute*.

ERWEIN, Johann
German, 16th century.
Active in Cologne in 1533.
Painter.

ERWIN DE STEINBACH
German, 13th - 14th century.
Born 1244, in Steinbach; died 1318, in Strasbourg.
Sculptor, architect.
In about 1275, De Steinbach was commissioned to design and direct work on the interior of Strasbourg Cathedral. His two sons, Jan and Winhing, who specialised in architecture rather than sculpture, continued this work after his death. All three of them were buried in Strasbourg Cathedral.

ERXLEBEN, August
German, 19th century.
Born to a family originally from Baden.
Painter.
August Erxleben studied in Munich.

ERXLEBEN, J.
Dutch, 19th century.
Active c. 1830.
Lithographer.
J. Erxleben executed the portraits of a number of eminent Dutch and German figures.

ERXLEBEN, Otto
German, 19th century.
Active in Munich c. 1860.
Painter.

Otto Erxleben could possibly be the same person as the painter August Erxleben.

ERYCHEV, Nikolai
Russian, 20th century.
Born 1936.
Painter. Scenes with figures.

Nikolai Erychev graduated from the school of art in Moscow in 1962. He was a member of the Union of Painters of the USSR from 1965 onwards. He lived and worked in Orenbourg.

ERZINGER, Lili
Swiss, 20th century.
Born 1908, in Zurich.
Painter, graphic designer.

Lili Erzinger studied in Switzerland and in Paris, with Lhote, Bissière and Léger. Between 1936 and 1937, she also benefited from the guidance of Severini and Arp. Having taught painting for a period in the USA, she decided to settle in Neuchâtel. Lili Erzinger took part in the Salon des Réalités Nouvelles in Paris from 1947 to 1955. Her abstract compositions had the precision of graphic exercises.

ES, Jacob Fopsen van, or Jakob Foppeus van, or Essen or Esch
Flemish, 17th century.
Born c. 1596, in Antwerp; died 1666; buried 11 March in Antwerp.
Painter. Still-lifes.
Flemish School.

Jacob Fopsen van Es was a master in Antwerp in 1617. He married Joanna Claessens and taught Jacob Gilles in 1621 and Jan van Thiemen in 1623. In 1646 he entered the Guild of St Luke. On occasion he collaborated with Jacob Jordaens.

A painter of descriptive still-lifes, he displays his tabletops strewn with grapes, lemons, and oysters. His representation of such meals with assorted crockery and glassware are evidence of his restraint and soberness of composition, which are intermingled with sensuality. He did not hesitate to bring out discordant greens and yellows.

IV· ES.

Bibliography:
Hairs, Marie-Louise, *Les Peintres de fleurs flamands au XVIIe siècle*, Lefebvre et Gillet, Brussels, 1985.

Museums and Galleries:
Antwerp: *Still-life* - Arras: *Cheeses and Desserts; Dishes of Oysters* - Augsburg: *Salt-water Fish* - Besançon: *Still-life with Quinces* - Brussels: *Oysters* - Frankfurt am Main: *Kitchen Bench with Fish* - Geneva: *Fish and Lobsters; Still-life* - Glasgow: *Game and Fruit* - Lille: *Still-life* - Madrid (Prado): *Lemons, Oysters and Wine; Oysters, Wine and Fruit; Apples and Carnations* - Nancy: *Crabs, Shrimps and Lemon* - Oxford (Ashmolean Mus.): *Still Life with Oysters* (oil/panel) - Prague: *Fruit* - Stockholm: *Breakfast Table* - Vienna (Liechtenstein Mus.): *Breakfast Table; Fruit; Remains of a Meal* - Vienna (Österreichische Gal. Belvedere): *Two Fish Markets*.

Auction records:
London, 30 March 1908, *Still-life*, GBP 11. Paris, 17 April 1920, *Oysters, a Knife, a Glass of Wine on a Table*, FRF 530. Paris, 28 June 1934, *Dish of Shrimps*, FRF 5,100. London, 9 May 1940, *Flowers*, GBP 6. Paris, 16 Oct 1940, *Oysters and Pitcher*, FRF 2,500. Paris, 8 Dec 1948, *Still-life*, FRF 190,000. Paris, 4 Dec 1954, *Still-life with Shrimps*, FRF 500,000. Paris, 3 Dec 1959, *Still-life with Carnation*, FRF 1,350,000. London, 27 June 1962, *Still-life with Fruit*, GBP 1,000. London, 1 May 1964, *Basket with Flowers* (panel on copper) Gns 1,000. London, 1 July 1966, *Still-life with Artichoke, Fruit and Pitcher* (oil/copper) Gns 1,300. London, 11 June 1969, *Still-life*, GBP 6,200. Cologne, 26 May 1971, *Still-life with Fruit*, DEM 24,000. London, 6 Dec 1972, *Still-life*, GBP 15,000. London, 21 March 1973, *Still-life with Fruit and Flowers*, GBP 2,800. London, 21 May 1976, *Basket of Fruit* (oil on panel, 25 1/2 x 34 ins / 64.7 x 86.3 cm) GBP 4,500. Zurich, 25 Nov 1977, *Still-life with Flowers* (oil, 19 1/2 x 14 1/2 ins / 49.5 x 37 cm) CHF 40,000. London, 1 Dec 1978, *Still-life* (oil on panel, 17 3/4 x 28 1/2 ins / 45 x 72.5 cm) GBP 6,500. New York, 9 Jan 1981, *Bowl of Strawberries and other Fruit* (oil on panel, 9 1/2 x 15 ins / 24 x 38 cm) USD 32,000. London, 11 Dec 1984, *Still-life with Oysters* (oil on panel, 20 1/4 x 28 3/4 ins / 51.5 x 73 cm) GBP 24,000. New York, 3 June 1987, *Basket of Flowers, Mulberries and Plums on an Entablature* (oil on mounted panel/canvas, 24 x 34 1/2 ins / 61 x 87.7 cm) USD 70,000. London, 8 July 1988, *Still-life with Chinese Porcelain Bowl filled with Fruit, Bunch of Grapes, Strawberries and Corn on an Entablature* (oil on canvas, 19 1/4 x 25 1/4 ins / 49 x 64 cm) GBP 99,000. New York, 21 Oct 1988, *Still-life with Seafood and Fruit in Dishes on an Entablature* (oil on panel, 21 1/4 x 39 1/4 ins / 54 x 99.6 cm) USD 66,000. London, 11 April 1990, *Still-life with a Glass of Wine, Peaches, a Salad Bowl of Strawberries and a Butterfly* (oil/copper, 10 3/4 x 14 ins / 27.5 x 35.5 cm) GBP 99,000. Paris, 16 May 1990, *Still-life with Lobster and Seafood on a Stone Entablature* (oil on canvas, 13 1/2 x 12 ins / 34.5 x 30.5 cm) FRF 81,000. New York, 31 May 1991, *Still-life with a Plate of Shrimps and a Cut Small Loaf, a Bowl of Olives, a Venetian Glass and a Goblet on a Table* (oil/copper, 12 3/4 x 15 3/4 ins / 32.2 x 40 cm) USD 77,000. Amsterdam, 10 Nov 1992, *Grapes in a Basket near Cake, an Ear of Corn and Bread in a Pewter Plate on a Table* (oil on canvas, 19 1/4 x 31 ins / 49 x 79 cm) NLG 50,600. New York, 14 Jan 1994, *Still-life of Grapes, Pear and Peaches on a Large Pewter Salver with Hazelnuts and an Insect on a Table* (oil/copper, 14 1/4 x 19 1/4 ins / 36.2 x 48.9 cm) USD 43,125. Paris, 31 Jan 1994, *Still-life with Lemon* (oil on canvas, 20 x 29 3/4 ins / 50.5 x 75.5 cm) FRF 175,000. Paris, 29 March 1994, *Still-life with Peaches, Grapes and Walnuts on an Entablature* (oil on panel, 10 x 13 1/2 ins / 25.5 x 34.5 cm) FRF 170,000. Paris, 9 Dec 1996, *Still-life with Basket of Grapes, Round Loaves and an Ear of Corn on an Entablature* (oil on panel remounted/canvas, 19 1/4 x 31 1/4 ins / 49 x 79.5 cm) FRF 290,000. New York, 30 Jan 1997, *Still-life with Fruit, Leaves, Strawberries and a Carnation in Wanli Dishes with other Fruit and an Ear of Corn on a Table* (oil on canvas, 19 1/2 x 24 3/4 ins / 49.5 x 62.9 cm) USD 68,500. London, 29 Oct 1999, *Fish on Terracotta Platter, Asparagus, Artichokes, Fish* (oil on canvas, 32 x 54 ins / 82 x 138 cm) GBP 55,000. London, 5 July 2000, *Plums, Grapes and a Vase of Carnations on a Table* (oil on panel, 13 x 18 ins / 34 x 46 cm) GBP 13,000. Amsterdam, 9 May 2001, *Hazelnuts in a Bowl with Grapes, Orange, and Peeled Lemon on a Table* (oil on panel, 11 x 14 ins / 27 x 35 cm) NLG 130,000. London, 13 Dec 2001, *Still-life of Grapes, Peach and Walnut. Still-life of Honey Melons, Grapes and Peach* (oil on panel, a pair, 13 x 18 ins / 33 x 46 cm) GBP 55,000. New York, 5 June 2002, *Still-life of Grapes, Plums and Apples on a Silver Platter, Vase of Flowers all Resting on a Ledge* (oil on panel, 14 x 24 ins / 36 x 61 cm) USD 40,000. London, 12 Dec 2002, *Still-life of Green Olives in a Bowl, Shrimps, Oyster, Roemer and Lemon* (oil on panel, 10 x 14 ins / 25 x 35 cm) GBP 20,000. Amsterdam, 13 May 2003, *Still-life with Oysters, Chestnuts and Roll with Fork on Pewter Plates* (oil on panel, 20 x 29 ins / 52 x 73 cm) EUR 14,000.

ES, Niclaes van
Flemish, 17th century.
Born before 1617.
Painter.

Flemish School.
Niclaes van Es was a master in 1648 and the son of Jacob van Es.

ESAIAS
German, 16th century.
Active in Mainz in 1550.
Painter.

ESAKI, Yoshiro
Japanese, 20th century.
Born in Tokyo.
Painter. Landscapes, urban landscapes.
Esaki was a pupil of Pougheon. In 1928, he exhibited a landscape at the Salon d'Automne, and in 1929 *Parisian Suburb* at the Salon des Artistes Français.

ESAKOV, Aleksei Ekimovich
Russian, 19th century.
Born 1787; died 1815.
Sculptor, medallist.
Aleksei Ekimovich Esakov trained at the academy of art in St Petersburg, which awarded him its gold medal, first class, in 1809 and accepted him as a member in 1813. Among his works known to have been in the Academy's collection until 1917 were the following low reliefs: *Marfa-Posadnitsa, Death of Hector, Dmitri Donskoy, Prince Poyarsky Addressing the People, Martyrdom of St Andrew.*

ESAKOV, Ermolai Ivanovich
Russian, 19th century.
Born 1791, in Luga.
Painter, lithographer. Landscapes.
Ermolai Ivanovich Esakov trained at the academy of art in St Petersburg. He made seven lithographs for the Imperial Society for the Encouragement of Artists, two of which were accepted.

ESBENS, Émile Étienne
French, 19th century.
Born 5 August 1821, in Bordeaux.
Painter. Figures, portraits, still-lifes.
MUSEUMS AND GALLERIES:
BAYONNE: *Gypsies from Alcala de Jenarez* - CAMBRAI: *Girl with Birds* - ORLÉANS: *Still-lifes* (two).
AUCTION RECORDS:
NEW YORK, 15 and 16 Feb 1906, *At the Palace Gate,* USD 65; *Palace Guard,* USD 85. PARIS, 27 March 1931, *On Guard,* FRF 155. LONDON, 21 March 1997, *Lazybones* (oil on panel, 15 1/2 x 11 3/4 ins / 39.5 x 30 cm) GBP 6,670. DETROIT, 14 April 2000, *Boy Resting with a Book, a Chunk of Bread and Glass of Water* (oil on panel, 15 x 13 ins / 38 x 33 cm) USD 4,000. ZURICH, 13 Dec 2000, *Scene from Carmen* (oil on panel, 8 x 6 ins / 21 x 16 cm) CHF 2,600. BRUSSELS, 13 May 2002, *Advertisement for the Corrida* (oil on panel, 8 x 6 ins / 21 x 15 cm) EUR 1,800. MICHIGAN, 11 June 2003, *Continental Street Scene with Young Man* (oil on panel, 15 x 11 ins / 38 x 28 cm) USD 3,000.

ESBJÖRNSSON, Torsten
Swedish, 20th century.
Born 1925.
Painter.
Esbjörnsson studied at the academy of fine arts in Copenhagen and in Paris. He made some study trips to the USA. He exhibited in Sweden, Denmark, Finland, the USA and France, in particular at the 30 gallery in Paris in 1986. His painting consists of geometrical lines that are sometimes structured as prisms.

ESBRARD
French, 19th century.
Active in Paris at the beginning of the 19th century.
Engraver (aquatint).
Esbrard is best known for his portraits of *Poniatowski* and *Eugène de Beauharnais.*

ESBRAT, Raymond Noël
French, 19th century.
Born 1809, in Paris; died 1856, in Paris.
Painter. Landscapes with figures, landscapes.
Raymond Noël Esbrat gained his artistic training from attending the studios of Guillon, Lethière and Watelet. He made his Salon début in 1831, gaining a third-class medal in 1844, followed by a second-class medal in 1847. His paintings depict motifs taken mainly from Switzerland and the Auvergne region of France, but also from the areas around Compiègne and Fontainebleau.
MUSEUMS AND GALLERIES:
CHARTRES: *Landscape with Animals* - CHAUMONT: *Banks of the River Seine* - ORLÉANS: *Coudray Farm; Château de la Source, near Orléans; Landscapes* (two) - ROANNE: *View of St-Cloud Park* - VERSAILLES (Trianon): *Cottage in the Nivernais Region.*
AUCTION RECORDS:
LONDON, 18 Jan 1980, *Wooded Landscape* (oil on canvas, 36 1/2 x 27 ins / 92.6 x 68.6 cm) GBP 1,000. BERN, 26 Oct 1988, *Livestock in a Meadow in a Coastal Landscape* (oil on canvas, 27 1/2 x 36 1/4 ins / 70 x 92 cm) CHF 4,500.

ESBREF UREN
Turkish, 20th century.
Born 1907, in Istanbul.
Painter. Still-lifes, flowers.
Esbref-Uren and Uren-Esbref may well be one and the same person. In 1946 his work was displayed at the exhibition organised by the United Nations at the museum of modern art in Paris.

ESBROECK, Égide or Édouard van
Belgian, 19th - 20th century.
Born 27 April 1869, in Londerzeel (Brabant); died 1949, in Schaerbeek.
Painter. Religious subjects, portraits, genre scenes. Murals.
At the Académie des Beaux-Arts in Brussels, Esbroeck was a student of Jean-François Portaels and Joseph van Severdonck; he won the Prix de Rome in 1892 and the Godecharle prize in 1894.
He mainly practised mural art, in particular in Schaerbeek with his decoration of the church of St Marie and his biblical scenes at the church of St Servais.
AUCTION RECORDS:
LOKEREN, 9 Dec 1995, *Kitchen Garden* (oil on canvas, 14 1/2 x 25 1/2 ins / 37 x 65 cm) BEF 185,000. PARIS, 3 April 2002, *Separation of Hops in an Interior* (1928, oil on canvas, 34 x 43 ins / 86 x 110 cm) EUR 2,100.

ESBROECK, Pol van
Belgian, 20th century.
Born 1912, in Londerzeel.
Sculptor.
Pol van Esbroeck was probably the son of Égide. He was a student of Ernest Wynants at the Koninklijke Academie voor Schone Kunsten in Antwerp. He won the Godecharle prize in 1933.
AUCTION RECORDS:
ANTWERP, 26 April 1983, *Nude Standing* (wood, h. 47 1/4 ins / 120 cm) BEF 28,000.

ESBROT, Jean, or Asbrout
French, 17th century.
Active in Avignon during the second half of the 17th century.
Painter.

ESBROT, Pierre
French, 16th century.

Died c. 1595.
Active in Avignon in 1545.
Painter. Historical subjects, portraits.
Pierre Esbrot was made a noble in 1556.

ESBROT, Pierre Joseph de, or Asborout
French, 17th century.
Active in Avignon c. 1693.
Painter.

ESCACENA, Juan
Spanish, 19th century.
Died 3 January 1814, in Seville.
Painter. History painting.
Juan Escacena was the father of Escacena y Daza.

ESCACENA Y DAZA, José Maria
Spanish, 19th century.
Born c. 1800, in Seville; died 1858, in Seville.
Painter. Portraits, genre scenes, still-lifes.
José Maria Escacena y Daza studied at the school of fine arts in Seville. He became director of the school in 1829.
AUCTION RECORDS:
LONDON, 23 April 1910, *Portrait of Sir John Machpherson Brackenbury*, GBP 19.

ESCADA, Guillermo. See **SCADA**

ESCADA, José
Portuguese, 20th century.
Born 1934, in Lisbon; died 22 August 1980, in Lisbon.
From 1959 active in France.
Painter.
José Escada completed a diploma in art at the school of fine arts in Lisbon. He was a member of the *KWY* group. He settled in Paris where he took part in various collective exhibitions; he also exhibited in Holland, Italy and Germany He travelled in Europe on several occasions, spending time in Munich in particular.

Escada painted compositions with elegant forms in silhouette and arabesques. He also produced contemporary sacred art.

ESCALANTE, Antonio de
Spanish, 16th century.
Born c. 1502.
Active in Valladolid in 1548.
Sculptor.
Antonio de Escalante was a witness in proceedings instituted by Berruguete in 1553.

ESCALANTE, Juan Antonio de Frías y
Spanish, 17th century.
Born 1633, in Cordova; died 1670, in Madrid.
Painter.
Juan Antonio de Frías y Escalante studied in Madrid under Francisco Ricci (or Rizi), who was painter to the king and gave him access to the palace to copy a number of paintings. Escalante studied the methods of Tintoretto and Titian very keenly and they became his guides; in certain of Escalante's paintings the style, coloration, drawing and composition echoes that of Tintoretto; Escalante's *Christ* in the church of the Holy Spirit at the monastery of the Minorites in Madrid echoes Titian's use of colour. He was not yet 24 when he received a commission from the Calced Carmelites to paint scenes from the *Life of St Gerard*. This work made his reputation at court where he became very highly regarded. Escalante is also known, together with Carreno and Ricci, to have worked on the holy week monument in Toledo. Another painting by Escalante in the Carmelite monastery in Madrid is perhaps his finest work, *Redemption of the Captive*; in this piece Escalante has painted himself among the captives. The 18 paintings in the refectory are also by Escalante, with the exception of *The Crossing of the Red Sea* which is by Juan Montero de Rossas. The church of Nuestra Señora de la Merced in Madrid also has some fine paintings by the artist; the parish church of S Miguel has a *St Catherine, Virgin and Martyr* which owes much to Tintoretto's palette.

Escalenté.

BIBLIOGRAPHY:
Lafuente Ferrari, E., '*Escalante en Navarra y otras otas su sobre el pintor*' in *Principe de Viana*, 1941. Buendía, José Rogelio, '*Recordando a Escalante en los trescientos años de su muerte*' in *Goya*, vol 99, 1970.
MUSEUMS AND GALLERIES:
BUDAPEST (Simu): *Immaculate Conception of the Virgin* - MADRID (Prado): *Prudent Abigail; Triumph of Faith over the Senses; Holy Family; St John and the Infant Jesus Seated; Andromeda and the Dragon* (c. 1659); *Elias and the Angel* (1667-68) - NEW YORK (Hispanic Society of America): *The Annunciation* (1663) - ST PETERSBURG (Hermitage): *St Joseph with the Infant Jesus*.
AUCTION RECORDS:
PARIS, 12 March 1919, *Road to Calvary*, FRF 100. PARIS, 28 March 1919, *Road to Calvary*, FRF 50. LONDON, 23 Nov 1962, *The Virgin Appearing to St Peter*, Gns 1,000.

ESCALAS, Juan
Spanish, 18th century.
Active in Palma (Majorca) in 1791.
Sculptor.

ESCALERA, Pio
Spanish, 19th century.
Born c. 1850.
Painter, illustrator. Landscapes.
Pio Escalera began work as an artist around 1880. He was made a 'Knight of Christ of Portugal'.

ESCALIER, Marguerite
French, 19th century.
Born 19th century, in Dijon.
Painter. Genre scenes, portraits.
A pupil of Éléonore Escallier, Marguerite Escalier exhibited mainly drawings at the Salon from 1873.

ESCALIER, Nicolas Félix
French, 19th century.
Born 1843, in Paris.
Painter. Portraits, genre scenes, landscapes.
Nicolas Félix Escalier was a pupil of André and Delaunay at the École des Beaux-Arts. He initially studied architecture before devoting himself to painting from 1873. He exhibited fairly regularly at the Salon, gaining two honourable mentions in 1876 and 1878, followed by a second-class medal in 1884. He was awarded the Légion d'Honneur in 1900 and was a member of the Société des Artistes Français.

Escalier was particularly renowned for his beautifully handled decorative panels.
AUCTION RECORDS:
LONDON, 30 Nov 1908, *Rialto, Venice*, GBP 48. LONDON, 7 Oct 1987, *Rialto Bridge, Venice* (1881, oil on canvas, 22 x 39¼ ins / 56 x 100 cm) GBP 4,500.

ESCALLIER, Éléonore
Maiden name: Légerot
French, 19th century.
Born 1827, in Poligny; died June 1888, in Sèvres.
Painter. Flowers, fruit.
A pupil of Ziegler, Éléonore Escallier excelled at flower painting. She exhibited at the Paris Salon from 1857 to 1880.

MUSEUMS AND GALLERIES:
DIJON: *Peaches and Grapes* - PARIS (MAM): *Chrysanthemums* - ST-ÉTIENNE: *Vase of Flowers*.

ESCALPERO, Miguel
Spanish, 19th century.
Born c. 1831; died September 1867, in Paris.
Painter.
Miguel Escalpero is known for his *Defence of Saragossa*.

ESCAMAING, Jacques d'
Flemish School, 14th century.
Born in Tournai.
Sculptor.
Jacques d'Escamaing worked in Lille and Tournai. He may be the same person as Jean d'Escamaing.

ESCAMAING, Jean d'
Flemish School, 14th century.
Born in Tournai.
Sculptor.
Jean d'Escamaing carved the decorations on the door of the church of St-Sauveur in Lille. He may be the same person as Jacques d'Escamaing.

ESCAMEZ, Julio
Chilean, 20th century.
Born 1930.
Painter. Murals.
Julio Escamez collaborated with Gregorio de la Fuente and worked with him in Concepción. He also worked on his own at the town hall of Chillán.

ESCAMILLA, Marcos de
Spanish, 16th century.
Active in Seville in 1575.
Painter.

ESCARDO, Valentín
Spanish, 19th century.
Active in Catalonia c. 1880.
Sculptor.

ESCASSUT, Anna
French, 20th century.
Born 26 October 1878, in Paris.
Painter. Landscapes, flowers.
Anna Escassut was a pupil of Montézin and Adler. She exhibited landscapes and flowers in Paris at the Salon d'Automne in 1935 and was awarded a medal in 1938.

ESCENDI, Franz Aloisius
German, 18th century.
Active in Landeshut in 1799.
Painter.

ESCH, Mathilde
Czech, 19th century.
Born 18 January 1820, in Klatovy.
Painter. Genre scenes.
Mathilde Esch studied under Waldmuller in Vienna, then worked in Düsseldorf and Paris.

ESCH, Thomas Thomasz. van
Dutch, 17th century.
Active in Delft in 1640.
Painter.

ESCH, von. See **ABESCH**

ESCHAPASSE, René
French, 20th century.
Born in Nantes.
Painter. Mythological subjects, local scenes, landscapes.
René Eschapasse, who lived in Brittany, exhibited local landscapes, paintings of religious festivals, portraits and a *Judgement of Paris* at the Salon des Artistes, Paris, of which he became a member. He was awarded a second-class medal in 1941.

ESCHARD, Aimé
French, 20th century.
Born in St-Denis.
Painter. Flowers.
Aimé Eschard exhibited from 1922 at the Salon des Artistes Français, Paris, and eventually became a member.

ESCHARD, Charles, or Échard
French, 18th - 19th century.
Born 1748, in Caen; died 1810.
Painter (gouache), watercolourist, engraver, draughtsman. Genre scenes, landscapes, animals.
A pupil of Descamps at Rouen, in 1782 Charles Eschard was registered at the Académie de Paris, but not having submitted his admission work his name was deleted in 1783. He visited Holland and Savoy which inspired the landscapes he sent to the Salon in 1791 and 1798.
MUSEUMS AND GALLERIES:
ALENÇON: *Landscape* - GDANSK: *Landscape* - GRENOBLE: pen drawings - ROUEN: three landscapes.
AUCTION RECORDS:
PARIS, 7-8 May 1923, *Three Studies of a Young Savoyard* (red chalk) FRF 650. PARIS, 2 June 1923, *Mountainous Landscapes with River and Figure* (two drawings in pierre d'Italie (black chalk)) FRF 350. PARIS, 6 Dec 1923, *Fiddler* (red chalk) FRF 1,600. PARIS, 20 March 1924, *Ruins in Mountainous Site* (pen and wash) FRF 1,000; *Dutch Peasant* (black chalk) FRF 200. PARIS, 20-21 June 1924, *Beggar* (Indian ink) FRF 55; *Peasant* (pen) FRF 50. PARIS, 20-21 April 1925, *Peasant Cart* (pencil) FRF 115. PARIS, 25 April 1927, *Village Square* (pencil and wash) FRF 320; *Farm with Thatched Roof* (pencil and wash) FRF 350; *Farmyard* (black chalk heightened) FRF 230. PARIS, 23 Nov 1927, *Village Gallant, Dutch Interior* (watercolour) FRF 900. PARIS, 21-22 May 1928, *Flock in Shade* (pencil) FRF 300. PARIS, 10 Dec 1943, *Pasture; Dale* (two gouaches, a pair) FRF 8,800. PARIS, 25 Nov 1946, *Beggar* (pen) FRF 1,150. PARIS, 2 Dec 1946, *Half-length Portraits of Beggars* (four pen drawings) FRF 750. NEW YORK, 16 June 1977, *Fishers on Beach* (oil on canvas, 28 x 37 1/2 ins / 71 x 95 cm) USD 6,750. PARIS, 16 March 1990, *Conversations in a Village Lane* (black chalk and grey wash, 9 1/4 x 10 3/4 ins / 23.3 x 27.6 cm) FRF 3,600. PARIS, 22 Nov 1991, *Oaks* (red chalk and lead pencil, 6 1/4 x 9 1/4 ins / 16 x 23.5 cm) FRF 5,800. PARIS, 4 July 1995, *Study of Man Seen from Behind* (lead pencil and red chalk, 9 x 7 3/4 ins / 22 x 19.5 cm) FRF 6,000. PARIS, 3 Dec 1999, *Old Beggar Sitting by his Dog among Roman Ruins* (pen, brush, beige wash heightened with white, 20 x 16 ins / 52 x 41 cm) FRF 10,500. PARIS, 27 March 2002, *View of a Building by an Estuary* (oil on panel, 6 x 9 ins / 16 x 22 cm) EUR 1,900.

ESCHAY, Veit. See **EHESCHEUH**

ESCHBACH, Louis
French, 19th century.
Born in Lons-le-Saunier.
Painter. Portraits.
Louis Eschbach exhibited at the Paris Salon from 1835 to 1839.

ESCHBACH, Paul André Jean, or Eschback, Eschbart
French, 20th century.
Born 1881, in Paris; died 10 August 1961, in Paris.
Painter. Portraits, genre scenes, interiors with figures, fishing scenes, landscapes, waterscapes, winter landscapes, seascapes, flowers.
Paul André Jean Eschbach was a pupil of Jean-Paul Laurens and Pharaon Abdon Leon de Winter. He exhibited regularly in Paris at the Salon des Artistes Français, of which he eventually became a member. In 1907, he won a third-class medal

and in 1920 a gold medal. He taught at the Académie Julian from 1912 to 1938. His works can be found in several provincial museums. After 1920, he tired of the interior and genre scenes to which he had confined himself, started painting portraits and made a reputation as a landscapist. He also painted seascapes and cloud effects.

AUCTION RECORDS:

NEW YORK, 12 Feb 1909, *Musketeer,* USD 140. SCEAUX, 8 Dec 1985, *Pond at Night* (1912, oil on canvas, 36½ x 59 ins / 93 x 150 cm) FRF 4,500. CALAIS, 8 Nov 1987, *Peonies and Earthenware Flower Pot* (oil on canvas, 19¾ x 24 ins / 50 x 61 cm) FRF 7,000. PARIS, 21 April 1988, *Fishing Boats in Port* (oil on canvas, 19¾ x 24 ins / 50 x 61 cm) FRF 5,500. PARIS, 27 April 1989, *Landscape in Snow* (oil on canvas, 21¼ x 25½ ins / 54 x 65 cm) FRF 7,000. LA ROCHELLE, 17 March 1990, *Fishing Boats Setting Off* (oil on canvas, 25½ x 36¼ ins / 65 x 92 cm) FRF 22,000. PARIS, 6 Feb 1991, *Church in Snow* (oil on canvas, 20¾ x 17¾ ins / 53 x 45 cm) FRF 7,000. PARIS, 4 March 1991, *Honfleur, the Harbour Exit at Low Tide* (oil on canvas, 20 x 24½ ins / 50.5 x 62 cm) FRF 8,100. PARIS, 12 Dec 1997, *Banks of the Dordogne* (oil on canvas, 18 x 15 ins / 46 x 38 cm) FRF 2,000. BREST, 14 May 2000, *Concarneau, Tuna Boats with Sails, Figures on the Dock* (oil on canvas, 26 x 39 ins / 65 x 100 cm) FRF 15,500. BREST, 20 May 2001, *Fishing Vessels with Sails at Anchor* (oil on canvas, 24 x 32 ins / 60 x 81 cm) FRF 19,200. BREST, 16 Dec 2001, *Return of the Fishermen* (oil on canvas, 21 x 26 ins / 54 x 65 cm) FRF 25,000. BREST, 12 May 2002, *Tuna Boats with Sails at Anchor* (oil on canvas, 32 x 45 ins / 81 x 115 cm) EUR 6,800. BREST, 11 May 2003, *Return from Fishing* (oil on canvas, 20 x 26 ins / 50 x 65 cm) EUR 1,700. BREST, 11 May 2003, *Fishing Boats Under Sail by the Dock* (oil on canvas, 22 x 43 ins / 55 x 110 cm) EUR 4,000. BREST, 24 July 2004, *Unloading the Tuna Boats at the port of Douarnenez* (oil on canvas, 26 x 32 ins / 65 x 81 cm) EUR 3,000. BREST, 24 July 2004, *Sailing Boats in the Sun, Concarneau* (oil on canvas, 24 x 29 ins / 62 x 73 cm) EUR 4,600.

ESCHEMANN, Jean Bernard

French, 19th - 20th century.
Born 19th century, in Paris.
Painter, draughtsman. Mythological subjects, genre scenes.

Jean Bernard Eschemann was a pupil of Jules Lefebvre and Tony Robert-Fleury. He exhibited regularly from 1903 to 1927 at the Salon des Artistes Français, Paris, of which he became a member.

AUCTION RECORDS:

NEW YORK, 18 April 1928, *Hylas Led by Nymphs,* FRF 220. PARIS, 18 Feb 1977, *Drunken Bacchus* (oil on canvas, 13 x 16¼ ins / 33 x 41 cm) FRF 1,300. LONDON, 23 Feb 1983, *The Temptation* (1900, oil on canvas, 80 x 62 ins / 203 x 157.5 cm) GBP 1,500.

ESCHENBACH, Johann

German, 18th century.
Active in Mainz during the second half of the 18th century.
Sculptor.

In 1771, Eschenbach was working for Mainz Cathedral.

ESCHENBACH, Paul, or Ashbrook

American, 20th century.
Born 3 January 1867, in New York; died 1949, in San Miguel de Allende, Mexico.
Painter.

Paul Eschenbach started his studies at the Art Student's League in New York, and then went to work with Frank Duveneck in Cincinnati. He won first prize from the city's art club in 1903.

ESCHENBRENNER, Émilie Louise

French, 20th century.
Born 11 May 1880, in Lyons.
Painter.

Émilie Louise Eschenbrenner was a pupil of E. Renard. She exhibited for a time in Paris at the Salon des Artistes Français.

ESCHENBURG, Marianne von

Austrian, 19th century.
Born 18 April 1856, in Vienna.
Painter.

A pupil of her uncle, Karl von Blaas, von Eschenburg painted mainly portraits.

ESCHER, Albert von

Swiss, 19th century.
Born 20 May 1839, in Zurich; died 16 May 1905, in Geneva.
Painter, watercolourist, draughtsman. Military subjects.

An officer, Albert von Escher owed his knowledge of Swiss military dress to his extensive studies of the archives and documents concerning Swiss military life.

Von Escher's best-known works among those cited by Dr Brun are: *Swiss Regiments Serving Abroad* (200 watercolours), *18th-century Swiss Military* (160 watercolours) and *19th-century Swiss Military* (530 watercolours).

AUCTION RECORDS:

ZURICH, 24 Nov 1993, *General Jakob Christoph Ziegler of Zurich Commanding the 30th and 31st Swiss Regiments* (pencil and watercolour/paper, 11½ x 16½in/29 x 42cm) CHF 7,475.

ESCHER, Gertrud

Swiss, 20th century.
Born 23 May 1875, in Zurich.
Painter, engraver. Landscapes.

Gertrud Escher was a student of Gattiker. She exhibited from 1900, mainly with landscape engravings.

AUCTION RECORDS:

ZURICH, 6 June 1980, *Still-life* (oil on canvas, 16 x 19 ins / 40.5 x 48 cm) CHF 2,000.

ESCHER, Gottschalk

German, 18th century.
Active in Lübeck c. 1700.
Painter.

Gottschalk Escher worked for the church of St Peter in Lübeck.

ESCHER, Hans Kaspar

Swiss, 19th century.
Born 10 August 1775, in Zurich; died 29 August 1859, in Zurich.
Engraver (copper), architect.

The collection of the art society in Zurich holds many engravings of horses and one drawing by Hans Kaspar Escher.

ESCHER, Martin Friedrich

French, 18th - 19th century.
Born 12 April 1772, in Lyons; died 4 February 1814, in Zurich.
Active in Nîmes.
Painter, engraver.

Martin Escher painted in the manner of Gessner. He engraved landscapes and signed them with his name or with his monogram.

ESCHER, Maurits Cornelis

Dutch, 20th century.
Born 1898, in Leeuwarden; died 1972.

Painter, draughtsman, engraver (wood), lithographer. Figures, interiors, landscapes, urban landscapes, architectural views. Wall decorations, postage stamps.

M.C. Escher was born into a family of artists, and began by studying engineering at the technical university in Delft, while also studying at the school of architecture and decorative arts in Haarlem. A keen traveller, he lived in Italy from 1923 to 1935 and returned to settle in Holland in 1937. With a wide following in many countries, this Dutch artist's works were not truly known and appreciated in France until 1972 onwards, despite some articles that had revealed his art to the French-speaking public prior to this.

He featured in the exhibition *De blijvende verlokking: Nederlandse kunstenaars in Italië, 1806-1940* (*Lasting Attraction: Dutch Artists in Italy, 1806-1940*), which showed the impact of Italian travels on Dutch artists, in the Kunsthal in Rotterdam in 2003.

Escher's engravings still attract keen interest from numerous collectors - from scientists and mathematicians to Fantastic Art enthusiasts. Escher's work can be divided into two distinct periods. His Latin period is characterised by the representation of reinvented landscapes and plant and animal forms in an intense fantastical realism with unusual perspectives. From 1937, a transitional year, he produced many engravings (black-and-white and colour), in which his technical virtuosity, combined with a unique way of playing with perspective, opens the door to an enclosed, lunatic world and plunges us into the heart of vertiginous citadels in which vision is often a source of morbid delight... but for the knowledge that Escher is often seeking to prove to us that nature abhors a vacuum. In other words, sometimes what we take to be images of another world should be regarded as a series of moves in a skilful game in which the rules are known only to its inventor. Escher excelled at creating structures that were definitively closed in on themselves, embellishing them with extraordinary imbricated forms (black and white birds, birds and fishes, lizards and human figures taking shape along pseudo-parallel planes). The mystery of Escher is this constant quest for the fourth dimension: 'In a three-dimensional world, it is impossible to show the back and the front simultaneously'. Finally, it should be noted that in addition to his engravings, Escher designed some postage stamps and produced a mural painting, *Metamorphosis*, for a post office in the Hague.

Bibliography:

Chapelot, Pierre, '*Une découverte: le visionnaire Escher*' in *Planète* no. 8, periodical, Paris, 1963. Flocon, Albert, '*À la frontière de l'art graphique et des mathématiques: Maurits Cornelis Escher*' in *Le Jardin des Arts* no. 131, periodical, Paris, 1965. Locher, J.L./Broos, C.H.A./Escher, M.C./Locher, G.W./Coxeter, H.S.M., *Le Monde de M.C. Escher*, Éd. du Chêne, Paris, 1972 (including a catalogue of his works). *Escher*, exhibition catalogue, Institut néerlandais, Paris, 1973. Erst, B., *The Magic Mirror of M.C. Escher*, Random House, New York, 1976. Coxeter, H./Emmer, M./Penrose, R./Teuber, M. (ed.), *M.C. Escher: Art and Science - International Congress Proceedings*, North-Holland, Amsterdam, 1986. Locher, J. (ed.), *Escher: The Complete Graphic Work*, Thames and Hudson, London, 1992. Hofstadter, D., *Gödel, Escher, Bach: An Eternal Golden Braid (20th Anniversary Edition)*, Penguin Books Ltd, Harmondsworth, 2000. Emmer, M./Schattschneider, D. (ed.), *Escher's Legacy: A Centennial Celebration*, Springer-Verlag, Berlin, 2001. Escher, Maurits Cornelis, *M. C. Escher: l'oeuvre graphique*, Taschen, Cologne, London Paris, 2001. *De blijvende verlokking: Nederlandse kunstenaars in Italië, 1806-1940*, exhibition catalogue, Kunsthal, Rotterdam, 2003. Schattschneider, D., *M.C. Escher: Visions of Symmetry*, Thames and Hudson, London, 2004.

Museums and Galleries:

The Hague (Gemeentemus.).

Auction records:

Amsterdam, 25 May 1976, *Day and Night* (woodcut, $15\frac{1}{2}$ x $26\frac{3}{4}$ ins / 39.3 x 67.8 cm) NLG 7,500. Amsterdam, 26 April 1977, *Metamorphoses II* (1939-1940, woodcut, on Japanese paper, 11 x $6\frac{3}{4}$ ins / 28 x 17 cm) NLG 6,200. New York, 3 May 1978, *Convex and Concave* (1955) USD 2,000. Los Angeles, 24 Sept 1979, *Three Spheres II* (1946, lithograph, $10\frac{1}{4}$ x $18\frac{1}{2}$ ins / 26.1 x 46.9 cm) USD 16,500. Los Angeles, 22 Sept 1980, *Study near St Peter's and the Sistine Chapel* (c. 1936, lead pencil, white pencil and brown chalk, 13 x $9\frac{1}{2}$ ins / 33 x 24 cm) USD 5,500. New York, 16 Feb 1982, *Bond of Union* (1956, lithograph, $10\frac{1}{4}$ x 13 ins / 26 x 33 cm) USD 3,000. New York, 2 May 1984, *Hand with Reflecting Sphere* (1935, lithograph, $12\frac{1}{2}$ x $8\frac{1}{2}$ ins / 31.8 x 21.6 cm) USD 20,500. New York, 16 Nov 1985, *Day and Night* (1938, woodcut in black and greenish-grey/thin Japanese paper, $15\frac{1}{2}$ x $26\frac{3}{4}$ ins / 39.3 x 67.8 cm) USD 11,000. New York, 15 May 1986, *Hand with Sphere* (1936, lithograph, $12\frac{1}{2}$ x $8\frac{1}{2}$ ins / 31.8 x 21.3 cm) USD 17,000. New York, 13 Nov 1987, *Day and Night* (1938, woodcut in black and greenish-grey/thin Japanese paper, $15\frac{1}{2}$ x $26\frac{3}{4}$ ins / 39.3 x 67.8 cm) USD 16,000. Zurich, 16 Oct 1991, *Encounters* (1944, lithograph, $15\frac{1}{4}$ x $19\frac{1}{2}$ ins / 38.7 x 49.5 cm) CHF 6,500. Amsterdam, 30 May 1995, *Three Spheres* (1945, woodcut, 11 x $6\frac{3}{4}$ ins / 28 x 17 cm) NLG 6,500. New York, 6 and 7 March 1998, *Flying Sorceress* (1931, woodcut, 9 x $6\frac{1}{2}$ ins / 22.9 x 16.8 cm) USD 402. Amsterdam, 10 June 1999, *Tekenen, Drawing Hands* (1948, lithograph, 11 x 13 ins / 28 x 33 cm) NLG 85,000. Amsterdam, 1 Dec 1999, *Reptiles* (lithograph, 13 x 15 ins / 33 x 39 cm) NLG 80,000. Vienna, 7 June 2000, *Day and Night* (1938, woodcut, 15 x 27 ins / 38 x 68 cm) ATS 250,000. Amsterdam, 8 June 2000, *Metamorphose II* (woodcut in red and black, 7 x 157 ins / 19 x 400 cm) NLG 150,000. San Francisco, 25 Oct 2000, *Still-life with Mirror* (lithograph, 20 x 15 ins / 50 x 39 cm) USD 20,000. New York, 31 Oct 2001, *Drawing Hands* (1948, lithograph, 16 x 18 ins / 41 x 46 cm) USD 50,000. New York, 1 Nov 2001, *Circle Limit IV* (colour woodcut) USD 35,000. New York, 1 May 2002, *Liberation* (lithograph, 22 x 11 ins / 56 x 29 cm) USD 30,000. New York, 1 May 2002, *Metamorphosis* (colour woodcut, three joined sheets, 13 x 157 ins / 33 x 400 cm) USD 80,000. Amsterdam, 3 June 2003, *Day and Night* (wood engraving, 15 x 27 ins / 39 x 68 cm) EUR 16,000. New York, 4 Nov 2003, *Drawing Hands* (1948, lithograph, 15 x 18 ins / 38 x 45 cm) USD 48,000. New York, 2 Nov 2004, *Magic Mirror* (lithograph, 11 x 18 ins / 28 x 46 cm) USD 17,000. New York, 2 Nov 2004, *Waterfall* (lithograph, 15 x 12 ins / 38 x 30 cm) USD 20,000.

ESCHER, Rudolf

Swiss, 17th - 18th century.

Born 1662, in Zurich; died 1721, in Zurich.

Painter.

Alongside his career as a politician, Rudolf Escher painted primarily portraits. Those of the burgomaster, J. Heinrich Escher (who, according to Dr Brun, was probably his father), and of L. Engeler were subsequently engraved by J. Bodmer.

Rolf Escher

ESCHER, W.

German, 19th century.

Died 13 June 1871, in Berlin.

Painter (including porcelain). Portraits, genre scenes.

W. Escher was working in Vienna in 1850. He executed portraits and genre scenes.

ESCHER VOM LUCHS, Heinrich
Swiss, 19th century.
Born 1799, in Zurich; died 1844, in Zurich.
Painter, engraver, decorative designer. Landscapes.
Escher vom Luchs is represented in the print collections of the art society in Zurich and at the federal polytechnic institute by some plates after Gessner. He exhibited in Zurich in 1826.

ESCHER ZUM ADLERBERG, Konrad
Swiss, 18th - 19th century.
Born 1756, in Zurich; died 1813, in Zurich.
Painter (gouache), draughtsman, engraver.
Landscapes.
Konrad Escher painted in the style of Gessner and exhibited in 1803. He is represented by two engravings and some landscapes in the collection of the art society in Zurich. Contrary to Siret's suggestion, Konrad and Martin Friedrich Escher are two different artists.

ESCHER-SCHULTHEISS
Swiss, 19th century.
Active in Zurich at the beginning of the 19th century.
Painter.
A pupil of Huber, Escher-Schultheiss exhibited watercolours of Swiss views in Zurich in 1802.

ESCHERICH, Catharina
Austrian, 19th century.
Active in Vienna at the beginning of the 19th century.
Painter.
Escherich is best known for her *Portrait of Archduke Charles of Austria*.

ESCHERICH, F.
American, 20th century.
Born 20 March 1888, in Davenport (Iowa).
Painter.

ESCHINI, Angelo Maria d'
Italian, 17th century.
Died 1678, in Modena.
Painter, engraver.
Eschini is noted for his excellent engravings of the *Virgin*.

ESCHKE, Oskar
German, 19th century.
Born 28 May 1851, in Berlin; died April 1892, in Chicago.
Painter. Landscapes, seascapes.
A son and pupil of Wilhelm Benjamin Hermann Eschke in Berlin, Oskar Eschke participated in an expedition to China in 1875.
AUCTION RECORDS:
COLOGNE, 23 March 1990, *River Bank at Sunset* (oil on canvas, 22 x 33¾in/56 x 86cm) DEM 4,000. GREENVILLE, 25 July 2004, *Chinese Harbour* (oil on canvas) USD 2,800.

ESCHKE, Richard Hermann
German, 19th - 20th century.
Born 1 September 1859, in Berlin; died 1944.
Painter. Scenes with figures, genre scenes, landscapes with figures, seascapes.
Richard Eschke was the son and student of Wilhelm Benjamin Hermann Eschke in Berlin. From 1883, he exhibited in Munich and Berlin.
AUCTION RECORDS:
VIENNA, 13 June 1978, *Fish Market* (oil on canvas, 22 x 32 ins / 55 x 81.5 cm) ATS 28,000. AMSTERDAM, 5-6 Nov 1991, *Goats in a Mountain Landscape* (oil on canvas, 36 x 43½ ins / 90.5 x 110.5 cm) NLG 1,610. LONDON, 18 March 1992, *Young Piper* (1901, oil on canvas, 24 x 30½ ins / 61 x 77.5 cm) GBP 2,200. AMSTERDAM, 2 Nov 1992, *Little Red Riding Hood* (oil on canvas, 28¾ x 43¾ ins / 73 x 111 cm) NLG 10,350. COPENHAGEN, 17 May 1995, *Seascape with Russian Coast and a Port in the Background at Sunset* (oil on canvas, 31 x 51¼ ins / 79 x 130 cm) DKK 15,000.

ESCHKE, Wilhelm Benjamin Hermann
German, 19th century.
Born 6 May 1823, in Berlin; died 15 January 1900, in Berlin.
Painter. Landscapes with figures, landscapes, seascapes.
A pupil of the seascape painter W. Krause in Berlin, and of Le Poittevin in Paris, Wilhelm Eschke travelled in England, Belgium, Holland and France. He settled in Berlin, where he received an award in 1879.
MUSEUMS AND GALLERIES:
MELBOURNE: *Freshwater Bay, Isle of Wight* - SYDNEY: *Sunrise, Isle of Wight*.
AUCTION RECORDS:
LONDON, 16 Feb 1979, *Seaside, Ostend* (oil on canvas, 28¼ x 43¼in/71.7 x 109.8cm) GBP 1,100. LONDON, 27 Oct 1993, *Landscape with Figures* (1874, oil on canvas, 30¾ x 53¼in/78 x 135cm) GBP 4,830.

ESCHLBAUER, Johann
Austrian, 18th century.
Active in Salzburg.
Sculptor (wood).
Eschlbauer worked for the church of St Sebastian around 1750.

ESCHLINSPERG, Konrad
German, 16th century.
Active in Isny c. 1502.
Sculptor.

ESCHLINSPERG, Melchior
German, 16th century.
Active in Munich c. 1500.
Painter.
Melchior Eschlinsperg was the brother of Konrad.

ESCHMANN
Swiss, 14th century.
Active in Basel c. 1357.
Sculptor.

ESCHOLIER, Claude
French, 20th century.
Painter. Nudes, flowers.
Claude Escholier exhibited in Paris at the Salon des Indépendants from 1928.

ESCHOLIER, Marie
French, 19th century.
Born 13 May 1856, in Bordeaux.
Painter, sculptor.
A pupil of Barrias, Marie Escholier exhibited at the Salon of the Société des Artistes Français, becoming a member in 1882.

ESCHOT, Jacques
Flemish School, 16th - 17th century.
Active in Antwerp.
Painter.
In 1582, Jacques Eschot was the pupil of Frans Miróí. In 1610, he was working at Antwerp Cathedral.

ESCHWEGE, Elmar or Esmar von
German, 19th century.
Born 22 August 1856, in Brunswick.
Painter. History painting, genre scenes.
Eschwege studied at the academy of art in Dresden and worked with Ferdinand Pauwels. He settled in Blaswitz, near Dresden, exhibiting from 1884 at the royal academy in Dresden, and in Berlin.

Museums and Galleries:
Wroclaw: *Major Count von Schmettow at the Battle of Thionville.*
Auction records:
London, 18 Feb 1970, *William II and the Empress in a Barouche,* GBP 3,000. London, 12 May 1972, *William II on his Way to Potsdam Castle,* Gns 1,900. Amsterdam, 17 Nov 1981, *King Frederick II and Princess Victoria in a Barouche at Potsdam* (oil on canvas, 36 3/4 x 63in/93.5 x 160cm) NLG 70,000. New York, 1 March 1984, *Frederick II and Princess Victoria on their Way to Potsdam* (oil on canvas, 37 1/2 x 64in/95.2 x 162.5cm) USD 45,000.

ESCHWEGE, Lucette
French, 20th century.
Born in Marnes-la-Coquette (Seine-et-Oise, now Hauts-de-Seine).
Painter. Landscapes.
Lucette Eschwege exhibited in Paris at the Salon d'Automne in 1931.

ESCLAIBES, Noémie d'
French, 20th century.
Born in Cambrai.
Watercolourist.
Landscapes of the Île-de-France and Provence by Noémie d'Esclaibes were exhibited at the Salon de l'Union des Femmes Peintres et Sculpteurs, Paris.

ESCOBAR, Alonso de
Spanish, 17th century.
Active in Seville at the end of the 17th century.
Painter. History painting.
Alonso de Escobar was a disciple of Murillo.

ESCOBAR, Antonio de
Spanish, 16th century.
Active in Seville in 1503.
Painter.

ESCOBAR, Blas
Spanish, 17th century.
Active in Seville.
Sculptor.
On 12 April 1651, Blas Escobar delivered a new cross made of pear-tree wood.

ESCOBAR, Carlos Lugo
Venezuelan, 20th century.
Born 1894, in Caracas.
Active in the USA.
Painter, sculptor.
Carlos Lugo Escobar began his training at the school of fine arts in Caracas. He held exhibitions and became a teacher at the school of fine and applied art in his native city of Caracas. He later went to work and exhibit in New York.

ESCOBAR, Jose de
Spanish, 17th century.
Sculptor.
José de Escobar was *maistre mayor* or senior master of the Seville guild in 1694.

ESCOBAR, Juan de
Spanish, 16th century.
Active in Seville c. 1534.
Sculptor.

ESCOBAR, Marisol
Franco-Venezuelan, 20th century.
Born 1930, in Paris, to Venezuelan parents.
From 1950 active in the USA.
Sculptor. Groups.
Born in Paris to Venezuelan parents, Marisol Escobar spent her childhood travelling between Paris, Caracas and the USA. In 1949, she began studies at the École des Beaux-Arts, Paris, and the following year went to New York, where she became a pupil at the Art Students League and the New School for Social Research. She then spent four years in the studio of Hans Hoffman. She settled in the USA, where she was successful and showed at important exhibitions in New York, Washington, etc. Initially, she produced Pop Art, but she soon found her own style. Her early works are related to Mexican and Colombian traditions of ludic sculpture, but progressively, social and political satire entered into her work.
Museums and Galleries:
Colorado Springs (Fine Arts Center): *John Wayne* (1963, mixed media).
Auction records:
New York, 3 May 1989, *Untitled* (1960, painted plaster and steel, 11 x 10 x 7 ins / 28 x 25.5 x 17.8 cm) USD 6,050. New York, 18 May 1994, *Figures* (bronze, h. 22 1/4 ins / 56.2 cm) USD 11,500.

ESCOBAR, Pedro de
Spanish, 16th century.
Active in Seville.
Sculptor.
Pedro de Escobar was the pupil of his brother-in-law, Alfon Martin, who he left in 1508.

ESCOBEDO, Helen
Mexican, 20th century.
Born 28 July 1934, in Mexico City.
Sculptor.
Helen Escobedo studied first in Mexico City at Universidad de las Américas before completing her training at the Royal College of Art in London in 1954. During this period she met several sculptors, such as Henry Moore, Jacob Epstein and Ossip Zadkine, who were to influence her style significantly. Back in Mexico she became director of the museum of the Universidad Nacional Autónoma de México (1958-1982). By 1966, Escobedo's work was abstract - her moulded, carved and painted sculptures and frescoes with their strong and lively construction often reminiscent of Le Corbusier. The monumental dimensions of her work earned her several major urban projects in Mexico and abroad, including Signals (1971) at Auckland Harbour, New Zealand. In 1971 she took part in the Antwerp Sculpture Biennale. She was director of the Museo de Arte Moderno in Mexico City from 1983-1985.
Bibliography:
Gorostiza, C., *Escultura mexicana contemporánea,* Mexico City, 1960. Eder, R., *Helen Escobedo,* Mexico City, 1982. *Helen Escobedo: Lawn Figures,* exhibition catalogue, MoMA, Oxford, 1992.

ESCOBEDO Y BOSCH, Simon
Spanish, 19th century.
Born in the 19th century, in Barcelona.
Painter. Genre scenes.
Simon Escobedo y Bosch studied at the Barcelona school of fine arts. He received a commendation in Madrid in 1864.

ESCOBEDO-LAZO, Eberto
Cuban, 20th century.
Born 1919, in Cuba.
Painter. Landscapes.
In 1937, Eberto Escobedo-Lazo was a student at the Academia Nacional de Bellas Artes San Alejandro in Havana. He was influenced by Fidelio Ponce de León.
Auction records:
New York, 19-20 May 1992, *Cuban Landscape* (1954, oil on canvas, 24 x 30 1/4 ins / 61 x 76.8 cm) USD 4,950. New York, 25 Nov 1992, *Cuban Landscape* (1951, oil on canvas, 36 1/4 x 42 1/4 ins / 92 x 107 cm) USD 7,150. Miami, 3 April 1998, *Afternoon Tea* (oil on canvas, 20 x 16 ins / 51 x 41 cm) USD 1,800.

ESCOCHOIS, Sandre
Flemish School, 15th century.
Active in Bruges in 1468.
Painter.

ESCOFFEY, Abraham Isaac Jakob
Swiss, 18th - 19th century.
Born 26 February 1763; died 8 April 1834.
Active in Geneva.
Enameller.

ESCOFFEY, Jean Jacques
Swiss, 18th century.
Active in Geneva.
Enameller.
Jean Escoffey was the father of Abraham Escoffey.

ESCOFFIER, Giorgio
French, 17th century.
Born in Savoy.
Active in Rome at the beginning of the 17th century.
Painter.

ESCOFFIER, Poncet, called Poncet l'Imagier
French, 15th - 16th century.
Active in Lyons.
Sculptor, architect.
Working under the painter Jean Perréal, Escoffier was involved in preparing for the celebrations organised by the city of Lyons for the entries of Anne of Brittany (1494), Louis XII (1499) and Cardinal d'Ambroise, the French papal legate (1501).

ESCOLA, Salvador
Spanish, 19th century.
Born c. 1850.
Painter.
Among other works, Salvador Escola is known for his genre paintings.

ESCORIAL Y MARTINEZ, José
Spanish, 19th century.
Born in the 19th century, in Madrid.
Painter. History painting, portraits.
José Escorial y Martinez was a pupil of Antonio Perez Rubio.

ESCOSURA, Ignacio León y. See **LEÓN Y ESCOSURA Ignacio**

ESCOT, Bernardin, or Estoc
French, 14th century.
Active in Avignon c. 1345.
Painter.
Avignon School.
Bernardin Escot was involved in the decoration of the Palais des Papes (Papal Palace) in Avignon.

ESCOT, Charles
French, 19th century.
Born 16 April 1834, in Gaillac; died 5 May 1902, in Gaillac.
Painter, pastellist. Portraits.
Charles Escot first studied with Prévost before joining the Toulouse Académie des Beaux-Arts. He specialised in portraits and exhibited at the Paris Salon from 1869 to 1881.
MUSEUMS AND GALLERIES:
TOURCOING: *Portrait of Abbé Hubert* - VERSAILLES: *Portrait of Mlle d'Epinay; J.-J. Rousseau* (pastel).

ESCOULA, Jean
French, 19th - 20th century.
Born 26 October 1851, in Bagnères-de-Bigorre; died August 1911, in Paris.
Sculptor.
Jean Escoula, who was taught by Gautherin, first exhibited at the Salon de Paris in 1876 and was a member of the Salon des Artistes Français from 1885. He won a third-class medal in 1881, a second-class in 1882, and a gold medal at the Expositions Universelles of 1889 and 1900. He was a Chevalier of the Légion d'Honneur.
MUSEUMS AND GALLERIES:
CHÂLONS-EN-CHAMPAGNE: *Young Women Bathing* - NANCY: *Angélique* - VALENCIENNES: *Suffering.*

ESCOULA-MAROT, Jean Marie
French, 19th century.
Born in Bagnères-de-Bigorre.
Sculptor. Portraits.
Jean Marie Escoula-Marot was probably the same person as Jean Escoula, but may have been his pupil. He exhibited for the first time in Paris in 1889.
MUSEUMS AND GALLERIES:
NICE: *Stonecutter.*

ESCRIBANO, Bartolomé
Spanish, 18th century.
Engraver.
Bartolomé Escribano was a pupil of P. Irala.

ESCRIBANO, Francisco de Paula
Spanish, 19th century.
Born in the 19th century, in Seville.
Painter. History painting.
Francisco de Paula Escribano studied at the school of fine arts in Seville. He also exhibited in Seville, Cádiz and Madrid between 1858 and 1878.

ESCRIBANO Y PAUL, María del Pilar
Spanish, 19th century.
Born in Seville.
Painter.
María del Pilar Escribano y Paul painted historical and religious subjects.

ESCRIBE, Ivan Marie Laurent
French, 20th century.
Born in Briatexte (Tarn).
Painter.
Ivan Marie Laurent Escribe was a pupil of P.A. Laurens, Aubry and L. Roger. He exhibited in Paris at the Salon des Artiste Français from 1934.

ESCRIVAN, Mme d'. See **D'ESCRIVAN**

ESCROYS, Domingo
French, 18th century.
Painter.
Domingo Escroys worked for the court of Spain at the end of the 18th century.

ESCUDÉ Y BARTOLI, José
Spanish, 19th century.
Born 24 February 1863, in Reus.
Painter.
José Escudé y Bartoli was a pupil of Simon Gomez in Barcelona.

ESCUDER DE MARCILLA, Gaspard
Spanish, 20th century.
Born at the end of the 20th century, in Barcelona.
Miniaturist. Portraits.
Gapard Escuder de Marcilla exhibited miniatures in Paris at the Salon des Artistes Français from 1928 to 1933.

ESCUDERO, Francisco Xavier or François Xavier
Spanish, 20th century.
Born in Huesca (Aragon).
Medallist.
François Escudero exhibited plaster and bronze tablets in Paris at the Salon des Artistes Français from 1928 to 1933.

ESCUDERO, María Pastora
Spanish, 19th century.
Born in the 19th century.
Painter. History painting.
María Pastora Escudero exhibited in Seville in 1858 and 1868.

ESCUDERO LOZANO, Francisco Xavier
Spanish, 19th century.
Born in the 19th century, in Huesca (Aragon).
Sculptor.
Francisco Escudero Lozano exhibited at the Salon des Artistes Français. He received a commendation in 1897 and a bronze medal at the Paris Exposition Universelle of 1900.

ESCUDERO Y ESPRONCEDA, José
Spanish, 19th century.
Painter.
José Escudero y Espronceda settled in Mexico.

ESCUDIÉ, Roger
French, 20th century.
Born 16 May 1920, in Carcassonne.
Painter. Landscapes, seascapes.
Roger Escudié exhibited in Paris from 1950 at the Salon des Artistes Indépendants, the Salon Comparaisons, and the Salon de la Société Nationale des Beaux-Arts, where in 1965 he won the Marret prize with one of his landscapes, the Salon de la Marine and the Salon des Terres Latines. The State and the City of Paris bought some of his works.
AUCTION RECORDS:
ST-JEAN-CAP-FERRAT, 16 March 1993, *Low Tide* (oil on canvas, 39 x 51 1/4 ins / 99 x 130 cm) FRF 7,500.

ESCUDIER, Charles Jean Auguste
French, 19th century.
Born 20 April 1848, in Paris.
Painter. Portraits, genre scenes.
A pupil of Giacometti and Pils, Charles Escudier sent portraits to the Salon from 1869.
AUCTION RECORDS:
PARIS, 12 March 1919, *Lunch,* FRF 100. PARIS, 23 Dec 1935, *Fishermen's Wives,* FRF 140. NEW YORK, 17 Feb 1993, *Children Fishing* (oil on canvas, 26 x 39 1/4 ins / 65.1 x 99.7 cm) USD 14,950. LONDON, 31 Oct 1996, *Young Japanese Women Teasing a Parrot* (1871, oil on canvas, 47 1/4 x 30 ins / 120 x 76 cm) GBP 6,900. STOCKHOLM, 16 May 2000, *Young Woman with Distaff* (1902, oil on canvas, 29 x 24 ins / 74 x 61 cm) SEK 27,000. STUTTGART, 22 Sept 2000, *Portrait of Southern Woman in Traditional Costume - Neapolitan* (oil on canvas, 25 x 32 ins / 63 x 82 cm) DEM 7,000.

ESCUYER, Jules
French, 19th century.
Born 1798, in Compiègne; died January 1870, in Manosque.
Painter. Landscapes.
Jules Escuyer exhibited landscapes at the Salon from 1835 to 1865.

ESCUYER, Pierre
Swiss, 18th - 19th century.
Born 30 August 1749, in Geneva; died 1 July 1834, in Geneva.
Engraver.

ESDALL, William
Irish, 18th century.
Died March 1795, in Dublin.
Engraver.
William Esdall illustrated books and magazines.

ESDERS, Madeleine
French, 20th century.
Born 29 May 1891, in Paris.
Sculptor.
Madeleine Esders first exhibited in Paris at the Salon des Artistes Indépendants in 1921.

ESEGRENIO
Italian, 14th century.
Active in Venice.
Painter. History painting.
Esegrenio is mentioned by Siret.

ESEL, Hans
Swiss, 15th century.
Active in Basel in 1494.
Painter. Maps.

ESENGREN, Philipp
Italian, 16th century.
Active in Venice at the end of the 16th century.
Painter, engraver.

ESHERICK, Wharton
American, 20th century.
Born 15 July 1887, in Philadelphia; died 1970.
Painter, sculptor, engraver (wood), draughtsman.
Son of a prosperous merchant, Wharton Esherick won a scholarship in 1909 to attend the Philadelphia Academy of Fine Arts. He produced illustrations for the *North American* newspaper in Philadelphia and numerous books including *Rhymes of Early Jungle Folk* by Mary E. Marcy (Charles H. Kerr & Company, Chicago, 1922), *Tristam and Iseult* by Amory Hare (Slide Mountain Press, Gaylordsville, 1930) and *Bright Mariner* by Katherine Garrison Chapin (Duffield and Green, New York, 1933). He turned to woodwork in the 1920s, creating organic 'free-form' sculptures, furniture and architectural interiors. A year after his death, he was awarded the National Craftsmanship Medal by the American Institute of Architects. The Wharton Esherick Museum, which houses more than 200 works produced between 1920 and 1970, was opened the following year in his former studio in Paoli.
BIBLIOGRAPHY:
Woodenworks; furniture objects by five contemporary craftsmen: George Nakashima, Sam Maloof, Wharton Esherick, Arthur Espenet Carpenter, Wendell Castle, Minnesota Museum of Art, St Paul, 1972. *The Wharton Esherick Museum: studio and collection*, The Museum, Paoli (PA), c. 1977. Rochberg, Gene (ed.), *Drawings by Wharton Esherick*, Van Nostrand Reinhold, New York, c. 1978.
MUSEUMS AND GALLERIES:
PAOLI (Wharton Esherick Museum): over 200 works.

ESHIN SOZU. See **GENSHIN**

ESINGER, Adèle
Austrian, 19th century.
Born 1846, in Salzburg.
Painter. Genre scenes, landscapes.
Esinger studied under Gude and Hansch.

ESIPOV, Dmitri Aleksandrovich
Russian, 19th century.
Born 1854.
Painter. Landscapes.
Dmitri Aleksandrovich Esipov trained at the academy of art in St Petersburg which twice awarded him its silver medal. Works of his were included in the Academy's 1887 and 1888 exhibitions.

ESKENA, Edrik, or Ekenas
French, 17th century.
Died 1677.
Active in Paris.
Miniaturist.
In about 1636, Edrik Eskena was painter to Gaston d'Orléans.

ESKENAZI, Roger
French, 20th century.
Born 18 April 1923, in Sarcelles.
Painter.

Roger Eskenazi was a pupil of the École du Louvre. In 1941, he entered the studios of André Lhote and Fernand Léger. He received encouragement from Édouard Pignon and André Masson and took part in many group exhibitions in Paris: Salon des Moins de Trente Ans; Salon de l'Automne de la Libération in 1944; his first Salon de Mai in 1945 and others later; Salon Comparaisons as part of the group *Réalité Seconde* (*Second Reality*); regularly at the Salon des Réalités Nouvelles; in 1963 at the *École de Paris* (*Paris School*), and group exhibitions in the provinces and abroad. His first solo exhibition was held in Limoges in 1943, and this was followed by many others, including: 1972, Musée de la Culture, Créteil; 1977, Maison de la Culture, Amiens, and the Musée des Beaux-Arts, Caen; 1983, the Musée des Beaux-Arts, Nantes; 1985, Centre d'Art Contemporain, Rouen; 1989, Centre Culturel Français, Luxembourg; 1989, Théâtre Romain Rolland, Villejuif; 1992, 1994, L'Isle-Adam; 2002, Bibliothèque Municipale, Sisteron (Alpes-de-Haute-Provence).

From the start, Eskenazi's painting was apparently abstract, modulated in colour, with characteristic rhythms, but behind it lay observation of nature and the outside world. Eskenazi's need for this preliminary glance at reality, where feeling is born, is such that he himself indicates the subjects that have moved him, such as slopes, forests, lavender pickers, flocks, dogs, markets, abattoirs, wood-cutters, the choreography of Merce Cunningham, and sometimes even the big subjects that would formerly have inspired history painting: 1963 *Homage to Delacroix*, 1964 *The Invasion*, 1981 *Arrival of the Spaniards*, and 1982 *Grande progression de la rage*.

Although always Lyrical Abstract, Eskenazi's painting is marked by periodic variations in style: from 1948 the forms are very defined, with juxtaposed planes of colour, while after 1953 the forms overlap, passing from one colour to another, creating light and space, and in his mature work Eskenazi adopted a fluid and transparent technique, similar to that of watercolour, that is applied to a range of bright and luminous colour and animates the drawing it underpins. According to the artist, the swirls that develop relate to primordial states and suggest 'lands I would like to identify, where one could know oneself, where one could exist'.

BIBLIOGRAPHY:

Roger Eskenazi, exhibition catalogue, Musée des Beaux-Arts, Caen, 1977. *Roger Eskenazi*, exhibition catalogue, Musée des Beaux-Arts, Nantes, 1983. *Réalité Seconde*, group exhibition catalogue, Gal. d'Art contemporain, Chamalières, 1986. Brisset, Pierre, '*Roger Eskenazi*' in *L'Œil*, periodical, Paris, May 1991.

ESKENS, Martin
Flemish School, 16th century.
Died before 16 November 1569, in Mechelen.
Painter.

ESKESEN, Odgar Erik Frode
Danish, 19th century.
Born 21 April 1863, in Rudme, near Svendborg.
Painter. Portraits, landscapes.

Eskesen moved to Copenhagen in 1881 to try to make a living from art. He showed several of his sketches to G. S. Kröyer, who liked them and encouraged him, and in 1887 he was admitted to the artists' study school as a student, which he attended for three years. In 1891 he first showed at the Paris Salon, and from then on exhibited a series of landscapes, some at Charlottenborg, and others at particular exhibitions. The most important of these was *View of Dybböl*. In 1894, Eskesen painted a full-size portrait of *Lieutenant Colonel Dalgas* (offered to Askov University).

ESKEY, William A.
American, 20th century.
Born 21 August 1891, in Sistersville (West Virginia); died 1937, in North Hollywood (California).
Engraver (etching).

ESKILSSON, Per or Peter
Swedish, 19th century.
Born 1820, in Billeberga Socken; died 29 January 1872, in Bremö.
Painter. Genre scenes, figures.

Eskilsson was an NCO in the artillery, then a bookkeeper, before financial help from a friend enabled him to travel to Düsseldorf in 1853 to study under Tidemand. By 1859 Eskilsson had returned to Stockholm, and he became a member of the academy in 1866. His paintings focus on the humorous side of Swedish life.

AUCTION RECORDS:

MALMÖ, 2 May 1977, *The Pipe Smoker* (1856, oil on canvas, 19 x 15 ins / 48 x 38 cm) SEK 10,000. STOCKHOLM, 22 April 1981, *Old Man Cutting the Hair of a Child in a Courtyard* (1858, oil on canvas, 12 1/4 x 11 ins / 31 x 27 cm) SEK 19,000. STOCKHOLM, 30 Oct 1984, *Old Woman with a Man in an Interior* (oil on canvas, 20 1/2 x 19 3/4 ins / 52 x 50 cm) SEK 41,000. STOCKHOLM, 4 Nov 1986, *The End of the Meal* (oil on canvas, 9 3/4 x 13 1/2 ins / 25 x 34 cm) SEK 35,000. GÖTEBORG, 1 Oct 1988, *The Gardener's Work* (oil on canvas, 8 1/4 x 7 1/2 ins / 21 x 19 cm) SEK 11,500. STOCKHOLM, 15 Nov 1988, *Gröna Lund* (oil, 10 1/4 x 14 1/4 ins / 26 x 36 cm) SEK 38,000. STOCKHOLM, 16 May 1990, *Tasting Punch outside the Inn* (oil on canvas, 10 1/4 x 14 1/4 ins / 26 x 36 cm) SEK 26,000. LONDON, 17 May 1991, *Portrait* (oil on canvas, a pair, 14 1/4 x 18 ins / 36 x 45.5 cm) GBP 2,200. STOCKHOLM, 19 May 1992, *The White Tablecloth* (1867, oil on canvas, 11 x 9 ins / 28 x 23 cm) SEK 8,500. LUND, 23 April 1999, *Relating to the Life of People* (1867, oil on canvas, 14 x 18 ins / 35 x 45 cm) SEK 22,000. STOCKHOLM, 20 Dec 1999, *Interior Scene with Man Playing Cello* (1869, oil on canvas, 16 x 14 ins / 40 x 35 cm) SEK 18,000. STOCKHOLM, 29 May 2001, *Midsummer Celebrations* (oil on canvas, 27 x 35 ins / 68 x 90 cm) SEK 62,000. STOCKHOLM, 9 June 2001, *The Happy Drinking Party* (oil on canvas, 15 x 19 ins / 37 x 47 cm) SEK 25,000.

ESKRICH, Pierre, called Cruche, Vase or Du Vase or Krug
French, 16th century.
Born c. 1530, probably in Paris; died after 1590.
Painter, draughtsman, embroiderer.
School of Lyons.

Pierre was the son of Jacob Eskrich, a native of Freiburg-im-Brisgau and engraver who worked in Paris in the first quarter of the 16th century and whose real name seems to have been Krug ('jug' in German, hence his nickname). Pierre Eskrich must have arrived in Lyons in about 1548. In 1552, he was in Geneva, being granted the right to live there in 1552 and becoming a burgher in 1560. In 1562, he was living in great poverty and seeking assistance. In 1564, he made a plan or view of Geneva for Admiral de Coligny, and was invited to Lyons for a month by the Consulate to work on 'certain portraits and models' on the occasion of the entry of the king there. In 1565, he made Lyons his permanent home, describing himself in 1572 as 'painter and embroiderer to Monseigneur de Mandelot, the king's governor in Lyons'. In 1574, he painted the ship that was to bring Henri III home from Poland. He was still living in Lyons in 1590. His work is only known today because of a few woodcuts signed with one version of his name: *The Promised Land* (of Canaan), a map with a cartouche and figures, signed *Faciebat Peyrus Eskricheus. Lugduni 1566*, published, as were the two following works, in Honorati's Bible (Lyons 1585). These were:

The Land of Canaan Divided Between the Twelve Tribes of Israel, signed *Faciebat Petrus Eskrichius, 1566*; *The Israelites in the Desert*, signed *P. Eskricheus inventor*. Other works are: *Plan of the Town and Suburbs of Paris*, signed *Cruche* ('Jug'), a copy of an anonymous plan dated 1551 which appeared in B. Arnouller's *Premier livre des figures... des villes* of 1552; *Monument with Wooden Front Used as a Pyre for an Emperor's Funeral*, signed *Cruche* in C. Guichard's *Funérailles... et manière d'ensevelir des Romains* published by J. de Tournes of Lyons in 1581. It is also known, through archive documents, that Eskrich made the 16 plates of the *New Papal Map of the World* which was published in Geneva in 1566. Attributed to Eskrich are a later and rather different series of prints and, more certainly, the decorative engraved frames signed P. V. (Pierre Vase) in *Emblemata A. Alciali* and *French and Latin Hours*, both printed in Lyons in 1549 by Maci Bonhomme for G. Bovlile, as well as other works. It has been established that Eskrich is the anonymous artist known as Master P.V., also called Jean Monni. The woodcuts mentioned earlier, very different in style and execution, cannot be by the same hand, and although Eskrich is described as a 'carver of histories', this does not prove that he actually engraved. Perhaps he drew and signed, as the artist, the pieces that bear his name. However, it can be said that Eskrich was an illustrator working in Geneva and Lyons, that he drew with care, with a flexible and natural line, and that he was a minor artist, lacking personality and elegance but well able to imitate or copy contemporary masters.

ESKRIDGE, Robert Lee
American, 20th century.
Born 1891, in Philipsburg (Montana); died 1975.
Painter.

Robert Eskridge exhibited in Paris at the Salon des Artistes Français from 1925.

ESLOY
French, 17th century.
Sculptor (wood).

Esloy worked on the decoration of the apartments of Versailles and the Trianon from 1684 to 1689.

ESMAN, Herman Jean
Dutch, 19th century.
Painter.

Herman Jean Esman was the son of Johannes Esman.

ESMAN, Johannes
Dutch, 19th century.
Born 13 December 1793, in Hilversum.
Painter. Still-lifes.

Johannes Esman was the son and pupil of his father H. Esman, and the father of Herman Jean Esman.

ESMANN, Noels Erik
Danish, 20th century.
Born in Copenhagen.
Painter.

Esmann exhibited at the Salon d'Automne in Paris in 1931.

ESMEIN, Maurice Marcel Marie
French, 19th - 20th century.
Born 1888; died 4 February 1918, in Le Mont-St-Nom, on the battlefield.
Painter, watercolourist. Portraits, genre scenes, landscapes, still-lifes.

Maurice Marcel Marie Esmein was initially a medical student, but, influenced by his childhood friend, the painter and engraver Jean Buhot, he soon turned to art. He began in 1908 and 1910 by sketching during travels in Belgium and the Netherlands, and in 1912 set up a studio in the Rue des Ursulines, Paris. He exhibited at the Salon des Indépendants, Paris, in 1914. Several of his paintings were included in the exhibition of the works of artists killed in World War I, held by the Salon d'Automne in 1919. He painted mainly portraits, landscapes, still-lifes and circus scenes, in which he showed a mastery of Cubist composition. He also painted watercolours and wrote manuscript notes on art.

ESMENARD, Inès d'
French, 19th century.
Born 19th century, in Paris.
Painter. Genre scenes, portraits.

Inès d'Esmenard studied under Colson, Franque and Hollier. From 1814 to 1851 she exhibited mainly portraits at the Paris Salon and was awarded a second-class medal in 1819.

AUCTION RECORDS:
PARIS, 22 and 23 Dec 1924, *Bust of a Young Blonde Girl*, FRF 430.

ESMÉNARD, Nathalie d'
French, 19th century.
Born in Paris.
Painter. Genre scenes, flowers.

A pupil of Redouté, Nathalie d'Esménard exhibited at the Paris Salon between 1822 and 1834.

ESMERALDO, Servulo
Brazilian, 20th century.
Born 27 February 1929, in Crato.
Painter, engraver.
Kinetic Art.

Servulo Esmeraldo went to France in 1957 and frequented Friedlaender's studio. In addition to his engravings - often produced by stamping to create a simple relief that breaks up the monochrome quality of the plate - Esmeraldo also created curious objects that moved on contact with the hand. These were boxes made of transparent plastic inside which were glued minute squares of paper attached to small threads which began to move with the static electricity generated by rubbing. Esmeraldo took part in various exhibitions of kinetic art. His work is characterised by a great simplicity of conception and execution and his 'natural' approach which, in the context of kinetic art as a whole, gives him an endearing, poetic quality. He returned to live in Brazil in the mid-1970s.

AUCTION RECORDS:
NEW YORK, 22 May 1986, *Untitled* (varnished steel, 47 1/4 x 7 1/2 ins / 120.2 x 19.2 cm) USD 1,500.

ESMOND, Diane
French, 20th century.
Born in London.
Painter.

Diane Esmond was a pupil of Mac-Avoy and exhibited at the Salon des Artistes Français in 1935.

ESNAULT, Maurice
French, 19th - 20th century.
Born in the second half of the 19th century, in Marolles-les-Braults (Sarthe).
Painter. Urban landscapes, landscapes, flowers.

AUCTION RECORDS:
PARIS, 19 May 1930, *Landscape in Pontoise*, FRF 1,000. PARIS, 19 Feb 1932, *Poppies*, FRF 500.

ESNÉE-PERRIN, Marthe (Mme)
French, 19th century.
Born 1845, in Paris.
Painter. Landscapes.

A pupil of Mademoiselle Dautel and of Ségé, Marthe Esnée-Perrin sent works to the Paris Salon from 1870 to 1880. She is best known for her *Valley of the Old Mill*, *Minaret Path at Esnoh* and *Garden Gate*.

ESNEUX, Henri d'
Flemish School, 16th century.

Died 1598, in Liège.
Painter.
Henri d'Esneux was a pupil of Lambert Laubart and was already working around 1550.

ESNEUX, Joseph Thomas d'
Flemish, 18th century.
Active in Liège c. 1750.
Sculptor.
Flemish School.
Joseph Thomas d'Esneux was the pupil of Panhay de Rendeux.

ESNOAL
French, 20th century.
Painter.
There are references to works Esnoal sent to the Salon des Peintres de Montagne.

ESNOT, Claude
French, 16th century.
Active in Paris in 1586.
Painter.

ESNOUL, Paul
French, 20th century.
Born 1882, in Rennes; died 1960.
Painter. Landscapes, seascapes.
Born into a St Malo familly that had its origins in the 15th century, Paul Esnoul did not become a full-time painter until 1930. He took part in many group exhibitions in Paris and the provinces (Rouen, Boulogne-sur-Mer, Lyons, Lille, Lorient and Quimper). He exhibited several times at the Salon d'Automne and the Salon d'Hiver des Peintres de Montagne, and became a member of the Salon des Artistes Français.

Esnoul's painting on panels reflects his passionate love of the natural world, and above all of Brittany, with its islands, its fishing villages inhabited by the divinities of Celtic tales and legend, its fish auctions, the dangerous and harsh life of the fishermen who live there, and its coastline, which has been carved into and broken up by the power of the sea and the savagery of the winds. Mountains were another source of inspiration for him and his work also shows enclosed valleys, overhanging villages, and summits where the stone is lit by the natural rays of the 'fiery' snow.

BIBLIOGRAPHY:
'*Paul Esnoul*' in *La Gazette de l'Hôtel Drouot*, periodical, Paris, January 1990.

MUSEUMS AND GALLERIES:
COLOMBES - FALAISE - PARIS (Mus. de la Ville) - RENNES.

ESPADA, Manuel
Spanish, 18th - 19th century.
Active in Saragossa.
Sculptor.
In 1797, Manuel Espada was a student at the San Luis academy in Saragossa.

ESPAGNAT, Georges d'
French, 20th century.
Born 14 August 1870, in Paris; died 1950.
Painter, draughtsman, illustrator, engraver. Religious subjects, figures, nudes, genre scenes, still-lifes.
Murals.
Symbolism.
Groupe Libre Esthétique.
From the beginning of his career it was a constant concern of Georges d'Espagne to assert his originality. His studies at the École des Arts Décoratifs, Paris, did not last very long, for he wanted immediate independence and decided to follow courses in the private academies of Montparnasse. In about 1900, he became acquainted with Maurice Denis, Bonnard and Vuillard, and his collaboration with Denis led to a renewal of religious art in France.

In 1903, d'Espagne was one of the founders of the Salon d'Automne, and was appointed professor in charge of studios at the École des Beaux-Arts, Paris, in 1934. He illustrated a number of books: Rémy de Gourmont's *Oraisons mauvaises* (*Evil Prayers*) (1896), *Les Saintes du paradis* (*The Saints of Paradise*) (1898), *Simone* (1907), *Sixtine* (*Sistine*) (1922); Alphonse Daudet's *L'Immortel* (*The Immortal*) (1930); André Gide's *La Symphonie pastorale* (*The Pastoral Symphony*); Francis Jammes' *Chairières dans le ciel* (*Clearings in the Sky*) (1948).

D'Espagne belongs to the group of artists who made the *Courrier Français* so successful. The drawings of his which are published in it are strongly expressive and some bear comparison with the designs of the great Renaissance masters. He also contributed to *L'Image*. He often placed cheerful nudes in a landscape, reminding us that, though he moved away from the Fauves, he retained their freedom of colour and arabesque. He painted many portraits, including those of Albert André, André Barbier, Victor Boucher, Déodat de Séverac, Albert Marque, André Marty and Albert Roussel. He also painted mural decorations, including a wall for the Palais de la Découverte (1937), the ceiling of the Victor Hugo Room in the Palais du Luxembourg (1939), a decorative panel for the Palais de Justice, Toulouse (1941) and interior decorations for private houses. His landscapes are Impressionist in inspiration, and work for a certain sobriety, an intimacy, both in their composition - one, two or three sketched figures and large open spaces - and in the choice of colours and treatment with the special hazy brushstroke that marks his style.

D'Espagne took part in a number of annual Parisian exhibitions, including the Salon des Indépendants, the Salon de la Société Nationale des Beaux-Arts, the Salon d'Automne (from 1903 to 1949, except in special circumstances), the Salon de la Libre Ésthétique, Brussels (1899, 1901), the Berlin Secessionists (1940). He also exhibited at the first Salon de la Société de la Gravure sur Bois. Among other exhibitions were 1912, *Centenaire de l'art français* (*A century of French Art*), St Petersburg; 1916, Kunstverein, Winterthur; 1918, 1926, Galerie M. Bertheim, Paris; 1930, *Art français contemporain* (*Contemporary French Art*), Tokyo. Among posthumous exhibitions have been 2001, *La Femme en Provence et en Méditerranée* (*Women in Provence and the Mediterranean*), and Fondation Regards de Provence, Château de Borély, Marseilles.

Solo exhibitions of d'Espagne's work were held in 1898, 1900, 1903, 1906, 1908, 1911, Galerie Durand-Ruel, Paris; 1902, Galerie Durand-Ruel, New York; 1922, 1923, 1926, Galerie Druet, Paris; 1944, Galerie Sagot-le-Garrec and M. Cordier. Among retropectives and posthumous exhibitions have been 1951, tribute exhibition at the Salon d'Automne, Paris; 1987, Musée des Beaux-Arts et de la Dentelle, Alençon; 1996, Musée de Marly-le-Roi, Louveciennes; 2001, Espace St-Jean, Melun.

BIBLIOGRAPHY:
Durand-Ruel, *Georges d'Espagnat (1870-1950)*, Gal. Durand-Ruel, Paris, 1962. Lux, Aude, *Georges d'Espagnat: 1870-1950*, exhibition catalogue, Musée des Beaux-Arts et de la Dentelle, Alençon, 1987. Osterwalder, Marcus (ed.), *Dic-*

tionnaire des illustrateurs 1800-1914, Ides et Calendes, Neuchâtel, 1989. Lecomte, Georges/Jacquemond, Jean-Dominique, *Georges d'Espagnat*, La Bibliothèque des Arts, Paris, 1990.

MUSEUMS AND GALLERIES:

ALBI (Mus. Toulouse-Lautrec) - BAGNOLS-SUR-CÈZE (Mus. Albert-André) - BOSTON (MFA) - BRUSSELS (Mus. royaux des Beaux-Arts de Belgique) - CÉRET (Mus. municipal d'Art moderne) - CHICAGO (AI) - DOUAI (Mus. de la Chartreuse) - GENEVA (Petit Palais) - INDIANAPOLIS (MA): *A Tea Party*; *The Peaceful Day* - LE HAVRE (Mus. Malraux) - METZ (La Cour D'or) - MOSCOW (Pushkin MFA) - NANCY (MBA) - NANTES (MBA): *Nude Dressing* - NEW YORK (Metropolitan Mus. of Art) - NICE (MAH) - NICE (MBA Jules-Chéret) - PARIS (Bibliothèque-Mus. de l'Opéra) - PARIS (MAM): *Women Bathing* - PARIS (Mus. d'Orsay) - ROUEN (MBA) - SANTA BARBARA (MA): *Banks of the Seine, near the Bridge of Meulan* (no date, oil on canvas) - SÈTE (Mus. Paul Valéry) - ST-ÉTIENNE (Mus. d'Art et d'Industrie) - ST-TROPEZ (Mus. de l'Annonciade) - TOKYO (National Mus. of Western Art) - TOLEDO (MA).

AUCTION RECORDS:

PARIS, 6 March 1900, *Reading*, FRF 480. PARIS, 15 May 1901, *Tea*, FRF 1,080. PARIS, 31 May 1906, *Landscape, Southern France*, FRF 500. PARIS, 22 May 1907, *Children in a Garden*, FRF 1,500. PARIS, 6 June 1921, *Fishing Boat at Sea*, FRF 380. PARIS, 11 May 1925, *Young Woman in a Tricolour Cap*, FRF 1,000. PARIS, 21 Dec 1925, *Still-life*, FRF 1,050; *Young Woman Dressing*, FRF 1,010. PARIS, 21 Jan 1928, *Still-life with Fruit and Flowers*, FRF 1,350. PARIS, 4 July 1928, *Reclining Nude*, FRF 3,000. PARIS, 2 March 1929, *Young Girl Reading*, FRF 2,200. PARIS, 26 April 1929, *Woman Putting On her Stockings*, FRF 2,650. NEW YORK, 10 April 1930, *Sailing Race (Mansfield Ferry)*, USD 220. PARIS, 12 April 1936, *Young Girl with a Flute*, FRF 1,000. PARIS, 18 March 1938, *Bust Portrait of a Young Woman* (pastel) FRF 250. PARIS, 30 Oct 1940, *Nude with Flowers*, FRF 500. PARIS, 2 April 1941, *Vase of Flowers with Apples*, FRF 2,750. PARIS, 30 June 1941, *Child with a Balloon*, FRF 305. PARIS, 1 April 1942, *Young Girl in Pink*, FRF 1,400. PARIS, 10 June 1942, *The Quays*, FRF 2,700. PARIS, 6 May 1943, *Nude in a Blue Nightgown*, FRF 19,000. PARIS, 15 Dec 1943, *Woman Reading on a Divan*, FRF 21,000. PARIS, 31 Jan 1944, *The Parc Monceau*, FRF 10,000. PARIS, 3 May 1944, *Concarneau* (watercolour) FRF 2,400. PARIS, 24 Jan 1945, *The Model*, FRF 9,100. PARIS, 5 March 1945, *La loge* (drawing) FRF 2,700. PARIS, 9 April 1945, *Little Girl Sitting by a Lake*, FRF 10,000. PARIS, July 1946, *At the Salle Pleyel*, FRF 14,500. PARIS, 18 Nov 1946, *Still-life*, FRF 12,500. PARIS, 24 Feb 1947, *Still-life with Clock*, FRF 7,000. PARIS, 24 March 1947, *Fishing Port, Boat on Shore* (watercolour) FRF 6,200. PARIS, 19 March 1958, *Sailing Boats*, FRF 160,000. NEW YORK, 25 Jan 1961, *Fruit*, USD 1,100. GENEVA, 27 Nov 1965, *Woman and Child on the Seashore*, CHF 19,000. PARIS, 28 May 1969, *Women on the Seashore*, FRF 43,000. VERSAILLES, 26 Nov 1972, *Portrait of Thadée Nathanson*, FRF 60,000. PARIS, 5 June 1974, *Flowers in a Vase*, FRF 113,000. VERSAILLES, 2 June 1976, *Women Bathing* (oil on canvas, 51 1/2 x 63 3/4 ins / 130.5 x 162 cm) FRF 19,000. ROUEN, 21 June 1977, *Fishing Boats* (watercolour, 9 1/2 x 12 1/4 ins / 24 x 31 cm) FRF 5,000. PARIS, 7 May 1980, *Young Girl with Bust Uncovered* (three-crayon drawing/paper, 22 x 16 1/2 ins / 55 x 42 cm) FRF 5,100. PARIS, 14 Nov 1984, *The Beach* (oil on canvas, 17 x 24 ins / 43 x 61 cm) FRF 175,000; *Port of La Rochelle* (pen, pencil and watercolour, 9 x 11 1/2 ins / 22.5 x 29.5 cm) FRF 6,200. PARIS, 14 Dec 1984, *Young Woman in a Red Sweater* (watercolour, 6 3/4 x 8 ins / 17 x 20.5 cm) FRF 4,800. PARIS, 11 Dec 1985, *Mother and Child in a Garden* (watercolour, 9 x 10 1/4 ins / 23 x 26 cm) FRF 4,500. LA VARENNE-ST-HILAIRE, 20 June 1987, *Afternoon in the Garden* (oil/canvas, 25 1/2 x 43 1/4 ins / 65 x 110 cm) FRF 280,000. ARGENTEUIL, 20 Nov 1987, *Portait of a Young Girl* (oil on canvas, 22 x 18 ins / 56 x 46 cm) FRF 80,000. NEW YORK, 18 Feb 1988, *Two Young Girls on the Seashore* (oil on canvas, 35 x 39 1/4 ins / 89 x 100 cm) USD 27,500. PARIS, 14 March 1988, *Anenomes on a Small Table* (oil on canvas, 22 x 18 ins / 55 x 46 cm) FRF 47,500. PARIS, 22 June 1988, *Return from Fishing* (1905, oil on canvas, 25 1/2 x 32 ins / 65 x 81 cm) FRF 275,000. PARIS, 23 June 1988, *Young Woman Seated, Wearing a Check Dress* (oil on canvas, 16 x 13 ins / 40.5 x 33 cm) FRF 20,000; *Sailing Boats at Sea* (watercolour, 6 1/2 x 9 ins / 16.5 x 22 cm) FRF 18,500. NEW YORK, 6 Oct 1988, *Still-life with Flowers* (oil on canvas, 36 1/2 x 29 ins / 92.7 x 73.6 cm) USD 35,200. LONDON, 21 Oct 1988, *Two Children* (oil on canvas, 13 1/4 x 20 3/4 ins / 33.5 x 53 cm) GBP 4,180. PARIS, 14 Dec 1988, *Young Girl Taking a Bath* (oil on canvas, 39 1/4 x 25 1/2 ins / 100 x 65 cm) FRF 180,000. PARIS, 21 Dec 1988, *Young Girl with a Bunch of Flowers*. NEW YORK, 16 Feb 1989, *Still-life with Flowers and Fruit* (oil on canvas, 21 3/4 x 18 1/4 ins / 55.2 x 46.3 cm) USD 28,600. LONDON, 22 Feb 1989, *Bouquet of Flowers* (oil on canvas, 24 1/4 x 19 3/4 ins / 61.5 x 50 cm) GBP 14,850. PARIS, 22 March 1989, *Woman Dressing* (oil on canvas, 36 1/4 x 29 ins / 92 x 73.5 cm) FRF 460,000. PARIS, 9 April 1989, *Painting Session in a Park* (oil on canvas, 28 3/4 x 36 1/2 ins / 73 x 93 cm) FRF 650,000. PARIS, 13 April 1989, *Women under a Tree* (oil on canvas, 19 3/4 x 24 ins / 50 x 61 cm) FRF 88,000. MONACO, 3 May 1989, *Nude Arranging her Hair* (oil on canvas, 51 1/4 x 33 3/4 ins / 130 x 86 cm) FRF 366,300; *Mademoiselle Jeanne, Milliner* (oil on canvas, 45 3/4 x 29 ins / 116.5 x 73.5 cm) FRF 777,000. NEW YORK, 11 May 1989, *Landscape in Cagnes* (oil on canvas, 25 3/4 x 31 3/4 ins / 65.4 x 80.7 cm) USD 77,000. LE TOUQUET, 14 May 1989, *Bust Portrait of a Nude* (oil on canvas, 18 1/2 x 15 ins / 47 x 38 cm) FRF 72,000. PARIS, 11 Oct 1989, *Wide-brimmed Hat, Portrait of a Young Girl* (oil on canvas, 39 1/4 x 31 1/2 ins / 100 x 80 cm) FRF 540,000. NEW YORK, 18 Oct 1989, *Woman Playing Patience* (oil on canvas, 23 1/2 x 28 3/4 ins / 60 x 73 cm) USD 110,000. NEW YORK, 15 Nov 1989, *Women with a Parrot* (1903, oil on canvas, 64 x 51 1/2 ins / 162.5 x 130.8 cm) USD 198,000. PARIS, 22 Nov 1989, *Vases of Flowers* (oil on canvas, 25 1/2 x 21 1/4 ins / 65 x 54 cm) FRF 170,000. CALAIS, 10 Dec 1989, *White Cat* (oil on canvas, 29 1/4 x 36 1/2 ins / 74 x 93 cm) FRF 350,000. NEW YORK, 26 Feb 1990, *Two Vases of Flowers* (oil on jute canvas, 28 3/4 x 36 1/2 ins / 73.3 x 92.4 cm) USD 60,500. PARIS, 3 April 1990, *Port* (watercolour, 9 x 11 3/4 ins / 23 x 30 cm) FRF 35,500. LONDON, 4 April 1990, *The Tide at Aubergeville* (oil on canvas, 27 3/4 x 36 1/4 ins / 70.5 x 92 cm) GBP 38,500. PARIS, 26 April 1990, *On the Beach* (oil on canvas, 13 x 16 1/4 ins / 33 x 41 cm) FRF 90,000. NEW YORK, 18 May 1990, *Children Playing* (oil on canvas, triptych, centre panel 57 x 17 1/2 ins / 144.8 x 44.4 cm, each side panel 47 x 17 1/2 ins/119.4 x 44.4 cm) USD 132,000. PARIS, 30 May 1990, *Young Girls with Baskets* (oil on canvas, 39 1/4 x 32 ins / 100 x 81 cm) FRF 435,000. LONDON, 26 June 1990, *Bouquet of Flowers* (oil on canvas, 28 3/4 x 23 1/2 ins / 73 x 60 cm) GBP 57,200. NEW YORK, 2 Oct 1990, *Children in a Park* (1899, oil on canvas, 32 1/4 x 39 1/4 ins / 81.6 x 100 cm) USD 154,000. LE TOUQUET, 11 Nov 1990, *Young Woman Dressing* (oil on canvas, 36 1/4 x 28 3/4 ins / 92 x 73 cm) FRF 410, 000. NEW YORK, 15 Feb 1991, *Hyacinths and a Bunch of Flowers* (oil on canvas, 32 x 25 3/4 ins / 81.3 x 65.4 cm) USD 27,500. NEW YORK, 25 Feb 1992, *House in St-Véran* (oil on canvas, 23 3/4 x 29 ins / 60.3 x 73.6 cm) USD 33,000. NEW YORK, 23-25 Feb 1993, *Vase of Flowers* (oil on canvas, 32 x 26 ins / 81 x 65.1 cm) USD 19,550. PARIS, 6 April 1993, *Still-life with Bunch of Flowers* (oil on panel, 16 1/4 x 12 1/2 ins / 41 x 32 cm) FRF 29,000. NEW YORK, 13 May 1993, *View of Triel in Spring* (oil on canvas, 23 1/2 x 28 3/4 ins / 59.7 x 73 cm) USD 21,850. CALAIS, 4 July 1993, *Afternoon in the Garden* (watercolour, 6 3/4 x 9 ins / 17 x 22 cm) FRF 13,500. LONDON, 13 Oct 1993, *Cagnes Seen from St-Véran* (oil on canvas, 23 1/2 x 28 3/4 ins / 60 x 73 cm) GBP 9,200. DEAUVILLE, 13 Nov 1993, *Woman Bathing* (oil on canvas, 24 x 39 1/4 ins / 61 x 100 cm) FRF 191,000. NEW YORK, 12 May 1994,

Walk by the Sea (oil on canvas, 15 x 21 3/4 ins / 38.1 x 55.2 cm) USD 61,900. Paris, 15 June 1994, *Women and Children Playing in a Garden* (oil on canvas, 130 x 56 ins / 330 x 142 cm) FRF 380,000. London, 29 June 1994, *Hyacinths and Bunch of Flowers* (oil on canvas, 32 x 25 3/4 ins / 81.3 x 65.4 cm) GBP 14,375. Le Touquet, 21 May 1995, *Spring in Provence* (oil on canvas, 59 3/4 x 63 3/4 ins / 152 x 162 cm) FRF 112,000. New York, 9 Nov 1995, *Reading in the Garden* (1898, oil on canvas, 55 1/2 x 42 ins / 141 x 106.7 cm) USD 54,625. Paris, 13 June 1996, *Fishermen at Sea* (c. 1905, oil on canvas, 23 1/2 x 28 3/4 ins / 60 x 73 cm) FRF 130,000. New York, 9 Oct 1996, *Reading in the Garden* (oil on canvas, 29 x 36 1/4 ins / 73.7 x 92.1 cm) USD 51,750; *Vase of Flowers and Books on a Table* (oil on canvas, 24 x 19 1/2 ins / 61 x 49.5 cm) USD 25,300. New York, 12 Nov 1996, *Bunch of Flowers* (oil on canvas, 28 3/4 x 23 1/2 ins / 73 x 60 cm) USD 9,200. London, 3 Dec 1996, *Fishermen with Rods* (oil on canvas, 38 1/4 x 51 1/4 ins / 97 x 130 cm) GBP 47,700. Paris, 8 Dec 1996, *Woman and Children under the Trees* (oil on canvas, 32 x 39 1/4 ins / 81 x 100 cm) FRF 190,000. Paris, 12 March 1997, *Young Girl Seated* (c. 1908, oil on canvas, 28 3/4 x 21 1/4 ins / 73 x 54 cm) FFR 130, 000. Tel Aviv, 26 April 1997, *Vase of Flowers* (oil on canvas, 18 x 15 ins / 46 x 38.2 cm) USD 6,900. Paris, 5 June 1997, *Woman Bathing* (oil on canvas, 76 3/4 x 51 1/4 ins / 195 x 130 cm) FRF 150,000. Paris, 6 June 1997, *Fruit, a Bottle and a Plate* (oil on canvas, 15 x 18 ins / 38 x 46 cm) FRF 16,000. London, 25 June 1997, *Hammock* (1906, oil on canvas, 25 3/4 x 21 1/4 ins / 65.5 x 54 cm) GBP 17,250. New York, 13 Nov 1997, *Children Playing* (oil on canvas, triptych, central panel 57 1/2 x 17 1/2 ins / 146.1 x 44.5 cm and each side panel 47 x 17 1/2 ins/119.4 x 44.5 cm) USD 34,500. Paris, 5 Dec 1997, *Still-life with Flowers* (oil on canvas, 36 1/4 x 28 3/4 ins / 92 x 73 cm) FRF 100,000. Paris, 1 April 1998, *Anenomes and Curtain* (oil on canvas, 22 x 18 1/2 ins / 56 x 47 cm) FRF 37,000. Paris, 8 April 1998, *Nude* (oil on canvas, 15 x 22 ins / 38 x 55 cm) FRF 24,000.

ESPALARGUES, Pedro

Spanish, 15th century.
Born c. 1490; died 1527.
Active in Molins de Rei and Lérida at the end of the 15th century.
Painter. Religious subjects.

Pedro Espalargues made an inscription on an altarpiece, part of which is in the Hispanic Society of America, New York and part in the Johnson Collection of the Philadelphia Museum of Art.

Bibliography:

Rathfon Post, Chandler, *A History of Spanish Painting*, Harvard University Press, Cambridge (MA), 1930-1966.

Museums and Galleries:

New York (Hispanic Society of America): *Altarpiece* (1490, fragment) - Philadelphia (MA, Johnson Collection).

Auction records:

Paris, 31 March 1995, *The Annunciation* (tempera/panel with gilt background, 56 1/4 x 29 1/2 ins / 143 x 75 cm) FRF 110,000. Paris, 13 June 1997, *St Michael and St Nicaise; St Fabian and St Sebastian* (panel, a pair, 18 1/2 x 21 1/4 ins / 47 x 54 cm) FRF 20,000. Amsterdam, 10 Nov 1997, *Crucifixion* (oil on panel, 40 3/4 x 32 1/4 ins / 103.8 x 81.8 cm) NLG 40,362.

ESPALIU, Pepe

Spanish, 20th century.
Born 1955, in Cordova; died 1993.
Also active in France.
Painter, draughtsman, sculptor, installation artist.

Pepe Espaliu lives in Seville and Paris. In Espaliu's work, words, concepts, signs and subject are used expressively to focus upon and form the 'corpus' of an uncapturable body. This body - which can be the object of much suffering, torment and injury - is only barely represented in Espaliu's work. Exploring the eternal contradictions between body and soul, matter and spirit, the perishable and the eternal, and formal and spiritual beauty, his installations make references that are private, uncontrollable and intimate. The objects he uses include pieces of leather, ropes equipped with handles, bells, palanquins, oval and undulating forms and figurative representations, such as heads and the lines of bending bodies. All these signs function through analogy to the body, which - as a key concept in Espaliu's work - becomes a metaphor for an entire system. Espaliu contracted AIDS, and, after 1992, his work becomes a more direct expression of his awareness of death. These are works in which the image of the body appears to have given way to intuition or, more generally, to the spirit. He sometimes works in collaboration with Guillermo Paneque. The two artists started out by founding a magazine entitled *Figura*, in which they explained their convictions, their choices and their critical attitude towards an artistic policy that they held to be too mercenary.

He has taken part in several group exhibitions, including: in 1986, *New Trends in Spanish Art* at the Brompton Gallery, London; in 1986, *4 Artists from Seville*, Amsterdam; in 1987, *Dynamiques et Interrogations* at the ARC (Art Research Confrontation at the Musée d'Art Contemporain de la Ville), Paris; in 1988, *Invitational* at the Curt Marcus Gallery, New York; in 1989 *Promises, Promises* at the Serpentine Gallery, London; and, in 1990, at the Venice Biennale. He has also held solo exhibitions of his work: in 1989, in Amsterdam and New York; and, in 1990, in Madrid.

Bibliography:

Aliaga, Juan Vicente, '*Pepe Espaliu, le corps insaisissable*' in *Art Press* n° 150, periodical, Paris, September 1990.

ESPALTER Y RULL, Joaquim

Spanish, 19th century.
Born 30 November 1809, in Sitges, near Barcelona; died 3 January 1880, in Madrid.
Painter. History painting, religious subjects, portraits.
Nazarenes group.

Joaquim Espalter y Rull studied in Paris under Baron Gros. In 1843 he was made a member of the Real Academia de San Fernando in Madrid and went on to become a teacher of painting and sculpture at the college. He travelled in Italy and Germany and exhibited regularly at exhibitions in Madrid. He also took part in the Paris Expositions Universelles of 1855 and 1867 and was awarded the cross of the order of Isabel the Catholic.

With Clavé, Espalter y Rull was one of the founders and leaders of the Nazarene group of Barcelona.

Museums and Galleries:

Madrid (Prado): *Moses Carried into Heaven; Samson Brandishing the Ass's Jaw; St John the Baptist.*

Auction records:

Madrid, 24 Jan 1991, *Portrait of Manuel and Matilde Alvarez Amoros* (1853, oil on canvas, 55 x 31 1/2 ins / 140 x 80 cm) ESP 1,680,000.

ESPANADA, Esteban

Spanish, 17th century.
Born 1626, in Altura.
Painter.

Esteban Espanada lived and worked in Valencia.

E Espanada.

ESPAÑOL, Gregorio

Spanish, 16th - 17th century.
Born in Cisneros (Leon).
Sculptor (wood).

Gregorio Espanol worked for the Cathedral of Santiago de Compostela in 1606.

ESPARBÈS, Jean d'
French, 20th century.
Born 1898, in Verneuil-sur-Seine; died 1968, in Verneuil-sur-Seine.
Painter. Genre scenes.

Jean d'Esparbès' father was the author of *Légende de l'aigle* (*The Legend of the Eagle*) and curator of paintings at the Palais de Fontainebleau. He exhibited regularly at the Salon d'Automne, of which he became a member. In 2002, he was represented in the exhibition *Marcel Aymé & les peintres* (*Marcel Aymé and the Painters*), held at the Galerie Roussard, Paris. He was one of the heads of the Montmartre School, and as a driving force in the fêtes of the old Butte de Montmartre he enjoyed conjuring up popular or legendary scenes.

AUCTION RECORDS:
PARIS, 2 July 1926, *Roundabout Horses,* FRF 260. PARIS, 16 March 1929, *Man Possessed,* FRF 1,000. PARIS, 6 April 1936, *Marriage in Robinson,* FRF 60. PARIS, 15 March 1945, *Young Woman and Mask,* FRF 7,100. GENEVA, 8 June 1972, *Theatre,* FRF 2,750. VERSAILLES, 4 April 1976, *Two-sided Mirror* (1927-1928, oil on canvas, 46 x 34 3/4 ins / 116 x 88.5 cm) FRF 3,000. PARIS, 29 June 1981, *Harlequin Playing the Guitar* (oil on canvas, 13 3/4 x 22 ins / 35 x 55 cm) FRF 10,500. PARIS, 16 Dec 1983, *Last Fête* (oil on canvas, 32 x 39 1/4 ins / 81 x 100 cm) FRF 8,100. PARIS, 23 June 1987, *The Muse's Inspiration* (oil on canvas, 23 1/2 x 28 3/4 ins / 60 x 73 cm) FRF 22,000. PARIS, 16 May 1988, *Child Approaching its Destiny* (oil on canvas, 19 x 21 1/4 ins / 48 x 54 cm) FRF 8,000. PARIS, 30 May 1988, *Procession* (oil on canvas, 25 1/2 x 21 1/4 ins / 65 x 54 cm) FRF 10,000. PARIS, 22 Nov 1988, *Rainy Street with Figures* (oil on canvas, 24 x 19 3/4 ins / 61 x 50 cm) FRF 9,000. PARIS, 22 Jan 1990, *Mothering the Doll* (oil on canvas, 22 x 17 3/4 ins / 55 x 45 cm) FRF 14,000. PARIS, 6 Oct 1990, *Marriage Feast* (oil on canvas, 18 x 22 ins / 46 x 55 cm) FRF 8,000. RHEIMS, 21 April 1991, *Mask Decorator* (oil on canvas, 24 x 19 3/4 ins / 61 x 50 cm) FRF 20,500. PARIS, 4 March 1992, *Chess Player* (oil on canvas, 25 3/4 x 21 1/4 ins / 65.5 x 54 cm) FRF 10,000. PARIS, 24 March 1995, *Pair of Musicians* (oil on canvas, 28 3/4 x 23 1/2 ins / 73 x 60 cm) FRF 6,500. PARIS, 8 Dec 1997, *Boxing* (oil on canvas, 25 1/4 x 21 1/4 ins / 64 x 54 cm) FRF 6,500.

ESPARBES, Louis
French, 19th century.
Born 5 March 1827, in Toulouse.
Sculptor.

In 1870 Louis Esparbes sent an allegorical bust in low relief to the Paris Salon.

ESPARZA ABAD, Lino
Spanish, 19th century.
Born 2 August 1842, in Valencia; died April 1889, in Valencia.
Sculptor.

Lino Esparza Abad studied at the fine arts academy in Valencia. He produced a number of busts of well-known figures.

ESPAYARTE, Rodrigo de
Spanish, 16th century.
Active in Toledo c. 1500.
Sculptor.

Rodrigo de Espayarte worked on the altarpiece of *St Ildefonsus* in the cathedral at Toledo.

ESPEJO, Antonio de
Spanish, 18th century.
Active in Seville in 1741.
Painter.

ESPÉJO, Jean
French, 20th century.
Painter. Scenes with figures.

AUCTION RECORDS:
PARIS, 23 Oct 1987, *Coach Arriving* (oil on canvas, 11 x 9 ins / 27 x 22 cm) FRF 8,000. PARIS, 6 May 1988, *Pig Seller* (oil on canvas, 11 x 9 ins / 27 x 22 cm) FRF 8,200. PARIS, 12 June 1988, *Boxers* (oil on canvas, 9 x 11 ins / 22 x 27 cm) FRF 5,000. VERSAILLES, 23 Oct 1988, *Grocer* (oil on canvas, 9 x 11 ins / 22 x 27 cm) FRF 7,600. VERSAILLES, 6 Nov 1988, *Slide* (oil on canvas, 11 x 9 ins / 27 x 22 cm) FRF 8,500. VERSAILLES, 11 Jan 1989, *Game of Skittles* (oil on canvas, 11 x 9 ins / 27 x 22 cm) FRF 8,000. STRASBOURG, 29 Nov 1989, *Winter Morning* (oil on canvas, 9 x 11 ins / 22 x 27 cm) FRF 11,000. NEUILLY, 12 Dec 1993, *Game of Pétanque* (oil on canvas, 23 1/2 x 32 ins / 60 x 81 cm) FRF 10,200.

ESPEJO SAAVEDRA Y AGUILAR, Isidro
Spanish, 19th century.
Born 15 May 1788, in Cordova; died 2 April 1876, in Cordova.
Painter, goldsmith.

Isidro Espejo Saavedra y Aguilar was a pupil of Diego Monroy. He worked in particular for the church of S Jago in Cordova.

ESPELOSIN, Édouard F. d'
French, 19th - 20th century.
Born 2 April 1863, in Tours.
Painter.

Édouard F. d'Espelosin exhibited at the Salon of the Société des Artistes Français from 1897, becoming a member in 1902.

ESPEN, C. F. van
Belgian, 19th century.
Born in Herent, near Louvain.
Active from 1836.
Painter. Landscapes, animals.

ESPEN, Félix van
Belgian, 20th century.
Born 1928, in Frasnes-lez-Couvin.
Painter. Religious subjects. Murals, designs for stained glass.

Van Espen was a student at the Académie des Beaux-Arts in Namur and at the Institut Supérieur in La Cambre. He was a founder member of the Axe 59 (Axis 59) and Axe 66 (Axis 66) groups. He lives and works in St-Servais, Namur.

ESPENAN-CRESSON, Marguerite
French, 19th century.
Born 1867, in Agen.
Painter.

A pupil of Barrias, Marguerite Espenan-Cresson made her début at the Salon of the Société des Artistes Français in 1889. Her best pastels are sometimes reminiscent of those of Degas.

ESPERANDEU, Roger
Spanish, 15th century.
Active in Valencia in 1419.
Painter.

ESPERCIEUX, Jean Joseph
French, 18th - 19th century.
Born 22 July 1757, in Marseilles; died 6 May 1840, in Paris.
Sculptor.

Jean Joseph Espercieux had no masters, but took pleasure in saying that he was the pupil of those who had given him good advice. He exhibited in the Salon de Paris between 1793 and 1836. For the king he executed *Philoctetes Prey to his Sorrow,* a statue in marble, and also made the statue of *Louis XVI* for the court of the Palais de Versailles. His other works include: *Peace,* a statue commissioned by the State,

Bust of Cardinal Maury, Envy Expiring on Racine's Tomb, marble, and *Bust of Lemercier, of the Académie Française.*
MUSEUMS AND GALLERIES:
AVIGNON: *Greek Woman Preparing to Enter the Bath* - COMPIÈGNE: *Philoctetes* - MARSEILLES: *Philoctetes Wounded; Young Bather; Nymph Getting Out of the Bath* - PARIS (Louvre): *Victory and Peace* - VERSAILLES: *Sulkowski, General Bonaparte's Aide-de-camp; François Roussel, Major General.*

ESPERLANC, Thierry
French, 15th century.
Born in Delft; died c. 1455, in Dijon.
Glass painter.
Thierry Esperlanc worked for the dukes of Burgundy, John the Fearless and Philip the Good.

ESPERLING, Joseph, or Esperlin, Esper
Swiss, 18th century.
Born 1707, in Ingoldingen, near Biberach; died probably in 1775, in Beromünster.
Painter, fresco artist, draughtsman. Religious subjects, portraits, architectural views, animals.
Esperling worked for private individuals and for the churches in and around Basel. He was living in Beromünster around 1774.

Esperling signed many of his paintings in Solothurn 'Joseph Esper', which subsequently caused his name to be split.
MUSEUMS AND GALLERIES:
SOLOTHURN (Cathedral of St Urs and Victor): paintings and frescoes; *Four Biblical Sacrifices.*
AUCTION RECORDS:
VIENNA, 17 Sept 1968, *Young Girl with Basket of Flowers,* ATS 50,000. BERN, 28 May 1985, *Flight to Egypt* (oil on canvas, 26 1/4 x 35 1/2in/66.5 x 90cm) CHF 14,000. BERN, 30 April 1988, *Roses, Carnations and Lilies in an Antique Vase* (oil on canvas) CHF 11,000. LYONS, 9 Oct 1990, *Adoration of the Magi; Adoration of the Shepherds* (oil on canvas, a pair, 23 1/2 x 16 1/2in/60 x 42cm) FRF 225,000. ZURICH, 14 April 1997, *Portrait of a Young Girl* (1761, oil on canvas, 42 1/4 x 33 3/4in/107 x 86cm) CHF 10,925. FRANKFURT, 2 Sept 2000, *Raising of Lazarus* (oil on canvas, 33 x 26 ins / 83 x 67 cm) DEM 8,000.

ESPERSTEDT, August Wilhelm
German, 19th century.
Born 1814.
Active in Berlin.
Painter. History painting, genre scenes.
A pupil of Wach, Esperstedt exhibited in Berlin from 1834.

ESPI, Francisco
Spanish, 17th century.
Active in Valencia in 1608.
Painter.
Francisco Espi worked for Valencia Cathedral.

ESPIE, Yvonne
French, 20th century.
Born in St-Maur-des-Fossés.
Painter.
Yvonne Espie, a pupil of Humbert and R. Renard, first exhibited at the Salon des Artistes Français in 1923.

ESPILIT, Jean-Louis
French, 20th century.
Born 9 November 1943, in Ginestas (Aude).
Painter, collage artist, engraver.
Jean-Louis Espilit lives and works in Paris. He composes his works by arranging non-geometrical shapes which, in the case of his collages, are cut out of lithographic paper. His abstract style is sensitive and delicate.

Espilit has had solo shows including: Galerie Forum, Paris (1974); Galerie Philippe Frégnac, Paris (1976); Nieuwe Weg Gallery, Doorn, Netherlands (1979, 1982, 1984, 1986); Galerie Olivier Nouvellet, Paris (1988); and Galerie Climats, Paris (1989, 1990, 1992). He was awarded the Prix Félix Fénéon in 1978 and the Prix Lubian for painting in 1980.
MUSEUMS AND GALLERIES:
BRIVE-LA-GAILLARDE (Musée Labenche) - PARIS (FNAC) - PARIS (MAMVP).

ESPINA
Spanish, 16th century.
Active in Granada in the middle of the 16th century.
Sculptor (wood).
Espina collaborated with Diego de Siloe on the decoration of Granada Cathedral.

ESPINA Y CAPO, Juan
Spanish, 19th - 20th century.
Born 1848, in Madrid; died 15 December 1933, in Madrid.
Painter, engraver. Landscapes, seascapes.
Juan Espina y Capo abandoned his secondary education to take up drawing and painting. At the age of 15 he made a trip to Paris to study the art trends of the period. On his return to Madrid he joined the studio of the Belgian painter Carlos de Haes who taught him painting, sculpture and engraving. In 1872 he was awarded a bursary to study in Rome and remained there for three years, returning to Paris for a time before eventually settling in Madrid. He became a member and later, in 1928, first secretary of the Association of Painters and Sculptors of Madrid. He also promoted the first Autumn Salon in Madrid.

Throughout his life, Espina y Capo was involved in hard and sometimes violent political struggles in support of the popular cause. However, this political engagement is not found in his works, an oasis of detachment and tranquillity. His paintings and engravings represent mainly Spanish landscapes and show skill in draughtsmanship and love of line work. Espina y Capo's works are reminiscent of Constable's landscapes with their Romantic spirit, closeness to nature, trees, roads, leaves often accompanied by cloud-filled skies and a pervasive sense of inaccessibility. His best-known works are *The Countryside at Torrelodones, The Last Reflection* and *Summer Clouds.*

From 1876 to 1932 he took part in nearly all the exhibitions of the national fine arts society of Madrid. He was also the Spanish representative at the international exhibitions of Berlin (1886), Vienna (1892) and Chicago (1893) and represented Spain at exhibitions in Sweden and Norway in 1890. In 1920 a special event was organised to acknowledge his role in the art world.

In 1881 he was awarded a bronze medal in Madrid, in 1884 and 1895 a silver medal and in 1885 a first class diploma at the exhibition of the Writers' and Artists' Association. He continued to produce engravings and etchings and received awards in this field including a gold medal in 1926.
BIBLIOGRAPHY:
Arnáiz, José Manuel/López Jiménez, Javier/Merchán Díaz, Manuel (ed.), *Cien años de pintura en Espana y Portugal (1830-1930),* Antiqvaria, Madrid, 1988 (One Hundred Years of Painting in Spain and Portugal (1830-1930)).
MUSEUMS AND GALLERIES:
MADRID (Prado): *Memory of Brittany; Light Effect, Madrid; After the Storm; Landscape.*
AUCTION RECORDS:
MADRID, 20 Dec 1976, *Twilight* (oil on canvas, 50 3/4 x 37 1/2 ins / 129 x 95 cm) ESP 105,000. MADRID, 26 May 1987, *House at the Foot of a Mountain* (oil on canvas, 23 1/4 x 14 3/4 ins / 59 x 37.5 cm) ESP 225,000.

ESPINABETE, Felipe
Spanish, 18th century.
Active in Valladolid.
Sculptor (wood).

ESPINADAL, Pedro
Spanish, 17th century.
Active in Valladolid.
Sculptor.

ESPINAL, Gregorio de
French, 18th century.
Died 1746, in Seville.
Painter.
Gregorio d'Espinal was the father of Juan.

ESPINAL, Isidro
Spanish, 18th century.
Born c. 1700, in San Juan de la Plana.
Sculptor.
Isidro Espinal worked in the Tarragona area.

ESPINAL, Juan de
Spanish, 18th century.
Born 1714, in Seville; died 8 December 1783, in Seville.
Painter, fresco artist. Religious subjects, allegorical subjects.
After spending some time studying under his father, Gregorio Espinal, Juan de Espinal joined the school of Domingo Martinez and eventually married Martinez's daughter. He was appointed director of the *Tres Nobles Artes* ('Three Noble Arts') academy in Seville, founded by Ceán Bermúdez and other art lovers. Bermúdez recounts that Espinal was more talented than any of his contemporaries and that he would have been the finest painter in Seville, following on from Murillo, were it not for the incurable laziness that prevented him putting his gifts to good use. After visiting Madrid towards the end of his life, Espinal realised with sadness that he had wasted his life.

However, abundant examples of his work survive. He is known in particular for the 26 paintings of *Scenes from the Life of St Jerome*, which he painted between 1770 and 1780 for the monastery of S Geronimo de Buenavista; the majority of these are now in the Seville museum. Between 1770 and 1780 he produced the architectural trompe l'œil tempera decorations of the dome over the stairs at the bishop's palace, as well as some fifteen paintings for the staircase. Espinal also painted frescoes in the church of the S Salvador college. Starting from a style close to that of Murillo, he went on to show the influence of Valdés Leal before finally moving in the direction of a more Rococo approach.

J de Espinal.

MUSEUMS AND GALLERIES:
MADRID (Real Academia de Bellas Artes de San Fernando): *Allegory of Seville Painting* - SEVILLE: *Scene from the Life of St Jerome*.

ESPINASSE, B.
French, 18th century.
Active at the end of the 18th century.
Draughtsman.
J.B. Simonet engraved *First Martyrs for Freedom* after Espinasse.

ESPINASSE, Jean-Claude
French, 20th century.
Born 12 April 1943, in Montpellier.
Painter, screen printer, illustrator. Nudes, portraits, scenes with figures, landscapes.
Jean-Claude Espinasse was a student of Camille Descossy and Georges Dezeuze at the École des Beaux-Arts in Montpellier from 1959 to 1961. He approaches his work boldly, laying the paint on thickly and using a range of strong colours. He likes to treat subjects typical of the region, such as the wine harvest, or rugby matches. He has exhibited at collective shows in his region, Provence and the Côte d'Azur, gaining distinctions and prizes. He has shown collections of his works in solo exhibitions since 1960, especially in Montpellier and Béziers.

ESPINASSE, Léon
French, 20th century.
Born c. 1870, in Paris.
Painter. Still-lifes.
Léon Espinasse, a pupil of Jules Lefebvre and Benjamin-Constant, first exhibited at the Salon des Artistes Français in 1896. His preferred subjects were still-lifes painted against mainly neutral backgrounds and without unnecessary details.

ESPINASSE, Raymond
French, 20th century.
Born 8 September 1897, in Toulouse; died 1985.
Painter.
Raymond Espinasse was a professor at the École des Beaux-Arts, Toulouse, and exhibited in Paris at the Salons des Indépendants, d'Automne and des Tuileries.
MUSEUMS AND GALLERIES:
CHOLET - GRENOBLE - PERPIGNAN - TOULOUSE.
AUCTION RECORDS:
TOULOUSE, 15 Dec 1982, *Road to Méreuil* (oil on canvas, 18 x 24 ins / 46 x 61 cm) FRF 6,000. TOULOUSE, 13 June 1985, *Desnoyer Painting in his Studio with Suza* (1952, oil on canvas, 35 3/4 x 24 3/4 ins / 91 x 63 cm) FRF 9,000. PARIS, 26 Feb 1992, *Cactus on a Window Sill* (oil on canvas, 24 x 19 3/4 ins / 61 x 50 cm) FRF 3,200.

ESPINASSY, Auguste Alexandre d'
French, 19th century.
Born in Trévoux.
Painter. Battles.
A pupil of Regnault, Auguste Alexandre d'Espinassy settled in Paris, where, from 1842 to 1853, he exhibited four paintings depicting the battles of the First French Empire (1804-1814), two of which were painted in collaboration with Jung.
MUSEUMS AND GALLERIES:
VERSAILLES (Mus.): *Battle of Marchiennes*; *Battle of Arlon*.

ESPINDOLA, Humberto
Brazilian, 20th century.
Born 1943.
Painter, installation artist.
Humberto Espindola is associated with the Brazilian art movement that arose out of Tropicalism and dominated the artistic scene from 1967 to 1969; he is also associated with *Nova Objetividade* (*New Objectivity*), an exhibition which took place in 1967 at the Museu de Arte Moderna in Rio de Janeiro. Tropicalism was not only present and alive in thematic and figurative painting, but also in music with artists such as Caetano, Veloso and Gilberto Gil, as well as in cinema.

Espindola worked in Mato Grosso and produced a series entitled *Bovinocultural* in this region. Originally two-dimensional, his painting took on a third dimension which led eventually to monumental installations.

ESPINE DE LA FRENIÈRE, Jean Baptiste François
French, 18th century.
Baptised 15 January 1727 in Saint-Malo; died 16 January 1799, in Geneva.
Enameller.
Jean Baptiste Espine de la Frenière took refuge in Geneva for religious reasons and became a citizen in 1766.

ESPINELVES, Master of. See **MASTERS**

ESPINET, Caroline (Mme)
French, 19th century.

Born 1844, in Lyons; died 1910, in Lorient (Brittany).
Active in Lorient (Brittany).
Painter.

Caroline Espinet was a pupil of the seascape painter Ernest Coroller, and of H. Lazerges. She was the sister of Élodie de la Villette. Espinet exhibited seascapes of Brittany and Algeria in Paris from 1875 to 1887. Although she also painted woods, marshland, paths and rustic houses, her favoured motifs were views of coasts, ships and burning shipwrecks, which she handled with an eye for rendering the atmosphere. She gradually abandoned the precise line of her early works in favour of a more allusive style and simplified forms. Her painting of *The Crowd* was included in the exhibition devoted to *L'Âge d'Or de la Peinture en Bretagne* (*The Golden Age of Painting in Brittany*) at the museum of Vannes in 2001.

BIBLIOGRAPHY:

Élodie La Villette, Caroline Espinet: la peinture à Lorient à la fin du XIXe siècle, exhibition catalogue, Gal. du Faouedic, Hôtel de Ville, Lorient, 1994. Delouche, Denise/Lainé, Claire/Nicolas, Brigitte, *L'Âge d'or de la peinture en Bretagne*, exhibition catalogue, Musée de Vannes, Conseil général du Morbihan, Vannes, 2001. Delouche, Denise/Le Saux, Marie-Françoise, *Bretagne, terre des peintres*, exhibition catalogue, Musée des Beaux-Arts, Vannes, 2003.

MUSEUMS AND GALLERIES:

LORIENT (Town Collection): *The Shore at Keroman at Low Tide* (1879, oil on canvas); *The Buckling of a Lugger* (oil on canvas).

ESPINO, Martin de

Spanish, 16th century.
Active in Seville in 1534.
Sculptor.

ESPÍNOLA GÓMEZ, Manuel

Uruguayan, 20th century.
Born 1921, in Lavalleja.
Painter (gouache).

Manuel Espínola Gómez lived and worked in Montevideo. He studied at the Círculo de Bellas Artes in Montevideo under Guillermo Laborde and José Cúneo. In 1946, he won his first medal at the Salón Nacional de Bellas Artes in Montevideo. He made a trip to Europe in 1957 which influenced his work greatly. His style explored the human form and landscape often adding an unreal dimension. He exhibited at the Mexican Biennale of 1958; at the São Paulo Biennale in 1957, 1959 and 1961; in Buenos Aires in 1960, and at the first Córdoba Biennale in Argentina in 1962.

BIBLIOGRAPHY:

Retrospectiva Espínola Gómez 1980, exhibition catalogue, Gal. Latina, Montevideo, 1980. Kalenberg, A., ed., *Arte contemporáneo en el Uruguay*, exhibition catalogue, Museo Nacional de Artes Plásticas y Visuales, Montevideo, 1982. Kalenberg, A., '*El transrealismo: La paralogía de Espínola Gómez*' in *Arte en Colombia*, 1986 (no. 30). Beeren, W., ed., *UABC*, exhibition catalogue, Stedelijk Museum, Amsterdam, 1989. Abbondanza, J., *Manuel Espínola Gómez*, Montevideo, 1991.

ESPINOS, Benito

Spanish, 18th - 19th century.
Born 23 March 1748, in Valencia; died 23 March 1818, in Valencia.
Painter, decorative artist, engraver. Still-lifes, flowers. Ornaments.

Benito Espinos was the son of José Espinos. He specialised in flower drawings and silk decoration. In 1784 he was appointed director of the *Escuela de Flores y Ornatos* ('School of Flowers and Ornamentation') at the royal academy of S Carlos in Valencia.

The lively tones of his flowers are usually highlighted against dark backgrounds and display a highly elegant sense of composition.

BIBLIOGRAPHY:

Aldana Fernández, S., '*Benito Espinos, pintor académico*' in *Archivo de Arte Valenciano*, 1968.

MUSEUMS AND GALLERIES:

BARCELONA (Real Acad. Catalana de Bellas Artes de Sant Jordi): *Branch of Orange Blossom* - MADRID (Prado): *Flowers* - SAN LORENZO DE EL ESCORIAL (Real Monasterio de San Lorenzo) - VALENCIA.

AUCTION RECORDS:

LONDON, 20 April 1988, *Still-life in a Stone Niche* (oil on canvas, 18 1/2 x 24 1/2 ins / 47 x 62 cm) GBP 29,700. MONACO, 2 Dec 1989, *Vase of Flowers* (1789, oil on panel, 28 3/4 x 18 1/2 ins / 73 x 47 cm) FRF 466,200. LONDON, 5 April 1995, *Still-life with Flowers with a Stone Low-relief on a Table* (oil on panel, 23 x 29 1/4 ins / 57.5 x 74 cm) GBP 42,200. MADRID, 3 April 2000, *Bunch of Flowers* (oil on canvas/tin, 19 x 14 ins / 48 x 35 cm) ESP 1,600,000. LONDON, 18 April 2000, *Bust of a Lady Surrounded by a Garland of Flowers* (1813, oil on panel, 13 x 10 ins / 32 x 25 cm) GBP 3,500. PARIS, 19 Dec 2001, *Still-life with Roses and Orange Flowers* (oil on canvas, 26 x 19 ins / 65 x 49 cm) FRF 70,000. MADRID, 9 April 2002, *Bust of Woman in Garland* (oil on board, 13 x 10 ins / 32 x 25 cm) EUR 16,000. PARIS, 26 June 2002, *Flowers in a Glass Vase* (oil on panel, 25 x 17 ins / 64 x 43 cm) EUR 115,000.

ESPINOS, José

Spanish, 18th century.
Born 5 January 1721, in Valencia; died 1784, in Valencia.
Painter, engraver.

José Espinos studied under Luis Martinez and Evaristo Munoz. He painted *Our Lady of Seven Sorrows and the Founders of the Order* for the Servite convent of the Foot of the Cross in Valencia. When he died he left a fine collection of engravings, drawings and books. As an engraver he produced a number of engravings of saints.

ESPINOSA

Spanish, 16th century.
Painter.

Espinosa's name is entered in the artists' account book in Valladolid in 1532.

ESPINOSA

Spanish, 16th century.
Painter.

Espinosa worked in Seville, possibly with the painter Fernando Gomez, around 1534.

ESPINOSA

Spanish, 16th century.
Active in Seville in 1571.
Painter.

ESPINOSA, Alonso

Spanish, 16th century.
Painter. History painting.

Alonso Espinosa lived in Burgos at the beginning of the 16th century and mostly worked in collaboration with his brother Andrés. With the assistance of Cristobal de Herrera they painted the Chapel of Our Lady in the cathedral at Palencia.

ESPINOSA, Andres de

Spanish, 16th century.
Painter. History painting.

Andres de Espinosa lived in Burgos at the beginning of the 16th century and often collaborated with his brother Alonso. They were helped by Cristobal de Herrera to decorate the Chapel of Our Lady in the cathedral at Palencia.

ESPINOSA, Carlos
Spanish, 18th century.
Painter. Portraits.

Carlos Espinosa held a scholarship at the Spanish academy in Rome in 1784 and copied a *Self-portrait* of Mengs.

AUCTION RECORDS:
NEW YORK, 7 June 1978, *Portrait of a Young Lawyer* (1791, oil on canvas, 37 3/4 x 28 1/2 ins / 96 x 72.5 cm) USD 3,100.

ESPINOSA, Francisco
Spanish, 16th century.
Painter, glass painter. History painting.

Francisco Espinosa worked at the Escorial during the reign of Philip II and for the cathedral at Burgos.

ESPINOSA, Jeronimo de
Spanish, 18th century.
Born 1724, in Dona Mencia; died 1791, in Cordova.
Painter.

Jeronimo de Espinosa died a Dominican monk at the monastery of S Pablo in Cordova. He decorated several of the city's historic buildings with religious paintings.

ESPINOSA, Jeronimo Jacinto de
Spanish, 17th century.
Born 7 May 1600, in Cocentaina (Valencia); died 7 May 1680, in Valencia.
Painter. Religious subjects, portraits.

Jeronimo Jacinto de Espinosa was the son of Jeronimo Rodriguez de Espinosa, a painter of historical subjects. Jeronimo Jacinto was taught first by his father before becoming a pupil of Nicolas Borras and Francisco Ribalta. He studied at the Spanish-Italian academy in Valencia, whose director was Vincent Joanes. Espinosa is believed to have studied in Italy at the Bologna School, whose style he imitated with great success. He was only 25 when he painted the famous *Christ* of Rescate at the convent of St Theresa. In 1638 the Calced Carmelites of Rescate commissioned several major pieces from him and these works established his reputation, placing him on a level with the celebrated masters of the Lombardy School. His *Mary Magdalene* and *Death of St Louis Beltran*, and other works decorate the churches of Valencia.

His bold draughtsmanship and chiaroscuro are very powerful and his figures are graceful in expression. The earth tones he employs, heightened with reds and his luminist effects make him the natural heir of his master Ribalta. Espinosa made a speciality of painting monks, and consequently is sometimes known as the 'Zurbarán of Valencia'.

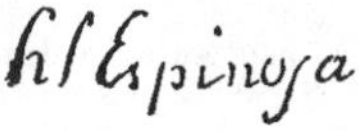

BIBLIOGRAPHY:
Pérez Sánchez, A.E., *Jeronimo Jacinto de Espinosa*, Madrid, 1972. Benito Domench, F., '*Jeronimo Jacinto Espinosa en sus comienzos como pintor*' in *Ars Longa 4*, 1993.

MUSEUMS AND GALLERIES:
ALPUENTE (Church) - BUDAPEST: *St Sebastian* - MADRID (Prado): *Mary Magdalene at Prayer; Christ at the Column; St John and the Lamb* - MONCADE (Church) - MORELLA (Church) - PUIG (Church) - SEGORBE (Church) - ST PETERSBURG: *Flight into Egypt* - TERUEL (Church) - VALENCIA: *Holy Family*.

AUCTION RECORDS:
NEW YORK, 15 Jan 1987, *Mystical Vision of St Bernard of Clairvaux* (oil on canvas, 46 1/2 x 35 3/4 ins / 118 x 91 cm) USD 12,000. NEW YORK, 10 Jan 1990, *Portrait of Godfrey of Bouillon Wearing a Red Habit, Armoured Breastplate and Emblazoned Chasuble* (oil on canvas, 61 1/2 x 45 3/4 ins / 156.2 x 116.2 cm) USD 20,900. MADRID, 18 May 1993, *Martyrdom of St Peter of Verona* (oil on canvas, 78 x 40 1/2 ins / 198 x 103 cm) ESP 4,000,000. MADRID, 23 April 1998, *Roman Figure* (oil on canvas, 61 x 46 ins / 156 x 116 cm) ESP 1,500,000. MADRID, 2 July 2001, *Our Lady of the Rosary* (oil on canvas, 60 x 44 ins / 153 x 111 cm) ESP 1,800,000.

ESPINOSA, Jeronimo Rodriguez de
Spanish, 16th - 17th century.
Born 1562, in Valladolid; died c. 1630, in Valencia.
Painter. History painting, religious subjects.
Valencian School.

After Jeronimo Rodriguez de Espinosa studied at Valladolid, he settled in Cocentaina (Valencia), where on 30 May 1596 he married Aldonze Lleo; she bore him a son, the painter Jeronimo Jacinto Espinosa. Espinosa subsequently settled in Valencia where he was a successful historical painter. In collaboration with the painter Jayme Ferol, he executed the paintings for the high altar of the church of John the Baptist in the town of Muro; the notary Don André Cister owned part of this high altar representing the saints Laurence, Hippolytus, Sebastian and Roch in Cocentaina.

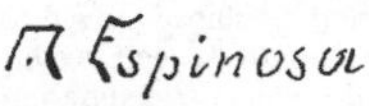

ESPINOSA, José Garcia
Spanish, 20th century.
Born 6 October 1922, in Callosa de Segura (Alicante).
From 1951 active in Brazil.
Painter, sculptor, engraver. Religious subjects, figures, portraits, landscapes, still-lifes. Groups.

In 1937, José Espinosa's family moved to Murcia because of the Spanish Civil War. In 1943 he studied at the Murcia school of fine arts and in 1948 exhibited for the first time at the 4th regional exhibition of artists of Murcia.

In 1951 he left for Brazil and settled in Rio de Janeiro where he taught painting and engraving. In 1957 he returned to Spain to learn restoration techniques for painting and sculpture at the Real Academia de Bellas Artes de San Fernando in Madrid. In 1969 he returned to Rio and pursued his career as a painter.

Espinosa adopted an old technique using blurred outlines. His subjects are often symbol-laden in a manner approaching the fantastical.

BIBLIOGRAPHY:
Margutti, Mario, *El Realismo magico de J.G. Espinosa*, Gavea, Rio de Janeiro, 1993 (The Magic Realism of J.G. Espinosa).

ESPINOSA, Juan Bautista de
Spanish, 16th century.
Active in Toledo.
Painter. Still-lifes.
Toledo School.

AUCTION RECORDS:
LONDON, 9 April 1990, *Still-life with Silverplate, Set Places and Earthenware etc.* (1624, oil on canvas, 39 x 47 ins / 99 x 119.5 cm) GBP 605,000. LONDON, 8 July 1992, *Still-life with Grapes, other Fruits and Jug on Table Top* (1676, oil on canvas, 26 1/2 x 26 3/4 ins / 67.5 x 68 cm) GBP 143,000.

ESPINOSA, Juan de
Spanish, 17th century.
Painter.

According to accounts records of 1603 from Valencia, Juan de Espinosa received payment, via Vicencio Carducho, for paintings he had executed on wooden chests, with Jusepe de Porras and Ambrosio de Caro.

ESPINOSA, Juan de
Spanish, 17th century.
Died in Puente de la Reyna (Navarre).
Painter. Religious subjects.

In 1653, Juan de Espinosa painted 24 *Scenes from the Life of St Millan* for the monastery of S Millan de la Cogolla. He only completed 12 of these himself; the rest were completed after his death by brother Juan Rizi.

ESPINOSA, Juan de
Spanish, 17th - 18th century.
Painter. Still-lifes (fruit).
Juan de Espinosa was active in the late 17th century and early 18th century.
MUSEUMS AND GALLERIES:
MADRID (Prado): two works.

ESPINOSA, Manuel
Argentinian, 20th century.
Born 1912, in Buenos Aires.
Painter.
Op Art.
Arte Concreto Invención Group.
Manuel Espinosa studied at the school of fine arts in Buenos Aires. In 1945, together with Tomás Maldonado, he was one of the founders of the Arte Concreto-Invención group. After a short Surrealist period, Espinosa moved towards geometric abstraction. In his paintings he employed the dual technique of transparency and opaqueness, superimposing geometric forms in different positions and giving them movement and dynamism. Optical effects and visual values are two of Espinosa's key pictorial pursuits. Like many of his contemporaries who also worked with geometric forms, his work also displays a keenness to give the impression of three-dimensional spatial volume. From 1959 he exhibited both in Argentina (at the museum of modern art in Buenos Aires) and in Europe. In 1967 he exhibited at the Salon Comparaisons in Paris.
BIBLIOGRAPHY:
Bayon, Damian, *Projection et dynamisme, six peintres argentins*, exhibition catalogue, Musée d'Art moderne de la Ville de Paris, Paris, 1973. Paz Castillo, F./Rojas Guardia, P., *Diccionario de las artes plásticas en Venezuela*, Caracas, 1973.
AUCTION RECORDS:
PARIS, 24 Feb 1982, *Couple from Martinique* (oil on panel, 10 3/4 x 7 3/4 ins / 27.5 x 19.5 cm) FRF 4,300.

ESPINOSA, Matias
Spanish, 16th century.
Painter.
In 1545, Matias Espinosa carried out a work by Rabuyate with Antonio de Avila at Valladolid.

ESPINOSA, Miguel de
Spanish, 16th century.
Born probably in Saragossa.
Painter.
Miguel de Espinosa was invited by the Benedictine fathers to decorate the monastery of San Millán de la Cogolla. Among the works carried out were *The Marriage at Cana* and *Miracle of the Loaves and Fishes*.

ESPINOSA, Miguel de
Spanish, 16th century.
Born c. 1513, in Palencia.
Sculptor.
Valladolid School.

ESPINOSA, Miguel Jeronimo
Spanish, 17th century.
Painter. Religious subjects.
Miguel Jeronimo Espinosa was the son of Jeronimo Jacinto de Espinosa; he worked in Aragon.
AUCTION RECORDS:
LONDON, 19 Feb 1910, *Virgin and Infant Jesus*, GBP 18; *St Peter*, GBP 30.

ESPINOSA, Vicente
Spanish, 16th century.
Sculptor.
Vicente Espinosa worked in Madrid, and in 1569 was in Segovia.

ESPINOSA DE CASTRO, Jacinto
Spanish, 17th century.
Born 1633, in Valencia.
Sculptor.
Jacinto Espinosa de Castro was the son of Jeronimo Jacinto de Espinosa.

ESPINOSA DE LOS MONTEROS, Antonio
Spanish, 18th century.
Born 1732, in Murcia.
Engraver.
Antonio Espinosa de los Monteros worked in Madrid and Segovia.

ESPINOSA-PACEDA, Romano, also known as Romano Espinosa Caceda
Peruvian, 20th century.
Born 18 November 1897, in San Mateo.
Sculptor. Statues.
Romano Espinosa-Paceda studied under A. Boucher. He painted works inspired by prehistory and the life of the Indians. He exhibited in Paris at the Salons des Artistes Français - where he was awarded a prize in 1928, and at the Salon des Indépendants

ESPINOSA-VIALE, Lia C. M. de
French, 20th century.
Painter.
Lia C.M. de Espinosa-Viale was a member of the Salon des Artistes Français, in Paris.

ESPINOUZE, Henri, pseudonym: Espinoza
French, 20th century.
Born 21 March 1915, in Perpignan; died 1982, in Vichy.
Painter, draughtsman, illustrator. Figure compositions, portraits, landscapes, still-lifes, animals.
Henri Espinouze was a pupil of the private studio in the Place Malesherbes of the poster designer Paul Colin. He took part in group exhibitions, including 1938 Paris, *Exposition Internationale Surréaliste* (*International Surrealist Exhibition*). There is a photograph of 1940 which shows him at the Château du Bel-Air, Marseilles, with the Surrealists who were leaving for the USA; he does not seem to have gone with them. After the war, he lived in the Rue Mazarine with Youki Desnos, until her death. It seems that he then moved to Perpignan. Until 1938, he signed himself *Espinoza*, without a forename. After that, there is no evidence of his artistic activity.

Before World War II Espinouze mixed in Surrealist circles and contributed to such publications as *Le Minotaure*. At the 1938 exhibition, he made one of the models for the *Surrealist Road*. He collaborated in the illustration of de Lautréamont's *Les Chants de Maldoror* (*The Songs of Maldoror*), published by G.L.M., and illustrated, or part-illustrated, André Breton's *Un Cahier sur le Rêve* (*A Notebook on Dreaming*) and R. Masset's *Méridiens encyclopédiques* (*Encyclopaedic Meridians*)
BIBLIOGRAPHY:
Monod, Luc, *Manuel de l'amateur de livres illustrés modernes 1875-1975*, Ides et Calendes, Neuchâtel, 1992.
AUCTION RECORDS:
PARIS, 8 Dec 1987, *Forest Walk* (1959, oil on canvas, 45 1/4 x 32 ins / 115 x 81 cm) FRF 7,000.

ESPINOZA. See **ESPINOUZE Henri**

ESPLEGHEM, Frans Crabbe Van. See **CRABBE VAN ESPLEGHEM**

ESPLENS, John and Charles
British, 18th century.

Active in Edinburgh c. 1740.
Engravers.
It is known that John and Charles Esplens engraved the *Portrait of the Goldsmith Heriot* by Scougal.

ESPONS-MORALÈS, Albert d'
French, 20th century.
Born in Paris.
Painter. Landscapes.
Albert d'Espons-Moralès, a pupil of Cormon, painted in Italy and Spain and exhibited at the Salon de la Société Nationale des Beaux-Arts, Paris.

ESPOSITO, Diego
Italian, 20th century.
Born 1940, in Teramo (Abruzzio).
Also active in the USA.
Painter.
Diego Esposito studied in Naples until 1964. He lived in New York from 1968 to 1971, and since 1972, has divided his time between Rome and New York. He has been exhibiting in the USA and Italy since 1969.

In his brushwork there is evidence of a reflective kind of craftsmanship. He works the canvas with *pliages* and *découpages*, which bring the creative process into relief.

ESPOSITO, Gaetano
Italian, 19th - 20th century.
Born 1858, in Salerno; died 8 April 1911, in Sala Consilina.
Painter (gouache), watercolourist, draughtsman.
Historical scenes, portraits, seascapes.
Gaetano Esposito exhibited in Naples and Turin from 1877.
AUCTION RECORDS:
MILAN, 12 June 1973, *Scugnizzo*, ITL 800,000. MILAN, 25 May 1978, *Water Carrier* (oil on canvas, 41 x 17 3/4 ins / 104 x 45 cm) ITL 2,000,000. MILAN, 19 March 1981, *Rock* (pastel, 9 3/4 x 7 1/2 ins / 25 x 19 cm) ITL 500,000. NEW YORK, 27 May 1983, *View of the Suez Canal with Moored Boats* (1901, gouache, 9 1/4 x 18 ins / 23.2 x 44.8 cm) USD 850. NEW YORK, 24 May 1984, *In Chiesa* (oil on canvas, 43 x 68 ins / 109 x 173 cm) USD 14,000. MILAN, 7 Nov 1985, *Elegant Woman with a Fan* (watercolour, 24 x 17 3/4 ins / 61 x 45 cm) ITL 3,300,000. ROME, 13 May 1986, *Young Woman Fishing* (1889, oil on canvas, 63 x 37 1/2 ins / 160 x 95 cm) ITL 38,000,000. ROME, 14 Dec 1988, *Self-portrait* (1927, oil on panel, 6 1/4 x 4 ins / 16 x 10 cm) ITL 1,700,000. NEW YORK, 25 Oct 1989, *Young Peasant Woman with a Horse* (oil on canvas, 40 1/4 x 22 ins / 102.2 x 55.8 cm) USD 28,600. ROME, 14 Dec 1989, *Bust of a Young Girl* (oil on canvas, 19 x 11 ins / 48 x 28 cm) ITL 2,070,000. BERN, 12 May 1990, *Rocky Shore* (tempera and chalk, 12 1/2 x 13 1/4 ins / 31.5 x 33.5 cm) CHF 3,000. ROME, 29 May 1990, *Puttino* (1886, oil on canvas, 9 x 11 1/2 ins / 22 x 29 cm) ITL 7,475,000. MILAN, 30 May 1990, *Donn'Anna Palace in Naples* (oil on canvas, 9 1/2 x 15 1/2 ins / 24 x 39.5 cm) ITL 13,000,000. LONDON, 17 July 1992, *Cruise Ship in the Mediterranean* (watercolour and gouache, 13 1/4 x 19 1/2 ins / 33.7 x 49.5 cm) GBP 770. AMSTERDAM, 3 Nov 1992, *Fishing Boats in the Bay of Naples* (oil on canvas, 19 x 11 ins / 48 x 28 cm) NLG 3,220. ROME, 29-30 Nov 1993, *Sailor* (1904, watercolour/paper, 22 x 15 1/4 ins / 56 x 39 cm) ITL 4,714,000. ROME, 6 Dec 1994, *Sweet Rest* (oil on canvas, 19 3/4 x 30 3/4 ins / 50 x 78 cm) ITL 21,213,000. MILAN, 29 March 1995, *Little Peasant Boys at a Fountain* (oil on canvas, 19 3/4 x 13 ins / 50 x 33 cm) ITL 15,525,000. ROME, 23 May 1996, *Young Girl of the People* (oil on canvas/paper, 20 1/2 x 12 1/4 ins / 52 x 31 cm) ITL 14,375,000. AMSTERDAM, 9 March 1999, *Rocky Coastal Landscape* (oil on canvas, 22 x 30 ins / 57 x 75 cm) NLG 5,500. MILAN, 20 Oct 1999, *Betrothed Couple* (oil on canvas, 23 x 39 ins / 58 x 100 cm) ITL 11,287,000. MILAN, 10 Nov 2000, *Portrait of a Young Lady* (1884, oil on canvas, 11 x 9 ins / 29 x 24 cm) ITL 6,500,000. ROME, 14 Nov 2000, *Palazzo Donna Anna* (oil on canvas, 13 x 21 ins / 33 x 54 cm) ITL 8,500,000. ROME, 4 June 2001, *Young Woman with Fan* (1892, mixed media on cardboard, 11 x 9 ins / 28 x 22 cm) ITL 4,000,000. ROME, 4 June 2001, *Portrait of Giuseppina Gemito* (oil on panel, 5 x 3 ins / 13 x 7 cm) ITL 4,500,000. BERN, 1 May 2002, *Faraglioni Cliffs* (oil on canvas, 26 x 26 ins / 66 x 67 cm) CHF 2,500. LUCERNE, 15 May 2002, *Yacht and Fishing Boat in Sunlight* (oil on canvas, 19 x 21 ins / 48 x 54 cm) CHF 3,100. FLORENCE, 9 Dec 2003, *Choir Boy* (oil on canvas, 63 x 39 ins / 160 x 100 cm) EUR 3,000. MILAN, 8 June 2004, *Bay of Naples* (oil on board, 9 x 13 ins / 22 x 34 cm) EUR 5,000.

ESPOSITO, Salvatore
Italian, 20th century.
Born 1937, in Gallipolo.
Painter.
Salvatore Esposito arrived in Milan in 1960, then went to Paris in 1964. He is an abstract painter: he covers the entire surface of the canvas with small marks and lines, which are sometimes reminiscent of Mark Tobey, but above all belong to the general trend of challenging the nature of painting. By presenting itself as a surface, and no longer as a language, nor an evocation of something that transcends it, painting becomes its own subject. He has been involved in collective exhibitions since 1963.

ESPOSITO-FARÈSE, Aimé
French, 20th century.
Born 1932, in Bône (now Annaba), Algeria.
Painter, illustrator.
Aimé Esposito-Farèse became a Protestant minister without giving up his artistic vocation. The subject of his 1957 thesis was *Peinture Contemporain et Art Sacré* (*Contemporary Painting and Religious Art*). From 1975 to 1979 he taught at the University of Paris-Nord, giving courses on the *Semiology of the Image, and the Philosophy of Art*. From 1975 to 1981 he travelled and tried to re-establish the technique and transparent effects of encaustic painting as it was practised in Pompeii. He settled in Paris in 1982.

From 1952, Esposito-Farèse took part in group exhibitions; in 1955, 1956 and 1959 he was selected for the Young Painters' Prize and he showed regularly at the Salon des Indépendents. His solo shows include 1952 to 1963, Montpellier; 1960, 1963, 1964, 1968, Marseilles; 1966, 1986, 1992, Paris; 1988, 1989, 1990, Tokyo, etc. In 1974, 1975 and 1976, he conducted three artistic operations in the mountains, involving the local population in the painting of monumental works; this was an experiment repeated in 1979, 1980 and 1981 on the banks of the Étang de Berre in Martigues. In 1991, he illustrated Tristan Cabral's *Requiem-Océan*.

After the figuration of his early works, Esposito-Farèse chose to use an abstract pictorial language, though in cases such as the monumental group paintings he returns quite naturally to figurative elements. It is not surprising to find the painting of this painter/pastor belongs with the Spiritual Abstraction practised by Bertholle, Manessier and Le Moal. He often designed stained glass, in which the darkness is structured by tall vertical lines and light obliques, interrupted by short horizontals or an intersecting circle - a grid through which the light and colours shine brightly. Esposito-Farèse the pastor, commenting on the painter in himself, said: 'Painting is not the clear expression of a world already known, but rather the search for a hidden world that one has a sense of. Paintings are only the marks of a hope not yet fulfilled, so it is necessary to go beyond them.'

ESPOUY, Hector Jean Baptiste
French, 19th century.
Born 8 May 1854, in Sables Adour.
Painter, architect.
Hector Espouy exhibited landscapes and views of monuments at the Salon from 1880 and lectured at the École des Beaux-Arts in Paris from 1895.

ESPOUY, Jean d'
French, 20th century.
Born 30 November 1891, in Paris; died 1921, in Paris.
Painter.

Jean d'Espouy, a pupil of Harpignies, exhibited for the first time at an early age at the Salon des Artistes Français of 1910.

ESPOY, Angel
American, 20th century.
Born 1879, in Villa Nueva, Spain; died 1963, in Seal Beach (California).
Painter. Landscapes, seascapes.

Espoy worked initially in the merchant marine, from which he later drew the inspiration to paint. He studied with Joaquin Sorolla, and emigrated to San Francisco, moving on to Los Angeles. He is best known for his rolling landscapes of California with wild flowers.

AUCTION RECORDS:
LOS ANGELES, 9 Feb 1982, *Stormy Sea* (oil on canvas, 28 x 40 ins / 71 x 101.5 cm) USD 600. NEW YORK, 28 Sept 1989, *Spring in the Mountains* (oil on canvas, 25 x 30 ins / 63.5 x 76.2 cm) USD 3,080. LOS ANGELES-SAN FRANCISCO, 12 July 1990, *Cypress on Dune* (oil on canvas, 20 x 24 ins / 51 x 61 cm) USD 1,210. NEW YORK, 20 March 1996, *The Oasis* (1948, oil on canvas, 28 x 38 ins / 71.1 x 96.5 cm) USD 2,070. NEW ORLEANS, 6 Feb 1999, *Beach Scene with Figures, Horse and Sailboat* (oil on canvas, 24 x 30 ins / 61 x 76 cm) USD 4,400. SAN FRANCISCO, 17 June 1999, *Cattle Grazing in Valley* (oil on canvas, 30 x 36 ins / 76 x 91 cm) USD 7,500. PASADENA, 14 Nov 2000, *Rolling Hills and Flower Fields* (oil on canvas, 8 x 9 ins / 20 x 24 cm) USD 9,000. LOS ANGELES, 13 Dec 2000, *California in Bloom* (oil on canvas, 24 x 30 ins / 61 x 76 cm) USD 6,500. DOWNINGTON, 30 Nov 2001, *Western Landscape with Snow-capped Mountains in Background* (oil on canvas, 19 x 35 ins / 48 x 89 cm) USD 4,250. SAN FRANCISCO, 12 Dec 2001, *Landscape with Poppies and Lupins* (oil on canvas, 20 x 30 ins / 51 x 76 cm) USD 7,500. PASADENA, 11 June 2002, *Flower Fields and Cattle in Foothill Landscape* (oil on canvas, 20 x 30 ins / 51 x 76 cm) USD 6,500. LOS ANGELES, 19 June 2002, *Poppies and Eucalyptus* (oil on canvas, 25 x 30 ins / 63 x 76 cm) USD 8,500. PASADENA, 18 Feb 2003, *Eucalyptus Landscape with Flower Field* (oil on canvas, 30 x 36 ins / 76 x 91 cm) USD 10,000. SAN FRANCISCO, 11 June 2003, *Along the Pacific* (oil on canvas, 30 x 40 ins / 76 x 102 cm) USD 12,000. SAN FRANCISCO, 8 June 2004, *California Landscape with Poppies and Oaks* (oil on canvas, 25 x 30 ins / 63 x 76 cm) USD 8,500. PASADENA, 15 June 2004, *Eucalyptus and Flower Field* (oil on canvas, 30 x 40 ins / 76 x 102 cm) USD 9,000.

ESPRIT, Anne Marie
French, 19th - 20th century.
Born in Lyons.
Painter.

Anne Marie Esprit, a pupil of Miciol and Tollet, exhibited in Lyons from 1889, showing portraits, flowers, figures, and history and genre paintings (paintings and watercolours). Among her works are *Autumn*, a decorative panel (1896), *Elijah Reproaching Jezebel for the Slaying of the Prophets* (1986), *The Thread of Life* (1900), *The Death of St Odile* (1901, first-class medal), and *Little Sisters* (1908). She signed herself *A.M. Esprit*.

ESPRIT, Raymonde
French, 20th century.
Born in Valence.
Painter.

Raymonde Esprit, a pupil of Biloul and Humbert, was a member of the Salon des Artistes Français.

ESQUARTE, Pablo
Spanish, 17th century.
Active during the second half of the 17th century.
Painter.

After studying in Valencia, Pablo Esquarte went to Venice, where he became a pupil of Titian. He is known primarily for his excellent portraits. He was also commissioned by the Duke of Villa Hermosa to decorate his palace and country house.

ESQUIVEL, Antonio Maria
Spanish, 19th century.
Born 8 March 1806, in Seville; died 9 April 1857, in Madrid.
Painter. Religious subjects, figure compositions, portraits.
Costumbrismo.

Antonio Maria Esquivel was a pupil of José Gutierrez. He went to Madrid around 1832 and was made a member of the Real Academia de San Fernando. Esquivel was a very prolific artist. He painted mainly portraits and subjects from religious history; these reveal him to be a somewhat servile imitator of Murillo. Nevertheless, he was a talented painter and one of the most famous artists of the 19th-century Spanish School.

Esquivel's life was more Romantic than his work. When he was aged just two, his father was killed at the Battle of Bailén and after a childhood of poverty he went to war himself at the age of 17, witnessing the siege of Cádiz and the defence of the Trocadero. He became known for his paintings of Andalusian life and was one of the founders of the artistic and literary group known as the Liceo, which became the centre for the Romantic movement in Madrid. He lost his sight to illness, and tried twice to commit suicide by jumping into the River Guadalquivir. He was much encouraged by the support he received and when he eventually recovered his sight he devoted himself to portrait painting.

BIBLIOGRAPHY:
Guerrero Lovillo, José, *Antonio Maria Esquivel*, Madrid, 1957. Gaya Nuño, J.A., '*Arte del siglo XIX*' in *A. Hisp.*, vol xix, Madrid, 1966.

MUSEUMS AND GALLERIES:
MADRID (Prado): *Group of Contemporary Poets* (1900); *The Saviour, Child Dying in the Christian Faith.*

AUCTION RECORDS:
PARIS, 25 May 1927, *The Most Celebrated Works of Murillo* (twelve canvases copied after Murillo) FRF 2,400. PARIS, 24 Feb 1928, *The Most Celebrated Works of Murillo* (twelve canvases copied after Murillo) FRF 1,500. BARCELONA, 26 May 1983, *Suzanna and the Elders* (oil on canvas, 24¾ x 33 ins / 63 x 84 cm) ESP 220,000. LONDON, 7 Oct 1987, *Portrait of an Elegant Horsewoman* (1848, oil on canvas, 82 x 57¾ ins / 208.5 x 147 cm) GBP 5,800. MADRID, 18 Feb 1999, *Portrait of D. Mariano Roca de Togores* (1841, oil on canvas, 40 x 32 ins / 102 x 82 cm) ESP 3,400,000. MADRID, 2 Dec 1999, *Reclining Nude* (oil on canvas, 41 x 64 ins / 105 x 163 cm) ESP 4,000,000. SEVILLE, 7 April 2000, *Portrait of Juan Perea* (1838, oil on canvas, 50 x 38 ins / 126 x 97 cm) ESP 1,000,000. SEVILLE, 7 April 2000, *Hagar and Ishmael in the Desert of Beersheba* (1856, oil on canvas, 83 x 57 ins / 210 x 146 cm) ESP 8,000,000. MADRID, 24 April 2001, *Lady by Piano* (1844, oil on canvas, 45 x 37 ins / 114 x 94 cm) ESP 370,000. MADRID, 21 May 2001, *Adam and Eve* (oil on canvas, 89 x 67 ins / 225 x 170 cm) ESP 1,800,000. SEVILLE, 14 Nov 2002, *Portrait of Antonio Gutierrez Solana* (1834, oil on canvas, 44 x 35 ins / 112 x 90 cm) EUR 7,000. LONDON, 19 Nov 2002, *Studio Chess Game* (oil on canvas, 22 x 24 ins / 55 x 61 cm) GBP 8,000. MADRID, 11 March 2003, *Portrait of Isabel II* (oil on canvas, 47 x 34 ins / 120 x 87 cm) EUR 11,000. MADRID, 30 June 2003, *Portrait of Gentleman* (1846, oil on canvas, 33 x 22 ins / 83 x 56 cm) EUR 7,500.

ESQUIVEL, Carlos Maria
Spanish, 19th century.
Born c. 1830, in Seville; died 20 July 1867, in Madrid.
Painter. History painting, portraits.
Carlos Maria Esquivel was the son and pupil of Antonio Maria Esquivel; he also worked in Paris under the direction of Léon Cogniet. In 1857 he was appointed to a teaching post at the Real Academia de San Fernando. He exhibited in Madrid from 1845 to 1867 and painted a series of portraits of the kings of Spain.
MUSEUMS AND GALLERIES:
MADRID (Prado): several portraits of the kings of Spain.

ESQUIVEL, Diego de
Spanish, 17th century.
Active in Seville in 1618.
Painter.
Diego de Esquivel worked on the decoration of the Alcazar and cathedral in Seville.

ESQUIVEL, Francisco de
Spanish, 16th century.
Active in Seville in the middle of the 16th century.
Painter.

ESQUIVEL, Jacques
Spanish, 16th century.
Active in Seville c. 1594.
Painter.

ESQUIVEL, Joaquin
Mexican, 18th century.
Painter. Religious subjects.
Joaquin Esquivel was active in Mexico City at the end of the 18th century. He decorated the church of Loreto in Mexico City with *Scenes from the Life of Ignatius Loyola*.
AUCTION RECORDS:
AMSTERDAM, 12 June 1990, *Penitent St Jerome* (1739, oil/copper, 15 1/4 x 11 3/4 ins / 38.8 x 30 cm) NLG 1,725.

ESQUIVEL, Miguel de
Spanish, 17th century.
Born c. 1595, in Seville; died 11 September 1621, in Seville.
Painter.
Miguel de Esquivel was the father of Lucas.
MUSEUMS AND GALLERIES:
SEVILLE (Cathedral): *Justa and Rufina* (c. 1620).

ESQUIVEL, Vicente
Spanish, 19th century.
Born in the 19th century, in Seville.
Sculptor, painter. Portraits, genre scenes.
Vicente Esquivel was the second son of Antonio Maria Esquivel. In 1867 he was appointed drawing teacher at the Real Academia de San Fernando in Madrid. He painted mainly portraits.
AUCTION RECORDS:
LONDON, 9 Dec 1907, *Visit of the Abbot,* GBP 16. LONDON, 15 June 1979, *Bullfighter's Preparations* (oil on panel, 19 1/4 x 26 ins / 48.8 x 66 cm) GBP 3,500.

ESQUIVEL DE SOTOMAYOR, Manuel
Spanish, 19th century.
Born 1777, in Madrid; died 1842, in Madrid.
Engraver.
Manuel Esquivel de Sotomayor was a pupil of the line engraver Montaner. In 1796 he was awarded the engraving prize at the Real Academia de San Fernando. He worked in Paris and Italy, having received a bursary from King Charles IV. He was made a member of the academy in 1829. His work is not extensive and consists mainly of portraits. His engravings were often after Raphael, Titian, Mengs and Velázquez.

ESQUIVEL PELAYO, Lucas de
Spanish, 17th century.
Active in Seville.
Painter.
Lucas de Esquivel Pelayo provided 'Paintings, Cases and Inventions' for the Corpus Christi floats on 20 May 1622.

ESS, Hans
German, 16th century.
Active in Nuremberg at the end of the 16th century.
Glass painter.

ESSAOULENKO, Evgueni
Russian, 20th century.
Born 1944, in Krasnodar.
Active in the USA.
Painter (mixed media).
Evgueni Essaoulenko studied at the school of fine arts in Moscow and at the Mukhina Institute in Leningrad (now St Petersburg). He emigrated to France in 1979 and then settled in the USA. He began participating in group exhibitions in 1974.

ESSCHE, Jean
Flemish School, 16th century.
Active in Mechelen in 1566.
Painter.

ESSCHE, Maurice van
Belgian, 20th century.
Born 1906, in Antwerp; died 1977, in Thonon-les-Bains, France.
Also active in South Africa.
Painter, draughtsman, lithographer. Figures, landscapes, still-lifes.
Maurice van Essche was a student at the Académie des Beaux-Arts in Brussels and worked with Henri Matisse in Nice. He was sent to the Congo in 1939. Prevented from returning to occupied Belgium in 1940, he settled in South Africa, where he was a part-time lecturer at the art school of the Witwatersrand technical college in Johannesburg, then became professor and director at the Michaelis art school in Capetown. His figures and characters are African in inspiration.
AUCTION RECORDS:
JOHANNESBURG, 17 March 1976, *Congolese Women* (oil on canvas, 23 1/4 x 28 1/4 ins / 59 x 71.5 cm) ZAR 1,450. JOHANNESBURG, 21 June 1983, *Congolese Women in a Village* (oil on card, 8 1/2 x 17 1/4 ins / 21.5 x 44 cm) ZAR 1,000.

ESSEGERN, Arendt
German, 17th century.
Died 1681, in Hamburg.
Painter.

ESSEGERN, Hinrich
German, 17th century.
Died 1668, in Hamburg.
Painter.

ESSEGERN, Johan
German, 17th century.
Died 1691, in Hamburg.
Painter.

ESSEGERN, Johan Matthes
German, 18th century.
Died 1759, in Hamburg.
Painter.

ESSEGERN, Kurt
German, 17th century.
Active in Lübeck c. 1660.
Painter.
Kurt Essegern worked for the Marienkirche in Lübeck.

ESSEGERN, Matthes
German, 18th century.
Died 1732, in Hamburg.
Painter.

ESSELENS, Jacob
Flemish, 17th century.
Born 1626, in Amsterdam; died 1687; buried 15 January in Amsterdam.
Painter, engraver, draughtsman. Landscapes.
Flemish School.

A painter of the Rembrandt School, Jacob Esselens travelled a great deal and probably went to Italy. On 20 April 1668 he married Janneken Jans, who bore him two children. He was a merchant as well. He was also active as an engraver and executed *Man and Woman Seated in front of a Hut with a Child* and *Group of Trees with a Shepherd and Sheep.*

He is mainly known for his beach scenes, the composition of which is not dissimilar to those of Simon de Vlieger and Adrian van de Velde.

J. E. J Esselens.

BIBLIOGRAPHY:
Bol, Laurens Johannes, *Die Holländische Marinemalerei des 17. Jarhunderts*, Klinkhardt & Biermann, Brunswick, 1973.

MUSEUMS AND GALLERIES:
AMSTERDAM: *Landscape; View of a Beach* - BRUNSWICK: *Mountainous Landscape with Satyrs and Ruins* - COPENHAGEN: *Fishermen Hiding their Catch* - GLASGOW: *Rendezvous after the Hunt* - LEIPZIG: *View of Haarlem* - LILLE: *Dutch Beach* - ROTTERDAM: *Castle by the Water.*

AUCTION RECORDS:
PARIS, 8 Feb 1904, *Beach at Low Tide,* FRF 650. PARIS, 7 March 1923, *Beach,* FRF 2,600. PARIS, 4 July 1929, *River in a Mountainous Landscape* (pen) FRF 400. PARIS, 8 Dec 1938, *Leaving for a Walk* (black chalk and pen, heightened with wash) FRF 750; *Sailing Boats in Port* (bistre wash) FRF 1,500. PARIS, 25 May 1949, *Fishermen at Low Tide,* FRF 310,000. PARIS, 5 April 1965, *View of a Beach,* FRF 15,500. LONDON, 25 Nov 1966, *Beach Scene near Scheveningen,* Gns 5,200. LONDON, 25 Nov 1970, *Seaside with Numerous Figures,* GBP 5,400. AMSTERDAM, 30 May 1978, *Elegant Company Fishing at Riverside* (oil on canvas, 17 1/4 x 20 1/2 ins / 43.5 x 52 cm) NLG 16,000. MONTE CARLO, 26 Oct 1981, *Seascape in Calm Weather* (oil on canvas, 24 1/2 x 33 1/2 ins / 62 x 85 cm) FRF 115,000. LONDON, 11 March 1983, *Horsemen at Rest in a Wooded Landscape* (oil on canvas, 23 1/4 x 28 1/4 ins / 59 x 71.8 cm) GBP 4,500. PARIS, 5 March 1986, *Fishermen on the Beach* (oil on canvas, 18 x 26 1/4 ins / 46 x 66.5 cm) FRF 72,000. PARIS, 16 March 1990, *View of a Castle in a Wooded Landscape* (pen and wash, 6 x 8 ins / 15.4 x 20.6 cm) FRF 25,000. MONACO, 14 June 1996, *Beach with Boats and Fishermen in Conversation* (oil on canvas, 39 1/2 x 50 1/2 ins / 100.5 x 128.5 cm) FRF 198,900. NEW YORK, 13 Nov 1997, *Landscape with Huntsman and Dog near a Fallen Tree; Italian Landscape with a Washerwoman* (oil on canvas, 30 1/2 x 30 1/2 ins / 77.5 x 77.5 cm) USD 4,830. NEW YORK, 28 Jan 1999, *Ships in Calm Sea* (oil on canvas, 42 x 39 ins / 107 x 98 cm) USD 30,000. ZURICH, 15 March 2000, *Portraits of Couple from Amsterdam* (oil on panel, a pair, 11 x 9 ins / 28 x 23 cm) CHF 22,000. ZURICH, 5 Oct 2001, *Beach Landscape with Fishermen and Peasants* (oil on canvas, 31 x 39 ins / 79 x 99 cm) CHF 28,000. VIENNA, 5 June 2002, *Beach at Scheveningen with Church of Scheveningen in the Background* (oil on wood, 24 x 33 ins / 60 x 84 cm) EUR 7,500. PARIS, 18 March 2004, *Landscape along the Rhine near Arnhem* (pen, brown ink, grey wash, 8 x 10 ins / 20 x 26 cm) EUR 2,400.

ESSEN, Cornelis van
Dutch, 18th century.
Active in Amsterdam between 1736 and 1757.
Painter, engraver. Battles, genre scenes, landscapes.

MUSEUMS AND GALLERIES:
STOCKHOLM: *Cavalry Engagement in front of a Ruined Castle.*

AUCTION RECORDS:
COLOGNE, 6 June 1973, *Travellers outside an Inn,* DEM 13,000. LONDON, 26 May 1978, *Horsemen and Peasants outside an Inn* (oil on canvas, 9 3/4 x 11 ins / 25 x 27 cm) USD 3,400. LONDON, 29 Oct 1980, *Travellers outside an Inn* (oil on panel, 14 3/4 x 20 1/2 ins / 37.5 x 52 cm) GBP 3,600. LONDON, 18 Dec 1987, *Stopping at the Inn* (two oils on canvas, 19 1/2 x 24 1/2 ins / 49.5 x 62.2 cm) GBP 11,000. LONDON, 15 Dec 1989, *Travellers outside an Inn* (oil on canvas, 28 x 38 3/4 ins / 71 x 98.5 cm) GBP 7,700. LONDON, 26 Oct 1990, *Stablemen Attending to Post Horses behind the Inn* (oil on canvas, 32 1/4 x 40 ins / 81.9 x 100.7 cm) GBP 4,400. LONDON, 3 July 1991, *Peasants and Horsemen outside an Inn* (oil on canvas, 23 x 29 ins / 58.5 x 73.5 cm) GBP 4,620. AMSTERDAM, 6 May 1993, *Travellers outside an Inn* (oil on panel, 7 3/4 x 9 ins / 19.8 x 23 cm) NLG 9,200. NEW YORK, 5 Oct 1995, *Peasants Dancing outside an Inn* (oil on canvas, 26 3/4 x 22 1/2 ins / 68 x 57 cm) USD 4,600. NEW YORK, 2 Oct 1996, *Travellers Buying Horses outside an Inn in a Mountainous Landscape* (oil on panel, 10 x 12 1/2 ins / 25.1 x 31.5 cm) USD 1,265. PARIS, 15 Dec 1997, *Horsemen Stopping outside an Inn* (pair of oils/canvas, 20 x 24 ins / 51 x 61 cm) FRF 45,000. ANTWERP, 13 Dec 1999, *Men on Horseback Resting by Dutch Village* (oil on canvas, 11 x 15 ins / 29 x 37 cm) BEF 185,000. LONDON, 24 April 2001, *Highway Robbery by a Cottage* (oil on canvas, 19 x 16 ins / 47 x 41 cm) GBP 3,500. BRUSSELS, 15 April 2002, *Huntsman with Hounds Crossing a Ford* (oil on canvas, 21 x 26 ins / 54 x 65 cm) EUR 12,000. VIENNA, 2 Oct 2002, *Resting Horsemen Outside an Inn* (oil on canvas, 18 x 24 ins / 45 x 61 cm) EUR 16,000.

ESSEN, F. H. A.
German, 18th century.
Painter.

Romsted engraved a portrait of the theologian, T. Pfanner, after a painting by Essen.

ESSEN, François van
Flemish, 17th century.
Active in Antwerp, in 1612.
Painter.
Flemish School.

ESSEN, Hans van
Flemish, 17th century.
Born before 1590, in Antwerp; died after 1642, probably in Amsterdam.
Painter. Still-lifes.
Flemish School.

Possibly related to Jacob van Essen, Hans van Essen was a pupil of Hack in Antwerp in 1601 and a member of the guild in 1609. He was married twice, in 1609 and 1636.

HESSEN.

ESSEN, Hans von. See also **LADENSPELDER Johann**

ESSEN, Jan van
Flemish, 17th century.
Active in Antwerp in 1660.
Painter, watercolourist. Landscapes with figures, landscapes.
Flemish School.

AUCTION RECORDS:
NEW YORK, 25 Feb 1987, *Ducks by a River in Woodland* (watercolour and gouache on outlines in black chalk, 10 1/4 x 15 1/4 ins / 26 x 39 cm) USD 1,300. AMSTERDAM, 5-6 Nov 1991,

Promenade along a Canal (1900, oil on canvas, 26 1/2 x 40 1/4 ins / 67 x 102 cm) NLG 5,750.

ESSEN, Johannes Cornelis van
Dutch, 19th - 20th century.
Born 25 January 1854, in Amsterdam; died 1936.
Painter. Genre scenes, landscapes, animals.
Van Essen was a student of Petrus Franciscus Greive. He was also influenced by Maris and Swan.
MUSEUMS AND GALLERIES:
AMSTERDAM: *Marabou* - HAARLEM: *Painting* - MUNICH: *Dutch Landscape* - THE HAGUE (Gemeentemus.): *Heron* - THE HAGUE (Mus. Mesdag): *In the Dunes around Bergen.*
AUCTION RECORDS:
LONDON, 30 April 1909, *Corn Sheaves,* GBP 11. LONDON, 13 May 1909, *Old Cottages,* GBP 37. LONDON, 15 July 1910, *Village Road,* GBP 10. LONDON, 9 June 1922, *Sheep in the Dunes,* GBP 5. AMSTERDAM, 27 April 1976, *Summer Landscape* (oil on panel, 9 x 12 1/4 ins / 22 x 31 cm) NLG 3,400. NEW YORK, 15 June 1977, *Huntsmen and Travellers before an Inn* (oil on canvas, 32 1/4 x 26 1/2 ins / 82 x 67.5 cm) USD 4,200. LONDON, 9 Oct 1987, *River Landscape with View of a Village* (1890, oil on canvas, 31 x 39 ins / 78.8 x 99 cm) GBP 4,000. AMSTERDAM, 30 Aug 1988, *Ploughed Fields* (1902, oil on canvas, 32 x 39 3/4 ins / 81 x 101 cm) NLG 1,035. LONDON, 21 June 1989, *Ice-Skating Trip* (oil on canvas, 23 1/2 x 36 1/4 ins / 60 x 92 cm) GBP 11,550. AMSTERDAM, 2 May 1990, *Observation of a Magpie* (1880, oil on canvas, 26 x 20 ins / 66 x 51 cm) NLG 3,220. AMSTERDAM, 11 Sept 1990, *Herd of Sheep in a Dune Landscape* (oil on canvas, 22 1/4 x 35 1/2 ins / 56.5 x 90 cm) NLG 2,300. AMSTERDAM, 19 April 1994, *Swans* (oil on canvas, 23 1/4 x 23 1/4 ins / 59 x 59 cm) NLG 9,200. AMSTERDAM, 11 April 1995, *Poultry in a Garden* (1910, oil on canvas, 39 x 53 1/4 ins / 99 x 135 cm) NLG 11,800. AMSTERDAM, 18 June 1996, *Burning Question* (1910, oil on panel, 9 1/4 x 12 1/2 ins / 23.5 x 31.5 cm) NLG 2,760.

ESSENHECK, J. van
Dutch, 17th century.
Born 1627, in Rotterdam; died 1678.
Painter.
Little is known about the life of J. van Essenheck.

ESSER, Anton
Austrian, 17th - 18th century.
Born in Innsbruck.
Painter.
Anton Esser was working in Vienna in 1712.

ESSER, Max
German, 20th century.
Born 16 May 1885, in Barth; died 23 December 1945, in Berlin.
Sculptor (bronze), medallist. Animals. Monuments (fountains).
Jugendstil, Art Deco.
Max Esser trained in wood sculpture at a young age and attended evening classes at the Kunstgewerbemuseum in Berlin. He was a pupil of, and assistant to, the animal sculptor August Gaul from 1904 to 1915, and made a medal in homage to his master. He was a member of the Prussian academy of arts. He lived in Barth.

In 1908, he started working for the Schwarzburg porcelain art workshops (Schwarzburger Werkstätten für Porzellankunst) and, between 1913 and 1926, designed pottery at the Meissen porcelain manufactory. This was where the production of totally original animal figures originated in 1903, after a stylistic revival which came from Copenhagen, and lasted until the 1920s. These animals were the subject of an exhibition at the Naturmuseum Senckenberg, Frankfurt, in 1996, entitled *Tiere aus Meissener Porzellan* (*Meissen Porcelain Animals*). Max Esser also worked for the royal porcelain manufactory in Berlin and the Lorenz Hutschenreuther manufactory in Hohenberg. He was represented in the 1937 international exhibition in Paris. Reputed as an animal specialist, his aesthetic style evolved from Neo-Rococo to the Art Deco style he made his own, notably with the chessboard design he made for the Meissen manufactory. Until 1939, he also sculpted several fountains in Berlin.

Esser began participating in international exhibitions in 1906, and was awarded a gold medal at the 1937 Exposition Universelle in Paris. His work was shown in the exhibition *Traumwelten: Portzellanfiguren zwischen Jugendstil und Art Deco* (*Dream Worlds: German Porcelain Figures from Jugendstil to Art Deco*) at the Museum Huelsmann, Bielefeld, in 1999.
BIBLIOGRAPHY:
Maltschew, Ulrike, '*Tierplastik von Max Esser: das Perlhuhn mit Kücken*' in *Dresdener Kunstblätter p. 52-55,* periodical, 1996. Zöller-Stock, Bettina, *Traumwelten: Porzellanfiguren zwischen Jugendstil und Art Deco,* exhibition catalogue, Kunstgewerbemuseum, Berlin, 1998.
MUSEUMS AND GALLERIES:
BARTH (Vineta Mus.) - BERLIN (Bröhan-Mus.) - BERLIN (Staatliche Mus.) - GLAUCHAU (Schloss Hinterglauchau).

ESSER, Theodor
German, 19th century.
Born 30 July 1868, in Bonn.
Painter.
Theodor Esser was a pupil of Ferdinand Keller in Karlsruhe. He painted landscapes and interiors that were strongly influenced by the French Impressionist School.

ESSER, V.P.
Dutch, 20th century.
Born 1914, in Baarn.
Sculptor. Busts, monuments.
Esser was a student of Bronner at the academy in Amsterdam and then worked in the former Yugoslavia with Ivan Mestrovic and Krsinic. Since 1946, he has been a professor at the Amsterdam academy.

His sculpture is figurative and distinctly expressionist. He seems to have been strongly influenced by Rodin's work. He produced many monuments, including war memorials in Ede and Hilversum. He also produced portraits and figurines and engraved some coins.

ESSERS, Bernard
Dutch, 20th century.
Born 3 November 1893, in Kraksaan (Indonesia); died 13 May 1945, in Scharsterburg.
Draughtsman, engraver (including wood), illustrator.
Bernard Essers was born on the island of Java, then a Dutch colony; he died in The Netherlands. He studied in Amsterdam and at the Royal College of Art in London. He took part in group exhibitions, including regular appearances at the Venice Biennale between 1924 and 1940. He also showed in 1925 at the *Exposition internationale des Arts décoratifs et industriels modernes* (*International Exhibition of Modern Decorative and Industrial Arts*) in Paris and in 1929, at the Art Institute in Chicago. R. Mahé and Ed. Joseph cite Essers as having illustrated a deluxe edition of Jean Moréas' 1927 work *Stances.*
BIBLIOGRAPHY:
Fierens, Paul, *L'Art Hollandais contemporain,* Le Triangle, Paris, 1933.
MUSEUMS AND GALLERIES:
AMSTERDAM (Stedelijk Mus.).

ESSESTEYN, Adriaen van, called den Lossen
Dutch, 17th century.
Active in Rome in 1647.
Painter.
A few portraits by Adriaen van Essesteyn are known.

ESSEX, John
British, 15th century.
Sculptor.
John Essex carved the tomb of Richard Beauchamp, Earl of Warwick.

ESSEX, Richard Hamilton
British, 19th century.
Born 1802; died 22 February 1855, in Bow.
Painter, watercolourist. Landscapes.
Richard Hamilton Essex exhibited at the Royal Academy and became an associate of the Society of Painters in Watercolours in 1823. He exhibited at the latter until 1836.
AUCTION RECORDS:
LONDON, 13 March 1986, *Clarence Terrace, Regent's Park, London* (1832, watercolour and pencil outlines, 7 1/2 x 11 ins / 19 x 27 cm) GBP 1,700. LONDON, 21 Jan 2004, *Old London Bridge* (oil on canvas, 27 x 46 ins / 68 x 116 cm) GBP 2,800.

ESSEX, Thomas R.
British, 19th century.
Active in London.
Sculptor. Figures. Busts.
Thomas R. Essex exhibited at the Royal Academy from 1888 onwards.
MUSEUMS AND GALLERIES:
BRISTOL: *Bust of Christopher James Thomas*.

ESSEX, William
British, 19th century.
Born 1784; died 29 December 1869, in Brighton.
Painter.
William Essex copied landscapes and genre subjects by old and modern Masters into enamel. Near the end of his life he executed several miniatures from life. He was appointed miniaturist to the Queen in 1839, and exhibited at the Royal Academy from 1818 to 1862.

ESSEX, William B.
British, 19th century.
Born 1822; died 19 January 1852, in Birmingham.
Painter. Portraits.
William B. Essex was miniaturist to the Queen and painted several portraits. He exhibited miniatures at the Royal Academy from 1840. He was the son of William Essex.

ESSIG, George Emerick
American, 19th century.
Born 2 September 1838, in Philadelphia; died 1926, in Atlantic City.
Active in Atlantic City.
Painter. Landscapes, seascapes.
George Emerick Essig was a pupil of Edward Moran. He had a reputation as a landscape painter.
AUCTION RECORDS:
NEW YORK, 5 April 1984, *Arctic Ice* (1877, oil on canvas, 20 x 49 1/4 ins / 50.8 x 125.3 cm) USD 1,600. NEW YORK, 2 Dec 1992, *Grounded Sailing Boat* (oil on canvas, 11 1/4 x 17 1/2 ins / 28.5 x 44.4 cm) USD 1,100.

ESSINGS, Dirk
Dutch, 17th century.
Active in Alkmaar in 1624.
Painter.

ESSINGS, Jan
Dutch, 17th century.
Died May 1645, in Alkmaar.
Painter.

ESSLINGER, Anna Barbara, later Mme G. Amberger
Swiss, 19th century.
Born 6 April 1792, in Glattfelden; died 9 January 1868, in Basel.
Draughtswoman.
A pupil of the engraver M. Pfenninger, Anna Esslinger taught drawing at a girls' high school in Zurich. She lived in Solingen, where her second son, the painter Gustav Adol-Amberger, was probably born. Sometime after 1844, she moved to Basel. The engraver Johann Martin Esslinger was her brother.

ESSLINGER, Johann Friedrich
Austrian, 18th century.
Born 1686; died 10 May 1738.
Sculptor.
Johann Esslinger lived mainly in Vienna.

ESSLINGER, Johann Martin
Swiss, 19th century.
Born March 1793, in Glattfelden; died 9 February 1841, in Zurich.
Engraver, painter.
Johann Martin Esslinger studied drawing with G.C. Oberkogler and engraving with J.H. Lips, before moving to Stuttgart (Germany). In Paris, he was advised by Fr Müller (1813). From the age of 11 until 1819, Esslinger exhibited frequently in Zurich. He provided the illustrations for novels, for the Swiss almanac *Alpenrosen* (*Alpine Roses*) and for other Zurich and Bern journals. His portrait of *Konrad Escher von der Linth* is at the central library in Zurich.

ESSLINGER-SCHULTHEISS, David
Swiss, 19th century.
Born 1779, in Zurich; died 1828, in Zurich.
Painter.
Esslinger-Schultheiss was also a businessman. He is best known for three drawings in an official book of the art society in Zurich.

ESSOC, Marie
French, 19th century.
Born 15 April 1867, in Paris.
Painter.
Marie Essoc exhibited at the Salon of the Société des Artistes Français, becoming a member in 1891.

ESSON REID, Tomas
Cuban, 20th - 21st century.
Born 1963, in Havana.
Painter.
Tomas Esson Reid paints 'the sexual and the dramatic... combined with essentially sensual, anthropomorphic, zoomorphic and phytobiological elements'. These barely identifiable animals, some of which resemble man, represent a way of criticising sexual prejudices head on, and in a form free from erotic mannerism.
BIBLIOGRAPHY:
'*Tomas Esson Reid*' in *Revue Noire* n° 6, periodical, Fondation pour la coopération culturelle CEE-ACP, Paris, autumn 1992.

ESSWURM, Johannes
German, 16th century.
Active in Würzburg in 1515.
Miniaturist.
Esswurm was a Benedictine monk.

ESTABROOK, Florence C. (Mrs)
American, 20th century.
Born in Lowell (Massachusetts).
Painter.
Florence Estabrook was a pupil at the School of the Museum of Fine Art in Boston.

ESTACE, Guillemin
French, 14th century.

Active in Poitiers in 1385.
Sculptor (wood).
Guillemin Estace worked at the château of the dukes of Berry.

ESTACHON, Louis Antoine
French, 19th century.
Born 15 July 1819, in La Tour-d'Aigues; died 15 May 1857, in Marseilles.
Painter. Landscapes, still-lifes.
A pupil of Camille, Louis Antoine Estachon exhibited landscapes and still-lifes at the Paris Salon from 1847.
AUCTION RECORDS:
NEW YORK, 14 Oct 1978, *Still-life with Flowers* (1852, oil on canvas, 21 x 17 1/4 ins / 53.5 x 43.5 cm) USD 5,000.

ESTACHY, Françoise Élisabeth
French, 20th century.
Born in Lamotte-Beuvron.
Painter, sculptor, draughtsman, illustrator. Figure compositions, figures, landscapes.
Françoise Élisabeth Estachy was a pupil of the École d'Art et Publicité and, in Hubey's studio, of the École Nationale des Beaux-Arts, Paris. She illustrated many children's books: *De quoi encore* (*What more*) by C. Aveline; *Esmeralda* and *Le roi errant* (*The Wandering King*) by A. Dubois-Millet; *Enfantines* (*Tales for Children*) by F. Marc; *Carafet-le-sage* (*Carafet the Wise*) by P. Dacquin, and *Dans le pré* (*In the Meadow*) by M. Soleillant. She also did advertising pages for the magazines *Femina* and *Vogue*, and illustrated C. Salvy's *Quai aux fleurs* (*Flower Quay*).
AUCTION RECORDS:
PARIS, 10 July 1983, *The Hunts of Gaston Phoebus, Comte de Foix* (oil on panel, 35 x 50 3/4 ins / 89 x 129 cm) FRF 8,000.

ESTAKIO, Pavel Aleksandrovich
Russian, 19th century.
Painter.
Estakio studied at the St Petersburg academy of fine arts in about 1860.

ESTALL, William Charles
British, 19th century.
Born 1857, in London; died 1897.
Painter, watercolourist, pastellist. Landscapes, animals.
William Charles Estall exhibited frequently in London, at the Royal Academy, and particularly at the Suffolk Street Gallery from 1874 onwards.
AUCTION RECORDS:
LONDON, 21 Nov 1908, *Windmill* (pastel) GBP 1; *Flock; Farm* (watercolour) GBP 2. LONDON, 24 May 1909, *Moorland*, GBP 15; *Autumn Morning*, GBP 7. LONDON, 3 April 1922, *Flock Feeding*, GBP 16. LONDON, 6 April 1923, *Shepherd and His Flock* (drawing) GBP 19; *Flock at Sunset*, GBP 10; *Three Cows*, GBP 5. LONDON, 22 June 1923, *While Watching the Flock*, GBP 32. LONDON, 1 April 1980, *Duck Pond* (oil on canvas, 19 x 29 1/2 ins / 48 x 75 cm) GBP 420. LONDON, 27 Jan 1986, *Shepherd and His Flock* (oil on canvas, 23 x 27 ins / 58.5 x 68.5 cm) GBP 2,100.

ESTANSAN, Raymond
French, 17th century.
Sculptor.
Raymond Estansan sculpted an altar in 1663 for the church of Ste-Croix at Bordeaux.

ESTAQUE, Claude Henry
French, 18th century.
Active in Paris in 1786.
Painter (?), sculptor (?).

ESTAQUE, Jean
French, 20th century.
Born 1945, in St-Girons (Ariège).
Painter, sculptor. Figures.
Jean Estaque is self-taught, and currently works in Creuse. He started as a sculptor in 1970; in his early work, he was strongly influenced by Romanesque art. This sacred dimension is found again, this time in a 'pagan' form, in the little polychrome sculptures of his later years: carved wooden statuettes like totems, and primitive-looking stylised heads on top of nested boxes. Around these, a nation of worshippers throngs, either carved or merely suggested. These works evoke reminiscences of the heads of primitive idols in pure, pale colours, or new contemporary divinities mocking our human weaknesses.
Estaque has exhibited regularly, including, in 1989, at the Musée Ingres in Montauban, and at *Délire de Livres*, Centre Culturel, Boulogne-sur-Seine. Solo exhibitions include: 1988, Musée de l'Évêché de Limoges; and 1989, Centre Jacques Prévert à Aix-sur-Vienne.
BIBLIOGRAPHY:
Chevrier, Jean Marie, '*Jean Estaque*' in *Artension*, periodical, Rouen, 1991.

ESTCOURT, T.H.S. Bucknall
British, 19th century.
Draughtsman.
A series of *Views of the Alhambra* are attributed to T.H.S. Bucknall Estcourt.

ESTE, Alessandro d'
Italian, 19th century.
Born 1787, in Rome; died 8 December 1826, in Rome.
Sculptor.
Alessandro d'Este was the son and pupil of Antonio Este, and studied with Canova at the same time.

ESTE, Antonio d'
Italian, 18th - 19th century.
Born 1754, in Venice; died 13 September 1837, in Rome.
Sculptor. Figures, portraits. Busts.
Father of Alessandro, he was the pupil and collaborator of Canova, and for many years Director of the Vatican Museums.
AUCTION RECORDS:
LONDON, 8 July 1981, *Bust of Sir John Francis Edward of Acton* (marble, h. 27 1/4 ins / 69 cm) GBP 1,300.

ESTÉ, Florence
American, 19th - 20th century.
Born in Cincinnati (Ohio).
Painter. Landscapes.
Florence Esté began by working in Philadelphia, before going to Paris to study with Nozal. She exhibited at the Salon de la Société Nationale des Beaux-Arts from 1913. In 2003 the Galerie Chantal Kiener in Paris showed a collection of her work, landscapes of the Britany coast.

ESTEBA, Berenguer
Spanish, 14th century.
Active in Catalonia c. 1316.
Painter.

ESTEBAN
Spanish, 16th century.
Active in Toledo in 1539.
Sculptor.
Esteban worked for Toledo Cathedral.

ESTEBAN
Spanish, 17th century.
Active in Aragon at the beginning of the 17th century.
Sculptor.

ESTEBAN, Alfonso
Spanish, 13th century.
Active in Valladolid.
Painter.

The murals painted on the orders of Don Sancho IV, King of Castille, in the Sta Barbara Chapel of Burgos Cathedral are attributed to Alfonso and Rodrigo Esteban.

ESTEBAN, Carlos
Argentinian, 20th century.
Born 15 May 1938, in Buenos Aires.
Active in France from 1970.
Painter. Figures, landscapes.
Symbolism.

Carlos Esteban was active first in Buenos Aires but settled in Paris in 1970. In the early part of his career, Esteban's work was closely associated with hyperrealism although the reality he depicted was often portrayed in an indirect manner. After leaving this movement he experimented with various techniques including collage and froissage before turning towards a style of painting that was simpler in technique but more ambitious in its intentions. His semi-realist, semi-naive figures are painted in tones of ochre and sienna brown and inspired by literature, music, ancestral myths and the collective imagination. Esteban depicts tribal dances, grandiose and mysterious landscapes and mother goddesses who represent the mythical and mystical.

He exhibited in Paris in 1972, 1973 and 1985 at the Salon de la Jeune Peinture; in 1973 and 1974 at the Salon Grands et Jeunes d'Aujourd'hui; in 1974 at the Salon Comparaisons, and in 1975 at the FIAC (Foire Internationale d'Art Contemporain). In 1984, he showed in the 1st Biennale in Havana and in 1986 at the Salon de Montrouge. He held solo exhibitions of his work in 1964, 1966 and 1968 at the Lirolay Gallery in Buenos Aires, and from 1975 he has held regular solo exhibitions in Paris.

BIBLIOGRAPHY:
Parent, Francis, *Kilimandjaro. Carlos Esteban,* exhibition catalogue, Gal. Duras, Paris, 1990.

ESTEBAN, Celestino
Spanish, 20th century.
Active in Paris.
Ceramicist.

Celestino Esteban exhibited *Cordova Amphora* at the Sèvres pavilion at the 1937 Exposition Universelle.He is known for his Indian jars and his Hispano-Moorish vases and dishes.

ESTEBAN, Felix
Spanish, 19th century.
Born in Granada.
Painter.

Felix Esteban exhibited in Madrid from 1866.

ESTEBAN, Geronimo
Spanish, 16th century.
Active in Valencia in 1584.
Sculptor.

ESTEBAN, Jorge
Spanish, 16th century.
Active in Seville in 1574.
Painter.

Jorge Esteban worked for Seville Cathedral.

ESTEBAN, Juan
Spanish, 15th century.
Active in Valencia.
Painter.

In 1432 Juan Esteban executed paintings for Valencia Cathedral.

ESTEBAN, Juan
Spanish, 16th century.
Active in Madrid.
Sculptor.

Juan Esteban collaborated with Jeronimo Trezo.

ESTEBAN, Juan
Spanish, 17th century.
Active probably in Madrid.
Painter, priest. Historical painting, perspectives, landscapes.

Juan Esteban worked mainly around 1650.

ESTEBAN, Juan
Spanish, 17th century.
Active probably in Jaén c. 1666.
Painter. History painting, portraits.

Juan Esteban worked for Baeza Cathedral and for the church of the Baeza hospice.

J Esteban.

ESTEBAN, Lydia
Spanish, 20th century.
Born 1932.
Ceramicist.

Lydia Esteban studied under her father, Celestino Esteban.

ESTEBAN, Paquita
Spanish, 20th century.
Born 1929.
Ceramicist.

Paquita Esteban studied under her father, Celestino Esteban.

ESTEBAN, Pedro
Spanish, 17th century.
Active in Valladolid in 1616.
Painter.

ESTEBAN, Rodrigo
Spanish, 13th century.
Painter.

There is no work known to be exclusively by this artist, who was painter to Don Sancho IV, King of Castille. We know of him through an accounts book of the period in the Real Library, Madrid. He was Alfonso's brother.

MUSEUMS AND GALLERIES:
MADRID (Biblioteca Nacional).

ESTEBAN FERNANDO, Hermenegildo
Spanish, 19th - 20th century.
Born 13 April 1851, in Maella (Aragon); died 1945, in Rome.
Active in Italy.
Painter. Landscapes.

Hermenegildo Esteban Fernando began to paint while studying law and soon abandoned his legal career in Madrid to enrol at the school for Watercolour painters and the Real Academia de Bellas Artes de San Fernando where Carlos de Haes was a teacher. In 1882 he was awarded a bursary to study at the Accademia delle Belle Arti in Rome. At the end of his study trip he decided to settle in Rome and in 1887 became academy secretary, a position he occupied until his retirement in 1933. He returned to Madrid for one year in 1934 and then went back to Rome, remaining there until his death in 1945. In Madrid he exhibited with the national fine arts society in 1876, 1878 and 1881; in Italy he exhibited in 1884, 1890, 1892, 1906, 1912 and 1915; he also showed his work in Paris, Berlin and Munich; two retrospective exhibitions of his work were held in 1934 to mark his return to Madrid - the first at the Madrid fine arts circle and the second entitled *The Hero of Saragossa* at the Saragossa Salon. During his career he received a number of awards and became a member of the San Fernando and Saragossa royal fine arts academies. He mainly painted landscapes of Spain and Italy (Rome and Venice). His Impressionist style is imbued with a certain Classicism.

Bibliography:
Arnáiz, José Manuel/López Jiménez, Javier/Merchán Díaz, Manuel (ed.), *Cien años de pintura en Espana y Portugal (1830-1930)*, Antiqvaria, Madrid, 1988 (One Hundred Years of Painting in Spain and Portugal (1830-1930)).

ESTEBAN Y LOZANO, José
Spanish, 19th century.
Born in the 19th century, in Madrid.
Sculptor, medallist.
José Esteban y Lozano was a pupil of José Piquer. He first exhibited in exhibitions in Madrid in 1862. He was the brother of Victor Esteban y Lozano.

ESTEBAN Y LOZANO, Victor
Spanish, 19th century.
Born in the 19th century, in Madrid.
Painter. Historical painting, portraits, genre scenes.
Victor Esteban y Lozano was the brother of the sculptor José Esteban y Lozano. He studied at the Real Academia de San Fernando. From 1856 to 1866 he exhibited paintings of historical subjects and genre pieces in Madrid.

ESTEBAN Y VINCENTE, Enrique
Spanish, 19th century.
Born in the 19th century, in Salamanca.
Painter.
Enrique Esteban y Vincente studied at the Madrid school of painting. He first exhibited in 1866. His work consisted mainly of genre paintings and historical subjects.
Museums and Galleries:
Madrid (Prado): *The First Shot.*

ESTEBANEZ, Isidro
Spanish, 19th century.
Born in Madrid.
Sculptor (wood).
Isidro Estebanez specialised in religious subjects.

ESTÈBE, Jean-Marie
French, 20th century.
Born 18 February 1929, in Paris.
Draughtsman, engraver. Figures, landscapes with figures, landscapes.
Jean-Marie Estèbe was a pupil of Bersier, Georg and Jaudon. In 1960, he became professor of engraving and drawing at the École des Beaux-Arts, Grenoble. Since 1960 he has also been a life member of the Société des Peintres-Graveurs Français, in Paris. In his engraved landscapes, light effects are paramount; objects, trees and figures function only as shade. It is light that provides atmosphere and the depth of the planes and gives the objects their reality.
Bibliography:
Les Peintres graveurs français - 80e anniversaire, Société des peintres-graveurs français, Paris, 1969.
Museums and Galleries:
Amsterdam - Paris (Louvre) - Poitiers.

ESTEL
French.
Engraver (aquatint/stippling).

ESTENSE, Baldassare. See **BALDASSARE Estense**

ESTEPHAN, Youssef
Lebanese, 18th - 19th century.
Active c. 1800.
Painter. Portraits.
It is not known whether he was a priest or a layman. A known work by him is the *Portrait of Bishop Mikhayil Fadel II*, painted in 1819. The composition and execution of this painting are traditional and timid. The priestly garments and attributes make it decorative.
Bibliography:
Liban. Le Regard des peintres. 200 ans de peinture libanaise, exhibition catalogue, Institut du Monde Arabe, Paris, 1989.

ESTERAS, Juan
Spanish, 18th century.
Born 26 November 1747, in Pueblo de Majorca.
Painter, sculptor.

ESTERBAUER, Balthasar
German, 18th century.
Born at the beginning of the 18th century, in Franconia.
Sculptor.
Esterbauer seems to have worked in Würzburg.

ESTERLE, Max von (Ritter)
Austrian, 20th century.
Born 16 October 1870, in Cortina.
Painter, lithographer.
Max von Esterle lived in Innsbruck after studying in Munich, Paris and Vienna.

ESTERNOD, Marcel d'
Swiss, 20th century.
Born in Geneva.
Painter. Landscapes.
Marcel d'Esternod was a student at the school of fine arts in Geneva. He exhibited at the Salon des Artistes Français and the Salon des Artists Indépendants in Paris from 1929, with landscapes of Switzerland, Provence and Tunisia.

ESTERREICH
Russian, 19th century.
Active at the beginning of the 19th century.
Portrait artist.
Might perhaps be one of the Œsterreichs. The Russian Museum in St Petersburg has two portraits by him.

ESTES, Richard
American, 20th century.
Born 1932, in Evanston (Illinois).
Painter.
Richard Estes studied at the Art Institute of Chicago, then in New York where he lived from 1968. He took part in the Kassel Documenta in 1972, then in numerous other group exhibitions, including ones in Europe in 1974 and 1975, which brought American Hyperrealism face-to-face with European Realists. In 2002 he featured in the exhibition *Les Années 70: l'art en cause* (*The Seventies: Art on Trial*), Capc Musée d'Art Contemporain, Bordeaux; in 2003, *USA Hyperrealism 1965-75*, Musée d'Art Moderne et Contemporain, Strasbourg.

It was around 1970 that Hyperrealism, in which he broadly participated, started to form the subject of exhibitions and gain public attention. Competing in terms of the accuracy of detail and in the abrupt description of reality, taken from earlier photographs, Hyperrealist works, and the canvases of Richard Estes in particular, started by seducing and surprising with their mastery of technique. Nevertheless, Estes' canvases break free most of the time from reality as it is conceived through the subtle use of reflections. He mainly tackles subjects from urban life: the metro, streets, cars, shops, but all of them void of human presence. In the case of the frontages and shop displays, he pays great attention to reflections such as reflections of the street in the glass window, that even shows the opposite window, in which the painted window is reflected, etc., closely combining the described reality and its image. The success achieved by this type of painting has caused questions to be asked as to the real motivations behind such painting. These questions were directly tackled at the 1972 Documenta in Kassel, which introduced and established American Hyperrealism in Europe as an avant-garde movement. A distinguishing feature of Hyperrealism is that unlike the photograph where only one plane is sharp and the others out-of-focus, in a Hyperrealist work the Hyperrealist artist can make everything sharp, as if everything where in focus. Estes, however, paints with small brushstrokes, thereby retaining a degree of pictorial sensitivity. Estes has earned a place alongside Close, Don Eddy, Morley or Maclean.

BIBLIOGRAPHY:

Arthur, John, *Richard Estes: the urban landscape*, Museum of Fine Arts, Boston, 1978. Meisel, Louis K., *Richard Estes: the complete paintings 1966 - 1985*, catalogue raisonné, Abrams, New York, 1986. *Richard Estes: the complete prints*, exhibition catalogue, catalogue raisonné, American Federation of Arts, New York, 1992. *Richard Estes, recent works*, exhibition catalogue, Marlborough Fine Art, London, 2000. Fréruchet, Maurice, et al., *Les Années soixante-dix: l'art en cause*, exhibition catalogue, Capc musée d'Art contemporain, Bordeaux, 2002. Lebensztejn, Jean-Claude, et al., *Hyperréalismes USA 1965-75*, group exhibition catalogue, Musée d'Art moderne et contemporain, Strasbourg, Hazan, Paris, 2003.

MUSEUMS AND GALLERIES:

BUDAPEST (Ludwig Múz.): *Rappaports Pharmacy* (1976) - COLOGNE (Mus. Ludwig): *Foodshop* (1967).

AUCTION RECORDS:

LOS ANGELES, 15 May 1972, *Women on the Streets of New York*, USD 5,000. LONDON, 4 Dec 1974, *Teleflorist*, GBP 21,000; *Urban Landscapes* (series of eight silk screen prints, 14 x 20 1/4 ins / 35.5 x 51.5 cm) GBP 2,200. NEW YORK, 14 Dec 1976, *Pizza Restaurant* (1969, watercolour and gouache, 9 3/4 x 12 ins / 25 x 30.5 cm) USD 3,600. NEW YORK, 10 Feb 1977, *Untitled* (1974, silk screen print in colour, 33 1/2 x 46 3/4 ins / 85 x 119 cm) USD 2,600. NEW YORK, 12 May 1977, *Storefront Reflections, Miami* (1969, oil on canvas, 35 1/4 x 43 3/4 ins / 89.5 x 111.1 cm) USD 16,000. NEW YORK, 23 May 1978, *Columbus Avenue* (1975, acrylic/card, 12 1/2 x 20 3/4 ins / 32 x 53 cm) USD 10,000. NEW YORK, 18 May 1979, *Forty-Sixth Street* (1968, oil on canvas, 16 x 24 ins / 40.5 x 61 cm) USD 28,000. NEW YORK, 8 Nov 1979, *Corner Window* (1974, gouache, 16 x 19 1/2 ins / 40.7 x 49.5 cm) USD 13,500. NEW YORK, 14 Nov 1979, *Urban Landscape: Grant's* (1972, silk screen print in colour, 15 x 20 ins / 38 x 50.5 cm) USD 1,400. NEW YORK, 19 Nov 1981, *The Bridge* (1974, gouache, 16 x 16 3/4 ins / 40.5 x 42.5 cm) USD 14,000. NEW YORK, 5 May 1983, *Qualicraft Shoes* (1974, silk screen print in colour, 33 1/4 x 47 ins / 84.6 x 119.3 cm) USD 3,750. NEW YORK, 1 Nov 1984, *Donohue's* (1967, hardboard, 48 1/4 x 30 ins / 122.5 x 76.2 cm) USD 65,000. NEW YORK, 4 Nov 1987, *Bus Reflections* (1972, oil on canvas, 39 3/4 x 52 ins / 101 x 132.2 cm) USD 440,000. NEW YORK, 4 May 1988, *Cadillac* (oil on canvas, 40 x 50 ins / 101.3 x 127 cm) USD 38,500. NEW YORK, 10 Nov 1988, *Food* (watercolour/paper, 11 3/4 x 14 1/2 ins / 30 x 36.6 cm) USD 16,500. NEW YORK, 2 May 1989, *Holland Hotel* (1984, oil on canvas, 45 x 71 1/2 ins / 114.3 x 181.5 cm) USD 539,000. NEW YORK, 9 Nov 1989, *U-Ban* (1980, acrylic/card, 14 x 20 ins / 35.5 x 50.8 cm) USD 93,500. NEW YORK, 18 Nov 1992, *Shop Window Lighting* (1968, oil/synthetic resin, 48 x 30 ins / 121.9 x 76.2 cm) USD 27,500. NEW YORK, 10 Nov 1993, *At Nedick's Place* (1970, oil on canvas, 48 x 66 ins / 121.9 x 167.6 cm) USD 464,500. NEW YORK, 4 May 1994, *Revolving Doors* (1968, oil/synthetic resin, 30 x 48 ins / 76.5 x 121.9 cm) USD 184,000. NEW YORK, 2 Nov 1994, *Teleflorist* (1974, oil on canvas, 36 x 52 ins / 91.4 x 132.1 cm) USD 211,500. NEW YORK, 2 May 1995, *Embarcation for Cythera II* (1989, oil/material, 36 x 73 ins / 91.4 x 185.4 cm) USD 217,000. NEW YORK, 5 May 1996, *Salzburg Cathedral* (1982, colour silk screen print, 20 x 14 1/2 ins / 50.6 x 37 cm) USD 747. NEW YORK, 9 Nov 1996, *Urban Landscapes III; Manhattan; Cafeteria; Vatican; Metro; Bus Interior; Eiffel Tower Restaurant; Images; Lakewood Mall* (1981, coloured lithograph, each 13 3/4 x 20 ins / 35 x 50.5 cm) USD 7,475. NEW YORK, 20 Nov 1996, *American Express in the City Centre* (1979, oil on canvas, 24 x 36 ins / 61 x 91.5 cm) USD 123,500. NEW YORK, 6 and 7 March 1998, *Cafeteria, Vatican* (1981, silk screen print in colour, 14 x 20 ins / 35.7 x 51 cm) USD 1,035. NEW YORK, 19 May 1999, *Broadway and 64th, Spring 84* (1984, oil on canvas, 39 x 71 ins / 100 x 180 cm) USD 320,000. NEW YORK, 18 Nov 1999, *Ice Cream* (oil and acrylic on board, 20 x 25 ins / 51 x 63 cm) USD 60,000. NEW YORK, 15 Nov 2000, *Number Five* (oil on canvas laid on masonite, 48 x 32 ins / 122 x 81 cm) USD 280,000. NEW YORK, 15 Nov 2000, *Gourmet Treats* (oil on canvas, 36 x 48 ins / 91 x 122 cm) USD 420,000. STOCKHOLM, 2 May 2001, *Qualicraft Shoes - The Chinese Lady* (colour silk screen print, 33 x 47 ins / 84 x 119 cm) SEK 31,000. NEW YORK, 4 May 2001, *Holland Hotel* (colour screenprint, 48 x 72 ins / 122 x 183 cm) USD 8,500. NEW YORK, 14 May 2002, *Times Square at 3.53 pm, Winter* (1985, oil on canvas, 27 x 49 ins / 69 x 124 cm) USD 300,000. NEW YORK, 14 May 2002, *Spirit* (1995, oil on canvas, 38 x 65 ins / 96 x 165 cm) USD 320,000. LONDON, 26 June 2003, *Paris Opera House* (2000, oil on canvas, 39 x 80 ins / 100 x 202 cm) GBP 190,000. PORTLAND, 8 Aug 2003, *Mt. Desert VII* (1996, oil on wood, 20 x 16 ins / 51 x 41 cm) USD 28,000. NEW YORK, 11 May 2004, *Baby Doll Lounge* (1978, oil on canvas, 36 x 60 ins / 92 x 152 cm) USD 370,000. NEW YORK, 12 May 2004, *34th Street, Manhattan, Looking East* (1982, oil on canvas, 91 x 91 ins / 231 x 231 cm) USD 500,000.

ESTEVAN, Hermenegildo. See **ESTEBAN FERNANDO Hermenegildo**

ESTEVE, Antonio

Spanish, 19th century.
Active in Toledo c. 1800.
Painter. History painting.

Antonio Esteve decorated a number of churches in Toledo and also worked on the decoration of Toledo University.

ESTEVE, Bautista

Spanish, 17th century.
Active in Valencia c. 1600.
Painter.

ESTEVE, Francisco

Spanish, 18th century.
Born 1682, in Valencia; died 1766, in Valencia.
Sculptor.

Francisco Esteve was a pupil of the painter Conchillos and the sculptor Cuevas. During the period of political turmoil in Spain he worked extensively on the Balearic island of Ibiza, and later returned to Valencia, where he produced numerous statues for various churches.

ESTEVE, Gabriel

French, 20th century.
Born in Valencia, Spain.
Painter.

Gabriel Esteve exhibited at the Salon des Artistes Français, Paris, in 1936.

ESTEVE, Jacinto

Spanish, 18th century.
Born 1766, in Liria; died in Valencia.
Painter. History painting.

MUSEUMS AND GALLERIES:

VALENCIA (PM): *King Alfonso V Receiving Cardinal de Fox.*

ESTÈVE, Jacques. See **ESTHOM Jacques**

ESTEVE, Jaime

Spanish, 15th century.
Active in Valencia in 1415.
Sculptor.

Jaime Esteve worked on the decoration of the façade of Valencia Cathedral.

ESTEVE, José

Spanish, 16th century.

Active in Valencia.
Sculptor.
In 1572, José Esteve worked for the church in Bocairente.

ESTEVE, Luciano

Spanish, 18th century.
Active in Valencia.
Sculptor.
Luciano Esteve carved a number of statues for the façade of Valencia Cathedral.

ESTÈVE, Maurice

French, 20th century.
Born 2 May 1904, in Culan (Cher); died 27 June 2001.
Painter (including gouache), watercolourist, pastellist, collage artist, lithographer, draughtsman. Figures, genre scenes, sporting subjects, still-lifes, urban landscapes. Designs for tapestries, and stained glass windows.
Poetic Reality.

Maurice Estève spent his childhood with his grandparents in his native town of Culan, and the countryside and nature were always to be for him a rich source of inspiration. His grandmother, the most important presence in his youth, was the first to encourage him in his artistic leanings. In 1913, he went to Paris to join his parents, his father (a shoemaker) and his mother (a dress designer). He soon felt at home in the capital and visited the Louvre (some biographers say on his own initiative) as an observer, where he was impressed by Courbet, Delacroix, Chardin, Tintoretto and Paolo Uccello's *Battle of San Romano*. He later said, 'I learnt everything by looking at painting. It was where I saw life.' In 1914, he returned to Culan for the summer holidays, but because of the war he had to stay there for four years and went to school there. In 1915, he began to paint and because of his obvious gifts, his mother encouraged him to train as an artist.

In 1919, Estève returned to Paris and enrolled in evening classes at the city's design school. He earned his living as a typographer at first, and then became an apprentice in the studio of a furniture designer. In 1919 he painted from the balcony of the family apartment a design, *The Boulevard de Belleville*, in a classical style. In the same year he discovered Cézanne. This was a period of conflict with his father, who was upset by his son's interest in painting and his determination to be an artist, as Monique Prudhomme-Estève reports. However, for a year he directed a studio designing shawls and fabrics in Barcelona.

Estève returned to Paris in 1924 and, once again among the painters he admired, his passion for painting revived and he attended the private Académie Colarossi in Montparnasse. In about 1927/1928 he was influenced by Surrealism, and in 1929 he showed at his first group exhibition, the Salon des Surindédependants. The following year he held his first solo exhibition at the Galerie Yvangot, Paris. It was not a success. He moved to a studio in Porte de Vanves. While still painting, he was attracted to cinema and theatre design. In 1936, the Spanish Civil War had a strong effect on him and for a short while, during which he painted *The Sisters of Barcelona*, he went through an Expressionist period. In 1939, he moved to the Rue Lepic in Montmartre. His military service ended in 1942. Always an admirer of Cézanne, he painted a *Homage* to the painter in 1942. He also signed an exclusive contract with the Galerie Louis Carré, Paris.

From 1952, Estève worked on colour lithography in the Clot studio, then in 1954 at the Desjobert studio, and finally in 1955 at the Fernand Moulot studio. In 1955 he moved again, this time to the 16th arrondissement of Paris, and decided to spend each summer in Culan, working mainly in watercolour, charcoal and collage. Pierre Francastel wrote the first monograph on the painter for the Éditions Galanis in 1956. Estève designed the windows for the church of Berlincourt (Swiss Jura) in 1957, did his first tapestry designs in 1963, and created his first collages in 1965. In 1970 he was awarded the Grand Prix National des Arts. On 4 August 1982, his friends founded an Association to help him set up a space to house and exhibit a large collection of his works that he wanted to donate. On 2 July 1985 the Municipality of Bourges, with the support of the Department of Historical Monuments and the Directorate of French Museums, undertook to exhibit the whole of the donation (50 oils on canvas, 34 drawings, 20 watercolours, 10 collages and two tapestries) in the Hôtel des Échevins, which was to be called the Estève Museum.

In the 1930s, Estève learned from some of the pictorial principles of Cubism and Léger, such as simple construction and the management of solid colour used for effects of contrast. Estève's pre-war and post-war painting always involves an analysis of the real world: he explores the function of objects, looking at how their shapes can be represented in simpler forms and the relationship between them and their surroundings, in compositions that are careful, thoughtful, and certainly structured. He painted an enormous number of still-lifes and his landscapes (1943(1944) clearly herald the abstract painter. Throughout this period, Estève gives colour a quite original role: it acts on form, which is not revolutionary at this time, but which is, above all, the reminder of a reality. He heightens the tones and they become more insistent and brighter, though always modulated and nuanced, in what could be called a lyrical use of colour.

Paintings such as *Painter in the Studio* (1948) or *The Pearl Fisher* (1949) and the work that marks Estève's turning point, when he began to produce work that is totally non-figurative, such as *Homage to Fouquet*, reveal that, for Estève, pure painting meant that the painting materials and strategies were essentially the subject of the composition. Consisting of coloured shapes that unfold, support each other, stand out, and extend according to a calculated and masterly logic, the surface of the canvas is lit by flat planes of colour that with nuance bring together every shade of red, orange, warm colours and greens. This painting develops in terms of rhythm and energy. In the 1950s, the arrangement tends to be loosely geometrical and answers to the formal and chromatic organisation of the paintings. The contours of the coloured surfaces are clear-cut, sometimes outlined, and most of the coloured sections are left solid. Nevertheless, the surface is very carefully worked, creating at each visual focal point a 'colour/form' clarity. In the 1960s, this kind of painting was followed by works in which the forms were looser, more irregular and lighter, where integration takes precedence over accumulation and stratification while the various coloured surfaces are related in a more nuanced way and the brushstroke reappears.

Estève deals with his investigations of material face-on, and they continue with his paintings of 1982-1990, in which the paint becomes thinner and lighter. There is an almost airy glow in the lively, warm colours, and the always balanced structures create and filter a near weightless space. Estève worked slowly, several years sometimes separating the first and last brushstrokes in a piece, and he sometimes painted several canvases simultaneously. His watercolour, drawing and collage form a separate body of work having its own characteristics. He also uses bright colours in his watercolours, but exploits the softer medium for transparent surfaces on backgrounds that are lighter, more flexible and very subtle in shading. He sometimes heightens his charcoal drawings with coloured crayon, and he manages black and white in a more architectural way than in his paintings. His collages are different in inspiration and idea: using pieces of newspaper or paper of various textures, Estève sometimes paints them to obtain washed colours, then sticks and combines them with other colours. The result indicates a greater liberty of action, which is less reflective and more impulsive than that shown in his drawings.

From the 1930s onwards, Estève took part in many group exhibitions including from 1929 to 1938 Salon des Surindépendants, Paris; 1937 a collaboration with Robert and Sonia Delaunay in the decoration of the Aviation and Railways pavilions at the Paris Exposition Universelle; between 1941 and 1944, Salon d'Automne, Paris; 1941, involvement in a large exhibition of *Jeunes peintres de tradition française* (*Young Painters of the French Tradition*); 1943, *Cinq peintres d'aujour'hui* (*Five Painters of Today*), in the company of Beaudin, Borès, Gischia and Pignon; between 1946 and 1961, Salon des Tuileries, Paris; travelling exhibition, *Bazaine, Estève, Lapique*, Stedelijk Museum, Amsterdam, and the National Art Museum, Copenhagen; 1949, *La Nouvelle Peinture française* (*New French Painting*), Musée de l'État, Luxembourg; 1949, *Peinture française 1938-1948* (*French Painting 1938-1948*); 1950, *Advancing French Art*, New York; 1950, *Peinture et sculpture française 1938-1948* (*French Painting and Sculpture 1938-1948*), Berlin; between 1950 and 1955, Salon de Mai, Paris; 1951, *L'École de Paris 1900-1950* (*The Paris School 1900-1950*), Royal Academy of Art, London; 1951, *Peintres parisiens de la deuxième génération* (*Parisian Painters of the Second Generation*), Kunsthalle, Basel; 1952, *Tendances actuelles de 'École de Paris* (*Current Trends in the Paris School*), Kunsthalle, Basel; 1953, *Onze peintres de paris* (*Eleven Parisian Painters*), Stedelijk Museum, Amsterdam; 1954, the Venice Biennale; 1955, the Carnegie Institute, Pittsburgh; 1957, *Pérennité de l'art français* (*The Continuity of French Art*), Musée de l'Athenée, Geneva; 1959, Documenta II, Kassel; 1967, Universal Exhibition, Montreal; 1981, Paris, *Paris 1937-1957*, Centre Georges Pompidou, Musée National d'Art Moderne. 2002, FIAC (Foire Internationale d'Art Contemporain), Paris; 2003, Galerie Claude Bernard, Paris.

Estève's first retrospective was held at the Galerie Carré in 1948, when thirty works painted between 1935 and 1947 were exhibited. He regularly showed at solo exhibitions in Paris, Copenhagen, Stokholm, and Geneva. In 1961, a large retrospective was held in Basel, Düsseldorf, Copenhagen and Oslo. Later, Estève exhibited collages, watercolours, drawings and lithographs. In 1977, there was an exhibition of recent paintings at the Galerie Claude Bernard and in 1981 a retrospective at the Musé Cantini, Marseilles, the Musée de l'Etat, Luxembourg, and the Museum of Metz. Other exhibitions included 1983, *Proposition pour une Rétrospective* (*Proposal for a Retrospective*), Maison de la Culture, Bourges; 1984, *Hommage à Estève* (*Homage to Estève*), organised by the Salon d'Automne; 1986, retrospective, Réunion des Musées Nationaux at the Grand Palais, Paris, which went on to Oslo and Tübingen; since then, many private exhibitions of works on paper (Galerie Claude Bernard, Galerie Tendances, Galerie du Luxembourg); 1990, exhibition of late paintings (1982-1990); 1994, exhibition of watercolours at the Galerie Louis Carré, Paris; 1998, *Estève insolite. Oeuvres inédites* (*Unknown Estève. Unpublished Works*); 2003, Galerie Claude Bernard, Paris; 2002, Musée Estève, Bourges.

Estève

BIBLIOGRAPHY:

Lescure, Jean, *Estève ou les Chemins silencieux de la réalité*, Gal. Louis Carré, Paris, 1945. Francastel, Pierre, *Estève*, Éd. Galanis, Paris, 1956. Franck, Elgar, *Estève, dessins*, Éd. Galanis, Paris, 1960. Muller, Joseph-Émile, '*Estève*', *Coll. Peintres d'aujourd'hui*, Hazan, Paris, 1961. Ragon, Michel/Seuphor, Michel, '*L'Art abstrait*', vol. 3, Hazan, Paris, 1973. Di San Lazzaro, Gualtieri, *Hommage à Maurice Estève*, Société internationale d'Art du XXe siècle, Paris, 1975. '*Maurice Estève*' in *Zodiaque* no. 120, periodical, Zodiaque, La-Pierre-qui-Vire, 1979. Acatos, Sylvio, *Conversation avec Maurice Estève*, Construire, Zurich, April 1982. Leymarie, Jean, *L'Aquarelle*, Skira, Geneva, 1984. Dobbels, Daniel, '*Maurice Estève*' in *Libération*, periodical, Paris, 16 December 1985. Leymarie, Jean/Peyré, Yves, *Rétrospective Estève*, exhibition catalogue, Réunion des musées nationaux, Paris, 1986. Prudhomme-Estève, Monique/Moestrup, Hans/Valier, Dora (introduction), *Estève. Catalogue de l'œuvre gravé*, catalogue raisonné, Forlaget Cordelia, Copenhagen, 1986 (text in French). Vézin, L., '*Aquarelles d'Estève*' in *Beaux-Arts Magazine*, periodical, Paris, January 1986. Muller, Joseph-Émile, *Estève, œuvres sur papier 1965-1985*, exhibition catalogue, Gal. du Luxembourg, Luxembourg, 1990. Prudhomme-Estève, Monique, *Catalogue du musée Estève*, catalogue, Musées de Bourges, Bourges, 1990. Maillard, Robert/Prudhomme-Estève, Monique, *Catalogue raisonné de l'œuvre peint*, Ides et Calendes, Neuchâtel, 1995. Chapon, François, *Collages: invention, subversion ou diversion?*, Musée Estève, Bourges, 1999. Harambourg, Lydia/Colson, Laurent, *Convergence spirituelle*, exhibition catalogue, Gal. Louis Carré, gal. Luohan, Paris, 2001 (text in French and English).

MUSEUMS AND GALLERIES:

BOURGES (Mus. Estève) - MARSEILLES (Mus. Cantini): *Women Harvesting* (1978) - PARIS (MNAM-CCI).

AUCTION RECORDS:

PARIS, 29 June 1955, *Boxers*, FRF 70,000. PARIS, 27 May 1959, *Composition* (watercolour) FRF 260,000. MILAN, 21 and 23 Nov 1962, *Still-life with Basket of Lettuce*, ITL 5,200,000. GENEVA, 25 May 1963, *Old Man*, CHF 62,000. COPENHAGEN, 9 May 1967, *Composition* (watercolour) DKK 15,100. HAMBURG, 6 June 1969, *Composition* (watercolour) DEM 6,800. VERSAILLES, 31 May 1972, *Orange, Blue and Red Composition* (watercolour) FRF 18,500. LONDON, 29 Sept 1972, *Rape*, GBP 6,600. PARIS, 24 Nov 1973, *Composition* (watercolour) FRF 22,000. VERSAILLES, 11 June 1974, *Composition* (watercolour) FRF 37,500. VERSAILLES, 8 Nov 1974, *Mask*, FRF 39,000. LONDON, 6 April 1976, *Bottle of Wine, Apples, Lemons and Pots on a Table* (1938, oil on canvas, 15 x 22 ins / 38 x 55 cm) GBP 4,500. BERN, 9 June 1976, *Abstract Composition* (1970, watercolour, 15 3/4 x 19 1/2 ins / 40.3 x 49.7 cm) CHF 21,000. LONDON, 30 June 1977, *Landscape* (1952, oil on canvas, 7 1/2 x 11 ins / 19 x 27 cm) GBP 2,000. NEW YORK, 16 March 1978, *Still-life* (1938, oil on canvas, 12 1/4 x 19 3/4 ins / 31 x 50 cm) USD 6,500. PARIS, 12 Dec 1979, *The Painter* (1937, oil on canvas, 46 x 32 ins / 116 x 81 cm) FRF 43,000. PARIS, 10 June 1980, *Amateur Fisherman* (1945, charcoal and blue pencil/paper, 12 1/2 x 15 1/4 ins / 31.5 x 39 cm) FRF 29,000. HAMBURG, 12 June 1981, *Composition* (1960, charcoal and pencil/paper, 5 1/2 x 7 1/2 ins / 14 x 19 cm) DEM 3,200. PARIS, 13 June 1983, *Amateur Fisherman* (1945, charcoal and blue pencil, 12 1/2 x 15 1/4 ins / 31.5 x 39 cm) FRF 33,000. LONDON, 26 June 1984, *Composition No. 981-1* (1967, watercolour/paper, 21 x 27 1/4 ins / 52.5 x 69.5 cm) GBP 4,800. LONDON, 6 Dec 1984, *Copse* (1948, oil on canvas, 15 1/2 x 12 1/2 ins / 39.6 x 31.7 cm) GBP 9,000. VERSAILLES, 23 March 1986, *Composition* (1964, charcoal, blue pencil and coloured ink, 13 x 19 3/4 ins / 33 x 50 cm) FRF 73,500. PARIS, 23 June 1986, *The Téméraire* (1952, oil on canvas, 46 x 35 ins / 116 x 89 cm) FRF 630,000. PARIS, 10 April 1987, *Composition 1962 Watercolour 730* (1962, watercolour, 24 x 19 ins / 61 x 48 cm) FRF 140,000. PARIS, 21 Oct 1987, *Composition* (1955, charcoal and colouring pencil, 9 3/4 x 12 1/2 ins / 25 x 31.5 cm) FRF 44,000. DENMARK, 2 March 1988, *Still-life with Jug* (18 x 24 ins / 46 x 61 cm) DKK 320,000. LONDON, 30 June 1988, *Round Table with Fruit* (1943, oil on canvas, 29 x 36 1/4 ins / 73.8 x 92 cm) GBP 55,000; *Tree on a Riverbank* (1949, oil on canvas, 25 1/2 x 36 ins / 65 x 91.5 cm) GBP 99,000. PARIS, 28 Oct 1988, *Arbre à cloches* (1965, watercolour and collage, 14 1/2 x 11 ins / 37 x 27 cm) FRF 135,000. PARIS, 16 Nov 1988, *Bodableu, tapestry* (1970, 96 1/2 x 70 3/4 ins / 245 x 180 cm) FRF 108,000. PARIS, 21 Nov 1988, *Biporelli* (1982, oil on canvas, 36 1/4 x 28 3/4 ins / 92 x 73 cm) FRF 450,000. COPENHAGEN, 30 Nov 1988, *Composition* (1963, watercolour, 9 3/4 x 13 ins / 25 x 33 cm) DKK 115,000. PARIS, 21 June 1989, *Composition* (1951, watercolour/paper, 25 1/2 x 19 3/4 ins / 65 x 50 cm) FRF 252,000. LONDON, 29 June 1989, *Brouclé* (1973, oil on canvas, 25 1/2 x 32 ins / 65 x 81 cm) GBP 77,000. PARIS, 8 Oct 1989, *Eclipse* (1950, oil on canvas, 7 1/2 x 9 1/2 ins / 19 x 24 cm) FRF 200,000. COPENHAGEN, 22 Nov 1989, *Erotic Scene* (1933, watercolour, 11 x 15 ins / 28 x 38 cm) DKK 75,000. PARIS, 22 Nov 1989, *Apple Trees* (1943, oil on canvas, 21 1/4 x 25 1/2 ins / 54 x 65 cm) FRF 540,000. PARIS, 25 March 1990, *Riverbank* (1918, watercolour and gouache, 9 1/2 x 12 1/4 ins / 24 x 31 cm) FRF 48,000; *Pipo Player* (1931, oil on canvas, 23 1/2 x 9 ins / 60 x 23 cm) FRF 95,000; *Weaver* (1948, oil on canvas, 31 1/2 x 25 1/2 ins / 80 x 65 cm) FRF 1,470,000; *Blois* (1953, oil on canvas, 36 1/4 x 28 3/4 ins / 92 x 73 cm) FRF 950,000; *Composition* (1961, gouache, 22 1/2 x 17 ins / 57 x 43 cm) FRF 420,000; *Bula* (1970, oil on canvas, diam. 25 1/2 ins / 65 cm) FRF 1,700,000; *Noirbel* (1957, oil on canvas, 31 1/2 x 39 1/4 ins / 80 x 100 cm) FRF 2,000,000. LONDON, 5 April 1990, *Trigourec* (1972, oil on canvas, 57 1/2 x 38 1/4 ins / 146 x 97 cm) GBP 297,000. PARIS, 18 June 1990, *Debredinoire III* (1971, collage, 26 x 20 1/2 ins / 66 x 52 cm) FRF 200,000. PARIS, 21 June 1990, *Motherhood* (graphite, 6 1/4 x 5 ins / 16 x 12.5 cm) FRF 50,000. LONDON, 18 Oct 1990, *Untitled* (1952, watercolour/paper, 16 1/4 x 12 1/4 ins / 41.3 x 31 cm) GBP 24,200. PARIS, 16 Dec 1990, *Mechanical Bouquet* (1974, oil on canvas, 20 x 24 ins / 50.5 x 61 cm) FRF 400,000. PARIS, 2 June 1991, *Light on the Window* (1942, oil on canvas, 28 3/4 x 23 1/2 ins / 73 x 60 cm) FRF 290,000. LONDON, 27 June 1991, *Tricorn* (1959, oil on canvas, 18 x 15 ins / 46 x 38 cm) GBP 37,400. PARIS, 12 Oct 1991, *Blois* (1953, oil on canvas, 36 1/4 x 28 3/4 ins / 92 x 73 cm) FRF 420,000. ZURICH, 16 Oct 1991, *Matinailles* (1956, coloured lithograph, 26 1/2 x 20 1/4 ins / 67 x 51.5 cm) CHF 4,200. COPENHAGEN, 4 Dec 1991, *Composition* (1963, watercolour, 9 3/4 x 13 ins / 25 x 33 cm) DKK 90,000. PARIS, 6 Dec 1991, *Cinétruc* (1970, soft pastel and charcoal, 20 1/2 x 19 1/2 ins / 52 x 49.5 cm) FRF 95,000. HONFLEUR, 19 April 1992, *Boulogne* (1957, oil on canvas, 26 x 36 1/4 ins / 66 x 92 cm) FRF 850,000. COPENHAGEN, 20 May 1992, *Composition* (1968, watercolour, 20 1/2 x 14 1/2 ins / 52 x 37 cm) DKK 125,000. LONDON, 15 Oct 1992, *Shrimp* (1983, oil on canvas, 28 3/4 x 39 1/4 ins / 73 x 100 cm) GBP 49,500. LONDON, 3 Dec 1992, 1958, oil on canvas, 39 1/4 x 32 ins / 100 x 81 cm) GBP 79,200. COPENHAGEN, 10 March 1993, *The Tall House* (1944, oil on canvas, 24 x 19 3/4 ins / 61 x 50 cm) DKK 200,000. PARIS, 3 June 1993, *Nohant Vicq* (1954, oil on canvas, 23 3/4 x 16 ins / 60.5 x 40.5 cm) FRF 350,000. NEW YORK, 3 Nov 1993, *1020-A* (1970, watercolour and gouache/paper, 25 x 19 1/2 ins / 63.2 x 49.5 cm) USD 23,000. LONDON, 2 Dec 1993, *Vermuse* (1958, oil on canvas, 39 1/4 x 32 ins / 100 x 81 cm) GBP 80,700. VERSAILLES, 27 March 1994, *Composition* (acrylic/paper, 20 x 17 1/4 ins / 51 x 43.5 cm) FRF 123,000. PARIS, 22 June 1994, *Weaver* (1948, oil on canvas, 32 x 25 1/2 ins / 81 x 65 cm) FRF 422,000. COPENHAGEN, 21 Sept 1994, *Pearl Fishers* (1950, oil on canvas, 22 x 25 1/2 ins / 55 x 65 cm) DKK 280,000. PARIS, 2 June 1995, *Untitled* (1967, watercolour/paper, 19 1/4 x 12 1/2 ins / 49 x 32 cm) FRF 90,000. ZURICH, 23 June 1995, *Black Stalks* (1948, oil on canvas, 13 x 9 1/2 ins / 33 x 24 cm) CHF 20,000. LONDON, 30 Nov 1995, *Tree on a Riverbank* (1949, oil on canvas, 25 1/2 x 36 ins / 65 x 91.5 cm) GBP 40,000. PARIS, 13 Dec 1995, *Troubadour, Landscape* (1954, oil on canvas, 46 x 32 ins / 116 x 81 cm) FRF 630,000. COPENHAGEN, 12 March 1996, *Composition* (1961, soft chalk, 9 x 6 3/4 ins / 22 x 17 cm) DKK 64,000. PARIS, 24 May 1996, *Parentis* (1955, oil on canvas, 46 x 35 ins / 116 x 89 cm) FRF 620,000. PARIS, 13 June 1996, *Lajoupée* (1973, lithograph, 25 1/2 x 19 3/4 ins / 64.7 x 50.3 cm) FRF 11,000. PARIS, 5 Oct 1996, *Composition* (1964, watercolour/paper, 19 1/4 x 24 1/2 ins / 49 x 62 cm) FRF 145,000. LONDON, 6 Dec 1996, *Untitled* (1962, watercolour/paper, 25 1/4 x 19 1/2 ins / 64 x 49.5 cm) GBP 8,280. LONDON, 6 Dec 1996, *Nude with Chevron* (1974, watercolour and pencil/paper, 18 1/2 x 14 ins / 46.7 x 35.5 cm) GBP 11,500. PARIS, 13 Dec 1996, *Composition* (1975, pastel and charcoal/paper, 16 1/4 x 12 3/4 ins / 41.5 x 32.5 cm) FRF 22,000. PARIS, 24 March 1997, *Bank Street* (1967, coloured lithograph, 25 3/4 x 18 ins / 65.5 x 46 cm) FRF 4,500. PARIS, 28 April 1997, *Composition* (1959, pastel /paper, 19 x 25 ins / 48 x 63.5 cm) FRF 70,000. LONDON, 23 Oct 1997, *The Black Causes* (1954, oil on canvas, 23 3/4 x 19 3/4 ins / 60.5 x 50 cm) GBP 51,000. PARIS, 14 Dec 1997, *Blue Yang* (1969, pastel/paper, 15 3/4 x 12 1/2 ins / 40 x 31.5 cm) FRF 70,000. LONDON, 24 June 1999, *Squirrel* (oil on canvas, 13 x 16 ins / 33 x 41 cm) GBP 28,000. STOCKHOLM, 26 Oct 1999, *Pole Star* (oil on canvas, 32 x 26 ins / 82 x 66 cm) SEK 1,025,000. PARIS, 1 Dec 2000, *Composition* (watercolour, 19 x 15 ins / 49 x 37 cm) FRF 165,000. PARIS, 30 March 2001, *Painter and Model* (oil on canvas, 46 x 35 ins / 116 x 89 cm) FRF 400,000. PARIS, 18 Dec 2001, *Young Girl with Ball* (oil on canvas, 26 x 18 ins / 65 x 46 cm) FRF 285,000. PARIS, 9 Dec 2002, *Glass Blower* (oil on canvas, 32 x 26 ins / 81 x 65 cm) EUR 132,000. PARIS, 10 Dec 2002, *Mitoi* (oil on canvas, 15 x 22 ins / 38 x 55 cm) EUR 200,000. PARIS, 2 April 2003, *Loxos* (oil on canvas, 39 x 29 ins / 100 x 73 cm) EUR 71,000. PARIS, 2 April 2003, *Bourriot* (oil on canvas) EUR 75,000. LONDON, 5 Feb 2004, *Forge* (oil on canvas, 13 x 22 ins / 33 x 55 cm) GBP 35,000. COPENHAGEN, 5 Oct 2004, *Jovius* (oil on canvas, 51 x 38 ins / 130 x 97 cm) DKK 800,000.

ESTEVE, Miguel
Spanish, 16th century.
Active in Valencia between 1507 and 1520.
Painter.

Miguel Esteve was one of the key figures among the group of artists in Valencia who gathered round Ferrando Yanez de la Almedina and were influenced by the Florentine school and Leonardo da Vinci. Along with Miguel de Prado he was commissioned to decorate the chapel of the town hall in Valencia in 1520.

MUSEUMS AND GALLERIES:
VALENCIA (MBA San Pío V): *St Vincent Ferrer* (altarpiece); *Holy Family*.

ESTEVE, Rafael. See **ESTÈVE Y VILLELA**

ESTEVE, Rémy
French, 20th century.
Born 17 May 1917, in Le Havre.
Painter.

Rémy Esteve was a self-taught, non-figurative painter.

R. ESTÈVE

ESTEVE ADAM, José
Spanish, 20th - 21st century.
Born 1946, in Algemesi (Valencia).
Painter. Interiors, landscapes.

José Esteve Adam has regularly taken part in group exhibitions in Spain, and, in 1991, in the Chicago international art exhibition. He has regularly exhibited his work in solo exhibitions in Valencia since 1973.

ESTEVE Y BONET, José
Spanish, 18th century.
Born 22 February 1741, in Valencia; died 17 August 1802, in Valencia.
Sculptor.

José Esteve y Bonet studied under Ignacio Vergara and Francisco Esteve. He was made a member of the Academy in

1772. He later held the posts of lecturer, deputy director and director in chief at the Academy. In 1782 he was appointed honorary sculptor to the king. Esteve y Bonet was a prolific artist but his work was somewhat lacking in original talent. He was one of the last sculptors to produce a polychrome piece in the Baroque tradition. He is known for his *Immaculate Conception* in Valencia Cathedral and another in the church of Santiago in Orihuela.

ESTEVE Y BOTTEY, Francisco
Spanish, 20th century.
Born 19 January 1884, in Sant Martí de Provençals (Barcelona); died 4 July 1959, in Sant Martí de Provençals (Barcelona).
Painter, engraver, writer. Landscapes, urban landscapes, seascapes.

Francisco Estevey y Bottey studied at the Real Academia de Bellas Artes de San Fernando. He was awarded two study bursaries and travelled in France, Italy, Belgium and Switzerland. On his return to Spain in 1941 he became an assistant teacher at the Academia de San Fernando. He taught drawing in 1923 at the school of arts and crafts in Madrid. He took part in a number of collective and solo exhibitions and received several awards including a first medal in 1920 and another in 1929. He also specialised in engraving and wrote several books on the subject.

BIBLIOGRAPHY:
Arnáiz, José Manuel/López Jiménez, Javier/Merchán Díaz, Manuel (ed.), *Cien años de pintura en Espana y Portugal (1830-1930)*, Antiqvaria, Madrid, 1988 (One Hundred Years of Painting in Spain and Portugal (1830-1930)).

ESTEVE Y MARQUES, Agustin
Spanish, 18th century.
Born 12 May 1753, in Valencia; died c. 1809, probably in Madrid, c. 1820 according to some sources.
Painter, copyist. Portraits.

Agustin Esteve y Marques studied in Valencia and Madrid. He was employed as a copyist by Goya, whose style he had assimilated, though he lacked Goya's power. He was appointed painter to the Chamber and a member of the academy of S Carlos in Valencia.

His portraits are of an individual style and have considerable delicacy and charm, particularly his portraits of children.

BIBLIOGRAPHY:
Soria, M.S., '*Agustin Esteve and Goya*' in *Art Bulletin*, vol xxv, 3, 1943.

MUSEUMS AND GALLERIES:
MADRID (Prado): *Don Moriano San Juan y Pineda; Doña Joaquina Tellez-Giron* - VALENCIA: *The Duchess of Alba* (1738).

AUCTION RECORDS:
NEW YORK, 18 Nov 1961, *Portrait of a Woman*, USD 5,000. NEW YORK, 6 June 1985, *Portrait of the Count of Torrejon with his Son* (oil on canvas, 80 1/2 x 50 ins / 204.5 x 127 cm) USD 33,000. NEW YORK, 7 April 1989, *Portrait of a Young Boy with his Dog* (oil on canvas, 35 1/2 x 27 1/2 ins / 90 x 70 cm) USD 77,000. LONDON, 17 Dec 1998, *Portrait of Lady Dressed in Pink with Feather Headdress* (oil on canvas, 44 x 30 ins / 112 x 77 cm) GBP 20,000. NEW YORK, 29 Jan 1999, *Don Manuel Godoy, Duke of Alcudia, Prince of the Peace* (oil on canvas, 49 x 37 ins / 124 x 93 cm) USD 70,000. MADRID, 22 May 2000, *Portrait of Gentleman* (oil on canvas, 40 x 30 ins / 101 x 75 cm) ESP 1,000,000. MADRID, 23 April 2002, *Portrait of Seated Gentleman* (oil on canvas, 46 x 33 ins / 117 x 83 cm) EUR 12,000. PARIS, 11 March 2003, *Portrait of the Duchess of Alba* (oil on canvas, after Goya, 81 x 48 ins / 206 x 121 cm) EUR 140,000.

ESTEVE Y ROMERO, Antonio
Spanish, 19th century.
Died 1 July 1859, in Valencia.
Sculptor.

Antonio Esteve y Romero was the son of José Esteve y Villela. He was director of the Real Academia de San Carlos in Valencia. There are works by the artist in Bilbao, Burgos, Madrid, Pamplona and Valencia.

ESTEVE Y VILLELA, José
Spanish, 18th century.
Born 1766, in Valencia.
Sculptor.

José Esteve y Villela was the son of José Esteve y Bonet. He was a member of the Real Academia de San Carlos in Valencia.

ESTEVE Y VILLELA, Rafael
Spanish, 18th - 19th century.
Born 1 July 1772, in Valencia; died 1 October 1847, in Madrid.
Engraver.

Rafael Esteve y Villela was the son and pupil of the sculptor José Esteve y Villela. Like his father, he also worked at the Academia de San Carlos in Valencia; he later went to Madrid where he was resident at the Real Academia de San Fernando. At that time he worked almost exclusively as a line engraver. He lived in Paris from 1802 to 1815. On his return to Spain he began to engrave works by the Spanish masters. His *Striking of the Rock* after Murillo won him a gold medal at the Paris Salon of 1839. He was appointed director of the Academia de San Carlos in Valencia and was made a member of the Academia in Madrid and decorated with the order of Charles III. He also produced numerous portraits and illustrations for an edition of Cervantes' *Don Quixote*. He was a remarkable engraver and his work is much sought after. He was a friend of Goya.

ESTEVÉNARD, Georges. See **LA SEIGNE**

ESTEVES, David
Danish, 17th century.
Active in Copenhagen.
Painter.

Esteves was a pupil of Jacques d'Agar.

ESTHOM, Jacques, pseudonym of Estève, Jacques
French, 20th century.
Born 1945.
Painter, sculptor.

Jacques Esthom studied at the Écoles des Beaux-Arts in Amiens and in Paris. His sculptures are heavily influenced by the works of Giacometti and Germaine Richier.

ESTIENNE, Auguste
French, 19th century.
Born 28 June 1794, in Paris; died 1865.
Painter. History painting, genre scenes.

Auguste Estienne joined the École des Beaux-Arts on 16 January 1817, studying under Gros. His works were well received at the Salon from 1831 to 1861. His best-known works are *Psyche Abandoned by Amor, Leaving Rome, Altar Boy Drinking the Dregs of a Flagon of Wine, Rendez-vous at the Fountain* and *Fanchon la Vielleuse*.

ESTIENNE, Christiane d'
French, 20th century.
Born 24 December 1915, in Pau.
Potter, engraver, draughtsman, illustrator. Designs for mosaics, de tapestries, murals.

Christiane d'Estienne was a pupil at the École des Beaux-Arts, Bourges, and later studied with Adam and Lesbounit. She went on to live and work in Paris. Her work has been shown since 1960 in Paris at the Salon des Indépendants and at the Salon Comparaisons, and in 1975 at the Salon de Mai. Solo exhibitions of her work since 1960 include 1962, Musée

Athénée, Geneva, the Institut Français, Ankara, and, 1976, the American Centre, Paris.

Primarily a potter, Estienne's figures and decorative pieces were turned and modelled in a popular style. She directed a workshop of young artisans, then moved towards sculpture and monumental mosaics. Her non-figurative metal sculptures are characterised by the use of acid applied to the material, which creates stains, shapes and subject matter.

MUSEUMS AND GALLERIES:

ANKARA (Resim Heykel Müz./MFA) - COPENHAGEN (Mus.) - CRACOW (Mus.) - FAENZA (Mus.) - MILAN (Mus.) - PARIS (BNF) - PARIS (MAMVP).

ESTIENNE, Clarisse (Mme)
French, 20th century.
Born in London.
Painter.

Clarisse Estienne was a pupil of H. Estienne and exhibited at the Salon des Artistes Français, Paris, in 1932.

ESTIENNE, Félicie d'
French, 20th century.
Born in Orléans.
Painter. Interiors.

Felicie d'Estienne exhibited at the Salon des Artistes Français in 1929.

ESTIENNE, Henry d'
French, 19th - 20th century.
Born 1 August 1872, in Conques (Aude); died 11 March 1949, in Paris.
Painter, pastellist. Genre scenes, landscapes. Orientalism.

Henry d'Estienne was a pupil of J.L. Gérôme and Joseph Paul Blanc. He exhibited in Paris at the Salon des Artistes Français, of which he became a member in 1899, and where he was awarded an honourable mention in 1897, a bronze medal and travel scholarship for the Exposition Universelle in 1900, a third-class medal and the Marie Bashkirtseff prize in 1903, and a second-class medal in 1904.

In 1908, d'Estienne's pastel *Young Arab Woman Bringing Coffee* was reproduced in Valérie Nicollier's *Der Offene Bruch* (*The Open Break*), published by the Institut Français, Munich.

BIBLIOGRAPHY:

Thornton, Lynne, *The Orientalists: Painter-Travellers*, Art Books International Ltd, London, 1996.

AUCTION RECORDS:

LONDON, 11-14 Nov 1921, *Preparations for the Meal*, GBP 27. PARIS, 11 Feb 1942, *Young Girl Writing a Letter* (pastel) FRF 390; *The Château de Tracy*, FRF 750; *Turkish Landscape with Canal*, FRF 380. PARIS, 16 March 1983, *Woman Reading in the Studio* (oil on canvas, 25 1/2 x 20 3/4 ins / 65 x 53 cm) FRF 7,000. LONDON, 21 March 1986, *The Good Mother* (oil on canvas, 23 x 38 1/4 ins / 58.4 x 97 cm) GBP 1,000. PARIS, 11 Dec 1995, *Young Arab Girl Bringing Coffee* (pastel, 25 1/4 x 17 3/4 ins / 64 x 45 cm) FRF 45,000. PARIS, 25 March 1998, *Woman Dressing* (oil on canvas) FRF 65,000.

ESTIENNE, Nicolas, called Le Brun
French, 18th century.
Active in Paris in 1735.
Sculptor.

ESTIET, Nicolas
French, 17th century.
Active in Paris in 1606.
Painter (?), sculptor (?).

ESTIEU, Renée
French, 20th century.
Born in Conflans Château (Yvelines).
Painter. Landscapes, flowers, fruit.

Renée Estieu exhibited in Paris at the Salon des Artistes Français between 1932 and 1938.

ESTIEVENART, Renée
French, 20th century.
Born in La Madeleine-les-Lille (Nord).
Painter.

Renée Estievenart was a pupil of Chanleur and Z. de Winter.

ESTIEVENART DARE. See **DARE**

ESTIGARRIBIA CACERES, Sila Antonio
Paraguayan, 20th - 21st century.
Born 25 September 1958.
Painter. Figures, landscapes, flowers.

Sila Antonio Estigarribia Cáceres studied at the Fundación de Arte Ouro Preto in Brazil in the early eighties. He uses a thick paste to depict dark coloured objects or flowers and creates a vaguely troubling atmosphere. A teacher and later principal of the Escuela de Bellas Artes in Asunción from 1992 to 1996, Sila Antonio Estigarribia Cáceres is also an engineer, geologist, poet and diplomat. He is now based in Paris. Collective exhibitions include the *Présence de la peinture paraguayenne contemporaine* (*The Influence of Contemporary Paraguayan Painting*), at the Musée École de la Perrine, in Laval, France in 2000. He won first prize at the 1998 International Biennale in Cairo.

ESTIGNARD, Albert
French, 19th century.
Born in Vaivre.
Painter. Landscapes with figures.

A pupil of Jeanneney, Albert Estignard exhibited landscapes at the Paris Salon from 1870 to 1877.

AUCTION RECORDS:

LUCERNE, 2 June 1981, *Peasants with Oxen in a Landscape* (1871, oil on canvas, 27 3/4 x 43 1/2 ins / 70.5 x 110.5 cm) CHF 1,500.

ESTIOT, Nicolas
French, 17th century.
Active in Paris c. 1610.
Painter (?), sculptor (?).

ESTIVAL, Germaine
French, 20th century.
Born in Brassac-les-Mines.
Painter. Figure compositions, portraits, landscapes.

From 1928, Germaine Estival exhibited in Paris at the Salon des Artistes Indépendants.

AUCTION RECORDS:

PARIS, 22 June 1945, *Portrait of a Woman*, FRF 70.

ESTIVAL, Jeanne
French, 20th century.
Born in Charenton (Val-de-Marne).
Pastellist.

From 1929 Jeanne Estival exhibited in Paris at the Salon de l'Union des Femmes Peintres et Sculpteurs.

ESTKO
Polish, 18th century.
Active in Vilna (now Vilnius, Lithuania).
Painter.

Estko was a painter at the court of Duke Charles Radzivill He produced a ceiling fresco for Radzivill Castle.

ESTLER, Georg Gustav
German, 19th century.
Born 3 March 1860, in Meissen (Saxony-Anhalt); died 1954, in Dresden.
Painter. Landscapes with figures, landscapes.

Estler studied at the academy of art in Dresden and was a pupil of P. Mohn, Jul Hübner and Fr Preller. In 1883, he was awarded a travel bursary. On his return from Italy, he settled in Dresden.

In 1887, Estler exhibited in Dresden. He is best known for his *Capri Landscape*.
AUCTION RECORDS:
COLOGNE, 15 June 1973, *Shepherd and Flock in a Landscape*, DEM 4,000. COPENHAGEN, 12 June 1985, *View of Circvice on the River Elbe* (oil on canvas, 13 x 18 1/2in/33 x 47cm) DKK 6,000. HEIDELBERG, 12 Oct 1991, *Children Picking Flowers on Capri; Children on the Beach on Capri* (watercolour, a pair, each 7 1/2 x 5 1/2in/19 x 14cm) DEM 1,700.

ESTLER, Richard
German, 19th - 20th century.
Born 28 September 1873, in Dresden.
Painter, draughtsman, decorative artist.
Estler began as a decorative painter in Berlin and later accepted a chair of drawing at the academy in Hanau-am-Main.

ESTOCHOIS, Alexandre
Flemish School, 15th century.
Painter.
Estochois is mentioned by Siret.

ESTOPINA, Cosme and Pedro (brothers)
Spanish, 15th century.
Painters.
The two brothers Cosme and Pedro Estopina worked for Valencia Cathedral in 1432. They may be the sons of Jaime Stopinyia.

ESTOPIÑÁN, Roberto
Cuban, 20th century.
Born 1920, in Havana.
Sculptor.
Roberto Estopiñán studied under Juan José Sicre at the Academia Nacional de Bellas Artes San Alejandro. He later travelled to Mexico, Portugal, the USA, France and Italy and abandoned the traditional methods he had learned in favour of the soldering iron. On his return to Havana he exhibited regularly and in 1956 was awarded first prize in the national sculpture competition. The forms he created with their bristling points and spines are perhaps inspired by the totemic sculptures of primitive civilisations.
AUCTION RECORDS:
NEW YORK, 13 May 1983, *The Prisoners* (1965, ink/paper, 16 x 21 ins / 40.6 x 53.4 cm) USD 650.

ESTOPPEY, David
Swiss, 19th - 20th century.
Born 14 July 1862, in Geneva; died 1952, in Geneva.
Painter, draughtsman, illustrator, lithographer.
Landscapes.
David Estoppey founded a studio in Geneva that had Alberto Giacometti among its students.

He exhibited his work in Paris, at the Salon des Indépendants in 1892, among the works of Seurat's disciples. He also featured at the Exposition Universelle of 1900, where he obtained an honourable mention.

He illustrated some luxury limited-edition books and contributed to the journal *Le Sapajou*, drawing political caricatures. His landscapes of the Parisian suburbs and his small-scale views of Paris by night demonstrate this painter's acute sensibility as a colourist.
MUSEUMS AND GALLERIES:
GENEVA (MAH): *November Landscape; Landscape in the Gruyère; Birches* - LAUSANNE (Cantonal MFA) - VEVEY.
AUCTION RECORDS:
GENEVA, 1 Nov 1984, *Landscape with Cornfields* (oil on canvas, 28 1/4 x 38 3/4 ins / 72 x 98.5 cm) CHF 2,000.

ESTOPPEY, Léonie
Swiss, 19th century.
Born 13 October 1852, in Payerne.
Painter.
Estoppey exhibited in Geneva in 1896.

ESTORACH, Antonio. See **CASANOVA Y ESTORACH Antonio**

ESTORGES, Jean
French, 17th century.
Painter, engraver.
There is a *Christ in the Garden of Gethsemane* by Jean Estorges.

ESTORNELL, Francisco Javier
Spanish, 19th century.
Born c. 1802; died 31 January 1854, in Valencia.
Engraver, medallist.

ESTORSÈME, Jean d'
French, 16th century.
Active in Zamora (Spain) in 1515.
Sculptor.

ESTOUILLY, O. d'
French, 19th century.
Painter.
O. d'Estouilly's *View of Cefala* is mentioned at the 1834 Salon, followed by his *Mares with their Foals in a Meadow* in 1836.

ESTOURE, Salhadin d'
Flemish School, 15th century.
Active in Bruges in 1468.
Painter (?), sculptor (?).

ESTOURNEAU, Jacques Mathieu
French, 16th century.
Born 1486, in La Flèche (Sarthe).
Sculptor, architect.
Estourneau's work was much admired by Françoise de Vendôme, duchess of Alençon, who took him into her service. In 1537, she commissioned him to make the funerary monument commemorating her husband, Charles of Bourbon, known as Charles the Magnanimous, which was erected at Vendôme. Estourneau was the architect of the duchess's château of Châteauneuf-sur-Cher, built in 1540.

ESTRADA, Anton de
Spanish, 15th - 16th century.
Active in Seville in the 15th and 16th century.
Painter.
A document pertaining to Anton de Estrada bears the date 1505.

ESTRADA, Ignacio de
Spanish, 18th century.
Born 21 March 1724, in Badajoz; died 19 December 1790, in Badajoz.
Painter, sculptor.
Ignacio de Estrada was the son and pupil of Manuel de Estrada. He collaborated with his brother Juan providing him with drawings for paintings in many of the churches of Valencia. He also produced some sculptural work.

ESTRADA, José
Spanish, 18th century.
Active in Huesca in 1759.
Engraver.

ESTRADA, José Maria
Spanish, 19th century.
Born in Valencia; died 1873, in Madrid.
Painter. Genre scenes, portraits.
José Maria Estrada studied at the Real Academia de San Fernando. He exhibited in Madrid from 1860.
MUSEUMS AND GALLERIES:
FOMENTO: two canvases.

ESTRADA, Juan Antonio de
Spanish, 17th century.
Died 28 November 1647, in Valladolid.
Sculptor.

ESTRADA, Juan de
Spanish, 18th century.
Born 30 August 1717, in Badajoz; died 28 July 1792, in Badajoz.
Painter.

Juan de Estrada studied under his father, Manuel de Estrada. For three years he received lessons from Pablo Pernicharo in Madrid. There are numerous paintings by the artist in the churches of Valencia, the drawings for which were provided by his brother Ignacio, with whom he almost always collaborated. Tradition has it that the two brothers were deeply devoted to their blind father.

ESTRADA, Manuel de
Spanish, 17th - 18th century.
Active in Badajoz.
Painter.

Manuel de Estrada was the father of Juan and Ignacio.

ESTRADA, Pablo de
Spanish, 17th century.
Active in Madrid in 1679.
Sculptor.

Pablo de Estrada worked on ceremonial decorations for the marriage of Charles II.

ESTRADA, Pedro de
Spanish, 18th century.
Born c. 1750, in Saragossa; died in Saragossa.
Sculptor.

Pedro de Estrada was a pupil of Juan de Mena and worked in Madrid.

ESTRADE, Christian
French, 20th century.
Born 20th century.
Painter.

The paintings of Christian Estrade are not highly coloured and are inspired by music. Using an automatist technique on a background of abstract painting, he achieves a lyricism that extends the musical atmosphere that is the point of departure.

ESTRADE, Léonie
French, 20th century.
Born in Dax (Landes).
Painter. Nudes.

From 1929, Léonie Estrade exhibited at the Salon de l'Union des Femmes Peintres et Sculpteurs.

ESTRADERE, Antonio
Spanish, 20th century.
Born 1911, in Barcelona.
Painter.

Antonio Estradere exhibited on many occasions in Spain, France and Italy. His work is in a realist vein but with a genuine interest in colour.

ESTRANY, Guillermo
Spanish, 14th century.
Died c. 1393, in Valencia.
Painter.

ESTRANY Y ROS, Rafael
Spanish, 20th century.
Born 14 October 1884, in Mataró near Barcelona; died 11 January 1958, in Barcelona.
Painter, draughtsman, watercolourist, engraver.
Religious subjects, figures, landscapes, urban landscapes.

Rafael Estrany y Ros studied at the Academia Baixas in Barcelona and later at the Académie Julian in Paris. He also spent time in Belgium where he was influenced by James Ensor and learned engraving. He worked in various countries including in Central and Latin America. In 1910 he became a teacher at the Escuela de Arte y Oficios in Mataró. He took part in various group exhibitions: Sala Parès, Barcelona (1913 engravings); Madrid Exposición Nacional (1915); Panama exhibition (1916). His engravings were shown in Barcelona (1926, 1920, 1922 and 1924). Other exhibitions include: watercolours (1934) and paintings (1942, 1943, 1944 and 1945). He was awarded a bronze medal in 1915, a gold medal in Panama in 1916 and another bronze medal in Mexico City, also in 1916.

Estrany y Ros was a technically skilled engraver and was highly accomplished in the rules of composition and chiaroscuro. In his paintings he sought to achieve harmony between colour and light. He occasionally produced religious scenes, notably showing the motherhood of the Virgin Mary. His approach to the representation of figures is often intimate. His best-known works include *View of Cadaqués* and *The Seven Words of the Redeemer.*

BIBLIOGRAPHY:
Arnáiz, José Manuel/López Jiménez, Javier/Merchán Díaz, Manuel (ed.), *Cien años de pintura en Espana y Portugal (1830-1930)*, Antiqvaria, Madrid, 1988 (One Hundred Years of Painting in Spain and Portugal (1830-1930)).

AUCTION RECORDS:
BARCELONA, 28 May 1987, *Children Playing* (watercolour and gouache, 25 3/4 x 32 ins / 65.5 x 81 cm) ESP 85,000.

ESTRÉES, Nicolas d'
French, 16th century.
Sculptor.

D'Estrées made six statues for the façade of Compiègne town hall between 1505 and 1508. He also carved an escutcheon bearing the coat of arms of France on the fireplace of the great hall of the same building.

ESTRÉES, Thérèse d'
French, 19th - 20th century.
Born 20 July 1874, in Ravenel Château (Vosges).
Painter, engraver. Genre scenes.

Thérèse d'Estrées was a pupil of Sain, Boutigny and Fournier. She first exhibited at the Salon des Artistes Français in 1909. Ed. Joseph mentions hunting scenes by her, and she also produced burin engravings.

ESTREICHER, Dominik
Polish, 18th century.
Born 1750, in Iglau (now Jihlava, Czech Republic); died 12 March 1809, in Cracow.
Painter.

Dominik Estreicher studied in Italy, and lived there for 10 years. In 1778, he settled in Cracow. He was invited by King Stanislas-Augustus of Poland to work at his court. He worked in Warsaw, where he produced portraits of members of the royal family. He lived in the Polish capital until 1781. In 1782, he returned to Cracow, where he taught at the fine arts academy. He also produced large-scale historical paintings, religious subjects, and several genre scenes. Some of his works are in churches in Cracow.

ESTREL, Auguste
French, 20th century.
Born in Paris.
Painter. Genre scenes.

Auguste Estrel exhibited in Paris at the Salon d'Automne and the Salon des Indépendants from 1923.

AUCTION RECORDS:
CALAIS, 24 March 1996, *Farmhouse in Brittany* (oil on canvas, 19 3/4 x 24 ins / 50 x 61 cm) FRF 4,000.

ESTREMBERC, Jacques d'
French, 15th century.
Active in Avignon c. 1452.
Painter.

ESTRICKE, Vincent van
Flemish School, 16th century.
Active in Bruges c. 1503.
Painter.

ESTRUCH, Jose
Spanish, 19th century.
Born February 1838, in San Juan de Enova (Valencia).
Painter. History painting, portraits.
Jose Estruch studied at the Real Academia de San Carlos in Valencia under Francisco Martinez. He worked a great deal in Italy.

ESTRUCH, Juan
Spanish, 19th century.
Born c. 1820, in Barcelona.
Engraver.
Juan Estruch was the son and pupil of the engraver Domingo Estruch y Jordan. He worked mainly on steel and produced a large number of portraits.

ESTRUCH Y JORDAN, Domingo
Spanish, 19th century.
Born 1796, in Muro; died 16 July 1851, in Madrid.
Engraver.
Domingo Estruch y Jordan studied under his uncle Francisco Jordan. He worked first in Barcelona and later Madrid. He left some rather fine engravings, mostly line engravings and drypoint work.

ESTURMES, Hernando d', or Sturmes
Flemish School, 16th century.
Born in Zierikzee (Showeven Island).
Active in Seville in 1539.
Painter. Religious subjects.
Esturmes was one of the artists who worked on a retable commissioned by the count of Urena, his contributions being the following: *St Jerome*; *St Gregory*; *St Augustine*; *St Ambrose*; *The Incarnation*; and *The Nativity*. For another retable, for the hospital of St Bartholomew, he painted: *Virgin with Four Angels*; *Christ holding a Crown*; *St Bartholomew with an Enchained Devil*; *St Andrew with his Cross*; *Our Lady of the Annunciation*; *Angel*; and *God the Father and the Four Evangelists*. Other works by him are: *Adoration of the Kings with Virgin and Child*; *A Hermit*; *St James the Apostle* and various other saints.

ESZABO. See **CRESSWELL Elizabeth**

ÉTAMPES, Master of. See **MASTERS**

ETANCOP, Enrique
Spanish, 14th century.
Active in Valencia c. 1376.
Glass painter.
Enrique Etancop worked for Valencia Cathedral.

ETARD
French, 19th century.
Active c. 1800.
Painter (porcelain).
Etard worked for the Sèvres porcelain factory, specialising in figure painting.

ETCHELLS, Frederick
British, 20th century.
Born 14 September 1886, in Newcastle; died 1973.
Painter.
Rebel Art Centre group, Group X.
From 1908 to 1911, Frederick Etchells studied at the Royal College of Art. He then spent time in Paris from 1911 to 1914, where he became interested in the Fauvist and Cubist movements. He formed part of the group of artists associated with Wyndham Lewis in the Vorticist movement, who were most active from 1914 to 1915 and whose ideas were similar to those of Italian Futurism. Shortly after World War I he abandoned painting in favour of architecture. He also translated several works by Le Corbusier into English.

Etchells took part in a number of group exhibitions, including the Second Post-Impressionist Exhibition of 1912 and the Post-Impressionist and Futurist Exhibition of 1913.

MUSEUMS AND GALLERIES:
LONDON (Tate Collection): *The Fair* (1911, tempera/canvas, fragment); *The Big Girl* (c. 1912, tempera/panel); *Still-life* (c. 1913, gouache/panel); *Inscription 'Let us now Praise Famous Men'* (1925, stone, relief).

AUCTION RECORDS:
NEW YORK, 19 May 1983, *Figure: Man Running* (1911-1919, watercolour and pencil, 11 1/2 x 8 3/4 ins / 29.1 x 22.5 cm) USD 38,000. LONDON, 9 March 1984, *Portrait of a Young Girl* (c. 1912, oil on canvas, 20 x 16 ins / 50.8 x 40.5 cm) GBP 4,500. LONDON, 18 April 1984, *Mediterranean Village* (1923, pencil and colour wash, 12 x 18 1/2 ins / 30.5 x 47 cm) GBP 900. LONDON, 13 May 1987, *Porthleven* (watercolour and pen, 13 x 18 1/2 ins / 33 x 47 cm) GBP 3,200. LONDON, 9 June 1989, *Portrait of a Young Woman* (oil on canvas, 20 x 16 ins / 50.8 x 40.7 cm) GBP 13,200. LONDON, 7 Nov 1991, *Cellular Composition* (1920, oil on panel, 10 1/4 x 13 1/2 ins / 26 x 34 cm) GBP 1,980. LONDON, 6 Nov 1992, *Porthleven* (1922, ink, watercolour and gouache, 13 1/2 x 18 1/2 ins / 34 x 47 cm) GBP 6,600. LONDON, 28 April 1999, *Portrait of Artist's Wife* (pencil and coloured chalk, 18 x 12 ins / 46 x 30 cm) GBP 1,600. LONDON, 7 June 2002, *Portrait of Young Girl* (c. 1911, oil on canvas, 20 x 16 ins / 51 x 41 cm) GBP 20,000. LONDON, 24 Nov 2004, *Gunwalloe* (pen, ink, watercolour and gouache, 17 x 12 ins / 44 x 30 cm) GBP 8,500.

ETCHETO, Jean François Marie
Spanish, 19th century.
Born 9 March 1853, in Madrid; died 10 November 1889, in Paris.
Sculptor.
Jean Etcheto first exhibited at the 1881 Salon with a statue of *François Villon*; two years later he received a commission from the government to produce a statue of *Democritus*.

ETCHEVERRY, Diego
French, 20th century.
Born 20 March 1933, in Casablanca, Morocco.
Painter.
Diego Etcheverry was a pupil of the École des Beaux-Arts, Nancy, and of that of Paris. He has taken part in group exhibitions: 1957 at Aix-les-Bains, Casablanca in 1958, Rome in 1960, Nancy in 1961, and since 1961 the Salon des Surindépendants and the Salon Comparaisons. His first solo exhibition was held in 1956 at the Maison des Beaux-Arts. He made reliefs consisting of several layers of white paper, cut out, torn, ripped, scratched, etc., and has also contributed to many opera and ballet set designs.

ETCHEVERRY, Hubert Denis
French, 19th - 20th century.
Born 21 September 1867, in Bayonne; died 3 April 1952, in Bayonne.
Painter, draughtsman. Religious subjects, portraits, genre scenes, flowers.
Hubert Denis Etcheverry was a pupil of Achille Zo at the municipal school of design and painting of Bayonne, and of Léon Bonnat and Albert Maignan at the École des Beaux-Arts, Paris. Initially, Etcheverry painted historical subjects, but he soon turned to portraits and genre scenes. The success of his *Vertigo* in 1903 earned him a considerable reputation. A skilful draughtsman and a successful colourist, he

was considered by many to be one of the best painters of his period. As a pupil of Bonnat he was considered by the Parisian art critics of the time to be a member of the 'Bayonne School'. He was appointed a professor at the École Spéciale d'Architecture, received the Henner prize from the Académie des Beaux-Arts, was invited to join the jury of the Salon des Artistes Français in 1927, and was awarded the Légion d'Honneur in 1906.

In 1892 Etcheverry came second in the Grand Prix de Rome with his painting *Philemon and Baucis*. He exhibited regularly in Paris at the Salon des Artistes Français, of which he became a member. He won a third-class medal in 1895, a second-class in 1899, and a gold medal in 1900, hors concours.

In 2001, the Musée Bonnat in Bayonne organised an exhibition around a painting of Henri Achille Zo, *Léon Bonnat et ses élèves basques et béarnais* (*Léon Bonnat and his Basque and Béarnaise Pupils*) (1914), which had been recently restored; it brought together the works of some of the artists who appeared in the painting, including Denis Etcheverry.

D. Etcheverry

Museums and Galleries:
Bayonne (Mus. Bonnat): *Philemon and Baucis; St Patrick Converting Two Irish Noblemen; Portrait d'une mondaine* (*Portrait of a Fashionable Lady*) (oil on canvas) - Toulouse: *Nannies* - Troyes: *St Michael Leading a Soul to Heaven.*

Auction records:
Los Angeles, 5 Oct 1981, *Market in Granada* (oil on canvas, 19 3/4 x 25 1/2 ins / 50 x 65 cm) USD 2,000. London, 28 Nov 1986, *Portrait, assumed to be of Anna de Noailles* (oil on canvas, oval, 78 x 63 ins / 198 x 160 cm) GBP 25,000. Paris, 17 June 1988, *Flowers in a Vase* (oil on canvas, two pendants, each 16 1/4 x 13 ins / 41 x 33 cm) FRF 8,500. Monaco, 17 June 1988, *Vase of Roses* (oil on panel, 13 3/4 x 11 ins / 35 x 27 cm) FRF 6,660. New York, 22 May 1990, *The Centre of Attraction* (oil on canvas, 86 1/2 x 49 1/4 ins / 220 x 125 cm) USD 30,800. New York, 21 May 1991, *Marigolds in a Vase* (oil on canvas, 16 1/4 x 13 ins / 41.3 x 33 cm) USD 1,650. New York, 16 July 1992, *Out-of-Competition* (1886, oil on panel, 8 1/2 x 6 ins / 21.6 x 15.2 cm) USD 2,860. Paris, 5 Nov 1993, *Market in Segovia* (1902, oil on canvas, 16 1/2 x 26 ins / 42 x 66 cm) FRF 9,000. Paris, 6 Dec 2002, *Portrait of Woman in Profile* (1886, oil on canvas, 25 x 22 ins / 64 x 55 cm) EUR 1,700. Paris, 9 Dec 2002, *Vanity* (1886, oil on canvas, 22 x 28 ins / 55 x 72 cm) EUR 1,900. Besancon, 31 Jan 2004, *White Roses in a White and Gold Porcelain Vase* (oil on canvas, 9 x 7 ins / 24 x 19 cm) EUR 3,500. Paris, 9 April 2004, *Still-life of Medicine* (1886, oil on canvas, 21 x 29 ins / 54 x 73 cm) EUR 4,000.

ETEROVIC, Josko

Yugoslav, 20th century.
Born 6 July 1943, in Split (now in Croatia).
Active in France.
Painter.

Josko Eterovic studied in Rijeka and arrived in France in 1969, where he had his first solo exhibition in 1970, followed by a second in 1973. His paintings are Abstract in style, often American, similar to both Newman and Hard Edge, and exploit the expressive possibilities of colour. Starting with a scheme made up of vertical stripes, the style maintains a certain degree of inaccuracy.

ETÈVE, Aline Marie

French, 20th century.
Born 11 November 1898, in Moulins-la-Marche (Orne).
Painter, engraver, watercolourist.

Aline Marie Etève first exhibited in Paris at the Salon des Artistes Français of 1920.

Auction records:
Paris, 24 April 1942, watercolour) FRF 180.

ETEVÉ, Félix Raoul

French, 20th century.
Born in Montmorillon (Vienne).
Painter. Landscapes.

Félix Raoul Etevé exhibited regularly in Paris at the Salon des Artistes Français, hors concours. He was awarded a second-class medal at the Exhibition of 1937 and the Corot prize in 1938.

ÉTEX, Antoine

French, 19th century.
Born 20 March 1808, in Paris; died 14 July 1888, in Chaville.
Painter, sculptor, engraver, architect. Local scenes. Orientalism.

Antoine Étex joined the Paris École des Beaux-Arts, studying sculpture under Pradier and Dupaty, painting under Ingres, and subsequently architecture under Duban. In 1829 he won second prize in the Prix de Rome for sculpture, and went to live in Italy for two years. During the summer of 1832, Étex spent three weeks in Algiers, during which he executed the best of his painted works from his sketches and rough drawings. In 1870 he moved to Nice. He exhibited and was awarded a first-class medal at the 1833 Paris Salon. In 1841 he was awarded the Légion d'Honneur.

Étex recounts his productive sojourn in Algiers in his *Souvenirs d'un Artiste* (*Recollections of an Artist*). He left a considerable number of works, but, despite his large painting of *The Glory of the United States* painted in 1853 for New York City Hall, it was not as a painter that he gained fame, but as a very prolific sculptor. His works include two of the reliefs on the Arc de Triomphe de l'Étoile in Paris; the *Tomb of Géricault; Monument to Ingres; Monument to General Lecourbe; Monument to Vauban* at Les Invalides; *Statue of Charlemagne* at the Senate; *Statue of Francis I* in Cognac; *Tomb of Brizeux* in Nantes; and his *Monument to Garibaldi* in Nice (completed by Deloye). He executed many sketches and models in honour of men of standing in the Nice region. His work was greatly appreciated by his contemporaries, although he was subsequently accused of lacking feeling and emotion.

Museums and Galleries:
Angers (MBA): *Apollo killed Hyacinthus with his Disc* (1829) - Caen: *Nice* - Lyons (MBA): *Cain and his Family; Death of a Misunderstood Man of Genius* (painting) - Metz: *Mme Amable Tastu* - Montauban: *Poliziano Educating the Three Medicis* (painting) - Nantes (MBA): *Hero* - Nice: *Garibaldi; Masséna* - Semur-en-Auxois: *M. de Franqueville; Léon de Montbéliard* - Toul: *Medallion of Dornès; Model of the Tomb of Géricault; Busts of Félix Liouville, Chanzy and P.-J. Proudhon* - Versailles: *Blanche de Castille; Marshal de Lescun* - Versailles (Mus. Lambinet): *Olympia.*

ÉTEX, Louis Jules

French, 19th century.
Born 20 September 1810, in Paris; died 7 July 1889, in Paris.
Painter, watercolourist, draughtsman. Religious subjects, portraits, genre scenes.

The brother of Antoine Étex, Louis Jules Étex joined the École des Beaux-Arts on 30 September 1826, studying there under Lethière and Ingres. He made his Salon début in 1833, when he was awarded a second-class medal. He continued to send works to the Salon until 1876.

Étex's best-known works are *Adam and Eve; Women from the Frontiers of the Kingdom of Naples; Portrait of Berryer; Portrait of Descamps; Portrait of Legentil; Le Religieux et le Philosophe; Lost Way; Stagecoach en Route during the*

Storm; and *Vestal Virgin Letting Herself be Led out of the Temple*.

MUSEUMS AND GALLERIES:

SOISSONS: *St Geneviève* - VERSAILLES: *Portrait of Henry I, Duke of Montmorency; Portrait of Brulart, Marquis of Sillery, Chancellor of France*.

AUCTION RECORDS:

PARIS, 16 Dec 1925, *On the Way to Market, around Beauvais*, FRF 620. PARIS, 2 and 3 June 1926, *Portrait of Lieutenant Dubosq with Bodyguards*, FRF 400. PARIS, 9 Feb 1927, *Biblical Scene* (watercolour) FRF 100. PARIS, 7 May 1943, *Fishermen's Wives Attending an Accident*, FRF 1,600. PARIS, 16 April 1945, *Jupiter and Leda* (two paintings forming a diptych) FRF 1,050. PARIS, 29 Jan 1947, *Bust of a Child* (graphite) FRF 250. PARIS, 22 Oct 1986, *The Blacksmith; The Writer* (two oils on canvas, 68½ x 32¾ ins / 174 x 83 cm) FRF 9,000.

ETGENS, Johann Georg
Moravian School, 18th century.
Born 1693, in Brno; died 21 January 1757, in Brno.
Painter.

After living in Rome, Johann Etgens worked for various churches, including the churches in Welebrad and Jihlava.

ETHENARD Y ABARCA, Francisco Antonio
Spanish, 17th century.
Born c. 1650, in Madrid; died c. 1701, in Madrid.
Painter, engraver.

Francisco Ethenard y Abarca had a German father. He served under Charles II in the German Lifeguards until 1701. Having been little more than a keen amateur until then, he went on to devote himself entirely to the arts. In 1676 he published a *Philosophy of War*, which he illustrated with numerous engravings.

ETHERINGTON, Edward
British, 19th century.
Active in Paris c. 1860.
Engraver (wood).

Edward Etherington was a friend and disciple of Gustave Doré.

ETHERINGTON, Lilian
British, 19th - 20th century.
Active in London.
Painter.

Lilian Etherington exhibited genre scenes at the Suffolk Street Gallery and the Royal Academy in London between 1885 and 1901.

ETHIOU, Adèle
French, 19th century.
Active in Paris.
Painter, engraver. Portraits.

Adèle Ethiou made an engraving after Jacques-Louis David's *Belisarius*.

ETHLE, Clemens
German, 17th century.
Active in Weilheim c. 1600.
Sculptor (wood).

ETHLER, Josef
Moravian School, 19th century.
Born 1796, in Brno; died 8 November 1880, in Brno.
Painter. Landscapes.

Josef Ethler produced a number of watercolours and drawings.

ETHOFER, Theodor Josef
Austrian, 19th century.
Born 29 December 1849, in Vienna; died 1915.
Painter. Portraits, genre scenes.

Ethofer worked for many years in Italy.

MUSEUMS AND GALLERIES:

GRAZ: design for a poster*Koffee Tomaselli*.

AUCTION RECORDS:

LONDON, 3 April 1909, *Umbrella Mender*, GBP 4. PARIS, 4 Dec 1933, *Studies of Women* (set of three watercolours) FRF 70. MUNICH, 15 March 1984, *Peasant Cottage near Frascati* (1874, oil on panel, 19¼ x 12½in/49 x 32cm) DEM 8,000. TORONTO, 7 Dec 2000, *Washing Day* (oil on panel, 11 x 17 ins / 29 x 44 cm) CAD 7,000. VIENNA, 4 April 2001, *Interior Scene with Man on Chair* (oil on panel, 11 x 8 ins / 29 x 21 cm) ATS 28,000. VIENNA, 28 May 2001, *Banco del'Lotto in the Via S Eustachio* (oil on panel, 21 x 13 ins / 54 x 34 cm) ATS 90,000. SALZBURG, 12 June 2002, *Flower Seller* (tempera, 19 x 12 ins / 49 x 30 cm) EUR 2,000. GRAZ, 12 June 2003, *Cairo Bazaar* (oil on panel, 20 x 12 ins / 50 x 31 cm) EUR 2,200. GRAZ, 12 June 2003, *Girl in Traditional Costume Knitting* (oil on panel, 22 x 13 ins / 55 x 32 cm) EUR 2,200. LONDON, 16 June 2004, *Courtyard in the Alhambra, Granada* (oil on canvas, 30 x 17 ins / 77 x 42 cm) GBP 6,000.

ETHUIN, Anne
French, 20th century.
Born 1921, in Le Cateau-Cambrésis (Nord).
Collage artist.
Phases group.

Anne Ethuin was the wife of Édouard Jaguer and co-founded the review *Phases* with her husband in 1952. Strictly speaking neither collages nor paintings, her works consist of everyday images taken from magazines and overwritten in black and gold. Slipping from animal to vegetable and human shapes, her compositions, which are Surrealist in style, have something of fantasy about them. She has been represented in a number of group exhibitions: 2000, *Les Ciseaux du rêve. Collages, assemblages, boîtes* (*The Scissors of Dreams. Collages, Constructions, Boxes*), Galerie 1900-2000, Paris; 2000, *Le Movement Phases de 1952 à l'horizon 2001* (*The Phases Movement from 1952 to the New Millennium*), the Kiosque Centre Culturel, Mayenne, and the Centre Noroit, Arras.

BIBLIOGRAPHY:

Galizot, Roger/Jaguer, Edouard/Kral, Petr, *Anne Ethuin, collages revêtus*, Librairie les mains libres, Paris, 1973. Rosemont, Penelope, *Surrealist Women. An international anthology*, University of Texas Press, Austin (TX), 1998.

ETIENNE
Italian, 10th - 11th century.
Painter.

This artist worked at S Elie in Nepi.

ETIENNE
French, 14th century.
Born to a family originally from Montpellier.
Painter.
Avignon School.

Etienne was working in Avignon in 1365.

ETIENNE
French, 15th century.
Painter.

Etienne worked at Troyes Cathedral, particularly in 1421.

ETIENNE
French, 16th century.
Painter.

This painter was in Lyons in 1516 and 1533. In 1516, he was engaged on preparations for an entry. There are references to several artists known only by the first name 'Etienne' living in Lyons during the period from 1342 to 1568.

ÉTIENNE
French, 20th - 21st century.
Born 1952.
Sculptor. Allegorical subjects.

In 1992, the Galerie Prazan-Fitoussi in Paris exhibited a collection of Étienne's works. His preferred medium is patinated bronze, and his sculptures often depict faces. Their expressions have a certain symbolic significance, and convey a range of emotions - tenderness as well as sadness. Étienne has also sculpted a number of outdoor monuments.

AUCTION RECORDS:
PARIS, 1 Feb 1988, *Magnificat: Homage to Monteverdi* (polished and patinated bronze, 12 1/4 x 12 1/2 x 8 1/2 ins / 31 x 31.5 x 21.5 cm) FRF 17,000. PARIS, 3 Oct 1988, *Thunderbolt* (1986, polished and patinated bronze, 13 3/4 x 13 3/4 x 6 1/4 ins / 35 x 35 x 16 cm) FRF 18,000. PARIS, 30 Jan 1989, *Fertility* (polished and polychrome-patinated bronze, 28 x 11 x 9 1/2 ins / 71 x 27 x 24 cm) FRF 34,000. PARIS, 22 May 1989, *Baroque Cello* (bronze, 22 x 4 3/4 x 14 1/2 ins / 55 x 12 x 37 cm) FRF 23,000. PARIS, 5 Feb 1990, *The Poet* (polished bronze, 7 3/4 x 10 1/4 x 3 1/4 ins / 20 x 26 x 8 cm) FRF 15,000. PARIS, 13 May 1996, *The Poet* (polished bronze, 7 3/4 x 10 1/4 x 3 1/4 ins / 20 x 26 x 8 cm) FRF 13,000.

ETIENNE, David
Swiss, 16th century.
Born in St-Machet.
Enameller.

In 1556, David Etienne was working in Geneva.

ÉTIENNE, Francis Paul, called Paolo
French, 20th century.
Born 23 February 1874, in Dôle; died 24 December 1960, in Neuilly-sur-Seine.
Painter, engraver.

Francis Paul Étienne, a pupil of Biloul and Adler, was a member of the Salon des Artistes Français, in Paris. According to Ed. Joseph, he collaborated in the restoration of 18th-century plates.

AUCTION RECORDS:
LONDON, 25 Nov 1992, *Arab Women in a Harem* (1912, oil on canvas, 27 1/4 x 41 3/4 ins / 69 x 106 cm) GBP 10,450.

ETIENNE, Gillot
Flemish School, 15th century.
Active in Tournai c. 1480.
Painter.

ÉTIENNE, Henri
French, 20th century.
Sculptor. Animals.

Henri Étienne was a member of the Salon des Tuileries from 1929.

ETIENNE, Jean
French, 16th century.
Sculptor, architect.

In 1541, Jean Etienne was commissioned to make the retable for the chapel of the Holy Spirit in the church in Vence (Alpes-Maritimes).

ÉTIENNE, Jules Auguste
French, 20th century.
Painter. Landscapes.

Jules Auguste Étienne exhibited at the Salon des Artistes Français in 1923.

ÉTIENNE, Marie Thérèse
French, 20th century.
Born 24 April 1945, in Lyons.
Painter. Designs for mosaics.

Marie Thérèse Étienne studied under Jean Bertholle and Roger Chapelain-Midy in Paris, and learnt mosaic technique with Riccardo Licata in Ravenna. She has been a participant in the Salon d'Automne in Paris since 1968. Most of her works are figurative mosaics.

ETIENNE, Marius
French, 19th century.
Painter. Landscapes.

AUCTION RECORDS:
PARIS, 30 Jan 1899, *Panorama*, FRF 98.

ETIENNE, Pierre, called Le Brun
French, 18th century.
Active in Paris in 1767.
Sculptor.

ETIENNE, René Ernest
French, 19th century.
Born 19th century, in Paris.
Painter. Genre scenes, landscapes.

René Ernest Etienne was a pupil of Jules Lefebvre, Gabriel Ferrier and C. Berlon. He exhibited at the Salon of the Société des Artistes Français, becoming a member and receiving an honourable mention in 1899. He was awarded a bronze medal at the Exposition Universelle of 1900.

AUCTION RECORDS:
LUCERNE, 20 May 1980, *Summer Landscape; Winter Landscape* (two paintings/panel, 10 1/2 x 18 3/4 ins / 26.5 x 47.5 cm) CHF 5,000.

ETIENNE D'AUXERRE
French, 13th century.
Active in Paris in 1292.
Painter.

This artist worked for the Count of Burgundy, Mahaut d'Artois, and then for Philippe le Bel, King of France.

ETIENNE DE BAR
French, 12th century.
Died 29 December 1163.
Sculptor. Religious subjects.

Architect and Bishop of Metz, this artist was also known as a sculptor. He decorated the high-altar choir of his cathedral and restored the churches of St-Pierre-aux-Images and Notre-Dame-la-Ronde.

ETIENNE DE FRANCHEVILLE
French, 15th century.
Painter.

Etienne de Francheville worked at Toul and was at the court of King René II of Lorraine in about 1495.

ÉTIENNE-MARTIN, pseudonym of Martin, Étienne
French, 20th century.
Born 4 February 1913, in Loriol (Drôme); died 21 March 1995, in Paris.
Sculptor, draughtsman. Busts, statues, architectural integration.

Étienne-Martin went to school in Valence and became a pupil at the École des Beaux-Arts, Lyons when he was sixteen. He studied there from 1930 to 1933 and met the art writer Marcel Michaud there. He then went to Paris and became a pupil of Malfray and Maillol at the Académie Ranson (from 1933 to 1939). He joined the sculptor Stahly and the painters Le Moal, Bertholle and Manessier of the Lyons group Témoinage (Testimony) that had been set up by Marcel Michaud. He served in World War II, was taken prisoner, was released in 1942, and settled first in Oppède (a community led by the architect Bernard Zehrfuss), then in Dieulefit (Orne) with Pierre-Henri Roché (who was to write *Jules et Jim* (Jules and Jim)), writer and art collector, and later, from 1944 to 1947, in Mortagne (Orne), with Manessier, whose calm spirituality impressed him. He went to Paris in 1947 and met the art critic Michel Tapié, Brancusi, Henri Michaux, Dubuffet and Gurdjieff. He was a professor and head of the sculpture workshop at the École Nationale des Beaux-Arts, Paris, from 1965 to 1983. He won many awards: 1948, the Blumenthal prize; 1949 the Young Sculptors' prize, Paris; 1966, the Grand Prix at the Venice Biennale; 1967, the Grand Prix National des Arts. He was elected to the Institute in 1971.

He preferred to work in wood (he assembled works that were made of wood and string), and his first works, on the theme of *Night*, moved between figuration and abstraction, refusing to admit there was any problem in doing so. Among the works of this period are *Painted Idol* (1934), in the shape of a staircase; *Alphabet Book* (1934), a clearly abstract form; *Seated Woman* (1935); the first *Night* (1935), massive and hieratic, perhaps a reference to the *Nights* of Gerard de Nerval or a response to the shock of meeting Marcel Duchamp. At this time he also made *The Knot* (1938), consisting of articulated abstract shapes. After the Liberation, he sculpted while staying with Pierre-Henri Roche a further *Night*, and with Manessier some *Pietà* (1944) that are expressionist in intention; the *Grand Couple* (1946); *Dragon (1946)*, and *Landscape* (1947). In 1956 he had extended the series *Couples* with the *Red Couple*. Between 1948 and 1956, in particular with *Boaz* of 1953, he continued to develop the theme of *Nights*. In 1963 he sculpted *The Cry*, a tree stump, which he often used, pruned and with its roots in the air.In 1948 he made sculptures from fabric, the *Soft Furnishings*, which terminate with the *Cloak* (1962) that is *Dwelling No. 5*. It was in 1954 that he began the series that is the backbone of his work, *Dwellings*, of which there are twenty. Whether they are fortified with long points, like that of 1959, divided into three parts like that of 1960, or include an internal winding staircase, like that of 1961, they have one point in common: they are habitable, or at least penetrable, sculptures that one views from inside, not objects to be seen from the outside, but hollowed matrices, receptacles, shelters for the whole being. These *Dwellings* were initially designed in and made of plaster, or, more rarely, in the case of the smaller ones with relative and symbolic proportions, of wood; only *No. 5* was made of fabric. In 1966 the Galerie Michel-Coutourier had these sculptures cast in bronze, and they then became transportable and saleable. However, casting bronze changed their character somewhat. 'They're like rhinoceroses, I don't like them,' Étienne-Martin said. In 1967 he published *Abécédaire et autres lieux* (*The Alphabet Book and Other Places*), a sort of catalogue of his works, prepared by himself. In 1962, he made *Dwelling No. 5* in the form of an enormous cloak made of heavy fabrics and soft furnishing materials.

Étienne-Martin continued to explore the theme of *Dwellings* until *House No. 10*, which he exhibited in 1968 for the inauguration of the Centre d'Art Contemporain in Paris.

Étienne-Martin's drawings were published with his writings. They are plans for the interior spaces of the *Dwellings*, simple diagrams drawn in colours, figures and letters, organising space and dividing it into compartments (*Room of the Birds, Room of the Books, Door to the Centre, Dark Staircase*, etc.). His last objects, the *Roots* series, continue his work in wood, the accent being on their anatomical and sensual characteristics, based as they are on a sexual symbology. He also built a new *Dwelling* in Bois-Orcan using the rooms, the park and the stretches of water of the 15th-century fortified château for the installation of various sculptures. Several times Étienne-Martin was requested to make works that were part of an architectural scheme: windows in the church of Baccarat, the Vatican Pavilion at the Brussels Exposition Universelle of 1958, designs for the cathedral of Algiers, a wall a hundred metres long for a power station near Fontainebleau, which he made by superimposing identical cubes (1966), and another *Dwelling* for the forecourt of the new Bibliothèque Nationale in Paris.

He took part in many group exhibitions, including the Salon de Mai, of which he was a committee member. He was invited to Documenta in Kassel in 1963, and in 1991 was represented in the exhibition *Les Artistes réfugiés à Dieulefit pendant la Seconde Guerre mondiale* (*The Refugee Artists of Dieulefit during the World War II*), held at the museum of Valence.

His first solo exhibition in France was held at the Galerie Breteau, Paris, in 1960, and there followed 1962-1963, a retrospective at the Kunsthalle, Bern, organised by the Swiss Harald Szeemann; 1963-1964, retrospective at the Stedeljick Museum, Amsterdam; 1963-1964, retrospective at the Van Abbemuseum, Eindhoven; 1965, retrospective at the Palais des Beaux-Arts, Brussels; 1966, Musée d'Art et d'Industrie, St-Étienne; 1972, Musée Rodin, Paris and Documenta V, Kassel; from 1977 regularly at the Galerie Artcurial, Paris, including a collection of wooden sculptures in 1984; 1984, Musée National d'Art Moderne, Paris, with a collection of *Dwellings*; 1988, sculptures at the Chapelle de la Salpêtrière, Paris, an exhibition organised by Harald Szeemann; 1991, retrospective at the Musée de l'Abbaye St-Croix, Les Sables d'Olonne. Posthumously, 1996, Fondation de Coubertin, St-Rémy-lès-Chevreuse; 1997, Musée des Beaux-Arts, Clermont-Ferrand; 2002, *Etienne-Martin: Paysage* (*Etienne-Martin: Landscape*), an exhibition centred round the eponymous sculpture, Musée de Picardie, Amiens.

Etienne Martin

BIBLIOGRAPHY:
Tapié, Michel, *Un art autre*, Girand, Paris, 1952. Seuphor, Michel, *La Sculpture de ce siècle*, Griffon, Neuchâtel, 1959. Étienne-Martin, *Abécédaire et autres lieux*, Éd. Claude Givaudan, Geneva, 1967. Ragon, Michel, *Étienne-Martin*, Éd. de la Connaissance, Brussels, 1970. Étienne-Martin, *Le Mur miroir*, Éd. Aréa, Paris, 1982 (poem by Dominique Le Buhan). Le Buhan, Dominique, '*Les Demeures-mémoires d'Étienne-Martin*' in *Coll. Format/Art*, Herscher, Paris, 1982. Bozo, Dominique/Michaud, Yves/Szeemann, Harald, *Étienne-Martin, les Demeures*, exhibition catalogue, Musée national d'Art moderne, Paris, 1984. Szeemann, H./Breerette, G., *Étienne-Martin*, exhibition catalogue, Chapelle Saint-Louis de la Salpêtrière, Paris, 1988 (documentation). Ammann, J.-Ch./Le Buhan, Dominique/Ragon, Michel/Szeemann, H., *Étienne-Martin*, Adam Biro, Paris, 1991. Szeemann, Harald/Le Buhan, Dominique/Ragon, Michel/Ammann, Jean-Christophe, *Étienne-Martin*, Adam Biro, Paris, 1991. '*Entretien avec Étienne-Martin*' in *Libération*, periodical, Paris, 25 August 1992. Faure, Fabien, *Étienne-Martin, Mario Merz, des Demeures et des 'Igloos', primitivisme et dimension anthropologique de la sculpture contemporaine*, L'Harmattan, Montreal, Paris, 2000. Etienne-Martin, *Etienne-Martin*, Henry Moore Institute, Leeds, c. 2000 (interviewed by Irmeline Lebeer; translated by Charles Penwarden).

MUSEUMS AND GALLERIES:
AMIENS (Maison de la Culture): *Lanleff* - AMIENS (Mus. de Picardie): *Landscape* (between 1936 and 1947, plaster) - AMSTERDAM (Stedelijk Mus.): *Man in the Style of Bernini* - BRUSSELS (Mus. royaux des Beaux-Arts de Belgique): *Opening Night* - CHICAGO (AI): *Dwelling No. IV* - GRENOBLE: *Opening Night* - LES SABLES-D'OLONNE (Musée de L'Abbaye Ste-Croix) - NEW YORK (MoMA) - NEW YORK (Solomon R. Guggenheim Mus.): *Anenome* - OTTERLO (Kröller-Müller Mus.): *Dwelling No. III* - PARIS (FNAC): *Dwelling No. IV* (1961, work on show in front of the Église St-Leu since 1993) - PARIS (MAMVP): *The Tower of Shadows*; *Large Couple* - PARIS (MNAM-CCI): *Alma*; *Opening Night* (1945-1955); *Three Soft Furnishings*; *Alphabet Book*; *Cloak or Dwelling No. 5*; *Mirror-Wall* (1979) - ST-ÉTIENNE (MAM): *Couple* - VIENNA (Mus. Moderner Kunst Stiftung Ludwig): *Large Couple*.

Auction records:
Paris, 9 June 1977, *Duck* (bronze, h. 17 1/4 ins / 44 cm, l. 13 1/2 ins/34 cm) FRF 19,000. Paris, 20 March 1979, *The Conquered* (patinated bronze, h. 18 ins / 46 cm) FRF 5,800. Paris, 23 Oct 1981, *The Knot* (1937, bronze, 20 3/4 x 20 3/4 x 17 3/4 ins / 53 x 53 x 45 cm) FRF 17,000. Paris, 6 June 1985, *Mandolin* (dark-patinated bronze, 35 x 10 x 5 1/4 ins / 88 x 25.5 x 13.5 cm) FRF 29,000. Paris, 6 Dec 1986, *Bitumen Couple* (1955, brown-patinated bronze, h. 17 3/4 ins / 45 cm) FRF 80,000. New York, 6 Oct 1988, *Head in Hands* (bronze, h. 23 1/2 ins / 59.5 cm) USD 17,600. London, 26 Oct 1989, *Head of Alma* (1956, lost-wax bronze, h. 7 3/4 ins / 20 cm) GBP 6,600. London, 22 Feb 1990, *The Knot* (1955, bronze, 18 1/2 x 17 x 18 ins / 47 x 43 x 46 cm) GBP 33,000. Paris, 21 May 1990, *Night Nina* (1951, bronze, 53 1/2 x 31 1/2 x 31 1/2 ins / 136 x 80 x 80 cm) FRF 1,000,000. Paris, 9 April 1991, *Dwelling IV* (bronze, 126 x 55 ins / 320 x 140 cm) FRF 1,550,000. Paris, 23 Nov 1994, *Study for the Unknown Political Prisoner* (1952, bronze, h. 20 ins / 51 cm) FRF 50,000. Paris, 15 Dec 1994, *Bitumen Couple* (bronze, 17 3/4 x 43 1/4 x 15 3/4 ins / 45 x 110 x 40 cm) FRF 185,000. Paris, 29 Nov 1996, *The Beak* (1964, black-patinated bronze, 26 x 59 x 25 1/4 ins / 66 x 150 x 64 cm) FRF 121,000. Paris, 20 March 1998, *Alphabet Book* (collage, 19 3/4 x 19 3/4 ins / 50 x 50 cm) FRF 1,800. New York, 23 Feb 1999, *Flame* (brown-patinated bronze, 44 x 12x11 ins / 112 x 30x29 cm) USD 4,200. London, 18 June 1999, *Tar Couple* (1950, black-patinated bronze, 18 x 42x15 ins / 46 x 107x38 cm) GBP 8,000. Paris, 19 April 2000, *Head of Alma* (patinated bronze, 8 x 7x9 ins / 20 x 17x22 cm) FRF 85,000. Paris, 21 Dec 2000, *Dragon* (wood, 39 x 79x31 ins / 100 x 200x80 cm) FRF 750,000. Paris, 25 June 2001, *Mandolin* (bronze, 34 x 9x6 ins / 87 x 24x14 cm) FRF 50,000. Paris, 25 June 2001, *Knot* (bronze, 20 x 22x20 ins / 50 x 55x50 cm) FRF 52,000. Paris, 14 June 2002, *Knot* (1938, bronze, 20 x 22x20 ins / 50 x 55x50 cm) EUR 12,500. Paris, 15 Nov 2002, *Nuit Nina* (1951, bronze, h. 54 ins / 136 cm) EUR 30,000. Paris, 9 Dec 2003, *Woman* (wood, h. 47 ins / 120 cm) EUR 15,000. Paris, 25 May 2004, *Claude with Long Neck* (bronze, h. 13 ins / 34 cm) EUR 5,000.

ETIENNERET

French, 20th century.
Born in Cusset (Allier).
Painter.

From 1928 Etienneret exhibited in Paris at the Salon d'Automne and the Salon des Tuileries.

ETIENNERET, Christophe

American, 20th century.
Born in New York.
Painter. Genre scenes.

ETIGNY, Annick d'

French, 20th century.
Born in Rheims.
Painter. Portraits.

Annick d'Etigny was a pupil of Bompart and P.-A. Laurens, and exhibited at the Salon des Artistes Français.

ETLINGER, Georg

German.
Active in Bamberg (Bavaria).
Engraver (wood).

There is a reference to an engraved portrait of Bishop Blaize by him.

ETNIER, Stephen Morgan

American, 20th century.
Born 1903, in York (Pennsylvania); died 1984.
Painter. Landscapes.

Stephen Etnier was a pupil at the Pennsylvania Academy of the Fine Arts; he later studied under Rockwell Kent and John Carol. A landscapist he painted landscapes of America in a Realist style sometimes evocative of Albert Marquet.

Museums and Galleries:
Boston - Dallas (MA): *Hibiscus Alley* (1951, oil on canvas) - Los Angeles - New York (Metropolitan Mus. of Art).

Auction records:
Portland, 7 April 1984, *July 4* (1934, oil on canvas, 25 x 30 ins / 63.5 x 76.2 cm) USD 950. New York, 31 March 1993, *Port Scene in New England* (oil on canvas, 30 x 40 ins / 76.2 x 101.6 cm) USD 3,220. Portland, 4 Aug 1999, *Stiff Breeze, Nassau* (oil on board, 22 x 36 ins / 56 x 91 cm) USD 12,000. Portland, 4 Aug 1999, *Bath Iron Works* (1937, oil on canvas, 40 x 50 ins / 102 x 127 cm) USD 15,000. Portland, 2 Aug 2000, *The Hudson Dealer, Bath, Maine* (oil on canvas, 18 x 30 ins / 46 x 76 cm) USD 15,000. Portland, 2 Aug 2000, *Winter's End* (1954, oil on canvas, 29 x 42 ins / 74 x 107 cm) USD 35,000. Portland, 8 Aug 2001, *Monhegan Harbour* (oil on canvas, 22 x 36 ins / 56 x 91 cm) USD 37,000. St Louis, 1 Dec 2001, *Beach Hotel* (oil on panel, 21 x 35 ins / 53 x 89 cm) USD 4,750. York, 23 Feb 2002, *Union Station, Portland* (1941, oil on canvas, 27 x 35 ins / 69 x 89 cm) USD 18,000. Portland, 31 July 2002, *Day's End* (1975, oil on canvas, 14 x 23 ins / 36 x 58 cm) USD 15,000. York, 16 May 2003, *In the Hanger* (1941, oil on canvas, 35 x 49 ins / 89 x 124 cm) USD 17,000. Portland, 8 Aug 2003, *Boulder* (oil on canvas, 22 x 36 ins / 56 x 91 cm) USD 30,000. Portland, 6 Aug 2004, *In Ash Cove, South Harpswell, ME* (oil on canvas, 16 x 24 ins / 41 x 61 cm) USD 6,500. Portland, 6 Aug 2004, *Hoisting Sail, Jewel Island Harbor* (oil on canvas, 20 x 36 ins / 51 x 91 cm) USD 32,500.

ETROG, Sorel

Romanian, 20th century.
Born 1933, in Iasi.
Active in Canada from 1963.
Sculptor, decorative designer, illustrator.

Sorel Etrog began studying art in 1945 and eventually left Romania to go to Israel in 1950, taking classes at the institute of painting and sculpture in Tel Aviv. He obtained a study grant in 1958 to go and work at the Institute of Art of the Brooklyn Museum, then opened a sculpture workshop in New York. He finally settled in Toronto in 1963. He was a sculptor but also produced illustrations for books by Eugène Ionesco, Samuel Beckett and Claude Aveline and published *Dream Chamber (Joyce and Dada Circus)* with John Cage in 1978, *Bridges* with a preface by Marshall McLuhan in 1983 and *Kite* in 1984. Etrog designed sets and costumes for the play *The Celtic Hero*.

Some of his works can be seen in the open air in public places. His sculptures place groups of geometric shapes such as cubes, cylinders, curves and right angles in tension with each other. These are compositions of an organic nature with interconnected masses and volumes symbolizing the forces of conflicting trends in humanity. He represented Canada at the Venice Biennale in 1966. His first exhibition in Israel was in 1958 and was followed by many others in Israel as well as in Canada, the USA, Italy, Switzerland and France (Canadian Cultural Centre in 1978).

Bibliography:
Heinrich, Theodore Allen, *The Painted Compositions 1952-1960 of Sorel Etrog*, Staempfl, Bern, 1968. Jianou, Ionel, *Romanian Artists and the West*, American Romanian Academy of Arts and Sciences, Los Angeles, 1986. Etrog, Sorel, *The Cult of the Head Sculptures*, National Heritage Board, Singapore, c. 1997. Etrog, Sorel, *Sorel Etrog*, Prestel, New York, c. 2001.

Museums and Galleries:
Chicago (Ravinia Park) - Los Angeles (County MA) - Otterlo (Kröller-Müller Mus.) - Washington DC (Hirshhorn Mus. and Sculpture Garden): *Africana* (bronze); *Barcarolle (Dance II)* (1960, painted wood).

Auction records:
New York, 6 June 1974, *Wave* (bronze) USD 3,200. New York, 21 Oct 1977, *Embrace* (brown and green-patinated

bronze, h. 40 ins / 101.5 cm) USD 2,250. NEW YORK, 28 March 1979, *Leitzan* (brown-patinated bronze, h. 25 1/2 ins / 65 cm) USD 3,600. LOS ANGELES, 23 June 1980, *Survivors are not always Heroes* (1965-1967, bronze, h. 73 ins / 185.5 cm) USD 10,500. LONDON, 8 Nov 1984, *Ceremonial Figure* (1962-1964, bronze, h. 65 1/4 ins / 165.5 cm) USD 9,500. NEW YORK, 27 Feb 1985, *Albq* (c. 1972, dark brown-patinated bronze, h. 55 1/2 ins / 141 cm) USD 6,000. NEW YORK, 13 Feb 1986, *Homage to Kodaly, Bronze* (pale green and black patinatas, h. 59 3/4 ins / 152 cm) USD 14,000. NEW YORK, 5 Nov 1987, *Study for Jester* (1962-64, bronze, h. 22 1/2 ins / 57.2 cm) USD 4,000. NEW YORK, 3 May 1988, *Leader* (bronze, h. 37 ins / 94 cm) USD 9,900. NEW YORK, 8 Oct 1988, *Croisé* (sheet of bronze, h. 43 1/4 ins / 109.7 cm) USD 13,200. NEW YORK, 3 May 1989, *Queen III* (1967, bronze, base 47 ins / 119.5 cm) USD 35,750. NEW YORK, 12 Nov 1991, *Untitled or Bacarole* (bronze, 22 x 18 x 5 ins / 55.9 x 45.7 x 12.7 cm) USD 5,280. NEW YORK, 25-26 Feb 1992, *Counter-Head* (1976, bronze, 17 1/2 x 22 1/2 ins / 44.5 x 57.2 cm) USD 5,500. NEW YORK, 30 June 1993, *Untitled* (bronze, h. 8 ins / 20.3 cm) USD 2,070. NEW YORK, 23 Feb 1994, *Dual-Key Head I* (bronze, 9 1/2 x 7 x 4 ins / 24 x 17.5 x 10 cm) USD 2,300. NEW YORK, 14 June 1995, *Memory of War* (bronze, h. 9 1/2 ins / 24.4 cm) USD 3,450. AMSTERDAM, 6 Dec 1995, *Composition* (bronze, h. 17 3/4 ins / 45 cm) NLG 5,520.

ETSCHMANN, Andreas
Austrian, 17th century.
Born in the Tyrol; died 2 July 1708, in Obermachtal.
Sculptor.

Andreas Etschmann decorated churches, including the church at Obermachtal.

ETSCHMANN, Paul
German, 17th century.
Active in Wiblingen at the end of the 17th century.
Painter.

Paul Etschmann decorated the Benedictine monastery in Wiblingen.

ETTEBEEK, Jean van
Flemish School, 15th century.
Active in Louvain in 1450.
Sculptor.

ETTEL, Georg
German, 19th century.
Born 21 September 1861, in Wirsitz.
Engraver.

Ettel engraved many plates after old masters.

ETTEN, Ferdinand von
Flemish, 17th century.
Born 14 May 1595, in Antwerp.
Engraver.
Flemish School.

Ferdinand von Etten executed a *Crowning with Thorns*.

ETTERAC, Marcelle
French, 20th century.
Born in Paris.
Painter. Flowers.

Marcelle Etterac exhibited in Paris at the Salon des Indépendants from 1925 to 1932.

ETTERBEKE, Antoine
Flemish School, 15th century.
Active in Antwerp in 1488.
Sculptor.

ETTERBEKE, Servais
Flemish School, 15th century.
Active in Antwerp in 1488.
Sculptor.

ETTING, E. P.
French, 20th century.
Painter. Portraits.

E.P. Etting exhibited at the Salon des Tuileries in 1930.

ETTINGER, Josef Carl
German, 19th century.
Born 1805, in Munich; died 1860, in Munich.
Painter. Landscapes.

Ettinger studied under Köbell and Wagenbauer.

ETTL, Alex J.
American, 20th century.
Born 12 December 1898, in Fort Lee (New Jersey).
Sculptor. Monuments.

Alex Ettl was a pupil of his father, John Ettl. He is credited with various monuments.

ETTL, Georg
German, 20th century.
Born 1940, in Bavaria.
Painter, installation artist, draughtsman. Murals.

Georg Ettl has featured in collective exhibitions, including: 2003, *Une collection de 'chefs-d'œuvre', emprunts, pastiches, copies, citations et interprétrations* (*A Collection of 'Masterpieces', Borrowings, Pastiches, Copies, Quotations and Interpretations*), an exhibition addressing the practice of appropriation in art, mainly from a European perspective, at the regional foundation of contemporary art in Limoges. He has shown his works in solo exhibitions, including: 1995, J.-F. Dumont gallery, Bordeaux; 1996, Château d'Angers then the Château d'Oiron; 2000, Decimus Magnus art gallery, Bordeaux.

Ettl works from a wide variety of historical and iconographic sources: the fall of Babylon, the detail from a fresco at Pompeii, the tapestry of the Apocalypse in Angers, horses in outline, signs of modernity and such like, which he interprets freely. In the context of art theory and irony, he seeks - like many others before him - to identify their element of truth.

BIBLIOGRAPHY:

Lasserre, Jean-Claude/Dumont, Jean-François, *Georg Ettl: art et architecture: entretiens*, exhibition catalogue, Château d'Oiron, Oiron, 1997. Arnaudet, Didier, *'Georg Ettl'* in *Art Press* no. 264 p 82, periodical, Paris, January 2001.

ETTL, John
Hungarian, 20th century.
Born 1 August 1872, in Budapest; died 1940.
Active and naturalised in the USA.
Sculptor.

John Ettl studied in Budapest and Vienna before settling in the USA. His best known works are: the memorial to *President Abraham Lincoln* at the Arsenal in New York; *Memorial to World War I* in East Ruthenford, New Jersey and a sculpture adorning the Place de la Justice in Bern, Switzerland.

ETTLE, Franz
Swiss, 19th century.
Born 24 January 1847, in Biberach.
Sculptor.

Ettle replaced Franz Bosinger as sculpture and drawing master in Interlaken, where he worked until 1876. He also exhibited in Bern, where he lived until 1881.

ETTLIN, Joseph
Swiss, 19th century.
Born 19 March 1826, in Sarnen; died 23 June 1870, in Sachseln.
Painter.

Joseph Ettlin took lessons with Schlatt in Lucerne, subsequently going on to study at the academy of art in Rome. He also went to Milan. He settled permanently in Sarnen after 1850.

ETTLIN, Joseph Maria
Swiss, 19th century.
Born 1791, in Kernsen; died 1 November 1874, probably in Sarnen or Kerns.
Sculptor.

Joseph Maria Ettlin studied with the sculptor Abart. He worked for churches, notably those at Sarnen and the monastery at Engelberg, as well as in other Swiss towns. He had two pupils, Nikolaus Ettlin (probably a relation) and Kuster.

ETTLIN, Nikolaus, the Elder
Swiss, 19th century.
Born 3 March 1830, in Kerns.
Sculptor.

Nikolaus Ettlin the Elder studied with the sculptor Joseph Maria Ettlin, acting as his apprentice, and went on to study at the school of drawing in Basel. He continued his artistic studies during a stay in Rome, where he joined the Swiss Guard, before returning to Switzerland to take a job as drawing master in Sachseln and Kerns. He created many works for churches and chapels.

ETTLIN, Nikolaus, the Younger
Swiss, 19th century.
Born 4 April 1869, in Kerns.
Draughtsman, sculptor (wood), stonemason.

The son of Nikolaus Ettlin the Elder, Nikolaus Ettlin the Younger worked in Paris and Fribourg and held the post of drawing master at the school of arts and crafts in Kerns. He studied drawing with his father and also in the German city of Karlsruhe.

ETTLIN, P. Lukas
Swiss, 19th century.
Born 1864, in Sarnen.
Draughtsman, painter, calligrapher.

A monk at the Monastery of the Conception in Engelberg, P. Lukas Ettlin took lessons with P. Emanuel Wagner. In 1886, he left for North America, where he entered a monastery of his order, and did not return to Europe until 1892. The paintings in the church of the Engelberg monastery are attributed to him.

ETTLIN, Simon
Swiss, 19th century.
Born 9 January 1818, in Sarnen; died 7 May 1871, probably in Sarnen.
Draughtsman, painter, architect.

A pupil of P. Leodegar Kretz at the Muri monastery, according to Dr Brun, Simon Ettlin was drawing master at the college in Sarnen for 25 years, while still pursuing his career as a doctor and architect. He is best known for a work at the Sarnen college. Some wash and watercolour drawings by him also remain.

ETTLINGER, Salomon
French, 20th century.
Born in Paris.
Sculptor.

Salomon Ettlinger was a pupil of Levasseur and a member of the Salon des Artistes Français, Paris. He was awarded an honourable mention in 1932.

ETTORE D'ALBA
Italian, 15th century.
Active in Lombardy at the end of the 15th century.
Sculptor.

Ettore d'Alba collaborated on the embellishment of the façade of the Certosa di Pavia.

ETTORI, Giambattista
Italian, 18th century.
Active in Ferrara c. 1780.
Painter.

Ettori painted a fresco for the Castello Estenze at Ferrara.

ETTY, William
British, 19th century.
Born 10 March 1787, in York; died 13 November 1849, in York.
Painter, watercolourist. Mythological subjects, figures, nudes, genre scenes.

William Etty was the son of a miller. At the age of 11 he was sent to Hull as an apprentice to his uncle, the printer Robert Peck, publisher of the *Hull Packet*, where he remained for seven years. His wish was to become a painter, and he used every opportunity that his hard apprenticeship allowed him to draw and paint. In 1806 he went to one of his uncles in London and worked fervently to be admitted to classes at the Royal Academy.

Having drawn the group *Cupid and Psyche* in the shop of an Italian called Gianelli, he showed his work to Opie, who introduced him to Fuseli. He was admitted to the Royal Academy in 1807, the same week as the landscape painter Collins, thanks to the generosity of his uncle. He chose Sir Thomas Lawrence as his teacher, but this fashionable portrait painter was so absorbed by his work that he left his pupil to his own devices and to make copies of his portraits. From Lawrence's studio he went to the British Institute, where he copied the Old Masters. He found little favour during the awarding of medals by the Academy, and the works he sent to the Exhibition were rejected year after year.

In 1811, *Sappho*, the first of his works to be exhibited, was bought by the British Institute for 25 guineas, and *Telemachus Rescuing Antiope* was acquired by the Royal Academy. In 1816, accompanied by his brother, he visited Paris and worked for Jean-Baptiste Regnault. In 1820 he achieved fame for his work *Coral Finders: Venus and her Youthful Satellites Arriving at the Isle of Paphos*, and his *Pandora Crowned by the Seasons* and *Arrival of Cleopatra in Cilicia* brought him increasing success.

At this point he decided to see the works of the great Italian Schools, though he did not visit Rome, Naples, Florence and Venice until 1822. He remained in Italy for 18 months, completely captivated by the masterpieces of Rubens and Titian that surrounded him. They gratified his partiality for expressing the sensuality of the female form, and it was with reluctance that he returned to England, bringing back with him around 50 paintings. During his travels from 1822 to 1824, he also went to Paris. In 1824 he was elected an associate member of the Royal Academy. In 1825 he painted *Woman Pleading for the Vanquished* and *Judgement of Paris*, a triptych entitled *Judith* - the story of the deliverance of Israel - and *Benaiah Killing the Two Strongest Men in Moab*. In 1828 he was elected a member of the Royal Academy. When someone remarked to him that, from now on, it was no longer appropriate for him to attend the afternoon classes, as he had been doing habitually, he replied that he 'would prefer to abandon the honour of being a member of the Royal Academy than give up continuing to educate myself.' He lived in London until 1848, then returned to York.

In his autobiography, Etty informs us that his goal had always been to impart some great moral lesson through his painting. His working life is attributed to influencing the formation of the French Romantic painters at the start of the 19th century. Eugène Delacroix, who was not afraid of borrowing from Bonington (as he did a great number of times), could not have been indifferent to an art as new as that of William Etty. His smooth and richly coloured impasto, highlighted by powerful drawing, even to the extent of outlining shapes and forms, was unheard of and audacious in its time. It contrasted so completely with productions by the pupils of David that artists such as Delacroix, searching for original means of expression, could not help but be strongly impressed by it. Through Delacroix's means of expression, this manner of painting (colour and paste) lasted quite a long time in the French School.

BIBLIOGRAPHY:

Gilchrist, Alexander, *Life of William Etty, R.A.*, D. Bogue, London, 1855. Monkhouse, William Cosmo, *Pictures by William Etty: with descriptions and a biographical sketch of the painter*, George Routledge and Sons, London; New York, 1874. Gaunt, William, *Etty and the nude: the art and life of William Etty, R.A., 1787-1849*, F. Lewis, Leigh on Sea, 1943 (limited). *Paintings by William Etty, R.A., 1787-1849*, Adams Gallery, London, 1946. *An exhibition of paintings by William Etty*, Arts Council of Great Britain, London, 1955. Farr, Dennis, *William Etty*, Routledge and Paul, London, 1958. Bailey, Brian J., *William Etty's nudes*, Inglenook Press, Pulloxhill, England, c. 1974. Curr, G.C., '*Who Saved York Walls?: The Roles of William Etty and the Corporation of York*' in *York Historian*, 1984. Postle, M./Wright, J., *The Artist's Model: It's Role in British Art from Lely to Etty*, exhibition catalogue, U. Nottingham, A.G., 1991.

MUSEUMS AND GALLERIES:

ABERDEEN (AG): *Somnolency* (1838, oil on canvas) - DUBLIN: *Duo* - EDINBURGH (Nat. Gal. of Scotland): *Benaiah Slaying Two Lion-like Men of Moab* (oil on canvas); *The Combat: Woman Pleading for the Vanquished* (oil on canvas); *Judith's Maid outside the Tent of Holophernes* (oil on canvas); *Judith and Holofernes* (oil on canvas); *Judith Coming Out of the Tent* (oil on canvas) - GLASGOW: *The Three Graces; Christ Appearing to Mary Magdalene* - LEEDS (City AG): *Pandora Crowned By the Seasons* (1824, oil on canvas) - LEICESTER: *Man in Persian Armour* - LIVERPOOL: *Bathers Surprised by a Swan* - LONDON (Royal Academy of Arts): *Sleeping Nymph and Satyrs* (1828, oil on canvas, competition piece) - LONDON (Tate Collection): *Miss Mary Arabella Jay* (exhibited in 1819, oil on canvas, portrait); *Study for `Pandora Crowned by the Seasons'* (c. 1824, oil and drawing/paper); *Youth on the Prow, and Pleasure at the Helm* (1830-1832, oil on canvas, exhibited in 1832); *Britomart Redeems Faire Amoret* (exhibited in 1833, oil on canvas); *Standing Female Nude* (c. 1835-1840, oil on canvas); numerous paintings - LONDON (Victoria and Albert Mus.): *Seated Female Nude* - LOS ANGELES (Getty Mus.): *Female Nude in a Landscape* (end 1820s - 1830s, oil/paper/Masonite) - MONTREAL (Learmont): *Triumphant Love* - MONTREAL (MBA): *Cupid's Bivouac* - NEW YORK (Metropolitan Mus. of Art): *The Three Graces* (sketch) - NOTTINGHAM (Castle Museum & AG): *The Afflicted; Study, Figure; Head of a Jew* - PARIS (Louvre): *Eve* - PRESTON: *Cupid in a Shell; Biblical Scene* - SHEFFIELD: *Study for a Head of Christ* - SUNDERLAND: *Aaron the High Priest* - WASHINGTON DC (Georgetown University): , c. 1830, oil on canvas).

AUCTION RECORDS:

NEW YORK, 23 Jan 1903, *Getting Ready,* USD 300. NEW YORK, 1906, *Lady Ellenborough* USD 275. LONDON, 8 Feb 1908, *The World before the Flood,* GBP 241. LONDON, 23 March 1908, *Combat,* GBP 14; *Study of a Female,* GBP 7; *Queen of the Amazons,* GBP 2; *Cupid and Psyche,* GBP 9. LONDON, 30 March 1908, *Nymph of the Fountain,* GBP 9. LONDON, 4 May 1908, *Gypsy,* GBP 2. LONDON, 8 May 1908, *Cave Dwellers* GBP 27. LONDON, 3 June 1908, *Pandora Crowned by the Seasons,* GBP 10; *Model Reading,* GBP 14. LONDON, 20 June 1908, *Young Girl Writing,* GBP 18. LONDON, 20 Feb 1909, *Study of a Female,* GBP 27. NEW YORK, 11-12 March 1909, *Evening Star,* USD 320; *Pirate,* USD 310. LONDON, 22 March 1909, *Widows and Cupids,* GBP 16. LONDON, 28 July 1909, *Spring,* GBP 39. LONDON, 19 March 1910, *Nymphs Dancing,* GBP 23. PARIS, 30 Nov-1-2 Dec 1920, *Odalisque* (watercolour) FRF 550. PARIS, 4 Dec 1920, *The Three Graces,* FRF 4,300. PARIS, 27 Jan 1921, *Young Bathers,* FRF 180. PARIS, 27 Jan 1921, *Female Bather from Behind,* FRF 1,575; *Vestal Virgin,* FRF 1,000. PARIS, 23 Feb 1921, *Bust of Young Girl* (attributed) FRF 210. LONDON, 27 Jan 1922, *Studies for Ariadne; Subject on Its Knees* (both) GBP 3. LONDON, 17 March 1922, *Model* (sketch) GBP 7. LONDON, 24 March 1922, *Nymph of the Woods Sleeping,* GBP 21. LONDON, 3 April 1922, *Still-life: Pheasant, Fruit and a Vase of Flowers,* GBP 23; *Man with Arms Open and Man Holding a Lance,* GBP 2; *Man Sitting on a Rock; Man with Cymbals,* GBP 1. LONDON, 21 April 1922, *Model Sleeping,* GBP 4. LONDON, 9 June 1922, *Judgement of Paris* (study) GBP 2; *Seated Female Nude,* GBP 6. LONDON, 26 June 1922, *Bather,* GBP 3. LONDON, 7 July 1922, *Diana and Endymion* (1839) GBP 346. LONDON, 24 July 1922, *Model Sleeping; Scene on the Shore with Figures,* GBP 9. LONDON, 19 Jan 1923, *The Combat, Mercy Interceding for the Vanquished,* GBP 5; *Innocence* GBP 54. LONDON, 23 March 1923, *Model,* GBP 3. LONDON, 11 May 1923, *Cupid and Psyche,* GBP 52. LONDON, 15 June 1923, *Aurora and Zephyr,* GBP 252. LONDON, 25 June 1923, *Model,* GBP 8. PARIS, 17-18 June 1924, *Ariadne Abandoned,* FRF 950. PARIS, 14 and 15 Dec 1925, *Mirror of the Nymph,* FRF 1,250. PARIS, 20-21 April 1932, *Young Female Nude from Behind* (attributed) FRF 490. PARIS, 8 April 1935, *Portrait of a Young Woman* (attributed) FRF 600. PARIS, 26 May 1937, *Study of a Female Nude with Raised Arms* (black and red chalk heightened with white, attributed) FRF 155. PARIS, 8 June 1937, *Dreamer,* FRF 1,400. PARIS, 24 March 1941, *Woman and Cupid Running* (attributed) FRF 480. PARIS, 29 Jan 1943, *Female Nude,* FRF 26,000. PARIS, 12 March 1943, *Woman in Pink Hat* (attributed) FRF 4,000. PARIS, 20 Dec 1944, *Venus Reclining* (attributed) FRF 45,000. PARIS, 21 Nov 1949, *Portrait of a Young Woman in a White Dress,* FRF 60,000. LONDON, 22 April 1959, *Golden Age,* GBP 250. LONDON, 13 April 1960, *Bather,* GBP 100. LONDON, 19 April 1961, *Model with Black Hair* (card) GBP 250. NEW YORK, 10 May 1961, *Three Wrestlers,* USD 550. LONDON, 14 March 1962, *Still-life,* GBP 700. LONDON, 20 Nov 1964, *Leda* (after Michelangelo) Gns 3,500. LONDON, 22 Nov 1967, *Abduction of Proserpina,* GBP 2,500. LONDON, 10 July 1973, *Venus and Cupid,* GBP 7,000. LONDON, 15 Oct 1976, *Venus and Cupid* (oil on card, 23 1/4 x 16 1/2 ins / 59 x 42 cm) GBP 1,100. LONDON, 29 July 1977, *Study of a Nude* (1837, oil on card, 15 x 13 ins / 38 x 33 cm) GBP 700. NEW YORK, 12 May 1978, *Hesperides* (gouache and chalk/canvas, 34 1/2 x 69 ins / 87.5 x 175 cm) USD 1,800. LONDON, 18 March 1980, *Study of Female with Breasts Bared* (black and white chalk/paper, 19 1/2 x 12 ins / 49.5 x 30.5 cm) GBP 500. LONDON, 26 Nov 1982, *To Arms, to Arms, Ye Brave!* (oil on canvas, 31 x 44 ins / 78.7 x 111.7 cm) GBP 5,000. LONDON, 5 July 1984, *Reclining Male Nude* (oil on card, 17 x 20 ins / 43 x 51 cm) GBP 6,500. LONDON, 24 July 1984, *Reclining Nude* (pencil heightened with white/brown paper, 20 x 12 ins / 50.4 x 30.6 cm) GBP 950. LONDON, 11 March 1987, *Ariadne* (oil on panel, 27 1/2 x 20 1/2 ins / 70 x 52 cm) GBP 10,000. LONDON, 29 Jan 1988, *Cupid* (oil on card, 19 1/2 x 15 1/2 ins / 49.5 x 39.4 cm) GBP 715. LONDON, 26 May 1989, *Study of a Female Nude* (oil on card, 18 1/2 x 15 ins / 47 x 38 cm) GBP 825. NEW YORK, 17 Jan 1990, *Flora* (oil on panel, 30 1/4 x 22 1/2 ins / 77 x 57.2 cm) USD 2,200. NEW YORK, 28 Feb 1990, *Lute Player* (oil on panel, 16 x 17 3/4 ins / 40.6 x 45.1 cm) USD 19,800. LONDON, 20 April 1990, *Bust-Length Portrait of a Young Indian Dressed in an Embroidered Red Waistcoat, with a White Cravate and Turban* (oil on canvas, 18 x 14 ins / 45.5 x 35.5 cm) GBP 15,400. LONDON, 26 Sept 1990, *Male Nude* (pencil, 15 x 10 1/4 ins / 38 x 26 cm) GBP 990. LONDON, 1 March 1991, *Female Nude Reclining in the Moonlight* (oil on canvas, 18 x 23 ins / 45.7 x 58.4 cm) GBP 1,430. LONDON, 10 April 1991, *Portrait of Rebecca Singleton and Elizabeth Her Sister, Faces and Shoulders* (oil on panel, 25 1/2 x 20 3/4 ins / 65 x 53 cm) GBP 4,400. NEW YORK, 23 May 1991, *Male Nude* (oil/card, 25 x 19 ins / 63.5 x 48.2 cm) USD 8,800. LONDON, 10 April 1992, *Bathers* (oil on canvas, 24 x 20 ins / 60.9 x 50.8 cm) GBP 1,980. NEW YORK, 27 May 1993, *Ariadne* (oil on card/synthetic resin, 19$^{3/4}$ x 26 ins / 50.2 x 65.8 cm) USD 9,200. LONDON, 13 April 1994, *Psyche with Cupid and Venus* (oil on canvas, 16 1/4 x 20 1/2 ins / 41.5 x 52 cm) GBP 5,750. LONDON, 5 June 1996, *War and Peace* (oil on canvas, after Rubens, 30 1/4 x 25 1/4 ins / 77 x 64 cm) GBP 2,300. LONDON, 9 Oct 1996, *Study of Model* (oil on panel, 9 x 8 1/4 ins / 22 x 21 cm) GBP 1,955. LONDON, 9 July 1997, *Studies of an Arab* (oil on canvas, 30 x 25 1/4 ins / 76 x 64 cm) GBP 13,800. LONDON, 12 Nov 1997, *Lady Godiva* (oil on panel, 27 1/4 x 19 1/4 ins / 69 x 49 cm) GBP 4,600. LONDON, 31 March 1999, *Portrait of Master Hardcastle* (oil on canvas, 53 x 43 ins / 135 x 110 cm) GBP 13,000. LONDON, 24 Nov 1999, *Female Nude* (oil on board, 16 x 10 ins / 40 x 26 cm) GBP 7,500. LONDON, 15 June 2000, *Bacchus* (oil on board on panel, 17 x 19 ins / 42 x 49 cm) GBP 5,000. LONDON, 1 Dec 2000, *Venus Reclining, Holding an Arrow, Looking towards a Full Moon* (oil on panel, 17 x 23 ins / 44 x 58 cm) GBP 26,000. LONDON, 26 June 2001, *Bather* (oil on board, 9 x 19 ins / 24 x 47 cm) GBP 11,500. LONDON, 26 June 2001, *Rose of Love* (oil on panel, 20 x 14 ins / 51 x 35 cm) GBP 36,000. LONDON, 11 June 2002, *Seated Tajik in an Interior with His Shield and Scabbard at His Side* (oil on board, 27 x 21 ins / 69 x 53 cm) GBP 4,500. TORONTO, 18 Nov 2002, *Musidora, the Bather at the Doubtful Breeze Alarmed* (oil on board, 12 x 9 ins / 30 x 23 cm) CAD 10,000. LONDON, 20 Feb 2003, *Despair. Nude Study* (oil on board, arched top, double-sided, 19 x 26 ins / 48 x 67 cm) GBP 10,000. LONDON, 20 Feb 2003, *Phaedria and Cymochles on the Idle Lake* (oil on canvas, arched top, 23 x 31 ins / 58 x 79 cm) GBP 17,000. NEW YORK, 27 May 2004, *Daydreams* (oil on board, 20 x 30 ins / 51 x 77 cm) USD 40,000. NEW YORK, 27 Oct 2004, *Venus and Her Satellites* (oil on panel, 26 x 20 ins / 67 x 51 cm) USD 17,500.

ETZLER, Martin
German, 17th century.
Born c. 1635; died 31 October 1709.
Active in Breslau (now Wroclaw, Poland).
Painter.

EUANTHES
Active in Thebes c. 5th century BC.
Painter.
Ancient Greek.
Euanthes decorated the temple of Zeus at Pelusium (near Port Said).

EUBELEN, Anne-Marie
Belgian, 20th century.
Born 1886, in Stavelot; died 1968, in Liège.
Painter, engraver, watercolourist.
Anne-Marie Eubelen worked on the Belgian coast and in Liège.

EUBERLOT, Dominique
French, 20th century.
Born in Ploërmel (Morbihan).
Painter. Portraits, landscapes.
Dominique Euberlot exhibited at the Salon des Indépendants from 1925.

EUBERT, Noël
French, 18th century.
Active in Paris in 1767.
Painter, sculptor.

EUBIUS
5th century BC.
Active In Thebes c. the 5th century BC.
Sculptor.
Ancient Greek.
Eubius, with his compatriot Xenocritus, made a statue of Heracles Promachus.

EUBULIDES I
3th century BC.
Active in Tanagra c. the 3rd century BC.
Sculptor.
Ancient Greek.
Eubulides' signature was found on a statue pedestal.

EUBULIDES II
2th century BC.
Born in Cropidae (Athens).
Sculptor.
Ancient Greek.
Eubulides, born in the Athenian deme of Cropidae, and his father Eucheir made several colossal statues that stood in the Inner Ceramicus district of Athens.

EUBULIDES III
2th century BC.
Active in Athens.
Sculptor.
Ancient Greek.
Eubulides, son of Eucheir and grandson of Eubulides II, was, like his grandfather, a member of the Athenian deme of Cropidae. A number of statue pedestals have been found in Athens bearing his signature. Amongst other works he made a statue of a priestess of Athena with his father. He is mentioned by Pausanias.

EUBULIDES IV
1th century.
Born in Piraeus.
Sculptor.
Ancient Greek.
Eubulides is said to have made a statue of the Roman emperor Claudius.

EUBULUS I
Sculptor.
Ancient Greek.
Eubulus is only known from a mention by Pliny the Elder.

EUBULUS II
1th century.
Sculptor.
Ancient Greek.
Eubulus' name appears on a pedestal found at the Propylaea.

EUCADMUS
4th century BC.
Sculptor.
Ancient Greek.
Eucadmus was the teacher of Androsthenes of Athens, according to Pausanias.

EUCADMUS
5th century BC.
Active in 450 BC.
Sculptor.
Ancient Greek.
Eucadmus, according to Pausanias, was the master of Androsthenes.

EUCAS, Pedro
Spanish, 16th century.
Active in Valencia in 1569.
Painter.

EUCHEIR I
7th century BC.
Born c. 7th century BC, in Corinth.
Sculptor, painter.
Ancient Greek.
Eucheir, according to Pliny the Elder, travelled with Damaratus and Eugrammus to Etruria. He was a potter, and can probably be identified with the artist who, according to Aristotle, invented painting in Greece.

EUCHEIR II
2th century BC.
Active in Athens.
Sculptor.
Ancient Greek.
Eucheir was either the father or the son of Eubulides II and is mentioned by Pausanias. There may be several sculptors of the same name. A number of statue pedestals inscribed with this name have been found in Athens and Megara.

EUCHEIRUS
6th century BC.
Active in Corinth.
Sculptor.
Ancient Greek.
Eucheirus was the pupil of Chartas and Syagras of Sparta, and the teacher of Clearchus of Rhegium, who in turn was the teacher of Pythagoras.

EUCLES
4th century BC.
Sculptor.
Ancient Greek.
Eucles was the contemporary of Lysippus, according to Pliny.

EUCLIDES
4th century BC.
Athenian, active 376 BC.
Sculptor.
Ancient Greek.
Euclides made a *Bacchus* for the town of Bura in Achaea.

EUCLIDES
4th century.
Active in Athens c. 373 BC.
Sculptor.
Ancient Greek.
Euclides made some marble statues for the temples of Achaea and Bura.

EUDE, Édouard Charles
French, 19th century.
Born 19th century, in Offranville.
Sculptor (ivory).
Édouard Charles Eude exhibited at the Paris Salon from 1877 to 1881. His best-known works are two low reliefs in ivory, *Coronation of Charles VII* and *Bianca-Capella*.

EUDE, Jean Louis Adolphe
French, 19th century.
Born 1818, in Arès; died 8 April 1889, in Paris.
Sculptor.
Jean Eude trained under David d'Angers. He was awarded a third-class medal in 1859 followed by a first-class medal in 1877. From 1847 he exhibited regularly at the Paris Salon, always with great success. In all of his works Eude demonstrated great qualities of form and grace. His most notable works are *Marshal Soult* (marble bust for the Colonne de la Grande Armée in Boulogne); *Omphale* (marble statue in the courtyard of the Louvre); *Mozart* (marble bust for the Conservatoire de Musique); and *Steadfastness* (statue for the commercial court). His other works include *Virgin with Rosary* (marble low relief); *Echo of the Flute* (marble statue); *Tossulus, Grand Master of Roman Decadence* (marble statue); and *Return of the Hunt* (marble statue).
MUSEUMS AND GALLERIES:
AMIENS: *Marble Bust of Jean Goujon* - BORDEAUX: *Echo of the Flute* - SAINTES: *Palissy Standing; Palissy Seated on a Stool; Palissy Seated on a Kiln.*

EUDEMUS
6th century BC.
Active in Ionia.
Sculptor.
Ancient Greek.
Eudemus is known from the signature on a headless statue found near Miletus.
MUSEUMS AND GALLERIES:
LONDON (British Mus.): headless statue.

EUDES
French, 13th century.
Active c. 1292.
Miniaturist, calligrapher.

EUDES, Eugène Jules
French, 19th - 20th century.
Born in the second half of the 19th century, in Choisy-le-Roi.
Watercolourist.
Eugène Jules Eudes is one of the very many artists of whom nothing is known after 1914.

EUDES DE GUIMARD, Louise
French, 19th century.
Born 9 May 1827, in Argentan.
Painter. Genre scenes, landscapes.
A pupil of L. Cogniet, Louise Eudes de Guimard exhibited at the Salon from 1847 to 1880. The state purchased her work *The Lake*.
AUCTION RECORDS:
PARIS, 18 March 1994, *Melancholy* (oil on canvas, 22 x 18 ins / 55 x 46 cm) FRF 7,000.

EUDES DE MONTREUIL
French, 13th century.
Born c. 1220; died 1289.
Sculptor, architect.
This artist is known above all as the architect of St Louis, for whom he worked in many churches in Paris and whom he accompanied to Palestine. As a sculptor, it is known that he carved in the Franciscan church a low relief for his own tomb.

EUDIDACTUS
3th century BC.
Active in Athens.
Sculptor.
Ancient Greek.
Eudidactus left his signature on a fragment of a statue found in the ruins of the Acropolis.

EUDIER, Pierre
French, 16th century.
Active c. 1560.
Glass painter.
In 1560, Pierre Eudier was working at the Abbey of Fécamp.

EUDORUS
Sculptor.
Ancient Greek.
Eudorus is said by Pliny to have decorated several theatres with statues. Nothing is known of his dates or birthplace.

EUDOXUS
5th century BC.
Sculptor.
Ancient Greek.
Eudoxus, born in the Athenian town of Alopece, was one of the sculptors to decorate the temple of Athena Polias on the Acropolis in Athens.

EUELPISTUS, Lucius Canidius, called Genareius
Active in Rome.
Sculptor.
Ancient Roman.

Euelpistus made small figures of genii (local or presiding spirits) in gold, silver and ivory.

EUENOR
Greek, 5th century BC.
Active in Ephesus.
Painter.
Euenor was one of the group of earliest Greek painters, according to Pliny.

EUENOR
6th century BC.
Sculptor.
Ancient Greek.
Euenor's name is found on several statue pedestals.

EUERTZ, Hans. See **EWOUTSZ**

EUGEN, Napoleon Nicholas Bern (Prince of Sweden)
Swedish, 19th - 20th century.
Born 1 August 1865, in Drottningholm, near Stockholm; died 17 August 1947, in Waldermarsudde.
Painter (gouache). Landscapes. Murals.
Symbolism.
Eugen Napoléon Nicholas Bern was the youngest of the four sons of King Oscar II and Queen Sophie of Sweden. He worked on his painting in Uppsala, with Von Gegerfelt, and then in Paris (1887-1889), with Léon Bonnat, Pierre Puvis de Chavannes and Henri Gervex. Making regular extended journeys to France and Italy, he also worked as an artist in Sweden. He worked mainly in Tyresö and Waldemarsudde, near Stockholm. He also found in the forests of western Sweden the vital force that he considered to be 'the source of the Nordic identity'. He bequeathed his property in Waldemarsudde (now a public museum), as well as the art collection that he had housed there, to the Swedish state. He took part in the Exposition Universelle in Paris in 1900, with *Stockholm Castle at Night*, then in many others, including the one organised in London that transferred to the Musée du Petit-Palais in Paris and, finally, to Düsseldorf, which was entitled *Northern Lights*, in 1987. In 2003, the Prins Eugens Waldemarsudde in Stockholm presented an exhibition on the subject of his life and artistic achievements.

His works, consisting exclusively of landscapes, mainly reflect the influences of Klinger, Böcklin and Friedrich. He had a 'symbolist' vision of the Swedish landscape, with forms simplified to the point of abstraction, a lyrical composition and dramatic colours. He especially liked to convey the poetic atmospheres of the Swedish landscape - both the dreamy silences of the bright nights and the sunlit days of the summer. The decorative quality of his art was reinforced at a very early stage by a departure from the architecture of landscape. The artist's best-known oil paintings are: *Spring, Old Castle, Cloud, Still Water, Summer Night* and *White Steamboat*. His talent as a decorative artist is demonstrated in several vast mural paintings, most of which are executed in fresco. The largest and best-known, *Town near the Water*, is on display at the city hall in Stockholm. He also gained a reputation as a gouache painter.

BIBLIOGRAPHY:
Wennerholm, Eric, *Prins Eugen: människan och konstnären: en biografi*, Bonnier, Stockholm, 1982. Zachau, Inga, *Prins Eugen: national romantikern*, Signum, Lund, 1989. Zachau, Inga, *Prins Eugen: det öppna landskapets skildrare*, Signum, Lund, 1991. Brummer, Hans Henrik, *Prins Eugen: minnet av ett landskap*, Norstedt, Stockholm, 1998. Zachau, Inga, *Eugen de Suède peintre et prince*, Michel de Maule, Paris, 2000.

MUSEUMS AND GALLERIES:
BRUSSELS (Mus. royaux des Beaux-Arts de Belgique): *Slopes* - COPENHAGEN (Statens Mus. for Kunst): *White Steamboat* - GÖTEBORG (Konstmus.): *Forest* (1892, oil on canvas); *Cloud* (replica) - HELSINKI (Ateneumin Taidemus.): *Church in Tyresö* - OSLO (Nasjonalgal.): *Lake* - PARIS (Mus. d'Orsay): *Old Castle* (replica) - STOCKHOLM (Kungliga Akademien): *Summer Landscape* - STOCKHOLM (Nationalmus.): *Summer Night; Still Water; Dawn* - STOCKHOLM (Thielska Gal.): *Night Cloud* - STOCKHOLM (Waldemarsudde): *Spring; Old Castle* (1893, oil on canvas); *Cloud* (1896, oil on canvas); *Windmill* (1908, oil on canvas); *Blue Villa; Illuminated Steamboat*.

AUCTION RECORDS:
STOCKHOLM, 8 Nov 1972, *Landscape*, SEK 11,400. STOCKHOLM, 30 Oct 1979, *View of a Small Port* (1937, oil on panel, 12 1/2 x 15 3/4 ins / 32 x 40 cm) SEK 25,500. STOCKHOLM, 26 Oct 1982, *Summer Landscape* (1929, gouache, 11 x 17 3/4 ins / 28 x 45 cm) SEK 15,500. STOCKHOLM, 16 May 1984, *Landscape* (1938, watercolour, 11 x 17 3/4 ins / 28 x 45 cm) SEK 21,500. STOCKHOLM, 30 Oct 1984, *View of Bergen* (1924, oil on canvas, 35 x 30 3/4 ins / 89 x 78 cm) SEK 70,000. STOCKHOLM, 20 Oct 1987, *Landscape with Cornfields* (oil on canvas, 22 x 43 1/4 ins / 55 x 110 cm) SEK 260,000. STOCKHOLM, 15 Nov 1988, *Park in the Frisians* (1926, oil, 18 x 15 ins / 46 x 38 cm) SEK 30,000. STOCKHOLM, 15 Nov 1989, *Road to Vadstena in Summer* (1929, oil, 16 1/4 x 25 1/4 ins / 41 x 64 cm) SEK 65,000. NEW YORK, 23 Oct 1990, *View of Gardens at Dala Manor* (1915, watercolour and gouache/paper, 12 1/2 x 22 1/2 ins / 31.8 x 57.2 cm) USD 8,800. STOCKHOLM, 30 Nov 1993, *Summer Landscape with Red House and Oaks in the Foreground* (oil on canvas, 22 x 29 1/2 ins / 55 x 75 cm) SEK 33,000. STOCKHOLM, 18 May 1999, *Oak Trees at Djurgarden* (1930, oil on canvas, 20 x 30 ins / 50 x 75 cm) SEK 125,000. STOCKHOLM, 25 Nov 1999, *Harbour at Waldemarsudde* (oil on canvas, 18 x 20 ins / 46 x 52 cm) SEK 122,000. STOCKHOLM, 29 May 2000, *Study for 'The Light Night'* (1899, oil on canvas, 23 x 19 ins / 58 x 47 cm) SEK 280,000. UPPSALA, 10 Dec 2000, *Brunnsviken* (1925, oil on canvas, 24 x 27 ins / 61 x 69 cm) SEK 92,000. STOCKHOLM, 29 May 2001, *The Town from Waldermarsudde* (1903, oil on canvas, 11 x 14 ins / 28 x 36 cm) SEK 82,000. STOCKHOLM, 29 May 2001, *Hazy Sunshine over the Town* (1929, oil on panel, 18 x 25 ins / 46 x 64 cm) SEK 200,000. STOCKHOLM, 29 May 2002, *The Town seen from Waldemarsudde* (1903, oil on canvas, 11 x 14 ins / 28 x 35 cm) SEK 175,000. STOCKHOLM, 4 Dec 2002, *Strandvagen, Stockholm - Boats at Quay* (oil on panel, 13 x 18 ins / 33 x 46 cm) SEK 95,000. STOCKHOLM, 4 June 2003, *Fenris at Finnboda, View from Waldemarsudde* (1940, oil on canvas, 15 x 22 ins / 38 x 55 cm) SEK 110,000. STOCKHOLM, 3 Dec 2003, *The Bay, Waldemarsudde* (1945, oil on panel, 19 x 22 ins / 48 x 57 cm) SEK 115,000. STOCKHOLM, 25 May 2004, *Rolling Landscape* (oil on canvas, 20 x 24 ins / 51 x 61 cm) SEK 43,000. STOCKHOLM, 14 June 2004, *Landscape with Clouds* (1930, watercolour, 11 x 17 ins / 28 x 44 cm) SEK 25,000.

EUGEN, Nöelle van, pseudonym of Noëlle van Oldenbaneveldstaat
Dutch, 20th - 21st century.
Born 1960.
Since 1981 until 1987 active in France.
Painter.
Art Cloche group.
Van Eugen lives and works in Amsterdam. In the 1980s, she belonged to the Art Cloche group in Paris which was a venue for artistic exchange and practices on the fringes of institutional organizations.

BIBLIOGRAPHY:
Art cloche. Éléments pour une rétrospective. Squatt artistique, auction catalogue, Maître Pierre Cornette de Saint-Cyr, Paris, 30 January 1989.

EUGÈNE. See **ALLARD Jean Pierre**

EUGÈNE, G.
French, 19th century.
Painter. Portraits, landscapes.

G. Eugène sent landscapes to the Paris Salon in 1827 and 1837. He is probably the same person as the artist who painted the *Woman's Head* owned by the museum of Bordeaux.
MUSEUMS AND GALLERIES:
BORDEAUX: *Woman's Head.*

EUGENIKOS, Manuel
14th century.
Active during the second half of the 14th century.
Painter.
He demonstrates an elegant and precise way of painting in the execution of the frescoes of the church of Tzalendjikhe, Georgia.

EUGRAMMUS
7th century BC.
Active in Corinth in 660 BC.
Sculptor.
Ancient Greek.
Eugrammus, according to Pliny and Pausanias, left Corinth along with Eucheir I when the Bacchiad dynasty was expelled. They followed Demaratus, the father of Tarquinius Priscus, and moved to Italy.

EUKHOUT, J. J.
French, 19th century.
Painter. Portraits.
The museum of Montpellier has *Portrait of the Actor Lafeuillade in the Role of Masaniello* listed under the name of J. J. Eukhout. The painting is probably by the artist J.-J. Eeckhout.
MUSEUMS AND GALLERIES:
MONTPELLIER: *Portrait of the Actor Lafeuillade in the Role of Masaniello.*

EULBERG, Veronica Appollonia
American, 20th century.
Born 20 August 1905, in Portland (Oregon).
Painter.
Veronica Eulberg was a pupil of Émil Jacques. She was a member of the Oregon Artists' Society.

EULENBURG, Felix
German, 19th - 20th century.
Born 13 July 1881, in Greifswald; died 1909.
Painter. Genre scenes, animals.
Felix Eulenburg studied in Düsseldorf and Berlin.

EULENBURG, Olga von (Countess)
German, 19th century.
Born 1 June 1848, in Rastenberg.
Painter. History painting.
Von Eulenburg studied with Rops in Dresden and Girot in Paris.

EULER
German, 18th century.
Active in Brzeg, Poland c. 1767.
Painter.

EULER, Carl
German, 19th century.
Born 9 March 1815, in Kassel.
Painter, lithographer. Landscapes, animals.
Carl Euler has left mainly animal paintings.
AUCTION RECORDS:
MUNICH, 29 May 1980, *Moonlit Landscape* (1860, oil on canvas, 25½ x 30in/65 x 76cm) DEM 2,600.

EULER, Eduard
German, 19th - 20th century.
Born 19 August 1867, in Düsseldorf.
Painter, lithographer. Urban landscapes, landscapes.
Euler studied in Düsseldorf and then in Karlsruhe. He was deeply influenced by Schönleber. In his lithographs, he mainly represents views of towns and the countryside.
AUCTION RECORDS:
COLOGNE, 20 Oct 1989, *Orchard in South Tyrol* (1911, oil on canvas, 27½ x 39¼ ins / 70 x 100 cm) DEM 1,100.

EULER, Emil Ludwig
German, 20th century.
Born 15 May 1878, in Wiesbaden (Hesse).
Painter, engraver.
Emil Euler mainly produced portrait engravings.

EULER, Henri Jean Albert
Swiss, 19th century.
Born 21 April 1814, in Rolle; died 29 June 1866, in Lausanne.
Painter, draughtsman.
Henri Euler studied in Munich before settling in Paris. He exhibited *Pandours' Post, on the Mountains of Herzegovina, Dalmatian Sailors, Daughters of Zara* and *Slovenian Shepherds* at the 1848 Paris Salon.

EULER, Johann Heinz
Swiss, 18th century.
Born 1720; died 1750.
Active in Basel.
Painter.
Johann Euler was admitted to the guild of painters in Basel in 1746. Dr Brun believes him to be the author of a series of portraits reminiscent of the School of Johann Rudolph Huber.

EULER, Margaret J.
British, 20th century.
Born in England.
Active in Kent from c. 1925.
Painter.
Margaret J. Euler exhibited *Lest We Forget* at the Salon des Artistes Français in Paris in 1934.

EULER, Pierre-Nicolas
French, 19th - 20th century.
Born 12 January 1846, in Lyons; died c. 1913.
Draughtsman (charcoal), painter. Still-lifes (flowers).
From 1860 to 1865 Pierre-Nicolas Euler was a pupil at the École des Beaux-Arts, Lyons, in the flower-painting class of Jean-Marie Reignier. He opened a drawing studio in Paris about 1876. From 1875 he exhibited at the Lyons Salon and was awarded a first-class medal in 1895. In the same year he began to exhibit at the Salon de Paris, where he won the medal in 1904. He painted canvases (and drew some heightened charcoal drawings) of flowers and fruit. His paintings were at first thought to be 'theatrical', his lighting effects 'flashy'. Later criticism was more favourable, praising his originality, his mastery in managing light and his integration of colour.
MUSEUMS AND GALLERIES:
ANGERS - CLERMONT-FERRAND - LYONS (MBA): *The Violet Season* - MONTPELLIER.

EULHOFER, Ignaz. See **ELHAFEN**

EULICH, Carl Friedrich
German, 18th century.
Active in Brieg (now Brzeg, Poland) in 1715.
Painter. Landscapes.

EULISSE, Vincenzo
Italian, 20th century.
Born 1936, in Venice.
Painter.
Vincenzo Eulisse is self-taught. He has regularly shown his work in Italy since 1959 in both Venice and Milan, and also

exhibited in Brussels in 1960 and Warsaw in 1970. He lives in Venice.

In his allusive scenes, which are sometimes close to a type of Surrealism, he juxtaposes a variety of figurative elements. He creates a world influenced both by Pop Art and by New Realism, in that he makes use of figuration and the freedoms obtained from the Dada and Surrealist movements.

EULRY, André
French, 20th century.
Born 1930, in the Champagne Region.
Painter, stained glass painter.

André Eulry was a pupil of the Académie de la Grande Chaumière in 1947 and 1948. He lived in Bastia, Corsica, where he painted from 1952 to 1955. His painting is abstract and uses a language of small signs, a gestural or automatic calligraphy.

EUMARES, or Eumarus
6th century BC.
Active in Athens c. 540 BC.
Painter.
Ancient Greek.

Eumares apparently introduced an element of chiaroscuro into his paintings. He was the first to differentiate between male and female figures, giving the flesh of the males a darker colour and making that of the female figures white. Pliny tells us that he was not afraid to paint his figures in a wide variety of poses.

EUMELUS I
5th century BC.
Born in Athens.
Sculptor.
Ancient Greek.

Eumelus, born in the Athenian district of Scambonidae, collaborated in the work on the temple of Athena Polias on the Acropolis in Athens.

EUMELUS II
3th century.
Active c. 220 AD.
Painter.
Ancient Greek.

Eumelus made a *Helen* for the Forum in Rome, according to Philistratus.

EUMNESTUS
Sculptor.
Ancient Greek.

Eumnestus was born in the Athenian deme of Paeania in the time of Augustus. He made a statue of the king of Thrace, Cotys son of Rhescuporis.

EUMOLPUS, Quintus Considius
Sculptor.
Ancient Roman.

Eumolpus, a Greek slave freed by the Considia family, is described in an inscription at the Villa Strozzi in Florence as *faber eborarius*, a carver in ivory.

EUMYTHIS
6th century BC.
Sculptor.
Ancient Greek.

Eumythis' name was found on the pedestal of a statue discovered near Sellasia in the Peleponnese.

EUN, Robert
French, 16th century.
Active in Rouen.
Sculptor.
Rouen School.

Robert Eun carried out some work in the large cemetery of the church of St-Maclou in Rouen in 1527.

EUNA, Pedro d'
Spanish, 15th century.
Born in Roussillon.
Active in Barcelona.
Painter.

EUNOSTIDES
6th century BC.
Active in Athens c. 500 BC.
Sculptor.
Ancient Greek.

Eunostides' name was found on the pedestal of a statue.

EUNUS
3th - 2nd century BC.
Active in Epidaurus.
Sculptor.
Ancient Greek.

Eunus' name was found on some pedestals at Epidaurus.

EUPALINUS
3th century BC.
Active in Megara.
Sculptor.
Ancient Greek.

Eupalinus worked in Athens. He should not be confused with famous architect of the 6th century.

EUPHILETUS
6th century BC.
Painter.
Ancient Greek.

Euphiletus may have worked in Eleusis.

EUPHORUS
5th century BC.
Sculptor.
Ancient Greek.

EUPHRANOR, called the Isthmian
4th century BC.
Born in Corinth.
Active from 375 to 335 BC.
Painter, sculptor.
Ancient Greek.

Euphranor learned his craft in the workshop of Aristides and lived in Athens, where most of his masterpieces of sculpture are to be seen. On one side of the porch of the Ceramicus in Athens, the 12 divinities are represented, while Theseus and other figures are shown on the other side. In the same spot there was also at one time a painting showing *The Battle of Mantinea between the Athenian and Boeotian Cavalry*, including portraits of Gryllus, the son of Xenophon, and Epaminondas.

Euphranor made some remarkable works in marble and metal. His heroes had an air of grave dignity and were highly praised by Pliny. He was known for his realistic rendering of human emotions. Other works mentioned as being by him are statues of *Paris, Heracles, Hephaestus, Dionysus, Philip* and *Alexander*. None of these works has survived.

BIBLIOGRAPHY:
Palagia, Olga, *Euphranor*, Brill, Leiden, 1980.

EUPHRON
5th century BC.
Born on Paros.
Sculptor.
Ancient Greek.

Euphron's signature has been found on several statue pedestals, including two from the Acropolis in Athens.

EUPHRONIUS
6th - 5th century BC.
Active between 510 and 490 BC.
Vase painter, potter.

Ancient Greek.

Euphronius both made and painted vases, as well as making vases for other artists to paint, including Onesimus, Pistoxenus and Panaetius. In his later years, he seems to have given up painting his vases in order to devote himself to creating new forms, particularly of cups. He liked to decorate the broad areas offered by such cups, as well as those of vases such as volute and calyx kraters. His themes include scenes from the Heracles cycle and Dionysus and his satyrs, and he was happy to provide the banqueting scenes that always proved popular with clients.

Euphronius' work, in the 'Severe Style', is notable for its balance, power and liveliness. These three qualities are well illustrated by the red-figure krater in the Louvre depicting *Heracles Struggling with Antaeus*. The two heroes confront each other, their bodies balancing one another to form a pyramidal composition. A feeling of power is produced by the bent position of Heracles' legs as he seeks to overcome the giant. A realistic expression of pain marks the giant's face and he seems to be gasping with his mouth half open. His wild beard and hair indicate both his defeat and his monstrousness. The artist gives a realistic rendering of the musculature of the fighters' limbs while at the same time paying attention to the decorative aspect of their bodies. This careful and detailed depiction of the human body is also found in the sculpture of this period. The reliefs on the Athenian Treasury at Delphi, for example, show many similarities to the work of Euphronius.

A volute krater (Arezzo), depicting a *Amazonomachy* (battle between Greeks and Amazons), has many similarities with the Heracles scene, with shortened limbs and identical muscular details. A cup in Berlin, attributed to Euphronius, exemplifies his gifts of accurate observation and his desire to portray the emotional states of his figures. In the interior of the cup is a scene showing *Achilles Binding Patroclus' Arm*, from which he has removed an arrow. Euphronius paints the details of the garments and anatomy of his figures with great care. He demonstrates his skill in foreshortening by depicting Patroclus front on, sitting with one leg bent and the other stretched out to the side, thereby giving shape to the composition - always a particularly complicated matter in the case of a cup. Patroclus' face, the mouth half open, expresses a stoical suffering.

Even in his own day, Euphronius was considered to be an unrivalled master of his art. Within the framework of his harmonious compositions, he is not afraid to attempt naturalistic foreshortenings and detailed anatomy, particularly in the rendering of the muscles, without neglecting the decorative aspect of the whole. He is able to express all the feelings and sufferings of his subjects, but always in a restrained way.

BIBLIOGRAPHY:

Boardman, John, *Athenian Red Figure Vases: The Archaic Period*, Thames and Hudson, London, 1975. Keuls, Eva, *'The Social Position of Attic Vase Painters and the Birth of Caricature'* in *Proceedings of the 3rd Symposium on Ancient Greek and Related Pottery, Copenhagen, August 31-September 4 1987, Nationalmuseet, Ny Carlsberg Glypotek, Thorvaldsens Museum*, Copenhagen, 1988.

EUPOMPUS

5th century BC.
Active in Sicyon c. 400 BC.
Painter.
Ancient Greek.

Eupompus was the founder of the Sicyon School and a contemporary of Zeuxis, Timanthes and Parrhasius.

EUPREPES

Active in Phrygia during the Roman Empire.
Sculptor.
Ancient Greek.

Euprepes made a statue of P. Aelius Agestratus in Rhodes.

EURICH, August

German, 19th century.
Active in Berlin.
Miniaturist.

EURICH, Richard Ernst

British, 20th century.
Born 14 March 1903, in Bradford (Yorkshire); died 1992.
Painter, draughtsman. Landscapes, seascapes.

Richard Eurich studied at Bradford College from 1920 to 1924 and then at the Slade School in London until 1926. During World War II he was appointed as an official war artist to the Admiralty. He became a member of the New English Art Club in 1943. He was also a member of the Royal Academy in London. He taught from 1949.

Eurich began exhibiting his drawings in 1929 and his paintings in 1933. He exhibited at the New English Art Club from 1927. In 1946 he showed *A Place on the Hampshire Coast* at the International Exhibition organised by UNESCO at the Musée d'Art Moderne de la Ville de Paris.

R. Eurich 1948

MUSEUMS AND GALLERIES:

LONDON (National Maritime Mus.): seascapes, war scenes - LONDON (Royal Academy of Arts): *Queen of the Sea, 1911* (1954, oil on canvas, harbour scene); *From Haworth, Yorkshire* (1965, oil on canvas); *The Mariner's Return* (1953, oil on canvas, competition piece, seascape) - LONDON (Tate Collection): *Night Raid on Portsmouth Docks* (1941, oil on canvas); *The Landing at Dieppe, 19th August 1942* (1942-1943, oil/wood) - NEW YORK (MoMA).

AUCTION RECORDS:

LONDON, 13 March 1981, *Dunkirk Beach, May 1940* (oil on card, 11 x 19 3/4 ins / 28 x 50.3 cm) GBP 900. LONDON, 9 Nov 1984, *Fawley Beach* (1939, oil on canvas, 25 x 30 ins / 63.5 x 76.2 cm) GBP 2,200. LONDON, 6 March 1987, *Boats on a Beach* (1938, oil on canvas, 15 1/2 x 19 1/2 ins / 39.5 x 49.5 cm) GBP 2,800. LONDON, 12 May 1989, *Children on a Beach* (1984, oil on card, 11 3/4 x 23 1/2 ins / 30 x 60 cm) GBP 1,980. LONDON, 21 Sept 1989, *At Sea* (1984, oil on card, 12 1/4 x 23 1/2 ins / 31.1 x 59.7 cm) GBP 1,210. LONDON, 3 May 1990, *Sword Dance in Northern Umbria* (1973, oil on card, 11 1/2 x 23 3/4 ins / 29 x 60.5 cm) GBP 3,520. LONDON, 6 Nov 1992, *Dorset Landscape* (1937, oil on canvas, 20 x 24 ins / 51 x 61 cm) GBP 3,740. LONDON, 5 Oct 1999, *Sunday Morning, Huddersfield* (1977, oil on board, 24 x 28 ins / 61 x 71 cm) GBP 1,800. LONDON, 21 Nov 2000, *Near Seaview, Isle of Wight* (1962, oil on board, 9 x 24 ins / 22 x 61 cm) GBP 9,000. LONDON, 22 Nov 2000, *Dunkirk 1940* (oil on board, 11 x 14 ins / 27 x 35 cm) GBP 22,000. LONDON, 17 Jan 2001, *Her Majesty the Queen visits Yarmouth on Britannia, July 1965* (1966-1967, oil on board, 12 x 30 ins / 30 x 76 cm) GBP 10,500. LONDON, 4 July 2002, *Cornwall* (1958, oil on board, 13 x 17 ins / 33 x 42 cm) GBP 11,000. LONDON, 16 Oct 2003, *Girl by a Window* (1930, oil on canvas, 16 x 12 ins / 41 x 31 cm) GBP 9,000. LONDON, 11 Feb 2004, *Harbour Scene, Penzance* (oil on panel, 15 x 18 ins / 37 x 45 cm) GBP 9,500. LONDON, 4 June 2004, *Northumbrian Sword Dance* (1973, oil on board, 12 x 24 ins / 30 x 61 cm) GBP 11,000.

EURIPIDES

5th century BC.
Born 480 BC; died c. 405 BC.
Painter.
Ancient Greek.

Euripides, the great playwright, is said to have also been a painter in his youth.

EUSEBI, Luis
Spanish, 19th century.
Born c. 1770, in Rome; died 16 August 1829, in Paris.
Active in Madrid.
Painter, miniaturist. Portraits.
Luis Eusebi spent some time in England. When he returned to Spain he was appointed curator of the Prado Museum.

EUSEBIO, Ferrari. See **FERRARI**

EUSEBIO DI JACOPO DA SAN GIORGIO
Italian, 15th - 16th century.
Born c. 1465, in Perugia; died c. 1550.
Painter. Religious subjects. Murals.
Eusebio di Jacopo da San Giorgo was instructed by Perugino at the same time as Giannicola Manni, his childhood friend. He belonged to the Matricola dei Pittori Porta Sant'Angelo (Perugian painters' guild) along with of Pinturicchio, under the name of Eusepius Jacobi Christofori, to which Vasari added that of San Giorgio. In 1501 he was commissioned with Fiorenzo di Lorenzo to paint the banners of the trumpets of Perugia. Shortly afterwards Pinturicchio took him, and a number of other young painters, to decorate the sacristy of the Duomo at Siena. It is recorded in a notarial deed dated 1506 that Pinturicchio recognises that he owes Eusebio 100 golden ducats.In 1507, in the cloisters of S Damiano, near Assisi, Eusebio painted two frescoes, one of which bears the inscription: *Eusebius Perusinus pinxit MDVII.* One is an *Annunciation* in a poor state of preservation: the Virgin kneeling, a book in her hand, and the angel bearing a lily reminiscent of the lily in the *The Angelic Salutation* by Raphael in the Vatican. The second fresco, likewise badly damaged, represents the *St Francis of Assisi Receiving the Stigmata* in the presence of Friar Rufino, his companion. Christ is winged like Giotto's Christ, the only difference being that he is crucified. The landscape is composed of strange rocks, obviously intended to be those of the Alverne, and is much more craggy than that of Giotto.Vasari ascribed to Eusebio the *Adoration of the Magi* in the Oddi Chapel in S Agostino, Perugia, today in the Galleria Nazionale, Perugia. However, some scholars, drawing attention to the gracefulness of the four musician angels, consider the work worthy of Raphael, while others detect the influence of Pinturicchio, whose pupil Eusebio was. An inscription of an incomplete date MDV... can only be 1505, 1506, 1507 or 1508; the two letters which follow S.I. are difficult to interpret. It is unlikely that the first initial is that of Raphael Sanzio. Interpreting it as Sinibaldo Ibi, it may have been completed by this contemporary of Eusebio. It is known that Eusebio and his friend Giannicola completed each other's paintings out of friendship. However, Ibi, a fairly mediocre pupil of Perugino, was not necessarily on close terms with Eusebio.The *Madonna* of the church of S Francesco at Mantelica, a Virgin with the Christ Child, a young St John and four saints is signed *Eusebius. de Sco. Georgio Perusianus. pinxit,* with the painter's monogram. As an imitation of Raphael can be detected, one could argue from its authenticity that the *Adoration of the Magi* is also by Eusebio. This Madonna is the last of the paintings by Eusebio. It is, however, unlikely that he stopped painting after 1512. Indeed, it is known that he was still alive in 1527 and passionate about his art, or so Pascoli tells us. On the other hand he seems to have been the father of several children whom he was scarcely able to feed and bring up. He was to survive by 10 years his friend Giannicola.

BIBLIOGRAPHY:
Crowe, J.A./Cavalcaselle, G.B., *A New History of Painting in Italy*, John Murray, London, 1903 (reprint AMS Press, New York, 1975). Joannidès, Paul, *Raphäel et son temps*, exhibition catalogue, Palais des Beaux Arts, Lille, 2002.

MUSEUMS AND GALLERIES:
LILLE (MBA, Wicar Collection): *Woman's Head* (c.1507, black chalk, attributed); *Bust of woman* (c.1507, black chalk, attributed); *Woman's Head* (c.1505, black chalk, attributed).

AUCTION RECORDS:
LUCERNE, 13 June 1970, *Christ on the Mount of Olives*, CHF 33,000. MILAN, 21 April 1986, *Virgin and Child with St John* (oil on panel, round, diam. 26 3/4 ins / 68 cm) ITL 31,500,000.

EUSTACE (Brother)
Flemish School, 15th century.
Active in Lille.
Illuminator.
Eustace copied and illuminated a book of hours for the bishop of Bethlehem, the illustrations to which included six figures of saints. He may be the same Brother Eustace who was working for the Duke of Burgundy in 1428.

EUSTACHE
Flemish School, 13th - 14th century.
Born to a family originally from Lisbourg.
Painter.
Eustache worked at the castle of Hesdin.

EUSTACHE
Flemish School, 15th century.
Active in Louvain.
Sculptor.
Eustache carried out work at the church of St Peter.

EUSTACHE
Italian, 15th century.
Active in Rome.
Sculptor (wood).
Under the guidance of Philippot Viart, Eustache collaborated in 1549 on the embellishment of the choir stalls in St Peter's, Rome.

EUSTACHE, André
French, 20th century.
Born in La Coucourde (Drôme).
Painter. Landscapes.
André Eustache exhibited in Paris at the Salon des Artistes Indépendants from 1925 to 1931.

EUSTACHE, Charles François
French, 19th century.
Born 6 December 1820, in Paris; died 24 April 1870, in Cherbourg.
Painter, pastellist, draughtsman. Local scenes, landscapes, waterscapes, seascapes.
Orientalism.
Charles François Eustache was a pupil of Prosper Marilhat, whom he accompanied on his travels in the Far East. He enjoyed a long friendship with the Romantic painter and writer Eugène Fromentin. Eustache travelled in Italy and Egypt, finally settling in Cherbourg around 1857. He had a small private fortune so could afford to neglect the commercial aspect of his chosen career, his work long being underrated as a result. He exhibited at the Paris Salon.

Eustache's best-known works are *Ruins of the Temple of Ermonthis, Upper Egypt* (1849); *Evening, Memory of the Banks of the Nile* and *Greek Ruins* (1851); and *Interior of the Fourchambault Factory* (1852). He executed many views of the Normandy countryside or the English Channel coasts, using charcoal or pastel. He also executed a lithograph of the *Ruins of the Temple of Luxor in the Plains of Thebes* from one of his drawings from life.

AUCTION RECORDS:
PARIS, 27 Sept 1990, *Rough Sea* (pastel, 22 x 40 1/2 ins / 56 x 103 cm) FRF 5,000; *Beach* (oil on panel, 8 1/2 x 16 1/4 ins / 21.5 x 41.5 cm) FRF 7,000; *View of The Hague* (oil on panel, 11 x 17 1/4 ins / 28 x 43.5 cm) FRF 6,200. PARIS, 28 June 2002, *Study of Clouds* (oil on paper on canvas, 7 x 11 ins / 17 x 28 cm)

EUR 6,000. PARIS, 28 June 2002, *Mountain Landscape* (oil on paper on canvas, 11 x 18 ins / 29 x 45 cm) EUR 6,000.

EUSTACHE, Claude
French, 17th century.
Active in Nantes.
Painter.

It was possibly Claude Eustache who in 1657 worked in Paris as painter to the royal household.

EUSTACHE, Georgette
French, 20th century.
Born 16 July 1874, in Fontenay-aux-Roses.
Sculptor.

Georgette Eustache was a pupil of Sicard and first exhibited in Paris at the Salon des Artistes Français in 1924.

EUSTACHE, Nicolas
French, 18th century.
Active in Paris in 1772.
Painter, sculptor.

EUSTACHE, Robert
Spanish, 19th century.
Painter. Interiors with figures, genre scenes, local scenes.
Orientalism.

Robert Eustache was the son of Charles François Eustache and accompanied him on his travels.

AUCTION RECORDS:
PARIS, 27 Sept 1990, *Black Cook and Serving Maid* (oil on canvas, 25 1/4 x 35 1/2 ins / 64 x 90 cm) FRF 27,000; *Atelier in Cairo* (1889, oil on canvas, 25 1/4 x 31 1/2 ins / 64 x 80 cm) FRF 10,500.

EUSTACHE, Sylla
French, 19th - 20th century.
Born 1 December 1856, in Paris.
Medallist. Portraits.

Initially an artisan engraver, Sylla Eustache became a pupil of Émile Laporte and Gabriel Guay in the Lequein studio. He was a member of the Salon des Artistes Français from 1891. Among his most famous works are medals and medallions including *Portrait of My Son* (1893), *Portraits of M. Loustau's Children* (1894), *Portraits of the Dog Tony* (1887), and his study for the *Souvenir Français Medal*.

EUSTACHE OF LIÈGE
Flemish School, 16th century.
Sculptor.

Eustache of Liège made the high altar of the church at Erckelenz in 1547.

EUSTACHE-LORSAY. See **LORSA Louis Alexandre Eustache**

EUSTACHI
Austrian, 16th century.
Active in Graz in 1539.
Painter.

EUSTACHIO (Fra)
Italian, 15th - 16th century.
Born 1473, in Florence; died 25 September 1555, in Florence.
Miniaturist.
Florentine School.

Eustachio was a monk in the Dominican convent of S Marco in Florence, having taken the habit at Villa Gondi when Savonarola was viceroy-general, at the time of the plague in Florence. Around 1502 he began to embellish an *Antiphonary of Saints* with miniatures for the monks of the convent of S Spirito in Siena, restoring and embellishing a number of manuscripts in their sacristy. Among his works are a *Psalter* of 1505 (now part of the collection in the Museo di S Marco, Florence), a *Gradual*, begun in 1518, and an *Antiphonary* running from the Advent of the eve of the Nativity and another *Antiphonary* which is now part of the collection in the Duomo at Florence. He also worked on the choir-books of the Duomo at Florence and the church of S Maria della Quercia in Viterbo.

EUSTACHIO DA UDINE, Celebrino
Italian, 16th century.
Active in Venice.
Engraver (wood), print publisher.

EUSTACHIUS
Bohemian School, 18th century.
Died 25 August 1779, in Prague.
Painter.

Eustachius belonged to the Carmelite order; there is a painting by him dated 1764.

EUSTATHIOS
Italian, 11th century.
Active in Southern Italy.
Fresco artist.

There are frescoes signed by this artist in the Otranto area.

EUSTON, Jacob Howard
American, 20th century.
Born 4 October 1892, in Lebanon near Philadelphia; died 1965.
Painter.

Jacob Euston was a member of the Illinois Academy of Fine Arts.

EUTELIDAS
6th century BC.
Argive, active in 516 BC.
Sculptor.
Ancient Greek.

Eutelidas and Chrysothemis made the statues of two victors at the Olympic Games, Demarates and his son Theopompus.

EUTHYCARTIDES
7th century BC.
Sculptor.
Ancient Greek.

Euthycartides' name was signed on a statue pedestal in Delos.

EUTHYCLES
6th century BC.
Active in Athens.
Sculptor.
Ancient Greek.

Euthycles' name was found signed on a statue pedestal on the Acropolis.

EUTHYCRATES I, or Euthychrates
4th century BC.
Sculptor. Statues.
Ancient Greek.

Euthycrates, the son and pupil of Lysippus and brother of Bedas and Daippus, was active in Sicyon in 312 BC. He is known to have made statues, in the Severe Style, of hunters and warriors and a portrait statue of Alexander the Great.

EUTHYCRATES II, or Euthychrates
2th century BC.
Sculptor.
Ancient Greek.

Euthycrates is thought to have worked in Rhodes where pedestals bearing his name have been found.

EUTHYMIDES
6th century BC.
Active 520 to 500 BC.
Vase painter.
Ancient Greek.

Euthymides was a contemporary of Phintias, with whom he has several points in common both in the variety of vases that he decorated and in the rounded depiction of the human body. He is known above all as being a rival of Euphronius, as we know from an inscription on a vase that reads: 'as never Euphronius [made like this]'. This rather naive boastfulness is evidence both of the fame of Euphronius and the rivalry between artists who worked with an eye on each others' achievements, always trying to outdo one another.

Euthymides' red-figure designs included scenes from the gymnasium, warriors taking leave and a number of mythological scenes, particular from the life of Theseus. At this period, Theseus was emerging as the most popular hero of the Attic world, as opposed to Heracles, the hero of the Dorians and Peloponnesians. Euthymides' rather stocky nudes show a good sense of volume and a desire to make the body's anatomy both decorative and realistic. These concerns give weight to the idea that Polias, whom Euthymides claimed was his father, was a sculptor. Although lacking the grace of Euphronius, he was skilled in using drapery to emphasise the form of the naked human body.

BIBLIOGRAPHY:

Boardman, John, *Athenian Red Figure Vases: The Archaic Period*, Thames and Hudson, London, 1975. Keuls, Eva, '*The Social Position of Attic Vase Painters and the Birth of Caricature*' in *Proceedings of the 3rd Symposium of Ancient Greek and Related Pottery, Copenhagen, August 31-September 4 1987, Nationalmuseet, Ny Carlsberg Glypotek, Thorvaldsens Museum*, Copenhagen, 1988.

EUTROPUS
Sculptor.
Ancient Roman.
Eutropus was a Christian sculptor making sarcophagi. A tombstone found in Rome, in the cemetery of the Capella Santa di Sant' Elena (The Holy Chapel of St Helena), shows him at work.

EUTYCHES
Sculptor.
Ancient Greek.
Eutyches' name is signed on a terracotta piece representing Heracles, found at Mirina.

EUTYCHIDES I
4th century BC.
Active in Sicyon in 318 BC.
Sculptor.
Ancient Greek, Hellenistic period.
Eutychides, a pupil of Lysippus, is known for his gilded bronze group of *Tyche* (Fortune) and of the river *Orontes* at Antioch. He was the originator of the type of Fortune crowned with city walls, generally symbolising the City and frequently copied. He also made a *Eurotas*, another depiction of a river, praised by Pliny for its fluid movement.

EUTYCHIDES II
2th century BC.
Active in Athens.
Sculptor.
Ancient Greek.
Eutychides' name has been deciphered on a number of statue pedestals from the Acropolis.

EUTYCHIDES III
2th - 1st century BC.
Active in Delos.
Sculptor.
Ancient Greek.

EUTYCHIDES IV
Born in Miletus, Ionia (Turkey).
Active during the Roman Empire.
Sculptor.
Ancient Greek.
Eutychides was the son of Zoilus.

EUTYCHUS
1th century.
Active in Rome AD.
Painter.
Ancient Roman.

EUVERLANDER, Klaas Lourisz.
Dutch, 17th century.
Born c. 1600, in Jisp.
Sculptor.
Klaas Lourisz. Euverlander travelled to France and Italy.

EUWOUTSONE, Jan
Dutch, 16th century.
Born in Emerik.
Engraver (wood, line-engraving), printer.
Jan Euwoutsone lived in Amsterdam.

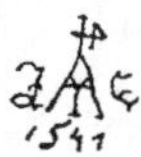

EUXENIDAS
5th - 4th century BC.
Theban, active c. 400 or 380 BC.
Painter.
Ancient Greek.
Euxenidas is unknown except as the teacher of Aristides.

EUXENUS
Sculptor.
Ancient Greek.
Euxenus, who dates from the Hellenistic period, is known from a statue pedestal found on the island of Telos.

EUZET, Jean Marie
French, 20th century.
Born 26 April 1905, in Sète; died 1980.
Painter. Designs for tapestries.
Musicalism (the attempt to interpret music in painting).
Jean Marie Euzet studied art at the École Nationale d'Art Décoratif, Limoges. In 1948 he became a professor in the same school and taught all disciplines. He took part in several group exhibitions: the Salon des Réalités Nouvelles, the Salon des Indépendants and the Salon Comparaisons; and exhibitions in Amsterdam, Prague, Vienna and The Hague.

In 1925 he turned to Cubism and Neo-Plasticism. His meeting with Louis Baudron, a member of the Musicalist group, and with Velensi led him to adopt Musicalist procedures. Valensi had organised Musicalist rooms at the Salon Comparaisons. Between 1949 and 1956 he showed in various salons abstract compositions in which the curve was predominant, but which had some reference to figuration. He also designed tapestries for the Aubusson Tapestry Company, including: *The Port, The Town, Three Movements of a Floral Suite* and *Summer Nocturne*.

AUCTION RECORDS:
PARIS, 4 July 1997, *Radiology* (oil on canvas, 76 3/4 x 45 1/4 ins / 195 x 115 cm) FRF 30,000.

EUZET, Juliette
French, 20th century.
Born 20th century, in Limoges.
Painter, potter, enameller.
Musicalism (the attempt to interpret music in painting).
The wife of Jean-Marie Euzet and a former pupil at the École d'Art Décoratif, Limoges, Juliette Euzet contributed with her husband to the renewal of *l'art du feu* (includes kiln-fired pottery, forging metals and artworks of wrought iron). She works according to Musicalist ideas.

EVANCE, Hans. See **EWOUTSZ**

EVANDER
1th century BC.
Active in Athens and Rome.
Sculptor.
Ancient Greek.

Evander, a slave freed by M. Avianius Evander, met Cicero in 51 BC. It is known that at this period he made statues of Bacchantes and an Ares. Mark Anthony summoned him to Alexandria whence he was sent to Rome as a prisoner of war. Once in Rome, he continued to work there.

EVANGELISTA
Italian, 15th century.
Born to a family originally from Sutri.
Active in Rome.
Painter.

EVANGELISTA
Italian, 15th century.
Active in Padua in 1461.
Painter.

EVANGELISTA (Fra)
Italian, 15th century.
Born in Reggio; died c. 1495, in Ferrara.
Miniaturist, writer.

Evangelista illustrated rituals for Ferrara Cathedral in collaboration with Jacobo Filippo d'Argenta. He worked for the Marchese Borso d'Este.

EVANGELISTA, Francesco Paolo
Italian, 19th century.
Born 1837, in Penne.
Sculptor.

Evangelista studied art in Naples and Florence. He exhibited allegorical subjects and genre figures in Naples and Rome from 1877.

EVANGELISTA, Roberto
Brazilian, 20th century.
Installation artist.

In 1996, Roberto Evangelista took part in the 23rd São Paulo Biennale.

EVANGELISTA DA MILANO
Italian, 16th century.
Active in Genoa in 1544.
Painter.

EVANGELISTA DAL FERRO. See **FERRO**

EVANGELISTA DI NICCOLO SARACENI
Italian, 15th century.
Active in Orvieto c. 1470.
Painter.

Evangelista di Niccolo Saraceni was a priest who worked for Orvieto Cathedral.

EVANGELISTA DI PIAN DI MELETO
Italian, 15th - 16th century.
Born c. 1458, in Pian de Meleto; died 18 January 1549, in Urbino.
Painter.

Evangelista di Pian di Meleto was the pupil of Giovanni Santi. He executed the altarpiece of *St Nicholas of Tolentino* (1501) for the church of S Agostino at Città di Castello. It is possible that he later worked for Timoteo Viti.

EVANGELISTI, Agostino
Italian, 17th century.
Born to a family originally from Ripatransone (Marche).
Sculptor (wood).

Father of Giovanni, with whom he collaborated at the cathedral in Ferrara.

EVANGELISTI, Benedetto
Italian, 17th century.
Active in Arcevia (Marche) in 1668.
Painter.

EVANGELISTI, Filippo
Italian, 18th century.
Born c. 1684, in Rome; died 16 March 1761, in Rome.
Painter. History painting.

Evangelisti was the valet to Cardinal Corradini; for a number of years he owed his success to the latter's patronage, and in particular to his collaboration with Benefal. He was a pupil of Luti.

EVANGELISTI, Giovanni Basilio
Italian, 17th century.
Born in Ripatransone (Marche).
Sculptor (wood).

Son of Agostino, he worked at the cathedrals of Ferrara and Ripatransone.

EVANO, Yvonne
French, 20th century.
Born in St-Brieuc.
Painter. Genre scenes.

Yvonne Evano was a pupil of Léon Félix.

EVANS
French, 18th century.
Painter. Landscapes.

Evans, a distinguished artist, was attached to the Sèvres porcelain factory.

EVANS
British, 20th century.
Born 1890, in London.
Painter.

Evans was a self-taught artist who worked in the Caledonian market in London. Works such as his *Omnibus* have led to him being classified among British Naive artists.

EVANS, Benjamin Beale
British, 19th century.
Died c. 1824.
Engraver.

Benjamin Beale Evans engraved genre scenes and series of portraits, including *Delia* (which formed part of the Boydell collection).

EVANS, Bernard Walter
British, 19th - 20th century.
Born 1848, in Birmingham; died 1922, in London.
Painter, watercolourist. Landscapes.

Bernard Walter Evans studied under Samuel Lines in Birmingham. He moved to London in 1869 and exhibited from 1871 at the Royal Academy, the Suffolk Street Gallery and the New Water-Colour Society. In 1880 he became a member of the Royal Society of British Artists and in 1887 was elected to the Royal Institute of Painters in Watercolours. He received a commendation in France at the Exposition Universelle of 1900.

MUSEUMS AND GALLERIES:
LONDON (Victoria and Albert Mus.): *Old House at Hendon; Near Barmouth; Moonlight; Cannock Chase, Staffordshire; Grasse de la Croix de Gardes; Cannes Seen from Cannet; Leaving Pasture* - MELBOURNE: *Sunset; Cannock Chase* - SYDNEY: two watercolours.

AUCTION RECORDS:
NEW YORK, 12 and 13 March 1903, *Returning Home* (watercolour) USD 80; *On the Plain* (watercolour) USD 55. LONDON, 7 Dec 1907, *Colwich Church* (watercolour) GBP 19; *Near Cannock Chase* (watercolour) GBP 10. LONDON, 21 Nov 1908, *Cannock Chase,* GBP 4. LONDON, 16 June 1922, *Barden Towers* (drawing) GBP 46. LONDON, 7 July 1922, *Cabra, near*

Grasse, GBP 44. LONDON, 23 April 1923, *Spa Town,* GBP 21. LONDON, 19 Feb 1981, *Bolton Abbey, Yorkshire* (watercolour, 16 x 30 ins / 40.5 x 76 cm) GBP 480. LONDON, 29 April 1986, *View of Harrogate* (watercolour, 15 x 28 1/2 ins / 37.2 x 72.5 cm) GBP 650. LONDON, 12 May 1993, *Antibes from the Cap d'Antibes (Alpes Maritimes)* (watercolour and gouache, 15 1/2 x 29 1/4 ins / 39.4 x 74.5 cm) GBP 2,127.

EVANS, Bob

British, 20th - 21st century.

Born 1947, in Cardiff.

Painter, draughtsman.

From 1964 to 1971, Bob Evans studied at the Cardiff College of Art, the Chelsea School of Art and the Hornsey College of Art. Using photography as a source and extending this with preliminary drawings, he gradually develops a form of art that through this process acquires an independent history. He has exhibited as group exhibitions since 1968, including the 9th Paris Biennale in 1975.

BIBLIOGRAPHY:

IXe Biennale de Paris, exhibition catalogue, Idea Books, Musée d'Art moderne de la Ville de Paris, Paris, 1975.

EVANS, David

British, 19th century.

Born 1793, in Montgomeryshire; died 17 November 1861, in Shrewsbury.

Glass painter.

David Evans trained under J. Betton in Shrewsbury.

EVANS, De Scott

American, 19th century.

Born 28 March 1847, in Boston (Wayne County, Indiana); died 4 July 1898.

Painter. Portraits, genre scenes, still-lifes.

After working in Cleveland around 1874, De Scott Evans went to Paris in 1877 and became a pupil of Bouguereau. When he returned to Cleveland he was appointed as a professor at the Academy of Fine Arts. He died on his way to Paris to paint a ceiling commission when the ship he was travelling in, the Burgundy, sank.

AUCTION RECORDS:

NEW YORK, 15 March 1906, *Idlers* (drawing) USD 100. LONDON, 19 Dec 1908, *Tenby* (1865, drawing) GBP 5. LONDON, 16 March 1979, *A Serious Question* (1896, oil on canvas, 23 3/4 x 19 3/4 ins / 60.3 x 50.2 cm) GBP 900. NEW YORK, 29 Jan 1981, *A Serious Question* (1896, oil on canvas, 24 x 20 ins / 61 x 50.8 cm) USD 2,500. NEW YORK, 21 Sept 1984, *Trompe l'Oeil: 'Leave Message'* (oil on canvas, 12 x 10 ins / 30.7 x 25.5 cm) USD 24,000. NEW YORK, 4 Dec 1986, *Pistol and Ace* (oil on canvas, 12 x 10 ins / 30.5 x 25.4 cm) USD 21,000. NEW YORK, 25 May 1989, *Still-life with Oranges and Grapes* (1891, oil on canvas, 10 x 12 ins / 25.5 x 30.5 cm) USD 19,800. NEW YORK, 12 March 1992, *Artist and his Model* (1891, oil on canvas, 20 x 16 ins / 50.8 x 40.4 cm) USD 6,600. NEW YORK, 14 Sept 1995, *'Goody Two Shoes'* (oil on canvas, 12 x 10 ins / 30.5 x 25.4 cm) USD 12,650. NEW YORK, 14 March 1996, *Connoisseur* (1887, oil on canvas, 43 1/4 x 24 ins / 109.9 x 61 cm) USD 29,900. NEW YORK, 3 Dec 1997, *Pears* (1888, oil on canvas, 12 x 10 ins / 30.5 x 25.4 cm) USD 11,500. NEW YORK, 11 March 1999, *Woman Playing the Mandolin* (oil on canvas, 26 x 14 ins / 66 x 36 cm) USD 6,500. NEW YORK, 15 March 2000, *Peanuts* (oil on canvas, 12 x 10 ins / 30 x 25 cm) USD 7,000. MILFORD, 26 April 2001, *Irish Question* (oil on canvas, 12 x 10 ins / 30 x 25 cm) USD 16,000. MILFORD, 26 April 2001, *Daisies in a Glass Mug* (oil on canvas, 12 x 10 ins / 30 x 25 cm) USD 20,000. NEW YORK, 4 March 2003, *Free Sample, Try One* (oil on canvas, 12 x 10 ins / 30 x 25 cm) USD 28,000. NEW YORK, 4 Dec 2003, *Irish Question* (oil on canvas, 12 x 10 ins / 30 x 25 cm) USD 24,000. MILFORD, 6 May 2004, *Mandolin and Roses* (oil on canvas, 24 x 20 ins / 61 x 51 cm) USD 7,000. NEW YORK, 26 May 2004, *Picking Wildflowers* (1891, watercolour over pencil, 23 x 16 ins / 58 x 41 cm) USD 2,250.

EVANS, Donald

American, 20th century.

Born 1945; died 1977.

Watercolourist.

AUCTION RECORDS:

NEW YORK, 11 Nov 1986, *Clog* (1977, watercolour/paper/philately paper, 11 1/2 x 8 ins / 29.3 x 20.4 cm) USD 8,000. NEW YORK, 10 Oct 1990, *Archterduk Pear* (1972, watercolour/paper, 6 x 4 ins / 15.2 x 10.1 cm) USD 4,125. NEW YORK, 1 May 1991, *Song-ting* (1975, four watercolours/paper folded as though in a stamp-collecting album, 11 1/2 x 20 1/4 ins / 29.5 x 51.4 cm) USD 6,600. AMSTERDAM, 22 May 1991, *Flora of Jantar* (watercolour/philately paper, postage stamps, 8 1/4 x 7 1/4 ins / 20.8 x 18.4 cm) NLG 18,400. AMSTERDAM, 10 Dec 1996, *Joisas* (c. 1975, watercolour/paper, ten stamps, 8 1/4 x 2 3/4 ins / 21 x 7 cm) NLG 6,342. AMSTERDAM, 3 Dec 2002, *Domino - 12 Stamps in One Frame* (1973, pen, ink and watercolour, 12 x 8 ins / 30 x 21 cm) EUR 2,200.

EVANS, Edmund

British, 19th century.

Born 23 February 1826, in London; died 21 August 1905, on the Isle of Wight.

Engraver.

Edmund Evans trained under Ebenezer Landells. He worked on many different newspapers, such as the *Illustrated London News,* and illustrated books, such as the *Chronicle of England* by J.E. Doyle.

EVANS, Edmund William

British, 19th century.

Born 14 January 1858.

Engraver.

Edmund William Evans exhibited eight times at the Royal Academy in London from 1879 to 1893.

EVANS, Edwin

American, 19th - 20th century.

Born 1860, in Lehi (Utah); died 1946.

Painter.

Edwin Evans was a pupil in Paris at the Académie Julian and of J.-P. Laurens, Jules Lefebvre and Benjamin-Constant.

EVANS, Étienne

French, 19th century.

Born 1793, in Paris.

Painter (porcelain).

Like his son, Étienne Evans was a painter for the Sèvres porcelain factory.

EVANS, F.

British, 18th century.

Engraver.

MUSEUMS AND GALLERIES:

LONDON (British Mus.): *Portrait.*

EVANS, Frederick McNamara

British, 19th - 20th century.

Active in London 1886-1928.

Painter, watercolourist. Genre scenes.

Frederick McNamara Evans first exhibited at the Royal Academy in London in 1891.

AUCTION RECORDS:

LONDON, 17 Oct 1984, *Home Hairdressing* (watercolour, 14 3/4 x 10 1/2 ins / 37.5 x 26.7 cm) GBP 2,200. LONDON, 16 Oct 1986, *Fisherman Telling a Tale* (watercolour on paper remounted on card, 20 x 30 ins / 51 x 76 cm) GBP 1,800. MONTREAL, 18 June 1996, *Fisherman's Tale* (watercolour, 26 x 33 ins / 66 x 83.8 cm) CAD 1,800. LONDON, 6 Nov 1996, *Storyteller* (watercolour, 25 1/2 x 32 ins / 65 x 81.5 cm) GBP 2,760.

EVANS, G.
British, 19th century.
Painter. Portraits.
G. Evans worked in London and exhibited at the Royal Academy in 1842.
MUSEUMS AND GALLERIES:
SALFORD (Museum and AG): *Robert Parren Livingston.*

EVANS, Garth
British, 20th century.
Born 1934, in Cheshire.
Sculptor, environmental artist, watercolourist.
Garth Evans studied at the Slade School of Art in London. He is known for creating geometric environments.

EVANS, George
British, 18th century.
Died before 1770.
Painter. Portraits.
George Evans exhibited portraits and decorations in London.

EVANS, George
British, 18th - 19th century.
Born 1763; died 18 April 1819, in Shrewsbury.
Painter, draughtsman. Landscapes.
George Evans exhibited Welsh landscapes at the Royal Academy in London in 1795.

EVANS, George H.
American, 20th century.
Born in Graton (Michigan).
Painter.
George Evans was an exhibitor at the Salon des Artistes Français from 1924.

EVANS, Grace French
American, 20th century.
Born in Davenport (Iowa).
Painter.
Grace Evans was a pupil of H. More and K.H. Miller and a member of the American Federation of Arts..

EVANS, J.
British, 18th century.
Active in Liverpool c. 1760.
Engraver.
Notable works by J. Evans are some bookplates.

EVANS, J.
British, 19th century.
Active in London c. 1800.
Engraver.
J. Evans trained under Charles Knight.

EVANS, Jessie Benton
American, 19th century.
Born 24 March 1866, in Akeroy (Ohio); died 1954.
Painter, engraver (etching).
A pupil at the Art Institute of Chicago and of Zanetti Zilla in Venice, Jessie Benton Evans was a member of the Chicago Society of Artists.

EVANS, Joe
American, 19th century.
Born 29 October 1857, in New York; died 22 April 1898, in New York.
Painter. Landscapes.
After studying in New York at the National Academy of Design and the Art Students League, Joe Evans went to Paris in 1877 and spent three years at the École des Beaux-Arts under Gérôme. On returning to America, he became the secretary of the Society of American Artists and took part in its exhibitions.

EVANS, John
British, 19th century.
Active in London.
Painter. Landscapes, urban landscapes.
John Evans exhibited in London from 1849 to 1891, and notably at the Royal Academy of Arts in 1888 with *View of Venice from the Lagoons.*

EVANS, John William
American, 19th - 20th century.
Born 27 March 1855, in Brooklyn.
Engraver (wood).
John William Evans was a pupil of P.R.B. Peterson and won bronze medals in Buffalo in 1901 and St Louis in 1904.

EVANS, Margaret
American, 20th century.
Born in Youngstown (Ohio).
Painter.
Margaret Evans was a pupil at the Art Students' League in New York and Director of the Butler Art Institute.

EVANS, Merlyn
British, 20th century.
Born 31 March 1910, in Cardiff; died 1973.
Painter, sculptor, engraver.
Merlyn Evans studied at the Glasgow School of Fine Arts and the Royal Academy in London. He continued his studies in Paris, Berlin, Copenhagen and Italy. From 1934 to 1936 he lived in Paris and studied engraving at S. W. Hayter's studio. He then went to South Africa and remained there until 1942, holding his first solo exhibition in Durban in 1939. Having returned to England during World War II, he served in North Africa, Syria and Italy and on his return settled in London. In 1952 Evans became a member of the London Group. He taught at the Central School of Art and Crafts.

Evans became part of the abstact art movement very early, around 1930, influenced at first by Wyndham Lewis's Vorticism and then by other abstact artists. Over time his own style evolved towards Surrealism.

Evans took part in many group exhibitions, including the International Surrealism Exhibition in London (1936), the São Paulo Biennale (1953, 1961), Kassel Documenta (1959) and the Venice Biennale (1960). He also held solo exhibitions of his work in London, the first being in 1949.

MUSEUMS AND GALLERIES:
LONDON (Tate Collection): *Souvenir of Suez* (1952, oil on canvas); other paintings, prints.
AUCTION RECORDS:
LONDON, 13 Dec 1967, *Standing Figure,* GBP 280. LONDON, 26 Sept 1985, *Landscape* (1952, watercolour and pen, 7½ x 10 ins / 19 x 25.5 cm) GBP 500. LONDON, 3 May 1990, *Abstraction* (1958, oil on canvas, 50 x 39½ ins / 127 x 100.5 cm) GBP 1,540. LONDON, 24 May 1990, *Two Figures* (1950, oil on canvas, 18 x 16¼ ins / 46 x 41 cm) GBP 3,300. LONDON, 7 June 1991, *Two Figures* (1950, oil on canvas, 18 x 16¼ ins / 46 x 41 cm) GBP 1,430. LONDON, 25 Nov 1993, *Conflict* (1949, oil on canvas, 40 x 50 ins / 101.5 x 127 cm) GBP 3,450. LONDON, 26 Oct 1994, *Large Interior* (1952, oil on canvas, 40 x 50 ins / 101.5 x 127 cm) GBP 7,475. LONDON, 2 Nov 1999, *Composition* (1933, oil on board, 30 x 60 ins / 76 x 152 cm) GBP 3,200. LONDON, 4 Nov 1999, *Study in Red and Green* (1965, oil on canvas laid on board, 16 x 20 ins / 40 x 50 cm) GBP 1,000. LONDON, 4 June 2003, *Interior with Red and Green* (1952, oil on canvas, 40 x 30 ins / 101 x 76 cm) GBP 9,000. LONDON, 19 Oct 2004, *Meeting* (1951, oil on canvas, 71 x 115 ins / 180 x 292 cm) GBP 9,200.

EVANS, Minnie

American, 20th century.

Born 12 December 1892, in Long Creek (North Carolina); died 16 December 1987.

Painter, draughtswoman. Religious subjects, still-lifes. Folk Art.

Minnie Evans worked as a maid and nanny on a plantation and did not start to draw until she was forty-three: she was self-taught. Her first drawing came to her in 1935, in a dream. 'Something told me to draw or die. It was shown to me what to do.' She made two drawings, and then waited five years before her next call to create again, always on impulse, always to relate her visions. She sold her drawings for a few cents at the gate of the property at Airlie Gardens, Wilmington, North Carolina, where she was taken on as nanny in 1948. Minnie Evans started by using ink and crayons before moving to oils. She depicted religious subjects, animals, angels, flowers, birds and plants, using the primary colours in symmetrical compositions. Her work is a synthesis of West Indian, African-American, Chinese and American myths.

After she died, her work was included in various thematic exhibitions such as in 1999, *To Conserve a Legacy. American Art from Historically Black Colleges and Universities*, Addison Gallery of Art, Phillips Academy, Andover, Massachusetts and in 2000, *Narratives of African Art and Identity*, High Museum of Art, Atlanta. She also had solo exhibitions including in 1931, Wilmington, North Carolina; 1966, New York; and in 1975 a retrospective at the Whitney Museum of American Art, New York. Her work was also included in retrospectives after her death, for example, in 1989, *Black Folk Artists: Minnie Evans and Bill Traylor from the African-American Museum*, African-American Museum, Hempstead, New York and in 1998, at Luise Ross Gallery, New York.

BIBLIOGRAPHY:

Kahan, Mitchell Douglas, *Heavenly Visions: the Art of Minnie Evans*, exhibition catalogue, North Carolina Museum of Art, Raleigh (NC), 1986. Lovell, Charles M./Hester, Erwin, *Minnie Evans: artist*, exhibition catalogue, Wellington B. Gray Gall., East Carolina University, Greenville (NC), 1993. Lyons, Mary E., *Painting Dreams: Minnie Evans, Visionary Artist*, Houghton Mifflin Company, Boston, 1996. Kernan, Nathan, '*Aspects of Minnie Evans*' in *On Paper* vol. 1 n° 6, periodical, New York, July-August 1997. *Minnie Evans: Five Decades of Paintings and Drawings*, exhibition catalogue, Luise Ross Gall., New York, 1998.

MUSEUMS AND GALLERIES:

AUGUSTA (Morris Mus. of Art): *Ark of the Covenant* (1966) - NEW YORK (Whitney Mus. of American Art) - RALEIGH (North Carolina MA): *The Lion of Judah* (1960) - WASHINGTON DC (Smithsonian American AM): *Design Made at Airlie Gardens* (1967, oil and mixed media/canvas/paperboard).

AUCTION RECORDS:

NEW YORK, 27 Jan 2003, *Untitled - Design with Angels and Sunset* (1972, graphite, coloured pencil and paint, 11 x 13 ins / 27 x 34 cm) USD 5,000. BUFORD, 15 Nov 2003, *My Home, My Home* (crayon and coloured pencil, 15 x 22 ins / 38 x 56 cm) USD 4,700. BUFORD, 24 April 2004, *Picture I Painted at Anlie Gate* (coloured pencil and wax crayon on poster paper, 15 x 22 ins / 38 x 56 cm) USD 3,100.

EVANS, Richard

British, 19th century.

Born 1784, in Hereford; died 1871, in Southampton.

Painter, fresco artist, copyist. Portraits.

Richard Evans was employed for a short time by Sir Thomas Lawrence to execute the backgrounds and draperies of his paintings. The copies of Raphael's arabesques in the Victoria and Albert Museum, and (in the style of Lawrence) portraits of Sir Thomas Lawrence, Lord Thurlow and Thomas Taylor, are also by him.

Evans lived for many years in Rome, practising fresco and copying the Old Masters, as well as painting some original portraits.

MUSEUMS AND GALLERIES:

LONDON (National Portrait Gal.): *Harriet Martineau* (exhibited in 1834, oil on canvas); *Thomas Taylor* (exhibited in 1812, oil on canvas, after Sir Thomas Lawrence) - LONDON (Victoria and Albert Mus.): *Ganymede Feeding the Eagle of Jupiter* (watercolour, imitation of a Roman fresco).

AUCTION RECORDS:

LONDON, 17 March 1978, *Portrait of Henry Christophe, King of Haiti* (oil on canvas, 33 1/2 x 25 1/2 ins / 85 x 65 cm) GBP 7,000. LONDON, 8 May 1985, *Portrait of Admiral Sir Thomas Masterman Hardy* (oil on canvas, 50 x 40 1/4 ins / 127 x 102 cm) GBP 2,600.

EVANS, Rudolph

American, 20th century.

Born 11 February 1878, in Washington DC; died 1960.

Sculptor. Busts, statues.

Rudolph Evans was a pupil of Falguière and of Rodin. He received awards including a medal for third place at the Salon des Artistes Français in 1914 in Paris and a gold medal Watrous of the National Academy of Design in 1919. He is credited with *General Bolivar* (marble) at the American Republics Bureau in Washington and a statue of *James Pierce* in New York.

MUSEUMS AND GALLERIES:

NEW YORK (Metropolitan Mus. of Art): *The Golden Hour*.

AUCTION RECORDS:

NEW YORK, 1 March 1980, *Winged Figure Riding a Dolphin* (bronze, h. 17 1/4 ins / 43.8 cm) USD 1,100. NEW YORK, 7 Oct 1997, *Precious Moment* (c. 1913-1914, marble, h. 66 1/2 ins / 168.7 cm) USD 13,800.

EVANS, Samuel

British, 19th century.

Born in Flintshire; died c. 1835, in Droxford.

Painter. Landscapes.

Samuel Evans was an art teacher at Eton College, and the father of William Evans (known as Evans of Eton).

EVANS, Samuel T. G.

British, 19th century.

Born 1829, in Eton; died 1 November 1904, in Eton.

Painter, watercolourist. Genre scenes.

Samuel T.G. Evans was the son of William Evans (known as Evans of Eton). He was a member of the Royal Society of Painters in Watercolours and taught art at Eton College for much of his life. He exhibited at the Royal Academy from 1854 to 1893.

MUSEUMS AND GALLERIES:

DUBLIN: *House near a Lake*.

AUCTION RECORDS:

PERTH, 13 April 1981, *Falls in the Highlands* (oil on canvas, 23 1/2 x 35 ins / 59.5 x 89 cm) GBP 340. LONDON, 21 July 1987, *Falls of Glen Tilt* (watercolour heightened with white, 20 1/4 x 26 3/4 ins / 51.4 x 68 cm) GBP 650. LONDON, 15 June 2000, *Market Boats on Lake Traun in the Salzkammergut, Austria* (watercolour heightened with gouache and scratching out, 26 x 48 ins / 65 x 121 cm) GBP 4,000. LONDON, 9 Nov 2004, *Salmon Leap* (watercolour heightened with white, 19 x 27 ins / 48 x 69 cm) GBP 1,000.

EVANS, Sarah

Canadian, 19th century.

Born 1870, in Brussels (Ontario).

Active in Chicago.

Painter.

EVANS, Sophie Wilhelmine
Dutch, 18th - 19th century.
Active probably in Rotterdam.
Engraver.
Sophie Wilhelmine Evans travelled between 1791 and 1828 and was a pupil of Nath. de Salieth.

EVANS, Wilfred Muir
British, 19th - 20th century.
Active in London.
Painter.
Wilfred Muir Evans exhibited landscapes at the Royal Academy in London.

EVANS, William, called Evans of Bristol
British, 19th century.
Born 1809, in Bristol; died 18 December 1858, in London.
Painter, watercolourist. Landscapes.
William Evans lived for many years in an isolated place in North Wales, where he found wonderful subjects for painting the wild mountains at which he excelled. He became a member of the Society of Painters in Watercolours in 1845. After 1852, he spent many years in Italy.
AUCTION RECORDS:
LONDON, 21 July 1987, *Falls of the Machno, North Wales* (1848, watercolour and pencil, 9 x 12 3/4 ins / 23.1 x 32.5 cm) GBP 450. LONDON, 25 Jan 1989, *Farm Yard in Frant in Sussex* (watercolour and gouache, 10 x 14 ins / 25.5 x 35.5 cm) GBP 572. LONDON, 25-26 April 1990, *Figure near an Old Water Mill* (1847, watercolour and gouache, 14 1/4 x 17 ins / 36.5 x 43 cm) GBP 495.

EVANS, William, called Evans of Eton
British, 19th century.
Born 4 December 1798, in Eton; died 31 December 1877, in Eton.
Painter, watercolourist. Landscapes.
William Evans succeeded his father as art teacher at Eton College in 1818. He was elected an associate of the Society of Painters in Watercolours in 1823, and a member in 1830. He continued to exhibit there until 1875.
MUSEUMS AND GALLERIES:
BLACKBURN: *Bolton Abbey* - LONDON (Victoria and Albert Mus.): *Windmill at Droxford; Guard's House.*
AUCTION RECORDS:
LONDON, 20 Dec 1909, *View of Wales; Pass of Glencoe* (watercolour) GBP 2. LONDON, 29 Jan 1910, *Near Stourbridge* (watercolour) GBP 7. LONDON, 7 March 1910, *Lake in the Tyrol* (watercolour) GBP 2. LONDON, 4 April 1910, *Italian Coastline* (watercolour) GBP 2. LONDON, 23 June 1972, *Eton High Street* Gns 6,000. LONDON, 19 Nov 1981, *The Thames at Windsor, Berkshire* (watercolour, 21 1/4 x 29 1/2 ins / 54 x 75 cm) GBP 2,100. LONDON, 10 May 1983, *Windsor from the River* (watercolour and pencil heightened with white, 11 1/2 x 16 1/2 ins / 29.5 x 42 cm) GBP 700. LONDON, 24 March 1987, *Romney Lock, near Windsor* (watercolour and pencil heightened with white, 12 1/4 x 19 ins / 31.1 x 48 cm) GBP 3,000. LONDON, 9 April 1992, *Urchins Bathing in a Stream with Windsor Castle in the Background* (watercolour and gouache, 16 1/2 x 26 1/4 ins / 42 x 66.5 cm) GBP 2,640. LONDON, 8 June 1999, *Figures and Boats on the Thames, below Windsor Castle* (pencil, watercolour and scratching out, 8 x 11 ins / 21 x 28 cm) GBP 2,800. BILLINGSHURST, 14 Sept 1999, *Eton College from the River with Eel Traps to the Right* (1837, watercolour, 16 x 12 ins / 40 x 31 cm) GBP 1,600. LONDON, 15 June 2000, *View of Clovelly, North Devon* (watercolour and pencil heightened with gouache and stopping out, 17 x 23 ins / 42 x 59 cm) GBP 4,800. LONDON, 28 Nov 2000, *Cliveden from Cookham Weir, Horse Ferry in the Foreground* (pencil, watercolour and gum arabic heightened with white and scratching out, 16 x 23 ins / 41 x 58 cm) GBP 3,500. LONDON, 7 Nov 2001, *Eton from the Thames. Thames at Windsor* (watercolour, a pair, 3 x 9 ins / 7 x 22 cm) GBP 1,400. LONDON, 5 June 2003, *Shooting Party outside Haddon Hall, Derbyshire* (1873, pencil, watercolour and gum arabic heightened with gouache, 22 x 30 ins / 56 x 77 cm) GBP 8,000. LONDON, 12 June 2003, *Windsor from the Locks* (watercolour, 14 x 17 ins / 35 x 44 cm) GBP 2,000.

EVANS, William
British, 19th century.
Active in London at the beginning of the 19th century.
Draughtsman, engraver.
William Evans produced the drawings for the publications by Cadell and Boydell, and worked with Benjamin Smith. In 1822, he engraved several panels for *Specimens of Ancient Sculpture by the Society of Dilettanti* and produced the drawings for the *Gallery of Contemporary Portraits.*

EVANS, William E.
British, 19th - 20th century.
Painter. Genre scenes.
William E. Evans exhibited at the Royal Academy in London from 1889.
AUCTION RECORDS:
LONDON, 1 Oct 1986, *Skipping Rope* (oil on canvas, 30 x 20 ins / 76 x 51 cm) GBP 2,000.

EVARD, André
Swiss, 20th century.
Born 1 June 1876, in Renan; died 1972, in Renan.
Painter.
Die Allianz Group.
André Evard worked in La Chaux-de-Fonds and was a founder member of Die Allianz group. He exhibited at the Salon d'Automne and the Salon des Artistes Indépendants in Paris from 1924.
From 1919 to 1939, he practised a form of painting that was initially Cubist, then abstract and fairly close to Constructivism.
AUCTION RECORDS:
MUNICH, 29 June 1983, *Spaces and Times* (1923, oil on canvas, 13 3/4 x 9 1/2 ins / 35 x 24 cm) DEM 10,500.

EVARD, Enea
Russian, 19th century.
Painter.
We know of his *Portrait of Edvard Grieg.*

EVARD, René
Swiss, 20th century.
Born in Biel (Bern).
Active in France.
Painter. Landscapes with figures.
René Evard, having settled in Béthune, exhibited views of northern France at the Salon des Artistes Français in Paris from 1934.

EVARISTO
Spanish, 20th century.
Born 1923, in Spain.
Active in France.
Painter (including gouache), sculptor (wood). Figures.
Evaristo and his family suffered the horrors of the Spanish Civil War, which marked him permanently. He went into exile in France, in St-Fons, where he became a labourer. He lives and works in Vallon-Pont-d'Arc. A self-taught artist, he began painting in the 1950s. His painting expresses suffering and tragedy: 'I paint for memory, for witnessing', he says. A solo exhibition was organised by the city of Villeurbanne (1996).
BIBLIOGRAPHY:
Brouan, Anne, *Evaristo. La Chambre des falaises*, S. Bachèse, Lyons, 2002.

EVDOKIMOV, Fektist
Russian, 17th century.
Born to a family originally from Pskov.
Icon painter.

EVDOKIMOV, Patrikei
Russian, 17th century.
Icon painter.
Patrikei Evdokimov worked on the murals of the Cathedral of the Archangel in the Kremlin in 1652.

EVE, George William
British, 19th century.
Born 4 July 1855, in London.
Engraver.
George Willliam Eve became a member of the Royal Society of Painter-Etchers. A great many bookplates are attributed to him.

EVE, Jean
French, 16th century.
Active in Caen at the end of the 16th century.
Painter.

ÈVE, Jean
French, 20th century.
Born 1900, in Somain (Nord); died 1968, in Louveciennes.
Painter. Landscapes, urban landscapes, flowers.
Designs for tapestries.
Jean Ève, a self-taught miner's son who became a fully educated artist, started painting watercolours at the age of seven and by fifteen had moved on to oil painting. At the apprenticeship school of Thiers (Puy-de Drôme) he painted to relieve the tedium of manual work. He was successively a pupil at the École Coloniale of Le Havre, a soldier (he volunteered for the Spahis in 1918), a railway worker, a foundry timekeeper, an industrial draughtsman and a customs officer, but he always painted.

The 1925 *Courbet* exhibition was a revelation to him. He came to notice when he began to paint the Île-de-France and the Parisian suburbs. Encouraged by Kisling and the Art Vivant group, he was able to hold his first solo show in Paris in 1930. However, like Henri (the Douanier) Rousseau, he wisely kept his job in the administration. After taking part in the exhibition *Maîtres de la Réalité Populaire* (*Masters of the Popular*) in Paris and Zurich, he was represented in many exhibitions in France, England and the USA. He exhibited regularly in Paris at the Salon des Indépendants and the Salon d'Automne, and in 2001 some of his works were included in the *Die Naïven, aufbruch ins verlorene Paradies* (*The Naïve Painters, Journey to a Lost Paradise*) at the Kunsthaus, Vienna. This exhibition brought together 200 works from the collection of the Charlotte Zander Museum. He won the Île-de-France prize in 1952. Bernard Dorival writes of him: 'His favourite subjects are suburbs, cathedrals and churches, which he treats in a lively, somewhat photographic, way'. He also designed tapestries for the Beauvais and Gobelins factories.

Jean Eve

BIBLIOGRAPHY:
Gauthier, Maximilien, '*Jean Eve*' in *coll. Peintres et sculpteurs d'hier et d'aujourd'hui*, Éd. Pierre Cailler, Geneva, 1971. Debroye, Anne, *Jean Eve, rétrospective, 1900-1968*, exhibition catalogue, Musée international d'Art naïf Anatole-Jakovsky, Nice, 1984.

MUSEUMS AND GALLERIES:
BÖNNIGHEIM (Mus. Charlotte Zander) - NEW YORK (MoMA) - PARIS (MAM).

AUCTION RECORDS:
PARIS, 5 June 1944, *Landscape Overlooking Limazy, near Mantes* (1930) FRF 3,000. PARIS, 24 March 1947, *The Waterside Restaurant 'Au Petit Poucet'*, FRF 13,000. PARIS, 14 June 1957, *Baudemont Hills with the Hamlet of Mauverand*, FRF 210,000. NEW YORK, 16 Feb 1961, *Château on the Epte (Eure)*, USD 725. TOKYO, 30 Oct 1969, *Landscape in Snow*, JPY 340,000. PARIS, 13 June 1974, *Autumn on the Baudemont Hills, near Bray-Lû (Val-d'Oise)*, FRF 13,000. LONDON, 20 Oct 1976, *Farm in Winter, Doubs* (1963, oil on canvas, 12 1/2 x 17 3/4 ins / 32 x 45 cm) GBP 340. NEW YORK, 18 Oct 1979, *Harvest Scene, Epte-sur-Eure* (1947, oil on canvas, 21 1/4 x 28 1/2 ins / 54 x 72.4 cm) USD 2,100. PARIS, 27 June 1983, *Menton, View of the Port with the Greyhound* (oil on canvas, 21 1/4 x 25 1/2 ins / 54 x 65 cm) FRF 18,500. PARIS, 11 June 1987, *View of the Celestine Church of Jimay* (1930, oil on canvas, 19 3/4 x 28 3/4 ins / 50 x 73 cm) FRF 30,000. PARIS, 29 June 1988, *Bunch of Wild Flowers* (oil on canvas, 28 3/4 x 21 1/2 ins / 73 x 54.5 cm) FRF 20,000. LE TOUQUET, 12 Nov 1989, *Village under Snow* (oil on panel, 7 1/2 x 9 1/2 ins / 19 x 24 cm) FRF 21,000. PARIS, 26 April 1990, *Harvest on the Road to Aveny (Eure)* (1952, oil on canvas, 18 x 22 ins / 46 x 55 cm) FRF 40,000. PARIS, 15 April 1991, *Trees Flowering in Spring* (oil on canvas, 13 x 18 ins / 33 x 46 cm) FRF 28,000. PARIS, 26 June 1991, *Avenue of Plane Trees* (1931, oil on canvas, 22 x 18 ins / 55 x 46 cm) FRF 38,000. NEW YORK, 24 Feb 1994, *View of Paris* (1959, oil on canvas, 16 1/4 x 10 3/4 ins / 41.3 x 27.3 cm) USD 3,910. CALAIS, 3 July 1994, *Flowering Chestnut* (1951, oil on canvas, 18 x 13 ins / 46 x 33 cm) FRF 25,000. NEW YORK, 14 June 1995, *Still-life with Oysters* (oil on canvas, 18 x 25 1/2 ins / 45.7 x 64.8 cm) USD 4,887. PARIS, 12 July 1995, *Snow, the Village of Berthenonville* (oil on canvas, 21 1/4 x 28 3/4 ins / 54 x 73 cm) FRF 52,000. PARIS, 28 Oct 1996, *Mantes Cathedral* (1930, oil on canvas, 15 x 22 ins / 38 x 55 cm) FRF 25,500. PARIS, 23 Feb 1997, *Landscape with Pond* (oil on canvas, 19 3/4 x 28 3/4 ins / 50 x 73 cm) FRF 50,000. PARIS, 12 Dec 1997, *Village of Pierrelaye* (oil on canvas, 19 3/4 x 28 3/4 ins / 50 x 73 cm) FRF 16,000. SAN FRANCISCO, 18 April 2000, *Harbour Entrance at Guibrinec* (oil on canvas, 15 x 22 ins / 38 x 55 cm) USD 2,750. CALAIS, 5 Nov 2000, *Le quartier de la cathedrale* (oil on canvas, 24 x 32 ins / 60 x 81 cm) FRF 27,000. PARIS, 8 Dec 2001, *Sacre-Coeur* (oil on canvas, 26 x 20 ins / 65 x 50 cm) FRF 14,000. CANNES, 30 Dec 2001, *Harbour Entrance at Guilvinec* (oil on canvas, 15 x 21 ins / 37 x 54 cm) FRF 14,000. PARIS, 24 April 2002, *Church of St-Ouen* (1929, oil on canvas, 19 x 25 ins / 48 x 64 cm) EUR 3,800. PARIS, 5 Nov 2002, *Spring in the Vallee de Chevreuse* (1945, oil on canvas, 22 x 29 ins / 55 x 73 cm) EUR 9,500. PARIS, 3 Dec 2003, *Edge of the Village, St Clairs/Epte* (1948, oil on canvas, 18 x 22 ins / 46 x 55 cm) EUR 4,000. PARIS, 3 Dec 2003, *House in the Forest* (oil on canvas, 13 x 16 ins / 32 x 40 cm) EUR 4,000.

ÉVEILLARD, Georges
French, 20th century.
Born in Nantes.
Painter.
From 1919 Georges Éveillard exhibited in Paris at the Salon des Artistes Français, where he figured in the special section for artists who had served in the war.

EVELDT, Christian
German, 18th - 19th century.
Painter.
Eveldt worked at Dyk Castle near Grevenbroich (North Rhine-Westphalia), Germany.

EVELEN, Hans van
Dutch, 17th century.
Active in Amsterdam c. 1650.
Painter.

EVELYN, John
British, 17th century.
Born 31 October 1620, in Wotton (Surrey); died 27 February 1706, in London.
Engraver.

In 1649, John Evelyn engraved five small plates in Paris, which dealt with his travels to Rome and Naples. He also engraved a view of his property in Wotton and a view of Putney. He was the author of *Sculptura*, one of the first English publications on sculpture, which was published in 1662.

EVEN, André
French, 20th century.
Born 16 May 1918, in Pont-Aven; died 1997.
Painter. Religious subjects, landscapes, urban landscapes, seascapes. Murals, designs for tapestries.

André Even studied in the Souverbie studio at the École Nationale des Beaux-Arts, Paris, and then with Maurice Denis. He also worked for some time as a restorer for the Department of Historical Monuments. He was a member of the Salon des Indépendants and of the Salon des Artistes Français, where he was awarded a silver medal. He also exhibited at the Salons des Terres Latines, Populistes and Comparaisons. In 1979 he took part in an exhibition organised by the poet Pierre Osenet and held at the Galerie Drouot, Paris, to mark the fiftieth anniversary of the review *Le Caducée*. He also showed in solo exhibitions, including his first in Paris in 1955 at the Galerie Guillerot, under the patronage of Raymond Cogniat, and exhibitions in Kuwait, New Caledonia, Australia, Germany, the USA and South America.

He painted murals in the churches of Névez (1950), Concarneau (1951) and Rocleng-sur-Geer, near Liège (1955). Influenced by the Pont-Aven School, he simplified colour planes, and this led to an art that is part pseudo-naïve, part decorative - an aspect that is more developed in his tapestries. Although he painted various regions of France, he above all took the landscape of Brittany as his subject.

André Even

BIBLIOGRAPHY:
Bouillot, Roger, *André Even*, Vision des arts, Paris.
MUSEUMS AND GALLERIES:
BREST - PARIS (FMAC) - PONT-AVEN - TOURCOING - VATICAN (Mus. Vaticani).
AUCTION RECORDS:
BREST, 18 Dec 1983, *Yellow Meadows* (oil on canvas, 15 x 22 ins / 38 x 56 cm) FRF 7,800. BREST, 17 May 1987, *Landscape with Blue Fields* (oil on canvas, 19¾ x 25½ ins / 50 x 65 cm) FRF 10,800. PARIS, 4 April 1989, *View of Chartres* (oil on paper, 24 x 18 ins / 61 x 46 cm) FRF 4,000. SCEAUX, 11 March 1990, *Yellow Valley* (oil on canvas, 9½ x 13¾ ins / 24 x 35 cm) FRF 3,800. PARIS, 6 Feb 1991, *Breton Village* (oil on paper remounted/canvas, 21¼ x 28¾ ins / 54 x 73 cm) FRF 4,200.

EVEN, Jean
French, 19th century.
Born 19th century, in Dinan.
Painter, watercolourist. Genre scenes, still-lifes.

From 1872 to 1880 Jean Even exhibited informal genre scenes and still-lifes in watercolour at the Paris Salon.

EVEN, Jean
French, 20th century.
Born 14 July 1910, in Paris; died 6 January 1986.
Painter, watercolourist, lithographer, poster artist. Figures, landscapes with figures.

In 1932 Jean Even entered the studios of Devambez and Charles Guérin at the École des Beaux-Arts, Paris. From 1935 he exhibited at the Salon des Artistes Français, where he won a silver medal in the same year, and various awards later, including a gold medal in 1939. In 1936 he won the Casa Velázquez prize and spent time in Fez in Morocco, because of the Spanish Civil War.

On his return to Paris he took up the post of professor of drawing with the Municipality of Paris. He exhibited at the Salon des Indépendants, Salon d'Automne, Salon de l'Imagerie, Salon de la Marine and others. During the 1940s he carried out many commissions for tourist posters, including some for Air France, the Moroccan Tourist Board, and Evian. He also painted murals for tourist premises. From 1959 he exhibited regularly at the Salon des Peintres Témoin de leur Temps. In 1968 he was elected to the jury of the Salon d'Automne, becoming a committee member in 1980. During these years he travelled widely, in Corsica, Morocco, Italy and Spain. From 1938 he showed in many solo exhibitions in Paris, the provinces, abroad, in the USA and elsewhere; but from 1938 he lived and worked mainly in Faou, Brittany. In 1986 the Musée de la Marine held a large retrospective of his work, and this was followed by retrospectives at the Salon d'Automne, in 1987 at the Salon de la Société Nationale des Beaux-Arts, Paris, and in 1988 at the Salon du Dessin et de la Peinture à l'Eau.

He painted portraits and figures, but these were mainly of members of his circle. His favourite subjects were port seascapes, beaches, forest hunts, and horses in general. From early on he demonstrated the technique that characterises his work: a rapid Post-Impressionist brush put to the service of unfailing sunlight.

BIBLIOGRAPHY:
Ikor, Roger, *Jean Even*, Rosay, Vincennes, 1985. *Jean Even*, retrospective exhibition catalogue, Crédit mutuel de Bretagne, 1988. *Jean Even 1910-1986*, exhibition catalogue, Musée de Pont-Aven, 1995.
MUSEUMS AND GALLERIES:
PARIS (MAMVP) - PARIS (MNAM-CCI).
AUCTION RECORDS:
VERSAILLES, 23 Nov 1986, *Boats Decked with Flags in Porto del Selva* (watercolour and gouache, 19¼ x 25¼ ins / 49 x 64 cm) FRF 5,500. VERSAILLES, 21 Feb 1988, *Sailing Boats in the Port of St Tropez* (oil on canvas, 25½ x 32 ins / 65 x 81 cm) FRF 9,000. PARIS, 14 Dec 1988, *Young Girl Reading* (oil on canvas, 22 x 18 ins / 55 x 46 cm) FRF 10,000. PARIS, 16 Oct 1996, *Table in the Sun* (oil on canvas, 35½ x 41¾ ins / 90 x 106 cm) FRF 20,500.

EVENEPOEL, Henri Jacques Édouard
Belgian, 19th century.
Born 4 October 1872, in Nice; died 27 December 1899, in Paris.
Painter, pastellist, draughtsman, lithographer. Figures, portraits, genre scenes, landscapes, urban landscapes.

Henri Jacques Édouard Evenepoel received his first artistic training at the academy in Brussels, in the studio of Blanc Gorin. He then studied in Paris, at first with Galland from 1892 and then with Gustave Moreau, who taught Rouault and Matisse. Towards the end of his short life he spent some time in Algeria in an attempt to recover his health. On his return to Paris and while preparing to return to Belgium, he suddenly died of a haemorrhage.

Evenepoel excelled in painting full-length figures, well situated in their setting. A few children's scenes of his are known, and he brought back some intensely coloured compositions from Algeria. But it is mainly by his figures, such as his vigorous *Spaniard in Paris*, that he should be judged. The canvas is solidly constructed, and in his sobriety of execution Manet springs to mind. The comparison with Manet could be extended, for Evenepoel was also impartial to all sentiment superfluous to the beauty of the lines, the solidity of the form and the harmony of the colours.

h. j. evenepoel

Museums and Galleries:

Brussels (MBA): *Portrait of the Painter Paul Baignières; Man in Red; Henriette in Large Hat* - Frankfurt am Main (Städel): *Harcourt Café* - Ghent: *Spaniard in Paris* - Ixelles: *Drowned Figure at the Pont des Arts* - Liège: *Sunday Walk* - Paris (Mus. d'Orsay): *Portrait of Milcendeau.*

Auction records:

Brussels, 30 May 1967, *Avenue de la Motte-Piquet,* BEF 60,000. Amsterdam, 10 Dec 1968, *Embroideresses,* NLG 9,000. Antwerp, 22 April 1969, *Sophie in a Red Dress,* BEF 900,000. Antwerp, 3 April 1973, *Woman with Red Pompom* (pastel) BEF 1,500,000. Brussels, 24 March 1976, *The Apparition of Christ* (oil on canvas, 13 3/4 x 9 1/2 ins / 35 x 24 cm) BEF 38,000. Brussels, 23 March 1977, *Arabian Beggar* (1897, oil on canvas, 32 1/4 x 21 1/4 ins / 82 x 54 cm) BEF 100,000. London, 4 April 1978, *Plan of a Poster for a Print Dealer* (gouache, coloured chalk and pen, 7 3/4 x 5 1/2 ins / 20 x 14 cm) GBP 800. Amsterdam, 24 Feb 1981, *The Case of Monsieur Valdemar* (black chalk/paper, 7 x 11 1/2 ins / 17.5 x 29 cm) NLG 2,000. Brussels, 23 March 1983, *Young Woman in Straw Hat* (oil on canvas, 22 x 18 ins / 55 x 46 cm) BEF 950,000. New York, 10 Oct 1984, *In the Square* (1897, coloured lithograph, 13 x 9 1/4 ins / 33.2 x 23.2 cm) USD 1,500. Brussels, 8 May 1985, *Little Duet, Henriette and Sophie* (1897, oil on canvas, 12 1/2 x 16 1/4 ins / 32 x 41 cm) BEF 900,000. London, 25 March 1987, *At the Folies-Bergère* (pastel, 13 1/2 x 17 1/2 ins / 34 x 44.5 cm) GBP 43,000. Lokeren, 8 Oct 1988, *Man Seated, Man Standing Seen from Back* (two drawings in black chalk, each 7 3/4 x 5 ins / 20 x 12.8 cm) BEF 36,000; *Outing* (black chalk, 6 3/4 x 5 ins / 17 x 12.5 cm) BEF 19,000; *Corner of my Studio in Paris* (black chalk, 7 3/4 x 5 ins / 20 x 13 cm) BEF 22,000. Brussels, 12 June 1990, *Outing* (oil on panel, 9 3/4 x 9 ins / 25 x 22 cm) BEF 220,000. Lokeren, 10 Oct 1992, *Charles in Arabia* (1898, oil on canvas, 28 3/4 x 19 3/4 ins / 73 x 50 cm) BEF 5,000,000. Paris, 2 April 1993, *Woman with Parasol and Small Daughter* (coloured lithograph, 13 x 9 ins / 33 x 23 cm) FRF 5,500. Lokeren, 15 May 1993, *Arabian Landscape, Small Fir Trees* (1898, oil on panel, 9 x 13 3/4 ins / 22 x 35 cm) BEF 320,000. Lokeren, 28 May 1994, *Small Arabian Cemetery in Blidah* (oil on canvas, 11 x 16 ins / 27 x 40.5 cm) BEF 650,000. Paris, 26 Feb 1996, *In the Square* (1897, lithograph) FRF 7,800. Brussels, 16 May 2000, *Musical Box* (1895, oil on canvas, 13 x 16 ins / 32 x 40 cm) BEF 1,500,000. Lokeren, 7 Oct 2000, *Dante* (crayon, 13 x 8 ins / 32 x 20 cm) BEF 105,000. Brussels, 8 May 2001, *The Cook* (oil on canvas, 15 x 10 ins / 38 x 26 cm) BEF 800,000. Lokeren, 8 Dec 2001, *Artist's Room* (c. 1891-1892, oil on canvas, 21 x 29 ins / 54 x 73 cm) BEF 1,500,000. London, 5 Feb 2002, *At the Moulin Rouge* (1897, oil on canvas, 29 x 23 ins / 73 x 59 cm) GBP 560,000. Lokeren, 7 Dec 2002, *Pier of the Port of Algiers* (1897, oil on panel, 9 x 13 ins / 24 x 33 cm) EUR 22,000. Brussels, 13 May 2003, *Gardens of the Rue Dupont in Summer* (c. 1891-1892, oil on canvas, 22 x 26 ins / 55 x 65 cm) EUR 15,000. Lokeren, 13 Dec 2003, *Pilgrims of Emmaus* (oil on canvas, after Veronese, 11 x 16 ins / 27 x 41 cm) EUR 5,000. Brussels, 7 June 2004, *Young Painter* (oil on canvas, 11 x 9 ins / 28 x 23 cm) EUR 98,000.

ÉVENO, Édouard Jules

French, 20th century.
Born 11 September 1884, in St-Aubin-du-Comier (Ille-et-Vilaine).
Painter. Animals.

Édouard Jules Éveno worked in Rouen in the 20th century.

EVENS

German, 19th century.
Active in Münster at the beginning of the 19th century.
Painter.

Evens painted a *Martyrdom of Saint Lambert* for the church of St Lambert in Münster around 1800.

EVENS, Otto Frederik Theobald

Danish, 19th century.
Born 16 February 1826, in Copenhagen; died 21 November 1895, in Copenhagen.
Sculptor. Groups.

The son of a copper foundry owner, Evens was apprenticed into his father's trade while at the same time taking art courses at the academy (1839). Once he had fully recognised his artistic vocation, however, he switched to the academy's art school proper. He was accepted into H. V. Bissen's studio, where he stayed for several years. In 1857 he won the Neuhausen prize for his group *Maternal Love,* and the following year was awarded a travel bursary by the academy. With this he spent three years in Rome, returning from there in 1865 after receiving the Ancher bequest scholarship.

Evens sculpted a statue of Christoffer Wilhelm Eckersberg for the 1865 exhibition in the hall of the academy. His later statues of Saxo and Grundtvig were also very well received. He was elected to the academy in 1871.

Museums and Galleries:

Copenhagen: *A Stablehand Watering his Horse; Tycho Brahe; Young Boy About to Take a Bath; A Fisherman Teaching a Boy to Play the Flute.*

Auction records:

London, 8 Nov 1984, *Bacchus Carrying a Young Satyr* (c. 1850, bronze, h. 51 1/2 ins / 131 cm) GBP 3,100.

EVERAARDS, N.

Flemish School.
Miniaturist. Portraits.

Was mentioned by Siret.

EVERAERT, Clemens Augustinus

Flemish, 18th century.
Active in Antwerp, at the beginning of the 18th century.
Painter.
Flemish School.

EVERAERT, M. X.

Flemish School, 19th century.
Active in Louvain c. 1850.
Painter.

M. X. Everaert executed a painting for the abbey of Vlierbeck in 1855.

EVERAERTS, D.

Flemish, 19th century.
Active c. 1845.
Painter. Landscapes, animals.
Flemish School.

D. Everaerts is mentioned by Siret.

EVERAERTS, Joannes

Flemish, 17th century.
Active in Antwerp, c. 1697.
Engraver.
Flemish School.

EVERAERTS, Johann

Dutch, 18th century.
Died c. 1766, in Cologne.
Engraver. Religious subjects.

EVERAERTSONE, Lambrecht

Flemish School, 16th century.
Active in Antwerp at the beginning of the 16th century.
Painter.

EVERARD
11th century.
Active in 1068 in Parma.
Painter.
Was a priest.

EVERARD
Flemish School, 16th century.
Active in St-Omer.
Painter. Historical subjects.
Sanderus mentioned one work by this artist, a retable depicting the *Flagellation* in the church of St-Bertin in Poperinghe.

EVERARD, Ruth
British, 20th century.
Born in Natal.
Painter. Landscapes.

EVERARD VON MONSTER
German, 15th century.
Active in Calkar in 1493.
Sculptor.
Everard von Monster is thought to have worked with members of the Arnold family, sculptors in Calkar from the 14th to the 16th century.

EVERARDI, Angiolo, called Fiaminghino
Italian, 17th century.
Born 1647, in Brescia; died 1678, in Brescia.
Painter. Landscapes with figures.
Of Flemish origin, Everardi was a pupil of Jan van Hert. He produced work for the church of S Giovanni Evangelista at Brescia.
AUCTION RECORDS:
MILAN, 16 Dec 1971, *Riverscape with Fishermen,* ITL 1,500,000.

EVERARDO
Italian, 11th century.
Active in Parma c. 1068.
Painter.
Parma School.

EVERART, Marthe
French, 19th - 20th century.
Born 20 November 1874, in Paris.
Painter.
Marthe Everart exhibited in Paris at the Salon des Artistes Français from 1905.

EVERASI, A.
Italian, 16th century.
Probably active at the end of the 16th century.
Painter. Religious subjects.
MUSEUMS AND GALLERIES:
AJACCIO: *Annunciation.*

EVERBAG, Frans
Dutch, 20th century.
Born 25 October 1877, in Amsterdam.
Painter, engraver. Still-lifes.
Frans Everbag produced a large number of plates after Hals and Rembrandt.
AUCTION RECORDS:
AMSTERDAM, 27 April 1976, *Still-life with Roses* (1934, oil on panel, 9 3/4 x 12 1/2 ins / 24.7 x 31.5 cm) NLG 1,350. AMSTERDAM, 18 March 1985, *Still-life* (1945, oil on canvas, 23 x 27 ins / 58.5 x 68.5 cm) NLG 1,650.

EVERBROECK, Carl Albert
Flemish, 17th century.
Active in Antwerp, in 1695.
Sculptor.
Flemish School.

EVERBROECK, Ferdinandus
Flemish, 17th century.
Active in Ghent in 1676.
Sculptor.
Flemish School.

EVERBROECK, Frans van
Flemish, 17th century.
Active in Antwerp in the second half of the 17th century.
Painter. Still-lifes (flowers/fruit).
Flemish School.
AUCTION RECORDS:
NEW YORK, 8 Jan 1981, *Still-life with Flowers and Fruit* (oil on canvas, 27 1/4 x 41 ins / 69 x 104 cm) USD 16,000. MONACO, 17 June 1989, *Bunches of Grapes* (oil on canvas, 32 1/4 x 22 ins / 82 x 55 cm) FRF 111,000. BOSTON, 29 May 1999, *Portrait of Lady amongst Chatelaine* (oil on canvas, 41 x 33 ins / 104 x 84 cm) USD 18,500. BERN, 7 May 2003, *Still-life of Flowers and Fruit* (oil on canvas, 30 x 25 ins / 75 x 64 cm) CHF 15,000.

EVERBROOT, Corneille
Belgian, 17th century.
Active in Brussels in 1610.
Painter.
Corneille Everbroot was a pupil of Crayer.

EVERDING, Hans
German, 19th century.
Active in Kassel.
Sculptor.
Hans Everding was awarded a bronze medal at the 1900 Exposition Universelle, having won first prize at the academy in Berlin the previous year.

EVERDING, Wilhelm
German, 19th century.
Born 18 July 1863, in Bremen.
Sculptor.
Wilhelm Everding studied under and worked with Robert Dorer. From 1894, he taught sculpture in Bremen, where he also created several monuments and many tombs.

EVERDINGEN, Adriaen or Adrianus van
Dutch, 19th - 20th century.
Born 22 June 1832, in Utrecht; died c. 1910 or 1919, in Utrecht.
Painter, engraver (etching). Landscapes with figures, landscapes.
Everdingen was a student of J.-W. Bilders.

A.v.Everdingen

MUSEUMS AND GALLERIES:
UTRECHT: *Landscape.*
AUCTION RECORDS:
AMSTERDAM, 16 Nov 1988, *Good Fishing Spot, with a Fisherman on a Grassy River Bank and a Mill in the Distance* (oil on canvas, 23 1/4 x 20 1/2 ins / 59 x 52 cm) NLG 7,475. AMSTERDAM, 30 Oct 1990, *Cows in a Meadow at Dawn* (oil on panel, 12 3/4 x 16 3/4 ins / 32.5 x 42.5 cm) NLG 3,910. AMSTERDAM, 17 Sept 1991, *Wooded River Landscape with an Angler and Cows* (1868, oil on canvas) NLG 4,370. AMSTERDAM, 14-15 April 1992, *Barge of Hay* (oil on canvas, 30 x 44 ins / 76 x 111.5 cm) NLG 20,125. AMSTERDAM, 21 April 1994, *River Landscape with Farm and Peasants in a Boat* (oil on panel, 14 1/4 x 22 3/4 ins / 36.5 x 58 cm) NLG 6,900. AMSTERDAM, 2 Sept 1997, *Cornfield with Windmill* (oil on panel, 14 1/4 x 10 3/4 ins / 36 x 27.5 cm) NLG 634. AMSTERDAM, 21 Jan 1998, *Peasants and Donkey Resting on River Banks in Autumn* (oil on panel, study, 22 x 15 1/2 ins / 56 x 39.5 cm; and six other landscape studies in oil) NLG 4,382.

EVERDINGEN, Albert or Allaert or Allart van

Dutch, 17th century.

Baptised 18 June 1621 in Alkmaar; died 1675; buried 8 November in Amsterdam.

Painter, watercolourist, draughtsman, engraver (etching). History painting, portraits, landscapes with figures, landscapes.

The first master of Albert van Everdingen was the landscape painter Roland Savery. On the death of this talented and influential painter, 18-year-old van Everdingen became the pupil of Pierre Molyn the Elder, a capable painter, engraver and landscapist. The influence of each of these masters is evident in van Everdingen's work: from Savery he inherited wild sites, fallen rocks and rushing torrents, and from Molyn, peaceful countryside. Little is known of the life of van Everdingen. His painted or engraved seascapes give the impression that he actually undertook sea voyages. It is further alleged that he was shipwrecked off the Norwegian coast, and that while his boat was being repaired he travelled through the country accumulating drawings and sketches which he later used to infuse life and variety into his landscapes and coast scenes. On his return he stopped in Denmark and was commissioned by King Frederik IV to carry out the large paintings which embellish the Christianborg palace in Copenhagen. A religious man, he was elected a deacon of the Reformed Church. He was outlived by two sons who were both painters.

His pictures are relatively rare and executed on wood. The paucity of extant signed works is attributed to the fact that his name was effaced and substituted by that of Jacques Ruysdael, as the paintings of his contemporary fetched a higher price. Only one van Everdingen painting is to be found in the Louvre, a *Landscape* signed *A. V. Everdingen*, and the museums in Antwerp and Brussels possess no works by him. Neither are there any in London, although there was one at Hampton Court Palace, the residence of Cardinal Wolsey, and another at the Hermitage in St Petersburg. In various auctions attention has been drawn to a *View of Tirol*, a *Waterfall*, a *Cascade*, a *Norwegian Site* and a *Village by a River* (view of storm).

Van Everdingen is possibly more famous for his etchings than his paintings. We know of two series of prints by him. The first, made up of 103 landscapes, all described by Adam Bartsch, is not very rare. This is not the case with the second series comprising 56 or 57 pieces. They are described in a manuscript by Mariette, bound together with a book of van Everdingen's engraving proofs which Mariette owned and which is now held by the Cabinet des Estampes de Paris. They represent the adventures of Reinecke-Fuchs (Reynard the Fox) of the famous old German folk tale, comparable to the French *Roman de Renart*. They were probably intended to illustrate an edition of this satire which was never published. Van Everdingen's work was shown at the exhibition *Twee gouden eeuwen: schilderkunst uit Nederland en Denemarken* (*Two Golden Ages: masterpieces of Dutch and Danish painting*) at the Rijksmuseum, Amsterdam, and at the exhibition on *Dessins hollandais du Musée Condé à Chantilly* (*Dutch Drawings at the Musée Condé in Chantilly*) at the Condé museum in 2001.

A: VAN: EVERDINGEN
A v. Everdingen 1647 AVE

BIBLIOGRAPHY:

Drugulin, William E., *Catalogue raisonné de toutes les estampes qui forment son oeuvre gravée*, W. Drugulin, Leipzig, 1873 (supplement from the Painter-engraver of Bartsch). Davies, Alice I./Duparc, Frédéric J., *Allart van Everdingen, 1621-1675: First Painter of Scandinavian landscape*, catalogue raisonné, Davaco, Doornspijk, 2001. Mandrella, David, *Dessins hollandais du Musée Condé à Chantilly*, exhibition catalogue, Musée Condé, Chantilly, Somogy, Paris, 2001.

MUSEUMS AND GALLERIES:

AMIENS: *Norwegian Landscape* - AMSTERDAM: *View of Norway* - AMSTERDAM (Rijksmus.): *Wooded Hill* - AVIGNON: *Seascape; Storm* - BORDEAUX: sketch of a landscape - BREMEN: *Swedish Landscape* - CAEN: *Northern Landscape* - CARCASSONNE: *Seascape* - CHANTILLY (Mus. Condé): *Storm in Snowy Weather; Fishing Boats by the Coast* (drawing); *Northern Landscape with Castle* (drawing); *The Months of June and October* (drawing) - COLOGNE: *Wooded Landscape; Mountainous Landscape with Waterfall* (1647) - CONSTANCE: *Landscape* - COPENHAGEN (Statens Mus. for Kunst): *Norwegian Landscape* - DRESDEN (Gemäldegal.): *Landscape* - FLORENCE (Gal.): *Large Waterfall* - FRANKFURT AM MAIN: *Mill; Storm; Norwegian Landscape; Cascade in Norway* - GRAZ: *Norwegian River Banks* - HAARLEM: *View of Haarlem* - HAMBURG: *Norwegian Landscape; Cascade in Norway; Landscape* - HANOVER: *Mountain Landscape; Same Subject* - KALININGRAD: *Gully with Lions* - LEIPZIG: *Northern Landscape* - LILLE: *Landscape* - LONDON (NG): *A Saw-mill by a Torrent* (c. 1670, oil/wood) - LONDON (Wallace Collection): *Landscape with Waterfall* (after 1660, oil on canvas) - LYONS: *Landscape* - MAINZ: *Wooded Landscape* - MUNICH (Pinakothek): *Landscape; Storm; Waterfall* - NANCY: *Cascade* - PARIS (Louvre): *Landscape* (two works) - ROTTERDAM (Mus. Boijmans Van Beuningen): *Swedish Landscape* - STRASBOURG: *Mountain Lake; Mountain Landscape* - STUTTGART: *Landscape with Stream and Castle* - VALENCIENNES: *Landscape* - VIENNA (Czernin'sche Gemäldegal.): *Landscape with Waterfall; Landscape with Waterfall* - WROCLAW: *Mountainous Landscape in Norway*.

AUCTION RECORDS:

PARIS, 1832, *Waterfall in Torrent*, FRF 5,210. PARIS, 30 April 1895, *View Taken in Norway*, FRF 2,200; *Everdingen and Albert Cuyp; The Prince of Orange at the Siege of Breda*, FRF 11,000. LONDON, 16 March 1908, *Rocky River*, GBP 11. LONDON, 27 May 1908, *Landscape* (watercolour) GBP 13. LONDON, 17 June 1908, *River*, GBP 35. LONDON, 20 Feb 1909, *River*, GBP 16. LONDON, 27 June 1909, *Horsemen at the Door of an Inn*, GBP 19. AMSTERDAM, 22 June 1910, *Small Landscape*, NLG 250. LONDON, 8 July 1910, *Mountain River*, GBP 39. PARIS, 3 March 1919, *Windmill*, FRF 3,600. PARIS, 3 June 1920, *Torrent*, FRF 1,700. PARIS, 20 Oct 1920, *Mountain Landscape with Waterfall* (attributed) FRF 450. PARIS, 28 Feb 1921, *Waterfall* (attributed) FRF 3,020. PARIS, 13 June 1921, *Torrent*, FRF 1,310. LONDON, 25 Nov 1921, *Mountain Landscape with Figures, Goats and Sheep*, GBP 31. LONDON, 3 Feb 1922, *Rocky Cascade*, GBP 5. LONDON, 26 June 1922, *Winter Landscape with Buildings, Figures and Fallen Trees*, GBP 10. LONDON, 25-26 July 1922, *Cascade Surrounded by Rocks and Trees amongst which are Huts*, GBP 4. LONDON, 16 April 1923, *Landscape with Farm Buildings and a Horseman Crossing a Bridge*, GBP 18. PARIS, 6 July 1928, *Norwegian Landscape*, FRF 820. PARIS, 9 March 1929, *View of a Port* (attributed) FRF 600. PARIS, 12 May 1937, *Torrent* (attributed) FRF 2,050; *Flotilla Crossing Reefs* (attributed) FRF 3,100. PARIS, 8 Dec 1938, *Seascape: Rough Sea* (bistre wash) FRF 1,000. PARIS, 4 Dec 1941, *Torrent* (school of Albert van Everdingen) FRF 5,500. PARIS, 4 June 1947, *Cascade in the Mountains* (pen and wash, attributed) FRF 950. PARIS, 5 Dec 1951, *Storm*, FRF 480,000. LONDON, 8 July 1959, *Royal Hunting Lodge*, GBP 320. LONDON, 17 May 1961, *Estuary with Fishing Boats*, GBP 350. LONDON, 26 June 1964, *Landscape with Waterfall and Figures on Craggy Headland*, Gns 750. PARIS, 31 March 1966, *Cascade*, FRF 14,000. LONDON, 7 July 1966, *River Landscape with Fishermen* (watercolour) GBP 800. VERSAILLES, 8 June 1967, *Seascape*, FRF 16,000. AMSTERDAM, 10 Nov 1970, *Craggy Landscape*, NLG 18,000. LONDON, 21

March 1973, *View of a Norwegian Fjord*, GBP 15,000. LONDON, 19 July 1974, *River Landscape with Mill*, Gns 2,000. LONDON, 19 May 1976, *River Landscape* (oil on canvas, 30 x 45 1/4 ins / 76 x 115 cm) GBP 1,200. AMSTERDAM, 21 March 1977, *Two Figures Drawing near a Mountain Stream* (5 3/4 x 8 3/4 ins / 14.5 x 22.3 cm) NLG 26,000. AMSTERDAM, 30 Oct 1979, *Huts near a Torrent* (oil on canvas, 25 3/4 x 24 1/2 ins / 65.5 x 62 cm) NLG 6,400. AMSTERDAM, 17 Nov 1980, *Figures on Frozen River* (pen and wash/paper, 2 x 3 1/4 ins / 4.7 x 8.4 cm) NLG 6,800. NEW YORK, 17 June 1982, *Sailing Boats on Rough Sea* (oil on panel, 16 3/4 x 23 1/4 ins / 42.5 x 59 cm) USD 5,250. NEW YORK, 7 Nov 1984, *Mountain Landscape with Cascade* (oil on panel, 18 x 25 1/2 ins / 45.5 x 64.5 cm) USD 8,000. AMSTERDAM, 26 Nov 1984, *View of Forest with Cascade* (pen and wash/black chalk outline, 17 1/4 x 22 ins / 43.5 x 55.8 cm) NLG 95,000. MONTE CARLO, 6 Dec 1987, *View of Estuary in Holland* (oil on canvas, 37 x 51 3/4 ins / 94 x 131.5 cm) FRF 254,000. NEW YORK, 14 Jan 1988, *Wooded Mountain Landscape with Figures and Animals* (oil on panel, 18 1/2 x 24 1/2 ins / 47 x 62.5 cm) USD 19,800. AMSTERDAM, 14 Nov 1988, *Landscape with Peasants* (wash, 4 x 4 ins / 10.3 x 10.1 cm) NLG 2,300. NEW YORK, 11 Jan 1989, *Mountain Landscape with Figures on a Headland and a Church in the Foreground* (ink and watercolour, 4 1/4 x 6 ins / 10.7 x 14.4 cm) USD 5,720. STOCKHOLM, 16 May 1990, *Figures in a Landscape* (oil on panel, 7 3/4 x 11 ins / 20 x 27 cm) SEK 12,500. AMSTERDAM, 13 Nov 1990, *Mill by a Torrent with a Steeple in the Background* (oil on panel, 15 x 13 ins / 37.8 x 33 cm) NLG 25,300. AMSTERDAM, 14 Nov 1990, *Mountain Landscape with Figures near a Torrent* (oil on canvas, 35 x 28 1/4 ins / 89 x 71.5 cm) NLG 13,225. LONDON, 3 July 1991, *Northern Landscape with Stream* (oil on panel, 16 x 20 3/4 ins / 40.6 x 52.8 cm) GBP 7,700. LONDON, 15 April 1992, *Travellers in Mountain Landscape* (oil on panel, 15 1/4 x 12 1/2 ins / 38.5 x 32 cm) GBP 7,200. NEW YORK, 22 May 1992, *Extensive Landscape with a Castle on a Cliff Overhanging a Cascade and Watermill with a Manor and Village in the Distance* (oil on canvas, 41 1/2 x 63 1/2 ins / 105.4 x 161.3 cm) USD 159,500. AMSTERDAM, 10 Nov 1992, *Scandinavian Landscape with a Peasant and Shepherds on a Track near a Watermill* (oil on canvas, 43 1/2 x 37 ins / 110.5 x 94 cm) NLG 20,700. AMSTERDAM, 16 Nov 1993, *Summer Landscape with Fishermen* (black chalk and wash, a pair, each 2 x 3 1/4 ins / 4.9 x 8.4 cm) NLG 51,750. NEW YORK, 11 Jan 1994, *Winter Landscape with Pigs, Swineherd and Farmer with Church and Mill in the Background* (black chalk, ink and wash, 4 x 3 1/2 ins / 10 x 9 cm) USD 4,600. PARIS, 28 Oct 1994, *Timber Raft on a River near a Mill* (watercolour and wash on a pencil drawing, 7 x 11 1/2 ins / 18 x 29.5 cm) FRF 170,000. AMSTERDAM, 12 Nov 1996, *Fishing Boats on a River in a Summer Landscape* (pencil, brown ink and wash/black chalk, 19 3/4 x 33 ins / 50 x 84 cm) NLG 5,900. RUMBEKE, 20-23 May 1997, *Landscape and Sheep in a Scandinavian Landscape* (oil on canvas, 43 1/2 x 37 ins / 110.5 x 94 cm) BEF 233,060. LUCERNE, 13 Oct 1999, *Hunters and Deer in Forest Landscape* (oil on canvas, 26 x 26 ins / 67 x 66 cm) CHF 4,600. AMSTERDAM, 10 Nov 1999, *Capriccio of Amsterdam seen from the Ij* (black lead/grey wash, 4 x 6 ins / 11 x 16 cm) NLG 9,000. LONDON, 14 Dec 2000, *Extensive Wooded Landscape with a Covered Wagon Approaching a Cottage, Distant View of Country House* (oil on canvas, 29 x 34 ins / 74 x 86 cm) GBP 72,000. NEW YORK, 23 Jan 2001, *Landscape with Cottages* (colour wash over black chalk, 4 x 5 ins / 10 x 13 cm) USD 4,000. PARIS, 21 Nov 2001, *Fishermen's House* (pen and ink wash, 4 x 6 ins / 11 x 16 cm) FRF 22,000. AMSTERDAM, 14 May 2002, *Rocky Nordic Landscape with Peasants on a Path by a Waterfall* (oil on canvas, 29 x 24 ins / 74 x 61 cm) EUR 28,000. AMSTERDAM, 14 May 2003, *Wooded River Landscape with Peasants Loading a Boat* (oil on canvas, 19 x 24 ins / 48 x 61 cm) EUR 9,000.

EVERDINGEN, Cesar Boetius van

Dutch, 17th century.
Born c. 1617, in Alkmaar; died 1678; buried 13 October in Alkmaar.
Painter. Religious subjects, mythological subjects, portraits, genre scenes.

Cesar Boetius van Everdingen was the brother of Albert van Everdingen and the pupil of Jan van Bronckhorst in Utrecht. In 1632 he entered the guild of Utrecht and in 1651 the guild in Haarlem, after having married Helena van Oosthorn. In 1661 he settled in Amsterdam. Hendrik Graan, van Hoorn, Adr. Wauneuhuysen, Ad. Dekker and Jan Teunisz. Blankhof were amongst his pupils.

He painted portraits of nobles including *The Regents* in 1634 in Alkmaar. In 1644 he executed the organ of the church of St Lawrence in Alkmaar. In 1648 and 1650 he decorated a residence of the House of Orange, the Huis ten Bosch in The Hague, with what is considered to be his key work, *Pegasus and the Muses*. The figures surrounding the horse exude elegance in an airy composition against a backdrop of foliage, enhanced by musical instruments. In Holland, Cesar van Everdingen continued the academic style inspired by antiquity.

BIBLIOGRAPHY:

Huys Janssen, Paul, *Caesar van Everdingen*, catalogue raisonné, monograph, Doornspijk, Davaco, 2002 (text in English).

MUSEUMS AND GALLERIES:

AMSTERDAM (Rijksmus.): *Portrait of Willem Jacobsz. Baert, Burgomaster of Alkmaar; Portrait of Elisabeth van Kessel, Wife of Willem Jacobsz. Baert; Lovers in a Park; Pan and Syrinx* - DOUAI: *Seamstress of Antwerp* - DRESDEN: *Bacchus and Two Nymphs in a Grotto* - HAARLEM: *Apollo Pursuing Daphne; Venus and Cupid; Woman with a Basket of Flowers* - LEIDEN: *Portrait of a Man; Anna Bloem* - ROUEN (MBA): *The Guitar Player* - STOCKHOLM: *Zeus and Semele* - STRASBOURG: *Socrates, Two Women and Alcibiades* - THE HAGUE: *Diogenes Seeking an Honest Man.*

AUCTION RECORDS:

LONDON, 31 May 1922, *Woman in a Brown Coat*, GBP 44. LUCERNE, 29 Nov 1969, *Pomona*, CHF 130,000. NEW YORK, 30 May 1979, *Christ Blessing the Children* (oil on panel, 30 x 50 ins / 76.5 x 127 cm) USD 25,000. LONDON, 11 Dec 1987, *Portrait of a Woman with a Large Ruff* (oil on panel, 28 1/4 x 23 1/2 ins / 71.5 x 60 cm) GBP 13,000. NEW YORK, 11 Jan 1989, *Young Boy Making Soap Bubbles* (oil on canvas, 28 x 22 ins / 71 x 56 cm) USD 8,800. NEW YORK, 1 June 1989, *Rape of Europa* (oil on canvas, 59 1/2 x 46 1/2 ins / 151.1 x 118.1 cm) USD 286,000. NEW YORK, 15 May 1996, *Three-quarter Portrait of a Young Man in Black Attire and White Shirt Standing before a Draped Green Curtain* (oil on canvas, 39 1/2 x 34 ins / 100.3 x 86.3 cm) USD 6,900. LONDON, 13 Dec 1996, *Portrait of Elizabeth Cromwell* (oil on canvas, 40 x 32 3/4 ins / 101.9 x 83.3 cm) GBP 18,400. LONDON, 8 July 1999, *Artemisia* (oil on canvas, 31 x 26 ins / 79 x 67 cm) GBP 60,000.

EVERDINGEN, Cornelis van

Dutch, 17th century.
Born 16 February 1646, in Haarlem.
Draughtsman.

Cornelis van Everdingen was the son of Albert van Everdingen. He married in Amsterdam on 16 June 1684. In 1670 he drew the title of his drama *De Slag in Vlaanderen* (*The Battle in Flanders*).

EVERDINGEN, Jan van

Dutch, 17th century.
Died 1656, in Alkmaar.
Painter. Still-lifes.

Jan van Everdingen was the older brother of Albert van Everdingen. He was a lawyer. By 1639 he was a notary. On 3 August 1642 he married and in 1644 he entered the guild in Alkmaar.

EVERDINGEN, Pieter van
Dutch, 17th - 18th century.
Born after 1651, in Amsterdam; died after 1715.
Painter. Urban landscapes.
Pieter van Everdingen was the son of Albert van Everdingen.
AUCTION RECORDS:
PARIS, 23 May 1928, *Bridge at the Entrance of the Village* (Indian ink wash) FRF 560.

EVERDT, Mathias
Polish, 17th century.
Active in Riga in 1683.
Painter. Portraits.

EVERDYCK, Mattheus van
Flemish, 17th century.
Active in Antwerp, in 1613.
Engraver.
Flemish School.

EVERE, Jan van
Flemish School, 15th century.
Active in Brussels during the first half of the 15th century.
Sculptor.
In 1439, Jan van Evere carved the retable, painted by Roger van der Weyden, in the church of the Recollects in Brussels.

EVEREN, Gillis
Flemish School, 16th century.
Died c. 1513.
Painter.
Antwerp School.
Gillis Everen died in Antwerp in 1477. We know that in 1465 a painter from Brussels by the name of Gillis van Everen painted an altarpiece for the high altar of the church at Brecht. A certain Adriaen Tack is mentioned in 1513 as being a pupil of Gillis van Everen. A work mentioned as being by Everen is a *Virgin Holding the Dead Christ in Her Lap,* signed *Aegid van Everen*. Formerly in Nuremberg, this picture is now lost.

EVERETT, Bruce
American, 20th century.
Born 1942, in California.
Painter.
Bruce Everett's paintings are highly characteristic: they depict greatly enlarged details of household hardware, such as door handles, coat racks, electric sockets and switches. The canvases are painted with a constant concern for photographic precision and a high level of technical skill. He owes his success in about 1970 to Hyperrealism, although the spirit of his works is closer to Pop Art.

EVERETT, Elisabeth
American, 20th century.
Born 20th century, in Toledo (Ohio).
Painter, sculptor, engraver (etching).
Elisabeth Everett was a pupil of Walter Isaacs and studied at the Ratt Institute. She won the Sweepstake prize in 1926 and first prize at the Washington Fair in 1927 and 1928.

EVERETT, Herbert Edward
American, 19th - 20th century.
Born in Worcester (Massachusetts).
Active in Philadelphia.
Sculptor.
Herbert Everett was a pupil at the Museum of Fine Arts in Boston and the Académie Julian in Paris.

EVERETT, Joseph Alma Freestone
American, 20th century.
Born 7 January 1884, in Salt Lake City; died 1945.
Painter, engraver (etching).

EVERETT, Lena (Mrs)
Maiden name: Mills
American, 19th - 20th century.
Born in Rhode Island.
Painter, pastellist.
Lena Everett was a pupil at the Académie Julian in Paris. On returning to New York, she made her reputation as a pastel portraitist.

EVERETT, Louise
American, 20th century.
Born 9 April 1899, in Des Moines (Iowa); died 1959.
Painter, sculptor.
Louise Everett was a pupil at various academies in the USA and at the Académie Julian in Paris and the École des Beaux-Arts in Fontainebleau (1925). She was a silver medal-winner for the sculpture in the Park Southwest Exhibition in 1928.

EVERETT, Mary, Mrs H. G. Everett
American, 20th century.
Born 1876, in Mifflinburg (Pennsylvania); died 1948, in Los Angeles.
Painter.

EVERETT, Raymond
American, 20th century.
Born 10 August 1885, in Englishtown (New Jersey); died 1948.
Painter, sculptor.
Raymond Everett taught design and painting at the University of Texas.

EVEREYNDE, Dirk
Dutch, 17th century.
Active in London c. 1670.
Painter.

EVERGHEM, Jan van, also known as Jan van der Eecke
Flemish School, 15th century.
Active in Brussels.
Sculptor.
In 1463, working with Godemaer de Boschere, Jan van Everghem constructed a tower for the hospital of Oudenaarde.

EVERGOOD, Philip
American, 20th century.
Born 26 October 1901, in New York; died 11 March 1973, in Bridgewater.
Painter, engraver, draughtsman. Religious subjects, scenes with figures. Murals.
American Magical Realism.
Philip Evergood was born Blashki, his parents legally changed their name in 1914. He studied at Eton College in England (1915-1919) and at Cambridge (1919). In 1921 he decided to become an artist, leaving Cambridge at that point to become a pupil of sculpture under Havard Thomas at the Slade School of Art in London. On returning to New York in 1923, he studied painting under George Luks and William von Schlegell at the Art Students' League. He started engraving during that same year. Between 1924 and 1926 he visited the Paris studio of André Lhote and attended the Académie Julian under the guidance of Jean-Paul Laurens. In 1925 he made a study trip to the British Academy in Rome and spent several weeks painting in the south of France. In 1930 he studied engraving with Stanley Hayter, earning his living as a carpenter and sparring partner for professional boxers. He finally returned to the USA in 1931. Evergood taught in several American Universities: New York, Iowa, Minnesota. From 1934 to 1937 he was entrusted with the management of the easel painting section in the Works of Art Project of the Federal Art Project. He was a member of the American Artists' Congress, president of the Artists'

Union, of the American Society of Painters, Sculptors and Engravers, etc.

After a period of concentrating on biblical subjects, his paintings were then inspired by dramatic elements of contemporary life. The most complete example of this period remains the composition *American Tragedy* (1936 or 1937) depicting the terrible repression of a street demonstration by the police, as well as *Don't Cry Mother* (1938-1944), which denounces poverty, or *Street Corner* (1936), which focuses on a strange collection of a district's inhabitants and workers.

His style owes much to the German Expressionist, Max Beckmann, but with a more narrative edge. His interest later moved on to entirely symbolic, surreal and allegorical images: *Sunny Side of the Street* (1950), *Happy Entrance* (1951), *Nude with Violin* (1957), but sometimes academic too. Evergood developed in his painting a figuration with a dreamlike quality, both disconcerting and strong. Any realistic perspective is absent from his compositions, the figures are larger than life and expressions of the faces exacerbated. In relation to the narration, it continuously circulates around the image. He was also a painter of murals: *The Story of Richmond Hill*, executed for the Public Library in Richmond Hill, New York, in 1937; *Gottom from Field to Mill*, for the Post Office in Jackson, Georgie, in 1938.

Looked upon and appreciated today, Evergood's painting is interesting on several levels and, finally, is not far removed from contemporary compositions with a certain 'free figuration'.

He took part in a number of group exhibitions, notably during his stay in Paris, including the Salon d'Automne in 1925 and, in the USA, the 2nd Biennale of the Whitney Museum in New York in 1934. His first solo exhibition took place in 1927 at the Dudensing Galleries in New York. Others followed, mainly in New York in 1929, 1933 and 1935 at the Montross Gallery, New York; 1936, Denver Art Museum, Denver; regularly from 1938 to 1961 at the ACA Gallery, New York; 1955, retrospective at the University of Minnesota, Duluth; 1960, Whitney Museum of New York. He gained numerous awards, notably: 1945, an honourable mention in the Carnegie Prize, Pittsburgh; 1946, second prize in the Franklin D. Roosevelt competition; 1946, the Alexander Shilling Purchase award; 1949, second prize at the Carnegie Institute; 1955, first prize at the Baltimore Museum of Art.

Philip Evergood

BIBLIOGRAPHY:

Baur, John I.H., *Philip Evergood*, Abrams, New York, 1975.

MUSEUMS AND GALLERIES:

NEW YORK (MoMA): *Don't Cry Mother* (1938-1944) - NEW YORK (Whitney Mus. of American Art): *The New Lazarus* - WASHINGTON DC (Corcoran Gal. of Art): *Sunny Side of the Street* (1950).

AUCTION RECORDS:

NEW YORK, 18 Feb 1960, *Ice Cream Cornets*, USD 825. NEW YORK, 9 Oct 1963, *Strollers in a Park*, USD 2,750. NEW YORK, 27 Jan 1965, *Mountaineers*, USD 1,250. NEW YORK, 8 Dec 1971, *Germinal, Hommage to Zola*, USD 3,000. NEW YORK, 12 Dec 1974, *Self-portrait*, USD 1,300. NEW YORK, 21 April 1977, *Nebuchadnezzar's Court, Scene in Babylon* (two watercolour and pencils, 17 1/4 x 22 ins / 43.5 x 56 cm and 13 1/4 x 18 1/4 ins/33.5 x 46.3 cm) USD 3,100. NEW YORK, 20 April 1979, *David and the Wife of Uriah, the Hittite* (c. 1955, oil on canvas, 32 x 21 1/4 ins / 81.3 x 54 cm) USD 10,500. NEW YORK, 19 June 1981, *Young Girl with Sunflowers* (ink wash and charcoal heightened with white/paper, 22 1/2 x 15 1/2 ins / 57.1 x 39.3 cm) USD 1,600. NEW YORK, 23 June 1983, *Slaves Bringing the Vessels to the Treasure House* (1927, watercolour and pencil, 14 3/4 x 17 3/4 ins / 37.5 x 45 cm) USD 1,100. NEW YORK, 23 March 1984, *American Beauty* (oil on canvas, 35 x 25 ins / 88.8 x 63.2 cm) USD 11,000; *Sampling Cotton* (1945, brush, black ink and gouache, 23 3/4 x 18 3/4 ins / 60.3 x 47.8 cm) USD 850. NEW YORK, 30 Sept 1985, *Men and Machines* (watercolour and pencil/paper, 39 1/2 x 30 ins / 100.5 x 76.2 cm) USD 2,000. NEW YORK, 3 Dec 1987, *The Bride (New York Suzana)* (oil on canvas, 37 x 31 1/2 ins / 94 x 80 cm) USD 35,000. NEW YORK, 17 March 1988, *Jerry Purtie's Chalet* (1935, gouache/paper, 13 1/2 x 19 3/4 ins / 34.3 x 50 cm) USD 16,500. NEW YORK, 24 Jan 1990, *Pub near the Harbour* (gouache/paper, 13 x 16 1/4 ins / 33 x 41.2 cm) USD 3,850. NEW YORK, 14 Feb 1990, *Nude* (pencil/paper, 18 1/4 x 14 ins / 46.2 x 35.5 cm) USD 715. NEW YORK, 16 March 1990, *Recruiting* (1960, oil on canvas, 18 x 28 ins / 45.8 x 71.2 cm) USD 9,350. NEW YORK, 30 May 1990, *Hesitation* (oil on canvas, 20 x 18 ins / 50.8 x 45.5 cm) USD 6,050. NEW YORK, 26 Sept 1990, *What's the Weather Going to be Like?* (oil on canvas, 35 x 25 ins / 88.9 x 63.5 cm) USD 15,400. NEW YORK, 17 Dec 1990, *Female Nude* (1963, gouache/paper, 29 1/4 x 21 ins / 74.3 x 53.3 cm) USD 5,500. NEW YORK, 18 Dec 1991, *Western Landscape* (1947, oil/synthetic resin, 10 3/4 x 12 1/4 ins / 27.3 x 31.1 cm) USD 1,650. NEW YORK, 25 Sept 1992, *Victorious Team* (1959, oil on reinforced canvas, 21 x 18 ins / 53.3 x 45.7 cm) USD 8,250. NEW YORK, 31 March 1993, *Three Mythological Characters* (pencil and watercolour/paper, 22 1/4 x 16 1/4 ins / 56.5 x 41.3 cm) USD 3,565. NEW YORK, 25 May 1994, *The Garage Track* (1936, oil on canvas, 36 x 27 ins / 91.4 x 68.6 cm) USD 63,000. NEW YORK, 20 March 1996, *Touching Future* (oil on panel, 29 x 21 ins / 73.7 x 53.3 cm) USD 5,750. NEW YORK, 27 Sept 1996, *Still-life with a Jug and Fruit* (oil on canvas, 30 1/2 x 25 1/2 ins / 77.5 x 64.7 cm) USD 9,200. NEW YORK, 25 March 1997, *Young American* (1949, oil on canvas, 28 x 22 1/4 ins / 71.1 x 56.2 cm) USD 6,325. NEW YORK, 11 March 1999, *Aftermath* (oil on canvas, 37 x 49 ins / 95 x 124 cm) USD 12,000. NEW YORK, 16 Sept 1999, *Cleaning Cotton* (1945, pencil and gouache on card, 19 x 25 ins / 47 x 64 cm) USD 2,200. SAN FRANCISCO, 24 Oct 2000, *Big Peter and the Oranges* (1964, oil on canvas, 36 x 30 ins / 91 x 76 cm) USD 4,250. NEW YORK, 5 Dec 2000, *Shrimp Girl* (c. 1953, oil on canvas) USD 6,000. DOWNINGTON, 20 April 2001, *Harbour Scene with Men Unloading a Boat* (oil on canvas, 12 x 20 ins / 30 x 51 cm) USD 2,000. NEW YORK, 13 June 2001, *Self-portrait* (1960, oil on masonite, 14 x 11 ins / 36 x 29 cm) USD 1,700. NEW YORK, 23 May 2002, *Portrait of a Boy* (1949, gouache, pastel and watercolour, 28 x 22 ins / 72 x 57 cm) USD 5,600. NEW YORK, 17 July 2002, *Modern Inquisitor* (oil on canvas, 28 x 20 ins / 70 x 51 cm) USD 9,500. CINCINNATI, 7 Sept 2003, *Marketplace* (oil on canvas, 19 x 16 ins / 48 x 41 cm) USD 3,000. CINCINNATI, 7 Dec 2003, *It'd Better Not Rain* (1966, oil on board, 15 x 11 ins / 38 x 28 cm) USD 4,250. NEW YORK, 18 May 2004, *Dog Bite Clinic* (c. 1933, oil on canvas, 40 x 50 ins / 102 x 128 cm) USD 60,000. NEW YORK, 27 Sept 2004, *Fruit* (1948, oil on panel, 30 x 23 ins / 77 x 59 cm) USD 24,000.

EVERHART, Adelaide

American, 20th century.

Born 1865, in Charlotte (North Carolina).

Painter, illustrator.

Adelaide Everhart illustrated Evaleen Stein's *Gabriel and the Hour Book* (Boston: Page Company, c. 1906), and Robert Neilson Stephens' *Clementina's Highwayman* (Boston: Page Company, 1907).

MUSEUMS AND GALLERIES:

AUGUSTA (Morris Mus. of Art): *Glass Bowl of Tiger Lilies*; *Still-life*.

EVERINGTON, Everel Alice

British, 20th century.

Born in England.

Painter.

EVERITT, Allen Edward
British, 19th century.
Born 1824, in Birmingham; died 11 June 1882.
Watercolourist, draughtsman, decorative designer.

Allen Edward Everitt trained under David Cox. He specialised in the decoration of country houses in the Midlands. He was a skilled archaeologist, and executed some very good archaeological watercolours both in England and on the continent. From 1858 to 1882 he was an honorary member of the Royal Society of Artists in Birmingham.

MUSEUMS AND GALLERIES:
BIRMINGHAM (Mus. and AG): *St. Kenelm's Church, Clent* (watercolour); *School House* (watercolour).

AUCTION RECORDS:
LONDON, 17 Nov 1995, *Oak Panelling in a Gallery Interior* (1844, pencil and watercolour, 11 1/4 x 17 1/4 ins / 28.8 x 43.5 cm) GBP 575. LONDON, 20 March 2003, *East Front of Aston Hall, Warwickshire* (watercolour over pencil heightened with gouache, 14 x 22 ins / 35 x 57 cm) GBP 5,200. LONDON, 20 March 2003, *Heathfield House, Handsworth, Birmingham* (watercolour over pencil heightened with white, 13 x 22 ins / 33 x 56 cm) GBP 9,000.

EVERITT, Edward
British, 19th century.
Active in Birmingham.
Painter.

Edward Everitt exhibited in London from 1819 onwards.

EVERS, Anton Clemens Albrecht
German, 19th century.
Born 1802, in Moritzberg; died 1 February 1848, in Hanover.
Painter. Portraits, genre scenes.

Anton Evers studied at the academy of art in Dresden until 1829 and subsequently worked in Munich and Hanover.

AUCTION RECORDS:
VIENNA, 4 Dec 1973, *Happy Family*, ATS 50,000.

EVERS, Gerrit
German, 18th century.
Probably active in Schaffhausen.
Potter.

MUSEUMS AND GALLERIES:
PARIS (Mus. National du Moyen Age): decorated dish.

EVERS, Hans
German, 19th - 20th century.
Born 13 June 1872, in Hanover.
Painter.

Hans Evers was a student of Kaulbach in Karlsruhe; he then settled in Munich in around 1895.

EVERS, Ivar Elis
American, 19th century.
Born 1866, in Sweden.
Active in New York.
Painter.

Ivar Elis Evers was a pupil of Napoleon Caesar, Joseph de Camp and J.-H. Twactman. He held an important post as an architect and engineer. He won a first prize at the Lennox Art Academy and was a member of the American Secessionists Group.

EVERS, J.
German, 19th century.
Active in Berlin at the end of the 19th century.
Painter. Landscapes.

EVERS, John
American, 19th century.
Born 17 April 1797, in New Town (Long Island); died 1884.
Active in New York.
Painter. Landscapes, street scenes.

John Evers began his career as an artist around 1816. He exhibited architectural drawings at the American Academy. During the 1840's and 1850's he was active as a panorama painter in New York City. He was a founding member and often exhibited at the National Academy.

EVERS, Tonnies, the Elder
German, 16th century.
Active in Lübeck at the end of the 16th century.
Sculptor (wood).

EVERS, Tonnies, the Younger
German, 17th century.
Died c. 1613, in Lübeck.
Sculptor (wood).

Like his father, Tonnies Evers the Younger worked for the churches in Lübeck.

EVERSDYCK, Cornelis Willemsz.
Dutch, 17th century.
Born in Goës; died probably before 1644.
Painter. Genre scenes.

Cornelis Willemsz. Eversdyck was a member of *La Noble Arquebuse* (*The Noble Arquebus*) in 1613 and went to Antwerp in 1619, returning to Goës in 1635. A Catholic, he offered shelter to priests, as there was intolerance of the Catholic minority in Goës and its environs at the time.

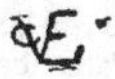

MUSEUMS AND GALLERIES:
ROTTERDAM: *Arquebusiers of Goës*; *Arquebusiers*; *Arquebusiers*.

AUCTION RECORDS:
NEW YORK, 9 Jan 1981, *Poultry Seller* (oil on canvas, 48 x 66 1/2 ins / 122 x 169 cm) USD 12,000. LONDON, 5 July 1991, *Cat Closely Watching Pieces of Game on a Cloth-covered Table* (oil on canvas, 64 1/4 x 81 1/4 ins / 162.9 x 206.6 cm) GBP 13,750.

EVERSDYCK, David
Dutch, 17th century.
Active in Amsterdam c. 1659.
Painter.

David Eversdyck was a pupil of J. Backer.

EVERSDYCK, Willem
Dutch, 17th century.
Born in Goës; died 1671; buried 14 March in Middelburg.
Painter. Group portraits, portraits.

Willem Eversdyck was the pupil of his father Cornelis Willemsz. Eversdyck, and subsequently of Cornelis de Vos in Antwerp in 1633. From 1652 onwards he lived in Middelburg. On 15 June 1653 he married Blasina van Ossewaade in Goës.

MUSEUMS AND GALLERIES:
AMSTERDAM: *Cornelis Fransz. Eversdyck, Mathematician; Nicolas Blancardus, Philologist; Maria Eversdyck, Wife of the Mathematician* - ROTTERDAM: *Twelve Members of the Arquebusiers of Goës*.

AUCTION RECORDS:
PARIS, 5 Dec 1892, *Portrait of a Man*, FRF 300.

EVERSEN, Adrianus
Dutch, 19th century.
Born 13 January 1818, in Amsterdam; died 1897; 1889 according to some sources.

Painter, watercolourist, draughtsman. Scenes with figures, landscapes with figures, urban landscapes, architectural views.

Adrianus Eversen was a pupil of Cornelis de Kruyff.

AUCTION RECORDS:

LONDON, 2 Dec 1907, *View of a Dutch Town*, GBP 13. LONDON, 6 April 1923, *View of a Dutch Town in Winter*, GBP 19. PARIS, 18 June 1930, *Church*, FRF 330; *Small Town in Winter*, FRF 330; *View of Town, Church in Background*, FRF 450. AMSTERDAM, 8 Feb 1966, *View of Amsterdam*, NLG 10,200. LONDON, 4 June 1969, *Street Scene in Amsterdam*, GBP 1,800. AMSTERDAM, 23 Nov 1971, *Street Scene*, NLG 24,000. LONDON, 12 May 1972, *Street Scene*, Gns 5,500. LONDON, 4 May 1973, *Market Scene in Amsterdam*, Gns 6,500. LONDON, 15 March 1974, *Street Scene*, Gns 4,800. AMSTERDAM, 15 Nov 1976, *Street Scene, Edam* (1881, oil on canvas, 22 x 18 ins / 56 x 46 cm) NLG 36,000. LONDON, 11 Feb 1977, *Street Scene in Winter in Amsterdam* (12 1/2 x 11 ins / 32 x 27 cm) GBP 3,200. COLOGNE, 1 June 1978, *View of a Small Dutch Town* (oil on panel, 9 1/2 x 11 ins / 24 x 28 cm) DEM 11,000. LONDON, 5 Oct 1979, *Street Scene, Amsterdam* (oil on canvas, 20 1/2 x 17 ins / 52 x 43.1 cm) USD 1,600. NEW YORK, 28 May 1981, *Street Scene in Winter* (oil on canvas, 26 x 20 ins / 66 x 51 cm) USD 18,000. NEW YORK, 29 Feb 1984, *Street Scene in a Small Dutch Town* (oil on canvas, 27 1/4 x 21 ins / 69 x 53.5 cm) USD 13,000. LONDON, 9 Oct 1987, *Street Scene in Holland* (oil on panel, 24 1/4 x 32 ins / 61.6 x 81 cm) GBP 20,000. AMSTERDAM, 10 Feb 1988, *Anglers in Boat on River* (oil on panel, 9 x 11 ins / 22 x 28 cm) NLG 6,325. NEW YORK, 25 Feb 1988, *Street in Amsterdam* (oil on canvas, 22 1/4 x 27 1/2 ins / 56.5 x 69.8 cm) USD 28,600. AMSTERDAM, 16 Nov 1988, *Villager at the Market behind the Church* (1854, oil on canvas, 18 3/4 x 15 3/4 ins / 47.5 x 40 cm) NLG 32,200. LONDON, 5 May 1989, *Street in Amsterdam* (oil on panel, 9 1/4 x 6 3/4 ins / 23.5 x 17 cm) GBP 3,300. LONDON, 22 Nov 1989, *Street Scene with Figures* (oil on panel, 22 x 29 1/4 ins / 56 x 74 cm) GBP 26,400. LONDON, 14 Feb 1990, *Figures on a Bridge Spanning a Canal* (oil on panel, 8 x 10 3/4 ins / 20.5 x 27.5 cm) GBP 7,150. AMSTERDAM, 2 May 1990, *Winter in a Street in Delft with the Old Church in the Background* (oil on canvas, 27 1/2 x 23 1/2 ins / 70 x 60 cm) NLG 126,500. NEW YORK, 23 May 1990, *Village in Winter* (1978, oil on panel, 13 3/4 x 17 1/4 ins / 35.2 x 43.6 cm) USD 18,700. AMSTERDAM, 6 Nov 1990, *Market in a Dutch Town* (oil on panel, 11 x 8 1/4 ins / 27 x 21 cm) NLG 15,525. LONDON, 22 Nov 1990, *Street with Figures* (oil on panel, 10 x 8 1/4 ins / 25.4 x 21 cm) GBP 2,200. AMSTERDAM, 5-6 Feb 1991, *Town's People Strolling in Town with a Church in the Background* (oil on canvas, 16 3/4 x 14 ins / 42.5 x 35.5 cm) NLG 32,200. NEW YORK, 28 Feb 1991, *Village Street* (oil on canvas, 12 3/4 x 16 1/2 ins / 32.4 x 42 cm) USD 20,900. AMSTERDAM, 24 April 1991, *Street in a Dutch Town with Figures* (1858, oil on panel, 17 x 22 ins / 43 x 55 cm) NLG 80,500. NEW YORK, 22 May 1991, *Dutch Village Street in Winter* (oil on canvas, 26 x 20 ins / 66 x 51.1 cm) USD 30,800. MONTREAL, 4 June 1991, *View of a Dutch Market Town* (oil on panel, 17 1/4 x 14 ins / 43.8 x 35.5 cm) CAD 16,500. AMSTERDAM, 30 Oct 1991, *Town's People behind the Village Church* (oil on panel, 6 1/4 x 5 ins / 16 x 12.5 cm) NLG 8,050. AMSTERDAM, 5-6 Nov 1991, *Village Square with Figures* (oil on panel, 10 3/4 x 14 3/4 ins / 27.5 x 37.5 cm) NLG 20,700. AMSTERDAM, 22 April 1992, *Wooded River Landscape with Fishermen in a Boat near a Castle* (oil on panel, 9 x 11 1/4 ins / 23 x 28.5 cm) NLG 5,175. AMSTERDAM, 28 Oct 1992, *Numerous Passers-by by a Canal in a Dutch Town* (1858, oil on canvas, 17 1/4 x 20 1/4 ins / 43.5 x 51.5 cm) NLG 59,800. AMSTERDAM, 2-3 Nov 1992, *Scene of a Dutch Town* (1862, oil on canvas, 16 3/4 x 22 3/4 ins / 42.5 x 58 cm) NLG 55,200. NEW YORK, 12 Oct 1993, *Street Running alongside a Canal with Numerous Passers-by* (oil on canvas, 28 x 23 3/4 ins / 71.4 x 60.3 cm) USD 51,750. AMSTERDAM, 9 Nov 1993, *Villager on a Road in Ransdorp* (oil on canvas, 17 1/2 x 24 ins / 44.5 x 61 cm) NLG 57,500. NEW YORK, 12 Oct 1994, *Shopping Street in Amsterdam* (oil on canvas) USD 107,000. LONDON, 18 Nov 1994, *Street in a Dutch Town with Figures* (oil on panel, 12 1/2 x 16 1/4 ins / 31.8 x 41 cm) GBP 25,300. AMSTERDAM, 3 Sept 1996, *View of a Town with Boats on a Canal* (pencil, brush, brown ink and watercolour/paper, 4 x 5 ins / 10 x 13 cm) NLG 1,729. AMSTERDAM, 5 Nov 1996, *Dutch Town in Winter* (oil on canvas, 17 1/2 x 14 1/4 ins / 44.5 x 36 cm) NLG 42,480. AMSTERDAM, 19-20 Feb 1997, *Workers Lingering in front of the Church* (oil on panel, 6 1/4 x 5 ins / 16 x 13 cm) NLG 9,225. NEW YORK, 23 Oct 1997, *Dutch Street with Figures* (oil on canvas, 17 1/4 x 14 3/4 ins / 43.8 x 37.5 cm) USD 31,050. LONDON, 19 Nov 1997, *Binnen Singel, Amersfoort* (1883, oil on panel, 10 1/2 x 14 1/4 ins / 26.5 x 36.5 cm) GBP 17,250. AMSTERDAM, 21 Jan 1998, *The Old Binnengasthuis in Zwolle* (pencil, pen, brown ink and watercolour/paper, 7 3/4 x 11 ins / 20 x 27 cm) NLG 2,075. AMSTERDAM, 27 April 1999, *View in Delft* (1885, oil on canvas, 27 x 33 ins / 68 x 83 cm) NLG 280,000. LONDON, 21 Oct 1999, *Figures in Snowy Village Street* (oil on canvas, 26 x 20 ins / 66 x 51 cm) GBP 45,000. VIENNA, 23 May 2000, *Town with Figures in Winter* (oil on panel, 17 x 14 ins / 44 x 35 cm) ATS 900,000. LONDON, 22 June 2000, *The Belfry at Bruges* (1853, oil on canvas, 45 x 39 ins / 115 x 100 cm) GBP 140,000. AMSTERDAM, 24 April 2001, *Straatje te Edam - Townsfolk in a Sunlit Street* (1881, oil on canvas, 22 x 19 ins / 57 x 47 cm) NLG 220,000. COLOGNE, 19 May 2001, *Cityscape* (oil on canvas, 16 x 23 ins / 41 x 58 cm) DEM 100,000. AMSTERDAM, 24 April 2002, *Townsfolk Conversing in Front of a Church* (oil on canvas, 22 x 18 ins / 56 x 46 cm) EUR 62,000. HAMBURG, 15 June 2002, *Town Scene with Various Figures in Front of Sunlit Ruin* (oil on canvas, 16 x 19 ins / 40 x 48 cm) EUR 52,000. AMSTERDAM, 29 April 2003, *Bustling Street by a Church in a Dutch Town* (1856, oil on canvas, 28 x 24 ins / 71 x 61 cm) EUR 72,000. AMSTERDAM, 21 Oct 2003, *Villagers in the Streets of a Dutch Town* (oil on canvas, 22 x 19 ins / 57 x 47 cm) EUR 60,000. AMSTERDAM, 20 April 2004, *View of the Dijkpoort, Hattem* (oil on panel, 15 x 12 ins / 39 x 30 cm) EUR 25,000. LONDON, 26 May 2004, *Dutch Town Scene* (oil on canvas, 13 x 16 ins / 34 x 41 cm) GBP 18,500.

EVERSEN, Johannes or Jan Hendrik, or Everson

Dutch, 20th century.

Born 1906.

Painter. Still-lifes.

AUCTION RECORDS:

AMSTERDAM, 5 Nov 1981, *Still-life* (1947, oil on panel, 12 x 18 ins / 30.5 x 45.5 cm) NLG 2,000. LONDON, 11 July 1983, *Still-life with Schoolbook* (1959, oil on canvas, 20 1/2 x 24 1/4 ins / 52 x 61.5 cm) GBP 700. AMSTERDAM, 28 Feb 1989, *Still-life with Eggs and a Jug* (oil on panel, 9 x 13 ins / 23 x 33 cm) NLG 3,680. AMSTERDAM, 5 June 1990, *Still-life with Bronze Pitcher, Glass of Wine, Bread and Cheese on an Entablature* (1956, oil on canvas, 16 1/4 x 20 ins / 41 x 51 cm) NLG 4,025. AMSTERDAM, 21 April 1993, *Still-life with a Rummer, Bronze Dish, Jug and Peaches on a Table* (1947, oil on panel, 12 1/4 x 19 3/4 ins / 31 x 50 cm) NLG 8,625. AMSTERDAM, 21 April 1994, *Still-life with Cherries in a Bronze Dish* (1962, oil on canvas, 16 x 24 ins / 40.5 x 61 cm) NLG 18,400. ST ASAPH, 2 June 1994, *Still-life* (1962, oil on canvas, 19 1/2 x 24 ins / 49.5 x 61 cm) GBP 3,910. AMSTERDAM, 7 Nov 1995, *Still-life with Grapes in a Glass Bowl* (1953, oil on panel, 15 3/4 x 11 3/4 ins / 40 x 30 cm) NLG 8,850. LONDON, 27 May 1999, *Celery and Red Pepper on a Pewter Dish. Wine Glass, Bottle, Bread and Cheese on a Table* (1966, oil on canvas, a pair, 14 x 18 ins / 36 x 45 cm) GBP 13,000. AMSTERDAM, 1 Sept 1999, *Still-life with Radishes, Bread and Pewter Jug* (1965, oil on canvas, 16 x 24 ins / 40 x 61 cm) NLG 45,000. LONDON, 27 Oct 2000, *Wine Bottle, Baguette and Cheeses on a Wooden Table* (1962, oil on canvas, 20 x 28 ins / 51 x 71 cm) GBP 15,500. LONDON, 27 Oct 2000, *Pewterware, Oysters and a Peeled Lemon on a Draped Table* (1962, oil on canvas, 20 x 28 ins / 51 x 72 cm) GBP 19,500. AMSTERDAM, 12 June 2001, *Still-*

life with Glass, Bread, Cheese on Pewter Plate (1957, oil on canvas, 20 x 24 ins / 51 x 61 cm) NLG 45,000. CALAIS, 1 July 2001, *Still-life with Cherries and Strawberries* (1984, oil on canvas, 16 x 24 ins / 40 x 60 cm) FRF 145,000. AMSTERDAM, 28 May 2002, *Still-life with Glass, Knife and Three Peaches* (1947, oil on panel, 12 x 16 ins / 30 x 40 cm) EUR 6,000. LONDON, 21 Nov 2002, *Lobster, Partly Peeled Lemon, Pewter Jug and Pewter Plate on Wooded Table* (1954, oil on canvas, 20 x 28 ins / 51 x 71 cm) GBP 13,000. PHILADELPHIA, 27 June 2004, *Tabletop Still-life with Books, Pewter Tankard, Candlestand and Pipe* (1963, oil on canvas, 20 x 28 ins / 51 x 71 cm) USD 37,500. LONDON, 14 July 2004, *Still-life with Cheese and Wine* (1959, oil on canvas, 16 x 20 ins / 41 x 51 cm) GBP 22,000.

EVERSHED, Arthur (Dr)
British, 19th century.
Born 18 January 1836, in Billingshurst.
Painter, engraver.

Dr Arthur Evershed was an associate of the Royal Society of Painter-Etchers. He exhibited landscapes at the Royal Academy in London from 1855 to 1892.

EVERSLEY, Frederick John
American, 20th century.
Born 1941, in Brooklyn (New York City).
Sculptor.

Frederick Eversley initially studied science at the Carnegie Institute of Technology and trained as an engineer. This undoubtedly influenced his work and his use of plastics. He uses methyl-metacrilate, in simple structures, which have a minimalist spirit, but in which, nevertheless, the internal role of colour is extremely important: indeed the sumptuous colours make these sculptures highly decorative.

Eversley has been exhibiting since 1970 in New York, Chicago and San Francisco. In 1970 he also participated in a collective exhibition entitled *Art and Technology* at the Los Angeles County Museum of Art.

EVERSON. See **EVERSEN**

EVERT VAN AMERSFOORT, or Evrard van Amersfoort
Dutch, 16th century.
Active in Amsterdam.
Painter.

In 1570, Evert van Amersfoort was a pupil of Frans Floris.

EVERTSZ., Dirck
Dutch, 17th century.
Active in Rotterdam in 1614.
Painter.

EVERTSZ., Harmen
Dutch, 17th century.
Active in Delft in 1636.
Painter.

EVERTSZ., Herman
Dutch, 17th century.
Active in Arnhem c. 1612.
Glass painter.

Herman Evertsz. is mentioned by Siret.

EVERTSZ., Jan
Dutch, 17th century.
Active in Amsterdam c. 1660.
Painter.

Jan Evertsz. was married twice.

EVERWIN
German, 13th century.
Active in Soest in 1231.
Painter.

This artist painted mural decorations for the chapel of St Nicholas in Soest.

EVERWINUS
Bohemian School, 12th - 13th century.
Active in Prague.
Miniaturist.

Everwinus illustrated a manuscript of St Augustin's the *City of God*.

EVERY, George H.
British, 19th - 20th century.
Born 28 August 1837, in London; died 1910.
Engraver.

George H. Every exhibited frequently at the Royal Academy in London from 1864.

EVES, Reginald Grenville
British, 19th - 20th century.
Born 24 May 1876, in London; died 13 June 1941, in Middleton-in-Teesdale (Durham).
Painter. Portraits.

After studying at the Slade School in London from 1891 to 1895, Reginald Grenville Eves moved to Yorkshire and painted many views, particularly of Holswick. In 1900 he returned to London and began a career as a portrait artist. He became a highly sought-after portraitist in a wide variety of circles from London high society to Parisian actors and executed many portraits of well-known figures. In 1940 he was appointed as a war artist.

He exhibited at the Royal Academy from 1901 and became a member of the academy in 1939. He also exhibited in Paris at the Salon des Artistes Français.

MUSEUMS AND GALLERIES:
LONDON (National Portrait Gal.): around 20 portraits; *Max Beerbohm* - LONDON (Tate Collection): *Thomas Hardy* (1924, oil on canvas); *Max Beerbohm* (1936, oil on canvas).

AUCTION RECORDS:
LONDON, 8 June 1984, *Portrait of Thomas Hardy, O.M.* (1923-1924, oil on canvas, 20 x 16 ins / 50.8 x 40.6 cm) GBP 1,000. LONDON, 6 Feb 1985, *Portrait of Miss Severn* (oil on canvas, 20 x 16 ins / 51 x 40.5 cm) GBP 460. LONDON, 12 May 1993, *Portrait of a Lady* (1912, oil on canvas, 50 x 40¼ ins / 127 x 102 cm) GBP 1,207. LONDON, 28 Nov 2000, *Lincoln's Inn Fields* (1930, oil on canvas, 18 x 24 ins / 45 x 60 cm) GBP 3,600.

EVESHAM, Epiphanius
British, 17th century.
Active in London.
Sculptor.

Epiphanius Evesham trained under Vlamen Steevens.

EVETTE, Christophe. See **BOCAL**

EVFIMEV, Ivan
Russian, 17th century.
Born to a family originally from Yaroslavl.
Icon painter.

In 1652 and 1660, Ivan Evfimev worked on the murals of the Cathedral of the Archangel in the Kremlin.

EVFIMOV, Anton
Russian, 17th century.
Icon painter.

In 1666, Anton Evfimov worked in Moscow on the murals of the Cathedral of the Archangel in the Kremlin and in 1675 on the Tsar's Palace.

EVOLA, Giulio or Julius
Italian, 20th century.
Born 19 May 1898, in Rome; died 1974.
Painter, engraver (wood).
Futurism, Dadaism.

Evola was initially part of the Futurist movement, but in 1918 he came into contact with Tristan Tzara and the Dada group in Zurich. He then joined the Dada movement, just as many Futurists were being influenced by the ideas expressed by

Mussolini. He wrote two books in the *Dada* collection, published in Rome: *Arte Astratta (Abstract Art)* in 1920, and *La Parole Obscure du Paysage Intérieur (The Obscure Words of the Interior Landscape)* in 1921.

He held exhibitions of his works in Zurich, Berlin, Stockholm and Paris between 1918 and 1921. From 1920 to 1921 he worked on the *Dada* review, *Blue*, in Mantua, and the Futurist review *Noi (Us)*, which was edited by Prampolini. He took part in the Dada Salon again in 1921, in Paris, after he had organised a Dada exhibition in Rome. Evola then abandoned art, devoting himself to studying the philosophy of civilisations and Orientalism.

His early period, spanning 1915 to 1918, which he described as his period of 'sensorial idealism', is characterised by works whose titles clearly express the concerns of the Futurists: the modern world, the notion of time and dynamism. *Five O'clock Tea* (1917) and *Forge: Study of Noises* (1918) are now in the Museo d'Arte Moderna in Brescia. The works from his second period (1918 to 1920) bridge Futurism and Dadaism. The same is true of his series of *Interior Landscapes*: they still tie in with the expression of 'states of mind', as advocated by Boccioni, whereas intellectually they belong to the Dada movement.

BIBLIOGRAPHY:
Dorival, Bernard/Hoog, Michel, *Dada*, exhibition catalogue, Musée national d'Art moderne, Paris, 1966-1967.

MUSEUMS AND GALLERIES:
BRESCIA (MAM): *Five O'clock Tea*; *Forge: Study of Noises*.

AUCTION RECORDS:
ROME, 25 Nov 1986, *Tendencies of Sensorial Idealism* (1918, oil on canvas, 11 x 18 1/2 ins / 28 x 47 cm) ITL 9,000,000. LONDON, 21 Oct 1987, *Composition No 3* (1919, pen, 17 1/4 x 12 1/2 ins / 43.7 x 32 cm) GBP 1,200. MILAN, 30 May 2000, *Untitled* (tempera on paper, 35 x 19 ins / 90 x 49 cm) ITL 30,000,000. MILAN, 30 May 2000, *Interior Landscape at 3am* (1918, oil on canvas, 44 x 26 ins / 112 x 65 cm) ITL 76,000,000. MILAN, 26 May 2003, *Dada Composition* (1919-1920, tempera on canvas, 45 x 20 ins / 115 x 50 cm) EUR 18,000.

EVORA ALTARPIECE, Master of the.
See **MASTERS**

EVRARD
French, 14th century.
Active in Paris.
Painter.

Evrard was employed to carry out some royal commissions in 1329.

EVRARD
Flemish School, 14th century.
Born to a family originally from Hennegau.
Painter.

Evrard worked in Paris in 1375.

EVRARD, Adèle
Flemish, 19th century.
Born 1792, in Ath-in-Hennegau; died 22 July 1889, in Ath-in-Hennegau.
Painter. Still-lifes (flowers/fruit).
Flemish School.

Adèle Evrard was a pupil of Ducorrou. Her works are in Amsterdam and Brussels.

AUCTION RECORDS:
NEW YORK, 24 May 1985, *Still-life with Flowers and Fruit* (oil on panel, 22 1/4 x 30 ins / 56.5 x 75.3 cm) USD 22,000. TORONTO, 22 Nov 1999, *Still-life with Eggs, Bacon and Onion* (oil on canvas, 20 x 27 ins / 52 x 69 cm) CAD 2,800. SAN FRANCISCO, 15 Nov 2000, *Still-life with Eggs, Bacon and Green Onions* (oil on canvas, 20 x 27 ins / 52 x 69 cm) USD 2,500.

EVRARD, André
Swiss, 20th century.
Born 1936, in La Chaux-de-Fonds.
Painter, engraver, illustrator.

André Evrard studied at the art school in La Chaux-de-Fonds and spent a year in Paris. He exhibits in Switzerland, Germany and Austria. He has taken part in various salons, in particular in 1969 at the Salon des Réalités Nouvelles in Paris. In 1970, he featured in the international graphic exhibition in Catana, Italy. He has won several awards, including the first Choquet prize in 1971 in Paris. Evrard has also illustrated poems by Baudelaire, Rimbaud and Éluard.

MUSEUMS AND GALLERIES:
BASEL - BREMEN (Kunsthalle) - BRUSSELS (Bibliothèque royale Albert Ier) - GENEVA (MAH, Prints Collection) - KARLSRUHE (Staatliche Kunsthalle) - LA CHAUX-DE-FONDS - NEUCHÂTEL - VEVEY - ZURICH.

EVRARD, André Charles Eugène
French, 20th century.
Born 26 August 1896, in Vincennes.
Designer.

André Charles Eugène Evrard studied at the École Germain-Pilon and exhibited at the Salon d'Automne, where he showed sets of furniture.

EVRARD, Ennemond, called Ennemond the Painter
French, 14th century.
Active in Lyons at the end of the 14th century.
Painter.

EVRARD, Eugène
French, 19th century.
Born 24 July 1835, in Paris.
Painter.

A pupil of J. Noël, Eugène Evrard sent *The Duchess of Berry's Ewer* to the Salon in 1869, followed by a *Still-life* in 1870.

EVRARD, Guillaume
Flemish, 18th century.
Born c. 1710, in Tilleur, near Liège; died 10 July 1793, in Tilleur.
Sculptor, engraver.
Flemish School.

Guillaume Evrard's father's first name was Gilles. Guillaume worked in Liège in the workshop of Rendeux, and he then entered J. B. Maini's workshop in Rome. In 1744 he returned to Liège where, from that time onwards, he worked for the churches in the region. The cathedral in Liège possesses his funerary monuments of Prince-Bishop Georges-Louis de Bergh, John Theodore of Bavaria and Charles d'Oultremont.

EVRARD, Gustave Grégoire
French, 19th century.
Born 19th century, in Magimont (Ardennes), Belgium.
Sculptor.

A pupil of Bosio, Gustave Grégoire Evrard exhibited at the Paris Salon from 1851 to 1868. He executed the busts of Collé and Désaugiers at the Théâtre du Vaudeville in Paris.

EVRARD, Henri
Belgian, 19th century.
Born c. 1850; died 1887.
Painter.

Henri Evrard taught at the academy in Brussels. The army museum in Brussels holds a work by him.

EVRARD, Jacques or Perpète, or Everard, Everards, Eurard
Flemish, 17th - 18th century.
Born 23 October 1662, in Dinant; died 1727, in The Hague.
Miniaturist.
Flemish School.

In 1708 Jacques Evrard was in the guild in The Hague. He also worked in Spain and Vienna. His works figure in the collections of the governor of the Low Countries and those of Prince Charles of Lorraine.

AUCTION RECORDS:

PARIS, 2 April 1897, *Childhood of Bacchus* (miniature) FRF 761.

EVRARD, Jean, the Elder,
called de Larche
French, 14th century.
Active in Lyons at the end of the 14th century.
Painter. Coats of arms.

EVRARD, Jean, the Younger
French, 14th - 15th century.
Died c. 1440.
Active in Lyons.
Painter, copyist. Coats of arms.

Jean Evrard painted coats of arms and worked as a copyist.

EVRARD, Jean III
French, 16th century.
Painter.

Active in Lyons in 1548.

EVRARD, Jean Marie
French, 19th century.
Born 16 April 1776, in Chauny; died November 1860, in Paris.
Painter. History painting, portraits.

A pupil of Regnault, Jean Marie Evrard exhibited mainly portraits at the Paris Salon from 1810 to 1836. He executed an *Immaculate Conception* for the church at Chauny and a *Sacred Heart* for the church at Compiègne.

AUCTION RECORDS:

PARIS, 18 Dec 1946, *Young Man Wearing a Black Suit and White Waistcoat in front of a Yellow Curtain; Young Man Wearing a Dark Suit and White Waistcoat* (two miniatures) FRF 8,400. PARIS, 27 March 1947, *Wooded Landscape,* FRF 1,200.

EVRARD, Jehan
French.
Painter.

Worked in the Château of Compiègne.

EVRARD, Louis Eugène
French, 20th century.
Born 9 February 1901, in Dunkirk.
Painter. Landscapes, portraits.

Louis Eugène Evrard studied at the Académie Julian with Laurens from 1931 to 1936 and exhibited several times in Paris at the Salon des Artistes Français, Société Nationale des Beaux-Arts and Salon d'Automne. His favourite subjects were interiors and seascapes. His figurative style is entirely traditional.

ÉVRARD, Paula
Belgian, 20th century.
Born 1878, in Charleroi; died 1927, in Montigny-sur-Sambre.
Painter. Landscapes, flowers.

Paula Évrard was a student of Herman Richir and Jean Delville at the Académie des Beaux-Arts in Brussels. She painted solidly structured compositions in rich and warm harmonies.

EVRARD, Pierre François
French, 20th century.
Born in Paris.
Painter.

Pierre François Evrard exhibited in Paris at the Salon d'Automne from 1926.

EVRARD, Pierre I
French, 15th century.
Died c. 1455.
Active in Lyons.
Painter.

EVRARD, Pierre II, called de Larche
French, 15th century.
Active in Lyons in 1470.
Painter.

EVRARD, Pierre III
French, 16th century.
Active in Lyons.
Glass painter.

Pierre III Evrard was commissioned by the rectors of the Aumône Générale (a charitable body) in 1557 or 1558 to restore the great window at the church of St Catherine in Lyons.

EVRARD, Pierre Paul
French, 20th century.
Born 22 October 1924, in Argenteuil.
Watercolourist, painter (gouache).

Pierre Paul Evrard lives and works in St-Jean-d'Angély and shows his work in local exhibitions in Argenteuil, Versailles and Enghien. He paints with some spontaneity in the Impressionist style, but also experiments with abstraction, automatism and concrete art.

EVRARD, René Hippolyte
French, 20th century.
Born in Le Havre.
Sculptor.

René Hippolyte Evrard exhibited in Paris at the Salon des Artistes Français from 1924.

EVRARD, Victor
French, 19th century.
Born 4 October 1807, in Aire.
Sculptor.

A pupil of Dantan the Elder, Victor Evrard exhibited at the Salon from 1838 to 1877. His best-known works are *Young Faun Intoxicating a Bacchante* (bronze group); *St Anthony the Hermit* (bronze statuette); *Homer* (bronze statuette); and *Christ* (silvered bronze).

EVRARD D'ESPINQUES
German, 15th century.
Active in the region of Cologne.
Miniaturist.

Evrard d'Espinques went to Paris in 1430, and entered the service of Jean d'Armagnac, Duke of Nemours. He copied and illustrated several manuscripts for the lords at the French court.

EVRARD D'ORLÉANS
French, 13th - 14th century.
Born c. 1270.
Active in Paris.
Painter, sculptor, architect.

Evrard d'Orléans bore the title of painter to the king although he worked for a number of different nobles at the French court, including the Countess of Burgundy, Mahaut of Artois. He worked on the Hôtel d'Artoise in Paris and at the abbey church of Maubuisson near Pontoise. He is thought to have died in 1357.

EVRARD VAN AMERSFOORT. See **EVERT VAN AMERSFOORT**

EVREINOV, Dmitri Ivanovich
Russian, 18th - 19th century.
Miniaturist.

Dmitri Ivanovich Evreinov trained under Jacques St-Ours in Geneva. In 1775 he was appointed member of the academy of art in St Petersburg and in 1799, councillor of the acade-

my. In 1812 he worked in Kazan Cathedral. He was often commissioned to paint works for the Court at Tsarskoe-Selo and at the Winter Palace.
MUSEUMS AND GALLERIES:
ST PETERSBURG (Academy): *Portrait of President Count AS Stroganov.*

EVRIER, T.
French, 18th century.
Active in Paris.
Draughtsman.
Evrier contributed to the illustrated edition of the *Description of Paris* by Piganiol de la Force.

EVRY, Jules d'
French, 19th century.
Born 1820, in Paris.
Painter.
Jules d'Évry made his Salon début in 1842, subsequently sending views and landscapes until 1852. In 1854 he became curator of Laval museum.
MUSEUMS AND GALLERIES:
LAVAL: *View of the Alps.*

EVSEEV, Artyushka
Russian, 17th century.
Icon painter.
Artyushka Evseev worked in the imperial palaces and churches in the Kremlin as well as in the palaces in the villages of Ismailovo, Preobazhenskoe and Vorobevo.

EVSEEV, Ivan
Russian, 17th century.
Born to a family originally from Novgorod.
Painter.
Ivan Evseev worked in 1660 on the murals in the Cathedral of the Archangel in Moscow.

EVSEEV, Yakov
Russian, 19th century.
Engraver.
Two engravings of views, by Yakov Eseev, are to be found in A.P. Sumarokov's *Leisure Hours of a Crimean Judge.* A *Portrait of Grand Duchess Bianca Capello of Tuscany* bears his signature.

EVSTAFIEV, Dmitri
Russian, 17th century.
Icon painter.
Dmitri Evstafiev worked in the Kremlin in 1666.

EVSTAFIEV, Kiril
Russian, 17th century.
Icon painter.
In 1665 Kiril Evstatfiev was commissioned by the Tsar to illuminate books in Moscow.

EVSTAFIEV, Mark
Russian, 17th century.
Icon painter.
In 1680, Mark Evstafiev painted murals in the Kremlin Golgotha.

EVSTAFIEV, Vasili Ivanovich
Russian, 19th century.
Born 1838, in Moscow.
Sculptor.
Vasili Ivanovich Evstafiev trained at the academy of art in St Petersburg, which four times awarded him a second class silver medal and in 1864 a first class medal for his low relief *Neoptolemos Preventing Philoctetes from Wounding Odysseus.* In 1865 he received the lesser gold medal. In 1874, he exhibited a plaster bust of *Kovrigin* at the academy.

EVSTRATI
Russian, 17th century.
Engraver (wood).
Evstrati's signature is to be found on the allegorical frontispiece of the *Key to Intelligence* (Kiev, 1659).

EWALD, Alois
Austrian, 19th century.
Born 2 June 1845, in Vienna; died 18 July 1889, in Innsbruck.
Painter, draughtsman. Landscapes, architectural views.
Alois Ewald studied at the Akademie der bildenden Künste in Vienna, then went on to teach drawing in the Tyrol. He worked mainly in Innsbruck.
MUSEUMS AND GALLERIES:
VIENNA: *The Taufer Ruins in the Tyrol.*

EWALD, Arnold Ferdinand
German, 19th century.
Born c. 1810, in Berlin.
Painter. History painting, genre scenes.
Arnold Ewald exhibited in Munich in 1854. He is best known for his painting *Elizabeth of England.*

EWALD, Clara
Maiden name: Philippson
German, 19th century.
Born 22 October 1859, in Düsseldorf.
Painter.
A pupil of Bouguereau, Clara Ewald exhibited portraits and genre scenes in Berlin.

EWALD, Ernst Deodat Paul Ferdinand
German, 19th century.
Born 17 March 1836; died 30 December 1904.
Active in Berlin.
Painter. History painting.
Initially a pupil of Steffeck, Ernst Ewald studied with Couture between 1856 and 1863, before going to work in Italy. On his return to Germany, he became director of the academy of fine art in Berlin.

EWALD, Louis
American, 20th century.
Born 19 December 1891, in Minneapolis.
Painter. Religious subjects. Murals.
Louis Ewald painted an *Annunciation* and a *Visitation* as well as other mural works for various churches.

EWALD, Pierre Albert
French, 20th century.
Born 5 June 1880, in Paris.
Painter. Landscapes.
Pierre Albert Ewald exhibited in Paris at the Salon des Artistes Français and the Salon d'Automne from 1910.

EWALD, Reinhold
German, 19th - 20th century.
Born at the end of the 19th century.
Painter. Nudes, portraits, interiors with figures, landscapes.
Reinhold Ewald constantly travelled to Paris, Florence, Naples and Venice, to paint and to visit museums. His art is deliberately atemporal, except for occasional non-figurative experiments in around the 1920s. Although he exhibited very rarely, he was often mentioned in that period. He settled in Hanau, near Frankfurt.

Wilhelm Hausenstein praises the general scope of Ewald's work, which ranges from black-and-white to compositions ablaze with colour and from the reproduction of nature to fantastical transposition. He paints interiors, female nudes, portraits and landscapes. Behind the realist surface, another reality - magical rather than surrealist - shows through. The things that he paints are at the same time both simply themselves and something else, as in fairy tales. His distance from the plastic concerns of his era makes him a very isolated artist.

Bibliography:

Hoffmann, Dieter, '*Trois oubliés*' in *Chroniques de l'Art Vivant*, periodical, Maeght, Paris, November 1970.

Auction records:

Cologne, 17 May 1980, *Young Woman, Seated* (oil on panel, 29 1/2 x 23 1/2 ins / 75 x 60 cm) DEM 3,000. Munich, 30 Nov 1999, *Landscape* (1919, oil on card, 32 x 42 ins / 81 x 106 cm) DEM 25,000. Frankfurt, 6 Sept 2003, *Woman* (oil on board, 14 x 10 ins / 36 x 25 cm) EUR 3,000. Frankfurt, 6 Sept 2003, *Women Skating* (1922, oil on card, 18 x 14 ins / 45 x 36 cm) EUR 5,000.

EWART, W.

British, 19th century.
Active in London.
Painter.

W. Ewart exhibited a portrait of the painter William Russell at the Royal Academy in 1846.

EWBANK, Johnn Wilson

British, 19th century.
Born c. 1799, in Gateshead; died 28 November 1847, in Edinburgh.
Painter. History painting, landscapes, seascapes.

Johnn Wilson Ewbank was destined for the priesthood and sent to Ushaw College. But it was not long before he switched vocation and entered the studio of a painter in Newcastle. From there, he went to Edinburgh with Coulson, a very skilled decorator. Finally, he received another section of training from Alexander Nasmyth.

Ewbank was one of the founder members of the Royal Scottish Academy in 1826, and from then on he produced some very ambitious works, including *George IV at Edinburgh Castle*, *Alexander the Great Entering Babylon* and *Hannibal Crossing the Alps*. His seascapes and landscapes are very beautiful; the limpidity of his skies has rarely been equalled. He fell on hard times towards the end of his life because of overindulgence, and lived in poverty in Sunderland for 12 years.

Museums and Galleries:

Edinburgh (Nat. Gal. of Scotland): *Harbour Scene with Shipping* (oil/card/panel) - Edinburgh (Royal Scottish Academy): *Coastal Scene* - Sunderland: *Calm Morning*.

Auction records:

New York, 10 and 11 April 1902, *Windsor Castle*, USD 220. London, 29 Feb 1908, *Scottish Mountains*, GBP 8; *River*; *Seascape*, GBP 7; *Two Views of Scotland* (drawing) GBP 1. London, 10 July 1908, *Kilchun Castle* GBP 5. London, 6 July 1983, *Richmond, Yorkshire* (oil on canvas, 29 1/2 x 44 1/2 ins / 75 x 113 cm) GBP 2,400. London, 18 Oct 1989, *Landscape with Ayr in the Distance* (oil on canvas, 39 1/4 x 49 1/4 ins / 100 x 125 cm) GBP 2,860. Perth, 26 Aug 1991, *Evening on Loch Tay in the Scottish Highlands* (oil on canvas, 20 x 27 ins / 51 x 68.5 cm) GBP 1,430. Perth, 31 Aug 1993, *Linlithgow Palace where Mary Queen of Scots Was Born at Sunrise*; *Water Mill at the Foot of Ben Ledi in the Highlands* (oil on card, each 7 x 9 3/4 ins / 18 x 25 cm) GBP 1,495. Perth, 29 Aug 1995, *Cistercian Monastery near Athol*; *Loch Tay, with Ben Lawers in the Distance* (oil on panel, a pair, each 7 1/4 x 11 ins / 18.5 x 27 cm) GBP 1,380. Bath, 12 April 1999, *William of Orange Landing at Liverpool after the Battle of the Boyne, 1690* (oil on canvas, 33 x 52 ins / 85 x 132 cm) GBP 4,000. London, 8 March 2001, *Richmond Castle at Dusk* (oil on canvas, 30 x 45 ins / 76 x 114 cm) GBP 6,500. Leyburn, 26 April 2001, *Mouth of the River Tyne, North and South Shields from the Black Middens* (1826, oil on canvas, 25 x 40 ins / 63 x 102 cm) GBP 1,800. Edinburgh, 22 Aug 2002, *Ardarden Old Watch Tower, Firth of Clyde, Morning Calm* (oil on canvas, 9 x 13 ins / 24 x 34 cm) GBP 1,300. London, 31 Oct 2002, *Shipping in the Harbour, South Shields* (oil on canvas, 40 x 62 ins / 102 x 157 cm) GBP 35,000. Edinburgh, 18 Aug 2004, *Stirling Castle* (oil on canvas, 24 x 36 ins / 61 x 92 cm) GBP 1,400.

EWBANK, Thomas John

British, 19th century.
Painter. Genre scenes.

Thomas John Ewbank was active in Liverpool from 1826 to 1862. He exhibited in London from 1860 onwards.

Auction records:

London, 26 May 1989, *Moment of Tenderness* (oil on canvas, 28 x 35 ins / 71 x 89 cm) GBP 2,420. London, 22 March 2000, *Rosina with Jockey up on Lincoln Racecourse* (1843, oil on canvas, 23 x 29 ins / 58 x 73 cm) GBP 5,500.

EWEL, Otto

German, 20th century.
Born 21 February 1871, in Trutenau (East Prussia).
Painter.

Otto Ewel studied in Königsberg (now Kaliningrad, Russia) and Dresden. Thereafter, he mainly worked in Königsberg.

EWEN, Paterson, or William Paterson

Canadian, 20th century.
Born 7 April 1925, in Montreal; died 17 February 2002, in London (Ontario).
Painter.

William Paterson Ewen was conscripted into the army at the age of eighteen and took part in World War II. On returning to Montreal he began studies in art, science and geology, and between 1948 and 1950 was a pupil at the city's School of Art and Design. In 1949 he married the dancer Françoise Sullivan. The following year he worked in a hat factory, while still continuing to paint. In 1965 he shared a studio with Molinari and Tousignant. In 1966 he separated from his wife and was hospitalised for severe depression, and in 1968 moved to London, Ontario, where he taught from 1969, except for one year that he spent in Toronto.

After his early figurative and expressionist painting he moved in the 1950s towards abstraction, and his work for a while was a kind of fusion between automatism and the figurative. Gradually the figurative elements disappeared, giving way to a freedom of gesture. He painted a series of abstracts entitled *Lifestream* that evoked landscapes or geological layers. At the start of the 1960s he became interested in the work of Capogrossi, Native American works and the dance costumes of Jean Paul Mousseau, and painted compositions based on successions of irregular horizontal bands, the colour contrasts of which suggested space and movement. Then black became the predominant colour in the *Blackout* series and *Alert*. About 1965, when he was working in the same studio as Molinari and Tousignant, an interest in constructivism led to monochrome works that he called 'hard edge'. Shortly after, about 1966 to 1967, he created canvases divided into several parts, each containing a variation on a simple linear theme; these are entitled *Diagrams of Multiple Personality*, and were followed by *Close-Ups*, depicting parts of the earlier series. At the end of the 1960s, when he was deeply depressed, he questioned everything, including his art, thought up new techniques and abandoned canvas for wood, which enabled him to add nailed elements. He then returned to a modified figuration because of his interest in natural phenomena such as rain, storms, lightning, and astronomical subjects such as galaxies and eclipses. Among these works are *Traces through Space*, *Rain Triptych* and other *Phenomascapes* through to his *Large Wave, Homage to Hokusai*.

Ewen exhibited from 1950 nat the Spring Show and the 'Rebels' exhibition in Montreal. He showed his abstract paintings for the first time at the Montreal Fine Arts Museum in 1955, and again in 1957, 1960 and 1961. From 1956 to

1960 he exhibited at the Association of Non-figurative Artists, Montreal. He took part in the New York exhibitions of Modern Canadian Painters in 1956, 1958 and 1959, the Watercolor Biennale at the Brooklyn Museum, New York, in 1959, and the exhibition of modern Canadian painting held in Spoleto in 1962. He was invited to show at the Biennale of Canadian Painters in Ottawa of 1968 and the Venice Biennale of 1982. He held regular solo shows in Montreal from 1950 to 1966, exhibited in New York in 1956 and 1958, in Vancouver in 1987 and 1996 and retrospectives of his work were held in 1968 in Toronto and in 1970 in London, Ontario.

BIBLIOGRAPHY:

Paterson Ewen, Recents Works, exhibition catalogue, Vancouver Art Gall., Vancouver, 1987. Monk, Philip, *Paterson Ewen, Paintings 1971-1987, Phenomena'*, Art Gall. of Ontario, Toronto, 1987. Teitelbaum, Matthew, *Paterson Ewen: the Montreal years,* Mendel Art Gall., Saskatoon, 1988. Teitelbaum, Matthew (ed.), *Paterson Ewen,* exhibition catalogue, Douglas & McIntyre, Vancouver, 1996.

MUSEUMS AND GALLERIES:

HAMILTON, NJ (AG): *Alert no. 28* (1961) - MONTREAL (MAC): *Untitled* (1956); *Current of Life* (1959); *Current of Summer* (1962); *Untitled* (1962); *Untitled no. 35* (1962); *The Star* (1962); *Untitled* (1963); *Diagrama of the Multiple Personality no. 1* (1966); *Star Trace* (1973) - MONTREAL (MBA): *Untitled* (1956); *Summer Night* (1958); *Solar Eruption* (1980) - OTTAWA (NG. of Canada): *Galaxy NGC 253* (1973); *Striped Man* (1973); *Rainbow* (1973); *Gibbous Moon* (1980) - QUEBEC: *Untitled* (1962) - TORONTO (AG of Ontario): *Clouds on Water* (1979); *Stones Rolling in a Water torrent* (1971); *Northern Lights* (1973); *Journey on the Shore* (1974); *Clouds on Water* (1979); *Moon over Tobermory* (1981) - VANCOUVER (AG): *Stormy Night* (1973); *Portrait of Vincent* (1974) - WINDSOR (Windsor Castle, Royal Collection): *Large Wave: Homage to Hokusai* (1974) - WINNIPEG (AG): *Iceberg* (1974).

AUCTION RECORDS:

MONTREAL, 20 Oct 1987, *Untitled* (1957, oil on canvas, 19 3/4 x 24 ins / 50 x 61 cm) CAD 5,800. MONTREAL, 25 April 1988, *Alert* (oil on canvas, 28 x 30 ins / 71 x 76 cm) CAD 4,200. MONTREAL, 17 Oct 1988, *Square Twilight* (oil on canvas, 35 3/4 x 46 ins / 91 x 117 cm) CAD 11,000. TORONTO, 13 Sept 1999, *Abstract* (1977, oil on canvas, 12 x 12 ins / 30 x 30 cm) CAD 7,000. TORONTO, 25 Feb 2002, *Summer Landscape* (1953, oil on canvas, 22 x 28 ins / 56 x 72 cm) CAD 3,250. TORONTO, 27 May 2003, *Life Stream with Time Intervals B* (1968, acrylic on canvas, 49 x 50 ins / 124 x 127 cm) CAD 13,000. TORONTO, 31 May 2004, *Full Moon* (1984, acrylic on gouged plywood, 48 x 50 ins / 122 x 127 cm) CAD 50,000.

EWERBECK, Ernst

German, 20th century.
Born 6 July 1872, in Aachen.
Painter, illustrator. Landscapes.

Ewerbeck studied at the academy in Munich, and later painted landscapes and contributed to Bavarian periodicals.

EWERS, Heindrich

German, 19th century.
Born 1817, in Wismar; died 13 March 1885, in Düsseldorf.
Painter. Portraits, interiors with figures, genre scenes.

Ewers studied at the academy of art in Düsseldorf and first exhibited in Berlin around 1866.

AUCTION RECORDS:

NEW YORK, 30 June 1981, *Interior* (oil on canvas, 31 x 27in/79 x 68.5cm) USD 3,100.

EWERT, Lukas

German, 16th century.
Active in Danzig (now Gdansk, Poland).
Painter.

EWERT, Per John Tage

Swedish, 19th century.
Born 1869; died 1894, in Paris.
Painter. Portraits, landscapes.

In Paris, Ewert was a pupil of J. P. Laurens and Benjamin Constant. He was active in Göteborg in 1869, and exhibited at the Salon from 1893 onwards.

MUSEUMS AND GALLERIES:

GÖTEBORG: *Winter Landscape*.

AUCTION RECORDS:

STOCKHOLM, 20 Oct 1987, *Nun Sitting at the Side of a Sunlit Avenue* (1893, oil on canvas, 23 1/4 x 17 1/4 ins / 59 x 44 cm) SEK 86,000. STOCKHOLM, 29 May 1991, *French Midi Landscape in Summer* (oil on canvas, 17 x 24 ins / 43 x 61 cm) SEK 12,500.

EWING, George Edwin

British, 19th century.
Born 1828, in Birmingham; died 26 April 1884, in New York.
Sculptor. Figures. Busts.

George Edwin Ewing exhibited at the Royal Academy in London from 1862 to 1877.

MUSEUMS AND GALLERIES:

LIVERPOOL: *Dr Norman Macleod* (bust); *James Newlands* (bust).

EWING, Hugh

British, 20th century.
Born in Glasgow.
Painter, watercolourist.

EWING, James A.

British, 19th century.
Born 1843, in Carlisle; died 1900, in Glasgow.
Sculptor.

James A. Ewing was the brother of and worked with George Edwin Ewing.

MUSEUMS AND GALLERIES:

GLASGOW: *Bust of Sir Michael Connal.*

EWING, William

British, 19th century.
Active in Rome during the first half of the 19th century.
Sculptor.

William Ewing exhibited at the Royal Academy in London from 1822 onwards.

EWOUTSZ., Hans, or Eworth, Eottes, Euertz, Huett, Evance

Flemish School, 16th century.
Born 1515, in Antwerp; died 1573.
Painter, draughtsman, decorative designer. Allegorical subjects, portraits.
Antwerp School.

Hans Ewoutsz. worked first in Antwerp, where he was a master in the Guild of St Luke in 1540. In about 1543, he emigrated to England, where he was to acquire a considerable reputation as a portrait artist. Little is known about his life. He is known to have been active in England from 1545 to 1574, being supported by the court from 1554 onwards, at which period he had some influence on the work of the English miniaturist Nicholas Hilliard. His works can be recongised from the artist's monogram, HE.

He designed costumes and decorations for festivals. His portraits included those of *Edward Shelley, Sir John Luttrell* and *Captain T. Wyndham*. In the portraits that have survived it is possible to see, in the more successful works, echoes of Holbein's style as well as that of Scorel and Metsys. Often the mannerism of the allegory leads to rather odd results, as in his *Queen Elizabeth Triumphing over Juno, Minerva and Venus,* where we are presented with a distinctly unusual version of the judgement of Paris. The more his portraits move away from allegory and over-fussy detail the better they are, and quite as good as those of Antonio Moro, who was then in favour at court.

Museums and Galleries:

London (Courtauld Institute of Art): *Allegorical portrait of Sir John Luttrell* (1550, oil/panel) - Ottawa (NG. of Canada): *Portrait of Lady Dacre* - Windsor (Castle): *Queen Elizabeth Triumphing over Juno, Minerva and Venus.*

Auction records:

London, 3 Feb 1922, *Lady in a Black Dress with White Embroidered Sleeves, a Gold Chain around Her Neck and Holding Gloves and a Book,* GBP 39. London, 2 March 1923, *Charles Brandon, First Duke of Suffolk, in a Black Suit with Embroidered Sleeves with a Fur Collar and a Black Cloak,* GBP 1,050. New York, 16 Nov 1935, *An English Court Lady,* USD 1,400. London, 2 July 1958, *Portrait,* GBP 1,000. London, 15 July 1960, *Portrait of a Man,* GBP 231. London, 25 June 1965, *Portrait of Queen Elizabeth I,* Gns 750. London, 7 July 1967, *Portrait of Joan Wakeman,* Gns 12,000. London, 5 July 1984, *Portrait of Margaret Clifford, Lady Strange, Later the Countess of Derby* (1560, oil on canvas, 38¼ x 24in/97 x 61cm) GBP 68,000. Lokeren, 22 Feb 1986, *Episode from the Life of Moses* (oil on panel, 50½ x 70in/128 x 178cm) BEF 850,000.

EWOUTSZON, Jan

Dutch, 16th century.
Active in Amsterdam c. 1536.
Engraver (wood).

EWYNS, Thomas

Dutch, 17th century.
Born 1620, in Amsterdam; died possibly in 1687.
Painter.

EXBRAYAT, Étienne Victor

French, 19th - 20th century.
Born 12 May 1879, in St-Étienne; died during World War I, on the battlefield.
Sculptor.

Étienne Victor Exbrayat exhibited regularly in Paris at the Salon des Artistes Français, of which he became a member in 1905. He was given an honourable mention in 1904 and awarded a third-class medal in 1911.

EXECESTUS

4th century BC.
Active during the second half of the 4th century BC.
Sculptor.
Ancient Greek.

Execestus' name appears on the pedestal of a statue of Athena Polias found to the north of the Parthenon in 1837.

EXEKIAS

6th century BC.
Active 550 to 520 BC.
Potter, vase painter.
Ancient Greek.

Execias may have worked with the potter Amasis, giving a very individual breadth to the amphorae painted by him. He was one of the masters of the black-figure style, most skilled in endowing even the most ordinary scenes of everyday life with a feeling of gravity. More often he depicted divinities and heroes, choosing his subjects from mythology, with a particular predilection for the story of Dionysus and his followers.

Many of his subjects are unusual, and the artist manages to give a dramatic intensity to apparently unimportant scenes, endowing them with implications that raise them to a heroic level. An example, on an amphora in the Vatican Museums, shows the Dioscuri being welcomed home by their parents. The circumstances of their brief visit are full of emotion, yet we seem to be present at a simple family scene, where Pollux, for example, is playing with the dog that is jumping up at him. The horses, on the other hand, have all the majesty of the archaic horses on the Acropolis in Athens. Once again we see connections between painting and sculpture. On the other side of the same amphora, Execias shows Ajax and Achilles playing at dice, an apparently anodyne scene, yet one full of a tension that reminds us of the underlying preoccupations that concern the two men - the Trojan War - and foretells the fate awaiting Ajax after the death of Achilles. Despite the ornamental details on the men's garments, the composition of the scene, consisting of only two figures, is quite austere.

Execias paints new themes and presents them in highly original ways. Beneath the handles of a cup in Munich, the interior of which depicts Dionysus in his boat, the artist has painted scenes of war. A dead warrior, stretched out under one of the handles, has just been killed by a small group of men standing to the right of the handle. On the other side the compatriots of the dead man try to pull him towards them. The greater part of the composition of the exterior surface, however, is occupied by rather alarming and schematic prophylactic eyes.

The interior decoration of this cup is both unusual and harmonious. Dionysus is sailing in his boat with its black sail and a mast culminating in a vine heavy with great bunches of grapes. The composition is entirely determined by the circular shape of the cup's interior, the vine shoots and grapes echoing the general form, while dolphins do the same thing below, representing the sea in the place of the absent waves. Everything seems part of a single whole, with no separation between sea and sky (as is often the case when out at sea). Thus through his figured evocation, Execias subtly conveys a rather abstract reality. Realism and myth are combined with observed details like the sail swollen by the wind set in a scene that seems unreal. It is the first time that the god is reduced to so small a figure. Here he can hardly be seen as he reclines in the bottom of his boat.

Execias depicts the most unexpected scenes with great clarity, making confident use of the wide surfaces provided by the vases he decorates. He makes much use of the technique of incised lines for the details, but without allowing them to harm the composition as a whole or become mannered. Most importantly, he gives a dramatic intensity to the scenes he depicts, conveying the state of mind of his characters.

Bibliography:

Boardman, John, *Athenian Black Figure Vases,* Thames and Hudson, London, 1974.

Museums and Galleries:

Munich (Staatliche Antikensammlung) - Vatican (Mus. Etrusco Gregoriano).

EXEL, Jean van

Flemish, 19th century.
Active in Antwerp.
Sculptor.
Flemish School.

Jean van Exel was a pupil of G. Geefs.

EXILIOUS, John G.

American, 19th century.
Active in Philadelphia.
Engraver.

Among the works of John G. Exilious is a view of the Pennsylvania Hospital.

EXIMENO, Joaquín, the Elder

Spanish, 17th century.
Born c. 1645, in Valencia.
Painter.

Joaquín Eximeno the Elder was a pupil of J. J. Espinosa.

EXIMENO, Joaquín, the Younger

Spanish, 17th - 18th century.
Born 1674, in Valencia; died 1754.
Painter.

Joaquín Eximeno the Younger was the son and pupil of Joaquín Eximeno the Elder. He painted still-lifes and demonstrated great precision in his painting of fish, birds, flowers and fruit. His works have been grouped with those of his father, since they share the same name. Their works are indeed strikingly similar and were very highly regarded by art lovers of the period. The church of Nuestra Señora del Pilar in Valencia has four of this artist's paintings.

EXLEY, James Robert Granville

British, 19th - 20th century.
Born 16 May 1878, in Great Horton (Bradford).
Engraver.

James Robert Granville Exley studied under Frank Short. He exhibited from 1906 in London at the Royal Academy and the Royal Society of Painter-Etchers.

EXNER, Adolph Sophus Aage

Danish, 20th century.
Born 4 July 1870, in Christianshavn; died 1951.
Painter. Interiors with figures, local scenes.

The son of J.J. Exner, Adolph studied at the academy from 1885 to 1892. He first exhibited at the Salon in 1892 with *Studio*, depicting his father's studio. He exhibited some *Interiors* in 1892 and, in 1894, *Bell-Ringer in the Tower*, in which he also portrayed a sunset.

AUCTION RECORDS:

LONDON, 6 Oct 1989, *At the Inn* (1910, oil on canvas, 31 x 40 3/4 ins / 79 x 103.5 cm) GBP 3,300.

EXNER, Johan Julius

Danish, 19th - 20th century.
Born 30 November 1825, in Copenhagen; died 15 November 1910, in Copenhagen.
Painter. Genre scenes.

The son of a musician from Bohemia, who had immigrated to Denmark at a very early age and was employed as an oboist in the royal regiment in Copenhagen, Johan Exner demonstrated a particular aptitude for drawing and painting. He was apprenticed to a painter and attended the academy from 1839. J.L. Lund noticed his artistic abilities and enabled him to dispense with the remaining period of his apprenticeship. Under the supervision of Lund and Eckersberg, Exner produced some studies of history paintings.

He first exhibited at the Salon in 1844 with a *Portrait of a Lady*. A generous gentleman came to his aid by providing him with a free studio and giving him a major commission: *Mark Stig's Daughters* (exhibited in 1851). One of the artist's best works was: *Portrait of an Elderly Woman*, which was acquired by the royal museum. Then, he exhibited *Visiting Grandfather* (1853), which won him an exhibition medal and which is on display at the royal museum of painting. From this period, he annually exhibited *tableaux de moeurs* (pictures depicting everyday behaviour and customs), of Amager and Zealand, and of Dalecarlie (in Sweden).

Exner

MUSEUMS AND GALLERIES:

COPENHAGEN: *Woman from Amager Counting Her Money; Visiting Grandfather on Sunday; Feast at a Peasant's House in Amager; Country Fair in the Jutland Heathland; Card-Players; Young Convalescent; Old Man Sealing a Letter; Dispatch.*

AUCTION RECORDS:

COPENHAGEN, 19 Nov 1957, *Interior*, DKK 11,400. COPENHAGEN, 4 April 1960, *Interior with Five Girls*, DKK 10,100. COPENHAGEN, 23 May 1962, *Young Girl Writing a Letter*, DKK 24,000. COPENHAGEN, 21 Feb 1963, *Interrupted Siesta*, DKK 35,000. COPENHAGEN, 16 May 1968, *Young Girl Reading*, DKK 25,000. COPENHAGEN, 5 Nov 1969, *Kitchen Interior*, DKK 24,000. COPENHAGEN, 23 March 1971, *Village Festivities*, DKK 30,000. COPENHAGEN, 23 Feb 1972, *Young Smoker*, DKK 16,200. COPENHAGEN, 12 June 1974, *Woman and Child in a Garden*, DKK 40,000. COPENHAGEN, 25 Feb 1976, *Children at a Church Door* (1867, oil on canvas, 22 x 16 1/2 ins / 55 x 42 cm) DKK 26,000. COPENHAGEN, 29 Nov 1978, *Country Scene* (1845, oil on canvas, 12 1/4 x 14 1/2 ins / 31 x 37 cm) DKK 23,000. COPENHAGEN, 20 Feb 1979, *Old Couple in an Interior* (1887, oil on canvas, 32 x 27 1/4 ins / 81 x 69 cm) DKK 34,000. COPENHAGEN, 8 Dec 1981, *Happy Family* (1867, oil on canvas, 14 1/2 x 18 1/2 ins / 37 x 47 cm) DKK 48,000. COPENHAGEN, 2 Oct 1984, *Midday Rest* (1877, oil on canvas, 24 1/2 x 20 1/2 ins / 62 x 52 cm) DKK 82,000. COPENHAGEN, 12 Aug 1985, *Sailors and Peasants in a Rustic Interior* (1884, oil on canvas, 35 3/4 x 53 1/4 ins / 91 x 135 cm) DKK 170,000. COPENHAGEN, 25 Oct 1989, *Pair of Lovers in a Barn* (1862, oil on canvas, 12 1/4 x 10 1/4 ins / 31 x 26 cm) DKK 20,000. COPENHAGEN, 6 March 1991, *Teasing during the Siesta* (oil on canvas, 12 1/4 x 14 1/2 ins / 31 x 37 cm) DKK 26,000. COPENHAGEN, 1 May 1991, *Children Playing in a Farmyard* (1877, oil on canvas, 11 x 14 1/2 ins / 28 x 37 cm) DKK 11,000. COPENHAGEN, 28 Aug 1991, *Girl Holding a Kitten and Making it Play with a Piece of Straw* (1895, oil on canvas, 9 x 12 1/4 ins / 22 x 31 cm) DKK 19,000. COPENHAGEN, 6 May 1992, *Mother and Her Children near a French Window* (1873, oil on canvas, 28 x 25 1/2 ins / 71 x 65 cm) DKK 37,000. COPENHAGEN, 18 Nov 1992, *Waiting for the Guests* (1880, oil on canvas, 14 1/2 x 20 3/4 ins / 37 x 53 cm) DKK 26,000. COPENHAGEN, 10 Feb 1993, *Mother Lydum Reading the Bible*. COPENHAGEN, 7 Sept 1994, *Rehearsing Songs for the Festival* (1906, oil on canvas, 11 3/4 x 15 ins / 30 x 38 cm) DKK 30,000. COPENHAGEN, 16 Nov 1994, *Young Servant Lighting his Cigar on a Candle* (1893, oil on canvas, 18 x 16 1/4 ins / 46 x 41 cm) DKK 21,000.

EXPERTON, Jean François

French, 19th century.
Born 1814, in Le Puy-en-Velay; died 1863, in Paris.
Sculptor.

Jean François Experton was a pupil of David d'Angers. His works have been included in a variety of exhibitions.

MUSEUMS AND GALLERIES:

LE PUY-EN-VELAY: *Antoinette Sennetère* (bust); *Bishop of Puy* (bust); *Baron of St-Vidal* (bust); *Cardinal Polignac* (bust and statuette); *Marshal de Vaux* (bust); *The Sculptor Julien* (bust); *The Fair* (statuette); two low reliefs.

EXPORT, Valie

Austrian, 20th century.
Born 1940, in Linz.
Sculptor, performance artist. Multimedia.

Valie Export has taken part in collective exhibitions since 1968, mainly at 'underground' or avant-garde film festivals, but also in: 1974, Institute of Contemporary Art, Philadelphia; 1975, International Women's Festival; Museum of the 20th century, Vienna; 1975, 9th Paris Biennale; 1996, *L'Art au corps. Le corps exposé de Man Ray à nos jours* (*Body Art: The Exposed Body from Man Ray to the Present*), Musée d'Art Contemporain, Marseilles; 1997, Biennale d'Art Contemporain, Lyons; 2001, exhibition on the unreal, the transreal and the reconstruction of reality, *Hypermental*, Kunsthalle, Hamburg; 2003, *Selbst und Andere. Das Bildnis in der Kunst nach 1960* (*Self and Others: Portraiture since 1960*), an exhibition on the theme of the portrait, Rupertinum, Salzburg. She has also shown her work in solo exhibitions, including in 1997 at the Museum Moderner Kunst, Vienna.

She is part of the Viennese actionist movement. Her political approach to art condemns mechanisms of domination and the patriarchal order in particular by presenting her own body. 'I try to show through my works that human beings experience reality through structures of preconditioned reference-points (those of space, time, moral systems and so on) and further that reality can be classified according to these systems of reference. This is why I am mainly concerned with the concept that is critical to these referential structures: identity'. Valie Export has produced many films: *Mann & Frau & Animal* (*Man & Woman & Animal*), videos: *Body actions, Raumsehen und Hören* (*Body Actions, Seeing and Hearing Space*), and has written some theoretical essays about her ideas.

BIBLIOGRAPHY:

IXe Biennale de Paris, exhibition catalogue, Idea Books, musée d'Art moderne de la Ville de Paris, Paris, 1975. Breerette, Geneviève, '*Les Installations et actions subversives de la pécheresse Valie Export*' in *Le Monde*, Paris, 9 October 2003 (interview with the artist).

MUSEUMS AND GALLERIES:

GRAZ (Landesmus. Joanneum) - VIENNA (Mus. Moderner Kunst Stiftung Ludwig).

EXSHAW, Charles

Irish, 18th century.
Born at the beginning of the 18th century, in Dublin; died 1771.
Painter, engraver. History painting.

Charles Exshaw's engravings, which were not without merit, were more often than not copies of works by Rembrandt. He trained in Rome, Amsterdam and probably Paris, and he did not go to London until around 1758. He engraved the portraits of the Van Loo family, and other works by him include *Christ and His Disciples on the Boat during the Storm*, *Bust of an Old Man with a Large Beard and Short Hair*, and *Joseph Accused by the Wife of Potiphar*, all in the style of Rembrandt, *Young Girl with a Basket of Cherries and Two Boys*, in the style of Rubens, and *Van Loo's Children*, in the style of Van Loo.

EXTER, Aleksandra Aleksandrovna, or Ekster

Maiden name: Grigorovich
Russian, 20th century.
Born 1882 or 1884, in Bielostok (Kiev); died 1949, in Fontenay-aux-Roses, France.
Active in France from 1924.
Painter and decorative artist. Stage sets, stage costumes.
Symbolism, Futurism, Constructivism.
Groups: Golubaya Roza (Blue Rose), Bubnovy Valet (Jack of Diamonds).

A student at the school of fine art in Kiev, Aleksandra Exter exhibited for the first time with the Golubaya Roza (Blue Rose) group in Moscow in 1907. The following year in Kiev she organised one of the first exhibitions of the Russian avant-garde, *Zveno* (*The Link*), which brought together Baranoff-Rossine, the Burlyuk brothers, Larionov, Goncharova and Lentulov.

She travelled extensively from 1903 to 1914 between Paris, Rome, Genoa and Florence. From 1908 onwards she spent long periods in Paris, where she joined the Cubist circle. In 1908 she also married her cousin Nicolai Eugenovitch Exter, a wealthy lawyer. She met Picasso, Apollinaire and Max Jacob and came under the influence of Léger and then of Sonia and Robert Delaunay.

In 1912, she painted a series of *Visions of Cities*, which encouraged Apollinaire to invent a new term to describe Cubism tending towards Abstraction, 'Orphic Cubism', practised by Robert Delaunay and Kupka among others. Exter returned to Russia periodically between 1910 and 1914 with photos of the latest Parisian pictorial innovations and established a link between France and Russia. Before the war in 1914, she joined all the avant-garde groups for a short time, including the Young People's Union in St Petersburg, the Bubnovy Valet (Jack of Diamonds) group in Moscow, founded in 1910 by Mikhail Fedorovich Larionov, and the Section d'Or group in Paris to which Archipenko, Survage and Baranoff-Rossine belonged. She also discovered Italian Futurism, particularly through the painter and writer Ardengo Soffici with whom she shared a workshop from 1914 onwards and took part in the *Esposizione Internazionale Futurista* in Rome. Having assimilated the lesson of the Cubists and Futurists, she took part in the exhibition *Tramway V* in St Petersburg in 1915 with Malevich, Tatlin, Popova and Klyun.

Aleksandra Exter played a vital role of in the history of Russian theatre. It is no exaggeration to say that she initiated the majority of innovations in sets and costumes in 1920s Russia. These novelties were widely disseminated through the teaching she so tenaciously provided in Kiev, Odessa, Moscow and, after 1924, in Paris. In her theatrical work, she showed particular interest in the movement of shapes in space in relation to the movement of the actors on stage. Together with Tairov, Director of the Chamber Theatre of Moscow, she established a general theatre formula in which costumes, sets and actors form a lively, dynamic unit. The majority of her costume designs, including those for *Salome* (1917) and *Romeo and Juliet* (1921) are examples of her Cubo-Futurist design for the rotating movement of shapes and planes. This experience was developed in some of her paintings, in particular those exhibited at the Venice Biennale in 1924.

In 1921, she became involved in Constructivism, and was represented at the *5 x 5 = 25* exhibition organised by Rodchenko. She left Russia in 1924 and settled in Paris where she started teaching in Léger's workshop and continued working for the theatre. In 1930, she became established in Constructivism with an illustration in the first edition of the journal *Cercle et Carré*, organised by Michel Seuphor. She ended her days in Fontenay-aux-Roses, apparently in semi-oblivion.

Her work is a synthesis between Cubism in its decomposition of forms, Futurism in its dynamics of composition and Constructivism and in the arrangement of its coloured, geometric shapes. Her pure colours show often touches of white, which give an effect of volume and depth to the whole.

Exter was represented in 2003 in three collective exhibitions: *Un été russe à Montmartre. Artistes de St-Pétersbourg à Paris au début du XXe siècle* (*A Russian Summer in Montmartre. St Petersburg Artists in Paris at the Beginning of the 20th century*), Musée de Montmartre, Paris; *Russian Paris 1910-1960*, itinerant exhibition on Russian art and artists organised by the Russian Museum, St Petersburg and shown at the Von der Heydt-Museum in Wuppertal and at the Museum of Fine Art in Bordeaux; *Aux origines de l'abstraction (1800-1914)* (*The Origins of Abstraction (1800-1914)*), Musée d'Orsay, Paris. In 1975, a gallery in New York exhibited a group of her works and in 1991, the exhibition *Alexandra Exter and the Chamber Theatre* was organised in Rovereto (Italy).

A Exter.

BIBLIOGRAPHY:

Nakov, Andrei B., *Alexandra Exter*, Galerie Jean Chauvelin, Paris, 1972. Weiss, E., *Russische Avant-garde 1910-1930*, Prestel, Munich, 1986. Bowlt, John E./Drutt, Matthew (ed.), *Amazons of the Avant-Garde: Alexandra Exter [et al]*, Guggenheim Museum/Thames and Hudson, New York, London, 2000. Gérard, Raphaël/Essaïan, Sergeï, et al., *Un été russe à Montmartre. Artistes de Saint-Pétersbourg à Paris au début du XXe siècle*, exhibition catalogue, Musée de Montmartre, Éditions Fragments, Paris, 2003. Marcadé, Jean-Claude/Pétrova, Evguénia, *Paris russe 1910-1960*, exhibition catalogue, Musée des Beaux-Arts, Bordeaux, 2003. Lemoine, Serge/Rousseau, Pascal, et al., *Aux origines de l'abstraction (1800-1914)*, exhibition catalogue, Musée d'Orsay, Paris, 2003. Chauvelin, Jean, *Alexandra Exter*, M. Milo, Paris, 2003.

AUCTION RECORDS:

LONDON, 12 April 1972, *Suprematist Composition* (gouache) GBP 2,800. LONDON, 4 July 1974, *Abstract Composition* (gouache) GBP 2,200; *Cubist Nude* (c. 1914) GBP 1,600. NEW YORK, 27 May 1976, *Stage Set* (gouache and collage, 7 x 9 ins / 17.8 x 22 cm) USD 750. NEW YORK, 15 Dec 1977, *Stage Set* (c. 1923, watercolour and pencil, 20¼ x 21¼ ins / 51.3 x 54 cm) USD 3,000; *Marionnette: Costume* (wood, card, plastic and fabrics, h. 21½ ins / 54.6 cm) USD 8,000. NEW YORK, 3 Nov 1978, *Figure* (c. 1924-25, gouache, 19 x 9 ins / 48.2 x 22 cm) USD 1,800. NEW YORK, 6 Dec 1979, *Tarantella* (c. 1920-21, watercolour, gouache and pencil, 5 x 5¼ ins / 13 x 13.3 cm) USD 1,400. LONDON, 29 Oct 1981, *Costume Design for The Circus* (gouache and pencil, 15 x 19¼ ins / 38 x 49.2 cm) GBP 1,500. LONDON, 28 June 1983, *Dynamic Vision for a City* (c. 1921, pencil and white gouache/paper, 17¾ x 19¾ ins / 45 x 50 cm) GBP 4,500. NEW YORK, 17 May 1984, *Set Design* (1925, gouache/pencil outlines, 19 x 14 ins / 48.2 x 35.3 cm) USD 7,500. LONDON, 13 Feb 1986, *City* (oil and gouache, 17¼ x 11¾ ins / 44 x 30 cm) GBP 1,800. LONDON, 2 April 1987, *Cafe Scene* (1925, watercolour, pen and pencil, 25 x 16½ ins / 63.5 x 42 cm) GBP 10,000. VARENNE-ST-HILAIRE, 6 Dec 1987, *Still-life and Sailing Boat* (1925, gouache/card, 24¾ x 19 ins / 63 x 48 cm) FRF 31,000. LONDON, 6 Oct 1988, *Costume Sketch: The Hunter* (gouache/paper, 18¼ x 12 ins / 464 x 30.2 cm) GBP 3,960; *Prancing Horse* (oil on canvas, 12½ x 15½ ins / 32 x 39.5 cm) GBP 6,600. LONDON, 6 April 1989, *Composition, Genoa* (1912, oil on canvas, 45½ x 34 ins / 115.5 x 86.5 cm) GBP 759,000. LONDON, 5 Oct 1989, *Paris Bridges* (1912, oil on canvas, 37½ x 60½ ins / 95 x 153.5 cm) GBP 330,000. VERSAILLES, 29 Oct 1989, *Woman in a Cloak* (gouache, 11½ x 8½ ins / 29 x 21.5 cm) FRF 5,000. NEW YORK, 21 Feb 1990, *Sketches for Set Designs: Don Juan and Death; Don Juan and Hell* (gouache and stencil, a pair, each 13 x 19¾ ins / 33.1 x 50 cm) USD 2,860. LONDON, 4 April 1990, *Romeo and Juliet, Costume Design* (oil, gouache and gold paint/card, 19 x 13¾ ins / 48 x 35 cm) GBP 143,000. LONDON, 5 April 1990, *Composition of Dynamic Colours* (58¼ x 32¼ ins / 148 x 82 cm) GBP 506,000. LONDON, 23 May 1990, *Chateau* (oil on canvas, 18 x 28¾ ins / 46 x 73 cm) GBP 15,400. LUGANO, 28 March 1992, *Costume Design for 'Romeo and Juliet'* (1920, pencil and tempera/paper, 23 x 17¼ ins / 57.5 x 43.5 cm) CHF 38,000. NEW YORK, 12 June 1992, *Set Designs for 'The Merchant of Venice' and 'Circus Big Top'* (gouache and stencil/paper, 13 x 15¾ ins / 33 x 40 cm and 13 x 19¾ ins/33 x 50.2 cm) USD 1,320. BOULOGNE-SUR-SEINE, 20 March 1994, *Concert* (oil on canvas, 23½ x 32 ins / 60 x 81 cm) FRF 168,500. NEW YORK, 9 June 1994, *Landscape and Architecture* (oil on canvas, decor design, 24¼ x 28¾ ins / 61.9 x 73 cm) USD 8,050. LONDON, 29 June 1994, *Castles Under the Sea* (1928, oil on canvas, 35½ x 43¾ ins / 90.2 x 111.1 cm) GBP 11,500. PARIS, 26 June 1995, *Costume Design for 'Salome' by Oscar Wilde* (varnished gouache, 18 x 12¼ ins / 46 x 31 cm) FRF 16,000. LONDON, 14 Dec 1995, *Costume Design for 'Romeo and Juliet'* (gouache heightened with gold, 19¾ x 19 ins / 50 x 48 cm) GBP 25,300. LONDON, 11-12 June 1997, *Figure Study* (oil on canvas, 21 x 17¾ ins / 53.5 x 45 cm) GBP 4,025. LONDON, 29 April 1999, *Stage Designs* (oil on card, two works, 22 x 20 ins / 56 x 50 cm) GBP 7,000. LONDON, 29 April 1999, *Set Designs* (oil on card, three works, 20 x 7 ins / 50 x 17 cm) GBP 9,000. LONDON, 23 Nov 2000, *Fisherwomen* (c. 1925, oil on canvas, 46 x 29 ins / 116 x 74 cm) GBP 60,000. PARIS, 30 May 2001, *Colour Dynamism* (1915, watercolour and gouache on card, 19 x 13 ins / 48 x 32 cm) FRF 420,000. LONDON, 31 May 2001, *Nude Bathers* (oil on canvas, 18 x 22 ins / 46 x 55 cm) GBP 40,000. LONDON, 22 May 2002, *Harbour Scene* (oil on panel, 23 x 15 ins / 58 x 39 cm) GBP 25,000. LONDON, 27 June 2002, *Stage Design* (1921, gouache, 19 x 25 ins / 48 x 64 cm) GBP 7,000. LONDON, 21 May 2003, *Costume Design for a Dancer* (gouache, 20 x 13 ins / 50 x 34 cm) GBP 28,000. LONDON, 25 Nov 2003, *Still-life of Fruit, Vegetables, Bowl of Eggs and Bottle of Milk* (oil on canvas, 32 x 21 ins / 82 x 54 cm) GBP 48,000. NEW YORK, 23 April 2004, *Costume Design for the Seven against Thebes* (pencil and gouache, 20 x 13 ins / 51 x 33 cm) USD 40,000. PARIS, 19 May 2004, *Costume Project* (gouache, 22 x 17 ins / 57 x 42 cm) EUR 31,000.

EXTER, Friedrich

German, 19th century.
Born 6 March 1820, in Theresienfeld; died 27 June 1860, in Vienna.
Engraver (wood). Landscapes.

A pupil of the engraver Höfe, in Vienna, and of C. Braun in Munich, Friedrich Exter was the pioneer of the first colour engraving processes.

EXTER, Julius

German, 19th century.
Born 20 September 1863, in Ludwigshafen am Rhein.
Painter, sculptor. Genre scenes.

Julius Exter first studied at the school of art in Nuremberg, from 1881 to 1887, before completing his studies at the academy of art in Munich. He subsequently worked for two years in the studio of Alexander von Wagner. He exhibited in Munich in 1888 and 1889, and was awarded a bronze medal at the 1900 Exposition Universelle in Paris.

MUSEUMS AND GALLERIES:

BREMEN: *Young Judith; Two Men* - BUCHAREST: *Small Girl Asleep* - MUNICH: *Good Friday*.

EYB, Gustav A.

German, 19th century.
Born 13 October 1863, in Wangen, near Stuttgart.
Engraver (wood), painter.

Gustav Eyb studied at the academy of art in Stuttgart.

EYB, Johann Paul von

German, 17th century.
Active in Nuremberg.
Engraver.

EYBE, Caspar

German, 17th century.
Active in Schleswig c. 1650.
Sculptor (wood).

EYBE, Claus

German, 17th century.
Died 1697, in Schleswig.
Sculptor.

In 1656, Claus Eybe was working for a monastery in Preetz. Subsequently, around 1666, he executed an altarpiece for Schleswig Cathedral.

EYBE, Karl Gottfried

German, 19th century.
Born 17 December 1813, in Hamburg; died 17 February 1893, in Blankenese.
Painter. History painting, genre scenes, portraits.

Karl Eybe studied at the academy of art in Düsseldorf in the studios of K. Sohn and Schadow. He travelled in Germany and Italy, exhibiting in Cologne and in Munich in 1854 and 1861. His best-known work is *Spring*.

MUSEUMS AND GALLERIES:

HAMBURG: *Children Bathing*.

EYBEL, Adolf

German, 19th century.

Born 24 February 1808, in Berlin; died 12 October 1882, in Berlin.
Painter. History painting, portraits, genre scenes.
Eybel studied at the academy of art in Berlin. In 1835, he joined Kolbe's studio while also studying with Delaroche in Paris. From 1850, he lectured at the academy of art in Berlin. He became a member of the academy in 1845 and a senator in 1854. In 1848, he was awarded the small gold medal in Berlin. His best-known work is *Child Musicians*.

EYBELWIESER, Hans Jacob
German, 17th century.
Born in Vienna; died 17 March 1694, in Breslau (now Wroclaw, Poland).
Painter.
Eybelwieser is known to have painted a *Crucifixion*. He was the father of Johann Jacob Eybelwieser.

EYBELWIESER, Johann Jacob
German, 17th - 18th century.
Born c. 1667, in Vienna; died c. 1744, in Breslau (now Wroclaw, Poland).
Painter.
Johann Eybelwieser married the widow of the composer, B.J. Lehmann. He studied under M.L.L. Willmann. K. Ertl engraved the frontispiece of Lesage de Richée's work *Kabinett der Lauten* (*Lute Cabinet*), which was published around 1695, after a drawing by Johann Eybelwieser.
BIBLIOGRAPHY:
Michael Willmann und sein Kreis: Johann Christoph Liska, Georg Wilhelm Neunhertz und Johann Jakob Eybelwieser: Zeichnungen, exhibition catalogue, Salzburger Barockmuseum, Salzburg, 2001.

EYBEN, H. L.
German, 18th century.
Painter.
Bernigeroth engraved a portrait of the theologian J.J. Bertram after Eyben.

EYBENSTOCK
Austrian, 15th century.
Sculptor. Monuments.
Eybenstock worked in Strasbourg, where he made a number of funerary monuments.

EYBL, Franz
Austrian, 19th century.
Born 1 April 1806, in Vienna; died 29 April 1880, in Vienna.
Painter, watercolourist. Portraits, genre scenes.
Eybl studied at the academy of art in Vienna, becoming a member in 1843.
MUSEUMS AND GALLERIES:
VIENNA (Österreichische Gal. Belvedere): *Old Austrian Peasant Woman Leaving Church* (1847); *Old Beggar in a Mountain Landscape* (1856); *Self-portrait and Portrait of Doctor Gross*.
AUCTION RECORDS:
VIENNA, 18 Sept 1962, *Hallstatt Peasant Woman with Basket of Strawberries*, ATS 130,000. VIENNA, 20 Jan 1981, *Portrait of a Man* (oil on canvas, 26¾ x 22in/68 x 56cm) ATS 22,000. MUNICH, 15 Sept 1983, *Portrait of an Austrian Officer* (oil on canvas, 31½ x 24¾in/80 x 63cm) DEM 10,000. VIENNA, 23 Feb 1989, *The Promise* (1856, oil on panel, 19¼ x 16¼in/49 x 41cm) ATS 1,320,000. PARIS, 5 April 1990, *Portrait of a Young Man* (oil on canvas, 21½ x 17¼in/54.5 x 44cm) FRF 30,000. LONDON, 20 May 1993, *Portrait of Anton Diabelli, Seated* (1842, watercolour heightened with white/paper, 8¼ x 6¾in/20.7 x 17.1cm) GBP 6,830. VIENNA, 20 April 1999, *Lady in Striped Dress* (watercolour, 11 x 9 ins / 28 x 23 cm) ATS 30,000. VIENNA, 20 May 1999, *Portrait of Young Boy Sitting on Bench, Landscape Beyond* (oil on canvas, 10 x 12 ins / 26 x 30 cm) ATS 45,000. LONDON, 6 April 2000, *Picture Book* (oil on canvas, 32 x 40 ins / 82 x 101 cm) GBP 1,800. VIENNA, 29 Nov 2001, *Courtship* (oil on panel, 20 x 15 ins / 50 x 39 cm) ATS 45,000. VIENNA, 24 Nov 2003, *Woman's Portrait* (oil on panel, 11 x 9 ins / 27 x 22 cm) EUR 7,000.

EYCHART, Paul
French, 20th century.
Born in Ségura.
Painter.
Paul Eychart was a member of the Salon des Artistes Français and in 1938 was awarded the Deldebat de Gonzalva prize.

EYCHART, Pierre
French, 20th century.
Born 1943.
Painter, engraver. Figure compositions, figures, nudes, portraits, interiors with figures, landscapes, waterscapes, urban landscapes, landscapes with figures, still-lifes.
Pierre Eychart studied under Chapelain-Midy at the École des Beaux-Arts in Paris, and went on to live in Madrid from 1969 to 1971, where he won the Casa de Velázquez prize.

As far as painting is concerned, Eychart is interested not in theoretical, but in practical challenges. He reflects not on any possible 'higher purpose' that painting might have, but on the more immediately relevant challenge of communicating his pleasure in his paintings. His style is inspired by the Impressionists: his subtle brushstrokes intertwine, juxtapose and superimpose colours to convey his sensations, and his appreciation of colour harmony turns these sensations into emotions.

He has taken part in group exhibitions in Paris, including the Salon d'Automne, where he won the Young Painters' Prize in 1967, and became an associate in 1973, a member of the jury in 1981 and a member of the committee in 1984; the Salon des Artistes Français, where he won the Young Painter's Prize in 1968 and the Gold Medal in 1970; and the Salon Comparaisons, the Salon du Dessin and the Salon de la Peinture à l'Eau. In addition, he was selected to exhibit at various Salons d'Automne and the Salons d'Artistes Français in Moscow, Leningrad (now St Petersburg), Warsaw and Tehran.

Eychart has also staged a number of solo exhibitions: in Tokyo in 1968 and 1976, in London and Paris in 1970, in Melbourne in 1971, and in Paris again in 1978 and 1980; Galerie Bernheim-Jeune, Paris, 1982 and 1985; Musée de Draguignan, 1988; and the 1991 Homage to the Salon d'Automne. He won the Prince Rainier III Prize in 1972, the Orthon Friesz Prize in 1973, and the Prix de l'Institut de France.
BIBLIOGRAPHY:
Clerval, J.P. (preface), *Pierre Eychart*, exhibition catalogue, Musée de Draguignan, Draguignan, 1988. Siméon, J.P., *Pierre Eychart ou la Réalité en Face*, Imprimerie P.J. Mathan, Boulogne-Billancourt, 1992.
MUSEUMS AND GALLERIES:
CLERMONT-FERRAND (Mus. Bargoin).
AUCTION RECORDS:
PARIS, 26 March 1990, *The Bank of the Seine* (oil on canvas, 23½ x 28¾ ins / 60 x 73 cm) FRF 7,500. PARIS, 8 Dec 1994, *The Loing on a Summer Morning* (1987, oil on canvas, 39¼ x 39¼ ins / 100 x 100 cm) FRF 7,600.

EYCHENNE, Gaston
French, 19th - 20th century.
Born 1873; died 13 May 1902, in St-Germain-en-Laye.
Painter, sculptor.
Gaston Eychenne exhibited in Paris at the Salon des Artistes Français in 1902.

EYCHUISE, Jean de
Flemish School, 14th century.
Active in Ghent.
Glass painter.

Jean de Eychuise made the glass for the windows of the chapel at the castle of Ninove.

EYCK, Artus van der
Flemish, 17th century.
Born to a family originally from Mechelen.
Painter.
Flemish School.

Artus van der Eyck married in Amsterdam in 1646.

EYCK, Barthélémy d', the Master of the Aix Annunciation
French, 15th century.
Active between 1440 and 1470.
Painter. Religious subjects.
Provencal School.

A recent suggestion for the identity of the Master of the Aix Annunciation is a certain Barthélemy d'Eyck, a name indicating someone of Flemish origin, and who may have worked as an illuminator for King René. If so he would be the author of the *Annunciation* painted for St Saviour's Cathedral, today the church of Ste-Marie-Madeleine, in Aix-en-Provence. Some scholars have concluded that this is the same artist as the Master of the Captured Loving Heart, also known as the Master of King René. Formerly thought to be by Enguerrand Quarton, a *Christ on the Cross*, influenced by the Sienese style and acquired by the Louvre in 1993, is now attributed to Barthélemy d'Eyck.

The central panel of the *Annunciation* is still in the church for which it was made. The right-hand panel, showing the prophet Jeremiah, is now in the museum in Brussels, while part of the left-hand panel with Isaiah is in the Boijmans van Beuningen Museum in Rotterdam. The section showing a still-life belongs to the Rijksmuseum in Amsterdam but is on loan to the Louvre. This means that it is not possible to see the exterior of the wings which, when closed, show *Christ Appearing to St Mary Magdalene*. As a whole the work has posed, and still poses, many questions of identification. The triptych was apparently painted to fulfil the last wishes of a draper, Pierre Courty or Corpici, whose will is dated 9 December 1442 and who died in 1449. It would seem logical to suppose that the work was painted between these two dates. The central Annunciation scene takes place against the background of the interior of a Gothic church in a style reminiscent of, although not identical to, Flemish compositions, and more specifically those of Van Eyck or the Master of Flémalle. Tolnay has attributed the triptych to an artist close to the Master of Flémalle. While it is true that the heavy draperies, the use of gold and the still-life of flowers in a vase in the foreground are all redolent of 15th-century Flemish art, Burgundian influence is equally present, and the statues that form part of the architecture are not unlike those by Sluter at Champnol. A curious detail is the lectern that is taken from a drawing by the Limbourg brothers. If we take all these points into consideration, the most likely attribution would seem to be that of Liebreich, who concludes that the artist was Flemish and influenced by Sluter and Van Eyck. The broken folds of the draperies are reminiscent of Conrad Witz, whose work has analogies with works from the south of France. The painter of the triptych has a subtle sense of colour, and favours particularly greys and mauves, as do a number of other artists from the Provence area. Thus equally plausible is Hulin de Loo's theory that the artist was a Flemish painter who was in contact with Conrad Witz before going to work in southern France. What we can safely assume is that the Master of the Aix Annunciation had assimilated Flemish art, is likely to have encountered the work of Conrad Witz (albeit probably indirectly), came into contact with Burgundian art, and was also familiar with Provençal art. As intriguing as the work's stylistic elements are some of its iconographic aspects. Space does not permit a proper exploration of this subject, but it is worth noting one or two details. A minute figure of the Christ Child appears in the ray of light extending from God the Father to the Virgin. This motif, representing the Incarnation, can already be found in the work of the Master of Flémalle. A much stranger detail is the tiny monkey, surrounded by demonic figures, perched on the lectern standing before the Virgin. The artist must have been sufficiently confident of his protected status to allow himself such liberties, which are worthy of the inventions of King René, an art lover who is thought to have been a painter himself. It is possible that the painter of the *Annunciation* was a member of this king's entourage. If so, it would lend credence to the theory put forward in 1948 by J. Boyer that the artist was Jean Chapus, who had worked in Avignon and Aix for King René. Boyer was later to abandon this idea, however. Tracing a rather more contorted line of contacts, Lionello Venturi attributes the triptych to Colantonio, who is said to have been influenced to some extent by King René. Boyer subsequently attributed the *Annunciation* to Guillaume Dombet because of stylistic similarities between the painting and the windows, commissioned from Dombet, in the chapel of the Holy Mitre in Aix Cathedral. This suggestion gave rise to many counterproposals. In 1963, A. Chatelet declared that the artist of the triptych was Arnolet de Gatz, Dombet's son-in-law, Charles Sterling going on to prove that Arnolet died before 1442 and hence before the commission to paint the *Annunciation*. While the painting has generally been considered to be the work of a single artist, Sterling suggests that the stained glass maker must have been younger than the principal artist of the *Annunciation*, and that he painted the exterior of the wings only. His candidate is Aubry Dombet, son and collaborator of Guillaume. None of these theories can be entirely proved or disproved, leaving the way still clear for further discoveries and suggestions. The problems posed by the painting neatly demonstrate the melting pot of influences coming from Flanders, Provence, Italy and Burgundy.

Work by this artist was shown in the exhibition *Jan van Eyck et les Primitifs flamands et le Sud* (Jan van Eyck and Flemish Art and the South) held at the Groeningemuseum in Bruges in 2002.

BIBLIOGRAPHY:

Liebreich, A., *'L'Annonciation d'Aix-en-Provence'* in *Gazette des Beaux-Arts*, periodical, Paris, February 1938. Lassaigne, Jacques, *Le XVe siècle. De Van Eyck à Botticelli*, Skira, Geneva, 1955. Boyer, J., *'Le Maître d'Aix enfin identifié'* in *Connaissance des Arts* n° 72, periodical, Paris, February 1958. König, Eberhard, *Das liebentbrannte Herz: der Wiener Codex und der Maler Barthélemy d'Eyck*, Graz, 1996. Châtelet, Albert, *'Pour en finir avec Barthélemy d'Eyck'* in *Gazette des Beaux-Arts* n° 131, periodical, Paris, 1998. Nishino, Yoshiaki, *'Le Triptyque de lAnnonciation d'Aix et son programme iconographique'* in *Artibus et historiae n°39*, periodical, Irsa, Vienna, 1999. *Le Siècle de Jan van Eyck. Le monde méditerranéen et les Primitifs flamands, 1430-1530*, exhibition catalogue, Groeningemuseum, Bruges, Flammarion, Paris, 2002.

MUSEUMS AND GALLERIES:

AIX-EN-PROVENCE (Ste-Marie-Madeleine): *Annunciation* - AMSTERDAM (Rijksmus.): *Books on a Shelf* - BRUSSELS: *The Prophet Jeremiah* (right-hand panel of the 'Annunciation') - FLORENCE (Uffizi): *Portrait of Lucrezia Panciatichi* - PARIS (Louvre): *Christ on the Cross* - ROTTERDAM (Mus. Boijmans Van Beuningen): *The Prophet Isaiah* (fragment of the left-hand panel of the 'Annunciation').

EYCK, Carel van
Flemish, 18th century.

Active in Antwerp, c. 1710.
Painter.
Flemish School.

EYCK, Charles Hubertus
Dutch, 20th century.
Born 1897, in Meersen (Limburg); died 1983.
Painter. Portraits, landscapes, urban landscapes.
Murals, designs for stained glass.

During his travels, Charles Eyck recorded his impressions and exhibited a series of landscapes of the Parisian suburbs, in particular at the Salon des Tuileries in Paris in 1930, to which he was invited. His landscapes of his native Limburg and his portraits are also considered worthy of note. With his stained glass windows, Eyck contributed to the renaissance of religious art in Holland.

MUSEUMS AND GALLERIES:
MAASTRICHT (Bonnefantenmus.): *Haystack* (1928) - OTTAWA (Nat. Gal. of Canada): *The Square*.

AUCTION RECORDS:
AMSTERDAM, 28 Sept 1987, *Houses in France* (1933, oil on canvas, 31 1/2 x 38 3/4 ins / 80 x 98.5 cm) NLG 2,800. AMSTERDAM, 11 Sept 1990, *Snowy Landscape* (oil on canvas, 25 1/2 x 21 1/4 ins / 65 x 54 cm) NLG 5,175. AMSTERDAM, 10 Dec 1992, *Azalea* (1941, oil on canvas, 22 x 17 3/4 ins / 55 x 45 cm) NLG 2,875. AMSTERDAM, 27-28 May 1993, *Parisian Boulevard* (1969, oil on canvas, 39 1/4 x 43 1/4 ins / 100 x 110 cm) NLG 6,325. AMSTERDAM, 7 Dec 1994, *Parisian Boulevard* (1944, oil on canvas, 37 1/4 x 39 1/4 ins / 94.5 x 100 cm) NLG 12,650. AMSTERDAM, 30 May 1995, *Church in Clamart* (1929, oil on canvas, 23 1/2 x 28 1/4 ins / 60 x 72 cm) NLG 9,375. AMSTERDAM, 10 Dec 1996, *Landscape* (1973, oil on canvas, 32 x 35 1/2 ins / 81 x 90 cm) NLG 10,378. AMSTERDAM, 19-20 Feb 1997, *Still-life with Bottles* (oil on panel, 19 1/4 x 19 1/4 ins / 49 x 49 cm) NLG 4,612. AMSTERDAM, 29 Nov 1999, *Boulevard St Germain, Paris* (1973, oil on canvas, 27 x 31 ins / 69 x 79 cm) NLG 6,500. AMSTERDAM, 4 July 2000, *Boulevard St Germain, Paris* (1973, oil on canvas, 27 x 31 ins / 69 x 79 cm) NLG 5,800. THE HAGUE, 24 April 2002, *Two Nudes* (1933, oil on canvas, 39 x 31 ins / 99 x 80 cm) EUR 9,000. AMSTERDAM, 7 June 2004, *Tuscany* (1925, oil on canvas, 31 x 23 ins / 80 x 59 cm) EUR 18,000. MAASTRICHT, 9 Dec 2004, *Geleenstraat in Heerlen* (oil on canvas, 31 x 24 ins / 80 x 60 cm) EUR 3,000.

EYCK, Huber van
Flemish School, 15th century.
Died probably on the 18 September 1426, in Ghent.
Painter. Religious subjects.

See the entry for Jan van Eyck.

EYCK, Jacques van
Flemish, 17th century.
Born 1601, in Antwerp; died 1648.
Painter.
Flemish School.

Jacques van Eyck executed portraits and paintings illustrating mythological and Biblical scenes.

EYCK, Jan
Flemish, 17th century.
Active in Antwerp.
Painter.
Flemish School.

Jan Eyck was a pupil of Jan Blanchaert.

EYCK, Jan Karel van
Flemish, 17th century.
Baptised 12 May 1649 in Antwerp.
Painter.
Flemish School.

Jan Karel van Eyck was the brother of Nicholas II and pupil of Jan Erasmus Quellinus in 1669. After he went travelling there is no trace of his whereabouts.

EYCK, Jan van or Jean
Flemish School, 15th century.
Born c. 1390; died 9 July 1441, in Bruges.
Painter, miniaturist. Religious subjects, portraits.

Any discussion of Van Eyck is inevitably problematic, for the artist and his work have always been surrounded by controversy. Jan seems to have had a brother who was a painter and who is mentioned in one or two documents as having the name of Hubert. However, the documents concerned spell the name in several different ways and, while it has been established that Jan did indeed have a brother, his name was in fact Lambert. Hubert's existence was discovered in 1822 when Waagen had the paint covering the frame of the Ghent Altarpiece removed, revealing the famous quatrain that mentions the painter Hubert van Eyck. Since no works had hitherto come to light signed with that name, ingenious attempts were made to find some trace of them. All those works hitherto attributed to Jan van Eyck, but not signed or dated, became objects of suspicion. Even among those paintings clearly signed and dated by Jan there appeared to be reasons for doubt, since Jan appears not to have started signing his works until 1432. Returning to earlier works, he added dates, but not always correctly. As a result it is difficult both to determine which are early works by Jan and to compare them with paintings that could be attributed to Hubert. The numerous inscriptions on Van Eyck's paintings, instead of providing valuable information, have given rise to endless debate since they are incomplete, imprecise or very worn, and consequently hard to read. Interpretations have varied, therefore, sometimes lacking in objectivity as they are enrolled to support one theory or another. In an attempt to prove the existence of Hubert, scholars have also sought documentary and other types of evidence which can be briefly summarised here. A damaged tile was discovered, believed to have come from Hubert's tomb, bearing the date of his death, 1426. The inscription was subsequently shown to be a 16th-century copy, although that is not to say that it was not an accurate one. Those scholars who support the idea of Hubert's existence have generally based their arguments on somewhat flimsy evidence: in 1424 a 'meester Luberecht' supplied two sketches to the Ghent town council; in 1424 and 1426, a Lubrecht van Heycke is mentioned; in 1426, the heirs of a Hubrecht den Scildere are recorded as having paid dues to remove some inherited property. Unfortunately, these documents neither prove that they refer to the Hubert who was the brother of Jan, nor show that he was a painter. The main proof remains the quatrain on the Ghent Altarpiece mentioned above. It consists of a Latin inscription in hexameters, and is now so worn as to be almost illegible. Depending on how some of the letters are interpreted, it may read: *Hubertus... Eyck. major quo nemo repertus incepit. pondusque. Johannes arte secundus... ecit. Judoci Vijd prece fretus VersV SeXta MaI Vos CoLLacat aCta tUerI.* This would mean something like: 'Hubert, than whom none was greater, began it; Jan finished it at the request of the donor Josse Vydt and asks you by this verse on 6 May to contemplate what has been done.' The last line is a chronostich containing the date 1432. There is some doubt about the quatrain's authenticity, however. A microchemical examination carried out in 1951 revealed that the inscription is painted onto a piece of silver leaf that had been substituted for the gold leaf present everywhere else on the frame of the retable. The style of the letters of the quatrain is clumsier than the elegant lettering used by Jan elsewhere, while the use of a chronogram at this period is unusual, whereas it is quite common in the 16th century. This evidence would suggest that the inscription was repainted in the 16th century. The second debatable feature of the inscription is the qualification of Hubert as the greatest painter. If the inscription is genuine, it would seem logical that it was written by Jan and consequently, as Hulin de Loo has written, a formula expressing the modesty of a younger brother towards his elder. If someone else wrote the words, conveying the true renown of this painter, one wonders - as R. Genaille has pointed out - why, if Hubert was such a great painter, he was not chosen by the dukes John of Bavaria and Philip the Good to be their court painter rather than Jan, who was apparently less esteemed. Some scholars have concluded, in view of these contradictions, that the quatrain must be a fake. But this leads one to speculate about the possible motive for falsifying such an inscription. Some writers have suggested that it was the idea of some learned inhabitants of Ghent who, in the sixteenth century, wished for patriotic reasons to increase the fame of their town by inventing an elder and more skilled brother for Jan. The response of art historian E. Renders to this theory is to deny that Hubert ever existed. While it seems reasonable enough to espouse Panofsky's view that Hubert did exist, and that he collaborated in the painting of the Ghent Altarpiece, to do so is to initiate endless debates over which parts were painted by Hubert. This question is rendered the more difficult because the piece been restored several times. It is entirely probable that Master Hubert existed, but it is unfortunate that we have no other works by him. A number of scholars, including Durant Gréville, have re-attributed to Hubert a considerable number of paintings that were originally attributed to Jan. The quality of these works is so similar to works signed and dated by Jan that it is difficult to follow the arguments of these writers. The problem still remains, however, and particularly in the case of the Ghent Altarpiece. Other paintings that have been more convincingly attributed to Hubert include *The Three Marys at the Tomb* in the Boymans Museum, and the *Friedsam Annunciation* (New York). The first of these is generally accepted as Hubert's (by Hulin de Loo, according to Panofsky, Beenken and Baldass), while Tolnay considers it to be a copy of a painting by Hubert. The archaic character of the work, its rather confused landscape, and its clumsy perspective lead Chatelet to conclude that it is indeed by Hubert. The *Friedsam Annunciation*, attributed by Panofsky to Hubert, in the view of Beeken is a copy of a work by Petrus Christus. The composition is still miniaturist in style with a somewhat stylised notion of space. In general, those works that reveal elements of archaism in comparison with the works known to be by Jan are either attributed to Hubert or to Jan's early period. Alternatively, they are either considered to be later copies of paintings by one or other of the Van Eyck brothers or attributed to another unknown artist. It is not at all surprising that so much controversy surrounds the name of Van Eyck when we realise that the first work signed and dated by the Van Eycks is the Ghent Altarpeice, which is undoubtedly a masterpiece. There is no doubt that it must have been the product of several or many years' experience, perhaps that of Hubert, but also that of Jan. But, before 1432, no work can be attributed with any certainty to Jan.

It is known that Jan was born sometime around 1390, but there is no certainty as to where. 16th-century sources say that he was born in Maaseik, in Limburg or Gelderland. Between 1390 and 1418, he seems to have been living in Liège where he is thought to have entered the service of John of Bavaria, who was then in the city. Three documents dating between 24 October 1422 and 11 September 1424 confirm the presence of the artist in The Hague, where he was probably still working for John of Bavaria, who had moved his court there. On 19 May 1425, Jan was in Bruges in the service of Philip III, Duke of Burgundy, who had engaged him as painter and valet de chambre, granting him an annual salary of 100 *livres parisis* (pound coins struck in Paris). Such an elevated position can only be explained if Jan was already by that date well known and esteemed as the author of paintings that we now have great difficulty in identifying, but which include the panels in New York, the *Crucifixion with the Virgin and St John* (Berlin) and the *Virgin in a Church* (Berlin). But both the dating of between 1420 and 1425, and the attribution of the latter works, are generally dependent on the dating and attribution of the *Turin Hours*, about which in turn there is considerable debate. To understand the problems surrounding the *Turin Hours*, it is necessary to say something about the history of this manuscript. In 1524, Summonte mentions in a letter to M.A. Michiel the great Johannes who 'first exercised the art of illumination, or art of the miniature as we call it today'. This clue suggests that, before achieving the level of his later works, Jan had very naturally turned his hand to try a style of painting that was very widespread at that time. In 1902, P. Durrieu published a series of illuminated pages from the national library in Turin - whence the name *Turin Hours* - some of which are very reminiscent of the Eyck style. The pages were taken from a book of hours which belonged to Jean duc de Berry around 1400, and was finished at a later date. In 1904, the miniatures were destroyed in a fire. In 1911, Hulin de Loo discovered some more miniatures in Milan that had belonged to the same book - giving the name *Milan-Turin Hours* - also in some cases Eyckian in style. Scholars studying the miniatures came up with a variety of different dates and attributions. Hulin de Loo, Beeken and Winkler put their dates at 1415 and 1417, attributing them to Hubert. Dvorak, followed by Baldass and Tolnay, proposed a date some twenty years later, about 1435-1437, and Dvorak attributed them to a Dutch painter, possibly Ouwater. Panofsky sees the miniatures as early works by Jan. One of them depicts *Prayer on the Shore*. Among the horsemen in the scene is the Duke of Bavaria, although it is unclear whether it is William, who died in 1417, or John, who died in 1425 and for whom Jan van Eyck is thought to have worked in The Hague between 1422 and 1424. The inclusion of this figure makes it possible that Jan executed some of the illuminations in the *Turin Hours* at that time. These differing attributions can be explained by the difference in styles between the miniatures that are unlikely to be all by the same hand. Taking the two publications together (the Milan collection and the Turin collection), it is possible to detect, as Chatelet did, four groups of miniatures: those in an earlier pre-Eyckian style; those by one or other or both of the Van Eycks; those showing an Eyckian influence; those that are of a later date. Of the miniatures generally attributed to the Van Eycks, Chatelet attributes five to Jan and two to a Master H, a close follower of Jan. It would appear that the miniatures that can be attributed to Jan are *St Julian and St Martha Ferrying Christ over the Mouth of a River, The Prayer on the Shore, The Birth of St John* and *The Mass for the Dead*. The stylistic features supporting this argument include the confident painting of the landscape in the first two and the successful rendering of space in the last two, which are both interiors. Nevertheless, it can be said that, overall, the details are still strongly influenced by the ideals of the International Gothic style. A similar stylistic assessment can be made of the Berlin *Virgin in a Church*, the New York panels and the Berlin *Crucifixion*. This is one of the reasons why these works are linked to the *Turin Hours*, with the solution adopted for the attribution of the Hours being applied almost automatically to the three paintings.

In 1425, Jan moved from Bruges to Lille. The following year he embarked on the first of the secret missions he was to make for the Duke of Burgundy. He left for Aragon, where he was to attempt to pave the way for his master's marriage. On St Luke's Day, 18 October 1427, however, Jan was in Tournai, where he is thought to have met Robert Campin (Master of Flémalle). From this supposed meeting, Tolnay develops a tortuous argument showing how a number of pictorial innovations until then attributed to Van Eyck were in fact invented by Campin. Nevertheless, at a later date, the Master of Flémalle was ready to show his admiration for Van Eyck by introducing motifs such as the convex mirror imitated from Jan's work. In 1428, Jan was sent on a new mission to the king of Portugal to seek the hand of his daughter Isabelle for the Duke of Burgundy. He went there ostensibly to paint the princess, who was married on 7 January 1430. Unfortunately the two portraits he executed have both been lost. During the year he was in Portugal, Jan must have done some other painting, as mention is made of a *St George*, which may have been in Spain, and a *Portuguese Girl*. He returned to Bruges in 1430, was summoned to Hesdin by Duke Philip, and returned again to Bruges where he probably made the acquaintance of Cardinal Nicola Albergati, of whom there is a portrait painting (in Berlin) and a drawing. Of the two, both of which are probably by Jan, the drawing more successfully captures the vigour and truth of the man.

The polyptych entitled the *Adoration of the Mystic Lamb*, often simply known as the Ghent Altarpiece, was presented to the church of St Bavo on 6 May 1432. It was an immense work, not least in its dimensions. It consists of 20 panels that must have taken several years not only to paint but also to prepare in the earlier stages. It represents a kind of synthesis or summary with an overarching theme of the redemption of sinners through Christ's sacrifice. The main problem for a work of this kind can be a lack of unity, particularly if it combines the work of more than one artist. Here the work is remarkable for its unity. With the wings closed, we can see the most homogenous of the compositions: corresponding to the *Erythrean Sibyl* is the *Cumean Sibyl*, while the figure of *Zaccharias* corresponds to that of *Michah*, each framed by a semi-circular arch. An *Annunciation* takes up the four panels below this with the *Angel* and the *Virgin* on the outer panels. The inner two panels show a landscape viewed through the windows of a twin bay and a trompe-l'oeil still-life that already demonstrates the artist's virtuosity. Below this, two figures painted in grisaille to simulate statues depict *St John the Evangelist and St John the Baptist* standing in niches with trilobed arches. On the outer side of each are represented the *Donor and Wife* who kneel facing inwards. Despite one or two mistakes of continuity in the representation of the room where the Annunciation is taking place, the outer wings present a composition of perfect homogeneity. The modelling, the rendering of the different materials, the weight and folds of the draperies, the skill of the still-life, the details of the landscape, the realism of the portraits of the donors, the vividness of the colours alongside the grisaille, all give the viewer the impression of standing before something quite new in art. The ornamental and flat preciousness of earlier painting has been left behind, making way for volume, colour and a sense of depth. All these innovations are startlingly present in the figures of *Adam and Eve* painted on the interior face of the wings of the altarpiece. Here the realism takes on a fantastic and almost surreal appearance which is characteristic of Jan van Eyck's painting. The lower portion of the central panel of the retable is taken up with the representation of the much discussed *Adoration of the Mystic Lamb*. This is an extraordinary and theatrical scene, in which the landscape not only plays a unifying role but also defines a new and airy space that also incorporates minute details: towns, trees and flowers of every kind. It is likely that not all of the altarpiece is by the same hand. The hieratic character of the *Christ in Glory*, presented as God on the upper level of the central panel, flanked by *The Virgin and St John*, could incline one to an attribution to Hubert. More difficult to determine is the artist of the *Musical Angels*, whose costly brocade garments are so skilfully painted. One thing is certain, the lower left wing depicting the *Righteous Judges* is a copy of the original stolen in 1934. Even if the work is of more than one artist, the altarpiece as a whole has a creative force that points the way to a new understanding of painting. Despite the large size of this masterpiece of religious art, Jan van Eyck appears to have preferred painting smaller works. On 10 October 1432, he dated and signed a portrait believed to be of *Gilles Binchois* (London), adding an inscription in Greek, 'Thymoteos'. Suggestions as to the significance of this inscription have led to much debate among scholars, including Panofsky and Münzel. A finer portrait from the following year is the *Portrait of a Man*, signed by Jan and dated 21 October 1433. This work too poses a number of iconographical questions. In the view of E. Durand Gréville, the picture is a self-portrait, even though Van Eyck would have been 47 at the time but looks older in the picture. Panofsky is of the same opinion, pointing out that the subject appears to be looking towards the viewer, the result of posing in front of a mirror. Panofsky also maintains that the absence of hands is another indication of a self-portrait. These arguments seem rather flimsy, and it could be objected that the portrait of *Jan de Leeuw* similarly looks towards the viewer. The question of the identity of the *Portrait of a Man* fades into insignificance before the quality of the painting. The artist has employed all his skills to bring to life the face of this man, whose pale complexion is rendered by the use of translucent glazes. Dark and solid colours in the background, the brown cloak and the red turban allow the light-bathed features to stand out from the surface of the painting. Van Eyck seems to have painted not only the surface but also the inner life of his subject, in a way that is almost surreal. Thus we begin to understand what it is that Van Eyck has introduced into his painting: volume, intensity, light and space, all accentuated by his use of rich and saturated colours. The painting of *The Arnolfini Portrait* dates from 1434, its subject innovative in its intimacy. The couple stand together in their bedroom, seeming to promise themselves one to the other for life. Their faces show all the gravity appropriate to the solemnity of the occasion. All the elements of the scene - the calm stillness of the composition, the iconographic symbols, the choice of colours and the light that is at once diffused and intense - combine to give it a serious intensity that still manages to be full of movement. The composition is based on verticals counterbalanced by opposing obliques that mirror one another. The symbolism of the painting, with its wealth of minute details that demonstrate so well Jan's technique, has given rise to numerous studies and a variety of interpretations, some rather more far-fetched than others. Yet it is clear that nothing in this picture is there by chance, and details such as the single lighted candle burning in the chandelier in the Arnolfinis' bedroom is no decorative whim but a symbol of the faith that the couple have promised to one another. Marriage, fidelity and faith are all symbolised in the many objects carefully arranged by the artist within this interior. Many have commented on the great virtuosity with which Van Eyck has shown the scene reflected in the mirror, thereby opening up the painting to the exterior world, and revealing the presence of two other people, perhaps the witnesses (one of whom may be the artist himself), outside the frame of the composition. Van Eyck demonstrates his ability to conquer a third dimension that he so skilfully suggests here. To speak of such a creation, so perfect in its way, as realist is clearly not enough. Through his use of light to suggest volume, Jan's painting creates space, and offers a reality that is more ideal than concrete, defining a spiritual world of great depth even when treating subjects that would otherwise be genre scenes. The artist puts the viewer in touch with something that exists outside perceptible reality, particularly in his religious subjects which often take the form of scenes of intimate family life as in his many versions of the Sacra Conversazione including the *Virgin and Child with the Chancellor Rolin* and the *Madonna of Canon George van der Paele*. The dating of the first of these two paintings presents more problems. Scholars have suggested dates of 1422-1425 or 1435-1436. There is equally some disagreement about the identity of the figure kneeling before the Virgin traditionally thought to be Rolin. Whatever the case, the important thing about this work is the quality of the painting. Once again, Van Eyck has surrounded his figures with light, showing all the richness of the brocade garment worn by the chancellor and skilfully rendering the feeling of weight in the Virgin's heavy red cloak. An almost supernatural serenity reigns, accentuated by the view of a landscape extending away into infinity through the window. Everything in the picture leads to this vanishing point, which starts from the floor tiles in the room where the two figures face one another, and continues along the river that winds through the town and vanishes far away in the mountains. Jan depicts in minute detail every aspect of the architecture of the room and then of the unknown, and probably imaginary, town beyond, where tiny figures can be seen moving about its streets.

Critics and painters, and particularly the Italians, have long been fascinated by Jan van Eyck's ability to depict details with such minute care. Vasari concluded that Van Eyck had invented oil painting, a medium that allowed him to give such transparency and warmth to his colours and to paint with such precise detail. Alexandre Ziloty in his work *La découverte de Jan van Eyck et l'évolution des procédés de la peinture à l'huile* (*The Discovery of Jan van Eyck and the Development of Oil Painting*) (1947) has shown that oil paint was being used well before Van Eyck. His original discovery was how to dilute these oil colours with essential oils in order to make them less sticky and easier to use in the depiction of details. The result was, both in Jan's work and in that of other contemporaries, an outbreak of accumulated detail. By using the normal preparation for oil painting on wood panels of a white base made of plaster and animal glue, the colour of the oil paints appeared brighter, absorbing the light without diminishing it, and then reflecting it back in all its clarity and brightness. All the qualities typically found in Van Eyck's work - beauty of tone, confidence in treatment, rendering of space and transparency - can be found in his painting of 1436, the *Madonna of Canon George van der Paele*. The sumptuous brocaded garments of St Donatian, the skilfully rendered reflections on the armour worn by St George, and the faces of the saints and the canon are depicted with the hand of a master. Van Eyck had reached the peak of his powers, with full mastery of his medium. It was at this period, 1434-1436, that Jan married Margaret, whose portrait he painted in 1439. When his first son was born, the Duke of Burgundy acted as the child's godfather while Jan's salary was increased from 100 to 360 livres, despite the misgivings of the exchequer in Lille. Duke Philip also sent him off again on a secret mission. His painting, the Antwerp *St Barbara*, signed and dated 1437, had been supposed by some scholars to be unfinished since it is merely sketched in brown with a fine brush on an oak panel covered with a layer of plaster. The technique used and the very precise details of the exterior of the church visible behind the Virgin, providing such a complete example of the architecture of the 15th century, makes the work seem finished. A work that was definitely unfinished, however, was his *Virgin of the Provost van Maelbeke*, the completion of which was interrupted by his death. The colours were added at a later date. In 1441, Jan was buried in the churchyard of St Donatian. On 21 March 1442, his brother Lambert asked to be allowed to exhume Jan's body and have it buried within the church itself, his request being granted in view of the artist's fame.

Many exhibitions have been devoted to Van Eyck himself, or Van Eyck and his times. These have included *Flämische Malerei von Jan van Eyck bis Pieter Bruegel* (Flemish Painters from Van Eyck to Pieter Breugel) Kunsthistorisches Museum, Vienna, 1981; *Early Netherlandish Painting in the Metropolitan Museum of Art* Metropolitan Museum of Art, New York, 1998; *Recognising Van Eyck* Philadelphia Museum of Art, Philadelphia, 1998; *Le Siecle de Van Eyck: le monde méditerranéen et les primitifs flamands 1430-1530* (*The Age of Jan Van Eyck: the Mediterranean world of early Netherlandish painting 1430-1530*), Groeningemuseum, Bruges, 2002.

The influence of Van Eyck was considerable and many-faceted. He gave a new impetus to European painting in the 15th century, pointing the way forward. His influence varied depending on the degree of development of painting in different countries and on their differing preoccupations. Flemish painting was influenced both by the spirit and the technique characteristic of Van Eyck's work, although in the work of Rogier van der Weyden there is already a noticeable change. In France, easel painting was in its infancy and it was thanks to Van Eyck that it began to develop at this period. Spanish and German artists absorbed particularly the interior intensity and seriousness of Van Eyck's work, these elements turning towards the dramatic in Spain and towards the fantastic in Germany. The country that was most greatly affected, however, was Italy. Italian artists were fascinated by the magic of Van Eyck's technique and his ability to render reflections, minute detail and the richness and shine of costly fabrics. At this period, it was the Italians who made the journey north to Flanders to see this new style of painting, so different from their own and which they were to try to imitate, seizing on its characteristic details such as the transparent glass vases, shiny armour reflecting scenes from miniature townscapes, and many other virtuoso displays. More importantly, however, the principal lesson that was taken and developed by the Italians, and the Venetians in particular, was the use of light. Thus each nation sought out and took from Van Eyck those things that they were best able to understand and so best able to develop in their own particular ways.

BIBLIOGRAPHY:

Panofsky, Erwin, *Early Netherlandish Painting*, Harvard University Press, Cambridge (MA), 1953. Châtelet, Albert, '*Les Enluminures eyckiennes des manuscrits de Turin et de Milan-Turin*' in *Revue des Arts*, periodical, Paris, 1956-1957. Dhanens, Elisabeth, *Van Eyck: The Ghent Altarpiece*, Penguin, London, 1973. Duverger, J., '*Jan van Eyck as Court Painter*' in *Connoisseur*, vol 194, 1977. Dhanens, Elisabeth, *Hubert and Jan van Eyck*, London, 1980. Purtle, Carol J., *The Marian Paintings of Jan van Eyck*, Princeton University Press, Princeton, 1982. Dhanens, Élizabeth, *Van Eyck*, Fonds Mercator, Antwerp, c. 1990. Elkins, J., '*On the Arnolfini Portrait and the Lucca Madonna: Did Jan van Eyck have a Perspectival System?*' in *Art Bulletin*, vol 73, 1991. Harbison, Craig, *Jan van Eyck: The Play of Realism*, Reatikon, London, 1991. Bosshard, E., '*Revealing van Eyck: The Examination of the Thyssen-Bornemisza Annunciation*' in *Apollo*, vol 136, 1992. Seidel, Linda, *Jan van Eyck's Arnolfini Portrait: Stories of an Icon*, Cambridge University Press, Cambridge, 1993. Hall, J.C., *The Arnolfini Betrothal: Medieval Marriage and the Enigma of Van Eyck's Double Portrait*, University of California Press, Berkeley, 1994. Van Asperen, J.R.J., *Jan van Eyck: Two Paintings of St Francis Receiving the Stigmata*, Philadelphia Museum of Art, Philadelphia, 1997. Ainsworth, Maryan W./Christiansen, Keith, *From Van Eyck to Bruegel: early Netherlandish painting in the Metropolitan Museum of Art*, Metropolitan Museum of Art, New York, 1998. Luber, K.C., '*Patronage and Pilgrimage: Jan van Eyck, the Adornes Family, and Two Paintings of St Francis' in Portraiture*' in *Bulletin of the Philadelphia Museum of Art*, vol 111, 1998. Pächt, Otto, *Van Eyck and the Founders of Early Netherlandish Painting*,

Harvey Miller, London, 1999. Rothstein, Bret, '*Visions and Devotion in Jan van Eyck's Virgin and Child with Canon Joris van der Paele*' in *Word and Image*, vol 15, 1999. Foister, S. (ed.), *Investigating Jan van Eyck*, Brepols, Turnhout, 2001. Borchert, Till-Holger, *The Age of van Eyck: The Mediterranean World of Early Netherlandish Painting, 1430-1530*, Thames and Hudson, London, 2002. Koreny, Fritz/Pokorny, Erwin, *Early Netherlandish Drawings from Jan van Eyck to Hieronymus Bosch*, Rubenshuis, Antwerp, 2002. Vandenbroek, Paul/Depuydt-Elbaum, Livia, *Jan van Eyck, Madonna at the Fountain*, Kononklijk Museum voor Schone Kunsten, Antwerp, 2002.

MUSEUMS AND GALLERIES:

ANTWERP (Koninklijk Mus. voor Schone Kunsten): *St Barbara; Virgin by the Fountain* - BERLIN (Staatliche Mus.): *Crucifixion with Virgin and St John; Virgin in the Church; Portrait of Badouin de Lannoy* - BRUGES (Groeningemus.): *Virgin of Canon Van der Paele; Margaret van Eyck* - DRESDEN: triptych - FRANKFURT AM MAIN: *Lucca Virgin* - GHENT (St-Baafskathedraal): polyptych - LONDON (NG): *Portrait of a Man (Léal Souvenir)* (1432, oil/wood, formerly identified as 'Portrait thought to be of Gilles Binchois'); *Portrait of a Man (Self Portrait?)* (1433, oil/wood); *Portrait of Giovanni (?) Arnolfini and his Wife (The Arnolfini Portrait)* (1434, oil/wood) - LUGANO: *Thyssen Annunciation* - MELBOURNE (Nat. Gal. of Victoria): *Virign and Child; Ince Hall Virgin* - NEW YORK (Metropolitan Mus. of Art): *The Crucifixion* (c. 1430); *Annunciation; The Last Judgement* (c. 1430) - PARIS (Louvre): *Autun Virgin; Virgin of Chanceller Rolin* - PARIS (Mus. des Arts décoratifs): *Fragment of Architecture* - PHILADELPHIA (MA): *St Francis of Assisi Receiving the Stigmata* (c. 1428-1430) - ROTTERDAM (Mus. Boijmans Van Beuningen): *The Three Marys at the Tomb* - TURIN: *Book of Hours* - VIENNA (Kunsthistorisches Mus.): *Cardinal Niccolò Albergati; Portrait of Jan de Keeuw* - WARWICK (Castle): *Virgin of Provost van Maelbeke (Ypres Virgin)* - WASHINGTON DC (NGA): *The Annunciation* (c. 1434-1436, oil/canvas/panel).

AUCTION RECORDS:

PARIS, 25 June 1892, *Wing of a Triptych*, FRF 88,400. LONDON, 2 July 1958, *Christ Blessing*, GBP 2,800. LONDON, 16 March 1966, *St George Slaying the Dragon* (attibuted to Hubert van Eyck) GBP 220,000.

EYCK, Johannes van

Dutch, 17th century.
Born 1580, in Ijsselmonde; died 1660, in Antwerp.
Painter. Portraits, landscapes, still-lifes.

Johannes van Eyck was born in Holland and travelled though Europe, spending a prolonged period in Rome. Focusing initially on still-lifes, it was only later that he turned to landscapes and portraits.

AUCTION RECORDS:

AMSTERDAM, 20 June 1989, *Vanitas with Books, a Violin Resting on a Skull, a Pistol and Other Objects on a Cloth-covered Entablature* (oil on panel, 27 1/4 x 39 3/4 ins / 69.3 x 101 cm) NLG 36,800.

EYCK, Kasper or Caspar van or Gaspar

Flemish, 17th century.
Baptised 6 February 1613 in Antwerp; died 1673, in Brussels.
Painter. Religious subjects, genre scenes, seascapes.
Flemish School.

Kasper van Eyck was the brother of Nicholas I and a pupil of van Eertveld in 1625. In 1633 he was a master in Antwerp, but after the death of his parents in 1656 he led such a dissolute life that he was placed under the guardianship of his brother, the priest Hendrik van der Eyck.

MUSEUMS AND GALLERIES:

LA FÈRE: *Seascape* - MADRID (Prado): *Galleys and Vessels before a Castle; Sea Battle between Christians and Turks; Frigates on High Seas.*

AUCTION RECORDS:

LONDON, 28 March 1923, *The Madonna and the Saviour, with Two Angels Holding a Crown above Them*, GBP 152. NEW YORK, 7 April 1989, *Scene with a Horse at the Farrier's surrounded by Figures before a House* (oil on canvas, 15 1/2 x 18 ins / 39.5 x 45.5 cm) USD 7,150. LONDON, 17 April 1996, *Sea Battle in the Mediterranean* (oil on canvas, 43 1/2 x 59 1/4 ins / 110.2 x 150.6 cm) GBP 8,280. AMSTERDAM, 11 Nov 1997, *Sea Battle between Turks and Christians* (oil on canvas/panel, a pair, 26 3/4 x 34 ins / 67.8 x 85.5 cm and 27 x 33 1/2 ins/68.4 x 85.4 cm) NLG 9,225. NEW YORK, 14 Oct 1999, *Ships in Calm Sea* (oil on panel, 15 x 28 ins / 37 x 71 cm) USD 9,500. LONDON, 9 July 2002, *Sea Battle between Moors and Christians* (oil on canvas, 43 x 59 ins / 110 x 151 cm) GBP 16,000.

EYCK, Lambert van

Flemish School, 15th century.
Painter.

Lambert was the brother of Hubert and Jan van Eyck. According to a document of 1430-1431, he too was a painter although this has been disputed. It was he who had his brother Jan's body moved from the cemetery of St Donatian into the church itself.

EYCK, Mathias van der

Dutch, 18th century.
Born c. 1710. Active in Leiden.
Painter. Portraits.

Mathias van der Eyck is documented in Leiden in 1737 and was a member of the guild there. The Stedelijk Museum De Lakenhal holds a group of sculptures by him entitled *Paul de Rieu, his Wife and their Three Children.*

EYCK, Nicolaas van I

Flemish, 17th century.
Baptised 9 February 1617 in Antwerp; died 1679, in Antwerp.
Painter. Figure compositions, portraits.
Flemish School.

Nicolaas van Eyck I was a pupil of Theodore Rombouts in 1633. He married Dymphana Heyman on 15 November 1643, was captain of the guard on 20 December 1658, and taught Michel Mylaer in 1641 and Peter Hofman in 1656. His sons Nicolaas and Carel were also painters. His repertoire consisted mostly of scenes from military life.

MUSEUMS AND GALLERIES:

ANTWERP (Town Hall): *Inspection of the Garrison* - LILLE: *Portrait of a Horseman* - MECHELEN: two paintings depicting the capture of Mechelen - NAPLES: *Peasant Dance* - TURIN: *Soldiers Crossing a River* - VIENNA: *Soldiers in a Village.*

AUCTION RECORDS:

PARIS, 1932, *Battle Scene*, FRF 800. VIENNA, 17 March 1964, *Battle of Calloo in 1638*, ATS 30,000.

EYCK, Nicolaas van II

Flemish, 17th century.
Born 5 April 1646, in Antwerp; died April 1692, in Antwerp.
Painter.
Flemish School.

Nicolaas van Eyck II was a pupil of his father Nicolaas van Eyck I. He was a captain of the guard in 1669, a master in Antwerp in 1671, and married Catharina van Essen on 5 June 1672.

EYCKELBEEK, Nicasius Jansz. van

Dutch, 17th century.
Active in Utrecht.
Sculptor.

EYCKEN, Alphonse van der

Belgian, 19th century.

Born in Brussels.

Painter. Genre scenes.

MUSEUMS AND GALLERIES:

DOUAI: *Hunters at Rest*.

EYCKEN, Charles van den or der, the Elder

Belgian, 19th century.

Born 1809, in Aerschoten or Alost; died 1891, in Louvain.

Painter. Genre scenes, landscapes.

Charles van den Eycken the Elder was the son of the decorative painter Frans van den (or der) Eycken. He studied initially in Holland and thereafter at the academy in Louvain. He travelled to Germany, Holland and the Ardennes, settling definitively in Louvain, where he executed a few oil paintings on which Charles Verboeckhoven intermittently collaborated.

He concentrated on winter landscapes with pronounced effects of shadow and light.

Ch. Van den Eycken

MUSEUMS AND GALLERIES:

KALININGRAD: *Winter Landscape*.

AUCTION RECORDS:

LONDON, 20 Oct 1978, *Wooded Landscape with Cascade* (oil on canvas, 17 x 14 1/4 ins / 43 x 36 cm) GBP 1,200. LONDON, 20 June 1979, *Cart Pulled by Dogs* (oil on panel, 10 x 13 1/4 ins / 25.5 x 33.5 cm) GBP 900. COLOGNE, 21 May 1981, *The Joys of Skating* (oil on panel, 13 1/2 x 18 1/4 ins / 34.5 x 46.5 cm) DEM 18,000. BRUSSELS, 15 Dec 1983, *Winter Landscape with Skaters* (1840, wood, 15 x 18 1/2 ins / 38 x 47 cm) BEF 260,000. NEW YORK, 28 Oct 1987, *Kittens Playing* (oil on canvas, 21 1/2 x 26 1/4 ins / 54.3 x 66.7 cm) USD 17,000. PARIS, 10 April 1989, *History of Bone* (1882, oil on canvas, 23 1/2 x 31 1/2 ins / 60 x 80 cm) FRF 24,000. BRUSSELS, 27 March 1990, *Romantic Scene in a Landscape* (1835, oil on panel, 15 x 19 ins / 38 x 48 cm) BEF 60,000. NEW YORK, 30 Oct 1992, *On the Farm Path* (1847, oil on panel, 17 x 23 1/4 ins / 42.9 x 59 cm) USD 8,800. AMSTERDAM, 16 April 1996, *Figures with Livestock on Wooded Track* (oil on panel, 13 1/4 x 19 ins / 33.5 x 48 cm) NLG 8,260. COLOGNE, 15 May 1999, *Winter Landscape* (1850, oil on panel, 11 x 15 ins / 27 x 37 cm) DEM 17,000. ANTWERP, 22 May 2000, *Interior with Two Dogs and a Cat* (1890, oil on panel, 15 x 18 ins / 37 x 46 cm) BEF 80,000. CLEVEDON, 7 Sept 2000, *Winter Landscape with Cottages, Figures and Animals* (oil on panel, 12 x 15 ins / 30 x 38 cm) GBP 4,900. AMSTERDAM, 29 April 2003, *Winter Fun in a Hilly Forest Landscape* (1840, oil on canvas, 16 x 19 ins / 41 x 48 cm) EUR 5,000. BRUSSELS, 10 Nov 2003, *Kittens Playing* (oil on panel, 14 x 11 ins / 35 x 27 cm) EUR 3,200.

EYCKEN, Charles van den or der, the Younger, pseudonym: Duchêne, Charles

Belgian, 19th - 20th century.

Born 1859, in Brussels; died 1923.

Painter. Portraits, genre scenes, animals.

Charles van den Eycken studied with his father, Charles the Elder, and at the Académie Royale in Brussels, then at the academy in Louvain. He was a member of the L'Essor (Development) group. He also featured at the Salon des Artistes Français in Paris, and received an honourable mention in 1895.

He specialised entirely in genre scenes, in which dogs are the protagonists of various episodes. He sometimes signed his works *Charles Duchêne*.

AUCTION RECORDS:

NEW YORK, 28 May 1981, *Cat and Kittens* (1892, oil on canvas, 26 1/4 x 21 1/2 ins / 66.5 x 54.5 cm) USD 5,000. NEW YORK, 25 Feb 1988, *Milkman's Cart* (1888, oil on panel, 10 3/4 x 13 3/4 ins / 27.3 x 34.9 cm) USD 3,300. NEW YORK, 25 Oct 1989, *Two Against One* (oil on canvas, 26 x 21 1/2 ins / 66 x 54.6 cm) USD 9,900. NEW YORK, 28 Feb 1990, *Family Portrait* (1890, oil on canvas, 13 1/2 x 18 ins / 34.3 x 45.7 cm) USD 14,300. NEW YORK, 1 March 1990, *Companions in Play* (1892, oil on canvas, 25 x 38 ins / 63.5 x 96.5 cm) USD 52,800. COLOGNE, 29 June 1990, *Two Dogs and some Tools in a Cart* (oil on wood, 7 1/4 x 9 3/4 ins / 18.5 x 25 cm) DEM 2,500. LONDON, 15 Jan 1991, *Kittens Playing with a Workbasket* (1905, oil on canvas, 14 x 17 3/4 ins / 34.7 x 45.2 cm) GBP 4,840. LONDON, 16 July 1991, *Circus Dogs* (1890, oil on canvas, 17 x 18 ins / 43.3 x 45.7 cm) GBP 6,600. AMSTERDAM, 5-6 Nov 1991, *Dogs' Bowl* (1886, oil on canvas, 14 1/2 x 21 ins / 37 x 53.5 cm) NLG 4,830. NEW YORK, 19 Feb 1992, *Intruder* (1904, oil on canvas, 26 3/4 x 39 1/2 ins / 67.9 x 100.3 cm) USD 9,350. NEW YORK, 27 May 1992, *Kittens in the Sewing Basket* (1909, oil on canvas, 13 3/4 x 18 ins / 35 x 45.7 cm) USD 9,900. AMSTERDAM, 9 Nov 1993, *Dog-Cart* (1879, oil on canvas, 17 1/2 x 12 3/4 ins / 44.5 x 32.5 cm) NLG 4,140. STOCKHOLM, 30 Nov 1993, *Two Dogs Stealing Cake from a Table* (1881, oil on canvas, 24 x 33 3/4 ins / 61 x 86 cm) SEK 82,000. LOKEREN, 8 Oct 1994, *Dog-Cart* (1880, oil on panel, 11 x 9 ins / 28 x 22 cm) BEF 95,000. LOKEREN, 11 March 1995, *Oh! What Women Cost!* (oil on panel, 9 1/2 x 7 ins / 24 x 17.5 cm) BEF 65,000. LONDON, 11 April 1995, *Idiocies* (1905, oil on canvas, 13 x 17 1/4 ins / 33 x 44 cm) GBP 5,175. AMSTERDAM, 7 Nov 1995, *Dogs* (1875, oil on panel, 7 x 9 3/4 ins / 17.5 x 25 cm) NLG 4,720. AMSTERDAM, 27 Oct 1997, *In the Boudoir* (oil on canvas, 31 x 23 1/4 ins / 79 x 59 cm) NLG 42,480. LONDON, 18 Dec 1997, *Torn Canvas* (1892, oil on canvas, 26 x 21 1/4 ins / 66 x 54 cm) GBP 5,750. NEW YORK, 10 Feb 1998, *Kittens Playing* (1907, oil on canvas, 13 1/2 x 18 ins / 34.2 x 45.8 cm) USD 11,500.

EYCKEN, Frans van den or der

Belgian, 18th - 19th century.

Painter, decorative artist. Murals.

Frans van den Eycken was the father and master of Charles van den Eycken the Elder. He was a decorative painter in the Louvain region.

EYCKEN, Henri van der

Flemish School, 15th century.

Active in Louvain in the middle of the 15th century.

Sculptor.

Henri van der Eycken worked from drawings by Hubert Stuerbouts.

EYCKEN, Jan van den. See **EGAS Anequin de**

EYCKEN, Jean Baptiste van

Belgian, 19th century.

Born 16 September 1809, in Brussels; died 19 December 1853.

Painter. History painting, genre scenes.

Jean Baptiste van Eycken was taught by Navez. A poet, he travelled to France, Switzerland, Italy and Germany. His wife Julie Anne Marie Noël, born on 19 August 1812, was a painter. An artist with the same name died in Brussels in 1861.

MUSEUMS AND GALLERIES:

AMSTERDAM: *To Make a Master out of Him* - BRUSSELS: *The Parmesan Surprised in his Workshop by the Soldiers of Charles the Fifth of Spain*; *Descent from the Cross* - LIÈGE: *Christ at the Tomb*.

AUCTION RECORDS:
LONDON, 13 June 1910, *Pigeon; Poultry* (two pendants) GBP 1. LONDON, 24 March 1982, *Peasants by a River* (oil on panel, 14¼ x 12¼ ins / 36 x 31 cm) GBP 800. COLOGNE, 29 June 1990, *Woman Giving Two Vagabonds a Drink* (oil on canvas, 14½ x 12½ ins / 37 x 32 cm) DEM 4,500. AMSTERDAM, 18 June 1996, *Family Drinking Coffee in an Interior* (oil on panel, 21 x 18 ins / 52.5 x 46 cm) NLG 1,955. ANTWERP, 21 June 1999, *Beautiful Venetian Lady* (1848, oil on canvas, 48 x 40 ins / 122 x 101 cm) BEF 400,000. ANTWERP, 22 May 2000, *The Pretty Venetian Lady* (oil on canvas, 48 x 40 ins / 122 x 101 cm) BEF 340,000. BRUSSELS, 5 Nov 2001, *Family Gathered round the Table* (oil on panel, 19 x 23 ins / 49 x 58 cm) BEF 150,000. ANTWERP, 28 May 2002, *Mother and Two Children* (1848, oil on canvas, oval, 43 x 49 ins / 108 x 124 cm) EUR 5,500.

EYCKEN, Julie Anne Marie van
Maiden name: Noël
Belgian, 19th century.
Born 1812.
Active in Brussels.
Painter. History painting.
Julie Anne Marie van Eycken was the wife of Jean Baptiste van Eycken.

EYCKEN, Robert Van der.
See **VANDEREYCKEN Robert**

EYCKENS. See also **IJKENS**

EYCKENS, Jakob
Flemish, 17th century.
Sculptor.
Flemish School.
Jakob Eyckens was a master in Antwerp in 1607.

EYCKENS, Karel, or Ykens
Flemish, 18th century.
Born 1719, in Brussels; died 1 May 1753.
Painter. History painting.
Flemish School.
Karel Eyckens was a pupil of Pieter Snayers and a master in Antwerp in 1745. He worked at the convent in Beggnerden.

EYCKENS, Pieter Abrahamsz. See **YKENS**

EYCKENWACK, Gérard Claesz.
Dutch, 16th century.
Died 13 February 1557, in Haarlem.
Sculptor.

EYCKERMANS, Lode
Belgian, 20th century.
Born 1919, in Antwerp.
Sculptor.
Eyckermans was a student at the higher institute in Antwerp. He became director of the academy in Mechelen. He received several prizes, including from the town of Antwerp in 1936 and from Rome in 1944. He made monuments in Wilrijk, Willebroek, Mechelen and Barvaux, as well as outside Belgium - in Bonn, Vienna, Helsinki, Milan, Zagreb and Denver.
AUCTION RECORDS:
LOKEREN, 28 May 1988, *Torso* (1972, bronze, h. 46½ ins / 118 cm) BEF 260,000.

EYCKMANS, Johannes
Flemish, 18th - 19th century.
Born 1749, in Breda; died 1815, in Antwerp.
Sculptor.
Flemish School.
Johannes Eyckmans was a pupil of Walter Pompe. He executed genre sculptures and illustrated religious subjects.

EYDEN, Jeremias van der
Flemish, 17th century.
Born in Brussels; died 1697, in England.
Painter.
Flemish School.
Jeremias van der Eyden was a pupil of Hannerman and subsequently collaborated with Sir Peter Lely on a series of portraits. He also worked for Count Rutland, Count Gainsbourough and Lord Sherard.

EYDOUX, Denis Charles
French, 20th century.
Born in Carpentras.
Engraver.
Denis Charles Eydoux exhibited in Paris at the Salon des Artistes Français from 1930.

EYDOUX, Leone
Italian, 19th century.
Active in Turin.
Painter. Historical scenes, genre scenes.
Eydoux was a pupil at the Accademia in Turin in 1853.

EYENBERGER, J. G.
French, 19th century.
Painter. Genre scenes.
MUSEUMS AND GALLERIES:
BORDEAUX: *After Lunch.*

EYERSCHÖTTEL, Johann Christof
German, 17th - 18th century.
Born 1674; died c. 1732.
Active in Husum.
Painter.
The son of Johann Eyerschöttel, Johann Christof Eyerschöttel created an altar painting for Kœting Church in 1712.

EYERWERYEN, Alexander van
Flemish, 17th century.
Active in Antwerp, c. 1622.
Painter.
Flemish School.

EYFFLENDER, Hans
German, 15th - 16th century.
Active in Leipzig.
Painter, sculptor (wood).
Dresden School.
In 1517, Eyfflender came to Dresden and worked there for a number of different churches. He is probably the same person as the Dresden painter *Meister Hans dem Maler* (Master Hans the Painter).

EYGELSHOVEN, Léon
Belgian, 20th century.
Born 11 April 1882; died 5 June 1967.
Painter.

EYGEN, Kaspar
Austrian, 18th century.
Born to a family originally from Brixen (now Bressanone, Italy).
Sculptor.
Eygen initially worked in Eichstädt (Brandenburg), Germany, before moving to Brussels.

EYK, Abraham van der
Dutch, 17th - 18th century.
Active in Leiden between 1709 and 1725.
Painter. Portraits, genre scenes.
Abraham van der Eyk was a pupil of Minje and an imitator of Willem von Mieris. The Meerman museum in The Hague holds a painting by him.
AUCTION RECORDS:
PARIS, 13 June 1997, *Portrait of a Man in Armour* (oak panel, 14¼ x 11½ ins / 36 x 29 cm) FRF 50,000.

EYK, Jan van
Dutch, 20th century.
Born 1927, in Helmond (Brabant).
Painter.
In 1960, Jan van Eyk took part in an exhibition of Dutch art in Charleroi. He has exhibited in various Dutch museums, in particular in Eindhoven in 1964. His abstract painting is close to what is known as *nuagisme* (from 'nuage' meaning 'cloud'), with strokes that sweep across the canvas to trace broad volutes resembling those of a cloudy sky.

EYKE, Margaret van
Flemish School, 15th century.
Miniaturist.
Perhaps the sister of the Van Eycks, this artist did not marry, becoming instead a nun. None of the works attributed to her are entirely certain and some scholars have doubted that she even existed. Some think she may have been the wife of Jan van Eyck.
MUSEUMS AND GALLERIES:
LILLE: *Holy Family* (attributed).

EYKELENBERG, Symon, or Eikelenberg
Dutch, 17th - 18th century.
Born 1663, in Alkmaar; died 23 November 1738.
Painter. Landscapes.
Symon Eykelenberg was an antiquarian and belonged to the guild in Alkmaar in 1702.

EYKEN, Carel
Flemish, 17th century.
Active c. 1692.
Painter. Religious subjects.
Flemish School.
MUSEUMS AND GALLERIES:
WROCLAW: *The Holy Family*.

EYKEN, Jan van
Flemish, 19th century.
Active c. 1842.
Painter. History painting.
Flemish School.
Jan van Eyken is cited by Siret.

EYKEN, Moritz van
German, 19th century.
Born 25 October 1865, in Elberfeld.
Painter, engraver.
Van Eyken studied at the academy of art in Berlin and went on to paint portraits, landscapes and paintings inspired by biblical scenes.

EYKENS, Pierre, the Elder
Flemish, 17th century.
Born 1599, in Antwerp; died 1649, in Mechelen.
Painter. History painting.
Flemish School.
Pierre Eykens the Elder was director of the academy in Antwerp in 1649.
MUSEUMS AND GALLERIES:
ORLÉANS: mythological subject.

EYLE VAN LÜBBEKE
German, 16th century.
Active in Lüneburg (Lower Saxony) in 1502.
Painter.

EYLENBERGER, Marten
German, 16th century.
Active in Breslau (now Wroclaw, Poland) in 1519.
Sculptor (wood).

EYLES, B.
British, 19th century.
Active c. 1850.
Engraver.
B. Eyles executed engraved portraits.

EYLES, Charles
British, 19th century.
Active in London.
Painter. Landscapes.
Charles Eyles exhibited at the Royal Academy from 1883 to 1899.

EYMAEL
Dutch, 19th century.
Active towards the middle of the 19th century.
Lithographer.
His portraits of officers are mentioned.

EYMAR, Joseph
French, 19th century.
Active in Paris at the beginning of the 19th century.
Engraver.
Joseph Eymar exhibited a series of vignettes after Devéria at the 1822 Salon.

EYMAR, Louis Charles
French, 20th century.
Born 1882, in Montpellier; died 1944, in Montpellier.
Painter (including wash), watercolourist.
Louis Charles Eymar, who worked as a court clerk, painted watercolours of young girls and landscapes. There are works by him in the museums of Sète and Montpellier.

EYMARD, Édouard
French, 20th century.
Born 25 May 1924, in Montbrison.
Painter.
Édouard Eymard studied initially at the École des Beaux-Arts, St-Étienne, and then in the MacAvoy studio at the Grande Chaumière, Paris. He exhibits mainly in the Lyons area, where he lives, and from 1958 to 1964 showed at the Salon Comparaisons. He also exhibits at the Salon du Sud-Est. His painting is abstract, but nevertheless evokes imaginary landscapes. In addition to his painting he has an interest in murals, and has worked using enamel on steel.
MUSEUMS AND GALLERIES:
ÉPINAL (Musée départemental d'Art ancien et contemporain): *Where the Winds Meet* (1958).

EYMARD DE LANCHATRE. See **DAVID DE MAYRÉNA**

EYMER, Anton Julius Christoph
German, 20th century.
Born 29 April 1884, in Frankfurt am Main.
Painter. Landscapes.
Anton Eymer was a student of J. Becker.
AUCTION RECORDS:
AMSTERDAM, 20 Oct 1981, *View of a Dutch Town* (oil on panel, 14 1/2 x 18 1/2 ins / 37 x 46.7 cm) NLG 4,400.

EYMER, Arnoldus Johannes, or Eijmer
Dutch, 19th century.
Born 17 June 1803, in Amsterdam; died 21 January 1863, in Haarlem.
Painter. Landscapes with figures, landscapes.
The museum in Haarlem holds five paintings by Arnoldus Johannes Eymer, who travelled in Germany.
MUSEUMS AND GALLERIES:
HAARLEM.
AUCTION RECORDS:
AMSTERDAM, 15 Nov 1976, *River Landscape* (1850, oil on canvas, 25 x 34 ins / 63.5 x 85.5 cm) NLG 15,000. NEW YORK, 29 May 1981, *Town by a River* (oil on panel, 12 3/4 x 17 1/4 ins / 32.5 x 43.8 cm) USD 3,200. AMSTERDAM, 15 May 1984, *Landscape* (1832, oil on canvas, 35 1/4 x 43 ins / 89.5 x 109 cm) NLG 5,000. AMSTERDAM, 25 April 1990, *Wooded Summer Land-*

scape with People Gathering Firewood (1838, oil on canvas, 24 3/4 x 30 3/4 ins / 63 x 78 cm) NLG 6,900. AMSTERDAM, 2 May 1990, *Wooded Landscape with Fishermen near a Watermill and a Peasant Woman and Child on the Path* (oil on canvas, 25 1/2 x 35 ins / 65 x 88 cm) NLG 10,925. AMSTERDAM, 6 Nov 1990, *Winter Landscape with Boats Moored and Figures with a Sledge on the Ice* (1850, oil on canvas, 24 3/4 x 33 ins / 63 x 84 cm) NLG 32,200. AMSTERDAM, 20 April 1993, *Large Gathering at the Restaurant 'Kraantje Lek'* (1840, oil on canvas, 11 1/2 ins / 29.39.5 cm) NLG 10,350. MUNICH, 4 Dec 2002, *View of a Canal with Train Bridge* (oil on panel, 10 x 13 ins / 26 x 33 cm) EUR 3,000. AMSTERDAM, 21 April 2004, *River Spaarne, Haarlem in the Distance* (1849, oil on panel, 17 x 24 ins / 44 x 60 cm) EUR 6,000.

EYMERLING, Entres
German, 16th century.
Active in Würzburg (Bavaria) c. 1554.
Painter.

EYMIEU, Léon Bernard
French, 19th - 20th century.
Born in Saillans.
Painter. Landscapes.
Léon Bernard Eymieu, a pupil of Sauvageot and Roullet, exhibited landscapes at the Salon de Paris from 1870 to 1906.
AUCTION RECORDS:
COPENHAGEN, 12 April 1983, *Seashore* (1882, oil on canvas, 18 x 14 1/2 ins / 46 x 37 cm) DKK 10,000.

EYMONNET, Jean
French, 19th century.
Born 11 October 1815, in Commette.
Painter. Religious subjects, genre scenes, portraits.
Jean Eymonnet was a pupil of Bonnefond at the École des Beaux-Arts in Lyons. He exhibited portraits and some genre paintings, including *A Budding Artist* (1866, Lyons) and *Little Girl at the Fountain* (1868, Lyons) in Paris and London.
AUCTION RECORDS:
PARIS, 20 Nov 1942, *Woman Playing the Harp*, FRF 2,600. PARIS, 26 Nov 1992, *Four Sisters* (oil on canvas, 32 x 25 1/2 ins / 81.5 x 65 cm) FRF 3,500. PARIS, 25 June 1993, *St Cecilia* (oil on canvas, 22 x 18 ins / 55 x 46 cm) FRF 3,800.

EYNARD, Henry André
French, 20th century.
Born 1904, in Paris.
Engraver.
Henry André Eynard, a pupil of Cormon and P. Laurens, exhibited in Paris at the Salon d'Automne and the Salon des Artistes Français in 1931.

EYNARD, Louis
French, 20th century.
Born 1881, in Lyons; died 1941.
Painter, draughtsman. Interiors, local scenes.
Louis Eynard was a pupil at the École des Beaux-Arts, Lyons. He exhibited mainly at the various Salons de Peinture of the Société Lyonnaise des Beaux-Arts, Lyons, from 1919 to 1935. He won a medal in 1920, and some of his works were acquired by the Municipality of Lyons in 1919.
MUSEUMS AND GALLERIES:
LYONS (MBA).

EYNARD CHATELAIN, Charles
Swiss, 19th century.
Born 1807, in Geneva; died 1876.
Painter.
The son of Suzanne Elisabeth Eynard Châtelain, Charles Eynard Châtelain completed several portraits.

EYNARD CHATELAIN, Suzanne Elisabeth
Swiss, 19th century.
Born 1775, in Amsterdam; died 24 March 1844, in Geneva.
Painter. Religious subjects, landscapes.
Suzanne Eynard Châtelain was a pupil of La Rives and Vanières, and the mother of Charles Eynard Châtelain.

EYNARD LULLIN, Anne Charlotte Adélaide
Swiss, 19th century.
Born 26 May 1793, in Geneva; died 30 October 1868, in Geneva.
Sculptor.
Eynard Lullin created several busts.

EYNARD-MERCIER, Marguerite
French, 20th century.
Born 10 June 1876, in Dormans (Marne); died 4 November 1955, in Toulon.
Painter.
Marguerite Eynard-Mercier, a pupil of Courtois, first exhibited in Paris at the Salon des Artistes Français in 1914. She was given an honourable mention.

EYNDE, Augustus Josephus Antonius van den
Flemish, 19th century.
Born 8 October 1822, in Mechelen; died 20 April 1861, in Mechelen.
Draughtsman, lithographer.
Flemish School.
Augustus van den Eynde was a pupil of Goetgebuer in Ghent, and subsequently became a professor at the institute of art in Mechelen.

EYNDE, Hubrecht van den
Flemish, 17th century.
Died 1661, in Antwerp.
Sculptor.
Flemish School.
Hubrecht van den Eynde was the father of Norbert and Sebastian van den Eynde. In 1629 he was commissioned to execute a marble altar for the church of Notre Dame in Termonde. He also worked for various churches in Antwerp.

EYNDE, Jan van den
Flemish School, 16th century.
Active in Mechelen.
Glass painter.
In 1590, Jan van den Eynde made a window depicting Philip II for the church of St-Jean in Mechelen. A painter of the same name was executed in Mechelen on 6 August 1568.

EYNDE, Jan van den
Flemish, 18th century.
Active in Antwerp, at the beginning of the 18th century.
Illuminator.
Flemish School.

EYNDE, Norbert van den I
Flemish, 17th century.
Active in the second half of the 17th century.
Sculptor.
Flemish School.
The son of Hubrecht van den Eynde, Norbert van den Eynde I worked for the chapel of St George and the church of St Nicholas in Antwerp.

EYNDE, Norbert van den II
Flemish, 17th century.
Active in Antwerp, during the second half of the 17th century.
Sculptor.
Flemish School.

EYNDE, Petrus van den
Dutch, 19th century.

Died 1849.
Active in Haarlem.
Draughtsman, lithographer.
Twelve lithograph portraits by Petrus van den Eynde are known.

EYNDE, Pieter van den
German, 16th century.
Active in Middelburg.
Painter.
It is known that Pieter van den Eynde sold a *View of Middelburg* in 1533.

EYNDE, Sebastian van den
Flemish, 17th century.
Active in Antwerp.
Sculptor.
Flemish School.
Sebastian van den Eynde was the son of Hubrecht van den Eynde.

EYNDE, Steven van
Flemish School, 16th century.
Active in Antwerp in 1560.
Painter.

EYNDEN, Frans van
Dutch, 18th century.
Born 1694, in Nijmegen; died 1742.
Painter. Landscapes.
Frans van Eynden was the uncle of Jacobus the Younger and a pupil of Bomborgh and Elias in Nijmegen. He assisted his master with paintings for the fireplaces and ceilings of apartments in Rotterdam. He also wrote a book on glass painting.
AUCTION RECORDS:
LONDON, 12 May 1910, *Adonis and his Dogs,* GBP 1.

EYNDEN, Hubertus van den
Flemish, 17th century.
Died 1661, in Antwerp.
Sculptor.
Flemish School.
Having become a master in 1620, Hubertus van den Eynden executed the high altar of the church in Dendermonde. He worked for the Infanta Isabelle-Claire-Eugénie, the Duke of Arenberg and for Rubens. His *St Gideon* (Antwerp cathedral) and *Marble Altar of the St Magdalene Chapel* (church of St James, Antwerp) are cited.

EYNDEN, Jacobus van, the Elder
Dutch, 18th century.
Painter.
Jacobus van Eynden the Elder was the father and master of Jacobus the Younger in Nijmegen.

EYNDEN, Jacobus van or Jacob, the Younger
Dutch, 18th - 19th century.
Born 23 December 1733, in Nijmegen; died 1824, in Nijmegen.
Painter, watercolourist. Landscapes, still-lifes, animals.
AUCTION RECORDS:
AMSTERDAM, 14 Nov 1983, *Branch of a Plum Tree* (watercolour and gouache/black chalk outline, 14 3/4 x 11 ins / 37.6 x 27 cm) NLG 6,500.

EYNDEN, Jan van den
Flemish, 17th century.
Active c. 1626.
Painter. History painting.
Flemish School.
Siret cites a mural by Jan van den Eynden in the church of Notre Dame in St Trond, a *Last Judgement* signed *Joes van der Eynden.*

EYNDEN, Pieter Tielmansz. van
Dutch, 17th century.
Active in Vlaerdingen c. 1617.
Painter.

EYNDEN, Roeland van
Dutch, 18th - 19th century.
Born 1747, in Nijmegen; died 28 August 1819, in Dordrecht.
Painter, draughtsman, engraver.
Roeland van Eynden was the brother of Jacobus van Eynden. He was also a biographer of art.

EYNGBERT
Dutch, 16th century.
Active in Gouda in 1552.
Painter.

EYNHOUDTS, Remoldus or Rombout
Flemish, 17th century.
Born 1 October 1613, in Antwerp or in Mechelen; died 1679 or 1680.
Painter, engraver.
Flemish School.
A pupil of Adam van Noort, Remoldus Eynhoudts worked in Rubens' workshop and became a master in Antwerp in 1636.

EYRAUD, Marguerite
French, 20th century.
Born in Paris.
Painter.
From 1920 Marguerite Eyraud exhibited landscapes and flower paintings at the Salon d'Automne, Paris.

EYRE, Edward
British, 18th century.
Painter, watercolourist. Genre scenes, landscapes.
Edward Eyre exhibited 15 times at the Royal Academy in London from 1771 to 1786.
AUCTION RECORDS:
LONDON, 18 June 1980, *Wild Boar Fair* (watercolour, pencil and pen, 14 1/4 x 20 1/4 ins / 36.5 x 51.5 cm) GBP 380.

EYRE, Ivan
Canadian, 20th century.
Born 1935, in Saskatoon.
Painter. Interiors, landscapes, still-lifes, figures.
Ivan Eyre studied at the Saskatoon Technical Collegiate under Ernest Linder, at the University of Saskatchewan under Eli Bornstein (1952), and at the University of Manitoba School of Art, obtaining a BFA in 1957. From 1958 to 1959, he taught at University of North Dakota in Grand Forks, and from 1959 to 1993 he taught painting and drawing at University of Manitoba.

Eyre has exhibited his work regularly in group and solo shows in Canada since 1962 and at the Canadian Cultural Center, Paris, in 1982. The Winnipeg Art Gallery held a retrospective in 2005.
MUSEUMS AND GALLERIES:
OTTAWA (Nat. Gal. of Canada).

EYRE, James
British, 19th century.
Born 1807, in Ashbourne; died 1838, in Derby.
Painter, watercolourist. Landscapes.
James Eyre trained under Creswick and De Wint.

EYRE, John
British, 19th - 20th century.
Died 1927.
Painter, watercolourist. Religious subjects, genre scenes.
John Eyre exhibited eight times at the Royal Academy in London between 1877 and 1893.

AUCTION RECORDS:
LONDON, 9 May 1984, *Chelsea Pensioners* (watercolour heightened with white, 10 x 14 1/4 ins / 25.3 x 36 cm) GBP 650. LONDON, 17 Nov 1999, *Dymchurch on Romney Marshes* (watercolour, 12 x 36 ins / 30 x 91 cm) GBP 1,700.

EYRE, Louisa
American, 19th - 20th century.
Born 16 January 1872; died 1953.
Painter.
Louisa Eyre, a pupil of Augustus St-Gaudens, lived in Philadelphia.

EYRE, Wilson
American, 19th - 20th century.
Active in Philadelphia.
Painter.
Wilson Eyre was awarded a silver medal at the World Fair in Saint Louis in 1904.

EYRES, John W.
British, 19th century.
Active in Walton-on-Thames.
Painter. Landscapes, flowers.
John W. Eyres exhibited frequently in London, notably at the Royal Academy from 1887.
AUCTION RECORDS:
LONDON, 5 Feb 1910, *Vase of Chrysanthemums*, GBP 3. NEWMARKET, 15 Nov 2002, *Children Playing with a Wooden Cart in a Yard* (oil on canvas, 25 x 30 ins / 63 x 75 cm) GBP 1,150.

EYRICH, Emil
German, 19th century.
Died 1 February 1897, in Berlin.
Painter, draughtsman.
Eyrich created historical paintings.

EYRIES, Gustave
French, 19th century.
Born 19th century, in Troyes.
Painter. Portraits.
Gustave Eyries exhibited at the Salon in 1846 and 1851.
MUSEUMS AND GALLERIES:
TROYES: *Portrait of Paillot de Montabert.*

EYROLLES, Paul
French, 20th century.
Born in Neuilly.
Painter.
From 1920 Paul Eyrolles exhibited landscapes and flower paintings at the Salon d'Automne, Paris.

EYROLLES-EVRARD, Jean-Pierre
French.
Painter.
He studied at the Versailles school of fine arts and architecture, and between 1971 and 1975 joined the Mirabelle Dors and Maurice Rapin's surrealist group. At the same time as working in advertising as a graphic artist, between 1972 and 1987, he continued to paint.

He has taken part in several group exhibitions and shown his work in solo exhibitions, notably at La Mandragore gallery, Paris, in 1982.

Figurative, dreamlike and symbolist, he later added an abstract gesture to his work.

EYRSCHÖTTEL, Christof
German, 17th century.
Born in Nuremberg.
Painter.
Christof Eyrschöttel was the father of Johann Eyrschöttel.

EYRSCHÖTTEL, Johann
German, 17th century.
Born 1640; died 1702.
Painter.
The son of Christof Eyrschöttel and probably born in Nuremberg, he lived mainly in Husum, frequently working for Duchess Maria Elisabeth. He executed a reredos for the church in Bau, near Flensburg.

EYS, Christoffel van
Flemish, 17th century.
Active in Antwerp, in 1650.
Painter.
Flemish School.

EYSDEN, Robert van
Dutch, 19th century.
Born 22 April 1810, in Rotterdam; died October 1890, in Apeldoorn.
Painter, lithographer. Portraits, genre scenes.
Robert van Eysden initially received his artistic education from G. de Meyer and in 1828 he was a pupil of F. de Braeker in Antwerp. The museum in Rotterdam holds his portrait of *Jean Hofman.*
AUCTION RECORDS:
AMSTERDAM, 2 Sept 1997, *The Silent Intruder* (1831, oil/paper, 19 1/4 x 14 3/4 ins / 49 x 37.5 cm) NLG 3,690. BREMEN, 12 April 2002, *Young Woman at Spinning Wheel Watched by Boy* (oil on panel, 18 x 22 ins / 46 x 56 cm) EUR 3,400.

EYSELT, J. Thomas
Czech, 18th century.
Active in Jablonne nad Orlici.
Painter.
J. Thomas Eyselt painted a *St Bernard of Clairvaux* for the convent of Marienthal, near Zittau in 1739.

EYSEN, Barend van
Dutch, 17th century.
Died c. 1702, in Haarlem.
Painter, sculptor. Still-lifes (including musical instruments).
AUCTION RECORDS:
PARIS, 17 Dec 1984, *Still-life with Books, Musical Instruments and Shells* (oil on canvas, 37 1/2 x 46 1/2 ins / 95 x 118 cm) FRF 145,000.

EYSEN, Johann Jacob
Austrian, 17th century.
Active in Vienna.
Painter.
In 1665, Prince Karl Eusebius of Liechtenstein bought ten paintings from Johann Eysen.

EYSEN, Louis
German, 19th century.
Born 24 November 1843, in Manchester, to German parents; died 2 July 1899, in Munich.
Painter. Portraits, landscapes.
Kronberg Artists' Colony.
After studying at the institute in Frankfurt am Main, Louis Eysen became a pupil of Bonnat and Schalderer in Paris. From 1870 to 1876, he lived again in Frankfurt, before travelling in Italy and finally settling in Meran, South Tyrol (now Merano, Italy).

Eysen's landscapes demonstrate the influence of Courbet's and Millet's realism.
BIBLIOGRAPHY:
Wiederspahn, August, *Die Kronberger Malerkolonie*, Verlag Waldemar Kramer, Frankfurt am Main, c. 1971.
MUSEUMS AND GALLERIES:
BERLIN: *Portrait of the Artist's Mother; Meadow* - FRANKFURT AM MAIN: *Chestnut Trees* - KASSEL: *Mountain Landscape.*
AUCTION RECORDS:
LUCERNE, 30 May 1979, *Flower Garden* (oil on canvas, 15 x 22in/38 x 55cm) CHF 11,000. HEIDELBERG, 11-12 April 1997, *View over a Range of Mountains Hidden beneath the Clouds* (1894, oil on canvas, 11 1/2 x 7 3/4in/29.2 x 19.7cm) DEM

17,000. MUNICH, 27 Feb 1999, *Still-life with Fruit* (oil on canvas, 20 x 28 ins / 50 x 70 cm) DEM 20,000. MUNICH, 27 Feb 1999, *Scene from Bad Kissingen in Spa Area with Houses and Trees* (1898, oil on canvas/board, 11 x 8 ins / 27 x 20 cm) DEM 21,000. MUNICH, 30 June 2004, *Landscape with Trees* (oil on board, 8 x 12 ins / 20 x 30 cm) EUR 4,000.

EYSENPLOSER, Andreas
German, 15th century.
Active in Nuremberg (Bavaria) during the first half of the 15th century.
Painter.
This artist may be the same person as Andres von Prewsen.

EYSERMANS, Gasper
Flemish, 17th century.
Active in Antwerp, at the end of the 17th century.
Illuminator.
Flemish School.

EYSERT, Eberhard
Austrian, 19th century.
Born 30 November 1860, in Lobositz (now Lovosice, Czech Republic).
Painter. History painting.
After studying at the academy of art in Vienna, Eysert went on to work in Leitmoritz (now Litomerice, Czech Republic).

EYSKENS, Félix
Belgian, 20th century.
Born 1882, in Antwerp; died 1968.
Painter. Landscapes.
Eyskens worked in Paris for some time and then spent a period in London. He was a student of F. Sabatté. He returned to Belgium in 1919, and painted landscapes from the Antwerp region. His work was influenced by Claus and Baertsoen. He featured frequently at the Salon des Artistes Français in Paris. He received an honourable mention in 1909.

AUCTION RECORDS:
BRUSSELS, 29 Sept 1982, *October Morning* (oil on canvas, 38 1/4 x 70 3/4 ins / 97 x 180 cm) BEF 34,000. BRUSSELS, 12 June 1990, *Sunlit Avenue with Figures* (oil on canvas, 31 1/2 x 23 1/2 ins / 80 x 60 cm) BEF 50,000. AMSTERDAM, 17 Sept 1991, *View of Antwerp in Winter* (1912, oil on canvas, 45 x 57 1/2 ins / 114 x 146 cm) NLG 7,475. ANTWERP, 1 March 2000, *Bloom in Spring* (oil on canvas, 35 x 47 ins / 90 x 120 cm) BEF 90,000.

EYSLER. See **EISLER**

EYSSENHARDT, Friedrich Albert
German, 19th century.
Born c. 1801, in Berlin; died 25 August 1832, in Berlin.
Painter. Landscapes.
Eyssenhardt studied at the academy of art in Berlin.

EYSSENHARDT, Mathilde
Maiden name: Arnemann
German, 19th - 20th century.
Born in Hamburg.
Painter.
Mathilde Eyssenhardt exhibited in Hamburg and Berlin.

EYSSERIC, Joseph
French, 19th - 20th century.
Born 20 November 1860, in Carpentras (Vaucluse); died 3 July 1932, in Carpentras.
Painter, watercolourist, draughtsman. Seascapes, landscapes.
Joseph Eysseric was a pupil of the two Laurens brothers, Jules and Jean Bonaventure. He travelled in Europe and the Middle East in 1890, and later in India, Japan, Mexico, the unexplored region of Bandama in the Ivory Coast, and Russia, keeping a sort of log made up of sketches and drawings. From 1890 he exhibited regularly at the Salon des Artistes Français, Paris, sending to it: 1895, *Ramparts of Beijing*; 1896, *The Himalayas* and *Midnight Sun in Norway*. He received an honourable mention in 1902.

His work is primarily an account of his thirst for exploration; he made over five thousand watercolours and drawings, including seascapes, that he donated to the Musée Duplessis of his native town, Carpentras. He also published a school geography textbook in three volumes, illustrated with documents brought back from his many travels.

MUSEUMS AND GALLERIES:
AVIGNON: *Baie de la Recherche, Spitzberg* (pastel) - CARPENTRAS (Mus. Comtadin-Duplessis): *Marabout in Sfax* (1905-1910, and important donation).

EYTH, Heinrich
German, 19th century.
Born 8 July 1851, in Schiltach.
Painter, engraver.
Heinrich Eyth taught drawing in Karlsruhe. He provided the illustrations for Von Oechelhäuser's work, *Führer durch das Heidelberger Schloss* (*Guidebook to Heidelberg Castle*).

EYTH, Karl
German, 19th century.
Born 30 January 1856, in Schiltach.
Painter.
Karl Eyth was a decorator and illustrator of books.

EYTH, Max von
German, 19th century.
Born 6 May 1836, in Kirchheim; died 25 August 1906, in Ulm.
Painter, draughtsman.
An engineer and writer, Max von Eyth made paintings and drawings to illustrate his works.

EYTINGE, Sol.
American, 19th century.
Born 1833; died 25 March 1905, in Bayonne (New Jersey).
Painter. Genre scenes.
Sol. Eytinge acquired a considerable reputation through the works he painted during the War of Secession. He was a friend of Charles Dickens.

EYTON, Anthony John Plowden
British, 20th century.
Born 17 May 1923, in Teddington.
Painter. Landscapes, still-lifes, interiors.
Anthony Eyton studied at Reading University in 1941 and at Camberwell School of Arts and Crafts in London from 1947 to 1950. He taught at Camberwell from 1957, at the Royal Academy Schools from 1965, and at St Lawrence College in Kingston, Ontario, from 1969. He has travelled in India and Italy, and has been particularly influenced by Italian Renaissance painting.

A favourite subject for him is the view from his studio in east London, as in his oil *Open Window: Spitalfields* (1976-1981). In 1994 he was invited, with a number of other artists, to paint in the interior of the Bankside Power Station (later the Tate Modern) on the South Bank of the Thames, where he produced such work as the oil *Bankside - The Turbine Hall* (1995-1996). Eyton believed that his art came from a regard for nature, and the need to balance fact and the abstract.

He first exhibited at the Royal Academy and with the London Group. In 1955, he had his first solo show at St George's Gallery. Retrospectives of his work include the South London Art Gallery (1980, touring); King's Road Gallery (2002); and Woodlands Art Gallery (2003). He was awarded an Abbey Major Scholarship in Painting (1951-1952); a prize at the John Moores Exhibition in Liverpool (1972); a Grocer's Company Fellowship (1973); first prize in the Second British International Drawing Biennial, Middlesbrough (1975); and a Charles Wollaston Award (1981). He was elected to the Royal Academy in 1987.

BIBLIOGRAPHY:

Anthony Eyton: A Sort of Touchability': Paintings 1938-1975, Exhibition catalogue, Austin/Desmond Fine Art Gallery Two, London, 1990.

MUSEUMS AND GALLERIES:

LONDON (Arts Council of Great Britain) - LONDON (Imperial War Mus.) - LONDON (Tate Collection): *The Tank, Bankside Power Station* (1995, pastel); *Bankside - The Turbine Hall* (1995-1996, oil); *Open Window: Spitalfields* (1976-1981, oil) - LONDON (UK Government Art Collection): *Biarritz* (watercolour); *Causeway Naxos* (1959, oil); *Christchurch, Spitalfields* (1972, oil); *Landscape: Exmoor* (oil); *Old Delhi* (1979, charcoal and pastel); *Raising the Flag of Liberty, Dubrovnik Festival* (1996, oil); *Trinity Selassie Church, Addis Ababa* (1997, oil); *Women at the Western Wall, Jerusalem* (oil); *Wooded Landscape* (oil) - PLYMOUTH (Plymouth Art Gallery).

AUCTION RECORDS:

LONDON, 2 March 1999, *Christchurch, Spitalfields, from a Window* (oil on canvas, 74 x 56 ins / 187 x 141 cm) GBP 2,600. LONDON, 7 March 2000, *Seated Female Nude* (oil on canvas, 50 x 40 ins / 127 x 102 cm) GBP 4,000. LONDON, 2 Nov 2000, *Revere Beach, Boston* (oil on canvas, 22 x 28 ins / 56 x 71 cm) GBP 1,400. LONDON, 1 March 2001, *Woman with Towel* (1994, pastel, 30 x 21 ins / 75 x 54 cm) GBP 1,200. LONDON, 12 March 2002, *Girl in front of a Mirror* (pastel, 43 x 31 ins / 109 x 79 cm) GBP 2,600. LONDON, 7 June 2002, *Wailing Wall* (oil on canvas, 73 x 59 ins / 185 x 149 cm) GBP 6,800. LONDON, 3 June 2003, *Chrys* (1995, oil on board, 47 x 43 ins / 119 x 110 cm) GBP 1,300. LONDON, 16 March 2004, *Bathing in the Ganges* (oil on canvas, 58 x 69 ins / 148 x 174 cm) GBP 5,200. LONDON, 14 May 2004, *Beach and Sea* (oil on canvas, 37 x 20 ins / 93 x 52 cm) GBP 2,700.

EYUBOGLU, Bedri Rahmi

Turkish, 20th century.

Born 1911 or 1913, in Trabzon; died 1975.

Painter, illustrator, decorative artist, poet. Genre scenes, landscapes. Wall decorations.

Bedri Eyuboglu studied painting in Istanbul and at the André Lhote academy in Paris. A distant follower of Matisse and Dufy, he was basically a modernist, although at the same time he was also heir to the tradition of ancient oriental miniaturists. He was a notable illustrator, and carried out several mural decorations in Turkey.

Eyuboglu exhibited in Turkey, Bucharest (1937) and New York. In 1946 his works *Pink House, Old Cafe* and *Itinerant Photographer* were shown at the exhibition of Turkish art at the Cernuschi museum in Paris.

EYUBOGLU, Eren, or Eyubogluereren

Turkish, 20th century.

Born 1913, in Jassy; died 1988.

Painter.

Eren Eyuboglu studied at the school of fine arts in Istanbul and at the André Lhote academy in Paris. She was the wife of Bedri Rahmi Eyuboglu and lived in Turkey. Her first exhibition dates from 1933, and in 1946 she was represented in the exhibition of Turkish art at the Cernuschi museum in Paris. Her work has also been shown in Edinburgh, Hamburg and Milan, and is noted for its strong colours.

EYVEAU, Pietro

Italian, 19th century.

Active in Chieri.

Painter. Genre scenes.

Eyveau exhibited in Venice and Turin.

EYWIG, Jonas

German, 17th century.

Active in Pirna.

Painter.

Eywig painted a reredos for the church in Schönfeld near Dresden in 1658.

EYZERE, Dierick

Flemish School, 16th century.

Born to a family originally from Zwolle.

Active in Antwerp.

Painter.

EZDORF, Christian Friedrich

German, 19th century.

Born 7 January 1807, in Pössneck; died May 1858, in Würzburg.

Painter, engraver. Landscapes with figures, landscapes, seascapes.

The younger brother of Johann Christian Michael Ezdorf, Christian Friedrich Ezdorf studied in Munich before settling in Kissingen in 1852. He is best known for his *Autumn Landscape*, and also engraved many of his brother's works.

AUCTION RECORDS:

GÖTEBORG, 7 Nov 1984, *Sailing Ship off the Cape of Good Hope* (oil on canvas, 40½ x 59in/103 x 150cm) SEK 10,500. MUNICH, 18 Sept 1985, *Riverscape* (1830, oil on canvas, 23½ x 33¾in/60 x 86cm) DEM 8,500. NEW YORK, 16 Oct 1991, *Figures in a Landscape before the Storm* (1831, oil on canvas, 39¾ x 54¼in/101 x 137.8cm) USD 8,250. VIENNA, 29-30 Oct 1996, *Wooded Landscape* (1837, 27 x 32in/68.5 x 81.3cm) ATS 63,250. MUNICH, 27 Feb 1999, *Forest Landscape with Carrier and Donkey-drawn Carriage* (oil on canvas, 24 x 30 ins / 62 x 77 cm) DEM 6,500. LUCERNE, 8 Nov 2000, *Stormy Weather over Lake Landscape* (1831, oil on canvas, 40 x 54 ins / 101 x 138 cm) CHF 35,000. VEJLE, 9 May 2001, *Landscape* (1829, oil on canvas, 20 x 17 ins / 52 x 43 cm) DKK 17,000. HEIDELBERG, 19 April 2002, *Landscape with Mountain Stream* (oil on canvas, 20 x 42 ins / 50 x 106 cm) EUR 2,800. HAMBURG, 5 Dec 2002, *Storm over the North Cape* (1823, oil on canvas, 12 x 17 ins / 30 x 42 cm) EUR 2,800. BERLIN, 27 Nov 2003, *Rock Archway in the Sea off Coast of Iceland* (oil on canvas, 24 x 33 ins / 61 x 85 cm) EUR 4,000.

EZDORF, Johann Christian Michael

German, 19th century.

Born 28 February 1801, in Pössneck; died 18 December 1851, in Munich.

Painter. Hunting scenes, landscapes.

The elder brother of Christian Friedrich Ezdorf, Johann Ezdorf studied at the academy of art in Munich. In 1821, he made a study trip to Hamburg, Copenhagen, Iceland and England. He was painter to the court and a member of the academy in Stockholm.

MUSEUMS AND GALLERIES:

LEIPZIG: *Magerae Island* - MUNICH: *Swedish Landscape* - STOCKHOLM: *Hare Hunt; Northern Landscape* - STUTTGART: *Norwegian Landscape.*

EZEKIEL, E. Abraham

British, 18th century.

Born 1757, in Exeter; died December 1806, in Exeter.

Engraver. Painted miniatures.

A great number of portraits and bookplates are attributed to E. Abraham Ezekiel.

EZEKIEL, Moses Jakob

American, 19th century.

Born 28 October 1844, in Richmond; died 1917.

Sculptor.

Moses Jakob Ezekiel went to Europe in 1869 and became a pupil of Albert Wolf at the Berlin Academy. He exhibited in Berlin, Rome, New York and Cincinnati. Among his best works are *Martyrs, Consolation* and *Pan and Cupid.*

EZHEVSKY, Nikifor, or Ezhev
Russian, 18th century.
Painter and decorative artist. Stage sets (?).
Nikifor Ezhevsky is known for works in the apartments of Empress Catherine the Great in the Winter Palace, in the Moscow Court Theatre and in Grand Palace at Pavlovsk.

EZHOV, Aleksei
Russian, 19th century.
Lithographer.
Aleksei Ezhov trained at the academy of art in St Petersburg. He is known for a portrait of the Metropolitan of Novgorod and *Mikhail*, a portrait dated 15 May 1820.

EZOCKI
Polish, 18th century.
Painter.
Ezocki painted a portrait of King Stanislas-Augustus Poniatowski.

EZPELETA
Spanish, 16th century.
Born in Alagón near Saragossa; died towards the middle of the 16th century, in Saragossa, at the age of about 60.
Painter.
Ezpeleta distinguished himself by his skilful painting of miniatures like those in his choir-books for Saragossa Cathedral.

EZQUERRA, Domingo
Spanish, 17th century.
Active in Madrid.
Painter. Portraits.
Domingo Ezquerra was a pupil of Carreno.

EZQUERRA, Geronimo Antonio de
Spanish, 18th century.
Painter. Religious subjects, mythological subjects.
Geronimo Ezquerra was a pupil of Antonio Palonimo. He produced a series of paintings of saints for the church of St Philip Neri in Madrid and various works for the Buen Retiro Palace.
MUSEUMS AND GALLERIES:
MADRID: *Neptune with Tritons and Nereids.*

EZZAT, Laïla
Egyptian, 20th century.
Born 1935, in Cairo.
Painter.
Ezzat is self-taught. She began exhibiting her work from 1970 onwards, notably in the Suzanne de Coninck gallery. Her work is characterized by its hazy, evanescent forms.
BIBLIOGRAPHY:
Badr El-Din Abou Ghazy, *Visages de l'Art contemporain égyptien*, exhibition catalogue, Musée Galliera, Paris, 1971.
MUSEUMS AND GALLERIES:
CAIRO (Egyptian MMA).

F.
Flemish School, 15th century.
Monogram of an engraver (burin). Religious subjects.
Bruges School.
Likely to have been active in Bruges at the end of the 15th century, little is known about this artist. His work *The Virgin Displaying the Body of Christ* was shown in the 1994 exhibition *Hans Memling* held at the Groeningemuseum in Bruges in the section devoted to precursors, contemporaries and followers of Memling.
BIBLIOGRAPHY:
De Vos, Dirk, *Hans Memling,* exhibition catalogue, Groeningemuseum, Bruges, 1994.
MUSEUMS AND GALLERIES:
LONDON (British Library): *Virgin Displaying the Body of Christ* (c. 1490, engraving).

F., J. H., or D. J. D.
French, 18th century.
Painter. Genre scenes.
The museum in Nancy has a painting of unknown origin signed *D.J.D.F.*or *J.H.F.F.* This painting, entitled *Romantic Conversation in a Park,* can be attributed either to Jean du Faget or to Jean-Honoré Fragonard.

F. A.
German, 16th century.
Monogram of an engraver.
A print dated 1561 by this engraver is known: *Grand Ball for Emperor Maximilian II.*

F. B.
German, 16th century.
Monogram of an engraver. Religious subjects, mythological subjects, military subjects.
A large number of pieces by this artist bear the dates 1559 and 1560.

F. B.
Italian, 16th century.
Monogram of an engraver (wood).
F.B. engraved an allegory representing *Fortune, Death and Time.*

F. B.
17th century.
Probably born in Germany.
Monogram of an engraver (burin).
He was working in about 1600, and is mentioned by Brulliot, who refers to an ornament on with a bird on it.

F. B.
Spanish, 17th century.
Monogram of an engraver (etching).
F. B. was active in the 17th century. He is mentioned by Brulliot, who refers to an engraving by him: *B Ceccadot Martire Vescovo.*

F. C.
British, 14th century.
Monogram of an engraver.
This was the monogram of the artist Craig, from the late 14th century.

F. C.
German, 16th century.
Monogram of an engraver.
An engraving of *St Jerome,* dated 1552, has been identified as being by this artist.

F. C. I.
German, 16th century.
Monogram of an engraver (wood).

F. H. B.
Dutch, 16th century.
Monogram of an engraver (etching).
Active in the second half of the 16th century, this artist is listed by Brulliot, who mentions his caricatures.

F.I.B. See **FIB**

F. M.
German, 16th century.
Monogram of an engraver.
This artist was active in Cologne in around 1525.

F. M.
Dutch, 17th (?) century.
Monogram of a painter.
The author of the *Catalogue of Brussels* infers that the monogram *F. M.* could be that of Frans Franken (1607-1667).

F. R.
16th century.
Monogram of a sculptor (ivory).

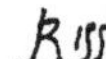

F. R.
17th century.
Monogram of an engraver.
This mark can be seen on engravings printed in Naples in 1607.

F. T.
German, 15th century.
Monogram of an engraver.
A print by this artist, dated 1473, shows *The Resurrection*.

F. V. B., MASTER OF THE INITIALS
Flemish School, 15th century.
Engraver. Religious subjects.
Born in Bruges at the end of the 15th century, this artist has been identified as Franz von Bocholt although this is not accepted by all scholars. More that 50 plates, showing the influence of Rogier Van der Weyden, have been attributed to him.

AUCTION RECORDS:
LONDON, 5 Dec 1985, *St George* (engraving/copper, 71/4 x 51/4 ins / 18.5 x 13.1 cm) GBP 30,000.

F. W. P.
Monogram of an engraver.

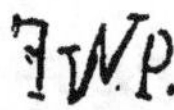

FA JO-CHEN. See **FA RUOZHEN**

FA RUOZHEN, or Fa Jo-chen, style name: Hanru, sobriquets: Huangshan, Huangshi
Chinese, 17th century.
Born 1613, in Jiaozhou (now Jiaoxiao, Shandong); died 1696.
Painter. Landscapes.
Fa Ruozhen passed his jinshi (acomplished scholar) examinations in 1646. He then went to the Hanlin academy. Later he became a 'Doctor of the Five Classics' and deputy governor of Fujian-Anhui. He is known as a poet and landscape painter of the Nanjing school and one of the group of individualist landscape painters. The landscapes of the 17th century individualists are often dark and of uncertain basis, owing perhaps to the severe treatment they received during the Manchu conquest (the advent of the Qing dynasty in 1644) and to their feeling of alienation from the new social order. This was found not only among monks and recluses, but even with high-ranking officials in the Manchu administration, such as Fa Ruozhen.

Fa Ruozhen's scroll in the Stockholm Östasiatiska Museet is a puzzling work with no equivalent in Chinese painting. Its entire surface depicts a landscape filled with rocks and trees in accentuated chiaroscuro that produces a rounded quality in the rocky mass and gives the impression that we are witnessing a terrible turmoil in nature, or an hallucination by the artist. Indeed, he does not seem to be in full control of his materials, nor to have the clarity or depth of a major artist. Nevertheless he is one of the most interesting artists of the period.

MUSEUMS AND GALLERIES:
KYOTO (Yurinkan): *Large Landscape* (signed) - SHENYANG (Liaoning Mus.): *Landscape* (1689, light colour on paper, dated from the colophon) - STOCKHOLM (Östasiatiska Museet): *Clouds and Fog in Mountains* - TOKYO (National Mus.): *Autumn Landscape in Huangshan*.

AUCTION RECORDS:
NEW YORK, 31 May 1990, *Poems in running script* (ink on paper, handscroll, 121/4 x 108 ins / 31 x 274.3 cm) USD 11,000. NEW YORK, 21 March 1995, *Autumn Landscape* (ink and colour on paper, hanging scroll, 31 1/4 x 15 ins / 79.4 x 38.4 cm) USD 2,875. NEW YORK, 22 Sept 1997, *Landscape* (ink on paper, hanging scroll, 47 x 23 ins / 119.4 x 58.4 cm) USD 23,000.

FABA, Girolamo
Italian, 16th century.
Active in Calabria.
Painter, engraver (wood).

FABARIUS, Friedrich Wilhelm
German, 19th century.
Born 25 January 1815, in Mülheim; died 31 December 1900, in Düsseldorf.
Painter. Landscapes, seascapes.
A pupil of A. von Wille in Düsseldorf, Fabarius exhibited at the royal academy in Berlin from 1868 to 1870. His best-known works include *View of the Beach* and *Seascape*.

AUCTION RECORDS:
COLOGNE, 21 Oct 1977, *Beach at Scheveningen* (1871, oil on canvas, 241/2 x 361/2in/62 x 93cm) DEM 4,000.

FABBI, Alberto
Italian, 19th century.
Born 1858, in Bologna; died 1906.
Painter, watercolourist. Figures, genre scenes.
Alberto Fabbi was the elder brother of Fabio Fabbi.

AUCTION RECORDS:
PARIS, 9 June 1993, *Two Oriental Women Making Soap Bubbles* (watercolour, 153/4 x 91/2 ins / 40 x 24 cm) FRF 10,500. PARIS, 17 Dec 1993, *Shower* (watercolour, 161/4 x 111/4 ins / 41 x 28.5 cm) FRF 4,200. LONDON, 14 June 1995, *Dancer* (oil on canvas, 743/4 x 331/4 ins / 190 x 84.5 cm) GBP 9,775. ROME, 12 Dec 2001, *Dancing Couple* (oil on canvas, 18 x 14 ins / 45 x 35 cm) ITL 4,200,000. NEW YORK, 30 Oct 2002, *Musical Interlude in the Harem* (oil on canvas, 40 x 27 ins / 102 x 68 cm) USD 18,000. PARIS, 16 June 2003, *Rocking Chair* (1880, oil on canvas, 27 x 41 ins / 69 x 103 cm) EUR 4,000. ROME, 1 Dec 2003, *Love Scene* (oil on canvas, 27 x 41 ins / 69 x 103 cm) EUR 4,760.

FABBI, Fabio
Italian, 19th - 20th century.
Born 1861, in Bologna; died 1946, in Casalecchio di Reno, near Florence.
Painter, watercolourist, pastellist, draughtsman.
Religious subjects, portraits, genre scenes, local scenes (harems).
Orientalism.

Fabio Fabbi studied painting and sculpture at the Accademia di Belle Arti in Florence, in the studio of Augusto Rivalta, and won several prizes in both disciplines during the early 1880s. He then visited Paris, Munich and Egypt. When he returned to Italy he devoted himself solely to painting. In 1893, he was teaching at the Accademia in Florence, and in 1894 he was a member of the Accademia di Belle Arti in Bologna. He was decorated with the title of knight of the crown of Italy in 1898.

Fabbi painted a few religious pictures, but he mostly chose Middle Eastern themes for his subjects: odalisques, markets, bazaars and harems. He also designed medals. The style of his paintings varies according to the technique used. In his pastel works, form and movement are merely suggested by a few strokes of the chalk, whereas his oil paintings on ivory are more boldly executed. He chose the medium of watercolour to illustrate new editions of the *Aeneid*, the *Iliad* and the *Odyssey*.

His best-known works include *The Seven Deadly Sins; Madonna of the Corn; Selling a Slave; Slave Market; In the Harem; Mammina!; A Terrace in Alexandria; Arab Woman; Old Muslim Man; Dance; Women on a Terrace.*

He took part in various exhibitions including exhibitions in Monaco, in Turin from 1884 where he won a prize in 1899, in Florence in 1888, and in Milan.

Bibliography:

Juler, Caroline, *Les Orientalistes de l'École Italienne*, ACR Édition, Paris, 1994.

Auction records:

London, 9-10 April 1946, *Slave Market in the East,* GBP 62. Florence, 7 June 1976, *Nuptial Procession* (oil on canvas, 26 x 32 ins / 66 x 81 cm) ITL 380,000. New York, 15 Dec 1978, *The Favourites* (oil on canvas, 23 1/2 x 31 1/2 ins / 59.5 x 80 cm) USD 6,000. London, 1 Oct 1980, *The Dance of the Seven Veils* (oil on canvas, 26 1/2 x 39 ins / 67 x 99 cm) GBP 2,800. London, 17 March 1983, *In the Harem; Capture of the Harem* (two watercolours, 17 1/4 x 11 ins / 44 x 28 cm) GBP 1,200. New York, 25 May 1984, *Capture* (oil on canvas, 27 3/4 x 15 3/4 ins / 70.8 x 40.3 cm) USD 11,000. New York, 15 Feb 1985, *Orange Seller* (watercolour, 25 x 18 ins / 63.5 x 45.7 cm) USD 2,200. London, 24 June 1987, *Slave Merchant* (oil on canvas, 82 3/4 x 39 1/4 ins / 210 x 99.5 cm) GBP 8,000. New York, 25 Feb 1988, *Women and a Carpet Merchant* (watercolour, gouache and ink, 16 1/2 x 10 1/4 ins / 41.6 x 26 cm) USD 2,860. London, 26 Feb 1988, *Slave Merchant* (oil on canvas, 46 1/2 x 33 ins / 118 x 84 cm) GBP 6,050. New York, 25 May 1988, *For the Little One* (oil on canvas remounted on board, 52 x 36 3/4 ins / 132.1 x 93.3 cm) USD 3,520. London, 5 May 1989, *Young Arab Dancers* (oil on canvas, 28 x 16 ins / 70.2 x 40.4 cm) GBP 2,750. New York, 23 May 1989, *Slave Market* (1910, oil on canvas, 34 x 23 1/2 ins / 85.5 x 60 cm) USD 13,200. London, 22 Nov 1989, *On the Patio of the Harem* (oil on canvas, 23 1/4 x 30 1/2 ins / 59 x 77.5 cm) GBP 13,200. Milan, 6 Dec 1989, *Oriental Dancers in a Bazaar* (oil on canvas, 11 3/4 x 8 1/4 ins / 30 x 21 cm) ITL 5,000,000. London, 22 June 1990, *Slave Market* (oil on canvas, 82 1/2 x 39 1/4 ins / 209.6 x 99.4 cm) GBP 14,300. New York, 23 Oct 1990, *Marriage Procession* (oil on canvas, 24 x 35 1/2 ins / 61 x 90.2 cm) USD 16,500. Milan, 7 Nov 1991, *Harem* (oil on canvas, 39 1/4 x 25 3/4 ins / 100 x 65.5 cm) ITL 10,000,000. Rome, 14 Nov 1991, *Odalisques in a Harem* (oil on canvas, 23 1/2 x 31 ins / 60 x 79 cm) ITL 17,250,000. London, 29 Nov 1991, *In the Harem* (oil on canvas, 28 1/2 x 43 1/2 ins / 72.4 x 110.5 cm) GBP 15,950. New York, 20 Feb 1992, *Harem Dancers* (oil on canvas, 28 3/4 x 41 1/2 ins / 73 x 105.4 cm) USD 18,150. Bologna, 8-9 June 1992, *Pigeon Feed* (watercolour, 12 3/4 x 9 3/4 ins / 32.5 x 25 cm) ITL 1,840,000. London, 19 June 1992, *Roman Slave Girl* (oil on canvas, 36 x 36 ins / 91.5 x 91.5 cm) GBP 8,800. Paris, 8 Nov 1993, *Slave Market* (oil on canvas, 27 1/4 x 15 1/4 ins / 69 x 39 cm) FRF 100,000. New York, 19 Jan 1994, *Oriental Dancer and Musicians* (oil on canvas, 18 1/2 x 27 ins / 47 x 68.6 cm) USD 10,925. London, 18 March 1994, *Dancer* (oil on canvas, 39 1/4 x 26 ins / 99.8 x 65.1 cm) GBP 28,750. New York, 12 Oct 1994, *Slave Market* (oil on canvas, 39 1/2 x 22 ins / 100.3 x 55.9 cm) USD 37,375. Paris, 6 Nov 1995, *Three Young Women on a Terrace* (watercolour, 17 1/4 x 11 1/2 ins / 44 x 29 cm) FRF 55,000. Paris, 18-19 March 1996, *Marriage in Cairo* (oil on canvas, 26 1/2 x 46 1/2 ins / 67 x 118 cm) FRF 290,000. New York, 23-24 May 1996, *Fabric Merchant* (oil on canvas, 27 1/4 x 15 1/4 ins / 69.2 x 38.7 cm) USD 21,275. Milan, 23 Oct 1996, *Odalisque* (watercolour/card, 17 3/4 x 11 3/4 ins / 45 x 30 cm) ITL 3,495,000. London, 21 Nov 1996, *Oriental Dancers on a Terrace* (oil on canvas, 28 1/4 x 36 ins / 71.7 x 91.5 cm) GBP 24,150. New York, 23 Oct 1997, *Young Women of the Harem* (oil on canvas, 32 1/2 x 38 1/2 ins / 82.6 x 97.8 cm) USD 57,500. Paris, 17 Nov 1997, *Women Selling Oranges* (watercolour, 18 x 12 1/2 ins / 46 x 32 cm) FRF 20,000. Paris, 26 March 1998, *The Dance of the Water Jugs* (c. 1885-1895, oil on canvas, 61 x 45 1/4 ins / 155 x 115 cm) FRF 400,000. New York, 5 May 1999, *Slave Auction* (oil on canvas, 28 x 16 ins / 70 x 41 cm) USD 31,000. New York, 1 Nov 1999, *Arab Market* (oil on canvas/board, 55 x 79 ins / 140 x 200 cm) USD 145,000. New York, 1 May 2000, *On the Terrace* (oil on canvas, 29 x 41 ins / 74 x 105 cm) USD 90,000. Paris, 14 Nov 2000, *Presentation of Young Slaves* (oil on canvas, 36 x 28 ins / 92 x 72 cm) FRF 580,000. Victoria, 1 May 2001, *Odalisque* (oil on panel, 10 x 7 ins / 26 x 19 cm) AUD 6,000. Paris, 19 Nov 2001, *Merrymaking on a Cairo Terrace* (oil on canvas, 26 x 34 ins / 65 x 86 cm) FRF 600,000. Ahlden, 30 Nov 2001, *Slave Market* (oil on canvas, 60 x 44 ins / 153 x 112 cm) DEM 140,000. North Bethesda, 16 March 2002, *In the Harem* (oil on canvas, 28 x 39 ins / 72 x 100 cm) USD 47,000. London, 20 June 2002, *Master's Choice* (oil on canvas, 39 x 22 ins / 100 x 55 cm) GBP 60,000. Paris, 16 June 2003, *Presentation of Slaves in an Oriental Port* (oil on canvas, 30 x 24 ins / 76 x 60 cm) EUR 55,000. London, 19 June 2003, *Lazy Afternoon on the Terrace* (oil on canvas, 35 x 59 ins / 90 x 150 cm) GBP 100,000. New York, 22 April 2004, *Orange Seller* (oil on canvas, 28 x 22 ins / 70 x 55 cm) USD 40,000. San Francisco, 18 May 2004, *Wedding Procession* (oil on canvas, 35 x 56 ins / 88 x 143 cm) USD 50,000.

FABBIANI, Juan Vicente

Venezuelan, 20th century.

Born 15 June 1910, in Caracas.

Painter.

Juan Vicente Fabbiani studied under Marcos Castillo at the Caracas academy of fine arts. He sent *Still-life with Guitar* to the exhibition held in Paris in 1946 by the United Nations Organisation.

FABBRI, Agenor, known erroneously as Fabri Agenore

Italian, 20th century.

Born 1911, in Barba.

Sculptor, potter. Figures, animals.

Fabbri was a pupil at the school of industrial art and design in Pistoia, then went on to study at the Accademia di Belle Arti in Florence, where he worked with terracotta. In 1935 he went to work as a model maker in a ceramics workshop in Albisola (Liguria), and was then mobilised until the end of the war.

In 1937, he took part in the *Nazionale* exhibition in Naples, with great success. At the Venice Biennale of 1952, an entire room was devoted to his work. He also participated in the Antwerp-Middelheim and São Paulo Biennales, and showed his works at numerous exhibitions of contemporary Italian sculpture in Europe and the USA.

In his early years he was influenced by the Futurist Constructivism espoused by Marino Marini, as can be seen in *The Battle* (1945), *Woman of the People* (1946) and *Dance Step* (1947). His use of terracotta, from 1950 to 1955, took him in an almost Expressionist direction. His output during this period also owes much to the work of the great Italian ceramist Arturo Martini. He created monstrous animals, and giant insects bristling with menacing limbs. He then returned to working with melted-down bronze, and the creatures of his imagination came closer to the human form, although they remained disturbing, as in the series *The Man of Hiroshima* (1957, 1959 and 1961).

The Cry, *The Monster of War*, *Homage to Fontana*, *The Wounded Woman* and his series of *Pietàs* express the suffering of human beings as an integral part of the human condition, but also as a result of man's inhumanity to man. Whether on a hand imprisoned in a cage of thorns, or on a screaming figure, the same scar brutally eats away at the limb, or the lower torso, right up to the head. The deep split exacerbates the pain felt in the flesh. The material, which is a symbolic medium in Fabbri's work, seems to be ready to explode under the pressure of the scream, the dramatic act or the pure idea.

BIBLIOGRAPHY:

Gassiot-Talabot, Gérald, '*Fabbri*' in *Opus international*, periodical, Paris, April 1972.

AUCTION RECORDS:

MILAN, 21 Dec 1982, *The Atomised Man* (1958, welded bronze, h. 38 1/4 ins / 97 cm) ITL 3,000,000. MILAN, 24 Oct 1983, *Il Monstro della Guerra* (1967, bronze, 32 3/4 x 18 x 9 ins / 83 x 46 x 23 cm) ITL 5,500,000. MILAN, 18 Dec 1984, *People* (gouache/mounted paper/canvas, 19 3/4 x 13 3/4 ins / 50 x 35 cm) ITL 1,200,000. MILAN, 12 Nov 1985, *Two Figures* (iron, h. 16 1/4 ins / 41 cm) ITL 2,200,000. MILAN, 11 March 1986, *Horse* (1948, terracotta, polychrome, 11 3/4 x 22 ins / 30 x 55 cm) ITL 9,500,000. NEW YORK, 6 Oct 1987, *Dancer* (1958, patinated bronze, h. 11 1/2 ins / 29.2 cm) USD 800. MILAN, 7 Nov 1989, *Form* (1959, multiple materials/panel painting, 37 3/4 x 33 3/4 ins / 96 x 86 cm) ITL 29,000,000. MILAN, 27 March 1990, *Untitled* (burnt wood, 48 x 21 1/2 x 10 1/4 ins / 122 x 54.5 x 26 cm) ITL 21,000,000. MILAN, 27 Sept 1990, *Composition* (wood/sheets of brass, 19 x 16 1/2 x 2 ins / 48 x 42 x 5 cm) ITL 2,200,000. ROME, 3 Dec 1990, *Composition* (1952, wood panel, 38 1/4 x 38 1/4 x 1 1/4 ins / 97 x 97 x 3 cm) ITL 29,900,000. ROME, 25 March 1993, *Untitled* (polychrome ceramic, diam. 20 ins / 51 cm) ITL 2,200,000. LOKEREN, 12 March 1994, *Composition* (bronze, h. 10 1/4 ins / 26 cm, w. 24 3/4 ins/63 cm) BEF 30,000. MILAN, 24 June 1994, *Person* (bronze, h. 14 1/4 ins / 36.5 cm) ITL 3,680,000. MILAN, 22 June 1995, *Person* (1962, bronze, 23 1/2 x 19 1/4 x 4 3/4 ins / 60 x 49 x 12 cm) ITL 11,500,000. MILAN, 28 May 1996, *Untitled* (bronze, h. 24 3/4 ins / 63 cm) ITL 3,450,000. MILAN, 22 June 1999, *Untitled* (bronze, 26 x 40x12 ins / 65 x 102x30 cm) ITL 6,500,000. ROME, 23 Nov 2000, *Seated Woman* (polychrome terracotta, h. 20 ins / 51 cm) ITL 4,500,000. ROME, 23 Nov 2000, *Horse and Rider* (polychrome terracotta, h. 16 ins / 40 cm) ITL 4,500,000. ROME, 12 April 2001, *Untitled* (1963, enamel on panel, 25 x 17 ins / 63 x 43 cm) ITL 6,000,000. MILAN, 30 May 2001, *Mother* (1953, polychrome terracotta, 14 x 4x3 ins / 36 x 10x8 cm) ITL 6,000,000. MILAN, 14 May 2002, *Untitled* (bronze, 9 x 7 ins / 22 x 17 cm) EUR 2,900. ROME, 18 Dec 2002, *Figure* (bronze, h. 25 ins / 63 cm) EUR 2,900. MILAN, 28 Oct 2003, *Composition* (1958, bronze, h. 46 ins / 115 cm) EUR 9,500. MILAN, 16 Dec 2003, *Man in Space* (bronze, h. 52 ins / 133 cm) EUR 10,000. CHICAGO, 28 March 2004, *Magnificent Ribbon* (enameled steel, 13 x 65x16 ins / 33 x 165x41 cm) USD 7,000. VERCELLI, 12 June 2004, *Seated Figure* (terracotta, 12 x 6x5 ins / 30 x 14x12 cm) EUR 5,500.

FABBRI, Ercole
Italian, 19th century.
Born in Faenza.
Painter (majolica).

He worked in Berlin, mostly for Prince Henry of Prussia.

FABBRI, Giovanni
Italian, 18th century.
Died 1777, in Bologna.
Engraver.

Fabbri is known for his illustrations, and copies after Guido Reni and the Carracci.

FABBRICA, Francesco
Italian, 17th century.
Painter.

Fabbrica painted a *St Anne* for the church of S Maria del Paradisio in Milan.

FABBRICOTTI, Annibale
Italian, 20th century.
Born in Carrara.
Sculptor.

Annibale Fabbricotti was a pupil of Biggi Alessandro. He exhibited at the Paris Salon of 1922.

FABBRINI, Cesare di Vinci
Italian, 16th century.
Born in Peretola, near Florence; died 17 January 1593.
Painter.
Florentine School.

Cesare di Vinci Fabbrini lived in Florence, where he was Vasari's pupil and later his collaborator.

FABBRINI, E.
Italian, 19th century.
Active in Italy.
Engraver (burin).

Fabbrini illustrated books by D'Azeglio and Bardi.

FABBRINI, Gaetano
Italian, 19th century.
Born in Florence.
Active in Ireland.
Painter.

Gaetano Fabbrini lived in Ireland, where he acquired a certain renown as a portrait artist.

FABBRINI, Giuseppe
Italian, 18th century.
Born 1740, in Florence.
Painter.

Fabbrini painted a *St Donato* for the cathedral in Arezzo, and is also noted for his portraits.

FABBRO, Giovanni Battista di Giacomo
Italian, 16th century.
Active in Bologna in 1529.
Painter.

FABBRO, Pippo del
Italian, 16th century.
Active in Florence at the beginning of the 16th century.
Sculptor.
Florentine School.

Pippo del Fabbro was one of Jacopo Sansovino's pupils.

FABBRONI, Atto
Italian, 17th century.
Active in Pistoia (Tuscany) in 1654.
Sculptor.

Fabbroni is known to have carved a crucifix for the church of S Vitale in Brescia.

FABBRUCCI, Aristide
Italian, 19th century.
Born in Florence.
Sculptor.

Aristide Fabbrucci exhibited at the Royal Academy in London from 1880 to 1885.

AUCTION RECORDS:
LONDON, 11 June 1987, *Two Putti* (c. 1870, patinated bronze, h. 32 ins / 81 cm) GBP 800.

FABBRUCCI, Francesco
Italian, 18th century.
Born c. 1687, in Cortona (Tuscany); died 1767, in Cortona.
Sculptor.

FABBRUCCI, Luigi
Italian, 19th century.
Born 1829, in Florence; died 1893, in London.
Sculptor. Figures. Busts.

Luigi Fabbrucci exhibited in Paris at the Salon of the Société des Artistes Français, where he was awarded an honourable mention in 1863. He also showed his work at the Royal Academy in London from 1870 to 1884.

MUSEUMS AND GALLERIES:
DIJON: *General Delaborde* (bust).

FABELTHIER
French, 20th century.
Painter.

AUCTION RECORDS:
PARIS, 30 May 1935, *Composition*, FRF 400.

FABER
German, 18th century.
Sculptor.

Faber was a monk who worked for the church in Utterweiler around 1700.

FABER
German, 19th century.
Miniaturist.

Faber was active around 1837 and is mentioned by Siret.

FABER, Christoffer
Danish, 19th century.
Born 18 September 1800; died 20 November 1869.
Painter.

A pupil and collaborator of J. L. Lund, Faber painted landscapes and religiously-inspired paintings.

FABER, Conrad, called de Creuznach, or Kreuznach
German, 16th century.
Born possibly c. 1500, in Kreuznach (Rhineland-Palatinate); died c. 1553, in Frankfurt am Main.
Painter, draughtsman. Portraits, landscapes. Cards.

Conrad Faber was known for his topographical drawings until the discovery in 1909 of his numerous and fine portraits of members of the Holzhaus family and others of the most prominent families in Frankfurt. They are painted on wood and signed with the monogram *C. v. C.*. Subsequently it has been possible to piece together Faber's career: he appeared in Frankfurt in around 1523, perhaps coming from Mainz where he may have met Matthias Grünewald. He was still a journeyman in 1526 in Frankfurt, working in the studio of Conrad Fyoll. In 1537, in Frankfurt, he took a second wife.

Scholars have detected the influence of Albrecht Altdorfer and the painters of the Danube School in the landscapes that he uses in the backgrounds of his paintings. He also painted the entourage of Cardinal Albert of Brandenburg. In 1551, he made a large woodcut depicting the *Siege of Frankfurt*, a work that is believed to give a faithful image of the town at this period.

AUCTION RECORDS:
LONDON, 11 May 1934, *Elizabeth Breun, Wife of Ulrich von Hynsberg*, GBP 577; *Ulrich von Hynsberg*, GBP 504. LONDON, 8-18 July 1940, *Young Man*, GBP 115. NEW YORK, 14-16 Jan 1943, *Margaret Schottin*, USD 700. NEW YORK, 26 Nov 1943, *Margaret Schottin*, USD 1,050. LONDON, 1 April 1966, *Portrait of a Man*, Gns 7,000. NEW YORK, 7 June 1978, *Portrait of Johann Reys; Portrait of his Wife Anna Uffstendern* (two oils on panel, 20 x 14 ins / 51 x 35.5 cm) USD 100,000. NEW YORK, 17 Jan 1985, *Portrait of Dorothea von Stalenburg* (1533, oil on panel, 20 x 13 3/4 ins / 50.5 x 35 cm) USD 45,000. NEW YORK, 11 Jan 1989, *Portrait of Dorothea von Stalenburg aged 26* (1533, oil on panel, 20 x 13 3/4 ins / 50.5 x 35 cm) USD 82,500.

FABER, Cornelis
Dutch, 17th century.
Born c. 1594.
Active in Seville and Amsterdam.
Painter.

FABER, Daniel
French, 17th century.
Active in Paris c. 1619.
Painter.

FABER, Daniel
German, 18th century.
Probably active in Saxony.
Painter.

Many works signed by Daniel Faber have been found in Saxony.

FABER, Franz
Austrian, 18th century.
Active in Arco (Tyrol).
Sculptor.

Franz Faber has sometimes been wrongly identified as Johann Faber.

FABER, Friedrich Theodor
Belgian, 19th century.
Born 4 June 1782, in Brussels; died 13 April 1844, in Brussels.
Painter, engraver (etching).

After having been taught by his father, Friedrich Theodor Faber went on to study under the guidance of Omeganck in Antwerp. Established in Brussels, he later abandoned oil painting to dedicate himself to running a porcelain factory, where his talent as a painter proved to be beneficial. Of his output as an engraver he is renowned for about 100 plates of landscapes and animals after his own drawings or those of Omeganck, De Roy and van Assche. The museum in Brussels holds his *Working Man's Meal*.

AUCTION RECORDS:
LUCERNE, 22 June 1968, *Child Playing Violin; Old Man and Child* (two pendants) CHF 4,500.

FABER, Gabriel
French, 16th - 17th century.
Born 1560, in Lyons; died 1637.
Engraver.

Le Blanc mentions an engraving by this artist: *Arbeer religionis graphice cupri incisa, dicato Carolo Barberino* (sic).

FABER, Gottlob
German, 19th century.
Born 1812, in Schwäbisch-Gmünd; died 1884, in Rome.
Painter.

Son of the miniaturist Josepha Faber, Gottlob Faber worked in Munich.

FABER, J.
German, 17th century.
Active in Bamberg in 1661.
Draughtsman.

FABER, J. G.
German, 19th century.
Active in Germany.
Engraver (burin).
J.G. Faber is best known for his engraving of *Wolfgang Dillis* after Kellerhoven.

FABER, Jakob
Swiss, 16th century.
Active in Basel, Lyons and in Paris.
Engraver (wood).
Jakob Faber was one of the first artists to make engravings from the works of Hans Holbein, with whom he collaborated until Holbein went to England. He lived for some time in France, where he was known as Jacques Lefèvre. While there he illustrated several religious books.

FABER, Jean
Flemish, 17th century.
Born in Berehem; died 1674; buried in Antwerp, in the Dominican church.
Painter. Landscapes.
Flemish School.
Jean Faber was a member of the academy of St Luke.

FABER, Johan
Dutch, 18th century.
Active in The Hague in 1754.
Painter, miniaturist. Portraits, landscapes.
Johan Faber may be the same person as John Faber the Younger.

FABER, Johann
Austrian, 18th century.
Active in the Tyrol c. 1750.
Sculptor. Interiors with figures.
Johann Faber worked for the cathedral in Brixen (now Bressanone, Italy).
AUCTION RECORDS:
NEW YORK, 26 Feb 1997, *Peasants Preparing Fruit in an Interior; Peasants Plucking Birds in an Interior* (oil on panel, a pair, 12 1/4 x 15 1/4in/31.2 x 38.7cm) USD 8,050.

FABER, Johann Joachim
German, 19th century.
Born 12 April 1778, in Hamburg; died 2 August 1846.
Painter, engraver.
A pupil of the painter Carl Waagen in Hamburg, Johann Joachim Faber exhibited in Leipzig in 1841. He spent several years in Dresden and Prague before returning to Hamburg, where he focused on history painting.
MUSEUMS AND GALLERIES:
BERLIN: *Capuchin Monastery near Naples* - HAMBURG: *Several Italian Landscapes* - KARLSRUHE: *Views around Sorrento.*
AUCTION RECORDS:
LONDON, 13 Oct 1967, *View of Dresden,* Gns 450.

FABER, Johann Ludwig
German, 17th century.
Active in Nuremberg.
Glass painter.
The Victoria and Albert Museum in London has a work that is very plausibly attributed to Johann Ludwig Faber and signed *J. L. F.*.
MUSEUMS AND GALLERIES:
LONDON (Victoria and Albert Mus.).

FABER, Johann Theodor Eusebius
German, 18th - 19th century.
Born 28 October 1772, in Gottleuba, near Pirna; died 2 September 1852, in Dresden.
Painter. Genre scenes, landscapes.
A pupil of Klengel and a member of the academy in Dresden, Johann Theodor Eusebius Faber lived in Dresden and is best known for his *Moonlit Landscape*.
AUCTION RECORDS:
LONDON, 22 Jan 1965, *View of Dresden,* Gns 500. COLOGNE, 12 Nov 1976, *View of Dresden* (oil on canvas, 37 x 52 3/4in/94 x 134cm) DEM 18,000. LONDON, 21 Oct 1984, *Italian Town in a Wooded Riverscape* (1817, oil on canvas, 17 1/2 x 24in/44.5 x 61cm) GBP 4,000. AMSTERDAM, 29 Nov 1988, *Tobacco Merchant Seated in Office with Two Workmen* (1760, oil on canvas, 33 1/2 x 39in/84.8 x 99.2cm) NLG 89,700.

FABER, Johannes, the Elder
German, 16th century.
Engraver (?).
This artist was the father of Johannes Faber the Younger and probably also an engraver. He worked in Leipzig.

FABER, Johannes, the Younger
German, 16th - 17th century.
Painter, engraver.
The son of Johannes the Elder, this artist worked in Leipzig. He made a number of illustrations for the publisher Henning Gross.

FABER, John, the Elder
Dutch, 17th - 18th century.
Born c. 1660, in The Hague; died 1721, in Bristol.
Active also in England.
Draughtsman, engraver (mezzotint).
John Faber the Elder is considered one of the foremost engravers to use the mezzotint technique. After having made a name for himself in the Netherlands through his portraits drawn on parchment, he went to London in about 1687 where he received similar acclaim as a draughtsman and engraver. He is especially mentioned for his 25 portraits of the founders of the Universities of Oxford and Cambridge.
AUCTION RECORDS:
LONDON, 27-28 June 1922, *Lieutenant-admiral Van Holland* (1696, pen) GBP 10. LONDON, 16 July 1928, *Francis I of Austria* (drawing) GBP 29. LONDON, 28 Feb 1945, *Charles I; James Francis Edward Stuart; William III in Armour* (three drawings) GBP 20. LONDON, 9 April 2001, *Nobleman in Robes* (ink on vellum, miniature, oval, 5 ins / 13 cm) GBP 1,500. LONDON, 12 Dec 2003, *Military Skirmish in a Wooded Pass* (oil on canvas, 33 x 45 ins / 85 x 114 cm) GBP 3,200.

FABER, John, the Younger
Dutch, 18th century.
Born c. 1684, in The Hague; died 2 May 1756, in London.
Active also in England.
Draughtsman, engraver.
John Faber the Younger was the son and pupil of John Faber the Elder and he also worked with Jan Vander Bank. Through his frank approach he rapidly achieved fame as a mezzotint engraver. His patrons included Lely and Kneller. He is known to have executed 165 plates, some of which are of exquisite workmanship.

FABER, John
American, 19th century.
Died 1906, in New York.
Painter, watercolourist.
John Faber was a member of the New York Watercolor Club.

FABER, Josef David
Austrian, 17th century.
Born in Hall (Tyrol).
Painter.
Josef David Faber worked in many places, including Schannis, Rottenburg and Spaichingen (Baden-Württemberg), Germany.

FABER, Josepha
Maiden name: Knoll
German, 19th century.
Born 1781, in Gmünd; died 1847.
Miniaturist.

Josepha Faber was the wife of Karl and mother of Gottlob Faber.

FABER, Jürgen
German, 17th - 18th century.
Active in Hamburg.
Painter.

In 1709, Jürgen Faber executed a *Portrait of Pastor J.F. Meyer.*

FABER, Karl
German, 18th - 19th century.
Active in Gmünd.
Painter.

Karl Faber painted miniature portraits.

FABER, Karl Gottfried Traugott
German, 19th century.
Born 10 November 1786, in Dresden; died 25 July 1863, in Dresden.
Painter, engraver, lithographer. Genre scenes, landscapes.

A pupil of Klengel, Karl Gottfried Traugott Faber became a member of the Dresden academy in July 1820. His best-known works include: *Autumn Evening* and *Waterfall*.

AUCTION RECORDS:
LONDON, 14 March 1969, *View of Dresden*, Gns 650. LONDON, 20 May 1993, *View of Dresden* (oil on canvas, 20 x 29 1/4in/50.5 x 74.6cm) GBP 47,700. CALAIS, 7 July 2002, *Women in Mountainous Landscape* (1849, oil on canvas, 15 x 20 ins / 38 x 52 cm) EUR 1,800. AMSTERDAM, 2 Sept 2003, *Dresden from the Right Bank of the Elbe Below the August Bridge* (oil on canvas, 43 x 60 ins / 108 x 153 cm) EUR 23,000.

FABER, Leopold
Austrian, 18th century.
Born c. 1760, in Salzburg.
Painter, draughtsman.

FABER, Ludwig E.
American, 19th - 20th century.
Born 21 October 1855, in Philadelphia; died 1913.
Painter, watercolourist, engraver (etching).
Landscapes.

Ludwig E. Faber was a pupil of Benjamin-Constant, T. Robert-Fleury, Jules Lefebvre, and the Munich Academy. He lived in Philadelphia and was President of the Philadelphia Society of Artists and a member of the New York Watercolor Club.

AUCTION RECORDS:
NEW YORK, 7 Nov 1980, *View of Chile* (oil on canvas, 15 x 19 ins / 38.3 x 48.5 cm) USD 1,150.

FABER, Martin
Flemish, 17th century.
Born 1587, in Emden; died 1648, in Emden.
Active between 1611 and 1629.
Painter, engraver.
Flemish School.

Martin Faber was a pupil of Finsonius in Bruges. He was also an architect.

FABER, Mauritius
German, 18th century.
Active in Prüm in the middle of the 18th century.
Painter.

Mauritius Faber decorated a monastery in Prüm (Rheinland-Pfalz).

FABER, Pierre
French, 17th century.
Born in Lyons.
Active in Lyons in the first quarter of the 17th century.
Engraver (burin).

Pierre Faber was a little-known artist who signed himself *Petrus Faber* and whose name was perhaps Fabre. With the burin he engraved a series of plates for works printed in Lyons from 1621 to 1624, including the frontispiece for the *Work of the Three Theological Virtues*, by the Jesuit Fr. Suarez (Lyons, 1621), *Portrait of Louis XIII Petrus Faber fecit Lugduni*; two plates (depicting fireworks) of which one is signed *P.F.*, in the *Reception of the Very Christian Monarch Louis XIII... by the Canons and Counts of Lyons* (Lyons, J. Roussin, 1623); a frontispiece signed *Petrus Faber Lugd. fecit sculp.* and four plates, of which one was signed *Petrus Lugdunensis sculp.* in *Sun of the Sign of the Lyons* (Lyons, J.Julliéus, 1623); and *King and Queen Entering the Town of Lyons* (same printer, 1624), as well as a *Portrait of Cardinal Maurice of Savoy*.

FABER, Sebastian
German, 17th century.
Born to a family originally from Nuremberg.
Painter.

It was probably Sebastian Faber who decorated the monastery in Zwettl (Niederösterreich), Austria, around 1675.

FABER, Theodor
Dutch, 17th century.
Active in the middle of the 17th century.
Painter.

Theodor Faber produced a number of portraits.

FABER, Thomas
German, 16th century.
Died c. 1590.
Painter.

Thomas Faber worked at the church of St Nicholas in Laub.

FABER DU FAUR, Christian Wilhelm von
German, 19th century.
Born 18 August 1780, in Stuttgart; died 6 February 1857, in Stuttgart.
Painter. History painting, genre scenes.

A lieutenant in Napoleon's *Grande Armée* (and later a general in the Württemberg army), Christian von Faber du Faur fought in Napoleon's Russian campaign and painted many pictures of that war.

MUSEUMS AND GALLERIES:
MUNICH: *Captured* - TRIESTE (Civico Mus. Revoltella): *Returning from the Russian Campaign*.

FABER DU FAUR, Hans von
German, 19th - 20th century.
Born 21 November 1863, in Stuttgart; died 1949.
Painter, watercolourist. Portraits, genre scenes.

The son of Otto, Hans von Faber du Faur served in the army like his grandfather and was an officer in the Uhlans. He lived in Paris for a few years, where he worked in Whistler's studio and exhibited in various salons from 1894.

AUCTION RECORDS:
HAMBURG, 11 June 1981, *Cavalrymen in a Landscape* (1912, watercolour, 7 1/2 x 9 1/2 ins / 18.9 x 24.2 cm) DEM 2,600. LONDON, 21 March 1984, *Morning Promenade* (1920, oil on paper, 27 1/4 x 37 1/2 ins / 69.5 x 95.5 cm) GBP 6,500. LONDON, 22 March 1984, *Cavalrymen* (1914, watercolour, 11 1/4 x 16 3/4 ins / 28.5 x 42.5 cm) GBP 2,000. LONDON, 5 Dec 1986, *Cavalrymen in a Park* (1915, watercolour/paper, 7 x 8 3/4 ins / 18 x

22.5 cm) GBP 6,200. COLOGNE, 9 Dec 1986, *Start of the Race at the Seaside* (oil on card, 27 1/2 x 39 1/4 ins / 70 x 100 cm) DEM 64,000. MUNICH, 7 June 1989, *Horse Race on the Beach* (watercolour, gouache and ink, 8 x 9 1/2 ins / 20.5 x 24 cm) DEM 7,150. COLOGNE, 29 May 1999, *Three Riders* (oil on board, 22 x 29 ins / 56 x 74 cm) DEM 8,500. HAMBURG, 6 Oct 2001, *Mounted Soldier with Shield* (oil on canvas, 32 x 26 ins / 82 x 65 cm) DEM 9,000. MUNICH, 28 March 2003, *Animal Tamer* (oil on board, 28 x 39 ins / 70 x 99 cm) EUR 2,400. HAMBURG, 28 April 2004, *Elegant Riders* (oil on canvas, 33 x 39 ins / 85 x 99 cm) EUR 1,575. HAMBURG, 28 April 2004, *Women Riding in Park* (oil on board, 32 x 35 ins / 81 x 89 cm) EUR 1,575.

FABER DU FAUR, Otto von
German, 19th century.
Born 3 June 1828, in Ludwigsburg, near Stuttgart; died 10 August 1901, in Munich.
Painter, watercolourist, draughtsman. Historical subjects, battles, genre scenes.

A son of General Christian Wilhelm von Faber du Faur, Otto von Faber du Faur also drew war scenes. He was a soldier like his father and did not leave the army until 1867. He studied under Yvon in Paris and under Piloty in Munich, where he settled. He exhibited in Vienna, Berlin and Munich from 1869.

MUSEUMS AND GALLERIES:
STUTTGART: *Two Episodes from the Battle of Champigny.*

AUCTION RECORDS:
PARIS, 7 March 1921, *The Sultan's Procession*, FRF 550. PARIS, 16 and 17 Oct 1922, *Arab Market*, FRF 110; *Arabs on Horseback in a Moroccan Landscape*, FRF 200. MUNICH, 27 May 1978, *Arab Warriors' Camp* (gouache, 6 x 14 1/4in/15 x 36cm) DEM 1,900. MUNICH, 26 Nov 1981, *Convoy of Prisoners* (oil on canvas, 24 x 35in/61 x 89cm) DEM 15,000. MUNICH, 29 Nov 1984, *Retreat from Russia* (1869, oil on canvas, 37 3/4 x 58 1/4in/96 x 148cm) DEM 29,000. MUNICH, 13 June 1985, *Cavalrymen at Rest* (watercolour, 4 1/4 x 6in/11 x 15cm) DEM 1,500. LONDON, 17 March 1989, *Napoleon Saluted by the Hussars* (watercolour, 4 3/4 x 14 1/4in/12 x 36.5cm) GBP 880. NEW YORK, 16 Feb 1994, *The Victors' Return* (oil on canvas, 38 1/2 x 109in/98.1 x 276.9cm) USD 28,750. MUNICH, 6 Dec 1994, *Franco-Prussian War Scene* (1874, oil on canvas, 29 1/4 x 48 1/2in/74 x 123cm) DEM 9,200. STUTTGART, 24 Sept 1999, *Horse and Rider Galoping* (oil on board, 19 x 14 ins / 49 x 36 cm) DEM 3,800. STUTTGART, 24 Sept 1999, *Extensive Meadow Landscape with Summer Flowers in Bloom* (oil on canvas, 43 x 176 ins / 110 x 447 cm) DEM 11,000. MUNICH, 29 June 2000, *Ophelia* (1871, oil on canvas, 31 x 44 ins / 78 x 113 cm) DEM 6,000. LONDON, 12 Oct 2000, *Fantasia* (oil on canvas, 31 x 49 ins / 79 x 124 cm) GBP 18,000.

FABERE, Jean
French, 15th - 16th century.
Sculptor (wood).

Jean Fabere was working at Amiens Cathedral (Somme) in 1506.

FABERT-GALLOIS, Edmond
French, 18th century.
Born in Grenoble.
Active in Nantes from 1764 to 1780.
Painter.

FABI, Cristoforo
Italian, 16th century.
Active in Parma.
Sculptor (wood).

Cristoforo Fabi was the son of Matteo Fabi.

FABI, Francesco, or Facci
Italian, 17th century.
Born to a family originally from Soave (near Verona, Veneto); died 1621.
Painter.

Fabi painted a *Virgin* for the church of S Anastasia in Verona, in 1619.

FABI, Matteo
Italian, 16th century.
Born c. 1500, in Parma.
Sculptor (wood).

Father of Cristoforo Fabi, Matteo Fabi worked for the church of S Giovanni Evangelista at Parma and was also an architect.

FABI-ALTINI, Francesco
Italian, 19th century.
Born 15 September 1830, in Fabriano; died March 1906, in San Mariano.
Sculptor.

Fabi-altini studied in Rome with Tadolini. He is known for a *Monumental Statue of St Romuald* and the *Tomb of Cardinal Bianchi* in the church of S Gregorio Magno in Rome.

FABIAEN, Adriaen
Flemish School, 16th century.
Died December 1545.
Painter, miniaturist.
Bruges School.

The son of a painter, Jean Fabiaen (probably the same person as Jan Fabiaen), Adriaen was received as a master painter in Bruges in 1519. In 1536, he was inducted into the Guild of St Luke, as a miniaturist. His wife, also a miniaturist, became a member of the guild in 1538.

FABIAEN, Donaes
Flemish School, 16th century.
Died 1521, in Bruges.
Painter.

Donaes was the son of Jan Fabiaen.

FABIAEN, Jan
Flemish School, 16th century.
Died 1520.
Painter.
Bruges School.

Jan Fabiaen was a master in Bruges in 1469. He had many pupils and was the father of Adriaen and Donaes.

FABIAEN, Ruberecht
Flemish School, 16th century.
Active in Bruges c. 1560.
Painter.

FABIAN
Swiss, 16th century.
Active in Zurich at the beginning of the 16th century.
Painter.

FABIAN
British, 18th century.
Miniaturist.

Fabian exhibited at the Society of Arts in London in 1762.

FABIAN, Gottfried
German, 20th century.
Born 1905, in Dresden.
Painter.

After studying at Leipzig University, Gottfried Fabian attended the academy in Dresden. He had many exhibitions - in Amsterdam, Vienna, Paris, Bern, Rome and London. An abstractionist, he produced tachiste (or action-painted) canvases, in which the splashes, sometimes applied in a way that recalls the work of Sam Francis, completely or partly fill the painted surface in a moment of action rather than a spatial presentation.

FABIAN, Hans
German, 15th - 16th century.

Born to a family originally from Glatz, Silesia (now Klodzko, Poland).
Painter.

FABIAN, Henri Adolphe Paulin
French, 20th century.
Born in Étampes.
Painter.
Henri Adolphe Paulin Fabian exhibited at the Salon des Indépendants from 1925.

FABIAN, Jacobus
German, 15th century.
Born to a family originally from Glatz, Silesia (now Klodzko, Poland).
Painter.

FABIAN, Johannes
German, 16th century.
Died 15 February 1558, in Glatz, Silesia (now Klodzko, Poland).
Painter.
This artist is probably the same person as the Hans Fabian who, in 1513, was the pupil of Niclas von Lemberg in Breslau (now Wroclaw).

FABIAN, Lydia Dunham
American, 19th century.
Born 12 May 1867, in Charlotte (Michigan); died 25 May 1947, in Chicago.
Painter.

FABIAN, Max
German, 20th century.
Born 3 March 1873, in Berlin.
Painter. Portraits, genre scenes.
Max Fabian was a student at the academy of fine arts in Berlin.
MUSEUMS AND GALLERIES:
DESSAU: *Student* - GDANSK: *Bathrooms.*

FABIAN DE CASTRO. See **CASTRO Fabian de**

FABIANI, Domenico
Italian.
Painter.
This signature is believed to have been read on a painting representing Christ and the Samaritan, kept somewhere outside Leningrad.

FABIANI, Federico
Italian, 19th century.
Active in Genoa in 1835.
Sculptor.
Fabiani studied under Isola and Varni. He made a name for himself with a work depicting the *Battle of Palestro*. He also sculpted a number of funeral monuments.

FABIANO, Fabien, pseudonym of Coup de Fréjac, Jules
French, 20th century.
Born 1883; died June 1962.
Watercolourist, pastellist, draughtsman, illustrator. Figures, nudes.
Fabien Fabiano, of Breton origin, travelled widely and worked for many publications, including *Life, Elegante Welt, La Nation, Le Rire* and above all *La Vie Parisienne*. He drew women for fifty years and was called the 'serious painter of frivolities' by André Thérive.
AUCTION RECORDS:
PARIS, 16-17 May 1939, *Express Passing*, FRF 380; *Hesitation*, FRF 400. PARIS, 10 Nov 1943, *Woman Aviator* (pen drawing) FRF 100. PARIS, 19 March 1945, *Rear View of Seated Nude* (pastel) FRF 1,400. VERSAILLES, 16 Oct 1988, *Bust of Young Brunette* (pastel, 24 3/4 x 19 ins / 63 x 48.5 cm) FRF 5,100. PARIS, 21 Nov 1988, *The Golden Carriage* (red chalk, 22 x 17 3/4 ins / 56 x 45 cm) FRF 1,300. PARIS, 12 Feb 1991, *Women Bathing* (1928, oil on panel, 16 1/4 x 13 1/4 ins / 41.5 x 33.5 cm) FRF 4,000. PARIS, 7 April 1995, *Paris* (1936, mounted poster, 63 x 94 1/2 ins / 160 x 240 cm) FRF 6,000.

FABIANO DA URBINO
Italian, 16th century.
Born in Urbino.
Painter.
A member of the Order of San Domenico, Fabiano da Urbino executed a series of paintings which is in Cancelli, near Fabriano.

FABIANO DI GIOVANNI
Italian, 16th century.
Active in Perugia at the beginning of the 16th century.
Painter, sculptor.

FABIANSOHN, Heinrich
Russian, 19th century.
Born near Wesenberg.
Painter.
This painter worked mostly in St Petersburg, where he produced paintings of animals and religious subjects.

FABIARIO, Giovanni Pietro
Italian, 17th century.
Born 1585, in Udine (Friuli Venezia Giulia); died c. 1660.
Painter.
Fabiario painted an altarpiece for the cathedral in Aquileia, showing the Virgin surrounded by saints, in a landscape.

FABIEN, Cécile
French, 18th century.
Active in Paris in 1751.
Painter.

FABIEN, Henri
Canadian, 19th century.
Born in Ottawa.
Active during the second half of the 19th century.
Painter. Portraits.
Henri Fabien was a pupil of Gérôme and Dijonnet and exhibited at the Salon des Artistes Français.

FABIEN, Louis, pseudonym of Pouilloux
French, 20th century.
Born 18 January 1924, in L'Isle-Jourdain (Vienne).
Painter, engraver. Figure compositions, landscapes.
Louis Fabien is a self-taught artist. He was invited to the first Paris Biennale des Jeunes Artistes in 1959 and won the prize for painting. He exhibits, or has exhibited, at many of the yearly Paris Salons: Salon d'Automne, Salon de la Jeune Peinture, Salon de Mai, Salon Comparaisons, Salon des Peintres Témoins de leur Temps. For the last sixty years he has taken part in collective exhibitions whose purpose is the re-establishment of Realism, and his name is often associated with that of Paul Rebeyrolle. He also shows at solo exhibitions in Paris (including 1974 with landscapes of St Tropez), Lausanne and New York. He lives in the South of France. Always faithful to reality and with an elegant pointillist technique, he aims above all to catch colourful and often charming moments.

fabien

AUCTION RECORDS:
NEW YORK, 17 July 1981, *Nude with Violet Irises* (39 1/4 x 28 3/4 ins / 100 x 73 cm) USD 600. ZURICH, 8 Nov 1985, *Nude Reclining in the Sun* (oil on canvas, 19 3/4 x 39 1/4 ins / 50 x 100 cm)

CHF 5,500. PARIS, 16 June 1987, *Street in Montmartre* (oil on canvas, 22 x 18 ins / 55 x 46 cm) FRF 2,100. NEW YORK, 10 Nov 1992, *Monte Carlo by Day* (1976, oil on canvas, 29 x 39 1/4 ins / 73.5 x 100 cm) USD 1,870. NEW YORK, 22 Feb 1993, *Monte Carlo by Night* (1977, oil on canvas, 28 3/4 x 39 1/4 ins / 73 x 100 cm) USD 1,650.

FABIEN DE FLESCHIÈRES. See **FLESCHIÈRES**

FABIENNE, pseudonym of Pan, Fabienne
French, 20th century.
Born in Paris.
Active in Venezuela.
Painter, sculptor. Landscapes.

Fabienne attended the Académie de la Grande Chaumière, Paris, and exhibited at the Salon des Artistes Indépendants on 1939. Since 1971 she has again exhibited in Paris, both at the Salon des Artistes Français and in solo shows. She settled in Venezuela and has exhibited in Latin America in group and solo shows. She also sculpts and makes jewellery.

Her move to Venezuela has been a determining factor in her painting of a poeticised reality in which she depicts the harshness of her adopted country, while making use of lessons learnt from the Impressionists.

FABIJANSKI. See **FABJANSKI**

FABIO, Pio. See **PAOLINI Pio**

FABIO DA BORGO SAN SEPOLCRO
Italian, 15th century.
Active in Milan in 1471.
Sculptor (wood).

FABIO DI GENTILE DI ANDREA
Italian, 15th century.
Active in San Ginesio (Macerata) in 1442.
Painter.

Fabio di Gentile di Andrea executed an altarpiece in the manner of Crivelli.

FABISCH, Joseph Hugues
French, 19th century.
Born 19 March 1812, in Aix; died 7 September 1886.
Sculptor. Religious subjects, figures. Busts.

Joseph Hugues Fabisch studied art at the École des Beaux-Arts in Aix. From 1846 to 1878 he exhibited at the Paris Salon. His best-known works include *Mary Magdalene* (marble statue) and *Beatrix* (marble statue). He was appointed lecturer at the Lyons École des Beaux-Arts on 28 February 1860 and was awarded a second-class medal the following year.

MUSEUMS AND GALLERIES:
AIX: *Jephtha's Daughter* - LYONS: *Bust of Hippolyte Flandrin; Bust of Professor Ozanam; Bust of Artaud, the Archaeologist; Beatrix; Bust of Jean-Jacques de Boissieu.*

FABISCH, Philippe
French, 19th century.
Born 12 August 1845, in Lyons; died 14 June 1881, in Lyons.
Sculptor.

The son and pupil of Joseph Fabisch, Philippe Fabisch also worked with Dumont. He made his début at the Paris Salon in 1868.

MUSEUMS AND GALLERIES:
LE HAVRE: *Rebecca.*

FABIUS, Caius, pseudonym: Pictor
4th century BC.
Active c. 300 BC.
Painter.
Ancient Roman.

Fabius, a member of the illustrious family of the Fabii, was criticised for dishonouring the family name by becoming a painter - it is thought that the epithet Pictor (the painter) was given to ridicule him. He is cited as the first Roman painter. In 304 BC he decorated the temple of Salus in Rome, probably with a scene showing the battle in which Bibulus defeated the Samnites. These paintings existed until the time of the emperor Claudius when the temple was destroyed by fire. He cannot have been very famous in his time for Pliny seems not to have known of him and makes no mention of him in his writings. An interval of some 150 years was to pass before the advent of the next named Roman painter.

FABIUS, Jan
Dutch, 19th century.
Born 1820; died 1889.
Painter. Genre scenes.

AUCTION RECORDS:
DORDRECHT, 14 June 1972, *Children Playing in a Lane,* NLG 6,400. AMSTERDAM, 14-15 April 1992, *Children Playing near a Well in Heiloo* (oil on canvas, 18 3/4 x 23 ins / 47.5 x 57.5 cm) NLG 4,600. AMSTERDAM, 9 Nov 1994, *Student in an Interior* (1868, oil on panel, 22 x 26 ins / 55 x 66 cm) NLG 1,610. AMSTERDAM, 22 June 2004, *Harmonious Family* (oil on canvas, 31 x 41 ins / 78 x 103 cm) EUR 2,000.

FABJANSKI, Erasmus Rudolf
Ukrainian, 19th century.
Born 1829, in Zhitomir; died 1891, in Cracow.
Painter. Landscapes.

After studying medecine, Fabjanski went to St Petersburg where he became interested in painting. During the war in 1870, he fought in France in the Foreign Legion.

MUSEUMS AND GALLERIES:
LVIV: several landscapes.

FABJANSKI, Stanislaw Poraj
Polish, 19th - 20th century.
Born 1865, in Paris; died 1947.
Painter (including gouache), watercolourist. Figures, local scenes, landscapes.

Son of the painter Erasmus Fabjanski, Stanislaw Fabjanski lived in Cracow and executed many landscapes during his trips across Europe. His work shows the life of the Jews in Poland before World War II. He is particularly known for *After the Pogrom* produced in 1910.

BIBLIOGRAPHY:
Encyclopaedia Judaïca, Jerusalem, 1918.

AUCTION RECORDS:
TEL AVIV, 26 April 1997, *View of the Old City of Cracow* (1917, gouache and watercolour/panel, 15 1/4 x 19 1/2 ins / 39 x 49.3 cm) USD 9,200. LONDON, 18 March 1999, *Army Officers Riding through Snow* (1890, oil on panel, 11 x 16 ins / 27 x 41 cm) GBP 2,200.

FABRA, Alberto
Argentinian, 20th century.
Born 2 February 1920, in Buenos Aires.
Active in France from 1946.
Painter, engraver, draughtsman. Designs for mosaics. Op Art.

After studying in Barcelona, in 1946 Alberto Fabra was awarded a travel bursary and moved to Paris. Fabra worked firmly within the spirit of Op Art. His geometric figures present a very slow optical development from one plane to another through a subtle interplay of gradations of colour and values. From 1943, he took part in various group exhibitions, including in 1947 the Salon des Surindépendants, from 1948 the Salon de Mai and the Salon des Réalités Nouvelles, in 1969 the *Artistes Latino-Américains* (*Latin American Artists*) exhibition at the Musée d'Art Moderne in Paris, from 1971 the Salon Grands et Jeunes d'Aujourd'hui and from 1974 the Salon Comparaisons. He has also held solo exhibitions of his work in Barcelona, Paris, Lausanne, Geneva, Luxembourg, Worms, Düsseldorf, Milan and Bergamo.

AUCTION RECORDS:

VERSAILLES, 22 April 1990, *Young Woman with Pitcher* (1964, oil on canvas, 39 1/4 x 32 ins / 100 x 81 cm) FRF 9,800.

FABRA, Marie-Hélène

French, 20th - 21st century.
Born 1961.
Painter, draughtswoman.

Marie-Hélène Fabra graduated from the École du Louvre and the École Nationale des Beaux-Arts in Paris, where she lives and works. Her paintings depict urban scenes, between périphériques (ring roads) and new towns. Painting either from memory or from photographs, she produces canvases with a chromatic range, of warm hues of pink, red and orange reminiscent of Klee. Her expressive, somewhat dreamlike endeavour to transform the suburbs, for all the soullessness of their architecture, into something new and vibrant. The countryside is part of this transformation into almost abstract units, as, here and there, a tower or a train disturbs its pastoral serenity.

She has taken part in group exhibitions, including: Vitry, 1986; the Salon de la Jeune Peinture, 1988; the Salon des Réalités Nouvelles, 1990; *Les Saisons* (*The Seasons*) (The Seasons), at the Galerie Eric Dupont, and the Centre Régional d'Art Contemporain Le 19, in Montbéliard, 1998; *Et Toutes Elles Réinventaient le Monde* (*And All These Women Are Reinventing the World...*), 2003. In the latter, Fabra was one of 27 female artists whose work could not be pigeonholed as 'women's art'. She has also staged a number of solo exhibitions, including one at the Centre Culturel Claude Monet, at Ste-Adresse in Le Havre, in 1990.

BIBLIOGRAPHY:

Et toutes elles réinventent le monde, exhibition catalogue, Centre Régional d'Art Contemporain Le 19, Montbéliard, 2003.

AUCTION RECORDS:

PARIS, 21 March 1992, *The Rabbits* (mixed media/sheet, 45 x 57 1/2 ins / 114 x 146 cm) FRF 3,000.

FABRE

French, 14th century.
Born in Montpellier; died 1390.
Glass painter.

According to Siret, Fabre worked in several churches in Montpellier.

FABRE, Abel

French, 19th century.
Born 19th century, in Blagnac.
Sculptor.

Abel Fabre exhibited at the Salon des Artistes Français, obtaining an honourable mention in 1897.

FABRE, Auguste Victor

French, 20th century.
Born 1882, in Montpellier; died 1939, in Paris.
Painter, designer.

From 1919 Auguste Victor Fabre exhibited regularly at the Salon d'Automne, of which he was a member, showing paintings and models of decoration. He also exhibited at the Salon des Artistes Indépendants in 1925.

AUCTION RECORDS:

NEW YORK, 26 May 1992, *Fashionable Women Admiring a Dove* (oil on canvas, 24 x 30 ins / 61 x 76.2 cm) USD 1,980.

FABRE, Charles

French, 19th century.
Painter. History painting, portraits.

Charles Fabre exhibited portraits at the Paris Salon from 1836 to 1842. Perhaps the best-known example of his other works is *Charles V of Spain at the Monastery of St-Just*.

FABRE, François Xavier, or Fr. Saverio

(Baron)
French, 18th - 19th century.
Born 1 April 1766, in Montpellier; died 16 March 1837, in Montpellier.
Also active in Italy.
Painter, engraver. Religious subjects, mythological subjects, portraits, landscapes.

From childhood, François Xavier Fabre proved himself gifted in the arts. In 1781, when still young, he sent works to the Exposition de Montpellier. His first master, Coustou, recommended him to Vien and David, in whose studios he continued his studies. In 1787 he won the Prix de Rome with *Nebuchadnezzar Ordering the Execution of Zedekiah's Children*.Receiving an allowance from the king in Rome, Fabre sent a *Death of Abel* to the Salon in 1791 and worked there till 1793. After a year in Naples he settled in Florence, where he taught at the art academy. It was in Florence that he produced the majority of his works, including *Penitent Magdalene, Sixth Eclogue of Virgil, Judgement of Paris* and other paintings which figured in exhibitions in Paris and in the Salons.Having struck up a friendship with Alfieri, the Italian poet, he got to know the Countess of Albany, whom he married after the death of his friend. In her will of 29 January 1824 she appointed Fabre sole legatee, leaving him her extensive and fine collections, now in the museum in Montpellier. On his return to his native country, Fabre continued to paint. He exhibited in *Infant Oedipus* in the 1827 Salon, and was named Chevalier of the Légion d'Honneur and made a baron by Charles X.In 2001 Fabre was represented at the *Un Paese incantato. Italia dipinta da Thomas Jones a Corot* (*An Enchanted Country. Italy Depicted by Artists from Thomas Jones to Corot*) at the Centre of International Art and Culture in the Palazzo Te Mantua.

F.x. Fabre. Flor.

BIBLIOGRAPHY:

Pellicer, Laure, *Le Peintre François-Xavier Fabre (1766-1837)*, Université Paris IV-Sorbonne, Paris, 1982. Pellicer, Laure (ed.), *François-Xavier Fabre*, exhibition catalogue, Palazzo Racani-Arroni, Spoleto, De Luca edizioni d'arte, Rome, 1988. Ottani Cavina, Anna (ed.), *Un Paese incantato. Italia dipinta da Thomas Jones a Corot*, exhibition catalogue, Electa, Milan, 2001. Dagorne, Richard (dir.), *Au-delà du maître Girodet et l'atelier de David*, exhibition catalogue, Somogy, Paris, 2005 (exhibition, musée Girodet, Montargis).

MUSEUMS AND GALLERIES:

CRACOW: *Portrait of Skotniky and Mme Skotnika* - FLORENCE: *Portrait of the Countess of Albany; Portrait of Victor Alfieri* - FLORENCE (Gal. d'Arte Moderna): *Portrait of Antonio Santarelli* - LYONS: *Death of Abel* - MADRID: *Forest of Etruria* - MONTAUBAN: *Landscape* - MONTPELLIER (Mus. Fabre): *Saul, Troubled by Remorse, Thinks He Sees the Shadow of the High Priest Abim Whom He Has Killed; Death of Narcissus; Portrait of Antonio Canova; Abel Dying; Holy Family; Oedipus and Antigone; St Jerome Praying; St Sebastian; Roman Soldier at Rest; Portrait of Lady Charlemont as Psyche; Portrait of Francesco Fornaccieri, Hermit; Great Dane of the Countess of Albany; Two Portraits of Vittorio Alfieri; Portrait of the Countess of Albany; Portrait of Louis XVIII; Portrait of J. Fabre, Father of the Artist; Portrait of the Artist* (two works); *Portrait of H. Fabre, Brother of the Artist; Portrait of Gache; Preaching of St John in the Desert; Entombment; Lucca Spas* (oil on paper) - NANTES (MBA): *Full-length Portrait of Maréchal Duc de Feltre* - NARBONNE: study; *St Jerome* - PARIS (Louvre): *Neoptolemus and Ulysses Divest Philoctetes of Hercules' Arrows* - VERSAILLES: *Portrait of Jacques Coiny, Engraver*.

AUCTION RECORDS:
LONDON, 20 May 1927, *Elizabeth Fabbiola Mascagni,* GBP 420. LONDON, 3 July 1935, *Four Rustic Subjects and Park Scenes,* GBP 65. PARIS, 18 June 1973, *Half-length Portrait of a Young Woman* (1814) FRF 12,700. LONDON, 23 June 1978, *Portrait of a Young Girl* (oil on canvas, 29 1/2 x 25 ins / 75 x 63.5 cm) GBP 750. LONDON, 25 Jan 1980, *Presumed Portrait of Luisa Paolina Angelica Cosway* (oil on canvas, 29 1/2 x 25 ins / 74.9 x 63.4 cm) GBP 700. LONDON, 21 June 1984, *Portrait of Henry Richard Fox, 3rd Lord Holland* (1795, oil on canvas, 41 x 32 1/4 ins / 104 x 82 cm) GBP 7,000. MONTE CARLO, 3 April 1987, *Presumed Portrait of Governor Delanoy with View of Florence in the Distance* (1809, oil on canvas, 45 1/4 x 32 1/4 ins / 115 x 82 cm) FRF 400,000. PARIS, 3 May 1988, *View of Monastery* (pen and wash, 8 x 11 3/4 ins / 20.5 x 29.7 cm) FRF 8,500. LONDON, 14 Nov 1990, *Portrait of John Henry Petty, Earl of Wycombe and later Marquis of Lansdowne* (1795, oil on canvas, oval, 28 3/4 x 23 3/4 ins / 73 x 60.5 cm) GBP 25,300. LONDON, 13 Dec 1991, *Madonna of the Throne* (1794, oil on canvas, after Raphael, 29 1/4 x 29 1/4 ins / 74 x 74 cm) GBP 8,800. LONDON, 15 April 1992, *Half-length Portrait of Jeanne-Robertine, Marquise d'Orvilliers, with Laced Scarf Tied in a Knot and Red Band in her Hair* (oil on canvas, oval, 29 1/4 x 24 1/4 ins / 74 x 61.6 cm) GBP 6,000. MONACO, 4 Dec 1993, *Portrait of Don Luigi Grimaldi, Prince of Santa-Croce, Marquis of Pietro Vajrana, of Monaco and Genoa, Leaning on the Tomb of his Fiancée Fanny, Marchioness of Grimaldi; Posthumous Portrait of the Marchioness Fanny Grimaldi, née Baronne von Bürkenwald on the Point of Joining her First Husband, the Marquis Giovanni Battista Grimaldi in his tomb* (oil on canvas, a pair, 31 1/2 x 19 3/4 ins / 80 x 50 cm) FRF 888,000. LONDON, 6 July 1994, *View of Florence from the North Bank of the Arno towards the East* (1813, oil on canvas, 37 3/4 x 53 ins / 95.9 x 134.6 cm) GBP 309,500. LONDON, 19 Nov 1997, *Clementina Incontri, Marquise de Prié* (1803, oil on canvas, 26 x 19 3/4 ins / 66 x 50 cm) GBP 166,500. NEW YORK, 25 May 1999, *Young Man Dressed as an Arcadian Shepherd* (oil on canvas, 28 x 20 ins / 70 x 52 cm) USD 62,000. LONDON, 29 Oct 1999, *Portrait of the Marquise de Groslier Wearing Cameo Pendant* (1800, oil on canvas, oval, 15 x 13 ins / 37 x 32 cm) GBP 6,000. PARIS, 17 Nov 2000, *Philoctetes on the Island of Lemnos having been Asked by Ulysses for the Arrows of Hercules* (oil on canvas, 11 x 17 ins / 28 x 44 cm) FRF 270,000. NEW YORK, 25 Jan 2001, *Oedipus and the Sphinx* (oil on canvas, 20 x 26 ins / 50 x 66 cm) USD 190,000. PARIS, 28 June 2002, *Oedipus and Antigone* (oil on paper/canvas, 7 x 9 ins / 18 x 22 cm) EUR 20,000. ZURICH, 28 March 2003, *Portrait of William Fitzgerald* (1815, oil on canvas, 13 x 11 ins / 34 x 27 cm) CHF 17,000.

FABRE, Gérard

French, 20th - 21st century.
Born 1955, in Marseilles.
Sculptor.

Gérard Fabre studied at the École des Beaux-Arts in Marseilles-Luminy. Some of his early works are in a conceptual, Borgesian style, based on the theme of the book. He also worked with papier mâché walls. Since 1984, he has worked as a sculptor in a variety of materials, including iron bars, metal sheets and painted wood.

He has taken part in a number of group exhibitions, notably in Marseilles and other southern French towns, since 1978, including: *Le Papier (Paper)*, Auch, 1979; *Papier, Papier (Paper, Paper)*, Musée Réattu, Arles, 1980; *Les Métiers de l'Art*, Musée des Arts Décoratifs, Paris; *La Jeune Peinture à Marseille (Young Painting in Marseilles)*, Galeries de la Vieille Charité, Marseilles; *Du Cubisme à Nos Jours (From Cubism to the Present Day)*, Musée Cantini; and at the Salon de Mai in Paris, among others. He has also staged a number of solo exhibitions in Marseilles, Nantes and Nancy.

BIBLIOGRAPHY:
Cantini 84, exhibition catalogue, Musée Cantini, Marseilles, 1984. Partouche, Marc/Cyroulnik, Philippe/Villain, Nicole, *Martine Diemer, Gérard Fabre, Didier Mencoboni*, group exhibition catalogue, Centre d'Art Contemporain, Ivry-sur-Seine, 1987.

MUSEUMS AND GALLERIES:
MARSEILLES (Mus. Cantini): *Wall 02* (1981); *Rebounding* (1986).

FABRE, Gilles

French, 20th century.
Born 7 October 1933, in Blâmont.
Painter. Portraits, interiors, landscapes, flowers.

Gilles Fabre was a pupil first at the École des Beaux-Arts, Nancy, and then at the École des Arts Décoratifs, Paris. Initially he had to take employment in an architectural design office. From 1957 he exhibited at the Salon des Artistes Français, of which he was a member, and at the Salon de la Société Nationale des Beaux-Arts. He also showed in solo exhibitions, the first of which was held in 1956 at the Maison des Jeunes et de la Culture, St-Cloud; he exhibited in Paris for the first time in 1967 and subsequently in Nancy again in 1967, and in Tokyo, Osaka, Yokohama, Kobe, London, Brussels, Kuwait, Sri Lanka, Moscow and St Petersburg. He won many awards and is a Chevalier of the Ordre des Arts et Lettres and of the Ordre du Mérite.

He painted a series of Parisian landscapes. He returned to live in Lorraine, at Repaix, and painted all aspects of its landscape. However, he made study journeys nearly every year, from which he came back with sketches and drawings. His painting is sound and sincere, uninfluenced by Impressionism, but in the traditional style of the 19th-century Realists.

BIBLIOGRAPHY:
'*Gilles Fabre*' in *L'Officiel des arts*, Éd. du Chevalet, Paris, 1988.

AUCTION RECORDS:
VERSAILLES, 11 Jan 1989, *Lorraine in Snow* (oil on canvas, 28 3/4 x 36 1/4 ins / 73 x 92 cm) FRF 5,000.

FABRE, J.

French, 18th century.
Active in Switzerland during the second half of the 18th century.
Miniaturist.

J. Fabre collaborated on the illustration of a book on the Zurlauben family, which is now in the possession of the Von Schuhmacher family in Lucerne.

FABRE, Jan

Belgian, 20th - 21st century.
Born 14 December 1958, in Antwerp.
Draughtsman, watercolourist, installation artist, performance artist, director, scenographer, film writer.

Jan Fabre attended the art academy and the arts and crafts institute in Antwerp. He is a visual artist, but also a choreographer, dancer and playwright (his first play was written in 1975). From 1977 to 1980 he designed scenographies and costumes at the new Flemish theatre in Antwerp. In 1980 he produced his first play, then became interested in classical dance and opera. He lives and works in Antwerp.

Fabre became well-known in Belgium, for which he has a particular affection. Formally, his style is similar to a ritual, which has arisen out of a fusion between sculpture and theatre. The provocative dimension of his artistic practice is often a subject for discussion. This dimension fuelled his initial works, the *Money Performances* (1979), during which he burnt dollars and wrote 'money' with the ashes. He often puts his own body at the centre of his artistic devices, notably in performances. Thus, a few weeks before the performance of his play *I Am Blood*, presented at the close of the Festival d'Avignon in 2001 and which established the event, he produced a performance with sacrificial nuances entitled *Sanguis/Mantis* at the international performance festival, the *Polysonneries de Lyon* (*Polysonneries de Lyons*). Dressed in 'praying mantis' knights armour, and provided with two large antennae, he spoke, letting his mind wander for seven hours; he had his blood taken six times by a nurse, with a view to producing 'red chalk drawings' on paper.

His name is also associated with 'Bic Art', drawings or collections of objects produced with a ball-point pen, and a blue colour which would become emblematic. He sometimes integrated dead insects into his works, creating a certain sense of unease, as in *Wall of the Ascending Angels* of 1994, a dress comprising 5,000 sacred insects of Asian origin. Effectively, they constitute the relationships between the human and animal worlds, particularly the insect world, and their metamorphosis, which are the basis of the main themes of his universe. Two environments which interpenetrate and mimic each other, protect themselves - one by carapaces or shells, the other by armour or suits.

In the film *A Meeting/Vstrecha*, with Fabre disguised as a beetle and the artist Ilya Kabakov as a fly, they discuss New York's cockroaches, armed with an insecticidal spray. His sculptures and watercolours celebrate the insect in all its forms. However, a poetic environment rules supreme in Fabre's work, which verges on the fantastic and gives free reign to his unconscious mind and imagination. His installations coexist and conflict: baths, a coat, a cross, a urinal resembling a laboratory are featured; animals and human beings, the representatives of reality, are subjected to the same organic composition. He also produces photographs.

He has participated in many group exhibitions, including: 1984, Venice Biennale, which made his name on the international scene; 1994, *Encounters Like Nothing Else*, at the Mukha in Antwerp; 1995, *Nature Mutante* (*Mutant Nature*), Auch (Gers); 2000, 5th Lyons Biennale. Solo shows include: 1995, Galerie der Stadt, Stuttgart; 1999, La Chaufferie, Galerie de l'École Supérieure des Arts Décoratifs de Strasbourg; 2000, Galerie Daniel Templon, Paris; 2001, Chapelle St-Charles, Avignon; 2002, a retrospective at the SMAK, Ghent; 2003, *L'Homme qui Donne du Feu. Choix dan l'Oeuvre Sculpturale de Jan Fabre* (*The Man who Gives Fire. Choice in the Sculptures of Jan Fabre*), Château d'Arenthon, Alex (Haute-Savoie).

BIBLIOGRAPHY:

'*Jan Fabre*' in *Artforum* vol. XXX n° 1, periodical, New York, September, 1992. Arvers, Fabienne, '*Jan Fabre. L'Homme-scarabée*' in *Beaux-Arts Magazine* n° 198 p. 64, periodical, Paris, November 2000. Fabre, Jan, *Umbraculum: un lieu ombragé hors du monde pour réfléchir et travailler*, Actes Sud, Arles, 2001. Frétard, Dominique, '*L'Outrance de Jan Fabre fêtée sur tous les fronts dans une Belgique conquise*' in *Le Monde*, periodical, Paris, 26 November 2002.

MUSEUMS AND GALLERIES:

DUNKIRK (FRAC Nord-Pas de Calais): *Vleech (Meat)* (1996) - METZ (FRAC Lorraine): *Tomb of the Unknown Computer* (1993).

AUCTION RECORDS:

LOKEREN, 23 May 1992, *I Would Like You to Get Dressed...* (ball-point pen and chalk, 11 x 8 1/4 ins / 28 x 20.8 cm) BEF 33,000. LOKEREN, 4 Dec 1993, *Leaves Swirling in the Wind* (1989, ball-point pen and collage, 82 3/4 x 59 ins / 210 x 150 cm) BEF 360,000. LOKEREN, 12 March 1994, *Swords* (1987, ball-point pen and collage, 83 3/4 x 60 1/4 ins / 213 x 153 cm) BEF 300,000. AMSTERDAM, 2-3 June 1997, *Sword* (1987, ball-point pen/paper, 84 1/4 x 59 ins / 214 x 149 cm) NLG 13,570. LOKEREN, 9 Oct 1999, *Sound of One Hand Clapping* (1990, watercolour, ball-point pen and crayon, three, 6 x 4 ins / 15 x 9 cm) BEF 90,000. ANTWERP, 24 Oct 2000, *Composition* (pen, 110 x 24 ins / 280 x 60 cm) BEF 180,000. LOKEREN, 6 Oct 2001, *Knight's Garland of Roses* (armour, wood, leather beetle, sculpture, 49 x 43 ins / 124 x 110 cm) BEF 500,000. LOKEREN, 8 Dec 2001, *Berlijn Morgend Wandeling* (1988, ball-point pen, 82 x 61 ins / 208 x 156 cm) BEF 330,000. LOKEREN, 11 May 2002, *House of Flames* (1991, wood and blue ball-point pen in plexi box on iron base, 26 x 13x15 ins / 65 x 33x39 cm) EUR 6,500. NEW YORK, 10 Dec 2003, *Untitled* (synthetic resin and skull organic material, 6 x 5x8 ins / 16 x 12x21 cm) USD 2,300. ANTWERP, 26 Oct 2004, *Design for Documenta, Self-portrait* (drawing, five in one frame, 8 x 6 ins / 21 x 16 cm) EUR 2,600. ANTWERP, 22 Nov 2004, *He wat een Plezierige Zottigheid* (1987, ball-point pen and watercolour, set of four, 10 x 8 ins / 26 x 20 cm) EUR 5,000.

FABRE, Jean
French, 17th century.
Painter.

Jean Fabre may be the same artist as Jean Fabre de Brioude. He lived in Puy-en-Velay in 1652-1683.

FABRE, Jean
French, 17th century.
Born in Brioude (Haute-Loire).
Active in Brioude in 1639.
Painter.

FABRE, Louis André
Swiss, 18th - 19th century.
Born 18 September 1750, in Geneva; died 15 February 1814, in La Chaux-de-Fonds.
Miniaturist.

A pupil of P.L. Bouvier, Louis Fabre painted miniatures.

FABRE, Madeleine
French, 20th century.
Active c. 1930-c. 1955.
Sculptor. Animals.

Madeleine Fabre was invited to exhibit at the Salon des Tuileries in 1930.

FABRE, Max
French, 20th century.
Born 6 March 1928, in Marseilles.
Painter (including gouache), pastellist, draughtsman, engraver.

Max Fabre was a pupil at the École des Beaux-Arts, Marseilles, from 1944 to 1948. He exhibited at various Paris salons, such as the Salon d'Automne, the Salon de la Jeune Peinture, the Salon Comparaisons; and in 1957 at the Menton Biennale, in 1958 at the Florence Museum, and in 1967 at the museum of St-Paul-de Vence. Since 1954 he has regularly shown in solo exhibitions in Nice, mainly at the Galerie Matarasso, since 1959 in Paris, and in 1970 at the Maison de la Culture, Bourges.

He initially produced illustrations and humorous drawings, but between 1956 and 1959 painted smooth canvases in subdued tones, later introducing strokes of strong colour into the plaster-like effects. Finally he used sand in his paintings, in which the various shades of one colour often predominate. Whether his works are abstract or contain human figures, the surface is always matt, rough and suggestive of fresco painting.

MUSEUMS AND GALLERIES:

ANTIBES (Mus. Picasso) - MARSEILLES (MBA) - NICE (Mus.).

FABRE, Pierre. See also **FABER Pierre**

FABRE, Renée
French, 20th century.
Born in St-Palais (Basses-Pyrénées).
Painter.

Renée Fabre exhibited landscapes and flowers, first in 1931 at the Salon des Artistes Français and later at the Salon de la Société Nationale.

FABRE, Véra, Mme Couve de Murville
French, 20th century.
Born 15 February 1912, in Paris.
Painter, engraver. Still-lifes.

Véra Fabre exhibited in Paris and Geneva. She used the soft-ground etching technique in still-lifes that stress contour and shape. Her style is reminiscent of Morandi.

FABRE, Yolande Georgette Jeannine
Maiden name: Legrand
French, 20th century.
Born 25 October 1928, in St-Étienne.
Painter. Landscapes, still-lifes, flowers.

Yolande Fabre was a pupil of the École des Beaux-Arts, St-Étienne. She has shown at group exhibitions, mainly in Paris: 1982, 1983, 1984 Salon des Artistes Français; and in solo shows: 1986, Prieuré de Champdieu. She paints nature with a concern for light, correctness of form and harmony of colour.

FABRE D'ÉGLANTINE, Philippe François Nazaire
French, 18th century.
Born 28 December 1755, in Carcassonne; died 5 April 1794, in Paris, guillotined.
Painter, pastellist. Portraits.

Philippe Fabre d'Églantine executed a few portraits in pastel. He was also a poet and politician.

FABRE D'OLIVET, Julie (Mlle)
French, 19th century.
Painter. Genre scenes, portraits.

A pupil of Mme Haudebourt, Julie Fabre d'Olivet exhibited the following paintings at the Paris Salon: *Mother and Sister*; *The Eve of First Communion*; *Olivia's Homecoming*; and *The Protestants of the Cévennes*.

FABRE PARIS, Antonio
Spanish, 20th century.
Born 1891, in Barcelona; died 1948.
Painter, draughtsman. Portraits, scenes with figures, landscapes.

Antonio Fabre Paris studied at the school of fine arts in Barcelona and continued his training in Italy. He took part in exhibitions in Barcelona as well as exhibiting at the Salon des Artistes Français and in London. He was awarded a bronze medal at the exhibition of the national fine arts society of Madrid in 1924. He also worked as a restorer.

His painting was very rich but with simplified forms.

Bibliography:
Arnáiz, José Manuel/López Jiménez, Javier/Merchán Díaz, Manuel (ed.), *Cien años de pintura en Espana y Portugal (1830-1930)*, Antiqvaria, Madrid, 1988 (One Hundred Years of Painting in Spain and Portugal (1830-1930)).

FABRE-BONIFAY, Mme Joseph
French, 20th century.
Born 1874, in Marseilles.
Painter.

Mme Joseph Fabre-Bonifay exhibited at the Salon des Artistes Français, of which she was a member from 1903.

FABREGAT, Joaquín
Spanish, 18th century.
Born 1748, in Torreblanca; died probably 3 January 1807, in Madrid.
Engraver.

Joaquín Fabregat studied at the Real Academia de San Carlos in Valencia. He produced engravings after Lucas Giordano.

FABREGAT, Juan
Spanish, 20th century.
Born in Barcelona.
Painter. Nudes.

Juan Fabregat studied in Paris under Jules Adler and exhibited at the Salon des Artistes Français in 1929.

FABRÈGE, pseudonym of Fourestier, Jacques
French, 20th century.
Born 5 May 1896, in Béziers; died 1974.
Painter, watercolourist, engraver, illustrator.

Fabrège was a pupil at the École des Beaux-Arts, Paris, and received advice from Maurice Denis and Édouard Vuillard. He also worked with Bonnard in Cannes. He exhibited at the Salon des Artistes Français, Paris.

Auction records:
Paris, 10 July 1984, *Woman from Tours* (oil on canvas remounted on hardboard, 44 x 28 1/4 ins / 112 x 72 cm) FRF 7,500.

FABREGUETTES, François Jean
French, 19th century.
Born 20 November 1801, in Privat.
Painter.

François Jean Fabreguettes joined the École des Beaux-Arts on 21 August 1819, studying under Girodet. He exhibited at the Paris Salon from 1833 to 1850. Cited works of his include *French Butterflies*; *Grapes from the Midi*; *Partridges Tied to a Window*; *Hanging Hare*; and *Maid Playing with a Cat*.

FABRES Y COSTA, Antonio Maria
Spanish, 19th - 20th century.
Born 1854, in Gracia (Barcelona); died 1938, in Rome.
Painter, watercolourist, illustrator, sculptor. Genre scenes (harems).

Antonio Fabres y Costa studied at the Barcelona art school. He was a great admirer of the work of Mariano Fortuny y Carbo. He received a bursary from the Barcelona authorities and went to Rome in 1874, shortly after Fortuny's death. He took part in exhibitions in Vienna and Munich and was awarded gold medals. He lived in Paris from 1894 and received a silver medal at the 1900 Exposition Universelle. There he met the Mexican sculptor Jesús Contreras who was inspector general of fine arts at the time and he invited him to teach in Mexico. Fabres y Costa remained in Mexico from 1902 to 1907 and returned to Rome in 1908.

He imitated Fortuny's work both in his conventional technique and in his typical or oriental subjects including genre scenes and scenes of flirtation and romance. He was keen to evoke the Rococo style, which he did successfully but with some additional sentimentality of his own.

Bibliography:
Juler, Caroline, *Les Orientalistes de l'École Italienne*, ACR Édition, Paris, 1994 (The Orientalists of the Italian School).

Auction records:
Paris, 18 May 1897, *Young Spanish Girl*, FRF 8,370. Paris, 18 May 1897, *Young Spanish Girl*, FRF 8,370. New York, 4-5 Feb 1904, *A New Piece of Jewellery*, USD 675. New York, 12 March 1908, *The Sultane Café*, USD 460. New York, 7-10 Nov 1945, *Bowls*, USD 220. London, 24 Nov 1976, *The Sentry and his Prisoner* (1894, oil on canvas, 35 3/4 x 27 1/4 ins / 91 x 69 cm) GBP 4,000. London, 10 Feb 1977, *Horseman Drinking* (oil on canvas, 37 1/2 x 23 1/2 ins / 95.3 x 59.7 cm) GBP 1,600. New York, 25 Oct 1977, *Reading the Koran* (watercolour, 39 1/4 x 25 3/4 ins / 99.5 x 65.5 cm) USD 1,600. New York, 31 Oct 1980, *The Guard* (watercolour, 38 3/4 x 26 ins / 98.4 x 66 cm) USD 7,000. New York, 23 Feb 1983, *Jewellery Merchant in a Harem* (1883, watercolour and pencil, 38 1/4 x 26 1/4 ins / 972 x 66.7 cm) USD 4,000. London, 24 June 1984, *The Prisoner* (1894, oil on canvas, 35 1/2 x 27 1/4 ins / 90 x 69.2 cm) GBP 25,000. New York, 13 Feb 1985, *Visit to the Antiquarian* (watercolour, 21 1/4 x 29 1/2 ins / 54 x 75 cm) USD 8,000. New York, 21 May 1987, *The Pasha's Repose* (oil on canvas, 33 1/2 x 57 1/2 ins / 85 x 146 cm) USD 67,500. Paris, 7 March 1988, *The Seraglio Guard* (oil on canvas, 63 3/4 x 32 3/4 ins / 162 x 83 cm) FRF 165,000. London, 23 Nov 1988, *The Picador's Refreshment* (oil on canvas, 15 x 11

ins / 38 x 28 cm) GBP 3,080. PARIS, 17 March 1989, *The Ambush* (watercolour/paper, 39 1/4 x 31 1/2 ins / 100 x 80 cm) FRF 90,000. NEW YORK, 23 May 1989, *Young Snake Charmer* (oil on panel, 18 x 21 3/4 ins / 45.7 x 55.2 cm) USD 29,700. LONDON, 22 Nov 1989, *The Millionaire* (oil on canvas, 65 x 87 1/2 ins / 165 x 222 cm) GBP 4,180. LONDON, 15 Feb 1990, *An Oriental Man* (oil on canvas, 21 3/4 x 16 ins / 55.3 x 40.6 cm) GBP 4,180. NEW YORK, 19 Feb 1992, *The Haleberdier* (oil on panel, 25 3/4 x 15 3/4 ins / 65.6 x 40 cm) USD 13,200. LONDON, 29 May 1992, *By the River* (oil on canvas, 30 x 22 ins / 76 x 55 cm) GBP 3,300. LONDON, 17 Nov 1993, *Arab Marksmen* (watercolour, 29 1/2 x 23 1/4 ins / 75 x 59 cm) GBP 3,910. PARIS, 11 Dec 1995, *The Favourite* (oil on panel, 10 x 16 1/4 ins / 25.3 x 41.3 cm) FRF 110,000. LONDON, 15 March 1996, *In the Harem* (pencil and watercolour/paper, 21 x 14 1/2 ins / 53.4 x 37 cm) GBP 7,475.

FABRI, A. E.
20th century.
Painter. Genre scenes.
He was mentioned by Florence Levy.
AUCTION RECORDS:
NEW YORK, 12 and 13 March 1903, *Japanese Interior,* USD 160. NEW YORK, April 1903, *The Favourite of the Harem,* USD 425.

FABRI, Aloisio
Italian, 19th century.
Born 1778, in Rome; died 1835, in Rome.
Engraver.
Fabri was a highly productive artist. He engraved a huge number of works, including four plates after Raphael's frescoes in the Vatican: *Constantine Offering Rome to the Pope; The Vow of Leo III; The Coronation of Charlemagne*; and *Charlemagne's Victory over the Saracens*. Other notable works include 11 plates after Michelangelo's paintings in the Sistine chapel; these are a continuation of some plates originally begun by Cunego. Fabri may also have engraved *The Magi*. According to Vallardi, Fabri is mentioned by Le Blanc, who gives his first name as Luigi.

FABRI, Antonio
Italian, 18th century.
Active in Bologna c. 1782.
Painter.
Antonio Fabri was a pupil of G. A. Calvi.

FABRI, Giovanni Battista di
Italian, 17th century.
Active in Bologna in 1618.
Painter.

FABRI, Giulio
Italian, 16th century.
Active in Ferrara in 1586.
Painter.

FABRI, Jean
French, 15th century.
Active in Limoges.
Miniaturist, calligrapher.
Jean Fabri may be the same person as the painter Jean Faure, known as 'The Writer'.

FABRI, Joannes
Flemish, 19th century.
Born to a family originally from Antwerp; died 8 December 1874, in Antwerp.
Painter. Landscapes.
Flemish School.

FABRI, Johann
German, 16th - 17th century.
Born at the end of the 16th century, in Mainz.
Sculptor.
Johann Fabri worked in Würzburg.

FABRI, Luigi. See **FABRI Aloisio**

FABRI, Pietro
Italian, 18th century.
Born in San Giovanni in Persiceto (Emilia-Romagna).
Painter. History painting, genre scenes.
Active around 1770, Pietro Fabri was a pupil of Vittorio Bigari. His most important works are to be found in Bologna.
AUCTION RECORDS:
LONDON, 17 Dec 1982, *Fashionable Couple Fishing 'alla Lampara'* (1777, oil on canvas, 20 3/4 x 25 1/2 ins / 52.7 x 64.8 cm) GBP 6,000.

FABRI, Pietro
Italian, 18th century.
Painter. Religious subjects.
This artist worked at the church of S Maria della Carità in Mantua.

FABRI, Ralph
Hungarian, 20th century.
Born 23 April 1894, in Budapest.
Painter, engraver (etching).
Ralph Fabri studied at the royal academy of fine art in Budapest.

FABRI, Rémi
French, 17th century.
Active in Marseilles in 1631.
Painter.

FABRI, Robrecht Jan
French, 19th century.
Born 1839, in Antwerp.
Sculptor.
Robrecht Jan Fabri won the Prix de Rome. The museum of Antwerp has his *Wine* (marble).

FABRI, Vincenza
Italian, 17th century.
Active in Bologna c. 1680.
Painter.
Vincenza Fabri was a pupil of E. Sirani.

FABRI-CANTI, Noëlle
French, 20th century.
Born 25 May 1916, in Tarbes.
Sculptor, mosaicist, potter. Designs for stained glass.
Noëlle Fabri-Canti, a musician as well as an artist, was a pupil at the École des Beaux-Arts, Paris, from 1939 to 1946, and received advice from Charles Despiau. She exhibited at several Paris salons: the Salon des Artistes Français, Salon des Artistes Indépendants, Salon d'Automne, Salon d'Art Sacré. From 1942 to 1963 she showed her work in solo exhibitions in Paris, the provinces and Switzerland. She carried out many commissions for mosaics and windows for chapels and several town halls: Marseilles, Valence, Le Mans, Clermont-Ferrand. She often carved *Virgin and Child* statues in a figurative and Classical style.

FABRI-CONTI, José
French, 20th century.
Born 1920, in Nice.
Painter. Landscapes with figures.
José Fabri-Conti exhibited regularly in Paris at the Salon des Artistes Français, of which he was a member. In 1941 he won the Jean Geoffroy prize, in 1942 a second-class medal and the James Bertrand prize, and in 1943 a travel scholarship.
AUCTION RECORDS:
LUCERNE, 30 Sept 1988, *Port of Bastia* (oil on canvas, 20 3/4 x 32 ins / 53 x 81 cm) CHF 2,200. BERN, 26 Oct 1988, *Woman Flower Seller* (oil on panel, 31 1/2 x 20 3/4 ins / 80 x 53 cm) CHF

2,400. VERSAILLES, 19 Nov 2000, *Erbalunga Village, Corsica* (oil on canvas, 20 x 29 ins / 50 x 73 cm) FRF 13,500.

FABRIANO, da. See first name

FABRIANO DE BOCCO
Italian, 14th century.
Active in Fabriano (Ancona) in 1306.
Painter.
Fabriano de Bocco painted a fresco after Lanzi in the church of S Maria Maddelena.

FABRICE, Ilka Freiin von, pseudonym: Carl Freibach
German, 19th century.
Born 1846, in Dresden; died 1907, in Florence.
Painter. Portraits, genre scenes.
Fabrice exhibited in Munich under the pseudonym of Carl Freibach.

FABRICIO
Spanish, 16th century.
Painter. History painting.
Fabricio is mentioned by Siret.

FABRICIUS, Johann Christian
German, 18th century.
Born 7 January 1748, in Tondern; died 3 March 1808, in Kiel.
Painter.
It was probably Johann Fabricius who settled in Danzig (now Gdansk, Poland) in the second half of the 18th century and painted the portrait of Grand Duke Paul of Russia.

FABRICIUS, Karl
German, 17th century.
Painter.
Karl Fabricius was active in the court of Bishop Ferdinand von Furstenberg. His best-known work is a *View of Paderborn*, which now belongs to the faculty of theology in Paderborn.

FABRICIUS, Richard
German, 19th century.
Born 23 February 1863, in Berlin.
Painter.
After studying at the academy of art in Berlin, Richard Fabricius first travelled in Italy before settling in Dresden. He is best known for his *Eve* and *St Paul the Apostle* at the church in Moritzburg-Eisenberg.

FABRICOTTI, Mazzia
Italian, 20th century.
Born in Florence.
Potter.
Fabricotti was awarded an honourable mention in Paris at the Salon of the Société des Artistes Français in 1931.

FABRIKANT
French, 20th century.
Born 20th century.
Painter.
Fabrikant won the second Grand Prix de Rome in 1945.

FABRIS
German, 17th century.
Active in Mähren in 1606.
Sculptor.

FABRIS, Antonio
Italian, 19th century.
Born 24 November 1792, in Udine; died 8 February 1865, in Venice.
Sculptor, medallist.
MUSEUMS AND GALLERIES:
UDINE (Musei Civici del Castello): *Canova* - VENICE (Gal. dell'Accademia): four statuettes (terracotta).

FABRIS, Carlo Alvise
Italian, 18th century.
Died 6 November 1803, in Venice.
Painter.
Carlo Alvise Fabris was a pupil of Longhi the Elder, and of Giuseppe Angeli. In 1793, he painted a *Martyrdom of St Sophia* for the cathedral at Lendinara.

FABRIS, Domenico
Italian, 19th century.
Born 8 June 1817, in Osoppo, near Udine; died August 1893, in Turin.
Painter, draughtsman, engraver.
Domenico Fabris was the son of Antonio Fabris. He decorated several palaces in Udine, and illustrated an edition of the *Divine Comedy* published in Florence in 1841.

FABRIS, Giovanni
Italian, 19th century.
Born in Bessica; died 1842, in London.
Engraver.
Giovanni Fabris was the pupil of A. Suntach.

FABRIS, Giuseppe
Italian, 19th century.
Born 19 August 1790, in Nove di Bassano (Veneto); died 22 August 1860, in Rome.
Sculptor.
Giuseppe Fabris was sent to Rome on a grant awarded by his home province. Once there, he was accepted as a member of the Accademia di San Luca after showing a sculpture of *Milo of Croton*. He is also known for various monuments. He was appointed correspondent of the Institut de France in 1846.

FABRIS, Jacino or Aiacino
Italian, 14th century.
Active in Cividale de Aquilèia in the middle of the 14th century.
Painter.

FABRIS, Jacopo
Italian, 18th century.
Born 1689, in Venice; died 1761, in Copenhagen.
Painter. Urban landscapes, architectural views.
Fabris specialised in highly unusual views of Rome and Venice; he also developed imaginary *capricci* ('caprices') based on these and his knowledge of the Roman ruins, which were often depicted as 'stone quarries' or workshops.
AUCTION RECORDS:
COPENHAGEN, 3 Nov 1981, *Capriccio with Views of the Arch of Titus and the Arch of Constantine* (oil on canvas, 38 1/4 x 51 1/4 ins / 97 x 130 cm) DKK 44,000. ROME, 15 March 1984, *Banks of the Tiber and the Castel Sant'Angelo* (oil on canvas, 20 x 54 3/4 ins / 51 x 139 cm) ITL 6,500,000. MILAN, 4 Nov 1986, *View of the Grand Canal and the Riva degli Schiavoni* (oil on canvas, 29 1/2 x 49 1/2 ins / 75 x 126 cm) ITL 36,000,000. ROME, 8 May 1990, *View of the Tiber and Castel Sant'Angelo* (oil on canvas, 30 x 36 1/4 ins / 76 x 92 cm) ITL 82,000,000. LONDON, 3 July 1991, *View of the Roman Forum* (oil on canvas, 28 x 39 ins / 71 x 99 cm) GBP 24,200. MILAN, 29 Nov 1994, *View of the Entrance to Cannaregio, with the church of St Jerome* (oil on canvas, 26 1/2 x 31 1/2 ins / 67.5 x 80 cm) ITL 43,700,000. PARIS, 7 Nov 2001, *St Mark's Square with Stage and Play, Venice* (oil on canvas, attributed, 35x43 ins / 88x110 cm) FRF 426,000. LONDON, 11 Dec 2002, *Piazza Navona, Rome* (oil on canvas, attributed, 22x35 ins / 55x90 cm) GBP 40,000. LONDON, 12 June 2003, *View of St Paul's Cathedral* (oil on canvas, 25x43 ins / 63x108 cm) GBP 10,000.

FABRIS, Pietro
Italian, 18th century.
Painter. Genre scenes, landscapes.

Active in Naples from 1754 to 1804, Pietro Fabris worked for the English plenipotentiary to Naples, Sir William Hamilton, who commissioned paintings from him (notably a series of gouaches in 1778), and encouraged him to exhibit in London, adding the words 'English painter' after his signature. He exhibited with the Free Society in London in 1768. Fabris' views of Naples were highly popular. One of his paintings, *Ruins of the Palace of Queen Giovanna II of Naples* was engraved by Robertson.

AUCTION RECORDS:

LONDON, 31 Jan 1930, *Rome Seen from the Tiber, and a River Scene,* GBP 48. LONDON, 8 Dec 1930, *Two Views of the Bay of Naples,* GBP 14. PARIS, 15 May 1942, *Crab-Fishers* (1778) FRF 4,000. LONDON, 5 Feb 1947, *Two Scenes on the Neapolitan Shore* (1773) GBP 75. LONDON, 24 March 1976, *View of Naples* (1778, oil on canvas, 35 3/4 x 60 1/4 ins / 91 x 153 cm) GBP 6,500. LONDON, 6 April 1977, *Views of Naples* (oil on canvas, two pendants, 24 1/2 x 51 1/4 ins / 62 x 130 cm) GBP 15,000. NEW YORK, 21 Jan 1982, *Village Fête* (1773, oil on canvas, 51 x 72 ins / 129.5 x 183 cm) USD 23,000. LONDON, 4 April 1984, *View of Naples* (oil on canvas, 21 1/2 x 39 3/4 ins / 54.5 x 101 cm) GBP 18,000. LONDON, 12 Dec 1986, *View of Rome with the Arco degli Argentari and the Arco di Jano* (oil on canvas, 28 x 42 1/4 ins / 71 x 107.3 cm) GBP 10,000. NEW YORK, 11 Jan 1989, *Temples of Paestum Seen from the South-East* (watercolour and gouache, 11 x 23 1/4 ins / 27.9 x 58.8 cm) USD 26,400. MARSEILLES, 30 Sept 1989, *Lively Scene before a Triumphal Arch* (oil on canvas, 25 1/4 x 29 1/4 ins / 64 x 74 cm) FRF 120,000. ROME, 14 Dec 1989, *Woman from the Town of Chiaja* (tempera, 8 1/2 x 6 ins / 21.5 x 15.5 cm) ITL 3,680,000. LONDON, 9 April 1990, *Views of Palermo with Figures: The Cathedral Square and Piazza Vigliena* (oil on canvas, a pair, each 26 x 34 1/4 ins / 65.2 x 87 cm) GBP 253,000. ROME, 23 April 1991, *Landscape with the Arch of Trajan and Figures* (oil on canvas, 24 3/4 x 30 ins / 63 x 76.5 cm) ITL 31,000,000. LONDON, 24 May 1991, *Figures and Carriages on the Seafront Promenade around the Bay of Naples, with S Lucia and the Castel dell'Ovo* (oil on canvas, 16 1/2 x 30 ins / 41.7 x 76.3 cm) GBP 53,900. MONACO, 21 June 1991, *Dancers Performing the Tarantella; Hunt Picnic in a Landscape* (oil on paper/canvas, a pair, each 15 1/4 x 17 1/4 ins / 39 x 44 cm) FRF 166,500. LONDON, 13 Dec 1991, *Panorama of the Gulf of Pozzuoli with the Town, the Bay, Cap Miseno, Procida and Ischia, seen from the Monastery of Caùaldolesi* (1776, oil on canvas, 40 3/4 x 81 1/2 ins / 103.5 x 207 cm) GBP 88,000. NEW YORK, 16 Jan 1992, *Vast Landscape with Peasants Dancing on the Beach at Posillipo, and the Ferryboat coming in to Land, a House on a Rock Overlooking the Bay of Naples, and Vesuvius in the Distance* (1777, oil on canvas, 41 x 61 3/4 ins / 104.2 x 157.1 cm) USD 495,000. NEW YORK, 21 May 1992, *Tarantella at Posillipo: Neapolitans Grilling Fish and Eating Shellfish in front of an Inn* (1772, oil on canvas, 50 1/2 x 71 ins / 128 x 180.3 cm) USD 242,000. NEW YORK, 14 Jan 1994, *Peasants on the Strand with Vesuvius in the Distance, seen from Posilipo; Peasants on the Shore, with Bay of Pozzuoli* (1773, oil on canvas, a pair, 17 1/2 x 27 ins / 44.5 x 68.6 cm) USD 343,500. PARIS, 11 April 1995, *View of Baia and the Temple of Diana* (a pair, 15 3/4 x 30 1/4 ins / 40 x 77 cm) FRF 200,000. NEW YORK, 12 Jan 1996, *Temple of Hera at Paestum with a Peasant Woman and her Child in the Foreground, and other Figures* (oil on canvas, 22 1/4 x 36 ins / 56.6 x 90.5 cm) USD 46,000. NEW YORK, 22 May 1997, *Game of Civetta* (oil on canvas, a pair, 34 1/4 x 48 3/4 ins / 87 x 123.8 cm) USD 112,500. NEW YORK, Jan 1998, *Naples seen from the Bay with Vesuvius in the Distance, Figures Eating and Playing Music in the Foreground* (oil on card, 20 1/2 x 30 3/4 ins / 51.8 x 78.1 cm) USD 156,500. NEW YORK, 29 Jan 1999, *Kitchen: Woman Spinning, Man Mending Shoes, Girl Feeding Hens* (oil on canvas, 20x16 ins / 50x41 cm) USD 18,000. LONDON, 6 July 2000, *Mediterranean Port Scene with Fishermen Drawing their Catch* (1777, oil on canvas, 41x62 ins / 103x157 cm) GBP 260,000. VENICE, 23 Sept 2000, *Women and Men in Popular Calabrese Costumes* (tempera, set of four, 13x10 ins / 32x26 cm) ITL 30,000,000. PARIS, 27 Nov 2002, *Spaghetti Eaters on the Bay of Naples, Vesuvius in the background* (gouache, 17x22 ins / 42x56 cm) EUR 23,000. NEW YORK, 23 Jan 2003, *Festival of the Madonna dell'Arco Naples* (1777, oil on canvas, 41x61 ins / 103x154 cm) USD 700,000. MILAN, 12 Nov 2003, *Pozzuoli Bay* (1776, tempera, 11x19 ins / 28x49 cm) EUR 42,000.

FABRIS, Placido

Italian, 19th century.
Born 26 August 1802, in Pieve d'Alpago; died 7 December 1859, in Venice.
Painter. Historical subjects, portraits.

Placido Fabris was a pupil at the Accademia di Belle Arti in Venice.

MUSEUMS AND GALLERIES:

VENICE (Gal. dell'Accademia): 11 paintings - VENICE (Gal. Reale): *Portrait of Captain Gaspard Graghetta; Episode from Jean Bernard; Madonna, Jesus, St John and Zacharias; The Parents of the Artist; Rape of Europa; Virgin and Child with St Antony of Padua and St Catherine; Antonio Canova; Cupid and Psyche; Virgin and Child.*

FABRIS, Toni

Italian, 20th century.
Born 1915, in Bassano del Grappa.
Sculptor.

Toni Fabris was a student at the Accademia di Brera in Milan. He creates abstract works, constructed according to a concept of space and emptiness that has its roots in Cubism. He also makes films about kinetic sculpture, and has executed a monumental sculpture for a school in Milan.

He has been involved in collective exhibitions since 1950, most notably in Italy, Holland, and at the 1963 exhibition *Galeries-pilotes du monde* (*Pilot Galleries of the World*) at the Musée Cantonal in Lausanne, Switzerland. He also exhibits his works in solo exhibitions, one of which was held in Milan in 1962.

FABRITIUS, Barent or Bernaert, or Fabricius

Flemish, 17th century.
Born 1624; died 1673.
Active between 1650 and 1672.
Painter, draughtsman. Religious subjects, mythological subjects, portraits.
Flemish School.

Barent Fabritius was probably a pupil of Rembrandt. He possibly lived in Amsterdam where he continued the work of his brother Carel, primarily executing Biblical scenes.

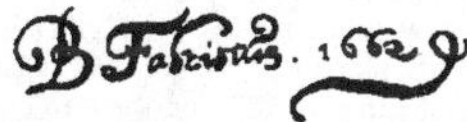

MUSEUMS AND GALLERIES:

AMSTERDAM: *Portrait of Willem van der Helm, Architect of Leiden, with his Wife and Child* - ARRAS: *The Three Angels at the House of Abraham* - BERGAMO (Accademia Carrara): *The Satyr and the Peasant* - BUDAPEST: *Portrait of a Man* - COPENHAGEN (Statens Mus. for Kunst): *Presentation of Christ at the Temple* - DRESDEN: *Portrait of a Young Woman* - KASSEL: *Mercury and Argus* - LONDON (NG): *The Adoration of the Shepherds* (1667, oil on canvas); *The Naming of St John the Baptist* (1650-1655, oil on canvas) - MUNICH: *Portrait of a Young Man* - ROHRAU (Schlossmuseum, Graf Harrach'sche Familiensammlung): *Head of an Old Man*; two works - STOCKHOLM: *Family at Table; Chemist in his Laboratory.*

AUCTION RECORDS:

PARIS, 27 Feb 1896, *Pythoness,* FRF 3,000. PARIS, 14 Oct 1896, *Portrait of a Military Man,* FRF 650. NEW YORK, 12-13 March 1903, *Philosopher,* USD 150. LONDON, 3 Feb 1922, *Monk*

Meditating, GBP 5. LONDON, 24 Feb 1922, *Christ before Pontius Pilate,* GBP 84. LONDON, 26 June 1922, *Landscape with Venus and Adonis,* GBP 445. PARIS, 27 Nov 1922, *David before the Fight* (school of B. F.) FRF 950. LONDON, 11 May 1923, *The Duet,* GBP 57. LONDON, 8 June 1923, *Young Girl Seated,* GBP 29. LONDON, 4 July 1924, *Young Boy Holding Dead Magpie,* GBP 42. LONDON, 19-20 May 1926, *Old Man in a Brown Coat,* GBP 13. LONDON, 5 July 1926, *Peasant and his Wife Seated under a Tree,* GBP 30. LONDON, 19 March 1928, *Departure of the Prodigal Son,* GBP 105. LONDON, 29 June 1928, *Moses Writing the Pentateuch* (1656) GBP 44. LONDON, 1 Feb 1929, *Young Boy Dressed in Black Silk* (1657) GBP 210. LONDON, 28 June 1929, *Adoration of the Shepherds,* GBP 105. LONDON, 29 Nov 1929, *Tobias and the Angel at the Stream,* GBP 42. LONDON, 16 June 1930, *Old Man Sharpening a Quill,* GBP 204. NEW YORK, 11 Dec 1930, *The Family of Dr Tulp,* USD 6,000. LONDON, 6 Feb 1931, *Two Children on a Terrace,* GBP 37. GENEVA, 27 Oct 1934, *Old Man Reading,* CHF 8,100. LONDON, 28 Feb 1936, *Belshazzar Holding a Cup,* GBP 11. LONDON, 10-14 July 1936, *Joseph Recounting his Dreams* (pen and bistre drawing) GBP 21. LONDON, 28 Oct 1936, *St Peter in Prison,* GBP 190. LONDON, 18 Dec 1936, *A Negro,* GBP 25. LONDON, 23 June 1937, *Elijah and Samuel,* GBP 2,900. PARIS, 16 Dec 1942, *The Adulteress* (painting in grisaille) FRF 16,000. LONDON, 4 March 1943, *Man with Long Hair,* GBP 31. PARIS, 25 May 1949, *Balaam's Ass,* FRF 125,000. LONDON, 29 June 1962, *Hippocrates Visiting Democritus in Abdera,* Gns 380. LONDON, 24 June 1964, *The Circumcision,* GBP 650. AMSTERDAM, 27 Sept 1966, *St Matthew,* NLG 5,400. NEW YORK, 22 Oct 1970, *Christ and the Woman Taken in Adultery,* USD 25,000. LONDON, 29 March 1974, *Elijah and the Widow of Zarephath,* Gns 1,900. LONDON, 9 April 1981, *Young Girl at a Window Plucking a Bird* (pen and wash/paper, 6¾ x 5¾ ins / 17.2 x 14.7 cm) GBP 7,500. STOCKHOLM, 19 May 1992, *Judas Iscariot Receiving the Thirty Deniers from the Hands of the High Priest* (oil on canvas, 39¾ x 59 ins / 101 x 150 cm) SEK 25,000. LONDON, 8 July 1999, *Self-portrait as St John the Evangelist* (print, 39 x 33 ins / 99 x 83 cm) GBP 30,000. LONDON, 16 Dec 1999, *Circumcision* (oil on panel, 18 x 18 ins / 46 x 46 cm) GBP 18,000. LONDON, 11 July 2001, *Abraham Entertaining the Three Angels. Compositional Sketch* (pen and brown ink wash over black chalk, double-sided, 7 x 9 ins / 17 x 23 cm) GBP 1,700.

FABRITIUS, Carel

Dutch, 17th century.

Born 1624 or 1625, possibly in Midden-Beemster; died 12 October 1654, in Delft.

Painter. Religious subjects, mythological subjects, portraits, genre scenes.

Delft School.

Carel Fabritius was a versatile artist who has frequently been confused with his brother Barent Fabritius. He entered the Delft painters' guild on 29 October 1652. He perished with the rest of his family in an explosion of the municipal arsenal in Delft, which also destroyed the works in his studio. He was the most gifted pupil of Rembrandt, whose influence was largely felt in the works of his youth. Very few of his pictures survive and his output was in any case scanty. Particularly noteworthy is his *Portrait of Abraham de Hotte.*

Depite the paucity of his paintings, Fabritius is notable for several reasons. Not only was he a pupil of Rembrandt, but he was also the master of Vermeer of Delft, on whom he exerted an important influence. One of the few works to come down to us is his *Goldfinch,* which aroused considerable contemporary interest, due mainly to the accuracy of the rendering, the psychological quality and the minute observation of light that informs the work. It is of note that the same phenomenon of exactitude pervades the entire output of Vermeer. Fabritius' work shared Rembrandt's Expressionist potential and foreshadowed the 'nouveau roman' Objectivism which was to constitute the mystery of the appearance of the paintings of his pupil Vermeer.

BIBLIOGRAPHY:

Brown, Christopher, *Carel Fabritius: complete edition with a catalogue raisonné,* Phaidon, Oxford, 1981. Liedtke, Walter, *A View of Delft: Vermeer and his contemporaries,* Waanders, Zwolle, 2000.

MUSEUMS AND GALLERIES:

AMSTERDAM: *The Beheading of John the Baptist* - BERLIN (National Mus.): *Study of a Man Praying* (attributed) - LONDON (NG): *A View of Delft, with a Musical Instrument Seller's Stall* (1652, oil on canvas); *Self Portrait* (1654, oil on canvas) - MUNICH: *Portrait of a Young Man* - ROTTERDAM (Mus. Boijmans Van Beuningen): *Portrait of a Man* - SCHWERIN: *The Sentinel* - THE HAGUE: *Goldfinch* - WARSAW: *The Raising of Lazarus.*

AUCTION RECORDS:

PARIS, 5 Oct 1890, *The Donkey of Balaam,* FRF 420; *Goldfinch,* FRF 5,500. PARIS, 25 June 1892, *Abraham,* FRF 5,070. PARIS, 27 Feb 1896, *Goldfinch,* FRF 6,200. NEW YORK, 7-8 April 1904, *The Lawyer,* USD 160. NEW YORK, 9-10 April 1908, *The Alchemist,* USD 200. LONDON, 23 July 1909, *Head of an Old Man,* GBP 78. LONDON, 18 July 1910, *Satyr and Peasant,* GBP 31. LONDON, 14 Dec 1923, *Old Man Praying,* GBP 19. PARIS, 13 Nov 1924, *Portrait of a Man* (school of Carel Fabritius) FRF 400. LONDON, 12 Dec 1924, *Young Man,* GBP 6,615. LONDON, 6 May 1925, *Ruth and Naomi,* GBP 830. PARIS, 7 July 1926, *Head of a Man* (attributed) FRF 3,000. LONDON, 22 March 1934, *Tobias and the Angel,* GBP 36. GENEVA, 25 May 1935, *Woman Reading,* CHF 5,450. LONDON, 16 Dec 1938, *Old Woman Reading a Book,* GBP 29. LONDON, 26 April 1939, *Saul and David,* GBP 95. LONDON, 19 June 1942, *A Man in Black Garb and Headgear,* GBP 94. PARIS, 25 Nov 1946, *Presumed Portrait of Rembrandt* (attributed) FRF 6,200. AMSTERDAM, 17-18 Dec 1946, *Portrait of an Elderly Woman,* NLG 675. PARIS, 7 Dec 1950, *Return of the Prodigal Son,* FRF 400,000. LONDON, 24 June 1959, *Double Portrait of Children,* GBP 3,400. LONDON, 1 April 1960, *Portrait of Rembrandt,* GBP 14,700. LONDON, 29 Nov 1961, *Young Woman with Oriental Hairstyle,* GBP 5,000. LONDON, 3 July 1963, *Portrait of a Young Woman,* GBP 3,400. LONDON, 1 April 1966, *Portrait of a Young Man,* Gns 3,600. LONDON, 30 Nov 1973, *Portrait of a Man* (1650) Gns 13,000. LONDON, 25 March 1977, *Portrait of a Man* (1650, oil on panel, oval, 11½ x 9 ins / 29.2 x 23 cm) GBP 6,500. MONTE CARLO, 22 June 1985, *Mercury and Argus* (oil on canvas, 29 x 41 ins / 73.5 x 104 cm) FRF 7,200,000.

FABRITIUS, Carl Ferdinand

Austrian, 17th century.

Born 1637, in Warsaw; died 21 January 1673, in Vienna.

Painter. Landscapes.

A pupil of J.L. Kegl in Vienna, Carl Fabritius went on to become painter to Emperor Leopold I.

FABRITIUS, Chillian

German, 17th century.

Died 1633, in Dresden.

Painter, engraver (etching).

Chillian Fabritius is best known for a *Holy Family* and some hunting scenes.

MUSEUMS AND GALLERIES:

MAINZ: *Landscape with River.*

AUCTION RECORDS:

LONDON, 19 Nov 1926, *St Cecilia* (drawing) GBP 12.

FABRITIUS, Gaaf Meynertsz.

Dutch, 17th century.

Died October 1666.
Engraver, goldsmith.
Gaaf Meynertsz. Fabritius belonged to the Haarlem guild in 1640.

FABRITIUS, Georg
Bohemian School, 16th century.
Active probably in Bohemia.
Miniaturist.
Georg Fabritius produced two miniatures dated 1585.

FABRITIUS, Jean
Dutch, 17th century.
Painter. Landscapes, still-lifes.
MUSEUMS AND GALLERIES:
LA FÈRE: *Flowers and Fruit.*
AUCTION RECORDS:
BRUSSELS, 21 Sept 1968, *Landscape and Ruins,* BEF 40,000.

FABRITIUS, Johann Jakob
German, 18th century.
Active in Danzig (now Gdansk).
Painter.
Johann Fabritius is best known for his portrait of the syndic Gottfried Lengnich.

FABRITIUS, Josef
Austrian, 18th century.
Born 1746, in Buchlovice; died 18 October 1799, in Vienna.
Painter.

FABRITIUS DE TENGNAGEL, Frederik Michael Ernst
Danish, 19th century.
Born 2 January 1781, in Fyn; died 27 May 1849.
Painter. Landscapes with figures.
This artist was a pupil of J. P. Möller, and mostly painted snowy landscapes.
MUSEUMS AND GALLERIES:
COPENHAGEN.
AUCTION RECORDS:
NEW YORK, 13 Feb 1985, *Winter Landscape at Sunset* (1837, oil on panel, 23 x 33 ins / 58.5 x 83.8 cm) USD 7,750. COPENHAGEN, 8 Feb 1995, *Winter Landscape with a Dolmen in the Foreground and Birds Overhead* (1841, oil/mahogany). LONDON, 12 June 1996, *The Dolmen in Winter; The Dolmen in Summer* (1841, oil on panel, a pair, 9½ x 11 ins / 24 x 27 cm and 11 x 15 ins/27 x 38 cm) GBP 5,750. AARHUS, 8 Jan 2001, *Landscape* (oil on canvas, 29 x 42 ins / 74 x 106 cm) DKK 21,000.

FABRIZI, Fabrizio
Italian, 16th century.
Active in Sant'Angelo c. 1500.
Painter.
Fabrizio Fabrizi executed a number of frescoes.

FABRIZIO, Andrea. See **PARMIGIANO**

FABRIZIO DA CAPUA
Italian, 16th century.
Active in Naples.
Sculptor.

FABRIZIO VENEZIANO
Italian, 16th century.
Active in Venice.
Painter.
According to Vasari, Fabrizio Veneziano painted a fresco in the church of S Maria Sobenigo.

FABRIZZI, Anton Maria
Italian, 16th - 17th century.
Born 1504, in Perugia; died 1549, in Perugia.
Painter.
Anton Fabrizzi went to Rome when young and was, according to Pascoli, the pupil of Annibale Carracci until the age of 15.

FABRO, Jean
French, 16th century.
Sculptor, architect.
Jean Fabro was the son-in-law of Jean Gaildé. Between 1515 and 1517, he worked on the rood screen of the church of the Ste-Madeleine in Troyes (Aube).

FABRO, Luciano
Italian, 20th century.
Born 1936, in Turin.
Sculptor, installation artist, environmental artist, performance artist.
Arte Povera.
Luciano Fabro lives and works in Milan. His creations may seem entirely disparate, to which he responds that coherence between different elements across all sections of a work seem unnecessary to him, and that a deeper coherence is provided by the very identity of the artist.His creations are enormously diverse in their appearance, but it has been suggested by Fabro himself that what links them is that they all fall within the domain of Arte Povera. This is convenient, given that the artists using this concept (first coined by Germano Celant in 1967) have never been able to agree on what it really means. The most widely accepted interpretation is that it involves using 'poor', uncommon materials. This does not apply to Fabro, however, as many of his works are made from large blocks of marble, or else sections of works are made of bronze, gold, and other expensive materials. Another interpretation of Arte Povera hinges on the fact that the materials used are not modified or refined. This is true of some of Fabro's works, but in fact the majority are either carefully executed, such as *Lo Spirato* (1968-1973) for example, or presented with research, as in his 1969 work *Edera.* Another version of Arte Povera interprets the term 'poor' as relating to spontaneous, intuitive art, operating within the space of life itself and not in the artificial space of art. This is in fact true of all Fabro's works. The artist himself regards his creations as Arte Povera in that he is seeking to uncover their 'nudity', or what lies beneath them. He explains:'When I create a work, my ambition is to make something extremely complex, rendered in an extremely simple way. But complexity must be reflected in this simplicity.'He means that an artistic creation falls outside the bounds of representation, but is above all an undertaking, an act of knowing and understanding as much for the artist himself as for the viewing public. Each one of his works demands analysis; this is new, different and difficult every time, and sometimes seems like a gloss. This cognitive demand is probably the true objective of his art: once again, this links Arte Povera with the wider movement of conceptual art. However, if we look at the many forms his output takes, any possible adherence to Arte Povera should not overshadow the creative expression manifested in his performance art. There are numerous examples, including *Cubo Specchiatto* (1967-1975), in which a participant is placed inside a cube made out of two-way mirrors, so that he sees infinite reflections of himself, while the spectators outside can only see a single reflection of themselves. Likewise, the following brief description of *Lo Spirato* demonstrates the luxurious nature and potential beauty of some of his creations. After some photographic work, Fabro wrapped himself in a sort of shroud and then made a mould of himself, allowing him to produce a recumbent statue of himself in plaster, which he then replicated in marble.

Fabro has been involved in various international collective exhibitions, most notably the Biennale des Jeunes Artistes in Paris in 1971; *Documenta* in Kassel in 1972; the Nouvelle Biennale de Paris in 1985; *Zero to Infinity: Arte Povera 1962-*

1971, Tate Modern, London; Walker Art Center, Minneapolis; Museum of Contemporary Art, L.A; Hirshhorn Museum and Sculpture Garden, Washington, D.C in 2001; *Les Années 70: l'art en cause* (*The 1970s: Art in Question*), at the Capc-Musée d'Art Contemporain in Bordeaux in 2002.

Fabro's creations have also been shown in solo exhibitions in Turin, Milan, Antwerp, the Sparta gallery in Chagny (Burgundy), Rome, Basel, Cologne, Brescia and New York. Many of these exhibitions have been held in museums, and some have been retrospectives. Examples include the Folkwang museum in Essen in 1981; the Boymans van Beuningen museum in Rotterdam in 1982; the Pinacoteca di Ravenna in 1984; at the Edinburgh Fruitmarket in 1987; the museum of modern art in Paris and the Nouveau Musée in Villeurbanne, eastern France; the Palais des Beaux-Arts in Brussels and the Kunstverein in Munich in 1988; the Rivoli museum in Turin in 1989; the Miró foundation in Barcelona in 1990; the Kunstmuseum in Lucerne and the Museum of Modern Art in San Francisco in 1991; and the Pompidou Centre in Paris in 1996.

BIBLIOGRAPHY:

Sanna, J., *Fabro*, Essegi, Ravenna, 1983. Fabro, Luciano, *Fabro, travaux - entretiens, 1963-1986*, Art Édition, Paris, 1987 (important documentation). Lageira, Jacinto, '*Luciano Fabro: le miroir des sens ou quelques tautologies sur l'expérience artistique*' in *Artstudio*, periodical, Gal. Templon, Paris, summer 1989. Rowell, Margit, '*Entretien: Luciano Fabro, questions d'identité*' in *Art Press*, periodical, Paris, February 1991. Sanna, Jole de, '*Luciano Fabro*' in *coll. Zeta Università Saggi*, Campanotto, Pasian di Patro, 1996. '*Luciano Fabro*' in *coll. Contemporains - Monographie*, exhibition catalogue, Éd. du Centre Georges-Pompidou, Paris, 1996. Ammann, Jean-Christophe/Celant, Germano/Szeemann, Harald/Trini, Tommaso, *Arte povera in collection*, exhibition catalogue, Castello di Rivoli-museo d'Arte contemporanea, Torino, Charta, Milan, 2000 (text in Italian and English). Zahm, Olivier (preface), et al., *Trésors publics, 20 ans de création dans les Fonds régionaux d'art contemporain*, Flammarion, Paris, 2003 (text in French and English).

MUSEUMS AND GALLERIES:

AMSTERDAM (Stedelijk Mus.) - CARQUEFOU (FRAC Pays de la Loire): *Etude pour Lo Spirato* (*Study for Lo Spirato*) (1971) - DIJON (FRAC Bourgogne): *Mezzo specchiato mezzo transparente* (*Mezzo Specchiato Mezzo Transparente*) (1965) - MAASTRICHT (Bonnefantenmus.): *Pavement* (1967-1988, printer's zinc) - NANTES (MBA) - NÎMES (Carré d'Art, MAC): *Drunken Flag* (1991, brass, fabric, electric cable, paint) - OTTERLO (Kröller-Müller Mus.): *The Two Sides of the Sky* (1986, marble) - PARIS (FNAC): *Sisyphus* (1994) - PARIS (MNAM-CCI): *Foot* (1968-69); *Infinito* (1989, marble) - ROCHECHOUART (Mus. Départemental d'Art Contemporain): *Habitat delle Erbe* (1980) - SAN FRANCISCO (MoMA): *Demetra* (1987, stone and steel cable).

AUCTION RECORDS:

MILAN, 10 Dec 1985, *Murano Glass and Natural Seta* (1972, Murano glass, h. 104 ins / 264 cm) ITL 36,000,000. NEW YORK, 5 May 1993, *Ephesus* (1986, marble, 138 x 38 x 15 ins / 350.5 x 96.5 x 38 cm) USD 74,000. ZURICH, 19 June 2001, *Caspar David Friedrich* (metal construction, 62 x 28 ins / 157 x 70 cm) CHF 50,000. LONDON, 22 Oct 2001, *Package Italy* (1970, lead, 20 x 47x24 ins / 50 x 120x60 cm) GBP 80,000. LONDON, 7 Feb 2002, *IT-ALIA* (1971, mirror and lead crystal on wood in two parts, 30 x 58x4 ins / 77 x 148x9 cm) GBP 100,000. LONDON, 22 Oct 2002, *Golden Italy* (gilt bronze and steel cable, h. 36 ins / 91 cm) GBP 145,000. LONDON, 6 Feb 2003, *Hole 8 mm* (1967, stainless steel, 76 x 39 ins / 194 x 99 cm) GBP 8,000. LONDON, 22 Oct 2003, *Effimero 3* (1986, pencil, cut-out paper, cardboard and blade, 39 x 24 ins / 100 x 60 cm) GBP 4,500. LONDON, 24 June 2004, *De Italia* (1972, leather, 39 x 35 ins / 99 x 90 cm) GBP 5,000. LONDON, 19 Oct 2004, *Circle and Rectangle* (1964, glass, 38 x 56 ins / 96 x 142 cm) GBP 16,000.

FABROL, Yehan

French, 16th century.
Active in Toulouse in 1520.
Painter, miniaturist. Cards.

FABRON, Luigi

Italian, 19th century.
Born 26 October 1855, in Turin; died 24 September 1905, in Pozzuoli.
Painter, watercolourist. Figures, portraits, genre scenes.

Luigi Fabron was a pupil of the sculptor Lista in Naples, then of Domenico Morelli. In Paris, where he lived for several years, he exhibited portraits at the Salon from 1877 to 1879.

AUCTION RECORDS:

NEW YORK, 10 Feb 1903, *Turkish Soldier*, USD 120. ROME, 13 May 1986, *Odalisque* (watercolour, 6 3/4 x 7 ins / 17 x 18 cm) ITL 1,500,000. AMSTERDAM, 30 Oct 1991, *Spanish Shepherds Talking* (oil on panel, 13 x 8 ins / 33 x 20.5 cm) NLG 3,450. AMSTERDAM, 22 April 1992, *Haymaking* (1877, oil on panel, 12 1/4 x 9 1/2 ins / 31 x 24 cm) NLG 3,450. AMSTERDAM, 29 April 2003, *Spanish Herdsmen Conversing* (oil on panel, 13 x 8 ins / 34 x 20 cm) EUR 1,900.

FABRY, Élisée or Élysée

Belgian, 20th century.
Born 1882, in Liège.
Painter. Landscapes.

Élisée Fabry was a student of Richard Heinz. He painted typical, sometimes anecdotal landscapes of the Belgian Ardennes.

AUCTION RECORDS:

BRUSSELS, 25 Feb 1981, *Corner of a Village in the Ardennes* (oil on canvas, 25 1/2 x 31 1/2 ins / 65 x 80 cm) BEF 8,500. PARIS, 3 Feb 1988, *Village of Targnon* (1924, oil on canvas, 36 1/4 x 46 ins / 92 x 117 cm) FRF 3,900. BRUSSELS, 12 June 2002, *Rocks at Sy* (oil on canvas, 21 x 26 ins / 54 x 65 cm) EUR 1,800. BRUSSELS, 15 Oct 2003, *Horizon* (oil on canvas, 32 x 39 ins / 82 x 100 cm) EUR 1,500.

FABRY, Émile Bartelemy

Belgian, 19th - 20th century.
Born 30 December 1865, in Verviers; died 1966, in St-Pieters-Woluwe.
Painter. Figure compositions. Murals.
Symbolism.

Émile Fabry was a student of Jean François Portaels at the Académie des Beaux-Arts in Brussels, where he was made a professor from 1900. He was one of the founders, with Jean Delville, of the Pour l'Art (For Art) circle. He exhibited at the Salon de l'Art Idéaliste in Brussels and the Salon de la Rose-Croix in Paris. He was made a member of the Académie Royale in Belgium.

In common with many Belgian painters of his generation, he was deeply influenced by Symbolist poetry, which was in favour with Belgian writers such as Maeterlinck, and by the painters William Blake, Henry Fuseli and Ferdinand Hodler. In the next generation, this adherence to Symbolism was followed by an active participation in the Surrealist movement, both by writers and artists. Symbolism and then Surrealism seemed to find congenial conditions in the Flemish unconscious, which was counterbalanced by an equal aptitude for Expressionism, when the two were not combined as in the case of James Ensor.

In technical terms, Émile Fabry practised a pointillist form of Post-Impressionism, like other artists of the Symbolist movement, such as Puvis de Chavannes, Henri-Martin and Maurice Denis. He produced a great many mural decorations: for the communal residence of St-Josse, the regional palace of Brabant, the museum of Central Africa in Tervuren, the Théâtre de la Monnaie (Theatre of the Mint) in Brussels, the communal residences of Laeken and St-Gilles in Brussels and part of the painting in the Palais du Cinquantenaire (palace of the golden jubilee) in Brussels. He was called to Cardiff to decorate University College. His compositions are rigorously constructed according to classical guidelines (Blake), with a symmetrical balance of masses and light in the two lateral parts in relation to the central theme, the depth of spacing in the planes, and so on, for example in *The Fates*. The drawing and the relief are deliberate and robust (Hodler). The lighting emphasises the action (Füssli). His nudes, frequently from mythology and allegory, are powerfully portrayed, with well-developed and dynamic anatomy and musculature, in chiaroscuro relief that is reminiscent of Rembrandt. In the early period of his life, he painted allegories of the dark forces oppressing a suffering humanity, in accordance with Maeterlinck's *Pelleas and Melisande*. Later, his themes and coloured harmonies blossomed in the brilliance of light with new allegories with a solar quality, in which fauns are charmed by poets. In his many monumental compositions, his rigorous sense of rhythmic composition is further reinforced in the style of Rubens.

MUSEUMS AND GALLERIES:

BRUSSELS (Mus. royaux des Beaux-Arts de Belgique): *Fiancée* - OSTEND (Mus. voor Schone Kunsten).

AUCTION RECORDS:

LONDON, 12 Nov 1970, *The Ages of Life,* GBP 900. PARIS, 4 April 1979, *Despair* (1892, red chalk, 15 1/2 x 12 1/2 ins / 39.5 x 31.5 cm) FRF 5,600. LONDON, 15 June 1982, *Journey* (1893, oil on canvas, 51 1/2 x 82 3/4 ins / 131 x 210 cm) GBP 13,000. LONDON, 27 March 1984, *Portrait of Miss Shakerley* (1918, pastel and pencil, 16 1/2 x 13 ins / 42 x 33 cm) GBP 650. ANTWERP, 3 April 1984, *Mythological Subject* (oil on canvas remounted on board, 41 x 22 3/4 ins / 104 x 58 cm) BEF 32,000. LONDON, 8 Feb 1985, *Temptation* (1912, oil on canvas, 49 1/4 x 38 1/4 ins / 125 x 97 cm) GBP 1,200. LONDON, 25 Nov 1987, *Call of the Sea* (1915, pastel, 24 x 31 3/4 ins / 61 x 80.5 cm) GBP 12,000. LONDON, 27 June 1988, *Poet* (1915, pastel/paper, 21 1/2 x 7 3/4 ins / 54.5 x 19.7 cm) GBP 18,700. LONDON, 22 Nov 1989, *Faun Playing the Pipe* (oil on canvas, 52 x 46 ins / 132 x 116 cm) GBP 7,150. LOKEREN, 21 March 1992, *Waiting* (oil on canvas, 47 1/4 x 78 3/4 ins / 120 x 200 cm) BEF 300,000. LOKEREN, 28 May 1994, *Thinker* (oil on card, 24 x 16 1/4 ins / 61 x 41 cm) BEF 50,000. NEW YORK, 20 July 1995, *Plinth* (oil on canvas, 30 3/4 x 48 1/2 ins / 78.1 x 123.2 cm) USD 9,200. AMSTERDAM, 25 Oct 1999, *Circle of Life* (oil on canvas, 53 x 68 ins / 135 x 173 cm) NLG 32,000. LONDON, 3 April 2001, *Dance* (1896, oil on canvas, 26 x 43 ins / 65 x 108 cm) GBP 10,000. BRUSSELS, 12 Nov 2001, *Young Woman, Black Period* (oil on canvas, 31 x 26 ins / 80 x 65 cm) BEF 190,000. ANTWERP, 23 April 2002, *Judith* (oil on canvas, 26 x 21 ins / 66 x 53 cm) EUR 7,000. LOKEREN, 5 Oct 2002, *Small Virgin* (1913, oil on panel, 18 x 16 ins / 46 x 40 cm) EUR 12,000. BUDAPEST, 4 Oct 2003, *Goddesses, Parks* (oil on canvas, 42 x 52 ins / 106 x 131 cm) HUF 5,500,000. BUDAPEST, 4 Oct 2003, *Women on the Shore* (oil on canvas, 33 x 46 ins / 83 x 117 cm) HUF 7,000,000. LONDON, 16 Nov 2004, *The Journey* (1893, oil on canvas, 83 x 52 ins / 211 x 132 cm) GBP 13,000. BRUSSELS, 6 Dec 2004, *Springtime* (1909, oil on canvas, 55 x 48 ins / 140 x 123 cm) EUR 9,500.

FABRY, François Gabriel

French, 18th - 19th century.

Born 25 January 1759, in Gex (Ain); died 29 September 1841, in Geneva.

Painter, engraver.

François Gabriel Fabry is remembered for a series of engravings after Van Dyck.

FABRY, Françoise

Belgian, 20th century.

Born 1939, in Wavre.

Painter, watercolourist, illustrator. Interiors, landscapes, urban landscapes, still-lifes.

From 1953 to 1958, Françoise Fabry attended Marcel Hastir's private academy, L'Atelier (The Studio). From 1955 to 1961, she studied at the École des Arts Décoratifs and the Académie des Beaux-Arts in Brussels, while continuing her training between 1959 and 1962 at the Académie de la Grande Chaumière in Paris. In 1972 to 1973, she worked for a second time in Edward Rizkallah's studio. She took part in collective exhibitions in Belgium, of which there were many, and also exhibited at the following: 1979, 1980, 1981, Paris, Salon des Femmes Peintres et Sculpteurs; 1979, *Sud 92* (*South 92*) salon in Issy-les-Moulineaux; also in 1979 and in 1981, at the Salon d'Automne, Paris. She has won various awards in regional competitions. She has exhibited individually: 1960, Wavre; 1961, Knokke-le-Zoute; 1978, Egmont gallery, Brussels; 1979, Paris; 1980, Musée Municipal, St-Paul-de-Vence; 1981, Namur and Nice; 1982, Présences gallery, Brussels; 1982, Maison de la Francité, Quebec, and elsewhere.

Her drawing, with clear and structured strokes, is tempered by subtle coloured harmonies. Her work as a whole, in which there are very few figures other than in sketch form, nevertheless comprises two distinct main categories: the light and floating or fluid watercolours, with echoes of Turner, contain the expanses - skies, wind, sea, waters, desert and light. By contrast, the oil paintings, which are certainly post-Cubist but perhaps better described as Post-Cézannian, depict constructions - steep villages, alleys and church towers, café terraces under sunshades, umbrellas in pouring rain, eroded mountainsides; everything evokes the Midi. The still-lifes do not constitute a separate category and belong with the constructions; more synthesised and bordering on abstraction, they recall the purity of the compositional lines of Ben Nicholson. What unites these two techniques and sets of themes in all their variety is a single sense of light, which details the horizontal strata of the watercolours and the vertical fractures of the oils, while filtering the colours that are crushed by the sun. This is still very much the Midi, contrary to the view expressed by crude sensibilities in the belief that they are seeing clashing colours.

BIBLIOGRAPHY:

Cruysmans, Philippe, *Françoise Fabry, poète de la lumière*, Éd. d'Art Associés, Brussels, 1981.

FABRY, Médy

Belgian, 20th century.

Born in Wasseiges (Belgium).

Painter.

Médy Fabry exhibited at the Salon des Indépendants in Paris in 1935.

FABRY, Pierre

French, 18th century.

Active in Paris during the first half of the 18th century.

Sculptor.

FABRY, Suzanne

Belgian, 20th century.

Born 1904, in Brussels; died 1985.

Painter, draughtswoman. Figures, scenes with figures. Stage costumes.

Symbolism.

Suzanne Fabry was a student of Isidore de Rudder, Jean Delville and Constant Montald at the Académie des Beaux-Arts in Brussels.

She took part in collective exhibitions: in 1930, at the triennial salon in Antwerp; 1931, the quadrennial salon of Belgium in Liège.

Her principal production was a large number of costumes for the Théâtre de la Monnaie (Theatre of the Mint) in Brussels.

AUCTION RECORDS:

PARIS, 6 Oct 1986, *Two Friends* (1948, oil on canvas, 59 x 55 ins / 150 x 140 cm) FRF 9,000. LOKEREN, 11 March 1995, *Return* (1936, oil on canvas, 31 1/2 x 46 ins / 80 x 116 cm) BEF 38,000. PARIS, 8 April 1998, *Head of Orpheus* (1930, oil on canvas, 39 1/4 x 50 ins / 100 x 127 cm) FRF 10,000.

FABRY, Thomas
German, 19th century.
Born c. 1810, in Cologne.
Painter.

Fabry produced a lithograph depicting *Princess Blanche of Amalfi*.

FABULLUS. See **AMULUS**

FABVRE, Jacques Jean Édouard
French, 19th century.
Died 1840, in Paris.
Painter.

Jacques Fabvre exhibited mainly views from 1819 to 1840. His best-known paintings include *View of the Château de Cognac, View on the Road to Malabry* and *View from near Le Plessis-Piquet*.

FACCENDA, Francesco
Italian, 18th - 19th century.
Born c. 1750, in Perugia; died 5 August 1820, in Rome.
Engraver.

Faccenda engraved the emblems and plates for Cesare Ripa's *Iconologia*.

FACCHETTI, Domenico
Italian, 17th century.
Active in Rome and in Bologna in the middle of the 17th century.
Sculptor, architect.

Facchetti worked at the church of S Paolo, in Bologna.

FACCHETTI, Pietro
Italian, 16th - 17th century.
Born 1535, in Mantua; died 27 February 1619, in Rome.
Painter, engraver.

The pupil of Girolamo and Ippolito Costa, Pietro Fachetti initially tried history painting, with some success, but then turned his attention to portrait painting. Few persons of quality did not have themselves painted by Fachetti, given his reputation for portraits of the nobility. Also an engraver, he made two plates remarkable for their purity of design. One represents *The Holy Family*, after Raphael and the other *Christ Carrying the Cross*. He visited Rome during the pontificate of Gregory XIII and died there.

Pietro f.

FACCHINETTI, Carlo, or Fachinetti
Italian, 19th - 20th century.
Born 1870.
Painter. Figure compositions, figures, landscapes.

Carlo Facchinetti often depicted and glorified motherhood in a tender, moving way.

AUCTION RECORDS:

CHESTER, 7 Oct 1984, *Maternal Love* (oil on canvas, 29 x 23 1/2 ins / 73.5 x 60 cm) GBP 1,250. LONDON, 19 June 1991, *A Young Mother's Pride* (oil on canvas, 27 1/4 x 19 1/4 ins / 69 x 49 cm) GBP 4,400. NEW YORK, 17 Feb 1993, *Motherhood* (oil on canvas, 31 x 22 1/2 ins / 78.7 x 57.2 cm) USD 9,488. NEW YORK, 18 Feb 1993, *Happy Family* (oil on canvas, 35 1/4 x 28 ins / 89.5 x 71 cm) USD 13,750. MILAN, 8 June 1994, *Animated Lakeside Landscape* (1898, oil on card, 7 x 9 1/2 ins / 18 x 24 cm) ITL 1,495,000.

FACCHINETTI, Giuseppe
Italian, 18th century.
Born in Ferrara; died 11 February 1777, in Ferrara.
Painter.

One of the most talented pupils of A.-F. Ferrari, Facchinetti excelled at history painting, perspectives and architectural subjects. His works may be found in the church of S Caterina of Siena, in Ferrara, and other churches in the surrounding region.

FACCHINETTI, Giuseppe
Italian, 18th century.
Active in Vienna in 1702.
Painter.

FACCHINETTI, Nicola Antonio, or Fachinetti
Italian, 19th century.
Born 1824; died 1900.
Painter, draughtsman. Portraits, landscapes.

AUCTION RECORDS:

LONDON, 12 Nov 1974, *The Bay of Rio de Janeiro*, GBP 1,500. SÃO PAULO, 26 June 1981, *Portrait of a Little Girl* (1888, oil on card, 22 x 14 1/4 ins / 55 x 36 cm) BRL 250,000. RIO DE JANEIRO, 8 Oct 1984, *Casa Grande da Fazenda March* (1900, oil on canvas, 4 3/4 x 14 1/2 ins / 12 x 37 cm) BRL 7,000,000. RIO DE JANEIRO, 17 June 1985, *Praia das Flexas* (1877, oil on panel, 7 3/4 x 13 3/4 ins / 20 x 35 cm) BRL 135,000,000. RIO DE JANEIRO, 31 July 1986, *View of Rio de Janeiro* (oil on panel, 10 1/4 x 15 3/4 ins / 26 x 40 cm) BRL 684,000. PARIS, 4 Dec 1992, *View of Moro Queimadu in Brazil* (pen, oval, 9 x 11 3/4 ins / 22 x 30 cm) FRF 10,000. LONDON, 18 April 2000, *House and Grounds of Dr A. C. Valdectaro, Gavea, Dous Irmãos, Rio de Janeiro* (oil on paper/panel, 5 x 11 ins / 12 x 29 cm) GBP 9,000. LONDON, 26 Sept 2002, *Bay of Rio seen from the Road to Petropolis* (1869, oil on canvas, 22 x 31 ins / 56 x 80 cm) GBP 45,000. RIO DE JANEIRO, 1 April 2003, *Waterfall on the Soberbo* (oil on panel, 9 x 7 ins / 23 x 19 cm) BRL 51,450. RIO DE JANEIRO, 2 Dec 2003, *Landscape with Sea* (oil on panel, 10 x 16 ins / 26 x 40 cm) BRL 98,000. RIO DE JANEIRO, 6 July 2004, *Souvenir de la rue Paissandu* (1880, graphite, 10 x 14 ins / 26 x 35 cm) BRL 19,000.

FACCHINETTI, Pietro
Italian, 17th century.
Born in Venice.
Painter.

Pietro Facchinetti settled in France, where he painted a *Portrait of Louis XIV*.

FACCI, Francesco. See **FABI Francesco**

FACCI-NEGRATTI, Francesco
Italian, 19th century.
Born 30 December 1810, in Bassano; died 27 May 1839.
Painter. Portraits.

Facci-Negratti worked for various churches in Gallio, Fozza and Villarasso Casoni.

MUSEUMS AND GALLERIES:

BASSANO DEL GRAPPA: *Portrait of G Peninetti*.

FACCINI, Bartolommeo
Italian, 16th century.
Born 1532, in Ferrara; died 22 July 1577.
Painter.

Bartolommeo Facini, brother of Girolamo Faccini, painted portraits and architectural pictures in the style of Girolamo da Carpi. He died after a fall from scaffolding.

MUSEUMS AND GALLERIES:

LILLE: *Martyrdom of St Agnes* (attributed).

FACCINI, Girolamo
Italian, 16th - 17th century.

Born 1547; died before 1616.
Active in Ferrara.
Painter.

Girolamo Faccini was the brother of Bartolommeo Faccini, whom he often helped, also specialising in architectural subjects and embellishment. He was taught by J. Carpi.

FACCINI, Pietro, or Facini
Italian, 16th century.
Born 1560 or 1562, in Bologna; died 1 April 1602, in Bologna.
Painter, draughtsman, engraver. Religious subjects, figures.
Bolognese School.

Pietro Faccini turned to painting a relatively advanced age. It is said that he often visited the workshop of Annibaldo Carracci out of curiosity, and following an impromptu caricature of Faccini done by one of the pupils of the great painter, Faccini grabbed a piece of charcoal and sketched a satirical portrait of the artist who had ridiculed him. This portrait was so convincing that Carracci persuaded him to become an artist, offering to teach him. Faccini set to work and made rapid progress.

However, Faccini fell out with his master over a trivial joke and set up a rival school in Bologna which for some time enjoyed considerable success. But criticism of inaccuracy in his drawings was not slow to come. His heads, however, are vigorously carried out and his handling of flesh tints is similar to that of Tintoretto. He attempted to foster a synthesis between elements borrowed from Barocci and the Carracci. His works include *St Jerome; Mystic Marriage of Saint Catherine* and *Holy Family*.

BIBLIOGRAPHY:
Cazort, M./Johnston, C., *Bolognese Drawings in North American Collections, 1500-1800*, exhibition catalogue, National Gallery, Ottawa, 1982. De Grazia, D., *Correggio and his Legacy: Sixteenth-century Emilian Drawings*, exhibition catalogue, National Gallery of Art, Washington, 1984.

MUSEUMS AND GALLERIES:
FLORENCE (Uffizi): *Self-portrait.*

AUCTION RECORDS:
LONDON, 1 July 1980, *Vision of St Francis* (etching and burin, 13 1/2 x 9 3/4 ins / 34.3 x 24.8 cm) GBP 260. LONDON, 1 Dec 1983, *Virgin and Child* (grey wash, 6 1/4 x 4 3/4 ins / 15.9 x 12.3 cm) GBP 1,500. LONDON, 5 Dec 1985, *Vision of St Francis* (c. 1590, etching/paper, 13 1/2 x 9 3/4 ins / 34 x 24.9 cm) GBP 1,400. NEW YORK, 13 Jan 1987, *Study of Man Seen from Behind* (black chalk/beige paper, 14 x 8 1/4 ins / 35.5 x 21.2 cm) USD 16,000. PARIS, 4 March 1988, *Christ Crucified* (black chalk heightened with white/beige paper, 16 x 9 3/4 ins / 40.8 x 25 cm) FRF 39,000. NEW YORK, 12 Oct 1989, *St Jerome in the Desert* (oil/copper, 18 1/2 x 13 3/4 ins / 47 x 35 cm) USD 71,500. NEW YORK, 12 Jan 1990, *Male Nude Standing with His Right Arm Raised and Head Turned to the Right* (red chalk, 16 1/4 x 10 1/2 ins / 41.4 x 26.7 cm) USD 29,700. NEW YORK, 13 Jan 1993, *Raising of Lazarus* (black chalk and brown ink and brown wash, 10 1/2 x 7 3/4 ins / 26.5 x 19.7 cm) USD 3,080. NEW YORK, 14 Jan 1993, *St Jerome in the Desert* (oil/copper, 18 1/2 x 13 1/2 ins / 46.7 x 34.5 cm) USD 33,000. MILAN, 31 May 1994, *Study of Figure* (pen and pink watercolour wash, 7 1/4 x 4 ins / 18.5 x 10 cm) ITL 1,035,000. LONDON, 12 Dec 1996, *Group of Praying Sts* (pen, brown ink and brown wash, 7 3/4 x 4 ins / 19.6 x 10.4 cm) GBP 1,552. LONDON, 6 July 1999, *Nude Leaning Forward. Kneeling Nude, his Hands Behind his Back* (chalk, double-sided, 18 x 14 ins / 45 x 35 cm) GBP 2,800. LONDON, 5 July 2000, *Young Man Seated, Reading a Book* (red chalk, 11 x 9 ins / 27 x 24 cm) GBP 1,200. LONDON, 3 Nov 2000, *Entombment* (oil on panel, 11 x 8 ins / 29 x 21 cm) GBP 13,000. MILAN, 16 May 2001, *Portrait of a Priest* (red chalk, 9 x 8 ins / 24 x 20 cm) ITL 4,800,000. LONDON, 11 April 2002, *Madonna and Child* (black chalk, 6 x 5 ins / 16 x 12 cm) GBP 3,000. LONDON, 10 July 2002, *Standing Male Nude. Head Studies* (black chalk heightened with white, double-sided, 22 x 14 ins / 56 x 35 cm) GBP 18,000. NEW YORK, 22 Jan 2003, *Two Elders Conversing* (pen and ink wash, 12 x 9 ins / 31 x 22 cm) USD 30,000.

FACCIOLI, Giovanni
Italian, 18th century.
Born 12 October 1729, in Verona; died 26 March 1809, in Verona.
Painter.

A pupil of Michelangelo Prunati in Verona, he later settled in Venice. He produced works for a number of churches in the two cities, as well as for those of Tiezzo, Taglio della Mira and Grisolara.

FACCIOLI, Girolamo. See **FAGIVOLI**

FACCIOLI, Giuseppe
Italian, 17th century.
Born c. 1629; died 1709.
Active in Bologna.
Engraver.

Noted for his *Holy Family*.

FACCIOLI, Raffaele
Italian, 19th century.
Born 23 December 1846, in Bologna; died 1916.
Painter. Genre scenes.

Faccioli was a pupil at the art institute of Venturoli, and a teacher at the Accademia di Belle Arti in Bologna. His best-known work is called *Agreeable Encounter in the Park*. He exhibited in Vienna and Munich between 1873 and 1883, and was awarded an honourable mention at the Paris Exposition Universelle of 1900.

AUCTION RECORDS:
MILAN, 11 Dec 1986, *Sad Journey* (oil on canvas, 16 1/2 x 12 1/2 ins / 42 x 31.5 cm) ITL 5,000,000. MILAN, 29 Oct 1992, *Village Street on a Festival Day* (1880, oil on panel, 5 1/4 x 9 ins / 13.5 x 23 cm) ITL 2,400,000. MILAN, 18 Dec 1996, *Sunday Stroll* (1880, oil on panel, 5 1/4 x 9 ins / 13.5 x 23 cm) ITL 2,446,000. ROME, 6 June 2000, *Winter Landscape* (oil on canvas, a pair, 19 x 13 ins / 47 x 32 cm) ITL 7,000,000.

FACCIOLI, Silvio
Italian, 19th century.
Active in Bologna.
Painter. Historical subjects.

MUSEUMS AND GALLERIES:
BOLOGNA: *The Oath of the Pazzi.*

FACCIOLI-LICATA, Orsola. See **LICATA-FACCIOLI**

FACE, Giuseppe La. See **LA FACE**

FACE, Jean
French, 16th century.
Active in Paris in 1597.
Painter.

FACEWICZ, Ludwik
Polish, 19th century.
Painter.

Ludwik Facewicz is known for a watercolour portrait.

FACHAI, Michele de
Italian, 16th century.
Active in Verona.
Painter.

FACHANG. See **MUQI**

FACHARD, Robert
French, 20th century.
Born 25 June 1921, in Paris.
Sculptor. Monuments.

Robert Fachard was a pupil at the École des Beaux-Arts, Toulouse, from 1941 to 1946, then later at the Académie de la Grande Chaumière, Paris. He also received advice from Henri Laurens in 1950. Also in 1950 he founded the abstract art group *Présence*, which exhibited for three years in succession at the Palais des Beaux-Arts, Toulouse. In 1953 he spent some time in Greece. Fachard made several low reliefs and monumental statues in the Toulouse region, in 1956 in Toulouse itself and in 1958 in Lourdes. In 1956 he collaborated with Jean Arp. In 1961 he carved a sculpture for Lille, in 1962 for Valenciennes, 1963 for Aubervilliers, 1964 for Liévin and Toulouse again, 1965 for Béthune and Rheims, 1966 for Aubenas, 1967 for Arras and Steny, 1968 for Rheims and Aubenas again, as well as for Privas and numerous other places.

He has taken part in group exhibitions in Paris: from 1954 at the Salon de la Jeune Sculpture, since 1959 at the Salon des Réalités Nouvelles (of which he was made a committee member in 1964), and in 1962 at the *Exposition Internationale du Petit Bronze* (*International Exhibition of Small Bronzes*). He has also shown in many provincial and international exhibitions: 1963, *De Rodin à nos jours* (*From Rodin to Today*) at the Gemeentemuseum, Arnhem; in Brussels, Brazil, Great Britain and elsewhere. He has also shown in solo exhibitions, his first in Toulouse in 1954, and subsequently at the Musée des Beaux-Arts, Vervier, in 1962; in Brussels and London in 1963; Paris in 1967, 1969, 1979, 1982; in Toulouse again in 1968; and at the Maison de la Culture, Nevers, in 1976.

His work became progressively more abstract and he used a great variety of materials, at one point creating sculptures that he called 'bivalent'. Very different from chryselephantine sculptures, these consisted of two contrasting materials such as marble and bronze, or volcanic rock and cut-out metal. From 1958 he also carved polychrome stone sculptures. In addition to their high technical quality, Fauchard's now classic abstract works are characterised by voids that create a sense of space at the centre of the volume.

Museums and Galleries:
Paris (MNAM-CCI) - Toulouse (MBA, Mus. des Augustins).

Auction records:
Paris, 6 Dec 1986, *J - 67* (1967, welded and patinated brass, h. 10 1/4 ins / 26 cm, Long. 11 ins/27 cm) FRF 7,000.

FACHE
French, 18th century.
Active in Paris at the end of the 18th century.
Miniaturist.

FACHE, René
French, 19th century.
Born 23 November 1816, in Douai; died March 1891, in Valenciennes.
Sculptor.

René Fache was a pupil of David d'Angers and Th. Bra before becoming a lecturer at the academy in Valenciennes. In 1874 he sent his bronze bust of Major General Lhériller and three bronze medallions depicting private individuals to the Paris Salon. His principal works are to be found at the church of St Peter in Douai: a marble group (memorial to *M. Duforest de Lewarde*, founder of the town's Christian schools) in the transept of the chapel of St Joseph; a group representing *St Joseph Carrying the Christ Child with Two Angels on Either Side* in the chapel of the Sacred Heart; *Our Lord Jesus Christ Surrounded by Two Angels* at the church in Anzin; and two stone statues of *St Eligius* and *St Barbara*. He executed the pulpit sculptures in the church of St-Géry in Cambrai and sculpted six stone caryatids for the Valenciennes town hall. He executed the high altar at Notre-Dame church in St-Cordon, with two low reliefs beneath the altar stone depicting scenes from the Passion. For the chapel of the Marist Fathers he executed a stone high altar, a low relief beneath the altar stone depicting the *Entombment*, a statue of the *Immaculate Conception* on the reredos above the tabernacle, eight angels in the recesses, and two statuettes at the pinnacle of the altar representing *St John the Baptist and St Elizabeth*. In Arras he executed a stone statue (*Angel Bearing the Holy Sacrament*) in the chapel of the Nuns of the Holy Sacrament, together with a statue of the *Virgin* and 14 statues of saints in the chapel of the Ursuline Nuns at the altar of the Immaculate Conception. At Ruitz castle near Béthune he executed stone statues of *Our Lady of Victories, St Louis, King of France* and *St Germaine* in the chapel. At Bryolle Castle (Belgium) he executed the marble font *Angel of Prayer Crushing the Evil Spirit*. At the town hall and law courts of the commune of Marcoing, he executed four caryatids. Fache also produced a large number of busts.

Museums and Galleries:
Douai: *Jean de Bologne; Malotau de Guerne; Doctor Taranget; Louis-Michel Huré; Douai Town Council Distributing Awards.*

FACHERIS, Agostino, called Agostino da Caversegno
Italian, 16th century.
Born 1500; died c. 1552.
Active in Bergamo.
Painter.

Tasso speaks of Agostino Facheris in his *Vite de' Pittori, Scultori e Architetti Bergamaschi* (*Lives of the Painters of Bergamo*) (1793) in which he says that the church of SS Trinità in Bergamo has one of his paintings dated 1528, *St Antony with Two Angels*. He was the pupil of Lorenzo Lotto. A *Virgin with St Roch* in the museum in Innsbruck (Austria) was attributed to him by Berenson.

FACHET, Paul René
French, 20th century.
Born 19 January 1885, in Tours.
Painter. Landscapes.

Paul René Fachet was a pupil of Ernest Laurent. In the 1920s he painted riverside landscapes of the Loire.

FACHINETTI, Carlo. See **FACCHINETTI Carlo**

FACHINETTI, Nicola Antonio.
See **FACCHINETTI Nicola Antonio**

FACHNLEIN, Jules
French, 19th century.
Born in the second half of the 19th century, in Mulhouse.
Painter.

A pupil of Henner and Gérome, Jules Fachnlein made his début at the Salon des Artistes Français in 1895.

FACIPONTE
Italian, 17th century.
Active in Sicily.
Painter.

Pupil of Pietro Novelli.

FACIS, Ange de
Italian, 15th century.
Active c. 1477.
Painter. History painting.

Siret mentions that Ange de Facis painted six religious subjects within a single frame.

FACITOLO, Pietro
Italian, 13th century.

Born in Bari.
Sculptor.
This artist worked in Apulia.

FACIUS, Angelica
German, 19th century.
Born 14 October 1806, in Weimar; died 17 April 1887, in Weimar.
Medallist, sculptor.
Angelica Facius' works include several *Portraits of Goethe* and a *Bust of Grand Duke Karl Friedrich.*

FACIUS, Georg Siegmund and Johann Gottlieb (brothers)
German, 18th century.
Born c. 1750, in Regensburg; died after 1802.
Also active in England.
Draughtsmen, engravers. Mythological subjects, historical subjects, religious subjects.
The biographies of the brothers Georg and Johann Facius, whose lives followed totally identical courses and who always worked together, are so similar that it is almost impossible to find a detail concerning Georg that does not apply equally well to Johann. They both studied in Brussels, where their father was the Russian consul. In 1776, they both went to work for Alderman Boydell in London, where they produced a great many plates. The prints of their etchings are sometimes black, sometimes brown or coloured. Their best works include: *Benjamin West and his Family* after West, 1777, *Hector and Paris* after Angelica Kaufmann, and *Abraham Conversing with the Three Angels* after Murillo. It should be noted, however, that Georg Siegmund Facius exhibited some miniatures at the Royal Academy in London from 1785 to 1788.

FACKERE, Jef Van De. See **VANDEFACKERE Jef**

FACKERT, Oscar William
American, 20th century.
Born 29 July 1891, in Jersey City (New Jersey).
Painter, illustrator.
Oscar William Fackert, a pupil of Frederick Clark Gottwald, won first prize at the Northern Indiana Exhibition in 1923 and 1925.

FACKLER, Johann Joseph
Austrian, 18th century.
Born 1698, in Salzburg; died 18 November 1745, in Salzburg.
Painter.
Fackler's *St Rupert* is in the church of St Peter in Salzburg (Austria).

FACONNET, Marie Anne Eugénie.
See **COLLOT Marie Anne**

FACONTI, Dionigi
Italian, 19th century.
Born in Bergamo; died 1865, in Turin.
Painter. Historical subjects.
Faconti taught at the Accademia in Turin. He is known for a painting of *Werther.*

FACQ, Gustave
Belgian, 20th century.
Born 1902, in Tournai.
Painter. Landscapes.
Gustave Facq was a student at the Académie des Beaux-Arts in Tournai and of Herman Richir at the academy in Brussels.
MUSEUMS AND GALLERIES:
TOURNAI.

FACTOR, Nicolás (Saint)
Spanish, 16th century.
Born 29 June 1520, in Valencia; died 23 December 1583, in Valencia.
Painter.
Nicolás Factor dedicated the first part of his life to study, distinguishing himself as a painter and poet. In 1537 he became a Franciscan and entered the monastery of Sta Maria de Jesus where he carried out many paintings, including *St Michael Defeating the Demon.* None of his works is known to survive. According to Caen Bermudez Factor's drawings were excellent if somewhat colourless. He painted several virgins and illuminated many missals. Among the numerous Spanish saints he was the only artist to be canonised.

FACUNDUS
Spanish, 11th century.
Illuminator.
MUSEUMS AND GALLERIES:
MADRID (Biblioteca Nacional): miniature.

FACUOL DALLE PALME, Giovanni Domenico di Antonio
Spanish, 17th century.
Active during the first half of the 17th century.
Miniaturist.
Most of the miniatures and decorations for a register of the brotherhood of S Niccolò in Venice were executed by Giovanni Facuol dalle Palme around 1636.

FADA, Annibale
Italian, 16th century.
Active in Rimini c. 1590.
Painter.
The cathedral at Rimini has a *Virgin* by Anibale Fada.

FADDA, Cosimo
Italian, 19th century.
Born 1858, in Cagliari (Sardinia).
Sculptor.
MUSEUMS AND GALLERIES:
CAGLIARI (Ospedale): several works.

FADEEV, Grigori Fadeevich
Russian, 18th century.
Born 1752; died 20 March 1778.
Active in Moscow.
Engraver.

FADEEV, Ivan
Russian, 18th century.
Active in Moscow.
Engraver.

FADEEV, Stepan
Russian, 18th century.
Active in Moscow.
Engraver.
In 1764, Stepan Fadeev was a student at the Moscow academy of arts.

FADEEV, Varlaami
Russian, 17th - 18th century.
Active in Moscow.
Draughtsman, engraver.

FADEGON, Jean Melchior
Dutch, 19th - 20th century.
Born 31 October 1871, in Amsterdam.
Active and from 1906 naturalised in France.
Sculptor, medallist.
Jean Fadegon lived mainly in Paris, where he was a student of the sculptors Ferdinand Leenhoff and (Gabriel?) Thomas.

FADEL, Makaroff
Lebanese, 20th century.
Born 1910, in Hamate; died 1945, in Hamate.
Painter. Portraits.

He settled in Beirut, where he met the painter César Gemayel. He went to stay in Italy, where he studied under Carlo Siviero at the Rome Institute of Fine Arts. On his return to Lebanon, he was made Gemayel's assistant at the Lebanese academy of fine arts.

A known work by him is the *Portrait of Archbishop Elia Saliby*, painted in about 1940. The composition is traditional, almost frontal; the technique is skilful, direct and energetic.

BIBLIOGRAPHY:

Liban. Le Regard des peintres. 200 ans de peinture libanaise, exhibition catalogue, Institut du Monde Arabe, Paris, 1989.

FADELLO, Pietro
Italian, 16th century.
Painter.

Pietro Fadello worked for the church of S Giovanni Ilarione, near Verona, where, in 1515, he painted a *Virgin and Four Saints*

FADER, Fernando
Argentinian, 20th century.
Born 1882; died 1935.
Painter. Landscapes with figures.

Originating in the provinces, Fernando Fader remained untouched by the internationalist trend and continued to adopt a regionalist approach in his work.

AUCTION RECORDS:

NEW YORK, 27 Nov 1984, *Dead Leaves* (oil on canvas, 38 x 46 1/4 ins / 96.5 x 117.4 cm) USD 30,000. MONTEVIDEO, 30 June 1987, *End of the Day* (oil on panel, 22 x 27 1/2 ins / 55 x 70 cm) UYU 3,094,000. NEW YORK, 8 May 1991, *Lady Looking at a Ploughing Scene* (1903, oil on canvas, 51 1/4 x 35 1/2 ins / 130 x 90 cm) USD 28,600. NEW YORK, 20 Nov 1991, *After the Rain* (1906, oil on canvas, 15 3/4 x 23 1/2 ins / 40 x 60 cm) USD 22,000. BUENOS AIRES, 24 Nov 1999, *Farmstead, Ischilin* (1923, oil on canvas, 35 x 43 ins / 89 x 110 cm) USD 100,000. BUENOS AIRES, 9 Aug 2000, *Closure* (oil on canvas, 31 x 39 ins / 80 x 100 cm) USD 70,000. BUENOS AIRES, 1 June 2004, *Pirca (Dry-stone Wall)* (oil on canvas, 22 x 31 ins / 55 x 78 cm) USD 56,000. BUENOS AIRES, 11 Aug 2004, *Herd in the Fields* (1908, oil on canvas, 53 x 67 ins / 135 x 170 cm) USD 179,360.

FADIER, Denis
French, 20th - 21st century.
Born 21 February 1949, in Boulogne-sur-Seine.
Painter. Scenes with figures.

Denis Fadier has exhibited at the Salon de Mai and the Salon des Grands et Jeunes. At these exhibitions, he presented canvases whose somewhat fantastical style is touched with surrealism.

AUCTION RECORDS:

PARIS, 13 June 1990, *Face Composition* (oil on canvas, 39 1/4 x 39 1/4 ins / 100 x 100 cm) FRF 27,000.

FADIGA, Domenico
Italian, 18th - 19th century.
Born in Verona.
Sculptor.

Son of Giuseppe, Domenico Fadiga was a pupil of Canova in Rome. He worked on the decoration of the tomb of Callemberg, in Padua, and carved the high altar of the church of S Giovanni Novo in Venice.

FADIGA, Giuseppe
Italian, 18th century.
Born in Venice.
Sculptor.

Father of Domenico.

FADINE, Igor
Russian, 20th century.
Born 1939, in Leningrad (now St Petersburg).
Painter. Landscapes with figures.

Igor Fadine attended the art school and then the academy of fine art in St Petersburg. He painted typical landscapes beautifully conveying the effects of sunlight on snow. He was a member of the Union of Soviet Artists.

AUCTION RECORDS:

PARIS, 18 Feb 1991, *Carriage Near the Volga* (1963, oil on canvas, 29 1/4 x 36 1/4 ins / 74 x 92 cm) FRF 7,800. PARIS, 26 April 1991, *Winter in Cherniavino* (oil on canvas, 16 3/4 x 26 ins / 42.5 x 66.2 cm) FRF 3,500. PARIS, 29 May 1991, *Morning Mist* (oil on canvas, 23 3/4 x 47 1/2 ins / 60.5 x 120.5 cm) FRF 6,000. PARIS, 9 Dec 1991, *In the Dandelions* (1975, oil on canvas, 39 1/4 x 46 ins / 100 x 117 cm) FRF 6,000. PARIS, 17 June 1992, *Lake in the Morning* (oil on canvas, 23 1/2 x 46 3/4 ins / 60 x 119 cm) FRF 6,500. PARIS, 5 Nov 1992, *Meeting in a Park* (oil on canvas, 21 1/4 x 18 1/2 ins / 54 x 47 cm) FRF 4,000.

FADINI, Giovanni Maria
Italian, 16th century.
Born 1513, near Brescia.
Active in Novara.
Painter.

Giovanni Maria Fadini was the brother of Lorenzo Fadini.

FADINI, Lorenzo
Italian, 16th century.
Born in Orzi Nuovi, near Brescia.
Painter.

Lorenzo Fadini was the brother of Giovanni Maria and worked with him in Novara.

FADRUSZ, János, or Fadswisz
Hungarian, 19th century.
Born 2 September 1858, in Pozsony (now Bratislava); died 26 October 1903, in Budapest.
Sculptor.

A remarkable artist, author of the statue of Maria Theresa in Bratislava, János Fadrusz was unknown internationally for much of his career. However, his submissions to the Exposition Universelle in Paris in 1900, entitled *Christ on the Cross* and *Matthias Corvinus* were much admired, and won him the Grand Prix for sculpture.

FADY-CAJANI, Louis E.
French, 19th - 20th century.
Born 6 April 1869, in Paris.
Sculptor.

Louis E. Fady-Cajani exhibited in Paris at the Salons des Artistes Français, of which he was a member from 1903.

FAEBER, Anton
German, 17th century.
Active in Halberstadt c. 1620.
Glass painter.

FAECX, Nicolaes
Flemish, 17th century.
Active in Antwerp, in 1625.
Painter.
Flemish School.

FAED, James, the Elder
British, 19th - 20th century.
Born 4 April 1821, in Burley Mill (Kirkcudbrightshire), Scotland; died 24 September 1911, in Edinburgh.
Painter, engraver. Genre scenes, landscapes.

James Faed the Elder was the brother of John and Thomas Faed and is best known as an engraver. He made engravings of his brothers' paintings and of some works by Sir Francis Grant. Faed exhibited from 1855 at the Royal Academy in London and the Royal Scottish Academy.

AUCTION RECORDS:

NEW YORK, 21 May 1987, *Landscape with Cottages* (oil on canvas, 22 x 30 ins / 56 x 76 cm) USD 3,000. EDINBURGH, 9 June 1994, *Dive Hole* (oil on canvas, 17 x 22 ins / 43.2 x 56 cm)

GBP 4,025. EDINBURGH, 15 May 1997, *Barholm Tower, Gatehouse-of-Fleet, Wigtonshire* (1871, oil on panel, 18 x 14 ins / 45.8 x 35.5 cm) GBP 2,530.

FAED, James, the Younger

British, 19th - 20th century.
Born 1856 or 1857; died 1920.
Active in Edinburgh and London.
Painter (gouache), watercolourist. Landscapes, waterscapes.

James Faed the Younger was the son of James Faed the Elder and the nephew of John and Thomas Faed. He exhibited at the Royal Academy in London from 1900.

AUCTION RECORDS:

SCOTLAND, 29 Aug 1978, *Spring Landscape* (1885, oil on canvas, 9 3/4 x 13 1/2 ins / 25 x 34.5 cm) GBP 1,200. SCOTLAND, 28 Aug 1984, *At the Edge of a Wood* (1881, oil on canvas, 22 x 30 ins / 56 x 76 cm) GBP 1,200. LONDON, 26 April 1988, *Copses* (oil on card, 5 x 4 1/2 ins / 12.5 x 11.5 cm) GBP 1,540. EDINBURGH, 30 Aug 1988, *Rocky Stream at Laggan* (1899, oil on canvas, 10 x 16 1/4 ins / 25.5 x 41 cm) GBP 1,870. PERTH, 28 Aug 1989, *Heather in the Highlands* (1900, oil on canvas, 7 x 9 3/4 ins / 18 x 25 cm) GBP 3,740. SOUTH QUEENSFERRY, 1 May 1990, *Flowing Torrent in a Small Valley* (1910, oil on canvas, 16 1/4 x 24 ins / 41 x 61 cm) GBP 2,750. PERTH, 27 Aug 1990, *November* (oil on canvas, 21 3/4 x 30 ins / 55.5 x 76 cm) GBP 3,080. GLASGOW, 22 Nov 1990, *Invercomrie Burn in Perthshire* (1908, oil on canvas, 14 x 21 ins / 35.6 x 53.3 cm) GBP 2,090. YORK, 12 Nov 1991, *Galloway* (1902, oil on panel, 7 x 9 3/4 ins / 18 x 25 cm) GBP 660. GLASGOW, 4 Dec 1991, *Garden Gate* (oil on card, 10 x 8 1/4 ins / 25.5 x 21 cm) GBP 825. EDINBURGH, 28 April 1992, *On a Hillside* (1901, oil on panel, 6 1/4 x 9 1/2 ins / 16 x 24 cm) GBP 770. GLASGOW, 1 Feb 1994, *On the Old Cramond Bridge* (1878, watercolour and gouache, 14 1/4 x 18 ins / 36.5 x 45.5 cm) GBP 977. GLASGOW, 16 April 1996, *Early Spring, Cramond* (1885, oil on canvas, 11 x 14 1/4 ins / 27 x 36.5 cm) GBP 2,760.

FAED, John

British, 19th century.
Born 1820, in Burley Mill (Kirkcudbrightshire), Scotland; died 22 October 1902, in Burley Mill.
Painter, miniaturist. Religious subjects, portraits, genre scenes.

John Faed's father was a farmer, miller and engineer. Four of his children became distinguished artists. John was self-taught and produced miniatures from the age of 12 until 1841, when he went to Edinburgh and achieved great success. He then enrolled for art classes at the Trustees Academy and trained in oil painting under Sir William Allan. He subsequently devoted himself almost entirely to oil painting. He was elected an associate of the Royal Scottish Academy in 1847 and a member in 1851 and exhibited there from 1841. In 1862 he went to London and lived there until 1880, sending regular consignments to the Royal Academy.

His main works include *Olivia and Viola, Catherine Leyton* and *Poet's Dream,* among others. He often drew upon subjects from the Bible, Shakespeare and especially Scottish songs, history and poetry.

MUSEUMS AND GALLERIES:

EDINBURGH (Royal Scottish Academy): *Annie's Tryste* (1864, oil/panel) - GLASGOW: *Meeting; Death of Burd Ellen* - LONDON (Victoria and Albert Mus.): *The Great Hall at Haddon.*

AUCTION RECORDS:

LONDON, 1 May 1908, *Haddon Hall in Times Past* (1868) GBP 21. LONDON, 25 June 1908, *Gypsy,* GBP 8. LONDON, 21 April 1910, *The Raid of Ruthven,* GBP 52. LONDON, 17 June 1910, *Tam O'Shanter,* GBP 110. LONDON, 21 July 1922, *Slave,* GBP 26. LONDON, 8 Dec 1922, *Rivals,* GBP 44. LONDON, 29 June 1923, *Catherine Seton and Roland Graene,* GBP 50. LONDON, 21 Dec 1923, *Thirsty Client,* GBP 25. LONDON, 5 June 1924, *When the 'Kye' Comes Home,* GBP 8. LONDON, 26 Nov 1926, *Youth and Old Age* (1867) GBP 21. LONDON, 18 July 1927, *Bonnie Scotland* (1871) GBP 28. LONDON, 2 Dec 1927, *Darby and Joan,* GBP 105. GLASGOW, 4 June 1936, *Shakespeare and His Friends,* GBP 15; *Walter Scott and His Friends,* GBP 37. LONDON, 30 and 31 July 1936, *Darby and Joan,* GBP 10. LONDON, 23 Oct 1942, *Slave,* GBP 36. LONDON, 27 June 1945, *Dispatch from Ruthven,* GBP 48. LONDON, 29 June 1945, *Old Gardener and His Granddaughter,* GBP 57. GLASGOW, 2 May 1947, *Young Lady,* GBP 26. LONDON, 29 May 1964, *Young Lady in a White Dress Seated beneath a Tree,* Gns 270. GLASGOW, 25 Aug 1972, *Royal Scottish Justiciary,* GBP 480. GLASGOW, 30 Nov 1976, *Harpist* (oil on card, 17 1/2 x 23 1/2 ins / 44.5 x 60 cm) GBP 600. LONDON, 21 Oct 1977, *Landscape Seen through an Arch* (1885, oil on canvas, 41 x 30 ins / 104 x 76 cm) GBP 950. NEW YORK, 28 May 1981, *Oliver Goldsmith Working* (1877, oil on canvas, 43 x 32 1/2 ins / 109 x 82.5 cm) USD 7,000. NEW YORK, 11 April 1984, *Portrait of George Washington on a Grey Charger* (oil on canvas, 55 1/2 x 40 ins / 141 x 101.5 cm) USD 43,000. AUCHTERARDER, 1 Sept 1987, *Evangeline; the Parting of Evangeline and Gabriel* (1869, oil on canvas, 23 x 17 ins / 58.5 x 43 cm) GBP 8,000. EDINBURGH, 30 Aug 1988, *What Will Happen Next?* (oil/card, 18 x 21 1/2 ins / 46 x 54.5 cm) GBP 1,980. EDINBURGH, 22 Nov 1989, *Raid of Ruthven* (oil on canvas, 20 x 27 ins / 50.8 x 68.6 cm) GBP 4,950. LONDON, 11 June 1993, *Haggling* (1981, oil on canvas, 28 x 36 ins / 71 x 91.5 cm) GBP 1,955. LONDON, 4 Nov 1994, *Shakespeare and His Friends at the Mermaid Inn* (1850, oil on card/panel, 15 x 18 1/2 ins / 38.1 x 46.7 cm) GBP 7,475. GLASGOW, 16 April 1996, *John Wesley and Maidservant* (1874, oil on canvas/card, 29 3/4 x 24 3/4 ins / 75.5 x 63 cm) GBP 1,725. NEW YORK, 31 Jan 1997, *Portrait of Georges Washington Reviewing the Troops at Trenton* (oil on canvas, 56 x 41 1/2 ins / 142 x 105.5 cm) USD 662,000. NEW YORK, 26 Feb 1997, *Family in an Interior* (oil on canvas, 36 x 47 1/4 ins / 91.5 x 120 cm) USD 27,600. GLASGOW, 25 Aug 1997, *Woode Landscape on Fire, Perthshire* (1871, watercolour heightened with white, 7 1/2 x 10 3/4 ins / 19 x 27.3 cm) GBP 368. LONDON, 10 June 1999, *Moment's Reflection* (oil on canvas, 30 x 23 ins / 76 x 58 cm) GBP 3,800. EDINBURGH, 25 Aug 2000, *Fleet at Gatehouse* (1882, oil on canvas, 13 x 19 ins / 34 x 47 cm) GBP 14,500. LONDON, 28 Nov 2000, *Guilty or Not Guilty* (oil on canvas, 42 x 36 ins / 107 x 92 cm) GBP 15,000. LONDON, 30 Oct 2001, *Gentleman with Side Whiskers* (miniature, h. 4 ins / 9 cm) GBP 2,000. LONDON, 8 Nov 2001, *Trout Pool* (oil on board, 12 x 14 ins / 31 x 36 cm) GBP 3,500. LONDON, 15 April 2002, *Their Eldest Hope, Their Jenny, Woman Grown, from the Cotter's Saturday Night* (oil on panel, 19 x 22 ins / 48 x 57 cm) GBP 30,000. LONDON, 28 Aug 2002, *Cotter's Saturday Night* (oil on board, 8 x 11 ins / 20 x 27 cm) GBP 9,000. LONDON, 19 Feb 2003, *Boyhood* (oil on canvas, 40 x 34 ins / 102 x 86 cm) GBP 210,000. EDINBURGH, 21 Aug 2003, *Scene from Burns' Cottar's Saturday Night* (watercolour over grisaille, 7 x 9 ins / 18 x 23 cm) GBP 1,150. LONDON, 11 June 2004, *Boaz and Ruth* (oil on board, 8 x 11 ins / 21 x 27 cm) GBP 15,000. EDINBURGH, 18 Aug 2004, *Catherine Seaton, from Sir Walter Scott's The Abbott* (1866, oil on canvas, 28 x 36 ins / 71 x 91 cm) GBP 8,800.

FAED, John Francis

British, 19th century.
Born c. 1860, in London.
Painter.

John Francis Faed exhibited at the Royal Academy from 1883. He was the son of Thomas Faed.

FAED, Thomas

British, 19th century.

Born 8 June 1826, in Barlae Mill (Kirkcudbrightshire), Scotland; died 17 August 1900, in London.

Painter (gouache), watercolourist. Portraits, genre scenes, landscapes, animals.

Thomas Faed began to practise the arts at a very young age under the supervision of his older brother John in Edinburgh. The latter had sent for Thomas upon the death of their father. Thomas attended the art school at the age of 15 and had Orchardson as a companion there. He devoted himself particularly to the representation of characteristic scenes from the lives of Scottish peasants. He was elected an associate of the Royal Scottish Academy at the age of 23, but being dissatisfied with the lack of success he had achieved so far, he went to London in 1852. He exhibited regularly at the Royal Academy in London and remained there until his death. He was elected an associate of the Royal Academy in 1859 and a member in 1864.

Faed was obliged to give up painting in 1893 because his sight began to fail; it soon failed him completely and he was blind for the last seven years of his life. The eminent qualities of this artist - strength, trueness to life and precision - emerge from his painting *Faults on Both Sides*, which is considered his masterpiece and is preserved at the Tate Gallery. Other outstanding works by him include *In Times of War, Hand to Mouth* and *Sunrise to Sunset*.

Museums and Galleries:

Aberdeen (AG): *The Reaper* (oil on canvas); *A Seaside Toilet; Highland Mary* (1857, oil on canvas) - Blackburn: *Silk Dress* - Brighton (Mus. & AG): *The Mitherless Bairn* (oil on canvas) - Edinburgh (Scottish National Portrait Gallery): *Sir Walter Scott and his Friends at Abbotsford* (1849, oil on canvas, imaginary portrait group) - Glasgow: *Violets and Primroses; Venus and Cupid; Spanish Brigands* - Hamburg: *Ray of Sunlight; Flower of Dumblanc* - Leicester: *Pot Luck* - Liverpool (Walker AG): *When the Children are Asleep* (1885); *In Time of War* (1876); *Gameskeeper's Cottage* (1846) - London (Royal Academy of Arts): *Ere Care Begins* (1865, oil on canvas, competition piece) - London (Tate Collection): *Poor Man and Friend of the Poor; The Silken Gown* (1860 or 1863, oil on canvas); *Faults on Both Sides* (1861, oil on canvas); *Highland Mother* (exhibited in 1870, oil on canvas) - London (Victoria and Albert Mus.): *Ravine; Riverscape and Mountainscape; Ship in an Inlet; Riverscape at Sunset; Surrounding Areas of Melrose; Riverscape in the Moonlight* - Melbourne: *Motherless Child* - Montreal (MBA): *Sunday in the Virgin Forests* - Salford (Museum and AG): *A Runaway Horse* - Sheffield: *Draughts; Robert Burns and Highland Mary; Auld Robin Gray* - Sunderland: *Why Have I Left My Hamlet?; With the Weight of Many Years.*

Auction records:

London, 6 May 1899, *Cradle,* FRF 5,500. London, 9 Dec 1907, *Family of Gypsies,* GBP 14; *In the Cornfield,* GBP 6. London, 15 Feb 1908, *Return from Market* (1881) GBP 78. London, 3 April 1909, *Arrival of Daddy,* GBP 26. London, 24 May 1909, *Scene from the Pretty Girl of Perth,* GBP 47. London, 24 June 1909, *Her Alone* (1869) GBP 199. London, 12 Feb 1910, *Milkmaid,* GBP 26. London, 27 May 1910, *Its Only Couple,* GBP 294. London, 27 April 1923, *Page of Burns,* GBP 351. London, 20 July 1923, *Fruit Girl,* GBP 10. London, 23 Nov 1923, *Nora Creina* GBP 27. London, 28 Jan 1924, *Well Chosen,* GBP 141. London, 20 June 1924, *Reading the Newspapers,* GBP 67. London, 23 June 1924, *Young Mother,* GBP 73. London, 14 Nov 1924, *Lesson from the Bible,* GBP 23. London, 15 May 1925, *On the Arran Coast,* GBP 162; *Returning from Work,* GBP 25. London, 1 Dec 1925, *Donald McTavish,* GBP 22. London, 30 April-3 May 1926, *Only Her,* GBP 52. London, 3 May 1926, *Listener,* GBP 13. London, 17 June 1926, *Two Children in a Farmyard* (1872, watercolour) GBP 40. London, 18 June 1926, *Fisherman's Daughter,* GBP 39. London, 18 July 1927, *Queen of Kirn,* GBP 21. London, 30 Nov 1928, *Fisherwoman,* GBP 29. London, 19 April 1929, *Red Rose,* GBP 23. London, 10 May 1929, *Only Her,* GBP 31. London, 16 May 1929, *Hand to Mouth* (1879, oil on canvas) GBP 622; *Day to Day,* GBP 65. London, 24 May 1935, *Reading the Bible,* GBP 81. London, 3 July 1942, *Happy While the Day Lasts,* GBP 54. London, 16 April 1943, *Reading Lesson,* GBP 78. Glasgow, 3 March 1944, *Little Gypsy,* GBP 19. New York, 18-19 April 1945, *Resting near the Staircase* (1869) USD 400. London, 30 Jan 1946, *Wee Auntie Jeanie* (1887) GBP 60. London, 22 Feb 1946, *Lady of High Rank,* GBP 52. London, 3 July 1964, *Sophia and Olivia,* Gns 520. London, 11 July 1969, *Portrait of Mary Allan,* Gns 600. Scotland, 30 Aug 1974, *Village School,* GBP 3,800. London, 14 June 1977, *Milkmaid* (oil on canvas, 19 3/4 x 13 1/2 ins / 50 x 34 cm) GBP 800. Scotland, 29 Aug 1978, *First Family Dispute* (1857, watercolour heightened with gouache, 31 x 43 ins / 79 x 109 cm) GBP 2,500. Scotland, 31 Aug 1982, *Courteous Meeting* (watercolour, 23 x 17 ins / 58.5 x 43 cm) GBP 550. Glasgow, 7 July 1984, *From Hand to Mouth* (1879, oil on canvas) GBP 26,000. London, 26 July 1985, *Forgiven - God be Praised!* (1874, oil on canvas, 51 x 67 ins / 129.5 x 170.2 cm) GBP 7,000. Glasgow, 4 Feb 1987, *Seeing Them Off* (watercolour and pencil heightened with gouache, 6 1/2 x 9 1/2 ins / 16.5 x 24 cm) GBP 1,500. London, 25 Jan 1988, *Illustration for The Jolly Beggars by Robert Burns* (watercolour, 7 3/4 x 11 ins / 20 x 28 cm) GBP 418. London, 25 March 1988, *Family Hit by Misfortune* (1857, oil on panel, 35 x 48 ins / 89 x 122 cm) GBP 93,500. Edinburgh, 30 Aug 1988, *Heat of the Hearth and the Homeless* (oil on panel, 14 x 20 ins / 35.5 x 51 cm) GBP 15,950. Toronto, 30 Nov 1988, *Morning Toilette* (1874, oil on canvas, 32 x 22 ins / 81 x 56 cm) CAD 18,500. Perth, 28 Aug 1989, *Fisherman's Daughter* (1866, oil on card, 7 x 4 1/2 ins / 17.5 x 11.5 cm) GBP 1,540. Stockholm, 15 Nov 1989, *The Dream: Young Girl Asleep in a Chair in an Interior* (oil on panel, 7 x 10 ins / 17.5 x 25.5 cm) SEK 39,000. London, 30 March 1990, *Stop at the Inn* (1870, oil on canvas, 20 x 27 ins / 50.7 x 68.8 cm) GBP 7,150. South Queensferry, 1 May 1990, *Friendly Bird* (1873, oil on canvas, 21 x 17 ins / 53.5 x 43 cm) GBP 3,080. Glasgow, 5 Feb 1991, *Solitude* (1868, oil on canvas, 20 x 14 ins / 51 x 35.5 cm) GBP 10,450. Edinburgh, 2 May 1991, *Mother and Child Picking Wild Fruit* (oil on canvas, 12 x 16 ins / 30.5 x 40.5 cm) GBP 3,300. London, 5 June 1991, *Homeless in a Welcoming Home* (oil on panel, 14 1/4 x 20 ins / 36 x 51 cm) GBP 9,900. Perth, 26 Aug 1991, *Proposal* (1866, oil on canvas, 24 1/2 x 17 ins / 62 x 43 cm) GBP 6,050. Glasgow, 4 Dec 1991, *Milkmaid* (oil on canvas, 20 x 14 ins / 51 x 35.5 cm) GBP 4,400. London, 12 June 1992, *Happy Family Taking in the Poverty-stricken* (1856, oil on canvas, 26 x 38 ins / 66 x 96.5 cm) GBP 27,500. New York, 29 Oct 1992, *Harvest* (1881, oil on canvas, 23 1/2 x 15 3/4 ins / 59.7 x 40 cm) USD 6,600. London, 13 Nov 1992, *A Little Different* (1867, oil on canvas, 31 1/2 x 21 3/4 ins / 80 x 55.3 cm) GBP 2,530. New York, 15 Feb 1994, *Happy All Day Long* (1872, oil on canvas, 27 1/4 x 36 1/2 ins / 68.9 x 92.7 cm) USD 29,900. Glasgow, 16 April 1996, *Pretty Milkmaid* (oil on canvas, 26 1/4 x 18 1/4 ins / 66.5 x 46.5 cm) GBP 8,050. Perth, 26 Aug 1996, *Wild Rose* (1870, oil on canvas, 29 3/4 x 20 1/4 ins / 75.5 x 51.5 cm) GBP 6,325. London, 6 Nov 1997, *Washerwomen* (1863, oil on canvas, 11 3/4 x 11 ins / 30 x 27.9 cm) GBP 4,025. Bury St Edmunds, 23 June 1999, *Sophia and Olivia* (1864, oil on panel, 11 x 9 ins / 29 x 23 cm) GBP 5,000. Malmö, 13 Nov 1999, *Proposal by the Well* (1864, oil on canvas, 20 x 17 ins / 51 x 43 cm) SEK 40,000. London, 10 April 2000, *Flirtation* (1847, oil on canvas, 20 x 17 ins / 51 x 42 cm) GBP 6,000. Stockholm, 5 Dec 2000, *Going Fishing* (oil on canvas, 56 x 79 ins / 142 x 200 cm) SEK 135,000. London, 8 March 2001, *Absent Thoughts* (1869, oil on canvas, 31 x 21 ins / 80 x 53 cm) GBP 9,000. London, 8 Nov 2001, *Cottage Bedroom* (oil on board, 12 x 16 ins / 30 x 41 cm) GBP

8,500. EDINBURGH, 24 May 2002, *Silken Gown* (oil on panel, 12 x 9 ins / 30 x 22 cm) GBP 6,000. EDINBURGH, 22 Aug 2002, *Lucy's Flittin* (1864, oil on canvas, 22 x 14 ins / 57 x 35 cm) GBP 10,000. LONDON, 19 Feb 2003, *Worn Out* (1868, oil on canvas, 42 x 57 ins / 106 x 145 cm) GBP 230,000. LONDON, 27 Aug 2003, *Orange Seller* (1884, oil on canvas, 31 x 20 ins / 78 x 51 cm) GBP 7,500. PARIS, 17 March 2004, *Coming Events Cast Their Shadows Before* (1857, oil on canvas, 28 x 19 ins / 72 x 48 cm) EUR 28,000. LONDON, 25 Nov 2004, *Catherine Seyton* (oil on canvas, 24 x 20 ins / 61 x 50 cm) GBP 5,000.

FAEDDERHOLDT, Ludvig Dominico Francisco
Danish, 19th century.
Born 1809, in Copenhagen; died 2 April 1830, in Copenhagen.
Painter.
Faedderholdt was a pupil of J. L. Lund.

FAEGERPLAN, Axel Johan. See **FAGERPLAN**

FAEHNLEIN, Louis
French, 19th century.
Born 19th century, in Mulhouse.
Painter.
Louis Faehnlein exhibited at the Salon des Artistes Français, obtaining an honourable mention in 1898.

FAELBEL, Franz Josef
Austrian, 18th century.
Active in Vienna at the beginning of the 18th century.
Painter.

FAEN. See **FAL Guillaem de**

FAENZA, da. See first name

FAENZA, Giovanni Battista da. See **BERTUCCI**

FAENZA, Marco Antonio da. See **ROCCHETTI**

FAENZA, Vinzenzo, II. See **VALDRE**

FAENZONI, Ferrau. See **FANZONI**

FAES, Jurg Jacobsz.
Dutch, 17th century.
Active in The Hague in 1616.
Engraver.
Jurg Jacobsz. Faez is believed to have executed a plan of The Hague.

FAES, Pieter
Flemish, 18th - 19th century.
Born 14 July 1750, in Meir; died 22 December 1814, in Antwerp.
Painter. Still-lifes (flowers/fruit), insects.
Flemish School.
Pieter Faes worked in the manner of Jacob van Huysum.

MUSEUMS AND GALLERIES:
ANTWERP (Smit van Gelder Mus.) - BARNARD CASTLE (Bowes Mus.): *A Marble Vase of Lilac with other Flowers on a Marble Shelf* (oil/panel) - BRUSSELS (MBA) - GHENT (Mus. voor Schone Kunsten) - TURNHOUT (Taxandria Mus.) - VIENNA (Kunstmus.).

AUCTION RECORDS:
LONDON, 30 July 1924, *Flowers in a Vase on a Marble Flagstone* (1790) GBP 73. LONDON, 3 Dec 1926, *Flowers in a Vase and Fruit on a Marble Flagstone,* GBP 178. LONDON, 29 May 1931, *Bedroom,* GBP 15. LONDON, 24 May 1935, *Flowers in a Bronze Vase,* GBP 99. LONDON, 12 April 1937, *Flowers in a Glass Vase,* GBP 10. PARIS, 23 March 1963, *Crystal Vase,* FRF 12,300. BRUSSELS, 5-7 May 1965, *Flowers and Fruit,* BEF 120,000. PARIS, 7 June 1968, *Vase of Flowers,* FRF 32,000. BRUSSELS, 12 Dec 1972, *Vase of Flowers,* BEF 200,000. PARIS, 6 April 1976, *Flowers Placed on an Entablature* (1796; *Fruit Placed on an Entablature* (two oils on panel, 10 1/2 x 14 3/4 ins / 26.5 x 37.5 cm) FRF 24,000. PARIS, 10 July 1984, *Bouquet of Flowers with Bunch of Grapes Placed on an Entablature* (oil on canvas, 26 x 20 ins / 66 x 50.5 cm) FRF 140,000. MONTE CARLO, 6 Dec 1987, *Bouquet of Flowers* (1789, oil on panel, 13 x 11 ins / 33 x 27 cm) FRF 350,000. MONACO, 2 Dec 1989, *Floral Composition on a Marble Entablature* (1795, oil on panel, 21 3/4 x 16 1/4 ins / 55.5 x 41.5 cm) FRF 832,500. MONACO, 19 June 1994, *Roses, Tulip and Other Flowers in a Glass Vase on a Ledge* (oil on canvas, 13 x 10 3/4 ins / 33 x 27.5 cm) FRF 75,480. LONDON, 6 July 1994, *Still-life of Flowers in a Terracotta Urn with a Nest and Fledglings on an Entablature* (1793, oil on panel, 26 1/2 x 19 1/2 ins / 67.3 x 49.4 cm) GBP 36,700. LONDON, 3-4 Dec 1997, *Still-life with Roses, a Tulip, Peonies, Daffodils, Hydrangeas, Hyacinths and Other Flowers in a Vase on a Marble Entablature with Insects; Still-life with Roses, Peonies, Daffodils, Tulips and Other Flowers in a Vase on a Marble Entablature with a Bird's Nest and Insects* (1789, oil on canvas, a pair, each 28 1/2 x 22 1/4 ins / 72.3 x 56.2 cm) GBP 133,500. NEW YORK, 29 Jan 1999, *Melon, Grapes, Peaches, Gooseberries, Flowers on Ledge* (1789, oil on panel, 20 x 15 ins / 50 x 38 cm) USD 18,000. LONDON, 14 Dec 2000, *Still-life of Mixed Flowers in a Stone Vase, Together with Bird's Nest* (oil on panel, 22 x 16 ins / 57 x 41 cm) GBP 35,000. NEW YORK, 5 June 2002, *Still-life of Roses, Peonies, Tulips and Other Flowers in a Terracotta Vase, Fruit Resting on a Ledge* (1782, oil on panel, 33 x 25 ins / 83 x 63 cm) USD 200,000. LONDON, 30 Oct 2002, *Tulips, Roses and Other Flowers with Butterfly in Urn on a Marble Ledge* (oil on canvas, 31 x 26 ins / 79 x 65 cm) GBP 14,000.

FAES, Pieter van der. See **LELY Peter**

FAES, Raymond
Belgian, 20th century.
Born 1905, in Antwerp.
Painter, draughtsman. Portraits, still-lifes, flowers.
Raymond Faes was a student of Jean de Graef and Joseph Posenaer at the academy of fine arts in Antwerp and of Albert Ciamberlani at the higher institute.

He produced an allusive form of painting that was nevertheless reinforced by some strong colours.

FAESCH, Johann Ludwig Wernhard
Swiss, 18th century.
Born c. 1738, in Basel; died 20 May 1778, in Paris.
Draughtsman, miniaturist.
Johann Faesch worked primarily in London and Paris.

FAESCH, Sebastian
Swiss, 18th century.
Active in Basel in the middle of the 18th century.
Draughtsman.

FAESI-GESSNER, Johann Konrad. See **FASI-GESSNER**

FAESTER, Hans Julius
Danish, 19th century.
Born 24 August 1856, in Nyborg.
Painter. Genre scenes, interiors with figures.
Faester exhibited at Charlottenborg castle from 1882 to 1888.

AUCTION RECORDS:
COPENHAGEN, 14 Nov 1986, *Interior Scene* (1887, oil on canvas, 24 x 19 1/4 ins / 61 x 49 cm) DKK 8,000.

FAETI, Giorgio
Italian, 17th century.
Active in Castel Durante.
Painter (majolica).
Noted for his *Holy Family*.

FAGALO, Guillem
Spanish, 14th century.
Active in Perpignan in 1337.
Painter.
Guillem Fagalo was the brother of Pere Fagalo.

FAGALO, Pere
Spanish, 14th century.
Active in Perpignan in 1337.
Painter.
Pere Fagalo worked with his brother Guillem.

FAGAN, Betty Maude
French, 19th - 20th century.
Died 1932.
Painter. Genre scenes.
AUCTION RECORDS:
LONDON, 31 March 1981, *Snip, Snip* (oil on canvas, 37 3/4 x 29 1/4 ins / 96 x 74 cm) GBP 480. NEW YORK, 29 Oct 1992, *Crystal Chandelier* (oil on canvas, 40 1/2 x 29 ins / 102.8 x 73.7 cm) USD 2,090. LONDON, 13 Nov 1992, *First Haircut* (oil on canvas, 38 x 29 ins / 96.5 x 73.7 cm) GBP 11,000.

FAGAN, James
American, 19th - 20th century.
Born 1864, in New York; died in New York.
Painter, engraver. Portraits, genre scenes.
MUSEUMS AND GALLERIES:
NEW HAVEN (Knights of Columbus Mus.): *Pope Leo XIII* (engraving).
AUCTION RECORDS:
NEW YORK, 10 March 1905, *Idealised Head,* USD 155.

FAGAN, Louis Alexander
British, 19th century.
Born 7 February 1845, in Naples, Italy; died 8 January 1903, in Florence.
Watercolourist, draughtsman, art critic.
Louis Alexander Fagan was an amateur artist who produced excellent watercolours and drawings. He was deputy director of the collection of engravings at the British Museum. He is known notably for his works on the art of Michelangelo, Correggio and several modern artists. He wrote the life of his close friend Panizzi. He was a distinguished diplomat who held official posts in Italy, Venezuela, Sweden and France, yet never stopped pursuing his artistic training. Later on, when he gave up his diplomatic career to take up an administrative position at the British Museum, he used his numerous connections for the benefit of his new role.
AUCTION RECORDS:
LONDON, 1 June 1945, *Anne Marie Fagan* GBP 52; *Self-portrait,* GBP 47.

FAGAN, Robert
British, 18th - 19th century.
Born c. 1745, in Cork, 5 March 1761 according to some sources; died 26 August 1816, in Rome.
Painter. Portraits.
Robert Fagan entered the Royal Academy Schools in 1781. He left for Rome via Paris in 1783. Of his work, little other than portraits is known, for example *Sophia, Lady Mainwaring* (1792). He exhibited at the Royal Academy in 1793 and from 1812 to 1816, for example *Sarah and Jeffrey, Children of Lord Amherst* (1812). Fagan was also a diplomat. In 1809 he was appointed Counsul General for Sicily and Malta and went to live in Palermo.
BIBLIOGRAPHY:
Crookshank, A./The Knight of Glin/Laffan, William, *Masterpieces by Irish Artists, 1660-1860,* exhibition catalogue, Pyms Gallery, London, 1999. Laffan, William, *Robert Fagan in Sicily - The Acton Family Portrait,* exhibition catalogue, Pyms Gallery, London, 2000.
MUSEUMS AND GALLERIES:
LIMERICK (Hunt Museum): *The Artist and his Wife* - LONDON (Tate Collection): *Anna Maria Ferri, the Artist's First Wife* (c. 1790-1792, oil on canvas).
AUCTION RECORDS:
LONDON, 18 March 1981, *Portrait of Anna Maria Ferri, the Artist's Wife* (oil on canvas, 28 1/4 x 23 1/2 ins / 72 x 60 cm) GBP 18,500. LONDON, 10 April 1991, *Portrait of Anna Maria Ferri, the Artist's First Wife, Dressed in a Yellow Dress and an Orange Stole Edged with Fur* (oil on canvas, 29 x 24 ins / 73.5 x 61 cm) GBP 26,400. BURY ST EDMUNDS, 24 March 1999, *Portrait of Young Man Holding a Bow* (oil on canvas, 36 x 26 ins / 91 x 66 cm) GBP 2,100. LONDON, 18 May 2000, *Emma Hamilton as a Bacchante* (oil on canvas, 38 x 30 ins / 96 x 76 cm) GBP 80,000. LONDON, 18 May 2001, *Portrait of Lady Wearing White Dress, Red Robes* (oil on canvas, 36 x 29 ins / 92 x 73 cm) GBP 50,000. LONDON, 23 Nov 2004, *Portrait of Lady Clifford* (1791, oil on canvas, 89 x 59 ins / 226 x 149 cm) GBP 39,000.

FAGAN, William B.
British, 19th century.
Born 1860, in London.
Sculptor.
William B. Fagan trained under Dalou and W.S. Frith. He exhibited at the Royal Academy in London from 1886.

FAGARD, Hugues
French, 16th century.
Active in Arras in 1552.
Painter.

FAGARD, Virginie
French, 19th century.
Born 29 December 1829, in Paris.
Painter.
A pupil of Mlle Dautel, Virginie Fagard exhibited portraits and several studies at the Salon from 1848 to 1866.

FAGE, Jean-Marie
French, 20th century.
Born 1925, in L'Isle-sur-la-Sorgue.
Painter (mixed media/gouache), lithographer, sculptor.
In 1947-1948 Jean-Marie Fage worked with the Candelié group in Avignon. Between 1946 and 1952 he also attended the André Lhote studio in Paris, and at the home of René Char he met Georges Braque in 1948. In Paris he was friendly with Ferdinand Desnos, whom he visited in his studio in the Rue Claude-Bernard. In Provence he regularly met Auguste Chabaud in Graveson, near Maillaine, until the artist died in 1955. Subsequently he was acquainted with Louis Latapie in Avignon, and for forty years he was a friend of Marcel Melot, who lived in Isle-sur-la-Sorgue. From 1961 he showed in group or solo exhibitions in Isle-sur-la-Sorgue, Avignon, Salon-de-Provence, Privas, Mulhouse, Aix-en-Provence, Calais in 1992, and Paris, where René Char wrote the introduction to his solo exhibition at the Galerie Arlette Chabaud. Since then he has had two exhibitions at the Galerie Peinture Fraîche, in 1984 and 1986, and one at the Galerie Hansma in 1992. During the 1980s he illustrated the work of several poets, including that of Eugène Guillevic, and in 1990 Jacques Kober's *Un pigment d'horizon* (*An Horizon Pigment*). In 1990 he made a monumental sculpture for the *La Vie Sociale* buildings.

Since 1980 Fage has painted abstracts. However, in 1985 he broke this continuity with a series of groups of nudes, his personal variations on the traditional subject of women posing or bathing. Some of his figurative paintings clearly benefit from the rigour of his abstract compositions. On the other hand, his abstract paintings do not try to hide any initial glance at the outside world that may have provoked them: *Blue Flight, Broken Flight* of 1979, or *The Château de*

Lacoste and *The Window* of 1991. These paintings, which demonstrate a Baudelairean 'correspondence' with reality, are spontaneous in feeling and treatment, not painted within a system, and each subject deploys its own strategy. Conversely, those that are more avowedly plastic constructions, such as *Opening, Balance* of 1991, are designed and carried out according to rigorous rules, the strong lines clearly marking out surfaces, largely at right angles; though this does exclude imagination in the combination of forms or sensuality in the treatment of texture and colour. As Jacques Kober quotes him, Fage assumes that his balance between representation and abstraction goes without saying: 'Colour by itself creates form, whether it is a silhouette or a nothing.'

Bibliography:

Char, René (preface), *J-M Fage*, exhibition catalogue, Gal. Arlette Chabaud, Paris, 1963. Kober, Jacques, *Un pigment d'horizon*, Gal. Annie Lagier, L'Isle-sur-la-Sorgue, 1990.

FAGE, Nicolas Raymond de La. See **LA FAGE**

FAGEL, Léon

French, 19th - 20th century.

Born 30 January 1851, in Valenciennes; died March 1913, in Paris.

Sculptor.

Léon Fagel, who was taught by Cavelier, won the Second Grand Prix de Rome with a low relief, *Homer Singing his Poems in a Greek City*, in 1875, and the First Grand prix with *Tobias Restoring his Father's Eyesight* in 1879. He won a third-class medal in 1882 and a second-class medal in 1883. From Rome he sent back a plaster low relief, *The Dying Poet*. Fagel was commissioned to sculpt the bronze statue of *Dupleix* erected in the Place d'Armes, Landricies (Nord). He was awarded gold medals in the USA in 1889 and 1900.

Museums and Galleries:

Copenhagen (Ny Carlsberg Glyptotek): *Young Carp* - Nantes (MBA): *Tree Grafter* - Valenciennes: *Bust of Chevreul; Abel's First Offering; Soldier from Wattignies.*

FAGER, H. von

German, 18th century.

Active in Xanten in 1762.

Painter.

There is a signed painting by Von Fager in the church of St Victor in Xanten (North Rhine-Westphalia).

FAGERBERBERG, Carl Vilhelm

Swedish, 20th century.

Born 1878.

Sculptor.

Fagerberberg studied in Stockholm. He also exhibited in Paris from 1906.

FAGERBERG, C. H.

Swedish, 19th century.

Born 1796; died 25 March 1831.

Miniaturist.

FAGERLIN, Ferdinand Julius

Swedish, 19th century.

Born 5 February 1825, in Stockholm; died 19 March 1907, in Düsseldorf.

Painter. Genre scenes.

Fagerlin was a pupil of Carl Sohn, and painted in the style of R. Jordans and H. Ritter. Before becoming a full-time artist, he was in the army. As a painter, he studied first at the academy in Stockholm, then in Düsseldorf, and finally in Paris under Thomas Couture. In 1865, he was elected a member of the academy in Stockholm.

Fagerlin visited Holland several times to study the coast, and indeed almost all his paintings are Dutch seascapes. The pictures he painted in the Netherlands are naive, typical scenes of the lives of fishermen and seamen in that country. They are all painted from life, with a clear, solid sense of colour; they are also imbued with a fitting seriousness and depth of feeling. His masterpiece is generally considered to be the painting *The Declaration of Love*.

Museums and Galleries:

Düsseldorf: *Come, Hans; The Timid Admirer; Jealousy; Study of an Interior* - Leipzig: *Young Fisherwoman* - Oslo: *The Enemies of a Celibate Life* - Stockholm: *Woman; Two Dutch Interiors; Little Fishermen Smoking; Jealousy; Recovery.*

Auction records:

London, 18 June 1928, *Without Hope* (1876) GBP 120. London, 2 March 1934, *The First Puff*, GBP 157. London, 25 Oct 1940, *The Twilight of Life*, GBP 27. London, 8 Nov 1946, *Young Musician*, GBP 1,260. London, 21 Feb 1947, *Melody of Other Times*, GBP 987. London, 7 March 1947, *Letter of Love*, GBP 714; *Old Man Filling His Pipe*, GBP 231; *The Child with Small Accordion*, GBP 31. Lucerne, 1 Dec 1956, *Fisherman's House*, CHF 13,600. Stockholm, 26 Oct 1960, *Interior with a Cupboard Bed to the Right*, SEK 1,000. Göteborg, 1 Nov 1972, *Reading the Letter*, SEK 13,000. Göteborg, 28 March 1974, *Interior Scene*, SEK 9,300. Göteborg, 5 April 1978, *Reading the Letter* (oil on canvas, 24 1/2 x 22 ins / 62 x 56 cm) SEK 34,500. Stockholm, 11 Nov 1981, *Young Girl at Her Mirror* (1871, oil on canvas, 18 x 25 1/2 ins / 46 x 65 cm) SEK 46,000. Cologne, 26 Oct 1984, *The Declaration of Love* (1866, oil on canvas, 31 1/2 x 39 1/4 ins / 80 x 100 cm) DEM 85,000. Stockholm, 29 Oct 1985, *Rustic Interior Scene* (1895, oil on canvas, 31 x 39 ins / 79 x 99 cm) SEK 135,000. Stockholm, 15 Nov 1988, *Fisherman's Family in Their Home* (oil, 29 1/4 x 39 ins / 74 x 99 cm) SEK 200,000. London, 16 March 1989, *The Declaration* (1881, oil on canvas, 22 1/4 x 19 3/4 ins / 56.5 x 50 cm) GBP 11,000. Stockholm, 15 Nov 1989, *Family Scene in a Fisherman's House* (1871, oil, 29 1/4 x 39 ins / 74 x 99 cm) SEK 175,000. Stockholm, 26 May 1999, *Young Girl with Basket of Vegetables* (oil on canvas, 20 x 34 ins / 52 x 86 cm) SEK 48,000. Uppsala, 5 Dec 1999, *Interior Scene with Figures - The Sailor's Return* (1870, oil on canvas, 16 x 19 ins / 40 x 49 cm) SEK 92,000. Stockholm, 29 May 2000, *A Mother's Love* (1865, oil on canvas, 29 x 35 ins / 73 x 89 cm) SEK 150,000. Stockholm, 5 Dec 2000, *Domestic Devotion* (1887, oil on canvas, 38 x 45 ins / 96 x 114 cm) SEK 250,000. Amsterdam, 23 Oct 2001, *Love Token* (1889, oil on canvas, 20 x 22 ins / 51 x 57 cm) EUR 5,200. Stockholm, 29 May 2002, *Reading Aloud - Interior Scene with Figures* (1890, oil on canvas, 35 x 31 ins / 90 x 78 cm) SEK 100,000. Stockholm, 26 May 2004, *Devotion at Home or The Recovery* (1868, oil on canvas, 32 x 39 ins / 81 x 100 cm) SEK 170,000. London, 15 June 2004, *Wishing it were She* (oil on canvas, 33 x 41 ins / 85 x 103 cm) GBP 12,000.

FAGERPLAN, Axel Johan

Swedish, 19th century.

Born 1788, in Vestergöttland; died 17 July 1865, in Stockholm.

Painter. History painting, genre scenes, still-lifes, fruit.

A student at the academy in Stockholm, Fagerplan later painted a portrait of King Gustavus IV Adolphus as a child.

Auction records:

Stockholm, 30 Nov 1993, *Farmers Drinking in an Inn* (oil on canvas, after a Dutch master, 15 1/4 x 17 1/4 ins / 39 x 44 cm) SEK 12,500.

FAGES, Arthur R.

French, 20th century.

Born 11 May 1902, in Toulouse.

Painter. Portraits, seascapes, still-lifes. Murals.

Poetic Reality.

After studying mathematics, Arthur R. Fages taught himself to paint and then joined the studio of Paul-Albert Laurens at the Académie Julian, where he met Jules Cavaillès. He exhibited at group exhibitions in Paris: the Salon des Artistes

Français, of which he was a member, from 1925, from 1929 the Salon d'Automne, of which he became a member in 1939, the Salon des Tuileries from 1932, and occasionally the Salon des Artistes Indepéndants. In 1937 he exhibited with Cavaillès and Limouse. He also showed his work in solo exhibitions: 1925, 1928, 1941 in Toulouse, 1931 and 1948 in Paris, and 1941 in Cannes. He travelled frequently in Spain, Portugal. Italy, Austria and Hungary, and was made a Chevalier of the Légion d'Honneur in 1949.

He was always a great admirer of Bonnard, Matisse and Dufy, and may be considered one of the 'poetic realist' painters. He painted many seascapes in Collioure, Argelès and Port-Vendres; his portraits of the clothes designer Paul Poiret (1942) and of Pierre Bonnard (1943) are two powerful, broadly brushed works. He painted murals for the Toulouse Chamber of Commerce and the École des Officiers d'Administration, Montpellier, and in 1950 decorations for the liner *Maréchal Joffre* and the École Polytechnique, Paris.

BIBLIOGRAPHY:

Gauthier, Maximilien, *Arthur Fages*, Les Gémeaux, Paris, 1951.

FAGES, Guy

French, 20th - 21st century.
Born 1948, in Cavaillon (Vaucluse).
Sculptor.

In the early part of his career, Guy Fages devoted his efforts to modelling, and to sculpting in stone. Since then, he has worked more with bronze, for which he uses a range of finishes, such as blue, dark red and jade green. His style is informed by the works of Carpeaux, Rodin and Volti. His works are based on nature, but he interprets the latter freely, and his desire to convey life and movement in his works lends them a certain abstract quality.

FAGET-BERNARD, Georges

French, 20th century.
Born 1944.
Painter.

While staying in London, Georges Faget-Bernard attended the Royal Academy. He has taken part in various group exhibitions.

AUCTION RECORDS:

PARIS, 31 Oct 1990, *La Piste du Temps* (*The Track of Time*) (oil on canvas, 51 1/4 x 38 1/4 ins / 130 x 97 cm) FRF 15,000.

FAGET-GERMAIN, Pierre

French, 20th century.
Born 1902, in Bordeaux; died 1961, in Algiers.
Painter. Seascapes.

Pierre Faget-Germain studied at the École des Beaux-Arts and the École des Arts Décoratifs in Bordeaux. He settled in Algeria around 1930. He painted using a thick texture.

He featured in *Lumineuse Algérie, sous le regard des peintres de marines (1830-1960)* (*Luminous Algeria, Through the Eyes of Seascape Painters (1830-1960)*), Musée National de la Marine, Toulon (2003).

BIBLIOGRAPHY:

Mourot, Marjolaine/Vidal-Bué, Marion/Cazenave, Elisabeth, et al., *Lumineuse Algérie, sous le regard des peintres de marines (1830-1960)*, exhibition catalogue, Musée National de la Marine, Toulon, 2003.

AUCTION RECORDS:

PARIS, 25 March 1991, *The Port of Algiers* (1930, oil/painting, 20 x 49 1/4 ins / 51 x 125 cm) FRF 9,000. PARIS, 29 June 1999, *Côte Djidjellienne, Algeria* (oil on canvas, 30 x 66 ins / 75 x 168 cm) FRF 19,000. PARIS, 7 Oct 1999, *Formentera* (oil on panel, 20 x 47 ins / 50 x 119 cm) FRF 12,000.

FAGG, Kenneth S.

American, 20th century.
Born 2 May 1901, in Chicago.
Painter, engraver, illustrator. Landscapes, arctic scenes, aviation, science fiction.

Kenneth S. Fagg, a pupil of Joseph Pennel, F. Du Mond, Frederick Bridgman, Daniel Garber and Édouard Vysekal, was a member of the Art Students League, New York, and the American Watercolor Society.

FAGGI, Alféo

Italian, 20th century.
Born 11 September 1885, in Florence.
Active in the USA.
Sculptor. Busts, statues, monuments.

Faggi sculpted a *Pietà* as a monument to commemorate World War I for the church of St Thomas in Chicago, as well as some other religious works.

FAGIVOLI, Girolamo, or Faccioli

Italian, 16th century.
Died 1573.
Active in Bologna c. 1560.
Engraver, goldsmith, medallist.

Girolamo Fagivoli published engravings in the style of Correggio, Cecchino de Salviati and Francesco Mazzuola.

FAGLI, Vicenzo

Italian, 17th century.
Painter.

Fagli was active in Florence in 1642, working on a chapel in the cloister of S Maria degli Angeli, now part of the Ospidale S Maria Novella.

FAGNANI, Giuseppe

Italian, 19th century.
Born 1819, in Naples; died 1873, in New York.
Painter. Portraits.

Fagnani was given a pension by Queen Isabella to study at the Accademia in Naples. He then travelled in Austria, France, Spain, Turkey and America. During his travels he painted portraits of some highly illustrious people. He is remembered for portraits of *The Duchess of Montpensier*, *Garibaldi*, *Sultan Abd-el-Aziz* and *Archduke Charles*.

MUSEUMS AND GALLERIES:

FLORENCE (Uffizi): *Portrait of the Artist* - LONDON (National Portrait Gal.): *Richard Cobden* (1865, oil on canvas, replica); *William Bulwer, Baron Dalling and Bulwer* (1865, oil on canvas) - NEW YORK (Metropolitan Mus. of Art): *The Nine Muses*.

AUCTION RECORDS:

PARIS, 15 June 1984, *Portrait of Princess Matilda* (1858, oil on canvas, 46 x 35 1/4 ins / 117 x 89.5 cm) FRF 4,500.

FAGNANI, Nina

American, 19th century.
Born in New York.
Miniaturist.

Nina Fagnani exhibited miniatures at the Royal Academy in 1892.

FAGNIEZ, François Xavier

French, 20th century.
Born 1936, in Salies-de-Béarn.
Painter. Designs for mosaics.

In 1954 François Xavier Fagniez entered the École des Beaux-Arts and the École des Métiers d'Art, Paris. Lung problems delayed his taking up his place at the École des Métiers d'Art until 1956. From 1956 to 1959 he attended various studios, including that of André Lhote, and in 1963 he was selected for the Prix Fénéon.

Fagniez's early paintings date from the late 1950s, since which time his line of development has been coherent. In addition to his admiration for the historical painters he discovered by chance during his travels (and although for his own purposes he had given attention to Cézanne, as the first landmark of modern painting, and to Bonnard, for his spirit of delight), it was from Bazaine that he developed his personal style. The first paintings fit perfectly into the context of the post-war Paris School, when Bazaine and Manessier were aiming to reconcile a realist flavour with the rigour of abstraction. That was exactly Fagniez's approach. He never tried to hide the fact that his work originated in the sensory world, and, indeed, his titles make this clear: *Night Under Trees, Festival in the Port, Pheasant Shooting*. In these early works, between 1957 and 1960, even the technique, with its small strokes of colour placed between the main lines of the drawing, is reminiscent of his predecessors.

From about 1967 he began to free himself from this slightly automatic treatment, the more so as his journeys in the very different landscapes of Brittany, Spain and even Vietnam became the source of his way of seeing and his creation of images - his imagination, in fact. Everything that he takes or 'abstracts' from what he is looking at provides him with rhythms, colour ranges and tastes. As a result there is an alternation between the resonant and varied travel paintings and the repetitive calm of works painted at home. However, during this regular routine of travel and homecoming the consistency of his expression and his essential subject matter is modulated not only by climatic variation, but a personal change: although contact with the sensory world is maintained, as in *Rainy, Corsica, Water*, the material aspect of the reality is gradually done away with, leaving only the essentials, rhythm, colour, materials, tastes. In this way Fagniez continually achieves a balance between abstract landscape painting and sensory abstraction.

He has taken part in many group exhibitions in Paris: from 1970 the Salon d'Automne, 1972, 1973 the Salon Grands et Jeunes d'Aujourd'hui, since 1986 the Salon des Réalités Nouvelles. He has showed at many solo exhibitions since 1968: in Switzerland, Denmark, Saigon, Belgium, Luxembourg, Toulouse, Troyes, Bordeaux, Lyons, the Netherlands, in 1988 *Fagniez, 20 ans de peinture* (*Fagniez, 20 Years of Painting*) at the Musée de Mont-de-Marsan, in 1991 he was invited to the Galerie de la Prévôté at the 44th Festival of Aix-en-Provence, in 1999 in Vence, etc., in 1969, 1976, and 1977 in Paris, and since 1979, including 1995 and 1997, very regularly at the Galerie Bellint.

BIBLIOGRAPHY:

Dunoyer, Jean-Marie, *Fagniez*, Le Sphinx, Paris, 1979. Le Sidaner, Jean-Marie, *Fagniez*, La Différence, Paris, 1985. Cluny, Claude Michel, *Fagniez*, La Différence, Paris, 1988. *Fagniez*, exhibition catalogue, Gal. P. J. Meurisse, Toulouse, 1989.

MUSEUMS AND GALLERIES:

LUXEMBOURG: two paintings.

AUCTION RECORDS:

PARIS, 27 Oct 1985, *Tower, New York* (oil on canvas, 36 1/4 x 23 1/2 ins / 92 x 60 cm) FRF 5,100. PARIS, 29 Jan 1988, *Untitled* (1970-1971, oil on canvas, 32 x 51 1/4 ins / 81 x 130 cm) FRF 17,200. PARIS, 13 Dec 1991, *Hen Bird* (1989, tempera/paper, 46 1/2 x 29 1/4 ins / 118 x 74 cm) FRF 18,000. PARIS, 5 Feb 1992, *Outdoor Theatre* (1987, oil on canvas, 36 1/4 x 28 3/4 ins / 92 x 73 cm) FRF 7,500.

FAGNION, Jules

French, 19th century.
Born 19th century, in Paris.
Engraver.

A pupil of C. Thompson, Jules Fagnion made his Salon début in 1861.

FAGO, Nicola or Niclaes

Flemish, 16th - 17th century.
Active in Antwerp, in 1600.
Sculptor.
Flemish School.

Nicola Fago was a master of the Guild of St Luke in Antwerp in 1595.

FAGOT, Alphonse

French, 18th century.
Active in Paris in 1785.
Painter (?), sculptor (?).

FAGOT, Nicolas

French, 16th century.
Active in Troyes in 1519.
Glass painter.

FAGOT, Nicolas

French, 16th century.
Painter.

Fagot was the son of the stained glass painter of the same name. He worked between 1547 and 1558 for the churches in Troyes (Aube).

FAGOT, Nicolas, or Fanyau

French, 17th century.
Sculptor.

Nicolas Fagot executed three statues for the façade of the town hall in Nantes from 1605 to 1608: *Faith, Hope* and *Charity*.

FAGUE, Paul

French, 18th century.
Enameller.

Paul Fague set up in Bern in 1758 and was still there in 1763.

FAGUET, Adrienne

French, 19th century.
Painter. Landscapes.

Adrienne Faguet exhibited landscapes at the Salon from 1827 to 1846. Her best-known works are *Pretty Spot in the Dauphiné Region*; *Gasny Mill, near Vernon*; *View of Normandy*; *View from the Banks of the River Epte at Gommecour*; *Ruins of the Château de Coucy*; and *View from La Roche-Guyon*.

FAGUNDES, Guiomar

Brazilian, 20th century.
Born 31 October 1896, in São Paulo.
Painter. Allegorical subjects, nudes, genre scenes, flowers.

Guiomar Fagundes took part in many group exhibitions in Latin America. In Paris she exhibited two nudes at the Salon of the Société Nationale des Beaux-Arts in 1929. She painted genre scenes and allegories such as *The Queen of Sheba in Her Youth* and flower paintings, including *White Roses*.

MUSEUMS AND GALLERIES:

MONTEVIDEO: several paintings.

FAHAD, Mosaad

Kuwaiti, 20th century.
Born 1945.
Painter.

Fahad's work has been shown in several group exhibitions.

FAHEY, Alfred

British, 19th century.
Active in England.
Painter. History painting.

AUCTION RECORDS:

LONDON, 19 July 1909, *Discovery of the Cross*, GBP 7.

FAHEY, Edward Henry

British, 19th - 20th century.
Born 1844, in Brompton; died 1907.
Painter, watercolourist, draughtsman. Genre scenes, landscapes, seascapes.

Edward Henry Fahey was the son of James Fahey. He studied at South Kensington, the Royal Academy in London and in schools in Italy. In 1872 he became a member of the Royal

Institution and in 1875 of the Royal Academy. He exhibited in Paris in 1878.

MUSEUMS AND GALLERIES:

MELBOURNE: *Sea Mist over Oulton Broad, Norfolk; Farm* - SALFORD (Museum and AG): *Still Waters Run Deep* (1877) - SYDNEY: *Dyer's Stream* (watercolour).

AUCTION RECORDS:

LONDON, 23 July 1923, *Sunset* (drawing) GBP 10. LONDON, 29 Feb 1984, *View of a Port* (oil on canvas, 50 x 40 ins / 127 x 101.5 cm) GBP 850.

FAHEY, James

British, 19th century.

Born 16 April 1804, in Paddington; died 19 December 1885, in London.

Painter, watercolourist, draughtsman, engraver.

Portraits, genre scenes, landscapes.

James Fahey studied engraving for some time with his uncle Swaine, then went to Munich and Paris, where he produced drawings for surgical art.

Having exhibited a portrait at the Royal Academy in London in 1825, he devoted himself to watercolours. Together with some important members of the former association of watercolourists, he founded the New Water-Colour Society, of which he was secretary for over 40 years.

MUSEUMS AND GALLERIES:

LONDON (British Mus.): watercolour.

AUCTION RECORDS:

LONDON, 14 Nov 1924, *Loch Lomond, Isle of Macfarlane* (drawing) GBP 5. EDINBURGH, 30 April 1985, *The Lawnmarket, Edinburgh* (watercolour heightened with gouache, 19¼ x 25½ ins / 49 x 65 cm) GBP 700. LONDON, 25 Jan 1989, *Return of the Reapers* (1859, watercolour and gouache, 20½ x 33½ ins / 52 x 85 cm) GBP 4,400. PARIS, 30 March 1998, *Bootle Fell, Cumberland* (watercolour varnished in parts heightened with white, 16½ x 29 ins / 42 x 73.5 cm) FRF 3,800. LONDON, 11 July 2000, *Figures in a River Valley* (1846, oil on canvas, 50 x 39 ins / 128 x 99 cm) GBP 2,700.

FAHL, F.

German, 19th century.

Active in Liegnitz (now Legnica, Poland) c. 1830.

Painter, miniaturist.

FAHLBERG, Arthur

German, 20th century.

Born 25 December 1874, in Merseburg.

Painter, illustrator. Religious subjects. Murals.

Arthur Fahlberg was a student at the school of arts and trades in Berlin. He began as an illustrator. He then became a painter, mainly of religious mural decorations, including at the evangelical church at the garrison in Berlin, the chapel at the castle in Plön (Holstein) and the fresco *Suffer the Little Children to Come unto Me* at the educational centre in Quedlinburg (Saxony).

FAHLCRANTZ, Axel Erik Valerius

Swedish, 19th - 20th century.

Born 1851, in Stockholm; died 1925.

Painter. Landscapes.

Fahlcrantz exhibited in Munich in 1909.

MUSEUMS AND GALLERIES:

GÖTEBORG: *Motala* - STOCKHOLM: *Stormy Day; Moonlight.*

AUCTION RECORDS:

STOCKHOLM, 29 Oct 1985, *Summer Day* (1892, oil on canvas, 29¼ x 43¾ ins / 74 x 111 cm) SEK 59,000. STOCKHOLM, 19 April 1989, *Summer Landscape with Sunlight on a Stream Bordered with Bushes* (oil on canvas, 9¾ x 15¾ ins / 25 x 40 cm) SEK 6,000. STOCKHOLM, 15 Nov 1989, *Trolldom, Lakeside Landscape* (oil on canvas, 25½ x 39 ins / 65 x 99 cm) SEK 7,000. STOCKHOLM, 13 April 1992, *Norrström and the Castle on a Summer Night* (oil on canvas, 37½ x 78¼ ins / 95 x 199 cm) SEK 4,000.

FAHLCRANTZ, Axel Magnus

Swedish, 19th century.

Born 1780, in Stora Tuna (Dalarna); died 7 October 1854, in Stockholm.

Sculptor.

The brother of Carl Johan Fahlcrantz and pupil of P. Ljung, Axel Fahlcrantz was elected to the academy in 1834.

FAHLCRANTZ, Carl Johan

Swedish, 18th - 19th century.

Born 1774, in Stora Tuna (Dalarna); died 1861, in Stockholm.

Painter. Landscapes.

Carl Johan Fahlcrantz was a pupil of Brussel and Limnell. He painted Norwegian landscapes, and among his best works are *The Legend of Frithiof* and *View of Kalmar Castle in Moonlight.*

Fahlcrantz was a very interesting landscape painter, whose work is full of Romantic sentiment. His portrayal of shadows and moonlight effects is quite remarkable.

MUSEUMS AND GALLERIES:

HELSINKI: *Forest Landscape with Domestic Animals* - OSLO: *Forest Location in the North* - STOCKHOLM: *View of Kalmar Castle in the Moonlight; Landscape*; two works.

AUCTION RECORDS:

STOCKHOLM, 25-27 Sept 1935, *Landscape*, SEK 1,185. STOCKHOLM, 27 Oct 1981, *Summer Landscape* (oil on canvas, 14½ x 21¼ ins / 37 x 54 cm) SEK 6,600. STOCKHOLM, 24 April 1984, *Panorama of Pau* (1836, oil on canvas, 23½ x 33¾ ins / 60 x 86 cm) SEK 28,000. STOCKHOLM, 17 April 1985, *Wooded Landscape with Mountain Stream* (oil on canvas, 36¼ x 50 ins / 92 x 127 cm) SEK 35,500. LONDON, 24 March 1988, *Watermill in a Wooded Landscape* (1811, oil on canvas, 19½ x 27½ ins / 49.8 x 69.8 cm) GBP 935. STOCKHOLM, 15 Nov 1988, *Mills near Valdemar* (1836, oil, 10¼ x 14¼ ins / 26 x 36 cm) SEK 50,000. STOCKHOLM, 19 April 1989, *Landscape with the Ruins of St Olof* (oil on canvas, 9¾ x 14¼ ins / 25 x 36 cm) SEK 6,500. STOCKHOLM, 14 Nov 1990, *Panorama of Spereholm* (1837, oil on canvas, 35½ x 46 ins / 90 x 117 cm) SEK 47,000. LONDON, 22 Nov 1990, *Windmill beside the Sea* (1836, oil on canvas, 10¾ x 14¾ ins / 27.5 x 37.5 cm) GBP 825. LONDON, 19 June 1991, *Wooded Landscape Overhanging a River* (oil on canvas, 33¾ x 45½ ins / 86 x 115.5 cm) GBP 3,850. STOCKHOLM, 19 May 1992, *Wooded Mountain Landscape in the South* (oil on canvas, 9¾ x 12½ ins / 25 x 32 cm) SEK 9,000. STOCKHOLM, 25 Nov 1999, *View of Stockholm from Soder's Hill* (oil on canvas, 39 x 52 ins / 100 x 132 cm) SEK 70,000. STOCKHOLM, 16 May 2000, *View across Stjernsund and Edo* (oil on canvas, 17 x 24 ins / 44 x 60 cm) SEK 20,000. MALMÖ, 19 Nov 2000, *Hunters Resting by Waterfall* (1810, oil on canvas, 23 x 31 ins / 59 x 80 cm) SEK 25,000. COPENHAGEN, 5 March 2001, *Mountain Landscape with Two Hunters and their Dogs near Waterfall* (1815, oil on canvas, 23 x 31 ins / 59 x 79 cm) DKK 31,000. STOCKHOLM, 26 May 2003, *Park Landscape with Manor House* (oil on canvas, 19 x 26 ins / 48 x 67 cm) SEK 14,000. STOCKHOLM, 3 Dec 2003, *Landscape with Castle* (oil on canvas, 49 x 67 ins / 124 x 170 cm) SEK 90,000.

FAHLCRANTZ, Karl Robert

Swedish, 19th century.

Born 1778; died 1833, in Stockholm.

Active in Värmdö, near Stockholm.

Miniaturist, engraver.

The Stockholm museum has a *Portrait of Charles XIII* by this artist.

FAHLEN, Charles

American, 20th century.

Born 1939, in San Francisco.
Engraver, sculptor.
Charles Fahlen studied first in Los Angeles and then at the Slade School of Art, London. From 1967 to 2000 he taught in Philadelphia. He exhibits in group exhibitions in the USA, Britain and Denmark, and has held solo shows in Chicago and New York but most frequently Philadelphia, including Charles Fahlen: Unexplained Mysteries at the Locks Gallery in 2003.

FAHLGREN, Karl August or Carl

Swedish, 19th century.
Born 8 March 1819, in Norrtälje; died 2 May 1905, in Stockholm.
Painter. Landscapes.
Karl Fahlgren studied at the academy in Stockholm for a time, and painted landscapes of the region around Stockholm.

Auction records:
Stockholm, 27 Oct 1981, *Seaside* (1872, oil on canvas, 19 x 25 1/2 ins / 48 x 65 cm) SEK 6,100. Stockholm, 26 April 1984, *Landscape* (1864, oil on canvas, 11 x 14 1/2 ins / 27 x 37 cm) SEK 4,500. Stockholm, 9 April 1985, *Summer Landscape* (1866, oil on canvas, 31 1/2 x 46 3/4 ins / 80 x 119 cm) SEK 18,500. Stockholm, 15 Nov 1988, *Forest Landscape with Structures* (1861, oil, 11 x 14 1/2 ins / 27 x 37 cm) SEK 8,500. Stockholm, 19 April 1989, *Mountain Landscape with a Chalet and Stream* (1883, oil on panel, 9 1/2 x 13 3/4 ins / 24 x 35 cm) SEK 7,700. Stockholm, 15 Nov 1989, *Lakeside Landscape with a Sailboat* (1897, oil, 13 3/4 x 22 ins / 35 x 55 cm) SEK 7,500. Helsinki, 11 Dec 1999, *Evening Light* (1860, oil on canvas, 20 x 28 ins / 52 x 72 cm) FIM 10,500. Stockholm, 28 Nov 2001, *Landscape with Farm in Sunshine* (1868, oil on canvas, 26 x 35 ins / 66 x 89 cm) SEK 16,000.

FAHLSTRÖM, Öyvind or Övind

Swedish, 20th century.
Born 1928, in São Paulo, Brazil; died 1976, in Stockholm.
Also active in the USA.
Painter. Scenes with figures.
Visual Poetry, Nouvelle Figuration, Figuration Narrative.
Fahlström's family, with his Swedish father and Norwegian mother, settled in Stockholm in 1939. He himself did not adopt Swedish nationality until 1947. He studied first art history and then archaeology from 1949 to 1952. He began with literary work - drama, poetry, journalism and criticism - publishing a *Manifesto for Concrete Poetry* in Stockholm in 1953. In 1952, he trained himself as a painter in Florence. In 1955, he planned the execution of three large paintings, only two of which he produced. From 1955 to 1960, he studied pre-Columbian art, cartoons, Matta's painting, Stockhausen's music and John Cage's various activities. As early as 1957, his painting developed towards composite assemblages. In 1961, he settled in New York, dividing his time between there and Stockholm. He took part in some collective exhibitions: in 1959, with the Phases group in Pittsburgh and at the São Paulo Biennale, where he received a mention; 1960, Surrealism exhibition in New York; 1961, the 2nd Biennale des Jeunes Artistes in Paris; 1962, *Twelve Swedish Painters* in the USA and in New York at the *New Realism* exhibition; 1964, Paris, *Mythologies Quotidiennes* (*Everyday Mythologies*); 1965, Paris, *La Figuration Narrative* (*Narrative Figuration*), organised by G. Gassiot-Talabot, and others. He also showed his paintings in solo exhibitions - in 1953 in Florence and in 1959, 1962 and subsequently in Paris - and in retrospectives: 1979, museum of modern art in Stockholm; 1980, Musée National d'Art Moderne in Paris; 1982, Guggenheim Museum in New York; 1990, Beaudoin-Lebon gallery in Paris, which displayed three of his masterpieces; 1995, Centre Culturel Suédois (Swedish cultural centre) in Paris; 2002, Institut d'Art Contemporain in Villeurbanne.

Certain sources suggest that he painted for a short period in the abstract expressionist style that was then dominant, with signs repeated in series. From 1957, on foundations that were still informal, he developed 'sign-figures' in a narrative mode. Then the informal foundations were replaced by drawings, often taken from cartoons. In the 'variable paintings', some of the compositional elements are figures cut out from metal that the spectator is invited to move around on a magnetic background. From his installation in New York onwards, he organised happenings, performances, films and radio plays. Producing his pictorial work simultaneously, he developed overtly towards Pop Art from 1962, proposing the use of the powers of the signifying image. His friends then were Andy Warhol, Jasper Johns and Peter Saul. His paintings that had featured in *La Figuration Narrative* (*Narrative Figuration*) in Paris in 1965 were among those that took inspiration from cartoons, elements of which could be moved around at the viewer's will. In some cumulative compositions, stemming from the principle of collage like those of Erro, he used popular figurative imagery, heroes from cartoons and science fiction, but also caricatured figures from the international political scene, for militant, antimilitarist, political and social purposes, with texts in speech bubbles explaining the message that is often blurred by the profusion of images, as in *The Cold War* of 1963-1965 and *Dr Schweitzer's Last Mission* of 1964-1966.

His installations, 'variable paintings', sometimes took on surprising metric and technical dimensions, as with *Little General*, in which the many characters - Che Guevara, Lyndon Johnson, animals and so on - are floating on a six-metre-long pool. In 1966, he gave a new or at least supplementary dimension to his compositions, which became *Do-It-Yourself* compositions to be completed by the viewer. Fahlström thus conferred practically infinite possibilities on his compositions, by 'staging' current or even fictional events, with the spectator becoming co-creator and having complete latitude to intervene in the works' later development. In these games, from which he constructed a microcosm of our universe, Fahlström retains the role of demiurge, as creator of a world in which he determines the moral rules, in a moralising role that was always at the heart of his preoccupations, but he accords the viewer and co-creator the right to free will.

Bibliography:
Gassiot-Talabot, Gérald, *Depuis 45*, Éd. de la Connaissance, Brussels, 1970. Pierre, José, *Pop art: an Illustrated Dictionary*, Eyre Methuen, London, 1977. Springfeldt, Björn/Hulten, Pontus, *Öyvind Fahlström*, travelling exhibition catalogue, Moderna Museet, Stockholm, Musée national d'Art moderne, Éd. du Centre Georges-Pompidou, Paris, 1980 (text in French, English and Swedish). *öyvind Fahlström*, exhibition catalogue, Instituto Valenciano de Arte Moderno (IVAM) Centro Julio González, Valencia, 1992 (text in Spanish and English). Avery-Fahlström, Sharon/Schmidt, Eva/Kittelmann, Udo, *öyvind Fahlström: die Installationen*, exhibition catalogue, Kölnischer Kunstverein, Köln, Cantz, Ostfildern, 1995 (text in German and English). *Öyvind Fahlström. Essais choisis*, Presses du réel, Paris, 2002 (collection of writings by the artist).

Museums and Galleries:
Cologne (Wallraf-Richartz Mus.): *Roulette, Game-Painting* (1966) - Paris (MNAM-CCI): *Planetarium* (1963) - Stockholm (Moderna Mus.): *Ade Ledic Nander II* (1955-1957).

Auction records:
Munich, 29 Nov 1976, *Column no. 2 (Picasso 90)* (gouache, 23 1/4 x 19 ins / 59 x 48.5 cm) DEM 5,700. Stockholm, 26 Nov 1981, *Composition* (Indian ink/paper, 17 1/4 x 20 3/4 ins / 44 x 53 cm) SEK 14,000. London, 20 May 1987, *Frame-Storm*

(1960, mixed media/paper, 19 1/4 x 25 1/2 ins / 49 x 64.5 cm) GBP 9,800. LONDON, 29 June 1989, *Suggestions for the Cold War* (1965, distemper and ink/card, 25 1/2 x 35 1/2 ins / 64.8 x 90.2 cm) GBP 48,400. LONDON, 22 Feb 1990, *Nothingness Roars On* (water paints/copper, 11 x 19 1/2 ins / 28 x 49.5 cm) GBP 26,400. LONDON, 5 April 1990, *Column no. 1 (Wonderbread)* (1972, acrylic and Indian ink, 23 1/4 x 19 ins / 59 x 48 cm) GBP 50,600. STOCKHOLM, 5-6 Dec 1990, *Frame-Storm* (mixed media, 19 1/4 x 25 1/2 ins / 49 x 64.5 cm) SEK 375,000. LONDON, 2 July 1992, *Sitting... Six Months Later* (1963, oil, gouache and collage with magnets, nylon string, beads, and iron wire/canvas/metal, 22 x 46 ins / 55.9 x 116 cm) GBP 40,700. LONDON, 3 Dec 1992, *Column no. 1 (Wonderbread)* (1972, acrylic and Indian ink/paper, 23 1/4 x 19 ins / 59 x 48 cm) GBP 20,900. STOCKHOLM, 10-12 May 1993, *Appointment* (oil on canvas, 11 3/4 x 16 1/2 ins / 30 x 42 cm) SEK 54,000. NEW YORK, 10 Oct 1996, *Study for Lifespan no. 3, Marilyn Monroe* (1968, tempera/paper/panel, 14 1/2 x 18 ins / 36.8 x 45.7 cm) USD 2,530. STOCKHOLM, 27 April 1999, *The Kvalster Song* (1958, gouache, 11 x 17 ins / 29 x 42 cm) SEK 40,000. STOCKHOLM, 27 April 1999, *Ingo-Floyd - Floyd Vainquer* (1959, mixed media, 10 x 15 ins / 26 x 37 cm) SEK 45,000. STOCKHOLM, 2 May 2000, *Hotel* (1961, tempera on paper/canvas, 57 x 51 ins / 146 x 130 cm) SEK 820,000. STOCKHOLM, 7 Nov 2000, *Sitting, Six Months Later* (1963, tempera on vinyl/paper, work with 18 movable elements, 22 x 46 ins / 56 x 116 cm) SEK 1,800,000. STOCKHOLM, 2 May 2001, *Sitting, Composition Dominoes* (1928, silk screen on vinyl with plexi magnets, 28 x 39 ins / 72 x 100 cm) SEK 50,000. STOCKHOLM, 2 May 2001, *The Grove of the Following Happy Events* (1958, varnish, Indian ink and tempera on paper/canvas, 22 x 26 ins / 56 x 67 cm) SEK 205,000. STOCKHOLM, 5 Nov 2002, *Steps* (1960, tempera, varnish and Indian ink, 13 x 17 ins / 33 x 42 cm) SEK 175,000. STOCKHOLM, 6 Nov 2002, *Study for Life - Span No.3 - Marilyn Monroe* (1968, tempera and Indian ink, 10 x 14 ins / 25 x 35 cm) SEK 77,000. STOCKHOLM, 7 May 2003, *Untitled* (pastel, 10 x 13 ins / 26 x 33 cm) SEK 29,000. STOCKHOLM, 7 May 2003, *You Believed That?* (mixed media, 11 x 14 ins / 27 x 35 cm) SEK 38,000. STOCKHOLM, 4 Nov 2003, *The Gift of Casalpusterlengo* (varnish and chalk on paper/canvas, 20 x 26 ins / 50 x 65 cm) SEK 255,000. LUND, 24 April 2004, *Composition II* (1959, mixed media, 10 x 14 ins / 26 x 36 cm) SEK 35,000. STOCKHOLM, 2 Nov 2004, *Untitled - Composition* (1962, Indian ink, watercolour and tempera, 8 x 11 ins / 20 x 29 cm) SEK 52,000.

FAHNE, Halvor, or Farden, Fanc
Norwegian, 18th century.
Active near Drammen c. 1700.
Sculptor (wood).

Fahne was born into a farming family. His children were also wood carvers.

MUSEUMS AND GALLERIES:
COPENHAGEN (Rosenborg Slot): *Busts of a Peasant and His Wife* (presumed to be Fahne and his wife).

FAHNENSCHMIDT
German, 19th century.
Active c. 1839.
Painter. Genre scenes.

Fahnenschmidt was a pupil of Dœege.

FAHNESTOCK, Wallace Weir
American, 20th century.
Born 15 January 1877, in Harrisburg (Pennsylvania); died 1962.
Painter. Landscapes.

AUCTION RECORDS:
NEW YORK, 17 Oct 1980, *New Mexico Landscape* (oil on canvas, 25 1/4 x 30 ins / 64.2 x 76.2 cm) USD 3,250. NEW YORK, 29 Jan 1981, *Rural Scene in New Jersey* (oil on canvas, 40 x 60 ins / 101.6 x 152.4 cm) USD 3,000. NEW YORK, 13 Oct 1999, *Vermont Farm in Autumn* (oil on canvas, 25 x 30 ins / 64 x 76 cm) USD 3,000. CAMBRIDGE, 17 May 2003, *Mountain Landscape with Birch* (1919, oil on canvas, 25 x 30 ins / 64 x 76 cm) USD 5,250. PORTLAND, 6 Aug 2004, *Snow-covered Mill, Vermont* (oil on canvas, 28 x 36 ins / 71 x 91 cm) USD 3,000.

FAHR-EL-NISSA-ZEID. See **ZEID Fahr-El-Nissa**

FAHRBACH, Carl Ludwig
German, 19th century.
Born 10 December 1835, in Heidelberg; died 26 January 1902, in Düsseldorf.
Painter, watercolourist, engraver (etching).
Landscapes.

Fahrbach first studied with J.W. Schirmer in Düsseldorf, and then in Munich. In 1877, he was awarded a silver medal. He exhibited in Munich and Vienna as well as at the royal academy in Berlin from 1873 to 1888.

Fahrbach's best-known works include: *Wooded Landscape, Waterfall in Bavaria, Heidelberg Castle* (watercolour), *Trout Stream* and *Eberstein Castle*.

MUSEUMS AND GALLERIES:
DÜSSELDORF: *Moon Rising in the Black Forest* - DÜSSELDORF (Malkasten): *Heidelberg Ruins in the Snow* - KARLSRUHE: *Heidelberg Forest*.

AUCTION RECORDS:
LUCERNE, 17 Nov 1976, *Wooded Landscape* (oil on canvas, 43 1/4 x 37 1/4in/110 x 94.5cm) CHF 9,000. LONDON, 18 March 1977, *The Clearing* (1896, oil on canvas, 33 x 45in/84 x 114cm) DEM 2,600. ZURICH, 26 May 1978, *Wooded Landscape* (oil on canvas, 44 x 33 1/4in/112 x 84.5cm) CHF 8,000. NEW YORK, 11 Feb 1981, *Stag in a Clearing* (oil on canvas, 45 x 34in/114 x 86.5cm) USD 6,500. BERN, 21 Oct 1984, *Winter Landscape* (1893, oil on canvas, 40 1/2 x 23 1/2in/103 x 60cm) CHF 2,200. LONDON, 10 Oct 1986, *Livestock in Wooded Landscape* (oil on canvas, 44 3/4 x 34in/113.5 x 86.5cm) GBP 4,000. HEIDELBERG, 9 Oct 1992, *Dense Forest* (oil on card, 19 x 15in/47.4 x 38cm) DEM 2,500. MUNICH, 6 Dec 1994, *Autumn Evening in a Beech Wood* (oil on canvas, 33 x 44in/84 x 112cm) DEM 3,450. HEIDELBERG, 11-12 April 1997, *Forest with a View over the Neckar Valley* (oil on card, 19 x 23 1/2in/48.5 x 60cm) DEM 4,000. VIENNA, 20 May 1999, *Evening Scene with Deer at Pond in German Castle Meadow* (oil on canvas, 31 x 52 ins / 79 x 132 cm) ATS 45,000. COLOGNE, 28 Oct 1999, *Late Autumn Landscape in Evening Light* (oil on canvas, 44 x 33 ins / 112 x 85 cm) DEM 5,000. HEIDELBERG, 13 Oct 2000, *Shepherd with Flock in Meadow* (oil on canvas, 35 x 24 ins / 88 x 61 cm) DEM 9,000. HEIDELBERG, 13 Oct 2000, *Bremen* (1888, oil on canvas, 33 x 44 ins / 85 x 113 cm) DEM 16,000. COLOGNE, 5 April 2001, *Wooded Landscape* (oil on canvas, 32 x 25 ins / 81 x 63 cm) DEM 5,800. COLOGNE, 11 April 2002, *View of the Rhine with Nonnenwerth Island from Siebengebirge* (1895, oil on canvas, 20 x 14 ins / 50 x 36 cm) EUR 2,500. LONDON, 21 June 2002, *In the Wood* (oil on canvas, 36 x 26 ins / 91 x 65 cm) GBP 3,000. STUTTGART, 25 Sept 2003, *Deer in Forest* (1899, oil on canvas, 33 x 44 ins / 85 x 112 cm) EUR 3,000. STUTTGART, 25 Sept 2003, *Forest near Bensberg* (oil on canvas, 44 x 33 ins / 112 x 85 cm) EUR 8,000. STUTTGART, 24 June 2004, *Extensive Wooded Landscape* (1870, oil on canvas, 31 x 52 ins / 79 x 131 cm) EUR 1,700. STUTTGART, 24 June 2004, *Stony Stream in Autumn Wood* (oil on board, 12 x 9 ins / 30 x 24 cm) EUR 1,700.

FAHRENHOLTZ, Georg
Danish, 18th - 19th century.
Born 1758, in Copenhagen; died 1816.
Engraver.

Most of Fahrenholtz's engravings were vignettes and satirical pictures, which caused him problems with the censors.

FAHRENHOLZ, J. H.
German, 18th century.
Active in Bockenem (Lower Saxony).
Sculptor.

There is an altarpiece and a lectern by Fahrenholz in Bültum (Lower Saxony), Germany.

FAHRENKROG, Ludwig Karl Wilhelm
German, 19th - 20th century.
Born 20 October 1867, in Rendsburg.
Painter, illustrator, sculptor. Figure compositions, religious subjects, figures, portraits, landscapes. Murals.

Ludwig Fahrenkrog was a student of Hugo Vogel and Anton Alexander von Werner at the academy of fine arts in Berlin, where he received many prizes. In 1893, he received the main national prize. In 1908, he founded a religious association. In 1913, he was made professor at the school of arts and trades in Barmen, where he then lived.

He painted mainly religious compositions, into which he introduced his 'inner visions'. He painted mural compositions in churches in Lüdenscheid, Gevelsberg, Herdecke and Langerfeld. At the girls' school in Barmen, he painted *Golden Days of Childhood*.

MUSEUMS AND GALLERIES:
KIEL.

FAHRENSCHON, Franz von
Bohemian School, 18th century.
Born 1726, in Chomutov; died 1796, in Prague.
Painter. Portraits.

Franz von Fahrenschon lived in Prague, where he painted a portrait of the family of count Pachtain in around 1778. He also produced a portrait of the Empress Maria Theresa with her family which featured in the *Maria Theresa Exhibition*, Vienna (1888), along with paintings of Eger Cathedral in Hungary.

FAHRENSCHON, Joh. Nepomuk
German, 19th century.
Painter. History painting, genre scenes.

Fahrenschon studied at the academy of art in Munich and became a member of the city's society of artists, where he exhibited religious paintings from 1843 to 1852. He also produced genre portraits and drawings and is known to have painted a *Portrait of Privy Counsellor Schlichting*, of which Blanz made a lithograph.

FAHRENSCHON, Paul Friedrich
Bohemian School, 18th century.
Active in Prague.
Painter.

Paul Friedrich Fahrenschon may have been the father of the portraitist Franz von Fahrenschon, who may have completed his commissions.

FAHRINGER, Karl
Austrian, 20th century.
Born 25 December 1874, in Wiener-Neustadt; died 1952.
Painter, watercolourist. Portraits, landscapes, animals.

Karl Fahringer was a student of August Eisenmenger at the academy of fine arts in Vienna and of Karl von Marr in Munich. He visited Italy, France, Egypt and Montenegro. He often exhibited in Munich, Berlin, Dresden and Rome.

He was principally a painter of exotic animals: *Tiger and Snake; Flamingoes; Young Lions at the Water's Edge*. His sketches are also noted, as are his watercolours of the East and some portraits, including one of his wife.

CFahringeh

AUCTION RECORDS:
VIENNA, 11 Feb 1976, *Landscape with Windmill* (oil on card, 13 1/2 x 16 1/4 ins / 34 x 41 cm) ATS 28,000. VIENNA, 17 Sept 1976, *Parrot* (gouache, 13 3/4 x 11 ins / 35 x 27 cm) ATS 10,000. VIENNA, 23 Sept 1977, *Port of Rotterdam* (oil on card, 12 1/2 x 15 ins / 32 x 38 cm) ATS 22,000. VIENNA, 16 June 1978, *Port* (watercolour and gouache, 11 3/4 x 16 1/4 ins / 30 x 41.5 cm) ATS 14,000. VIENNA, 14 March 1980, *Piraeus* (1942, oil on canvas, 20 x 25 1/4 ins / 51 x 64 cm) ATS 55,000. VIENNA, 22 March 1984, *Carriage in a Snowy Landscape* (oil on canvas, 13 x 28 ins / 33 x 71 cm) ATS 80,000. VIENNA, 10 April 1984, *Livestock Market* (watercolour, 9 x 13 ins / 23 x 33 cm) ATS 16,000. VIENNA, 4 Dec 1984, *Study of Tigers* (1925, chalk, brush and Indian ink wash, 16 1/2 x 12 1/2 ins / 42 x 32 cm) ATS 11,000. VIENNA, 10 Dec 1985, *Livestock in Pasture* (oil on canvas, 33 1/2 x 39 ins / 85 x 99 cm) ATS 90,000. VIENNA, 17 March 1987, *Pig Market in Holland* (gouache, 18 x 26 ins / 46 x 66 cm) ATS 45,000. AMSTERDAM, 18 Feb 1992, *Livestock Market in Hoorn* (1949, oil on canvas, 16 1/4 x 22 ins / 41 x 55 cm) NLG 9,775. AMSTERDAM, 19 Oct 1993, *Livestock Market in Hoorn* (1949, oil on canvas, 16 1/4 x 22 ins / 41 x 55 cm) NLG 6,325. MONTREAL, 23-24 Nov 1993, *Livestock Market* (1938, mixed media, 14 1/4 x 18 1/4 ins / 36.2 x 46.2 cm) CAD 1,700; *Market in Hoorn, Holland* (1932, mixed media, 17 3/4 x 22 ins / 45 x 55.8 cm) CAD 2,400. VIENNA, 9 March 1999, *Study of Leopard* (oil on canvas/board, 15 x 17 ins / 38 x 44 cm) ATS 25,000. VIENNA, 1 Dec 1999, *Market in Java* (watercolour and gouache, 13 x 19 ins / 34 x 49 cm) ATS 50,000. ST GALL, 10 May 2000, *Farmhouse in Lustenau* (oil on canvas, 20 x 25 ins / 50 x 63 cm) CHF 12,000. VIENNA, 29 Nov 2000, *A Day at the Market* (oil on canvas, 31 x 22 ins / 78 x 57 cm) ATS 180,000. VIENNA, 20 March 2001, *Mountain Landscape* (watercolour, 10 x 14 ins / 26 x 35 cm) ATS 30,000. VIENNA, 12 June 2001, *Market Scene* (oil on board, 12 x 15 ins / 30 x 38 cm) ATS 40,000. VIENNA, 13 May 2002, *Country Market* (oil on canvas, 20 x 27 ins / 52 x 69 cm) EUR 15,260. VIENNA, 27 Nov 2002, *Cattle Market in Holland* (oil on canvas/panel, 18 x 22 ins / 45 x 55 cm) EUR 9,000. VIENNA, 11 March 2003, *Bison* (oil on canvas, 33 x 33 ins / 83 x 85 cm) EUR 12,000. VIENNA, 25 March 2003, *Cattle Market* (oil on canvas, 13 x 17 ins / 33 x 44 cm) EUR 10,000. AMSTERDAM, 16 March 2004, *Klung Kung* (1927, watercolour and gouache, 13 x 18 ins / 32 x 45 cm) EUR 5,000. SINGAPORE, 3 April 2004, *Pasar Scene* (1929, mixed media on board, 13 x 19 ins / 32 x 47 cm) SGD 16,000.

FAHRLANDER, Franz
German, 19th century.
Born 1793, in Ettenheim (Breisgau, Baden-Württemberg).
Miniaturist.

Having entered the academy of art in Vienna in 1814, Fahrlander received a prize in 1820 for his painting of *Pan and Apollo* and showed miniature portraits at the academy exhibition in 1822. One of his best-known works is his portrait of *Grand Duchess Sophie of Austria*, which was shown in the exhibitions of miniatures at Troppau (now Opava, Czech Republic) in 1905 and Berlin in 1906, and that of *Countess Friederike Monzynska*.

FAHRMANN, P.
German, 18th century.
Active in Hamburg.
Draughtsman.

The Hamburg Kunsthalle owns six plates of drawings and some watercolour plans for a hospital by Fahrmann.

FAHRNBAUER, J. G.
Austrian, 19th century.
Born 1 March 1841, in Vienna.
Lithographer, engraver (etching).

Fahrnbauer made etchings of objects in the treasury of the royal residence in Vienna, and some lithographs after items in the armoury collection at the army museum.

FAHRNI, Otto
Swiss, 19th century.
Born 15 September 1856; died 1887, in Dürrenast, near Thoune.
Active in Eriz (Bern canton).
Landscape artist.

Fahrni exhibited in Biel in 1880. He lived in Thoune and Iseltwald before finally settling in Dürrenast, near Thoune.

FAIBISSOVITCH, Semion Nathanovitch, or Simyon, Simon
Russian, 20th - 21st century.
Born 1947 or 1949, in Moscow.
Painter. Figure compositions.

Utilising unusual and subjective framing shots, Semion Nathanovitch Faibissovitch first photographs the subjects he wants to depict, often taking the risk of photographing scenes that point to the financial or social shortcomings of the official regime, for example queues outside a food store, crowds jostling through the Metro, or the mediocrity of beach scenes on the shores of the Black Sea. He then projects them using a slide projector and copies them in minute detail, even going so far as to reproduce any yellowing of the original photographs. A morbid atmosphere is introduced into the painting which, he claims, accords with his vision of the world.

BIBLIOGRAPHY:
'L'Art au pays des Soviets, 1963-1988' in *Les Cahiers du Musée National d'Art Moderne,* no. 26, periodical, Paris, winter 1988. Makhroff, Olga, *'Les Dossiers des Cahiers'* in *Les Cahiers du Musée National d'Art Moderne,* no. 26, periodical, Paris, winter 1988. *'Berlin-Moskau/Moskau-Berlin 1950-2000'* in *2 volumes,* exhibition catalogue, Martin-Gropius-Bau, Berlin, 2003 (text in German).

FAICHTMAIR. See **FEICHTMAYR**

FAIDHERBE. See **FAYDHERBE**

FAIDIDE, Jean
French, 20th century.
Born in Chalon-sur-Saône.
Painter. Genre scenes.

Jean Faidide exhibited in Paris at the Salon des Indépendants from 1940.

FAÏF, Garry
Georgian, 20th century.
Born 12 June 1942, in Tbilisi.
Active in France from 1973, naturalised in 1979.
Sculptor.
Neo-Constructivism.
Mir group.

Garry Faïf first trained at the institute of architecture in Moscow, where he was especially interested in Suprematism and Constructivism. In 1966-1967 he founded the kineticist-constructive Mir group with Koleitchouk and Rikounoff ('mir' means both 'peace' and 'world' in Russian). In 1973 he left the USSR for France, where he studied at the École des Beaux-Arts in Paris and then at the Unité Pédagogique d'Architecture in Vincennes. He undertook many architectural projects in Russia, France, Japan and Germany.

Faïf's assemblages (which can be dismantled) are negotiations of form that aspire to defy the laws of gravity, even though they obey a geometric spirit rather than the more ludic spirit of Calder's mobiles. The majority of the works are called *The World,* which clearly translates the artist's preached vocation of achieving universality. His overriding desire is that his works might access an autonomous life in the cosmos through the dynamism of the shapes he uses, and the way that light and colour play on the planes, tubes and cables. His work is an expression of Suprematism with its spatial, abstract, orthogonal, coloured constructions that look more like Constructivism, the definition of which is wider than that of Suprematism.

Faïf participated in group exhibitions from 1976 onwards in France, Germany, Austria, Switzerland, Italy, the USA, Canada and Japan, and most notably at the Salon de la Jeune Sculpture, the Salon de Mai, the Salon des Réalités Nouvelles and the Salon des Grands and Jeunes d'Aujourd'hui in Paris. His first solo exhibition was held at the East-West Gallery in Tokyo in 1981.

BIBLIOGRAPHY:
Jianou, Ionel/Lardera, Aube/Xuriguera, Gérard, *La Sculpture moderne en France depuis 1950,* Arted, Paris, 1983.

FAÏF, Simone
French, 20th century.
Born 8 February 1942, in Paris.
Painter.

Having graduated in applied arts from the École Boulle, Simone Faïf worked for some years as an interior designer. It was in this capacity that she spent three years (1970-1973) in the former Soviet Union. In 1973 she moved to Paris with her husband, Garry Faïf, himself an artist, and since then has been a full-time painter. Faïf's representative style is playful, arranging silhouettes, symbolic elements and fragments of texts on abstract themes. She describes her style as 'iconographic and constructivist'.

She has taken part in a number of group exhibitions in galleries and salons, including: the Salon des Femmes Peintres et Sculpteurs of 1979, 1981 and 1988; the Salon de la Jeune Peinture of 1979, 1980 and 1982; the Salon de la Figuration Critique from 1979; and the Salon de Mai in 1989, 1990 and 1991. She has also staged solo exhibitions, notably at the Galerie Grambilher in Paris (1986-90).

FAIG, Frances Wiley (Mrs)
American, 20th century.
Painter. Wall decorations.

Frances Wiley Faig painted mural decorations in the Technical Library of the University of Cincinnati.

FAIGNART, Mathis
Flemish School, 16th century.
Active in Tournai.
Sculptor.

FAIJA, Guglielmo
French, 19th century.
Painter, miniaturist.

Guglielmo Faija exhibited at the Paris Salon from 1831 to 1837. He is best known for his portraits of *Count Rod. d'Aponi* and *M. Massinimo* in Hungarian court costume, his *Mystical Marriage of St Catherine* after Correggio, and *Mona Lisa* after Leonardo da Vinci.

FAILER, Peter, clerical name Brother Fidelis
German, 19th - 20th century.
Born 28 May 1870, in Jungnau (Hohenzollern).
Sculptor. Religious subjects.

Peter Failer was a lay brother at the Benedictine abbey in Beuron. He was a student of Baptiste Franz Xavier Marmon in Sigmaringen and of Peter (Desiderius by religious name) Lenz at the school of fine arts in Beuron. The Benedictine monasteries of Beuron, St-Gabriel-Prag and Monte Cassino hold some of his works, along with those of Lenz.

FAILLE, Carl Arthur
American, 20th century.
Born 17 February 1883, in Detroit (Michigan).
Painter, engraver.

Carl Arthur Faille made etchings.

FAILLON, Pierre
French, 16th century.
Painter, glass painter.
Faillon worked in Lyons for the *Aumône Générale* (a charitable almsgiving institution) and was commissioned by the town to carry out work on the decorations for the entry of the queen into Lyons in 1533.

FAILLOT, Edme Nicolas
French, 19th century.
Born 5 August 1810, in Auxerre; died 9 June 1849, in Paris.
Sculptor.
Edme Nicolas Faillot made his début at the Paris Salon in 1838 and received a medal in 1843. His works include *Scene from the Flood* and *Sign of the Sabbath* (plaster group).
MUSEUMS AND GALLERIES:
AUXERRE: *St Jerome* (plaster); *Combat between a Gladiator and a Lion* (plaster); *Statue of Fourier* (bronze) - DIJON: *The Sculptor, V. Couchery* (plaster, medallion).
AUCTION RECORDS:
NEW YORK, 13 March 1984, *America* (bronze, h. 18 1/2 ins / 47 cm) USD 1,200.

FAILLY, Oscar de (Baron)
French, 19th century.
Active in Paris.
Painter. Landscapes.
Oscar de Failly exhibited at the Salon in 1857 and 1859.

FAIN, Giulio
Italian, 20th century.
Born 1933, in San Vito al Tagliamento (Friuli-Venezia Giulia).
Painter.
Fain has been involved in various collective exhibitions, including some in Paris, at the Salon Grands et Jeunes d'Aujourd'hui, for example. He paints what he calls 'chromatic structures'.

FAIN, Pierre
French, 16th century.
Active in Rouen.
Sculptor, architect.
Gaillon School, Rouen School.
From 1501 to 1507, Pierre Fain worked on the bishop's palace in Rouen and at the abbey manor of St-Ouen. He was summoned to Gaillon in 1508 by the cardinal of Amboise to collaborate on the construction of the high chapel at the Château there. In 1509, he constructed the portal of the courtyard in Vernon stone that today is in the École des Beaux-Arts in Paris. He also made two windows and a dormer window for the main body of the building at Gaillon.

FAIN, Yvonne
Belgian, 20th century.
Born 1910, in Mechelen.
Sculptor.
Yvonne Fain was a student of a sculptor called Jacobs (Constant?) and of Lambert Lemmes, the painter, at the academy of fine arts in St-Josse-ten-Noode.

FAINA, Giuseppina
Maiden name: Anselmi
Italian, 19th century.
Born in Turin; died 8 March 1872, in Florence.
Painter.
Giuseppina Faina was a pupil of Giambattista Biscarra at the Accademia in Turin. She continued her studies in Rome, where she painted religious pictures for churches, and some portraits. In 1842, she exhibited a painting entitled *Three Children on Swings*, which was subsequently reproduced as a lithograph.

FAINA, Lorenzo
Italian, 19th century.
Painter.
Lorenzo Faina worked for the cloister of S Domenico, and for the churches of S Maria di Colle and S Filippo Neri in Perugia.

FAINA, Lorenzo del
Italian, 16th century.
Painter.
In 1505 Lorenzo del Faina worked on the Sala del Gran Consiglio of the Palazzo della Signoria in Florence.

FAINARDI, Riccardo
Italian, 19th - 20th century.
Born 1865, in Collecchio (Parma); died 1969, in Gaiano-Taro (Parma).
Painter. Portraits, seascapes, landscapes.
Fainardi was a student of Guido Carmignani at the Accademia di Belle Arti in Parma.
MUSEUMS AND GALLERIES:
PARMA (Accademia Nazionale di Belle Arti): *View of the Church of Fornovo del Taro*; other works.

FAINMEL, Charles
Polish, 20th century.
Born in Warsaw.
Active and naturalised in Canada.
Sculptor.
Charles Fainmel exhibited a *Nude* at the Salon des Indépendants in Paris in 1932.

FAINO, Alfred
Italian, 20th century.
Born in Bergamo.
Sculptor.
Faino has exhibited at the Salon of the Société des Artistes Français in Paris.

FAIR, Hannah
American, 18th - 19th century.
Painter, watercolourist. Portraits.
Hannah Fair may be the same as Hannah Fairfield.
AUCTION RECORDS:
NEW YORK, 26 Oct 1985, *George Washington* (1796, watercolour and pen, 7 x 9 ins / 17.7 x 23 cm) USD 4,500.

FAIR, Robert
American, 19th century.
Born 1847, in Ireland; died May 1907, in Philadelphia.
Painter.
Robert Fair went to live in New York in 1876, and a few years later settled in Philadelphia, where he became well known. Several of his works are owned by regional museums.

FAIRAM. See **FAYRAM**

FAIRBAIRN, Hilda
British, 19th - 20th century.
Born in Henley-on-Thames (Oxfordshire).
Active in London 1893-1903.
Painter, pastellist, watercolourist. Figures, portraits, flowers.
Hilda Fairbairn studied at the Herkomer School of Art in Bushey and for a time in Paris. In 1896 she showed *Little Mermaid* at the Royal Academy in London and continued exhibiting there on a number of occasions, mainly showing pastel and watercolour portraits of children.
AUCTION RECORDS:
LONDON, 6 Oct 1980, *Love the Pedlar* (1903, oil on canvas, 25 1/2 x 15 ins / 65 x 38 cm) GBP 1,800. LONDON, 17 June 1987, *The Cagrants* (1908, oil on canvas, 50 x 30 ins / 127 x 76 cm) GBP 2,000. LONDON, 29 March 1996, *These Lovely Children Go Wandering off Hand in Hand* (oil on canvas, 50 3/4 x 38 ins / 1277 x 96.5 cm) GBP 10,580. LONDON, 9 Oct 1996, *Wild*

Hyacinth (oil on canvas, 20 x 14 ins / 51 x 35.5 cm) GBP 10,120.

FAIRBAIRN, Thomas
British, 19th century.
Born 1820, in Stirling; died 1884, in Glasgow.
Painter, watercolourist. Landscapes.

Thomas Fairbairn worked in Hamilton and exhibited his watercolours at Suffolk Street Gallery from 1865 to 1877.

AUCTION RECORDS:

PERTH, 26 Aug 1986, *Hamilton Palace* (oil on canvas, 15 x 24 ins / 38 x 61 cm) GBP 1,100.

FAIRBANKS, Avard Tennyson
American, 20th century.
Born 2 March 1897, in Provo (Utah); died January 1987, in Salt Lake City.
Sculptor. Statues, monuments.

Avard Tennyson Fairbanks, a pupil of the Art Students League in New York and of Injalbert at the École des Beaux-Arts in Paris, was a member of the National Sculpture Society and the American Federation of Arts. He carved many sculptures for public and private buildings, including the door of the tabernacle of Eugene Cathedral, Oregon, and a fountain in the same city.

MUSEUMS AND GALLERIES:

SALT LAKE CITY (MFA, University of Utah) - WASHINGTON DC (National Cathedral).

FAIRBANKS, Frank P.
American, 20th century.
Born 1875, in Boston.
Painter. Murals.

Frank P. Fairbanks was primarily an architect. He studied art in Boston and among other distinctions was awarded the Page travel scholarship of the Boston Museum of Fine Arts. In 1922 he became a professor at the American School in Rome. He was a member of several architectural and fresco-painting societies.

FAIRBANKS, J. Leo
American, 19th - 20th century.
Active at the end of the 19th and at the beginning of the 20th century.
Painter, engraver.

J. Leo Fairbanks, a pupil at the Académie Julian in Paris, was a member of a number of art associations, mainly in Oregon. He decorated churches and the Library Building at Oregon State College where he was head of the Department of Art and Mural Architecture.

FAIRBANKS, John B.
American, 19th century.
Born December 1855, in Payson (Utah); died 1940.
Painter, teacher.

John B. Fairbanks finished his art studies in Paris. He was a member of many artistic societies and won many prizes, especially for seascapes and landscapes, from 1899.

FAIRCHILD, Charles Willard
American, 20th century.
Born 18 November 1886, in Marinette (Wisconsin); died 4 January 1946, in New York.
Illustrator.

Charles Willard Fairchild, a pupil at the Chicago Academy of Fine Arts, was a member of the Society of Illustrators.

FAIRCHILD, Louis
American, 19th century.
Born 1800, in Farmington (Connecticut).
Engraver (including etching), painter.

Louis Fairchild was a pupil of A. Willard in New Haven. He engraved mainly landscapes, but also painted a few miniatures.

FAIRCHILD, Mary Louise (Mrs).
See **MACMONNIES**

FAIRCHILD, May
American, 20th century.
Born 1872, in Philadelphia; died 1959.
Painter, miniaturist. Portraits.

May Fairchild was a pupil of the Boston School of Art and the American Students League, New York, of which she became a member, as she did of several other societies.

FAIRCLOUGH, Bernard
British, 20th century.
Born 1915, in Manchester.
Painter. Landscapes.

Bernard Fairclough was a member of the Manchester Group, founded in 1946. Their first exhibition took place in London in 1948 and Fairclough exhibited two landscapes there, including *Barn Door.*

FAIRFIELD, Charles
British, 18th century.
Born c. 1759; died 1804, in Brompton.
Painter, copyist. Landscapes.

Charles Fairfield is particularly well-known for his excellent copies of Dutch artists.

AUCTION RECORDS:

AMSTERDAM, 7 May 1996, *Capriccio of a Mediterranean Coast and the Castel Sant' Angelo, with Merchants, Fishermen and Washerwomen* (1799, oil on panel, 11 x 15 ins / 27.8 x 37.9 cm) NLG 5,750.

FAIRFIELD, Hannah T.
American, 19th century.
Born 1808; died 1894.
Active in New York City from 1836 to 1839.
Painter. Portraits.

Hannah Fairfield studied under Alexander Robertson at the National Academy.

AUCTION RECORDS:

NEW YORK, 26 Oct 1985, *Ellen Nichols Tracy and Lucy Adams Tracy* (c. 1839, oil on canvas, 35 x 30 ins / 89 x 76 cm) USD 42,500.

FAIRHOLT, Frederick William
British, 19th century.
Born 1818, in London; died 1866, in London.
Draughtsman, writer.

Frederick William Fairholt was of Prussian origin, and after a few futile attempts to find work was employed by Charles Knight to illustrate various different books. He contributed both as an author and artist to the *Art Journal* from the time of its foundation. He also wrote several works on morals and English costume, a part of which he bequeathed to the Society of Antiquities.

FAIRLAND, Thomas
British, 19th century.
Born 1804, in London; died 1852.
Engraver, lithographer.

Thomas Fairland trained under Fuseli at the Royal Academy. He was awarded a silver medal for a design in the style of antiquity, then became a pupil of Charles Heath. He achieved great popularity by copying the works of Landseer and Hunt, and Queen Victoria honoured him by bestowing her favour on him.

FAIRLAND, W.
British, 19th century.
Active in London.
Engraver.

W. Fairland exhibited at Suffolk Street Gallery in 1828.

FAIRLESS, Thomas Ker
British, 19th century.

Born c. 1825, in Hexham (Northumberland); died 1853, in Hexham.
Painter. Landscapes.

Thomas Ker Fairless trained as a wood engraver under Nicholson, then went to London and exhibited at the Royal Academy from 1848 to 1853.

AUCTION RECORDS:

MUNICH, 29 June 1982, *Sailing Ships off the Coast* (1848, oil on canvas, 16 1/4 x 24 1/2 ins / 41 x 62.5 cm) DEM 4,500.

FAIRMAN, David
American, 19th century.
Born 1782; died 1815, in Philadelphia.
Active in Philadelphia.
Engraver.

David Fairman was the brother of Gideon and Richard Fairman. None of his works are known.

FAIRMAN, Frances C., or Francis
British, 19th - 20th century.
Born 1836; died 1923.
Painter. Animals.

Frances C. Fairman took part in many exhibitions in London from 1865, showing oil paintings and watercolours, often of dogs. In 1910 the Queen commissioned her to paint portraits of her four favourite dogs.

AUCTION RECORDS:

LONDON, 30 Sept 1987, *Maru, Hisa, Fifi and Yum-Yum* (1894, oil on canvas, 28 x 36 ins / 71 x 91.5 cm) GBP 5,700. LONDON, 15 Jan 1991, *Litter of Young Spaniels* (pencil and watercolour, 14 x 20 ins / 35.6 x 50.8 cm) GBP 660. NEW YORK, 16 July 1992, *Impudence* (1893, pencil and watercolour/paper, 19 3/4 x 14 1/2 ins / 50.2 x 36.8 cm) USD 880. LONDON, 25 March 1994, *English Dwarf Terrier and Affenpincher* (1903, oil on canvas, 24 x 20 ins / 60.9 x 50.8 cm) GBP 4,600. LONDON, 14 June 1996, *Jaffa* (1974, oil on canvas, 32 1/4 x 45 ins / 81.6 x 114.5 cm) GBP 21,850. LONDON, 10 July 1997, *Portraits of Two Bulldogs, a Hound and a Terrier* (1911, pencil and watercolour, four works, 9 x 7 1/2 ins / 23 x 19 cm) GBP 920. LONDON, 18 Dec 1997, *Cairn Terrier with Scottie* (oil on canvas, 9 x 12 ins / 22.8 x 30.5 cm) GBP 460.

FAIRMAN, Gideon
American, 18th - 19th century.
Born 26 June 1774, in Newtown (Connecticut); died 18 April 1827, in Philadelphia.
Active in Philadelphia.
Engraver.

Gideon Fairman studied in Albany, went to Philadelphia, and then worked in London with Heath and, on his return to Philadelphia, with Cephas G. Childs.

FAIRMAN, James
American, 19th century.
Born 1826, in Glasgow; died 12 March 1904, in Chicago.
Painter. History painting, genre scenes, landscapes. Orientalism.

James Fairman, the son of a Swedish officer, went to New York on his father's death and entered the National Academy of Design, where he was a pupil of Frederick Agate. He devoted himself to painting and in 1867 won a prize for his *Androscoggin Valley*. He spent a long time in Europe, living in Düsseldorf, Paris and London. When he returned to America he settled in Chicago. Among his works are *Stratford-upon-Avon, Pleasant River Valley, Maine* and *Carnarvon Castle, North Wales*.

AUCTION RECORDS:

NEW YORK, 18 Nov 1976, *Maine Landscape* (1866, oil on canvas, 27 x 48 1/4 ins / 68.5 x 122.5 cm) USD 1,100. NEW YORK, 29 Jan 1981, *Mount of Olives at Twilight* (1875, oil on canvas, 32 x 45 ins / 81.3 x 114.3 cm) USD 1,400. NEW YORK, 20 Sept 1984, *Shipwreck at Twilight* (oil on canvas, 10 1/4 x 14 1/4 ins / 26 x 36 cm) USD 550. NEW YORK, 4 Dec 1987, *Hudson River* (oil on canvas, 31 1/4 x 52 1/4 ins / 79.5 x 132.7 cm) USD 11,000. GLASGOW, 22 Nov 1990, *Entrance of Bonnie Prince Charlie into Edinburgh on the Morning of 17 September 1745* (1883, oil on canvas, 32 1/4 x 45 1/2 ins / 81.9 x 115.5 cm) GBP 8,250. NEW YORK, 17 Dec 1990, *River Landscape with Figures and a Classical Temple* (1877, oil on canvas, 32 x 45 ins / 81.4 x 114.3 cm) USD 3,850. NEW YORK, 28 May 1992, *Stormy Sky above Echo Lake in the White Mountains* (oil on canvas, 31 3/4 x 45 ins / 80.7 x 114 cm) USD 15,400. NEW YORK, 11 March 1993, *Mounts Madison and Adams, near Gorham in New Hampshire* (1870, oil on canvas, 19 3/4 x 36 ins / 50 x 91.2 cm) USD 27,600. NEW YORK, 14 Sept 1995, *View of Jerusalem* (oil on canvas, 32 x 45 ins / 81.3 x 114.3 cm) USD 13,800. LONDON, 9 Oct 1996, *Little Brat* (1820, oil on canvas, 15 3/4 x 13 ins / 40 x 33 cm) GBP 1,265. NEW YORK, 24 May 2000, *Sunset on the Coast of Corsica* (oil on canvas, 32 x 45 ins / 81 x 114 cm) USD 7,500. EAST DENNIS, 17 Nov 2000, *Shore View near Venice* (oil on canvas, 36 x 46 ins / 91 x 117 cm) USD 8,000. LONDON, 21 Nov 2002, *Camel Trail in Evening Sunlight* (oil on canvas, 32 x 45 ins / 81 x 114 cm) GBP 4,500.

FAIRMAN, Richard
American, 19th century.
Born 1788; died 1821, in Philadelphia.
Active in Philadelphia.
Engraver.

Richard Fairman was the brother of Gideon Fairman and worked with him.

FAIRWEATHER, Ian
British, 20th century.
Born 29 September 1891, in Bridge of Allan (Perthshire), Scotland; died 1974.
Active also in Australia.
Painter (including gouache).

Ian Fairweather originally studied agriculture and forestry. During World War I he was taken prisoner in Germany. On his return to England, while working in forestry, he sporadically studied at the Slade School in London. For two years he lived alone on an island that was a nature reserve. Around 1933 Fairweather travelled to Bali, Beijing, the Philippines, India and Australia. After World War II he went by raft to Timor, one of the Sonda Islands of Indonesia. He eventually returned to Australia and settled there.

Fairweather was an adventurer but also a genuine artist who brought back paintings from his travels. His work, which always borders on the abstract, is a synthesis of early 20th-century trends in Western painting, from Cubism to Abstraction, as well as including the calligraphy of the Far East.

BIBLIOGRAPHY:

Creating Australia: 200 Years of Art 1788-1988, exhibition catalogue, Art Gall. Board of South Australia, Adelaide, 1988.

MUSEUMS AND GALLERIES:

CANBERRA (Nat. Gal. of Australia): *Monastery* (1961) - LONDON (Tate Collection): *Bathing Scene, Bali* (c. 1933-1934, tempera/paper).

AUCTION RECORDS:

SYDNEY, 1 Oct 1974, *Figures* (gouache) AUD 3,800. SYDNEY, 6 Oct 1976, *Mother and Child* (1970, oil on canvas, 38 1/2 x 29 1/2 ins / 98 x 75 cm) AUD 2,300. MELBOURNE, 19 June 1978, *Four Figures* (gouache, 23 1/4 x 19 1/2 ins / 59 x 49.5 cm) AUD 2,800. SYDNEY, 10 Sept 1979, *Figures in a Monastery* (gouache, 10 x 13 1/2 ins / 24.5 x 34.5 cm) AUD 1,400. LONDON, 15 March 1985, *Figure* (pen and wash/beige paper, 9 x 7 ins / 22.8 x 17.8 cm) GBP 1,300. MELBOURNE, 26 July 1987, *Figures* (gouache, 14 x 9 ins / 35.5 x 22 cm) AUD 10,000; *Three Heads II* (oil on card, 32 x 27 1/2 ins / 81 x 70 cm) AUD 44,000. SYD-

NEY, 2 Dec 1991, *Family* (oil on card, 13 3/4 x 18 ins / 35 x 46 cm) AUD 2,750. MELBOURNE, 20-21 Aug 1996, *Three Heads II* (mixed media/card/panel, 31 1/2 x 27 1/4 ins / 80 x 69.5 cm) AUD 55,200. PADDINGTON, 16 Aug 1999, *Cyclops* (1963, synthetic polymer on composition board, 36 x 26 ins / 92 x 67 cm) AUD 74,000. MELBOURNE, 28 June 2000, *Performing Elephants* (oil on paper laid on board, 29 x 38 ins / 73 x 96 cm) AUD 130,000. MELBOURNE, 28 June 2000, *Chi-tien Goes Begging* (oil on card on board, 35 x 59 ins / 89 x 150 cm) AUD 230,000. MELBOURNE, 20 Aug 2001, *Dervish* (gouache on card, 25 x 20 ins / 63 x 50 cm) AUD 55,000. MELBOURNE, 28 Aug 2002, *Birdcage* (gouache, 21 x 15 ins / 53 x 38 cm) AUD 82,500. MELBOURNE, 6 May 2003, *Queen of Diamonds* (synthetic polymer on composition board, 37 x 28 ins / 95 x 71 cm) AUD 162,000. SYDNEY, 26 Aug 2003, *Composition in Orange and Yellow* (synthetic polymer, paint and gouache on card on hardboard, 37 x 54 ins / 95 x 136 cm) AUD 135,000. MELBOURNE, 3 May 2004, *Tea Garden, Peking* (oil on compressed card, 35 x 35 ins / 88 x 90 cm) AUD 480,000. SYDNEY, 23 Aug 2004, *Outside the Walls of Peking* (oil and pencil on board, 19 x 22 ins / 49 x 57 cm) AUD 180,000.

FAÏS VAN DYCK, Corsy de

Dutch, 20th century.
Born in Helmond (Brabant).
Painter, sculptor, decorative artist. Religious subjects, figure compositions.

At the salon of the national society of fine arts in 1936, Faïs van Dyck exhibited many works, including a decorative panel entitled *And... Solomon in All His Glory Was Not Clothed Like One of These.*

FAISCHE, Joseph

French, 17th century.
Active in Paris.
Sculptor.

FAISTAUER, Anton

Austrian, 20th century.
Born 1887, in St Martin bei Lofer (Salzburg); died 1930, in Vienna.
Painter. Figure compositions, nudes, portraits, landscapes, still-lifes, flowers. Murals.

Anton Faistauer was a student at the school of fine arts in Vienna from 1906 to 1909. He was one of the co-founders, with Egon Schiele among others, of the New Art Group. After settling in Salzburg in 1919, he founded the Wassermann New Association of Artists. He then wrote a book entitled *Neue Malerei in Oesterreich* (*New Painting in Austria*). He settled in Vienna in 1926. Apart from his participation in groups, he had some solo exhibitions: in Vienna in 1909, and in 1911 with Kokoschka.

He was one of the artists who worked in opposition both to academicism and the Secession movement, criticising its development towards the decorative arts while acknowledging its historic role. Using a technique of oily strokes, he constructed form through colour. From around 1920, drawing took over the construction of his works, while the colour became lighter. In 1922-1923 he painted frescoes depicting the life of Mary for the parish church in Morzg, near Salzburg, and in 1926 the frescoes of symbolic subjects for the festival centre, which were removed by the Nazis in 1939 and restored in 1956.

MUSEUMS AND GALLERIES:
VIENNA (Österreichische Gal. Belvedere): *Nude on Red Sofa* (1913); *Portrait of Hugo von Hofmannstahl* (1928); *Landscape of Salzburg* (1929).

AUCTION RECORDS:
VIENNA, 24 March 1965, *Vase of Flowers*, ATS 22,000. VIENNA, 18 Sept 1968, *Still-life*, ATS 35,000. VIENNA, 28 May 1974, *Bunch of Flowers*, ATS 80,000. VIENNA, 3 Dec 1976, *Portrait of a Woman* (1927, oil on canvas, 40 1/2 x 29 1/2 ins / 103 x 75 cm) ATS 45,000. VIENNA, 17 March 1978, *View of Salzburg* (1922, oil on canvas, 22 1/2 x 36 1/2 ins / 57 x 92.8 cm) ATS 180,000. VIENNA, 12 Nov 1980, *Portrait of a Young Woman* (1920, brown chalk, 18 1/4 x 13 3/4 ins / 46.5 x 35 cm) ATS 25,000. BERN, 23 June 1982, *Portrait of Idschi, the Artist's Wife* (1916, pastel, 18 1/4 x 12 1/4 ins / 46.4 x 30.8 cm) CHF 3,000. BERN, 20 June 1984, *Study for the Birth of the Virgin* (1925, red chalk, 19 x 13 1/2 ins / 48 x 34 cm) CHF 3,300; *Portrait of the Artist's Wife* (1916, pastel, 18 1/4 x 12 1/4 ins / 46.4 x 30.8 cm) CHF 10,000. VIENNA, 4 Dec 1984, *Johannes Faistauer in Green* (oil on canvas remounted on board, 10 3/4 x 11 ins / 27.5 x 27 cm) ATS 60,000. VIENNA, 22 Sept 1987, *Young Woman Putting on Her Shoes* (1918, pastel, 17 3/4 x 11 1/2 ins / 45 x 29 cm) ATS 40,000. MUNICH, 3 Dec 1996, *Bearded Man with Pipe, the Artist's Father-in-Law* (1918, oil on wood, 29 1/2 x 22 ins / 75 x 56 cm) DEM 189,600. LONDON, 7 Oct 1999, *Still-life of Flowers* (1922, oil on canvas, 24 x 19 ins / 60 x 49 cm) GBP 55,000. VIENNA, 11 Oct 1999, *View of Salzburg from Moenchsberg, Kapuzinerberg and Gaisberg beyond* (oil on canvas, 22 x 31 ins / 55 x 80 cm) ATS 1,150,000. VIENNA, 25 Sept 2001, *Still-life of Fish with Stone Jug* (1929, oil on canvas, 24 x 30 ins / 60 x 75 cm) ATS 800,000. VIENNA, 27 Nov 2001, *Still-life of Fruit in Ceramic Dish* (woodcut, 13 x 10 ins / 34 x 26 cm) ATS 420,000. VIENNA, 26 Nov 2002, *Lakeside Town* (watercolour, 5 x 8 ins / 13 x 21 cm) EUR 5,500. COLOGNE, 4 Dec 2002, *Reclining Female Nude* (1919, oil on canvas, 29 x 41 ins / 74 x 103 cm) EUR 60,000. LONDON, 3 June 2003, *Two Nudes* (1913, oil on canvas, 80 x 66 ins / 203 x 168 cm) GBP 35,000. VIENNA, 28 Oct 2003, *Still-life with Apples and Bottle* (oil on canvas, 19 x 24 ins / 47 x 61 cm) EUR 60,000. LONDON, 23 June 2004, *Flowers in a Vase* (1918, oil on canvas/board, 20 x 16 ins / 50 x 40 cm) GBP 38,000. LONDON, 23 June 2004, *Flowers in a Vase* (1917, oil on canvas/board, 20 x 16 ins / 50 x 40 cm) GBP 40,000.

FAISTENAUER, Andreas. See **FEISTENAUER**

FAISTENAUER, Hans

German, 17th century.
Born to a family originally from Berchtesgaden.
Painter.

Hans Faistenauer may have been the father of Andreas Feistenauer and is possibly the same person as Johann Faistenauer.

FAISTENAUER, Johann

German, 17th century.
Active in Seeon (Bavaria).
Draughtsman.

Johann Faistenauer may be the same person as Hans Faistenauer. He produced drawings of views of the monastery at Seeon attached to a handwritten chronicle by Abbot Honorat Kolb.

FAISTENBERGER, Andreas I

Austrian, 17th century.
Born 1588, in Hall (Tyrol); died 1652; buried 13 February in Kitzbühl.
Painter.

A burgher of the town of Kitzbühl, in 1620 Andreas Faistenberger I married Barbara Hüber in Salzburg. He imitated the Italian and Flemish styles, and several oil paintings are attributed to him, including a copy of the *Judgement of Solomon* after Rubens, which is kept at Kitzbühl Town Hall. He was probably the son of Balthasar Faistenberger, a stucco worker in Hall, and was the father of Benedikt Faistenberger I, a sculptor, and Wilhelm Faistenberger, a painter.

FAISTENBERGER, Andreas II
German, 17th - 18th century.
Born 1647, in Kitzbühl; died 8 December 1736, in Munich.
Sculptor.

Andreas Faistenberger II studied under his father, Benedikt Faistenberger I. He then travelled to Italy before settling in Munich in 1674. An extremely prolific artist, he sculpted stone, marble, wood and ivory, and produced crucifixes, as well as statues of madonnas and saints. He erected many altarpieces in Munich and other towns. His main works are in Munich and include: *Christ in the Tomb, Sacrifice of Abraham* and *Descent from the Cross* in the church of St Kajetan, the statues of *St Gabriel* and *St Raphael* in the church of the Holy Spirit, and an *Ecce Homo* in the chapel of the Passion. He was master to Egid Quirin Asam.

FAISTENBERGER, Anton
Austrian, 17th century.
Born 1663, in Salzburg; died 29 February 1708, in Vienna.
Painter, engraver (etching). Landscapes.

The son of Wilhelm Faistenberger, Anton Faistenberger's master was only an unknown artist, named Bouritzsch, who lived in Salzburg or Passau. Anton profited greatly from the opportunity to study some of the works of Gaspard Poussin, and went on to become an excellent landscape artist.

The emperor of Austria called Faistenberger to Vienna and employed him for several years. The Imperial and Liechtenstein collections in Vienna have his best works. Some of his landscapes can also be seen in Dresden and in Weimar. Hans Graf and Van Bredael assisted him with the figures, which he was not so skilled at depicting.

AUCTION RECORDS:
VIENNA, 18 March 1969, *Watering Place in the Roman Countryside,* ATS 40,000. LUCERNE, 19 June 1972, *Riverscape,* CHF 30,000. VIENNA, 22 June 1976, *Fishermen by a Mountain Stream* (oil/metal, 10 x 14 1/4in/24.5 x 36.5cm) ATS 120,000. LUCERNE, 19 Nov 1977, *Riverscape* (oil on canvas, 37 1/2 x 53 1/4in/95 x 135cm) CHF 31,000. LUCERNE, 6 Nov 1986, *Mountain Village with Bridge and Figures* (oil on canvas, 37 1/2 x 53 1/4in/95 x 135cm) CHF 22,000. ROME, 4 April 2000, *Shepherds in Landscape* (oil on canvas, 41 x 73 ins / 103 x 185 cm) ITL 23,010,000. VIENNA, 12 June 2001, *An Extensive Mountainous Landscape with a Torrent and Travellers* (oil on canvas, 42 x 54 ins / 107 x 138 cm) ATS 110,000.

FAISTENBERGER, Benedikt I
Austrian, 17th century.
Born 1621, in Kitzbühl; died 1693; buried in Kitzbühl.
Sculptor.

The son of Andreas Faistenberger I, Benedikt Faistenberger I erected a high altar in the parish church of St Andrew. The high altar in the parish church of Oberndorf, near Kitzbühl, is also attributed to him, as is the altarpiece with eight statues and the crucifix in the church of St Andrew in Sankt Johann (Tyrol). He drew his inspiration from the precepts of Palladio. He had many sons who became artists.

FAISTENBERGER, Benedikt II
Austrian, 17th century.
Born 12 March 1653, in Kitzbühl; died 1708.
Sculptor.

The son of Benedikt Faistenberger I, Benedikt Faistenberger II lived in Prague.

FAISTENBERGER, Dominikus
German, 17th - 18th century.
Born 1651, in Kitzbühl; died 1722; buried 1 March in Munich.
Painter.

The son of Benedikt Faistenberger I, Dominikus Faistenberger became a burgher of Munich in 1685 and was admitted as a master of the guild in 1686. The church of St Kajetan in Munich has several decorative paintings by Dominikus Faistenberger.

FAISTENBERGER, Erasmus
Austrian, 17th - 18th century.
Born 9 September 1666, in Kitzbühl; died 1718, in Kitzbühl.
Sculptor.

Erasmus Faistenberger painted a portrait of Ignaz Faistenberger I.

FAISTENBERGER, Franz
Austrian, 18th century.
Born c. 1710, in Kitzbühl; died 1786, in Salzburg.
Painter.

Initially taught by his older brothers, Franz Faistenberger subsequently studied in Munich before going on to work in Salzburg, where he produced religious paintings and reredos.

FAISTENBERGER, Georg I
Austrian, 18th century.
Baptised 24 July 1656 in Kitzbühl; died c. 1711 or 1730.
Sculptor.

Georg Faistenberger I was the son of Benedikt Faistenberger I, and is credited with the statues of *St Peter* and *St Paul* in the parish church of Sankt Johann (Tyrol).

FAISTENBERGER, Georg II
Austrian, 18th century.
Born 1707, probably in Kitzbühl; died c. 1766.
Painter.

A pupil of his father, Ignaz Faistenberger I, and of his brother, Simon Benedikt Faistenberger, Georg Faistenberger II lived in Weissenkirchen, near Krems (Niederösterreich), in Austria.

FAISTENBERGER, Ignaz I
Austrian, 17th - 18th century.
Baptised 9 September 1667; died 1718; buried 10 May in Kitzbühl.
Painter.

The son of Benedikt Faistenberger I, Ignaz Faistenberger I painted portraits and frescoes, including the *Scourging of Christ* and the *Crown of Thorns,* which used to be kept by the Capuchin monks in Kitzbühl. A farm near Kitzbühl has the portrait of *Sebastian Jäger,* a copy of which, made by the artist, is at the museum of the local art association in Kufstein (Tyrol), Austria.

FAISTENBERGER, Ignaz II
Austrian, 18th century.
Born 1692, in Kitzbühl.
Painter.

The son of Ignaz Faistenberger I, Ignaz Faistenberger II worked as a portraitist in Kitzbühl until he became blind.

FAISTENBERGER, Johann
Austrian, 18th century.
Born 1709, in Kitzbühl; died 1770.
Painter.

The son of Ignaz Faistenberger I, Johann Faistenberger painted landscapes, shepherds, and Paul the Apostle. He was also a topographer and made a map of Berchtesgaden (Bavaria), Germany. He is possibly identical with Johann Georg Faistenberger.

FAISTENBERGER, Johann Georg
Austrian, 18th century.
Painter.

Johann Georg Faistenberger produced decorative paintings, frescoes and murals. Works by him are mentioned as being in Hohenbrunn and Trinstein-an-der-Donau (Lower Austria). He is perhaps the same person as Johann Faistenberger.

FAISTENBERGER, Joseph Franz
Austrian, 17th - 18th century.
Born 1675, probably in Salzburg; died 30 August 1724, probably in Salzburg.
Painter.

Joseph Franz Faistenberger was a pupil and brother of Anton Faistenberger, whom he assisted in some of his works. Some of his paintings are at the abbey of St Florian in Austria. A gallery in Vienna has two landscapes by Faistenberger.

MUSEUMS AND GALLERIES:
GRAZ: *Landscape* - VIENNA: two landscapes - WROCLAW: *Landscape*; *Southern River*; two works.

FAISTENBERGER, Paul
Austrian, 17th century.
Born 16 September 1654, in Kitzbühl; died 1707.
Painter.

Paul Faistenberger was a son of Benedikt Faistenberger I.

FAISTENBERGER, Sebastian
Austrian, 17th century.
Active in Kitzbühl.
Painter, sculptor.

The youngest son of Benedikt Faistenberger I, Sebastian Faistenberger is possibly identical with a person of the same name who became a burgher of Rattenberg (Tyrol), and who died there.

FAISTENBERGER, Simon Benedikt
Austrian, 18th century.
Baptised 27 October 1695, in Kitzbühl; died 22 April 1759, in Kitzbühl.
Painter.

The son of Ignaz Faistenberger I, Simon Benedikt Faistenberger first studied art with his father before going on to study in Munich with J. Anton Gumpp and J.M. Rottmayr. He produced frescoes in many churches in the Tyrol, though many have now been lost. Most important of these frescoes are those in the parish church for Sankt Johann, Reith and Oberndorf; the ceiling paintings in the church of Our Lady in Kitzbühl; and the chancel paintings at Rattenberg. Three of his oil paintings are held by the Ferdinandeum in Innsbruck, while others can be found at the museum in Kufstein and in the churches and chapels in and around Kitzbühl. The Ferdinandeum also has over 30 plates of drawings by Faistenberger, as well as plans for ceiling paintings and reredos.

MUSEUMS AND GALLERIES:
INNSBRUCK (Tiroler Landesmus. Ferdinandeum) - KUFSTEIN (Heimatmus.).

FAISTENBERGER, Wilhelm
Austrian, 17th century.
Born 1623, in Kitzbühl; died probably c. 1690, in Salzburg.
Painter.

The son of Andreas Faistenberger I, Wilhelm Faistenberger settled in Salzburg, where he produced altarpieces and portraits. He is best known for a portrait of *Archbishop Maximilien* in the refectory of St Peter.

FAITDIEU, Charles Joseph
French, 18th century.
Active in Paris in 1764.
Painter.

FAITDIEU, Pierre Philmen. See **FILMENT-FAITDIEU Pierre Germain**

FAITHFULL, Leila
British, 20th century.
Born in Woolton; died 1994.
Painter. Genre scenes.

Leila Faithfull exhibited at the Salon des Artistes Français in Paris in 1933.

FAITHORNE, William, the Elder
British, 17th century.
Born 1616, in London; died 1691, in London.
Engraver, pastellist.

Until the start of the English Civil War, William Faithorne the Elder trained under Robert Peake, a painter and seller of engravings who was knighted by Charles I and then took up arms for the King, dragging his pupil along with him. Fairthorne was captured during the seige of Basing House and imprisoned for quite some time in Aldersgate. However, he benefited from his incarceration by practising his art. The plates he engraved included *Villiers, Duke of Buckingham*.

Released on condition that he left England, he went to France, where he was advised by Robert Nanteuil. After 1650 he was allowed to return to his homeland. He then set himself up as an engraver and seller of Italian, English and Dutch engravings, and continued to engrave and produce pencil drawings, abandoning his first style for the French method. He excelled particularly at portraits.

His many works include *Lady Paston*, in the style of Van Dyck (1649), *William Sanderson*, in the style of Joust (1658), *John Kersey*, also in the style of Joust, and *Henry Cary, Earl of Monmouth*. He signed with his own name or *F.F.* Some of his engravings were presented at *Painted Ladies, Women at the Court of Charles II* at the National Portrait Gallery in London in 2001.

F·F

BIBLIOGRAPHY:
MacLeod, Catharine/Marciari Alexander, Julia/Sharpe, Kevin/Dethloff, Diana/Wynne, Sonya, *Painted Ladies. Women at the Court of Charles II*, exhibition catalogue, National Portrait Gall., London, 2001.

MUSEUMS AND GALLERIES:
CAMBRIDGE (Sydney Sussex College): *Oliver Cromwell* (pastel) - LONDON (British Mus.): *Sir Orlando Bridgman* (drawing); *Sir Edmund King* (pastel); *John Ray* (pastel); *Caxton* (Indian ink); *Catherine of Braganza* (1662, engraving/paper, after Dirck Stoop); *Barbara Villiers, Countess of Castlemaine* (1666, engraving, after Sir Peter Lely) - OXFORD (Ashmolean Mus.): *John Aubrey* (pencil).

FAITHORNE, William, the Younger
British, 17th - 18th century.
Born 1656, in London; died c. 1710.
Painter.

William Faithorne the Younger trained under his father, the great William Faithorne the Elder. He executed mainly mezzotint portraits, the best of which include *Mary, Princess of Orange*, in the style of Hanneman, and *Queen Anne, Sophie, Wife of the Elector of Hannover* and *Charles XII of Sweden*, in the style of Ehrenstrahl.

FAIVE, Annette Suzanne, Mme Fontanarosa
French, 20th century.
Born 22 February 1911, in Paris; died 12 November 1988, in Paris.
Painter, watercolourist, pastellist, sculptor.

Having always lived in Paris, Annette Suzanne Faive graduated from the Collège Technique pour Jeunes Filles, Centre Élisa Lemonnier, where she later taught for several years. She entered the Lucien Simon studio at the École des Beaux-Arts, where she won several prizes and met Lucien Fontanarosa, whom she married and with whom she had three children who became well-known musicians. She spent some time in Morocco in 1936 and lived in Italy from 1937 to 1939.

In 1985 she founded the Association Lucien Fontanarosa in Paris. She was a professor at the Union Centrale des Arts Décoratifs from 1961 to 1971.

She exhibited at the Salon de la Société Nationale des Beaux-Arts and very regularly in various French salons and galleries from 1976 to 1987. A retrospective of her works was held at the Fondation Taylor, Paris, in 1994.

In technique, subject matter and psychological atmosphere, her paintings are quite different from those of Lucien Fontanarosa. Her landscapes, with their tense backlighting and chiaroscuro, are reminiscent of the neo-Romantic tenor of Victor Hugo's wash drawings.

FAIVRE. See also **FAVRE**

FAIVRE, Abel, for Jules Abel

French, 19th - 20th century.

Born 30 March 1867, in Lyons; died August 1945.

Painter, watercolourist, pastellist, draughtsman, illustrator. Genre scenes, portraits, figures, nudes, interiors, still-lifes (fruit). Humorous cartoons.

Abel Faivre was a pupil of Jean-Baptiste Poncet at the École des Beaux-Arts, Lyons, which he entered in 1886, and then of Benjamin-Constant and Jules Lefebvre in Paris. He also received advice from Renoir. He exhibited regularly at the Salon de Lyons, in 1899 with *Return from Wagram*, winning the Salon medal in 1897, and at the Salon de Paris from 1982, with *Woman Musing* in 1898, *The Virgin with Children* in 1899, *Woman with a Fan* in 1901, *Child with a Book* in 1906, and *Portrait of Maurice Donnay* in 1907. At this salon he won a third-class medal in 1894, and he was awarded an honourable mention at the Exposition Universelle of 1900 and the Légion d'Honneur in 1906.

Although his portraits of women are charming, it is as an illustrator rather than a painter that he is remembered. His drawing, which contrasts white with flat blocks of black, is forceful, deliberate and cruel. He contributed caricatures to many periodicals of the period: *L'Assiette au beurre, La Baïonnette, Candide, L'Écho de Paris, Figaro, Gazette du bon ton, Le Journal,* and *Le Rire*. His targets were mainly the world of medicine and the bourgeoisie - especially mature middle-class women with animal-like and lecherous faces.

MUSEUMS AND GALLERIES:

LYONS (MBA): *Portrait of a Young Girl; Woman in Blue* - PARIS (Mus. d'Orsay): *Woman with a Fan* (1901).

AUCTION RECORDS:

PARIS, 21 Nov 1901, *Nude Women,* FRF 200. PARIS, 6 Nov 1924, *Young Woman with a Garland,* FRF 500; *Nude,* FRF 1,750; *Portrait of a Young Woman* (pastel) FRF 24,000. PARIS, 11 Dec 1925, *Cup of Milk,* FRF 5,100. PARIS, 29 June 1927, *Woman with Roses,* FRF 2,000. PARIS, 5 May 1928, *Young Woman with a Rose* (pastel) FRF 2,300. PARIS, 7 Dec 1931, *Young Girl* (drawing in black, red and white chalk) FRF 360. PARIS, 12 April 1935, *Modern Bacchante,* FRF 1,380. PARIS, 20 March 1942, *Dress Fitting; Unbelievable Gentleman* (oil on canvas, a pair) FRF 3,000. PARIS, 22 July 1942, *Hideous Satyr* (heightened with wash) FRF 220. PARIS, 3 March 1943, *Artist's Studio* (watercolour) FRF 600. PARIS, 21 April 1943, *Young Woman Seated* (drawing in colouring pencil) FRF 1,200. PARIS, 29 June 1945, *Still-life,* FRF 600. PARIS, 12 March 1973, *The Virgin with Children* (1894) FRF 8,200. ENGHIEN-LES-BAINS, 14 June 1981, *Gowned Nude in a Landscape* (oil on canvas, 33 3/4 x 21 1/4 ins / 86 x 54 cm) FRF 13,100. PARIS, 5 March 1984, *Fortune Teller and Demi-mondaine* (oil on canvas, 39 1/4 x 82 3/4 ins / 100 x 210 cm) FRF 25,500. PARIS, 17 June 1985, *Landscape with Lake* (oil on canvas, 15 1/4 x 18 1/4 ins / 38.5 x 46.5 cm) FRF 11,000. PARIS, 6 May 1988, *Model in an Armchair* (mixed media, 11 x 7 3/4 ins / 28 x 20 cm) FRF 3,000. PARIS, 21 Nov 1988, *Portrait of a Young Woman* (oil on canvas, 11 x 9 ins / 27 x 22 cm) FRF 6,500. PARIS, 22 Nov 1988, *Portrait of a Child wearing a Lace Collar* (pastel, 18 x 15 ins / 46 x 38 cm) FRF 20,000. VERSAILLES, 18 Dec 1988, *Young Woman Nude in a Landscape* (1920, oil on canvas, 16 1/4 x 12 1/2 ins / 41 x 32 cm) FRF 10,200. PARIS, 1 Feb 1989, *Woman with a Dog* (pastel, 29 1/4 x 22 ins / 74 x 56 cm) FRF 10,000. PARIS, 21 Nov 1989, *Portrait of a Child Wearing a Lace Collar* (pastel, 18 x 15 ins / 46 x 38 cm) FRF 20,000. PARIS, 9 July 1992, *Portrait of a Woman Wearing a Red Turban* (pastel, 31 1/2 x 25 1/4 ins / 80 x 64 cm) FRF 5, 000. PARIS, 25 March 1994, *Peace Treaties* (Indian ink, 8 1/4 x 7 ins / 21 x 17.5 cm) FRF 10,000. CALAIS, 25 June 1995, *Portrait of a Young Woman* (oil on canvas, 18 x 15 ins / 46 x 38 cm) FRF 4,500. PARIS, 19 Dec 1997, *Young Woman Leaning* (oil on panel, oval, 14 1/2 x 11 1/4 ins / 37 x 28.5 cm) FRF 3,800. NEW YORK, 17 Feb 1999, *Parisian Woman* (oil on panel, oval, 15 x 11 ins / 37 x 29 cm) USD 5,000. CALAIS, 12 Dec 1999, *Portrait of an Elegant Lady* (oil on canvas, 9 x 7 ins / 24 x 18 cm) FRF 14,000. PARIS, 15 Dec 2000, *Woman Bathing on the Shore* (oil on canvas, 13 x 8 ins / 32 x 20 cm) FRF 43,000. LONDON, 13 Feb 2002, *Beach Scene* (1904, oil on canvas, 15 x 24 ins / 38 x 62 cm) GBP 2,500. PARIS, 17 Dec 2002, *Bather with Cherries* (oil on canvas, 18 x 15 ins / 46 x 38 cm) EUR 3,200. PARIS, 26 June 2003, *Woman* (pastel, 32 x 26 ins / 81 x 65 cm) EUR 1,700.

FAIVRE, Antoine Jean Étienne, called Tony

French, 19th century.

Born 24 May 1830, in Besançon; died 1905, in Paris.

Painter, watercolourist. Genre scenes, portraits, figures, interiors with figures. Decorative panels, fans, decorative designs.

Antoine Faivre exhibited at the Paris Salon from 1848, being awarded a medal in 1864. He executed many portraits of private individuals, including that of *Nessim-Bey*. An excellent watercolorist, he executed charming decorative panels and pretty fans.

MUSEUMS AND GALLERIES:

BESANÇON: *Pomona and Flora* (design for a ceiling).

AUCTION RECORDS:

PARIS, 19 March 1928, *The Kill* (watercolour) FRF 125. LONDON, 25 Feb 1929, *Mirror,* GBP 19. PARIS, 2 and 3 July 1929, *Warming Pan,* FRF 1,200. LONDON, 19 Feb 1934, *The Toilette,* GBP 5. PARIS, 12 March 1941, *Young Woman in a Blue Dress with a Red Poppy in her Hair,* FRF 120. LONDON, 21 Feb 1945, *Young Woman Washing her Hands* (1873) GBP 34. LONDON, 21 March 1984, *Nun and Children in an Interior* (1888, oil on canvas, 24 3/4 x 20 1/2 ins / 63 x 52 cm) GBP 1,800. NEW YORK, 22 May 1986, *Portrait of Nessim-Bey, Asian Campaign* (1855, oil on canvas, 59 x 47 ins / 150 x 119.5 cm) USD 45,000. LONDON, 18 March 1992, *Young Servant* (1865, oil on canvas, 60 1/4 x 47 1/4 ins / 153 x 120 cm) GBP 7,480. NEW YORK, 13 Sept 2000, *Preparing for an Afternoon Stroll* (1876, oil on panel, 17 x 11 ins / 42 x 28 cm) USD 9,500. PARIS, 5 April 2001, *Servant-girl with Warming Pan* (1875, oil on canvas, 18 x 13 ins / 45 x 32 cm) FRF 70,000. NEW ORLEANS, 26 May 2001, *Putti Serenading a Reclining Maiden. Paris stencil* (1883, oil on panel, 11 x 16 ins / 28 x 41 cm) USD 2,000.

FAIVRE, Benoît. See **FAIVRE François**

FAIVRE, Claude

French, 19th century.

Engraver (etching).

Claude Faivre was a pupil of Boulanger, Courtry and Jules Lefebvre.

MUSEUMS AND GALLERIES:

DIEPPE: *House in the Country* (etching, after Peter de Hooch).

FAIVRE, Claude

French, 20th century.

Born 14 November 1943, in Paris.

Sculptor, painter, engraver, illustrator, installation artist.

Claude Faivre studied in Paris at the École des Arts Appliqués, the École Normale Supérieure de l'Enseignement Technique, and at the École des Beaux-Arts. In 1979, he won a research scholarship. He has homes in Clamart and La Roche-Posay, and teaches at the École des Beaux-Arts d'Orléans.

He has displayed his work in a number of group exhibitions, including: the Salon de Mai from 1973 to 1978, the Salon Grands et Jeunes d'Aujourd'hui in 1978, *Livres d'Art et d'Artistes* (*Books of Art and of Artists*), at the Galerie N.R.A. in 1983, and *Livres Gravés* (*Engraved Books*), at the Nicaise bookshop in 1997, all in Paris. His work has more often been shown in solo exhibitions, such as: *Ventes et Sentes*, at the Galerie N.R.A. in Paris, in 1979; Dijon, 1981; Lyons, 1984; Bibliothèque de Beaune, 1986; Poitiers, 1990; Institute of Art in Canberra, 1993; and *Ouvertures et Portes de Toile* (*Cloth Doors and Openings*), in Dijon in 1995.

FAIVRE, Claude Léonard
French, 18th century.
Active in Besançon.
Sculptor (wood), architect.

Claude Léonard Faivre worked for the abbey in Bellevaux and the church in Baume-les-Dames.

FAIVRE, Ferdinand
French, 19th century.
Born 8 October 1860, in Marseilles.
Sculptor.

A pupil of Cavelier, Ferdinand Faivre exhibited at the Salon des Artistes Français. He received an honourable mention in 1889, a third-class medal and a travel bursary in 1892, and a second-class medal in 1899, followed by a bronze medal at the 1900 Exposition Universelle.

MUSEUMS AND GALLERIES:
SÈTE: *Decorative Fountain*.

AUCTION RECORDS:
NEW YORK, 21 Sept 1981, *Jean* (bronze, h. 52 1/2 ins / 133.5 cm) USD 7,500.

FAIVRE, François, sometimes Benoît
French, 19th century.
Born c. 1830, in Dôle.
Painter. Genre scenes.

A pupil of Thomas Couture, François Faivre made his début at the Paris Salon in 1850 with *Don't Forget the Poor Blind Man*. Thereafter, he regularly sent pictures to the Salon, including *Poet in his Garret* in 1852 and *Reprimand* in 1855.

Faivre painted mainly genre scenes, the themes of which show the effects of the sentimentality of the period. He avoided excessive pathos when painting figures by the fireside: he used neutral tones and was skilled at exercising expressive restraint.

FAIVRE, Jean Alexis
French, 18th century.
Born c. 1710, in Besançon.
Sculptor (wood).

Jean Alexis Faivre was the son of the woodcarver Jean Baptiste Faivre. In 1778 he executed carvings in the sacristy of St-Jean in Besançon, after the plans by Cl. J. A. Bertrand.

FAIVRE, Jean Baptiste
French, 18th century.
Active in Besançon.
Sculptor (wood).

Jean Baptiste Faivre executed woodcarvings in a chapel of the cathedral in Besançon in 1743.

FAIVRE, Maxime, for Léon Maxime
French, 19th - 20th century.
Born 5 January 1856, in Paris; died 5 January 1941, in Paris.
Painter. Allegorical subjects, genre scenes, landscapes, still-lifes.
Symbolism.

Maxime Faivre was a pupil of Gustave Boulanger and Gérome at the École des Beaux-Arts, Paris. He exhibited at the Salon de Paris from 1877 to 1881, and then at the Salon des Artistes Français, of which he became a member in 1886. He was awarded an honourable mention in 1879, a third-class medal in 1884, a bronze medal at the Exposition Universelle of 1889, and a silver medal at that of 1900. In 2003 he was represented in *Vénus et Caïn. Figures de la préhistoire 1830-1930* (*Venus and Cain. Prehistoric Figures 1830-1930*), an exhibition showing the emergence of prehistory as a scientific discipline and a source of artistic inspiration, held at the Musée d'Aquitaine, Bordeaux.

BIBLIOGRAPHY:
Lafont-Couturier, Hélène/Dagen, Philippe/Loizeau, Sigolène, *Vénus et Caïn. Figures de la préhistoire 1830-1930*, exhibition catalogue, Musée d'Aquitaine, Bordeaux, 2003.

MUSEUMS AND GALLERIES:
CABOURG (ville): *Flower Seller* - LISIEUX: *Women of the Revolution; Last Victory* - PARIS (Mus. d'Orsay): *Two Mothers* - VERSAILLES (Mus. d'Histoire de France): *Mort de la duchesse de Lamballe* (*Death of the Duchesse de Lamballe*).

AUCTION RECORDS:
PARIS, 3-4 May 1923, *Playing the Viola d'Amore*, FRF 260; *Still-life with Game*, FRF 1,100. GRENOBLE, 9 May 1977, *Street with Figures in Dax* (oil on panel, 11 x 7 ins / 27 x 18 cm) FRF 1,500. PARIS, 8 June 1982, *Young Woman with a Muff* (1897, oil on panel, 11 x 7 1/4 ins / 28 x 18.7 cm) FRF 14,000. ZURICH, 30 Nov 1984, *Walkers on a Beach* (oil on card, 11 1/2 x 18 ins / 29.5 x 46 cm) CHF 10,000. ZURICH, 21 Nov 1986, *Seacoast Scenes* (two oils on card, 4 x 11 ins / 10.3 x 27 cm and 4 1/4 x 10 ins/10.8 x 24.5 cm) CHF 11,000.

FAIVRE, Paul Émile Denis
French, 19th century.
Born 1 March 1821, in Metz; died 29 January 1868, in Metz.
Painter.

Paul Faivre exhibited at the Paris Salon from 1855 to 1866.

MUSEUMS AND GALLERIES:
METZ: *Fruit and Flowers; Vulture Swooping Down on a Stork; Flowers* - NANCY: *Dead Game; Fruit and Crockery*.

AUCTION RECORDS:
PARIS, 14 Oct 1946, *Hunting Still-life*, FRF 1,100.

FAIVRE, Tony. See **FAIVRE Antoine Jean Etienne**

FAIVRE-DUFFER, Louis Stanislas
French, 19th century.
Born 1818, in Nancy; died 1897.
Painter, watercolourist, pastellist, miniaturist, lithographer. Religious subjects, portraits, genre scenes, animals. Murals.
Symbolism.

Louis Stanislas Faivre-Duffer studied under Claude Bonnefond and Victor Orsel at the Lyons École des Beaux-Arts before joining the École des Beaux-Arts in Paris, where he won many awards. He then travelled to Rome. In 1836 he made his début at the Lyons Salon with *Prodigal Son*. From 1847 he exhibited at the Paris Salon with *Italian Woman with her Child* and *Woman's Head*. At the 1855 Exposition Universelle he exhibited a pastel of *Spring*. He exhibited the following works in Paris: *Pilgrimage* in 1863; *Consequences of an Error* in 1865; *Isabelle and the Pot of Basil* in 1879; *Mater Dolorosa* in 1881; *Potiphar* in 1894; and the watercolours *Herodias* and *Bathers* in 1896. He was awarded a third-class medal in 1851, followed by a further medal in 1861.

Faivre-Duffer painted genre scenes and animals, but he devoted a good part of his work to religious murals. He received various commissions, including decorative paintings at the Château d'Anet in Eure-et-Loire from 1873. Together with other former pupils of Victor Orsel, he was commissioned to finish the paintings in the chapel of the Eucharist at Notre-Dame-de-Lorette in Paris. He subsequently executed the decorations at the Château de Coyolles in the Aisne region, together with a cartoon for the mosaics decorating the tympanum of Notre-Dame-de-la-Garde in Marseilles. He executed many lithographs after V. Orsel. Faivre-Duffer had an extremely realistic eye for detail and used acid tints to prevent his religious painting from appearing faded. Having specialised in society portraits intended for the salons of the Second French Empire, he painted hundreds of portraits of the Lyons middle classes. Handling this genre in many different ways, in oil, watercolour, pastel or wax, sometimes even in miniature, he was adept at flattering the features of his models while still ensuring that there was a true resemblance.

L FAIVRE - DUFFER

MUSEUMS AND GALLERIES:

LYONS: *Pilgrimage to the Madonna; Study of a Female Nude* - NANCY: *Italian Peasant Woman and her Child.*

AUCTION RECORDS:

ZÜRICH, 9 Nov 1984, *Young Woman with Red Parasol* (oil on canvas, 27 1/2 x 19 3/4 ins / 70 x 50 cm) CHF 3,200. SAN FRANCISCO, 16 May 2001, *Portrait of a Young Girl Holding a Bouquet of Flowers* (1862, pastel, paper/canvas, oval, 31 x 25 ins / 79 x 63 cm) USD 1,500. LONDON, 5 July 2001, *Portrait of Gentleman, Wearing Morning Suit. Portrait of his Wife in laborate Dress* (1854, oil on canvas, a pair, 43 x 31 ins / 109 x 80 cm) GBP 1,000.

FAIVRE-VALLÉE, Euphémie (Mme)
French, 20th century.
Miniaturist.

Euphémie Faivre-Vallée exhibited in Paris at the Salon des Artistes Français from 1922.

FAIX, Andras
Hungarian, 19th century.
Painter. History painting, portraits.

Andras Faix spent time in Temesvár (now Timisoara, Romania) where he painted a *Baptism of St Stephen, King of Hungary*. This work was exhibited in the cathedral.

FAIZAN, Jenny von
German, 19th century.
Active c. 1800.
Miniaturist.

A miniature on ivory depicting *Electress Wilhelmine Caroline of Hesse* is attributed to Von Faizan.

FAIZANT, Jacques
French, 20th century.
Born 1918, in Laroquebrou; died 14 january 2006.
Cartoonist.

Jacques Faizant's first drawings date from 1945 and his first political cartoons appeared in *Paris Presse* in 1959. From the end of the 1960s he contributed a daily drawing to *Figaro*. He also worked for *Le Point, Jour de France, Paris Match, France-Dimanche, Samedi soir* and *La Vie Catholique*.

AUCTION RECORDS:

PARIS, 13 Nov 1986, *For What You Do with Your Old Toys* (watercolour, 11 1/2 x 9 ins / 29 x 23 cm) FRF 4,000. PARIS, 27 Nov 1993, *You Should Find a Desert Island with Lots of Girls and Free Bars* (1982, black ink and colour/paper, illustration for 'Jour de France', 8 x 10 1/2 ins / 20.5 x 26.5 cm) FRF 5,500.

FAJANS, Maximilian
Polish, 19th century.
Born 5 May 1827, in Sieradz; died 26 July 1890, in Targówko, near Warsaw.
Draughtsman, lithographer.

Maximilian Fajans studied at the art academy in Warsaw, and went to Paris in 1849, where he worked in Ary Scheffer's studio. He studied lithography under Émile Lasalle, and chromolithography at the Lemercier institute. On his return to Warsaw he published a work entitled *Polish Portraits*, featuring effigies of famous people and lithographs in black, and chromolithographs in a work entitled *Flowers and Poems*.

FAJARDO, Alonso
Spanish, 17th century.
Painter.

Alonso Fajardo settled in Seville in 1646. He was the brother of Juan and Nicolas Fajardo.

FAJARDO, Carlos
Brazilian, 20th century.
Born 1941.
Painter, draughtsman.

Carlos Fajardo was one of the founder members of the Rex group inspired by Wesley Duke Lee in São Paulo around 1965. The group's work centred around a gallery and a journal, and was outside the traditional art circuit. Fajardo shared the effervescence characterising this period of Brazilian art and challenging the constraints and censorship of the dictatorial regime. Around 1975, he was part of a powerful movement that returned to drawing as an effective means of gaining ascendancy over and opposing a close and threatening reality.

FAJARDO, Juan Antonio
Spanish, 17th century.
Active in Seville.
Painter.

FAJARDO, Nicolás
Spanish, 17th century.
Active in Seville.
Painter.

Nicolás Fajardo was the brother of Juan and Alonso Fajardo.

FAJEN, Gebert
German, 17th century.
Painter.

Fajen worked for the church of St Mary in Lübeck (Schleswig-Holstein), Germany.

FAJFROWSKA, Sylvie
French, 20th - 21st century.
Born 1959.
Painter.

Sylvie Fajfrowska lives and works in Paris. She was an artist in residence at the Villa Arson in Nice in 1994. Her paintings consist of diverse, graphic, non-geometric signs, systematically combined and distributed upon their backgrounds. The colours themselves are also symbolic. She has even applied this style to portraits, in which, as in her other works, 'colour-shapes' become entities unto themselves, deliberately estranged from the reality upon which they are based. Since 2000, she has used individual figurative motifs, such as a branch, a teddy bear's head, or a piece of corrugated iron. She also depicts objects which evoke, or bear traces of, the human body, like a bed, or women's underwear, distorting viewers' perspective so as to draw their attention to the absence of the body itself. Their colours are vividly contrasted, their contours realistic, and their composition almost decorative in its simplicity.

She has participated in a number of group exhibitions, including; the Salon de Montrouge, 1992, 1993; Galerie Eric Dupont, Toulouse, 1992; *Vraiment Peintres* (*Now, These Are*

Painters), Galerie Zürcher, Paris, 1994; Galerie Regards, Paris, 1995; and the International Contemporary Art Fair, Galerie Eric Dupont, Paris, in 1997.

She has also displayed her work in a number of solo exhibitions, including: Galerie Regards, Paris, 1993; Maison d'Art Contemporain, Chailloux, 1994; Galerie Eric Dupont, Toulouse, 1994; Galerie Jordan-Devarieux, Paris, 1996; Galerie Eric Dupont, Paris, 1997; Espace d'Art Contemporain C. Lambert, Juvisy-sur-Orge, 1997; Chapelle St-Jacques, St-Gaudens, 2002; and the Abbaye St-André, Centre d'Art Contemporain, Meymac, in 2003.

BIBLIOGRAPHY:

Chassey, Éric de, *L'Objet de la peinture*, exhibition catalogue, Espace d'Art contemporain, C. Lambert, Juvisy-sur-Orge, 1997. Ottinger, Didier, *Sympathy for the Devil*, exhibition catalogue, Chapelle Saint-Jacques, St-Gaudens, 2002.

FAJOL, Pierre
French, 20th century.
Born 26 April 1920, in Bordeaux.
Painter. Figure compositions, figures, portraits, landscapes.

Pierre Fajol was a self-taught painter, but he did attend the free courses at the École des Beaux-Arts, Bordeaux, from 1935 to 1938. After World War II, in which he served in Leclerc's Second Armoured Division, he took part in group and solo exhibitions: from 1945 to 1963 in Morocco, from 1963 to 1965 in Algeria, from 1965 to 1969 in Corsica, on the Côte d'Azur in 1969-1970, at the Salon d'Automne between 1970 and 1975, from 1975 in Bordeaux and Arcachon, and in many American cities. He won a number of awards. Using a variety of techniques, he paints pictures in which figures appear to be taking part in mysterious, sometimes mystical, ceremonies.

FAJON, Rose Jeanne (Mme)
Maiden name: Boquet
French, 19th century.
Born 1798, in Marseilles.
Painter.

A pupil of M. and Mme Hersent, Rose Jeanne Fajon exhibited watercolour flowers and portraits at the Paris Salon in 1833 and 1834.

FAKITS, Erno
Hungarian, 20th century.
Born 30 January 1883, in Budapest.
Sculptor.

Erno Fakits studied at the arts and crafts School in Budapest and later went to Vienna. He executed the *Memorial to the Heroes of Branyiszko* in Szepesvaralja.

FAL, Guillaem de, or Faen
Flemish, 17th century.
Born to a family originally from Liège.
Active in Amsterdam.
Painter.
Flemish School.

Guillaem de Fal married in Amsterdam.

AUCTION RECORDS:

LONDON, 19 Feb 1937, *Family Gathering*, GBP 8.

FALAIZE, Richard
French, 16th century.
Born in Paris.
Sculptor (wood).

Falaize sculpted the 54 carved choir stalls of the collegiate church of St Martin in Champeaux in the canton of Mormant (Seine-et-Marne) in 1522.

FALAMPIN, Jean Baptiste Louis
French, 18th century.
Active in Paris in 1769.
Painter, sculptor.

FALANDER, Ida Amanda Maria
Swedish, 19th century.
Born 6 September 1842, in Stockholm.
Engraver (wood).

A pupil of E. Skill and the Stockholm academy, Ida Falander produced woodcuts, including a large number for the magazine *Ny Illustrerad Tidning*. In 1878, she worked in London for the journal *The Graphic*.

FALANGE, Enrico, or Falangè
17th century.
Flemish or German by birth.
Painter. Allegorical subjects.

Worked in Venice, in 1650, in particular for the oratory of the church of S Bartolomeo.

AUCTION RECORDS:

NEW YORK, 5 April 1990, *Allegory of Minerva and Time* (1641, oil on canvas, 44 1/2 x 34 ins / 113 x 85.5 cm) USD 1,650.

FALASSO, Silvestro
Italian, 17th century.
Active in Rome.
Painter.

FALAT, Julian
Austrian, 19th - 20th century.
Born 30 July 1853, in Tuliglovy (Ukraine); died 1929, in Bystra.
Watercolourist, painter (gouache), draughtsman, illustrator. Genre scenes, landscapes, landscapes with figures, urban landscapes, architectural views.
Symbolism.
Sztuka Group.

Julian Falat studied at the school of fine arts in Cracow from 1869 to 1871, then was a student of Josef von Brandt at the academy in Munich. In 1885, he embarked on a tour of the world, and particularly Europe. From 1886, he entered the service of the crown prince of Prussia, the future Wilhelm II, for whom he portrayed hunting scenes. He lived in Berlin from 1894 to 1896 and painted, with W. Kossak, *Napoleon Crossing the Berezina*. He was a professor and director of the school of fine arts in Cracow (which became an academy in 1900) from 1895 to 1905. He was a member of the Sztuka group of artists from 1897. He contributed to the journals: *Tygodnik Ilustrowany* (*Illustrated Weekly*), *Klosy*, *Liberum Veto*, and *Ver Sacrum* (*Sacred Spring*), the journal of the Austrian Secession movement.

He took part in many exhibitions from 1874. His picture, *Bear Hunt in Russia*, now housed at the museum in Berlin, won a silver medal at the Exposition Universelle in Paris in 1900. In 2001, some of his works were presented at the exhibition *L'Avant-printemps. Pologne 1880-1920* (*Early Spring. Poland 1880-1920*) at the Palais des Beaux-Arts in Brussels.

His pictures of note include *Party in a Forest Interior near Munich* and *Ash Wednesday in a Church in Northern Italy*. He also produced a series of 28 watercolours and drawings, including *Emperor Wilhelm II Returning from a Bear Hunt*. Belonging to the Polish Impressionist school, he drew his inspiration from the landscapes that surrounded him, which he sometimes interpreted in a Symbolist vein, in particular in his winter scenes. He also produced some architectural studies.

BIBLIOGRAPHY:

Malinowski, Jerzy, *Julian Falat*, Krajowa Agencja Wydawnicza, Warsaw, 1985. Lubasiowa, Anna, '*Pamietniki. Julian Falat*' in *coll. Série Silesiana*, Pslaski Instytut Nauk., Katowice, 1987. Morawinska, Agnieszka/Clegg, Elisabeth/Poprzecka, Maria/Crugten, Alain van, *L'Avant-printemps. Pologne 1880-1920*, exhibition catalogue, Palais des Beaux-Arts, Tempera, Brussels, 2001.

Museums and Galleries:
Berlin: *Bear Hunting in Russia* - Cracow (Muz. Narodowe): *Sermon at the Patronal Festival at Kalwaria* (1906, oil on canvas) - Warsaw (Muz. Narodowe): *Winter Landscape with River* (1907, oil on canvas).
Auction records:
New York, 24 Sept 1969, *Hunting Scene*, USD 2,000. New York, 2 April 1976, *Snowy Landscape* (gouache and watercolour, 21 1/4 x 44 1/2 ins / 54 x 113 cm) USD 1,600. New York, 25 May 1984, *Polish Wife* (1888, watercolour and gouache, 29 1/4 x 22 1/2 ins / 74 x 57.1 cm) USD 7,000. Vienna, 12 Sept 1984, *Winter Sun* (1906, oil on canvas, 30 1/4 x 78 3/4 ins / 77 x 200 cm) ATS 130,000. Munich, 2 Dec 1997, *Easter Blessing* (1881, watercolour/paper, 30 1/2 x 44 1/4 ins / 77.5 x 112.5 cm) DEM 50,400.

FALBE, Joachim Martin
German, 18th century.
Born 1709, in Berlin; died 1782, in Berlin.
Painter, engraver.

A pupil of J. Harper and A. Pesne, Falbe's best-known engravings are plates depicting figures, such as *Adoration of the Shepherds* after Rembrandt, *Presentation in the Temple* after C.W. Dietrier, *The Philosopher in his Study*, *Child on Reins* and *Old Man with Book of Hours*.

Auction records:
London, 30 Nov 1907, *Little Fishermen on the Shore*, GBP 1.

FÄLBEL, Franz Joseph
Austrian, 18th century.
Died c. 1760.
Active in Vienna.
Painter.

FALBESONER, Joseph
Austrian, 18th - 19th century.
Born 1769, in Nassereith (Tyrol); died 1849, in Nassereith.
Sculptor (wood), architect.

Having decorated the monastery at Einsiedeln in Switzerland, Falbesoner worked with the sculptor Franz Speicher in Freisingen, producing 18 statues of the Bavarian electors. Churches in the Tyrol have many of his works, including altars, tabernacles and crucifixes.

FALC, Nora
Russian, 19th - 20th century.
Born at the end of the 19th century, in Moscow.
Painter.

Nora Falc exhibited at the Salon d'Automne in Paris in about 1920.

FALCAZ, Alphonse Auguste
French, 19th century.
Born 19 April 1813, in Paris.
Painter.

A pupil of Léon Cogniet, Alphonse Auguste Falcaz joined the École des Beaux-Arts on 2 October 1837. He exhibited at the Salon from 1840 to 1846. He is best known for his *Portrait of Mlle Anaïs Aubert*, *Holy Women at the Tomb of Christ* and *Christ on the Cross*.

FALCH, Georg Friedrich
German, 18th century.
Born 1694; died 1723.
Painter.

Georg Friedrich Falch worked with his father, Georg Ulrich Falch, on the decoration of the castle of Warthausen, near Biberach.

FALCH, Georg Ulrich
German, 17th - 18th century.
Born 1655; died 1735.
Active in Biberach (Württemberg).
Painter.

Georg Ulrich Falch worked with his son, Georg Friedrich Falch, on the decoration of the castle of Warthausen, near Biberach.

FALCH, Johann, or Falk
German, 18th century.
Born 1687; died 1727.
Painter. Animals.

Johann Falch imitated W. Hamilton and worked in Augsburg.
Museums and Galleries:
St Petersburg (Hermitage): *Insects*; *Reptiles*.

FALCHETTI, Alberto
Italian, 20th century.
Born 1878, in Caluso; died 1951.
Also active in France.
Painter. Mountainscapes, landscapes.

Alberto Falchetti lived and worked in Turin. He worked in France for many years, chiefly painting landscapes of high mountain peaks.

His work has appeared in exhibitions in Venice, Turin (in 1898 and 1911), the Nymphenburg palace in Munich (1909 and 1913) and the Salon of the Société des Artistes Français in Paris (1914).

Museums and Galleries:
Paris (Mus. d'Orsay): *Ouragan in the Mountains*.
Auction records:
Rome, 13 May 1986, *Peasants in a Landscape* (1908, oil on canvas, 57 3/4 x 92 1/4 ins / 147 x 234 cm) ITL 14,000,000. Rome, 12 Dec 1989, *Mountain Pasturelands* (oil on canvas, 29 1/4 x 50 1/2 ins / 74 x 128 cm) ITL 11,000,000. Milan, 14 June 1995, *Sunset over Pizzo di Sciora* (oil on canvas, 23 1/2 x 39 1/4 ins / 60 x 100 cm) ITL 6,325,000. Milan, 18 Dec 1996, *Still-life with Fruit* (1898, oil on canvas, 11 1/2 x 22 1/2 ins / 29.5 x 57 cm) ITL 6,058,000. Lymington, 19 May 1999, *Still-life with Oranges* (oil on canvas, 26 x 17 ins / 65 x 43 cm) GBP 1,500. Rome, 21 Nov 2000, *Still-life with Oranges* (1897, oil on canvas, 26 x 17 ins / 65 x 44 cm) ITL 6,500,000. Vercelli, 24 Feb 2001, *Nioslet Lake* (oil on cardboard, 14 x 18 ins / 35 x 46 cm) ITL 3,200,000. London, 28 Nov 2001, *Bunches of Grapes* (1891, oil on canvas, a pair, 19 x 13 ins / 49 x 34 cm) GBP 7,000. Turin, 26 June 2003, *Still-life with Grapes* (1898, oil on canvas, 22 x 11 ins / 56 x 28 cm) EUR 2,800. Vercelli, 1 Nov 2003, *Frassinetto Mountains* (oil on cardboard, 13 x 17 ins / 33 x 44 cm) EUR 2,200. Vercelli, 1 May 2004, *In the Mountains* (oil on cardboard, 13 x 18 ins / 34 x 45 cm) EUR 2,800. Vercelli, 1 May 2004, *Riva del Carbon, Venice* (oil on cardboard, 13 x 17 ins / 34 x 44 cm) EUR 2,900.

FALCHETTI, Giuseppe
Italian, 19th century.
Born 1843, in Caluso.
Painter. Landscapes with figures, still-lifes.

Giuseppe Falchetti exhibited a *Still-life* in Turin in 1898.
Museums and Galleries:
Turin (Gal. Civica d'Arte Moderna e Contemporanea) - Turin (Palazzo Reale).
Auction records:
London, 23 July 1976, *Still-life* (1878, oil on canvas, 21 1/2 x 14 ins / 54.5 x 35.5 cm) GBP 300. Los Angeles, 22 June 1981, *Still-life with Fruit* (1878, oil on canvas, 31 1/2 x 23 1/4 ins / 80 x 59 cm) USD 1,700. Rome, 26 Oct 1984, *Peasant Woman in a*

Riverscape, Woman Collecting Firewood in a Landscape (two oil on canvas, 27 1/2 x 39 1/4 ins / 70 x 100 cm) ITL 7,000,000. ROME, 16 Dec 1987, *Still-life with Basket of Apples; Still-life with Bunches of Grapes* (two oil on canvas, 26 3/4 x 17 3/4 ins / 68 x 45 cm) ITL 9,000,000. MILAN, 6 Dec 1989, *The Canavese* (oil on panel, 10 3/4 x 15 3/4 ins / 27.5 x 40 cm) ITL 3,600,000. MONACO, 21 April 1990, *Still-life with Grapes and Corn* (oil on canvas, 27 1/2 x 18 ins / 70 x 46 cm) FRF 22,200. MILAN, 17 Dec 1992, *Bunches of Grapes* (oil on canvas, 23 1/2 x 15 3/4 ins / 60 x 40 cm) ITL 5,700,000. MILAN, 20 Oct 1999, *Lake Landscape* (1862, oil on canvas, 17 x 22 ins / 43 x 56 cm) ITL 5,130,000. SWITZERLAND, 3 Dec 1999, *Upper Italian Mountain Landscape with Figure and Animals* (1910, oil on canvas, 24 x 34 ins / 61 x 87 cm) CHF 2,600. TURIN, 21 March 2000, *Still-life* (oil on canvas, 40 x 28 ins / 102 x 70 cm) ITL 18,000,000. VERCELLI, 20 May 2000, *Flock Returning from Pasture* (oil on canvas, 39 x 55 ins / 100 x 140 cm) ITL 20,000,000. LONDON, 5 April 2001, *Grapes, Peaches, Figs and a Melon with a Wine Flask against a Wall* (oil on canvas, 23 x 15 ins / 58 x 39 cm) GBP 4,000. ROME, 4 June 2001, *Still-life with Fruit* (1885, oil on canvas, 25 x 33 ins / 64 x 85 cm) ITL 24,000,000. LONDON, 21 March 2002, *Camel Train Leaving a Mosque* (oil on canvas, 32 x 54 ins / 81 x 138 cm) GBP 1,750. MILAN, 22 May 2002, *Montecarlo* (1897, oil on canvas, 20 x 29 ins / 52 x 73 cm) EUR 6,000. TURIN, 10 Dec 2002, *Landscape* (oil on canvas, 17 x 23 ins / 44 x 58 cm) EUR 2,800. MILAN, 27 May 2003, *View of Lake Como* (1887, oil on canvas, 26 x 35 ins / 65 x 88 cm) EUR 8,000. VERCELLI, 1 Nov 2003, *View of Lake Como* (1887, oil on canvas, 26 x 35 ins / 65 x 88 cm) EUR 10,000. FRANKFURT, 5 June 2004, *Coast and Fishing Boat* (1887, oil on canvas, 15 x 19 ins / 38 x 47 cm) EUR 2,600. TURIN, 14 June 2004, *Still-life* (1894, oil on canvas, 35 x 24 ins / 90 x 60 cm) EUR 8,000. SHERBORNE, 16 July 2004, *Landscape near Turin* (oil on canvas, 20 x 31 ins / 50 x 80 cm) GBP 2,400.

FALCHI, Ange Ethoré
French, 20th century.
Born 26 October 1913, in Vence; died 1989.
Sculptor, painter (gouache), pastellist, lithographer.

Ange Falchi, a pupil at the École des Arts Décoratifs, Nice, graduated in sculptural art and has a degree in art history. In 1958 a scholarship enabled him to visit Italy to study its monuments and museums and in 1959 he was awarded a scholarship to study in Spain. He takes part in many group exhibitions and has shown his paintings and sculptures in solo exhibitions since 1955 in Nice, Paris, Rennes, Poitiers, São Paulo, Brasilia, Bahia (El Salvador), Rio de Janeiro and more. As a result of undertaking several large works in Brazil he became a professor at the Alliance Française of Brasilia.

In his paintings he combines smooth areas of strong colour with broad impasto, creating deep planes and varied rhythmic surfaces. In 1961 he entered an international sculpture competition to create a sculpture to represent France in Brasilia. He won this competition with his 52-foot (16-metre) sculpture *Solarius*, which was erected in 1967 after being exhibited in Nice, where it was made. Subsequently the government of Brasilia commissioned from him a monument, *O Proféta*, 16 feet (5 metres) high and weighing a tonne, in memory of Don Bosco; and later a *Mercury*, 30 feet (9 metres) high and weighing 3 tonnes, for the La Salle College, Brasilia. He exploits a variety of techniques in his sculptures, using heavy bases and a sort of spiderweb netting; but the common factor between them, and with the paintings, is an almost gestural rhythm, an airy lightness.

BIBLIOGRAPHY:
Ange Falchi, auction catalogue, Drouot, Paris, 1 March 1988.

AUCTION RECORDS:
PARIS, 12 July 1990, *Composition* (oil on canvas, 32 x 21 1/4 ins / 81 x 54 cm) FRF 39,000. PARIS, 22 Nov 1990, *Composition* (oil on canvas, 20 3/4 x 25 1/4 ins / 53 x 64 cm) FRF 12,100.

FALCHI, Ettore
Italian, 20th century.
Born 1913, in Rome.
From 1935 also active in France.
Painter. Murals.

Ettore Falchi initially found fame as a music-hall performer. He began to paint in 1939, frequenting the free academies. He painted his first abstract works in 1946 and 1947. His paintings are derived from the classicism of abstraction and use diverse materials, with an occasional tendency towards relief. In 1963, he created some murals in Legnano.

He has taken part in some collective exhibitions in Paris: at the Salon des Réalités Nouvelles from 1949; fairly regularly at the Salon de Mai; and at the Salon Comparaisons since 1961. He exhibited in New York in 1947, Paris in 1948, Copenhagen in 1950 and Lausanne in 1954. In 1960, he was awarded the UFIB Grand Prix at the exhibition *Some Italian Painters Living in Paris*.

FALCHINI, Giovanni
Italian, 19th century.
Born 1790, in Montorio al Vomano (Abruzzo); died in San Benedetto del Tronto (Marches).
Painter (enamel), draughtsman. Portraits.

Giovanni Falchini's best known work is a copy of Raphael's *Transfiguration*.

FALCIANI, Paolo
Italian, 19th century.
Born c. 1780, in Samo; died 18 February 1872, in Naples.
Painter.

Paolo Falciani taught at the institute of fine arts in Naples.

FALCIANO, Rocco
Italian, 20th century.
Born 30 November 1933, in Potenza.
Painter. Interiors with figures, landscapes, landscapes with figures, still-lifes, flowers, fruit. Murals.

Rocco Falciano was a regular visitor to Marino Mazzacurati's studio in Rome from 1963 to 1965. In 1965, he worked in collaboration with Ettore de Conciliis on a mural for the church of S Francesco in Avellino. He later produced other murals in Mantua and Trappeto. In 1969, he began teaching at a high school for the arts in Frosinone before moving to a similar institution in Rome in 1975. In 1972, he was a founder member of the Gruppo Arte Pubblica Popolare (Public Popular Art group), along with Ettore de Conciliis, Wendy Fieldman and Pio Valeriani.

Falciano's works come from a well-established figurative tradition. His luminous, immobile interiors, depicted as momentary snapshots, are executed with precision and lightness, particularly in the case of his watercolours. The human figure is excluded from his works: indicators of their presence, close to but outside the canvas, are the only things that seem to count. His still-lifes have neutral backgrounds, and tend to show very few elements at a time: oranges in a bowl, some sparse medlars or some apples on a plate. Beneath an appearance of simplicity, the artist often gives his works greater complexity, summoning up where necessary the charms of nature.

He has taken part in various collective exhibitions, including *One Hundred Painters for Socialism* at the Parco Ruffini in Turin (1971). He has also shown his works in some solo exhibitions, including the Spazio gallery in Rome (1976); the Italian Institute of Culture in Toronto (1979); the Trifalco gallery in Rome (1980); the Modulo gallery in Terni (1982); and *Watercolours 1980-1992* at the Indicatore gallery in Rome (1993).

FALCIATORE, Filippo
Italian, 18th century.
Born 1718, in Naples; died 1768, in Naples.

Painter, fresco artist. Religious subjects, genre scenes. Initially a pupil of Paolo de Matteis, Falciatore later studied under D.A. Vaccaro. He is noted for his frescoes at the palace of the dukes of Monteleone and Brunasso in Naples, the *Sacrifice of Elijah* in the sacristy of the Carmine, and his picture of the *Virgin with St Sebastian, St Charles Borromeo and St Amelia*. He also produced small history paintings and genre scenes. A *Revolt in Naples* was exhibited in 1877.

MUSEUMS AND GALLERIES:

LINZ (Gal.): *Moses Saved from the Waters*.

AUCTION RECORDS:

MILAN, 30 Nov 1982, *Figure Studies* (pen, 12 x 10 ins / 30.5 x 25.3 cm) ITL 1,600,000. MILAN, 21 May 1991, *Rustic Concert; Society Concert* (oil on canvas, a pair, oval, each 23¾ x 17 ins / 60.5 x 43 cm) ITL 192,100,000. NEW YORK, 17 Jan 1992, *Fashionable Figures Dancing, Walking in a Garden, Talking* (oil on canvas/card, series of four oval panels, each 25¼ x 19¼ ins / 64.1 x 48.9 cm) USD 165,000. ROME, 21 Nov 1995, *Annunciation* (oil/copper, 13½ x 11 ins / 34 x 27 cm) ITL 24,748,000. LONDON, 3-4 Dec 1997, *Elegantly Dressed Men Sitting Outside an Inn* (oil on canvas, 30 x 40 ins / 76 x 101.7 cm) GBP 52,100. ROME, 4 Dec 2000, *Erminia's Dream* (oil on canvas, attributed, 15x15 ins / 38x38 cm) ITL 9,000,000. BERLIN, 18 May 2001, *Fallen Figures* (pen and wash over chalk, 10x9 ins / 26x22 cm) DEM 2,200. LONDON, 11 July 2001, *Elegant Company at a Fair with a Fortune Teller* (oil on canvas, 24x36 ins / 61x91 cm) GBP 20,000. ROME, 12 Dec 2001, *Rinaldo Leaving Armida* (oil on canvas, 44x35 ins / 113x89 cm) ITL 50,000,000.

FALCIERI, Biagio

Italian, 17th century.
Born 1628, in Brentonico (Trentino-Alto Adige); died 1703, in Verona.
Painter, engraver.

Falcieri worked under Locatelli in Verona, and Pietro Liberi in Venice. Only one engraving by him is known, a *St Jerome in the Wilderness*. His most notable pictures include a large history painting of the *Council of Trent* in the Dominican chapel in Verona. The upper part of the scene features *St Thomas Triumphing over the Heretics*.

FALCINI, Bettina

Maiden name: Battista Hartmann
Swiss, 19th century.
Born 1805, in Lucerne.
Draughtswoman.

Falcini drew an *Idyll* (in the collection of Mr Karl Mahler in Lucerne). The art society in Lucerne also has one of her drawings, which dates from 1822.

FALCINI, Domenico

Italian, 16th century.
Active in Siena at the end of the 16th century.
Engraver.

Domenico Falcini made wood engravings in the style of Raphael and other masters. He also worked in metal. One of his plates is signed *DFF* and all the others bear his monogram *D.F.F.*

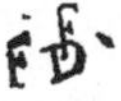

FALCINI, Louis

Brazilian, 20th century.
Born in Buenos Aires.
Sculptor.

Falcini was a member of the Sociedade Nacional de Belas Artes.

FALCK, Bernard

German, 17th century.
Active in Saarbrücken.
Sculptor.

In 1611, Falck created a large crucifix and a cross for the rood screen of the church in Bitche (Lorraine), France.

FALCK, Jeremias. See **FALK**

FALCK, Martin

German, 16th century.
Draughtsman.

Martin Falck illustrated part of a manuscript from the monastery of Etenheim with drawings in pen and ink. The manuscript is kept in the regional library at Karlsruhe.

FALCK, Steffen

German, 17th century.
Active in Pforzheim.
Sculptor.

FALCKE, Tobias, or Falke

German, 19th century.
Active in Nuremberg.
Engraver.

In addition to producing printing plates, Falcke made a copy of *Faith, Hope and Charity* by H.M. Hess, signed *T. Falke*; a *Portrait of Duke Alexander Frederick Christian of Anhalt Bernburg*, signed *Falke*, a *Portrait of Tsarina Alexandra Feodorovna* and a *Portrait of Prince Paskevitch-Erivanski* as well as many other portraits of the Russian and Polish nobility.

FALCKEISEN, Theodor, or Falkeisen

Swiss, 18th - 19th century.
Born 1765, in Basel; died 1814, in Basel.
Draughtsman, engraver (burin).

A pupil of Holzhall, Mechel and Ch. Guttenberg, Falckeisen's best-known engravings include: *Study of a Tree, Nightmare*, after Henry Fuseli (Johann Heinrich Füssli), and *Death of General Wolfe*, after Benjamin West, an engraving Falckeisen produced during his stay in London.

FALCKENBURG. See **VALKENBORCH**

FALCKENER, Johann, or Falckner

German, 18th century.
Born at the beginning of the 18th century, in Augsburg.
Painter.

Johann Falckener worked with his brother Polycarp at the academy of art in Vienna.

FALCKENER, Polycarp

German, 18th century.
Born at the beginning of the 18th century, in Augsburg or in Bude.
Painter.

A pupil at the academy of art in Vienna in 1728, Polycarp Falckener may also have studied under Peter Strude.

FALCO, Angelo

Italian, 17th century.
Born 1600, in Naples; died 1665.
Painter, engraver (etching).

A rather crude and clumsily executed etching bears the name of Angelo Falco, depicting the story of Apollo and Daphne. The drawing is extremely faulty, and the style indifferent, but it does seem to be the work of a painter. Falco was a pupil of Giuseppe Ribera. His signature is also found on three further etchings: *Sirens, Naiads and Tritons, A Philosopher's Tomb*, and *Naked Men in Combat*. He has often been confused with Aniello Falcone, notably by Nagler.

FALCO, Carlo de

Italian, 19th century.
Born 26 November 1798, in Naples; died 15 October 1882, in Pagani (Salerno).
Painter. Portraits.

Carlo de Falco started out as a pupil of his father, Filippo de Falco, before becoming a student of Angelini at the institute of fine arts in Naples. He exhibited a *Portrait of Queen Isabella de Bourbon* in 1826, and was subsequently appointed court painter. He also painted portraits of *Francis I*, the royal princes, *Marie-Christine of Savoy*, and various other personalities, including *The Minister Marquis Tanucci; General Clary; Captain D'Andrea;* and *The Poet Giulio Genoino.*

FALCO, Félix
Italian, 17th century.
Born 17th century, in Valenza (Piedmont).
Painter. Genre scenes.
Pupil of Espinosa, his works are to be found in Venice.

FALCO, Filippo de
Italian, 19th century.
Born 1852, in Naples; died 1891.
Painter. Genre scenes, landscapes.
Filippo de Falco started out as a student at the Accademia in Naples. When he finished his education, he devoted himself to genre and landscape painting. In Naples in 1877, he exhibited a painting entitled *Lake at Dusk*, whose diffuse light and hazy reflections earned him critical acclaim.

He sent *In the Countryside* to an exhibition in Rome in 1883, *Luisa* to Turin in the same year, and *The Newspaper of Everywhere* to Venice in 1887.

AUCTION RECORDS:
ROME, 31 May 1990, *Woman in a Garden* (oil on canvas, 11 x 16 1/2 ins / 27 x 42 cm) ITL 4,000,000. ROME, 4 Dec 1990, *Town Hall Square in Naples* (oil on panel, 11 3/4 x 14 3/4 ins / 30 x 37.5 cm) ITL 3,000,000.

FALCO, Giuseppe de
Italian, 19th century.
Miniaturist.
Giuseppe de Falco painted a *Madonna of the Graces*, which was exhibited in Naples in 1877, and two *Portraits*, which were shown in Turin in 1884.

FALCO, Juan. See **CONCHILLOS Y FALCO**

FALCO, Nicola de
Italian, 17th century.
Died 8 October 1700.
Painter.
Nicola de Falco was admitted to the painters' guild in Naples in 1683.

FALCÓ, Nicolás, the Elder
Spanish, 16th century.
Painter.
In 1502 Nicolás Falcó worked on the high altars of the monastery of S Clara and Isabella in Valencia. He participated in the works of the cathedral chapter and painted *Our Lady of Wisdom* for the university chapel. He often completed the works of the Master of Perea.

MUSEUMS AND GALLERIES:
VALENCIA: *Scenes from the Life of the Virgin.*

FALCÓ, Nicolás, the Younger
Spanish, 16th century.
Painter.
Valencian School.
Nicolás Falcó was the son of Onofre Falcó whom he succeeded as painter of the kingdom of Valencia on 9 March 1560.

FALCÓ, Onofre
Spanish, 16th century.
Painter.
Valencian School.
In 1556 Onofre Falcó succeeded Juan Cardona as painter of the kingdom of Valencia. He was the father of Nicolas Falcó the Younger.

FALCO, Paolo di
Italian, 18th century.
Active in Naples.
Priest, painter.
A pupil of Solimena, he painted frescoes for the churches of Naples and the surrounding region, as well as a great many religious pictures. He exhibited an allegorical painting glorifying the Bourbon Prince Charles III upon the latter's entry into Naples.

FALCO, Pietro
Italian, 17th century.
Born to a family originally from Savoy; died 1616, in Rome.
Painter.

FALCON, Bartolomeo
Spanish, 15th century.
Active in Seville.
Painter.

FALCON, Carlos (Brother)
Spanish.
Painter.
He was a Franciscan monk and worked in the Aranzazu monastery in Guipúzcoa.

FALCON, Nicola
Italian, 15th century.
Of Venetian origin.
Painter.
Paduan School.
In 1441, Nicola Falcon was a member of the guild of Padua.

FALCON DE CIMIER (Mme)
Maiden name: Laporte
French, 19th century.
Active in Paris.
Painter.
Falcon de Cimier became a member of the Société des Artistes Français in 1888.

FALCONE, Andrea
Italian, 17th century.
Born c. 1630, in Naples; died c. 1675, in Naples.
Sculptor.
Great-nephew of the painter Aniello Falcone, Andrea was initially a pupil of Fansago, and studied later in Rome. His works include a number of marble statues in Naples: *Madonna, Charity and Mercy* at Monte della Misericordia, and four marbles of *Prudence, Temperance, Indulgence* and *Justice* at S Paolo Maggiore. Together with other sculptors, Falcone initiated a new genre which became a Neapolitan speciality in the 18th century - that of Christmas crib figures.

FALCONE, Aniello or Angelo, called l'Oracolo delle Battaglie
Italian, 17th century.
Born 1607, in Naples; died 1656, in Naples.
Painter, fresco artist, engraver, draughtsman. Religious subjects, allegorical subjects, genre scenes, battles, landscapes.
Neapolitan School.
Son of Vincenzo Falcone, Aniello was a pupil of Giuseppe Ribera, known as Il Spagnoletto. He was captain of the so-called 'Compania della Morte' (the Company of Death), during the Masaniello uprising in Naples in 1647 against Spanish rule; after the suppression of the revolt and Masaniello's assassination, he took refuge in France, where he was given a warm welcome by Louis XIV's finance minister (and patron of the arts) Jean-Baptiste Colbert. Falcone gained an enviable reputation, and a sizable fortune, before returning to Naples, where he founded an influential school of painting whose pupils included the pre-Romantic Salvatore Rosa.

Most his surviving works (scarce and highly valued) are in France. Falcone was a particularly accomplished painter of battles and cavalry skirmishes. His best works in the genre are second only to those of Borgognone. He also produced a number of religious compositions, such as the *Rest on the Flight into Egypt* for the cathedral in Naples, *St Lucy Distributing Alms*, and a *Virgin and Child*. He is also noted for his frescoes at S Paolo Maggiore and the Gesù Nuovo. He produced 20 engravings, including *Apollo and Mars* after Parmigianino, the *Adoration of the Magi* after Raphael, and *St George and the Dragon*. He inherited Caravaggio's technique of representing sacred scenes in terms of everyday reality, thereby conveying the Christian message to those that the established church had come to overlook - the humblest, most dispossessed members of society. His Caravaggism is nonetheless tempered by the influence of Roman painters of *bambocciate* (burlesque rustic scenes). Influenced by Caravaggio, and familiar with the Italian paintings of Velázquez, he had a profound influence on the Neapolitan school, and an indirect influence on the work of Bernardo Cavallino.

Museums and Galleries:
Bourges: *Martyrdom of St Barbara* - Madrid (Prado): *Combat between Turks and Christians; Roman Soldiers Entering the Circus; Concert* - Naples (Mus. di Capodimonte): *Rest on the Flight into Egypt; St Lucy Distributing Alms; Battle Scene* (two works); *Studies for a Head of David, and a Child* (drawing) - St-Marin: *Battle* (two works).
Auction records:
Milan, 11 May 1966, *St Lucy*, ITL 6,200,000. London, 3 Dec 1969, *Battle Scene*, GBP 5,800. Milan, 17 Dec 1971, *Battle Scene*, ITL 6,500,000. Vienna, 12 March 1974, *Amazons Fighting*, ATS 50,000. London, 7 July 1981, *Landscape with Trees and a Waterwheel* (red chalk/paper, 6 1/4 x 8 1/2 ins / 15.9 x 21.7 cm) GBP 1,800. New York, 6 June 1984, *Army Attacking a Town* (oil on canvas, 40 1/4 x 61 ins / 102 x 155 cm) USD 23,000. London, 4 July 1984, *The Bronze Serpent* (red chalk and wash, 8 x 10 1/2 ins / 20.1 x 26.6 cm) GBP 1,700. London, 22 May 1985, *Virgin and Child* (oil on canvas, 22 x 16 1/2 ins / 55 x 42 cm) GBP 5,800. London, 26 June 1985, *St George and the Dragon* (etching, 6 x 10 ins / 15.5 x 25.2 cm) GBP 750. London, 8 Dec 1987, *Landscape with Trees and a Waterwheel* (red chalk, 6 1/4 x 8 1/2 ins / 15.9 x 21.7 cm) GBP 1,800. Monaco, 16 June 1989, *Battle Scenes* (oil on canvas, two pendants, each 40 1/2 x 56 1/4 ins / 103 x 143 cm) FRF 377,400. Amelia, 18 May 1990, *Joshua Making the Sun Disappear During the Battle of Gabaon* (oil on canvas, 24 3/4 x 29 3/4 ins / 63 x 75.5 cm) ITL 30,000,000. New York, 10 Oct 1991, *Battle Scene* (oil on canvas, circular and square canvases, 59 1/4 x 59 1/4 ins / 150.5 x 150.5 cm) USD 77,000. New York, 17 Jan 1992, *Cleopatra Fleeing the Battle of Actium* (oil on canvas, 34 1/2 x 44 1/2 ins / 87.6 x 113 cm) USD 27,500. Milan, 3 Dec 1992, *Battle Scene* (oil on canvas, 30 1/4 x 36 1/2 ins / 77 x 93 cm) ITL 60,000,000. Rome, 22 Nov 1994, *Battle of Ponte Milvio* (oil on canvas, 49 1/2 x 61 ins / 126 x 154 cm) ITL 86,250,000. Rome, 9 May 1995, *Battle of Clavijo* (oil on canvas, 50 x 60 1/4 ins / 127 x 153 cm) ITL 89,700,000. London, 2 July 1996, *A Battle* (black chalk, ink and wash, 5 x 10 ins / 12.8 x 25.2 cm) GBP 1,610. London, 7 July 1999, *Study of Male Nude with Left Arm Outstretched, Facing Left* (red chalk, 10x7 ins / 25x19 cm) GBP 1,050. London, 14 Dec 2000, *Cavalry Engagement between Turks and Christians* (oil on canvas, 29x44 ins / 74x113 cm) GBP 30,000. Rome, 7 June 2001, *Jerusalem under Siege* (oil on canvas, 41x51 ins / 104x130 cm) ITL 145,000,000. New York, 23 Jan 2003, *Standing Oriental Salesman* (red chalk, 8x4 ins / 21x11 cm) USD 600. London, 12 Dec 2003, *Five Women; Kneeling Man* (red chalk, double-sided, 7x6 ins / 19x14 cm) GBP 900. New York, 29 Jan 2004, *Cavalry Skirmish; Portrait Study* (pen and brown ink, red chalk, double-sided, 5x8 ins / 12x20 cm) USD 1,000.

FALCONE, Bernardo
Swiss, 17th century.
Born 17th century, to a family originally from Lugano (Ticino), Switzerland.
Sculptor, caster.
Many of Falcone's works are in Venice, including his statues of the *Virgin* and of *St Dominic* above the high altar in the church of SS Giovanni e Paolo; the statues of *St Theodore with Four Angels* on the façade of the school of St Theodore; and four bronze statues in the church of the Frari. In Padua, the church of St Justine also has several of his works.

FALCONE, Giovanni, or Falconi
Italian, 15th century.
Active in the first half of the 15th century.
Miniaturist.
Giovanni Falcone was employed about 1434 by Niccòlo III d'Este. A manuscript of the *Commentaries of Caesar*, now in the Biblioteca Estense in Modena (Emilia Romagna), is decorated with 14 miniatures by Falcone.

FALCONE, Nicola
Italian, 17th century.
Active in Naples.
Painter.
Relative of Aniello Falcone. He was also an architect, and designed the façade of S Maria Maddalena in Naples.

FALCONE, Pietro
Italian, 17th century.
Died c. 1656; of plague.
Painter.
Active in Naples, he was apprenticed to Aniello Falcone.

FALCONE, Silvio
Italian, 16th century.
Born 16th century, to a family originally from Magliano Sabina (Lazio).
Sculptor.
Silvio Falcone worked with Michelangelo.

FALCONE, Tommaso dal
Italian, 16th century.
Sculptor.
In 1542, Tommaso dal Falcone took part in the construction of the church of S Domenico in Bologna.

FALCONE, Vincenzo
Italian, 17th century.
Died 1648.
Active in Naples.
Painter, gilder.

FALCONER, György. See **FALKONER**

FALCONER, John M.
British, 19th century.
Born 22 May 1820, in Edinburgh; died 12 March 1903, in New York.
Active in the USA.
Painter, watercolourist, engraver. Architectural views.
John M. Falconer went to the USA and trained at the National Academy of Design in New York. He travelled a great deal in Europe and enjoyed reproducing numerous historical monuments from the old and new continents in his paintings. Watercolours, paintings on porcelain, enamels and etchings are also attributed to him. He was a member of the American Watercolors Society.
Auction records:
San Francisco, 21 June 1984, *Washington's Home, Newburgh, New York* (oil on card, 8 1/4 x 12 1/4 ins / 21 x 31 cm)

USD 1,800. NEW YORK, 3 Dec 1996, *William Penn's House, Philadelphia* (1864, watercolour and paper/paper/card, 17 1/4 x 23 1/2 ins / 43.8 x 59.7 cm) USD 4,600.

FALCONET, Étienne Maurice

French, 18th century.
Born 1 December 1716, in Paris; died 24 January 1791, in Paris.
Sculptor, draughtsman. Allegorical subjects, nudes. Groups, statues, statuettes.

Étienne Maurice Falconet may be considered as one of the masters of French Neo-Classical sculpture in the 18th century. A pupil of Lemoyne, he was recognised quite quickly, as the date on which he was elected to the Académie (29 August 1744) shows. He made his debut at the Salon in 1745 with a plaster maquette, *Milo of Crotona Devoured by a Lion*, a subject which he reworked in marble ten years later for his diploma work at the Académie. Between these two dates he mainly exhibited Classical models and allegories such as *The Genius of Sculpture, Science, Music* and *The Four Seasons*. The success obtained by his *Milo of Crotona* was confirmed by his *Pygmalion at the Feet of his Statue*, one of his best works and one into which he put the most charm and personality.

He had known Mme d'Étiolles, the future Mme de Pompadour and mistress of Louis XV, for whom he executed the group *Music* in 1751. The sculpture, now in the Louvre, was intended for her Château de Bellevue, and depicts her in the role of Egle, which she had played before the King. Falconet retained Mme de Pompadour's favour and she commissioned other works from him, including *The Threatening Cupid* of 1757. She asked him to direct the sculpture studio of the ceramics factory called the Manufacture de Sèvres, which she had founded at the far end of her park. Until 1766 Falconet supplied about 100 patterns, either originals or after Boucher, for the production of highly prized 'bisques'. The writer and philosopher Diderot felt his group *Pygmalion and Galathea* of 1763 to be an unsurpassable masterpiece.

Among the other statues by Falconet, mention should be made of *Christ in Agony* (church of St-Roch), *Woman Bathing*, and *Sweet Melancholy*. The vogue he enjoyed caused him to be appointed successively as assistant professor on 5 July 1755, professor on 7 March 1761 and assistant rector on 26 April 1783. In the meantime, in 1766, Catherine II of Russia had summoned him to St Petersburg to execute the colossal statue of Peter the Great. However, the Empress paid rather poorly and Falconet left Russia in 1778 or 1781 to return to Paris. Noting the change in taste which had taken place in his absence, he decided to give up sculpture. He devoted the rest of his life to writing numerous works on art.

Falconet was undoubtedly a great artist, and a sculptor of considerable skill who was well served by a deep knowledge of drawing.

In 2001 the Musée de la Céramique de Sèvres devoted an exhibition to him on the theme of *Falconet ou l'Art de plaire* (*Falconet or the Art of Pleasing*), bringing together a large number of statuettes in bisque.

BIBLIOGRAPHY:

Weinshenker, A. B., *Falconet: His Writings and his Friend Diderot*, Geneva, 1966. Sahut, M.-C./Volle, N. (eds.), *Diderot et l'Art de Boucher à David, pp. 448-454*, exhibition catalogue, Hôtel de la Monnaie, Paris, 1984-1985. Faÿ-Hallé, Antoinette/Pinot de Villechenon, Marie-Noëlle/Scherf, Guilhem, et al., *Falconet à Sèvres 1757-1766 ou l'Art de plaire*, exhibition catalogue, Musée national de la Céramique, Sèvres, Réunion des musées nationaux, Paris, 2001.

MUSEUMS AND GALLERIES:

ANGERS: *Bust of Dr Camille Falconet* (marble) - BAGNOLS: *Woman Bathing* - BAYONNE (Mus. Bonnat): *Painting* (terracotta, statuette) - BERLIN: *Cupids and a Billy-goat; Dancer* (bronze) - CHÂLONS-EN-CHAMPAGNE: *Woman Bathing* - FRANKFURT AM MAIN (Liebighaus): *Girl* (gilt bronze) - LA ROCHELLE: *Woman Bathing; Woman Sensitive to the Cold* - LIBOURNE: *Allegory* - LYONS: *Bust of Dr Camille Falconet* (marble) - PARIS (Louvre): *Mask of a Man* (terracotta); *Flora* (marble, seated statuette); *Music* (marble); *Woman Bathing* (marble, statuette); *The Threatening Cupid* (marble); *Milo of Crotona* (red marble) - PARIS (Mus. Jacquemart-André): *The Glory of Catherine II* (marble) - SENS: *Woman Bathing* - ST PETERSBURG (Hermitage): *Pygmalion* (marble, group).

AUCTION RECORDS:

PARIS, 21-22 Feb 1919, *First Plan for the Statue of Peter the Great* (sepia) FRF 150. PARIS, 8-10 June 1920, *Plan for a Group* (red chalk) FRF 520. PARIS, 1-2 Dec 1932, *Cupid Asks Venus to Return his Quiver* (terracotta, group) FRF 67,000; *Venus Correcting Love* (white marble, group) FRF 210,000; *Young Woman* (white marble, statuette) FRF 60,000. PARIS, 10 Dec 1964, *Venus Breastfeeding Love* (terracotta) FRF 14,000. PARIS, 14 June 1983, *Male Study* (red chalk, 13 1/2 x 14 3/4 ins / 34.5 x 37.5 cm) FRF 7,500. GENEVA, 24 Nov 1985, *Study of a Man Seen from Behind* (lead pencil heightened with white/grey paper, 22 3/4 x 16 1/2 ins / 58 x 42 cm) CHF 6,500. PARIS, 28 June 1988, *Love Punished* (1760, white marble, h. 19 ins / 48 cm) FRF 15,500. LOKEREN, 10 Oct 1992, *Woman Bathing* (brown-patinated bronze, h. 32 ins / 81 cm, w. 9 3/4 ins/25 cm) BEF 80,000. PARIS, 12 July 1993, *Hunting; Fishing* (1788, stone, a pair, 74 3/4 x 76 3/4 ins / 190 x 195 cm and 74 3/4 x 70 3/4 ins/190 x 180 cm) FRF 800,000. LOKEREN, 9 Dec 1995, *Woman Bathing* (bronze, h. 20 1/4 ins / 51.5 cm) BEF 50,000. ANTWERP, 22 March 1999, *The Bather* (white marble, 33 ins / 83 cm) BEF 85,000. MONACO, 28 April 2000, *Woman Seated in Neo-classical Style* (1760-1770, terracotta, 5 x 27x8 ins / 12 x 69x21 cm) FRF 380,000. PARIS, 20 June 2001, *Woman Seated Naked with Draped Cloth* (brown patinated bronze, 11 ins / 28 cm) FRF 16,000. VIENNA, 29 April 2002, *Standing Female Nude* (brown patinated bronze, 32 ins / 81 cm) EUR 2,400. PARIS, 3 Dec 2003, *Love among Doves. Young Girl with Basket of Flowers* (1753, terracotta, a pair, 7 ins / 17 cm) EUR 18,500. ILKLEY, 16 June 2004, *Female Bather* (brown and green patinated bronze, 32 ins / 81 cm) GBP 2,500.

FALCONET, György. See **FALKONER**

FALCONET, Jean François

French, 18th century.
Active in Paris.
Sculptor.

Jean François Falconet became a member of the Académie de St-Luc on 23 September 1742.

FALCONET, Marie Anne (Mrs). See **COLLOT**

FALCONET, Pierre Étienne

French, 18th century.
Born 1741; died 25 June 1791, in Paris.
Active also in England.
Painter. Portraits.

Pierre Étienne Falconet was the son of Étienne Maurice Falconet and survived his father by only a few months. He studied painting in England under Reynolds and soon became one of the most well-known portraitists in London. He was made a member of the Incorporated Society of Artists in 1766, to whose exhibitions he sent a large number of portraits between 1767 and 1773. He also exhibited at the Royal Academy. He is known to have painted some historical compositions. He returned to France around 1778 and his return seems to have coincided with his father's. It also seems probable that he married Marie Anne Collot after this return.

AUCTION RECORDS:
PARIS, 8-9 Dec 1919, *Young Woman Seated on a Stone Plinth* (pencil) FRF 380. PARIS, 18 Nov 1920, *Miss Harriet Parrot*, FRF 10,900. PARIS, 15 Dec 1922, *Young Woman Seated on a Stone Plinth* (pencil heightened with white) FRF 280. NEW YORK, 20 Nov 1931, *Child Playing with Cards*, USD 275. PARIS, 22 Feb 1934, *Study of a Statue of a Clothed Woman, Left Profile, and Two Children* (red chalk, attributed) FRF 120. LONDON, 10 Dec 1943, *A Woman*, GBP 357. PARIS, 26 March 1974, *Portrait of Miss Nanette Thellusson*, FRF 25,000. PARIS, 25 June 1996, *Portrait of Miss Nanette Thellusson* (1768, oil on canvas, 28 x 26 ins / 71 x 66 cm) FRF 200,000. LONDON, 2 July 1996, *Self-portrait* (1764, graphite and black chalk/primed paper, 4 1/4 x 3 3/4 ins / 10.9 x 9.4 cm) GBP 2,300. PARIS, 21 Nov 2001, *Head of an Emperor* (red chalk, 10 x 5 ins / 25 x 13 cm) FRF 32,000.

FALCONET, Pierre François
French, 18th century.
Active in Paris.
Sculptor.

FALCONETTI, Angelo
Italian, 16th century.
Died before 1572.
Painter, engraver (etching).
Angelo Falconetti lived and worked in the Trentino. His key works are the frescoes of a tabernacle in the church of S Roch at Rovereto and some etchings: *The Young Tobias and the Archangel*; *Apollo and Daphne* and *Judas and Tamar*.

FALCONETTI, Antonio I
Italian, 15th century.
Painter.
Antonio Falconetti I was the half-brother of Stefano di Verona and probably lived in Beverara.

FALCONETTI, Antonio II
Italian, 16th century.
Born c. 1531.
Active in Verona.
Painter.
Antonio Falconetti II married several times, and one of his wives was Margherita Marangoni.

FALCONETTI, Bartholus. See **BARTHOLUS**

FALCONETTI, Giambattista
Italian, 16th - 17th century.
Born c. 1574; died before 1625.
Painter.
Giambattista Falconetti lived in Beverara and decorated a few rooms in the canonry of S Lorenzo. None of his works has survived.

FALCONETTI, Jacopo
Italian, 15th century.
Born c. 1447.
Active in Beverara.
Painter.

FALCONETTI, Jacopo
Italian, 17th century.
Active in Beverara (near Bologna) c. 1600.
Painter.
The son of Giacomo Falconetti, Jacopo assisted his father in decorative works at the canonry of St Lawrence.

FALCONETTI, Margherita
Maiden name: Marangoni
Italian, 16th century.
Born c. 1539; died before 1600.
Painter.
Margherita Falconetti was the wife of Antonio Falconetti II, whom she assisted.

FALCONETTI, Ottaviano
Italian, 16th century.
Born c. 1508.
Active in Verona.
Painter, decorative designer.
Ottaviano Falconetti was probably the son of Gian Maria Falconetto. He carried out works in stucco.

FALCONETTI, Provolo
Italian, 16th century.
Born c. 1502.
Active in Beverara.
Painter, decorative designer, potter.

FALCONETTI, Stefano
Italian, 17th century.
Born c. 1582.
Active in Beverara (near Bologna).
Painter.

FALCONETTI, Tomaso
Italian, 16th century.
Active in Verona and the Trentino.
Painter.

FALCONETTO, Gian Antonio
Italian, 15th century.
Born c. 1470, in Verona; died in Roveredo.
Painter.
Gian Antonio Falconetto was the pupil of his father Jacopo Falconetto, nephew of Stefano da Verona. He mostly painted fruit and animals, and some of his works survive in and around Verona.

FALCONETTO, Gian Maria or Giovanni Maria
Italian, 15th - 16th century.
Born c. 1458 or 1468, in Verona; died 1534, in Padua.
Painter, fresco artist, draughtsman, architect. Religious subjects, allegorical subjects. Church decoration.
Veronese School.
Gian Maria Falconetto was the brother of Gian Antonio and was also instructed by their father, Jacopo Falconetto; he was probably the father of Ottaviano Falconetti. After dedicating the first part of his life to painting, he turned his attention to architecture and was employed by Alvise Cornaro (Corner) in Padua, where most of his architectural works are to be found. He was a successor to Liberale and imitator of Melozzo da Forlì, decorating a number of churches in Verona.

Falconetto's skill as an architect is evident in his handling of perspective, in particular the decoration of the dome and drum of the chapel of S Biagio in the church of S Nazaro e Celso. He is best known for his religious allegories, executed between 1509 and 1516, in the church of S Pietro Martire in Verona. His frescoes survive: a *Virgin and Child with St Augustine and St Joseph*, painted in 1523 at the basilica of S Giuseppe, Verona and an *Annunciation* at the church of S Zeno Maggiore di Verona.

BIBLIOGRAPHY:
Carpeggiani, P., '*Giovanni Maria Falconetto: Temi ed eventi di una nuova architettura civile*' in *Padova, case e palazzi, eds L. Puppi/F. Zuliani*, Neri Pozza, Vicenza, 1977.

MUSEUMS AND GALLERIES:
BERLIN: *The Assumption* - VERONA (Pinacoteca): *Augustus and the Sibyl*.

AUCTION RECORDS:
MONACO, 2 July 1993, *The Temptation of Christ in the Wilderness* (brown ink, 6 1/4 x 9 1/4 ins / 16.1 x 23.3 cm) FRF 11,100.

FALCONI, Bernardo di Nello di Giovanni, or Vanni
Italian, 14th century.
Active at the end of the 14th century.
Painter.

Bernardo Falconi studied in the workshop of Andrea Orcagna in Pisa, where he executed a series of altarpieces for the cathedral. Supino attributes to him the frescoes of the Campo Santo in Pisa and the paintings of two saints (in the municipal museum of Pisa).

FALCONI, Giovanni. See **FALCONE**

FALCONNIER, Léon

French, 19th century.

Born 10 March 1811, in Ancy-le-Franc (Yonne); died 1876.

Painter, pastellist, sculptor.

After serving a brief apprenticeship in Michel Picquenot's Caen studio, Léon Falconnier joined the Paris École des Beaux-Arts. In 1837 he started a painting course run by Michel Drolling while at the same time studying sculpture with Étienne Ramey and later Augustin Dumont. He exhibited at the Paris Salon from 1841 to 1874, receiving a third-class medal in 1851.

Falconnier was involved in the decoration of the church of the Madeleine in Paris and then the Arc de Triomphe de l'Étoile. He executed several paintings, such as his *St Sebastian*, but he made his career primarily as a sculptor. His best-known works include *Stella Salutis* (*Virgin*); *Mucius Scoevola*; *Jesus Chasing the Merchants from the Temple*; *Peace in Strength*; and some marble groups and statues such as *Cain Cursed* and *Young Burgundian Woman*.

MUSEUMS AND GALLERIES:

AUXERRE: *Cain Cursed* (marble); *President Lincoln Freeing the American Slaves*.

FALCOU, Jacques

French, 20th century.

Born 9 May 1912, in Neuilly-sur-Seine; died 26 March 1975, in Paris.

Painter (gouache), lithographer, illustrator. Figures, portraits, still-lifes, flowers, landscapes, seascapes.

Jacques Falcou, the son of Raphael Falcou, was a pupil of Lucien Simon at the École des Beaux-Arts, Paris. From 1934 to 1942 he taught art in the schools of Paris. In 1937 he was selected to compete for the Prix de Rome. He served in World War II and was awarded the Croix de Guerre and the Resistance Medal. He exhibited in group exhibitions in the provinces, abroad and in Paris: from 1932 at the Salon des Artistes Français, of which he was a member, and at the Expositions Universelles of 1937 and 1938, where he won silver medals. He also exhibited at the Salon de la Société Nationale des Beaux-Arts and the Salon d'Automne, of which he was a member. He won several prizes, including the Institute's Prix Roux. He held solo exhibitions in Paris in 1943 and 1968, and in various cities in the USA and Switzerland. As an illustrator he contributed to the encyclopedias published by Jean Grassin: 1970 *Windmills*, 1971 *The Moon*, 1972 *The Native Country*, 1973 *Happiness*.

Technically, he paints by juxtaposing thick, sensuous strokes, generally slightly different in colour, one providing a generalised colour, the other, lighter and warmer, lighting up objects, or, deeper and colder, forming the shadows. Like many painters of his generation, on the one hand he treated various traditional subjects, on the other, going beyond the influence of Late Impressionism, he turned to Cézanne for inspiration, with occasional incursions, especially in still-lifes, into the calm Cubism of Georges Braque.

BIBLIOGRAPHY:

Barotte, René, *Falcou*, Éd. de la Revue moderne, Paris, 1981.

AUCTION RECORDS:

CANNES, 29 Jan 1981, *Les Martigues* (oil on canvas, 19 3/4 x 24 3/4 ins / 50 x 63 cm) FRF 2,400.

FALCOU, Pierre Jean

French, 20th century.

Born in Paris.

Painter. Landscapes.

Pierre Jean Falcou, a painter mainly of Breton landscapes, exhibited at the Salon des Artistes Indépendants from 1925.

FALCOU, Raphaël

French, 19th - 20th century.

Born 1862, in Paris; died 1949.

Painter. Landscapes.

Raphael Falcou, the father of Jacques Falcou, exhibited in Paris at the Salon de la Société Nationale des Beaux-Arts from 1921. He was director of the Beaux-Arts and Commissioner for Festivals of the City of Paris.

FALCOYANO, Alesi J.

Romanian, 19th century.

Born 19th century, in Bucharest.

Painter, engraver. Portraits.

Alesi Falcojano's work featured in the Exposition Universelle of 1900 in Paris, where she received a commendation.

AUCTION RECORDS:

PARIS, 7 April 1987, *Portrait of Three Children* (1896, oil on canvas, 21 1/4 x 32 ins / 54 x 81 cm) FRF 14,000.

FALCOZ, Alphonse Auguste

French, 19th century.

Born 19 April 1813, in Paris.

Painter. History painting, portraits.

Alphonse Auguste Falcoz was a pupil at the École des Beaux-Arts in 1837 and a student of Léon Cogniet. He made his Salon début in 1840, exhibiting portraits and religious paintings there until 1846.

FALCUCCI, Robert

French, 20th century.

Born 10 April 1900, in Châteauroux; died 13 May 1989, in St-Aubin-Châteauneuf.

Painter, watercolourist, draughtsman, illustrator, designer, poster artist, sculptor. Religious subjects, military subjects, battles, figures, nudes, figure compositions. Wall decorations.

Robert Falcucci trained in Paris at the École des Beaux-Arts and the École des Arts Décoratifs, and he was also taught by Cécile and Émmanuel Cavaille-Coll. In 1922 he joined the Renault company as a commercial artist and designed many posters for it. While pursuing this career he also painted and exhibited regularly in Paris at the Salon des Artistes Français, the Salon des Indépendants, the Salon des Peintres de l'Armée and the Salon de la Marine. He won a gold medal at the Colonial Exhibition of Marrakech in 1967 and a number of other distinctions followed: gold medal in the Grand Prix of the Salon de l'Armée, gold medal at the Salon des Artistes Français, the Vermeil medal of the City of Paris, the Corot landscape prize and the Bonnat prize at the Académie. From 1970 he lived in St-Aubain-Châteauneuf.

He decorated the battleship *Dunkerque*, the first Caravelle, the Boeing *Château de Compiègne*, the Air Japan rooms at Orly and the reception area in Le Bourget airport. He also carried out works for the Paris churches of St Francis of Assisi, the Chœur Eucharistique and Notre-Dame de l'Éspérance, and carved a monumental statue for the Sacré-Coeur Basilica. He illustrated R. Hervouin's *Guynemer, héros légendaire* (*Guynemer, Legendary Hero*), Paul Ribers' *Flèches ouvrantes* (*Opening Arrows*) (Opening Arrows), Prosper Mérimée's *Colomba*, and R.P. Ranson's *Présences Sacrées* (*Sacred Presences*) (Sacred Presences).

He used the techniques of painting and sculpture with rare energy. His works fall into several categories. Among his large religious paintings are a *Last Supper*, a *Resurrection of the Body*, and several moving images of Christ painted with dramatic chiaroscuro. Falcucci was also an official military painter, painting many French war heroes and a monumental work on the subject of World War I. He also painted sensual female nudes.

Museums and Galleries:

Verdun (Mémorial).

Auction records:

Paris, 15 May 1985, *Guynemer* (oil on canvas, 28¾ x 23½ ins / 73 x 60 cm) FRF 7,900. Paris, 23 April 1993, *In the Open Air* (oil on canvas, 57½ x 38¼ ins / 146 x 97 cm) FRF 20,000.

FALDA, Giovanni Battista, or Johan Baptist Falti

Italian, 17th century.

Born 1648, in Valduggia; died 1678, in Rome.

Draughtsman, engraver (etching/burin), architect. Architectural views.

His master is unknown, but Falda's style is very similar to that of Israël Silvestre. He was active in Rome from 1669 to 1678, where he produced a number of engravings of the city's churches, gardens, fountains and public buildings, peopled with figures and demonstrating a scientific mastery of perspective.

Auction records:

London, 18 June 1982, *Nuova pianta et alzata della citta di Roma* (1676, series of 12 etchings and engravings, 15½ x 20¼ ins / 39.5 x 51.3 cm) GBP 950.

FALDI, Arturo

Italian, 19th - 20th century.

Born 27 July 1856, in Florence; died 30 May 1911, in Florence.

Painter. Historical subjects, figures, genre scenes, interiors with figures, flowers.

Arturo Faldi started out exhibiting history paintings in Milan, Florence and Monaco, and at the Paris Salon in 1881. He then abandoned history painting and started to paint interiors.

His best known works include *Joseph Sold by His Brothers* (1873); *Artite e Sesostris* (1879); *In the Garden* (1882); *On the Mountain* (1888); *Waiting* (1896); *Rainy Weather*; and *Jalousie*.

He won bronze medals at the Expositions Universelles in both 1889 and 1900 in Paris.

Museums and Galleries:

Rome (Gal. Nazionale): *May God Be with Them; Winter in Tuscany* - Turin (Gal. Civica d'Arte Moderna e Contemporanea): *Honeymoon*.

Auction records:

Milan, 6 Nov 1980, *Calore Domestico* (oil on canvas, 16½ x 12¼ ins / 42 x 31 cm) ITL 4,600,000. Rome, 1 Dec 1982, *Temptation* (oil on canvas, 20 x 23½ ins / 50.5 x 60 cm) ITL 2,200,000. London, 24 June 1987, *People on a Terrace Overlooking the Hills of Tuscany* (oil on canvas, 27¼ x 34½ ins / 69 x 87.5 cm) GBP 10,500. Milan, 7 Nov 1991, *Flowers of the Fields* (oil on canvas, 25 x 18 ins / 63.5 x 45.5 cm) ITL 20,500,000. New York, 15 Oct 1993, *Feeding a Fire* (1895, oil on canvas, 92¼ x 82 ins / 234.3 x 208.2 cm) USD 19,550. London, 16 March 1994, *Artite e Sesostris* (1879, oil on canvas, 45¾ x 33¾ ins / 116.5 x 86 cm) GBP 8,050. New York, 29 Nov 1999, *Mother's Pride* (oil on canvas, 20 x 28 ins / 51 x 70 cm) USD 8,000.

FALDONI, Antonio Giovanni

Italian, 18th century.

Born c. 1690, in Asolo (Friuli); died c. 1770.

Painter, engraver.

Faldoni studied landscape painting with Antonio Luciani, but his painted works are little known. He devoted himself to engraving, at first copying the style of Gilles Sadler, and later (with greater success) that of Mellan. He produced a series of portraits of the Doges of Venice and the Procurators of S Marco.

A.F.

FALENS, Carel van

Flemish, 17th - 18th century.

Baptised 24 November 1683 in Antwerp; died 27 May 1733, in Paris.

Painter. Genre scenes, hunting scenes, landscapes with figures.

Flemish School.

Carel van Falens was a pupil of Constantin Francken until 1697. He went to Paris in 1703 where he married the daughter of the sculptor Sébastien Slodtz. On 29 November 1726 he became a member of the Académie de Paris. He signed his works with the initials *C. F. F.*

c. vanfalens

Museums and Galleries:

Courtrai: *Horsemen Resting* - Dresden: *Leaving for the Hunt* - Glasgow: *Departure* - Göttingen: *Scene of Looting* - La Fère: *Stag Hunt; Return from the Hunt* - Le Puy-en-Velay: *Leaving for the Hunt* - Lübeck: *Vegetable Market* - Montpellier: *Horsemen Resting* - Moscow (Rumiantsev Mus.): *Resting on the Hunt; Return from the Hunt* - Naples (Mus. Civico Gaetano Filangieri): *Venus and Cupid* - Nice: *Departure* - Paris (Louvre): *Hunt Rendezvous; Horsemen Resting* - Rouen: *Falconer* - St Petersburg (Hermitage): *Leaving for the Hunt; Falcon Hunt* - Stuttgart: *Horsemen Fighting*.

Auction records:

Paris, 8 May 1900, *Leaving for the Falcon Hunt*, FRF 175. Paris, 29 June 1905, *Leaving for the Falcon Hunt*, FRF 2,000. London, 27 Nov 1909, *Horseman Pausing; Herdsman and Livestock*, GBP 2. London, 21 Feb 1910, *Falcon Hunter Stopping*, GBP 17. Paris, 17 Nov 1919, *Halting on the Hunt* (attributed) FRF 700. Paris, 8 Nov 1922, *Landscape with Horseman* (attributed) FRF 380. Paris, 7 March 1923, *Halt at the Inn*, FRF 820. Paris, 9-10 March 1923, *Stag Hunt* (pen) FRF 85. Paris, 15 March 1923, *Halt on the Hunt* (school of Van Falens) FRF 1,500. London, 5 July 1926, *Landscape in Winter* (drawing) GBP 10. London, 20 July 1927, *Group of Huntsmen in front of an Inn*, GBP 52. Paris, 27-28 Dec 1927, *Huntsman Giving Alms* (attributed) FRF 2,510. Paris, 17 Feb 1928, *Skating Scene; Stopping among the Ruins* (collection) FRF 3,200. Paris, 1 June 1928, *Departure* (attributed) FRF 1,250. Paris, 24 Nov 1928, *Horsemen and Figures at the Fountain* (school of C. van F.) FRF 480. London, 27 June 1930, *Leaving for the Hunt; Hunting Party* (collection) GBP 35. London, 22 Dec 1936, *Horsemen*, GBP 8. Paris, 25 Nov 1937, *Stag Hunt; Halt at the Inn* (two sepia drawings heightened with white, two pendants) FRF 310. London, 1 April 1938, *Falcon Hunt*, GBP 8. London, 6 May 1938, *River Scene*, GBP 8. Paris, 1 July 1938, *Crossing the Ford*, FRF 190. London, 28 April 1939, *Sporting Party* (1730) GBP 9. London, 31 May 1940, *Two Horsemen*, GBP 10. London, 9 Oct 1941, *Horsemen*, GBP 6. London, 7 July 1943, *Cavalry Engagement* (two paintings) GBP 21. Paris, 25 Nov 1946, *One for the Road* (pen and wash, attributed) FRF 3,250. Paris, 10 June 1954, *Falcon Hunt Scenes* (two pendants) FRF 166,000. Paris, 11 Dec 1961, *Leaving for the Hunt; Hunt* (two pendants) FRF 5,200. Cologne, 21 Oct 1966, *Horsemen in Wooded Landscape*, DEM 3,500. New York, 21 March 1969, *Military Encampment*, USD 2,000. Paris, 9 Nov 1970, *Horse Market*, FRF 23,500. Paris, 16 June 1972, *Return from the Hunt*, FRF 9,100. London, 9 Feb 1973, *Hunt Rendezvous*, Gns 3,000. London, 7 July 1976, *Falconer on a White Horse* (oil on panel, 14¼ x 24½ ins / 36 x 62.5 cm) GBP 3,800. Versailles, 27 March 1977, *Leaving for the*

Hunt (oil on canvas, 24 x 30 ins / 61 x 76 cm) FRF 12,500. AMSTERDAM, 2 June 1981, *Horsemen and Peasants in a Landscape* (oil on panel, 11 x 13 3/4 ins / 27 x 35 cm) NLG 15,000. AMSTERDAM, 15 May 1984, *Hunting Scene* (oil on panel, 11 1/2 x 14 3/4 ins / 29.5 x 37.5 cm) NLG 30,000. PARIS, 11 July 1985, *Horsemen Halting* (oil/copper, 10 1/2 x 12 1/2 ins / 26.5 x 31.5 cm) FRF 52,000. PARIS, 4 Dec 1987, *Leaving for the Hunt* (oil on canvas, 21 x 27 1/4 ins / 52.5 x 69 cm) FRF 20,000. LONDON, 8 July 1988, *Huntsmen Resting by a Fountain and Ruins in an Extensive Landscape* (oil on canvas, 13 1/4 x 17 ins / 33.5 x 43 cm) GBP 5,500. TROYES, 19 Nov 1989, *Horsemen Returning from Falcon Hunt* (oil on canvas, 6 1/4 x 8 1/4 ins / 16 x 21 cm) FRF 20,500. NEW YORK, 16 Jan 1992, *Extensive Landscape with Horsemen Taking Refreshment in a Tent and Travellers on a Track in the Background* (oil/copper, 14 1/2 x 19 ins / 36.8 x 48.3 cm) USD 13,200. PARIS, 11 Dec 1992, *Le Manège de Chevaux* (oil on panel, 14 x 18 ins / 35.5 x 45.5 cm) FRF 20,000. NEW YORK, 14 Jan 1994, *Horsemen Pausing after the Hunt* (oil on canvas, 26 x 20 3/4 ins / 65.1 x 53 cm) USD 13,800. PARIS, 16 March 1994, *Leaving for the Falcon Hunt* (oil on oak panel, 19 1/4 x 25 1/2 ins / 49 x 64.5 cm) FRF 135,000. PARIS, 13 Dec 1995, *Return from the Hunt* (oil on canvas, 21 1/4 x 25 1/2 ins / 54 x 65 cm) FRF 60,000. NEW YORK, 16 May 1996, *Return of Huntsmen* (oil on canvas, 20 3/4 x 24 3/4 ins / 53 x 62.9 cm) USD 25,300. ICKWORTH, 12 June 1996, *Departure* (oil on canvas, 19 3/4 x 23 1/2 ins / 50 x 60 cm) GBP 13,800. LONDON, 3-4 Dec 1997, *Falcon Hunt with Elegant Figures on Horseback in an Extensive Landscape* (oil on panel, a pair, each 12 3/4 x 18 ins / 32.5 x 46 cm) GBP 17,250. VIENNA, 6 Oct 1999, *Military Encampment with Tents by River* (oil on panel, 17 x 26 ins / 44 x 65 cm) ATS 130,000. LONDON, 14 Dec 1999, *Departure for the Hunt* (oil on canvas, 17 x 23 ins / 42 x 59 cm) GBP 80,000. AMSTERDAM, 9 May 2000, *Peasant Woman Meeting a Shepherd on a River Bank in Summer Landscape* (oil on canvas, 21 x 26 ins / 54 x 65 cm) NLG 42,000. VIENNA, 4 Oct 2000, *Return from Hawking* (oil on copper, 15 x 13 ins / 39 x 33 cm) ATS 150,000. PARIS, 31 Jan 2001, *Stopping at the Blacksmith's* (oil on canvas, 14 x 16 ins / 35 x 40 cm) FRF 52,500. LONDON, 14 Dec 2001, *Hunting Party Halting after the Chase* (oil on canvas, 21 x 25 ins / 54 x 64 cm) GBP 12,000. LONDON, 17 April 2002, *Extensive Landscape with Hunting Party* (oil on copper, 15 x 19 ins / 37 x 48 cm) GBP 12,000. GENEVA, 17 Nov 2002, *Falconer on Horseback* (oil on panel, 14 x 13 ins / 36 x 32 cm) CHF 30,000. PARIS, 1 July 2003, *Riders Halting* (oil on panel, 12 x 17 ins / 30 x 44 cm) EUR 3,300. PARIS, 15 Oct 2003, *Setting off Hawking* (oil on copper, 18 x 22 ins / 45 x 56 cm) EUR 21,500. MADRID, 26 Jan 2004, *Hunting Scenes* (oil on board, a pair, 17 x 20 ins / 42 x 51 cm) EUR 18,000. PARIS, 5 June 2004, *Village Fair, the Magician. Hunting with Hounds, the Stag* (oil on panel, two, 9 x 13 ins / 24 x 34 cm) EUR 12,000.

FALERI, Domenico

Italian, 17th century.
Born 1595; died 1640.
Painter.

The church of the Monagnese hospice in Siena houses Faleri's *Nativity*. Further examples of his work are to be found in the neighbouring Benedictine priory.

FALERO, Luis Ricardo

Spanish, 19th century.
Born 1851, in Granada; died 1896, in London.
Painter, watercolourist. Figures, nudes, genre scenes.

Luis Ricardo Falero began his career in the Spanish navy; he later studied in Paris before moving to London. He was well-versed in astronomy and the subjects he painted were mainly related to this. They include *Marriage of a Comet, Twin Stars* and *Faust's Dream*. He also painted many studies of female nudes.

MUSEUMS AND GALLERIES:
NEW YORK (Metropolitan Mus. of Art): *Twin Stars* (watercolour).

AUCTION RECORDS:
PARIS, 9 March 1891, *Biblis*, FRF 600; *Tokay Wine*, FRF 1,500. PARIS, 27 April 1897, *The Snake Charmer*, FRF 205. PARIS, 30 June 1904, *Gypsy Woman*, FRF 620. NEW YORK, 22 and 23 April 1907, *Music*, USD 110. NEW YORK, 1-3 April 1908, *The Engagement Ring*, USD 180. PARIS, 3-4 May 1923, *Gypsy Woman*, FRF 500. PARIS, 6 May 1925, *Serenade*, FRF 250. LONDON, 9 July 1928, *Sea Nymph*, GBP 14. LONDON, 13 Feb 1931, *The Favourite*, GBP 15. VERSAILLES, 15 May 1977, *Snake Charmer* (oil on canvas, 22 x 16 1/4 ins / 56 x 41 cm) USD 4,250. LONDON, 18 June 1980, *Portrait of Mrs M G Spinelli Falero* (oil on canvas, 32 3/4 x 25 1/4 ins / 83 x 64 cm) GBP 400. NEW YORK, 25 May 1984, *The Show-Off* (1879, oil on canvas, 63 1/4 x 33 1/2 ins / 160.7 x 85.1 cm) USD 11,000. NEW YORK, 26 Feb 1986, *The Offering* (1892, oil on canvas, 29 x 15 1/4 ins / 73.5 x 38.7 cm) USD 12,000. LONDON, 15 Feb 1990, *Moment of Idleness* (1896, oil on canvas, a pair, each 16 x 8 ins / 40.5 x 20.3 cm) GBP 4,400. NEW YORK, 23 May 1990, *Female Nude Sculpting Marble* (1892, oil on canvas, 41 1/2 x 66 ins / 105.5 x 167.6 cm) USD 20,900. LONDON, 30 Nov 1990, *The Coquette* (1879, oil on canvas, 63 1/4 x 33 ins / 160.7 x 83.8 cm) GBP 14,300. NEW YORK, 27 May 1993, *Dance of the Minstrels* (oil on canvas, 13 3/4 x 27 1/2 ins / 35 x 69.8 cm) USD 9,200. LONDON, 17 June 1999, *The Favourite* (1880, oil on canvas, 29 x 16 ins / 74 x 41 cm) GBP 17,000. NEW YORK, 2 Nov 1999, *The Balance of the Zodiac* (oil on panel, 30 x 20 ins / 75 x 52 cm) USD 37,500. MADRID, 20 June 2000, *Nymphs* (oil on copper, 15 x 25 ins / 38 x 63 cm) ESP 3,000,000. GODALMING, 7 Feb 2001, *Spanish Beauty* (1877, oil on canvas, 26 x 21 ins / 66 x 54 cm) GBP 4,000. LONDON, 11 Oct 2001, *Artist's Model* (oil on canvas, 12 x 9 ins / 30 x 23 cm) GBP 1,000. NEW YORK, 30 Oct 2002, *An Oriental Beauty* (oil on canvas, 29 x 16 ins / 74 x 41 cm) USD 28,000. NEW YORK, 28 Oct 2003, *Falero's Dream* (1880, oil on canvas, 32 x 59 ins / 81 x 150 cm) USD 32,500. NEW YORK, 28 Oct 2003, *Faust's Vision* (1878, oil on canvas, 57 x 46 ins / 145 x 118 cm) USD 90,000.

FALET, Eugène

French, 20th century.
Born in Paris.
Painter.

Eugène Falet exhibited in Paris at the Salon de la Société Nationale des Beaux-Arts.

FALETRO, Joannis. See **FALIER Giovanni**

FALEZZA, Giuseppe

Italian, 19th century.
Active in Verona c. 1850.
Painter. Still-lifes.

Giuseppe Falezza was also a priest.

FALGANI, Guasparre

Italian, 17th century.
Born at the beginning of the 17th century, in Florence.
Landscape artist.

Guasparre Falgani was a pupil of Valerio Marucelli. Examples of his work are housed in various museums and galleries throughout Italy.

FALGAS

French, 18th - 19th century.
Born in Rodez.

Active at the end of the 18th century or the beginning of the 19th century.

Sculptor, painter, lithographer. Sculpted frames.

Falgas, who spent his life in Rodez, was first a barber and then a museum attendant. He was one of the first exponents of lithography, and his sculpted frames are remarkable.

Museums and Galleries:

Rodez: engravings; sculpted frames.

FALGER, Anton

Austrian, 19th century.

Born 1791, in Elbigenalp (Tyrol).

Draughtsman, engraver (etching), lithographer.

Falger worked in Munich and Weimar around 1820, making engravings and lithographs of maps, vignettes (text illustrations), landscapes and genre scenes. He is best known for his copies of engravings by Callot.

FALGUIÈRE, Henriette

French, 20th century.

Born 19 January 1888, in Suresnes; died 8 October 1956, in Paris.

Painter, pastellist.

Henriette Falguière was a pupil of Jules Levebvre and Tony Robert-Fleury in Paris. She first exhibited at the Salon des Artistes Français in 1908.

FALGUIÈRE, Jean Alexandre Joseph

French, 19th century.

Born 7 September 1831, in Toulouse; died 1900, in Paris.

Sculptor, draughtsman. Religious subjects, genre scenes. Monuments, groups, statues, busts.

A pupil of Jouffroy at the Paris École des Beaux-Arts, Jean Falguière made his début at the Paris Salon in 1857. In 1859 he won the Prix de Rome. In 1864, while still in Rome, he sent his *Winner of the Cockfight* to the Salon, winning his first award, followed three years later by a further medal for his statue of *Tarcisius the Martyr*. In the same year he obtained a first-class medal at the Paris Exposition Universelle (1867), followed in 1868 by the medal of honour at the Salon for a marble replica of his *Tarcisius*. He suffered no lack of official awards or commissions. A lecturer at the Paris École des Beaux-Arts, he was made a Chevalier of the Légion d'Honneur in 1870, subsequently being promoted to officer in 1878.

Falguière began his artistic career by studying Classical art and the effect of this training can be seen in his early works, most notably in his *Theseus as a Child* from the 1857 Salon, and in the group that gained him the Prix de Rome, *Wounded Mezentius Saved by his Son Lausus*. During the next few years, Falguière confirmed his inclination towards Realist art with sufficient vigour for some critics to accuse him of a lack of refinement. His best works from this stage in his career are *Egyptian Dancer* (1872); *Statue of Pierre Corneille*; *Cardinal Lavigerie*; *Woman with Peacock*; *Statue of La Rochejaquelin*; and a statue of *Eve*, together with many monuments.

In 1878 he was commissioned to execute the *Triumph of the Republic* (installed in 1881 at the top of the Arc de Triomphe de l'Étoile, only to be removed in 1886), the *Courbet Monument* and the *Statue of La Fayette*.

Falguière was also a talented painter, and his paintings reveal a vigorous technique and striking palette. His best paintings include *Fan and Dagger*; *Fighters* and *Cain and Abel*. Falguière may be considered as one of the creators of Realism in sculpture in the French School of the 19th century.

A Falguière

Museums and Galleries:

Amiens: *Gambetta* - Angers: *Sphynx* - Antwerp: *Beheading of St John the Baptist* (painting) - Berlin: *Young Centaur* - Bucharest: *Diana the Hunter* - Copenhagen (Ny Carlsberg Glyptotek): *Bust of Paul Dubois* - Grenoble: *Quadriga of Victory* (wax model) - Paris (Louvre): *Baroness Daumesnil, Wife of the General* (marble, bust); *Winner of the Cockfight* (bronze) - Paris (Maison de Victor Hugo): *Victor Hugo on his Deathbed* (drawing) - Paris (MAM): *Dwarfs* (painting); *Fan and Dagger* (painting); *Tarcisius the Martyr* (marble) - Paris (Mus. d'Orsay): *Fighters* - Paris (Mus. de la Comédie-Française): *Pierre Corneille* (marble) - Toul: *Diana*; *Young Martyr* - Toulouse: *Switzerland Welcoming the French Army* (plaster).

Auction records:

Paris, 24 Nov 1922, *Portrait of a Young Girl* (pastel) FRF 110. Paris, 4 May 1923, *Portrait of a Woman*, FRF 115. Paris, 1 Dec 1923, *The Fight* (pen) FRF 38; *Portrait of a Young Man* (charcoal) FRF 100; *Old Man*, FRF 60. Paris, 9 Feb 1924, *Bust of a Young Man* (pencil, heightened) FRF 55; *Study* (red chalk) FRF 100. Paris, 1 July 1932, *Cicada* (silvered bronze) FRF 250. Paris, 26 Jan 1941, *Nude Study* (pen drawing) FRF 250. Paris, 18 and 19 April 1945, *Nude Reclining*, FRF 2,700. Paris, 19 May 1947, *Young Girl Seated, Hands Crossed* (pastel) FRF 1,100. New York, 4 April 1968, *Diana* (patinated bronze) USD 1,600. Versailles, 3 Dec 1978, *Face of a Young Woman* (terracotta, h. 17 ins / 43 cm) FRF 4,500. London, 14 May 1980, *Diana* (bronze, h. 16 1/4 ins / 41.5 cm) GBP 420. Paris, 1 March 1982, *Cléo de Mérode* (bronze, h. 15 1/4 ins / 39 cm) FRF 4,800. New York, 25 May 1984, *Study of a Centaur and Satyr* (black chalk/blue paper, 12 1/2 x 11 1/4 ins / 31.7 x 28.8 cm) USD 4,500. Paris, 9 Nov 1984, *Diana the Hunter* (bronze, h. 41 ins / 104 cm) FRF 17,000. New York, 30 March 1985, *Juno with a Peacock* (bronze with dark brown patina, h. 30 ins / 76.2 cm) USD 1,700. Paris, 2 June 1986, *Strength Leaning on a Rock* (white marble, h. 23 ins / 57.5 cm) FRF 15,000. Paris, 9 March 1987, *Diana the Hunter* (patinated bronze, h. 34 ins / 86.5 cm) FRF 19,900. New York, 24 May 1989, *Pegasus Leading the Poet into the Realm of Dreams* (bronze, h. 28 3/4 ins / 73 cm) USD 6,050. London, 21 Nov 1989, *Phryné* (brown-patinated bronze, h. 32 3/4 ins / 83 cm) GBP 9,900. New York, 24 Oct 1990, *Bust of Honoré de Balzac* (bronze with gold-brown patina, h. 15 1/2 ins / 39.4 cm) USD 6,600; *Diana the Hunter Standing* (patinated bronze, h. 68 3/4 ins / 174.6 cm) USD 49,500. New York, 27 May 1992, *Diana* (bronze, h. 18 1/4 ins / 46.4 cm) USD 3,300. Paris, 22 March 1994, *Young Woman at the Piano* (terracotta, low relief, 11 1/2 x 6 1/2 ins / 29 x 16.5 cm) FRF 17,000. Le Touquet, 22 May 1994, *Sweetheart Playing the Mandolin* (bronze, 35 ins / 88 cm) FRF 14,000. New York, 26 May 1994, *Diana* (bronze, h. 69 ins / 175.3 cm) USD 46,000. New York, 1 Nov 1995, *Egyptian Woman* (1867, bronze, h. 25 1/4 ins / 64.1 cm) USD 18,400. Paris, 15 Dec 1995, *Woman Reading* (white marble, h. 30 3/4 ins / 78 cm, w. 28 1/4 ins/72 cm, depth 13 3/4 ins/35 cm) FRF 37,000. St-Brieuc, 29 March 1998, *Leda and the Swan* (1873, green patinated bronze, h. 41 1/4 ins / 105 cm) FRF 70,000. New York, 5 May 1999, *Diana* (brown patinated bronze, 41 ins / 103 cm) USD 8,500. Pontoise, 16 Oct 1999, *The Spring or Eve* (1880, gold tinged patinated bronze/lacquer, 30 ins / 75 cm) FRF 56,000. London, 5 Oct 2000, *Music, Lady holding Violin* (black and brown patinated bronze, 30 ins / 75 cm) GBP 5,500. London, 12 Oct 2000, *Egyptian Dance* (1887, bronze, 65 ins / 165 cm) GBP 23,000. Paris, 22 June 2001, *Bust of Diana* (brown patinated bronze, 18 ins / 45 cm) FRF 31,000. London, 11 July 2001, *Clytie* (dark brown patinated bronze, 20 x 31 ins / 52 x 78 cm) GBP 9,000. London, 5 Nov 2002, *Guitar Player* (silvered bronze, 15 ins / 38 cm) GBP 3,200. New York, 10 Dec 2002, *Bust of Diana, Goddess of the Hunt* (green and brown patinated bronze, 7 ins / 17cm) USD 5,500. Chester, 27 Feb 2003, *Victory in the Cockfight* (bronze, 69 ins / 174 cm) GBP 17,000. LONDON, 8 July 2003, *Study for the Monument to Balzac* (terracotta, 28 x 17x15 ins / 72 x 42x37 cm) GBP 45,000. SYDNEY, 15 May 2004, *Bust of Diana* (marble, 24 ins / 60 cm) AUD 15,000.

FALI, Giuseppe
Italian, 18th century.
Born c. 1697; died 1772.
Active in Brescia.
Painter.
Giuseppe Fali studied under G. G. del Sole. Examples of his work housed in the church of S Maria dei Miracoli, in Brescia, include a *Noli me tangere* and a *Descent from the Cross*.

FALIER, Clément
French, 20th century.
Painter.
AUCTION RECORDS:
PARIS, 4 March 1893, *Dawn*, FRF 220.

FALIER, Giovanni, also known as Faletro Joannis
Italian, 16th century.
Medallist, engraver.
We know of two medals by Giovanni Falier: one of the Presbyterian Marcus and one of the procurator of St Mark's in Venice. He is probably Giovanni Faller, the engraver of decoration and grotesques, cited by Florent Le Comte.

FALIES, Jean Pierre Victor
French, 19th century.
Born 12 January 1849, in Montpellier; died 18 March 1901, in Montpellier.
Painter. Genre scenes, landscapes.
MUSEUMS AND GALLERIES:
MONTPELLIER: *Landscape*; *Caravan*.
AUCTION RECORDS:
PARIS, 27 Jan 1943, *Village in the Midi*, FRF 2,200.

FALIGUM, J.
Austrian, 18th century.
Engraver.
In 1723, Faligum engraved a view of the church of the Calvary in Graz (Styria), Austria.

FALILEEV, Vadim Dmitrievich
Russian, 20th century.
Born 13 January 1879, in Pensa; died 1948.
Engraver, draughtsman, copyist. Portraits, landscapes.
Vadim Dmitrievich Falileev studied at the school of design in Pensa, then at workshops of the Princess Tanichev school of arts and crafts in St Petersburg and at the academy of fine art in that city. He travelled to Berlin, Munich and Paris in around 1907. Culturally he was an eclectic and admired works by Gauguin, Van Gogh, Cézanne and Matisse. He is known for a series of landscapes of the Volga engraved in colour. Falileev also reproduced as engravings the *Portrait of Inghirami* after Raphael and the *Miracle of St Mark* after Tintoretto.
MUSEUMS AND GALLERIES:
MOSCOW (Rumiantsev Mus.): almost complete works.

FALILELA, Antonio Raffaele
Italian, 17th century.
Sculptor (wood).
Antonio Falilela produced ornamental sculptures for the sacristy of the church of Gravedona on Lake Como in 1628.

FALIP, Charles Antoine Étienne
French, 19th century.
Born 19th century, in Perpignan.
Painter.
Charles Falip exhibited some pen-and-ink drawings at the Paris Salon in 1878 and 1879: *Cows in Pasture*; *Returning to the Abandoned House*; and *Winter at Auderghen*.

FALIZE, André
French, 19th - 20th century.
Born 21 May 1872, in Montereau.
Worker in precious metals.
André Falize won the Art Workers competition. Among other works he designed and made the ceremonial swords presented to French marshals after World War I, Marshal Lyautey's baton, a laurel wreath for President Venizelos of Greece and *France's Homage to the Unknown American Soldier* in gold.

FALIZE, Pierre
French, 19th - 20th century.
Born 1876; died 1953.
Painter, sculptor, enameller, draughtsman, illustrator. Landscapes.
Pierre Falize studied at the École des Beaux-Arts, Paris, and exhibited at the Salon de la Société Nationale des Beaux-Arts, of which he was a member.

His work included gouaches, sepias and heightened drawings, but early on he moved to decorative sculpture and created ornamental shapes for the goldsmith's shop that belonged to his family. His bronzes, such as the trophy he made in 1913 for the Society of Breton Lifeboatmen, are in the Belle Époque style. However, he developed a quite different style in his painting and had a strong interest in illustration, as we can see from his posters (*Prunier Delivers Fast and Efficiently* and *Sport and the Future*), his caricatures of actors, and his sketches of landscapes with figures drawn in Breton villages; all of these are spare in style and delineated with confident, incisive and rapid strokes.

FALIZE, Robert
French, 20th century.
Born in Paris.
Painter.
Robert Falize exhibited in Paris at the Salon des Artistes Français in 1932.

FALK. See also **FALCK**

FALK, Gathie
Canadian, 20th century.
Born 31 January 1928, in Alexander (Manitoba).
Sculptor, painter.
Gathie Falk studied at the University of British Columbia. In the early 1960s her paintings were abstract. In around 1964 she studied pottery and ceramics and made sculptures using the objects in her environment: shirts, shoes, fruit. In 1974 she made *Herds One*, an installation of 24 horses carved in wood and painted in oils. After a series of photographs taken in her garden, she returned to painting with the *Borders Series* and the triptych *Lawn in Three Parts*, the left section of which is pure green, the middle section also green, but scattered with a few small flowers that seem to extend the flower border that fills the whole of the right section. Painted with small brushstrokes in a Post-Impressionist style, this painting is only exceptional in its layout. In 1978-1979 she painted a number of series, including *Night Skies*, variations on a colour, essentially midnight blue, heightened with stars, and *Pieces of Water*, abstract compositions varying in colour from cobalt blue to pearly pink to lemon green. The series *Cement Sidewalks* consists of views of sections of pavement, with leaves or a shadow. The last in the series was a large composition, *Beautiful British Columbia Multiple Purpose Thermal Blanket*, which was made up of nine squares containing views of flowers and pavement edges, similar to those of the previous works and surrounded by a green border. Plants were one of her favourite subjects, and she compared watching a plant grow to watching the performance of a play. This is why she called one of the series *Theater in*

B/W and Colour (1983), a contrast between a black and white version of the floral subject and a coloured version.

Gathie Falk held a solo show of her works at the National Gallery of Canada, Ottawa, in 2002.

BIBLIOGRAPHY:

Gathie Falk: Paintings 1978-1984, exhibition catalogue, Art Gall. of Greater Victoria, Victoria (CAN), 1985. *Gathie Falk*, illustrated book, Douglas and McIntyre, Vancouver, 2000.

MUSEUMS AND GALLERIES:

OTTAWA (NG. of Canada) - STRATFORD (Rothman's AG) - TORONTO (AG of Ontario) - VANCOUVER (AG) - VICTORIA (AG of Greater Victoria).

FALK, Hans

Swiss, 20th century.
Born 1918, in Zurich; died 2002.
Painter (including gouache), collage artist.

AUCTION RECORDS:

ZURICH, 7 Nov 1982, *Stromboli* (1962, gouache, 8 1/4 x 10 3/4 ins / 20.7 x 27.3 cm) CHF 1,000. ZURICH, 21-22 June 1985, *Still-life* (c. 1960, oil on card, 11 x 15 1/4 ins / 28 x 38.5 cm) CHF 5,000; *Cornwall* (1959, gouache, charcoal, tearing, 23 x 27 1/2 ins / 57.5 x 70 cm) CHF 6,000. LUCERNE, 23 May 1992, *Violin Concert* (coloured chalks and charcoal, 9 x 6 1/2 ins / 22 x 16.5 cm) CHF 1,350. ZURICH, 9 June 1993, *Stromboli 46* (plans and oil on paper, 29 1/2 x 40 1/2 ins / 75 x 103 cm) CHF 9,775. ZURICH, 24 Nov 1993, *Wall with Fossils* (1960, oil on canvas, 37 x 52 ins / 94 x 132 cm) CHF 13,800. ZURICH, 26 March 1996, *Flashy New Dancing* (1971, acrylic and collage/canvas, 60 1/4 x 78 3/4 ins / 153 x 200 cm) CHF 19,000. ZURICH, 12 Nov 1996, *Stromboli* (1965, mixed media/paper, 29 1/2 x 41 1/4 ins / 75 x 104.5 cm) CHF 10,000. ZURICH, 14 April 1997, *Mauerkreisel* (1960, oil on canvas, 37 x 52 ins / 94 x 132 cm) CHF 9,200. LUCERNE, 5 June 1999, *Stromboli* (1960, mixed media, tempera, chalk and sand, 29 x 40 ins / 73 x 101 cm) CHF 4,000. ZURICH, 21 Nov 2000, *Old Man* (oil on canvas, 35 x 50 ins / 90 x 128 cm) CHF 7,000. ZURICH, 15 May 2001, *Work Year* (mixed media over lithograph, 29 x 39 ins / 74 x 98 cm) CHF 4,500. ZURICH, 15 May 2001, *Work Year* (1985, ink, acrylic, pencil and aluminium on panel, 34 x 43 ins / 86 x 110 cm) CHF 9,500. ZURICH, 18 March 2002, *Aeolus Lied* (1960, oil on canvas, 26 x 37 ins / 67 x 95 cm) CHF 5,500. ZURICH, 25 Nov 2002, *Untitled* (oil on panel, 20 x 26 ins / 51 x 67 cm) CHF 7,500. ZURICH, 24 June 2003, *Stromboli* (collage, acrylic, oil and chalk over colour lithograph, 39 x 27 ins / 100 x 69 cm) CHF 2,400. LUCERNE, 22 Nov 2003, *Reclining Female Nude* (1967, mixed media, oil, pencil and tempera, 9 x 15 ins / 23 x 39 cm) CHF 2,800. BERN, 12 Nov 2004, *Nude* (1967, charcoal and coloured pencil, 19 x 16 ins / 47 x 41 cm) CHF 2,500.

FALK, Jeremias, or Falck

Polish, 17th century.
Born 1609 or 1610 or 1610, in Gdansk; died 1677; buried the 7 February in Gdansk.
Painter, engraver, draughtsman. Mythological subjects, portraits.

Jeremias Falk studied in Paris under Chauveau and then went to Holland, where he worked for several years. He returned to Poland, where he painted the King's portrait. He was also invited to the Swedish court, and appointed draughtsman and engraver to the Danish royal court.

AUCTION RECORDS:

MUNICH, 29 June 1982, *Venus* (pen, 15 1/4 x 10 1/4 ins / 39 x 26 cm) DEM 1,000. MUNICH, 21 June 2002, *Flowers in Glass Vase* (oil on panel, 17x14 ins / 44x35 cm) EUR 19,000.

FALK, Johann. See **FALCH**

FALK, Karl

Swiss, 19th century.
Active in Sankt Fiden.
Lithographer.

In 1828-1829, Falk exhibited a lithograph portrait and a *Holy Family* (watercolour) in St Gall.

FALK, Lars Erik

Swedish, 20th century.
Born 1922.
Sculptor.
Neo-Constructivism.

Lars Falk took part in collective exhibitions from around 1942. He then took part in the ninth Swedish demonstration of *Art in the Street* in 1976, in the exhibition *Art Construit. Current Trends in France and Sweden*, which took place at the 30 gallery in Paris (at 30, rue Rambuteau, adjoining the Beaubourg), then at the French institute in Stockholm in 1987 and other places. His first solo exhibition took place in Sweden in 1952.

He uses various materials, usually metallic, in sculptures that he describes as 'modular'. He conceives them as monumental, from the perspective of integration with architecture. They often consist in geometrical, simple and repetitive elements. The elements indicate the general dynamic of the works - their repetition creates the internal rhythm.

MUSEUMS AND GALLERIES:

STOCKHOLM (Moderna Mus.).

AUCTION RECORDS:

STOCKHOLM, 14 June 1990, *Composition* (1955, grey and yellow gouache on a black card background, 17 1/4 x 8 ins / 43.8 x 20.5 cm) SEK 24,000. STOCKHOLM, 30 May 1991, *Composition* (metal painted black and red, h. 21 3/4 ins / 55.5 cm) SEK 24,000. STOCKHOLM, 19 May 1992, *Module-Sculpture for Colour 24* (black lacquered metal, h. 19 1/4 ins / 49 cm) SEK 10,000. STOCKHOLM, 11 March 1999, *Module Sculpture in Black - 63* (1988, varnished steel, h. 33 ins / 84 cm) SEK 18,000. STOCKHOLM, 27 May 1999, *Module Sulpture in Colour* (1997, painted metal, h. 30 ins / 75 cm) SEK 20,000. STOCKHOLM, 2 May 2001, *Module Sculpture in Colour* (1989, varnished aluminium, h. 49 ins / 125 cm) SEK 25,000. STOCKHOLM, 5 Nov 2003, *White Sculpture* (1957, white marble, h. 19 ins / 49 cm) SEK 24,000. STOCKHOLM, 5 Nov 2003, *Untitled* (1950-1983, oil on canvas, 28 x 18 ins / 72 x 45 cm) SEK 34,000. STOCKHOLM, 26 April 2004, *Window-sash II* (1956-1977, metal, 39 x 25 ins / 100 x 63 cm) SEK 16,000. STOCKHOLM, 3 Nov 2004, *Module Sculpture in Colour - B20* (1990, varnished aluminium, h. 29 ins / 74 cm) SEK 16,500.

FALK, Robert Rafailovich

Russian, 20th century.
Born 1886, in Moscow; died 1958.
Also active in France.
Painter. Portraits, landscapes, still-lifes.
Bubnovy Valet (Jack of Diamonds) group.

Before deciding on art, Robert Falk had studied music. In Moscow he was a pupil of Constantin Yuon, Valentin Serov and Ilya Mashkov, then of Constantin Korovin and Valentino Serov at the college of arts, from which he was excluded with some of his friends for being non-conformist. In 1909 Falk was one of the founding members, with Aristarkh Lentulov, Mashkov and Piotr Konchalovsky, of the Bubnovy Valet (Jack of Diamonds) group, which came to public notice with an exhibition in 1912. In 1917, he helped set up the Mir Iskusstva (World of Art) group. He became acquainted with Larionov, Natalya Goncharova, Malevich and others in the Bubnovy Valet (Jack of Diamonds) group. He taught painting from 1918 to 1928 and was a member of the Pan-Russian college of fine arts where he was in charge of organising artwork on new social bases and was appointed dean of the faculty of art in 1928. He was in Paris from around 1928 to 1937 and exhibited at the Salon d'Automne, Salon des Artistes Indépendants, Zack gallery and the Salon des Tuileries. He returned to Moscow in 1937 and lived there until 1944 when he was evacuated to Samarkand.

Falk was introduced by Konstantin Alekseevich Korovin to the technique, at that time a novelty, of Impressionism which influenced many of the works of his youth. From Korovin, Falk discovered Van Gogh and particularly Cézanne, who influenced him to such an extent that he, Mashkov and Lentulov were known as the 'Cézannians' when they exhibited with the Bubnovy Valet (Jack of Diamonds) group. Despite his active involvement with this group, Falk did not follow the Abstraction path and his painting remained within the general style of Central European Expressionism, although included some of the achievements of Cubism in his post-Cézanne period. On his return to Moscow from Paris, he only took back the 'optimistic' works, having destroyed almost all those of a melancholic nature, fearing that they would be badly received in Stalinist Russia. In this dark period he had to spend his time on stage sets, particularly for the Kamerni and Mossoviet theatres. In his last years he designed sets for Sartre's *Nekrassov* to be staged in Moscow. Although politically uncommitted, Falk's painting was able to retain some aspects of modernity in this regressive era.

Robert Falk held an individual exhibition in 1924 at the Tretyakov Gallery but since he did not follow the 'Socialist Realism' party line in his painting, he had to work virtually in secret. In 1962, one of his paintings appeared in Moscow in the exhibition of the *Arena* with other non-conformist painters. At the time of this exhibition Kruschev turned violently against non-academic art and had the exhibition closed. Falk was represented in the exhibition *Art Russe: Des Scythes à nos jours* (*Russian Art: from the Scythians to Today*), Paris (1967) and at *Un été russe à Montmartre. Artistes de St-Pétersbourg à Paris au début du XXe siècle* (*A Russian Summer in Montmartre. St Petersburg Artists in Paris at the Beginning of the 20th Century*), Musée de Montmartre in Paris (2003).

R.F 47

R. Falk

BIBLIOGRAPHY:

Falk, Robert, *Lettres et souvenirs*, Sovetskii Khudozhnik, Moscow, 1981. Gérard, Raphaël/Essaïan, Sergeï, et al., *Un été russe à Montmartre. Artistes de Saint-Pétersbourg à Paris au début du XXe siècle*, exhibition catalogue, Musée de Montmartre, Éditions Fragments, Paris, 2003.

MUSEUMS AND GALLERIES:

MOSCOW (State Tretyakov Gal.): *Landscape at Kosy, in the Crimea*; *Portrait of Midhad Refatov* (1915); *Woman in White* (1923).

AUCTION RECORDS:

LONDON, 29 March 1973, *Bunch of Flowers*, GBP 650. BRUSSELS, 15 March 1978, *Landscape* (oil on canvas, 39 1/4 x 37 ins / 100 x 94 cm) BEF 100,000. LONDON, 23 Feb 1984, *View of a City* (oil on canvas, 21 1/4 x 32 ins / 54 x 81 cm) GBP 520. LONDON, 6 Oct 1988, *House in the Forest* (oil on canvas, 20 3/4 x 32 ins / 53 x 81 cm) GBP 6,600. LONDON, 6 April 1989, *Young Hindu Man* (oil on canvas, 39 x 28 ins / 99 x 71 cm) GBP 11,550. LONDON, 5 Oct 1989, *Bread* (1932, oil on canvas, 25 1/4 x 31 1/2 ins / 64.1 x 80 cm) GBP 5,500. PARIS, 19 June 1991, *Zagorsk Monastery* (1957, oil on card, 19 1/4 x 22 ins / 49 x 56 cm) FRF 11,000. PARIS, 31 Oct 1991, *Buildings* (oil on canvas, 35 3/4 x 29 1/2 ins / 91 x 75 cm) FRF 17,000. LONDON, 15 June 1995, *Still-life of Apples and Grapes* (oil on canvas, 25 1/4 x 31 1/4 ins / 64 x 79.5 cm) GBP 7,820. LONDON, 14 Dec 1995, *Notre-Dame in Paris* (oil on canvas, 28 1/2 x 35 1/4 ins / 72.5 x 89.5 cm) GBP 11,500. LONDON, 17 July 1996, *Still-life with Fruit and Bottle of Wine* (oil on canvas, 24 3/4 x 25 1/2 ins / 63 x 65 cm) GBP 6,900. LONDON, 19 Dec 1996, *Village* (oil on canvas, 11 1/2 x 17 ins / 29.3 x 43 cm) GBP 7,130. LONDON, 11-12 June 1997, *Landscape with Village and Lavander Tree* (oil on canvas, 16 3/4 x 26 3/4 ins / 42.5 x 68 cm) GBP 4,370. LONDON, 29 April 1999, *Still-life with Red Onions and Fruit* (oil on canvas, 21 x 25 ins / 54 x 64 cm) GBP 3,600. LONDON, 18 Nov 1999, *The Blue Mountains* (oil on canvas, 25 x 30 ins / 64 x 77 cm) GBP 7,500. LONDON, 20 Nov 2001, *Summer Time* (oil on canvas, 25 x 36 ins / 64 x 91 cm) GBP 85,000. LONDON, 21 Nov 2001, *Landscape* (oil on canvas, 13 x 16 ins / 33 x 41 cm) GBP 7,500. LONDON, 21 May 2003, *Portrait of an Indian Boy* (oil on canvas, 39 x 28 ins / 99 x 71 cm) GBP 60,000. PARIS, 17 Nov 2003, *Still-life with a Bottle and Fish* (1922, oil on canvas, 36 x 25 ins / 91 x 64 cm) EUR 30,500. PARIS, 21 Jan 2004, *Trees and Houses* (1929, oil on canvas, 27 x 17 ins / 68 x 44 cm) EUR 26,000. HELSINKI, 8 May 2004, *The House behind the Forest* (oil on canvas, 21 x 32 ins / 53 x 81 cm) EUR 54,000.

FALKA, Samuel

Hungarian, 18th - 19th century.

Born 4 May 1766, in Fagaras; died 20 January 1826, in Buda.

Engraver.

Samuel Falka produced engravings for a *History of Hungary*, by Engel.

FALKÉ, Pierre

French, 20th century.

Born 24 May 1884, in Paris; died June 1947, in Coutevroult (Seine-et-Marne).

Painter, watercolourist, engraver, illustrator.

In his early youth Pierre Falké travelled in Australia and the Indies and brought back from his journeys a heightened sense of colour and the exotic. He exhibited at the former Salon de l'Araingée. He provided illustrated papers with studies of peasant dress and customs, and also illustrated a wide variety of books, including Poe's *Adventures of Arthur Gordon Pym*, Chadoune's *Le Pot au Noir* (*In the Doldrums*), Jules Renard's *Poil de Carotte* (*Redhead*), Daniel Defoe's *Robinson Crusoe*, and, in 1931, Claude Farrère's *Les Civilisés* (*The Civilised*). He published some of the many sketches he made during his travels, as well as mezzotints and watercolours.

BIBLIOGRAPHY:

Mornand, Pierre/Thomé, Jules-René, *Vingt artistes du livre*, A. Cymboliste, Paris, 1950.

FALKE, Tobias. See **FALCKE**

FALKEISEN, Johann Jakob

Swiss, 19th century.

Born 1804, in Basel; died 15 February 1883, in Basel.

Engraver, painter. Landscapes.

After studying in Paris, Falkeisen went to Milan, where he worked under Migliara and Louis Cherbuin until 1838. Around 1843, he set himself up as a businessman in Asia Minor, returning to Switzerland some years later to take up the post of curator at the museum in Basel, which still has his *View over the Bosphorus*.

FALKEISEN, Theodor. See **FALCKEISEN**

FALKENBERG, Christian Friedrich von

German, 18th century.

Born c. 1675, in Copenhagen; died 8 July 1745, in Danzig (now Gdansk, Poland).

Painter. History painting.

A pupil of Andreas Stech in Danzig, Von Falkenberg is best known for his *Cyrus and the Amazon Queen* and 10 drawings of the Passion, possibly after Dürer.

FALKENBERG, George Richard
German, 19th century.
Born 14 March 1850, in Berlin.
Painter. Religious subjects, genre scenes, portraits.
Falkenberg worked in Munich, exhibiting there and in Vienna from 1888 to 1889. He is best known for his *Ave Maria* and his *Portrait of Prince Ludwig of Bavaria*.
MUSEUMS AND GALLERIES:
ZURICH (Kunsthaus): two genre scenes.
AUCTION RECORDS:
LONDON, 24 June 1988, *In the Garden* (1892, oil on canvas, 55 x 34$^{1/2}$in/140 x 87.5cm) GBP 12,100. LONDON, 27 Oct 1993, *Shellfish Gatherers* (1888, oil on canvas, 34$^{1/4}$ x 53$^{1/2}$in/87 x 136cm) GBP 4,370.

FALKENBERG, Richard
German, 20th century.
Born 20 September 1875, in Elberfeld.
Painter. Seascapes, landscapes, interiors.
Falkenberg was a student at the academy of fine arts in Düsseldorf. From 1904, he featured in collective exhibitions in Düsseldorf and Berlin.

As a landscape artist, he showed sensitivity to the atmosphere of the seasons, moments of the day and weather conditions, as seen in *March Morning; Moonlight.*

FALKENBURG. See **VALKENBORCH** and **VALKENBURG**

FALKENER, Erhart
German, 15th - 16th century.
Born to a family originally from Abensberg (Bavaria).
Sculptor (wood).
In 1496, Falkener carved the choir stalls in the parish church of Bechtolsheim (Oppenheim) and, in 1510, those of the church at Kiedrich (Rheingau).

FALKENSTEIN, Claire
American, 20th century.
Born 1908, in Coos Bay (Oregon); died 1997.
From 1950 also active in France.
Sculptor.
Claire Falkenstein graduated in literature and then taught for a while at Mills College, Oakland, and the California School of Fine Art, San Francisco, before she started painting. She subsequently took up sculpture in 1942. In 1950 she settled in Paris and visited Belgium, Germany, Spain and Italy, where in 1954 she set up a studio in Rome. After 1959 she worked mainly in New York, but exhibited in Californian cities.

Initially she made fairly traditional studies, mainly portraits in wood and stone, and later in plastic materials and bronze. From 1948, when she had moved to abstraction, she used metal - steel, iron, copper, silver and bronze - and glass melted at a high temperature. She became very proficient at welding together different metals. She then began to collaborate with architects in the San Francisco area. During her time in Paris, after 1955, she carried out many building commissions, including a gate for Santa Marinella, the home of Princess Pignatelli, near Rome, and a railing for the Peggy Guggenhiem Foundation in Venice. In abstract, but still classical, works, she used wood, but finally she found her own style in the working of iron or other forged metals. In the interstices of metal bars, twisted and welded like knots, she fitted coloured glass or other objects that caught her fancy. These works are like great insects carrying jewels in their tapered claws.

Falkenstein took part in the Salon des Réalités Nouvelles in Paris in 1950 and 1952, and other group exhibitions, including the Salon de la Jeune Sculpture. Her numerous solo shows have included: the Museum of Art, San Francisco, the Chicago Art Institute, the Galerie Stadler, Paris, and private galleries in San Francisco, New York, London, Berlin, Milan and elsewhere.
BIBLIOGRAPHY:
1er Salon des Galeries pilotes, exhibition catalogue, Musée cantonal, Lausanne, 1963.
MUSEUMS AND GALLERIES:
MARSEILLES (Mus. Cantini): *Le Couple* (*The Couple*) (1956).
AUCTION RECORDS:
LOS ANGELES, 9 Feb 1982, *Fusion* (glass and copper, 4$^{3/4}$ x 6 ins / 12 x 15 cm) USD 500. SAN FRANCISCO, 24 Oct 2000, *Untitled, Moving Point Painting* (1966, oil on canvas, 76 x 76 ins / 193 x 193 cm) USD 6,000. SAN FRANCISCO, 23 April 2002, *Living Curve, Fountain* (copper, h. 48 ins / 122 cm) USD 12,000. CHICAGO, 28 March 2004, *Untitled* (copper and patinated glass, 84 x 42x12 ins / 213 x 107x30 cm) USD 27,000. CHICAGO, 6 June 2004, *Untitled, Fusion* (c. 1968, copper and Murano glass, 48 x 16x33 ins / 122 x 41x84 cm) USD 23,000.

FALKINI
Italian (?), 19th century.
Probably born in Italy.
Painter. Landscapes.
MUSEUMS AND GALLERIES:
SARATOV (Raditschev Gal.): *Winter Landscape*; two works.

FALKMAN, Severin Gabriel
Swedish, 19th century.
Born 25 April 1831, in Stockholm; died 9 July 1889, in Helsinki.
Also active in Italy.
Painter.
Falkman was a pupil of Thomas Couture in Paris, and subsequently spent several years in Rome. He did historical genre paintings and paintings with subjects drawn from everyday Roman life. The Helsinki gallery holds a number of the latter.

FALKNER, Anne L.
British, 20th century.
Born in Dorset.
Painter. Local scenes, landscapes.
Anne L. Falkner painted mainly scenes of peasant life in the country. She exhibited in Britain and in Paris at the Salon d'Automne from 1921.

FALKNER, Harold
British, 20th century.
Draughtsman, architect.
Harold Falkner exhibited in 1900 and 1902 at the Royal Academy in London, showing drawings of houses he had designed on the outskirts of Farnham in Surrey.

FALKNER, Johann Friedrich
German, 19th century.
Born 20 December 1828, in Nuremberg; died 29 December 1866, in Munich.
Draughtsman, engraver (including etching).
A pupil of F. Geissler, Falkner worked in Munich and Venice. He produced a series of drawings of views of Nuremberg as well as engravings after R. von Alt, J.C. Erhard and L. Kachel.

FALKONER, Anna Elisabetha
Hungarian, 18th century.
Born 23 October 1714; died 26 September 1790.
Painter.
Anna Eliisabetha Falkoner was the daughter of Gyorgy Falkoner, and became a nun of the Clare order under the name of Sophia. She decorated the old church of her order with frescoes and altarpieces. She also painted images of saints and decorated the album of the Sorority of the Clare monastery with watercolours, which are now in the National Archives in Budapest.

FALKONER, Ferencz
Hungarian, 18th century.
Born 1736; died 20 April 1792.
Painter.

The son of Polycarp Falkoner, Ferencz Falkoner probably studied under his grandfather, Gyorgy. He produced frescoes, one of which is in the garrison church in Budapest, and another of which is in the parish church of Budapest. Some of his oils are held in a private collection in Budapest, and include a *Crucifixion*, a self-portrait and a *Portrait of the Painter's Wife, Barbara*.

MUSEUMS AND GALLERIES:
BUDAPEST (Szépmuvészeti Múz.): *Joseph Interpreting Dreams*.

FALKONER, György, or Falconer or Falconet
Hungarian, 17th - 18th century.
Born 1646; died 14 February 1741.
Painter.

Gyorgy Falkoner was probably of Scottish origin. He studied in Vienna under Guido Cagnacci, and settled in Budapest. He produced a painting of the *Virgin*, a votive canvas which is now in the parish church of Budapest, and *St Anne with Mary as a Child and St Joachim*, which is now in the church of the parish of Viziváros, a district of Budapest. He also produced *St John the Baptist, St Paul, Angelic Greeting* and *Our Lady of Perpetual Mercy*.

FALKONER, Henrik Josef, clerical name Julianus
Hungarian, 18th century.
Born 2 February 1708.
Painter.

A member of the Carmelite order, Henrik Falkoner took part in the production of decorative paintings in the old Carmelite church in Buda. He was the son of Gyorgy Falkoner.

FALKONER, Jozsef Ferencz
Hungarian, 18th century.
Baptised 22 March 1765; died 23 October 1808.
Painter.

The son of Ferencz Falkoner, Jozsef Falkoner studied under his father. In 1797, he painted frescoes for the sanctuary of the parish church of St Christina in Budapest. He also produced the altarpiece of the church, a *St Joseph*.

FALKONER, Polycarp
Hungarian, 18th century.
Born 26 January 1706; died 18 January 1739.
Painter.

Polycarp Falkoner was the eldest son of Gyorgy Falkoner as well as his student.

FALL, Obéye
Senegalese, 20th - 21st century.
Born 11 September 1962, in St Louis, Senegal.
Painter.

Obèye Fall studied modelling at the École Nationale des Beaux-Arts de Dakar in 1978, painting at the Atelier de Recherche d'Arts Plastiques de Pierre Lods in 1985, and pictorial art at the same school from 1986 to 1988.

Fall's research inspired him to write an essay on Black African statue craft. This influenced his style to evolve towards the abstract. He contorts a vertical line upwards or downwards, thus conveying his perception of 'space-time' and describing concave or convex forms, always in accordance with the traditions of Black African statue craft. He has also researched heraldic imagery, as found on African statues and sanctuaries. This inspired him to imbue animals in his works with a communicative significance, bringing humans, animals, minerals and nature together. He expresses this unity in *Totem*. Here, his representations of animals recall artworks originating in Africa or in the Caribbean, and they serve as a medium of expression and communication, evoking the intimate relationship between humans and their environment.

Since 1982, he has taken part in several group exhibitions, notably in Dakar, in the *Littérature, Art et Architecture de l'Islam* (*Islamic Literature, Art and Architecture*) exhibition in 1991. He also exhibited in Oslo in 1993, at the *Black History Week* exhibition.

FALLANI, Giuseppe
Italian, 19th century.
Born 1859, in Rome.
Sculptor, decorative artist.

Fallani's masters were Ettore Ferrari and Ercole Rosa. He mostly made sculptures for churches and decorated the Pinacoteca in the Vatican, the church of the Rosary, the church of S Helena, and some palazzi. He won a prize in Rome for a statue of *St Sebastian*.

FALLARO, Jacopo
Italian, 16th century.
Painter. History painting.

Jacopo Fallaro was a contemporary of Titian. According to Vasari, the Chiesa dei Gesuati in Venice has his painting, *Giovanni Colombini Receiving the Monastic Habit from the Pope*, intended for the door of the organ box.

MUSEUMS AND GALLERIES:
VENICE (Church of the Gesuati).

FALLENBÖCK, Alfred
Austrian, 19th century.
Born 17 June 1849, in Vienna.
Painter.

Like his brother Richard, Alfred Fallenböck was a pupil of Canon. He also studied with Engerth.

FALLENBÖCK, Richard
Austrian, 19th century.
Born 15 August 1859, in Vienna; died 21 December 1891, in Paris.
Painter, decorative designer. Flowers.

Richard Fallenböck studied in Vienna. In 1889, he was awarded a bursary to stay in Paris, where he studied the use of flower painting in industry. Throughout his life, he was a regular contributor to the exhibition of the conservatoire of arts and crafts in Vienna.

FALLENTER, Franz, or Falleter
Swiss, 16th - 17th century.
Born in Lucerne; died 1612, in Lucerne.
Glass painter.
Lucerne School.

Noteworthy among Fallenter's works, listed in Brun, is a stained glass window, now in the historical museum in Lucerne, representing *The Judgement of Solomon* (dated 1598) and another with *Arms of Sonnenberg and Zurgilgen*. Another 33 works are mentioned, mainly executed in collaboration with his assistants and now dispersed among the collections in Basel, Zurich and Mainz. He also painted the miniatures in Rudolf Pfyfer's *Romreise* (Journey to Rome) published in 1592.

MUSEUMS AND GALLERIES:
BASEL - LUCERNE (Historisches Mus.): *Judgement of Solomon* (1598, stained glass window); *Arms of Sonnenberg and Zurgilgen* (stained glass window) - MAINZ - ZURICH.

FALLENTER, Jost
Swiss, 17th century.
Born 1586, in Lucerne.
Glass painter.

According to Pfyffer, Fallenter produced stained glass windows of great artistic merit. He was the son of Franz Fallenter.

FALLER, Emily
French, 19th century.
Born in New York, to French parents.
Painter. Genre scenes.

The daughter and pupil of Louis Clément Faller, Emily Faller regularly exhibited portraits, watercolours, drawings and paintings on porcelain at the Salon from 1874.

FALLER, Felix
German, 19th century.
Born in Lenzkirch (Baden-Württemberg).
Painter.

Faller's drawings of the *Black Forest* are held in Lenzkirch (Baden-Württemberg).

FALLER, Giovanni. See **FALIER**

FALLER, Karl
Swiss, 19th - 20th century.
Born 8 May 1875, in Meggen; died 30 November 1908, in Paris.
Sculptor. Religious subjects, genre scenes.

Karl Faller began his studies at the school of industrial arts in Lucerne and completed them at the academy of fine arts in Munich, as well as in Paris. He exhibited at the academy of fine arts in Munich in 1899, receiving a silver medal, and at the Salon des Artistes Français in Paris in 1900 for the Exposition Universelle.

His career was a very short one. He often created sculptures on biblical themes: *Christ on the Cross* for the choirstall at the Franciscan church in Lucerne, *Adam and Eve*, which he exhibited in Paris in 1900 and *Prodigal Son*. He also produced works on genre subjects, such as *Poor Woman*.

MUSEUMS AND GALLERIES:
BERN: *Miner; Firedamp Explosion* - GENEVA: *Homeless* - LUCERNE: *Adam*.

FALLER, Louis Clément
French, 19th century.
Born 1 June 1819, in Habsheim; died 27 February 1901, in Paris.
Also active in the USA.
Painter, watercolourist, draughtsman. Portraits, genre scenes, landscapes.

Louis Clément Faller ran away from the Jesuit college in Fribourg, Switzerland, to take up art studies in Paris. He joined the studio of Paul Delaroche in 1838, subsequently moving on to that of Eugène Delacroix. Meanwhile, Faller had become involved with the Fourierist movement (promoting communal associations of producers) and, after the events that led to the 1848 French Revolution, he left for the USA. He set up a studio in St Louis, then in New York, which he ran for six years. In 1858 he returned to Alsace, initially settling in Ribeauvillé, then moving in 1863 to Orsay in the Chevreuse valley. He exhibited at the Paris Salon, where his contributions were noticed by only a few friends and compatriots.

Faller's biographers allude to his difficult, solitary nature, due to his rejection of compromise both on an artistic level and in daily life, a misanthropy which is barely reflected in the light, clear, pleasing nature of his paintings of cattle grazing, farm interiors, landscapes and portraits.

MUSEUMS AND GALLERIES:
MULHOUSE: *Chevreuse Valley; Shepherds* - STRASBOURG: *Peasant House*.

AUCTION RECORDS:
PARIS, 5 Dec 1923, *Chicken Food* (charcoal/paper) FRF 150. PARIS, 17-18 June 1928, *Portrait of a Little Girl*, FRF 110. PARIS, 29 Jan 1931, *Child and Toad* (drawing) FRF 40. PARIS, 4 Dec 1941, *Man with Beard; Fauve Study* (two pencil drawings) FRF 110. PARIS, 17 Dec 1943, *House by the Water* (watercolour/paper) FRF 210. PARIS, 3 May 1945, *Cowgirls*, FRF 420. PARIS, Oct 1945-July 1946, *Young Girl Seated under a Tree*, FRF 1,200. PARIS, 8 Nov 1980, *Edge of the Forest* (oil on canvas, 12 1/2 x 9 ins / 32 x 22 cm) FRF 650. PARIS, 22 Jan 1988, *Twilight* (black chalk and stump heightened with white/yellow paper, 10 x 14 1/2 ins / 25.5 x 37 cm) FRF 3,500. NEW YORK, 26 May 1992, *Riverscape in France* (1879, oil on canvas, 9 1/4 x 13 ins / 23.5 x 33 cm) USD 1,320. PARIS, 18 Nov 1994, *Clouds* (oil on canvas, 32 3/4 x 42 1/4 ins / 83 x 107 cm) FRF 20,000.

FALLEUR, family of artists
Flemish, 17th - 18th century.
Of German origin.
Active in Liège and Namur.
Glass painters.
Flemish School.

FALLIGAN, Henri
Flemish, 17th century.
Painter.
Flemish School.

Henri Falligan qualified as a master in Tournai on 20 April 1701.

FALLOISE, Jean François
French, 19th century.
Active in Paris c. 1820.
Engraver.

FALLOISE, Joseph
Belgian, 19th century.
Born 22 October 1812, in Liège; died 17 January 1886, in Liège.
Engraver (steel), metal worker.

Joseph Falloise attended the academy in Liège and subsequently Paris. Landscapes and animals predominate in his works.

MUSEUMS AND GALLERIES:
LIÈGE (Army Mus.): *Decoration of Arms*.

FALLON, Melchior
French, 16th century.
Painter. Architectural views.

MUSEUMS AND GALLERIES:
CAMBRAI: *General View of the Old Church of St-Géry in 1543* (1543, oil).

FALLORIUS, Simon Peter
Hungarian, 17th century.
Draughtsman.

Simon Fallorius was a curate in Csejthe, and produced a drawing of the old church in the town.

FALLOT, Nicolas. See **FALOT**

FALLOT, Pierre
French, 20th century.
Born in Paris.
Painter.

Pierre Fallot exhibited Spanish scenes at the Salon des Artistes Indépendants and the Salon d'Automne about 1927.

FALLOT, Robert
French, 20th century.
Born in Paris.
Painter. Landscapes.

From 1928 Robert Fallot exhibited in Paris at the Salon des Artistes Français.

FALLOURS, Samuel
Dutch, 18th century.
Active in the Moluccas.
Painter, engraver.

Samuel Fallours painted insects, shells and fish and published these works as engraved reproductions under the title *Natural Curiosities*.

FALLS, Charles Buckles
American, 20th century.
Born 10 December 1874, in Fort Wayne (Indiana); died 15 April 1960, in Falls Village.
Painter, engraver, illustrator. Wall decorations, stage sets, posters.

Charles Buckles Falls was a member of the Society of Illustrators and the National Society of Mural Painters and was awarded a number of distinctions.

He began as an illustrator for the *Chicago Tribune*. In 1923 he wrote and illustrated an *ABC Book* for children. He also illustrated literary works, including Walter Bowie's *When Jesus was Born* (1928) and *Vast Horizons* by Mary Seymour Lucas (1943).

BIBLIOGRAPHY:
Hammond, Wayne G,, *The Graphic Art of C. B. Falls: an Introduction*, exhibition catalogue, Chapin Library, Williams College, Williamstown, 1982.

FALLS, Clinton De Witt
American, 19th century.
Born 1864, in New York.
Painter, illustrator.

Clinton De Witt Falls was a pupil of Walter Satterlee. He often painted military subjects and did comic illustrations.

FALLSTEDT, Ingel
Danish, 19th century.
Born 1848, in Copenhagen; died 1899, in Stockholm.
Sculptor.

A student at the academy in Stockholm, Fallstedt subsequently studied in Munich and Paris.

MUSEUMS AND GALLERIES:
GÖTEBORG: *Bust of G. von Rosen; Bust of King Oscar II* (marble); *Bust of Count A. Ehrensvärd; Bust of J. Dickson; copy of Donatello's low relief at the Bargello in Florence* (marble) - HELSINKI: *Bust of A. von Becker* - STOCKHOLM (Kungliga Akademien): *Bust of G. Cederstrom* - STOCKHOLM (Nationalmus.): *Bust of H. Salmon* (bronze); *Bust of A. von Becker* (bronze); *Bust of G. von Rosen* (bronze); *Bust of Baron J. Nordenfalk* (marble); *Bust of Princess Louisa of Denmark*.

FALMAGNE, Louis
Belgian, 19th century.
Born 1829, in Namur; died 1871, in Brussels.
Engraver.

Louis Falmagne was a pupil of Calamatta. He executed engravings after the works of French and Walloon painters. Seven of his works are to be found in the British Museum.

FALOCCO, Niccolò
Italian, 18th century.
Born in Oratino, near Campobasso.
Active c. 1740.
Painter.

Niccolò Falocco was a skilful copyist of the work of Francesco Solimena, his teacher.

FALOPPI, Cesare de
Italian, 15th century.
Active in Bologna in 1441.
Painter.

Cesare de Faloppi was the son of Giovanni di Pietro de' Faloppi.

FALOPPI, Giovanni di Pietro de'
Italian, 15th century.
Born in Modena.
Active in Bologna from 1428 to 1441.
Painter.
Bolognese School.

In the church of S Francesco at Bologna Giovanni di Pietro de'Faloppi executed a fresco of *The Birth of John the Baptist*. He was the father of Cesare de Faloppi and is perhaps identical with Giovanni da Modena.

FALOT, J.
French, 18th century.
Painter (including porcelain). Genre scenes.

J. Falot was working in 1770 for the royal porcelain factory at Sèvres and was in the service of Louis XV. The royal castle in Stockholm has a Service on which he worked.

MUSEUMS AND GALLERIES:
LONDON (Wallace Collection).

FALOT, Nicolas
French, 16th - 17th century.
Active between 1576 and 1627 in Paris.
Painter. History painting.

Nothing is known about the life and work of this artist.

FALSA, Farid
Algerian, 20th century.
Born 11 April 1940, in Tlemcen.
Active in Spain since 1963.
Painter, watercolourist. Figures, landscapes. Symbolism.

Farid Falsa has had solo exhibitions in the Spanish cities of Salamanca, Málaga and Valladolid. He paints watercolour landscapes using generous brush strokes.

MUSEUMS AND GALLERIES:
AYLLON (MCA) - GRANADA (MBA).

FALSARESI
Italian, 17th century.
Painter.

The parish church of S Martino in Celone, in Pontignano, houses his small altarpiece depicting St Romuald.

FALSEN, Marie Bolette Wilhelmine, called Mimi
Norwegian, 19th - 20th century.
Born 29 May 1861, in Bergen.
Painter.

Marie Falsen went to Paris in 1888 and was a student of Courtois, Collin, Dagnan-Bouveret and Puvis de Chavannes. She then studied in Stockholm with Richard Berg and Zorn. After travelling in Italy, she settled in Christiania (now Oslo) in 1906, where since 1891 she had regularly featured at the annual exhibition. Her works include: *Once Upon a Time* and *The Greatest Sorrow* (mother and child). She exhibited in Copenhagen, at the Universal Exhibition in Chicago in 1893, at the Norwegian exhibition in Brighton in 1913, and then in Bergen.

FALTER, John Philip
American, 20th century.
Born 28 February 1910, in Plattsmouth (Nebraska); died 16 May 1982, in Philadelphia.
Painter, illustrator. Genre scenes of American life. Posters and magazine covers and illustrations, portraits.

John Philip Falter studied at the City Art Institute, Kansas (1928-1930) and the Grand Central School of Art and Art Students League, New York (1930-1931). His teachers included Ivan Olinsky, George Brandt Bridgman, George Wright, Mahonri Young and Monte Crews.

He is among America's best-known and popular illustrators, and was allegedly called 'America's most gifted illustrator' by Norman Rockwell. He began his career as an illustrator working for popular magazines, receiving his first commission from *Liberty* magazine in 1933. He subsequently worked for a number of clients in advertising. His most famous work includes his covers for the widely-read *Saturday Evening Post*: Falter produced over 183 covers for the magazine between 1943 and 1969, depicting a range of panoramic scenes from American life, provincial and urban, as well as some portraits. During World War II Falter joined the Navy and created over 300 recruiting posters. He also received a commission from *Esquire* magazine for a series of posters of war heroes.

Falter is also known for his interest in Jazz, which led him to create portraits of Jazz legends, such as Louis Armstrong, and scenes from club life in Harlem. Noted for his skill in portraiture, he also produced paintings of famous stars such as Clark Cable and Olivia de Haviland. In the 1970s and 1980s, Falter's work included historical scenes from 'Western' American life, notably of the migration between 1843 and 1880 from the Missouri River to the Rocky Mountains, and the life of the Pioneers.

BIBLIOGRAPHY:

Crawford, A.R., *Posters of World War I and World War II in the George C. Marshall Research Foundation*, University of Virginia Press, 1988. Reed, Walt, *The Illustrator in America: 1880-1980: A Century of Illustration*, HarperCollins, New York, 1993. Cohn, J./Rutt, J., *Covers of the Saturday Evening Post: Seventy Years of Outstanding Illustration from America's Favorite Magazine*, Smithmark, U.S., 1998.

MUSEUMS AND GALLERIES:

INDEPENDENCE (Harry S. Truman Library) - LINCOLN (Nebraska State Museum of History) - LINCOLN, NE (Sheldon Memorial AG, University of Nebraska): *Windy Day in Atchison* (1952, oil on canvas) - LONG BRANCH (Herbert Hoover Museum) - NEW YORK (Museum of the City).

AUCTION RECORDS:

NEW YORK, 6 Nov 1999, *Children Waiting for Bus in Snowy Rural Landscape* (oil on board, 24 x 20 ins / 61 x 51 cm) USD 40,000. CEDAR FALLS, 20 Nov 1999, *Old Gold Advertisement* (oil on canvas, 28 x 22 ins / 71 x 56 cm) USD 35,000. NEW YORK, 4 Oct 2000, *Huckleberry Finn* (oil on gessoed masonite, 9 x 9 ins / 22 x 23 cm) USD 13,000. NEW YORK, 30 Nov 2000, *Visit* (oil on board, 19 x 19 ins / 49 x 47 cm) USD 25,000. NEW YORK, 10 Nov 2001, *Bombadier Shot Through Turret During Bombing Run* (oil on canvas, 22 x 29 ins / 56 x 74 cm) USD 11,000. NEW YORK, 28 Nov 2001, *Night Game Yankee Stadium* (oil on board, 24 x 20 ins / 61 x 51 cm) USD 130,000. PORTLAND, 31 July 2002, *After a Nor' Easter, Oqunquit* (gouache, 20 x 22 ins / 51 x 56 cm) USD 2,000.

FALTER, Marcel
French, 20th century.
Born 17 April 1866, in Dieuze.
Painter. Animals.

It was not until 1923 that Marcel Falter first exhibited, initially at the Salon d'Automne, and later at the Salon des Artistes Indépendants. He always painted animals, his subjects ranging from slaughtered cattle to circus scenes.

AUCTION RECORDS:

VERSAILLES, 29 Oct 1989, *Circus Rider* (oil on canvas, 25 1/2 x 32 ins / 65 x 81 cm) FRF 14,500; *Circus* (oil on canvas, 36 1/4 x 28 3/4 ins / 92 x 73 cm) FRF 23,000. PARIS, 22 March 1990, *Circus Rider* (oil on canvas, 25 1/2 x 31 3/4 ins / 64.5 x 80.5 cm) FRF 19,000. VERSAILLES, 21 Oct 1990, *Cows and Peasant* (oil on canvas, 25 1/2 x 31 3/4 ins / 65 x 80.5 cm) FRF 4,000. VERSAILLES, 25 Nov 1990, *Cattle* (1949, oil on canvas, 28 3/4 x 39 1/4 ins / 73 x 100 cm) FRF 8,000.

FALTI, Johan Baptist. See **FALDA Giovanni Battista**

FALTIN, Margarete
German, 19th - 20th century.
Born 3 October 1865, near Aue (Saxony).
Painter.

Margarete Faltin was a student of H. Herterich in Munich and studied in Dresden with F. Kops and A. Pepino. She painted watercolour interiors and also oil and watercolour landscapes, including *Pilnitzallee in Autumn* and *On the Canal*. She also made some attempts at lithographs, such as *Stream*. This artist exhibited at the major exhibition in Dresden from 1901.

FALTZ, Raimund, or Falz
Swedish, 17th - 18th century.
Born 4 July 1658, in Stockholm; died 21 May 1713, in Berlin.
Medallist, modeller, sculptor (ivory). Historical subjects, portraits. Medallions, miniatures.

After studying gold and silverwork and spending time in Copenhagen and Augsburg, Raimund Faltz went to Paris to do intaglio engraving with C. Chéron. He then settled in Berlin, where he produced a large number of medals of historical figures, including *Frederick I and His Wife*, *Charles XII of Sweden*, *Louis XIV* and *Elector Georg Augustus of Hanover*, as well as ivory portrait medallions and miniature portraits. The Kaiser Friedrich museum in Berlin holds wax medallions by Faltz that were probably created as maquettes for his medals.

FALUS, Elek
Hungarian, 20th century.
Born 1883, in Orosháza.
Draughtsman, illustrator.

Elek Falus lived for a few years in London where he worked on book illustrations before settling in Budapest, where he continued to produce illustrations for books and magazines. He illustrated the poetry of Josef Kiss, *Levelek Hullasa*.

FALUSE, Aert van den
Flemish School, 15th century.
Born to a family originally from Louvain.
Painter.

Faluse is mentioned in 1468 as one of those participating in the preparation of the decorations for the celebration of the marriage of Charles the Bold of Burgundy in Bruges.

FALVARD, Maurice Gabriel
French, 20th century.
Born 30 December 1899, in La Ferté-Macé (Orne).
Painter, illustrator. Landscapes, landscapes with figures, seascapes.

Maurice Gabriel Falvard exhibited in Paris at the Salon des Artistes Indépendants from 1929. He won the Gustave Doré prize in 1927 and 1928. He illustrated Marcel Prévost's *Nouvelles lettres à Françoise* (*New Letters to Françoise*), and painted seascapes with figures (*Shellfish Gatherers*) and characterised landscapes (*Night Visions*).

FALVAT, Julian
Polish, 20th century.
Born in Torun.
Painter, watercolourist. Figures, portraits, landscapes.

Julian Falvat showed work in Paris at the Salon de la Société Nationale des Beaux-Arts, of which he was a member. In 1921 he contributed watercolours of portraits (*Portrait of the Artist, Montagnard*), urban landscapes (*Courtyard of Dembuo Castle, Cracow; Old Country Church*) and landscapes with figures (*Bear Hunt*) to an exhibition of Polish artists organised by the Société Nationale des Beaux-Arts in Paris.

FALVEY, Thomas
Irish, 19th century.
Active in Cork.
Painter.

Thomas Falvey appeared at the Royal Hibernian Academy in 1832 with two portraits. Other notable works by him are *Young Boys Bathing* and *Institution of the Order of St Francis*.

FALYD, Raimund, or Falyt
Italian, 18th century.
Active in Milan.
Sculptor.
Raimund Falyd is recorded as being in Vienna in 1729 and acquiring citizenship rights in Prague on 18 September of the same year.

FALZAGALLONI, Stefano, called Stefano da Ferrara
Italian, 15th century.
Born before 1430, in Ferrara; died 17 January 1500, in Padua.
Painter. History painting.
Paduan School.
Stefano Falzagolloni, known as Stefano di Ferrara, is mentioned by Vasari as a close friend of Andrea Mantegna. He carried out a number of major commissions of which little trace remains. It is thought that several of his works were attributed to Giovanni Bellini, whose style his resembles.

Falzagolloni was commissioned to decorate the old Cappella dell'Arca di S Antonio in the Basilica del Santo at Padua. Vasari called these frescoes, now lost, a masterpiece. They were executed before 1445, for they are cited by Michele Savonarola at this date, but were covered in the 16th century by a series of low reliefs representing the miracles of St Anthony of Padua. In the same basilica he painted on a pillar the *Madonna of the Pillar*. The painting on wood in the Pinacoteca di Brera, Milan measuring 8 x 10 feet (248 x 320 cm) represents *The Virgin and Child* seated on a throne decorated with low reliefs with a saint on each side and lower down *St Augustine* and *Saint Bonaventura*.

Falzagolloni's death is recorded in the 'Libri' (books) of the Archiconfraternità della Morte (Brotherhood of Death) in Ferrara, where mention is made of six torches 'to accompany the corpse of Stefano Falzagalloni to the church of S Apollinare at Farrara'.
MUSEUMS AND GALLERIES:
MILAN (Pinacoteca di Brera): *Virgin and Child enthroned with Sts, St Augustine and St Bonaventura.*

FALZONI, Giulio
Italian, 20th century.
Born 1900, in Marmirolo.
Painter, watercolourist. Scenes with figures, local figures, interiors with figures, landscapes, urban landscapes, architectural views.

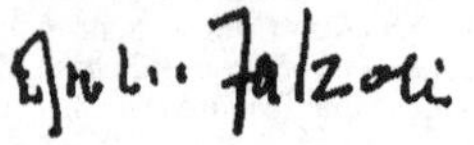

AUCTION RECORDS:
MILAN, 7 Nov 1985, *Tower Bridge, London* (watercolour, 19 3/4 x 27 1/2 ins / 50 x 70 cm) ITL 1,400,000. MILAN, 16 Dec 1987, *Il Palio di Siena* (1954, oil on canvas, 27 1/2 x 39 1/4 ins / 70 x 100 cm) ITL 3,000,000. MILAN, 12 Dec 1991, *Interior of the Carminati Restaurant in Milan; Ballroom of the Carminati Restaurant in Milan* (watercolour/paper, a pair, each 19 3/4 x 27 1/2 ins / 50 x 70 cm) ITL 3,900,000. MILAN, 16 June 1992, *Gypsies* (1959, watercolour/card, 19 1/2 x 27 1/2 ins / 49.5 x 70 cm) ITL 1,600,000. LUGANO, 8 May 1993, *The Sant'Ambrogio Festival* (1913, watercolour/paper, 20 x 27 1/2 ins / 51 x 70 cm) CHF 5,000. MILAN, 10 Dec 1996, *Old Milan: Piazza Vetra* (watercolour/card, 19 3/4 x 27 1/2 ins / 50 x 70 cm) ITL 2,330,000. MILAN, 18 March 2003, *My Garden* (oil on cardboard, 22 x 22 ins / 55 x 55 cm) EUR 4,800.

FAMARS, Charles Alexandre François Joseph Le Hardy de. See **LE HARDY DE FAMARS**

FAMARS TESTAS, Willem de
Dutch, 19th century.
Born 30 August 1834, in Utrecht; died 24 March 1896, near Arnhem.
Painter, illustrator, engraver (etching). Landscapes with figures, landscapes.
Willem de Famars Testas was a pupil of J. E. J. van den Berg.
MUSEUMS AND GALLERIES:
AMSTERDAM: *Interior of a House in Cairo* - UTRECHT: *Street in Jerusalem.*
AUCTION RECORDS:
LONDON, 5 Oct 1983, *Family of Nomads* (oil on canvas, 23 3/4 x 55 ins / 60.5 x 140 cm) GBP 1,800. AMSTERDAM, 15 April 1985, *Arab Street Scene* (1861, oil on panel, 21 1/4 x 16 3/4 ins / 54.2 x 42.7 cm) NLG 11,500. LONDON, 6 Oct 1989, *Street of an Arab Town* (oil on canvas, 31 1/2 x 22 1/2 ins / 80 x 57 cm) GBP 5,280. AMSTERDAM, 10 April 1990, *View of an Arab Town* (1865, watercolour and gouache/paper, 5 x 7 ins / 12.4 x 17.6 cm) NLG 2,990. AMSTERDAM, 5-6 Nov 1991, *Street of an Eastern Town* (1865, watercolour, 4 3/4 x 6 3/4 ins / 12 x 17 cm) NLG 3,450. AMSTERDAM, 30 Oct 1996, *Parade in Petra* (1868, oil on canvas, 32 3/4 x 23 ins / 83 x 58.2 cm) NLG 12,685. AMSTERDAM, 19-20 Feb 1997, *Arab Saddling a Horse* (oil on canvas, 6 x 7 1/2 ins / 15 x 19 cm) NLG 7,495.

FAMBRINI, Ferdinando
Italian, 18th century.
Active in Lucca.
Engraver (burin).
Ferdinando Fambrini is remembered for having engraved plates for the *Illustrated Album of the Very Beautiful Town and Port of Livorno* and *View of Pisa.*

FAMCHON, Alphonse Adolphe Onésime
French, 19th century.
Born 10 March 1821, in Boulogne-sur-Mer.
Painter.
Alphonse Famchon studied under Gobert. From 1864 to 1880 he exhibited still-lifes of flowers, fruit and game at the Paris Salon.

FAMEI, Giovanni Maria
Italian, 16th century.
Active in Reggio Emilia.
Painter.

FAMEL, Marie (Mme)
French, 19th - 20th century.
Born 27 January 1874, in Paris.
Enameller.
Marie Famel exhibited from 1906 at the Salon des Artistes Français, of which she was a member.

FAMELLA, Pietro
Italian, 15th century.
Painter.
Pietro Familla painted the armorial bearings in the abbey of SS Flora and Lucia in Arezzo.

FAMIBUS, Magno de (Fra)
Italian, 15th century.
Painter.
In 1479, with Johann Lanfelder, Magno de Famibus made an altarpiece for the abbey of Santo Spirito at Solmena.

FAMIN, Auguste Pierre
French, 19th century.
Born 1776; died 1859.
Sculptor, watercolourist. Figures. Statues, busts.
Auguste Pierre Famin gained his artistic training in the studio of David d'Angers. From 1842 to 1852 he exhibited at the Paris Salon. His best-known works include *Pandora* (plaster statue); *Billiard Player* (marble statue); *Medallion of General*

Thouvenel (marble); *Bust of Doctor Fornari* (marble); *Amazone Blessée* (plaster); and *Jacques Callot* (marble bust at the French ministry of the interior).
MUSEUMS AND GALLERIES:
CHARTRES: *Perfect Christmas* (bust).
AUCTION RECORDS:
PARIS, 18 Nov 1994, *Villa Medici* (watercolour, 6 x 8 1/2 ins / 14.4 x 21.5 cm) FRF 13,000.

FAMIN, Charles Victor
French, 19th century.
Born 1809, in Paris; died 1909, in Chartres.
Painter, architect, photographer (?).
Charles Victor Famin won the Grand Prix de Rome in 1835. He died at the age of 100. Many questions concerning Famin's identity have yet to be answered. He may have been the landscape and architectural photographer of the same name whose first attempts appeared in 1862. Some sources, notably those of the Cleveland Museum of Art, would be tempted to attribute the authorship of these photographic clichés to a certain Constant Alexandre Famin (1827-1888), asserting the existence of a different person of the same name.

Famin's work has been included in various collective themed exhibitions, including *Orte des Impressionismus: Gemälde und Fotografien* (*Locations of Impressionism: Paintings and Photographs*), an exhibition focusing on the aesthetic approach of painting and photography to the same subjects, at the Kunstmuseum, Basel, in 2003.
BIBLIOGRAPHY:
Fischer, Hartwig, et al., *Orte des Impressionismus. Gemälde und Fotografien*, exhibition catalogue, Kunstmuseum, Basel, 2003.

FAMIN, Pierre
French, 20th century.
Born 1890, in Algeria; died March 1988, in Marseilles.
Painter (including gouache), draughtsman.
Pierre Famin did not leave Algeria until just before 1980. He directed a gallery, *The Minaret*, which was the cultural and artistic centre of Algeria between 1925 and 1955, and was frequented by Camus, Cocteau, Le Corbusier, Jean Sénac and Jean de Maisonseul. It was he who acted as guide to Marquet's crossing of the Sahara.

FAMINIUS
French, 16th century.
Painter. Urban landscapes.
MUSEUMS AND GALLERIES:
MARSEILLES (Archives Municipales): *View of Marseilles.*

FAMINS, François, or Jamins
French, 16th century.
Active in Melun (Seine-et-Marne).
Painter.

FAMOL
Czech, 18th century.
Painter.
The inventory of the Prague treasury contains references to two of his works, namely two head portraits of the philosophers *Heraclitus* and *Democritus*.

FAMPA
Italian, 18th century.
Active in Naples.
Painter.
Fampa is recorded as having worked together with Mario Gioffredo on decorations for the Palazzo Gravina.

FAMULUS. See **AMULUS**

FAN AN-JEN. See **FAN ANREN**

FAN ANREN, or Fan An-jen, called Fan Laizi
Chinese, 13th century.
Born in Qiantang (Zhejiang).
Painter. Fish.
Song dynasty.
Fan Anren specialised in painting fish. He was a member of the Imperial Painting Academy from 1253 to 1258.
MUSEUMS AND GALLERIES:
BOSTON (MFA): *Two Carp Jumping in Waves* (attributed).

FAN CH'I. See **FAN QI**

FAN CH'IUNG. See **FAN QIONG**

FAN CHI. See **FAN JI**

FAN CHING-WEN. See **FAN JINGWEN**

FAN HIUE-I. See **FAN XUEYI**

FAN JI, or Fan Chi
Chinese, 19th century.
Active during the first half of the 19th century.
Painter.
Fan Ji's skill in authenticating antiques was unequalled. Also a painter, he sold his works on street corners in order to meet the needs of his aged mother. He wrote a treatise on painting, *The Guoyunlu Hualun*, consisting of three sections (theory on landscapes, theory on flowers and plants and theory on figures). The work groups together a collection of discontinuous, fair and sober comments, which although not particularly original, are not without interest.
BIBLIOGRAPHY:
Ryckmans, Pierre, *Les Propos sur la peinture de Shitao. Traduction et commentaires pour servir de contribution à l'étude terminologique et esthétique des théories chinoises de la peinture*, Institut belge des hautes études chinoises, Brussels, 1970.

FAN JINGWEN, or Fan Ching-wen, style name: Mengzhang, sobriquets: Zhigong, Siren
Chinese, 17th century.
Born 1587, in Suzhou; died 1644.
Painter.
Fan Jingwen was a poet and high-ranking official. Although he is not mentioned in the biographies of the painters, two works by him are known to exist: *Five Pines*, signed and dated 1639, and *Man Pulling Barge*, an album leaf after Fang Congyi dated 1642.

FAN K'I. See **FAN QI**

FAN K'IONG. See **FAN QIONG**

FAN KI. See **FAN JI**

FAN KUAN, or Fan K'uan, real name: Fan Zhongzheng, style name: Zhongli
Chinese, 10th - 11th century.
Born towards the mid- 10th century, in Huayuan, now Yaoxian (Shanxi).
Active c. 990-1030.
Painter. Landscapes.
Fan Kuan's biographical details are not well known. He was a landscape painter from northern China. It appears that he did not hold any official position and, after a peripatetic youth, he retreated into the mountain range of Mount Hua to devote himself to Daoism and the contemplation of nature. His work conveys the austere grandeur of the Shanxi mountains. Indeed, it represents the apogee of Chinese landscape painting and is among the most sublime in its entire history.

Having for some years adopted the style of his illustrious predecessor Li Cheng, and following a sudden interior revelation, Fan decided to change his own style: 'My predecessor's method consisted in an immediate approach to that which reveals itself in nature. Yet I am adopting the lessons of a man; to aspire to find them in the things themselves would be better. Better still would be to ask them from my own heart.' His contemporary critics attributed to him, as to Li Cheng, a creative power close to that of nature and the only authentic landscape to have reached us, *Travellers amidst Mountains and Gorges*, the signature on which was discovered in 1958, confirms this. 'This work represents an historic milestone, marking the first (and most complete) development of the landscape, conceived as much as a spiritual as a plastic experience.' (P. Ryckmans). The artist has reached the level where rocks, trees, torrents and mountains are no longer the simple image of a given landscape but are microcosmic realities parallel to the elements of the macrocosm. Man hardly impinges on this monumental universe but is an integral part of the whole; he is not crushed by it, he merges with it. Technically, all the resources in ink and painting are devoted to this contribution: each line seems possessed by an internal tension, the powerful contours are animated by irregular accents whose cross-hatching and innumerable small marks produce subtle tonal values. The brush strokes belong to the genre of 'raindrop wrinkles', whose density produces a tactile impression and translates the spontaneity of nature itself. This simple and serene composition, majestic and austere, still remains unequalled. However, all other works linked to the name of Fan Kuan are still no more than attributions.

BIBLIOGRAPHY:

Sirén, O, *Chinese Painting: Leading Masters and Principles I*, London, 1956. Cahill, James, *Chinese Painting*, Skira, Geneva, 1960. T. Miyagawa, T. (ed.), *Chinese Painting*, Chin. Lit, 1980. Linsheng, Wu, *Fu Baoshi's Contribution to Traditional Chinese Painting*, Tokyo, 1983. Yang Xin and others, *Three Thousand Years of Chinese Painting*, Yale University Press, 1997.

MUSEUMS AND GALLERIES:

BOSTON (MFA): *Temple in Snowy Hills* (fan-shaped album leaf, light colour on silk, attributed); *Palace in Snowy Hills* (hanging scroll, ink and light colour on silk, attributed) - NEW YORK (Metropolitan Mus. of Art): *Temple in Mountain* (hanging scroll, late copy) - TAIPEI (National Palace Mus.): *Travellers by Streams and Mountains* (c. 1000, ink and light colour on silk, hanging scroll, several imperial seals, inscription by Dong Qichang in the mounting, signature discovered bottom right in 1958); *Muleteers Approaching tream at Foot of Steep Mountains* (poem by Emperor Qianlong, colophons by Wang Shimin and Song Junye, attributed); *Isolated Temple in Snowy Hills* (hanging scroll, inscriptions by Wang De and Dong Qichang, attributed); *Sitting by Stream at Foot of Mountains in Clouds* (hanging scroll, inscriptions from the Yuan, Ming and Qing dynasties, attributed); *Woods and Waterfalls in Autumn* (c. 1050, hanging scroll, attributed, probably of the school of Li Tang) - WASHINGTON DC (Freer Gal. of Art): *Clear Peaks of Mount Hua* (hanging scroll, attributed).

FAN LI, also known as Zongsi
Chinese, 15th century.
Born in Changshu (Jiangsu).
Painter.

Fan Li worked in the style of Ma Yuan (c.1325-1365).

FAN LONG, style name: Maozong, sobriquet: Wuzhu
Chinese, 12th century.
Born in Wuxing (Zhejiang).
Active during the first half of the 12th century.
Painter. Landscapes.

Fan Long, a pupil of Li Gonglin (1040-1165), is one of the great literati painters of the 12th century. He is known for his *bai miao* style (ink-drawings with very fine outlines), the origin of which dates back to Wu Daozi (worked in c.720-760). As a Chan Buddhist monk, he specialised in portraits of *arhats* (disciples of the Buddha who have attained nirvana). Ascribed to him is a long scroll of such portraits, shown in the traditional manner as lonely old people in a landscape. The figures are painted in a fluid and delicate style; the landscapes are less well-defined, occasionally scratched in with a half-dry brush. These features contrast with the elegant and solid graphic tradition of the Imperial Academy. This scroll is one of the rare examples of Chan painting of the 12th century.

MUSEUMS AND GALLERIES:

WASHINGTON DC (Freer Gal. of Art): *Arhats in Forests and Crossing the Sea* (1279-1368 or later, ink on paper, handscroll, attributed, probably Ming dynasty).

FAN QI, or Fan Ch'i, sobriquets: Huigong, Qiagong
Chinese, 17th century.
Born 1616, in Jiangning, near Nanjing; died c. 1695.
Painter. Landscapes.

Fan Qi was one of the 'Eight Masters of Nanjing', the second most important after Gang Xian (c.1620-1689). Little is known of his life other than that he was born and earned a living from his work in the Nanjing region. Like many professional artists, he worked in varying styles, particularly that of Zhao Mengfu (1254-1322). Yet he was also receptive to new ideas and some of his works show that he even had some knowledge of western painting. During the last two decades of the 16th century, the Jesuit Matteo Ricci had brought prints and paintings to Nanjing, where they could be seen by Chinese artists and scholars. From this time on, Western influence can be seen in Chinese works, in terms of ideas, conceptions, motifs previously unfamiliar in China, the use of line and colour, the way of representing the sun and the rain, which led to a new interest in chiaroscuro. Fan Qi's landscapes bristle with this ferment of new ideas.

BIBLIOGRAPHY:

Yang Xin and others, *Three Thousand Years of Chinese Painting*, Yale University Press, 1997.

MUSEUMS AND GALLERIES:

BEIJING (Palace Mus.): *Fishing Village, Figures on Shore and in Boats* (dated 1669, handscroll) - BERLIN: *View of River* (handscroll, seal of the artist) - COLOGNE (Mus. für ostasiatische Kunst): *Scholar Leaning on Tree near Stream* (signed and dated 1659, fan painting, light colour on gold-flecked paper) - SHANGHAI: *Walk in Mountains in Springtime* (colour on gold-flecked paper).

AUCTION RECORDS:

NEW YORK, 29 Nov 1993, *Album of Landscapes* (1657, ink and colour on silk, eight leaves, each 13 x 8 1/2 ins / 32.1 x 21.9 cm) USD 31,050.

FAN QIONG, or Fan Ch'iung
Chinese, 9th century.
Active in the middle of the 9th century in Chengdu (Sichuan).
Painter. Religious subjects. Murals.

Fan Qiong was a painter of religious subjects. He produced many mural paintings after Buddhism was restored in China in 850. His brushstrokes were said to be like wire.

MUSEUMS AND GALLERIES:

TAIPEI (National Palace Mus.): *Guanyin of a Thousand Arms Sitting on Lotus Throne* (colour on silk, with an inscription attributing it to the artist and stating it was executed at the Shengxing temple in Chengdu in the first month of 850); one colophon, attributed.

FAN TCHUNPI. See **FANG JUNBI**

FAN TSEU-MIN. See **FAN ZIMIN**

FAN TZU-MIN. See **FAN ZIMIN**

FAN XUEYI, or Fan Hsüeh-i
Chinese, 18th century.
Painter.

Fan Xueyi was a specialist flower painter in the style of Yun Shouping (1633-1690). Several portraits are also attributed to him.

FAN YUN, or Fan Yün, style name: Qingruo
Chinese, 17th century.
Painter.
Fan Yun was the son of the painter Fan Qi.

FAN ZENG, or Fan Tseng
Chinese, 20th century.
Born 1938.
Painter. Figure paintings.
Fan Zeng is a noted calligrapher.
BIBLIOGRAPHY:
Zhongmin, Xu/Zhou Daguang (ed.), *Selected Paintings by Fan Zeng*, Foreign Languages Press, Beijing, 1985.
AUCTION RECORDS:
NEW YORK, 2 June 1988, *Zhong Kui* (ink on paper, hanging scroll, 53 1/4 x 26 1/2 ins / 135.3 x 67.3 cm) USD 2,420. HONG KONG, 18 May 1989, *Old Man with Monkeys* (ink and colour on paper, 17 1/2 x 20 1/2 ins / 44.5 x 52 cm) HKD 46,200. HONG KONG, 15 Nov 1989, *Asking One's Way Under Pine Tree* (1975, ink and colour on paper, hanging scroll, 70 x 37 1/2 ins / 177.5 x 95.1 cm) HKD 93,500. NEW YORK, 6 Dec 1989, *Cockerel* (1979, ink and colour on paper, hanging scroll, 33 x 19 1/2 ins / 83.8 x 49.5 cm) USD 2,750. NEW YORK, 16 June 1993, *Enlightenment of Lu Dongbin* (1979, ink and colour on paper, 54 3/4 x 97 ins / 139.1 x 246.4 cm) USD 25,300. STUTTGART, 30 May 2003, *Portrait of the Poet Li Taibo* (ink and colour, hanging scroll, 37 x 24 ins / 94 x 61 cm) EUR 2,400.

FAN ZHANGSHOU, or Fan Chang-shou
Chinese, 7th century.
Painter.
Fan Zhangshou was an officer and painter, and a pupil of Zheng Sengyu (active 500-550). He painted scenes of country life and domestic animals.

FAN ZIMIN, or Fan Tzu-min
Chinese, 13th century.
Monk-painter. Animals.
Fan Zimin was a Taoist monk. He was hardly known as a painter.
MUSEUMS AND GALLERIES:
CHICAGO (AI): *Oxen in Pasture* (handscroll, ink on paper, signed, colophon).

FAN-LUNG. See **FAN LONG**

FANAR, Simon
French, 17th century.
Active in Bruyères (Aisne).
Sculptor.
Simon Fanar executed two statues in walnut depicting *Our Lady* and *St John* in 1624 for a master painter in Laon called Pierre Le Long.

FANARD, Jehan. See **FAVART**

FANART, Clément Alphonse Antonin, or Fanard
French, 19th century.
Born 18 January 1831, in Besançon; died 2 September 1903, in Besançon.
Painter, lithographer. Genre scenes, landscapes.
Clément Fanart studied painting under François Diday in Geneva. After settling in Paris, he exhibited at the Salon from 1847 to 1879, receiving an honourable mention at the 1861 Salon.

He followed in the line of the 1830 School, but, rather than the Barbizon School, it was the undulating landscapes of the Savoy, Jura and Franche-Comté regions of France that inspired him to create his light effects. His best-known works include *Oak Forest in Savoy; Burst of Sunshine before the Storm; Twilight in the Rocailles Plain; Harvest in Jura; Nanette Going to the Fields; Harvest in Franche-Comté; A Stream in the Jura Valleys;* and *Banks of the River Doubs in Beaume.*
MUSEUMS AND GALLERIES:
BESANÇON: *Evening on the Banks of the River Ognon; Harvest; Pasture.*
AUCTION RECORDS:
PARIS, 12 Feb 1923, *Trees by a Pond* (oil on canvas) FRF 80. ENGHIEN-LES-BAINS, 14 June 1981, *Fishermen by a Mill in the Montains* (1854, oil on canvas, 27 3/4 x 38 1/4 ins / 70.5 x 97 cm) FRF 8,600. BERN, 21 Oct 1984, *Peasant Woman at the Well* (oil on card, 17 1/4 x 27 1/4 ins / 44 x 69 cm) CHF 6,500. LUCERNE, 13 Oct 1999, *Cattle in Landscape* (oil on canvas, 26 x 43 ins / 66 x 110 cm) CHF 7,000. CALAIS, 12 March 2000, *Fishermen by Lake* (oil on canvas, 15 x 24 ins / 38 x 61 cm) FRF 25,000. BELFORT, 2 March 2002, *Franche-Comté Landscape with Flock of Sheep* (*Paysage franc-comtois avec troupeau de moutons*) (oil on canvas, 18 x 26 ins / 46 x 65 cm) EUR 4,500. BESANCON, 8 Nov 2003, *Village by River* (oil on paper on canvas, 17 x 26 ins / 44 x 66 cm) EUR 1,600.

FANCATI
British, 18th century.
Born c. 1700, of Italian origin.
Draughtsman.
Fancati worked in England. Notable works by him include pen-and-ink drawings and copies of the *Portraits of King James II* and *Queen Mary*, in the style of Kneller.

FANCÉ
French, 17th century.
Active in Portugal.
Sculptor.
Fancé executed the statues of *St Peter* and *St Paul* on either side of a portal of the church of Sta Maria de Loretta in Lisbon, which was destroyed by an earthquake in 1755.

FANCELLI
Spanish, 17th century.
Active in Valladolid.
Sculptor, painter.
Fancelli enjoyed great popularity in Spain and was one of the outstanding artists of the Spanish Renaissance. However, his talent and efforts were not sufficient to prevent the rapid decline into decadence of his country's art. The exaggeration of the model, the pursuit of 'morbidezza' (delicacy of flesh tones) and of grace led his contemporaries and successors to bring a new stringency to their compositions. Convention took the place of reality, prettiness that of beauty and the grandeur of earlier works was replaced by a more mannered style. The power, boldness and somewhat austere and lofty nobility that had been the very essence of Spanish art collapsed, and along with these qualities, the movement and the relationship between living beings and the clothes they wore, also disappeared. Studies were based on mannequins instead of live models and all genuine expression of life vanished, giving way to the artificial and the unreal.

Most of Francelli's work is religious in content. He worked a great deal with the sculptor Vilmereate, known as Vemereado, and also got to know Valentin Díaz who became his friend and lent him support. The earliest date we have for Fancelli is 1605. He carved the main retable for the church of S Miguel in Valladolid, which had been rebuilt by order of the king. This retable is not in the present-day church of S Miguel, which was in fact originally the church of S Ignacio and underwent a change of name. In 1621 he executed a sculpture of the Holy Family for the church of S Lorenzo, which was painted by Díaz, and shortly after two retables for the convent of the Concepción in Vitoria. In 1624 he made a retable for the Discalced Franciscans and in 1629, the main retable for Valladolid Cathedral. One of his finest pieces is a Christ he made for the church of S Benito; this is now in Valladolid museum. The museum also boasts a very fine portrait of Fancelli himself.

FANCELLI, Antonio
Italian, 17th century.
Born 1606; died 1646.
Sculptor.

Antonio Fancelli lived and worked in Siena. He sculpted altars in the cathedral of Siena and started work on the magnificent altar of St Francis subsequently completed by Dionisio Mazzuoli.

FANCELLI, Bartolo
Italian, 16th century.
Born probably in Mantua.
Painter.

Bartolo Fancelli was a pupil of Perugino and made a copy of a picture by his master.

FANCELLI, Carlo I
Italian, 16th - 17th century.
Born c. 1566, to a family originally from Settignano (Florence); died 7 October 1640.
Sculptor.

Carlo Fancelli I worked in Rome for the Vatican, various churches and the Quirinal.

FANCELLI, Carlo II
Italian, 17th century.
Born 1661; died 19 April 1698.
Sculptor.

He was the son of Francesco Fancelli II.

FANCELLI, Chiarissimo
Italian, 17th century.
Born in Settignano; died 23 May 1632, in Florence.
Sculptor.

Chiarissimo Fancelli's body of work includes statues of *Mary Magdalene* and *St Christina* for the cathedral of Pisa and three marble busts of *Grand Duke Cosimo II* in Florence. He also sculpted four allegorical statues for Maria de' Medici and a statue of *Vulcan* for the Boboli gardens.

FANCELLI, Cosimo
Italian, 17th century.
Born 1620, in Rome; died 3 April 1688, in Rome.
Sculptor.

The son of Carlo Fancelli I, he studied under Bernini and worked alongside Pietro da Cortona until the latter's death. Examples of his decorative work are housed in the churches of St Peter's (under Bernini), SS Luca e Martina (under Cortona), S Maria della Pace, S Carlo al Corso, S Maria in Via Lata, La Chiesa Nuova, and S Nicolò da Tolentino. Cosimo Fancelli also produced models of angels for the papal chapel, the tomb of Cardinal Widmann in St Mark's, and a series of statues for the cathedral of St Luke. In collaboration with Ferrata, he sculpted an *Angel with a Saintly Face* on the Ponte S Angelo, the statue for the tomb of Pope Clement IX at S Maria Maggiore, Rome, two busts of Cardinal Altieri at S Maria sopra Minerva, Rome, and numerous other statues, busts and low reliefs.

FANCELLI, Francesco I
Italian, 17th century.
Sculptor.

Francesco Fancelli I worked on the construction of the church of S Pietro in Florence. He was also a member of the Accademia di San Luca.

FANCELLI, Francesco II
Italian, 17th century.
Born 23 January 1624, in Rome; died 14 May 1681.
Sculptor.

The son of Carlo Fancelli I, he worked on the decoration of the Villa and Casino Borghese in Rome and the Villa Mondragone in Frascati. He was also commissioned by Cardinal Borghese to provide ornamentation for the church of Monteporzio Catone, and he worked in Rome in the churches of S Maria Maggiore and S Marta.

FANCELLI, Francesco III
Italian, 18th century.
Born c. 1691; died 19 September 1750.
Sculptor.

He was the son of Giacomo Fancelli.

FANCELLI, Giacomo, also known as Fiorentino
Italian, 17th century.
Died 15 December 1614.
Sculptor.

FANCELLI, Giacomo
Italian, 17th - 18th century.
Born 25 July 1658; died 25 November 1738.
Sculptor.

He was the son of Francesco Fancelli II.

FANCELLI, Giacomo Antonio
Italian, 17th century.
Born 1619, in Rome; died 1671, in Rome.
Sculptor.

The son of Carlo Fancelli I, he studied under Bernini and was retained by the latter to help produce the statue of the *Nile* for the Piazza Navona in Rome and to work on the basilica of St Peter's.

FANCELLI, Giovanni di Paolo, or Giovanni di Stocco, or Fancegli
Italian, 16th century.
Born in Settignano (Florence) in 1st decade of the 16th century; died 1 July 1586.
Sculptor, goldsmith.
Florentine School.

Giovanni di Paolo Fancelli was a member of the academy of drawing and the pupil of B. Bandelli, who engaged him to work on the decorative sculpture of the Grotticina di Madonna in the Giardini di Boboli (Boboli Gardens) in Florence. Under the guidance of Vasari he carried out a statue of *Religion*, a fountain, satyrs and decorative works for the marriage celebrations of Francesco de' Medici with Joanna of Austria. In Pisa he carried out sculptural works for the church of the Cavalieri of the Order of S Stefano.

FANCELLI, Giuseppe
Italian, 18th century.
Architectural draughtsman.

G. de Pian subsequently engraved Giuseppe Fancelli's two views of the Doge's Palace in Venice.

FANCELLI, Giuseppe
Italian, 19th century.
Active in Bologna.
Painter.

Fancelli studied in Venice. He is known for the frescoes on tombs in the Certosa di Bologna.

FANCELLI, Luca
Italian, 15th century.
Born 1430, in Florence; died 1495, in Florence.
Sculptor, engineer, architect.

Luca Fancelli worked primarily in Mantua where he was architect at the court of Ludovico de Gonzaga. Among his sculptural works only the relief of a fireplace from the Palazzo di Revere, now in the museum of Mantua, appears to survive.

BIBLIOGRAPHY:
Carpeggiani, P., *Il Palazzo Gonzaghesco di Revere*, Mantua, 1974.

FANCELLI, Pandolfo
Italian, 16th century.
Born in Mantua; died July 1526, in Pisa, of the plague.
Sculptor.

Pandolfo Fancelli is probably identical with Pandolfo Fiorentino, who worked in Carrara with B. Ordonez in 1521. In 1523 he carried out decorative work for the cathedral of Pisa.

FANCELLI, Petronio
Italian, 18th century.
Born 1734; died 1800.
Painter, decorative artist. Church decoration, frescoes.

Petronio Fancelli studied under Mauro Tesi and was a member of the academy in Bologna, where he worked. He is credited with paintings in the Palazzo Bianchi and Palazzo Scarselli, and in the churches of S Isaia, S Marino and S Antonio. He also provided decorative frescoes for the Villa Bentivoglio in Pontecchio.

FANCELLI, Pietro
Italian, 18th - 19th century.
Born 1764, in Bologna; died 1850.
Painter, decorative artist. History painting.

Pietro Fancelli worked on various churches in Bologna.

AUCTION RECORDS:

MILAN, 17 Dec 1987, *Discovery of an Ancient Monument* (pen and brown ink/traces of pencil, 20¼ x 25½in/51.2 x 64.5cm) ITL 1,800,000. PARIS, 17 Dec 1999, *Christ before Pontius Pilate* (charcoal ink/colour wash/colour ink squared, 11 x 7 ins / 27 x 19 cm) FRF 20,000. LONDON, 13 Dec 2001, *Design for a Ceiling Decoration with Apollo and Allegorical Figures* (pen/ink wash, 26 x 19 ins / 67 x 47 cm) GBP 4,000.

FANCELLI, Tomaso
Italian, 15th - 16th century.
Born to a family originally from Prato.
Painter.

Tomaso Fancelli was a member of the Accademia de San Luca in Rome.

FANCELLI DI ALESSANDRO, Domenico, or Domenico Alejandro
Italian, 15th - 16th century.
Born 1469, in Settignano (Florence); died 1519, in Saragossa.
Sculptor.

The funerary monument to Cardinal Cisneros is one of the finest works of Castilian sculpture. It was executed by two sculptors, Fancelli di Alessandro, and the Castilian, Bartolomeo Ordóñez. These two great sculptors were also responsible for carrying out the funerary monuments of Ferdinand and Isabella and of Philip of Burgundy and Joan the Mad, in the royal chapel of Granada Cathedral. A Dane, J. Gayer, and the German Dr Juris attempted to prove that these masterpieces had no link with the Spanish sculptor Ordóñez. This question of attribution was definitively settled by the discovery of a document which revealed that in 1518 the bishop of Avila and the rector of the Colegio de S Ildefonso in Alcalá de Henares ordered Bartolomeo Ordóñez de Burgos to erect a funerary monument to the memory of Cardinal Cisernos. They specified that it was to be of even greater perfection than the double tomb of the Catholic kings in the royal chapel in Granada. Fancelli died in 1519 so it was in reality Bartolomeo Ordóñez who was responsible for Cisneros' tomb. Biguerny stated that the sculptor had indeed surpassed himself, as required.

Fancelli carried the style of the Italian Renaissance into Spanish sculpture, in the spirit of Donatello and Michelangelo, in whose tradition he worked. Some of the tombs which he executed in his workshop in Genoa were later transported to Spain, including those of Archbishop Diego Hurtado de Mendoza (1508-1510), Prince John (1513) at the church of Sto Tomás in Avila, and the Catholic Monarchs (1517), in the royal chapel of Granada Cathedral. He also sculpted the fonts of the cathedrals of Valencia and Toledo.

BIBLIOGRAPHY:

Hernandez Perera, J., *Escultores Florentinos en España*, Madrid, 1957. Azcárate, J.M., *'Escultura del siglo XVI'* in *Arte Hispánico*, Madrid, 1958.

FANCHER, Luis
American, 20th century.
Born 25 December 1884, in Minneapolis; died 1944.
Active in New York.
Painter.

Luis Fancher was a pupil of Mowbray, Henri, W.A. Clark and Kenyon Cox.

FANCHON, Sylvie
French, 20th - 21st century.
Born 1953.
Painter.

Sylvie Fanchon lives and works in Paris. In her paintings, she avoids immediate aesthetic appeal. Her works consist of simple and sparse forms, drawn from an existing reality and distorted, such as a cave from a Mickey Mouse comic, or a label from a book about technology. They have a modernistic lightness to them, and their colours are quiet and undemonstrative.

She has taken part in a number of group exhibitions, including: the Salon d'Art Contemporain in Montrouge, 1991; *Bleu Pour Les Filles. Rose pour les Garçons* (*Blue for Girls, Pink for Boys*), École des Beaux-Arts de Paris, 1995; *Couleurs, Couleurs* (*Colours, Colours*) Galerie Jordan-Devarrieux, Paris, 1997; and *L'Abstraction et Ses Territoires* (*Abstraction and its Territories*) at the Centre d'Art Contemporain in Montbéliard Le 19, in 1998. She has also staged a number of solo exhibitions, including: Galerie Françoise Palluel, 1987; Galerie du Haut-Pavé, 1990; Galerie Bernard Jordan, 1993 and 1998, all in Paris; Maison d'Art Contemporain, Fresnes, 1994; at the Fonds Régional d'Art Contemporain Basse-Normandie in Caen, 2001; and at the Abbaye St-André Centre d'Art Contemporain in Meymac, in 2003.

BIBLIOGRAPHY:

Blanc, Dominique, *'Sylvie Fanchon'* in *Connaissance des Arts*, n° 522, periodical, Paris, November 1995. Ghaddab, Karim, *'Sylvie Fanchon'* in *Art Press*, n° 232, periodical, Paris, 1998.

MUSEUMS AND GALLERIES:

CAEN (FRAC Basse-Normandie) - MARSEILLES (FRAC Provence-Alpes-Côte d'Azur) - PARIS (FNAC) - SÉLESTAT (FRAC Alsace).

FANCIULLACCI, Giovanni
Italian.
Miniaturist.

MUSEUMS AND GALLERIES:

GENEVA (MAH): *Portrait of Rubens* (after Rubens); after Raphael*La Fornarina*; *Portrait of Raphael* (after Raphael).

FANCIULLI, Felice
Italian, 17th century.
Sculptor.

Felice Fanciulli provided a marble relief for the cathedral of Orvieto in 1618.

FANCK, Ferdinand. See **FENAK**

FANCONY, Pascal
French, 20th - 21st century.
Born 26 February 1949, in Lemé (Aisne).
Environmental artist.

Pascal Fancony studied at the Écoles des Beaux-Arts in Aix-en-Provence, Nice, Rheims and St-Étienne. In his work, he lays claim to space and the environment by occupying it. Most often, he uses long, multicoloured twill ribbons to create large, hanging curtains.

He took part in the 1971 Biennale des Jeunes Artistes. He has also participated in a few street exhibitions: in La Rochelle in 1972, and in St-Étienne in 1973.

FANCOURT, E.
British, 19th century.
Painter.
E. Fancourt exhibited portraits of women at the Royal Academy in London in 1820 and 1821. The British Museum houses a portrait of the missionary Joseph Wolff, reproduced in mezzotint by H. Meyer after one of his works.

FANDA, J.
German, 19th century.
Of Silesian origin.
Sculptor.
After studying with Rauch in Berlin, Fanda exhibited a wooden statuette of *Shakespeare* at the Great Exhibition in London in 1851.

FANE
British, 18th century.
Active in Staines near London.
Miniaturist.
Fane exhibited a portrait at the Royal Academy in London in 1776.

FANELLI, Francesco
Italian, 17th century.
Sculptor, draughtsman, founder. Groups, statues.
Francesco Fanelli lived and worked in Genoa, England and Paris. His wooden carving of the *Dead Christ* is housed in the church of S Luca in Genoa, and two small bronze angels by him adorn the main altar in the church of S Maria della Neve, also in Genoa. In 1610, Fanelli travelled to England, where he was retained in Richmond, Surrey, by Henry, Prince of Wales, principally to sculpt bronze, marble and ivory urns and vases. He found favour with Charles I and was officially designated royal sculptor. Examples of his work include an ivory *Pygmalion*, 18 Florentine statues in bronze, a bronze bust of *Charles, Prince of Wales* (signed and dated 1640), and a whole series of bronze statuettes, including a *St George* and a *Centaur*. Francesco Fanelli's work is liberally scattered throughout England: a gilded bronze bust of *Lady Cottington* is housed in Westminster Abbey; marble funerary sculptures are preserved in Gloucester Cathedral; and a bronze fountain is to be found at Hampton Court. Fanelli travelled to Paris after leaving England; there, engravings were produced from his fountain designs, including a series entitled *Fountains and Waterspouts from the Most Beautiful Sites in Italy* and *Drawings of Grottoes*.
MUSEUMS AND GALLERIES:
LONDON (Victoria and Albert Mus.): *Charles I*.
AUCTION RECORDS:
LONDON, 22 March 1966, *Rearing Horse* (bronze) GBP 750. LONDON, 17 April 1969, *Dog Attacking a Deer* (bronze) GBP 820. LONDON, 8 July 1981, *St George and the Dragon; Turk Hunting Lion* (two bronzes, 7 1/4 x 9 1/4in/18.5 x 23.5cm) GBP 6,500. LONDON, 13 April 1983, *Horse* (bronze, h. 6in/15.5cm) GBP 2,000. LONDON, 20 April 1988, *Horse at Rest; Horse Trotting* (bronze, two statuettes, h. 6 1/4in/16cm) GBP 16,500. LONDON, 11 July 2001, *Group of Nessus and Deianara* (bronze, h. 8 ins / 20 cm) GBP 28,000. LONDON, 14 Dec 2001, *St. Catherine of Alexandria* (bronze, h. 6 ins / 15 cm) GBP 1,300. LONDON, 10 Dec 2002, *Group of Venus and Cupid* (brown patinated bronze, h. 7 ins / 19 cm) GBP 12,000. LONDON, 10 Dec 2002, *Nessus and Deianara* (bronze, 7 x 6 ins / 19 x 14 cm) GBP 32,000.

FANELLI, Francesco
Italian, 19th - 20th century.
Born 1863, in Livorno; died 1924, in Torre del Lago.
Painter. Religious subjects, figures, portraits, local scenes, landscapes with figures, landscapes.
Orientalism.
Fanelli was a pupil of Norfini at the Accademia in Lucca, then studied with Fattori in Florence. An Orientalist, his works are engagingly serene, and are executed with delicacy and a precise eye for detail, with luminous, limpid colours and strong contrasts between sombre foregrounds and brightly-lit backgrounds.

He showed three canvases in 1896 in Florence: *Dead Branches; Marshes; The Call*. In 1898 he exhibited in Turin, and in 1900 he presented *Washerwomen* in Milan.
MUSEUMS AND GALLERIES:
CLERMONT-FERRAND: *Eliezar and Rebecca*.
AUCTION RECORDS:
ROME, 1 Dec 1982, *Portrait of Giuseppe Bandi* (oil on canvas, 30 1/4 x 17 1/4 ins / 77 x 44 cm) ITL 800,000. MILAN, 19 Oct 1989, *Lakeside Landscape* (oil on canvas, 79 1/4 x 67 1/4 ins / 201 x 170.5 cm) ITL 15,000,000. MILAN, 6 Dec 1989, *Sails in the Wind* (oil on canvas, 74 3/4 x 46 ins / 190 x 117 cm) ITL 12,000,000. MILAN, 21 Nov 1990, *Young Girl Collecting Wood* (oil on canvas, 26 x 16 1/4 ins / 66 x 41 cm) ITL 2,400,000. ROME, 11 Dec 1990, *Lakeside Landscape* (oil on panel, 9 x 12 1/2 ins / 23 x 32 cm) ITL 2,300,000.

FANELLI, Pier Simon
Italian, 17th century.
Born in Ancona; died 1703, in Recanati.
Painter. History painting.
He studied under G. Peruzzini. Numerous examples of his work are to be found throughout the Marche region of Italy.

FANELLI, Virgilio
Italian, 17th century.
Born c. 1600, in Florence; died 1678, in Toledo.
Goldsmith, sculptor.
Virgilio Fanelli was probably the son of Francesco Fanelli. He travelled to Spain at the request of the Spanish ambassador in Genoa, who commissioned work at the Escorial. Fanelli was so well received in Spain that he decided to settle there. Examples of his work include a silver statue of *St Ferdinand* and a *Throne of the Virgin* in Toledo, together with a *Christ* in Casarubias.

FANELLI-SEMAH, Louis Joseph
French, 19th century.
Born 28 May 1804, in Toulon; died 1875.
Painter. History painting, religious subjects, portraits, genre scenes.
Louis Joseph Fanelli-Semah joined the École des Beaux-Arts on 19 November 1825 and studied under Gros. In 1844 he was awarded a third-class medal. His best-known works are *Neapolitan Bandits; Major Visiting Advanced Posts; Henri IV Sparing the Defeated after the Battle of Ivry; Portrait of M. Dupin in Public Prosecutor's Garb at the Court of Appeal; Christ in the Garden of Gethsemane; Education of the Virgin; Holy Family with Lily; The Three Marys at the Tomb of Christ; Christ Mourned by the Angels; Judith's Prayer*; and *Grandfather's Party*.
MUSEUMS AND GALLERIES:
TOULON: *Duke of Savoy Raising the Siege of Toulon in 1707* - VERSAILLES: *François-Louis de Bourbon, Prince de Conti; Thomas Corneille*.
AUCTION RECORDS:
PARIS, 23 April 1993, *Courtesan* (1831, oil on canvas, 18 x 15 ins / 46 x 38 cm) FRF 11,500.

FANET, Anne-Marie, Mme Viellard
French, 19th - 20th century.
Born 22 May 1866, in Caen.
Painter. Genre scenes.

Anne-Marie Fanet was a pupil of Jean-Paul Laurens and Benjamin-Constant. She exhibited regularly in Paris at the Salon des Artistes Français, of which she was a member from 1905.

FANFANI, Enrico
Italian, 19th century.
Painter. Historical scenes, genre scenes.
Enrico Fanfani worked in Italy.
MUSEUMS AND GALLERIES:
FLORENCE (Gal. Antica e Moderna): *Scenes from the Revolution of 27 April 1859 in Florence; The Widow's Offering; The Blind Poet Milton.*
AUCTION RECORDS:
NEW YORK, 25 Oct 1984, *Visit to the Monastery* (oil on canvas, 48 1/2 x 36 1/4 ins / 123.1 x 92 cm) USD 2,000. NEW YORK, 16 Feb 1995, *Water Carriers* (oil on canvas, a pair, each 21 1/2 x 36 ins / 54.6 x 91.4 cm) USD 17,250. PARIS, 15 Dec 1995, *Bedouin Woman by a Well* (oil on canvas, 27 1/2 x 19 3/4 ins / 70 x 50 cm) FRF 40,000. LONDON, 25 March 1999, *Leaving the Encampment* (oil on canvas, 31 x 21 ins / 79 x 54 cm) GBP 1,200. BOSTON, 2 Oct 1999, *Contemplation before Altar Flame* (oil on canvas, 26 x 18 ins / 66 x 46 cm) USD 2,000. NEUILLY, 12 June 2001, *Painter and Model in the Studio* (oil on canvas, 17 x 22 ins / 42 x 56 cm) FRF 23,000. LONDON, 26 Sept 2001, *Entering the Monastery* (oil on canvas, 39 x 31 ins / 100 x 78 cm) GBP 1,300. DETROIT, 19 July 2002, *Encampment* (oil on canvas, 32 x 21 ins / 81 x 53 cm) USD 1,800. ELGIN, 17 May 2003, *Hagar and Ishmael* (oil on canvas, 31 x 21 ins / 79 x 53 cm) USD 3,000. COPENHAGEN, 9 Dec 2003, *Female Artist in front of an Easel with Palette in Her Hand* (oil on canvas, oval, 29 x 22 ins / 73 x 57 cm) DKK 22,000. STOCKHOLM, 26 May 2004, *Woman at the Well* (oil on canvas, 31 x 22 ins / 80 x 55 cm) SEK 27,000.

FANFANI, Paolo
Italian, 19th century.
Born 12 June 1823, in Florence.
Sculptor (wood).
Paolo Fanfani was a pupil of Luigi Sani at the Accademia in Florence. He created the large chandelier made of wood and iron in the throne room at the Pitti Palace. He sculpted furniture, altars and candelabra, working for foreign clients. A few of his works were exhibited in Florence and Rome: a frame for the portrait of Count Francesco Larderello (which is now in the Palazzo Larderello in Livorno), and some crucifixes and chandeliers.

FANFOJA
Italian, 16th century.
Painter. History painting.
Fanfoja was a pupil of Leonardo da Vinci.

FANG BI, or Fang Pi, style name: Huanshan
Chinese, 16th century.
Active during the Jiajing period (1522-1566).
Painter.
Fang Bi was a painter during the Ming dynasty but is not mentioned in the annals.

FANG BINGSHAN
Chinese, 20th century.
Born 1940.
Painter. Landscapes.
Fang Bingshan graduated from the Nanjing Academy, where he teaches. His works have been shown at numerous exhibitions and widely reproduced.
AUCTION RECORDS:
HONG KONG, 30 April 1996, *Spring Morning* (1995, oil on canvas, 41 3/4 x 30 3/4 ins / 106 x 78.1 cm) HKD 46,000.

FANG CH'IEN. See **FANG QIAN**

FANG CHE-CHU. See **FANG SHISHU**

FANG CHI. See **FANG JI**

FANG CHIN-SHIH. See **FANG JINSHI**

FANG CHÜN-JUI. See **FANG JUNRUI**

FANG CHUN-PI. See **FANG JUNBI**

FANG CHUXIONG
Chinese, 20th century.
Born 1925.
Painter, calligrapher. Flowers, animals.
Fang Chuxiong taught at the Guangzhou Municipal College of Art. His work was shown in Paris in 1980 at the exhibition *Peintres traditionnels de la République Populaire chinoise* (*Traditional Painters of the People's Republic of China*).

FANG CONYI, or Fang Ts'ung-i, style name: Wuyu, sobriquets: Fanghu, Jinmen Yuke, Bumang Doaren
Chinese, 14th century.
Born in Guixi (Jiangxi).
Active during the second half of the 14th century.
Painter.
Fang Congyi, a Taoist monk at the Shangqing temple in his native province, is known as a landscape artist and for his spontaneous, splashy style and his rapid execution with a loaded brush. He gives a very subtle rendering of misty landscapes. Highly appreciated in his time, his style is reminiscent of that of the great landscape painter Gao Kegong (c.1245-1310), while his brushwork evokes the manner of the Two Mis (Mi Fu 1051-1107 and Mi Youren 1086-1165). In his landscapes, rugged mountains rise up with force above the valleys like so much living matter; tortured pines heighten the impression of severity and the bold areas accentuate the general movement. The distribution of the patches of fog is also reminiscent of Fan Kuan (mid 10th century) and Li Tang (c.1050-1130).
BIBLIOGRAPHY:
Yang Xin and others, *Three Thousand Years of Chinese Painting*, Yale University Press, 1997.
MUSEUMS AND GALLERIES:
BEIJING (Palace Mus.): *Mountains in Fog and Clouds, Traveller Followed by Attendant Carrying Lute* (signed and dated 1378, signed, poems by four contemporaries, colophon by Dan Shao dated 1385); *Mountains in Clouds* (1365, signed) - OSAKA (Municipal Mus. of Art): *Bright Sunlight on Waterfall in Autumn* - SHANGHAI: *In the Depths of Cloudy Mountains* (dated 1392 from the colophon, ink on paper, hanging scroll) - TAIPEI (National Palace Mus.): *On a Boat at Huishan; Immortal Mountains and Luminous Woods* (1364, ink and colour on paper, hanging scroll, signed, painted for a Taoist friend of the artist).

FANG DAYOU, or Fang Ta-yu, style name: Oyu, sobriquets: Yanlan, Yunsheng
Chinese, 17th century.
Born 1596, in Wucheng (Zhejiang); died 1677.
Painter.
Fang Dayou was governor of Shandong at the beginning of the Qing dynasty (1644-1911). He painted landscapes in the style of Dong Yuan (10th century).

FANG GUOQI, or Fang Kuo-ch'i, style name: Nangong
Chinese, 17th century.
Born in Kunshan (Jiangsu).
Active at the beginning of the Qing dynasty (1644-1911).
Painter.
Fang Guoqi painted bamboo in the style of Xia Chang (1388-1470).

FANG HENGXIAN, or Fang Heng-hsien
Chinese, 17th century.
Active at the beginning of the Qing dynasty (1644-1911).
Painter.

Fang Hengxian worked with the landscape painter Chang Xun (mid-17th century).

FANG HIAO-JU. See **FANG XIAORU**

FANG HSIAO-JU. See **FANG XIAORU**

FANG HSUN. See **FANG XUN**

FANG I-CHIH. See **FANG YIZHI**

FANG I-TCHE. See **FANG YIZHI**

FANG JEN-TING. See **FANG RENDING**

FANG JI, or Fang Chi, style name: Juchuan, sobriquet: Xiyuan
Chinese, 18th century.
Active during the second half of the 18th century.
Painter. Landscapes.

Fang Ji travelled to Japan in 1772.

MUSEUMS AND GALLERIES:

LONDON (British Mus.): *Two Magpies in Plum Tree* (signed); *Album of Landscapes*.

FANG JINSHI, or Fang Chin-Shih
Chinese, 17th century.
Probably active at the end of the Ming dynasty (second half of the 17th century).
Painter.

FANG JUNBI, or Fang Chun-pi
Chinese, 20th century.
Born 1898, in Fujian; died 1986.
Also active in France and the USA.
Painter. Portraits, landscapes.

Fang Junbi went to France when still a child and studied in Paris and Bordeaux. From 1924 to 1928, she returned to China, teaching at Guangdong University, and returning to France in 1926. In 1927, 1928 and 1929, she exhibited in Paris at the Salons des Tuileries and Salon de la Société Nationale des Beaux-Arts. After 1949 she moved to France and afterward to the USA.

AUCTION RECORDS:

HONG KONG, 17 Nov 1988, *Portrait of Zhao Shao'ang* (ink and colour on paper, 33 3/4 x 22 ins / 86 x 55 cm) HKD 82,500; *Autumn Landscape* (ink and colour on paper, hanging scroll, 47 1/4 x 23 1/4 ins / 120 x 59 cm) HKD 33,000.

FANG JUNRUI, or Fang Chün-jui
Chinese, 14th century.
Born in Wujin (Jiangsu).
Active at the beginning of the 14th century.
Painter.

Fang Junrui in painting grass and insects in the style of the monk-painter Juning.

FANG K'IEN. See **FANG QIAN**

FANG KIN-CHE. See **FANG JINSHI**

FANG KIUN-JUEI. See **FANG JUNRUI**

FANG KIUN-PI. See **FANG JUNBI**

FANG KUO-CH'I. See **FANG GUOQI**

FANG KUO-K'I. See **FANG GUOQI**

FANG NANYUN, or Fang Nan-yün
Chinese, 17th century.
Active towards the end of the 17th century.
Painter.

Although Fang Nanyun is not mentioned in the biographies of painters, he is known for a fan painting, *Man in Grove by River*, signed and dated 1697.

FANG PI. See **FANG BI**

FANG QIAN, or Fang Ch'ien, style names: Yuqian, Xixian
Chinese, 17th century.
Active in Xiexian (Anhui) at the beginning of the Qing dynasty (1644-1911).
Painter.

Fang Qian was a specialist painter of landscapes and flowers.

FANG RENDING, or Fang Jen-ting
Chinese, 20th century.
Born 1901, in Zhongshan, Guangdong; died 1975.
Also active in the USA.
Painter.
Lingnan school.

Fang Rending was a pupil of Gao Jianfu. He lived in Japan from 1929 to 1935, and in 1939 he left for the USA. He took part in the *Golden Gate Exhibition* held in San Francisco.

AUCTION RECORDS:

HONG KONG, 29 April 1996, *Goat Eating Leaves* (ink and colour on paper, hanging scroll, 65 x 29 1/4 ins / 165 x 74 cm) HKD 34,500. HONG KONG, 28 April 2003, *Lake Xuanwu* (1947, ink and colour, hanging scroll, 68 x 37 ins / 173 x 94 cm) HKD 50,000. HONG KONG, 27 Oct 2003, *Crossing the River on a Buffalo's Back* (1946, ink and colour, hanging scroll, 67 x 37 ins / 169 x 94 cm) HKD 100,000. HONG KONG, 26 April 2004, *Milkmaid* (1941, ink and colour, hanging scroll, 67 x 38 ins / 170 x 96 cm) HKD 150,000.

FANG SHISHU, or Fang Shih-shu, style name: Dunyuan, sobriquets: Huanshan, Xiaoshi Daoren
Chinese, 18th century.
Born 1692, in Xiexian (Anhui); died 1751.
Painter. Landscapes.

Fang Shishu was a pupil of Huang Ding (1660-1730). He painted mainly portraits.

MUSEUMS AND GALLERIES:

BERLIN: *Album of Twelve Landsacapes after the ancient masters* (signed and dated 1733) - KANSAS CITY (Nelson-Atkins MA): *Summer Mountains before Rain* (after Mi Youren, signed with a poem dated 1738) - TAIPEI (National Palace Mus.): *Two Leaves from a Landscape Album* (after the Yuan masters, signed).

AUCTION RECORDS:

NEW YORK, 4 Dec 1989, *Isolated House by Clear Stream* (ink on paper, hanging scroll, 49 1/2 x 24 ins / 125.5 x 61 cm) USD 11,000. NEW YORK, 1 June 1993, *Landscape Album* (1747, ink and colour on paper and ink on paper, eight leaves, each 19 x 12 3/4 ins / 48.3 x 32.4 cm) USD 79,500. HONG KONG, 25 April 2004, *Landscape* (ink and colour, hanging scroll, 52 x 24 ins / 133 x 62 cm) HKD 160,000.

FANG SIUN. See **FANG XUN**

FANG TA-YEU. See **FANG DAYOU**

FANG TA-YU. See **FANG DAYOU**

FANG TS'ONG-I. See **FANG CONGYI**

FANG TS'UNG-I. See **FANG CONGYI**

FANG TSI. See **FANG JI**

FANG TSONG. See **FANG ZONG**

FANG TSUNG. See **FANG ZONG**

FANG WANYI, or Fang Wan-i, sobriquet: Bolian jushi
Chinese, 18th century.
Born 1732, in Xiexian (Anhui); died after 1784.
Painter.

Fang Wanyi was the wife of the painter Luo Ping. She is known as a woman of letters and poet. She specialised in painting plum blossom, orchids, bamboo and landscapes.

FANG XIAORU, or Fang Hsiao-ju, style names: Xizhi, Xigu, also known as Master Zhengxue
Chinese, 14th century.
Born 1357, in Ninghai (Zhejiang); died 1402.
Painter.
Ming dynasty.

Fang Xiaoru was a painter and a high-ranking official. He was executed by order of Emperor Yongle (1402-1425).

FANG XUN, or Fang Hsün, style name: Landi, sobriquets: Lanshi, Changqing
Chinese, 18th century.
Born 1736, in Shimen (Zhejiang); died 1799.
Painter. Birds, landscapes, flowers.

Fang Xun was very gifted. He is known as a poet, calligrapher and painter of landscapes, flowers and birds. Of a proud and independent nature, he kept aloof from public life and devoted himself exclusively to the arts. He wrote a treatise on painting, the *Shanjingju Hualan*, the failings of which - discontinuity, dispersed remarks, repetition, truisms, and a lack of synthesis - are common to most works of the time. It does, however, include a number of personal views that are not without interest. Fang opposed fixed rules and set forms, and stressed the need for a new personal creation, one no longer modelled on the ancient masters. He also criticised prejudice and the rivalry between schools.

BIBLIOGRAPHY:
Ryckmans, Pierre, *Les Propos sur la peinture' de Shitao. Traduction et commentaires pour servir de contribution à l'étude terminologique et esthétique des théories chinoises de la peinture*, Institut belge des hautes études chinoises, Brussels, 1970.

MUSEUMS AND GALLERIES:
BEIJING (Palace Mus.): *Scholar's Garden on River-bank* (dated 1801) - KYOTO (National Mus.): *Young Bamboo, Chrysanthemums and Rocks.*

AUCTION RECORDS:
NEW YORK, 31 May 1994, *Flowers* (ink/silk, Album of twelve leaves, 9 1/2 x 8 ins / 24.4 x 19.4 cm) USD 3,450. NEW YORK, 21 March 1995, *Flowers of the Four Seasons* (ink and colour on silk, four hanging scrolls, each 58 3/4 x 15 ins / 149.2 x 38.4 cm) USD 2,875.

FANG XUN, or Fang Hsun
Chinese, 20th - 21st century.
Born 1954, in Xinzhu, Taiwan.
Painter. Genre scenes, interiors with figures.

Fang Xun graduated in 1978 from the journalism department of the Chinese Culture University, Taipei, and then started her artistic career. In 1986, she began to take part in exhibitions and in 1991, a solo exhibition was held of her work at the Taizhong Art Center. Her paintings attempt to depict scenes from everyday life with some realism.

AUCTION RECORDS:
HONG KONG, 30 March 1992, *Door* (1989, oil on canvas, 30 x 20 ins / 76 x 51 cm) HKD 20,900.

FANG YIZHI, or Fang I-chih, style name: Changgong, sobriquets: Luqi, Zhike, Mizhi
Chinese, 17th century.
Born in Tongcheng (Anhui).
Active towards the middle of the 17th century.
Painter, monk. Landscapes.

Fang Yizhi passed the jinshi (accomplished scholar) examinations in Beijing in 1640. After the collapse of the Ming dynasty, he became a monk under the name of Hongzhi, using the style name Wuke and the sobriquet Yaodi. He painted landscapes in the style of the great Yuan masters.

MUSEUMS AND GALLERIES:
BEIJING (Palace Mus.): *Man Riding Donkey near Wutong Tree* (ink on paper, signed with the monk's name Hongzhi).

FANG YONG, or Fang Yung
Chinese, 20th century.
Born 26 December 1900, in Chengdu (Sichuan).
Active in France.
Painter, lacquerer. Landscapes.

Fang Yong was taught traditional Chinese painting from an early age. He continued to paint in this style after moving to France in 1919, but also taught himself to paint in a western style, while retaining certain Chinese elements through his lacquer work. He rarely exhibited. In 1948, he became a member of the Association des Artistes Chinois en France (Association of Chinese Artists in France).

There is often a strong hint of romanticism in his paintings, after the manner of Corot. His new concept of painting produced great vigour and freshness in his better works, at that time still rare among Chinese artists.

BIBLIOGRAPHY:
Sullivan, Michael, *Chinese Art in the Twentieth Century*, University of California Press, Berkeley, 1959.

FANG ZHAOLIN, or Fang Zhaoling
Chinese, 20th century.
Born 1914.
Painter. Landscapes with figures.

Fang Zhaolin painted traditional subjects, such as scenes with figures, using traditional techniques. His drawings, however, are more obscure and more lively. Using lightly varying shades of grey for the landscapes, he uses bright colours to paint little, amusingly anecdotal figures.

AUCTION RECORDS:
HONG KONG, 17 Nov 1988, *Landscape with Figures* (1983, ink and colour on paper, 26 1/2 x 27 1/4 ins / 67.5 x 69 cm) HKD 396,000. HONG KONG, 18 May 1989, *Huang Shan* (1986, ink and colour on paper, hanging scroll, 39 x 27 ins / 98.8 x 68.5 cm) HKD 528,000. HONG KONG, 15 Nov 1989, *Inhabited Cave* (1986, ink and colour on paper, hanging scroll, 69 3/4 x 37 3/4 ins / 177 x 96 cm) HKD 770,000. HONG KONG, 2 May 1991, *Year Of Universal Peace* (1986, ink and colour on paper, 44 1/4 x 37 3/4 ins / 112.7 x 96 cm) HKD 594,000. HONG KONG, 31 Oct 1991, *Travellers Admiring Waterfall* (1988, ink and colour on paper, hanging scroll, 69 3/4 x 37 3/4 ins / 177 x 96.2 cm) HKD 605,000. HONG KONG, 30 April 1992, *Steps Leading to Top of Hill* (1986, ink and colour on paper, hanging scroll, 53 1/2 x 26 3/4 ins / 136 x 68 cm) HKD 660,000. HONG KONG, 29 Oct 1992, *Painting in Grotto* (ink and colour on paper, hanging scroll, 51 1/2 x 31 1/4 ins / 130.5 x 79.5 cm) HKD 616,000. HONG KONG, 4 May 1995, *Icy Atmosphere* (ink and colour on paper, 38 x 28 1/2 ins / 96.5 x 72.4 cm) HKD 230,000. HONG KONG, 28 April 1997, *Painting(calligraphy diptych)* (1996, ink and colour on paper and ink on paper, two items, 27 1/4 x 22 3/4 ins / 69.2 x 58.1 cm and 49 1/2 x 11 ins/126 x 27.9 cm) HKD 230,000.

FANG ZONG, or Fang Tsung, style name: Huangshan, sobriquets: Shidian, Youhuang
Chinese, 18th century.
Painter.
Qing dynasty.

Fang Zong was a pupil of Zhang Zongcang (1686-1756). He painted landscapes and was a court painter in the reign of Emperor Qianlong (1736-1796).

FANGARETTI, Francesco
Italian, 18th century.
Painter.

Francesco Fangaretti painted frescoes for the Naples church of S Caterina a Formello.

FANGER, Simon, or Fangert
Dutch, 17th century.
Painter.

Simon Fanger qualified as a master in Delft on 16 October 1647.

FANGER, Wolfgang
Swiss, 17th century.
Active in Sarnen.
Painter, sculptor.

Fanger is mentioned in Dr Brun's dictionary of artists as having made six paintings of saints and some altarpieces for the church of Giswil (Unterwalden).

FANGYA, or Fang-Yai
Chinese, 14th century.
Painter.

Fangya is only known through the inscriptions on his work. He was a monk at the Chongyu temple, Suzhou, during the second half of the 14th century and a friend of the painter Ni Zan (1301-1374). He painted mostly trees, bamboo and rocks in the style of the poet and painter Su Dongpo. His paintings of bamboo are uncomplicated and his work has a naturally profound quality. He painted branches and stems with a loaded brush, and leaves with diluted ink, producing varying shades in tone.

MUSEUMS AND GALLERIES:
TAIPEI (National Palace Mus.): *Delicate Bamboo in Stony Ground* (seal of the artist, poem and colophon of Ma Zhi dated 1382); *Bamboo in Ink* (hanging scroll, ink on paper, inscription).

FANIA, Giuseppe
Italian, 18th century.
Born 18th century, in Foggia (Apulia).
Painter, decorative artist. Stage sets.

Giuseppe Fania worked mainly at the theatre of S Carlo in Naples.

FANIEL, Stéphane Axel Jean
French, 20th century.
Born 30 April 1909, in Paris; died June or July 1978, in Paris.
Painter.

Stéphane Axel Jean Faniel came from a Dutch family of antique dealers and precious metal workers, from whom he inherited both taste and knowledge in a wide range of artistic fields. He was a pupil of Lucien Simon at the École des Beaux-Arts, Paris. In 1928 he exhibited a portrait in Paris at the Salon des Artistes Français, and was later represented at the Salon d'Automne and invited to show at the Salon des Tuileries. He took part in other group exhibitions, and in 1992-1993 the Galerie de l'Échaudé, Paris, included some of his works in the exhibition *Francis Ponge et les artistes* (*Francis Ponge and the Artists*). He also held solo exhibitions in Paris in 1954, 1956 and 1960. While at the same time investigating form, especially in precious metal work, in 1951 he collaborated with Jean Prouvé, Charlotte Perriand and Fernand Léger in organising the French section of the Milan Triennale, where some of his own works won awards. He wrote books on the history of French style, the Louvre Museum, and more, and contributed to many artistic and literary journals.

Initially he painted in the traditional figurative style, but he was influenced by the powerful presence of Post-Cubism, especially in his still-lifes, which are elegantly constructed and exploit rich and sensuous materials. Finally he moved to Painting without Form and Tachisme.

FANIEST, Pierre
French, 20th century.
Born 7 July 1926, in Frignicourt (Marne).
Painter. Stage sets.

Pierre Faniest was a pupil in the studio of Fernand Léger from 1946 to 1950. He lives and works in Biot. He takes part in collective and solo exhibitions: the first in Biot in 1953, then at the Menton Biennale in 1955 and 1957, at the Musée des Ponchettes, Nice, in 1956, the Musée du Bastion St-André, Antibes, in 1969, at the Musée d'Art Moderne, Céret, in 1977, at the Villa Arson, Nice, in 1984, and in Paris, Lyons and St-Paul-de-Vence. Since 1988 he has refused to exhibit. He covers his canvases with coloured signs, similar to hieroglyphics, in a sort of Lyrical Tachiste style that creates a poetic space.

MUSEUMS AND GALLERIES:
ANTIBES (Mus. Picasso) - CÉRET (Mus. municipal d'Art moderne): *Homage to Ornette Coleman*.

FANISCH
French, 18th century.
Active c. 1793.
Painter.

MUSEUMS AND GALLERIES:
COUTANCES: *Portrait of Captain Lhermitte*.

FANJANS, Jaume
French, 14th century.
Active in Perpignan.
Painter.

FANNER, Alice Maud, Mrs Taite
British, 19th - 20th century.
Born 1865, in Surrey; died 1930.
Painter. Landscapes, seascapes.

Alice Maud Fanner studied at the Slade School in London under Brown, Wilson Steer and Henry Tonks. She also studied for a time in Paris. She was a member of the New English Art Club in London, where she exhibited landscapes and seascapes, and also showed her work at the Royal Academy in London and the Carnegie Institute in Pittsburgh in the USA.

MUSEUMS AND GALLERIES:
BRIGHTON: *Chestnut Tree* - BRIGHTON (Mus. & AG): *Seaside* (c. 1920, oil on canvas) - DUDLEY: *Ornamental Lake in the Luxembourg Gardens; Stormy Weather in the Solent*.

AUCTION RECORDS:
LONDON, 13 Feb 1931, *Watering Place,* GBP 6. LONDON, 6 Dec 1935, *Mist Lifting in the Crouch Valley,* GBP 10. LONDON, 9 June 1981, *Spring Landscape* (oil on canvas, 15 1/4 x 19 1/4 ins / 39 x 49 cm) GBP 220. LONDON, 20 June 1984, *Luxembourg Gardens, Paris* (oil on canvas remounted on panel, 8 1/4 x 11 1/2 ins / 21 x 29 cm) GBP 500. LEWES, 20 July 1999, *Versailles from the Fountain* (oil on canvas, 25 x 32 ins / 64 x 81 cm) GBP 2,600. BURY ST EDMUNDS, 28 Sept 2000, *In the Luxemburg Gardens* (oil on board, 7 x 11 ins / 19 x 29 cm) GBP 2,100. HAVERHILL, 18 Oct 2000, *Heeled Over, Yacht before a Bay and Cliff* (oil on canvas, 36 x 28 ins / 91 x 71 cm) GBP 12,500. LONDON, 1 Nov 2001, *Yachts Racing in a Good Breeze* (oil on canvas, 28 x 36 ins / 71 x 91 cm) GBP 2,500.

FANNER, Henry George
British, 19th century.
Active in London.
Watercolourist. Portraits.

Henry George Fanner exhibited at the Royal Academy and Suffolk Street Gallery in 1854.

MUSEUMS AND GALLERIES:
GLASGOW: *Portrait of a Child*.

AUCTION RECORDS:
LONDON, 25 June 1909, *Spanish Beauty* (1865, watercolour) GBP 2.

FANNIATCHO, Fanny Louise Bennet.
See **BENNETT-NIATCHO Fanny Louise**

FANNIÈRE, Auguste François
French, 19th century.
Born 24 November 1818, in Longwy; died 29 November 1900, in Paris.
Sculptor, goldsmith.

Auguste François Fannière joined the École des Beaux-Arts on 2 October 1838 and studied under Drolling. He exhibited at the Paris Salon from 1841 to 1876, most notably medallions and busts. His brother François-Joseph-Louis Fannière assisted him, especially with his work as a goldsmith.

FANNING, Nettie B.
American, 19th century.
Born 12 March 1863, in Delhi.
Active in Norwich.
Painter, illustrator.

Nettie B. Fanning was a pupil at the School of Design in Norwich and that in Boston. She was also a teacher.

AUCTION RECORDS:
LONDON, 20 March 1963, *Houses by a River*, GBP 380.

FANNING, Ralph
American, 20th century.
Born 29 November 1889, in New York; died 1971.
Painter.

Ralph Fanning graduated at Cornell University and the University of Illinois. He was also an architect, a writer, a professor of art history at Ohio State University, and a member of many art societies.

FANNING, William Sanders
American, 20th century.
Born 10 May 1887, in Detroit (Michigan).
Painter.

William Sanders Fanning was also an architect. After starting his studies in the USA, he completed them in Paris in the studio of Othon Friesz. He was a member of the Detroit Society of Independent Artists.

FANO, da. See **MORGANTI**

FANO, Giovanni
Austrian, 17th century.
Active in Vienna.
Painter.

Fano is mentioned as being in Rome in 1606-1607.

FANO, Lodovico
Italian, 17th century.
Painter.

Lodovico Fano was a monk credited with having painted a *St Francis and St Anthony* for the Verona church of S Fermo Maggiore in 1631.

FANO, Tesandra
French, 20th century.
Born in Venice.
Miniaturist.

Tesandra Fano exhibited in Paris at the Salon des Artistes Français.

FANOLI, Michele
Italian, 19th century.
Born c. 1807, in Cittadella; died 1876, in Milan.
Lithographer, engraver.

Fanoli studied at the Accademia in Venice, and was a pupil of Cicognara. He then went to France, and lived in Paris for many years. He was recalled to Italy by the Italian government in 1860 to found a school of lithography in Milan. He died there in poverty, bequeathing a collection of engravings to the Accademia in Venice.

His reproductions include *Orpheus*, after Jalabert; *Holy Women at the Tomb* and *Christ with St Peter and St John*, after Landelle; *The Willis*, after Gendron; and *The Two Foscaris*, after Grigoletti.

FANSAGA, Carlo, or Fanzago
Italian, 17th century.
Died in Spain.
Sculptor.

He was the son and collaborator of Cosimo Fansaga. Examples of his own work include sculptures for the *Fonseca Fountain* and a low relief of the *Dead Christ* for the main altar of the church of S Maria degli Angeli in Naples.

FANSAGA, Cosimo, or Fanzago
Italian, 17th century.
Born 1591, in Clusone, near Bergamo; died 1678, in Naples.
Painter, sculptor, architect.

Cosimo Fansaga studied in Rome under Pietro Bernini and worked predominantly in Naples, where he was responsible for a large number of buildings in a muted Baroque style. These were often adorned with his own statues and paintings - as was the case, for example, with his *St Francis* for the church of S Maria degli Angeli and his *Immaculate Conception* in the chapel of the royal palace.

FANSHAW, Catherine Maria
British, 19th century.
Born c. 1775, in London; died c. 1834.
Engraver (including etching), poet.

Catherine Maria Fanshaw very skilfully engraved plates on historical and genre subjects, such as the *Game of Chess*.

MUSEUMS AND GALLERIES:
LONDON (British Mus.): numerous etchings and drawings.

FANSHAW, Penelope
British, 19th century.
Died April 1833.
Engraver (etching).

Penelope Fanshaw was the older sister of Catherine Fanshaw. She also tried her hand at engraving, but did not achieve much success. A *View of the Church at Chipstead (Surrey)* is attributed to her.

FANSHAW, S. R.
American, 19th century.
Born 1814; died 1888.
Painter.

From 1841 S.R. Fanshaw was a member of the National Academy of Design in New York.

FANSHAWE, Irène
French, 20th century.
Born 14 March 1912, in St Petersburg.
Painter, watercolourist, illustrator. Portraits, landscapes.

Irène Fanshawe was born into a very ancient family of English origin that was forced to leave Russia at the Revolution. After travelling around she finally took refuge with her compatriots at the Villa Baron, Cannes. She was a pupil at the École des Beaux-Arts, Paris, and her work was noted by Robert Vrinat and Renée Carvalho.

In Paris she was a member of the Salon d'Hiver and the Salon des Femmes Peintres, and she exhibited regularly at the Salon des Artistes Indépendants and the Salon des Artistes Français. She also exhibited several times in Nancy.

She has held solo shows of her work: initially in 1930 at the Cercle Nautique, Cannes; regularly in Denmark; 1969, the Galerie J.-M. Gauthier, Épernay; 1981, *Aquarelles du Danemark* (*Watercolours from Denmark*), Galerie Dany Thibaud. In Paris in 1973 she exhibited the illustrations she did for Hans Christian Anderson's Fairy Tales. Her work is eclectic in style, somewhere between Realism and Post-Impressionism.

MUSEUMS AND GALLERIES:
DAGENHAM (Valencia House Mus. and AG): *Portrait of Reine Fanshawe*.

FANTACCHIOTTI, Cesare
Italian, 19th - 20th century.
Born December 1844, in Florence; died 1922.
Sculptor.

Cesare Fantacchiotti was the son and pupil of Odoardo Fantacchiotti. He was a highly prolific artist, and his output is extremely diverse. He is best known for his statuettes and groups *The Thorn, Shepherdess, The Goat Herder* and *Morning*.

He sculpted numerous busts of well-known people of his time, including one of *Victor Emmanuel*. There are also other groups: *Bacchants, Romeo and Juliet* and a group for a fountain in Kansas City. Statues executed by him include *Meditation* and *Young Girl Awakening*; the funeral monument to his father at San Miniato, near Florence; works on the façade of Florence Cathedral; and finally, busts of *Dante* and *Leonardo da Vinci*. He exhibited in Florence, Turin, Venice, London (at the Royal Academy) and Berlin.

MUSEUMS AND GALLERIES:
ROME (Gal. Nazionale): *Savonarola; Molière*.

FANTACCHIOTTI, Odoardo
Italian, 19th century.
Born 1809, in Rome; died 1877, in Florence.
Sculptor. Religious subjects, figures. Statues, monuments.

Odoardo Fantacchiotti quickly built a reputation for himself, earning him admission into several academies. His major works are considered to be his statue of *Boccaccio*; his monument to the engraver Raphael Morghen in S Croce in Florence; the monument to Spence, in Fiesole; and the *Angel of Prayer*, in Cincinnati, Ohio.

MUSEUMS AND GALLERIES:
TURIN (Gal. Civica d'Arte Moderna e Contemporanea): *Eve*.

FANTACCINI, Carlo
Italian, 18th century.
Active in Rome.
Painter.

Carlo Fantaccini studied under B. Lamberti and A. Amorosi. His body of work includes a *Virgin of the Gonfalonier* for a church in the Marche region of Italy, a *St Lucy* for a church in Portugal, and a *St Peter and St Paul* for a church on Corsica.

FANTAGUZZI, Giovanni, or Fantagucci, called il Pittor Paniza
Italian, 17th century.
Born to a family originally from Faenza; died 1663.
Painter. Architectural views.

FANTAGUZZI, Giuseppe
Italian, 19th century.
Active in Modena c. 1800.
Painter, draughtsman.

Fantaguzzi produced drawings after some church paintings in Modena for a few of the engravings made by B. Eredi.

MUSEUMS AND GALLERIES:
MODENA (Cathedral): *St Eloi and St Lucy* - MODENA (Church of St Charles): *St Rosalia in the Desert*.

FANTAGUZZI, Pietro
Italian, 17th century.
Born to a family originally from Faenza.
Painter.

The son of Giovanni Fantaguzzi, Pietro Fantaguzzi was a painter who went on to take holy orders and become a priest in Felisio. He corresponded with Pater Orlandi, the author of the *ABC of Painting*.

FANTAGUZZI, Savino I, or Fantagucci
Italian, 17th century.
Died 1629.
Active in Faenza.
Painter.

He was the brother of Giovanni Fantaguzzi.

FANTAGUZZI, Savino II, or Fantagucci
Italian, 17th century.
Died 1709.
Active in Faenza.
Engraver, goldsmith, painter. Architectural views.

The son of Giovanni Fantaguzzi, Savino Fantaguzzi II painted decorations for churches and palazzi in several towns in Italy, including Faenza and Florence. He subsequently had figures added to his work by painters such as the French artist C. de Bock and G. Neri of Bologna. He collaborated with de Bock on a ceiling fresco entitled *Virgin and Angels*, painted in 1678 for the Porta Imolese in Faenza.

FANTASIA, Antonio
Italian, 18th century.
Sculptor.

Antonio Fantasia was commissioned by Pope Clement XI to sculpt one of the statues of the saints for the piers of St Peter's in Rome.

FANTASIA, Giovanni
Italian, 15th century.
Born to a family originally from Lucca (Tuscany).
Sculptor.

Giovanni Fantasia made a door with marble sculptured decoration in the church of S Maria in Cosmedin, Naples, in 1482 with Bernardino di Martino.

FANTASIA, Giovanni. See also **CIAMBELLA DI FRANCESCO Giovanni**

FANTASTICI, Bernardino
Italian, 18th century.
Painter.

Several paintings by Fantastici can be found in churches in the area around Siena, notably a *Virgin with St Michael and St Sebastian* in the church of S Magno in Simignano; a *Virgin with St Anthony of Padua* in the church of S Pietro in Gallena; and a *Decapitation of St John the Baptist* in the church of S Caterina in Pienza.

FANTASTICI, Giuseppe
Italian, 18th century.
Active in Siena.
Painter.

Two paintings by Giuseppe Fantastici, dated 1764, hang in the church of S Michelangelo in Ponte a Tressa.

FANTASTICO, Il. See **AVANZARANI Francesco**

FANTAUZZO, Carmelo
Italian, 20th century.
Born in Barrafranca, Sicily.
Sculptor.

FANTEINE, Johann Christian
Austrian, 18th century.
Miniaturist.

Fanteine is mentioned as being in Graz (Styria), Austria in 1752.

FANTEL, Sophie
French, 19th century.
Active in Paris.
Portrait artist.

Sophie Fantel exhibited at the Salon in 1836 and 1838.

FANTELLI, Domenico
Italian, 18th century.
Active in Rome.
Painter.

Domenico Fantelli exhibited a *Venus* after Titian at the Free Society, London, in 1778.

FANTETTI, Cesare
Italian, 17th century.
Born c. 1660, in Florence.
Draughtsman, engraver.

Cesare Fantetti lived and worked predominantly in Rome, where he engraved several plates from his own drawings and those of old masters. In collaboration with Pietro Aquila, he engraved Raphael paintings at the Vatican. He also worked from originals by Francesco Rosa (*Agrippina Contemplating the Ashes of Tiberius*), by Annibale Carracci (*Latona Offended by Niobe*), and by Andrea Sacchi (*Death of St Anne*).

FANTI, Ercole Gaetano
Italian, 18th century.
Born 1687, in Bologna; died 1759, in Vienna.
Painter. Self-portraits.

A pupil of M. A. Chiarini, Ercole Fanti was initially a decorative artist who later moved to Vienna as curator of the Liechtenstein gallery.

MUSEUMS AND GALLERIES:
FLORENCE (Uffizi): *Self-portrait.*

FANTI, Erminio
Italian, 19th century.
Born 16 January 1821, in Parma; died 2 October 1888.
Painter. Landscapes.

Erminio Fanti studied at the Accademia di Belle Arti in Parma, then lived in Rome from 1856 to 1860. When he returned to his home town, he was taken on as a teacher at the Accademia. He painted various landscapes for the Duchess of Parma and Duke Charles III, views of the *Village of Bagnone*, and of *Berceto Castle* and *Malgrate Castle*.

MUSEUMS AND GALLERIES:
PARMA (GA): *View of Enza and Montechiarugolo Castle.*

AUCTION RECORDS:
MILAN, 28 Oct 1986, *The Old Town* (oil on card, 17¼ x 22 ins / 44 x 56 cm) ITL 850,000.

FANTI, Girolamo
Italian, 19th century.
Born 21 April 1818, in Parma; died 1860.
Engraver, draughtsman.

Girolamo Fanti worked with Paolo Toschi on Correggio's frescoes in Parma. He made engravings for the Bardi family's Pitti gallery, and produced watercolour copies of works by Correggio with Raimondi and Toschi.

MUSEUMS AND GALLERIES:
PARMA (Gal. Nazionale): after Correggio (watercolour).

FANTI, Lucio
Italian, 20th century.
Born 20 November 1945, in Bologna.
Also active in France.
Painter. Scenes with figures. Stage sets.

Fanti's choice of subjects in his paintings, in a figurative, realist style, seems to have been stamped by his 18-month stay in a Soviet Pioneers camp. He used photos from Russian magazines extolling the benefits of the régime to create montages reflecting his own critical sensitivities and political attitude scoffing at bourgeois society. He is also known for his paintings of fragile-looking labyrinths bathed in light and shade. His theatrical work includes sets for Peter Stein, Klaus Michael Grüber (*La Traviata*, 1993) and Jean-Pierre Vincent (*Woyzeck*, 1994).

He exhibited in Italy and from 1968 also in France, where he participated in the Salon de la Jeune Peinture at the Musée d'Art Moderne, notably in 1968 at the *Salle rouge pour le Viet-Nam* (*Red Room for Vietnam*). In 2003, he participated in the thematic exhibition *Déchirures de l'histoire* (*Ruptures in History*), a look at slavery and the Paris Commune, at Le 19, the Centre régional d'art contemporain in Montbéliard. His solo shows include Musée d'Art Moderne, Paris (1973), Galleria Gastaldelli, Milan (1975, 1980), Galerie Visconti, Paris (1977, 1980, 1981, 1985).

BIBLIOGRAPHY:
Lucio Fanti, exhibition catalogue, Galerie Krief-Raymond, Paris, 1977. Deutsch, Michel, *Lucio Fanti*, exhibition catalogue, Galerie Krief-Raymond, Paris, 1983. Chapuis, Bernard, *Lucio Fanti*, exhibition catalogue, Galerie Dambier Masset, Paris, 1993. Fanti, Lucio, *Lucio Fanti, Tout sauf la peinture*, exhibition catalogue, Maison d'art contemporain Chaillioux, Fresnes, 2002. *Déchirures de l'histoire*, exhibition catalogue, Le 19, Centre régional d'art contemporain, Montbéliard, 2003. Semprun, Jorge (preface)/Chapuis, Bernard, *Lucio Fanti. Paysage*, exhibition catalogue, Gal. Lavignes-Bastille, Paris, 2003.

AUCTION RECORDS:
PARIS, 25 Oct 1982, *Official Poets* (1976, acrylic, 78¾ x 78¾ ins / 200 x 200 cm) FRF 13,500.

FANTI, Pietro Santi
Italian, 17th century.
Active in Rome.
Painter.

A priest at S Simeone and master of ceremonies for the Pope, Pietro Fanti painted a copy of Ventura Salimbeni's *Circumcision of Christ* for the altar of his own parish church. Pietro Aquila subsequently engraved Fanti's *Pilgrimage to St Peter's*, and F. Aquila engraved his *St Venantius*.

FANTI, Settimio
Italian, 19th century.
Born 1852, in Parma.
Painter.

Settimio Fanti was the son and pupil of Erminio Fanti.

MUSEUMS AND GALLERIES:
PARMA (GA): *Architectural Views* (two paintings).

FANTI, Vinzenz Anton Joseph
Italian, 18th century.
Born 1719, in Vienna; died 1776, in Vienna.
Painter. Portraits.

Vinzenz Fanti studied under Altomonte before moving to Rome, Turin and, in 1744, to Vienna, where he took over from his father Ercola Gaetano Fanti as curator of the Liechtenstein gallery.

FANTIN-LATOUR, François Victor
French, 19th century.
Born 7 March 1803, in Luxembourg; died 25 June 1886, in Paris.
Painter. Landscapes.

François Victor Fantin-Latour was the uncle of Henri Fantin-Latour and the brother of Théodore Fantin-Latour. He exhibited at the Grenoble Salon. His views of the Isère region are of undoubted historical and anecdotal interest.

He was represented in the exhibition *L'École de la Nature en Dauphiné au XIXe Siècle* (*The Natural School in Dauphiné in the 19th Century*) at Grenoble museum in 1982.

MUSEUMS AND GALLERIES:
GRENOBLE: *View of the Porte de France; River Isère and the St-Laurent Quarter; Ruins at Champ; River Isère, the Old Stone Bridge and Le Rabot.*

FANTIN-LATOUR, Ignace Henri Jean Théodore
French, 19th century.
Born 14 January 1836, in Grenoble; died 25 August 1904, in Buré.
Painter, pastellist, engraver, lithographer, draughtsman. Mythological subjects, religious subjects, allegorical subjects, genre scenes, portraits, nudes, seascapes, interiors, flowers, fruit, still-lifes (including flowers/fruit).
Japonisme.

The son of the painter Théodore Fantin-Latour, Henri Fantin-Latour initially worked under his father's direction before moving to study under Lecoq de Boisbaudran and Courbet. He joined the École des Beaux-Arts on 6 October 1854, making his Salon début in 1861. Even his earliest works reveal his talent as a draughtsman and colourist and his eye for charm and the ideal. He became friends with Manet in 1857, having met him at the Louvre, and in 1862 Manet portrayed him in his *Music at the Tuileries*. He also got to know Whistler during the latter's stay in Paris. In 1859, together with Manet, Whistler and other artists, Fantin-Latour was rejected from the Salon. Following this rejection, he joined the group that exhibited with Bonvin and met at the Café Guerbois, a group of friends which he portrayed in his *Studio in the Batignoles*. Although he was accepted at the 1861 Salon, he was part of the first Salon des Refusés in 1863 and also exhibited at the Salon of the Brussels Société des Beaux-Arts in 1900. Fantin-Latour did not receive any official recognition until 1870, with his *Studio in the Batignolles*. In 1878 he was awarded a second-class medal for two portraits and in 1897 he was given the Légion d'Honneur.

Fantin-Latour was one of the most sensitive painters of the second half of the 19th century. His technique was extremely soft and used a diffuse light. His portraits are wonders of grace, while his studio views give a superb impression of intimacy. His best paintings include *La Lecture* (*Reading*), *Homage to Delacroix* and *The Toast* (1865). He also tried a wide variety of genres and handled portraits, genre paintings, flowers and allegorical paintings with equal mastery. He was also a superb pastellist and an extremely talented lithographer. A contemporary and friend of the Impressionists, he was more of a successor to Delacroix, although he showed his sympathy with the Impressionists' cause by painting portraits of Baudelaire, Rimbaud, Delacroix, Manet, Monet, Renoir, Zola and Whistler.

Fantin-Latour himself is difficult to place. His situation at the end of the 19th century resembles that of Bonnard in the 20th century. Both of them liked to think of themselves as standing apart from the competition, mere painters, and accepting the condition that they would be judged solely by the quality of their work, regardless of their historical position in the development of the means of plastic expression. While still belonging to the Romantic movement, he painted visions of ethereal beings dancing in a fantastical landscape, preferring to exercise his imagination in the studio rather than to observe nature. Art history holds him in high esteem primarily for the peerless iconographic testimony of the many portraits he painted of his fellow painters and poets. Art enthusiasts liked him primarily for his many flower paintings, which they were quick to buy from a very early stage and which accounted for nearly all of his output between 1864 and 1896. Several exhibitions were organised after his death, including one at the Paris École des Beaux-Arts in 1906, and *'Hommes de Valeur': Henri Fantin-Latour, Odilon Redon en Tijdgenoten (and their Contemporaries)* at the Kröller-Müller Museum in Otterlo, the Netherlands, in 2002.

Fantin 58

Fantin

Fantin

BIBLIOGRAPHY:

Wedmore, Frederick, '*Fantin-Latour*' in *Pall-Mall Magazine*, vol 30, 1903. Wedmore, Frederick, '*The Art of Fantin-Latour*' in *Magazine of Fine Arts*, vol 1, 1906. Fantin-Latour, Madame, *Catalogue de l'œuvre complet de Fantin-Latour*, catalogue raisonné, H. Floury, Paris, 1911 (Gal. Antoine Laurentin, Paris, 2000). Gibson, Frank F., *The Art of Henri Fantin-Latour: His Life and Work*, London, 1924. Lucie-Smith, Edward, *Fantin-Latour*, Phaidon, Oxford, 1977. Lucie-Smith, Edward, *Henri Fantin-Latour*, Rizzoli, New York, 1977. Druick, Douglas W., *Fantin-Latour*, National Gallery of Canada/National Museums of Canada, Ottawa, 1983. Bal, Danielle, *Fantin-Latour: œuvres graphiques*, exhibition catalogue, Musée des Beaux-Arts, Grenoble, 2004.

MUSEUMS AND GALLERIES:

ALENÇON: *Still-life Study* - AMIENS (Mus. de Picardie): *Figures in a Wood* - ANTWERP: *Study for a Portrait* - ATHENS (Ethnikí Pinakothíki): *Flowers, Melon, Strawberries and Cherries* (1866, oil on canvas) - BERLIN: *Portrait of the Artist*; *The Artist's Wife* - BRUSSELS: *Drawing Lesson* - DALLAS (MA): *Fleurs de Printemps* (*Spring Flowers*) (1863, oil on canvas); *Fleurs d'Automne* (*Fall Flowers*) (1863, oil on canvas); *Still-life with Bunch of Hawthorn, Bowl of Cherries, Japanese Bowl, and Cup and Saucer* (1872, oil on canvas); *Flowers and Bunches of Grapes* (1875, oil on canvas, lithographs and drawing) - DOUAI: *Grapes* - FLORENCE: *Portrait of the Artist* - GRENOBLE (Mus. de Grenoble): *Portrait of the Artist's Mother*; *Portrait of the Artist Aged 23*; *Birthday*; *Temptation* - LONDON (NG): *Still Life with Glass Jug, Fruit and Flowers* (1861, oil on canvas, on loan since 1979 at the Hugh Lane Municipal Gallery of Modern Art, Dublin); *Roses* (1886 and 1890, oil on canvas, two paintings); *Self Portrait* (1860, oil on canvas); *A Plate of Apples* (1861, oil on canvas); *The Judgement of Paris* (c. 1863, oil on canvas, study); *Mr and Mrs Edwin Edwards* (1875, oil on canvas, exhibited at the Salon in 1875); *Roses* (1864, oil on canvas, five paintings on loan from the Tate Gallery since 1997) - MELBOURNE: *Petunias*; *Dahlias* - MONTREAL (MBA): *Fairy* (1863) - NANCY: *Odalisque* - PARIS (Louvre): *Corner of the Table*; *Portrait of Verlaine*; *Portrait of Rimbaud* - PARIS (MAM): *Portrait of Madame Fantin-Latour*; *Studio in Batignolles*; *Night*; *Rhine Gold*; *Portrait of the Artist*; *Around the Piano*; *Portrait of M. Adolphe Julien*; *Portrait of Mlle Charlotte Dubourg*; *Carnations* - PARIS (Mus. d'Orsay): *Homage to Delacroix*; *Narcissi and Tulips*; *Nude Study* - PARIS (Mus. du Petit Palais): *Faustus*; *Temptation of St Anthony* - RHEIMS: *Judgement of Paris*.

AUCTION RECORDS:

Roses, FRF 405,000; *Young Female Nude*, FRF 201,000; *Semi-nude Bather Seated by the River*, FRF 195,000; *Copy after Rubens*, FRF 19,500; *Copy after an Old Master*, FRF 14,800; *Copy after Titian*, FRF 13,000. *Copy after Rubens*, FRF 21,000; *Female Nudes* (six studies) FRF 2,850. PARIS, 1 May 1899, *Andromeda*, FRF 2,950. PARIS, 6 March 1900, *Violet*, FRF 13,000; *Ariadne Abandoned*, FRF 5,300. PARIS, 24 March 1900, *Manet's Studio*, FRF 900. PARIS, 10 May 1900, *Nymph*, FRF 3,150. PARIS, 14 May 1900, *Woman Bathing*, FRF 3,090. PARIS, 11 May 1901, *Nymphs at their Toilette* (painting) FRF 9,000. PARIS, 2 May 1905, *La Danse d'Almée* (painting) FRF 21,300. LONDON, 1 Feb 1908, *Mixed Bouquet* (painting) GBP 304. LONDON, 23 March 1908, *Portrait of the Artist's Sister* (painting) GBP 105. LONDON, 30 March 1908, *Spring Flowers* (painting) GBP 40. LONDON, 12 May 1908, *Dahlias in a Vase*; *Grapes and Peaches* (paintings) GBP 420. LONDON, 3 June 1910, *Roses in a Glass* (1886) GBP 346. PARIS, Oct 1918-July 1919, *Study of a Woman*, FRF 1,550; *Roses*, FRF 6,900; *Nymphs at their Toilette* (painting) FRF 22,800; *Apotheosis of Berlioz* (painting) FRF 4,000; *Almah's Dance*, FRF 6,000; *Flowers*, FRF 7,250; *Pears, Apples and Flowers*, FRF 34,000; *Oranges, Strawberries and Flowers*, FRF 36,500. PARIS, 7 Dec 1922, *Fairy*, FRF 49,200. LONDON, 8 Dec 1922,

Apple Blossom, GBP 157. LONDON, 9 March 1923, *The Model,* GBP 31. PARIS, 20 March 1923, *Peach,* FRF 3,100; *Temptation of St Anthony,* FRF 2,600. LONDON, 6 April 1923, *Still-life,* GBP 567. LONDON, 27 April 1923, *Flowers in a Glass Bowl,* GBP 472. PARIS, 11 May 1923, *Nymph Caressed by a Cupid,* FRF 41,000. PARIS, 25 May 1923, *Temptation of St Hilarion,* FRF 46,500; *The Bath,* FRF 19,500. LONDON, 1 June 1923, *Narcissi in a Glass,* GBP 162; *Judgement of Paris,* GBP 94; *Two Water Sprites,* GBP 462. LONDON, 22 June 1923, *Roses,* GBP 336; *Spring Flowers in a Glass,* GBP 309. LONDON, 23 Nov 1923, *Idyll,* GBP 882; *Roses in a Glass Vase,* GBP 1,008. LONDON, 9 May 1924, *Decorated Table* (1866) GBP 2,305; *Roses,* GBP 997; *Mixed Flowers,* GBP 472; *Roses* (1891) GBP 2,310. PARIS, 28 Nov 1924, *Still-life: Basket of Grapes and Apples,* FRF 27,500. LONDON, 24 April 1925, *Roses in a Glass Vase,* GBP 75; *Bouquets of Roses* (1883) GBP 630; *Roses in a Glass Bowl* (1883) GBP 1,123. LONDON, 4 May 1925, *Flowers in a Glass Jar,* GBP 131. PARIS, 5 and 6 June 1925, *Bathers* (pencil) FRF 970. PARIS, 23 June 1925, *Still-life with Orange and Lemon,* FRF 5,750. LONDON, 8 July 1925, *White Roses and Red Roses* (1883) GBP 265. PARIS, 9-10 Nov 1925, *Sketch,* FRF 900. PARIS, 3 Dec 1925, *Venus at her Toilette,* FRF 26,000; *Venus Embraced by Amor,* FRF 25,500. LONDON, 18 Dec 1925, *Dahlias in a Bowl,* GBP 913. PARIS, 1-3 June 1927, *Temptation of St Anthony,* FRF 4,000; *Roses in a Glass,* FRF 29,000. PARIS, 17-18 June 1927, *Portrait of a Woman,* FRF 4,100. PARIS, 29 June 1927, *Shepherdess* (pastel) FRF 1,500; *Flower Girl* (pastel) FRF 1,500. PARIS, 29 and 30 June 1927, *Beatrice and Benedict* (pastel) FRF 19,500; *Woman Bathing,* FRF 48,100. LONDON, 28 July 1927, *Flowers in a Vase* (1878) GBP 320; *Mixed Flowers in a Vase* (1877) GBP 260. LONDON, 2 Dec 1927, *Narcissi in a Glass,* GBP 81. PARIS, 3 Dec 1927, *Allegory,* FRF 32,000; *White Carnations in a Glass,* FRF 30,100; *Woman Bathing,* FRF 17,600; *Fruit,* FRF 20,000; *Fruit,* FRF 25,000. PARIS, 16-17 March 1928, *Evocation of Kundry* (lead pencil) FRF 650. PARIS, 5 May 1928, *The Three Graces* (graphite) FRF 650. PARIS, 14 May 1928, *The Valkyrie,* FRF 850. PARIS, 31 May 1928, *Woman Bathing* (Conté crayon) FRF 3,750; *Nude Studies* (two drawings) FRF 1,400; *Self-portrait* (wash) FRF 3,050; *Album with 53 Sheets* (including 92 sketches) FRF 19,100. LONDON, 19 April 1929, *Still-life,* GBP 1,627; *Dawn; Nymph,* GBP 651. LONDON, 10 May 1929, *Roses in a Basket,* GBP 1,522; *The Bath,* GBP 252. PARIS, 24 May 1929, *La Toilette* FRF 5,200. LONDON, 21 June 1929, *Madame L. Cassini,* GBP 152. PARIS, 26 June 1929, *Woman Bathing,* FRF 85,000. LONDON, 26 July 1929, *Roses and a Dish of Strawberries,* GBP 73; *Dahlias and Other Flowers in a Glass Vase,* GBP 483. LONDON, 6 Dec 1929, *Gladioli and Roses,* GBP 1,522. LONDON, 6 Dec 1929, *Flowers in a Bowl,* GBP 882. PARIS, 2-3 June 1932, *The Trojans at Carthage,* FRF 45,000; *Still-life,* FRF 27,100. LONDON, 17 June 1932, *Yellow Roses in a Glass Vase,* GBP 52. LONDON, 26 July 1932, *Artist's Despondency* (black chalk) GBP 6; *Flowers,* GBP 73. PARIS, 15 Dec 1932, *Landscape at Bure,* FRF 1,000; *Woman Embroidering,* FRF 35,000. PARIS, 16 Dec 1933, *Tea Roses in a Vase,* FRF 61,100. PARIS, 19-20 Feb 1934, *Roses in a Glass Vase,* FRF 28,000. PARIS, 26 Feb 1934, *La Source* FRF 14,500. NEW YORK, 7 Nov 1935, *Vase of Flowers,* USD 550; *Venus at her Toilette,* USD 2,300; *Queen of the Night,* USD 350. LONDON, 9 July 1936, *Chrysanthemums* (drawing) GBP 180. LONDON, 30 Oct-2 Nov 1936, *Flowers and Fruit,* GBP 1,155. PARIS, 23 Nov 1936, *Fame* (black chalk) FRF 450; *Nymph Reclining in the Woods* (black chalk) FRF 325; *Studies of Female Nudes* (black chalk, two drawings in the same frame) FRF 510; *Garden Flowers,* FRF 30,000. PARIS, 17 June 1938, *Broken Lyre: Homage to Victor Hugo* (charcoal) FRF 2,100; *Bathers* (charcoal) FRF 2,350; *Young Fitz-James,* FRF 10,800; *Roses,* FRF 41,000; *Carnations,* FRF 44,000; *Still-life,* FRF 27,200. LONDON, 15 July 1938, *Dahlias in a Glass Vase,* GBP 241. LONDON, 28 July 1938, *Narcissi on a Dish,* GBP 18. LONDON, 2 Dec 1938, *Wallflowers and Cherry Blossom,* GBP 294. PARIS, 15 Dec 1941, *Roses* (1890) FRF 205,000; *Fame,* FRF 55,000. PARIS, 9 Feb 1942, *Bouquet of Country Flowers,* FRF 246,000. LONDON, 12 Feb 1942, *Still-life* (attributed) GBP 8. PARIS, 12 March 1942, *Bouquet of Flowers* (pastel) FRF 3,100. PARIS, 20 May 1942, *After the Bath,* FRF 106,000. PARIS, 15 and 16 June 1942, *Meal with Music,* FRF 81,100. PARIS, 22 June 1942, *Vase of Flowers* (pastel) FRF 2,000. PARIS, 24 June 1942, *Homage to Victor Hugo,* FRF 25,000; *Three Women Bathing,* FRF 41,000. PARIS, 13 July 1942, *Woman with Pink Scarf,* FRF 35,000. LONDON, 18 Sept 1942, *Flowers,* GBP 178. LONDON, 21 Oct 1942, *Flowers,* GBP 33. PARIS, 20 Nov 1942, *Sheet of Nude Studies* (graphite) FRF 6,000. PARIS, 23 Dec 1942, *Study of Nudes* (graphite) FRF 4,000; *Balthazar* (pencil) FRF 2,500; *Seated Bather,* FRF 38,000. PARIS, 25-26 Jan 1943, *Composition,* FRF 90,000. PARIS, 24 Feb 1943, *Copy after Giorgione,* FRF 60,000. NEW YORK, 25 Feb 1943, *Zinnias,* USD 5,100. GLASGOW, 3 March 1943, *Woman with Cat,* GBP 19. LONDON, 14 April 1943, *Branch of Lilac,* GBP 22. NEW YORK, 29 April 1943, *Vase of Flowers,* USD 2,000. NEW YORK, 14 Oct 1943, *Flowers,* USD 450. PARIS, 10 Nov 1943, *The Apparition,* FRF 3,000. PARIS, 31 Jan 1944, *Daffodils and Nasturtiums* (1881) FRF 345,000. PARIS, 20 March 1944, *Woman Bathing,* FRF 52,000; *Faun Abducting a Nymph,* FRF 6,000. NEW YORK, 30 March 1944, *Ariadne* (lead pencil) USD 60; *Cupid's Whisperings,* USD 400; *Carnations,* USD 950. LONDON, 14 April 1944, *The Dream,* GBP 63. PARIS, 24 May 1944, *Homage to Berlioz* (1886, lead pencil) FRF 12,000. NEW YORK, 22 Nov 1944, *Calypso,* USD 1,100. PARIS, 23 April 1945, *Draped Woman Bathing by the River,* FRF 38,500. NEW YORK, 4 May 1945, *Andromeda,* USD 160. LONDON, 6 June 1945, *Temptation of St Anthony,* GBP 125. PARIS, 15 June 1945, *Studies for the Rhine Maidens* (lead pencil) FRF 2,000. PARIS, Oct 1945-July 1946, *White Roses in a Champagne Glass,* FRF 355,000. NEW YORK, 18-19 Feb 1946, *Sara la Baigneuse* (*Sara the Bather*) (drawing) USD 70. LONDON, 31 May 1946, *Venus and Cupid,* GBP 35; *Two Wood Nymphs,* GBP 39. AMSTERDAM, 26 Nov-2 Dec 1946, *White Roses,* NLG 3,700; *Nymph,* NLG 775. PARIS, 16 Dec 1946, *Head of the Man with a Glove* (after Titian) FRF 15,000. LONDON, 29 Jan 1947, *Female Nude,* GBP 35. PARIS, 24 Feb 1947, *Female Nudes* (drawing) FRF 3,600. NEW YORK, 9-10 April 1947, *Charity* (lead pencil) USD 70. PARIS, 30 June 1947, *Bathers,* FRF 43,500; *Rêverie* FRF 190,000; *Water Sprite* (pastel) FRF 26,000. LONDON, 2 July 1947, *Sprig of Lilac,* GBP 78. AMSTERDAM, 1-4 July 1947, *Episode from the Valkyrie,* NLG 220. LONDON, 28 Nov 1956, *Roses,* GBP 6,500. LONDON, 1 Dec 1957, *Carnations,* GBP 3,360. NEW YORK, 15 Jan 1958, *Still-life,* USD 1,800. LONDON, 3 Dec 1958, *Night* (pastel/canvas) GBP 480; *Portrait of Madame Fantin-Latour,* GBP 1,200. VERSAILLES, 16 March 1959, *Spiraea in a Vase,* FRF 3,800,000. PARIS, 18 March 1959, *Spiraea without Vase,* FRF 3,800,000. PARIS, 20 March 1959, *Japanese Lilies in a Vase,* FRF 3,220,000; *Spray of Narcissi,* FRF 2,600,000. LONDON, 1 July 1959, *Two Water Nymphs,* GBP 720; *Still-life with a Pot of White Azalea,* GBP 15,000. NEW YORK, 9 Dec 1959, *Still-life with Roses,* USD 11,000. PARIS, 29 March 1960, *Dawn,* FRF 6,000. LONDON, 23 Nov 1960, *White and Yellow Roses in a Glass,* GBP 5,000. LONDON, 28 June 1961, *Larkspur in a Large Crystal Vase,* GBP 21,000. LONDON, 6 Dec 1961, *Peonies,* GBP 12,500. LONDON, 11 June 1963, *Branch of Rhododendrons,* GBP 18,800. NEW YORK, 19 May 1966, *Bouquet of Flowers,* USD 77,500. LONDON, 26 April 1967, *All the Garden's Roses,* GBP 23,000. LONDON, 3 July 1968, *Vase of Peonies,* GBP 54,000. LONDON, 6 July 1971, *Fruit,* Gns 5,000. LONDON, 28 June 1972, *White and Pink Roses,* GBP 34,000. PARIS, 4 Dec 1972, *Flowers and Bunches of Grapes* (1875) FRF 205,000. LONDON, 3 April 1974, *Vase of Flowers,* GBP 31,000. PARIS, 5 June 1974, *Homage to Venus,* FRF 32,000; *Homage to R. Schumann, H. Berlioz, R. Wagner and Brahms* (drawing) FRF 8,000. LONDON, 1 July 1974, *Roses in a*

Stemmed Glass, Gns 35,000. LONDON, 6 April 1976, *Spring Flowers* (1869, oil on canvas, 15 3/4 x 13 ins / 40 x 33 cm) GBP 22,000. LONDON, 27 June 1977, *Ranunculus and Narcissi* (1880, oil on canvas, 13 1/2 x 12 ins / 34 x 30.5 cm) GBP 22,000. LONDON, 6 Dec 1978, *Carnations* (1887, oil on canvas, 16 3/4 x 13 3/4 ins / 42.5 x 35 cm) GBP 55,000. NEW YORK, 17 May 1979, *Vision* (1876, pastel/paper, 17 1/4 x 11 1/2 ins / 43.5 x 29.2 cm) USD 6,750. PARIS, 1 Feb 1980, *Self-portrait* (soft lead pencil, 9 x 7 1/2 ins / 22 x 19 cm) FRF 8,600. NEW YORK, 16 Nov 1983, *Drawing Lesson* (1879, pen/paper mounted on card, 5 1/2 x 6 1/2 ins / 14 x 16.3 cm) USD 18,000. BERN, 20 June 1984, *Bouquet of Roses* (1879, lithograph) CHF 21,000. NEW YORK, 15 Nov 1984, *Geraniums* (1888, oil on canvas, 17 1/4 x 14 1/4 ins / 44 x 36.2 cm) USD 150,000. LONDON, 29 June 1987, *White Roses, Chrysanthemums in a Vase, Peaches and Grapes on a Table with a White Cloth* (1876, oil on canvas, 24 x 28 3/4 ins / 61 x 73 cm) GBP 1,300,000. PARIS, 10 Dec 1987, *Painter's Despair* (lead pencil, 9 1/4 x 9 ins / 23.5 x 23 cm) FRF 42,000. LONDON, 29 March 1988, *Narcissi and White and Pink Peonies* (1878, oil on canvas, 18 3/4 x 17 1/2 ins / 47.5 x 44.5 cm) GBP 374,000. NEW YORK, 11 May 1988, *Roses in a Vase* (1892, oil on canvas, 16 1/4 x 14 1/4 ins / 41.2 x 36.2 cm) USD 385,000. NEW YORK, 24 May 1988, *Danaë* (1898, oil on canvas, 11 x 14 ins / 27 x 35.3 cm) USD 46,750. PARIS, 8 June 1988, *Allegory of the Muse* (1869, paper mounted on canvas, 12 3/4 x 9 1/2 ins / 32.5 x 24.3 cm) FRF 25,000. LONDON, 28 June 1988, *Seascape, Impression of Morning* (oil on canvas, 6 1/4 x 9 ins / 15.9 x 22.9 cm) GBP 9,900; *White Narcissi in an Opaline Vase* (1875, oil on canvas, 20 x 18 1/2 ins / 50.5 x 47 cm) GBP 198,000; *Carnation Flowers* (1872, oil on canvas, 15 x 10 3/4 ins / 38 x 27.5 cm) GBP 88,000. LONDON, 29 Nov 1988, *Pink Roses* (1886, oil on canvas, 15 3/4 x 13 3/4 ins / 40 x 35 cm) GBP 297,000. LONDON, 4 April 1989, *Aimé-Viebert Roses*. PARIS, 8 April 1989, *Woman with Cat* (1876, oil on canvas, 12 1/2 x 10 1/2 ins / 32 x 26.4 cm) FRF 490,000. NEW YORK, 9 May 1989, *Asters and Fruit on a Table* (1868, oil on canvas, 22 1/4 x 22 ins / 56.5 x 55 cm) USD 1,870,000; *Larkspur* (1888, oil on canvas, 28 1/2 x 24 ins / 72.5 x 61 cm) USD 1,100,000. LONDON, 27 June 1989, *Still-life with Flowers and Fruit* (1872, oil on canvas, 15 1/4 x 11 ins / 39 x 28 cm) GBP 132,000. NEW YORK, 18 Oct 1989, *Zinnias* (1891, oil on canvas, 19 3/4 x 23 1/4 ins / 50 x 59 cm) USD 1,430,000. NEW YORK, 24 Oct 1989, *Holy Family Resting* (1896, oil on canvas, 13 1/2 x 13 1/2 ins / 34.3 x 34.3 cm) USD 27,500. NEW YORK, 14 Nov 1989, *Bouquet of Flowers* (1894, oil on canvas, 18 1/2 x 24 1/2 ins / 47.3 x 62.5 cm) USD 990,000. MONACO, 3 Dec 1989, *Spring* (1896, oil on canvas, 17 1/2 x 21 1/4 ins / 44.7 x 54 cm) FRF 777,000. PARIS, 30 March 1990, *Mixed Flowers* (1902, oil on canvas, 13 1/2 x 15 3/4 ins / 34.3 x 40 cm) FRF 2,250,000. LONDON, 3 April 1990, *Anemones and Ranunculus* (1890, oil on canvas, 17 1/4 x 14 1/4 ins / 44 x 36 cm) GBP 220,000. PARIS, 3 May 1990, *Woman with Mirror* (oil on canvas, 22 x 25 1/2 ins / 55 x 65 cm) FRF 700,000. NEW YORK, 23 May 1990, *Water Sprite* (oil on card/canvas, 12 1/4 x 17 1/2 ins / 30.8 x 44.5 cm) USD 71,500. LONDON, 25 June 1990, *Bouquet of Roses in a Glass* (1881, oil on canvas, 16 1/4 x 12 1/2 ins / 41.3 x 32 cm) GBP 297,000. NEW YORK, 14 Feb 1991, *Cyclamen Flowers* (oil on canvas, 8 x 6 ins / 20.2 x 15.2 cm) USD 30,800. CANNES, 26 Feb 1991, *Andromeda* (1904, oil on canvas, 32 x 25 1/2 ins / 81 x 65 cm) FRF 450,000. NEW YORK, 7 May 1991, *French Marigolds* (1893, oil on canvas, 18 1/4 x 19 1/2 ins / 46.2 x 49.7 cm) USD 374,000. PARIS, 20 June 1991, *Temptation of St Anthony* (oil on canvas, 24 1/2 x 30 ins / 62.5 x 76 cm) FRF 600,000. LONDON, 24 June 1991, *Bouquet of Flowers with Pansies* (1883, oil on canvas, 10 1/4 x 12 ins / 26 x 30.5 cm) GBP 82,500. NEW YORK, 6 Nov 1991, *Flowers and Fruit* (1868, oil on canvas, 21 3/4 x 21 1/2 ins / 55.5 x 54.5 cm) USD 1,540,000. LONDON, 3 Dec 1991, *Roses and Mimosa* (1873, oil on panel, 11 x 7 1/4 ins / 27 x 18.6 cm) GBP 121,000. NEW YORK, 12 May 1992, *Mixed Bouquet* (1881, oil on canvas, 19 3/4 x 24 1/4 ins / 50.2 x 61.9 cm) USD 990,000. MONACO, 18-19 June 1992, *Holy Family Resting* (charcoal, 17 1/4 x 12 1/4 ins / 44 x 31.3 cm) FRF 44,400. LONDON, 29 June 1992, *Roses in a Basket on a Table* (1876, oil on canvas, 17 1/4 x 17 1/2 ins / 43.7 x 44.5 cm) GBP 165,000. NEW YORK, 10 Nov 1992, *Vase of Dahlias* (oil on canvas, 19 3/4 x 24 3/4 ins / 50.2 x 62.9 cm) USD 1,100,000. PARIS, 31 March 1993, *Study of Female Nudes* (black chalk/paper, 4 3/4 x 9 ins / 12 x 22 cm) FRF 3,500. LONDON, 22 June 1993, *Still-life* (1872, oil on canvas, 16 1/2 x 12 3/4 ins / 42 x 32.5 cm) GBP 144,500. NEW YORK, 15 Feb 1994, *Diana* (1871, oil on panel, 9 3/4 x 8 1/2 ins / 24.8 x 21.6 cm) USD 18,400. AMSTERDAM, 19 April 1994, *The Last Supper* (1853, oil on canvas, 11 x 14 1/2 ins / 27 x 37 cm) NLG 11,500. NEW YORK, 11 May 1994, *Fecundity* (1877, oil on canvas, 23 x 20 1/2 ins / 58.4 x 52.1 cm) USD 965,000. PARIS, 15 Nov 1994, *Young Woman with Cat* (1876, oil on canvas, 12 1/2 x 10 1/4 ins / 32 x 26 cm) FRF 135,000. LONDON, 28 Nov 1994, *Roses in a Basket on a Table* (1876, oil on canvas, 17 1/4 x 17 1/2 ins / 43.7 x 44.5 cm) GBP 232,500. NEW YORK, 24 May 1995, *Almah's Dance* (oil on canvas, 24 1/2 x 30 ins / 62.2 x 76.2 cm) USD 123,500. LONDON, 28 Nov 1995, *Dahlias* (1896, oil on canvas, 235 3/4 x 29 1/4 ins / 599 x 74 cm) GBP 881,500. PARIS, 13 Dec 1995, *Roses* (oil on canvas, 11 x 15 3/4 ins / 27 x 40 cm) FRF 440,000. NEW YORK, 1 May 1996, *Flowers, Large Bouquet with Three Peonies* (1879, oil on canvas, 16 1/2 x 13 1/4 ins / 41.6 x 33.5 cm) USD 266,500. NEW YORK, 13 Nov 1996, *Portrait of the Artist* (1860, oil on canvas, 14 x 11 1/2 ins / 35.6 x 28.9 cm) USD 87,750. PARIS, 22 Nov 1996, *Woman Bathing* (graphite, 5 x 3 1/4 ins / 13 x 8 cm) FRF 28,000. LONDON, 3 Dec 1996, *Vase of Peonies* (1902, oil on canvas, 16 1/4 x 14 1/2 ins / 41 x 37 cm) GBP 199,500. LONDON, 19 March 1997, *Portrait of Fantin* (1865, oil on canvas, 14 1/2 x 13 ins / 37 x 33 cm) GBP 29,900. PARIS, 24 March 1997, *Judgement of Paris* (c. 1894, oil on canvas, 16 3/4 x 13 1/2 ins / 42.5 x 34 cm) FRF 72,000. LONDON, 11 June 1997, *Judgement of Paris* (oil on canvas, 16 1/2 x 13 1/2 ins / 42 x 34 cm) GBP 10,350. PARIS, 17 June 1997, *Birthday* (c. 1876, pastel/paper, 24 1/2 x 19 3/4 ins / 62 x 50 cm) FRF 400,000. NEW YORK, 23 Oct 1997, *Solitude* (1884, oil on canvas, 9 3/4 x 17 1/2 ins / 24.8 x 44.5 cm) USD 17,250. LONDON, 21 Nov 1997, *Dream* (1871, oil on paper/canvas, 12 x 9 ins / 30.5 x 22.9 cm) GBP 10,350. NEW YORK, 8 Nov 1999, *Mixed Bouquet, Garden Flowers* (oil on canvas, 16 x 24 ins / 40 x 61 cm) USD 820,000. NEW YORK, 8 Nov 1999, *Vase of Peonies* (1879, oil on canvas, 22 x 26 ins / 55 x 66 cm) USD 900,000. NEW YORK, 8 May 2000, *Bouquet of Peonies* (1878, oil on canvas, 20 x 19 ins / 52 x 49 cm) USD 820,000. NEW YORK, 8 Nov 2000, *Bouquet of Flowers* (oil on canvas, 20 x 24 ins / 51 x 62 cm) USD 3,200,000. NEW YORK, 9 May 2001, *Marguerites* (1872, oil on canvas, 18 x 16 ins / 46 x 41 cm) USD 1,200,000. NEW YORK, 6 Nov 2001, *Flowers, Malmaison Roses* (oil on canvas, 19 x 16 ins / 48 x 40 cm) USD 550,000. LONDON, 25 June 2002, *Roses* (oil on canvas, 22 x 17 ins / 55 x 42 cm) GBP 720,000. NEW YORK, 6 Nov 2002, *Still-life, Dahlias, Grapes and Peaches* (1868, oil on canvas, 20 x 19 ins / 51 x 49 cm) USD 780,000. LONDON, 4 Feb 2003, *Carnations* (oil on canvas, 18 x 20 ins / 46 x 51 cm) GBP 420,000. NEW YORK, 4 Nov 2003, *Vase of Flowers with a Cup of Coffee* (1865, oil on canvas, 19 x 15 ins / 48 x 39 cm) USD 1,400,000. NEW YORK, 4 May 2004, *Flowers; Carnations and Hyacinths In a Champagne Glass* (oil on canvas, 15 x 11 ins / 38 x 27 cm) USD 260,000. NEW YORK, 5 May 2004, *Roses* (1903, oil on canvas, 13 x 13 ins / 34 x 33 cm) USD 300,000.

FANTIN-LATOUR, Théodore

French, 19th century.

Born 1805, in Metz; died 1872, in Paris.

Painter, pastellist. Religious subjects, genre scenes, portraits.

Théodore Fantin-Latour first worked in Grenoble, living there until he left for Paris in 1841. From 1842 to 1866 he exhibited several works at the Paris Salon. His last exhibited work was *Christ on the Cross*. He executed a large number of charming portraits, mainly in pastel.

MUSEUMS AND GALLERIES:

GRENOBLE: *Portrait of the Artist's Eldest Daughter as a Child*.

AUCTION RECORDS:

PARIS, 11-13 June 1923, *Young Girl at the Fountain; Little Flower Girl* (pastel, a pair) FRF 1,000. PARIS, 18 June 1923, *Portrait of a Young Woman in Oriental Costume* (pastel) FRF 255. MONACO, 16 June 1989, *Bust Portrait of a Little Girl Holding her King Charles Spaniel in her Arms* (pastel/paper, 21 1/2 x 18 1/4 ins / 54.5 x 46.5 cm) FRF 133,200. GRANDVILLE, 15 July 1990, *Nymph on the Swing* (oil on canvas, 18 x 13 3/4 ins / 46 x 35 cm) FRF 500,000. CANNES, 27 April 1991, *Woman Bathing* (oil on canvas, 16 1/2 x 13 1/2 ins / 42 x 34 cm) FRF 210,000. PARIS, 9 April 1999, *Renown* (black crayon scratching out, 15 x 11 ins / 39 x 28 cm) FRF 60,000. AMSTERDAM, 26 Oct 1999, *Portrait of Young Lady in 18th Century Costume* (pastel, 31 x 25 ins / 80 x 64 cm) NLG 9,000. LONDON, 6 April 2000, *Seascape, Morning* (oil on canvas, 6 x 9 ins / 16 x 23 cm) GBP 4,800. LONDON, 22 June 2000, *Reclining Maiden with her Dog* (pastel, 21 x 27 ins / 53 x 68 cm) GBP 3,800. PARIS, 7 Nov 2001, *Portrait of Vicomte de Matharel* (1854, oil on canvas, oval, 32 x 26 ins / 81 x 65 cm) FRF 34,000. LONDON, 9 July 2002, *Shepherd and Shepherdess with Dogs in a Landscape. Young Lovers Seated by a Fountain* (pastel, oval, 29 x 24 ins / 73 x 61 cm) GBP 13,000. LONDON, 20 March 2003, *Pensive Moment. Passage of Time* (pastel, oval, a pair, 16 x 13 ins / 41 x 33 cm) GBP 4,500. LONDON, 18 Nov 2003, *Dream of Poet* (oil on canvas, 24 x 29 ins / 60 x 73 cm) GBP 3,000.

FANTIN-LATOUR, Victoria (Mme)

Maiden name: Dubourg
French, 19th - 20th century.
Born 1 December 1840, in Paris; died 1926.
Painter. Genre scenes, interiors with figures, flowers, still-lifes (including fruit).

Victoria Fantin-Latour was the wife of Henri Fantin-Latour. In 1895 she was awarded a medal by the Société des Amis des Arts at the Salon de Grenoble. From 1869 she sent still-life paintings depicting flowers and fruit to the Salon de Paris. In 1895 and 1899 she took part in the exhibition of the Société des Amis des Arts at the Salon de Grenoble. In 2003 she was represented in the exhibition *Peintres et artistes dans le Perche, 19e - 20e siècles* (*Painters and Artists in the Perche Region, 19th-20th Centuries*), held at the Château St-Jean, Nogent-le-Rotrou.

V Dubourg

BIBLIOGRAPHY:

Arpentinier, Jean, *Peintures et Artistes du Perche 1560-1960*, Editions de la Reinette, Le Mans, 2003.

MUSEUMS AND GALLERIES:

ALENÇON: *Fantin-Latour's Studio in Buré* - CHÂTEAU-THIERRY: *Flowers* - GRENOBLE (Mus. de Grenoble): *Still-life* (1899) - PARIS (MAM): *Corner of a Table*.

AUCTION RECORDS:

LONDON, 9 Feb 1923, *Fish in a Basket* (drawing) GBP 9. PARIS, 18 June 1924, *Pinks in a Glass*, FRF 950. PARIS, 19 Jan 1925, *Young Girl with a Bird*, FRF 680. LONDON, 19 June 1925, *Roses in a Vase*, GBP 15; *Apple Blossom*, GBP 8. LONDON, 25 June 1937, *Flowers in a Vase*, GBP 50. LONDON, 6 May 1969, *Still-life with Flowers*, Gns 1,200. MONTE CARLO, 21 June 1987, *Basket of Flowers* (oil on canvas, 16 x 22 1/4 ins / 40.5 x 56.5 cm) FRF 70,000. AMSTERDAM, 16 Nov 1988, *Still-life with Fish in a Wicker Basket and Syringa Flowers on a Table* (1874, oil on canvas, 17 1/2 x 19 3/4 ins / 44.5 x 50 cm) NLG 43,700. LONDON, 21 Feb 1989, *Basket of Flowers* (oil on canvas, 11 1/4 x 17 ins / 28.5 x 43 cm) GBP 19,800. NEW YORK, 23 Feb 1989, *Still-life with White Flowers, Plums and Peaches on a Table* (oil on canvas, 16 x 18 1/4 ins / 39.7 x 46.3 cm) USD 49,500. NEW YORK, 25 Oct 1989, *Still-life with an Apple beside a Plate of Grapes on a Ledge* (oil on canvas, 6 3/4 x 14 1/4 ins / 17 x 36 cm) USD 22,000. PARIS, 1 July 1992, *Basket of Roses* (oil on canvas, 11 3/4 x 16 1/4 ins / 30 x 41 cm) FRF 49,000. NEW YORK, 12 Oct 1994, *Vase of Roses* (oil on canvas, 14 x 7 ins / 35.6 x 17.8 cm) USD 4,025. PARIS, 26 June 1995, *Flowers* (oil on canvas, 9 3/4 x 12 1/4 ins / 25 x 31 cm) FRF 53,000. LONDON, 23 June 1997, *Basket of Flowers* (oil on canvas, 20 1/2 x 24 3/4 ins / 52 x 63 cm) GBP 69,700. PARIS, 22 Nov 1999, *Woman and Child* (oil on canvas, 11 x 8 ins / 27 x 21 cm) FRF 51,000.

FANTINANTI, Francesco

Italian, 15th century.
Born to a family originally from Rome.
Active in Cesena and Ferrara in 1490.
Painter.

FANTINI, Bonifazio

Italian, 17th century.
Born to a family originally from Reggio (province of Emilia).
Painter.

In 1617, Bonifazio Fantini decorated the façade and portico of the law courts of Correggio. It seems probable that he is the same painter as Bonifacio Pittore, who painted the *Four Apostles* for the cupola of the cathedral of Reggio.

FANTINI, Matteo

Italian, 18th - 19th century.
Born to a family originally from Murano.
Glass painter.

Matteo Fantini lived and worked in Venice, producing mostly engravings on crystal and paintings on glass and enamel.

FANTINO

Italian, 15th century.
Painter.

With other artists from Verona and Pisa, Fantino decorated rooms of the Castello Vecchio and Palazzo Pubblico in Verona for the entry of Duke Fr. Carrara.

FANTINO DA BEVAGNA. See **SPACCA Ascensidonio**

FANTITTO, Cesare

Italian, 17th century.
Active in L'Aquila.
Painter, engraver.

Cesare Fantitto painted frescoes portraying popes and cardinals for the town hall in L'Aquila.

FANTO, Leonhard

Austrian, 19th - 20th century.
Born 8 September 1874, in Vienna.
Also active in Germany.
Painter, watercolourist, draughtsman, engraver (wood), director. Figures, local figures, costume studies. Stage sets.

Leonhard Fanto studied at the academy of fine arts in Vienna and the Académie Julian in Paris. He also spent a period in Rome. Having worked in Vienna, he was called to the theatre in Dresden, where he acquired a strong reputation for his stage sets. In 1904, he painted in watercolour a series of historical uniforms for the German Emperor and for Leopold, the Prince Regent. He also painted typical figures representing the Magyar and Galician peoples. From 1909, he produced colour wood engravings, representing typical figures from Dalmatia, and an engraving that portrayed *Grete Wesenthal Dancing Liszt's Rhapsody*.

MUSEUMS AND GALLERIES:

VIENNA (Kunsthistorisches Mus.): *Portrait of Eduard Bauernfeld*.

FANTON, Joseph L.
French, 19th century.
Active in Val-d'Oise.
Painter.
Joseph L. Fanton exhibited at the Salon of the Société des Artistes Français, becoming a member in 1890.

FANTON, Madeleine
French, 19th century.
Born in the second half of the 19th century.
Engraver (wood).
A pupil of J. Breton, Madeleine Fanton was a member of the Société des Artistes Français.

FANTON-LEKEU, Henri Ferdinand
Flemish, 19th century.
Born 1791, in Liège; died 1858, in Liège.
Painter. Landscapes.
Flemish School.
Henri Ferdinand Fanton-Lekeu was taught by Hennequin, Viroux and Verbocken. His wife's name was Lekeu.
MUSEUMS AND GALLERIES:
LIÈGE (Ansembourg): *The Ruins of St-Lambert Cathedral in Liège* (sepia wash); *Interior of an Inn*; *River Bank*; *Walker and Dog*; *Landscape near a Bridge*.

FANTONE, Francesco da Norcia
Italian, 16th century.
Active at the beginning of the 16th century.
Painter.
Francesco da Norcia Fantone's *Virgin, Christ Child and Various Saints* is in the Pinacoteca di Brera, Milan.

FANTONI, Andrea
Italian, 17th - 18th century.
Born 25 August 1659, in Rovetta, near Bergamo; died 25 July 1734, in Rovetta.
Sculptor (wood/ivory), engraver.
Andrea Fantoni was the son of Grazioso Fantoni I and a pupil of Pietro Rame, the German artist who settled in Brescia. Andrea Fantoni is the most important member of the Fantoni dynasty of sculptors. He developed numerous church architecture projects. His principal work is to be found in the church of S Martino in Alzano Maggiore near Bergamo, where Fantoni sculpted and carved virtually the entire ornamentation for the sacristy - sumptuous cabinets and prie-dieux, and low reliefs portraying scenes from the Old and New Testaments. He was assisted by his four brothers, Donato, Giovanni Antonio, Giambettino and Giovanni. In the rosary chapel of the church, he sculpted a marble angel and a low relief of the *Birth of Mary*. Other examples of his work include a carved chair for the parish church of Ardesio; a marble statue of the *Immaculate Virgin* for the church of S Michele in Alzano; a confessional, low reliefs of *Our Lady of the Seven Sorrows* and two statues of angels for the church of S Maria Maggiore in Bergamo; and a low relief, *Last Supper*, for the Annunciation altar in the church of S Alessandro della Cruce. Fantoni is also recorded as having sculpted the ivory crucifixes preserved in the Carrara academy in Bergamo.

FANTONI, Andrea I
Italian, 17th century.
Born 24 June 1628.
Active in Rovetta.
Sculptor.
He was the son of Donato Fantoni.

FANTONI, Andrea II
Italian, 17th century.
Born 15 November 1633; died 6 June 1683.
Active in Rovetta.
Sculptor.
He was the son of Giovanni Fantoni.

FANTONI, Andrea III
Italian, 17th century.
Born 28 October 1635.
Active in Rovetta.
Sculptor.
He was the son of Giovanni Fantoni.

FANTONI, Bertulio or Bertulino
Italian, 15th century.
Active in Rovetta.
Sculptor (wood).
Bertulio Fantoni is the first known representative of the Fantoni family.

FANTONI, Donato Andrea
Italian, 18th - 19th century.
Born 20 August 1746, in Rovetta; died 31 August 1817.
Sculptor.
He was the son of Grazioso Fantoni III, and the last active member of the Fantoni sculptor dynasty. Little is known of his work other than an altar in Castione.

FANTONI, Donato I
Italian, 16th century.
Active in Rovetta between 1562 and 1580.
Sculptor.

FANTONI, Donato II
Italian, 17th century.
Born 24 August 1594.
Active in Rovetta.
Sculptor.

FANTONI, Donato III
Italian, 17th century.
Born 9 December 1661; died 16 March 1683.
Active in Rovetta.
Sculptor.
He was the son of Donato Fantoni II.

FANTONI, Francesca
Italian, 18th century.
Died c. 1772.
Painter.
The niece and pupil of Giovanni Giuseppe del Sole, she went on to study under Cavazzoni.

FANTONI, Francesco Donato
Italian, 18th century.
Born 14 June 1726; died 22 February 1787.
Active in Rovetta.
Sculptor.
The son of Giambettino Fantoni, he worked alongside his cousin Grazioso Fantoni III at the church of S Martino in Alzano Maggiore, and on a large number of other churches.

FANTONI, Giambettino
Italian, 17th - 18th century.
Born 26 November 1672; died 20 July 1750.
Active in Rovetta.
Sculptor.
The son of Grazioso Fantoni I, he worked alongside his brothers.

FANTONI, Giovanni
Italian, 17th - 18th century.
Born 24 December 1674; died 15 May 1745.
Active in Rovetta.
Sculptor.
The son of Grazioso Fantoni I, he worked alongside Andrea Fantoni III and his other brothers.

FANTONI, Giovanni Antonio I
Italian, 17th - 18th century.
Born 12 January 1669; died 7 April 1748.

Active in Rovetta.
Sculptor.
The son of Grazioso Fantoni I, he worked alongside his brother Andrea Fantoni III.

FANTONI, Giovanni Antonio II
Italian, 17th century.
Born 29 October 1641.
Active in Rovetta.
Sculptor.

FANTONI, Giuseppe
Austrian, 19th century.
Born to a family originally from Frioul (Tyrol).
Painter.
In 1805, Fantoni decorated the dome and apse of the cathedral of Gemona.

FANTONI, Giuseppe Grazioso
Italian, 18th century.
Born 20 February 1731; died 17 February 1781.
Active in Rovetta.
Sculptor.
He was the son of Giambettino Fantoni.

FANTONI, Grazioso I
Italian, 17th century.
Born 28 November 1630; died 5 April 1693.
Active in Rovetta.
Sculptor (wood).
The son of Donato Fantoni II, he worked in the sacristy of the church of S Martino in Alzano Maggiore, where he decorated a series of cabinets with carvings, groups and low reliefs. He also carved decorations for the organ loft in the parish church of Castione.

FANTONI, Grazioso II
Italian, 17th century.
Born 11 June 1638.
Active in Rovetta.
Sculptor.
The father of Donato Andrea Fantoni, he worked alongside his cousin Francesco Donato Fantoni to sculpt marble low reliefs for the pulpit in the church of S Martino in Alzano Maggiore. The two also collaborated on decorations for the parish church in Adro, as well as in various churches in Salo, Vezza, Vilminore, Grumello and Angolo.

FANTONI, Grazioso III
Italian, 18th century.
Born 30 April 1713; died 21 March 1798.
Sculptor. Religious subjects. Low reliefs.

FANTONI, Luigi Andrea
Italian, 18th century.
Born 30 July 1759, in Rovetta; died 22 December 1788.
Sculptor.
The son of Francesco Donato Fantoni, he studied under the Milanese sculptor G. Franchi and worked alongside the latter on the tomb of Count Firmian in Milan. His own body of work includes a marble low relief, *Story of Jephthah*, for the cemetery in Milan.

FANTONI, Peter
British, 20th century.
Painter, watercolourist. Landscapes.
During his adolescence, Peter Fantoni travelled from London to Latin America by boat. This was the start of a journey that would last 10 years. He studied art at the Hoffman School of Art in Buenos Aires and on his return to England exhibited regularly. After World War II he abandoned painting but began to earn a living from painting again in the 1960s. He painted many views of Las Palmas, Venice and Florence.

FANTONI, Pietro
Italian, 19th century.
Born to a family originally from Gémone.
Sculptor. Busts.
MUSEUMS AND GALLERIES:
VERSAILLES (Château): *King Ferdinand II of Naples and His Wife Marie Christine* (busts in plaster).

FANTONI, Venturino di Giovanni
Italian, 16th century.
Born to a family originally from Bergamo.
Sculptor.
Venturino di Giovanni Fantoni worked in Venice where, with his sons Giovanni, Bernardo and Giacomo, he carried out the seven marble sculptures which decorate the high altar of the church of S Roch.

FANTOSE, Antoine. See **FANTUZZI Antonio**

FANTOZZI, Francesco, called il Parma
Italian, 17th century.
Born 17th century, probably in Parma.
Painter.
Francesco Fantozzi studied under F. Costanzo Catanio in Ferrara. He worked in Ferrara, where he painted a *Christ Carrying His Cross* for the church of S Nicolò, an *Annunciation* for the great organ of the church of S Stefano, and an *Archangel St Michael* for the façade of the church of S Michele. He is also credited with frescoes painted in the Oratorio della Penitenza.

FANTUZZI, Antonio, or Fantose, Antoine
Italian, 16th century.
Born in Bologna; died after 1550, in Fontainebleau.
Active in France from 1537.
Painter, engraver (etching), draughtsman, designer.
First School of Fontainebleau.
For a long time, Antonio Fantuzzi was confused with the chiaroscuro engraver Antonio da Trento, on account of the similarity of their monograms and the fact that they both engraved chiaroscuros from designs by Le Parmesan. He was identified in 1964 by Henri Zerner, who established a chronology of his engravings and was sometimes known by the name of Antoine Fantose. He lived in Fontainebleau from 1537 until his death. From 1542 to 1547, he worked with Léon Davent in the engraving studio 'atelier bellifontain' on the design programme that Francis I entrusted first to Rosso Fiorentino, then, after the latter's death in 1540, to Francesco Primaticcio (known as Le Primatice).

He was employed as a painter at Fontainebleau from January 1537 to December 1540, and from January 1540 to September 1550, both for his painting and for the creation of patterns and grotesques for the decoration of the Ulysses Gallery, which was carried out by other artists. From 1541, when Rosso Fiorentino died, he was given wider responsibilities. He decorated the bedroom that projected out above the Golden Door. This room has since been destroyed along with the Ulysses Gallery. In 1542-1543, he reproduced many drawings by Giulio Romano and Rosso Fiorentino, especially some works that have since been lost. He then made engravings in the manner of Le Primatice. Within the 'atelier bellifontain', Fantuzzi gradually departed from a rather violent style of structuring light and shade, and began to adopt the lighter and more uniform line of Léon Davent. The two artists shared the same sources - in particular Giulio Romano, Le Parmesan and Le Primatice - and consequently each was influenced by the other during these years. The Georg Baselitz Collection at the Cabinet des Estampes in Geneva has preserved a significant stock of works by this artist. The *catalogue raisonné* of his engravings includes almost a hundred etchings.

He has featured in themed group exhibitions, including: 1999, *Old Masters Prints from the Museum's Collection*, Los Angeles County Museum of Art, Los Angeles; 2002, the personal collection of Georg Baselitz, *La bella maniera. Collection d'estampes maniéristes* (*La Bella Maniera. Collection of Mannerist Prints*), École Nationale Supérieure des Beaux-Arts, Paris, then at the Cabinet des Estampes, Geneva, the Boijmans van Beuningen Museum, Rotterdam, and the Carnegie Museum of Art, Pittsburgh. In 2003, the Cabinet des Estampes in Geneva put on an exhibition both of his work and of the other leading engraver of the same school, Léon Davent, under the heading, *Les Lumières du maniérisme français: Antonio Fantuzzi et Léon Davent, 1540-1550* (*Leaders of French Mannerism: Antonio Fantuzzi and Léon Davent, 1540-1550*).

BIBLIOGRAPHY:
Zerner, Henri, '*L'eau-forte à Fontainebleau. Le rôle d'Antonio Fantuzzi*' in *L'Art de France*, 1964. Zerner, Henri, *École de Fontainebleau, Gravures*, Arts et métiers graphiques, Paris, 1969. Brugerolles, Emmanuelle/Strasser, Nathalie/Mason, Rainer Michael (ed.)/Baselitz, Georg, *La Bella maniera. Gravures maniéristes de la collection Georg Baselitz*, École nationale supérieure des beaux-arts, Paris, 2002.

MUSEUMS AND GALLERIES:
GENEVA (MAH, Prints Collection): *Large Bowl* (1543, engraving) - SAN FRANCISCO (FAM): *Achilles bids farewell to Deidamia* - ZURICH (Graphische Sammlung, EHT): *Melpomene* (c. 1545, engraving).

FANTUZZI, Eliano
Italian, 20th century.
Born 1909, in Verona.
Painter. Scenes with figures, landscapes with figures.

AUCTION RECORDS:
ROME, 2 Dec 1980, *Station Platforms* (1947, oil on canvas, 15 3/4 x 19 3/4 ins / 40 x 50 cm) ITL 800,000. ROME, 20 April 1982, *Portrait of Carra* (1953, charcoal, 11 x 7 3/4 ins / 28 x 20 cm) ITL 500,000. ROME, 12 June 1986, *La Fioraia* (oil on canvas, 31 3/4 x 25 3/4 ins / 80.5 x 65.5 cm) ITL 800,000. ROME, 7 April 1988, *Versailles* (1940, oil on canvas, 27 1/2 x 23 1/2 ins / 70 x 60 cm) ITL 3,200,000. MILAN, 20 March 1989, *Tomcats* (1967, oil on canvas, 23 1/2 x 20 ins / 60 x 50.5 cm) GBP 800,000. ROME, 17 April 1989, *Street in Rome* (1946, oil on canvas, 19 3/4 x 15 3/4 ins / 50 x 40 cm) ITL 2,200,000. ROME, 28 Nov 1989, *Fishermen No 1* (1954, oil on canvas, 19 3/4 x 39 1/4 ins / 50 x 100 cm) ITL 1,700,000. ROME, 10 April 1990, *At the Hippodrome* (oil on canvas, 19 3/4 x 27 1/2 ins / 50 x 70 cm) ITL 1,200,000. MILAN, 27 Sept 1990, *View of Venice* (oil on canvas, 23 1/2 x 35 1/2 ins / 60 x 90 cm) ITL 950,000. ROME, 3 June 1993, *In the Cafe* (1980, oil on canvas, 31 1/2 x 31 1/2 ins / 80 x 80 cm) ITL 2,000,000. ROME, 30 Nov 1993, *At the Market* (1984, oil on canvas, 19 3/4 x 15 3/4 ins / 50 x 40 cm) ITL 1,380,000. PRATO, 7 June 2002, *Coffee* (1955, oil on canvas, 20 x 16 ins / 50 x 40 cm) EUR 1,900. ROME, 21 Nov 2002, *At the Tailor's* (oil on canvas, 31 x 47 ins / 80 x 120 cm) EUR 2,400. ROME, 13 Nov 2003, *Venice* (oil on cardboard, 20 x 28 ins / 50 x 70 cm) EUR 1,500.

FANTY-LESCURE, Emma
French, 19th - 20th century.
Born in La Rochelle; died 1935.
Painter (including gouache). Genre scenes, flowers. Fans.

Emma Fanty-Lescure, a pupil of Eugène Claude, exhibited at the Salon de Paris from 1876 and won a third-class medal at the Exposition Universelle of 1900.

AUCTION RECORDS:
PARIS, 2-3 June 1926, *Roses*, FRF 200; *Basket of Pansies*, FRF 120.

FANTY-LESCURE, Gaston
French, 19th - 20th century.
Born in Paris; died July 1914, in Paris.
Painter. Local figures, genre scenes, local scenes.

Gaston Fanty-Lescure, a pupil of Fernand Cormon, exhibited in Paris at the Salon des Artistes Français, of which he was member from 1903, and where he was awarded an honourable mention in 1905 and a third-class medal in 1910.

MUSEUMS AND GALLERIES:
CASTRES: *In Trégor*; *The Image Maker* - CHÂTEAU-THIERRY: *Woman with Plums* - ORAN: *Washerwomen* - SOISSONS: *Normandy Lace-Maker*.

FANYAU, Nicolas. See **FAGOT**

FANZAGO. See **FANSAGA**

FANZELLI
Italian, 19th century.
Born in Bologna.
Painter. Historical subjects.

Fanzelli's fresco of *Alexander in Babylon* is mentioned by Siret.

FANZELT. See **PFANDZELT**

FANZERES, Evany
Brazilian, 20th century.
Born 1940, in Rio de Janeiro.
Painter, sculptor, mixed media.

In 1957 and 1958 Evany Fanzeres studied history of art, drawing and architecture at the fine arts institute in Rio de Janeiro. In 1961 she spent time in Great Britain and later travelled to Germany where, in Düsseldorf, in 1964 she met Joseph Beuys. She also spent time in Paris and in 1970-1971 travelled around Europe. Fanzeres's painting is based on the concept of signs, which she transposes into multi-dimensional spaces. She has also produced pieces in flexible materials such as foam-filled plastic fabrics and has worked with cement applied to canvas-covered structures.

FANZONI, Ferrau, or Faenzoni or Fenzoni
Italian, 16th - 17th century.
Born 1562, in Faenza; died 1645, in Faenza.
Painter, fresco artist. Religious subjects.

According to Abbot Titi, Ferrau Fanzoni studied in Rome with the knight Vanni and made frescoes. From his output conserved in Ravenna it is tempting to think he studied in the workshop of Lodovico Carracci. Out of envy he murdered the young painter Monzoni de Faenza, who showed an aptitude for painting.

MUSEUMS AND GALLERIES:
FAENZA (Confraternity of S Giovanni): *Probatica* - FAENZA (Dominican Church): *Descent from the Cross* - FAENZA (Pinacoteca Comunale d'Arte Antica e Moderna): *The Pool of Bethesda*; *Descent from the Cross*; *Death of the Virgin*; *Christ Carrying the Cross* - ROME (Church of S Giovanni In Laterano): frescoes - ROME (Church of S Maria Maggiore): frescoes - ROME (Scala Santa): frescoes.

AUCTION RECORDS:
LONDON, 22 May 1928, *The Bronze Serpent of the Holy Staircase, Rome* (red chalk, study) GBP 7. MUNICH, 27 Nov 1980, *Virgin and Child* (red chalk/paper, 11 x 7 1/2 ins / 27 x 19 cm) DEM 2,700. NEW YORK, 3 June 1981, *Martyrdom of St Sebastian* (pen and white gouache/blue paper, 12 x 8 1/2 ins / 30.2 x 21.9 cm) USD 2,400. PARIS, 17 Nov 1983, *Angel Measuring a Globe* (black chalk heightened with white/greyish-green paper, 12 1/4 x 7 1/2 ins / 31 x 19 cm) FRF 24,000. ROME, 20 March 1986, *Conversion of St Paul* (oil on canvas, 63 x 46 ins / 160 x 116 cm) ITL 16,000,000. LONDON, 6 July 1987, *St Simon Seated* (black chalk heightened with white/blue paper, 12 x 8 1/2 ins / 30.7 x 21.8 cm) GBP 2,800. MONACO, 2 Dec 1989, *The Entombment* (oil on canvas, 31 x 34 3/4 ins / 79 x 88.5 cm) FRF 61,050. MONACO, 20 June 1992, *St John the Evangelist* (red chalk, design for a pendentive, 8 1/4 x 7 ins / 21.1 x 16.9 cm) FRF 57,720. LONDON, 6 July 1992, *The Deposition* (ink height-

ened with white/beige paper, 15¾ x 12 ins / 40.3 x 29.6 cm) GBP 55,000. NEW YORK, 7 Oct 1994, *Assumption of the Virgin* (oil/copper, 19¾ x 11½ ins / 50.2 x 28.9 cm) USD 8,050.

FAR SI, Georges
French, 19th - 20th century.
Born 15 February 1866, in Paris.
Painter.

Far Si was a pupil of both Cormon and Bompard. From 1921 he exhibited at the Salon des Artistes Français, of which he was a member. He received the gold medal in 1926 and exhibited non-competitively in 1927. In 1928 he was made a Chevalier of the Légion d'Honneur.

FARABOLLINI, Elvidio
Italian, 20th century.
Born 21 July 1930, in Treia; died 1 July 1971, in Treia.
Engraver (etching). Figures, nudes, landscapes, urban landscapes.
Symbolism.

Farabollini was a frequent visitor to the art institute of Urbino and the Accademia di Belle Arti in Rome. His black and white etchings are executed in a traditional style, highlighting the marks of the needle at the first glimpse. However, there is also evidence of deliberate figuration with a Symbolist accent, built up around the offerings and communion of souls.

His work has appeared in various collective exhibitions, including Milan (1950); the Galerie Nationale d'Art Moderne in Paris (1952); Maratea (1962, 1963, 1964 and 1965); the Taranto Biennale of engraving (1964, 1965 and 1966); the international exhibition of graphic art in Arezzo (1970); and the Tolentino Biennale (1996). He has also held a number of solo exhibitions, including Arco (1965); Studio Margutta 13 in Rome (1965); Padua (1965); University of Washington (1966); Cagliari (1968); Macerata (1968); and Bologna (1969). There have been several retrospective exhibitions of his work, most notably in 1990 at the church of S Paolo in Macerata, and the church of S Filippo in Treia.

BIBLIOGRAPHY:

Volpini, V./Binni, G./Melloni, C., *Elvidio Farabollini*, exhibition catalogue, Macerata, Église S. Filippo, Treia. Appella, Giuseppe/Del Gobbo, Lucio, *Quatro incisori marchigiani del novecento. Vitalini, Mainini, Pace, Farabollini*, exhibition catalogue, Commune di Tolentino, Tolentino, 1996.

FARAFONTEEV
Russian, 18th century.
Painter.

This artist might be Yacob Gerassimovich Farafonteev. A portrait of Baron A. Ivanovich Cherkassov, signed by this artist and dated 1771, appeared at the St Petersburg Portrait Exhibition of 1870.

FARAFONTEEV, Mikhaïl Yacovlevich
Russian, 18th century.
Sculptor.

Son of Yacob Gerassimovich, he was a pupil of the St Petersburg School of Sculpture, and received several wards for his studies from life and compositions from Russian history.

FARAFONTEEV, Yacob Gerassimovich
Russian, 18th century.
Born 20 October 1758, in Peterhof; died 6 June 1798, in St Petersburg.
Painter.

Son of a court gardener, Farafonteev was a pupil at the Imperial Academy in St Petersburg. For his painting *Battle of Dniester*, he received an award, then later a scholarship to travel. This allowed him to spend four years in Paris, where he studied in the studio of the architectural painter A. de Machy. The collection of the St Petersburg academy of fine arts, included a vivid representation by this artist of the stairway of the Palace of the St Petersburg academy, with figures dressed in Louis XVI style costumes.

FARAFONTOV, Fedor Timofeivich
Russian, 18th century.
Born 8 February 1770, in St Petersburg.
Painter, illustrator.

This artist studied at the St Petersburg academy of fine arts, where he received several awards, including a gold award for his painting *Justinian and Belisarius*. Engravings were made of some of his drawings.

FARAGO, Geza
Hungarian, 19th - 20th century.
Born 1877, in Budapest; died 1928.
Painter, draughtsman, decorative painter. Patterns (fabrics), stage costumes, posters.

Geza Farago was initially a fabric designer in a cotton fabric factory, then went to Paris where he was apprenticed as a painter, draughtsman and decorator in several workshops, notably at the Académie Colarossi.

Farago specialised in costume design and worked in this field for theatres in Vienna and Budapest. He drew his set designs and his costumes in a soft style, his arabesques are refined and his ornamental lines stylised. This flowery style marking his posters, and his entire production, emerged from his admiration for Alphonse Mucha, with whom he was associated. Geza Farago won the Harkanyi Prize in Budapest in 1905 and organised an individual exhibition of his works at the Salon Nemzeti in 1910 in Budapest.

FARAGO, Jozsef
Hungarian, 19th century.
Born probably in 1822, in Ujbánya.
Sculptor.

Jozsef Farago worked in Budapest with the sculptor Ferenczy, and then with Casagrande in Esztergom on the construction of the basilica. In 1840 he submitted a work entitled *Armenia* to the Budapest Exhibition. He spent time in Vienna and Munich, where he exhibited a sculpture of *The Spirit of Hungary*. On returning to Ujbanya, he produced a *Holy Trinity with St Stephen, St Helen, St Ladislas and the Virgin* for the town.

FARAGO, Jozsef
Hungarian, 19th century.
Born 1866, in Esztergom; died 2 September 1906, in Berlin.
Painter, draughtsman, caricaturist, illustrator. Nudes, genre scenes.

Jozsef Farago studied under Hollósy in Munich then at the academy. In 1889 he went to Paris, from where he sent his first canvas, *A Difficult Lesson*, to Budapest. On returning to Budapest, his work consisted mainly of caricatures for humorous reviews, which attracted the attention of the New York publication *Puck*, where he was offered a job. After a stay in America, he returned to his home country, where he worked regularly for the humorous newspapers *Borsszem Janko* and *Kakas Marton* in Budapest.

AUCTION RECORDS:

VIENNA, 23 June 1982, *Nude Looking into the Distance* (oil on canvas, 30¾ x 22½ ins / 78 x 57 cm) ATS 10,000.

FARAGUET, H. (Mme)
French, 19th century.
Active in Sèvres.
Painter (porcelain).

MUSEUMS AND GALLERIES:

DIEPPE: painted vase, Sèvres porcelain.

FARAGUET, Marie
French, 19th - 20th century.
Born 16 September 1872, in Dijon.
Painter.

Marie Faraguet exhibited in Paris at the Salon des Artistes Français from 1899.

FARAILL, Gabriel Emmanuel
French, 19th century.
Born 1838, in St-Marsal; died 1892, in Paris.
Sculptor.

Gabriel Emmanuel Faraill studied under Oliva and Farachon. From 1866 to 1882 he exhibited at the Salon de Paris, most notably busts and medallions of private individuals. His best-known works include *Young Roman* (marble bust); *Shepherd's Awakening* (plaster statue); *Graziella* (marble bust); *Young Girl* (marble statue); *Young Flautist* (bronze statue); *Poverty* (group in plaster); *Young Girl with Snail*; *Bust of Doctor Companyo*; *Bust of Antoine Guiraud*; and *Bust of the Artist's Mother*. Most of these works are to be found in the museum of Perpignan.

FARALICQ, Laurence (Mrs). See **DELOBEL-FARALICQ**

FARALICQ-MÉRY, Renée
French, 20th century.
Born 27 April 1877, in Sens; died 1 June 1925, in Paris.
Painter, miniaturist.

Renée Faralicq-Méry exhibited in Paris at the Salon des Artistes Français from 1906 until her death.

FARAMA, Constantin
Romanian, 20th century.
Born in Romania.
Sculptor.

Costantin Farama exhibited at the Salon d'Automne in Paris in 1929.

FARAONI, G.
Italian, 19th century.
Sculptor.

MUSEUMS AND GALLERIES:
LE PUY-EN-VELAY: *France Standing*.

FARASIO, Stefano
Italian, 15th - 16th century.
Born c. 1450, to a family originally from Parma.
Miniaturist.

In 1496, 1500 and 1511, Stefano Farasio carried out various works for the cathedral in Parma.

FARASYN, Edgard
Belgian, 19th - 20th century.
Born 11 August 1858, in Antwerp; died 1938.
Painter, watercolourist, engraver. Interiors with figures, scenes with figures, genre scenes, fishing scenes, harbour views, landscapes, seascapes. Murals.

Edgard Farasyn was a student at the academy of fine arts in Antwerp, at which he then became a professor. He was one of the founder-members of the De XIII (The Thirteen) group and a member of the Wees Uzelf group. He also exhibited in Paris and won a bronze medal at the Exposition Universelle in 1889. He painted very varied subjects, with a predilection for the typical scenes of the daily lives of peasants and fishermen. He executed some mural decorations at the town hall in Antwerp.

Edg. Farasyn
ANTWERPEN

Edg-Farasyn

Edg. F.

MUSEUMS AND GALLERIES:
ANTWERP: *Covered Fish Market in Antwerp in 1882*; *Market in Étaples* (watercolour); *Doctor's Visit* - BERLIN: *Widow* - BRUSSELS: *Shipwreck* - COURTRAI: *Catching Shellfish* - NAMUR: *Father's Boat*.

AUCTION RECORDS:
LONDON, 10 July 1908, *Broken Jug*, GBP 17. PARIS, 7 Nov 1946, *Peasant Interior*, FRF 650. LOKEREN, 13 March 1976, *Mussel-pickers* (oil on canvas, 50 1/2 x 78 3/4 ins / 128 x 200 cm) BEF 120,000. NEW YORK, 14 Oct 1978, *Little Girl and Parrot* (1879, oil on canvas, 55 x 31 1/2 ins / 139.5 x 80 cm) USD 5,000. NEW YORK, 24 Feb 1987, *Artist's Daughter with Her Dog* (oil on canvas, 56 3/4 x 43 1/4 ins / 144.2 x 109.8 cm) USD 21,000. PARIS, 11 April 1989, *Fisherman's Wife* (oil on canvas, 47 1/4 x 31 1/2 ins / 120 x 80 cm) FRF 20,000. BRUSSELS, 27 March 1990, *Child and Flowers* (oil on canvas, 19 3/4 x 27 1/2 ins / 50 x 70 cm) BEF 160,000. AMSTERDAM, 24 April 1991, *Young Hero* (oil on canvas, 32 3/4 x 39 1/2 ins / 83 x 100.5 cm) NLG 13,800. AMSTERDAM, 14-15 April 1992, *On the Way to Church* (oil on canvas, 34 1/4 x 53 1/4 ins / 87 x 135 cm) NLG 4,370. LOKEREN, 5 Dec 1992, *Veere by Moonlight* (oil on canvas, 23 1/2 x 31 1/2 ins / 60 x 80 cm) BEF 25,000. AMSTERDAM, 19 Oct 1993, *Boats at Low Tide* (oil on panel, 9 1/4 x 12 1/2 ins / 23.5 x 32 cm) NLG 2,070. LOKEREN, 10 Dec 1994, *Fishing Boats by Moonlight* (oil on canvas, 15 x 22 ins / 38 x 55 cm) BEF 48,000. AMSTERDAM, 30 Oct 1996, *Netmenders in the Dunes* (oil on canvas, 5 1/4 x 7 ins / 13.5 x 18 cm) NLG 16,144.

FARASYN, L.
Belgian, 19th century.
Born 1822; died September 1899, in Antwerp.
Painter.

FARAUT, Charles
French, 20th century.
Born in the Alpes-Maritimes.
Painter.

Charles Faraut exhibited in Paris at the Salon des Artistes Indépendants.

FARB, Adrian or Adrienne
American, 20th - 21st century.
Born 1956, in Chicago.
Since c. 1980 active in France and in Great Britain.
Draughtswoman, painter (gouache).

Adrian Farb has studied the French colourists - Fragonard, Delacroix, Monet and Matisse - with passion, and draws inspiration from the big Paris parks and her impressions of Turkey and Egypt. She has taken the route of abstract landscape painting, in series with explicit titles (such as *Tuileries*, *Luxembourg*). In her large-format works, she entangles multicoloured, generally vertical lines which recreate the impressions she has memorised in situ.

Farb takes part in collective exhibitions, which have included: 1985, *La Voie Abstraite* (*The Abstract Way*) in Paris; 1992, the Salon Découvertes in Paris, presented by the Galerie Zurcher; and a 1997 show at the '19' Centre Régional d'Art Contemporain in Montbéliard. She also regularly shows her paintings in solo exhibitions in Paris, at the Galerie Zurcher.

FARBA, Isaac
Polish, 20th century.
Born 23 December 1914, in Warsaw.
Active since 1964 in France, naturalised in Israel.
Painter. Figure compositions, figures.
Symbolism.

Having studied painting in Poland, Isaac Farba studied at the Académie de la Grande Chaumière in Paris where he frequently spent time from 1938 onwards, settling there permanently in 1964. He exhibited in Paris frequently from 1954 onwards, as well as in Rome, New York and Tel-Aviv.

A mystical individual as well as a writer, the central theme of his painting is Man, his nature, origin and destiny. In *Man, that Unknown Person, Man and Matter*, the subject is shown with subtle means and a perfect command of form, in a Biblical style geared to a symbolism with an Expressionist tendency.

FARBER, Manny
American, 20th century.
Born 1917, in Douglas (Arizona).
Painter, draughtsman, art critic. Still-lifes.

Manny Farber studied in California at Berkeley, Stanford, the California School of Fine Arts, the Rudolf Schaefer School of Design in San Francisco. Professor emeritus of the University of California, San Diego, he began his career as film critic. He brought his film reviewer's eye to his drawing and painting. After experimenting with Abstraction, he painted objects or plants, organising in his canvases as if for filming from classical cinema angles. He makes no apologies for using cinematic language as, he says, the object is the same, in essence: to select the best possible way to offer a full view of a piece, picking the best angles, in effect to progress horizontally in all possible directions. He has written numerous reviews and critical writings, including *Negative Space*. He began taking part in collective exhibitions in 1951 with the *Peggy Guggenheim Group Show*, in New York. Among other exhibitions, he took part in the Whitney Annual Painting Exhibition; in *19 Artists: Emergent Americans*, at the Guggenheim Museum, New York; in *American Still-life 1945-1983*, Contemporary Arts Museum, Houston, and in *Made in California: Art, Image, and Identity, 1900-2000*, Los Angeles County Museum of Art. He has shown his works in solo exhibitions, often in La Jolla (California). He had retrospectives in 1978 in San Diego and La Jolla, in 1993 in La Jolla (*Manny Farber: Works on Paper from the Seventies*), in 2003 in La Jolla (*Two for the Road: Sketchbooks of Patricia Patterson and Manny Farber*) and solo exhibitions in New York, Los Angeles and Pitsburg.

BIBLIOGRAPHY:
Goldin, Amy/Armstrong, Richard, *Manny Farber*, exhibition catalogue, La Jolla Museum of Contemporary Art, La Jolla (CA), 1978. Gorin, Jean-Pierre, et al., *'Manny Farber Critique et Peintre du Cinéma'* in *Cahiers du Cinéma*, periodical, Paris, April 1982. Crary, Jonathan, et al., *Manny Farber*, exhibition catalogue, Los Angeles Museum of Contemporary Art, Los Angeles, 1985. Smith, Elizabeth, *'Manny Farber: An Interview'* in *The Contemporary (The Museum of Contemporary Art Los Angeles)*, periodical, Los Angeles, Fall 1985. Parker, Kevin, *'Manny Farber and Landscape'* in *Artforum*, periodical, New York, February 1985. Yard, Sally, *Manny Farber: Paintings of the Eighties*, exhibition catalogue, Quinto Krichman Projects, La Jolla (CA), 1991. Matthieussent, Brice, *'Manny Farber, critique termite'* in *Art Press* n° 300, periodical, Paris, April 2004.

MUSEUMS AND GALLERIES:
BOSTON (MFA) - LOS ANGELES (County MA) - LOS ANGELES (MCA) - NEW YORK (Solomon R. Guggenheim Mus.): *The Red Can, the Push Pin, and the White Label* (1976, oil on paper) - NEW YORK (Whitney Mus. of American Art) - NEWPORT BEACH (Newport Harbor Art Mus.) - PITTSBURGH (Carnegie MA): *Endgame* (1992, oil/board) - SAN DIEGO (MCA) - SAN DIEGO (MCA Downtown) - WALTHAM (Rose AM, Brandeis University).

FARCAS, Johannes de, or Farius
Flemish, 17th century.
Painter.
Flemish School.

Johannes de Farcas became a member of the guild in Antwerp in 1622-1623.

FARCHINI
Italian, 19th century.
Painter.

Farchini worked in Germany with Cremonini.

FARCY, Alphonse
French, 19th century.
Born 1817, in Rouen.
Painter. Portraits.

Alphonse Farcy exhibited at the Paris Salon in 1845 and 1848. His best-known work is a portrait of Pope Pius IX.

FARCY, Andry
French, 20th century.
Born 18 May 1882, in Charleville; died 5 July 1950, in Grenoble.
Draughtsman, caricaturist, poster artist. Advertising art.

Andry Farcy was a student in Paris at the École des Arts Décoratifs and the École des Beaux-Arts. He was curator of the museum of Grenoble from 1919 to 1950 and through his contacts managed to get modern art into its collection. He was a talented draughtsman, very much attached to the Dauphiné, and he contributed many caricatures to the *Petit Dauphinois*. *Père Lustucru* was probably the most famous of his advertisement posters. He also designed posters for museum exhibitions of painting. In 1980 he was represented by a *Self-portrait* in the exhibition *150 ans de peinture dauphinoise* (*150 Years of Painting in the Dauphiné*), held at the Château de la Condamine, Corenc (Isère).

MUSEUMS AND GALLERIES:
GRENOBLE.

FARCY, Victor Marius
French, 19th - 20th century.
Born 30 May 1858, in Poilly-sur-Serein (Yonne); died 12 April 1942, in Boulogne-Billancourt.
Painter. Landscapes, still-lifes.

Victor Marius Farcy was a pupil of Fernand Sabatté and exhibited in Paris at the Salon des Artistes Français. He painted landscapes of his native region and of Brittany. His still-lifes depict local objects, and ancient or exotic statues.

FARDEL, Alice Andrée
French, 20th century.
Born 11 February 1890, in Mons.
Painter.

Alice Andrée Fardel exhibited in Paris at the Salon des Artistes Français from 1922.

FARDEL, Robert
French, 20th century.
Born in Besançon; died 14 March 1931, in Paris.
Painter. Landscapes.

Robert Fardel exhibited in Paris at the Société Nationale des Beaux-Arts and the Salon d'Hiver, of which he was a member.

FARDELLA, Giacomo
Italian, 17th century.
Painter. Still-lifes (fruit/vegetables).

AUCTION RECORDS:
ROME, 12 Oct 1978, *Still-life* (oil on canvas, 28 x 36¼in/71 x 92cm) ITL 4,400,000. MILAN, 20 May 1982, *Still-life with Fruit*

(oil on canvas, 19 3/4 x 26 1/2in/50 x 67cm) ITL 10,000,000. MILAN, 12 Dec 1988, *Still-life with Fruit, Salads, Mushrooms and Fish; Still-life with Melons, Pears, Apples, Almonds and Mushrooms* (oil on canvas, each 31 1/2 x 39 1/4in/80 x 100cm) ITL 100,000,000. MILAN, 4 April 1989, *Still-life with Various Summer Fruits, an Ear of Corn and a Cloth on a Marble Flagstone* (oil on canvas, 28 1/4 x 63 1/2in/72 x 161cm) ITL 46,000,000. ROME, 21 Nov 1989, *Still-life with Fruit, Mushrooms and a Marrow* (oil on canvas, 28 1/4 x 63 1/2in/72 x 161cm) ITL 56,000,000.

FARDELLA, Giuseppe or D. Joseph
Italian, 17th century.
Painter. Genre scenes.
Giuseppe Fardella was active around 1680 and was perhaps the same artist as Giacomo Farelli, who is known to have worked around the end of the 17th century.
MUSEUMS AND GALLERIES:
MULHOUSE: *Market Scene.*

FARDEN, Halvor. See **FAHNE**

FARÉ, Paul
French, 20th century.
Painter. Figures.
AUCTION RECORDS:
PARIS, 5 Nov 1923, *Young Pilferers,* FRF 155.

FARELLE, Lilian
British, 20th century.
Born 17 January 1918, in London.
Active also in France.
Painter, watercolourist.
Lilian Farelle trained at the Académies Libres in Paris. After a figurative period, she became attracted by abstraction which allowed her greater freedom and dynamism. Her approach was close to the post-war French abstraction associated with Bazaine. She exhibited in Paris at the Salon des Femmes Peintres et Sculpteurs and at the Société Nationale des Beaux-Arts. She also took part in the Trouville Biennale.
MUSEUMS AND GALLERIES:
TROUVILLE-SUR-MER: a watercolour.

FARELLI, Giacomo
Italian, 17th century.
Born 1624, in Rome; died 1701 or 1706, in Naples.
Painter. Religious subjects, portraits.
Giacomo Farelli painted initially in the style of Andrea Vaccaro, his first teacher, but was more successful imitating the style of Guido. His *Fall of the Angels* and *Ascension* are preserved in the church of S Maria Maggiore in Naples. Many further examples of his work are to be seen in other churches in Naples.
BIBLIOGRAPHY:
Spinosa, Nicolà, et al., *Les Mystères de Naples. Sublime et triviale: la peinture napolitaine,* collective exhibition catalogue, Musée Fesch, Ajaccio, 2003.
MUSEUMS AND GALLERIES:
NANTES (MBA): *Portrait of Artist* (oil on canvas) - NAPLES (Church of S Maria Maggiore): *The Fall of Angels; Ascension.*
AUCTION RECORDS:
PARIS, 24 June 1929, *Moses Causing Manna to Fall from Heaven* (pen) FRF 180. ROME, 13 April 1989, *St John the Baptist Beheaded* (oil on canvas, 17 3/4 x 25 1/2in/45 x 65cm) ITL 3,000,000. MONACO, 2 Dec 1989, *St Sebastian Stretched Out* (oil on canvas, 35 x 46 3/4in/89 x 119cm) FRF 66,600. LONDON, 9 Dec 1994, *Samson and Delilah* (oil on canvas, 36 x 44 3/4in/91.5 x 113.9cm) GBP 5,980. LONDON, 31 Oct 1997, *The Penitent Mary Magdalene* (oil on canvas, 48 x 67 1/4in/121.7 x 171cm) GBP 5,520. ROME, 5 June 2000, *David with the Head of Goliath* (oil on canvas, 54 x 39 ins / 136 x 99 cm) ITL 17,000,000.

FARENHOLZ. See **FAHRENHOLZ**

FARENSCHON, Franz von.
See **FAHRENSCHON**

FARÈSE, Esposito. See **ESPOSITO-FARÈSE Aimé**

FARESLITZ, Aegidius
German, 18th century.
Sculptor.
Fareslitz was court painter in Munich.

FAREY, Hélène, or Farey-Nivelt
French, 20th century.
Born 21 January 1909, in Algiers.
Painter (gouache). Local figures, portraits, interiors with figures, still-lifes, landscapes, seascapes.
Hélène Farey started painting in 1930 and went to Paris in 1937. In 1941 she married the painter Roger Nivelt and in 1949 they bought a house in St-Vinnemer (Yonne), and, apart from their many travels, they worked in this region.

From 1938 she took part in the annual Paris salons: Salon de la Société Nationale des Beaux-Arts, Salon des Artistes Français, Salon d'Automne, Salon Comparaisons, Salon des Femmes Peintres. She won many distinctions and prizes (at the Académie des Beaux-Arts in 1948, 1969, and 1973, and the Foundation Taylor), the Charles Cottet prize in 1968, and travel scholarships: 1946 for Tunisia, 1952 Morocco, and 1956 Egypt.

From 1948 she exhibited her paintings in solo shows in Paris (1953, 1955, 1959, Galerie de l'Institut), North Africa, Copenhagen (1959, Marya Gallery) and New York (1959 Paris Art Gallery). In 1994 the town of Tonnerre organised a retrospective of her works from 1930 to 1993, and her paintings have been bought by the State and the Municipality of Paris.

Primarily a landscape artist, her travels provided subjects and new atmospheres for her painting; in France, Drôme or Brittany; outside France, Spain, Italy and Venice, Greece; in the Middle East, Tunisia, Morocco, Egypt. However, especially in Tunisia, she took a great interest in the life of the people and local figures. Léon-Paul Fargue praised her view of the south of Tunisia. She had mastery of a compact draughtsmanship that caught the essentials and a confident technique, and used a range of bright colours that she knew how to adapt to her subjects.
MUSEUMS AND GALLERIES:
ARRAS: *The Port of Volendam, Holland* (1957) - NOYERS-SUR-SEREIN: collection of paintings of Spain, Tunisia, portraits and self-portraits - PARIS (Municipal Collection) - TONNERRE (Mus. Marguerite-de-Bourgogne): *Storm in St-Vinnemer.*

FARFA, pseudonym of Tommasini Vittorio
Italian, 20th century.
Born 1881, in Trieste; died 1964, in San Remo.
Painter, collage artist, potter.
Futurism.
Farfa's early years were uneventful, until he met the Futurists on the evening of 12 January 1910 in Trieste. He forged a lasting bond with Marinetti in 1919, and this marked the beginning of his strictly Futurist period. He participated in the activities of the Turin group, led by Fillia, and then settled in Savona. In 1929 he exhibited his first Futurist ceramics, and from that point on he took part in all the key events of the group until 1934. He was forgotten until after World War II, when he was rediscovered by Enrico Baj and Asger Jorn.He also made a large number of collages, the most famous being his *Cartopittura*, a collage of coloured paper. In 2003 his works appeared in a collective exhibition held at the museum in Lodève, south-west France, entitled *De Chirico et la peinture italienne de l'entre-deux guerres* (*De Chirico and Italian Painting of the Interwar Period*).

Bibliography:

Bonito Oliva, Achille/Iovane, Giovanni/Lista, Giovanni, et al., *De Chirico et la peinture italienne de l'entre-deux guerres*, exhibition catalogue, Musée de Lodève, 2003.

Auction records:

Rome, 20 April 1982, *Portrait of Carra* (charcoal, 11 x 7 3/4 ins / 28 x 20 cm) ITL 500,000. Rome, 25 Nov 1986, *Man in a Grey Hat* (c. 1935, pencil, 11 1/2 x 9 ins / 29.5 x 22 cm) ITL 2,000,000. Rome, 24 Nov 1987, *Self-portrait* (11 x 9 ins / 28 x 22 cm) ITL 2,000,000. Milan, 14 Dec 1988, *Massacre of the Hearts* (mixed media/newsprint, 17 3/4 x 23 ins / 45 x 58.5 cm) ITL 2,200,000. Milan, 27 March 1990, *Domino 3* (1933, tempera and collage/card, 24 3/4 x 30 3/4 ins / 63 x 78 cm) ITL 5,700,000. Milan, 12 June 1990, *Family Joy or the Happy Couple at the Masquerade* (1953, collage/card, 10 3/4 x 12 1/4 ins / 27.5 x 31 cm) ITL 3,600,000. Milan, 20 May 1996, *Girotondo, nell'Asilo* (collage and tempera/paper, 11 1/2 x 9 1/2 ins / 29 x 24 cm) ITL 9,200,000.

FARFALLA, Gioseffo
Italian, 16th century.
Active in Rome.
Painter.

FARFAN, Juan
Spanish, 15th century.
Active in Seville in 1489.
Painter.

FARFANICO
Italian, 17th century.
Probably born in Milan.
Painter.

Farfanico worked alongside G. B. Crespi on frescoes for a chapel in Varallo.

FARFUSOLA, Bartolomeo
Italian, 17th century.
Born in Verona.
Active in 1640.
Painter. History painting.

The church of S Ursula in Verona boasts a Farfusola painting, as do other churches in that city.

FARFUSOLA, Giulio
Italian, 16th century.
Born c. 1565.
Active in Verona.
Painter.

FARGAUDIE, Yvonne Camille Marie
French, 20th century.
Born in Paris.
Watercolourist.

Yvonne Camille Marie Fargaudie was a member of the Union des Femmes Peintres et Sculpteurs.

FARGE, Henri
French, 20th century.
Born January 1884, in Paris.
Painter, engraver, illustrator. Scenes with figures, genre scenes.

Henri Farge studied for five years in Venice and Rome. He exhibited in Paris at the Salon de la Société Nationale des Beaux-Arts and the Salon des Artistes Français, where he won a silver medal in 1966. He illustrated books by Claude Farrère, including *L'Homme qui assassina* (*The Man who Killed*), Devambez, 1926, and Pierre Loti.

His painting, proof of lively powers of observation, depicts picturesque scenes that are a testimony to the times and places that inspired them: Deauville in 1925, Paris in 1930 and the Holy Year in Rome in 1950. He also painted music halls, art galleries, views of Paris and Venice, and, generally speaking, crowds.

Auction records:

Paris, 12 March 1969, *Public Meeting*, FRF 4,000. Paris, 18 June 1984, *Break-in* (oil on panel, 20 3/4 x 25 1/4 ins / 53 x 64 cm) FRF 5,000.

FARGE, Pierre
French, 20th century.
Born in the Corrèze region.
Painter, watercolourist. Urban landscapes.

Pierre Farge exhibited in Paris at the Salon des Artistes Indépendants and then at the Salon des Tuileries in 1930. Although he specialised in local and touristic Paris landscapes, he also painted views of Venice, Bruges and, more rarely, his native Corrèze.

Auction records:

Paris, 16 Jan 1928, *Church of St-Séverin*, FRF 125. Paris, 4 May 1928, *The Place du Tertre*, FRF 410. Paris, 24 Feb 1936, *Fishing Boats in the Port of Venice* (watercolour) FRF 45. Paris, 14 May 1943, *Church of St-Nicolas-des-Champs, Paris* (1929) FRF 1,350. Paris, 2 Dec 1946, *The Place de la Concorde*, FRF 2,000. Paris, 23 April 1947, *The Place du Tertre*, FRF 10,500. Versailles, 17 Nov 1985, *Rue St-Vincent, Montmartre* (oil on canvas, 28 3/4 x 36 1/4 ins / 73 x 92 cm) FRF 4,200. Paris, 22 March 1988, *Church of St-Nicolas-des-Champs, Paris* (1929, oil on canvas, 28 3/4 x 39 1/4 ins / 73 x 100 cm) FRF 4,500. Versailles, 25 Sept 1988, *Village in the Corrèze* (oil on canvas, 32 x 25 1/2 ins / 81 x 65 cm) FRF 5,000. Paris, 11 July 1989, *The Palais de Justice* (oil on canvas, 41 3/4 x 39 1/4 ins / 106 x 100 cm) FRF 7,500. Versailles, 21 Oct 1990, *The Place du Tertre, Paris* (oil on card, 20 x 24 1/2 ins / 51 x 62 cm) FRF 7,100. Amsterdam, 30 Nov 2000, *Silk Mills* (1939, oil on canvas, 32 x 39 ins / 81 x 100 cm) NLG 12,000.

FARGE, Yves
French, 20th century.
Born 18 August 1899, in Salon; died 1953, in Moscow.
Painter.

Yves Farge was a well-known politician who was at one time a pupil at the École des Beaux-Arts, Marseilles. He travelled in North Africa.

Museums and Galleries:

Rabat (Résidence de France).

FARGEAU. See also **NORBLIN Eugène**

FARGEAU, Raymond
French, 18th century.
Active in Paris in 1748.
Sculptor.

FARGELL, F.
18th century.
Engraver (etching).

There is a reference to a signed plate by him, dated 1766, representing *Three Soldiers Carrying a Corpse to the Pyre.*

FARGEOT, Ferdinand
French, 20th century.
Born 17 September 1880, in Lyons; died 1957.
Painter, pastellist, illustrator. Genre scenes, landscapes.

Ferdinand Fargeot was a pupil at the École des Arts Décoratifs, Paris, and exhibited at the Salon des Artistes Français, where he was declared hors concours. He also showed at the Salon d'Automne and many group exhibitions abroad. He illustrated the novels of Paul de Kock and painted a decorative panel for the liner *Île-de-France*. He served in World War I and was made a Chevalier of the Légion d'Honneur.

Auction records:

Paris, 20 Jan 1988, *Little Girl in an Armchair* (pastel, 10 x 9 1/2 ins / 25.5 x 24 cm) FRF 5,200. Paris, 14 March 1994, *Reading* (pastel, 14 1/2 x 10 1/4 ins / 37 x 26 cm) FRF 4,200. Paris, 21 March 1994, *Crinoline and Top Hat* (1920, oil on canvas, 23 1/2 x 23 1/2 ins / 60 x 60 cm) FRF 6,000. Paris, 21 June 2000, *Cafe Concert* (oil on canvas, 24 x 28 ins / 60 x 72 cm) FRF 70,000.

FARGIS, Alexandre
French, 19th century.
Born 19th century, in Périgueux.
Painter, draughtsman. Architectural views.
Alexandre Fargis was drawing master at the college of Périgueux.
MUSEUMS AND GALLERIES:
PÉRIGUEUX: *Roman Ruins.*

FARGUE. See also **LA FARGUE**

FARGUE, Claire
Russian, 20th century.
Born in Russia.
Active in France.
Painter.
Claire Fargue exhibited in Paris, at the Salon d'Automne in 1921 to begin with, then at the Salon des Tuileries.

FARGUE, Léon-Paul
French, 20th century.
Born 4 March 1878, in Paris; died 1947, in Paris.
Painter.
Léon-Paul Fargue was the son of a potter. There is, however, some question about how serious a painter he was before he turned to poetry and wrote *Tancrède* (*Tancred*) and *Pour la Musique* (*For Music*). He said himself that he 'won quite a few prizes for drawing at school', and we know of some very sensitive paintings from his youth. He also said that he 'had never been held up by any material difficulty' and 'believed in himself' until he visited the Salon des Artistes Indépendants, where 'in that year Cézanne, Van Gogh, Gaugin, Lautrec and Seurat were exhibiting'; then he 'gave it all up'. Nevertheless, he did paint and draw afterwards 'with a desolate feeling it was too late'. His wife painted under the pseudonym Chérianne. For Paul Fort's *Paris sentimental ou le Roman de nos vingt ans* (*Sentimental Paris or the Novel of Our Twenties*) Fargue drew a cover wash drawing (vignette pasted on green canvas) that depicted the Seine and Notre-Dame. Because of the identical initials *P.F.* this has been wrongly attributed to Paul Fort.

FARHAT, Amar, for Ammar
Tunisian, 20th century.
Born 5 January 1911, in Bejar; died 21 March 1987, in Tunis.
Painter. Figures, local scenes, still-lifes.
Amar Farhat, who is considered to be one of Tunisia's most important painters, was self-taught, and almost certainly acquired his familiarity with Western art by imitating paintings that he came across. Perhaps owing something to the Cubist artist Georges Braque, the faces of his figures reveal hints of what might be called 'full-on profiles' (a contour of the profile being incorporated into a depiction of the face seen from the front). He first exhibited at the Tunisian Salon in 1937 and continued to do so until 1979. He also took part in group exhibitions of the Tunis School. His first individual exhibition was in Tunis in 1940. In 1949 he was chosen for the young painting prize in Paris, and in 1956-57 he travelled to Sweden. In 1981 his work appeared at the Salon of La Marsa. In 1982 and 1983 he had three new solo exhibitions in Tunis, one of which was staged in the Roman amphitheatre at Carthage.

Farhat's draughtsmanship is very straightforward; he draws principally by simply outlining the forms. He knows how to temper colour and has a preference for the colours of the sun and heat - yellow, orange, ochre and brown. The economy of his style is akin to the rustic simplicity of a Mathieu Verdilhan. His figures are skilfully fashioned into the poses of the action in progress. As a serious storyteller, he held ordinary people in great affection and his work reflects their essential dignity; he customarily portrays them with a gentle humour. At times he attains an epic vision, even entering the realms of the fantastic, but above all he depicts the activities of everyday life, such porters carrying water, bread, or jars. He has also tackled subjects such as a young woman bather wearing a bikini lying on a crowded beach in a sensuous pose. In his work, still-lifes are unusual.
BIBLIOGRAPHY:
Lumières tunisiennes, exhibition catalogue, Association française d'action artistique, Pavillon des arts, Paris, 1995.
MUSEUMS AND GALLERIES:
TUNIS (MAM): *Sidi Bou Saïd* (1946).
AUCTION RECORDS:
PARIS, 21 April 1996, *Preparing Fish* (1944, oil on canvas, 28 3/4 x 23 1/2 ins / 73 x 60 cm) FRF 102,000. PARIS, 9 Dec 1996, *Musicians* (oil on panel, 16 1/4 x 14 ins / 41.5 x 35.5 cm) FRF 83,000. PARIS, 10-11 June 1997, *Tunisian Bride* (1941, oil on canvas, 24 1/2 x 20 3/4 ins / 62 x 53 cm) FRF 70,000. PARIS, 17 Nov 1997, *Naiads* (1948, oil on canvas, 26 3/4 x 19 1/4 ins / 68 x 49 cm) FRF 40,000. PARIS, 12 March 1999, *Evening in Ramadan* (1954, oil on canvas, 29x24 ins / 73x60 cm) FRF 138,000. PARIS, 29 Nov 1999, *Tourbet el Bey, Tunis* (1944, oil on cardboard, 15 x 18 ins / 37x46 cm) FRF 60,000. PARIS, 16 June 2003, *In the Cafe, Tunis. Still-life with Jug* (1966, oil on canvas, double-sided, 20 x 24 ins / 50x62 cm) EUR 7,700. PARIS, 15 Dec 2003, *Young Women Taking Tea* (1951, oil on canvas, 18x13 ins / 46x32 cm) EUR 6,000.

FARHAT, Sedigheh
Iranian, 20th - 21st century.
Born 1946, in Lahijan.
Painter.
Sedigheh Farhat obtained a diploma from the school of fine art in Teheran in 1971 and went on to teach design at a high school in the city. She travelled to Paris in 1974 and enrolled at the Sorbonne, obtaining a masters degree in aesthetics in 1976. Thereafter, she followed courses at the advanced school of fine arts in Paris and in 1979 returned to Teheran and took up a teaching post at the school of fine arts.

FARHI, Jean-Claude
French, 20th century.
Born 1940, in Paris.
Painter, sculptor.
Op Art.
After travelling in Latin America, Spain, Algeria and Scandinavia, Jean-Claude Farhi settled in Nice in 1958 and attended the École des Arts Décoratifs. In 1964 he won the Prix de la Jeune Peinture Méditerranéenne with paintings on the subject of machinery. In Paris he was represented in the Biennale des Jeunes Artistes and also exhibited at the Salon des Grands et Jeunes d'Aujourd'hui in 1966, Salon Comparaisons 1967, the group exhibition *L'Âge du Jazz* (*The Jazz Age*) at the Musée Galliéra 1968, Salon de Jeune Sculpture 1968, Salon de Mai 1969, etc.

In 1968 he gave up painting for sculpture, making use of coloured plastic materials fixed together and into which he introduced assemblages of chrome mechanical elements. Still in a somewhat Baroque style, he exhibited in Paris in 1968 under the generic title *Chromplexes*, sculptures referring to the history of technology and machinery. Shortly after, Farhi began progressively to reduce the external volume of the sculptures to basic geometric forms such as parallelograms, cones, truncated cones and cylinders, made in methylacrylate and making visible internal strata of varied colour, transparent effects and points of intersection. Usually made in factories to detailed plans that Farhi supplied, these works are of a high technical quality. These simple shapes are, in fact, internal sculptures - what is to be viewed is inside. After 1970 Farhi began to work again in two dimensions with a series of 'anthropometries' that he made into a silkscreen album.

Auction records:
Paris, 23 April 1980, *Rays of Colour* (1969, block of Plexiglas) FRF 2,000. Paris, 6 June 1985, *Stretches of Light* (1969, cube in Plexiglas, 11 1/2 x 14 1/4 ins / 29.5 x 36.5 cm) FRF 8,500. Paris, 12 Feb 1989, *Multicoloured Column* (1979, sculpture in Plexiglas, h. 24 3/4 ins / 63 cm) FRF 4,000. Paris, 21 Sept 1989, *Column* (1981, sculpture) FRF 6,500. Paris, 14 Dec 1997, *Column* (1974, polymethacrylate, 38 1/4 x 9 x 7 3/4 ins / 97 x 22 x 20 cm) FRF 9,500.

FARIA
Portuguese, 18th century.
Sculptor.
Faria was an imitator of Antonio Ferreira and, like Ferreira, worked in terracotta.

FARIA, Cavalheiro
Portuguese, 18th century.
Engraver.
Cavalheiro Faria executed an engraving of *St Anthony Preaching to the Fish*, after Raczynski. He is also believed to have produced pen and ink drawings.

FARIA, Estrela
Portuguese, 20th century.
Born 9 October 1910, in Évora (northern Portugal).
Painter, illustrator, decorative designer.
After first studying art in Portugal, Estrela Faria attended the Paris fine arts school in 1939. In 1948 he was awarded a bursary by the Portuguese government to continue his studies in Paris.
Faria has taken part in many exhibitions both in France and Portugal and received a number of awards including a gold medal at the international exhibition of 1937 and various prizes for displays.
He has executed illustrations for Portuguese and Brazilian magazines and also produced sets for the Portuguese ballet *Verde Gaie*.
Museums and Galleries:
Lisbon (MM) - Lisbon (Mus. do Chiado).

FARIA, Isodoro de
Spanish, 16th century.
Born 16th century, in Francosa.
Painter.
Isidoro de Faria is known for a *St Peter* surrounded by fine embellishments in the church of S Pedro de Francosa.

FARIA, Luisa de
Portuguese, 17th century.
Active at the end of the 17th century.
Painter.
Luisa de Faria was the daughter of the writer Emmanuel de Faria y Sousa. She painted a portrait of her father, which was engraved in 1733 for the book *Portrait of Manoel de Faria y Sousa*.

FARIA, Severino de
Portuguese, 18th - 19th century.
Engraver.
According to Nagler, Severino de Faria engraved a portrait of Camoëns.

FARIA, Silvestre de
Portuguese, 18th century.
Died c. 1800.
Sculptor.
Silvestre de Faria is probably the same individual as the sculptor Silvestre de Faria Lobo who, in 1758 with Manoel Alves, produced the marble group *Winged Heralds on Winged Horses* in the gardens of the Queluz Castle. He also made sculptures in wood.

FARIGOULE, Antoine
French, 17th century.
Died c. 1678, in Le Puy-en-Velay (Haute-Loire).
Painter.

FARINA, Achille
Italian, 19th century.
Born 1804, in Faenza; died 1879, in Faenza.
Painter.
Farina started out as a history painter and portrait artist, and painted the decorations in the chapel of the Immaculate Conception in Faenza. He then turned to ceramics, and set up a company that employed some highly talented artists. Their works were exhibited in London, Paris and Vienna.

FARINA, Baldassare
Italian, 17th century.
Painter.
Baldassare Farina worked together with M. Coda on a *Congregation of the Cross* that hangs in the church of S Giovanni Maggiore in Naples.

FARINA, Fabbrizio
Italian, 17th century.
Sculptor.
Fabbrizio Farina sculpted in porphyry. He is best known for a bust of *Grand Duke Cosimo II*.

FARINA, Isidoro
Italian, 19th century.
Born 1857, in Naples; died 1898.
Painter. Genre scenes, seascapes.
Isidoro Farina worked in Milan. In 1885 he exhibited three seascapes at the Brera in Milan, then in 1886 showed *Sic Vos Non Vobis* and *Flirtation*. In 1887 he exhibited two paintings in Venice, *Mountain Dweller* and *Violin Players*.

Auction records:
Milan, 29 May 1986, *The Little Beggar and the Violinist* (oil on canvas, 31 1/2 x 15 3/4 ins / 80 x 40 cm) ITL 9,000,000. New York, 25 Oct 1989, *The Red Umbrella* (oil on canvas, 36 3/4 x 24 1/2 ins / 93.4 x 62.5 cm) USD 17,600.

FARINA, Pasquale
Italian, 19th century.
Born 2 November 1864, in Naples.
Also active in Argentina.
Painter.
Pasquale Farina studied at the Accademia di Belle Arti in Naples. He managed a ceramics factory and taught a sculpture class near Naples. He later emigrated to Argentina, where he taught drawing and perspective. He belonged to a number of artistic associations in the USA.
Museums and Galleries:
Buenos Aires (National Mus.): several works.

FARINA, Pietro Francesco
Italian, 17th century.
Active at the end of the 17th century.
Painter, designer of ornamental architectural features.
Pietro Francesco Farina studied under the Roli brothers. He decorated the palace of Karlsruhe, in Germany, and several churches in Bologna.

FARINA, Ubaldo (Fra)
Italian, 18th century.
Monk, sculptor.
Ubaldo Farina is credited with two terracotta *Busts of the Apostles* sculpted in 1716 for the choir of the church of S Giovanni in Monte, Bologna.

FARINATI, Giambattista, called Battista da Verona (after Vasari), and erroneously known as Battista Zelotti and Battista Fontana
Italian, 16th century.
Born 1526, in Verona; died 1578, in Mantua.
Fresco artist.

According to some sources Giambattista Farinati was the pupil of Paolo Farinati, to others the pupil of Antonio Badile. He was the journeyman and friend of Paul Veronese, with whom he collaborated on a number of important works in the public buildings of Venice and Villa Soranzi at Castelfranco. Vasari places him among the disciples of Titian.

It was primarily as a frescoist that Farinati made a name for himself. Some of his works are in the cathedral at Vicenza: *The Conversion of Saint Paul* and *The Miraculous Draught of Fishes* and in Venice, the ceiling fresco of the Sala del Consiglio dei Dieci at the Doge's Palace.

BIBLIOGRAPHY:
Brugnolo Meloncelli, Katia/Puppi, Lionello (preface), *Battista Zelotti*, Berenice, Milan, 1992.

MUSEUMS AND GALLERIES:
BERGAMO (Gal. Lochis): *The Holy Family* - BERLIN (Bodemus.): *The Holy Family* - DRESDEN: *Venus and Adonis* - FLORENCE: *Mass* - GRAZ: *The Annunciation* - ROME (Mus. e Gal. Borghese): *Christ on the Cross* - ROME (Palazzo Doria Pamphili): *Descent from the Cross* - STUTTGART: *Allegory of Prosperity and Poverty* - VENICE (Gal. dell'Accademia): *Pietà* - VERONA (Mus. Civico): *Portrait of Unknown Man* - VIENNA (Kunsthistorisches Mus.): *Pietà*; *Portrait of Woman and Child*.

AUCTION RECORDS:
LONDON, 4 July 1924, *Marc Antonio Barbaro*, GBP 25. LONDON, 11 Dec 1979, *Study of Seated Woman* (black chalk, pen and wash heightened with white, 9 1/4 x 5 1/2 ins / 23.5 x 13.7 cm) GBP 1,100. PARIS, 1 Dec 1997, *Rhetoric and Dialectics* (removed fresco/canvas, 72 3/4 x 93 3/4 ins / 185 x 238 cm) FRF 350,000. LONDON, 28 Oct 1998, *Cloelia Escaping across the Tiber* (oil on canvas, feigned oval, 17 x 13 ins / 42 x 33 cm) GBP 3,600.

FARINATI, Giovanni Battista I, or Farinato
Italian, 16th century.
Born c. 1493.
Active in Verona in 1529.
Painter.

FARINATI, Giovanni Battista II, or Farinato
Italian, 16th century.
Born 1570; died after 1605.
Active in Verona.
Painter.

Giovanni Battista Farinati II was the son and possibly the pupil of Paolo Farinati.

FARINATI, Orazio, or Farinato
Italian, 16th - 17th century.
Born 1559; died after 1616.
Active in Verona.
Painter, engraver. History painting.

Orazio Farinati was the son and disciple of Paolo Farinati. Some of his works can be seen in Verona: in the church of S Paolo, *The Descent from the Cross* (copy of a work by his father); in the church of S Maria del Paradiso, *St James*, 1607 and in the church of S Stefano: *The Descent of the Holy Spirit*, his masterpiece. He engraved a few plates in the style of the drawings of his father with whom he is sometimes confused, due to the similarity of their signatures.

MUSEUMS AND GALLERIES:
VERONA: *St Bartholomew Heals a Man Possessed*.

FARINATI, Paolo, or Farinato
Italian, 16th century.
Born 1524, in Verona; died 1606.
Painter, draughtsman, engraver, architect. Religious subjects, allegorical subjects, mythological subjects, figures, portraits.

Paolo Farinati was a descendant of the Florentine Farinata degli Uberti, or Urbiti, who participated in the struggle between the Guelfs and Ghibellines. The son of Giovanni Battista I, his first master, he was also taught by Niccolo Giolfino and Antonio Badile, studying in addition the works of Parmigiano, Titian, Giorgione and Giulio Romano. He was still working at the age of 79.

Farinati's drawings are held in high esteem and, according to Mariette, an enthusiastic collectioner of drawings, he was a gifted draughtsman whose compositions show the influence of Paolo Veronese, though he fails to match Veronese's expressiveness of light and refinement. In the corner of some of his paintings a snail, his emblematic figure, can be deciphered. His works are scattered in Italy and abroad.

Farinati executed his most interesting and original works in the earlier part of his career. A number of engravings in a bold style survive, and he engraved *St John* (1567); *The Magdalene Reading with Book and Crucifix*; *Angels with Instruments of the Passion* and *Venus and Cupid* from his own drawings.

BIBLIOGRAPHY:
Dal Forno, F., *Paolo Farinati, 1524-1606*, Verona, 1965. Rearick, W.R., *Maestri veneti del Cinquecento*, Alinari, Florence, 1980. DeGrazia Bohlin, D., '*Paolo Farinati in the Palazzo Giuliari: Frescoes and Preparatory Drawings*' in *Master Drawings*, vol 20, 1982.

MUSEUMS AND GALLERIES:
BERGAMO (Accademia Carrara, Pinacoteca d'Arte Antica): *Adoration of the Shepherds* - BERLIN: *Presentation in the Temple* - BOURGES: *Moses Receiving the Tables of the Law* - DRESDEN: *Presentation in the Temple* - GRENOBLE: *Descent from the Cross* - MONTAUBAN: *St John* - MOSCOW (Rumiantsev Mus.): *St John* - PRAGUE (Rudolfinum Gal.): *Penitent Magdalene* - ROUEN: *Adoration of the Magi* - ST PETERSBURG: *Adoration of the Magi* - THE HAGUE (Mauritshuis): *Adoration of the Shepherds* - VERONA: *Tomb of Christ Watched over by two Angels*; *Christ Shown to the People*; two works; *St Batholomew, St Jerome and St Anne*; *Holy Trinity*; *Virgin with Saints and Donors*; *Marriage of St Catherine*; *Adoration of the Magi* - VIENNA: *St Sebastian*; *St John the Baptist*; *Adam and Eve after their Expulsion from Paradise*; *Lucretia's Suicide*; *Hercules and Dejanire*; *Venus and Adonis*; *Mystic Marriage of St Catherine*; *Resurrection of Christ*; *Sacrament of David*; *Body of Christ*.

AUCTION RECORDS:
PARIS, 22 Dec 1923, *St Mary Magdalen* (pen and sepia) FRF 370. LONDON, 28 Nov 1945, *Mounted Man* (drawing) GBP 44. LONDON, 16 Oct 1946, *Martyrdom of Saint* (drawing) GBP 50. LONDON, 15 April 1980, *The Adoration of the Shepherds* (1589, pen and wash heightened with white/grey paper, 16 1/2 x 13 1/2 ins / 41.8 x 34.3 cm) GBP 1,200. LONDON, 25 March 1982, *Standing Warrior (Mars?)* (ink and wash heightened, 11 1/2 x 5 1/4 ins / 29.3 x 13.4 cm) GBP 1,250. NEW YORK, 16 Jan 1985, *Athena and sketch of a Niche* (blue wash heightened with white and pen, 8 1/4 x 7 3/4 ins / 21.1 x 20 cm) USD 2,500. MILAN, 21 April 1986, *St Jerome* (oil on canvas, 38 1/4 x 27 1/4 ins / 97 x 69 cm) ITL 3,500,000. MONTE CARLO, 20 June 1987, *Triumph of Galatea* (pen, brown ink and wash heightened with white/ochre washed paper, 16 1/4 x 11 1/4 ins / 41.5 x 28.7 cm) FRF 170,000. MILAN, 27 March 1990, *Christ Supported by St John the Baptist and St Francis on his Descent from the Cross* (oil/touchstone, 22 3/4 x 11 1/2 ins / 58 x 29 cm)

ITL 12,000,000. NEW YORK, 8 Jan 1991, *The Dead Christ Supported by Putti* (ink and wash heightened with white, 16 3/4 x 14 ins / 42.5 x 35.5 cm) USD 72,600. NEW YORK, 11 Jan 1991, *The Forge of Vulcan* (oil/copper, 13 x 17 1/4 ins / 33 x 44.1 cm) USD 121,000. LONDON, 23 April 1993, *Portrait of the Artist* (oil on panel, 8 x 5 3/4 ins / 20.3 x 14.6 cm) GBP 9,200. NEW YORK, 10 Jan 1995, *The Judgement of Paris* (ink and wash heightened with white, 16 x 11 ins / 40.7 x 27.9 cm) USD 7,762. LONDON, 3 July 1996, *Allegory of Love* (ink and wash/blue paper, 6 1/4 x 10 1/4 ins / 16 x 26 cm) GBP 6,325. MILAN, 9 June 1999, *Group of Warriors Before Burning Castle* (ink heightened with white, 11 x 17 ins / 29 x 43 cm) ITL 32,000,000. LONDON, 8 July 1999, *Entombment* (oil on panel, 20 x 15 ins / 50 x 38 cm) GBP 48,000. NEW YORK, 28 Jan 2000, *Bust of Woman Flanked by Male and Female Satyrs* (black chalk, pen, brown ink, brown wash heightened with white, 6 x 9 ins / 15 x 23 cm) USD 7,000. NEW YORK, 3 Feb 2000, *Study for a Spandrel with a Nymph and Satyr* (black and white chalk, 11 x 17 ins / 29 x 42 cm) USD 1,600. MUNICH, 17 May 2001, *Penitent Mary Magdalene* (etching, 8 x 6 ins / 20 x 15 cm) DEM 7,000. NEW YORK, 22 Jan 2003, *St Barbara with St Anthony* (chalk, pen and ink wash heightened with white, 17 x 10 ins / 43 x 25 cm) USD 16,000. NEW YORK, 23 Jan 2003, *Lamentation over the Dead Christ* (oil on slate, 12 x 9 ins / 30 x 24 cm) USD 13,000.

FARINATI, Vittoria, or Farinato
Italian, 16th century.
Born 1565.
Active in Verona.
Painter, copyist.

Vittoria Farinati was the daughter of Paolo Farinati and possibly his pupil. She worked mainly as a copyist.

FARINELLO, S. di
17th century.
Painter.

This artist is known for only three paintings: *Jupiter and Semele, Bacchante Dancing* and *Bacchante Resting*, which appeared in an auction in Berlin in 1913. He may be the painter Foi di Farinello, some of whose mythological paintings were mentioned in the collections of the castles of Sagan and Hohenzollern-Hechingen.

FARINGTON, George
British, 18th century.
Born 1752, in Warrington; died 1788, in Moorshedabad (Bengal).
Painter. History painting, portraits.

George Farington was the son of the rector in Warrington. He worked with West and was awarded a gold medal at the Royal Academy for his painting of *Macbeth*. He then went to the West Indies, where he died prematurely.

AUCTION RECORDS:
LONDON, 18 Nov 1987, *Portrait of Richard Atherton Farington, Brother of the Artist* (oil on canvas, 28 3/4 x 24 1/4 ins / 73 x 61.5 cm) GBP 4,500.

FARINGTON, Joseph
British, 18th - 19th century.
Born 1747, in Leigh (Lancashire); died 30 December 1821, near Manchester.
Painter, watercolourist, draughtsman. Landscapes with figures, landscapes.

Joseph Farington was the elder brother of George Farington and trained under Richard Wilson. He was elected a member of the Royal Academy in 1785; he exhibited there from 1778 to 1813 and exerted considerable influence. In 1794 he published 76 views of the Thames. His works have been engraved by Byrne, Pouncey, Medland and others.

MUSEUMS AND GALLERIES:
LONDON (British Mus.): *Landscape with Riders; Town Hall in King's Lynn* - LONDON (Victoria and Albert Mus.): *Lake and Mountains; Old Manor House; Landscape; Peasants Chopping Wood; Lady Oak, Shropshire.*

AUCTION RECORDS:
LONDON, 30 Nov 1923, *View in the Highlands* (drawing) GBP 8; *Welsh Landscape* (drawing) GBP 11. PARIS, 6 Dec 1924, *View of London Bridge; View of Westminster Bridge* (two pendants) FRF 3,800. LONDON, 7 Dec 1925, *View of St Paul's from Blackfriars Bridge* (drawing) GBP 15. LONDON, 5 March 1926, *London and the Thames* (drawing) GBP 4. LONDON, 15 April 1929, *View of Oxford,* GBP 29. LONDON, 16 March 1934, *At Bewdley* (drawing) GBP 7. LONDON, 20 July 1934, *Carnavon Castle,* GBP 18. LONDON, 10 June 1936, *Upper Section of Loch Gair* (watercolour) GBP 5. LONDON, 11 July 1938, *London* (drawing) GBP 10. LONDON, 10 May 1939, *View of Cumberland,* GBP 8. LONDON, 25 May 1939, *Bridgnorth,* GBP 50. LONDON, 24 June 1960, *View of Flooding in Valenciennes* (watercolour) GBP 231. LONDON, 24 Nov 1972, *Carnavon Castle,* Gns 800. LONDON, 31 March 1976, *View of Lancaster* (oil on canvas, 18 1/2 x 24 3/4 ins / 47 x 63 cm) GBP 260. LONDON, 25 Sept 1980, *Basildon Church and Friary Mount* (1792, pencil and wash/paper, 8 1/4 x 12 ins / 21 x 30.5 cm) GBP 450. LONDON, 21 Nov 1984, *View of Blenheim Palace from across the Lake* (1792, pen and wash/pencil outlines, 12 1/4 x 18 3/4 ins / 31 x 47.5 cm) GBP 800. LONDON, 17 July 1987, *Roslyn Castle* (oil on canvas, 40 1/4 x 50 1/2 ins / 102.3 x 128.3 cm) GBP 6,000. LONDON, 28 Feb 1990, *Malvern Chapel* (oil on canvas, 15 1/4 x 19 3/4 ins / 39 x 50 cm) GBP 2,750. LONDON, 20 April 1990, *Extensive Rocky Italian Landscape with the Ruins of a Castle near a Waterfall and Figures in the Foreground* (oil on canvas, 38 x 48 ins / 96.5 x 122 cm) GBP 8,800. LONDON, 31 Oct 1990, *Landscape with Lincoln Castle and Lucy Tower from the West* (oil on canvas, 23 3/4 x 28 1/4 ins / 60.5 x 72 cm) GBP 5,940. LONDON, 14 July 1999, *Extensive View of Loch Lomond* (oil on canvas, 21 x 40 ins / 53 x 102 cm) GBP 9,500. LONDON, 19 March 2003, *Figures by a Cottage in a Wooded Landscape* (pen, ink and grey and brown wash over pencil, 22 x 18 ins / 56 x 45 cm) GBP 1,000. LONDON, 25 Nov 2003, *Gatehouse on the Bridge over the River Severn at Bridgnorth, Shropshire* (1791, oil on canvas, 27 x 44 ins / 69 x 113 cm) GBP 12,000. LONDON, 18 Nov 2004, *Views of Bruges, Belgium* (1793, pencil, pen, brown ink and grey wash, a pair, 13 x 15 ins / 32 x 39 cm) GBP 2,200. LONDON, 25 Nov 2004, *View of London Bridge* (oil on canvas, 35 x 27 ins / 90 x 69 cm) GBP 8,000.

FARINOS, Carmelo
Spanish, 19th century.
Born in the 19th century, in Valencia.
Sculptor.

Carmelo Farinos is known for his *Bust of a Slave, Gipsy Woman* and *The Surprise.*

FARINOS Y TORTOSA, Felipe
Spanish, 19th century.
Born 1826, in Valencia; died 1888, in Valencia.
Sculptor.

Felipe Farinos y Tortosa studied at the Real Academia de San Carlos in Valencia under the sculptor Antonio Marzo. He worked for Valencia Cathedral and for churches in Hellin and Orihuela in Murcia.

FARIS, Benjamin H.
American, 19th century.
Born 21 July 1862, in Cincinnati; died 1935.
Painter.

Benjamin H. Faris was a pupil at the Cincinnati Academy and a member of the Cincinnati Art Club.

FARIUS, Johannes de. See **FARCAS**

FARJAS, Jean-Claude
French, 20th century.

Born 31 May 1924, in Paris; died 21 February 2002, in Paris.
Painter. Landscapes with figures.

Jean-Claude Farjas studied ethnology and anthropology at the Science Faculty of the University of Paris. He volunteered to serve in the French Army in 1944. After the Liberation he began work as a journalist with *Arts-Spectackes, Paris-Match, Paris-Presse*, and then became a radio producer at the ORTF (French Radio and Television). In 1961 he became an information manager and Director of the Press Centre of the Government of Monaco. He had begun to paint in 1957, but only gave himself to it full-time when he decided to leave his former employments in the 1970s. In 1996 he was made a Chevalier of the Légion d'Honneur.

He took part in many group exhibitions, mainly in Paris, where he was a member of the Salon des Artistes Français, the Société Nationale des Beaux-Arts, the Salon d'Automne (of which he was a member of the Board of Directors and Secretary General from 1990), the Salon Comparaisons and the Salon de Dessin et de la Peinture à l'eau.

He also showed in solo exhibitions, the first in Paris in 1961, then subsequently at the Musée de la Marine de Seine, Caudebec-en-Caux, in Brussels, Amsterdam, Tokyo and elsewhere. The Salon d'Automne devoted an exhibition to him in 1990 and he was guest of honour at the Salon de Printemps in the Town Hall of the 5th arrondissement of Paris in 2002.

Farjas was a good technician who painted delicate, precise pictures at the crossroads of figurative, Surrealist and naive art. He painted mainly small-format landscapes. Initially fairly classical in style, his paintings move towards a very personal dreamscape: imaginary, highly-coloured landscapes, often interspersed with hills and cliffs that are scattered with familiar or exotic animals.

BIBLIOGRAPHY:

Jean Claude Farjas, Shoin Co., Kyoto, 1993.

FARJAT, Benoît

French, 17th century.
Born 1646, in Lyons; died at the beginning of the 18th century.
Active in Italy.
Engraver (burin). History painting, mythological subjects, religious subjects, portraits. Frontispieces.

Benoît Farjat was the pupil of Guill. Château, whom he followed to Italy. He set up there and married the daughter of the landscape painter G.-Fr. Grimaldi, called Le Bolognèse. He engraved religious or mythological subjects and portraits after the Carrache family, Albano, Pietro da Cortona and other Italian masters, and frontispieces for theses. His main works are *The Communion of St Jerome* (after D. Zampieri), *The Marriage of St Catherine* and *Portrait of Cardinal Cibo* (after C. Maratta, 1688).

FARJAT, Severino de

Portuguese, 19th century.
Active at the beginning of the 19th century.
Engraver (burin).

Le Blanc refers to a *Portrait of Camoëns* by Severino de Farjat.

FARJEON, Elliott Emmanuel

American, 19th - 20th century.
Born in New York.
Painter. Portraits.

Elliott Emmanuel Farjeon studied art in New York and then with Bouguereau and Bonnard in Paris. He was a member of the Pittsburgh Art Association.

FARJON, Eugène

French, 20th century.
Born in Ambert.
Sculptor.

Eugène Farjon exhibited at the Salon des Artistes Français.

FARJON, Jean François

French, 19th century.
Born 19th century, in Naples, to French parents.
Painter.

From 1864 to 1880 Jean François Farjon sent landscapes to the Paris Salon. His best-known works include *Impression of Setting Sun after Rain; Normandy Orchard; Sunken Lane in Les Trembleaux; Forest Interior; Return of the Shepherd;* and *Setting Sun in the Forest of Fontainebleau.*

FARKAS, Aladar

Hungarian, 20th century.
Born 1909.
Sculptor.

Aladar Farkas studied at a school of technical drawing, probably in Budapest. He worked in Paris from 1937 to 1939 and when he returned to Hungary in 1940, he was one of the leaders of the Socialist artists. He sculpted memorials and works devoted to the Korean and Vietnamese wars. A retrospective exhibition was held at the Ernst Museum in 1960. He was awarded the Munkácsy Prize.

BIBLIOGRAPHY:

Hongrie 68, Pannonia, Budapest, 1968.

FARKAS, André, known as André-François

Romanian, 20th century.
Born 9 November 1915, in Timisoara; died 11 April 2005, in Grisy-lès-Plâtres (Val-d'Oise), France.
Active in France from 1934.
Painter, sculptor of assemblages, draughtsman, illustrator, poster artist. Landscapes, figures. Comic cartoons, stage costumes and sets.

André Farkas studied at the school of art in Budapest. He arrived in France in 1934, and attended the École des Beaux-Arts in Paris before becoming Cassandre's student.

He became famous very quickly for his advertising posters (*Citroën, Esso, Le Printemps*), his magazine covers and comic cartoons (for the *The New Yorker* from 1963 onwards, *Punch, Télérama, Graphis, VST-Social Life and Treatment.* He also illustrated many works by Alfred Jarry (*Ubu Roi*), Queneau, Prévert (*Letters from the Baladar Islands*) and Boris Vian. In 1956 he published a children's book *The Crocodile.* He is also known for his stage costumes and sets: *Valentine and the Bike* for Roland Petit's ballets, Gene Kelly's *Pas de Deux, The Merry Wives of Windsor* at the Royal Shakespeare Theatre. Since the 1960s, he has also devoted himself more specifically to his painting, which often includes collage, and to his painted sculptures or assemblages full of gags.

Farkas appears to be defy classification, yet there is no difference between Farkas the painter and sculptor and Farkas the designer of advertising material, stage sets and illustrations. There is an undeniable poetry about his work, whatever it may be. His world André Farkas is a dreamy, sometimes blackly comical world, visited by farce and hoax, but also a world of tenderness, innocence and candour.

Farkas featured in collective exhibitions including the Salon de Mai (1968). From 1955 he held a number of solo exhibitions, including: Musée des Arts Décoratifs and Palais de Tokyo, Paris; Palais des Papes, Avignon; Stedelijk Museum, Amsterdam; Vilanova Museum, Warsaw; Museum of Fine Art, Brussels; *Fou de vous. Illustrations d'André François pour la revue VST* (*Crazy about you. Illustrations by André François for the magazine VST*) as part of the Graphic Arts Month, Échirolles (1999); Forney library, Paris (2003); Milieu du Monde gallery, St-Paul-de-Vence (2003). A gold medallist of the Arts Directors Clubs in New York and Philadelphia and the Warsaw Poster Biennale (1972), he won the national graphics arts prize in France in 1980.

In December 2002, a fire destroyed his workshop and all his work.

BIBLIOGRAPHY:

Roy, Claude, '*François André*' in *Graphis*, periodical, Zurich, 1958. Ragon, Michel, *Catalogue du Musée des Arts décoratifs*, Musée des Arts décoratifs, Paris, 1970. Goldine, Georges, *Catalogue du Musée Saint-Georges*, Crédit communal de Belgique, Brussels, 1977. Mathey, François, *Introduction à André François*, Herscher, Paris, 1989. Bazin, Pierre, *Catalogue du Musée de Dieppe*, Musée de Dieppe, Dieppe, 1989. Souchaud, Pierre, '*André François*' in *Artension* n° 10, periodical, Rouen, 1989. Pachès, Vincent/Vallon, Serge, *Fou de Vous. André François*, Éd. Alternatives, Paris, 1999. Lelieur, Anne-Claude/Bachollet, Raymond, *André François: affiches et graphismes*, exhibition catalogue, Bibliothèque Forney, Paris, 2003.

MUSEUMS AND GALLERIES:

BASEL (Mus. für Gegenwartskunst, Christoph Merian-Stiftung) - BRUSSELS (MAM) - CAEN (FRAC Basse-Normandie): *The Day the Marchioness went Mad* (1990) - HANOVER (Wilhelm-Busch Mus.) - NEW YORK (MoMA) - PARIS (FRAC Île-de-France): *The Aura of the Blue and Red Dinghy* (1978-1979); *Woman with Pears* (1981) - PARIS (MNAM-CCI) - PARIS (Mus. des Arts décoratifs) - TOKYO (MMA) - TOYAMA (Mus. of Posters).

AUCTION RECORDS:

PARIS, 2 June 1991, *Battleship* (assemblage, graphite, watercolour, shingle and hand written document, 11 x 9 ins / 27 x 22 cm) FRF 8,000.

FARKAS, Étienne or Istvan

Hungarian, 20th century.
Born 1887, in Budapest; died 1944.
Also active in France.
Painter, illustrator.

Étienne Farkas lived in Paris for a long time, exhibiting at the Salon des Tuileries. He was closely associated with literary circles and composed a series of gouaches to accompany text by the poet André Salmon.

Two periods can be distinguished in his work: in the first, from 1925 to 1932 when he spent time in Paris, he was influenced by Cubism; in the second he was influenced by Vaszary and he painted figure compositions with a profound feeling of tragedy. This talented artist was not able to achieve his full potential because he was killed by the Nazis during World War II.

BIBLIOGRAPHY:

Németh, Lajos, *Moderne ungarische Kunst*, Corvina Kiadó, Budapest, 1969.

AUCTION RECORDS:

LONDON, 3 July 1987, *On the Terrace, Pimeno* (1935, watercolour and pencil, 11½ x 10 ins / 29 x 25.5 cm) GBP 450. BUDAPEST, 12 Oct 2001, *Letter* (c. 1930, oil on canvas, 32 x 39 ins / 81 x 99 cm) HUF 26,000,000. BUDAPEST, 7 Dec 2001, *Lunch* (1929, tempera on panel, 39 x 53 ins / 100 x 134 cm) HUF 28,000,000. BUDAPEST, 11 Sept 2002, *At the Level Crossing* (1934, oil on card, 32 x 39 ins / 81 x 100 cm) HUF 26,000,000. BUDAPEST, 6 Dec 2002, *Woman by the Window* (tempera on card/canvas, 39 x 39 ins / 100 x 100 cm) HUF 7,500,000. BUDAPEST, 16 May 2003, *By a Garden Table* (1930, oil on canvas, 18 x 21 ins / 45 x 54 cm) HUF 7,000,000.

FARKAS, István

Hungarian, 18th century.
Engraver.

István Farkas engraved the frontispiece for the Debrecen edition of *Cicero's Letters* (1767).

FARKAS, Jozsef, or de Frakasfalva

Slovak, 19th - 20th century.
Painter, engraver, illustrator.

Jozsef Farkas worked initially in Pest, near Bratislava. He is known for a portrait of the writer *Janos Nagy-Vathy*, a portrait of *Mihaly Kenderessy*, *Genius*, an engraved frontispiece, and other illustrations for religious works.

AUCTION RECORDS:

PARIS, 30 Jan 1995, *Woman in a Flowery Hat* (1932, oil on canvas, 32 x 21¼ ins / 81 x 54 cm) FRF 25,000.

FARKASHAZY, Nicolas

Hungarian, 20th century.
Born in Budapest.
Painter.

Nicolas Farkashazy exhibited in Paris at the Salon des Indépendants in 1932.

FARKHONDEH, Reza

20th century.
Painter.

She took part in the FIAC (Foire Internationale d'Art Contemporain), Paris, in 1994. She has also shown her work in solo exhibitions in Paris, notably in 1995 at the Philippe Rizzo gallery. She applies herself to the painstaking reproduction of children's toys, such as clowns and lorries, in bright colours.

FARL, Hermann

German, 17th century.
Sculptor (wood).

Farl is mentioned in guild documents as having worked in Rheine (North Rhine-Westphalia) from 1656 to 1669.

FARLEIGH, John

British, 20th century.
Born 16 June 1900; died 1965.
Painter, engraver, watercolourist.

John Farleigh studied at the Central School of Arts and Crafts. He exhibited with the London Group and was an associate member of the Royal Society of Painters.

FARLET, Georges

French, 19th century.
Born 10 February 1860, in Paris.
Engraver (wood).

Georges Farlet became a member of the Société des Artistes Français in 1884 and received an honourable mention in 1886.

FARLEY, Richard Blossom

American, 20th century.
Born 24 October 1875, in Poultney (Vermont); died 1951.
Painter. Portraits.

Richard Blossom Farley, a pupil of Whistler, Chase and Cecilia Beaux, was awarded the Charles Toppen Prize in 1888 and a travel scholarship in 1889. He lived in Trenton, New Jersey.

AUCTION RECORDS:

NEW YORK, 22 Sept 1987, *Along the Shore* (1928, oil on canvas, 17¾ x 19½ ins / 45 x 49.5 cm) USD 3,000.

FARLINGER, James Schackleton

American, 20th century.
Born 8 July 1881, in Buffalo (New York State).
Painter.

FARLOW, Harry

American, 20th century.
Born 11 April 1882, in Chicago; died 1956 or 1957.
Painter. Portraits.

Harry Farlow was a pupil of Duvench, Benson and Tarbell, and a member of the Salmagundi Club.

AUCTION RECORDS:

BOLTON, 20 Nov 1984, *Portrait of a Lady* (oil on canvas, 60¼ x 28 ins / 153 x 71.2 cm) USD 2,200. NEW YORK, 23 May 2000, *The Blue Vase* (oil on canvas, 40 x 27 ins / 102 x 69 cm) USD

4,000. BOSTON, 22 March 2002, *Portrait of Lady in Yellow* (oil on canvas, 36 x 30 ins / 91 x 76 cm) USD 1,800.

FARMBERGER, Georg
Austrian, 19th century.
Painter (porcelain).
Farmberger was a flower painter at the Vienna porcelain factory around 1822.

FARMER, Alexandre (Mrs)
British, 19th century.
Painter. Genre scenes.
Alexandra Farmer worked in Porchester in Hampshire. She exhibited at the Royal Academy in London and elsewhere between 1855 and 1867.
MUSEUMS AND GALLERIES:
LONDON (Tate Collection): *Anxious Time; Everyone Knows Where the Shoe Pinches.*

FARMER, Brigitta Moran
American, 20th century.
Born in Lyons (New York).
Miniaturist.
Brigitte Moran Farmer, a pupil at Syracuse University and at the Académie de la Grande Chaumière in Paris, was a member of the American Federation of Arts.

FARMER, Emily
British, 19th century.
Born c. 1826; died 8 May 1905, in Porchester.
Painter, watercolourist, miniaturist. Genre scenes.
Emily Farmer was the daughter of John Biker Farmer. She exhibited at the Royal Academy in London in 1847 and was elected a member of the Royal Institute in 1854. She exhibited regularly at the Royal Institute from 1854 to 1905.
MUSEUMS AND GALLERIES:
LONDON (Victoria and Albert Mus.): *Kitty's Lunch.*
AUCTION RECORDS:
PARIS, 2 Nov 1992, *Young Dancer* (oil on canvas, 22 x 15 ins / 55 x 38 cm) FRF 12,000. LONDON, 8-9 June 1993, *Picking Flowers in the Garden* (watercolour, 10 1/2 x 7 ins / 26.5 x 18 cm) GBP 2,070. BATH, 23 July 2001, *Way to School* (1884, watercolour heightened with white, 10 x 7 ins / 25 x 17 cm) GBP 1,100. LONDON, 1 July 2004, *Necklace Maker* (watercolour heightened with white, arched top, 12 x 15 ins / 31 x 39 cm) GBP 2,600.

FARMER, John
Australian, 19th - 20th century.
Born in Australia.
Painter. Figures.
John Farmer exhibited his work in Paris at the Salon des Artistes Français from 1924.
AUCTION RECORDS:
NEW YORK, 19 July 1990, *Lady in Pink at her Mirror* (1934, oil on canvas, 13 1/4 x 16 1/4 ins / 33.7 x 41.3 cm) USD 2,200.

FARMILOE, Edith
Maiden name: Parnell
British, 19th century.
Active in London.
Draughtswoman.
Edith Farmiloe was the wife of a clergyman in a poor district of London. She used to watch the children left to their own devices on the streets and made them the subject of her sketches. These appeared in *Little Folks* in November 1895. In the case of the *Child's Pictorial,* she wrote several impressions of a journey to France and illustrated them. Other notable children's books by her include *Rag, Tag and Bobtail* and *All the World Over.*

FARN, J.
British, 18th century.
Active in Newington Butts (Surrey).
Engraver, painter.
J. Farn executed portraits in mezzotint for the *European Magazine,* including portraits of the politician W. Burton Conyngham, after G. Stuart; the actress Mrs Susanna Maria Cibber, after J. Giles Eccardt; the writer Sir Herbert Croft; and the botanist Th. Martyn and the clergyman J. Towers, both after S. Drummond.

FARNBOROUGH, Amelia (Lady), or Long
Maiden name: Hume, Baroness
British, 18th - 19th century.
Born 1772, in Wormley; died 1837, in Bromley Hill.
Watercolourist. Landscapes.
Lady Amelia Farnborough was a skilful amateur artist. She exhibited a great number of works at the Royal Academy in London.
MUSEUMS AND GALLERIES:
HANOVER: *Landscape near Bromley Hill* - LONDON (British Mus.): same subject.

FARNDON, Walter
British, 19th - 20th century.
Born 13 March 1876, in England; died 1964.
Painter, draughtsman. Landscapes, winter landscapes, village views, seascapes.
Walter Farndon went to the USA as a young man and studied at the National Academy of Design in New York.

WALTER FARDON

AUCTION RECORDS:
NEW YORK, 21 Nov 1945, *Port Washington Beach,* USD 120. NEW YORK, 21 April 1977, *Landscape with Lighthouse* (oil on canvas, 30 x 36 ins / 76.2 x 91.5 cm) USD 2,000. NEW YORK, 30 Sept 1988, *Tranquil Cove* (oil on canvas, 26 x 32 ins / 66 x 81.5 cm) USD 3,850. NEW YORK, 15 May 1991, *House by a Stone Bridge in Winter* (oil on card, 20 x 24 ins / 50.8 x 61 cm) USD 2,090. NEW YORK, 28 Nov 1995, *Near a Port* (oil on canvas, 30 x 36 1/4 ins / 76.2 x 92.1 cm) USD 6,612. NEW YORK, 7 Oct 1997, *Village on Cliffs* (oil/Masonite, 18 x 14 ins / 45.7 x 35.5 cm) USD 16,100.

FARNERIUS. See **FURNERIUS**

FARNET, Claude
French, 15th century.
Born to a family originally from Salins (Jura), France.
Painter.
In 1489, Farnet was working in the studio of Jean Changenet in Avignon.

FARNETI, Stefano
Italian, 19th century.
Born 1855, in Pisa.
Active in Naples.
Painter.
Stefano Farneti was an associate of the Salon de la Nationale des Beaux-Arts in Paris. In 1900, he entered the Alinari competition with a painting entitled *Mother with Her Child.*

FARNETZ, I.
Painter. Landscapes.
Mentioned by Florence Levy.
AUCTION RECORDS:
NEW YORK, 23 Jan 1903, *On the River,* USD 225.

FARNHAM, Sally James
American, 20th century.
Born 1876; died 1943.
Sculptor. Figures, animals.
Sally James Farnham taught herself sculpture, though she received advice from Frederick Remington, the painter and sculptor of the animals of the American West. She was as

well-known for her portraits, some equestrian, as for her sculptures of animals.

BIBLIOGRAPHY:

Broder, Patricia Janis, *Bronzes of the American West*, Abrams, New York, 1974.

AUCTION RECORDS:

NEW YORK, 29 Sept 1977, *Mounted Policeman* (patinated bronze, h. 11 3/4 ins / 30 cm) USD 1,200. NEW YORK, 24 April 1981, *The Feather Dance* (bronze, h. 13 ins / 33.3 cm) USD 1,900. NEW YORK, 1 Oct 1987, *Nymph* (dark-green patinated bronze, h. 14 ins / 35.3 cm) USD 1,200. NEW YORK, 12 March 1992, *Two Elephants* (bronze, h. 7 3/4 ins / 19.7 cm) USD 2,860. NEW YORK, 28 May 1992, *Will Rogers on his Horse* (bronze, h. 21 1/2 ins / 54.6 cm) USD 13,200. NEW YORK, 12 Sept 1994, *Mounted Policeman* (bronze, h. 12 ins / 30.5 cm) USD 2,300. ASHVILLE, 23 Feb 2002, *Horse in Prancing or Trotting Posture* (dark brown patinated bronze, 10 x 11x4 ins / 25 x 28x10 cm) USD 2,600. HAYDEN, 24 July 2004, *Horse and Rider* (bronze, 8 x 13x6 ins / 20 x 33x15 cm) USD 37,500.

FARNSWORTH, Jerry

American, 20th century.
Born 31 December 1895, in Dalton; died 1993.
Painter.

Jerry Farnsworth's works can be found in the Delgado Museum and the Pennsylvania Academy of Fine Arts.

AUCTION RECORDS:

BOLTON, 26 Nov 1985, *The Young Girl* (oil on canvas, 37 x 30 ins / 94 x 76.2 cm) USD 1,600. NEW YORK, 31 May 1990, *Duet, Man at the Piano, Young Woman Beside* (oil on canvas, 38 x 28 ins / 96.5 x 71.1 cm) USD 660. NEW YORK, 26 Sept 1990, *Spring Hat* (oil on canvas, 20 x 16 1/2 ins / 50.8 x 41.9 cm) USD 5,500. NEW YORK, 17 Dec 1990, *Thoughtful Child* (1944, oil on canvas, 24 x 20 ins / 61 x 50.8 cm) USD 1,650. NEW YORK, 12 Sept 1994, *Duet* (oil on canvas, 38 1/4 x 28 1/4 ins / 97.2 x 71.8 cm) USD 1,380. NEW YORK, 7 Oct 2003, *Calypso* (1933, oil on canvas laid on board, 76 x 40 ins / 193 x 101 cm) USD 9,000. MILFORD, 23 Oct 2003, *Truro Child* (oil on canvas, 18 x 15 ins / 46 x 38 cm) USD 3,250. PROVINCETOWN, 10 Oct 2004, *Three Friends and Jeffer* (oil on canvas, 28 x 32 ins / 71 x 81 cm) USD 12,000.

FARNUM, Suzanne

Belgian, 20th century.
Born 29 May 1898, in Maeseyck.
Sculptor.

Suzanne Farnum signed some busts, mainly in Belgium, in particular that of the Princess Josephine-Charlotte, and the baptismal fonts for a church in Connecticut. She won the fine arts prize in 1927, then the prize of the Rome academy in 1928.

FARNY, Émilienne

Swiss, 20th century.
Born 1938, in Neuchâtel.
Since 1964 active in France.
Painter. Urban landscapes, landscapes with figures.

Émilienne Farny exhibited a collection of her paintings at the Centre Culturel Suisse (Swiss cultural centre) in Paris in 1992.

While working in Paris, she depicted the streets, with their hoardings covered in poster advertisements, and building sites with their tall cranes standing out against the sky, using a very precise ruler-drawn technique with meticulously applied colours. The passers-by are hiding behind dark glasses or only showing themselves from the back. Everything is clean and glossy. This would be a painting of record, if it reflected reality.

FARNY, Henry François

French, 19th - 20th century.
Born 15 July 1847, in Ribeauvillé (Haut-Rhin); died 23 December 1916, in Cincinnati.
Active in America from 1865.
Watercolourist, painter (gouache), illustrator. Portraits, genre scenes, scenes with figures.

Henry François Farny studied in Munich. His French family emigrated and settled in western Pennsylvania. His mother often cared for members of the neighbouring Onandaigua tribe, which fascinated the child. Later, when living in Illinois, he maintained this interest in Native American culture and often painted Native Americans.

Between 1865 and 1893 he made a large number of illustrations for *Harper's Weekly* and other periodicals. From 1893 he gradually painted more oils and gouaches, concentrating on them entirely as his reputation for this kind of work increased. He won a bronze medal at the Paris Exposition Universelle of 1889 and was a jury member at the Chicago Exhibition of 1893.

MUSEUMS AND GALLERIES:

CINCINNATI (AM): *The Last of the Herd* (painting); *The Captive* (gouache); numerous other works - CINCINNATI (Taft MA): *The Song of the Talking Wire* (1904, oil on canvas); *The Song of the Talking Wire* (c. 1904, oil/panel, study) - OKLAHOMA CITY (National Cowboy and Western Heritage Mus.): *Morning of a New Day* (1907, oil on canvas).

AUCTION RECORDS:

PARIS, 11-13 June 1923, *Head of a Young Peruvian Woman* (watercolour) FRF 160. NEW YORK, 19 and 20 Jan 1945, *Rattlesnakes' Cave* (watercolour) USD 2,300. NEW YORK, 24 Oct 1968, *An Indian Holding a Rifle* (watercolour and gouache) USD 8,250. NEW YORK, 22 Oct 1969, *Indian Village* (gouache) USD 10,000. NEW YORK, 27 Oct 1971, *Over the Divide*, USD 34,000. NEW YORK, 19 Oct 1972, *Indian in a Snowy Landscape* (gouache) USD 31,000. NEW YORK, 21 April 1977, *In Luck* (1913, gouache/paper, 9 3/4 x 8 ins / 25 x 20.3 cm) USD 28,000. NEW YORK, 21 April 1978, *Crossing the Divide* (1907, oil on canvas, 28 1/4 x 18 1/4 ins / 71.8 x 46.4 cm) USD 195,000. NEW YORK, 25 April 1980, *Indian Encampment* (pen/paper mounted/card, 5 x 9 ins / 12.7 x 22.8 cm) USD 7,000. NEW YORK, 29 Jan 1981, *The Drowsy Member from Tennessee* (pen heightened with white/paper, 7 1/2 x 12 ins / 19 x 30.5 cm) USD 4,750. NEW YORK, 8 Dec 1983, *Good-bye* (pen, 9 1/2 x 14 1/4 ins / 24.1 x 36.2 cm) USD 5,000; *On the Move* (1901, gouache/paper mounted/card, 11 3/4 x 18 1/4 ins / 29.9 x 46.4 cm) USD 200,000. NEW YORK, 8 Dec 1984, *After the Hunt* (1904, oil on canvas remounted on board, 13 3/4 x 7 ins / 35 x 17.8 cm) USD 70,000. SAN FRANCISCO, 28 Feb 1985, *Indian with his Family* (1908, gouache/paper, 14 1/4 x 10 ins / 36 x 25.5 cm) USD 90,000. NEW YORK, 29 May 1986, *Portrait of a Brave* (1895, gouache/mounted paper/card, 9 3/4 x 7 ins / 24.8 x 17.8 cm) USD 38,000. NEW YORK, 26 May 1988, *Buffalo Grazing at Dusk* (1913, gouache/paper, 4 1/2 x 16 1/2 ins / 11.6 x 42 cm) USD 28,600. NEW YORK, 24 May 1989, *The Obsidian Mountain in the Yellowstone Region* (1897, gouache/paper, 23 1/4 x 17 1/4 ins / 59 x 43.7 cm) USD 203,500. NEW YORK, 31 May 1990, *Portrait of a Man* (1907, oil on canvas/card, 9 x 6 ins / 22.8 x 15.5 cm) USD 4,950. NEW YORK, 6 Dec 1991, *Indian Encampment* (1892, gouache/paper, 8 1/2 x 14 1/4 ins / 21.5 x 36.2 cm) USD 148,500. NEW YORK, 27 May 1992, *Moonlit Indian Encampment* (1911, gouache/drawing paper, 9 3/4 x 6 1/4 ins / 24.8 x 15.9 cm) USD 55,000. NEW YORK, 28 May 1992, *Trail over the Pass* (1910, oil on canvas, 16¼ x 24 ins / 41 x 61 cm) USD 165,000. NEW YORK, 3 Dec 1992, *The Sioux Ukchekekaskan Minneconjue* (watercolour/card, 9½ x 6¼ ins / 24.1 x 15.9 cm) USD 16,500. NEW YORK, 27 May 1993, *Indian Brave with a Rifle* (ink/paper, 15¼ x 9¼ ins / 38.7 x 23.5 cm) USD 14,950. NEW YORK, 2 Dec 1993, *The Courtship* (1890, gouache/paper, 9 x 6 ins / 22.9 x 15.2 cm) USD 57,500. NEW YORK, 23 May 1996, *Painting Pots* (1880, gouache/paper, 13¾ x 20 ins / 34.9 x 51.1 cm) USD 123,500. NEW YORK, 26 Sept 1996, *After the Hunt* (1906, gouache/panel, 10½ x 7¾ ins / 26.7 x 19.7 cm) USD 51,750. NEW YORK, 5 June 1997, *Danger* (1902, oil on canvas, 22¼ x 40 ins / 56.5 x 101.6 cm) USD 629,500. NEW YORK, 3 Dec 1997, *Plains Indian* (1902, gouache/card, 10 x 7 ins / 25.4 x 17.8 cm) USD 63,000.

FAROCHON, Jean Baptiste Eugène

French, 19th century.
Born 10 March 1812, in Paris; died 1 July 1871, in Paris.
Sculptor, medallist.

Jean Farochon is known primarily as a medal engraver, and won the Prix de Rome in this category in 1835. However, he was also a talented sculptor, and executed the statues at the law courts in Châlons-sur-Marne, the statue of *St John the Baptist* in the church of St-Vincent-de-Paul in Paris, and many busts of famous men.

MUSEUMS AND GALLERIES:
PARIS (Louvre): *Bust of J.-B. Rousseau* (marble); *View of the Vatican* (watercolour); *Ingres* (bronze, medallion); *Corot* (bronze, medallion).

FAROUX, Charles

French, 19th - 20th century.
Born 24 or 25 December 1861, in Compiègne; died 22 May 1946, in Magny-en-Vexin.
Painter, draughtsman, watercolourist, pastellist.
Landscapes with figures, urban landscapes.

Charles Faroux was born into a very old family from Compiègne and like his father was a rope-maker. During military service, from 1881 to 1886, he met Jean-François Millet in Paris and Eugène Boudin in Eu - or, more precisely, on the beach at Le Tréport. He returned to Paris in 1897 and met Luc-Olivier Merson, with whom he collaborated on theatre sets at the Opéra Comique. He went to live in Pontoise in 1899, where, painting in the Auvers-sur-Oise area, he met Harpignies. Together with Dr Gachet, he was a member of the Société Française Artistique (French Society of Artists).

Between the two World Wars he exhibited in Paris at the Salon des Artistes Indépendants. From 1942 he lived in Magny-en-Vexin. He only left the Île-de-France for a journey to the Dauphiné. In 1975-1976 the Musée Vivenel in Compiègne held a retrospective of his work entitled *Impressions au fils de l'Oise* (*Impressions by the Oise*).

Although he worked in Paris and the Dauphiné a little, he was primarily a faithful painter of the landscapes of the Oise valley, from Noyan to Conflans, and of the Île-de-France, before industrialisation had disfigured them. He also painted the banks of the Oise, with its barges, boats, fishermen and walkers, and the streets and buildings of the towns and villages bordering it. In his technique and feeling we find a mixture of the romantic influence of the Barbizon School and the Impressionists, who also often painted his favourite subjects.

BIBLIOGRAPHY:
Impressions au fil de l'Oise, par Charles Faroux, exhibition catalogue, Musée Vivenel, Compiègne, 1975-1976.

MUSEUMS AND GALLERIES:
BEAUVAIS - COMPIÈGNE - GRENOBLE.

FARQUHAR, Lizzi. See **VIVIAN**

FARQUHARSON, David

British, 19th century.
Born 1839 or 1840, in Perth, Scotland; died 12 July 1907, in Birnam.
Painter. Landscapes with figures, landscapes.

David Farquharson was elected a member of the Royal Scottish Academy in 1879. He went to London in 1882, then settled in Sennen Cove near Penzance in Cornwall. He exhibited at the Royal Academy in London in 1904 and was elected a member in 1905.

David Farquharson

MUSEUMS AND GALLERIES:
GLASGOW: *View of Arran from the Ayrshire Coast*; *On the River Achray* - LONDON (Tate Collection): *In a Fog* (1897, oil on canvas); *Birnam Wood* (1906, oil on canvas) - MELBOURNE (Nat. Gal. of Victoria): *View of Dundee from Harecraigs*.

AUCTION RECORDS:
LONDON, 7 Dec 1907, *Invermark Castle* GBP 52. LONDON, 14 March 1908, *Glen Falloch* GBP 31; *Dunkeld* GBP 29. LONDON, 4 April 1908, *Bank of the Dee*, GBP 59; *Moray Estuary*, GBP 44. LONDON, 11 April 1908, *Haymaking in the Landales*, GBP 110. LONDON, 6 Feb 1909, *Hilly Path near Castletown*, GBP 36; *May Morning* (1903) GBP 39; *Field of Barley*; *Pilchard Season* (1907) GBP 86; *Field of Beans*, GBP 39; *Brown Mare*, GBP 60; *News from the War*, GBP 63; *Ardlui, Loch Lomond* (1901) GBP 148; *Evening* (1906) GBP 115. LONDON, 10 June 1909, *Rapids on the Spey*, GBP 63. LONDON, 29 Jan 1910, *Sunset on the Hills* (1905) GBP 89. LONDON, 23 April 1910, *Aberdelfy*, GBP 94. LONDON, 24 Nov 1922, *In the Hills towards Abenfoyle*, GBP 53. LONDON, 27 April 1923, *Berwick-upon-Tweed* GBP 37; *Grudie Bridge*, GBP 34. LONDON, 21 Dec 1923, *In the Marshes*, GBP 22. LONDON, 28 Jan 1924, *Evening in Stirling*, GBP 8. LONDON, 21 March 1924, *Kilchum Castle*, GBP 31. LONDON, 25 April 1924, *Cornish Path*, GBP 18. LONDON, 2 May 1924, *On the Bank of the Dee*, GBP 50. LONDON, 28 Nov 1924, *Shade and Sun*, GBP 52. LONDON, 19 Dec 1924, *Guddling* GBP 32. LONDON, 17 April 1925, *Haymaking*, GBP 52. LONDON, 20 April 1925, *West Suburb*, GBP 23. LONDON, 28 May 1925, *Summer Evening*, GBP 22. LONDON, 28 May 1926, *Full Moon*, GBP 105. LONDON, 28 and 29 July 1926, *Shady Pasture*, GBP 13. LONDON, 10 Dec 1926, *Achrais Marshes, Winter*, GBP 12; *Harvest Time in Galloway*, GBP 22. LONDON, 11 Feb 1927, *Eventide* GBP 23. LONDON, 1 and 2 June 1927, *Autumn Day on the Tummel*, GBP 32; *Argyll Highlanders*, GBP 15. LONDON, 9 July 1928, *Peat Moss in Galloway*, GBP 57. LONDON, 26 Oct 1928, *Harvest Day*; *On the Bank of Allanwater* (collection) GBP 35. EDINBURGH, 27 Oct 1928, *Riverbank*, GBP 18. LONDON, 3 Dec 1928, *Flowering Pastures*, GBP 15. EDINBURGH, 15 Dec 1928, *Winter Morning*, GBP 12. EDINBURGH, 23 March 1929, *Drummond Forest*, GBP 15; *The Clyde*, GBP 14. LONDON, 16 May 1929, *Tail of the Grey Mare*, GBP 11. EDINBURGH, 13 July 1929, *Port of Aberdeen*, GBP 14. EDINBURGH, 8 March 1930, *Dalmellington* GBP 18. EDINBURGH, 29 Nov 1930, *Near Gonda*, GBP 5. EDINBURGH, 29 Nov 1930, *In Doonfort*, GBP 18. EDINBURGH, 25 April 1931, *Durch Market Boat*, GBP 7; *Autumn in Perthshire*, GBP 24. EDINBURGH, 5 March 1932, *Sennen Cove*, GBP 17. LONDON, 12 March 1932, *Trout Stream in the Highlands*, GBP 11. EDINBURGH, 28 Oct 1933, *On the Tummel*, GBP 11; *'Wayside' in Summer*, GBP 9. GLASGOW, 25 Oct 1934, *Mountain and Loch*, GBP 20. LONDON, 8 March 1935, *Sad Winter Day*, GBP 43. LONDON, 26 April 1935, *Herring Boats*, GBP 13. GLASGOW, 10 May 1935, *River Un*, GBP 14. LONDON, 6 March 1936, *Cape Cornwall*, GBP 9; *Scottish Lowlands*, GBP 22; *Clearing in Birhan Wood*, GBP 23; *Killicronkies Pass*, GBP 14; *Near the Loch*, GBP 8. GLASGOW, 4 June 1936, *Breezy Day*, GBP 16. EDINBURGH, 28 Nov 1936, *Entrance to Gleneagles*, GBP 6. LONDON, 11 Dec 1936, *Burning Weeds*, GBP 6. LONDON, 12 Feb 1937, *Newport-upon-Tay*, GBP 14. GLASGOW, 1 Oct

1943, *Harvest Time,* GBP 40. LONDON, 14 Jan 1944, *Hilly Road,* GBP 30. LONDON, 30 June 1944, *On the Way to the Fishing Locations,* GBP 44. GLASGOW, 4 Sept 1946, *Harvest Field,* GBP 51. GLASGOW, 2 July 1947, *Muirtown* GBP 19; *Men on the Scrap Heap,* GBP 19. LONDON, 22 May 1973, *Sennen Cove, Cornwall* (1897) GBP 650. GLASGOW, 30 Nov 1976, *Entrance to Gleneagles* (1878, oil on canvas, 11 x 14 3/4 ins / 27 x 37.5 cm) GBP 800. AUCHTERARDER, 30 Aug 1977, *Return of the Fishermen* (1901, oil on canvas, 17 1/4 x 29 1/2 ins / 44 x 75 cm) GBP 720. GLASGOW, 9 April 1981, *Herring Fishermen Leaving Dee* (1888, oil on canvas, 22 x 35 1/2 ins / 55 x 90 cm) GBP 11,000. GLASGOW, 19 April 1984, *'Among the Withies'* (1894-1895, oil on canvas, 34 x 54 1/2 ins / 86.3 x 138.4 cm) GBP 11,000. AUCHTERARDER, 1 Sept 1987, *Gathering in the Reeds* (1873-1885, oil on canvas, 20 3/4 x 35 ins / 53 x 89 cm) GBP 10,000. EDINBURGH, 30 Aug 1988, *Berwick-upon-Tweed* (oil on card, 7 3/4 x 13 3/4 ins / 20 x 35 cm) GBP 2,860. PERTH, 29 Aug 1989, *Fieldwork in Midlothian* (1906, oil on canvas, 60 1/4 x 40 1/4 ins / 153 x 102 cm) GBP 5,500. LONDON, 3 Nov 1989, *Moonlight over a Spring Tide* (1904, oil on canvas, 65 x 96 ins / 165 x 244 cm) GBP 8,800. GLASGOW, 6 Feb 1990, *Field of Broad Beans* (oil on canvas, 32 1/4 x 53 1/2 ins / 82 x 136 cm) GBP 8,800. PERTH, 27 Aug 1990, *Raking the Fields* (1883, oil on canvas, 12 1/4 x 20 ins / 31 x 51 cm) GBP 4,400. PARIS, 16 Nov 1990, *Snowy Landscape* (oil on panel, 8 x 12 1/2 ins / 20.5 x 31.5 cm) FRF 10,000. GLASGOW, 22 Nov 1990, *Morning Breeze in Dordrecht* (1889, oil on canvas, 40 x 72 ins / 101.6 x 182.8 cm) GBP 9,900. SOUTH QUEENSFERRY, 23 April 1991, *Hoddum Castle on the River Annan* (1889, oil on canvas, 16 1/4 x 24 ins / 41 x 61 cm) GBP 2,640. LONDON, 14 June 1991, *View of the Seine from St-Cloud* (1883, watercolour, 8 1/2 x 13 1/4 ins / 21.6 x 33.7 cm) GBP 495. PERTH, 26 Aug 1991, *Dan the Region of Glenlyon* (1881, oil on canvas, 24 x 38 1/4 ins / 61 x 97 cm) GBP 5,500. NEW YORK, 16 July 1992, *Canty Bay at Sunrise* (1883, oil on panel, 8 1/4 x 13 1/2 ins / 21 x 34 cm, 3 1/2 ins/9 cm) USD 2,200. LONDON, 3 Feb 1993, *Breaker of Stones* (1879, oil on card, 12 1/4 x 8 ins / 31 x 20.5 cm) GBP 517. GLASGOW, 1 Feb 1994, *Autumn Sun on the Tweed near Melrose* (oil on canvas, 20 x 30 ins / 51 x 76 cm) GBP 4,830. EDINBURGH, 9 June 1994, *After Dinner Training* (1894, oil on canvas, 20 x 30 ins / 50.8 x 76.2 cm) GBP 7,475. PERTH, 30 Aug 1994, *At the Foot of Ben Lomond* (1887, oil on canvas, 16 1/2 x 24 1/2 ins / 42 x 62 cm) GBP 8,050. GLASGOW, 14 Feb 1995, *Summer Afternoon near Blaigowrie* (1878, oil on canvas, 10 x 14 ins / 25.5 x 35.5 cm) GBP 4,830. PERTH, 26 Aug 1996, *River Spey in October* (1901, oil on canvas, 18 x 30 ins / 46 x 76 cm) GBP 8,625. LONDON, 5 Sept 1996, *Flock Grazing in a Sunny Meadow* (1886-1887, oil on canvas, 30 x 50 ins / 76.2 x 127 cm) GBP 11,500. GLASGOW, 11 Dec 1996, *Sowing Time* (1878, oil on canvas, 9 x 13 1/4 ins / 23 x 33.5 cm) GBP 2,645. LONDON, 14 March 1997, *Cows Grazing in a Meadow* (oil on canvas, 29 1/4 x 50 ins / 74 x 127.3 cm) GBP 19,550. LONDON, 28 Oct 1999, *Sheep among the Roots* (1884, oil on board, 9 x 15 ins / 22 x 37 cm) GBP 3,200. LONDON, 29 Nov 1999, *River Track* (1876, oil on canvas, 20 x 30 ins / 51 x 76 cm) GBP 7,500. LONDON, 10 April 2000, *Lousing Time near Dumfries* (oil on canvas, 22 x 36 ins / 56 x 91 cm) GBP 13,000. LONDON, 26 Oct 2000, *Shore of Canty Bay* (1883, oil on canvas, 14 x 24 ins / 36 x 61 cm) GBP 7,500. LONDON, 9 April 2001, *Auld Brig O'Ayr* (1886, oil on canvas, 16 x 24 ins / 40 x 61 cm) GBP 7,500. LONDON, 5 Sept 2001, *Game of Football* (oil on canvas, 14 x 18 ins / 35 x 45 cm) GBP 26,000. EDINBURGH, 22 Aug 2002, *Loch Coruisk, Isle of Skye* (oil on canvas, 9 x 13 ins / 22 x 32 cm) GBP 1,650. LONDON, 28 Aug 2002, *Lily Pond in the Park, Castle Kennedy, Stranraer* (1901, oil on canvas, 12 x 20 ins / 30 x 51 cm) GBP 3,200. LONDON, 14 April 2003, *At Loch Maree-Side* (oil on canvas, 16 x 22 ins / 41 x 56 cm) GBP 5,000. LONDON, 30 Oct 2003, *Seedtime* (1878, oil on canvas, 9 x 12 ins / 23 x 31 cm) GBP 4,800. EDINBURGH, 8 April 2004, *Home from the Harvest* (1887, oil on canvas, 14 x 24 ins / 35 x 60 cm) GBP 6,600. LONDON, 28 Oct 2004, *Morning Breeze, Dordrecht* (1889, oil on canvas, 40 x 72 ins / 101 x 183 cm) GBP 14,000.

FARQUHARSON, Joseph

British, 19th - 20th century.

Born 4 May 1846, in Finzean (Aberdeenshire); died 15 April 1935.

Painter. Portraits, genre scenes, local scenes, landscapes.

Orientalism.

Joseph Farquharson studied at the Board of Manufacture School in Edinburgh with Peter Graham. He enjoyed great success with *Joyless Winter Day* in 1877 and was considered to be a painter of 'snow and sheep' during the 1880s. Wishing to escape this classification, he left for the continent and attended the studio of Carolus-Duran in Paris from 1880 to 1884 and began painting compositions with figures. During the winter of 1885-1886 he made a trip to Egypt and painted scenes of life in Cairo. His work has been compared with that of Frederick Goodall and the French artist Gérome.

Farquharson exhibited at the Royal Scottish Academy in 1859, the Royal Academy in London from 1886 to 1893, and at the Royal Institution in 1896. In 1900 he was elected as an assiociate of the Royal Academy, and as a member in 1915.

J. Farquharson

MUSEUMS AND GALLERIES:

ABERDEEN (AG): *Self-portrait* - LEEDS (City AG): *Yon Yellow Sunset Dying in the West* (oil on canvas) - LIVERPOOL: *Dawn* - LIVERPOOL (Walker AG): *And All the Air a Solemn Silence Holds* (c. 1900, oil on canvas) - LONDON (Royal Academy of Arts): *'When snow the pasture sheets'* (1915, oil on canvas, competition piece) - LONDON (Tate Collection): *The Joyless Winter Day* (exhibited in 1833, oil on canvas).

AUCTION RECORDS:

LONDON, 7 Dec 1907, *Calm and Gentle Sun,* GBP 141. LONDON, 18 Jan 1908, *Prowler,* GBP 23. LONDON, 21 Nov 1908, *Snow Effect,* GBP 26. LONDON, 10 June 1909, *Winter,* GBP 682. LONDON, 3 June 1910, *Birse Forest,* GBP 81. LONDON, 12 March 1923, *Return of the Livestock,* GBP 126. LONDON, 11 May 1923, *To Winter Quarters,* GBP 326; *Through Mist and Rain,* GBP 230. LONDON, 20 July 1923, *Winter Night,* GBP 131. LONDON, 7 March 1924, *Homeward Bound,* GBP 157. LONDON, 25 April 1924, *A Corner of my Garden,* GBP 22. LONDON, 13 June 1924, *Loch Ailort,* GBP 126. LONDON, 20 June 1924, *Bass Rock,* GBP 31. LONDON, 19 Dec 1924, *Salmon-fishing on the Dee,* GBP 68. LONDON, 27 Feb 1925, *In Cairo,* GBP 42. LONDON, 15 May 1925, *Egyptian Market,* GBP 24. LONDON, 22 Jan 1926, *Moonrise over the Sea,* GBP 19. LONDON, 19 Feb 1926, *Homeward Bound,* GBP 16. LONDON, 19 April 1926, *Spring Evening,* GBP 10. LONDON, 13 Dec 1926, *In the Highlands,* GBP 16. LONDON, 11 Feb 1927, *Ferry on the Nile,* GBP 31. LONDON, 28 March 1927, *Evening,* GBP 57. LONDON, 30 March 1927, *Rocky Coastal Landscape by Moonlight,* GBP 12. LONDON, 13 May 1927, *Sheep in the Snow,* GBP 194. LONDON, 16 May 1927, *Homeward Bound,* GBP 13. LONDON, 22 June 1928, *Sheep in the Snow,* GBP 136. LONDON, 30 July 1928, *Fox in the Snow,* GBP 27. EDINBURGH, 20 April 1929, *Snow Storm,* GBP 42. LONDON, 26 July 1929, *Sunset in the Highlands,* GBP 94. LONDON, 25 April 1930, *Snow Storm,* GBP 12. LONDON, 7 July 1930, *Watercourse in the Highlands,* GBP 17. LONDON, 25 July 1930, *Entrance to a Turkish Bath,* GBP 8. LONDON, 2 March 1932, *End of the Wood; Leaving the Hills* (collection) GBP 84. PHILADELPHIA, 30 and 31 March 1932, *Willow by a Stream,* USD 27.50. LONDON, 12 May 1932, *Prayer Time,* GBP 6. GLASGOW, 2 Nov 1933, *View over Loch Etion,* GBP 22. LONDON, 17 Nov 1933, *In Glen Derry,* GBP 7. LONDON, 2 July 1934, *Iona,* GBP 6. LONDON, 11 July 1934,

Winter Landscape, GBP 35; *Salmon-fishing on the Dee*, GBP 4. LONDON, 16 Dec 1935, *Changing Pasture*, GBP 39. LONDON, 14 Feb 1936, *Thintel Castle*, GBP 8. LONDON, 25 May 1936, *Highland Loch*, GBP 9. GLASGOW, 4 June 1936, *In Cairo*, GBP 29. LONDON, 8 March 1937, *Landscape with Loch in the Highlands*, GBP 75. LONDON, 19 July 1937, *Sheep*, GBP 31. LONDON, 17 Dec 1937, *Homeward Bound*, GBP 15. LONDON, 11 Feb 1938, *Ready to Go Riding*, GBP 5. LONDON, 25 March 1938, *Winter Day Growing Shorter*, GBP 15. LONDON, 15 July 1938, *Totaig, Loch Duigh*, GBP 39. LONDON, 2 Dec 1938, *Winter Comes to End the Varied Year*, GBP 50; *Sun and Shade*, GBP 71. LONDON, 18 Sept 1942, *When Mist Sparkles in the Evening*, GBP 52. LONDON, 25 July 1945, *Through the Calm and Icy Air*, GBP 115. GLASGOW, 5 Sept 1945, *Air Laden with Snow*, GBP 80. LONDON, 21 Nov 1945, *When the West Sparkles in the Evening*, GBP 44. LONDON, 27 Sept 1946, *Sheep in the Snow*, GBP 65. LONDON, 7 Feb 1947, *Winter Day*, GBP 42. LONDON, 28 July 1972, *Snowy Landscape*, Gns 2,000. LONDON, 26 July 1974, *Winter Landscape*, Gns 2,500. NEW YORK, 7 Oct 1977, *Sheep in a Landscape* (oil on canvas, 36 1/4 x 28 1/4 ins / 92 x 72 cm) USD 2,500. CHESTER, 31 July 1981, *Homeward Thro' the Glistening Snow* (oil on canvas, 39 1/2 x 60 ins / 100.5 x 152.5 cm) GBP 10,500. SCOTLAND, 28 Aug 1984, *Evening at Finzean* (oil on canvas, 42 1/4 x 59 ins / 107 x 150 cm) GBP 14,000. PERTH, 27 Aug 1985, *Highland Raiders* (1900, oil on canvas, 39 3/4 x 59 3/4 ins / 101 x 152 cm) GBP 16,500. LONDON, 26 March 1988, *Sunset in the Highlands* (oil on canvas, 26 x 40 1/4 ins / 66 x 102 cm) GBP 4,180. EDINBURGH, 22 Nov 1988, *A Corner of my Garden* (oil on canvas, 31 x 21 3/4 ins / 78.8 x 55.2 cm) GBP 10,000. GLASGOW, 7 Feb 1989, *Snowy Path* (oil on canvas, 20 x 30 ins / 51 x 76 cm) GBP 37,400. LONDON, 2 June 1989, *The Artist's Garden* (oil on canvas, 18 1/4 x 12 ins / 46.5 x 30.5 cm) GBP 3,850. PERTH, 28 Aug 1989, *Loch Maree Road* (oil on canvas, 24 x 36 ins / 61 x 91.5 cm) GBP 9,350. MONTREAL, 30 Oct 1989, *Winter Landscape* (1910, oil on canvas, 20 x 30 ins / 51 x 76 cm) CAD 4,400. EDINBURGH, 22 Nov 1989, *Transhumance* (1874, oil on canvas, 24 x 48 ins / 61 x 121.9 cm) GBP 24,200. GLASGOW, 6 Feb 1990, *Sheep in a Snowy Landscape* (oil on canvas, 20 x 30 ins / 51 x 76 cm) GBP 20,900. PERTH, 27 Aug 1990, *Sheep in the Snow* (oil on canvas, 19 3/4 x 29 1/2 ins / 50 x 75 cm) GBP 48,400. GLASGOW, 22 Nov 1990, *Sad Winter Day* (oil on canvas, 24 x 42 ins / 61 x 106.7 cm) GBP 17,600. GLASGOW, 5 Feb 1991, *Egyptian Market* (oil on canvas, 18 x 28 1/4 ins / 46 x 72 cm) GBP 5,720. LONDON, 8 Feb 1991, *A Corner of the Garden* (oil on canvas, 18 x 12 ins / 46 x 30.5 cm) GBP 3,850. SOUTH QUEENSFERRY, 23 April 1991, *A Corner of the Garden at Finzean* (oil on canvas, 19 1/4 x 14 ins / 49 x 35.5 cm) GBP 6,050. EDINBURGH, 2 May 1991, *Flock of Sheep on a Sunken, Snowy Path* (oil on canvas, 19 1/4 x 17 ins / 48.9 x 43.2 cm) GBP 4,400. PERTH, 26 Aug 1991, *Soft Light of Evening* (oil on canvas, 16 x 12 ins / 40.5 x 30.5 cm) GBP 9,900. PERTH, 1 Sept 1992, *Snowy Path* (oil on canvas, 12 x 18 ins / 30.5 x 46 cm) GBP 6,160. LONDON, 13 Nov 1992, *Young Stag and Man Collecting Firewood on a Forest Path* (1900, oil on canvas, 60 1/4 x 44 ins / 153 x 111.8 cm) GBP 15,400. EDINBURGH, 13 May 1993, *First Snow of Winter* (oil on canvas, 20 x 30 ins / 50.8 x 76.2 cm) GBP 8,800. NEW YORK, 26 May 1993, *Chrysanthemum Borders* (oil on canvas, 20 x 24 ins / 50.8 x 61 cm) USD 25,300. LONDON, 3 Nov 1993, *In Cairo: Ferries from the Island of Gazirie to Boulach, Port of Cairo* (oil on canvas, 44 x 78 ins / 112 x 198 cm) GBP 27,600. PERTH, 30 Aug 1994, *To Winter Quarters* (oil on canvas, 40 x 60 1/2 ins / 101.5 x 153.5 cm) GBP 49,900. GLASGOW, 14 Feb 1995, *Joyless Winter Day* (oil on canvas, 20 x 36 ins / 51 x 91.5 cm) GBP 14,950. PERTH, 29 Aug 1995, *End of a Freezing Day* (oil on canvas, 20 x 30 ins / 51 x 76 cm) GBP 45,500. LONDON, 29 March 1996, *When Frost Comes at Nightfall* (oil on canvas, 39 1/2 x 54 ins / 100.3 x 137.1 cm) GBP 109,300. PERTH, 26 Aug 1996, *Sheep on a Snowy Path* (oil on canvas, 30 x 40 ins / 76 x 101.5 cm) GBP 35,600. EDINBURGH, 27 Nov 1996, *Summer Days: Peter Hill, Finzean, near Banchory* (oil on canvas, 37 x 60 ins / 94 x 152.3 cm) GBP 73,000. LONDON, 15 April 1997, *Winter Afternoon at Finzean* (oil on canvas, 36 x 28 ins / 91.5 x 71 cm) GBP 38,900. EDINBURGH, 15 May 1997, *Letterfearn on Loch Duich, Kintail* (oil on canvas, 30 x 40 ins / 76 x 101.5 cm) GBP 7,475.

FARQUIN, Ernest
French, 19th century.
Born 19th century, in Châtelet.
Painter.

In 1865 Ernest Farquin exhibited his *View of the Maisons-Laffitte Mill* at the Salon, followed in 1866 by his *Île Laborde Farm at Maisons-Laffitte*.

FARR, A. F.
German, 19th century.
Lithographer.

Possibly the son of Daniel Farr, A.F. Farr is known to have produced three views of Überlingen.

FARR, Daniel
German, 19th century.
Born 2 February 1782, in Ulm.
Lithographer.

A pupil of Senefelder, Daniel Farr founded the first institute of lithography in Ulm. He produced a series of portraits, including one of the king of Württemberg and another of Dr F. Palm. Other important works include his *Capitulation of Ulm in 1805* and *Laying the First Stone of the Ludwig Wilhelm Bridge in Ulm in 1829*.

FARRA, Mario Dal, or Dal-Farra
French, 20th century.
Born 6 October 1937, in Thorigny.
Painter. Figure compositions, landscapes, landscapes with figures, flowers.

Mario Dal Farra is a self-taught painter who has painted continuously since 1980. He first exhibited in Chelles in 1982. He has taken part in group exhibitions in many provincial cities. In Paris he has exhibited since 1981 at the Salon des Indépendants, of which he is a member, and since 1987 at the Société des Beaux-Arts, to which he also belongs. He shows collections of his work in solo exhibitions in the Paris area (in 1986 and 1989 at the Galerie L'Atelier), in provincial cities, where he has won various awards, and abroad, in Barcelona, Brussels and elsewhere.

FARRADESCHE, Paul
French, 19th - 20th century.
Born 19th century, in Le Raincy.
Engraver (etching).

A pupil of Charles Delaye, Paul Farradesche exhibited at the Salon of the Société des Artistes Français, becoming a member in 1903.

FARRAR, Charles Brooke
British, 20th century.
Born in Bedford.
Painter. Landscapes.

Charles Farrar exhibited at the Salon des Indépendants in Paris in 1927 and 1928.

FARRAR, Frances
American, 19th century.
Born 25 October 1855, in Elmira.
Active in Chicago.
Painter, teacher. Portraits.

FARRAR, Frederica E. W.
British, 20th century.
Miniaturist.

FARRE, Antoine
Spanish, 20th century.

Born in Barcelona.
Painter. Interiors.
Antoine Farre exhibited in Paris at the Salon des Artistes Français from 1924.

FARRÉ, Henry
French, 20th century.
Born 13 July 1871, in Foix (Ariège).
Painter. Genre scenes, landscapes.
Farré was a pupil of Thirion, Cormon and of Paul Sain. From 1898 he was a member of the Salon des Artistes Français in Paris. He received a third-class medal in 1907. He is best known for his works *The Beach at Trouville* and *Afternoon of a Faun*.
AUCTION RECORDS:
PARIS, 8 June 1931, *Landscape Near Foix*, FRF 32; *View of the Bridge in Foix*, FRF 90. NEW YORK, 11 April 1981, *The Shot-down Fokker* (1916, oil on canvas, 27 1/2 x 39 ins / 70 x 99 cm) USD 1,750. LONDON, 19 March 1986, *Nymphs in the Forest* (1909, oil on canvas, 71 x 90 1/4 ins / 179.5 x 229 cm) GBP 7,500. VERSAILLES, 8 July 1990, *Figures in a Boat on the Pond* (1919, oil on canvas, 21 1/4 x 28 3/4 ins / 54 x 73 cm) FRF 19,000.

FARRÉ, Jean
French, 16th century.
Active c. 1550.
Painter.
Farré worked with B. Salomon on the refectory of the Augustinian monastery in Lyons.

FARREL, Malachi. See **FARRELL**

FARRELL, Francis
Irish, 18th century.
Died January 1785, in Dublin.
Active in Dublin.
Painter. Portraits.
J. Wilson engraved the *Portrait of Louisa Williams* in 1771 in the style of Francis Farrell.

FARRELL, James
Irish, 19th century.
Born 1821; died 20 November 1891.
Active in Dublin.
Sculptor.
James Farrell was the son and pupil of Terence Farrell. He worked on the decoration of churches in Ireland. An *Annunciation* by him can be found in the church of St Francis-Xavier in Dublin; there is a *Sacred Heart* in the convent at Sion Hill, Blackrock; and an *Our-Lady-of-Misericord* and a *Christ in the Temple* in the church of Rathmines. He appeared at the Hibernian Academy in 1846 with two busts and at the Dublin exhibition in 1853 with *Hunter Resting*. *Return of the Favourite Dove* was awarded a prize by the Royal Irish Art Union.

FARRELL, John
Irish, 19th century.
Born 1829; died 1901.
Active in Dublin.
Sculptor.
John Farrell was the son of Terence Farrell and trained at the Royal Dublin Society. He exhibited at the Royal Academy in London and the Royal Hibernian Academy. His works include *Sweet Slumber of a Happy Childhood* and *Judith*.

FARRELL, Joseph
Irish, 19th century.
Born 1823; died 1904.
Active in Dublin.
Sculptor.
Joseph Farrell was the son of Terence Farrell. He executed a great number of works for churches. His *The Holy Virgin* was frequently copied. He exhibited at the Royal Hibernian Academy from 1839 to 1896. He also produced genre sculptures, including *Bard*, *Looking towards the Sea* and *Rescued from the Shipwreck*.

FARRELL, Katherine Levin
American, 20th century.
Born 1857; died 1951.
Active in Philadelphia.
Painter, engraver.

FARRELL, Malachi
Irish, 20th - 21st century.
Born 1970, in Dublin.
Active in France.
Sculptor, assemblage artist, installation artist.
Malachi Farrell studied at the Rijksakademie in Amsterdam from 1994 to 1995, at the École des Beaux-Arts in Rouen from 1987 to 1992 and at the Institut Supérieur des Hautes Études in Paris, where he was taught by Buren in 1993. Farrell's work has a social and political dimension, addressing issues such as ecology, consumer society, exclusion, intolerance and militarization and uses means borrowed from performance and spectacle such as movement and sound and light, all computer programmed. He produces infernal machines, extremely complex robots driven by technology which recall Tinguely's work. His machines are confronted with nature in a combination of craftsmanship and advanced technology. His articulated robots electrify, transform into trees, dance and sing an Irish jig. His masks are grotesque versions of the heroic features of cartoon strip figures. They use and show violence and collective hysteria, conveying the difficulty of daily life in today's world from an implacable viewpoint. In a morbid vein, he invites the viewer to experience unlikely adventures with a socio-political dimension, relating, for example, to the troubles in Northern Ireland or the violence surrounding football matches.

He took part in group exhibitions in 1992 at the gallery of the fine arts academy in Rouen; in 1993 at the Kerguéhennec art centre; in 1994 at the Musée d'Art Moderne de la Ville de Paris; in 1994 and 1995 at the Rijksakademie in Amsterdam; in 1995 at Le Magasin, Grenoble; in 1996 at the Wiener Secession in Vienna and the CAPC in Bordeaux, and in 1997 at the Musée du Luxembourg, Paris. He has also shown his work in solo exhibitions: in 1996 in Utrecht; in 1997 at the Caisse des Dépôts et Consignations and the Galerie Anne de Villepoix, Paris, and in 2003 at the Galerie Xippas, Paris.
BIBLIOGRAPHY:
Colard, Jean Max, '*Malachi Farrell, ses patates, ses robots, ses machines*' in *Beaux-Arts Magazine* n° 156, periodical, Paris, May 1997. Francblin, Catherine, '*Malachi Farrell*' in *Art Press* n° 258 p. 30, Paris, June 2000.
MUSEUMS AND GALLERIES:
PARIS (FNAC): *It Didn't Have to Be Like That (A Million Ways of Dying, Chose One)*.

FARRELL, Michael
Irish, 19th century.
Born 1834; died 1855.
Sculptor.
Michael Farrell was the son of Terence Farrell. He worked with his brother Thomas on an allegorical statue *Prudence* for the church on Marlborough Street in Dublin.

FARRELL, Michael
Irish, 20th century.
Born 1940, in Kells (County Meath); died 7 June 2000.
Painter.
Michael Farrell studied at St Martin's School of Art in London. His painting is in fact an assemblage of carefully cut-out shapes in a variety of forms which often suggest a fountain or some composite spurting material in painted wood which may overflow on to the ground. His work has been shown in Ireland, England, France, Belgium, the USA and Yugoslavia.

He took part in the *Exposition d'Art Contemporain Irlandais* (*Exhibition of Contemporary Irish Art*) in Paris in 1973. He has had a number of solo exhibitions in London, Paris, Munich and Dublin. Farrell was awarded the Carroll Prize in 1964, 1965, 1967 and 1968.

BIBLIOGRAPHY:

Art irlandais actuel, exhibition catalogue, Musée d'Art moderne de la Ville de Paris, Paris, 1973.

MUSEUMS AND GALLERIES:

BELFAST (Ulster Mus.): *Study Monochrome* (1967, acrylic/canvas); *Pressé Series with Cream* (1970, acrylic/canvas) - DUBLIN (Douglas Art Gallery, Trinity College) - DUBLIN (Hugh Lane Gallery) - PARIS (MNAM-CCI).

FARRELL, Terence

Irish, 19th century.

Born 1798, in Creve (Longford); died 19 March 1876, in Dublin.

Sculptor.

Terence Farrell trained under Edward and John Smyth, then Thomas Kirk in Dublin. He sculpted busts, particularly miniatures, and statues. A notable statue by him is the statue in memory of *Sir L. Cole*, which can be found in Enniskillen. He also executed works for churches, such as the Tomlinson funeral monument in St Patrick's Cathedral in Dublin, and that of the wife of his benefactor, Earl Grey, in the church at Flitton (Bedfordshire). He appeared at the Royal Hibernian Academy from 1826 onwards.

AUCTION RECORDS:

MILAN, 26 Nov 1968, *Woman and Children at Prayer in a Church*, ITL 3,400,000.

FARRELL, Thomas

Irish, 19th century.

Born 1827, in Dublin; died 2 July 1900, in Redesdale.

Sculptor.

Thomas Farrell was the son of Terence Farrell and trained under Panormo at the Royal Dublin Society School. In 1843, 1844 and 1846, he was awarded prizes from the Royal Irish Art Union for his groups *Young Boys with a Dog, Young Boys with a Goat, Nisus and Euryale* and *Young Bather Surprised*. He appeared at the Royal Academy in London with *Little Favourite* and a statue of *Lord O'Hagan*, and frequently at the Royal Hibernian Academy. After a stay in Italy, he executed a great many works in Dublin, including the statues of Lord Ardiloun (Lord Ardiloun), Cardinal Cullen (Cullen) in the church on Marlborough Street, and Archbishop Whateley (Whateley) and Captain McNeill Boyd.

FARRELL, William

Irish, 19th - 20th century.

Active in Dublin.

Sculptor.

William Farrell was the son of Terence Farrell.

FARREN, Robert

British, 19th century.

Born 5 March 1832, in Cambridge.

Painter, watercolourist, engraver. Figure compositions, figures, genre scenes.

Robert Farren exhibited in London, notably at the Royal Academy and Suffolk Street Gallery, from 1868 to 1880.

MUSEUMS AND GALLERIES:

CAMBRIDGE (Fitzwilliam Mus.): *Teacher Adam Sedgwich*.

AUCTION RECORDS:

LONDON, 28 Sept 1976, *Reapers* (1877, oil on canvas, 39 x 52 ins / 99 x 132 cm) GBP 300. LONDON, 24 May 1984, *Cymbeline, Act II, Scene II* (1872, watercolour heightened with gouache, 24 x 35 3/4 ins / 61 x 91 cm) GBP 550. BILLINGSHURST, 18 May 1999, *March Idyll in the Fens* (1885, oil on paper, 24 x 50 ins / 61 x 127 cm) GBP 4,500. LONDON, 1 Aug 2000, *Fisherfolk on the Shoreline* (oil on canvas, 24 x 36 ins / 61 x 91 cm) GBP 1,600. CAMBRIDGE, 11 Feb 2004, *Farmer's Daughter* (oil on paper on canvas, 19 x 13 ins / 47 x 32 cm) GBP 1,200.

FARRER, Henry

American, 19th century.

Born 23 March 1843, in London, England; died 24 February 1903, in Brooklyn.

Painter, watercolourist, engraver. Landscapes.

Henry Farrer emigrated to the USA in 1861 and made himself a place among its artists. He was a member of a number of artistic groups, including the Royal Society of Engravers and Etchers in London, and the Engraving Club of New York, of which he later became president. He exhibited at the National Academy of Design in New York from 1867 to 1881.

AUCTION RECORDS:

NEW YORK, 3 Feb 1904, *Dead Leaves*, USD 105. NEW YORK, 24 Sept 1981, *Summer Landscape at Twilight* (watercolour, 11 1/4 x 17 1/4 ins / 28.6 x 43.8 cm) USD 1,300. NEW YORK, 28 Sept 1983, *Clearing Skies* (watercolour, 15 x 20 1/2 ins / 38 x 51.8 cm) USD 2,800. NEW YORK, 30 Sept 1985, *A Southern Harbour* (1881, watercolour, 27 1/2 x 41 1/4 ins / 70 x 105 cm) USD 5,000. NEW YORK, 20 March 1987, *Landscape at Sunset* (1901, watercolour, 9 x 13 3/4 ins / 22.9 x 35.2 cm) USD 6,000. NEW YORK, 17 March 1988, *Silhouette in a Landscape* (watercolour/paper, 11 3/4 x 17 ins / 30 x 43 cm) USD 2,090. NEW YORK, 25 May 1989, *Two Dead Birds Hanging on a Nail* (1867, watercolour and ink/paper, 9 3/4 x 8 ins / 24.8 x 19.4 cm) USD 18,700. NEW YORK, 28 Sept 1989, *Last Light of the Setting Sun* (1899, watercolour/paper/card, 25 x 36 1/2 ins / 63.5 x 93 cm) USD 17,600. NEW YORK, 24 Jan 1990, *Twilight* (1892, watercolour/paper/card, 8 1/4 x 13 1/4 ins / 20.9 x 33.6 cm) USD 2,420. NEW YORK, 28 May 1992, *Twilight over the Port of New York* (1880, watercolour and pencil/paper, 25 x 37 1/2 ins / 63.5 x 95.4 cm) USD 20,900. NEW YORK, 3 Dec 1992, *Light of the Setting Sun* (1900, watercolour/paper, 18 1/4 x 25 1/4 ins / 46.4 x 64.1 cm) USD 8,250. NEW YORK, 10 March 1993, *End of a Grey Day* (1887, watercolour/paper, 24 x 36 1/2 ins / 61 x 92.7 cm) USD 14,950. NEW YORK, 28 Nov 1995, *Overcast Weather* (watercolour/paper, 16 1/2 x 24 3/4 ins / 41.9 x 62.8 cm) USD 2,875. NEW YORK, 3 Dec 1996, *Cottage by the Sea* (1880, watercolour and pencil/card, 16 1/2 x 27 ins / 42 x 68.5 cm) USD 3,680. MILFORD, 21 Oct 1999, *Summer Sunset* (watercolour, 11 x 17 ins / 28 x 43 cm) USD 3,500. LOS ANGELES, 9 Dec 1999, *Sunset on a Farm near a Lake* (watercolour, 12 x 18 ins / 30 x 46 cm) USD 7,000. NEW YORK, 22 May 2001, *Wetlands* (oil on canvas) USD 2,000. PORTSMOUTH, 18 Aug 2001, *Sailboat at Sunset in New York Harbour* (1875, watercolour, 6 x 9 ins / 14 x 22 cm) USD 43,000. MILFORD, 25 April 2002, *Mellow Reflections* (watercolour, 18 x 30 ins / 46 x 76 cm) USD 7,500. SAN FRANCISCO, 9 June 2002, *Small Farm Cottage with a Stream at Sunset* (watercolour and gouache on paper on board, 14 x 22 ins / 36 x 56 cm) USD 5,000. NEW YORK, 5 March 2003, *Sunlit Landscape* (1894, watercolour, 9 x 15 ins / 23 x 38 cm) USD 3,000. EAST DENNIS, 31 July 2003, *Still-life with Three Eggs* (1868, oil on paper, 5 x 10 ins / 13 x 25 cm) USD 4,900.

FARRER, Henry

British, 19th century.

Born in London.

Painter. Portraits.

Henry Farrer may have been the son of T. Farrer. J. Egan engraved *The Actor Denvil in the Role of Manfred* after him. Farrer exhibited a portrait of his wife on ivory and a self-portrait on paper in 1865.

FARRER, Julia

British, 20th century.

Painter.

Julia Farrer produces abstract pieces of a geometrical nature dominated by the use of line and pastel tones. In 1995, she took part in the FIAC (Foire Internationale d'Art Contemporain) in Paris with the Graham Dixon Gallery of London.

FARRER, Nicholas

British, 18th century.
Born 1750, in Sunderland; died 1805.
Painter. Portraits.

Nicholas Farrer was a friend of Reynolds and Northcote and studied under Pine. Although his portraits are not copies of Reynolds, they resemble those of Reynolds so much that they have been attributed to him. Farrer painted portraits of the Duke of Richmond and his family.

FARRER, T.

British, 19th century.
Active in London.
Miniaturist.

T. Farrer exhibited portraits at the Royal Academy in London from 1805 to 1820, including one of *The Actress Miss O'Neill in the Role of Juliet.*

FARRER, Thomas Charles

British, 19th century.
Born 16 September 1839, in London; died 16 June 1891, in London.
Painter. Landscapes.

Thomas Charles Farrer was the brother of Henry Farrer. He initially worked in New York, and was one of the first members of the American Society of Painters in Watercolor. In 1871 the art press classed him as one of the notable painters in the New World. He went to London in 1872, and from that time on took part in the main exhibitions there, notably at the Royal Academy and the Suffolk Street Gallery.

AUCTION RECORDS:

LONDON, 25 Jan 1908, *Wheat Field,* GBP 4. LONDON, 10 June 1910, *Royal Windsor Castle,* GBP 37. LONDON, 20 Jan 1928, *Royal Windsor Castle,* GBP 28. NEW YORK, 7 June 1979, *Self-portrait with Violin* (1859, pencil heightened with white, 10 x 73/4 ins / 25.2 x 19.8 cm) USD 2,200. LONDON, 3 June 1988, *The Silver Birches in Burnham* (1874-1876, oil on canvas, 36 x 48 ins / 91.5 x 122 cm) GBP 1,210. MILFORD, 25 Oct 2001, *Quiet Read* (oil on panel, 9 x 7 ins / 23 x 18 cm) USD 4,000.

FARRERAS RICART, Francisco

Spanish, 20th century.
Born 1927, in Barcelona.
Painter, collage artist. Designs for stained glass, murals.

Francisco Ferreras Ricart trained in Madrid with Stolz and Vásquez Díaz. He lives and works in Madrid and has produced mural decorations.

He has participated in the Venice Biennale in 1954, 1958 and 1960 and other collective and solo exhibitions.

After being influenced by Picasso, Ferreras Ricart turned to abstraction, firstly geometric abstraction and later, from 1958, lyrical abstraction, using a scratching technique on to pigment.

BIBLIOGRAPHY:

Catálogo nacional de arte contemporáneo 1990-1991, Ibérico 2Mil, Barcelona, 1990-1991 (National Catalogue of Contemporary Art 1990-1991).

MUSEUMS AND GALLERIES:

ALICANTE (Mus. de La Asegurada) - ATLANTA (High Mus. of Art) - BILBAO (MBA) - CARACAS (Fundación Eugenio Mendóza) - CUENCA (Mus. De Arte Abstracto Español, Fundación Juan March) - DOWNEY (MA) - GRANADA (Fundación Rodríguez Acosta) - HELSINKI (Ateneumin Taidemus.) - HONOLULU (Academy of Arts) - LANZAROTE (Mus. del Castillo de San José) - LONDON (Tate Collection): *No. 139* (1961, mixed media on wood) - MADRID (Areces Foundation) - MADRID (Fundación Juan March) - MADRID (Mus. Nacional Centro de Arte Reina Sofía) - MONTREAL (MAC) - NEW YORK (MoMA) - NEW YORK (Solomon R. Guggenheim Mus.) - OKLAHOMA CITY (Art Center) - PÁMANES (Mus. de Elsedo) - PARIS (MNAM-CCI) - PEDRAZA (Castillo) - PITTSBURGH (Carnegie MA): *Acuatinta No. 4, 1962* (1962, ink and watercolour on paper) - SEVILLE (Centro Andaluz de Arte Contemporáneo) - SOFIA (Nacionalna chudozestvena galerija) - STOCKHOLM (Moderna Mus.) - TENERIFE (Art Collection) - THE HAGUE (Gemeentemus.) - TOKYO (National MMA) - VIENNA (Mus. Moderner Kunst Stiftung Ludwig) - VILLAFAMÉS (Mus. Popular de Arte Contemporáneo) - VITORIA (MMA).

AUCTION RECORDS:

MADRID, 24 Feb 1984, *Composition* (1965, collage, 45 x 45 ins / 114 x 114 cm) ESP 275,000. MADRID, 27 Feb 1985, *No. 145* (1961, collage/panel, 471/4 x 391/4 ins / 120 x 100 cm) ESP 391,000. MADRID, 28 Nov 1991, *Collage 421* (1970, acrylic/paper/panel, 783/4 x 55 ins / 200 x 140 cm) ESP 1,792,000. MADRID, 5 July 1999, *Pozuelo* (1975, collage on panel, 55 x 79 ins / 140 x 200 cm) ESP 2,000,000. MADRID, 24 Jan 2000, *Painting 227-A* (1988, wood, paint, panel, relief, 20 x 20x4 ins / 50 x 50x9 cm) ESP 550,000. MADRID, 21 Feb 2000, *Painting no. 55* (1960, oil on canvas, 46 x 35 ins / 116 x 90 cm) ESP 300,000. MADRID, 6 Feb 2002, *174-A* (1987, acrylic and collage on board, 39 x 39 ins / 100 x 100 cm) EUR 7,800. MADRID, 17 Dec 2002, *Collage 254* (1965, collage on panel, 36 x 29 ins / 91 x 73 cm) EUR 5,400. MADRID, 24 June 2003, *Collage no. 236* (1965, collage and mixed media on panel, 36 x 29 ins / 91 x 74 cm) EUR 6,000. MADRID, 16 Sept 2003, *Perseus* (1973, oil and collage on board, 47 x 39 ins / 120 x 100 cm) EUR 7,500. MADRID, 29 June 2004, *Collage* (1983, collage and ink wash on paper, 16 x 10 ins / 40 x 26 cm) EUR 2,000. MADRID, 6 Oct 2004, *Untitled* (1981, collage on board, 20 x 20 ins / 50 x 50 cm) EUR 3,000.

FARRET

Dutch, 18th century.
Active in Amsterdam.
Draughtsman.

Farret illustrated a translation of Homer which was published between 1712 and 1716 in Amsterdam. He is probably the same person as Coenraad Farret.

FARRET, Coenraad

Dutch, 18th century.
Born in Dordrecht.
Painter.

Coenraad Farret became a citizen of Amsterdam on 10 February 1724. The museum in Haarlem holds his portraits of *Aletta-Henrietta d'Hendrick* and *Willem Meulenaer.*

FARREY, Pierre Francis

French, 20th century.
Born 1896, in Paris.
Painter. Landscapes, portraits.
School of Algiers.

Pierre Farrey exhibited regularly in Paris, at the Salon des Tuileries, from 1924. It is likely that he was the same artist as Pierre-Alexis, who was included in the 2003 exhibition, *L'École d'Alger* (*The School of Algiers*), at the Musée des Beaux-Arts in Bordeaux.

BIBLIOGRAPHY:

Cazenave, Elisabeth/Dalia, Mahammed-Orfali/Vidal-Bué, Marion, *L'École d'Alger*, exhibition catalogue, Musée des Beaux-Arts, Bordeaux, 2003.

MUSEUMS AND GALLERIES:

ALGIERS (Mus. National des Beaux-Arts).

AUCTION RECORDS:

PARIS, 20 March 1923, *Young Woman,* FRF 180. PARIS, 9 April 1927, *St-Tropez* FRF 110. PARIS, 16 Feb 1929, *Hill,* FRF 800. PARIS, 30 May 1945, *St-Tropez* FRF 400. ENGHIEN-LES-BAINS, 26 June 1984, *The Men of St-Tropez* (oil on canvas, 68 x 541/4 ins / 173 x 138 cm) FRF 22,000.

FARRIER, Charlotte
British, 19th century.
Active in London.
Painter. Portraits.
Charlotte Farrier exhibited in London at the Royal Academy and Suffolk Street Gallery from 1826 to 1875.

FARRIER, Robert
British, 19th century.
Born 1796, in Chelsea (London); died 1879, in Chelsea.
Painter, miniaturist. Genre scenes.
Robert Farrier executed miniatures and genre paintings. He exhibited at the Royal Academy for the first time after 1818, yet still featured in the catalogue brought out in 1872.
AUCTION RECORDS:
LONDON, 21 Nov 1908, *Fortune Teller and Dutch Interior in Meyerbeem* (1850) GBP 1. LONDON, 25 Jan 1924, *Work and Rest,* GBP 10. LONDON, 28 June 1937, *St Valentine's Day,* GBP 6. LONDON, 5 Dec 1941, *Who Shall Serve the Queen!,* GBP 19. LONDON, 18 March 1980, *Pursuit of Knowledge under Difficulties* (oil on panel, 20 x 17 1/4 ins / 51 x 44 cm) GBP 1,200. LONDON, 14 March 1990, *Brutal Awakening; Village Market* (oil on canvas, a pair, each 19 1/2 x 23 1/2 ins / 49.5 x 59.5 cm) GBP 12,100. LONDON, 3 June 1992, *Tame Rabbit* (oil on canvas, 22 x 20 ins / 56 x 51 cm) GBP 1,870. LONDON, 8-9 June 1993, *Pedlar* (oil on panel, 20 3/4 x 18 ins / 53 x 46 cm) GBP 2,645. LONDON, 20 July 1994, *Pastoral Symphony* (oil on canvas, 20 x 24 ins / 50.5 x 61 cm) GBP 1,380. LONDON, 29 March 1995, *Ready for the War 'Si vis pacem, para bellum'* (oil on panel, 22 3/4 x 24 1/2 ins / 58 x 62 cm) GBP 4,600. ROME, 21 Nov 2000, *Interiors with figures* (oil on board, 26 x 21 ins / 67 x 54 cm) ITL 5,500,000. CAMBRIDGE, 21 April 2004, *Who Shall Serve the King? - The Recruit* (oil on board, 20 x 24 ins / 50 x 62 cm) GBP 7,000.

FARRIER, T.
French, 20th century.
Painter. Animals.
AUCTION RECORDS:
LONDON, 5 June 1924, *Favourite Rabbits,* GBP 6. LONDON, 2 June 1989, *The Tamed Rabbits* (oil on canvas, 22 x 20 ins / 56 x 50.5 cm) GBP 3,300.

FARRIGOLA Y FERNANDO, Isidoro
Spanish, 19th century.
Born in Sans.
Painter. Genre scenes.
Isidoro Farrigola y Fernando studied at the school of fine arts in Barcelona.

FARRINGTON, Richard, or Ffarrington
Dutch, 17th century.
Active in Dordrecht from 1648 to 1670.
Painter. Landscapes.
Descendants of Richard Farrington are known in England as painters.

FARRINUSA ZIED
Turkish, 20th century.
Born 1904, in Istanbul.
Painter.
This artist is thought to be the same person as the princess Fahr-El-Nissa-Zeid. Zied Farrinusa studied at the school of fine arts in Istanbul, and exhibited her work in the official exhibitions in Ankara. In 1946, she submitted two canvases, one of which was a view of *Golden Horn* to the exhibition of modern art organised by the United Nations at the museum of modern art in Paris.

FARRIOL, Guillermo
Spanish, 15th century.
Active in Valencia.
Painter.

FARRO, Judith
French, 20th - 21st century.
Born 1947.
Painter.
In 1986 and 1988, Judith Farro exhibited at the Salon des Réalités Nouvelles in Paris.

FARROUKH, Moustafa or Moustapha
Lebanese, 20th century.
Born 1901, in Beirut; died 16 February 1957, in Beirut.
Painter, watercolourist. Portraits, landscapes.
From 1924 to 1927 he studied at the Royal Academy of Decorative Arts in Rome, where he was taught by Coromaldi and Calcagnadoro. He stayed in Paris in 1930-1932, where he was given advice by Bompard and Paul Chabasse, president of the Association des Artistes Français. From 1935 to 1954 he taught at the American University in Beirut. He was the author of four books on art published in Arabic. He took part in several group exhibitions in Lebanon, as well as in Italy, New York and Paris, notably at the Salon des Artistes Français in 1930, with *Turkish Café,* and in 1931, with *Mon Professeur* (*My Teacher*). In 1955 he was awarded first prize by the President of the Lebanese Republic at the Spring Salon in Beirut. He also received the Lebanese order of merit and the national order of the Cedar.

Farroukh has played an important role in introducing Western art to Lebanon. His highly colourful landscapes denote a post-impressionist influence. He has often painted typical Lebanese villages, with their inhabitants and their customs. His numerous portraits are characterized by their attempt to show an individual's 'inner expression', often captured in a glance.
BIBLIOGRAPHY:
Liban. Le Regard des peintres. 200 ans de peinture libanaise, exhibition catalogue, Institut du Monde Arabe, Paris, 1989.
AUCTION RECORDS:
PARIS, 5 April 1993, *Portrait of Chibli Bek El-Mallat* (pen drawing, 6 3/4 x 4 1/4 ins / 17 x 10.5 cm) FRF 10,000.

FARROW, William McKnight
American, 20th century.
Born 13 April 1885, in Dayton (Ohio); died 1967.
Painter, engraver.
William McKnight Farrow studied at the Chicago Art Institute. He won a number of prizes in different competitions and exhibitions.

FARRUGIA, Giovanni
Italian, 19th century.
Born 1810.
Active in Malta.
Engraver.
Giovanni Farrugia was a pupil of Longhi. He engraved *The Madonna of the Carnation* after Raphael.

FARSCHIK, Sargis
11(?)th century.
Painter.
A fresco in the Church of the Saviour, built in Ani in 1036, carries a signature that is probably by this artist.

FARSHCHIAN, Mahmoud
Iranian, 20th century.
Born 1929, in Esfahan.
Miniaturist.
Mahmoud Farshchian studied with other Iranian miniaturists, after which he travelled to Europe. He depicts the folklore and legends of the Middle East in a precise style.

FARTHING, Stephen
British, 20th - 21st century.
Born 16 September 1950, in London.
Active in New York.
Painter, collage artist.

Stephen Farthing studied at St Martin's School of Art in London (1969-1973) and then at the Royal College of Art in London (1973-1976) for an MA in Painting. In 1976 he went to the British School in Rome on an Abbey Major Scholarship. He was a lecturer in painting at the Canterbury College of Art (1977-1979) and tutor in painting at the Royal College of Art in London (1980-1985). From 1985 to 1987 he was head of painting and then from 1987 to 1989 departmental head at the West Surrey College of Art and Design. From 1990 to 2000 he was Ruskin Master at the Ruskin School of Fine Art and a fellow of St Edmund Hall in Oxford. In 2002 he took up the post of executive director of the New York Academy of Art in Manhattan. He was elected a Member of the Royal Academy in 1998.

As a student Farthing produced the painting *Louis XV Rigaud* (1975, in Walker Art Gallery in Liverpool), a reinterpretation of a painting of Louis XV of France by the 18th-century court painter Hyacinthe Rigaud. The painting is an example of Farthing's mixing of styles, including Pop Art, Cubism, collage, caricature and graffiti, and of Farthing's interest in both Figurative painting and the subject of history or historical figures and art history. The National Portrait Gallery of London holds *Historians of 'Past and Present'* (1999), a group portrait of 20th-century British Marxist historians, for which Farthing visited each historian separately for sittings in 1999. In 1982 he began a series of paintings based on and inspired by Balzac's novel *Eugénie Grandet*.

Bibliography:

Livingstone, Marco, *Stephen Farthing: Mute Accomplices*, exhibition catalogue, Modern Art Oxford, 1987. Bonaventura, P., *'Falsifying the Log'* in *Modern Painters*, vol 7, no. 4, 1994. *Stephen Farthing: Absolute Monarchy*, exhibition catalogue, Anne Berthoud, London, 1996. Farthing, Stephen, *The Intelligent Person's Guide to Modern Art*, London, 2000.

Museums and Galleries:

London (National Portrait Gal.): *Historians of 'Past and Present'* (1999) - London (UK Government Art Collection): *Museum No. 12* (1988); *Writing About* (1984).

FARTUSSOV, Victor Dormidontovich

Russian, 19th century.
Painter.

Fartussov was a pupil at the Moscow school of fine arts, then the St Petersburg academy, where he won several diplomas. In 1869 and 1874, his work appeared at the academy exhibitions, mostly in the form of religious paintings, among which can be cited a *Virgin* and a *Holy Spirit Descending to the Apostles*, for the church of St Sophia in Moscow.

FARUFFINI, Federico

Italian, 19th century.
Born 1831, in Sesto San Giovanni near Milan; died 1869, in Perugia.
Painter, watercolourist. Religious subjects, allegorical subjects, portraits, genre scenes.

Faruffini studied in Pavia, Venice, Milan and Rome. He was friends with Giovanni Carnovali and was a fellow pupil of Tranquillo Cremona.

He produced altar paintings and historical pictures that were original in their design, notably the *Prayer of St Dominic* for the charterhouse in Pavia, and *Titian's Gondola*. His painting of *Machiavelli and Borgia*, which he later reproduced as an engraving, was enormously successful. He won a medal in 1866.

Museums and Galleries:

Milan (Gal. d'Arte Moderna): *Sordello*; *Titian's Gondola* - Pavia (Musei Civici del Castello Visconteo, Pinacoteca Malaspina): *Machiavelli and Borgia* - Rome (Gal. Nazionale): *Sacrifice on the Nile*.

Auction records:

Milan, 17 Oct 1972, *Boys on a Roof*, ITL 2,800,000. Milan, 21 April 1984, *The Poison of the Borgias* (oil on canvas, 9 1/2 x 12 3/4 ins / 24 x 32.5 cm) ITL 5,000,000. Milan, 18 Dec 1986, *Idyll in Venice* (oil on canvas, 31 1/4 x 57 3/4 ins / 79.3 x 147 cm) ITL 27,000,000. Rome, 25 April 1988, *The Dwarf of Philip II* (oil on panel, 6 1/4 x 9 1/2 ins / 16 x 24 cm) ITL 3,000,000. Rome, 14 Dec 1989, *Page* (watercolour, 12 x 8 1/4 ins / 30.7 x 20.7 cm) ITL 3,680,000. Milan, 8 March 1990, *Female Figure Dressed in Green* (oil on canvas, 13 3/4 x 10 ins / 35 x 24.5 cm) ITL 12,000,000. Rome, 11 Dec 1990, *Page Playing the Lute* (1856, oil on card/canvas, 13 1/2 x 9 1/4 ins / 34.5 x 23.5 cm) ITL 7,475,000. Rome, 13 Dec 1995, *Oriental Costume* (oil on canvas, 14 1/4 x 10 3/4 ins / 36.5 x 27.5 cm) ITL 34,500,000. Rome, 25 May 1999, *Elegant Company in a Gondola* (1853, oil on canvas, 39 x 61 ins / 100 x 155 cm) ITL 20,000,000. Rome, 23 May 2000, *Rivals in Love in Venice* (oil on canvas, 15 x 12 ins / 38 x 30 cm) ITL 26,000,000. Milan, 22 May 2001, *Roman Farmer with Jug. Roman Farmer Standing. Roman Farmer Sitting* (watercolour, three, 13 x 9 ins / 32 x 22 cm) ITL 7,500,000.

FARVEZE, François

French, 20th century.
Born 19 February 1912, in Esperaza (Aude).
Painter, sculptor. Designs for tapestries.

Farveze was a pupil of Gleizes. He lived in Africa for many years, exhibiting there from 1951, before leaving in 1959. He later returned to Paris for two years, before settling in the South of France. He worked with architects, creating sculptures and tapestries.

FARZAT, Sakher Abdulrahman

Syrian, 20th century.
Born 6 January 1943, in Syria.
Also active in France.
Painter.

Sakher Farzat obtained a diploma from the faculty of fine arts in Damascus in 1965. He was a founder member both of the fine arts association in Damascus, and of the association of Arab artists. In 1976, he travelled to Brazil on a scholarship.

Farzat took part in most official exhibitions of Syrian art from 1961 onwards. He was regularly commissioned to decorate several halls of the International Trade Fair in Damascus. Farzat participated in many collective exhibitions: Syria in 1961, 1972, and 1975, the 1971 Biennale in Alexandria, the 1975 São Paulo Biennale, the exhibition of the Arab League in Cyprus in 1972, the Arab biennale in Kuwait in 1973 and 1975, official exhibitions of Syrian artists (1975-1977), the exhibition of Syrian art in 1976, the exhibition of contemporary Arab art held at the Espace Cardin in Paris (1978) and regular contributions to the Salon de Réalités Nouvelles. He also mounted solo exhibitions: in 1972, 1973 and 1974 at the Umina gallery (Damascus), at the Carlton gallery in Beirut in 1974, a retrospective exhibition in Syria in 1978, and in Paris in 1987. Farzat paints by using small touches of ochre, yellow and brown. By playing with light and the simulation of movement, the artist seems to deconstruct and then put together again forms that are made up of graphic motifs, as if resembling a prism and almost giving them a 'readable' quality.

Museums and Galleries:

Al-Dawha (Mus. Nat. de L'État) - Damascus (Coll. of the Foreign Ministry) - Damascus (Coll. of the Ministry of Culture) - Paris (Collection of the Ministry of Culture) - Tunis (MAM).

FASANINO, Emile Dominique

Swiss, 19th - 20th century.
Born 10 July 1851, in Sostogno (Piedmont); died 15 January 1910, in Geneva.

Sculptor, stucco artist.

Emile Fasanino studied at the school of arts and trades in Geneva and, after a study trip to France and Italy, he settled in Geneva, where he carried out decorative works for various buildings, both in Lausanne and in Bern.

Museums and Galleries:

Geneva (Conservatoire des Arts et Métiers): several models of sculptures.

FASANO, Antonio

Italian, 16th century.

Of Mantuan origin.

Sculptor.

In 1563, Antonio Fasano sculpted the marble sculptures of the Fountain of Neptune designed by Tomaso Laureti.

FASANO, Clara

Italian, 20th century.

Born 1900, in Castellaneta; died 1990, in America.

Sculptor. Portraits. Busts, monuments.

Clara Fasano went with her family from Italy to the USA when she was three years old. She studied at the Cooper Union Art School, the Art Students League, New York, in Rome with Professor Arturo Dazzi, and in Paris at the Académie Julian and the Académie Colarossi. She taught sculpture in various educational institutions in New York, including the School of Industrial and Fine Arts and the Manhattanville College of the Sacred Heart.

She sculpted portrait busts of personalities such as Tito Schipa (tenor at the Metropolitan Opera), Luigi Pirandello, and General Battley, and made sculptures for administrative and educational establishments (the Post Office of Middleport, Ohio, Richmond High School, Staten Island, the Brooklyn Technical High School, New York, etc.).

Fasano took part in many group exhibitions, including: the Rome Biennale, the Salon d'Automne, Paris, exhibitions in various museums in the USA such as The Whitney Museum of Art and the Metropolitan Museum of Art, New York, the Pennsylvania Academy of Fine Arts and the Art Alliance, Philadelphia, the Art Institute of Chicago and the Cleveland Museum. She also held solo shows outside the USA.

Bibliography:

Schnier, Jacques, *Sculpture in Modern America*, University of California Press, Berkeley, 1948. Brummé, C. Ludwig, *Contemporary American Sculpture*, Crown Publishers, New York, 1948. Soria, Regina, *American Artists of Italian Heritage 1776-1945: A Biographical Dictionary*, Fairleigh Dickinson University Press, Associated University Presses, London and Toronto, 1993.

Museums and Galleries:

New York (Metropolitan Mus. of Art) - Norfolk (Khouri Memorial Collection) - Purchase (Manhattanville College) - Washington DC (Smithsonian American AM): *Penelope* (terracotta/wood base).

FASANO, Lorenzo

Italian, 18th century.

Active in Naples.

Painter.

In 1728, Lorenzo Fasano became a member of the artists' guild.

FASANO, Michelangelo

Italian, 18th century.

Active in Naples.

Painter.

Michelangelo Fasano worked together with Bonito and Langlois from 1758 to 1760 on a tapestry project portraying the life of Don Quixote.

FASANO, Tommaso, called l'Abate Fasano

Italian, 18th century.

Died c. 1716.

Painter. History painting.

He was a pupil of Luca Giordano.

FASANOTTI, Gaetano

Italian, 19th century.

Born 1831, in Milan; died 7 February 1882, in Milan.

Painter, watercolourist. Historical subjects, landscapes, seascapes.

Gaetano Fasanotti was a pupil of G. Renica, and taught at the Accademia di Brera in Milan. He exhibited in Milan from 1850. His most frequently mentioned works are *Molino* and his Lake Como landscapes.

Museums and Galleries:

Milan (Mus. Poldi Pezzoli): *Landscape* (watercolour).

Auction records:

Milan, 28 Oct 1976, *Falconer* (1879, oil on canvas, 17 1/2 x 29 1/2 ins / 44.5 x 75 cm) ITL 900,000. New York, 30 Sept 1982, *Fisherman in a Riverscape* (1893, watercolour and pencil, 12 1/2 x 19 3/4 ins / 31.8 x 50.1 cm) USD 1,100. Milan, 21 April 1984, *Seascape* (oil on canvas, 15 1/2 x 25 3/4 ins / 39.5 x 65.5 cm) ITL 2,000,000. Milan, 4 June 1985, *Episode from the War of 1859* (watercolour, 3 x 9 ins / 7.8 x 23 cm) ITL 650,000. Milan, 10 Dec 1987, *View of Belgirate* (1882, oil on canvas, 16 1/4 x 34 ins / 41 x 85.5 cm) ITL 8,000,000. London, 29 April 1988, *Alpine Landscape* (9 3/4 x 14 1/2 ins / 25 x 37 cm) GBP 1210. Milan, 14 March 1989, *Fishermen's Huts on the Edge of the Lake* (oil on canvas, 18 x 29 1/4 ins / 46 x 74.5 cm) ITL 7,000,000. London, 22 June 1990, *The Gulf of Palermo* (oil on canvas, 39 1/2 x 56 ins / 100.5 x 142.2 cm) GBP 12,650. Rome, 11 Dec 1990, *Landscape* (oil on canvas, 9 x 18 1/2 ins / 22 x 47 cm) ITL 2,990,000. Milan, 6 June 1991, *Returning from the Fields* (1876, oil on canvas, 15 1/2 x 26 1/4 ins / 39.5 x 66.5 cm) ITL 5,200,000. Milan, 19 March 1992, *Volla in Brianza* (oil on card, 10 x 14 3/4 ins / 24.5 x 37.5 cm) ITL 5,000,000. Milan, 29 Oct 1992, *Lombardy Landscape* (1876, oil on canvas, 15 1/2 x 26 1/4 ins / 39.5 x 66.5 cm) ITL 11,500,000. Milan, 19 Dec 1995, *Fishermen on a Lake in Lombardy* (oil on canvas, 15 1/4 x 23 1/2 ins / 38.5 x 59.5 cm) ITL 10,350,000. Milan, 16 June 1999, *Peasants in a Landscape* (1878, oil on canvas, 11 x 17 ins / 29 x 42 cm) ITL 6,000,000. Ahlden, 28 Sept 2001, *Arrival of the Fishing Boat* (1874, oil on canvas, 36 x 65 ins / 92 x 165 cm) DEM 32,000. Rome, 5 June 2002, *Figures, with Vesuvius beyond* (oil on canvas, 17 x 14 ins / 44 x 35 cm) EUR 4,400. Turin, 26 June 2003, *Seascape* (1874, oil on canvas, 17 x 29 ins / 44 x 73 cm) EUR 7,000. Bern, 5 Nov 2003, *Coast* (1874, oil on canvas, 13 x 20 ins / 32 x 51 cm) CHF 3,300.

FASCE, Gianfranco

Italian, 20th century.

Born 1927, in Genoa.

Painter, sculptor.

Fasce studied at the art school and the Accademia in Genoa. He has been exhibiting since 1947, most notably at the Venice Biennale, in 1958 and 1962, and the Rome Quadriennale in 1959. In 1950, he won a prize for painting in Genoa, and a sculpture prize in Rome. In 1953, he joined the Genoan Concretist group. Later his art evolved towards a more informal, lyrical style.

Auction records:

Milan, 18 June 1987, *Landscape* (1956, oil on canvas, 19 3/4 x 28 3/4 ins / 50 x 73 cm) ITL 1,600,000. Milan, 1 Dec 1987, *Landscape* (1954, gouache, 13 3/4 x 18 3/4 ins / 35 x 47.5 cm) ITL 600,000. Milan, 24 March 1988, *Town* (oil on canvas, 13 x 22 ins / 33 x 55 cm) ITL 1,700,000. Vercelli, 29 April 2000, *Composition* (1956, oil on canvas, 24 x 18 ins / 60 x 46 cm) ITL 3,600,000. Vercelli, 21 April 2001, *Colours* (1972, oil on canvas, 38 x 29 ins / 97 x 73 cm) ITL 3,900,000.

FASCH, Johann Ludwig

Swiss, 18th century.

Born c. 1750, in Basel; died 1778, in Paris.

Miniaturist, watercolourist.

Fasch worked in Basel, Paris and England. He was particularly skilled at painting miniature watercolour medallion portraits on parchment. In Paris, he produced many portraits of famous actresses.

FASCINA, Ignazio. See **FASSINA**

FASEL, Georg Wilhelm
German, 19th century.
Active in Karlsruhe.
Painter. History painting.

Fasel exhibited in Vienna in 1836. His best-known works include his *Holy Family*, *Apotheosis of Goethe*, *Young Roman* and *Wallenstein*.

FASI-GESSNER, Johann Konrad
Swiss, 19th century.
Born 1796, in Zurich; died 1870, in Zurich.
Draughtsman, painter. Flowers.

Probably a descendant of the Gessner family of Zurich, Fasi-Gessner exhibited in Zurich from 1811. An amateur artist, he painted portraits, genre scenes and flower paintings. J. Brodtmann made engravings of many of his portraits, most of which were drawn in pencil.

FASINI, Aleksandr, Alexander Fainsilberg or Saul Finesilber
Ukrainian, 20th century.
Born 1892, in Kiev; sent to Auschwitz in 1942.
Active in France from 1922.
Painter.

Aleksandr Fasini studied at the academy of fine art in Odessa with the Impressionist painter Kiriac Kostandi and settled in Paris in 1922. His painting was particularly influenced by a desire for new experiences and earned him a special place among the painters of the Paris School. His figures are set in strange places, recalling the atmosphere of Surrealist painting. He exhibited at the Salon d'Automne (1926) and Salon des Indépendants (1927) and was invited that same year to the Salon des Tuileries. He was also a photographer and his snapshots were displayed at the Exposition Internationale in Paris in 1937. For two years he exhibited at the Galerie Vavin alongside Picasso, Lurçat and Papazoff.

BIBLIOGRAPHY:

Nieszawer, Nadine/Boyé, Marie/Lanzmann, Claude (preface), *Peintres juifs de lécole de Paris 1905-1939*, Denoël, Paris, 2001.

AUCTION RECORDS:

PARIS, 19 Nov 1932, *Still-life*, FRF 85. PARIS, 5 Nov 1937, *Houses and Tunnel*, FRF 150. PARIS, 27 Feb 1976, *Abstract Composition* (1929, oil on canvas, 13 x 22 ins / 33 x 55 cm) FRF 1,450. VERSAILLES, 5 Oct 1980, *Composition* (1930, oil on canvas, 21 x 28¾ ins / 53.5 x 73 cm) FRF 3,000. ZURICH, 13 May 1984, *Entrance to the Park* (oil on canvas, 22 x 18 ins / 55 x 46 cm) CHF 3,600. PARIS, 28 June 1985, *Figures* (two oil paintings on canvas, 18 x 22 ins / 46 x 55 cm and 18 x 24 ins/46 x 61 cm) FRF 8,500. VERSAILLES, 17 April 1988, *Entrance to the Park* (oil on canvas, 18 x 22 ins / 46 x 55 cm) FRF 2,000. PARIS, 4 July 1991, *Man Near a Boat* (1934, oil on canvas, 14¾ x 18 ins / 37.5 x 45.5 cm) FRF 7,800. PARIS, 17 May 1992, *On the Bridge of a Boat* (c. 1920, oil on canvas, 15 x 18 ins / 38 x 46 cm) FRF 7,000. PARIS, 27 June 1994, *Composition* (1929, oil on canvas, 18 x 22 ins / 46 x 55 cm) FRF 7,500; *Figures* (1930, oil on canvas, 21¼ x 28¾ ins / 54 x 73 cm) FRF 19,000. PARIS, 20 Dec 1995, *Figure and Boat* (oil on canvas, 25½ x 36¼ ins / 65 x 92 cm) FRF 22,000. PARIS, 19 June 1996, *Composition No. 3* (1929, oil on canvas, 23½ x 36¼ ins / 60 x 92 cm) FRF 22,000. PARIS, 23 June 1997, *Architects* (1930, oil on canvas, 13 x 22 ins / 33 x 55 cm) FRF 20,000. AMSTERDAM, 12 June 2001, *Two Men Standing* (1929, oil on canvas, 36 x 26 ins / 92 x 65 cm) NLG 6,000. VERSAILLES, 7 April 2002, *Painter* (1929, oil on canvas, 36 x 25 ins / 92 x 64 cm) EUR 3,300. PARIS, 16 April 2002, *Women in an Interior* (1930, oil on canvas, 13 x 18 ins / 33 x 46 cm) EUR 4,690.

FASMER, Dankert Peters
Danish, 18th century.
Sculptor.

Dankert Peters Fasmer is mentioned as having executed a marble bust of King Frederick V of Denmark in 1763.

FASOLA, C.
19th - 20th century.
Painter. Urban landscapes, winter landscapes.

AUCTION RECORDS:

PARIS, 18 March 1929, *Milan Cathedral; A Street in Milan in the Snow* (two canvases) FRF 240; *The Adige in Verona, a Night Piece*, FRF 140.

FASOLATO, Agostino
Italian, 18th century.
Active in Padua.
Sculptor.

Agostino Fasolato worked in 1753 on a series of low reliefs for the choir stalls in the church of S Antonio. He also sculpted *Fall of the Angels* for the Palazzo Papafava, a group of 60 statues hewn from a single block of marble.

FASOLATO, Giovanni
Italian, 18th century.
Died 6 May 1729, in Padua.
Sculptor.

Giovanni Fasolato lived and worked in Rovigo, and sculpted the marble main altar for the church of S Antonio, together with a tabernacle and two statues of angels. He was also responsible for the altar depicting St Anthony in the church of S Francesco, with its four columns of red Verona marble.

FASOLD
German, 18th century.
Born to a family originally from Saalfeld.
Painter.

Around 1775, Fasold painted scenes from *The Apocalypse* and *Jacob's Dream* on the ceiling of the nave in the church of Graba, near Saalfeld.

FASOLD, Johann
German, 17th century.
Born to a family originally from Radeberg; died c. 1620, in Dresden.
Painter.

Johann Fasold worked for the electors of Saxony, Christian II and Johann Georg I, and was appointed painter to the court. He is best known for his portraits of Johann Georg and of his wife. Some of his works are to be found in Dresden, including his pulpit paintings in the church of St Sophie.

FASOLO, Bernardino, or Fazoli
Italian, 16th century.
Active in Pavia in 1518.
Painter. History painting, portraits.

In 1520, Bernardino Fasolo was a member of the board of the guild of Genoa. He was taught by his father Lorenzo Fasolo and Leonardo da Vinci, and specialised in mythological subjects. He was the brother of Raffaelo Fasolo.

MUSEUMS AND GALLERIES:

BERLIN: *The Holy Family* - FONTAINEBLEAU: *The Virgin and Christ Child* (1518, signed) - PARIS (Louvre): *The Virgin and Child*.

FASOLO, Giovanni Antonio
Italian, 16th century.
Born c. 1530, in Vicenza; died 1572, in Vicenza.

Painter, fresco artist. Historical subjects, religious subjects, portraits. Murals, theatre decoration.

After studying with Battista Zelotti, Giovanni Antonio Fasolo was attracted by the reputation of Paolo Veronese and entered his studio. He gained success as a historical painter. His paintings *Mucius Scaevola before Porsenna, Horatius Defending the Bridge* and *Marcus Curtius* are in the prefecture of Padri Servi. A fine *Epiphany* is in the church of the same town.

Fasolo collaborated with Paolo Veronese on the ceiling of the church of S Sebastiano in Venice, and carried out the decoration of a number of constructions by A. Palladio at Vicenza, including the Theatro Olimpico (Olympic Theatre) (1552-1562). His frescoes for the Porto-Colleoni at Thiene (1552) are also noteworthy.

BIBLIOGRAPHY:

Zorzi, G., '*Giovanni Antonio Fasolo pittore lombardo-veneto emulo di Paolo Veronese*' in *Arte Lombarda*, vol 6, 1961.

MUSEUMS AND GALLERIES:

DRESDEN: *Portrait of Venetian Lady* - VENICE (Gal. dell'Accademia): *Fish Pond* - VICENZA (Pinacoteca): *The Vigin and Child with St Rose.*

AUCTION RECORDS:

LONDON, 5 July 1991, *Young Girl Adoring Christ on the Virgin's Lap with Landscape in Background* (oil on canvas, 38 x 32 1/2 ins / 96.5 x 82.5 cm) GBP 29,700.

FASOLO, Lorenzo da Pavia, or Fazoli

Italian, 15th - 16th century.

Born 1463, in Pavia; died 1518, in Genoa.

Painter.

Lorenzo da Pavia Fasolo went to Genoa early in his career where he was among the artists employed by Ludovico Sforza to decorate the Palazzo Porta Giovia in Milan. In 1502 he collaborated on the frescoes in the Duomo di S Lorenzo at Genoa and the Chiesa del Carmine (church of Mount Carmel). The following year he painted the altarpiece of *St Sebastian* and *St Roch* for the church at Viarreggio and the *Life of Christ* (now in the Louvre) for the church of S Giacomo. His *The Family of the Virgin*, dated 1513, is also in the Louvre, but his masterpiece, a *Descent from the Cross*, dated 1508, is in the convent of Chiavari.

AUCTION RECORDS:

PARIS, 25 March 1965, *The Nativity*, FRF 9,000.

FASOLO, Pietro, or Fasoli

Italian, 15th century.

Active in Reggio Emilia.

Painter.

FASOLO, Raffaelo, or Fazoli or Fasoli

Italian, 16th century.

Active in Pavia.

Painter.

Raffaelo Fasolo was the brother of Bernardino Fasolo. He made a door for a shrine for a chapel of the church of S Agostino.

FASONI, Anthoni

German, 16th century.

Active in Nuremberg (Bavaria) from 1538 to 1555.

Sculptor.

FASQUET, Marguerite Claude

French, 18th century.

Active in Paris in 1753.

Painter, sculptor.

FASSAUER, Johann Adam

French, 19th century.

Painter, engraver. Genre scenes, animals.

Johann Adam Fassauer was probably the son of the Leipzig painter J. A. Fassauer. He painted in the 17th-century Dutch style, his preferred subjects being poultry, groups of chickens, ducks, turkeys, and also horned animals and sheep. He also painted humorous scenes peopled with beggars and peasants.

AUCTION RECORDS:

PARIS, 14 Jan 1902, *Roosters*, FRF 200.

FASSBENDER, Joseph

German, 20th century.

Born 1903, in Cologne; died 1974.

Painter. Designs for tapestries, murals.

Joseph Fassbender studied painting only from 1926 to 1929, in Richard Seewald's studio at the school of fine arts in Cologne. He made study trips to Italy and Munich. Under the Nazi regime his paintings were confiscated. After having being mobilised and taken prisoner during World War II, he became one of the founders of the Thursday Meetings in Bornheim near Bonn, where the German artists were resuming their place in contemporary movements. In 1949, he was also one of the founders of the Zen group. He had been made a professor at the school of fine arts in Hamburg, and in 1955 he was made director of the graphic arts department at the school of fine arts in Krefeld. From 1958, he taught at the academy in Düsseldorf. He took part in exhibitions of German art, and was represented at *Documenta I* in Kassel in 1955. Some of his works appeared at the exhibition of *Non-Figurative German Art* in 1955 at the Volney circle in Paris. He received the Villa Romana prize in 1929; the main arts prize of Cologne in 1957; the main arts prize of North Rhine-Westphalia and the second Marzotto prize in 1960. He produced paintings and large-scale tapestries, in particular in Cologne.

His painting belongs in the category of abstract landscape art and makes allusive borrowings from external reality, using a rich spectrum of colours in sombre and deep tones. He likes to give his paintings titles with a poetic humour that intentionally evokes those of Paul Klee. His vast mural painting of *The Signs of the Zodiac* (1954) for the Ernst Moritz Arndt secondary school in Bonn, is a good illustration of his works as a whole.

BIBLIOGRAPHY:

Josef Fassbender, Stedelijk Museum, Amsterdam, 1961.

MUSEUMS AND GALLERIES:

AMSTERDAM (Stedelijk Mus.).

AUCTION RECORDS:

COLOGNE, 17 May 1980, *Robinson Crusoe's Adventure* (1947, monotype and watercolour, 16 1/2 x 22 ins / 42 x 55.8 cm) DEM 1,600. COLOGNE, 4 June 1983, *Stone* (1953, mixed media, 25 1/2 x 35 1/2 ins / 65 x 90 cm) DEM 3,200. COLOGNE, 6 Dec 1984, *Black on Ochre* (1954, oil on card, 26 1/2 x 37 3/4 ins / 67 x 96 cm) DEM 3,200. COLOGNE, 29 May 1987, *Serious Cake* (1953, tempera/paper, 25 1/2 x 38 1/4 ins / 65 x 97 cm) DEM 5,400. LONDON, 30 June 1988, *Yellow Portrait* (1957, oil on paper, 24 x 34 ins / 61 x 86.5 cm) GBP 4,400. COLOGNE, 28 April 1999, *Still-life with Corn on Cob, Picture Book* (1947, oil on canvas, 30 x 47 ins / 75 x 119 cm) DEM 12,000. COLOGNE, 2 June 2001, *Untitled* (1957, oil on paper/masonite, 24 x 36 ins / 61 x 92 cm) DEM 4,800. COLOGNE, 3 Dec 2002, *Composition II* (1949, oil on canvas, 35 x 53 ins / 90 x 135 cm) EUR 4,000. COLOGNE, 26 Nov 2003, *Old City of Cologne* (oil on canvas, 40 x 35 ins / 102 x 90 cm) EUR 15,000. DÜSSELDORF, 25 Sept 2004, *For Sellers of the Moon I* (oil on canvas, 79 x 55 ins / 200 x 140 cm) EUR 5,500.

FASSBENDER, P. J.

German, 19th century.

Active in Cologne.

Lithographer.

A pupil of Levy Elkan, Fassbender is known to have made a plate after E. Bourel: *Doors of the Main Entrance to St Mary in the Capitol of Cologne.*

FASSBIND, Anton
Swiss, 18th century.
Active in Schwyz c. the end of the 18th century.
Engraver (copper).
An engraving by Fassbind, *Gessler and Werner Stauffacher*, appeared in Lucerne in 1790.

FASSBINDER, Andreas
German, 18th century.
Born in Duisdorf, near Bonn; died 7 September 1713, in Munich.
Sculptor.
After studying in Duisdorf and travelling throughout Germany, Andreas Fassbinder settled in Munich, where he was admitted as a burgher and as master of the guild in 1697. His works include *Christ Bidding Farewell to Mary*, a *Crucifixion*, an *Ecce Homo* and *Christ Falling under the Cross*, together with various decorative ornaments, such as capitals, foliage and angels' heads.
MUSEUMS AND GALLERIES:
MUNICH.

FASSBINDER, Wilhelm
German, 19th century.
Born 20 April 1858, in Cologne.
Sculptor.
Wilhelm Fassbinder first studied in Cologne with his father-in-law, the sculptor J. Nothen. His many works are to be found in the public spaces and cemeteries of the Rhineland, but particularly in Cologne. He is best known for his monuments to the dead at Euskirchen, Bernkastel and Arzfeld; the monuments to Emperor William I at Altenkirchen and Heinsberg; the William II fountains in Dortmund and Daun; and the Bismarck fountain in Dortmund-Dorstfeld. Cologne has his bust of Mayor Becker and the gravestone of Prof Bardenheuer, and his monument to the actor L. Teller can be found in Meiningen.

FASSETT, C. Adele (Mrs), or Adeline
American, 19th century.
Born 1831, in Owasko (New York); died 4 January 1898, in Washington DC.
Painter. History painting, portraits.
After studying watercolour painting in New York with J.B. Wandesforde, C. Adèle Fassett went to Paris to work with Castiglione, La Tour and Matthieu. She spent two years there and in Rome. In about 1855 she settled in Chicago, where she worked for 20 years. In 1875 she went to Washington DC, and painted a large number of official portraits. She took part in the decoration of the Capitol and painted a large work, *The Electoral Committee*, which included more than 200 life-size figures. She also painted a portrait of President Garfield.

FASSETT, Truman Edmund
American, 20th century.
Born 9 May 1885, in Elmira (New York State).
Painter.
Truman Edmund Fassett was a pupil of the Boston School, Richard Miller and L. Simon. He became a member of the Salmagundi Club.
AUCTION RECORDS:
NEW YORK, 26 April 1988, *Spanish Dancer* (oil on canvas, 41 1/4 x 32 ins / 105 x 81.3 cm) USD 14,300.

FASSETTI, Giovanni Battista
Italian, 18th century.
Born 1686, in Reggio; died after 1772.
Painter.
Apprenticed initially as a colour-grinder in Giuseppe Dallamano's studio, Giovanni Fassetti started painting at the age of 18 (or, according to Siret, 28). He subsequently studied under Francesco Bibiena and emerged as one of the best decorative artists of his day.

FASSHAMB
Czech, 18th century.
Sculptor.
Fasshamb is recorded as having produced sculptures in Telc in Moravia.

FASSIANOS, Alexander or Aleco
Greek, 20th century.
Born 1935, in Athens.
Active in France from 1962.
Painter (including gouache), pastellist, engraver, lithographer, illustrator. Scenes with figures, figures, nudes, still-lifes. Stage sets.
Alexander Fassianos was a pupil of Moralis at the school of fine art in Athens from 1954 to 1960 and absorbed ancient culture through frequent visits to the National Museum. He received a grant from a French institution enabling him to learn lithography at the École des Beaux-Arts in Paris. He settled in Paris in 1962 and has since produced several sets for the Festival at Epidaurus.

His style is very individual, a rich, firm style that underlines contours with pure colours (blue, red and yellow). His modern interpretations of Ulysses and Calypso recreate a familiar mythology, showing them on bikes with cigarettes and hair flying in the wind; Greek soul and memory are recaptured in the folklore of modernity, amid the light of the Athens streets and the freedom of life of the Mediterranean people.

Lying beyond trends and fashions in art, Fassianos' painting portrays atmosphere of tender poetry and a very engaging vision of things and people. As in antique vases, he paints silhouettes on plain backgrounds, often in terracotta red, on which subtle effects of white and silver play, set off here and there with a bright stroke. He often reverses the process: black figures stand out against light backgrounds, his economic, firm stroke adding the occasional detail.

He exhibited in Paris (regularly especially at the Fachetti and Iolas galeries) as well as in Athens, Tokyo, Milan, Stockholm, London, São Paulo Biennale (1971) and Venice Biennale (1972). The Château de Chenonceau held a retrospective of his work in 1985. The city of Athens plans to devote a museum to him.
BIBLIOGRAPHY:
'*Aleco Fassianos*' in *Art et Métiers du Livre* n° 191 p. 56-57, periodical, Paris, 1995. Analis, Dimitri T./Cabanne, Pierre, *Fassianos*, La Différence, Paris, 2003.
AUCTION RECORDS:
PARIS, 9 June 1976, *Figure* (1970, oil on canvas, 16 1/4 x 13 ins / 41 x 33 cm) FRF 3,500. PARIS, 31 May 1978, *Figures* (1969, oil on canvas, 70 3/4 x 35 1/2 ins / 180 x 90 cm) FRF 7,000. PARIS, 23 Oct 1981, *Two Figures* (oil on canvas, 31 1/2 x 23 1/2 ins / 80 x 60 cm) FRF 4,000. PARIS, 23 May 1984, *Man and the City* (1969, oil on canvas, 85 3/4 x 47 1/4 ins / 218 x 120 cm) FRF 27,000. PARIS, 17 April 1985, *Cyclists* (1972, gouache, 25 1/2 x 20 1/4 ins / 65 x 51.5 cm) FRF 4,000. PARIS, 9 Dec 1985, *Apollo* (1968, gold leaf/canvas, 59 x 59 ins / 150 x 150 cm) FRF 41,000. PARIS, 8 Feb 1988, *Meeting* (mixed paint /panel, 16 1/2 x 33 3/4 ins / 42 x 86 cm) FRF 10,800. PARIS, 20 March 1988, *Upside Down Glass* (1985, gouache/paper/canvas, 57 1/2 x 38 1/4 ins / 146 x 97 cm) FRF 35,000. PARIS, 23 March 1988, *Bath* (oil on canvas, 51 1/4 x 46 3/4 ins / 130 x 119 cm) FRF 20,000. PARIS, 11 April 1988, *After the Rain* (gouache/canvas, 13 3/4 x 8 1/4 ins / 35 x 21 cm) FRF 5,500. PARIS, 5 May 1988, *Different Fruits* (1980, acrylic/canvas, 23 1/2 x 27 1/2 ins / 60 x 70 cm) FRF 11,000. PARIS, 29 Sept 1989, *Young Greek* (gouache, 35 1/2 x 24 3/4 ins / 90 x 63 cm) FRF 52,000. PARIS, 20 Nov 1989, *Young Greek with Hat* (1967, oil and gold paint/canvas, 12 1/4 x 14 1/2 ins / 31 x 37 cm) FRF 33,000. PAR-

IS, 15 Feb 1990, *The Lamp will Tell No Tale* (1972, oil and silver leaf/wood, 31 1/2 x 24 ins / 80 x 61 cm) FRF 60,000. LA VARENNE-ST-HILAIRE, 20 May 1990, *Couple* (1973, oil on canvas, 35 x 46 ins / 89 x 116 cm) FRF 70,000. PARIS, 10 Feb 1991, *The Two Red Cyclists* (1968, gouache/paper/canvas, 46 x 30 ins / 116 x 76 cm) FRF 51,000. PARIS, 16 Feb 1992, *My Home for Eternity* (1968, oil on canvas, 57 1/2 x 45 ins / 146 x 114 cm) FRF 50,000. PARIS, 15 June 1992, *Blue Cyclist* (1968, oil on canvas, 59 x 59 ins / 150 x 150 cm) FRF 105,000. PARIS, 23 June 1993, *Major Player* (1971, oil on canvas, 63 3/4 x 45 ins / 162 x 114 cm) FRF 75,000. PARIS, 7 Oct 1995, *Man in the City* (acrylic/canvas, 17 1/4 x 12 3/4 ins / 44 x 32.5 cm) FRF 19,000. PARIS, 12 Dec 1995, *Athena* (1979, oil on canvas, 47 1/4 x 47 1/4 ins / 120 x 120 cm) FRF 94,600. PARIS, 28 March 1996, *Poetic Panorama of 1975* (oil on canvas, 31 1/2 x 39 1/4 ins / 80 x 100 cm) FRF 91,000. PARIS, 13 June 1996, *My Dear Smoker* (1971, gold leaf and oil on canvas, 39 1/4 x 32 ins / 100 x 81 cm) FRF 75,000. CALAIS, 7 July 1996, *Horse Rider* (mixed media, 21 1/4 x 17 1/4 ins / 54 x 44 cm) FRF 15,000. PARIS, 30 Sept 1996, *Blue Nude with Scarf and Dove* (pencil/paper); *Smoker with Palm* (pastel and pencil/paper, 25 1/4 x 19 1/4 ins / 64 x 49 cm) FRF 19,000. PARIS, 16 Dec 1996, *Man on Bicycle* (gouache/paper, 14 1/2 x 11 1/2 ins / 37 x 29 cm) FRF 9,000; *Couple* (1977, oil on canvas, 43 1/4 x 61 ins / 110 x 154 cm) FRF 74,000. PARIS, 28 April 1997, *Figures with Birds* (oil on canvas, 23 x 17 1/4 ins / 58.5 x 44 cm) FRF 26,000. PARIS, 5 Dec 1997, *Smoker* (gouache and collage of gold leaf, 30 x 22 1/2 ins / 76 x 57 cm) FRF 15,500.

FASSIN, Adolphe Ferdinand
Belgian, 19th century.
Born 14 July 1828, in Seny, near Liège; died 1900, near Brussels.
Sculptor.

Adolphe Ferdinand Fassin took part in the exhibition in Philadelphia in 1876 where he obtained a medal.

FASSIN, Nicolas Henri Joseph de
Flemish, 18th - 19th century.
Born 1728, in Liège; died 1811, in Liège.
Painter. Landscapes with figures, animals.
Flemish School.

After having served in the French army, Nicolas Henri Joseph de Fassin devoted himself to painting at the age of 34. He attended the academy in Antwerp. He travelled in Italy and Switzerland and spent a long time in Geneva. After working for the Emperor of Russia he settled in his native town.

MUSEUMS AND GALLERIES:
BUDAPEST: *Shepherds* - GENEVA: *Landscape and Animals* - LIÈGE: *Landscape with Livestock*.

AUCTION RECORDS:
PARIS, 17 Feb 1928, *Crossing the Ford*, FRF 2,150. AMSTERDAM, 30 Nov 1981, *Shepherdess and Flock in a Landscape* (oil on canvas, 33 x 43 3/4 ins / 84 x 111 cm) NLG 10,000. LONDON, 9 Dec 1994, *Italian Landscape with Peasants Resting near Classical Ruins* (oil on canvas, 39 x 52 3/4 ins / 98.2 x 134.2 cm) GBP 19,550.

FASSIN, Victor Charles Alexandre
Belgian, 19th century.
Born 1826, in Liège; died 1906, in Liège.
Painter. History painting.

The museum in Liège holds *The Good Samaritan* by Victor Charles Alexandre Fassin.

FASSINA, Ignazio, or Fascina
Italian, 18th century.
Died c. 1767.
Active in Carmagnola.
Painter.

Ignazio Fassina was a member of the congregation of the Philippine fathers. He painted a *Trinity* and other altarpieces for the church of that order in Carmagnola, together with a *St Anne* for the church of Mondovi.

FASSLER, Johann
Austrian, 17th century.
Painter.

Fassler became a burgher of Vienna in 1724.

FASSNACHT, Joseph
German, 19th - 20th century.
Born 11 June 1873, in Mittelstreu.
Sculptor. Religious subjects, allegorical subjects.

After working in Würzburg with a wood sculptor, Fassnacht studied at the academy in Munich, where he was a student of Eberle and Schmidt. He received the Prix de Rome, with a travel scholarship for Italy. He then settled in Munich.

His renowned works include: *Maternal Happiness - St Barbara*, the patron saint of artillerymen, a bust of *Prince Leopold of Bavaria*, the monuments to the dead at Altmannstein and Heidenheim, the group of the *Crucifixion* at the church of St Elizabeth in Nuremberg, a statue of a woman, *Blossoming*, a *Young Bacchus* (both these statues are in marble) - *Young Sparrowhawk* (bronze), *Mother of the Saviour* and *Behold the Lamb of God*.

FASSNAUER
Austrian, 17th century.
Active in Vienna.
Painter, engraver, engineer.

FASTO, Cristofaro
Italian, 15th century.
Active in Naples.
Painter.

Cristofaro Fasto may be identical with Cristofaro Fusco, who is mentioned in 1487 in connection with a drawing: *Granada and the Siege of Malaga*.

FASTOVITCH, Vladimir de
Russian, 20th century.
Born in Theodosia.
Painter. Genre scenes.

Vladimir Fastovich exhibited in Paris at the Salon des Indépendants from 1937 to 1939.

FASUOLO, Giovanni Antonio. See **FASOLO**

FATATTI, Antonio
Italian, 17th century.
Born c. 1640, in Rome.
Painter.

FATEEVA, Irina Anatolevna
Ukrainian, 20th century.
Born 1908, in Kiev; died 1978 or 1981.
Painter. Scenes with figures, figures.

Irina Anatolevna Fateeva was a pupil of Kuzma Petrov-Vodkin and graduated from the Russian academy of fine art in 1937. Her avant-garde experiments were interrupted in 1940 when she was imprisoned; later she practised a scholarly painting, traditional in concept, even dealing with subjects in keeping with Socialist Realism. She took part in exhibitions from the 1930s onwards both in her home country and abroad.

AUCTION RECORDS:
PARIS, 15 Dec 1989, *Donbass, the Festival* (oil on canvas, 19 1/4 x 27 1/2 ins / 49 x 70 cm) FRF 21,000. PARIS, 14 May 1990, *Preparations for the Festival* (1963, gouache/paper, 15 1/4 x 20 1/2 ins / 39 x 52 cm) FRF 6,500.

FATH, René Maurice
French, 19th - 20th century.
Born 22 November 1850, in Paris; died 1922.

Painter. Portraits, genre scenes, landscapes with figures, landscapes.

René Fath was a pupil of both Alexandre Cabanel, and Camille Bernier. He made his debut in 1870 at the Salon de Paris, and then exhibited at the Salon des Artistes Français, where he continued to show his work on a regular basis, becoming a member in 1883. He received numerous awards, including: honourable mention in 1887, honourable mention at the Exposition Universelle in 1889, Prix Raigecourt-Goyon in 1891, third-class medal in 1897, and bronze medal at the Exposition Universelle in 1900. He was made a Chevalier of the Légion d'Honneur in 1906.

His evocations of underbrush and park scenes, executed in his Maisons-Laffitte studio, show solid composition and a rich use of texture, and were immediately appreciated by the Salon public. He also executed several academic portraits and genre scenes.

Museums and Galleries:

Amiens: *The Frozen Stream; The Hallier; Mouth of a Wood* - Autun: *Underbrush in April* - Calais: *The Flowering Pool* - Draguignan: *Gorge in the Forest of Fontainebleau; The Duck Pond* - Limoges: *The Clearing* - Montpellier: *The Duck Pond; Forest in St-Germain-en-Laye; September Morning.*

Auction records:

New York, 13 May 1904, *Lake in the Forest* (oil on canvas) USD 250. Paris, 24 Nov 1922, *River Banks* (oil on canvas) FRF 210. Paris, 19 Nov 1924, *Underbrush* (oil on canvas) FRF 100. Paris, 24 Jan 1947, *Landscape* (oil on canvas) FRF 1,300. Paris, 17 Feb 1947, *The Seine in Maisons-Laffitte* (oil on canvas) FRF 250. London, 24 June 1987, *Banks of the Seine* (oil on canvas, 27 1/2 x 38 1/4 ins / 70 x 97 cm) GBP 2,600.

FATH, Richard

French, 20th century.

Born 1900, in Paris; died 1952.

Sculptor, medallist, painter, engraver. Animals.

From 1922 to 1926, Richard Fath was a pupil of Jean Boucher at the École des Beaux-Arts in Paris. He was also a friend of Paul Belmondo. He made his first real debut around 1925. He exhibited at the Salon des Artistes Français, where he received honourable mention in 1932. In 1927 and 1928 he exhibited at the Salon des Indépendants. Fath kept his distance from the trends of the time. Instead, his character drew him to painting nature and he created several thousand works, which may be found throughout the world. He was very attracted to animals, and among his works is a unique collection of more than a hundred portraits of racing dogs.

Auction records:

New York, 4 June 1993, *Two Hounds* (bronze, h. 12 ins / 30.5 cm x l. 28 ins/71.1 cm) USD 2,300. Paris, 8 Nov 1995, *Trotting* (bronze, h. 8 1/4 ins / 21 cm) FRF 12,000.

FATHWINTER, pseudonym of Winter, Franz Alfred Theophil

German, 20th century.

Born 1906, in Mainz-Castel; died 27 June 1974, in Düsseldorf.

Painter.

Fathwinter was a factory worker who taught himself to paint. From 1926 to 1928, he made journeys to Belgium, Holland and Poland. He had his first exhibition in 1931, which was immediately followed by a prohibition on his work by the Nazi regime. Having settled in Krefeld, from 1945 he took part in many exhibitions, in particular in Munich, Cologne, Hanover and Wuppertal. A bursary from the French government enabled him to spend a period in Paris, during which he featured at the Salon des Réalités Nouvelles, in 1954 and 1955, with works that had some features of classical abstraction but were nevertheless fairly free and tended towards a minimum of gestural lyricism.

Auction records:

Cologne, 27 Nov 1987, *In-formation 'Yar-the'* (1965, mixed media/panel, 27 1/2 x 39 1/4 ins / 70 x 100 cm) DEM 2,900.

FATI, pseudonym of Ipaktchi Fatemeh

Iranian, 20th - 21st century.

Born 21 November 1952.

Active in France.

Painter.

Fati studied at the school of decorative arts in Teheran and then from 1980 to 1983 at the school of fine arts in Paris, where her teacher was Yankel. She has shown her work in collective exhibitions from 1982 onwards in Paris, notably at the Salon des Indépendents (1987) Salon des Artistes Français (1988) Salon Comparaisons (1988, 1992), and the Salon d'Automne (1989). She has also had solo exhibitions in Paris. Fati applies colour in flat patches, deconstructing surfaces in the Cubist manner. Her works are like puzzles containing familiar shapes, but at the same time tending towards abstraction.

FATIGATI, Andrea

Italian, 18th century.

Born in Chiari, near Brescia.

Painter.

Andrea Fatigati painted an altarpiece of *St Jerome and the Prophet Elijah* for the church of S Girolamo in Brescia.

FATIN, Édouard

French, 17th century.

Active in Paris in 1675.

Painter.

FATIN, Jean Antoine

French, 19th century.

Born 19 September 1824, in Lyons.

Draughtsman.

A pupil at the Lyons École des Beaux-Arts between 1839 and 1842, Jean Antoine Fatin exhibited pen-and-ink landscapes (views of the city and its environs) in Lyons from 1840 to 1847-1848. He also executed gouache flower paintings.

FATIO, Antonin. See **MOREL-FATIO Antoine**

FATJO Y BARTRA, Ángel

Spanish, 19th century.

Born in Reus; died 1889, in Barcelona.

Engraver.

Ángel Fatjo y Bartra studied at the school of fine arts in Barcelona. He engraved the illustrations for a luxury edition of *Don Quixote* by Cervantes, the illustrations for a guide to the city of Barcelona, *Barcelona Old and New*, as well as numerous religious plates, including the *Virgin of Monserrat*.

FATOU, Julien

French, 18th century.

Engraver.

Julien Fatou executed an engraving in coloured stippling of the painter *Maria Cosway*, after a drawing by Richard Cosway. Cosway himself was inspired by a self-portrait of the artist.

FATOURE, Pierre, pseudonym: G. Giovanne

French, 17th century.

Died 1629, in Malta.

Active in Paris at the beginning of the 17th century.

Draughtsman, engraver.

Pierre Fatoure is said to have worked with a certain G. Giovanne, but according to Le Blanc these two artists were in fact one and the same person. He is remembered for some allegories and religious subjects.

FATRET, A.

French, 20th century.

Painter.

AUCTION RECORDS:
NEW YORK, 11 March 1943, *Painter of Turkish Canvases*, USD 120.

FATT, Johann Peter
Latvian, 18th century.
Active in Riga and Mitau (now Jelgava).
Painter.
His work, *The Portrait of a Stranger*, dated 1791, was cited in the catalogue of a private collection in Riga.

FATTORE, Il. See **PENNI Giovanni Francesco**

FATTORETTO, Giovanni Battista
Italian, 18th century.
Active in Venice.
Sculptor, architect.
In 1715, Giovanni Fattoretto worked on the façade of the Jesuit church in Venice.

FATTORI, Giovanni
Italian, 19th century.
Born 25 October 1825, in Livorno; died 30 August 1908, in Florence.
Painter, pastellist, watercolourist, engraver. Military subjects, figures, portraits, genre scenes, animals.
Macchiaioli group.
Giovanni Fattori is considered to be the principal representative of the Macchiaioli movement. Impressionism did not make much of a mark on Italy during the 19th century, its place was occupied by the Macchiaioli (the name coming from the Italian 'macchia', meaning 'patch' or 'blot'). The Macchiaioli held their first exhibitions in Florence. Rather than following any specific aesthetic doctrine, they were more of a social movement, expressing their ideas through art. This is perhaps why they did not ally themselves with the Impressionists, even though they admired them: because they felt that the pure aestheticism of the Impressionists did not suit the expression of their own political and social convictions. Almost all of the Macchiaioli were from working-class backgrounds, and their concern was to speak out about the life and work of the Italian working classes, and their battle for social emancipation.

Giovanni Fattori was of humble origin. He started to paint in his home town, but never took formal lessons. Then in 1846, he went to Florence where he worked for a year in the studio of Giuseppe Bezzuoli, before enrolling at the Accademia. From that moment on he started to take note of all his observations via countless sketches, set down in notebooks that never left his side. Echoes of these sketches would later appear in his etchings.

He fought in the revolution and only returned to Florence in 1850, when he became close to Giovanni Costa. In 1869 Fattori was appointed as a member of the teaching staff at the Accademia in Florence, and in 1886 he began to teach the advanced class. In 1875 he went on a brief trip to Paris, where he became interested in the work of the Impressionists, although this did not modify his own ideas about art. He exhibited in Munich, Vienna, and in Philadelphia, where he won medals. He also exhibited in Paris, receiving a mention in 1889, and a gold medal in 1900 at the Exposition Universelle.

Fattori did not immediately adhere to the ethos of the Macchiaioli; for many years he remained faithful to traditional ideas about composition and subject, attempting a balanced synthesis between *plein-air* painting and the centrality of the subject, putting him closer to Manet than the Impressionists. These were the aims behind the paintings *French Soldiers* and *Patrol along the Seashore* of around 1860, which are made up of lively but composed blots. He also took on more ambitious subjects: *Mary Stuart at Crookstone Camp* in 1861 and *The Italian Camp after the Battle of Magenta*, for which he won a government competition in 1862.

Fattori regarded these carefully planned compositions as his finest works. However, modern critics prefer his more spontaneous works, in particular *The Rotunda of Palmieri* (1866); *Woman with an Umbrella* (1866); *Diego Martelli in Castiglioncello*; *Woman in the Open Air*; *The Stone Breaker*; his landscapes of the Florentine countryside, then of the Roman countryside, between 1873 and 1880; and his landscapes of the *maremme* of Tuscany, painted between 1880 and 1895.

MUSEUMS AND GALLERIES:
FLORENCE (Uffizi): *The Italian Camp at the Battle of Magenta*; *Portrait of the Artist* - LIVORNO: *Attack on the Madonna della Scoperta* (*L'Attaco alla Madonna della Scoperta*) - MILAN (Pinacoteca di Brera): *Prince Amedeo Wounded at Custozza* - NAPLES (Mus. di San Martino): *The Battle of Custozza* - PRATO: *Filippo Brunelleschi*; *Battle of Custozza*; *Episode from the Battle of Magenta*; *Mary Stuart*; *St John the Baptist Rebuking Herod* - ROME (Gal. Nazionale): *Le Macchiajole*; *Wardroom of the 49th Regiment at Custozza* - TRIESTE (Civico Mus. Revoltella): *Bivouac*.

AUCTION RECORDS:
PARIS, 19 March 1945, *Horses in the Meadow*, FRF 2,500. CAIRO, 14-23 March 1947, *Charge*, EGP 25,500. PARIS, 19 June 1950, *Keeper of the Horses*, FRF 200,000. LONDON, 2 June 1964, *Scene of War and Animals*, GBP 400. MILAN, 3 March 1966, *Study for 'The Indifferent Man'*, ITL 1,400,000. MILAN, 10 May 1967, *Horse Dying on a Beach* (pastel) ITL 1,000,000. MILAN, 8 Nov 1967, *Country Landscape*, ITL 2,400,000. MILAN, 26 Nov 1968, *The Soldier and the Peasant Woman*, ITL 6,500,000. MILAN, 11 Nov 1969, *Carabineer on Horseback*, ITL 8,000,000. MILAN, 10 Nov 1970, *Cavaliers*, ITL 14,000,000. MILAN, 16 Nov 1972, *Lancer*, ITL 5,500,000. MILAN, 28 May 1974, *On Manoeuvres* (pastel and charcoal) ITL 36,000,000. MILAN, 14 Nov 1974, *Attack*, ITL 7,500,000. ROME, 27 Feb 1976, *Seaside* (oil on panel, 5 x 9 ins / 13 x 22 cm) ITL 13,000,000. MILAN, 26 May 1977, *Cavalier* (oil on canvas, 9½ x 8¼ ins / 24 x 21 cm) ITL 11,500,000. LONDON, 1 July 1977, *Peasant with Two Oxen* (watercolour and pen, 12½ x 15¾ ins / 32 x 40 cm) GBP 1,100. MILAN, 25 May 1978, *Military Camp* (watercolour, 13¼ x 8¾ ins / 33.5 x 22.5 cm) ITL 3,600,000. MILAN, 12 March 1980, *Battle Scene* (pencil/paper, 10 x 14½ ins / 25 x 36.7 cm) ITL 2,000,000. MILAN, 12 Dec 1983, *Donkey* (etching, 7½ x 10½ ins / 19 x 26.5 cm) ITL 1,300,000. MILAN, 23 March 1984, *Idyll* (oil on canvas, 41¾ x 20¾ ins / 106 x 53 cm) ITL 180,000,000. MILAN, 13 Dec 1984, *The Artillery in the Countryside* (pastel/mounted paper/canvas, 18¼ x 53¾ ins / 46.5 x 136.5 cm) ITL 100,000,000. MILAN, 18 March 1986, *Fishermen in Antignano near Livorno* (oil on canvas, 17¾ x 38½ ins / 45 x 98 cm) ITL 200,000,000. LONDON, 27 March 1987, *Military Camp* (1898, watercolour and pen, 17¾ x 13¾ ins / 45 x 35 cm) GBP 36,000. MILAN, 23 March 1988, *Steam Ships in the Port of Livorno* (oil on panel, 5¼ x 9 ins / 13.5 x 23 cm) ITL 19,000. ROME, 14 Dec 1988, *Forest* (watercolour/paper, 11¾ x 9 ins / 30 x 22 cm) ITL 6,200,000. ROME, 25 April 1989, 12½ x 9¾ ins / 32 x 25 cm) ITL 40,000,000. MILAN, 14 June 1989, *Halt of the Lancers* (1898, oil on canvas, 16¼ x 35 ins / 41 x 89 cm) ITL 520,000,000. MILAN, 8 March 1990, *House among the Trees* (1900, oil on panel, 5 x 9 ins / 13 x 23 cm) ITL 60,000,000. MONACO, 21 April 1990, *In the Fields* (ink and watercolour, 11½ x 15¼ ins / 29 x 38.5 cm) FRF 139,860. ROME, 29 May 1990, *Foot Soldiers in a Landscape* (1865, oil on panel, 3¼ x 5 ins

/ 8.5 x 13 cm) ITL 23,000,000. ROME, 31 May 1990, *Charge of the Cavalry* (oil on canvas, 19 3/4 x 39 1/4 ins / 50 x 100 cm) ITL 350,000,000. MILAN, 18 Oct 1990, *Buildings at the Port of Livorno* (oil on panel, 7 1/2 x 12 3/4 ins / 19 x 32.5 cm) ITL 130,000,000. MILAN, 5 Dec 1990, *View of Castiglioncello* (watercolour/paper, 4 3/4 x 15 ins / 12 x 38 cm) ITL 46,000,000. MILAN, 12 March 1991, *Artillery Manoeuvres* (oil on canvas, 12 x 23 1/2 ins / 30.5 x 59.5 cm) ITL 350,000,000. MILAN, 6 June 1991, *Seascape in Livorno* (oil on panel, 5 1/4 x 9 1/4 ins / 13.5 x 23.5 cm) ITL 22,000,000. MILAN, 7 Nov 1991, *Study of Soldiers* (1860, pencil/paper, 3 1/4 x 5 ins / 8 x 12.5 cm) ITL 1,500,000. ROME, 14 Nov 1991, *Portrait of a Man with a Cigarette Holder* (etching, 6 x 4 1/4 ins / 15.5 x 10.5 cm) ITL 2,185,000. PARIS, 2 Dec 1991, *Artillery Train* (oil on card, 12 x 16 ins / 30.5 x 40.5 cm) FRF 80,000. MILAN, 12 Dec 1991, *Horses in a Prairie* (etching, 17 1/2 x 24 3/4 ins / 44.5 x 63 cm) ITL 5,500,000. MILAN, 19 March 1992, *Fishermen in Antignano near Livorno* (oil on canvas, 17 1/4 x 37 1/2 ins / 44 x 95 cm) ITL 305,000,000. MILAN, 16 March 1993, *Call after the Charge* (1895, oil on canvas, 32 1/4 x 77 1/4 ins / 82 x 196 cm) ITL 600,000,000. LUGANO, 8 May 1993, *Halt of a Cavalry Regiment* (oil on canvas, 32 1/2 x 56 ins / 82.5 x 142.5 cm) CHF 530,000. MILAN, 22 March 1994, *A Man in the Woods* (oil on canvas, 17 3/4 x 38 1/4 ins / 45 x 97 cm) ITL 460,000,000. LONDON, 15 June 1994, *Halt of the Lancers* (oil on canvas, 15 1/4 x 11 ins / 39 x 28 cm) GBP 205,000. NEW YORK, 12 Oct 1994, *Cavalry Manoeuvre* (pencil and oil on panel, 6 3/4 x 10 ins / 17.1 x 25.4 cm) USD 57,500. MILAN, 14 June 1995, *Peasant Women near the Seashore* (watercolour/paper, 10 3/4 x 13 1/2 ins / 27.5 x 34.5 cm) ITL 46,000,000. MILAN, 25 Oct 1995, *Young Blonde Woman in Profile* (oil on panel, 20 x 13 ins / 50.5 x 33 cm) ITL 120,750,000. LONDON, 14 June 1996, *Standing Sentry* (oil on panel, 6 1/2 x 10 ins / 16.5 x 25.3 cm) GBP 35,600. ROME, 28 Nov 1996, *View of Montenegro* (1880-1885, oil on panel, 3 3/4 x 7 ins / 9.5 x 18 cm) ITL 21,000,000. MILAN, 18 Dec 1996, *Portrait of a Woman* (oil on canvas, 20 3/4 x 16 1/4 ins / 53 x 41 cm) ITL 38,445,000. MILAN, 25 March 1997, *The Arno in Spate* (oil on panel, 7 1/4 x 12 1/2 ins / 18.5 x 32 cm) ITL 36,115,000. LONDON, 13 June 1997, *Patrol of Lancers* (c. 1880-1885, oil on canvas, 10 3/4 x 23 1/2 ins / 27.3 x 60 cm) GBP 100,500. LONDON, 9 Dec 1999, *Horses Fleeing* (pastel on board, 28 x 39 ins / 71 x 98 cm) GBP 38,000. LONDON, 7 April 2000, *L'arno all'Indiano* (oil on board, 5 x 5 ins / 12 x 12 cm) GBP 12,000. MILAN, 15 June 2000, *Soldier on Horseback* (watercolour, 11 x 4 ins / 27 x 10 cm) ITL 26,500,000. MILAN, 28 May 2001, *Knight by Seafront* (watercolour, 16 x 21 ins / 40 x 53 cm) ITL 28,000,000. MILAN, 27 Nov 2001, *Picking Leaves* (oil on canvas, 44 x 31 ins / 113 x 80 cm) ITL 190,000,000. VENICE, 12 May 2002, *Three Impressions on a Rainy Day* (oil on board, 10 x 6 ins / 25 x 15 cm) EUR 75,000. FLORENCE, 4 June 2002, *Back Home* (engraving, 13 x 8 ins / 34 x 21 cm) EUR 2,600. ROME, 11 June 2003, *Knight on Horseback* (oil on canvas, 23 x 26 ins / 59 x 67 cm) EUR 40,000. NEW YORK, 29 Oct 2003, *Soldiers on the March* (oil on panel, 7 x 10 ins / 17 x 25 cm) USD 24,000. PARIS, 30 April 2004, *Roman Peasants in the Village* (oil on panel, 12 x 6 ins / 31 x 15 cm) EUR 55,000. ROME, 10 June 2004, *Soldier on Horseback with Two Horses* (oil on canvas, 11 x 6 ins / 29 x 16 cm) EUR 40,000.

FATTORI, Giovanni Battista

Italian, 18th century.
Died 1778.
Active in Trento.
Sculptor (including wood).

The cathedral of Trento houses Fattori's two marble statues of angels and a wooden carving of *Christ on the Mount of Olves*.

FATTORI, Giuseppe

Italian, 19th century.
Born 1818; died 20 December 1888.
Active in Florence.
Painter.

Giuseppe Fattori was a teacher at the Accademia in Florence. He painted a portrait of *Filippo Brunelleschi*.

FATTORINI, Eliseo Tuderte

Italian, 19th century.
Born to a family originally from Todi.
Painter, copyist. Religious subjects.

Fattorini was a pupil of Silvestro Valeri in Perugia. He made copies of the *Resurrection* by Piero della Francesca and the frescoes in the Sistine chapel for the Arundel Society.

AUCTION RECORDS:

AMSTERDAM, 28 Oct 1992, *Virgin and Child after Fra Angelico* (1877, oil on panel, ogival upper, 30 1/4 x 18 1/4 ins / 77 x 46.5 cm) NLG 5,175. AMSTERDAM, 9 Nov 1993, *Adoration* (1842, oil on panel, 27 1/4 x 15 3/4 ins / 69 x 40 cm) NLG 2,185.

FATTORINI, Eugène Justin

French, 19th century.
Born 19th century, in Paris.
Engraver (burin).

A pupil of Lamotte and Patricot, Eugène Justin Fattorini became a member of the Société des Artistes Français in 1899. He received an honourable mention in 1897, followed by a further honourable mention at the Exposition Universelle of 1900.

AUCTION RECORDS:

LONDON, 15 July 1910, *The Stop* (1882) GBP 4.

FATTORUSO, Giuseppe

Italian, 17th century.
Active in Naples.
Painter.

Nothing remains of Fattoruso's body of work. It is on record, however, that he painted a *St Peter* for the church of S Gennaro, together with frescoes for the churches of Carmine Maggiore and S Diego.

FAU, André

French, 20th century.
Born 13 November 1896, in Les Lilas (Hauts-de-Seine).
Painter.

Fau was a pupil of Gabriel Ferrier at the École des Beaux-Arts in Paris. He showed at the major Parisian exhibitions. He was first influenced by a kind of Post-Cubist tendency, after which his style veered progressively towards a measured Classicism.

AUCTION RECORDS:

PARIS, 24 June 1986, *The Couple* (faience, pair of trophies, h. 19 3/4 ins / 50 cm) FRF 6,000. PARIS, 9 March 1998, *Woman with a Comb* (oil on canvas) FRF 11,000.

FAU, Fernand

French, 19th - 20th century.
Draughtsman, illustrator, writer.

Fau collaborated in 1907 on Paul Iribe's satirical review, *Le Témoin* (*The Witness*). He illustrated *La Guerre sous l'eau* (*The War Under Water*) (1892) by G. Le Faure, *Une lune de miel à Monte Carlo* (*A Honeymoon in Monte Carlo*) (1887) by Adolphe Belot, and *The Woman in Breeches* (1899) by John Grand-Carteret. He was also a writer, and wrote a play, *Cruel Enigma*, which was presented at the Chat-Noir cabaret in Montmartre.

FAU, Joseph Pierre

French, 19th century.
Born 19th century, in Gibraltar, to French parents.
Painter.

A pupil of Decamps, Joseph Pierre Fau made his Salon début in Paris in 1831 with *Wreck of a Brig*. He went on to exhibit his *View of Flanders* in 1835, followed by *Persian Objects* in 1875, *16th-century Crockery* in 1876, and *Oriental Objects* and *Bric-à-brac Display* in 1877.

Auction records:
Paris, 19 April 1926, *Small Port*, FRF 200.

FAUBERT, Jean
French, 20th century.
Born 1942 or 1946.
Painter. Genre scenes, interiors, still-lifes.
Jean Faubert lives and works in and around Toulouse. He began painting full-time in around 1975.
Auction records:
Paris, 26 Oct 1990, *Interior Scene* (oil on panel, 25 1/2 x 8 1/2 ins / 65 x 21.5 cm) FRF 2,500; *Le Fumeur à la Palette* (*The Smoking Painter*) (oil on panel and collage, 36 1/2 x 25 1/2 ins / 92.5 x 65 cm) FRF 2,400. Paris, 26 May 1997, *Cigar Smoker* (oil on canvas, 18 x 13 ins / 46 x 33 cm) FRF 5,000. Paris, 5 Dec 1997, *Flautist* (watercolour, 11 3/4 x 7 3/4 ins / 30 x 20 cm) FRF 2,600. Paris, 7 Dec 1997, *Still-life with a Cat* (oil on canvas, 15 x 18 ins / 38 x 46 cm) FRF 3,800. Paris, Jan 1998, *Smoker* (gouache/paper, 31 1/2 x 19 3/4 ins / 80 x 50 cm) FRF 4,000. Paris, 22 Nov 1998, *Duet for Guitar and Double Bass* (oil on canvas laid on panel, 31 x 24 ins / 80 x 60 cm) FRF 9,500.

FAUBERT, Pierre
French, 17th century.
Died 1681, in Paris.
Painter.

FAUBLÉE, Michel
French, 20th century.
Born in Morzine (Haute-Savoie).
Watercolourist, painter (gouache), draughtsman, sculptor. Figures, flowers.
Faublée has participated in the following collective exhibitions: 1982, 1985, Basel Fair; 1982 FIAC (Foire Internationale d'Art Contemporain) in Paris; 1984, 1986 Zurich international fair; 1988, 1989 ARCO, Madrid international fair. His solo exhibitions since 1972 include: 1983, 1990, 1991 Paul Schulz gallery in Flein; 1984, 1987, 1988, 1989 Bastille gallery in Paris; 1988 Del Palau gallery in Valencia; 1990, 1991 I.S. Thomas Galerie in Paris. In 1966 he received the Fénéon prize.

Faublée paints figures, flowers and leaves in a free, figurative style. Often figures and vegetation are interwoven in a frenzied dance, bodies exploding, and nature enveloping them, as in the series *Picture Puzzles, Head Flowers*, and *Couples*.
Bibliography:
Michel Faublée, exhibition catalogue, Gal. I.S. Thomas, Paris, 1991.

FAUCAS, Georges, or Focus
French, 17th century.
Born 1641, in Châteaudun; died 1708, in Paris.
Painter, engraver (etching), draughtsman. Religious subjects, landscapes.
Georges Faucas spent time in Italy at the end of the 1660s and was a member of the Académie Royale in 1675. He suffered from schizophrenia and is said to have died insane. He specialised in landscape painting and in particular produced a series of six etchings, *Various Views of Italy*. None of his paintings appear to have survived.

His work was displayed at the following themed exhibitions: *Le Dessin en France au XVIIe Siècle dans les Collections de l'École des Beaux-Arts* (*Drawing in France in the 18th Century in the Collections of the École des Beaux-Arts*) in the École des Beaux-Arts, Paris, in 2001, and *Les Mystérieux du XVIIe siècle: Une Enquête au Cabinet d'Art Graphique* (*Mysteries of the 17th century: An Exploration of the Graphic Art Collection*) at the Musée des Beaux-Arts, Nancy, in 2002. The latter exhibition covered a group of forgotten artists from the 17th century whose output is only known from prints of works stated as being by or after them.
Bibliography:
Paul, Céline/Harent, Sophie, '*Les Mystérieux du XVIIe siècle. Une enquête au cabinet d'art graphique*' in *coll. Lire en filigrane*, Musée des Beaux-Arts, Nancy, 2002.
Auction records:
Paris, 25 April 1997, *The Holy Family and St John the Baptist* (pen, black ink and brown wash heightened with white, 13 x 18 1/2 ins / 33.2 x 47.3 cm) FRF 16,500.

FAUCCI, Carlo
Italian, 18th century.
Born 1729, in Florence; died c. 1784, in Florence.
Engraver.
Carlo Faucci studied under Carlo Gregori and was recognised as a skilful engraver of portraits and historical subjects. He furnished several plates for Marchese Gerini's gallery collection prior to visiting England, where he worked under Boydell. Examples of his work include engravings from Pietro da Cortona's *Birth of the Virgin*, Carlo Dolci's *Martyrdom of St Andrew*, Rubens' *Bacchic Theme* and Guido Reni's *Madonna and Child*.

FAUCCI, Raimondo
Italian, 18th century.
Engraver.
Raimondo Faucci assisted his uncle Carlo in the great majority of his work.

FAUCHÉ, Jacques
French, 20th century.
Born 1927, in the Ariège.
Painter. Interiors.
Fauché studied in the workshop of Raoul Bergougnan in Toulouse at the École des Beaux-Arts, where he also became professor. He has had solo exhibitions, including in 1995-1996, at the Sollertis gallery in Toulouse. After producing a number of abstract works, he returned to his meticulously rendered figurative works (notably the *Windows* series), in which he pursued his research into the formal aspect of colour.
Bibliography:
Vingt-cinq ans d'acquisitions (1959-1984), exhibition catalogue, Musée d'Art et d'Histoire, Narbonne, 1984. Cabidoche, Laurence, '*Jacques Fauché*' in *Art Press* n° 211, periodical, Paris, March 1996.
Museums and Galleries:
Narbonne (MAH).

FAUCHÉ, Léon
French, 19th - 20th century.
Born 1868, in Briey (Meurthe-et-Moselle).
Painter.
Léon Fauché first studied at the École des Beaux-Arts in Nancy and then in Paris, with Aimé Morot and Chartran. Along with his studio colleagues Anguetin, Toulouse-Lautrec and Dethomas, he exhibited at the Salon des Indépendants. He also showed at the Salon of the Société Nationale des Beaux-Arts. In 1901, he and Anquetin organised the Salon des Refusés at the Pavillon des Arts Décoratifs, and founded the Association *L'Atelier* (*The Studio*) with Armand Point. From 1906 he showed his portraits, interiors and still-lifes at the Salon of the Société Nationale des Beaux-Arts. He had previously exhibited landscapes, still-lifes and peasant genre scenes.
Auction records:
Paris, 14 May 1943, *Still-life*, FRF 100. Alençon, 27 Sept 1987, *The Stock-Exchange* (oil on paper tracing remounted/panel, 16 1/4 x 16 1/4 ins / 41 x 41 cm) FRF 5,500. Paris, 16 Dec 1987, *The Port of Honfleur* (1868, brown ink wash heightened with gouache, 15 x 15 ins / 38 x 38 cm) FRF 2,500. Paris, 17 Feb 1988, *Street Scene* (1868, oil on cardboard, 13 x 16 1/4 ins / 33 x 41 cm) FRF 7,500.

FAUCHER, Denis
French, 16th century.
Born c. 1480, in Arles; died 1562, in Cloître de Lérins.
Miniaturist.
Faucher illustrated his own books on history.

FAUCHER, Guillaume
French, 19th century.
Born 1827, in Paris.
Sculptor, medallist.
Guillaume Faucher studied under Dumont and Meusnier. From 1868 to 1870 he exhibited mainly medallion portraits of private individuals at the Salon.

FAUCHER, Jean Charles
Canadian, 20th century.
Born 1907, in Montreal.
Painter.
MUSEUMS AND GALLERIES:
QUEBEC (Mus. du Quebec): *School Playground.*

FAUCHER, Jules
French.
Draughtsman.
MUSEUMS AND GALLERIES:
BOURGES: drawing.

FAUCHER, Lisa (Mme)
Maiden name: Quitrel
French, 19th century.
Born 19th century, in Rouen.
Painter, pastellist.
Having studied under Lazerges, Perret and Madame O'Connell, Lisa Faucher sent views and several portraits to the Paris Salon from 1866 to 1870.

FAUCHER, Pierre
French, 20th - 21st century.
Born 1960, in Paris.
Painter (mixed media).
Pierre Faucher won two successive 'Hors Les Murs' prizes from the Villa Medici (travel bursaries from the French Academy in Rome), in 1988 and 1989. The first took him to Naples, the second to Rome.

Among Faucher's works are a series of paintings depicting the Battle of Monte Cassino, which took place in 1944 in Frosinone, Italy. They are a homage to those who died in this battle, soberly deploring their loss of human identity as anonymous soldiers of war.

Since 1981, he has taken part in several group exhibitions, including: at the Centre Culturel, Villeparisis, 1981; *Atelier 81-82* (*Studio 81-82*) Musée d'Art Moderne de la Ville de Paris, 1982; *Terre* (*Earth*) Centre Georges Pompidou, 1982; *Perspective 83 Art Bassel* Galerie Yvon Lambert, 1983; at the Deuxième Biennale d'Art Contemporain de Tours in 1985; and, in 1986 and 1987, at the Salon de Montrouge.

He has also staged a number of solo exhibitions, including: at the Espace Avant-Première Paris, 1982; Galerie Arlogos, Nantes, 1984 and 1986; Foire Internationale d'Art Contemporain (International Contemporary Art Fair), Grand Palais in Paris, 1986 and 1989; Institut Français de Cologne, 1988; and the Galerie Maeght in Paris in 1995.
BIBLIOGRAPHY:
Acquisitions 1989, Fonds National d'Art Contemporain, Paris, 1989.
MUSEUMS AND GALLERIES:
PARIS (FNAC).
AUCTION RECORDS:
PARIS, 8 Oct 1989, *Material* (oil on canvas, 39 1/4 x 39 1/4 ins / 100 x 100 cm) FRF 11,000.

FAUCHERY, Augustine (Mme)
French, 19th century.
Born 1803, in Paris.
Painter, lithographer.
A pupil of Regnault, Augustine Fauchery is best known for her *Death of Hippolyte* and *Sappho Meditating on the Eve of her Death.*

FAUCHERY, Jean Claude Auguste
French, 19th century.
Born 2 April 1798, in Paris; died 15 April 1843, in Paris.
Painter, engraver.
Jean Fauchery joined the École des Beaux-Arts in 1813, studying under Regnault and Guérin. He exhibited at the Paris Salon from 1827 to 1834 and was awarded a second-class medal in 1831.
MUSEUMS AND GALLERIES:
NARBONNE: *Mona Lisa* (after Leonardo da Vinci).

FAUCHET, Charlotte. See **TOTY**

FAUCHET, Raymond
French, 20th century.
Born 8 January 1896, in Bruyères-le-Châtel (Essonne).
Painter.
Raymond Fauchet was of very French Classical inspiration, with a Modern accent. He exhibited in Paris at the Salon des Tuileries. He was also a writer.
AUCTION RECORDS:
PARIS, 3 May 1928, *Seated Nude* (drawing) FRF 100.

FAUCHET, René
French, 20th century.
Painter. Urban landscapes.
AUCTION RECORDS:
PARIS, 4 June 1926, *Part of a Suburb,* FRF 140.

FAUCHEUR
French, 18th century.
Active in Paris.
Sculptor.

FAUCHEUR. See also **RIPOULINS, brothers**

FAUCHEUR, Arthur
French, 19th century.
Died 1904.
Painter.
Arthur Faucheur exhibited at the Salon of the Société des Artistes Français, of which he was also a member.

FAUCHEUR, Jean
French, 20th - 21st century.
Born 1956.
Active in Normandy.
Painter, sculptor. Busts.
Jean Faucheur graduated from the École Nationale des Beaux-Arts in Paris, and won the Prix de Dessin P. David Weill and the Prix Sculpteur de la COPRIM. He also won a Villa Medici 'Hors Les Murs' travel bursary, which took him to New York.

He has twice been commissioned to sculpt important monuments, one in homage to La Bruyère (the celebrated moralist) in 1998, and one for the Europlaza Towers, in La Défense (in Paris), in 1999.

He has taken part in a number of group exhibitions, including: *Un Regard sur l'Art Contemporain* (*A Look at Contemporary Art*), at La Collection Agnès B. in Paris, in 1992; *Complicité d'Évasion* (*Complicity in Escapism*), at the ELAC in Lyons, 1992; *Terres* (*Soil*), Musée de Soissons, 1994; and *Sculptures dans la Ville* (*Town Sculptures*) in St-Étienne in 2000.

He has also displayed his work in a number of solo exhibitions, including at La Galerie Pascal Polar in Brussels, in 1994 and 1995, the Galerie Art et Patrimoine in Paris in 1995, and *Trahisons* (*Betrayals*), at the Galerie Les Singuliers in Paris, in 1999.

BIBLIOGRAPHY:
Chevalier, Pierre, *Jean Faucheur, 24 dessins*, exhibition catalogue, Gal. du Jour Agnès B., Paris, 1989.
AUCTION RECORDS:
PARIS, 25 June 1986, *Freefall* (acrylic/canvas, 69¼ x 47¼ ins / 176 x 120 cm) FRF 6,000.

FAUCHEUR, Léonie Eugénie
French, 19th - 20th century.
Born 7 April 1873, in Paris.
Painter, watercolourist. Still-lifes.

Léonie Fauchuer was a pupil of Rivoire. She made her debut in Paris in 1908, at the Salon des Artistes Français.
AUCTION RECORDS:
PARIS, 14 Dec 1942, *Vase of Tulips* (watercolour) FRF 140.

FAUCHEUR, Yves
French, 20th century.
Painter.

Yves Faucheur was an artist in Paris. He was the pupil of Fernand Léger in 1948, and was strongly influenced by him. Faucheur's paintings are figurative, with large areas of flat colour and simplified, often geometric forms. The ensemble is monumental, solid, brightly coloured, giving a vigorous character to his work.

FAUCHIER, Herminie. See **GUDIN**

FAUCHIER, Joseph François
French, 18th century.
Born 1687, in Peyrius (Alpes-de-Haute-Provence); died 1751.
Potter, ceramicist. Religious subjects.

From 1710, Joseph François Fauchier was in charge of the pottery factory of Anne Clérissy-Héraud in Marseilles. He set up on his own in 1732. He should not be confused with his nephew Joseph Fauchier II, who succeeded him. Both of them were among the leading practitioners of the pottery revival in Marseilles in the course of the 18th century. He created a *Virgin and Child* in the parish church of Peipin (Alpes-de-Haute-Provence).
MUSEUMS AND GALLERIES:
MARSEILLES (Mus. de la Faïence).

FAUCHIER, Joseph II
French, 18th century.
Born 1725, in Peyruis (Alpes-de-Haute-Provence); died 1789 (?).
Potter, painter, sculptor.

Fauchier was the nephew of Joseph François Fauchier, and suceeded him as head of the manufactory in Marseilles. He developed original models. He was a member of the Académie de Peinture et de Sculpture in Marseilles.
MUSEUMS AND GALLERIES:
MARSEILLES (Mus. de la Faïence).

FAUCHIER, Laurent or Léon
French, 17th century.
Born 11 March 1643, in Aix-en-Provence; died 25 March 1672, in Aix-en-Provence.
Painter, engraver.
Provencal School.

Laurent Fauchier, the son of a goldsmith, excelled in portraiture. This is all the more surprising because he was self-taught. He studied and copied the portraits of Finsonius, as well as drawing after antiquity and the prints of Raphael and the Carracci School. The Cardinal, Duke of Vendôme and Governor of Provence, brought him to Paris and introduced him to Mignard, who put him under his protection and had him work on many of his paintings. Fauchier completely understood the exaggerations and faults of his teachers, in particular the mannerism of Mignard. Pierre Puget had him give lessons to his son François. In spite of the offers made to him, Fauchier refused to appear at court. He died at the age of 29, the victim of overwork, whilst painting Madame de Forbin, known under the name of the *Beauty from Le Canet*, for the fifth time. Although he died young, Fauchier executed a large number of works, including *Councillor at Aix Parliament, Guitarist* and *Portrait of Mme de Grignan*.
BIBLIOGRAPHY:
Sterling, Charles/Jamot, Paul, *Les Peintres de la réalité en France au XVIIe siècle*, exhibition catalogue, Musée de l'Orangerie, Paris, 1934.
MUSEUMS AND GALLERIES:
BRUSSELS (MBA): *Portrait of a Young Man* - CHARTRES: *Portrait Presumed to be of Princess Farnèse* - MARSEILLES: *Portrait of a Woman; Portrait of an Abbot* - MONTPELLIER: *Portrait of a Man* - ORLÉANS (Mus. Fourché): *Portrait Presumed to be of Prince Mario Piccolomini* - TOULON: *Portrait of a Magistrate*.
AUCTION RECORDS:
PARIS, 13 May 1904, *Adhémar de Monteil, Count of Grignan; Françoise-Marguerite de Sévigné* (two) FRF 3,850.

FAUCHIER, N., or Fouchier
Dutch, 18th century.
Born 18th century, in Bergen op Zoom.
Painter. History painting.

N. Fauchier revealed considerable talent and was successful in all genres. Unfortunately, he had a wild nature which led to his death by drowning.

FAUCHIER, Robert, or Fouchier
French, 14th century.
Born 1358, in Melun (Seine-et-Marne).
Sculptor, architect.

Fauchier was commissioned, in 1383, by Jean, duke of Berry, to direct the work on the palace at Poitiers in the place of Guy de Dammartin. When he returned to Melun he was made master of the works for the town. King Charles VI entrusted him with the restoration of his castle in 1403.

FAUCHIER, Serge
French, 20th century.
Born in Perpignan.
Painter.

Fauchier exhibited collectively on several occasions, notably at the Salon de Montrouge (Paris), in 1992. He has also had solo exhibitions since 1984, including: Perpignan, Bordeaux; 1985 Institut Français in Barcelona; 1988 Jacques Girard gallery, in Toulouse; 1988, the Priory in Serrabona, in Ile-sur-Têt; 1988 Regards gallery in Paris; 1995 Jean Fournier gallery in Paris. Fauchier's painting appears to be a continuation of that of Newman and Rothko, but it centres on a classic problem: 'How to achieve a painting with colour, almost nothing but colour, and a painting that escapes the monochromatic and the repetition of one single modulation?' This question was asked in reference to Fauchier's work by the art historian and critic, Philippe Dagen.
BIBLIOGRAPHY:
Dagen, Philippe, '*Serge Fauchier, peintre américain*' in *Art Press*, periodical, Paris, 1988.

FAUCHON, Hippolyte Auguste
French, 19th century.
Born 19th century, in Paris.
Painter, engraver.

A pupil of Ettebert and A. Morot, Hippolyte Auguste Fauchon made his Salon début in 1877 and became a member of the Société des Artistes Français in 1885. He was awarded a third-class medal in 1888, followed by a further third-class medal in 1892 and an honourable mention at the 1900 Exposition Universelle. He executed lithographs after Ribot, Berton and Fortuny.

FAUCHOT-BAILLION, Juliette
French, 19th century.
Born in the second half of the 19th century, in Paris.
Painter.

FAUCIGNY
British, 18th century.
Active in London.
Miniaturist.
Faucigny exhibited five portraits at the Royal Academy in London in 1797.

FAUCK, François Raymond
French, 20th century.
Born at the beginning of the 20th century, in Lille.
Painter.
Fauck was a pupil of Sabatté and Simon, and a member of the Salon des Artistes Français in Paris.
AUCTION RECORDS:
PARIS, July 1946, *The Canal,* FRF 5,000.

FAUCON, Claude
French, 17th century.
Sculptor (wood).
In 1647 Claude Faucon undertook the decoration of the altar of the Ursulines in Beaucaire with a low relief depicting *The Annunciation.*

FAUCON, Édith
French, 20th century.
Born 24 May 1919, in Carentan (Manche).
Painter.
Faucon exhibited in Paris at the Salon des Artistes Français. In 1942 she won the T. Ralli prize; in 1943 she obtained a mention and the Valérie Havard prize.

FAUCON, Jacques
French, 18th century.
Active in Paris in 1763.
Painter.

FAUCON, Jean Claude
Belgian, 20th century.
Born 1939, in Berchem-Ste-Agathe (Antwerp).
Painter, sculptor.
Faucon was a student at the academy in Brussels. He is a professor at the academy in Molenbeek. He won the S.H. Hirshorn Foundation prize in the USA. In 2003, he was represented in the collective exhibition *Peindre en trois dimensions* (*Painting in Three Dimensions*) at the Ingres museum in Montauban.
BIBLIOGRAPHY:
Duchein, Paul/Vidal, Éric/Viguier, Florence, *Peindre en trois dimensions,* exhibition catalogue, Musée Ingres, Montauban, 2003.

FAUCON, Jules André
French, 19th - 20th century.
Born 30 November 1870, in Lyons.
Painter. Interiors, figures, still-lifes.
Faucon was a pupil at the École des Beaux-Arts in Lyons, which he entered in 1887. He received a third-class medal in 1904 with *Pancakes, Pomegranates and Grapes.*

FAUCON, Marie Célestine, Mme Pigault
French, 19th century.
Born 1811, in Honfleur; died 1859.
Painter. Genre scenes.
MUSEUMS AND GALLERIES:
CAEN: *Young Woman at her Toilette; La Veilleuse.*
AUCTION RECORDS:
NEW YORK, 2 Dec 1986, *Summer Landscape with Pond* (oil on panel, 10 x 16 ins / 25.3 x 40.5 cm) USD 2,300.

FAUCONNET, Alexis
French, 18th century.
Active in Lyons.
Sculptor.

FAUCONNET, Augustin
French, 18th century.
Born 1701, in Liévremont (Doubs); died 1770, in Goux.
Sculptor (wood).
Augustin Fauconnet executed various works in the churches of Doubs and Jura. In Bannans, Doubs, he carved altars and fonts and in Goux-lez-Usier the high altar and the panelling of the choir, pulpit and lectern. In Lisine he worked on the high altar, pulpit and fonts, and in Mignovillars, Jura, he executed panelling and altars.

FAUCONNET, Guy Pierre
French, 20th century.
Born 1882, in Paris; died 1920, in Paris.
Painter, draughtsman, designer, engraver.
Fauconnet was a contemporary of La Fresnaye and Dunoyer de Segonzac. He was a painter of delicate nudes in light tones. Fauconnet was also a designer and a decorator, and made costumes and masks for the theatre.

g. fauconnet

g. fauconnet

G.P. FAUCONNET

MUSEUMS AND GALLERIES:
LUXEMBOURG (Mus. national d'histoire et d'art).
AUCTION RECORDS:
PARIS, 18 Nov 1927, *Black and White Cat,* FRF 1,250. MONTE CARLO, 9 Oct 1977, *The Sleeping Shepherd* (oil on canvas, 38 1/4 x 51 1/4 ins / 97 x 130 cm) FRF 12,000. LONDON, 27 June 1988, *The Sleeping Shepherd* (oil on canvas, 37 3/4 x 51 1/4 ins / 96 x 130 cm) GBP 10,450.

FAUCONNIER
French, 19th century.
Active in Paris.
Engraver, lithographer.
Fauconnier is known to have produced six plates, *The King of Siam's Elephant,* and the lithograph *Tyrolean Singers.*

FAUCONNIER, Berthe. See **FAUCONNIER-CLERGET**

FAUCONNIER, Édouard
Flemish, 19th century.
Active c. 1842.
Painter. History painting, portraits.
Flemish School.
Siret mentions a *Judith* by Édouard Fauconnier.

FAUCONNIER, Émile Eugène
French, 19th - 20th century.
Born 1857, in Paris.
Painter. Genre scenes.
A pupil of Cormon, Émile Eugène Fauconnier became a member of the Société des Artistes Français in 1894. He received an honourable mention in 1894, a second honourable mention at the 1900 Exposition Universelle, followed by a third-class medal in 1903. The Lycée Michelet owns his *Martyrdom of St Nicasius and St Eutropius.*

FAUCONNIER, Johannes
French, 15th century.
Active in Lille.
Painter.

In 1453, Johannes Fauconnier worked on the preparations for a banquet to be held in honour of Philip the Good.

FAUCONNIER, Laurence (Mme)
French, 16th century.
Died after 1567.
Active in Bourges (Cher).
Glass painter.

This female artist made the beautiful stained glass window in the chapel founded by her in the church of St-Bonnet in Bruges, as well as *Scenes from the Life of the Virgin* in the church at Écouen. She married the municipal magistrate (*échevin*) Pragneau in 1528.

FAUCONNIER-CLERGET, Berthe
French, 20th century.
Born 13 February 1882, in Paris.
Miniaturist.

Fauconnier-Clerget made her debut in Paris in 1901 at the Salon des Artistes Français, of which she became a member in 1903.

FAUCQ, Jean
Belgian, 20th century.
Born 1900, in Brussels; died 1978.
Painter.

Jean Faucq was a self-taught artist. A café-owner by profession, he only began painting at the age of 60.

FAUDACQ, Louis Marie
French, 19th - 20th century.
Born 1840, in Givet; died 1917, in Paimpol (Côtes-d'Armor).
Painter, watercolourist, engraver, draughtsman, illustrator. Landscapes, seascapes.

Faudacq was a pupil of Alfred Foullongne. He entered into administration as a customs officer, and was able to reconcile his customs functions with his passion for watercolour. He exhibited at the Salon de Paris as early as 1878.

He painted the seaside locations of Goëlo and Trégor. He collaborated on the magazine *L'Illustration* in 1875, the paper *Le Yacht* from 1885 to 1894, and on the review *Le Salon* in 1880, in which a large number of his drawings were reproduced.

BIBLIOGRAPHY:
Prigent, Guy (ed.), *Louis Faudacq: dessin et croquis marins*, Apogée, Rennes, 2002.

FAUDOT, Bernard
French, 20th century.
Born in Flogny (Yonne).
Sculptor.

Faudot exhibited in Paris at the Salon des Artistes Français from 1921.

FAUDRAN, Jean Baptiste
French, 17th century.
Born c. 1630, in Lambesc; died c. 1694, in Marseilles.
Painter. History painting, religious subjects.

Jean Baptiste Faudran was a gentleman and scion of the noble house of Faudran de Lambesc. He had a natural gift for painting and was fêted for it by his contemporaries. Unfortunately his works no longer exist or are not now known. He may be the Jean Baptiste de Faudran, born in 1611 and died in 1669, whose *Adoration of the Magi* was sold in Paris in 1982.

AUCTION RECORDS:
PARIS, 5 March 1982, *Adoration of the Magi* (oil on canvas, 36 1/4 x 44 1/2 ins / 92 x 113 cm) FRF 330,000.

FAUE, Maryn
Flemish School, 16th century.
Active in Bruges.
Painter.

FAUERHOLDT, Viggo, or Faurholt
Danish, 19th century.
Born 1832, in Copenhagen; died 7 August 1883, in Düsseldorf.
Painter. Seascapes.

Viggo Fauerholdt was a pupil at the academy of Copenhagen. He exhibited seascapes at the palace of Charlottenborg from 1854 to 1867. He received a bursary on which he travelled to Germany, and settled in Düsseldorf.

MUSEUMS AND GALLERIES:
STOCKHOLM: *On the Beach*.

AUCTION RECORDS:
COPENHAGEN, 10 Feb 1976, *Summer Landscape* (oil on canvas, 16 1/2 x 24 3/4 ins / 42 x 63 cm) DKK 3,100. COLOGNE, 20 March 1981, *Shoreline with Figures and Boats* (oil on canvas, 16 1/2 x 24 1/2 ins / 42 x 62 cm) DEM 4,000. COPENHAGEN, 7 Nov 1984, *Fishermen on the Beach at Gudhjem* (1860, oil on canvas, 20 x 30 3/4 ins / 51 x 78 cm) DKK 28,000. COPENHAGEN, 1 June 1999, *Figures by Beached Boat at Fano* (1855, oil on canvas, 12 x 16 ins / 30 x 40 cm) DKK 25,000. COPENHAGEN, 30 May 2000, *Summer's Day by Rocky Coast* (oil on canvas, 17 x 25 ins / 42 x 63 cm) DKK 20,000. COPENHAGEN, 6 Sept 2000, *Loading the Steam Ship off the Coast on a Clear Day in Summer* (1857, oil on canvas, 18 x 29 ins / 45 x 73 cm) DKK 35,000. COPENHAGEN, 5 March 2001, *Seascape with Caledonia off Klampenborg* (oil on canvas, 10 x 14 ins / 25 x 35 cm) DKK 16,000. VEJLE, 25 Sept 2001, *Entrance to Town by Fjord* (1860, oil on canvas, 14 x 19 ins / 35 x 48 cm) DKK 14,500. MUNICH, 18 April 2002, *Northern Harbour with Sailing Ships* (1855, oil on canvas, 19 x 24 ins / 47 x 62 cm) EUR 4,500. COPENHAGEN, 27 Aug 2002, *Entrance by Copenhagen's Customs House* (1855, oil on canvas, 19 x 25 ins / 47 x 63 cm) DKK 120,000. COPENHAGEN, 9 Dec 2003, *Entrance to Oslo* (1859, oil on canvas, 23 x 36 ins / 59 x 92 cm) DKK 36,000. COPENHAGEN, 9 Dec 2003, *Busy Traffic at Knippelsbro* (1861, oil on canvas, 26 x 38 ins / 66 x 97 cm) DKK 130,000. AMSTERDAM, 3 Feb 2004, *Sailing Vessels Moored by a Coast at Dusk* (1870, oil on canvas, 16 x 24 ins / 40 x 61 cm) EUR 2,600.

FAUGERON, Adolphe
French, 19th - 20th century.
Born 6 January 1866.
Painter. Landscapes, urban landscapes.

Faugeron exhibited regularly in Paris at the Salon des Artistes Français, of which he became a member in 1883. He received honourable mention in 1907, and a third-class medal at the Salon in 1911.

AUCTION RECORDS:
PARIS, 17 May 1987, *Nude, Arms Raised* (oil on canvas, 38 1/2 x 22 ins / 98 x 55 cm) FRF 6,100. TROYES, 24 Jan 1988, *The Dolls* (oil on canvas, 28 3/4 x 39 1/4 ins / 73 x 100 cm) FRF 28,000. NEW YORK, 25 Oct 1989, *Water Nymph* (oil on canvas, 57 1/2 x 38 ins / 146 x 96.5 cm) USD 9,900.

FAUGINET, Jacques Auguste
French, 19th century.
Born 22 April 1809, in Paris; died 1847, in Paris.
Sculptor. Animals. Busts, statues.

Jacques Auguste Fauginet was a pupil of Gatteaux. From 1831 he exhibited busts, statues, statuettes, groups, animals and other sculptures at the Salon, being awarded a third-class medal in 1838. The collection of the Comédie-Française owns a marble bust of the French playwright *Marivaux* by Fauginet.

AUCTION RECORDS:

LONDON, 14 May 1980, *Stallion* (bronze, h. 7 3/4 ins / 19.5 cm) GBP 400. PARIS, 8 Dec 1987, *Gentleman on Horseback* (brown-patinated bronze, 21 1/4 x 19 3/4 ins / 54 x 50 cm) FRF 15,000. NEW YORK, 3 June 1994, *Horse* (1836, bronze, h. 13 1/4 ins / 33.7 cm, l. 13 3/4 ins/34.9 cm) USD 8,625. BILLINGSHURST, 29 Jan 2001, *Pacing Horse* (dark brown patinated bronze, 7 x 10 ins / 19 x 25 cm) GBP 1,050. LE HAVRE, 21 April 2002, *Horse, Right Forefoot Lifted* (brown patinated bronze, 7 x 10x3 ins / 19 x 25x8 cm) EUR 2,100.

FAUGUET, Richard

French, 20th - 21st century.
Born 1963, in La Châtre (Indre).
Draughtsman, collage artist, assemblage artist.

Richard Fauget lives and works in Châteauroux. His work is laced with humour, and an irreverent disregard for the traditional notion of 'art as creation'. He draws women's underwear on raw lasagne, makes portraits out of straw on bed linen, arranges funnels and lace, and constructs robots to look after chimneys. His work also contains many references, whether biographical, cinematic (as to the *Star Wars* movies), journalistic (as to *L'Équipe*, a French soccer newspaper), or art-historical. He also makes references to advertisements.

He has taken part in various group exhibitions, including: *Ateliers* (*Studios*), at the Centre de Création Contemporaine in Tours, 1988; *Coïncidences, Coïncidences*, Fondation Cartier, Paris, 1997; *Transit - 60 Artistes Nés Après 60* (*Transit - 60 Artists Born After 60 - Works from the National Collection of Contemporary Art*), École des Beaux-Arts de Paris, 1997; *Nouvelles Collections: des Oeuvres à Vivre* (*New Collections: Works to Experience*), at Les Abattoirs in Toulouse, in 2002; *La Vie, au Fond, se Rit du Vrai* (*In Essence, Life Laughs at Reality*), at the CAPC Musée d'Art Contemporain in Bordeaux, 2002; *En Forme. La Forme*, Le Quartier Centre d'Art Contemporain in Quimper, 2003; and *Une Collection de 'Chefs-d'Oeuvre', Emprunts, Pastiches, Copies, Citations et Interprétrations* (*A Collection of 'Masterpieces', Borrowings, Pastiches, Copies, Quotations and Interpretations*), at the Fonds Régional d'Art Contemporain in Bordeaux, also in 2003. The latter exhibition explored, primarily from a European point of view, the way in which artists appropriate ideas from each other.

He has also displayed his work in a number of solo exhibitions, including: Centre d'Art Contemporain, Châteauroux, 1987; Galerie Jean-François Dumont, Bordeaux, 1989, 1991 and 1994; Espace Artpool, Lauret, 1990; Frac Limousin, Limoges, 1993; *Aquarelle = Jus de Fille*, at Le Creux de l'Enfer in Thiers, in 1994; Galerie du Progrès, Lauret, 1995; Espace Jules Verne, Bretigny-sur-Orge, 1995; Centre d'Art Contemporain, Vassivière-en-Limousin, 1996; Galerie Art: Concept, Paris, 1997; La Chaufferie École Supérieure des Arts Décoratifs, Strasbourg, 2002; Musée de l'Abbaye St-Croix, Les Sables d'Olonne, 2002; *Richard Fauguet et Daniel Schlier: Oeuvres à Quatre Mains* (*Richard Fauguet and Daniel Schlier: the Works of Four Hands*), Centre Régional d'Art Contemporain, Montbéliard, 2002; and at the Le Quartier Centre d'Art Contemporain in Quimper, in 2003.

BIBLIOGRAPHY:

Acquisitions 1989, Fonds National d'Art Contemporain, Paris, 1989. Ainardi, Dolène, '*Top 50*' in *Art Press* n° 157, periodical, Paris, 1991. *Richard Fauguet*, exhibition catalogue, Espace Jules-Verne, Brétigny-sur-Orge, 1995. Paul, Frédéric, '*Richard Fauguet, un hippocampe dans les étangs de la Brenne*' in *Art Press*, n° 203, periodical, Paris, June 1995.

MUSEUMS AND GALLERIES:

ANGOULÊME (FRAC Poitou-Charentes): *Untitled* (1992, two drawings) - BORDEAUX (FRAC Aquitaine): *Untitled* (1995) - MARSEILLES (FRAC Provence-Alpes-Côte d'Azur): *Molecule of a Dog* (1993) - PARIS (FNAC): *Selection among key works of modern sculpture* - RHEIMS (FRAC Champagne-Ardenne): *La boucle* (1996).

FAUJAERT, S.

17th century.
Probably born in Holland.
Painter. Portraits.

A known work by this artist is a painting in Riga Cathedral of the senator of Riga, *Johann Kocken* (died 1656), with his family at the foot of the Cross.

FAUKEMBERGHE, Bauduin de.

See **BAUDUIN DE FAUKEMBERGHE**

FAULCHEUR, Michel

French, 17th century.
Active in Paris in 1611.
Painter (?), sculptor (?).

FAULCON, Louise Adèle (Mme)

later Madame Aug. Gemin
Maiden name: Guichard
French, 19th century.
Born 1817, in Crémieu; died March 1897, in Crémieu.
Painter.

A pupil of Lessore, Louise Adèle Faulcon exhibited flower paintings and still-lifes in Lyons from 1878, having exhibited *Christmas Roses* in Paris in 1877. Her drawings have a good style depicting the landscapes and views of Crémieu, where she lived and knew the French painter François Auguste Ravier.

MUSEUMS AND GALLERIES:

GRENOBLE (Mus. de Grenoble): *Thistles and Everlasting Flowers.*

FAULE, Adolphe

French, 19th - 20th century.
Born 19th century, in Paris.
Engraver (wood).

A pupil of Émile Lemaire, Adolphe Faule became a member of the Société des Artistes Français in 1904, having received an honourable mention in 1894.

FAULER

Czech, 17th century.
Sculptor.

Fauler sculpted a stone *Crucifixion* in Trebová in Moravia with the sculptor Gatschke d'Eibenschitz.

FAULEY, Albert C.

American, 19th century.
Born 20 May 1858, in Fultonham; died 1919.
Painter.

Albert Fauley was a pupil of Boulanger, Benjamin-Constant and Blanc in Paris.

FAULHABER, Urban

German, 18th century.
Born 26 May 1711; died 17 May 1780.
Active in Schömberg (Württemberg).
Sculptor. Religious furnishings (altars).

Faulhaber installed and decorated the altars, stalls and pulpit at the church in Schörzingen and the altars of the church at Palmbühl, near Schömberg. The archives of the presbytery in Schömberg have some altar drawings by him.

FAULKNER, Amanda

British, 20th - 21st century.
Born 1953, in Dorset.
Active in London.
Painter (mixed media).

Amanda Faulkner studied at the Bournemouth College of Art (1978-1979), the Ravensbourne College of Art (1979-

1982) and, for an MA in Print-making, the Chelsea School of Art (1982-1983). Prior to this Faulkner lived in South America among the Indian peoples of the Andes, and worked and travelled in Europe.

Faulkner stands out for her bold paintings which are often described as 'deeply personal', 'Expressionist' and 'vigorous' and even as 'imbued with a religious intensity' (Norbert Lynton in *Picturing People*, The British Council, 1989). The subjects of Faulkner's paintings are human interaction and relationships from a woman's point of view. They particularly focus on women and the roles they play in society. Her work has thus often attracted the label 'feminist'.

Faulkner held her first solo exhibition at the Woodlands Art Gallery in Blackheath in 1983, followed by others in London, Wigan, Manchester and Kendal. Her work has featured in many group exhibitions in London, Germany, New York and Hungary, including: *Artists Against Apartheid* at the Merz Gallery in London (1989); *Images of Hope and Disquiet: Expressionism in Britain in the Nineties* at the Castlefield Gallery in Manchester (1991); *Marie R: Many Images of a Queen* at the Bourne Fine Art Gallery in Edinburgh (2000); and *Dreaming* and *Spiritus Mundi*, both held at Flowers East in London (2004).

BIBLIOGRAPHY:

Lynton, Norbert, *Human Interest: 50 Years of British Art About People*, 1985. Edward, Lucie-Smith, et al., *The New British Painting*, Phaidon, Oxford, 1988.

MUSEUMS AND GALLERIES:

MANCHESTER (Whitworth Art Gallery): *Mangas Obscuras* (1990, etching); *Big Red Journey* (1990, pastel, charcoal and chalk).

FAULKNER, Barry

American, 20th century.
Born 12 July 1881, in Keine (New Hampshire); died 1966.
Painter. Murals.

Barry Faulkner, a Harvard graduate, studied painting in New York at the Art Students League, then in Rome at the American Academy. He was also a pupil of Abbott H. Tayer and Georges de Forest Brush. He painted a mural for the house of Mrs E.K. Harriman in Arden, New York, which won him a gold medal from the Architectural League of New York in 1914.

FAULKNER, Benjamin Rawlinson

British, 19th century.
Born 1787, in Manchester; died 1849, in London.
Painter. Portraits.

Benjamin Rawlinson Faulkner trained for a time in London and began to exhibit at the Royal Academy in 1821. His most important clientele was located in Manchester. His portraits included those of *John Dalton* (1841) and *John Nic. Culloch*.

MUSEUMS AND GALLERIES:

EDINBURGH (Scottish National Portrait Gallery): *Admiral Sir John Ross* (oil on canvas) - LONDON (British Library, Oriental and Indian Office Collections): *Portrait of General W. Nott* - SALFORD (Mus. and AG): *Portrait of William Nield (second Mayor of Manchester 1840-1842)*.

AUCTION RECORDS:

LONDON, 27 Nov 1936, *Portrait of a Woman*, GBP 29. LONDON, 10 April 1992, *Portrait of Louisa, Countess of Kintore, Standing, Dressed in a White Satin Dress with a Guitar at Her Feet* (oil on canvas, 94 1/2 x 58 ins / 240.3 x 147.3 cm) GBP 7,920. SHREWSBURY, 10 Nov 1999, *Portrait of a Lady in a Red Dress Holding a Fan* (1835, oil on canvas, 36 x 27 ins / 91 x 69 cm) GBP 1,800. LONDON, 14 May 2002, *Portrait of an Officer* (1835, oil on canvas, 30 x 24 ins / 76 x 62 cm) GBP 1,850. LONDON, 11 May 2004, *Portrait of a Gentleman* (1831, oil on canvas, 30 x 25 ins / 75 x 63 cm) GBP 2,200.

FAULKNER, Florence

British, 20th century.
Born in London.
Miniaturist.

Florence Faulkner exhibited in Paris at the Salon des Artistes Français from 1925.

FAULKNER, Frank

British, 20th century.
Painter (mixed media).

AUCTION RECORDS:

LONDON, 2 Dec 1980, *Untitled* (1977, mixed media, 62 1/4 x 45 ins / 158 x 114 cm) GBP 1,000. NEW YORK, 11 Nov 1986, *Narcissus* (1981, acrylic/canvas, 72 x 72 ins / 182 x 183 cm) USD 7,000. NEW YORK, 10 Oct 1990, *Untitled* (1979, acrylic/canvas, 64 1/2 x 41 1/4 ins / 164.1 x 104.7 cm) USD 3,300. NEW YORK, 30 June 1993, *Ariadne* (1983, mixed media/canvas, 72 x 72 ins / 182.9 x 182.9 cm) USD 3,450. NEW YORK, 7 May 1996, *Mirror* (1978, acrylic/paper/sacking, 60 x 72 ins / 152.4 x 182.9 cm) USD 1,840. NEW YORK, 10 Oct 1996, *Untitled* (1978, mixed media/panel, 71 3/4 x 59 3/4 ins / 182.3 x 151.8 cm) USD 2,070.

FAULKNER, Herbert W.

American, 19th century.
Born 8 October 1860, in Stamford (Connecticut); died 1940.
Active in Paris.
Painter, illustrator. Urban landscapes, architectural views.

Herbert W. Faulkner studied initially in New York with Carroll Beckwith and then worked in Paris with R. Collin. He specialised in Venetian subjects.

MUSEUMS AND GALLERIES:

DALLAS (MA): *Gondolier's Kitchen* (1898, oil on canvas) - INDIANAPOLIS (MA): *San Giorgio, Venice* (1860) - MINNEAPOLIS: *Settling Accounts* - ST LOUIS: *Palazzo on the Grand Canal*.

FAULKNER, John

Irish, 19th century.
Born 1803 or 1830; died 1888.
Painter (gouache), watercolourist, draughtsman.
Landscapes with figures, landscapes, seascapes, animals.

John Faulkner was active in Dublin and a member of the Royal Hibernian Academy. He exhibited a painting entitled *Deer* at the Royal Academy in London in 1865.

There is possibility of confusion between the two John Faulkners, especially regarding the auction records.

AUCTION RECORDS:

LONDON, 15 July 1910, *The Avon near Leamington* (watercolour) GBP 4. LONDON, 19 Dec 1978, *Landscape* (1878, watercolour heightened with white, 25 3/4 x 46 1/2 ins / 65.5 x 118 cm) GBP 1,600. NEW YORK, 7 Jan 1981, *On Lough Corrib, County Galway* (watercolour and pencil, 8 3/4 x 19 1/4 ins / 22.5 x 48.9 cm) USD 2,600. LONDON, 24 May 1984, *Near Rickmansworth, Hertfordshire* (watercolour heightened with gouache, 18 1/2 x 38 1/2 ins / 47 x 98 cm) GBP 1,500. LONDON, 22 Feb 1985, *Fishermen Pullling up the Nets* (1869, oil on canvas, 25 1/2 x 35 ins / 64.8 x 89 cm) GBP 2,800. LONDON, 30 May 1985, *Farm in the Outskirts of Donegal* (1875, watercolour and pencil heightened with gouache, 25 1/2 x 35 1/4 ins / 64.5 x 89.5 cm) GBP 2,200. LONDON, 25 Jan 1988, *The Path at Little Flaunden in the Valley between the Hills* (watercolour, 18 3/4 x 38 3/4 ins / 47.5 x 98.5 cm) GBP 2,640. ROME, 25 April 1988, *Sharmbrook Bed* (watercolour/paper, 18 1/2 x 38 1/2 ins / 47 x 98 cm) ITL 1,800,000. LONDON, 25 Jan 1989, *Old Church at Rickmansworth* (watercolour, 18 1/2 x 38 1/2 ins / 47 x 98 cm) GBP 2,200; *Shooting Party on the Moors* (watercolour and gouache, 30 1/2 x 52 1/4 ins / 77.5 x 133 cm) GBP 2,860. LONDON, 15 June 1990, *Approach of the Storm* (1885, oil on canvas, 42 x 70 3/4 ins / 106.7 x 180 cm) GBP 10,450. PERTH, 27 Aug 1990, *Grouse Shooting* (watercolour heightened with white, 30¼ x 52 ins / 77 x 132 cm) GBP 3,850. DUBLIN, 12 Dec 1990, *Postern Gate at Rathfarnham Castle* (oil on canvas, 18 x 25¾ ins / 45.9 x 65.5 cm) IEP 2,000. LONDON, 8 Feb 1991, *Houses of Cambus O'May in Aberdeenshire* (1878, pencil and watercolour, 17 x 30¼ ins / 43.3 x 77 cm) GBP 1,650. LONDON, 12 May 1993, *Pinner, Middlesex* (watercolour, 18 x 38½ ins / 46 x 98 cm) GBP 1,495. DUBLIN, 26 May 1993, *Cliffs at Blacksod Bay* (watercolour heightened with white, 26¼ x 46¼ ins / 66.7 x 117.5 cm) IEP 3,520. NEW YORK, 28 May 1993, *Morning Breeze* (watercolour/paper, 22½ x 39½ ins / 57.2 x 100.3 cm) USD 1,150. PERTH, 30 Aug 1994, *Ballater from the Glen of Muick; The Dee near Cambus O'May* (1879, watercolour heightened with white, a pair, each 17¼ x 30 ins / 43.5 x 76 cm) GBP 4,945. EDINBURGH, 7 May 1999, *Between Kenilworth and Coventry. Crossing the Stream* (watercolour, a pair, 19 x 39 ins / 48 x 99 cm) GBP 2,500. DUBLIN, 8 Dec 1999, *Approach to Galway Harbour* (watercolour, 16 x 28 ins / 41 x 71 cm) IEP 6,000. LONDON, 19 May 2000, *Sailing Boats on a Rough Sea* (oil on canvas, 22 x 36 ins / 56 x 91 cm) GBP 3,200. BELFAST, 7 June 2000, *Between Kenworth and Canterbury* (watercolour, 20 x 40 ins / 51 x 102 cm) GBP 2,750. LONDON, 18 May 2001, *Mountain Landscape* (1866, oil on board, 24 x 41 ins / 62 x 104 cm) GBP 3,000. DUBLIN, 5 Dec 2001, *Fisherfolk on a Pier* (watercolour, 19 x 33 ins / 48 x 84 cm) IEP 6,000. LONDON, 16 May 2002, *Coastal Road* (watercolour heightened with gouache, 17 x 37 ins / 44 x 94 cm) GBP 3,000. DUBLIN, 3 Dec 2002, *Valley of the Chess, Herts* (watercolour, 19 x 39 ins / 48 x 99 cm) EUR 6,000. DUBLIN, 26 March 2003, *Landscape with Cottages and Figures on a Path, Dorking* (watercolour, 18 x 30 ins / 46 x 75 cm) EUR 2,400. LONDON, 16 May 2003, *Cottage near Roundwood, County Wicklow* (watercolour, 17 x 28 ins / 42 x 71 cm) GBP 3,500. DUBLIN, 31 March 2004, *Figure in an Extensive Lake and Mountain Landscape* (oil on canvas, 30 x 47 ins / 77 x 120 cm) EUR 2,800. LONDON, 14 May 2004, *Crookhaven, Co. Cork* (pencil and watercolour heightened with gouache and scratching out, 11 x 18 ins / 27 x 46 cm) GBP 5,500.

FAULKNER, John
Irish or British, 19th century.
Born c. 1830; died 1894.
Painter. Landscapes.

John Faulkner exhibited at the Royal Academy and Suffolk Street Gallery between 1884 and 1890.

MUSEUMS AND GALLERIES:
MANCHESTER: *Loch Sheil; Slievemore, Isle of Achill* - SHEFFIELD: *Off Cape Slear.*

AUCTION RECORDS:
NEW YORK, 11 April 1984, *Landscape with Lake and Figures* (1889, oil on canvas, 26 x 40¼ ins / 66 x 102.5 cm) USD 3,000. NEW YORK, 9 March 1996, *Off the Harbour of Horoth near Dublin* (watercolour/paper, 19½ x 36½ ins / 49.5 x 92.8 cm) USD 2,530. LONDON, 6 Nov 1996, *View of Harrow Hill, Middlesex* (watercolour heightened with gouache, 17 x 28¼ ins / 43 x 72 cm) GBP 1,150. GLASGOW, 11 Dec 1996, *Loch Sheil, Argyllshire* (watercolour heightened with white, 24½ x 40¼ ins / 62 x 102.5 cm) GBP 1,035.

FAULKNER, Joshua Wilson
British, 19th century.
Born in Manchester; died after 1820.
Miniaturist. Portraits.

Joshua Wilson Faulkner was the brother of Benjamin Faulkner. He spent the greater part of his life in Manchester. From 1809 to 1820 he exhibited at the Liverpool Institution and occasionally at the Royal Academy.

AUCTION RECORDS:
LONDON, 20 Dec 1940, *Simplicity,* GBP 262.

FAULKNER, Mary
British, 19th century.
Active in London.
Painter.

Mary Faulkner was probably the daughter of B.R. Faulkner. She featured at the Royal Academy in London and British Institution with portraits, studies of heads and genre scenes from 1838 to 1842.

FAULKNER, Robert
British, 19th century.
Painter. Portraits.

Robert Faulkner is probably the son of Benjamin Rawlinson Faulkner. He exhibited at the Royal Academy in London and Suffolk Street Gallery from 1847 to 1849.

FAULL, Emma
British, 20th - 21st century.
Born 1956.
Painter, watercolourist, draughtswoman, illustrator. Birds.

Emma Faull is an ornothologist and paints endangered species of birds. She has exhibited in the UK and abroad and illustrated *Endangered Birds* by James Ferguson-Lees (London, 1992).

AUCTION RECORDS:
LONDON, 15 March 1994, *Golden Eagle* (1991, ink and watercolour, 47 x 34¾ ins / 119.4 x 88.2 cm) GBP 2,530. LONDON, 14 May 1996, *Golden Eagles* (pencil, ink and watercolour heightened with white, 51½ x 39½ ins / 130.7 x 100.3 cm) GBP 3,680. LONDON, 30 Sept 1997, *Partridge among Poppies* (pencil, pen and ink and watercolour, 38 x 32 ins / 96.5 x 81.2 cm) GBP 2,875.

FAULQUE, Louise
French, 19th century.
Active in Paris.
Painter.

Louise Faulque exhibited at the Salon of the Société des Artistes Français, becoming a member in 1888.

FAULSTICH, Johannes
Swiss, 15th century.
Active in St Gall at the end of the 15th century.
Painter, miniaturist.

In 1496, Faulstich decorated some choir books for the parish church of Bischofzell. They are now kept in the Biobliothèque Nationale in Paris.

FAULTE, Michel
French, 17th century.
Active in Paris.
Painter, engraver.

Michel Faulte engraved portraits and religious and historical subjects.

FAULX, Henri
French, 17th century.
Born 17th century, in Dijon.
Painter.

Henri Faulx is mentioned by De Marolles.

FAUNER, Josef
Austrian, 18th century.
Born 1756, in Vienna.
Painter.

Fauner studied at the academy of art in Vienna and was a painter at the porcelain factory there.

FAUQUER, Jean Baptiste
French, 17th century.
Active in Paris.
Sculptor.

FAUQUET, Édith
French, 20th century.
Born at the beginning of the 20th century, in Paris.
Painter.
Édith Fauquet was a pupil of Sabbaté. She exhibited from 1934 in Paris at the Salon des Artistes Français. There she won the T. Ralli prize in 1936, a second-class medal in 1937, and the Paul Liot prize in 1937, as well as a travel grant in 1938.

FAUQUET, Firmin B.
French, 19th century.
Died 1902.
Active in Paris.
Engraver.
Firmin B. Fauquet exhibited at the Salon of the Société des Artistes Français, of which he became a member.

FAUQUET, Louise (Mme)
Maiden name: Saint-Edme
French, 19th century.
Born 19th century, in Milan, to French parents.
Painter.
From 1847 to 1852 Louise Fauquet sent miniature and pastel portraits to the Paris Salon.

FAUQUET, Pierre
French, 18th century.
Active in Paris in 1723.
Painter.

FAUQUEZ, J. B.
French, 18th - 19th century.
Born 1778, in Valenciennes; died 1843, in Tournai, Belgium.
Painter. History painting, animals.
J. B. Fauquez left his collections of work to the Belgian city of Tournai.

FAUQUIGNON
French, 19th century.
Engraver (wood).
Fauquignon provided the illustrations for works including *Les Français Peints par Eux-mêmes* (*The French Painted by Themselves*) and *Physiologie du Fumeur* (*Physiology of the Smoker*).

FAURANT, Philippe
French, 20th century.
Born 16 July 1945, in Versailles.
Painter.
Philippe Faurant studied drawing from 1961 to 1963, at the Académie Charpentier and the Académie de la Grande Chaumière, both in Paris. Subsequently, from 1963 to 1966, he studied sculpting and painting at the Académie du Feu, where he worked under the noted sculptor, Zabo. He has been exhibiting his work since 1966.

FAURAY, Antoine de (Chevalier). See **FAVRAY**

FAURE. See also **FAVRE**

FAURE, A. (Mme)
Maiden name: Octavie Delorme
French, 19th century.
Born c. 1810, in Bordeaux.
Painter, pastellist.
From 1835 to 1857 A. Faure sent several works to the Paris Salon, mostly anonymous portraits. She is perhaps best known for her *Witch from the Scottish Mountains*.

FAURE, Aimée
French, 20th century.
Born 9 March 1880, in St-Étienne.
Painter, miniaturist.
Aimée Faure was probably the sister-in-law of Anne Faure, née Fuarez. She exhibited in Paris at the Salon des Artistes Français from 1919 to 1956, and was also a member of that society. She received a silver medal in 1936, and a gold medal in 1949. She painted mostly miniatures.

FAURE, Alphonse
French, 19th - 20th century.
Born in Toulouse.
Painter, engraver.
Faure was a member of the Société des Artistes Français from 1905. He received an honourable mention in 1902.
AUCTION RECORDS:
VERSAILLES, 22 June 1980, *Dancer in her Dressing Room* (1913, oil on canvas, 21 1/2 x 18 ins / 54.5 x 46 cm) FRF 3,200.

FAURE, Amandus
German, 20th century.
Born 1874, in Hamburg; died 1931, in Stuttgart.
Painter, engraver. Genre scenes.
MUSEUMS AND GALLERIES:
BUCHAREST (Muz. National de Arta al României): *In a Circus* - STUTTGART: *Goldoni Arena; Porta Romana; Flowers* - VENICE (Ca' Pesaro, Gal. Internazionale d'Arte Moderna): *Cake Walk*.
AUCTION RECORDS:
PORTLAND, 6 Nov 1981, *Still-life* (1917, oil on card, 28 1/4 x 18 ins / 72 x 46 cm) DEM 5,000. COLOGNE, 26 Oct 1984, *Circus Scene* (1909, oil on card, 27 1/2 x 35 1/2 ins / 70 x 90 cm) DEM 4,500. BREMEN, 7 Nov 1987, *Turkish Bath* (1919, oil on card, 12 x 16 1/4 ins / 30.5 x 41.5 cm) DEM 5,200. MUNICH, 10 Dec 1991, *In the Caravan* (1913, oil on canvas, 59 x 74 3/4 ins / 150 x 190 cm) DEM 46,000. STUTTGART, 23 Oct 1999, *Market in Morocco* (1950, oil on board, 13 x 21 ins / 34 x 53 cm) DEM 4,000. STUTTGART, 6 April 2000, *Assembly at Night in Stuttgart* (1918, oil on canvas/board, 11 x 14 ins / 27 x 36 cm) DEM 3,400. STUTTGART, 27 Sept 2001, *In the Variety* (1916, oil on canvas, 31 x 42 ins / 80 x 106 cm) DEM 3,500. LUCERNE, 9 Nov 2002, *Odalisque* (1923, oil on canvas, 51 x 79 ins / 130 x 201 cm) CHF 4,000. VIENNA, 19 Dec 2003, *Still-life of Flowers* (1923, oil on canvas, 35 x 39 ins / 90 x 100 cm) EUR 1,600. WARSAW, 26 Sept 2004, *Bouquet of Flowers in a Vase* (oil on card, 19 x 13 ins / 49 x 34 cm) PLN 8,500.

FAURE, André Baptiste
French, 19th century.
Born 19 January 1806.
Painter.
Having joined the École des Beaux-Arts on 13 October 1829, André Baptiste Faure exhibited portraits, many of them in pastel, of private individuals at the Salon.

FAURE, Angelica
French, 20th century.
Born in Le Puy.
Sculptor.

FAURE, Anne
Maiden name: Fuarez
French, 20th century.
Born 21 May 1878, in St-Étienne.
Painter.
Anne Faure was a pupil of Fernand Humbert. She exhibited regularly in Paris, at the Salon des Artistes Français, from 1909 until 1956. She exhibited under her maiden-name, Fuarez, until 1913, and afterwards under the name of Faure.

FAURE, Antoine. See **FAVRE**

FAURE, Antoine Ferdinand
French, 19th century.
Born 19th century, in Marseilles.
Sculptor. Statues.

Antoine Ferdinand Faure studied at the École des Beaux-Arts in Marseilles before becoming a pupil of Cavelier at the Paris École des Beaux-Arts. He made his Salon début in 1882. His principal works are *Portrait of Mlle B. and Mme Clovis Hugues* (1882-83); *Young Mother and her Child; Childhood of Bacchus* (1889); and *Last Games* (1892). He was awarded a third-class medal and a travel bursary. Other works include *Youth* (bronze, 1893); *Primrose* (marble); a full-length portrait of *Jean Ehrard* (1895); a marble bust (1896); and *Psyche* (1897). In 1888 he was employed to renovate the sculptures in the Cour d'Honneur of Versailles palace. Further works include *Cupid Fishing* (Brasserie du Pêcheur in Strasbourg, 1890), together with various sculptures in the museum of Egyptian antiquities (Cairo, 1897).

FAURE, Elisabeth
French, 20th century.
Born 1906, in Ferryville; died 1964.
Painter. Landscapes, flowers.

Elisabeth Faure was a pupil of Lucien Simon. From 1933, she exhibited in the Salon des Artistes Français in Paris. There she received a second-class medal in 1935, and, in the same year, the national prize. Faure painted landscapes of Brittany, Auvergne and Africa around 1930. She also painted flowers in delicate strokes and colours. She does not seem to be the same person as Élisabeth Dodel-Faure.

BIBLIOGRAPHY:
Thornton, Lynne, *Les Africanistes, peintres voyageurs*, ACR Édition, Paris, 1990.

AUCTION RECORDS:
PARIS, 27 April 1990, *Boutique in Moroni, Grande Comore* (watercolour and gouache, 12 3/4 x 20 ins / 32.5 x 50.5 cm) FRF 7,500. PARIS, 22 June 1990, *Part of Foulpointe, Madagascar* (watercolour and gouache, 12 x 18 ins / 30.5 x 46 cm) FRF 6,000. NEW YORK, 15 Nov 1990, *The Anemones* (1955, oil and sand/canvas, 33 1/2 x 22 ins / 85 x 56 cm) USD 88,000. PARIS, 22 June 1992, *Village of Imerina in Madagascar* (oil on canvas, 25 3/4 x 32 ins / 65.5 x 81 cm) FRF 10,000. PARIS, 17 Dec 2001, *Woman at Market, Brazzaville* (oil on canvas, 24 x 29 ins / 60 x 73 cm) FRF 27,000. PARIS, 14 June 2004, *Fruit Seller* (oil on panel, 20 x 26 ins / 50 x 65 cm) EUR 3,500.

FAURE, Émilia
French, 20th century.
Born 16 November 1924, in Lomme.
Painter.

Faure participated in Paris in the Salon des Réalités Nouvelles from 1961 to 1967, and in the Salon Comparaison from 1960 to 1963. Her painting is aligned with lyrical abstraction.

FAURE, Emmanuel
French, 19th century.
Draughtsman.

MUSEUMS AND GALLERIES:
DIEPPE: *Head of Beethoven.*

FAURE, Eugène
French, 19th century.
Born 1822, in Seyssinet (Isère); died 1879, in Bourg-St-Andéol (Ardèche).
Painter. Portraits, genre scenes, hunting scenes, landscapes.

Eugène Faure started studying sculpture in the studio of David d'Angers, and then in Rude's studio. He then, however, moved to painting and exhibited in the Paris Salon from 1847 to 1879, winning a medal in 1864. His work was exhibited at the 1981 exhibition *Le portrait en Dauphiné au XIXe siècle* (*The Portrait in the Dauphiné Region in the 19th century*) at the Fondation Hébert d'Uckermann in La Tronche.

He produced many landscapes based on his trips to Italy. Some of his genre paintings show hunting scenes, as well as more romantic subjects, such as *Dreams of Youth, Education of Love, The Secret*. He seemed to favour painting portraits of his friends and especially women, whom he presented in traditional allegories. Works include *Eve, Venus, Chloë, Italian Woman*.

MUSEUMS AND GALLERIES:
GRENOBLE: *First Days of Love; Eve; Negress; Spring; In the Mountains* (1846) - GRENOBLE (Mus. Dauphinois): *A. Albert; C. L. Reynaud; Craponne du Villard; Portrait of general Debelle; Portrait of U. Basset (sculptor)* - GRENOBLE (Mus. de Grenoble): *Self-portrait; Portrait of Théodore Ravanat; Portrait of Jean Alexis Achard.*

AUCTION RECORDS:
GRENOBLE, 18 Feb 1980, *Torrent in the Forest* (oil on canvas, 13 x 9 1/2 ins / 33 x 24 cm) FRF 2,000. LONDON, 6 Oct 1989, *Flower Seller* (oil on canvas, 78 1/2 x 39 ins / 199.5 x 99 cm) GBP 15,400. LONDON, 19 June 1992, *Woodland Idyll* (oil on canvas, 86 x 48 ins / 218.5 x 122 cm) GBP 11,000. LONDON, 18 Sept 2003, *Woodland Idyll* (oil on canvas, 86 x 48 ins / 218 x 123 cm) GBP 14,000.

FAURE, Francis
French, 20th - 21st century.
Born 1951.
Painter, draughtsman.

Francis Faure studied at the Académie de Port-Royal in Paris, and now works in Paris. As Alain Pizerra writes, Faure paints whirlpools, 'underwater waves, dream-like landscapes crammed with plant life, African tribal motifs, or even volcanoes spewing forth pointillist colours. [They are like] streamers and multicoloured confetti in an extravaganza.'

Since 1980, he has put on a number of exhibitions in his studio, and also displayed his work at the Galerie Lamaignère St-Germain in 1991. He also produces prints.

AUCTION RECORDS:
PARIS, 11 Oct 1989, *Untitled* (acrylic/canvas, 51 1/4 x 38 1/4 ins / 130 x 97 cm) FRF 10,500.

FAURE, Gabrielle
French, 20th century.
Born in Lumbin (Isere).
Painter, engraver, illustrator.

Gabrielle Faure worked with Maurice Denis, K.X. Roussel and P. Vers. She was a member of the Salon de la Société Nationale des Beaux-Arts in Paris, and also exhibited at the Salon des Tuileries.

AUCTION RECORDS:
PARIS, 8 May 1936, *Afternoon in the Garden*, FRF 35. PARIS, 23 June 1943, *Tea Time*, FRF 1,000.

FAURE, Georges
French, 20th - 21st century.
Born 14 October 1946.
Sculptor, decorative designer, designer. Designs for stained glass.

Georges Faure studied at the École des Beaux-Arts in Lyons, and the École des Beaux-Arts in Paris. He creates wooden sculptures, and also uses bronze, welded metal and concrete resin. His work has a primarily decorative function.

FAURE, Germain Christophe
French, 20th century.
Born 1884, in Marseilles.
Watercolourist, draughtsman, architect. Architectural views.

Faure entered the École des Beaux-Arts d'Architecture in Paris with the class of 1902. He received his diploma of architecture in 1909.

BIBLIOGRAPHY:
Delaire, E., *Les Architectes élèves de l'École des Beaux-Arts*, Librairie de la Construction moderne, Paris, 1907.

AUCTION RECORDS:
PARIS, 5 April 1991, *Facade design for a City Hall* (drawing in watercolour, 18¼ x 30 ins / 46.5 x 76.5 cm) FRF 22,000.

FAURE, Hélène
French, 19th - 20th century.
Born 19th century, in Montbrison.
Miniaturist.
Hélène Faure was a pupil of Mrs Pelletier-Dupont, Debillemont-Chardon and F. Humbert. On several occasions she exhibited at the Salon des Artistes Français and received an honourable mention in 1910.

FAURE, Jean, called The Writer
French, 15th century.
Painter.
In 1484, Jean Faure was working at the château in Limoges. He may be the same artist as the miniaturist Jean Fabri.

FAURE, Jean
French, 16th century.
Born 16th century, in Grenoble.
Painter.
This artist's signature appears on a deed drawn up in 1535.

FAURE, Jean
French, 19th century.
Active in Rome c. 1820.
Painter, draughtsman.
MUSEUMS AND GALLERIES:
LONDON (British Mus., Department of Prints and Drawings): drawings.

FAURE, Jean. See also **FAVRE**

FAURE, Jean François
French, 18th - 19th century.
Born 1750, in Toulouse; died 1824, in Toulouse.
Painter.
Jean Faure was the pupil of Despax and a member of the Académie Royale de Peinture.
MUSEUMS AND GALLERIES:
TOULOUSE: several works.

FAURE, Jean Victor Louis
French, 19th century.
Born 1786, in Berlin, to French parents; died 1879, in Paris.
Painter. Landscapes.
Jean Victor Faure was a pupil of J.V. Bertin. Between 1814 and 1834 he exhibited landscapes at the Paris Salon.
MUSEUMS AND GALLERIES:
ST-OMER: *View of the Mourg Torrent.*

FAURE, Joanny
French, 19th century.
Born 1832, in St-Étienne; died 1906, in St-Étienne.
Painter.
Joanny Faure was a pupil of Gleyre, Soulary and Gérôme. He taught at the École Municipale des Beaux-Arts in St-Étienne and painted very idealised and poetic portraits and landscapes. He also produced many landscapes in charcoal.

FAURÉ, Léon
French, 19th century.
Born 1819, in Toulouse; died 1887, in Paris.
Painter. History painting, portraits, genre scenes.
Fauré studied under Eugène Delacroix and exhibited at the Paris Salon from 1857 to 1876. Works include: *L'Offrande, Cabaret at Subiaco, Plainsong, Jean Huss before Emperor Sigismund, Last Kiss, Abraham Receiving the Three Travellers, Philip the Good Giving his Mistress the Toison d'Or Necklace* and *The Cardinal's Godson.*
MUSEUMS AND GALLERIES:
BÉZIERS: *Return of the Young Tobias* - TOULOUSE: *Jean Huss before Emperor Sigismund; Portrait of F. Mailhol; Inside a Roman Tavern.*
AUCTION RECORDS:
PARIS, 1 March 1984, *Coming out of the Opera* (oil on canvas, 20¾ x 28¾ ins / 53 x 73 cm) FRF 6,500. BERN, 1 May 2002, *Blind Isaac with Jacob* (oil on canvas, 31 x 39 ins / 80 x 100 cm) CHF 3,000.

FAURE, Mathieu. See **FAVRE**

FAURE, Paul Émile
French, 20th century.
Born 2 August 1898, in Rabastens.
Painter.
Paul Faure exhibited at the Salon des Indépendants in Paris.

FAURE, Pierre
French, 15th century.
Active towards the middle of the 15th century.
Copyist.
A manuscript entitled *Boccacio de Casibus*, dated 1458, was copied by Pierre Faure. The miniatures of this very well-known book were for many years attributed to Jean Fouquet. It is now thought that they are the work of several hands, probably Fouquet's pupils. One or two of the better miniatures may, according to Laborde, be by Jean Fouquet himself.

FAURE, Pierre
French, 20th century.
Born c. 1932.
Painter (mixed media/gouache), pastellist, draughtsman. Interiors with figures, still-lifes.
After a solo exhibition in 1964, the École des Beaux-Arts in Paris, where Faure has taught since 1970, showed an ensemble of his paintings in 1995. Using a discreet and refined technique, Faure depicts the most quotidian of themes, and the most insignificant details, with sensitivity. His subjects include anonymous interiors in filtered semi-darkness, a chair or stool, a broom, a radiator, and a crab.

FAURE, Thierry
French, 20th century.
Born 1944, in Nevers (Nièvre).
Watercolourist. Equestrian subjects, animals.
Thierry Faure was a professional horse rider, and ran a riding school from 1969 to 1977, when, inspired by his artistic family, he turned to painting. Although Faure has painted other subjects, most of his works are watercolour depictions of horses, either portraying sporting competitions or reconstructing historical events.

He staged his first exhibition in 1983, and became a professional painter in 1985. Since then, he has staged numerous exhibitions in his home, 'La Boulaye', and has also displayed his work in galleries in Rennes, St Malo, Paris and Versailles, as well as Cirencester, in England, and Naas, in Ireland. Most of his exhibitions have coincided with equestrian competitions.

FAURE, Urbain
French, 20th century.
Painter.
Urbain Faure painted in Sanary, in around 1920. He was a traveller, and became a curator of the Musée de Tananarive. He exhibited in Paris at the Salon d'Automne. He tried to introduce three dimensional depictions to naive art.

FAURE, Victor Amédée
French, 19th century.
Born 5 February 1801, in Paris; died 1878, in Paris.
Painter, draughtsman, lithographer. History painting, portraits.

Victor Faure entered the École des Beaux-Arts in Paris in 1824 and was taught by Hersent. He exhibited at the Paris Salon from 1831 to 1864, and received a second-class medal in 1833. Much of his work was devoted to ceremonial portraits, including those of the entire Orléans family.

MUSEUMS AND GALLERIES:

VERSAILLES (Château): *Portrait of Antoine-Philippe of Orléans, Duke of Montpensier; Portrait of Louis-Charles of Orléans, Count of Beaujolais; Portrait of Napoleon Bonaparte, General in Chief of the Italian Army; Portrait of Édouard-Auguste, Duke of Kent; The Duke of Orléans and the Duke of Chartres Returning to the Royal Palace; Portrait of Antoine-Philippe of Orléans, Duke of Montpensier, Wearing Sergeant-Major's Uniform; Battle of Johannisberg, 30 August 1762; The Duke of Nemours in the Trenches during the Siege of Anvers Citadel.*

AUCTION RECORDS:

PARIS, 10 March 1971, *Portrait of HRH Louis Charles of Orléans, Count of Beaujolais* (oil on canvas) FRF 14,500. PARIS, 18 Feb 1977, *During the Barricades, in 1830* (graphite/paper, two pages, 11 3/4 x 8 ins / 30 x 20 cm) FRF 500. PARIS, 29 April 1994, *The Duke of Orléans and the Duke of Chartres Leading the First Regiment of Hussars as They Return to the Royal Palace* (1830, oil on card, 10 x 7 1/4 ins / 25.5 x 18.5 cm) FRF 15,000.

FAURE DE BROUSSÉ, Vincent Désiré

French, 19th century.
Born in Paris.
Sculptor. Figures. Busts.

A pupil of Salmson, Vincent Désiré Faure de Broussé sent his marble bust of a *16th-century Florentine Patrician* to the Salon in 1876, followed by his bronze bust of *A 16th-century Young Florentine Lady* in 1877, and his marble statuettes of *Nyssia* and *A Young Florentine Lady* in 1878.

AUCTION RECORDS:

LONDON, 14 Oct 1976, *Young Girl Seated* (white marble, h. 36 ins / 91.5 cm) GBP 880. BARCELONA, 23 April 1980, *Pan* (bronze, h. 23 1/4 ins / 59 cm) ESP 60,000. LONDON, 10 Nov 1983, *Marie-Antoinette* (c. 1880, bronze, h. 22 ins / 55 cm) GBP 550. NEW YORK, 19 Jan 1994, *Bust of a Noble Lady Wearing a Crown* (1878, bronze, h. 26 1/2 ins / 67.3 cm) USD 3,450. NEUILLY, 22 June 1999, *Pandora and Mercury* (brown patinated bronze, 30 ins / 75 cm) FRF 13,500. BRUSSELS, 13 Nov 2000, *Improviser* (patinated bronze, 28 ins / 72 cm) BEF 140,000. LONDON, 11 July 2001, *Maiden Feeding Chicks* (1885, white marble, 37 ins / 93 cm) GBP 12,000. LOKEREN, 6 Oct 2001, *Cellist* (brown patinated bronze, 28 x 13 ins / 72 x 33 cm) BEF 120,000. ANTWERP, 22 April 2002, *Figure of a Seated Lady with a Harp* (brown patinated bronze, 17 ins / 42 cm) EUR 7,500. PARIS, 4 June 2003, *Female Musician* (gold brown patinated bronze, 23 ins / 58 cm) EUR 2,600.

FAURE-BEAULIEU, Émile

French, 19th century.
Born 19th century, in Nevers.
Painter.

Émile Faure-Beaulieu exhibited at the Paris Salon from 1864. He is best known for his *Farm near New York, Sunken Lane in Berry, American Tumbledown Houses in New Jersey* and *Green Bridge at Vaux-de-Cernay in Autumn.*

FAURE-DELCOURT, Henri

French, 19th century.
Active in Lille.
Painter, engraver (etching).

A pupil of Corot, Henri Faure-Delcourt executed 12 etchings after paintings by his master, including *The Three Haymakers* and *The River Scarpe near Arras.*

FAURE-DUJARRIC, Louis Lucien

French, 19th - 20th century.
Born 1872, in Paris.
Painter.

Faurre-Dujaric was a pupil of Moyaux and Bonnat and the son of Lucien Faure-Dujarric.

FAURE-VINCENT, Julien

French, 20th century.
Born in Cervière (Hautes-Alpes).
Sculptor.

Faure-Vincent was a pupil of Niclausse. He exhibited in Paris at the Salon des Artistes Indépendants. He received an honourable mention in 1936 for *The Call*, a statue in plaster.

FAURET, Jean Joseph Léon

French, 19th - 20th century.
Born 25 December 1863, in Mugron (Landes); died 12 April 1955, in Neuilly-sur-Seine.
Painter. Genre scenes, urban landscapes.

Fauret was a pupil of A. Dupuy at the École des Beaux-Arts in Bordeaux. He also studied with J.P. Laurens, Benjamin Constant and Gabriel Ferrier at the Académie Julian. He was a member of the Société des Artistes Français from 1897, and was awarded a third-class medal in 1896.

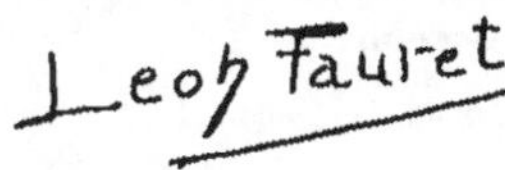

MUSEUMS AND GALLERIES:

BORDEAUX: *Holy Waif.*

AUCTION RECORDS:

PARIS, 11 July 1989, *Place de l'Étoile* (oil on canvas, 28 3/4 x 21 1/4 ins / 73 x 54 cm) FRF 19,000. PARIS, 20 Nov 1989, *The Automobile Fair* (oil on canvas, 21 1/4 x 28 3/4 ins / 54 x 73 cm) FRF 30,000. AMSTERDAM, 24 April 1991, *Old Couple Seated; Proclamation* (grey monochrome, a pair, 13 3/4 x 11 ins / 35 x 27 cm) NLG 2,070. LONDON, 22 Nov 1996, *Refreshment at the Petit Trianon* (1898, oil on canvas, 37 x 52 ins / 94 x 132.2 cm) GBP 5,520. LONDON, 22 Sept 2000, *Conversation* (oil on canvas, 20 x 24 ins / 50 x 61 cm) GBP 3,000.

FAURETI, Francesco Jacopo. See **FAVRETO**

FAURHOLT, Viggo. See **FAUERHOLDT**

FAURON, Émile César

French, 19th century.
Born 19th century, in Lormes (Nièvre).
Painter.

Émile Fauron was a pupil of Paul Delaroche. He exhibited the following works at the Paris Salon: *Return from the Wash House*, in 1859, *Christ on the Cross*, in 1864, *Old Woman from Morvan Knitting* in 1868 and *Morvan Landscape*, also in 1868.

FAURON, M. (Mlle)

French, 19th century.
Painter.

Mlle Fauron exhibited portraits at the Paris Salon in 1894 and 1895.

FAUSSIG, Aurelia

Hungarian, 20th century.
Born in Budapest.
Painter, decorative designer.

FAUST, Carl

German, 20th century.
Born 30 October 1874, in Reyershausen, near Göttingen.
Painter. Genre scenes, portraits.

Carl Faust began as a decorative painter, and studied at the academy in Düsseldorf, where he was the student of Peter Janssen, Claus Myer and H. Lauenstein. His well-known works include: *For the Good Bread*, some sketches of Berlin society and the portrait of *Cardinal von Hartmann, Archbishop of Cologne*.

FAUST, Heinrich
Swiss, 17th century.
Painter.

Heinrich Faust was active in Basel at the end of the 17th century. In 1678, he was admitted to the brotherhood of painters in Basel.

AUCTION RECORDS:
LONDON, 11 Oct 1985, *Young Girl Gathering Flowers* (oil on canvas, 8 1/2 x 6 1/4in/21.5 x 16cm) GBP 1,100.

FAUST, Heinrich
German, 19th century.
Born 6 October 1843, in Reinsdorf; died 4 January 1891, in Kassel.
Painter. Portraits, genre scenes, landscapes.

Heinrich Faust studied at the academy of art in Kassel, then in Antwerp with Van Lerius. He later returned to settle in Kassel after spending many years in Italy.

MUSEUMS AND GALLERIES:
KASSEL: *Autumn Landscape*.

FAUST, Joseph
French, 19th century.
Born 28 June 1868, in Toulon.
Painter.

Faust was a pupil of L. Bonnat and Maignan. He was a member of the Société des Artistes Français (Society of French Artists).

FAUST, Matthaus
Swiss, 17th century.
Painter.

Matthaus Faust was admitted to the brotherhood of painters in Basel in 1686.

FAUST, Otmar S., or Othmar
Czech, 20th century.
Born 10 October 1876, in Jarmeritz (Moravia).
Painter. Landscapes.

Otmar Faust studied at the academy in Vienna. He is known for: *On Lake Geneva, In the Vienna Woods* and *In Luther's Pulpit in Iena*.

FAUST, Sebastian
Swiss, 17th century.
Active in Basel at the end of the 17th century.
Painter, decorative designer.

Faust was admitted to the brotherhood of painters in Basel in 1679.

FAUSTA VITTORIA, Nicoletti Mengarini
Italian, 20th century.
Born in Rome.
Sculptor.

Fausta Vittoria exhibited two sculptures at the Salon of the Société des Artistes Français in 1921: *Dancer* (in bronze) and *Little Boy* (a bronze bust).

FAUSTIN, real name: Faustin Betbeder
French, 19th - 20th century.
Born 1847, in Soissons; died c. 1914.
Active in Great Britain.
Draughtsman, caricaturist.

The war of 1870 surprised Faustin, a spiritual artist attending the École des Beaux-Arts in Paris, and momentarily made a caricaturist of him. A drawing of Napoleon III, *The Habit Does Not Make the Monk*, garnered an enormous success and 12,000 francs for its author. It was followed by a series of amusing popular engravings executed in a quick, powerful pencil. Having gone to London, Faustin collaborated on the *London Figaro*. He married and founded a colour printing establishment, and his artistic production was of first-class calibre, comparing with that of Chéret. Among others, Faustin produced a certain number of paintings of world renown, notably *The Lord's Prayer* and *The Coronation of King George V*, as well as some charming pastels. He also furnished numerous costumes for the Alhambra, the Lyceum and the Comic Opera in London.

MUSEUMS AND GALLERIES:
ROCHEFORT: *Portrait of Doctor P.A. Lesson (benefactor of Rochefort)*.

AUCTION RECORDS:
PARIS, 14 Dec 1925, *Flowers; Fruit* (pastel, a pair) FRF 100.

FAUSTIN, Obes
Haitian, 20th - 21st century.
Born 1959.
Painter. Genre scenes.

Obes Faustin's work is far from prolific but he has gained a reputation in Canada and the USA.

AUCTION RECORDS:
PARIS, 14 Dec 1992, *Request to Dambalha* (1988, oil on canvas, 14 x 10 ins / 35.5 x 25.5 cm) FRF 4,000.

FAUSTIN-BESSON. See **BESSON Faustin**

FAUSTINA, James Kelley
American, 20th century.
Born 1876, in Dyerburg; died 1 August 1928, in Chicago.
Painter, illustrator.

FAUSTINETTI, Giacomo
Italian, 16th century.
Active in Brescia.
Sculptor.

It is generally accepted that Giacomo Faustinetti executed the funerary monument to Martinengo della Pallata, who died in 1526, after the designs by Stefano Lamberti. Originally intended for the church of S Cristo in Brescia, the monument is now in the museum of that town.

FAUSTINI, Modesto
Italian, 19th century.
Born 1839, in Brescia; died 1893, in Rome.
Painter, watercolourist. Genre scenes.

MUSEUMS AND GALLERIES:
ROME (Gal. Nazionale d'Arte Moderna): studies - TRIESTE (Civico Mus. Revoltella): *Morning Caresses; Unexpected Visit*.

AUCTION RECORDS:
NEW YORK, 15 and 16 April 1909, *Matrimonial Celebration in Pompeii*, USD 325. LONDON, 4 May 1928, *Yeghen Var*, GBP 19. EAST DENNIS (MASSACHUSETTS), 14 Aug 1980, *Idyll in Pompeii* (oil on panel, 40 1/4 x 29 1/2 ins / 102 x 75 cm) USD 4,500. MILAN, 21 Dec 1993, *Gallant Scene* (watercolour/paper, 15 x 22 ins / 38 x 56 cm) ITL 1,840,000. MILAN, 20 Oct 1999, *Pompeiian Idyll* (oil on board, 8 x 7 ins / 21 x 18 cm) ITL 3,283,000. NEW YORK, 8 March 2000, *Suitor* (oil on canvas, 20 x 40 ins / 51 x 102 cm) USD 28,000. LONDON, 21 March 2002, *Bold Entrance. Studious Courtier* (watercolour, a pair, 18 x 12 ins / 46 x 30 cm) GBP 1,550.

FAUSTINO
Italian, 16th century.
Active in Perugia.
Painter.

Faustino was a monk and worked in 1590 and 1591 for the churches of S Gualtiero and S Pietro in Perugia.

FAUSTINO-LAFETAT, Maurice
French, 20th century.
Born 10 September 1925, in Paris.
Painter (gouache), watercolourist. Figures, still-lifes, flowers, landscapes.

Faustino-Lafetat was a pupil at both the École du Louvre and the École des Beaux-Arts in Paris. In Paris, he participated in the Salon d'Automne, the Salon de la Société Nationale des Beaux-Arts, the Salon des Artistes Français (where he was made laureate and won a gold medal), the Salon des Indépendants and the Salon de la Marine. His solo exhibitions include: 1975, Palais des Arts et de la Culture in Brest; and 1986, Musée de Montbard.

The work of Faustino-Lafetat is impregnated with the lessons of the Neo-Cubism of André Lhote and Jacques Villon, and is highly ordered. Though less structured than that of his elders, it is distinguished by the vivacity of its coloured planes.

BIBLIOGRAPHY:
Faustino-Lafetat, exhibition catalogue, Palais des Arts et de la Culture, Brest, 1975.

MUSEUMS AND GALLERIES:
CASTRES (Mus. Goya) - LAGNY-SUR-MARNE (Mus. Gatien-Bonnet) - PARIS (FNAC): *The Casbah* (oil on canvas) - ST-DENIS (MAH).

AUCTION RECORDS:
PARIS, 8 April 1991, *Istanbul* (oil on canvas, 35 x 45$^{1}/_{4}$ ins / 88 x 115 cm) FRF 7,800.

FAUSTNER, Leonhard
German, 19th century.
Born 16 February 1815, in Munich; died 1 April 1884, in Munich.
Painter. Architectural views, landscapes.

A pupil of Hinmiller, Leonhard Faustner studied at the academy of art in Munich. On Hinmiller's death, Faustner was appointed to run a glass-painting school.

MUSEUMS AND GALLERIES:
MUNICH: *In the Church of Our Lady in Munich*.

FAUSTNER, Luitpold
German, 19th century.
Born 10 July 1845, in Munich.
Painter. Genre scenes, landscapes.

The son of Leonhard Faustner, Luitpold Faustner studied at the academy of art in Munich, where he was influenced primarily by C. von Piloty, with whom he travelled in Italy. He studied landscape under Jules Lange. Faustner exhibited in Munich in 1881. His best-known works are: *After Lunch* and *In the Forest.*

AUCTION RECORDS:
NEW YORK, 12 May 1978, *View of the Dachstein* (1915, oil on canvas, 36$^{1}/_{2}$ x 28in/92.5 x 71cm) USD 2,900. VIENNA, 19 May 1981, *Alpine Landscape* (1915, oil on canvas, 36$^{1}/_{2}$ x 28in/93 x 71cm) ATS 80,000. ARHUS, 11 Dec 2001, *Mountain Landscape* (1894, oil on canvas, 57 x 46 ins / 146 x 118 cm) DKK 18,000. MUNICH, 20 March 2002, *Fishing Huts on Shore of Upper Bavarian Lake* (1874, oil on panel, two, 5 x 13 ins / 12 x 32 cm) EUR 2,200.

FAUSTO, Cadorro
Brazilian, 20th century.
Born in Rio de Janeiro.
Painter.

Cadorro Fausto exhibited two portraits at the Salon of the Société Nationale des Beaux-Arts in Paris in 1932.

FAUT, Ernest
Belgian, 20th century.
Born 1879, in Ghent; died 1961, in Louvain.
Painter. Religious subjects, nudes, church interiors.

AUCTION RECORDS:
LOKEREN, 10 Dec 1994, *Nude* (oil on panel, 13$^{3}/_{4}$ x 13$^{3}/_{4}$ ins / 35 x 35 cm) BEF 36,000. LOKEREN, 11 March 1995, *Beguine Convent* (oil on canvas, 27$^{1}/_{2}$ x 23$^{1}/_{2}$ ins / 70 x 60 cm) BEF 26,000.

FAUT, Kuntz
German, 16th century.
Active in Würzburg (Bavaria).
Painter.

FAUT, Peter
German, 16th century.
Active in Würzburg (Bavaria).
Painter.

Brother of Kuntz Faut.

FAUTEPEAU DE LA CARTE, Arthur de (Vicomte)
French, 19th century.
Active in Montmorillon (Vienne).
Sculptor.

He exhibited two busts of women at the Paris Salons of 1878 and 1879.

FAUTEREL, Pierrequin
French, 16th century.
Active in Nancy.
Painter.

Fauterel worked on the tomb of René II in the church of the Cordeliers between 1509 and 1511.

FAUTEUX, André
Canadian, 20th - 21st century.
Born 1946, in Dunnville (Ontario).
Sculptor.

André Fauteux began working with metal during the early 1970s. His initial works were composed of a few simple geometric elements - triangles, rectangles and circles - strictly arranged along vertical and horizontal axes. Then, midway through the 1970s, his forms became more complex and his axes less rigid and more flexible, with changing and varying points of view. He is primarily influenced by the sculptor Anthony Caro and the painter Kenneth Noland.

MUSEUMS AND GALLERIES:
OTTAWA (Nat. Gal. of Canada): *Untitled* (1967, monotype).

FAUTIER, Jean
French, 18th century.
Active in Bordeaux.
Painter.

Jean Fautier executed paintings for the triumphal arches erected on the occasion of the entry of the Queen of Spain to Bordeaux in 1722. He may be identical to the decorative painter Fautier mentioned on a list of payments for *Menus Plaisirs*.

FAUTRAS, Albert
French, 19th century.
Born 25 July 1832, in Tours.
Sculptor.

Fautras was a pupil of Préault. He exhibited at the Paris Salon from 1864.

FAUTRIER, Jean
French, 20th century.
Born 16 May 1898, in Paris; died 21 July 1964, in Châtenay-Malabry (Hauts-de-Seine).
Painter (gouache), watercolourist, pastellist, sculptor, engraver, lithographer, draughtsman, illustrator.
Nudes, still-lifes, flowers, landscapes.

Fautrier was born in Paris, to parents from the Béarn region. He was an illegitimate child, and was given his mother's surname. Upon the death of his father, and when he was just ten years old, his mother took him to London. At the age of 14 he entered the Royal Academy, where he studied with Sickert. He then took classes at the Slade School of Fine Art. In 1917 he was summoned to France to be conscripted into the army. During the war he was gassed and wounded. At the end of the war, he settled in Paris. He was unable to achieve any kind of success in the 1930s, especially as the national economy was in the grip of the Depression. Fautrier left for the Alps, where he worked in the hotel business and as a ski instructor from 1935 to 1939. At that time he ceased to paint, and only took it up again during the war.

He began to exhibit his paintings when he was about 14, and showed them in Paris from 1923. He had already been spotted by dealers, including Jeanne Castel since 1921, as well as Paul Guillaume, and others. During the 1920s he took part in several collective exhibitions, notably in Paris. From 1922 he exhibited at the Salon d'Automne, where he showed his *Skinned Wild Pig* in 1927, and a *Christ on the Cross* in 1929. He showed at the Salon des Tuileries from 1924. In 1960, he was awarded the Grand Prize in Painting at the Biennale in Venice, and in 1961, that of the Biennale in Tokyo. Among the collective exhibitions in which he took part are: 1993, *Paris Post-War: Art and Existentialism, 1945-1955*, Tate Gallery, London; 1996, *Face à l'Histoire* (*Facing History*), Centre National d'Art et de Culture Georges-Pompidou, Paris.

Fautrier had solo exhibitions on a regular basis, including: in 1928, light-coloured paintings and less severe subjects than those of his 'black' period, such as nudes, still-lifes and flowers at the Georges Bernheim gallery; in 1939, a suite of lithographs for Dante's *Inferno*, still-lifes and bouquets at the Galerie de la Nouvelle Revue Française; in 1945, an ensemble of paintings entitled *Hostages*, a historic exhibition at the Galerie Drouin in Paris which was prefaced by André Malraux; in 1955, his *Objects* series, with a preface by Jean Paulhan in Paris and New York; *Nus* (*Nudes*) in 1956, an exhibition prefaced by Francis Ponge; in 1957, an exhibition in New York bringing together many elements of his work, principally the Supporters series, but also works previously at the Galerie André Schoeller; in 1964, the first retrospective exhibition of his work, which illness hindered him from seeing, at the Musée d'Art Moderne de la Ville in Paris. After his death, retrospective exhibitions have included: 1980, Cologne; 1985-1986, *Fautrier 1925* at the Musée de Calais, and *Fautrier 1925-1935* at museums in Amsterdam and in Zurich; 1987, a programmed retrospective at the Centre Georges Pompidou, which was cancelled with no explanation (at the same time, a donation from a German collector was rejected by the national cultural authority); 1989, retrospective, at the Musée d'Art moderne de la Ville de Paris; 1996, Musée Fernand Léger, Biot; and 1998, *Hommage pour le centenaire* (*Homage to the Centenarian*), Musée de l'Île-de-France, Sceaux Castle.

Fautrier drew a great deal, especially nudes in outline, over different periods. He also worked in pastel, and painted in watercolour. He began engraving in 1923, but it was not until after 1940 that he produced numerous etchings, especially of nudes. He also worked as an illustrator in 1928, commissioned by Malraux for the Éditions Gallimard, to create a series of lithographs for an edition of Dante's *Inferno*. It was not published, but was instead only exhibited in 1939. He illustrated two erotic texts by Georges Bataille: *Madame Edwarda* (*Mrs Edwarda*) and *L'Alleluiah* (*The Hallelujah*), published by Blaizot, Paris, in 1947. Other illustrated works were: *Orénoque* (*Orinoco*) by Robert Ganzo, and *La Femme de ma vie* (*The Woman of My Life*), by André Frénaud.

According to Malraux, Fautrier also sculpted a great deal, but these works remained hidden for a long time. Nothing was done to exhibit them, until they reappeared during the retrospective exhibition of 1989. He executed 20 small sculptures, showing diverse influences, from Maillol to Henri Laurens, from 1927 to 1929, and then between 1935 and 1943. He is known for his great *Tragic Head* in copper, dated 1943, of which half of the face is torn off, a mutilation recalling the *Hostages* paintings.

Biographers have always insisted that Fautrier enjoyed two careers and two different kinds of success. Fautrier himself largely encouraged this point of view, intensely disdaining the works of his first period. Yet such an entrenched view begs to be called into question.

It is true that as well as the paintings of his black period, he also represented subjects that were considerably easier and more accessible. However, it is important to look more carefully at his somewhat excessive reaction to his earlier work. The 45-year-old Fautrier could not completely deny what he had been at the age of 27. His radical attempt to deny it might be explained by one of two reasons. The first could have been a desire to block out a period of his work which later seemed to him to cast a pall over his stance as an inventor of a new, three-dimensional language. Yet the opposite might be true as well. He may have wished to suppress a certain tenderness he might have had for these works, which were produced more spontaneously, and in a somewhat purer manner. Under closer scrutiny, this interior conflict does not bear out a contradiction between his two periods, but rather serves to prepare the way for them, already manifesting the power found in the later works.

Regardless, Fautrier was hardly someone who easily gave himself away. He spent the end of his life in a bohemian home, whose ambiguous atmosphere was both familial and erotic. If one remarked that there was no visible studio or painting materials, he would respond that he did as the cats, burying his excrement in the ground. Indeed, after finishing working on any given corner of a painting, he would hide his material and works in the closets. As he had the same attitude to his own life, his biographers have had their work cut out for them.

Not enough is known about the works of his first period and how they linked to those that followed. Around 1920, he executed several satirical paintings, such as *The Sunday Stroll*. It would seem that he first painted nudes, with soft forms which were already suggested more by the sensual, flesh-tinted texture of the paint, with its provocative iridescence, rather than by his drawing. These nudes, along with the portraits and still-lifes, can be viewed as belonging to Derain's anti-Cubist reaction. At the same time, he also depicted lighter subjects, scenes of brothels, in red chalk and watercolour. From 1921 to 1928, he made numerous trips to the Tyrol, the Causses, Brittany, Port-Cros, the Alps and Chamonix. They provided him with themes for landscapes, notably the lakes and glaciers in 1925-1926, and Port-Cros in 1928. In the *Glaciers* series, he achieved a balance in the piling up of the blocks of ice, not through drawing, but through working up the layers of white. This was followed no doubt by the *Rabbit Skins* series, by the *Game* series of all kinds, killed or skinned, of wild boars, and his *Head of a Skinned Sheep*. These works show a debt to Soutine, which was continued through the work of Paul Rebeyrolle, already making Fautrier one of the rare French Expressionists.

The only quality that Fautrier himself recognized in these old works was that they owed nothing to Cubism, whose vestiges made up an important part of French painting in between the wars. For him, this latter fact represented an abomination of the facile and the vulgar. His style would darken progressively in his treatment of the same themes, mainly of dead game, reaching for the darkest browns and blues of night. This extreme darkening of his palette might also perhaps explain the public's disenchantment with him at that time, even though in 1927, he still enjoyed considerable success with the paintings of his so-called 'black' period. Shortly before 1929, he painted two versions of a *Christ on the Cross*, recalling somewhat Gauguin's *Yellow Christ*. In these works, he foregrounded in a radical way the problem of the flatness of painting. He excluded, perhaps for the first time, all illusion of depth and volume. The rendering of his Christ was totally primitive, all flat and yellow, on a summarily right-angled cross, outlined in stormy black.

During the 1939 exhibition at the *Nouvelle Revue Française* (*New French Review*), he showed mostly large *Bouquets* in muted blues, and *Bunches of Grapes* painted in a thick, enamelled material. From 1930-1932, Fautrier abandoned the technique of oil painting on canvas. He took up working in pastel and tempera, and began to develop a new technique that would become the mark of his second period. He painted onto paper, and the ensemble was then remounted onto a more solid canvas. The substance of the paint, on generally sombre preparations, was made up of an important paste of accumulated papers, and of large thicknesses of pastel powders, all bound together with glue. These thicknesses were at first crushed, ground together, shaped with a spatula, and then scratched. After they were dry, he applied light glazes in delicate tones, and finished off with some kind of acronym, in idiogram of one part for the whole, allowing the identification of the theme of each work. His distaste for his pre-1939 works is even less understandable, given that some of his *Nudes, Rabbit Skins*, or his *Head of a Skinned Sheep*, or even some *Glaciers*, already revealed a synthetic simplicity of form and expressiveness of substance that is also evident in the *Hostages* that introduced his second period. This is true to the extent that he himself sometimes inserted old paintings into subsequent exhibitions. It was after Fautrier's *Hostages*, the first *High Paws* by Dubuffet, and the spottings of Wols, that Michel Tapié developed the category of *Art Informel*. He was correct. It is clear that Fautrier's method, which made him create form before understanding its meaning, brought something entirely new to painting, if one excludes the advice of da Vinci to draw after stains of humidity on walls, and some Surrealist experiments of automatic creation. Nevertheless, Fautrier in the end detested *art informel*. Contrary to all the production ascribed to him, to each of his works Fautrier attributed a very precise meaning, even if it was at the end. The creator of *Art Informel* was not abstract, and did not want to be. Even in his *informel* period, he could continue to be considered an Expressionist. It is true that in his work between the wars, he was already attracted to the morbid, as evidenced by his disembowelled wild boar, and bloody butchered head of a sheep. During World War II, when he took up painting again, his attraction for blood, sensual pleasure and death was strangely linked, as it was for the writer Georges Bataille, with a profound horror of crime, massacres and war, from which, nevertheless, an erotic perception of violent death is not absent. He then painted the long *Hostages* series, in which Malraux saw 'the hieroglyphs of suffering', which Michel Ragon thus described: 'Each painting is painted in the same manner. On a watergreen background, a pool of thick white is laid out. A brushstroke indicates the form of the face. That was all, but a painter, in finding his subject had found his style... The models of *Hostages* are these shot hostages, with faces deformed by torture, riddled by bullets, these faces that are no more than a muddied, pink wound'.

Subsequently, Fautrier painted the *Nudes*. These, despite the implied derision in their titles - *For My Hands, His Beautiful Eyes, Plump One, Guili-guili* - are not so different from his preceding tortured figures. The forms are perhaps fuller and more fleshed-out than those in *Hostages*, yet eroticism is the instrument of enquiry into suffering and death. From 1949 to 1954, Fautrier developed a process of the reproduction of paintings in thicknesses. He also developed a process, an extension of the first process, of *Multiple Originals*, by which artists could produce a work in several copies, signed and numbered, which made their price affordable to a broader public. At the time, it did not become a widespread practice, even though this preoccupation of the multiple, which relates to the sociology of the distribution of art, took on considerable importance, beginning in the 1960s. It was in 1954 that Fautrier painted the *Objects* series, but, when he exhibited them in Paris and New York, one of the paintings was dated 1942, one 1945, some from 1946 to 1949, and most strikingly, one was dated 1928. This was a new indication that his old work was not entirely without a bearing on his new manner. The objects in question were made up of all and everything: an old can of food, a wrinkled paper bag, a crate. Indeed, in Fautrier's painting, these different objects could just as well be perceived as being *Hostages* or *Nudes*. It would seem that their role came to be principally to manifest against the abstraction that he was credited with creating at the same time as that of *Art Informel*. It should be observed nevertheless that the very 'insignificance' of these objects tends to prove the uselessness of their identification when they are unable to provide a specific meaning that could distinguish them from other themes. Extending the rare landscaped vein of the old *Port-Cros Landscapes*, the *Glaciers* of the end of the first period, some of the works of around 1955 are entitled *Trees, Landscapes, Forests*. The importance accorded to the 'landscape' motif is of the same order as that in the *Objects*. In 1957, Fautrier created the *Supporters* series, with which, echoing the 1945 *Hostages*, he used his means as a painter to commemorate the massacre of the rebels in Budapest when Stalin had seized control of Hungary.

What was the use to him of these verbal supports? Was he beginning with the word and its image, or did the word instead name the image once it had been settled upon? Regardless of its title, a painting by Fautrier, before being a crushed head, a nude, an old can of food or a tree, is above all a Fautrier. It is ultimately an image of himself. Fautrier would appear to have been preoccupied on several occasions with the suffering of man. Too great a moralising dimension should perhaps not be given to this compassion. There where they struck, violent death and torture were of concern to him, not so much in his real perception of injustice and crime, as by the fascination they exerted on one of the most authentically erotic minds of the time, for whom the annihilation of love was inseparable from death, and the refinements of torture insoluble from those of the flesh.

F. Fautrier

Fautrier

BIBLIOGRAPHY:
Restany, Pierre, *Fautrier*, Hazan, Paris. Malraux, André, *Les Otages de Fautrier*, Gal. René Drouin, Paris, 1945. Paulhan, Jean, *Fautrier l'enragé*, Blaizot, Paris, 1949 (2nd edition, 1962). Paulhan, Jean, *Les Objets de Fautrier*, Gal. Rive Droite, Paris, 1955. Tapié, Michel, *'Fautrier paints a picture'* in *Art News*, periodical, New York, December, 1955. Ponge, Francis, *Paroles à propos des nus de Fautrier*, Gal. Rive Droite, Paris, 1956. Ragon, Michel, *'Fautrier'* in *coll. Musée de Poche*, Georges Fall, Paris, 1957. Melville, Robert, *'Jean Fautrier'* in *Art International*, no. 3, Lugano, 1960. Paulhan, Jean, *L'Art informel: éloge*, Gallimard, Paris, 1962. *Catalogue raisonné de l'œuvre gravé de Fautrier*, Musée d'Art et d'Histoire, Cabinet des estampes, Geneva, 1986. *Fautrier*, exhibition catalogue, Musée d'Art moderne de la Ville de Paris, Paris, 1989. Cabanne, Pierre, *Fautrier*, La Différence, Paris, 1989. Breerette, Geneviève, *'Fautrier, tragique et dandy'* in *Le Monde*, periodical, Paris, 11 June 1989. Peyré, Yves, *Fautrier ou les Outrages de l'impossible*, Éd. du Regard, Paris, 1990. Fautrier, Jean, *Ecrits publics*, L'Échoppe, Paris, 1995. *Fautrier*, exhibition catalogue, Musée Fernand-Léger, Biot, 1996. Dupont-Logié, Cécile/Peyré, Yves/Berne-

Joffroy, André, *Hommage pour le centenaire*, exhibition catalogue, Musée de l'Île-de-France, château de Sceaux, 1998.

Museums and Galleries:

New York (MoMA) - Paris (MAMVP): *The Great Black Boar* (1926); *The Pretty Girl* (1927); *Bust with Breasts* (1927-1929, sculpture); *The Eyes* (1940, plaster); *Diversion,- 1960*; an important donation - Paris (MNAM-CCI): *Christ on the Cross* (before 1929); *The Great Torso* (1927-1929, sculpture); *Great Tragic Head* (1942, sculpture) - Sceaux (Mus. de l'Île-de-France): *Otages (Hostages)* (collection of works) - Vatican (Mus. Vaticani): *Christ on the Cross* (c. 1929).

Auction records:

Paris, 6 June 1929, *Head,* FRF 620. Paris, 5 Dec 1940, *Flowers,* FRF 330. Paris, 24 Nov 1941, *Still-life,* FRF 1,500. Paris, 28 Jan 1942, *Guinea Fowl,* FRF 3,300. Paris, 22 Feb 1943, *The Bowl of Fruit,* FRF 2,800. Paris, 2 July 1943, *The Two Ducks,* FRF 6,200. Paris, 5 Feb 1945, *Portrait of Odette,* FRF 12,600. Paris, 24 April 1947, *The Bouquet* (pastel) FRF 8,500. Paris, 15 Dec 1958, *Small Precious Object* (1956) FRF 380,000. New York, 30 Nov 1960, *Abstraction* (watercolour and gouache) USD 525. Versailles, 3 Dec 1961, *Composition* (gouache) FRF 5,500. Stuttgart, 3-4 May 1962, *Coloured Lines II,* DEM 32,000. Geneva, 27 Nov 1965, *Composition* CHF 52,000. New York, 24 March 1966, *Mujeres (Women)* (oil and plaster/canvas) USD 5,000. Paris, 8 June 1966, *Nude, Arm Raised* (green-patinated bronze) FRF 10,800. London, 29 Nov 1967, *Algae,* GBP 2,000. Geneva, 7 Nov 1969, *Flowers,* CHF 83,000. Paris, 19 March 1971, *The Stem Glass,* FRF 67,000. Paris, 26 Feb 1973, *The Pretty Girl* (1944) FRF 130,000. Milan, 10 June 1974, *Composition* (gouache) ITL 4,400,000. Milan, 29 Oct 1974, *Tangles,* ITL 33,000,000. Paris, 31 March 1976, *Still-life with Flowers and Fruit* (oil on canvas, 32 x 39¼ ins / 81 x 100 cm) FRF 27,000. Paris, 4 May 1976, *Nude with Arms Raised* (bronze, h. 19¾ ins / 50 cm) FRF 13,000. Versailles, 17 March 1977, *The Man with the Cigarette* (1926, oil on canvas, 16¼ x 13 ins / 41 x 33 cm) FRF 8,000. Milan, 24 Nov 1977, *Variations* (1960, tempera and watercolour/cardboard, 20 x 25½ ins / 50.5 x 65 cm) ITL 2,600,000. Paris, 12 Dec 1979, *The Fairy Lantern Family* (1925, charcoal, pen and watercolour, 9½ x 11¾ ins / 24 x 30 cm) FRF 4,800. Paris, 14 Dec 1981, *The Model* (1977, red chalk/paper, 39¾ x 27½ ins / 101 x 70 cm) FRF 33,000. Milan, 15 Nov 1984, *Nude* (pen, 10¼ x 7¾ ins / 26 x 20 cm) ITL 2,600,000; *Composition* (coloured lithograph with watercolour, 20 x 14¼ ins / 51 x 36 cm) ITL 1,500,000. Paris, 23 Nov 1984, *Nude with Arms Raised* (1927, bronze, h. 17¼ ins / 44 cm) FRF 95,000. London, 6 Dec 1984, *Better than Nothing* (1953, oil on paper remounted/canvas, 24¾ x 35¾ ins / 63 x 91 cm) GBP 44,000. Paris, 26 Sept 1986, *Bust with Breasts* (1929, bronze with antique patina, h. 15¾ ins / 40 cm) FRF 132,000. Versailles, 21 Dec 1986, *Nude* (pen, 12½ x 13¾ ins / 32 x 35 cm) FRF 22,000. Paris, 9 Feb 1987, *Nude with Arms Raised* (1927, greenish-patinated bronze, h. 17¼ ins / 44 cm) FRF 180,000. Milan, 9 Nov 1987, *Pastures* (1959, oil on paper remounted/canvas, 35½ x 51¼ ins / 90 x 130 cm) ITL 295,000,000. Paris, 3 Dec 1987, *Composition* (oil on canvas, 11 x 13¾ ins / 27 x 35 cm) FRF 90,000. Milan, 18 Dec 1987, *Composition* (1963, gouache, 19¾ x 25½ ins / 50 x 65 cm) ITL 15,000,000. London, 25 Feb 1988, *Scratches* (ink and oil on paper, 25½ x 39¼ ins / 65 x 100 cm) GBP 10,450; *Fruit* (mixed media, 11 x 14 ins / 28 x 35.5 cm) GBP 44,000. Paris, 20 March 1988, *Composition* (1957, watercolour and gouache, 19¾ x 24¾ ins / 50 x 63 cm) FRF 60,000. Paris, 28 March 1988, *Still-life* (oil on card, 15¼ x 21 ins / 38.5 x 53.5 cm) FRF 78,000. Milan, 8 June 1988, *Vase of Flowers* (tempera and pastel/paper, 7¾ x 6¾ ins / 20 x 17 cm) ITL 16,000,000. Paris, 12 June 1988, *Composition* (1959, gouache/blotting paper, 19¾ x 25½ ins / 50 x 65 cm) FRF 60,000; *Composition* (1958, gouache/blotting paper, 19¾ x 25½ ins / 50 x 65 cm) FRF 90,000; *The Trees* (gouache/mounted paper/canvas, 14¼ x 19¾ ins / 36 x 50 cm) FRF 42,000; *City* (1951, oil and gouache/mounted paper/canvas, 1951, 11 x 13¾ ins / 27 x 35 cm) FRF 31,000; *American Landscapes* (1951, gouache and oil on paper/canvas, 11 x 13¾ ins / 27 x 35 cm) FRF 45,000; *The Dominos* (gouache and oil on paper remounted/canvas, 12½ x 15¾ ins / 32 x 40 cm) FRF 42,000. Paris, 17 June 1988, *Composition* (1958, gouache, charcoal and chalk/blotting paper, 17¾ x 25¼ ins / 45 x 64 cm) FRF 66,000. London, 30 June 1988, *Construction: Four-sided Table* (1958, mixed media, 18 x 21½ ins / 45.5 x 54.3 cm) GBP 63,800; *Construction* (1958, mixed media, 32 x 39¼ ins / 81 x 100 cm) GBP 104,500. Paris, 28 Oct 1988, *Composition* (1958, gouache, 6¼ x 9½ ins / 16 x 24 cm) FRF 45,000; *Seated Nude with Legs Crossed* (1925, red chalk, 11 x 8¼ ins / 27 x 21 cm) FRF 21,000. Paris, 22 Nov 1988, *Nude from the Back* (pencil drawing, 15 x 6½ ins / 38 x 16.5 cm) FRF 24,000. London, 1 Dec 1988, *Composition* (1962, oil and pigment/paper/canvas, 19¾ x 25½ ins / 50 x 65 cm) GBP 82,500. Lucerne, 3 Dec 1988, *Red and Black Construction* (oil on paper/synthetic resin, 48 x 35¾ ins / 122 x 91 cm) CHF 1,000. Paris, 17 Feb 1989, *Trees* (pastel and gouache, 8¼ x 9 ins / 21 x 22 cm) FRF 58,000. London, 23 Feb 1989, *Dusk* (1958, oil and pigments/paper/canvas, 13 x 15¾ ins / 33 x 40 cm) GBP 79,200; *Small Mask* (1935, bronze, h. 6¼ ins / 16 cm) GBP 7,480. Paris, 7 April 1989, *Composition* (charcoal and pastel, 14¼ x 19¾ ins / 36 x 50 cm) FRF 65,000. London, 29 June 1989, *Processions* (1963, oil and pigments/paper/canvas, 25½ x 39¼ ins / 65 x 100 cm) GBP 286,000. Paris, 8 Nov 1989, *Nude* (1961, oil and watercolour, 19¼ x 24¾ ins / 49 x 63 cm) FRF 280,000. Paris, 15 Feb 1990, *Small Seated Nude* (1929, bronze, h. 5½ ins / 14 cm) FRF 140,000. Paris, 25 March 1990, *Head of a Hostage* (1944, oil on paper/canvas, 25½ x 21¼ ins / 65 x 54 cm) FRF 16,200,000. Paris, 29 March 1990, *Portrait of a Young Girl* (oil on canvas, 22 x 18¼ ins / 55 x 46.5 cm) FRF 460,000. London, 5 April 1990, *The Box* (1945, oil and pigment/paper/canvas, 18 x 22 ins / 46 x 55 cm) GBP 330,000. Paris, 10 June 1990, *Head of a Hostage* (oil on paper, 10¾ x 9 ins / 27.5 x 22 cm) FRF 1,660,000. Paris, 10 June 1990, *Reclining Nude* (1944, pen, 12½ x 14¾ ins / 32 x 37.5 cm) FRF 100,000. Paris, 6 Oct 1990, *Kneeling Nude Model* (1944, brown wash and stump, 13½ x 11¾ ins / 34 x 30 cm) FRF 75,000. London, 18 Oct 1990, *Still-life* (oil on canvas, 15 x 18¼ ins / 38 x 46.4 cm) GBP 47,300. Paris, 29 Oct 1990, *Composition* (c. 1960, gouache/blotting paper, 19½ x 25½ ins / 49.5 x 64.5 cm) FRF 180,000. Paris, 26 Nov 1990, *Small Seated Nude* (1929, brown-patinated bronze, h. 5½ ins / 14 cm) FRF 180,000. London, 6 Dec 1990, *Orange Slices* (1944, oil and pigments/paper/canvas, 11 x 13¾ ins / 27 x 35 cm) GBP 110,000. Paris, 14 Feb 1991, *Nude Resting* (graphite, 9 x 13½ ins / 22 x 34 cm) FRF 62,000. London, 21 March 1991, *Untitled* (ink and charcoal/paper, 8 x 13¾ ins / 20.4 x 34.8 cm) GBP 6,600. Paris, 2 June 1991, *Head* (1942, oil on paper/canvas, 11 x 9 ins / 27 x 22 cm) FRF 250,000. Milan, 20 June 1991, *Claudette* (1926, oil on canvas, 10 x 11 ins / 24.5 x 27 cm) ITL 21,000,000. London, 27 June 1991, *Great Spaces* (1957, oil and pigments/paper/sacking, 28¾ x 36¼ ins / 73 x 92 cm) GBP 407,000. St-Dié, 13 Oct 1991, *Young Nude Woman* (1925, Indian ink, 11 x 7¾ ins / 27 x 19.5 cm) FRF 41,000. Paris, 23 Nov 1992, *Still-life with a Facetted Glass* (1956, oil on canvas, 13½ x 16¼ ins / 34 x 41 cm) FRF 500,000. Paris, 24 Nov 1992, *Face (Supporter)* (1956, oil on paper/canvas, 11 x 9 ins / 27 x 22 cm) FRF 700,000. London, 3 Dec 1992, *Streaks of Colour* (1959, oil, pigments and mixture/paper/canvas, 19¾ x 24 ins / 50 x 61 cm) GBP 107,800. Paris, 3 Dec 1992, *Self-portrait* (1921, oil on canvas, 24 x 20 ins / 61 x 51 cm) FRF 80,000. Paris, 21 June 1993, *Coffee-maker* (1955, oil on paper/canvas, 21¼ x 25¼ ins / 54 x 64 cm) FRF 810,000. London, 24 June 1993, *Young Roman Woman* (1940, bronze, h. 6½ ins / 16.5 cm) GBP 11,500. Paris, 14 Oct 1993,

Reclining Nude (1944, pen and charcoal, 11¾ x 13½ ins / 30 x 34.5 cm) FRF 16,000; *Johanna* (1957, oil on paper/canvas, 36½ x 28½ ins / 93 x 72.5 cm) FRF 1,150,000. LONDON, 2 Dec 1993, *The Bouquet* (1926, oil on canvas, 23½ x 28¾ ins / 60 x 73 cm) GBP 47,700; *Pink Nude* (oil on canvas, 32 x 51 ins / 81 x 129.5 cm) GBP 177,500. PARIS, 22 Dec 1993, *The Supporters* (watercolour and gouache, 16¾ x 17¼ ins / 42.5 x 44 cm) FRF 75,000. PARIS, 29 April 1994, *Series of Small, Dark Landscapes VI* (1958, oil on panel, 15 x 24 ins / 38 x 61 cm) FRF 600,000. MILAN, 21 June 1994, *Composition* (1957, tempera/mounted paper, 19¾ x 25½ ins / 50 x 65 cm) ITL 16,675,000. LONDON, 30 June 1994, *The Naked Breasts* (1945, oil and pigments/paper/canvas, 18 x 22 ins / 46 x 55 cm) GBP 298,500. PARIS, 12 Oct 1994, *Nude Woman with Long Hair* (1926, pastel/paper, 23¼ x 17 ins / 59 x 43 cm) FRF 46,000. LOKEREN, 11 March 1995, *Wagtail* (1942, etching, 4¼ ins / 11 cm, 2 x 5¼ ins/5 x 13.5 cm) BEF 120,000. PARIS, 13 June 1995, *Scatterbrain* (oil and crushed pastel/paper, 25¼ x 32 ins / 64 x 81 cm) FRF 800,000. LONDON, 26 Oct 1995, *Bust with Breasts* (1929, bronze, h. 15½ ins / 39.5 cm) GBP 56,500. PARIS, 22 Nov 1995, *Composition* (mixed media/paper/canvas, 18 x 21½ ins / 46 x 54.5 cm) FRF 510,000. MILAN, 23 May 1996, *Composition* (1957, mixed media/mounted paper, 12 x 9½ ins / 30.5 x 24 cm) ITL 8,625,000. LONDON, 27 June 1996, *Death of the Wild Boar* (1927, oil on canvas, 63¾ x 51½ ins / 162 x 130.5 cm) GBP 298,500. PARIS, 5 Oct 1996, *Untitled* (charcoal/paper, 10¼ x 19¼ ins / 26 x 49 cm) FRF 12,500. LONDON, 24 Oct 1996, *Still-life with Bottles* (1924-1925, oil on canvas, 42½ x 64¼ ins / 108 x 163 cm) GBP 144,500; *Tall Standing Nude* (1928, bronze, h. 20 ins / 51 cm) GBP 32,200. LONDON, 4 Dec 1996, *Plants* (1957, pigment and oil on paper/canvas, 32 x 39¼ ins / 81 x 100 cm) GBP 133,500. PARIS, 24 March 1997, *Still-life with Onions* (1926, oil on canvas, 24 x 23¼ ins / 61 x 59 cm) FRF 80,000. PARIS, 11 April 1997, *Nude Resting* (1942, pen, 11¾ x 13¾ ins / 30 x 35 cm) FRF 14,000. LONDON, 26 June 1997, *Head of Hostage n°3* (1944, pigment and oil on paper/canvas, 22 x 18 ins / 55 x 46 cm) GBP 441,500. LONDON, 26 June 1997, *Orange Landscape* (1956, oil and pigment/paper/canvas, 15 x 22 ins / 38 x 55 cm) GBP 51,000. PARIS, 14 Dec 1997, *Port-Cros Landscape* (1940, oil/paper remounted/canvas, 6¼ x 9 ins / 16 x 22 cm) FRF 95,000. PARIS, 15 Dec 1997, *Untitled* (1954, gouache, ink wash/blotting paper, 19½ x 25½ ins / 49.5 x 65 cm) FRF 21,000. LONDON, 30 June 1999, *Entanglements* (1959, oil pigment on paper laid on canvas, 26 x 36 ins / 65 x 92 cm) GBP 110,000. LONDON, 30 June 1999, *Fruit* (1947, oil pigment on paper laid on canvas, 21 x 26 ins / 54 x 65 cm) GBP 130,000. LONDON, 28 June 2000, *Pink Nude* (oil on canvas, 32 x 51 ins / 81 x 129 cm) GBP 110,000. LONDON, 29 June 2000, *All Alone* (oil and mixed media on paper laid on canvas, 35 x 57 ins / 89 x 146 cm) GBP 320,000. LONDON, 27 June 2001, *Three Trees* (1944, oil pigment on paper laid on canvas, 24 x 36 ins / 60 x 92 cm) GBP 240,000. PARIS, 18 Dec 2001, *Composition* (1956, oil and mixed media on paper laid on panel, 35 x 46 ins / 89 x 116 cm) FRF 1,600,000. STOCKHOLM, 23 April 2002, *Composition* (1960, mixed media on paper laid on canvas, 36 x 26 ins / 92 x 65 cm) SEK 1,200,000. NEW YORK, 11 Nov 2002, *Head of Partisan, Budapest* (1957, oil on paper laid on canvas, 11 x 9 ins / 27 x 22 cm) USD 105,000. PARIS, 2 April 2003, *Fruit* (1943, oil pigment on paper laid on canvas, 11 x 14 ins / 27 x 35 cm) EUR 120,000. LONDON, 25 June 2003, *Composition* (1961, oil on paper laid on canvas, 29 x 46 ins / 73 x 116 cm) GBP 80,000. LONDON, 4 Feb 2004, *Ile be happy* (1960, oil on paper laid on canvas, 35 x 58 ins / 90 x 147 cm) GBP 190,000. VERSAILLES, 25 April 2004, *Head* (c. 1954, oil pigment on paper laid on canvas, 11 x 9 ins / 27 x 22 cm) EUR 128,000.

FAUVEAU, Eustache Germain

French, 18th century.

Active in Paris.

Painter.

Fauveau was a member of the Académie de St-Luc and a Lancer of the King's Stables. He worked for the Château de Meudon, where he is mentioned in 1711.

FAUVEAU, Félicie de (Mlle)

French, 19th century.

Born 1799, in Florence, to French parents; died 1886.

Sculptor.

Mlle Félicie de Fauveau loved the so-called Neo-Gothic with a predilection for the Middle Ages; she incorporated in her works symbolic details to illustrate ancient thoughts, maxims or mottos. She was a sculptor of the Romantic school. She was born in Florence to Breton parents in 1799, and her childhood was barely over when her father, a banker, left Italy, ruined, to settle in Besançon in France, where he had obtained a job as a civil servant. Wild, opinionated and undisciplined, she was sent down from several boarding schools. She began to model in wax, and became passionate about the Middle Ages, Dante and Walter Scott, who at that time was enormously popular in France. Her refusal to marry or to become a nun is evidence of her independent temperament. Her father, a so-called Ultra-Royalist, died in 1822, and she went to Paris with her mother. She was welcomed to the Court of Charles X and into high society. Admired and spoilt, she remained determined to become an artist. Delaroche and Ingres visited her studio in Rue La Rochefoucauld and advised her; Hersent gave her lessons. Finding the paintbrush altogether too feminine a tool, she turned to the chisel and mallet and intended to become a sculptor. She communicated her enthusiasm to Delaroche, just two years her senior, several of whose highly successful pieces from this period are still extant including both plasters and bronzes and sketches of his paintings such as *Head of Charles the First* and *Deposition*. She encouraged him to study the ancient chronicles. Ary Scheffer produced a portrait of Félicie de Fauveau in riding habit with her hair cut short. Mlle de Fauveau greatly admired the Duchess of Berry who was about her age and sported that hair style for a while. On the other hand she strongly disliked George Sand who never wore her hair short and was five year her junior. She was an ardent royalist and an intransigent legitimist, which twice led her to potentially disastrous experiences in Vendée. She exhibited at the Salon as early as 1827 with two low reliefs based on *The Abbot*, the novel by Walter Scott, whose works had fired her in her gifted but unstudious youth. She won a second medal with *Queen Christina of Sweden and Monaldeschi*, now in the Louvre. She had a passion for Dante and, in 1830, planned a monument to his glory. She may have begun it in that year since the finished work bore an inscription on its pedestal saying 'begun in 1830, finished in 1836'. Louis-Philippe, proclaimed 'King of the French' on 7 August 1830, was to Fauveau, a Breton royalist, nothing but a usurper; for a time politics and insurrection made her forget sculpture. Her first trip to Vendée with the Countess of La Rochejaquelein, in the autumn of 1830, seems to have been for the sole purpose of fleeing Louis-Philippe's Paris and, instead, drawing, hunting and spending time among faithful royalists, that is, legitimists. However few in number, the legitimists were plotting. Louis Charles Boisnormand de Bonnechose, a young man of 21, who had come to bring them secret instructions from Charles X, was fatally injured by the police who had been ordered to arrest him. Naturally Félicie was angry and became impassioned for the cause. Disguised as a man she travelled the region barefoot at the service of the Countess of La Rochejaquelein. The château where the two friends stayed was searched. The women, uneasy, hid in a neighbouring farm. They were discovered huddled in an oven, removed from this uncomfortable refuge and sent to Angers. At their first stop, the Countess managed to escape during the night by exchanging clothes with a servant at the inn where the party had stopped. Félicie was jailed for a few days in Angers and subsequently in Fontenay-le-Comte prison, where she was kept for seven months. She obtained books, pencils, painting and sculpture tools; her mother joined her. There she began several medium-sized works, including *The Battle of Jarnac and de la Chataigneraie*. In January 1832, she painted on the wall of the prison a satirical composition about the death of Charles the tenth's page, the younger brother of the cardinal of Bonnechose. The painting, using gold, silver, blue and very colours, is a curious and interesting display of gothic architecture, coats of arms and escutcheons belonging to those who had achieved fame during the Vendée wars. On the top of the building, an angel holding the Bonnechose shield, hides his face. On the pedestal the archangel Michael, with threatening eyes and ruffled feathers, brandishes a blazing, bloody sword with which he has just killed a dragon with a cock's head (Louis-Philippe, the usurper) in his right hand and scales in his left. One of the scale pans holds judges, prosecutors and magistrates and the other, heavier, contains a single drop of blood. Underneath is the explanation of this rebus: *Quam Gravis Est Sanguis Justi Inultus* (how heavy is the innocent's blood which is shed unpunished). Between the columns are two texts in gothic characters and in medieval French. The text on the right recalls the captivity of the noble and fearless lady Félicie de Duras, Countess of La Rochejaquelein, of the noble women Anne de la Pierre de Fauveau and Mlle Félicie, her daughter. The text on the right refers to several prisoners in the same jail and undertakes to avenge them on the battlefield and to serve their dear master the king. Of course, over time this pseudo-fresco disappeared from the prison wall, but the artist kept the drawing of it, which was later reproduced as a lithograph, a good example of her style. She was judged and acquitted in Poitiers, and able to take up her work again. She refused to see her former friends who were allied to the new regime and treated Delaroche and Scheffer as cowards and traitors. She herself had barely reopened her studio when, in April 1832, her fighting spirit was revived by news of the arrival in Vendée of the Duchess of Berry, mother of the Duke of Bordeaux. She dropped everything and, without hesitation, sped to Vendée. She was reunited with the Countess of La Rochejaquelein and they both joined in the attempted uprising on horseback and armed with sabres and pistols. The uprising was quickly suppressed by the authorities. After two small skirmishes near Clisson, the group dispersed. This time, however, it was more serious for Fauveau. After hiding for some time she managed to get to Belgium. Sentenced in absentia to life imprisonment, she decided to go to Italy with the Countess. She had previously risked a trip to Paris with false papers to empty her studio. Apparently the police were not particularly interested in her capture since, after she had emptied her studio, she was able to go to Switzerland then to Italy without problems.

She settled in Florence, the town where she was born, and mingled with the exiled Bourbons. She set up a studio in a former convent which became a destination for well-to-do tourists. Félicie designed stained glass windows for Ussé château. She sculpted in wood a *Vanity Mirror*, reproduced in the French publication *Magasin Pittoresque* (Picturesque Magazine) in 1839. Apparently Paris did not hold a grudge against her for her adventure in Vendée, since she sent there in 1842 *St George Slaying the Dragon, The Martyrdom of St Dorothy* and *Judith Showing the Head of Holofernes to the People*. When she showed the latter work to her visitors in Florence, she apparently said that it represented the Duchess of Berry and Louis-Philippe. She also sent to Paris *The Battle of Jarnac and de la Chataigneraie*, to be cast in bronze; unfortunately the work suffered an accident at the customs in Marseilles. She produced portraits (*Duchess of Berry* and *Duke of Bordeaux*), and carried out commissions for exiled princes (a marble *St Genevieve* for the Duchess, and *St George Delivering Cappadocia* for the Countess of La Rochejaquelein). She was back in France in 1852 and showed several of her works at the Exhibition of 1875, including *St Dorothy* and *St Elizabeth*. The Count of Pourtalès purchased her famous monument *To the Glory of Dante* completed in Florence in 1836. Like the composition for the death of Louis Charles de Bonnechose, it typifies her method, her love of symbolic detail and even of rebus. For the Count of Pourtalès she had already produced the very intricate *St Michael's Lamp*, with which she tried to elaborate on the words of Christ predicting the end of the world, *Vigilate et Orate*, written on the pedestal with the medieval cry *Valiant and Vigilant; Vigilant and Valiant*. The words *Non Dormit Qui Custodit* (the sentinel never sleeps) appear on the sculpted oak panel supporting the work. Her monument to Dante is a composition in marble, measuring 7 feet 10 inches (2.40 metres) in height, comprising pinnacles, wreathed columns, escutcheons, coats of arms and winged angels, side by side with Minos, the judge of Hell, an owl, a devil with huge bat wings and the inevitable quotation, a verse by Dante: *Di Qua, Di Là, Di Qui, Di Su Li Mena* (Hither and Thither, Upwards and Downwards It Carries Them), explaining the punishment meted out to the two lovers, the central theme of the sculpture. Paolo and Francesca were unable to resist in life their passion and are therefore condemned in death to be forever in the whirlwind of a storm. Between the wreathed columns and below a kind of gothic dais, sits indeed Francesca da Rimini with Paolo Malatesta, her husband's young brother, at her feet. The work is undoubtedly a masterpiece in ingenuity and patience. It has been said that Mlle Fauveau had the soul of a goldsmith. She died aged 87, having designed her tombstone with the inscription: *Vendée, Labeur, Honneur, Douleur* (*Vendée, Work, Honour, Pain*). She sculpted her mother's tomb, now in the Carmes cloisters in Florence. The tomb of Louise Favreau can be seen in the Medici Chapel in the church of Santa Croce. Besides the low relief *Queen Christina of Sweden and Monaldeschi* in the Louvre, and the font in Douai Museum, *Angel Emerging from Holy Water* (otherwise known as *Soul Becoming Free of Earthly Bonds*), the small number of her works in France include the monument to Baron Gros in Toulouse, and a *Virgin and Child* at Hyères (Var), in the church of St Louis, in the south aisle, above the altar, a copy of the original in Florence.

MUSEUMS AND GALLERIES:

DOUAI: stoup - PARIS (Louvre): *Queen Christina of Sweden and Monaldeschi* (low relief).

FAUVEAU, Hippolyte de

French, 19th century.

Born in Florence, to French parents.

Sculptor, architect.

Hippolyte de Fauveau was a pupil of his sister, Félicie de Fauveau.

FAUVEL, Auguste

French, 19th century.

Born 1 May 1822, in Bapaume (Pas-de-Calais).

Painter. Genre scenes, landscapes with figures, still-lifes, animals.

Auguste Fauvel exhibited at the Paris Salon from 1848 to 1875. His paintings include *Game, Fruits, Vegetables, Wild Boar, A Funny Story, Love of Animals* and *The Bird Charmer*.

AUCTION RECORDS:

PARIS, 6 Feb 1932, *Dogs* (no forename given) FRF 100. COLOGNE, 2 June 1967, *Landscape with a Shepherd and his Flock*, DEM 900. PARIS, 20 Nov 1981, *Woman Making a Bouquet* (1870, oil on canvas, 17 3/4 x 12 1/4 ins / 45 x 31 cm) FRF 3,600.

FAUVEL, Georges Henri
French, 19th century.
Born 1890, in Le Havre.
Painter. Animals.

Georges Fauvel received a third-class medal in 1889.

AUCTION RECORDS:
VIENNA, 20 Nov 1981, *Flock in Pasture* (oil on canvas, 21 1/4 x 28 3/4 ins / 54 x 73 cm) ATS 13,000. LONDON, 9 Oct 1987, *Hunting Dogs at Rest* (1896, oil on canvas, 56 x 47 1/4 ins / 142.2 x 120 cm) GBP 4,000.

FAUVEL, Hippolyte
French, 19th century.
Born 1835, in Amiens.
Painter. Landscapes with figures, landscapes.

Hippolyte Fauvel was a pupil of Yvon. He exhibited at the Paris Salon from 1861 onwards.

MUSEUMS AND GALLERIES:
AMIENS: *Footpath in Capri.*

AUCTION RECORDS:
PARIS, 18 April 1928, *L'abreuvoir* FRF 155. PARIS, 7 July 1982, *Haymaker* (oil on panel, 21 3/4 x 13 3/4 ins / 55.5 x 35 cm) FRF 5,500.

FAUVEL, Louis François Sébastien
French, 18th - 19th century.
Born 14 September 1753, in Clermont-en-Beauvaisis; died 12 March 1838, in Smyrna.
Draughtsman, painter, engraver, archaeologist.

Fauvel is known to have produced an engraving in colour, as well as *The Philosopher* after Janinet and a *Portrait of the Poet Delille* engraved by L. Guyot. A view of *Sarratoya* was engraved after Fauvel by Geoffroy for the *Collection of Prints of the War of South America*. F. L. Couché engraved *The Bed of Victory and the Death of Toiras*, and Macret *The Reception of Voltaire on the Champs-Élysées* after Fauvel's works. He accompanied Choiseul-Gouffiers, ambassador to Turkey, first of all to Greece and then to Constantinople, and was appointed vice-consul in Athens. He collaborated on the work by Choiseul-Gouffiers entitled *Illustrated Journey to Greece,* for which he drew three views of Constantinople and a *View of the Harem*. The Bibliothèque Nationale in Paris has some of his works.

FAUVEL, Louise
French, 19th century.
Born in Constantinople, to French parents.
Painter.

Louise Fauvel was a pupil of Mme Colin-Libour. She exhibited flowers and pottery at the Paris Salon, from 1876 onwards.

FAUVEL, Mathieu
17th century.
Painter.

Mentioned by Marolles.

FAUVEL, Pierre
French, 15th century.
Active in Amiens.
Sculptor, metal worker, goldsmith.

In 1485, in collaboration with Pierre de Dury, Fauvel executed a silver altarpiece with statuettes and low reliefs showing scenes from the Old and New Testaments for the high altar of Amiens Cathedral (Somme).

FAUVELET, Jean-Baptiste
French, 19th century.
Born 9 June 1819, in Bordeaux; died 14 March 1883, in Chartres.
Painter, lithographer. Genre scenes, landscapes, still-lifes.

Fauvelet exhibited at the Paris Salon from 1845 to 1870, receiving a second-class medal in 1848. He pained landscapes, still-lifes and, especially, genre scenes where the background is merely suggested.

MUSEUMS AND GALLERIES:
CHARTRES: *Rigolo* - LA ROCHELLE: *Young Girl* - LONDON (Wallace Collection): *Pheasants* (before 1855, oil/panel) - PARIS (Mus. d'Orsay): *Ascanio the Engraver; The Plaintiffs* - SZCZECIN: *Scientist at Work.*

AUCTION RECORDS:
PARIS, 7 April 1896, *Artist in a Studio,* FRF 680; *Engravings Collectors,* FRF 700. PARIS, 7 Feb 1903, *Young Woman by the Fire,* FRF 600. PARIS, 20 Nov 1918, *Bass Player,* FRF 605. PARIS, 10 Dec 1920, *In front of the Mirror,* FRF 680. PARIS, 21-22 Nov 1922, *Portrait of the Duchess Decazes* (watercolour/paper) FRF 300. PARIS, 4 June 1924, *Smoker,* FRF 600. PARIS, 17-18 Nov 1924, *Woman in Interior Putting on Shoes,* FRF 1,620. PARIS, 27-28 Nov 1924, *Meeting; Reading over Coffee,* FRF 1,400. PARIS, 30 Dec 1925, *Smoker,* FRF 3,000. PARIS, 14 Dec 1933, *Drawing Class,* FRF 1,000; *Visiting,* FRF 1,150. PARIS, 22 Feb 1943, *Writer,* FRF 3,000. LONDON, 29 Sept 1976, *Success* (oil on panel, 9 1/4 x 7 1/4 ins / 23.5 x 18.5 cm) GBP 550. LOS ANGELES, 17 March 1980, *Art Lovers* (1860, oil on panel, 8 1/2 x 6 ins / 21.3 x 15.5 cm) USD 2,500. NEW YORK, 1 March 1984, *Art Lover* (oil on panel, 9 1/2 x 7 1/4 ins / 24.1 x 18.5 cm) USD 1,000. NEW YORK, 13 Feb 1985, *Women in Interior* (1863, oil on canvas, 15 1/2 x 18 1/4 ins / 39.4 x 46.4 cm) USD 3,000. AMSTERDAM, 30 Oct 1991, *Moments of Idleness* (oil on canvas, 14 1/4 x 11 3/4 ins / 36 x 30 cm) NLG 4,140. AMSTERDAM, 5-6 Nov 1991, *Young Girl Listening at a Door* (1831, oil on panel, 10 x 7 1/4 ins / 24.5 x 18.5 cm) NLG 2,875. LONDON, 2 Oct 1992, *Connoisseur* (oil on panel, 8 1/4 x 6 1/4 ins / 21 x 16 cm) GBP 1,980. NEW YORK, 22-23 July 1993, *Gentleman smoking Pipe* (oil on panel, a pair, 8 1/2 x 6 1/2 ins / 21.6 x 16.5 cm) USD 4,888. BOSTON, 29 May 1999, *Ladies at Table* (1863, oil on canvas, 15 x 18 ins / 38 x 46 cm) USD 4,000. PARIS, 16 Nov 2001, *Two Gentlemen in a Cabaret* (oil on panel, 11 x 8 ins / 27 x 21 cm) FRF 15,000. COPENHAGEN, 2 March 2004, *Young Couple Conversing* (oil on panel, 8 x 10 ins / 20 x 25 cm) DKK 21,000.

FAUVERGE, Caroline Stéphanie
French, 19th century.
Born 19th century, in Strasbourg.
Painter.

She exhibited landscapes painted in Germany and Normandy at the Paris Salon from 1834 to 1839.

FAUVILLE, Daniel
Belgian, 20th - 21st century.
Born 1953, in Charleroi.
Painter, draughtsman, sculptor (bronze), pastellist.

Fauville lives and works in Charleroi.

He produces sculptures in bronze using the lost-wax technique. He draws his inspiration from a recent past, when the technological structures of the steelworks and collieries dominated the Belgian landscape; he evokes this through metaphors and by likening these structures to religious sculpture, the mausoleum falling into a state of neglect, with broken columns, wide open exits and eroded flying buttresses. Some of his works have been purchased by the French Ministry of Culture. He has participated in many Belgian and international group exhibitions, including: 1982, Salon de Montrouge; 1984, Salon Figuration Critique, Paris; 1985,

Musée des Beaux-Arts in Brussels; 1989, São Paulo Biennale. In addition, he has held solo shows in Brussels, particularly at the Palais des Beaux-Arts in 1992 and also at La Louvière in Paris; and in 2002 at the Gallery Roselyn Koener, Westhampton, New York.

FAUVILLE, Marie Ange
French, 20th century.
Born in Léo-St-Amand.
Sculptor.

Fauville exhibited at the Salon d'Automne in Paris in 1924.

FAUX-FROIDURE, Eugénie Juliette
French, 20th century.
Born 23 August 1866, in Noyen-sur-Sarthe; died 14 February 1942.
Painter, watercolourist. Landscapes, flowers.

Faux-Froidure was a pupil of Albert Maignan, Saintpierre, Quost, and of Léon Bonnat. She was made Chevalier of the Légion d'Honneur. She regularly exhibited at the Salon des Artistes Français, of which she became a member in 1893. She received an honourable mention there in 1898, as well as at the Exposition Universelle in 1900, where she also received a third-class medal in 1903 and received a non-competitive nomination in 1906. She was also a member of the Société des Aquarellistes Français.

MUSEUMS AND GALLERIES:
AMIENS - DIJON - PARIS - ROUEN: *Chrysanthemums; Autumn Foliage* - TUNIS.

AUCTION RECORDS:
PARIS, 21 Feb 1924, *Bundle of Roses* (watercolour) FRF 470. PARIS, 24 April 1942, *Nasturtiums* (watercolour) FRF 350. PARIS, 18 Feb 1944, *Gilliflowers* (watercolour) FRF 220. PARIS, 21 March 1947, *Flowers* (watercolour) FRF 4,700. NEW YORK, 25 Oct 1984, *Geraniums* (watercolour, 33½ x 23½ ins / 85.1 x 59.6 cm) USD 1,300. PARIS, 7 April 1987, *Flower-stand* (watercolour, 20½ x 25¼ ins / 52 x 64 cm) FRF 8,200. VERSAILLES, 18 March 1990, *Flowers in a Blue Vase* (watercolour, 15 x 22 ins / 38 x 55 cm) FRF 24,000. VERSAILLES, 25 Nov 1990, *Bouquet of Geraniums* (watercolour, 32¾ x 23½ ins / 83 x 60 cm) FRF 25,000. PARIS, 16 Dec 1993, *Bunch of Hortensias on a Pedestal Table* (watercolour, 22 x 28½ ins / 55 x 72.5 cm) FRF 13,500. AMSTERDAM, 21 April 1994, *Roses, Margueritas and Other Summer Flowers in a Basket* (1886, watercolour/paper, 19 x 23¼ ins / 48 x 59 cm) NLG 4,370. PARIS, 5 June 1996, *Still-life with Basket of Roses and Eyelets* (watercolour/paper, 21 x 28 ins / 52.5 x 71 cm) FRF 6,000. PARIS, 14 March 1997, *Bouquets of Roses and Dahlias in Oriental Pitcher* (watercolour, 58¼ x 30¾ ins / 148 x 78 cm) FRF 22,000. BRUSSELS, 4 April 2000, *Abundance* (watercolour, 51 x 28 ins / 129 x 70 cm) BEF 85,000. BRUSSELS, 20 Jan 2003, *Elegant Woman Smiling with Bunch of Roses* (watercolour, 50 x 27 ins / 128 x 68 cm) EUR 3,400.

FAVA, Brigida (Contessa)
Maiden name: (Marchesa) Tanari
Italian, 19th century.
Active in Bologna.
Painter.

Brigida Fava was a pupil of Pietro Fancelli. She exhibited miniatures, including a copy of Guido Reni's *Virgin*, and some portraits. She was also a history painter.

FAVA, Carlo Luigi
Italian, 19th century.
Born in San Prospero, near Parma.
Sculptor.

Carlo Luigi Fava was a student of Tommaso Bandini at the Accademia in Parma. He exhibited a series of high and low reliefs that were engraved by Bigola as a frontispiece for an edition of works by the writer Pietro Giordani.

FAVA, Giuseppe
Italian, 17th century.
Born 29 May 1611, in Ugozzolo, near Parma.
Painter, copyist.

In 1653, Fava produced a drawing based on a fresco of St Francis of Assisi; he also made two copies of works by Michele Raineri and Michele Desubleo that were kept in the Palazzo del Giardino during the time of the Farnese.

FAVA, Pietro Ercole da (Count)
Italian, 17th - 18th century.
Born 1667, in Bologna; died 1744.
Painter.

A patron of the arts and an occasional painter in his own right, Count Pietro Ercole da Fava worked with L. Pasinelli and sponsored his friends Donato Creti and Ercole Graziani. Carracci was his mentor of choice, however, and he studied the latter's work avidly. He was also a member of the academy of Clementina. He painted an altarpiece entitled *Virgin and Child with St Albert, St Paul and Others* for the church of S Tommaso dal Mercato in Bologna; his *Epiphany* and *Resurrection* hang in the cathedral of Ancona.

FAVAI, Gennaro
Italian, 20th century.
Born 1879, in Venice; died 1958.
Painter. Urban landscapes, architectural views.

Gennaro Favai mainly painted views of Venice, and exhibited at the Salon of the Société Nationale des Beaux-Arts in Paris.

AUCTION RECORDS:
PARIS, 6-7 Dec 1944, *Caravel*, FRF 1,600. PARIS, 21 March 1947, *Canal in Venice*, FRF 420. NEW YORK, 21 Aug 1981, *Desdemona's Place* (oil on panel, 39¼ x 47¼ ins / 99.5 x 120 cm) USD 800. PARIS, 6 Feb 1991, *Venetian Palace* (oil on panel, 18½ x 20¾ ins / 47 x 53 cm) FRF 7,000. NEW YORK, 26 May 1992, *View of St Mark's Square in Venice* (oil on panel, 38¾ x 53 ins / 98.4 x 134.6 cm) USD 7,700. NEW YORK, 28 May 1993, *View of S Maria della Salute at Night* (oil on panel, 28¼ x 34½ ins / 71.6 x 87.9 cm) USD 2,300. VENICE, 7-8 Oct 1996, *Church in Messina* (oil on card, 14 x 16¼ ins / 35.5 x 41 cm) ITL 2,300,000. NEW YORK, 15 June 1999, *Mattino seen from on high. Ducal Palace at Mattino* (1939, oil on panel, a pair, 15 x 19 ins / 38 x 48 cm) USD 4,500. VENICE, 13 Nov 1999, *Il Bucintoro* (1909, oil on canvas, 43 x 55 ins / 109 x 140 cm) ITL 13,900,000. NEW YORK, 30 Oct 2001, *Venetian Canal* (oil on canvas, 26 x 31 ins / 65 x 79 cm) USD 2,400. ROME, 27 May 2002, *Celebration of the Redemptor* (1909, oil on canvas, 43 x 60 ins / 110 x 152 cm) EUR 5,000. ROME, 26 Nov 2002, *Celebration of the Redemptor* (1909, oil on canvas, 43 x 60 ins / 110 x 152 cm) EUR 4,800.

FAVANNE, Henri Antoine de
French, 17th - 18th century.
Born 3 October 1668, in London, to French parents; died 27 April 1752, in Paris.
Painter. History painting, allegorical subjects, mythological subjects.

Henri Antoine de Favanne was the pupil of Houasse. On 28 August 1704 he was admitted as an academician, became a professor on 28 September 1725, assistant rector on 26 March 1746, and rector on 6 July 1748. In 1695, in Rome, De Favanne became friends with D'Aubigny, secretary to the Princesse des Ursins. As a result of this connection he was summoned to Spain by Philip V in 1705. He returned to France in the company of M. d'Aubigny in 1714, when his protectress had lost her influence. Between 1704 and 1715 Henri de Favanne sent several works to the Salon.

The best known of his paintings are *Ceres Finding the Girdle of her Daughter Proserpine, Abducted by Pluto; Naiads; Thetis Forced to Consent to Marry Peleus; Separation of Telemachus and Eucharis* (in Rome); *The Nymphs, Excited by*

Love, Set Fire to the Vessel to Prevent Telemachus from Escaping; Venus Puts Love in the Hands of Calypso and *Chaste Susanna and the Elders.* Henri de Favanne was painter in ordinary to the King of France and premier huntsman to the King of England, Charles II.

MUSEUMS AND GALLERIES:
ORLÉANS: *Philip of France, King of Anjou Recognised as King of Spain; Sketch for a Portrait* - PARIS (ENSBA): *Portrait of the Artist* - PARIS (Louvre): *Pen and Ink Drawing* - TOULOUSE: *Interior* - VERSAILLES: *Allegory, with Cardinal Alberoni.*
AUCTION RECORDS:
PARIS, 12-14 May 1924, *Venus on the Waters* (attributed) FRF 2,600. PARIS, 17 June 1994, *Two Studies of a Male Nude* (black chalk and white chalk highlights/beige paper, 10 x 15 3/4 ins / 24.5 x 40 cm) FRF 6,200. PARIS, 10 April 1995, *Allegory to the Glory of Philip V, King of Spain* (oil on canvas, 15 x 18 1/4 ins / 38 x 46.5 cm) FRF 12,000. NEW YORK, 30 Jan 1998, *The Seasons* (oil on canvas, four works, 28 3/4 x 23 1/4 ins / 73 x 59.1 cm) USD 79,500. PARIS, 18 March 2001, *Birth of Adonis* (oil on canvas, 22 x 22 ins / 57 x 57 cm) FRF 39,000. LONDON, 11 Dec 2001, *Meleager and Atalanta* (oil on canvas, 41 x 33 ins / 103 x 83 cm) GBP 11,000.

FAVANNE, Jacques de
French, 18th century.
Born 1716, in Paris; died 1770.
Engraver.
Jacques de Favanne was the son of Henri de Favanne. He was the pupil of F. Thomassin, and established himself in Paris around 1760. He engraved after Watteau, Lancret and Le Maine.

FAVANNE, Jean Henry de
French, 18th century.
Active in Paris.
Painter, engraver.
Jean Henry de Favanne was the son of Henri de Favanne.

FAVANT, Gabrielle
French, 20th century.
Born 1889, in Agde.
Painter. Seascapes, landscapes.
Gabrielle Favant lived in St-Henri, near Marseilles. She was introduced to painting by the seascape artist, Louis Nattero. She exhibited in Marseilles around 1914. Her most representative works are those which she created on the Marseilles coastline, such as the seascapes of La Pointe Rouge, La Redonne and L'Estaque.

FAVARD, Antoine Gabriel
French, 19th century.
Born 14 February 1829, in Lyons.
Painter, watercolourist.
In 1853 Favard entered the École des Beaux-Arts in Paris. From 1863 to 1877, he exhibited in Paris watercolours and gouaches in the style of the Italian and German masters, and religious and genre scenes. Works exhibited include *Abel Dying* (1863), *Memory of Italy,* a watercolour (1867), *Last Moments of Christ* (1874) and *Four Friends* (1877). At this point, the artist was in Rome. In 1867 he received a medal in Paris.

FAVARD, Philippe
French, 19th - 20th century.
Born in Berlin.
Painter.
Favard was a pupil of both J. Lefebvre and T. Robert-Fleury.

FAVARD, Ville
British, 18th century.
Active in London.
Miniaturist.
Ville Favard exhibited four miniature portraits and a *Cupid* at the Royal Academy in London from 1794 to 1797.

FAVART, Antoine Pierre Charles
French, 19th century.
Born 1784, in Paris; died 28 March 1867.
Painter, engraver. History painting.
Favart was a pupil of Suvée, and exhibited at the Paris Salon from 1806 to 1839. Works include *Heroic Action of Henry II, Duke of Montmorency, General View of Jerusalem* and *Bayard Injured beneath the Walls of Brescia.*

AUCTION RECORDS:
PARIS, 27 Jan 1943, *Portrait of a Man Leaning against a Fireplace* (watercolour) FRF 2,050.

FAVART, Geneviève (Mme)
Maiden name: Bellot
French, 18th - 19th century.
Painter.
Geneviève Favart was the pupil of Bachelier. In 1800 and 1808 she exhibited several portraits at the Salon de Paris.
AUCTION RECORDS:
PARIS, 22 June 1939, *Charles-Simon Favart Writing the Comedy 'The Englishman in Bordeaux'* (pastel) FRF 4,500.

FAVART, Jehan or Little Jehan, or Favert or Fauvert or Fanart
French, 16th century.
Active in Amboise (Indre-et-Loire).
Painter.
Gaillon School.
Favart was involved in the preparations for the entry of Anne of Brittany into Amboise and the staging of the Mystery Play of *Julius Caesar.* In 1508, together with the sculptor Juste, he made the low relief showing the battle of Gennes for the Château of the cardinal of Amboise in Gaillon. In 1523, he directed the preparations for a staging of the Passion, and in 1530 those for the entry of Queen Éléonore into Amboise.

FAVAS, Jean Daniel
Swiss, 19th century.
Born 11 October 1813, in Geneva; died 1864, in Geneva.
Active in France as a naturalised Frenchman.
Painter.
On 7 October 1835, Favas entered the École des Beaux-Arts in Paris, where he studied under Hornung and P. Delaroche. From 1842 to 1861, he exhibited regularly at the Paris Salon, gaining a third-class medal in 1845. His best-known works include: *Mariocetta, Young Shepherd in the Roman Countryside, Costumes of Mola di Gaeta, View from Acquacetosa, Roman Countryside, Studio Interior* and *Young Woman Removing her Mask.* He also painted portraits, including his *Portrait of General Dufour,* held by the Rath Museum in Geneva.

FAVAZZA, Alessandro
Italian, 17th century.
Born to a family originally from Foligno.
Painter.
Alessandro Favazza was listed in the register of the Accademia di San Luca, Rome, in 1635.

FAVÉ, Paul
French, 20th century.
Born 20th century, in Montereau.
Painter. Landscapes, still-lifes.
Favé showed for the first time in Paris at the Salon des Indépendants in 1926. He also participated in the Salon d'Automne and had a solo exhibition in Paris in 1925. Mainly a

landscapist, his painting has primitive and spontaneous qualities.
AUCTION RECORDS:
PARIS, 27 Dec 1926, *Moret Church*, FRF 360.

FAVEL
French, 18th century.
Painter, draughtsman. Landscapes.
Favel was active in Toulon, where in 1782 he executed paintings for the navy and was appointed professor of marine painting. The engraver J. N. Laugier was his pupil.
AUCTION RECORDS:
PARIS, 24 Nov 1995, *View of the City and Roads of Toulon* (watercolour and black ink, a pair, 14 x 25 ins / 35.4 x 63.5 cm and 14 x 24 1/2 ins/35.5 x 62.5 cm) FRF 20,000.

FAVÉN, Antti Yrjo
Finnish, 20th century.
Born 20 May 1882, in Helsinki.
Active in France.
Painter, draughtsman. Portraits, genre scenes, landscapes.
Favén was a caricaturist as well as a painter. He exhibited at the Salon d'Automne in Paris from 1903.
MUSEUMS AND GALLERIES:
HELSINKI: *Portrait of Two Ladies* - TURKU: *Portrait of the Artist's Three Brothers.*
AUCTION RECORDS:
STOCKHOLM, 13 April 1992, *Rainbow and Factories by a River in Österbotten* (oil on panel, 15 3/4 x 19 1/4 ins / 40 x 49 cm) SEK 5,200. HELSINKI, 11 Dec 1999, *Harvest Time* (1928, oil on canvas, 19 x 16 ins / 47 x 40 cm) FIM 14,500. HELSINKI, 11 Dec 1999, *Cloudy Summer Landscape* (1938, oil on canvas, 20 x 17 ins / 51 x 44 cm) FIM 22,000. HELSINKI, 3 Dec 2000, *The Trip - Landscape with Horse, Cart and Figures* (1911, oil on canvas, 47 x 38 ins / 119 x 97 cm) FIM 40,000. HELSINKI, 3 Dec 2000, *Midsummer Dance* (1911, oil on canvas, 47 x 47 ins / 120 x 120 cm) FIM 82,000. HELSINKI, 12 May 2001, *The Meeting* (1904, oil on canvas, 12 x 11 ins / 31 x 28 cm) FIM 22,000. HELSINKI, 12 May 2001, *After the Rain* (1947, oil on canvas, 39 x 52 ins / 100 x 132 cm) FIM 42,000. HELSINKI, 28 April 2002, *Clouds above the Sea* (1940, oil on board, 20 x 17 ins / 52 x 43 cm) EUR 2,700. UPPSALA, 8 Dec 2002, *Landscape in Evening Light* (1911, oil on panel, 7 x 9 ins / 19 x 24 cm) SEK 26,000. HELSINKI, 10 May 2003, *After the Rain* (1901, oil on canvas, 28 x 21 ins / 70 x 53 cm) EUR 5,000. HELSINKI, 29 Nov 2003, *View from Brunnsparken towards the Ocean* (1931, oil on canvas, 36 x 52 ins / 91 x 131 cm) EUR 7,000. HELSINKI, 15 May 2004, *Autumn Landscape* (1927, oil on canvas, 24 x 19 ins / 60 x 47 cm) EUR 3,600. HELSINKI, 15 May 2004, *Landscape* (oil on canvas/board, 15 x 11 ins / 38 x 29 cm) EUR 4,800.

FAVENZA, V.
Italian, 19th century.
Active in Venice c. 1850.
Sculptor (wood), marquetry worker.
Favenza's work can be seen in the municipal museum in Venice. It has some items of furniture by this artist which have decorative carvings and are encrusted with ebony and ivory.
MUSEUMS AND GALLERIES:
VENICE (Mus. Civico).

FAVEREAU, Adrien
French, 17th century.
Active in Paris in 1690.
Painter, sculptor, engraver.

FAVEREAU, Gabriel
French, 16th century.
Died 1576.
Active in Troyes.
Sculptor, architect.
The son-in-law of Dominique Florentin, Favereau collaborated with his father-in-law on a stone rood screen in the collegiate church of St-Étienne in Troyes between 1549 and 1555. The remains of this work, which was demolished during the French Revolution, are scattered in different places. He was appointed as master mason of the cathedral in 1559, a post he held until his death.

FAVERET, Claude
French, 17th century.
Active in Angers.
Painter.

FAVERGE, Georges
French, 17th - 18th century.
Born c. 1654; died 14 December 1734.
Active in Grenoble.
Sculptor.

FAVERGE, Siméon
French, 18th century.
Sculptor.

FAVERI, Flavio de, or Flaveri
French, 20th century.
Born 11 July 1930, in Codogno.
Sculptor.
Faveri studied at the École des Beaux-Arts in Toulouse from 1949 to 1954 and taught drawing in Montauban. His work consisted of classical sculptures of women, which he exhibited in the Toulouse region.

FAVERIC, Étienne, or Faverle
French, 15th century.
Glass painter.
Between 1452 and 1476, Faveric worked on the windows of the church of St-Sulpice in Fougères (Ille-et-Vilaine).

FAVERIE, Nadine (Mme)
Maiden name: Ollivier
French, 19th century.
Active in Paris.
Portrait artist.
Faverie exhibited portraits at the Paris Salon from 1844 to 1849.

FAVERJON, Jean Marie
French, 19th century.
Born 3 January 1823, in St-Étienne; died 1873.
Painter. Religious subjects, mythological subjects, portraits, genre scenes, landscapes.
Faverjon entered the École des Beaux-Arts on 7 October 1846 and became the pupil of Flandrin. He exhibited at the Paris Salon from 1848 to 1872. His works include *View of Paris from a Park in Clamart, Banks of the Bièvre, Christ on the Cross, Spring, Summer, Deliverance of St Peter, Forge Interior, Autumn, Battle Scene, Amphitrite* and *Wash House on the Bank of the Furens*.
MUSEUMS AND GALLERIES:
ST-ÉTIENNE: *View from Fontenay-aux-Roses; Interior of Turner's Studio; Haute-Loire Lacemaker; Self-portrait.*
AUCTION RECORDS:
LONDON, 6 Feb 1987, *Seasons* (1855, set of four oils on canvas, 32 1/4 x 67 3/4 ins / 81.9 x 172.1 cm) GBP 4,500.

FAVERLE, Étienne. See **FAVERIC**

FAVERO, Andrea
Italian, 19th - 20th century.
Born 1837, in San Zenone degli Ezzelini (Treviso); died 1914.
Painter. Genre scenes, architectural views. Decorative schemes, theatre decoration.
Andrea Favero studied in Venice where he won a gold medal for a painting entitled *Ancient Moorish Structures* in 1856.

In Bologna he decorated the Palazzo Belardini and produced paintings for the Matelica and Camerino theatres.

AUCTION RECORDS:

MILAN, 10 Dec 1987, *Children's Games* (oil on canvas, 24 1/2 x 17 3/4 ins / 62 x 45 cm) ITL 7,000,000. MILAN, 21 Dec 1999, *Female Figure* (1887, ink heightened with white, 8 x 6 ins / 21 x 14 cm) ITL 5,000,000. LONDON, 7 April 2000, *Dead Brother* (oil on board, 9 x 11 ins / 22 x 29 cm) GBP 7,200. ROME, 4 June 2001, *Male Nude* (oil on canvas, 16 x 11 ins / 40 x 28 cm) ITL 9,000,000. ROME, 27 May 2002, *Lady with Hat* (1884, watercolour on card, 9 x 6 ins / 24 x 15 cm) EUR 7,800. ZURICH, 16 Sept 2002, *Study of the Lottery Draw* (oil on canvas, 16 x 12 ins / 41 x 30 cm) CHF 15,000. VIENNA, 28 March 2003, *Young Girl with Birdcage* (sketch, 11 x 7 ins / 28 x 19 cm) EUR 5,000. PRATO, 14 Nov 2003, *Confidences* (oil on canvas, 26 x 37 ins / 65 x 95 cm) EUR 400,000. BERN, 12 May 2004, *Young Flower Girl* (oil on canvas, 23 x 14 ins / 59 x 36 cm) CHF 10,000.

FAVERO, Antonio dal

Italian, 19th century.
Born 1844, in Ceneda.
Painter, sculptor.

Antonio dal Favero began his studies at the Accademia in Venice, where he won several prizes. His early works include a relief of *Esmeralda*; a *Deposition* (life-size), which is now in the church of S Michele di Vittorio; two statues *(Rebecca* and *Fioraia)*, for the palace of Prince Giovanelli in Venice; two statues *(The Immaculate Conception* and *St Lucy)* for a church in Conegliano, and many others.

The works considered to be Antonio dal Favero's masterpieces are two monuments: one erected in honour of *Victor Emmanuel*, and one to *Garibaldi*, both in Vittorio. For these monuments he was decorated with the cross of the Crown of Italy.

His best-known paintings include *The Pupils* and *The Grandmother's Cow*, which were exhibited in Turin in 1884; and *Assumption*, a chalice pall in the church of Covolo.

FAVEROT, Joseph B.-B.

French, 19th century.
Born May 1862, in Paris.
Painter. Genre scenes, animals, farmyard scenes.

Faverot worked in Gérome's studio. He exhibited at the Paris Salon from 1887 to 1900, and at the Salon of the Société Nationale des Beaux-Arts. He painted genre scenes, generally of farmyard animals, such as *Cocks and Hens*. He spent his youth among circus people and specialised in decorative panels depicting clowns and acrobats which he painted in night clubs in the Paris district of Montmartre.

AUCTION RECORDS:

PARIS, 20-21 April 1928, *On the Fortifications*; *The Open-air Café* (ensemble) FRF 300. PARIS, 12-13 Nov 1928, *Clown Line Fishing*, FRF 65; *Clown Playing a Guitar*, FRF 170. PARIS, 4 June 1941, *Henhouse*, FRF 390. PARIS, 22 July 1942, *Cock and Hens*, FRF 700. PARIS, 17 May 1943, *Dog and Circus Scene* (two oils on canvas) FRF 1,000. PARIS, 28 March 1947, *Entrance of the Clowns*, FRF 1,500. PARIS, 23 June 1947, *Henhouse*, FRF 2,900. BARBIZON, 31 Oct 1982, *Wedding* (oil on canvas, 75 1/2 x 63 ins / 192 x 160 cm) FRF 3,000. VERRIÈRES-LE-BUISSON, 14 Dec 1986, *Weight Lifter* (oil on canvas, 18 x 24 3/4 ins / 46 x 63 cm) FRF 7,500. PARIS, 19 June 1989, *Circus Scene* (oil on panel, 16 1/4 x 13 ins / 41 x 33 cm) FRF 13,000. PARIS, 30 March 1992, *Farmyard* (oil on panel, 15 x 11 ins / 38 x 27 cm) FRF 3,500. LE TOUQUET, 30 May 1993, *Good Lunch* (oil on canvas, 36 1/4 x 28 3/4 ins / 92 x 73 cm) FRF 8,500. PARIS, 16 June 1997, *Cock and Hens* (oil on canvas, 53 1/4 x 39 3/4 ins / 135 x 101 cm) FRF 15,000. BERN, 6 Nov 2002, *Poultry Yard* (oil on canvas, 13 x 16 ins / 33 x 41 cm) CHF 2,300.

FAVET, Charles

French, 20th century.
Engraver. Urban landscapes.

Favet produced numerous exhibitions both in France and abroad. He was a laureate of the Institut, and received the prize of the Société Française de Gravure in 1960. He designed around 500 ex-libris plates. He specialised in depicting the historic city of Troyes.

FAVIER, Annie

French, 20th century.
Painter.

Annie Favier exhibited her works in a solo exhibition in 1994 at the Kandler gallery in Toulouse.

She draws inspiration from her travels, creating feeling through colour in her abstract compositions.

FAVIER, Cécile

French, 20th century.
Born 1906, in the Puy-de-Dôme.
Painter.

Cécile Favier travelled to Argentina when she was young. She was of modest means, and began to paint relatively late, showing her first paintings in 1950. Her art can be linked to naive painting.

FAVIER, Claude François

French, 17th century.
Active in St-Claude (Jura).
Sculptor.

FAVIER, Eugène

French, 19th - 20th century.
Born 1860, in Paris.
Painter, pastellist. Nudes, portraits, flowers.

Eugène Favier was a pupil of Gérome. He exhibited at the Salon des Artistes Français in Paris, of which he became a member in 1892. He received an honourable mention in 1902. He focused on flowers, nudes and, predominantly, portraits, either in oil or pastel. He painted the portraits of all the actors at the Théatre de l'Odéon.

AUCTION RECORDS:

BARBIZON, 22 April 1979, *Little Girl in Blue Dress* (oil on canvas, 16 1/4 x 11 ins / 41 x 27 cm) FRF 3,100. PARIS, 10 June 1987, *Portrait of a Young Brown-haired Girl with Lace Dress* (1924, pastel) FRF 3,000.

FAVIER, Jeanne Magdeleine

French, 19th century.
Born in Vichy (Allier); died 1902.
Painter, pastellist. Portraits, genre scenes.

Jeanne Favier's works include *Portrait of My Mother* (1888), *Portrait of M. E. M.* (1892), *Portrait of the Author* (1895), *En fraude* (*Secrecy*), *At Work* and *Portrait of Maurice Faure* (1897).

AUCTION RECORDS:

PARIS, 23 April 1945, *Seated Woman, Undressed* (1902, pastel, no forename given) FRF 400.

FAVIER, Nicolas

French, 18th century.
Active in Paris in 1758.
Painter, sculptor.

FAVIER, Philippe

French, 20th - 21st century.
Born 1957, in St-Étienne.
Engraver, painter, draughtsman.

Philippe Favier studied under Gérard Pascual at the École des Beaux-Arts de St-Étienne, graduating in 1981. He lives and works in St-Étienne.

Favier has produced his works in series, frequently changing the media in which he works; his representational style has thus developed rapidly. From 1980 to 1985, he drew tiny figures on paper, which he coloured in by hand; from 1985 to 1987, he produced drawings and oil paintings on broken glass or glass boxes; and, since 1989, he has painted in gloss and solvent on metal (in particular, on the lids of jam jars and sardine tins). In addition, he has produced engravings in a more traditional style. His *Winds* series and still-lifes are prime examples of his paintings on glass, a material which he works with care: in recovering all the smashed fragments, painting their backs, scraping and engraving them, and playing upon the effects of their transparency, he creates an impression of space. His paintings on sardine and mackerel tins include the *Parisiana* series, evocative of night-time in the city. Sometimes, as in his engravings of Flemish and German masterpieces from the 15th and 16th centuries, and of works from the Far East, Favier makes mythological or art-historical quotations. His works are essentially narrative, and they often contain a story for viewers to read, or a meaning for them to interpret. His imaginative world is one of anecdotes, swarming with small creatures and objects. These are chosen not at random, but to convey memories, desires, emotions and fears.

Favier also shows a certain intellectual playfulness in his work, hence his series of engravings paradoxically entitled *Grande Excursion en Casanie*: 'Casanie' derives from the adjective, 'casanier', meaning 'unadventurous', or 'stay-at-home'. This title is also typical of his defiantly unobtrusive attitude. While his contemporaries constantly push the boundaries, he is always trying to produce works on a smaller scale than theirs, often only a few square centimetres in area. His paintings have been reproduced on a larger scale, but this runs contrary to his approach, since he avoids the bravado, and vulgar ostentation, typical of a generation which wants to 'see everything'. He does produce some works in a larger format: 4 x 5 foot (1.2 x 1.6 metre) paintings, as well as various silkscreen prints and engravings. In these works, Favier draws various objects or plants, or engraves pastoral scenes; but, even in these large formats, he still depicts his subjects on a small scale, whether on dark or black backgrounds (like those used in his paintings on broken glass), or on white backgrounds, as in his series of engraved pastoral scenes, entitled *Les Ambassades Verticales* (*Vertical Embassies*).

In 1982, he staged a solo exhibition in the Musée d'Art et d'Industrie de St-Étienne, and later exhibited in a number of prestigious venues, both in France and elsewhere.

Favier has taken part in a number of group exhibitions, including: *Atelier 81-82* (*Studio 81-82*), at the Musée d'Art Moderne de la Ville de Paris, in 1981; *The 12th Biennale Paris Exhibition*, at the same venue in 1982; *12 French Artists*, at the Venice Biennale in 1984; *French Painting 1960-1980*, at the Zagreb Art Museum, 1985; *12 French Artists in Space*, at the Saibu Museum in Tokyo, in 1985; *Angle of Visions*, at the Guggenheim Museum in New York, in 1986; *Emerging Artist 1978-1986*, at the same venue in 1987; *Leçons de Peinture* (*Painting Lessons*), at the Hôtel de Ville in Paris in 1988; *Correspondence*, at the Berlin Modern Art Museum, 1989; *French Spring*, at the Scottish National Gallery in Edinburgh, 1990; *Biennale d'Art Contemporain* (*Biennale Exhibition of Contemporary Art*), in Lyons in 1991; and *Lato Sensu*, in Copenhagen, Hamburg, Freiburg and Mulhouse, in 1991.

He staged a number of solo exhibitions, including: his first, in the Galerie Napalm de St-Étienne; Musée d'Art et d'Industrie, St-Étienne, 1982; Galerie Farideh Cadot, Paris and New York, between 1983 and 1986; regular exhibitions since 1987 at the Galerie Yvon Lambert; at the Galerie Pierre Hubert in Geneva, in 1987 and 1990; a retrospective of his engravings in 1988 at the Galerie La Hune; at the Blum Helman Gallery in New York, in 1989; a 1990 retrospective, at the Musée du Dessin et de l'Estampe in Gravelines; at the Musée de Beaux-Arts in Carcassonne in 1990; Galerie Pierre Hubert, 1991; Galerie La Hune-Brenner, 1991; *L'Archipel des Pacotilles* (*The Bogus Archipelago*), at the Galerie Yvon Lambert in Paris, 1994; *Les Cases Conjuguées* (*Combined Squares*), a homage to Teeny Duchamp, at the Galerie Nationale du Jeu de Paume, 1996; and, in 2000, in the French National Library.

BIBLIOGRAPHY:

Lascault, Gilbert, *Philippe Favier*, Musée d'Art et d'Industrie, St-Étienne, 1982. Darragon, Éric, *Capitaine Coucou*, exhibition catalogue, Gal. Alma, Lyons, 1985. Ferrari/Michaud, E./Bonnaval, J., *'Philippe Favier'* in *Cahiers de l'abbaye Sainte-Croix*, periodical, Musée de l'abbaye Sainte-Croix, Les Sables d'Olonne, 1986. Abadie, Daniel (preface), *Les Noirs Secrets de Philippe Favier*, exhibition catalogue, Musée de Carcassonne, Carcassonne, 1990. Abadie, Daniel, *Philippe Favier. Œuvres récentes 1988-1989*, exhibition catalogue, Musée des Beaux-Arts, Carcassonne, 1990. Roche, Maurice/Stoullig, Claire/Adams, Brooks, *Philippe Favier*, travelling exhibition catalogue, Gal. nationale du Jeu de Paume, Paris, Réunion des musées nationaux, Paris, 1995. Arrouye, Jean/Chabot, Jacques/Duborgel, Bruno, et al., '*Une Œuvre de Philippe Favier: `L'Archipel des pacotilles' 1991*' in *coll. Iconotexte*, Muntaner, Marseilles, 1995. *Favier*, exhibition catalogue, Gal. nationale du Jeu de Paume, Paris, 1996. Ceysson, Bernard/Darragon, Éric/Favier, Philippe, *Philippe Favier*, Éd. Printer, St-Étienne, 1997. Tossato, Guy, *Philippe Favier*, exhibition catalogue, Carré d'art-Musée d'Art Contemporain, Nîmes, Actes Sud, Arles, 1999.

MUSEUMS AND GALLERIES:

DUNKIRK (FRAC Nord-Pas de Calais): *Captain Cuckoo* (1984) - MARSEILLES (Mus. Cantini): *The Aquarium*; *Castle 'Chasse Spleen'* - MONTREAL (MAM) - NEW YORK (Solomon R. Guggenheim Mus.) - NÎMES (Carré d'Art, MAC) - PARIS (FNAC): *Micro-climate* (1994-1995) - PARIS (MNAM-CCI): *Multicoloured Wind* (1986); *Yellow Wind* (1986) - ROCHECHOUART (Mus. Départemental d'Art Contemporain): *Les Majorettes* (1981) - ST-ÉTIENNE (MAM).

AUCTION RECORDS:

PARIS, 15 Feb 1986, *Parallaxis 108* (1985, paint/glass, 5 x $4^1/_4$ ins / 13 x 11 cm) FRF 4,000. PARIS, 20 Nov 1988, *The Screens* (1985, paint/glass, triptych, 7 x 5 ins / 17.5 x 12.5 cm) FRF 32,000. PARIS, 30 Jan 1989, *Composition* (1985, paint/glass, $6^1/_4$ x $4^3/_4$ ins / 16 x 12 cm) FRF 18,000. PARIS, 19 March 1989, *The Minor Arts* (1985, paint/glass) FRF 8,000. PARIS, 17 Dec 1989, *The Screens No. 7* (1985, paint/glass, in three parts, 5 x $7^3/_4$ ins / 12.5 x 20 cm) FRF 30,000. PARIS, 18 June 1990, *The Toothpick* (1988, paint/glass, in three parts, $3^1/_2$ x $4^3/_4$ ins / 9.2 x 12 cm and $3^1/_2$ x 1 ins/9.2 x 2.4 cm and $3^1/_2$ x 2 ins/9.2 x 4.2 cm) FRF 20,000. PARIS, 26 Oct 1990, *Blue Wind* (1988, enamel paint/glass, 6 x 9 ins / 15 x 22 cm) FRF 41,000. PARIS, 30 May 1991, *Homage to Young Ladies* (1986, collage and oil/glass, triptych, in all $4^1/_2$ x $7^1/_2$ ins / 11.5 x 19.2 cm) FRF 60,000. PARIS, 10 July 1991, *Untitled* (1986, oil/glass, $5^1/_4$ x 3 ins / 13.5 x 7.5 cm) FRF 38,000. PARIS, 11 March 1992, *The Screens* (1985, oil under glass, triptych, 5 x $2^1/_2$ ins / 12.5 x 6.2 cm, 5 x 1 ins/12.8 x 2.6 cm and 5 x $3^1/_2$ ins/12.8 x 9.1 cm) FRF 28,000. PARIS, 26 Nov 1992, *The Water Lilies* (oil under glass, 6 x 4 ins / 15.5 x 10 cm) FRF 35,000. PARIS, 18 June 1993, *The Lemon* (1986, enamel and oil under glass, triptych, $5^1/_4$ x $9^3/_4$ ins / 13.5 x 25 cm) FRF 55,000. PARIS, 25 March 1994, *Beans III* (1986, oil under glass, triptych, $4^3/_4$ x 7 ins / 12 x 18 cm) FRF 14,000. PARIS, 24 June 1994, *Peeled Oranges* (1987, enamel and glazed ceramic on glass, 5 x $4^1/_4$ ins / 11.8 x 10.8 cm) FRF 23,000. PARIS, 21 June 1995, *Composition* (1984, acrylic/cut paper, $7^1/_2$ x $11^3/_4$ ins / 19 x 30 cm) FRF 20,500. PARIS, 7 Oct 1996, *The Screens* (1985, paint fixed under glass, $5^1/_4$ x $8^1/_4$ ins / 13.5 x 21 cm) FRF 22,000. PARIS, 20 June 1997, *Untitled* (1985, varnish/glass, $4^1/_2$ x $3^1/_2$ ins / 11.5 x 9 cm) FRF 15,000. PARIS, 23 Nov 1997, *Redcurrants* (1992, paint/glass, triptych, $4^1/_4$ x $6^3/_4$ ins / 11 x 17 cm) FRF 28,000. PARIS, 3 April 1998, *Three Apricots* (1988, Conté pencil and enamel/screen-printed paper, $39^1/_4$ x $39^1/_4$ ins / 100 x 100 cm) FRF

15,000. PARIS, 21 March 1999, *Pentimento* (1992, collage on slate, 7 x 10 ins / 18 x 25 cm) FRF 12,000. PARIS, 11 July 2000, *Paravent* (1990, oil on canvas, 7 x 4 ins / 19 x 10 cm) FRF 37,000. PARIS, 28 Oct 2000, *Numero 3178841172999* (paint on sardine tin, 5 x 4 ins / 12 x 10 cm) FRF 29,000. PARIS, 10 May 2001, *Artichoke* (1995, oil on panel, 39 x 39 ins / 98 x 98 cm) FRF 19,000. PARIS, 21 Nov 2001, *Untitled* (1986, ball-point pen and enamel on glass, 7 x 11 ins / 18 x 29 cm) FRF 28,000. PARIS, 21 Oct 2003, *Roma Capriciosa* (1993, mixed media under glass, 15 x 15 ins / 37 x 37 cm) EUR 4,500. PARIS, 18 Dec 2003, *Lieu dit* (watercolour, collage, ink and crayon, 9 x 9 ins / 24 x 24 cm) EUR 20,000. PARIS, 9 June 2004, *L'Archipel des Pacotilles* (1992, collage and paint under glass, 11 x 11 ins / 27 x 27 cm) EUR 3,500.

FAVIER, Pierre
French, 20th century.
Born 13 July 1899, in St-Just-sur-Loire.
Painter.

Pierre Favier first studied at the École des Beaux-Arts in St-Étienne, and then studied with Le Fauconnier. He exhibited in Paris at the Salon des Artistes Indépendants from 1925, as well as at the Salon Populiste, and the Salon Violet. His painting is figurative.

FAVIER, Robin
French, 15th century.
Active in Avignon.
Painter.

In 1426, Favier was contracted to execute 'in good and fine colours' paintings for the tribune in Grenoble Cathedral.

FAVIER, Roger
French, 20th century.
Born 1 August 1881, in Versailles; died 14 August 1925.
Engraver (etching).

Roger Favier studied with Waltner, Jacquet and Cormon. He was a member of the Société des Artistes Français from 1907. He received honourable mention in 1907, a third-class medal in 1910, and a silver medal and *hors-concours* recognition in 1911.

FAVIER, Victor
French, 19th century.
Born 18 November 1824, in Versailles.
Painter. Portraits, landscapes.

Victor Favier was a pupil of Horace Vernet and Wachsmuth. He was the drawing master at Agen School. He exhibited views and portraits at the Salon from 1848 to 1879.

AUCTION RECORDS:
PARIS, 14 Dec 1980, *View of Constantinople* (1873, oil on canvas, 8 1/2 x 12 3/4 ins / 21.5 x 32.5 cm) FRF 2,700.

FAVIERES, Didier
French, 17th century.
Active in Paris.
Engraver.

Favieres worked between 1620 and 1644 and is mentioned as 'engraver to the King and Monsieur'.

FAVIN, Roger
French, 20th century.
Born in Deauville.
Sculptor. Busts.

Favin exhibited busts of women at the Salon de la Société Nationale from 1929.

AUCTION RECORDS:
PARIS, 18 Nov 1996, *Maternity* (bronze, h. 10 1/2 ins / 26.5 cm) FRF 6,000.

FAVORSKAYA, Maria
Russian, 20th century.
Born 10 June 1928, in Moscow.
Sculptor, ceramicist.

Maria Favorskaya was the daughter of Vladimir Favorsky. She trained at the school of modern art in Moscow from 1948 to 1956. She creates figurative work in ceramic.

FAVORSKY, Nikita
Russian, 20th century.
Born 10 May 1915, in Moscow.
Draughtsman.

Nikita Favorsky was the son of Vladimir Favorsky. He was a pupil of Pavel Yacovlevich Pavlinov from 1932 to 1938.

FAVORSKY, Vladimir Andreevich
Russian, 20th century.
Born 15 March 1886, in Moscow; died 1964.
Engraver, illustrator.
Socialist Realism.
Obshchestvo Khudoznikov 4 Iskusstva (Four Arts Society of Artists).

Vladimir Andreevich Favorsky studied in Munich from 1905 to 1908 in the Hollósy workshop and in the faculty of philosophy. Then he travelled to Italy, Germany and Austria. Having returned to Moscow, he worked in the faculty of arts from 1908 to 1913, then left for the front. He taught at the Higher Artistic and Technical Institute in Moscow in 1921 and was rector there in 1923, an important figure in the world of education. He decorated the *Komsomol Skaja* underground station in Moscow (1959).

His style is Realist and typically represents the ideal of Russian art remote from the effects of contemporary art. Favorsky was one of the official artists of the regime and was honoured in many portraits.

He started exhibiting in 1910 in Moscow. He was represented at *L'Art Russe des Scythes à nos jours* (*Russian Art from the Scythians to Today*), Paris (1967). He was awarded a prize at the Exposition des Arts Décoratifs, Paris (1925), a gold medal at the International Exhibition of Graphic Art, Leipzig (1959) and the Lenin Prize (1962).

FAVORY, André
French, 20th century.
Born 29 March 1888, in Paris; died 5 February 1937, in Paris.
Painter, draughtsman, illustrator, pastellist, watercolourist. Figures, nudes, portraits, genre scenes.

André Favory was a pupil of Baschet and Royer at the Académie Julian, where he made contact with A. Lhote, Gleizes and La Fresnaye. His own work began in 1913. In Paris, he exhibited at the Salon des Artistes Indépendants and at the Salon des Tuileries. He was a member of the Salon d'Automne.

Favory was one of the few of his generation who were able to attempt large compositions which, quite often, are absent from the art of our time. He was a spirited artist, of sensualist inspiration, and was invigorated by his admiration for Rubens. He could sometimes lack taste, although his attention never tired. He always showed a lively sense of composition. Due to an illness, he was half-paralysed for many months before his death. He befriended writers, and illustrated: *L'Humour triste* (*Sad Humour*) by J. Supervielle; *Ouvert la nuit* (*Open All Night*) by Paul Morand; *Le Festival* by A. Erlande, and also *L'Éducation sentimentale* by G. Flaubert. Some of his major works include: *The Abduction of Europa, The Joy of Living, The Village Bath, Nude on a Bed, Afternoon in Quercy, Crystal Palace in Antwerp, Summer (Nude), Bather, Nude Resting, Nude in a Landscape*. E. Jaloux wrote of Favory: 'One sees forming in him a painter uniquely sensual, violent, even brutal, but whose power was real, and who needed great impetus to accomplish his journey'.

C.R. Marx noted that Favory 'benefitted from the crises he faced' (including that of Cubism).

A.FAVORY.

A.FAVORY

Bibliography:

Jaloux, E., *André Favory*, La Nouvelle Revue Française, Gallimard, Paris, 1926. *André Favory (1889-1937)*, Imprimerie Jean Riss, Paris, 1971.

Museums and Galleries:

Le Havre (Mus. Malraux).

Auction records:

Paris, 22 Oct 1920, *Landscape* (watercolour) FRF 100. Paris, 9 June 1921, *Landscape*, FRF 510. Paris, 21 Jan 1924, *Nude Study* (Indian ink) FRF 30. Paris, 4 Nov 1924, *Figure* FRF 400. Paris, 23 April 1925, *Young Woman in Yellow*, FRF 420. Paris, 4 June 1925, *The Woman in Blue*, FRF 950. Paris, 18 June 1925, *The Bather*, FRF 1,010. Paris, 21 Dec 1925, *Nude Young Woman* (pastel) FRF 950. Paris, 19 May 1926, *The Flowering Headland*, FRF 2,900. Paris, 4 June 1926, *Young Woman with Red Turban*, FRF 580. Paris, 2 July 1926, *Standing Nude Woman* (red chalk) FRF 300. Paris, 22 Nov 1926, *Boats in a Port*, FRF 340. Paris, 2 March 1929, *Houses of Pleasure*, FRF 1,100. Paris, 24 April 1929, *Standing Nude in a Landscape*, FRF 820. Paris, 3 May 1929, *Nude with Hat*, FRF 2,000. Paris, 30 May 1929, *Bathers*, FRF 2,500. Paris, 14 June 1929, *Seated Nude* (drawing) FRF 225; *Resting Female Nude* (pastel) FRF 1,020. Paris, 13 Feb 1932, *Nude from the Back*, FRF 800. Paris, 23 April 1932, *Rustic Venus*, FRF 250. Paris, 24 Feb 1934, *Nude Torso of a Woman* (red chalk) FRF 80. Paris, 2 July 1936, *Red House in a Landscape of the Midi*, FRF 105. Paris, 28 April 1937, *Landscape with Bridge* (watercolour) FRF 65. Paris, 29 Dec 1941, *Undressed Woman on her Knees*, FRF 760. Paris, 30 Nov 1942, *Entrance to the Village*, FRF 1,100. Paris, 24 Dec 1942, *Resting Nude Turned to the Right and Resting Nude Turned to the Left*, FRF 720. Paris, 22 Feb 1943, *Bust of a Woman*, FRF 1,500. Paris, 7 April 1943, *Bust of a Nude Woman*, FRF 2,300; *The Old Bridge*, FRF 10,000. Paris, 14 May 1943, *Bathers*, FRF 2,000; *Landscape*, FRF 2,400. Paris, 1 July 1943, *Seated Nude*. Paris, 2 July 1943, *The Model from the Back*, FRF 4,150; *Europa*, FRF 5,000. Paris, 17 Dec 1943, *Bather*, FRF 7,200. Paris, 23 March 1944, *Pastoral Scene* (watercolour) FRF 1,000. Paris, 3 May 1944, *Landscape*, FRF 4,100. Paris, 13 Nov 1944, *Head of a Woman* (red chalk) FRF 220. Paris, 5 March 1945, *Flowers*, FRF 10,000. Paris, 9 April 1945, *Bust of a Woman*, FRF 7,200. Paris, 29 June 1945, *Nude Woman*, FRF 6,000. Paris, 20 Nov 1946, *Portrait of a Woman with Black Hair*, FRF 6,000. Paris, 23 Dec 1946, *Resting Nude*, FRF 12,500. Paris, 24 Jan 1947, *The Garden*, FRF 2,300. Paris, 21 Feb 1947, *Nude* (red chalk) FRF 2,800. Paris, 23 April 1947, *Private Interview*, FRF 7,500. Paris, 23 April 1947, *Verlaine Drinking Absinthe at the 'Soleil d'Or' in 1898* (pastel) FRF 1,100. Stockholm, 24 April 1947, *Aqueduct*, SEK 4,300. Paris, 19 May 1947, *Head of a Woman*, FRF 850. Paris, 20 June 1947, *Portrait of a Young Boy*, FRF 700. Paris, 2 July 1947, *Underbrush* (watercolour) FRF 1,050. Paris, 25 Feb 1955, *Afternoon in Quercy*, FRF 51,000. Versailles, 14 Dec 1969, *Pastoral Scene*, FRF 4,000. Geneva, 18 Nov 1976, *Standing Nude* (oil on canvas, 22 x 12 1/2 ins / 55 x 32 cm) CHF 3,400. Paris, 4 March 1981, *Landscape* (oil on canvas, 15 x 24 ins / 38 x 61 cm) FRF 5,000. Versailles, 18 June 1986, *Bather at the River* (oil on canvas, 32 x 25 1/2 ins / 81 x 65 cm) FRF 15,000. Paris, 3 June 1987, *Bather in a Landscape* (oil on canvas, 28 3/4 x 23 1/2 ins / 73 x 60 cm) FRF 8,500. Paris, 21 Feb 1988, *Nude Reclining with Red Cushions* (pastel, 18 x 23 1/2 ins / 45.5 x 60 cm) FRF 3,500. Paris, 20 March 1988, *Seated Woman* (oil on canvas, 32 x 21 1/4 ins / 81 x 54 cm) FRF 10,000. Paris, 23 March 1988, *Feminine Figure* (oil on cardboard, 18 x 15 ins / 46 x 38 cm) FRF 7,000. Paris, 8 June 1988, *Nude Bust* (oil on canvas, 17 1/4 x 20 1/2 ins / 44 x 52 cm) FRF 6,300. Paris, 7 Nov 1988, *Provence Landscape* (oil on canvas, 21 1/4 x 32 ins / 54 x 81 cm) FRF 6,400. Neuilly, 22 Nov 1988, *Nude with Parasol* (oil on canvas, 21 1/4 x 28 3/4 ins / 54 x 73 cm) FRF 11,000. Versailles, 18 Dec 1988, *Road at the Entrance to the Village* (oil on canvas, 15 x 22 ins / 38 x 55 cm) FRF 10,500. Versailles, 20 June 1989, *The Bridge* (oil on canvas, 28 3/4 x 21 1/4 ins / 73 x 54 cm) FRF 20,000. Paris, 27 Nov 1989, *Bather* (oil on canvas, 13 x 22 ins / 33 x 55 cm) FRF 9,500. Paris, 29 Nov 1989, *The Little Window, Valenciennes* (1923, oil on cardboard, 13 3/4 x 11 ins / 35 x 27 cm) FRF 4,000. Versailles, 10 Dec 1989, *Nude Resting* (oil on canvas, 15 1/4 x 24 ins / 38.5 x 61 cm) FRF 13,500. Paris, 20 Feb 1990, *Landscape with Bridge* (oil on canvas, 31 1/2 x 24 3/4 ins / 80 x 63 cm) FRF 18,500. Le Touquet, 11 Nov 1990, *Seated Nude with Hat* (oil on canvas, 25 1/2 x 18 ins / 65 x 46 cm) FRF 19,000. Neuilly, 3 Feb 1991, *Nude in a Landscape* (oil on canvas, 32 x 49 1/4 ins / 81 x 125 cm) FRF 36,000. Calais, 5 April 1992, *Young Woman at the Bath* (oil on canvas, 22 x 13 ins / 55 x 33 cm) FRF 11,000. Paris, 5 Nov 1994, *Mont Ste-Victoire* (oil on canvas, 19 3/4 x 28 3/4 ins / 50 x 73 cm) FRF 5,800. Paris, 28 June 1995, *Landscape* (oil on canvas, 25 1/2 x 18 ins / 65 x 46 cm) FRF 4,800. Paris, 20 June 1996, *Nude on the Bank of the River* (oil on canvas, 34 1/4 x 28 1/4 ins / 87 x 72 cm) FRF 6,200. Neuilly, 27 Nov 1997, *Bathers* (oil on canvas, 39 1/4 x 32 ins / 100 x 81 cm) FRF 28,500. Paris, 10 Dec 1997, *Provence Landscape* (oil on canvas, 19 3/4 x 28 3/4 ins / 50 x 73 cm) FRF 4,600. Calais, 4 July 1999, *Model Resting* (oil on canvas, 20 x 26 ins / 50 x 65 cm) FRF 15,000. Paris, 28 Nov 1999, *Tall Woman Bathing* (oil on canvas, 55 x 41 ins / 140 x 105 cm) FRF 34,000. Paris, 29 May 2000, *Tall Woman Bathing* (oil on canvas, 55 x 41 ins / 140 x 105 cm) FRF 18,000. Paris, 17 Nov 2000, *Sleeping Bather* (oil on canvas, 15 x 22 ins / 38 x 55 cm) FRF 17,000. Paris, 16 March 2001, *Woman in Blue Dress* (oil on canvas, 36 x 29 ins / 92 x 73 cm) FRF 22,000. Paris, 28 March 2001, *Beach* (oil on canvas, 18 x 22 ins / 46 x 55 cm) FRF 16,000. Paris, 30 Jan 2002, *Portrait of a Woman in a Landscape* (c. 1912, oil on canvas, 32 x 24 ins / 81 x 60 cm) EUR 2,410. Paris, 30 Jan 2002, *Sleeping Nude* (oil on canvas, 18 x 26 ins / 46 x 65 cm) EUR 2,410. Neuilly, 20 Nov 2003, *Bathers in the Meadow* (oil on canvas, 29 x 21 ins / 73 x 54 cm) EUR 1,500. London, 4 March 2004, *Reclining Female Nude* (pastel on paper/board, 19 x 24 ins / 48 x 62 cm) GBP 2,400.

FAVRAY, Antoine de (Chevalier), or Fauray

French, 18th century.

Born 8 September 1706, in Bagnolet; died 1791, in Malta.

Painter, draughtsman. Religious subjects, portraits, scenes with figures, genre scenes.

Orientalism.

Antoine de Favray was taken by his master Jean-François de Troy to Rome when the latter was appointed director of the Académie, obtaining for his pupil a position as a boarding student. During his stay in Rome Favray made the acquaintance of some Knights of Malta who engaged him to follow them to their island. On 30 October 1762 Favray was admitted as an academician. During the same year he went to Constantinople to paint Turkish scenes, but was unable to stay long because of the war openly declared a few years later between Russia and Turkey.

His most notable works include *Interior of the Church of St-John of Malta, Decorated with Ceilings Painted by Calabrese*; *A Maltese Family in an Apartment*; *Women of Malta of*

Different Stations, Distinguished by the Kinds of Materials; and *The Audience Given to the Knight of St-Priest by the Grand Master.*

MUSEUMS AND GALLERIES:

FLORENCE (Uffizi): *Self-portrait* - GOTHA: *Portrait of a Man* - PARIS (Louvre): *Ladies of Malta Making Visits; Portrait of a Young Maltese Woman* - PARIS (Mus. Carnavalet): *Fanchon the Hurdy-gurdy Woman* - TOULOUSE (Capitole): *Turkish Dance; Portrait of Two Levantines.*

AUCTION RECORDS:

PARIS, 30-31 Jan 1894, *Visit to the Convalescent Woman,* FRF 290. PARIS, 28 Oct 1922, *Portrait of a Young Girl* (attributed) FRF 450. PARIS, 6 Dec 1923, *Portrait of a Lady of Malta* (pencil) FRF 100. LONDON, 4 Dec 1935, *The Artist* (drawing) GBP 70. PARIS, 14 Dec 1935, *Examining the Portrait,* FRF 2,250. PARIS, 26 May 1937, *Maltese Women* (black chalk and red chalk) FRF 200. PARIS, 13 Feb 1939, *Maltese Women* (black chalk and red chalk) FRF 410. VERSAILLES, 13 Feb 1977, *View of the Golden Horn, Constantinople, Site of the Sultan's Seraglio* (1762, oil on canvas, 34 1/4 x 81 ins / 87 x 206 cm) FRF 26,000. PARIS, 10 June 1984, *The Frigate 'L'Oiseau', Commanded by M. de Mariès, Bringing back from Malta the Turkish Vessel 'Le Capitaine' Flying the Admiral's Flag, Enters the Port of Constantinople* (1770, oil on canvas, 37 x 98 ins / 94 x 249 cm) FRF 276,000. MONTE CARLO, 22 June 1986, *Portrait of the Countess of Vergennes Dressed as a Sultana* (1766, oil on canvas, 32 3/4 x 26 ins / 83 x 66 cm) FRF 30,000. MONACO, 7 Dec 1990, *Ladies of Malta Making Visits* (oil on canvas, 19 x 25 1/4 ins / 48 x 64 cm) FRF 521,700. LONDON, 15 April 1992, *St John the Baptist Indicating to Christ the Jordan behind Him* (1759, oil on canvas, 30 3/4 x 41 1/2 ins / 78.2 x 105.5 cm) GBP 9,000. AUBAGNE, 24 May 1992, *Portrait of a Dignitary Dressed as a Turk* (oil on canvas, 57 1/2 x 46 3/4 ins / 146 x 119 cm) FRF 202,000. PARIS, 25 Oct 1994, *Portrait of a Turkish Dignitary in front of an Inscription in Greek* (1765, oil on canvas, 31 3/4 x 24 3/4 ins / 80.5 x 63 cm) FRF 300,000. LONDON, 11 Oct 1996, *A Turkish Woman and her Child* (1769, oil on canvas, 38 1/4 x 30 ins / 97 x 76.5 cm) GBP 25,300. NEW YORK, 29 Jan 1998, *A View of Constantinople Dominating the Bosphorus* (1770, oil on canvas, 37 1/2 x 98 ins / 95 x 248 cm) USD 607,500. NEW YORK, 3 Nov 1999, *Portrait of an Artist in Green Fur-lined Coat* (1763, oil on canvas, 28 x 22 ins / 71 x 57 cm) USD 4,000. NEW YORK, 29 May 2001, *Asclepius, the God of Healing and Medicine, Seated at a Table, Reading a Book* (1771, oil on canvas, 31 x 25 ins / 79 x 64 cm) USD 7,000. WEST TWO, 11 Dec 2001, *Portrait of an Oriental Gentleman, Standing in his Study Pointing at an Open Book* (oil on canvas, 29 x 24 ins / 73 x 60 cm) GBP 3,500. PARIS, 10 Dec 2003, *Portrait of Charles Gravier, Comte de Vergennes* (1766, oil on canvas, 55 x 44 ins / 140 x 112 cm) EUR 260,000. PARIS, 10 Dec 2003, *Portrait of the Comtesse de Vergennes in Oriental Dress* (1768, oil on canvas, 51 x 37 ins / 129 x 93 cm) EUR 290,000.

FAVRE, Adam, or Faivre, Fèvre, Le Fèvre
French, 16th century.
Died 1523 or 1524.
Painter.

In 1426, Adam Favre was living in Lyons. He worked on preparations for various entries between 1499 and 1516. He painted, in 1507, *Representations of Histories Performed in Lyons before Louis XII.*

FAVRE, Antoine, or Faure
French, 16th - 17th century.
Active in Lyons from 1588 to 1619.
Painter.

Antoine Faure was a guild master six times between 1592 and 1616.

FAVRE, Charles
French, 18th century.
Born 18th century, in St-Jean-de-Maurienne.
Painter.

Charles Favre executed numerous paintings for the Oratorians of Arc-Tal, including a *St Mary Magdalene* dated 1741.

FAVRE, François Edmond
Swiss, 19th century.
Born 26 July 1812, in Geneva; died 26 May 1880, in Geneva.
Painter.

A pupil of A. Calame, Favre exhibited landscape drawings and paintings in Geneva from 1841.

FAVRE, Jean, or Faure
French, 16th century.
Died c. 1528.
Active in Lyons in 1523.
Painter.

FAVRE, Jean, or Faure
French, 16th century.
Active in Lyons in 1548.
Painter.

Jean Favre worked in Lyons on preparations for the entry into the town of Henri II.

FAVRE, Jean François
Swiss, 18th century.
Born 4 July 1751, in Geneva; died 3 March 1807, in Geneva.
Enameller.

Jean Favre studied enamel painting with the illustrator M.T. Bourrit. In 1772, he went to Paris, where he worked in the studio of the enamel painter Loehr. He became friends with Jacques Thouron, working with him to produce enamels for jewellery, portraits and copies of the old masters. On his return to Geneva, he executed mainly portrait drawings.

MUSEUMS AND GALLERIES:

GENEVA (MAH): *Portrait on Enamel of M. Arnoux.*

FAVRE, Louis
Swiss, 19th century.
Born 17 March 1822, in Boudry (Vaud); died 13 September 1904, in Neuchâtel.
Draughtsman, illustrator.

A lecturer in technical drawing in Neuchâtel, Louis Favre illustrated *Musée Neuchâtelois* and some scientific works.

FAVRE, Louis
French, 19th century.
Born 1824, in Lyons.
Painter.

Louis Favre was a pupil of Mélin. He exhibited landscapes and seascapes in Paris from 1864 to 1869.

FAVRE, Louis
Swiss, 19th century.
Born 4 December 1830, in Geneva.
Draughtsman.

Having studied at the school of drawing in Geneva, Louis Favre devoted himself to landscape drawing late on in life and left some views of the French Riviera.

FAVRE, Louis
French, 20th century.
Born 15 September 1892, in Annemasse; died 17 April 1956, in Annemasse.
Painter, lithographer, illustrator. Figure compositions, figures, nudes, portraits, interiors, landscapes, still-lifes. Designs for stained glass.

Louis Favre was first a surveyor, and then an industrial designer. Drafted for the war of 1914-1918, he was wounded in Verdun. He settled in Paris in 1919, and devoted himself to painting. He was self-taught. In 1927 he travelled to Morocco, and to Algeria in 1929. From 1930 to 1933 he interrupted his painting activity, but resumed it in 1934. He settled in Lyons during the war in 1940, where, from 1946, he devoted himself entirely to colour lithography. In 1947 he stayed and worked in Holland. He spent time in London in 1949.

He participated in collective exhibitions: in Paris at the Salon d'Automne from 1949, and at the Salon des Indépendants. In 1954 he was part of the French selection at the Biennale in Venice. He also exhibited in London, New York, Geneva, Rotterdam and Milan. He showed ensembles of his works in solo exhibitions, amongst others at Paris in 1926 and 1927, and at Lyons in 1940 and 1942.

In his paintings, and later in his lithographs on diverse themes, Favre showed the influence of Matisse, and to a more subtle degree, Braque's synthetic Cubism. He illustrated Arthur Rimbaud's *Une Saison en Enfer* (*A Season in Hell*) and Edgar Allan Poe's *The Raven*. In 1955 he executed cartoons for the windows of Thusy.

BIBLIOGRAPHY:

Cailler, Pierre, *Louis Favre 1892-1956*, Éd. Pierre Cailler, Geneva, 1963.

MUSEUMS AND GALLERIES:

BOSTON (Public Library, Fine Arts Department) - CINCINNATI (AM): numerous engravings - GENEVA (MAH) - LONDON (Victoria and Albert Mus.) - PARIS (BNF, Prints Collection) - PARIS (MAMVP).

FAVRE, Marcel Auguste

French, 20th century.
Born 16 December 1907, in Dingy-St-Clair (Haute-Savoie).
Painter.

Marcel Auguste Favre was self-taught. He exhibited in Paris at the Salons des Artistes Indépendants and the Salon Comparaisons.

FAVRE, Mathieu, or Faure

French, 16th century.
Active in Lyons from 1571 to 1591.
Painter.

FAVRE, Maurice

French, 19th - 20th century.
Born in Paris.
Sculptor, medallist.

Maurice Favre exhibited in Paris, at the Salon des Artistes Français. He received an honourable mention in 1896 and a second-class medal in 1907. That same year he was named a member, and received a travel grant.

AUCTION RECORDS:

LONDON, 15 Nov 1976, *The Song of the One who Grinds* (bronze and ivory, h. 23 3/4 ins / 60.5 cm) GBP 350. MONTE CARLO, 25 Oct 1982, *Spinning-woman's Song* (c. 1890, bronze and ivory, h. 15 1/2 ins / 39.5 cm) FRF 5,500. NEW YORK, 17 May 1983, *Bull and Dog* (bronze, h. 41 ins / 104 cm) USD 2,800.

FAVRE, Nicolas

French, 17th century.
Active in Paris.
Miniaturist.

FAVRE, Pierre

Swiss, 16th century.
Born 16th century, in Geneva.
Painter, glass painter.
Geneva School.

A burgher of Geneva in 1546, Pierre Favre worked at the church of the Magdalene, the town house, the town hall and the church of St Peter. In 1562, he produced a map of the area around Geneva.

FAVRE, Pierre

French, 20th century.
Born 28 February 1906, in Paris.
Painter. Landscapes, seascapes.

Pierre Favre was a pupil at the École des Arts Décoratifs in Paris. He received a grant from the City of Paris in 1939. He exhibited at the Salon des Artistes Indépendants in Paris from 1952, and at the Salon d'Automne from 1960. In 1945 the City of Marseilles bought his *Market in Provence*. He sometimes signed his works *Pierre-Favre*. His landscapes are mainly those of Provence.

AUCTION RECORDS:

PARIS, 17 March 1974, *On the Terrace*, FRF 1,320. PARIS, 20 June 1985, *Landscape* (oil on paper, 14 1/2 x 17 3/4 ins / 37 x 45 cm) FRF 6,000.

FAVRE, Pierrette, later Mme Bédié

French, 19th century.
Born 19 August 1827, in Challex (Savoy).
Miniaturist.

Pierrette Favre worked in Paris where she exhibited portraits at the Salon from 1857 to 1864, including her self-portrait and a portrait of her children.

FAVRE, Valérie

Swiss, 20th - 21st century.
Born 1959, in Evilard.
Since 1985 active in Paris, since 1998 in Berlin.
Painter, installation artist, video artist, performance artist.
Neo-Conceptual Art.

Favre settled in Paris in 1985, then in Berlin in 1998. Her work, which draws on different sources, is eclectic and even seems contradictory. She divides her time between performance, sound, video, theatre, writing and painting. Generally, she produces work in series revolving around a chosen object, such as a chair, a pillow or a cupboard. Using a single colour, white, she then invites us to reflect.

She presented a series of paintings entitled *Bedroom with Wardrobes* at her exhibition in Marseilles in 1992. In 1994, her exhibition at the Centre d'Art Contemporain, Basse-Normandie, presented installations which questioned painting itself through symbols. In her 1997 exhibitions she combined various techniques with video installations, allowing her to draw on extracts from famous works of the past and the exhilaration of using the most dazzling colours. In 2002 she exhibited landscape paintings with tones inspired by Fauvism, in which fantasy figures move around, evoking the pictorial tradition as well as a modern, visionary world.

She has participated in several group exhibitions: 1987, Salon d'Art Contemporain, Montrouge; 1998, *Le Chiffre* (*The Figure*), Carré des Arts, Paris; 1988, Usine Éphémère; 1989, *Paysages dans l'Art Contemporain* (*Landscapes in Contemporary Art*), École des Beaux-Arts, Paris; 1997, *Transit - 60 Artistes Nés après 60 - Oeuvres du Fonds National d'Art Contemporain* (*Transit - 60 Artists Born After 60 - Works from the National Collection of Contemporary Art*), École des Beaux-Arts, Paris.

She has also held solo shows: 1988, Usine Éphémère, Paris; 1989, Galerie Transit, Strasbourg; 1992, Galerie de Marseilles; 1994, *Range Ta Chambre* (*Tidy your Room*), Centre d'Art Contemporain, Basse-Normandie; 1995, Galerie Natacha Knapp, Lausanne; 1997, Caisse des Dépôts et Consignations (French public and investment organisation), Paris; then the Musée de Picardie in Amiens; Galerie Nathalie Obadia, Paris; Crédac in Ivry-sur-Seine; Centre Culturel Suisse, Paris; 2003, *Valérie Favre, Oeuvres Récentes* (*Valérie Favre, Recent Works*), Musée de Picardie, Amiens.

BIBLIOGRAPHY:

Jarton, Cyril, '*Les Restes de la peinture selon Valérie Favre*' in *Beaux-Arts Magazine* n° 160, periodical, Paris, September 1997. Piguet, Philippe, '*Valérie Favre ou l'art de la collusion*' in *L'Œil* n° 545, periodical, Paris, March 2003. Leydier, Richard, '*Valérie Favre*' in *Art Press* n° 289 p. 73, periodical, Paris, April 2003.

Museums and Galleries:
Paris (FNAC): *Red Dress* (1995).
Auction records:
Paris, 16 June 1988, *Untitled* (1988, mixed media/canvas, 38 1/2 x 63 3/4 ins / 98 x 162 cm) FRF 6,500. Paris, 20 May 1989, *Untitled* (1989, mixed media/canvas, 44 x 53 1/4 ins / 112 x 135 cm) FRF 7,000. Paris, 7 March 1990, *Hunting Scene* (1989, oil and Indian ink/canvas, 39 1/4 x 39 1/4 ins / 100 x 100 cm) FRF 9,000.

FAVRE DE THIERRENS, Jacques
French, 20th century.
Born 18 February 1895, in Nîmes; died 17 October 1973, in Paris.
Painter. Nudes, portraits, landscapes.

After having developed his painting during his youth, Favre de Thierrens' active but traditional life led him away from it until 1952, when he was able to put together a fine collection. An exhibition in Paris in 1955 revealed a robust talent and bold sense of colour. He painted in a traditional, sometimes intimate manner.

Bibliography:
George, Waldemar, *Jacques Favre de Thierrens*, Éd. Orféa, Paris, 1955.
Auction records:
Lausanne, 28 Oct 1965, *Young Woman with Collar*, CHF 5,000. Versailles, 15 June 1976, *Landscape of the Midi* (1958, oil on panel, 21 1/4 x 28 3/4 ins / 54 x 73 cm) FRF 4,000. New York, 1 May 1981, *Sleeping Young Girl* (oil on panel, 23 3/4 x 28 3/4 ins / 60.5 x 73.2 cm) USD 2,100. Versailles, 18 June 1986, *Studies of Nude Young Girls* (oil on panel, 22 x 18 ins / 55 x 46 cm) FRF 7,500. New York, 13 April 1988, *Reclining Young Girl* (oil on canvas, 20 x 28 1/2 ins / 50.7 x 72.7 cm) USD 2,200. Paris, 24 June 1988, *The Model Seated* (oil on panel, 13 x 9 1/2 ins / 33 x 24 cm) FRF 6,000. St-Jean-Cap-Ferrat, 16 March 1993, *Nude with White Sheet* (oil on panel, 13 3/4 x 17 1/4 ins / 35 x 44 cm) FRF 11,000. Chicago, 30 March 2003, *Theime Square* (oil on board, 23 x 29 ins / 58 x 74 cm) USD 3,000.

FAVRE-BERTIN, Charles Maurice
French, 20th century.
Born 13 November 1887, in Paris.
Sculptor, medallist.

Favre-Bertin was a pupil of G. Greber and C. Monnin. He made his debut at the Salon des Artistes Français in Paris in 1920. In 1929 he received a gold medal and was declared *hors concours*.

FAVRE-GUILLARMOD, Marie
Swiss, 19th century.
Born 10 March 1824, in La Chaux-de-Fonds; died 17 December 1872, in Neuchâtel.
Painter, illustrator. Still-lifes.

Favre-Guillarmod was the wife of the drawing lecturer Louis Favre, and sister of the painter Jules-Jacot Guillarmod. From 1860 to 1872, she contributed still-lifes to exhibitions in Neuchâtel. She also drew the illustrations for the journal *Le Rameau de Sapin* (*The Fir Tree Branch*).

Museums and Galleries:
Neuchâtel.
Auction records:
Zurich, 6 June 1986, *Still-life with Fruit* (1860, oil on canvas, 16 1/2 x 22in/42 x 56cm) CHF 2,000.

FAVRE-LANOA, Marie Thérèse. See **LANOA**

FAVRE-THOUVENIN
French, 18th century.
Active in Paris.
Sculptor.

Favre-Thouvenin was rector of the Académie de St-Luc in 1746.

FAVREAU, Yvan
French, 20th century.
Born 29 June 1933, in Les Sables-d'Olonne.
Painter.

Favreau studied painting and drawing with Cathelin in 1953. He paints abstract landscapes, impressions of the sun on the sea, and snowy roads. He exhibits at the Salon des Réalités Nouvelles.

FAVREL, Marcelle
French, 20th century.
Born 9 February 1901, in Paris.
Painter, pastellist.

Favrel was a member of the Salon des Artistes Français in Paris from 1921.

FAVRESSE, Marc
French, 20th century.
Painter.

Favresse creates and uses the effects of materials such as sand, cement, gold leaf, metal plate, in abstract compositions. He has exhibited in Paris since 1970.

FAVRETO, Francesco Jacopo, or Faureti
Italian, 17th century.
Painter.

Francesco Favreto was active in Treviso around 1675. His portrait was painted by G. Lazzari.

FAVRETTO, Giacomo
Italian, 19th century.
Born 1849, in Venice; died 1887, in Venice.
Painter, watercolourist, pastellist, draughtsman.
Portraits, genre scenes, landscapes.

Giacomo Favretto was influenced by French artists, yet did not stray far from certain trends peculiar to Italian art. It is important to take both factors into account in order to understand the nature of his talent.

Alberto Pasini was certainly an early influence on him, and Favretto knew his work particularly well. Pasini had lived in Paris and worked with the French masters, and was highly regarded there. He returned to Italy familiar with the trends and ideas in French painting, and it is likely that his ideas, just as much as his talent, had a profound effect on the young Favretto.

Favretto learned to paint by following the modern ideas that were established by Manet. This is where he strays from the truly Italian style. Favretto's principles are clear; he takes his inspiration from the present day, even when the work involves alteration; and above all, he retains only what he sees, while allowing himself to imagine what could be. This represents a resolute break with Romanticism.

Sometimes he arranges a scene, assembling the pleasing elements capable of entertaining the spectator, while at other times he is more of a realist, content with removing the anecdotal element and skilfully grouping his figures in the manner of Degas or Manet. From a technical point of view, Favretto's works, which are small in size, are always drawn with great care. The artist searches for the nature of his forms, but without recourse to sweeping simplifications, and retains the ability to reproduce the truth of a pose or a face. His colours are smooth and discreet but also bold, and rather cheerful; he avoids tones that are too light or too dark, often sticking to a palette of resonant greens and browns. His paste is neither too smooth nor too thin, and he refrains from overloading the canvas, which was so much in favour with the artists of the Italian School.

Favretto distanced himself from the type of painting that dazzles in an artificial, deceptive and, ultimately, transitory way. His compositions have a truth about their presentation that effectively retains all the teachings of Manet, even though he did not have any direct contact with French painting.

MUSEUMS AND GALLERIES:
BERLIN: *The Sleeping Servant* - MILAN (Pinacoteca di Brera): *Anatomy Lesson; Vandalism* - MUNICH (Pinakothek): *Venetian Artist* - ROME (Gal. Nazionale): *After the Bath; Walking in St Mark's Square in the 18th century* - TRIESTE (Civico Mus. Revoltella): *Declaration* - VENICE (Gal. Nazionale): *18th century Venetian Woman; Portrait of the Artist's Father.*
AUCTION RECORDS:
LONDON, 11 April 1908, *Playing with Baby,* GBP 22. PARIS, 2 and 3 July 1929, *People on a Balcony,* FRF 42,000. LONDON, 6 Feb 1947, *Landscape,* GBP 210. MILAN, 21 Oct 1969, *Street in Venice,* ITL 2,600,000. MILAN, 16 March 1972, *Nursery School,* ITL 10,500,000. MILAN, 28 Oct 1976, *Blue Kimono* (oil on panel, 10 x 8 1/4 ins / 25.5 x 21 cm) ITL 5,500,000. MILAN, 26 May 1977, *Cup of Coffee* (oil on panel, 17 1/4 x 24 1/2 ins / 44 x 62 cm) ITL 7,500,000. LONDON, 12 July 1977, *Young Italian Women Admiring an Umbrella* (watercolour, 10 1/4 x 15 1/4 ins / 26 x 38.8 cm) GBP 800. MILAN, 10 June 1981, *Portrait of a Woman* (oil on canvas, 30 3/4 x 25 1/2 ins / 78 x 65 cm) ITL 11,000,000. MILAN, 29 May 1984, *Bust-length Portrait of a Peasant Woman: Venice* (1883, oil on canvas, diam. 14 1/2 ins / 37 cm) ITL 66,000,000. ROME, 29 Oct 1985, *Portrait of Bressanin the Painter* (1880, oil on panel, 15 1/4 x 11 3/4 ins / 39 x 30 cm) ITL 24,000,000. MILAN, 9 June 1987, *Reading* (pastel, 24 1/2 x 17 1/4 ins / 62.5 x 44 cm) ITL 2,400,000. NEW YORK, 24 April 1988, *While Leafing through the Books on the Antiquarian's Stall* (watercolour/paper, 8 1/2 x 12 1/2 ins / 21.3 x 31.7 cm) USD 17,600. ROME, 14 Dec 1988, *Woman in an Interior* (Indian ink/paper, 83 1/4 x 12 1/4 ins / 211.2 x 31 cm) ITL 850,000. MILAN, 14 March 1989, *Portrait of a Young Woman Seated* (pencil/paper, 13 1/4 x 9 1/2 ins / 33.5 x 24 cm) ITL 6,000,000. PARIS, 5 June 1989, *Italian Lake* (oil on canvas, 18 x 23 1/2 ins / 46 x 60 cm) FRF 11,000. MILAN, 19 Oct 1989, *Liston Moderno* (1887, oil on canvas, 32 1/2 x 64 ins / 82.5 x 162.5 cm) ITL 670,000,000. VERSAILLES, 19 Nov 1989, *Gallant Conversation* (oil on canvas, 20 x 33 3/4 ins / 51 x 86 cm) FRF 14,000. MILAN, 6 Dec 1989, *The San Paolo Quarter in Venice* (ink, 7 x 9 3/4 ins / 18 x 25 cm) ITL 18,000,000. MILAN, 8 March 1990, *Needlework* (1881, watercolour/paper, 9 3/4 x 6 1/4 ins / 25 x 16 cm) ITL 36,000,000. MILAN, 12 Dec 1991, *Woman in Profile* (watercolour/paper, 15 1/4 x 12 1/4 ins / 39 x 31 cm) ITL 17,000,000. MILAN, 19 March 1992, *Portrait of the Artist's Father* (1884, oil on panel, 11 x 7 ins / 28 x 18 cm) ITL 22,000,000. MILAN, 3 Dec 1992, *Portrait of an Elderly Lady* (oil on canvas, 25 x 32 1/4 ins / 63.5 x 82 cm) ITL 20,340,000. MILAN, 18 Dec 1996, *Popular Scene in a Street in Venice* (1883, oil on panel, 9 1/2 x 24 ins / 24 x 61 cm) ITL 180,575,000. ROME, 2 Dec 1997, *The Father and Sister of the Painter* (oil on canvas, 9 1/2 x 11 ins / 24 x 28 cm) ITL 244,250,000.

FAVRIN, Louis
French, 18th - 19th century.
Active in Paris.
Painter.
Favrin is known to have executed some miniatures on ivory between 1789 and 1813.

FAVRIOU, Suzanne Marie
French, 20th century.
Born in Souvigné.
Painter.
Suzanne Favriou exhibited in Paris in 1933, at the Salon des Artistes Français.

FAVRO, Murray
Canadian, 20th century.
Born 1940, in Huntsville.
Installation artist.
Murray Favro works in two fields: installations that make use of projectors, and constructions of objects reproduced to scale. His installations with projections explore the relationship between seeing and understanding, between illusion and the creation of illusion. Thus, *Synthetic Lake* (1973) consists of a film of waves projected on to a canvas fixed to a mechanical device that raises and lowers it, giving the illusion of movement. By reproducing in three dimensions a famous work like *Van Gogh's Room,* in which the objects retain the perspective distortions of the picture, he is not recreating the original, but making tangible the reality and the illusion. Nor is it a desire to reproduce that led him to build a model of the F.86 Sabre plane when he made his sculpture *Sabre Jet,* the transparent body of which makes visible the construction methods; rather, a wish to celebrate the creative capacity of man.

Favro has exhibited solo since 1968 in Canada, notably in 1996, 1998, 200 and 2002 at the Christopher Cutts Gallery in Toronto.
BIBLIOGRAPHY:
Lucie-Smith, Edward, *Art in the Seventies,* Phaidon, Oxford, 1980. Burnett, David, *Masterpieces of Canadian Art from the National Gallery of Canada,* Hurtig, Edmonton, 1990.
MUSEUMS AND GALLERIES:
OTTAWA (NG. of Canada): *Synthetic Lake* (1973) - TORONTO (AG of Ontario): *Van Gogh's Room* (1973-1974).

FAVROT, Louis Sébastien
Flemish, 19th century.
Active in Brussels c. 1836.
Painter. Genre scenes.
Flemish School.

FAWCETT, Emily Addis (Miss)
British, 19th century.
Active in London.
Sculptor.
Emily Addis Fawcett exhibited frequently at the Royal Academy in London from 1883 onwards.

FAWCETT, George
British, 20th century.
Born 8 April 1877, in London.
Active in the USA.
Engraver, illustrator.
George Fawcett studied in England and exhibited in Chicago and Canada.

FAWKES, Lionel Grimston (Colonel)
British, 19th - 20th century.
Born 1849; died 1931.
Painter, draughtsman. Interiors with figures.
He was at the Royal Military Academy in Woolwich in 1868. From 1878 to 1884 he was an attaché at the house of the governor of Barbados and visited other Caribbean Islands.
AUCTION RECORDS:
LONDON, 17 Nov 1995, *The sitting rooms of 'The Queen's House' in Barbados* (pencil and watercolour, 9 1/2 x 14 3/4 ins / 24.4 x 37.3 cm) GBP 1,725. LONDON, 29 April 1999, *Queen's House, Barbados. Queen's House Windmill* (watercolour, six, 6x9 ins / 15x23 cm) GBP 2,400.

FAWORSKI, Jozef
Polish, 18th - 19th century.
Painter.
Jozef Faworski worked in Warsaw between 1790 and 1805, and probably also in Berlin. His portraits were painted in the Sarmatian tradition; in the style of funerary portraits, whose popularity peaked in the 17th century. They show Polish

people in national costume, with a dignity that emphasises their high social position. The colours are vivid, and the faces express each subject's individuality.

FAWZI, Hussein
Egyptian, 20th century.
Born in Cairo.
Painter.
This artist exhibited at the Salon in 1933.

FAX, Elton Clay
American, 20th century.
Born 1909, in Baltimore; died 1993.
Painter, draughtsman, print artist, illustrator, art historian, writer. Figures, portraits, genre scenes, scenes with figures, landscapes. Comic strips.
Elton Clay Fax studied at Clafin University, Orangeburg, South Carolina, and Syracuse University, Syracuse, New York. He was taught by Augusta Savage.

Fax illustrated many children's books, such as Harold Lamb's *Genghis Khan and the Mongol Horde* (Random House, New York, 1954) and Verna Aardema's *More Tales from the Story Hat* (Coward-McCann, New York, 1966). During the 1930s Depression, he also illustrated school books such as George P. Lipscomb's *The Pygmies* and Natalie Hughes' *Two-Step Tom* (Board of Education of the City of New York, 1940), for the Work Progress Administration. Among his prints, the portfolio *Black and Beautiful* stands out.

Elton Fax's political involvement can also be seen in a series of books illustrating his travels in Africa and the USSR: *Through Black Eyes; Journeys of a Black Artist to East Africa and Russia* (New York, Dodd Mead, 1974), *Hashar* (Moscow, Progress Publishers, 1980), and *Soviet People as I Knew Them* (Moscow, Progress Publishers, 1988). During the 1940s he created the comic strip *Susabelle* for the Black Press (1942-1943). It depicted the adventures of a little black girl in the street, its frames almost without dialogue. Fax was also known for two works in the 1970s introducing black artists: *Seventeen Black Artists* and *Black Artists of the New Generation*, and black figures: *Contemporary Black Leaders*.

He took part in various group exhibitions, such as in 1933, Harmon Foundation, New York; 1939, *Contemporary Negro Art*, Museum of Art, Baltimore, Maryland, and solo exhibitions, including 1968, *Elton C. Fax: Drawings from Africa*, Fisk University, Nashville, Tennessee.

BIBLIOGRAPHY:
Fax, Elton, *West Africa vignettes*, American Society of African Culture, New York, 1963 (text in English and French). Driskell, David C., *Elton C. Fax: Drawings from Africa*, exhibition catalogue, Fisk University, Nashville (TN), 1968. Fax, Elton, *Contemporary Black Leaders*, Dodd Mead, New York, 1970. Fax, Elton, *Seventeen Black Artists*, Dodd Mead, New York, 1971. Fax, Elton, *Black Artists of The New Generation*, Dodd Mead, New York, 1977.

MUSEUMS AND GALLERIES:
WASHINGTON DC (Navy Art Collection).

FAXARDO, Juan Antonio
Spanish.
Born in Seville.
Painter.
It was he who gave painting lessons to Alonzo Miguel de Tobar as a child

FAXOÉ, Nikolaj Christian
Danish, 18th - 19th century.
Born 1762; died 15 May 1810.
Painter.
Nikolaj Christian Faxoé worked at the royal porcelain factory in Copenhagen from 1783 until his death. One of his portraits was exhibited in 1811.

FAXOÉ, Peder Madsen
Danish, 18th - 19th century.
Born 13 February 1761, in Faxinge; died 27 February 1840.
Active in Copenhagen.
Painter, decorative designer. Portraits.
MUSEUMS AND GALLERIES:
HILLERØD: *Portrait of the Poet Oehlenschläger as a Child.*

FAXON, Amélie (Mme)
French, 19th century.
Born 19th century, in Bordeaux.
Painter.
Amélie Faxon was a pupil of Steuben. She exhibited the following works at the Paris Salon: *Easter in Bloom* in 1865, *Courtyard in Pont-l'Abbé* in 1868 and *Strawberries* and *Breton Children* in 1870.

FAXON, Richard
French, 19th century.
Born c. 1830, in Bordeaux.
Painter. Landscapes, seascapes.
Richard Faxon was a pupil of Jean-Baptiste Durand-Brager. He exhibited at the Paris Salon from 1859 to 1875. He painted landscapes and seascapes, inspired by the region of his birth and by the Breton coast. His works include *Royan Regatta, The Verdon Region, Broken down ship, Boat on the Garonne, Boat in a Squall.*
MUSEUMS AND GALLERIES:
BREST: *Battle between an English Cutter and a Spanish Schooner; Port Entrance.*
AUCTION RECORDS:
PARIS, 9 June 1980, *Yacht at Sea* (oil on canvas, 28¼ x 43¼ ins / 72 x 110 cm) FRF 5,000. LONDON, 5 June 1985, *Boat in Two Positions* (oil on canvas, 20½ x 24 ins / 52 x 61 cm) GBP 1,700. LONDON, 13 May 1999, *Two-master Heading into Royan, France* (oil on canvas, 22 x 32 ins / 55 x 81 cm) GBP 2,600. BREST, 11 May 2003, *Seascapes* (oil, two oils, one on paper, 7 x 9 ins / 18 x 23 cm) EUR 3,600.

FAXON, William Bailey
American, 19th century.
Born 1849, in Hartford (Connecticut); died 1941.
Painter. Figures.
William Bailey Faxon was a pupil of Jacquesson de la Chevreuse and worked in New York.
AUCTION RECORDS:
SAN FRANCISCO, 24 June 1981, *Peasant Girl* (oil on canvas, 28 x 39¼ ins / 71 x 100 cm) DEM 14,000.

FAY, A.
German, 19th century.
Active in Frankfurt am Main.
Lithographer.
A. Fay lithographed *The Players* after G. Flüggen, with the assistance of Jakob Fay, and then worked on his own to lithograph *The Wine Tasting* after Hasenclever, and *The Fiancée* and *Coming Back from Church* after H. Rustige. He also made lithographs after C. Schröder and H. Kretschmer.

FAY, Albert
Hungarian, 19th century.
Active c. 1848.
Painter.
Albert Fay produced drawings for the illustrated review *Kepes Ujsag*. The museum of Košice owns one of his paintings showing the Grand Duke Stephen entering the town on an official visit.

FAY, Alexis
French, 19th century.
Born 19th century, in Paris.
Painter.

Fay was a pupil of Navez. He exhibited portraits at the Salon in 1850 and 1853.

FAY, Charlotte
Dutch, 19th century.
Miniaturist.

There is a portrait of a woman held in the Van Arkel collection in Abcoude by Charlotte Fay.

FAY, Clark
American, 20th century.
Born in the USA.
Lithographer.

Fay Clark exhibited *The Circus, Nice* at the Salon des Artistes Français in 1928.

FAY, François
French, 17th century.
Active in Le Mans in 1695.
Painter.

FAY, Frank
French, 20th century.
Born 23 November 1921, in Paris.
Painter, sculptor, mixed media. Murals.

Of Algonquin origin, Fay left France in 1949 for Polynesia and Melanesia. He returned to the city in 1987. He first exhibited in Paris after the war, and then in Tahiti and São Paulo. In Paris he participated in the Salon des Indépendants until 1949, and after 1973 he exhibited at the Salons des Grands et Jeunes d'Aujourd'hui and at the Salon des Réalités Nouvelles. Among his exhibitions and retrospectives are: 1970, Musée Gauguin, Tahiti; 1955, Musée de l'Abbaye St-Germain, Auxerre; 1995, Bibliothèque Municipale, Auxerre; 2002, Musée de Sens, a retrospective of paintings and sculptures from 1962 to 2001. Fay has worked in pottery since 1940 and has more recently begun sculpting in wood and plaster. In 1960 he discovered his own way of sculpting, which he called *cloutage* (nailing). This was a system of assembling driftwood and roots. In painting, he systematised a sign language. Around 1956, he expressed his somewhat geometric sculptural preoccupations in painting fabrics.

BIBLIOGRAPHY:
Frank Fay, exhibition catalogue, Musée Gauguin, Papeete (Tahiti), 1970. Winkler, S.W., *Frank Fay. Sculptures 1958-1973, Peintures 1978*, exhibition catalogue, Fare Manihini, Papeete (Tahiti), 1978.

FAY, Fred
Swiss, 20th century.
Born 7 July 1901, in Basel.
Painter, draughtsman, engraver, illustrator, decorative artist. Figures, portraits, landscapes, urban landscapes. Designs for stained glass.

Fred Fay acquired some technical knowledge of painting from his father, who was a picture restorer. While still a student, he exhibited as early as 1918 in Geneva, with the Puits d'Or (Gold Mine) group. He continued his art studies in Florence. In 1923, he made study trips to Berlin and Stuttgart. He was a founder member of the Société des Graveurs de la Suisse Latine in 1930 and later became its president. He worked in Paris in 1932, in Italy in 1933 and in Greece and the Lebanon in 1935. In 1949, he founded the École des Beaux-Arts in Le Valais. He received a medal from the city of Paris in 1965. In 1946, he painted four murals for the church of the Holy Family in Erde (Le Valais). In 1952, he made the stage sets and costumes for the opera *Le Ballet du Soleil* (*Sun Ballet*) in Lyons. He also illustrated around fifty books.

He has taken part in collective exhibitions in all the major European countries, and regularly at L'Art Libre (Free Art), of which he is a society member. He was also a member of the fine arts societies in Milan, Basel and Paris and a member of the society of the Salon des Artistes Français in Paris, where he exhibited in this capacity. He has held an impressive number of solo exhibitions, in particular a major retrospective of his work for his 70th birthday, in Sion, at the Musée Cantonal des Beaux-Arts in La Majorie in 1971.

Although when young Fay was initially influenced by Cubism and Futurism, he never moved towards abstraction in its formal distancing of the subject. On the contrary, abandoning the 'modern' ideas of the period, he preferred to use the more traditional expressiveness of form and representation. Nevertheless, certain Cubist influences have remained in his work. Landscapes, portraits and nudes illustrate the 'art of serenity' (Arnold Kohler) practised by this artist and untiring champion of reality, established by a composition that is reflective and illuminated by colours. It is to him that we owe the renaissance of wood engraving in Switzerland.

BIBLIOGRAPHY:
Fred Fay, exhibition catalogue, Musée de la Majorie, Sion, 1971.

MUSEUMS AND GALLERIES:
BERN (Schweizerische Landesbibliothek).

AUCTION RECORDS:
BERN, 12 May 1990, *View of Bern* (1933, oil on canvas, 33 1/2 x 41 3/4 ins / 85 x 106 cm) CHF 1,800.

FAY, J. B.
French, 18th century.
Active in Paris c. 1785.
Engraver (etching).

J. B. Fay is remembered for 12 sketchbooks containing 72 drawings of ornamental decoration.

FAY, Jakob
German, 19th century.
Active in Frankfurt am Main.
Lithographer.

Jakob Fay executed lithographs after R. Jordan, A. Rethel, J.B. Sonderland, P. Vogel and Steinle. His best-known lithographs include: *Gretchen* after A.V.D. Embde, *Knight at Rest in the Forest* after C.F. Lessing, and *Death of Gustave Adolphe* after D. Monten.

FAY, Joseph, or Fey
German, 19th century.
Born 10 August 1813, in Cologne; died 27 July 1875, in Düsseldorf.
Painter. History painting, religious subjects, mythological subjects, genre scenes.

From 1833 to 1841, Joseph Fay studied painting at the academy of art in Düsseldorf. He continued his studies in Munich, before going on to study under Paul Delaroche at the École des Beaux-Arts in Paris. He exhibited at the Paris Salon in 1845 and 1846.

Fay produced many paintings depicting the small trades of the suburbs, and peasant life, all inspired by a long stay in Italy. The council in Elberfeld commissioned various cartoons from him to decorate the assembly hall. He found his inspiration primarily in biblical texts and in classical antiquity.

MUSEUMS AND GALLERIES:
BREMEN: *Romans Bathing* - COLOGNE: *Samson and Delilah* - HAMBURG: *Christmas Eve* - HANOVER (Niedersächsisches Landesmus.): *Monk Begging* - MANNHEIM: *Young Girls Bathing*.

AUCTION RECORDS:
COLOGNE, 14 Nov 1974, *Roman Country Scene*, DEM 8,500.

FAY, Ludwig Benno
German, 19th century.
Born 24 March 1859, in Gerresheim, near Düsseldorf; died September 1906, in Düsseldorf.
Painter. Genre scenes, animals.

A son and pupil of Joseph Fay, Ludwig Fay worked in Düsseldorf. He is best known for his *In the Morning* and *Horses Returning Before the Storm*.

Museums and Galleries:

Rostock: *Coming Back from Market by Sledge*.

Auction records:

Cologne, 2 June 1965, *Children and Grazing Horses*, DEM 3,300. Cologne, 23 Oct 1981, *Hunting Dog Holding a Hare in its Mouth* (oil on canvas, 30¼ x 39¼in/77 x 100cm) DEM 14,000. London, 21 March 1986, *Return of the Draught Horses* (oil on canvas, 22 x 17¼in/55.8 x 43.7cm) GBP 5,000. Bremen, 29 Nov 2002, *Hunting Dog in the Snow with Slain Hare* (oil on canvas, 22 x 28 ins / 57 x 70 cm) EUR 5,100. Cologne, 1 July 2004, *Grandfather and his Grandson Riding Together on a Horse-drawn Sleigh* (oil on canvas, 25 x 38 ins / 64 x 96 cm) EUR 8,900.

FAY D'HERBE, Antoine, or Faydherbe
Flemish, 17th century.
Born before 1580, in Mechelen; died 8 October 1653.
Sculptor.
Flemish School.

Antoine Fay d'Herbe was the brother of Henri Fay d'Herbe. He qualified as a master in Mechelen in 1605.

FAY D'HERBE, Henri, or Faydherbe
Flemish School, 16th - 17th century.
Born 1574, in Mechelen; died 30 April 1629, in Mechelen.
Sculptor, illuminator.
Mechelen School, Antwerp School.

Brother of Antoine Fayd'herbe and pupil of Melchior d'Hassonville in the Mechelen guild in 1588, Henri was received as a master in 1599. He worked in Mechelen until 1603 and thereafter in Antwerp.

FAY D'HERBE, Lukas, or Faydherbe
Flemish, 17th century.
Born 19 January 1617, in Mechelen; died 31 December 1697, in Mechelen.
Sculptor.
Flemish School.

The son of Henri Fay d'Herbe, Lukas Fay d'Herbe, who was also an architect, worked for a long time on drawing with Rubens. Among his sculptures are *Fountain* after Rubens, and *St Joseph and the Child* in Brussels. He also worked in ivory. His works are to be found in a number of Belgian churches, especially in Mechelen, where he erected the church of Notre Dame d'Hanswyck between 1663 and 1681, adorning the dome with large high-reliefs representing the *Nativity* and *Bearing of the Cross*. He also executed a high-relief in black and white marble and a high altar for the church of the Beguine convent, as well as a monument for Archbishop André Cruesen in the church of St-Rombaut. He helped define Flemish Baroque sculpture.

Museums and Galleries:

Copenhagen (Rosenborg Slot): *Venus, Ceres and Bacchus* (low relief) - Mechelen: *Hercules and Omphale; Christ on the Terrestrial Globe; St George on Horseback; St James the Less* (statue); *Descent from the Cross* (low relief); *St Roch Healing the Plague-stricken* (low relief) - Vienna: *Judgement of Solomon* (low relief); *Venus, Ceres and Bacchus* (low relief).

Auction records:

London, 2 April 1971, *Virgin and Child* (marble) Gns 2,500.

FAY D'HERBE, Marie, or Faydherbe
Flemish, 17th century.
Born 22 January 1611, in Mechelen.
Active in the Netherlands.
Sculptor.
Flemish School.

Marie Fay d'Herbe was the daughter of Antoine Fay d'Herbe.

FAYA, G.
20th century.
Painter.

Auction records:

London, 19 June 1942, *Susannah and the Elders*, GBP 7.

FAYARD, Georges
French, 20th century.
Born in Algiers.
Sculptor.

Georges Fayard exhibited in Paris at the Salon des Artistes Français from 1913.

FAYARD, Jean
French, 20th century.
Born 20 June 1919, in Marseilles.
Painter. Urban landscapes, still-lifes.

Jean Fayard lives and works in Marseilles. He also exhibits in Paris at the Salon d'Automne. He participates in collective exhibitions, mainly on the Côte d'Azur, but also, in 1983, at the Salon des Indépendants in Paris. The Marcel Bernheim gallery in Paris showed an ensemble of his works in 1981. He works in a very realistic style, with a heavy use of paint.

FAYAU
French, 17th century.
Active in Le Mans c. 1617-1626.
Painter.

FAYDHERBE, Anne Barbe
Flemish, 17th century.
Baptised 4 December 1643 in Mechelen.
Sculptor.
Flemish School.

The daughter of Faydherbe, Anne Barbe Faydherbe married one of her father's pupils, Jan van Delen, in 1666. Two statuettes representing *Minerva* and *Diana* are attributed to her.

FAYDHERBE, Jean
Flemish, 17th century.
Sculptor.
Flemish School.

Jean Faydherbe was sculptor to Duke Henry of Orléans and the Duke of Longueville.

FAYDHERBE, Jean Lukas
Flemish, 17th century.
Born 28 August 1654, in Mechelen; died 1704, in Mechelen.
Sculptor.
Flemish School.

Jean Lukas Faydherbe was the son and pupil of Lukas Fay d'Herbe. He was also an architect.

FAYDHERBE, Rombaut
Flemish, 17th century.
Born 12 December 1649, in Mechelen; died 1673, in Naxos, Greece.
Painter.
Flemish School.

Rombaut Faydherbe was the son of Lukas Fay d'Herbe and was taught by Abraham von Diepenbeck and Jacques Jordaens. In 1673 he accompanied the Marquis of Nointel, ambassador to Louis XIV, to the Levant, but died near the beginning of the journey.

FAYE, Alice
French, 19th century.
Born 19th century, in Bordeaux.
Painter.

Alice Faye was a pupil of Lefebvre, Tony Robert-Fleury and F. Humbert. She was a member of the Société des Artistes Français from 1902 and exhibited at the society's Salon.

FAYE, Balthazar
Senegalese, 20th - 21st century.
Born 1964, in Dakar.
Painter (mixed media), designer.

Balthazar Faye lived in Senegal for almost twenty years, then came to Europe via Geneva. He studied at the École des Beaux-Arts de Besançon, moving to the École des Arts Décoratifs in Paris in 1989. Faye believes that 'error is a driving force,' and never erases the mistakes in his artworks. In fact, he uses the tension between them and the composition itself for artistic effect. In his works, he exploits space and materials, particularly the latter, and is just as confident a designer as he is a painter. Indeed, he designed the bar and the furniture for the *African Suites* exhibition, which took place in 1997 at the Couvent des Cordeliers in Paris, and in which he also formally participated.

FAYE, J. de
Flemish, 18th century.
Active in The Hague in 1739.
Painter.
Flemish School.

J. de Faye distinguished himself by imitating the great artists Teniers and Rickaert.

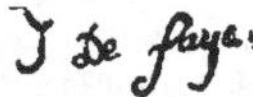

FAYE, Marie (Mme)
French, 19th century.
Born in Chablis (Yonne).
Painter.

Marie Faye was a pupil of L. Cogniet. She exhibited some portraits of private individuals at the Paris Salon in 1875.

FAYE, Mor
Senegalese, 20th - 21st century.
Born 16 March 1947, in Dakar.
Painter.

Mor Faye studied at the École Nationale des Arts du Sénégal, in the Visual Arts department. His paintings are abstract and lively, with splashes of colour.

In 1966, he received a certificate in artistic education, and has taught the visual arts in a number of schools.

He took part in the following group exhibitions: the work of 44 American modellers at the American Cultural Centre in Dakar in 1964. *Premier Festival Mondial des Arts Nègres* (*The First World-wide Festival of Black Art*), in Dakar in 1966; *Semaine Sénégalaise* (*Senegalese Week*) in Morocco, and, later, *Dix Ans d'Art au Sénégal* (*Ten Years of Senegalese Art*), both in 1970; at the Quinzaine de la SAC-SEN in Dakar, and the Festival d'I.F.E., in 1972; at the Premier Salon des Arts Sénégalais, in 1973; at the Senegalese Exhibitions in Rome and Tunis, and the Exposition des Arts Plastiques Contemporains in the Musée des Beaux-Arts de Liège, 1973; and at the Deuxième Salon des Artistes Sénégalais, at the Musée Dynamique in Dakar, in 1974.

Faye also won the Prix de Peinture, Décoration et Modelage (Prize for Painting, Decoration and Modelling) at the Maison des Arts.

FAYE, Ousman
Senegalese, 20th century.
Born 23 November 1940, in Dakar.
Painter. Designs for tapestries.

Ousman Faye was a former pupil of the École Nationale des Arts in Senegal (in the department of sculptural research), and was a former painter and cartoon artist at the Manufacture Nationale de Tapisseries de Thiès in Sénégal. He then did an apprenticeship at the École des Arts Décoratifs d'Aubusson. In 1973 he set up his own weaving studio in Dakar. He took part in the following exhibitions: 1966, *Premier Festival Mondial des Arts Nègres* (*First World Festival of Negro Arts*), where he came third in the poster competition; 1967, Cinquième Biennale des Jeunes Artistes in Paris; 1969, first pan-African cultural festival of Algiers; 1970, laureate of the Grand Prize in Painting in Cagnes-sur-Mer; 1971, several collective exhibitions in Normandy; 1973 and 1974, the first and second Salon des Artistes Sénégalais in Dakar. His works are figurative, highly coloured, and perceivably influenced by the style of Jean Curçat.

FAYE M'BOR
Senegalese, 20th century.
Born 28 October 1900, in Dakar.
Painter.

Faye M'bor was drafted in 1920 for the Levant campaign, which he was involved with until 1922. He was then employed at the Dakar city hall, and later as a transporter and consignee of cutters. He was a self-taught, popular painter, who never exhibited either by himself or collectively until the second Salon des Artistes Sénégalais in Dakar in 1974. His painting is figurative, and shows a use of vivid colours.

FAYEIN-CHABANON
French, 20th century.
Born 20 October 1920, in Paris.
Painter, engraver.

Fayein-Chabanon was born in Beaujolais. He studied at the École Nationale Supérieure des Beaux-Arts in Paris from 1945 to 1952. He studied painting with Nicolas Untersteller, engraving with Cami and Goerg, and fresco art with Ducos de la Haille. Since 1968 he has worked as a conservator of historic monuments.

Fayein-Chabanon began his career by exhibiting in Paris at the Salon des Artistes Français from 1948, as well as at that of the Société Nationale des Beaux-Arts. He received a gold medal at the Salon des Artistes Français, and several prizes at the Salon of the Société Nationale des Beaux-Arts. He also received a medal from the City of Paris and another from the City of Versailles. He has deposited his work as an engraver at the Cabinet des Estampes in Paris.

BIBLIOGRAPHY:
'*Fayein-Chabanon*' in *Les Nouvelles de l'estampe* n° 73, periodical, Bibliothèque nationale de France, Paris, 1984.

MUSEUMS AND GALLERIES:
BOULOGNE-BILLANCOURT - PARIS (Mus. de la Ville).

FAYEN, Etienne. See **FAYN**

FAYERMAN, Anne Charlotte.
See **BARTHOLOMEW**

FAYET, Antoine Gilbert
French, 20th century.
Born 1924, in Andance.
Painter, pastellist. Figures, nudes, portraits, scenes with figures, landscapes.

Antoine Fayet lived in Roanne for many years. As a young man, he belonged to a group of painters who aligned themselves with the Lyons school, and he met and befriended Jean Puy. Jean Puy encouraged him, allowing him to work in his studio. The friendship and trust of Puy endured throughout Fayet's career. For several years,he resided in Casablanca. Upon his return to France, an industrial career distanced him from exhibitions, although not from painting. Since 1982 he has lived in Bandol.

Fayet participated in collective exhibitions in Roanne from 1943, in Casablanca in 1949 and 1968, from 1980 in Roanne once again, and later in Bandol and the whole Mediterranean region. He has participated in the Salon des Indépendants in Paris since 1988 and has shown ensembles of his work in solo exhibitions in Roanne, Casablanca and Bandol, as well as in Cassis in 1991. His figures, nudes and portraits show a sureness of line and a balance of composition. Since settling in Bandol, he has painted pastel Mediterranean landscapes and shores with sensitivity.

FAYET, François
French, 17th century.
Born 1630, in Rheims; died 1708, in Toulouse.
Painter. Religious subjects.

Museums and Galleries:
Toulouse: *Adoration of the Shepherds; Rest during the Flight into Egypt.*

FAYET, Gustave
French, 19th - 20th century.
Born 1865, in Béziers; died 1926, in Carcassonne.
Painter, designer, potter. Landscapes. Designs for tapestries.

Gustave Fayet was a wine grower who used his fortune to collect works of modern art, notably those of Gauguin and Redon. He was helped by the art critic, Maurice Fabre. In 1910, his collection of Gauguin included 31 paintings and wood sculptures, 56 engravings and 12 ceramics. He had 37 of Redon's works, in addition to 7 Renoirs, 29 Monticellis, 17 Bonnards and 8 Van Goghs, including *Self-portrait with Bandaged Ear*. In 1908 he bought and renovated the Fontfroide abbey. Odilon Redon helped with the decoration, and the stained glass artist Richard Burgsthal worked on the windows. Having become curator of the museum in Béziers, he organised the annual exhibition of the Société des Beaux-Arts in 1901. Maurice Fabre wrote the preface to the catalogue, and the exhibition was significant in the number of important artists invited. They included Redon, Degas, Renoir, Cézanne, Pissaro, Gauguin, Rodin, Maurice Denis, Jacques Villon and Picasso. Gustave Fayet was particularly linked with Daniel de Monfreid. He was the intermediary through whom Fayet took up a correspondence with Gauguin, and through whom Fayet came to know Maillol in 1900.

Fayet exhibited at the Salon de la Société Nationale des Beaux-Arts in Paris. He was included in the 1998 exhibition, *1894-1908. Le Roussillon à l'origine de l'art moderne* (*1894-1908. Le Roussillon at the Beginnings of Modern Art*), at the Palais des Congrès in Perpignan. He devoted himself to decorative works and chose themes of stylised flowers, fruits and butterflies for his tapestries. With Louis Paul, he created about a hundred ceramics between 1897 and 1899, which were exhibited notably at the Galerie Bing in Paris.

Bibliography:
Valaison, Marie-Claude/Barou, Jean-Pierre, *1894-1908. Le Roussillon à l'origine de l'art moderne*, exhibition catalogue, Ville de Perpignan, 1998.

FAYET, Henri
French, 20th century.
Born 13 October 1888, in Lezoux.
Painter.

Henri Fayet was a pupil of Cormon, and a member of the Salon des Artistes Français.

FAYET, Jacqueline
French, 20th century.
Sculptor.

Jacqueline Fayet received her university diploma in Fine Arts in 1956. A sculptor, she was a resident at the Casa Velázquez in Madrid in 1959. She exhibited in several Parisian salons, including the Salon des Artistes Français, and the Salon Comparaisons. She also showed at the salons in Boulogne, Montgeron and Garches and exhibited in several galleries in Paris. In 1949 she received the Chevanard prize, and in 1960 the Grand Prix des Beaux-Arts de la Ville de Paris.

Bibliography:
Ateliers de Boulogne, auction catalogue, Maître Cheval, Drouot, Paris, 1989.

FAYET, Léon
French, 19th century.
Born 22 April 1826, in Béziers; died 1880, in Béziers.
Painter.

Léon Fayet exhibited landscapes at the Paris Salon from 1864 to 1870.

Museums and Galleries:
Béziers: *Farm beneath Trees*; charcoal.

Auction records:
Paris, 21 and 22 May 1928, *River Bank in the Morning; River Bank in the Evening* (pair) FRF 1,500.

FAYET, Marie-Thérèse
Spanish, 20th century.
Born 5 June 1934, in Madrid.
Active and naturalised in France.
Painter, engraver, sculptor, mixed media.

Marie-Thérèse Fayet studied at the school of fine arts in Lyons and Paris from 1954 to 1959.

In Paris she has exhibited regularly since the late 80s at the Salon des Réalités Nouvelles and the Salon des Grands et Jeunes d'Aujourd'hui, the Salon de Mai and at the Espace Latino-Américain. She has also shown work at the Biennale in Ljubljana, Varna and Cadaqués and in 1990 at the Kyoto museum. She has had solo exhibitions in Paris and Lyons.

The titles of Fayet's works draw attention to her use of texture: *L'Écorce Terrestre* (*The Earth's Crust*) and *Grottes Basaltiques* (*Basalt Caves*). She works on hand-made paper manufactured from natural textiles, stamping and imprinting to create low reliefs and sculptures.

Museums and Galleries:
Annecy (Mus.-Château) - Ferrol (Mus.) - Mulhouse (MBA, Prints Collection) - Sofia (Mus.) - Vénissieux (Mus.).

FAYET, Pierre Antoine Gabriel
French, 19th century.
Born 17 December 1832, in Béziers; died 1899, in Béziers.
Painter. Landscapes, urban landscapes.

Pierre Antoine Fayet exhibited landscapes at the Paris Salon from 1865 to 1870. Works include *Rocomolatio* and *Colombières*.

Museums and Galleries:
Béziers: *Banks of the Agout; Fountain, Sète.*

FAYET, Pierre Antoine Gustave
French, 19th - 20th century.
Born 19 May 1865, in Béziers; died 1925.
Painter. Landscapes, village views.

Pierre Antoine Gustave was a pupil of his father Gabriel Fayet, and was curator at the museum in Béziers.

Museums and Galleries:
Béziers: *View of St-Mandrier near Toulon* - Narbonne: *The Brooms* - Sète: *Wood of Tabarka.*

FAYETON, Joseph
French, 19th century.
Born 31 January 1826, in Lyons.
Painter, draughtsman. Portraits, still-lifes (flowers/fruit). Textiles.

Fayeton was a pupil at Lyons École des Beaux-Arts and started to design church ornaments. He exhibited paintings of flowers and fruit at the Lyons Salon in 1868, and went on to exhibit still-lifes of flowers and fruits and his self-portrait in 1869. He designed silks.

FAYMOREAU, Renée de
French, 20th century.
Born in Château-Gontier.
Watercolourist.
Faymoreau exhibited in Paris at the Salon d'Automne and at the Salon des Tuileries.

FAYN, Étienne, or Fayen
Flemish, 18th century.
Born 3 September 1712, in Liège; died before 1790.
Engraver, architect.
Flemish School.
Étienne Fayn executed drawings and engravings of Liège and the principality among which the following are notable: *Château d'Hex; Abbey of Neumoustier; Abbey of Val St-Lambert; Views of Chèvremont;* and *Chaudfontaine.* He also drew historical subjects, such as *The Death of Cleopatra.*
MUSEUMS AND GALLERIES:
LIÈGE (Ansembourg): *Portrait of Jacques de Hubin; Portrait of Benjamin Franklin; Portrait of the Burgomaster Fabry.*
AUCTION RECORDS:
PARIS, 22 March 1928, *View of the Great Observatory and the French Pantheon* (pen) FRF 1,550.

FAYNOT, Émile
French, 20th century.
Born in Levrezy.
Watercolourist.
Faynot exhibited in Paris at the Salon, beginning in 1931.

FAYOD, Charles
Swiss, 19th century.
Born 1 March 1857, in Bex (Vaud).
Painter.
Having initially drawn illustrations for scientific works, Fayod went on to paint flowers and landscapes. In 1881, he settled in Nervi (Liguria), Italy, and contributed to Swiss and Italian exhibitions.

FAYOL, Marianne
French, 20th century.
Born 9 May 1908, in Strasbourg.
Painter, collage artist.
Fayol was a pupil at the Académie André Lhote and exhibited in Paris, at the Salon des Femmes Peintres et Sculpteurs, of which she was president. She also exhibited at the Salon d'Automne, the Salon des Grands et Jeunes d'Aujourd'hui and the Salon Comparaisons. She structured her compositions with long and high verticals, which animated subtle harmonies of light greys in an almost musical manner. In her collages she used a rich diversity of materials, inciting herself to greater freedom of expression.
BIBLIOGRAPHY:
'*Marianne Fayol*' in *L'Officiel des arts*, Éd. du Chevalet, Paris, 1988.

FAYOLLE, Amélie Léonie
French, 19th century.
Born 19th century, in Paris.
Painter.
Amélie Fayolle was a pupil of L. Cogniet. She exhibited portraits and genre and historical scenes at the Paris Salon, from 1848 to 1870. Works include *Portrait of General Maizière, Portrait of Mme Maizière, Portrait of Monsieur Fayolle, Artist's Father, Portrait of Mme Fayolle, Artist's Mother* and *Roman Woman.*
MUSEUMS AND GALLERIES:
LA ROCHE-SUR-YON: *Country Girls.*

FAYOLLE, Étienne
French, 19th century.
Born 22 June 1805, in Lyons.
Painter.
Étienne Fayolle was a pupil of Thierriat at the École des Beaux-Arts in Lyons. He exhibited numerous portraits at the Paris Salon.

FAYOLLE, Marie Eugénie
French, 19th century.
Born in Paris.
Miniaturist, enameller, painter (porcelain).
Marie Fayolle was a pupil of Mme D. de Cool and first exhibited at the Salon in 1876.

FAYOLLE, Pierre Gabriel
French, 19th century.
Painter.
Pierre Fayolle exhibited regularly at the Paris Salon from 1839 to 1848. Works include *Monk Meditating in His Cell, The Painter, In a Quarry, Murder in a Quarry* and *Souvenir of Morlaix.*

FAYOLLE-LAPLANCHE, Sally
French, 20th century.
Born in St-Étienne.
Painter, lithographer.
Fayolle-Laplanche was a pupil of both A. Leleu and L. Jonas, and exhibited at the Salon des Artistes Français.

FAYRAM, John
British, 18th century.
Painter. Portraits.
Known works by John Fayram are a portrait of *Lord John Hervey, First Earl of Bristol, and His Children, Tom, Nan and Felton;* two copies of female portraits after G. Kneller and J. Richardson; and two portraits of *Sir Thomas* and *Sir Roger Twysden.* In 1742 a portrait by him of *W. Stanhope, Earl of Harrington* was copied by J. Faber the Younger and J. Simon. He is probably the same as John Fayram the engraver.
AUCTION RECORDS:
LONDON, 20 Nov 1931, *Portrait of Elizabeth Streynsham,* GBP 44. PARIS, 7 and 8 June 1933, *Portrait of a Man,* FRF 7,400. LONDON, 23 Feb 1934, *Portrait of George Pretyman,* GBP 21. LONDON, 26 Feb 1937, *Portrait of George Pretyman,* GBP 10. LONDON, 9 Oct 1981, *Portrait of a Gentleman* (oil on canvas, 48 x 38 3/4 ins / 122 x 98.4 cm) GBP 300.

FAYRAM, John
British, 18th century.
Painter, engraver. Portraits, landscapes.
John Fayram worked in London around 1740. Known works by this artist include views and sketches of the surrounding areas of Chelsea and Battersea.

FAYS, Béatrice de
French, 20th century.
Painter, illustrator.
In 1986, Fays participated with the *Ripolins* group in its wild postering on the Circuit Opéra in Paris, and took part in the collective exhibition *Palettes pauvres, images riches* (*Poor Palettes, Rich Images*). In 1988 she exhibited at the Ministère de la Culture et de la Communication. She produced numerous illustrations for journals, newspapers and other publications.
AUCTION RECORDS:
PARIS, 9 March 1987, *Boomerang of the Stimul'acrum* (acrylic/canvas, 78 x 59 ins / 198 x 150 cm) FRF 7,600. PARIS, 12 Feb 1989, *Sweet Little Sexy Lady* (acrylic/canvas, 63 x 35 1/2 ins / 160 x 90 cm) FRF 7,000. PARIS, 26 April 1990, *A Dedication for Fred and his Bride 'Cat Zoubix'* (acrylic/canvas, 32 x 14 1/4 ins / 81 x 36 cm) FRF 4,500.

FAYTTAN, Claude, or Fetan
French, 18th century.
Active in Lyons.
Sculptor.

FAZANO
Italian, 14th century.
Active in Cherasco (Piedmont) in 1347.
Painter.

FAZIO (Fra)
Italian, 14th century.
Died 1340.
Active in Pisa.
Monk, sculptor.
Fazio was perhaps a pupil and assistant of Fra Guglielmo. The low reliefs of the old pulpit of the church of S Michele in Borgo (Corsica) are attributed to him.

FAZIO DI DIETISALVI
Italian, 13th century.
Active in Siena.
Painter.

FAZOLI. See **FASOLO**

FAZY, Michel Marie
Swiss, 19th century.
Born 31 December 1798, in Sécheron, near Geneva; died 31 May 1826, in Paris.
Painter.
Fazy was the son of the art collector Jean Samuel Fazy, and brother of the writer and statesman James Fazy. After studying with J.L. David in 1814, he became a pupil of Girodet-Trioson. We know of a painting of a ball by Fazy.

FAZZI, Arnaldo
Italian, 19th century.
Born to a family originally from Lucca.
Sculptor.
Fazzi was a pupil of Giovanni Dupré and worked in Florence. In 1881, he exhibited a marble statuette entitled *Falcon Hunter* at the Salon of the Société des Artistes Français in Paris, and his work was regularly shown at the Florence Salon. He made a bronze statuette of the sculptor *Matteo Civitali*, which is now in Lucca. In 1910 he won first prize in a competition to build a monument to *Garibaldi* in Genoa.

FAZZINI, Pericle
Italian, 20th century.
Born 4 May 1913, in Grottamare (Ascoli Piceno); died 1987, in Rome.
Painter (including gouache/mixed media), sculptor.
Figures, portraits, animals.
School of Rome group.
Fazzini studied drawing at a free Accademia in Rome, where he began to sculpt in 1929. Before that, his first initiation into the world of sculpture was through his father, who was a carpenter and cabinetmaker.

His early works were expressive portraits: *Orazio Costa* and *Renato Birolli* (1931). His next works were *Coming out of the Ark* (1932); *The Tempest*, in stone, and *The Dance*, in wood - both high reliefs from 1934, a milestone year for Fazzini; *Portrait of Ungaretti* (1936); *Sybil* (1947); *Acrobats* (1950); *The Little Runaway Horse* (1953); *Cats* in 1958, the year in which he won the competition to build the *Auschwitz Memorial*; and a *Portrait* for a church at the junction of the Sun Route and Florence motorways. His works were figurative, particularly after the war, and were liberated from reality through the dynamic lyricism of the form in space.

He regularly participated in the Biennales in Venice, Antwerp and São Paulo. He also held numerous solo exhibitions, notably in Paris in 1934; Rome in 1943 and 1951; and New York in 1952. In 1954, he won the sculpture prize at the Venice Biennale, and in 1955 he won the international prize at the Tokyo Biennale.

MUSEUMS AND GALLERIES:
NEW HAVEN (Knights of Columbus Mus.): *The Redeemer* (plaque in relief in silvered bronze) - NEW YORK (MoMA): *Sybil* - PARIS (former Mus. du Jeu de Paume): *Portrait of Anita*.

AUCTION RECORDS:
NEW YORK, 4 April 1968, *Bather* (gold patina) USD 15,500. MILAN, 19 Oct 1974, *Cats* (bronze) ITL 1,800,000. LOS ANGELES, 9 Nov 1977, *Dancer* (1958, bronze and copper, h. 22 ins / 56 cm) USD 2,500. ROME, 2 Dec 1980, *Recumbent Nude* (bronze, 4 x 7¾ x 4¾ ins / 10 x 20 x 12 cm) ITL 1,600,000. NEW YORK, 4 Nov 1982, *Dancer* (bronze, h. 52 ins / 132 cm) USD 6,500. PARIS, 23 Nov 1984, *Young Girl* (bronze, 5¾ x 9¾ x 5¾ ins / 14.5 x 25 x 14.5 cm) ITL 1,300,000. ROME, 23 April 1985, *Standing Nude, Arched* (1949, gold-patinated silver, h. 12¼ ins / 31 cm) ITL 3,600,000. NEW YORK, 14 Nov 1986, *Dancer* (1953, bronze, h. 12½ ins / 32 cm) USD 3,200. ROME, 29 April 1987, *Portrait of Maria Pia* (1933, wood, h. 23½ ins / 60 cm) ITL 20,000,000. ROME, 15 Nov 1988, *Portrait of a Young Woman Smiling* (1954, plaster, h. 13¾ ins / 35 cm) ITL 2,000,000; *St Sebastian* (1948, bronze, 28 x 9¾ x 9 ins / 71 x 25 x 23 cm) ITL 21,000,000. ROME, 28 Nov 1989, *Dancer* (1947, brown-patinated bronze, h. 10¼ ins / 26 cm) ITL 15,000,000. NEW YORK, 9 May 1992, *Gymnast* (brown-patinated bronze, h. 8¾ ins / 22.5 cm) USD 6,600. ROME, 12 May 1992, *Portrait of Baroness Anita Blanc* (1938, wood from olive tree, 8¼ x 7¾ x 5 ins / 21 x 20 x 12.5 cm) ITL 12,500,000. NEW YORK, 29 Sept 1993, *Acrobat* (bronze, h. 5 ins / 12.7 cm) USD 1,955. ROME, 30 Nov 1993, *Flute Player in a Wood* (1955, mixed media/paper/canvas, 49½ x 23¼ ins / 126 x 59 cm) ITL 5,750,000. NEW YORK, 24 Feb 1994, *Man Falling* (bronze, h. 15½ ins / 39.4 cm) USD 8,050. ROME, 19 April 1994, *Cat* (1956, bronze, 18 x 30¾ x 11 ins / 45.5 x 78 x 27 cm) ITL 25,300,000. NEW YORK, 24 Feb 1995, *Two Cats Playing* (bronze, h. 15 ins / 38.4 cm) USD 10,925. ROME, 28 March 1995, *Self-portrait with Pipe* (1944, Indian ink/paper, 11 x 8¼ ins / 27 x 21 cm) ITL 2,530,000. MILAN, 20 May 1996, *Two Figures* (1950, ink/card); *Untitled* (1935, ink/card, 11 x 8¼ ins / 28 x 21 cm) ITL 1,495,000; *Acrobat and Horse* (1948, Indian ink and gouache/paper, 30¼ x 22½ ins / 77 x 57 cm) ITL 6,900,000. ROME, 8 April 1997, *Head of a Man* (1929, brown patinated bronze, h. 12¼ ins / 31 cm) ITL 22,135,000. VENICE, 13 Nov 1999, *Portrait of Parizzi* (1943-1944, bronze, h. 10 ins / 26 cm) ITL 4,600,000. ROME, 25 Nov 1999, *Scene from Rural Life* (1930, terracotta, 7 x 19x3 ins / 18 x 48x8 cm) ITL 5,000,000. MILAN, 29 May 2001, *Nude* (bronze, 6 x 9x5 ins / 16 x 24x12 cm) ITL 6,500,000. PRATO, 8 June 2001, *Resurrection* (1975, wax crayon, 24 x 39 ins / 62 x 99 cm) ITL 4,000,000. NEW YORK, 26 Sept 2002, *Bust of a Woman* (brown and black patinated bronze, h. 28 ins / 71 cm) USD 7,000. NEW YORK, 26 Sept 2002, *Seated Man* (1956, grey patinated bronze, h. 39 ins / 99 cm) USD 8,500. NEW YORK, 25 Sept 2003, *Nude* (gold patinated bronze, h. 8 ins / 20 cm) USD 2,200. MILAN, 28 Oct 2003, *Cat Scratching Itself* (1954, bronze, 11 x 54 ins / 28 x 138 cm) EUR 8,000. NEW YORK, 29 Sept 2004, *Male Nude* (gold patinated bronze, h. 12 ins / 30 cm) USD 4,000.

FÉ, Jacob Louis
Swiss, 18th century.
Born 19 November 1732, in Paris; died after 1790, in Geneva.
Engraver, enameller.
The son of Pierre Fé, Jacob Fé joined the firm of *Lalime, Cussin and Colondre Frères* in 1762.

FÉ, Juan Facundo (Fray)
Spanish, 18th century.
Born 25 March 1713, in Torrente, near Valencia; died 29 May 1750, in Palma (Majorca).
Sculptor, embroiderer.
Juan Facundo Fé was a brother of the Order of St Augustine. He travelled widely in France, Spain and Italy and studied sculpture in Rome. He spent the last years of his life at the Augustinian monastery in Palma and carved a large crucifix

for the choir of Palma cathedral. He also carved a sculpture of *The Adoration of the Shepherds* for the convent of the Consolation in Palma.

FÉ, Pierre, also known as Lalime
Swiss, 18th century.
Born 6 February 1698, in Geneva; died 23 October 1774, in Geneva.
Engraver, enameller.

Fé was co-owner of the company 'Lalime, Cussin, and Colondre Brothers', which produced enamel paintings for the jewellers of Geneva.

FEA, Antonio, Francesco and Giovanni.
See **CERRUTI**

FEA, Pietro
Italian, 19th century.
Born to a family originally from Casale Monferrato (Piedmont).
Painter.

Fea was a pupil of G. Galliari. He mostly painted architectural views with figures.

FEARNLEY, Thomas
Norwegian, 19th century.
Born 1802, in Frederikshald (now Halden); died 1842, in Munich.
Painter, engraver (etching). Hunting scenes, landscapes.

Thomas Fearnley first studied at the royal school of freehand drawing, then entered the Kunstakademi in Copenhagen. Throughout the 1820s he enjoyed the protection of Prince Oscar, for whom he painted a view of the city. From 1829 to 1830 he was a pupil of Dahl in Dresden. From 1828 to 1836 he travelled across Europe from Germany to Italy, passing through Paris in 1835. The following year he travelled to London, where he showed *A Norwegian Waterfall* at the British Institution.During the course of his stay in Dresden, he discovered the art of Caspar David Friedrich, whose Romanticism would influence his own work. Among his paintings are *The Blue Grotto of Capri* and *The Grindelwald Glacier*. His larger works were painted in a fluid palette after his real-life studies. He then reworked the plays on light and shade in his workshop.

In 2001 he was included in the exhibition *Un Paese Incantato: Italia Dipinta da Thomas Jones a Corot* (*An Enchanted Country. Italy Depicted by Artists from Thomas Jones to Corot*) at the Centro Internazionale d'Arte e di Cultura di Palazzo Te in Mantua, and in the exhibition *Da Dahl a Munch: Romanticismo, Realismo e Simbolismo nella Pittura di Paesaggio Norvegese* (*From Dahl to Munch: Romanticism, Realism and Symbolism in Norwegian Landscape Painting*) at the Palazzo dei Diamanti in Ferrare.

Th. Fearnley 1837

BIBLIOGRAPHY:
Thomas Fearnley 1802-1842: Stiftelsen Modums blaafarveværk, exhibition catalogue, Blaafarveværk, Modum, 1986. Munro, Jane, *Nature's way: Romantic landscapes from Norway: oil studies, watercolours and drawings by John Christian Dahl (1788-1857) and Thomas Fearnley (1802-1842)*, exhibition catalogue, Whitworth Art Gall., University of Manchester, Manchester, 1993. Strohbehn, Birte, *Thomas Fearnleys Malerei im Urteil von Kunsgeschichte und Kunskritik 1845 bis heute*, Kiel, 2000. Ottani Cavina, Anna (ed.), *Un Paese incantato. Italia dipinta da Thomas Jones a Corot*, exhibition catalogue, Electa, Milan, 2001. Lange, Marit (ed.), *Da Dahl a Munch. Romanticismo, realismo e simbolismo nella pittura di paesaggio norvegese*, exhibition catalogue, Palazzo dei Diamanti, Ferrara Arte editore, Ferrara, 2001.

MUSEUMS AND GALLERIES:
BERGEN: *Landscapes* - COPENHAGEN (Statens Mus. for Kunst): *Landscapes* - HAMBURG: *Dolmen* - LONDON (NG): *Coast Scene, possibly Capri* (1833?, oil/paper/panel, on loan from a private collection) - OSLO (Nasjonalgal.): *Waterfall at Labro; Waterspout in the Bay of Naples* (oil on paper mounted on cardboard); *Terrace in Sorrento* (oil/pap.?); *Seascape at Capri, 13 September 1833* (1833, oil on paper mounted on canvas); *The Grindelwald Glacier in Switzerland* (c. 1837, oil on canvas); *Dawn in the Wengern Alps, Switzerland* (1838, oil on canvas); *Mount Jordalsnuten in the Sogn Region* (1839, oil on paper mounted on cardboard) - STOCKHOLM: *Landscapes* - WEIMAR: *Mountain Landscape*.

AUCTION RECORDS:
ROUEN, 14 June 1981, *Hunt for Water Game* (1828, oil on canvas, 29 1/4 x 38 1/2 ins / 74 x 98 cm) FRF 80,000. LONDON, 22 June 1984, *Autumn Morning, Königsee* (1835, oil on canvas, 34 1/4 x 28 1/4 ins / 87 x 71.6 cm) GBP 12,000. NEW YORK, 27 Feb 1986, *Fishermen Pulling their Nets in the Bay of Sorrento* (1837, oil on canvas, 23 x 31 1/2 ins / 58.4 x 80 cm) USD 61,000. LONDON, 24 March 1988, *View of Vesuvius* (oil on cardboard, 10 1/2 x 14 ins / 26.5 x 35.5 cm) USD 6,050. LONDON, 27-28 March 1990, *Hunter near a Waterfall in the Forest* (1825, oil on panel, 33 1/2 x 26 1/2 ins / 85 x 67.5 cm) GBP 18,150. LONDON, 28 Nov 1990, *Norwegian Landscape with River* (1820, oil on canvas, 24 1/2 x 31 1/2 ins / 62 x 80 cm) GBP 27,500. LONDON, 17 Nov 1993, *Farm in a Mountain Landscape* (1830, oil on canvas, 11 3/4 x 15 3/4 ins / 30 x 40 cm) GBP 4,370. LONDON, 14 June 1996, *Castle of Vadstena on Lake Vättern in Sweden* (1831, oil on canvas, 19 1/4 x 31 1/2 ins / 49.2 x 79.8 cm) GBP 23,000. LONDON, 26 March 1997, *Etna Seen from the Sea* (1833, oil on paper/canvas, 10 1/4 x 15 1/4 ins / 26 x 38.5 cm) GBP 8,280. COPENHAGEN, 23 Feb 1999, *Alpine Landscape with Foaming River, Switzerland* (1835, pastel, 49 x 33 ins / 124 x 83 cm) DKK 75,000. OSLO, 26 April 1999, *Hunter in Wooded Landscape near Waterfall* (1825, oil on panel, 33 x 26 ins / 85 x 67 cm) NOK 560,000. LONDON, 7 April 2000, *En plein air, Sorrento* (1841, oil on paper/canvas, 15 x 18 ins / 38 x 45 cm) GBP 35,000. OSLO, 25 May 2000, *From Ramsau* (1830, oil on canvas, 11 x 11 ins / 28 x 27 cm) NOK 360,000. OSLO, 29 Oct 2001, *Norwegian Mountain Landscape with Waterfall* (1822, oil on canvas, 52 x 74 ins / 132 x 187 cm) NOK 700,000. OSLO, 10 Dec 2001, *Landscape from Sorento* (1834, oil on paper/panel, 11 x 17 ins / 29 x 44 cm) NOK 220,000. LONDON, 13 June 2002, *Elbe Valley* (1830, oil on canvas, 31 x 45 ins / 79 x 114 cm) GBP 70,000. OSLO, 21 Nov 2002, *View of Procida and Ischia with Epomeo Mountain* (c. 1833, oil on paper/panel, 10 x 15 ins / 26 x 39 cm) NOK 110,000. OSLO, 17 March 2003, *Fisherman near Sorrento* (1834, oil on paper/canvas, Oil Painting, 11 x 15 ins / 27 x 39 cm) NOK 200,000. OSLO, 26 May 2003, *Landscape from Sorrento* (1840, oil on canvas, 15 x 22 ins / 39 x 55 cm) NOK 200,000.

FEARNSIDE, W.
British, 18th century.
Painter. Genre scenes, landscapes.

W. Fearnside exhibited at the Royal Academy between 1791 and 1801.

MUSEUMS AND GALLERIES:
LONDON (Victoria and Albert Mus.): *Country Inn; Landscape, Mill and Cattle; Landscape with Seascape and Cattle*.

FEARON, Hilda
British, 20th century.
Born 14 September 1878, in Banstead (Surrey); died 2 June 1917, in London.
Painter. Portraits, landscapes.

Hilda Fearon studied at the Slade School from 1899 to 1904 after beginning to draw and model at a very young age. She went on to exhibit at the Royal Academy in London, the Salon des Artistes Français in Paris and the Carnegie Institute in Pittsburgh.

MUSEUMS AND GALLERIES:

LONDON (Tate Collection): *The Tea Party* (1916, oil on canvas).

AUCTION RECORDS:

LONDON, 12 Nov 1987, *The Picture Book* (1911, oil on canvas, 29 1/2 x 24 1/2 ins / 75 x 62.5 cm) GBP 2,350. LONDON, 9 Oct 1996, *Boating* (1907, oil on canvas, 24 x 30 ins / 61 x 76.5 cm) GBP 3,105.

FEARSON, J.

British, 18th century.
Active in London.
Painter.

J. Fearson appeared at the Royal Academy in London in 1786 with a miniature portrait, in 1788 with a history painting and in 1789 with a *Resurrection of the Daughter of Jairus*.

FEART, Adrien

French, 19th century.
Born 11 April 1813, in Sedan.
Sculptor, draughtsman, medallist.

Feart was trained by H Dantan. He sent works to the Salon from 1845 to 1879. His most notable works, all low relief in bronze, are *The Marriage of the Virgin*, in the style of Raphael, and *Summer, Winter, Spring, Feast, Dance, Music, Autumn*. *Ewer and Bowl* is silver-plated bronze.

FEART, Jérôme

French, 17th century.
Painter.

Feart is mentioned by Siret.

FEARY, John

British, 18th century.
Born c. 1745; died 1788.
Painter. Landscapes with figures, architectural views, landscapes.

John Feary regularly exhibited at the Royal Academy from 1772 to 1788, and was awarded a grant from the Society of Arts in 1775.

AUCTION RECORDS:

LONDON, 15 Feb 1939, *Camping Scene*, GBP 10.

FEASSE, Paul

French, 18th century.
Active in Paris in 1786.
Painter, sculptor.

FEATHERSTON, William

Canadian, 20th century.
Born 1927, in Toronto.
Active in England since 1961.
Sculptor.

William Featherstone studied in Ontario and taught there until 1961, when he went to England. The influence, indeed the near monopoly, of the *Group of Seven* in Canada certainly inhibited the development of some Canadian artists, and after leaving Canada Featherston was able to take much from new currents in British and American art. He created both large and more modest sculptures in basic geometrical forms.

FEAU, Amédée

French, 20th century.
Born 11 February 1872, in Paris.
Painter, engraver. Genre scenes.

Amédée Feau was a pupil of Richemont, Gabriel Ferrier and Guillemet. Beginning in 1908, he was a member of the Salon des Artistes Français. He received an honourable mention in 1907.

FEAUSSÉ, Jean

French, 17th century.
Active in Boulogne.
Painter.

FEBBRARI, Giovan Battista

Italian, 18th century.
Active in Cremona.
Sculptor (wood).

He worked alongside the lay brother G. B. Gasparini to carve most of the choir stalls in the church of S Domenico in Cremona, together with the main altar in the collegiate church of S Bartolomeo in Busseto, an elaborate piece comprising wood carvings painted in imitation bronze.

FEBBRARI, Giuseppe

Italian, 18th century.
Born c. 1725; died 10 February 1785.
Active in Cremona.
Sculptor (wood).

The son of Giovan Battista Febbrari, he carved several coloured-wood statues for churches in Cremona.

FEBLAND, Harriet

American, 20th century.
Born in New York.
Painter, sculptor, engraver, mixed media.

Harriet Febland began her studies at the Pratt Institute, the University of New York, the American Artists School, and the Art Students League, and then completed them in England and France, where she lived for eleven years. When she returned to the USA in the early 1960s she opened a studio in New York and Westchester and taught in several centres and art schools. She makes geometric constructions out of a variety of materials, including Plexiglas, acrylic, nails and electricity.

Febland has exhibited regularly in group exhibitions, including at the Carnegie Institute, Pittsburgh, the Cultural Center, New York, the Musée d'Art Moderne, Paris, and the Modern Art Center, Mexico. She held solo shows mainly in New York, at the Riverside Museum, the University, and the Bruce Marshall Gallery, but also in Yonkers, Katonah, Chicago, Atlanta, Sweet Briar, and elsewhere. Retrospectives of her work were held at the Municipal Art Center Galleries, White Plains, New York, in 1976, and at the Brainerd Art Gallery Museum, State University of New York, Potsdam, New York, in 1986.

MUSEUMS AND GALLERIES:

DULUTH (Tweed MA, University of Minnesota) - YONKERS (Hudson River Mus.).

FEBRER, Franck William

French, 20th century.
Born 1926, in Angers, of Catalan origin.
Painter (gouache). Figures, nudes, still-lifes, landscapes.

Franck Febrer was self-taught. He participated in collective exhibitions, notably from 1945, at the Parisian Salon des Indépendants, Salon de la Société Nationale des Beaux-Arts and the Salon des Terres Latines. His solo exhibitions include: 1962, Soulanges gallery in Paris; 1968, Centre Culturel d'Ivry-sur-Seine; and 1973, 1976, Le Procope gallery in Paris. He was first strongly inspired by Cubism but progressively detached himself from it, adopting a strongly contrasting palette, with rich tones and a more supple line. He favoured scenes of families, couples, still-lifes and landscapes. His figurative style was solidly constructed, suggesting his subjects with flat zones of colour surrounded by a black outline. These were integrated into an abstract background, composed of large square planes of variously coloured geometric colours.

FEBRIMONT, Arnould

Flemish, 17th century.
Died before 1650.

Active in Tournai.
Sculptor.
Flemish School.

In 1625 Arnould Febrimont worked on the chapel in the cathedral of St-André and in 1626 on the altar of the Notre Dame-du-Bon-Secours in the church of St-Brice.

FEBRUITSKI, Grigori Féodorovitch.
See **SREBRENITSKI**

FÉBUIMONT, Nicolas de
French, 17th century.
Active in Tournai.
Sculptor.

Nicolas de Fébuimont worked on the chapel of the hospital in Séclin from 1619 to 1623. In the choir of the chapel he executed a tabernacle in Avesnes stone.

FEBUS
Italian, 16th century.
Active in Mantua.
Painter.

A fresco by Febus is in the monastery of Gradaro at Mantua. He is perhaps the same artist as Franciscus de Wit.

FEBVRE, Édouard
French, 20th century.
Painter, watercolourist, pastellist. Scenes with figures, landscapes, urban landscapes.

Febvre rarely painted very far from Paris and its suburbs. The few times that he did, it was to paint landscapes with water, riverbanks, canals or ports. In Paris, his favourite views were taken from the picturesque old Montmartre. He continued to paint the picturesque in his animated composition with clowns in the circus, lovers on the dance floor, or figures seeking rare finds at the scrap-iron fair.

AUCTION RECORDS:
PARIS, 30 March 1925, *Riverbanks*, FRF 150. PARIS, 22 March 1926, *The Fratellini in the Ring* (pastel) FRF 175; *Market in Brittany*, FRF 250. PARIS, 4 June 1926, *Landscape*, FRF 110. PARIS, 2 July 1926, *Fortifications*, FRF 170. PARIS, 9 Feb 1929, *Palais du Luxembourg*, FRF 240. PARIS, 22 July 1942, *Banks of a Canal* (watercolour) FRF 120. PARIS, 20 Nov 1942, *Public Park*, FRF 400. PARIS, 15 Jan 1943, *Banks of the Seine*; *Parisian Suburb* (two pastels) FRF 800. PARIS, 24 May 1943, *The Ham Fair* (1904) FRF 700; *Place Clichy* (1923) FRF 450; *The Pollet Reservoir in Dieppe*, FRF 300. PARIS, 25 and 26 Oct 1944, *On the Zone* (watercolour) FRF 220. PARIS, 10 Nov 1944, *Travelling Fair: the Merry-go-rounds* (watercolour) FRF 1,000. PARIS, 27 June 1945, *Montmartre: Place du Tertre*, FRF 550. PARIS, 19 June 1946, *Street in Montmartre*, FRF 700. PARIS, 14 Feb 1947, *Suburb*, FRF 3,800. PARIS, 13 June 1947, *The Sacré-Cœur*, FRF 1,400. GRENOBLE, 8 Nov 1976, *The Trône Fair* (oil on canvas, 21 1/4 x 25 1/2 ins / 54 x 65 cm) FRF 2,200. PARIS, 24 Feb 1982, *Riverbanks* (oil on canvas, 21 1/4 x 25 1/2 ins / 54 x 65 cm) FRF 3,000. LINDAU, 2 Oct 1985, *Beach Scene* (1925, oil on canvas, 19 3/4 x 25 1/2 ins / 50 x 64.5 cm) DEM 6,000. PARIS, 6 May 1988, *The Red Caravan* (watercolour and charcoal, 22 1/2 x 17 3/4 ins / 57 x 45 cm) FRF 4,000. VERSAILLES, 25 Sept 1988, *Snowy Landscape* (oil/hardboard, 23 1/2 x 28 3/4 ins / 60 x 73 cm) FRF 3,600. LE TOUQUET, 12 Nov 1989, *Jardin du Luxembourg* (oil on canvas, 15 x 22 ins / 38 x 55 cm) FRF 16,000. PARIS, 1 Dec 1989, *Ball on the 14th July* (oil on canvas, 18 x 22 ins / 46 x 55 cm) FRF 13,000. VERSAILLES, 28 Jan 1990, *Caravans* (1957, oil on canvas, 15 x 18 ins / 38 x 46 cm) FRF 9,800. PARIS, 13 June 1990, *Street Scene* (oil on canvas, 21 1/4 x 25 1/2 ins / 54 x 65 cm) FRF 7,000. NEW YORK, 10 Oct 1990, *Jardin du Luxembourg* (1924, oil on canvas, 15 x 21 1/2 ins / 38.2 x 54.6 cm) USD 3,740. VERSAILLES, 25 Nov 1990, *The Orchard* (1922, oil on canvas, 23 1/2 x 35 3/4 ins / 60 x 91 cm) FRF 16,000. CALAIS, 10 March 1991, *Riverbank* (1925, oil on canvas, 21 1/4 x 25 1/2 ins / 54 x 65 cm) FRF 21,500. PARIS, 21 March 1995, *Paris, the Jardin du Luxembourg* (oil on canvas, 22 x 25 1/2 ins / 55 x 65 cm) FRF 8,500. PARIS, 14 June 1999, *Place de l'Opéra* (oil on canvas, 24 x 29 ins / 60 x 73 cm) FRF 10,500. PARIS, 31 March 2000, *Beach Scene* (oil on panel, 20 x 25 ins / 50 x 64 cm) FRF 18,200. CALAIS, 28 May 2000, *14 July 1924* (oil on canvas, 26 x 32 ins / 66 x 81 cm) FRF 25,000. PARIS, 29 May 2002, *Bohemian Camp* (oil on masonite, 18 x 24 ins / 46 x 61 cm) EUR 1,600. VERSAILLES, 7 July 2002, *Place de la Bastille* (1924, oil on canvas, 20 x 29 ins / 50 x 73 cm) EUR 2,400.

FECCHIA, Vincenzo
Italian, 18th century.
Active in Sulmona.
Painter.

Vincenzo Fecchia painted representations of saints for churches in Sulmona.

FECHELM, Carl Traugott
German, 18th - 19th century.
Born 1748, in Dresden; died 1819, in Riga.
Painter, decorative designer. Landscapes, architectural views.

In 1786, 1789 and 1791, Fechelm featured in the exhibition of the academy in Berlin, gaining membership with his *Views of Berlin* (in oil). In 1790, he was involved in executing the fresco of *Apollo and the Muses* in the reception hall of Minister von Heinitz' house on Berlin's Pariser Platz. In Riga, where he was employed as a scene painter, he created the stage set for *The Magic Flute*.

MUSEUMS AND GALLERIES:
BERLIN (Märkisches Mus.): *View of Berlin* (five works) - RIGA (Cathedral Mus.): *View of Riga* (numerous works).

FECHHELM, Christian Gottlob
German, 18th - 19th century.
Born 1732, in Dresden; died 1816, in Dresden.
Painter, miniaturist. Religious subjects, allegorical subjects, portraits.

A pupil of Mengs, Manjocky and Hutin, Christian Fechhelm is best known for his portraits and miniatures. His paintings include: *Apollo Teaching the Nymphs to Dance*; *The Holy Trinity*; *St John the Baptist*; *The Entombment* (wash drawing); *Apollo and Psyche* and *Allegory of Love*.

FECHHELM, Georg Friedrich or Georg Wilhelm
German, 18th century.
Born 1740, in Dresden.
Painter, decorative designer. Landscapes.

A brother and pupil of Carl Friedrich Fechhelm, Georg Fechhelm has often been confused with Johann Friedrich or Carl T. Fechhelm. He worked in Berlin. His paintings frequently took prisons as their subject. In 1789, he showed a *Passage* and a *Prison* at the exhibition of the academy in Berlin.

FECHHELM, Johann Friedrich
German, 18th century.
Born 14 May 1746, in Dresden; died 3 March 1794, in Berlin.
Painter. Landscapes, urban landscapes.

The son of Carl Friedrich Fechhelm, Johann Fechhelm became a member of the academy in Berlin in 1789. He produced paintings at the castle of Rossewitz (Mecklenburg-Vorpommern).

MUSEUMS AND GALLERIES:
SCHWERIN: *Landscape with Livestock* - SCHWERIN (Schloss): *Cattle* - WROCLAW (Muz. Narodowe): *Landscape with Livestock*; same subject.

Auction records:
London, 4 July 1997, *Berlin Viewed from the South East* (1781, oil on canvas, 21 3/4 x 30 1/2in/55.4 x 77.7cm) GBP 69,700.

FECHHELM, Karl Christian

German, 18th - 19th century.
Born 1770, in Dresden; died 1826.
Painter.

The son of Christian Gottlob Fechhelm, Karl Christian Fechhelm painted mainly portraits and history paintings.

FECHHELM, Karl Friedrich

German, 18th century.
Born 1725, in Dresden; died 1785, in Berlin.
Painter. Architectural views.

After studying with Muller in Prague, Karl Fechhelm went to Berlin, where he carried out decorations at the royal palace.

Museums and Galleries:
Florence (Palazzo Pitti): *Portrait of Prince Philip of Bourbon-Parma.*

FECHIN, Nikolai Ivanovich

Russian, 20th century.
Born 28 November 1881, in Kazan; died 5 October 1955, in Santa Monica (California).
Active in the USA.
Painter. Local figures, portraits, still-lifes.

Nikolai Fechin painted female figures in particular.

Fechin

Museums and Galleries:
Oklahoma City (National Cowboy and Western Heritage Mus.): *Joe* (c. 1930) - San Diego (MA): *Portrait of Mademoiselle Sapolnikov* (1908, oil on canvas); *Manuelita with Kachina* (1932, oil on canvas); *Torrey Pines* (undated, oil on canvas).

Auction records:
New York, 14 Oct 1943, *Isabella,* USD 220. New York, 24-28 Sept 1946, *Young Girl in Black,* USD 450. Los Angeles, 9 June 1976, *Head of Young Mexican Girl* (1937, oil on canvas, 17 x 14 ins / 43 x 35.5 cm) USD 9,500. New York, 27 Oct 1978, *Landscape* (oil on canvas, 14 3/4 x 24 1/4 ins / 37.4 x 61.5 cm) USD 20,000. New York, 22 Oct 1981, *Mexican Girl* (oil on canvas, 13 3/4 x 10 1/2 ins / 34.9 x 26.7 cm) USD 30,000. San Francisco, 8 Nov 1984, *Portrait of the Artist's Daughter* (graphite heightened with white, 17 x 14 ins / 43 x 35.5 cm) USD 4,750. New York, 6 Dec 1984, *Russian Girl* (1924-1925, oil on canvas, 35 x 30 ins / 88.9 x 76.2 cm) USD 52,000. New York, 29 May 1986, *Juan the Peon* (oil on canvas, 24 x 20 ins / 61 x 50.8 cm) USD 50,000. New York, 17 March 1988, *Portrait of Rose K L Davis* (1952, oil on canvas, 19 3/4 x 15 3/4 ins / 50 x 40 cm) USD 9,350. New York, 1 Dec 1988, *Girl in Red Shawl* (oil on canvas, 30 x 25 ins / 76.2 x 63.5 cm) USD 115,500. New York, 17 Dec 1988, *Rio Grande* (oil on canvas, 15 x 12 3/4 ins / 38 x 32.5 cm) USD 11,000. New York, 25 May 1989, *Tuppy with a Cat* (oil on canvas, 30 x 25 ins / 76.4 x 63.7 cm) USD 121,000. New York, 23 May 1990, *Gypsy Girl* (1912, oil on canvas, 45 1/2 x 35 ins / 115.5 x 88.9 cm) USD 176,000. New York, 6 Dec 1991, *Relics* (oil on canvas, 25 x 30 ins / 63.5 x 76.3 cm) USD 143,000. New York, 3 Dec 1992, *Still-life of Flowers* (1945, oil on canvas, 20 x 16 ins / 50.8 x 40.6 cm) USD 55,000. New York, 22 Sept 1993, *Woman's Head* (1926, charcoal and pastel/grey paper/card, 16 1/2 x 12 1/2 ins / 42 x 32 cm) USD 2,990. New York, 25 May 1995, *Tuppy with a Cat* (oil on canvas, 30 x 25 ins / 76.2 x 63.5 cm) USD 112,500.

FECHNER, Eduard Clemens

German, 19th century.
Born 1799, in Gross-Sarchen (Saxony); died 1861, in Paris.
Portrait artist, draughtsman.

In 1814, Fechner studied in Dresden under Grassi and Retsch. He then became a pupil of Stieler in Munich. After having worked for a while for the Duke of Leuchtenberg, he went to Paris in 1825, where he remained until his death. He produced eleven etchings with great dexterity and was a good painter of women and children. He made his debut at the *Salon de Paris* of 1835 and regularly exhibited portraits there, mostly in watercolour.

FECHNER, Fritz

German, 19th century.
Active in Berlin.
Painter. Seascapes, landscapes.

Fritz Fechner received an honourable mention in Berlin in 1889. His best-known works include: *The North Sea* and *Evening near Dordrecht.*

FECHNER, Hans

German, 19th - 20th century.
Born 7 June 1860, in Berlin; died 30 November 1931, in Schreiberhau.
Painter. Portraits, genre scenes.

Hans Fechner was a writer who also painted portraits.

Auction records:
Munich, 6 Dec 1994, *Good News* (1884, oil on canvas, 19 1/4 x 15 1/4 ins / 49 x 38.5 cm) DEM 7,475.

FECHNER, Johann Friedrich

German, 18th century.
Active in Breslau (now Wroclaw, Poland).
Painter.

A pupil of George Drescher, Johann Friedrich Fechner was admitted as a master in 1710. He is best known for his *Birth of Christ.*

FECHNER, Johann Gottlieb

German, 18th century.
Baptised 21 September 1721.
Active in Breslau (now Wroclaw, Poland).
Painter.

Johann Gottlieb Fechner studied with his father, Johann Friedrich Fechner.

FECHNER, Johannes, the Younger

German, 19th century.
Born 7 June 1860, in Berlin.
Painter, lithographer. Portraits, genre scenes.

The son of Wilhelm Fechner, Johannes Fechner the Younger studied at the academy of art in Berlin and was a pupil of Defregger. In 1887, he was awarded a travel study bursary. He worked in Berlin and was appointed painting lecturer and curator of the lithography collection of the duchy of Anhalt in Dessau. His painted and engraved portraits are of great artistic merit.

Museums and Galleries:
Berlin: *Portrait of Count von Kirchbach* - Berlin (Märkisches Mus.): *Portrait of Theodor Fontane* (study) - Brunswick: *Portrait of Wilhelm Raabe.*

FECHNER, Wilhelm

German, 19th century.
Born 30 November 1835, in Sprottau (now Szprotawa, Silesia, Poland); died 8 April 1909, in Berlin.
Painter.

Wilhelm Fechner studied at the academy of art in Berlin, subsequently showing portraits, mostly in pastel, and genre paintings at its exhibitions in 1856 and 1862.

FECHTER, Emerich

Austrian, 19th - 20th century.

Born 27 September 1854, in Friedberg, Bohemia; died 1912, in Vienna.

Painter. Landscapes.

Fechter studied first at the academy in Prague and then was a student of Lichtenfels at the academy in Vienna. The subjects of his pictures are mostly drawn from the Bohemian forests. His works include: *Meadow by the Krottenbach* and *View of Gmünd.*

AUCTION RECORDS:

NEW YORK, 30 June 1981, *Steep River Landscape* (1901, oil on canvas, 31 1/2 x 41 1/4 ins / 80 x 105 cm) USD 1,300.

FECKERT, Gustav Heinrich Gottlob

German, 19th century.

Born 1820, in Cottbus; died 1899, in Berlin.

Lithographer, portrait artist.

After studying at the academy of art in Berlin, Feckert became a member in 1869. He lived in Berlin and was awarded the small gold medal in Berlin in 1859, the gold medal in Cologne in 1861 and the silver medal in Munich in 1876. He is best known for his *Portrait of a Woman.*

FECTEAU, Vincent

American, 20th - 21st century.

Born 1969.

Sculptor of assemblages.

Vincent Fecteau's sculptures have similarities with baroque furniture. He has been exhibiting regularly in the USA since the early 1990s, particularly at Feature Inc. in New York. He has participated in various collective exhibitions, including: 2002, the Whitney Biennial at the Whitney Museum of American Art, New York; 2002, *Artists Imagine Architecture* at the Institute of Contemporary Arts, Boston (an exhibition about the links between sculpture and architectural models); and 2004, a show at the Van Abbemuseum, Eindhoven.

BIBLIOGRAPHY:

Farquharson, Alex, '*Vincent Fecteau*' in *Frieze,* periodical, January-February, 2001. Hainley, Bruce, '*A Thousand Words*' in *Artforum p. 127,* periodical, March, 2001.

FEDDEN, A. Romilly

British, 20th century.

Born 5 February 1875, in Stoke Bishop, near Bristol; died 1939.

Painter. Genre scenes.

MUSEUMS AND GALLERIES:

BRISTOL: *Brittany Pastoral.*

AUCTION RECORDS:

LONDON, 20 Jan 1981, *A Ball by Lantern Light* (1912, watercolour, 11 1/4 x 15 1/4 ins / 28.5 x 38.5 cm) GBP 240. MELBOURNE, 26 July 1987, *Figures beneath Chinese Lanterns* (1908, watercolour, 23 1/2 x 29 1/2 ins / 60 x 75 cm) AUD 4,000. NEW YORK, 14 Oct 1993, *Market Place, Tangiers* (1920, watercolour/paper, 6 1/2 x 8 1/4 ins / 16.5 x 21 cm) USD 920.

FEDDEN, Mary

British, 20th century.

Born 14 August 1915, in Bristol.

Painter (gouache), watercolourist. Still-lifes (including flowers/fruit), cats.

Mary Fedden studied at the Slade School of Art in London from 1932 to 1936 under the theatre designer Vladimir Polunin. During World War II she served in the Land Army and Women's Volunteer Service and in 1944 as a driver for the Navy, Army and Air Force Institutes. After the war she settled in London. The first woman to work as a tutor at the Painting School, she taught at the Royal College of Art in London from 1958 to 1964 and then at the Yehudi Menhuin School from 1965 to 1970. Her career as an artist has been extremely varied: she initially painted sets for professional performances at Sadler's Wells before deciding not to pursue a career in stage design; this was followed by a period painting portraits (in Bristol). In 1964 she returned to easel painting in earnest - she is well known for her still-lifes and flower paintings, often positioned before a landscape and reminiscent of Matisse and Braque. After her marriage to the artist Julian Trevelyan she also painted murals: for the Festival of Britain, Television Pavilion (1951), for the shipping company P&O (1961), and with her husband for Charing Cross Hospital (1980) and Colindale Hospital (1981). Fedden travelled widely with her husband including travels in Europe, Africa, India, Russian and the USA.

She held her first exhibition at the Mansard Gallery in Heal's department store in 1947. This was followed by a number of solo shows including: Redfern Gallery, London (regularly from 1953); New Grafton Gallery, London (from the 1960s); Hamet Gallery (from 1970) and Arnolfini Gallery, Bristol, and Beaux Arts Gallery, London (in the 1990s). She was elected a Royal Academician in the Senior Order in 1992 and is a recipient of the Order of the British Empire.

BIBLIOGRAPHY:

Gooding, Mel, *Mary Fedden,* Aldershot, 1995. Lester, Anthony J., '*Contemporary British Artists*' in *Antique Collecting,* June 1998 (vol. 33, no. 2.). Munn, Geoffrey, '*Painters and Sculptors of East Anglia*' in *Antique Collecting,* 2003 (vol. 37, no. 8, pp. 6-11).

MUSEUMS AND GALLERIES:

BRISTOL (City Mus. & AG): *Still-life in Gozo; Sicilian Flowers* - CARDIFF (National Museum of Wales): *Fruit and Flowers* (1946, oil on canvas); *Farm, Penne du Tarn* (1958, oil on canvas) - CARLISLE (Tullie House Museum) - CHICHESTER (Pallant House) - DURHAM (University Art Gallery) - HEREFORD (City Art Gallery) - LONDON (Contemporary Art Society) - LONDON (Tate Collection): *The Staffordshire Horse* (1948, oil on board); *Fritillaries* (1972, lithograph on paper); *Mauve Still-life* (1968, oil on board); *Basket of Lemons* (1971, lithograph on paper); *Shells and Pebbles* (1971, lithograph on paper); *Straw Plate* (1971, lithograph on paper); *The Etching Table* (1971, oil on canvas); *Ginger Beer Bottle* (1972, lithograph on paper); *Etching Table* (1972, lithograph on paper); *Figs* (1972, lithograph on paper); *Ivy* (1972, lithograph on paper); *The Lamp* (1972, lithograph on paper) - SHEFFIELD (Museum and Art Gallery) - WELLINGTON (National Gallery of New Zealand).

AUCTION RECORDS:

LONDON, 5 March 1980, *Vase of Flowers* (oil on canvas, 17 1/2 x 14 ins / 44.5 x 35.5 cm) GBP 300. LONDON, 22 July 1986, *Yellow Still-life* (1966, oil on canvas, 30 x 40 ins / 76 x 101.5 cm) GBP 700. LONDON, 29 July 1988, *Spanish Still-life* (1984, oil on canvas, 24 1/2 x 22 ins / 62.5 x 55 cm) GBP 715; *Black Umbrella* (1965, oil on canvas, 23 1/2 x 19 3/4 ins / 60 x 50 cm) GBP 1,430. LONDON, 10 Nov 1989, *Black Teapot* (1989, oil on canvas, 19 1/2 x 29 ins / 49.4 x 73.7 cm) GBP 2,420. LONDON, 9 March 1990, *Fruit in Albatax* (1956, oil on canvas, 15 3/4 x 23 1/4 ins / 40.1 x 59 cm) GBP 7,150. LONDON, 8 June 1990, *Still-life with Fruit* (1984, oil on canvas, 24 x 19 3/4 ins / 61 x 50 cm) GBP 3,850. LONDON, 20 Sept 1990, *Lulu the Cat* (1989, oil on card, 19 3/4 x 16 ins / 50 x 40.5 cm) GBP 3,520. LONDON, 9 Nov 1990, *Still-life of Flowers and Fruit on a Blue Table* (1952, oil on canvas, 18 x 21 1/2 ins / 46 x 54.5 cm) GBP 4,950. LONDON, 25 Jan 1991, *Cat on a Harbour Wall* (1981, watercolour and gouache, 8 1/4 x 6 1/4 ins / 21 x 16 cm) GBP 1,045. LONDON, 8 March 1991, *Still-life with Fruit* (1988, oil on canvas, 24 x 20 ins / 61 x 51 cm) GBP 2,750. LONDON, 27 Sept 1991, *Suzi* (1988, watercolour and gouache, 6 3/4 x 7 3/4 ins / 17 x 20 cm) GBP 638. LONDON, 18 Dec 1991, *Island of Gozo* (1950, oil on canvas, 19 x 23 ins / 48 x 58.5 cm) GBP 1,078. LONDON, 14 May 1992, *Viaduct* (1970, oil on canvas, 24 x 20 ins / 61 x 51 cm) GBP 1,045. SONNING (BERKSHIRE), 22 June 1994, *Tabby Cat* (1993, oil on card, 23 x 29 ins / 58.5 x 73.7 cm) GBP 2,530.

LONDON, 3 March 1999, *Black Cat Cafe* (1994, oil on canvas, 30 x 36 ins / 76 x 91 cm) GBP 17,000. LONDON, 23 June 1999, *Harlequin Coffee Pot* (1964, oil on canvas, 39 x 52 ins / 98 x 131 cm) GBP 18,000. LONDON, 28 June 2000, *Mediterranean Idyll* (1955, oil on canvas, 24 x 30 ins / 61 x 76 cm) GBP 13,000. LONDON, 24 Nov 2000, *Still-life with Pears and Onions* (1990, oil on canvas, 30 x 36 ins / 76 x 91 cm) GBP 14,500. LONDON, 4 July 2001, *Jocelyn's Egg Stand* (1989, oil on canvas, 30 x 36 ins / 76 x 91 cm) GBP 15,000. LONDON, 5 Dec 2001, *Woman by a Window* (1993, oil on canvas, 30 x 36 ins / 76 x 91 cm) GBP 25,000. LONDON, 7 June 2002, *Basket of Lemons* (1982, oil on canvas, 20 x 24 ins / 51 x 61 cm) GBP 14,000. LONDON, 27 Nov 2002, *Still-life with Flowers and Fruit* (1989, oil on board, 36 x 30 ins / 91 x 77 cm) GBP 25,000. LONDON, 6 June 2003, *Gull's Eggs* (1901, oil on canvas, 30 x 40 ins / 76 x 101 cm) GBP 11,000. LONDON, 3 Dec 2003, *Arranging Flowers* (1989, oil on canvas, 24 x 36 ins / 61 x 91 cm) GBP 9,000. LONDON, 1 July 2004, *Zechariah's Dream* (1951, oil on canvas, 20 x 24 ins / 51 x 61 cm) GBP 9,000. LONDON, 1 July 2004, *Still-life with Lemons* (1960, oil on board, 18 x 24 ins / 46 x 61 cm) GBP 20,500.

FEDDER, Otto

German, 20th century.
Born 1873, in Schwerzin; died 1919, in Wildschweige.
Painter. Genre scenes, landscapes.

Some pictures by Otto Fedder were mentioned in the auction sales in Berlin at the beginning of the 20th century.

Otto Fedder

AUCTION RECORDS:

NEW YORK, 14-15 Nov 1941, *Landscape with Livestock*, USD 45. COLOGNE, 26 March 1976, *Harvest Scene* (1907, oil on panel, 3 x 5 1/2 ins / 7.5 x 14 cm) DEM 2,600. COLOGNE, 23 Nov 1978, *Harvest Scene* (oil on panel, 3 1/4 x 5 1/4 ins / 8.5 x 13.5 cm) DEM 8,000. LINDAU, 7 Oct 1981, *Return from the Market* (oil on panel, 4 3/4 x 7 ins / 12 x 17.5 cm) DEM 9,000. MUNICH, 17 May 1984, *Spring Landscape* (oil on canvas, 7 1/2 x 15 1/4 ins / 19 x 39 cm) DEM 3,500. LONDON, 27 Feb 1985, *Huntsmen in a Winter Landscape* (1896, oil on canvas, 18 1/2 x 30 1/2 ins / 47 x 77.5 cm) GBP 3,500. LONDON, 8 Oct 1986, *Conversation by the Roadside* (1905, oil on panel, 7 x 5 3/4 ins / 18 x 14.5 cm) GBP 2,700. STUTTGART, 19 March 1999, *Sledge Ride in Winter* (oil on panel, 4 x 5 ins / 9 x 12 cm) DEM 4,600. NEW YORK, 7 Dec 1999, *Haymakers. Winter Landscape* (1902, oil on panel, a pair, 3 x 5 ins / 8 x 13 cm) USD 5,500. DÜSSELDORF, 31 Jan 2000, *Landscape with Brook* (oil on panel, 8 x 16 ins / 20 x 40 cm) DEM 5,500. MUNICH, 23 March 2000, *Harvest* (oil on panel, 3 x 6 ins / 7 x 15 cm) DEM 4,400. MUNICH, 26 Sept 2001, *Hunting Party in Winter Wood* (1900, oil on panel, 5 x 7 ins / 12 x 19 cm) DEM 4,000. PARIS, 14 May 2003, *Arrival in the Village* (oil on panel, 5 x 7 ins / 13 x 19 cm) EUR 2,900. AHLDEN, 19 Sept 2003, *Fishermen, Chiemsee* (oil on canvas, 11 x 15 ins / 28 x 37 cm) EUR 4,000. MUNICH, 24 March 2004, *Hunters Returning Home in Winter Landscape* (oil on panel, 4 x 4 ins / 10 x 10 cm) EUR 1,600. MUNICH, 26 March 2004, *Moor Landscape* (1901, oil on panel, 8 x 10 ins / 20 x 26 cm) EUR 1,600.

FEDDER, Yuliy Ivanovich, or Fedders Julius

Russian, 19th century.
Born 7 or 19 June 1838, in Kokenhusen (Livonia); died 1 or 14 February 1909, in Niejin (Russia).
Painter.

Fedder was a pupil of the painter S.M. Vorob'ev at the St Petersburg academy of arts, where he received a number of awards and where his work appeared in the exhibitions of 1862 and 1875, with landscapes of Livonia and Norway. He also exhibited at the Great Exhibition of London in 1875. After a stay in Düsseldorf, where he continued his artistic training, he returned to Russia and took part in exhibitions at the St Petersburg academy, as well as the National Exhibition of Moscow in 1852, the Berlin Academy Exhibition of 1886 and at the Exposition Universelle in Paris in 1889, with his painting *Cemetry of those who Have Committed Suicide*. Works also painted by him include: *The Fishermen's Hut, My Country House, Along the River Luga* and *Pine Trees on the Hill*.

MUSEUMS AND GALLERIES:

RIGA: *By the Sea*.

FEDDERG

Painter. Landscapes.

AUCTION RECORDS:

PARIS, 25 and 26 April 1910, *The Little Wooden Bridge*, FRF 105.

FEDDERSEN, Ann Katrin

German, 20th - 21st century.
Born 1965.
Active in France.
Sculptor.

Feddersen lives and works in Sète. In 1994 she was invited to stay at the Centre d'Art Contemporain, Pougues-les-Eaux. In 1993 and 1995 she exhibited at the Fonds Régional d'Art Contemporain, Languedoc-Roussillon.

BIBLIOGRAPHY:

Leguillon, Pierre, '*Trois jeunes artistes en résidence*' in *Le Journal des arts* n° 6, periodical, Paris, September 1994.

FEDDERSEN, Hans Peter, the Elder

Danish, 19th century.
Born 9 January 1788, in Wester-Schnatebüll (Schleswig-Holstein); died 1860, in Wester-Schnatebüll.
Painter, miniaturist. Portraits.

Hans Peter Feddersen the Elder was a soldier in the Danish army from 1808 to 1815, and then worked as a hotel keeper in Schnatebüll. He executed a large number of miniature portraits, all in profile. His subjects were a diverse representation of society, including peasants, bourgeois and members of high society. He executed the portrait *King Christian VIII of Denmark* and those of many members of the court of Copenhagen, including the ducal family *Von Augustenburg*, the marshall's father *Lieutenant von Moltke*, and the singer *Catalani*. Other portraits included those of distinguished foreigners. He was also a writer, and with his brother he wrote a volume of poetry, *Diary of a Danish Soldier from 1812 to 1813, or The Most Remarkable Year of My Life*.

FEDDERSEN, Hans Peter, the Younger

German, 19th - 20th century.
Born 29 May 1848, in Wester-Schnatebüll; died 1941.
Painter. Portraits, genre scenes, interiors, landscapes.

The son of Hans Peter the Elder, Hans Peter Feddersen was a student at the academy in Düsseldorf and of Oswald Achenbach. He then attended the art school in Weimar. He worked in Düsseldorf.

MUSEUMS AND GALLERIES:

BERLIN: *Church Interior* - DESSAU: *Portrait of the Artist's Daughter* - WROCLAW: *Polish Pasture*.

AUCTION RECORDS:

HAMBURG, 10 June 1987, *River Landscape by Moonlight* (oil on panel, 10 1/4 x 20 ins / 26 x 50.5 cm) DEM 3,200. MUNICH, 26-27 Nov 1991, *Fishermen Mending the Nets by a Canal* (oil on canvas, 22 x 32 ins / 56 x 81.5 cm) DEM 19,550.

FEDDERSEN, Martin Peter Georg

German, 19th century.
Born 1 April 1849, in Altona.
Painter, sculptor.

Feddersen studied at the school of arts and crafts in Hamburg before becoming a pupil of Widmann in Munich. He painted landscapes, and many of his works are now in private collections in Hamburg. The Hamburg Kunstverein acquired a landscape, *Finkenwarder,* and his *Moonlight.* His best-known sculptural work is the *Monument to Professor Deutschmann* at the Ohlsdorf cemetery.

FEDDES, Pieter van Harlingen
Dutch, 17th century.
Born 1586, in Harlingen; died 1634.
Painter, glass painter, engraver.

Pieter van Harlingen Feddes usually signed his works *P. Harliensis.* His engravings of portraits and historical subjects total 119 pieces.

FEDDES, S.
Dutch.
Painter. Flowers, fruit.

He is mentioned by Siret, who says that his name appears on a painting of fruit, owned by an amateur collector from Dresden.

FEDE, Annunzio
Italian, 16th - 17th century.
Miniaturist.

Annuncio Fede, who seems to have been the son of Annuncio Galizia, was active in Trento and enjoyed a considerable reputation during his lifetime.

FEDE, Galizia
Italian, 17th century.
Born in Trento.
Painter. History painting, landscapes.

Galizia Fede studied under her father Annunzio Fede, and is almost certainly the same artist as Fede Galizia. She was active around 1616, living and working in Milan.

FEDE DI FRANCESCO
Italian, 14th century.
Painter.

Fede di Francesco became a member of the Accademia di San Luca in Florence in 1397.

FEDE DI NALDUCCIO
Italian, 14th century.
Died 13 December 1389, in Siena.
Active in Pisa in 1374.
Painter.

FEDELE, Tommaso del Porfido
Italian, 17th century.
Active in Rome.
Painter.

Fedele's preferred material was porphyry, hence his sobriquet 'del Porfido'. He produced a *Children's Bacchanale* in the manner of Francesco Fiammingo, commissioned by Cardinal Barberini as a gift for King Philip IV of Spain; the work is now in Madrid. A low relief of cherubs in the Villa Borghese is also attributed to Fedele.

FEDELE DA CARONA. See **CASELLA Fedele** and **CASELLA Scipione**

FEDELE DA NORCIA
Italian, 16th century.
Active in Rome.
Painter.

Fedele da Norcia was a member of the Università delle Arti between 1534 and 1535.

FEDELER, Carl
German, 19th century.
Born 7 November 1837, in Bremen; died 18 March 1897, in Bremerhaven.
Painter, illustrator. Seascapes.

A pupil and son of Carl Justus Harmen Fedeler, Carl Fedeler settled in Bremen. He produced works painted on glass for the town hall in Bremen, as well as many illustrations for journals. Ships formed the principal subject for his paintings.

MUSEUMS AND GALLERIES:
BREMEN (Focke-Mus.).

AUCTION RECORDS:
COPENHAGEN, 7 Dec 1977, *Three-masted Ships at Sea* (1866, oil on canvas, 24 1/2 x 36 1/4in/62 x 92cm) DKK 20,000. NEW YORK, 24 Jan 1980, *Ship in the Moonlight* (1870, oil on canvas, 20 x 30in/51 x 76cm) USD 1,300. NEW YORK, 8 March 2000, *Bringing in the Catch* (1889, oil on canvas, 26 x 43 ins / 67 x 110 cm) USD 8,000. TOESTORF, 10 May 2003, *Winter Wood with Ruins, Frozen Water, Hunter and Dog* (1859, oil on canvas, 32 x 42 ins / 81 x 107 cm) EUR 3,300.

FEDELER, Carl Justus Harmen
German, 19th century.
Born 25 January 1799, in Bremen; died 23 January 1858, in Bremen.
Painter, engraver, lithographer. Seascapes.

MUSEUMS AND GALLERIES:
HANOVER: *Whaling.*

FEDELI, Francesco
Italian, 20th century.
Born 1911, in Milan; died 26 January 1998.
Painter.

Francesco Fedeli was a student at the Accademia di Belle Arti di Brera in Milan. He has been exhibiting since 1931, and has taken part in a large number of group exhibitions and salons in Italy. In 1942 he was represented at the Venice Biennale.

Fedeli's style of painting is abstract, and close to the Art Informel and Matter Painting movements. He works his materials onto the canvas in thick layers, using stamps and graffiti. He seems to be fascinated by primitive and prehistoric civilisations.

MUSEUMS AND GALLERIES:
ROME (Gal. Nazionale d'Arte Moderna).

FEDELI, Gian Antonio de
Italian, 16th century.
Active in Milan.
Painter.

Gian Antonio de Fedeli was the son of Matteo de Fedeli and is mentioned in 1505.

FEDELI, Matteo de'
Italian, 15th century.
Active in Milan.
Painter.

Matteo de' Fedeli became a member of the guild in 1481. He executed the paintings of the wooden tabernacle of S Satiro, with Marco dei Lombardi, and those of the altar of St Joseph in the cathedral.

FEDELI, Ortensia
Italian, 17th century.
Active in Florence.
Painter.

Ortensia Fedeli was a nun. Around 1620, she was painting in the convent of S Agata, which today is a hospital.

FEDELI, Stefano de'. See **STEFANO DE' FEDELI**

FEDER, Adolphe
Ukrainian, 20th century.
Born 1886, in Odessa; died between 1943 and 1945; sent to Auschwitz in 1943.
Active and naturalised in France.

Painter, watercolourist, illustrator. Portraits, landscapes.

Adolphe Feder settled in Paris in 1910, after attending the school of fine art in Berlin, and enrolled at the Académie Julian. At the beginning of the 1920s, he travelled in the south of France and Algeria, then in Palestine in 1926. Close to Modigliani, he came into contact with the group of Montparnasse artists in Paris. He illustrated various works by Joseph Kessel and Arthur Rimbaud. His works reveal a certain formal influence from Cubism. He exhibited in the main Salons in Paris, notably at the Tuileries. In 1912, he was elected a member of the Salon d'Automne in Paris.

BIBLIOGRAPHY:

Nieszawer, Nadine/Boyé, Marie/Lanzmann, Claude (preface), *Peintres juifs de lécole de Paris 1905-1939*, Denoël, Paris, 2001.

AUCTION RECORDS:

PARIS, 9 April 1927, *Houses at the Water's Edge*, FRF 140. PARIS, 14 Nov 1927, *Peasant Woman with Pitcher*, FRF 150. PARIS, 24 Nov 1928, *Cagnes*, FRF 280. PARIS, 3 May 1930, *Algerian Woman* (watercolour) FRF 85. PARIS, 28 Feb 1944, *Flowers*, FRF 400. PARIS, 24 Jan 1945, *Algerian Woman* (watercolour) FRF 200. PARIS, 31 March 1954, *Schoolboy in Jerusalem* (watercolour) FRF 15,000. LA FLÈCHE, 25 Oct 1981, *Young Moor* (oil on canvas, 28 3/4 x 21 1/4 ins / 73 x 54 cm) FRF 3,000. PARIS, 6 April 1987, *Cubist Cathedral* (1920, oil on canvas, 25 1/2 x 19 3/4 ins / 65 x 50 cm) FRF 30,000. VERSAILLES, 7 Feb 1988, *Bare-breasted Dancer* (oil on canvas, 18 x 15 ins / 46 x 38 cm) FRF 2,600. PARIS, 20 March 1988, *Banks of the Seine at Notre-Dame* (oil on canvas, 24 1/2 x 34 1/4 ins / 62 x 87 cm) FRF 10,000; *Edge of Lake* (oil on canvas, 19 3/4 x 25 1/2 ins / 50 x 65 cm) FRF 13,000. PARIS, 8 June 1988, *Family in Jerusalem* (pencil drawing/paper) FRF 2,000. PARIS, 16 April 1989, *Village Square* (oil on canvas, 22 x 18 ins / 55 x 46 cm) FRF 9,000. TEL AVIV, 30 May 1989, *Village Street* (oil on canvas, 23 1/2 x 2 3/4 ins / 60 x 7 cm) USD 5,500. PARIS, 8 April 1990, *Cubist Still-life* (oil on canvas, 36 1/4 x 28 1/4 ins / 92 x 72 cm) FRF 50,000. PARIS, 8 April 1990, *Little Trader* (oil on canvas, 35 x 21 1/4 ins / 89 x 54 cm) FRF 13,500. PARIS, 13 June 1990, *Young Woman Sitting in an Interior* (oil on canvas, 39 1/4 x 32 ins / 100 x 81 cm) FRF 6,500. PARIS, 10 Oct 1990, *Still-life with Tulips* (1938, oil on canvas, 39 1/4 x 26 ins / 100 x 66 cm) FRF 12,200. PARIS, 17 June 1991, *Menu for 28/04/28* (gouache, 23 1/4 x 17 ins / 59 x 43 cm) FRF 5,000. PARIS, 18 June 1991, *Woman's Portrait* (oil on canvas, 39 1/4 x 32 ins / 100 x 81 cm) FRF 14,000. PARIS, 14 April 1992, *Entertainer Seated* (oil on canvas, 18 x 15 ins / 46 x 38 cm) FRF 11,000. PARIS, 26 March 1995, *Houses and Trees in Provence* (oil on canvas, 21 1/4 x 25 1/2 ins / 54 x 65 cm) FRF 5,800.

FEDER, Alex

Finnish, 19th century.
Active in Helsinki.
Painter, draughtsman.

The museum in Helsinki holds the following drawings by Alex Feder: *Torrent in Nokia, Hovasland Landscape, Tavesland, Birkkale*, and *Summer*.

FEDER, Georg

German, 19th century.
Born 19th century, in Ansbach.
Painter. Portraits, landscapes.

Feder, who worked in Bremen, Hamburg and Berlin, painted in oil and pastel and executed miniatures. The library in Bremen has his portrait of his father, *Professor J.G.H. Feder*.

FEDERER, Friedrich

German, 19th century.
Born in Ludwigsburg; died 1853, in Stuttgart.
Lithographer, watercolourist.

Federer drew landscapes and portraits as well as his *Ten Parables of Jesus* after Gross. He also painted watercolour landscapes.

FEDERHAUSER, Peter

German, 18th century.
Active in Ingolstadt c. 1754.
Miniaturist.

FEDERICH, Antoine Bernard

French, 17th century.
Active in Paris.
Painter.

FEDERICI, Antonio

Italian, 19th century.
Born 4 June 1790, in Belluno (Veneto); died 16 March 1869, in Belluno.
Painter.

As well as being an artist, Antonio Federici also taught drawing.

FEDERICI, Giuseppe

Italian, 19th century.
Born c. 1806, in Genoa.
Painter, fresco artist. Landscapes.

Giuseppe Federici studied in Rome and worked mostly in Genoa. He spent some time in France and Tunis, where he was official painter at the court of the Bey.

MUSEUMS AND GALLERIES:

GENOA (Palazzo Garibaldi): frescoes.

AUCTION RECORDS:

MILAN, 10 Dec 1987, *Mountain Landscape* (oil on panel, 39 1/4 x 56 ins / 100 x 142 cm) ITL 4,000,000. SWITZERLAND, 31 May 2002, *Peasant Girl with Goats* (oil on canvas, 28 x 24 ins / 70 x 60 cm) CHF 3,100.

FEDERICO, Juan

Spanish, 18th century.
Active in Murcia.
Painter.

Juan Federico produced the statues of *St Philip Neri* and *St Charles Borromeo* in the Oratory of St Philip Neri in Murcia.

FEDERICO, Michele

Italian, 20th century.
Born 1884; died 1966.
Painter. Landscapes, seascapes.

Michele Federico mostly painted Neapolitan landscapes.

AUCTION RECORDS:

MILAN, 5 Nov 1981, *Capri* (oil on canvas, 31 1/2 x 39 1/4 ins / 80 x 100 cm) ITL 1,400,000. NEW YORK, 21 May 1987, *The Capri Coast* (oil on canvas, 44 1/2 x 57 1/4 ins / 113 x 145.4 cm) USD 4,000. COLOGNE, 15 Oct 1988, *In the Bay of Naples* (oil on canvas, 15 1/4 x 22 1/4 ins / 39 x 56.5 cm) DEM 1,000. LONDON, 16 Feb 1990, *Mount Vesuvius from Mergellina in the Bay of Naples* (oil on canvas, 15 1/4 x 22 1/4 ins / 39 x 56.5 cm) GBP 3,850. LONDON, 4 Oct 1991, *Faraglione and Capri* (oil on canvas, 10 x 13 ins / 25.3 x 33 cm) GBP 1,320. NEW YORK, 26 May 1992, *Calm Sea at Dusk* (oil on canvas, 21 1/4 x 28 ins / 53.9 x 71.1 cm) USD 2,750. LONDON, 28 Oct 1992, *Rocks at Faraglione and Monacone in Capri* (oil on canvas, 24 x 43 3/4 ins / 61 x 111 cm) GBP 4,400. LONDON, 7 April 1993, *Coastal Landscape in Capri* (oil on canvas, 21 1/2 x 27 1/2 ins / 54.5 x 70 cm) GBP 690. NEW YORK, 22-23 July 1993, *Capri* (oil on canvas, 22 x 27 3/4 ins / 55.9 x 70.5 cm) USD 863. ROME, 6 Dec 1994, *Boats in Capri* (oil on wood, 11 3/4 x 15 3/4 ins / 30 x 40 cm) ITL 1,768,000. NEW YORK, 17 Jan 1996, *Coasts of Capri* (oil on canvas, a pair, 22 x 27 3/4 ins / 55.9 x 70.5 cm) USD 3,450. LONDON, 30 May 1996, *Sunrise over Capri* (oil on canvas, 21 1/4 x 27 1/4 ins / 54 x 69 cm) GBP 517. LONDON, 4 Feb 1999, *Rocky Coastline on Capri. Sunlit Coastline on Capri* (oil on canvas, a pair, 22 x 28 ins / 56 x 70 cm) GBP 1,400. TORONTO, 12 June 2000, *Summer's Day, Capri* (oil on canvas, 20 x 30 ins / 51 x 76 cm) CAD

4,800. TORONTO, 7 Dec 2000, *Calm Sea at Capri* (oil on canvas, 25 x 30 ins / 64 x 77 cm) CAD 3,000. LONDON, 29 Nov 2001, *Rough Sea off the Coast of Capri* (oil on canvas, 22 x 28 ins / 55 x 70 cm) GBP 2,000. LONDON, 29 Nov 2001, *Coast off Capri* (oil on canvas, 27 x 35 ins / 69 x 89 cm) GBP 2,400. VIENNA, 19 Feb 2002, *On the Coast of Capri* (oil on canvas, 28 x 35 ins / 70 x 90 cm) EUR 2,200. LONDON, 21 June 2002, *Coast of Capri* (oil on canvas, 21 x 36 ins / 53 x 91 cm) GBP 1,500. LONDON, 13 Feb 2003, *Waves Crashing on the Coast at Capri* (oil on canvas, 27 x 39 ins / 69 x 98 cm) GBP 1,600. LONDON, 20 March 2003, *Capri Coastline at Dusk* (oil on canvas, 20 x 28 ins / 51 x 71 cm) GBP 1,200. TRIESTE, 12 May 2004, *Fishermen Returning* (oil on canvas, 21 x 16 ins / 53 x 40 cm) EUR 2,100. TURIN, 25 Oct 2004, *Seascape in Capri* (oil on canvas, 16 x 10 ins / 40 x 26 cm) EUR 1,800.

FEDERICO DI LAMBERTO. See **SUSTRIS**

FEDERICO DI MARCO

Italian, 17th century.
Born to a family originally from Cefalù (Sicily).
Sculptor.

Federico di Marco worked alongside Giacomo Mangio in decorating the choir stalls in the church of Isnello.

FEDERICO DI QUONDAM VALCONE

Italian, 14th century.
Born to a family originally from Gemona (Friuli).
Miniaturist.

Federico di Quondam Valcone is mentioned in 1340 as having received a payment for the miniature of a crucifix.

FEDERICO TEDESCO

German, 15th century.
Born in Germany.
Painter.

Federico Tedesco worked in Padua where he embellished the choir of the church of S Agostino (now demolished) with frescoes. He also executed an altar painting in this church.

FEDERIGHI, Antonio. See **ANTONIO FEDERIGHI DEI TOLOMEI**

FEDERIGO FIAMMINGO. See **SUSTRIS**

FEDERL, Andreas Gotthard, or Foderl

Austrian, 18th century.
Active in Vienna.
Painter.

Andreas Federl belonged to the guild of painters, but was expelled in 1721.

FEDERL, Anton, or Foderl

Austrian, 18th century.
Born c. 1680; died 9 June 1723.
Active in Vienna.
Painter.

FEDERL, Johann

Austrian, 17th century.
Active in Regensburg.
Engraver.

Some of Johann Federl's works are to be found in the collection of the town hall in Regensburg (Bavaria), Germany.

FEDERL, Johann Georg, or Foderl

Austrian, 18th century.
Born 1737; died 4 October 1807.
Active in Vienna.
Painter.

The son of Andreas Gotthard, Johann Georg Federl entered the academy of art in Vienna on 3 July 1752 under the name of Federl von Au.

FEDERL, Joseph

Austrian, 18th century.
Born 1764, in Vienna.
Sculptor.

FEDERL, Martin

Austrian, 18th century.
Active in Vienna.
Painter.

Martin Federl entered the academy of art in Vienna on 27 November 1754.

FEDERLE, Aegidius

Swiss, 19th century.
Born 10 October 1810, in Stühlingen; died 21 March 1876, in Fribourg.
Painter. Landscapes.

Federle learned gouache painting as a pupil of Heinrich Uster in Feuerthalen. He exhibited at the Swiss Turnus between 1848 and 1858, and taught drawing in schools in Fribourg. He also stayed at the castle of Lauffen, at Schaffhouse, and in Constance.

AUCTION RECORDS:

PARIS, 19 May 1927, *View of Lake Zug; Views of the village of Capitale, Glarus and Glärnisch* (gouache, a pair) FRF 1,500.

FEDERLE, Helmut

Swiss, 20th century.
Born 1944, in Solothurn.
Since 1985 active in Austria.
Painter, draughtsman, engraver. Artists' books.

After completing his studies at the Kunstgewerbeschule in Basel (1964-1969), Helmut Federle stayed in Paris for a year at the Cité Internationale des Arts. Then he lived in New York before settling in Zurich. From 1985 he lived and worked in Vienna. He has made trips to Tunisia, Afghanistan, India and Nepal.

His initial works were representations of mountains and the sun, verging on Symbolism. From the end of the 1970s, notably with the various *Black Series*, his works were undoubtedly in the tradition of some of the fathers of Abstraction, such as Mondrian and Malevich, and were influenced by the more recent tradition of artists such as Russian- Mark Rothko, Barnett Newman and Agnès Martin. There is a dryness, a rigidity, but also a working drawing of the geometric form etched in a space, which also feeds it in return; a decisive confidence in the line (which is often the line on the edges of the picture), and pale colours generally worked out in a binary vein (Naples grey-yellow; Naples black-yellow), are from the outset characteristic features of Federle's painting. Federle claims to be an advocate of *Über das Geistige in der Kunst* (*On the Question of the Spiritual in Art*) (an essay published in 1912 by Wassily Kandinsky) in search of a mystical balance beyond the world of objects and forms. With Federle, there is a correlation between this quest for transcendence and the use of signs and esoteric symbols. 'Today, signs have broken away from their original models. Signs have become available, which necessitates a great sense of responsibility'.

The interpretation of a painting by Federle reveals, in the superimposed layers and brushmarks signs of a search for something other than the simple representation of its plane. In addition, his drawings show us his different preoccupations, his particular interest in decorative motifs, and also acronyms or letters of the alphabet, such as 'H', his first initial, which is repeated several times and never completely represented.

He has participated in many group exhibitions, including: 1975, Biennale de Paris; 1984, *Peinture Abstraite* (*Abstract Painting*), Geneva; 1986, *Abstraits* (*Abstracts*), Dijon; 1986, *Tableaux Abstraits* (*Abstract Paintings*), Villa Arson, Nice; 1988, *The Image of Abstraction*, Museum of Contemporary Art, Los Angeles; 1989, *Prospekt 1989* (*Prospect 1989*), Kunstverein, Frankfurt; 1989, *Bilderstreit* (*Picture Conflict*), Museum Ludwig, Cologne; 1991, Donald Young Gallery, Seattle; 1992, *Federle, Fulton, LeWitt* (*Federle, Fulton, LeWitt*), Galerie Franck + Schulte, Berlin; 1992, *Face-à-Face* (*Face to Face*), Espace de l'Art Concret, Mouans-Sartoux; 1993, *Abstrakt* (*Abstract*), Deutscher Künstlerbund, Dresden; 1993, *Équilibre* (*Balance*), Aargauer Kunsthaus, Aarau; 1994, *Praxis*, Centre d'Art du Domaine de Kerguéhennec, Locminé; 1997, *Abstraction/Abstractions - Géométries Provisoires* (*Abstraction/Abstractions - Provisional Geometry*), Musée d'Art Moderne, St-Étienne; 2001, *Abstracción: El Paradigma Amerindio* (*Abstraction: The American-Indian Paradigm*), IVAM, Centre Julio González, Valencia; 2003, *Un Tableau dans le Décor. Peintures 1970-2000* (*A Painting in the Décor: Paintings 1970-2000*), an exhibition to celebrate 20 years of the FRAC (Fonds Nationaux d'Art Contemporain - regional contemporary art collections), Château des Ducs de Bretagne, Nantes.

His first solo show was held in 1971 in Basel. Then he exhibited his works in many countries: 1972, Fribourg; 1973, Lucerne; 1974, Basel; 1975, Olten; 1979, the Kunsthalle, Basel; 1983, the Musée Cantonal des Beaux-Arts, Lausanne; 1985, the Museum für Gegenswartskunst, Basel (contemporary art); 1985, the Gemeentemuseum, The Hague; 1988, the Donald Young Gallery, Seattle; 1989, *Helmut Federle. Bilder und Zeichnungen 1975-1988* (*Helmut Federle. Paintings and Drawings 1975-1988*), a travelling exhibition: the Museum Hans Lange in Krefeld, the Kunsthalle in Bielefeld, the Kunstverein in Hamburg; 1989, *Helmut Federle. Peintures, Dessins* (*Helmut Federle. Paintings, Drawings*), Musée de Grenoble; 1991, the Secession, Vienna; 1992, *Helmut Federle* (*Helmut Federle*), a travelling exhibition: the Kunsthalle in Zurich, the Moderna Museet in Stockholm, the Museum Fridericianum in Kassel; 1992, the Galerie Durand-Dessert, Paris; 1993, the Museum Folkwang, Essen; 1994, Peter Blum, New York; 1995, the Galerie Nationale du Jeu de Paume, Paris; 2002, the Musée des Beaux-Arts, Nantes.

BIBLIOGRAPHY:

Lemoine, Serge/Monery, Jean-Paul, *Helmut Federle, peintures, dessins*, exhibition catalogue, Musée de Grenoble, Grenoble, 1989. Federle, Helmut/Dickhoff, Wilfried/Röder, Sabine, *Helmut Federle, Bilder und Zeichnungen, 1975-1988*, travelling exhibition catalogue, Kunstverein, Hamburger, Kunsthalle, Karl Kerber Verlag, Bielefeld, 1989. Badura-Triska, Eva/Meschede, Friedrich/Lores, Veit, et al., *Helmut Federle*, exhibition catalogue, Wiener Secession, Vienna, 1991. Schrenk, Klaus/Franz, Erich, et al., *Helmut Federle*, exhibition catalogue, Kunstmuseum, Bonn, Richter, Düsseldorf, 1995 (text in German and English). Ceysson, Bernard/De Andrés, Alberto, *Helmut Federle*, exhibition catalogue, Gal. nationale du Jeu de Paume, Paris, 1995. Wismer, Beat/Jonas-Edel, Justus/Gachnang, Johannes, *Helmut Federle. Black series I +II und Nachbarschaft der Farben*, travelling exhibition catalogue, Staatliche Kunsthalle, Karlsruhe, Kunstverein, Braunschweig, Aargauer Kunsthaus, Aarau, 1998. Bonet, Juan Manuel/Abadie, Daniel/Boehm, Gottfried, *Helmut Federle*, exhibition catalogue, Instituto Valenciano de Arte Moderno (IVAM) Centre Julio González, Valencia, 1998 (text in Spanish and English). Yau, John/Schmatz, Ferdinand/Samsonow, Elisabeth, *Helmut Federle*, exhibition catalogue, Kunsthaus, Bregenz, König, Cologne, 1999. Paternosto, César/Frame, Mary/Lippard, Lucy R., et al., *Abstracción: El paradigma amerindio*, exhibition catalogue, Instituto Valenciano de Arte Moderno (IVAM), Valencia, 2001. *Helmut Federle*, exhibition catalogue, Musée des Beaux-Arts, Nantes, 2002.

MUSEUMS AND GALLERIES:

AARAU (Aargauer Kunsthaus) - DIJON (FRAC Bourgogne) - DUNKIRK (FRAC Nord-Pas de Calais) - GRENOBLE (Mus. de Grenoble): *MacArthur Park* (1987) - PARIS (FNAC): *MacArthur Park* (1987); *Destructive Zero Limit III* (1990); *Sign of the Earthly Centre* (1990); *Indian Painting* (1993).

AUCTION RECORDS:

PARIS, 23 March 1988, *Untitled* (black felt/paper, 11 3/4 x 8 ins / 29.8 x 20.1 cm) FRF 7,000; *Mechanical Arm* (gouache and pencil/paper, 11 x 8 1/2 ins / 28 x 21.5 cm) FRF 7,500. NEW YORK, 6 May 1992, *Large Wall* (oil/fabric, 107 1/2 x 72 3/4 ins / 273 x 184.7 cm) USD 26,400. NEW YORK, 8 Oct 1992, *Okinava* (acrylic/canvas, 90 1/2 x 128 1/4 ins / 229.9 x 325.7 cm) USD 55,000. NEW YORK, 19 Nov 1992, *Two Undefined 'Is'* (1985, oil on canvas, 112 x 70 1/2 ins / 284.6 x 179.3 cm) USD 30,800. LONDON, 25 March 1993, *Line of Desolation* (1984, acrylic/canvas, 80 3/4 x 132 3/4 ins / 205 x 337 cm) GBP 19,550. STOCKHOLM, 10-12 May 1993, *Abstract Composition* (ink, 11 1/2 x 8 1/4 ins / 29.5 x 21 cm) SEK 6,700. LUCERNE, 15 May 1993, *Leopard* (1969, mixed media, tempera and collage, oil on card, 20 x 26 1/2 ins / 51 x 67 cm) CHF 2,200. LONDON, 26 Oct 1995, *Principle about Forms* (1986, oil on canvas, 19 3/4 x 15 3/4 ins / 50 x 40 cm) GBP 7,475. NEW YORK, 18 Nov 1997, *Basic Forms IV* (1987, oil on linen, 48 x 36 ins / 121.9 x 91.5 cm) USD 10,925. NEW YORK, 17 Feb 1999, *Nach Unten abnehmende Form* (1988, oil on canvas, 16 x 24 ins / 40 x 60 cm) USD 13,000. LUCERNE, 5 June 1999, *Leopard* (1969, oil and collage on board, 20 x 26 ins / 51 x 67 cm) CHF 4,200. LONDON, 27 June 2001, *Tree of Inside and Outside* (1988, oil on canvas, 107 x 69 ins / 271 x 176 cm) GBP 23,000. COLOGNE, 5 Dec 2001, *Basics on Composition XXXXI* (dispersion, 16 x 20 ins / 40 x 50 cm) DEM 25,000. ZURICH, 24 June 2003, *Mountain Lake* (1973, pencil and gouache, 28 x 39 ins / 70 x 100 cm) CHF 3,800. NEW YORK, 14 May 2004, *Three Forms, 1/4, 1/8, 1/16* (colour dispersion, 110 x 173 ins / 280 x 440 cm) USD 72,000. BERLIN, 12 June 2004, *Untitled* (1982, oil on canvas, 73 x 55 ins / 186 x 140 cm) EUR 25,000.

FEDERLEY, Alexander Thiodolf

Finnish, 19th century.

Born 1864.

Painter, watercolourist, illustrator.

Alexander Thiodolf Federley studied in Helsinki, and then in Paris from 1891 to 1893. In 1893 he became superintendant of the artists' association of Helsinki. The Atheneum in Helsinki has two of his landscapes.

FEDERLIN, Karl

German, 19th century.

Sculptor.

Federlin was court painter in Ulm. He made statues of the apostles *St Matthew* and *St Bartholomew*, and of *Emperor Konrad III* and *A.H. Franke*, which were placed on the pillars of the central nave of the cathedral at Ulm. His busts of *King Charles of Württemberg* are in the König-Karl-Haus and in the Staatsgalerie in Stuttgart. He also fulfilled plans for several altars in the church of the seminary at Ehingen.

FEDERSPIEL, Pierre

Luxembourg, 19th - 20th century.

Born 1864, in Luxembourg; died 1924, in Luxembourg.

Sculptor. Statues, busts.

Pierre Federspiel was a student at the academy of fine arts in Munich, the Académie Julian and Alfred Boucher's private studio in Paris. In 1894, he took part in the first exhibition of the artistic circle in Luxembourg.

He represents his contemporaries in their bourgeois period clothes; the women wearing showy hats and the men holding their gloves. Skilled at official consecrations, he created various monumental sculptures in Luxembourg: the *Monument Dicks et Lentz* (*Dicks-Lenz Monument*) at the Place d'Armes; the *Frise de la Comtesse Ermesinde* (*Frieze of the Countess Ermesinde*) that decorates the façade of the Cercle Municipal; and the heads of the historical figures on the façade of the Central Station.

Bibliography:

Cent cinquante ans d'Art luxembourgeois, exhibition catalogue, Musée national d'Histoire et d'Art du Luxembourg, Luxembourg, 1989.

Museums and Galleries:

Luxembourg (Mus. national d'histoire et d'art): *Stone-Thrower* (1890, plaster); *Constant Mersch* (1891, bronze); *Grand Duke Adolphe* (c. 1890-1894, terracotta); *Young Norwegian Woman Painter* (1894, marble); *Countess Ermesinde* (before 1914, plaster, model of the relief in the Central Station); *Emperor Charles IV* (before 1914, plaster, model of the relief in the Central Station); *Vendelin Jurion* (before 1914, plaster, model of the relief in the Central Station); *Emmanuel Servais* (before 1914, plaster, model of the relief in the Central Station); *King William III, Grand Duke* (before 1914, plaster, model of the relief in the Central Station); *Prince Henry of the Netherlands* (before 1914, plaster, model of the relief in the Central Station); *Princess Henry of the Netherlands* (before 1914, plaster, model of the relief in the Central Station); *Mme Émile Metz, née Tesch* (marble); *Émile Metz* (1919, plaster).

FEDI, Antonio I

Italian, 18th century.
Active in Florence.
Draughtsman, engraver, collector. Portraits. Vignettes, decorative designs.

Antonio Fedi I published two series of engravings, *Bronze Low-reliefs* and *Marble Group*, and drew vignettes for G. Buganza's *Treasury of Latin Verse*. Three of his engravings from 1788 are preserved in the national library of Florence. F. Rainaldi engraved some of Fedi's portraits of celebrated composers.

FEDI, Antonio II

Italian, 18th - 19th century.
Born 1771; died 1843.
Painter.

His self-portrait hangs in the Uffizi gallery in Florence.

FEDI, Pio

Italian, 19th century.
Born 1816, in Viterbo (Lazio); died 1 June 1892, in Florence.
Sculptor, engraver. Religious subjects.

Pio Fedi started out as an apprentice goldsmith in Florence, then became a copper engraver in Vienna. He returned to Florence and entered the academy, where he studied sculpture. He made his debut in Rome and produced several works that established his reputation, notably *Christ Healing the Sick*. When Fedi returned to Florence in 1844, Grand Duke Leopold II entrusted him with some major works. *The Rape of Polyxena*, in the Loggia dei Lanzi, Florence, is considered to be his masterpiece.

Museums and Galleries:

Liverpool (Walker AG): *Florentine Woman* - Verona (Mus. Civico): *Poetry*.

Auction records:

London, 12 Feb 1976, *Young Fisherman* (1864, white marble, h. 54 ins / 137 cm) GBP 1,850. London, 23 Feb 1981, *Pia de Tolomei and Nello della Pietra* (1862, marble, h. 33 3/4 ins / 86 cm) GBP 1,200. London, 6 Nov 1986, *Pia de Tolomei e Nello della Pietra* (1862, white marble, h. 32 1/2 ins / 82.5 cm) GBP 3,300. Sevenoaks, 18 July 2000, *Cupid* (1875, marble, h. 31 ins / 79 cm) GBP 4,800. London, 27 April 2001, *Bust of Minerva* (1850, white marble, h. 19 ins / 49 cm) GBP 1,400. London, 9 April 2003, *Supreme Fisher Boy* (1864, white marble, h. 53 ins / 135 cm) GBP 46,000. New Orleans, 4 Oct 2003, *Bust Portrait of a Gentleman* (1868, marble, 25 x 21x10 ins / 64 x 53x25 cm) USD 2,000.

FEDIAEVSKAYA, Vera Konstantinova

Russian, 20th century.
Born 1911, in St Petersburg.
Draughtswoman.

Vera Konstantinovna Fediaevskaya studied in Moscow with Vladimir Favorsky from 1931 to 1938. Evacuated to Kazan between 1941 and 1943, she then returned to Moscow.

FEDIER, Franz

Swiss, 20th century.
Born 1922, in Erstfeld (Uri).
Active in France.
Painter.

Franz Fedier was a student at the school of arts and trades in Lucerne in 1941-1942, and then worked as an advertising executive in Bern. From 1949 to 1952, he travelled to Algeria, Spain, France, and in particular to Paris, where he studied at the Académie de la Grande Chaumière. In 1953, he attended S.W. Hayter's engraving courses. He lives in Paris.

He has taken part in many group exhibitions in Paris, Rome, Brussels, Berlin and other German cities, in particular at Documenta in Kassel in 1959, as well as in many Swiss towns, and in the fifth São Paulo Biennale in 1959. Fedier has also held some solo exhibitions, including: 1959, Basel and Düsseldorf; 1961, Bern and Frankfurt; 1962, Geneva; 1966, Zurich, and others.

An abstract painter, he expresses himself with great subtlety while exploiting the possibilities of the interplay between materials.

Auction records:

Bern, 24 June 1981, *Alp* (1956, oil on canvas, 48 x 26 3/4 ins / 121 x 68 cm) CHF 2,800. Lucerne, 25 May 1991, *Untitled* (1980, acrylic/plywood, 31 1/2 x 22 ins / 80 x 55 cm) CHF 1,700. Lucerne, 21 Nov 1992, *Composition* (1956, oil on jute canvas, 13 1/2 x 12 1/2 ins / 34 x 32 cm) CHF 1,600; *Untitled* (1960, oil on canvas, 77 1/4 x 61 1/2 ins / 196 x 156 cm) CHF 4,800. Zurich, 24 Nov 1993, *Doris* (1960, oil on canvas, 63 3/4 x 51 1/4 ins / 162 x 130 cm) CHF 4,600. Lucerne, 26 Nov 1994, *Untitled* (1958, oil on canvas, 31 1/2 x 25 1/2 ins / 80 x 65 cm) CHF 2,200. Zurich, 15 May 2001, *Vertical-horizontal-diagonal* (1961, acrylic, 64 x 51 ins / 162 x 130 cm) CHF 2,600. Zurich, 3 Dec 2001, *Spring* (1955, oil on canvas, 16 x 22 ins / 41 x 57 cm) CHF 5,000.

FEDINI, Giovanni

Italian, 16th century.
Active in Florence.
Painter.

Giovanni Fedini painted the frescoes in the chapel of the painters of the Accademia di San Luca with Montorsoli, A. Fei and other artists.

FEDIT, Gaston

French, 20th century.
Born in Bordeaux.
Painter.

Fedit exhibited in Paris, at the Salon of the Société Nationale des Beaux-Arts, from 1922 to 1928.

FEDOR, also known as Rostovski

Russian, 14th century.
Active in Rostov (region of Yaroslavl).
Painter.

Fedor was an archimandrite. He painted a portrait of his uncle *Sergei Radonejski*.

FEDOR, or Novgorodtseff

Russian, 16th century.

Born to a family originally from Novgorod.
Painter.
Fedor produced works in conjunction with other artists and icon painters for the monastery of Volokolamsk in the Moscow region.

FEDOR, A.
Russian, 18th century.
Engraver (wood).
A. Fedor worked in Kiev and engraved the illustrations for a book of the Gospels, printed in the monastery in Pechersk in the Kiev region and sixteen illustrations for a book of the Gospels printed in Kiev in 1703.

FEDOR IVANOVICH. See **IVANOVICH**

FEDOROV, Boris Grigorievich
Russian, 19th century.
Born 24 March 1793; died 1831.
Engraver.
Fedorov studied at the St Petersburg academy of fine arts, then under the engraver N.J. Utkin. While still a student he engraved two landscapes with goats and sheep. Two battle scenes: the battle of Leipzig, from a drawing by A.I. Mamonov, and at Fère Champenoise, bear his signature.

FEDOROV, Dmitri
Russian, 19th century.
Painter.
Dmitri Fedorov was active in St Petersburg. This does not seem though to be a good enough reason for identifying him with Fedor Fedorov.

FEDOROV, Fedor
Russian, 19th century.
Painter.
In 1808 and 1809 Fedorov he received a gold and silver award from the St Petersburg academy of arts for his portraits.

FEDOROV, Ilarion Fedorovich
Russian, 19th century.
Lithographer.
Fedorov produced lithographs of engravings for a great number of prayer sheets, for the Moscow editor V. Loguinov.

FEDOROV, Ivan Kusmich
Ukrainian, 19th century.
Born 1853, in Odessa.
Painter.
I.K. Fedorov studied at the St Petersburg academy of fine arts, where he received several awards, including a gold award for his painting *Prometheus Chained to a Rock in the Caucasus*. He continued his artistic training in Paris, where he painted a *St Alexis* and a *St John Chrysostom*, in Ivan Yakoviev's Byzantine chapel in the Père Lachaise cemetry. On his return to Russia, he exhibited his painting *Catherine the Great at the Lomonossov's* at the St Petersburg academy exhibition. He also exhibited other genre paintings and portraits.
MUSEUMS AND GALLERIES:
MOSCOW (State Tretyakov Gal.): *Model Posing in an Artist's Studio*.

FEDOROV, Ivan Panteleemonovich
Russian, 19th century.
Painter.
Fedorov was a pupil of A.T. Markov, at the St Petersburg academy of fine arts, he exhibited a painting here in 1888 entitled *The Arrival of Prince Alexei Alexandrovich in Odessa in 1887 aboard the Elbrouz.*

FEDOROV, Leonti
Russian, 18th century.
Painter.
In 1720, Leonti Fedorov produced paintings for the Monplaisir Palace at the Peterhof near St Petersburg and in 1725, icon paintings for the chapel at the new Summer Palace in St Petersburg.

FEDOROV, Lev
Russian, 18th century.
Painter.
Was active in St Petersburg at the Winter Palace in 1765. Perhaps identical to Leonti Fedorov.

FEDOROV, Mikhail or Michel
Russian, 19th century.
Painter, engraver, illustrator. Portraits, genre scenes.
This artist may be perhaps identical to the engraver who worked in St Petersburg from 1812 to 1820 as master minter. We know of his vignettes, book illustrations and portraits.
AUCTION RECORDS:
PARIS, 27 June 1991, *Dancers in front of a Datcha; Young Girls Playing on a Swing in front of a Datcha* (1843, oil/metal, a pair, each 10 1/4 x 13 3/4 ins / 26 x 35 cm) FRF 14,000.

FEDOROV, Nikolai
Russian, 20th century.
Born in Bobrov.
Painter. Landscapes.
Nikolai Fedorov exhibited in Paris at the Salon des Indépendants before 1939.

FEDOROV, P.
Russian, 19th century.
Painter, watercolourist. Flowers.
MUSEUMS AND GALLERIES:
ST PETERSBURG (Gosudarstvennyj Russkij Muz.): *Bunch of Flowers* (two watercolours).

FEDOROV, Petr
Russian, 19th century.
Engraver, draughtsman.
Petr Fedorov was probably a student at the St Petersburg academy. We know of his portraits of the Russian actor *AS Yakovlev*, Tsar *Nicholas I, Alexander Nicolaievich aged 7*, (later Tsar Aleksandr II), then historical subjects which he engraved from his own drawings, such as *Death of the Tsars' Mother, Maria Fedorovna; Tsar Nicholas Visiting the Tombs of the Soldiers Who Fought at Brailov, Scenes from the Life of Peter the Great*, and also to be mentioned are *Glory of Tsar Nicholas I and Tsarina Alexandra Fedorovna After the Defeat of the Turks in 1831* and religious subjects *Christ Blessing the Children* and an *Ascension*.

FEDOROV, Sergei
Russian, 19th century.
Engraver.
Fedorov engraved from the drawings of D. de Scotti, plates illustrating six battles for S. Cardelli's series *Twelve Russian Victories During the French Campaign*. A known work of his is *Aurora*, a vignette for a music score.

FEDOROV, Stepan
Russian, 18th century.
Painter. Genre scenes. Theatre decoration.
In 1736, Fedorov worked on the decoration of the hall of the Theatre of the Winter Palace in St Petersburg.
AUCTION RECORDS:
LONDON, 15 June 1995, *Pastoral Idyll* (oil on canvas, 24 1/4 x 38 1/4 ins / 61.5 x 97 cm) GBP 2,300.

FEDOROV, Vasili
Russian, 18th century.
Active in St Petersburg.
Painter.
Vasili Fedorov carried out, with Andrei Ivanov, the decoration of the state apartments of the Grand Palace at Peterhof, near St Petersburg.

FEDOROV, Vladimir
Russian, 20th century.
Born at the beginning of the 20th century, in the Crimea.
Active in France.
Painter.
Vladimir Fedorov lived in Paris and exhibited a landscape at the Salon d'Automne in 1913.
MUSEUMS AND GALLERIES:
ST PETERSBURG (Academy of Fine Art): *Landscape with River*.
AUCTION RECORDS:
AMSTERDAM, 24 April 1991, *Spring* (1922, oil on panel, 3 1/2 x 4 1/2 ins / 9 x 11.5 cm) NLG 1,035.

FEDOROVA, Mariya Alekseeva
Russian, 19th - 20th century.
Born 1859; died 1916.
Painter. Landscapes, flowers.
Mariya Alekseeva Fedorova studied at the academy in St Petersburg. She exhibited from 1887 onwards with landscapes including *The Dniepr, Fast-flowing River* and *Flowers*.
MUSEUMS AND GALLERIES:
MOSCOW (State Tretyakov Gal.): *Fog on the Volga; In the Storm; In St Petersburg During Bad Weather* - ST PETERSBURG (Gosudarstvennyj Russkij Muz.): *Banks of the Volga*.
AUCTION RECORDS:
STOCKHOLM, 10 April 1985, *Summer Landscape* (oil on canvas, 14 1/4 x 20 3/4 ins / 36 x 53 cm) SEK 9,500. LONDON, 5 Oct 1989, *Door of a Russian Monastery* (oil on canvas, 14 1/4 x 10 1/2 ins / 36.2 x 26.7 cm) GBP 2,750.

FEDOROVICH, Sophia, or Fedrovich
Russian, 20th century.
Born in Minsk.
Painter. Seascapes.
Sophia Fedorovich exhibited in Paris from 1925 to 1929 at the Salon des Artistes Indépendants and the Salon d'Automne from 1928 onwards.
AUCTION RECORDS:
LONDON, 4 June 1981, *Costume Design for Michael Somes in Dante Sonata* (gouache and pencil, 15 1/2 x 9 ins / 39.5 x 22.7 cm) GBP 240.

FEDOSSEEV, Ielissei Iemelianovich
Russian, 18th century.
Born 1745, in St Petersburg.
Engraver.
A pupil of J. Stenglin, Fedosseev became court engraver. With his tutor he produced a portrait of the physician *F.W. Richman*; attributed to him is the engraving of the portrait of the engineer *J.G. Leutman*, from W. Sokolov's work. Two other known works are two plates, showing a firework display given in St Petersburg to celebrate peace between Russia and Turkey in 1775.

FEDOSSEEV, S.
Russian, 18th century.
Engraver.
Fedosseev was probably the brother of Ielissei I. Fedosseev. He engraved a vignette *Minerva*, as a frontispiece for the *Annual Report of the Russian Free Society* and a medallion portarait of *Count Marshal B.P. Sheremeteev*, for the first volume of his correspondence with Peter the Great.

FEDOTOV, Aleksei
Russian, 18th century.
Painter.
Fedotov studied at the St Petersburg academy of fine arts in about 1780. He was probably the uncle of Paul Andreevich Fedotov.

FEDOTOV, Paul Andrevitch or Pavel Andreevich
Russian, 19th century.
Born 1815, in Moscow; died 1852, in St Petersburg.
Painter, watercolourist. Military subjects, portraits, genre scenes, still-lifes, satire.
Son of a soldier and himself an officer in the Finnish regiment of the Imperial Guard, Fedotov spent a long time at the St Petersburg academy, but waited until his retirement, in 1843, before devoting himself entirely to painting. He died insane.

He was initially attracted to military scenes, with which he had a great success. He then painted genre scenes with the critical approach of the naturalist school and filled with enough satire to provoke great scandals. In particular he mocked the self-importance of the Muscovite middle-class in works such as *The morning of a Civil Servant who has been promoted, The Major's Engagement* and *The Choosy Bride*. He has been compared to Boilly and Gavarni. His still-lifes are highly regarded.
MUSEUMS AND GALLERIES:
MOSCOW (ostruchov Mus.): *Infantry of the Russian Guard Crossing a Ford* - MOSCOW (Rumiantsev Mus.): *A Widow; A Lunch; The Indebted Major's Marriage Request; A New Knight of the Order with Holes in his Soles* - MOSCOW (State Tretyakov Gal.): *Injustice Under Kirasnoie, Injustice under Smolensk; A Servant Buying Brushes in a Haberdashery; Cholera in St Petersburg; P.A. Fedotov and Friends; An Officer near a Funeral Urn; Three Unknown Figures; I was mistaken!; At the Shop; The Fate of a Painter who, Believing in his Talent, Marries without a Dowry; Fidelka's Illness; The Death of Fidelka; Players; Portrait of the Painter's Father; A Street Scene During the Rain; The Widow; Portarit of the Countess E.P. Rostopchin, the Writer; Portrait of Th. E. Yakolev; The Anteroom of a Police Station during a Large Party; Portrait of the Artist* (watercolour); *Portrait of the Aged Artist* - OXFORD (Ashmolean Mus.) - ST PETERSBURG (Gosudarstvennyj Russkij Muz.): *Portrait of Mlle de Moncal Kneeling; The Jdanovitch Sisters; The Young Widow; The Indebted Major's Marriage Request*.
AUCTION RECORDS:
LONDON, 10 Oct 1990, *Portrait of a Young Man* (oil on card, 10 x 8 ins / 25.3 x 20.4 cm) GBP 6,600.

FEDRIANI Y CAMPS, Emilia (Doña)
Spanish, 19th century.
Active in Cádiz.
Painter.
Emilia Fedriani y Camps studied painting in Cádiz, and exhibited still-lifes and landscapes there in 1879.

FEDRIANI Y RAMIREZ, Manuel
Spanish, 19th century.
Born in Cádiz.
Painter. Historical painting, genre scenes.

FEDRIANI Y RAMIREZ, Tomás
Spanish, 19th century.
Born in the 19th century, in Cádiz.
Painter. History painting, still-lifes.
Tomás Fedriani y Ramirez studied at the academy of fine arts in Cádiz.

FEDRICHETTI
Italian, 18th century.
Probably born in Verona.
Painter. Religious subjects.
Since there is no record of his having been active in Verona, it is conceivable that this artist is the same person as Federico Bencovitch, whose first name was transliterated as Ferighetto and, ultimately, Fedrichetti. He is credited with an *Ecstasy of St Juliana* for the church of S Maria dei Servi in Milan.
MUSEUMS AND GALLERIES:
VIENNA (Albertina Mus.): *Virgin Appearing to St Francis* (pen, drawing).

FEDROVICH, Sophia. See **FEDOROVICH**

FEDUCCI, Michele

Italian, 17th century.
Died 1608; buried 12 April in Florence.
Active in Florence.
Painter.

FEDULLO, Nelida

Argentinian, 20th century.
Born 20th century, in Buenos Aires.
Active in France from 1964.
Painter, engraver.

Nelida Fedullo belonged to the Arte Concreto Invención group, Argentina's first geometric abstract art movement. In 1964 she went to Paris where she worked at S.W. Hayter's engraving studio. Fedullo's early work is a variation on the theme of the straight line, but she went on to create networks of crystallised forms behind which fantastical images appear. Her abstract forms show a tendency towards fetishism with the image rising to the surface of the pictorial construction to produce a surreal, ambiguous representation not devoid of eroticism - the surface becoming an 'enclosed field of hallucination and fantasy'. She exhibited in Buenos Aires from 1948 to 1963.

FÉE, Floris de La. See **LA FÉE**

FEEDERLE, Karl

German, 19th century.
Born 1832, in Donaueschingen; died 12 March 1881, in Munich.
Lithographer. Landscapes.

In 1854, Feederle went to study art in Munich, exhibiting there in 1879. He is best known for his *Winter Landscape*.

FEELEY, Paul

American, 20th century.
Born 1910 or 1913, in Des Moines (Iowa); died 1966, in New York.
Painter, sculptor.
Minimal Art.

Paul Feeley studied at Menlo College in California from 1930 to 1931, and at the Art Students League in New York from 1931 to 1934. He taught at Bennington College of Vermont, where his stated policy on the teaching of art included the idea that the study of art was a way of life, rather than a vocational pursuit; that the encouragement of primitive and elementary things in art is necessary; and that absolutism must be avoided. Feeley was influenced by Jackson Pollock, saying that he had learned to escape 'tradional taste'. His work drew upon Mediterranean traditions, such as Greek sculpture and Moorish tiles, and his use of colour evoked qualities of Mediterranean light. His work typically blended abstraction with biomorphic form.

In 2002 the Matthew Marks Gallery in New York exhibited a collection of Paul Feeley's paintings and sculptures.

BIBLIOGRAPHY:

Alloway, Lawrence, '*Paul Feeley: Introduction and Interview*' in *Living Arts*, periodical, London, April, 1964. Goossen, E.C., '*Paul Feeley*' in *Art international*, periodical, Zurich, December 1964. Baro, Gene, '*Paul Feeley: The Art of the Definite*' in *Arts Magazine*, periodical, New York, February, 1966. Relyea, Lane/Alloway, Lawrence/Garo, Gene, *Paul Feeley: Painting and Sculpture*, exhibition catalogue, Marks Gallery, New York, 2002.

MUSEUMS AND GALLERIES:

WASHINGTON DC (Smithsonian American AM): *Alruccambam* (1964, oil on canvas); *Jack* (1966, fibreglass).

AUCTION RECORDS:

NEW YORK, 28 May 1976, *Caesarea* (1962, plastic paint/canvas, 60 x 48 ins / 152.5 x 122 cm) USD 2,200. NEW YORK, 9 Nov 1984, *Akerena* (1963, enamel/canvas, 65 3/4 x 51 ins / 167 x 129.5 cm) USD 3,800. NEW YORK, 6 May 1987, *Apyu* (1963, oil on canvas, 60 x 48 ins / 152.4 x 121 cm) USD 8,000. NEW YORK, 5 Oct 1990, *Acrab* (1964, acrylic/canvas, 60 1/4 x 59 3/4 ins / 152.8 x 151.8 cm) USD 8,800. NEW YORK, 10 Nov 1993, *Maia* (1963, acrylic/canvas, 30 x 25 ins / 76.2 x 63.5 cm) USD 13,800. NEW YORK, 15 May 2003, *Apyu* (1963, oil on canvas, 60 x 48 ins / 152 x 122 cm) USD 16,000. NEW YORK, 23 Sept 2003, *Untitled* (oil on canvas, 60 x 48 ins / 152 x 122 cm) USD 22,000. LAMBERTVILLE, 24 April 2004, *Etamin* (1965, enamel on canvas, 24 x 24 ins / 60 x 60 cm) USD 9,500. NEW YORK, 15 Sept 2004, *Untitled* (1961, oil on canvas, 60 x 48 ins / 152 x 121 cm) USD 24,000.

FEELINGS, Tom

American, 20th century.
Born 19 May 1933, in Brooklyn; died 25 August 2003.
Painter, draughtsman, sculptor, illustrator. Figures, figure compositions, scenes with figures.

Tom Feelings trained at the Cartoonists and Illustrators' School, New York (1951-1953) and the School of Visual Art, New York, (1957-1960). He enrolled in the US Air Force in 1953 and worked as an illustrator in the Graphics Division of the Third Air Force in London. He later lived in Africa before returning to the USA. In 1989 he took up a post as artist in residence at the University of South Carolina, Columbia, SC, remaining there until 1995.

In the early 1960s, Feelings set out to depict the life of the rural blacks in the Southern states. Some of his drawings were reproduced in an article entitled 'The Negro in the US', in *Look magazine*. When living in Ghana from 1964 to 1966, he worked as an illustrator for *Africa Review*. He also illustrated some twenty books, including Julius Lester's *To Be a Slave*, the 1969 Newberry Honor Book, as well as works of children's literature, including Muriel Feelings' introductory Swahili texts, *Moja Means One* and *Jambo Means Hello*. Feelings worked with Maya Angelou on her *Now Sheba Sings the Song* and *Soul Looks Back in Wonder* (1993), which won him the Coretta Scott King Award. Feelings' drawings are classical in style but with an element of fantasy in them. He puts the accent on individual suffering and living in tension with the outside world, which he shows in taut musculature. He always regarded himself as an African who lived in America, and devoted his work to reconstituting the history of the black diaspora and to reforging links with African culture.

He took part in various group exhibitions, including in 1980, *The Child: Paintings, Drawings, Sculpture*, Gallery 62, New York. Posthumous retrospectives of his work were organised, such as 2004, a book of drawings *Tom Feelings: The Middle Passage. White Ships, Black Cargo*, DuSable Museum, Chicago.

BIBLIOGRAPHY:

Dover, Cedric, *American Negro Art*, New York Graphic Society, Greenwich (CT), 1972. *The child: paintings, drawings, sculpture*, group exhibition catalogue, Gall. 62, National Urban League, New York, 1980. Feelings, Tom, *The Middle Passage: White Ships, Black Cargo*, Penguin Putnam, New York, 1995.

FEENEY, Patrick M.

British, 19th century.
Painter. Landscapes, seascapes.

In 1868 Patrick M. Feeney enrolled at the Carey Academy and subsequently attended the Royal Academy Schools. He exhibited at the Royal Academy in London in 1888, 1889 and 1903, as well as at the Birmingham Royal Society of Artists, of which he was a member.

MUSEUMS AND GALLERIES:

BIRMINGHAM: *Llyn Idwal*.

FEER, Cambon (Mme)

French, 19th century.

Active in Paris.
Sculptor.
Feer became a member of the Société des Artistes Français in 1888 and exhibited at the society's Salon.

FEER, Lisette
Swiss, 19th century.
Born 1794, in Zurich; died 29 July 1866.
Painter, lithographer.
Feer exhibited in Zurich between 1820 and 1829. She produced a series of lithographs of alpine plants, which were collated and published under the title *Souvenirs*.

FEERMANS, Cornille and Jan.
See **FEREMANS**

FEFFERI, Angelo
Italian, 17th century.
Active in Ravenna.
Painter.
Angelo Fefferi worked alongside Giulio Costa around 1680, painting frescoes for the church of S Nicandro e S Marciano in Ravenna.

FEGALY, Louis, called Luigi
Lebanese, 20th - 21st century.
Born 18 May 1949, in Beirut.
Active in France and naturalised in 1990.
Painter, scenographer. Stage sets, murals.
Both a painter and a teacher, he has also produced stage sets and scenery. He has taken part in group exhibitions: at the Palazzo Strozzi, Florence (1975-1976), and from 1985 in Paris, at the Salon d'Automne and Salon des Indépendants, drawing and watercolour biennials and the Salon d'Art Sacré (1991). He has had solo exhibitions at the Beirut academy of fine arts (1982-1983) and at the Centre Culturel, Villemomble (1987-1989).

He describes himself as a 'metaphysical expressionist', his paintings being in the fantastic style.

FEGATELLI. See also **FIGATELLI**

FEGATELLI, Stefano, or Ficatelli
Italian, 18th century.
Born 1687.
Painter.
The son of Giuseppe Maria Fegatelli, he painted portraits, religious subjects and architectural themes. Two of his drawings are housed in the Uffizi, and an altarpiece by him can be found in the church of S Rosa in Ferrara.

FEGDAL, Suzanne
French, 20th century.
Born in Paris.
Painter.
Fegdal exhibited in Paris from 1924 at the Salon d'Automne and the Salon des Indépendants.

FEGELY, Philippe de
Swiss, 19th century.
Born 8 October 1790, in Fribourg; died 16 June 1831, in Baden.
Draughtsman.
Fegely drew architectural views and landscapes, which he then lithographed and published himself or used to illustrate other works. He also painted in oil and contributed to exhibitions in Switzerland.

FEGER, Stefan, or Foger
Austrian, 18th century.
Born 1726, in Imst; died 1770, in Innsbruck.
Sculptor.
After studying in Innsbruck, Feger travelled to Italy, spending many years in Rome. He returned to settle in Innsbruck, where he sculpted stone, wood and ivory. St John's Church in Innsbruck has a high altar that he executed with Peter Trolf, as well as a crucifix and several statues of saints sculpted in wood. The Ferdinandeum museum in Innsbruck has four small statuettes by Feger of travelling musicians in ivory and wood, while the cathedral in Bressanone has some ornamental works.

FEGHALI, Louis
Lebanese, 20th - 21st century.
Born 18 May 1949, in Biblos.
Painter, illustrator. Religious subjects.
He obtained his degree at the Beirut school of fine arts, where he taught from 1980 to 1983 in the architecture, decorative arts and graphics departments.

He has taken part in regular group exhibitions, since 1972 in Beirut, 1975 in Florence and 1985 in Paris, notably at the Salon d'automne. He has had solo exhibitions in Beirut. A number of his paintings are inspired by or pay homage to the work of El Greco. He illustrated the great book of the *Epic of Lebanese Emigration*, in 1979.

FEGRETIN, Pierre
French, 16th century.
Active in Paris.
Painter.

FEHDMER, Richard
German, 19th - 20th century.
Born 14 December 1860, in Königsberg (now Kaliningrad, Russia).
Painter. Landscapes.
Fehdmer studied at the academies in Düsseldorf and Antwerp, and was also a pupil of J. Van Luppen. He settled in Antwerp. He took part in the *Jubilee Exhibition* in Vienna in 1888, the Exhibition at the Glaspalast in Munich in 1900, the Grosse Berliner Kunstausstellung in Berlin in 1893 and in exhibitions of watercolours in Dresden in 1909, 1911 and 1913.
MUSEUMS AND GALLERIES:
AARAU (Aargauer Kunsthaus): *Two Landscapes* (watercolours) - BAUTZEN (Stadtmus.) - BERLIN (Nationalgal.) - KREFELD: *A Winter Landscape*.
AUCTION RECORDS:
LONDON, 26 Nov 1986, *The Return One Winter's Evening* (1889, oil on canvas, 26 1/2 x 37 1/2 ins / 67 x 95 cm) GBP 5,000. AMSTERDAM, 21 April 1994, *Elegant Skaters on a Frozen Lake Bordering a Forest* (1895, oil on canvas, 29 1/4 x 22 ins / 74 x 56 cm) NLG 3,450.

FEHER, Ennery Alexander
Hungarian, 20th century.
Born in Budapest.
Painter.
Ennery Feher was a student of Cormon and a member of the Salon des Artistes Français, where he first exhibited in 1923.

FEHER, Georges
Hungarian, 20th century.
Born 22 January 1929, in Miskolc.
Active in France from 1954.
Painter, illustrator.
Geoges Feher studied at the school of fine art in Budapest from 1946 to 1949. He travelled in Europe then settled in France. His paintings normally represent everyday objects and fruit, occasionally integrated in sequences in the same picture. He also practised lithography and illustrated texts by St-Exupery and Verlaine including *Sagesse* and *Jadis et Naguère*.

Feher participated in several collective exhibitions including: *Huit peintres de trente ans* (*Eight Thirty-year-old Painters*), Galerie Pierre Loeb, Paris (1959); Galerie de Seine, Paris (1960); Morgan Knotte Gallery, Dallas (from 1961); Salon d'Automne, (1967); for the *International Figurative Exhibition*, Tokyo (1968). Solo exhibitions include: Galerie de Seine,

Paris (1959); Falerie J.-C. Bellier, Paris (1965),; Tokyo (1968); Osaka (1973); Galerie Anne Colin, Paris (1973 and 1979); Galerie Corianne, Paris (1988); Concarneau (1990); Galerie Claude Hémery, Paris (1991); Dinan (1993).

Feher

Auction records:
Brussels, 27 Oct 1976, *Seascape* (oil on canvas, 28¼ x 20¾ ins / 72 x 53 cm) BEF 16,000. Paris, 30 May 1990, *Yellow Ochre Composition* (1955, oil on canvas, 25½ x 39¼ ins / 65 x 100 cm) FRF 5,000.

FEHER, Laszlo

Hungarian, 20th - 21st century.
Born 1953, in Székesfehérvár.
Painter. Scenes with figures.

Laszlo Feher won a Derkovits Scholarship and studied at the school of fine arts in Budapest. He is a representative of the 'New Sensitivity' movement and a member of a group that regularly exhibits at the Feszek Gallery. His work is represented in the Ludwig Collections in Germany. He builds up his poetic compositions through the application of wide areas of flat synthetic paints in contrasting colours. As he is a recognised artist, the Hungarian state has devoted several major exhibitions to his work, notably at the Kunsthalle in Budapest in 1988. He also exhibited at the museum in Graz in the same year.

Auction records:
Paris, 14 Oct 1991, *Fête* (1991, oil on canvas, 47¼ x 35½ ins / 120 x 90 cm) FRF 20,000. Budapest, 7 Dec 2001, *On the Bridge* (oil on canvas, 28 x 39 ins / 70 x 100 cm) HUF 700,000.

FEHLING, Carl Heinrich Jacob

German, 18th century.
Born 1683, in Dresden; died December 1753, in Meissen.
Painter, architect.

The son of H.C. Fehling, Carl Fehling taught at the school of drawing at the Meissen porcelain factory. His drawings and the engravings he made from them were held in the Dresden print collection.

FEHLING, Heinrich Christoph

German, 17th - 18th century.
Born 1657, in Sangerhausen; died 1725, in Dresden.
Painter.

A pupil of Samuel Bottschild, Heinrich Fehling worked for many years in Italy, before becoming director of the academy of art in Dresden, where he also painted many ceilings in the residential palace.

H Fehling.

Museums and Galleries:
Berlin: *Portrait of Colonel W. Caspar von Klengel* - Wroclaw (Miejska Biblioteka): *Study of Children* (drawing); *Study of a Head* (drawing); *Male Nude* (drawing); *Tree Study* (drawing).

FEHLING, Ilise

German, 20th century.
Born 1896, in Danzig (now Gdansk, Poland); died 1982.
Painter, sculptor. Stage sets.

Ilise Fehling studied at the Reimannschule and the Kunstgewerbeschule in Berlin from 1918 to 1921, continuing her studies in the theatre department at the Bauhaus from 1921 to 1923. She worked successively in Berlin, Munich and Hamburg, from 1925 to 1943. From 1950, back in Munich, she was a teacher in the Volkshochschule.

Bibliography:
Leymarie, Jean/Herzogenrath, Wulf/Grote, Ludwig/Gropius, Walter, *Le Bauhaus*, exhibition catalogue, Württembergischer Kunsteverein, Stuttgart, Musée national d'Art moderne, Paris, 1969.

Auction records:
Munich, 2 June 1987, *Head of Elisabeth Bergner* (1931, bronze, h. 12¾ ins / 32.5 cm) DEM 4,300.

FEHLING, Julius

German, 19th century.
Born 29 July 1869, in Mariendorf, near Berlin.
Painter.

After studying at the academy of art in Berlin, Julius Fehling went on to become a pupil of Marr and Zügel in Munich. He worked in Berlin, where from 1887 he regularly featured in the Grosse Kunstausstellung, showing genre paintings such as *The Nun* and *In Front of the Mirror*, although he showed mainly portraits. He occasionally exhibited at the Glaspalast in Munich.

FEHLING, Zacharias

German, 17th - 18th century.
Born c. 1658; died 9 September 1743, in Dresden.
Painter.

B. Cratz engraved two *Views of Ruins* painted by Zacharias Fehling, who worked in Dresden.

FEHR

German, 18th century.
Watercolourist, draughtsman.

Fehr painted a watercolour portrait of *Sir Ralph Woodford* in a landscape, which is now in a collection in Hamburg.

FEHR

German, 19th century.
Painter (porcelain).

A painter at a porcelain factory, he showed vases, plates and other porcelain objects, painted with figures or portraits, at the Berlin exhibitions.

FEHR, Charles de

French, 18th century.
Died 1774.
Active in Denmark.
Engraver.

Charles de Fehr is mentioned by Nagler.

FEHR, F.

German, 19th century.
Lithographer.

F. Fehr made six plates of flower drawings, which Major L. von Reiche had published in his lithograph workshop in Berlin around 1817. He is possibly identical with Friedrich Fehr.

FEHR, Friedrich

German, 19th century.
Born 24 May 1862, in Werneck (Bavaria).
Painter, engraver. Genre scenes, landscapes.

Friedrich Fehr worked in Karlsruhe, Italy and Munich, and produced many lithographs.

Museums and Galleries:
Karlsruhe: *Twilight* - Mannheim: *Woman Playing the Lute* - Mulhouse: *The Presbytery* - Munich: *End of the Working Day*.

Auction records:
London, 18 Feb 1984, *Two Fashionable Young Women* (1901, oil on card, 18½ x 12in/47 x 30.5cm) GBP 800. New York, 1 Nov 1995, *Choosing the Wedding Dress* (oil on canvas, 46½ x 35in/118.1 x 88.9cm) USD 12,650.

FEHR, Georg Konrad

Swiss, 19th century.
Born 19 June 1784, in St Gall; died 10 August 1844, in St Gall.

Draughtsman. Hunting scenes, natural history (animals).

A pupil of G.L. and Wilhelm Hartmann, Georg Fehr lived for a time in Lyons and dabbled in painting hunting scenes and wild animals. He left his natural history collection to the town of St Gall.

FEHR, Henri

Swiss, 20th century.

Born 1890, in Geneva; died 1974, in Geneva.

Painter. Figures, nudes, portraits.

Henri Fehr mainly painted female figures.

MUSEUMS AND GALLERIES:

LA CHAUX-DE-FONDS (MBA).

AUCTION RECORDS:

ZURICH, 30 Oct 1982, *Vase of Flowers* (oil on canvas, 25 1/2 x 22 1/2 ins / 65 x 57 cm) CHF 1,500. BERN, 26 Oct 1984, *Reverie* (pastel, 25 1/4 x 19 1/4 ins / 64 x 49 cm) CHF 1,200. GENEVA, 24 Nov 1985, *Portrait of an Elegant Woman* (oil/hardboard, 25 1/4 x 19 ins / 64 x 48 cm) CHF 2,600. BERN, 2 May 1986, *Portrait of a Woman with a Large Hat* (c. 1930, oil on canvas, 49 1/2 x 37 1/2 ins / 126 x 95 cm) CHF 8,000. BERN, 30 April 1988, *Seated Nude Young Woman* (oil on canvas, 28 3/4 x 23 1/2 ins / 73 x 60 cm) CHF 3,100. BERN, 26 Oct 1988, *Girl in the Garden* (oil/plywood, 19 3/4 x 27 1/2 ins / 50 x 70 cm) CHF 2,000. BERN, 9 Nov 2001, *Standing Female Nude* (oil on canvas, 29 x 21 ins / 73 x 54 cm) CHF 3,000. ZURICH, 11 Dec 2001, *Sitting Lady in Profile* (oil on canvas, 25 x 21 ins / 64 x 53 cm) CHF 3,000. BERN, 16 May 2002, *Young Woman at her Toilette* (oil on canvas, 26 x 21 ins / 65 x 54 cm) CHF 2,600. BERN, 8 Nov 2002, *Young Ballerina at her Make-up* (oil on canvas, 36 x 28 ins / 91 x 72 cm) CHF 2,600.

FEHR, Henry Charles

British, 19th - 20th century.

Born 4 November 1867; died 13 May 1940, in London.

Sculptor, designer. Portraits. Busts, monuments.

Henry Fehr exhibited at the Royal Academy from 1887. He produced many memorials, including one of Queen Victoria in Hull, and monuments to the fallen. He also produced a decorative piece for Cardiff Town Hall. In 1898 he created a coloured low relief frieze showing scenes from the War of the Roses for Wakefield County Hall.

MUSEUMS AND GALLERIES:

BRADFORD (Cartwright Hall AG): *Dr Edmund Cartwright; Lord Masham* - LONDON (Tate Collection): *The Rescue of Andromeda* (1893, bronze).

AUCTION RECORDS:

LONDON, 2 Oct 1985, *Young Girl Blown by a Sea Breeze* (brown-patinated bronze, h. 31 1/2 ins / 80 cm) GBP 3,200.

FEHR, Julius

German, 19th century.

Born c. 1860, in Grosseicholzheim; died 1900, in Mannheim.

Painter, draughtsman. Portraits, landscapes.

Julius Fehr studied in Karlsruhe before settling in Mannheim, where he ran a painting school. Some of his portraits and landscapes are in private collections in Mannheim.

FEHR, Karl Friedrich Bartholomaus

Swiss, 19th century.

Active in St Gall.

Draughtsman, watercolourist.

Karl Fehr taught drawing in Lyons and at St Gall, where he exhibited in 1834 and 1841. He travelled to Algiers.

FEHR, Konrad

German, 19th century.

Born 19 November 1854, in Toftlund, near Hadersleben.

Painter. Portraits, genre scenes.

Konrad Fehr studied at the academy of art in Munich under Benczur, Gabb, A. Wagner and Löfftz, before going on to teach at the drawing school of the circle of women artists in Berlin. He was awarded a bronze medal in London in 1884. He is best known for his *Bedroom Interior* and his *Portrait of Minister Maybach*.

MUSEUMS AND GALLERIES:

COLOGNE (Wallraf-Richartz Mus.): *Vampire* - KIEL: *Portrait of Councillor Forchhammer* - OSNABRÜCK: *Choir* - ROSTOCK: *The Dunes on Sylt*.

FEHR, Ludwig

Norwegian, 19th century.

Born in Germany.

Active in Christiania (now Oslo).

Lithographer.

Ludwig Fehr studied in Copenhagen. In 1821 he founded a lithography workshop in Christiania, where he produced a large number of portraits and city landscapes.

FEHR, Pieter

German, 18th century.

Born 1681; died 1740.

Active in Frankfurt am Main.

Engraver.

Pieter Fehr illustrated various works.

FEHRENBACH, Eduard Ludwig

German, 19th century.

Born 1855, in Villingen (Baden-Württemberg); died 24 January 1886, in Munich.

Draughtsman.

Fehrenbach worked in Munich for illustrated magazines and for editors such as Alphons Dürr, Lipperheide, Braun and Schneider. His best-known works are: *In the Fields and Plains; From Home and School; All Sorts of Bright and Cheerful Things; Springtime; Child's Life; Returning Home; The Four Seasons; Some Cheer during the Hard Winter; At the Carnival* and the booklet, *All Sorts of Images in Black* in collaboration with Henri Braun and Karl Fröhlich, with verses by Heinrich Seidel.

FEHRENBACH, Gerson

German, 20th century.

Born 18 February 1932, in Villingen (Black Forest).

Sculptor.

Fehrenbach studied in the studio of Karl Hartung, at the Hochschule für Bildenden Künste in Berlin. In 1959 he exhibited at the Symposium of European Sculptors in Berlin. He most often executes his sculptures in bronze, but also works in stone and cement. His sculptures are monumental, with robust shapes, which sometimes evoke natural formations, and sometimes recall human forms. He subsequently took part in group exhibitions, notably *German Sculpture in the 20th century* (1964), at the Musée Rodin in Paris, and *Documenta III* in Kassel. He held solo exhibitions in 1961 in Frankfurt and in 1963 in Berlin. He was awarded a prize at the Berlin Exhibition, and in 1962 received the Villa Romana Prize in Florence.

MUSEUMS AND GALLERIES:

DARMSTADT (Hessisches Landesmus.) - KASSEL (Staatliche Kunstsammlungen).

FEHRENBACH, Lucy

French, 19th century.

Born 19th century, in Paris.

Painter.

Fehrenbach was a pupil of Mme Chéron. She exhibited miniature portraits at the Salon from 1875 to 1880.

FEHRENBERG, Hans

German, 19th century.

Born 2 November 1868, in Kassel; died 1902, near Bremen.

Painter. Landscapes.

MUSEUMS AND GALLERIES:
KASSEL: *Forest Landscape*.
AUCTION RECORDS:
VIENNA, 14 Sept 1982, *Spring Landscape* (1893, oil on canvas, 26 x 18 1/2in/66 x 47cm) ATS 12,000.

FEHRLE, Wilhelm Jakob
German, 20th century.
Born 27 November 1884, in Schwäbisch-Gmünd; died 1974.
Sculptor. Figures, animals.

Fehrle was a student at the academies in Berlin and Munich. He spent time in Rome and Paris, and showed bronze animal sculptures at the Grosse Berliner Kunstausstellung in Berlin in 1907 and 1908. In 1913, in Stuttgart and Paris, he exhibited wooden sculptures of *The Virgin* and *St Mary Magdalene*.

AUCTION RECORDS:
HEIDELBERG, 8 April 1995, *Seated Female Nude* (wash and charcoal, 17 1/4 x 14 1/4 ins / 44 x 36 cm) DEM 1,500. STUTTGART, 30 Jan 1999, *Yvonne* (bronze) DEM 4,000. STUTTGART, 24 April 1999, *Female Nude Emerging from Bath* (1946, terracotta, h. 20 ins / 52 cm) DEM 6,500. STUTTGART, 14 April 2000, *Head of White Woman* (1912, plaster, h. 13 ins / 33 cm) DEM 5,300. STUTTGART, 20 Oct 2000, *Seated Female Nude* (brown patinated bronze, h. 9 ins / 22 cm) DEM 5,300. STUTTGART, 18 Oct 2002, *Female Nude Wearing Cape* (brown and green patinated bronze, h. 29 ins / 73 cm) EUR 3,500. LINDAU, 6 Dec 2002, *Standing Female Figure* (bronze, h. 19 ins / 47 cm) EUR 1,600. STUTTGART, 27 Sept 2003, *Nude Woman Stepping into Bath* (1922, brown patinated bronze, h. 14 ins / 35 cm) EUR 2,400. HAMBURG, 24 Oct 2003, *Standing Female Figure* (dark patinated bronze, 11 x 3x2 ins / 27 x 7x6 cm) EUR 2,500. STUTTGART, 30 April 2004, *The Four Seasons* (clay, 47 x 28 ins / 120 x 70 cm) EUR 19,000. LINDAU, 23 Sept 2004, *Lion* (bronze, 6 x 11 ins / 16 x 28 cm) EUR 2,900.

FEHRMANN, A.
German, 19th century.
Active in Hamburg.
Lithographer.

A. Fehrmann set up a lithography workshop that published popular works.

FEHRMANN, Jacob
German, 19th century.
Baptised 27 January 1760 in Bremen; died 27 August 1837, in Bremen.
Painter, engraver.

Jacob Fehrmann studied in Copenhagen and Kassel, where he apparently settled around 1788, and produced a large number of portraits and history paintings. These included *The Conversion of Villehad*, which won him a gold medal. His engraved works include an etching after Tischbein and his self-portrait.
MUSEUMS AND GALLERIES:
BREMEN (Kunsthalle) - BREMEN (StadtBibliothek).

FEHRT, A.J. de
Engraver (burin).

He engraved *Portraits*, in particular for the Odieuvre Collection, and *Genre subjects*.

FEHRT, Carl de
French, 18th century.
Died 1774, in Norway.
Engraver.

FEI, Alessandro di Vincenzio, also known as Alessandro del Barbiere
Italian, 16th century.
Born 1543, in Florence; died 1592, in Florence.
Painter, fresco artist. History painting, religious subjects.
Florentine School.

The pupil of Ridolfo del Ghirlandaio, Pier Francesco di Jacopo Foschi and Maso da San Frediano, Alessandro di Vincenzio Fei carried out a number of large works in fresco, also handling their architectural context. He was noted for adding constructions and grotesque figures.
MUSEUMS AND GALLERIES:
FLORENCE (Church of S Croce): *The Flagellation*.
AUCTION RECORDS:
PARIS, 9 April 1990, *Beheading of St John the Baptist* (oil on canvas, 30 1/2 x 21 ins / 77.5 x 53.5 cm) FRF 130,000.

FEI, Paolo. See **PAOLO DI GIOVANNI FEI**

FEI CHENG, or Fei Ch'eng
Chinese, 16th - 17th century.
Active at the end of the Ming dynasty (1368-1644).
Painter.

Fei Cheng is mentioned as a landscape painter in the *Tuian xinshanglu*.

FEI CHENGWU, or Fei Ch'eng-wu
Chinese, 20th century.
Active in England.
Painter. Architectural views.

Fei Chengwu studied at National Central University, Nanjing. He went to England in 1947 and settled in London, where he made a living as a *guohua painter*.
AUCTION RECORDS:
TAIPEI, 18 April 1993, *Canterbury Cathedral* (1947, oil on card, 20 x 15 1/4 ins / 51 x 38.6 cm) NT$ 195,500.

FEI DANXU, or Fei Tan-hsü, style name: Yutiao, sobriquets: Xiaolou, Huanqi, Huanxisheng, Zitiao
Chinese, 19th century.
Born 1801 or 1802, in Wucheng (Zhejiang); died 1850.
Painter. Portraits, landscapes, flowers.

Although a gifted painter of landscapes, flowers and plants, Fei Danxu is known above all for his portraits of scholars and beautiful women, whose beauty and grace he conveys with meticulous detail. His technique influenced the painters of women's portraits at the end of the 19th century. We know of several signed works by him.
MUSEUMS AND GALLERIES:
PARIS (Mus. National des Arts asiatiques-Guimet): *Young Woman Dancing in Water* (ink and colour on paper, hanging scroll, inscription dated 1833).
AUCTION RECORDS:
NEW YORK, 4 Dec 1989, *Young Woman Walking by Moonlight* (ink and colour on paper, hanging scroll, 38 1/2 x 11 1/4 ins / 98 x 28.5 cm) USD 990. NEW YORK, 31 May 1994, *Reading by Evening* (ink and colour on paper, hanging scroll, 46 x 18 1/2 ins / 116.8 x 47 cm) USD 3,450. NEW YORK, 21 March 1995, *Woman and Children in Interior* (ink and colour on silk, hanging scroll, 32 3/4 x 13 3/4 ins / 83.5 x 35.2 cm) USD 2,415. HONG KONG, 4 May 1995, *Gathering of Scholars at Yu Shan* (1848, ink on paper, hanging scroll, 11 3/4 x 51 1/2 ins / 30 x 130.8 cm) HKD 48,300.

FEI ERQI, or Fei Erh-ch'i, style name: Gepo
Chinese, 18th century.
Born in Hangzhou (Zhejiang).
Active c. 1700.
Painter.

Fei Erqi painted flowers and birds in the style of the Southern Tang master Xu Xi (died before 975). He also painted landscapes.

FEI MINGJIE, pseudonym: Ming Fay
Chinese, 20th - 21st century.

Born 1949, in Shanghai.
Sculptor.

Ming Fay was from an artistic family. He began his studies in Hong Kong in 1961 and went on to continue in the USA, studying design at Ohio State University, Columbus, and sculpture at the University of California at Santa Barbara and the Kansas Institute of Art. After briefly returning to Hong Kong, he finally settled in New York. Since 1971, his series of realistic bronze sculptures, representing fruit and vegetables and arranged on trompe-l'œil backgrounds, make up the bulk of his work.

AUCTION RECORDS:

TAIPEI, 22 March 1992, *A Pear* (1990, bronze, h. 19 ins / 48.2 cm, diam. 9 ins/22.8 cm) NT$ 308,000.

FEI TAN-HIU. See **FEI DANXU**

FEI TCH'ENG. See **FEI CHENG**

FEI TCH'ENG-WU. See **FEI CHENGWU**

FEIBUSCH, Hans Nathan

German, 20th century.
Born 15 August 1898, in Frankfurt am Main; died 17 June 1998, in London.
Painter. Religious subjects, figures. Murals.

Feibusch began by studying medicine in Munich, but in 1920, he moved to Berlin to attend the courses of the Hochschule für Bildenden Künste under the direction of Carl Hofer. In 1923, he completed his training in Paris with André Lhote, then returned to Frankfurt in 1925. Excluded as a Jew from the Frankfurter Künstlerbund (Association of Frankfurt Artists) in 1933, he went into exile in London where he became a member of the London Group. He took British nationality in 1941. He was the author, in 1946, of an important work: *Mural Painting*. He became a well known painter of church murals.

Feibusch featured in Paris in 1925 at the Salon des Indépendants and exhibited at the Sezession in Berlin. In 1937, one of his works was displayed at the exhibition of 'degenerate art' organised by the Nazis. He was represented in 2001 at the exhibition *Verfemt. Vergessen. Wiederentdeckt. Schicksale expressiver Bildkunst im 20. Jahrhundert* (*Condemned. Forgotten. Rediscovered. The Fate of Expressive Art in the 20th century*), an exhibition at the Kulturgeschichtiches Museum, Osnabrück, setting out to rediscover a generation of German and Austrian artists who appeared in the 1920s and 1930s, but who were subjected to the cultural and political repression of the Nazis and were forgotten after the War. A solo exhibition was devoted to him in Frankfurt in 1986.

BIBLIOGRAPHY:

Rücker, Rita/Feibusch, Hans, *Hans Feibusch: ein Frankfurter Maler*, exhibition catalogue, Histor. Museum, Frankfurt, 1986. Henzel, Rita, *Hans Feibusch: Biographie und Werk*, 1996. *Verfemt. Vergessen. Wiederentdeckt. Schicksale expressiver Bildkunst im 20. Jahrhundert. Sammlung Gerhard Schneider*, exhibition catalogue, Kulturgeschichtiches Museum, Osnabrück, 2001.

AUCTION RECORDS:

MUNICH, 30 June 1982, *The Drum* (oil on canvas, 41 1/4 x 28 1/4 ins / 105 x 72 cm) DEM 5,300. LONDON, 10 Sept 2003, *Architects prefer Shell* (gouache on card, 15 x 22 ins / 39 x 55 cm) GBP 1,500. BERLIN, 29 Nov 2003, *Telephone Kiosk* (oil on canvas, 28 x 34 ins / 71 x 86 cm) EUR 7,500.

FEICHTINGER, Angela, Married name Astuto-Palli

Hungarian, 19th - 20th century.
Active in Budapest.
Painter.

FEICHTINGER, Carl

Austrian, 19th century.
Born 1 November 1838, in Stubenberg (Styria); died 15 January 1877, in Wiltern.
Sculptor.

A pupil of Gschiel in Graz, Carl Feichtinger worked in Vienna, Munich and Wiltern. His statue of *St Joseph* is in Graz, as is a sculpture at a small altar exhibited in 1865.

FEICHTINGER, Joseph

German, 18th century.
Born 1765, in Altenmarkt.
Painter.

Joseph Feichtinger worked in Erding (Bavaria), Germany.

FEICHTINGER, Jozsef

Hungarian, 19th century.
Born 1840, in Budapest; died 28 December 1907, in Budapest.
Painter.

Jozsef Feichtinger studied under K. Lotz, and then at the school of industrial arts in Budapest. He painted watercolours of architectural subjects, including *The Interior of Pécs Cathedral*.

FEICHTMAYR, Franz Joseph

German, 17th century.
Born to a family originally from Schongau.
Active during the second half of the 17th century.
Sculptor (wood).

In 1687, together with Johann Michael Feichtmayr, Franz Feichtmayr produced 23 statues of saints for Abbot Augustin of Einsiedeln, most of which are still to be found in the choir of the church.

FEICHTMAYR, Johann Michael

German, 17th century.
Born to a family originally from Schongau (Bavaria).
Active in Einsiedeln.
Sculptor (wood).

Johann Feichtmayr collaborated with F.J. Feichtmayr on the wooden statues for Abbot Augustin of Einsiedeln.

FEICHTMAYR, Joseph Anton, or Feuchtmayer

German, 18th century.
Born 1696, in Linz, near Pfullendorf; died 2 January 1770, in Mimmenhausen.
Sculptor, draughtsman.

Joseph Feichtmayr studied in Schongau and Salmansweiler, before working for the churches in Weingarten, St Gall and Salmansweiler. He also spent time in Solothurn and Einsiedeln.

Feichtmayr's most important works were his sculptures on the east façade of the cathedral of St Gall, as well as the seats and balustrades of the choir. He directed all the decorative works for the church at Birnau, which were carried out in a Mannerist style with a flowing, dancing movement. Feichtmayr was also a stucco worker.

AUCTION RECORDS:

MUNICH, 4 June 1981, *Library Plan* (1755, pen and wash, 14 1/4 x 20 1/4in/36 x 51.5cm) DEM 8,500.

FEID, Joseph

Austrian, 19th century.
Born 21 February 1806, in Vienna; died 8 April 1870, in Weidling near Vienna.
Painter. Landscapes with figures, landscapes.

Feid was a talented painter of rural and forest scenes.

MUSEUMS AND GALLERIES:

VIENNA (Gal.): *Nymphs Bathing; Landscape with Approaching Storm.*

AUCTION RECORDS:

VIENNA, 12 Dec 1978, *Wooded Landscape with Figures* (1867, oil on panel, 28 1/4 x 36in/71.5 x 90.5cm) ATS 160,000. VIEN-

NA, 15 Sept 1981, *Viennese Forest Landscape* (oil on paper, 12 1/2 x 19in/32 x 48cm) ATS 80,000. HEIDELBERG, 15 Oct 1984, *View of Halstatt* (1858, oil on card, 16 1/4 x 21 1/2in/41 x 54.5cm) DEM 16,500. NEW YORK, 26 Feb 1986, *Livestock in an Alpine Landscape* (1849, oil on panel, 18 x 22 3/4in/46 x 58.1cm) USD 11,500. HEIDELBERG, 9 Oct 1992, *Landscape with Two Cows* (1845, oil on card, 6 1/2 x 5in/16.5 x 12.6cm) DEM 2,800. VIENNA, 2 Dec 1999, *Summer Landscape with Woman and Son on Path* (1833, oil on canvas, 16 x 20 ins / 40 x 50 cm) ATS 50,000. DÜSSELDORF, 31 Jan 2000, *Wooded Landscape with Shepherds and Cows* (oil on canvas, 18 x 22 ins / 46 x 57 cm) DEM 14,000. VIENNA, 23 May 2000, *Extensive Mountain Landscape with Figures* (1850, oil on panel, 18 x 25 ins / 46 x 64 cm) ATS 35,000. VIENNA, 29 Nov 2001, *Fishing Hut by Worther See, Karnten* (oil on panel, 18 x 24 ins / 46 x 60 cm) ATS 250,000. VIENNA, 28 Nov 2002, *Landscape with Deer on the Ford* (1832, oil on canvas, 30 x 37 ins / 76 x 94 cm) EUR 5,000. VIENNA, 16 June 2003, *Wooded Landscape* (1859, oil on canvas, 41 x 55 ins / 103 x 139 cm) EUR 5,000. VIENNA, 16 June 2003, *Cows in Meadow* (1852, oil on panel, 17 x 22 ins / 44 x 55 cm) EUR 5,500.

FEIDE, H.
German, 16th century.
Active c. 1570.
Engraver.

Two portrait engravings are known by this artist. One shows *Elector Joachim II of Brandenburg in Military Uniform*, while the other is of the same subject but in ceremonial dress.

FEIDE, Hans Peter
German, 17th century.
Active in Breslau (now Wroclaw, Poland).
Painter.

FEIDEAU, Ambroise
17th century.
Painter, sculptor.

Cited by Marolles.

FEIEREISEN, Marie Paule
Luxembourg, 20th - 21st century.
Born 1955, in Luxembourg.
Active in France.
Painter.

Feiereisen studied fine arts at the Université de la Sorbonne, then attended the École Nationale des Beaux-Arts. She produces work which represents reality through symbols: geometric figures, imaginary plans, coupled with allusions to human feelings.

She has participated in group exhibitions, including: 1977-1989, Salon du Cercle Artistique, Luxembourg; 1982, *Trente Artistes Luxembourgeois* (*30 Artists from Luxembourg*) and *La Femme dans la Peinture Luxembourgeoise* (*Women in Luxembourg Painting*), the Villa Vaubon, Luxembourg; 1983, *L'Autoportrait* (*The Self-portrait*), the Musée des Beaux-Arts, Pau; 1986, the Painting Festival, Ostend; 1987, the Cité Internationale des Arts, Paris; 1988, *Quarante Artistes Luxembourgeois* (*40 Artists from Luxembourg*), the town hall, Cologne; 1988, *12 Peintres Européens* (*12 European Painters*), the Musée de Roubaix; 1989, *150e Anniversaire de l'Indépendance du Grand Duché de Luxembourg* (*150th Anniversary of the Independence of the Grand Duchy of Luxembourg*), the Cercle Municipal, Luxembourg. Feiereisen has held solo shows: 1984, the Centre Culturel Français, Luxembourg; 1987 and 1989, the Galerie Beaumont, Luxembourg.

BIBLIOGRAPHY:
Acquisitions 1989, Fonds National d'Art Contemporain, Paris, 1989.

MUSEUMS AND GALLERIES:
PARIS (FNAC).

FEIGE, Johann Christian, the Elder
German, 18th century.
Born 4 February 1689, in Zeitz; died 11 February 1751, in Dresden.
Sculptor.

Johann Christian Feige the Elder became a burgher of Dresden in 1728. His principal work is an altar in the church of Our Lady in Dresden, on which he worked for six years. He also made the pulpit for the church of Radeberg, together with the pulpit, baptismal fonts and lectern for the church in Plauen, near Dresden. He held the title of 'court sculptor'.

FEIGE, Johann Christian, the Younger
German, 18th century.
Born 1720, in Dresden; died 26 October 1788, in Dresden.
Sculptor.

The elder son of J.C. Feige the Elder, Johann Christian Feige the Younger produced sculptures for the church of the Crucifixion in Dresden and for the *Landtag* (state parliament) building. He also carried out the sculpted decorations of one room in Stösitz castle, together with many gravestone monuments.

FEIGE, Johann Ferdinand, the Elder
German, 18th century.
Born 12 July 1733, in Dresden; died 13 May 1783, in Dresden.
Sculptor.

The younger son of Johann Christian Feige the Elder, Johann Ferdinand Feige the Elder was probably also his pupil. Much younger than his brother, Johann Christian Feige the Younger, he worked under his direction in Helle, near Pirna, and in Dresden. He is best known for a golden lion that used to adorn a Dresden pharmacy.

FEIGE, Johann Ferdinand, the Younger
German, 18th - 19th century.
Born 25 November 1766, near Pirna (Saxony); died 16 April 1827, in Dresden.
Sculptor.

Johann Ferdinand Feige the Younger was initially a pupil of his father, J.F. Feige the Elder, before going on to study at the academy of art in Dresden. He became a burgher of Dresden in 1800. He is responsible for the black Saxon marble and white Carrara marble baptismal fonts in the church of the Crucifixion in Munich. He also made gravestone monuments.

FEIGE, Johann Friedrich
German, 18th century.
Born 9 September 1728, in Dresden; died 19 April 1788, in Dresden.
Sculptor.

Johann Friedrich Feige was the third son and a pupil of J.C. Feige the Elder. He went on to work in the court at Zerbst (Saxony-Anhalt), Germany, and at the small academy of art there, before settling in Dresden. He produced the memorial to the actress C. Neuber.

FEIGEL, Johann, or Feigl
German, 18th century.
Active in Vienna until 1775.
Engraver (burin).

A pupil of Schmutzer and Wille, Feigel is best known for a plate after G. Dou, dated 1776: *Old Woman Washing a Small Boy's Head*. Other works that should be mentioned include six plates for *The Cries of Vienna*, after Ch. Brand (1775), *Washerwoman* and *Young Girl wearing a Blouse Looking for Fleas* after Bolognini, and two pendants after Freudenberger.

FEIGL, Anton, or Veigl
Austrian, 18th century.
Active in Vienna.
Sculptor.

Anton Feigl was possibly the brother of Franz Joseph Feigl.

FEIGL, Franz Joseph, or Veigl
Austrian, 18th century.
Born c. 1679, in Habern (Bohemia); died 7 May 1757.
Sculptor.

Franz Feigl was a pupil of S. de Caradea.

FEIGL, Johann Karl, or Veigl
Austrian, 18th century.
Born 1720, in Vienna; died 18 July 1770, in Gumpendorf.
Sculptor.

The son of Franz Joseph Feigl, Johann Feigl entered the university of Vienna in 1744 'pro cive academico', which earned him the title of 'university sculptor'.

FEIKS, Alfred
Slovene, 20th century.
Born 27 October 1880, in Brod; died 1953.
Painter.

Alfred Feiks studied in Munich, Paris and London. A painter, he was also an art critic for Hungarian newspapers.

FEIKS, Jeno
Hungarian, 20th century.
Born 1878, in Kaposvár.
Painter, draughtsman.

Jeno Feiks studied in Paris and Munich. A large number of his cartoons appeared in the weekly journals in Budapest.

FEILER, Max
17th - 18th century.
Painter.

There is a painting attributed to him, *Still-life with Fruit and Musical Instruments*, in the Wiesbaden Gallery, and two *Landscapes* in the Benedictine monastery in Melk (Lower Austria).

FEILER, Paul
British, 20th century.
Born 1918, in Frankfurt am Main, Germany.
Painter.

Paul Feiler studied at the Slade School. He became an art teacher and painted in a geometric abstract style. His first exhibition took place in London in 1953. He also exhibited at a group exhibition at the Tate Gallery, at the Institute of Contemporary Art, in the USA, in Australia and in China. A solo exhibition of his work was held at the Tate St Ives in 2005.

MUSEUMS AND GALLERIES:
BATH (Victoria AG) - CAMBRIDGE (Kettle's Yard, University of Cambridge) - CHICHESTER (University College): *Boats and Sea* (1952-1953, oil on canvas) - GLASGOW (AG and Mus.) - LONDON (Tate Collection): *Portheras Grey* (1959-1961, oil on canvas) - MANCHESTER (City AG) - PARIS (BNF) - TOLEDO (OH Mus. of Art) - TORONTO (AG) - WASHINGTON DC (Phillips Memorial Gal.) - WORCESTER (City Museum).

AUCTION RECORDS:
LONDON, 13 Nov 1985, *Green Table with Ocean Window* (oil on card, 33 3/4 x 39 ins / 86 x 99 cm) GBP 1,000. LONDON, 9 June 1988, *Atlantic Island* (oil on card, 21 x 29 1/2 ins / 52.5 x 75 cm) GBP 902. LONDON, 24 May 1990, *Intersected Ovals* (1963, oil on canvas, 36 1/4 x 36 1/4 ins / 92 x 92 cm) GBP 9,350. LONDON, 8 March 1991, *Small Orange Rocks III* (1953, oil on card, 9 1/4 x 12 ins / 23.5 x 30.5 cm) GBP 1,540. LONDON, 26 March 1993, *Godrevy Pink I* (1962, oil on card with gesso, 15 1/2 x 14 3/4 ins / 39.5 x 37.5 cm) GBP 1,495. LONDON, 25 Oct 1995, *Porthglaze* (1962, oil on canvas, 36 x 36 ins / 91.5 x 91.5 cm) GBP 2,875. LONDON, 28 April 1999, *Newlyn, August* (oil on board, 24 x 30 ins / 61 x 76 cm) GBP 3,200. LONDON, 4 Nov 1999, *Floating Form, White* (1963-1965, oil on canvas, 22 x 18 ins / 56 x 46 cm) GBP 4,400. LONDON, 21 Nov 2000, *Samphire Blue* (1958-1961, oil on board, 60 x 36 ins / 153 x 91 cm) GBP 8,500. LONDON, 24 Nov 2000, *Enclosed Verticals* (1964-1965, oil on canvas, 66 x 72 ins / 168 x 184 cm) GBP 14,000. LONDON, 8 June 2001, *Porth Eras White, 1961* (1961, oil on canvas, 40 x 24 ins / 102 x 61 cm) GBP 5,500. LONDON, 8 June 2001, *Broken Form, 1964* (1964, oil on canvas, 30 x 28 ins / 76 x 71 cm) GBP 7,500. LONDON, 4 Dec 2002, *Seawall* (1951, oil on canvas, 17 x 21 ins / 43 x 53 cm) GBP 9,000. LONDON, 16 Dec 2002, *Winter Coast, Cornwall* (1955, oil on board, 20 x 33 ins / 50 x 84 cm) GBP 12,000. LONDON, 4 June 2003, *Lamorna Harbour* (1952, oil on board, 26 x 30 ins / 66 x 76 cm) GBP 17,000. PENZANCE, 10 June 2003, *Morning Harbour, Mousehole* (1954, oil on board, 26 x 38 ins / 66 x 97 cm) GBP 20,000. LONDON, 11 March 2004, *Orbis L1* (1970, oil on canvas, 10 x 10 ins / 25 x 25 cm) GBP 4,000. LONDON, 2 June 2004, *Boskenna* (1962, oil on canvas, 16 x 16 ins / 40 x 40 cm) GBP 13,000.

FEILER, Thomas
Czech, 18th century.
Sculptor.

In 1765 Thomas Feiler produced the altarpiece of the church of the Virgin of Sorrows as well as a statue of *St Barbara* for the village church of Nemcic.

FEILHAMMER, Franz Anton
Moravian School, 19th century.
Born 30 March 1817, in Brno; died 14 February 1888, in Brno.
Painter, watercolourist. Landscapes, still-lifes, flowers.

Franz Anton Feilhammer produced a large number of watercolours and oil paintings of flowers and landscapes, as well as flowers painted on glass.

MUSEUMS AND GALLERIES:
BRNO (Moravská Gal.): *Flowers; November*.

AUCTION RECORDS:
VIENNA, 16 Feb 1982, *Stag in the Undergrowth* (1884, oil on canvas, 26 3/4 x 35 ins / 68 x 89 cm) ATS 8,000. LINDAU, 5 Oct 1984, *Still-life with Flowers* (1874, oil on canvas remounted on board, 8 1/4 x 11 1/2 ins / 21 x 29.5 cm) DEM 2,600. VIENNA, 13 June 2001, *Still-life of Flowers* (1876, oil on board, 12x11 ins / 30x27 cm) ATS 13,000. MUNICH, 4 July 2001, *Ruins in a Landscape* (oil on canvas, 31x25 ins / 80x63 cm) DEM 1,800.

FEILITZSCH-WOLFF, Benita (Baroness)
Latvian, 20th century.
Born in Hinzenberg.
Miniaturist.

Baroness Benita Feilitzsch-Wolff exhibited miniatures on ivory at the Salon de la Société Nationale from 1929 onwards.

FEILL, Joseph
German, 18th century.
Sculptor.

Feill worked with J.C. Schlaun in Münster and with J. Seiz in Trier. He lived in St Petersburg and in Osnabrück, where he executed the Hanover armorial bearings on the gable of the episcopal chancellery.

FEILLET, Hélène
French, 19th century.
Born 1812, in Paris; died 9 December 1889, in Biarritz.
Painter, lithographer. Historical subjects, local figures, portraits, landscapes, seascapes.

Hélène Feillet exhibited at the Paris Salon from 1836 to 1848. Works include *Portrait of Juana Cano, First Bolera at the Principo Theatre, Madrid, Spanish Woman at Church, Gypsy Woman, Arrival of the Duke and Duchess of Orléans at Bayonne* and *Lafayette boarding in 1777*.

FEILLET, Pierre Jacques
French, 19th century.
Born 16 December 1794, in Imeray (Eure-et-Loir); died 16 December 1855, in Biarritz.
Painter.

Pierre Feillet was a pupil of his father-in-law Pernotin and of Girodet. He sent a portrait of a woman to the Paris Salon in 1841. He was director of the academy of drawing in Bayonne.

FEILNER, Johann Everhard
German, 19th century.
Born 28 March 1802, in Cologne; died 27 May 1869, in Bremen.
Lithographer, painter.

Feilner produced some lithographs for J.W. Brever's *National Chronicle*. He is also best known for his plates, such as *The Correction House* and *Scene from the Bremen Flood of 1841*.

FEINBERG, Hirsch Bernarovich
Russian, 19th century.
Born 19th century, in Georgenburg.
Active and naturalised in France.
Sculptor.

His work appeared at the Salon des Artistes Français in 1893, where he received an honourable mention.

FEINGOLD, Ken
American, 20th - 21st century.
Born 1952.
Sculptor, video artist. Multimedia.

Ken Feingold took part in the 1995 Lyons Biennale, with an interactive sculpture entitled *Childhood/Hot and Cold Wars*.

FEININGER, Lyonel
American, 20th century.
Born 17 July 1871, in New York; died 31 July 1956, in New York.
Painter, watercolourist, engraver, illustrator, decorative designer.
Novembergruppe, Die Blauen Vier.

Lyonel Feininger was born of German immigrant parents. He initially studied music and gave violin recitals at the age of twelve. He studied composition and in 1887 went to Hamburg to continue his musical training. He also took an interest in decoration and entered the Hamburg school of decorative arts and then, until 1891, studied painting at the Berlin academy together with Hancke and Waldemar Freidrich. In 1892-1893 he spent some months in Paris, where he worked at the Académie Colarossi for six months. He went back to Berlin and from 1893 to 1906 contributed cartoons and satirical drawings to *Ulk, Lüstige Blätter, Narrenschiff* and the *Berliner Illustrierte Zeitung*. In Paris from 1906-1907 he continued to draw for papers such as *Témoin* and the *Chicago Sunday Tribune*. For the latter he drew humorous and poetic 'stories in pictures' (forerunners of strip cartoons): *Kin-der-Kids* (Éitions Pierre Horay) and *Wee Willie Winkie's World*. In 1906 he went to live in Weimar, then went to Paris again, where he met Pascin and Goetz. He returned yet again to Berlin, and it seems he began to paint again seriously in 1908, though it was not until 1911-1912 that he produced a significant work. He became friendly with Julia Berg, Pascin Iribe, and, most importantly, in 1911 he met Delaunay, whose influence was crucial for him, even though this is only evident in the appearance of his works, which were to remain inferior to Delaunay's; however, the meeting introduced him to Cubist painting. In 1912 he joined Die Brücke and met Schmidt-Rottluff. In 1913 Franz Marc invited him to exhibit at the first Berlin *Erbstsalon* (Autumn Salon) organised by the journal *Sturm* and he sent *Der Blaue Reiter* (*The Blue Rider*). In 1918 he rejoined the Novembergruppe. In 1919 Gropius invited him to teach at the Bauhaus in Weimar as head of the engraving workshop. It was he who made the woodcut of the Bauhaus manifesto of 1919, *Cathedral of the Future*. In 1924 he joined Kandinsky, Klee and Jawlensky to form Die Blauen Vier (The Blue Four), successors to the Blaue Reiter group, and exhibited with them in Dresden and Wiesbaden. His teaching at the Bauhaus did not continue for long; from 1925 he was professor without a chair, but he continued to live there and share its fate until it was closed by the Nazis in 1933. In the same year his works were included in the exhibition *Entartete Kunst* (*Degenerate Art*) that the Nazis sent all round Germany. In 1937 Feininger was able to leave Germany and he settled in the USA. In 1938 he taught first at a summer school at Mills College, Oakland, California. From 1939 he lived in New York. In 1945 he taught at a summer school at Black Mountain College, North Carolina, and in 1955 he was appointed Honorary Vice-President of the American Federations of Painters and Sculptors. In 1938 he painted murals for the New York World's Fair and for the Maine Transport Company.

During his first period, from 1908 to 1911, Feininger painted a series of 54 canvases, anecdotal in subject matter and bright in colour, depicting figures in movement and seen from above. The draughtmanship of these paintings betrays the cartoonist of earlier years. For a long time this series was unknown. In 1937 Feininger had to leave Germany to escape the Nazi persecution of non-academic artists, and he entrusted the paintings to his friend Herman Klump. When he got to New York he asked for the canvases to be sent to him, but they never arrived. Even after the war was over Klump, who lived in East Germany, refused to return them and claimed them as his own property. Feininger died in 1956, and, after much litigation, in 1976 the claims of Feininger's heirs were recognised, though another eight years of negotiation were needed between the East German Democratic Republic and the USA before the collection was sent to New York in 1984. The paintings, until then unseen, at first seemed surprising in their oddness, which contrasted with the coherence of his later work. He had used celebratory movement instead of the sombre colours he was to adopt later, and arabesques where he later used straight lines and right angles. It was about 1910 that Feininger found his own style. In complete contradiction to Analytical Cubism, one of the rules of which was that all the elements must be brought into the two-dimensional plane of the canvas, Feininger aimed at the opposite, even to the point of giving an illusion of space. Not only did he transpose all the solid forms into simple planes that overlapped each other like the facets of a crystal, he used the same procedure for empty spaces such as air and sky, perhaps basing this 'solidifying' of voids on the rays of the sun, which we sometimes see geometrically distributed in space: for example, inside a church, in a forest, in a street. Space and light soon become the only subject of his paintings; the solid elements, made transparent, dissolve in the fluidity of the air and create a poetic climate very special to his work -though one finds it sometimes, in a more virile form, in Delaunay (*Eiffel Towers, Window*) or Jacques Villon. From 1919 to 1924 he took for the subject of his paintings streets with Gothic buildings in the towns and villages around Weimar and Dessau. The cathedral and churches of Halle inspired some of his best canvases. His reconstruction of space by the solidification of voids fitted well the spirit of Gothic architecture, in which the invention of intersecting ribs enabled the building to be freed from the constraint of solid walls and opened it on all sides to rays of light that reconstructed a non-material space, but nevertheless clearly defined it. From 1939 he lived in New York, and the skyscrapers of Manhattan provided him with a theme for his reconstruction of space by light, reflected endlessly from wall to wall and from edge to edge. In the USA he rediscovered his earlier love of the sea and, often in watercolours, he painted its immensity and its changing aspects under different skies with transparent effects that evoked both veils of mist and the rays of the sun piercing the clouds.

Feininger's solo exhibitions include: 1917, the first, at the Der Sturm Gallery, Berlin; 1931, a retrospective, Nationalgalerie, Berlin; 1944, retrospective, Museum of Modern Art, New York; 1949-1950, Paris. Retrospectives since his death include: 1967, Museum of Modern Art, New York; 1968, University of Delaware, Newark; 1981, travelling exhibition in Germany; 1994, collection of works presented by the Galerie du Musée de la Seita, Paris; 1998, Neue Nationalgalerie, Berlin; 2003, *Lyonel Feininger. Human Portraits. An Unfamiliar World*, Kunsthalle, Hamburg.

Lyonel Feininger

Feininger

BIBLIOGRAPHY:

Klump, H., *Abstraktion in der Malerei: Kandinsky, Feininger, Klee*, Berlin, 1932. Muller, H.B., *Lyonel Feininger*, exhibition catalogue, Museum of Modern Art, New York, 1944. Hess, Hans, *Lyonel Feininger*, Kholhammer, Stuttgart, 1959. Ruhmer, E., *Lyonel Feininger, Zeichnungen, Aquarelle, Grafik*, Bruckmann, Munich, 1961. Feininger, T. Lux, *Lyonel Feininger: City at the Edge of the World*, Praeger, New York, 1965. Prass, L.E., *Lyonel Feininger. A Definitive Catalogue of his Graphic work*, Geb Mann, Berlin, 1972. Ness, J.L., *Lyonel Feininger*, A Lane, London, 1974. *Lyonel Feininger: Figurative Drawings, 1908-1912*, exhibition catalogue, Achim Moeller Fine Art, New York, 1990. Blackbeard, Bill (ed), *The Comic Strip Art of Lyonel Feininger*, Kitchen Sink Press, Northampton (MA), 1994. Barnett, Vivian Endicott/Helfenstein, Josef, *The Blue Four: Feininger, Jawlensky, Kandinsky, and Klee in the New World*, Yale University Press, London, 1998. *Lyonel Feininger. Menschenbilder. Eine Unbekannte Welt*, exhibition catalogue, Hamburger Kunsthalle, Hamburg, 2003.

MUSEUMS AND GALLERIES:

BASEL (Richard Doetsch-Benziger Collection): *Schooner in the Baltic* (1924) - BOSTON (MFA): *Blue Boat* (1944) - COLOGNE (Wallraf-Richartz Mus.): *Bridge III*; *Tower over Halle* - DETROIT (IA): *Paddle Boat* (1913) - DÜSSELDORF (Kunstsammlung Nordrhein-Westfalen): *Umpferstedt* (1914) - EDINBURGH (Scottish Nat. Gal. of Modern Art): *Gelmeroda II* - ESSEN (Folkwang Mus.): *Gelmeroda IX*; *Light Buoy* (1913); *Kolberg* - HAMBURG (Kunsthalle): *The Choir of Halle Cathedral* (1930) - HOUSTON (University of Houston): *Self-portrait* (1915) - MINNEAPOLIS (Walker Art Center): *Church of the Minorites II* (1926, oil on canvas) - MONTREAL (MBA): *Yellow Road* (1918) - MUNICH (Neue Pinakothek): *Halle Cathedral* (1930) - NEW YORK (Metropolitan Mus. of Art): *The Church of Gelmeroda* - NEW YORK (MoMA): *Viaduct* (1920); *Riot* (1910); *Steamship Odin II* (1927); *Manhattan* (set) - NEW YORK (Solomon R. Guggenheim Mus.): *Gelmeroda IV* (1915); *Sunset by the Sea I* (1927); *Cloud* (1936, drawing) - PARIS (MNAM-CCI) - ST LOUIS (AM): *Bridge* (1913) - THE HAGUE (Gemeentemus.): *Italian Landscape* (1912); *Monchröda* (1922); *Kunstfort* (1932) - WASHINGTON DC (GA, Howard University) - WASHINGTON DC (NGA): *The Bicycle Race* (1912, oil on canvas); *Storm Brewing* (1939, oil on canvas); other paintings, a drawing, prints - WASHINGTON DC (Phillips Collection): *Village* (1927).

AUCTION RECORDS:

STUTTGART, 21 May 1959, *Man Standing in front of Rocks*, DEM 23,000. STUTTGART, 20 May 1960, *Sailing Boat in a Rough Sea*, DEM 83,000. NEW YORK, 25 Jan 1961, *Rue St-Jacques, Paris*, USD 7,000. STUTTGART, 3 May 1961, *Landing Stage*, DEM 120,000. MILAN, 21 and 23 Nov 1962, *Blue Seascape* (watercolour) ITL 1,800,000. HAMBURG, 18 May 1963, *Sailing Boats* (watercolour) DEM 12,200. NEW YORK, 6 April 1967, *Cammin*, USD 10,000. NEW YORK, 19 Nov 1969, *Town Roofs at Night* (watercolour/pen outline, study) USD 10,500. NEW YORK, 27 April 1972, *Village* (watercolour) USD 16,000. LONDON, 2 May 1974, *Zottelstedt II*, USD 140,000. ZURICH, 28 May 1976, *Last Journey* (1940, oil on canvas, 19 x 30 3/4 ins / 48 x 78 cm) CHF 240,000. MUNICH, 28 May 1976, *Church, Tower and Apse* (woodcut) DEM 3,700. HAMBURG, 3 June 1976, *The Mill of Swinemünd* (1916, pen/charcoal, 8 3/4 x 10 ins / 22.4 x 25.6 cm) DEM 24,000. NEW YORK, 12 May 1977, *Benz* (1933, watercolour and Indian ink, 9 1/2 x 12 1/4 ins / 24.3 x 31 cm) USD 5,500. BERN, 8 June 1977, *Bridge* (1912, etching and dry-point) CHF 6,400. NEW YORK, 19 Oct 1977, *Alert or Church in Winter* (1942, oil on canvas, 36 3/4 x 25 1/4 ins / 93.3 x 64 cm) USD 50,000. LONDON, 26 April 1978, *Paris Street* (1978, woodcut, 21 1/2 x 16 1/4 ins / 54.5 x 41.2 cm) GBP 1,850. HAMBURG, 8 June 1979, *Nieder Grunstedt* (1912, gouache, 8 1/4 x 10 ins / 21 x 24.5 cm) DEM 22,000. LONDON, 2 Dec 1980, *Promenade* (1914, pen/paper, 5 x 9 ins / 13 x 22 cm) GBP 8,500. NEW YORK, 18 May 1983, *The Ship Wayward Lass in a Gale in the Gulf of Arabia* (1933, watercolour and black ink, 11 x 12 1/2 ins / 28.2 x 32 cm) USD 22,000. HAMBURG, 9 June 1983, *Mill* (1912, charcoal, 8 x 10 ins / 20.1 x 25.1 cm) DEM 26,000. BERN, 22 June 1984, *Gelmerode II* (oil on canvas, 39 1/4 x 31 1/2 ins / 100 x 80 cm) CHF 365,000. NEW YORK, 7 Nov 1984, *The Old Locomotive Windspiel* (1906, lithograph, 6 1/4 x 12 3/4 ins / 15.9 x 32.4 cm) USD 9,500. BERN, 19 June 1985, *Taubch* (1934, coloured chalk/outline in black chalk, 9 1/4 x 12 ins / 23.4 x 30.4 cm) CHF 24,500. NEW YORK, 14 Nov 1985, *Village* (1912, watercolour and Indian ink, 8 1/2 x 10 ins / 21.9 x 25.4 cm) USD 50,000. NEW YORK, 9 Oct 1986, *Figurines and Houses* (set of 10 figurines and 7 painted wooden houses, h. 1 1/2 ins / 3.7 cm à 3 3/4 ins/9.7 cm) USD 15,000. HAMBURG, 12 June 1987, *Rauchfane II* (1931, pen, Indian ink and chalk, 11 x 17 3/4 ins / 27.7 x 45.1 cm) DEM 32,000. NEW YORK, 11 Nov 1987, *Promenade, Arcueil II* (1915, oil on canvas, 35 1/4 x 28 1/4 ins / 89.5 x 72 cm) USD 310,000. NEW YORK, 18 Feb 1988, *A Memory II* (1955, watercolour and ink/paper, 12 1/4 x 18 3/4 ins / 31.1 x 47.6 cm) USD 15,400. LONDON, 29 March 1988, *Velocipedists* (oil on canvas, 37 1/2 x 33 1/2 ins / 95.5 x 85 cm) GBP 781,000. LONDON, 30 March 1988, *Vallersroda* (watercolour, pen and pencil, 9 1/4 x 12 1/2 ins / 23.5 x 31.8 cm) GBP 5,720. LONDON, 18 May 1988, *Ghost Games* (1955, Indian ink and watercolour, 3 1/4 x 6 ins / 8 x 15.5 cm) GBP 3,300. MUNICH, 8 June 1988, *Boat* (1931, watercolour and ink, 11 3/4 x 18 1/2 ins / 30 x 46.9 cm) DEM 55,000. LONDON, 28 June 1988, *Ruins on a Cliff II* (1940, oil on canvas, 19 x 28 1/2 ins / 48.2 x 72.3 cm) GBP 82,500; *Figures at Twilight* (1909, oil on canvas, 16 1/4 x 14 1/4 ins / 41.3 x 36.2 cm) GBP 192,500. MUNICH, 26 Oct 1988, *Dune IV* (watercolour, 10 3/4 x 17 3/4 ins / 27.5 x 45 cm) DEM 33,000. NEW YORK, 12 Nov 1988, *The Church of Treptow* (1933, ink and watercolour/paper, 14 1/2 x 18 1/2 ins / 37 x 47 cm) USD 44,000. LONDON, 29 Nov 1988, *Cliffs* (1912, oil on canvas, study, 18 x 23 3/4 ins / 45.7 x 60.3 cm) GBP 198,000. MILAN, 14 Dec 1988, *Deliveries* (1955, ink and watercolour/paper, 9 x 12 1/4 ins / 22 x 31 cm) ITL 12,000,000. NEW YORK, 16 Feb 1989, *The Church of Heringsdorf* (1916, watercolour and ink/paper/card, 11 3/4 x 9 1/4 ins / 29.8 x 23.2 cm) USD 35,200. NEW YORK, 10 May 1989, *Belgian Railways* (1911, oil on canvas, 28 3/4 x 35 3/4 ins / 73 x 91 cm) USD 495,000. LONDON, 24 May 1989, *Sailing Boats* (1934, ink and watercolour, 8 x 11 ins / 19.4 x 28.1 cm) GBP 28,600. LONDON, 28 June 1989, *Sailing Boats and Red Sun*

(1924, oil on canvas, 10 1/2 x 16 ins / 26.5 x 40.5 cm) GBP 88, 000. NEW YORK, 5 Oct 1989, *Topaz Sun II* (1947, watercolour and ink/paper, 9 1/4 x 11 1/2 ins / 23.8 x 28.9 cm) USD 17,600. NEW YORK, 6 Oct 1989, *Spanker off the Coast* (1939, oil on canvas, 18 x 30 3/4 ins / 45.7 x 78 cm) USD 264,000. LONDON, 27 Nov 1989, *Village Church* (oil on canvas, 33 3/4 x 39 1/4 ins / 86 x 100 cm) GBP 550,000. NEW YORK, 26 Feb 1990, *Cloud II* (1925, oil on canvas, 16 1/4 x 27 ins / 41.5 x 68.5 cm) GBP 297,000. LONDON, 4 April 1990, *Westward Ho!* (1936, ink and watercolour, 8 1/2 x 11 3/4 ins / 21.5 x 30 cm) GBP 27,500. NEW YORK, 17 May 1990, *Sunny Day* (1943, watercolour and ink/paper, 12 1/2 x 19 ins / 31.7 x 48.2 cm) USD 27,500. MUNICH, 31 May 1990, *Lüneburg II* (1924, ink and watercolour, 10 3/4 x 13 1/2 ins / 27.5 x 34.3 cm) DEM 83,600. NEW YORK, 3 Oct 1990, *Composition Gables 5* (1953, oil and pencil/sacking, 15 x 24 ins / 38 x 61 cm) USD 126,500. PARIS, 23 Oct 1990, *Locomotive* (1953, watercolour and Indian ink/paper, 3 1/4 x 6 ins / 8 x 15 cm) FRF 60,000. ZURICH, 7-8 Dec 1990, *Part of a Village with Church at Sunset* (1955, watercolour charcoal and ink/paper, 9 x 12 ins / 23 x 30.7 cm) CHF 15,000. NEW YORK, 15 Feb 1991, *Street in Treptow* (1952, watercolour and ink/paper, 12 1/4 x 9 1/2 ins / 31 x 24 cm) USD 17,600. NEW YORK, 8 May 1991, *Houses in Paris* (1912, ink/paper, 12 1/2 x 9 1/4 ins / 31.7 x 23.5 cm) USD 71,500. BERLIN, 30 May 1991, *Eichelborn (Thuringia) no. 2* (ink and watercolour/vellum/Japanese paper, 9 1/2 x 12 1/2 ins / 24.2 x 32 cm) DEM 666,000. NEW YORK, 5 Nov 1991, *Four Elements of a Model Train for Children* (painted wooden model, locomotive l. 8 ins / 20.5 cm, coal truck l. 4 1/4 ins/11 cm, Pullman car l. 8 1/2 ins/21.5 cm, luggage car l. 3 1/2 ins/9 cm) USD 7,700. HEIDELBERG, 11 April 1992, *The Hanseatic Fleet* (1918, woodcut, 6 1/2 x 8 1/2 ins / 16.4 x 21.8 cm) DEM 1,100. NEW YORK, 12 May 1992, *Pieces of Glass* (1927, oil and pencil/canvas, 28 1/2 x 25 1/2 ins / 72.5 x 65 cm) USD 209,000. MILAN, 21 May 1992, *Liner with Flag Flying* (1939, watercolour, 7 x 9 ins / 18 x 22 cm) ITL 28,000,000. NEW YORK, 11 Nov 1992, *Boat* (1940, watercolour and ink/paper, 11 ins / 27 cm, 3 1/2 x 15 3/4 ins/9 x 40 cm) USD 33,000. LUCERNE, 21 Nov 1992, *Coast with Small Boats* (1925, pencil/paper, 5 1/4 x 8 1/4 ins / 13.3 x 21 cm) CHF 2,600. BERLIN, 27 Nov 1992, *Hottelstedt* (watercolour and ink, 10 3/4 x 16 3/4 ins / 27.5 x 42.8 cm) DEM 22,600. ZURICH, 21 April 1993, *Houses and Church* (1921, woodcut, 7 3/4 x 11 3/4 ins / 19.6 x 30 cm) CHF 6,000. NEW YORK, 13 May 1993, *Blue Mist* (1938, watercolour and ink/beige paper, 12 1/2 x 18 3/4 ins / 31.7 x 47.9 cm) USD 25,300. LONDON, 20 May 1993, *Walkers with a Small Child in Blue* (1946, watercolour and ink/paper, 11 1/2 x 15 1/4 ins / 28.9 x 38.7 cm) GBP 14,375. MILAN, 12 Oct 1993, *Village* (1922, pencil, 7 3/4 x 6 1/4 ins / 20 x 16 cm) ITL 16,100,000. NEW YORK, 2 Nov 1993, *Figures with Dandy-horses* (1910, oil on canvas, 37 1/2 x 33 1/2 ins / 95.5 x 85 cm) USD 1,542,500. NEW YORK, 11 May 1994, *Mariage Proposal* (1907, oil on canvas, 26 3/4 x 21 ins / 67.9 x 53.3 cm) USD 387,500. PARIS, 8 June 1994, *The Church of Hailigenhafen* (1922, pen and watercolour, 9 3/4 x 14 ins / 25 x 35.5 cm) FRF 101,000. LONDON, 28 June 1994, *Sailing Boats at Sea* (1953, oil on canvas, 18 x 30 ins / 45.7 x 76.2 cm) GBP 67,500. NEW YORK, 8 Nov 1995, *The Lightship* (1920, watercolour and ink/paper, 9 1/4 x 12 1/4 ins / 23.8 x 30.8 cm) USD 43,700. ZURICH, 14 Nov 1995, *Setting Off West* (1943, watercolour and ink, 11 1/2 x 18 ins / 29.5 x 46 cm) CHF 26,000. PARIS, 13 Dec 1995, *Houses by a River I* (oil on canvas, 20 x 30 ins / 50.5 x 76 cm) FRF 635,000. LONDON, 9 Oct 1996, *Sailing Boat and Steamer in front of an Iceberg* (watercolour and ink/paper, 9 1/4 x 12 1/4 ins / 23.5 x 31.4 cm) GBP 14,950. NEW YORK, 14 Nov 1996, *Summer Afternoon I* (1937, watercolour, pen and black ink/paper, 12 1/2 x 19 ins / 31.5 x 48.2 cm) USD 29,900. NEW YORK, 14 May 1997, *Windmill* (1925, watercolour and pen and ink/paper, 11 1/2 x 16 ins / 28.9 x 40.6 cm) USD 26,450. LONDON, 9 Oct 1997, *Road to the Château* (1915, oil on canvas, 39 1/4 x 32 ins / 100 x 81 cm) GBP 463,500. LONDON, 7 Oct 1999, *Afternoon Light I - Strasse in Treptow* (1932, oil on canvas, 31 x 39 ins / 80 x 100 cm) GBP 180,000. LONDON, 7 Oct 1999, *Cloud II* (1925, oil on canvas, 16 x 27 ins / 41 x 68 cm) GBP 240,000. LONDON, 17 Oct 2000, *Jesuiten I* (1908, oil on canvas, 24 x 22 ins / 60 x 55 cm) GBP 650,000. LONDON, 18 Oct 2000, *Battlefield* (1915, watercolour, pen, ink and pencil, 8 x 10 ins / 21 x 25 cm) GBP 125,000. LONDON, 25 June 2001, *Green Bridge* (1909, oil on canvas, 40 x 32 ins / 101 x 81 cm) GBP 2,200,000. NEW YORK, 5 Nov 2001, *Das Rathaus von Swinemunde* (1912, oil on canvas, 28 x 23 ins / 71 x 59 cm) USD 3,000,000. LONDON, 25 June 2002, *Carnival in Gelmeroda II* (1908, oil on canvas, 27 x 22 ins / 69 x 55 cm) GBP 650,000. NEW YORK, 4 Nov 2002, *Newspaper Readers* (1909, oil on canvas, 20 x 25 ins / 50 x 63 cm) USD 2,000,000. HAMBURG, 2 Dec 2003, *Steam Engine* (1915, Indian ink and watercolour, 9 x 12 ins / 24 x 31 cm) EUR 38,000. LONDON, 2 Feb 2004, *Newspaper Readers II* (1916, oil on canvas, 41 x 37 ins / 104 x 93 cm) GBP 2,200,000. NEW YORK, 4 Nov 2004, *Green Bridge* (1909, watercolour, pen and ink, 13 x 10 ins / 33 x 25 cm) USD 200,000.

FEINLEIN, Johann Christoph

German, 17th century.

Active in Waldshut-am-Rhein.

Engraver, cabinet maker.

Feinlein published a book on cabinetmaking and one artwork, *The Arrangement of Columns*, engraved on copper.

FEINSTEIN, Guy

French, 20th century.

Born 15 February 1929, in Alexandria.

Painter. Interiors, still-lifes.

Feinstein settled in Paris in 1946. After a year of study at the Faculty of Science, he took courses in the Atelier Fernand Léger and at the Institut d'Art et d'Archéologie. He took part in a number of collective exhibitions, including: 1954, Salon de la Jeune Peinture, Paris; 1958, *École de Paris*, Charpentier gallery, Paris; 1958, 1959, Salon des Réalités Nouvelles, Paris; 1958, 1959, 1972, 1975, Salons Grands et Jeunes d'Aujourd'hui, Paris; 1972, 1976, 1978, 1984, 1986, Salon Comparaisons, Paris; 1976, *Promenade à travers l'art contemporain* (*Promenade Through Contemporary Art*), American Center, Paris; 1977, Salon de mai, Paris; 1983, *Les Figurations* (*Figurative Elements*), Maison de la Culture des Hauts de Belleville, Paris. His solo exhibitions included: 1951, Breteau gallery, Paris; 1953, 1955, Jeanne Castel gallery, Paris; 1968, Jacob gallery, Paris; 1972, Riestal gallery, Arnheim (Holland); 1975, Presbytère de Montmaur (Aude); 1985, 1987, Sculptures gallery, Paris.

Speaking of his own painting, Feinstein said: 'The essential in my work is focused on the expression of the feeling I have for space'. After experimenting with non-figurative art he returned to perceiving space with a kind of unambiguous figurativeness, taking up the problem in his compositions of the figure in his environment. Waldemar George, Georges Boudaille, Pierre Descargues, Jacques Lacarrière and Gérard Xuriguera have all written about his work.

MUSEUMS AND GALLERIES:

LAUSANNE (Cantonal MFA) - PARIS (BNF) - REHOVOT (Centre d'Art Contemporain).

AUCTION RECORDS:

PARIS, 26 Jan 1990, *Composition* (1959, oil on canvas, 23 1/2 x 28 3/4 ins / 60 x 73 cm) FRF 3,500.

FEINSTEIN, Rachel

American, 20th - 21st century.

Born 1971, in Fort Defiance (Arizona).

Active in New York.

Sculptor.

Rachel Feinstein is a graduate of Columbia University (1993) and in the same year attended the Skowhegan School of Painting and Sculpture in Maine, a school established in

1946 by artists for artists and still governed by artists. She is married to painter John Currin.

Feinstein produces a variety of freestanding 'sculptures' in painted wood but also works in other materials including plaster, beads, rhinestones, velvet and rope. *Mirrored Ball* (1998) is rather like an elaborate and fanciful chandelier in plaster and mirrors and hangs from the ceiling. Reviewers unfailingly refer to the 'Rococo' and 'Baroque' aspects of Feinstein's sculptures. In 2000 she visited the 18th-century Nymphenburg Palace in Munich, Germany and this visit, coupled with her childhood years spent in the vicinity of Disneyworld and the fairy-tale architecture of South Florida have apparently left an indelible mark on Feinstein's aesthetics.

Rachel Feinstein has participated in group exhibitions in New York, London, Manchester, Denmark, Greece, Austria and Switzerland, including: 2001, *The Visitors*, Printemps de Septembre, Toulouse; *The Americans*, The Barbican Centre, London and *The Love of the Look*, the Kerstin Engholm Galerie, Vienna; 2002, *John Currin and Rachel Feinstein*, Hydra Workshop, Hydra, Greece; *Landscape*, the Derek Eller Gallery, New York; 2003, *Self Portraits*, Deitsch Projects, New York; *Roll Out*, the Karyn Lovegrove Gallery, Los Angeles; 2004, *Seeing Other People*, the Marianne Boesky Gallery, New York; *Art Fortnight London*, London; *Candyland*, the Herbert Read Gallery, Kent Institute of Art and Design. She held her first solo exhibition in 1999 at White Columns, New York, followed by others at the Robert Prime Gallery, London (1999), Corvi Mora, London (2002), and the Marianne Boesky Gallery (2001, 2004).

BIBLIOGRAPHY:

in *Artnews*, September 2002 (Interview with the artist). Dannatt, Adrian, *'When Arte Povera Meets Rococo'* in *Flash Art*, May-June 2003. Celant, Germano, *'John Currin and Rachel Feinstein'* in *Interview*, September 2003.

FEINT, Adrian
Australian, 20th century.
Born 1894, in Sydney.
Painter. Landscapes, flowers.

AUCTION RECORDS:

SYDNEY, 6 Oct 1976, *Still-life with Flowers* (1942, oil on canvas, 19 x 30 3/4 ins / 48 x 78 cm) AUD 800. SYDNEY, 29 June 1981, *Still-life* (oil on canvas, 19 3/4 x 15 3/4 ins / 50 x 40 cm) AUD 1,600. SYDNEY, 29 Oct 1987, *Floral Still-life in Nautilus Shell Vase* (1959, oil on canvas, 12 x 15 ins / 30.5 x 37.8 cm) AUD 7,500. SYDNEY, 2 July 1990, *Spring Shrubs at Whale Beach* (oil on canvas, 5 x 9 ins / 13 x 23 cm) AUD 1,700. SYDNEY, 15 Oct 1990, *Floral Still-life* (1961, oil on card, 5 x 7 3/4 ins / 13 x 20 cm) AUD 1,500. MELBOURNE, 26 April 1999, *Still-life* (1945, oil on wood panel, 17 x 15 ins / 44 x 39 cm) AUD 9,500. MELBOURNE, 15 Aug 2000, *Summer at Pittwater* (1951, oil on canvas, 20 x 17 ins / 51 x 43 cm) AUD 12,000. MELBOURNE, 27 Nov 2000, *Little Farm, Bungarby* (1947, oil on canvas laid on board, 13 x 1 ins / 33 x 3 cm) AUD 13,000. MELBOURNE, 28 Nov 2001, *Basket of Flowers* (1945, oil on canvas, 20 x 22 ins / 51 x 56 cm) AUD 7,500. MELBOURNE, 30 April 2002, *Hibiscus and Mixed Flowers in a Japanese Vase* (1951, oil on board, 19 x 15 ins / 49 x 39 cm) AUD 7,500. MELBOURNE, 24 Nov 2003, *Banksias in a Jug* (1959, oil on canvas, 18 x 9 ins / 45 x 24 cm) AUD 5,500. SYDNEY, 23 Aug 2004, *Nocturnal Visitor* (1945, oil on canvas, 19 x 22 ins / 49 x 55 cm) AUD 7,500.

FEINTEL, Jean
French, 16th century.
Born in Amboise (Indre-et-Loire).
Painter.

Feintel worked for François de Longueville in around 1511.

FEISS, Jorg
Italian, 16th century.
Active in Bolzano (Trentino-Alto Adige).
Sculptor (wood).

FEISSOLLE, François
French, 18th century.
Active in Toulon.
Painter.

FEIST, Otto
German, 20th century.
Born 18 November 1872, in Karlsruhe.
Sculptor. Allegorical subjects, figures. Busts.

Feist worked at the Hochschule für Gestaltung in Karlsruhe, where he specialised in sculpted portraits. He featured from 1904 at the Glaspalast in Munich and in the Grosse Berliner Kunstausstellung in Berlin. His portraits include: *Professor Göhler; Professor F.S. Meyer* (bronze); *Professor Groh; Grand Duke Frederick I; Grand Duchess Louise* (low relief, bronze). His other works include: *Dream* (marble); *Nymph* (tomb low relief); *Spirit of the Sudeten Mountains* (alabaster); *Busts of Children* (wood); *Statuette of a Woman* (bronze).

FEISTEL-ROHMEDER, Bettina
German, 20th century.
Born 24 August 1873, in Heidenheim (Bavaria).
Also active in Switzerland.
Painter, draughtswoman, watercolourist. Figures, urban landscapes.

Bettina Feistel-Rohmeder studied in Dachau, Karlsruhe and Stuttgart, then in 1905 and 1906 in Venice. In 1909 she founded the Mannheim Studios in Heidelberg, then set up in Switzerland. From her stay in Dachau came works like: *Edge of the Forest, near Dachau; Farm in the Region of Dachau; The Park of Castle at Dachau* and from her stay in Venice: *Evening on the Lido; On the Balcony; Light is His Clothing; Saint Mark's School in Chiogga*. In Heidelberg, she executed oil paintings and watercolours: *Courtyard of the Castle at Erbach; Portrait of My Mother; Town Hall at Michetstadt*. The Mannheim Studios produced numerous plates for business, ex-libris, letterheads and a series of 25 pen-and-ink drawings with views of Heidelberg and Mannheim for postcards.

FEISTENAUER, Andreas, or Faistenauer
German, 17th century.
Born in Rosenheim.
Painter.

A pupil of Stoll in Vienna, Feistenauer subsequently moved to Munich, where he carried out many decorations for the city's churches and worked for the elector of Bavaria. He produced a *St Thomas of Villanueva* for the Augustinian church and a *St Francis in Ecstasy* for the Franciscan church.

FEISTENBERGER. See **FAISTENBERGER**

FEISTER, Carl
Austrian, 18th - 19th century.
Born 1742, in Vienna; died in Vienna.
Draughtsman.

In 1881, drawings and engravings by Feister were included in the collection of prints and paintings that had recently opened in Baden, near Vienna.

FEISTHAMEL, J. J.
French, 19th century.
Draughtsman, watercolourist. Landscapes, mountainscapes, church interiors.

MUSEUMS AND GALLERIES:

ORLÉANS: *Interior of Church of St-Euverte* (watercolour) - VIENNA: *Mountain Landscape* - WROCLAW: *Italian Landscape*; same subject; *Italian Coast; Italian Landscape; Southern Landscape*.

FEISTKORN
German, 19th century.

Active in Göttingen.
Painter. Genre scenes.

FEIT, Franz

Czech, 18th century.
Born to a family originally from Pilhrimov.
Sculptor.

Franz Feit took part in work on the high altar of the church of the Monastery of the Assumption in Bechyne.

FEIT, Nicolaus

Hungarian, 15th century.
Active in Cassovia (now Košice).
Painter.

Nicolaus Feit was made citizen of Cassovia in 1465.

FEITAMA, Sybrand

Dutch, 18th century.
Born 10 December 1694, in Amsterdam; died 3 June 1758, in Amsterdam.
Draughtsman, poet.

Sybrand Feitama drew a portrait of *King Augustus II of Poland.*

FEITELBERG, Zina

Russian, 20th century.
Born in Kazan.
Painter.

Zina Feitelberg exhibited from 1924 onwards in Paris at the Salon d'Automne and from 1926 onwards at the Salon des Tuileries.

FEITELSON, Lorser or I. Lorser

American, 20th century.
Born 11 February 1898, in Savannah; died 24 May 1978, in Los Angeles.
Painter, watercolourist, muralist. Figures, still-lifes.

Lorser Feitelson studied in the Art Students League in New York City and independently in Paris from 1919 to 1927. He settled in Los Angeles in 1927 where he was influential in the artistic community there. He taught at the Art Center School, where his students included Reuben Kadish, Philip Guston and Helen Lundeberg (whom he later married). In 1934 Feitelson and Lundeberg founded Post-Surrealism. From 1937 to 1943, as area supervisor of murals for the new Deal's Federal Art Project, he designed a number of murals for public spaces, including Edison Junior High School and Hooper's Avenue School in south-central Los Angeles; Cedars of Lebanon Hospital (now Cedars-Sinai) in West Hollywood; and Patriotic Hall in downtown Los Angeles. Unfortunately, not one of his murals is extant. Feitelson also ran an art gallery and gave many public lectures on topics concerning contemporary art. Feitelson exhibited at the California Palace, San Francisco (1928-1929); the Museum of Modern Art, New York (1936-1937); *Contemporary American Painting,* Whitney Museum of American Art, New York (1965-1966); a retrospective at the Municipal Art Gallery, Los Angeles (1972); a commemorative solo exhibition, Whitney Museum of American Art (1978-1979); retrospectives at the Tobey C. Moss Gallery, Los Angeles (1987, 1988); the San Francisco Museum of Art; Scripps College; Brooklyn Museum; the Metropolitan Museum of Art, New York; and Los Angeles County Museum of Art.

BIBLIOGRAPHY:
Lorser Feitelson 1898-1978, exhibition catalogue, Municipal Art Gallery, Los Angeles, 1972. Longstreet, Stephen (ed.), *Drawings on Classic Themes and Others,* Illustrated book, Los Angeles Art Association, Los Angeles, 1979. Moran, Daine de Gasis, *Feitelson: Three Analytical Essays,* Illustrated book, L. Feitelson and H. L. Feitelson Arts Foundation, Los Angeles, 1981. *Lorser Feitelson 1898-1978: Magical Space Forms - Boulder Series,* exhibition catalogue, Tobey C. Moss Gallery, Los Angeles, 1987. *Lorser Feitelson 1898-1978,* exhibition catalogue, Tobey C. Moss Gallery, Los Angeles, 1988. Hopkins Henry T./Duncan, Michael, *Lorser Feitelson and the invention of hard edge painting 1945-1965,* exhibition catalogue, Louis Stern Fine Arts, Hollywood, 2004. Peter Selz (introduction), *Lorser Feitelson, the Kinetic Series - works from 1916-1923,* exhibition catalogue, Louis Stern Fine Arts, Hollywood, 2005.

MUSEUMS AND GALLERIES:
CHICAGO (AI) - LOS ANGELES (County MA): *Life Begins* (1936, oil and collage); *Seated Nude Woman* (1918, red chalk); *Study of Female Nudes* (1920, watercolour and graphite); *Untitled* (1971, silk screen); *Studies of Figure Movement* (1952, ink) - NEW YORK (Brooklyn Mus.) - NEW YORK (Metropolitan Mus. of Art) - NEW YORK (MoMA) - SAN FRANCISCO (MoMA): *Genesis First Version* (1934, oil on celotex); *Magical Space Forms* (1963, enamel on canvas); *Magical Forms* (1948, oil on canvas) - WASHINGTON DC (NGA): *Untitled* (1964, enamel on canvas) - WASHINGTON DC (Smithsonian American AM): *Genesis #2* (1934, oil); *Post-Surreal Configuration: Biological Symphony* (1939/72, lithograph); *Seated Figure* (1919, oil); *Untitled* (1969, acrylic).

AUCTION RECORDS:
SAN FRANCISCO, 27 Feb 1986, *Woman Reading* (1920, oil on card, 18 x 10 1/4 ins / 46 x 26 cm) USD 3,750. NEW YORK, 25-26 Feb 1994, *Untitled* (1962, oil and varnish/canvas, 60 x 50 ins / 152.4 x 127 cm) USD 23,000. NEW YORK, 22 Feb 1996, *Untitled* (1965, varnish and Liquitex/canvas, 60 x 60 ins / 152.5 x 152.5 cm) USD 7,475. NEW YORK, 8 May 1996, *Magical Space Forms* (1962, oil on canvas, 60 x 52 ins / 152.4 x 132 cm) USD 18,400. PASADENA, 19 Oct 1999, *Goblet in Modernist Still-life* (oil on particleboard, 11 x 9 ins / 28 x 23 cm) USD 1,900. SAN FRANCISCO, 24 Oct 2000, *Portrait of a Girl* (oil on board, 23 x 19 ins / 59 x 47 cm) USD 8,000. SAN FRANCISCO, 19 Nov 2002, *Seated Female Nude. Reclining Female Nude* (oil on board on board, a pair, 30 x 24 ins / 75 x 60 cm) USD 2,500. SAN FRANCISCO, 22 April 2003, *Untitled* (1964, enamel and oil on paper, 60 x 40 ins / 152 x 102 cm) USD 11,000.

FEITKNECHT, Peter

Swiss, 17th century.
Died 15 August 1645, in Pfäffer.
Active in Biel.
Glass painter.

An artist and statesman, Feitknecht is mentioned as having produced six coats of arms in 1612.

FEITO, Luis, or Feito-López Luis

Spanish, 20th century.
Born 31 October 1929, in Madrid.
Also active in France from 1954.
Painter (including gouache/mixed media), lithographer.
El Paso Group.

After studying at a seminary in Spain, Luis Feito became interested in bullfighting. He later studied at the Real Academia de Bellas Artes de San Fernando in Madrid and was awarded a drawing teaching diploma in 1954. The same year he received a bursary from the French and Spanish governments and moved to Paris. In 1957 he became a founder member of the *El Paso* group with Saura, Canogar and Millarès. He then divided his time between Paris and Madrid. In 1985 he was made an Officier des Arts et Lettres in France.

In his early career, in 1953-1954, Feito was influenced by the Post-Cubism that dominated the way in which painting was taught in the academies. However, he soon turned towards abstraction while still preserving a style of construction which relied on the generous application of colour. Around 1955-1956 he made a firm transition to a form of expression linked to *art informel* and which now relied on the use of colour alone. In these works an enormous, thick splash of red stands out in a highly individual way against dark, almost black backgrounds. Around 1963 he began concentrating more on form and organised his compositions around the notion of concentric layers. Around 1965-1966 he developed a new manner of working: he divided each of his canvases like diptychs. One side was reserved for flat tints of bright colour and on the other with a more action-based approach he produced a powerful, contrasting balance that appears to be underpinned by an analytical view of the world. Pierre Restany describes Feito's work with these words: 'The blacks of coal seams, the greys of peat bogs, the whites of whitewashed roughcast in the sunlight, the ochres of Horta de Ebro and the clays of Andalusia, all the soils of Spain, even the sand of the bullring bathed in the blood of a dead bull'.

Feito was awarded a number prizes: Mediterranean Art Biennale (1956); 1st Paris Biennale (1959); Documenta 2 in Kassel and the Lissone Prize (1959); David Bright Prize, the 30th Venice Biennale (1960); outstanding merit in the Lissone prize (1961).In 1954, Feito became the first Spanish painter of his generation to hold an exhibition of abstract painting; this was in Madrid in the post-Civil War period at a time when official art still dominated.

He took part in a large number of group exhibitions, including: Salon des Réalités Nouvelles, Salon Comparaisons and Salon d'Automne in Paris; *L'École de Paris* (*The Paris School*) exhibition at the Galerie Charpentier (1960); Mediterranean Art Biennale in Cairo and Athens (1956); São Paulo Biennale and 10th Lissone prize (1957); 29th Venice Biennale (the Spanish Pavilion, 1958) where, in a striking manner, he demonstrated the re-emergence of Spanish painting after a long period of eclipse. In 1961 his work was selected for the Carnegie Prize international exhibition in Pittsburgh.

Feito has exhibited his work in many solo exhibitions including: the first in 1954 at the Bucholz gallery; regularly in Paris at the Galerie Arnaud; in Milan, New York, Helsinki, Tokyo, Basel, Copenhagen, Montreal and Seattle; in 1964 at the Hamburg museum; in 1965 at the Tacoma museum; in 1968 in San Francisco, Liège and the Verviers museum; in 1968 at the Montreal Museum of Contemporary Art; in 1982 at the Egam gallery in Madrid (a retrospective); in 1988 in Madrid; in 1988 at the Museo Español de Arte Contemporáneo; and in 1991 at the Louis Carré gallery in Paris.

Feito

Bibliography:

Restany, Pierre, *Luis Feito, le lyrisme castillan et la tradition mystique*, Gal. Arnaud, Paris, 1960 (Luis Feito, Castilian Lyricism and the Mystic Tradition). *Catálogo nacional de arte contemporáneo 1990-1991*, Ibérico 2Mil, Barcelona, 1990-1991 (National Catalogue of Contemporary Art 1990-1991).

Museums and Galleries:

Alexandria (Royal Mus.) - Atlanta (Georgia State University AG) - Buffalo (Albright-Knox AG) - Cuenca (Mus. De Arte Abstracto Español, Fundación Juan March) - Helsinki (Ateneumin Taidemus.) - Lissone (Civica Gal. d'Arte Contemporanea) - Madrid (Mus. de Arte Moderno) - Marseilles (Mus. Cantini): *Diptych 563* (1966) - Montreal (MAM) - Nagaoka (Niigata MMA) - New York (Solomon R. Guggenheim Mus.) - Paris (CNAC) - Paris (MAM) - Rio de Janeiro (MAM) - Rome (Gal. Nazionale d'Arte Moderna) - Tokyo (Bridgestone MA) - Tokyo (MMA) - Toronto (AG of Ontario).

Auction records:

Madrid, 21 Dec 1976, *Composition* (1973, oil on canvas, 59 x 59 ins / 150 x 150 cm) ESP 105,000. Madrid, 24 May 1977, *Infinity* (1959, mixed media, 35 x 46 ins / 88 x 116 cm) ESP 260,000. Antwerp, 23 April 1980, *Composition* (1971, oil on canvas, 57 x 44 1/2 ins / 145 x 113 cm) BEF 14,000. Barcelona, 17 March 1983, *228 Base* (1961, mixed media/canvas, 32 x 39 1/4 ins / 81 x 100 cm) ESP 125,000. Milan, 14 June 1984, *Painting 620* (1968, oil on canvas, 25 1/2 x 42 1/2 ins / 65 x 108 cm) ITL 1,300,000. Paris, 5 Dec 1985, *Composition with Yellow Background* (1974, oil on canvas, 51 1/4 x 38 1/4 ins / 130 x 97 cm) FRF 4,800. London, 20 Oct 1988, *Red with Black* (1961, gouache/card, 18 1/4 x 26 1/4 ins / 46.4 x 66.7 cm) GBP 5,280. London, 23 Feb 1989, *Red with Black II* (gouache and oil on paper/card, 18 1/4 x 23 1/2 ins / 46.5 x 59.5 cm) GBP 4,400. Copenhagen, 10 May 1989, *Composition* (1961, oil on canvas, 45 x 57 1/2 ins / 114 x 146 cm) DKK 150,000. Paris, 26 Jan 1990, *Untitled* (oil on canvas, collage and mixed media, 10 x 7 3/4 ins / 24.5 x 19.5 cm) FRF 18,000. London, 22 Feb 1990, *Frame 210* (1960, oil and mixture/canvas, 10 x 13 3/4 ins / 25.5 x 34.9 cm) GBP 10,450. Milan, 27 March 1990, *Untitled* (1970, oil on canvas, 17 3/4 x 21 1/2 ins / 45 x 54.5 cm) ITL 11,000,000. London, 5 April 1990, *Frame 522* (1965, oil and mixture/canvas, two parts, 39 1/4 x 64 1/4 ins / 100 x 163 cm) GBP 35,200. Paris, 30 May 1990, *Composition* (1970, oil on canvas, 39 1/4 x 31 1/2 ins / 100 x 80 cm) FRF 175,000. Douai, 11 Nov 1990, *Composition* (oil on paper, 17 1/4 x 24 ins / 44 x 61 cm) FRF 50,000. Rome, 3 Dec 1990, *Untitled* (1959, tempera/paper/canvas, 17 3/4 x 21 3/4 ins / 45 x 55.5 cm) ITL 28,750,000. Milan, 13 Dec 1990, *Composition* (1969, oil on canvas, 17 3/4 x 21 1/4 ins / 45 x 54 cm) ITL 11,000,000. Madrid, 13 Dec 1990, *Frame 830* (1971, oil on canvas, 57 1/2 x 45 ins / 146 x 114 cm) ESP 3,136,000. London, 21 March 1991, *Composition* (oil on paper, 25 1/2 x 20 ins / 65 x 51 cm) GBP 3,740. Paris, 30 May 1991, *Composition* (1975, oil on canvas, 51 1/4 x 77 1/4 ins / 130 x 196 cm) FRF 100,000. London, 17 Oct 1991, *Untitled* (oil on canvas, 57 3/4 x 44 3/4 ins / 147 x 113.5 cm) GBP 16,500. Madrid, 28 Nov 1991, *Frame 397* (1963, oil on canvas, 28 3/4 x 36 1/4 ins / 73 x 92 cm) ESP 2,464,000. London, 29 May 1992, *Frame 196* (1960, oil on canvas, 35 1/2 x 31 1/2 ins / 90 x 80 cm) GBP 7,700. Paris, 28 Sept 1992, *Composition 166* (1959, oil on canvas, 31 1/2 x 35 1/2 ins / 80 x 90 cm) FRF 37,000. Rome, 14 Dec 1992, *Composition* (1970, oil on canvas, 21 1/2 x 17 3/4 ins / 54.5 x 45 cm) ITL 5,175,000. London, 3 Dec 1993, *Frame 346* (1962, oil and mixed media/canvas, 51 1/4 x 64 ins / 130 x 162.5 cm) GBP 11,500. Paris, 24 June 1994, *Composition No. 1127* (1975, oil on canvas, 51 1/4 x 38 1/4 ins / 130 x 97 cm) FRF 25,000. London, 30 Nov 1995, *Frame 158* (1959, oil and sand/canvas, 29 x 39 1/2 ins / 73.5 x 100.5 cm) GBP 13,800. Milan, 2 April 1996, *Composition* (1968, oil/two canvases joined together, 23 3/4 x 35 3/4 ins / 60.5 x 91 cm) ITL 6,670,000. London, 23 May 1996, *Painting 153* (1959, oil and sand/canvas, 35 x 46 ins / 89 x 116 cm) GBP 14,950. Lucerne, 8 June 1996, *Composition* (gouache and oil on thick paper, 21 1/4 x 26 3/4 ins / 54 x 68 cm) CHF 4,500. Paris, 5 Oct 1996, *Painting* (1969, oil on canvas, diptych, 57 1/2 x 90 1/2 ins / 146 x 230 cm) FRF 58,000. Paris, 29 Nov 1996, *Composition* (1967, oil on canvas, 57 3/4 x 39 1/4 ins / 147 x 100 cm) FRF 32,000. London, 5 Dec 1996, *Painting XII* (1958, oil on canvas, 45 x 57 1/2 ins / 114 x 146 cm) GBP 13,225; *Picture No. 194* (1960, oil on canvas, 33 3/4 x 43 1/4 ins / 86 x 110 cm) GBP 9,200. Paris, 29 April 1997, *Untitled* (mixed media/canvas, 44 3/4 x 57 1/4 ins / 113.5 x 145.5 cm) FRF 84,000. Lokeren, 11 Oct 1997, *No. 539* (1966, oil on canvas, 57 1/2 x 39 1/4 ins / 146 x 100 cm) BEF 130,000. Paris, Jan 1998, *Composition* (oil on canvas, 45 x 57 1/2 ins / 114.5 x 146 cm) FRF 15,000. Madrid, 27 April 1999, *Painting 394* (1962, mixed media on paper, 39 x 39 ins / 100 x 100 cm) ESP 2,500,000. Lucerne, 27 Nov 1999, *Composition 283* (1961, oil and cement on canvas, 57 x 45 ins / 146 x 114 cm) CHF 18,000. Madrid, 29 May 2000, *Number 332* (oil on canvas, 45 x 57 ins / 114 x 146 cm) ESP 2,800,000. Paris, 4 July 2000, *Composition No. 283* (1961, oil on canvas, 57 x 45 ins / 146 x 114 cm) FRF 100,000. London, 6 April 2001, *Painting no. 316* (1962, oil and sand on canvas, 38 x 51 ins / 96 x 130 cm) GBP 8,000. Prato, 25 May 2001, *Painting Number 897* (1971, oil on canvas, 59 x 59 ins / 150 x 149 cm) ITL

36,000,000. STOCKHOLM, 23 April 2002, *Base* (1959, oil on canvas, 24 x 32 ins / 60 x 81 cm) SEK 200,000. LONDON, 5 Dec 2002, *Painting 847* (1971, acrylic on canvas, 38 x 51 ins / 97 x 130 cm) GBP 8,000. LONDON, 26 June 2003, *Painting 139* (1959, oil and mixed media on canvas, 45 x 57 ins / 114 x 145 cm) GBP 30,000. PARIS, 9 Dec 2003, *Composition* (1963, oil on canvas, 32 x 39 ins / 81 x 100 cm) EUR 25,000. PARIS, 18 May 2004, *Untitled* (1957, mixed media on paper, 24 x 37 ins / 60 x 93 cm) EUR 21,000. LONDON, 21 June 2004, *Painting 383* (1963, mixed media on canvas, 35 x 46 ins / 89 x 116 cm) GBP 17,000.

FEITOSA, Roberto
Brazilian, 20th century.
Painter. Landscapes.

Roberto Feitosa specialised in imaginary landscapes of Amazonia.

AUCTION RECORDS:
NEW YORK, 9 July 1981, *Moonrise* (1980, acrylic, 25 1/2 x 31 3/4 ins / 65 x 80.6 cm) USD 800. NEUILLY, 6 June 1989, *Landscape* (oil on panel, 18 1/2 x 24 ins / 47 x 61 cm) FRF 7,200.

FEITU, Pierre Luc
French, 20th century.
Born 16 April 1868, in Mûr-de-Bretagne.
Sculptor. Allegorical subjects, mythological subjects.

In Paris, Feitu was a member of the Salon des Artistes Français, and later of the Salon National des Beaux-Arts. He also exhibited in New York, Philadelphia, Pittsburgh, Mexico, and elsewhere. His best-known works include: *Glory, Salome, Sisyphus*. He created the sword of Albert I, King of the Belgians.

AUCTION RECORDS:
NEW YORK, 17 May 1983, *Fading Dream* (1900, bronze, h. 41 ins / 104 cm) USD 2,800.

FEJES, Claire
American, 20th century.
Active in Alaska.
Painter.

Claire Fejes was influenced by Gauguin.

FEJES, Emerik
Croat, 20th century.
Born 1904, in Osijek; died 1969, in Novi Sad.
Painter.

A button and comb cutter, Emerik Fejes subsequently opened a bric-à-brac shop. In 1949 he started painting his highly distinctive 'city portraits'. He lived in Novi-Sad. He executed portraits of houses or streets and recounted the daily life of these dwellings with total freedom in relation to perspective and with the narrative gifts of a child, not hesitating to remove a construction, if necessary, to show what was going on within.

Exhibitions include: *Primitive Artists*, Dubrovnik (1956); Belgrade (1957); *Naive Painting from the Douanier Rousseau to Today*, Knokke-Le-Zout (1958); *Die Naïven, aufbruch ins verlorene Paradies* (*The Naïve Painters, Journey to a Lost Paradise*), which brought together some 200 works from the Charlotte Zander Museum in Bönnigheim, Kunsthaus, Vienna (2001).

BIBLIOGRAPHY:
Bihalji-Merin, Oto, *Les Peintres naïfs*, Delpire, Paris, 1960. Maxim, Julia/Crnkovic, Vladimir, *Emerik Fejes*, exhibition catalogue, Museum Charlotte Zander, Wachter, Bönnigheim, 1997 (text in German and Englsih).

MUSEUMS AND GALLERIES:
BÖNNIGHEIM (Mus. Charlotte Zander).

AUCTION RECORDS:
NEW YORK, 24 Sept 1981, *Piccolo Teatro, Milan* (tempera, 16 1/2 x 23 1/4 ins / 42 x 59 cm) USD 2,000. VIENNA, 23 June 1987, *Trogir* (watercolour and gouache, 13 1/4 x 17 1/2 ins / 33.5 x 44.5 cm) ATS 18,000. VIENNA, 25 May 2000, *Monastery, Prizren* (tempera on paper, 11 x 16 ins / 29 x 41 cm) ATS 25,000.

FEKE, Robert
American, 18th century.
Born between 1705 and 1710, in Oyster Bay (Long Island); died 1750 or 1767.
Painter. Portraits.

There are different accounts of Robert Feke's origins and early life. Some say he was descended from a Dutch family that settled in Oyster Bay, and according to information that seems almost legendary he is said to have been captured and taken to Spain as a prisoner, where he learnt to paint. He seems to have spent some time in England and been influenced by the English portrait painters. When he returned to the USA he went to live in Newport in about 1741, and settled in Boston in around 1750.

He became a portrait painter, his sitters being mainly aristocratic. In 1741 he painted the family of Isaac Royall, a group inspired by the *Bermudas* of John Smibert. The surface quality of his pictures, the contrast of colours and the treatment of fabrics give Feke's work a distinctly American character. However, he also attempted to imitate the art of English portraiture. His manner of relating the figures to the background by lines is reminiscent of the work of Ralph Earl.

MUSEUMS AND GALLERIES:
BOSTON - NEWPORT (Redwood Library and Athenaeum): *Portrait of Governor Wanton's Wife*.

AUCTION RECORDS:
NEW YORK, 3 Nov 1960, *Captain William Stoddard*, USD 6,200. NEW YORK, 22 March 1978, *Portrait of Captain William Stoddard* (c. 1740, oil on canvas, 30 x 25 ins / 76.2 x 63.5 cm) USD 12,500.

FEKLISTOV, Vasili
Russian, 19th century.
Painter.

Feklistov studied at the St Petersburg academy of fine arts where he received several silver awards for his portraits and his genre paintings. In 1850 he was given a gold award for his painting *The Legend of Tobias*.

FEL, William
French, 20th century.
Engraver, draughtsman.

Fel is known for his illustrations of Gustave Flaubert's *Madame Bovary* (original etchings, 1927) and of *Douze sonnets* (*Twelve Sonnets*) by C. Guérin, as well as of the poems of H. de Régnier and A. Samain.

AUCTION RECORDS:
PARIS, 16 May 1924, *Study of a Woman* (pencil) FRF 330. PARIS, 15 May 1931, *Scene of Antiquity*, FRF 20.

FELAERT, Dirk Jacobsz., or Vellert or Vellaert or Fielart, also known as Dietrich Tierry or Dierich Jacobssone
Flemish School, 16th century.
Painter, painter (glass), engraver. Religious subjects.
Antwerp School.

It is thought that this artist was one of the first to paint on glass. Guicciardini, who described him as a grand master, refers to him by the name Fielart. He is probably the same artist as the Dietrich Tierry mentioned by Durel in his account of his journey to the Netherlands. He appears under the name of Tierry as the dean of the Guild of St Luke in Antwerp in 1518 and 1526. He was received as a master in 1511 and was still living in 1540.

AUCTION RECORDS:
NEW YORK, 15 Feb 1980, *Vision of St Bernard* (engraving/copper, 6 3/4 x 5 ins / 17.2 x 12.5 cm) USD 1,000. LONDON,

18 June 1982, *Temptation of Christ* (1525, etching, 4 1/2 x 3 ins / 11.2 x 7.7 cm) GBP 520. LONDON, 7 Dec 1984, *Drummer Boy and Child* (etching, 3 1/2 x 2 1/2 ins / 8.9 x 6.3 cm) GBP 3,000. LONDON, 5 Dec 1985, *St Luke Painting the Virgin* (1526, etching/watermarked paper, 6 3/4 x 5 ins / 17.2 x 12.4 cm) GBP 8,000. AMSTERDAM, 20 June 1989, *Holy Family with Angels (central panel), St Catherine and St Barbara (on wings)* (oil on panel, triptych, centre 30 x 22 3/4 ins / 76.5 x 58 cm, wings 30 x 10 ins/76.5 x 25.7 cm) NLG 414,000.

FELB, Josias
Swiss, 16th century.
Active in Basel in 1566.
Painter.

FELBER, Carl Friedrich
Swiss, 20th century.
Born 21 September 1880, in Wädenswil; died 1932, in Dachau.
Painter, draughtsman. Urban landscapes, landscapes.

Felber studied at the Hochschule für Gestaltung in Karlsruhe, the Académie Julian in Paris, the Hollosy school in Munich and the Hölsel school in Dachau, and finished by setting up in Dachau. He painted landscapes in the area around Dachau and in Upper Bavaria, as well as snow-covered landscapes in Switzerland, and views of Venice. He exhibited, from 1906, in particular at the Glaspalast in Munich, and sometimes at the Salon de la Société Nationale des Beaux-Arts in Paris.

MUSEUMS AND GALLERIES:
BERLIN (Kupferstichkabinet) - MUNICH (Staatliche Graphische Sammlung).

AUCTION RECORDS:
LUCERNE, 25 June 1976, *Landscape in Engadine* (1920, oil on canvas, 31 1/2 x 23 1/2 ins / 80 x 60 cm) CHF 1,300. LUCERNE, 13 Nov 1982, *Winter's Evening, Engadine* (1921, oil on canvas, 24 x 36 ins / 61 x 90.5 cm) CHF 900. BERN, 2 May 1986, *Mountain Landscape in Winter* (1920, oil on canvas, 19 3/4 x 35 3/4 ins / 50 x 91 cm) CHF 3,600. MUNICH, 1-2 Dec 1992, *Polish House in Autumn* (oil on paper, 23 1/2 x 27 1/2 ins / 60 x 70 cm) DEM 7,475. MUNICH, 11 Nov 1999, *Winter River Landscape, Schleissheimer Canal* (1910, oil on canvas, 27 x 24 ins / 68 x 60 cm) DEM 10,000. COLOGNE, 4 Dec 1999, *Late Summer Landscape near Dachau* (1918, oil on canvas, 35 x 35 ins / 90 x 90 cm) DEM 7,000. MUNICH, 22 March 2000, *Farmstead in Dachauer Land* (1902, oil on canvas, 25 x 31 ins / 63 x 80 cm) DEM 3,300. MUNICH, 15 Nov 2001, *Pollnhof near Dachau* (oil on canvas, 28 x 20 ins / 71 x 51 cm) DEM 4,500.

FELBER, Johann Carl
German, 18th century.
Born 1743, in Berlin; died 1768, in Dresden.
Painter, engraver.

A pupil of N.B. Le Sueur, Felber engraved portraits and genre scenes.

FELBER, Marguerite Lucie
French, 20th century.
Born 30 May 1878, in Paris.
Painter, watercolourist.

FELBERMEYER, Johann
Austrian, 19th century.
Active in Graz.
Painter.

Felbermeyer studied at the academy of art in Graz and painted many religious pictures. In 1853, he was awarded an academy prize for his painting *Extreme Unction.*

FELBIER, Maurice
Belgian, 20th century.
Born 1903, in Antwerp.
Painter, engraver (wood). Nudes, still-lifes.

Felbier was the son of a painter and decorative artist. He was a student at the Academie voor Schone Kunsten and the Nationaal Hoger Instituut voor Schone Kunsten in Antwerp. He was a lecturer at the Academie voor Schone Kunsten in Antwerp between 1950 and 1968. He won the Van Lerius prize in 1925.

MUSEUMS AND GALLERIES:
ANTWERP.

AUCTION RECORDS:
ANTWERP, 8 April 1976, *Sunflowers* (1938, oil on canvas, 35 3/4 x 32 ins / 91 x 81 cm) BEF 22,000. LOKEREN, 17 Oct 1981, *Still-life with Flowers* (1945, oil on canvas, 20 x 17 1/4 ins / 51 x 44 cm) BEF 18,000. ANTWERP, 21 Oct 2003, *Roses and Peonies* (1944, oil on canvas, 33 x 30 ins / 85 x 75 cm) EUR 1,600.

FELBINGER, Franz von (Ritter)
Austrian, 19th century.
Born 8 July 1844, in Hainburg (Lower Austria); died 15 July 1906, in Trebitsch (Moravia).
Painter. Figures, portraits, scenes with figures, genre scenes, interiors with figures, church interiors.

An engineer, Von Felbinger did not devote himself to painting until late in his life. After studying in Brünn (now Brno, Czech Republic), he went on to complete his training in Munich.

MUSEUMS AND GALLERIES:
BRNO (Heinrich Gomperz Gal.): *The Beggar; The Grass Market in Brünn (now Brno); Interior of the Jesuit Church; Portrait of the Artist;* same subject - BRNO (Moravské zemské Muz.): *Portrait of the Artist* - MORAVIA (Art Association): *The Player.*

AUCTION RECORDS:
NEW YORK, 24 Jan 1980, *Young Woman Knitting* (oil on panel, 21 3/4 x 17 1/2in/55.3 x 44.5cm) USD 5,500.

FELD, Hans von, or Johann von Feldt
Bohemian School, 17th century.
Active in Prague.
Painter.

Hans von Feld was an official painter to the Emperor Mathias. He produced banners for the church at Prague castle for the funeral of Rudolph II. He was given responsibility for protecting paintings in Prague cathedral from the iconoclasts in 1619.

FELD, Julius
Romanian, 20th century.
Born 29 June 1871, in Botosani.
Active and naturalised in France.
Painter.

Juluis Feld was a student of Gerome, Bonnat and Cormon. He received an honourable mention in 1902.

FELD, Otto
German, 19th - 20th century.
Born 26 February 1860, in Breslau (now Wroclaw, Poland); died 21 March 1911, in Neubabelsberg, near Potsdam.
Painter. Landscapes.

Feld studied at the Akademie in Berlin, then spent a period of time in Paris, where he exhibited a *Portrait of a Woman* at the Salon of the Société des Artistes Français in 1896. On returning to Germany he painted almost exclusively landscapes from the Berlin region and frequently showed them at the exhibitions in Berlin, but also in Dresden, in 1899 and 1901, and Düsseldorf in 1904. In Berlin he was the Director of the Association called *Art in the Life of the Child.*

MUSEUMS AND GALLERIES:
WROCLAW: *Evening.*

FELDBAUER, Max
German, 19th - 20th century.
Born 14 February 1869, in Neumarkt (Palatinate); died 1948.
Painter, illustrator.

Die Scholle group.

Feldbauer worked in Munich, where he was an illustrator for the magazine *Die Jugend* (*Youth*) and a member of *Die Scholle* (*The Glebe*). He also featured in the exhibitions at the Glaspalast in Munich and Berlin.

Feldbauer executed paintings in oils, taking his subjects from the lives of soldiers and the Bavarian people. He also executed paintings of horses, female nudes, peasant girls and serving girls.

MUSEUMS AND GALLERIES:

BERLIN (Nationalgal.) - DRESDEN (Prints Collection) - MUNICH (Stuck Mus.): *Horses* (study).

AUCTION RECORDS:

MUNICH, 26 May 1978, *Horse and Jockey* (1917, oil on canvas, 17¼ x 19¼ ins / 44 x 49 cm) DEM 3,200. MUNICH, 14 May 1986, *Reclining Nude* (1908, oil on canvas, 21¾ x 39¼ ins / 55.2 x 100 cm) DEM 4,000. STUTTGART, 30 Jan 1999, *Mountain Farmer* (1932, oil on canvas, 28 x 22 ins / 71 x 56 cm) DEM 3,500. MUNICH, 18 May 2000, *Horse with Slave* (1913, oil on canvas, 26 x 34 ins / 65 x 86 cm) DEM 4,200. MUNICH, 18 May 2000, *Bathers in River Amper* (1915, oil on canvas, 9 x 18 ins / 23 x 46 cm) DEM 16,000. ERLANGEN, 25 Oct 2003, *Horse Portrait* (oil on panel, 26 x 31 ins / 65 x 79 cm) EUR 5,000. ERLANGEN, 25 Oct 2003, *Girl's Portrait* (1905, oil on canvas, 21 x 16 ins / 54 x 40 cm) EUR 6,300.

FELDER, Carl

German, 18th century.

Active in Breslau (now Wroclaw, Poland).

Painter.

The second son of Franz Anton Felder, Carl Felder initially studied with his father, before entering the academy of art in Vienna in 1769.

FELDER, Franz Anton

German, 18th century.

Died 16 August 1782.

Active in Breslau (now Wroclaw, Poland).

Painter.

In the cathedral in Breslau, Franz Felder painted an altarpiece in the chapel of the Grand Elector, and in the same building, after the fire of 1759, he replaced several images of apostles painted by G.A. Mainardi. In 1781, he painted an altarpiece depicting the apostle *Judas Thadeus* in the church in Prausnitz (now Brusnice, Czech Republic).

FELDER, Johann

German, 18th century.

Born 18th century, in Breslau (now Wroclaw, Poland).

Painter.

The son of Johann Franz Felder, Johann Felder entered the academy of art in Vienna in 1799.

FELDER, Johann Franz

German, 18th century.

Active in Breslau (now Wroclaw, Poland).

Painter.

A pupil of his father, Franz Anton Felder, Johann Felder also studied at the academy of art in Vienna. He painted a portrait of the Grand Elector Franz Ludwig of Palatine for the chapel of the Grand Elector in the cathedral in Breslau.

FELDER, Katharina Maria

German, 19th century.

Born 15 January 1816, in Ellenbogen, near Bezau; died 13 February 1848, in Berlin.

Sculptor.

Despite displaying an early talent for sculpting, Katharina Felder went on to study drawing in Constance, before joining the academy in Munich. She then worked in Schwantal's workshop, where she produced a group in sandstone, *Faith, Hope and Charity*. She settled in Berlin, where she created an equestrian statue of *St George* for General Knesebeck. Her wooden sculpture of *St Sebastian* is in the church in Oberbezau.

MUSEUMS AND GALLERIES:

INNSBRUCK (Tiroler Landesmus. Ferdinandeum): *Virgin Kneeling before the Christ Child*.

FELDER, Marguerite

Belgian, 20th century.

Born in Huy (Liège).

Painter.

Marguerite Felder was an exhibitor, in Paris, at the Salon des Artistes Français from 1924.

FELDERER, Christian

German, 18th century.

Born 1709, in Schwäbisch-Gmünd; died 12 September 1778, in Schwäbisch-Gmünd.

Sculptor (wood), cabinet maker.

Felderer was a lay brother (going by his new first name of Andrea), at the Dominican monastery in Wimpfen. He carried out the entire Rococo decoration of the Dominican church in Wimpfen, with its ornate stalls, communion grille and organ stool. He also created the high altar of the collegiate church in Wimpfen-im-Tal.

FELDERHOFF, Reinhold

German, 19th century.

Born 25 January 1865, in Elbing (now Elblag, Poland).

Sculptor.

A pupil of Begas at the academy of art in Berlin, Felderhoff travelled to Italy in 1885, before finally settling in Berlin. The museum in Berlin has his *Diana*.

FELDHAAS, Anton, or Feldhans

Austrian, 18th century.

Active in Vienna.

Painter.

Having entered the academy of art in Vienna on 7 February 1756, Feldhaas was still a student at the engraving academy founded by Schmutzer in 1767. The church in Kelca (Moravia) has altarpieces created by Anton Feldhaas and his brother, Louis Adolphe.

FELDHUTTER, Ferdinand

German, 19th century.

Born 7 April 1842, in Munich; died 8 December 1898, in Munich.

Painter. Landscapes, waterscapes.

Feldhutter exhibited in Munich and Berlin in 1888-1889. He is best known for his *View over the Lake*.

AUCTION RECORDS:

MUNICH, 28 March 1973, *Tegernsee*, DEM 8,000. COLOGNE, 25 June 1976, *View of Königsee* (oil on canvas, 12¾ x 16¼in/32.5 x 41cm) DEM 3,200. MUNICH, 26 Oct 1978, *Bay of Naples* (oil on canvas, 27¼ x 35in/69 x 89cm) DEM 3,200. MUNICH, 27 Nov 1980, *Return from the Hunt* (1890, oil on panel, 9½ x 14¼in/24 x 36cm) DEM 8,800. VIENNA, 23 June 1982, *View of Isabella Bella on Lake Maggiore* (oil on canvas, 9¼ x 14¼in/23.5 x 36cm) ATS 28,000. LINDAU, 5 Oct 1984, *View of Lake Garda* (oil on panel, 9¼ x 14¼in/23.5 x 36cm) DEM 10,000. NEW YORK, 29 Oct 1986, *Gypsy Camp* (oil on canvas, 29¼ x 46in/74.3 x 116.9cm) USD 4,800. BERN, 30 April 1988, *Waterfall near Mantendorf* (oil on canvas, 20½ x 16½in/52 x 42cm) CHF 5,300. COLOGNE, 15 June 1989, *Boats on a Lake in the Alps* (oil on canvas, 16½ x 26in/42 x 66cm) DEM 2,200. AMSTERDAM, 19 Sept 1989, *Alpine Landscape with a Peasant Woman by a Stream at Dusk* (oil on canvas, 10 x 7in/24.5 x 17.5cm) NLG 4,370. NEW YORK, 29 Oct 1992, *Mountain Chalet* (oil on canvas, 17¼ x 23in/43.7 x 58.4cm) USD 2,420. MUNICH, 27 Feb 1999, *Castle Neuschwanstein as Seen from Pollat Gorge* (1886, oil on canvas, 15 x 22 ins / 37 x 55 cm) DEM 30,000. AHLDEN, 23 April 1999, *Summer Afternoon on a Lake* (oil on canvas, 30 x 45 ins / 75 x 114 cm) DEM 8,500. MUNICH, 22 March

2000, *Eibsee in Morning Light* (oil on panel, 9 x 14 ins / 24 x 36 cm) DEM 14,000. MUNICH, 26 Sept 2001, *Konigssee* (oil on canvas, 22 x 30 ins / 55 x 75 cm) DEM 6,500. LONDON, 29 Nov 2001, *Austrian Town in a Mountainous Lake Landscape* (oil on canvas, 37 x 54 ins / 95 x 137 cm) GBP 5,500. MUNICH, 20 Sept 2002, *Herder with Cattle in High Mountain Valley* (1866, oil on canvas, 29 x 35 ins / 73 x 88 cm) EUR 2,700. MUNICH, 20 Sept 2002, *Berchtesgaden* (oil on canvas, 24 x 30 ins / 61 x 76 cm) EUR 4,000. NUREMBERG, 6 Feb 2003, *Königssee with Figures* (1892, oil on canvas, 27 x 39 ins / 69 x 98 cm) EUR 2,700. ERLANGEN, 25 Oct 2003, *Starnberger See* (1881, oil on panel, 6 x 11 ins / 16 x 27 cm) EUR 2,100. ESSEN, 27 March 2004, *Alpine View with Lake* (1896, oil on canvas, 31 x 43 ins / 80 x 110 cm) EUR 4,000. LINDAU, 6 May 2004, *Waterfall near Bad Gastein* (oil on canvas, 19 x 16 ins / 48 x 41 cm) EUR 2,800.

FELDMAN, Charles

American, 20th century.

Born 27 January 1893, in Lublin, Russia (now in Poland).

Painter.

Charles Feldman was a pupil of the National Academy of Design, and studied under R. Henri and G. Bellows. He was also a writer and lecturer.

FELDMAN, Hilda

American, 20th century.

Born 22 November 1899, in Newark (New Jersey).

Painter.

Hilda Feldman studied under Ida Wells Stroud and Anna Fisher. She was also a craftswoman.

FELDMANN, Eduard

German, 19th century.

Active in Hamburg.

Lithographer.

In 1846, Eduard Feldmann published his colour print of the *Panorama of the Old and the New Jungfernstieg*. His other works include a lithograph of *The Church of St Mary Magdalene in Hamburg*.

FELDMANN, Hans-Peter

German, 20th century.

Born 1941, in Düsseldorf.

Assemblage artist, painter, draughtsman, photographer. Artists' books.

Conceptual Art.

A conceptual artist who was recognised in the 1960s, Hans-Peter Feldmann left the art world in 1976 and only resurfaced in the 1980s. He lives and works in Düsseldorf. He works from reproductions, photocopies or plaster busts, which he might paint and retouch. In his unsigned images and objects produced as series, he increases the references to his own culture. His work could also draw on the concept of plagiarism as a criticism of the world of art and culture, invaded by these mass-produced images.

From 1968 to 1969, Feldmann published a series of booklets composed of images on different themes called the 'Bilder' (Pictures), which are similar to the artists' books: *Der Überfall* (*The Raid*) (1975), about the hold-up of a bank; *Eine Stadt: Essen* (*A Town: Essen*) 1977, about the town; *Der Schwarze Sternehimmel* (*The Black Spangled Sky*) 1989; *Das Museum im Kopf* (*The Museum in the Head*); *Eine Firma* (*A Firm*) 1991, about the company Siemens; *Kunstgeschichten* (*Stories of Art*) 1992; *Enzyklopädie* (*Encyclopaedia*) 1994; *Porträt* (*Portrait*) 1994: *Voyeur* (*Voyeur*) 1994; *1,000 Frauen* (*1,000 Women*) 1998, 1,000 portraits of women.

100 Jahre (*100 Years*) is the work he exhibited at the exhibition *Voilà* (*Voilà*) at the Musée d'Art Moderne de la Ville de Paris in 2000, on the theme of memory. It consists of 100 photographs of women and men, one for each age, ranging from 0 - 100 years. His use of photography is considered to have influenced a large number of artists.

He has participated in group exhibitions, including: 2000, *Voilà* (*Voilà*), at the Musée d'Art Moderne de la Ville de Paris; 2002, *Sans Commune Mesure. Image et Texte dans l'Art Actuel* (*Without Common Measure: Image and Text in Contemporary Art*), the Musée d'Art Moderne Lille Métropole, Villeneuve d'Ascq; 2003, *Une Collection de 'Chefs-d'Oeuvre', Emprunts, Pastiches, Copies, Citations et Interprétations* (*A Collection of 'Masterpieces', Borrowings, Pastiches, Copies, Quotations and Interpretations*), an exhibition tackling the practice of appropriation in art, mainly from the European point of view, at the Fonds Régional d'Art Contemporain, Limoges; 2003, *Berlin-Moscow/Moscow-Berlin 1950-2000*, an exhibition overview which, following the exhibition covering the period 1900 - 1950, opened up for debate 50 years of German-Russian artistic and cultural relations, marked by political change, and was held at the Martin-Gropius-Bau in Berlin and the Tretyakov Gallery in Moscow.

Solo shows include: 1992, Musée d'Art Moderne de la Ville de Paris; 1994, La Flèche; 2001, Fundació Antoni Tàpies, Barcelona; 2002, Museum Ludwig, Cologne.

BIBLIOGRAPHY:

Leguillon, Pierre, *'L'Art épinglé'* in *Le Journal des arts* n° 4, periodical, Paris, June 1994. *Hans-Peter Feldmann*, exhibition catalogue, Neues Museum Weserburg, Bremen, 1999. Feldmann, Hans-Peter/Tatay, Helena/Durand, Régis, et al., *Hans-Peter Feldmann*, exhibition catalogue, Fundació Antoni Tàpies, Barcelona, 2001. Durand, Régis, et al., *Sans commune mesure. Image et texte dans lart actuel*, exhibition catalogue, Éd. Léo Scheer, Paris, 2002. *Hans-Peter Feldmann*, exhibition catalogue, Fotomuseum Winterthur, Winterthur (CHE), 2002. Wetterwald, Elisabeth, *'Hans-Peter Feldmann, passeur d'images'* in *Art Press* n° 277, Paris, March 2002. *'Berlin-Moskau/Moskau-Berlin 1950-2000'* in *2 vol.*, exhibition catalogue, Martin-Gropius-Bau, Berlin, 2003 (text in German).

MUSEUMS AND GALLERIES:

CARQUEFOU (FRAC Pays de la Loire): *Pin Ups* (1977, five retouched photocopies); *Portraits of Holbein* (1977, six photocopies); *David* (1990, painted plaster); *Caesar* (1989, painted plaster); *Children* (1977, five photocopies); *Encyclopaedia* (1990, five photocopies); *Mountain - 1990* (six photocopies); *Eiffel Tower* (1990, 24 photocopies); *Jacket and Shoes* (1991, one photocopy, a jacket and shoes); *Girls in Underclothes* (1991, three photocopies); *Bakery* (1991, 10 photocopies); *Dishes* (1991, five photocopies); *Washing Machines - 1990* (nine photocopies); *Carpet* (1990, nine photocopies); *Installation* (1992, six handwritten pages) - LIMOGES (FRAC Limousin): *Objects/Photocopies* (1992-1994, installation); *Untitled* (1995).

FELDMANN, Kaspar

Swiss, 19th century.

Born 1805, in Glarus; died 1866, in Stuttgart.

Painter. Architectural views, landscapes.

Kaspar Feldmann was a businessman and as an artist was entirely self-taught. He lived in St Petersburg, Tägerwilen, Constance, Munich and Stuttgart.

FELDMANN, Konon

Russian, 20th century.

Born 1870, in Krinitchnoie on the Don.

Painter. Portraits, genre scenes, landscapes.

Koon Feldmann studied initially at the school of fine art in Odessa and was then a student of Pavel Petrovich Chistyakov at the academy in St Petersburg. He exhibited in the spring exhibition in that city in 1900, his works including *Wood Drive on the Dnieper*, *Leaves and Roots*, *Mother* and *Scene*.

AUCTION RECORDS:

LONDON, 2 Nov 1979, *Portrait of Ali Haider, Emir of Mecca* (1921, pastel, 23 3/4 x 18 ins / 60.3 x 45.7 cm) GBP 3,200.

FELDMANN, Louis
German, 19th century.
Born 12 June 1856, in Itzehoe (Schleswig-Holstein); died 1938.
Painter. Religious subjects, genre scenes.
Louis Feldmann worked in Düsseldorf. In 1889, he received an honourable mention in Berlin. His best-known works include: *Doubting Thomas; The Last Supper; Holy Family; Gethsemane* and *St Valentine Curing a Young Epileptic.*
AUCTION RECORDS:
DÜSSELDORF, 6 Oct 1982, *Opening the Will* (oil on canvas, 29 1/2 x 34 1/4in/75 x 87cm) DEM 3,600.

FELDMANN, Peter
German, 19th century.
Born 27 August 1790, in Krefeld; died 8 October 1871, in Krefeld.
Painter. Landscapes.
From 1819 to 1822, Peter Feldmann studied in Paris, where he exhibited several landscapes at the salon, including *Sunset* and *Moonlight.* He also exhibited further landscapes at the academy in Berlin. Following time spent in southern Germany and Switzerland, and a journey through Italy, he painted views of the north Italian lakes, Mount Pilatus, and the Roman countryside.
MUSEUMS AND GALLERIES:
KREFELD (Kaiser Wilhelm Mus.): *Lake Maggiore.*

FELDMANN, Valentin Augustovitch
Russian.
Active in St Petersburg.
Painter, watercolourist. Seascapes.
MUSEUMS AND GALLERIES:
ST PETERSBURG (Gosudarstvennyj Russkij Muz.): *Seaside* (watercolour).

FELDMANN, Wilhelm
German, 19th century.
Born 1 December 1859, in Lüneburg; died 1932.
Painter, watercolourist, engraver. Landscapes.
Wilhelm Feldmann exhibited and received an award for his watercolours in Dresden in 1887. In 1889, he was awarded the Menzel Foundation prize. He settled in Berlin in 1886 and was principally an etcher.
MUSEUMS AND GALLERIES:
BERLIN: *Moonrise* - KALININGRAD: *Village on the Heath* - LÜBECK: *The Heath at Sunset.*
AUCTION RECORDS:
STUTTGART, 9 May 1981, *Wooded Landscape* (oil on canvas, 39 1/4 x 31 1/2in/100 x 80cm) DEM 4,800. BREMEN, 30 March 2001, *In the Sunshine* (oil on canvas, 22 x 30 ins / 56 x 75 cm) DEM 3,700. BREMEN, 29 Nov 2002, *After the Storm* (1916, oil on canvas, 39 x 51 ins / 100 x 130 cm) EUR 2,000.

FELDMULLER, Tilman Joseph
German, 18th century.
Born 20 July 1737, in Ahrweiler; died 1788, in Cologne.
Painter.
Feldmuller studied at the art academies in Antwerp and Vienna, becoming a master painter in Vienna in 1764. He was a history and portrait painter and also produced frescoes.

FELDNER, Reinhold
German, 19th century.
Born 12 January 1855, in Frankfurt an der Oder; died 1906, in Hamburg.
Painter. Architectural views.
Feldner worked for many years in Hamburg.

FELDTRAPPE, Henri
French, 19th century.
Born 19th century, in Paris.
Painter.
Feldtrappe was taught by Bonnegrâce. He became a member of the Société des Artistes Français in 1893. He first exhibited at the Salon in 1876.

FELDWEG, Joh. Christ. Gustav
German, 19th century.
Born 1814, in Leipzig.
Active in Leipzig.
Lithographer, engraver.
Feldweg's preferred field was architectural plates. He engraved views of German towns for C.A. Menzel's book *Works of Art from Antiquity to the Present Day.*

FELEDI, Tivadar or Theodor, or Flesch
Hungarian, 19th century.
Born 8 October 1852, in Budapest; died 6 February 1896, in Budapest.
Painter.
Tivadar Feledi began his studies in Budapest and then spent six years in Paris, where he worked with Bonnat, Munkácsy and Zichy. In 1879 and 1880 his work featured in the Salon de la Société des Artistes Français.
MUSEUMS AND GALLERIES:
BUDAPEST (Szépmuvészeti Múz.): *Shepherd.*

FELEDY, Gyula
Hungarian, 20th century.
Born 1928.
Engraver.
Gyula Feledy was a pupil of Karoly Koffan, Janos Kmetty and Bertalan Por. He completed his studies at the academy of fine art in Cracow. He was awarded a three-year Derkovits grant. He lived in Miskole after 1955. Feledy used direct printing and texture processes with a modern emphasis in his engravings. He participated in the Biennales in Lugano, Tokyo, Cracow and, in 1966, Venice. He held solo exhibitions in Cracow (1953) and Budapest (1965).
BIBLIOGRAPHY:
Csorba, Géza, *L'Art hongrois contemporain,* exhibition catalogue, Musée Galliera, Paris, 1970.

FELETTI, Giacomo Filippo
Italian, 17th century.
Born to a family originally from Comacchio.
Fresco artist.
Giacomo Feletti worked in Ferrara alongside Cesare Mezzogori, decorating the nave of the church of the monastic order known as the Theatines with oil paintings depicting episodes from the life of St Cajetan, one of the order's founders.

FÉLEZ, Fernando Jesus, pseudonym of San Martin Félez
Spanish, 20th century.
Born 4 September 1930, in Saragossa.
From 1955 active in France.
Painter, engraver, illustrator.
Groupe Mouvement.
Fernando Félez studied at the school of arts and crafts at the Barcelona fine arts academy between 1941 and 1950. He was awarded a study bursary and went to Paris in 1950. In 1957 he enrolled at the Paris school of fine arts to study lithography. In 1970 he travelled to New York.

In 1955 he began his first experiments with abstract painting. He participated in the training of several groups of artists including the Mouvement (Movement) group with Albertini, Canes, Fiaux, Plaza, E. Valles, Guzman and the writer Charles Juliet. In 1964 he came into contact with the 'lifestyle group' Panic formed by Arrabal, Jodorowsky and Topor and produced a first series of portraits of Fernando Arrabal. He abandoned abstract painting in 1965. 'Panic' according to Jodorowsky was perceived as a 'euphoric blend' of things and events and above all 'a rejection of gravity'. Félez's paintings with their sustained and careful realism are interesting for their Surrealist element and often show nude women and carnal desire in a way that is very appealing to the eye. Later in time, Fernando Arrabal describes them thus: 'Félez's art is a superb creation of desire and not a sordid demand that comes from need'.

Félez took part in many collective exhibitions including: in 1950 an exhibition of Spanish engravers that toured Latin America; in 1963, the Salon Option organised by the art critic Deroudille in Lyons. He also held solo exhibitions of his work: in 1962 at the Galerie de Beaune in Paris; in 1963 at the Galerie de Verneuil in Paris; in 1971 in New York; in 1975 in Barcelona among others.

FELGENTREFF, Paul

German, 19th century.

Born 3 August 1854, in Potsdam; died 1933, in Munich.

Painter, draughtsman. Genre scenes, landscapes.

Initially a pupil of Nieper in Leipzig, Felgentreff then moved to Munich to continue his studies with Seitz and Defregger. He executed studies of landscapes inspired by the Bavarian mountains, brought to life with local characters. His best-known works include: *A Refreshing Drink* and *Arrival of the Holidaymakers in the High Mountain Pasture*. A collective exhibition of his works was held at the Kunstverein in Munich in 1914.

AUCTION RECORDS:

LINDAU, 8 Oct 1980, *Seated Nude Viewed from Behind* (oil on canvas, 33 1/4 x 27in/84.5 x 68.5cm) DEM 4,200. COLOGNE, 25 June 1982, *Portrait of a Young Peasant* (oil on panel, 5 1/4 x 4 1/4in/13.5 x 10.5cm) DEM 1,600. NEW YORK, 27 Oct 1984, *Coming Back from Market* (oil on canvas, 20 x 13 1/2in/50.8 x 34.3cm) USD 3,800. MUNICH, 6 Dec 1994, *Young Woman* (oil on panel, 10 x 7 1/4in/24.5 x 18.5cm) DEM 2,070. MUNICH, 27 June 1995, *Monk Preaching at a Young Peasant Woman* (oil on canvas, 24 1/2 x 19 3/4in/62.5 x 50cm) DEM 5,175. PARIS, 21 March 1996, *Coming Back from the Market* (oil on canvas, 19 3/4 x 13in/50 x 33cm) FRF 31,000. ERLANGEN, 16 Sept 2000, *Interior Scene with Woman and Old Man* (oil on canvas, 27 x 22 ins / 69 x 55 cm) DEM 3,600. MUNICH, 27 Sept 2000, *Italian Flower Girl from Rome* (oil on canvas, 49 x 37 ins / 125 x 93 cm) DEM 10,000. NEW YORK, 2 Oct 2002, *Rest after the Hunt at an Alpine Tavern* (oil on canvas, 31 x 27 ins / 80 x 69 cm) USD 16,000. MUNICH, 6 Nov 2002, *Boy with Beer Tankard and Radishes* (oil on canvas, 20 x 12 ins / 51 x 31 cm) EUR 2,000. SAN FRANCISCO, 18 May 2004, *Einkehr* (oil on canvas, 27 x 22 ins / 68 x 56 cm) USD 4,000.

FELGENTREU, Max

German, 20th century.

Born 13 June 1874, in Luckenwalde (Brandenburg).

Painter. Landscapes.

Felgentreu was the pupil of J. Bergmann at the Kunstakademie in Düsseldorf. He featured in the National Exhibition in Zurich. He is known to have painted landscapes in Ticino.

FELGUÉREZ BARRA, Manuel

Mexican, 20th century.

Born 12 December 1928, in Hacienda de Valparaíso, Zacatecas.

Painter, sculptor.

Manuel Felguérez Barra studied in Mexico City at the Escuela Nacional de Pintura y Escultura ('La Esmeralda'). After a visit to Europe in 1947, Felguérez returned to Mexico having decided to pursue a career in art. He won a French Government grant to study in Paris for two years. He studied sculpture in Paris with Ossip Zadkine and exhibited at the 1st Biennale des Jeunes. He started painting by transposing his sculptural assemblages, created from pieces of soldered metal, into pictorial form. He was the first Mexican artist to practise total abstraction. Returning to Mexico in 1956, he began teaching sculpture at the Escuela de Arte y Diseño in the Universidad Iberoamericana and subsequently at the Universidad Nacional Autónoma de Mexico (UNAM). From the fairly strict geometricism of his early work, he developed towards compositions in warm colours, close to the subject, the medium generously applied with the knife. He also worked in silk-screen printing and computer art. His first solo exhibition was held in Mexico City in 1958.

BIBLIOGRAPHY:

Manuel Felguérez: El espacio múltiple, exhibition catalogue, Museo de Arte Moderno, Mexico City, 1973 (introduction by Octavio Paz). Manrique, J. A., et al., *El geometrismo mexicano*, Mexico City, 1977. Felguérez, Manuel, *La máquina estética*, Mexico City, 1983. Del Conde, T./Schneider, L.M., *Manuel Felguérez: Muestra antológica*, exhibition catalogue, Instituto Nacional de Bellas Artes, Mexico City, 1987. García Ponce, J., *Manuel Felguérez*, Mexico City, 1992. González Gortázar, F. (ed.), *La arquitectura mexicana del siglo XX*, Mexico City, 1994. Villoro, J., *Manuel Felguérez: El límite de una secuencia*, Mexico City, 1997.

AUCTION RECORDS:

NEW YORK, 19 May 1987, *Untitled* (1960, oil and mixed media/canvas, 31 3/4 x 39 1/4 ins / 80.7 x 100 cm) USD 2,000. NEW YORK, 21 Nov 1988, *Personal Iconography* (1966, oil on canvas, 45 1/4 x 50 1/4 ins / 115 x 127.5 cm) USD 9,350. NEW YORK, 1 May 1990, *La Cintura de la Andreida* (1967, oil on canvas, 49 1/4 x 55 ins / 125.3 x 140 cm) USD 5,500. NEW YORK, 18-19 May 1992, *Entrañas de Piedra* (*Heart of Stone*) (1989, oil, resin, wax, gold paint and sand on canvas, 45 1/4 x 53 ins / 115 x 134.6 cm) USD 16,500. NEW YORK, 18 May 1994, *Poza Rica* (1965, oil on canvas, 47 1/4 x 39 1/4 ins / 120 x 99.7 cm) USD 13,800. NEW YORK, 15 Nov 1994, *Kid on a Toboggan* (jute canvas and stainless steel sculpture, h. 15 ins / 38.1 cm) USD 2,300. MEXICO, 10 Aug 2000, *Archer* (terracotta, 16 x 13x19 ins / 40 x 34x47 cm) MXP 18,000. MEXICO, 30 Oct 2003, *Untitled* (oil on panel, 11 x 19 ins / 29 x 48 cm) MXP 24,000. MEXICO, 30 Oct 2003, *Untitled* (1975, oil on panel, 48 x 63 ins / 122 x 160 cm) MXP 68,000.

FÉLIBANT, Barthélémy

French, 17th century.

Active in Paris.

Sculptor.

FELICE

Italian, 17th century.

Active in Naples.

Painter, engraver.

Felice was a member of the order of Friars Minor (Minorites). He is remembered for three plates engraved for a prayer-book: *All the Saints*, *Ascension* and *St Clare in Heaven*. B. Thibout engraved his *St Anthony of Padua with the Infant Jesus* from an original by Felice.

FELICE (Fra)

Italian, 18th century.

Born to a family originally from Teramo.

Sculptor (wood).

A lay brother of the Capuchin order, Felice carved the main altar and a reliquary for the Capuchin church in Chieti in 1700.

FELICE. See also first name

FELICE, Alessandro de

Italian, 16th - 17th century.

Sculptor.

Alessandro de Felice collaborated with his brother Felice de Felice on the decoration of the monastery of S Martino in Naples.

FELICE, Felice de
Italian, 16th - 17th century.
Born to a family originally from Carrara.
Sculptor.
Felice de Felice worked on the monastery of S Martino in Naples with his brother Alessandro de Felice.

FELICE, Niccolò di Bernardino de
Italian, 17th century.
Born 17th century, to a family originally from Pesaro.
Painter.
He studied under A. Tasso and worked in Rome and Siena.

FELICE, Simone
Italian, 17th century.
Active in Rome.
Engraver.
Simone Felice collaborated with Giovanni Battista Falda on a collection of engravings entitled *Gardens of Rome*.

FELICE D'ARVANO
Italian, 16th century.
Active in Naples.
Engraver (wood).

FELICE DA BORNATO
Italian, 16th century.
Active in Brescia.
Sculptor.
Felice da Bornato worked after 1554 on the loggia of the Palazzo Municipale (town hall) in Brescia.

FELICE DA SIENNA
Italian, 15th century.
Active in Bologna.
Painter.
With Ranuccio da Imola, Felice da Sienna painted the miniatures of an antiphonary for the church of S Petronio in Bologna.

FELICE DE'FIORI. See **BIGGI Felice Fortunato**

FELICE DI FRANCESCO
Italian, 15th century.
Active in Perugia.
Miniaturist.

FELICE DI GIOVANNI DI SER PIETRO ZABOYE, or Ciaboie
Italian, 15th century.
Died 1481.
Active in Perugia.
Painter.
Felice was chancellor of the guild, director and lastly prior. He is probably identical with the chancellor of the guild in 1449, Felice di Pietro.

FELICE DI MICHELE
Italian, 15th - 16th century.
Born c. 1442; died 1518.
Active in Florence.
Miniaturist.
In 1473, Felice di Michele embellished, in the style of Girolamo da Cremona, part of a psalter conserved in the sacristy of the hospital of Santa Maria Novella in Florence.

FELICELLO, Giacomo
Italian, 17th century.
Of Sienese origin.
Painter.
Giacomo Felicello is recorded as being active in Rome around 1613.

FELICETTI, Giovanni
Italian, 18th century.
Born to a family originally from Predazzo; died 1727, in Bologna.
Painter.
Giovanni Felicetti studied under Cignani.

FELICI, Augusto
Italian, 19th century.
Born 1851, in Rome.
Sculptor.
Augusto Felici was a student at the institute of fine arts in Rome. In 1887 he showed *Bust of a Venetian Woman* and *Head of a Child* at exhibitions in Rome and Venice, with great success. Next, he exhibited six marble low reliefs in Venice (allegories of science for the Franchetti Palace). During a trip to Vadodara in India he was appointed court sculptor to a Hindu prince in 1892, and made numerous works for him, some in India and some in Venice. The best-known of these are low reliefs and statues, including *Violin Player Crouching*; *Bayadère Dancing*; and *Brahmin*; as well as a bronze group entitled *Hunting with Tamed Leopard*. For his patron in Vadodara Felici also sculpted some bronze busts and a monumental statue of the prince's wife. He travelled to Buenos Aires, where he sculpted a monument in memory of three Argentine poets. Felici's monumental statue of *St Anthony* can be seen in Padua.
MUSEUMS AND GALLERIES:
ROME (Gal. Nazionale d'Arte Moderna): *Turbine*.

FELICI, Sperandio
Italian, 16th century.
Active in Brescia.
Sculptor.
Sperandio Felici is mentioned in Munich in 1567 in connection with the restoration of antiques, and worked on the Palazzo Comunale in Brescia.

FELICI, Vincenzo
Italian, 17th - 18th century.
Active in Rome.
Painter, sculptor. Statues, busts.
School of Rome.
Vincenzo Felici studied in Rome under Domenico Guidi. Various works by Felici are to be found in the churches of S Maria in Trastevere, S Silvestro and S Maria dell'Umiltà. Felici also contributed a statue to the colonnade of St Peter's Square in Rome.

FELICIANO D'ALMEIDA. See **ALMEIDA Féliciano**

FELICIANO DA FOLIGNO, or Feliciano di Giacomo de Muti or Mutis
Italian, 16th century.
Painter.
The majority of Feliciano da Foligno's works are to be found at Foligno, where he seems to have worked between 1473 and 1518. They include a *Virgin and Christ Child with Two Angels Praying* in the Palazzo Candiotti; *Scenes from the Life of the Virgin* and *Christ and God the Father between the Cardinal Virtues*, frescoes in the Monastero di Santa Anna, Foligno. Also attributed to him is a *Virgin with St Antony and St François* in the Pinacoteca Comunale of the same town.

FELICIATI, Francesco
Italian, 18th century.
Active in Siena.
Painter.

FELICIATI, Lorenço
Italian, 18th century.
Born 1732, in Siena; died 1779.

Painter. History painting.
Several of his paintings are preserved in and around Siena.

FELIKER, C.
Sculptor. Mythological subjects.
MUSEUMS AND GALLERIES:
LIMOGES: *Venus Seated Surrounded by Putti.*

FELINI. See also **FELLINI**

FELINI, Egidio
Italian, 18th century.
Born 3 March 1704, in Parma.
Painter.
Egidio Felini is remembered as the source of an engraving by G. Ramis entitled *Virgin and Flower*, a copy of which is in the municipal library of Parma.

FELINO, Agostino. See **FELLINI**

FELIPE (Fray)
Spanish, 16th century.
Active during the first half of the 16th century.
Illuminator.
Felipe collaborated with Bernardino Canderron and Alonso Vasquez on the miniatures and embellishments of the *Missal* of Cardinal Francisco Jiménez Cisernos (1514-1518). Composed of seven volumes, it is conserved in the cathedral library in Toledo.

FELIPE, Juan
Spanish, 17th century.
Active in Valencia.
Engraver. Frontispieces.
Juan Felipe is known for the frontispieces of works by L. Mateu y Sanz and C. de Vega.

FELIPE, Pablo
Spanish, 16th century.
Active in Valencia.
Miniaturist.

FELIU, Francisco
Spanish, 15th century.
Of Catalan origin.
Painter.
A citizen of Manresa, near Barcelona, in 1412, Francisco Feliu worked for the Brotherhood of the Holy Spirit of Manresa, in the chapel of the Holy Spirit in the basilica.

FELIU, Guillermo
Spanish, 15th century.
Of Catalan origin.
Active in Barcelona.
Painter. Banners.
Guillermo Feliu is perhaps identical with an artist mentioned in Barcelona in 1394 as a painter of banners.

FELIU, Manuel
Spanish, 19th century.
Born 19 February 1865, in Barcelona.
Painter. Genre scenes.
Manuel Feliu was an associate of the exhibition of the national fine arts society from 1894 and exhibited at the society's exhibitions. He received a commendation at the Paris Exposition Universelle of 1900.
MUSEUMS AND GALLERIES:
BARCELONA: *Last Resort; The Kiss.*

FELIX
Painter.
Ancient Roman.
Felix, an artist from Pompeii, is attested by a signature on a mosaic in the House of Siricus.

FELIX
Polish, 16th century.
Active in Cracow.
Glass painter.

FÉLIX
German, 16th century.
Active in Liegnitz, Silesia (now Legnica, Poland).
Painter.

FÉLIX, Alexandre Florentin
French, 19th century.
Born in Paris.
Engraver (wood).
Alexandre Félix exhibited at the Salon des Artistes Français and received an honourable mention in 1888.

FÉLIX, Anna Désirée
French, 19th century.
Born 1827, in Bourg (Ain); died 6 January 1863, in Lyons.
Painter.
Anna Félix was a pupil of Elisa Blondel and of L. Cogniet. She exhibited figures, portraits, genre scenes and interiors in Paris in 1846 and in Lyons from 1846 to 1859. She lived in Lyons towards the end of her life, where she painted *Visit of the Virgin to St Elizabeth* for the nuns of St-Joseph.
MUSEUMS AND GALLERIES:
BOURG.

FELIX, Anthoine
French, 16th century.
Painter.
Fontainebleau School.
Anthoine Felix carried out some decorative work at Fontainebleau between 1540 and 1550.

FELIX, Auguste
French, 19th - 20th century.
Born 2 February 1860, in Bernin; died 1936, in Grenoble.
Painter. Portraits, landscapes.
Auguste Felix was a pupil of Hébert and Achard. He attended the École Nationale des Beaux-Arts in Paris, and participated in the Salon de Paris in 1884. He was included in the exhibition, *Le Portrait en Dauphiné au XIXe siècle* (*The Portrait in the Dauphiné Region in the 19th century*), at the Fondation Hébert d'Uckermann in La Tronche in 1981. In his portraits he attempted to reveal the souls or the hidden soul of his contemporaries, and would work on each painting for a long time.
MUSEUMS AND GALLERIES:
GRENOBLE (Mus. de Grenoble): *Portrait of a Woman* (1901, pastel).
AUCTION RECORDS:
GRENOBLE, 12 Dec 1984, *Grenoble, Quai Jongkind, Pont de la Citadelle and le Moucherotte* (oil on canvas, 23 1/2 x 36 1/4 ins / 60 x 92 cm) FRF 6,000.

FELIX, Charles
French, 18th century.
Active in Nancy.
Sculptor (wood).
In 1728 he sculpted the coats of arms of the city of Nancy for the church of Notre-Dame and an altar for the church in Amance, near Nancy.

FÉLIX, Claudius
French, 20th century.
Born 11 November 1875, in Paris.
Painter.
Claudius Félix was a pupil of Carolus-Duran. He exhibited in Paris at the Salon des Artistes Français.

FÉLIX, Dominique
French, 19th century.
Born in Paris.

Painter. Genre scenes.

Dominique Félix was a pupil of L. Cogniet. He first exhibited at the Salon in 1846, with *Cavalry Division Crossing a River*.

MUSEUMS AND GALLERIES:

MARSEILLES: *Episode during the Siege of Zaatcha.*

FELIX, Eugen

Austrian, 19th - 20th century.

Born 27 April 1837, in Vienna; died 21 August 1906, in Vienna.

Painter. Portraits, genre scenes.

Eugen Felix studied under the direction of Waldmüller; according to Siret, he was the pupil of Rahl. He completed his studies during journeys and in Paris. He lived in Vienna. He exhibited in Munich and Vienna from 1869 to 1873. Among his works are *After the Bath* and *Portraits of Children*.

MUSEUMS AND GALLERIES:

VIENNA: *The First Friend.*

AUCTION RECORDS:

LONDON, 28 Nov 1990, *The Baby-sitter* (oil on canvas, 25 1/2 x 31 ins / 65 x 79 cm) GBP 4,620. LONDON, 28 Oct 1992, *Portrait of a Small Boy with His Dog* (1875, oil on panel, 56 3/4 x 37 ins / 144 x 94 cm) GBP 1,705.

FÉLIX, Henri André

French, 19th century.

Born in Noyon.

Painter.

Henri Félix exhibited portraits at the Paris Salon in 1872 and 1873.

FELIX, Jean Pierre

Belgian, 20th century.

Born 1938, in Bouge.

Painter.

Jean Pierre Felix became a lecturer in fine art, and also created compositions in fantasy art.

FELIX, Johann

German, 18th century.

Sculptor.

Johann Felix created a Calvary, which he erected on the right bank of the River Erst at the entrance to the town of Bergheim.

FÉLIX, Juliette

French, 20th century.

Born 20 July 1869, in Paris.

Painter.

Juliette Félix was a pupil of Carrière, Brindeau and Mrs Boyer-Breton. She exhibited regularly in Paris, at the Salon des Artistes Français, of which she later became a member.

AUCTION RECORDS:

RHEIMS, 18 March 1990, *Portrait of a Young Woman with a Coral Necklace* (1919, pastel, 23 1/2 x 17 3/4 ins / 60 x 45 cm) FRF 3,000.

FÉLIX, Léon Pierre

French, 19th - 20th century.

Born 17 August 1869, in Périgueux.

Painter. Genre scenes.

He was a pupil of Bonnat, Cormon and Tony Robert-Fleury. In Paris, he was a member of the Salon des Artistes Français from 1894. He received a third-class medal in 1898, an honourable mention at the Exposition Universelle in 1900 in Paris, and the Marie-Bashkirtseff prize in 1908. He also exhibited *hors concours* in the Salon des Artistes Français.

FELIX, Leopold

Czech, 18th century.

Born to a family originally from Policka.

Painter.

Leopold Felix produced paintings of scenes from the life of St James, which are in the church of the deanery of St James in Policka in Bohemia.

FÉLIX, Marie Émélie

French, 19th century.

Active in Paris.

Engraver.

Marie Félix became a member of the Sociéte des Artistes Français in 1883. She exhibited at the society's Salon.

FÉLIX, Maurice

French, 20th century.

Born 26 June 1895, in Suresnes.

Painter.

Maurice Félix was a pupil of Cormon. He exhibited regularly in Paris at the Salon des Artistes Français, of which he became a member. He received a second-class medal in 1920.

FELIX, Nannette

18th century.

Engraver (etching), draughtsman. Landscapes.

Known works by her are etchings of landscapes, after Schütz and Waterloo, and a sepia drawing of a Russian landscape after J.B. Le Prince.

FÉLIX, Nelson

Brazilian, 20th century.

Draughtsman.

Nelson Félix has taken part in various group exhibitions including the 1996 Biennale in São Paulo. He produces extremely elaborate drawings based on images of the human body seen through the microscope which give rise to mysterious abstractions.

BIBLIOGRAPHY:

Farias, Agnaldo, '*Brésil: petit manuel d'instructions*' in *Art Press* n° 221, periodical, Paris, February 1997.

FÉLIX, Rebecca

French, 19th century.

Born in Paris.

Active during the second half of the 19th century.

Painter.

Rebecca Félix was a pupil of F. Humbert, and exhibited at the Salon des Artistes Français.

FELIX OF RAGUSA, or Felix Plianens of Ragusa or Felix Ragusinus

Croat, 15th - 16th century.

Born c. 1450, in Ragusa (now Dubrovnik); died after 1517.

Miniaturist, copyist.

This remarkably talented artist was put in charge of the group of miniaturists and copyists employed by Mattias Corvinus in Budapest.

FELIXMÜLLER, Conrad, real name: Felix Conrad Müller

German, 20th century.

Born 21 May 1897, in Dresden; died 1977, in Berlin.

Painter, watercolourist, engraver, draughtsman, illustrator. Figures, nudes, portraits, landscapes.

Felixmüller studied at the Kunstakademie in Dresden, where he was the pupil of F Dorsch and C Bantzer. From 1913 he began to engrave and to use the lithographic process. As a politically committed individual, he was active in Berlin in the Sturm circle and among the Expressionists in Dresden. He illustrated the newspaper *Die Aktion* using woodcuts. He exhibited for the first time in Berlin, in 1916, at the Sturm Gallery, which had introduced Cubism into Germany in 1911. Until 1913 Berlin was the centre of German artistic life, notably through the presence of *Die Brücke*. Felixmüller was influenced by the style of this group, by the very popular negro art in the creations of the avant-garde, by Cubism and, more prosaically, by the industrial landscape of the Ruhr. He produced many beautiful woodcuts, in black and white, featuring portraits, certain of which are near to caricature. In 1914 he produced portraits using a heavy, coarse line. In 1915 he introduced into his paintings colours applied in the Expressionist manner, such as rose-red scarlet flesh colour. His work often denounced the hard working conditions; the backgrounds of his compositions illustrated the dark, steel grey urban landscapes of the industrial complexes, where men are overwhelmed, and children are emaciated. People are depicted as deformed - over-large heads, bulging eyes - in saturated colours. In around 1932 he produced a series of well formed nudes, bathed in sensuality and with an ambiguous eroticism. From 1935, he expresses a more traditional realism. His scenes are almost rustic, if it were not for the 'workers' burden' which is still present: women are working in the fields, for example. Felixmüller's Expressionism was nevertheless blunted from the years 1948-1950 onwards, becoming a somewhat dry academicism.

BIBLIOGRAPHY:

Söhn, Gerhart/Heckmanns, Friedrich, *Conrad Felixmüller. Das graphische Werk 1912-1974*, Graphik-Salon Gerhart Söhn, Düsseldorf, 1975. Guenther, Peter W./Thesing, Susanne/Söhn, Gerhart, *Conrad Felixmüller, Werke und Dokumente*, exhibition catalogue, Germanisches Nationalmuseum, Nürnberg, 1981. Heckmanns, Friedrich W., *Conrad Felixmüller: das druckgraphische Werk 1912 bis 1976 im Kunstmuseum Düsseldorf: Schenkung Titus Felixmüller und Luca Felix Müller*, exhibition catalogue, catalogue raisonné, Das Kunstmuseum, Düsseldorf, 1986. Rathke, Chritian/Barth, Peter/Felixmüller, Titus/Frenzel, Ursula, *Conrad Felixmüller. Gemälde, Aquarelle, Zeichnungen, Druckgraphik, Skulpturen*, exhibition catalogue, Schleswig-Holsteinisches Landesmuseum Schloss Gottorf, Schleswig, 1990. Spielmann, Heinz/Felixmüller, Titus/Kobbe, Heinz/Frenzel, Ursula, *Conrad Felixmüller*, catalogue raisonné, monograph, Wienand, Cologne, 1996.

MUSEUMS AND GALLERIES:

BERLIN (Berlinische Gal.): *The Prizefighter* (1921) - DRESDEN (Gemäldegal.): *Portrait of a Woman; Young Worker* - DRESDEN (Stadtmus.): *Portrait of the Beloved; Portrait of the Artist; Happy Marriage* - ELBERFELD: *In the Studio* - HEILBRONN: *Noon in Winter* - STUTTGART: *Citizen* - WIESBADEN: *Father and Son; Librarian; Winter Landscape; Portrait of the Artist with His Sons; In the Spring Wind; The Kirschhoff Family.*

AUCTION RECORDS:

NEW YORK, 15 April 1959, *Winter*, USD 550. COLOGNE, 24 Dec 1972, *Unloading Barges in Dresden*, DEM 7,500. COLOGNE, 21 May 1976, *The Miner* (lithograph, 23 x 17 ins / 58.5 x 43 cm) DEM 2,200. HAMBURG, 3 June 1976, *Newborn Baby* (1921, oil on canvas, 23 x 26 1/2 ins / 58.2 x 67.3 cm) DEM 30,000. MUNICH, 26 May 1978, *Three Friends* (1919, woodcut) DEM 2,600. COLOGNE, 3 Dec 1980, *Max John* (1919, pen/paper, 19 1/4 x 16 ins / 49 x 40.2 cm) DEM 5,000. COLOGNE, 1 Dec 1982, *Still-life of Flowers with Cat* (1922, oil on canvas, 35 1/2 x 29 1/2 ins / 90 x 75 cm) DEM 32,000. ROME, 22 May 1984, *The Miner* (1922, Indian ink, 25 1/4 x 19 ins / 64 x 48 cm) ITL 3,500,000; *Summer's Night* (1918, pastel, 21 1/4 x 15 1/2 ins / 54 x 39.5 cm) ITL 6,000,000. HAMBURG, 9 June 1984, *Man by the Sea* (1918, oil on canvas, 26 1/2 x 22 3/4 ins / 67 x 58 cm) DEM 36,000. LONDON, 26 June 1984, *Coal Miner* (1920, coloured lithograph heightened with pastels, 22 1/2 x 15 1/2 ins / 57 x 39.2 cm) GBP 4,800. LONDON, 25 June 1985, *Auration* (1922, brush and ink, 25 1/2 x 19 3/4 ins / 64.5 x 50 cm) GBP 6,000. LONDON, 23 June 1986, *In the Spring Wind* (1920, oil on canvas, 37 x 29 ins / 94 x 73.6 cm) GBP 70,000. LONDON, 2 Dec 1986, *Small Town in Saxony* (c. 1918-1922, watercolour/paper, 23 x 18 ins / 58.5 x 46 cm) GBP 22,000. MUNICH, 26 Oct 1988, *Portrait of Hermann Kühn* (1923, oil on canvas, 23 1/2 x 23 1/2 ins / 60 x 60 cm) DEM 52,800. LONDON, 29 Nov 1988, *The Castle at Schleinitz* (1937, oil on canvas, 23 1/2 x 26 ins / 60 x 66 cm) GBP 12,100. MUNICH, 7 June 1989, *Leipzig, View of the Albertina Library and the Law Courts* (1935, oil on canvas, 19 3/4 x 15 3/4 ins / 50 x 40 cm) DEM 25,300. LONDON, 28 Nov 1989, *Portrait of Georgette Maire* (1921, oil on canvas, 31 1/2 x 33 1/2 ins / 80 x 85 cm) GBP 49,500. HEIDELBERG, 12 Oct 1991, *Draught Horse in Berlin* (1936, woodcut, 16 x 20 ins / 39.7 x 50.5 cm) DEM 1,500. ZURICH, 16 Oct 1991, *Max John* (1920, woodcut, 22 x 17 1/2 ins / 56 x 44.5 cm) CHF 4,800. MUNICH, 26-27 Nov 1991, *Portrait of Karin Lehmann* (1917, pencil, 18 x 15 1/4 ins / 46 x 39 cm) DEM 4,025. MUNICH, 26 May 1992, *Young Woman from Prachatice* (1924, woodcut, 19 3/4 x 15 3/4 ins / 50 x 40 cm) DEM 1,955. HEIDELBERG, 3 April 1993, *Portrait of Max Liebermann* (1926, woodcut, 19 1/2 x 15 1/2 ins / 49.8 x 39.5 cm) DEM 3,000. HEIDELBERG, 5-13 April 1994, *Young Woman near a Window* (1916, woodcut, 19 1/2 x 16 ins / 49.5 x 39.8 cm) DEM 11,000. LONDON, 13 Oct 1994, *Clemens Braun* (1931, oil on canvas, 45 1/2 x 30 ins / 115.5 x 75.3 cm) GBP 95,000. AMSTERDAM, 8 Dec 1994, *Woman Feeding a Baby* (1918, ink/paper, 23 1/2 x 18 ins / 60 x 45.5 cm) NLG 6,325. HEIDELBERG, 8 April 1995, *Head of a Woman* (1922, lithograph, 11 x 7 ins / 28 x 18 cm) DEM 3,500. LONDON, 9 Oct 1996, *Miner* (1920, coloured lithograph, 23 x 17 ins / 58.7 x 43 cm) GBP 27,600. LONDON, 4 Dec 1996, *Man out of Work* (1922, pen, brush and ink/paper, 25 1/2 x 19 3/4 ins / 64.5 x 50 cm) GBP 25,300. HEIDELBERG, 11-12 April 1997, *Couple in a Forest* (1918, woodcut, 10 x 11 3/4 ins / 25.2 x 30 cm) DEM 15,500; *On a Boat* (1920, coloured lithograph, 22 1/4 x 16 1/4 ins / 56.5 x 41 cm) DEM 34,000. PARIS, 10 June 1997, *Return from the Mine* (1920, lithograph, 25 1/2 x 19 ins / 64.6 x 48.2 cm) FRF 58,000. LONDON, 9 Oct 1997, *Madame Matil and Her Son* (1922, lithograph, 22 x 10 1/4 ins / 56 x 26 cm) GBP 1,265. NEW YORK, 6 and 7 March 1998, *Otto Dix Painting* (1920, engraving, 11 3/4 x 9 3/4 ins / 29.7 x 24.7 cm) USD 3,450. LONDON, 7 Oct 1999, *Injured Workers* (1922, pen, 26 x 20 ins / 65 x 50 cm) GBP 26,000. LONDON, 7 Oct 1999, *Autumn Evening in Klotzsche* (1921, oil on canvas, 39 x 47 ins / 99 x 120 cm) GBP 115,000. LONDON, 17 Oct 2000, *Self-portrait with My Wife Londo and My Son Titus* (1923, gouache, watercolour and pencil, 25 x 20 ins / 64 x 50 cm) GBP 158,000. LONDON, 18 Oct 2000, *Portrait of Otto Ritschl, Painter from Wiesbaden* (1920, oil on canvas, 33 x 30 ins / 85 x 75 cm) GBP 150,000. COLOGNE, 1 June 2001, *View from Balcony with Biblioteca Albertina, Leipzig* (1935, oil on canvas, 20 x 16 ins / 50 x 40 cm) DEM 26,000. BERLIN, 30 Nov 2001, *Love - Landscape* (1915, oil on canvas, 30 x 26 ins / 75 x 65 cm) DEM 210,000. MUNICH, 16 May 2002, *Portrait of Frau Else Oswald* (1923, watercolour, 18 x 13 ins / 46 x 33 cm) EUR 32,000. COLOGNE, 7 Dec 2002, *Study No 214* (1920, watercolour and gouache, 23 x 18 ins / 59 x 46 cm) EUR 9,000. LONDON, 3 Feb 2003, *Woman Reading* (1923, oil on canvas, 27 x 38 ins / 68 x 97 cm) GBP 160,000. LONDON, 3 Feb 2003, *Way Home* (1921, oil on canvas, 37 x 37 ins / 95 x 95 cm) GBP 510,000. LONDON, 22 June 2004, *Flower Girl. Praising the Model* (1925 and 1934, oil on canvas, double-sided, 31 x 33 ins / 80 x 85 cm) GBP 50,000.

BERLIN, 26 Nov 2004, *Bouquet of Dahlias* (1925, oil on canvas, 31 x 33 ins / 80 x 85 cm) EUR 32,000.

FELIZYN, Rostislaff
Russian, 19th century.
Painter. Portraits, genre scenes.
This artist was a pupil of Bruyllov at the St Petersburg academy. Two genre paintings *Two Young Female Friends* and *Death announced* won him a nomination as academician.

FELKER, Ruth Kate
American, 20th century.
Born 16 May 1889, in St Louis (Missouri).
Painter.
Ruth Kate Felker was a pupil of Washington University and the Saint Louis School of Fine Arts. Among her works is a fresco in St John's Hospital, Saint Louis.

FELL, F.
French, 20th century.
Painter.
AUCTION RECORDS:
LONDON, 8 July 1930, *Portrait of a Young Woman,* GBP 5.

FELL, Herbert Granville
British, 20th century.
Born 1872, in London; died 1951.
Painter, illustrator, stained glass painter.
Herbert Fell studied in London at Heatherley's, in Brussels and in towns in Germany. He produced drawings for the *Pall Mall Magazine, The Ludgate Monthly, The Windmill,* the *English Illustrated,* the *Ladies Field* (of which he was artistic director) and other magazines. From 1924, he edited the *Queen.* Fell taught painting and drawing at the Royal Albert Memorial College in Exeter. His work as an illustrator was influenced by Art Nouveau. Fell also illustrated a large number of books, including children's books, collections of short stories and poetry such as: *The Book of Job; The Song of Solomon; Arabian Nights Entertainments: Ali Baba and the 40 Thieves; Cinderella; Fairy Gifts and Tom Hickathrift; The Wonder Book* by N. Hawthorne; *The Wonder Book and Tanglewood Tales; Our Lady's Tumbler; Wagner's Heroes, Poems;* and *Poems* by Yeats. In Bath, he collaborated with Cedric Chivers on the colour decoration of leather book bindings. He exhibited his work at the New Gallery and the Royal Academy.
BIBLIOGRAPHY:
Osterwalder, Marcus (ed.), *Dictionnaire des illustrateurs 1800-1914,* Ides et Calendes, Neuchâtel, 1989.

FELL, Sheila
British, 20th century.
Born 20 July 1931, in Aspatria (Cumberland); died 1979.
Painter. Figures, landscapes.
Sheila Fell studied at St Martin's School of Art from 1950 to 1953 with Vivian Pitchforth. She settled in London and taught at the Chelsea School of Art. Fell held her first exhibition in 1955. She painted mainly landscapes of the Cumberland region.

MUSEUMS AND GALLERIES:
LONDON (Tate Collection): *Snowscape IV* (1961, oil on canvas); *Maryport, Cumbria* (1965, oil on canvas); *Haystack in a Field* (1967, oil on canvas).
AUCTION RECORDS:
LONDON, 11 March 1981, *Farm in Cumberland* (oil on canvas, 39¼ x 49½ ins / 100 x 126 cm) GBP 680. LONDON, 10 June 1983, *Farm in Cumberland* (oil on canvas, 40 x 50 ins / 101.5 x 127 cm) GBP 1,050. LONDON, 28 July 1987, *Farm in a Field* (oil on canvas, 30 x 40 ins / 76 x 101.5 cm) GBP 1,300. LONDON, 20 Sept 1990, *Woman* (1977, oil on canvas, 12 x 16¼ ins / 30.5 x 41 cm) GBP 1,705. LONDON, 26 Oct 1994, *Cumberland under Snow* (1962, oil on canvas, 40 x 49 ins / 101.5 x 124.5 cm) GBP 2,875. LONDON, 5 Nov 1999, *Farmhouse, Yorkshire Moors* (oil on canvas, 20 x 24 ins / 51 x 60 cm) GBP 5,500. LONDON, 2 Nov 2000, *Hillside with Farms* (1958, oil on board, 66 x 40 ins / 168 x 101 cm) GBP 5,800. LEYBURN, 19 July 2002, *Farmland at Aspatria* (oil on canvas, 28 x 35 ins / 70 x 90 cm) GBP 15,000. LONDON, 5 Sept 2002, *Farm in a Field* (oil on canvas, 30 x 40 ins / 76 x 101 cm) GBP 11,000. LONDON, 26 Feb 2003, *Potato Picking at Aigle Ghyll 1* (oil on canvas, 29 x 39 ins / 74 x 100 cm) GBP 13,000. LONDON, 16 Oct 2003, *Wheat Harvest at Mechi Farm, Cumberland I* (1968, oil on canvas, 20 x 24 ins / 51 x 61 cm) GBP 17,000. LONDON, 17 Nov 2004, *Harvest Field, Skinburness* (1966, oil on canvas, 20 x 24 ins / 51 x 61 cm) GBP 5,500.

FELLE, Hans Jacob
German, 17th century.
Active in Altdorf near Weingarten.
Painter.

FELLECCHIA, F
Italian, 19th century.
Active in Naples.
Engraver.
In 1846 Fellecchia engraved two plates for a book by D. del Re, entitled *Historic Memories... of Naples.*

FELLENBAUM, Marx
German, 16th century.
Painter.
Nuremberg School.
Marx Fellenbaum was a painter and pattern-maker in Nuremberg, Bavaria, and became a burgher of the town in 1526.

FELLENBAUM, Simon
German, 16th century.
Painter.
Nuremberg School.
A painter and pattern-maker in Nuremberg, Simon Fellenbaum became a burgher of the town in 1524.

FELLENBERG, Hans Conrad
Swiss, 17th century.
Baptised 15 February 1621; died 1657.
Painter.
Fellenberg painted a picture of the two sculpted stags' heads kept at the town hall in Bern. He was also a statesman.

FELLENGIEBEL, Georg, or Fellengibl
Austrian, 17th century.
Born in Liegnitz, Silesia (now Legnica, Poland); died before 27 November 1613, in Innsbruck.
Active in Innsbruck.
Painter, draughtsman. Cards.
Fellengiebel was court painter to Grand Duke Ferdinand II and produced paintings at Rotholz castle, near Brixlegg (Tyrol). He drew a genealogical tree of the House of Austria for Grand Duke Maximilian, and also drew and painted cards of the Upper and Lower Inn valleys.

FELLER, Albert
Swiss, 19th century.
Active in Geneva.
Enameller.

FELLER, F. T.
German, 18th century.
Active in Jena.
Engraver.
F.T. Feller engraved the portraits of *Duke Wilhelm Heinrich of Saxe-Eisenach* and *Elector Friedrich III of Saxony.*

FELLER, Frank
Swiss, 19th century.
Born 28 October 1848, in Bumplitz; died 6 March 1908, in London.
Painter, illustrator.
A pupil in Geneva of the enamel painter Albert Feller, Frank Feller went on to study for a year at the academy of art in Munich, before going to Paris and London, where he produced pen-and-ink drawings for illustrated journals and books. He chose mainly war subjects for his paintings and exhibited *An Advanced Post, Bushey Park* and *Faithful to the Last* at the Royal Academy in London.

FELLER, P. F.
Painter, watercolourist. Genre scenes.
AUCTION RECORDS:
LONDON, 9 Dec 1907, *Race for Life* (watercolour) GBP 7.

FELLERMEYER, Josef
German, 19th century.
Born 10 January 1862, in Ingolstadt.
Painter.
A pupil of Lindenschmidt at the academy of art in Munich and of Benjamin Constant and Gérôme in Paris, Fellermeyer went on to work in Munich, Milan and Berlin and showed genre paintings such as *Astarte, In the Shade* and *Bathing* at the annual exhibition in Munich in 1891 and 1908, the great exhibitions in Berlin and Dresden and, in 1898, at the national exhibition in Turin.

FELLINGA
Dutch, 19th century.
Active in Friseland.
Painter. Genre scenes.
Mentioned by Siret, Fellinga was perhaps an amateur painter.

FELLINI, Agostino, or Felino
Italian, 15th century.
Probably born in Bologna.
Painter.
Agostino Fellini worked on the Palazzo del Quirinale.

FELLINI, Giovanni Battista
Italian, 17th century.
Active in Bologna in 1600.
Painter, designer of ornamental architectural features.

FELLINI, Giulio Cesare
Italian, 17th century.
Born c. 1600; died 1656.
Painter. Genre scenes, animals.
The son of Giovanni Battista Fellini, he studied under Gabriel Ferrantini and Annibale Carracci. Fellini excelled particularly at painting horses and people. He was frequently assisted by his brother, Marco Antonio Fellini.

FELLINI, Marco Antonio
Italian, 17th century.
Died 1660, in Bologna.
Painter.
The son of Giovanni Battista Fellini, he worked frequently with his brother, Giulio Cesare Fellini.

FELLMANN, Aloys
Swiss, 19th century.
Born 11 January 1855, in Oberkirch (Baden-Württemberg), Germany; died 9 March 1892, in Düsseldorf.
Painter, engraver. Portraits, genre scenes, history painting.
Fellmann was probably first taught by the sculptor Sales Amlehm, whom he know in Sursee. He went on to the workshop of George Kaiser in Stans, before studying with Seraphin Weingartner at the school of drawing in Lucerne and finally entering the academy of art in Düsseldorf.
MUSEUMS AND GALLERIES:
BERN: *Man's Head* (study) - DRESDEN: *Vows of a Benedictine Monk.*

FELLNER
German, 19th century.
Active in Erfurt (Thuringia).
Painter.
Fellner's painting *Woman at the Piano* is kept at the Museum in Erfurt.

FELLNER, Ferdinand August Michael
German, 19th century.
Born 12 May 1799, in Frankfurt am Main; died 14 September 1859, in Stuttgart.
Painter, draughtsman, illustrator. History painting, figures, portraits.
After studying law, Ferdinand Fellner went to Munich, where he studied painting with Cornelius until 1831. He then settled in Stuttgart. His best-known works include *Emperor Conrad III* and *St Cecilia.* He also illustrated works such as *Die Niebelungen, Gudrun, Don Quixote, William Tell, The Maid of Orleans, Faust, Romeo and Juliet* and *Macbeth.*

Fellner specialised in the Middle Ages and was interested in old paintings, which at that time were still much neglected. Following the example of his tutor Cornelius, he was true to the Gothic-Romantic spirit so typical of that period in Germany.

AUCTION RECORDS:
MUNICH, 26 Nov 1981, *Meeting between Margaret and Mephistopheles* (1855, watercolour, 9¾ x 7in/25 x 17.5cm) DEM 1,350. MUNICH, 10 Dec 1992, *Portrait of a Lady* (pencil/paper, 10¼ x 7¼in/26 x 18.6cm) DEM 1,695.

FELLNER, Kolomanus (Father)
Austrian, 18th - 19th century.
Born 1750, in Bistorff; died 1818, in Lambach.
Draughtsman, engraver (etching/burin).
Kolomanus Fellner was a member of the Order of Benedictines. He engraved religious and genre subjects.

FELLOWES, C.A. (Miss)
British, 19th century.
Active in Wolverhampton.
Sculptor.
Miss C.A. Fellowes exhibited at the Royal Academy in London from 1867 to 1872.

FELLOWES, Frank Wayland
American, 19th century.
Born 1833; died 16 June 1900, in New Haven.
Painter.

FELLOWES, James
British, 18th century.
Painter. Portraits.
The Last Supper in the church of St Mary in Whitechapel (London) is attributed to one James Fellowes.
AUCTION RECORDS:
LONDON, 24 Nov 1922, *Sir Holland Egerton; Miss Legh* (collection) GBP 21. LONDON, 9 July 1926, *Naval Officer in Uniform,* GBP 10. LONDON, 18 Dec 1933, *Portrait of John Puleston,* GBP 5. LONDON, 5 July 1937, *Woman,* GBP 42. LONDON, 1 July 1938, *Elisabeth Pennant* GBP 31. LONDON, 4 Sept 2003, *Portrait of a Young Boy in Roman Costume* (oil on can-

vas, 30 x 25 ins / 76 x 63 cm) GBP 1,900. LONDON, 4 Sept 2003, *Portrait of Margaret Aldersey in a Yellow Dress and Blue Wrap* (oil on canvas, 36 x 30 ins / 91 x 76 cm) GBP 3,500.

FELLOWES, William Dorset
British, 19th century.
Draughtsman, engraver.
William Dorset Fellowes drew the plates engraved by J. Clark for his work *Visit to the Monastery of La Trappe in 1817*, published in London in 1818, and for *The Antiquities of Westminster* by J.T. Smith. He also published *Historical Drawings on the Last Part of the Reign of Charles I* in London in 1828, with a great number of original portraits.

FELLOWES-PRYNNE, Edward A.
See **PRYNNE Edward A. Fellowes**

FELLOWS, Albert P.
American, 19th century.
Born 1864, in Cahaba (Alabama).
Painter, engraver (etching).
Albert P. Fellows, the husband of the painter Cornelia Fellows, studied and settled in Philadelphia, where he frequently exhibited.

FELLOWS, Cornelia
Maiden name: Faber
American, 19th century.
Born 1857, in Philadelphia.
Painter.
Cornelia Fellows, the wife of the artist Albert P. Fellows, painted mainly portraits and miniatures.

FELLOWS, William K.
American, 20th century.
Born 1870, in Winona (Minnesota).
Painter.
William K. Fellows was pupil of Edward Ertz in Paris and taught architecture.
AUCTION RECORDS:
PARIS, 15 Dec 1995, *Tarantella with Vesuvius in the background* (oil on canvas, 39¼ x 29½ ins / 100 x 75 cm) FRF 46,000.

FELLY, Joseph
French, 19th century.
Born in Paris.
Painter, sculptor. Architectural interiors, landscapes.
Felly exhibited at the Salon from 1834 to 1863, especially views. Works include *Interior of a Ruined Cloister, Interior of a Courtyard in Fuorigrotta, near Naples, View from Montalais* and *View from the Park of St-Cloud*.
AUCTION RECORDS:
PARIS, 22 June 1981, *Young Woman* (white marble, h. 24¾ ins / 63 cm) FRF 2,700. VERSAILLES, 29 Nov 1981, *View of Montfort-Lamaury from the Towers* (1844, oil on canvas, 40¾ x 57½ ins / 103.5 x 146 cm) FRF 10,000. VERSAILLES, 6 Nov 1988, *Tower of the Castle of Anne of Brittany, Dominating Montfort-L'Amaury* (1944, oil on canvas, 40¾ x 57¾ ins / 103.5 x 147 cm) FRF 25,000.

FÉLON, Charles François
Belgian, 19th century.
Born 19th century
in Brussels.
Painter. History painting, genre scenes.

FÉLON, Jean Pierre Maurice
French, 18th century.
Active in Paris in 1760.
Painter.

FÉLON, Joseph
French, 19th century.
Born 21 August 1818, in Bordeaux; died 1896, in Nice.
Painter, sculptor, ceramicist, lithographer. Allegorical subjects, genre scenes. Designs for stained glass.
Félon was self-taught. He exhibited at the Paris Salon from 1840 to 1882, receiving honourable mentions in 1857, 1861 and 1863. Sculptures include *Galatea* and *Amphitrite*, bronze low reliefs, *Andromeda*, a bronze statuette, *Woman Bathing*, a plaster statuette, *Vanity*, a marble bust, *Sailing*, a marble produced for the Emperor, *St Sigebert, King of Austrasia*, a stone statue for the façade of Nancy Cathedral, *Gerson*, a stone statue for the façade of the Sorbonne, *Nélaton*, a marble bust for the Institute and *Woman from the South Seas*, a stone statue. Paintings include *Guardian Angel; Shipwrecked People on Cap Seret; Shepherds in Les Landes; Awakening at the End of the Day; Young Woman Carrying a Child* and *Death of Bishop Monseigneur Affre*, a painting commissioned by the Ministère de l'Intérieur. He made many designs for stained glass windows for the church of Ste-Perpétue in Nîmes.

MUSEUMS AND GALLERIES:
ANGERS: *Faun* - BORDEAUX: *Nymph Huntress; History Consulting Truth* - DUNKIRK: *Andromeda* - LE HAVRE: *Sailing* - MONTPELLIER (Mus. Fabre): *Death of Bishop Monseigneur Affre* - NICE: *Andromeda; Monochrome; Oceania; Music; Spring; Prudence* - PARIS (Institut de France): *Bust of Combes; Bust of Nélaton* - PARIS (Mus. d'Orsay): *Bust of Baron Gros*.
AUCTION RECORDS:
SCEAUX, 9 April 1995, *Kneeling Man, Nude* (1872, graphite, 11¾ x 9½ ins / 30 x 24 cm) FRF 3,800. PARIS, 25 Oct 1999, *The Water-Diviners* (1888, oil on canvas, 17 x 24 ins / 43 x 61 cm) FRF 17,000. NEW YORK, 25 Oct 2000, *Four Seasons* (1873-1874, oil on panel, set of eight, 64 x 32 ins / 162 x 82 cm) USD 51,000. AHLDEN, 9 May 2003, *City on Canal* (1838, oil on panel, 9 x 13 ins / 23 x 33 cm) EUR 1,800.

FELOT, Auguste
Czech, 20th century.
Painter.
Auguste Felot showed *Prisoners* at the 1926 Salon d'Automne in Paris.

FELPACHER
Dutch, 17th century.
Painter.
The Nostitz gallery in Prague holds a landscape with *Diana and Actaeon* by Felpacher. He is identical with J. Felpacker whose painting, *Shepherd and Shepherdess with their Sheep*, is mentioned in an inventory in Amsterdam in 1678.

FELS, Elias
Swiss, 17th century.
Born 1614, in Emmishofen; died 1655, in Heidelberg (Baden-Württemberg, Germany).
Painter. History painting, portraits.
It is thought that Fels, who lived in St Gall for a short time, studied at the art schools in the Netherlands, and returned to Germany when he took up the post of painter at the Court of the Elector of Heidelberg. His works include *Portrait of Dean Locher* (kept in the city library at St Gall), an allegorical painting dated 1643, and an imaginary composition dated 1647, which is kept at the museum of history in Mulhouse (Bas-Rhin, France).

MUSEUMS AND GALLERIES:
MULHOUSE (Mus. Historique): *Composition* (1647) - ST GALL (City Library): *Portrait of Dean Locher.*

FELS, Jan Jacob
Dutch, 19th century.
Born 1816, in Campen; died 1883.
Painter. Landscapes with figures.
Jan Jacob Fels was a pupil of J. Pluger.
AUCTION RECORDS:
AMSTERDAM, 11 April 1995, *Figures on a Path along a Stream* (oil on panel, 15 3/4 x 21 1/2 ins / 40 x 54.5 cm) NLG 5,900.

FELSBURG, Albrecht Steiner von
Austrian, 19th century.
Born 25 February 1838, in Vienna; died 31 October 1905, in Innsbruck.
Painter, architect. History painting.
Felsburg studied under Schlotthauer and Schraudolph at the academy in Munich. After making several journeys to study in Italy, he settled in Innsbruck. He painted altar paintings for churches in Marburg (Hesse) Germany, *Death of St Elizabeth*, and Wieliczka (Galicia, East central Europe), and undertook the restoration of a large number of frescoes. He also painted some frescoes himself.

FELSENBERG (Frau). See **FISCHER Maria Anna**

FELSENHELD, Lise Suzanne
French, 20th century.
Born in Paris.
Painter, engraver.
Felsenheld was a pupil of Sabatté. She exhibited in Paris at the Salon des Artistes Français from 1931, as well as at the Salon des Artistes Indépendants.

FELSER, Heinrich
German, 17th century.
Active in Munich c. 1600.
Sculptor.
Together with other artists such as Krumpper, Weinhart and Türfelder, Felser carved the stone statues of Bavarian princes on the façade of the Michaelskirche (church of St Michael) in Munich.

FELSING, Georg Jakob
German, 19th century.
Born 1802, in Darmstadt; died 1883, in Darmstadt.
Engraver.
Felsing was the son and pupil of Johann Konrad Felsing, the engraver. He went to Italy, where he studied under Longhi in Milan. He lived in turn in Naples and Florence, where he was a teacher at the academy. He was then made a member of the academy in Milan. He returned to Darmstadt in 1832, where he was appointed as teacher at the academy, then court engraver. Felsing was also a member of the academies in Berlin, Vienna and St Petersburg, and a corresponding member of the Paris Institute. He engraved the works of the classical Italian masters.

FELSING, Johann Heinrich
German, 19th century.
Born 1800, in Darmstadt; died 1875, in Darmstadt.
Engraver (burin), printer.

FELSING, Johann Konrad
German, 18th - 19th century.
Born 1766, in Giessen (Hesse); died 1819, in Darmstadt (Hesse).
Engraver.
Felsing worked mainly in Darmstadt as an engraver of portraits.

FELSKO, Oskar Eduard Daniel
Russian, 19th century.
Born 17 June 1848, in Riga.
Painter.
Felsko initially studied sculpture at the St Petersburg academy of fine arts, then painting at the Düsseldorf Academy and settled in Mitau (now Jelgava). The Jelgava Guild House has a portrait by him of *Zander*, a member of the Corporation, and the Riga Stock Exchange has that of the commercial advisor *R. Kerovius*.

FELSTEAD
British, 20th century.
Painter.
AUCTION RECORDS:
LONDON, 26 Oct 1945, *Ara with a Rabbit and Fruit*, GBP 42.

FELTER, W. D.
American, 19th century.
Active at the beginning of the 19th century.
Engraver (wood).
W.D. Felter engraved many illustrations in the style of Bewick.

FELTESSE, Émile Henri
French, 20th century.
Born 7 February 1881, in Paris.
Engraver.
Émile Feltesse was a pupil of Sulpis, Deschamp and Dubouchet. He exhibited in Paris at the Salon des Artistes Français, the society of which he became a member in 1904. He engraved in burin and received an honourable mention in 1905.

FELTRE. See first name

FELTRIN, Victor
French, 20th century.
Born 5 May 1905, in Italy.
Sculptor.
Feltrin studied in Paris at the Académie de la Grande Chaumière from 1947 to 1949, and then at the Académie Julian until 1952. He exhibited in Paris at the Salon des Artistes Indépendants from 1952, and at the Salon de la Jeune Sculpture from 1953 to 1957. His sculptures are abstract and synthetic in their form.

FELTRIN DI LORENZO, Giambattista
Italian, 19th century.
Died 1863.
Active in Belluno (Lazio).
Painter.

FELTRINI, Andrea, known as Andrea di Cosimo, or del Fornajo
Italian, 16th century.
Born c. 1490; died c. 1554.
Painter.
Florentine School.
Andrea Feltrini's name is a result of his having studied with the painter Morto da Feltre and his sobriquet stems from his master Cosimo Roselli. He specialised in burlesque paintings on the walls, ceilings and façades of the houses in Florence. He worked on the Palazzo Strozzi and with Ridolfo Ghirlandaio on the Palazzo Vecchio.

FELTSCH, Jakob
German, 16th century.
Active in Zittau (Saxony).
Sculptor (wood).
Feltsch carved several statues for the church of St John in Zittau. Destroyed in a fire in 1737, the works are only known through a surviving description.

FELTZ, Franz Anton
German, 17th century.
Active in Strasbourg.
Potter.

Feltz is mentioned in 1731 as the 'porcelain maker to the Margrave of Baden'.

FELU, Charles François
Belgian, 19th century.
Born 1830, in Waarmaerde; died 5 February 1900, in Antwerp.
Painter. Portraits.

Charles François Felu was born without arms and attended the academy in Antwerp, the town where he settled and painted excellent portraits, including those of *Victoria Lafontaine* and *King Massala*. He also copied various works in the museum in Antwerp and the Victoria and Albert Museum in London.

AUCTION RECORDS:
PARIS, 30 Jan 1947, *Head of a Woman*, FRF 700.

FELY-MOUTTET
French, 20th century.
Born 1893, in Collobrières; died in Toulon.
Painter.

Fely-Mouttet was a pupil in the studio of Cormon, at the École des Beaux-Arts in Paris and at the École des Arts Décoratifs. He was director of the École des Beaux-Arts in Toulon. In 1952 he organised an important exhibition of abstract art. He exhibited in numerous salons, notably in Paris at the Salon d'Automne. His work evolved towards abstraction, and he exhibited at the Salon des Réalités Nouvelles, which organised a retrospective exhibition of his work in 1954. His abstract works are highly constructed, whether based on combinations of angular and rectilinear surfaces, or combinations of curved surfaces. They occupy space in the spirit of a mural decoration, which emerges from constructivism and sometimes recalls Auguste Herbin.

BIBLIOGRAPHY:
Réty, L., *Fély-Mouttet*, À la Tête d'Or, Lyons.

FELYER, Johannes
Dutch, 17th century.
Active in The Hague.
Sculptor.

FEMADES, Francisco
Spanish, 15th century.
Active in Valencia.
Painter.

FEMALE HALF-LENGTHS, Master of the.
See **MASTERS**

FEMENIA, Gabriel
Spanish, 17th century.
Born in the 17th century, on Majorca (Balearic Islands).
Painter. Landscapes.

There are paintings by Gabriel Femenia in Geneva. He is one of those Spanish artists who deserves to be better known; indeed, in Spain at the time he was working, he was considered one of the country's foremost landscape artists.

FEMES-BECK, Vilmos
Hungarian, 20th century.
Born 1885; died 1918.
Sculptor, decorative designer.
Nyolcak Group (The Eight).

Vilmos Femes-Beck studied in Budapest, Darmstadt, Munich, Paris and London. At the invitation of the Eight, he exhibited with them. Executed sculptural decorative details for the Villa Schiffer in Budapest.

BIBLIOGRAPHY:
Passuth, Krisztina/Szabó, Júlia, *L'Art en Hongrie 1905-1930. Art et révolution*, exhibition catalogue, Musée d'Art et d'Industrie, Saint-Étienne, Musée d'Art moderne de la ville de Paris, Paris, 1980.

MUSEUMS AND GALLERIES:
BUDAPEST (Magyar Nemzeti Gal.) - SZÉKESFEHÉRVÁR (Szent Istvan Kiraly Museum).

FEMI, Cesare, called Il Norcino
Italian, 19th century.
Active in Bergamo.
Painter.

Cesare Femi was a pupil of the portrait painter Fra Vittore Ghislandi. He made his living copying paintings of people and animals and, most often, landscapes by Zuccarelli. His most famous portraits are of *Father Giulio Oderi*, who died in Bergamo in the odour of sanctity; and the *Capuchin Gaetano Migliorini*. Femi was also a surgeon.

FEMINE, Giulio Cesare de
Italian, 18th century.
Born in Genoa; died probably in 1736, in Lisbon.
Painter.

He painted numerous oils of major public buildings and monuments in Lisbon. Much of his work was unfortunately lost in the Lisbon earthquake of 1755. He was received into the Lisbon artists' guild in 1720.

FEN, Jan
Flemish, 17th century.
Of English origin.
Active in Antwerp.
Painter.
Flemish School.

Jan Fen qualified as a master of the guild and became a citizen of Antwerp in 1614.

FEN, Robbert
Flemish, 17th century.
Active in Antwerp.
Painter.
Flemish School.

Probably the son of Jan Fen, Robbert Fen qualified as master of the guild in 1620.

FENACOLIUS, Johannes
Dutch, 17th century.
Active in Dordrecht.
Painter.

FENAEM, Gerrit Gerritsz. van
Dutch, 17th century.
Active in Dordrecht between 1633 and 1671.
Engraver (line-engraving).

G.v.F. *sculp.*

FENAILLON, Madeleine
French, 20th century.
Born 8 May 1889, in Paris.
Miniaturist.

Madeleine Fenaillon exhibited in Paris at the Salon des Artistes Français, beginning in 1909.

FENAK, Ferdinand, or Fanck or Fenk
Czech, 18th century.
Born 1737, in Nový Zámek; died 18 January 1787, in Vienna.
Sculptor.

Ferdinand Fenak worked mainly in Vienna.

FENARD, Gaston
French, 20th century.
Born in Goupillières.
Painter.

Fenard exhibited landscapes at the Salon des Indépendants in Paris from 1925.

FENAROLI, Flavia
Italian, 20th - 21st century.

Born 1955.
Sculptor.
Fenaroli exhibited at the Salon des Réalités Nouvelles in Paris in 1988.

FENASSE, Paul
French, 20th century.
Born in Algiers.
Painter. Landscapes.
Fenasse exhibited at the Salon des Artistes Français from 1926.
AUCTION RECORDS:
PARIS, 6 April 1990, *The Bay of Algiers* (oil on canvas, 29 1/4 x 64 1/2 ins / 74 x 164 cm) FRF 160,000. PARIS, 13 March 1995, *The Bay of Algiers* (oil on canvas, 30 x 64 1/2 ins / 76 x 164 cm) FRF 128,000. PARIS, 14 Nov 2000, *Moorish Villa on the Heights of Algiers* (oil on canvas, 13 x 16 ins / 33 x 41 cm) FRF 20,000. PARIS, 14 Nov 2000, *Bay of Algiers* (oil on canvas, 29 x 65 ins / 74 x 164 cm) FRF 280,000. PARIS, 19 Nov 2001, *El Kantara Gorges* (oil on panel, 16 x 39 ins / 41 x 100 cm) FRF 14,000. PARIS, 17 Dec 2001, *Wadi in Flower in Spring* (oil on panel, 24 x 52 ins / 60 x 131 cm) FRF 20,000.

FENCY, Johannes Baptista Josefus
Flemish, 18th century.
Born c. 1756.
Active in Brussels.
Painter.
Flemish School.
Johannes Baptista Josefus Fency became a member of the academy in Leiden on 4 August 1783.

FEND, Peter
20th century.
Painter.
MUSEUMS AND GALLERIES:
MARSEILLES (FRAC Provence-Alpes-Côte d'Azur): *Beach Party; Europe, Germany, America, Asia, Southern Oceans* (1992, silk screen print on fabric, series of five flags).

FENDERICH, Charles
German, 19th century.
Draughtsman, lithographer.
In 1841 Fenderich published a series of portraits of important people in Washington. He is probably the same person as the artist Fendrich, who reproduced the paintings of Ludwig Vogel of Zurich.

FENDERSON, Annie M.
American, 20th century.
Born in Spartansburg (Pennsylvania).
Painter, miniaturist.

FENDERSON, Mark
American, 19th - 20th century.
Born in the second half of the 19th century, in the USA.
Illustrator.
Mark Fenderson was a member of the Society of Illustrators in 1913.

FENDI, Peter
Austrian, 19th century.
Born 4 September 1796, in Vienna; died 28 August 1842, in Vienna.
Painter, sculptor, engraver, draughtsman. History painting, portraits, genre scenes.
Fendi studied art in Vienna with Fischer, Maurer and Lampi. He was one of the painters of the Vienna Biedermeier era, and his style was fluid and colourful. In 1836 he was appointed member of the academy of fine arts. He worked as a draughtsman at the imperial coin and antiquities collection.

In 1994 some of Fendi's works were exhibited at the Marmottan museum in Paris, in the exhibition dedicated to *Chefs-d'oeuvre du Belvédère de Vienne* (*Masterpieces from the Belvedere in Vienna*). Many of his works belong to private collections.
MUSEUMS AND GALLERIES:
RIGA: *Little Violinist* - VIENNA: *Girl; Baptism; Sower; Indiscreet Woman; Open Air Mass; Brother of the Artist; Emperor Francis I; Maternal Blessing; Burial; Storm; Sad News* - VIENNA (Österreichische Gal. Belvedere): *Girl at the Lottery* (1829).
AUCTION RECORDS:
PARIS, 7 April 1896, *Maternal Love*, FRF 1,450. VIENNA, 4 Dec 1962, *Maternal Joy* (watercolour) ATS 25,000. LONDON, 12 May 1972, *Morning Work*, Gns 2,600. MUNICH, 29 May 1976, *Illustration of a Poem by Schiller* (watercolour, 8 3/4 x 12 ins / 22.5 x 30.5 cm) DEM 3,000. VIENNA, 19 May 1981, *Das Krampusfest* (*Festival of Krampus*) (pen/paper, 4 1/4 x 7 ins / 11 x 17.5 cm) ATS 22,000. BERN, 23 June 1982, *Carriage Pulled by Two Horses* (c. 1830, pencil, 7 1/4 x 7 3/4 ins / 18.4 x 20 cm) CHF 2,000. MUNICH, 27 June 1984, *Blind Man's Buff* (oil on panel, 18 1/2 x 24 ins / 47 x 61 cm) DEM 36,000. STUTTGART, 6 March 1999, *Nun Praying before Writing Table in Cell* (1823, oil on panel, 9 x 7 ins / 23 x 19 cm) DEM 4,800. LUCERNE, 19 May 1999, *The Charitable Queen* (watercolour, 6 x 6 ins / 14 x 15 cm) CHF 5,000. VIENNA, 20 March 2001, *The Post Station* (pencil and watercolour, 5 x 8 ins / 13 x 20 cm) ATS 60,000. VIENNA, 11 June 2002, *Two Women with Children* (1839, watercolour, 4 x 5 ins / 10 x 12 cm) EUR 22,000. VIENNA, 26 Nov 2002, *Interior of Apartment at Alserstrasse 19, Vienna IX* (1831, oil on panel, 9 x 13 ins / 23 x 32 cm) EUR 20,000. VIENNA, 30 Sept 2003, *The Diver* (watercolour, 3 x 4 ins / 7 x 10 cm) EUR 1,500. LINZ, 27 Nov 2003, *Warden Boy* (pencil, 4 x 3 ins / 10 x 8 cm) EUR 1,600.

FENDT, Bernhard
German, 16th century.
Died 1515.
Active in Augsburg (Bavaria).
Painter.
Bernhard Fendt belonged to the school of Hans Holbein the Elder. He executed work for churches and hospitals.

FENDT, Tobias
German, 16th century.
Died 1576, in Breslau (now Wroclaw, Poland).
Active in Breslau.
Painter, engraver (burin).
Tobias Fendt engraved 125 plates for the work *Monumenta Sepulcrorum cum epigraphis ingenio et doctrina excellentium Verorum*.

FENEAU
French, 18th century.
Sculptor.
Feneau exhibited a bust of Marat, from life, at the Salon in 1793.

FÉNÉRA, Bertrand de. See **BERTRAND DE FÉNÉRA**

FENESI, Paolo
Italian, 18th century.
Painter. Landscapes.
An archive catalogue of the guild of St Luke attributes two landscapes to Fenesi.
MUSEUMS AND GALLERIES:
TOULOUSE: two landscapes.

FENESTRE, Robert de La. See **LA FENESTRE**

FENESTREAULX, Nicolas de
Flemish School, 16th century.
Born in Antwerp.
Active in Orléans c. 1527.
Painter.

The naturalisation documents of this artist survive in the Archives of French art.

FENET, Pierre
French, 18th century.
Active in Paris in 1771.
Painter, sculptor.

FENG CH'AO-JAN. See **FENG CHAORAN**

FENG CHAORAN, or Feng Ch'ao-Jan, Feng Chaoren
Chinese, 20th century.
Born 1881 or 1882, in Lujin (Jiangsu); died 1954.
Painter, calligrapher. Landscapes, animals.

Feng Chaoran worked in Suzhou and Shanghai. His academic style sometimes demonstrates a certain vigour and freedom.

AUCTION RECORDS:
HONG KONG, 18 May 1989, *Landscape after Yan Ciping* (ink and colour on paper, hanging scroll, 42 3/4 x 18 1/2 ins / 108.6 x 46.7 cm) HKD 121,000. HONG KONG, 15 Nov 1989, *Album of Landscapes after Wang Hui* (ink and colour on silk, twelve leaves, each 15 x 13 1/2 ins / 38 x 34 cm) HKD 132,000. NEW YORK, 31 May 1990, *Lady in Garden* (ink and colour on paper, hanging scroll, 29 1/4 x 14 3/4 ins / 74.3 x 37.5 cm) USD 1,760. HONG KONG, 15 Nov 1990, *Landscape of the Four Seasons* (1941 to 1943, ink and colour on paper, set of four hanging scrolls, each 52 x 25 3/4 ins / 132.3 x 65.5 cm) HKD 176,000. NEW YORK, 26 Nov 1990, *Mandarin Ducks, Flowering Tree and Rocks* (1929, ink and colour on paper, hanging scroll, 29 3/4 x 16 ins / 75.5 x 39.8 cm) USD 1,760. HONG KONG, 31 Oct 1991, *Scholar playing Weiqi in Landscape* (1951, ink and colour on paper, hanging scroll, 49 x 25 1/2 ins / 124.4 x 64.8 cm) HKD 143,000. HONG KONG, 30 April 1992, *Lotus Pond* (1946, ink and colour on paper, hanging scroll, 33 1/4 x 16 ins / 84.3 x 40.5 cm) HKD 46,200. HONG KONG, 29 April 1993, *Two Rabbits* (ink and colour on paper, 16 x 26 ins / 40.5 x 66.3 cm) HKD 17,250. HONG KONG, 3 Nov 1994, *Various Subjects* (ink and colour on silk, album of eight leaves, each 11 x 12 1/2 ins / 27 x 32 cm) HKD 97,750. HONG KONG, 4 May 1995, *Lake in Spring* (ink and colour on paper, hanging scroll, 42 1/4 x 20 3/4 ins / 107 x 52.9 cm) HKD 48,300. HONG KONG, 28 April 1997, *Landscape* (1906, ink and colour on paper, handscroll, 16 1/4 x 104 1/4 ins / 41.3 x 264.8 cm) HKD 59,800. HONG KONG, 25 April 2004, *Lady by Willow* (ink and colour, folding fan, 7 x 22 ins / 19 x 56 cm) HKD 65,000. HONG KONG, 26 April 2004, *Flower Goddesses* (1921, ink and colour, hanging scroll, 55 x 31 ins / 140 x 78 cm) HKD 500,000.

FENG CHI. See **FENG JI**

FENG FA-SSU. See **FENG FASI**

FENG FASI, or Feng Fa-Ssu
Chinese, 20th century.
Painter.
Modern School.

Fang Fasi was a pupil of Xu Beihong (1896-1953) at National Central University, Nanjing. He settled in Nanjing after the war.

FENG HSIEN-SHIH. See **FENG XIANSHI**

FENG JI, or Feng Chi, style name: Ziyang, sobriquet: Qixia
Chinese, 19th century.
Active c. 1820 in Qiantang (Zhejiang) and Suzhou (Jiangsu).
Painter.

Feng Ji was a specialist painter of people and landscapes.

FENG MIAN. See **LIN FENG MIAN**

FENG NING
Chinese, 18th century.
Painter.
Qing dynasty.

Feng Ning was a court painter during the reign of Emperor Qianlong (1736-1796).

FENG SIZUO
Chinese, 18th - 19th century.
Painter. Landscapes.

Feng Sizuo was born in Nanhai in Guangzhou. He painted accidents of nature.

AUCTION RECORDS:
NEW YORK, 6 Dec 1989, *Battle Scene* (ink and colour on silk handscroll, 19 1/4 x 348 ins / 48.9 x 884 cm) USD 5,500.

FENG TSÙ-K'AI. See **FENG ZIKAI**

FENG XIANSHI, or Feng Hsien-shih, style name: Zilan
Chinese, 18th century.
Born in Shanxi (Zhejiang).
Painter.

Feng Xianshi worked in about 1700. He wrote a treatise on painting entitled *Tuhui baojian Xucuan*.

FENG ZHENGJIE
Chinese, 20th - 21st century.
Born 1968, in Sichuan Province.
Painter, illustrator. Portraits.

Feng Zhengjie graduated as a master of fine arts from the oil painting department of the Sichuan academy of arts in 1995 and began teaching in the fine arts department of the Beijing Normal Institute. Feng's work borders on kitsch-like caricature. He uses the garish colours of Pop Art and popular culture, as well as traditional Chinese iconography. In his eyes, woman is an allegorical figure symbolising the metamorphosis currently underway in China, and he transforms her into a monstrous figure, perverse and menacing. His work is essentially a kind of parody, a mix of tradition and modernism that plays on stereotyped scenes of gallantry, as for instance in the series *Butterfly in Love*. He has also illustrated the book *La rêveuse et la dragueuse* by Xi Yang (Éditions Bleu de Chine, Paris, 2002).

He has taken part in various group exhibitions, including 2003, *Chinese Avant-garde*, Foundation Culturegest, Lisbon; among his solo exhibitions are 1996, *Skin Stories*, Art Museum of Beijing Normal University, and 2003, Galerie Albert Benamou and Véronique Maxé, Paris.

FENG ZHONGRUI, or Fong Chung-Ray
Chinese, 20th century.
Born 1933, in Henan.
Painter.

Fong Chung-Ray moved to Taiwan in 1949 and in 1956 joined the Fifth Moon Group. He took part in numerous international group exhibitions such as the 1959, 1963 and 1969 São Paulo Biennale; 1963, the first Paris Biennale; 1964, a travelling exhibition in Africa of contemporary Chinese painting; 1965, *Exhibition of Modern Chinese Art*, Rome; *Major Asian Painters*, a travelling exhibition in Asia. Other exhibitions include 1966 to 1968, *The New Country Of China* a travelling exhibition in the USA; 1967 to 1970, *New Voices of China*, a travelling exhibition to North American museums; 1970, *Exhibition of Calligraphy and Painting of the Republic of China*, National History Museum, Taipei. In 1960, he received the silver award at the first *International Painting Exhibition*, Hong Kong. He has also shown his work in solo exhibitions: 1965, National Art Center, Taipei; 1967, Taipei; 1970, San Francisco.

MUSEUMS AND GALLERIES:
SAN FRANCISCO (De Young Mus.).

FENG ZIKAI, or Feng Tsù-K'ai
Chinese, 20th century.
Born 1898, in Zongde (Zhejiang); died 1975.
Painter, cartoonist, essayist.

Feng Zikai studied with Li Shutong. In 1920, together with Liu Zhiping, he founded the Shanghai Private Arts University. In 1921 he went to Japan to study western art. He later taught at Zhejiang University and the National Art Academy, Chongqing. After the war he was director of the Chinese Artists Association.

BIBLIOGRAPHY:

Sullivan, Michael, *Chinese Art in the Twentieth century*, University of California Press, Berkeley, 1959.

AUCTION RECORDS:

HONG KONG, 16 Jan 1989, *Buddha* (ink and colour on paper, hanging scroll, 20 1/4 x 13 1/2 ins / 51.4 x 34.3 cm) HKD 26,400. NEW YORK, 31 May 1990, *Figures* (ink on paper, album of fifteen leaves, each 10 x 6 1/2 ins / 24.5 x 16.2 cm) USD 8,800. HONG KONG, 15 Nov 1990, *Winter* (ink and colour on paper, 22 x 17 3/4 ins / 55 x 45 cm) HKD 39,600. NEW YORK, 29 May 1991, *Figures* (ink and colour on paper, album of ten leaves, 9 1/2 x 13 ins / 24.3 x 33.2 cm) USD 7,700. HONG KONG, 29 Oct 1992, *Children Carrying Watermelons* (ink and colour on paper, fan, 6 3/4 x 19 3/4 ins / 17 x 50 cm) HKD 22,000. NEW YORK, 16 June 1993, *Scenes from Everyday Life* (ink and colour on paper, album of twelve leaves, each 16 3/4 x 11 1/2 ins / 42.5 x 29.2 cm) USD 23,000. HONG KONG, 3 Nov 1994, *West Lake* (1947, ink and colour on paper, hanging scroll, 40 1/2 x 22 ins / 102.9 x 55.9 cm) HKD 55,200. HONG KONG, 29 April 1996, *Celebrating New Year* (1963, ink on paper, 13 1/2 x 10 1/2 ins / 34.2 x 26.5 cm) HKD 46,000. HONG KONG, 4 Nov 1996, *Voyage* (1948, ink and colour on paper, 26 x 13 ins / 66 x 33 cm) HKD 103,500. HONG KONG, 28 April 1997, *Scenes from the Postwar Period* (1938-1939, ink on paper, album of six leaves, 13 x 9 ins / 33.1 x 22.8 cm) HKD 82,800. HONG KONG, 26 April 1999, *Dream* (ink, 13 x 14 ins / 33 x 36 cm) HKD 25,000. HONG KONG, 26 April 1999, *Gathering by Waterfront* (1947, ink and colour, hanging scroll, 28 x 15 ins / 72 x 38 cm) HKD 52,000. HONG KONG, 28 Oct 2001, *Gathering at a Riverside Pavilion* (ink and colour, scroll, 25 x 11 ins / 63 x 29 cm) HKD 65,000. HONG KONG, 28 Oct 2001, *Playing Football* (ink and colour, 27 x 14 ins / 69 x 35 cm) HKD 85,000. HONG KONG, 6 May 2002, *Running Horse* (ink, 13 x 11 ins / 34 x 27 cm) HKD 35,000. HONG KONG, 6 May 2002, *Two Bats Flying around Candle* (1956, ink, 13 x 9 ins / 33 x 22 cm) HKD 38,000. HONG KONG, 6 July 2003, *Chinese New Year* (ink, scroll, 27 x 13 ins / 68 x 34 cm) HKD 160,000. HONG KONG, 27 Oct 2003, *Green Hills with Figures* (1942, ink and colour, hanging scroll, 24 x 19 ins / 62 x 48 cm) HKD 120,000. HONG KONG, 26 April 2004, *Goddess of Mercy* (ink and colour, hanging scroll, 26 x 11 ins / 65 x 29 cm) HKD 140,000. HONG KONG, 26 April 2004, *Amitabha, the Eternal Buddha* (1948, ink and colour, 52 x 26 ins / 131 x 66 cm) HKD 700,000.

FENGLER, Anton I
Austrian, 18th century.
Born 1694, in Weidenau (Silesia); died 20 June 1770.
Active in Vienna.
Sculptor.

Fengler was awarded citizenship of Vienna in 1722 and produced the sculptures for the Archives building, erected in 1755.

FENGLER, Anton II
Austrian, 18th century.
Active in Vienna.
Sculptor.

Anton II was the son of Anton Fengler.

FENGLER, Johann Georg
Austrian, 18th century.
Born 1734.
Active in Vienna.
Sculptor.

The son of Anton Fengler I, Johann Georg Fengler was a student at the academy in Vienna.

FENGLER, Michael
Austrian, 18th century.
Active in Vienna in 1756.
Sculptor.

FENGLER, Peter
Austrian, 18th century.
Born 1726; died 9 November 1771.
Active in Vienna.
Sculptor.

The son of Anton Fengler I, Peter Fengler was a student at the academy in Vienna in 1743.

FENGLER, Wenzel
Austrian, 18th century.
Active in Vienna.
Sculptor.

Wenzel Fengler was the son of Johann Georg Fengler. He studied at the academy in Vienna and with Martin Fischer.

FENICE, Nicolò or Nicolas, or Fénis
Italian, 17th century.
Of French origin.
Active in Modena c. 1660.
Painter.

The church of S Agostino in Modena houses Fenice's painting of *St Casimir of Poland surrounded by Three Angels.*

FENINGER, Franz
Austrian, 18th century.
Active in Vienna c. 1750.
Engraver.

Feninger is attributed with producing decorative bookplates and the portrait of Count *Franz of Barkoczy*, the archbishop of Gran.

FENIS, Barthélémy or Bartolomeo
Italian, 17th century.
Active in Modena from 1653 to 1669.
Engraver.

He engraved several plates in the manner of Callot.

FENITZER. See **FENNITZER**

FENIZZI, Ascanio. See **AMBROSI Ascanio**

FENN, Harry
American, 19th - 20th century.
Born 1845, in Richmond (London), England, or 1838 according to some sources; died 21 April 1911, in Montclair (New Jersey).
Painter, watercolourist. Local scenes, landscapes.

Harry Fenn received a gold medal at the Chicago Exhibition of 1893 and was one of the founders of the Watercolours Society. He was an important figure among watercolour painters in the USA.

MUSEUMS AND GALLERIES:

CHICAGO (AI).

AUCTION RECORDS:

SAN FRANCISCO, 19 March 1981, *Birthplace of Mark Hopkins* (1894, watercolour and wash, 10 1/2 x 14 1/4 ins / 26.5 x 36 cm) USD 650. NEW YORK, 7 Dec 1984, *Pelham Bay Park, NYC* (1884, watercolour, 12 x 18 1/4 ins / 30.5 x 46.2 cm) USD 1,800. NEW YORK, 15 March 1986, *Market Place, Damascus* (watercolour heightened with white gouache, 30 x 24 ins / 76.2 x 61 cm) USD 1,400. NEW YORK, 30 Sept 1988, *Lily Pond* (watercolour/card, 7 x 21 ins / 18 x 53.2 cm) USD 4,400. NEW YORK, 17 Dec 1990, *Hudson River near Cornwall* (watercolour/paper, 9 x 16 1/4 ins / 22.9 x 41.3 cm) USD 880. NEW YORK, 4 May 1993,

Busy Oriental Market Place (watercolour/card, 27 1/4 x 20 ins / 69.2 x 50.8 cm) USD 2,875.

FENN, William Wilthieu
British, 19th century.
Born c. 1827, in England; died 19 December 1906, in London.
Painter. Landscapes.
William Fenn exhibited in London from 1848 to 1880, notably at the Royal Academy, Suffolk Street and the British Institution.

FENNEBRESQUE-MORING, Marie Félicie
French, 19th century.
Born 19th century, in Montamisé (Vienne).
Painter, watercolourist.
Fennebresque-Moring was taught by E. Lafon and Mme D. de Cool. She exhibited at the Paris Salon *Judith Returning to Bethulia*, in 1878, and *The Satyr and the Passer-by*, in 1879.

FENNEKOHL, Jacob
German, 17th century.
Active in Hamburg in 1695.
Sculptor.

FENNEL, Friedrich
German, 19th - 20th century.
Born 12 August 1872, in Kassel.
Painter, draughtsman, engraver. Nudes, portraits, landscapes.
Fennel, who was a student at the Kunstakademie in Kassel and the pupil of the lecturer Wünnenberg, also worked in Italy and at the Académie Julian in Paris. He showed his work at the principal German exhibitions.

He specialised in landscape painting, but nevertheless executed studies of nudes and portraits. His lithographs, like indeed his paintings, take their inspiration in particular from the landscapes of Hessen.

FENNEL, John Greville
British, 19th century.
Born 1807; died 1885.
Painter, engraver.
John Fennel was a pupil at the London Royal Academy. He also studied under Henry Sass. He produced a large number of newspaper illustrations and humorous genre scenes, and exhibited landscapes at Suffolk Street from 1851 to 1874.

FENNER
British, 17th century.
Painter.
MUSEUMS AND GALLERIES:
BURY ST EDMUNDS (Guildhall): *Portrait of James I* (before 1616).

FENNER, Charles
British, 19th century.
Active in Hampton Wick.
Painter. Genre scenes, landscapes.
Charles Fenner exhibited at the British Institution and the Royal Academy from 1858 to 1866.

FENNER, Johann Baptist
German, 18th century.
Painter.
Fenner is believed to have lived in Munich. He was painter to the Court in 1713.

FENNER, Maud Richmont
American, 19th century.
Born 24 May 1868, in Bristol.
Painter, decorative artist.

FENNER-BEHMER, Hermann
German, 19th - 20th century.
Born 8 June 1866, in Berlin; died 3 February 1913, in Berlin.
Painter. Portraits, genre scenes, landscapes.
Fenner-Behmer was the pupil of Lefebvre and Boulanger in Paris. After studying at the Akademie in Berlin, and with Hellqvist, he travelled in Europe. On returning to Berlin, he sent his works to different exhibitions in Paris, Munich and Berlin.
AUCTION RECORDS:
LONDON, 4 Nov 1977, *Confidences on the Telephone* (oil on panel, 36 x 22 ins / 91.4 x 56 cm) GBP 1,500.

FENNITZER, Georg, or Venitzer
German, 17th century.
Active in Nuremberg (Bavaria).
Engraver.
Fennitzer mainly engraved portraits.

FENNITZER, Johann Philipp
German, 17th century.
Active in Nuremberg (Bavaria).
Engraver.
Fennitzer's known works include his self-portrait, engraved in a sombre style, and portraits of famous men of the 15th century.

FENNITZER, Michael, or Venitzer
German, 17th century.
Born 1641, in Nuremberg; died 25 February 1702, in Wittenberg (Saxony-Anhalt).
Engraver.
Michael Fennitzer engraved portraits of famous people of Nuremberg.

FENOLLABBATE, Frédéric
French, 20th - 21st century.
Born 1959.
Painter, draughtsman.
Frédéric Fenollabbate lives and works in Nice. He has produced pictures in a number of different styles, including Neo-Geo and Figuration Libre. He uses a meticulously calculated and premeditated system, involving curves and parallelepipeds, and his preparatory drawings are filled with numbers. Following this system, and using different supports (wood, canvas or metal) and media (oil, gloss or varnish), Fenollabbate experiments with visual effects in his works.

He has taken part in exhibitions: *Caution: Wet Paint*, at the Galerie d'Art Contemporain des Musées de Nice, in 1985; at Art Jonction in 1986; and at the Villa Arson in 1987.
BIBLIOGRAPHY:
Frédéric Fenollabbate, exhibition catalogue, Villa Arson-Centre national des Arts plastiques, Nice, 1988. Dampérat, Marie-Hélène, '*Frédéric Fenollabbate*' in *Art Press*, periodical, Paris, 1988.
AUCTION RECORDS:
PARIS, 26 Jan 1987, *Untitled* (varnish lacquer/canvas, 78 3/4 x 65 ins / 200 x 165 cm) FRF 7,850.

FENOLLERA Y IBANEZ, Vicente or José
Spanish, 19th century.
Born c. 1850, in Valencia.
Painter. Religious subjects, figures, portraits.
Vicente Fenollera y Ibanez studied at the school of fine arts in Valencia and was awarded a bursary by the province to go to Rome in 1872. He exhibited regularly at exhibitions in Madrid.
MUSEUMS AND GALLERIES:
VALENCIA: *St Francis of Paula*; *Odalisque*; *Fisherman*.

FENOLLIET, Marc Antoine, pseudonyms: Carroys or La Rose
French, 17th century.
Born 17th century, in Lyons.
Painter.

Fenolliet was master of the painters in Lyons in 1660 and 1675. He also worked in Grenoble.

FENOSA, Apelles, or Apelles
Spanish, 20th century.
Born 16 May 1899, in Barcelona; died 25 March 1988, in Paris.
Also active in France.
Sculptor. Figures, animals. Monuments.

Apelles Fenosa trained under Casanovas. He lived in Paris from 1921 to 1929, returning to Spain from 1929 to 1939 before finally settling in France in 1939. During his first period in France, Fenosa quickly became integrated into the active colony of Spanish artists there who, at this period, gravitated around Picasso. It is interesting to note that when in 1945 the Musée d'Art Moderne wanted to commission a monument to commemorate the devastation of the French town of Oradour during the German retreat of 1944, it was to Fenosa that they turned, an indication of how completely integrated he had become in his adopted country. However, for aesthetic reasons - the bronze sculpture showing the body of a pregnant, naked woman engulfed in flame was found shocking by the clergy - it was 30 years before the statue was taken out of storage at the national collection and erected at the crossroads leading from Limoges to Oradour. Fenosa was awarded the Légion d'Honneur in 1983.

Fenosa first worked directly in stone and marble but gradually abandoned these media in favour of modelling. His art shows great sensitivity: his bronzes carry the marks of the feverish caresses of the his creative touch. The form, however, bears the mark of our time, revealing a visible memory of Surrealism here and a more modern sense of the arabesque there, but most of all a synthetical vision of the whole. His work can be divided into several periods: his early works *The Guitarist* of 1925 and the *Bust of Pilar Supervielle* of 1927 are tinged with Classicism; his terracotta pieces such as *Reclining Woman* and *Crouching Woman* date from his return to Spain; while the busts of poets and writers like Cocteau (1939), *Picasso* and *Éluard* (1942), *Michaux* (1949) and *Colette* (1948) date from the period of his return to France. He executed a large statue of *Christ* for Freiburg and a monument for Guingamp. Many of his sculptures were inspired by music: *Violinist, Flautist* (1946) and by mythology and the work of Homer: *Ulysses and Nausicaa* (1946) and *Blind Polyphemus* (1949). Nature and the fusion of human and plant species were also sources of inspiration for Fenosa particularly in his depictions of nudes.

Fenosa took part in many collective exhibitions including: the sculpture Biennale in Antwerp (1954) and Carrara (1957 when he was awarded a prize, and in 1959 and 1965); Yverdon (1958); Musée Rodin, Paris (1966 and 1968). He also exhibited at solo exhibitions: his first exhibition, in Paris either in 1925 or 1926 was prefaced by Max Jacob, then Paris again in 1928; Spain between 1929 and 1939; in 1939 Picasso organised in his studio an exhibition of the sculptures by Fenosa that he had purchased. Fenosa exhibited in Paris in 1946, 1952, 1956, 1961 and 1965 with introductory texts by Paul Éluard, Jean Cocteau, Jules Supervielle and Francis Ponge. In 1954 he exhibited in London; in 1960 and 1961 in New York; in 1965 and 1969 in Barcelona; in 1966 in Tokyo; in 1972 a retrospective of his work was held at the Château de Rochechouart; in 1980 a retrospective was held at the Musée Rodin in Paris; and in 2003, the exhibition *Fenosa et la Littérature, de l'Antiquité à la Modernité* (*Fenosa and Literature, from Antiquity to Modernity*) was held at the Musée Bossuet in Meaux.

BIBLIOGRAPHY:

Leymarie, Jean, *Fenosa*, Skira, Geneva, 1993. Tillier, Bertrand, *Fenosa sculpteur, 1899-1988: de l'identité à l'évanescence*, Séguier, Paris, 2001 (The Sculptor Fenosa, 1899-1988: from Identity to Evanescence). Fenosa, Nicole (ed.), *Apelles Fenosa: catalogue raisonné de l'œuvre sculpté*, Flammarion, Paris, 2002 (Appelles Fenosa: Critical Catalogue of his Sculptural Work). *Fenosa et la littérature de l'Antiquité à la modernité*, exhibition catalogue, Musée Bossuet, Meaux, 2003 (Fenosa and Literature from Antiquity to Modernity).

MUSEUMS AND GALLERIES:

BARCELONA (MAM del Mus. Nacional d'Art de Catalunya): *Flora* (1938); *Head of Montserrat* (1931) - BARCELONA (Town Hall): *Monument to Pablo Casals* (1976-1977); *Fine Weather Driving Away the Storm* (1979) - CÉRET (Mus. municipal d'Art moderne): *Head of Nicole* (1949) - DIJON (MBA): *Ophelia* (1956) - FREIBURG (Church of Christ the King): *Christ* - MADRID (Mus. de Arte Moderno): *Orlando Furioso* (1971-1973) - MONTPELLIER (Ville): *Orlando Furioso* (1971-1973) - PARIS (FNAC): *The Four Seasons* (1947, group); *Woman Speaking* (1952); *Plant Motif* (1955); *Sphinx* (1973); *Polyphemus* (1949); *Volute* (1967) - PARIS (MAMVP): *The Three Kingdoms* (a fountain); *Liberty* (1950) - PARIS (MNAM-CCI): *Mantelina* (1966); *Kimono* (1957); *Oradour* (1945); *The Three Kingdoms* (1950); *Small Torso* (1960); *Small Cabbage Leaf* (1960); *Fig Leaf, 1958*; *Rocking Chair* (1958); *William* (1955) - RHEIMS (MBA): *Harpist* (1967); *Beach* (1960); *Longue* (1961); *Friend* (1964); *Little Woman from Valls* (1964) - ST-DENIS (MAH): *Head of Paul Éluard* (1942, times three) - SYDNEY (MA): *Head of Paul Éluard* (1942).

AUCTION RECORDS:

PARIS, 2 June 1980, *Nude with Arms Raised* (bronze, h. 23 1/4 ins / 59 cm) FRF 5,000. PARIS, 19 Oct 1982, *The Violinist* (bronze, h. 17 3/4 ins / 45 cm) FRF 8,500. PARIS, 9 Feb 1987, *Woman Running* (black-patinated bronze, h. 5 ins / 12.5 cm) FRF 15,500. PARIS, 3 Oct 1988, *Chrysanthemum* (1960, green-brown-patinated bronze, 11 x 5 x 3 1/2 ins / 28 x 13 x 9 cm) FRF 35,000; *Woman Speaking* (1948, golden-brown-patinated bronze, 6 x 2 x 1 1/2 ins / 15 x 5 x 4 cm) FRF 14,000; *Fig Leaf* (1958, shaded-brown-patinated bronze, 11 x 6 1/4 x 4 1/4 ins / 27 x 16 x 11 cm) FRF 81,000. PARIS, 16 March 1989, *Woman Beseeching* (brown-patinated bronze, h. 6 1/2 ins / 16.5 cm) FRF 21,000. PARIS, 6 April 1989, *Woman in Drapery* (bronze, h. 7 1/2 ins / 19 cm) FRF 30,000. PARIS, 22 May 1989, *Woman* (green-brown-patinated bronze, 6 1/4 x 2 x 2 1/4 ins / 16 x 5 x 5.5 cm) FRF 37,000. PARIS, 19 June 1989, *The Conversation* (lost-wax bronze, h. 6 1/2 ins / 16.5 cm) FRF 28,000. PARIS, 28 Nov 1990, *Pliés* (1976, bronze, h. 9 ins / 22 cm) FRF 47,000; *Liberty* (1950, bronze, h. 29 1/2 ins / 75 cm) FRF 355,000. PARIS, 3 June 1991, *Acanthus Leaf Skirt* (bronze, 7 1/2 x 2 1/4 x 2 ins / 19 x 5.5 x 5 cm) FRF 30,000. NEW YORK, 26 Feb 1993, *Lady of the Court* (1965, dark-patinated bronze, h. 7 3/4 ins / 19.7 cm) USD 1,955. PARIS, 16 March 1993, *Portrait of Roger Caillois* (1970, bronze, 6 1/4 x 4 x 5 ins / 16 x 10 x 13 cm) FRF 13,500. PARIS, 6 April 1994, *Woman in Drapery* (bronze, h. 5 1/2 ins / 14 cm) FRF 23,000. NEW YORK, 14 June 1995, *Dancers* (bronze, collection of six, approx. each h. 7 ins / 17.8 cm) USD 6,325. ZURICH, 3 April 1996, *Coral* (bronze, h. 8 1/2 ins / 21.5 cm) CHF 3,200. PARIS, 15 April 1996, *Back View of Woman in Drapery* (bronze, h. 8 1/4 ins / 21 cm) FRF 28,000. PARIS, 16 Sept 1996, *Andalusian Woman* (black-patinated bronze, 7 x 2 x 2 1/2 ins / 18 x 5 x 6.5 cm) FRF 11,000. ZURICH, 12 Nov 1996, *St John's Wort* (bronze, 9 x 3 1/2 x 2 1/4 ins / 22 x 9 x 5.5 cm) CHF 2,600. PARIS, 16 June 1997, *Woman with Arm Extended* (black-patinated bronze, h. 7 ins / 18 cm) FRF 16,000. PARIS, 18 June 1997, *Psyche* (1959, green-brown-patinated bronze, h. 9 3/4 ins / 25 cm) FRF 30,000. PARIS, 31 May 1999, *Woman with Long Shawl* (brown-patinated bronze, h. 16

ins / 41 cm. PARIS, 21 June 1999, *Harpist* (c. 1959, black patinated bronze, h. 18 ins / 45 cm) FRF 47,000. PARIS, 30 Jan 2000, *Long Woman* (green patinated bronze, h. 17 ins / 42 cm) FRF 30,000. PARIS, 18 Dec 2000, *Head of Paul Éluard* (patinated bronze, h. 7 ins / 17 cm) FRF 30,000. PARIS, 19 Nov 2001, *Woman at a Mirror* (brown-patinated bronze, h. 9 ins / 23 cm) FRF 20,000. PARIS, 12 Dec 2001, *Tall Woman* (bronze, h. 6 ins / 15 cm) EUR 3,660. LILLE, 20 Oct 2002, *Bust of a Girl* (brown-patinated bronze, h. 14 ins / 35 cm) EUR 5,500. PARIS, 27 June 2003, *Centaur* (bronze) EUR 3,000. CALAIS, 9 Nov 2003, *Small Violonist* (bronze, h. 6 ins / 15 cm) EUR 3,300.

FENOUIL, Jean César
French, 18th century.
Born in Marseilles.
Painter.

Jean César Fenouil was painter to the king. He seems to have spent a long time in Lyons where he is mentioned in 1738 and 1746. His works are often confused with those of Paul Fenouil.

AUCTION RECORDS:
PARIS, 21 Nov 1919, *Portrait of a Gentleman,* FRF 1,720. PARIS, 7 April 1941, *Self-portrait,* FRF 500. PARIS, 16 June 1972, *Portrait Presumed to be of Préville,* FRF 10,600. PARIS, 2 March 1994, *Portrait of Louis Philippe of Orléans, Prince of Joinville, and Henrietta of Bourbon Conti, Dressed as Hercules and Omphale* (1750, oil on canvas, 32 x 39 3/4 ins / 81 x 101 cm) FRF 32,000.

FENOUIL, Paul or A. P., or Paolo Fenollo
French, 18th century.
Born 18th century, in France.
Painter. History painting.

Paul Fenouil may be the brother of Jean César Fenouil. He was elected to the Académie Royale in 1740. In Paris he executed a series of portraits and some scenes from everyday life. A large number of engravings were made after his work.

MUSEUMS AND GALLERIES:
MADRID (Prado): *Bacchanalian Scene.*

AUCTION RECORDS:
PARIS, 15 June 1929, *Portrait of a Man; Portrait of a Young Woman* (two oils on canvas) FRF 51,500. NEW YORK, 30 Jan 1998, *The Pyramids of Giza; The Statue of Zeus at Olympia; The Lighthouse in Alexandria; The Colossus of Rhodes* (oil on canvas).

FENOUILLET
French, 20th century.
Painter.

Fenouillet received the second Prix de Rome in 1906.

FENS, Wilhelm Christian Heinrich
German, 19th century.
Born 1821, in Hamburg; died July 1840, in Enge, near Zurich.
Painter.

Fens was a student of J.J. Faber, and worked principally in Munich. One of his works is *Young Tobias Says Farewell*

FENSTERER, Christoph
German, 17th century.
Active in Magdeburg (Saxony-Anhalt).
Painter.

Known works by Fensterer include *Portrait of the Artist by Himself,* and *Resurrection, Crucifixion* and *Last Supper* in the Johanneskirche (St John's Church) in Magdeburg.

FENTON, Annie Grace
British, 19th century.
Active in London.
Painter. Genre scenes.

Annie Fenton exhibited in London, notably at the Royal Academy, from 1875 to 1885.

FENTON, Beatrice
American, 20th century.
Born 12 July 1887, in Philadelphia; died 1983.
Sculptor. Figures. Busts.

Beatrice Fenton began her art studies with the intention of becoming an animal painter, but she was advised by Thomas Eakins, himself a painter and sculptor, to take up sculpture. She went to the School of Industrial Art, where she was taught by Alexander Stirling Calder, the father of 'Sandy' Calder. She was also a pupil Charles Grafly at the Pennsylvania Academy of Fine Arts. She won the Stewardson prize for Sculpture in 1908, an honourable mention at the San Francisco Exhibition of 1915, and a Widener medal from the Pennsylvania Academy in 1922.

At the start of her career she carved mainly busts, but then became popular by making fairy figures for the fountains of public gardens and parks and private residences.

AUCTION RECORDS:
NEW YORK, 5 Dec 1991, *Nereid Fountain* (1928, bronze, h. 108 ins / 274.3 cm) USD 88,000. PHILADELPHIA, 27 June 2004, *Dancers* (1924, brown patinated bronze, h. 16 ins / 40 cm) USD 2,900.

FENTON, Hallie Champlin
American, 20th century.
Born October 1880, in St Louis (Missouri); died 1935.
Painter.

Hallie Champlin Fenton was a pupil of Jacques Blanche in Paris and a member of the National Association of Women Painters and Sculptors.

FENTON, John
American, 20th century.
Born in the second half of the 19th century.
Engraver.

John Fenton exhibited in New York from 1958. His engravings are symbolic, often doom-laden, sometimes leaning towards a kind of Surrealism.

FENTON, John William
American, 20th century.
Born 6 July 1875, in Couewango Valley (New York); died 1939.
Painter.

John William Fenton taught art in the high schools of New York City and was a member of the Salmagundi Club.

FENTZEL, Gregor
German, 17th century.
Born in Nuremberg.
Active c. 1650.
Engraver.

Fentzel engraved portraits and historical pictures after A. Tempesta, F. Cleyn and J. Sadeler.

FENWICK, Thomas
British, 19th century.
Born in the North of England; died c. 1850.
Painter. Landscapes, seascapes.

Thomas Fenwick was a friend of John W. Ewbank, with whom he worked in the studios of Coulson and Nasmyth. He painted mostly seascapes.

AUCTION RECORDS:
LONDON, 27 March 1973, *Ravenscraig,* GBP 1,400. LONDON, 10 Oct 1980, *Mountain Landscape* (1846, oil on canvas, 17 1/4 x 26 1/2 ins / 44 x 67 cm) GBP 500. LONDON, 10 April 2000, *Highland Loch* (1842, oil on canvas, 18 x 24 ins / 46 x 61 cm) GBP 1,400. EDINBURGH, 17 Oct 2002, *On the Dutch Coast* (oil on canvas, 20 x 25 ins / 50 x 63 cm) GBP 2,000.

FENYES, Adolph
Hungarian, 19th - 20th century.
Born 1867, in Kescskemet; died 1945.
Painter. Genre scenes.
Szolnok Artists' Colony, School of La Plaine.

Adolph Fenyes was a pupil of Szekely, Bouguereau, Ferrier and J. Benczur. He took part in the 1900 Exposition Universelle, winning a bronze medal.

He left the Nagbanya group and founded the Szolnok group.

MUSEUMS AND GALLERIES:
BUDAPEST (Szépmuvészeti Múz.): *Klastch; Widow; Old Man* - SZEGED: *Old Woman* - WEIMAR (Schlossmus.): *Old Woman*.

AUCTION RECORDS:
ZURICH, 14 May 1982, *Hungarian Farmyard* (oil on canvas, 21 1/4 x 26 3/4 ins / 54 x 68 cm) CHF 4,500. TEL AVIV, 11 April 1996, *Street Scene* (oil on canvas, 23 3/4 x 16 ins / 60.4 x 40.4 cm) USD 5,750. BUDAPEST, 27 April 2001, *Early Spring in Szolnok* (oil on canvas, 29 x 33 ins / 73 x 84 cm) HUF 1,600,000. BUDAPEST, 27 April 2001, *Early Spring* (oil on canvas, 16 x 20 ins / 40 x 50 cm) HUF 2,600,000. BUDAPEST, 11 Sept 2002, *Spring by the River Zagyva* (oil on canvas, 30 x 38 ins / 77 x 97 cm) HUF 2,800,000. BUDAPEST, 13 Sept 2002, *In the Garden* (oil on canvas, 12 x 16 ins / 31 x 41 cm) HUF 1,600,000. BUDAPEST, 11 April 2003, *Woman in Hat, Sitting in Shadowy Courtyard* (oil on canvas, 17 x 24 ins / 43 x 61 cm) HUF 10,000,000. BUDAPEST, 12 Dec 2003, *Celebration Day - In the Room* (1909, oil on card, 35 x 27 ins / 90 x 68 cm) HUF 22,000,000. BUDAPEST, 28 April 2004, *Rocking the Cradle* (oil on canvas/card, 22 x 18 ins / 57 x 45 cm) HUF 5,000,000. BUDAPEST, 26 May 2004, *River Landscape* (oil on canvas, 25 x 37 ins / 64 x 95 cm) HUF 2,400,000.

FENYO, A. Endre
Hungarian, 20th century.
Born 1904.
Painter. Figure compositions, landscapes.

Endre Fenyo was one of the founders of the Socialist Artists group and executed figurative paintings, generally with a political message. He was awarded the Munkácsy prize and mounted special exhibitions in 1930, 1948, 1956 and 1964.

FENZONI, Ferrau. See **FANZONI**

FEO, Luigi de
Italian, 19th century.
Born in the 19th century, in Austria.
Active in Paris and in Venice.
Painter, sculptor, medallist.

Luigi de Feo exhibited two sculptures at the Société des Artistes Français in 1907, and a bronze entitled *Adolescent* at the International Exhibition in Venice in 1909.

FEODOR, Ivanovich Charles Frédéric. See **IVANOVICH Fedor**

FEODOROV. See also **FEDOROV**

FEODOROV, John
American, 20th - 21st century.
Born 1960, of Native-American and Euro-American descent.
Active in Seattle.
Installation and performance artist, painter, musician.

John Feodorov has a BFA from California State University at Long Beach (1990). His mixed parentage (he is part Navajo part Euro-American) continues to inform the thematic choices of his work, in particular his concern to address what he sees as the commodification or usurping of Navajo spirituality and ritual by Western consumerism, especially New Age spiritualism.

He works in a variety of media. He is a painter, video and installation artist, filmmaker, and musician. His paintings with titles such as *Heaven, Offering, The Origin Of Religion* and *Urban Myth* all feature bold and somewhat grotesque human figures, in either dull or lurid colours, who are variously confused or satirised - satirised when they appear to represent human icons or symbols of corporate power, confused as people in search for higher meanings and reality. In a similar vein, his performance *Office Shaman* mocks the efforts of corporate culture to 'look after' the spiritual well being of its employees, in the hope of improving their productivity and performance at work. As a musician he was part of the band *Skinwalkers* named after Navajo witches who according to Navajo legend could transform themselves into animal forms and back to human ones. His new band is *Left Wing Party*.

Feodorov has held solo exhibitions, including: 1994, *Myths etc*, at Truckee Meadows Community College, Reno; 1995, *What Makes the Red Man Red?*, at King County Art Commission Gallery, Seattle; 2001, *Office Shamans and Other Mythologies*, Sacred Circle Gallery, Seattle; and 2002-2003, *Myths and Prophecies*, Howard House, Seattle.

BIBLIOGRAPHY:
Boyland, John, *Artist Uses his Craft to Examine Portrayal of Indians in America*, December 1995. *Seattle Collects Seattle*, exhibition catalogue, Seattle Arts Commission, 1997 (Exhibition curated by Beth Sellars). Bryant, Elizabeth, '*Sacred Circle of American Indian Art Hosts the Dream Hat Ritual and What Makes the Red Man Red?*' in *Art Access*, July-August 1997.

FEODOTOV. See **FEDOTOV**

FEOFAN, K.
Russian, 17th century.
Engraver.

FEOFILATOFF, Ivan. See **FILATEEV**

FEOLI, Vincenzo
Italian, 19th century.
Active in Rome.
Engraver (burin).

Vincenzo Feoli illustrated various books.

FER, Édouard de
French, 20th century.
Born 1887, in Nice; died 1959, in Nice.
Painter, watercolourist, illustrator, poster artist, designer. Landscapes. Murals, designs for tapestries.

Édouard de Fer settled in Paris, enrolling at the École des Arts Décoratifs, and then at the École des Beaux-Arts and exhibiting, from 1925, at the Salon des Artistes Indépendants in Paris. In 1923 he decorated the Bibliothèque Municipale in Nice with a canvas entitled: *Nice: Muse to Arts and Letters*. Other projects included the saloon of the steamboat 'Ile de France' in 1928, and the Hall of Nations in the Palace of Peace, in New Jersey, USA, with an enormous painting: *The Tree of Minerva*. He executed landscapes, and in a large part of his work, he painted with luminous, almost blinding tints. Indeed, he created numerous posters praising the sun of the Riviera. Édouard de Fer wrote a theoretical work, *Solfège de la couleur* (*Solfeggio of Colour*), in which he clearly developed the scientific principles of Neo-Impressionism. He wrote the following: 'Given that the resulting optical effect is exact, it matters little the manner in which the Neo-Impressionist positions his brushstroke: let us try to see farther than the formula' Showing a certain independence with regard to the theories of his friends Maximilien Luce, Louis Valtat and Paul Signac, he often spaced his strokes, allowing the underneath of the canvas to appear in his paintings.

AUCTION RECORDS:
PARIS, 4 June 1987, *House by Lake Geneva* (oil on canvas remounted on board, 9 1/4 x 6 ins / 23.5 x 15.5 cm) FRF 30,000. PARIS, 15 Feb 1988, *Dahlias, Garden My Rest* (oil on panel, 9 1/2 x 7 ins / 24 x 18 cm) FRF 12,000. PARIS, 18 June 1989,

Provence House (oil on canvas, 13 3/4 x 11 ins / 35 x 27 cm) FRF 9,500. PARIS, 6 July 1990, *Man with the Helmet, St-Cloud* (oil on cardboard, 9 x 6 1/4 ins / 22 x 16 cm) FRF 6,500. CALAIS, 14 March 1999, *Terrace on the Mediterranean* (oil on canvas, 20 x 26 ins / 50 x 65 cm) FRF 20,500. PARIS, 27 Oct 2000, *Clouds over Lake Geneva* (oil on panel, 6 x 8 ins / 16 x 21 cm) FRF 17,000.

FER, de. See also **DEFER**

FER, Faivre Louis Stanislas. See **FAIVRE-DUFFER**

FER, Nicolas de
French, 17th - 18th century.
Born 1646; died 15 October 1720.
Engraver, geographer. Maps.
Nicolas de Fer had the title of geographer to the king and engraved about 600 maps, especially memorable for the rich ornamentation of the plates. He also produced plates of portraits for the *History of the Kings of France from Pharamond to Louis XV*.

FERA, Bernardino
Italian, 18th century.
Died c. 1714.
Active in Naples.
Painter.
Bernadino Fera was a pupil of Solimena and is remembered for his fresco work. The church of S Francesco di Paola in Pozzano (near Castellammare) houses two oils by Fera: a *Rebecca* and a *Joseph in the Well*.

FERA, Matteo
Italian, 18th century.
Painter.
The brother of Bernardino Fera, he studied under Solimeno and subsequently joined the Dominican order.

FERABECH, Giovanni, or Ferrabech
Italian, 14th century.
Active in Venice at the end of the 14th century.
Sculptor.
Giovanni Ferabech participated, with other artists, in sculptural works in the church of S Petronio at Bologna.

FERABOSCHI, Antonio Maria
Italian, 17th - 18th century.
Born 16 March 1663, in Parma; died 1738.
Sculptor.
Antonio Feraboschi is recorded as having worked on the cathedral of Carpi (near Modena) in 1724, and at Reggio nell'Emilia, where he sculpted two altar statues for the former church of S Francesco.

FERABOSCO, Girolamo. See **FERRABOSCO**

FERABOSCO, Martino
Italian, 17th century.
Active at the beginning of the 17th century.
Engraver, architect.
Martino Ferabosco lived in Rome and engraved plates for *Architettura della Basilica di San Pietro in Vaticano* (*Architecture of St Peter's Basilica, Vatican City*), published in Rome in 1620.

FERABOSCO, Pietro, or Ferrabosco
Italian, 16th century.
Born 1513, in Laino, near Como.
Painter, architect.
Pietro Ferabosco spent the early part of his career as a painter of war subjects in Hungary, while a soldier in the imperial army. He was then employed as painter to the court of Ferdinand I in Vienna, where he decorated a number of Hofbourg apartments, but it was in architecture that he specialised.

FERABOSCO, Pietro
Italian, 17th century.
Born probably in Lucca.
Active c. 1616.
Painter.
Pietro Ferabosco spent most of his life in Portugal, where the majority of his work is to be found.

FERADINY. See **FERRANDINI**

FÉRAGU, Auguste François Joseph
French, 19th century.
Born 24 May 1816, in Lille; died 1892, in Amiens.
Painter.
Féragu entered the École des Beaux-Arts on 2 October 1837, and was trained under Abel de Pujol and L. Cogniet. He exhibited at the Paris Salon from 1841 to 1880. Works include *Almsgiving, Christ on the Cross, Flooding of the Loire in 1846, Roadsweeper, St Louis and His Brother Robert Taking the Holy Crown of Thorns to Notre-Dame in Paris, Bonaparte and Josephine Visiting Amiens Cathedral, Christ in the Garden of Gethsemane* and *Monk from the Dominican Monastery in Abbeville, Rescuing a Child from the Somme River*.
MUSEUMS AND GALLERIES:
CAMBRAI: *Portrait of Dr Fenin*.

FERAIL, Edmond
French, 19th century.
Born to a family originally from Cambrai
in Paris.
Painter.
Ferail was taught by Joseph Berger at Cambrai École de Dessin.

FERAJUOLI. See **FERRAJUOLI**

FÉRAL, Bert
French, 20th century.
Painter.
Since the 1980s, Féral has exhibited regularly in Paris at the Salon des Réalités Novuelles. His paintings are composed of a juxtaposition of non-geometric forms of a somewhat curved nature. They are lightly sculpted in sombre tones, and positioned before a neutral background, much in the same way as the figures and decorative accessories are arranged on a stage foreground.

FERAND
French.
Engraver.
Mentioned by Nagler. He engraved two plates of *Portraits*.

FERARA, Carel de. See **FERRARA**

FERARE, Jacques Maurice
French, 18th century.
Active in Paris in 1787.
Painter, sculptor.

FERARI. See **FERRARI**

FERAT, Jules Descartes
French, 19th century.
Born 27 November 1829, in Ham (Somme).
Painter.
Ferat entered the École des Beaux-Arts on 4 April 1850 and became the pupil of J. Cogniet. He exhibited at the Paris Salon from 1857 to 1871. His major works include *Interior of Stables at Montfort-l'Amaury, Summer, Dissection Room, First Plough after the War* and *The Pit and the Pendulum*

FÉRAT, Serge, pseudonym of Serge Jastrebzoff, (Count)
Russian, 20th century.
Born 28 May 1881, in Moscow; died 13 October 1958, in Paris.
Active in France from 1901.

Painter (including gouache), engraver, collage artist, decorative painter, illustrator. Designs for tapestries.

Serge Férat travelled extensively in his youth to England, France, Italy and Germany. In 1901-1902 he settled, with his sister Baroness d'Oettingen, in Paris, where he took classes with Bouguereau at the Académie Julian. He was also a pupil of Baschet and Schommer. Wealthy and ostentatious, the young Count was surrounded by poets and painters and often attended the night club Le Lapin Agile in Montmartre. He bought many paintings, notably a dozen by the Douanier Rousseau, to whose home in Montparnasse he went for musical evenings. He also acquired works by Picasso and Braque and other Cubist artists. In 1911 he got to know Picasso who introduced him to Apollinaire who became his friend and coined his pseudonym, Férat.

It is reputed that Férat bought *Soirées de Paris* from André Billy, Dalize and Salmon in 1913, and that he financed this journal, in which new ideas were defended. Férat became director and Apollinaire took over the literary direction, and the administration was moved into Férat's sister's apartment at 278 Boulevard Raspail, Paris. The name Jean Cerusse (from 'Ces Russes' = These Russians: Serge and Hélène) appeared on the cover. The Italian Futurists, in their journal *Lacerba*, established close relations at that time with *Les Soirées de Paris*.

In 1914 he signed up as a volunteer at the Italian Hospital in Paris and witnessed the wounded Apollinaire arrive there not long afterwards. Ruined by the Russian Revolution, he found himself abandoned by people who had formerly flocked to his parties, where they might meet Picasso, Léger, Cendrars, Jacob, Modigliani and so on. He continued to see only Survage, Gleizes and Delaunay. Disheartened, he destroyed a number of his works but still just managed to continue to live from his art after 1917. Henri Pierre Roché, a man who understood the art of the time, was one of the few people to help him, and Jean Cocteau devoted a monograph to him in 1924. Férat died penniless and unknown in 1958.

His paintings from 1910 onwards were inspired by the Italians of the Quattrocento and won favour with Maurice Denis; later Férat became influenced by Cézanne. He knew Picasso, Braque and the other Cubist painters and adopted their aesthetics, Férat made them his own, becoming a Cubist of charm and sophistication. His gouaches are particular noteworthy. He produced the programme, sets and costumes for the unique performance of Apollinaire's *Mamelles de Tirésias* in 1917, which attracted some jealousy from the other Cubists, with the exception of Picasso, and also provided illustrations for Albert Birot's magazine *Sic* in gouache. The Government commissioned three cartoons for tapestries from him for the Factory in Beauvais.

Férat exhibited in Paris under the name of Jastrebzoff at the Salon des Artistes Français, winning an award in 1906, and at the Salon des Artistes Indépendants in 1910, 1911 and 1912 under the pseudonym of Roudniev. He took part in the exhibition of the Section d'Or in Paris in 1920 and exhibited with Max Jacob in 1924. After he took part in the exhibition on Cubism at the Musée d'Art Moderne de la Ville de Paris in 1935, some interest in him re-emerged. He exhibited solo first in 1917 in Paris and in 1938.

Férat was represented in 2003 at the collective exhibition *Russian Paris 1910-1960*, an exhibition on Russian art and artists in Paris organised by the St Petersburg Russian Museum and shown at the Von der Heydt Museum, Wuppertal and at the Museum of Fine Art, Bordeaux. A retrospective was organised at the Galerie Michèle Heyraud in Paris in 1989.

S. FERAT

Bibliography:

Cocteau, Jean, *Serge Férat*, Valori Plastici, Rome, 1924. Marcadé, Jean-Claude/Pétrova, Evguénia, *Paris russe 1910-1960*, exhibition catalogue, Musée des Beaux-Arts, Bordeaux, 2003.

Museums and Galleries:

Paris (MNAM-CCI): *Still-life: Glass, Pipe and Bottle* (1914-1915).

Auction records:

Paris, 29 Oct 1927, *Circus Parade* (gouache) FRF 300. Paris, 5 Nov 1937, *Musical Attributes* (gouache) FRF 200. Paris, 18 May 1945, *Circus* (watercolour) FRF 1,700. Paris, 28 March 1955, *Parade*, FRF 55,000. Zurich, 16 May 1974, *Viaduct*, CHF 13,000. Paris, 12 June 1974, *Composition* (watercolour and gouache) FRF 20,000. Paris, 22 June 1976, *Composition* (watercolour and gouache, 4 1/4 x 20 ins / 11 x 51 cm) FRF 3,500. New York, 22 Oct 1976, *Horses Near a Village* (oil on canvas, 32 x 23 1/2 ins / 81 x 60 cm) USD 800. New York, 19 May 1978, *Still-life* (oil/collage /card, 15 1/2 x 11 ins / 39.5 x 28 cm) USD 4,000; *Still-life with Fruit Bowl* (c. 1918, gouache/paper, 9 1/4 x 6 1/2 ins / 23.5 x 16.2 cm) USD 1,200. New York, 17 May 1979, *Still-life No. 2* (1929, gouache and pencil/beige paper, 10 3/4 x 7 1/4 ins / 27.6 x 18.4 cm) USD 1,500. Paris, 24 Nov 1980, *Still-life with Mandolin* (gouache, 10 3/4 x 9 ins / 27.5 x 23 cm) FRF 11,500. Paris, 23 June 1983, *Harvest* (gouache, 15 x 11 3/4 ins / 38 x 30 cm) FRF 13,000. Paris, 21 June 1984, *Composition with Fruit Bowl* (oil on canvas, 25 1/2 x 31 1/2 ins / 64.5 x 80 cm) FRF 33,500. London, 26 Feb 1986, *Sailing Boats in the Harbour* (oil on canvas, 32 x 23 1/2 ins / 81 x 60 cm) GBP 5,000. Versailles, 13 Dec 1987, *Saxophonist* (watercolour and gouache, 8 3/4 x 6 1/2 ins / 22.5 x 166 cm) FRF 26,500. Paris, 17 Feb 1988, *Two Figures* (watercolour and gouache, 8 1/4 x 6 3/4 ins / 21 x 17 cm) FRF 14,000. Paris, 15 June 1988, *Pink House* (oil on canvas, 32 x 24 ins / 81 x 61 cm) FRF 77,000. London, 22 Feb 1989, *Two Harlequins* (gouache, 14 1/2 x 8 3/4 ins / 37 x 22.5 cm) GBP 3,080. Douai, 3 Dec 1989, *Musician* (gouache, 4 3/4 x 3 1/4 ins / 12 x 8.5 cm) FRF 20,100. Calais, 10 Dec 1989, *Horses Near Bridle Paths* (oil on canvas, 32 x 23 1/2 ins / 81 x 60 cm) FRF 52,000. Paris, 18 Feb 1990, *Landscapes with Factories* (oil on canvas, 31 1/2 x 23 1/4 ins / 80 x 59 cm) FRF 85,000. London, 29 March 1990, *Cubist Harlequin* (watercolour and pencil with collage/paper, 11 1/2 x 7 3/4 ins / 29 x 20 cm) FRF 5,500. Amsterdam, 10 April 1990, *Landscape* (gouache/paper, 12 1/2 x 8 1/2 ins / 31.5 x 21.5 cm) NLG 7,475. Versailles, 6 June 1990, *Woman on Bridge* (oil on canvas, 32 x 23 1/2 ins / 81 x 60 cm) FRF 45,000. Paris, 11 Oct 1990, *Still-life* (c. 1915, gouache, 4 1/4 x 6 ins / 11 x 15 cm) FRF 32,000. Paris, 18 April 1991, *Harbour* (drawing in lead pencil, 8 1/4 x 5 1/2 ins / 21 x 14 cm) FRF 12,000. Amsterdam, 30 Oct 1991, *Breakfast Table with a Still-life of Fruit on a Sunny Table* (oil on canvas, 32 x 33 3/4 ins / 81 x 86 cm) NLG 6,900. Paris, 23 March 1992, *Family* (1919, gouache/card, 7 1/2 x 2 1/4 ins / 19 x 6 cm) FRF 12,000. London, 15 Oct 1992, *Fishermen at the Edge of the Lake* (gouache and Indian ink, 4 1/2 x 5 1/2 ins / 11.2 x 13.7 cm) GBP 880. Paris, 4 Nov 1992, *Harlequin's Head* (colouring pencil/paper, 5 x 4 3/4 ins / 12.5 x 12 cm) FRF 4,500. Amsterdam, 10 Dec 1992, *River Landscape* (gouache/paper, 4 x 5 1/4 ins / 10 x 13.5 cm) NLG 4,370. Paris, 21 Dec 1992, *Landscape* (oil on canvas, 31 1/2 x 23 1/2 ins / 80 x 60 cm) FRF 15,000. New York, 10 May 1993, *Still-life with Fish and Fruit* (oil on canvas, 36 x 29 ins / 91.5 x 73.5 cm) USD 3,220. Paris, 5 July 1994, *At the Circus* (oil on canvas, 16 1/4 x 13 ins / 41 x 33 cm) FRF 18,000. New York, 8 Nov 1994, *Figures* (1926, gouache/paper, 6 1/2 x 5 ins / 16.5 x 12.7 cm) USD 1,150. Paris, 10 April 1995, *Composition with Flowers and Fruit* (oil on canvas, 36 1/4 x 25 1/2 ins / 92 x 65 cm) FRF 17,500. London, 25 Oct 1995, *At the Circus* (gouache and pencil/paper, 11 x 8 1/4 ins / 28 x 21 cm) GBP 1,150. Paris, 26 Feb 1996, *Harlequin* (gouache and charcoal, 9 1/4 x 7 1/4 ins / 23.5 x 18.5 cm) FRF 4,500. Paris, 23 June 1997, *Village* (oil on canvas,

23$\frac{1}{2}$ x 32 ins / 60 x 81 cm) FRF 5,500. PARIS, 22 March 1998, *Harlequin's Head* (colouring pencil/paper, 5 x 4$\frac{3}{4}$ ins / 13 x 12 cm) FRF 6,500. PARIS, 8 July 1999, *Harlequine* (gouache, 6 x 4 ins / 14 x 10 cm) FRF 23,000. PARIS, 11 Dec 1999, *Cubist Composition* (oil on canvas, 17 x 20 ins / 43 x 50 cm) FRF 56,000. PARIS, 22 Oct 2000, *Harvest* (oil on canvas, 32 x 24 ins / 81 x 60 cm) FRF 24,000. LONDON, 25 Oct 2000, *Man with a Guitar and Dog* (gouache and oil, 11 x 7 ins / 27 x 18 cm) GBP 4,200. PARIS, 17 Oct 2001, *Still-life with Guitar, Coffee-pot and Jug* (gouache, 12 x 8 ins / 31 x 21 cm) FRF 22,000. PARIS, 8 Dec 2001, *Cubist Still-life with Fruit Bowl* (c. 1920, oil on canvas, 31 x 26 ins / 80 x 65 cm) FRF 85,000. PARIS, 5 June 2002, *Seated Woman* (gouache, 11 x 7 ins / 28 x 17 cm) EUR 10,500. MADRID, 12 June 2002, *Composition* (oil on canvas, 17 x 20 ins / 43 x 50 cm) EUR 14,000. PARIS, 19 June 2003, *Still-life with Vase of Flowers* (oil on canvas, 32 x 24 ins / 81 x 60 cm) EUR 5,500. CALAIS, 9 Nov 2003, *Musical Composition* (oil on panel, 10 x 8 ins / 25 x 20 cm) EUR 9,000. LONDON, 4 Feb 2004, *Still-life* (oil on canvas, 17 x 20 ins / 43 x 50 cm) GBP 8,000. CALAIS, 30 May 2004, *Circus* (gouache, 15 x 9 ins / 37 x 22 cm) EUR 6,000.

FERAU Y ALSINA, Enrique

Spanish, 19th century.

Born c. 1825, in Barcelona; died 5 August 1887, in Barcelona.

Painter (?), goldsmith. Landscapes.

Enrique Ferau y Alsina exhibited in Barcelona from 1847 to 1878.

FERAUD (Mme)

French, 19th century.

Painter. Flowers.

Mme Feraud exhibited at the Paris Salon in 1833 and 1835.

FÉRAUD, Albert

French, 20th century.

Born 21 November 1921, in Paris.

Sculptor.

Albert Féraud was the son of a Nobel Prize winner in Medicine and a singer at the Opéra. He spent his childhood in Paris, at Cap d'Ail and in Nîmes, near his uncle. He returned to Paris just before the war to finish his secondary studies. He left for Nîmes during the hostilities and entered the École des Beaux-Arts in Montpellier, where he met Lelouët. He then went to Marseilles in 1942-1943, before returning to Paris, where he attended Janniot's studio. As early as 1949, the latter saw the state purchase Féraud's *Women at the Fountain*. In 1951 he received the Grand Prix de Rome, and went to Italy. He returned to France in 1954.

Since 1957, he has produced numerous monumental works, often commissioned by the state, including: 1962, Pontarlier; 1965, Toulouse; 1967, Arles, Marseilles, Grenoble; 1968, Nice; 1970, Loudun and Skôde (Sweden); 1971, Conflans-Ste-Honorine; 1972, the platform of the RER station in St-Germain-en-Laye; 1974, Mulhouse, Rheims; 1977, Neuilly-sur-Seine; 1981, Bastia; 1984, the Général Koeinig monument, Porte Maillot, Paris; 1986, Washington; and 1986, the Victor Hugo monument, Créteil.

Féraud has participated in numerous collective exhibitions in Paris, notably: from 1960, Salon des Réalités Nouvelles; Salon Grands et Jeunes d'Aujourd'hui; Salon Comparaisons; Salon de Mai. He is also a member of the committee of the Salon de la Jeune Sculpture. His solo exhibitions include: 1960, 1961, Galerie 7, Paris; shows in Germany, Switzerland, and more occasionally in Spain, in 1962; 1962, Austria; Rome, Naples and Turin; 1965, 1967, Canada; 1972, Sweden; 1974, Soleil gallery, Paris; 1977, Naples; 1978, Paul Brück gallery, Luxembourg; 1979, Centre Culturel, Montbéliard; 1985, Jean-Pierre Lavignes gallery, Paris; 1986, Galerie du Luxembourg, Luxembourg; 1987, Hélène Trintignan gallery, Montpellier; 1988, Arlette Gimaray gallery, Paris; 1996, Lavignes-Bastille gallery, Paris; 2001, Galerie de l'Europe, Paris.

By 1954 the Grand Prix de Rome had become burdensome, and Féraud was feeling his way. He veered away from the classical expression that came naturally to him, and experimented with various materials. He used molten lead, evoking the influence of Giacometti, whom he had met, and he also used stainless steel, which his friend César had also just 'discovered'. He had at his disposal a vast studio of unused mechanical materials, still full of machines. Féraud then began a new career, folding, assembling, soldering, twisting, shredding, and adjusting the metal, in compositions which, if they showed nothing of his classical training, nevertheless remained powerfully expressive. Beginning with volumes, and putting the emphasis on the grooves and voids contained in relief, Féraud at once invested the sculptures with monumental dimensions. He had freed himself from his Prix de Rome label, and could, in all liberty, exhibit what he had created. 'To use force to give form, to choose that which is a relic, cast-off, allows him a new adventure: to make the unoxydized metal vibrate with the strangest sensations', Michel Faucher wrote about him in 1988.

BIBLIOGRAPHY:

Chabrun, Jean-François, *'Féraud'* in *coll. Musée de poche*, Georges Fall, Paris, 1974. Testanière, Geneviève/Moulin, Raoul-Jean, *Féraud*, exhibition catalogue, Musée des Beaux-Arts, Le Havre, 1976. Xuriguera, Gérard (preface), *Féraud*, travelling exhibition catalogue, Paris, Sarcelles, St-Nazaire, St-Omer, Montbéliard, 1979. Jianou, Ionel/Xuriguera, Gérard, *La Sculpture moderne en France depuis 1950*, Arted, Paris, 1982.

MUSEUMS AND GALLERIES:

MARSEILLES (Mus. Cantini) - PARIS (MAMVP) - PARIS (MNAM-CCI).

AUCTION RECORDS:

PARIS, 14 Dec 1976, *Composition* (stainless steel, 11$\frac{1}{2}$ x 4$\frac{1}{4}$ x 9 ins / 29 x 11 x 23 cm) FRF 2,200. PARIS, 6 April 1981, *Figure* (welded iron, h. 36$\frac{1}{2}$ ins / 93 cm) FRF 2,800. PARIS, 24 April 1983, *Untitled* (1963, stainless steel sculpture, h. 39$\frac{1}{4}$ ins / 100 cm) FRF 8,000. PARIS, 17 Dec 1985, *Composition* (steel, 90$\frac{1}{2}$ x 31$\frac{1}{2}$ x 31$\frac{1}{2}$ ins / 230 x 80 x 80 cm) FRF 34,000. PARIS, 1 Feb 1988, *Mask* (stainless steel, 11$\frac{3}{4}$ x 5$\frac{1}{2}$ x 11 ins / 30 x 14 x 27 cm) FRF 5,000. PARIS, 15 Feb 1988, *Composition* (iron, h. 12$\frac{1}{2}$ ins / 32 cm) FRF 3,200. PARIS, 20-21 June 1988, *Composition* (1967, iron sculpture, h. 13 ins / 33 cm) FRF 6,500. PARIS, 3 Oct 1988, *Untitled* (painted steel, sculpture, h. 22$\frac{3}{4}$ ins / 58 cm) FRF 9,000. PARIS, 26 Oct 1988, *Composition* (1974, h. 27$\frac{1}{2}$ ins / 70 cm) FRF 4,500. DOUAI, 23 April 1989, *Composition* (steel, sculpture, h. 30$\frac{3}{4}$ ins / 78 cm) FRF 12,000. PARIS, 22 May 1989, *Untitled* (stainless steel, 11$\frac{3}{4}$ x 12$\frac{1}{4}$ x 7$\frac{1}{2}$ ins / 30 x 31 x 19 cm) FRF 7,000. PARIS, 26 Sept 1989, *Liberty* (metal, h. 17$\frac{1}{2}$ ins / 44.5 cm and w. 7 ins/18 cm) FRF 9,500. DOUAI, 3 Dec 1989, *Composition* (1988, steel, sculpture, h. 16$\frac{1}{4}$ ins / 41 cm) FRF 11,500. PARIS, 14 March 1990, *Mask* (unique piece in steel, 18 x 17$\frac{3}{4}$ ins / 46 x 45 cm) FRF 15,000. PARIS, 25 April 1990, *Composition* (metal, h. 19 ins / 48 cm, and w. 19 ins/48 cm) FRF 9,500. PARIS, 13 June 1990, *The Chandelier* (sculpture, h. 35 ins / 88 cm) FRF 16,000. PARIS, 15 April 1991, *Untitled* (1974, stainless steel, draft model for the monument to Maréchal Koenig representing the battle scene at Bir-Hakeim, 26$\frac{3}{4}$ x 20$\frac{3}{4}$ x 17$\frac{3}{4}$ ins / 68 x 53 x 45 cm) FRF 5,000. PARIS, 19 April 1991, *Composition* (1960, stainless steel, 98$\frac{1}{2}$ x 49$\frac{1}{4}$ ins / 250 x 125 cm) FRF 58,000. PARIS, 25 June 1993, *Cock* (1960, iron, h. 33$\frac{3}{4}$ ins / 86 cm) FRF 8,100. PARIS, 17 Dec 1993, *Standing Figure* (1958, steel with bronze) FRF 10,500. PARIS, 23 Jan 1995, *Untitled* (welded aluminium, 17$\frac{3}{4}$ x 13$\frac{3}{4}$ ins / 45 x 35 cm) FRF 10,000. PARIS, 19 June 1996, *Figure* (sculpture in welded steel plates, 65$\frac{1}{4}$ x 19$\frac{3}{4}$ x 14$\frac{1}{2}$ ins / 166 x 50 x 37 cm) FRF 6,000. PARIS, 28 Oct 1996, *Composition* (steel, h. 14$\frac{3}{4}$ ins / 37.5 cm) FRF 4,800. PARIS, 17 May 2000, *Totem* (stainless steel, h. 71

ins / 180 cm) FRF 15,000. VERSAILLES, 25 June 2000, *Untitled* (bronze, 35 x 17x7 ins / 88 x 42x18 cm) FRF 20,000. PARIS, 27 June 2001, *The Betrothed* (stainless steel, h. 52 ins / 131 cm) FRF 19,000. PARIS, 9 July 2001, *Great Wing* (1969, welded iron, 20 x 41 ins / 51 x 105 cm) FRF 24,000. PARIS, 17 March 2002, *Composition* (iron, h. 30 ins / 75 cm) EUR 1,800. PARIS, 24 Nov 2002, *Untitled* (welded metal, 41 x 31 ins / 105 x 80 cm) EUR 3,000. PARIS, 18 May 2004, *Untitled* (1975-1976, steel, 35 x 27x18 ins / 88 x 68x45 cm) EUR 1,600.

FERAUD, Vincent, or Féréaud
French, 19th century.
Born 1800, in Marseilles.
Painter, lithographer.

Vincent Feraud exhibited at the Paris Salon from 1834 to 1851, mainly portraits. Works include *Justice, Ruins in Scotland, Jesus Being Presented to the Jews by Pilate, Deposition* and *Virgin and Mary Magdalene*. He received a third-class medal in 1836.

FERAY (Mme)
Maiden name: Oberkampf
French, 19th century.
Active c. 1820.
Draughtswoman, engraver.

Feray engraved *Views*.

FERAZZO
Italian, 17th century.
Born in Venice.
Active c. 1675.
Painter. Animals.

He was admitted to the academy of painting in Paris in 1675.

FERBACH, Hans von
German, 14th century.
Sculptor.

The door of a sacristy (south) in Milan, dating from the end of the 14th century, is by Hans von Ferbach. Earlier he had worked in Venice and Bologna.

FERBER
Austrian, 19th century.
Active in Vienna.
Painter.

One of Ferber's known works is a portrait of the opera singer G. Walter, which was exhibited at the Kunstverein (art association) in Vienna in 1860 and at the school of artists (*Schubert Exhibition*) in 1897.

FERBER, A.C.
German, 18th century.
Engraver (etching).

Two prints by Ferber are referred to: *Busts of Two Bearded Men with Fur Hats*, and *Busts of Men and Women with Fur Hats*. These prints are dated 1750 and 1766 respectively.

FERBER, Hans
German, 16th century.
Sculptor (wood).

Between 1559 and 1564, Hans Ferber was working at the castle of Güstrow (Mecklenburg).

FERBER, Herbert
American, 20th century.
Born 1906, in New York; died 1991, in North Egremont (Massachusetts).
Sculptor.
School of New York.

Herbert Ferber initially trained to be a dental surgeon before studying sculpture at the National Academy of Design, New York, from 1927 to 1930. Until 1950 his sculptures were based on a recognisable reality, even though this was recreated for expressive purposes. After that, using cast bronze or lead, he created three-dimensional calligraphies that evoked vegetable growth, consisting of graceful elements intersecting in space. Some were monumental, could be entered, and were supported inside by partitions that broke up the empty volume that each of these strange flowerings occupied.

Ferber took part in many group exhibitions, and his first solo show was held at the National Academy of Design in 1930. A large retrospective was held at the Walker Art Center, Minneapolis. His public commissions include a large work for the Milburn Synagogue, New Jersey (1952) and a living space for Rutgers University, New Jersey (1958).

BIBLIOGRAPHY:

'Trois sculpteurs américains, Ferber, Hare, Lassaw' in *coll. Musée de Poche*, Georges Fall, Paris. Reynolds, Donald Martin, *Masters of American Sculpture: The Figurative Tradition*, Abbeville Press, New York, 1994. Herskovic, Marika (ed.), *American Abstract Expressionism of the 1950s*, New York School Press, New York, 2000.

AUCTION RECORDS:

NEW YORK, 12 May 1981, *Disc II* (1978, wrought copper, 63 x 57 ins / 160 x 144.8 cm) USD 12,000. NEW YORK, 8 May 1984, *Marl II* (1971, forged steel, 45 x 34 x 35 ins / 114.3 x 86.3 x 89 cm) USD 8,000. NEW YORK, 20 Feb 1987, *Williams II B* (copper, 36 x 36 x 26 ins / 91.5 x 91.5 x 66 cm) USD 7,000. NEW YORK, 24 Jan 1989, *The Couple at no. 40* (1940, gouache/paper, 15 x 11 1/2 ins / 37.2 x 29.4 cm) USD 550. NEW YORK, 17 Nov 1992, *Williams 2B* (1976, welded copper, 36 x 36 x 26 ins / 91.5 x 91.5 x 66 cm) USD 5,280. NEW YORK, 23 Feb 1994, *Pointer* (brass, 24 1/4 x 10 x 7 3/4 ins / 61.5 x 25.4 x 19.6 cm) USD 2,990. NEW YORK, 26 Sept 2002, *Homage to Piranesi II a2* (1962, oil on copper, 37 x 18x17 ins / 95 x 46x44 cm) USD 8,000. NEW YORK, 23 Sept 2003, *Calligraphic Mercury II* (1955, bronze, 51 x 44x16 ins / 129 x 111x41 cm) USD 10,000.

FERCH, Adam Pankratz. See **FERG**

FERCH, Theodorich
German, 17th century.
Active in Buchau (Württemberg) c. 1631.
Painter.

FERDEN, H. von
German, 16th century.
Painter.

The town hall in Lüneburg (Lower Saxony) houses a large oil painting by this artist showing *St Peter Preaching*. Also attributed to him was *A Reindeer*, owned by the family of the painter Jurgen Oven.

FERDENAND. See **FERDINAND** and **FERDINANDUS**

FERDI
Dutch, 20th century.
Born 1927, in Arnhem.
From 1950 active in France.
Sculptor.
Pop Art.

Ferdi studied sculpture in 1952 with Zadkine. He made a long journey to South Africa in 1954. In 1968 he exhibited at the Stedelijk Museum in Amsterdam, then in Brussels, and at the Van Abbe Museum in Eindhoven.

Ferdi often took bright and colourful flowers as his theme.

FERDI-PARIS, Abélard
French, 19th century.
Born 12 April 1857, in Vincennes.
Engraver (etching).

Ferdi-Paris was a pupil of Gervex and Humbert. He was a member of the Société du Salon des Artistes Français.

FERDIANI, Giuseppe
Italian, 17th century.
Active in Naples.
Sculptor.

Giuseppe Ferdiani was a signatory to the statutes of 1618, which established the corporation.

FERDINAND. See **ELLE Ferdinand, ELLE Louis the Elder, ELLE Louis the Younger, ELLE Pierre**

FERDINAND
Lithuanian, 17th century.
Born in Vilnius.
Fresco artist.

Ferdinand produced frescoes from the church of Vilnius in 1610.

FERDINAND
French, 18th century.
Active in Marseilles.
Sculptor.

In 1794, Ferdinand executed a plaster *Statue of Liberty* in Marseilles for the altar called the Autel de la Patrie.

FERDINAND
French, 19th century.
Engraver.

Ferdinand produced some plates for the costume museum, Musée des Costumes, and some engraved portraits: *Nicholas I of Russia*, in the style of the painting by Krüger, dating from 1835 and in the style of the drawings by Jeanson, in the book *The Mysteries of Russia*; *Nikon, Patriarch of Moscow*, in the style of R. de Moraine in *The Martyrs of Freedom*, and *General Moreau* and *Napoleon III*, in the style of Eugène Lami.

FERDINAND, Andreas Niklas
German, 18th century.
Active in Zerbst (Anhalt Dessau, now Saxony-Anhalt).
Painter (porcelain).

Ferdinand worked at J. Wolff's porcelain factory in Copenhagen, then in Stockholm, where he became manager of the factory newly opened by Wolff at Rörstrand.

FERDINAND, Dominicus
German, 18th century.
Born to a family originally from Arnstorf (Lower Bavaria).
Painter.

In 1739 Dominicus Ferdinand painted a religious picture for Reith (Dingolfing), Germany.

FERDINAND, Eugène
French, 19th century.
Born 19th century, in Bordeaux.
Painter. History painting, genre scenes, landscapes.

Eugène Ferdinand was a pupil of Vincent. He worked for the Paris hospital Hôpital de Bicêtre and for the church of St-Roch in Paris.

FERDINAND, Georg
Austrian, 18th century.
Active in Vienna.
Sculptor (wood).

Georg Ferdinand was the son of Johann Ferdinand, painter of miniatures.

FERDINAND, Jakob
Austrian, 18th century.
Active in Vienna.
Painter.

Ferdinand was the brother of the miniaturist Johann Ferdinand.

FERDINAND, Jean
Belgian, 20th century.
Born 1898, in Brussels; died 1972; committed suicide.
Painter.

Ferdinand was a hairdresser until 1951. Subsequently he became the painter of a particular world, imbued with the echoes of the *Belle Époque*.

FERDINAND, Johann
Austrian, 17th century.
Born 1633 or 1634; died 22 February 1704, in Vienna.
Active in Vienna.
Miniaturist.

Ferdinand is believed to have worked at the castle of Ratibor in Silesia (now Racibórz, Poland) around 1670.

FERDINAND, Johann
Croat, 18th century.
Born 1679, in Karlstadt.
Painter.

FERDINAND D'ORLEANS (Duc)
French, 19th century.
Born 3 September 1810, in Palermo, Italy; died 13 July 1842, in Paris.
Engraver (etching), lithographer.

Ferdinand d'Orléans was the son of Louis Philippe, King of France.

FERDINAND DE VIZEU. See **FERNANDES Vasco**

FERDINAND II (King Regent of Portugal), or Ferdinand of Saxe-Coburg-Gotha
Portuguese, 19th century.
Born 29 October 1816, in Vienna; died 15 December 1881, in Lisbon.
Painter, watercolourist, sculptor, engraver. Portraits, genre scenes. Statues.

Ferdinand II married Maria II of Portugal while he was Duke of Braganza and was King Regent of Portugal until the accession of his son Pedro V. He was a keen lover of all the arts. His works include an equestrian statue of *Marshal J. von Rantzau*, watercolour landscapes for the queen's boudoir in the Palacio das Necessidades in Lisbon, and numerous pen and ink drawings, which he engraved himself on copper.

His drawings include studies of animals from nature, scenes of children, Portuguese costumes, recollections of his life in Hungary, caricatures of court life in Lisbon, and portraits such as those of *Baron Eschwege* and of his two eldest sons and his father. His monogram consisted of the letters F and E intertwined.

BIBLIOGRAPHY:
Hermano Saravia, José, *Historia de Portugal*, Alianza Editorial, Madrid, 1989.

FERDINAND III (Emperor)
German, 17th century.
Born 13 July 1608, in Graz; died 2 April 1657.
Sculptor.

Ferdinand III was Emperor of Germany and Holy Roman Emperor. He produced sculptures in ivory.

MUSEUMS AND GALLERIES:
VIENNA (Treasure Room).

FERDINAND MARIA OF BAVARIA (Elector)
German, 17th century.
Born 3 October 1636, in Schleissheim (Bavaria); died 26 May 1679, in Schleissheim.
Sculptor (ivory).

The lid of an oval bowl by Ferdinand is kept in the Munich collection.

FERDINAND OF BRUNSWICK (Duke)
German, 18th century.
Born 1721; died 1792.
Engraver.

One of Ferdinand of Brunswick's known works is *Landscape with Cottages*, after A. Bloemert.

FERDINAND-AUGUSTE (Ferdinand of Saxe-Coburg-Gotha). See **FERNANDO II**

FERDINAND-OLIVIER. See **OLIVIER Ferdinand**

FERDINANDI, Francesco. See **FERNANDI**

FERDINANDO D'ORVIETO
Italian, 16th century.
Active in Rome.
Painter.

Ferdinando d'Orvieto was the pupil of C. Nebbia. He painted two evangelists in front of the chapel of Sixtus V in S Maria Maggiore in Rome.

FERDINANDO DA VICE MORCOTE
Swiss, 17th century.
Miniaturist.

Ferdinando da Vice Morcote was a Franciscan monk. He painted the folios of books of canticles for the monastery of S Maria degli Angeli in Lugano with Brother Bonaventura da Varese.

FERDINANDUS, Alexandre
French, 19th century.
Died 1888.
Painter. Scenes with figures.

Ferdinandus was a member of the Sociéte des Artistes Français and exhibited at the society's Salon.

AUCTION RECORDS:
PARIS, 25 Jan 1929, *Horseriders, Cars, People Walking* (drawing) FRF 450.

FERDINANDUS, Philips
Flemish School, 16th century.
Born to a family originally from Antwerp.
Painter.

Philips Ferdinandus is probably the same person as a Ferdinandus, painter and burgher of the town of Prague, who painted a *Sacellum corporis Christis* in 1603. The Franzenmuseum in Brünn owns his *Christ Crowned with Thorns* with portraits of the family of Michael Reich of Brünn.

FERDOMNACH
Irish, 9th century.
Died 846.
Miniaturist.

Illuminator of the *Book of Armagh* in Trinity College, Dublin.

MUSEUMS AND GALLERIES:
DUBLIN (Trinity College Library): *Book of Armagh.*

FERÉ
French, 18th century.
Active in Alençon.
Sculptor (wood).

Feré sculpted the pulpit of the church of St-Paterne in Alençon in 1775.

FÉRÉAUD, Vincent. See **FÉRAUD**

FERÉE
French, 19th century.
Active c. 1800.
Engraver.

Ferée's name is found on three illustrations designed by Clavereau for Montesquieu's work *Gnide Temple*. He worked for Herhan and Mame.

FÉRELLE, Pierre Antoine
French, 18th century.
Active in Paris in 1719.
Sculptor.

FERELST. See **VERELST**

FEREMANS, Cornille, or Feermans
Flemish, 17th century.
Active in Mechelen from 1600 to 1619.
Painter.
Flemish School.

Cornille Feremans was summoned to Brussels with other painters in 1603 to execute a painting for the infante.

FEREMANS, Jan, or Feermans
Flemish School, 16th century.
Active in Mechelen from 1559 to 1588.
Painter.

FERENCZ (Baron). See **HATVANY Ferencz von**

FERENCZY, Beni
Hungarian, 20th century.
Born 18 June 1890, in Szentendre; died 1967, in Budapest.
Sculptor, draughtsman.

Beni Ferenczy, the son of Karoly Ferenczy, began his art training in Nagybanya. He subsequently continued his studies in Florence, Munich and Paris where he was Bourdelle's and Archipenko's student. He was in Vienna in 1919 and lived in Moscow from 1932 to 1935, returning to his native land in 1936. After his initial Neo-Classical and Cubist tendencies resulting from the successive influences of Bourdelle and Archipenko, he worked on sculptures that were small but had monumental power, evoking the spirit of both Greek and Maillol's sculpture. A very good draughtsman, he produced portraits including that of *Bela Bartok*. He was awarded the Kossuth Prize and was regarded as the best Hungarian sculptor of his generation.

BIBLIOGRAPHY:
Németh, Lajos, *Moderne ungarische Kunst*, Corvina Kiadó, Budapest, 1969.

FERENCZY, István
Hungarian, 19th century.
Born 23 February 1792, in Rimavská Sobota; died 4 July 1856, in Rimavská Sobota.
Sculptor.

István Ferenczy studied in Budapest and at the Akademie der Bildenden Künste in Vienna. He spent time in Rome, where he was influenced by Canova, before entering Thorvaldsen's workshop. During his stay in Rome, he sculpted the marble bust of the Hungarian poet *Csokonai*, which he donated to the town of Debrecen. On returning to Hungary, he settled in Budapest, where he made efforts to revive the art of sculpture. He sculpted a *Eurydice* in Rimavská Sobota which was buried with him and then exhumed and placed in the church in the same town.

MUSEUMS AND GALLERIES:
BUDAPEST (Szépmuvészeti Múz.): *The Origin of Fine Arts* (marble); *Bust of Kazinczy, the Poet*; *Allegory of Science and Strength.*

FERENCZY, Jozsef
Hungarian, 20th century.
Born 17 December 1866, in Marosvásárhely (now Tîrgu-Mures, Romania); died 1925.
Painter.

Jozsef Ferenczy studied in Budapest, then in Paris and finally with J. Benczur in Budapest. Settled in Temesvár (now Timisoara, Romania) where he adorned the Piarist church with four pictures. In 1911, he organised a collective exhibition of his works.

AUCTION RECORDS:
LONDON, 17 Nov 1993, *Serenade* (oil on canvas, 26 x 20¾ ins / 66 x 53 cm) GBP 1,035.

FERENCZY, Karoly
Hungarian, 19th - 20th century.

Born 8 February 1862, in Vienna, to Hungarian parents; died 1917.
Painter. Religious subjects, figures, portraits, genre scenes.

Karoly Ferenczy was a student of Bouguereau and of Tony Robert-Fleury in Paris for three years. His early work was marked by his sensitive feeling for nature. In 1896 he founded the Nagybanya group, which was to Hungary what Barbizon was in France. His painting evolved from Naturalism to a measured Impressionism. Biblical compositions painted in familiar mode succeeded intimate genre scenes and the landscapes of the preceding period: *The Three Magi* (1898), *Joseph Being Sold by His Brothers* (1900) and *The Sacrifice of Abraham* (1901). As with the French Symbolists, his paintings and the illustrations at this time did not always manage to shake off the decorative style predominant throughout Europe in the 1900s. Ferenczy is considered the creator of modern Hungarian painting. He was awarded a bronze medal at the Exposition Universelle in Paris in 1900.

BIBLIOGRAPHY:
Németh, Lajos, *Moderne ungarische Kunst*, Corvina Kiadó, Budapest, 1969.

MUSEUMS AND GALLERIES:
BUDAPEST (Szépmuvészeti Múz.): *Painter and a Model; Lumberjack.*

AUCTION RECORDS:
LONDON, 19 June 1985, *Peasant by a River* (oil on canvas, 38 1/2 x 34 1/4 ins / 97.5 x 87 cm) GBP 3,000. AMSTERDAM, 5 Nov 1996, *Teasing a Little Girl* (oil on canvas/panel, 46 x 34 1/4 ins / 117 x 87 cm) NLG 6,844. BUDAPEST, 12 Oct 2001, *Scene* (oil on canvas, 31 x 39 ins / 78 x 100 cm) HUF 900,000. AHLDEN, 30 Nov 2001, *Girl and Goat* (oil on canvas, 24 x 32 ins / 61 x 81 cm) DEM 3,500. BUDAPEST, 11 April 2003, *Venus Still-life* (oil on canvas, 22 x 13 ins / 57 x 34 cm) HUF 5,000,000. BUDAPEST, 12 Dec 2003, *My Studio in Nagybanya - House among Trees* (oil on canvas, 33 x 45 ins / 85 x 115 cm) HUF 24,000,000. BUDAPEST, 28 April 2004, *Landscape in Nagybanya* (oil on canvas, 17 x 19 ins / 42 x 48 cm) HUF 3,400,000.

FERENCZY, Noemi
Hungarian, 20th century.
Born 1890, in Szentendre; died 1957, in Budapest.
Watercolourist, draughtsman. Scenes with figures, figures, landscapes. Designs for tapestries.

Noemi Ferenczy was the twin sister of Beni Ferenczy. She studied at the Manufacture des Gobelins in Paris.

Her early works were influenced by the French 'Verdure' (greenery) of the 17th century, which she had seen at the Gobelins. She then moved towards the natural, open-air style which her father, Karoly Ferenczy, had introduced to Hungary known as 'Nagybanya' after a village. Her tapestries were based on preliminary watercolour studies with a cool simplicity not without a certain monumental meaning.

MUSEUMS AND GALLERIES:
BUDAPEST (Magyar Nemzeti Gal.): *Shepherd; Vineyards in Autumn.*

AUCTION RECORDS:
LONDON, 21 Oct 1987, *Figure and House in a Field* (tempera, 22 x 19 1/4 ins / 56 x 49 cm) GBP 1,200. BUDAPEST, 11 Sept 2002, *Sleeping Shepherd* (1937, oil on canvas, 31 x 68 ins / 80 x 173 cm) HUF 10,000,000. BUDAPEST, 13 Sept 2002, *Abundance* (watercolour, 87 x 48 ins / 221 x 123 cm) HUF 1,000,000.

FERENCZY, Valer
Hungarian, 20th century.
Active in Vienna.
Painter.

Son of Karoly Ferenczy.

FERENZ, Anton
Hungarian, 19th century.
Died 19 July 1874, in Brno.
Painter. Religious subjects, portraits.

Anton Ferenz produced mainly portraits, as well as religious works for churches.

AUCTION RECORDS:
LONDON, 24 Feb 1982, *Portrait of a Young Girl* (1850, oil on canvas, 13 1/2 x 11 ins / 34 x 28 cm) GBP 550.

FÉRÉOL, Auguste
French, 19th century.
Painter. Landscapes.

Auguste Féréol exhibited at the Paris Salon from 1833 to 1848. Works include *Mill in the Wood, Mort-Chêne Valley, Stormy Weather, View from Batignolles, Sologne Stable* and *Sologne Cowshed.*

FÉRÉOL, Louis, called Second
French, 19th century.
Born in Amiens.
Painter. Genre scenes, landscapes.

Louis Féréol was a pupil of Xavier Le Prince, and exhibited landscapes at the Paris Salon in 1824 and 1827. His most important works are *Scotsman Sitting on the Edge of a Torrent, Mist on the Loire, Orléans Courtyard, Young Clovis Discovered in the Marne by a Fisherman* and *View of Part of Orleans Bridge*

AUCTION RECORDS:
PARIS, 28 Oct 1932, *Drinking Trough*, FRF 135.

FERER MORGADO, Horacio. See **FERRER MORGADO**

FERET, Alexandre
French, 19th century.
Born 19th century, in Paris.
Lithographer.

Alexandre Feret was a pupil of Lemoine and exhibited at the Salon from 1866 to 1880. Most notable works are *Portrait of Mr Garnier-Pagès, Portrait of Mr Louis Jourdan, Portrait of Havin, Portrait of Mr Quatrefages* and *For the Little Birds.*

FERET, Amédée
French, 19th century.
Painter, pastellist, draughtsman, lithographer.

The Museum of Dieppe holds two pastels by Amédée Feret, representing the château of Arques-la-Bataille and several lithographs, notably *Attempted Bombardment by the English in 1803*, in the publication *Mémorial Dieppois* (*Chronicles of Dieppe*).

MUSEUMS AND GALLERIES:
DIEPPE: *View of the Castle from Arques-la-Bataille* (pastel); several lithographs.

FERET, Armand
French, 19th century.
Painter.

MUSEUMS AND GALLERIES:
ST-LÔ: *Souvenir from Holland.*

FERET, Baptiste
French, 17th century.
Active in Avignon in 1677.
Painter, priest.

FERET, C.
French, 17th century.
Engraver.

C. Feret's signature, *C. Feret fecit* 1697, is on an engraving depicting *Mars and Two Slaves.*

FERET, Jean Baptiste
French, 17th - 18th century.
Born 1664, in Évreux; died 1 February 1739, in Paris.
Painter. Landscapes.

Jean Baptiste Feret was admitted as an academician on 26 October 1709.

Museums and Galleries:
Grenoble (Mus. de Grenoble): *Landscape with Shepherds* (oil on canvas) - Munich (Schloss Nymphenburg): *The Valley of the Seine River* (oil on canvas, two landscapes).

FERETTI, Alessandro and Giorgio.
See **FERRETTI**

FEREY, Louise Renée
French, 19th century.
Born in Nantes.
Miniaturist.

Louise Ferey was a pupil of Hortense Richard, Jules Lefebvre and Robert-Fleury. She received a honourable mention in 1900 at the Exposition Universelle.

FEREY, Prosper
French, 19th century.
Painter. Genre scenes, landscapes with figures.

Prosper Ferey exhibited views of Normandy at the Paris Salon in 1847 and 1848.

Auction records:
Paris, 8 Dec 1924, *Sunrise; Sunset* (two panels) FRF 150. Paris, 21 Jan 1928, *Landscape with Figure and Animals, towards Evening,* FRF 380. Enghien-les-Bains, 24 Feb 1980, *Skating Scene* (oil on canvas, 13 x 18 ins / 33 x 46 cm) FRF 4,500,. Paris, 15 Dec 1999, *Market Scene in Normandy* (oil on canvas, 22 x 40 ins / 56 x 102 cm) FRF 61,000.

FEREYS, Wills
British, 13th century.
Sculptor.

A monument in the church of Beres Ferrers, Devon, is inscribed *Wills Fereys me fecit* (*Wills Fereys made me*).

FERG, Adam Pankratz, or Ferch
Austrian, 17th - 18th century.
Born 1651, in Linz; died 8 April 1729, in Vienna.
Painter. Landscapes.

Ferg was the father of Franz de Paula Ferg.

FERG, Franz de PAULA
Austrian, 18th century.
Born 1689, in Vienna; died 1740, in London.
Also active in England.
Painter, engraver. Genre scenes, local scenes (including village fairs), landscapes, landscapes with figures, seascapes.

The son and student of Adam Pankratz Ferg, Ferg was also a student of Joseph Orient and Hans Graff in Vienna. He was quick to establish a reputation and spent several years at the court in Dresden. In 1718 he left Vienna and went to Bamberg, Brunswick and then in around 1720 to London, where he lived for twenty years.

Ferg's landscapes, often very detailed and containing many figures, bring to mind those by Poelenborch, while his scenes of everyday life are reminiscent of those by Van Ostade. He produced a series of etchings in London in 1726, representing peasants in the countryside, entitled: *Capricci Fatti per F.F.*

Museums and Galleries:
Brunswick: *Four Seasons; Rural Fair; Market Scene* - Budapest: *Port* (two paintings of the same subject) - Dresden: *Market near a Bridge; People Relaxing on the Riverbank; Village Square; Day Out at the Ruins; Market in front of an Old Castle* - Florence (NG): *Landscape with Figures; Landscape* - Graz: *Landscape* - Hamburg (Kunsthalle): *Market Day* - Nottingham: *Two Landscapes* - Schwerin: *Four Landscapes* - Vienna: *Fair* (two paintings) - Wroclaw: *Mountain Fair; Shore of a Calm Lake.*

Auction records:
Paris, 11 April 1874, *Village Fête,* FRF 990. London, 9 May 1910, *Landscape with Figures,* GBP 27. London, 4 Feb 1927, *Seasons,* GBP 30. New York, 28 Nov 1941, *Market Scene,* USD 30. Paris, 15 Dec 1949, *Village Fête,* FRF 110,000. Vienna, 2 June 1964, *Local Fair,* ATS 30,000. Vienna, 16 March 1971, *Monument in Mountain Landscape,* ATS 100,000. London, 8 March 1972, *Landscape with Figures,* GBP 2,000. Cologne, 27 June 1974, *Italianate Landscape with Figures,* DEM 17,000. Vienna, 30 Nov 1976, *Landscape with Figures* (oil on canvas, 4 1/4 x 6 ins / 10.5 x 15.5 cm) ATS 75,000. Vienna, 12 Dec 1978, *Children Playing near an Old Well* (oil/copper, 12 3/4 x 18 ins / 32.5 x 46 cm) ATS 200,000. Vienna, 17 March 1981, *Village Dance* (oil on paper, 10 1/2 x 14 1/4 ins / 26.5 x 36.5 cm) ATS 200,000. London, 15 June 1983, *River Landscape with Figures* (oil on canvas, 16 3/4 x 24 1/2 ins / 42.5 x 62 cm) GBP 12,500. London, 8 July 1987, *Village Fête* (oil/copper, 13 3/4 x 18 1/2 ins / 35 x 47 cm) GBP 33,000. Milan, 17 Dec 1987, *Village Scene* (pen and wash, 9 x 13 1/2 ins / 23 x 34.5 cm) ITL 1,800,000. New York, 7 April 1988, *Farmers at Work in a Farmyard* (oil on canvas, 12 1/2 x 9 ins / 31.5 x 23 cm) USD 4,125. Paris, 23 Jan 1989, *Villagers in front of Tavern* (oil on canvas, 13 x 10 ins / 33 x 24.5 cm) FRF 32,000. New York, 31 May 1989, *Village Fair* (oil on panel, 10 1/2 x 15 1/2 ins / 26.8 x 39.4 cm) USD 17,600. Cologne, 15 June 1989, *River Landscape with Rider* (oil on paper/canvas, 6 3/4 x 9 ins / 17 x 22 cm) DEM 2,600. Monaco, 16 June 1989, *Landscapes with Travellers and Shepherds* (oil/copper, a pair, 10 1/4 x 13 1/4 ins / 26 x 33.5 cm) FRF 310,800. London, 27 Oct 1989, *Village Fête in front of the Inn; Locals at the Village Pier* (oil/copper, a pair, each 9 1/4 x 12 1/4 ins / 23.6 x 31 cm) GBP 20,900. Rome, 21 Nov 1989, *Landscape with Bridge; Landscape with Woods* (oil on panel, a pair, 6 x 8 3/4 ins / 15.2 x 22.5 cm) ITL 13,500,000. London, 8 Dec 1989, *River Landscape with Passengers on a Ferry, with the Mast at the Stern* (oil/copper, forming a pair, 14 1/4 x 16 1/2 ins / 36.5 x 42 cm) GBP 41,800. New York, 5 April 1990, *Vast Landscape with Classical Ruins* (oil on panel, 11 1/4 x 15 1/2 ins / 28.5 x 39.5 cm) USD 7,150. Paris, 31 Jan 1991, *Shephers near Obelisk* (gouache, 10 3/4 x 15 1/4 ins / 27.5 x 38.5 cm) FRF 22,000. London, 19 April 1991, *Gipsy Encampment with Traveller being Robbed by Children whilst having his Fortune Told* (oil/copper, 11 x 15 1/2 ins / 27.7 x 39.5 cm) GBP 7,700. Stockholm, 29 May 1991, *People and Animals on Ferry* (oil/copper, 12 1/2 x 18 ins / 32 x 46 cm) SEK 200,000. New York, 31 May 1991, *Mountain and River Landscape with Figures* (oil on canvas, a pair, 30 1/2 x 25 1/2 ins / 77.5 x 64.8 cm) USD 82,500. London, 3 July 1991, *Italianate Landscape with Virgil's Tomb* (oil on canvas, 30 x 53 1/4 ins / 76 x 135 cm) GBP 29,700. Paris, 31 Oct 1991, *Riders Listening to Fortune Teller* (oil/copper, 9 3/4 x 14 1/4 ins / 25 x 36 cm) FRF 90,000. London, 13 Dec 1991, *Italianate Landscapes with Local Families in Foreground* (oil on canvas, a pair, 17 1/4 x 22 ins / 43.5 x 56 cm) GBP 25,300. London, 15 April 1992, *Bandits Attacking a Convoy near a Ford; Riders at the Walls of a Town* (oil/copper, a pair, each 8 1/2 x 10 1/2 ins / 21.5 x 26.5 cm) GBP 9,000. Bologna, 8-9 June 1992, *River Landscape with Mill* (oil on canvas, 15 x 18 3/4 ins / 38 x 47.5 cm) ITL 16,100,000. Amsterdam, 10 Nov 1992, *Officer Inspecting Troups on their Departure* (oil on canvas/panel, 13 1/2 x 15 1/2 ins / 34 x 39.5 cm) NLG 6,900. London, 11 Dec 1992, *Rhenish Landscape with People Waiting for Ferry* (oil/copper, a pair, 12 3/4 x 17 ins / 32.2 x 42.3 cm and 12 3/4 x 16 1/2 ins/32.4 x 42 cm) GBP 39,600. New York, 15 Jan 1993, *Christ Calling the Children to Him* (oil/copper, 9 x 11 1/2 ins / 22.9 x 29.2 cm) USD 8,625. London, 10 Dec 1993, *People Relaxing among Ruins in Italian Countryside* (oil/copper, 13 x 16 1/2 ins / 33.3 x 42.2 cm) GBP 13, 800. Paris, 17 June 1994, *Mountainous Landscape with Figures and Buildings* (oil/copper, a pair, each 6 3/4 x 8 1/4 ins / 17.3 x 21.2 cm) FRF 52,000. Paris, 8

March 1995, *Landscape with Figures* (oil/copper, a pair, each 6 3/4 x 9 ins / 17 x 22 cm) FRF 98,000. LONDON, 3 July 1996, *Market Scene with Riders; Village Fair* (oil/copper, a pair, 15 x 18 3/4 ins / 38 x 47.5 cm) GBP 47,700. LONDON, 11 Dec 1996, *Classical Landscape with Travellers and Local People* (oil/copper, a pair, each 12 1/4 x 15 ins / 31 x 37.8 cm) GBP 13,800. LONDON, 4 July 1997, *River Landscape with People Embarking on Ferry, with Castle and Hilltop in the Distance* (oil/copper, 13 1/2 x 18 1/2 ins / 34 x 47.3 cm) GBP 14,375. CASTLECOMER, 27 July 1999, *The Village Dance. Strolling Players* (oil on copper, a pair, 13 x 17 ins / 33 x 42 cm) IEP 25,500.

FERG, Xaver
German, 19th century.
Born 1812, in Reinstetten; died 1844, in Biberach (Württemberg).
Painter. Birds.

FERGIONE, Bernardino, or Fergioni
Italian, 18th century.
Born 1675; died after 1736, according to Zani.
Painter. Hunting scenes, seascapes, animals.

He welcomed Claude-Joseph Vernet to his studio when Vernet arrived in Rome in 1732.

MUSEUMS AND GALLERIES:
ROME (Villa Albani Torlonia): *Stag-hunt.*

FERGOLA, Alessandro
Italian, 19th century.
Born 1812, in Naples; died 1864.
Painter. Figure compositions, landscapes.

In 1839 Alessandro Fergola exhibited a painting of a fair, in Naples. He may have been the brother of Salvatore Fergola.

AUCTION RECORDS:
LONDON, 15 Nov 1995, *View of Naples* (oil on canvas, 11 x 14 1/2 ins / 27 x 37 cm) GBP 6,325.

FERGOLA, Luigi
Italian, 18th - 19th century.
Active in Naples.
Painter.

Luigi Fergola was a pupil of Hackert. V. Alloja engraved a *Collection of the Most Pleasing Views of Naples* from Fergola originals.

FERGOLA, Salvatore
Italian, 19th century.
Born 1799, in Naples; died 1874 or 1877.
Painter. Scenes with figures, landscapes, seascapes.

Salvatore Fergola's father was the painter Luigi Fergola. Salvatore was a landscape painter in the service of the Bourbon court, and in this capacity accompanied King Francesco I of Naples on a journey to Sicily and Spain, for the marriage of the King's daughter to Ferdinand VII of Spain. (Luigi Fergola was given the task of painting the official ceremonies.) Salvatore showed his work at the National Exhibition in Naples, in 1877.

He related contemporary events in Naples through his paintings, for example his *Inauguration of the Train between Naples and Portici*. Occasionally, he also painted seascapes.

MUSEUMS AND GALLERIES:
NAPLES (Mus. di San Martino): *Inauguration of the Train between Naples and Portici.*

AUCTION RECORDS:
MILAN, 6 April 1966, *View of a Harbour Town,* ITL 800,000. PARIS, 11 March 1971, *Peasant Family at Prayer* (1838, oil on canvas, 28 3/4 x 37 3/4 ins / 73 x 96 cm) FRF 950. MILAN, 26 May 1977, *Seascape; Nocturnal Eruption* (two canvases, 11 x 15 1/4 ins / 28 x 38.5 cm) ITL 1,900,000. MILAN, 20 March 1980, *Flight into Egypt* (1867, oil on canvas, 16 1/4 x 22 1/2 ins / 41 x 57 cm) ITL 1,700,000. ROME, 6 March 1984, *Sorrento* (oil on canvas, 11 3/4 x 19 ins / 30 x 48 cm) ITL 3,400,000. NEW YORK, 16 June 1984, *Battery Park* (1817, gouache, 15 1/4 x 21 1/2 ins / 38.6 x 54.5 cm) USD 2,300. ROME, 21 March 1985, *View of Naples with Mount Vesuvius; View of the Bay of Naples* (two oils on canvas, 10 1/4 x 12 3/4 ins / 26 x 32.5 cm) ITL 17,000,000. ROME, 19 May 1987, *Adoration of the Shepherds (back); Rest on the Flight into Egypt (front)* (watercolour and pencil, 11 x 9 ins / 27 x 22.6 cm) ITL 1,600,000. PARIS, 16 June 1987, *View of the Sicilian Countryside* (1838, oil on canvas, 29 1/4 x 38 1/2 ins / 74 x 97.5 cm) FRF 70,000. ROME, 25 May 1988, *Fish Sellers* (distemper/paper, 9 1/2 x 15 1/4 ins / 24 x 38.5 cm) ITL 8,500,000. ROME, 31 May 1990, *View of Paestum* (watercolour and tempera/paper, 10 1/4 x 12 3/4 ins / 26 x 32.5 cm) ITL 3,000,000. ROME, 4 Dec 1990, *Abbey of Trinità di Cava dei Tirreni* (oil on canvas, 20 3/4 x 26 ins / 53 x 66 cm) ITL 16,500,000. ROME, 5 Dec 1995, *Figures on the Shore* (1856, oil on card, 5 3/4 x 7 1/2 ins / 14.5 x 19 cm) ITL 5,893,000. MILAN, 31 May 1999, *Maria Sofia of Bavaria Hunting. Country Road with Figures* (1857, oil on canvas, a pair, 16 x 23 ins / 41 x 58 cm) ITL 44,000,000. ROME, 30 Nov 1999, *Naples from the Mountaintop with Figures* (oil on canvas, 12 x 17 ins / 30 x 42 cm) ITL 18,000,000. BERN, 9 Nov 2000, *Eremitage della Stella Albano near Rome* (oil on canvas, 18 x 22 ins / 46 x 55 cm) CHF 3,600. NEW YORK, 5 June 2002, *View of the Castello Di Baia, Naples* (oil on board, 12 x 18 ins / 30 x 45 cm) USD 6,500. MILAN, 3 April 2003, *Capri* (oil on canvas, 11 x 13 ins / 27 x 33 cm) EUR 9,000.

FERGUSON, Alice L. L.
American, 20th century.
Born in Washington.
Painter.

FERGUSON, D.
British, 19th century.
Painter.

D. Ferguson is mentioned in Art Prices Current.

AUCTION RECORDS:
LONDON, 25 April 1908, *Spring Sun,* GBP 17.

FERGUSON, Dorothy H.
American, 20th century.
Born 9 December 1896, in Alton.
Painter, engraver.

Dorothy H. Ferguson, a pupil of Charles W. Hawthorne, won the first prize at the Saint Louis Artists Guild in 1928.

FERGUSON, Duncan
American, 20th century.
Born 1 January 1901, in Shanghai, China; died 1974.
Sculptor.

FERGUSON, Eleonor M.
American, 20th century.
Born 30 June 1876, in Hartford (Connecticut).
Sculptor.

Eleonor M. Ferguson began her training in Hartford with Charles Noel Flagg and then went to New York to work under Daniel Chester French.

FERGUSON, Henry, or Heindrich or Hendrik Vergazoon or Vergazon
Dutch, 17th - 18th century.
Born c. 1655; died 1730, in Toulouse.
Active in England then in France.
Painter. Figures, landscapes, ruins.

Henry Ferguson was the son of the painter William Gouw Ferguson. He set up in Toulouse, and while in France he worked with the painter Adrian van der Cabel, a Dutchman who had established himself in Lyons.

Ferguson is mainly remembered as a painter of landscapes with ruins, painted in dark tones with contrasted light effects. Occasionally he painted genre scenes such as groups of soldiers feasting and travellers being held up. According to Horace Walpole, Ferguson also painted small portraits while he was employed by the portrait artist Godfrey Kneller to paint his backgrounds, but none of these have survived. Several of his paintings are signed *W. J. Ferguson*.

BIBLIOGRAPHY:

Eidelberg, Martin, '*Reintroducing Henry Ferguson*' in *Apollo* n° 463 p. 27, periodical, London, September 2000.

MUSEUMS AND GALLERIES:

ALBI (Mus. Toulouse-Lautrec): *Landscape with Ruins* (oil on canvas) - EDINBURGH (Nat. Gal. of Scotland): *Grotto with Music-making Peasants and Ruins* (oil on canvas) - PORTLAND (AM): *Bacchic Frieze* (fragment of a larger scale work) - ST PETERSBURG (Hermitage): *Landscape with Ruins* (1680, oil on canvas) - TOULOUSE: *Dice Players; Attack.*

FERGUSON, Henry Augustus

American, 19th - 20th century.
Born 14 January 1842, in Glens Falls; died 22 March 1911, in New York.
Painter, watercolourist. Landscapes, waterscapes, architectural views.

Henry Augustus Ferguson taught himself to paint in Glens Falls. He settled in New York, where he was a member of the National Academy of Design and the century Association. In his maturity he travelled in Europe and North Africa. He specialised in painting the landscape of New York State, and when travelling he produced views of a number of sites and cities, including Venice and Cairo. He took part in several exhibitions in the 1860s, including one at the National Academy of Design in 1867.

AUCTION RECORDS:

MILAN, 28 May 1974, *Venice,* ITL 1,100,000. NEW YORK, 10 July 1980, *Canal Scene, Venice* (oil on canvas, 19 x 14 ins / 48.2 x 35.5 cm) USD 1,500. NEW YORK, 23 Sept 1981, *By the Lake* (oil on canvas, 30 x 22 ins / 76.2 x 55.9 cm) USD 3,750. NEW YORK, 4 April 1984, *Upland Pasture* (oil on canvas, 16 1/2 x 26 ins / 42 x 66 cm) USD 1,800. NEW YORK, 26 Sept 1990, *Glens Falls on the Hudson* (oil on canvas, 15 1/4 x 25 1/2 ins / 38.7 x 64.8 cm) USD 22,000. NEW YORK, 22 May 1991, *Near Troy, New York* (oil on canvas, 10 1/4 x 18 1/4 ins / 26 x 46.2 cm) USD 3,080. NEW YORK, 27 May 1992, *Mountain Lake in Autumn* (1867, oil on canvas, 24 x 42 ins / 61 x 106.7 cm) USD 14,300. NEW YORK, 4 May 1993, *View of S Giorgio Maggiore, Venice* (oil on canvas, 10 1/4 x 17 ins / 26 x 43.2 cm) USD 2,760. NEW YORK, 9 March 1996, *Landscape in New York State* (1867, oil on canvas, 24 x 42 ins / 61 x 106.6 cm) USD 17,250. NEW YORK, 3 Dec 1996, *After the Rain, Sails up to Dry, Venice* (oil on card, 12 1/2 x 19 ins / 32 x 48.5 cm) USD 4,600. NEW YORK, 25 March 1997, *Pyramids from the Banks of the Nile* (oil on canvas, 16 x 28 ins / 40.6 x 71.1 cm) USD 5,750.

FERGUSON, James

British, 18th century.
Born 1710, near Keith; died 1776, in London.
Painter.

A self-taught artist, James Ferguson was best known as an astronomer. He earned a living painting miniatures in Edinburgh and England, for a number of years.

FERGUSON, James

British, 19th century.
Painter. Landscapes.

James Ferguson was active in London, Edinburgh and Keswick (the Lake District, Cumberland). He submitted works to the Royal Academy in London, the Suffolk Street Gallery and exhibitions at the British Institution.

FERGUSON, John Duncan. See FERGUSSON

FERGUSON, Lillian Prest

Canadian, 20th century.
Born 18 August 1877, in Windsor (Ontario); died 1955. Active in the USA.
Painter.

Lillian Prest Ferguson was a pupil at the Académie Julian, Paris, worked also in the Netherlands, and received advice from the Impressionist William Chase, probably in New York. She was a member of the California Art Club.

FERGUSON, Nancy Maybin

American, 20th century.
Born 1869 or 1872, in Philadelphia; died 1967.
Painter. Landscapes, street scenes..

Nancy Maybin Ferguson studied at the Pennsylvania Academy of the Fine Arts as well as at the Philadelphia School of Design for Women (now Moore College of Art and Design), where she was influenced by, among others Elliot Daingerfield. She was a member of The Philadelphia Ten, a group of women artists who exhibited together between 1917 and 1945.

AUCTION RECORDS:

NEW YORK, 27 March 1985, *Oqunquit, Maine* (oil/hardboard, 25 1/4 x 30 ins / 64.2 x 76.2 cm) USD 800. WINDSOR, 2 Jan 2000, *Girl with Striped Skirt* (oil on board, 12 x 12 ins / 30 x 30 cm) USD 14,000. MILFORD, 11 May 2000, *Two Fishing Boats* (oil on masonite, 16 x 19 ins / 41 x 48 cm) USD 2,500. MILFORD, 26 April 2001, *Road to the Monument, Provincetown* (oil on canvas, 28 x 36 ins / 71 x 91 cm) USD 4,000. PHILADELPHIA, 8 Dec 2002, *Church, Provincetown* (oil on board, 13 x 13 ins / 34 x 34 cm) USD 5,500. PROVINCETOWN, 19 July 2003, *Excursion* (oil on board, 12 x 16 ins / 30 x 41 cm) USD 3,200. FAIRFIELD, 20 Aug 2003, *Road to the Monument, Provincetown, Massachusetts* (oil on canvas, 30 x 36 ins / 76 x 91 cm) USD 11,000. DOWNINGTON, 21 May 2004, *Fairmount Park, Philadelphia* (oil on canvasboard, 12 x 16 ins / 30 x 41 cm) USD 3,400.

FERGUSON, William Gouw

British, 17th century.
Born c. 1622 or 1632, in Scotland; died c. 1695, in London.
Painter, watercolourist. Still-lifes.

William Gouw Ferguson studied art in Britain and subsequently spent a number of years in The Netherlands, where he became a master of the Utrecht Guild of St Luke in 1648. He lived in The Hague, Amsterdam and London. Ferguson has now been identified as the father of Henry Fergusson (prior to this, the two artists' lives and works were often confused). His remarkably fine still-lifes have also sometimes been incorrectly attributed to the Dutch painter Weenix. He also painted a small number of portraits.

W. Gouw. Ferguson fec.

BIBLIOGRAPHY:

Eidelberg, Martin, '*Reintroducing Henry Ferguson*' in *Apollo* n° 463 p. 27, periodical, London, september 2000.

MUSEUMS AND GALLERIES:

AMERSFOORT (Mus. Flehite): *Flowers* - AMSTERDAM: *Dead Birds; Still-life* - BERLIN: *Still-life with Partridge* - EDINBURGH (Nat. Gal. of Scotland): three versions*Still-life: Dead Game* (oil on canvas); *A Ruined Altar and Figures* (oil on canvas) - GENEVA: *Dead Game* - GLASGOW: *Still-life* - HAMBURG: *Dead Birds.*

AUCTION RECORDS:

LONDON, 19 Dec 1908, *Dead Bird on a Table-top,* GBP 21. LONDON, 24 Nov 1924, *Two Girls and a Boy,* GBP 12. LONDON, 12 March 1926, *Dead Birds,* GBP 7. LONDON, 4 March 1927, *Dead Birds,* GBP 16. LONDON, 2 Aug 1928, *Flowers in a Glass Vase,* GBP 11. LONDON, 8 March 1929, *Dead Birds,* GBP 16. LONDON, 27 July 1931, *Dead Birds,* GBP 3. EDINBURGH, 7 May 1932, *Pheasant and Other Dead Game Birds,* GBP 7. LONDON, 22 Feb 1935, *Dead Birds,* GBP 10. LONDON, 13 March 1936,

Flowers in a Glass Vase, GBP 8. PARIS, 7 Dec 1950, *Still-life with Birds,* FRF 70,000. LONDON, 14 May 1965, *Still-life with Wildfowl,* Gns 350. LONDON, 25 Nov 1966, *Still-life with Game* (two pendants) Gns 1,300. AMSTERDAM, 20 Nov 1973, *Hunting Trophies,* NLG 14,000. VIENNA, 30 Nov 1976, *Still-life* (oil on canvas, 23¼ x 18¼ ins / 59 x 46.5 cm) ATS 75,000. AMSTERDAM, 18 May 1981, *Still-life* (oil on canvas, 24 x 21 ins / 61 x 52.5 cm) NLG 10,000. LONDON, 15 June 1983, *Still-life with Wildfowl* (oil on panel, 15¼ x 11 ins / 39 x 27 cm) GBP 2,600. LUCERNE, 11 Nov 1987, *Still-life with Game* (oil on canvas, 25½ x 22 ins / 64.5 x 55 cm) CHF 24,000. EDINBURGH, 30 Aug 1988, *Shooting from a Hide in the Highlands* (watercolour, 19 x 27 ins / 48 x 68.5 cm) GBP 1,870. PARIS, 30 June 1989, *Hunting Trophies* (oil on canvas, 26½ x 21¼ ins / 67 x 54 cm) FRF 45,000. LONDON, 9 Feb 1990, *Still-life with a Pheasant Hanging above a Counter-top with a Red Curtain in the Background* (oil on canvas, 31 x 25 ins / 78.8 x 63.5 cm) GBP 1,980. LONDON, 10 April 1991, *Still-life with a Pigeon, Chaffinch, Bullfinch, Greenfinch and Grey Partridges* (1661, oil on canvas, 24 x 29¼ ins / 61 x 74 cm) GBP 3,300. LONDON, 17 April 1991, *Still-life with Game* (1684, oil on canvas, 23¼ x 18¾ ins / 59 x 47.5 cm) GBP 5,720. AMSTERDAM, 14 Nov 1991, *Sparrows Hanging from a Cord and Partridges on a Tabletop beside a Gamebag* (1670, oil on canvas, 24¾ x 21 ins / 63 x 53.5 cm) NLG 6,325. LONDON, 1 April 1992, *Still-life with Game Birds and Hunting Equipment on a Tabletop* (oil on canvas, 24½ x 19¾ ins / 62.3 x 50 cm) GBP 1,485. PARIS, 26 June 1992, *Hunting Trophies* (oil on panel, each 14½ x 12½ ins / 36.7 x 31.5 cm) FRF 70,000. PARIS, 26 June 1992, *Hunting Trophies: Duck, Pigeon, Goldfinch and Clothing on a Tabletop* (oil on canvas, 23 x 27¼ ins / 58.5 x 69 cm) FRF 60,000. ROME, 24 Nov 1992, *Still-life with Game Birds on a Stone Balustrade* (oil on canvas, 24 x 20 ins / 61 x 51 cm) ITL 10,350,000. AMSTERDAM, 6 May 1993, *Game Birds and a Gamebag on a Tabletop* (oil on canvas, 20¾ x 16½ ins / 53 x 42 cm) NLG 5,750. PARIS, 28 June 1993, *Still-life with Birds* (oil on canvas, 29¼ x 25¼ ins / 74 x 64 cm) FRF 50,000. LONDON, 22 April 1994, *Partridge and Sparrows Hanging above a Tabletop Partly Covered by a Drape* (1684, oil on canvas, 23 x 18¾ ins / 58.7 x 47.7 cm) GBP 9,775. COPENHAGEN, 16 May 1994, *Still-life with Dead Birds on a Stone Tabletop* (oil on canvas, 22½ x 18½ ins / 57 x 47 cm) DKK 25,500. NEW YORK, 7 Oct 1994, *Still-life with Game on a Marble Tabletop* (oil on canvas, 21½ x 28 ins / 54.6 x 71.1 cm) USD 6,900. AMSTERDAM, 13 Nov 1995, *Sparrows Hanging from a Cord; Partridge, Falcon and Other Birds on a Tabletop* (oil on canvas, a pair, 22¼ x 18 ins / 56.6 x 45.8 cm) NLG 10,925. LONDON, 14 April 1999, *Dead Partridge and Dead Snipe Hanging from Nails* (oil on canvas, a pair, 18 x 15 ins / 46 x 37 cm) GBP 3,000. LONDON, 6 July 1999, *Still-lifes with Finch, Partridge, Kingfisher and Other Birds* (oil on canvas, a pair, 25 x 21 ins / 64 x 53 cm) GBP 2,300. AMSTERDAM, 5 Nov 2002, *Hunting Still-life with Partridge, Woodcock and Other Birds on a Marble Ledge* (oil on canvas, 29 x 24 ins / 73 x 60 cm) EUR 5,500. VIENNA, 27 March 2003, *Hunting Still-life* (oil on canvas, 25 x 20 ins / 64 x 51 cm) EUR 4,500. NEW YORK, 30 April 2003, *Still-life with Birds on a Marble Ledge* (1661, oil on canvas, 25 x 30 ins / 63 x 76 cm) USD 5,000. LONDON, 4 March 2004, *Gamebirds by a Plinth in a Wooded Landscape* (oil on canvas, 50 x 40 ins / 127 x 102 cm) GBP 2,500.

FERGUSON, William Hugh

American, 20th century.
Born 8 September 1905, in Reading (Pennsylvania).
Painter, engraver.

William Hugh Ferguson was a pupil of the Pennsylvania Academy of Art and also studied in Paris.

FERGUSON, William J.

British, 19th century.
Painter. Landscapes.

William J. Ferguson exhibited in London from 1849 to 1886, notably at the Royal Academy, Suffolk Street and the British Institution.

MUSEUMS AND GALLERIES:
CAPE TOWN: *Landscape.*

AUCTION RECORDS:
LONDON, 23 July 1981, *Cattle Watering* (watercolour, 15 x 24 ins / 38 x 61 cm) GBP 300. NEW YORK, 15 Oct 1993, *View of Amalfi from the Positano Road* (1874, oil on canvas, 16½ x 23¼ ins / 42 x 59 cm) USD 1,725. NEW YORK, 25 Jan 2002, *Gathering Hay* (watercolour and gouache, 6 x 9 ins / 15 x 24 cm) USD 4,000.

FERGUSON-TEPPET, Louis Édouard Guillaume

French, 19th century.
Sculptor.

Ferguson-Teppet was a pupil of M.J. Oliva. He exhibited at the Paris Salon from 1869 to 1873. Works include the marble bust of *E. Colombet de l'Isère,* the bronze bust of *Gustave Lambert,* the bronze bust of *Frédérick Lemaître* and the terracotta bust of *Jacques Gros.*

FERGUSSON, John Duncan, or Ferguson

British, 19th - 20th century.
Born 9 March 1874, in Leith (Edinburgh); died 30 January 1961, in Glasgow.
Also active in France.
Painter, watercolourist. Figures, nudes, portraits, landscapes with figures, still-lifes.
Scottish Colourists.

After studying medicine at Edinburgh University, John Fergusson decided to follow a career as a surgeon in the Royal Navy. However, he failed the competitive selection process and decided to devote himself to art. He travelled in Spain and Morocco. During a period in Paris in 1898, he enrolled at the private Académie Colarossi and Académie Julian and studied the painting of Bonnington at the Louvre and the Impressionists in the Caillebotte bequest at the Musée de Luxembourg. Fergusson was made a member of the Royal Society of British Artists in 1903. In 1905 he moved to Paris. During World War I, he returned to London and was appointed a war artist to the Royal Navy. He continued his career in England until 1929 when he moved back to France, remaining there until 1940. When World War II broke out he moved back to Glasgow where he was made an honorary member of the university.

After coming under the influence of Impressionism during his first period of study and then during his time in Paris from 1905, Fergusson became very aware of the graphical spontaneity and the striking colours of the Fauvists. Although he did not belong to any group, he lightened his palette considerably and adopted a more synthetic style of drawing. His work of this period, though by no means a servile imitation, shows traces of his admiration for Matisse, Friesz and Dufy. Around this time, he met the American artist Anne Estelle Rice, whom he painted on a number of occasions. From 1910, while his work continues to reveal the arabesque style characteristic of Fauvism between 1905 and 1908, he brings to it his own style of drawing, giving it a rhythmical function clearly linked to colour and which is most noticeable in his nudes, which were numerous at the time: *Three Nudes on the Shore* of around 1912; *Summer in the South* around 1913; continuing up to *Women Bathing* from Eden Roc to the Cap d'Antibes in 1929 and *Nudes in the Forest* of 1930, although the latter were painted in a range of muted browns.

Fergusson tackled a wide diversity of subjects including portraits and figure paintings: *Miss Anne Estella Rice, Miss Elisabeth Dryden, The Lady with the Oranges, The Red Shawl, The Chinese Cloak,* the caricaturist *Joseph Simpson,* as well as many still-lifes, including *After Dinner, The Japanese Statuette,* and landscapes, often painted during his travels or trips abroad: *A Square in Cádiz, Dieppe, 14th July 1905, Night.* His landscapes with figures, often nudes or women bathing on beaches, represent an important part of Fergusson's work in terms of quantity and interest. Whatever he painted and throughout his career, Fergusson always displayed a strong sense of curiosity and a meticulous approach.

Fergusson took part in group exhibitions in London in 1912 and 1925; at the Royal Society of British Artists; at the Allied Artists Association; in *Peintures de Six Artistes Écossais (Paintings by Six Scottish Artists)* in 1932 in Paris; in *Les Peintres de l'Ecosse Moderne (Painters of Modern Scotland)* in 1924; in *Les Peintres Écossais (Scottish Painters)* in 1931; and at the Salon d'Automne, of which he was a member, and the Salon des Indépendants. In Glasgow he exhibited in the fine art section at the Empire Exhibition of 1938, at the Scottish Painting exhibition of 1961 and in Edinburgh at the *Four Scottish Colourists* exhibition of 1952. Since his death, Fergusson's work has featured in group and thematic exhibitions, including in 2000, *The Scottish Colourists 1900-1930: Peploe, Fergusson, Hunter and Cadell* at the Royal Academy in London, which was later shown at the Scottish National Gallery of Modern Art in Edinburgh.

BIBLIOGRAPHY:

Morris, Margaret, *The Art of J. D. Fergusson*, Blackie and Son Ltd, Glasgow, 1974. *Colour, Rythm and Dance: Paintings and Drawings by J. D. Fergusson and his Circle in Paris, 1907-1914*, exhibition catalogue, Scottish Arts Council, Edinburgh, 1985. Billcliffe, Roger, *The Scottish Colourists: Cadell, Fergusson, Hunter, Peploe*, John Murray, London, 1989. *John Duncan Fergusson (1874-1961): Malerei und Zeichnung*, exhibition catalogue, Gal. der Stadt, Aschaffenburg, 1996. Long, Philipp/Elliot, Patrick, *The Scottish Colourists 1900-1930. Peploe, Fergusson, Hunter and Cadell*, exhibition catalogue, Royal Academy of Arts, London, 2000.

MUSEUMS AND GALLERIES:

EDINBURGH (Scottish Nat. Gal. of Modern Art): *Dieppe, 14th July 1905: Night* (1905, oil on canvas) - EDINBURGH (Scottish National Portrait Gallery): *Self Portrait* (c. 1902) - GLASGOW (Hunterian): *Le Voile Persan* (1909, oil on canvas) - LONDON (Tate Collection): *Café-Concert des Ambassadeurs* (1907, oil/panel); *Blue Beads, Paris* (1910, oil/panel); *Oak Rhythm* (1925, wood, sculpture).

AUCTION RECORDS:

LONDON, 22 June 1923, *The White Hat*, GBP 11. LONDON, 2 July 1926, *Still-life*, GBP 21. LONDON, 26 Nov 1969, *Submarines and Camouflaged Battleship*, GBP 1,600. LONDON, 14 March 1973, *Vase of Flowers*, GBP 1,700. PERTH, 13 April 1976, *Where the Glen Begins* (1922, oil on canvas, 22 x 24 ins / 56 x 61 cm) GBP 600. PERTH, 19 April 1977, *Still-life* (oil on card, 23 1/2 x 20 ins / 60 x 51 cm) GBP 1,100. SCOTLAND, 31 Aug 1982, *Chez Maxim* (1908, watercolour, 15 x 11 ins / 38 x 28 cm) GBP 1,700. EDINBURGH, 27 March 1984, *Study of Margaret Morris* (black chalks and coloured wash, 13 x 10 ins / 33 x 25.5 cm) GBP 520. GLASGOW, 19 April 1984, *A Storm round Ben Ledi* (1922, oil on canvas, 21 1/2 x 22 ins / 54.6 x 55.8 cm) GBP 13,000. EDINBURGH, 30 April 1986, *The Bouquet* (1909, oil on canvas, 22 x 15 ins / 55.9 x 38 cm) GBP 16,000. GLASGOW, 11 Dec 1986, *Café Dameseuil, Gare Montparnasse* (1907, watercolour heightened with white, 15 3/4 x 12 1/4 ins / 40 x 31.1 cm) GBP 4,800. EDINBURGH, 30 Aug 1988, *Standing Female Nudes* (wash on white chalk, 13 x 9 3/4 ins / 33 x 25 cm) GBP 2,860; *Silk Hat* (1903, oil on canvas, 24 x 20 ins / 61 x 50.5 cm) GBP 9,900. TORONTO, 30 Nov 1988, *Aberdour on the Forth* (oil on card, 7 x 8 3/4 ins / 17.8 x 22.3 cm) CAD 46,000. GLASGOW, 8 Dec 1988, *Bathers, Antibes* (1925, watercolour, 12 1/2 x 10 1/4 ins / 31.7 x 26 cm) GBP 7,150; *Off Antibes* (pencil and watercolour, 9 x 7 ins / 22.8 x 17.8 cm) GBP 10,450; *Nudes in a Forest* (oil on card, 7 1/2 x 9 1/4 ins / 19 x 23.8 cm) GBP 7,700; *On Juan Beach* (1926, oil on canvas, 20 x 18 ins / 50.8 x 45.7 cm) GBP 55,000. GLASGOW, 7 Feb 1989, *Reclining Female Nude* (black chalk and wash, 7 3/4 x 5 ins / 19.5 x 12.5 cm) GBP 1,430; *Cassis* (oil on canvas, 21 1/4 x 25 1/2 ins / 54 x 65 cm) GBP 48,400. PERTH, 29 Aug 1989, *Portrait of a Young Girl* (1914, oil on card, 13 3/4 x 11 ins / 35 x 28 cm) GBP 9,900. GLASGOW, 22 Nov 1989, *Girl in Grey Hat, Possibly Anne Estelle Rice* (oil on card, 12 1/2 x 9 3/4 ins / 31.7 x 24.7 cm) GBP 10,450. GLASGOW, 7 Dec 1989, *The Raft, Eden Rock, Antibes* (1929, watercolour, 9 1/2 x 6 3/4 ins / 24.2 x 17.2 cm) GBP 4,400; *The Rosette, Portrait of Miss Elizabeth Dryden* (oil on card, 26 x 22 1/2 ins / 66 x 57.2 cm) GBP 352,000. GLASGOW, 6 Dec 1990, *Bouquet de fleurs* (c. 1910, oil on card, 24 x 20 ins / 61 x 50.8 cm) GBP 55,000. GLASGOW, 5 Feb 1991, *Antibes, 1925* (watercolour and black chalk, 6 1/4 x 4 1/4 ins / 16 x 11 cm) GBP 2,200. EDINBURGH, 2 May 1991, *Nude on a Divan* (1910, mixed media, 10 1/2 x 15 ins / 26.7 x 38.1 cm) GBP 5,500. GLASGOW, 4 Dec 1991, *The Young She-goat 'Trousers'* (copper, h. 4 ins / 10 cm) GBP 990. EDINBURGH, 28 April 1992, *Villa 'Stella Maris'* (1907, oil on panel, 7 3/4 x 10 ins / 20 x 24.5 cm) GBP 17,600. PERTH, 1 Sept 1992, *Boulevard Saint Michel* (1907, oil on panel, 7 3/4 x 9 1/2 ins / 19.5 x 24 cm) GBP 17,600. EDINBURGH, 23 March 1993, *Yachts* (1927, oil on canvas, 22 x 24 ins / 56 x 61 cm) GBP 25,300. NEW YORK, 15 Feb 1994, *View through a Forest Interior* (oil on canvas, 30 x 40 ins / 76.5 x 101.6 cm) USD 1,955. EDINBURGH, 23 May 1996, *Roses* (1938, oil on canvas, 25 1/2 x 21 1/2 ins / 64.7 x 54.6 cm) GBP 33,350. EDINBURGH, 27 Nov 1996, *Seascape, Pier and Two Boats* (oil on panel, 13 1/2 x 10 1/2 ins / 34.2 x 26.7 cm) GBP 18,400. GLASGOW, 11 Dec 1996, *Nude in Wood* (1915, oil on panel, 13 1/2 x 10 1/2 ins / 34 x 26.5 cm) GBP 8,050. GLASGOW, 20 Nov 1997, *Ruby, Portrait of R* (1911, oil on panel, 24 x 20 ins / 61 x 50.8 cm) GBP 84,000; *The Dressing Table, Antibes* (1929, watercolour, 8 x 6 1/4 ins / 20.3 x 15.6 cm) GBP 2,300. PARIS, 20 March 1998, *Tree* (1942, charcoal and watercolour, 11 x 9 ins / 28 x 22 cm) FRF 4,500. LONDON, 28 Oct 1999, *Summer in the South, Margaret Morris* (1924, oil on canvas, 16 x 16 ins / 41 x 41 cm) GBP 22,000. EDINBURGH, 3 Dec 1999, *St Jacques Studio* (oil on panel, 15 x 15 ins / 37 x 37 cm) GBP 82,000. LONDON, 30 Aug 2000, *Creme de Menthe, Café d'Harcourt* (oil on canvas, 20 x 18 ins / 51 x 45 cm) GBP 125,000. EDINBURGH, 8 Dec 2000, *Yellow Bowl* (1911, oil on board, 24 x 20 ins / 61 x 51 cm) GBP 108,000. LONDON, 5 Sept 2001, *Craig Coinach* (1922, oil on canvas, 22 x 24 ins / 56 x 61 cm) GBP 68,000. LONDON, 1 Nov 2001, *Paris, Plage, France* (1904, oil on board, 7 x 9 ins / 19 x 24 cm) GBP 38,000. COLOGNE, 4 June 2002, *Still-life* (c. 1903-1907, oil on canvas, 18 x 20 ins / 45 x 51 cm) EUR 171,000. LONDON, 28 Aug 2002, *Cassis through the Trees* (oil on canvas, 26 x 30 ins / 66 x 76 cm) GBP 62,000. LONDON, 14 April 2003, *Near La Canche, Picardy* (oil on panel, 7 x 9 ins / 18 x 23 cm) GBP 15,000. EDINBURGH, 4 Dec 2003, *Nude and Cliff* (oil on canvas, 22 x 24 ins / 56 x 61 cm) GBP 25,000. LONDON, 28 Oct 2004, *The Rocky Glen* (1922, oil on canvas, 22 x 24 ins / 55 x 61 cm) GBP 27,000. LONDON, 28 Oct 2004, *Fête Cassis* (1913, oil on panel, 13 x 10 ins / 34 x 26 cm) GBP 43,000.

FERGUSSON-LEBRETON, Laure Madeleine Eugénie

French, 19th century.

Born 6 December 1857, in St-Pierre-Lacour (Mayenne).

Painter.

Fergusson-Lebreton first exhibited at the Salon des Artistes Français in 1880.

FERIE, or Fery

Flemish, 18th century.

Active in Mons.

Sculptor.

Flemish School.

Ferie executed works in the church of Notre Dame-de-Belle-Direction in 1741. He is also mentioned with Ph. J. Couder and Goffiaux as the sculptor of an altar in the chapel of the École Dominicale.

FERIER, Jean, known as Grosjean
French, 16th century.
Sculptor.

Ferier executed some works at the town hall in Cambrai in around 1534.

FERIGOULE, Claude André
French, 19th - 20th century.
Born 20 April 1863, in Avignon; died 6 August 1946, in Arles.
Sculptor. Statues.

Ferigoule was a pupil of Falguière at the École des Beaux-Arts. He is known for works including: *The Woodsman* (1892), *Thank You* (1894), *Guinean Negro Fighting a Snake* (1895), the Hall of Honour at the Avignon City Hall, statues for the restoration of the façade of the St. Peter church, and the bust of *Antony Réal* (1897). In collaboration with Félix Charpentier in 1891, he built the commemorative monument to the annexation of Comtat Venaissin to France. He was a curator at the Musée d'Arles, and director of the drawing classes in that city. He received an honourable mention in 1890.

MUSEUMS AND GALLERIES:
AVIGNON: *The Woodsman*; bust*Melle Favart* - CARPENTRAS: *The Reef*.

FERIGOULE, Jeanne Vincent Douci (Mme)
French, 19th century.
Active at the end of the 19th century.
Painter, pastellist.

MUSEUMS AND GALLERIES:
AVIGNON: *Head of a Camargue Herdsman* (watercolour); *Portrait of a Girl from Avignon* (pastel).

FÉRIL
French, 19th century.
Active c. 1820.
Miniaturist.

A woman's portrait, on ivory, signed by Féril, was discovered during an auction in Cologne in 1905.

FERITTER, K.
French, 19th century.
Miniaturist.

A portrait of a child, dated 1850 and bearing Feritter's signature, was discovered during an auction in Munich in 1911.

FERKH, Ambros
Austrian, 17th century.
Sculptor.

In 1680 Ferkh created the stone statues of *St Joseph* and *St Leopold* and also a fountain on the Grabenplatz in Vienna.

FERLAND, Christian
Hungarian, 18th century.
Sculptor.

Christinan Ferland was made a citizen of Košice in 1775.

FERLATO, J.
French, 16th century.
Engraver (wood).

Works known by this artist include a *Beheading of St John the Baptist* and 29 small engravings illustrating a book that was published in Paris in 1543 by Denys Janot: *Cebes Le Tableau: auquel est paincte de ses couleurs la vraye ymaige de la vie humaine, etc., exposé en rythme Francoyse par Gilles Corrozet* (*Table of Cebes: in which is painted in its colours the true image of human life, etc., presented in the French language by Gilles Corrozet*). Ferlato also made illustrations for a *New Testament* published by AJ Bonhomme in 1551 in Paris.

FERLENGA, Franco
Italian, 20th century.
Born 1916, in Castiglione delle Stiviere (Mantua, Lombardy).
Painter, mosaicist, fresco artist.

Franco Ferlenga was a student at the Accademia di Belle Arti di Brera in Milan. He exhibited in a great many towns around Italy, and in the USA and Paris too, notably in 1970.

Ferlenga's paintings are reminiscent of Francis Grüber, although more so in terms of colour than emotion.

FERLET, Adolphe Auguste
French, 19th century.
Born 9 March 1867, in Paris.
Sculptor, medallist.

Ferlet was a pupil of Carlus, Hiolin and Claudius Marioton. He became a member of the Société des Artistes Français in 1906 and exhibited at the society's Salon from 1887.

FERLHAUSE, Heinrich, or Pferlshussen or Verlshauser
German, 15th century.
Active in Nuremberg (Bavaria).
Painter.

FERLIN, Paulette
French, 20th century.
Born 1921; died 22 March 1972.
Painter.

Ferlin was a self-taught painter. She produced numerous works using ink on canvas, creating a kind of automatic writing, evoking the technique and manner of Henri Michaux.

FERLOV-MANCOBA, Sonja
Danish, 20th century.
Born 1 November 1911, in Copenhagen; died 1985.
From 1936 active in France.
Sculptor.
CoBrA group.

Sonja Ferlov-Mancoba was a student at the Kunstakademi in Copenhagen from 1933, where she met Richard Mortensen, Ejler Bille and Vilhelm Bjerke Petersen, figures prominent at that time in Danish art. In 1937 she attended the École des Beaux-Arts in Paris, where she met, and in 1942 married, Ernest Mancoba, returning to Denmark from 1947 to 1952. In Copenhagen she collaborated in the review *Linien* (*Lines*), which was directed by Asger Jorn, and took part in the Group's exhibition in 1937, being a member of the Group from 1937 to 1939. She was a member of the Cobra Group from 1948 to 1951, of *Höst-udstillingen* (*Autumn Exhibition*) in 1949, and of *Den Frie* (*The Free*) from 1968.

Ferlov-Mancova's first sculptures were reminiscent of some of the stylised figures of pre-Columbian art. She then moved on to more abstract forms, which nevertheless conveyed some anthropomorphic echoes. It has been suggested that the relative abstraction of her anthropomorphic creations symbolises the dehumanisation of the modern world. At the 1973 Art Danois exhibition in Paris she showed five works whose titles demonstrate the humanist dimension of her inspiration: *Confidence*, *Joint Efforts* and *Impetus Towards the Future*.

In 1961 Sonja Ferlov-Mancoba took part in the exhibition of the Cobra Group. In Paris she featured at the Salon des Réalités Nouvelles in 1962 and 1963, in the Salon de la Jeune Sculpture at the Musée d'Art Moderne in 1962 and 1964, and in the *Esquisse d'un Salon* (*Attempt at a Salon*) at the Galerie Denise René in 1963. In 1964 she took part in the Salon de la Jeune Peinture at the Musée d'Art Moderne in Paris, the *Louisiana Visits Middelheim* in Antwerp, and in *Danish Abstract Art* in five cities in the USA. She featured in an exhibition in the Aarhus Kunstmuseum in 1969, and in the exhibition *Art*

Danois, 1945-1973 at the Galeries Nationales du Grand Palais in 1973. She held a solo exhibition at the Birch gallery in Copenhagen in 1952, and another one in Copenhagen in 1960.
BIBLIOGRAPHY:
Galy-Carles, Henry, *Art danois, 1945-1973*, exhibition catalogue, Gal. nationales du Grand Palais, Paris, 1973. Stokvis, Willemijn, *Cobra*, Gallimard, Paris, 2001.
MUSEUMS AND GALLERIES:
AALBORG (Nordjyllands Kunstmus.) - COPENHAGEN (Statens Mus. for Kunst) - HUMLEBÆK (Louisiana Mus. for Moderne Kunst) - STOCKHOLM (Moderna Mus.).
AUCTION RECORDS:
COPENHAGEN, 25 Sept 1985, *Sculpture* (1949, bronze, h. 11 ins / 28 cm and l. 15 ins/38 cm) DKK 51,000. COPENHAGEN, 27 Nov 1985, *Composition* (1938-1939, oil on canvas, 28¼ x 21¼ ins / 72 x 54 cm) DKK 31,000. COPENHAGEN, 25 Feb 1987, *Figure* (1969, bronze, h. 30¾ ins / 78 cm) DKK 93,000. COPENHAGEN, 24 Feb 1988, *Bird with Its Young in the Nest* (1935, stone, h. 20¾ ins / 53 cm) DKK 18,000. COPENHAGEN, 8 Nov 1988, *Mask* (1977, bronze, h. 32¾ ins / 83 cm) DKK 100,000. COPENHAGEN, 13-14 Feb 1991, *Rough Sketch for 'Joint Effort'* (bronze, h. 11½ ins / 29 cm and l. 13½ ins/34 cm and w. 7½ ins/19 cm) DKK 37,000. COPENHAGEN, 3 Nov 1993, *Sculpture* (1969, bronze, h. 30¾ ins / 78 cm) DKK 135,000. COPENHAGEN, 1 Dec 1993, *The Agreement* (1967, bronze, h. 15¾ ins / 40 cm) DKK 75,000. COPENHAGEN, 6 Dec 1994, *Livsmod* (*Courage to Face Life*) (1964, bronze, h. 60¼ ins / 153 cm) DKK 92,000. COPENHAGEN, 7 June 1995, *Bronze Sculpture* (1959, bronze, h. 11 ins / 27 cm) DKK 18,000.

FERMANS, Petrus
Flemish, 18th century.
Active in Antwerp.
Sculptor.
Flemish School.
Petrus Fermans qualified as a master of the Antwerp Guild of St Luke in 1763.

FERMARIELLO, Sergio
Italian, 20th century.
Painter.
Sergio Fermariello exhibits his work in Italy and France. He customarily covers the entire surface of his canvases, either black on white or white on black, with small figures, warriors, horsemen and archers, drawn with minute detail. His painstaking work rests on a single motif, and has the obsessive character of the works of the Polish conceptual artist Roman Opalka.

FERMEPIN, Alphonse
French, 19th century.
Active in Paris.
Painter.
Fermepin exhibited portraits in 1835, 1836 and 1848. In 1848 he also exhibited a self-portrait.

FERMET, Nicolás
Spanish, 15th century.
Miniaturist.
Nicolás Fermet is mentioned in 1497 as a citizen of Barcelona.

FERMEUS, Victor
Belgian, 20th century.
Born 25 December 1894, in Laeken; died 13 April 1963.
Painter.

FERMIN, Jehan
French, 15th century.
Sculptor.
Fermin carried out some work at the church of St-Aubert in Cambrai in 1459.

FERMINE, Philippe
French, 17th century.
Active in Angers.
Painter.

FERMO. See also **GHISONI Fermo di Giovanni, GUISONI Fermo di Stefano,** and **STELLA Fermo da Caravaggio**

FERMO, Anton
German, 17th century.
Painter.
Fermo executed decorative paintings for the pulpit in the chapel of St Michael in Mergentheim.

FERMOUT, Gilliam or Wilhelm Jansz., called Strazio Voluto
Dutch, 17th century.
Born 17th century.
Active in Dordrecht.
Painter. History painting.
Gilliam Fermout is mentioned by van Hoogstraaten. His paintings include *A Giant* and *Dutch Kitchen*.

FERNACH, Hans von. See **GIOVANNI DI FERNACH DA DI CAMPION**

FERNALD, Helen Elizabeth
American, 20th century.
Born 24 December 1891, in Baltimore.
Painter.
Helen Elizabeth Fernald also published studies of Chinese art.

FERNAN, Jacques
French, 19th century.
Active in Paris.
Painter.
Fernan became a member of the Société des Artistes Français in 1893 and exhibited at the society's Salon.

FERNAND-DUBOIS, Émile
French, 19th - 20th century.
Born 27 July 1869, in Paris; died 1952.
Sculptor (including bronze). Allegorical subjects.
Statues, funerary monuments.
Fernand-Dubois was a pupil of Jean Sul-Abadie and of Jules Dalou. He was honorary curator of the Musée de la Loire, in Cosne-Cours-sur-Loire. In Paris, he presided in the role of 'supreme chief' of an association of artists, La Horde. Their libertine parties made history between the wars in the Montparnasse district.

Fernand-Dubois exhibited in Paris, at the Salon des Artistes Français. He was a member from 1902, received an honourable mention and a third-class medal in 1910, a medal in 1911 for his marble *Before Love*, which was acquired by the State, and won first medal in 1922, when he also exhibited *hors concours*. In 2003 the museum presented an exhibition of his works under the title *Emile Fernand-Dubois: l'homme et le sculpteur* (*Emile Fernand-Dubois: The Man and the Sculptor*) at the Musée de la Loire, Cosne-Cours-sur-Loire. Other than statues, he executed several monuments to the dead of the Great War (notably in Cosne-sur-Loire, Issy-les-Moulineaux and Avion).
BIBLIOGRAPHY:
Roudier, Jean-Michel, *Émile Fernand-Dubois. L'homme et le sculpteur*, exhibition catalogue, Association des Amis du musée de Cosne, Cosne-sur-Loire, 2003.
AUCTION RECORDS:
ENGHIEN-LES-BAINS, 24 Oct 1982, *Nude Woman Hiding her Face* (bronze, h. 14½ ins / 37 cm) FRF 9,000.

FERNAND-RENAULT, Albert
French, 20th century.
Born in Paris.
Painter.

Fernand-Renault was a pupil of Fernand Cormon. He exhibited in Paris at the Salon des Artistes Français, receiving a silver medal in 1928, and a gold medal in 1931.

FERNAND-TROCHAIN, Jean, pseudonym of Tronchain, Jean Fernand
French, 20th century.
Born 21 February 1879, in Rueil-Malmaison; died 8 May 1969, in Paris.
Painter. Figures, nudes, interiors, landscapes, urban landscapes, mountainscapes, seascapes, waterscapes, architectural views. Wall decorations.

Fernand-Trochain exhibited regularly in Paris: as a member of the Salon d'Automne from 1919, at the Salon des Artistes Indépendants and the Salon des Tuileries. He also showed at the Salon de la Société Nationale des Beaux-Arts. He was a friend of Valtat, Fujita, Zingg, Girieud and Marie Vassilieff.

Fernand-Trochain attended to the example of the Impressionists, to whom he owed his tastes for light harmonies, vibrant tones, and the vivacity of spontaneous notations, but his temperament distanced him from excesses of expression. He often painted landscapes of the valley of the Epte, and he executed decorations, including those of the Hôtel de la Poste in Murols in Auvergne and the wedding room of the city hall in Étrpagny (Eure). Around 1925, he painted one of the pillars of *La Coupole* (*The Cupula*) in Montparnasse.

Museums and Galleries:
Aurillac - Paris (MAM): *Snow in Vauréal* - Tananarive.

Auction records:
La Varenne-St-Hilaire, 23 Oct 1988, *Barges at the Quay on the Seine, in Levallois* (1911, oil on canvas, 17 x 28 3/4 ins / 43 x 73 cm) FRF 24,000. Paris, 21 Nov 1989, *Provence Landscape* (1913, oil on canvas, 38 1/2 x 56 3/4 ins / 98 x 144 cm) FRF 35,000. Versailles, 25 March 1990, *The Old Castle on the Edge of the Mediterranean* (1913, 38 1/2 x 57 3/4 ins / 98 x 147 cm) FRF 61,000.

FERNANDE, Joseph, or Fernandi
Flemish, 18th century.
Born 1 October 1741, in Bruges; died 10 August 1799, in Bruges.
Sculptor.
Flemish School.

Joseph Fernande was instructed by Mathias de Visch and Jan van Hecke in Bruges and in 1763 went to Paris where he attended the Académie St-Luc and the Académie Royale. The next three years of his career were spent in Rome where he executed a bust of Archduke Maximilian, son of Empress Marie Theresa. On his return to his native land he became sculptor in Brussels to the court of Duke Alexandre de Lorraine. In 1779 in Paris he exhibited a bust of Queen Marie-Antoinette and allegorical sculptures. Worthy of comment among these sculptural groups are a *Flora* for Duchess Marie-Christine, statues for the abbey of Bonne-Espérance near Mons and, for the church of Vlierbeck near Louvain, *Faith, Hope, Charity* and *St Peter and St Paul*.

FERNANDE, Lucien
French, 20th century.
Born in Paris.
Painter.

Fernande exhibited landscapes at the Salon d'Automne in Paris from 1928.

FERNANDES. See also **FERNÁNDEZ, FERRANDES, HERNÁNDEZ**

FERNANDES, Bernardo
Portuguese, 18th century.
Engraver.

The signature of Bernardo Fernandes, *Bernardo Frz Lisboa*, can be seen below a portrait engraving of the Benedictine friar J. Vahia that serves as the frontispiece to Vahia's poem *Elisabetha Triumphans*. A portrait engraving dated 1733 of the poet Manuel de Faria e Sousa is also attributed to Fernandes.

FERNANDES, Constantino
Portuguese, 20th century.
Born 29 September 1878, in Lisbon; died 21 June 1920, in Lisbon.
Painter. Figure compositions, portraits, genre scenes.

In 1892, Constantino Fernandes studied at the Lisbon fine arts academy. In 1901 he began to exhibit at the Lisbon Salon showing *The Lisbon Plague of 1385*. The same year he was awarded a state bursary and went to Paris where he studied under Fernand Cormon and exhibited male portraits at the Salon des Artistes Français in 1903 and 1904. In 1905 he went to Rome and in 1906 travelled around Italy, Belgium, Holland, England and Spain. In 1908 he took part in the Rio de Janeiro exhibition and in 1911 entered a competition to create a figure symbolising the new Portuguese Republic. In 1912 he exhibited at the national exhibition of the fine arts society of Madrid where he showed *The Abandoned Women*. In 1913 he was awarded a medal of honour at the Lisbon national fine arts Salon for his triptych *The Sailor*.

Bibliography:
Arnáiz, José Manuel/López Jiménez, Javier/Merchán Díaz, Manuel (ed.), *Cien años de pintura en Espana y Portugal (1830-1930)*, Antiqvaria, Madrid, 1988 (One Hundred Years of Painting in Spain and Portugal (1830-1930)).

FERNANDES, Diego
Portuguese, 16th century.
Illuminator.

Diego Fernandes worked for the monastery of Thamar with Jorge Vieira in 1537. He is perhaps identical with Diego Fernandez and Diego Hernandes.

FERNANDES, Domingo
Portuguese, 16th century.
Active c. 1554.
Painter.

Domingo Fernandes figures in a register of Queen Catherine as having received eight crusados for a painting on wood, which was given to the convent of Abrantès.

FERNANDES, Francisco
Portuguese, 16th century.
Active in Viseu.
Painter.

FERNANDES, Garcia. See **GARCIA Fernandes**

FERNANDES, Maria Teresa or Theresa
Brazilian, 20th century.
Born 1926, in Jaboticabal.
Painter, watercolourist, pastellist. Portraits, landscapes, seascapes, still-lifes.

Maria Teresa Fernandes lives and works in São Paulo, where she also trained. Principally a painter of still-lifes, Fernandes also paints glass compositions, skilfully and faithfully reproducing the effects of transparency and reflection. She has exhibited at numerous group exhibitions and received a number of awards.

FERNANDES DE SA, Antonio
Portuguese, 19th century.
Born in Portugal.
Sculptor.

Antonio Fernandes de Sa received a commendation in 1898 at the Salon des Artistes Français for his *Abduction of Ganymede*.

FERNANDES VASCO
Portuguese, 15th century.
Painter.

Fernandes Vasco is mentioned in a document of 1459 as a citizen of Tortosa in Catalonia.

FERNANDES VASCO, also known as Fernandes de Viseu, Grão Vasco de Viseu, Ferdinand de Viseu, Fernandez Vasco de Cazal, Vasco Pereira or Pereyra, Vasco Fernandez, etc, called Grão Vasco
Portuguese, 16th century.
Born c. 1475-1480, in Viseu; died c. 1541-1542, probably in Viseu.
Painter.

For some time the Portuguese heralded 'Grão Vasco' as their greatest painter, ascribing to him all fine unattributed paintings in Portugal. According to Zani he was active in 1594, though he confused him with Vasco Pereyra, also Portuguese, but active in Seville as well. Cean Bermudez, who classified him as a Spanish painter, must have made the same mistake. It is now virtually certain that he was predominantly active in Viseu (Beira Alta) at the beginning of the 16th century, where he probably led the most important provincial workshop in Portugal. About his training we are completely in the dark.

Vasco's career seems to have begun before 1502 and to have lasted over 40 years. While he was indirectly exposed to Flemish or Dutch influences through contact with Dutch artists resident in Portugal or their works, his work is marked by a decorative sense of the South and a quintessentially Spanish expressive force.

It is now accepted that Flemish influence permeates his initial phase, evident in the high altar of the Cathedral of Viseu (1500-1506), today in the Museu Grão Vasco in Viseu; the *Assumption of the Virgin* in the Museu Nacional d'Arte Antiga in Lisbon; and in the museum of Lamego: *The Annunciation, The Visitation, The Circumcision, The Creation of the Animals*, the remaining wings of the altarpiece which he painted between 1506 and 1511 for the cathedral of the same town; the triptych (around 1520) of the Museu Nacional d'Arte Antiga in Lisbon: *Descent from the Cross; St Francis; St Antony*.

Dutch influence (Lucas van Leyden) is evident in the lighter works of Vasco's later period. Attributed to him are the 16 panels on the *Life of the Virgin*, the *Passion of Christ* (both around 1520-1525) of the altarpiece of the church of Freixo-de-Espada-à-Cinta; the triptych of the *Last Supper* (about 1530-1535) of the episcopal palace of Fontelo, today in the Museu Grão Vasco in Viseu; *Pentecost* around 1535 in the sacristy of Santa Cruz, Coimbra, arguably his most famous work due to the dynamic complexity of the composition and its dramatic character. The *Christ on the Cross*, in the church of the Misericórdia of Oporto, previously attributed to Holbein is sometimes ascribed to Vasco.

Among the key compositions of his final period (1535-1542) are the *St Sebastian*, today housed in the museum of Viseu, and the five large altarpieces with predellas from the cathedral of Viseu, including a *St Peter* and *Calvary*. All these works are tinged with a panoply of influences and marked by regional naturalism evinced in the figures and landscapes. It was this indigenous element which was to contribute to the appearance of a specifically Portuguese style during the Manoeline Renaissance.

BIBLIOGRAPHY:

Raczynski, A., *Les Arts en Portugal*, Paris, 1846.

MUSEUMS AND GALLERIES:

LAMEGO: *Annunciation, Visitation, Circumcision, Creation of the Animals* (c. 1506-1511, panels from an altarpiece) - LISBON (Mus. Nacional de Arte Antiga): *Assumption of the Virgin; Descent from the Cross, St Francois, St Antony* (c. 1520, triptych) - VISEU (Mus. de Grão Vasco): *High Altar* (1500-1506); *The Last Supper* (c. 1530-1535).

FERNÁNDEZ. See also **FERNANDES, FERRANDES, FERRÁNDEZ, HERNÁNDEZ**

FERNÁNDEZ, Agustín
Cuban, 20th century.
Born 1928, in Havana.
Active in the USA.
Painter (gouache). Scenes with figures, still-lifes.

Agustín Fernández studied at the Academia San Alejandro in Havana and then at the Art Students' League in New York, where he was taught by Kasuo Kuniyoshi. He later went to Paris where he became part of the Surrealist group before finally settling in New York. Fernández's composition and drawing and his mastery of colour - contrasting the purest accents of yellow, orange and red against dark blue and green backgrounds - are reminiscent of Matisse. Towards the end of the 1950s his painting became more erotic and included nudes alongside inanimate forms.

MUSEUMS AND GALLERIES:

NEW YORK (MoMA).

AUCTION RECORDS:

NEW YORK, 30 May 1984, *Apples* (1953, oil on canvas, 55 x 35 ins / 139.8 x 89 cm) USD 2,750. NEW YORK, 29 May 1985, *Portrait of a Woman* (1949, oil on canvas, 30 x 25 ins / 76.2 x 63.5 cm) USD 600. NEW YORK, 17 May 1988, *Untitled* (oil on canvas, 50 x 55 ins / 127 x 140 cm) USD 16,500. NEW YORK, 21 Nov 1988, *Snake Coiled around a Dreamer* (1986, oil on canvas, 52 x 42 ins / 132 x 106.6 cm) USD 17,600. NEW YORK, 17 May 1989, *Untitled* (1960, oil on canvas, 43 x 43 ins / 109.5 x 109.5 cm) USD 3,850. PARIS, 21 June 1989, *Composition* (gouache, 24 3/4 x 28 1/4 ins / 63 x 72 cm) FRF 18,000. NEW YORK, 21 Nov 1989, *Composition* (pencil, watercolour and gouache/paper/canvas, 24 1/2 x 28 ins / 62.5 x 71 cm) USD 3,520. NEW YORK, 1 May 1990, *Razor Blade* (1975, oil on canvas, diam. 37 1/2 ins / 95 cm) USD 3,300. NEW YORK, 18 May 1993, *Table* (1952, oil on canvas, 46 1/2 x 37 1/4 ins / 118.4 x 94.6 cm) USD 20,700. NEW YORK, 23-24 Nov 1993, *Tennis Players* (1952, oil on canvas, 38 x 59 ins / 95.6 x 149 cm) USD 17,250. NEW YORK, 18 May 1994, *Pair* (oil on canvas, 43 3/4 x 35 ins / 111.1 x 88 cm) USD 17,250. NEW YORK, 18 May 1995, *Nude* (1952, oil on canvas, 47 1/4 x 30 3/4 ins / 119.7 x 78.4 cm) USD 9,200. WASHINGTON, 13 Nov 1999, *Ariadne* (1963, oil on canvas, 48 x 49 ins / 123 x 124 cm) USD 3,200. WASHINGTON, 13 Nov 1999, *Origin* (1964, oil on canvas, 55 x 50 ins / 140 x 128 cm) USD 5,500. NEW YORK, 30 May 2001, *Untitled* (1966, oil on canvas, 57 x 44 ins / 144 x 112 cm) USD 4,200. NEW YORK, 20 Nov 2002, *Still-life of Fruit* (oil on canvas, 38 x 48 ins / 96 x 122 cm) USD 6,500. NEW YORK, 20 Nov 2002, *Seated Woman* (c. 1950, oil on canvas, 4 x 37 ins / 10 x 95 cm) USD 13,000. HAMBURG, 24 Oct 2003, *Untitled* (oil on canvas) EUR 2,000.

FERNÁNDEZ, Alejo, or Hernandez
Spanish, 15th - 16th century.
Born c. 1470; died 1543, in Seville.
Painter.
Andalusian School (Seville).

Alejo Fernández did a number of paintings for the rood screen of the major chapel at the convent of St Jerome at Cordova (where he stayed until 1508), representing scenes from the life of Christ and St Jerome. In 1508 he embellished the high altar of Seville Cathedral. In the church of St Anne in Seville is his *Madonna Surrounded by Angels*. He painted the *Altarpiece of Nicolas Durango* (1509-1513) in Seville Cathedral and the altarpiece of *Maese Rodrigo* (1516-1523) for the university chapel. For the Alcázar he painted *Virgin of the Navigators* and *Good Air*.

On the occasion of the entry of Charles V in Seville in 1526 Fernández decorated the town with triumphal arches and allegorical figures. His art hovers between late Gothic and Renaissance; while he places his figures in an architectural setting of classical antiquity, they radiate Umbrian charm. The church of Santiago at Écija has his paintings for a high altar and the cathedral at Saragossa a triptych with a *Last Supper* as the central motif.

BIBLIOGRAPHY:

Valdivieso, E., *Historia de la Pintura Sevillana*, Seville, 1986.

MUSEUMS AND GALLERIES:

CORDOVA: *The Flagellation*.

FERNÁNDEZ, Alfon I
Spanish, 16th century.
Active in Seville in 1503.
Painter.

FERNÁNDEZ, Alfon II
Spanish, 16th century.
Active in Seville c. 1519.
Painter.
School of Seville.

Alfon Fernández II is perhaps identical to Alonso Hernandez.

FERNÁNDEZ, Alonso
Spanish, 16th century.
Active in Montilla near Cordova.
Painter.

FERNÁNDEZ, Andrés
Spanish, 16th century.
Active in Seville in 1515 and 1557.
Painter.

FERNÁNDEZ, Andrés
Spanish, 16th century.
Born 1555, in Cordova.
Painter, sculptor (wood).

Andrés Fernández produced the high altar and tabernacle of the parish church of Obejo, near Cordova and, for the church of Santa Maria de Guijo near Cordova, painted a wooden statue of *Christ Resuscitated with the Cross*.

FERNÁNDEZ, Andrés, or Hernandez
Spanish, 16th century.
Sculptor.

Andrés Fernández made the candelabra for the Puerta del Claustro (cloister door) at Toledo Cathedral.

FERNÁNDEZ, Antonio
Spanish, 16th century.
Active in Cordova.
Painter.
School of Cordova.

The guild of Cordova recognised Antonio Fernández as a painter of altarpieces and decorations in 1549.

FERNÁNDEZ, Antonio Arias. See **ARIAS FERNÁNDEZ**

FERNÁNDEZ, Aristides
Cuban, 20th century.
Born 1904, in Havana; died 1934.
Painter, watercolourist, draughtsman. Scenes with figures.

Aristides Fernández was a student at the Academia San Alejandro but did not complete his studies. The small number of works - paintings, watercolours and drawings - exhibited in 1935, after his death, have achieved cult status among Cuban artists. His short stories were also published the year after his death. Both a painter and writer, Fernández was a politically committed artist who addressed alienation and the hardship and troubles of manual workers at a time of right-wing dictatorship, representing this in a synthetic style reminiscent of Gauguin, with the peasants bent under the weight of their loads and their labours.

BIBLIOGRAPHY:

Lezama Lima, José, *Aristides Fernández*, Ministerio de Educacion, Havana, 1950. Carreño, Enrique, *Transmutaciones relacionables en Aristides Fernández*, Editorial Letras Cubanas, Havana, 1994.

AUCTION RECORDS:

NEW YORK, 19-20 May 1992, *Untitled* (ink and watercolour/paper, 9 x 12 3/4 ins / 22.9 x 32.7 cm) USD 17,600. NEW YORK, 17 May 1994, *Untitled* (watercolour and ink/reinforced paper, 8 3/4 x 12 3/4 ins / 22.5 x 32.5 cm) USD 17,250. NEW YORK, 25-26 Nov 1996, *Rest* (c. 1930, oil on panel, 11 1/4 x 12 1/4 ins / 28.3 x 31.4 cm) USD 31,050.

FERNÁNDEZ, Armand. See **ARMAN**

FERNÁNDEZ, Bartolomeo
Spanish, 16th century.
Active in Segovia.
Sculptor.

Bartolomeo Fernández made the double-tier Renaissance stalls for the monastery of S Jeronimo del Paral near Segovia. Of the upper tier, 26 seats are now integrated into the choir stalls of the church of San Francisco el Grande at Madrid, while another 17 of this tier and 28 of the lower tier are in the Museo Nacional Arqueológico in Madrid.

MUSEUMS AND GALLERIES:

MADRID (Mus. Arqueológico Nacional).

FERNÁNDEZ, Blas
Spanish, 16th century.
Active in Seville in 1509.
Sculptor.

Blas Fernández may be identical with Blas Hernandez.

FERNÁNDEZ, Diego, or Ferrandez
Spanish, 15th century.
Painter.

Diego Fernández is probably identical with the miniaturist Diego Farrández de los Pilares. In 1433 and 1434 he was responsible for painting the paschal candle at Seville Cathedral.

FERNÁNDEZ, Diego, or Hernandez Campoverde
Spanish, 16th century.
Active in Seville in the first half of the 16th century.
Painter.

FERNÁNDEZ, Diego
Spanish, 16th century.
Active in Seville from 1511 to 1528.
Miniaturist.

FERNÁNDEZ, Diego
Spanish, 17th century.
Sculptor (wood).

In 1674, Diego Fernández executed statues of *St Joseph, St Michael* and *St John the Baptist* for the stalls of Malaga Cathedral.

FERNÁNDEZ, Diego I
Spanish, 15th century.
Sculptor.

Diego Fernández I worked with his brother Juan on the main portal of Toledo Cathedral in 1418.

FERNÁNDEZ, Domingo. See **FERNÁNDEZ Y GONZÁLEZ Domingo**

FERNÁNDEZ, Domingo, or Hernàndez
Spanish, 17th century.
Engraver. Religious subjects.

Domingo Fernández worked in Seville. He is known for his *Virgin of Bethlehem*, his *Immaculate Conception* for a book by Dr Lucas de Gongora, and his *Virgin of the Rosary*.

FERNÁNDEZ, Enrique, or Ferràndez
Spanish, 16th century.
Died before 23 March 1547, in Barcelona.
Painter.

FERNÁNDEZ, Francisco
Spanish, 16th century.
Active in Cordova.
Painter.

Francisco Fernández painted eight plates for the *Life of S Juan de Dios*, which were engraved by Villafranca and Pautrel.

FERNÁNDEZ, Francisco
Spanish, 16th century.
Painter.

In 1529 Francisco Fernández was a prisoner in Seville. Permission was granted by the prison governor to remove his chains so that he might paint in a church.

FERNÁNDEZ, Francisco
Spanish, 16th century.
Died before 1520.
Active in Seville.
Sculptor.

f fernandez.

FERNÁNDEZ, Francisco
Spanish, 16th century.
Active in Granada.
Painter.

Francisco Fernández painted decorative paintings in the audience chamber in the chapter of the cathedral.

FERNÁNDEZ, Francisco, or Ferrandez
Spanish, 16th century.
Active in Seville in 1504.
Illuminator.

FERNÁNDEZ, Francisco
Spanish, 17th century.
Born 1605, in Madrid; died 1646.
Painter, engraver.

Francisco Fernández studied at the school of Vincenzo Carducho. He was one of the most gifted painters of the period and established a reputation while still very young. Philip IV commissioned him to decorate various palaces in Madrid. The Vitoria convent has a number of his works: *Death of St Francis of Paula*; *St Joachim*; and *St Anne*. He engraved five allegorical plates for Carducho's *Dialogues on Painting*, which was published in 1633. Fernández was killed by Francisco de Baras during a quarrel.

FERNÁNDEZ, Francisco, or Hernández
Spanish, 19th century.
Active in Madrid.
Engraver, medallist.

Francisco Fernández provided the engravings for the zodiac medallion for the accession of King Ferdinand VI and for the first coins issued under his monarchy.

FERNÁNDEZ, Garcia
Spanish, 15th century.
Painter.

Garcia Fernández worked in Seville in 1407 and is perhaps identical with Garcia Ferrandez.

FERNÁNDEZ, Garcia. See also **FERRANDEZ**

FERNÁNDEZ, Geronimo
Spanish, 15th century.
Active in Toledo.
Painter.

FERNÁNDEZ, Gil
Spanish, 16th century.
Of Flemish origin.
Active in 1500.
Painter.

FERNÁNDEZ, Gomez, or Ferrandez
Spanish, 16th century.
Active in Seville from 1514 to 1525.
Painter.

FERNÁNDEZ, Gomez
Spanish, 16th century.
Active c. 1580.
Painter.

FERNÁNDEZ, Gonzalo
Spanish, 15th century.
Active in Seville between 1480 and 1496.
Painter.

FERNÁNDEZ, Gonzalo
Spanish, 16th century.
Active in Valladolid.
Painter.

Gonzalo Fernández was prolific between the years 1553 and 1556. His key work was a life-size *Madonna* of 1558.

FERNÁNDEZ, Gonzalo, or Hernandez
Spanish, 16th century.
Active in Seville in the early 16th century.
Painter.

Gonzalo Fernández drew up his will in 1555 and is perhaps the brother of Jac Fernández.

FERNÁNDEZ, Gonzalo. See also **FERNÁNDEZ Jac**

FERNÁNDEZ, Gregorio
Spanish, 17th century.
Died 1689.
Active in Valladolid.
Sculptor.

Though a reasonable artist, Gregorio Fernández cannot be compared with Gregorio Fernández known as Hernández, who was one of the great masters of Spanish art. The confusion that often occurs among historians and art lovers between the two artists is due only to the similarity of their names. Gregorio Fernández/Hernández died 53 years before Gregorio Fernández

FERNÁNDEZ, Gregorio, known as Gregorio Hernández
Spanish, 17th century.
Born c. 1576, in Galicia; died 22 Jan 1636, in Valladolid.
Active in Valladolid.
Sculptor, painter. Religious subjects. Religious furnishings, statues.
Valladolid School.

Gregorio Fernández, known as Hernández, was a pupil of Francisco Rincón and lived his entire life in Valladolid. He specialised in polychrome sculpture and endeavoured to bring a new originality to the genre through the introduction of Baroque realism. His treatment of drapery is generous, large in form but careful in decoration and revealing a certain spiritedness. His entire body of work is a reflection of his deep religious spirit, with the emphasis on sorrow. Many of his pieces were on a large scale, which he could not have executed alone; he therefore employed assistants, which resulted in a certain unevenness in his sculptural oeuvre. He produced a series of *Retables*, including those at the church of S Miguel in Valladolid (1616), at the collegiate church of Lerma (1615), the Franciscan church of the Conception (1621) and the church of S Miguel in Vitoria (1624-1632). He carved altars and high altars in Valladolid in 1616 and in Plasencia between 1624 and1634. He produced dramatic works representing scenes from the Passion of Christ - the *Pasos* that were paraded through the streets during Holy Week. Of these *Pasos* only a few single statues remain. Fernández also carved individual statues, always on sorrowful themes such as *Christ at the Column* (Church of Vera Cruz in Valladolid, 1623; Convent of the Incarnation, Madrid), *Christ Recumbent* and the *Virgen de las Angustias (Virgin of the Anguish).*

BIBLIOGRAPHY:

Plaza Santiago, F.J. de la, '*El pueblo natal de Gregorio Fernández*' in *Boletín del Seminario de estudios de arte y arqueología*, 1973. Fernández de Hoyo, M.A., '*Oficiales de Gregorio Fernández y ensembladores que trabajaron con el*' in *Boletín del Seminario de estudios de arte y arqueología*, 1983. Urrea, J., '*Escultores coetaneos y discipulos de G. Fernández en Valladolid*' in *Boletín del Seminario de estudios de arte y arqueología*, 1984.

MUSEUMS AND GALLERIES:

VALLADOLID: *Relief of the Virgin and St Simon; St Theresa and St Magdalene of Pazzi; Christ Recumbent; Virgin of the Anguish; St Veronica; Simon of Cyrene* - VALLADOLID (Mus. Nacional de Escultura): *St Teresa* (before 1625); *St Peter* - VALLADOLID (San Pablo): *St Paul* (1624); *St Dominic* (1625).

FERNÁNDEZ, Guillen. See **FERNÁNDEZ Jac**

FERNÁNDEZ, Isabel

Spanish, 15th century.
Active in Seville.
Miniaturist, embroiderer (?).

Isabel Fernández worked for Seville Cathedral as 'maestra de los ornementos' (master of the ornamentation).

FERNÁNDEZ, Jac, or Hernandez

Spanish, 16th century.
Active c. 1535.
Painter. History painting.

Jac Fernández is mentioned in the records of Seville Cathedral, together with Guillen and Gonzalo Fernández, who were probably his brothers.

FERNÁNDEZ, Jeronimo. See **HERNÁNDEZ**

FERNÁNDEZ, Jorge, also known as Aleman

Spanish, 15th - 16th century.
Born c. 1470; died before 1553.
Active in Seville.
Sculptor.

Perhaps the brother of Alejo Fernández, Jorge Fernández carried out important sculptures for Seville Cathedral and the Alcázar around 1508. He is recorded again at the cathedral in 1515 and 1530. He sculpted a crucifix on a pedestal on which the *Fifth Mystery* and several other works were represented.

FERNÁNDEZ, José

Spanish, 18th century.
Active in Seville.
Engraver.

The church of Sta Catalina in Seville has a copperplate engraving showing St Francis of Paola which bears the name José Fernández.

BIBLIOGRAPHY:

Las edades del hombre: la música en la iglesia de Castilla y León, exhibition catalogue, Valladolid, 1991.

FERNÁNDEZ, José

Venezuelan, 20th century.
Born 1918, in Caracas.
Painter.

FERNÁNDEZ, Juan

Spanish, 16th century.
Sculptor (wood).

Juan Fernández made ceiling decorations for the Curia Ecclesiastica in Granada.

FERNÁNDEZ, Juan, or Hernandez

Spanish, 16th century.
Active in Seville.
Painter. Playing cards.

Juan Fernández was son of the painter Pedro Fernández.

FERNÁNDEZ, Juan

Spanish, 17th century.
Sculptor, architect. Statues.

In 1616, Juan Fernández worked on statues of *St Peter* and *St Paul* for the chapel of Nuestra Señora del Sagrario at Toledo Cathedral.

FERNÁNDEZ, Juan, called El Labrador

Spanish, 17th century.
Painter. Still-lifes (fruit and flower pieces).

Juan Fernández 'El Labrador' is listed as being in Madrid from 1629 to 1636. Though a 'rustic' painter, he was also very successful at Court, being pursued by royalty and wealthy individuals.

BIBLIOGRAPHY:

Ponz, Antonio, in *Viaje de España, 3*, Aguilar, Madrid, 1988. Jordan, William B./Cherry, Peter, *Spanish Still-life, from Velázquez to Goya*, exhibition catalogue, National Gallery, London, 1995.

MUSEUMS AND GALLERIES:

LONDON (Hampton Court, HM The Queen's Collection): *Still-life with Apples, Grapes, Chestnuts and Acorns* (1630, oil on canvas) - MADRID (Prado): *Vase of Flowers* (1630, oil on canvas).

AUCTION RECORDS:

LONDON, 6 Dec 1995, *Still-life with Grapes, Acorns, Hazelnuts, Chestnuts and Apples with a Small Jug and Glass of Wine on a Table* (oil on canvas, 25 1/4 x 19 ins / 64 x 48 cm) GBP 166,500.

FERNÁNDEZ, Juan

Spanish, 18th century.
Engraver.

Juan Fernández made a copperplate engraving for the frontispiece of the book *Ecclesiastical and Secular Annals of the City of Seville, Drawn by Don Pedro Tortolero in 1747.*

FERNÁNDEZ, Juan. See also **FERNÁNDEZ Diego I**

FERNÁNDEZ, Juan Antonio

Spanish, 16th century.
Died before 1536.
Active in Seville.
Painter.

Juan Antonio Fernández is probably identical with Fernández de Alcala.

FERNÁNDEZ, Juan de Dios

Spanish, 18th century.
Died c. 1801, in Seville.
Painter. Portraits.

The museum in Seville has the portraits executed by Juan de Dios Fernández: *Don Francisco de Bruna y Ahumada* and *Fernán Cortés in Mexico*.

BIBLIOGRAPHY:

Ponz, Antonio, in *Viaje de España, 4*, Aguilar, Madrid, 1988.

FERNÁNDEZ, Lorenzo, or Ferrandez

Spanish, 15th century.
Active in Seville.
Painter.

In 1462 and 1464 Lorenzo Fernández did the paintings for the paschal candle of Seville Cathedral

FERNÁNDEZ, Luis, or Hernandez
Spanish, 16th century.
Active in Seville.
Painter.

Luis Fernández executed a number of decorative works at the Alcázar and the Palacio del Lomo de Grullo as well as paintings for Seville Cathedral.

FERNÁNDEZ, Luis, the Elder
Spanish, 16th century.
Born in Cordova.
Active in Seville in 1580.
Painter.

The pupils of Luis Fernández the Elder included Francisco Herrera, Francisco Pacheco and Augustin del Castillo.

FERNÁNDEZ, Luis
Spanish, 17th century.
Born 1596, in Madrid; died 1654, in Madrid.
Painter. History painting.

Luis Fernández was a pupil of Eugenio Caxes. He worked in oils but also painted frescoes. The convent of Merced Calzada has some scenes of the life of San Ramón, which he painted in 1625. Several frescoes and paintings by Fernández were at Santa Cruz, but were destroyed in a fire in the 17th century.

BIBLIOGRAPHY:

Ponz, Antonio, in *Viaje de España, 3*, Aguilar, Madrid, 1988.

FERNÁNDEZ, Luis
Spanish, 18th century.
Born 1745, in Madrid; died soon after 1766, in Madrid.
Painter.

Luis Fernández was a pupil of A. Gonzalez Velázquez at the Academia de San Fernando, where he received a number of awards.

BIBLIOGRAPHY:

Ponz, Antonio, in *Viaje de España, 3*, Aguilar, Madrid, 1988.

FERNÁNDEZ, Luis or Louis
Spanish, 20th century.
Born 1900, in Oviedo (Asturias); died 1973.
Active in France from 1924.
Painter, engraver, sculptor.
Abstraction-Création group.

Luis Fernández began drawing as a child. After moving to France he began to study painting and also started experimenting with engraving and sculpture.

As an artist Fernández felt that drawing was more important than painting; he also considered sculpture to be the culmination of drawing and for several years worked directly in stone. His early paintings were noticed by Braque. At that time he was more interested and influenced in his painting, which was abstract and totally geometric using ruler and compass, by the purism of Jeanneret and Ozenfant and by the cold abstraction of Mondrian than by Cubism; sculpturally he was interested in the work of Brancusi and Lipchitz. In 1934 he became friends with Picasso and saw him every day up to 1940. In 1936 Picasso asked Fernández to produce from a small gouache painting, the 18 metres by 11 stage curtain for a play by Romain Rolland entitled *Quatorze Juillet* (*The Fourteenth of July*). For a time Picasso's powerful personality had an influence on Fernández's painting to such an extent that his *Bullfight* of 1940 seems almost a pastiche inspired by *Guernica*. From 1938 to 1941 his painting came under the influence of Surrealism with the series *Murders and Rapes* following his association with artists such as André Breton, Paul Éluard and René Char.

After this he developed his own, definitive style of expression. His technique reverted to older methods such as egg tempera and glazes to create still-lifes. These are bare and geometrical, with objects cut out and painted in flat tints in tired, impoverished tones of black, white and grey. The volume is barely suggested by dry, graduated shadow as on a metal object. The objects he assembled for these still-lifes accentuate their strangeness: candles, dried out roses, joints of ham and skulls (as in *Skulls* of 1964) on which dust has been allowed to gather to depersonalise them still further and achieve a unified outer surface. Although his painting technique and style, inspired by the Spanish masters of the 16th and 17th centuries and by Zurbarán in particular, remained constant during this period, he also painted in other genres: other works include portraits such as his *Portrait of the Freedom Fighter* dated 1944 and a large number of landscapes reduced to their essential elements with horizontal lines and bands punctuated by identifiable points of reference as in *Bordeaux Landscape* of 1948. Although largely unrecognised, Fernández did capture the attention of a wide variety of important figures including Braque, Henri Laurens, Breton, Éluard, Mirò, Ozenfant, Jeanneret, Mondrian, Brancusi, Arp, Pevsner, Picasso, Cristian Zervos (director of *Cahiers d'Art*) and Alberto Giacometti as well as Victor Brauner and René Char, who both wrote studies of his paintings.

He did not exhibit in Paris very often: *Abstraction-Création* (1931); Salon des Surindépendants (1933); first Salon de Mai (1945) where he showed *Motherhood*. In 1978 his work featured at the commemorative *Abstraction-Création* exhibition at the Musée d'Art Moderne in Paris. He also showed collections of his work in solo exhibitions: the first in 1950 at the Galerie Pierre in Paris; in 1956 at the *Cahiers d'Art* gallery in Paris; in 1965 in Turin; and in 1968 at the A. Iolas gallery in Paris and the V. Iolas gallery in Madrid. In 1972, shortly before his death, the Centre National d'Art Contemporain in Paris organised a retrospective exhibition of his work. Fernández was an unusual and much underrated painter and was honoured by his native Oviedo in 1984.

MUSEUMS AND GALLERIES:

MARSEILLES (Mus. Cantini): *Seascape No. 4* (watercolour and gouache); *Seascape No. 5* (gouache) - PARIS (FNAC) - ST-ÉTIENNE (MAM).

AUCTION RECORDS:

PARIS, 30 March 1982, *Head of a Dead Bull* (1939, oil on panel, 28 3/4 x 40 1/2 ins / 73 x 103 cm) FRF 26,000. MADRID, 17 March 1987, *La Inmensa Boca* (*The Immense Mouth*) (1939, oil on canvas, 7 1/2 x 12 3/4 ins / 19 x 32.5 cm) ESP 1,600,000. PARIS, 11 Oct 1989, *Médoc Landscape* (15 3/4 x 13 ins / 40 x 33 cm) FRF 36,000. PARIS, 22 Nov 1993, *Composition* (oil on wood, 7 1/4 x 58 3/4 ins / 18.5 x 149.5 cm) FRF 180,000. PARIS, 13 April 1994, *Portrait of Francis Jourdain* (1940, oil on canvas, 13 x 9 1/2 ins / 33 x 24 cm) FRF 60,000. PARIS, 28 Nov 1994, *Landscape* (oil on canvas, 23 1/2 x 28 3/4 ins / 60 x 73 cm) FRF 70,000. PARIS, 1 July 1996, *Still-life* (1955, oil on paper/canvas, 7 x 8 1/2 ins / 18 x 21.8 cm) FRF 100,000. PARIS, 20 June 1997, *Untitled* (1944, oil on canvas, 19 x 15 1/4 ins / 48 x 39 cm) FRF 60,000. PARIS, 13 Dec 1997, *Bullfight* (1940, oil on canvas, 76 3/4 x 51 1/4 ins / 195 x 130 cm) FRF 400,000.

FERNÁNDEZ, Manuel Santos
Spanish, 18th century.
Born in Madrid.
Active c. 1709.
Painter. History painting.

Manuel Santos Fernández was a pupil of Ezquerra. He painted a *Death of St Francis Xavier* for Madrid Cathedral in 1715, and is also known for his *St Francis* and *St Anthony* which were in the chapel of Nuestra Señora del Puerto in Madrid.

FERNÁNDEZ, Mariusa
Argentinian, 20th century.

Born in Buenos Aires.
Painter.
Mariusa Fernández painted in tempera. She exhibited at the open exhibition organised by the United Nations at the Musée d'Art Moderne in Paris in 1946.

FERNÁNDEZ, Pedro, or Ferrandez
Spanish, 15th century.
Active in Seville c. 1422.
Painter.

FERNÁNDEZ, Pedro, or Ferrandez
Spanish, 15th century.
Active in Cordova.
Painter.
Pedro Fernández, son of Yuste Lopez, in about 1490 made an altar for the church of San Francisco at Écija, near Cordova.

FERNÁNDEZ, Pedro, or Ferrandez
Spanish, 15th - 16th century.
Died before 19 June 1513, in Seville.
Miniaturist.
Pedro Fernández is mentioned in 1513 in connection with a contract signed with the Dominican painter Pedro de Córdoba, 'vicaire de las Indias' (Vicar of the Indies), for the illumination of two psalters.

FERNÁNDEZ, Pedro
Spanish, 16th century.
Active in Seville from 1509 to 1526.
Painter.
Pedro Fernández must have had a fortune at his disposal, for it is documented that he sold a slave on 21 May 1520.

FERNÁNDEZ, Pedro
Spanish, 16th century.
Active in Seville.
Glass painter.
Pedro Fernández worked for the chapter of Seville Cathedral in 1526.

FERNÁNDEZ, Pedro, or Ferrandez
Spanish, 16th century.
Active in Cordova.
Painter.
The son of Diego Lopez, Pedro Fernández did the paintings for a Sagrario (memorial chapel) embellished with wooden statues in the church of Montilla, near Cordova.

FERNÁNDEZ, Pedro, or Hernandez
Spanish, 16th century.
Active in Seville.
Painter. Playing cards.

FERNÁNDEZ, Pedro, or Hernandez
Spanish, 16th century.
Died 1534, in Seville.
Painter.
Pedro Fernández is perhaps identical to the Pedro Fernández mentioned as an illuminator in 1503. He was the husband of Isabel Fernández.

FERNÁNDEZ, Pedro
Spanish, 17th century.
Died 1641, in Seville.
Painter.

FERNÁNDEZ, Pedro
Spanish, 19th century.
Painter. Landscapes.
Pedro Fernández taught at the school of fine arts in Malaga. He exhibited in Madrid in 1871 and in Malaga in 1884.
BIBLIOGRAPHY:
Ponz, Antonio, in *Viaje de España, 1, 3,* Aguilar, Madrid, 1988.

FERNÁNDEZ, Sebastián Alejos
Spanish, 16th century.
Active in Seville.
Painter.
Sebastián Alejos Fernández was the son of Alejo Fernández and imitated the painting of his father.

FERNÁNDEZ, Thomas
Spanish, 16th century.
Active in Seville from 1503 to 1509.
Painter.
Thomas Fernández took on a pupil in 1508.

FERNÁNDEZ AGUANEVADA, Lope
Spanish, 16th century.
Active in Seville.
Sculptor.
In 1513, Lope Fernández Aguanevada sculpted a wooden crucifix for the church and in 1516 contributed a few decorative works to the Corpus Christi and Easter celebrations and those of the Holy Ghost. On 8 October 1517 he received payment for a sculpted slab for the chapter house. He may be identical with Lope Ruiz Agua Nevada.

FERNÁNDEZ ALVARADO. See **ALVARADO Fernandez**

FERNÁNDEZ ARDAVÍN, César
Spanish, 20th century.
Born c. 1880, in Madrid.
Painter. Genre scenes.
Cesar Fernández Ardavin studied under Cecilio Plà y Gallardo in Madrid. He took part in collective exhibitions and was awarded medals in Madrid and Barcelona. He painted the genre scenes *The Rosary* and *The Fiancée and her Friends*.

FERNÁNDEZ BENDICHO, Pedro, or Ferrandez Bendicho or Fernández Pedro
Spanish, 16th century.
Active in Seville c. 1520.
Painter.

FERNÁNDEZ CARPIO, Manuel
Spanish, 19th century.
Born in the 19th century, in Jaén.
Painter.
Orientalism.
Manuel Fernández Carpio studied under M. de la Paz at the school of fine arts in Madrid. One of his earliest works was *Está Muerto*. He exhibited genre paintings in Madrid, such as *Bullfight*, and obtained a number of awards.
MUSEUMS AND GALLERIES:
MADRID (Mus. de Arte Moderno): *17th-Century Studio Interior*.

FERNÁNDEZ CRUZADO, Joaquín Manuel
Spanish, 19th century.
Born 24 December 1781, in Jerez de la Frontera (Andalusia); died 31 January 1856, in Cádiz.
Painter. History painting, portraits.
Joaquín Fernández Cruzado was a very highly regarded artist of his period. He is known for some remarkable portraits and fine paintings, including an *Assumption*; *Adam and Eve Mourning Abel*; and *Guardian Angel*.

FERNÁNDEZ CUESTA Y PALAFOX, Eusebio
Spanish, 19th century.
Born 26 July 1847, in Madrid.
Painter.
Eusebio Fernández Cuesta y Palafox studied at the school of fine arts in Madrid under P. Gonzalvo. He painted copies of works in the Prado Museum and portraits, including those of the *Duke of Valencia* and the *Marquess de los Castillejos*.

He also painted genre pieces inspired by everyday life in Spain, such as *Card Players* and *Village Wedding*, which were exhibited in Madrid in 1871.

FERNÁNDEZ DE ALCALA, Juan
Spanish, 16th century.
Active in Seville in 1515.
Painter.
Juan Fernández de Alcala is probably identical with Juan-Antonio Fernández.

FERNÁNDEZ DE AYORA, Pedro
Spanish, 16th century.
Active in Cordova in 1579.
Painter.
Pedro Fernández de Ayora was master of the guild of painters.

FERNÁNDEZ DE BARCELONA, Diego
Spanish, 16th century.
Active in Barcelona c. 1525.
Sculptor.
Diego Fernández de Barcelona took over from Pedro Baco as master engraver of the Mint in Seville.

FERNÁNDEZ DE BIEDMA, Diego
Spanish, 15th century.
Active in Seville.
Illuminator.

FERNÁNDEZ DE CASTRO VILLAVICENCIO, Antonio
Spanish, 18th century.
Died 1739, in Cordova.
Painter.
Antonio Fernández de Castro Villavicencio was a canon in Cordova. He painted a *St Ferdinand* and an *Immaculate Conception* for the chapterhouse of Cordova Cathedral.

FERNÁNDEZ DE CONCA, Marcos
Spanish, 17th century.
Born in Burguillos.
Painter.
Marcos Fernández de Conca is mentioned in Seville in 1676.

FERNÁNDEZ DE GUADALUPE, Pedro
Spanish, 16th century.
Active in Seville at the beginning of the 16th century.
Painter.
Andalusian School.
Between 1500 and 1512, Pedro Fernández de Guadelupe painted a series of wooden figures for Seville Cathedral. For the same church he painted, in 1527, *A Descent from the Cross* and several other paintings including *The Repentance of St Peter*. The museum at Seville has his *Entombment of Christ*.

FERNÁNDEZ DE LA OLIVA, Francisco
Spanish, 19th century.
Born in the 19th century, in Valladolid.
Landscape painter.
Francisco Fernández de la Oliva was a pupil of Carlos de Haes. He exhibited in Madrid between 1875 and 1881.
Museums and Galleries:
Madrid: *View of Villalba*.

FERNÁNDEZ DE LA OLIVA, Manuel
Spanish, 19th century.
Born in the 19th century, in Madrid.
Sculptor.
Manuel Fernández de la Oliva was the son of the artist Nicolás Fernández and worked with his father. He studied at the Academia de San Fernando and is known for his *Andromeda* (1862) and *First Disenchantment*. He taught sculpture at the schools of fine arts in Cádiz and Seville.

FERNÁNDEZ DE LA OLIVA, Nicolás
Spanish, 19th century.
Sculptor.
Nicolás Fernández de la Oliva studied at the Academia de San Fernando. One of the creators of the Madrid artistic and literary circle, he is known for his *Statue of Cervantes*, erected in Valladolid in 1877 and a statue of *Christopher Columbus*, also for Valladolid.

FERNÁNDEZ DE LA VEGA, Luis
Spanish, 17th century.
Born c. 1600, in Lantone; died 1675, in Oviedo.
Sculptor.
Luis Fernández de la Vega studied in Valladolid under Gregorio Hernández. He worked in Oviedo Cathedral around 1640.
Bibliography:
Ramallo Asensio, Germán, *Luis Fernández de la Vega, escultor asturiano del siglo XVII*, Comisión Diocesana del Patrimonio Artístico-Religioso y Documental, Consejería de Educación y Cultura del Principado de Asturias, Oviedo, 1983.

FERNÁNDEZ DE LAREDO, Juan
Spanish, 17th century.
Born 1632, in Madrid; died 1692, in Madrid.
Painter.
Juan Fernández de Laredo was a pupil of Francisco Rizi; he assisted Rizi in his work at the Retiro and became one of the best fresco painters of the period. He produced a large number of paintings for churches in Madrid.
Bibliography:
Buendía, José Rogelio, *Dos pintores madrileños en la época de Carlos II: Francisco Lizona y Juan Fernández de Laredo*, Diputación Foral de Navarra, Institución Príncipe de Viana Consejo de Cultura, Pamplona, 1965.

FERNÁNDEZ DE NAVARRETE, Juan, called El Mudo
Spanish, 16th century.
Born c. 1526, in Logroño (Rioja); died 1579, in Toledo.
Painter.
A childhood illness left Juan Fernández de Navarrete deaf-mute, which accounts for the name 'El Mudo'. His first master was Fray Vicente de Santo Domingo. It is maintained that Navarrete went to Italy where he worked under the guidance of Titian in Venice. His reputation reached Philip II who summoned him to Madrid to work on the decorations of the Escorial, the painting of which was just commencing. In 1568 he was appointed royal painter, receiving a stipend of 200 ducats a month in addition to the fees for his works.

Fernández de Navarrete's key works are: *The Assumption*; *The Martyrdom of St James the Greater*; *St Philip and St Jerome*; a *Nativity*; a *Holy Family* and *St John Writing the Apocalyse*. For these last paintings, completed in 1575, he received 800 ducats. Unfortunately *The Assumption*, *St Philip* and *St John* were destroyed in a fire.

Fernández de Navarrete's major work, *Abraham and the Three Angels* was painted in 1576. At the same time he signed a contract with the prior-treasurer of the Escorial for the production of 32 paintings in four years, but death intervened before he was able to complete them. Between 1577 and 1578 he painted the first eight pictures. The remaining paintings were assigned to Alonso Sánchez Coello and Luis de Carajal. Fernández de Navarrete was a somewhat unorthodox painter who stripped his religious pictures of all superfluous emphasis. In his handling of the effects of tenebrism he foreshadowed Caravaggio.
Bibliography:
Mulcahy, Rosemarie, '*Abraham and the Three Angels by Juan Fernández de Navarrete El Mudo*' in *Apollo*, vol 107,

1978. Mulcahy, Rosemarie, ' *The High Altarpiece of the Basilica of San Lorenzo de el Escorial: An unpublished document*' in *Burlington Magazine,* vol 122, 1980. Davidson, B., '*Navarrete in Rome*' in *Burlington Magazine,* vol 135, 1993. Mulcahy, Rosemarie, *Juan Fernàndez de Navarrete el Mudo': Pintor de Felipe II,* Sociedad Estatal Conme, Madrid, 1999.

MUSEUMS AND GALLERIES:

LONDON (British Mus.): *Male Nude* - MADRID: *Baptism of Christ; Saints Peter and Paul.*

FERNÁNDEZ DE PEDRAXAS, Tomás

Spanish, 18th century.

Sculptor.

Two low reliefs - one an *Incarnation,* the other an *Assumption* - found in the house of Don R. Diaz de Morales in Cordova, demolished around 1890, carry the date 3 August 1749, Cordova, and the name Tomás Fernández de Padraxas.

FERNÁNDEZ DE PENALOSA, Pedro

Spanish, 16th century.

Died 1523, in Seville, according to some sources.

Painter.

FERNÁNDEZ DE QUESADA, Gabriel

Spanish, 16th century.

Active in Seville in 1534.

Sculptor.

FERNÁNDEZ DE SAHAGUN, Alfonso

Spanish, 15th century.

Sculptor.

In 1418, Alfonso Fernández de Sahagun executed sculptures on the main portal of Toledo Cathedral.

FERNÁNDEZ DE SANTOS, Sinforiano

Spanish, 19th century.

Born 8 November 1858, in Valladolid; died 21 July 1876, in Valladolid.

Painter.

In 1875, while still very young, Sinforiano Fernández de Santos won first prize in a competition. He showed great promise as a painter.

FERNANDEZ DE VILLASANTE, Julio Moisés. See **MOISÉS FERNANDEZ DE VILLASANTE Julio**

FERNÁNDEZ DEL MORAL, Lesmes

Spanish, 16th century.

Born in Burgos (Castilla y León).

Active in Valladolid.

Sculptor, painter, goldsmith.

One of the great Spanish sculptors, Lesmes Fernández del Moral married one of the daughters of the sculptor Juan de Arfe and had a hand in virtually all the works executed by his father-in-law who, in turn, worked with Juan de Juni and the Florentine Pompeiio Léoni on two statues of *D. Francisco de Sandoval,* Duke of Lerma, and *Doña Catalina de la Cerda,* his wife, portrayed kneeling in prayer on their tomb. These statues were conceived by Léoni, who at the outset collaborated on them with Arfe. Léoni later withdrew, leaving Arfe to continue the work assisted by Fernández del Moral. Arfe then died and the statues were successfully completed single-handed by Fernández del Moral under the guidance of Leoni. The history of these sculptures, now in Museo Nacional de Escultura, has made their attribution somewhat problematic. Moral also worked on the statues of the cardinal of Lerma and the archbishop of Toledo and a number of others.

FERNÁNDEZ GUERRA Y ORBE, Luis

Spanish, 19th century.

Born 1818; died 1890.

Active in Madrid.

Painter, writer.

Luis Fernández Guerra y Orbe studied at the fine arts school in Granada and from 1839 exhibited watercolour portraits, drawings and oil paintings of military scenes. He also produced lithographs for the journal *El Semanario Pintoresco Español.* He published his lectures as *Discursos leídos ante la Academia Española en la recepción pública de don Luis Fernández-Guerra y Orbe* in 1875.

FERNÁNDEZ GUERRERO, José

Spanish, 19th century.

Sculptor.

José Fernández Guerrero studied at the school of fine arts in Cádiz. In 1819 he was made an honorary member of the Academia de San Fernando in Madrid for a monumental statue he produced for the funeral of Maria Isabella of Braganza.

FERNÁNDEZ HIDALGO, Eulalio

Spanish, 19th - 20th century.

Painter. Figures, portraits, genre scenes, landscapes.

Eulalio Fernández Hidalgo studied at the Real Academia de Bellas Artes de San Fernando in Madrid. He exhibited at the Madrid national fine arts society in 1906 and received a commendation.

Fernández Hidalgo was inspired by religious subjects in the classical 17th century style and by Zurbarán in particular.

BIBLIOGRAPHY:

Arnáiz, José Manuel/López Jiménez, Javier/Merchán Díaz, Manuel (ed.), *Cien años de pintura en Espana y Portugal (1830-1930),* Antiqvaria, Madrid, 1988 (One Hundred Years of Painting in Spain and Portugal (1830-1930)).

FERNÁNDEZ MUÑOZ, Teodoro

Spanish, 19th century.

Born in the 19th century, in Jaén.

Painter.

Teodoro Fernández Muñoz studied and worked in Madrid as a seascape and landscape painter. His work was exhibited in Cádiz in 1856 and Madrid in 1860.

FERNÁNDEZ OLMOS, José

Spanish, 19th century.

Born in Valencia.

Painter.

José Fernández Olmos studied at the Academia de San Carlos in Valencia. His painting of Cervantes' *Don Quixote* featured in the Madrid exhibition of 1866.

BIBLIOGRAPHY:

Fernández Olmos, José, *Bosquejo del origen progreso y decadencia de las Artes llamadas del diseño,* Manuel Alufre, Valencia, 1878. Navarrete y Fos, Fedérico, *San Antonio de Padua,* Manuel Tello, Madrid, 1885.

FERNANDEZ PATTO, Lucien

French, 19th century.

Born in Paris.

Sculptor.

Fernandez Patto became a member of the Société des Artistes Français in 1902. He received a honourable mention in 1906.

FERNÁNDEZ PESCADOR, Eduardo

Spanish, 19th century.

Born 1836, in Madrid; died 26 May 1872, in Madrid.

Engraver, sculptor.

Eduardo Fernández Pescador studied at the Academia de San Fernando and under his uncle José Sanchez Pescador. He went to Paris around 1855 and exhibited in Madrid from 1860 to 1866.

BIBLIOGRAPHY:

Fernández Pescador, Eduardo, *Discursos leídos ante la Academia de Nobles Artes de San Fernando en la recepción pública de Don Eduardo Fernández Pescador el dia 18 de Abril de 1869*, M. Tello, Madrid, 1869.

FERNÁNDEZ SANAHUYA, Manuel
Spanish, 19th century.
Born in the 19th century, in Madrid.
Painter. History painting, genre scenes, seascapes.

Manuel Fernández Sanahuya studied at the Academia de San Alejandro in Havana. He exhibited in Madrid from 1864.

FERNANDEZ VASCO DE CAZAL. See **FERNANDES VASCO**

FERNÁNDEZ Y GONZÁLEZ, Domingo, or Fernández
Spanish, 19th - 20th century.
Born 1862, in Seville; died c. 1918.
Painter, illustrator. History painting, religious subjects, figure compositions, harbour scenes, church interiors.

Domingo Fernández y González studied at the school of fine arts in Seville where he was awarded a number of prizes. In 1886 he was granted a bursary to study at the Spanish academy in Rome. He travelled in Germany, France, Spain and especially Latin America, where he spent many years, particularly in Buenos Aires where he held official positions. He took part in many exhibitions including in Cádiz, Berlin, Munich, London, Madrid, Santiago de Chile and Rosario de Santa Fe.

BIBLIOGRAPHY:
Arnáiz, José Manuel/López Jiménez, Javier/Merchán Díaz, Manuel (ed.), *Cien años de pintura en Espana y Portugal (1830-1930)*, Antiqvaria, Madrid, 1988 (One Hundred Years of Painting in Spain and Portugal (1830-1930)).

MUSEUMS AND GALLERIES:
ROME (Mus. d'Arte Contemporanea) - SEVILLE: *Jupiter and Leda; The Sentencing of St Stephen.*

AUCTION RECORDS:
NEW YORK, 25 Jan 1980, *A Toast to the Guitarist* (oil on panel, 9 x 13 ins / 22 x 33 cm) USD 9,000. BARCELONA, 17 Dec 1987, *Interior of St Mark's Basilica in Venice* (oil on canvas, 27 1/2 x 20 ins / 70 x 51 cm) ESP 1,850,000. LONDON, 23 March 1988, *At the Fountain* (oil on canvas, 19 1/4 x 11 ins / 49 x 27 cm) GBP 4,400. LONDON, 23 Nov 1988, *The Port of Barcelona* (oil on card, 10 1/4 x 7 3/4 ins / 26 x 20 cm) GBP 2,200. LONDON, 15 Feb 1990, *Asking the Way* (oil on panel, 8 x 6 ins / 20.5 x 15 cm) GBP 550. MILAN, 23 Oct 1996, *Capri, Steps by the Shore* (oil on canvas, 8 3/4 x 13 1/2 ins / 22.5 x 34 cm) ITL 9,087,000.

FERNANDEZ Y JIMÉNEZ. See **JIMÉNEZ Y FERNANDEZ**

FERNÁNDEZ Y RODRÍGUEZ, Rosendo
Spanish, 19th century.
Born 24 September 1840, in Antequera; died 8 December 1909, in Cartagena.
Painter. Genre scenes.

Rosendo Fernández y Rodríguez studied at the school of fine arts in Seville. He first exhibited in 1864 with *Resignation*. His painting *View of the Monastery of St Paul and St Francis* is in the museum in Seville.

FERNÁNDEZ Y RODRÍGUEZ, Silvio
Spanish, 19th century.
Born c. 1850, in Ribadavia (Galicia).
Painter.

Silvio Fernández y Rodríguez studied under José Marti y Monso at the Valladolid academy, where he received an award for his *Mozo de Cuadra*; the academy also purchased the work. He also studied in Madrid and Rome and exhibited his historical painting, *Torquemada*, at the exhibition of the national fine arts society of Madrid. His genre studies of life in Galicia appeared at the regional exhibition in Madrid in 1912.

FERNÁNDEZ-MURO, José Antonio
Spanish, 20th century.
Born 1920, in Madrid.
From 1938 active in Argentina, from 1962 active in the USA and from 1969 active in Spain.
Painter (mixed media).

José Antonio Fernández Muro's family emigrated to Buenos Aires in 1938 and he began to study painting there. In 1948 he returned to Spain for two years. Back in Buenos Aires in 1957 he formed a group with four other painters and two sculptors; in the same year he was awarded a UNESCO bursary to study museography at the Louvre Museum in Paris with Germain Bazin and at the Sorbonne with Pierre Francastel. He also visited the major museums of Europe and the USA.

In his early career Fernández Muro went through different phases and displayed a variety of influences including Neo-Impressionist pointillism and Die Brücke's Expressionism. From about 1955 he began to define his personal style with a marked reference to Constructivism. Over the years the paintings of his mature years borrowed stylistically from the modern repertoire of a variety of artists belonging mainly to the modern American School. These include key figures of minimalism such as Rothko and Sol Lewitt with his squares and hatchings but also Spanish artists like Tapies with his rustic 'marks'. He was inspired to use typographic letters, figures and the chromatic spectrum of television test cards from the American Rauchenberg, the Yugoslav Velickovic and the Japanese Tabuchi. The stereotypes so openly adopted by Fernández Muro can be seen as the basic vocabulary of a future, impersonal, international plastic language of which he became a master.

He took part in numerous collective exhibitions including: Latin-American artists exhibition organised by UNESCO (1948); Rio de Janeiro museum of modern art with the Buenos Aires group and at the Stedelijk Museum in Amsterdam (1952); São Paulo Biennale (1953); Venice Biennale (1956); Carnegie Institute *Pittsburgh International* and the Brussels international exhibitions (1958); Chicago Art Institute and the Dallas Art Museum groups of Latin-American painters (1959); *Tapies and Fernández Muro* at the national fine arts museum of Buenos Aires and the 6th São Paulo Biennale (1961); *Art Concret and the Nouvelle Tendance* at the Buenos Aires museum of modern art (1963); the Guggenheim International Award in New York (1964); *Latin-American Art* at the Pennsylvania Academy in Philadelphia (1967); a selection from the collections of the Guggenheim museum in New York (1970); *Art of the Present in Argentina* at the Basel Kunsthalle, the Rhineland museum in Bonn and the Hamburg Kunsthaus (1971). He received numerous honours: gold medal at the Brussels international exhibition (1958); the Herbert Read prize at the inter-American Biennale in Córdoba, Argentina (1962); prize at the Coltejer Medellín Biennale (1968). He also showed collections of his paintings in many solo exhibitions.

BIBLIOGRAPHY:
Messer, Thomas M., *Fernández-Muro 1979-1985*, exhibition catalogue, Museo español de arte contemporáneo, Madrid, 1985 (extensive documentation).

MUSEUMS AND GALLERIES:
AMSTERDAM (Stedelijk Mus.) - AUSTIN (Jack S. Blanton MA, University of Texas): *Al gran pueblo argentino..* (*To the Great Argentinian People...*) (1964); *Campo de plata* (*Silver Field*) (1966); *Gris plomizo* (*Leaden Gray*) (1969) - BUENOS AIRES (Mus. Nacional de Bellas Artes) - CARACAS (MBA) - CUENCA (Mus. De Arte Abstracto Español, Fundación Juan March) - DALLAS (MA): *Violet Red on Grey* (1958, oil on canvas) - MADRID (Mus. Nacional Centro de Arte Reina Sofía) - MIAMI (Metropolitan Mus.) - NEW YORK (MoMA) - NEW YORK (So-

lomon R. Guggenheim Mus.) - OAKLAND (AM) - PONCE (MA) - WASHINGTON DC (Art Mus. of the Americas).

AUCTION RECORDS:

NEW YORK, 7 Nov 1980, *N.Y.C. Electrical* (1966, mixed media/canvas, 36 x 31 ins / 91.5 x 78.7 cm) USD 1,000. NEW YORK, 30 May 1984, *Transico-Verde-Entrada (Transico-Green-Entrance)* (1960, oil on canvas, 51 x 38 1/2 ins / 129.6 x 98 cm) USD 1,500.

FERNANDI, Francesco, or Ferdinandi, called Imperiali
Italian, 18th century.
Born 1679; died 1740.
Painter. History painting, religious subjects.
School of Rome.

Francesco Fernandi was working in Rome in 1730. Like Maratti, he eschewed fashionable Rococo influences on his work and adhered strictly to Classical models.

MUSEUMS AND GALLERIES:

ROME (Church of S Eustachio): *Martyrdom of St Eustace* - ROME (Church of S Gregorio Magno): *Martyrdom of St Romuald of Ravenna*.

AUCTION RECORDS:

LONDON, 25 Nov 1970, *Hector and Andromache*, GBP 800. LONDON, 6 July 1978, *Alexander the Great Rewarding his Generals* (oil on canvas, 21 1/2 x 30 1/4in/54.5 x 77cm) GBP 2,200. LONDON, 24 Oct 1986, *Eliezer and Rebecca at the Well* (oil on canvas, 48 3/4 x 62 1/4in/123.9 x 158cm) GBP 23,000. NEW YORK, 7 April 1989, *Adoration of the Magi* (oil on canvas, 28 3/4 x 34in/73 x 86.5cm) USD 9,350. LONDON, 9 April 1990, *Herminia Carving Tancredi's Name on a Tree Trunk* (oil on canvas, 34 1/2 x 29 1/4in/87.7 x 74cm) GBP 16,500. LONDON, 19 April 1991, *Mythological Fishing Party* (oil on canvas, 37 1/4 x 48in/94.5 x 121.8cm) GBP 6,600.

FERNANDINOV, Nicholas
Russian, 20th century.
Active in Venezuela.
Painter.

Little is known about Nicholas Fernandinov. Completely uprooted, he spent his life in Venezuela and was influenced by the painting of the Venezuelan Armando Reveron.

FERNANDO
Spanish, 15th century.
Active in Seville c. 1480.
Painter.

FERNANDO, Francisco
Spanish, 17th century.
Active in Valladolid.
Sculptor.

In 1630, Francisco Fernando was responsible for moving the main retable in Tuleda.

FERNANDO, Gomez
Spanish, 16th century.
Active in Seville c. 1533.
Painter.

FERNANDO, José
Spanish, 19th century.
Active in Seville.
Engraver.

FERNANDO DE ALCALA
Spanish, 15th century.
Died before April 1505.
Active in Seville.
Painter.

FERNANDO DE CORDOBA
Spanish, 16th century.
Active in Seville.
Sculptor.

FERNANDO DE REVILLA. See **REVILLA Fernando de**

FERNANDO DE TOLEDO, also known as Hernando de Toledo
Spanish, 15th - 16th century.
Active in Seville during the 15th and 16th centuries.
Painter.

FERNBACH, Agnes B.
American, 20th century.
Born 29 June 1877, in New York.
Engraver (etching).

FERNBACH, Alfred
Italian, 20th century.
Born 1866, in Verona, declared 27 February 1867; died 21 March 1941, in Montréjeau, France.
Active then naturalised in France.
Painter.

Alfred Fernbach was the son of Guglielmo Fernbach, and the brother of Ermanno. He went to live in Marseilles, and thereafter Toulon (Var département, southern France) in around 1900, where he worked as an art photographer. He was also an amateur painter.

BIBLIOGRAPHY:

FERNBACH, Ermanno
Italian, 19th - 20th century.
Born 6 December 1859, in Verona; died 12 December 1933, in Turin.
Painter, pastellist. Portraits, genre scenes.

The son of Guglielmo Fernbach, Ermanno studied at the Accademia di Belle Arti di Brera in Milan, in 1877, under Giuseppe Bertini. He taught painting in Turin, where he lived and worked.

Ermanno Fernbach exhibited at the fine arts society in Milan and Turin from 1884 to 1886. He painted a fresco in the Marquis of Calabiana's private chapel in the archbishopric of Milan. His self-portrait is often referred to as being in the tradition of Toulouse-Lautrec and Monet. He was also an art critic.

BIBLIOGRAPHY:

FERNBACH, Franz Xaver, real name: Fehrenbach
German, 19th century.
Born 14 October 1793, in Waldkirch, near Freiburg (Breisgau); died 27 February 1851, in Munich.
Painter, draughtsman, miniaturist. Religious subjects, figures, portraits, still-lifes. Porcelain.

Franz Xaver Fernbach began to decorate clock faces at an early age, while at the same time taking an interest in chemistry. He went to the Akademie der Bildenden Künste in Munich in 1816, where he was awarded a silver medal at the Kunstausstellung of 1819 for his tabletop lacquerwork imitating oil-painted mosaics. Thanks to the support of King Maximilian Joseph I, who bought some of his works, he was able to study mineralogy, physics and chemistry at the Universities of Landshut and Vienna. There he gained valuable technical experience, which he used in the writing of his books, *Kenntniss und Behandlung der Ölfarben (Knowledge and Treatment of Oil Paints)*, Munich, 1834; *Lehr und Handbuch über die Ölfarbe (Handbook of Oil Painting for Artists and Art Lovers)*, Munich, 1843; *Die Enkaustiche Malerei (Encaustic Painting)*, Munich, 1845. He became a founder member of the first Society of Fine Arts in Munich in 1823, and in 1837 was appointed Royal Curator of the former Pinakothek in Munich.

He created tables in imitation mosaic (for King Maximilian Joseph I, his wife Queen Caroline and Eugène de Beauharnais) and decorated porcelain. He also painted the portraits of the King and Queen of Bavaria, family scenes and still-lifes. He was perhaps more of a researcher and theorist than a painter, and is recognised today for having invented a type of encaustic mural painting close to that which was employed in antiquity. It was a technique that was much used by, among others, Julius Schnorr von Carolsfeld, in his paintings of the Royal Residenz in Munich, and by Hiltensperger and Carl Rottmann. Fernbach also perfected a varnish to protect copper from the damp, and a type of tempera painting.

BIBLIOGRAPHY:

André, Michel, *Les Peintres Fernbach de 1793 à 1992* (private notes).

FERNBACH, Odette
French, 20th century.
Born 21 March 1905, in Toulon; died 15 February 1992, in La Celle (Var).
Painter, sculptor. Religious subjects, scenes with figures. Murals.

Odette Fernbach was the grand-daughter of the painter Gugliemo Fernbach and the daughter of Alfred. She studied at the École des Beaux-Arts in Toulon. A Dominican nun, she produced murals, sculptures (plaster, terracotta, wood) at Montréjeau and in other cities in the South and on the coast. She is known for a *Portrait of Yvonne Fernbach with a Headscarf*, produced in 1926.

BIBLIOGRAPHY:

André, Michel, *Les Peintres Fernbach de 1793 à 1992* (private notes).

FERNBACH, Wilhelm, called Guglielmo
German, 19th century.
Born 23 February 1826, in Munich; died 16 March 1884, in Milan.
Active in Italy from 1856.
Painter, sculptor.

The son of Franz Xaver Fernbach, Wilhelm Fernbach was a student at the academy of fine arts in Munich. In 1856 he moved to Verona, and in 1870 to Milan. He produced sculptures and frescoes for churches.

MUSEUMS AND GALLERIES:

DONAUESCHINGEN: *Two Women in front of the Cross.*

FERNE, Hortense T.
American, 20th century.
Born 1885, in New York; died 1975.
Painter, engraver (etching).

Hortense T. Ferne was awarded the first honourable mention given by the Plastic Club in 1927.

FERNEAUT, Charles
French, 18th century.
Born c. 1693; died July 1759.
Active in Paris.
Sculptor.

FERNEL, Clémence
French, 19th century.
Born 19th century.
Painter.

Fernel exhibited at the Paris Salon in 1837, 1838 and 1839.

FERNEL, Fernand
Belgian, 20th century.
Born c. 1872, in Brussels; died c. 1934, in Paris.
Painter, humorist artist, poster artist.

As a painter, Fernel devoted a good number of his works to the circus and the world of the theatre. He drew albums for children: *Mr Bob et son Rataplan, Estampes sportives, Les jolies poupées,* and in 1913 *Les enfants s'amusent* (*The Children Are Playing*). He published drawings in *La Caricature, Le Rire, Le Sourire,* and other magazines. He also created posters, notably for the department store *La Belle Jardinière.* Fernel exhibited in Paris, in 1903 at the Salon d'Automne, then at the Salon des Humoristes from 1907 to 1914 and 1920 to 1923, and from 1925 onwards at the Salon des Artistes Indépendants.

BIBLIOGRAPHY:

Osterwalder, Marcus (ed.), *Dictionnaire des illustrateurs 1800-1914*, Ides et Calendes, Neuchâtel, 1989.

FERNEL, Jacques, or Fernelle
French, 18th century.
Born to a family originally from Caen.
Painter.

FERNELEY, Claude Lorraine
British, 19th century.
Born 1822; died 1891 or 1892.
Painter. Hunting scenes, landscapes with figures, animals.

Claude Lorraine Ferneley's paintings (mostly equestrian scenes) were exhibited from 1851 to 1853 in London, and at the Royal Hibernian Academy in Dublin. He exhibited at the Royal Academy in 1868.

AUCTION RECORDS:

LONDON, 16 May 1928, *Two Hunters,* GBP 10. LONDON, 25 May 1934, *The Bangor Coach,* GBP 11. LONDON, 30 July 1947, *Hunting Scene,* GBP 170. LONDON, 17 March 1961, *Slawston, Magnum Bovum and Sultan,* GBP 294. LONDON, 16 July 1976, *Horses in their Box* (1877, two oils on canvas, 23 3/4 x 30 3/4 ins / 60.5 x 78 cm) GBP 400. LONDON, 19 July 1978, *Lord Newport with his Favourite Hunter Rowton* (1862, oil on canvas, 17 1/2 x 23 1/2 ins / 44.5 x 60 cm) GBP 1,400. LONDON, 26 June 1981, *Landscape with a Pure-blood and Dog* (1850, oil on canvas, 25 1/4 x 30 1/4 ins / 64 x 77 cm) GBP 3,000. LONDON, 11 July 1984, *Saddled Horse held by a Huntsman with a Hound* (1852, oil on canvas, 25 x 30 ins / 63.5 x 76 cm) GBP 2,400. NEW YORK, 7 June 1985, *Horse and Terrier in the Stables* (1846, oil on card, 12 x 14 ins / 30.5 x 35.5 cm) USD 4,500. LONDON, 14 July 1989, *Saddled Pony with a Rifle and Gamebag Either Side of a Door* (1879, oil on canvas, 20 x 30 1/2 ins / 51 x 77.5 cm) GBP 8,250. LONDON, 15 Nov 1989, *A Gunner in G Battery of the Royal Artillery* (1848, oil on canvas, 19 1/2 x 24 1/2 ins / 49.5 x 62 cm) GBP 4,950. NEW YORK, 7 June 1991, *The Earl of Jersey's Horse Riddleworth Ridden by J. Robinson* (1841, oil on canvas, 10 x 12 ins / 25.4 x 30.5 cm) USD 6,600. LONDON, 3 Feb 1993, *Landscape with the Horses Dragon and Black Prince* (1852, oil on card, 9 x 11 ins / 22 x 28 cm) GBP 862. NEW YORK, 3 June 1994, *Little Peter in his Stable* (1875, oil on canvas, 19 x 25 ins / 48.3 x 63.5 cm) USD 6,325. NEW YORK, 11 April 1997, *Chestnut Hunter in a Box* (oil on canvas, 24 x 31 ins / 61 x 78.7 cm) USD 3,450. BUENOS AIRES, 24 Nov 1999, *Horses in a Landscape* (oil on canvas, 35 x 49 ins / 90 x 125 cm) USD 20,000. LONDON, 15 June 2000, *Chestnut Horse with Jockey up, Horses Exercising beyond* (1849, oil on canvas, 14 x 19 ins / 36 x 47 cm) GBP 5,800. LONDON, 14 June 2001, *Duncan's Horses, Scene from Macbeth* (1849, oil on board, 13 x 17 ins / 33 x 44 cm) GBP 4,500. LONDON, 17 July 2002, *Dark Bay Hunter in Grounds of a Country House* (1865, oil on canvas, 24 x 31 ins / 60 x 78 cm) GBP 1,500. LONDON, 27 Nov 2003, *Bay Hunter in the Park of a Country House* (1862, oil on canvas, 20 x 25 ins / 51 x 63 cm) GBP 3,000. AMSTERDAM, 10 Dec 2003, *Bess and Polly in a Stable* (1879, oil on canvas, 24 x 31 ins / 61 x 78 cm) EUR 2,000. DORCHESTER, 8 July 2004, *Horses in a Wooded Landscape* (1850, oil on canvas, 19 x 15 ins / 48 x 38 cm) GBP 1,100. LONDON, 3 Nov 2004, *Bay Horse in a Landscape* (1864, oil on canvas, 19 x 25 ins / 49 x 64 cm) GBP 2,800.

FERNELEY, John E.
British, 19th century.
Born 1782; died 1860 or 1862, in Melton Mowbray.
Painter. Hunting scenes, animals.

John E. Fernley exhibited hunting scenes at the Royal Academy, the British Institution and Suffolk Street from 1809 to 1855.

J Ferneley

Auction records:
Paris, 23 March 1878, *The Racehorse Lancelot,* FRF 320. London, 4 June 1923, *Racehorse,* GBP 3. London, 25 June 1923, *Hunter,* GBP 21. London, 21 Dec 1923, *The Racehorse Jolly Roger,* GBP 10; *Three Hunters: Coriander, Zanga and Don Pedro,* GBP 13; *Lord Lismore,* GBP 110. London, 4 Feb 1924, *Beeswing with her Foal,* GBP 73. London, 22 Feb 1924, *Cesario with a Mare,* GBP 52. London, 30 June 1924, *Conjuror in his Stable-box,* GBP 27. London, 27 Feb 1925, *Hunters,* GBP 8. London, 18 Dec 1925, *William Michener Max Field,* GBP 60; *Groom,* GBP 10. London, 12 Feb 1926, *Fox-hunting,* GBP 199. London, 13 April 1927, *O'Callaghan,* GBP 294. London, 9 May 1927, *Grey Horse,* GBP 10. London, 4 July 1927, *Hunter at the Stable Door,* GBP 13; *Three Horses,* GBP 18. London, 13 July 1928, *Two Hunters Grazing,* GBP 546. London, 5 Dec 1928, *Henry Villebois,* GBP 820. London, 7 Dec 1928, *Wycombe Abbey,* GBP 378. London, 14 Dec 1928, *Portrait of a Hunter,* GBP 304. London, 14 June 1929, *Fox-hunting* (three paintings) GBP 1,102. London, 19 July 1929, *Fox-hunting* (three paintings) GBP 609. London, 16 July 1930, *Hounds at a Meet,* GBP 740. London, 3 July 1931, *Caro,* GBP 6. London, 17 July 1931, *Benedict,* GBP 33. Philadelphia, 30 and 31 March 1932, *Huntsman with Hounds,* USD 105. London, 8 April 1932, *White Horse,* GBP 19. London, 7 Dec 1933, *Richard William Penn,* GBP 525. New York, 18 and 19 April 1934, *Gustavus with his Jockey,* USD 225. London, 25 April 1934, *Major Healy,* GBP 78. London, 19 June 1936, *Rockingham,* GBP 7. London, 17 March 1937, *Clinker,* GBP 25. London, 24 May 1937, *Horse,* GBP 18; *Grey Horse*; *Bay* (collection) GBP 10. London, 23 July 1937, *Three Horses,* GBP 147; *Two Horses,* GBP 120; *Landscape with Three Horses,* GBP 152. London, 2 June 1938, *Banquet after the Hunt,* GBP 19. Paris, 20 June 1938, *Landscape with a Greyhound Bitch and Dead Hares* (1829) FRF 3,000. London, 7 Dec 1938, *Huntsman,* GBP 25. London, 25 May 1939, *Huntsman,* GBP 68. London, 28 July 1939, *Fox-hunting,* GBP 52; *Clinker,* GBP 6. London, 9 May 1940, *Huntsman,* GBP 5. London, 25 Oct 1940, *Three Horses,* GBP 31. London, 18 Dec 1940, *Hunting Scene,* GBP 6. London, 5 Dec 1941, *Portrait of H. W. Pennestone,* GBP 10. London, 24 June 1942, *The Horse Melbourne,* GBP 32. London, 26 Aug 1942, *The Rufford Hunt,* GBP 270; *The Rufford Hunt,* GBP 55. London, 25 Nov 1942, *The Rufford Hunt,* GBP 50. London, 17 June 1943, *Boy with Two Horses,* GBP 78. London, 26 July 1943, *John Foster Giles,* GBP 325. London, 24 May 1944, *White Horse,* GBP 115. New York, 15 and 16 May 1946, *Horse with Hounds,* USD 1,600. London, 19 March 1947, *Hunter,* GBP 30. London, 28 March 1947, *John Drummond,* GBP 1,680; *Fox-hunting,* GBP 1,312. London, 30 May 1947, *Man,* GBP 630; *The Horse Baronet,* GBP 504; *The Horse Crossbow,* GBP 73; *Horse,* GBP 220; *Defiance,* GBP 210. London, 29 Nov 1957, *Portrait of Chorister, a Bay Racehorse,* GBP 1,627. London, 6 Nov 1959, *Hunting Scene with a Portrait of Captain John White,* GBP 945. New York, 6 April 1960, *Blue Beret,* USD 800. London, 30 Nov 1960, *Portrait of Sir Wilfrid Lawson,* GBP 2,000. London, 16 June 1961, *Captain Frank Hall,* GBP 2,100. London, 20 Nov 1963, *Landscape with Horse,* GBP 1,700. London, 19 Nov 1965, *Stable-boy Holding Two Horses in a London Street,* Gns 7,200. London, 18 Nov 1966, *Thoroughbred,* Gns 9,500. London, 22 Nov 1967, *Landscape with Thoroughbred,* GBP 17,000. New York, 25 Sept 1968, *Landscape with Three Horses,* USD 44,000. London, 20 June 1969, *The Ferneley Children,* Gns 28,000. London, 13 Dec 1972, *Landscape with Three Thoroughbreds,* GBP 16,000. London, 22 Nov 1974, *Burton Hunt,* Gns 55,000. London, 26 March 1976, *Hunting Scene* (1831, oil on panel, 18 x 23 ins / 45.7 x 58.4 cm) GBP 1,700. London, 24 June 1977, *Gentleman Holding a Saddled Horse by the Bridle* (1807, oil on canvas, 27 1/2 x 35 1/2 ins / 70 x 90 cm) GBP 4,000. London, 27 March 1981, *Sir Harry Goodrick Deer-stalking* (1836, oil on canvas, 43 1/2 x 58 ins / 110.5 x 147.3 cm) GBP 22,000. London, 26 June 1981, *Landscape with a Pure-blood and Pony* (1849, oil on canvas, 24 1/2 x 29 1/2 ins / 62.2 x 75 cm) GBP 4,500. London, 13 July 1984, *Equestrian Portrait of Captain Joseph Smyth-Windham* (1816, oil on canvas, 40 x 50 1/4 ins / 101.6 x 127.5 cm) GBP 48,000. London, 23 Nov 1984, *8th King's Irish Hussars on a Field Day* (oil on canvas, 27 x 38 ins / 68.6 x 96.5 cm) GBP 12,000. New York, 6 June 1985, *Melton Mowbray Statute Fair* (1838, oil on canvas, 23 1/4 x 33 ins / 59 x 84 cm) USD 22,000. New York, 4 June 1987, *The Cur, a Chestnut Racehorse with Jockey up on Newmarket Heath* (1848, oil on canvas, 40 x 50 ins / 101.6 x 127 cm) USD 290,000. London, 15 July 1988, *Mr George Marriott on his Bay Trotter Jumping a Fence* (1845, oil on canvas, 34 x 45 ins / 86.4 x 114.2 cm) GBP 77,000. London, 18 Nov 1988, *Retriever Running with a Partridge* (1836, oil on canvas, 39 3/4 x 50 ins / 101.2 x 126.7 cm) GBP 9,350. New York, 24 May 1989, *The Thoroughbred Harkaway* (1840, oil on canvas, 28 x 33 1/2 ins / 71.1 x 85.4 cm) USD 39,600. London, 14 July 1989, *Portrait of George Payne of Sulby Galloping on his Chestnut Trotter The Clipper* (1827, oil on canvas, 35 x 44 ins / 89 x 112 cm) GBP 88,000. London, 14 July 1989, *Hyde Park Corner* (oil on canvas, 30 x 60 ins / 76.2 x 152.3 cm) GBP 49,500. Perth, 28 Aug 1989, *Butcher Skinning a Stag* (oil on canvas, 30 x 25 ins / 76 x 63.5 cm) GBP 5,720. London, 20 April 1990, *Mrs Meakin Holding a Hunter by the Bridle in a Stable-box, with the Hounds Hector and Jem* (1853, oil on canvas, 34 x 44 ins / 86.3 x 111.8 cm) GBP 30,800. London, 20 April 1990, *Marquis of Westminster's Brown Foal Lancelot, Ridden by W. Scott, with Maroon and Gibraltar in the Background* (1840, oil on canvas, 28 3/4 x 36 3/4 ins / 73 x 93.4 cm) GBP 19,800. London, 11 July 1990, *Landscape with the Master of Hounds Peter Christie on his Chestnut* (1817, oil on canvas, 33 x 41 1/4 ins / 84 x 105 cm) GBP 17,600. New York, 24 Oct 1990, *Golden Chestnut Hunter in a Landscape* (1853, oil on canvas, 34 1/4 x 44 1/4 ins / 87 x 112.4 cm) USD 19,800. London, 10 April 1991, *Thoroughbred Bay with his Lad, in his Stable-box* (oil on canvas, 24 x 29 ins / 61 x 73.5 cm) GBP 2,090. London, 12 April 1991, *Mr Sterling Crawford's Trotter Cigar in his Stable* (1841, oil on canvas, 33 x 43 1/2 ins / 83.8 x 110.5 cm) GBP 27,500. New York, 7 June 1991, *Thoroughbred Ridden by a Jockey in the Colours of Lord Elcho* (1838, oil on canvas, 34 x 42 ins / 86.4 x 106.7 cm) USD 154,000. London, 10 July 1991, *Mr Markwell, Master of the Cheshire Hounds, on Magic* (oil on canvas, 17 x 23 1/2 ins / 43 x 60 cm) GBP 5,500. New York, 16 Oct 1991, *Start of a Twelve-horse Race at York; Finish of a Twelve-horse Race at York* (oil on canvas, a pair, each 18 1/4 x 40 ins / 46.6 x 101.6 cm) USD 41,800. London, 10 April 1992, *Panoramic Landscape With a Saddled Bay Hunter, Hunstmen and Hounds in the Distance* (1824, oil on canvas, 34 x 42 ins / 86.3 x 106.7 cm) GBP 31,900. London, 18 Nov 1992, *Landscape with a Mare and Foal* (1856, oil on canvas, 24 1/4 x 29 1/4 ins / 61.5 x 74 cm) GBP 7,150. London, 20 Nov 1992, *The Thoroughbred Bay Priam Ridden by Sam Day, Before a Race* (1830, oil on canvas, 33 1/2 x 42 ins / 85.4 x 106.4 cm) GBP 71,500. London, 6 April 1993, *Lord Robert Manners of Benefit, Lord Charles of Featherlegs and the Duke of Rutland Hunting near Belvoir Castle* (1838, oil on canvas, 35 x 56 ins / 89 x 142.4 cm) GBP 132,400. London, 14 July 1993, *Hunt Breaking Cover with a Distant View of Melton Mowbray* (oil on canvas, 13 1/2 x 25 1/4 ins / 34 x 64 cm) GBP 6,900. New York, 12 Oct 1994, *Landscape with a Portrait of the Bay Sultan* (1831, oil on canvas, 28 x 36 ins / 71.1 x 91.4 cm) USD 27,600. New York, 9 June 1995, *Meet in Front of the*

Hunting Lodge at Garendon Park (oil on canvas, 23 3/4 x 62 1/2 ins / 60.3 x 158.8 cm) USD 48,875. LONDON, 12 July 1995, *Lord Elcho's Thoroughbred Bay Philip, Ridden by his Jockey* (1838, oil on canvas, 34 x 42 ins / 86.5 x 106.7 cm) GBP 67,500. PARIS, 29 March 1996, *Soldier of the 15th Dragoon Guards Leading Colonel Colqhoun Grant's Horse at Canterbury* (1826, oil on canvas, 31 x 42 1/4 ins / 79 x 107 cm) FRF 200,000. PERTH, 20 Aug 1996, *Heading for Home* (1833, oil on canvas, 20 x 25 ins / 51 x 63.5 cm) GBP 4,830. LONDON, 13 Nov 1996, *Waiting for the Master: Horses, Grooms and John Morant's Hounds* (1820, oil on canvas, 41 1/2 x 50 1/2 ins / 105.5 x 128 cm) GBP 194,000. LONDON, 13 Nov 1996, *Landscape with the Thoroughbred Bay Shamrock and a Distant View of Belvoir Castle* (1829, oil on canvas, 28 x 35 3/4 ins / 71 x 91 cm) GBP 28,750. NEW YORK, 11 April 1997, *Emilius, Winner of the 1832 Derby* (oil on canvas, 24 1/2 x 30 ins / 62.2 x 76.2 cm) USD 34,500; *Three Hunters Belonging to Robert Myddelton-Biddulph* (1830, oil on canvas, 44 x 63 ins / 111.8 x 160 cm) USD 96,000. LONDON, 12 Nov 1997, *Ralph John Lambton with his Master of Hounds, and the Pack* (1832, oil on canvas, 43 1/4 x 61 1/2 ins / 110 x 156 cm) GBP 397,500. NEW YORK, 9 April 1999, *Captain Horatio Ross on Clinker with Lord Kennedy's Radical* (1826, oil on canvas, 43 x 62 ins / 109 x 157 cm) USD 1,000,000. LONDON, 27 May 1999, *Mountebank and Albion, Grooms and Hunters in a Landscape* (1826, oil on canvas, 42 x 59 ins / 107 x 151 cm) GBP 201,000. LONDON, 26 May 2000, *Chestnut Racehorse with Trainer and Jockey on a Racecourse* (1824, oil on canvas, 33 x 45 ins / 85 x 115 cm) GBP 140,000. NEW YORK, 6 Dec 2000, *Lord Lowther's Spaniel, Winner of the 1831 Derby, with Jockey up, on a Racecourse* (1831, oil on canvas, 35 x 43 ins / 88 x 108 cm) USD 220,000. NEW YORK, 1 June 2001, *Lord Robert Grosvenor's Hunters at Moor Park, Rickmansworth, Hertfordshire* (1853, oil on canvas, 42 x 57 ins / 107 x 145 cm) USD 210,000. NEW YORK, 1 June 2001, *Squire Wormald with a Hunt in Full Cry* (1828, oil on canvas, 55 x 119 ins / 140 x 302 cm) USD 370,000. LONDON, 13 June 2002, *Marvel, Kingfisher and the Lad, Three Hunters Belonging to William Angerstein* (oil on canvas, 44 x 72 ins / 113 x 182 cm) GBP 60,000. LONDON, 13 June 2002, *Sir John Thorold's Bay Hunter with Groom in a Stable* (oil on canvas, 40 x 51 ins / 102 x 130 cm) GBP 150,000. LONDON, 25 Nov 2003, *Two Bay Mares with a Terrier by a Tree in a Landscape* (1842, oil on canvas, 50 x 40 ins / 127 x 102 cm) GBP 90,000. NEW YORK, 5 Dec 2003, *Two Hunters at Grass* (1827, oil on canvas, 44 x 63 ins / 112 x 160 cm) USD 220,000. LONDON, 21 May 2004, *Bay Hunter in an Extensive Landscape with Lake beyond* (oil on canvas, 28 x 41 ins / 72 x 104 cm) GBP 20,000. LONDON, 23 Nov 2004, *Fox in Shrubbery* (oil on canvas, 26 x 33 ins / 65 x 85 cm) GBP 9,000.

FERNEMAN, Albin Verner

Swedish, 20th century.

Born 1894, in Filipstad.

Painter. Scenes with figures, portraits, landscapes.

Ferneman featured in 1921 in the Salon d'Automne in Paris.

AUCTION RECORDS:

STOCKHOLM, 20 Oct 1987, *A Village in Alsace* (1922, oil on canvas, 19 1/4 x 15 3/4 ins / 49 x 40 cm) SEK 28,000.

FERNER

German, 18th century.

Active in Meissen (Saxony).

Painter (porcelain).

FERNET, Richard Joseph

French, 18th - 19th century.

Born 18 April 1735, in Valenciennes; died 31 March 1810, in Valenciennes.

Sculptor (wood).

Fernet was admitted as the master of a studio before 1757, and was several times master of his corporation in Valenciennes. He worked for churches and monasteries in his native town, in particular for the chapel of the Holy Sacrament in St-Géry, and for St-Nicholas, where he sculpted the organ casing. With J. P. Gillet he executed the decoration of the boxes at the theatre in Valenciennes. He also carved a tabernacle for the church of Marquette-en-Ostrevent.

FERNEX, Jean Baptiste, or Jean Baptiste de.
See **DEFERNEX**

FERNEZ, Louis

French, 20th century.

Born 1 August 1900, in Avignon; died 1984, in Savigny-sur-Orge.

Painter. Figures, landscapes, seascapes, still-lifes, flowers. Murals.

Orientalism.

School of Algiers.

Louis Fernez came to Paris from Algeria, where his family had settled. He studied under Fernand Cormon at the École des Beaux-Arts in Paris, as well as Léon Cauvy, who ran the École des Beaux-Arts of Algiers. Fernez won a studentship from the Casa Velázquez in Madrid. He taught painting at the École des Beaux-Arts of Algiers in 1941, moving on to Bourges in 1942, then to the École Camondo. He was made a Chevalier of the Ordre des Arts et Lettres. After winning the Prix de l'Art for Algeria, he continued his career there.

Attached to the Musée d'Alger, he realised mural compositions in a number of public buildings. He also designed the first stamp bearing an effigy of Marianne, symbol of the French Republic. Created during World War II, it was in use from 1944 to 1947. A Review in *L'Écho d'Alger* asserted that his style combined a conceptual approach and sensuous colours.

Fernez began to exhibit in Paris in 1920, at the Salon des Artistes Français and the Salon d'Automne, of which he was an associate member. He also featured in the Salon des Tuileries. He showed in many collective exhibitions in Prague, Rome, Brussels, Bucharest, The Hague and in many North-African cities. In 2003, he featured in the collective exhibitions *Lumineuse Algérie, sous le regard des peintres de marines (1830-1960)* (*Luminous Algeria, Through the Eyes of Seascape Painters (1830-1960)*) at the Musée National de la Marine in Toulon and *L'École d'Alger* (*The School of Algiers*) at the Musée des Beaux-Arts in Bordeaux.

BIBLIOGRAPHY:

Barrucand, Victor, *L'Algérie et les Peintres orientalistes*, B. Arthaud éditeur, Grenoble, 1930. Mourot, Marjolaine/Vidal-Bué, Marion/Cazenave, Elisabeth, et al., *Lumineuse Algérie, sous le regard des peintres de marines (1830-1960)*, exhibition catalogue, Musée national de la Marine, Toulon, 2003. Cazenave, Elisabeth/Dalia, Mahammed-Orfali/Vidal-Bué, Marion, *L'École d'Alger*, exhibition catalogue, Musée des Beaux-Arts, Bordeaux, 2003.

MUSEUMS AND GALLERIES:

ALGIERS (Mus. National des Beaux-Arts): *La Place d'Isly à Alger*.

AUCTION RECORDS:

PARIS, 9 Dec 1996, *The Amirauté (Admiralty), Algiers* (gouache, 17 3/4 x 23 1/2 ins / 45 x 60 cm) FRF 7,500. PARIS, 6 Dec 2000, *Landscape with Figures* (1925, oil on canvas, 32 x 39 ins / 81 x 100 cm) FRF 17,000. PARIS, 18 June 2001, *Agha Harbour, Algiers* (oil on canvas laid on panel, 20 x 15 ins / 52 x 37 cm) FRF 22,000.

FERNHOUT, Edgar

Dutch, 20th century.

Born 1912, in Bergen; died 1976, in Bergen.

Painter. Portraits, landscapes, interiors, still-lifes.

Edgar Fernhout was the grandson of the Symbolist painter Jan Toorop and the son of Expressionist painter Charley Toorop, daughter of Jan. He frequently spent time working in Amsterdam, France and Italy. He started painting at the beginning of the 1930s in Amsterdam, having his first solo exhibition there in 1932, followed by others in the Netherlands and abroad. After the death of his mother in 1955, he set up again in Bergen.

In his first period, influenced by the paintings of his mother, he painted deserted interiors, often based on the theme of the *Open Window* such as his work of that title of 1933, and portraits, such as *Self-portrait with Rachel* of 1932. His landscapes of this period show strange tormented vegetation, in a register of bluish-green tones, in which there is an echo of the work of Jan Toorop, in spite of his Realist method of working which is near to the German *Neue Sachlichkeit* (*new objectivity*). In the following period, back in Bergen after the death of his mother, he painted happier compositions, inspired by the landscapes of dunes under blue skies. Using a Pontillist technique and harmonies of tones near to monochrome these works leaned towards a personal geometric abstraction. Certain sources, several of which diverge on the whole course of his work, mention a return to Realism in his last years.

BIBLIOGRAPHY:

Van der Berk, Aloys/Moerbeek, Jozien/Steen, John, *Fernhout Schilder: Schilderr*, exhibition catalogue, SDU, Amsterdam, 1990.

MUSEUMS AND GALLERIES:

UTRECHT (Centraal Mus.): *Self-portrait with Rachel* (1932).

AUCTION RECORDS:

AMSTERDAM, 1 Nov 1977, *Still-life* (1944, oil on panel, 13 3/4 x 16 1/2 ins / 35 x 42 cm) NLG 5,400. AMSTERDAM, 19 Nov 1984, *Autumn* (1967, oil on canvas, 35 1/2 x 39 1/4 ins / 90 x 100 cm) NLG 16,000. AMSTERDAM, 10 April 1989, *Self-portrait* (1937, oil on canvas, 15 3/4 x 13 3/4 ins / 40 x 35 cm) NLG 21,850. AMSTERDAM, 24 May 1989, *White Roses* (1936, oil on canvas, 11 3/4 x 9 3/4 ins / 30 x 25 cm) NLG 6,325. AMSTERDAM, 11 Sept 1990, *Young Woman with a Hat* (1949, oil on canvas, 23 1/2 x 19 3/4 ins / 60 x 50 cm) NLG 4,600. AMSTERDAM, 12 Dec 1990, *Spring Landscape* (1941, oil on canvas, 23 1/2 x 28 1/4 ins / 60 x 72 cm) NLG 7,475. AMSTERDAM, 13 Dec 1990, *Landscape in the Area around Bergen* (1955, oil on canvas, 25 3/4 x 39 1/4 ins / 65.5 x 100 cm) NLG 14,950. AMSTERDAM, 12 Dec 1991, *Sheep's Skull* (1940, oil on canvas/panel, 11 1/2 x 15 3/4 ins / 29.5 x 40 cm) NLG 19,550. AMSTERDAM, 9 Dec 1992, *Shellfish* (1937, oil on canvas, 13 3/4 x 13 3/4 ins / 35 x 35 cm) NLG 13,800. AMSTERDAM, 26 May 1993, *Self-portrait in front of Trees in Spring* (1938, oil on canvas, 24 x 21 ins / 61 x 52.5 cm) NLG 10,925. AMSTERDAM, 30 May 1995, *Self-portrait* (1948, oil on canvas, 31 1/2 x 20 3/4 ins / 80 x 53 cm) NLG 93,750. AMSTERDAM, 4 June 1996, *Winter* (1964, oil on canvas, 32 x 29 1/2 ins / 81 x 75 cm) NLG 44,840. AMSTERDAM, 17-18 Dec 1996, *Still-life with Little Bottles and Tubes of Paint* (1943, oil on panel, 9 x 8 3/4 ins / 23 x 22.5 cm) NLG 51,920. AMSTERDAM, 1 Dec 1997, *Spring Landscape* (1949-1950, oil on canvas, 22 1/2 x 27 3/4 ins / 57 x 70.5 cm) NLG 11,800. AMSTERDAM, 10 June 1999, *Stilleven met verflap* (1946, oil on canvas, 21 x 15 ins / 54 x 38 cm) NLG 42,000. AMSTERDAM, 1 Dec 1999, *Autumn* (1973, oil on canvas, 31 x 31 ins / 80 x 80 cm) NLG 200,000. ROTTERDAM, 23 April 2002, *Still-life with Artist's Canvas and Bottles* (1949, oil on canvas, 19 x 15 ins / 48 x 38 cm) EUR 33,000. AMSTERDAM, 26 Nov 2002, *Flowers* (1948, oil on panel, 16 x 18 ins / 40 x 45 cm) EUR 7,000. AMSTERDAM, 8 June 2004, *Still-life with Pears* (1932, oil on canvas, 16 x 16 ins / 40 x 40 cm) EUR 35,000. AMSTERDAM, 30 Nov 2004, *Skull* (1935, oil on canvas, 22 x 18 ins / 55 x 46 cm) EUR 82,000.

FERNICKEN. See **VERNUCKEN**

FERNIER, Gabrielle

French, 19th century.
Born 19th century, in Paris.
Painter.

Fernier exhibited gouaches for fans and small watercolours of flowers at the Salon from 1868 to 1878.

FERNIER, Robert

French, 20th century.
Born 26 July 1895, in Pontalier; died 27 March or May 1977, in Goux-les-Usiers.
Painter, watercolourist, illustrator. Landscapes. Orientalism.

Robert Fernier studied under Fernand Cormon. When in Paris, between 1923 and 1949, he exhibited at the Salon des Artistes Français, gaining a gold medal in 1932; from 1950 onwards, he exhibited at the Salon des Artistes Indépendants. In 1953, he was awarded the Prix de Madagascar. He was also a writer and had a cultural impact in his capacity as president of the Association des Amis de Gustave Courbet and organizer of the *Salon des Annonciades de Pontarlier*. He illustrated Alphonse Gaillard's *L'Amour au village. Nouvelles et récits du Haut-Jura* (*Country Love. Stories and Tales from the Haut-Jura*); Jules Mathez' *Annales du château de Joux et de la Seigneurerie de ce nom* (*Annals of the Castle of Joux and the Fiefdom of that Name*) (1932); *Histoire de la ville de Pontarlier des origines à 1790* (*A History of the City of Pontarlier from its Origins to 1790*) (1930).

He is best remembered for his depiction of his native Jura landscapes, but he also worked in Tahiti and Madagascar (1953-1958), and toured Morocco and Algeria.

Solo exhibitions include one in Pontarlier (1969); and, in 1955, *Fernier 'Racines'* (*'Roots'*) in the Musée Gustave Courbet, Ormans. Collective thematic exhibitions include one in 2002, *Ils furent tous attirés par le Sud et par l'Orient. Les Artistes comtois voyageurs* (*All were Drawn to the South and the East. Comtois Artists on their Travels*), Musée d'Art et d'Histoire, Montbéliard.

ROBERT FERNIER

BIBLIOGRAPHY:

Bailly, Auguste, *Robert Fernier, peintre de la neige, peintre du Jura*, Laboratoire Chantereau, Paris, 1955. *50 ans de peinture par Robert Fernier*, exhibition catalogue, Chapelle des Annonciades, Pontarlier, 1969. Humbert, Chantal/Fernier, Robert, *Robert Fernier racines'*, exhibition catalogue, Musée Gustave-Courbet, Ornans, 1995.

AUCTION RECORDS:

PARIS, 18 June 1990, *View of Vuittebœuf in the Swiss Jura* (oil on canvas, 15 x 18 ins / 38 x 46 cm) FRF 5,000. LONS-LE-SAUNIER, 19 June 1994, *Snowfall at Noirvaux* (oil on canvas, 19 3/4 x 25 1/2 ins / 50 x 65 cm) FRF 35,000. PARIS, 29 March 1996, *The Grand'combe* (oil on panel, 13 x 16 1/4 ins / 33 x 41 cm) FRF 12,500. ZURICH, 12 Nov 1996, *Still-life* (oil on canvas, 19 3/4 x 24 ins / 50 x 61 cm) CHF 2,600. BERN, 1 May 2002, *Peonies* (oil on canvas, 20 x 24 ins / 50 x 61 cm) CHF 4,000. BERN, 1 May 2002, *Les Hopitaux Neufs* (oil on board, 13 x 16 ins / 32 x 41 cm) CHF 4,000. MONTREAL, 12 Feb 2003, *Tide Coming In, Moroni, May 1954* (oil on panel, 20 x 24 ins / 50 x 61 cm) CAD 2,900. BERN, 7 May 2003, *Landscape at Betafo* (1953, oil on panel, 13 x 16 ins / 33 x 41 cm) CHF 2,600.

FERNKORN, Anton von

German, 19th century.
Born 1813, in Erfurt; died 1878, in Vienna.
Sculptor.

The Hamburg museum holds one of Fernkorn's works: *Bust of Emperor Franz-Joseph of Austria.*

FERNLAY

Norwegian, 19th century.
Born in Frederikshald (now Halden).
Active c. 1805.
Painter. Landscapes.

FERNLUND, Peter Petrovich
Russian, 19th century.
Painter.
A student, then professor of drawing at the St Petersburg academy of fine arts, Ferlund exhibited some portraits at the academy exhibition of 1872.

FERNOW, B.
American, 20th century.
Born 17 December 1881, in Jersey City (New Jersey).
Painter, miniaturist. Portraits.

FERNOW, Carl Ludwig
German, 18th century.
Born 19 November 1763, in Blumenhagen; died 4 December 1808, in Weimar (Thuringia).
Painter, art writer.
Fernow was librarian to the Duchess Amelia in Weimar. His work *Life of the Artist A.J. Carsten* is illustrated by a portrait of the master, drawn by C.L. Fernow and printed by H. Lips.

FERNSTEIN, Joseph von
Luxembourg, 18th century.
Born to a family originally from Luxembourg.
Engraver.
Joseph von Fernstein is documented as having attended the academy in Vienna in 1759, and the specialist school of engraving, founded by Schmutzer, in 1766.

FERNY, A. van
Dutch, 18th century.
Active in Middelburg.
Painter.

FEROGIO, François Fortuné Antoine
French, 19th century.
Born 2 April 1805, in Marseilles; died 1888, in Paris.
Painter, watercolourist, pastellist, engraver. Scenes with figures.
Ferogio entered the École des Beaux-Arts on 2 April 1825 and trained under Gros. He exhibited at the Paris Salon from 1831 to 1880. He painted mainly in pastels and watercolours. He also produced steel engravings and lithographs and occasional paintings on earthenware.
MUSEUMS AND GALLERIES:
LA ROCHELLE: *Village Fair* - MONTPELLIER: *Donkey Fair.*
AUCTION RECORDS:
PARIS, 13 June 1934, *Sheet with Ten Subjects* (sepia wash) FRF 60. VERSAILLES, 10 Oct 1981, *People by Ruins* (watercolour, 16 1/4 x 23 1/2 ins / 41.5 x 59.5 cm) FRF 2,200. PARIS, 15 April 1996, *Snack* (pastel, 9 x 16 3/4 ins / 22 x 42.5 cm) FRF 6,000. LUCERNE, 2 May 2001, *River Landscape with Stone Bridge* (oil on canvas, 9 x 13 ins / 24 x 32 cm) CHF 2,500.

FEROLDI, Charles Henri, called Carlo
French, 19th - 20th century.
Born in Lyons.
Painter.
From 1897, Charles Feroldi exhibited portraits, figures and landscapes in Lyons.

FEROLZ, Hanns
Austrian, 17th century.
Active in Vienna.
Sculptor.

FERON, Caroline
Flemish, 19th century.
Born in Brussels.
Active c. 1845.
Painter. Genre scenes, portraits.
Flemish School.
Caroline Feron studied under Navez.

FÉRON, Éloi Firmin
French, 19th century.
Born 1 December 1802, in Paris; died 1876, in Conflans-Ste-Honorine.
Painter. History painting, portraits, genre scenes, landscapes.
Feron entered the École des Beaux-Arts on 27 August 1818 and trained under Gros. In 1823 he received the second prize in the competition *Concours de Rome*, with *Aegisthus, Expecting to Recover the Body of Orestes, Finds the Body of Clytemnestra*. In 1826 he won the first prize with *Pythias, Damon and Denis the Tyrant.* He received a first-class medal in 1835. On 19 January 1841, he received the Cross of the Légion d'Honneur. He exhibited at the Paris Salon from 1833 to 1855.
MUSEUMS AND GALLERIES:
ARRAS: *Winning Athlete Dying in the Amphitheatre; Pompey Soldier* - MARSEILLES: *Hannibal Crossing the Alps* - STRASBOURG: *Kleber's Funeral in Egypt* - VERSAILLES: *Full-length Portrait of Du Guesclin; Triumphant Entrance of Charles the Eighth into Naples on 12 May 1495; Battle of Guntersdorf on 16 November 1805; Battle of Fornovo on 16 July 1485; Capture of Rhodes on 15 August 1310; Battle of Arsar in 1191; Battle of Putaka in 1159; Battle of Hanau on 30 October 1813; Full-length Portrait of Marshall Gilles de Laval; Portrait of Marshall Montfort de Laval on Horseback; Portrait of Marshall Charles de Choiseul; Full-length Portrait of Marshall Adrien-Maurice, Duke of Noailles; Portrait of the Count of Montgommery; Portrait of Gaspard de Guzman, Count of Olivarez; Portrait of Henry the Second of Lorraine.*
AUCTION RECORDS:
PARIS, 14 Feb 1931, *Roman Countryside* (attributed) FRF 110. ENGHIEN-LES-BAINS, 14 June 1981, *Cottage by a River* (oil on canvas, 15 x 22 ins / 38 x 55 cm) FRF 4,000. LONDON, 5 Oct 1990, *Ambush* (1844, oil on canvas, 13 x 16 1/4 ins / 33 x 41.2 cm) GBP 4,180. PARIS, 18 June 2001, *Retour du marche* (1845, oil on canvas, 9 x 13 ins / 24 x 33 cm) FRF 11,000. PARIS, 27 June 2002, *Scenes from the Conquest of Algeria* (1846, oil on canvas, a pair, 18 x 24 ins / 45 x 60 cm) EUR 12,000.

FÉRON, Julien Hippolyte
French, 19th - 20th century.
Born 1864, in St-Jean-du-Cardonnay (Seine-Maritime); died 1945.
Painter. Landscapes, waterscapes, urban landscapes, architectural views, still-lifes.
School of Normandy.
Julien Féron studied to be an engineer, and his art was self-taught, inspired by nature. He travelled and worked in Holland, England, Tunisia and Algeria. A painting prize bearing his name was created in 1991 in Normandy.

Féron exhibited at the Salon des Artistes Rouennais from 1906, in Paris at the Salon des Artistes Indépendants from 1908, and at the Salon d'Automne from 1911. He figured posthumously in 2003 in the collective exhibition *Autour de l'Impressionnisme: dix-neuf peintres de l'école normande* (*Around Impressionism: Nineteen Painters from the School of Normandy*) at the Maison des Arts in Antony. He specialised in the representation of Normandy sites he knew well. His broad manner, seeking to account for light through strong oppositions, is reminiscent of Guillaumin. He had a good eye for the changes in light brought about by the time of the day, the weather, or the seasons.
BIBLIOGRAPHY:
Dubosc, Georges, *L'École de Rouen, ses peintres et ses ferronniers*, Lecerf fils, Rouen, 1914. Fournier, Philippe, *Atelier de Marcel Couchaux (1877-1939), dessins, pastels, gouaches, aquarelles, tableaux modernes de lécole rouennaise*, auction catalogue, Rouen, 1968. *L'École de Rouen*, BDS, Rouen, 1972. *École normande, École de Rouen 1870-1930*, exhibition catalogue, Centre culturel du Palais Bénédictine, Fécamp, 1989. Lespinasse, François, *L'École de Rouen*, Lecerf, Rouen, 1995. *L'École de Rouen, de l'impressionnisme à Marcel Duch-*

amp 1878-1914*, exhibition catalogue, Musée des Beaux-Arts, Rouen, 1996. *Autour de l'Impressionnisme: dix-neuf peintres de l'école normande*, exhibition catalogue, La Maison des Arts, Antony, 2003.
AUCTION RECORDS:
LUCERNE, 20 May 1983, *Riverscapes* (two oils on canvas, 7 x 14 1/4 ins / 18 x 36 cm) CHF 2,900. NEUILLY, 20 May 1992, *Landscapes* (1930, oil on canvas, 25 1/2 x 32 ins / 65 x 81 cm) FRF 14,000. NEW YORK, 28 May 1992, *Vase of Flowers and Apples* (1898, oil on canvas, 31 1/2 x 39 ins / 80 x 99.1 cm) USD 11,000. NEUILLY, 9 May 1996, *Rue de l'Épicerie and Rouen Cathedral* (oil on canvas) FRF 4,000.

FÉRON, Paul
French, 20th century.
Painter, watercolourist. Urban landscapes, flowers.
Paul Féron painted very popular views of old Paris, and especially Montmartre.
AUCTION RECORDS:
PARIS, 30 May 1945, *Rue de l'Abreuvoir,* FRF 3,000. PARIS, 24 Feb 1947, *Snow Montmartre,* FRF 5,000. PARIS, 15 March 1988, *Rue des Ursins* (watercolour, 7 x 5 1/2 ins / 18 x 14 cm) FRF 1,500.

FÉRON, Sylvie. See **BAUCHER-FÉRON**

FÉRON, Thomas
French, 18th century.
Active in Paris in 1757.
Painter, sculptor.

FÉRON, William
Swedish, 19th century.
Born 25 October 1858, in Stockholm; died 25 June 1894, in Stockholm.
Painter. Figures, landscapes.
William Féron studied in Stockholm and in Paris, where he exhibited at the Salon de la Société des Artistes Français with *Washerwomen from Brittany* (1881), *Italian Woman* (1882) and *Norman Peasant* (1885). He also showed at exhibitions in Stockholm and Göteborg.
MUSEUMS AND GALLERIES:
STOCKHOLM: *Young Girl in the Garden.*
AUCTION RECORDS:
GÖTEBORG, 9 Nov 1983, *Woman with Parasol* (1886, oil on canvas, 35 1/2 x 51 1/4 ins / 90 x 130 cm) SEK 22,000. STOCKHOLM, 13 Nov 1987, *Young Courtier* (oil on canvas, 43 x 28 1/4 ins / 109 x 72 cm) SEK 25,000. STOCKHOLM, 15 Nov 1988, *The Break, Young Woman Standing Holding a Shovel* (oil, 21 1/4 x 14 1/2 ins / 54 x 37 cm) SEK 15,000. LONDON, 17 June 1994, *Mama's Party* (1886, oil on canvas, 35 1/4 x 51 1/4 ins / 89.5 x 130.2 cm) GBP 11,500. NEW YORK, 12 Oct 1994, *Elegant Woman in Paris* (oil on canvas, 21 1/4 x 12 1/4 ins / 54 x 31 cm) USD 10,350. LONDON, 21 Nov 1997, *Madeleine* (1882, oil on canvas, 51 1/2 x 32 1/4 ins / 130.8 x 81.9 cm) GBP 8,625. COPENHAGEN, 3 March 1998, *Sailing Boats in the Lagoon off Venice* (oil on canvas, 26 x 36 ins / 65 x 92 cm) DKK 18,000. STOCKHOLM, 3 Dec 2002, *At the Garden Plot* (oil on canvas, 22 x 32 ins / 57 x 81 cm) SEK 50,000. CREWKERNE, 22 April 2004, *Figures on a Beach* (oil on canvas, 9 x 13 ins / 23 x 34 cm) GBP 3,800.

FERONI, Caterina (Marchioness)
Italian, 19th century.
Painter.
Caterina Feroni is known for a painting of the *Virgin* in the chapel of S Maria e S Giovanni in Malcavolo, and a *Mother of the Seven Sorrows* in the parish of San Galgano, Monte Siepi (in the province of Siena).

FERONI, Paolo (Marquis)
Italian, 19th century.
Died c. 1864.
Painter.
MUSEUMS AND GALLERIES:
FLORENCE (Gal. d'Arte Moderna (Palazzo Pitti)): *Portrait of the Painter Antonio Marini.*
AUCTION RECORDS:
LUCERNE, 30 Sept 1988, *Romeo and Juliet* (1841, oil on canvas, 34 1/4 x 46 ins / 87 x 117 cm) CHF 3,800.

FERRABECH, Giovanni. See **FERABECH**

FERRABOSCO. See also **FERABOSCO** and **FORABOSCO**

FERRABOSCO, Girolamo or Gerolamo, or Ferabosco, Forabosco
Italian, 17th century.
Born in Padua; died after 1675, in Venice.
Painter. Religious subjects, allegorical subjects, portraits.
Girolamo Ferrabosco is recorded as living and working in Venice from 1631 to 1659. His contemporary, Boschini, described him (and Cavaliere Liberi) as among the first rank of painters in his day. His particular forte was portraiture, where he exhibited an uncommon degree of expressiveness and sensitivity. He worked extensively for private collections.
MUSEUMS AND GALLERIES:
DRESDEN: *Young Woman Saved from Death* - FLORENCE (Uffizi): *Self-portrait; Rest during the Flight into Egypt* (pen drawing) - ROVIGO (Pinacoteca): *Joseph and Potiphar* - VENICE (Gal. dell'Accademia): *David Holding the Head of Goliath* - VIENNA (Liechtenstein Mus.): *David Holding the Head of Goliath.*
AUCTION RECORDS:
LONDON, 2 Aug 1939, *Woman,* GBP 8. MILAN, 27 Nov 1984, *Allegory of Temptation* (oil on canvas, 55 x 69 1/4in/140 x 176cm) ITL 12,000,000. ROME, 24 May 1988, *Portrait of a Young Woman with Rosebud* (oil on canvas, 22 3/4 x 20in/58 x 51cm) ITL 8,000,000.

FERRACCI, Antoine
French, 20th century.
Born 10 October 1890, in Bonifacio, Corsica.
Painter.
Antoine Ferracci studied under Luc-Olivier Merson, Fernand Cormon and Raphaël Collin. He made his debut in Paris at the Salon des Artistes Français in 1920 and gained an honourable mention in 1921.

FERRACINA, Giovanni Battista
Italian, 19th century.
Born in Salagna, near Bassano (Veneto); died 1830.
Painter.

FERRACINO, Francesco
Italian, 16th century.
Active in Padua.
Sculptor.

FERRACUTI
Italian, 18th century.
Painter.
He worked in Austria around 1870. His *Society Figures in the Park* can be found at the castle of Neuwaldegg near Vienna.

FERRACUTI, Giovanni Domenico
Italian, 17th century.
Born in Macerata, according to Lanzi.
Painter.
Giovanni Ferracuti was highly regarded in his day as a landscape painter, notably of winter views.

FERRADO, Cristóbal
Spanish, 17th century.
Born 1620, in Anieva; died 1673, in Seville.
Painter. Religious subjects.

School of Seville.
Cristóbal Ferrado received excellent instruction from an unknown master and went on to train alone. In 1640 he became a monk and entered the order of Sta Maria de las Cuevas near Seville. He painted a number of works for altars at his monastery. Several of his paintings are now in the monastery of S Miguel in Seville, others have been transferred to the Alcazar.

FERRAGSANI
Italian.
Draughtsman.
MUSEUMS AND GALLERIES:
RENNES: a study.

FERRAGUTI, Arnaldo
Italian, 19th - 20th century.
Born 17 April 1862, in Ferrara; died 1925, in Forlì.
Painter. Genre scenes.
Arnaldo Ferraguti lived and worked in Rome. He participated in various group exhibitions and won silver medals in Nice in 1884 and Ferrara in 1885. He also exhibited in Dresden, Munich and Vienna between 1887 and 1889.

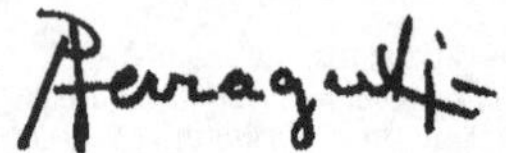

AUCTION RECORDS:
LONDON, 8 Oct 1982, *Washerwoman* (oil on canvas, 25 3/4 x 16 ins / 65.4 x 40.6 cm) GBP 500. LONDON, 20 June 1985, *In the Wings* (pastel and charcoal, 25 1/2 x 21 ins / 64.5 x 52.5 cm) GBP 1,300. MILAN, 8 March 1990, *Ballerinas in a Dressing Room* (pastel/paper, 32 x 22 1/2 ins / 81.5 x 57 cm) ITL 18,000,000. MONACO, 21 April 1990, *Family on a Country Road* (oil on canvas, 26 1/2 x 32 1/4 ins / 67 x 82 cm) FRF 105,450. NEW YORK, 22-23 July 1993, *Little Girl in the Woods* (oil on canvas, 29 1/4 x 19 3/4 ins / 74 x 50.2 cm) USD 5,175. LONDON, 1 Dec 1999, *Ballerinas in the Dressing Room* (pastel on card, 31 x 22 ins / 80 x 57 cm) GBP 12,000. LONDON, 1 Nov 2001, *Roman Campagna* (oil on canvas, 29 x 66 ins / 74 x 168 cm) GBP 2,300. MILAN, 28 Oct 2002, *Bather* (mixed media, 19 x 14 ins / 47 x 35 cm) EUR 4,000. ROME, 11 June 2003, *Povera Nini* (oil on canvas, 29 x 49 ins / 73 x 125 cm) EUR 25,000. MILAN, 29 Oct 2003, *Portrait of a Lady* (mixed media, 18 x 21 ins / 45 x 54 cm) EUR 2,700. LONDON, 16 June 2004, *Children in a Meadow* (oil on canvas, 16 x 12 ins / 40x31 cm) GBP 3,227. LONDON, 16 June 2004, *Children in a Meadow* (oil on canvas, 16 x 12 ins / 40 x 31 cm) GBP 2,700.

FERRAJUOLI, Nunzio, or Ferraioli, also known as Nunzio degli Afflitti
Italian, 17th - 18th century.
Born 1661, in Nocera dei Pagani; died 1735, in Bologna.
Painter. History painting, landscapes with figures.
He worked with Luca Giordano and Giuseppe del Sole. Initially a painter of historical subjects, he later turned to landscape work.
AUCTION RECORDS:
MILAN, 27 March 1990, *Landscape with Figures at Sunset* (oil on canvas, 48 x 59 3/4in/121 x 152cm) ITL 20,000,000.

FERRAMOLA, Benedetto
Italian, 16th century.
Born 1541; died after 1588.
Painter.
The son of Giovanni Giacomo Ferramola II, Benedetto Ferramola worked in Brescia.

FERRAMOLA, Floriano or Fioravante
Italian, 16th century.
Born before 1480, in Brescia; died 1528, in Brescia.
Painter. History painting.
Floriano Ferramola was the son of Lorenzo Ferramola, father of Giovanni Giacomo II and Giovanni Antonio, and master of Alessandro Bonvicini (Moretto). Rossi relates that at the time of the sacking of Brescia by Gaston de Foix in 1512 Ferramola continued to paint while soldiers looted his home. When they demanded a ransom, he told them they could help themselves, which they did, causing considerable damage. Luckily for Ferramola, Gaston de Foix heard of his fame and commissioned him to carry out his portrait, compensating him for the losses he suffered.

Very little of Ferramola's output survives. In 1514, he painted the *Apostles* in S Maria in Valvendra di Lovere (Bergamo) and between 1515 and 1518 decorated the chest and shutters of the organ of the Duomo Vecchio at Brescia. In 1527 he completed the frescoes at the church of S Giulia at Brescia with a painter named Paolo. In the same year he collaborated with his pupil Moretto on the Cappella delle SS Croci in the Duomo Vecchio. Several other works in Brescia have been attributed to him; in the church of S Maria in Valvendra di Lovere are frescoes dated 1514 and an *Annunciation* of 1518.

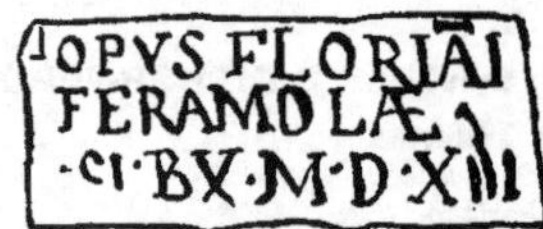

BIBLIOGRAPHY:
Morassi, A., *Brescia; Catalogo delle Cose d'Arte*, Libreria dello Stato, Rome, 1939. Vannini, L., *Brescia nella Storia e nell'Arte*, Brescia, 1971. *Nel Lume del Rinascimento. Dipinti, Sculture ed Oggetti dalla Diocesi di Brescia*, exhibition catalogue, Museo diocesano d'arte sacra, Brescia, 1997.
MUSEUMS AND GALLERIES:
BERLIN (Bodemus.): *Madonna and Saints* (1513).

FERRAMOLA, Giovanni Antonio
Italian, 16th century.
Born 1516.
Active in Brescia.
Painter.
Giovanni Antonio Ferramola was the younger son of Floriano Ferramola.

FERRAMOLA, Giovanni Giacomo I
Italian, 15th - 16th century.
Active in Brescia in 1513.
Painter.
Giovanni Giacomo Ferramola I was probably the brother of Floriano Ferramola.

FERRAMOLA, Giovanni Giacomo II
Italian, 16th century.
Born 1508; died after 1568.
Active in Brescia.
Painter.
Giovanni Giacomo Ferramola II was the elder brother of Floriano Ferramola.

FERRAMONTI, Lorenzo
Flemish, 18th century.
Died 1715, in Piacenza, Italy.
Painter.
Flemish School.
Lorenzo Ferramonti was a painter attached to the Palazzo Farnese.

FERRAN, Adriano
Spanish, 19th century.
Sculptor.
Adriano Ferran studied at the school of fine arts in Barcelona and moved to Palma, Majorca, where he produced many

statues of saints and altars for the churches of Sta Eulalia and S Nicholas and the high altar of the church of the Carthusian monastery of Valldemossa near Palma. He received an award at the Barcelona exhibition of 1815.

FERRAN, Antonio
Spanish, 19th century.
Born 1786, in Barcelona; died 1857, in Barcelona.
Painter. History painting.

Antonio Ferran studied drawing at the Casa Lonja and later became a teacher there. He is known for his *Socrates Drinking Hemlock*; *Bacchante*; and *Petrarch and Laura*. He exhibited in Madrid, Barcelona and Paris in 1855. Five of his works are in the museum in Barcelona. they include *Vulcan's Forge*; *St Jerome*; and *Othello Recounting his Exploits*.

FERRAN, Augusto
Spanish, 19th century.
Born 1813, in Palma, Majorca; died 28 June 1879, in Havana.
Sculptor. Historical figures. Busts.

Augusto Ferran produced many busts and exhibited regularly in Madrid.

MUSEUMS AND GALLERIES:
MADRID (Art School): *Queen Maria Cristina of Spain* (bust).

FERRAN, Manuel, or Ferrant
Spanish, 19th century.
Born in the 19th century, in Barcelona.
Painter. History painting, genre scenes.

Manuel Ferran studied under T. Couture in Paris. He is known for his *Liberation of Antonio Perez* and *Carnival in the Latin Quarter*.

MUSEUMS AND GALLERIES:
BARCELONA: several paintings - MADRID: *Philip III of France on his Death Bed Blessing his Sons*.

FERRAND, Adèle (Mme)
Maiden name: Marcel
French, 19th century.
Born 20 April 1807, in Massieu (Ain).
Miniaturist.

Adèle Ferrand was a pupil of Juine and Mme Jacotot and a painter at the Manufacture de Sèvres. She exhibited oil paintings and paintings on porcelain (portraits, historical subjects and genre scenes) in Paris from 1831 to 1846. Works include the portrait *Marie-Antoinette*.

FERRAND, Alexandre Jean Baptiste
French, 19th century.
Born 19 February 1786, in Versailles.
Painter.

Alexandre Ferrand entered the École des Beaux-Arts on 28 August 1810 and became the pupil of Regnault.

FERRAND, Arnould
French, 17th century.
Born to a family originally from Tours.
Painter, glass painter.

In 1601 Arnould Ferrand executed paintings in the tabernacle of the church of Ligré, near Chinon, as well as paintings on glass for the chapel and château of Champigny.

FERRAND, Ennemond
French, 19th century.
Born 29 January 1829, in Lyons.
Painter.

Ennemond Ferrand was a pupil of Régnier at the École des Beaux-Arts in Lyons. He exhibited still-lifes at the Paris Salon in 1878 and in Lyons in 1881.

FERRAND, Ernest Justin
French, 19th - 20th century.
Born 6 November 1846, in Paris; died 1932.
Sculptor. Statues.

Ernest Ferrand studied under Levasseur and Mathurin Moreau. He became a member of the Société des Artistes Français in 1891.

MUSEUMS AND GALLERIES:
CLAMECY: *Morning* (terracotta) - ROUEN: *By the Sword and by the Plough shares*.

AUCTION RECORDS:
LOS ANGELES, 21 June 1977, *The Fisherman* (bronze, h. 44 ins / 112 cm) USD 1,400. LONDON, 20 June 1985, *The Huntsman* (green-patinated bronze, h. 46 ins / 117 cm) GBP 1,800. LOKEREN, 9 Dec 1995, *Harpoon Fisherman* (bronze, h. 31 1/2 ins / 80 cm) BEF 48,000. NEW YORK, 9 Jan 1997, *Neptune* (brown-patinated bronze, h. 43 1/2 ins / 110.5 cm) USD 6,037.

FERRAND, Étienne
French, 19th century.
Active in Paris.
Painter.

Étienne Ferrand became a member of the Société des Artistes Français in 1886 and exhibited at the society's Salon.

FERRAND, Francis
French, 20th century.
Born in Paris.
Painter, engraver. Local scenes.

After 1926, Francis Ferrand exhibited in Paris, at the Salon d'Automne and at the Salon des Artistes Indépendants.

He mostly treated cafés and circus scenes.

FERRAND, François
French, 18th century.
Born to a family originally from Nantes.
Engraver.

François Ferrand engraved after J. A. Portail a portrait of *Gérard Mélier*, Mayor of Nantes.

FERRAND, François Augustin
French, 20th century.
Born 28 August 1877, in St-Sétiers (Corrèze); died 7 February 1953, in Paris.
Engraver (burin).

François Ferrand exhibited at the Salon des Artistes Français, of which he had been a member in 1906, the same year he received an honourable mention.

FERRAND, Gabrielle
French, 20th century.
Born 1887, in Bordeaux; died 1984.
Painter, watercolourist, engraver. Landscapes with figures.

Gabrielle Ferrand studied at the Académie des Beaux Arts in Bordeaux. A great traveller and a painter, she cut an unusual figure in the France of her days. Reaching Indonesia in 1922, she travelled over Java and Bali for three years. The paintings she took home enabled her to popularise Indonesian culture through exhibitions, talks and newspaper articles.

From 1923 to 1936, she featured in the Bataviasche Kunstkring exhibitions. She had been exhibiting in Paris, from 1926, at the Salon of the Société Nationale des Beaux Arts and the Salon d'Automne. She produced watercolours, drawings and paintings, engraved wood, and wrote several books.

AUCTION RECORDS:
SINGAPORE, 5 Oct 1996, *Main Street of a Town in Asia* (oil on card, 15 1/2 x 20 1/2 ins / 39.5 x 52 cm) SGD 8,200.

FERRAND, Jacques
French, 20th century.
Born 18 April 1911.
Illustrator, miniaturist.

Jacques Ferrand grew up under the spell of *Images d'épinal* (19th-century prints depicting stereotypical scenes of everyday life) and romantic picture books, and he became an illustrator in whose work technique and poetry are mingled. He has illustrated: by Gérard de Nerval, *Sylvie* (Librairie de l'Arc, 1937) and *Poèmes* (Librairie Marceau, 1944); by Louise Faure-Favier, *Notre Île St-Louis* (Éd. Montjoie, 1946); by Aubry, *Lady Hamilton* (Éd. françaises, 1946) and *Monsieur Poivre* (Plaisir de France, 1946); by Charles Nodier, *La Fée aux miettes* (*The Crumbs Fairy*) (José Corti, 1947); by Sacha Guitry, *Le Soir d'Austerlitz* (*The Night of Austerlitz*) (Éd. du Trèfle, 1947) and *N'écoutez pas Mesdames* (*Ladies, Do Not Listen*) (1950); by La Fontaine, *Fables* (1948); two works by Gisèle d'Assailly, including *Savoir-vivre tous les jours* (*Everyday Good Manners*) (Mame, 1951); by Daniel de Foe, *Robinson Crusoë* (Mame, 1951); and, by Oscar Wilde, *L'Enfant étoile* (*The Star-Child*) (Mame, 1952).

BIBLIOGRAPHY:

'*Chez Jacques Ferrand*' in *Plaisir de France*, periodical, Paris, Jan-Feb 1946. '*Le Monde à l'envers*' in *Art et Industrie* n° 14, periodical, Paris, 1949. Laran, Jean, *L'Estampe*, Presses universitaires de France, Paris, 1959.

FERRAND, Jacques Philippe

French, 17th - 18th century.
Born 25 July 1653, in Joigny (Yonne); died 5 January 1732, in Paris.
Painter.

Jacques Philippe Ferrand was the pupil of Mignard and of Samuel Bernard, and was admitted as an academician on 27 May 1699. He made several journeys to Germany and England. In 1699 he went to Turin and executed several works for the Duke of Savoy. War obliged him to return to France where he remained until the peace of 1696. Recalled to Savoy by the Duke, he painted a fine portrait of him. From Turin he went to Genoa where he was showered with honours. He then went to Florence and on to Rome. He stayed in Rome for 13 months, during which time he painted portraits of *Pope Innocent XII* and *Princess Pamphila*, as well as other dignitaries of note, which increased his reputation. When returning to France he again stopped in Turin for some months and finally arrived in Paris on Christmas Day, 1699.

FERRAND, Jean-Pierre

French, 20th century.
Born 1902, in Libourne; died 18 May 1983, in Ponthierry (Seine-et-Marne).
Painter. Landscapes.

Jean-Pierre Ferrand studied at the École des Beaux-Arts in Bordeaux, then under Fernand Cormon in Paris. He has painted the landscapes of many French regions and, more particularly, of the Seine-et-Marne near Paris. He exhibited in Paris at the Salon des Artistes Français, of which he was a member. In 1952, he won a silver medal, and, in 1956, a gold medal hors concours (as he was ineligible to compete on account of the number of distinctions he had already received). He has shown his work in numerous personal exhibitions in Paris, Lyons, St-Étienne, Lille, Amiens, Marseilles and Dijon.

AUCTION RECORDS:

AUXERRE, 2 July 1989, *Corn Field* (oil on canvas, 13 1/4 x 16 1/4 ins / 33.5 x 41 cm) FRF 24,000; *Interior Scene* (oil on canvas, 23 1/2 x 28 1/4 ins / 60 x 72 cm) FRF 34,000.

FERRAND, Jules Georges

French, 19th century.
Born 19th century, in Nancy.
Painter.

Jules Ferrand was a pupil of Paul Delaroche and exhibited landscapes and some portraits of private individuals at the Paris Salon from 1837 to 1857. Works include *View around Nancy*, *View near St-Maur* and *Farm Valley*

FERRAND, Louis

French, 20th century.
Born 8 January 1905, in Belle-Île (Morbihan); died 4 April 1992, in Nantes.
Painter (gouache), pastellist, draughtsman, engraver.
Religious subjects, landscapes.

Louis Ferrand was admitted (in 1921) to the Nantes École des Beaux-Arts, where he would teach from 1951 to 1974.

As early as 1939, his figuration took a religious turn, and his familiar visions of Christ owed something to Maurice Denis. Soon, the Franciscan themes Ferrand was to explore would appear in many of his canvases and wood engravings. Until 1957, he developed a very personal technique using diluted oil, treated in such a way as to create the illusion of charcoal drawings. However, Louis Ferrand did not neglect other techniques, be they oil, acrylics or pastel; in many paintings, he employed India ink and charcoal (such as his *Circus Series*, 1955-1975). In the 1960s, he also performed line-engraving on copper and zinc. In 1964, he shifted to abstract landscapes, inspired by islands, sea and brooks, as in his canvases *Sea Foams*, *Signs of the Rock* and *Salted Stream*. Painted in sets, sometimes over several years, many canvases bear the name of a village or port of Belle-Île, a testimony to Ferrand's love of his native soil. His *Domois*, from 1975-1976, a set of 14 paintings of the Kerguelen islands produced towards the end of his life, verge on monochromy.

In Nantes, he showed in Galerie Mignon Massard from 1927 to 1939, then in Galerie Michel Colomb nearly every year from 1949 to 1979. Nantes Musée des Beaux-Arts dedicated a major exhibition to him in 1976. His last exhibitions took place in Paris in Galerie Galarté in 1983 and 1986, and in Galerie Convergence in 1984, 1988 and 1991.

BIBLIOGRAPHY:

L'Écume de l'air, Les Amis de l'Archipel, Nantes, 1973 (with twelve drawings by Louis Ferrand). *Louis Ferrand*, exhibition catalogue, Musée des Beaux-Arts, Nantes, 1976.

FERRAND, Nicolas Robert

French, 18th century.
Active in Paris in 1748.
Painter, sculptor.

FERRAND, P. A.

Swiss, 20th - 21st century.
Born 1952, in Geneva.
Painter.

Ferrand lives and works in Geneva and La Chaux-de-Fonds. His painting is based on the notion of poverty. One or two vertical forms respect those in the picture plan, which he would sometimes make concave or convex in the 1990s, whilst subtle shades, almost colourless, hazy and solemn, nevertheless attract the light.

He has participated in group exhibitions, including: 1991, *Extra Muros* at the Musée des Beaux-Arts de La Chaux-de-Fonds and the Espace Lyonnais d'Art Contemporain, Lyons; 1997, *Abstraction/Abstractions. Géométries Provisoires* (*Abstraction/Abstractions - Provisional Geometry*) at the Musée d'Art Moderne, St Étienne. He also has held private shows: 1989, Kunsthalle, Winterthur; 1996, Galerie Patrick Roy, Lausanne.

BIBLIOGRAPHY:

Ceysson, Bernard/Chassey, Éric de/Morineau, Camille, *Abstraction/Abstractions. Géométries provisoires*, exhibition catalogue, Musée d'Art moderne, St-Étienne, 1997.

FERRAND, Patrice

French, 20th - 21st century.
Born 9 July 1946, in Paris.
Intervention artist, sculptor.
Kinetic Art.

Patrice Ferrand has staged kinetic art shows, and has exhibited inflatable structures.

FERRAND, Pierre François
French, 18th century.
Born 1722, in Paris; died 12 February 1800, in Paris.
Sculptor.
Pierre François Ferrand is probably identical to the sculptor Pierre Ferand or Ferrand admitted to the Académie de St-Luc in Paris on 14 August 1753.

FERRAND, V.
French, 18th century.
Draughtsman, engraver.
V. Ferrand is possibly identical to the engraver of vignettes Ferrand who engraved the frontispiece of the *Manuel Typographique* (*Typographical Manual*) by Fournier. He published *Un Cahier de Fleurs Utiles aux Dessinateurs* (*A Sketchbook of Useful Flowers for Illustrators*) which includes five plates.

FERRAND DE MONTHELON, Antoine
French, 18th century.
Born 11 April 1686, in Paris; died 20 March 1752, in Paris.
Painter, draughtsman.
Ferrand de Monthelon, when already a lecturer at the Académie de St-Luc in Paris, was appointed professor of drawing in Rheims on 9 April 1748. He was the son and pupil of Jacques Philippe Ferrand de Monthelon.
MUSEUMS AND GALLERIES:
RHEIMS: *Portrait of the Abbé Jean Godinot; Portrait of Jean-François Rogier; Portrait of Philippe Ferrand, Father of the Artist; Portrait of the Abbé Pierre de Saulx.*

FERRANDES. See **FERNANDES** and **FERRANDEZ**

FERRANDEZ. See also **FERNANDES** and **HERNANDEZ**

FERRANDEZ, Garcia, or Fernandez
Spanish, 15th century.
Active in Seville in 1543.
Painter. Religious subjects.
Don Manuel Gomez Moreno discovered a panel by Garcia Ferrandez in the church at Salamanca. Divided into two parts, the *Presentation at the Temple* is represented in the upper, while the *Massacre of the Innocents*, signed *G. Frrz Painter of Seville* is shown in the lower.

FERRANDEZ, Garcia, or Fernandez
Spanish, 15th - 16th century.
Active in Seville from 1480 to 1500.
Painter.
Garcia Ferrandez had a number of pupils, was twice married and enjoyed a comfortable lifestyle.

FERRANDEZ, Garcia. See also **FERNÁNDEZ**

FERRANDEZ, Luis
Spanish, 16th century.
Active in Seville in 1515.
Painter.
Luis Ferrandez is perhaps identical to Luis Fernández.

FERRANDEZ, Pedro
Spanish, 16th century.
Active in Seville in 1515.
Painter.
This Pedro Ferrandez may be a Pedro Fernández.

FERRÁNDEZ, Raúl
Spanish, 20th - 21st century.
Born 1960.
Draughtsman, newspaper cartoonist, illustrator. Comic strips.
Ferrández was a cartoonist for the Spanish newspaper *El Pais* for 12 years. He has no specific style to speak of. He experiments with the shapes necessary to create a narrative framework. Thus, *Window on the West* (published by Amok, 1995) is an album produced following a trip to Russia during Gorbachev's era, comprising a mixture of four narratives each composed in a different style. He has illustrated several children's books. He also works as a visual artist.

FERRANDEZ BENDICHO, Pedro.
See **FERNÁNDEZ BENDICHO Pedro**

FERRANDIER, Gisèle
French, 20th century.
Born 16 September 1909, in Paris.
Painter.
Gisèle Ferrandier studied at the École des Beaux-Arts in Paris. From 1935, she exhibited at the Salon des Tuileries and the Salon des Femmes Peintres et Sculpteurs (for women artists), as well as in Algiers, Geneva and Lyons.

FERRANDINA, Leonardo
Italian, 17th century.
Active in Genoa.
Sculptor, architect.
Leonardo Ferrandina studied under Taddeo Carlone. He is remembered for a marble statue of the Virgin made for an altar in the Serra chapel in the church of Nunziata del Guastato in Genoa.

FERRANDINI, Giovanni Battista, or Feradini or Feratini
Italian, 18th century.
Painter.
Giovanni Ferrandini painted two church pictures commissioned by the Duke of Württemberg and produced further paintings for the churches of Sontheim and Güglingen.

FERRANDINI, Jean François, or Feradiny
French, 18th century.
Born 1724.
Active in Paris and Toulon.
Engraver.
Ferrandini engraved landscapes, seascapes and views after Claude Lorraine, J. Vernet and Teniers.

FERRANDINO, Giovanni Battista
Italian, 17th century.
Born to a family originally from San Fedele (Lake Como).
Sculptor.
Giovanni Ferrandino sculpted the Maria delle Grazie altar in the cathedral of Cremona in 1668.

FERRANDIZ TERAN, Federico
Spanish, 19th - 20th century.
Born 1870, in Málaga; died 1957, in Madrid.
Painter. Landscapes.
Federico Ferrandiz Teran was the son of Bernardo Ferrandiz y Badenes. He received advice from his father and studied at the school of fine arts in Málaga. Jaime Sabartes describes him as a friend of Picasso's father, J. Ruiz Blasco. He took part in collective exhibitions: at the national fine arts society of Madrid in 1890 where he showed *Park of Los Gaitanes* in 1890, *Ronda* in 1892 and *Tarde de Málaga* (*Málaga Afternoon*) in 1901; he was awarded bronze medals at the Málaga regional exhibition of 1899 and at provincial exhibitions in 1901 and 1915. He taught at the school of arts and crafts in Madrid.
BIBLIOGRAPHY:
Arnáiz, José Manuel/López Jiménez, Javier/Merchán Díaz, Manuel (ed.), *Cien años de pintura en Espana y Portugal (1830-1930)*, Antiqvaria, Madrid, 1988 (One Hundred Years of Painting in Spain and Portugal (1830-1930)).

FERRANDIZ Y BADENES, Bernardo, or Ferrando y Badenes
Spanish, 19th century.

Born 1835, in Valencia; died 1885, in Malaga.
Painter. Genre scenes.

Bernardo Ferrandiz y Badenes studied at the Academia de San Carlos in Valencia, the Academia de San Fernando in Madrid and lastly, from 1859, at the École des Beaux-Arts in Paris. In Paris he met Mariano Fortuny who exerted a certain influence on his work. They left for Italy together, staying first in Rome and in 1874 in Portici.

He exhibited from 1860 in Madrid and Paris and in 1868 was appointed to teach at the school of fine arts in Malaga.

BIBLIOGRAPHY:

González Anaya, D./Gónzalez Martí, J./García Sanchíz, Federico, *Bernardo Ferrándiz maestro de los pintores de Málaga: Homenaje en el primer centenario de su nacimiento 21 de Julio de 1835. Estudios de su arte y anecdotario de su vida por los disciplos del maestro José Moren*, Ibèrica, Málaga, 1935. Peña Hinojosa, Baltasar, *Fortuny y Ferrándiz, el genio y la amistad*, Caja de Ahorros Provincial, Obra Cultural, Málaga, 1969. Carmen, Gracia, *El Tribunal de las Aguas: Ferrándiz ante la modernidad*, Institució Alfons el Magnànim, Valencia, 1986. Sauret Guerrero, Teresa, *Bernardo Ferrándiz Bádenes y el eclecticismo pictórico del siglo XIX*, Benedito, Málaga, 1996.

MUSEUMS AND GALLERIES:

BORDEAUX: *The Valencia Water Tribunal in 1800* - MADRID (Prado): *The Political Charlatan; The Horses, The Horses!; Like a Fish in Water.*

AUCTION RECORDS:

PARIS, 15 March 1976, *Illusions of an Idiot* (1870, oil on panel, 12 1/2 x 8 1/2 ins / 31.5 x 21.5 cm) FRF 3,750. MADRID, 24 May 1977, *Marriage in Valencia* (1879, oil on canvas, 25 1/2 x 37 1/2 ins / 65 x 95 cm) ESP 625,000. LONDON, 19 April 1978, *Valencia Militia* (1867, oil on panel, 8 1/2 x 11 ins / 21.5 x 28 cm) GBP 1,300. NEW YORK, 31 Oct 1981, *Fortuny's Studio* (1874, oil on canvas, 19 x 31 3/4 ins / 48.2 x 80.6 cm) USD 9,000. CHESTER, 18 Jan 1985, *Spanish Gallant* (1866, oil on panel, 7 3/4 x 5 ins / 20 x 12.5 cm) GBP 920. LONDON, 21 June 1991, *In the Court* (oil on canvas, 18 1/4 x 28 ins / 46.3 x 71.1 cm) GBP 24,200. NEW YORK, 18 March 1998, *Santa Lucia Mergellina, Naples* (1874, (24,1x36,8)) USD 26,450. MADRID, 18 Dec 2000, *A Terrible Haircut* (oil on board, 13 x 20 ins / 33x52 cm) ESP 5,500,000. MADRID, 21 May 2001, *Elderly Man* (drawing, 10x5 ins / 25x12 cm) ESO 110,000.

FERRANDO, Augustin

French, 20th century.
Born 14 April 1880, in Miliana, Algeria; died 7 or 8 April 1957, in Oran, Algeria.
Painter. Figure compositions, figures, nudes, portraits, local scenes, landscapes, still-lifes. Designs for mosaics. Orientalism.
School of Algiers.

Augustin Ferrando's parents came from Italy. He studied at the École des Beaux-Arts in Algiers before gaining a scholarship to the École des Beaux-Arts in Paris from 1902 to 1908, studying under Fernand Comon from 1906. Back in Algeria, he shared his time between the capital and the countryside. He married in Algiers in 1913. After World War I, he was appointed head of the École des Beaux-Arts in Oran. He was a founding member of the Association Amicale des Artistes Africains, a grouping of African artists. In 1930, the art school was moved to a new, purpose built building with a museum, of which he became curator. During the Spanish Civil War, he took in a few fugitive artists, including Orlando Pelayo. In 1937, he resigned from his positions and retired to Oued Taria, while also making some time to go and work in Southern France and the Alps.

His early works are indebted to the Nabis and, specifically, Maurice Denis. He continued to use flat colour, as did the Nabis after Gauguin, but his practice of Sahel landscapes boosted his colours: purple and blue for the mountains, green in the gardens, and red for the land and autumn vineyards. He was later influenced by Cézanne, foregoing flat colours for a construction mediated by volume, whilst keeping his vibrant range of colours in deference to the Fauves and his friend Charles Camoin. He was, from an early age, interested in murals, producing (while he was still a student) a 8 x 16 feet (2.5 x 5 metres) composition. His work includes many character compositions: *The Pilgrimage, Women at a Balcony, Women Bathing, Women by a Rock, Persian Tales* and, above all, the theme he returned to, *Arab Feast*. He decorated (besides the houses of friends) the theatre and courts at Sidi-bel-Abes with great allegorical mosaics. He also designed a 13 x 33 feet (4 x 10 metres) mosaic for the courts at Tlemcen. This, he prepared with 200 detailed drawings, 10 general studies and three installation cartoons. Ferrando's work has been held back by Algerian remoteness, then by the War of Independence, during which many of his works were abandoned in the turmoil. The bequest his daughter made to the Musée Rollin in Autun released a body of work in the tradition of Cézanne that is fit to figure alongside Friesz' or Derain's.

From 1910 Ferrando began to exhibit notably: in Algiers with the Salon de la Société des Orientalistes; in 1931 at the Institut Français in Prague; in 1937 at the l'Hôtel-de-Ville in Oran; in 1941 at the Crédit Municipal d'Alger; and in 1953 at the Académie des Arts in Oran. After his death, his works featured in several collective exhibitions: in 1990 in *Les Coloniales* (*Colonials*), at the Musée Municipal, Boulogne-Billancourt; in 1992 in *Algérie heureuse* (*Happy Algeria*), at the Palais des Congrès, Versailles; in 1992 at the Salon des Artistes Français Repliés d'Afrique du Nord, Mairie of the third Arrondissement, Paris; in 2003 in *Lumineuse Algérie, sous le regard des peintres de marines (1830-1960* (*Luminous Algeria, Through the Eyes of Seascape Painters (1830-1960)*), at the Musée National de la Marine, Toulon; and also in 2003 at the *L'École d'Alger* (*The School of Algiers*), Musée des Beaux-Arts in Bordeaux. His personal posthumous exhibitions include: in 1959, a Retrospective at Salle P. Bordes, Algiers; and, in 1977, a Retrospective at the musée Rollin, Autun.

BIBLIOGRAPHY:

Jacquemin, Pierre, *Augustin Ferrando*, exhibition catalogue, Salle Pierre-Bordes, Algiers, 1959 (extensive documentation). *Augustin Ferrando*, exhibition catalogue, Musée Rolin, Autun, 1977. Blandinières, Muriel, *Monographie, catalogue raisonné des peintures, catalogue raisonné des gouaches, aquarelles, pastels, dessins, grands décors*, dissertation, Université de Paris IV Sorbonne, Paris, September 1997 (Masters in History of art). Mourot, Marjolaine/Vidal-Bué, Marion/Cazenave, Elisabeth, et al., *Lumineuse Algérie, sous le regard des peintres de marines (1830-1960)*, exhibition catalogue, Musée national de la Marine, Toulon, 2003.

MUSEUMS AND GALLERIES:

ALGIERS (Mus. National des Beaux-Arts): *Arab Horsemen; Still-life; Bou-Hanifia; Arab Shepherd with his Flock* - AUTUN (Mus. Rolin): important legacy - ORAN (Mus. Zabana).

FERRANDO, Bartolomé

Spanish, 20th - 21st century.
Born 1951, in Valencia.
Performance artist, installation artist.
Visual Poetry.

Bartolomé Ferrando teaches performance and mixed media arts at the fine arts faculty in Valencia. He has held exhibitions and installations of 'visual poetry' and 'object poetry' in Spain, Italy and France (in 2001, at the Lara Vincy gallery and a performance piece executed as part of the *Revue Parlée* event at the Pompidou Centre). An 'object poem' shows us the hidden side of an object that conceals a silent sound that can be heard, whereas a 'visual poem' constructs its architecture on the basis of its own de-structuring.

FERRANDO, Francesco. See **FERNANDI**

FERRANDO, Manuel
Spanish, 16th century.
Active in Palma (Majorca).
Painter.

The museum of the Lonja in Palma has an oil painting by Manuel Ferrando of *The Foundation of the Charterhouse of Valldemosa near Palma*.

FERRANDO, Niccolo
Italian, 16th century.
Born to a family originally from Galatina (Apulia).
Sculptor.

Niccolo Ferrando produced a number of sculptures for Archbishop Serafino di Squillace at the cathedral of Otranto, including some statues of the archbishop himself.

FERRANDOUX, Paul
French, 20th century.
Born in Blois.
Painter.

Paul Ferrandoux showed at the Salon d'Automne and the Salon des Indépendants (from 1924).

FERRANDUS, Petri de Funes
Spanish, 12th century.
Miniaturist.

In 1197 this artist decorated with more than a thousand miniatures a Bible for King Sancho of Navarre. This is now in Amiens.

MUSEUMS AND GALLERIES:
AMIENS: *Bible* (miniature).

FERRANT, Ángel, or Ferrant-Vasquez
Spanish, 20th century.
Born 1891, in Madrid; died 1961, in Madrid.
Sculptor, draughtsman. Nudes. Groups, statues.
Kinetic Art.

Ángel Ferrant studied at the Real Academia de Bellas Artes de San Fernando in Madrid and was also self-taught. In 1913 he spent time in Paris, Belgium and Germany. He often returned to Paris. Ferrant was part of the very active artistic life of Barcelona during the early years of the 20th century and belonged to two avant-garde groups, The Evolutionists and the Friends of Art Nouveau.

Ferrant's early period was figurative with a tendency towards the monumental and he produced female figures and nudes. Soon, by the time of the exhibition of 1949, and alongside these early works, he began creating abstract sculptures based on natural forms, reducing these to their essential elements: his *Cyclopean Groups* of the 1940s and 1950s recall prehistorical megaliths. Even before 1950 he had begun creating new pieces composed of mobile wooden elements that could be altered in space as the viewer chose. He continued to develop the idea of mobile sculpture but began working in metal. His many drawings, preparatory sketches for sculptures or drawings in their own right, demonstrate clearly his analytical approach to form. He only became known outside Spain after the Pittsburgh International Exhibition of 1958.

Although Ferrant did not achieve the same status as Picasso or Miró within Catalan sculpture, he played a role comparable to that of Julio González, whom he did not know, in the development of Spanish sculpture of the period.

He took part in numerous collective exhibitions in Spain. In 1949 the Palma gallery in Madrid held an exhibition of his sculptures. In 1958 he was selected to take part in the Pittsburgh International Exhibition and in 1960 in the Venice Biennale where he showed *Infinite Sculpture*. In 1961 the museum of modern art in Barcelona held a solo exhibition of his work.

AUCTION RECORDS:
BARCELONA, 25 May 1983, *Seated Nude* (bronze, h. 7 ins / 18 cm and l. 11 1/2 ins/29 cm) ESP 145,000. MADRID, 28 Nov 1991, *Banderillas* (1939, bronze, relief, 12 3/4 x 20 ins / 32.5 x 51 cm) ESP 504,000. MADRID, 19 Dec 2000, *Hitting the Bull with a Muleta* (green patinated bronze, 13 x 20 ins / 33 x 52 cm) ESP 1,100,000. MADRID, 17 Dec 2001, *Bull Scene* (1939, green patinated bronze, 13 x 21 ins / 34 x 53 cm) EUR 6,610. MADRID, 17 June 2002, *Study for Sculpture* (1955, ink drawing, 8 x 7 ins / 21 x 17 cm) EUR 1,600.

FERRANT, Antoine
French, 18th century.
Active in Paris in 1719.
Painter.

FERRANT, Charles
French, 17th century.
Painter.

Charles Ferrant was admitted to the Académie de St-Luc in Paris in 1664.

FERRANT, Francisco
Spanish, 19th century.
Painter.

Francisco Ferrant is sometimes confused with Fernando Ferrant y Llausas. He painted nocturnal scenes inspired by German landscape artists. When Jenaro Perez died in 1853, Ferrant replaced him as master of landscape painting at the Academia de San Fernando in Madrid.

FERRANT, Nicolas Robert
French, 18th century.
Painter (porcelain).

Nicolas Robert Ferrant worked at the Sèvres porcelain factory from 1758 to 1790.

FERRANT Y FISCHERMANS, Alejandro
Spanish, 19th - 20th century.
Born 1843, in Madrid; died 1917, in Madrid.
Painter. History painting, portraits.

In 1874 Alejandro Ferrant y Fischermans was awarded a travel bursary and went to Rome. A talented artist, he became a well-known painter in late 19th-century Spain and in 1903 was appointed director of the national museum of modern art. A painter and watercolour artist, he also executed decorative pieces for the church of S Francisco el Grande, the Pardo Palace and the Barcelona law courts. He began exhibiting around 1860 and exhibited regularly in Madrid, Cádiz and Barcelona and in Munich in 1883.

MUSEUMS AND GALLERIES:
CÁDIZ (Mus.): *Martyrdom of St Servais and St Germain; Moorish Pirates Defeated near Cádiz in 1574; Murillo's Fall at the Capuchin Convent in Cádiz* - MADRID (Mus. de Arte Moderno): *The Burial of St Sebastian in the Catacombs in Rome; Interior from the Barber of Seville; Concert.*

FERRANT Y LLAUSAS, Fernando, or Ferrant y Llamas
Spanish, 19th century.
Born in Palma, Majorca; died 21 August 1856, in the Escorial (Madrid).
Painter. Landscapes.

Fernando Ferrant y Llausas studied at the Academia de San Fernando. He first exhibited in Madrid around 1843 and also took part in the Exposition Universelle in Paris in 1855.

MUSEUMS AND GALLERIES:
MADRID: *Landscape.*

AUCTION RECORDS:
PARIS, 8 Dec 1987, *Roman Landscape with Animals Returning Home* (1838, oil on canvas, 39 1/4 x 54 1/4 ins / 100 x 138 cm) FRF 36,000.

FERRANT Y LLAUSAS, Luis, or Ferrant y Llamas
Spanish, 19th century.
Born 1806, in Barcelona; died 28 July 1868, in Madrid.
Painter. History painting, portraits.

Luis Ferrant y Llausas studied under Ribera and received a bursary for Rome from the Infante Gabriel. In 1848 he returned to Spain and settled in Madrid where he was appointed painter to the court and later a teacher at the Academia de San Fernando. He worked mainly for the gallery of the Infante Gabriel. Ferrant y Llausas was an artist of real talent and left some fine historical paintings and remarkable portraits.

MUSEUMS AND GALLERIES:

MADRID: *Portrait of King Don Sancho IV, the Brave*; *Portrait of King Alfonso X*.

FERRANTE
Italian, 16th century.
Born 16th century, to a family originally from Cerreto Sannita.
Sculptor.

In 1537, Ferrante sculpted the portal of the church of St Nicolas at Cusano Mutri near Benevento.

FERRANTE, Alessio de
Italian, 17th century.
Active in Naples.
Painter.

He was admitted to the artists' guild in 1686.

FERRANTE, Decio. See **DECIO Ferrante**

FERRANTE, Francesco
Italian, 17th century.
Painter.
Messina School.

Francesco Ferrante probably studied under Guido Reni. He was invited to Messina by the Viceroy of Sicily, who commissioned him to produce a decorative marble piece for the cathedral of Messina. The work was subsequently completed by G. B. Quagliata.

FERRANTE, Paolo
Italian, 17th century.
Of Sicilian origin.
Painter.

Paolo Ferrante was active in Rome in 1607.

FERRANTE, Pietro Francesco, called il Cavaliere Ferrante
Italian, 17th century.
Born c. 1600, in Bologna; died 1652, in Pisa.
Painter.

Pietro Ferrante studied under Gessi and painted several oils and frescoes in Bologna, Pisa and Piacenza.

FERRANTINI, Gabriele, also known as Gabriele dagli Occhiali
Italian, 17th century.
Born 17th century, in Bologna.
Painter.
Bolognese School.

Gabriele Ferrantini studied under Dionysius Calvaert and painted historical compositions which, for the most part, are preserved in churches in Bologna. The best-known and admired of these include a *St Francis of Padua* in the church of S Benedetto, a *St Jerome* in S Mattia, a *St Francis Receiving the Stigmata* in the Chiesa della Carità, and a *Descent from the Cross* and a *Birth of the Virgin* in the church of the order of the Servants of Blessed Mary (Servites).

FERRANTINI, Giuseppe
Italian, 18th century.
Active in Rome c. 1700.
Sculptor.

Giuseppe Ferrantini is credited with one of the statues of saints which Pope Clement XI ordered to be positioned under the colonnades of St Peter's Square in Rome.

FERRANTINI, Ippolito
Italian, 17th century.
Painter. History painting, religious subjects.
Bolognese School.

The brother of Gabriele Ferrantini and a member of the Accademia degli Incamminati group, Ippolito Ferrantini studied under Carracci and imitated the latter with considerable success. A *St Michael* by him is housed in the church of S Mattia in Bologna.

FERRANTINI, Orazio
Italian, 17th century.
Of Florentine origin.
Painter.

Orazio Ferrantini was a member of the guild in Bologna around 1600.

FERRAPIANO, Carlo
Italian, 18th century.
Active in Naples.
Painter.

Carlo Ferrapiano was a guild member in 1723.

FERRARA, Antonio
Italian, 17th century.
Active in Naples.
Sculptor (wood).

Antonio Ferrara worked together with Nicola Montella on the decoration of the choir stalls in the church of S Andrea delle Dame in Naples.

FERRARA, Bono da. See **BONO DA FERRARA**

FERRARA, Carel de, or Ferara
Flemish, 17th century.
Died c. 1667, in Antwerp.
Active in Antwerp.
Painter.
Flemish School.

Carel de Ferrara worked with Kerstiaen de Coninck and became a master in 1612.

FERRARA, da. See first name

FERRARA, Daniel
French, 20th century.
Born 8 July 1906, in Mers-el-Kebir, Algeria; died 21 April 1990, in Marseilles.
Painter. Landscapes with figures, urban landscapes.

Daniel Ferrara showed an artistic bent from a very early age. Born in Algeria to a family of sailors from Italy, he started earning a living at the age of 11. He worked as a ship's boy, sailor, electrician, engineer, lorry driver and docker. In 1946, his wife persuaded him to show his first paintings, some harmonious Provence or Biblical landscapes. In 1960, Galerie Herbinet presented his first solo exhibition. Thereafter, he took part in group exhibitions with other naive artists in France and abroad, while featuring regularly at the Salon d'Automne and the Salon des Artistes Français. In 2001, he figured in *Die Naive, aufbruch ins verlorene paradies* (*The Naïve Painters, Journey to a Lost Paradise*), Kunsthaus Vienna. In 1965 and 1969, some of his works were bought by the Nation. Ferrara's paintings are naive, balanced composition boasting fresh, harmonious, gentle colours and a rich imagination.

BIBLIOGRAPHY:

Jakovsky, Anatole, *Lexique des peintres naïfs du monde entier*, Basilius Presse, Basel, 1967 (text in French, German and English). Gavelle, Madeleine, *Les Peintres naïfs illuminés de l'instinct*, Éd. Filipacchi, Paris, 1977. *Guide naïf des provinces de France*, Hervas, Paris, 1985. Bihalji-Merin, Oto, *Encyclo-*

pédie naïve du monde entier, La Bibliothèque des Arts, Paris, 1985. Drot, J.M., *Voyage au pays des naïfs*, Hatier, Paris, 1986.

MUSEUMS AND GALLERIES:

LAVAL (Mus. d'Art naïf) - NICE (Mus. International d'Art Naïf Anatole-Jakovsky) - PARIS (Mus. d'Art Naïf Max-Fourny) - VICQ (Mus. International d'Art Naïf).

FERRARA, Jackie

American, 20th century.
Born 1929.
Sculptor.

Jackie Ferrara has worked in wood, metals, stone and concrete, sometimes incorporating water, trees and grass, assembling with great care and precision constructions perhaps inspired by pyramids or mastabas.

Her major architectural or landscape projects include 65,000 square feet (20,000 square metres) of ceramic flooring for Pittsburg International Airport (1992-6); a 106 feet (32.6 metre) granite, concrete and grass amphitheatre for the Los Angeles County Museum of Art (1999); and a 60 feet (18.5 metre) copper and concrete tower for the University of Connecticut (2000).

She has held solo exhibitions regularly since 1973, notably *In Focus: Jackie Ferrara* at the Museum of Contemporary Art in Chicago in 1998, and at the Frederieka Taylor Gallery, New York, in 1998, 2000, 2002 and 2003.

AUCTION RECORDS:

NEW YORK, 2 Nov 1984, *Untitled* (1977, wood, 21 x 2 1/4 x 40 ins / 53 x 6 x 101.5 cmx24 ins/61 cm) USD 6,000. NEW YORK, 8 May 1990, *A233 Borbek* (wood and nails, 49 x 34 1/2 x 34 1/2 ins / 124.7 x 87.6 x 87.6 cm) USD 16,500. NEW YORK, 6 May 1992, *A209 Zogg* (pine construction, 112 1/2 x 31 1/2 x 41 1/2 ins / 285.7 x 80.3 x 105.4 cm) USD 18,700. NEW YORK, 16 Nov 1995, *A233 Borbek* (assemblage of wood and nails in six parts with a drawing on graph paper, sculpture, 49 1/4 x 34 1/2 x 34 1/2 ins / 124.8 x 87.6 x 87.6 cm, drawing 18 1/2 x 23 1/4 ins/47 x 59 cm) USD 10,350.

FERRARA, Onofrio

Italian, 19th century.
Born 1859, in Naples.
Active in Posilippo near Naples.
Painter.

In 1892 Onofrio Ferrara exhibited a painting entitled *Il Piccolo Guappo Napolitano* at the Palace of Fine Arts in Rome; in Paris he showed a landscape entitled *Sadness* at the Salon of the Société Nationale in 1912; and *Dressing Room of a Spanish Dancer* at the Salon des Artistes Indépendants in 1914.

FERRARA, Orazio

Italian, 19th century.
Born 15 October 1853, in Naples.
Painter.

Orazio Ferrara is known for his works: *Good Friday at the Certosa di San Martino*, which was exhibited in Naples in 1893; *At the Spring* (Turin, 1898); and a *Still-life* (Nymphenburg Palace, Munich, 1901).

FERRARA, Raffaele

Italian, 19th century.
Born 7 March 1814, in Chieti (Abruzzi); died before 1883, in Rome.
Painter.

Raffaele Ferrara studied in Naples. In Rome he worked for the restored church of the Holy Trinity in 1853, describing *The History of the Church* in four paintings. He also painted the vault of the Chapel of Succour in the Church of the Trinity in Naples, and an oil painting of the *Death of Joseph* for the Church of the Seven Sorrows.

FERRARA, Stefano da. See **FALZAGALLONI Stefano**

FERRARA, Taddeo da. See **CRIVELLI Taddeo**

FERRARESI, Adriano

Italian, 19th century.
Born 25 February 1851, in Rome; died 15 January 1892, in Rome.
Painter. Genre scenes.

In 1888 Ferraresi exhibited in Munich. He is known for a work entitled *Bird Market in the 15th century*.

MUSEUMS AND GALLERIES:

ROME (Gal. Nazionale d'Arte Moderna): *Falconer*.

FERRARI, Adelaïde

Italian, 19th century.
Born 16 July 1850; died 17 February 1893.
Painter. Landscapes.

Adelaïde Ferrari was the daughter of Carlo Ferrari (known as Il Ferrarin), and was taught to paint by her sister Elisabetta.

FERRARI, Agostino

Italian, 14th century.
Painter.

A fresco of the *Crucifixion*, dated 1376 and bearing the signature of Agostino Ferrari, is in the church of S Antonio di Combo at Bormio.

FERRARI, Agostino

Italian, 20th century.
Born 1938, in Milan.
Painter.

Agostino Ferrari has lived, worked and exhibited in Milan since 1962. He has also participated in group exhibitions in Italy, Spain, New York, Brussels and elsewhere.

Ferrari's paintings are made up of linear or rectilinear segments, with few variations, which divide the space by highlighting disconnected planes against a uniform background.

AUCTION RECORDS:

MILAN, 10 March 1986, *Nell'azzuro* (1985, sand and acrylic/canvas, 31 1/2 x 39 1/4 ins / 80 x 100 cm) ITL 1,400,000. MILAN, 27 March 2001, *Event F* (acrylic and sand, 43 x 20 ins / 108 x 50 cm) ITL 3,500,000. MUNICH, 16 May 2002, *In the Centre* (acrylic, graphite, lava and sand, 63 x 47 ins / 160 x 120 cm) EUR 2,200. VERCELLI, 12 June 2004, *Composition* (1991, acrylic and sand, 39 x 31 ins / 100 x 80 cm) EUR 2,000. VERCELLI, 12 June 2004, *Untitled* (acrylic and sand, 63 x 30 ins / 160 x 75 cm) EUR 3,000.

FERRARI, Antoine

French, 20th century.
Born 1 February 1910, in Marseilles; died 7 January 1995.
Painter. Portraits, landscapes, still-lifes. Murals.

Antoine Ferrari studied at the École des Beaux-Arts in Marseilles, then under Lucien Simon in Paris. In 1939, he obtained a residency at Villa Abd El Tif in Algiers, where he stayed until 1939, when he was called up into the military. Ferrari painted portraits and landscapes of Paris, Marseilles and the French Riviera. He carried out the composition *Sea Bathing* for the Pavilion on Hygiene of the 1937 Paris international fair and *Family Scene* for the School complex at Pré-St-Gervais.

Ferrari exhibited in Paris, making his debut at the Salon d'Automne in 1928, and continued showing until 1935. He was later asked to show at the Salon des Tuileries, notably in 1937 and 1943.

MUSEUMS AND GALLERIES:

ALGIERS: *Moorish Café*; *View of Marseilles Harbour*; *Still-life* (two canvases) - MARSEILLES (MBA): *Self-portrait* - PARIS (MAM): *Le Trayas Landscape*.

Auction records:
Versailles, 29 Oct 1989, *Mediterranean Port* (oil/hardboard, 21¼ x 28¾ ins / 54 x 73 cm) FRF 7,000. Versailles, 21 Jan 1990, *Nude* (oil on canvas, 21¼ x 25½ ins / 54 x 65 cm) FRF 6,800. Versailles, 8 July 1990, *Place de la Concorde* (oil/hardboard, 10¾ x 14 ins / 27.5 x 35.5 cm) FRF 4,500. Neuilly, 7 April 1991, *Place des Lices, St-Tropez* (oil on canvas, 21¼ x 25½ ins / 54 x 65 cm) FRF 10,000. Paris, 12 Feb 1992, *Street Scene* (oil on canvas, 21¼ x 25½ ins / 54 x 65 cm) FRF 9,500. Neuilly, 12 Dec 1993, *Landscape with a Tree* (oil/hardboard, 24½ x 15 ins / 62 x 38 cm) FRF 5,600. Paris, 19 April 2000, *Landscape at Puy Loubier* (oil on hardboard, 29 x 24 ins / 73 x 60 cm) FRF 12,000. Neuilly, 29 April 2004, *Almond Trees* (oil on panel, 26 x 36 ins / 65 x 92 cm) EUR 2,800.

FERRARI, Antonio. See **AGRATE Antonio Ferrari da**

FERRARI, Antonio de'. See **ANTONIO** and **ANTONINO DE' FERRARI**

FERRARI, Arturo
Italian, 19th - 20th century.
Born 1861, in Milan; died 1932.
Painter, watercolourist. Church interiors, waterscapes, urban landscapes, architectural views.

Arturo Ferrari's master was the Milanese painter Giuseppe Bertini. His work frequently appeared at exhibitions held at the Accademia di Belle Arti di Brera in Milan. He also exhibited in Paris (where he won a silver medal at the Exposition Universelle of 1900), Dresden and Munich.

Bibliography:
Cesura, Guido/Borgese, Leonardo/Fauser-Sartirana, Gioconda, *Arturo Ferrari: Pittore*, Cavalotti, Milan, 1980.

Museums and Galleries:
Rome (Gal. Nazionale): *Interior View of S Paolo in Milan*.

Auction records:
Milan, 16 March 1971, *Church of S Stefano*, ITL 1,600,000. Milan, 14 March 1978, *Lake Como* (oil on card, 11¾ x 9 ins / 30 x 23 cm) ITL 500,000. Milan, 10 Nov 1982, *Village* (watercolour, 13½ x 12½ ins / 34 x 32 cm) ITL 700,000. Milan, 29 May 1984, *Antiquarian's Shop, Via S Bernardino, Milan* (oil on canvas, 11¾ x 17½ ins / 30 x 44.5 cm) ITL 3,000,000. Milan, 4 June 1985, *Il Duomo di Milano* (oil on panel, 11¾ x 9¼ ins / 30 x 23.5 cm) ITL 1,700,000. Milan, 1 June 1988, *Raging Sea at Pegli* (1918, oil on canvas, 33½ x 54¾ ins / 85 x 139 cm) ITL 6,500,000. Milan, 14 June 1989, *River Landscape* (oil on card, 10 x 13¾ ins / 25.5 x 35 cm) ITL 1,900,000. Milan, 8 March 1990, *View of the Landing Stage at Como* (oil on canvas, 13½ x 19¾ ins / 34 x 50 cm) ITL 10,000,000. Milan, 5 Dec 1990, *St Mark's Square in Venice* (oil on canvas, 12¾ x 19 ins / 32.5 x 48 cm) ITL 10,500,000. Milan, 6 June 1991, *Hunting Lodge on the Southern Bank of the Lambro* (watercolour/card, 20¾ x 27¼ ins / 53 x 69.5 cm) ITL 3,000,000. Milan, 21 Dec 1993, *The Lambro at Canzo* (oil on card, 9¾ x 13¾ ins / 25 x 35 cm) ITL 1,725,000. Milan, 26 March 1996, *The Gentilino, Porta Ticinese, in Old Milan*; *The Little Morivione Bridge in Old Milan* (watercolour/paper, a pair, 8 x 6 ins / 20.5 x 15.5 cm and 9¾ x 13½ ins/25 x 34 cm) ITL 2,530,000. Milan, 20 Dec 2000, *Naviglio in Milan* (oil on canvas, 12 x 18 ins / 30 x 45 cm) ITL 16,000,000. Rome, 11 Dec 2003, *Naviglio in Milan* (oil on cardboard, 10 x 15 ins / 25 x 39 cm) EUR 3,500. Rome, 11 Dec 2003, *Milan Disappearing* (1911, watercolour on card, 28 x 50 ins / 72 x 126 cm) EUR 24,000. Milan, 15 Sept 2004, *Gentlemen Meeting* (1906, watercolour, 39 x 28 ins / 100 x 72 cm) EUR 4,000.

FERRARI, Bartolomeo
Italian, 19th century.
Born 18 July 1780, in Marostica, near Vicenza; died 8 February 1844, in Venice.
Sculptor, caster.

Bartolomeo Ferrari was the nephew and pupil of Giovanni Ferrari (who was known as Torretti). Among his many works, some of the best known are: the decorative sculptures on the triumphal arches erected in Milan for the arrival of Napoleon; crucifixes for churches on the Adriatic island of Losinj, and in Cologna; two monumental angels for S Maria del Carmino in Padua; funeral monuments for cemeteries in Ferrara and Vicenza; a low relief for Countess Sangiovanni in Vicenza; busts of patricians in Venice; and a work called *Sculpture* on Canova's tomb in the church of S Maria dei Frari, Venice.

FERRARI, Benedetto
Italian, 16th century.
Active in Mantua.
Painter.

Benedetto Ferrari is mentioned in 1518 for rebuilding works in a number of apartments in the castle of Marmirolo.

FERRARI, Bernardino de'. See **BERNARDINO DE' FERRARI**

FERRARI, Bernardo
Italian, 16th century.
Born c. 1495, in Vigevano (Lombardy); died c. 1574.
Painter. History painting.

Bernardo Ferrari primarily imitated the style of Gaudenzio Ferrari and painted the chapels of SS Jacopo and Filippo and the church of S Ambrogio in Vigevano.

FERRARI, Bernardo
Italian, 18th century.
Born 1689; died 1718.
Active in Piacenza (Emilia).
Painter.

Bernardo Ferrari was a pupil of G. B. Draghi. He painted a picture of St Anthony for the chapel of S Opilio in the church of S Antonio.

FERRARI, Berto
Italian, 20th century.
Born 1887, in Bogliasco; died 1965, in Genoa.
Painter. Landscapes.

Berto Ferrari continued to paint in the 19th-century Realist style, and was not particularly influenced by the Macchiaioli.

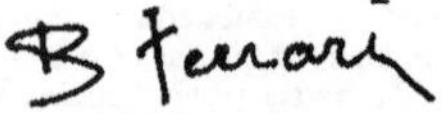

Auction records:
Milan, 6 June 1991, *First Hot Days in Nervi* (1939, oil on card, 16½ x 19¾ ins / 42 x 50 cm) ITL 3,000,000. Milan, 12 Dec 1991, *On the River* (oil on canvas, 18¾ x 33¼ ins / 47.5 x 84.5 cm) ITL 4,900,000. Rome, 7 June 1995, *Desert at Dawn* (oil on panel, 11¾ x 23½ ins / 30 x 60 cm) ITL 2,760,000. Milan, 26 March 1996, *Marina in Nervi* (oil on card, 11¾ x 15½ ins / 30 x 39.5 cm) ITL 4,370,000. Milan, 18 Dec 1996, *Morning by the Sea, Nervi* (1947, oil on card, 11¾ x 15½ ins / 30 x 39.5 cm) ITL 3,262,000. Genoa, 26 Feb 2004, *Landscape in Liguria* (oil on cardboard/canvas, 14 x 20 ins / 35 x 50 cm) EUR 1,600. Genoa, 26 Feb 2004, *Orero Church Square* (oil on board, 14 x 20 ins / 35 x 50 cm) EUR 4,000.

FERRARI, Carlo
Italian, 19th century.
Born in Bergamo.
Painter.

Carlo Ferrari won a bronze medal at the 1900 Exposition Universelle in Paris.

FERRARI, Carlo, called Il Ferrarin or Carlo da Verone
Italian, 19th century.

Born 30 September 1813, in Verona; died 28 January 1871, in Verona.
Painter. Religious subjects, portraits, architectural views.

Carlo Ferrari lived in Rome. He is known for the following works: *Street in Verona*; *Piazza di Spagna in Rome*; *Piazza Navona*; *Baptism of Clovis*; and *Apparition of the Virgin*. His work featured in numerous exhibitions in Italy, Vienna and Warsaw.

MUSEUMS AND GALLERIES:

VERONA (Pinacoteca): *Portrait of the Artist*.

AUCTION RECORDS:

PARIS, 8 Dec 1941, *Excavations at the Forum*, FRF 8,500. LONDON, 26 Nov 1985, *Bridge Builder in Verona* (1853, oil on canvas, 29 1/2 x 49 ins / 75 x 124.5 cm) GBP 17,000. NEW YORK, 25 Feb 1987, *Chi Dorme non Piglia Pesci* (1913, oil on canvas, 22 x 30 ins / 55.9 x 76.4 cm) USD 10,000. LONDON, 28 Nov 2000, *View of a Market Town and possibly the Fair of S Allessandro* (1839, oil on canvas, 20 x 28 ins / 51 x 71 cm) GBP 60,000.

FERRARI, Carlo
20th century.
Painter. Landscapes with figures.

AUCTION RECORDS:

ROME, 25 May 1988, *The Nemi Wood and a Little Girl* (1927, oil on panel, 17 1/4 x 23 1/4 ins / 44 x 59 cm) ITL 1,600,000. LONDON, 25 Nov 1992, *Busy Italian Square* (oil on canvas, 29 x 38 ins / 73.5 x 96.5 cm) GBP 16,500.

FERRARI, Cesare, also known as Cesare Augusto Ferrarese
Italian, 17th century.
Born to a family originally from Este.
Painter.

Cesare Ferrari worked in Padua and Venice. His pictures representing *Scenes from the Life of St Filippo Benizi* can be found in a church in Venice. G. L. Valesio subsequently engraved his *Deposition*.

FERRARI, Cristoforo de'. See **CRISTOFORO DE' FERRARI**

FERRARI, Daniele
Italian, 17th century.
Active in Milan c. 1600.
Sculptor.

Daniele Ferrari was a Jesuit priest who completed wood carvings started by his teacher, Ricciardo Taurino, for the church of S Fidele. Four silver statues of saints produced to Ferrari's designs are preserved in the church. Ferrari also carved the tabernacle above the main altar in S Fidele.

FERRARI, Defendente, called Defendente Ferrari da Chivasso
Italian, 16th century.
Born c. 1490, in Chivasso; died after 1535.
Painter. Religious subjects, genre scenes.

Defendente Ferrari's master was Martino Spanzotti. He worked in the region of Turin and from 1509 had Girolamo Giovenone as a follower. A contemporary of Giangiacomo Marcrino, he carried out a large number of religious paintings and predellas in a Gothic style. Worthy of mention are a *Pietà* in the cathedral of Chivasso, some altapieces in the cathedral at Ivrea, executed between 1519 and 1521, a *Nativity with Saints* of 1531 in the church at Ranverso and the triptych of S Giovanni d'Avigliana (1535).

BIBLIOGRAPHY:

Berenson, Bernard, *Italian Pictures of the Renaissance: Central Italian and North Italian Schools, 3 vols*, Phaidon, London, 1968. Mazzini, F., *Opere darte a Vercelli e nella sua provincia: Recuperi e restauri, 1968-1976*, exhibition catalogue, Museo Civico Borgogna, Vercelli, 1971.

MUSEUMS AND GALLERIES:

AMSTERDAM (Rijksmus.): *Virgin and Child with St Anne* - BERGAMO (SFA): *The Flagellation*; *The Crucifixion*; *The Adoration of the Shepherds*; *Concert* - BERLIN (Bodemus.): *Adoration of the Christ Child* - BOURG-EN-BRESSE: *Nativity of St John the Baptist*; *The Deposition* - DENVER (AM): *Christ in the House of Marta and Mary* - MILAN (Castello Sforzesco): *Saints and Donors* - MILAN (Pinacoteca di Brera): *St Sebastian and St Catherine*; *St Andrew*; *St Jerome* - NEW YORK (Metropolitan Mus. of Art): *St John the Evangelist and St Lawrence* - OLDENBURG (Augusteum): *Virgin and Child with St Anne* - STUTTGART (Staatsgal.): *Christ at the Temple, St Joseph and Mary* - TURIN (Accademia Albertina di Belle Arti): *Adoration of the Christ Child*; *A Donor with St Francis and St Agatha* - TURIN (Gal. Civica d'Arte Moderna e Contemporanea): *The Birth of Christ* - TURIN (Gal. Sabauda): *Marriage of St Catherine*; *The Virgin with the Christ Child at Breast*; *St Barbara*; *St George* (triptych) - VERCELLI (Mus. Camillo Leone): triptych; *The Glorification of the Virgin* - VERONA: *The Virgin* - VICENZA: *Adoration of the Magi*.

AUCTION RECORDS:

LONDON, 6 Dec 1937, *St Jerome*, GBP 7. LONDON, 26 April 1939, *Bishop*, GBP 48. LONDON, 28 April 1939, *The Madonna*, GBP 33. NEW YORK, 15-16 May 1946, *St Stephen*, USD 225. LONDON, 26 June 1970, *Salome with the Head of St John the Baptist*, Gns 1,400. PARIS, 11 Dec 1991, *Dormition of the Virgin* (tempera/panel, 11 x 25 1/4 ins / 27 x 64 cm) FRF 110,000. NEW YORK, 19 May 1995, *Adoration of the Magi* (oil and tempera/panel, 15 3/4 x 23 1/4 ins / 40 x 59.1 cm) USD 156,500. VENICE, 14 Feb 1999, *SS John the Baptist and Francis of Assisi* (oil on panel, 52 x 30 ins / 132 x 76 cm) ITL 110,000,000. LYONS, 4 March 2001, *Soldiers Before a Crucified Man* (oil on canvas) FRF 31,000.

FERRARI, Elisabetta
Italian, 19th century.
Born 24 August 1841.
Painter.

Elisabetta Ferrari was the daughter of Carlo Ferrari (known as Il Ferrarin), and married Gaetano Cristiani, one of her father's pupils. She exhibited a *Holy Family* in 1858.

FERRARI, Ettore
Italian, 19th - 20th century.
Born 25 March 1845, in Rome; died 1929.
Painter, watercolourist, pastellist, sculptor. Landscapes.

Ettore was the son of Filippo Ferrari. He won the Grand Prix at the 1889 Exposition Universelle in Paris. He built a large number of monuments and statues of famous men for towns in Italy, including Rome, Rovigo, Pisa, Pavia and Milan, and for towns in other countries too.

BIBLIOGRAPHY:

Mantura, B., *'Ettore Ferrari: Sculture tra il 1867 e il 1889'* in *Capitolium, no.49*, 1974. Mantura, B./Rosazza-Ferraris, P., *Ettore Ferrari 1845-1929*, Pal. Cult. Lat., Milan, 1998.

MUSEUMS AND GALLERIES:

NEW YORK (Metropolitan Mus. of Art): *President Lincoln* - ROME (Academia Nazionale di S Luca): *Jacopo Ortis* - ROME (Gal. Nazionale d'Arte Moderna): *Cum Spartaco Pugnavit*.

AUCTION RECORDS:

MILAN, 11 Dec 1986, *Garibaldi on Horseback* (terracotta, h. 11 ins / 28 cm) ITL 3,400,000. MILAN, 14 June 1989, *View of Venice* (watercolour/paper, 10 3/4 x 8 ins / 27.5 x 20.5 cm) ITL 1,300,000. MILAN, 21 Nov 1990, *Courtyard of a Palace in Verona* (1885, watercolour/paper, 11 x 8 1/4 ins / 28 x 21 cm) ITL 1,300,000. ROME, 28 May 1991, *Landscape* (pastel/paper, 27 3/4 x 21 ins / 70.5 x 53.5 cm) ITL 900,000. ROME, 24 June 2002, *Gypsum* (bronze, 28 x ?x? ins / 72 x ?x? cm) EUR 5,950.

FERRARI, Eusebio
Italian, 16th century.
Active from 1508 to 1533.

Painter. Religious subjects.
A. Griseri attibutes to Eusebio Ferrari an small altarpiece of meticulous workmanship intended for a private worshipper.
BIBLIOGRAPHY:
Romano, Giovanni, '*Eusebio Ferrari e gli affreschi cinquecenteschi di Palazzo Verga a Vercelli Giovanni Romano*' in *Prospettiva an. 1983-1984* n° 33-36, periodical, 1983-1984.
Romano, Giovanni, *Nuove indicazioni per Eusebio Ferrari e per il primo Cinquecento a Vercelli*, Longanesi, Milan, 1990.
MUSEUMS AND GALLERIES:
MAINZ: altarpiece triptych.
AUCTION RECORDS:
MILAN, 21 April 1988, *Adoration of the Christ Child* (oil on panel, 26 x 15 3/4 ins / 66 x 40 cm) ITL 83,000,000.

FERRARI, Evangelista
Italian, 18th century.
Born in Torrechiara (Parma); died September 1779.
Architect, painter. Landscapes.
Evangelista Ferrari studied landscape painting under Bossi. He is known for portraits and medallions of princes from the House of Savoy, as well as for illustrations of works by Bodoni, which were published in Parma in 1785 and are known by the collective title of *Epithalamia Linguis Exoticis Reddita*, a collection of songs 'in exotic tongues' celebrating nuptials.

FERRARI, Febo
American, 19th century.
Born 4 December 1865, in Pallanza, Italy.
Sculptor.
Febo Ferrari, a pupil at the Accademia Reale in Turin, became an American citizen and specialised in architectural sculpture in the USA.

FERRARI, Federico
Italian, 18th century.
Born 18th century, in Milan.
Painter. History painting.
Federico Ferrari studied under Pietro Maggi. He painted oils and frescoes for churches in Milan and elsewhere, notably in Piacenza (ceiling frescoes in the church of S Vincenzo), in Lodi (frescoes for the cupola of the church of S Filippo), in Bergamo (the churches of S Alessandro and S Rocca), and in Pavia (for the cathedral, the church of S Tommaso and other churches). His *Fifteen Mysteries of the Rosary* is housed in the rosary chapel of the church of S Martino in Alzano Maggiore.

FERRARI, Felice Antonio
Italian, 17th - 18th century.
Born 1667, in Ferrara; died 1720, in Ferrara.
Painter. Architectural views.
The son of Francesco Ferrari, he made a name for himself through his grandiose decoration of palazzi in Ferrara, Venice, Padua and Ravenna.

FERRARI, Filippo
Italian, 19th century.
Born 1819; died 1897, in Rome.
Sculptor, watercolourist.
Filippo Ferrari worked in Rome where, in 1880, he exhibited a statue entitled *Rebecca*. He was involved in sculpting the studies for the monument to Victor Emmanuel, and he made low reliefs for the façade of the Palazzo delle Esposizioni in Rome.
AUCTION RECORDS:
ROME, 8 March 1994, *Regional Dress* (watercolour/paper, series of five, each 10 x 6 ins / 24.5 x 15.5 cm) ITL 3,220,000.

FERRARI, Francesco
Italian, 17th century.
Born 1634, in Castello della Fratta, near Rovigo; died 1708, in Ferrara.
Painter, draughtsman. Religious subjects, landscapes, architectural views. Theatre decoration.
Initially a figure painter, Francesco Ferrari went on to study decoration under Gabriel Rossi. Ferrari decorated theatres in Vienna and San Lorenzo and worked for the Marquis degli Obizzi. He also painted several pictures for various churches in Bologna and Ferrara.
AUCTION RECORDS:
NEW YORK, 11 Jan 1994, *Door Surmounted by an Urn next to an Altar Flanked by Angels and a Cherub* (black chalk, ink and watercolour, 16 x 11 1/4in/40.6 x 28.3cm) USD 1,610.

FERRARI, Francesco
Italian, 18th century.
Active in Cremona.
Painter.
He studied under Francesco Chiozzi and worked in Cremona, in particular for the Casa Rizzola. He also decorated theatres.

FERRARI, Francesco
Italian, 18th century.
Active in Rome.
Painter, architect.
Francesco Ferrari enrolled at the Accademia di S Luca in 1721. He is credited with painting a *St Nicholas and St Vincent Ferrerio* for an altar in the church of S Nicola dei Prefetti, together with a painting portraying the founder of the order of the Servites (Servants of Blessed Mary), which was formerly displayed in the church of S Nicola in Arcione.

FERRARI, Francesco de, or Deferrari, also known as Francesco da Pavia
Italian, 15th century.
Born to a family originally from Pavia.
Painter.
Francesco de Ferrari worked in Genoa where he carried out alone or with other artists a number of works: in 1480 he frescoed the choir of the church of S Ambrogio and decorated the chapel of S Sebastiano in the cathedral. In 1484 he made an altarpiece for the large hall of the Palazzo della Repubblica and a painting *Doge Paolo Fregoso Dressed as Cardinal Kneeling before St George Flanked by St John the Baptist and St Lawrence*. His participation in the Palazzo di San Giorgio with his fellow citizen Francesco Grasso is mentioned in 1490.

FERRARI, Francesco de Bianchi.
See **BIANCHI-FERRARI Francesco de'**

FERRARI, Franciscus, or Ferari
Flemish, 17th century.
Active in Antwerp.
Painter.
Flemish School.

FERRARI, Gaetano
Italian, 19th century.
Sculptor. Groups, statues, busts, low reliefs.
The son of Giovanni Ferrari (known as Torretti), Gaetano studied under Rinaldo Rinaldi and worked in Venice. He sculpted the marble bust of *Moschini*, after studies by Rinaldi, in the seminary of S Maria delle Salute in Venice. He is also known for the bronze lion above the main window on the façade of St Mark's in Venice. He exhibited the heads of three nymphs, and the head of Christ crowned by thorns in low relief, at the 1820 exhibition in Venice.
AUCTION RECORDS:
NEW YORK, 14 Oct 1993, *Arab Lifting a Woman up onto a Camel* (bronze, h. 16 3/4 ins / 42.7 cm) USD 1,495. STUTTGART, 10 Dec 1999, *Roman War-chariot* (gold patinated bronze, h. 17 ins / 44 cm) DEM 4,000.

FERRARI, Gaudenzio, also known as Gaudenzio de Vince, or Vincio, and Gaudenzio Milanese by Vasari
Italian, 16th century.
Born 1480 or 1484, most probably in Valduggia; died 1546, in Milan.
Painter, sculptor.
Lombard School.

Gaudenzio Ferrari was probably for some time the pupil of Luini, and worked with Stefano Scotto, a painter of arabesques in Milan. Siret says that he was taught by Pietro Perugino, carried out important works at Varallo in 1504 and was the friend and journeyman of Raphael, whom he followed to Florence and later Rome where he assisted in the Farnesina and the Vatican. He was later the collaborator of Giulio Romano and Perino del Vaga. In 1521 Ferrari returned to Varallo where he did paintings and sculptures in his new style. He was master of the painter and writer Lomazzo. However, Bryan is not in agreement with Siret.

Ferrari was so precocious that in 1504 he was summoned to paint *The Sacrifice of Christ* in the Cappella del Sacro Monte de Varallo. In 1508 we find him in Vercelli. He was particularly productive in Varallo, where he produced several sculptures and paintings. From 1527 he resided in Milan where he executed oil paintings and frescoes for the various churches of the town and neighbourhood. For the decoration of the dome of S Maria dei Miracoli at Saronno he was inspired by Correggio's dome at Parma Cathedral. While he is situated in the category of Gothic frescoists, his style is Baroque. He died before having completed *The Last Supper* in the church of S Maria della Passione.

Ferrari also worked on pictures with his master in 1532, finishing these works alone in 1535, three years after the death of Bernardino Luini, at S Cristoforo de Vercelli and the church of Busto Arsizio near Milan.

BIBLIOGRAPHY:
Romano, Giovanni, *Gaudenzio Ferrari e la sua scuola*, exhibition catalogue, Accademia Albertina delle Belle Arti, Turin, 1982. Romano, G., *Gaudenzio Ferrari e la sua Scuola: I. Cartoni Cinquecenteschi dell'Accademia Albertina*, exhibition catalogue, Accademia Albertina, Turin, 1982. Ferro, F.M., '*Gaudenzio a Romagnano Sésia*' in *Paragone*, vol 34, 1983. Romano, G., '*Eusebio Ferrari e Gli Affreschi Cinquecenteschi di Palazzo Verga a Vercelli*' in *Prospettiva*, vol 33-36, 1983-4. Lazzaroni, L., et al., *Il Concerto degli Angeli: Gaudenzio Ferrari e la Cupola del Santuario di Saronno*, Milan, 1994. Nova, A., '*Popular Art in Renaissance Italy: Early Response to the Holy Mountain at Varallo*' in *Reframing the Renaissance: Visual Culture in Europe and Latin America, 1450-1650, ed C. Farago*, Yale University Press, New Haven and London, 1995.

MUSEUMS AND GALLERIES:
BERGAMO (Accademia Carrara, Pinacoteca d'Arte Antica): *The Virgin and the Christ Child; Small Cupids Dancing*; same subject; *Small Cupids Dancing*; same subject - BERLIN (Bodemus.): *Annunciation* - FLORENCE (NG): *Salvador Mundi* - LONDON (NG): *The Resurrection* - MILAN (Mus. Poldi Pezzoli): *Virgin and Saints* - MILAN (Pinacoteca di Brera): *Catherine of Alexandria; The Virgin and Christ Child; The Presentation of Mary; Isear Expelling St Joachim from the Temple; Angels Heralding the Birth of the Virgin to Anne; The Consecration of Mary; The Angel of the Annunciation; The Annunciation; Adoration of the Magi; The Assumption; Angel with Mandoline; Angel with Harp; Angel with Violin; The Visitation* - MOSCOW (Rumiantsev Mus.): *Adoration of the Shepherds* - NOVARA: *Angels Kneeling* - PARIS (Louvre): *St Paul* - TURIN (Pinacoteca): *God the Father; St Joachim Expelled from the Temple; The Visitation; St Anne; Pietà; The Crucixion; St Peter and Donors* - VARALLO: Fragments of frescoes; *St François Receiving the Stigmata* - VERCELLI (Mus. Borgogna): *Pietà*.

AUCTION RECORDS:
LONDON, 26 March 1908, *Fragment of Decoration*, GBP 44. LONDON, 19 Feb 1910, *The Virgin and Christ Child*, GBP 48. PARIS, 19 March 1919, *The Nativity* (attributed) FRF 1,850. LONDON, 11 Feb 1929, *Angel with Saints* (sepia) GBP 7. LONDON, 29 March 1929, *Adoration of the Magi* (drawing) GBP 8. LONDON, 10 June 1931, *Adoration of the Magi*, GBP 21. PARIS, 20 and 21 April 1932, *The Holy Family and St John* (pen and wash, attributed) FRF 520. LONDON, 21 Nov 1958, *Angel Playing Violin* (wash) GBP 630. GENEVA, 13 June 1960, *The Virgin and Child* (pen drawing, bistre wash) CHF 1,000. LONDON, 30 March 1962, *St Catherine of Alexandria and St Apollonia*, Gns 4,000. MILAN, 12 and 13 March 1963, *The Kiss of Judas; Ecce Homo; The Flagellation* (four temperas/wood) ITL 2,300,000. LONDON, 24 May 1963, *Christ in the Temple*, Gns 2,600. LONDON, 5 Dec 1969, *Virgin and Child*, Gns 2,500. NEW YORK, 16 Jan 1985, *Head of Young Woman* (black and white chalks/blue paper, 12 3/4 x 9 ins / 32.4 x 22 cm) USD 12,000. NEW YORK, 23 Jan 2001, *Holy Family* (colour ink, 5 x 5 ins / 12 x 12 cm) USD 5,500. MILAN, 17 Dec 2001, *Birth of the Virgin* (oil on board, 73 x 52 ins / 186 x 132 cm) EUR 537,815.

FERRARI, Giacinto
Italian, 18th century.
Active in Rome at the beginning of the 18th century.
Sculptor, painter.

Giacinto Ferrari worked on the decoration of the church of S Maria della Libertà.

FERRARI, Giacomo
Italian, 17th century.
Active in Cremona.
Painter.

The church of S Pietro in Cremona holds four paintings by Giacomo Ferrari, including a *Martyrdom of St Alexander* and a *St Dominic during the Albigensian Crusade*.

FERRARI, Giacomo Giuseppe, known in Russia as Jacopo Ferrari
Italian, 18th century.
Born 1747, in Torrechiara (Parma); died 1 May 1807, in St Petersburg.
Architect, architectural draughtsman.

Giacomo Ferrari studied at the academy in Parma, where he was awarded a prize for his project for a town square. He was retained in St Petersburg as an architect in the service of the tsar.

FERRARI, Gian Francesco. See **AGRATE Gian Francesco Ferrari d'**

FERRARI, Gio Andrea de. See **FERRARI Giovanni Andrea de**

FERRARI, Giovan Battista Antonio, Gio Batta Ferrari
Italian, 19th century.
Born 13 October 1829, in Brescia; died 26 April 1906, in Milan.
Painter. Landscapes, landscapes with figures, seascapes.

Giovan Battista Antonio Ferrari studied at the Municipal School of Art (la Scuola Communale di Disegno) founded by Gabriele Rottini in Brescia, then became a student of Giuseppe Sogni and Albert Zimmerman at the Accademia di Brera, Milan, from 1856. In 1849, he fought at Brescia, and in 1859 he joined the Corps of Lombard Volunteers, fighting in the Second War of Independence. He lived in London and then the USA from 1862 to 1865, then returned to Brescia and finally settled in Milan in 1868. There, he taught at the Municipal School of Art, where one of his students was Francesco Rovetta.

He painted mainly landscapes of Lombardy, in which lakes and rivers figured prominently, as well as seascapes in the style of the first Lombard Naturalism, meticulous and detailed. In 1873, he carried out a commission for Emperor Meiji of Japan.

Group exhibitions in which his paintings were shown included: 1857-1905, *Esposizione nazionale di Belle Arti* (*National Exhibition of Fine Arts*), Accademia di Brera, Milan; awarded Prix Mylius in 1879 with *Veduta di Brescia* (*View of Brescia*); 1861, *Esposizione nazionale* (*National Exhibition*), Florence; 1862, International Exhibition, London; around 1858, regularly, Società Promotrice delle Belle Arti, Turin; 1881, Società Promotrice delle Belle Arti, Genoa, with *La Salvatrice ai bagni di San Giuliano, Genova* (*The Female Lifesaver at the San Giuliano Baths, Genoa*); 1934, *Mostra di Pittura Bresciana dell'Ottocento* (*Exhibition of Nineteenth century Brescian Painting*), Brescia; 1993, *Il paesaggio del Garda, evoluzione di un mito* (*The Landscape of Lake Garda, Evolution of a Myth*); 1999, *Scoperta del Mare. Pittori lombardi in Liguria tra 1800 e 1900.* (*Discovering the Sea: Lombard Painters in Liguria between 1800 and 1900*), Palazzo Ducale, Genoa; 2000, *Francesco Filippini e la pittura bresciana dell'Ottocento: la memoria figurativa* (*Francesco Filippini and Nineteenth century Brescian Painting: the Visual Memory*), Galleria Aab, Brescia.

His solo exhibitions included: 1900, Milan Retrospective Exhibition (including his *Alpine Landscape*); 1990, Sale ex Monte di Pietà, Brescia; 1996, Galleria Gio Batta, Brescia; 2000, Commune di Caldes, Brescia.

Bibliography:

Ferrari, Roberto, et al., *Gio Batta Ferrari*, exhibition catalogue, Grafo, Brescia, 1990 (exhibition held at the Sale ex Monte di Pietà in Brescia, 1990). Ferrari, Roberto, *Gio Batta Ferrari: il fascino del paesaggio*, exhibition catalogue, Grafo, Brescia, 1993 (Desenzano exhibition, 1993). Ginex, Giovanna/Rebora, Sergio, *Scoperta del Mare. Pittori lombardi in Liguria tra 1800 e 1900*, group exhibition catalogue, Palazzo Ducale, Genoa, Mazzetta, Milan, 1999. Ferrari, Roberto/Ferrari, Salvatore/Iacobelli, Silvia, *Gio Batta Ferrari la magia della luce*, exhibition catalogue, Commune di Caldes, Grafo, Brescia, 2000.

Museums and Galleries:

Brescia (Pinacoteca Tosio-Martinengo): *Val di Ledro* (*Ledro Valley*) (1877); *Alpine Landscape*; *Paesaggio* (*Landscape*) (1862) - Milan (Galleria d'Arte moderna) - Milan (Pinacoteca di Brera): *Veduta di Brescia* (*View of Brescia*) (1879).

Auction records:

Milan, 16 Dec 1982, *Arona, Lago Maggiore* (oil on panel, 7 1/4 x 13 1/4 ins / 18.5 x 33.5 cm) ITL 1,500,000. Milan, 27 March 1984, *Arco della Pace in Milano*; *Lake Lombardy* (two panels, 8 x 13 3/4 ins / 20.5 x 35 cm) ITL 3,800,000. London, 9 Oct 1987, *Flock and Shepherd in a Wooded River Landscape* (1869, oil on canvas, 33 3/4 x 51 1/2 ins / 86 x 131 cm) GBP 6,500. Milan, 8 June 1993, *Lakeside Landscape with Peasants and Their Cattle* (1878, oil on canvas, 18 1/4 x 27 3/4 ins / 46.5 x 70.5 cm) ITL 14,000,000. Milan, 21 Dec 1993, *Isola Bella on Lake Maggiore* (1883, oil on canvas, 14 1/4 x 19 3/4 ins / 36.5 x 50 cm) ITL 13,225,000. Milan, 14 June 1995, *Arco della Pace in Milan*; *Island of San Giorgio in Venice* (oil on panel, a pair, 8 x 14 ins / 20.5 x 35.5 cm) ITL 13,225,000. Rome, 23 May 1996, *Walking along the Canal* (1866, oil on canvas, 22 x 31 1/2 ins / 56 x 80 cm) ITL 21,275,000. Rome, 11 Dec 1996, *Mountain Pasture* (oil on canvas, 41 3/4 x 59 3/4 ins / 106 x 152 cm) ITL 32,620. Milan, 20 Oct 1999, *Porto di Stresa* (1882, oil on panel, 7 x 13 ins / 17 x 32 cm) ITL 5,130,000. New York, 13 Sept 2000, *Summer Day* (oil on board, 8 x 14 ins / 21 x 36 cm) USD 2,400. Versailles, 3 Feb 2002, *Eastern Villa* (1880, oil on panel, 7 x 13 ins / 17 x 32 cm) FRF 12,460. Milford, 25 April 2002, *Canal in New York* (1864, gouache, 9 x 13 ins / 23 x 33 cm) USD 3,250. Paris, 25 April 2003, *Bundle of Corn and Faggot Carrier* (oil on canvas, 22 x 34 ins / 56 x 86 cm) EUR 7,800. Paris, 25 June 2003, *View of Isola Bella* (1880, oil on panel, 7 x 13 ins / 17 x 33 cm) EUR 3,500. Boston, 5 March 2004, *Canal in New York* (gouache, 8 x 13 ins / 21 x 32 cm) USD 4,500.

FERRARI, Giovanni
Italian, 16th century.
Active c. 1585.
Painter.

Two of Giovanni Ferrari's paintings are in the church of St Laurence at Morbegno (Como): *St Joachim and the Angel* and *The Meeting of St Joachim and Anne*

FERRARI, Giovanni, also known as Giovanni Torretti.
Italian, 18th - 19th century.
Born 1744, in Crespano; died 1826, in Venice.
Sculptor.

He was also known as Torretti, after his uncle Giuseppe Torretti II, Canova's first mentor. Giovanni Ferrari also studied under his uncle before going on to work in Mantua, Modena, Bologna, Rome and, ultimately, Venice. His body of work includes several statues on the Victor Emmanuel II square in Padua - including those of *Andrea Mantegna*, *Antonio Canova* and popes *Pope Alexander VIII* and *Pope Clement XIII* - together with statues of *St Peter and St Jerome* for the main altar of the Venetian church of S Geremia, statues of *Prudence* and *Wisdom* in the gardens of the Palazzo Trepolo in Carbonara, and a funerary monument to *Admiral Angelo Emo* in Venice.

FERRARI, Giovanni Andrea de
Italian, 17th century.
Died 1657 of the plague.
Painter. Religisous subjects, portraits.

The son of Orazio de Ferrari, he died of the plague, together with the rest of his immediate family. Giovanni Andrea de Ferrari started painting at an early age; a portrait of an Augustinian monk he painted when only 12 years old was kept for many years in Ventimiglia's Aprosiana library.

FERRARI, Giovanni Andrea or Gio Andrea de, or Deferrari
Italian, 17th century.
Born 1598, in Genoa; died 25 December 1669.
Painter. Religious subjects.

Giovanni Andrea Ferrari's mentors were Bernardo Castello and Bernardo Strozzi. He painted numerous altarpieces for churches in Genoa and elsewhere, including a *Death of St Joseph* for the church of S Rocco, a *St Thomas Professing his Faith before the King of the Moors* for the oratory of the Five Wounds, a *St Ambrose Driving the Emperor Theodosius from the Temple* a *Miracle of St Ignatius* for the church of S Ambrosiano, and a *Joseph Sold into Slavery by his Brethren* for the Durazzo-Pallavicini gallery. In 1619 - which is to say when only 21 years old - Ferrari painted ten compositions to frame a niche in the church of the Sisters of St Joseph; among these, two in particular (a *Marriage of the Virgin* and a *St Joseph the Carpenter*) attest to Ferrari's mastery of Caravaggio-like chiaroscuro and his exceptional sensitivity and virtuosity. His work as a whole bears evidence of the influence of Velázquez and Murillo as well as that of Caravaggio, Bassano and Titian.

Bibliography:

Salmi, Mario/Bazin, Germain, *Le Caravage et la Peinture italienne au XVIIe siècle*, exhibition catalogue, Musée du Louvre, Paris, 1965.

Museums and Galleries:
Chambéry (MBA): *Head of a Man* - Genoa (Mus. dell'Accademia Ligustica di Belle Arti): *Saint Resurrecting a Stonemason* - Genoa (Palazzo Bianco): *St Peter Delivered from his Bonds; Feast at Emmaüs* - Parma (Pinacoteca Giuseppe Stuard): *Noah's Shame; Joseph Sold into Slavery by his Brethren* - Rome (Gal. Nazionale): *Joseph's Brethren.*
Auction records:
London, 10 April 1981, *Joseph Refusing his Brothers' Gifts* (oil on canvas, 687 1/2 x 82 1/2in/1746 x 209.6cm) GBP 24,000. Milan, 8 May 1984, *Biblical Scene* (oil on canvas, 55 1/2 x 45in/141 x 114.5cm) ITL 19,000,000. London, 4 July 1986, *Adoration of the Shepherds* (oil on canvas, 44 1/4 x 55 3/4in/112.4 x 141.5cm) GBP 19,000. Rome, 10 May 1988, *St John the Baptist in the Wilderness* (oil on canvas, 56 3/4 x 46 3/4in/144 x 119cm) ITL 18,000,000. Rome, 24 May 1988, *Abraham Kneeling before the Three Angels* (oil on canvas, 75 1/2 x 95 1/4in/192 x 242cm) ITL 16,000,000. London, 21 April 1989, *Adoration of the Shepherds* (oil on canvas, 44 x 55 3/4in/112 x 141.5cm) GBP 19,800. Rome, 8 April 1991, *Lamenting the Dead Christ* (oil on canvas, 38 x 48in/96.5 x 121cm) ITL 3,680,000. Paris, 26 June 1991, *Apostle's Head* (oil on canvas, 19 x 15 1/4in/48 x 39cm) FRF 5,000. London, 31 March 1992, *Christ and the Samaritan* (oil on canvas, 42 3/4 x 51in/108.7 x 129.5cm) GBP 9,000. Milan, 14 June 1995, *The Island of San Giorgio, Venice* (oil on panel, 8 x 13 3/4in/20.5 x 35cm) ITL 11,500,000. Paris, 30 March 1998, *Christ Bearing His Cross* (oil on canvas, 29 1/4 x 42 1/2in/74 x 108cm) FRF 70,000. Vienna, 4 Oct 2000, *St John the Baptist* (oil on canvas, 47 x 39 ins / 120 x 98 cm) ATS 670,000. New York, 24 Jan 2002, *Massacre of the Innocents* (oil on canvas, 56 x 62 ins / 141 x 157 cm) USD 20,000. Paris, 28 Feb 2003, *Joseph and the Lady from Potiphar* (oil on canvas, 42 x 57 ins / 107 x 144 cm) EUR 20,000. Paris, 27 March 2003, *Baptism of Christ* (chalk, 12 x 8 ins / 31 x 21 cm) EUR 2,800.

FERRARI, Giovanni Battista
Italian, 17th century.
Born to a family originally from Novara (Piedmont).
Painter.
He is recorded as having been in Rome, where in 1608 he worked at the church of S Maria Maggiore.

FERRARI, Giovanni Battista
Italian, 17th century.
Painter.
A painting of three saints by Giovanni Battista Ferrari is preserved in the baptistery in Parma. This Ferrari may be related to the sculptor Giovanni Battista Ferrari, who is commonly known as Fornari Piccapietro.

FERRARI, Giovanni Battista
Italian, 17th century.
Active in Siena.
Engraver.
In 1633, he engraved plates for a volume on gardening (*De Florum Cultura*) illustrated by Guido Reni, Pietro da Cortona and A. Sacchi.

FERRARI, Giovanni Battista. See also **FORNARI PICCAPIETRO**

FERRARI, Giovanni Francesco
Italian, 16th century.
Active in Bologna.
Painter.
Giovanni Francesco Ferrari was a pupil of Carraccio and worked around 1590.

FERRARI, Girolamo, called Riccamador
Italian, 15th century.
Active in Ferrara.
Painter.
Attributed to Girolamo Ferrari is a large painting, *The Meeting of Mary and St Elizabeth*, from the church of the Madonnina, held in the university collection of Ferrara.

FERRARI, Girolamo
Italian, 16th century.
Active in Ferrara.
Painter.
Attributed to Girolamo Ferrari is a picture painted for the parish of Tamara near Ferrara. He also painted a banner (gonfalon) for the Compagnia della Morte.

FERRARI, Girolamo
Italian, 16th century.
Of Genoese origin.
Active in Rome.
Painter.
Girolamo Ferrari's only extant work is a drawing in the Prints Collection in Berlin.

FERRARI, Giulia
Italian, 19th century.
Born 30 December 1845; died 10 August 1901.
Painter. Portraits.
Guilia Ferrari was the daughter of Carlo Ferrari.

FERRARI, Giulio Cesare
Italian, 19th century.
Born 1813 or 1818, in Bologna; died c. 1899.
Painter. History painting, portraits.
Giulio Cesare Ferrari's best-known works include: *Tasso Reading His Poetry to Eleonora*; *Jephthah's Daughter*; and *Linda de Chamounix.*
Museums and Galleries:
Bologna (Pinacoteca Nazionale): *The Bronze Serpent; Esmeralda.*
Auction records:
Bologna, 27 Sept 1986, *Esmeralda* (oil on canvas, 35 1/2 x 25 1/2 ins / 90 x 65 cm) ITL 3,500,000.

FERRARI, Giuseppe
Italian, 18th - 19th century.
Born 1773; died 1864.
Active in Ferrara.
Sculptor.
Giuseppe Ferrari studied under Tenerani and went on to teach at the University of Ferrara. He sculpted a large number of funerary monuments in his native town, including statues of the poet *Vincenzo Monti*, the poet-philosopher *Alfonso Varano* and the philosopher *D. Bartoli*. Ferrari also sculpted allegorical statues and low reliefs.

FERRARI, Giuseppe
Italian, 19th century.
Active in Genoa.
Painter. Genre scenes, landscapes.
In 1863 Giuseppe Ferrari published an album of lithographed views of the Riviera di Ponente.

FERRARI, Giuseppe
Italian, 19th century.
Born 1840 or 1843, in Rome; died 4 August 1905, in Rieti (Lazio).
Painter, watercolourist. Religious subjects, figures, genre scenes, landscapes with figures, seascapes.
Giuseppe Ferrari exhibited in Munich between 1879 and 1888. He was awarded an honourable mention at the Exposition Universelle in Paris in 1900.
Museums and Galleries:
Rome (Gal. Nazionale): *The Three Maries; Christ in Gethsemane*; seascape; *Civitavecchia.*
Auction records:
London, 16 March 1979, *Morning Prayer* (1881, watercolour, 52 x 55 1/2 ins / 132.2 x 140.8 cm) GBP 900. London, 30 Jan

1980, *Horseman* (1878, oil on panel, 19 x 14 ins / 48 x 35.5 cm) GBP 1,000. LONDON, 29 April 1982, *Revenge* (1877, watercolour, 29 1/2 x 21 1/4 ins / 75 x 54 cm) GBP 1,100. ROME, 29 Oct 1985, *Young Girls in a Wooded Landscape* (oil on canvas, 40 1/4 x 43 1/4 ins / 102 x 110 cm) ITL 1,600,000. SAN FRANCISCO, 19 Nov 2003, *Domestic Bliss* (oil on canvas/panel, 28 x 37 ins / 71 x 94 cm) USD 3,000. PARIS, 3 June 2004, *Bull Scene* (patinated bronze, 15 x 19x8 ins / 38 x 49x21 cm) EUR 4,200.

FERRARI, Giuseppe
Italian, 19th century.
Born 1846, in Piacenza.
Sculptor (wood).

Giuseppe Ferrari was a pupil of Gregori and worked in Milan and Naples. He sculpted a crib for Victor Emmanuel, the heir to the Italian throne. He then moved to America, where he produced numerous decorative sculptures which earned him honours at the Universal Exhibition of 1876 in Philadelphia.

FERRARI, Gregorio de
Italian, 17th - 18th century.
Born 1644 or 1647, in Porto Maurizio; died 1726, in Genoa.
Painter, fresco artist, copyist, draughtsman. Religious subjects.
Genoese School.

Gregorio de Ferrari studied in Genoa under Domenico Fiasella (Il Sarzana) and worked extensively in Turin and Marseilles before returning to Genoa to work with Domenico Piola, whose daughter he subsequently married.

Gregorio de Ferrari's style was substantially more expansive than that of his original mentor Sarzana. His style changed radically after his study of Correggio's work in Parma, during which he went as far as to paint a faithful and very well-executed copy of Correggio's view of the cathedral dome. From that point on, his style tends to recall that of Allegri, although it could be said that, while Ferrari's heads and lone figures are on a par with those of Allegri in terms of tonal clarity and form, his overall compositional strength falls short of Allegri, as does the colour palette used in his fresco work. Gregorio de Ferrari produced numerous substantial works in Genoa, including a fresco for the Palazzo Cambiaso Centurione; a *Glory of St Andrew Avellino*, a *Rest during the Flight into Egypt* and an *Ecstasy of St Francis* for the church of S Siro; a *Spring* for the Palazzo Rosso; and a *Warrior's Triumph* for the royal palace in Turin.

Gregorio de Ferrari's imaginative decorative work is representative of Italian painting in the latter half of the 18th century to the extent that it forms a counterpart to the sculptural work of some of Bernini's disciples, notably Pierre Puget and Daniel Solaro, both of whom were also active in Genoa.

MUSEUMS AND GALLERIES:

GENOA (Palazzo Bianco) - GENOA (Palazzo Rosso): *Project for the Decoration of a Cupola: The Immaculate Conception with Two Pendentives of a Prophet and a Sibyl* (drawing).

AUCTION RECORDS:

PARIS, 21 Feb 1919, *Allegory for a Ceiling Fresco* (pen and Indian ink) FRF 30. LONDON, 13 Dec 1984, *Heads of Two Angels* (black chalk, 12 3/4 x 8in/32.4 x 20.5cm) GBP 450. ROME, 24 May 1988, *Christ Appearing to St Catherine* (oil on canvas, 53 1/4 x 37in/135 x 94cm) ITL 32,000,000. LONDON, 2 July 1991, *Our Lady of Loreto Appearing to Two Saints* (black chalk, brown ink and grey wash, 12 1/2 x 12 3/4in/32 x 32.7cm) GBP 10,450. ROME, 1 June 1999, *Narcissus* (oil on canvas, 45 x 65 ins / 115 x 166 cm) ITL 188,000,000. LONDON, 7 July 1999, *Bishop Saint with Three Putti* (pen/brown ink heightened with white over black chalk, 11 x 8 ins / 29 x 21 cm) GBP 2,400. LONDON, 6 July 2000, *The Rest on the Flight into Egypt* (oil on canvas, 39 x 29 ins / 98 x 74 cm) GBP 130,000. MILAN, 22 Nov 2000, *Deposition* (brown Chinese ink/grey watercolour, 19 x 12 ins / 49 x 30 cm) ITL 5,000,000.

FERRARI, Jacopo. See **FERRARI Giacomo Giuseppe**

FERRARI, Jan Baptista I, or Ferari
Flemish, 17th century.
Active in Antwerp.
Painter.
Flemish School.

Jan Baptista Ferrari I qualified as a master in 1696-1697.

FERRARI, Jan Baptista II, or Ferari
Flemish, 18th century.
Active in Antwerp.
Painter.
Flemish School.

Jan Baptista Ferrari II qualified as a master in 1725-1726.

FERRARI, Juan M.
Uruguayan, 20th century.
Born 21 May 1874, in Montevideo; died 31 October 1916, in Buenos Aires.
Sculptor. Busts, groups, monuments.

As a young man, Juan Ferrari was awarded a bursary to train in Europe. He studied in Rome under Ettore Ferrari and Ercole Rosa. From his Italian teachers Ferrari learned a style of sculpture that was still very objective but which he brought to life through his own sensibility, carving busts of his friends and monuments that have now become classics in Latin America. His most famous work is the *Monument Erected to Mendoza to Commemorate the Crossing of the Andes by General San Martín*, in which bronze statues and low reliefs arise from Andean stone with a fine, Romantic flourish.

FERRARI, Leonardo, also known as Leonardino
Italian, 17th century.
Born in Bologna; died 1648.
Painter. History painting.

Leonardo Ferrari studied under Lucio Massari. Although Ferrari is often referred to by Massari as a 'festivals painter', he enjoyed a solid reputation as a painter of historical subjects, primarily for churches in his native Bologna. Examples of his work include *Virgin of the Rosary with Mary Magdalene and other Saints* for the church of SS Gervasio e Protasio, a *Death of St Joseph* for the church of S Francesco, and a *St Anthony of Padua* for the church of Madonna delle Neve.

FERRARI, Lorenzo
Italian, 18th century.
Born in Sissa (Parma).
Painter, modeller.

The son of Paolo Ferrari I, he studied painting at the academy in Rome under Paolo Ferrari II and modelling under Lorenzo Guiard. He is remembered for a drawing of the *Communion of St Lucy* (based on a painting by S. Ricci for the church of S Lucia in Parma) which was subsequently engraved by G. Patrini.

FERRARI, Lorenzo de, called l'Abate de Ferrari
Italian, 18th century.
Born 1680, in Genoa; died 1744, in Genoa.
Painter, fresco artist, draughtsman. Religious subjects, allegorical subjects.

He was the son and pupil of Gregorio de Ferrari. Like his father, Lorenzo imitated the style of Correggio, albeit with more pronounced Roman overtones. He was best-known for his fresco work, but he also produced a number of fine paintings for churches. His style could be said at times to be somewhat languid, but his best work - such as the work he did for the Palazzo Doria in San Matteo - demonstrates a lively sense of colour.

MUSEUMS AND GALLERIES:

GENOA (Mus. dell'Accademia Ligustica di Belle Arti): *Courage* (drawing).

AUCTION RECORDS:

LONDON, 9 Dec 1980, *Two Sibyls* (black and white chalks/grey paper, two drawings, 24 x 15 ins / 61 x 37.8 cm and 24 x 15 1/4in/61 x 38.8cm) GBP 4,500. NEW YORK, 12 Jan 1988, *Ecstasy of a Saint* (black chalk, ceiling design, 16 1/4 x 10 1/4 ins / 41 x 26 cm) USD 3,080. NEW YORK, 12 Jan 1989, *Adam and Eve with their Children Cain and Abel* (oil on canvas, 36 x 37 1/4 ins / 91.5 x 94.5 cm) USD 30,800. PARIS, 16 June 1993, *Study for a Draped Caryatid* (black chalk with traces of white chalk/grey-blue paper, 21 x 9 1/4 ins / 53.5 x 23.8 cm) FRF 50,000. NEW YORK, 12 Jan 1995, *St Francis Xavier Standing on a Rock and Preaching* (black chalk, 17 1/4 x 11 1/2 ins / 43.7 x 29.5 cm) USD 3,680. NEW YORK, 26 Jan 2000, *Flying Figure and Putto. Sketches of a Kneeling Figure* (red/black chalk, double-sided, 11 x 16 ins / 27 x 41 cm) USD 7,000. PARIS, 27 March 2003, *Reclining Man* (chalk, 16 x 22 ins / 41 x 55 cm) EUR 8,000. PARIS, 27 March 2003, *Young Man* (chalk, 24 x 13 ins / 61 x 33 cm) EUR 12,000.

FERRARI, Luca, also known as Luca da Reggio
Italian, 17th century.
Born 1605, in Reggio nell'Emilia; died 1654, in Padua.
Painter. Religious subjects, mythological subjects, portraits.

A pupil of Guido Reni, Luca Ferrari essentially imitated Reni's style, not least in his graceful representation of figures and facial expressions. Ferrari himself went on to instruct Minorello and Cirelli. One of his best works - an admirably coloured and highly expressive *Pietà* - is in the church of S Antonio in Padua.

MUSEUMS AND GALLERIES:

BORDEAUX: *Allegory of Painting Crowned by Fame* - FLORENCE (Uffizi): *Self-portrait* - MODENA (Gal. Estense): *St Mary Magdalene; Death of Cleopatra; Tomyris Plunging the Head of Cyrus into a Goatskin Filled with Blood* - PADUA (Dominican church): *Plague* (1630).

AUCTION RECORDS:

ROME, 24 May 1973, *Scene from Antiquity*, ITL 6,000,000. ROME, 29 March 1977, *Noli Me Tangere* (oil on canvas, 44 x 57 1/2in/112 x 146cm) ITL 3,150,000. LONDON, 11 March 1983, *Paris* (oil on canvas, 27 1/4 x 23 1/4in/69.2 x 59cm) GBP 5,000. MILAN, 26 Nov 1985, *Lucretia* (oil on canvas, 48 3/4 x 43 1/4in/124 x 110cm) ITL 14,000,000. LONDON, 11 April 1990, *St Catherine* (oil on canvas, 41 1/4 x 34in/105 x 85.5cm) GBP 19,800. AMELIA, 18 May 1990, *St John the Baptist* (oil on canvas, 36 1/2 x 26 1/2in/93 x 67cm) ITL 9,500,000. ROME, 8 April 1991, *St John the Baptist as a Youth* (oil on canvas, 36 1/2 x 26 1/2in/93 x 67cm) ITL 3,220,000. MILAN, 28 May 1992, *Clemency of Scipio* (oil on canvas, 57 x 86 1/2in/145 x 220cm) ITL 210,000,000. NEW YORK, 25 May 1999, *Lucretia* (oil on canvas, 28 x 21 ins / 70 x 53 cm) USD 7,000. VIENNA, 30 March 2000, *King David Crowned by Angel after Victorious Battle* (oil on canvas, 46 x 35 ins / 116 x 88 cm) ATS 380,000. LONDON, 11 Dec 2002, *Agamemnon Refusing to Allow Chryses to Ransom his Daughter Chryseis* (oil on canvas, 51 x 56 ins / 130 x 141 cm) GBP 90,000.

FERRARI, Luigi
Italian, 19th century.
Born 21 June 1810, in Venice; died 13 May 1894, in Venice.
Sculptor, watercolourist. Religious subjects. Groups, statues, busts, low reliefs.

Luigi Ferrari's father, the sculptor Bartolomeo Ferrari, was also his master. He made a name for himself at a very young age, with an impressive statue of *The Virgin*, but achieved fame primarily through his *Laocoön* group. In 1851 he was engaged to teach sculpture at the Accademia di Belle Arti in Venice. He is best known for: *David and Goliath, Endymion*, and some low reliefs and busts.

MUSEUMS AND GALLERIES:

BOLOGNA: *The Immaculate Conception* (plaster) - BRESCIA: *Joseph I, Emperor of Austria* - BRESCIA (Correr): *Bust of General Giuglielmo Pepe* - BRESCIA (Ducal Palace): *Bust of Galileo; Bust of Paruta*.

AUCTION RECORDS:

ROME, 8 March 1994, *Regional Dress* (watercolour/paper, series of six, each 6 3/4 x 6 ins / 17 x 15 cm) ITL 3,450,000.

FERRARI, Marcel Jacques
French, 20th century.
Born in St-Maur-des-Fossés.
Painter.

Marcel Ferrari exhibited at the Salon d'Automne.

FERRARI, Moysio
Italian, 19th century.
Active in Venice.
Engraver (burin).

FERRARI, Nicola
Italian, 14th century.
Born to a family originally from Caravaggio.
Active in Bergamo.
Painter.

FERRARI, Nunzio
Italian, 19th - 20th century.
Born 25 March 1832, in Guardiagrele (Abruzzi); died 10 May 1910, in Guardiagrele.
Sculptor (wood).

Nunzio Ferrari was the pupil of Cataldi, Tenerani and Protesti at the academy in Rome. He worked in his native country, mostly for churches. There are four statues by him, representing the *Fathers of the Church*, in Lanciano Cathedral. Many churches in the Abruzzi mountains were decorated after his original designs.

FERRARI, Orazio de
Italian, 17th century.
Born 1605, in Voltri, in 1606 according to some sources; died 1657, in Genoa.
Painter, fresco artist. Religious subjects.

Orazio de Ferrari was a relative and pupil of Andrea Ansaldo. His reputation brought him to the attention of the prince of Monaco, who retained him in his service over a period of years. He died during the plague epidemic in Genoa in 1657.

Ferrari painted both frescoes and oils. Examples of his work include a *Last Supper* for the oratory of S Siro in Genoa; an *Apparition of the Virgin* and a *Consecration of the Martyred St Peter* for the oratory of S Giacomo della Marina in the same city; two episodes from the *Life of Christ*; and several paintings entitled *Ecce Homo*.

MUSEUMS AND GALLERIES:

GENOA (SFA): *St Augustine* - MILAN (Pinacoteca di Brera): *Ecce Homo*.

AUCTION RECORDS:

NEW YORK, 5 Nov 1982, *St Peter, St Paul and St Batholomew* (oils on canvas, three, 16 3/4 x 13 3/4in/42.5 x 35cm) USD 3,000. LONDON, 8 July 1987, *Old Testament Scene* (oil on canvas, 45 1/4 x 57 3/4in/115 x 147cm) GBP 200,000. MILAN, 10 June 1988, *St Cecilia* (oil on canvas, 48 1/2 x 35in/123 x 89cm) ITL 22,500,000. ROME, 8 April 1991, *Adoration of the Shepherds* (oil on canvas, 44 x 36 1/2in/112 x 93cm) ITL 3,450,000. MILAN, 3 Dec 1992, *Martyrdom of S Biagio* (oil on canvas, 61 x 68 3/4in/155 x 174.5cm) ITL 53,000,000. LONDON, 15 April 1999, *The Holy Family with a Donor* (oil on canvas, 44 x 51 ins / 111 x 130 cm) GBP 16,000. MILAN, 24 Nov 1999, *Biblical Scene* (oil on canvas, 46 x 62 ins / 117 x 158 cm) ITL

44,000,000. NEW YORK, 26 Jan 2001, *David and Abigail* (oil on canvas, 56 x 72 ins / 142 x 182 cm) USD 110,000.

FERRARI, Paolo I

Italian, 18th century.
Born c. 1700, in Sissa (Parma).
Architect, painter.

Paolo Ferrari's body of painted work includes medallions for the church of Trecasali, near Parma; an allegorical *Temperance* for a chimney-breast in a room in the city hall in Parma; and six plates for the catafalque in the church of the Annunciation in the same city.

FERRARI, Paolo II

Italian, 18th century.
Born c. 1730.
Active in Parma.
Painter.

Paolo Ferrari II taught at the academy in Parma. Examples of his work include an *Angel Offering St Cecilia the Palm and Crown of Martyrdom* for a chapel in the church of S Giuseppe, and a *Virgin with St Bernard and St Roch* for a small chapel at Ponte Caprazucca.

FERRARI, Pietro Melchiorre

Italian, 18th century.
Born 1735, in Parma; died 1787.
Painter. History painting, religious subjects, portraits.

A pupil of Giuseppe Baldrighi, Pietro Ferrari taught at the academy in Parma. He is best remembered as a copyist of the old masters.

Ferrari p.

MUSEUMS AND GALLERIES:

PARMA: *Male Nude* (two studies); *Portrait of Bertoluzzi*; *Portrait of Bertoluzzi's Wife*; *Self-portrait with Giuseppe Baldrighi and Gaetano Callani*; *Portrait of Ferdinand de Bourbon*; *Education of the Virgin*; *St Vincent Ferrer*; *Innocenzo Frugoni and the Arcadia Parmense*.

AUCTION RECORDS:

PARIS, 18 May 1942, *Coronation of the Poet* (pen and bistre wash) FRF 1,250. PARIS, 3 Feb 1943, *Scene from Antiquity* (pen and sepia wash) FRF 420. LONDON, 7 Dec 1987, *Annunciation* (pen and colour wash, 13¼ x 10in/33.6 x 25.6cm) GBP 1,000. ROME, 10 May 1994, *Portrait of a Gentleman* (oil on canvas, 41 x 32¾in/104 x 83.5cm) ITL 6,900,000.

FERRARI, Teodoro Wolf

Italian, 20th century.
Born 26 June 1878, in Venice; died 1945, in Zenone degli Ezzelini, near Treviso (Veneto).
From 1898 also active in Germany.
Painter, decorative designer. Nudes, portraits, landscapes.

Teodoro Wolf Ferrari studied under Guglielmo Ciardi at the academy of fine arts in Venice. He went to live in Munich in 1898, where he became known as Teodoro Wolf-Ferrari. He took part in many group exhibitions in Italy and Bavaria, notably at the International Exhibition in Turin in 1902, and the Venice Biennale.

Ferrari designed a large number of decorative panels, screens and stained glass windows, which evoke the fin-de-siècle style of the Nabis. He was also involved in decorating the Lido Baths in Venice. Generally speaking, his works reveal a talent for observation, and are drawn to an extremely high standard with a delicate colour palette. Although he preferred landscape painting, he also painted portraits and nudes. He followed the various artistic movements of his day, and assimilated the influence of the Impressionists, of Van Gogh and Cézanne, and also the Divisionist/Tachiste style of the Macchiaiolo painter Segantini.

BIBLIOGRAPHY:

Wolf Ferrari, Teodoro, *Opere giovanili di Teodoro Wolf Ferrari*, catalogue, Sala Napoleonica, Venice, 1968.

MUSEUMS AND GALLERIES:

BRIGHTON (Mus. and AG): *Lo Spitz di Mezzodi da brusa adaz a zolno alto* (oil/panel).

AUCTION RECORDS:

MILAN, 10 June 1981, *Mountain Landscape* (1925, oil on panel, 22 x 28 ins / 55 x 71 cm) ITL 600,000. LONDON, 24 Oct 1984, *Landscape* (oil on panel, 30¾ x 38½ ins / 78 x 98 cm) GBP 1,100. MILAN, 18 March 1986, *Landscape* (oil on panel, 23½ x 31½ ins / 60 x 80 cm) ITL 2,200,000. ROME, 31 May 1990, *Mountain Landscape* (oil on panel, 10 x 14¼ ins / 24.5 x 36 cm) ITL 2,000,000. ROME, 28 May 1991, *Landscape* (1930, oil on panel, 19¾ x 23½ ins / 50 x 60 cm) ITL 3,200,000. MILAN, 6 June 1991, *Willows and Cypresses* (1917, oil on canvas, 22½ x 34¾ ins / 57 x 88.5 cm) ITL 11,000,000. MILAN, 8 June 1993, *Venetian Canal* (oil on panel, 25¼ x 29½ ins / 64 x 75 cm) ITL 9,000,000. MILAN, 28 May 2001, *Summer Sunset at Sant'Elena with Riva degli Schiavoni in the background* (oil on board, 14 x 18 ins / 35 x 45 cm) ITL 5,500,000. TRIESTE, 4 Dec 2001, *Mount Grappa in the Morning* (oil on board, 23 x 30 ins / 58 x 75 cm) ITL 11,000,000. VENICE, 8 June 2002, *Woman in Pink with White Bear* (tempera on card, 10 x 7 ins / 26 x 17 cm) EUR 2,900. VENICE, 8 June 2002, *Evening* (oil on canvas, 52 x 79 ins / 132 x 200 cm) EUR 13,000. MILAN, 18 March 2003, *Wood* (1906, oil on board, 10 x 17 ins / 25 x 42 cm) EUR 2,000. MILAN, 18 March 2003, *Mountainous Landscape with Houses* (1906, oil on board, 9 x 16 ins / 24 x 41 cm) EUR 2,800.

FERRARI, William

Argentinian, 20th century.
Born in Rosario.
Engraver (burin).

William Ferrari studied under E. Léon. He exhibited at the Salon des Artistes Français in 1930.

FERRARINI, Agostino

Italian, 19th century.
Born 1828, in Moletolo (province of Parma, Emilia-Romagna).
Sculptor.

Agostino Ferrarini began his artistic studies at the age of nine with Tomaso Bandini, and ended up at the academy in Parma, where he became a teacher in 1865. His best-known works include: at Piacenza, the *Monument to Doctor Guglielmo da Saliceto* and a marble group entitled *Charity*, at the monastery of S Giovanni; in Parma, the statue of *Correggio*, in a niche at the Palazzo Communale, and the statues on the façade of the Tiburtius Oratory. Another famous work by Ferrarini is a group representing the *Descent from the Cross*, in Campiano near Parma.

FERRARINI, Giuseppe

Italian, 19th century.
Born 30 April 1846, in Parma.
Painter. Landscapes. Murals.

In 1871 Giuseppe Ferrarini exhibited three works at the gallery of fine arts in Parma, two of which were views of the Po; and in 1872 he showed *In the Middle of the Wood* at the Royal Gallery. He later moved to Australia, where he remained for many years. When he returned to Italy he brought back with him a large number of studies of Australian landscapes. He settled in Rome, and exhibited 32 sketches of Caprera Island there. Then, in 1891, he exhibited a view of the Roman countryside at the International Exhibition in Berlin.

MUSEUMS AND GALLERIES:

GOULBURN: *After the Bushfire* - NICE (Casino): *The Four Seasons* (murals) - PARMA (GA): *S Quintino Monastery in Parma.*

AUCTION RECORDS:
ROME, 16 Dec 1987, *Banks of the Tiber at Sunset* (1887, oil on canvas, 35 1/2 x 63 ins / 90 x 160 cm) ITL 8,000,000. MILAN, 20 Oct 1999, *Lake Landscape* (oil on canvas, 25 x 43 ins / 64 x 110 cm) ITL 7,695,000.

FERRARINI, Pier Giuseppe
Italian, 19th century.
Born 30 March 1852, in Parma; died 1887.
Painter. Figures, landscapes.

Pier Giuseppe Ferrarini exhibited two paintings at the Venice Exhibition of 1887: *The Coast near Finale Marina* and *Ruit Hora*.

MUSEUMS AND GALLERIES:
PARMA (GA): *Cul-de-sac near the Church of S Giovanni Evangelista in Parma.*

AUCTION RECORDS:
LONDON, 7 May 1976, *Return to Naples* (1882, oil on canvas, 28 1/4 x 38 1/4 ins / 72 x 97 cm) GBP 950. LONDON, 20 April 1978, *Dante and Beatrice* (oil on canvas, 4 3/4 x 37 3/4 ins / 12 x 96 cm) GBP 2,200.

FERRARIO, Bruno
Italian, 20th century.
Born in Italy.
Painter.

The Gallery of Modern Art in Florence has a painting entitled *Anatra* by Bruno Ferrario.

FERRARIO, Carlo
Italian, 19th century.
Born 8 September 1833, in Milan; died 11 May 1907, in Milan.
Painter, watercolourist. Landscapes, architectural views, church interiors. Stage sets, theatre decoration.

In 1867 Carlo Ferrario decorated La Scala in Milan, and also designed stage sets there, particularly for the works of Verdi. From 1870 onwards he showed watercolours of architectural views (mostly of Lombardy) at exhibitions in Italy, which he had published under the title *Beauties of Italy*.

MUSEUMS AND GALLERIES:
MILAN (Pinacoteca di Brera): twelve watercolours.

AUCTION RECORDS:
MILAN, 19 March 1992, *Stream in a Wood* (1905, oil on card); *Interior of St Mark's in Venice* (1879, watercolour/card, 11 1/2 x 7 3/4 ins / 29.5 x 19.5 cm) ITL 2,600,000.

FERRARIO, Giovanni Battista
Italian, 19th century.
Born 1845, in Milan.
Painter. Genre scenes.

Giovanni Battista Ferrario exhibited in Munich in 1883. He is known for a painting entitled *Goodbye Kiss*.

FERRARIO, Helvetio
Swiss, 19th - 20th century.
Born 23 March 1872, in Geneva.
Painter. Interiors with figures, genre scenes, still-lifes, fruit.

Ferrario was a native of Ticino. He studied in Geneva, Marseilles and Paris. He exhibited in Geneva from 1895.

MUSEUMS AND GALLERIES:
GENEVA (MAH): *Corner of a Studio*.

FERRARIS, Arthur von
Hungarian, 19th - 20th century.
Born 1856, in Galkovitz; died after 1928.
Active in Austria.
Painter. Portraits, local scenes, still-lifes, flowers. Orientalism.

Arthur von Ferraris studied at the workshop of the famous portrait painter Joseph Matthaus in Vienna, then settled in Paris where he was the pupil of Jean Léon Gérome and Jules Lefebvre. He painted mainly Orientalist pictures and portraits and a number of high-society figures posed for him in Paris, Budapest and Vienna. His works include: *Smoking a Hookah, At the El A'Hazar Mosque, Cairo, Descendant of the Prophet, Reading the Koran* and *Bedouins at the Armourer's*. Von Ferraris has a significant position in the Hungarian School.

Arthur von Ferraris exhibited from 1881 onwards at the Salon des Artistes Français in Paris, winning an honourable mention at the Expositions Universelles in 1889 and 1900. He also took part in many exhibitions in Berlin in 1894 and in Düsseldorf and Munich between 1904 and 1908.

BIBLIOGRAPHY:
Thornton, Lynne, *Les Orientalistes, peintres voyageurs, 1828-1908*, ACR Édition, Paris, 1993.

AUCTION RECORDS:
NEW YORK, 8-9 Jan 1903, *Cairo*, USD 1,400. NEW YORK, 8-9 Jan 1903, *Cairo*, USD 1,400. NEW YORK, 10-11 Jan 1907, *Street in Cairo*, USD 1,025. LONDON, 11 Dec 1925, *Student*, GBP 32. LONDON, 11 Dec 1925, *Student*, GBP 32. LONDON, 3 Nov 1934, *Visit of the Great Sheikh*, GBP 73. LONDON, 3 Nov 1934, *Visit of the Great Sheikh*, GBP 73. GLASGOW, 16 Nov 1945, *Mosque Door*, GBP 51. GLASGOW, 16 Nov 1945, *Mosque Door*, GBP 51. LONDON, 24 May 1946, *Interesting Book*, GBP 68. LONDON, 24 May 1946, *Interesting Book*, GBP 68. NEW YORK, 14 May 1976, *Turks Playing Dominoes* (1892, oil on canvas, 18 x 21 3/4 ins / 46 x 55.5 cm) USD 1,900. NEW YORK, 12 May 1978, *Egyptian Bazaar* (c. 1887, oil on panel, 25 x 18 ins / 63.5 x 46 cm) USD 3,500. LONDON, 25 Nov 1981, *Arab Minstrel* (1889, oil on panel, 25 x 19 1/4 ins / 63.5 x 49 cm) GBP 17,000. VIENNA, 18 Jan 1984, *Vase of Flowers* (oil on canvas, 35 1/2 x 28 1/4 ins / 90 x 72 cm) ATS 20,000. LONDON, 14 June 1995, *Bedouins at the Armourer's* (1893, oil on canvas, 23 1/2 x 31 1/2 ins / 60 x 80 cm) GBP 58,700. NORTH BETHESDA, 14 Feb 2001, *Recital* (1915, oil on canvas, 71 x 50 ins / 181 x 127 cm) USD 16,000. LONDON, 21 June 2001, *Negotiations in the Market Place* (1893, oil on canvas, 33 x 50 ins / 85 x 127 cm) GBP 115,000. LINZ, 27 May 2002, *Flowers on Shore* (1921, oil on card, 16 x 20 ins / 40 x 51 cm) EUR 2,000.

FERRARIUS, Bassa. See **BASSA Ferrer**

FERRARO, Agostino
Italian, 17th century.
Active in Naples c. 1680.
Sculptor.

Agostino Ferraro was a pupil and collaborator of Pietro Ceraso, and was also retained by the Viceroy of Naples. He sculpted numerous funerary monuments.

FERRARO, Antonio
Italian, 16th century.
Of Sicilian origin.
Painter, sculptor.

Antonio Ferraro was probably the pupil of the painter Orazio Alfani who worked in Sicily. With Giuseppe Spadofora he executed a marble font for Palermo Cathedral. He worked for the church of S Lorenzo at Caltabellotta where his *Pietà* group has life-size statues of the Virgin and St John, Mary Magdalene, the holy women, St Joseph and St Nicodemus. In the church of S Domenico at Castelvetrano he executed the decoration of the choir, of which the main elements comprised 14 monumental statues of the *Tree of Jesse*, dominated by a statue of the Virgin.

FERRARO, Bartolomeo
Italian, 16th century.
Active in Messina, Sicily, c. 1506.
Painter.

FERRARO, Giuseppe
Italian, 16th - 17th century.
Of Sicilian origin.
Sculptor.
Giuseppe Ferraro sculpted an *Ecce Homo* in the sacristy of the church of Sant'Ignazia all'Olivella, Palermo.

FERRARO, Matteo del
Italian, 16th century.
Born to a family originally from Carrara.
Sculptor.
Matteo del Ferraro is mentioned in Palermo in 1512 where he worked in the workshop of A. Cagini.

FERRARO, Orazio
Italian, 16th - 17th century.
Of Sicilian origin.
Painter, stucco artist.
The son of Antonio Ferraro, Orazio Ferraro did the stucco decorations of the chapel of the church of S Lorenzo in Caltabellota and those of the church of Burgio, where he also executed the ceiling frescoes. For the high altar of S Cataldo at Erice he made a statue of the *Virgin* and a low relief of *The Birth of Christ*. Altar paintings by Ferraro are in Castelvetrano, Mazàra, Marsala and Erice.

FERRARO, Salvatore
Italian, 17th century.
Active in Naples.
Sculptor.
He is recorded as having worked between 1598 and 1622 at the Carthusian church of S Martino.

FERRARO, Tomaso
Italian, 17th century.
Of Sicilian origin.
Painter.
The son of Antonio Ferraro, he is known exclusively for his decorative work on the chapel of St Mary Magdalene in the cathedral of Castelvetrano.

FERRARY, Désiré Maurice
French, 19th - 20th century.
Born 1852, in Embrun (Hautes-Alpes); died 1904, in Neuilly-sur-Seine.
Sculptor. Groups, statues.
Désiré Ferrary studied under Cavelier. He is remembered for: *Narcissus, Charmer* and *Gladiator Teasing a Panther*. In 1882, he was awarded the Grand Prix de Rome. At the Salon des Artistes Français, he received a third-class medal in 1879, a second-class medal in 1886, and a silver medal in 1889 for the International Fair. He received the Légion d'Honneur in 1891.
MUSEUMS AND GALLERIES:
AMIENS: *Léon Cogniet* - TOURS: *Mercury and Cupid* (plaster).
AUCTION RECORDS:
BRUSSELS, 25 Nov 1982, *Tiger Tamer* (bronze, h. 26 1/2 ins / 67 cm) BEF 18,000.

FERRAT, Charles Hippolyte Marcelin
French, 19th century.
Born 26 April 1830, in Aix-en-Provence; died 27 February 1882, in Aix-en-Provence.
Sculptor.
Charles Ferrat entered the École des Beaux-Arts on 31 March 1853 and was taught by Duret.
MUSEUMS AND GALLERIES:
AIX-EN-PROVENCE: *Cyparissus Weeping for the Death of His Stag* (bronze statue).

FERRAT, Jean Joseph Hippolyte Romain
French, 19th century.
Born 9 August 1822, in Aix-en-Provence; died 24 October 1882, in Aix-en-Provence.
Sculptor. Mythological subjects, figures.
Jean Ferrat entered the École des Beaux-Arts on 8 April 1841 and trained under Pradier. In 1850 he won second prize in the competition *Concours de Rome*. He exhibited at the Paris Salon from 1849 to 1870. His most important works are *Fall of Icarus*, the bust of *Tibullus*, commissioned by the Ministre de l'Intérieur, the marble bust of *Granet* commissioned by the town of Aix, the bronze statuette *Death of Achilles*, the marble bust of the president, *Belleyme*, the marble statue *Tronchet* at the Palais du Conseil d'État, the marble bust of *Paul Borde* and the marble statue *Joan of Arc*.
MUSEUMS AND GALLERIES:
AIX-EN-PROVENCE: *Corydon; Phalantes Receiving the Ashes of Hippias; Aix Foundation; J.B.E. Loubon; Bourguignon de Fabregoules; De l'Épée, the Abbot* - PARIS (ENSBA): *Antigone* - VERSAILLES: *General Desmichels*.

FERRAT DE GAUDE, Joseph
French, 20th century.
Died during World War I (1914-1918), on the battlefield.
Painter.
Joseph Ferrat de Gaude exhibited in Paris, at the Salon des Artistes Français, of which he was a member.

FERRATA
Italian, 17th - 18th century.
Painter.
He is credited with having painted a banner, a *St Michael* and a *Virgin of the Rosary* for the church of S Giorgio in Como, together with copper tablets decorated with the *Mysteries of the Rosary*, which formerly adorned the church's altar of the Virgin.

FERRATA, Ercole
Italian, 17th century.
Born 1610, in Pellio Inferiore (Como); died 1686, in Rome.
Sculptor. Mythological subjects.
Ercole Ferrata was possibly a pupil of L'Algarde. It is believed he worked alongside Bernini on sculptures for the pulpit of St Peter's in Rome, and Bernini was certainly an influence on his work. He is recorded as working around 1677 for Duke Como III of Tuscany. He was also a member of the Accademia di S Luca in Rome.

Ferrata's body of work is found chiefly in Rome, where he sculpted an allegorical *Charity* for the tomb of Pope Clement IX at S Maria Maggiore, a statue of the Apostle St Andrew for the façade of the church of S Andrea della Valle, and a *St Agnes Surrounded by Flames* for the church of S Agnese in Agone.
AUCTION RECORDS:
NEW YORK, 8 May 1969, *Man Astride a Lion* (terracotta) USD 7,000. LONDON, 10 Dec 1987, *Young Hercules in Combat with the Serpent* (white marble, width 24in/61cm) GBP 100,000.

FERRATER FELIU, Antonio de
Spanish, 19th - 20th century.
Born 1868, in Barcelona; died 1942, in Barcelona.
Painter. Landscapes.
Antonio de Ferrater Feliu studied at the school of fine arts in Barcelona. He took part in many collective exhibitions including: Barcelona fine arts exhibitions; the *Exposición Gallega* (*Galician Exhibition*) (1909); the Mexico City exhibition of (1910); the Buenos Aires international exhibition (1910); and the Barcelona 6th international exhibition (1911) and was awarded several medals.
BIBLIOGRAPHY:
Arnáiz, José Manuel/López Jiménez, Javier/Merchán Díaz, Manuel (ed.), *Cien años de pintura en Espana y Portugal (1830-1930)*, Antiqvaria, Madrid, 1988 (One Hundred Years of Painting in Spain and Portugal (1830-1930)).

FERRATI, Astolfo
Italian, 17th century.
Painter.
In 1603, Astolfo Ferrati produced a painting of *Two Saints and Angels* for the high altar of the church of S Gennaro in Sessa (near Capua).

FERRATI, Vincenzo
Italian, 18th century.
Active in Siena.
Painter, engraver (etching). Architectural views.
Vincenzo Ferrati collaborated with Francesco Franci to paint the ceiling of the oratory of the rosary in Siena. Vincenzo Ferrati is also remembered for a series of etchings of architectural plates and a drawing for the catafalque of Duchess Vittoria della Rovere in the cathedral of Siena.

FERRATTINI, Gaetano
Italian, 18th century.
Born 1697; died 1765.
Active in Bologna.
Painter.
Gaetano Ferrattini was a pupil of Marc'Antonio Franceschini and a member of the academy in Bologna. He produced numerous paintings for churches in Bologna, including a *St Francis* for the church of S Colombiano, a *Martyred St Peter* and a *St Anthony* for the church of S Michele, a *St Dominic* for the church of S Domenico, and a *St Francis Preaching to the Fishes* for the church of S Maria della Vita.

FERRAÙ DA FAENZA. See **FANZONI Ferrau**

FERRAUDI, Giuseppe
Italian, 19th century.
Born in the 19th century, in Turin.
Painter. Landscapes.
Giuseppe Ferraudi was the son and pupil of the watercolourist Maurizio Ferraudi. He exhibited landscapes, including *Last Rays* and *Morning Peace*, at exhibitions around Italy from 1884 onwards.

FERRAUDI, Maurizio
Italian, 19th century.
Active in Turin.
Painter, watercolourist.

FERRAUDY, Berthe
French, 20th century.
Born 15 April 1878, in Paris.
Sculptor.
Berthe Ferraudy studied under J.F. Coutan, Max Blondat and Paul Moreau-Vauthier. She exhibited in Paris at the Salon des Artistes Français, of which she had been a member in 1906.

FERRAZZI, Ferruccio
Italian, 20th century.
Born 15 March 1891, in Rome; died 8 December 1978.
Painter (including gouache), copyist. Figure compositions, figures, portraits, animals, still-lifes. Murals.
Symbolism.
Ferruccio Ferrazzi was the son of Stanislas Ferrazzi, a sculptor renowned as an excellent copyist of works of antiquity who started teaching drawing and modelling to his son when he was still a child. Ferruccio took part in various group exhibitions, starting with the Venice Biennale in 1910, followed by the International Exhibition of 1911 in Rome.

In 1912 he produced a large-scale painting entitled *Adolescent Girl*, which is also known as *Motherhood* or *Allegory*: although Ferrazzi was still very young at the time, it is executed with remarkable skill. His precocious talent was first revealed at the Venice Biennale in 1910. He predominantly painted portraits. When he painted groups of figures, he ordered them with symbolic significance. The critics of the day praised the young painter's ability to assimilate a range of techniques and aesthetic trends, such as Divisionism, Secessionism and Expressionism. However, within this cultural melting pot, a highly individual personality shines through.

BIBLIOGRAPHY:
Ragghianti, C.L./Recupeo, J./Ferrazzi, N.C., *Ferruccio Ferrazzi*, Rome, 1974. Mantura, B., *Ferruccio Ferrazzi dal 1916 al 1946: Catalogo della Mostra*, Spoleto, 1989. D'Amico, F./Guadagnini W./Roganti, G., *Ferruccio Ferrazzi: Il Disegno: Catalogo della Mostra*, Modena, 1993.

MUSEUMS AND GALLERIES:
ROME (Gal. Nazionale).

AUCTION RECORDS:
ROME, 11 June 1981, *Self-portrait* (1910, oil on canvas, 20 1/4 x 22 1/2 ins / 51.5 x 57 cm) ITL 1,700,000. MILAN, 18 June 1987, *Tied Bull* (1927, oil on panel, 39 1/4 x 31 1/2 ins / 100 x 80 cm) ITL 28,000,000. ROME, 7 April 1988, *Still-life with Figures and Coffee Pot* (oil on canvas, 15 3/4 x 10 1/2 ins / 40 x 26.5 cm) ITL 7,000,000. MILAN, 14 May 1988, *Study for a Fresco* (distemper, 12 3/4 x 16 1/4 ins / 32.5 x 41.5 cm) ITL 2,400,000. MILAN, 14 Nov 1991, *The Oppio Pass: the Road to Dette Dale* (1929, oil on canvas, 48 3/4 x 38 1/2 ins / 124 x 98 cm) ITL 30,000,000. ROME, 12 May 1992, *Portrait of Lisa* (1972, oil on canvas, 15 3/4 x 13 3/4 ins / 40 x 35 cm) ITL 1,900,000. MILAN, 15 March 1994, *Self-portrait* (oil on card mounted, 15 3/4 x 13 3/4 ins / 40 x 35 cm) ITL 2,760,000. MILAN, 2 April 1996, *Self-portrait with Ilaria and Milu* (1954, oil on canvas, 52 x 29 1/2 ins / 132 x 75 cm) ITL 16,675,000. MILAN, 20 May 1996, *Still-life* (1936, oil on panel, 9 3/4 x 9 3/4 ins / 25 x 25 cm) ITL 3,220,000. MILAN, 17 May 1999, *Nude* (oil on panel, 14 x 21 ins / 35 x 54 cm) ITL 10,000,000. ROME, 18 April 2000, *Presage, first version* (1912, oil on canvas, 45 x 38 ins / 115 x 96 cm) ITL 88,000,000. ROME, 13 May 2000, *Cosmic Rhythms: Lava at Catania* (1947, oil on panel, 16 x 19 ins / 41 x 47 cm) ITL 8,000,000. ROME, 12 April 2001, *Night Cry* (1944, oil on board, 31 x 37 ins / 80 x 95 cm) ITL 46,000,000. STUTTGART, 10 May 2001, *Portrait of a Man* (oil on panel, 28 x 16 ins / 72 x 40 cm) DEM 3,700. MILAN, 21 May 2002, *Morning in Leman* (1917, oil on canvas, 30 x 30 ins / 76 x 75 cm) EUR 12,000. MILAN, 21 May 2002, *Tiber at Via Ripetta* (1915, oil on canvas, 54 x 41 ins / 136 x 103 cm) EUR 52,000. MILAN, 25 Nov 2003, *Self-portrait* (1925, oil on board, 11 x 9 ins / 29 x 22 cm) EUR 7,500. ROME, 22 April 2004, *Storm in Aniene Valley* (1925, oil on canvas, 19 x 13 ins / 47 x 33 cm) EUR 20,000. MILAN, 24 May 2004, *Spring Night* (1936, oil on canvas, 64 x 79 ins / 162 x 201 cm) EUR 38,000.

FERRAZZI, Luigi
Italian, 19th century.
Painter. Genre scenes.
Luigi Ferrazzi exhibited in Munich in 1883.

AUCTION RECORDS:
LONDON, 23 July 1976, *Little Girls Decorating a Calvary with Flowers* (1887, oil on canvas, 49 x 19 1/4 ins / 124.5 x 49 cm) GBP 1,000. NEW YORK, 28 May 1980, *The Doll's New Dress* (oil on canvas, 25 1/2 x 20 ins / 64.7 x 50.8 cm) USD 3,000.

FERRAZZOLI, Antonio
Italian, 17th century.
Born 1586, in Rome; died 12 March 1622, in Rome.
Miniaturist.
Antonio Ferrazzoli was a member of the Accademia di S Luca in Rome.

FERRAZZOLI, Rotilio
Italian, 15th century.
Active in Rome c. 1458.
Miniaturist.

FERRAZZOLI, Rotilio
Italian, 17th century.
Active in Rome in 1615.
Miniaturist.

FERRÉ, Camille Alphonsine
French, 20th century.
Born in Angers.
Painter. Still-lifes (flowers/fruit).
Camille Ferré studied under Montézin. She exhibited in Paris, from 1928, at the Salon des Artistes Français, of which she was a member; she received an honourable mention in 1931.

FERRÉ, Édouard Bizi
French, 20th century.
Born 25 September 1891, in Tours.
Painter. Nudes, landscapes, still-lifes.
Édouard Ferré exhibited in Paris, at the Salon des Artistes Indépendants, from 1931, and also at the Salon de la Société Nationale des Beaux-Arts and the Salon des Tuileries.

FERRÉ, Fanny
French, 20th - 21st century.
Born 1963, in Évreux.
Sculptor, potter. Statuettes, groups.
Fanny Ferré studied at the École des Beaux-Arts d'Angers from 1980 to 1983, and later studied under Georges Jeanclos at the École des Beaux-Arts de Paris.

Ferré's works are mostly earthenware and waxed bronze. Her close attention to small but essential details, such as curls in a subject's hair, or folds in their tunic, reflects Jeanclos' influence upon her technique. She creates small figures, such as child musicians and mischievous young girls, which she distorts for expressive effect.

Since 1984, she has exhibited in a number of group exhibitions, including: *4e Biennale de la Céramique Contemporaine* (*The 4th Biennale Exhibition of Contemporary Pottery*), in Châteauroux in 1987; *Céramiques et Terres Contemporaines* (*Contemporary Pottery and Earthenware*), in Le Mans in 1988; *Hommage à Bernard Palissy* (*Homage to Bernard Palissy*), at the Musée des Arts Décoratifs in Paris, in 1991; at the Museum am Burghof, in Lörrach, Germany, in 1992; *Céramistes Contemporains* (*16 Contemporary Potters*), in Treigny; and *Courant d'Art* (*A Current of Art*), in Deauville in 1994.

She has also shown her work in solo exhibitions, including: at the Galerie Lavignes-Bastille, Paris, 1991; Brussels, 1992, at the Musée Mandet in Riom, 1993; *Les Bronzes de Fanny Ferré* (*Fanny Ferré's Bronzes*) in Deauville, in 1994; and at the Galerie Capazza in Nancay, Cher, in 2003.

BIBLIOGRAPHY:
Avila, Alin, '*Le Souffle des bronzes de Fanny Ferré*' in *Les Bronzes de Fanny Ferré*, exhibition catalogue, Open Art International, Deauville, 1994.

FERRÉ, Georges
French, 19th century.
Born c. 1860, in Paris.
Painter. Genre scenes, landscapes.
Ferré took a painting course in the studios of Émile Bin and Désiré Laugée. He became a member of the Société des Artistes Français in 1886 and exhibited at the society's Salon in Paris. He painted landscapes and many genre scenes, including *Potato Lifters, Harvesters, Washerwomen, Washing Done.*

MUSEUMS AND GALLERIES:
PONTOISE: *Harvesters.*

AUCTION RECORDS:
PARIS, 10 May 1900, *Potato Harvest,* FRF 145.

FERRÉ, Jacques
French, 17th century.
Active in Le Mans.
Sculptor (wood).
Jacques Ferré executed a tabernacle for the church in Lombron in 1638.

FERRE, Marguerite Emma. See **VION Maguy de**

FERRÈ, Natale
Italian, 19th century.
Born 24 February 1817, in Canegrate; died 27 August 1879, in Canegrate.
Painter, architect. Architectural views.
Natale Ferrè began exhibiting at the Accademia di Belle Arti di Brera in 1852.

FERRÉ, Pierre Baptiste
French, 18th century.
Active in Angers.
Sculptor.

FERREIRA, Antonio
Portuguese, 18th century.
Sculptor.
Antonio Ferreira was the son and probably also the pupil of Dionizio Ferreira. He worked in Lisbon and produced mainly terracotta works: Christmas mangers with lots of small statues and landscape backgrounds. He also made group pieces of peasants and shepherds, some examples of which could be found in the museum in Lisbon.

FERREIRA, Dionizio
Portuguese, 18th century.
Active in Lisbon.
Sculptor.

FERREIRA, Gustavus Adolphus
British, 19th century.
Of Portuguese origin.
Active in Exeter.
Painter. Landscapes.
Gustavus Ferreira exhibited in London, notably at the Royal Academy and Suffolk Street from 1845 to 1856.

AUCTION RECORDS:
LONDON, 24 Feb 1908, *Head of an Old Man; Seville Cathedral* (drawings) GBP 4.

FERREIRA, Henrique
Portuguese, 18th century.
Active in Lisbon c. 1720.
Painter.
Henrique Ferreira painted full-length, life-size portraits of the Portuguese kings, taken from earlier drawings, in the royal chamber of the St Jerome monastery in Belem.

FERREIRA, Jesus Reyes. See **REYES-FERREIRA Jesús**

FERREIRA, José
Portuguese, 19th - 20th century.
Born in Chaves (northern Portugal).
Painter.
José Ferreira lived in Lisbon around 1878. He studied under F.A. Metrass at the Lisbon academy and travelled in Spain, France and England. He painted portraits, military scenes and flowers.

MUSEUMS AND GALLERIES:
LISBON (Acad.): *Flowers* (several paintings).

FERREIRA, José Francisco I
Portuguese, 19th century.
Active in Belem.
Painter.
Ferreira painted landscapes and flower paintings.

FERREIRA, José Francisco II
Portuguese, 18th century.

Born in the 18th century, in Belem.
Painter.
José Francisco Ferreira II lived in Lisbon around 1820 and was taught by his father, José Ferreira I. Like his father, he painted landscapes and flower paintings and was also a decorative artist.

FERREIRA, Lucy C.
Brazilian, 20th century.
Born 20th century, in São Paulo.
Engraver (wood).
Lucy Ferreira worked in France and is known for a piece entitled *Refugees*.

FERREIRA, Rodrigo
Portuguese, 20th - 21st century.
Born 1951, in Paris.
Active in France.
Painter. Landscapes.
Symbolism.
From 1968 to 1975, Rodrigo Ferreira trained at the École Nationale Supérieure des Beaux-Arts in Paris. From 1984 to 1985, he was the recipient of a bursary awarded by the French Ministry of Foreign Affairs and the Franco-Egyptian Centre of the Temples of Karnak; this gave rise to some bare, luminous works, which he exhibited in 1986 at the Galerie Étienne de Causans in Paris. Since then, he has exhibited at numerous group and solo exhibitions, both in France and abroad.

Ferreira's compositions often consist of juxtapositions of small views of architectural remains, either Graeco-Roman or Arab-Egyptian, which are contemplated by figures in togas with their backs to the viewer. Bathed in golden light, these scenes convey a strong sense of calm and stability.

FERREIRA DA COSTA, João or Jean
Portuguese, 20th century.
Born in Lisbon.
Painter.
Ferreira da Costa exhibited in Paris from 1911 at the Salon des Artistes Français.

FERREIRA DA SILVA, Roberto
Portuguese, 19th century.
Painter.
Roberto Ferreira da Silva lived in Rio de Janeiro around 1827. He studied under the engraver E.M. de Barros in Lisbon. He painted and drew many views of Rio de Janeiro and the surrounding area, some of which were engraved by Paola.

BIBLIOGRAPHY:
Ferreira da Silva, Roberto, *Elementos de desenho e pintura com regras geraes de perspectiva*, Laemmert, Rio de Janeiro, 1841.

FERREIRA-ROCHA, Raoul
Portuguese, 20th - 21st century.
Born 10 August 1951, in Mozambique.
Active since 1976 in France.
Painter.
Raoul Ferreira Rocha graduated with a degree in fine arts from the Université de Paris VIII. In the early 1980s, Ferreira Rocha produced a series of paintings on world hunger, entitled *Glace Now*. In 1983-1984, he produced another series, entitled *The Immaterial*, which explores man's presence in space via memory and technological reality.

Rocha has taken part in various group exhibitions, including: regularly since 1978 at Salons, such as the Salon de la Jeune Peinture; in 1979, *Réalismes et Imageries* (*Realism and Imagery*) at the Galerie Alos, Toulouse; in 1983, *Exhibition in Solidarity with Political Prisoners in Turkey* in Basel; regularly since 1985, at the Salon des Grands et Jeunes d'Aujourd'hui; and, in 1988, the *12 Portuguese Painters from Paris* exhibition at the Gilde gallery, Guimarães. He has also shown his work in solo exhibitions, including: in 1985, 1986 and 1987, at the Salon Mac 2000 in Paris, where he had an individual stand; and, in 1989, at the Gilde gallery, Guimarães.

AUCTION RECORDS:
PARIS, 21 March 1992, *Composition* (1987, acrylic/canvas, 45 x 57 1/2 ins / 114 x 146 cm) FRF 8,000.

FERREN, John Millard
American, 20th century.
Born 1905, in Pendleton (Oregon); died July 1970, in Long Island.
Painter, sculptor, engraver.
Action Painting, Post-painterly Abstraction.
American Abstract Artists (AAA).
John Millard Ferren worked as an artisan sculptor in San Francisco after initial studies in Los Angeles. He only began to paint in 1930. From 1931 to 1938 he worked in the independent academies of Paris and studied engraving in Stanley William Hayter's Atelier 17. He returned to the USA in 1938 and became one of the founder members of the American Association of Abstract Artists.

An experimental artist, he played an important role in the development of modern art in the USA. In France, between 1936 and 1938, he painted simple forms reminiscent of the then abstract geometric constructions of Hélion or the paper cut-outs of Matisse. When he reurned to the USA he engaged resolutely with Abstract Expressionism and the Action Painting of the new American school, before moving on to Colour Field Painting on large canvases. As a man he was generous and open, and his work, with its sometimes disconcerting diversity, reflects this.

Ferren exhibited at the main exhibitions of contemporary American art. After 1930 he showed the phases of his work in numerous solo exhibitions, both in Paris and the USA: in New York in 1936, 1937, 1938, 1942, at the Santa Barbara Museum of Modern Art in 1952, in Washington and elsewhere. He taught from 1946, gave many lectures and wrote articles.

BIBLIOGRAPHY:
Carnduff Ritchie, Andrew, *Abstract Painting and Sculpture in America*, Museum of Modern Art, New York, 1951.

MUSEUMS AND GALLERIES:
NEW YORK (MoMA) - NEW YORK (Whitney Mus. of American Art).

AUCTION RECORDS:
NEW YORK, 15 June 1972, *Untitled* (1936) USD 1,600. NEW YORK, 23 May 1979, *Abstraction* (1938, pastel, 18 1/2 x 24 1/2 ins / 47 x 62 cm) USD 2,800. NEW YORK, 27 Feb 1980, *Mandola Amarilla* (1966, oil on canvas, 50 x 45 ins / 127 x 114.3 cm) USD 2,500. NEW YORK, 16 Feb 1984, *The Windows* (1958, oil on canvas, 63 1/4 x 75 ins / 160.5 x 190.5 cm) USD 1,600. NEW YORK, 6 Dec 1985, *Abstraction* (1935, oil on canvas, 25 1/2 x 36 ins / 65 x 90.5 cm) USD 10,000. PARIS, 27 Nov 1987, *Untitled* (1933, oil on canvas, 21 1/4 x 27 1/2 ins / 54 x 70 cm) FRF 29,000. NEW YORK, 30 Sept 1988, *Abstraction* (1932, oil on paper, 8 3/4 x 10 3/4 ins / 22.2 x 27.6 cm) USD 2,420. PARIS, 26 Oct 1988, *Blue and Black* (1951, oil, watercolour and pastel/paper, 20 x 26 ins / 51 x 66 cm) FRF 10,500. PARIS, 23 June 1989, *Composition* (1931-1932, oil on canvas, 19 3/4 x 23 1/2 ins / 50 x 60 cm) FRF 54,000. NEW YORK, 23 Feb 1990, *Untitled* (1962, acrylic/canvas, 50 x 30 ins / 127 x 76.2 cm) USD 7,150. PARIS, 8 April 1990, *Untitled* (oil on canvas, 25 x 30 ins / 63.5 x 76.5 cm) FRF 40,000. NEW YORK, 18 Dec 1991, *Yellow Field* (1960, oil on canvas, 36 x 36 ins / 91.4 x 91.4 cm) USD 1,980. NEW YORK, 15 April 1992, *Untitled* (oil, sand and cork/canvas, 11 3/4 x 23 3/4 ins / 29.8 x 60.3 cm) USD 5,775. NEW YORK, 25 Sept 1992, *Summer III* (1958, oil on canvas, 24 x 20 ins / 61 x 50.8 cm) USD 1,760. NEW YORK, 31 March 1993, *Untitled* (1942, casein/card, 10 1/2 x 8 1/4 ins / 26.7 x 21 cm) USD 2,300. NEW YORK, 31 March 1994, *Upright Form* (painted wood, h.

73 ins / 185.4 cm) USD 2,875. PARIS, 5 Oct 1996, *Summer Night* (1933, oil on canvas, 13 x 18 ins / 33 x 46 cm) FRF 5,000. PARIS, 24 Nov 1996, *Composition with Pink Lips* (1931, 24 x 19¾ ins / 61 x 50 cm) FRF 12,000. PARIS, 5 June 1997, *Composition* (1936, oil on canvas, 39¼ x 39¼ ins / 100 x 100 cm) FRF 29,000. NEW YORK, 3 Dec 1997, *Abstraction* (1938, pastel/paper, 18½ x 24½ ins / 47 x 62.2 cm) USD 14,950. NEW YORK, 7 Nov 2000, *Medeanus* (1955, oil on canvas, 72 x 55 ins / 184 x 140 cm) USD 3,000. CHICAGO, 19 Nov 2002, *Untitled* (oil on canvas, 12 x 14 ins / 31 x 36 cm) USD 1,800. ENGLEWOOD, 5 Nov 2003, *Souvenir of Spain* (oil on board, 32 x 23 ins / 81 x 58 cm) USD 1,700. NEW YORK, 19 Dec 2003, *Untitled* (1933, oil on canvas, 15 x 22 ins / 38 x 57 cm) USD 9,500.

FERRÉOL, Maurice
French, 20th century.
Born 10 September 1906, in Villeurbanne (Rhône); died 4 November 1969.
Painter. Figure compositions, figures, still-lifes. Designs for tapestries.

Maurice Ferréol was born to a working class family and lost his parents at an early age. At 16, he was sailing first in the merchant navy, then on board the battleship Jean Bart, roaming the seas and discovering the exotic landscapes and indigenous people who would fill his compositions. Back in Lyons, he became a steel worker living on a labourer's income and painting during his moments of leisure. The major social changes brought about by the 1936 socialist government stirred up his urge to paint. Though self-taught, his technique developed to the extent of designing tapestry cartoons, to-scale and numbered according to the range of colours. For the last two years of his life, he was able to make a living from his art.

In the tapestries produced from 1949 (but published much later), he gave full scope to the world of feasts and heavenly dreams he had harboured.

The Musée des Hospices Civils in Lyons acquired one of his tapestries: *Paradise Regained* 6 x 10 feet (1.75 x 3.50 metres). State incentives made possible the 646 square feet (60 square metres, tapestry *Horsemen,* which he produced for the École Centrale, the Lyons school of engineering. In these representations, the profusion of images and colours serves as composition. In less ambitious projects, his common touch and innocence set him in the naive tradition. The catalogue of the 1979 retrospective exhibition describes him as appreciating the poetry of the Bible: 'Genesis and the Book of Revelation, the beginning and the end of the world fuelled his more ambitious projects as a universe crammed with birds and fishes of many colours... springs before us'.

Ferréol featured in collective exhibitions in Lyons and others cities in France and abroad. He showed his paintings and tapestries in personal exhibitions in Lyons. The Espace Lyonnais d'Art Contemporain organised a major posthumous retrospective exhibition of his work in 1979.

BIBLIOGRAPHY:
Ferréol, exhibition catalogue, Espace lyonnais d'Art contemporain, Lyons, 1979.

MUSEUMS AND GALLERIES:
LYONS (MBA): *Little Girl with the Red Sunshade* (1963) - ST-ÉTIENNE (Mus. d'Art et d'Industrie): *The red Violin* (1963).

AUCTION RECORDS:
LYONS, 9 Dec 1980, *Masons* (oil on canvas, 28¾ x 23½ ins / 73 x 60 cm) FRF 2,200.

FERRER, Alberto
Italian, 19th - 20th century.
Born 1870, in Florence.
Sculptor. Figures, animals. Busts.

Alberto Ferrer was a Neapolitan who studied art in Naples. In 1901 he exhibited a bust in Venice, entitled *Misanthrope;* and in 1907 showed his bronze genre sculpture *Serenella* in Florence. He also exhibited in Munich in 1909. In Florence he worked with another sculptor on the two sphinxes outside the university.

FERRER, Antoine
Dutch, 16th - 17th century.
Painter.

In his description of his travels, *Voyage Pittoresque,* Descamps mentions two altarpieces by this artist in the parish church of Nieuwpoort in West Flanders, one showing *Herod with the Head of St John the Baptist* and the other *Martyrdom and Death of St Sebastian.*

FERRER, Bardina
Spanish, 14th century.
Of Catalan origin.
Painter.

Bardina Ferrer is mentioned in Barcelona in 1374.

FERRER, Bassa. See **BASSA**

FERRER, Bonifacio
Spanish, 14th century.
Painter.

The brother of Vincent Ferrer, Bonifacio Ferrer withdrew to the Charterhouse of Portacoeli on the death of his wife and seven children, following an epidemic in 1396. He is the probable painter of the *San Carlos Altarpiece* of Valencia. Although the work is sometimes attributed to an Italian painter (Gererdo di Jacopo el Starina), the simplified forms of the *Conversion of St Paul* confirm the Catalan nature of this artist. It is, however, likely that the predella of this altarpiece was executed by another painter, possibly Sienese in origin.

FERRER, Domingo
Spanish, 18th century.
Sculptor.

In 1717, Domingo Ferrer started work on the retable for the high altar of the church of Banalbufar in Majorca.

FERRER, García, called El Licenciado
Spanish, 17th century.
Born in Alcorisa, near Alcañiz; died 1659, in Toledo.
Active in Valencia.
Painter, sculptor, architect.

García Ferrer was a priest who executed some paintings for the altar of S Vincent Ferrer at the monastery of Sto Domingo. He worked mainly in Madrid. Cean Bermudez refers to a *Crucifixion* by Ferrer dated 1632. He also worked for Toledo Cathedral, where he was a chaplain.

FERRER, Geronimo
Spanish, 17th century.
Active in Rome in 1651.
Sculptor.

Geronimo Ferrer returned to Spain with Velázquez around 1649 to work on the sculptures at the Alcazar in Madrid.

FERRER, Guillermo, the Younger.
See **FERRER Y PUIG**

FERRER, Guillermo, the Elder
Spanish, 18th century.
Born c. 1700, in Palma.
Painter.

Guillermo Ferrer the Elder studied and worked in Palma and carved the monumental statue of *St Eulalia* above the main door the church of Sta Eulalia and the statue of *St Helena* in the doorway of the church of Santa Cruz. Palma Cathedral also has some friezes carved by Ferrer.

FERRER, Jaime I
Spanish, 15th century.
Born in Catalonia.
Painter. Religious subjects.
Catalan School.

Jaime Ferrer I was perhaps the pupil of Bernardo Martorell (unless he is identical with the other artist called Jaime Ferrer). He is mentioned in Barcelona in 1436 in connection with paintings of armorial bearings. Together with an *Epiphany*, conserved in the museum at Lerida, a few altarpieces have been attributed to Ferrer, including the *Saviour* at the church of Albatarech and *St Lucy* at Tamarit de Litera, also a *Last Supper*.

While Ferrer was initially influenced by the Serra brothers, he dissociates himself from their style in his pursuit of greater symmetry in his compositions, which were articulated by figures in movement and a more precise rendering of objects.

Museums and Galleries:

Lérida: *The Epiphany* - Solsona: *The Last Supper* - Vic (Episcopal Mus.): *The Flight into Egypt*.

Auction records:

London, 9 April 1990, *St Andrew Preaching before the Proconsul Egeas, the Crucifixion and Saving a Bishop from Temptation* (tempera/panel with gilt background, two wings of an altarpiece recounting the Life of St Andrew, 60 1/4 x 24 1/2 ins / 153 x 62 cm and 60 1/4 x 25 1/4 ins/153 x 64 cm) GBP 154,000.

FERRER, Jaime II

Spanish, 15th century.
Active between 1439 and 1457.
Painter. Religious subjects.

It is likely that Jaime Ferrer II collaborated with Bernardo Martorell on the altarpiece of the high altar of the cathedral at Lerida in 1441. He is mentioned in 1457 as having carried out the altarpiece of the church of Alcover, on the strength of which other works have been attributed to him. His urban landscapes and objects display great precision which can be attributed to Flemish influence. He is to be compared to Jaime Ferrer I.

Ferrer appeared in the exhibition *La pintura gótica hispano flamenca: Bartolomé Bermejo y su época* (*Hispano-Flemish Gothic Painting. Bartolomé Bermejo and his Time*), Museo de Arte de Catalunya, Barcelona, in 2003.

Bibliography:

Hispano-Flemish Gothic Painting. Bartolomé Bermejo and his time, group exhibition catalogue, Museu Nacional d'Art de Catalunya, Barcelona, 2003 (text in Spanish, Catalan and English).

Museums and Galleries:

Lérida: *St Julian* - Vic: *The Virgin*.

FERRER, Joaquín

Cuban, 20th century.
Born 4 July 1929, in Manzanillo.
Active in France from 1960.
Painter.

Joaquín Ferrer first worked for the railway but in 1948 joined the Academia San Alejandro in Havana, remaining there for two years. He first exhibited in 1954 at the Cuba national painting exhibition. After the revolution he was awarded a government grant and went to study in Paris and settled there. Ferrer's early paintings evoke exuberant tropical vegetation and are reminiscent of the world of Wilfredo Lam. He then came under the influence of Surrealism, creating non-figurative forms which embraced the often ambiguous and even erotic rhythms of organic life. His compositions are constructed from very fine, curved, often parallel lines, blueprints that define juxtaposed surfaces, segments painted in transparent, refined and gentle colours. Later, but still employing the same gossamer style and the same airy colours, he transformed these plastic constructions from their original, rigorous abstraction into what he refers to as 'attempts at landscape'.

Ferrer has taken part in various group exhibitions including: in 1962 the Latin American art exhibition at the Musée d'Art Moderne; in 1963 the Biennale des Jeunes Artistes in Paris; the Salon de Mai from 1968; the Menton Biennale in 1970, and the *Peintres d'Amérique latine* (*Painters of Latin America*) international festival of contemporary art in Royan. He held his first solo exhibition in Paris in 1968 at the Le Point Cardinal Gallery, introduced by Max Ernst. Others include: the Le Point Cardinal Gallery in Paris in 1971, 1972, 1974 and 1977; the Moderne Gallery in Silkborg, Denmark, in 1978 and 1980; the Farber Gallery in Brussels in 1980; and the Engelberts Gallery in Geneva, also in 1980.

Bibliography:

Joaquin Ferrer, exhibition catalogue, Le Point Cardinal, Paris, 1977. Ray, Lionel/Bosquet, Alain, *Joaquin Ferrer. L'Imaginaire absolu*, Éd. Palantines, Quimper, 2001.

Auction records:

Paris, 14 April 1986, *When the Sky Was Not Yet Born* (1977, oil on canvas, 51 1/4 x 63 ins / 130 x 160 cm) FRF 7,000. Paris, 15 Feb 1988, *Obstacle* (1969, oil on canvas, 44 1/2 x 36 1/4 ins / 113 x 92 cm) FRF 8,000. New York, 17 May 1989, *Untitled* (1970, oil on canvas, 31 1/2 x 31 1/2 ins / 80 x 80 cm) USD 1,870. Paris, 25 March 1990, *Light as Hostage* (1989, acrylic/canvas, 15 3/4 x 15 3/4 ins / 40 x 40 cm) FRF 12,000. Paris, 13 Dec 1991, *Oblivion Passes through the Town* (1980, oil on paper/wood, 28 3/4 x 21 1/4 ins / 73 x 54 cm) FRF 7,000. New York, 23 Nov 1998, *Carnac - Private Visit* (1993, oil on canvas, 59 x 59 ins / 150 x 150 cm) USD 23,000. Lokeren, 15 May 2004, *The Absent Visitor* (1983, oil on canvas, 46 x 35 ins / 116 x 89 cm) EUR 2,000. Lokeren, 15 May 2004, *Capital of Vertigo IV* (1988, oil on canvas, 51 x 51 ins / 130 x 130 cm) EUR 3,000.

FERRER, José

Spanish, 18th century.
Born December 1715, in Palma.
Painter.

José Ferrer was driven out of Spain in 1731 because he was a Jesuit postulant. He went to Rome where he studied painting. There has been reference to some of his paintings at the Augustinian monastery at Felanitx, Majorca, including *Blessed Catalina Tomás* and a painting of *San Luis de Gonzaga* at the Felanitx presbytery. He is probably the same artist as Giuseppe Ferrer.

FERRER, José

Spanish, 18th - 19th century.
Born 1746, in Alorca; died 4 December 1815.
Painter. Flowers.

José Ferrer was awarded his first major prize for painting in 1776. He was probably the son of Vicente Ferrer.

Museums and Galleries:

Barcelona: *Flowers*; same subject; *Flowers* (several versions); same subject - Valencia: *The Merchants Driven from the Temple*; *St Thomas Visiting the Sick*.

FERRER, Juan

Spanish, 15th - 16th century.
Active in Valencia.
Painter.
Catalan School.

FERRER, Juan de Dios

Spanish, 19th century.
Born 8 March 1817, in Madrid; died 1856, in Shanghai.
Sculptor.

Juan de Dios Ferrer is known for a *Flight into Egypt*. He studied in Naples and entered the Jesuit order; in 1847 he was sent to China.

FERRER, Micaela

Spanish, 18th century.
Died 23 April 1804, in Valencia.
Painter.

Micaela Ferrer was an honorary member of the Academia de San Carlos in Valencia.

Bibliography:

Ferrer, Micaela, *Academia de Maestros de Primera Enseñanza Pública de Madrid/Observaciones presentadas por... Dª Micaela Ferrer de Otálora... al tema... ¿Conviene acelerar en las escuelas la enseñanza de la niñez?*, José Noguera, Madrid, 1873.

FERRER, Miguel
Spanish, 15th century.
Active in Valencia.
Painter.

FERRER, Pedro
Spanish, 14th century.
Active in Valencia.
Painter.

Pedro Ferrer worked on the cathedral in Valencia in 1380.

FERRER, Pedro
Spanish, 16th century.
Born c. 1555.
Active in Valladolid in 1589.
Sculptor.

Pedro Ferrer was held in high esteem by the best artists of his time for his fine sculptures and memorials in alabaster.

FERRER, Pedro
Spanish, 19th century.
Born in Mirambel; died 1875, in Mirambel.
Sculptor.

Pedro Ferrer was the son of the sculptor Ramón Ferrer. He first exhibited at the Madrid Salon of 1866.

FERRER, Pedro Juan
Spanish, 18th century.
Born in Majorca.
Active c. 1730.
Painter.

Pedro Juan Ferrer was a pupil of G. Mesquida.

FERRER, Rafaël
American, 20th century.
Sculptor, environmental artist.
Arte Povera.

Rafaël Ferrer exhibited in New York in 1970. He created environments in the style of Arte Povera by assembling a variety of materials - wood, corrugated iron, neon bulbs.

FERRER, Ramón
Spanish, 19th century.
Sculptor.

In 1835, Ramón Ferrer was made a member of the Academia de San Fernando.

FERRER, Tomás
Spanish, 18th century.
Active in Granada.
Painter.

In 1753, Tomás Ferrer painted a fresco in the sacristy of the Carthusian church in Granada; he painted other frescoes in the city's churches.

FERRER, Vera L.
American, 20th century.
Born 13 January 1895, in New York.
Painter, miniaturist.

FERRER, Vicente
Spanish, 18th century.
Potter.

Vicente Ferrer collaborated with Joseph Olery de Moustiers at the Alcora ceramics factory in the province of Valencia. Various pieces of faience from the Alcora works signed *Fer* and decorated with ornamental paintings and figures can be seen in museums in Berlin and Sèvres.

Museums and Galleries:

Berlin (Kunstgewerbemus.) - Paris (Mus. National de Céramique Sèvres).

FERRER, Vicente
Spanish, 19th century.
Born c. 1850, in Castellon de la Plana (Valencia).
Painter. Architectural views.

Vicente Ferrer lived in Madrid and was a pupil of P. Gonzalvo. He exhibited views of the Alhambra in Madrid in 1886 and architectural pieces at the Suffolk Street Gallery in London. He may be the same artist as Vicente Ferrer y Alambillaga.

FERRER CALATAYUD, Pedro
Spanish, 19th - 20th century.
Born 1860, in Valencia; died 1944, in Valencia.
Painter. Seascapes.

Pedro Ferrer Calatayud studied under Vicente Borras at the Academia de San Carlos in Valencia where he later became a teacher and eventually director. He took part in many collective exhibitions: at the Madrid national fine arts society from 1878 and in Valencia in 1909 and 1910. He was awarded several medals.

Although he is sometimes described as a painter of portraits and flowers, he was primarily a seascape painter who particularly enjoyed showing the sea in bad weather. He became a master of the genre, displaying great virtuosity and an outstanding technique.

Bibliography:

Arnáiz, José Manuel/López Jiménez, Javier/Merchán Díaz, Manuel (ed.), *Cien años de pintura en Espana y Portugal (1830-1930)*, Antiqvaria, Madrid, 1988 (One Hundred Years of Painting in Spain and Portugal (1830-1930)).

Museums and Galleries:

Madrid (Mus. Nacional Centro de Arte Reina Sofía): *Seascape.*

FERRER CALATAYUD, Salvador
Spanish, 20th century.
Born in Valencia.
Painter. Landscapes.

Salvador Ferrer Calatayud was the brother of Pedro Ferrer Calatayud and studied under him. He began exhibiting in 1896 in Madrid.

FERRER CARBONELL, Juan
Spanish, 20th century.
Born 5 June 1892, in Madrid.
Painter, watercolourist. Landscapes.

Juan Ferrer Carbonell studied at the Real Academia de Bellas Artes de San Fernando in Madrid. He was awarded a bursary to study abroad and spent time in Belgium, France and Holland. From 1929 he often visited Africa, particularly Spanish Guinea (now Equatorial Guinea). He took part in many group exhibitions including the national exhibitions of the fine arts society of Madrid where he was awarded a travel bursary in 1930 and a bronze medal in 1934. He also exhibited in Bilbao, Barcelona, Paris, Brussels, Amsterdam, Rotterdam, Buenos Aires and Rio de Janeiro.

Bibliography:

Arnáiz, José Manuel/López Jiménez, Javier/Merchán Díaz, Manuel (ed.), *Cien años de pintura en Espana y Portugal (1830-1930)*, Antiqvaria, Madrid, 1988 (One Hundred Years of Painting in Spain and Portugal (1830-1930)).

FERRER MORGADO, Horacio
Spanish, 20th century.
Born 1894, in Cordova; died 1978, in Madrid.
Painter. Religious subjects. Murals, decorative schemes.

Horacio Ferrer Morgado studied at the school of fine arts in Madrid and later spent time in Paris. He exhibited in Madrid and also at the Salon des Indépendants in 1929 and 1930 in Paris and at the international exhibition of 1937. He was a militant artist heavily engaged intellectually and painted propaganda pieces during the Spanish Civil War. He also executed many decorative works for public buildings and churches.

BIBLIOGRAPHY:

Pagé, Suzanne/Winock, Michel/Michaud, Éric/Vidal, Aline, *Les Années trente en Europe. Le Temps menaçant*, exhibition catalogue, Musée d'Art moderne de la Ville de Paris, Paris musées, Flammarion, Paris, 1997.

MUSEUMS AND GALLERIES:

MADRID (Mus. Nacional Centro de Arte Reina Sofía): *Madrid 1937, the Black Aeroplanes* (1937).

FERRER Y ALAMBILLAGA

Spanish, 19th - 20th century.
Painter.

Ferrer y Alambillaga exhibited at the national exhibitions in Madrid in 1910 and 1912.

FERRER Y CORRIOL, Antonio

Spanish, 19th century.
Born c. 1850, in Vic (Catalonia).
Painter.

Antonio Ferrer y Corriol was a pupil of José Serra y Porson in Barcelona. He worked and exhibited his work there, including *Popular Catalan Fiesta around 1800* and *Parade*. He also exhibited works at the national fine arts exhibitions of Berlin in 1891 and 1896; these included genre pieces such as the *Guitar Player*.

MUSEUMS AND GALLERIES:

GERONA: *Bagpipe Player*.

FERRER Y CRESPI, Asunción

Spanish, 19th century.
Died 17 April 1818, in Valencia.
Painter.

Asunción Ferrer y Crespi was made an honorary member of the Academia de San Carlos in Valencia on 26 October 1795. She is known for her pastels.

FERRER Y MIRÓ, Juan

Spanish, 19th century.
Born c. 1850, in Vilanova i la Geltrú.
Painter.

Juan Ferrer y Miró studied and worked in Barcelona. He presented his *Art Exhibition Interior* at the Barcelona Universal Exhibition of 1888 and his *Eve of Epiphany* at the national exhibition in Paris in 1900.

AUCTION RECORDS:

LOS ANGELES, 9 April 1973, *Crowd outside a Picture Gallery*, USD 2,500.

FERRER Y PUIG, Guillermo, also known as Ferrer Guillermo the Younger

Spanish, 18th - 19th century.
Born 27 March 1759, in Palma; died 24 December 1833, in Palma.
Painter.

Guillermo Ferrer y Puig was a pupil of F. Montaner the Elder and completed his studies in France, mainly in Montpellier. He painted many portraits in Palma, as well as religious pieces such as *Visitation of St Elizabeth* in the church of Nuestra Señora de Gracia on Mont Randa near Palma, and an altarpiece of James the Apostle in the church of S Jaime in Alcúdia.

FERRER-COMAS, Eduardo

Spanish, 19th - 20th century.
Born in Barcelona.
Painter. Genre scenes, landscapes with figures.

Edouard Ferrer Comas exhibited in France, notably in 1921 and 1922 in Paris at the Salon of the Société Nationale des Beaux-Arts.

AUCTION RECORDS:

NEW YORK, 22 May 1990, *The Flower Cutters* (1916, oil on canvas, 29 1/2 x 25 3/4 ins / 75 x 65.4 cm) USD 16,500.

FERRERAS, José

Spanish, 16th century.
Born 16th century, in Saragossa.
Sculptor (wood).

In Segovia, José Ferreras sculpted the Renaissance high altar of the church of S Miguel.

FERRÈRE, Cécile, later Mme Guérin

French, 19th century.
Born 5 May 1847, in Paris.
Painter.

Ferrère was trained by Lefebvre, Amaury-Duval and Chaplin. She exhibited still-lifes, portraits and genre scenes at the Salon from 1863. Works include *Angelino, Sunday in Lower Brittany, Portrait of the Prince of Asturias, Sleeping Woman, Huntress* and *Ballad*.

AUCTION RECORDS:

NEW YORK, 10 and 11 April 1920, *Flower Seller*, GBP 375. PARIS, 11 March 1925, *Breton Girl*, FRF 270. PARIS, 23 June 1939, *Cripple*, FRF 380. LONDON, 22 Nov 1996, *Summer Flowers* (1870, oil on canvas, 34 x 43 ins / 86.4 x 109.2 cm) GBP 4,025. BRUSSELS, 1 Dec 2003, *The First Fencing Lesson* (1870, oil on canvas, 24 x 20 ins / 60 x 50 cm) EUR 2,600. NEW YORK, 22 April 2004, *Flower Seller* (oil on canvas, 58 x 36 ins / 147 x 91 cm) USD 10,000.

FERRÈRE, Jean

French, 17th century.
Active in Asté (Bigorre).
Sculptor.

Ferrère worked around 1667 on the tabernacle of the church of St-Brice in Guchon and restored the retable of the church of St-Martin in Cadéac, adding a few statues.

FERRERI, Andrea, or Ferrari

Italian, 17th - 18th century.
Born 1673, in Milan; died 1744, in Ferrara.
Painter, sculptor. Religious subjects.

Andrea Ferreri studied in Bologna under Giuseppe Maza, but worked principally in Ferrara, where he settled in 1722. He is better known for his sculpture and stucco work than for his painting.

AUCTION RECORDS:

MONTE CARLO, 21 June 1987, *Christ Affronted* (oil on canvas, 33 x 27 1/2in/84 x 70cm) FRF 60,000.

FERRERI, Cesare

Italian, 19th century.
Born 31 March 1802, in Pavia; died 13 November 1859, in Pavia.
Engraver (burin).

Cesare Ferreri engraved portraits and genre subjects.

FERRERI, Domenico, or Ferrerio or Ferrero

Italian, 17th century.
Died November 1630, in Rome.
Sculptor, founder.

Domenico Ferreri studied under Torrigiani. He produced numerous statues, tabernacles and low reliefs for churches in Rome, together with a bronze tabernacle encrusted with precious stones for the Jesuit church of Palermo. He also sculpted and cast six silver statues designed by A. Buonvicini and destined for Cracow, plus two statues of saints based on Mariani models that were commissioned by Cardinal Sannesio.

FERRERI, Enrico
Italian, 20th century.
Painter.
Enrico Ferreri lives and works in Rome, and exhibits in Milan.

Until 1965 his paintings were Expressionist in style. His work then rapidly evolved towards abstraction, with repeated motifs providing a serial effect. Ferreri has continued to paint in this way ever since, using a single form, module or pattern, by means of stamps or moulds, which he assembles and applies in layers, playing with the effects of both relief and coloration.

FERRERI, Giovanni Antonio
Italian, 17th century.
Of Genoese origin.
Painter.
Giovanni Ferreri is recorded as having been active in Rome around 1611.

FERRERI, Giovanni Battista
Italian, 17th century.
Active in Rome.
Painter. History painting, religious subjects.
School of Rome.
A pupil of Carlo Maratti, Giovanni Battista Ferreri is best remembered for his ceiling and mural frescoes of *Episodes from the Lives of St Charles and St Philip*, painted for the church of the Trinità dei Pellegrini in Rome.

FERRERI, Giuseppe
Italian, 18th century.
Born 1702.
Active in Ferrara.
Sculptor.
He was the son of Andrea Ferreri.

FERRERI, José
Spanish, 19th century.
Born in the 19th century, in Lérida.
Sculptor.
José Ferreri studied at the school of fine arts in Barcelona and produced the ornamental carvings of the high altar of the Carmelite church in Barcelona, the altar of S Bruno in the church of the monastery of Montealegre, and the altar in the monastery of Montserrat.

FERRERI, Victor
French, 20th century.
Born 1 October 1915, in Ferryville, Tunisia.
Painter. Portraits, landscapes, seascapes, still-lifes.
Victor Ferreri took part in collective exhibitions, especially on the French Riviera, where he showed sets of his works in local town halls.

FERRERI, Vincenzo
Italian, 18th century.
Active in Perugia.
Painter.
Vincenzo Ferreri studied in Perugia under Marcello Leopardi, then at the academy in Perugia, where he was awarded a prize in 1793 for his painting of *Polyxena Slain by Pyrrhus on the Tomb of Achilles*, a work now housed in the Pinacoteca in Parma. He is also remembered for a *St Andrew* painted for the oratory of SS Andrea e Bernardino in Perugia, and for a *St Bernard of Siena*.

FERRERI, Vincenzo
Italian, 19th century.
Active in Rome.
Engraver.
In 1845 Vincenzo Ferreri engraved a folio edition of 20 plates of frescoes by Domenichino in Grottaferrata.

FERRERIO, Domenico. See **FERRERI**

FERRERIO, Pietro
Italian, 17th century.
Born c. 1600, in Rome; died 10 March 1654, in Rome.
Architect, draughtsman.
Pietro Ferrerio is known for 44 plates of architectural views in a volume published in 1655 by G. G. Rossi entitled *Palazzi of the Most Celebrated Roman Architects*. He was a member of the Accademia di S Luca in Rome.

FERRERIS, Bartholomeüs
Dutch, 16th - 17th century.
Painter, collector.
Ferreris, who lived in Leiden, was a pupil of Antonio Moro and of Peeter and Frans Pourbus. His collection of paintings included works by Hans Holbein, Lucas van Leyden, Cornelis van Haarlem and others.

FERRERIS, Heindrick
Dutch, 17th century.
Active in Leiden c. 1655.
Painter.
Heindrick Ferreris was the son of Bartholomeüs Ferreris.

FERRERO, Giovanni Francesco
Italian, 19th century.
Painter, draughtsman, engraver.
Giovanni Francesco Ferrero worked in Rome where, in 1830, he published *The Finest Compositions by Raphael, Poussin, etc: Drawings and Engravings by G.F. Ferrero*. There is an altar painting by him, depicting *The Virgin and Saints*, in the church of S Pietro in his home town of Romano d'Ivrea (Piedmont).

FERRERO, Roger
Swiss, 20th century.
Born 11 August 1915, in Geneva.
Painter, illustrator.
Ferrero was a student at the École des Beaux-Arts in Geneva, from 1932 to 1935. He moved to France in 1948, then travelled in Greece, Arabia, Syria and Lebanon in 1953. Between 1943 and 1952 he exhibited in Geneva, Zurich, Venice, Paris and Brussels. He illustrated the works of Maupassant and Verlaine.
MUSEUMS AND GALLERIES:
PARIS (Mus. de la Ville).

FERRERS, Benjamin
British, 18th century.
Died 1732.
Painter. Portraits, genre scenes.
Benjamin Ferrers was a deaf-mute artist. His portraits of *Bishop Beveridge* and the *Bishop Hoadly* are among his finest works.
MUSEUMS AND GALLERIES:
OXFORD (Bodleian Library): *Portait of Bishop Beveridge*.
AUCTION RECORDS:
LONDON, 27 May 1938, *Thomas Macclesfield*, GBP 11. LONDON, 21 July 2003, *Portrait of a Lady* (oil on canvas, 50 x 40 ins / 127 x 101 cm) GBP 4,000.

FERRET, J. B.
French, 18th century.
Sculptor.
In 1771 J. B. Ferret executed the pulpit and the panelling of the choir and the nave, as well as two plaster statues of angels on the high altar, for the church of St-Brice and St-Roch in Beaulieu-sur-Loire.

FERRET, Pierre César
French, 19th century.
Born 1801, in St-Germain-en-Laye.
Painter.
Ferret exhibited at the Paris Salon from 1834 to 1852. In 1839, he received a third-class medal. Works include *Charles*

II, King of Spain, Having the Tomb of His Father, Philip IV, Opened, The Puritan, John Balfour of Burley, Lazarus the Monk, Jean d'Aubigné, Jesus in Egypt, Battle of Rocroi, Coenobite, St Cecilia and *Victory of Maccabeus.*

FERRET DE LA CHATAIGNERAY, Denise
French, 18th century.
Active in Paris in 1738.
Painter.

FERRETTI, Adeodato
Italian, 18th century.
Painter.
Adeodato Ferretti painted a *St Martin* for the church of S Martino in Chiusdino, a *Pietà* for S Miniato in Fonterutoli, and a *Madonna with St Simon* for the church of S Maria delle Grazie in Montepulciano.

FERRETTI, Alessandro, or Feretti
Italian, 18th century.
Painter.
Alessandro Ferretti painted frescoes and an *Annunciation* for the oratory of Restello at Val d'Intelvi (Lake Como) in 1748. He is probably the same artist as the Ferretti who worked alongside D. Francis to paint scenes representing the *Triumph of Virtue* on the banqueting hall ceiling in the castle in Stockholm.

FERRETTI, Antonio
Italian, 18th century.
Born to a family originally from the Intelvi Valley (Lake Como).
Sculptor.
He worked alongside his father Giorgio Ferretti to sculpt marble figures for the façade of the cathedral of Cremona. He is also remembered for statues in the choir of the church of S Girolamo and for statues entitled *Faith* and *Charity* for the church of S Clemente. The Queriniana library in Cremona houses four statues by Antonio Ferretti representing *The Sciences* and *Cherubs.*

FERRETTI, Camillo
Italian, 17th century.
Active in Rome in 1697.
Painter.

FERRETTI, Carlo
Italian, 18th century.
Born to a family originally from Castiglione.
Sculptor.
Around 1717, Carlo Ferretti worked with the architect Paolo Retti at the castle of Ludwigsburg, where he sculpted two statues of *River Gods*, and at the castle of Ansbach, where he sculpted a bust of *Margrave Karl Wilhelm Friedrich von Ansbach-Bayreuth.*

FERRETTI, Domenico
Italian, 18th century.
Born 1701, in Castiglione, on Lake Como; died 26 January 1774, in Stuttgart.
Sculptor.
The son of Carlo Ferretti, he was invited to work in Württemberg, where he made allegorical groups representing *War and Peace, Science and the Arts* and *Commerce and Agriculture*, together with trophies sculpted for the Residenz in Stuttgart and the castle of Ludwigsburg. Later he was retained by the porcelain works in Ludwigsburg. Porcelain statues produced from models by Domenico Ferretti include *Adonis and the Wild Boar, Good Samaritan, Latona with the Young Apollo and Diana, Mars in Vulcan's Forge,* and *Vulcan and Venus.*

FERRETTI, Gian Domenico or Giovanni Domenico, also known as Giovanni Domenico da Imola
Italian, 18th century.
Born 1692, in Florence; died between 1766 and 1769.
Painter, fresco artist, draughtsman. Religious subjects, mythological subjects, genre scenes.
Gian Domenico Ferretti studied under Giovanni Giuseppe del Sole. Oils and frescoes by him are to be found predominantly in palazzi and churches in Imola, Livorno, Siena and Florence; he also painted the cupola of the Filippini in Pistoia. In addition to these grandiose frescoes, Ferretti left drawings and sketches of mythological subjects and harlequinades exhibiting a lighter touch and somewhat Rococo mannerisms.

MUSEUMS AND GALLERIES:
CHAMBÉRY: *Descent from the Cross* - FLORENCE (Uffizi): *Self-portrait* - PISA (Church of S Bartholomeo): *Martyrdom of St Bartholomew* - PISA (Mus. Civico): *Transfer of the Corpse of St Guy; Portrait of Emperor Francis II; Portrait of Emperor Ferdinand II.*

AUCTION RECORDS:
NEW YORK, 8 Feb 1935, *Vanity Ridiculed; Futility of War* (collection) USD 200. LONDON, 29 Nov 1963, *Harlequin Painting the Portrait of a Lady of Substance; Harlequin Approaching a Beautiful Woman on his Return from War* (oil/copper, a pair, 13¾ x 11½in/35 x 29.2cm) Gns 700. MILAN, 10 May 1967, *St Catherine Appearing to a Monk,* ITL 750,000. MILAN, 1 Dec 1970, *Carnival Scene,* ITL 1,700,000. NEW YORK, 11 March 1978, *Dwarfs in Dialogue* (oil on canvas, 20 x 26¼in/51 x 66.5cm) USD 6,750. BARI, 5 April 1981, *Harlequin as a Painter* (oil on canvas, 37¾ x 30¼in/96 x 77cm) ITL 3,200,000. LONDON, 2 July 1984, *Group of Satyrs, Nymphs and Cherubs Drinking* (black chalk and grey wash, 8¾ x 7¾in/22.5 x 19.8cm) GBP 800. LONDON, 11 April 1986, *Harlequin Painting the Portrait of a Lady of Substance; Harlequin Approaching a Beautiful Woman on his Return from War* (oil/copper, a pair, 13¾ x 11½in/35 x 29.2cm) GBP 15,000. ROME, 27 Nov 1989, *Olympus* (oil on canvas, 24 x 19¼in/61 x 49cm) ITL 36,800,000. MILAN, 27 March 1990, *Harlequin and Columbine* (oil on canvas, 27¼ x 22in/69 x 56cm) ITL 7,000,000. LONDON, 18 May 1990, *Glory of St Philip Neri* (oil on canvas, 14½ x 12¼in/36.8 x 31.4cm) GBP 8,580. MONACO, 7 Dec 1990, *Scene from the Commedia dell'Arte* (oil on canvas, 18 x 12½in/45.5 x 32cm) FRF 38,850. LONDON, 8 July 1992, *Harlequin in the Role of a Father Nurturing his Child* (oil on canvas, 38½ x 31¼in/98 x 79.5cm) GBP 11,000. PARIS, 20 Dec 2000, *Harlequin and Colombine* (oil on canvas, 26 x 21 ins / 65 x 53 cm) FRF 350,000. LONDON, 9 July 2002, *Justinian Giving the Tablets of the Law* (oil on canvas, 28 x 22 ins / 72 x 57 cm) GBP 12,000. LONDON, 29 Oct 2003, *Dwarves in a Rocky Landscape* (oil on panel, 35 x 28 ins / 88 x 72 cm) GBP 7,000. MILAN, 15 Nov 2003, *Still-life with Pans* (1713, oil on canvas, 6 x 10 ins / 15 x 25 cm) EUR 32,000. VIENNA, 24 March 2004, *Venus and Diana with Putti* (oil on canvas, 25 x 20 ins / 64 x 52 cm) EUR 7,000. SAN FRANCISCO, 18 May 2004, *Masquerade Ball* (oil on canvas, 29 x 39 ins / 74 x 98 cm) USD 8,000.

FERRETTI, Giorgio, or Feretti or Ferrata
Italian, 18th century.
Born 18th century, to a family originally from the Intelvi Valley (Lake Como).
Sculptor.
Examples of Giorgio Ferretti's work include statues for the fountain and gardens of the Palazzo Avogradi in Brescia. Statues on the Michaelstor in Bonn are possibly his, and a G. Ferretti is on record as having worked in Mannheim, Germany in 1723. What is certain, on the other hand, is that he was working alongside his son Antonio Ferretti in Cremona in 1758.

FERRETTI, Giovanni Battista
Italian, 17th century.

Born 17th century, to a family originally from Alfedena (Abruzzo).
Painter. Religious subjects.
Giovanni Battista Ferretti was a pupil of C. Maratti. His *St Peter Martyr* is to be found in the church at Alfedena, and he also painted the ceiling and the pictures in four side chapels of the church of S Trinità dei Pellegrini in Rome.

FERRETTI, Giuseppe
Italian, 19th century.
Active in Rome.
Engraver (burin).
Giuseppe Ferretti engraved costume plates.

FERRETTI, Lodovico
Italian, 19th century.
Active in Rome.
Engraver.
Lodovico Ferretti engraved *The Testament of Moses* (a fresco in the Sistine Chapel) after Signorelli; *The Triumph of David* and a *St Cecilia* after Domenico; a *Holy Family with St John* after Garofalo; and 14 plates depicting the *Way of the Cross*, after Overbeck. He also engraved the works of Luini, Raphael, Michelangelo and L. Giordani.

FERRETTI, Orazio dei (Count)
Italian, 17th - 18th century.
Born 16 February 1639, in Perugia; died 1 January 1725, in Perugia.
Painter, architect.
Orazio dei Ferretti studied painting in Rome under Bernardino Gagliardi.

FERRETTI, Paolo
Italian, 19th - 20th century.
Born 1866, in Rome.
Painter. Landscapes.
Paolo Ferretti was a pupil of Nino Costa and, like him, was interested in unusual lighting effects. He exhibited in Rome at the *Promotrice* in 1901, then again in Rome in 1909, 1913 and 1914, and in Venice. He also worked in Switzerland.

The titles of his landscapes reveal his interest in the climactic conditions of light, for example: *Autumn Afternoon; Morning Vision; Golden Rays (Sunset in the Roman Countryside).*
MUSEUMS AND GALLERIES:
ROME (Gal. Nazionale): *Last Rays.*

FERRETTI, Stefano
Italian, 19th century.
Born 23 February 1807, in Parma.
Painter.
In 1841 Stefano Ferretti exhibited a head of *Peter the Apostle*, which was severely criticised in the Facchino.

FERREY, Coralie
French, 19th century.
Born in Rennes.
Painter. Portraits, animals.
Ferrey was a pupil of Lebour and first exhibited at the Salon in 1848. She continued to take part in Parisian exhibitions for many years.

FERREY, Fanni, also called (the) Citizen
French, 18th century.
Painter.
Fanni Ferrey was the pupil of Citizen Thonnesse, her father-in-law. She exhibited at the Salon de Paris in 1793 (*Two Young Women at their Lunch*) and 1796 (*Terrible News*).

FERREY, Raoul
French.
Painter.
MUSEUMS AND GALLERIES:
PARIS (Mus. de la Poste): *Portrait of Marc Pierre d'Argenson.*

FERREYRA, Rose Malvina
Argentinian, 20th century.
Born in Córdoba.
Painter.
Rose Ferreyra studied under Paul Albert Laaurens, Paul A. J. Eschbach and Louis Roger. She began exhibiting in Paris in 1927 at the Salon des Artistes Français.

FERREYRO, José Antonio Mauro
Spanish, 18th - 19th century.
Born 14 November 1738, in Noja; died 1830, in Hermisende (Zamora).
Sculptor.
José Antonio Mauro Ferreyro's best works include *Minerva*, a *Crucifix* for the church of S Martino in Santiago and *Virgin of Mount Carmel* which he produced for a convent in Santiago.

FERREZ, Jeanne
French, 20th century.
Born in Lyons.
Painter. Landscapes.
Jeanne Ferrez studied under Cagniart and Grosjean. She was a member of the Salon des Artistes Français.

FERRI. See **FERRY**

FERRI, Andrea
Italian, 14th century.
Active in Florence.
Painter.

FERRI, Antonio
Italian, 19th century.
Draughtsman.
Antonio Ferri taught drawing at Mirandola (Emilia-Romagna). He drew the study for the engraved portrait of *Ferdinand II de Medici*, for Pio Canossini (after Susterman), for the Pitti Gallery of the Bardi family.

FERRI, Augusto
Italian, 19th century.
Born 1829, in Bologna; died 1895, in Pesaro (Marche).
Painter, fresco artist, decorative designer. Landscapes, still-lifes (flowers/fruit). Frescoes, stage sets, church decoration, murals.
Augusto Ferri was the son of Domenico Ferri. After a trip to Paris with his father, he was taken on as a painter at the Teatro Regio in Turin. He spent time in Madrid too, designing sets for numerous operas. He also painted decorative frescoes in many churches, palaces and cafes in Madrid, Barcelona and Valladolid. Ferri is known in Turin for his decorative works in the palace of the Duke of Aosta.
AUCTION RECORDS:
MILAN, 6 June 1985, *Still-life*; *Seashore* (oil on canvas, a pair, 9 3/4 x 14 1/2 ins / 25 x 37 cm) ITL 1,600,000. MILAN, 14 June 1989, *Still-life with Roses* (1895, oil on canvas, 35 1/2 x 15 3/4 ins / 90 x 40 cm) ITL 1,900,000. MILAN, 6 June 1991, *Medlars and Cherries in Fruit Bowls* (oil on canvas, 12 1/4 x 19 3/4 ins / 31 x 50 cm) ITL 3,300,000. MILAN, 7 Nov 1991, *Lagoon in Venice* (oil on canvas, 14 x 21 3/4 ins / 35.5 x 55.5 cm) ITL 3,600,000. MILAN, 14 Oct 2003, *Still-life with Plums and Peaches* (oil on canvas, 20 x 28 ins / 50 x 70 cm) EUR 1,800.

FERRI, Ciro
Italian, 17th century.
Born 1634, in Rome; died 1689, in Rome.
Painter, fresco artist, sculptor, decorative artist, draughtsman, illustrator. Religious subjects, allegorical subjects.
Ciro Ferri was Pietro da Cortona's outstanding pupil. He frequently worked alongside da Cortona and was retained

on a regular basis by Pope Alexander VII and Prince Borghese. Grand Duke Cosimo III invited him to the Palazzo Pitti in Florence to complete frescoes left unfinished by da Cortona. By all accounts, Ferri did an excellent job and was soon entrusted with additional decorative work, including *Seasons* for the Villa Falconieri in Frascati and frescoes for the church of S Maria Maggiore in Bergamo (1667). Among his other works are frescoes in the cupola of S Agnese in the Piazza Navona in Rome.

Ferri's work in other disciplines is also worthy of note. He executed sculptures, notably four pieces for the sacristy of Gésu; and he illustrated a publication presented to Queen Christina of Sweden to celebrate her conversion to Catholicism in 1654.

Ferri was so skilled at imitating Pietro da Cortona's work that it has at times proved difficult to distinguish between the two artists.

MUSEUMS AND GALLERIES:

AJACCIO: *Holy Family at Rest* - CAEN: *Christ on the Cross* - COPENHAGEN (Statens Mus. for Kunst): *David Declining to put on Armour* - DARMSTADT: *Abduction of Helen of Troy* - ERLANGEN: *Virgin and St Martha* - FLORENCE (Uffizi): *Alexander Reading Homer; Self-portrait; Annunciation; Christ Crucified* - GOTHA: *Saints* - LILLE (MBA, Wicar Collection): *Martyr Appearing before the Proconsul* - MONTPELLIER: *Holy Virgin* - MUNICH: *Rest during the Flight into Egypt* - NUREMBERG: *Rebecca and Laban* - OLDENBURG (Augusteum): *St Theresa* - POTSDAM (Schloss Sanssouci): *Coriolanus at the Gates of Rome* - POZNAN: *Moses Striking Water from the Rock* - RENNES: *Roman Sacrifice; Allegory* - ROHRAU (Schlossmuseum, Graf Harrach'sche Familiensammlung): *Adoration of the Shepherds* - SPEYER: *Holy Family* - ST PETERSBURG: *Vision of St Catherine of Siena* - TURIN (Pinacoteca): *Jesus on the Mount of Olives* - VENICE (Gal. dell'Accademia): *Mystic Marriage of St Catherine* - VERSAILLES: *Triumph of Louis XIV* - VIENNA: *Christ and Mary Magdalene* - VIENNA (Liechtenstein Mus.): *Christ and the Samaritan* - VIRE: *Adoration of the Shepherds* - WARSAW: *Holy Virgin between St Ambrose and St Augustine.*

AUCTION RECORDS:

LONDON, 20 Feb 1909, *Isaac's Sacrifice,* GBP 4. LONDON, 24 Nov 1922, *Moses,* GBP 15. PARIS, 9 March 1929, *Julius Caesar* (drawing) FRF 100. PARIS, 20-22 April 1932, *Episode from Tasso's 'Jerusalem Delivered'* (pen and wash) FRF 400. LONDON, 29 Nov 1974, *Jesus and the Woman of Samaria,* Gns 3,000. LONDON, 29 Nov 1974, *Jesus and the Woman of Samaria* (oil on canvas, 27 x 21in/68.6 x 53.3cm) Gns 3,000. LONDON, 11 Dec 1980, *Mary Magdalene in Adoration of the Cross* (black chalk/paper, 8 x 7 1/4in/20.5 x 18.5cm) GBP 2,000. PARIS, 10 Oct 1983, *Holy Family during the Flight into Egypt* (red chalk, 16 3/4 x 11in/42.5 x 28cm) FRF 7,200. LONDON, 12 Dec 1985, *Resurrection* (black chalk and brown wash heightened with white/greyish-brown paper, 12 1/4 x 7 3/4in/30.8 x 19.6cm) GBP 8,500. LONDON, 10 Dec 1986, *Jesus and the Woman of Samaria* (oil on canvas, 27 x 21in/68.6 x 53.3cm) GBP 33,000. MONTE CARLO, 20 June 1987, *Baptism of St Ambrose* (pen, brown ink and wash heightened with white/outlines in black chalk, 6 3/4 x 7 3/4in/17.3 x 19.8cm) FRF 90,000. LONDON, 2 July 1991, *St Francis Meeting St Dominic* (black and red chalk heightened with white, 10 1/4 x 15 1/4in/25.9 x 39cm) GBP 38,500. LONDON, 15 April 1992, *Noli Me Tangere* (oil on canvas, 29 1/4 x 22 3/4in/74 x 58cm) GBP 7,000. NEW YORK, 19 May 1993, *Elijah and the Widow of Sarepta* (oil on canvas, 47 1/2 x 43 1/4in/120.6 x 109.8cm) USD 18,400. ROME, 29-30 Nov 1993, *Judah and Tamar* (oil on canvas, 46 1/2 x 52ins / 118 x 132cm) ITL 30,641,000. LONDON, 18 April 1994, *Allegory of the Papacy (recto); Compositional Study (verso)* (black chalk, 7 3/4 x 10in/20 x 25.3cm) GBP 2,530. ROME, 22 Nov 1994, *Allegory of Summer* (oil on canvas, 57 3/4 x 57 3/4in/147 x 147cm) ITL 25,300,000. NEW YORK, 10 Jan 1996, *Angels Carrying a Candelabra* (ink and wash, 7 1/2 x 10in/19 x 25.4cm) USD 2,530. LONDON, 16-17 April 1997, *Section of Arch Supported by Satyrs* (pen and brown ink on black chalk, study, 5 x 5in/11.8 x 12.7cm) GBP 805. PARIS, 3 April 1998, *Recto: Bacchus' Cortège; Verso: Male Nude and Three Studies for a Nativity* (black chalk, 16 x 10 1/2in/40.4 x 26.7cm) FRF 25,000. LONDON, 16 Dec 1999, *Madonna and Child with Infant St John the Baptist* (oil on canvas, 59 x 59 ins / 151 x 151 cm) GBP 42,000. NEW YORK, 28 Jan 2000, *Triumph of Bacchus* (oil on canvas, 56 x 81 ins / 141 x 206 cm) USD 120,000. LONDON, 4 July 2000, *The Martyrdom of a Saint. Studies of Attacking Soldiers* (chalk/pen/ink wash, double-sided, 8 x 6 ins / 21 x 15 cm) GBP 13,000. LONDON, 11 July 2001, *Angels among Clouds* (pen/brown ink wash, 7 x 9 ins / 19 x 24 cm) GBP 5,000. LONDON, 11 July 2001, *Madonna and Child in Glory, Appearing to a Kneeling Young Man* (black chalk/brown wash heightened with white, 5 x 4 ins / 13 x 10 cm) GBP 15,000. VENICE, 19 Feb 2003, *Cleopatra* (oil on canvas, 31 x 26 ins / 80 x 67 cm) EUR 35,000. LONDON, 9 Dec 2003, *Design for the High Altarpiece of St Agnese, Rome* (pen/brown ink wash/watercolour over black chalk, 28 x 20 ins / 71 x 51 cm) GBP 15,000. NEW YORK, 22 Jan 2004, *Resurrection* (black chalk/pen/brown ink wash, 12 x 8 ins / 31 x 20 cm) USD 22,000. ROME, 16 June 2004, *Judah and Tamar* (oil on canvas, 37 x 40 ins / 93 x 101 cm) EUR 13,800.

FERRI, Cristoforo

Italian, 16th century.
Active in Rome.
Sculptor.

FERRI, Domenico

Italian, 19th century.
Born 25 April 1857, in Castel di Lama (Ascoli Piceno).
Painter.

Domenico Ferri studied initially at the Accademia di Belle Arti in Florence, and subsequently in Naples with Domenico Morelli. He is known in Ascoli for his decorations in the Palazzo Ferretti and the Council Chamber, and for a triptych on an altar in the crypt of the cathedral in Montelupone (Macerata). In Bologna he decorated the ceiling of the town theatre, and was taken on as a teacher at the Bologna Accademia. In the church of St Mary Magdalene he decorated the apse and cupola with frescoes and painted the high altar. He also painted scenes from peasant life, including *Return of the Fishing Boats* and *White Butterflies*. Ferri exhibited in Rome, Vienna, Turin, Munich and Florence.

FERRI, Domenico

Italian, 19th century.
Born 1797; died 1869.
Painter, architect. Landscapes. Stage sets.

In around 1830 Domenico Ferri was working as a set designer in Paris, at the Théâtre des Italiens, making the stage sets for a production of Rossini's *William Tell.* He exhibited two landscapes at the Paris Salon of 1836. He was also an architect.

AUCTION RECORDS:

LONDON, 6 Oct 1989, *Covered Cart on a Path in a Rocky Landscape* (oil on canvas, 15 3/4 x 22 ins / 40 x 56 cm) GBP 1,650. MILAN, 17 Dec 1992, *View of Oggebio on Lake Maggiore* (1831, oil on card, 13 1/2 x 15 1/4 ins / 34 x 39 cm) ITL 2,600,000. NEW YORK, 26 May 1994, *View of Paris with the Pont-Neuf, the Île de la Cité and the Place Dauphine* (1832, oil on canvas, 21 x 29 1/2 ins / 53.3 x 74.9 cm) USD 20,700.

FERRI, Félice

Italian, 19th century.
Engraver (burin).

Félice Ferri was a pupil of Giuseppe Longhi. He engraved *The Holy Virgin Swooning,* after Bernardino Luini.

FERRI, Félix
Spanish, 18th century.
Painter.
Félix Ferri was trained in and worked in Valencia.
MUSEUMS AND GALLERIES:
VALENCIA: *Perseus; Virgin with Fish* (after Raphael).

FERRI, Gaetano
Italian, 19th century.
Born 1822, in Bologna; died 1896, in Oneglia.
Painter. History painting, portraits, genre scenes.
Gaetano Ferri won a third-class medal at the 1855 Exposition Universelle in Paris. Well-known works of his include: *Death of Princess de Lamballe; News of the Death of King Charles Albert*; and *Portrait of the Painter.*
AUCTION RECORDS:
ROME, 9 June 1992, *Mother and Child* (oil on canvas, 12 1/4 x 7 1/2 ins / 31 x 19 cm) ITL 2,000,000.

FERRI, Gesualdo Francesco
Italian, 18th century.
Born 1728, in San Miniato; died 1788, in San Miniato.
Painter. History painting.
Gesualdo Francesco Ferri was a pupil of Pompeo Batoni; his work is to be found in Florence and other Italian towns and cities. His *Exaltation* is preserved in the church of Carmine in Florence.
MUSEUMS AND GALLERIES:
FLORENCE (Uffizi): self-portrait; several drawings - LILLE (MBA, Wicar Collection): several drawings.

FERRI, Girolamo
Italian, 17th century.
Active in Perugia.
Painter.
Girolamo Ferri painted a *St Anthony of Padua* in 1650 for the chapel of the Palazzo Comunale in Perugia.

FERRI, Girolamo
Italian, 17th century.
Died 1670.
Active in Bologna.
Painter.
A pupil of F. Albani, Girolamo Ferri painted frescoes for the Bologna church of S Maria della Vita, together with a *St Thomas* and an *Albertus Magnus* for the church of the Dominican friars in Cremona.

FERRI, Giuseppe
Italian, 18th century.
Active in Bologna.
Painter, decorative artist, architect.
Giuseppe Ferri decorated a chapel in the church of SS Vitale e Agricola in Bologna.

FERRI, Nicodemo
Italian, 19th century.
Born in Siena.
Sculptor (wood).
Nicodemo Ferri was a pupil of L. Mussini at the academy of fine arts in Siena. He decorated a piano that was given as a gift from the town of Siena to the king of Italy, on the occasion of his marriage in 1896. He also decorated the king's bedroom at the Quirinale in Rome, and a bedroom for the Emperor of Germany. Ferri also worked in leather, and made a cover for the visitors' book at the tomb of Victor Emanuel II at the Pantheon in Rome.

FERRI, Simone
Italian, 16th century.
Painter.
Simone Ferri was a pupil of Mantegna and worked in Mantua and in Pietole for the Gonzaga family. The church of the delle Murate monastery in Florence has his ceiling paintings depicting the *Assumption* and ten scenes from the *Life of Mary*.

FERRI, Tommaso
Italian, 14th century.
Active in Modena.
Sculptor.
Tommaso Ferri carved the pulpit in Modena cathedral in 1322.

FERRI, Vincenzo or Vincent, or Ferry
French, 19th century.
Born 1787, in Gazzuolo; died after 1837.
Sculptor.
Ferri was a pupil at the École de Toulouse, and later became a teacher of sculpture at the École des Arts in Auch. His main works consist of four large low reliefs, for the churches of Ste-Marie and St-Orens at the college and seminary in Auch, several statues for churches in the department of Gers and a colossal group above the main door to the archbishop's palace in Auch.

FERRIÉ, Blanche
French, 19th - 20th century.
Painter. Flowers.
Blanche Ferrié studied under flower painter Pierre Adrien Chabal-Dussurgey.
MUSEUMS AND GALLERIES:
DRAGUIGNAN: *A Bunch of Roses.*

FERRIER, André Gabriel
French, 19th - 20th century.
Painter. Genre scenes.
André Ferrier exhibited in Paris at the Salon des Artistes Français and was awarded a third-class medal in 1911.
AUCTION RECORDS:
PARIS, 21 Jan 1942, *Apparition,* FRF 320; *The Broken Idol,* FRF 510; *Nymph at her Toilette,* FRF 650.

FERRIER, André Pierre
French, 20th century.
Born in Paris.
Sculptor.
André Ferrier exhibited at the Société Nationale des Beaux-Arts in Paris.

FERRIER, Bernard
French, 15th century.
Sculptor. Monuments.
In 1495, Ferrier sculpted the funerary monument of Antoine de Comis for the church of St-Didier in Avignon.
MUSEUMS AND GALLERIES:
AVIGNON (Mus. Calvet): *Funerary Monument of Antoine de Comis* (fragments).

FERRIER, Denise
French, 20th century.
Painter.
Denise Ferrier exhibited at the Salon des Réalités Nouvelles in 1950 and 1953.

FERRIER, Gabriel Joseph Marie Augustin
French, 19th - 20th century.
Born 27 September 1847, in Nîmes; died 6 June 1914, in Paris.
Painter. Religious subjects, mythological subjects, portraits, genre scenes, figures, still-lifes.
Orientalism.
Gabriel Ferrier studied under Pils, Lecoq de Boisbaudran and E. Hébert. He featured at the Paris Salon from 1869. He was awarded the Prix de Rome in 1872, a second-class medal in 1876, a first-class medal in 1878, a gold medal in 1889 for the International Exhibition, and the Médaille d'Honneur in 1903. As Commandeur of the Légion d'Honneur and a member of the Institut, he would have been a respected master at

the École des Beaux-Arts, where he taught Bissière (among others).

Salammbô, Spring, and *L'École* are among the best-known of Ferrier's paintings.

GABRIEL-FERRIER

GABRIEL-FERRIER

Museums and Galleries:

Algiers: *Kif Smokers* - Amiens: *Mothers Cursing War* - Munich: *Portrait of Baronne d'Akermann* - Nîmes: *David and Goliath* - Paris (MAM): *Portrait of General André; Portrait of the Alvéar Ladies; Young Girl on a Donkey* - Paris (Mus. du Petit Palais): *Scene from the Flood; Perfumes; Flowers* - Rouen: *Dead Sniper; War Scene; St Agnes.*

Auction records:

Paris, 1897, *Salammbô,* FRF 5,100. New York, 13-14 Feb 1900, *Thoughts of the Absent One,* USD 485. Paris, 25 May 1905, *Daphnis and Chloe,* FRF 300. Paris, 7 May 1906, *The Fair Nape,* FRF 100. Paris, 26-27 Nov 1923, *The Guardian Angel* (oil on canvas, diam. 42¼ ins / 107 cm) FRF 2,850. Paris, 26-27 Nov 1923, *Portrait of Pius X,* FRF 10,000; *Head of a Red Haired Woman in a Venetian Bonnet,* FRF 4,700; *Head of a Blond Young Woman,* FRF 1,600; *Girl of Flowers,* FRF 1,080; *Woman with the Fan,* FRF 1,000; *Woman at her Mirror,* FRF 1,050; *Reading,* FRF 2,500; *Child with Kid,* FRF 980; *Young Red-Head in a Venetian Bonnet,* FRF 1,250; *Woman with the Rose,* FRF 980; *Bacchanale* (sketch) FRF 1,000; *Young Flower Girl,* FRF 980; *The Guardian Angel,* FRF 2,850; *Velleda,* FRF 2,000; *Page Boy at the Court of Henry II of France,* FRF 980; *The Tea Party,* FRF 2,020. Paris, 19 Dec 1923, *Motherhood,* FRF 280. Paris, 26 May 1924, *The Star,* FRF 900. Paris, 30 May 1924, *The Working Girl* (attributed) FRF 130. Paris, 4 March 1925, *Girl of Flowers,* FRF 705. Paris, 14 and 15 Dec 1925, *Night,* FRF 320. Paris, 5 May 1928, *Lady with Locket or Happy Memory,* FRF 1,250. Paris, 4 Dec 1933, *Profane Love* (study after the painting by Titian kept in the Villa Borghese, in Rome) FRF 40. Paris, 20 Dec 1943, *Woman and Child,* FRF 4,300. Paris, 17 April 1944, *Spes invicta manet* (*Hope Stands Undefeated,* FRF 3,600. Paris, 2 Dec 1946, *Hope Stands Undefeated,* FRF 5,200. Los Angeles, 8 April 1973, *Couple Fording a River,* USD 1,900. Paris, 26 Nov 1976, *Young Red-Headed Girl* (oil on panel, 25½ x 21¼ ins / 65 x 54 cm) FRF 3,200. Paris, 10 June 1980, *The Tea Party* (oil on canvas) FRF 46,500. London, 3 June 1983, *The Lost Goat* (oil on canvas, 28 ins / 71 cm, ¾ x 19¼ ins/2 x 49 cm) GBP 2,800. London, 19 March 1986, *The Guardian Angel* (oil on canvas, round, diam. 42¼ ins / 107 cm) GBP 7,000. Paris, 10 Feb 1988, *Portrait of a Girl* (1909, oil on canvas, 22 x 18 ins / 56 x 46 cm) FRF 9,000. London, 26 Feb 1988, *Red-Headed Girl* (oil on canvas, 25½ x 21¼ ins / 65 x 54 cm) GBP 2,200. Copenhagen, 29 Aug 1990, *Still-life of Poppies in an Earthenware Vase* (1880, oil on canvas, 23½ x 19¾ ins / 60 x 50 cm) DKK 6,200. New York, 15 Feb 1994, *A Harem Beauty Holding a Fan* (oil on canvas, 60 x 42¼ ins / 152.4 x 107.3 cm) USD 55,200. Paris, 7 Nov 1994, *The Favourite at her Toilette* (1877, oil on canvas, 32¼ x 22 ins / 82 x 55 cm) FRF 90,000. Paris, 22 Nov 1996, *Woman with Birds* (oil on wood, 15¼ x 11¾ ins / 39 x 30 cm) FRF 4,000. New York, 23 Oct 1997, *John (Saint John the Baptist Young)* (1910, oil on canvas, round, diam. 35½ ins / 90 cm) USD 35,650.

FERRIER, George Straton

British, 20th century.

Born in Edinburgh; died 26 February 1912, in Edinburgh.

Painter, engraver.

George Ferrier exhibited at the Salon des Artistes Français and received a commendation in 1899. He also exhibited at the Royal Academy and the New Water-Colour Society. He was the son of James Ferrier.

Auction records:

Edinburgh, 13 July 1929, *Dordrecht* (watercolour) GBP 8.

FERRIER, Henry

French, 19th century.

Born in Nevers (Nièvre).

Painter.

Ferrier exhibited *Scarecrow* and *Young Greek Woman* at the Paris Salon in 1868 and *Flowers* in 1869.

FERRIER, Henry René

French, 20th century.

Born 19 February 1928, in Marseilles.

Painter. Landscapes.

Henry Ferrier has been able to live by his art since 1979.

He has featured in collective exhibitions since the early 1960s: notably, from 1987, in the Salon d'Automne in Paris and the New York Contemporary Art Fair, Osaka's International Festival and the France-Quebec Biennale exhibition.

Bibliography:

Ferrier, exhibition catalogue, Conseil régional de Provence-Alpes-Côte d'Azur, Musée Vouland, Avignon, 1990.

Auction records:

Lyons, 7 April 1994, *Village Roofs* (1987, oil on canvas, 19¾ x 25½ ins / 50 x 65 cm) FRF 11,000.

FERRIER, James

British, 19th century.

Painter (gouache), watercolourist. Genre scenes, landscapes.

James Ferrier was active in Edinburgh and exhibited a landscape of *Glen Cannick, Invernesshire* at the Royal Academy in 1873.

Auction records:

New York, 7 Jan 1981, *Trout Anglers* (watercolour and pencil, 24½ x 39¼ ins / 62.2 x 99.7 cm) USD 1,400. London, 16 Oct 1986, *Washday at the Mill* (watercolour heightened with gouache, 12½ x 20¾ ins / 32 x 53 cm) GBP 1,000. Perth, 1 Sept 1992, *Glencoe* (1866, watercolour and gouache, 27¼ x 23 ins / 69.5 x 57.5 cm) GBP 1,100. London, 5 Nov 2001, *On the Dee at Moulin near Pitlochrie* (watercolour and gouache, 13 x 21 ins / 32 x 53 cm) GBP 2,400.

FERRIER, Maurice Henry Franck, called Henry

French, 20th century.

Born in Mustapha (in Algiers).

Painter. Landscapes.

Henry Ferrier exhibited in Paris from 1931 at the Salon des Artistes Indépendants.

He mostly painted Algerian landscapes.

FERRIÈRE, Francis or François

Swiss, 18th - 19th century.

Born 11 July 1752, in Geneva; died 25 December 1839, in Morges.

From 1770 to 1822 active in France, then in England.

Painter, miniaturist.

Ferrière went to Paris in 1770 and stayed there for twenty years. Fleeing the revolution, he then went to live in England. He settled permanently in Geneva in 1822. He exhibited at the Royal Academy, London, from 1793 until 1822, where he established his reputation as a painter of portraits in miniature.

Museums and Galleries:

Geneva (MAH): two allegorical paintings.

FERRIÈRE, Louis

Swiss, 19th century.

Born 1792, in Geneva; died 1866.
Miniaturist.
Like his father Francis, Louis Ferrière worked in London and exhibited miniatures at the Royal Academy between 1817 and 1828.
MUSEUMS AND GALLERIES:
GENEVA (MAH): *Miniature Portrait of the Painter Adam Wolfgang Töpfer.*

FERRIÈRE, René
French, 20th century.
Born in Paris.
Painter. Landscapes.
René Ferrière exhibited in Paris from 1934, at the Salon de la Société Nationale des Beaux-Arts. In 1950, he showed at the Salon des Artistes Indépendants.

FERRIÈRES, Armand de
French, 19th - 20th century.
Born 14 July 1873.
Sculptor, painter. Interiors.
Armand de Ferrières studied under his father, the animal sculptor Louis de Ferrières. He made his debut in Paris in 1905 at the Salon des Artistes Français, where he showed sculptures. He is probably the same artist who exhibited paintings of interiors from 1933.

FERRIÈRES, Louis François Georges de
(Comte)
French, 19th - 20th century.
Born 10 November 1837, in Paris; died 1907.
Sculptor. Animals. Statues.
Louis de Ferrières featured at the Salon from 1865 to 1893. He is remembered for *Greyhound, Pointer, Horse and Dogs* and *Dog Pointing.*
AUCTION RECORDS:
PARIS, 28 Oct 1990, *Two Hounds* (brown-patinated bronze, h. 11 1/4 ins / 28.5 cm, l. 8 3/4 ins/22.5 cm) FRF 25,000. PARIS, 8 Nov 1995, *Whipper-in Jumping* (bronze, h. 13 1/2 ins / 34 cm) FRF 40,500.

FERRIERS
French, 18th century.
Painter.
In 1781, Ferriers exhibited *Portrait of the Queen, Children's Games* and *Seascape* at the Salon de la Correspondance.

FERRIEU, Jean
French, 20th century.
Born 2 March 1900, in Rodez.
Engraver (wood).
Jean Ferrieu exhibited in Paris at the Salon des Artistes Français, gaining an honourable mention in 1927.

FERRIGNO, Antonio
Italian, 19th century.
Born December 1863, in Maiori (Amalfi Coast, Campania).
Painter. Genre scenes, landscapes with figures, landscapes.
Antonio Ferrigno was a pupil of Di Chirico, and also studied at the Naples Institute of Fine Arts. His work appeared in national and international exhibitions. In 1893 he went to Brazil, where he painted landscapes with figures: six of these depict the coffee harvest. When he returned to Europe, Ferrigno went to live in Paris where, in 1914, he exhibited some landscapes at the Salon des Indépendants.
His best-known works include: *To the Gallant King; An Old Sergeant; In My Country; March Sun*; and *One Evening.*
BIBLIOGRAPHY:
Tarasanti, Ruth S., *Pintores Paisagistas: São Paulo 1890 a 1920*, Edusp, São Paulo, 2002.
AUCTION RECORDS:
SÃO PAULO, 21 Oct 1980, *Antiquarian* (oil on canvas, 16 1/4 x 9 1/4 ins / 41.4 x 23.5 cm) BRL 160,000. ROME, 12 Dec 1989, *St Lucy* (oil on canvas, 16 x 31 1/2 ins / 40.5 x 80 cm) ITL 8,500,000. RIO DE JANEIRO, 2 Dec 2003, *Washerwomen* (oil on panel, 5 x 10 ins / 13 x 25 cm) BRL 10,000.

FERRILLO, Giuliano
Italian, 15th century.
Active in Naples.
Miniaturist.

FERRINI, Agnolo
Italian, 15th century.
Illuminator, writer, binder.
Florentine School.
Agnolo Ferrini was a priest and chaplain at Capraia, near Empoli (Arno valley), in the 15th century. The archives in Florence record that he bound a large number of Florentine manuscripts and incunabula, painting and decorating the bindings himself.

FERRIOL, Guillem
Spanish, 15th century.
Active in Valencia.
Painter.

FERRIOL, Louis
French, 16th - 17th century.
Active in Nevers (Nièvre).
Sculptor, architect.
In 1590, Ferriol sculpted ten stone escutcheons bearing the arms of Louis of Gonzaga and Henriette of Clèves, duke and duchess of Nevers. They were decorated with the orders of St Michael and the Holy Spirit and placed on the gates of the town. On the occasion of the entry into Nevers of the duchess of Mantua, in 1606, he modelled three large clay figures. In 1610, in consultation with the municipal magistrates (*échevins*) and an architect called Jean Portier, he sought to find the most suitable place for the building of a bridge over the Loire.

FERRIOL, Ramon
Spanish, 13th century.
Of Catalan origin.
Painter.
This artist is mentioned in Barcelona in 1297.

FERRIOT, Lucien
French, 20th century.
Born 22 November 1905, in Paris.
Painter. Seascapes, landscapes.
Lucien Ferriot began to paint in 1943. He exhibited at the Salon des Artistes Français from 1946, and was made an associate member the following year.
A landscape artist, he mostly painted seascapes in the classical manner.

FERRIS, Berenice Branson
American, 20th century.
Born in Astoria (Illinois).
Illustrator.

FERRIS, Edith
American, 20th century.
Born 21 June 1897, in Riverton (New Jersey).
Painter, illustrator.

FERRIS, Jean Leon Jerome
American, 19th - 20th century.
Born 8 August 1863, in Philadelphia; died 1930.
Active in Philadelphia.
Painter, engraver. Genre scenes.
Jean Leon Jerome Ferris was a pupil of his father Stephen Ferris and of Bouguereau.

AUCTION RECORDS:
NEW YORK, 6-7 April 1909, *The Girl I Left Behind Me,* USD 145. NEW YORK, 28 Oct 1981, *Chess Game; Puzzling Story* (oil on canvas and oil on panel, 13 1/2 x 16 1/4 ins / 34.3 x 41.3 cm) USD 5,500. NEW YORK, 25 May 1989, *Her Weight in Gold* (oil on canvas, 25 1/4 x 35 1/2 ins / 64 x 90 cm) USD 13,750. NEW YORK, 15 April 1992, *Courtship* (oil on card, 16 x 20 ins / 40.6 x 50.8 cm) USD 2,750.

FERRIS, Stephen James
American, 19th century.
Born 25 December 1835, in Plattsburg (Ohio); died 1915, in Philadelphia.
Active in Philadelphia.
Painter, engraver.
Stephen James Ferris was a pupil of C. Schnesel and S. B. Wongh. He visited Europe on a travel scholarship and taught drawing for many years.

FERRIS, Wanen Wesley
American, 20th century.
Born 22 June 1890, in Rochester (New York).
Painter, illustrator.
Wanen Wesley Ferris was awarded first prize by the Decorative Art League, New York, in 1923.

FERRISS, Hugh
American, 20th century.
Born 12 July 1889, in St Louis (Missouri); died 1962.
Illustrator.

FERRIZ Y SICILIA, Cristóbal
Spanish, 19th - 20th century.
Born c. 1850, in Madrid; died c. 1912, in Madrid.
Painter. Genre scenes, landscapes.
Cristóbal Ferriz y Sicilia studied under Carlos de Haes. He first exhibited in Madrid in 1876 and continued to exhibit regularly at Salons in Madrid.
MUSEUMS AND GALLERIES:
MADRID: *After the Shower; Fishpond at a House in the Country; Lake at El Retiro; The Racecourse.*
AUCTION RECORDS:
MADRID, 6 March 1986, *In the Tagus at Aranjuez* (1877, oil on canvas, 27 1/4 x 18 ins / 69 x 46 cm) ESP 500,000.

FERRNA, Philipp
Austrian, 17th century.
Active in Vienna.
Painter.

FERRO, Cesare
Italian, 19th - 20th century.
Born in Turin.
Painter.
Cesare Ferro exhibited in Italy and in Paris, at the Salon of the Société des Artistes Français, where he won a third-class medal in 1904.

FERRO, Dario
Italian, 17th century.
Active in Rome.
Painter.

FERRO, Evangelista dal
Italian, 16th century.
Active in Ferrara.
Painter.

FERRO, Gabriel Marc Louis
French, 20th century.
Born 1 September 1903, in Paris; died 7 October 1981.
Painter. Urban landscapes, interiors.
Gabriel Ferro attended the académies libres (free art schools) in Montparnasse. He exhibited in Paris, from 1942, at the Salon d'Automne, of which he was appointed a member that same year. He was also a member of the Salon des Artistes Indépendants and exhibited at the Salon des Peintres Témoins de leur Temps.

Fittingly for a 'painter witnessing his age', his canvases bore out the wretchedness of desolate suburbs, miserable shacks weighed down by equally foreboding skies. These works, with downbeat titles like *Fried Roach Fish, The Carpenter's House* and *The Garret,* are nonetheless less penetrated by a singular beauty.

FERRO, Giacomino de
Italian, 14th century.
Active in Pinerolo (Piedmont).
Painter.
Giacomino de Ferro is documented as one of the painters who worked on the church of S Giorgio in Chieri around 1349.

FERRO, Giacomo
Italian, 17th century.
Born to a family originally from Balma d'Alagna (Sesia Valley).
Sculptor.
Giacomo Ferro worked together with Giovanni d'Enrico on the Calvary at Varallo and produced numerous terracotta sculptures.

FERRO, Giovanni Battista or Johann Baptist
Italian, 16th century.
Of Paduan origin.
Active in Poland, Austria and Bohemia.
Painter, architect.
Giovanni Battista Ferro worked in Warsaw and Vienna and later in Prague, where he completed designs for the great hall of the castle, which featured portraits of the kings of Bohemia.

FERRO, Gregorio
Spanish, 18th - 19th century.
Born 1742, in Santa Maria de Lamas; died 1812, in Madrid.
Painter. History painting.
Gregorio Ferro studied at the Academia de San Fernando and became its director in 1804. He worked mainly for convents, monasteries and churches in Madrid. His work was a pale imitation of that of Mengs.
BIBLIOGRAPHY:
Ponz, Antonio, in *Viaje de España, 1, 2,* Aguilar, Madrid, 1988. *Carlos III y La Ilustración,* exhibition catalogue, Lunwerg, Madrid, 1988-1989. Morales y Marín, José Luis/Coruña, A., *Gregorio Ferro (1742-1812),* Fundación Pedro Barrié de la Maza, 1999. *Gregorio Ferro,* exhibition catalogue, Fundación Pedro Barrié de la Maza, July-September 1999; Academia de Bellas Artes de San Fernando, Madrid, October-November 1999. *Gregorio Ferro: pintor de Boqueixón: exposición-homenaxe, Santa María de Lamas, 23 de xaneiro a 13 de febreiro do 2002,* exhibition catalogue, Concello de Boqueixón, Boqueixón, La Coruña, 2002. Fernández Castiñeiras, Enrique/López Vázquez, José Manuel B., *Gregorio Ferro, pintor de Boqueixón: vida y obra,* Concello de Boqueixón, Boqueixón, La Coruña, 2002.

FERRO, Gudmundur. See **ERRO**

FERRO, Nicola
Italian, 19th century.
Active in Naples c. 1810.
Painter.

FERRO, Tommaso
Italian, 17th century.
Active in Genoa.
Painter.
A pupil of G. B. Carlone, Tommaso Ferro painted emblems of the arts and sciences for the Augustine library in Genoa.

FERRO LA GRÉE, Georges
French, 20th century.
Born 30 July 1941, in Poissy.
Painter. Landscapes with figures, seascapes, still-lifes, flowers.

Georges Ferro la Grée studied music and engineering, and became a thermal engineer. On encountering the work of Van Gogh during a trip to Amsterdam, he was so impressed that he decided to quit his job, and to teach himself to paint.

Ferro la Grée generally works with a blade, and makes broad strokes on his canvas. There is a joyous brightness in his pastoral scenes, and he takes a somewhat divisionistic approach to colour combinations. His style is Post-Impressionist.

He has taken part in several group exhibitions in Paris and its suburbs, including the following: at the Salon des Artistes Indépendants since 1969; at the Salon des Artistes Français; at the Salon of Populist Art; and in Taverny, Bougival and L'Isle-Adam. He has won a number of awards at these exhibitions, including the silver medal at the Salon des Artistes Français in 1974. He has also staged a number of solo exhibitions. His earliest were in Paris, but he has also exhibited in numerous French provincial towns and, among others, in New York, San Francisco, Chicago, Boston, Tokyo and Geneva.

Ferro la grée

BIBLIOGRAPHY:
Georges Ferro La Grée - Œuvres récentes 1981-1982, exhibition catalogue, Paris, 1982. *Georges Ferro La Grée - Œuvres récentes*, exhibition catalogue, Paris, 1990.

AUCTION RECORDS:
BREST, 13 Dec 1981, *Grey skies in Brittany* (oil on canvas, 19¾ x 24 ins / 50 x 61 cm) FRF 2,700. LE RAINCY, 14 June 1987, *Flowering Apple Tree in Bagatelle* (1977, oil on canvas, 18 x 25½ ins / 46 x 65 cm) FRF 9,000. CALAIS, 8 Nov 1987, *Barge by the Bank of the Eure* (oil on canvas, 19¾ x 24 ins / 50 x 61 cm) FRF 5,200. PARIS, 8 June 1988, *The Flowering Prairie* (oil on canvas, 19¾ x 24 ins / 50 x 61 cm) FRF 18,000. VERSAILLES, 22 April 1990, *People on the River Bank* (oil on canvas, 18 x 21¾ ins / 46 x 55.5 cm) FRF 6,500. PARIS, 25 May 1992, *By the Lake* (oil on canvas, 19¾ x 24 ins / 50 x 61 cm) FRF 3,200. NEUILLY, 17 June 1992, *The Beloved in Montrichard* (oil on canvas, 19 x 24 ins / 48 x 61 cm) FRF 4,000. PARIS, 17 May 1993, *Poppies at St-Amand in l'Yonne* (oil on canvas, 11¾ x 24 ins / 30 x 61 cm) FRF 4,000. PARIS, 20 June 1999, *Nasturtiums* (oil on canvas, 18 x 22 ins / 46 x 55 cm) FRF 17,500.

FERROCCI, Alberto
Italian, 16th century.
Active in Ferrara, between 1533 and 1564.
Painter.

FERROCCI, Ginesio
Italian, 16th century.
Active in Genoa.
Painter.

FERRON, Marcelle
Canadian, 20th century.
Born 29 January 1924, in Louiseville (Quebec); died 19 November 2001, in Montreal.
Painter. Designs for stained glass.
Groupe des Automatistes.

Marcelle Ferron was a pupil at the École des Beaux-Arts in Quebec City in 1941-1942. In 1945 she met Paul Émile Borduas and took part in exhibitions of the Automatistes from 1946 to 1953. In 1948 she was a co-signatory of the manifesto of the Automatistes, *Refus global* (*Total Refusal*), in which they dissociated themselves from the art market and its middle-class ethos. She lived in Paris from 1953 to 1964, working from 1958 to 1960 in Stanley William Hayter's Atelier 17. When she returned to Canada she was appointed a professor in the School of Architecture at Laval University, Quebec. From 1965 she created designs for windows, including one for a pavilion at the Montreal International Exhibition of 1967, and panels for the station *Champ de Mars* on the Montreal underground. She won the Paul-Émile-Borduas Prize in 1983.

Ferron initially painted contorted landscapes. After she joined the Automatist movement she held to the credo of spontaneous gesture and acceptance of chance effects, and developed a gestural abstraction of drips and eddies furiously applied. She painted, 'at arm's length' and with exuberance, abstracts that were heavy with pigment and dark in colour. When she returned to Quebec in 1964 she gave attention to the transparency of 'antique' glass that she had come across in Paris. In addition to the large windows that were commissioned from about 1965, she painted a series in oil on the subject of transparency and light, lightening her palette until it was pure white; then, about 1970, she made small, very sparkling pictures in actual glass. After 1972-1973 she returned to abstract gestural painting, but introduced an infrastructure that had its basis in stained-glass technique. She participated in numerous group exhibitions, including the retrospective Borduas et les Automatistes at the Grand Palais in Paris in 1971. A personal retrospective was held at the Musée d'art contemporain de Montréal in 1970, which was mounted again at the Canadian Cultural Centre in Paris in 1972.

BIBLIOGRAPHY:
Marcelle Ferron de 1945 a 1970, exhibition catalogue, Musée d'Art contemporain, Montreal, 1970. Roberge, Gaston, *Autour de Marcelle Ferron*, Loup de Gouttière, Quebec, 1995. Lussier, Réal, *Marcelle Ferron*, Musée d'art contemporain, Montreal, 2000.

MUSEUMS AND GALLERIES:
MONTREAL (MAC): *Cerce Nacarat* (1948).

AUCTION RECORDS:
LONDON, 26 June 1984, *Hermitage* (oil on canvas, 25½ x 32 ins / 65 x 81 cm) GBP 700. MONTREAL, 24 Feb 1987, *Solitary Walker* (1979, oil on canvas, 72 x 30 ins / 183 x 76 cm) CAD 4,500. MONTREAL, 17 Oct 1988, *Untitled* (1960, oil on canvas, 32 x 39¾ ins / 81 x 101 cm) CAD 6,000. MONTREAL, 30 Oct 1989, *Abstract* (1956, oil on canvas, 18½ x 29½ ins / 47 x 75 cm) CAD 8,800. MONTREAL, 5 Nov 1990, *Abstraction* (1963, mixed media, 25¼ x 19 ins / 64 x 48 cm) CAD 1,980. MONTREAL, 16 Oct 2000, *Abstraction* (1958, oil on panel, 8 x 10 ins / 21 x 26 cm) CAD 4,200. MONTREAL, 12 Dec 2001, *Forty Figures* (oil on canvas, 30 x 37 ins / 76 x 93 cm) CAD 5,500. TORONTO, 14 May 2002, *Untitled Composition* (oil on canvas, 28 x 35 ins / 72 x 90 cm) CAD 13,000. TORONTO, 3 Dec 2002, *Painting* (1961, oil on canvas laid on board, 19 x 24 ins / 49 x 60 cm) CAD 5,500. MONTREAL, 15 Dec 2003, *Untitled* (1952, oil on canvas, 8 x 11 ins / 21 x 27 cm) CAD 3,700. OTTAWA, 9 June 2004, *Abstract Composition* (mixed media on board, 25 x 19 ins / 64 x 49 cm) CAD 4,000.

FERRON DE LA VILLAUDON, Louise
French, 17th century.
Active in Rennes c. 1650.
Painter. Portraits. Medallions.

Louise Ferron de la Villaudon was a nun. The museum in Rennes has by her the first page of an antiphony intended for the abbey of St-Georges, *Medallion with the Portrait, Held by Angels, of the Foundress.*

MUSEUMS AND GALLERIES:
RENNES: *Medallion with the Portrait, Held by Angels, of the Foundress.*

FERRONI, Alessandro
Italian, 16th century.
Active in Pisa.
Painter.
Alessandro Ferroni executed graffiti designed by Vasari in the Palazzo della Carovana in Pisa around 1652.

FERRONI, Egisto
Italian, 19th - 20th century.
Born 1835, in Signa (Florence); died 26 May 1912, in Florence.
Painter. Portraits, genre scenes, landscapes with figures.
Egisto Ferroni studied at the Accademia in Florence. He won a medal at the International Exhibition in Nice, and another at the Naples Exhibition. In 1900 he took part in the Alinari competition with a painting entitled *Young Mother*.

BIBLIOGRAPHY:

Farinella, Vincenzo, *Pittura dei Campi: Egisto Ferroni e il Naturalismo europeo*, Pacini, Pisa, 2002.

MUSEUMS AND GALLERIES:

FLORENCE (Gal. d'Arte Moderna): *In the Fields; The Visit; Woodcutter* - PRATO: *In the Fields* - ROME (Gal. Nazionale): two paintings - ROME (Gal. Nazionale d'Arte Moderna): *The Father's Return; Travelling Merchant; Braids.*

AUCTION RECORDS:

MILAN, 15 March 1977, *Young Girl on a Terrace* (oil on canvas, 35 3/4 x 24 ins / 91 x 61 cm) ITL 3,800,000. MILAN, 10 June 1981, *Head of a Little Girl* (oil on canvas, 14 1/4 x 11 3/4 ins / 36 x 30 cm) ITL 1,800,000. MILAN, 27 March 1984, *Two Sisters* (1887, oil on canvas, 24 x 22 ins / 61 x 55 cm) ITL 11,000,000. MILAN, 28 Oct 1986, *Peasant in His Field* (oil on canvas, 72 x 35 1/2 ins / 183 x 90 cm) ITL 8,500,000. NEW YORK, 20 Feb 1992, *Motherhood* (1897, oil on canvas, 36 1/4 x 53 1/2 ins / 92.1 x 135.9 cm) USD 17,600. MILAN, 26 March 1996, *Lively Banter* (oil on panel, 14 1/4 x 11 3/4 ins / 36 x 30 cm) ITL 18,975,000. ROME, 23 May 2000, *Butterfly and Flowers* (1907, oil on canvas, 44 x 28 ins / 112 x 70 cm) ITL 7,500,000. MILAN, 7 Nov 2000, *Happy Return from the Source* (oil on canvas, 19 x 10 ins / 47 x 25 cm) ITL 33,000,000. NEW YORK, 5 Dec 2001, *Three Generations* (1874, oil on canvas, 58 x 47 ins / 147 x 119 cm) USD 30,000. PARIS, 15 May 2002, *Princess with Taj Diadem* (oil on canvas, 41 x 27 ins / 105 x 69 cm) EUR 23,000. ROME, 26 Nov 2002, *Here is Dad!* (oil on canvas, 71 x 35 ins / 181 x 90 cm) EUR 18,000. BERN, 7 May 2003, *Florentine Woman* (oil on canvas, 36 x 19 ins / 92 x 47 cm) CHF 4,000. LONDON, 16 July 2003, *Girl with Guitar* (oil on canvas, 32 x 14 ins / 82 x 35 cm) GBP 1,900.

FERRONI, Gianfranco
Italian, 20th century.
Born 22 February 1927, in Livorno.
Painter, draughtsman, engraver, lithographer. Scenes with figures, still-lifes.
Gianfranco Ferroni arrived in Milan at an early age, and enrolled as a pupil at the school of fine arts. He taught himself engraving in 1957, and in 1963 won the Biella Prize.

During the 1950s Ferroni allied himself with the Existential Realism movement, which had certain things in common with the French political realism of Rebeyrolle and the Beehive group (La Ruche). In terms of form, his work during this time owed something to Pop Art; but he also borrowed layout techniques from the world of advertising, and used superimposed cinematic images, while still exhibiting a highly personal form of Expressionism. In all his different periods, he has always used drawing as the laboratory in which his paintings are prepared. He stopped working between 1960 and 1970, but did not give up thinking around his work. After this hiatus, his drawing skills provided the basis for a new direction, towards Hyperrealism. During this period he skilfully played with all kinds of lighting, from all white to chiaroscuro. This allowed him poetically and dramatically to transgress the gratuitous illusionism of photographic realism, through a disturbing presentation of light, depth of field and the surrounding space.

Ferroni has participated in various group exhibitions of work by young Italian painters, both national and international. These include: the Venice Biennale, in 1958, 1964, 1968 and 1982; the Rome Quadriennale, in 1959 and 1972; the Mediterranean Biennale in 1969; the Tokyo Biennale in 1964; the Salon de la Jeune Peinture in Paris, in 1966; and the travelling exhibition *Italian Painting 1950-1970*, which was held from 1975 to 1977 in various museums around Europe. He has staged solo exhibitions in Milan, Rome, Turin, Parma, Modena, Bologna and other cities. In 1970 he exhibited in Paris alongside Antonio Ségui and Gérard Titus-Carmel. From 1990 to 1991 a retrospective exhibition of his work was held at the Galerie Comunale d'Arte Moderna in Conegliano, under the title *Ferroni Opere 1957-1990 (Ferroni: Works from 1957-1990)*.

BIBLIOGRAPHY:

Polli, Francesco, et al., *Gianfranco Ferroni*, exhibition catalogue, Galleria Philippe Daverio, Milan, 1987. *Gianfranco Ferroni: Opera grafica*, exhibition catalogue, Casa della Cultura, Livorno, Lubrina, Bergamo, 1989. *Ferroni - Opere 1957-1990*, exhibition catalogue, Gall. comunale d'arte moderna, Conegliano, 1990-1991.

AUCTION RECORDS:

MILAN, 1 Dec 1964, *La Stanza Liberty* ITL 800,000. MILAN, 25 May 1971, *Composition*, ITL 1,400,000. ROME, 27 Nov 1973, *La Trappola* (1969) ITL 2,400,000. MILAN, 9 Nov 1976, *Crowd in a Street* (1958, oil on card mounted, study, 18 3/4 x 28 3/4 ins / 47.5 x 73 cm) ITL 1,000,000. MILAN, 22 May 1980, *Window and Vegetation* (1965, oil on canvas, 16 1/2 x 20 ins / 42 x 51 cm) ITL 2,300,000. MILAN, 27 April 1982, *Interior* (1974, pen, 6 x 7 ins / 15 x 18 cm) ITL 600,000. ROME, 22 May 1984, *Urban Landscape* (1963, oil on canvas, 24 1/2 x 24 1/2 ins / 62 x 62 cm) ITL 3,500,000. MILAN, 24 March 1988, *Familiar Objects* (1970, oil on canvas, 18 1/4 x 22 1/4 ins / 46.5 x 56.5 cm) ITL 18,000,000. MILAN, 14 Dec 1988, *Figure* (1961, oil on canvas, study, 35 1/2 x 27 1/2 ins / 90 x 70 cm) ITL 19,000,000. MILAN, 20 March 1989, *Interior with Table and Bed* (1959, oil on canvas, 47 1/4 x 47 1/4 ins / 120 x 120 cm) ITL 21,000,000. MILAN, 6 June 1989, *Still-life with Pink Cloth* (1985, mixed media/panel, 16 1/2 x 16 1/2 ins / 42 x 42 cm) ITL 26,000,000. ROME, 28 Nov 1989, *Hunter with a Duck* (1949, oil on canvas, 27 1/2 x 19 3/4 ins / 70 x 50 cm) ITL 8,000,000. MILAN, 19 June 1991, *Untitled* (1963, mixed media/paper/canvas, 18 3/4 x 20 1/2 ins / 47.5 x 52 cm) ITL 7,000,000; *Story of an Interior* (1962, oil on canvas, 27 1/2 x 35 1/2 ins / 70 x 90 cm) ITL 15,000,000. MILAN, 19 Dec 1991, *Disorder* (1971, oil and mixed media/paper/canvas, study, 67 1/4 x 57 ins / 171 x 145 cm) ITL 40,000,000. MILAN, 20 May 1993, *Return to the Village* (1972, pencil, 13 1/2 x 16 1/4 ins / 34 x 41.5 cm) ITL 6,000,000. MILAN, 14 Dec 1993, *Exploration of Objects* (1965, oil on canvas, 20 3/4 x 24 1/2 ins / 53 x 62 cm) ITL 16,100,000. ROME, 8 Nov 1994, *Bottle and Paper Cone in a Halo of Light* (pencil and pastel/paper, 13 1/2 x 11 1/2 ins / 34 x 29.5 cm) ITL 23,000,000. MILAN, 9 March 1995, *Interior* (1958, oil on canvas, 27 1/2 x 35 1/2 ins / 70 x 90 cm) ITL 20,125,000. MILAN, 10 Dec 1996, *Lake Massaciuccoli* (1964, oil on canvas, 20 x 15 1/4 ins / 51 x 38.5 cm) ITL 21,552,000. ROME, 8 April 1997, *Vertical Space* (1988, oil on panel, 22 x 11 1/4 ins / 56 x 28.5 cm) ITL 29,707,000. MILAN, 15 April 1999, *Hebrew's Memory* (1962, Indian ink and colour ink, 15 x 11 ins / 37 x 28 cm) ITL 4,500,000. MILAN, 22 June 1999, *Interior* (1959, oil on canvas, 20 x 24 ins / 50 x 60 cm) ITL 6,000,000. ROME, 23 Nov 2000, *Secular Light Blue Altar* (1990, mixed media, 11 x 9 ins / 29 x 24 cm) ITL 19,000,000. PRATO, 24 Nov 2000, *Objects* (1966, oil on canvas, 38 x 50 ins / 96 x 127 cm) ITL 25,000,000. ROME, 21 May 2001, *Objects in Light* (1984, oil on pastel, 11 x 13 ins / 29 x 34 cm) ITL 18,000,000. ROME, 21 May 2001, *Objects on Coffee Table* (1984, mixed media on paper/board, 15 x 15 ins / 38 x 37 cm) ITL 27,000,000. MILAN, 14 May 2002, *Autumn Reminders* (1962, oil on canvas, 39 x 31 ins / 100 x 80 cm) EUR 15,000. ROME, 19 May 2002, *In the Garden* (1966, oil on canvas, 20 x 24 ins / 50 x 60 cm) EUR 16,000. MILAN, 26 March 2003, *Landscape with Fire* (1965, oil on canvas, 15 x 15 ins / 38 x 38 cm) EUR 7,500. MILAN, 11 June 2003, *Objects* (1963, oil on canvas, 29 x 24 ins / 74 x 61 cm) EUR 13,000. MILAN, 8 June 2004, *Garden in Tradate* (1963, mixed media, 7 x 11 ins / 19 x 29 cm) EUR 2,400. MILAN, 8 June 2004, *Landscape in Quiesa* (1962, mixed media on card, 9 x 13 ins / 24 x 34 cm) EUR 2,400.

FERRONI, Girolamo
Italian, 18th century.
Born 1687, in Parma; died c. 1730, in Milan.
Painter, engraver.

At the start of his career, Girolamo Ferroni painted a *Death of St Joseph* for the church of S Eustorgio in Milan. He visited Rome to study under Carlo Maratti and produced a number of tasteful engravings of Maratti's work, among which are *Joshua Halting the Sun*, *Joseph's Chastity*, and *Judith and the Head of Holofernes*.

FERRONI, Guido
Italian, 20th century.
Born 1888, in Siena; died 1979, in Florence.
Painter. Genre scenes.

BIBLIOGRAPHY:
Costantini, Vincenzo, *Pittura italiana contemporanea*, A. Vallardi, Milan, 1958.

MUSEUMS AND GALLERIES:
FLORENCE (Gal. d'Arte Moderna): *Jousting*; *The Humble Life*.

FERRONI, Leonardo, called il Bigino
Italian, 17th century.
Active in Florence.
Painter.

Leonardo Ferroni studied under F. Furini and painted several portraits of monks that are to be found in the Casa Buonarroti.

FERRONI, Pietro
Italian, 19th century.
Born to a family originally from Arosio.
Sculptor.

Pietro Ferroni sculpted the statues on the façade of a high school in Como, and altars in the churches of Sonvico and Agno.

FERRONI, Riccardo Tommasi
Italian, 20th century.
Born 1934, in Pietrasanta (Tuscany); died 22 February 2000, in Camaiore (Tuscany).
Painter, draughtsman. Mythological subjects, genre scenes, landscapes, urban landscapes.

Born into a family of artists, Riccardo Ferroni was taught to draw at a very young age by his father, the sculptor Leone Tommasi. He studied at the faculty of arts and philosophy in Viareggio, and at the academy of fine arts in Florence. In 1959 he moved to Rome, where he lived for 20 years. He then moved back to Tuscany, and settled in the Camaiore countryside. He was a member of the Accademia di San Luca.

Ferroni was an extremely talented draughtsman, as evidenced by his red chalk drawing *Rearing Horse with Nude Rider*. He painted and drew numerous views of Rome, and a large number of landscapes: they are Surrealist compositions rich in fantasy, presented with an acute sense of drama.

Ferroni showed his works in exhibitions in Italy and abroad, notably at the Venice Biennale in 1982; the Rome Quadriennale; the Paris Biennale; and the Art Expo in New York.

BIBLIOGRAPHY:
Valeri, Franca, *Le Regine di Riccardo Tommasi Ferroni*, Borgobello, Parma, 1982 (text in Italian, French and English). Almansi, Guido, *Riccardo Tommasi Ferroni: il volo dell'Ippogrifo*, exhibition catalogue, Valle d'Aosta cultura, Fabbri, Milan, 1989 (text in Italian, French and English). Goldin, Marco/Gori Sassoli, Mario, *Riccardo Tommasi Ferroni*, Grafis, Casalecchio di Reno, 1992.

AUCTION RECORDS:
ROME, 3 Dec 1985, *Apollo* (mixed media/mounted paper/canvas, 26 x 12½ ins / 66 x 32 cm) ITL 1,800,000; *Metamorphoses* (oil on canvas, 22 x 22 ins / 55 x 55 cm) ITL 2,000,000. ROME, 17 April 1989, *Leda* (1984, oil on canvas, 59 x 86½ ins / 150 x 220 cm) ITL 33,000,000. ROME, 6 Dec 1989, *Panorama of Rome* (oil on canvas, 19¾ x 27½ ins / 50 x 70 cm) ITL 9,775,000. MILAN, 15 March 1994, *Apollo and Daphne* (oil on canvas, 39¼ x 39¼ ins / 100 x 100 cm) ITL 12,650,000. MILAN, 5 May 1994, *Rape of Proserpina* (oil on canvas, study, 30¼ x 43¼ ins / 77 x 110 cm) ITL 8,050,000. MILAN, 9 March 1995, *Venus and Cupid* (oil on canvas, study, 25½ x 35½ ins / 65 x 90 cm) ITL 4,600,000. ROME, 28 March 1995, *Rape of Proserpina* (oil on canvas, 30¼ x 43¼ ins / 77 x 110 cm) ITL 10,350,000.

FERRONI, Violante
Italian, 18th century.
Born 1720, in Florence.
Painter, copyist. Portraits.

A copyist and portraitist, Violante Ferroni is remembered for her medallion of St John painted for the church of S Giovanni di Dio.

FERROVERDE, Filippo
Italian, 17th century.
Draughtsman, engraver (wood).

Filippo Ferroverde made woodcut engravings from his own drawings for Vincent Catari's *Images of the Ancient Gods*, published in Padua in 1615.

FERROZZI. See **FERROCCI**

FERRU, Félix
French, 19th century.
Born 1831, in Limoges; died 1877.
Sculptor.

Ferru was a pupil at the École des Beaux-Arts and exhibited at the Paris Salon from 1866 to 1877. His more important works are *Scornful Girl*, *Mlle Sabine de Gosselin*, wax bust, *Love Taming the Sphinx*, *Bust of J. Offenbach*, *Marble Bust of Adrien Balny* and several works in Limoges Museum.

MUSEUMS AND GALLERIES:
LIMOGES: *Awakening Love*; *Gustave Ricard* (marble bust); *Charmer*; *Athenian Girl Watering Myrtle*.

FERRU, Marceau
French, 20th century.
Born in Algiers.
Sculptor.

Marceau Ferru studied under Paul Lambrovski. From 1933, he exhibited at the Salon des Artistes Français.

FERRU, Martinus
Swiss, 15th century.
Probably born in Sotto-Cenere.
Painter. History painting.

Frescoes showing *Scenes from the Life of St John the Baptist* in the parish church in Sonvico, near Lugano, are probably the work of this artist.

FERRUCCI, Andrea, also known as Andrea di Piero or Andrea da Fiesole
Italian, 15th - 16th century.

Born 1465, in Fiesole; died 1526, in Florence.
Sculptor, architect.
Florentine School.

Andrea Ferrucci was the son of Pietro di Marco Ferrucci, and one of the finest sculptors of the late 16th century. He worked in Florence and Pistoia and his pupils included Silvio Cosini and Bascoli. The cathedral in Florence has his bust of *Marcilio Ficino*, while his tomb of *A. Strozzi* is in the church of S Maria Novella; the baptismal fonts in the cathedral in Pistoia are also his work.

BIBLIOGRAPHY:
Pope-Hennessy, John, *Catalogue of Italian Sculpture in the Victoria and Albert Museum*, H M Stationery Office, London, 1964. Apfelstadt, E., *'Andrea Ferrucci's Crucifixion Altarpiece in the Victoria and Albert Museum'* in *Burlington Magazine*, vol 135, 1993.

MUSEUMS AND GALLERIES:
FLORENCE (Mus. Nazionale): *Virgin* (marble, low relief).

FERRUCCI, Andrea di Michelangelo, or Ferruzzi
Italian, 17th century.
Died 1626.
Sculptor.

The son of Michelangelo di Bastiano, he worked in Florence, providing sculptures for the Boboli gardens.

FERRUCCI, Bastiano. See **BASTIANO DI FRANCESCO**

FERRUCCI, Bernardo di Simone
Italian, 15th century.
Born 1434, in Fiesole.
Sculptor.

Bernardo di Simone Ferrucci was the son of Simone di Nanni Ferrucci. He worked with his brother, Francesco di Simone, at the monastery of S Maria de Servi in Florence from 1467 to 1478.

FERRUCCI, Cesare di Romolo
Italian, 16th century.
Died 1596; buried 12 September in Florence, in S Pier Maggiore.
Sculptor.

Cesare di Romolo Ferrucci was the son of Romolo di Francesco del Tadda Ferrucci.

FERRUCCI, Francesco di Nicodemo
Italian, 17th century.
Died 12 July 1678, in Florence.
Sculptor.

He was the son of Nicodemo Ferrucci.

FERRUCCI, Francesco di Simone da Fiesole
Italian, 15th century.
Born 1437, in Fiesole; died 24 March 1493, in Florence.
Sculptor, architect.

The son of Simone di Nanni and father of Bastiano di Francesco, Francesco di Simone da Fiesole Ferrucci worked in Fiesole, Florence, Bologna and Rome, and probably also in Venice. His notable works in Florence include the monument for the tomb of *Lemno Balducci* for the Ospedale di San Matteo and five small columns for an altar, and in Bologna the monument for the tomb of Alessandro Tartagni in the church of S Domenico and the portal of the Palazzo Bevilacqua. Decorative works in the Viviani chapel in the church of S Giobbe in Venice are attributed to him, and he also executed a ciborium for Prato Cathedral.

BIBLIOGRAPHY:
Darr, A.P., *Italian Renaissance Sculpture in the Time of Donatello*, exhibition catalogue, Michigan Institute of Art, Detroit, 1985. Wolohojian, S., *'Francesco di Simone Ferrucci's Fogg Virgin and Child and the Martini Chapel in S Giobbe, Venice'* in *Burlington Magazine*, vol 139, 1997.

MUSEUMS AND GALLERIES:
PARIS (Mus. Jacquemart-André): *Child Standing, Holding an Escutcheon* (terracotta, statuette).

FERRUCCI, Francesco or Cecco, called del Tadda, also known as Francesco di Giovanni
Italian, 16th century.
Born 1497, in Fiesole; died 1585.
Sculptor.

Francesco Ferrucci was the son of Giovanni Ferrucci, possibly the 15th-century artist Giovanni Ferrucci di Taddeo, and the father of Romolo Ferrucci and perhaps also of Giovanni Battista Ferrucci, called del Tadda. He worked mainly in Florence, where he produced various decorative works for the dukes Cosimo I and Francis I. His masterpiece is the *Tomb of G.F. Vogio* in the Campo Santo in Pisa. He also executed the *Tartagni Tomb* in the church of S Domenico in Bologna, the tomb of *Barbara Manfredi* in the church of S Mercuriale in Forlì, the high altar in the cathedral in Fiesole and the *Tabernacle* in the church of S Maria di Monteluce in Perugia. He also worked on a number of projects at the Palazzo Pitti in Florence.

BIBLIOGRAPHY:
Di Castro Moscati, D., *'The Revival of the Working of Porphyry in Sixteenth-century Florence'* in *Apollo*, vol 126, 1987.

MUSEUMS AND GALLERIES:
BERLIN (Bodemus.): *Head of Christ* - LONDON (Victoria and Albert Mus.): *Cosimo I* (low relief) - PRAGUE (Rudolfinum Gal.): *Head of Christ*.

FERRUCCI, Giovanni Battista, called del Tadda
Italian, 17th century.
Died 1617; buried 5 May in Florence, in S Maria del Carmine.
Sculptor.

The son of Francesco Ferrucci, Giovanni Battista Ferrucci worked under Vasari's direction and alongside a number of other sculptors to prepare decorations for the wedding ceremony of Francesco de' Medici and Jeanne of Austria, held at the Palazzo Vecchio in Florence. Ferrucci was also involved in the restoration of the church of S Maria del Pontenovo (now renamed S Maria della Spina) in Pisa.

FERRUCCI, Giovanni di Taddeo, perhaps del Tadda
Italian, 15th century.
Born 1461, in Fiesole or Florence.
Sculptor.

Giovanni di Taddeo Ferrucci, the grandson of Simone di Nanni Ferrucci, is mentioned in Carrara in 1521.

FERRUCCI, Giovanni Domenico
Italian, 17th century.
Born 17th century, of Florentine origin.
Painter.

A pupil of Cesare Dandini, Giovanni Domenico Ferrucci lived and worked in Lucca.

FERRUCCI, Michelangelo di Bastiano
Italian, 16th century.
Died 1593; buried 15 August in Florence, in S Ambrogio.
Active in Florence.
Sculptor.

Michelangelo di Bastiano was the father of Nicodemo Ferrucci.

FERRUCCI, Michele di Simone
Italian, 17th century.
Active in Florence.
Sculptor.

FERRUCCI, Nanni di Sandro
Italian, 14th century.

Born 1362, in Fiesole.
Sculptor.
Nanni di Sandro Ferrucci was the first of a long line of artists in the Ferrucci family.

FERRUCCI, Nicodemo, also known as Niccolo di Michelangelo
Italian, 16th - 17th century.
Born 1574, in Fiesole; died 1650, in Florence.
Painter, fresco artist. History painting.
The son of Michelangelo di Bastiano Ferrucci, Nicodemo Ferrucci was the friend and favourite disciple of Domenico Passignano, whose fluent, spiritual style he imitated. He followed Passignano to Rome and worked there as his assistant on a number of important projects. A fine fresco painter, his work can be seen in public buildings in Florence, Fiesole and the area around Rome.

FERRUCCI, Pietro di Marco
Italian, 15th century.
Born 1437.
Active in Fiesole.
Sculptor.
The grandson of Nanni di Sandro, and father of Andrea Ferrucci, Pietro di Marco Ferrucci is mentioned in Florence in 1487.

FERRUCCI, Pompeo
Italian.
Painter. History painting, portraits.

FERRUCCI, Pompeo di Giovanni Battista
Italian, 16th - 17th century.
Born c. 1566, in Florence; died July 1637, in Rome.
Sculptor.
The son of Giovanni Battista del Tadda Ferrucci, Pompeo di Giovanni Battista Ferrucci worked in Rome from 1605 onwards and was a member of the Accademia di San Luca. His works include a high relief depicting the *Assumption, St Jerome* and *St John* and two monuments for tombs in the Vidoni chapel in the church of S Maria della Vittoria; he also collaborated with Buzio on the monument for the tomb of Paul V in S Maria Maggiore.

FERRUCCI, Romolo, also called Romolo di Francesco del Tadda
Italian, 16th - 17th century.
Died 3 March 1621, in Florence.
Sculptor.
Romolo Ferrucci was the son of Francesco Ferrucci, called del Tadda, who taught him the art of sculpting porphyry, and the father of Cesare di Romolo Ferrucci. He was also the pupil of Andrea di Michelangelo Ferrucci, to whom he was related. He sculpted animals in porphyry for the Boboli Gardens, where lions and a dog survive, and also executed the capital of a column for the Antonine baths, in addition to a statue of Justice. Other works in the Grotto of the Palazzo Pitti, the Villa Pratolina, the Palazzo Gianfigliazzi (coats of arms) and his own home in S Maria Nuova are attributed to him.

FERRUCCI, Salvestro di Michelangelo, also known as Salvatore da Fiesole
Italian, 16th - 17th century.
Sculptor.
Salvestro di Michelangelo Ferrucci, the son of Michelangelo di Bastiano and brother of Nicodemo, was active in Florence in 1601.

FERRUCCI, Sandro or Alessandro di Marco
Italian, 15th century.
Sculptor.
The grandson of Nanno di Sandro Ferrucci, Sandro Ferrucci is mentioned in Florence in 1487.

FERRUCCI, Simone di Nanni
Italian, 15th century.
Born in Fiesole; died 4 March 1469, in Florence.
Sculptor.
Florentine School.
Simone di Nanni Ferrucci was the son of Nanni di Sandro and father of Bernardo di Simone and Francesco di Simone da Fiesole Ferrucci. He worked on a door for the Baptistery in Florence in the studio of L. Ghiberti, after 1427. He worked with Jacopo di Bartolomeo da Fiesole on a large marble frame for an altar of the Virgin by Fra Angelico, designed by Ghiberti for the guild of weavers; in 1467 he completed a low relief of the *Lamb of God* for the church of S Maria del Carmine. He also worked on the decorations of the church of S Francesco in Rimini and decorated the façade of the church of S Jacopo in Vicovaro, near Rome.

FERRUCCI, Vincenzo di Nicodemo
Italian, 17th century.
Died 1626; buried 2 November in Florence, in S Felice.
Active in Florence.
Painter.
He was the son of Nicodemo di Michelangelo.

FERRUCCIO, Domenico
Italian, 17th century.
Engraver.
Domenico Ferruccio engraved figures for Giuseppe Morsicato Pallavicini's *Illustrated Swordsmanship.*

FERRUH BASAGA
Turkish, 20th century.
Born 1915, in Istanbul.
Painter. Portraits.
Ferruh Basaga was a pupil of the French painter Léopold Lévy at the school of fine arts in Istanbul. He exhibited his works in official exhibitions in Ankara. In 1946 he was represented at the exhibition of modern art in Paris, organized by the United Nations, at which he showed his *Portrait of a Child.*

FERRUZZI, Andrea di Michelangelo. See **FERRUCCI**

FERRUZZI, Nanni di Sandro. See **FERRUCCI**

FERRUZZI, Roberto Felix
Croat, 19th - 20th century.
Born 1853 or 1854, in Sibenik; died 1934.
Painter, watercolourist, pastellist. Portraits, genre scenes.
Roberto Ferruzzi studied only painting and participated in the Turin Exhibition in 1883 with studies of heads, then in Venice in 1887 with *First Penance* and in 1897 with *Little Madonna* and a pastel painting *Towards the Light.*
AUCTION RECORDS:
MILAN, 10 Nov 1982, *Portrait of Young Girl* (1895-1896, watercolour, 14 3/4 x 11 1/4 ins / 37.5 x 28.5 cm) ITL 1,200,000.

FERRY, Adrien, or Ferri
French, 19th century.
Died before 1885.
Active in Auch.
Sculptor.
Adrien Ferry was probably the son of Vincenzo (also known as Vincent) Ferri. He produced the sketch for the statue *Vice-admiral Villaret-Joyeuse,* executed by Ed. Nelli in Auch in 1885.

FERRY, Didier
French, 16th - 17th century.
Active in Paris.
Sculptor.

FERRY, Isabelle H.
American, 19th century.

Born in the second half of the 19th century, in Williamsburg (Massachusetts).
Painter.
Isabelle H. Ferry was a pupil of William Bouguereau, Tony Robert-Fleury and Boutet de Monvel in Paris.

FERRY, Jean Georges
French, 19th - 20th century.
Born 22 June 1851, in Paris; died 1926.
Painter. Genre scenes, figures.
Jean Ferry studied under Hillemacher and Cabanel and made his debut at the Paris Salon in 1875. He is remembered for *Capri Girl, Easter Monday in Andalusia, Human Weakness* and *Spanish Serenade.* He became an associate member of the Artistes Français in 1888 and was awarded an honourable mention in 1900.
MUSEUMS AND GALLERIES:
COPENHAGEN (Ny Carlsberg Glyptotek): two paintings.
AUCTION RECORDS:
BREST, 13 Dec 1981, *Norman Woman in her Bonnet, Boulogne-sur-Mer* (oil on panel, 13 3/4 x 11 ins / 35 x 27 cm) FRF 2,700. PARIS, 10-11 June 1997, *Fruit Seller* (1890, oil on panel, 10 x 7 1/4 ins / 25.7 x 18.2 cm) FRF 10,000.

FERRY, Jules Jean
French, 19th century.
Born 1 January 1844, in Bordeaux.
Painter, draughtsman. Genre scenes, hunting scenes.
Jules Ferry was taught by Cabanel and J.L. Brown. He exhibited at the Paris Salon from 1869 to 1880. He received a honourable mention in 1887, a third-class medal in 1886, and bronze medals at the Exposition Universelle in 1889 and 1900. He was an associate of the Société Nationale des Beaux-Arts.
MUSEUMS AND GALLERIES:
PARIS (Mus. du Petit Palais): *Sketches for the Decoration of the Hôtel de Ville in Paris; Sketches for the Decoration of the Town Hall in Suresnes.*
AUCTION RECORDS:
LONDON, 6 April 1966, *Walk in the Woods,* GBP 900. LONDON, 18 Nov 1994, *Hunting Dog Scenting a Duck* (1862, oil on canvas, 56 1/4 x 85 ins / 142.9 x 215.9 cm) GBP 2,760.

FERRY, Marie-Alfred René
French, 20th century.
Born in Nancy.
Engraver (etching).
Marie-Alfred Ferry studied under Eugène Gauguet. He exhibited at the Salon des Artistes Français, of which he was an associate member. He received an honourable mention in 1932.

FERRY, Michel
French, 17th century.
Active in Verdun.
Glass painter.
Michel Ferry executed a window dated 1633 in the cathedral of Verdun.

FERRY, Pierre Augustin
French, 18th century.
Born 1742.
Painter. Flowers.
Pierre Ferry was the pupil of Bachelier, and worked from 1757 to 1763 at the Sèvres porcelain factory.

FERRY, René
French, 20th century.
Born in Joinville-le-Pont.
Painter.
René Ferry exhibited at the Salon d'Automne in 1926 and at the Salon des Artistes Indépendants from 1927 onwards.

FERRY, Vincent. See **FERRI**

FERRY-HUMBLOT, Guite
French, 20th century.
Born 22 May 1897, in Joinville.
Painter.
Guite Ferry Humblot exhibited at the Salon des Artistes Français, of which she was a member. She obtained a honourable mention in 1928.

FERSTL, Anton
German, 19th century.
Born 1844; died 23 March 1875.
Active in Munich.
Glass painter.
Ferstl was a student at the Munich academy and completed his education by travelling to Belgium, Paris, Switzerland and Vienna. The churches of Karlstadt, Burghausen (Bavaria), Murau (Styria, Austria), the Marienkirche in Esslingen (Baden-Württemberg), and the chapel of Grand Duke Charles in Vienna all own examples of his work.

FERSTLER, Heinrich
Austrian, 19th century.
Born 1800, in Vienna.
Miniaturist, watercolourist.
Ferstler was a student at the academy in Vienna and took part in the exhibitions at the academy in 1824 and 1828 where he presented a miniature in the style of J.B. von Lampi.

FERSTLER, Johann
Austrian, 18th century.
Active in Vienna.
Engraver.

FERSTLER, Johann
Austrian, 18th - 19th century.
Born 1776, in St Pölten.
Painter.
Ferstler was a student at the Akademie der Bildenden Künste in Vienna and worked from 1797 to 1820 as a painter of figurines at the porcelain factory.

FERSTLER, Johann Michael
Austrian, 18th century.
Born 1770, in St Pölten.
Active in Vienna.
Engraver.
Ferstler studied at the academy in Vienna and worked for Assner the engraver. He was the nephew of Johann Ferstler.

FERTBAUER, Leopold
Austrian, 19th century.
Born 1802, in Vienna; died 17 February 1875.
Painter. History painting, portraits, landscapes.
Fertbauer painted landscapes, historical pictures and portraits.
MUSEUMS AND GALLERIES:
VIENNA (Akademie der Bildenden Künste): *Church of St Mary.*
AUCTION RECORDS:
VIENNA, 29-30 Oct 1996, *Portrait of Woman Dressed in White and Pink* (oil on panel, 14 1/2 x 12 ins / 37 x 30.5 cm) ATS 126,500. VIENNA, 23 May 2000, *Couple in Alpine Landscape* (1827, oil on panel, 17 x 14 ins / 43 x 36 cm) ATS 110,000. VIENNA, 29 Nov 2001, *Young Woman in Morning Jacket* (oil on panel, 10 x 8 ins / 26 x 21 cm) ATS 75,000.

FERTE, Corinne
French, 20th century.
Painter.
Between 1981 and 1986, Corinne Ferte exhibited at the Montrouge Salon; in 1984, at *Un nouveau monde: jeunes artistes* (*A New World: Young Artists*) at the Musée des Arts Décoratifs in Paris; at *10 grands - 10 jeunes* (*10 Great Artists - 10 Young*

Artists) at the Grand Palais; in 1985, at *Émergence 85* (*Emergence 85*) at the CAPC in Bordeaux and *10 jeunes pour demain* (*10 Young Artists for Tomorrow*) at Amiens Museum; and, in 1986, in the exhibition *Art Here and Now* organised in Berlin.

Her personal approach to abstraction complements her generation's infatuation with action painting and matterism with a touch of 1980s Bad Painting.

AUCTION RECORDS:

PARIS, 25 June 1986, *Painting 250* (1985, acrylic/canvas, 94 1/2 x 78 3/4 ins / 240 x 200 cm) FRF 12,000. PARIS, 13 April 1988, *Untitled* (1985, oil on canvas, 80 1/4 x 94 1/2 ins / 204 x 240 cm) FRF 12,500. PARIS, 12 Feb 1989, *Untitled* (1984, oil on canvas, 86 1/2 x 78 3/4 ins / 220 x 200 cm) FRF 21,000.

FERTÉ, Papillon de La. See **PAPILLON DE LA FERTÉ**

FERTIG, Ignaz
German, 19th century.
Born 1809, near Aschaffenburg (Bavaria); died 1858, in Munich.
Lithographer.

Fertig first studied at an art school in Germany, then at a lithographic studio in Hanau (Hesse), and finally in Munich with G. Bodmer. He produced a great number of lithographic portraits of famous people of his time: *King Maximilian II*; *King Louis I and Queen Theresa with the Princes and Princesses*; *Prince Leopold II and his Wife*; *Family of the Duke of Leuchtenberg*, and of diplomats, poets and singers. He also did reproductions of famous paintings from the Alte Pinakotek in Munich.

MUSEUMS AND GALLERIES:

MUNICH (Stadtmus.).

FERTL, Johann
Czech, 18th century.
Born in the 18th century, to a family originally from Dünkelscherben.
Painter.

Johann Fertl lived and worked in Brno in Moravia.

FERTSCH, Johann Peter
German, 18th century.
Died 26 February 1791.
Active in Zerbst (Anhalt Dessau, now Saxony-Anhalt).
Potter.

Fertsch worked at the duke's earthenware factory at Zerbst.

FERVILLE-SUAN, Charles Georges
French, 19th century.
Born in Le Mans (Sarthe).
Sculptor. Animals. Groups, statues.

Ferville-Suan first exhibited at the Paris Salon in 1872, showing medallions and statuettes, and obtained a honourable mention. Works include *Villager and Snake*, *Noblewoman at End of 15th century*, a marble statuette, *17th century Dancer* and *Cicada*. It is certain that he is a descendant of the painter Charles Suan.

AUCTION RECORDS:

NEW YORK, 14 Nov 1980, *Fright* (bronze, h. 36 ins / 91.5 cm) USD 2,200. LONDON, 23 June 1983, *Discovery* (c. 1890, bronze, h. 32 1/2 ins / 82.5 cm) GBP 2,600. LOKEREN, 22 Feb 1986, *Sulking* (brown-patinated bronze, h. 31 ins / 79 cm) BEF 600,000. ST LOUIS, 2 Dec 2000, *Fairy with Butterflies* (sculpture, bronze on columnar base, h. 31 ins / 79 cm) USD 4,750.

FERWER
German.
Painter. Waterscapes.

MUSEUMS AND GALLERIES:

KALININGRAD: *River Landscape*.

FERY. See also **FERIE**

FÉRY, Cécile Amélie
French, 20th century.
Born in Paris.
Watercolourist, painter (gouache).

Cécile Féry exhibited at the Salon des Artistes Français from 1929.

FERY, John
American, 19th - 20th century.
Born 1859; died 1934.
Painter. Landscapes with figures.

John Fery painted typical American landscapes.

AUCTION RECORDS:

SAN FRANCISCO, 24 June 1981, *Red Eagle Lake* (oil on canvas, 35 3/4 x 72 ins / 91 x 183 cm) USD 4,250. NEW YORK, 25 Oct 1985, *Iceberg Lake, Glacier National Park* (oil on canvas, 52 x 57 ins / 132 x 145 cm) USD 6,750. NEW YORK, 17 March 1988, *Moose on Lake Shore* (oil on canvas, 13 3/4 x 23 1/2 ins / 35 x 60 cm) USD 1,430.

FÉRY, Louise Lucie
French, 19th century.
Born 6 November 1848, in Metz.
Painter.

Féry was a pupil of Mlle Houssaye and Mme Faye, and at the Paris Salon she exhibited *Gem Engraver*, in 1868, *Ewer and Bowl*, in 1870, and *Books, Mandolins, Flowers*, in 1874.

FESCA, A
German, 19th century.
Active in the middle of the 19th century.
Engraver.

FESCHAL, Jacques and Léonard
French, 16th century.
Painters.
Rouen School, Gaillon School.

The Feschal brothers worked for several churches in Rouen and at the Château of Gaillon in around 1510.

FESCHOTTE, Henri
French, 20th century.
Born in Lyons.
Painter. Landscapes.

Henri Feschotte exhibited at the Salon des Indépendants in Paris from 1925.

FESEL, Caspar Carl
German, 19th century.
Born 1775, in Würzburg (Bavaria); died 1820, in Würzburg.
Painter, copyist, art restorer.

Caspar was the son of Christoph Fesel, and worked mainly as a copyist and restorer. Most of his commissions came from his native town and Vienna.

FESEL, Christoph
German, 18th century.
Born 1737, in Ochsenfurt (Bavaria); died 25 October 1805, in Würzburg (Bavaria).
Painter. History painting, portraits.

Fesel studied under Adolf Mengs and Battoni in Rome. On returning to Germany, he painted many religious pictures. He was a teacher at the academy of St Luke in Rome, then court painter in Würzburg.

FESEL, Franz
Austrian, 19th century.
Born in Vienna.
Painter.

FESEL, Johann
Austrian, 18th century.
Born in Vienna.
Painter.

FESELEN, Melchior
German, 16th century.
Born possibly in Passau (Bavaria); died 10 April 1538, in Ingolstadt (Bavaria).
Painter. History painting.
Danube School.
Melchior Feselen worked in Ingolstadt between 1522 and 1532. His style is similar to that of Albrecht Altdorfer, but less accomplished.

MUSEUMS AND GALLERIES:
MUNICH: *Lars Porsena, King of the Etruscans, Laying Siege to Rome; The Town of Alesia in Burgundy Besieged by Julius Caesar.*

FESIERS, Joseph
Flemish, 17th century.
Active in Antwerp, in the middle of the 17th century.
Painter.
Flemish School.

FESLOV, P.
Russian, 19th century.
Active in Riga c. 1800.
Engraver.
Felsov engraved in 1793, from a work by Rotari, the *Portrait of Count Suvorof.*

FESNEAU, Auguste Henri
French, 19th - 20th century.
Born 21 January 1873, in Paris.
Painter.
Auguste Fesneau exhibited at the Salon d'Hiver and at the Salon des Artistes Français.

FESQUET, Jules
French, 19th century.
Born 11 July 1836, in Charleval.
Sculptor, engraver.
Fesquet entered the École des Beaux-Arts on 8 April 1858 and became the pupil of Dantan the elder. In 1862 he won second prize in the competition *Concours de Rome* with *Aristeus the Shepherd Loses his Bees.* He received a third-class medal in 1861, and was commended in 1863. He exhibited at the Paris Salon from 1861 to 1867. Works include *Faun Playing with a Goat, Biblis, Child Bacchus, Worker on the Capitoline, New York City,* a bronze statue, *Bust of Mr Montrouge, Cassandra in Agamemnon's Palace* and *Bust of Mr Carlier.* He also made a stone statue of St John for the church of La Trinité in Paris.
MUSEUMS AND GALLERIES:
AIX-EN-PROVENCE: *Biblis* - LONDON (Victoria and Albert Mus.): *Aragon Smugglers.*

FESSARD, Claude Mathieu
French, 18th century.
Born 1740, in Fontainebleau.
Engraver (burin).
Claude Mathieu Fessard was the pupil of Longueil. He engraved views, flowers and animals.

FESSARD, Étienne
French, 18th century.
Born 1714, in Paris; died 2 May 1777, in Paris.
Engraver.
Étienne Fessard was engraver in ordinary to the king's collection. On 26 May 1753 he was elected to the Académie, and from 1753 to 1763 he exhibited at the Salon.

FESSARD, Madeleine Henriette Louise
French, 20th century.
Born 7 October 1873, in Fécamp; died 1995, in Paris.
Sculptor. Religious subjects, figures, nudes, portraits, animals. Busts.
Madeleine Fessard was admitted to the École des Beaux-Arts in Paris in 1917. She studied under Victor Ségoffin, Henri Gauquié, François Sicard and Auguste Carli. Fessard exhibited in Paris at the Salon des Artistes Français from 1924. She gained an honourable mention in 1928 with *Woman with a Parrot* and a bronze medal in 1966. In 1934, she entered her *St Michael the Archangel* for the exhibition *L'Art religieux d'aujourd'hui* (*Religious Art Today*) at the Hôtel de Rohan in Paris.

Fessard sculpted female figures - first in a naturalistic vein, and later turning to mannerism. These works include *Woman with a Parrot* and *Lady and Doe.* After the war, she worked on animal subjects (rabbits, donkeys, cockerels and ducks) and produced busts, including *Girl from Martinique* and *Joan of Arc.*

FESSARD, Pierre Alphonse
French, 19th century.
Born 10 July 1798, in Paris; died 16 February 1844, in Paris.
Sculptor.
Fessard entered the École des Beaux-Arts on 23 February 1813 and was taught by Stouf, Bridan and Bosio. He exhibited at the Salon from 1822 to 1843. His major works are *Marble Bust of Valentine, Capaneus, Adonis, Bust of the Count of Lanjuinais, Bust of G. Rossini, Bust of Mme Rogerson-Cotter, Bust of Mr Nicodami, Bust of Baron Fourrier* and *Bust of the Marquess Amelot de Guépeau.* He received a second-class medal in 1844.
MUSEUMS AND GALLERIES:
GRENOBLE: *Adonis* - RENNES: *Lanjuinais* - VERSAILLES: *Simon Vouet.*

FESSEL, Pietrequin
French, 15th century.
Active in Rouen.
Sculptor (wood).
Probably Flemish in origin, this artist collaborated on the carving of the choir stalls in Rouen Cathedral in 1462, working under the direction of Philippot Viart.

FESSER, Edward
American, 19th century.
Born 1 November 1863, in New York.
Active in New York.
Miniaturist, watercolourist.
Edward Fesser was a pupil of Robert Bier. His miniature watercolour portraits are much admired.

FESSER-BORRHÉE, Joséphine
Maiden name: Borrhée
Dutch, 19th century.
Born 15 March 1819, in Namur; died 1891, in La Côte-St-André (Isère), France.
Active in France.
Painter. Landscapes, landscapes with figures, urban views.
Joséphine Borrhée married Alexandre Fesser, who pre-deceased her. She lived in Paris, where she became a teacher of drawing. Around 1860, she formed an association with Jean-Barthold Jongkind and became his companion. With him, she travelled to Belgium and Holland from 1866 to 1869. In 1873, her son Jules Fesser accepted employment at the Château de Pupetière, in the Dauphiné region. She and Jongkind often travelled to the region and spent time there. In 1878, Jules bought a house at La Côte St André, where all three lived together. Influenced by Jongkind, her art tends to convey the impression of picturesque landscapes bathed in soft light.

She exhibited in Paris, at the Salon des Refusés, in 1863, and showed regularly in Paris Salons, and at Nevers in 1872. In 2003, she featured in the themed group exhibition *Femmes peintres en Dauphiné XIXe et XX siècles* (*Women Painters of the Dauphiné in the 19th and 20th Centuries*), Musée de Mainssieux, Voiron.

BIBLIOGRAPHY:

Femmes peintres en Dauphiné XIXe et XXe siècles, group exhibition catalogue, Musée de Mainssieux, Voiron, 2003.

MUSEUMS AND GALLERIES:

GRENOBLE (Mus. de Grenoble): *View of Grenoble* (1867, oil on canvas).

AUCTION RECORDS:

LONDON, 1 July 1976, *Windmill in the Moonlight* (1888, oil on canvas, 9 1/2 x 15 3/4 ins / 24 x 40 cm) GBP 850.

FESSLER, Johann
Austrian, 19th century.
Born 29 August 1803, in Bregenz; died 14 March 1875, in Vienna.
Sculptor.

Johann Fessler, the father of Otto and Leo Fessler, was a student of Anton Peter and Anton Schaller at the academy in Vienna. His works include religious busts and sculptures, such as the important *Christ on the Cross with Mary* that he carved for the church of St Elizabeth in Vienna.

FESSLER, Leo
Austrian, 19th century.
Born 22 November 1840, in Vienna; died 14 November 1893, in Budapest.
Sculptor.

Leo was the son of Johann Fessler. He was a student of Bauer at the academy in Vienna and also, much later, studied under Melnitzky. Among his noted works are the bust of *Sculptor Emmanuel Vogel* and 38 portraits of musicians for the opera house in Budapest.

FESSLER, Otto
Austrian, 19th century.
Born 17 October 1853, in Vienna.
Painter.

Otto was the son of Johann Fessler and the brother of Leo Fessler. He specialised in religious paintings. The reredos in the church at Beuthen in Silesia (now Bytom, Poland) is one of his works.

FEST, Martin
German, 17th century.
Died 15 March 1642.
Active in Breslau (now Wroclaw, Poland).
Painter.

One of Fest's noted works is *Nativity*.

FEST, Wilhelm
German, 19th century.
Active in Vienna and in Berlin.
Miniaturist.

Wilhelm Fest's works include his *Portrait of Frederick William III, King of Prussia*.

FESTA, Agostino
Italian, 18th - 19th century.
Active in Vicenza.
Painter.

Agostino Festa painted several religious pictures in Vicenza.

FESTA, Bianca
Italian, 19th century.
Active in Rome c. 1830.
Miniaturist.

Bianca Festa was the daughter of Felice Festa, and taught drawing at the Accademia di San Luca in Rome.

FESTA, Domenica. See **MONVOISIN Domenica**

FESTA, Felice
Italian, 19th - 20th century.
Born in Turin; died 16 October 1926, in Turin.
Sculptor.
Symbolism.

Felice Festa lived in Rome for many years, making numerous funeral monuments and sculptures on symbolic subjects.

FESTA, Franz
Austrian, 18th century.
Born 1771; died 18 October 1800, in Vienna.
Painter.

Festa was the son of Johann Michaël the Elder and twin brother of Johann Michaël the Younger.

FESTA, Giovanni
Italian, 17th century.
Active in Orzinuovi, near Brescia, c. 1646.
Painter.

FESTA, Johann Michaël, the Elder
Austrian, 18th century.
Born in Presburg (now Bratislava, Slovakia); died 22 May 1804, in Vienna.
Painter.

FESTA, Johann Michaël, the Younger
Austrian, 18th - 19th century.
Born 1771, in Vienna.
Painter.

Festa was the son of Johann Michaël the Elder.

FESTA, Mathilde. See **PIACENTINI FESTA**

FESTA, Pietro Giovanni
Italian, 16th century.
Active in Piacenza at the end of the 16th century.
Sculptor.

FESTA, Raffa
Italian, 20th century.
Born 1927, in Bari (Puglia).
Painter.

Raffa Festa has been exhibiting since 1945, notably in Milan, at the *Exhibition of Italian Artists*, and at the Salon des Artistes Indépendants in Paris, where he lived for a time. His compositions are based around brightly-coloured circles.

FESTA, Tano
Italian, 20th century.
Born 1938, in Rome; died 1987, in Rome.
Painter, collage artist. Scenes with figures, urban landscapes.

Tano Festa made extensive use of collage, taking a normal canvas as his medium and embellishing it with pieces of wood and fragments of paper. He also painted on other media, such as wood panels. He used a wide variety of techniques, from acrylic to varnish to coloured felt. These processes combined give his compositions a Baroque character. They sometimes contain an architectural or landscape detail, or else there is an unusual confrontation between two unlikely objects, or between an object and a fragment of landscape.

BIBLIOGRAPHY:

Soligno, Francesco, *Tano Festa, Catalogo generale, Vol. I*, Canale Arte, 1997.

AUCTION RECORDS:

MILAN, 8 June 1976, *Danger* (1961, oil on mounted card, 18 3/4 x 23 1/2 ins / 47.5 x 60 cm) ITL 500,000. MILAN, 6 April 1982, *Louvred French Window* (1964-1972, painted wood, 39 1/4 x 31 1/2 ins / 100 x 80 cm) ITL 900,000. ROME, 22 May

1984, *Red and Black No 40* (1961, oil on canvas, wood and paper, 43 3/4 x 48 3/4 ins / 111 x 124 cm) ITL 3,800,000. MILAN, 10 Dec 1985, *Le Stanze del Vaticano* (1962, painted wood, 32 x 25 1/2 ins / 81 x 65 cm) ITL 4,400,000. ROME, 25 Nov 1987, *Door No 3* (1962, enamel/wood, 78 3/4 x 39 1/4 ins / 200 x 99.5 cm) ITL 21,000,000. ROME, 7 April 1988, *Original Sin* (1966, oil on canvas, 35 1/2 x 18 ins / 90 x 46 cm) ITL 14,500,000; *Michelangelo* (1969, acrylic/canvas, 31 1/2 x 39 1/4 ins / 80 x 100 cm) ITL 7,000,000. MILAN, 14 May 1988, *Monuments* (1962, felt and mixed media/card, 19 3/4 x 27 1/2 ins / 50 x 70 cm) ITL 1,500,000. MILAN, 8 June 1988, *From Original Sin: Eve* (1968, acrylic/canvas, 46 x 35 ins / 116 x 89 cm) ITL 7,000,000. ROME, 15 Nov 1988, *Dimensions of the Sky* (1965, acrylic/canvas, 39 1/4 x 32 ins / 100 x 81 cm) ITL 8,500,000. ROME, 15 Nov 1988, *Original Sin* (1968, acrylic/canvas, 63 x 51 1/4 ins / 160 x 130 cm) ITL 17,000,000. MILAN, 14 Dec 1988, *Lavatory 2* (1962, painted wood, 59 1/4 x 47 1/2 ins / 150.5 x 120.5 cm) ITL 28,000,000. MILAN, 8 Nov 1989, *Via Veneto No 1* (1961, acrylic and collage of wood/canvas, 59 x 78 3/4 ins / 150 x 200 cm) ITL 32,000,000. MILAN, 27 March 1990, *Red No 21* (1960, oil and collage of canvas and paper/canvas, 47 1/4 x 31 1/2 ins / 120 x 80 cm) ITL 30,000,000. MILAN, 13 June 1990, *Cupboard with Sky* (1964, varnish/wood, 63 x 51 1/4 ins / 160 x 130 cm) ITL 37,000,000; *Detail of the Sistine Chapel* (1963, oil and collage/wood, 76 1/2 x 51 1/4 ins / 194 x 130 cm) ITL 77,000,000. ROME, 30 Oct 1990, *Untitled* (1985, acrylic and confetti/canvas, 63 x 51 1/4 ins / 160 x 130 cm) ITL 7,000,000; *Window* (1963, felt/panel, 39 1/4 x 31 1/2 ins / 100 x 80 cm) ITL 20,000,000. MILAN, 26 March 1991, *Figures* (1986, oil on canvas, 27 1/2 x 31 1/2 ins / 70 x 80 cm) ITL 4,500,000. ROME, 9 April 1991, *Untitled* (acrylic and confetti/canvas, 63 x 51 1/4 ins / 160 x 130 cm) ITL 6,500,000. ROME, 13 May 1991, *Pink Period No 4* (1968, varnish and acrylic/canvas, 32 x 25 1/2 ins / 81 x 65 cm) ITL 8,050,000. MILAN, 20 June 1991, *Black and Red No 28* (1961, acrylic, paper and wood/canvas, 51 1/4 x 58 1/2 ins / 130 x 148.5 cm) ITL 23,500,000. MILAN, 14 April 1992, *Desert and Oasis* (1982, acrylic/canvas, 55 x 55 ins / 140 x 140 cm) ITL 4,000,000. ROME, 12 May 1992, *Studio per Pianoforte* (1963, felt/wood, 44 1/2 x 36 1/4 ins / 113 x 92 cm) ITL 25,000,000. MILAN, 23 June 1992, *Pink Period No 8* (1968, oil on canvas, 63 3/4 x 51 1/4 ins / 162 x 130 cm) ITL 17,000,000. ROME, 19 Nov 1992, *Untitled* (1987, acrylic and confetti/canvas, 63 x 51 1/4 ins / 160 x 130 cm) ITL 3,200,000. ROME, 14 Dec 1992, *From Original Sin* (1978, varnish/emulsion coated canvas, 19 3/4 x 43 1/4 ins / 50 x 110 cm) ITL 8,625,000. ROME, 25 March 1993, *Untitled* (1985, acrylic and confetti/canvas, 63 x 51 1/4 ins / 160 x 130 cm) ITL 4,500,000. MILAN, 6 April 1993, *Homage to Michelangelo* (oil on canvas, 20 x 39 1/4 ins / 51 x 100 cm) ITL 7,000,000. ROME, 19 April 1994, *Three-Coloured Sky* (1965, felt/canvas, 46 x 35 ins / 116 x 89 cm) ITL 14,950,000. ROME, 28 March 1995, *Extract from a Work by Michelangelo* (1966, varnish/canvas, 31 1/2 x 39 1/4 ins / 80 x 100 cm) ITL 15,525,000. MILAN, 20 May 1996, *Red No 29* (1961, oil on paper/canvas, 39 x 59 ins / 99 x 150 cm) ITL 25,300,000. MILAN, 25 Nov 1996, *Red and Black No 27* (1961, wood and oil on paper/canvas, 51 1/4 x 59 ins / 130 x 150 cm) ITL 21,850,000. MILAN, 19 May 1997, *From Mondrian to Michelangelo* (1966, acrylic/canvas, 39 1/4 x 32 ins / 100 x 81 cm) ITL 19,550,000. ROME, 27 April 1999, *Red and Black no.40* (1961, enamel and paper on wood/canvas, 44 x 49 ins / 111 x 124 cm) ITL 31,000,000. MILAN, 17 Nov 1999, *Black and Red* (1961, acrylic, wood and paper on panel, 51 x 59 ins / 130 x 150 cm) ITL 58,000,000. MILAN, 11 April 2000, *Collage No.12* (1960, oil, collage and paper on canvas, 28 x 39 ins / 70 x 100 cm) ITL 22,000,000. MILAN, 28 Nov 2000, *Red no. Twelve* (1960, oil and collage on canvas, 31 x 47 ins / 80 x 120 cm) ITL 23,000,000. MILAN, 21 June 2001, *Waterway* (1969, enamel on canvas, 36 x 29 ins / 92 x 73 cm) ITL 16,000,000. FLORENCE, 19 Nov 2001, *Piazza Sacnderberg 46* (1961, acrylic, wood and collage on canvas, 55 x 71 ins / 140 x 180 cm) ITL 46,000,000. MILAN, 19 Nov 2002, *After Michelangelo* (1976, acrylic on canvas, 31 x 24 ins / 80 x 60 cm) EUR 7,000. PRATO, 29 Nov 2002, *Interior* (1962, acrylic on panel, 46 x 32 ins / 116 x 81 cm) EUR 14,000. MILAN, 26 May 2003, *Bi-coloured Sky* (1964, enamel on wood, 55 x 39 ins / 140 x 99 cm) EUR 20,000. ROME, 18 Nov 2003, *Cardinal* (1973, oil on canvas, 63 x 71 ins / 160 x 180 cm) EUR 11,300. MILAN, 25 May 2004, *Monument 5* (1962, pastel, watercolour and oil on paper, 39 x 28 ins / 100 x 70 cm) EUR 6,000. LONDON, 19 Oct 2004, *Figure and Landscape* (1969, enamel on canvas, 39 x 39 ins / 100 x 100 cm) GBP 22,000.

FESTE, David
Slovak, 17th century.
Born in Banská Bystrica.
Painter.

In 1656 David Feste was working in Breslau (now Wroclaw).

FESTERSEN, Friedrich
German, 19th - 20th century.
Died 1916.
Ceramicist, decorative designer.
Jugendstil.

Friedrich Festersen had a pottery studio in Berlin in 1909. He worked for Deutsche Werkstätten. His pottery was noted for its decorative portrayal of peacocks.

BIBLIOGRAPHY:
Franzke, Irmela, *Jugendstil. Glas, Graphik, Keramik, Metall, Möbel, Skulpturen und Textilien von 1880 bis 1915*, exhibition catalogue, Badisches Landesmuseum, Karlsruhe, 1987. Kern, Andrea, et al., *Jugendstil in Dresden, Aufbruch in die Moderne*, exhibition catalogue, Staatliche Kunstsammlungen, Dresden, 1999.

MUSEUMS AND GALLERIES:
KARLSRUHE (Badisches Landesmus.): *Vase*.

FESTORAZZO, Theodor
Austrian, 19th century.
Born c. 1800, in the Tyrol; died 14 May 1862, near Vienna.
Painter, draughtsman, lithographer.

Festorazzo mainly illustrated historical or genre scenes.

FESTU, Jean
French, 15th century.
Active in Paris in 1413.
Painter.

FESZTI, Arpad
Hungarian, 19th - 20th century.
Born 25 December 1856, in Ogyalla; died 1 June 1914, in Lovrana in Istria.
Painter. Genre scenes, architectural views.

Arpad Feszti studied at the academy in Munich and illustrated a large number of mythological subjects. He is known for *Mine Disaster*, exhibited in Munich in 1888.

AUCTION RECORDS:
PARIS, 18 Feb 1924, *Magyar Seated, in Fur-Lined Cloak*, FRF 380.

FETAN, Claude. See **FAYTTAN**

FETEL, Pierre
French, 20th century.
Born in Loon-Plage (Nord).
Painter. Landscapes.

Pierre Fetel exhibited in Paris, at the Salon des Artistes Indépendants, from 1931.

FETI, Domenico, or Fetti
Italian, 17th century.
Born 1589, in Rome; died 1624, in Venice.
Painter. History painting, portraits, genre scenes.

Venetian School.

Domenico Feti studied under Civoli (or Cigoli) and, while still very young, painted an altarpiece entitled *Virgin Adored by Two Angels and Supported by Two Children* for the church of S Lorenzo in Damaso. That painting and a *Magdalene* are the only two works he is known to have painted in Rome, his native city.

Feti subsequently accompanied Cardinal Ferdinand de Gonzaga to Mantua. Cardinal Ferdinand was also Duke of Mantua, and he moved not only Feti but his entire family to that city. Domenico's sister Lucrina, who took holy orders at the Ursuline convent there, was also a painter of some talent; some of her paintings were retouched by her brother, notably a *Nativity*. Feti himself painted a large *Miracle of the Loaves and Fishes* for the Ursuline convent refectory, and he also decorated the convent staircase, the chapel of the law courts of Mantua and the canoness church of Latran, where he is credited with a *Mystic Marriage of St Catherine*. It is not known how long he lived in Venice, only that he died there in 1624 at the age of 35, the victim of a turbulent lifestyle.

Feti's talent was nurtured less by his mentor Civoli than by his study of the works of his near contemporary Giulio Romano; nevertheless, his frescoes could be described as less accomplished than his oils. This might be partly because the fresco medium did not allow him to give full rein to his bold use of colour. Perhaps as a result, his work tends to incorporate an abundance of elements that appear to have little relevance to the actual subject matter. Feti has frequently been taken to task over this, although he may have been judged too harshly. A painting commonly known as *Melancolia* (now in The Louvre) is a prime example: it contains all manner of seemingly disparate elements (a dog, a tattered book, a sand-glass, a palette, and so on) which seem extraneous to the central theme of a woman meditating on a death's head. At the beginning of the 18th century, Feller assigned another title to this 17th century work, calling it *Reflections on the Transience of Earthly Vanities*, a title that better justifies the presence of such a variety of objects.

Subsequently, art historians have been at pains to identify a wide variety of influences in Feti's body of work, including Elsheimer and Rubens. Those artists, together with Bassano, no doubt influenced Feti; not directly perhaps, but as conduits to the style of Caravaggio, which Domenico Feti espoused from the very start and sustained throughout his short career in Rome, Mantua and Venice. Chiaroscuro and contrived light effects are an integral part of his Caravaggio-inspired theatricality, of which his *Parable of the Lost Drachma* (now in the Palazzo Pitti in Florence) must rank as a shining example. When Feti eschews the heavy philosophical undertones implicit in his *Melancolia*, his style becomes more intimate and congenial; examples of work in this vein can be found in the series of small paintings entitled *Parables*.

Feti's oft-criticised tendency to cram too much detail into his work can arguably be interpreted as a technical device to enable him to explore the effects of light on a wide variety of objects and surface textures. His intrinsically modernist outlook, his dramatic sense of the distribution of light and his vibrant technique were long misunderstood, although he found willing imitators in the guise of artists such as the Florentine Mazzoni, the German Liss, or Maffei and Carneo. Of late, critics have started to rehabilitate him, not least in terms of his status as a follower of Caravaggio.

D Feti.

Bibliography:

Salmi, Mario/Bazin, Germain, *Le Caravage et la Peinture italienne du XVIIe siècle*, exhibition catalogue, Musée du Louvre, Paris, 1965.

Museums and Galleries:

Bergamo (Accademia Carrara, Pinacoteca d'Arte Antica): *Tobias and the Angel* - Berlin: *Elijah in the Wilderness* - Budapest: *Young Girl Sleeping; The Blind* - Caen: *Birth of the Virgin* - Compiègne: *Peasant; Soldier* - Dresden: *David with the Head of Goliath; Young Tobias with the Angel; Parable of the Prodigal Son; Parable of the Lost Drachma; Parable of the Poor Servant; Beheading of a Saint; Parable of the Lost Sheep; Parable of the Blind; Parable of the Vine; Parable of the Great Banquet; Good Samaritan* - Florence (NG): *Artemisia* - Florence (Palazzo Pitti): *Parable of the Vine; Parable of the Lost Drachma* - La Fère: *The Cenci* - Milan (Ambrosiana): *Sower of Seeds* - Munich: *Ecce Homo; St Paul the Apostle* - Nancy: *Archangel; Melancolia* - Paris (Louvre): *Nero; Country Life; Melancolia; Guardian Angel* - Rennes: *Dead Christ; Melancolia; Landscape with Figures* - Rome (Mus. e Gal. Borghese): *Holy Virgin, the Infant Jesus, St Elisabeth and St John* - Rome (Palazzo Doria Pamphili): *St Mary Magdalene* - St Petersburg: *David; Young Tobias Tending to his Father; Immaculate Conception; Adoration of the Shepherds; Portrait of an Actor; Daedalus and Icarus* - Venice (Gal. dell'Accademia): *Two Old Men* - Venice (Gal. Reale): *Old Man Wearing a Turban; Head of Old Man; Good Samaritan; Reading; Parable of the Wheat and Chaff* - Vienna: *Triumph of Galatea; Market Square; Peter Asleep; Moses and the Burning Bush; Flight into Egypt; Dead Leander; Queen Artemisia; Mystic Marriage of St Catherine; St Margaret* - Vienna (Kunsthistorisches Mus.): *Jacob's Ladder.*

Auction records:

St Agatha, GBP 15. Paris, 6 Feb 1865, *Tobias and his Father,* FRF 2,750. London, 23 May 1924, *Parable of the Mote and Beam,* GBP 57. London, 1 June 1928, *Mary Magdalene Contemplating a Skull,* GBP 47. London, 28 Nov 1928, *Mary Magdalene Meditating,* GBP 20. New York, 27 and 28 March 1930, *Words of Condolence,* USD 425. London, 19 April 1944, *Market Scene,* GBP 165. London, 17 Oct 1945, *Young Singer,* GBP 380. London, 21 Nov 1958, *Head of Young Boy Resting on his Hand* (red chalk) GBP 992. London, 11 Nov 1959, *Good Samaritan,* GBP 620. London, 30 June 1961, *Portrait of a Man,* GBP 3,675. Milan, 16 May 1962, *Martyrdom of Two Saints,* ITL 2,800,000. Milan, 29 Oct 1964, *St Paul,* ITL 1,600,000. Milan, 1 Dec 1970, *Parable of the Miser,* ITL 3,800,000. London, 1 Dec 1978, *Grape Harvesters* (oil on panel, 22 3/4 x 17in/58 x 43cm) GBP 20,000. Milan, 29 May 1981, *Ecce Homo* (oil on canvas, 34 x 26 3/4in/85.5 x 68cm) ITL 8,000,000. London, 11 Dec 1984, *Crates of Thebes, the Cynic Philosopher* (oil on canvas, 67 1/2 x 49 3/4in/171.5 x 126.3cm) GBP 60,000. Monte Carlo, 20 June 1987, *Mary Magdalene Leaning on a Skull* (double-sided drawing in black chalk heightened with white/blue paper, 8 x 7 1/4in/20.2 x 18.1cm) FRF 80,000. London, 8 July 1988, *Temptation of Christ* (oil on panel, 34 x 27 3/4in/85.5 x 70.5cm) GBP 57,200. Stockholm, 16 May 1990, *David with the Head of Goliath* (oil on canvas, 56 1/4 x 40 1/4in/143 x 102cm) SEK 65,000. New York, 10 Jan 1995, *Study for the Holy Trinity (recto); Study of a Figure (verso)* (black chalk/sheets of paper joined together, 8 1/4 x 8 3/4in/21.1 x 22.1cm) USD 3,450. New York, 24 Jan 2003, *Parable of the Treasure Hidden in the Field* (oil on panel, 24 x 18 ins / 61 x 45 cm) USD 45,000.

FETIVO, pseudonym of Fetiveau, André
French, 20th century.
Born 19 July 1908, in the Morbihan.
Painter, sculptor.

Fetivo studied at the Paris École des Beaux-Arts from 1926 to 1930. He exhibited in Paris at the Salon des Surindépendants and at the Salon d'Automne, and he also exhibited in the USA.

FETT, Maximilian
German, 18th - 19th century.
Born 1773.
Painter.
In 1810 Fett was living at Tölz in Bavaria.

FETT, William
American, 20th century.
Born in the USA.
Painter.

FETTI, Domenico. See **FETI**

FETTI, Giovanni di Francesco
Italian, 14th century.
Sculptor.
Giovanni di Francesco Fetti worked on the Loggia dei Priori in Florence and on the decorations of the cathedral.

FETTI, Lucrina
Italian, 17th century.
Painter.
The sister and pupil of Domenico Feti, she painted portraits and religious subjects. She took holy orders at an early age.

FETTI, Mariano
Italian, 17th - 18th century.
Active probably in Mantua.
Painter.
The Kaiser Friedrich Museum in Berlin housed two *Still-lifes* by Mariano Fetti.

FETTING, Rainer
German, 20th - 21st century.
Born 1949, in Wilhelmshaven.
Painter (mixed media).
New Fauves.
From 1969 to 1972, Fetting trained as a carpenter while simultaneously, completing his professional training in stage design at the Landesbühne (country theatre) in Wilhelmshaven. He went to Berlin and studied under Hans Jaenisch at the art academy until 1978. In 1977, with three other contributors, he had co-founded the Galerie am Moritzplatz, near the Berlin wall that divided East and West Germany. In 1978 Fetting obtained a German Exchange Grant (DAAD) to stay in New York. When he returned, he collaborated on many group paintings, and from 1976 to 1981 produced several films.

Baselitz, Lüpertz and Penck were considered to be the first New Fauves; without any significant links with the Fauvist movement of the past, this label tends to distinguish them from the vast Neo-Expressionist movement, in Germany and elsewhere; thus, Fetting belongs to the second wave of these New Fauves. Like the Fauves of the past, he follows Van Gogh's example: he uses and often combines various techniques including charcoal, watercolour, acrylic and oil. He feels compelled to paint very large pictures; 6 feet (2 metres) is a minimum unit of measurement, and he uses a makeshift technique of colourwashing, spatters and splashes, which produces an unfinished effect. He sometimes makes concessions to mixed media collage by inserting bits of wood in faces.

He paints figures, often nudes in erotic poses, recumbent, caricatured and informed; evocations of town settings, for example *Hudson River* of 1984; animals, and birds; he paints everything which passes in front of his eyes or through his head, with his fingers like a child; he paints his actual and ideal daily life. In *West Night* of 1984, which measures 108 x 251 in (275 x 640 cm), the ill-defined, heavy graphic construction is compensated for by a rich diversity of chromatic harmonies, from which suggestions of figures, violently lit in red, yellow-orange, green and blue, as if electric, loom up from among dull-coloured shadows.

Other compositions, such as those from the *Icarus with Iron* series, are comparable to the sub-trend of 'figuration libre' (spontaneous figurative painting), by virtue of their 'bad painting' appearance - really badly drawn and badly painted. By mixing his qualities with all his shortcomings, Fetting's painting establishes itself within one of the trends which have contributed to the modernity of the 1980s.

Fetting

BIBLIOGRAPHY:
Davvetas, Demosthène, '*Neuf + Un, notes pour une composition musicale sur le travail de Rainer Fetting*' in *Artstudio*, periodical, Gal. Templon, Paris, autumn 1986. *Rainer Fetting, peintures, aquarelles, dessins*, exhibition catalogue, Gal. Kaj Forsblom, Helsinki, 1988. *L'Art moderne à Marseille. La Collection du Musée Cantini*, exhibition catalogue, Musée Cantini, Marseilles, 1988. *'Berlin-Moskau/Moskau-Berlin 1950-2000'* in *2 vol.*, exhibition catalogue, Martin-Gropius-Bau, Berlin, 2003 (text in German).

MUSEUMS AND GALLERIES:
MARSEILLES (Mus. Cantini): *Gary Head* (1986).

AUCTION RECORDS:
NEW YORK, 11 May 1983, *Figure and Overhead Railway* (1981, acrylic/canvas, 78 1/2 x 98 1/4 ins / 199.5 x 249.5 cm) USD 6,500. NEW YORK, 6 May 1986, *Indian 2* (1982, tempera/canvas, 98 1/2 x 67 ins / 250.2 x 170.2 cm) USD 16,000. LONDON, 26 June 1986, *Van Gogh at the Wall* (1983, acrylic/canvas, 118 x 88 1/2 ins / 300 x 225 cm) GBP 14,000. NEW YORK, 4 May 1988, *Man with Angular Face (Green II)* (1981, acrylic/canvas, 86 1/2 x 63 ins / 220 x 160.2 cm) USD 12,100. NEW YORK, 10 Nov 1988, *Man with Candle* (1984, oil and wood/canvas, 90 x 81 ins / 228.6 x 205.8 cm) USD 30,800. STOCKHOLM, 21 Nov 1988, *Man and Bird* (1983, gouache and watercolour, 26 3/4 x 39 ins / 68 x 99 cm) SEK 6,000. PARIS, 12 April 1989, *Magic Flute I* (1984, oil on canvas, 90 1/4 x 72 ins / 229 x 182 cm) FRF 110,000. NEW YORK, 3 May 1989, *Child-Wolf* (1983, oil on canvas and wood, 90 x 72 ins / 228.5 x 183 cm) USD 27,500. NEW YORK, 5 Oct 1989, *Hallucination* (1984, acrylic and wood/canvas, 90 x 72 ins / 228.5 x 182.8 cm) USD 34,100. LONDON, 22 Feb 1990, *Van Gogh the Mason* (1983, acrylic/canvas, 118 x 88 1/2 ins / 300 x 225 cm) GBP 50,600. NEW YORK, 7 May 1990, *Van Gogh in New York* (1978, watercolour and charcoal/paper, 15 x 10 3/4 ins / 38.1 x 27.5 cm) USD 6,050. NEW YORK, 4 Oct 1990, *Prisoner* (1983, oil on canvas, 90 1/2 x 63 ins / 230 x 160 cm) USD 17,600. LONDON, 18 Oct 1990, *Green Indian Mountain* (1982, oil on canvas, diptych, each 98 1/2 x 47 1/4 ins / 250 x 120 cm) GBP 16,500. NEW YORK, 7 Nov 1990, *Wood Portrait* (1983, wood and oil on canvas/card, 89 3/4 x 72 ins / 228 x 182.8 cm) USD 25,300. PARIS, 9 Dec 1990, *Tuxedo Man and Dobermann* (1984, oil and wood/canvas, 90 1/4 x 72 1/2 ins / 229 x 184 cm) FRF 155,000. LONDON, 21 March 1991, *Mad Max* (1983, oil on canvas, 70 3/4 x 98 1/2 ins / 180 x 250 cm) GBP 13,200. PARIS, 16 June 1991, *Desmond - Profile* (1987, bronze, 41 1/4 x 44 x 13 ins / 105 x 112 x 33 cm) FRF 130,000. LONDON, 27 June 1991, *Man with Iron VII* (1983, acrylic/canvas, 90 1/2 x 78 3/4 ins / 230 x 200 cm) GBP 15,400. NEW YORK, 7 May 1992, *Goat* (1986, oil on canvas, 90 1/4 x 97 1/4 ins / 229.2 x 247 cm) USD 23,100. LONDON, 2 July 1992, *Large Shower II* (1980, acrylic/two panels with canvas, in all 106 x 120 ins / 269 x 305 cm) GBP 28,600. PARIS, 27 Oct 1992, *Magic Flute I* (1984, oil on canvas, 90 1/4 x 72 ins / 229 x 182 cm)

FRF 58,000. NEW YORK, 19 Nov 1992, *Man and Monkey* (1982, pigments/canvas, 106 1/4 x 82 3/4 ins / 270 x 210 cm) USD 28,600. NEW YORK, 4 May 1993, *Dancers III* (1982, dry spray/fabric, 82 1/2 x 110 1/4 ins / 209.6 x 280 cm) USD 23,000. LONDON, 2 Dec 1993, *Arab and Camel* (1983, oil on canvas, 90 1/2 x 63 ins / 230 x 160 cm) GBP 12,650. NEW YORK, 3 May 1995, *Nude with Fan* (1989, oil/plywood, 81 1/2 x 49 1/4 ins / 207 x 125.1 cm) USD 10,350. NEW YORK, 16 Nov 1995, *Halloween Van Gogh* (1983, oil on canvas, 48 x 35 3/4 ins / 121.9 x 91.1 cm) USD 12,650. LONDON, 15 March 1996, *Grey and Red Nude* (1981, acrylic/canvas, 67 x 53 1/4 ins / 170 x 135.3 cm) GBP 7,130. NEW YORK, 21 Nov 1996, *Orange Eater* (1984, oil, driftwood and ironmongery/canvas, 90 x 72 ins / 228.6 x 182.8 cm) USD 13,800. AMSTERDAM, 10 Dec 1996, *Salome* (c. 1978-1979, oil on canvas, 37 1/2 x 29 3/4 ins / 95 x 75.5 cm) NLG 8,072. NEW YORK, 18 Nov 1997, *Brush Head* (1984, oil, brushes and tubes of paint/canvas, 48 x 36 ins / 121.9 x 91.5 cm) USD 4,600. LONDON, 6 Oct 1999, *The Kiss IV* (1981, acrylic and resin on canvas, 94 x 79 ins / 240 x 200 cm) GBP 28,000. MUNICH, 11 Nov 1999, *Dandelions* (1990, oil on canvas, 79 x 63 ins / 200 x 160 cm) DEM 60,000. NEW YORK, 7 Nov 2000, *Van Gogh in Subway* (1985, oil on canvas, 84 x 104 ins / 214 x 265 cm) USD 26,000. BERLIN, 23 Nov 2000, *Street Workers* (1985, oil on canvas, 104 x 95 ins / 264 x 242 cm) DEM 55,000. NEW YORK, 8 May 2001, *Duscher II - Bleu* (1980, tempera, 98 x 79 ins / 250 x 200 cm) USD 30,000. MUNICH, 15 Nov 2001, *CNN* (1991, oil on canvas, 60 x 89 ins / 152 x 226 cm) DEM 100,000. LONDON, 8 Feb 2002, *Shower Room II* (1980, dispersion on linen, 10 x 80 ins / 25 x 202 cm) GBP 17,000. MUNICH, 16 May 2002, *World Trade Center-appearance, NY* (oil on canvas, 60 x 89 ins / 152 x 226 cm) EUR 45,000. COLOGNE, 27 Nov 2003, *Field of Rapeseed* (1990, oil on canvas, 98 x 91 ins / 250 x 230 cm) EUR 21,000. MUNICH, 5 Dec 2003, *Self at Green Table* (1980-1983, acrylic, oil and sand on canvas, 69 x 47 ins / 175 x 120 cm) EUR 35,000. COLOGNE, 4 June 2004, *Times Square* (1991, oil on jute, 60 x 85 ins / 152 x 216 cm) EUR 25,000. COLOGNE, 4 June 2004, *Self-portrait with Yellow Hat II* (1982, oil on canvas, 59 x 55 ins / 150 x 140 cm) EUR 29,000.

FETTU, Germaine
French, 20th century.
Born in Paris.
Painter.
Germaine Fettu shows at the Salon des Artistes Français.

FETZ, Leonhard
Austrian, 17th century.
Died 1657, in Graz.
Painter.
After having travelled in Italy, Fetz was chosen by Emperor Ferdinand III of Germany to be his personal painter.

FEU, Jaume de, or dez. See **DUFEU Jaume**

FEU, Ramon dez. See **DUFEU Ramon**

FEUARDENT, Georges François
French, 19th - 20th century.
Born 14 September 1873, in Paris.
Painter. Landscapes.

FEUCCIO DI PAOLO
Italian, 14th century.
Active in Pisa c. 1315.
Painter.
Feuccio di Paolo may also have worked as a goldsmith.

FEUCHÈRE, Jean-Jacques
French, 19th century.
Born 26 August 1807, in Paris; died 25 July 1852.
Painter, sculptor, engraver. History painting, portraits.
Feuchère was a pupil of Jean-Pierre Cortot and Claude Ramey. He exhibited at the Paris Salon from 1831 to 1852, receiving a second-class medal in 1834. He was decorated with the Légion d'Honneur in 1846. He was known mainly for his work as a sculptor. Sculptures include *David Showing Goliath's Head to the Israelites, Judith, Having Saved her Country, Thanks God for Her Victory, Nymph on a Shell, Raising of Lazarus, Angel Playing an Instrument, Young Man Entreating Monks to Receive Him into Their Order*, a low relief, *The Bridge at Arcole*, one of the low reliefs which decorates the Arc de Triomphe in Paris and *Benvenuto Cellini*, a bronze statue.

BIBLIOGRAPHY:
Nouvelles acquisitions du département des sculptures 1988-1991, exhibition catalogue, Musée du Louvre, Paris, 1992.

MUSEUMS AND GALLERIES:
DUNKIRK: *Raising of Lazarus* - ROUEN (MBA): *Raphael; Joan of Arc at the Stake* - VERSAILLES: *Olivier Castelan, Field Marshal of the King's Army; Mme Marie-Adélaide de France; Mme Clotilde, Queen of Sardinia; Simon, Count of Montfort; Count Jacques de Douglas.*

AUCTION RECORDS:
AMSTERDAM, 20 Feb 1980, *Horsewoman* (1843, bronze, h. 17 3/4 ins / 45 cm) NLG 4,300. COLOGNE, 29 June 1984, *Satan, the Fallen Angel* (1833, bronze, h. 13 1/2 ins / 34 cm) DEM 2,600. PARIS, 5 June 1987, *Pensive Devil* (1833, brown-patinated bronze, h. 13 3/4 ins / 35 cm) FRF 15,000. NEW YORK, 25 May 1988, *Daphnis and Chloë* (bronze, h. 21 ins / 53.4 cm) USD 3,850. LOKEREN, 4 Dec 1993, *Sailing Allegory* (bronze, h. 12 1/4 ins / 31 cm, w. 11 1/2 ins/29 cm) BEF 34,000. NEW YORK, 26 May 1994, *Satan* (1833, bronze, h. 13 1/2 ins / 34.3 cm) USD 8,625. NEW YORK, 9 Jan 1997, *Satan* (brown-patinated bronze, h. 8 1/2 ins / 21.6 cm) USD 4,025. DERBY, 14 April 1999, *Figure of a Lightly Draped Maiden, Standing with Arms Raised* (c. 1850, sculpture, bronze, h. 30 ins / 76 cm) GBP 1,400. PARIS, 7 April 2000, *Satan* (1833, sculpture, brown patinated bronze, h. 14 ins / 35 cm) FRF 68,000. LONDON, 5 July 2000, *Satan* (1833, sculpture, dark brown patinated bronze, h. 13 ins / 34 cm) GBP 7,200. PARIS, 25 June 2001, *The Fallen Angel* (sculpture, brown patinated bronze, black marble base, h. 18 ins / 45 cm) FRF 27,000. LONDON, 13 March 2002, *Dancing Harvester* (sculpture, dark brown patinated bronze, h. 18 ins / 45 cm) GBP 2,000. PARIS, 30 April 2003, *Satan, Fallen Angels* (sculpture, patinated bronze, h. 13 ins / 34 cm) EUR 9,000. PARIS, 2 Oct 2003, *Amazon* (1843, sculpture, patinated bronze, h. 17 ins / 44 cm) EUR 8,500. LONDON, 17 June 2004, *Satan* (sculpture, dark brown patinated bronze, variegated green marble plinth, h. 8 ins / 21 cm) GBP 4,200.

FEUCHÈRES, Anne Marie
French, 20th century.
Born in St-Brieuc.
Pastellist.
Anne Feuchères exhibited in Paris, at the Salon des Artistes Français, from 1930.

FEUCHOT, Pierre
French, 19th century.
Born in Dijon; died 1830, in Dijon.
Painter, draughtsman. Landscapes.
Feuchot was a pupil of Friar and A. Devosge.

FEUCHT, Georg Gottfried
German, 18th century.
Active in Bamberg in 1734.
Sculptor.

FEUCHT, Theodore
German, 19th century.
Born 8 November 1867, in Ludwigsburg (Baden-Württemberg).
Painter, draughtsman. Portraits, landscapes.

After studying in Stuttgart, Munich and Vienna, Feucht settled in Paris.

MUSEUMS AND GALLERIES:

PARIS (Mus. Carnavalet): *Landscape studies* - PHILADELPHIA: *Portrait of Woman.*

AUCTION RECORDS:

MUNICH, 29 May 1976, *Ploughman* (oil on canvas, 15 x 22 ins / 38 x 55 cm) DEM 1,000. MUNICH, 29 May 1980, *View of a Village* (1913, oil on canvas, 21 1/2 x 25 1/2 ins / 54.5 x 65 cm) DEM 1,600.

FEUCHTE, Hans

German, 16th century.

Active in Breslau (now Wroclaw, Poland) at the beginning of the 16th century.

Painter.

FEUCHTMAIR. See **FEICHTMAYR**

FEUDEL, Alma L. M. A. (Mrs)

American, 19th - 20th century.

Born 1 November 1867, in Leavenworth.

Active in New York.

Painter.

Alma L.M.A. Feudel was the wife of Arthur Feudel.

FEUDEL, Arthur

German, 19th - 20th century.

Born 27 March 1857, in Harthau, near Chemnitz (Saxony); died 1929.

Active and naturalised in the USA.

Painter. Portraits, genre scenes, landscapes, still-lifes.

Arthur Feudel was a pupil of Fedor Flinzer, Julius Benezer and the art schools of Dresden and Munich. He emigrated to the USA, living first in Chicago, where he made his mark in the artistic world. He was naturalised in 1892 and settled in New York in 1897. He painted scenes of rural life.

AUCTION RECORDS:

COLOGNE, 4 June 1985, *Spring Landscape* (1925, oil on canvas remounted/panel, 19 3/4 x 27 1/2 ins / 50 x 70 cm) DEM 3,400. NEW YORK, 20 Jan 1993, *Moonlight on Katwijk Beach* (watercolour/paper, 18 x 25 1/2 ins / 45.7 x 64.8 cm) USD 863. AMSTERDAM, 4 June 1996, *Still-life with Flowers* (oil on card, 13 3/4 x 13 3/4 ins / 35 x 35 cm) NLG 1,534.

FEUDEL, Constantin

German, 19th century.

Born 24 September 1860, in Harthau, near Chemnitz (Saxony).

Painter. Genre scenes.

Feudel studied at the academy in Dresden and at the studio of the teacher Pauwels. He then travelled in Italy. He exhibited in Dresden between 1884 and 1887. One of his known works is *Family Chronicle*.

FEUERBACH, Anselm or Anselme

German, 19th century.

Born 12 August 1829, in Speyer (Rhineland-Palatinate); died 4 January 1880, in Venice.

Painter, draughtsman. History painting, mythological subjects, portraits.

Munich School.

Anselm Feuerbach worked initially in Germany (in Düsseldorf and Munich), then in Amiens (Somme, France), and finally with Thomas Couture in Paris. In 1873 he was appointed as a teacher at the academy in Vienna, a post which he held for only three years. Feuerbach was independent and adventurous, and liked to travel. He cannot be associated with any one school. Some of his works show Couture's influence, while others very closely resemble the techniques of the Belgian masters of the period. During the final years of his life, which he spent in Venice, he tried, almost excessively, to imitate the art of the old masters of the Venetian school.

His paintings of groups of figures (*Hafiz, Platonic Banquet, Battle of the Amazons*) lack unity; he sometimes became discouraged and did not complete them. Similarly, his representations of figures of antiquity (*Medea, Iphigenia*) are considered rather cold. Feuerbach's portraits are considered to be his best works.

A. Feuerbach

BIBLIOGRAPHY:

Ecker, J., *Anselm Feuerbach, Leben und Werk*, Hirmer, Munich, 1991.

MUSEUMS AND GALLERIES:

BASEL: *Death of Pietro Aretino; Portrait of Allgeyer, the Sculptor; Nymphs Listening to Children Making Music* - BERLIN: *In the Mountains of Castell Toblino; Spring; The Artist's Mother-in-Law; Rocky Area with Three Cows Grazing; Ricordo di Tivoli; Heroic Landscape; Self-portrait; Medea Preparing to Flee; Battle of the Amazons; Concert; Platonic Feast* - BREMEN: *Mandolin Player* - DARMSTADT: *Iphigenia* - FRANKFURT AM MAIN: *Lucretia* - HAMBURG: *Gipsy Dance; Mandolin Player; Judgement of Paris* - LEIPZIG: *Children's Serenade* - MUNICH: *Giants; Self-portrait* - MUNICH (Neue Pinakothek): *Medea* - STRASBOURG: *Beach in Italy* - STUTTGART: *Portrait of Man; Portrait of Woman* - STUTTGART (Staatsgal.): *Iphigenia* - WEIMAR: *Study of Head* - WROCLAW: *Medea.*

AUCTION RECORDS:

NEW YORK, 6 April 1960, *Portrait of Nanna*, USD 2,000. COLOGNE, 14 Nov 1963, *Poetry*, DEM 18,000. COLOGNE, 16 Nov 1967, *Nanna*, DEM 10,000. LUCERNE, 27 Nov 1971, *Mother and Child*, CHF 13,500. MUNICH, 28 Nov 1974, *Head of Young Girl*, DEM 13,000. MUNICH, 29 Nov 1979, *Caliban Kneeling* (pen/pencil outlines, 11 x 15 1/4 ins / 27 x 39 cm) DEM 2,700. MUNICH, 27 Nov 1980, *Head of Young Girl* (oil on canvas, 12 1/2 x 9 3/4 ins / 32 x 25 cm) DEM 5,300. MUNICH, 29 June 1982, *Naked Child Seen from Behind* (c. 1858, charcoal, 12 1/2 x 6 1/4 ins / 32 x 16 cm) DEM 3,700. COLOGNE, 27 March 1987, *Courtesan with Servant* (1852, oil on canvas, 42 x 34 ins / 106.5 x 86.5 cm) DEM 44,000. HEIDELBERG, 14 Oct 1988, *Pierrot Standing* (pencil, 16 3/4 x 10 3/4 ins / 42.4 x 27.2 cm) DEM 2,200. MUNICH, 10 May 1989, *Italian Mother with Child* (pencil, charcoal and coloured pastels, 15 3/4 x 10 3/4 ins / 40 x 27.5 cm) DEM 25,300. MUNICH, 12 Dec 1990, *Peonies* (oil on canvas, 39 x 30 3/4 ins / 99 x 78 cm) DEM 88,000. LONDON, 13 Oct 1994, *Blindness of Samson* (oil on canvas, 13 3/4 x 22 ins / 35 x 55.8 cm) GBP 4,025. NEW YORK, 1 Nov 1995, *Head of Christ* (oil on canvas, 15 3/4 x 12 ins / 40 x 30.5 cm) USD 5,750. VIENNA, 29-30 Oct 1996, *Portrait of Lady with Pearl Necklace* (oil on canvas, 30 1/4 x 23 ins / 77 x 57.5 cm) ATS 299,000. LONDON, 21 Nov 1996, *Young Musicians near a Fountain* (c. 1855-1860, oil on canvas, 10 x 12 3/4 ins / 24.5 x 32.4 cm) GBP 6,900. MUNICH, 3 Dec 1996, *Orlando and Angelica* (oil on canvas, 25 1/4 x 30 ins / 64 x 76 cm) DEM 24,000. MUNICH, 27 Feb 1999, *Two Women and Child* (oil on canvas/board, 18 x 15 ins / 46 x 37 cm) DEM 60,000. MUNICH, 23 June 1999, *Portrait of Young Roman Girl* (oil on canvas, 18 x 14 ins / 46 x 36 cm) DEM 20,000. VENICE, 19 Feb 2000, *Young Woman Crowned with Laurel* (oil on canvas, 18 x 14 ins / 45 x 36 cm) ITL 12,500,000. STUTTGART, 6 April 2000, *Il Concerto Campestre* (oil on canvas, 15 x 18 ins / 38 x 46 cm) DEM 23,000. HEIDELBERG, 6 April 2001, *Naked Boy Playing Flute - Satyr* (oil on canvas, 32 x 19 ins / 82 x 47 cm) DEM 20,000. ZURICH, 10 Dec 2001, *Portrait of a Girl* (1852, oil on canvas, 17 x 13 ins / 43 x 34 cm) CHF 20,000. NEW YORK, 23 Jan 2002, *Four Studies of a Standing Woman Playing a Rebec* (black and white chalk, 13 x 17 ins / 33 x 44 cm) USD 3,800. NEW YORK, 29 Oct 2002, *Portrait of a Young Man* (pencil, black and white chalk, 8 x 6 ins / 21 x 15 cm) USD 16,000. MUNICH, 24 Sept 2003, *Study of*

Bearded Man (oil on canvas, 18 x 14 ins / 45 x 35 cm) EUR 4,000. PARIS, 17 Nov 2003, *Shipwrecks* (oil on canvas, 37 x 49 ins / 95 x 124 cm) EUR 4,000. RADOLFZELL, 3 July 2004, *The Death of Pietro Aretino* (1853, oil on canvas, 39 x 32 ins / 100 x 81 cm) EUR 8,000. RADOLFZELL, 3 July 2004, *Young Girls Bathing* (c. 1856, oil on card, 15 x 19 ins / 37 x 47 cm) EUR 10,000.

FEUERBACH, Johann Anselm
German, 18th - 19th century.
Born 19 February 1755, in Frankfurt am Main; died 1 March 1827.
Draughtsman, engraver.

Johann Feuerbach was the great-grandfather of Anselm Feuerbach.

FEUERER, Hanns
German, 15th century.
Active in Würzburg (Bavaria) around the middle of the 15th century.
Painter.

FEUERHAHN, Hermann
German, 19th - 20th century.
Born 20 May 1873, in Hildesheim.
Sculptor. Monuments.

Feuerhahn was the pupil of Karl Gundelach in Hanover and of Christian Behrens in Breslau (now Wroclaw, Poland). After long study trips to France, Italy and America, he finally set up in Berlin, where, amongst other things, he decorated the façade of the German National Library.

FEUERLE, Johann
Austrian, 18th century.
Active in Vienna.
Painter.

Johann was the son of Josef Benedikt Feuerle.

FEUERLE, Josef Benedikt
Austrian, 18th century.
Born c. 1719; died 17 July 1780, in Vienna.
Painter.

FEUERLEIN, Johann Peter
German, 17th - 18th century.
Born 12 October 1668, in Boxberg (Baden-Württemberg); died 16 September 1728, in Ansbach.
Painter.

After studying under Ongher at Würzburg, Feuerlein spent a long period in Vienna and Venice. He is particularly known for his portraits of members of the German imperial family, including one of King Joseph.

FEUERMAN, Carole Jean
American, 20th century.
Born 1945.
Painter, sculptor. Figures, scenes with figures.

Carole Feuerman paints familiar subjects with freshness and humour.

AUCTION RECORDS:
NEW YORK, 5 Oct 1989, *Brooke and the Beach Ball* (polyester resin and oil, 20½ x 25 x 19 ins / 52 x 63.5 x 48.2 cm) USD 23,100. NEW YORK, 9 May 1990, *Diver* (1984, polyester resin and oil, 35 x 19 x 15 ins / 88.9 x 48.2 x 38 cm) USD 35,750. NEW YORK, 4 Oct 1990, *Little Raincoat* (1987, polyester resin and paint, h. 17 ins / 43.2 cm) USD 14,300. NEW YORK, 12 June 1991, *Swimmer* (painted polyester resin, h. 17 ins / 43.2 cm) USD 8,800. NEW YORK, 12 June 1992, *Blue Beret* (1983, polyester resin, h. 16 ins / 40.6 cm) USD 6,600. NEW YORK, 15 Nov 1995, *Capri* (1991, acrylic on polyester resin mannequin with a wig, 35 x 18 x 12 ins / 89 x 45.7 x 30.4 cm) USD 19,550. NEW YORK, 8 May 1996, *Noël de Courtney* (acrylic/polyester resin, hair and acrylic foam, 23½ x 18 x 10 ins / 59.7 x 45.7 x 25.3 cm) USD 8,625.

FEUERRING, Maximilian, or Feuerring-Emefowicz
Polish, 20th century.
Born 16 November 1896, in Lviv; died 1985.
Active in Australia from 1950 and naturalised in 1955.
Painter. Stage sets.

Maximilian Feurring studied after World War I in Berlin and then trained in Rome, graduating in 1926. He visited Paris and came into contact with modern painting. During the six years of World War II, he was interned in the German camps. He later taught in Munich and then emigrated to Australia. He took part in collective exhibitions including: Rome (from 1926); Poland; Prague; Berlin and Paris after 1928 at the Salon de la Société Nationale des Beaux-Arts and the Salon d'Automne. Later he exhibited in collective exhibitions in the main Australian cities and an entire hall was devoted to him at the São Paulo Biennale in 1965. He held numerous solo exhibitions including: Sydney (1950, 1951, 1954, 1958, 1960, 1966 and 1969) and at Museum of Modern Art, Melbourne (1958 and 1970).

MUSEUMS AND GALLERIES:
ROME (Gal. dell'Accademia Nazionale di S Luca).

FEUERSTEIN, Émile
French, 19th century.
Born 17 February 1856, in Provins (Seine-et-Mane).
Painter (gouache), watercolourist, engraver. Flowers.

Émile Feuerstein was the pupil of T. Jourdain and J. Martin. He received a silver medal at the Paris Salon in 1926. He produced many lithographs.

AUCTION RECORDS:
RHEIMS, 18 March 1990, *Bunches of Flowers* (1922, watercolour and gouache, 24½ x 19 ins / 62 x 48 cm) FRF 7,500.

FEUERSTEIN, Georg
Austrian, 19th century.
Born 16 October 1840, in Hinterreuthe, near Bezau; died 26 October 1904, in Bregenz.
Sculptor.

A student of Knabl at the academy of Munich, Feuerstein was first noticed for a sculpture in wood: *Good Shepherds*. Subsequently he carved pictures and a large number of religious subjects.

FEUERSTEIN, Johann Martin
French, 19th century.
Active in Alsace.
Sculptor.

Johann Feuerstein was the father and teacher of Martin.

FEUERSTEIN, Martin
French, 19th - 20th century.
Born 5 January 1856, in Barr; died February 1931, in Barr.
Painter. History painting, religious subjects.

Martin Feuerstein studied first under his father in Alsace, then under Alexandre Strähuber, Ludwig Löfftz and Wilhelm Diez in Munich, and finally under Luc-Olivier Merson in Paris. He travelled to Italy, and he exhibited at the Paris Salon between 1879 and 1882 and in the 1898 travelling Turnus exhibition in Switzerland. He finally settled in Munich, where he got married. From 1898, he taught at the art academy in Munich.

Among his works are *Suffer the Little Children to Come unto Me*, *Scenes in the Life of St Anthony* (ten pieces painted on copper for the church of St Katharine in Munich), along with the set of 14 Stations of the Cross for the same church. Among other paintings, two (*Dance* and *Music*) are located at Winterthur, an *Allegory of the Mediterranean Sea* is in San Remo and, in the basilica at Marienthal (painted between 1888 and 1890), *Procession of the Coronation of*

our Lady of Marienthal, The Baptism of Christ and *Transfiguration.*
MUSEUMS AND GALLERIES:
STRASBOURG: *The Miracle of the Loaves and Fishes; The Erection of the First Church at Marienthal.*

FEUERSTEIN, Noël
French, 20th century.
Born in Sceaux.
Sculptor.
Noël Feuerstein studied under René Debarre. He exhibited in Paris at the Salon des Artistes Français, of which he was a member; he received a third-class medal in 1930.

FEUGERAY, Pierre, the Elder
French, 17th century.
Active in Caen.
Painter.
Pierre Feugeray the Elder executed several pictures for the church of St-Germain-la-Blanche-Herbe.

FEUGERAY, Pierre, the Younger
French, 17th century.
Active in Caen during the second half of the 17th century.
Painter.

FEUGÈRE, Marguerite, later Feugère-Mouton
French, 20th century.
Born 12 July 1876, in Longjumeau; died 20 February 1971, in Ivry-sur-Seine.
Painter.
Marguerite Feugère exhibited in Paris from 1896 at the Salon des Artistes Français, of which she became a member in 1903.

FEUGÈRE DES FORTS
French, 19th century.
Painter, draughtsman, illustrator. Religious subjects, landscapes.
Feugère des Forts was an amateur painter who exhibited landscapes at the Paris Salon in 1824 and 1834. He produced some church paintings and a series of vignettes for the French encyclopedia *Encyclopédie portative.* These were engraved by Girardot.

FEUGÈRE DES FORTS, Vincent Émile
French, 19th century.
Born 17 November 1825, in Paris; died March 1889, in Paris.
Sculptor.
Vincent Feugère des Forts was a pupil of Heim and Duseigneur. He exhibited at the Paris Salon from 1849 to 1870 and received medals in 1864 and 1866 and also at the Exposition Universelle of 1867.

He is remembered for his *Le denier de la veuve, St Clotilde, Marguerite, Woman from Castel-Madama, Negress, Goatherd, Archer, Christian Martyr, Dr. Bouchet* and *Christ on the Cross surrounded by the Virgin, St. John and Mary Magdalen.*
MUSEUMS AND GALLERIES:
CHÂLONS-EN-CHAMPAGNE: *Beethoven* - CHARTRES: *Abel, Dead.*

FEUGEREUX, Jean
French, 20th century.
Born 25 September 1923, in Fresnay-l'Évêque (Eure-et-Loir); died 1992.
Painter, engraver. Landscapes.
Jean Feugereux exhibited from 1944, both in the provinces and in Paris at the Salon Comparaisons, on whose committee he sat from 1954.

Essentially a landscape artist, he also produced compositions involving figurative elements and objects.
BIBLIOGRAPHY:
'Les gravures sur bois' in *Art et Métiers du Livre* no. 196, periodical, Paris, 1996.

FEUGEY, Jean
French, 20th century.
Born in Douai.
Painter.
Jean Feugey exhibited at the Salon d'Automne.

FEUILLAGE
French, 18th century.
Active in Paris in 1718.
Painter, sculptor.

FEUILLAS-CREUSY, Caroline
French, 19th century.
Born 19 March 1861, in Paris.
Painter, miniaturist.
Feuillas-Creusy was a pupil of Henner and Jules Lefebvre, and was also advised by Donzel and Camino. She started by exhibiting portraits on ivory, in 1880 and 1882. She became a member of the Société des Artistes Français in 1883 and received a bronze medal at the Exposition Universelle in Paris in 1889.

FEUILLAT, Julien
Flemish School, 18th century.
Born in Namur.
Sculptor.

FEUILLAT, Marcel
Swiss, 20th century.
Born 2 March 1896, in Geneva.
Sculptor, goldsmith, enameller.
Feuillat was a student at the École des Arts Industriels in Geneva. He took part in the decoration of the Maurice Denis Chapel at St-Germain-en-Laye.

FEUILLATE, Raymond
French, 20th century.
Born 13 May 1901, in Neuilly-sur-Seine; died 4 July 1971, in Neuilly-sur-Seine.
Painter, illustrator. Figures, landscapes. Designs for tapestries.
Raymond Feuillate studied at the École des Arts Décoratifs in Paris. He exhibited regularly at the Salon des Artistes Indépendants from 1919, at the Salon d'Automne from 1924 and at the Salon de la Société Nationale des Beaux-Arts from 1927. He was active in the Salon Populiste, of which he was vice-president from 1951. In 1933, the Prix de la Ville de Paris award enabled him to visit North Africa, travelling around Algeria, Tunisia and Morocco. In 1936, his canvas *Horsemen* was on display for France during the Berlin Olympic Games.
AUCTION RECORDS:
VERSAILLES, 21 Oct 1990, *Tugs on the River* (1928, oil on canvas, 18 x 22 ins / 46 x 55 cm) FRF 4,200. PARIS, 12 March 1999, *Young Moroccan Woman* (1933, oil on canvas, 29 x 21 ins / 73 x 54 cm) FRF 33,000.

FEUILLATRE, Eugène
French, 19th - 20th century.
Born 30 April 1870, in Dunkirk; died 17 September 1916.
Sculptor.
Eugène Feuillatre exhibited in Paris at the Salon des Artistes Français, of which he became an associate member in 1899. He gained an honourable mention in 1898, a third-class medal in 1904 and a second-class medal in 1905.

FEUILLET
French, 19th century.
Active in Paris.
Painter (porcelain).

FEUILLET, François
French, 17th century.
Active in Paris c. 1660.
Painter.

François Feuillet seems to have specialised in the painting of monuments, and received the title of painter to the king.

FEUILLET, G.
French, 17th century.
Active in Paris c. 1675.
Draughtsman.

G. Feuillet received commissions for the king's buildings.

FEUILLET, Jean Baptiste
French, 18th century.
Died 1806, in Provins.
Active in Paris.
Sculptor.

Jean Baptiste Feuillet was the director of the Académie de St-Luc. In 1762 he exhibited *Artemis Swallowing the Ashes of her Husband so as to Act, Herself, as his Tomb* and several low reliefs. In 1774 he showed *The Glory of the Princes* (statue of a winged woman), *Painting, Architecture, Music* (statues in terracotta) and *Modesty* (statue).

FEUILLOUX, Camille
French, 20th century.
Born in Chessy (Seine-et-Marne).
Engraver (etching).

Camille Feuilloux studied under Théophile Chauvel. She exhibited in Paris at the Salon des Artistes Français, of which she was a member from 1901. She received an honourable mention in 1908.

FEULARD, Alexandre Louis
French, 19th century.
Born 23 February 1813, in Paris; died 1886.
Painter.

Alexandre Feulard entered the École des Beaux-Arts on 2 April 1831, and was taught by Gros and Millet. He was best known for his miniatures. He exhibited at the Salon from 1840 to 1882. He was the son of Jean-Pierre Feulard.

MUSEUMS AND GALLERIES:
LE HAVRE: miniatures.

FEULARD, Jean Pierre
French, 19th century.
Born 15 November 1790, in Châteaudun; died 12 May 1849, in Le Havre.
Painter.

Jean Feulard was a pupil of Aubry. He exhibited miniatures at the Paris Salon from 1819 to 1848.

MUSEUMS AND GALLERIES:
LE HAVRE: *Portrait of Joseph Morlent.*

AUCTION RECORDS:
PARIS, 27-29 May 1929, *Portrait of Young Man in Uniform with Blue Lapels* (miniature, no forename given) FRF 460. PARIS, 24 March 1947, *Portrait of Changarnier, Wearing Staff Officer's Uniform* (1828, miniature) FRF 3,100.

FEULIEN, Marc
Belgian, 20th century.
Born 1943, in Courcelles.
Sculptor, potter.

Feulien attended the Académie des Beaux-Arts in Charleroi, and later became professor of ceramics there. He has participated in international group exhibitions. He won a medal in Gdansk in 1973, and a gold medal at the international competition for ceramics in Faenza in 1976. He is a member of the Académie Internationale de la Céramique in Geneva.

MUSEUMS AND GALLERIES:
BRUSSELS (Collection de l'État Belge) - FAENZA (Mus. Internazionale delle Ceramiche).

FEURE, Georges de, pseudonym of Van Sluijters Georges Joseph
French, 19th - 20th century.
Born 6 September 1868, in Paris, to Belgian and Dutch parents; died 26 November 1943, in Paris.
Painter (gouache), watercolourist, engraver, lithographer, sculptor, draughtsman, illustrator, designer. Scenes with figures, figures, landscapes. Designs for tapestries, and stained glass windows.
Symbolism, Japonisme, Art Nouveau.

Born of Belgian and Dutch roots, Georges de Feure studied under Jules Chéret in Paris in 1890. He contributed drawings for the periodicals *Le Courrier français, Le Boulevard* and *L'Image*. He illustrated, among other works, *The Gate to Dreams* by Marcel Schwob in 1899, he created an engraving after Georges Rodenbach's novel *Bruges-the-Dead*, and he produced posters for Loïe Füller in *Jeanne d'Arc* (*Joan of Arc*) for the Salon des Cent. As symbolism ebbed away, he became a key figure in the introduction of a Art Nouveau, a style he employed in the *Art Nouveau* pavilion for the 1900 International Fair. He was also the decorator of the cabaret *Le Chat Noir*, a famous artists' haunt. He formulated new shapes for furniture in what has become known as 'Modern Style', painted china and taught at the École des Beaux-Arts in Paris. In 1903, the Gallery Bing brought out a compilation of his works. A retrospective of his work was shown in the Van Gogh Museum in Amsterdam in 1993, then in 1995 at the Musée Départemental Maurice Denis in St-Germain-en Laye.

Although much of his energy was directed at interior decoration, his tapestry *La Fée Caprice* (*Caprice the Fairy*) was exhibited in 1896. He designed functional objects that are a credit to his times and style. He produced at least 400 lithographs, and he was a prolific painter, exhibiting with the Secession of Munich. Though he treated a variety of subjects, the female figure takes pride of place in his work; often shown in a contemplative mood, his women meet symbolist purposes in such compositions as *In Search of Infinite*, or *Red Vision*, an 1892 piece showing a forest scene he frequently returned to in his early works but the subtitle of which (*Woman in the Woods*) hardly accounts for the terror inhabiting the woman - a task left to the reds symbolistically pervading the scene.

BIBLIOGRAPHY:
Weisberg, Gabriel P., '*La Femme mystérieuse de Georges de Feure: une étude des sources symbolistes dans les écrits de Charles Baudelaire et de Georges Rodenbach*' in *Gazette des Beaux-Arts*, periodical, Paris, October 1974. Osterwalder, Marcus (ed.), *Dictionnaire des illustrateurs 1800-1914*, Ides et Calendes, Neuchâtel, 1989.

AUCTION RECORDS:
PARIS, 2 Dec 1946, *Dream*, FRF 8,000; *Young Woman Holding Flowers*, FRF 6,000; *Dance on the Waterside*; *Young Woman on the Riverside* (two gouaches) FRF 3,500. PARIS, 3 Dec 1969, *Seascape*, FRF 7,850. PARIS, 25 May 1970, *In Search of the Infinite* (watercolour) FRF 11,500. PARIS, 15 Nov 1971, *Stroll in the Woods* (watercolour and gouache) FRF 51,000. PARIS, 25 Nov 1974, *Woman in the Black Hat*, FRF 44,500. PARIS, 14 June 1976, *The Painter and his Model* (gouache, 26 x 28 ins / 66.3 x 71.4 cm) FRF 22,000. PARIS, 8 Dec 1976, *Country Scene* (oil on panel, 32 3/4 x 16 1/2 ins / 83

x 42 cm) FRF 3,100. PARIS, 25 Nov 1977, *Woman in the Undergrowth* (gouache, 23¼ x 28¼ ins / 59 x 72 cm) FRF 36,000. ENGHIEN-LES-BAINS, 28 Oct 1979, *The Spring* (gouache, watercolour and charcoal, 25½ x 9 ins / 65 x 23 cm) FRF 10,000. LYONS, 29 Oct 1981, *Portrait Supposed to be of Madame de Feure* (charcoal heightened with gouache and watercolour/paper, 16¼ x 11 ins / 41 x 28 cm) FRF 5,100. LONDON, 30 June 1983, *Return of the Knight* (1897, coloured lithograph, 12¾ x 10 ins / 32.6 x 25.5 cm) GBP 600. LONDON, 6 Dec 1983, *Fisherman and Windmill* (c. 1906, oil and tempera/canvas, 13 x 18¼ ins / 33 x 46.5 cm) GBP 4,000. VERSAILLES, 11 Dec 1983, *Elegant Lady at the Paddock* (gouache and watercolour, 12½ x 6 ins / 32 x 15.5 cm) FRF 28,000. ENGHIEN-LES-BAINS, 25 Oct 1987, *Lady in a Big Black Hat* (oil on canvas, 23½ x 28¼ ins / 60 x 72 cm) FRF 460,000; *The Botanist* (1894, gouache, 35½ x 28 ins / 90 x 71 cm) FRF 220,000. PARIS, 28 Nov 1988, *The Forbidden Fruit* (1895, watercolour and gouache/paper/canvas, 28½ x 22¾ ins / 72.5 x 58 cm) FRF 145,000. PARIS, 21 Nov 1989, *Circus Folks* (gouache, 13¾ x 9½ ins / 35 x 24 cm) FRF 41,000. LONDON, 1 Dec 1989, *L'Écu du diable* (black ink and gouache, frame designed by the artist, 26¾ x 19 ins / 68 x 48 cm) GBP 46,200. MONACO, 3 Dec 1989, *A Visit* (watercolour and gouache, 14½ x 11 ins / 37 x 28 cm) FRF 111,000. PARIS, 29 March 1990, *Madman with an Apple* (pencil, Indian ink and watercolour, 13¼ x 8¼ ins / 33.5 x 21 cm) FRF 5,000. PARIS, 10 June 1990, *Woman and Bird* (lithograph/vellum) FRF 5,200. PARIS, 6 Nov 1992, *Couple* (gouache/card, 18 x 15 ins / 46 x 38 cm) FRF 20,000. PARIS, 23 June 1993, *Femme Fatale* (oil on canvas, 23½ x 28¾ ins / 60 x 73 cm) FRF 180,000. PARIS, 24 June 1994, *Bungalow in Indonesia* (oil on panel, 29¼ x 46 ins / 74 x 116 cm) FRF 600,000. LONDON, 16 Nov 1994, *Glassworks* (oil on canvas, 109¾ x 40¼ ins / 279 x 102 cm) GBP 5,175. PARIS, 21 Dec 1994, *Elegant Ladies* (gouache, 13¼ x 9¾ ins / 33.5 x 25 cm) FRF 107,000. PARIS, 6 March 1996, *Solitude* (gouache, 17 x 10 ins / 43 x 25.5 cm) FRF 45,000. PARIS, 14 Oct 1996, *Mad Woman* (1901-1903, gouache/paper, 25¼ x 8¾ ins / 64 x 22.5 cm) FRF 50,000. PARIS, 29 Nov 1996, *Seascape* (gouache, 12½ x 17½ ins / 31.5 x 44.5 cm) FRF 7,000. PARIS, 16 May 1997, *Fine Sand Quarries near l'Isle-Adam* (watercolour heightened with gouache, 16 x 21 ins / 40.5 x 52.5 cm) FRF 10,000. PARIS, 8 April 1998, *Original Lithographs* (c. 1898, lithograph, poster) FRF 28,000. PARIS, 10 Dec 1998, *Candle Holder in the Shape of a Floral Stem Resting on a Broad Leafy Corolla* (a pair, h. 11¾ ins / 30 cm and 12 ins/30.5 cm) FRF 7,800. PARIS, 30 June 1999, *Fisherman* (c. 1891, oil on canvas, 18 x 32 ins / 46 x 81 cm) FRF 40,000. PARIS, 6 Dec 1999, *Dispatch* (colour lithograph, 78 x 31 ins / 198 x 80 cm) FRF 38,000. PARIS, 12 Dec 2001, *On the Bridge* (gouache, 12 x 7 ins / 30 x 19 cm) FRF 31,000. NEUILLY, 26 March 2002, *Female Nude with Chrysanthemums* (Indian ink heightened with colour pencil, 16 x 10 ins / 41 x 26 cm) EUR 3,500. PARIS, 3 June 2002, *Woman's Face before Opulent Foliage and Fantastic Birds* (c. 1893, gouache on paper on canvas, 39 x 32 ins / 100 x 81 cm) EUR 40,000. LONDON, 18 Nov 2003, *Nuns and the Devil* (gouache over pencil, 14 x 10 ins / 35 x 25 cm) GBP 3,800. PARIS, 27 Nov 2003, *Corsican Shore* (oil on canvas, 26 x 32 ins / 65 x 81 cm) EUR 8,500. BERLIN, 11 June 2004, *Original Lithographs* (1896, colour lithograph, 23 x 17 ins / 59 x 43 cm) EUR 6,000.

FEURER, Michael

French, 19th century.

Born 11 October 1862, in Merzweiler.

Painter, glass painter.

Feurer studied in Strasbourg then in Munich, and worked in Germany.

FEURER, René

Swiss, 20th century.

Born 1940, in St Gall.

Painter.

Feurer paints on large formats, placed flat on the ground. He covers the surface of the canvases with a pigmentary material, deliberately thick, which might appear monochrome if it were not 'flecked' with several very closely related tones. He claims that this technique is linked to the painting of fields by Mark Rothko or to Barnett Newman or Tobey. Where Rothko defines his fields by delicately shaded-off lines, Feurer marks off precise geometric areas on the surface of the painting, generally vertical rectangles sometimes surmounted by a triangle, as in the compartmentalising of ancient polyptychs. In fact he often paints diptychs or triptychs, which he explains has a reference to Fra Angelico. His painting obviously originates in a mystical spirituality, finding its inspiration as much in the Christian contemplation of the Quattrocento, as in the Zen meditation of the Pacific Coast painters.

Feurer has taken part in group exhibitions since 1965, notably: 1979 at the Musée Rath in Geneva, 1981 *La lumière et sa peinture* (*Light and Its Painting*) at the Centre d'Art Visuel in Geneva, 1982 Bilbao, 1986 Montreal, 1987 Salon de Montrouge. He has also shown his paintings in solo exhibitions, including, since the first in 1980 in Paris: 1981 Galerie Numaga in Auvernier-Neuchâtel; 1984 Centre d'Art Contemporain in Geneva; 1988-1989 *Sur les chemins de St-Jacques-de-Compostelle en Limousin* (*On the Roads to Santiago in Limousin*), a travelling exhibition shown in churches in Limoges 1989 Musée Municipal of the Diocese of Limoges, in Dorat, Eymoutiers, St-Léonard-de-Noblat, Solignac and Moustiers de St-Yrieix-la-Perche; 1990 Galerie Franka Berndt in Paris and 1992 in L'Isle-sur-la-Sorgue.

BIBLIOGRAPHY:

Tronche, Anne, '*René Feurer*' in *Opus international* n° 80, periodical, Paris, spring 1981. Bataillon, Françoise, '*Connection 87*' in *Art Press*, periodical, Paris, 1987. Magnol, Jacques, '*René Feurer, tout art digne de ce nom est religieux*' in *Impact* n° 241, periodical, Geneva, 1988. *René Feure, peintures 1978-1987. Sur les chemins de Saint-Jacques-de-Compostelle en Limousin*, travelling exhibition catalogue, Musée de Limoges, Limoges, 1988. '*Feurer rentre en collégiales*' in *La Croix*, periodical, Paris, 21 February 1989.

FEURGARD, Julie. See **DELANCE-FEURGARD**

FEURSTEIN, Leopold

Austrian, 18th century.

Born 1725, in Bezau; died 11 March 1807, in Bezau.

Sculptor (wood).

Feurstein decorated, among others, the church at Schnepfau.

FEUSTINGH, Johann

German, 17th century.

Active in Coesfeld (North Rhine-Westphalia) at the end of the 17th century.

Glass painter.

FEUTER, Lowis de

Dutch, 17th century.

Born to a family originally from The Hague.

Painter.

In 1639 he lived in Amsterdam.

FEUZ, Werner

Swiss, 20th century.

Born 10 June 1882, in Seftigen.

Active in Gsteigwiter, near Interlaken.

Painter. Figures, landscapes.

Feuz studied in Bern and Geneva, and exhibited in Bern in 1902 and 1903.

FEVER, Johannes Le. See **LE FEVER**

FÉVIN, Jean de. See **JEAN DE FÉVIN**

FEVOLA, Félix Pascal
French, 20th century.
Born 16 September 1882, in Poissy; died 7 February 1953, in Paris.
Sculptor.

Felix Fevola studied under Jean-Antoine Injalbert, and may have been taught by Gabriel Thomas. He exhibited in Paris at the Salon des Artistes Français, receiving an honourable mention in 1906 and a gold medal hors concours in 1927.

FÈVRE, Adam. See **FAVRE**

FÈVRE, Paul
French, 20th century.
Born in Méry-sur-Seine.
Painter. Landscapes.

Paul Fèvre exhibited in Paris at the Salon des Artistes Français and at the Salon des Indépendants from 1931.

FÈVRE, Simone
French, 20th century.
Born September 1915, in Langres.
Painter, pastellist. Figures, landscapes, still-lifes.

Simone Fèvre studied at the École des Beaux-Arts in Dijon. She has shown in collective exhibitions - in particular, in Paris at the Salon des Artistes Français, of which she was made a member. She taught at the École de Dessin in Langres.

Fèvre treats her figures in pastels and paints her landscapes and still-lifes. Dijon Museum has acquired her drawing of a *Lacemaker* and, in her native Haute-Marne, Chaumont Museum owns two of her drawings of the old town.

FEVRET DE SAINT-MEMIN, Charles Balthasar Julien. See **SAINT-MEMIN Charles**

FÉVRIER, L. J.
Dutch, 18th century.
Active during the second half of the 18th century.
Painter (?), draughtsman (?).

Cordon engraved a *Portrait of the Theologian J. Willemsen* executed by L. J. Février.

FEXIS, Dimitri
Greek, 20th century.
Born in Athens.
Painter. Still-lifes.

Dimitri Fexis showed at the Salon de la Société Nationale in Paris in 1938.

FEY, Joseph. See **FAY**

FEYDEAU, Anne de
French, 19th century.
Born in Guingamp.
Miniaturist.

Anne de Feydeau became an associate of the Salon of the Société Nationale des Beaux-Arts in 1901, and showed works at the society's exhibitions.

FEYDEAU, Diane
French, 19th century.
Active at the end of the 19th century.
Painter, watercolourist. Flowers.

MUSEUMS AND GALLERIES:
DIEPPE: *Bunch of Flowers* (watercolour).

FEYEAU, Maurice
French, 19th century.
Born in Rochefort.
Painter. Seascapes.

MUSEUMS AND GALLERIES:
ROCHEFORT: *Seascape*.

FEYEN, Eugène, for Jacques Eugène
French, 19th - 20th century.
Born 13 November 1815, in Bey-sur-Seille (Meurthe-et-Moselle); died June 1908, in Bey-sur-Seille.
Painter. Portraits, genre scenes, landscapes with figures, seascapes.

Eugène Feyen was François Feyen-Perrin's elder brother. He was admitted at the École des Beaux-Arts in Paris in 1837, studying under Léon Cognet and Paul Delaroche. He exhibited at the Paris Salon from 1841 to 1882, obtaining medals in 1866 and 1880, and he was made a Chevalier of the Légion d'Honneur in 1881.

In 2003, he featured in the collective exhibition *Bretagne, terre des peintres* (*Brittany, Land of Painters*) at the Musée des Beaux-Arts in Vannes.

Feyen first produced portraits, then genre paintings. The Breton scenes he and his brother liked treating, and his predilection for Cancale fishermen, earned him public favour. In 1872, he received a public commission for the *Sea Gleaners*. He is remembered for *The Fisherman's Return*, *The Sailor's Betrothed*, and *The Fisherman's Soup*.

EUC.FEYEN

BIBLIOGRAPHY:
Delouche, Denise/Michaud, Jean-Marc, et al., *Bretagne, terre des peintres*, exhibition catalogue, Musée des Beaux-Arts, Vannes, 2003.

MUSEUMS AND GALLERIES:
LILLE - MULHOUSE - NANCY: *Fishwives*; *Departure of the Fishermen* - RENNES: *Sailor*.

AUCTION RECORDS:
PARIS, 10 April 1899, *Mussel Pickers*, FRF 255. NEW YORK, 12-14 April 1909, *Harvest*, USD 70. PARIS, 29-30 Dec 1924, *Shrimp Pickers*, FRF 250. PARIS, 16 Dec 1925, *After Bathing*, FRF 500. PARIS, 15 June 1934, *Country Girl Sitting on the Seafront*, FRF 320. PARIS, 5 Dec 1941, *Cancale Girls Shell Picking*, FRF 420. VIENNA, 16 March 1971, *Net Menders*, ATS 55,000. COLOGNE, 15 June 1973, *Dunes*, DEM 5,000. VERSAILLES, 11 May 1975, *Waiting for the Tide* (oil on canvas, 26 x 37 1/2 ins / 66 x 95 cm) FRF 3,000. LONDON, 20 April 1978, *Girls Shell Picking* (oil on canvas, 24 x 38 ins / 61 x 96.5 cm) GBP 1,100. COLOGNE, 21 March 1980, *Shell Pickers* (oil on canvas, 22 x 31 1/2 ins / 56 x 80 cm) DEM 13,000. LONDON, 12 Oct 1984, *The Wash House at La Houle* (oil on canvas, 36 1/2 x 25 1/2 ins / 92.6 x 64.7 cm) GBP 2,800. BOURG-EN-BRESSE, 2 March 1986, *Oyster Picker* (oil on panel, 12 1/2 x 9 1/2 ins / 32 x 24 cm) FRF 34,000. NÎMES, 25 Feb 1989, *Washerwomen* (oil on panel, 9 x 19 3/4 ins / 23 x 50 cm) FRF 20,000. PARIS, 5 March 1989, *Young Girls with Baskets Full of Apples* (oil on canvas, 37 1/4 x 25 1/2 ins / 94.5 x 65 cm) FRF 25,000. VERSAILLES, 19 Nov 1989, *Seascape* (oil on card, 7 x 9 3/4 ins / 18 x 25 cm) FRF 7,500. PARIS, 13 Dec 1989, *Shell Picker* (oil on panel, 6 x 9 3/4 ins / 15 x 25 cm) FRF 38,000. VERSAILLES, 7 June 1990, *Breton Women Awaiting the Fishermen's Return* (oil on card, 12 1/2 x 20 ins / 32 x 50.5 cm) FRF 46,000. PAU, 21 July 1990, *Cancale Girls Back from Fishing* (oil on canvas, 35 1/2 x 59 ins / 90 x 150 cm) FRF 228,000. LONDON, 5 Oct 1990, *Shell Pickers* (oil on canvas, 24 x 38 1/2 ins / 61 x 97.8 cm) GBP 3,300. PARIS, 24 May 1991, *Apple Picking* (oil on canvas, 22 x 26 ins / 56 x 66 cm) FRF 28,000. NEW YORK, 15 Oct 1991, *Street Players Asleep* (oil on panel, 7 1/2 x 10 1/4 ins / 19 x 26 cm) USD 3,080. PARIS, 12 Dec 1991, *Girl on the Seafront* (oil on card, 12 1/2 x 19 3/4 ins / 32 x 50 cm) FRF 26,000. PARIS, 5 Nov 1993, *Boats on the Shore* (oil on panel, 6 1/4 x 9 3/4 ins / 16 x 25 cm) FRF 12,000. NEW YORK, 19 Jan 1995, *Departure of the Fishermen* (oil on canvas, 37 1/4 x 26 ins / 94.6 x 66 cm) USD 6,900. PARIS, 23 April 1996, *Women Fishing* (oil on canvas, 37 1/2 x 26 ins / 95 x 66 cm) FRF 20,000.

FEYEN, Justin Jean François
French, 19th century.
Born in Bar-sur-Seine.
Painter.

Feyen exhibited *Cancale Cliffs* and *Twilight Song* at the Salon in 1877 and 1878.

FEYEN-PERRIN, François Nicolas Augustin
French, 19th century.
Born 12 April 1826, in Bey-sur-Seille (Meurthe-et-Moselle); died 14 October 1888, in Paris.
Painter, draughtsman. Religious subjects, figures, nudes, portraits, genre scenes, local scenes, landscapes with figures, waterscapes, seascapes.
Symbolism.

Feyen-Perrin entered the École des Beaux-Arts in Paris in 1848 where he was taught by Léon Cogniet and Adolphe Yvon. He exhibited at the Paris Salon from 1848 to 1882, receiving medals in 1865 and 1867. His works created a sensation at the Salon and for many years, he was one of France's most popular painters. Along with his brother Jacques Eugène Feyen, he was the appointed painter of Cancale fishermen. His constant preoccupation with his subjects often reveals an artificial element in his art. Supposedly an artist devoted to realism his female figures are, however, manifestly too elegant ever to have been the wives of fishermen exposed to the rough work of the sea. Works include *Women from the Ile de Batz Waiting for the Rowing Boat to Go by, Fisherman's Wife, Cancale Woman at the Spring, Parisian Woman at Cancale, Fishing on Foot, Corniche Road, Knitter by the Seaside, Return to the Cottage,* and also *Charon's Boat, Wealth of the Arétin, Old Dance, Lesson in Anatomy, The Damned.* Feyen-Perrin's work was not limited to the customs of Cancale and its people and he painted the full range of subjects. Some paintings are historical: *Discovery of the Body of Charles the Bold after the Battle of Nancy,* or depict religious history: *Deposition,* mythology: *Charon's Boat,* allegory: *Elegy,* events: *Shipwreck of the Evening Star,* literary history: *Wealth of Aretino,* or celebrate female beauty: *Nude Lying on a Beach. Old Dance,* at the Chateau of Cormatin, near Cluny, was acquired by Raoul Gunsbourg, then director of the Opera at Monte Carlo, and a fervent collector, who owned the chateau from 1898 onwards. The painting was apparently seen by Henri Matisse, probably at an exhibition before its acquisition and not during the lifetime of Feyen-Perrin, who exhibited at the Salon only until 1882 (Matisse was born in 1869). Matisse would have recalled the rhythmic garland of naked young women when he created the various versions of *La Danse* (*The Dance*) in 1910. For Feyen-Perrin, as grace became compatible with his subject, his work took on a new dimension. Stylistically closer to Symbolism than to Impressionism, he found his place in history with a characteristic style which bears witness to the tastes of the bourgeoisie at that time.

A. Feyen-Perrin

BIBLIOGRAPHY:

Delouche, Denise/Michaud, Jean-Marc, et al., *Bretagne, terre des peintres,* exhibition catalogue, Musée des Beaux-Arts, Vannes, 2003.

MUSEUMS AND GALLERIES:

AIX-EN-PROVENCE (Mus. Granet): *Parisian Woman in Cancale* - ANGERS: *Shipwreck of the Evening Star* - ARRAS: *Cancale Women at the Seaside* - ÉPINAL (Mus. départemental d'Art ancien et contemporain): *Elegy* - LE MANS (Musée de Mans): *Coming-Back from Fishing* (1874, oil on canvas) - MOULINS: *Childhood of the Ship's Boy* - NANCY (MBA): *Charon's Boat; Deposition; Aretino; Discovery of the Body of Charles the Bold after the Battle of Nancy* - PARIS (Mus. d'Orsay): *Return from Fishing, Cancale* - RHEIMS (MBA): *Return of the Oyster Catchers* - TOULON: *Song* - TOURS (MBA): *The Knitter of Canale* (1882, oil on canvas) - TROYES: *Sketch.*

AUCTION RECORDS:

PARIS, 6-7 April 1892, *Cancale Woman,* FRF 330. PARIS, 27 Feb 1893, *Cancale Fisherwoman,* FRF 600; *Harbour at Dusk,* FRF 700. NEW YORK, 14 Nov 1903, *Rising Tide,* USD 190. PARIS, 18 Dec 1922, *Death of Charles the Bold,* FRF 190; *Portrait of Mr C. Lepère,* FRF 360. PARIS, 23 Feb 1925, *Portrait of Juana Romani,* FRF 200; *Model with Red Background,* FRF 1,050. PARIS, 5 May 1928, *Countrywoman and Dog by a River,* FRF 600. PARIS, 13 May 1942, *Nude in the Forest* (sketch) FRF 620. PARIS, 24 Nov 1944, *Three Fisherwomen on Donkeys, Returning from Fishing,* FRF 2,200. PARIS, July 1946, *Fishermen's Wives and Merchant at the Port,* FRF 11,800; *Nude Lying by the Port,* FRF 10,000. PARIS, 12-13 March 1947, *Little Girl in Grey Dress* (1823) FRF 2,300. PARIS, 16 March 1976, *Return of the Fishermen* (oil on canvas, 39 1/2 x 28 3/4 ins / 100.5 x 73 cm) FRF 3,000. PARIS, 27 April 1983, *Return from Fishing* (charcoal, 78 3/4 x 54 3/4 ins / 200 x 139 cm) FRF 11,500. NEW YORK, 19 Oct 1984, *Awaiting the Return of the Fishermen* (oil on canvas, 65 x 87 ins / 165 x 221 cm) USD 3,500. CANNES, 21 July 1987, *Fisherman's Wife as a Child, by the Sea* (oil on canvas, 49 1/4 x 71 1/4 ins / 125 x 181 cm) FRF 56,000. CALAIS, 28 Feb 1988, *Dance Scene* (1860, oil on canvas) FRF 11,500. PARIS, 15 April 1988, *Fishing on Foot* (oil on canvas, 32 1/4 x 23 1/4 ins / 82 x 59 cm) FRF 14,600. STOCKHOLM, 29 April 1988, *Young Girls at the Beach,* SEK 15,500. MORLAIX, 31 Oct 1988, *Countrywoman* (oil on paper remounted/canvas, 78 3/4 x 44 1/2 ins / 200 x 113 cm) FRF 19,000. NEW YORK, 23 Feb 1989, *Return from Oyster Fishing* (oil on canvas, 51 1/2 x 38 1/2 ins / 130.8 x 98.1 cm) USD 6,600. PARIS, 29 Nov 1989, *Cancale Women* (oil on canvas, 33 x 19 ins / 84 x 48 cm) FRF 28,500. NEW YORK, 21 May 1991, *Fishermen on River Bank* (oil on canvas, 29 1/2 x 42 ins / 75 x 106.8 cm) USD 2,420. NEW YORK, 17 Oct 1991, *Return from Fishing* (1877, oil on canvas). PARIS, 2 Nov 1992, *Cockle Harvesters* (oil on canvas, 32 x 25 1/2 ins / 81 x 65 cm) FRF 8,000. NEW YORK, 28 May 1993, *Looking across the Sea* (oil on canvas, 24 x 18 ins / 61 x 45.7 cm) USD 1,150. PARIS, 18 Nov 1994, *Young Country Girl, Sitting* (1888, oil on canvas, 28 1/4 x 20 1/2 ins / 72 x 52 cm) FRF 6,000. PARIS, 6 March 1996, *Fishermen's Wives* (oil on panel, 9 1/2 x 12 3/4 ins / 24 x 32.5 cm) FRF 5,000. PARIS, 16 Dec 1996, *Country Woman Lying on the Beach* (oil on canvas, 2 1/4 ins / 6.000 cm) FRF 6,000. RHEIMS, 24 Oct 1999, *Shell-collector on the Beach* (oil on board, 16 x 13 ins / 41 x 32 cm) FRF 25,500. GENEVA, 14 Nov 1999, *Young Peasant with a Donkey* (1881, oil on canvas, 21 x 16 ins / 54 x 41 cm) CHF 5,000. PARIS, 23 May 2000, *Self-portrait* (oil on canvas, 16 x 12 ins / 41 x 31 cm) FRF 20,000. PARIS, 28 June 2000, *Portrait, presumed to be of Manet* (oil on panel, 13 x 11 ins / 33 x 28 cm) FRF 21,000. BREST, 16 Dec 2001, *Fisherwomen on the Beach* (1878, oil on canvas, 28 x 20 ins / 72 x 51 cm) FRF 22,000. CALAIS, 15 Dec 2002, *Return of the Fisherwomen* (oil on panel, 13 x 17 ins / 32 x 42 cm) EUR 4,100. CALAIS, 14 Dec 2003, *Nude Reclining by a River* (oil on panel, 6 x 9 ins / 15 x 22 cm) EUR 1,800.

FEYENS, Augustin Joseph
Belgian, 19th century.
Born 1789, in Turnhait; died 6 November 1854, in Brussels.
Sculptor.

Augustin Joseph Feyens was a pupil at the academies in Antwerp and Godecharle. At the Brussels Salon in 1811 he exhibited a bust of Napoleon and in 1816 a statue of *Ariadne Abandoned* which attracted considerable attention. In Paris he worked on the Arc de Triomphe and on the statue of Henri IV on the Pont-Neuf. He also exhibited busts in Brussels.

FEYERABEND, Augustin
Swiss, 18th century.
Born 1745; died 1790.
Active in Basel.
Painter, decorative artist.

Augustin Feyerabend was the brother of Samuel and Franz Feyerabend. Almost all his works are landscapes and copies of reliefs.

FEYERABEND, Benedikt
Austrian, 19th century.
Born 1792, in Vienna; died 9 May 1825, in Vienna.
Painter.

FEYERABEND, Franz
Swiss, 18th century.
Born 1755, in Basel; died 1800, in Basel.
Painter (gouache), watercolourist, caricaturist, engraver.

Franz Feyerabend gave up the study of sculpture and decorative painting and became a portrait artist in around 1780, and then a caricaturist. His cartoons of the private lives of the bailiffs of Basel, published in around 1798, are the most well known of his works. His engravings include 26 illustrations of uniforms, produced in 1792.

MUSEUMS AND GALLERIES:
COLMAR: gouaches.

FEYERABEND, Jean Jacob
German, 18th century.
Active at the beginning of the 18th century in Danzig (now Gdansk, Poland).
Draughtsman.

Feyerabend probably came from a German family, although he is not the same person as the following artist.

FEYERABEND, Jean Jacob
Swiss, 18th century.
Born in the 18th century, in Basel.
Painter.

FEYERABEND, Johann Rudolff
Swiss, 19th century.
Born 1779, in Basel; died 1814, in Basel.
Painter, watercolourist. Portraits, flowers.

The son of Franz Feyerabend, Johann Rudolff followed the same profession as his father. He painted in gouache and watercolour, and left among others a landscape with figures, kept by the art association of Basel. An engraving in his style *The Dance of the Dead in Basel* was drawn from life.

AUCTION RECORDS:
PARIS, 29-30 Nov and 1 Dec 1927, *Still-life* (gouache, attributed) FRF 1,000. PARIS, 11 Oct 2002, *Still-lifes* (gouache, a pair, 6 x 8 ins / 15 x 20 cm) EUR 3,800. PARIS, 19 Dec 2002, *Still-lifes* (gouache, a pair, 7 x 9 ins / 17 x 22 cm) EUR 3,400. PARIS, 28 April 2004, *Still-lifes* (gouache, three, 6 x 8 ins / 15 x 21 cm) EUR 12,500.

FEYERABEND, Samuel
Swiss, 18th century.
Born 1746, in Basel; died 1787, in Basel.
Painter, gilder.

The brother of Franz Feyerabend, Samuel painted landscapes and decorations.

FEYERABEND, Sigmond
German, 16th century.
Born 1528, in Heidelberg (Baden-Württemberg); died 22 March 1590, in Frankfurt.
Painter, engraver.

Sigmond Feyerabend is mainly known as a publisher.

FEYGUINE, Grégoire
French, 20th century.
Born in Moscow.
Painter.

Grégoire Feyguine exhibited in Paris at the Salon des Indépendants in 1931 and 1932.

FEYHAMAN DURAN. See **DURAN Feyhaman**

FEYKEN, Jacob
Dutch, 17th century.
Active in Amsterdam.
Painter.

FEYSINGER, Jean
German, 16th century.
Painter.

FEYTAUD, Sophie Tavel (Mme)
French, 19th century.
Painter.

Feytaud exhibited portraits and genre scenes at the Paris Salon from 1835 to 1843.

MUSEUMS AND GALLERIES:
BORDEAUX: *Two Chimney-sweeps Sharing the Remains of a Meal* - VERSAILLES: *Portrait of the Surveyor the Marquess of Laplace*.

FEYTCH, G.S.
British, 19th century.
Born in England.
Active in London.
Painter. Figures.

G.S. Feytch exhibited in London from 1839 to 1847, notably at the Royal Academy, Suffolk Street and the British Institution.

FEYZDJOU, Choreh
Iranian, 20th century.
Born 1955, in Tehran; died 17 February 1996, in Paris.
Active in France from 1975.
Painter, draughtsman, sculptor, installation artist.
Neo-Conceptual Art.

Feyzdjou attended the national school of fine arts in Paris from 1975 onwards, at the same time as studying aesthetics at the Sorbonne. She displayed her work in various group exhibitions, including that at the Jeu de Paume gallery in Paris in 1994. Her work has also been shown in solo exhibitions: 1987 Hourian Art Gallery, Oakland; 1989 91 Quai de la Gare (91 Station Quay) Paris; 1992 Patricia Dorfmann gallery, Paris; 1992 Renate Schröder gallery, Cologne; 1993 Ludwig Museum, Koblenz; 1994 museum of contemporary art, St-Étienne; 1994 Kröller-Müller Museum, Otterlo, Holland; 1996 world of art gallery, Paris.

1994 was an important year for the artist, during which she had several exhibitions at prestigious locations. The work she presented at the Jeu de Paume in Paris had a dramatic and immediate impact. The exhibition area was filled with a large number of objects of various kinds that were grouped together according to their affinity of form. Heaped up against the walls or stored in installations of monumental dimensions, her installations comprised a multiplicity of canvases: stuck together in layers, heaped one on top of the other, unopened rolls of canvas, and some scrunched into balls and bundles. The rooms seemed as though they were jealous guardians of their contents. When closed they were covered with black pigment, carefully labelled 'Product of Chohreh Feyzdou' and the contents meticulously catalogued.

BIBLIOGRAPHY:
Choreh Feyzdjou, exhibition catalogue, Gal. nationale du Jeu de Paume, Paris, 1994.

FIACCO, Orlando, known as Il Moro
Italian, 16th century.

Born in Verona.
Active c. 1560.
Painter. History painting, religious subjects, portraits.
Orlando Fiacco was a pupil of Francesco Torbido. Vasari praised his portraits and Lanzi likened his paintings to those of Caravaggio.

MUSEUMS AND GALLERIES:
STOCKHOLM: *Portrait of Titian as an Old Man* - VERONA (Church of S Nazario): *Crucifixion; Ecce Homo.*

FIACRE, Fiacre
French, 17th century.
Died 1650, in Nancy.
Sculptor.

FIACRE, Martin
Belgian, 17th century.
Active in Liège.
Sculptor.
Martin Fiacre erected the tomb of Archbishop Reginard (died c. 1030) in the church of St-Laurent in Liège.

FIALA
German, 19th century.
Active in Berlin c. 1800.
Engraver.
The prints collection in Berlin has one of Fiala's prints.

FIALA, Jean
Austrian.
Painter (porcelain).
Worked in the Vienna porcelain factory.

FIALA, Sebastian
Austrian, 19th century.
Painter.
Fiala worked at the Vienna workshop from 1800 until 1812.
MUSEUMS AND GALLERIES:
WROCLAW (Mus. of Arts and Crafts): Breakfast Service.

FIALA, Vaclav
Czech, 20th century.
Born in Prague.
Engraver.
A student of Svabinsky, Vaclav Fiala exhibited two lithographs (portraits) at the Salon des Artistes Français in Paris in 1928.

FIALETTI, Bartolomeo
Italian.
Engraver.
Referred to by Nagler as having engraved a plate representing *The Ceremony of Agnus Dei*, which is in fact by Odoardo Fialetti.

FIALETTI, Odoardo, real name: Édouard Viallet
Italian, 16th - 17th century.
Born 18 July 1573, in Bologna, of Savoyard descent; died 1638.
Painter, engraver. Religious subjects, portraits.
The engraver Bartolomeo Fialetti, first mentioned by Marolle and later by Nagler, never actually existed, and is really Odoardo Fialetti. Fialetti's father, born at Beaufort-sur-Dozon into a noble family of lawyers, was a professor at the university in Padua and later also dean and rector of the university in Bologna. Édouard Viallet, called Odoardo Fialetti, was a pupil of Giovanni Battista Cremonini in Bologna; he then went to Rome and to Venice, where he entered the studio of Tintoretto, and was made executor of Tintoretto's will. Fialetti himself trained several pupils, including François Nigri of Bologna.
Bartsch describes 243 plates engraved by Fialetti from his own drawings and from those of other masters, but in fact they numbered more than 300, including a series depicting different national costumes and the dress of various religious orders as well as various decorative motifs. The latter were much sought after in France in the 18th and early 19th century by the earthenware makers of Nevers, who drew inspiration from them.

BIBLIOGRAPHY:
Welshreed, S., *Venice after 1600', Italian Etchers of the Renaissance and Baroque*, exhibition catalogue, Museum of Fine Art, Boston, 1989.
MUSEUMS AND GALLERIES:
LONDON (Royal Collection): *Doge Leonardo Donato Giving Audience to Sir Henry Wootton* (attributed); *Portrait of the Doge* (four portraits, attributed) - MURANO (S Marco) - MURANO (Sant'Andrea).
AUCTION RECORDS:
LONDON, 6 Dec 1983, *St Sebastian* (etching, copied after Tintoretto, 9 1/2 x 6 ins / 24.3 x 15.2 cm) GBP 750. PARIS, 14 Dec 1989, *Portrait of the Doge Leonardo Donato* (oil on canvas, 24 1/4 x 18 ins / 61.5 x 46 cm) FRF 20,000.

FIALEX
French, 19th century.
Glass painter.
Fialex made stained glass windows for the churches of Moncresson and Gy-les-Nonnains (Loiret) and for the church of St-Gumgalois in Château-du-Loir (Sarthe).

FIALIN, Georges
French, 20th century.
Born in Moulins (Allier).
Painter. Landscapes.
Georges Fialin exhibited in Paris at the Salon des Artistes Indépendants. He is known for his St-Tropez landscapes.

FIAMBERTI, Tomaso
Italian, 16th century.
Died between 7 September 1524 and 21 January 1525, in Cesenare.
Active in Campione.
Sculptor.
Tomaso Fiamberti worked in the same studio as Giovanni Ricci de Sala, from whom he parted in 1508. He worked with Ricci and Giovanni Cenni on the tomb of Luffo Numaï in the church of S Maria de Servi, and with Vincenzo Gottardi on three marble statues in St Leonard's chapel in the cathedral at Cesena.

FIAMINGHI, Hermelindo
Brazilian, 20th century.
Born 1920.
Painter.
Neo-Constructivism.
The first São Paulo Biennale was held in 1951. It suddenly offered young Brazilian and Latin-American artists a panoramic overview of art during the first half of the 20th century, and the impact was considerable. First it was Constructivist art that caught the imagination of the new audience. By 1952 the Ruptura group, of which Fiaminghi was one of the first members, had been formed. The same year the São Paulo museum of modern art held an exhibition of work by the group, thus announcing the beginning of a transformation in Brazilian art. Fiaminghi later belonged to the New Trends group which first appeared in São Paulo in

1963. The aim of this group was to give Constructivism a new and longer-lasting dimension through optical phenomena and kinetics.

BIBLIOGRAPHY:
Catlin, S. L./Grieder, T., *Art in Latin America since Independence*, exhibition catalogue, Yale University AG, New Haven, 1966. Bardi, P.M., *Profile of the New Brazilian Art*, Rio de Janeiro, 1970. Harrison, M.J./Sá Rego, S. de, *Modern Brazilian Painting*, Albuquerque, 1980. Marino, J. (ed.), *Tradição e ruptura: Síntese de arte e cultura brasileiras*, São Paulo, 1984. Ades, Dawn, *Art in Latin America: The Modern Era, 1820-1980*, exhibition catalogue, Hayward Gallery, London, 1989. Mesquita, I., *'Brazil'* in *Latin American Art in the Twentieth century*, London, 1996 (ed. E. Sullivan).

FIAMINGHINO. See **EVERARDI Angiolo**

FIAMINGO. See also first name

FIAMMINGO, Giorgio
Italian, 17th century.
Active in Florence.
Painter, glass painter.

FIAMMINGO, Gualtieri
Italian, 17th century.
Active in Florence.
Painter, glass painter.

FIAMMINGO, Guglielmo
Italian, 17th century.
Painter.

Guglielmo Fiammingo lived in Bologna around 1660 and painted mostly landscapes after the manner of his teacher, Francesco Albani.

FIAMMINGO, Michele. See **DESUBLEO**

FIAMMINGO, Paolo. See **FRANCESCHI Paolo dei**

FIANI, Giovanni Francesco
Italian, 18th century.
Born 18th century, in Lucca.
Mosaicist.

Giovanni Francesco Fiani worked in St Peter's Basilica in Rome, and was partly responsible for the altarpiece of the Archangel Michael.

FIASCHI, Angelo
Italian, 18th century.
Painter, engraver.

Angelo Fiaschi was retained from 1757 to 1791 by the Doccia porcelain factory near Florence. Of his engravings, a *Body of Christ* and *Death of a Christian* are known.

FIASELLA, Domenico, called Il Sarzana or Sarazana
Italian, 17th century.
Born 1589, in Sarzana (Liguria); died 14 October 1669, in Genoa.
Painter, fresco artist. Religious subjects, portraits.

Domenico Fiasella was a goldsmith's son who, under the direction of his father, took up drawing at an early age. Before leaving for Genoa, Fiasella experimented with painting, making several copies of an Andrea del Sarto composition housed in the church in his home town of Sarzana. He went on to live and work in Rome for a period of ten years or so before returning to Genoa, where the Lomellini family commissioned him to decorate their palazzo and, subsequently, the vaults of their chapel of the Annunziata. He produced numerous paintings for churches in Genoa, among them a *St Anthony Discovering the Body of St Paul the Hermit*, which was described at length by Soprani and hailed by Lanzi as a genuine masterpiece. In 1635, Princess Maria of Mantua, who had always refused to have her portrait painted, summoned him to Mantua; Prince Carlo di Massa, the Duke of Mantua, tried in vain to retain his services on a more permanent basis. Fiasella declined the most generous of offers, however, preferring to retain his independence. A commission came from Spain, when Count Sirvelo retained Il Sarzana, as Fiasella was known, to paint a *Hero Mourning the Death of Leander*, a painting presented as a gift to the Spanish monarch and housed in the Buen Retiro.

Age did not appear to diminish Fiasella's capacities or constrain his output: in 1647, at the age of 74, he embarked on a composition depicting the plague that had ravaged Genoa that year; his *Miracles of St Facius* was completed in his 76th year.

Fiasella taught a relatively large number of pupils, among them his nephew (according to some sources) or (according to others) his brother-in-law Giovanni Battista Fiasella, who went on to paint a *Madonna and Saints* for the church of Our Lady of the Vines. He also taught Valerio Castello, Francesco Capuro and Gregorio de Ferrari (1644-1726), who painted in Genoa, Turin, Porto Maurizio and Marseilles; Luca Saltarello, a painter who died very young in Rome and whose *St Benedict Bringing a Peasant's Son back to Life* and *St Peter Healing the Lame* now hang in Genoa; and Giovanni Paolo Oderico and Francesco Merano, two young artists who died during the plague of 1657.

It has been said of Fiasella that he was influenced variously by Van Dyck, Caravaggio, Raphael, Strozza and the Carracci family of painters. This might suggest that he was something of an artistic chameleon. Perhaps so, but he did enjoy an outstanding reputation in his day.

MUSEUMS AND GALLERIES:
CARIGNANO (Church of S Maria): *Alessandro Sauli, Bishop of Genoa, Healing the Sick* (wrongly attributed to Cambiaso) - FLORENCE (Uffizi): *Head Studies for a Madonna* - GENOA: *St Mary; Marriage of Mary; Angelica and Medoro* - GENOA (Basilica di S Stefano): *Christ's Nativity* - GENOA (Chruch of SS Annunziata del Guastato, sacristy): *Marriage of the Virgin; Rest during the Flight into Egypt; Wedding Feast at Cana; Baptism of Christ; St Andrew Worshipping the Cross; St Paul Preaching; Isaac Going to Meet his Bride-to-Be; Jacob Blessing his Sons* (frescoes) - GENOA (Church of S Agostino): *St Thomas of Villeneuve* - GENOA (Church of S Ambrogio): *St Francis Xavier* - GENOA (Church of S Bartolomeo): *Miracles of St Facius* - GENOA (Church of S Domenico): *Christ among the Teachers; Madonna of Loreto; St Hyacinth before the Holy Virgin; St Vincent Ferrier* - GENOA (Church of S Francesco di Castellotto): *Death of the Virgin* - GENOA (Church of S Marco): *St Barbara* - GENOA (Church of S Maria del Monte sul Bisagno): *St Anne; St Francis Presenting The Nun's Habit to St Clare; Assumption* - GENOA (Church of S Sebastian): *Annunciation* - GENOA (Church of S Silvestro): *St Sylvester* - GENOA (Church of S Siro): *Assumption; Death of St Andrew of Avellino* - GENOA (Church of SS Cosma e S Damiano): *Souls in Purgatory* (monochrome painting) - MILAN (Church of S Maddalena): *Assumption* - MILAN (Diocesan Mus.): *Christ as a Child* - MILAN (Sacristy of L'Annunziata): *Esau Selling his Birthright* - PARMA: *Madonna and Three Saints* (red chalk) - PAVERANO SOPRA IL BISAGNO (Church of S Giovanni Decollato): *Life of St John the Baptist* (fresco) - SARZANA (Cathedral): *Massacre of the Innocents.*

AUCTION RECORDS:
MILAN, 29 Oct 1964, *Nativity*, ITL 1,200,000. LONDON, 24 March 1971, *Rebecca and Eliezer*, GBP 2,000. ROME, 27 March 1980, *La Negozione di San Petro* (oil on canvas, 48 x 67 1/4in/121 x 171cm) ITL 8,500,000. LONDON, 18 Nov 1982, *Martyrdom of St Andrew* (red chalk, 11 x 16 1/2in/27 x 42cm) GBP 2,200. MILAN, 27 Nov 1984, *The Drunkenness of Noah* (oil on canvas, 80 x 57 1/2in/203 x 146cm) ITL 20,000,000. ROME, 20 March 1986, *Adoration of the Shepherds* (oil on canvas, 4 3/4 x 61 3/4in/12 x 157cm) ITL 18,000,000. MILAN, 12

Dec 1988, *Judith and Holofernes* (oil on canvas, 46 x 51¼in/117 x 130cm) ITL 14,000,000. ROME, 13 April 1989, *Portrait of an Old Man (presumed to be Bernardino Barengo of Siena)* (oil on canvas, 28¾ x 22¾in/73 x 58cm) ITL 9,500,000. NEW YORK, 31 May 1991, *Carlo and Ubaldo Rescuing Rinaldo from the Charms of Armida* (oil on canvas, 73½ x 100¾in/186.7 x 255.9cm) USD 148,500. MILAN, 28 May 1992, *Judith with the Head of Holofernes* (oil on canvas, 45 x 51¼in/114 x 130cm) ITL 24,000,000. NEW YORK, Jan 1998, *Portrait of a Young Man with a Sketchbook* (oil on canvas, 40½ x 33½in/102.9 x 85.1cm) USD 101,500. VENICE, 16 June 2000, *Justice* (oil on canvas, 58 x 43 ins / 147 x 108 cm) ITL 63,000,000. LONDON, 6 July 2000, *The Stoning of St Stephen* (oil on canvas, 59 x 68 ins / 149 x 173 cm) GBP 20,000. NEW YORK, 23 May 2001, *Abduction of Helen* (oil on canvas, 74 x 81 ins / 189 x 206 cm) USD 27,500. LONDON, 13 Dec 2001, *Portrait of a Young Man with a Sketchbook* (oil on canvas, 41 x 33 ins / 103 x 85 cm) GBP 45,000. LONDON, 30 Oct 2002, *Queen Artemisia* (oil on canvas, 40 x 30 ins / 101 x 76 cm) GBP 8,000. LONDON, 9 July 2003, *Madonna and Child with St Dominic, St Catherine and St John the Baptist* (oil on canvas, 56 x 65 ins / 141 x 166 cm) GBP 45,000. GENOA, 26 Feb 2004, *Nativity* (oil on canvas, 59 x 47 ins / 150 x 120 cm) EUR 6,000. ROME, 16 June 2004, *Samson and Delilah* (oil on canvas, 48 x 83 ins / 121 x 211 cm) EUR 38,000.

FIASELLA, Giovanni Batista or Battista
Italian, 17th century.
Active in Genoa.
Painter.

Giovanni Batista Fiasella studied under his uncle Domenico Fiasella. He inherited his uncle's works in 1669, and bequeathed them to the city of Genoa when he died.

FIAT, Auguste
French, 19th century.
Born 19th century, in Taninges.
Painter.

Fiat exhibited at the Salon des Artistes Français and received a honourable mention in 1903.

FIAULT, Henri Alexandre
French, 19th century.
Born 19th century, in Paris.
Engraver (etching).

Fiault was a pupil of H. Lefort. He became a member of the Société des Artistes Français in 1905 and exhibited at the society's Salon.

FIAUX, Jean-Claude
French, 20th century.
Born 15 November 1938.
Painter, draughtsman.
Group: Mouvement.

Jean-Claude Fiaux was admitted at the École Nationale des Beaux Arts in Paris, but also studied under Joseph Rivière at the Académie Julian. In 1960, he qualified as an art teacher. Fiaux joined the group Mouvement (Movement) along with Albertini, Canès, Plaza, Guzman and Felez, who exhibited together on a number of occasions. He would also join forces with the Nuagiste group. In 1987, he received the prize of the cultural association *Les Compagnons de Feu* (*Companions of Fire*) in Paris.

He figured in group exhibitions, many of them in Paris; in particular: in 1963, in the Salon des Indépendants; in 1979, in the Salon de Mai; in 1983, in the Salon de la Société Nationale des Beaux-Arts; in 1963, with the *Nuagistes*, in Galerie de Beaune in Paris; in *Option 63*, organised by art reviewer Déroudille in Lyons; in 1979, at the Galerie Art contemporain in Paris; and also in many Salons in the provinces.

His first solo exhibition took place at Verdun Town Hall, followed by several in Paris.

Over the years, Fiaux evolved from abstract expressionism and action art, characterised by angry dashes on white surfaces, to a more sedate research of absolute formal values, orbs and ovals. He starts from the fluctuation of light-colour accounting for silent moods in light, translucent shades.

MUSEUMS AND GALLERIES:
CHERBOURG.

FIB
German, 17th - 18th (?) century.
Monogram of a painter. Genre scenes, still-lifes.

The museum in Wroclaw (formerly Breslau) owns two *Still-lifes* by FIB, which were previously thought to be the work of the painter Franz Karl Palcko, who was in Breslau from 1724-1767. The artist FIB may possibly be the same person as the genre and animal painter Francis Barlow 1626-1702.

F. I. B.

FIBARDEL, Jean
French, 17th century.
Born 17th century, in Orléans.
Sculptor (wood).

Jean Fibardel finished off the sculptures of the portal of the Cathedral of the Holy Cross in Orléans. In 1702 he supplied the seats for the choir, with Degoulon carving the sculptures.

FIBICH, Johann
Austrian, 18th - 19th century.
Born 1771, in Vienna.
Painter (?).

Fibich entered the academy on 27 November 1786, during his father Kaspar's lifetime.

FIBICH, Kaspar
Austrian, 18th century.
Active in Vienna between 1760 and 1790.
Painter.

FIBICHOVA, Zdena
Czech, 20th century.
Born 9 December 1933, in Prague.
Sculptor.
Symbolism.

A student at the school of decorative art in Prague from 1948 to 1957, Zdena Fibichova exhibited in Paris in 1968 at the Musée Rodin with a selection of Czech sculptors.

FIBICKH, Hanns
Bohemian School, 16th century.
Active in Prague.
Sculptor.

Hanns Fibickh produced decorative sculptures for Maximilian II.

FIBICKH, Matthes
Bohemian School, 16th century.
Active in Prague.
Sculptor.

In 1570, Matthes Fibickh received payment for a wooden sculpture of the Emperor's coat of arms.

FIBING, Christian
Czech, 19th century.
Painter.

Christian Fibing is known for a statue of *St Matthew*.

FIBO, Giorgio
Italian, 17th century.
Active in Bologna.
Sculptor.

Giorgio Fibo completed a statue of the *Madonna del Carmine* for the church of S Giovanni on Capri in 1638.

FICATELLI, Stefano. See **FEGATELLI**

FICH, A. E.
Danish, 18th century.
Painter.
A. E. Fich is known for having sculpted a statue of a bishop.

FICH, Erik Carl Frederik
Danish, 19th century.
Born 17 February 1816, in Copenhagen; died 13 August 1870.
Painter.
Erik Fich was a pupil at the school of fine arts in Copenhagen. He exhibited several landscapes and scenes from the war of 1848-1850, in which he also took part.

FICHARD, Maximilian von (Baron)
Polish, 19th century.
Born 10 May 1836, in Leopol (now Lviv, Ukraine).
Painter, engraver. Landscapes.
Baron Maximilian von Fichard was a captain in the engineering corps before becoming an artist and working at the school of fine arts in Venice. He exhibited widely, including in Vienna, Berlin and Turin.
MUSEUMS AND GALLERIES:
PALLANZA: *Lago Maggiore* (two).

FICHAUX, Robert
French, 20th century.
Painter.
Robert Fichaux showed in 1952 and 1953 at the Salon des Réalités Nouvelles in Paris with abstract compositions akin to Auguste Herbin's Constructivist paintings.

FICHEFET, Georges
Belgian, 19th - 20th century.
Born 5 January 1864, in Bruges; died 1954, in Ukkel.
Painter. Figures, portraits, landscapes.
Fichefet was a student at the École des Beaux-Arts in Namur, and then the pupil of Portaels at the Académie in Brussels. He was the co-founder of *Soaring* and of the *For Art* Group.
MUSEUMS AND GALLERIES:
IXELLES: *Young English Woman* - NAMUR: *Girl with a Racquet*.
AUCTION RECORDS:
LONDON, 22 June 1983, *An Artist in His Studio* (1883, oil on canvas, 34 3/4 x 26 3/4 ins / 88.5 x 68 cm) GBP 4,000. LOKEREN, 16 May 1987, *Landscape with a Pond at Dusk* (oil on canvas, 31 x 25 1/4 ins / 79 x 64 cm) BEF 85,000. NEW YORK, 17 Feb 1993, *At the Café-Théâtre* (oil on canvas, 47 1/4 x 67 ins / 120 x 170.2 cm) USD 46,000.

FICHEL, Benjamin Eugène
French, 19th century.
Born 30 August 1826, in Paris; died 2 February 1895, in Paris.
Painter. History painting, religious subjects, portraits, genre scenes, interiors with figures.
Fichel entered the École des Beaux-Arts in Paris in 1841 and was trained under Paul Delaroche and Martin Drolling. He exhibited at the Paris Salon from 1849 to 1895. He received a medal in 1857 and in 1869 and was awarded the Légion d'Honneur in 1870.

Among his many works, Fichel is remebered for *The Holy Family, Portrait of Hadji-Add-Hamid-Bey, Guillaume Harwey Demonstrating Blood Circulation to Charles I, King of England, The Encylopaedists, The Gold Weigher, The Toilette, The Café, Sunrise, An Intimate Morning, Collation.*

E. FICHEL. E. FICHEL.

MUSEUMS AND GALLERIES:
AMSTERDAM: *Chess Players* - GRENOBLE: *Amateurs at Painter's Studio* - KALININGRAD: *Genre Scene* - LILLE: *Lunch* - MONTPELLIER: *Night of 24 August 1572* - MULHOUSE: *Gourmet; Smoker* - PARIS (Mus. d'Orsay): *Arrival at the Inn.*
AUCTION RECORDS:
PARIS, 11 March 1891, *Cuvier in his Surgery,* FRF 850. PARIS, 7 April 1896, *Innkeeper,* FRF 740. PARIS, 27 March 1897, *Interior of an Inn in the Times of Louis XVI,* FRF 1,730. PARIS, 9 May 1898, *Joyful Reunion,* FRF 1,555. LONDON, 29 June 1908, *Reading a Message* (watercolour) GBP 54. LONDON, 12 June 1910, *Reading News* (1871) GBP 50. PARIS, 26 Nov 1920, *Picture Lovers,* FRF 2,200; *New Clerk,* FRF 1,450. PARIS, 23-24 Nov 1923, *Church Collection,* FRF 1,855. PARIS, 23 May 1924, *Drinking Song,* FRF 5,100. LONDON, 1 July 1927, *Napoleon, Josephine, Eugene and Hortense,* GBP 115. PARIS, 16 Nov 1928, *Amateurs at a Painter's Studio,* FRF 5,800. PARIS, 23 Dec 1936, *Conjuror,* FRF 5,600. NEW YORK, 14-16 Jan 1943, *In a Tavern,* USD 200. PARIS, 7 May 1943, *Nude Male in Mirror,* FRF 12,000. PARIS, 1 Feb 1945, *Rebuke,* FRF 18,200. PARIS, July 1946, *Gold Weigher* (1851) FRF 27,000. GLASGOW, 26 July 1946, *Ornithologists,* GBP 336. LONDON, 21 Feb 1947, *Cardinal Richelieu,* GBP 157. PARIS, 15 June 1954, *Christening of Mlle Clairon,* FRF 150,000. LONDON, 12 Feb 1969, *Cabaret Scene,* GBP 500. LONDON, 7 May 1971, *Conjuror* (oil on canvas, 14 1/2 x 21 1/4 ins / 37 x 54 cm) FRF 18,000. LONDON, 23 July 1976, *Toast* (1863, oil on panel, 8 1/2 x 6 1/4 ins / 21.5 x 16 cm) GBP 1,400. LONDON, 16 June 1978, *Drawing Class* (oil on card, 5 1/2 x 3 1/2 ins / 14 x 9 cm) GBP 240. COLOGNE, 20 Nov 1980, *Girl Collecting Sticks* (1857, oil on panel, 13 x 11 ins / 33 x 27 cm) DEM 9,000. NEW YORK, 19 Oct 1984, *Gentlemen Feasting* (1888, oil on panel, 13 x 16 ins / 33 x 40.7 cm) USD 4,500. NEW YORK, 29 Oct 1987, *Mass at St-Sulpice, Paris* (1874, oil on panel, 31 x 53 1/4 ins / 79 x 135 cm) USD 20,000. LONDON, 6 Oct 1989, *Recital* (1853, oil on panel, 10 1/2 x 8 1/4 ins / 26.5 x 21 cm) GBP 1,760. NEW YORK, 25 Oct 1989, *Reading the Newspaper* (1866, oil on panel, 12 1/2 x 16 1/4 ins / 31.8 x 41 cm) USD 7,150. LONDON, 5 Oct 1990, *Music Meeting; Card Game* (oil on panel, a pair, each 8 1/2 x 10 3/4 ins / 21.3 x 27.4 cm) GBP 6,380. VERSAILLES, 25 Nov 1990, *Gentleman with Sword* (oil on panel, 9 1/2 x 6 1/4 ins / 24 x 16 cm) FRF 5,000. PARIS, 4 March 1991, *Military Parade* (gouache, 15 x 11 ins / 38 x 28 cm) FRF 10,000. NEW YORK, 21 May 1991, *Guard* (oil on panel, 9 1/2 x 5 1/2 ins / 24.1 x 14 cm) USD 1,650. AMSTERDAM, 5-6 Nov 1991, *Billet* (1883, oil on panel, 12 1/4 x 18 ins / 31 x 45.5 cm) NLG 16,100. LONDON, 18 March 1992, *Ultimatum* (1890, oil on panel, 13 x 16 1/4 ins / 33 x 41.5 cm) GBP 2,640. NEW YORK, 29 Oct 1992, *Musicians* (oil on card, 9 3/4 x 13 1/4 ins / 24.8 x 33.5 cm) USD 1,980. LONDON, 25 Nov 1992, *Helping Hands* (1854, oil on panel, 9 x 7 ins / 23 x 17.5 cm) GBP 2,200. NEW YORK, 20 Jan 1993, *Connoisseur* (1871, oil on panel, 8 3/4 x 6 1/4 ins / 22.2 x 15.9 cm) USD 3,738. LONDON, 17 Nov 1993, *Smoking Corner* (oil on panel, 8 1/2 x 11 ins / 21.5 x 27 cm) GBP 2,875. NEW YORK, 20 July 1994, *Interval at the Opera* (watercolour and chalk/paper, 12 1/4 x 9 1/4 ins / 31.1 x 238 cm) USD 6,900. LONDON, 14 June 1995, *Pipe Smokers in an Inn* (oil on panel, 8 1/4 x 6 ins / 21 x 15.5 cm) GBP 3,220. LOKEREN, 9 Dec 1995, *Joyful Reunion* (1858, oil on panel, 11 x 13 3/4 ins / 27 x 35 cm) BEF 220,000. PARIS, 21 March 1996, *Payment of Bets* (oil on canvas, 19 x 24 ins / 48 x 61 cm) FRF 32,000. NEW YORK, 5 May 1999, *Soiree in a Rococo Interior* (1855, oil on panel, 17 x 22 ins / 42 x 57 cm) USD 16,000. LONDON, 30 Nov 1999, *Daubenton in his Laboratory* (1873, oil on panel, 15 x 25 ins / 39 x 64 cm) GBP 10,000. LONDON, 4 April 2000, *The Next Move* (1859, oil on panel, 8 x 6 ins / 21 x 16 cm) GBP 4,500. TORONTO, 12 June 2000, *The Toast* (1867, oil on panel, 11 x 8 ins / 28 x 21 cm) CAD 5,000. LONDON, 6 June 2001, *Santé!* (1869, oil on panel, 9 x 6 ins / 22 x 16 cm) GBP 8,800. NEW YORK, 28 June 2001, *Soiree in an Elegant Interior* (1855, oil on panel, 17 x 22 ins / 42 x 57 cm) USD 11,000. LON-

DON, 26 March 2002, *Musical Entertainment at the Inn* (1882, oil on panel, 15 x 21 ins / 37 x 54 cm) GBP 8,000. NEW YORK, 23 April 2002, *Song of Long Ago* (1874, oil on panel, 13 x 16 ins / 32 x 41 cm) USD 17,000. LONDON, 18 March 2003, *Game of Chess* (1881, oil on panel, 9 x 13 ins / 24 x 34 cm) GBP 7,000. NEW YORK, 29 Oct 2003, *Music Concert* (1891, oil on panel, 18 x 22 ins / 45 x 55 cm) USD 32,000. ANTWERP, 8 March 2004, *L'animateur d'antiques* (1860, oil on panel, 8 x 6 ins / 21 x 16 cm) EUR 4,400. AMSTERDAM, 21 April 2004, *Choosing the Right Colour* (1854, oil on panel, 10 x 7 ins / 25 x 19 cm) EUR 3,000.

FICHEL, Jeanne. See **SAMSON**

FICHER, Julien
Belgian, 20th century.
Born c. 1888, in Brussels; died c. 1990, in Anderlecht.
Painter, watercolourist, engraver. Landscapes.

Ficher lived for six years, between 1914 and 1920, in Bolivia and Cuba, as a member of an educational mission. In Belgium he received the Prix de l'Oeuvre Nationale des Beaux-Arts.

It was in Latin America that he began to paint landscapes. His sense of composition and colour is particularly appreciated.

FICHERELLI, Felice, also known as Felice Riposo, or Il Riposo
Italian, 17th century.
Born 1605, in San Gimignano; died 1660 or 1669, in Florence.
Painter, draughtsman. Mythological subjects, religious subjects.

Felice Ficherelli studied under Jacopo da Empoli and, as of 1629, at the academy of drawing in Florence. A close friend of Cristoforo Allori, he earned his nickname, Il Riposo, through a taciturn nature and his legendary indolence - as a result of which he produced very few paintings. Even so, his body of work - such as it is - suggests he had genuine talent. His copies of Perugino, Andrea del Sarto and others were frequently accepted as originals. He had a predilection for scenes of violence.

BIBLIOGRAPHY:
Grigori, N., *Il Seicento fiorentino. Arte a Firenze da Fernandino I a Cosimo III. Biografie*, Palazzo Strozzi, Florence, 1986.

MUSEUMS AND GALLERIES:
BERLIN (Kupferstichkabinet) - CHAMBÉRY (MBA): *Jonah* - FLORENCE (Church of S Maria Novella): *St Antoninus* - FLORENCE (Palazzo Rinucci): *Adam and Eve Banished from the Garden of Eden* - LILLE (MBA, Wicar Collection): drawings.

AUCTION RECORDS:
PARIS, 6 Dec 1924, *Hercules and Omphalos; Hercules Returning Alcestis to Admetus* (two canvases) FRF 580. LONDON, 28 May 1982, *Sophonisbe Holding the Poisoned Chalice* (oil on canvas, 28 3/4 x 23 3/4in/73.1 x 60.4cm) GBP 2,200. LONDON, 11 Dec 1991, *Salome with the Head of St John the Baptist* (oil on canvas, 38 1/4 x 48 1/2in/97 x 123cm) GBP 27,500. LONDON, 15 April 1992, *Rinaldo in the Enchanted Forest* (oil on canvas, 91 1/4 x 137 1/4in/232 x 348.5cm) GBP 90,000. LONDON, 10 July 1992, *St Catherine* (oil on canvas, 38 1/2 x 29in/97.8 x 73.5cm) GBP 4,950. LONDON, 8 Dec 1993, *Tarquin and Lucretia* (oil on canvas, 39 1/4 x 58 1/4in/99.6 x 148cm) GBP 84,000. LONDON, 22 April 1994, *St Catherine of Alexandria* (oil on canvas, 29 x 38in/73.5 x 96.5cm) GBP 10,925. FLORENCE, 9 Oct 2001, *Mary Magdalene* (oil on canvas, 28 x 22 ins / 70 x 57 cm) ITL 31,000,000.

FICHEROUX, Mathieu
Dutch, 20th century.
Born 22 April 1926, in Rotterdam.
Sculptor (mixed media).

Ficheroux has exhibited regularly in Rotterdam since 1961. In 1965 he received the Prix Lissone. In 1971 he took part in the Antwerp Middelheim Biennale. He produces objects from chrome tubes, glass and plastic.

FICHET. See **BRAMA**

FICHET, Alexandre
French, 20th century.
Born 1881, in Paris; died 1968.
Active in Tunisia.
Painter. Portraits, landscapes. Murals.

Alexandre Fichet left Paris for Tunis, where he was soon fully engaged: teaching drawing at Émile-Loubet school, Sadiki college and Alaoui College in Tunis, and decorating public buildings (among others, the Palmarium auditorium and the Belvédère Casino). He also organised theatre shows and wrote for the daily *Tunis socialiste* (*Socialist Tunis*), the mouthpiece of anti-colonial politics. He served fine arts in his capacity as president of the Tunisian Salon from 1912 to 1968, with two interruptions due to the World Wars, and his attendant internment in a Silesian concentration camp for the duration of World War II. In pictorial terms, Alexandre Fichet remained rather academic, especially when he worked with oil, firmly underscoring contours; whereas his landscapes (especially his watercolours) were treated more freely, sometimes relying on pointillist techniques.

Fichet featured in several colonial exhibitions, notably in Marseilles in 1922, at the Salon des Indépendants, the French Africa exhibitions and the Tunisian Salon.

BIBLIOGRAPHY:
Lumières tunisiennes, exhibition catalogue, Association française d'action artistique, Pavillon des arts, Paris, 1995.

MUSEUMS AND GALLERIES:
TUNIS (MAM): *Portrait of Jules Lellouche*.

FICHET, Jean
French, 19th century.
Born 17 April 1822, in Lyons; died c. 1889.
Sculptor, draughtsman, mosaicist. Furniture, religious furnishings, objets d'art.

Fichet was a pupil of Legendre Héral at the École des Beaux-Arts in Lyons from 1835 to 1837. He exhibited drawings, sculptures and *Vessel for Holy Oil* in Lyons from 1842 to 1843, and devoted himself to church furnishing and decoration. He designed and made altars, pulpits, Stations of the Cross, friezes, tympanums, panels and tabletops in mosaics of enamelled glass for chapels and private homes. His style was reminiscent of ancient Rome and enabled him to demonstrate his knowledge of decoration and colour. He achieved fame in 1884 at the Exposition des Arts Décoratifs in Lyons. Some of his main works are in the church of St-Augustin and at the Oratorians in Paris, at the church of St-Louis, the Hôtel-Dieu hospital and the Réparation convent in Lyons, in the cathedral at Chambéry and in churches in Tassin, Dardilly, Iassam and Voiron.

MUSEUMS AND GALLERIES:
LYONS (Mus. des Tissus): drawings and sketches.

FICHET, Pierre
French, 20th century.
Born 10 August 1927, in Paris.
Painter.

Pierre Fichet trained between 1948 and 1950 to be an art teacher. When he gave up on that prospect, he continued to attend the art studio until 1952.

In 1947-1948, Fichet showed abstract leanings. However, between 1948 and 1951, he favoured figuration in the treatment of often religious themes (for example, in his *Pietà* and *Annunciation*), harping back to Philippe de Champaigne and Zurbaran. Having indulged his baroque vein, he reverted to abstraction in the 1950s. Fichet's works are representative of the 1950s' lyrical (sometimes called international) abstraction. With some similarities to action painting, Fichet uses monochrome backdrops (often in red or yellow), over which he lays sweeping, usually white, strokes, spreading them over larger black ones, scratched here and there with a blue smear or a slash of red.

Pierre Fichet exhibited at the Salon des Artistes Indépendants from 1948 to 1954, the Salon d'Automne regularly from 1951 (which, in return, paid tribute to him in 1987), and the Salon des Réalités Nouvelles from 1952 onwards. From 1954, he participated in many collective exhibitions, including: *Divergence 2*, Galerie Arnaud, Paris (1954); *Divergence 3*, *Éloge du petit format* (*In Praise of Small Sizes*) at Galerie La Roue in Paris; *19 French Painters* at the Kunsthalle in Mannheim (1955); *Divergence 4* (1956); *Divergence 5* (1957); *50 ans de peinture abstraite* (*50 Years of Abstract Painting*), introduced by Michel Seuphor at Galerie Greuze (1958); *Divergence 6* (1959); the Paris Biennale (1960 and 1963); an exhibition for the Prix Lissone (1966); the Menton Biennale (1967); *Une aventure de l'art abstrait* (*An Adventure in Abstract Art*) at Musée Galliéra in Paris; and also in Nantes, Brest, Orléans, Salon de Mai (since 1987), and (in 1988) *Aspect de l'abstraction des années 50* (*Aspects of 50s Abstraction*) in Créteil, Lille, Bordeaux, Lyons, Rouen, Toulouse, Marseilles, Grenoble, Nantes, Royan and Nancy. He mostly showed sets of paintings in his many solo exhibitions from 1952, including about 20 in Paris from 1954 to 1969, as well as in Brussels in 1955, in Toulouse from 1965 to 1985, in Nantes in 1977 and 1981, in Montreal in 1978, in Cannes in 1979, in St-Nazaire in 1985, in Lyons in 1986, in La Chaux de Fonds in 1988, and in Ghent in 1989. He created a mural for the mortuary hall in the Hospital St-Antoine, mosaics for the colleges of Auch and Blois, a tapestry for the Mobilier National, and sets for *King Lear* at the Grenier de Toulouse Theatre.

BIBLIOGRAPHY:

Boudaille, Georges, *P. Fichet*, Gal. Arnaud, Paris, 1961. *Pierre Fichet*, exhibition catalogue, Treffpunkt Kunst, Saarlouis, 1990 (good documentation).

MUSEUMS AND GALLERIES:

PARIS (MAMVP) - PARIS (MNAM-CCI) - SOTTEVILLE-LÈS-ROUEN (FRAC Haute-Normandie) - TOULOUSE (MBA, Mus. des Augustins).

AUCTION RECORDS:

PARIS, 6 Dec 1986, *Composition no. 23* (1955, oil on canvas, 25 1/2 x 32 3/4 ins / 65 x 83 cm) FRF 22,000. PARIS, 28 March 1990, *Composition, Yellow Background* (oil on canvas, 31 x 59 ins / 79 x 150 cm) FRF 58,000. DOUAI, 1 July 1990, *Composition no. 4086* (1986, oil on canvas, 19 3/4 x 19 3/4 ins / 50 x 50 cm) FRF 12,000. PARIS, 20 Nov 1991, *Le linge de la flagellation* (1957, oil on canvas, 63 x 31 1/2 ins / 160 x 80 cm) FRF 22,000. PARIS, 1 July 1992, *Composition no. 2* (1978, oil on canvas, 39 1/4 x 39 1/4 ins / 100 x 100 cm) FRF 3,200. PARIS, 19 March 1993, *Composition no. 39-88* (oil on canvas, 23 1/2 x 23 1/2 ins / 60 x 60 cm) FRF 4,000. PARIS, 25 May 1994, *Composition* (1959, oil on canvas, 39 1/4 x 39 1/4 ins / 100 x 100 cm) FRF 8,000. PARIS, 26 June 1995, *Gloria in excelsis deo* (1960, oil on canvas, 39 1/4 x 39 1/4 ins / 100 x 100 cm) FRF 6,500.

FICHI, Ercole

Italian, 17th century.
Born 1595, in Castel Bolognese; died 1665, in Bologna.
Sculptor, painter.

Ercole Fichi studied under Emilio Savonanzi and was responsible for completing the statues of St Charles and St Philip Neri which decorate the upper sections of the façade of the church of S Paolo in Bologna. He also worked as an architect.

FICHON, Jacques François

French, 17th century.
Sculptor.

Jacques François Fichon was the brother of Philippe Fichon and the son of the sculptor of the same name.

FICHON, Philippe

French, 18th century.
Died 25 November 1729, in Paris.
Sculptor.

FICHOT, Albert Lucien

French, 20th century.
Born in Nevers.
Painter. Genre scenes.

Albert Fichot exhibited at the Salon des Artistes Français in 1925.

FICHOT, Jean-Michel

French, 20th - 21st century.
Born 1959.
Sculptor. Figures, nudes. Groups.

Jean-Michel Fichot lives and works near Paris, where he obtained diplomas at the École des Arts Appliqués Duperré in 1980 and 1982, and at the École des Beaux-Arts in 1984.

Fichot produces collections of themed works, such as masks showing the same face contorted into 100 different grimaces. Mostly, he creates figures of women, or women 'hybrids'. For example, one of his figures is part woman, part leaf, while another is part woman, part panther. His figures are either solitary or in small groups; some are graceful, though buxom nudes; some are dancing folk dances; while others (as a homage to Titian) are flying through the air.

Since 1985, he has taken part in a number of group exhibitions, including the following: a symposium of contemporary sculpture in Sylt, Germany, in 1986; *Hommage à Jean Arp* (*Homage to Jean Arp*) in Clamart, where he won the Contemporary Art Prize; the Salon de la Jeune Peinture, in Paris in 1987; the International Contemporary Art Fair, in Tokyo in 1990; and the Los Angeles International Art Fair.

He has also exhibited collections of his works in a number of solo exhibitions, including the following: at the Mairie of the 10th arrondissement, in Paris in 1985; at the Centre Albert Chanot, in Clamart in 1987; at the Galerie Furstenburg, in 1988, 1991 and 1994; *Espace et Toiles* (*Space and Canvases*), at Paris City Hall and the Maison de la Culture de Metz, in 1989; and at the Musée de St-Denis, in 1990.

BIBLIOGRAPHY:

Sueur, Mireille, *Fichot*, exhibition catalogue, Gal. Furstenberg, Paris, 1988. Gilbert Lascault (preface), *Jean-Michel Fichot*, exhibition catalogue, Gal. Furstenberg, Paris, 1991.

MUSEUMS AND GALLERIES:

CLAMART (Centre d'Arts Plastiques Albert-Chanot) - ST-DENIS (MAH).

AUCTION RECORDS:

PARIS, 18 Feb 1990, *Woman-Leaf* (green-patinated bronze, 14 1/4 x 18 ins / 36 x 46 cm) FRF 20,000.

FICHOT, Michel Charles

French, 19th century.
Born 1817, in Troyes; died 7 July 1903, in Paris.
Painter, draughtsman, illustrator, lithographer, architect. Landscapes.

Fichot studied architecture at the École des Beaux-Arts in Paris. He exhibited at the Paris Salon from 1841 to 1875 and received an honourable mention in 1887. He was awarded the Légion d'Honneur. He illustrated a book *Voyage archéologique dans le département de l'Aube* (*Architectural Journey through the Aube*), using drawings of ancient monuments especially from the region of his birth. He then moved to Paris where he worked for *L'Illustration* (*The Illustration*) and for *Le Magasin Pittoresque* (*Picturesque Magazine*).

MUSEUMS AND GALLERIES:

PONTOISE: *Écouen Chateau*.

FICHTEL, J.N.
German, 19th century.
Active in Nuremberg (Bavaria).
Sculptor.
Fichtel's *Profiles of Meixner the Brewer and his Wife* and his portraits of *Elisabeth Schröppel* and *Georg Ulrich Friesser,* along with statuettes representing Napoleonic soldiers and officers after the retreat from Russia in 1812, are kept at the Germanic museum in Nuremberg.

FICHTEL, Johann Konrad
German, 18th century.
Active in Biberach (Baden-Württemberg).
Sculptor (wood).
Fichtel fashioned the great organ at the Protestant church in Biberach, Germany, in 1780.

FICHTENBERGER, Bartholomeus
German, 16th century.
Died February 1592.
Painter.
Breslau School.
Fichtenberger was a master of the guild in 1561 and was accepted as a citizen of the town of Breslau (now Wroclaw, Poland) on 23 January 1562. He painted the backs of the wings of the retable in the choir of the town's Cathedral.

FICHTENBERGER, Jacob
German, 17th century.
Born 1581.
Painter.
Fichtenberger was a student of the painter D. Moder.

FICHTENBERGER, Peter
German, 16th - 17th century.
Born 1570; died between 30 April and 7 May 1611.
Painter.
Breslau School.
For five years Peter Fichtenberger was the pupil of his father Bartholomeus. He was granted the title of master in 1591 in Breslau (now Wroclaw, Poland) and trained six followers.

FICHTHORN, Johann Abraham
German, 18th century.
Painter.
In 1747 Fichthorn was living in Bayreuth (Bavaria), and painted for the porcelain factory there. He also painted stoneware.
MUSEUMS AND GALLERIES:
HAMBURG - SÈVRES - STUTTGART - WÜRZBURG (Mainfränkisches Mus.): painted porcelain.

FICHTL, Joseph
German, 18th century.
Born in Adlzhausen, near Landsberg (Bavaria); died 18 May 1732, in Munich.
Sculptor.
Fichtl worked at Krems in Austria, and Munich, where he was appointed master of the painters' guild on 16 August 1714. He undertook work for the church of the Trinity, producing a large angel and a carved picture.

FICHTNER, Hugo de
Austrian, 19th - 20th century.
Born 6 September 1872, in Vienna.
Active and naturalised in France.
Painter. Military subjects.
Fichtner was the pupil of Benjamin-Constant and of Léon Bonnat in Paris. He exhibited at the Salon des Artistes Français, notably in 1921 with *Charge of the Dragoons at Montdidier.*
AUCTION RECORDS:
RHEIMS, 26 Oct 1980, *Hussars Mounted; The Cavalry Charge* (two oils on panel, 11 x 9 ins / 27 x 22 cm) FRF 4,500.

FICHTNER, Rochus
German, 16th - 17th century.
Born c. 1560, in Innsbruck; died c. 1610, in Munich.
Glass painter.
Munich School.
Fichtner was the pupil of Nicolaus Schinober in Innsbruck, later moving to Munich, where he was made a master of the guild in 1590.

FICHU (Mme)
French, 19th century.
Born 19th century, in Lille.
Painter.
Fichu was a pupil of Mme Coeffier. She exhibited miniature portraits at the Paris Salon in 1876 and 1880.

FICK, Andrès
Dutch, 17th century.
Painter. Still-lifes, vanitas.
Worth mentioning by Andrès Fick is a *Vanitas* framed in ebony.

FICK, Christian François
German, 18th century.
Active at the end of the 18th century.
Draughtsman.

FICK, Niels
Danish, 18th century.
Painter.
Niels Fick is cited as having been a painter in Faaborg (Fünen). He is known to have painted portraits and Bacchanalia.

FICKAERT, Cornelis
Flemish, 16th - 17th century.
Died before 17 October 1616.
Painter.
Flemish School.
Cornelis Fickaert was elected member of the Academy of St Luke in 1595.

FICKAERT, Hans
Flemish, 17th century.
Died c. 1634.
Painter.
Flemish School.
Hans Fickaert became a master of the Académie de St-Luc in Antwerp on the strength of being the son of a member of that academy.

FICKE, Nicolaes or Nikolaus
Flemish, 17th century.
Born 1642; died c. 1702.
Painter, engraver. Landscapes with figures.
Flemish School.
Taught by the painter Philips Wouverman in Haarlem, Nicolaes Ficke is known to have executed three landscapes with horses.
AUCTION RECORDS:
VIENNA, 16 March 1976, *Huntsman Resting* (oil on panel, 17 1/4 x 21 1/4 ins / 44 x 54 cm) ATS 90,000.

FICKER, Florian. See **FÜCKER**

FICKLER, Sebastian
German, 18th century.
Sculptor (wood), cabinet maker.
Fickler carried out work for the Protestant church in Dösingen, Bavaria, from 1785 until 1795.

FICO, Giovanni del
Italian, 18th century.
Painter.
Giovanni del Fico was a member of the guild of Naples in 1723.

FICQUENET
French, 19th century.
Active in Sèvres.
Painter (porcelain).

FICQUET, Adam
French, 17th century.
Sculptor.

Adam Ficquet was admitted to the Académie de St-Luc in Paris on 23 April 1666.

FICQUET, Antoine
French, 18th century.
Sculptor.

Antoine Ficquet was appointed warden of the studio of Michel-Ange Sledtz in Paris in 1764.

FICQUET, Étienne
French, 18th century.
Born 1719, in Paris; died 1794, in Paris.
Engraver.

Étienne Ficquet was the pupil of G. F. Schmidt and Le Bas. He executed the engravings of the *Lives of the Flemish and Dutch Painters* by Descamps. He is also remembered for numerous portraits, including one of Mme de Maintenon after Mignard. He was an excellent engraver with a delicate touch.

FICQUET, Jean
French, 18th century.
Active in Paris.
Sculptor.

FIDANI, Orazio
Italian, 17th century.
Born c. 1610, in Florence; died soon after 1656.
Painter. Mythological subjects, religious subjects, portraits.

Orazio Fidani studied under and adopted the style of Giovanni Biliverti; several examples of his work can be found in his native Florence.

MUSEUMS AND GALLERIES:
FLORENCE (Gal. Corsini): *Portrait* (two paintings) - FLORENCE (Mus. della Certosa): *Four Doctors; Four Apostles* - FLORENCE (Uffizi): *Self-portrait.*

AUCTION RECORDS:
LONDON, 15 April 1992, *Nymphs Playing Blind Man's Buff, with Corsica Pushing Mirtillo* (1654, oil on canvas, 91 1/4 x 137 1/4in/232 x 348.5cm) GBP 110,000. NEW YORK, 15 Jan 1993, *Narcissus near a Lake* (1647, oil on canvas, 67 1/2 x 80in/171.5 x 203.2cm) USD 10,925. ROME, 4 Dec 2000, *Jael and Sisara* (oil on canvas, 47 x 71 ins / 120 x 180 cm) ITL 55,000,000. LONDON, 12 Dec 2002, *Entombment* (oil on canvas, 70 x 56 ins / 179 x 142 cm) GBP 28,000.

FIDANZA
Italian, 13th century.
Painter.

The name of this artist occurs in a Florentine document of 1224.

FIDANZA, Filippo
Italian, 18th century.
Born 1720, in Sabino; died 1790, in Rome.
Painter.

Filippo Fidanza studied in Rome under Marco Benefial and went on to study and copy the works of the old masters. The Prato gallery houses his *Mountain Landscape* and a *Sea Harbour.*

FIDANZA, Francesco
Italian, 18th - 19th century.
Born 1747, in Rome; died 1819, in Milan.
Painter. Landscapes with figures, landscapes, seascapes.

The son of Filippo Fidanza, he studied under Vernet and Lacroix. He was an accomplished landscape artist who worked for Eugène de Beauharnais.

MUSEUMS AND GALLERIES:
FLORENCE (Uffizi): drawings - MILAN (Pinacoteca di Brera): *Snowfall; Rooftops in Ancona; Rooftops in Chioggia; Rootops in Rimmi* - ROHRAU (Schlossmuseum, Graf Harrach'sche Familiensammlung): two landscapes - ROME (Gal. dell'Accademia Nazionale di S Luca): two seascapes.

AUCTION RECORDS:
MILAN, 27 April 1978, *Fire by the Sea at Night* (oil on canvas, 29 3/4 x 41 1/4in/75.5 x 105cm) ITL 3,800,000. MILAN, 18 June 1981, *Night Fishing* (oil on canvas, 38 1/2 x 30in/98 x 76cm) ITL 2,600,000. MILAN, 8 May 1984, *Seascape in a Squall* (oil on canvas, 24 x 36 1/2in/61 x 93cm) ITL 9,000,000. LONDON, 11 Dec 1986, *Vesuvius Erupting* (1768, oil on paper, 35 1/4 x 25 1/2in/89.5 x 64.8cm) GBP 6,500. ROME, 23 May 1989, *Seascape with Fishermen* (oil on canvas, 25 1/4 x 37 1/2in/64 x 95cm) ITL 30,000,000. MONACO, 3 Dec 1989, *Figures in a Vaulted Cavern* (oil on canvas, 22 x 31 1/2in/55 x 80cm) FRF 77,700. ROME, 8 April 1991, *Village on Fire at Night* (oil on canvas, 28 3/4 x 23 1/2in/73 x 60cm) ITL 8,050,000. MILAN, 30 May 1991, *Seascape with Fishermen and a Fishing Vessel* (oil on canvas, 22 1/2 x 29 1/2in/57 x 75cm) ITL 15,000,000. MILAN, 16 March 1994, *Seascape with Fishing Vessels and Fishermen* (oil on canvas, a pair, each 9 1/4 x 14in/23.5 x 35.5cm) ITL 17,250,000. LONDON, 6 July 1994, *Beggar and Other Figures in front of a Waterfall Capriccio in Tivoli* (oil on canvas, 12 1/2 x 15 3/4in/32 x 40cm) GBP 3,220. LONDON, 30 Oct 1996, *Capriccio: Mediterranean Port with Fishermen* (oil on canvas, a pair, each 13 3/4 x 17 3/4in/35 x 45.2cm) GBP 14,950. LONDON, 13 Dec 1996, *Mediterranean Port at Dawn with Fishermen in the Foreground and a Merchant in the Middle Distance* (oil on canvas, 39 1/4 x 58 1/2in/99.7 x 148.4cm) GBP 43,300. LONDON, 30 Oct 1997, *Seascape with Boat on a Calm Sea and Fishermen Hauling in their Nets; Rocky Landscape with a Raging Sea and Figures Escaping from a Shipwreck* (oil on canvas, a pair, 24 1/4 x 29 3/4 ins / 61.8 x 75.8 cm and 24 1/4 x 29 1/4in/61.6 x 74.5cm) GBP 11,500. VIENNA, 24 March 2004, *Southern Port with Grotto of Posilippo near Naples* (oil on canvas, 14 x 21 ins / 35 x 53 cm) EUR 13,000.

FIDANZA, Giuseppe
Italian, 18th - 19th century.
Born c. 1750, in Rome; died c. 1820.
Painter. Landscapes.

Giuseppe Fidanza set up a landscape-painting school in Milan. He was a member of the academies in Florence, Rome and Padua.

FIDANZA, Gregorio
Italian, 18th - 19th century.
Born 1759, in Collevecchio; died 10 January 1823, in Rome.
Painter. Landscapes with figures, landscapes.

The brother of Francesco, Gregorio Fidanza studied in Paris under Lacroix and went on to become official court painter to Stanislaus August, King of Poland. He drew his inspiration from the work of Claude Lorraine and Salvator Rosa, whose landscapes he imitated. His landscapes and seascapes of Italy had the greatest appeal to foreign buyers.

MUSEUMS AND GALLERIES:
PARMA.

AUCTION RECORDS:
ZURICH, 22 May 1987, *Fishermen by the Sea at Dawn* (oil on canvas, 31 1/2 x 15in/80 x 38cm) CHF 7,000.

FIDANZA, Paolo
Italian, 18th century.

Born 1731, in Camerino.
Painter, engraver.

Paolo Fidanza studied the old masters in Rome and produced a series of head studies after them. He also engraved a series of plates from originals by Raphael, Guido Reni and Annibale Carracci, including Raphael's *Mount Parnassus* and Carracci's *Descent from the Cross* and *St Peter and St Paul Appearing to St Francis*.

FIDANZA, Raffaele
Italian, 19th century.
Born 10 December 1797, in Matelica (near Fabriano, Marche); died 23 November 1846, in Matelica.
Painter, lithographer.

Raffaele Fidanza studied art in Rome under P. Podesti. He exhibited in Paris and London, and mostly painted portraits. His works can be seen in churches around Matelica. Fidanza was one of the first artists to introduce lithography to Italy.

FIDANZIO, Prospero
Italian, 17th century.
Painter.

Prospero Fidanzio entered the Accademia di San Luca in Rome on 30 October 1663.

FIDE
Italian, 19th century.
Lithographer.

One lithograph known to be by this artist is entitled *View of Klosterneuburg*.

FIDE-FISNEGER, Johann
Austrian, 18th century.
Born 1753, in Trient, South Tyrol (now Trento, Trentino-Alto Adige, Italy); died 1 December 1807, in Vienna.
Sculptor.

FIDE-FISNEGER, Joseph
Austrian, 19th century.
Born 1790.
Sculptor.

Joseph Fide-Fisneger was the son of Johann Fide-Fisneger and was made a member of the academy of St Luke on 28 April 1802.

FIDELE, C.
Italian, 20th century.
Born in Vallerotonda, near Cassino (Lazio).
Sculptor.

Fidele exhibited a bust made of Siena marble at the Paris Salon of 1923.

FIDELIS (Brother). See **FAILER Peter**

FIDERLE, Isidore Coridon
Engraver (etching).

Mentioned by Nagler.

FIDLER, Constance Louise
British, 20th century.
Born 11 July 1904.
Painter (including wash), draughtswoman. Portraits.

FIDLER, Eugène
Russian, 20th century.
Born 1910, in Russia; died 30 September 1990, in Roussillon, France.
Active in France.
Painter, collage artist, ceramicist.

Eugène Fidler studied in Nice, then in Paris where he was admitted to the École d'Architecture. He dropped this subject and concentrated on painting and pottery. He settled in Vallauris after World War II and continued his work as a ceramicist. From 1957 onwards, he spent long periods in Spain, Portugal and the Azores.

His meeting the Post-Cubist Henri Hayden seems to have been a defining influence on his own development as a painter. He adopted the 'papier collé' (pasted paper) and assemblage techniques.

AUCTION RECORDS:
PARIS, 16 March 1989, *Riders in the Forest* (1932, oil on canvas, 1/4 x 1/4 ins / 0.60 x 0.70 cm) FRF 4,500.

FIDLER, Harry or Harold
British, 19th - 20th century.
Born in Salisbury; died 1935.
Painter. Genre scenes, landscapes with figures, waterscapes.

Harry Fidler specialised in painting rural landscapes, rivers and agricultural work.

AUCTION RECORDS:
LONDON, 2 Feb 1923, *The Plough is our Hope*, GBP 9; *Unloading Boats at St Ives*, GBP 3. LONDON, 19 Feb 1926, *The Hay Wain*, GBP 10. JOHANNESBURG, 17 March 1976, *Farm Horses* (oil on canvas, 16 x 18 ins / 40.5 x 45.5 cm) ZAR 650. LONDON, 10 Nov 1981, *Horse Fair* (oil on canvas, 30 1/2 x 36 ins / 77.5 x 91.5 cm) GBP 3,200. LONDON, 2 Nov 1983, *Volendam, Holland* (oil on canvas, 40 x 60 ins / 101.5 x 152.5 cm) GBP 2,600. LONDON, 23 May 1984, *Home from the Fields* (oil on canvas, 24 x 36 ins / 61 x 91.5 cm) GBP 1,750. LONDON, 19 March 1986, *Promenaders by the Gallop, Hyde Park* (watercolour) GBP 1,300. LONDON, 22 July 1987, *Going Home* (oil on canvas, 18 x 22 ins / 46 x 56 cm) GBP 6,500. LONDON, 9 June 1988, *The Port* (oil on canvas, 17 3/4 x 22 ins / 45 x 55 cm) GBP 6,600. LONDON, 29 July 1988, *Farmyard* (oil on panel, 27 1/2 x 35 1/2 ins / 70 x 90 cm) GBP 6,380. LONDON, 3 May 1990, *River Bank* (oil on canvas, 9 x 11 ins / 23 x 28 cm) GBP 880. SALISBURY, 19 April 1999, *Poacher* (oil on canvas, 30 x 26 ins / 76 x 66 cm) GBP 1,000. LONDON, 4 July 2001, *Haycart* (oil on canvas, 32 x 37 ins / 82 x 95 cm) GBP 17,000. VANCOUVER, 4 Dec 2001, *Homeward* (oil on canvas, 10 x 12 ins / 25 x 30 cm) CAD 11,500. PENZANCE, 30 May 2002, *Vegetable Seller* (oil on canvas, 15 x 19 ins / 39 x 49 cm) GBP 5,600. LONDON, 13 June 2002, *Returning Home* (oil on canvas, 31 x 37 ins / 79 x 93 cm) GBP 6,000. TORONTO, 10 June 2003, *Down the Nadder, Wiltshire* (1925, oil on canvas, 15 x 16 ins / 38 x 41 cm) CAD 4,750. NEWBURY, 19 May 2004, *Ploughing. Drawing the Cart* (oil on canvas, two, 8 x 10 ins / 20 x 26 cm) GBP 4,000.

FIDLER, Jean
French, 20th century.
Painter.

Jean Fidler exhibited still-lifes at the Salon des Indépendants in 1942 and 1943.

FIDLER, Michel, the Elder
German, 16th century.
Died before 1569.
Sculptor.

The tomb of Henry Ribisch in the church of St Elizabeth and that of Canon Stanilas Sauer in the church of the Holy Cross in Breslau (now Wroclaw, Poland) were the work of this sculptor.

FIDLER, Michel, the Younger
German, 16th century.
Sculptor.

This artist was the son of Michael Fidler the Elder.

FIDRIT, Charles André
French, 20th century.
Born 12 May 1881, in Paris; died April 1927.
Painter.

Charles Fidrit studied under Bonnat in Paris, where he exhibited at the Salon des Artistes Français. He received an honourable mention in 1906, and a second-class medal in 1922. He also won the prize offered by an association of Bonnat's former students in 1924 and 1926.

FIDRIT, Louis
French, 20th century.
Born in Paris.
Painter. Landscapes.

Louis Fidrit exhibited at the Salon des Artistes Français. He received an honourable mention in 1909.

AUCTION RECORDS:

PARIS, 22 Jan 1945, *Rocks on the Seafront,* FRF 150.

FIDUCCIO, Marco
Italian, 17th century.
Engraver.

Marco Fiduccio is remembered for a series of engravings, predominantly studies of horses.

FIDUS, pseudonym of Hugo Höppener
German, 19th - 20th century.
Born 8 October 1868, in Lübeck; died 23 February 1948, in Woltersdorf.
Painter, pastellist, watercolourist, draughtsman, illustrator. Figures, landscapes. Posters, ex-libris. Jugendstil.

Fidus studied the decorative arts in Lübeck, then at the Akademie der Bildenden Künste in Munich, where for two years he learnt from Karl Wilhelm Diefenbach, the unsociable hermit from Höllrigelskreuth on the Isar. Diefenbach had a powerful influence on him, was a believer in the unity of art and life and practised a form of primitive Christianity in which he saw himself as the defender of naturism. Höppener was nicknamed 'Fidus' (faithful) because he stood by his mentor even when the latter was condemned to eight days imprisonment for refusing to wear any clothing. In 1889, he returned to the Munich academy, where he became a student of the Greek painter Nikolaus Gysis. In 1892, he settled in Berlin.

He was particularly active as an artist for a number of newspapers and periodicals, such as *Berliner Illustrierte Zeitung* and *Die Jugend,* the periodical published in Munich that from 1896 promoted the new Jugendstil; also, *Pan,* a periodical published in Berlin by Julius Meier-Graefe and *Sphinx.* He also worked as an illustrator or designer for a number of books, including: *Das Buch des Kindes* (*Book of the Child*); *Aber die Liebe* (*But Love*) by Dehmel; *Hohe Lieder* (*Praise Songs*) by F. Evers; *Theosophische Erzählungen* (*Theosophical Tales*) by E. Stucken; *Nächte* (*Nights*), 1897, by K. Geuke; *Gedichte* (*Poems*) by K. Henckell; *Offenbarungen des Wacholderbaums* (*Revelations of the Juniper Bush*) by Bruno Wille (Eugen Diederichs, 1903). At the same time he was active as a painter and watercolourist.

His themes, as both illustrator and painter, often borrow from Symbolism, and his style seems to hover between the Symbolism of the Secession and the floral decorative art of Jugendstil. Taking an interest in Theosophy and Germanic mythology, he created esoteric and erotic figures, chiefly of nude girls and boys that he linked with abstract shapes. For his illustrations of K.W. Diefenbach's tales, *Per aspera ad astra,* he had the original idea of using a variety of cutout figures as a shadow show against a white background, representing women and children dancing. By far the best known and most frequently reproduced of his works is *Lichtgebet* (*Prayer to the Light*), which was produced in several different versions. The art of Fidus enjoyed great popularity. He promoted his work by means of postcards showing photographs of his works, and these postcards became highly prized by collectors.

BIBLIOGRAPHY:

Frecot, Janos, *Fidus: Zur ästhetischen Praxis bürgerlicher Fluchtbewegungen,* Rogner & Bernhard, Munich, 1972. Osterwalder, Marcus (ed.), *Dictionnaire des illustrateurs 1800-1914,* Ides et Calendes, Neuchâtel, 1989. Wermer, Ute/Witte, Klaus, *Bekanntes und Unbekanntes über das Exlibrisschaffen von Fidus mit revidierter Exlibriswerkliste,* Exlibristen, Frederikshavn, 1991. De Bruyn, Wolfgang, *Fidus - Künstler alles Lichtbaren,* Frölich und Kaufmann Verlag, Berlin, 1998.

MUSEUMS AND GALLERIES:

BERLIN (Akademie der Künste): *Selbstbildnis* (*Self-portrait*) (c. 1880) - BERLIN (Berlinische Gal.) - BERLIN (Deutsches Historisches Mus.).

AUCTION RECORDS:

LONDON, 26 Nov 1980, *Der Gottsucher* (1918 and 1943, oil on paper, 25 3/4 x 35 ins / 65.5 x 89 cm) GBP 3,200. LONDON, 21 Oct 1988, *Adam and Eve* (1905, watercolour/paper, 11 1/2 x 16 1/2 ins / 29.2 x 41.9 cm) GBP 1,430. MUNICH, 29 Nov 1989, *Evening in a Park* (1892, oil on card, 19 x 18 ins / 48 x 45.5 cm) DEM 7,700. LONDON, 1 Dec 1989, *On a Bridge in Zurich* (1906, watercolour, 12 1/2 x 19 ins / 32 x 48 cm) GBP 1,980. VIENNA, 29-30 Oct 1996, *Naiad* (1894, chalk and pastel/paper, 19 1/4 x 24 3/4 ins / 49 x 63 cm) ATS 460,000. HAMBURG, 23 March 2002, *Der Wolkenmann!* (1899, colour pastel and chalk over watercolour, 20 x 28 ins / 51 x 71 cm) EUR 6,800. COPENHAGEN, 5 March 2003, *Morning Mood* (1895, oil on canvas, 31 x 47 ins / 80 x 119 cm) DKK 17,000. VIENNA, 25 May 2004, *Fulfilment* (1912, pencil, charcoal and watercolour, 16 x 19 ins / 40 x 47 cm) EUR 3,000.

FIE-FIEUX, Madeleine
French, 20th century.
Born in Varenne-en-Gâtinais (Loiret).
Painter.

Madeleine Fie-Fieux exhibited at the Salon des Artistes Français. She received an honourable mention in 1943.

FIEBICH, Jan
Czech, 18th century.
Born in the 18th century, in Ronov nad Doubravou; died 1785.
Painter.

Jan Fiebich worked at the Akademie der Bildenden Künste in Vienna and painted frescoes for his patron, the Prince of Auersperg, for his castle at Slatinan, near Chrudim, Bohemia.

FIEBIG, Adam
German, 16th century.
Born 1555; died 11 January 1605, in Breslau (now Wroclaw, Poland).
Sculptor, architect.

It is known that this artist worked at the church of St Christopher in Breslau.

FIEBIG, Carl Rudolph
Swedish, 19th century.
Born 10 February 1812, in Eckernförde; died 23 February 1874, in Copenhagen.
Painter. Portraits.

Carl Rudolph Fiebig was a pupil of the portrait painter Baasch in Eckernförde and entered the Copenhagen school of fine arts in 1832. He also worked with J. L. Lund.

He was most appreciated as a portrait painter, and painted in particular Prince Frederik Ferdinand, Princess Caroline and Frederik VII.

AUCTION RECORDS:

COPENHAGEN, 27 Jan 1981, *Portrait of a Woman* (1855, oil on canvas, 27 1/4 x 20 3/4 ins / 69 x 53 cm) DKK 6,600. VEJLE, 13 Jan 2003, *Portrait of a Young Girl in a Blue Dress with a Dog at her Side* (1856, oil on canvas, 29 x 22 ins / 74 x 56 cm) DKK 86,000.

FIEBIG, Frederic
Latvian, 20th century.
Born 17 May 1885, in Talsi; died 6 February 1953, in Sélestat, France.
From 1907 active in France.
Painter, engraver (wood). Landscapes, figures.

Frédéric Fiebig studied at a school of art in St Petersburg in 1905-1906, then at the Académie Julian in Paris from 1907 onwards. He went to Italy on a study trip in 1911. During World War I he retreated to St-Georges-de-Didonne (Charente-Maritime). He spent some time in the Gers region in 1925 and in the Northern Pyrenées in 1926. Finally he settled in Sélestat (Lower Rhine) in 1929. Frédéric Fiebig used a knife and executed robust, earthy painting, more along the lines of Courbet than in debt to Impressionism. However, some of his landscapes show synthetic simplifications in the planes and spaces which seem to refer to the Puteaux group and to Jacques Villon in particular.

He exhibited in Paris at the Salon des Artistes Indépendants from 1908 until 1921, and at the Salon d'Automne, of which he was made a member in 1921, from 1910 to 1928. He also exhibited in London, New York, Riga, Barcelona and Moscow. His solo exhibitions included: Galerie Bernheim Jeune, Paris (1912); Riga where the museum made several purchases (1929) and Colmar (1936).

Bibliography:

Rheims, Maurice (preface), *Frédéric Fiebig, des plaines de Courlande au Ried alsacien*, monograph, Éd. Oberlin, Strasbourg, 1984.

Museums and Galleries:

Riga: several works.

Auction records:

Paris, 20 Feb 1990, *Young Woman in a Field* (oil on canvas, 27 1/2 x 47 1/4 ins / 70 x 120 cm) FRF 28,000.

FIEBIGER, Julius

German, 19th century.

Born 5 September 1813, in Bautzen; died 29 January 1883, in Dresden.

Watercolourist, engraver. Landscapes, mountainscapes, architectural views.

Fiebiger was an honorary member of the academy of Dresden. He exhibited in Dresden between 1837 and 1881. One of his known works is *Evening Landscape*.

Museums and Galleries:

Bautzen: *Landscapes* (watercolour); *View of Part of Ortenburg Castle in Bautzen* (engraving) - Dresden: *Mountain Landscape in Bohemia*; watercolours - Görlitz: *Wendish Church* - Schwerin: *Rainbow over a Hill*.

FIEBIGER, Moritz

German, 19th century.

Born 11 February 1810, in Görlitz; died 4 November 1834, in Munich.

Painter. History painting, portraits.

Moritz Fiebiger studied under F. Milde in Munich and worked with him in the style of Correggio and Batoni. He entered the Dresden school of fine arts, where he was said to be an excellent student. Fiebiger also worked with Fritz Overbeck.

Museums and Galleries:

Görlitz (Städtische Kunstsammlungen): *Daniel in the Lions' Den*.

FIECHTER. See **VIECHTER**

FIECHTNER

German, 17th century.

Died 6 March 1692.

Sculptor.

Fiechtner was made a citizen of Nuremberg on 6 March 1689.

FIEDLER, Arnold

German, 20th century.

Born 1 March 1900, in Hamburg; died 6 March 1985, in Hamburg.

Also active in France.

Painter, engraver, lithographer. Figures.

Arnold Fiedler studied under A. Illies and J. Wohlers at the Lerchenfeld Arts and Crafts College in Hamburg from 1916 to 1918. His studies were interrupted by World War I. Subsequently, he was awarded an Erwin-Amsinck Foundation scholarship which enabled him to complete his studies between 1925 and 1929 under the pre-Abstract Expressionist painter Hans Hofmann. He visited Paris as early as 1930, but it was not until 1938 that he elected to move to the French capital permanently. As things turned out, he was interned in France for part of World War II, initially by the French and later by the Americans.

He returned to his native Hamburg in 1946 and went on to become a member of the free academy of fine arts in 1955. He was awarded the Edwin-Scharff Prize in 1957. Between 1959 and 1969, he maintained a studio in Paris.

In the course of his career as a painter, Fiedler successfully made the transition from one style to another, starting out as a Surrealist, then turning to socially aware Expressionism, then reverting to Surrealism before finally espousing Tachism. Additionally, he produced a large number of etchings.

He showed his work regularly between 1919 and 1934 at the Fine Arts Gallery in Hamburg and within the framework of the Secession group, of which he became a member in 1932. Several solo exhibitions of his work are on record, including those in Hamburg, starting with the Fine Arts Association in 1922. Following World War II, he exhibited solo on numerous occasions. Following his death in 1985, several posthumous exhibitions of his work were organised, most notably in 1993 at the Richard-Haizmann Museum in Niebüll; in 2000 at the Haspa (Hamburger Sparkasse) Gallery in Hamburg; and in 2000 at the Herold Gallery in Hamburg.

Bibliography:

Arnold Fiedler, Christians, Hamburg, 1980. *Arnold Fiedler: Retrospektive*, Richard-Haizmann-Museum, Niebüll, 1993. Schoop, Uta/Weiss, Christina, *Arnold Fiedler: der Maler 1900-1985. Ein Werkverzeichnis*, catalogue raisonné, Wachholtz, Neumünster, 1995. *Arnold Fiedler (1900 - 1985): Arbeiten auf Papier*, exhibition catalogue, Galerie in der Haspa, Hamburg, 2000.

Museums and Galleries:

Darmstadt (Mus.) - Hamburg (Kunsthalle) - Hamburg (Mus. für Kunst und Gewerbe).

Auction records:

Paris, 10 April 1989, *Human Landscape* (1961, mixed media, 22 1/2 x 30 1/4 ins / 57 x 77 cm) FRF 13,500. Douai, 11 Nov 1990, *Composition* (1965, mixed media/paper, 28 1/4 x 19 3/4 ins / 72 x 50 cm) FRF 4,200.

FIEDLER, Bernhard

German, 19th century.

Born 23 November 1816, in Berlin; died 28 March 1904, in Trieste.

Painter, decorative artist, draughtsman. Landscapes.

Bernhard Fiedler was a student at the academy in Berlin; he also studied under the painter Gerst, and then the seascape painter Krause. He made study visits to Italy, Dalmatia and the Orient. Fiedler became a member of the academy of Venice. His known works include the decoration of the castle at Miramar, near Trieste.

Museums and Galleries:

Berlin: paintings - Cologne: *Marsh in Egypt* - Frankfurt am Main: paintings - Trieste (Civico Mus. Revoltella): *Ruins at Thebes*; *Ruins of Temple of the Sun at Baalbeck* - Vienna: *Cloister*; *View of Cairo from the Citadel*.

Auction records:

Cologne, 23 March 1973, *View of Jerusalem*, DEM 4,400. New York, 5 March 1981, *View of Constantinople* (1896, oil on paper, 15 1/2 x 13 ins / 39.5 x 33 cm) USD 1,000. London, 18 Feb 1983, *Trieste* (1870, oil on canvas, 18 x 30 ins / 45.8 x 76.2 cm) GBP 2,600. London, 17 May 1985, *Arabs on the Sea-*

shore (oil on canvas, 10 3/4 x 16 ins / 27.3 x 40.6 cm) GBP 3,200. LINDAU, 6 May 1987, *Summer Landscape* (1850, oil on canvas, 26 3/4 x 41 1/4 ins / 68 x 105 cm) DEM 5,000. LONDON, 13 March 1996, *View of Luxor in Egypt* (oil on canvas, 39 3/4 x 76 1/2 ins / 101 x 194 cm) GBP 7,130. LONDON, 12 Oct 2000, *Oriental Travellers* (oil on canvas, 16 x 21 ins / 41 x 54 cm) GBP 1,000. MUNICH, 17 May 2003, *Trieste Bay* (1850, oil on canvas, 12 x 20 ins / 30 x 51 cm) EUR 1,900. VIENNA, 10 Dec 2003, *Rowers in Trieste Bay* (1850, oil on canvas, 12 x 20 ins / 30 x 51 cm) EUR 1,500. VIENNA, 24 Feb 2004, *Valley Crossing near Trieste* (1852, oil on canvas, 17 x 25 ins / 43 x 63 cm) EUR 3,000. MUNICH, 24 March 2004, *Southern Park Landscape in Moonlight* (oil on panel, 23 x 19 ins / 58 x 49 cm) EUR 2,200.

FIEDLER, Carl Christian

German, 19th century.
Born 1789, in Schkeuditz, near Leipzig (Saxony); died 26 January 1851, in St Petersburg.
Painter, miniaturist.

Fiedler worked in Leipzig under the direction of Tiselibem and Schnorr. He exhibited in Leipzig in 1812.

FIEDLER, François

Hungarian, 20th century.
Born 15 February 1921, in Kassa (now Košice, Slovakia). Active from 1945-1950 in France.
Painter, engraver, illustrator.

François Fiedler started to learn about the academic portrait at a very young age and copied the masters. After university, was admitted to the academy of fine art in Budapest. After settling in France after World War II, he moved towards Abstraction. He practised gestural painting and collage at that time, then experimented with very thick materials, creating genuine relief paintings. Later he returned to very light, broad washes that made the colours run over each other like woven fabrics. From 1962 onwards he painted directly with colours as they come out of the tubes. He applied his experiments with materials to engraving, etching, aquatint and carborundum. Throughout his different periods, he always played with the notion of reduction of the symbol.

Fiedler illustrated various works: the *Bible*, *Spiritual Songs* by St John of the Cross, *Fragments* by Heraclitus and *Du fond des âges* by Claude Ollier. He exhibited at the Salon des Réalités Nouvelles in 1950 and at the Salon de Mai in 1968. Solo exhibitions include a few in Paris from 1956 and: *Paintings 1955-1965* (April 1989); *Paintings 1965-1975* (September 1989); *Paintings 1959-1961* (1994) and *Recent Works* (1997) at various venues of the Maeght galleries. The museum in Vevey exhibited a group of his engravings in 1995.

BIBLIOGRAPHY:

Nadal, Octave, *Fiedler*, exhibition catalogue, Gal. Maeght, Paris, 1983. Dobbels, Daniel, *Fiedler*, exhibition catalogue, Gal. Maeght, Paris, 1990.

MUSEUMS AND GALLERIES:

LAUSANNE (Bibliothèque cantonale et universitaire) - NEW YORK (Solomon R. Guggenheim Mus.) - PARIS (FNAC) - PARIS (MNAM-CCI) - ST-PAUL-DE-VENCE (Fondation Maeght) - VEVEY (musée Jenisch, cabinet cantonal des estampes).

AUCTION RECORDS:

PARIS, 21 June 1987, *Night Watch* (oil on canvas, 57 1/2 x 37 3/4 ins / 146 x 96 cm) FRF 10,000. MILAN, 19 Dec 1989, *Missing Memory* (1971, oil on canvas, 46 x 28 3/4 ins / 116 x 73 cm) ITL 3,800,000. PARIS, 10 June 1990, *Untitled* (1961, oil on canvas, 76 1/2 x 38 1/4 ins / 194 x 97 cm) FRF 30,000.

FIEDLER, Herbert Herman

German, 20th century.
Born 1891, in Leipzig; died 1962.
Painter. Figure compositions, nudes, portraits, genre scenes, landscapes.

Fiedler left Germany in the face of the Naziism. After a period in Paris, he settled in the Netherlands. In Germany Fiedler had known Max Beckmann, with whose painting his own had affinities, marked both by the aftermath of Cubism in its construction and by the expressionism of its colour. He is particularly known for his landscapes of Holland, his views of the Port of Amsterdam, and his scenes of dancing and the circus.

AUCTION RECORDS:

AMSTERDAM, 24 Oct 1983, *Café-concert in Paris* (oil on canvas, 44 1/4 x 23 1/2 ins / 112.5 x 60 cm) NLG 3,000. AMSTERDAM, 10 April 1990, *Gypsy Dancers* (oil on canvas, 14 3/4 x 18 1/4 ins / 37.4 x 46.5 cm) NLG 3,450. AMSTERDAM, 23 May 1991, *Winter Landscape with Cyclists* (oil on canvas, 20 x 31 1/2 ins / 50.5 x 80 cm) NLG 2,990. AMSTERDAM, 17 Sept 1991, *Portrait of a Young Boy in a Blue Suit* (oil on canvas, 16 1/4 x 10 ins / 41 x 25.5 cm) NLG 2,530. AMSTERDAM, 11 Dec 1991, *Woman with a Parrot* (gouache/paper, 20 3/4 x 19 ins / 53 x 48.5 cm) NLG 1,150. AMSTERDAM, 18 Feb 1992, *Pierrette/Figures Conversing* (oil on panel, 9 x 7 3/4 ins / 23 x 20 cm) NLG 1,840. AMSTERDAM, 19 May 1992, *Pieta* (oil on canvas, 32 1/4 x 46 1/2 ins / 82 x 118 cm) NLG 6,325. AMSTERDAM, 30 May 1995, *Landscape in Edam* (oil on canvas, 29 1/2 x 32 ins / 75 x 81 cm) NLG 7,500. AMSTERDAM, 4 June 1996, *A Bunch of Flowers* (oil on card, 17 3/4 x 20 ins / 45.2 x 50.5 cm) NLG 1,298. AMSTERDAM, 18 June 1996, *Portrait of a Young Boy* (oil on canvas/card, 16 3/4 x 10 1/4 ins / 42.5 x 26 cm) NLG 1,840. AMSTERDAM, 10 Dec 1996, *Nudes Bathing* (oil on canvas, 20 1/2 x 25 1/4 ins / 52 x 64 cm) NLG 2,998. AMSTERDAM, 7 June 2000, *Tulips in Amsterdam* (oil on canvas, 45 x 24 ins / 115 x 60 cm) NLG 8,000. AMSTERDAM, 11 June 2001, *View of the Village of Laren* (oil on paper, 19 x 25 ins / 47 x 63 cm) NLG 4,800. AMSTERDAM, 11 June 2001, *Landscape* (oil on board, 8 x 10 ins / 21 x 26 cm) NLG 10,500. AMSTERDAM, 27 May 2003, *Cafe Concert in Paris* (1913, oil on canvas, 45 x 25 ins / 115 x 63 cm) EUR 10,000. AMSTERDAM, 25 Nov 2003, *Circus Parade I* (c. 1940, oil on burlap, 42 x 29 ins / 107 x 74 cm) EUR 6,000. AMSTERDAM, 9 June 2004, *Clown Musicians* (oil on canvas, 32 x 26 ins / 81 x 65 cm) EUR 3,000. AMSTERDAM, 9 June 2004, *Clowns with Musical Instruments* (oil on board, 49 x 24 ins / 124 x 62 cm) EUR 3,500.

FIEDLER, J.H.

German, 19th century.
Active in Hanau (Hesse) c. 1828.
Engraver.

Fiedler's known works include engraved portraits of *Tsar Alexander I*, and the Russian general *A. J. Tschernyscheff.*

FIEDLER, Johann Christian

German, 18th century.
Born 31 October 1697, in Pirna (Saxony); died 5 September 1765, in Darmstadt (Hesse).
Painter. Portraits, genre scenes.

Johann Fiedler was the protégé of the duke of Brunswick, who sent him to study for a time in Paris.

MUSEUMS AND GALLERIES:

DARMSTADT: *Darmstadt Society*; *Self-portrait.*

AUCTION RECORDS:

LONDON, 5 July 1995, *Head and Shoulder Portrait of Sculptor Georg Friedrich Donett, with Marble Head engraved in Antique Style* (1756, oil on canvas, 33 1/2 x 26 1/4 ins / 85 x 66.8 cm) GBP 6,325. PARIS, 13 Dec 2000, *Princess de Hesse-Darmstadt in an Ivory Silk Gown in a Landscape* (c. 1750, Miniature, oval, 3 x 2 ins / 7 x 6 cm) FRF 18,000.

FIEDLER, Katharina

German, 19th century.
Painter. Landscapes.

Katharina Fiedler was the daughter of Bernhard Fiedler.

FIEDLER, Marianne

German, 19th century.

Born 29 April 1864, in Dresden; died 14 February 1904, in Mainburg (Bavaria).
Painter, lithographer.
Marianne Fiedler worked first with Ludwig Herterich in Munich, and then in Italy. She was influenced by Otto Greiner. She is especially known for her watercolours, such as: *Landscape on the Bank of the River Main, View of Loschwitz, near Dresden.*

FIEDLING, Thomas, or Fielding
British, 18th century.
Born c. 1758.
Painter, engraver. Hunting scenes, landscapes.
A pupil of F. Bartolozzi and W.W. Ryland, Thomas Fielding is noted for four series of landscapes and hunting scenes. He also engraved a number of *Historical Scenes.*

FIEGEL, Carl
German, 19th century.
Born 20 January 1824, in Munich; died 16 May 1869.
Painter, glass painter. Genre scenes.
Fiegel is particularly known for his sketches for glass paintings. One of his known works is *Adoration of the Magi.*

FIEGLIN, Jorg
German, 16th century.
Born in the 16th century, in Blaubeuren (Württemberg).
Sculptor.
Fieglin worked on the choir of the church at Oberlenningen between 1513 and 1540.

FIEHNE, J. M.
Dutch, 18th century.
Engraver.
J. M. Fiehne is known to have executed a landscape.

FIELD, Edward Loyal
American, 19th - 20th century.
Born 1856, in Galesburg; died 1914.
Painter. Landscapes.
Edward Loyal Field studied in Paris with Carolus-Duran. He won the Iuness Prize and the Samuel Shaw Prize, and was a member of the Salmagundi Club.
AUCTION RECORDS:
NEW YORK, 26 May 1904, *September Afternoon,* USD 135. NEW YORK, 25-26 March 1909, *Twilight,* USD 60. LOS ANGELES, 24 June 1980, *Landscape with Houses* (oil on canvas, 12 x 16 1/4 ins / 30.5 x 41.3 cm) USD 900.

FIELD, Erastus Aeneas Salisbury
American, 19th century.
Born 1807, in Leverett (Massachusetts); died 1900, in Sunderland.
Painter. Portraits, scenes with figures, mythological subjects.
Erastus Aeneas Salisbury Field, a Naive painter, was self-taught, although he did spend a few months in Samuel Morse's studio. He painted portraits and a series of Fantastic paintings.
AUCTION RECORDS:
NEW YORK, 13 Nov 1974, *Mary (Polly) Coomes; Abiel Coomes* (oils on canvas, a pair) USD 14,000. NEW YORK, 30 April 1981, *Deacon Joshua Smith; Jerusha Foote Smith* (c. 1825-1830, oils on canvas, a pair, 35 1/2 x 29 ins / 90.2 x 73.7 cm) USD 21,000. NEW YORK, 21 Jan 1984, *Aeneas Disembarking in Carthage* (c. 1865, oil on canvas, 33 x 38 3/4 ins / 83.8 x 98.4 cm) USD 65,000. NEW YORK, 26 Oct 1985, *Portrait of a Little Girl* (oil on canvas, 34 x 26 ins / 86.3 x 66 cm) USD 60,000.

FIELD, Hamilton Easter
American, 19th - 20th century.
Born 21 April 1873, in Brooklyn; died 1922.
Painter.
Hamilton Easter Field was in Paris a pupil of J.L. Gérôme, Raphael Collin and Fantin-Latour.

FIELD, John M.
British, 18th - 19th century.
Born 1771; died 1841, in Molesey, near London.
Active in London.
Painter. Portraits, landscapes.
John Field exhibited with the Royal Academy from 1800 to 1836. The British Museum holds two drawings by Field after a bust of William Pitt the Younger by Joseph Nollekens.
MUSEUMS AND GALLERIES:
LONDON (British Mus.).

FIELD, Louise Blodgett (Mrs)
American, 20th century.
Active in Boston.
Painter.
Louise Blodgett Field was a pupil of Rose Turner and Tomasso Juglaris in Boston.

FIELD, Robert
British, 19th century.
Born in Gloucester; died 9 August 1819, in Jamaica.
Painter, engraver. Portraits.
Robert Field exhibited with the Royal Academy in London in 1810. He was active in Halifax.
MUSEUMS AND GALLERIES:
LONDON (British Mus.): *Engraving after a Portrait of Thomas Warton* (after Reynolds) - LONDON (National Portrait Gal.): *Charles Inglis* (1810, oil on canvas).
AUCTION RECORDS:
NEW YORK, 5 April 1944, *Man,* USD 150. NEW YORK, 4 Nov 1987, *Portrait of a Naval Officer* (1818, oil on canvas, 30 x 24 3/4 ins / 76 x 63 cm) GBP 6,800.

FIELD, Walter
British, 19th - 20th century.
Born 1 January 1837; died 23 December 1901, in Hampstead.
Painter, watercolourist. Genre scenes, landscapes.
Walter Field studied under John Rogers Herbert and John Pye. He exhibited at the Royal Academy and the Royal Society of Painters in Watercolours between 1856 and 1899.
MUSEUMS AND GALLERIES:
HAMBURG: *Bad Weather on the Thames; Sunlight; Henley Regatta* - LONDON (Victoria and Albert Mus.): *Young Boy in a Cornfield; Young Girl Carrying a Pitcher.*
AUCTION RECORDS:
LONDON, 25 June 1909, *Bathing Place on the Coast* (watercolour) GBP 17. LONDON, 8 March 1977, *Henley Regatta* (1884, oil on canvas, 55 x 95 1/4 ins / 140 x 242 cm) GBP 400. LONDON, 23 June 1981, *Wargrave on Thames* (oil on canvas, 28 x 46 3/4 ins / 71 x 119 cm) GBP 2,200. LONDON, 11 Oct 1983, *Ploughing Scene* (1895, watercolour and pencil, 17 1/2 x 24 1/2 ins / 44.5 x 62.3 cm) GBP 500. LONDON, 30 Jan 1991, *Harvest* (1881, watercolour, 13 3/4 x 20 1/2 ins / 35 x 52 cm) GBP 2,090. LONDON, 14 June 1991, *The Breath of a Gentle Breeze...* (1870, oil on canvas, 30 x 48 ins / 76 x 122 cm) GBP 4,180. LONDON, 13 March 1992, *Philimore Island, Shiplake; Shiplake Overflow* (1882, oil on canvas, a pair, each 39 x 60 ins / 99 x 152.5 cm) GBP 13,200. LONDON, 4 Nov 1994, *Henley Regatta* (1884, oil on canvas, 55 x 95 1/4 ins / 139.7 x 242 cm) GBP 135,700. LONDON, 9 May 1996, *On the Bank of a River* (1879, oil on canvas, 13 3/4 x 24 ins / 35 x 61 cm) GBP 690.

FIELD-EMMETT, Lydia. See **EMMETT Lydia Field**

FIELDE, Jakob
Danish, 19th century.
Born 10 April 1859, in Aalesund; died 5 May 1896, in Minneapolis, USA.
Sculptor.

Jakob Fielde was a pupil at the Kunstakademi in Copenhagen and also worked with C.G.V. Bissen. The gallery in Bergen possesses his *Primavera* and *Portrait of Consul C. Sundt and his Wife*.

FIELDER

British, 18th century.
Died 1800, in Birmingham.
Miniaturist.

FIELDER, L.

British, 20th century.
Active in London.
Painter. Still-lifes.

AUCTION RECORDS:
LONDON, 13 June 1928, *Still-life*, GBP 21.

FIELDING, Anthony Vandyke Copley

British, 19th century.
Born 22 November 1787, in East Sowerby; died 3 March 1855, in Worthing, near Brighton.
Painter, watercolourist, draughtsman. Seascapes, landscapes.

The second son of Nathan Theodore Fielding, Anthony Vandyke Copley Fielding studied under John Varley and became a member and later president of the Society of Painters in Watercolours, where he often exhibited. He won a gold medal at the Salon des Artistes Français of 1824, in Paris. He also painted in oils, exhibiting with the Royal Academy in London. Through his brother Thales, Copley Fielding met the French painter Eugène Delacroix during the latter's visit to London in 1825, in the company of Bonington and Alexander Colin. Copley Fielding is best known for his broad, panoramic scenes. An excellent painter of seascapes and skies, he is one of a number of early 19th-century artists whose powerful natural scenes influenced French painters of the École de 1830.

Copley-Fielding

MUSEUMS AND GALLERIES:
AVIGNON: *Seascape, Sunset* - BERLIN: drawings - BIRMINGHAM: *Arundel Park* - BIRMINGHAM (Mus. and AG): *Packet Boat Entering Harbour* (oil on canvas) - BLACKBURN: *Sandgate* - CARDIFF: *Cardiff Castle; Arundel Castle* - DUBLIN: *View of the Port of Westminster; Landscape in Cumberland; The Harbour at Shoreham* - HAMBURG: *Seascape* - LONDON (Victoria and Albert Mus.): *Ship in Distress; Boat Passing under a Bridge; Seascape; Brougham Castle; Castle on a Rock; Mountain Landscape; The Irthing Valley; South Downs; The Rydal Mountains; Ramoch Heath; River and Mountain; Windsor Great Park; Loch Lomond; Carnavon Castle; Seashore at Sunset; Rievaulx Abbey; Scene on a Lake; Beccles on the River Waveney, Suffolk; Cowherds and Cattle; Wheatfield; Landscape* (1843); *Landscape* (1849); *Landscape* - LONDON (Wallace Collection): *Langdale Pikes* (1839, watercolour/paper); *Bridlington Harbour* (1837, watercolour/grey paper); *Crowborough Hill* (1838, watercolour/paper) - MANCHESTER: *Old Harbour; Loch Lomond; Staffa; View From Loch Etive; Boats Returning to Port at Dover; View of Ben Varlich from Loch Lomond* - NOTTINGHAM: *View of a Castle Beside the Sea; Ploughing; View of Stone Castle* - SHEFFIELD: *Seascape* - SYDNEY: *Off the Coast near Eddystone Harbour; Aftermath of a Shipwreck*.

AUCTION RECORDS:
LONDON, 6 May 1899, *The Sussex Dunes; Arundel Castle*, FRF 46,200. LONDON, 30 Nov 1907, *View of Towy* (watercolour) GBP 44; *Mountains at Glencoe* (watercolour) GBP 48. LONDON, 18 Jan 1908, *Kithurn Castle* (1826) GBP 54. LONDON, 4 April 1908, *Pembroke Castle*, GBP 325. LONDON, 21 May 1908, *View Near Lendfield*, GBP 33. LONDON, 19 June 1908, *Bolton Abbey*, GBP 336. LONDON, 27 Feb 1909, *Strath Bychan Near Tremador*, GBP 96; *Aeneas and the Sibyll*, GBP 47. LONDON, 7 May 1909, *Seascape*, GBP 39. LONDON, 21 May 1909, *View Near Lewes*, GBP 57. LONDON, 7 March 1910, *View of Liverpool*, GBP 37. LONDON, 17 June 1910, *Wooded Landscape; Peasant Driving his Herd*, GBP 126. PARIS, 16 and 17 Dec 1919, *Valley Road* (watercolour) FRF 400; *At Pasture* (watercolour) FRF 220. PARIS, 20-22 May 1920, *English Landscape* (watercolour) FRF 1,000. PARIS, 30 Nov-2 Dec 1920, *Loch in the Scottish Highlands* (watercolour) FRF 600; *Hen Pheasant; Two Ducks; Pheasant* (three pencils) FRF 410. LONDON, 26 Nov 1923, *Storm at Sea* (drawing) GBP 18. LONDON, 21 Dec 1923, *An Old Mill; Highway Scene; Dead Game* (three drawings) GBP 7. LONDON, 25 Jan 1924, *Bolton Abbey* (drawing) GBP 136. LONDON, 20 June 1924, *Loch Katrine* (drawing) GBP 231; *Storm at Sea* (drawing) GBP 52; *Loch in the Highlands* (drawing) GBP 672. LONDON, 18 July 1927, *Loch in the Highlands* (drawing) GBP 168; *Dolbauden Castle*, GBP 65. LONDON, 22 June 1928, *Loch Katrine* (drawing) GBP 483; *Loch Nemi* (drawing) GBP 304; *Bolney, Sussex* (drawing) GBP 199; *Warleigh Castle* (drawing) GBP 178. LONDON, 25 Oct 1928, *Groyim Valley* (watercolour) GBP 73. LONDON, 10 May 1929, *Cintra Spa* (drawing) GBP 273; *Loch Awe and Ben Cruachan* (drawing) GBP 52. LONDON, 29 May 1929, *Wooded Landscape* (watercolour) GBP 21; *Landscapes* (two watercolours) GBP 24. LONDON, 8 July 1930, *Snowdon* (watercolour) GBP 135; *Snowdon* (watercolour) GBP 74. LONDON, 3 Nov 1937, *Dindarrah Castle*, GBP 60. LONDON, 9 May 1938, *Low Tide* (drawing) GBP 35. LONDON, 6 March 1939, *Landscape* (drawing) GBP 24. LONDON, 26 April 1939, *Landscape around Cuckfield*, GBP 40. LONDON, 26 June 1940, *Landscape* (drawing) GBP 18. LONDON, 21 March 1941, *Glen Lockhy* (drawing) GBP 23. LONDON, 26 June 1941, *Conway* (drawing) GBP 11; *Highland Loch* (drawing) GBP 147; *Highland Loch* (drawing) GBP 63. LONDON, 14 Jan 1944, *Loch Lomond* (drawing) GBP 84. LONDON, 11 Feb 1944, *Goodrich Castle* (drawing) GBP 44; *Ross-on-Wye* (drawing) GBP 39; *Lake Bala* (drawing) GBP 14; *Conway Castle* (drawing) GBP 39; *Rossenah Marshes* (drawing) GBP 29. LONDON, 17 March 1944, *Loch Achray*, GBP 94. LONDON, 23 June 1944, *Glen Orchy* (drawing) GBP 231; *Loch Lomond* (drawing) GBP 37; *Near Maidstone* (drawing) GBP 78. LONDON, 23 June 1944, *View of Arundel* (drawing) GBP 262; *View of Lancaster* (drawing) GBP 294; *Goodrich Castle* (drawing) GBP 89. LONDON, 2 Aug 1944, *Loch Fyne* (drawing) GBP 38. LONDON, 25 Oct 1944, *Loch Fyne* (drawing) GBP 48. LONDON, 5 Oct 1945, *Ben Vorlich* (drawing) GBP 89. LONDON, 5 Oct 1945, *Scarborough* (drawing) GBP 36; *Dover* (drawing) GBP 26; *Sunset in the Highlands* (drawing) GBP 273. LONDON, 9 Nov 1945, *Ben Starine* (drawing) GBP 63; *Goodrich Castle* (drawing) GBP 31; *Lancaster Castle* (drawing) GBP 120. LONDON, 21 Nov 1945, *Ben Lomond* (drawing) GBP 135; *Coniston Water* (drawing) GBP 26; *Landscape* (drawing) GBP 98. LONDON, 21 Nov 1945, *Loch Katrine* (drawing) GBP 44; *Loch Lomond* (drawing) GBP 46; *Landscape* (drawing) GBP 60; *Kentish Woman* (drawing) GBP 18; *Landscape* (drawing) GBP 110; *Landscape* (drawing) GBP 120; *Lake* (drawing) GBP 130; *Ben Nevis* (drawing) GBP 85; *Patterdale* (drawing) GBP 45; *Goodrich Castle* (drawing) GBP 28; *Landscape* (drawing) GBP 34; *Port* (drawing) GBP 32. LONDON, 30 Nov 1945, *Whitby* (drawing) GBP 178; *Bay* (drawing) GBP 136; *Arundel Castle* (drawing) GBP 162. LONDON, 11 Jan 1946, *Arundel Castle* (drawing) GBP 136. LONDON, 16 Oct 1946, *Cintra Spa* (drawing) GBP 55; *Loch Leven* (drawing) GBP 35. LONDON, 29 Nov 1946, *Sussex Downs* (drawing) GBP 48. LONDON, 21 Feb 1947, *Highland Landscape* (drawing) GBP 47. LONDON, 25 April 1947, *Wooded Landscape*, GBP 39. LONDON, 11 July 1947,

Bolton Abbey (drawing) GBP 57. LONDON, 17 Nov 1971, *Byland Abbey*, GBP 1,400. LONDON, 8 June 1976, *Loch Tay* (watercolour, 10 x 14 1/4 ins / 25.5 x 36 cm) GBP 700. LONDON, 24 Nov 1977, *Chepstow Castle, Monmouthshire* (1832, watercolour, 9 3/4 x 12 3/4 ins / 25 x 32.5 cm) GBP 1,000. LONDON, 24 March 1981, *Loch Lomond* (1850, watercolour, 7 1/4 x 10 1/4 ins / 18.1 x 26.3 cm) GBP 1,000. NEW YORK, 1 March 1984, *Cumberland Landscape* (oil on canvas, 33 x 38 3/4 ins / 83.8 x 98.4 cm) USD 65,000. LONDON, 20 Nov 1984, *Arundel Castle from the Park* (watercolour, 11 x 15 1/2 ins / 28 x 39.5 cm) GBP 7,500. LONDON, 19 Nov 1987, *Shipwreck off the Yorkshire Coast* (1831, watercolour and pencil heightened with gouache, 27 3/4 x 45 ins / 70.5 x 114 cm) GBP 7,200. AMSTERDAM, 16 Nov 1988, *Rocky Landscape with a Shepherd Looking Down into a Valley* (1810, watercolour/paper, 15 x 21 1/4 ins / 38 x 54 cm) NLG 1,610. LONDON, 31 Jan 1990, *Shipwreck off the Sussex Coast at Seaford Cliffs* (1834, watercolour and gouache/paper, 8 1/2 x 12 3/4 ins / 21.5 x 32.5 cm) GBP 2,640. LONDON, 9 Feb 1990, *Fisherman in a Boat on the Wye with a Distant View of Goodrich Castle* (1838, oil on canvas, 17 1/4 x 24 1/4 ins / 43.5 x 61.5 cm) GBP 8,250. PARIS, 25 March 1991, *Capel Curig* (watercolour, 7 3/4 x 11 1/2 ins / 20 x 29.5 cm) FRF 3,500. LONDON, 10 July 1991, *Panoramic Landscape with a Distant View of Rievaulx Abbey, Yorkshire* (1847, oil on panel, 13 3/4 x 17 1/2 ins / 35 x 44.5 cm) GBP 18,700. LONDON, 9 April 1992, *Fishing Boats Heading for the Coast* (1842, watercolour and gouache, 19 1/2 x 29 1/2 ins / 49.5 x 75 cm) GBP 3,410. LONDON, 13 July 1993, *Shoreham* (pencil and watercolour, 11 1/2 x 15 3/4 ins / 29.2 x 40 cm) GBP 3,680. LUDLOW, 29 Sept 1994, *The Glydder Mountains in North Wales* (watercolour, 18 1/2 x 27 1/2 ins / 47 x 70 cm) GBP 2,760. CALAIS, 25 June 1995, *Sailing-boats in Venice* (oil on canvas/panel, 21 1/4 x 39 3/4 ins / 54 x 101 cm) FRF 15,000. LONDON, 11 March 1999, *Travellers on a Track, Snowdon, Wales* (oil on board, 10 x 12 ins / 25 x 30 cm) GBP 2,000. LONDON, 9 Nov 1999, *Shipwreck on the Yorkshire Coast* (1831, pencil, watercolour and scratching out, 28 x 46 ins / 72 x 116 cm) GBP 14,000. NORTH BETHESDA, 10 March 2000, *Travellers in a Landscape* (oil on canvas, 11 x 16 ins / 28 x 41 cm) USD 3,900. LONDON, 8 June 2000, *Distant View of the Cumberland Hills from Eskdale* (1833, pencil, watercolour and gum arabic with scratching out, 25 x 35 ins / 63 x 88 cm) GBP 7,000. LONDON, 15 June 2001, *Distant View of Rievaulx Abbey, near Helmsley, Yorkshire* (1842, oil on panel, 14 x 17 ins / 35 x 44 cm) GBP 4,500. LONDON, 4 July 2001, *Distant View of Arundel Castle, Sussex* (1834, watercolour over pencil heightened with gouche, 11 x 16 ins / 28 x 41 cm) GBP 2,900. LONDON, 4 July 2002, *Showery Weather near Arundel* (watercolour over pencil heightened with stopping out and scratching out, 9 x 13 ins / 22 x 33 cm) GBP 5,000. LONDON, 28 Nov 2002, *Loch Tay, Perthshire* (watercolour over pencil heightened with gouache and scratching out, 7 x 10 ins / 17 x 25 cm) GBP 3,200. LEEDS, 4 Feb 2003, *Folkestone, Kent* (watercolour, 16 x 23 ins / 41 x 58 cm) GBP 8,000. LONDON, 5 June 2003, *Extensive View of Greenwich, London* (1821, pencil, pen, ink, watercolour and gum arabic with scratching out, 22 x 43 ins / 56 x 110 cm) GBP 21,000. PARIS, 17 March 2004, *Bolton Abbey, Looking Down Wharfdale* (1841, watercolour, 24 x 39 ins / 62 x 98 cm) EUR 14,500. PARIS, 17 March 2004, *Scarborough Castle* (1854, watercolour and gouache, 15 x 24 ins / 39 x 60 cm) EUR 14,500.

FIELDING, John

British, 18th century.
Born c. 1758.
Engraver.

John Fielding studied intially under Bartolozzi and later Ryland, with whom he enjoyed a prolific collaboration, to the extent that few of his works are signed with his own name. He is known for his *Jacob and Rachel* after Stothard, and *Moses Saved by the Pharaoh's Daughter*.

FIELDING, John

British, 18th century.
Active in London.
Engraver.

John Fielding produced a number of engravings after Hogarth from 1746 to 1756.

FIELDING, Mary Ann (Mrs)

Maiden name: Mary Ann Walton
British, 19th century.
Painter, watercolourist, draughtswoman. Flowers, animals.

Mary Ann Walton was the wife of Theodore Henry Adolphus Fielding, with whom she collaborated on *A Picturesque Tour of English Lakes*. An accomplished watercolourist, she became a member of the Society of Painters in Watercolours in 1821, and exhibited drawings and paintings of flowers, birds and insects until 1835.

FIELDING, Nathan Theodore

British, 18th - 19th century.
Born c. 1747; died 1814 or 1818.
Painter, watercolourist. Portraits, landscapes.

Nathan Fielding was the father of Theodore, Copley, Thales and Newton Fielding, whom he also taught painting. He was active mainly in the northern English town of Halifax. In 1775 he became a member of the Society of Artists, with whom he exhibited in 1791. He also exhibited with the Free Society, the British Institution and the Society of Painters in Watercolours. He is best known for his portraits.

MUSEUMS AND GALLERIES:

LONDON (Victoria and Albert Mus.): *Portrait.*

AUCTION RECORDS:

LONDON, 19 Nov 1986, *Portrait of Two Little Girls* (1794, oil on canvas, 44 x 35 1/2 ins / 112 x 90 cm) GBP 9,000. LONDON, 18 Nov 1988, *View of a Town with Mills and a Viaduct, with Figures in the Foreground* (1764, oil on canvas, 39 1/2 x 52 ins / 100.3 x 131.8 cm) GBP 68,200. LONDON, 7 April 1993, *Two Children on a Black Pony* (oil on canvas, 40 x 46 ins / 101.6 x 116.9 cm) GBP 41,100. LONDON, 3 Dec 2002, *Extensive Landscape with Figures Crossing a Bridge* (1796, oil on canvas, 20 x 26 ins / 52 x 65 cm) GBP 2,100.

FIELDING, Newton Smith Limbird

British, 19th century.
Born 1799, in Huntington (Yorkshire); died 16 June 1856, in Paris.
Also active in France.
Painter, watercolourist, engraver, lithographer.
Landscapes, landscapes with figures, animals.

Newton Fielding was the youngest son and pupil of Nathan Theodore Fielding. He exhibited with the Royal Society of Watercolourists in London, but was best known as an engraver and lithographer, especially in France where he was drawing teacher to the family of Louis-Philippe. He was the author of two theoretical treatises on drawing.

MUSEUMS AND GALLERIES:

BALTIMORE (Peabody Art Collection): *Garden Scene with Rabbits* - CAEN: *Ducks* - LONDON (British Mus.): *Ducks* - LONDON (Victoria and Albert Mus.).

AUCTION RECORDS:

LONDON, 9 Dec 1907, *Landscape* (watercolour) GBP 2. PARIS, 30 Nov, 1 and 2 Dec 1920, *River with Overhanging Trees* (watercolour) FRF 605. PARIS, 3 May 1923, *Riverbank* (watercolour) FRF 100. PARIS, 15 Dec 1927, *Roe Deer Spared* (watercolour) FRF 430. PARIS, 22 Feb 1932, *Sleeping Huntsman*, FRF 500. PARIS, 31 June 1935, *Beach with the Wreck of a Dutch Warship* (watercolour) FRF 65. PARIS, 21 Dec 1938, *Birds and Animals* (two watercolours) FRF 1,410; *Hare* (watercolour) FRF 400. PARIS, 24 April 1942, *Boar* (1831, watercolour) FRF 550. PARIS, 8 Jan 1947, *Riverbank with Mountains on the Horizon* (1832, watercolour) FRF 2,300. VERSAILLES, 19 Oct 1969, *Landscape with Three Ducks* (watercolour) FRF 700. PARIS, 31 May 1972, *Peacock and a Golden Pheasant; Swans* (1830, watercolour, 7 x 10 1/4 ins / 18 x 26 cm) FRF 1,050. LONDON, 19 March 1981, *Pheasant and Two Cocks* (watercolour and gouache, 6 x 9 1/4 ins / 15 x 23.5 cm) GBP 400. LONDON, 7 July 1983, *Ducks on the Banks of a Stream; Farmyard* (two watercolours/pencil outlines, 6 1/2 x 10 ins / 16.5 x 24.5 cm and 6 3/4 x 9 3/4 ins/17 x 25 cm) GBP 1,050. LONDON, 19 Feb 1987, *Swans by a River Bank* (1830, watercolour, 7 1/4 x 10 1/4 ins / 18.5 x 26 cm) GBP 680. PARIS, 11 June 1997, *Weasel and Pheasant in a Wood; Ducks on the Edge of a Pond* (watercolour, two pendants, 4 3/4 x 7 ins / 12.3 x 18 cm) FRF 27,000. LONDON, 3 Feb 2000, *Vasley Road, Lyme Regis* (pencil and watercolour with scratching out, 6 x 9 ins / 16 x 23 cm) GBP 1,000. LONDON, 27 Nov 2003, *Golden Pheasant and Moorhens* (watercolour over pencil heightened with gouache, 6 x 8 ins / 14 x 21 cm) GBP 1,400. LONDON, 27 Nov 2003, *Hunter with Dogs* (watercolour over pencil heightened with gouache and gum arabic, 6 x 9 ins / 15 x 22 cm) GBP 2,000.

FIELDING, Thales Angelo Vernet
British, 19th century.
Born 1793, in Stamford, Lincolnshire; died 20 December 1837, in London.
Painter, watercolourist. Historical subjects, genre scenes, landscapes, animals.

Thales Fielding was the son of Nathan Theodore Fielding. He travelled to Paris in about 1820, where he befriended Eugène Delacroix, with whom he shared a garret on Place de la Sorbonne. He taught drawing at the military academy in Woolwich. Thales is best known for his genre scenes, landscapes (often featuring animals) and history paintings based on the writings of Sir Walter Scott. He exhibited with the Society of Painters in Watercolours (of which he became an associate, and a member on 12 February 1820), and at the Salon des Artistes Français of 1823-1824 in Paris.

MUSEUMS AND GALLERIES:
LONDON (British Mus.) - LONDON (Victoria and Albert Mus.): *The Hillside at Greenwich, the Observatory and the Thames; Landscape with Animals.*

AUCTION RECORDS:
LONDON, 1 Dec 1922, *Cattle,* GBP 3. LONDON, 30 July 1924, *Near Abergavenny,* GBP 18. LONDON, 18 March 1982, *Fishermen on a Beach* (watercolour, 7 3/4 x 11 1/4 ins / 20 x 28.5 cm) GBP 500. PARIS, 4 June 1999, *Portrait of Eugene Delacroix* (c. 1824, oil on canvas laid on board, 13 x 11 ins / 34 x 27 cm) FRF 77,000. LONDON, 15 March 2000, *Fisherfolk on the Beach* (1830, watercolour over pencil, 9 x 12 ins / 23 x 30 cm) GBP 1,600. LONDON, 15 June 2000, *Cows Watering from a Stream* (watercolour heightened with stopping out and scratching out, 20 x 24 ins / 51 x 61 cm) GBP 1,800.

FIELDING, Theodore Henry Adolphus
British, 19th century.
Born 1781; died 11 July 1851, in Croydon.
Painter, watercolourist, engraver. Landscapes.

Theodore Henry Adolphus Fielding, the elder son of Nathan Theodore Fielding, was an occasional exhibitor with the Royal Academy and a teacher of drawing at the military academy in Addiscombe. He was the author of a number of theoretical and practical works on painting, engraving and perspective. He also published collections of landscapes in aquatint such as: *A Picturesque Tour of the English Lakes* (1821), *Picturesque Illustrations of the River Wye* (1822), and *Cumberland, Westmoreland and Lancashire Illustrated* (1822).

MUSEUMS AND GALLERIES:
LEEDS (City AG): *The Entrance to the Wood* (watercolour) - LONDON (British Mus.) - LONDON (Victoria and Albert Mus.): *Manorbier Castle, Pembrokeshire.*

FIELDS, Mitchell
American, 20th century.
Born 28 September 1900, in Romania; died 1966.
Sculptor.

Mitchell Fields was awarded the Bornet Prize by the National Academy of Design and was a member of the Society of Sculptors and Modellers of America.

FIELDSKOV, Niels Voldemar
Danish, 19th century.
Born 2 April 1826, in Copenhagen; died 1903.
Sculptor.

Niels Voldemar Fieldskov was a pupil at the school of fine arts in Copenhagen and worked with H. W. Bissens. He is noted for his copies of Thorvaldsen and antique sculpture. Known works by him are *Pan, King Christian IV, Thor* and *The Four Seasons*. He decorated many churches, castles and official monuments.

MUSEUMS AND GALLERIES:
COPENHAGEN (Ny Carlsberg Glyptotek): *Thor.*

FIELDSTED, S., or Fjeldsted
Danish, 18th - 19th century.
Lithographer. Figures, historical subjects.

A lithograph by S. Fieldsted depicting *Jens, the Old Organ Blower* is at the cathedral of Roskilde.

AUCTION RECORDS:
COPENHAGEN, 6 May 1992, *Death of Napoleon on St Helena* (1835, oil on canvas, after C. von Steubens, 29 1/4 x 39 1/4 ins / 74 x 100 cm) DKK 5,200.

FIELGRAF, Karl
German, 19th century.
Born 1804, in Berlin.
Painter. Religious subjects, portraits, genre scenes.

Fielgraf was a student of Wach in Berlin and Schadow in Düsseldorf. He settled in Berlin, where he exhibited between 1826 and 1844. His works include *Abraham's Sacrifice.*

FIELING, Lodewyk, or Tieling
Italian, 18th century.
Painter. Landscapes with figures, landscapes, animals.

AUCTION RECORDS:
LONDON, 21 April 1993, *Italian Landscape with Peasant Women Milking Cows* (oil on canvas, 40 x 43 3/4 ins / 101.5 x 111 cm) GBP 4,830.

FIELISCH, Christoph
German, 18th century.
Died c. 1757.
Active in Goldberg, Silesia (now Zlotoryja, Poland).
Painter.

FIELITZ, Ida A.
Russian, 19th century.
Born 1847, in Riga.
Painter. Figures, local figures.

A pupil of Luc-Olivier Merson's, Ida Fielitz showed her work at the Salon des Artistes Français, where she received an honourable mention in 1892. After a successful debut, Ida Fielitz rejected the compromises so often required behind the scenes of artists of the Salons in order for their work to be exhibited. She stopped sending her paintings to the exhibitions at the Grand Palais, and merely sent engravings.

MUSEUMS AND GALLERIES:

RHEIMS: *Greek Nun* - RIGA: *Portrait of the Artist's Mother.*

FIELIUS, Johannes. See **TIELIUS**

FIENE, Ernest

German, 20th century.

Born 2 November 1894, in Elberfeld; died 10 August 1965, in Paris.

From 1910 active and from 1928 naturalised in the USA.

Painter, pastellist, draughtsman. Landscapes, urban landscapes, landscapes with figures, figures, portraits.

Fiene studied at the National Academy of Design in New York from 1914 to 1918, as well as at the Beaux-Arts Institute of Design from 1916 to 1918, and at the Art Student's League in 1923. He travelled to Europe, working in Paris in 1929 and Florence in 1932. He also travelled to Mexico. He was a member of several associations, a lecturer at the Cooper Union in 1938-1939, at the Art Student's League from 1938 to 1965, and at the National Academy of Design from 1960 to 1965. He received several prizes and distinctions, notably at the Carnegie Institute in 1938, and the Edwin Palmer Memorial Prize of the National Academy of Design in 1944.

Fiene executed some commissions for portraits, but he was especially noted for solidly constructed landscapes and realistic street scenes. He exhibited particularly in New York from 1923, notably at the Whitney Museum for American Art from 1930 to 1945, at the National Academy of Design, as well as at the Carnegie Institute in Pittsburgh and at the Pennsylvania Academy of Art between 1930 and 1945.

AUCTION RECORDS:

NEW YORK, 1 May 1946, *Winter's Evening,* USD 625. NEW YORK, 5 Dec 1982, *Pittsburgh* (oil on canvas, 22 x 28 ins / 56 x 71.4 cm) USD 5,200. NEW YORK, 18 March 1983, *Flowers in a Vase* (pastel, 24 1/4 x 19 3/4 ins / 61.8 x 50 cm) USD 550. NEW YORK, 23 March 1984, *Flowers* (oil on canvas, 27 1/2 x 35 1/4 ins / 70 x 89.5 cm) USD 600. WASHINGTON DC, 6 Dec 1985, *After the Bath* (1931, oil on canvas, 21 1/4 x 27 ins / 53.7 x 68.8 cm) USD 4,000. NEW YORK, 20 March 1987, *Madison Square Park* (charcoal and porcelain white/paper) USD 1,600. NEW YORK, 25 May 1989, *Pittsburgh* (oil on canvas, 30 x 36 ins / 76.2 x 91.4 cm) USD 28,600. NEW YORK, 14 Feb 1990, *Night Falling on the Village of Woodbury* (oil on canvas, 20 x 28 ins / 50.7 x 71 cm) USD 1,100. NEW YORK, 31 May 1990, *The Petrol Refinery* (oil on card, 32 x 23 3/4 ins / 81.2 x 60.3 cm) USD 8,250. NEW YORK, 27 Sept 1990, *First Snow* (oil on canvas, 26 x 36 1/4 ins / 66.3 x 92 cm) USD 7,700. NEW YORK, 14 March 1991, *The Woman with the Black Hat* (oil on canvas, 24 x 16 ins / 61 x 40.6 cm) USD 8,800. NEW YORK, 6 Dec 1991, *The East River by Night* (oil on card, 25 1/4 x 30 ins / 63.9 x 76.3 cm) USD 8,800. NEW YORK, 25 Sept 1992, *Dancer* (oil on card, 16 x 11 ins / 40.6 x 27.9 cm) USD 1,320. NEW YORK, 11 March 1993, *Nocturne* (1948, oil on canvas, 60 x 40 1/4 ins / 152.5 x 102 cm) USD 13,800. NEW YORK, 25 May 1994, *The Night Shift at the Aliquippa Factory* (oil on canvas, 36 x 48 ins / 91.4 x 121.9 cm) USD 20,700. NEW YORK, 28 Nov 1995, *On the Farm* (watercolour and pencil/paper, 14 1/2 x 21 1/2 ins / 37 x 54.4 cm) USD 1,725. NEW YORK, 26 May 1999, *Sunday* (oil on canvas, 14 x 17 ins / 36 x 43 cm) USD 4,250. NEW YORK, 11 Nov 1999, *Empire State Building* (lithograph, 14 x 9 ins / 36 x 22 cm) USD 4,200. NEW YORK, 15 June 2000, *Malbaie* (oil on canvas, 22 x 28 ins / 56 x 71 cm) USD 4,500. NEW YORK, 4 Oct 2000, *Safe Harbour* (oil on canvas, 25 x 30 ins / 63 x 76 cm) USD 5,500. CLEVELAND, 22 Jan 2001, *New England Hills* (22 x 35 ins / 56 x 89 cm) USD 3,900. NEW YORK, 13 June 2001, *Fishermen Cleaning the Day's Catch, Native Boy, Jamaica* (watercolour and gouache on paperboard, two, 22 x 28 ins / 56 x 71 cm) USD 2,400. OAK PARK, 3 March 2002, *Nudes in a Landscape* (1929, oil on canvas, 20 x 16 ins / 51 x 41 cm) USD 2,900. BOSTON, 10 May 2002, *Winter in Connecticut* (oil on canvas, 22 x 34 ins / 56 x 86 cm) USD 3,000. CHICAGO, 1 June 2003, *Cityscape* (1930, oil on canvas, 36 x 30 ins / 91 x 76 cm) USD 14,000. NEW YORK, 5 June 2003, *Manhattan Construction* (1932, pencil, 21 x 14 ins / 54 x 35 cm) USD 6,000. NEW YORK, 26 May 2004, *Nocturne* (oil on canvas on masonite, 7 x 15 ins / 18 x 38 cm) USD 3,500. BOSTON, 10 Sept 2004, *Autumn Farm* (1920, oil on canvas, 20 x 24 ins / 51 x 61 cm) USD 2,100.

FIENLES, Jean de

Flemish School, 14th century.

Painter.

In 1513, Jean de Fienles was working at the castle of Hesdin (Artois).

FIENNES, Jean Baptiste or Désiré de

Belgian, 19th century.

Born c. 1800, in Anderlecht.

Active still in 1842.

Painter. History painting, genre scenes.

In Antwerp in 1829 and in Brussels in 1830 Jean Baptiste Fiennes exhibited *Faun and Bacchante* and *Beggar with Child* as well as a portrait. In 1823 he showed *The Good Mother* and in 1836 *Death of Egmont.*

AUCTION RECORDS:

LONDON, 19 March 1980, *Seamstress* (1858, oil on panel, 18 x 13 1/2 ins / 46 x 34.5 cm) GBP 1,200.

FIENVILLIER, Thomas de

French, 14th century.

Parisian artist, active c. 1373.

Sculptor (ivory).

FIÉRARD, Clémentine

French, 20th century.

Painter.

Clémentine Fiérard lived and worked in St-Denis, a suburb of Paris. She exhibited at the Salon des Artistes Français, of which she was an associate member. She was granted a bronze medal in 1900 for the International Fair, and an honourable mention in 1901.

FIERAVINO, Francesco, called il Maltese or le Chevalier Maltais

Italian, 17th century.

Born in Malta.

Painter. Still-lifes (including fruit/musical instruments).

Francesco Fieravino worked in Rome from 1640 till about 1680. He featured in a themed group exhibition on the subject of the still-life in Italy: *Stille Welt. Italienische Stilleben aus drei Jahrhunderten (Still World: Three Centuries of Italian Still-life Painting),* Kunsthalle der Hypo-Kulturstiftung, Munich, 2003.

BIBLIOGRAPHY:

Gregori, Mina/Prinz, Johann Georg, *Stille Welt. Italienische Stilleben aus drei Jahrhunderten,* exhibition catalogue, Kunsthalle der Hypo-Kulturstiftung, Munich, 2003.

MUSEUMS AND GALLERIES:

AIX: *Still-life* - NANCY: *Carpets and Weapons* - RENNES: *Two Still-lifes* - ST-BRIEUC: *Still-life.*

AUCTION RECORDS:

MILAN, 12-13 March 1963, *Still-lifes* (two pendants) ITL 1,800,000. VERSAILLES, 3 June 1965, *Still-life,* FRF 10,000. LONDON, 1 July 1966, *Still-life with Fruit,* Gns 700. ROME, 7 May 1974, *Still-life,* ITL 4,000,000. MILAN, 5 Dec 1977, *Still-life* (oil on canvas, 37 3/4 x 48 1/2 ins / 96 x 123 cm) ITL 4,000,000. NEW YORK, 5 June 1982, *Still-life with Fruit* (oil on canvas,

36$^{3}/_{4}$ x 48$^{1}/_{2}$ ins / 93.3 x 123.3 cm) USD 8,000. LONDON, 9 March 1983, *Still-life with a Globe and a Vase of Flowers* (oil on canvas, 67 x 51$^{1}/_{4}$ ins / 170 x 130 cm) GBP 15,500. MONTE CARLO, 22 June 1985, *Still-life with Precious Metal Objects and a Guitar* (oil on canvas, 56$^{1}/_{4}$ x 81 ins / 143 x 206 cm) FRF 300,000. NEW YORK, 17 Jan 1992, *Still-life with a Gilded Bowl Full of Cakes Placed on a Richly Draped Table* (oil on canvas, 36 x 49$^{1}/_{2}$ ins / 91.4 x 125.7 cm) USD 42,900. MILAN, 13 May 1993, *Still-life with a Musical Score and Instruments on an Oriental Rug* (oil on canvas, 35 x 50 ins / 89 x 127 cm) ITL 40,000,000. NEW YORK, 12 Jan 1994, *Jewellery Box, Clock, Cushion and Urn on a Table Covered in a Tablecloth Embroidered with Gold* (oil on canvas, 39$^{3}/_{4}$ ins / 101 cm, x 30 ins/76.5 cm) USD 43,700. LONDON, 3 July 1997, *Still-life with Gilt and Silver Ewers, a Mirror, a Chest, Sweetmeats on a Gilt Platter and Embroidered Material* (oil on canvas, 38$^{1}/_{4}$ x 51$^{1}/_{2}$ ins / 97 x 130.5 cm) GBP 41,100. NEW YORK, 30 Jan 1998, *Still-life with Arms; Still-life with Musical Instruments* (oil on canvas, a pair, each 28$^{1}/_{2}$ x 38 ins / 72.7 x 96.8 cm) USD 32,200. MILAN, 9 June 1999, *Still-life* (oil on canvas, 33 x 45 ins / 83 x 115 cm) ITL 25,000,000. MILAN, 10 June 1999, *Still-lifes with Guitar, Fruit and Flowers* (oil on canvas, pair, 38 x 53 ins / 97 x 134 cm) ITL 98,000,000. LONDON, 14 Dec 2000, *Still-life of Gilt and Silver Ewers, Mirror, Chest, Sweetmeats and Cloths* (oil on canvas, 38 x 51 ins / 97 x 130 cm) GBP 50,000. VENICE, 19 April 2001, *Still-life with Little Dog on Cushion and Cat* (oil on canvas, 29 x 38 ins / 74 x 97 cm) ITL 35,000,000. MILAN, 2 Dec 2003, *Still-life with Pottery and Rugs* (oil on canvas, 25 x 31 ins / 64 x 78 cm) EUR 3,500.

FIERENS, Cornelis
Flemish, 18th century.
Painter.
Flemish School.

FIERENS, Jan F.
Flemish, 17th - 18th century.
Painter.
Flemish School.

Jan F. Fierens was the son of Jaques Fierens and a member of the guild. Between 1695 and 1708 he taught four students, of whom one was his son.

FIERENS, Jaques
Flemish, 17th century.
Died 1669.
Painter.
Flemish School.

Jaques Fierens was a member of the guild of Middelburg in 1652.

FIERENS, Jaques and Jodocus. See **FIRENS**

FIÉRET, Antoine
Flemish School, 15th century.
Painter.
Tournai School.

Antoine was the pupil of Pierre Fiéret in 1488. In 1503, he was named master of the guild in Tournai. Some of his drawings survive.

FIÉRET, Jennin
Flemish School, 16th century.
Painter.
Tournai School.

In 1496, Jennin became his father Pierre's pupil and, four years later, was made a member of the Tournai guild. He may identical to the painter known as Jehan Ferret, who was artist to the *connétable* (supreme military commander) of France.

FIÉRET, Philippot
Flemish School, 16th century.
Painter.
Tournai School.

The son of Antoine Fiéret, he was named as a master of the Tournai guild in 1525.

FIÉRET, Pierre
Flemish School, 15th century.
Born in the 15th century, in Bruges.
Painter.

Pierre Fiéret was named as a master of the Tournai guild on 11 January 1483. The painting in the choir of the Augustinian chapel there, dated 17 August 1498, was his work.

FIERLANT, Herman de
Flemish, 19th century.
Born 4 April 1835, in Antwerp; died 9 February 1872, in Lyons.
Sculptor.
Flemish School.

Herman de Fierlant was a pupil of Geerts. He is recorded as being in Rome.

MUSEUMS AND GALLERIES:
LYONS: *Ruth Gleaning* (statue).

FIERLANTS, Nicolaas Marten (Captain)
Flemish, 17th century.
Born 1622, in 's Hertogenbosch; died 1694; buried 14 May in Antwerp.
Painter. History painting.
Flemish School.

Nicolaas Marten Fierlants became a member of the Antwerp Guild of St Luke in 1651 or 1652. Siret mentions his painting representing *Painting Complaining to Jupiter*, which was offered to the guild. Genoels the Younger learned the principles of perspective from Nicolaas, who was considered first-rate in that area at the time.

FIERMAISTRE, François, or Fieremestre
French, 18th century.
Active in Paris c. 1700.
Painter.

FIERO, Emilie
American, 20th century.
Born in Joliet (Illinois).
Sculptor. Figures, animals.

Émilie Fiero was a pupil of Antoine Injalbert in Paris, where she exhibited plaster models and bronzes at the Salon des Artistes Français from 1925 to 1927.

FIERROS, Dionisio
Spanish, 19th century.
Born c. 1827, in Ballota (Asturias); died 1894.
Painter.

Dionisio Fierros worked at the Academia de San Fernando in Madrid with Federico de Madrazo. He exhibited genre paintings and portraits at the exhibition of the national fine arts society of Madrid in 1860-1861.

BIBLIOGRAPHY:
Exposición del pintor Dionisio Fierros: del 27 de junio al 27 de julio de 1992, Centro de Cultura, Casa Rectoral de Soto de Luiña, Cudillero, exhibition catalogue, Centro de Cultura, Soto de Luiña, 1992. *Cuatro pintores asturianos del XIX*, exhibition catalogue, Gijón, Tioda, 1993. *Homenaje a Dionisio Fierros, XXV Certamen Nacional de Pintura de Luarca; organizado por Ayuntamiento de Valdés y Caja de Asturias*, exhibition catalogue, Consejería de Educación, Valdés, 1994. López Vázquez, José Manuel B./García Quirós, Rosa María, *Dionisio Fierros, 1827-1894: íntimo y mundano: Centro Cultural Caixavigo, marzo-abril 2000*, Caixavigo e Ourense, Vigo, 2000.

MUSEUMS AND GALLERIES:
MADRID (Mus. de Arte Moderno): *Fountain* (genre painting) - MADRID (Prado): *Portrait of Alfonso V.*

FIERS, Edouard
Flemish, 19th century.
Born 27 May 1826, in Ypres; died 23 December 1894, near Brussels.
Sculptor.
Flemish School.

Edouard Fiers was a pupil at the academy of Geefs and Simonis in Brussels. The Order of Leopold was later bestowed on him.

MUSEUMS AND GALLERIES:
YPRES: *First Love; Daisy* (plaster); *Daisy* (marble); *Night; Satyr and Cupid; The Child Bacchus; Sciences and Arts; Commerce and Industry; The Negress Slave; Cupid with Shell; Innocence; Bust of M. Baedt; M. de Brouckère; Baron Sentin; M. Rodenbach; Painting; Sculpture; Architecture; Poetry; Music; Blind Man's Buff; Love Forlorn; Young Neapolitan Fisherman; Child Playing with a Dog; Victory; Fontaine de Brouckère; Past, Present, Future; Girl.*

FIERTMAIR, Joseph
German, 18th century.
Born 18 February 1702, in Schwandorf; died 24 June 1738, in Rothenburg (Bavaria).
Painter.

Fiertmair was a student of C.D. Adams. A Jesuit himself, he painted frescoes in the Jesuit chapels and schools in Ellwangen and Rottweil (Baden-Württemberg). Fiertmair executed the altar painting in the chapel of St Ignatius at Rottweil, while at Rothenburg he did the altar paintings for the churches of St Francis-Regis and St Xavier.

FIERZ, Albert
German, 19th - 20th century.
Born 31 October 1861, in Reutlingen.
Painter. Landscapes, still-lifes.

Albert Fierz was the pupil of Hermann Baisch and Gustav Schönleber at the Akademie der Bildenden Künste in Karlsruhe. He exhibited from 1886, and in 1902 spent time in Paris. In 1904 he took part in the setting up of an art school in Zurich. From his two masters, he has retained the attention to the effects of light on landscape, for example: *Morning Effect.*

AUCTION RECORDS:
LONDON, 15 June 1994, *Still-life of Flowers, Fruit and Various Objects on a Table* (1895, oil on canvas, 31 x 21 1/4 ins / 79 x 54 cm) GBP 4,600.

FIERZ, Mathilde
Swiss, 19th - 20th century.
Born 18 February 1873, in Zurich.
Painter. Still-lifes (flowers/fruit).

Mathilde Fierz was the pupil of Gioachimo Galburera and A. Barzaghi in Lugano. She exhibited in Geneva between 1896 and 1900. In 1902 she left for South America.

FIESCHI, Giannetto
Italian, 20th century.
Born June 1921, in Zogno (Bergamo).
Painter (mixed media). Scenes with figures.

Giannetto Fieschi lives and works in Genoa, where he held his first exhibition in 1947. Fieschi's style has evolved considerably over the years, towards a sort of conspicuous abstraction, but of a kind that is still inspired by reality - an imagined reality, sustained by a sensual, sumptuous use of paint pigments. Fieschi has taken part in a number of group exhibitions, including: *Figuration narrative* (*Narrative Figuration*), an exhibition staged by Gérald Gassiot-Talabot in Paris, in 1965, which grouped together artists working towards a return to figuration, following the wave of Pop Art; and the 1995 exhibition *Attraverso l'Immagine* (*Through the Image*), at the Centro culturale in Cremona. In 1965 the Municipal Museum of Bologna organised a retrospective exhibition of his works; and in 1966 the Botti Gallery in Cremona held an exhibition of his paintings.

BIBLIOGRAPHY:
Bossaglia, R./Giubbini, G., *Giannetto Fieschi*, Mazzotta, Milan, 1986. Crispolti, Enrico, *Giannetto Fieschi: Pittore*, Silvana Editoriale, Milan, 2000.

AUCTION RECORDS:
MILAN, 9 Nov 1982, *Devotion II* (oil/hardboard, 27 1/2 x 22 ins / 70 x 56 cm) ITL 900,000. MILAN, 9 April 1987, *Couple Getting Dressed Again* (1966, oil on canvas, 100 x 38 1/2 ins / 254 x 98 cm) ITL 4,200,000. MILAN, 14 April 1992, *Chalice and Flower* (oil on panel, 27 1/2 x 13 1/2 ins / 70 x 34 cm) ITL 2,600,000. ROME, 12 May 1992, *Kid* (1966, oil on canvas, 78 3/4 x 39 1/4 ins / 200 x 100 cm) ITL 6,000,000.

FIESCO, Tommasina del
Italian, 15th - 16th century.
Born 1448, in Genoa; died 1534.
Painter.

Tommasina del Fiesco was also an embroiderer. She took holy orders after the death of her husband, first entering the convent of S Maria delle Grazie and later that of SS Giacomo e Filippo. A number of her small pictures on parchment are in the convent of S Silvestro.

FIESINGER, Franz Gabriel
German, 18th century.
Born 11 March 1723, in Offenburg (Breisgau, Baden-Württemberg); died 2 February 1807, in London.
Engraver.

Fiesinger, a Jesuit, worked in Germany, Switzerland, France and England. He studied under the painter Franz S. Stöber. Fiesinger engraved portraits of members of the French National Convention, and of several of Napoleon's generals (Bernadotte, Régnier, Masséna, Kléber).

FIESOLE, da. See first name

FIESOLE, Giovanni
Italian, 17th century.
Born in Italy.
Active in Valladolid.
Sculptor.

Giovanni Fiesole often worked for the great sculptors of his period.

FIESS, Mathias
Austrian, 18th century.
Sculptor.

Fiess worked at the church in Horn, Austria, in 1723.

FIESSO, da. See first name

FIETURSKY, Nikon
Russian, 18th century.
Sculptor, engraver.

We know of his illustrations for two prayer-books which were printed in Chernikov in 1703. Fiertusky was a clergyman.

FIETZ, Gerhard
German, 20th century.
Born 1910, in Breslau (now Wroclaw, Poland).
Painter.
Zen 49 group.

Fietz was the pupil of Oskar Schlemmer in Breslau from 1930 to 1932, then studied at the academies in Düsseldorf and Berlin. He was mobilised during World War II. Afterwards, he lived in Munich, then Hamburg, where he became a guest lecturer at the Hochschule für Bildende Künste in 1956.

In 1948 he took part in the Salon des Réalités Nouvelles in Paris. He was a member of the *Zen 49* group. In 1950 he took part in the Venice Biennale, and in 1955 in the exhibition of German Abstract Painters in Paris.

Auction records:
HEIDELBERG, 11 April 1992, *Linear Composition* (1952, oil/synthetic resin, 15 1/4 x 20 ins / 39 x 50.5 cm) DEM 2,300. COLOGNE, 28 April 1999, *Untitled* (1956, tempera on paper, 15 x 20 ins / 39 x 51 cm) DEM 6,500. MUNICH, 20 Nov 1999, *Composition 1949/61* (1949, egg tempera, 28 x 38 ins / 71 x 96 cm) DEM 35,000. HAMBURG, 8 June 2000, *Composition* (1950-1958, tempera, 37 x 33 ins / 95 x 85 cm) DEM 5,500. STUTTGART, 20 Oct 2000, *Composition 1950/4* (1950, tempera, 26 x 33 ins / 66 x 84 cm) DEM 14,000. STUTTGART, 27 Jan 2001, *Composition* (1951, tempera on board, 25 x 19 ins / 63 x 49 cm) DEM 13,000. HAMBURG, 28 Sept 2002, *Picture 1952/90* (1952, egg tempera on masonite, 16 x 25 ins / 40 x 64 cm) EUR 2,500.

FIEULLIEN, Bonaventure
Belgian, 20th century.
Born 1903, in Schaerbeek (Brussels); died 1961, in Regniowez (French Ardennes).
Engraver (wood).
Fieullien was a Franciscan monk who illustrated the *Fioretti* of St Francis of Assisi.

FIEUZAL, Pierre Léonce Narcisse Félix
French, 18th - 19th century.
Born 20 September 1768, in Paris; died 1844, in Valenciennes.
Sculptor.
Pierre Fieuzal was the son of Madeleine Céleste Fieuzal, the actress known in the theatre under the name of Durancy. Protected by the Marquis de Deandrouin, he became the pupil of Godecharle, a lecturer at the Académie de Bruxelles. Later, in 1809, the Marquis had Fieuzal appointed professor of sculpture at the Académie de Valenciennes, a post he held until 1840. Fieuzal sculpted the marble tomb of the Marquis de Deandrouin, chamberlain to the emperor of Austria, and the monument to Desfontaines, erected at the hospital. Bellier de la Chavignerie mentions the following works by him in the museum in Valenciennes: *Louis XVIII* (marble bust), *Louis-Philippe I* (marble bust), *Momal* (plaster bust), and *Coliez* (terracotta bust). The current catalogue, however, does not mention any of his works.
Museums and Galleries:
VALENCIENNES (?).

FIÉVÉ, Nicolas
Flemish, 17th century.
Born in Ypres.
Active c. 1623.
Painter.
Flemish School.
Nicolas Fiévé executed portraits of sovereigns to decorate the town hall in Ypres.

FIÉVÉE, Adolphe Joseph Louis Théodore
French, 19th century.
Painter. Military subjects.
Fiévée exhibited at the Paris Salon from 1846 to 1849. Works include *Cavalrymen Removing a Russian Artillery Battery, Hussar of the Spanish Army, on Watch* and *Billet*.
Museums and Galleries:
NIORT: *Cavalrymen Crossing a River*.
Auction records:
NEW YORK, 3 June 1994, *Morning Horse Ride* (1846, oil on canvas, 19 1/4 x 29 1/4 ins / 48.6 x 74 cm) USD 9,200.

FIEVET, Carel
Flemish, 17th century.
Painter.
Flemish School.
Carel Fievet was the pupil of R. Serin in 1672-1673 and a master in Antwerp in 1676-1677.

FIÉVET, Nadine
Belgian, 20th - 21st century.
Born 1947, in Brussels.
Painter, draughtswoman, screen printer.
Fiévet studied under Edmond Dubrunfaut at the Académie des Beaux-Arts in Mons. Having started with murals, she later devoted herself to screen printing. She tends to synthesize the principal lines of photographic images.

FIÈVRE, Yolande
French, 20th century.
Born 25 January 1907, in Paris; died 1983, in Paris.
Painter, sculptor, sculptor of assemblages.
Yolande Fièvre grew up in a worldly, artistic family. She started painting at a very young age, and was well travelled - visiting the USA and living three years in Alexandria before studying at the École des Beaux-Arts in Paris. She taught for some time at the École des Beaux-Arts in Orléans. Married, and well off, she cut a striking figure at art events and private viewings.

Her association with the Surrealists - particularly with André Breton, Dubuffet, Réquichot and Jean Paulhan - greatly shaped her orientations. It is thought that she met Breton very early, and that her first paintings in 1933 resulted from automatic drawing. These early works, springing from poems by Paulhan, Jouve and Soupault, were abstract portraits technically indebted to action painting and a growing interest in textures. She then stopped painting altogether.

In 1957, she resumed her activities with her *Oniroscopes*, flimsy dream machines made up with the odd sand grains, threads, tinsel and foil star, signed in variations on her name (Yol-Han). She also used silks in sets, like *Silk-Fictions* and *Organzines*. Also in 1957, she began creating the *storage boxes*, which became her hallmark and in which she assembled small fragments and bones, bits of bark, driftwood, polished pebbles and perforated flint nodules. Set in racks inside boxes or in larger compositions, in low reliefs or in sculptures, these assemblages always suggest a very sensual approach to matter. Her work post-1957 has been classified by Jean-Paul and Isabelle Ledeur. Though comparable to Réquichot's reliquaries in conception, Yolande Fèvre's compositions differ in that, with the exception of a few toy soldiers or animals, she uses exclusively natural, often untreated natural materials. She barely intervened, merely adding in the 1960s some volume and colour to the elements of her polyptychs whilst tightly controlling their layout, sorting this trivia with great exactness. Her world, delicate, meticulous without ever becoming twee, veers on Fantasy.

Her biography and chronology remain tentative. The name 'Yolande Fèvre' could be an alias. She figured in a number of group and thematic exhibitions, as well as having solo exhibitions in Paris. There is a 10-year discrepancy over the date given for her first exhibition at the Galerie Simon Collinet (1948/1957), introduced by Jean Paulhan. It was followed by shows at the Galerie Daniel Cordier in Paris and the Künstlerhaus in Vienna (in 1962); at the Galerie Iris Clert in Paris (in 1964); at the Galerie Lucien Durand in Paris (in 1968); in Stockholm (in 1969); in Galerie Daniel Gervis in Paris (in 1973); and at the Galerie Bonnier in Geneva (in 1974). In 1991, the Galerie Di Méo in Paris exhibited a body of her work.
Bibliography:
Isabelle, Jean-Paul Ledeur, *Catalogue raisonné de l'œuvre de Yolande Fièvre*, Paris (in preparation). Planche, Jean, '*Yolande Fièvre*' in *Artension* no. 20, periodical, Rouen, c. 1980.
Auction records:
PARIS, 27 March 1980, *Attentive* (1962, assemblage of clay and pebbles, 9 1/2 x 9 1/2 x 2 1/4 ins / 24 x 24 x 6 cm) FRF 2,900. PARIS, 3 July 1992, *My Castle for a Dream!* (assemblage of pebbles, debris, wood and mirror, 9 1/2 x 9 1/2 ins / 24 x 24 cm) FRF 13,000. LONDON, 15 Oct 1992, *Glorification of Death*

(1961, framed construction of wood, 10 1/2 x 50 x 2 3/4 ins / 26.5 x 127 x 7.2 cm) GBP 4,400. PARIS, 31 May 1995, *Nocturne in Paris' Pit* (1966, assemblage of pebbles, clay and wood in a box, 13 3/4 x 13 3/4 x 4 ins / 35 x 35 x 10 cm) FRF 18,300. LONDON, 21 March 1996, *The Fishermen's Town* (painted clay/wooden plinth in a glass box, 16 3/4 x 6 1/2 ins / 42.5 x 16.5 cm) GBP 2,300. PARIS, 1 July 1996, *Oniroscope* (sand, fabric, wood, beads and wire mesh in a box, 14 1/2 x 17 3/4 ins / 37 x 45 cm) FRF 6,000. PARIS, 12 Dec 1996, *Un foyer pour les rêves* (1973, wood in Plexiglas, sculpture, 13 3/4 x 17 3/4 ins / 35 x 45 cm) FRF 16,500. PARIS, 18 June 1997, *Gloria (I)* (1967, wood/panel in Plexiglas box, 9 1/2 x 9 1/2 x 1 1/2 ins / 24 x 24 x 4 cm) FRF 20,000. PARIS, 18 Dec 1997, *Silk-Fiction* (1960, (44x36)) FRF 4,000. PARIS, 11 March 1998, *Untitled* (1960, sand, vegetable matter, fabric/card under glass, 14 1/4 x 17 1/4 ins / 36 x 44 cm) FRF 5,500. PARIS, 3 April 1998, *Cat Whales or Impromptu Wounds* (1959, silk-fiction, sand, vegetable matter and fabric on card under glass, 19 1/4 x 23 1/4 ins / 49 x 59 cm) FRF 15,000. PARIS, 15 Dec 1999, *Little Dream Palace* (objects in box, 14 x 14x4 ins / 35 x 35x10 cm) FRF 42,000. PARIS, 1 July 2003, *Dream Miserere* (mixed media and box, 14 x 14x4 ins / 36 x 35x11 cm) EUR 5,800. PARIS, 1 July 2003, *Ocean Demons and Angels* (1966, mixed media and box, 26 x 8x3 ins / 65 x 20x8 cm) EUR 6,300. PARIS, 13 Feb 2004, *Demons no. 49* (1962, driftwood, pebbles and plexiglas box, 49 x 26x2 ins / 125 x 65x6 cm) EUR 15,500. PARIS, 17 Oct 2004, *Fireworks* (mixed media, 19 x 15 ins / 47 x 39 cm) EUR 1,500.

FIFFA, Annibale

Italian, 17th century.
Active in Verona in 1605.
Painter.

FIGARELLA, Dominique

French, 20th - 21st century.
Born 1966.
Painter.

Dominique Figarella studied at the Villa Arson in Nice in 1992, and at the École Internationale d'Art.

He has taken part in group exhibitions since 1993, including the following: Salon de Montrouge; Villa Arson; in Paris and New York; *Nouvelle Vague* (*New Wave*), at the Musée d'Art Moderne et Contemporain de Nice, in 1994; and at the Galerie Les Filles du Calvaire in Paris, in 2002.

He has also exhibited in solo exhibitions: in Boulogne in 1992; at the Galerie du Forum St-Eustache in Paris, in 1995; and at the Villa Arson in Nice, in 1995.

BIBLIOGRAPHY:

Bernard, Christian, *Dominique Figarella*, exhibition catalogue, Villa Arson-Centre national des Arts plastiques, Nice, 1993.

FIGARI, Andrea

Italian (?), 19th - 20th century.
Born 1858, in Sassari (Sardinia), Italy; died 1945, in Genoa.
Painter. Landscapes, seascapes.

MUSEUMS AND GALLERIES:

GENOA (Palazzo Rosso): *Small Beach*.

AUCTION RECORDS:

NEW YORK, 25-26 Nov 1929, *Spanish Party*, USD 30. MILAN, 6 June 1991, *The Ligurian Coast* (oil on panel, 7 1/2 x 10 ins / 19 x 25.5 cm) ITL 2,500,000. MILAN, 12 Dec 1991, *Winter Morning in the Port of Genoa* (oil on card, 18 x 21 1/2 ins / 46 x 54.5 cm) ITL 9,500,000. MILAN, 16 June 1992, *Nocturnal Seascape* (oil on canvas, 29 1/2 x 35 3/4 ins / 75 x 91 cm) ITL 4,500,000. NORTH BETHESDA, 14 Feb 2001, *Coast at Genoa* (oil on board, 5 x 13 ins / 13 x 34 cm) USD 1,800. ROME, 10 June 2004, *Sea Storm* (oil on canvas, 55 x 71 ins / 140 x 180 cm) EUR 8,000. ROME, 10 June 2004, *Sea Storm on the Cliffs* (oil on canvas, 55 x 71 ins / 140 x 180 cm) EUR 14,000.

FIGARI, Pedro

Uruguayan, 19th - 20th century.
Born 29 June 1861, in Montevideo, to Italian parents; died 24 July 1938, in Montevideo.
Also active in France.
Painter. Genre scenes, local scenes.

A brilliant lawyer, man of public affairs, well-known politician, writer, philosopher, aesthetician and portrayer of the Uruguayan identity through his many activities and through his painting, Pedro Figari played a role of paramount importance in his country's development in the early part of the 20th century and particularly in the 'nativist' movement which stood for maintaining the racial and cultural diversity that created the country of Uruguay.

In 1886, Figari became a barrister and went on to work on some famous court cases. He also travelled in Europe. In 1895 he took on the defence of Second Lieutenant Enrique Almeida, who was finally acquitted after a national controversy. Figari later became a politician, was elected to Parliament in 1896, appointed to the Council of State in 1898 and elected vice-president of the Chamber of Deputies in 1899. He was given numerous official duties and chosen as a candidate for the presidency of the republic. A writer and aesthetician, he wrote several works on art including, in 1912, his *Essay on Biological Philosophy*, a 500-page work *Arte, Estética, Ideal* (*Art, Aesthetics and the Ideal*). In 1913 he spent six months in France. In 1915 he was appointed director of the Arts and Crafts Institute of Montevideo, where he reformed the teaching and played an important role in improving awareness and understanding of contemporary artists, before resigning from this post in 1917.

Figari had painted in his youth and continued to make watercolour sketches as a relaxation from public life. He signed these discreetly, using the pseudonyms P. Merlin and P. Weber. In 1920, at the age of 50, he withdrew completely from public life to pursue a long-held aspiration to focus on painting. He sold his property in Montevideo and moved to Buenos Aires, where he lived from 1921 to 1925, becoming one of the best-known Latin-American painters of the period. Figari had no followers in Uruguay, his influence being mainly felt in Argentina. He spent eight years, from 1925 to 1933, in Paris, where he was warmly received and painted the majority of his work, returning home with almost 2,000 paintings executed in oils on card.

Although a passionate admirer of the work of Diego Rivera, he was not influenced by the latter's style. His is closer to that of Vuillard and Bonnard at the time of the *Revue Blanche*, which he particularly admired; Figari used a delicate yet striking palette of pinks, yellows, soft green, sky blue and lilac over cursory drawing, with faces highlighted in tones of dark brown. With the exception of a rather humorous series devoted to cavemen, most of Figari's work revisits, entirely from memory, the recollections of his youth. His approach is not some historical reconstruction but a poetic, almost naive view showing lively domestic scenes in both town and countryside and includes black people and the first gauchos, accompanied by horses, dogs and bulls. He depicts these scenes frontally, as if in a theatre. In town he paints scenes in patios, a high-ceilinged red living room or a street. In the countryside he paints scenes outside a house, the entrance gates, by a wagon, and with the *ombu* - the typical tree of the area - and the small moon over the pampas.

His first exhibition took place in Buenos Aires in 1921 and was followed by others in 1923, 1924 and 1925. In 1923, prior to his stay in Paris, the Druet Gallery showed his paintings in a solo exhibition prefaced by his compatriot Jules Supervielle. The exhibition was admired by Bonnard and Vuillard and warmly acknowledged by André Lhote in the *Nouvelle Revue Française*. Later, in 1928 he was appointed ambassador to London and exhibited in several cities in Europe and

America before returning to Montevideo in 1933 as artistic advisor to the ministry of public education. In 1930 Figari was awarded the grand prix for painting at the Uruguay centenary exhibition in Montevideo. In 1938 he held his last exhibition in Buenos Aires and returned to Montevideo where he died three days later. In 1960, the Musée Nationale d'Art Moderne in Paris devoted a posthumous retrospective to Figari's work, again prefaced by Jules Supervielle. In 1992 the Pavillon des Arts de la Ville de Paris organised an exhibition of an important collection of the artist's work, accompanied by a very complete catalogue.

P. Figari

BIBLIOGRAPHY:

Figari, Pedro, *Essai de philosophie biologique. Art, esthétique, idéal,* Éd. de la Revue de l'Amérique latine, Paris, 1926 (3rd edition). Pillement, Georges, *Pedro Figari,* G. Crès, Paris, 1930. Borges, J.L., *Figari,* Buenos Aires, 1930. Kalenberg, A., '*Pedro Figari: El escenario americano*' in *América: Mirada interior,* exhibition catalogue, Bib. Luis-Angel Arango, Bogotá, 1985. Grant, K., '*The Candombe Paintings*' in *Latin American Art,* vol 3 no 2, 1991. Nelson Di Maggio, Gabriel Peluffo Linari, Jules Supervielle, Alejo Carpentier, Jorge Luis Borges, et al., *Pedro Figari,* exhibition catalogue, Pavillon des Arts, Paris, 1992 (extensive documentation). Peluffo Linari, G., *Historia de la pintura uruguaya: De Blanes a Figari,* Montevideo, 1993. Pini, Ivonne, '*Pedro Figari: The Search for Roots*' in *Art Nexus,* vol 18, 1995. Pereda, R., *Pedro Figari,* Montevideo, 1995. *Figari de luz de luna,* exhibition catalogue, Galería Sur, Montevideo, 1996.

MUSEUMS AND GALLERIES:

MONTEVIDEO (MBA Juán Manuel Blanes): *The Little Horse of All Trades* (1921); *Brutality; Uncertainty; Federal Meeting; Indecision; Las Quitanderas; Nightfall; Condolences; After the Capture; Creole Duel; Pericón (Peasant Dance) under the Ombu Trees; Palito (Popular Dance); Fond Recollections of Africa; The Lowering of the Coffin; Who Will Take Care of the Dead Man?; The Quest for the Cross* (triptych); *Apotheosis* (triptych); *Flowers for the Dead Man* (triptych); *The Old Negro; The Kiss; Victoria Ocampo; Stupidity; Greed* - MONTEVIDEO (Mus. de la Casa de Gobierno): numerous works - MONTEVIDEO (Mus. Histórico Nacional): *The Old Market, Montevideo, 1890; The Refusal; Colonial Ball; The Lance; The Wager; Visit to the Governor; The Inn; Fantasy; Don't Go, Old Chap; In the Village; Regret* - MONTEVIDEO (Mus. Nacional de Artes Visuales): *Vigilance; The Stagecoach; On the Pampas; The Cry of Asencio; At the Farm; Gato (Peasant Dance)* - PARIS (Mus. d'Orsay): *Differences* (1921); *Creole Scene.*

AUCTION RECORDS:

PARIS, 29 Oct 1926, *Creole Dance,* FRF 6,700. PARIS, 22 June 1945, *Negro Dance* (1921) FRF 4,000. LONDON, 28 Nov 1972, *La Plaza de Pueblo* (*Pueblo Main Square,* Gns 1,100. LONDON, 20 Oct 1976, *Farmyard* (oil on card, 7 1/4 x 9 1/4 ins / 18.5 x 23.5 cm) GBP 210. MONTEVIDEO, 23 Nov 1977, *Peasants and Horses* (oil on canvas, 15 3/4 x 11 3/4 ins / 40 x 30 cm) UYU 14,000. NEW YORK, 5 May 1981, *The Visit* (pencil/paper, 5 x 7 3/4 ins / 12.5 x 19.5 cm) USD 1,000. NEW YORK, 31 May 1984, *Creole Dance* (oil on card, 19 1/2 x 27 1/4 ins / 49.5 x 69.5 cm) USD 13,000. PARIS, 20 March 1985, *Guitarists and Dancer* (gouache, 19 x 23 1/2 ins / 48 x 60 cm) FRF 25,500. MONTEVIDEO, 14 Aug 1986, *Candombe* (oil on card, 23 1/2 x 31 1/2 ins / 60 x 80 cm) UYU 4,770,000. NEW YORK, 17 May 1988, *After the Dance* (oil on card, 15 3/4 x 13 ins / 40 x 33 cm) USD 13,200. NEW YORK, 21 Nov 1988, *The Conquest of El Chaco* (oil on card, 13 3/4 x 19 3/4 ins / 35 x 50.2 cm) USD 13,200; *The Family* (oil on card, 13 1/2 x 19 1/2 ins / 34.4 x 49.5 cm) USD 7,150; *Country Fair* (oil on card, 19 3/4 x 27 1/2 ins / 50 x 70 cm) USD 55,000. PARIS, 11 April 1989, *Leaving for the Concert* (oil on card, 13 1/2 x 19 1/4 ins / 34 x 49 cm) FRF 95,000. NEW YORK, 17 May 1989, *La Naticia* (15 3/4 x 23 1/4 ins / 40 x 59 cm) USD 19,800. NEW YORK, 20 Nov 1989, *The Cat* (1927, oil on card, 20 1/2 x 26 3/4 ins / 52 x 68 cm) USD 44,000. NEW YORK, 21 Nov 1989, *Traditional Dance in a Patio* (oil on card, 27 1/4 x 39 1/4 ins / 69 x 99.6 cm) USD 82,500. NEW YORK, 1 May 1990, *Gaucho Guitar Player* (oil on card, 19 3/4 x 27 1/2 ins / 50 x 70 cm) USD 77,000. NEW YORK, 19-20 Nov 1990, *The Wait* (oil on card, 27 1/2 x 39 1/4 ins / 69.6 x 100 cm) USD 52,250; *On the Way to the Bullring* (oil on card, 38 1/2 x 13 1/2 ins / 98 x 34.5 cm) USD 46,200. PARIS, 4 March 1991, *Lavanderas* (*Washer Women*) (1919, oil on card, 13 x 15 3/4 ins / 33 x 40 cm) FRF 50,000. NEW YORK, 8 May 1991, *Rounding up the Herd* (oil on card, 20 3/4 x 27 ins / 53 x 68.5 cm) USD 44,000. NEW YORK, 15-16 May 1991, *Colonial Reception* (oil on card, 27 1/4 x 39 1/4 ins / 69 x 99.6 cm) USD 30,800. NEW YORK, 20 Nov 1991, *The Walk* (oil on card, 15 3/4 x 23 1/2 ins / 40 x 60 cm) USD 33,000. NEW YORK, 18-19 May 1992, *Piety* (oil on card, 18 1/2 x 24 1/4 ins / 47.3 x 61.6 cm) USD 19,800. NEW YORK, 24 Nov 1992, *Ball in the Patio* (oil on card, 24 1/4 x 32 1/4 ins / 61.6 x 81.6 cm) USD 37,400. PARIS, 14 June 1993, *The Incident* (1933, oil on card, 12 1/4 x 18 1/2 ins / 31 x 47 cm) FRF 75,000. NEW YORK, 23-24 Nov 1993, *Halt in the Countryside* (oil on card, 23 1/2 x 31 1/2 ins / 60 x 80 cm) USD 68,500. NEW YORK, 16 Nov 1994, *Creole Celebration* (oil on card, 20 1/2 x 32 1/4 ins / 52 x 82.2 cm) USD 79,500. NEW YORK, 16 May 1996, *First Love* (1984, oil on card, 13 3/4 x 19 3/4 ins / 35 x 50 cm) USD 11,500. NEW YORK, 25-26 Nov 1996, *Walk* (c. 1930, oil on reformed panel, 12 1/4 x 32 1/4 ins / 30.8 x 81.9 cm) USD 24,150. NEW YORK, 28 May 1997, *Celebration in Camp* (oil on panel, 24 x 31 1/2 ins / 60.7 x 80.3 cm) USD 99,300. NEW YORK, 24-25 Nov 1997, *Creole Dance* (oil on panel, 19 1/2 x 27 1/2 ins / 49.8 x 69.8 cm) USD 46,000. MONTEVIDEO, 5 Jan 1999, *Arriving at the Bullring* (oil on board, 13 x 38 ins / 33 x 97 cm) USD 40,000. NEW YORK, 22 Nov 1999, *Insult* (1922, oil on board, 20 x 28 ins / 50 x 70 cm) USD 85,000. MONTEVIDEO, 5 Jan 2000, *Candombe* (*African Dance*) (oil on board, 16 x 20 ins / 40 x 50 cm) USD 50,000. NEW YORK, 1 June 2000, *Requiebro* (*Flirtatious Remark*) (c. 1920, oil on board, 19 x 24 ins / 48 x 61 cm) USD 50,000. NEW YORK, 30 May 2001, *Candombe* (*African Dance*) (oil on canvas, 24 x 31 ins / 60 x 80 cm) USD 40,000. NEW YORK, 19 Nov 2001, *La Media Caña* (c. 1932, oil on board, 19 x 28 ins / 49 x 70 cm) USD 40,000. NEW YORK, 28 May 2002, *Miriñaques* (*Crinolines*) (c. 1925, oil on board, 19 x 27 ins / 49 x 69 cm) USD 39,000. NEW YORK, 19 Nov 2002, *Coloured People* (c. 1930, oil on board, 14 x 19 ins / 35 x 49 cm) USD 22,000. NEW YORK, 18 Nov 2003, *Meeting on the Path* (c. 1935, oil on board, 16 x 24 ins / 40 x 60 cm) USD 40,000. MONTEVIDEO, 25 Nov 2003, *Candombe* (*African Dance*) (oil on card, 13 x 16 ins / 33 x 40 cm) USD 35,000. BUENOS AIRES, 30 March 2004, *Dusk in the Farm* (oil on card, 20 x 28 ins / 50 x 70 cm) USD 47,000. PARIS, 10 June 2004, *Visits* (c. 1935, oil on card, 19 x 24 ins / 48 x 61 cm) EUR 40,000.

FIGAS, Marcel, real name Pierre-Jean Figasso
French, 20th century.
Born 9 August 1935, in Nice.
Painter, engraver.

Marcel Figas studied from 1945 to 1955 at the École des Beaux-Arts in Nice, and his meeting in 1956 with Pierre Demaria was a watershed. Figas was always interested in the mechanisms of sensation, alternative sciences and particle physics. He defined his compositions as 'mazelike, intertwined with symbol': monsters, mass graves and metamorphoses. His *Opus Magnum* (1966) alluded to a nuclear holocaust. In 1975, he explored *Infinite Horizons,* achieved from tricks of light and matter. Other sets would follow: *Enthralled Venices, Metaflora* and *Paris Luminaissants* (*Paris Coming to Light*).

Figas featured in the exhibitions *Les Figuratifs de l'imaginaire* (*Figurative Painters of Imaginary Worlds*) (1965) and *Les Enfers* (*Underworld*) at the Bastion St-André in Antibes.

In 1956, he showed his work in a double exhibition in Nice at Galeries Gerber and Jacques Matarasso. He exhibited for the first time in Paris at Galerie Jacques-Henry Perrin.

Figas has since withdrawn from the traditional art distribution networks.

BIBLIOGRAPHY:

Habans, Brigitte F./Noël, Bernard (preface), *Marcel Figas: peintures 1958-1988: catalogue raisonné*, M. Figasso, Nice, 1990.

FIGATELLI, Giuseppe Maria, or Fegatelli
Italian, 17th century.
Born to a family originally from Cento.
Painter. Religious subjects.

Giuseppe Maria Figatelli studied under Cesare Gennari and was also influenced by Guerchino. He painted numerous altarpieces in Bologna and Cento during the latter half of the 17th century.

FIGATELLI, Paolo Antonio, or Fegatelli
Italian, 17th - 18th century.
Born 1672, in Bologna; died 18 February 1724, in Cento.
Painter, sculptor, architect.

Paolo Antonio Figatelli was the son of Giuseppe Maria Figatelli. He is known principally for his portraits, usually of saints. He was also an architect. A series of drawings by him is in the Uffizi in Florence.

FIGDOR DEPOSITION, Master of the.
See **MASTERS**

FIGGEMEIER, Bernd
German, 20th century.
Born 1940.
Painter.

Figgemeier paints in large, flat areas of solid colour.

FIGINO, Ambrogio
Italian, 16th century.
Born 1548, in Milan; died 1608.
Painter, draughtsman. History painting, religious subjects, portraits.

Ambrogio Figino's dates are not known, although we do know that he was still alive in 1595. However, Lomazzo records that he was his pupil, which means that he must have begun working as a painter at the very latest in 1571, the year in which Lomazzo went blind at the age of 33. Ambrogio is not to be confused with his contemporary Girolamo Figino.

Figino had a reputation as a portraitist and history painter; according to Lomazzo his works, almost all of which were in oils, included few figures and consequently distinguished themselves by their clarity. Figino was a great admirer of Michelangelo, especially towards the end of his life, and was ultimately so successful in imitating his work that quite a large number of his drawings have been attributed to Michelangelo or to his pupils.

Surviving paintings by Figino are few, however, the praise lavished upon him in verses by the Italian poet Marini or Marino testifies to his talent as a portraitist. This poet, known in France at the court of Marie de' Medici as the 'cavalier Marin', speaks of Ambrogio Figino as a contemporary, which, given that Marini was born in 1569 and died in 1605, gives us approximate dates for Figino's life.

BIBLIOGRAPHY:

Turnure, J.H., '*The Late Style of Ambrogio Figino*' in *Art Bulletin*, vol 47, 1965. Ciardi, R.P., *Giovane Ambrogio Figino*, Marchi & Bertolli, Florence, 1968. Pouncey, P., '*Studies by Figino for his St Matthew Altarpiece*' in *Master Drawings*, 1968. Perissa Torrini, Annalisa, *Disegni del Figino*, Electa, Milan, 1987. Gregori, Mina/Prinz, Johann Georg, *Stille Welt. Italienische Stilleben aus drei Jahrhunderten*, exhibition catalogue, Kunsthalle der Hypo-Kulturstiftung, Munich, 2003.

MUSEUMS AND GALLERIES:

HILDESHEIM: *Virgin with Saints* - MILAN (Ambrosiana): *Portrait of St Charles Borromeo* - MILAN (Church of S Antonio Abate): *Virgin Treading on the Serpent's Head* - MILAN (Church of S Eustorgio): *St Ambrose* - MILAN (Church of S Fedele): *Assumption* - MILAN (Church of S Raffaello): *St Matthew; St Paul* - MILAN (Municipal Mus.): *Design for a Banner with St Ambrose* - MILAN (Pinacoteca di Brera): *Portrait of Marshal Lucio Foppa; Virgin with Child between St John the Evangelist and St Michael Slaying Lucifer* - PARIS (Louvre): drawing.

AUCTION RECORDS:

PARIS, 10 Feb 1926, *Study of Heads of Orientals* (pen) FRF 100. LONDON, 28 June 1974, *Portrait of Bearded Man*, Gns 8,000. LONDON, 2 July 1984, *Christ and Angels for the Agony in the Garden (recto); Figures (verso)* (pen and brown ink, studies, 5 1/2 x 7 1/2 ins / 14.1 x 18.8 cm) GBP 1,050. NEW YORK, 25 Jan 2001, *Portrait of Giovanni Angelo Dannona Holding Gloves and Letter* (1570, oil on panel, 24 x 18 ins / 60 x 46 cm) USD 1,300,000.

FIGINO, Camillo
Italian, 19th century.
Died 25 November 1835.
Active in Mantua.
Painter.

FIGINO, Girolamo
Italian, 16th century.
Active in Milan during the second half of the 16th century.
Painter.

Girolamo Figino was the pupil of Giovanni Paolo Lomazzo, who extolled his art in a poem.

FIGINO, Jérôme
Flemish, 18th century.
Active c. 1795.
Painter, miniaturist. History painting.
Flemish School.

Jérôme Figinot is mentioned by Siret.

FIGLIOLINI, Vincenzo
Italian, 18th century.
Active in Naples c. 1775.
Painter.

FIGON
French, 16th century.
Active in Spain.
Sculptor.

From 1512 to 1513 this sculptor worked at Zamora Cathedral.

FIGUEIREDO, Cristovao de
Portuguese, 16th century.
Active between 1515 and 1543.
Painter. Religious subjects.

Cristovao de Figueiredo worked in the studio of Jorge Afonso and collaborated with him on the courts of justice in Lisbon. He was the official painter at the court of Manuel I. In 1522, he worked on the altar in the church of Sta Cruz in Coimbra where an *Ecce Homo* is attributed to him.

Figueiredo worked with Gregorio Lopes and Cristovao de Utreque on the *Ferreirim Retable* between 1533 and 1534 and in 1540 was appointed official painter to the cardinal Infant Dom Alfonso. As Figueiredo worked so much with Gregorio Lopes and Garcia Fernandes, it is often difficult to distinguish between the work of these artists, but works such as the *Ecce Homo* and the *Martyrdom of St Andrew and*

St Hippolytus can be attributed to him with a fair degree of certainty. He imbued his compositions with an almost expressionist quality, far removed from the mannered elegance of an artist such as Gregorio Lopes. His dense and dramatic composition is based on splashes of colour, which are handled with great skill.

MUSEUMS AND GALLERIES:

LISBON (Mus. Nacional de Arte Antiga): *Martyrdom of St Andrew and St Hippolytus; Entombment* (c. 1529-1530); *Scenes from the Childhood of Christ* (fragments of an altarpiece) - SETUBAL: *Retable*.

FIGUEIREDO, Francesco de

Portuguese, 18th century.

Born in Oporto; died shortly before 1800, in Lisbon.

Painter.

Francesco de Figueiredo painted a number of pious works in the Sta Ela cloister in Évora. He also painted murals and ceilings in the church of Joao da Praça in Lisbon.

FIGUEIREDO, Luiz Carlos

Brazilian, 20th century.

Born 1944, in Cuiaba (Mato Grosso).

Painter, sculptor. Religious subjects, figures, scenes with figures, local scenes. Designs for tapestries.

Figueiredo paints in a picturesque style, in bright but harmonious colours, showing scenes of daily life or imaginary scenes; he also sculpts papier mâché figures of people in movement. For many years his main source of inspiration was the town of Conservatoria in the state of Rio. He founded an open art studio for children.

He has taken part in group exhibitions, including: Salon des Indépendants, Paris (1982 and 1985); annual salon of naive art in Buenos Aires, where he received first prize (1983); French cultural centre in Abidjan (1986); Salon des Artistes Naïfs, Jacovsky Museum, Nice (1989); Musée d'Art Naïf Max Fourny, Paris (1991); Salon Comparaisons, Paris (1992).

Since 1966 he has held numerous solo exhibitions of his work in Brazil including: historical museum of Rio de Janeiro, museum of arts and popular traditions at Niteroi, museum of fine arts in Mococa and the museum of contemporary art in Campinas (1990). He has also exhibited in Europe: Brazilian Consulate, Berlin (1981); Brazilian Embassy in The Hague (1986); Dutch international museum of naive art, Rotterdam (1990).

BIBLIOGRAPHY:

Luiz Figueiredo, exhibition catalogue, Gal. Bonino, Rio de Janeiro, 1989. *Luiz Figueiredo*, exhibition catalogue, Gal. Debret, Musée d'Art naïf Max Fourny, Paris, Gal. Bonino, Rio de Janeiro, Durini Gall., London, 1993.

MUSEUMS AND GALLERIES:

AUVERS-SUR-OISE (Mus. Daubigny) - CAMPINAS (MAC) - JAÉN (Mus. Internacional de Arte Naif) - LAVAL (Musée du Vieux Château) - NICE (Mus. International d'Art Naïf Anatole-Jakovsky) - PARIS (Mus. d'Art Naïf Max-Fourny) - RIO DE JANEIRO (Mus. Histórico) - SHERBROOKE (MBA) - VICQ (Mus. International d'Art Naïf) - ZWOLLE (Mus. de Stadshof).

FIGUEIRERO, Hélène

Brazilian, 20th century.

Painter. Figure compositions, local scenes.

Hélène Figueirero studied under André Lhote in Paris and retained from his teaching a strong sense of constructional rigour. In her work, the juxtaposition of smoothly painted areas with others worked with the spatula creates an impression of collage. Her painting is figurative and evokes daily life in Rio de Janeiro through a vision that is filled with humour and invention.

FIGUERAS, Alfred

Spanish, 20th century.

Born 13 September 1898, in Sant Fruitós de Bages, near Manresa (Catalonia); died 9 June 1980, in Barcelona.

Painter, engraver, draughtsman. Landscapes, urban landscapes, urban views, still-lifes.

School of Algiers.

Alfred Figueras studied at evening classes at the La Llotja school of fine art until 1924, under the direction of Francesc Labarta. He then went to Paris around 1919 where he met Picasso and Miró. He got into trouble with the police under General Primo de Rivera's regime and left Spain to go to Algeria with his friend the sculptor Rafel Tona in 1925. He lived at the Abd-el Tiff villa where he associated with many French artists including Le Corbusier and Albert Camus. With Rafel Tona he founded an academy that taught up to 200 students. From 1930 to 1947 he lived in Spain and returned to Algeria in 1947. In 1951 he was awarded a French government bursary to paint in Morocco.

Figueras turned away from Academicism after visiting a French art exhibition in Barcelona in 1917 which opened his eyes to the possibilities offered by Cézanne's aesthetic approach. He remained faithful to this, constructing landscapes and townscapes which also reveal the influence of Fauvism. His highly linear etchings, notably the album *Images d'Alger (Images of Algiers)*, which contains 20 etchings and extracts from the writings of André Gide, are quite remarkable. Figueras is considered to occupy a key place in the history of Catalan painting and its links with the Paris School.

He exhibited in Barcelona before his departure for Algeria in 1925 and exhibited there again between 1930 and 1947. He took part in collective exhibitions including: *Aura Mediterránea - Catalan Masters of the 20th century*, National Gallery, Amann; *L'École d'Alger (The Algiers School)*, Musée des Beaux-Arts, Bordeaux (2003). He also held a solo exhibition in Oran (now Warhan) in 1930. In 1998 his home town celebrated the centenary of his birth, as did Barcelona in 1999, holding a solo exhibition of his work at the Sala Parés.

BIBLIOGRAPHY:

Exposició homenatge Alfred Figueras 1898-1980, exhibition catalogue, Sala Parés, Barcelona, 1981. Cazenave, Elisabeth/Dalia, Mahammed-Orfali/Vidal-Bué, Marion, *L'École d'Alger*, exhibition catalogue, Musée des Beaux-Arts, Bordeaux, 2003.

MUSEUMS AND GALLERIES:

ALGIERS (Mus. National des Beaux-Arts): *Images d'Alger (Images of Algiers)* (etchings, entire album).

FIGUERAS Y VILA, Juan

Spanish, 19th century.

Born 15 July 1829, in Gerona; died 28 December 1881, in Madrid.

Sculptor.

Juan Figueras y Vila was a pupil of José Piquer y Duart at the Academia de San Fernando in Madrid. He was awarded the Prix de Rome in 1858 for his *Suzanna Bathing* and exhibited at the Madrid international exhibition in 1860. He also painted a large number of portraits.

MUSEUMS AND GALLERIES:

MADRID (Mus. de Arte Moderno): *Conversion of a Native Woman to the Catholic Faith; Marriage*.

FIGUEROA, Baltazar de

Spanish, 17th century.

Died 19 April 1659.

Active in Seville.

Painter.

FIGUEROA, Diego de

Spanish, 16th century.

Sculptor.

Diego de Figueroa made six wooden moulds for the decoration of the exterior galleries of the chapter houses in Seville around 1564.

FIGUEROA, Francisco de
Spanish, 17th century.
Painter. History painting.
Francisco de Figueroa was a Dominican monk who worked for his monastery.

FIGUEROA, Francisco de
Spanish, 18th century.
Active in Galicia.
Landscape painter.
Francisco de Figueroa studied with the Prince de Pio y Miranda.

FIGUEROA, José Luis
Spanish, 20th century.
Born 1923, in Madrid.
Painter. Still-lifes.
José Luis Figueroa studied at the Real Academia de Bellas Artes de San Fernando in Madrid. He produced still-lifes of great simplicity showing restraint in both subject and tone.

He showed his work at solo exhibitions: since 1951 in Buenos Aires; 1954 at the museum of modern art in Caracas; 1954 at the Casa de la Cultura in Quito and the national library in Bogotá; 1963 at the museum of modern art in Rio de Janeiro; 1970 at the national library in Lisbon; 1977, 1978 and 1979 at the Venice Cadre gallery in Casablanca; and 1981 at the Guigné gallery in Paris.

MUSEUMS AND GALLERIES:
BUENOS AIRES (Mus.) - CARACAS (Mus.) - LIMA (Mus.) - QUITO (Mus.) - SÃO PAULO (MA).

FIGUEROA, Juan de
Spanish, 16th century.
Active in Seville.
Sculptor.
Around 1568, Juan de Figueroa was among those working on the Alcázar palace in Seville; in 1579, he collaborated with Bautista Vazquez on an organ case for the cathedral.

FIGUEROA, Luis
Spanish, 17th century.
Died 10 December 1642, in Seville.
Active in Seville.
Sculptor.
Luis Figueroa is known for a crucifix he made for the brotherhood of Vera Cruz, dated 23 May 1622.

FIGUEROLA
Spanish, 14th century.
Painter.
Barcelona School.
Figuerola was in Barcelona between 1378 and 1389.

FIGURES, Master of the. See **MASTERS**

FIGURINO. See **ROCCHETTI Marco Antonio**

FIHLER, Merten
German, 16th century.
Painter.
Breslau School.
Until 1579, Fihler was a pupil of J. Twenger. He was named master in Breslau (now Wroclaw, Poland) in 1581.

FIJALKOWSKI, Stanislaw
Polish, 20th century.
Born 4 November 1922, in Zdolbunov (now in Ukraine).
Painter, engraver.
Stanislaw Fijalkowski lived and worked in Lódz where he studied at the school of fine art from 1946 to 1951 and then taught. His paintings, generally small in format, employ very simple repetitive elements (points, circles, lines, squares) in a style reminiscent of a child's first attempts at writing. The slightest variation is introduced almost inadvertently: a circle smaller than the others or not in its logical place, an apparently accidental brush stroke or any other incongruous element that has a surprising irritating value on the viewer. As he progressed, Fijalkowski introduced more elements borrowed from reality into his painting.

Fijalkowski participated in very many collective exhibitions in Europe, Japan and the USA, including: Engraving Biennale, Cracow (1966, 1968 and 1970); 7th Engraving Biennale, Ljubljana (1967); 6th Engraving Biennale, Tokyo; 1st International Engraving Exhibition, Florence; *Xylon V*, Geneva, Berlin, Klagenfurt; and 10th Biennale, São Paulo (1969); 2nd International Original Drawings Exhibition, Rijeka; International Roudnice-nad-Labern and Eisendstadt Symposia (1970). Solo exhibitions include: Lódz (1957, 1959, 1961 and 1964); Cracow (1961 and 1967); Warsaw (1961 and 1967); Paris (1965); Wroclaw and Poznan (1967); Torun (1969); Graz (1970). He was awarded the 9th International Joan Miró Dibuix Prize in Barcelona.

FIJT, Jan. See **FYT**

FIKENTSCHER, Jenny
Maiden name: Nottebohin
German, 19th - 20th century.
Born 1 June 1869, in Kallowitz.
Painter, draughtsman.
Jenny Fikentscher was the wife of the painter Otto Fikentscher, and worked extensively at Grötzingen near Karlsruhe. She exhibited in Dresden in 1899 and 1901, and in Munich in 1900.

FIKENTSCHER, Otto
German, 19th - 20th century.
Born 6 July 1862, in Zwickau; died 1945, in Baden-Baden.
Painter, sculptor, engraver. Animals.
Otto Fikentscher worked at the Hochschule für Bildende Künste in Dresden, at the Akademie in Munich and at the Hochschule für Gestaltung in Karlsruhe. He travelled extensively and specialised in painting animals. He exhibited in Berlin in 1897 and 1908, at the International Exhibition in Düsseldorf in 1904, in Munich in 1900 and in Karlsruhe in 1906.

AUCTION RECORDS:
HEIDELBERG, 5-13 April 1994, *Stag on the Edge of a Sunny Valley* (oil on canvas, 28 3/4 x 26 1/2 ins / 73 x 67 cm) DEM 1,400. HEIDELBERG, 8 April 1995, *Stags in Woods* (oil on canvas, 20 x 25 1/4 ins / 50.5 x 64 cm) DEM 1,200.

FIKENTSCHER, Otto Clemens
German, 19th century.
Born 28 February 1831, in Aachen (North Rhine-Westphalia); died 11 November 1880, in Düsseldorf.
Painter. History painting, animals.
Fikentscher was a student of Theodore Hildebrandt. His sketch *Wild Cats Fighting* is kept at the Düsseldorf Museum.

FIKRET, Mualla or Mowalla. See **MUALLA Fikret**

FILA, Rudolf
Czech, 20th century.
Born 19 July 1932, in Príbram.
Painter.
Rudolf Fila studied in Brno in 1951-1952 and Bratislava from 1952 to 1958. He exhibited from 1962 onwards, particularly in the major Czech cities as well as in Hungary and Italy and at the Paris Biennale. He was represented at the major exhibition of *Fifty years of Czechoslovak Painting from the Collections of the Galleries, 1918-1958* organised in 1968 for the 50th anniversary of the founding of the Republic.

FILARET
Russian, 18th century.
Sculptor (wood).
Filaret was a monk and worked on a Book of the Apostles, printed in Kiev in 1784, for which he did twenty-two illustrations.

FILARETE, Antonio di Pietro Averlino
Italian, 15th century.
Born c. 1400, in Florence; died after 1465, in Rome.
Sculptor.
Filarete is also known as an architect and theorist. He was summoned to Rome by Pope Eugenius IV to sculpt and cast the bronze door of the Basilica of St Peter's in 1433, receiving the commission because he had worked on the doors of the Baptistery in Florence, in the studio of Ghiberti. He executed a *Virgin and Child*, also in bronze, now in the Louvre, and is said to have taught Fouquet the technique of applying enamel directly to copper before painting.

Most of Filarete's architectural work was commissioned by Francesco Sforza in Milan, where he moved in 1450, apparently after having been accused of stealing some relics in Rome. He built the clock tower at the castello Sforzesco on the site of the Visconti fortress, and also designed the ideal town of Sforzinda (although the plans were not executed) for the Sforza dynasty.

Filarete drew the plans for the hospital in Milan, built in the 18th century, but is better known for his *Treatise on Architecture*, a work in 25 volumes which contains architectural designs combining pagan and Christian forms with an occasional strong element of fantasy.

BIBLIOGRAPHY:
Röder, Helen, *'The borders of Filarete's bronze doors to St. Peter's'* in *Journal of the Warburg and Courtauld Institutes*, vol 10, 1947. Spencer, J.R. (ed), *Filarete, Treatise on Architecture: Being the Treatise by Antonio di Piero Averlino, Known as Filarete*, Yale University Press, New Haven, 1965. Lang, Susanne, *'Sforzinda, Filarete and Filelfo'* in *Journal of the Warburg and Courtauld Institutes*, vol 35, 1972. Seymour, C., *'Some Reflections on Filarete's Use of Antique Visual Sources'* in *Arte Lombarda*, vol 38-39, 1973. Lord, C., *'Solar Imagery in Filarete's Doors to Saint Peter's'* in *Gazette des Beaux-Arts*, vol 87, 1976. Spencer, J.R., *'Filarete the Medallist of the Roman Emperors'* in *Art Bulletin*, vol 41, 1979.

MUSEUMS AND GALLERIES:
BERLIN (Bodemus.): *Madonna with Angels* - LONDON (Victoria and Albert Mus.): *Self-portrait* (medallion) - PARIS (Louvre): *Triumph of Caesar; Madonna with Angels* - ROME (Mus. di Propaganda Fide): *Bust of Emperor John VI Paleologus* - VIENNA (Court Mus.): *Odysseus and Iros* (plaque).

FILARSKI, Dirk Hermann Wilhem
Dutch, 20th century.
Born 15 October 1885, in Amsterdam; died 1964.
Painter. Landscapes, still-lifes.
School of Bergen.
Filarshki was a student at the Hogeschool voor de Kunsten in Amsterdam. He featured in the Amsterdam International Exhibition in 1912. He made working trips to Switzerland, Paris and Spain.

D·H.W. FILARSKI.

AUCTION RECORDS:
AMSTERDAM, 7 Sept 1976, *View of Corte* (watercolour, 31 x 38 1/2 ins / 78.5 x 98 cm) NLG 2,100. AMSTERDAM, 7 Nov 1978, *Landscape in the South of France* (oil on canvas, 46 3/4 x 62 1/2 ins / 119 x 159 cm) NLG 6,000. AMSTERDAM, 20 May 1981, *Wooded Landscape* (oil on canvas, 25 1/2 x 21 ins / 65 x 53.5 cm) NLG 2,100. AMSTERDAM, 24 Oct 1983, *Town in the South of France* (oil on canvas, 25 1/4 x 31 1/2 ins / 64 x 80 cm) NLG 1,750. AMSTERDAM, 28 Sept 1987, *View of Corte, Corsica* (1931, oil on canvas, 46 1/2 x 62 1/2 ins / 118 x 159 cm) NLG 6,600. AMSTERDAM, 10 Feb 1988, *View of a Mountain Village* (oil on canvas, 33 1/4 x 25 3/4 ins / 84.5 x 65.5 cm) NLG 2,070. AMSTERDAM, 30 Aug 1988, *The Pont-Neuf in Paris* (oil on canvas, 32 x 25 1/2 ins / 81 x 65 cm) NLG 2,300. AMSTERDAM, 8 Dec 1988, *Haystacks* (oil on canvas, 13 3/4 x 20 3/4 ins / 35 x 53 cm) NLG 3,450. AMSTERDAM, 10 April 1989, *Still-life of Flowers* (1930, oil on canvas, 47 1/4 x 39 1/4 ins / 120 x 99.5 cm) NLG 4,370. AMSTERDAM, 13 Dec 1989, *Mountains in Snow* (1916, oil on canvas, 29 x 39 1/4 ins / 73.5 x 100 cm) NLG 17,250. AMSTERDAM, 10 April 1990, *The Diablerets* (1916, oil on canvas, 24 3/4 x 34 1/4 ins / 63 x 87 cm) NLG 8,625. AMSTERDAM, 22 May 1990, *Mountainous Landscape in Switzerland* (1917, oil on canvas, 25 1/2 x 35 1/2 ins / 65 x 90 cm) NLG 13,800. AMSTERDAM, 5 June 1990, *A Hamlet beside a Road through Woodland* (1940, oil on canvas, 19 3/4 x 27 1/2 ins / 50 x 70 cm) NLG 3,220. AMSTERDAM, 12 Dec 1990, *A Castle in the South of Spain* (oil on canvas, 26 1/2 x 32 1/4 ins / 67 x 82 cm) NLG 6,900. AMSTERDAM, 22 May 1991, *Still-life with Artist's Materials* (1911, oil on canvas, 22 x 27 1/2 ins / 55 x 70 cm) NLG 8,050. AMSTERDAM, 23 May 1991, *The Waterfall in the Valley* (1940, oil on canvas, 21 1/4 x 25 1/2 ins / 54 x 65 cm) NLG 12,650; *The Old Park in Bergen* (1940, oil on canvas, 21 1/4 x 25 1/2 ins / 54 x 65 cm) NLG 31,050. AMSTERDAM, 12 Dec 1991, *Winter* (1913, oil on canvas, 21 1/2 x 27 1/4 ins / 54.5 x 69 cm) NLG 8,050; *Landscape of Dunes* (1913, oil on canvas, 13 1/2 x 20 ins / 34 x 51 cm) NLG 21,850. AMSTERDAM, 21 May 1992, *Paris Café* (oil on canvas, 31 1/2 x 26 ins / 80 x 66 cm) NLG 13,800. AMSTERDAM, 10 Dec 1992, *Les Avants* (oil on canvas, 29 1/4 x 46 1/2 ins / 74 x 118 cm) NLG 11,500. AMSTERDAM, 26 May 1993, *Red Mountains in Spain* (1925, oil on canvas, 31 1/2 x 39 1/4 ins / 80 x 100 cm) NLG 12,650. AMSTERDAM, 9 Dec 1993, *Mountain Lake in Switzerland* (1914, oil on canvas, 13 3/4 x 20 3/4 ins / 35 x 53 cm) NLG 11,270. AMSTERDAM, 7 Dec 1994, *A Farm* (1942, oil on canvas, 39 1/4 x 31 1/2 ins / 100 x 80 cm) NLG 8,625. AMSTERDAM, 31 May 1995, *View of Lake Geneva* (1913, oil on canvas/panel, 17 1/4 x 23 1/2 ins / 43.5 x 60 cm) NLG 8,496. AMSTERDAM, 31 May 1995, *View of Lake Geneva* (1913, oil on canvas/panel, 32 1/4 x 25 1/2 ins / 82 x 65 cm) NLG 4,600. AMSTERDAM, 10 Dec 1996, *Swiss Landscape near Busier* (1916, oil on canvas, 25 1/2 x 35 1/2 ins / 64.5 x 90 cm) NLG 17,298. AMSTERDAM, 17-18 Dec 1996, *Mountain Village* (oil on canvas, 32 x 25 3/4 ins / 81.5 x 65.5 cm) NLG 6,844; *Partenkirchen Landscape* (c. 1917, oil on canvas, 23 x 32 3/4 ins / 57.5 x 83.5 cm) NLG 10,030. AMSTERDAM, 1 Dec 1997, *Road from Sospel* (oil on canvas, 43 x 51 1/4 ins / 109.5 x 130 cm) NLG 12,390. AMSTERDAM, 2 Dec 1997, *Farm at Drente* (1915, oil on canvas, 35 x 25 1/4 ins / 88 x 64 cm) NLG 25,370. AMSTERDAM, 10 June 1999, *Snowy Mountainous Landscape* (1916, oil on canvas, 27 x 21 ins / 68 x 54 cm) NLG 28,000. AMSTERDAM, 1 Dec 1999, *Bridge at Giethoorn* (oil on canvas, 21 x 26 ins / 54 x 66 cm) NLG 30,000. AMSTERDAM, 8 June 2000, *Alpenglooien, St Moritz* (1917, oil on canvas, 21 x 27 ins / 53 x 68 cm) NLG 18,000. AMSTERDAM, 30 Nov 2000, *Ruthli, Switzerland* (1917, oil on canvas, 16 x 22 ins / 41 x 57 cm) NLG 34,000. AMSTERDAM, 20 March 2001, *Farm with a Haystack* (1940, oil on canvas, 16 x 20 ins / 40 x 50 cm) NLG 16,000. AMSTERDAM, 12 June 2001, *Mountainous Landscape near Wassergrat, Berner Oberland* (1916, oil on canvas, 26 x 35 ins / 65 x 90 cm) NLG 28,000. AMSTERDAM, 25 Nov 2002, *View of a North African Landscape* (oil on canvas, 26 x 33 ins / 65 x 83 cm) EUR 10,000. AMSTERDAM, 3 Dec 2002, *Shipyard in Spain* (oil on canvas, 30 x 39 ins / 75 x 100 cm) EUR 15,000. AMSTERDAM, 10 March 2003, *Still-life with Flowers in a Vase and Flowers in a Bottle* (oil on canvas, 39 x 34 ins / 98 x 87 cm) EUR 5,500. AMSTERDAM, 29 Sept 2003, *City behind the Wall* (oil on canvas, 31 x 39 ins / 80 x 100 cm) EUR 7,500. AMSTERDAM, 21 Dec 2004, *Glass Vase with Red and Yellow Freesias* (oil on canvas, 21 x 26 ins / 54 x 65 cm) EUR 3,800. AMSTER-

DAM, 21 Dec 2004, *View of Menton* (oil on canvas, 22 x 28 ins / 55 x 70 cm) EUR 4,000.

FILASTRE, Ambroise
French, 18th century.
Active in Houdan.
Sculptor.
Ambroise Filastre worked for the churches in Nogent-le-Roi, Boutigny and Boué.

FILASTRE-DUMONT, Gérard
French, 20th century.
Born 1891, in Cussac (Gironde).
Painter. Portraits, genre scenes, seascapes, still-lifes.
Gérard Filastre-Dumont exhibited in Paris at the Salon d'Automne and the Salon des Artistes Indépendants.

FILATEEV, Ivan
Russian, 17th century.
Died 5 August 1678, in Moscow.
Painter.
Filateev painted icons for churches and monasteries in Moscow and produced work for the Kremlin.

FILATEEV, Tikhon Ivanovich
Russian, 17th century.
Active in Moscow.
Painter.
This artist was the son and most probably the pupil of Ivan Filateev. After the latter's death, he was nominated as painter attached to the Kremlin's studios. We know of his religious paintings in the church of Metropolitan Alexei.

FILATOV, Nikolai Vadimovitch
Ukrainian, 20th - 21st century.
Born 1951, in Lviv.
Active in Moscow from 1982.
Painter.
Nikolai Vadimovitch Filatov graduated from the institute of decorative arts in Lviv in 1977. In 1984 he was made a member of the Union of Soviet Artists. He joined a collective of artists' studios set up in a former children's kindergarten, which was later chased out by the police. His painting style is gestural, expressionist, and comparable to free Western Figurative art. Such paintings have been allowed to exist and be shown only since the second half of the 1980s.
BIBLIOGRAPHY:
'L'Art au pays des Soviets, 1963-1988' in *Les Cahiers du Musée National d'Art Moderne,* no. 26, periodical, Paris, winter 1988. Makhroff, Olga, *'Les Dossiers des Cahiers'* in *Les Cahiers du Musée National d'Art Moderne,* no. 26, periodical, Paris, winter 1988.
AUCTION RECORDS:
MOSCOW, 7 July 1988, *Minotaur* (1987, oil on canvas, 78 3/4 x 59 ins / 200 x 150 cm) GBP 12,100.

FILCZ, Joachim
German, 16th century.
Painter.
Breslau School.
In 1518, Filcz was a pupil of Nicolaus von Lemburg. In 1521 he was named a master in Breslau (now Wroclaw) and, in 1523, granted citizenship of the town.

FILDES, Fanny (Lady)
Maiden name: Woods
British, 19th century.
Painter. Genre scenes, landscapes, fruit.
Fanny Fildes, the wife of Sir Luke Fildes, exhibited with the Royal Academy from 1875.
AUCTION RECORDS:
LONDON, 24 June 1909, *Venetian House on the Grand Canal,* GBP 17. LONDON, 15 June 1923, *Fruit; Flowers* (collection) GBP 12. BRUSSELS, 16 Dec 1986, *Young Woman Peeling Potatoes* (1878, oil on canvas, 13 x 11 ins / 33 x 27 cm) GBP 2,500.

FILDES, Luke (Sir)
British, 19th century.
Born 18 October 1844, in Liverpool; died 27 February 1927, in London.
Painter. Portraits, genre scenes.
Sir Luke Fildes studied art at the South Kensington schools and, later, at the Royal Academy, where he exhibited for the first time in 1867. He was a noted illustrator for the periodicals *London Graphic, Cornhill Magazine* and *Once a Week,* and produced drawings for editions of Dickens and Lever. He enjoyed a considerable reputation as a social-realist painter. He was a frequent visitor to Venice, and produced a number of scenes of Venetian life. He was an associate of the Royal Academy, and became a full member in 1887. He took part in a number of exhibitions overseas, notably the Paris Expositions Universelles of 1878 and 1889 (when he won a silver medal).
BIBLIOGRAPHY:
Catalogue Raisonné of the Published Reproductions of Luke Fildes's Drawings: Typescript, National Art Library, London, 1960-1968. Fildes, Luke V., *Luke Fildes, a Victorian Painter,* Joseph, London, 1968. Wood, Christopher, *Paradise Lost: Paintings of English Country Life and Landscape, 1850-1914,* Trafalgar square Pub., North Pomfret (VT), 1988.
MUSEUMS AND GALLERIES:
ABERDEEN (AG): *Self Portrait* - BRIGHTON (Mus. & AG): *Venetian Girl with a Flask* (1870, oil on canvas); *A Venetian Market Girl* (1876, oil on canvas) - HAMBURG: *Young Flower-Seller in Venice* - LIVERPOOL (Walker AG): *The Widower* (1902, copy); *Fanny, Lady Fildes* - LONDON (National Portrait Gal.): *King Edward VII* (1902, oil on canvas, replica of the coronation portrait) - LONDON (Royal Academy of Arts): *Self-portrait of Sir Luke Fildes* (1911, oil on canvas) - LONDON (Tate Collection): *The Doctor* (exhibited in 1891, oil on canvas); *Applicants for Admission to a Casual Ward* (after 1908, oil on canvas) - SYDNEY (National Gallery of New South Wales): *The Widower* - WARRINGTON: *Daughter of the Lagoon.*
AUCTION RECORDS:
LONDON, 8 May 1886, *Village Wedding* (1883, oil on canvas, 60 x 100 ins / 152.4 x 254 cm) Gns 105. LONDON, 15 Feb 1908, *Dolly* (1881) GBP 210. LONDON, 21 March 1908, *Head of a Young Girl,* GBP 86. LONDON, 1 May 1908, *Waiting,* GBP 99. LONDON, 25 June 1908, *Young Englishwoman,* GBP 420; *Young Irish Woman,* GBP 231; *Nin,* GBP 168. LONDON, 10 July 1908, *Devotion,* GBP 220. LONDON, 24 June 1909, *Return of a Penitent,* GBP 266; *Venetian,* GBP 210; *Venetian Peasant Woman* (1876) GBP 252. LONDON, 12 Feb 1910, *In Love,* GBP 94. LONDON, 8 Dec 1922, *The Empty Chair* (drawing) GBP 39. LONDON, 9 March 1923, *Roses,* GBP 70. LONDON, 15 June 1923, *Head of a Little Girl,* GBP 47. LONDON, 15 Feb 1924, *Head of a Little Girl,* GBP 8. LONDON, 23 Jan 1925, *Contemplation,* GBP 27. LONDON, 15 March 1925, *Time Off,* GBP 35. LONDON, 1 Dec 1925, *Dairywoman,* GBP 92. LONDON, 5 Feb 1926, *Venetian Beauty,* GBP 52. LONDON, 4 June 1926, *Marianina,* GBP 60. LONDON, 24 June 1927, *Norah,* GBP 31; *Yellow Rose,* GBP 115; *Toilette* GBP 48; *Contemplation,* GBP 16; *Nina Knitting,* GBP 60; *Adoration,* GBP 16; *Naomi,* GBP 147; *The Green Shawl,* GBP 52; *Louis,* GBP 22; *The Mantilla,* GBP 115; *Brigitta,* GBP 10; *Irma no 2,* GBP 12; *Anna no 1,* GBP 33; *The Florist,* GBP 29; *Meditation,* GBP 23; *Catherine,* GBP 47; *The Black Shawl,* GBP 48; *Catarina,* GBP 47; *Irma,* GBP 39; *Rebecca,* GBP 25; *Maria no 2,* GBP 10; *The Red Shawl,* GBP 37; *Gina,* GBP 18; *Blonde,* GBP 27; *Nina,* GBP 13. LONDON, 12 Dec 1927, *Young Woman of the Red Cross,* GBP 13. LONDON, 4 June 1928, *Young Venetian Woman,* GBP 81. LONDON, 30 Nov 1928, *Time Off,* GBP 25. LONDON, 3 Dec 1928, *Netta,* GBP 11. LONDON, 10 May 1929, *Marietta,* GBP 14. LONDON, 30 May

1930, *Portrait of Williamina Margaret Ellen*, GBP 17. LONDON, 1 May 1931, *Sisters*, GBP 29. LONDON, 24 July 1931, *Young Venetian Woman*, GBP 17. LONDON, 2 March 1932, *Betty*, GBP 30. LONDON, 17 June 1932, *Marianina*, GBP 8. LONDON, 30 Nov 1934, *The Yellow Rose* (drawing) GBP 21. LONDON, 3 May 1935, *La Gardiniera* GBP 78; *Venetian Fruit Seller*, GBP 18. LONDON, 3 April 1936, *Venetian*, GBP 71. LONDON, 24 April 1936, *Feeding Pigeons* (drawing) GBP 5. LONDON, 25 May 1936, *Marietta*, GBP 6. LONDON, 21 May 1937, *Sylvia*, GBP 31. LONDON, 19 July 1937, *Vivienne*, GBP 10. LONDON, 14 Feb 1941, *Venetian Florist* (drawing) GBP 35. LONDON, 10 July 1970, *The Poor*, Gns 1,600. LONDON, 16 Nov 1976, *The Doctor* (oil on canvas, 20 1/4 x 29 1/2 ins / 51.5 x 75 cm) GBP 1,700. LONDON, 26 Nov 1982, *Village Wedding* (1883, oil on canvas, 60 x 100 ins / 152.4 x 254 cm) GBP 35,000. LONDON, 14 July 1983, *Daydream at the Edge of a Pond* (1876, oil on canvas, 24 x 16 ins / 61 x 40.5 cm) GBP 8,500. LONDON, 11 June 1986, *Fair Quiet and Sweet Rest* (oil on canvas, 24 x 36 ins / 61 x 91.5 cm) GBP 5,000. LONDON, 15 June 1988, *Gathering Roses* (oil on canvas, 20 3/4 x 14 1/2 ins / 53 x 37 cm) GBP 4,840. LONDON, 24 Nov 1989, *Life in Venice* (1884, oil on canvas, 84 1/4 x 62 1/4 ins / 214 x 158 cm) GBP 101,200. LONDON, 13 March 1992, *Study for 'The Widower'* (oil on canvas, 21 1/2 x 15 ins / 54.6 x 38.1 cm) GBP 6,270. LONDON, 12 June 1992, *Village Wedding* (1883, oil on canvas, 59 3/4 x 100 1/2 ins / 151.7 x 255.3 cm) GBP 275,000. LONDON, 12 Nov 1992, *Simpletons* (oil on canvas, 15 3/4 x 26 1/4 ins / 40 x 66.5 cm) GBP 12,100. LONDON, 13 Nov 1992, *Portrait of the Artist's Sister* (1891, oil on panel, 11 1/2 x 8 1/4 ins / 29.2 x 21 cm) GBP 8,580. LONDON, 8-9 June 1993, *Moments of Idleness* (1876, oil on canvas, 24 1/2 x 16 1/4 ins / 62.5 x 41 cm) GBP 10,925. LONDON, 6 Nov 1995, *Betty the Dairywoman* (1875, oil on canvas, 12 1/4 x 9 ins / 31 x 22 cm) GBP 3,220. LONDON, 7 June 1996, *Portrait of Josephine Agnew* (1892, oil on canvas, 21 1/2 x 17 ins / 54.7 x 43.2 cm) GBP 10,350. LONDON, 12 March 1997, *Rose Siega, Venetian Peasant Woman* (1876, oil on canvas, 34 x 22 3/4 ins / 86.5 x 58 cm) GBP 11,500. SYDNEY, 10 Aug 1999, *Making Flower Garland, Yorkshire* (watercolour and gouache, 10 x 18 ins / 26 x 45 cm) AUD 3,000. SHREWSBURY, 7 Nov 2001, *Fair Flower* (oil on canvas, 14 x 12 ins / 36 x 30 cm) GBP 3,000. LONDON, 11 June 2002, *Head of a Girl* (oil on canvas, 17 x 15 ins / 44 x 37 cm) GBP 1,200. LONDON, 20 Feb 2003, *Homeless and Hungry* (pencil, watercolour, gouache and gum arabic, 7 x 10 ins / 17 x 25 cm) GBP 8,500. LONDON, 19 Nov 2003, *Sisters, Double Portrait of Misses Renton* (1889, oil on canvas, 74 x 56 ins / 188 x 142 cm) GBP 36,000. ASHBURTON, 13 May 2004, *Portrait of Sir George Sutton, Former Chairman of Henley's* (oil on canvas, 52 x 39 ins / 132 x 99 cm) GBP 1,500.

FILDIER, Robert
French, 20th century.
Born in Avallon.
Watercolourist.

Robert Fildier exhibited at the Salon des Artistes Français from 1927.

FILELA, Jaime
Spanish, 14th century.
Sculptor.

In 1382, Jaime Filela worked on the sculptures adorning the portal of the cathedral in Barcelona.

FILGER, Conrad, or Filgher
Italian, 17th century.
Active in Venice c. 1660.
Painter. Landscapes.

Conrad Filger is mentioned in a text by Marco Boschini, written in 1660.

FILHASTRE, Paul Louis Georges
French, 19th - 20th century.
Born 18 September 1859, in St-Bazeille (Lot-et-Garonne); died 5 January 1948, in Villeneuve-sur-Lot.
Sculptor.

Paul Filhastre studied under Chappy and Puech. He made his debut at the Salon des Artistes Français in 1884.

FILHER, Julien
Belgian, 20th century.
Born 1888, in Brussels.
Painter, engraver.

Filher was a student at the Académie des Beaux Arts in Brussels. From 1914 to 1920 he travelled in South America, from where he brought back numerous studies. He exhibited in Brussels from 1922. Influenced at first by Impressionism, his style subsequently evolved in a more purely decorative direction.

FILHO, Joâo Camara. See **CAMARA-FILHO**

FILHOL, Antoine Michel
French, 18th - 19th century.
Born 1759, in Paris; died 5 May 1812, in Paris.
Engraver, print publisher.

Antoine Filhol was the pupil of F.-D. Née. Although he engraved landscapes, he is especially remembered as a publisher, and in particular for his publication of the *Cours élémentaire de peinture* (*Elementary Course in Painting*) or *Galerie du Musée Napoléon* (*Picture Gallery of the Musée Napoléon*), a work of 120 installments in 10 volumes with an explanatory text by Caroffe and J. Lavallée. In 1827 his widow, with the collaboration of Jal, completed the work with *Musée Royal de France* or *Collection gravée de chefs-d'œuvre de peinture et de sculpture dont il s'est enrichi depuis la Restauration* (*Engraved Collection of Masterpieces of Painting and Sculpture with which the Museum has been Enriched since the Restoration*).

FILHOL, Sophie Antoinette
French, 19th century.
Born 4 March 1806, in Paris; died 1854.
Painter.

Filhol was trained by Mme de Mirbel and received a second-class medal in 1839 and a first-class one in 1846. She exhibited at the Salon from 1836 to 1853. Her production was mainly miniatures.

FILHON, Bertrand
French, 17th century.
Active in Angoulême.
Painter.

FILHOS, Jean
French, 20th century.
Born 10 March 1921, in Le Mas-d'Agenais (Lot-et-Garonne); died 25 August 2002, in Bourges (Cher).
Sculptor, worker in precious metals. Objets d'art, jewels.

Jean Filhos's study of architecture was interrupted by World War II, and by his activity in the French Resistance from 1942. Between 1948 and 1958, he worked with architect Fernand Pouillon. His momentous meeting with Henri Laurens lead to his leaving his profession to become a full time sculptor and goldsmith.

In 1960, he discovered resins, which very soon became the medium through which he found a ready expression (the flexibility of the material allowing for his baroque aesthetics, where polychromy plays a major part). He has created pieces for Christofle, the goldsmiths, and for the Sèvres China Works, as well as some jewellery.

Filhos started to show in 1959 and took part in many Salons in Paris, including: Réalités Nouvelles, Salon de Mai, and Comparaisons.

FILIBERTI, Francesco
Italian, 15th century.
Born in Alessandria (Piedmont).
Sculptor.

Francesco Filiberti was the pupil of Jacopino da Tradate. His only known work is a terracotta *Virgin and Child*, dated 25 June 1462, found in an antique dealer's in 1910.

FILIBERTI, Georges Guido
Italian, 20th century.
Born 12 March 1881, in Milan; died 1970.
Active from 1900 and naturalised in France in 1924.
Painter, engraver. Landscapes.
Musicalism (the attempt to interpret music in painting).

Georges Filiberti studied in Paris, at the École des Arts Décoratifs and the École des Beaux-Arts; Louis Biloul was one of his masters. He spent all his life working in France. Filiberti was skilled in a wide variety of techniques, and his works are delicate and bold. Many contemporary engravers were influenced by him.

Filiberti regularly exhibited in Paris: first at the Salon of the Société des Artistes Français; occasionally at the Salon des Artistes Indépendants; at the Salon des Tuileries from 1934 to 1943; at the Salon d'Automne from 1942 to 1971; at the Salon des Réalités Nouvelles, with the 'Musicalists', in 1954 and 1955; at the Salon Comparaisons from 1956 to 1959; and finally, at the 1963 exhibition *Valensi and Musicalism*, at the Musée de Lyon.

AUCTION RECORDS:
HONFLEUR, 9 Nov 1986, *Mrs Filibert Seated* (1945, oil on canvas, 32 x 25 1/2 ins / 81 x 65 cm) FRF 15,000. PARIS, 12 July 1988, *Composition* (1937, oil on panel, 25 1/2 x 21 ins / 65 x 53.5 cm) FRF 4,000. PARIS, 11 July 1989, *Snow over Montmartre* (1946, oil on canvas, 13 x 16 1/2 ins / 33 x 42 cm) FRF 11,500. CALAIS, 8 July 1990, *Nice - The Baie des Anges* (1938, oil on panel, 13 x 16 1/4 ins / 33 x 41 cm) FRF 5,000.

FILICAJA, Simone da
Italian, 16th - 17th century.
Born at the end of the 16th century, in Florence.
Painter.

Simone da Filicaja was the pupil of Jacopo Vignali.

FILICCHI, Camilla
Italian, 18th - 19th century.
Born 1771, in Gubbio; died 1848.
Painter.

FILIDONI, Gioacchino
Italian, 19th century.
Active at the beginning of the 19th century.
Engraver (burin).

Filidoni made religious engravings. He is known for a work entitled *Charles V Entering Bologna*.

FILIE
French, 17th century.
Active at the end of the 17th century.
Ivory worker. Historical figures. Medallions.

MUSEUMS AND GALLERIES:
DIEPPE: *The Princess Palatine* (before 1700, medallion).

FILIGER, Charles, or Filliger
French, 19th - 20th century.
Born 28 November 1863, in Thann (Alsace); died 11 January 1928, in Plougastel or Brest.
Painter (gouache), engraver. Religious subjects, figures, landscapes.
School of Pont-Aven.

In 1886, Charles Filiger headed for Paris in order to paint, where he absorbed Seurat's Pointillism and Van Gogh's turbulent manner. After a brawl, he left Paris for Brittany, where he worked alongside Gauguin at Le Pouldu in 1890. He figured in Rémy de Gourmont's *L'Ymagier* and, in 1892, took part in the first Salon de la Rose-Croix. He would remain in Brittany, where he often led a nomadic existence in utmost poverty; he was prone to alcoholism until his violent death. In 1990, Strasbourg Museum organised a retrospective exhibition of his work.

BIBLIOGRAPHY:
Schneider, Pierre, '*Filiger: l'amer picon de l'absolu*' in *L'Express*, periodical, Paris, 31 August 1990. Puget, François, *Charles Filiger, 1863-1928*, Le Télégramme, Morlaix, 2001.

MUSEUMS AND GALLERIES:
PARIS (Mus. d'Orsay): *Head of a Breton Woman* - QUIMPER (MBA): *Le Pouldu Landscape* (c. 1892).

AUCTION RECORDS:
LONDON, 8 April 1976, *Portrait of a Man* (oil on paper remounted on board, 8 1/4 x 6 ins / 21 x 15 cm) GBP 1,200. VERSAILLES, 15 June 1976, *Fresh Search For a Unifying Primary Motive* (watercolour and gouache, 9 x 11 1/2 ins / 23 x 29 cm) FRF 6,200. VERSAILLES, 18 June 1980, *Still-life with a Pumpkin* (gouache, 6 1/4 x 8 ins / 16 x 20.5 cm) FRF 10,000. ENGHIEN-LES-BAINS, 22 April 1982, *Angel by a Chapel* (oil on canvas, 13 x 16 1/4 ins / 33 x 41.5 cm) FRF 118,000. PARIS, 19 June 1984, *Le Pouldu: the Chapel of St Maudez* (gouache, 10 1/4 x 14 1/4 ins / 26 x 36 cm) FRF 68,000. PARIS, 24 June 1988, *Christ on the Moor* (c. 1890, study in watercolour and ink on tracing paper, 14 1/2 x 9 3/4 ins / 37 x 25 cm) FRF 65,000; *Breton Shore* (c. 1892, gouache/card, 9 x 7 ins / 23 x 18 cm) FRF 320,000; *Bust of Christ between Two Angels and the Virgin Mary* (gouache/paper heightened with gold, 6 1/4 x 5 1/2 ins / 15.7 x 13.8 cm) FRF 160,000. PARIS, 21 June 1989, *The Spirit in the Garland* (1892, gouache/plaster, 13 3/4 x 28 1/4 ins / 35 x 72 cm) FRF 90,000. PARIS, 22 Nov 1989, *Still-life with Walnuts* (oil on panel, 3 1/2 x 4 1/4 ins / 9 x 10.5 cm) FRF 50,000. DOUAI, 3 Dec 1989, *Composition with a Figure* (watercolour, 5 1/2 x 5 1/2 ins / 14 x 14 cm) FRF 41,000. PARIS, 3 April 1990, *Angel* (collage with gouache, 54 x 54 ins / 137 x 137 cm) FRF 60,000. PARIS, 11 March 1991, *Virgin and Child* (watercolour, gouache and gold paint, 3 x 2 1/2 ins / 7.8 x 6.5 cm) FRF 19,000. PARIS, 8 Nov 1991, *Christ and the Virgin Mary* (1892, reproduction heightened with gouache, illustration for 'Le Lutin mystique', 3 1/4 x 3 1/2 ins / 8 x 9.2 cm) FRF 9,500. PARIS, 24 June 1992, *St in Prayers* (gouache, 9 1/4 x 6 1/2 ins / 23.5 x 16.5 cm) FRF 200,000. PARIS, 4 March 1994, *Study of Figures (portrait of la Rochefoucault) and of Ornamental Motives* (three pen drawings on tracing paper, 5 1/2 x 5 ins / 14 x 12.5 cm; 5 1/2 x 5 1/2 ins/14 x 14 cm, and 4 1/2 x 6 1/4 ins/11.5 x 15.8 cm) FRF 30,000. PARIS, 24 June 1994, *Portrait of a Man, Inset* (watercolour, 6 x 5 3/4 ins / 15.5 x 14.5 cm) FRF 6,500. PARIS, 15 Dec 1994, *Mosaic and Portrait* (watercolour, 6 x 5 3/4 ins / 15 x 14.5 cm) FRF 11,000. PARIS, 26 March 1995, *Study for Madonna with a Glow-worm* (watercolour and gouache heightened with gold on tracing paper/card, 9 1/4 x 12 ins / 23.5 x 30.5 cm) FRF 48,000. PARIS, 19 June 1995, *Le Génie à la guirlande* (1892, gouache/plaster panel, 14 1/4 x 28 ins / 36 x 71 cm) FRF 200,000. LONDON, 28 June 1995, *Angels near the Chapel of St Maudez, Le Pouldu* (1892, oil on canvas, 13 1/2 x 16 1/2 ins / 34 x 42 cm) GBP 8,050. PARIS, 16 Dec 1997, *Ora pro Nobis (Pray for Us)* (1894, heightened with gouache and gold, illustration, 3 1/4 x 2 1/4 ins / 8 x 6 cm) FRF 35,000. CALAIS, 5 Nov 2000, *Ile de Seine* (watercolour, 6 x 11 ins / 16 x 29 cm) FRF 30,000. BREST, 10 Dec 2000, *Portrait of an Adolescent Boy* (1886, oil on panel, 7 x 6 ins / 17 x 16 cm) FRF 39,000. PARIS, 22 June 2001, *Breton Landscape* (gouache, 13 x 19 ins / 32 x 48 cm) FRF 570,000. LONDON, 28 Sept 2001, *Breton Landscape* (oil on canvas, 13 x 17 ins / 33 x 43 cm) GBP 10,000. PARIS, 11 Oct 2002, *Male Nude* (1890, gouache on cardboard, 14 x 9 ins / 36 x 23 cm) EUR 10,500. PARIS, 26 March 2003, *Pointillist Landscape* (gouache on paper on panel, 7 x 11 ins / 17 x 29 cm) EUR 74,000. PARIS, 14 April 2003, *Madonna and Two Angels* (gouache, 9 x 11 ins / 23 x 29 cm) EUR 170,000.

PARIS, 30 June 2004, *Chromatic Notation* (c. 1903, gouache over pencil, 9 x 11 ins / 24 x 28 cm) EUR 9,000.

FILIMONOV, Vladimir
Russian, 20th century.
Born 1873; died 1934.
Painter. Still-lifes.

Vladimir Filimonov studied at the academy of fine art in St Petersburg. He painted hackneyed subjects in a controlled academic technique. He took part in national and international exhibitions including Vienna, Amsterdam, Rome and Paris and was awarded the title of People's Artist.

AUCTION RECORDS:
PARIS, 19 June 1991, *Still-life with Watermelon* (1929, oil on canvas, 38 1/4 x 47 1/4 ins / 97 x 120 cm) FRF 6,500.

FILIMONOV, Yacob Yakovlevich
Russian, 18th century.
Born 10 April 1771, in St Petersburg; died 2 April 1795, in Nadjeshidino, near Saratov.
Painter.

Filimonov went in 1786 to the Imperial School of Fine Arts and was the pupil of Semen Fedorovich Shchedrin. In 1793, he was won a first class award. The Alexander III Museum in St Petersburg has two of his Italian landscapes.

FILIPEPI, Alessandro. See **BOTTICELLI Sandro**

FILIPKIEWICZ, Stephan or Stefan
Polish, 20th century.
Born 1879, in Cracow; died 1944.
Painter. Landscapes, landscapes with figures.

Stephan Filipkiewicz was a pupil of Florian Cynk and Joseph Mehoffer at the academy of fine art in Cracow. He was specifically a landscape painter sensitive to particular atmospheres as seen in *Winter, Dew* and *Autumn Sky*; he also painted town streets including *View of Kasimiec*, and views with figures such as *Fair on Szczepauski Square in Cracow*. Filipkiewicz exhibited annually in Cracow, Lódz and Warsaw and appeared at collective exhibitions in Berlin, Munich, Vienna and Rome.

FILIPOV, Afanasii
Russian, 17th century.
Active in Moscow.
Painter.

Filipov was a pupil of Ivan Bogdanovich Saltanov. He worked with him on several of Moscow's churches.

FILIPOV, Konstantin Nicolaevich
Russian, 19th century.
Born 1830; died 12 July 1878, in Yalta.
Painter. Military subjects, figures, scenes with figures.

After 1850, Filipov was a pupil of the painter of battle scenes, B.P. Villevalde at the St Petersburg Imperial Academy. He received several awards. He exhibited in St Petersburg in 1863.

MUSEUMS AND GALLERIES:
MOSCOW (State Tretyakov Gal.): *The Military Road from Simferopol to Sebastopol at the Time of the Crimean War* - MOSCOW (Zvietkov Gal.): *Scene from the Crimean War; A Cossack* (watercolour); *Caucasian Cavalryman* (red chalk) - ST PETERSBURG (Gosudarstvennyj Russkij Muz.): *Bulgarian Migrants on their way to Russia; Russian Peasant Migrants going to the Caucasus.*

FILIPOVA, Katia
Russian, 20th century.
Painter, assemblage artist.

Katia Filipova incorporated into provocative Neo-Constructivist clothing characteristic images taken from 'sots' culture, the equivalent at the end of Soviet Russia of 'pop' culture in America.

FILIPOVIC, Franjo
Croat, 20th century.
Born 1930, in Hlebine.
Painter. Local scenes.
School of Hlebine.

Franjo Filipovic was always a small farmer and remained so, painting only in his spare time. He was born in Hlebine, a village that had become the capital of Naive painting because of the strong example set by Generalic. Filipovic showed him his drawings in 1945 and Generalic encouraged him to take up painting. He painted in broad, coloured flat tints in a style of decorative imagery. His favourite subjects were scenes of the daily life of small farmers: baking bread, shelling corn and churning butter. He exhibited his first paintings in regional shows from 1946 onwards and featured in the exhibition of Yugoslavian naive painters in Belgrade in 1957. He held a solo exhibition of his works in Zagreb in 1949.

BIBLIOGRAPHY:
Bihalji-Merin, Oto, *Les Peintres naïfs*, Delpire, Paris, 1960.

MUSEUMS AND GALLERIES:
ZAGREB (Hrvatski Muzej Naivne Umjetnosti): *Duck Hunt* (1957).

AUCTION RECORDS:
ZURICH, 23 Nov 1978, *Easter Eggs* (1962, fixed under glass, 12 1/2 x 17 3/4 ins / 32 x 45 cm) CHF 2,500.

FILIPOVIC-FILO, Branko
Montenegrin, 20th century.
Born 7 July 1924, in Cetinje; died 7 November 1997, in Belgrade.
Painter.

Branko Filipovic lived in Belgrade from 1936 to 1941, then returned to Cetinje. After being imprisoned in Kavai during the war in Albania, he enrolled at the school of art in his native town, Cetinje. He continued his training in Herceg Novi, then graduated from the academy of fine art in Belgrade in 1955. He stayed in France and Italy on several occasions. He was one of the representatives of Montenegrin Modernism after the War in pursuit of informally inspired pure painting.

He took part in collective exhibitions, including: *Contemporary Art of Montenegro 1945-1970*, Belgrade (1970); *Abstract Painting in Serbia 1951-1971*, cultural centre gallery, Belgrade (1971); Venice Biennale (1990); *50 Years of Art in Central Europe 1949-1999: Aspects, Positions*, Museum Moderner Kunst Stiftung Ludwig, Vienna (1999). Solo exhibitions include: Ulus Gallery (Association of Serb Artists), Belgrade (1957); Galerie Rive Gauche, Paris (1978); Galerie Yvon Lambert, Paris (1980); Museum of Contemporary Art, Belgrade (1997); Retrospective, Museum of Contemporary Art, Belgrade (1997).

BIBLIOGRAPHY:
Bosquet, Alain (preface), *Les oeuvres récentes de Filo Filipovic*, exhibition catalogue, Gal. Rive Gauche, Paris, 1978. *Branko Filipovic-Filo, Izlozba, 1957-1987*, exhibition catalogue, Muzej savremene umetnosti (musée d'Art moderne), Beograd, 1987. Blazevic, Dunja/Hegyi, Lóránd/Pejic, Bojana, *50 Years of art in Central Europe 1949-1999, Aspects, positions*, exhibition catalogue, Museum Moderner Kunst Stiftung Ludwig Wien, Vienna, 1999.

FILIPOWICZ, San-Joseph
Polish, 18th century.
Engraver (copper). Religious subjects, portraits.

According to the records Joseph Filipowicz lived in Lublin in 1742 and in Lemberg (now Lviv, Ukraine) in 1745. He engraved portraits of his contemporaries and religious pictures on copper. These include; *Madonnas*, images of *Saints*, and *Scenes from the Life of Christ*. His engraved portraits include those of *Prince Janusz Lubartowicz Sanguszko*, and the bishops *Leon* and *Athanase Szeptycki*, and also *Anna de Ossy Wielhorska* and *Stephan Studzinski*.

FILIPPELLI, Cafiero
Italian, 20th century.
Born 1889, in Livorno; died 1973.
Painter. Nudes, figures, genre scenes, interior scenes, rustic scenes, landscapes with figures, landscapes.

In his interior scenes, Filippelli exhibited a great fondness for genre painting, choosing local themes and characters as his subjects.

AUCTION RECORDS:
MILAN, 17 June 1981, *Lo Sincaldino* (oil/hardboard, 9 3/4 x 7 3/4 ins / 25 x 20 cm) ITL 1,700,000. MILAN, 16 Dec 1982, *Family around a Table* (oil on panel, 7 1/2 x 9 1/4 ins / 19 x 23.5 cm) ITL 1,400,000. MILAN, 2 April 1985, *Rustic Landscape, Tuscany* (1937, oil on panel, 17 3/4 x 13 ins / 45 x 33 cm) ITL 3,600,000. MILAN, 18 March 1986, *Interior Scene* (oil on card, 13 1/2 x 15 1/4 ins / 34 x 39 cm) ITL 2,800,000. ROME, 24 May 1988, *By the Hearth* (oil/plywood, 7 x 9 1/2 ins / 18 x 24 cm) ITL 2,200,000. ROME, 14 Dec 1988, *Table* (oil on panel, 7 3/4 x 11 3/4 ins / 20 x 30 cm) ITL 2,000,000. ROME, 14 Dec 1988, *Middle-class Interior* (oil on panel, 6 x 7 3/4 ins / 15 x 20 cm) ITL 1,400,000. ROME, 14 Dec 1989, *Evening at Home* (oil/plywood, 16 1/2 x 18 1/2 ins / 42 x 47 cm) ITL 2,875,000. MILAN, 30 May 1990, *Choirboys in the Sacristy* (1944, oil on panel, 23 1/2 x 20 3/4 ins / 59.5 x 53 cm) ITL 6,000,000. ROME, 31 May 1990, *The Umbrella Mender* (oil on panel, 13 3/4 x 18 ins / 35 x 45.5 cm) ITL 5,500,000. MILAN, 6 June 1991, *Village* (1952, oil on panel, 11 1/2 x 15 1/2 ins / 29 x 39.5 cm) ITL 1,900,000; *Female Nude Viewed from behind* (1940, oil on panel, 44 x 27 3/4 ins / 112 x 70.5 cm) ITL 4,000,000. MILAN, 19 March 1992, *Red Cart in the Olive Grove* (oil on panel, 10 x 13 1/2 ins / 24.5 x 34.5 cm) ITL 4,200,000. BOLOGNA, 8-9 June 1992, *By the Hearth* (oil/synthetic resin, 8 3/4 x 11 3/4 ins / 22.5 x 30 cm) ITL 2,300,000. NEW YORK, 29 Oct 1992, *Little Girl by a Fountain* (oil on panel, 13 1/2 x 19 1/2 ins / 34.2 x 49.5 cm) USD 2,200. MILAN, 3 Dec 1992, *Village Street* (oil on canvas, 26 3/4 x 45 1/4 ins / 68 x 115 cm) ITL 17,688,190. MILAN, 8 June 1993, *Patch of Country* (oil on panel, 15 x 10 1/2 ins / 38 x 26.5 cm) ITL 4,000,000. MILAN, 29 March 1995, *Waiting* (1913, oil on card, 7 1/4 x 5 3/4 ins / 18.5 x 14.5 cm) ITL 2,300,000. ROME, 5 Dec 1995, *At the Table* (oil on wood, 12 1/4 x 13 ins / 31 x 33 cm) ITL 4,478,000. ROME, 30 Nov 1999, *Tuscan Garden* (1935, oil on panel, 13 x 17 ins / 32 x 44 cm) ITL 4,200,000. ROME, 30 Nov 1999, *Sea Voyage* (oil on panel, 12 x 16 ins / 30 x 40 cm) ITL 5,500,000. MILAN, 28 March 2000, *Country Village Scene* (1926, oil on masonite, 11 x 15 ins / 29 x 39 cm) ITL 7,500,000. PRATO, 10 Nov 2000, *Life at the Seaside* (1954, oil on board, 6 x 9 ins / 16 x 23 cm) ITL 7,000,000. PRATO, 30 March 2001, *View of Livorno* (oil on board, 7 x 9 ins / 19 x 23 cm) ITL 6,000,000. MILAN, 27 Nov 2001, *Bather* (1952, oil on board, 11 x 15 ins / 27 x 38 cm) ITL 6,500,000. ROME, 27 May 2002, *Interiors with figures* (oil on board, 9 x 11 ins / 23 x 28 cm) EUR 2,600. PRATO, 15 Nov 2002, *Interior in the Evening* (oil on board, 9 x 11 ins / 24 x 28 cm) EUR 2,000. PRATO, 28 March 2003, *Evening Homework* (1922, oil on board, 11 x 10 ins / 27 x 26 cm) EUR 3,900. PRATO, 14 Nov 2003, *Coastal Road* (oil on board, 8 x 10 ins / 21 x 26 cm) EUR 2,800. MILAN, 8 June 2004, *Ardenza with Figures* (oil on board, 10 x 14 ins / 25 x 35 cm) EUR 6,000. PRATO, 11 June 2004, *Evening at Home* (oil on canvas, 15 x 20 ins / 37 x 50 cm) EUR 4,200.

FILIPPI, Agostino
Italian, 18th century.
Born c. 1680, in Parma; died after 1760.
Painter. Architectural views.

FILIPPI, André
French, 20th century.
Born 26 July 1902, in Toulon; died 14 April 1962.
Sculptor, engraver.

André Filippi sculpted many *Santons* (Christmas crib figures).

FILIPPI, Biagio di Lorenzo de
Italian, 16th century.
Died 22 September 1510.
Miniaturist.

Biagio di Lorenzo di Filippi was employed to work on the church of S Maria Novella in Florence.

FILIPPI, Camillo
Italian, 16th century.
Born c. 1500, in Ferrara; died 1574.
Painter. History painting, portraits.

Camillo Filippi, a pupil of Dosso Dossi, worked for the Este family. His painting of the *Annunciation* hangs in the church of S Maria del Vado in Ferrara, while the church of Il Gesù contains a *Trinity*; a painting of the *Battle of Marignano* can be found in the villa at Copparo. He also made a large number of cartoons for tapestries.

AUCTION RECORDS:
NEW YORK, 29 Jan 1998, *Virgin and Child with St John the Baptist Revealed by God the Father and Angels* (oil on panel, 21 1/4 x 13 3/4 ins / 54 x 35.2 cm) USD 32,200.

FILIPPI, Cesare
Italian, 16th century.
Born 1536, in Ferrara; died after 1602.
Painter.

The son and pupil of Camillo Filippi, Cesare Filippi worked as an assistant to his father and his brother Sebastiano, and executed a number of history paintings, such as the *Crucifixion* in the church of La Morte. He excelled at painting heads and grotesques in the ornamental style. His other works include the *Last Judgement* (on the façade of the church of St Sylvester) and *Resurrection of Christ in the Presence of St Bernard*, now in the Pinacoteca.

FILIPPI, Fernando de
Italian, 20th century.
Born 1940, in Lecce (Apulia).
Painter. Scenes with figures.

Fernando de Filippi was a pupil at the Accademia di Belle Arti di Brera in Milan, where he held his first exhibition in 1963. He went on to exhibit in various towns around Italy.

Filippi's work has links with the Figuration Narrative movement, which came out of Pop Art and its interest in stereotypical images. His paintings are drawn from photographs, and respect the 'anonymity' of the target, while striving to avoid the temptations of Impressionism or Expressionism. However, as Renato Barelli observes, far from simply making an observation, 'Filippi makes modifications...He works with scissors, making cuts and juxtapositions. Armed to some degree with newspaper and magazine cuttings, he allows the magnetic force of a secret preference to guide him in assembling or separating them in a lively kaleidoscope of colour. In this sense his painting can be considered a narrative or story '.

BIBLIOGRAPHY:
De Filippi, Fernando, *L'Enigma metafisico*, Fabbri RCS, Milan, 1995.

AUCTION RECORDS:
MILAN, 27 March 1990, *The Strange Story of Gregory* (1963, oil on canvas, 27 1/2 x 39 1/4 ins / 70 x 100 cm) ITL 2,400,000. MILAN, 9 Nov 2000, *Formal Opposites or Similar Things* (acrylic on canvas, 39 x 31 ins / 100 x 80 cm) ITL 3,500,000.

FILIPPI, Francesco
Italian, 16th century.

Active in Ferrara.
Painter.

Francesco Filippi, the brother of Gasparo Filippi, worked for the Confraternity of Death. His work includes a *Crucifixion* in the church of S Apollinare.

FILIPPI, Gasparo
Italian, 16th century.
Active in Ferrara.
Painter.

Like his brother Francesco Filippi, Gasparo Filippi worked for the Confraternity of Death and painted a *Crucifixion*, now in the church of S Apollinare.

FILIPPI, Giacomo
Italian, 18th century.
Born 1692, in Ferrara; died 3 August 1743.
Painter. Architectural views, landscapes.

Giacomo Filippi was a pupil of Francesco Ferrari. He worked in numerous churches (S Stefano, S Rosa, S Lorenzo) and on the Palazzo Paradiso in Ferrara.

FILIPPI, Giovanni Battista
Italian, 15th century.
Active in Bologna.
Sculptor.

FILIPPI, Giovanni Maria
Italian, 16th - 17th century.
Born in Dasindo.
Sculptor.

The main portal in Dasindo parish church, together with two windows in red and white marble, are the work of Giovanni Maria Filippi.

FILIPPI, Giuseppe
Italian, 18th century.
Died 28 July 1757.
Painter, decorative artist. Stage sets, church decorations.

Giuseppe Filippi was the nephew of Giacomo Filippi. He worked on the Ferrara churches of S Domenico and S Francesco.

FILIPPI, Jeanne de
French, 19th century.
Born 19th century, in Paris.
Painter.

Jeanne de Filippi was a pupil of Chaplin. She exhibited portraits at the Salon from 1876 to 1882. One of her most important works is the portrait of *Mme Élise Picard of the Odeon*.

FILIPPI, Lucienne
French, 20th century.
Born 23 July 1928, in Mandelieu.
Painter. History painting, local scenes, landscapes, flowers. Miniatures.

Lucienne Filippi trained in Paris at the Académie de la Grande Chaumière. She featured in many collective exhibitions, in particular in Paris at the Salon des Indépendants and the Salon de la Société Nationale des Beaux-Arts, as well as in venues in Greater Paris, receiving numerous awards. She taught art in the Centres Culturels at Bry-sur-Marne and Villers-sur-Marne, where she lives, works and has created an artists' society.

Floral compositions are her preferred theme, but she has also treated landscapes, provincial life scenes and the *Guinguettes*, modest restaurants with music and dancing on the Marne riverside. She has produced meticulous renderings of scenes from the French Revolution, as well as some miniature portraits.

BIBLIOGRAPHY:
Riousset, Michel, *Les Environs de la Marne et leurs peintres*, Amatteis, Dammarie-les-Lys, 1986.

MUSEUMS AND GALLERIES:
NOGENT-SUR-MARNE: *Arrest of Millin du Perreux in 1794*; *Pierre Marjolin Cuts off the Cross on the Steeple of St Saturnin in Nogent in 1794*; *Removal of the Lead Coffins from the Church at Nogent in 1794*; *Josephine and Hortense de Beauharnais* (miniature); *Miniature of Jérôme Millin du Perreux*; *Sophie Legrand* (miniature); *Château at Le Perreux in the 18th century* (miniature).

FILIPPI, Niccolo
Italian, 16th century.
Active in Siena.
Sculptor.

FILIPPI, Paolo
Italian, 18th - 19th century.
Born 4 September 1755; died 27 August 1830.
Painter, engraver.

Paolo Filippi painted a picture for the altar in the church of S Gervasio in Belluno.

FILIPPI, Paris
Polish, 19th century.
Born 1836, in Cracow; died 1874, in Warsaw.
Sculptor.

Paris Filippi studied under his father, and then at the art academy in Munich. His works include busts, low reliefs and funerary monuments.

FILIPPI, Pietri
Italian, 18th century.
Painter.

Pietri Filippi was the brother of Giuseppe Filippi, with whom he worked in Ferrara.

FILIPPI, Sebastiano, the Elder
Italian, 16th century.
Died before 1523, in Ferrara.
Active in Lendinara near Rovigo.
Painter.

Sebastiano Filippi the Elder was the grandfather of Sebastiano Filippi the Younger and of Cesare Filippi.

FILIPPI, Sebastiano, the Younger, known as il Bastianino, and sometimes Gradella
Italian, 16th century.
Born 1532, in Ferrara; died before 19 December 1602, in Ferrara.
Painter, draughtsman. History painting, religious subjects, portraits.

Sebastiano Filippi the Younger's father, Camillo Filippi, was also his master. At the age of 18, Sebastiano moved to Rome and was admitted to the school of Michelangelo, but was forced by the Roman climate to return to his native city.

He proved to be one of Michelangelo's best imitators.

MUSEUMS AND GALLERIES:
FERRARA (Cathedral): *Last Judgement* (1577-1584); *Circumcision of Christ*; *Annunciation* (seven versions) - FERRARA (Church of S Benedetta): *Dead Christ Borne by Angels* - FERRARA (Church of S Caterina): *Martyrdom of St Catherine* - FERRARA (Church of S Maria de Servi): *Epiphany* - FERRARA (Pinacoteca Nazionale): *Annunciation*; *Birth of Christ*; *St Cecilia*; *Madonnas*; *Portrait of Alfonso II*; *Portrait of Marquis Hippolyte Villa*.

AUCTION RECORDS:
MILAN, 8 May 1984, *Madonna in Gloria con Devoto* (oil on canvas, 15 3/4 x 9 1/2 ins / 40 x 24 cm) ITL 6,000,000. NEW YORK, 10 Jan 1996, *Two Putti and an Angel Blowing Trumpets* (black and white chalk/blue paper, 10 1/4 x 16 1/2 ins / 26.2 x 42 cm) USD 26,450.

FILIPPI, Theodoro
Engraver.

Mentioned by Nagler.

FILIPPINI, Achille
Italian, 19th - 20th century.
Died 16 November 1910.
Painter.
Achille Filippini fell from the scaffolding while painting the ceiling of the Paganini Theatre in Genoa.

FILIPPINI, Andrea
Italian, 18th century.
Born 18th century, in Trento.
Sculptor.
Andrea Filippini executed a marble altar in Trento Cathedral in celebration of the Immaculate Conception.

FILIPPINI, Antonio
Italian, 18th century.
Born near Bologna; died 1710.
Painter.
Antonio Filippini is cited exclusively by Zani.

FILIPPINI, Francesco
Italian, 17th - 18th century.
Born 1670; died after 1718.
Active in Verona.
Sculptor.
Francesco Filippini studied under Don Tommezzoli and Giov. Bonazza. He sculpted a large number of statues for churches and public gardens in Verona. Examples of his work include statues of *St Ignatius, St Francis Xavier* and *Francesco Borgia,* together with pieces decorating the chapel and gardens of the Villa Persico-Poggi in Affi.

FILIPPINI, Francesco
Italian, 19th century.
Born November 1853, in Brescia; died 6 March 1895, in Milan.
Painter. Religious subjects, landscapes.
Francesco Filippini worked with Luigi Campini, and with Giuseppe Bertini in Milan. He started out as a history painter, with *Caligula* and *Christian Martyr,* then devoted himself to landscape painting.
BIBLIOGRAPHY:
Ferrai, Roberto, *Francesco Filippini: Un Protagonista del Naturalismo Lombardo,* Skira, Milan, 1999-2000.
AUCTION RECORDS:
MILAN, 21 Oct 1969, *The Lagoon in Venice,* ITL 1,400,000. MILAN, 18 May 1971, *Sago d'Iseo* ITL 1,600,000. MILAN, 17 Oct 1972, *Fishermen,* ITL 3,400,000. MILAN, 12 June 1973, *Alpine Landscape,* ITL 1,700,000. MILAN, 15 March 1977, *Mountain Lake* (oil on panel, 13½ x 23½ ins / 34.5 x 59.5 cm) ITL 1,900,000. MILAN, 19 March 1981, *Women's Heads* (two watercolours, 15 x 14½ ins / 38 x 37 cm) ITL 2,400,000. MILAN, 12 Dec 1983, *Landscape* (oil on canvas, 45¼ x 31½ ins / 115 x 80 cm) ITL 17,000,000. MILAN, 28 Oct 1986, *Steep Landscape* (oil on canvas, 14¼ x 21¼ ins / 36.5 x 54 cm) ITL 12,000,000. MILAN, 14 March 1989, *Peat Bog beneath the Snow* (oil on canvas, 15¼ x 23½ ins / 39 x 60 cm) ITL 19,000,000. MILAN, 19 March 1992, *Steamship on the Lagoon* (oil on panel, 9½ x 18¼ ins / 24 x 46.5 cm) ITL 24,500,000. MILAN, 12 Dec 2000, *Rainy Day* (oil on canvas, 39 x 20 ins / 100 x 50 cm) ITL 70,000,000. MILAN, 22 May 2002, *City Covered in Snow* (oil on canvas, 5 x 10 ins / 12 x 25 cm) EUR 4,200.

FILIPPINI, Orlando
Italian, 18th century.
Painter.
In 1737 Orlando Filippini moved from Florence to Naples, where he was appointed principal of the Piccola Accademia. He also did tapestry work.

FILIPPINI, Pietro
Italian, 19th century.
Born c. 1789; died 6 April 1869.
Active in Brescia.
Painter, lithographer.
Pierto Filippini studied under Giuseppe Bezzuoli in Florence. He was an excellent restorer (he restored a Fra Angelico in the church of S Alessandro) and a talented mosaic artist. He introduced lithography to Brescia.

FILIPPIS, August de
American, 20th century.
Born 8 September 1906, in Jersey City (New Jersey).
Painter. Landscapes.
August de Fillipis was a pupil of Nicolai Féchin. He took part in the annual New Jersey exhibition, where he was awarded an honourable mention in 1935.

FILIPPIS, Nicolas de
Italian, 18th century.
Born c. 1697, in Triggiano (Apulia); died after 1740.
Painter.
Nicolas de Filippis studied under his painter cousin Vitantonio de Filippis de Triggiano and under Paolo de' Matteis. He took holy orders. He painted a *St Clare* for the church of that name in Bari, together with an *Exodus of the Israelites* in Sorrento.

FILIPPO
Italian, 13th century.
Sculptor.
This artist worked in Ancona from 1210 to 1225 on the churches of S Maria-di-Piazza and S Pellegrino; also an architect, he built the church of S Giovanni Profiamma in Foligno. The Christian Museum of Foligno Cathedral has statues by him.

FILIPPO
Italian, 15th century.
Active in Sulmona (L'Aquila) in 1408.
Painter.

FILIPPO
Italian, 15th century.
Active in Ferrara in 1430.
Painter.

FILIPPO
Italian, 15th century.
Active in Forlì in 1491.
Painter.

FILIPPO
Italian, 16th century.
Active in Pisa in 1540.
Sculptor.
Filippo, a sculptor whose medium was clay, executed a *Christ Flanked by Two Angels,* now lost, for the church of S Maria de Pontenovo.

FILIPPO, Napoletano. See **NAPOLETANO Filippo**

FILIPPO DA BISSONE
Italian, 16th century.
Active in Bissone.
Sculptor.
Filippo da Bissone was one of the three Bissone brothers, sons of Antonello Gaggini, who worked around 1558 on the sanctuary of the Madonna de Macerato, near Visso in the Apennine mountains.

FILIPPO DA BORSANO
Italian, 15th century.
Active in Milan in 1473.
Painter.

FILIPPO DA CAMPI
Italian, 14th century.
Active in Florence c. 1366.
Painter.

FILIPPO DA CARONA
Italian, 16th century.
Sculptor.
In 1509, Filippo da Carona executed a portal for the church of S Francesco in Udine.

FILIPPO DA CASTELLO
Italian, 15th century.
Sculptor.
Filippo da Castello worked on the altar of St Joseph in the cathedral in Milan in 1475.

FILIPPO DA COMO
Italian, 16th century.
Sculptor.
Filippo da Como made the tabernacle for the statue of Julius II erected by Michelangelo on the façade of the church of S Petronio in Bologna.

FILIPPO DA FIESOLE
Italian, 15th - 16th century.
Died 1540.
Sculptor.
Filippo da Fiesole worked on the royal palace in Cracow and in 1495 took part in the construction of the Sant' Angelo palace in Rome. He was better known as an architect.

FILIPPO DA FIESOLE, Florian
Italian, 16th - 17th century.
Sculptor.
Florian Filippo da Fiesole, the son of Filippo da Fiesole and pupil of Giovanni Cini, worked chiefly in Cracow.

FILIPPO DA FIRENZE
Italian, 15th century.
Monk, miniaturist.
Florentine School.
Filippo da Firenze lived in the monastery of S Miniato al Monte near Florence from 1488 to 1491, and in the convent of S Benedetto in Gubbio from 1494 to 1502. Miniatures taken from a missal, originally from the convent of Monte Olivetto, are now in the Museo di San Marco in Florence.

FILIPPO DA MANTU
Italian, 16th century.
Sculptor (wood).
In 1515, Filippo da Mantu produced a carved wooden crucifix depicting *St John between the Virgin Mary and Mary Magdalene* for the society of the Holy Cross in Urbino.

FILIPPO DA MARTINENGO
Italian, 16th century.
Active in Bergamo.
Painter.

FILIPPO DA MELEGNANO
Italian, 15th century.
Painter.
Lombard School.
On 4 March 1402, Filippo da Melegnano received payment for continuing and completing the main window in the chancel in Milan Cathedral.

FILIPPO DA MENDERISIO
Italian, 15th century.
Sculptor.

FILIPPO DA MONTERCALE
Italian, 15th century.
Painter.
Filippo da Montercale worked at the cathedral in L'Aquila in 1490.

FILIPPO DA SETTIGNANO
Italian, 16th century.
Sculptor.
Filippo da Settignano worked on the exterior of St John's chapel in the cathedral in Siena, following the designs of Peruzzi.

FILIPPO DA VENEZIA
Italian, 14th century.
Sculptor.
It is likely that Filippo da Venezia is the artist also known as Filippo De'Santi da Venezia. In 1332, he executed the tomb of the blessed Odorico de Pordenone, installed in the chapel of St Louis of Toulouse in the church of S Francesco in Udine. This is one of the major Venetian sculptural works of the first half of the 14th century. The fragments which survive include Odorico healing the sick, the burial of Odorico in the presence of the patriarch of Aquileja and Castaldus d'Udine, and seven figures of saints.

FILIPPO DA VERONA
Italian, 16th century.
Active at the beginning of the 16th century.
Painter.
Filippo da Verona is noted for his frescoes in the church of S Antonio in Padua, the *Madonna with St Felix and St Catherine, Annunciation with Angels, St Anthony* and the *Betrothal of St Catherine*, while a *Virgin with a Bishop* is in Bergamo.

FILIPPO DE POLA
Italian, 15th century.
Born to a family originally from Monteleone.
Active in Urbino in 1428.
Painter.

FILIPPO DEL AQUILO, Beato
Italian, 14th century.
Born in Abbruzzia.
Miniaturist.

FILIPPO DI ANDREA
Italian, 15th century.
Painter.
Filippo di Andrea is mentioned in documents in Venice from 1481 to 1486.

FILIPPO DI CELO
Italian, 14th century.
Active in Avignon in 1336.
Painter.
Avignon School.

FILIPPO DI CRISTOFANO
Italian, 15th century.
Sculptor.
In 1412 and 1413, Filippo di Cristofano worked on tabernacles in the Residenza dei Capitani del Bigallo in Florence.

FILIPPO DI DOMENICO
Italian, 14th - 15th century.
Sculptor.
From 1394 to 1396 and also in 1423, Venetian Filippo di Domenico worked on the windows of the first eight chapels in the church of S Petronio in Bologna. From 1416 to 1421 he worked at the Palazzo Malatestiano in Fano and erected the funeral monument of Paola Malatesta in the church of S Francisco.

FILIPPO DI GIOVANNI
Italian, 16th century.
Sculptor.
Florentine Filippo di Giovanni worked in Siena. In 1591, he produced an ornate tabernacle and an angel for the di Maggiano charterhouse.

FILIPPO DI GIULIANO
Italian, 15th century.
Painter.
Florentine School.

Filippi di Giuliano is mentioned in documents in Florence in 1480 and 1491; in 1480, he was sharing a studio with Jacopo del Sellajo.

FILIPPO DI GORO
Italian, 15th century.
Active at the beginning of the 15th century.
Painter.

FILIPPO DI JACOPO
Italian, 15th century.
Active in Pisa in 1493.
Sculptor.

FILIPPO DI LAZZARO
Italian, 13th century.
Painter.
This artist worked in 1280 in the cathedral of Pistoia and painted, in collaboration with Taddeo Gaddi, a picture for the altar of S Giovanni Fuorcivitas. He was the brother of Jacopo and Tommaso di Lazzaro.

FILIPPO DI MAESTRO GIOVANNI SCUTARIO. See **SCUTARIO**

FILIPPO DI MARCO
Italian, 15th century.
Painter.
Florentine School.
In 1447, Filippo di Marco was made a member of the guild in Florence.

FILIPPO DI UGOLINO DI ROBERTO
Italian, 15th century.
Died 1468.
Painter.
In 1415, Filippo di Ugolino di Roberto was admitted to the painters' guild in Perugia; he was elected a magistrate in 1468.

FILIPPONI, Giuseppe and Luigi (brothers)
Italian, 19th - 20th century.
Born in Udine.
Painters.
Giuseppe and Luigi Filipponi worked together. They studied in Rome, and were particularly interested in religious painting. They left behind numerous works in Treviso and Venice. The two brothers won prizes at exhibitions in Turin and, during the late 19th century, they took part in the SS Leo XIII competition. In 1900 they entered a painting entitled *Mystic Rose* in the Alinari competition.

FILIPPOV, Ilja
Russian, 17th century.
Painter.
Filippov was a pupil of Simon Ushakov in Moscow and from 1678 to 1685, painted, with other pupils of this master, icons and frescoes in Moscow's churches

FILIPPOV, Oleg
Russian, 20th century.
Born 1937.
Painter. Figure compositions, landscapes, still-lifes.
Oleg Filipov studied at the Repin Institute of Art and the academy of fine art in Leningrad (now St Petersbug). He became a member of the Association of Painters in Leningrad.
AUCTION RECORDS:
PARIS, 23 March 1992, *Autumn Wedding* (oil on canvas, 23 1/2 x 31 1/2 ins / 60 x 80 cm) FRF 4,000.

FILIPS
French, 20th - 21st century.
Born 9 November 1958, in Versailles.
Draughtsman, illustrator.
Filips graduated from the École des Beaux-Arts in Versailles, and has regularly contributed to *Bitro, Rock and Folk, l'Écho des Savanes, Actuel* and *Télérama*.
AUCTION RECORDS:
PARIS, 5 April 1991, *France-Colonie* (1988, coloured inks/paper, 8 1/2 x 6 1/2 ins / 21.5 x 16.5 cm) FRF 3,500.

FILIPSZ., Hans
Flemish, 17th century.
Active in Amsterdam.
Painter.
Flemish School.

FILISPONIO, Domenico
Italian, 18th century.
Painter.
Domenico Filisponio is on record as a member of the guild of Naples in 1709.

FILKO, Stano
Czechoslovak, 20th century.
Born 15 July 1937, in Velké-Hradné.
Assemblage artist, environmental artist, happenings artist.
Conceptual Art.
Stano Filko studied at the higher college of fine art in Bratislava. He began exhibiting in his country, Italy and France.

Filko attracted attention with complex assemblages of religious images and erotic photographs *Contemporary Altars* from 1963 to 1966, deals with the demystification of various taboos of the society of the time. He made painted, ornate costumes and made them available to the public so that they could actually take part in these sacrilegious celebrations. He organised the 'hapsocs', sort of happenings with political intentions, with Alex Miynarcik in 1965. In 1967, he produced a *Universal Environment*, a habitable structure that played with the effects of multiple mirrors showing silhouettes and reflections. This environment was displayed in Grenoble at the Community Arts Centre in 1968, at a time when these sorts of interactive events were in fashion.

FILKUKA, Anton, or Filkula
Austrian, 20th century.
Born 1888, in Vienna; died 1947.
Painter, pastellist. Portraits, landscapes, landscapes with figures.
Filkuka exhibited in Düsseldorf, Geneva, Stockholm, Melbourne and New York.
MUSEUMS AND GALLERIES:
VIENNA.
AUCTION RECORDS:
VIENNA, 20 May 1981, *Landscape with Chalet* (1912, oil on canvas, 35 1/2 x 47 1/4 ins / 90 x 120 cm) ATS 11,000. VIENNA, 13 Sept 1983, *Leopoldsberg* (pastel, 26 1/2 x 34 1/2 ins / 67 x 87.5 cm) ATS 12,000. VIENNA, 11 Sept 1984, *Alpine Lake* (oil on canvas, 59 x 67 ins / 150 x 170 cm) ATS 35,000. VIENNA, 23 June 1987, *Winter Landscape* (oil on canvas, 39 1/4 x 53 1/2 ins / 100 x 136 cm) ATS 13,000. BERN, 26 Oct 1988, *Chalets in a Mountain Village in Austria* (oil on canvas, 23 1/2 x 32 ins / 60 x 81 cm) CHF 1,000. LONDON, 30 Nov 1990, *The Ice-breakers in a Winter Landscape in the Mountains* (oil on canvas, 79 3/4 x 118 1/4 ins / 202.5 x 300.4 cm) GBP 6,820. BERN, 7 Nov 2001, *Reclining Female Nude* (oil on canvas, 45 x 61 ins / 115 x 156 cm) CHF 6,500. VIENNA, 22 Jan 2002, *Spring in Salzkammergut* (oil on canvas, 31 x 35 ins / 78 x 89 cm) EUR 3,000. VIENNA, 12 Nov 2002, *Sledge Ride* (oil on canvas, 39 x 51 ins / 100 x 130 cm) EUR 2,800. VIENNA, 28 Jan 2003, *Landscape with Birch Trees* (mixed media on board, 29 x 41 ins / 74 x 104 cm) EUR 1,600. VIENNA, 23 Sept 2003, *Bad Aussee* (oil on canvas, 32 x 41 ins / 81 x 104 cm) EUR 1,500. VIENNA, 12 Oct 2004, *Birch Tree in the Winter Landscape* (oil on canvas, 47 x 47 ins / 120 x 120 cm) EUR 1,600.

FILL, Phillip Josef

German, 18th century.

Active during the second half of the 18th century.

Engraver.

Fill worked in the Rhine valley. His known works include a portrait of the Prince Elector of Trier *Clemens Wenceslas* and *Departure of the French from Mannheim in 1795*.

FILLA, Emil

Czech, 20th century.

Born 4 April 1882, in Chropyne; died 7 October 1953, in Prague.

Painter, sculptor.

Groups: Osma (The Eight), Mánes, Skupina Vytvarnych Umelcu (Group of Plastic Artists).

Between 1903 and 1906, Emil Filla was a student at the school of art in Prague. He was interested at that time in El Greco, Goya, Daumier, Munch, Max Liebermann, the forerunners of Expressionism and Cézanne. Between 1907 and 1914, Filla took frequent and lengthy study trips across Germany, Italy and especially France. On these trips, he came into contact with Cubist painting. It seems that he had not become aware of Italian Futurism, or of the emergence of abstraction, even later when he took refuge in Holland during World War I, making friends with Mondrian and Van Doesburg and contributing to the first edition of *De Stijl*. He had exhibited in 1907 and 1908 with the group Osma (The Eight), which had Expressionist leanings and which he had co-founded with old art school friends. He became a member of the group Skupina Vytvarnych Umelcu (Group of Plastic Artists) after 1911, which placed greater importance on Cubist trends. At this time, notably through his contributions to magazines, he acted as intermediary between Czech artists and the French Cubists.

Returning to Prague in 1920, he became the leader of the Mánes association, named after the most important Czechoslovak Romantic painter, whose new exhibition hall, built by Novotny in 1930 on the banks of the Vltava, was still in existence in the 1970s and which, like Die Brücke in Munich in 1909, brought together artists with forward-looking tendencies, from the Expressionists to the Cubists and Surrealists. As administrator, Filla organised exhibitions representative of all the new trends in national and international art. In 1936, he published in *Art and Reality*. Apart from his well-known anti-Fascist activities, it was probably also because of his 'degenerate' art that the Nazis interned him in Buchenwald in 1939 after the annexation of Czechoslovakia and during World War II. After the war, Filla wrote a great deal about art. A professor at the school of applied art in Prague, he spent his last years living in Peruc castle north-west of Prague, where a museum of his works was subsequently established.

Many Czech painters, including Vaclav Spala, Frantisek Tichy and Jindrich Prucha, worked in the Expressionist atmosphere prevalent in Germany and Central Europe, whereas Vincenc Benes took a strong interest in the intimists and Frantisek Janousek was heavily influenced by the Surrealists. Emil Filla, like Kubista and Prochazka, had started painting in this Expressionist atmosphere, as his works from the Osma (Group of Eight) period (around 1907) show. Colour, pushed to its intense extremes, then moved his own Expressionism closer to French Fauvism, while he exploited its symbolic potential to express the spirituality of a certain existential tragedy. Cubism's influence, which Filla absorbed when he was around 30, was a determining factor on the final direction of the rest of his work. He was the leader of the Czech Cubist-Expressionist movement, which brought together outstanding artists including Bohumil Kubista, Antonin Prochazka, Josef Capek, Pravoslav Kotik, Alfred Justitz and Frantisek Muzika and was one of the most important developments from Cubism outside France, along with Italian Futurism.

Filla soon broke away from this trend which, though undeniably Cubist, was still tinged with Expressionism, and between 1912 and 1914 moved closer to pure Analytical Cubism, painting still-lifes in sober colours, perhaps because he was keen to express the physical nature of objects, with a taste for the tactile of which Braque was more aware than Picasso. He chose to continue with these characteristics during his Dutch period, with his feel for the physical strengthened by the study of 17th-century Dutch painters. His subjects, made uniform by Cubist writing, then diversified. When he returned to Prague, he continued to paint still-lifes in a stronger palette while his subjects grew so excited they became almost aggressive. From the 1930s onwards, and particularly in the years just prior to annexation and war, he painted large compositions illustrating both life in Czechoslovakia and industrial strife and soon after conflicts and allegories on violence and horror; at the same time he also produced his small bronzes. His painting remained anchored to Cubism though for circumstantial reasons he participated in 1932 in *Poetry 32*, a prelude to the formation of the Czechoslovak Surrealist group. After World War II, Filla painted a series of large landscapes, always constructed according to his initial Cubist principles. While Filla's work might sometimes have been too close Georges Braque's, his part in helping Czech art attain 20th-century modernity remains crucial.

BIBLIOGRAPHY:

Fifty years of Czechoslovak Painting from the Collections of the Galleries, 1918-1958, exhibition catalogue, Slovenska Narodna Gal., Bratislava, 1968 (in commemoration of the 50th anniversary of the Republic of Czechoslovakia).

MUSEUMS AND GALLERIES:

HADREC KRALOVE: *Painter* (1934) - PERUC (Castle-Museum): large collection - PRAGUE (Národní Muz.): *Person Reading Dostoievsky* (1907); *Ace of Hearts* (1908); *The Good Samaritan* (1910); *Still-life with Map* (1914); *Basket of Fruit* (1916-1917); *Still-life with Boar's Head* (1927); *Death of Orpheus* (1937).

AUCTION RECORDS:

LONDON, 2 Dec 1971, *Man Sitting Reading a Newspaper*, GBP 2,600. LONDON, 4 July 1974, *Head* (bronze) GBP 1,800. ZURICH, 9 Nov 1984, *BOL Composition* (1949, oil on canvas, 26 3/4 x 42 1/2 ins / 68 x 108 cm) CHF 11,000. LONDON, 25 Feb 1987, *Still-life with Ace of Hearts* (1928, oil on canvas, 15 1/4 x 18 ins / 39 x 46 cm) GBP 18,500. PARIS, 22 June 1988, *Cubist Still-life* (1926, oil on canvas, 18 x 22 ins / 46 x 55 cm) FRF 59,000. LONDON, 28 June 1988, *Still-life with Lute* (1946, oil on canvas, 38 1/4 x 51 1/4 ins / 97 x 130 cm) GBP 13,200. LONDON, 19 Oct 1988, *Pensive Young Girl* (1933, oil on canvas, 39 1/4 x 32 ins / 99.5 x 81 cm) GBP 16,500. BERN, 26 Oct 1988, *Composition with Clown, Princess and Ram* (oil on canvas, 22 x 17 3/4 ins / 56 x 45 cm) CHF 3,000. LONDON, 27 June 1989, *Cubist Composition* (1926, oil on canvas, 18 x 27 1/2 ins / 46 x 70 cm) GBP 13,200. PARIS, 11 March 1990, *Composition with Ace of Hearts* (1928, oil on canvas, 15 1/4 x 18 ins / 38.5 x 46 cm) FRF 232,000. SAUMUR, 22 April 1990, *Figure with Birds* (1932, oil on canvas, 39 1/4 x 19 3/4 ins / 100 x 50 cm) FRF 202,000. LONDON, 3 Dec 1991, *Still-life with Pears* (1927, oil on panel, 12 3/4 x 16 1/4 ins / 32.5 x 41 cm) GBP 14,300. LONDON, 24 March 1992, *Cubist Still-life* (oil on canvas, 39 1/4 x 32 ins / 100 x 81 cm) GBP 44,000. PARIS, 24 Nov 1992, *Still-life* (oil on canvas, 45 1/4 x 29 1/2 ins / 115 x 75 cm) FRF 280,000. AMSTERDAM, 10 Dec 1992, *Group of Soldiers around a Fire* (1949, oil on canvas, 77 1/4 x 61 ins / 196 x 155 cm) NLG 40,250. NEW YORK, 12 May 1993, *Zena* (1917, oil on canvas, 39 1/2 x 29 1/4 ins / 100.4 x 74.5 cm) USD 107,000. NEW YORK, 13 Nov 1996, *Artists in the Workshop* (1946, oil on canvas, 47 1/4 x 31 1/4 ins / 120 x 79.1 cm) USD 96,000. PARIS, 9 Dec 1996, *Composition with Fruit and Bowl* (1936, watercolour and ink/paper, 12 x 15 1/4 ins / 30.5 x 39 cm) FRF 33,000. LONDON, 19 March 1997, *Wood near Brno* (1906, oil on canvas/panel, 26 3/4 x 36 1/2 ins / 68 x 92.5 cm) GBP 12,650. NEW YORK, 13 Nov 1997, *Woman in an Armchair* (1946, oil on canvas, 38 1/2 x 28 3/4 ins / 97.8 x 73 cm) USD 63,000. NEW YORK, 17 Feb 1999, *Still-life with Alfred Flechtheim* (1928, watercolour and ink, 10 x 13 ins / 26 x 32 cm) USD 3,250. PRAGUE, 27 May 2000, *Still-life with Aquarium and Flowers* (1933, oil on canvas, 23 x 31 ins / 59 x 79 cm) CZK 1,000,000. LONDON, 28 June 2000, *Zena* (1917, oil on canvas, 39 x 29 ins / 100 x 73 cm) GBP 70,000. LYONS, 4 Feb 2001, *Figure with Birds* (1932, oil on canvas, 39 x 20 ins / 100 x 50 cm) FRF 95,000. LUND, 17 Nov 2001, *Cubist Painting with Dogs and Figures* (1945, oil on canvas, 64 x 51 ins / 162 x 130 cm) SEK 280,000. NEW YORK, 21 Feb 2002, *Figure and Birds* (1932, oil on canvas, 39 x 20 ins / 100 x 50 cm) USD 15,000. PRAGUE, 18 May 2002, *Still-life with Cup and Bottle* (1947, oil on canvas, 11 x 14 ins / 27 x 35 cm) CZK 500,000. BERLIN, 31 May 2003, *Untitled* (tempera, chalk and collage on canvas, 15 x 19 ins / 38 x 47 cm) EUR 7,500. LOS ANGELES, 9 Nov 2003, *Still-life* (1928, oil on canvas, 15 x 18 ins / 37 x 45 cm) USD 19,000. AMSTERDAM, 8 June 2004, *Weiblicher Akt* (1935, bronze, h. 15 ins / 39 cm) EUR 3,000. LONDON, 22 June 2004, *Still-life* (1928, oil on canvas, 15 x 18 ins / 37 x 45 cm) GBP 13,000.

FILLACIER, Jacques
French, 20th century.
Born 3 February 1913, in Paris.
Painter (including gouache), draughtsman, designer.

Jacques Fillacier studied at the École des Beaux-Arts in Paris and exhibited at the Salon des Artistes Français, winning a silver medal in 1939 and the Marie Bashkirtseff award. From 1950 to 1958, he taught at the Gobelins, Beauvais and La Savonnerie Tapestry Works. From 1962, he taught industrial aesthetics at the École des Arts Appliqués. His seminal theoretical and practical research on the aesthetics of colour earned him his professor's chair at the École des Arts Décoratifs in Paris.

AUCTION RECORDS:
PARIS, 24 April 1947, *Harbour* (gouache) FRF 1,300.

FILLACIER, Sophie
French, 20th century.
Born 20 June 1888, in Paris.
Painter.

Sophie Fillacier was a member of the Salon des Artistes Français in Paris.

FILLANS, James
British, 19th century.
Born 27 March 1808, in Lanarkshire, Scotland; died 27 September 1852, in Glasgow.
Sculptor.

Initially a stonemason, James Fillans later became an ornamental sculptor, and was the author of a number of interesting portrait busts. He travelled to Paris in 1835, where he studied at the Louvre, and returned to England in 1837, where he exhibited with the Royal Academy until 1850. He also produced a small number of statues, and visited Germany and Italy.

MUSEUMS AND GALLERIES:
EDINBURGH (Scottish National Portrait Gallery): bust *William Motherwell, Poet* (plaster) - GLASGOW: *Rachel Mourning for her Children* (plaster).

FILLATREAU, Benoist
French, 19th century.
Born 15 May 1843, in Cambrai.
Painter, engraver.

Fillatreau entered the École des Beaux-Arts on 31 March 1863 and was the pupil of Marius Cival. He exhibited landscapes at the Paris Salon from 1864 to 1880. Works include *Evening, Reuss, Page, Ravine near the Grande Chartreuse* and *Banks of the Marne*.

FILLET
17th century.
Painter.

Mentioned by Marolles.

FILLET, Pierre Hippolyte
French, 19th century.
Born 19th century, in Paris.
Painter.

Fillet was a pupil of Picot and painted mainly in pastels. He exhibited at the Salon from 1874 to 1878. Works include *Mender, Message* and *Young Italian Girl*.

FILLETTE, Ange Édouard
French, 19th century.
Born 3 July 1814, in Paris; died 18 March 1870.
Painter.

Fillette was a pupil of Mulard and attended the École des Beaux-Arts. Six round paintings of saints by him are at the church of St-Marcel de la Salpétrière.

FILLETTE, Pierre
French, 20th century.
Born 19 November 1926, in Le Mont-St-Aignan (Seine-Maritime).
Painter, potter, engraver, illustrator, lithographer.
Portraits, landscapes, still-lifes. Murals.

Pierre Fillette studied literature and fine arts, and he taught fine arts at two prestigious Paris schools: Henry IV and Janson de Sailly. He sits on the management committee of the Société des Artistes Indépendants and is a member of many organisations including the Salon d'Art Libre, the Société des Artistes Français, the Société Nationale des Beaux-Arts and the Salon des Terres Latines. He participated in group exhibitions in France and also abroad, in Brussels, Pittsburgh, New York and London. He has had solo exhibitions in France since 1950 (Galerie Saluden, Brest). In 1976, he exhibited at the Orangerie in Paris. A painter, a lithographer, and an engraver, he also tried his hand at ceramics and silk printing. Taking on a range of subjects, he conveys, in a naive style, a poetic universe, open to dream.

BIBLIOGRAPHY:
Bouillot, Roger, *Pierre Fillette*, Vision sur les arts, Paris, 1977.

AUCTION RECORDS:
ST-BRIEUC, 7 April 1980, *Flowers* (oil on canvas, 23 1/2 x 11 3/4 ins / 60 x 30 cm) FRF 2,000. VERSAILLES, 10 Dec 1989, *The Concert* (oil on canvas, 39 1/4 x 39 1/4 ins / 100 x 100 cm) FRF 4,600. VERSAILLES, 28 Jan 1990, *Don Quixote* (mixed media, 19 3/4 x 24 ins / 50 x 61 cm) FRF 3,100.

FILLEUL, Anne Rosalie (Mme)
Maiden name: Bocquet
French, 18th century.
Born 1752; died 1794.
Painter. Portraits.

Anne Rosalie Filleul was a pupil, with the future Madame Vigée-Lebrun, in the studio of Gabriel Briard, and was appointed a member of the Académie de St-Luc in 1773. She went to the scaffold at the same time as Madame Chalgrin.

MUSEUMS AND GALLERIES:

VERSAILLES (Mus.): *Louis, Count of Artois, and his Children* (portraits).

FILLEUL, Charles Alexandre

French, 19th century.
Born in Le Mans (Sarthe).
Sculptor.

Charles Filleul was a pupil of Cavalier and A. Millet. He was a member of the Société des Artistes Français and received a honourable mention in 1887.

FILLEUL, Clara

French, 19th century.
Born 1822, in Nogent-le-Rotrou (Eure-et-Loir); died 1878, in Nogent-le-Rotrou.
Painter, pastellist.

Clara Filleul was taught by Monvoisin and exhibited portraits, still-lifes and paintings of fruits at the Paris Salon from 1842 to 1878.

BIBLIOGRAPHY:

Arpentinier, Jean, *Peintures et Artistes du Perche 1560-1960*, Editions de la Reinette, Le Mans, 2003.

FILLEUL, Louis

French, 20th century.
Born 5 March 1891, in Le Mans.
Sculptor.

Louis Filleul studied under Charles Filleul. He exhibited regularly at the Salon des Artistes Français, of which he became a member.

FILLEUL, Paul

French, 20th century.
Born in Paris.
Painter.

Paul Filleul studied under P.A. Laurens. He made his debut at the 1926 Salon des Artistes Français.

FILLEY, G.

French, 20th century.
Painter. Genre scenes.

AUCTION RECORDS:

PARIS, 24 Feb 1934, *Woman with Sunshade*, FRF 30.

FILLIA, pseudonym of Colombo, Luigi Enrico

Italian, 20th century.
Born 3 October 1904, in Revello; died 9 February 1936, in Turin.
Painter, photomontage artist, writer, illustrator.
Murals, ceramics.
Futurism.

Luigi Enrico Colombo took the pseudonym Fillia, which was his mother's maiden name. Although he died at the age of only 32, he was one of the most far-sighted thinkers to influence the evolution of artistic expression between the two World Wars. In fact, in the course of the many journeys he made right up to his death in Paris, he was in contact with the pioneers of abstract art, which was at that time ignored by everyone, and this was how he came to be linked with the leaders of the Circle and Square Group in Paris. As early as 1922, he published a collection of poetry, *1+1+1=1. Dinamite. Poesie prolatarie. Rosso+Nero* (*1+1+1=1. Dynamite. Proletarian Poetry. Red+Black*), which reflected his political and aesthetic preoccupations. At the age of nineteen, together with T.A. Bracci, he began to take part in activities linked with the Futurist Movement, especially in the periodicals *Futurismo* (*Futurism*) in 1924, and *Vetrina futurista* (*Futurist Showcase*) in 1927. He became the chief creator of the Second Futurism, in Turin. This was a very active centre that brought together artists such as Alimandi, Oriani, Franco Costa, Ugo Pozzo, the sculptor Mino Rosso, and the architect Nicolas Diulgheroff. He created the publishing house *Sindacati Artisti Futuristi* (*Futurist Artistic Unions*). He was also the founder of the periodical *Citta Futurista* (*Futurist City*) in 1929, *Città Nuova* (*New City*), which he edited in collaboration with Prampolini, in the same year, and *Nuova Architettura* (*New Architecture*) in 1931. As a leader of the Futurist Movement, Fillia was also a theorist, publishing essays such as *Il futurismo: ideologie, realizzazioni e polemiche del Movimento futurista italiano* (*Futurism: Ideologies, Achievements and Controversies of the Italian Futurist Movement*), Milan, 1932, the year in which he also published, with Marinetti, *La cucina futurista* (*The Futurist Cuisine*) (Ed. Sonzogno, Milan). In 1928, Fillia organised the Futurist Pavillion at the Turin International Exhibition, for which Prampolini designed the architecture. In about 1932, he began work on monumental paintings, of which a notable example was the mural he painted for the Town Hall of La Spezia in 1933.

In 1925, his own painting, as in the series of *Mechanical Nudes*, was close to that of Prampolini in his mechanist period. It then evolved in various directions. He was influenced by the purism of Ozenfant in 1927. In 1928, a more personal psychological impulse inspired him to paint *Femininity*, a painting in which he depicted one of the states of mind classified by Boccioni. In 1929, with Balla, Marinetti, Prampolini and others, he enthusiastically signed the *Aéropeinture* (*Aeropainting*) Manifesto, which formed the cornerstone of the Second Futurist generation, and which, from the machinist and dynamic perspective of the First Futurism, advocated expressing the contemporary world from the distance and height afforded by the view from an aeroplane. He then painted: *Aerial Spirituality* and *Spirituality of the Aviator*. At the same time, he did not abandon his psychological preoccupations, producing, in 1931, *Lovers*, and *Woman, Sky and Landscape*. His mystical tendencies developed openly towards the end of his life, with the *Manifeste de l'art sacré futuriste* (*Manifesto of Futurist Sacred Art*), which he put his name to with Marinetti in 1931. He then discovered photography and produced photomontages. He illustrated several books, including Ruggero Vasari, *Flugmalerei, moderne Kunst und Reaktion* (*Aerial Painting, Modern Art and Reaction*) (published Max Mohring, Leipzig, 1934).

Group exhibitions at which his work has been shown include: 2002, *Noi futuristi* (*We Futurists*), Fonte d'Abisso Arte, Milan; 2003, *De Chirico et la peinture italienne de l'entre-deux guerres* (*De Chirico and Italian Painting of the Interwar Period*), Musée de Lodève; 2005, *Futurist Skies: Italian Aeropainting*, Estorick Collection of Modern Italian Art, London.

Solo shows devoted to his work have included: 1938, *Aeropittura, aeroscultura, arte sacra futuriste e mostra postuma Fillia* (*Aeropainting, Aerosculpture, Futurist Sacred Art and Fillia Posthumous Exhibition*), Salone della Gazzetta del Popolo, Turin; 1966, Galleria d'arte Mercurio, Biella; 1969, *Fillia: dipinti ad olio, tempere e disegni* (*Fillia: Oil Paintings, Tempera Paintings, and Drawings*), Il Vicolo Galleria d'Arte, Genoa; 1976, All'Insegna del Pesce d'Oro, Milan; 2001, *Fillia e il manifesto dell'Arte Sacra Futurista* (*Fillia and the Manifesto of Futurist Sacred Art*), Galleria d'Arte Narciso, Turin; 2004, *Sensibilità futurista. Fillia, l'avanguardia inquieta* (*Futurist Sensibility. Fillia, the Restless Avantgarde*), Sala Espositiva 'Le Casane', Asti (on the occasion of the centenary of the artist's birth).

BIBLIOGRAPHY:

Crispolti, Enrico/Galvano, Albino, *Aspetti del secondo Futurismo torinese: cinque pittori ed uno scultore: Fillia, Mino Rosso, Diulgheroff, Oriani, Alimandi, Costa*, exhibition catalogue, Galleria Civica d' arte moderna, Turin, 1962. Baldacci, Paolo/Evangelisti, Silvia/Pinottini, Marzio, *Fillia e l'avanguardia futurista negli anni del fascismo*, Mondadori, Milan, 1986. Crispolti, Enrico, et al., *Fillía: fra immaginario meccanico e primordio cosmico*, exhibition catalogue, San Francisco,

Cuneo, Mazzotta, Milan, 1988. Pinottini, Marzio/Massioli, Don Natale/Dalle Ore, Anna, *Fillia e il manifesto dellArte Sacra Futurista*, exhibition catalogue, Galleria d'Arte Narciso, Turin, 2001. Bonito Oliva, Achille/Iovane, Giovanni/Lista, Giovanni, et al., *De Chirico et la peinture italienne de l'entre-deux guerres*, exhibition catalogue, Musée de Lodève, 2003. *Futurist Skies: Italian Aeropainting*, group exhibition catalogue, Estorick Collection of Modern Italian Art, London, Mazzotta, Milan, 2004. Faussone, Marida /Pinottini, Marzio, *Sensibilita futurista. Fillia, l'avanguardia inquieta*, exhibition catalogue, Daniela Piazza Edizioni, Turin, 2004. Miracco, Renato, *Futurist skies. Italian aeropainting*, group exhibition catalogue, Estorick Collection of Modern Italian Art, London, Mazzotta, Milan, 2005 (text in English).

MUSEUMS AND GALLERIES:

GRENOBLE: *Man and Woman* - ROME (Gal. Nazionale d'Arte Moderna): *The Lovers* - TURIN (Gal. Civica d'Arte Moderna e Contemporanea): *Plasticity of Objects*.

AUCTION RECORDS:

MILAN, 4 Dec 1969, *Landscape* (tempera) ITL 950,000. MILAN, 25 Oct 1977, *Builder* (c. 1932, oil on card, 24 3/4 x 19 ins / 63 x 48 cm) ITL 6,200,000. MILAN, 18 April 1978, *Waiting* (1930, oil on canvas, 15 1/4 x 19 3/4 ins / 39 x 50 cm) ITL 2,400,000. PARIS, 24 Feb 1982, *Couple* (oil on canvas, 28 3/4 x 23 1/2 ins / 73 x 60 cm) FRF 6,000. LYONS, 23 Oct 1984, *Spiritual Tendencies* (1929, oil on canvas, 39 1/4 x 32 1/4 ins / 100 x 82 cm) FRF 110,000. MILAN, 11 June 1985, *Pezzo Rotante* (1925, tempera, 13 3/4 x 19 3/4 ins / 35 x 50 cm) ITL 9,000,000. MILAN, 18 June 1987, *L'Incontro* (1930, oil on canvas, 38 1/2 x 31 ins / 98 x 79 cm) ITL 34,000,000. MILAN, 27 March 1990, *Plastic Values of Today; Geometric Composition* (1928, oil on panel, a pair, each 12 1/2 x 9 1/2 ins / 32 x 24 cm) ITL 28,000,000. MILAN, 26 March 1991, *Waiting* (oil on canvas, 15 3/4 x 19 3/4 ins / 40 x 50 cm) ITL 17,000,000. MILAN, 14 April 1992, *Village* (oil on canvas, 9 3/4 x 13 1/4 ins / 25 x 33.5 cm) ITL 17,000,000. MILAN, 14 Dec 1993, *Still-life with Guitar* (oil on canvas, 21 x 18 3/4 ins / 52.5 x 47.5 cm) ITL 24,150,000. MILAN, 27 April 1995, *Path* (1930, oil on canvas, 32 x 25 1/2 ins / 81 x 65 cm) ITL 77,050,000. MILAN, 16 Dec 1999, *Holy Family* (oil on panel, 18 x 13 ins / 46 x 33 cm) ITL 12,000,000. AHLDEN, 22 Sept 2000, *Abstract Composition* (oil on panel, 9 x 14 ins / 24 x 35 cm) DEM 4,400. MILAN, 28 Nov 2000, *Figure in Space* (oil on canvas, 49 x 41 ins / 125 x 105 cm) ITL 90,000,000. ROME, 10 April 2003, *Drummer* (tempera on card, 10 x 7 ins / 25 x 18 cm) EUR 6,500. MILAN, 27 May 2003, *Plastic Patterns in a Nude* (oil on canvas, 23 x 19 ins / 59 x 47 cm) EUR 36,000. MILAN, 25 May 2004, *Coeur poilu* (1929, tempera on card, 27 x 20 ins / 69 x 50 cm) EUR 11,000.

FILLIAN, John

British, 17th century.
Died c. 1680, young.
Engraver.

A pupil of Faithorne the Elder, John Fillian worked in the latter's style, and produced a number of engravings: *Thomas Cromwell, William Faithorne, Head of Paracelsus* and others.

FILLIARD, Ernest

French, 19th - 20th century.
Born 1868, in Chambéry; died 1933.
Painter, watercolourist. Flowers.

Ernest Filliard studied under B. Molin, gaining an honourable mention in 1908 and a third-class medal at the Salon des Artistes Français in Paris in 1911. He was a Chevalier of the Légion d'Honneur.

MUSEUMS AND GALLERIES:

AVIGNON: *Carnations* - CHAMBÉRY: *Flowers* (watercolour).

AUCTION RECORDS:

PARIS, 11 and 12 May 1925, *Red Roses in a Glass Vase* (watercolour) FRF 1,020. PARIS, 9 Feb 1927, *Carnations in a Persian Vase* (watercolour) FRF 520; *Dahlias in a Blue Vase, Nasturtium and Bowl* (watercolour) FRF 2,050. PARIS, 30 May 1929, *Vase of Flowers* (four watercolours) FRF 900; *Flowers in a Vase* (watercolour) FRF 160. PARIS, 17 Dec 1934, *Carnations and Various Flowers* (watercolour) FRF 480. PARIS, 16 and 17 May 1939, *Mandarins and Blue Pot* (watercolour) FRF 1,400; *Sweet Peas* (watercolour) FRF 1,600. PARIS, 25 and 26 Jan 1943, *Small Watercolour,* FRF 700. PARIS, 14 May 1943, *Vase of Flowers,* FRF 2,000. PARIS, 24 May 1943, *Bowl of Cherries* (watercolour) FRF 1,500; *Flowers and Fruit* (watercolour) FRF 1,800. PARIS, 18 Feb 1944, *Red Roses in a Vase* (watercolour) FRF 7,300. PARIS, 15 Dec 1944, *Red Roses in a Vase,* FRF 2,600. PARIS, 7 Oct 1946, *Flowers,* FRF 3,100. PARIS, 9 June 1947, *Flowers* (watercolour) FRF 1,500. GRENOBLE, 18 May 1981, *Vase of Dahlias* (watercolour, 25 3/4 x 18 1/4 ins / 65.5 x 46.5 cm) FRF 5,000. NEUILLY, 7 April 1991, *Bunch of Carnations* (watercolour, 11 x 15 ins / 27 x 38 cm) FRF 4,200. PARIS, 4 March 1992, *Dahlias* (watercolour, 23 1/2 x 17 ins / 60 x 43 cm) FRF 13,000. AMSTERDAM, 21 April 1993, *Blue Gentians in a Vase* (watercolour/paper, 5 x 6 ins / 12.5 x 15.5 cm) NLG 4,025. PARIS, 12 Dec 1997, *Anemones in a Vase* (watercolour, 13 1/2 x 10 1/4 ins / 34 x 26 cm) FRF 3,500. PARIS, 21 June 1999, *White Peonies on an Entablature* (watercolour, 34 x 27 ins / 87 x 69 cm) FRF 23,000. AMSTERDAM, 1 Sept 1999, *Poppies in Bloom* (watercolour, five, 26 x 15 ins / 67 x 38 cm) NLG 11,000. AMSTERDAM, 18 Jan 2000, *Zinnias in a Vase. Roses in a White Vase* (watercolour, a pair, 6 x 7 ins / 14 x 17 cm) NLG 8,500. PARIS, 4 July 2000, *Still-life with Poppies* (watercolour, 21 x 18 ins / 54 x 45 cm) FRF 19,000. THE HAGUE, 25 April 2001, *Yellow Roses* (watercolour, 15 x 18 ins / 38 x 45 cm) NLG 6,400. NEUILLY, 28 March 2003, *Bouquet of Flowers in a Green Pot* (watercolour, 18 x 19 ins / 46 x 48 cm) EUR 1,500.

FILLIAU, Charles Édouard

French, 19th century.
Born 18 May 1812, in Livry.
Painter.

Filliau entered the École des Beaux-Arts on 3 April 1830 and exhibited a landscape and several portraits at the Salon from 1831 to 1840.

FILLINGER, Sebastian

German, 17th century.
Active in Würzburg (Bavaria).
Sculptor.

FILLION, John

Canadian, 20th century.
Born 1933, in Little Current.
Sculptor.

John Fillion's sculptures are figurative and Expressionist and their subject is often truncated human bodies. The internal surfaces in particular are cracked and contrast with the polished parts.

BIBLIOGRAPHY:

Reeves, John, *John Fillion: Thoughts about my Sculpture*, Martlet Press, Toronto, 1968.

FILLIOU, Robert

French, 20th century.
Born 1926, in Sauve; died 2 December 1987, in Les Eyzies (Dordogne).
Also active in Germany.
Installation artist, performance artist, video artist.
Multimedia.
Neo-Dadaism, Fluxus, Conceptual Art, Mail Art (forerunner).

The French artist Robert Filliou was closely associated with the Fluxus group, his career embracing French, German and American developments. Having moved to the USA in 1949, he read economics at the University of California, Los Angeles. From 1951 to 1954, he worked for the United Nations Korean Reconstruction Agency in South Korea, before leaving to live in Japan, where he had discovered Buddhism some years before, then moving on to Egypt and Spain. Back in France in 1959, he taught economics and started to write for the theatre. In 1964, in New York, he made contact with George Brecht and the leading exponents of the Fluxus group. In 1967, he was in Düsseldorf, teaching at the city's art academy. Later, in post at the Kunstakademie in Hamburg, he wrote a text book with J. Beuys, G. Brecht, J. Cage and A. Kaprow: *Teaching and Learning as Performing Arts*. In 1985, he started his three-year retreat in a Tibetan Studies centre at Chanteloube (Dordogne).

His work often used words (often in English; he had American citizenship). In 1960, he staged a play of 'auto-théâtre' dedicated to Daniel Spoerri, *Immortal Death of the World*. In the 1960s, he realised his *Suspense-Poems*, the *Low Speed Poems*, *Mummifications* and *Life Statistics*. In 1962, he opened his *Legitimate Gallery*. In 1963, with architect Joachim Pfeuffer, he brought out the *Poïpoïdrome*, an institute of 'permanent creation', the results of which would be shown in 1978 in Paris, at the Musée National d'Art Moderne. In 1965, he set up (with George Brecht) *La Cédille qui sourit* (*The Smiling Cedilla*) in Villefranche-sur-Mer, an 'anti-workshop', the first *Centre of Continuous Creativity*, where objects were created and tested and the book *Games at the Cedilla or the Cedilla takes off* (*Games at the Cedilla or the Cedilla Takes off*) (1967) came into being. The *Cedilla* closed in 1968, the year of his *Principle of Equivalence*. In 1971-1972, he undertook a *Research in Art and Astrology*; in 1973, a *Research on Pre-Biology*; from 1977 to 1981, he filmed a set of video clips in Canada (*Portafilliou* in 1977 and *Video Universe-City* in 1978-1981); and, in 1982-1984, with his pupils from the Kunstakademie in Hamburg, he developed his programme *Artists-in-Space*. Filiou produced his works during short periods of time without paying much attention to their presentation or aesthetic appearance. For many compositions he used mixed media such as cartons, bits of wood, cut out words, bricks, and paper. Other works focus entirely on a concept or an idea such as Ample Food for Stupid Thought (1965) which was made up by a set of 96 white cataloguing cards printed in black ink each with a different question.

Filliou has featured in many collective exhibitions, from the fringes to the most official. He participated in Fluxus performances, most memorably in Wiesbaden in September 1962. In 2003, he featured in the exhibition *L'état des choses* (*The State of Things*), which assessed the status of everyday objects in contemporary art, on the occasion of *Trésors publics, 20 ans de création dans les Fonds régionaux d'art contemporain (FRAC)* (*Public Treasury, 20 Years of Creation in the Regional Collection of Contemporary Art (FRAC)*) at the Musée des Beaux-Arts, Nantes.

His first personal exhibition, *PoïPoï*, took place in Gallery Köpcke in 1961. He subsequently exhibited widely, above all in France and Germany. A particularly notable exhibition is *Robert Filiou, Génie sans talent* at MACBA (Barcelona, Spain), Museum Kunst Palast (Düsseldorf, Germany) and Musée d'Art Moderne (Lille Métropole, France), 2003-2004.

BIBLIOGRAPHY:

Filliou, Robert, *Ample Food For Stupid Thought*, Something Else Press, New York, Cologne, Paris, 1965. Spoerri, Daniel, *An Anecdoted Topography of Chance (re-anecdoted version)*, Something Else Press, New York, 1966. Filliou, Robert, *Research at the Stedelijk, Nov. 5 - Dec. 5, 1971*, Amsterdam, Stedelijk Museum, 1971. *Continuous Creation: rooms by Robert Filliou, Bruce Lacey and Jill Bruce, Anna Oppermann, Paul Thek*, Arts Council of Great Britain, London, 1981. *Robert Filliou*, exhibition catalogue, Sprengel Museum, Hannover, ARC Musée d'Art moderne de la ville de Paris, Paris, 1984. *Qu'est-ce que l'art français?*, Centre régional d'Art contemporain Midi-Pyrénées, Toulouse, 1986. *Luxe, calme et volupté: aspects of French art, 1966-1986. Daniel Buren, Robert Combas, Robert Filliou, Gérard Garouste, Pierre Klossowski, Jean LeGac, Annette Messager, Martial Raysse*, Vancouver Art Gallery, Vancouver, 1986+. Abou-Isaac, Nathalie, *L'Art moderne à Marseille. La Collection du Musée Cantini*, exhibition catalogue, Musée Cantini, Marseilles, 1988. *Robert Filliou 1926-1987: Zum Gedächtnis*, Städtische Kunsthalle, Düsseldorf, 1988. Cuvelier, Pascaline, '*Robert Filliou, l'art économe*' in *Libération*, periodical, Paris, 18 December 1990. B., F., '*Filliou, de la folie au fou rire*' in *Beaux-Arts Magazine*, periodical, Paris, 1991. Recht, Roland, '*Un homme sans qualités*', *Parsy, Paul-Hervé*: '*Histoires de Filliou*' in *Robert Filliou*, exhibition catalogue, Musée national d'Art moderne, Paris, 1991. Partouche, Marc, '*Robert Filliou*' in *Art Press* n° 154, periodical, Paris, January 1991. Tilman, Pierre, *On recherche le dénommé Filliou*, Coprah, Paris, 1994. *Robert Filliou: from political to poetical economy*, exhibition catalogue, Morris and Helen Belkin Art Gallery, University of British Columbia, Vancouver, 1995. *Robert Filliou poet*, exhibition catalogue, Galerie der Stadt Remscheid, Remscheid, 1997. *Premiers mouvements, fragiles correspondances*, exhibition catalogue, Le Plateau, Fonds régional d'art contemporain d'Ile-de-France, Paris, 2002. Jouval, Sylvie/Martin, Jean-Hubert, et al., *Robert Filliou, genio sin talento*, exhibition catalogue, Museu d'art contemporani, Barcelona, 2003 (exhibition held at the Museum Kunst Palast in Dusseldorf). *Robert Filliou: génie sans talent*, exhibition catalogue, Musée d'Art moderne, Villeneuve d'Ascq, 2004. Ardenne, Paul, '*Robert Filliou, pour une création permanante*' in *L'Oeil* no. 556, periodical, March 2004.

MUSEUMS AND GALLERIES:

ANGOULÊME (FRAC Poitou-Charentes): *Work as Play. Art as Thought* (c. 1974) - BREMEN (Neues Mus. Weserburg, Sammlung Dobermann): *Principle of Equivalence: Well-made, Ill-made, Not-made* (1968) - DORTMUND (Mus. am Ostwall): *Marcel Broodthaers, Marianne and Me, Walking* (1970) - DUNKIRK (FRAC Nord-Pas de Calais): *Sun Book* (1972-1973) - LYONS (MBA): *Study on the Origin* - MARSEILLES (Mus. Cantini): *Daily Miracle-Daily Void* (1983) - MÖNCHENGLADBACH (Mus. Abteiberg): *Continuous Creation*; *General Semantics* (1962); *Poïpoïdrome* (1963) - NÎMES (Carré d'Art, MAC): *The Upside-down World* (1968); *General Semantics* (1962) - PARIS (MNAM-CCI): *Installation* (1970); *Telepathic Music: From Madness to Nomad-ness* (1979); *Telepathic Music No. 5* (1976-1978); *Briquolages, Brickings and Kueens 1* (1982); *Seven Childike Uses of Warlike Material* (1970) - RHEIMS (FRAC Champagne-Ardenne): *La Joconde est dans l'escalier* (*The Mona Lisa is in the Staircase*) (1969); *Infraduction* (1979, video); *Trilogy (Video-Univercesity: Thanks to Fourrier)* (1979, video) - STRASBOURG (Mus. d'Art Moderne et Contemporain): *The Last Time I Felt Sad* (1970) - TOULOUSE (FRAC Midi-Pyrénées) - VIENNA (Mus. Moderner Kunst Stiftung Ludwig): *It Would Give me Joy to Give Joy* (1970).

AUCTION RECORDS:

PARIS, 6 March 1989, 1976, wooden box, with a photograph inside the lid, and a game board, playing cards, a rake, two felt masks, a visor and a game rule book in the box, 12 3/4 x 14 1/2 x 2 3/4 ins / 32.5 x 37 x 7 cm) FRF 8,000. PARIS, 14 Jan 1991, *Telepathic Music Calling the Big Cats* (score in brick, pebble and collage/strip of paper, 8 1/2 x 4 1/4 x 2 3/4 ins / 21.5 x 11 x 7 cm) FRF 13,000. PARIS, 2 June 1991, *Optimistic Box no. 1, Thank You Oh Lord for Modern Weaponry* (wooden box containing a stone, 4 1/4 x 4 1/4 x 4 1/4 ins / 11 x 11 x 11 cm) FRF 8,000. PARIS, 17 Oct 1994, *La tour de Seine sans Rien Savoir* (1976, music stand supporting an open box containing three passport photos, 47 1/4 x 17 ins / 120 x 43 cm) FRF 13,500. AMSTERDAM, 8 Dec 1994, *Five Signs (of Time)* (1974, cardboard box with drawing in pencil and soft chalks/photos, card and wood, 16 1/4 x 11 3/4 ins / 41.5 x 30 cm) NLG 4,025. PARIS, 1 July 1996, *Couvre Chef(s) d' Œuvre* (1965, Béret, box containing five gilt vowels, box with six gilt items, small book in the shape of a head, small stamp painting, two pieces of writing, sculpture) FRF 7,500. COLOGNE, 28 May 1999, *Raining Cats and Dogs* (1964-1969, umbrella and plastic, 9 x 9x2 ins / 22 x 24x5 cm) DEM 10,200. COLOGNE, 28 May 1999, *Four Permanent Creators* (1970, wood and wire, 23 x 39x3 ins / 59 x 99x7 cm) DEM 11,000. PARIS, 18 March 2002, *Poet's Poor Privilege* (1977, pastel, graphite and collage, 27 x 38 ins / 68 x 97 cm) EUR 2,500. PARIS, 28 April 2003, *New Card Game* (various objects, wood, suitcase and photo, 13 x 15x2 ins / 32 x 37x6 cm) EUR 2,000. COLOGNE, 4 June 2004, *Green Boxes* (panel, three, h. 7 ins / 17 cm, w. 24 ins/60 cm) EUR 11,000.

FILLISCH, Christoph
German, 17th century.
Born c. 1628; died after 1679.
Painter.

Fillisch painted the portrait of *Councillor Lorenz Eyselin.*

FILLISCH, Johann Christoph
German, 18th century.
Died after 1738 and before 9 March 1743.
Painter, engraver, draughtsman.

Johann Fillisch was the son of Christoph Fillisch, and was attached to the court of the Margrave of Brandenburg at Ansbach. Two sketchbooks of his drawings, depicting the memorials at the church of Gumpertus in Ansbach, are kept at the municipal library in Munich. Another of his known works is the portrait of the margrave *George Frederick IV.*

FILLISCH, Johann David F.
German, 17th century.
Active during the second half of the 17th century.
Painter.

Fillisch painted the portraits of *J. L. Loelius, J. Ch. Rehm, Maria Sidonia of Erffa* and *The Benedictine Joh. Heuber.*

FILLOEUL, Gilbert
French, 17th century.
Born 1644, in Abbeville; died after 1697.
Engraver.

Gilbert Filloeul was the son of a surgeon and the pupil of Pierre Daret. He is remembered for a series of engravings after the funerary monuments of the architect and sculptor Nicolas Blassel, a *St Magdalene* after Charles Le Brun, a *St Theresa* and an *Annunciation* after Michel Corneille, a *St Joseph with Jesus*, and a *St Dominic* after Jean Restout the Elder. He engraved several portraits after Henri Rigaud: *Claude de Vert, Dominican; Anne-Marie-Louise of Orléans, Duchess of Montpensier;* and *The Abbot of La Trappe, Butler of Rancé.*

FILLOEUL, Pierre
French, 18th century.
Active in Paris.
Engraver, painter.

Pierre Filloeul was the son and pupil of Gilbert Filloeul. He illustrated the *Fables* of La Fontaine, and is also known for a collection of 60 portraits of the kings of France, the illustrations for the *Nouvel Abrégé* (*New Summary*) by President Hénault, and a series of engravings after the paintings of Pater (*The Cobbler, The Defeated and Contented Cuckold, Love and Banter, The Happy Lovers, The Beautiful Flower-girl* and *Pleasant Company*). After Chardin he engraved *Soap Bubbles, Knucklebones, Houses of Cards,* and *Lady Taking her Bath;* after Fontaine, *Stanislas Leczinski;* and after Watteau *Lunch, The Penitent, Winter, Book of Different Kinds of Heads, La Polonaise, The Doctor* and *The Woman from the Village.*

AUCTION RECORDS:

PARIS, 4-5 June 1926, *Touch; Smell* (gouache, a pair) FRF 2,450. PARIS, 20 March 1941, *Young Women in Landscapes* (gouache, two pendants) FRF 2,750.

FILLOL, Jaime
Spanish, 15th century.
Died c. 16 November 1476, in Valencia.
Painter.

Jaime Fillol worked at the court of Juan II, where he painted banners from 1437 to 1469.

FILLOL, Léon A.
French, 19th century.
Active in Paris.
Engraver.

Fillot became a member of the Société des Artistes Français in 1893 and exhibited at the society's Salon.

FILLOL GRANELL, Antonio
Spanish, 19th - 20th century.
Born 3 January 1870, in Castellnovo (Valencia); died August 1930, in Castellón de la Plana near Valencia.
Painter, illustrator. Genre scenes. Murals.

Antonio Fillol y Granel studied at the Academia de San Carlos in Valencia under Ignacio Pinazo and later became a teacher at the school of arts and crafts there. He took part in a number of collective exhibitions including at the Société Nationale des Beaux-Arts in Paris where he received medals in 1895 and 1897, a gold medal in 1901 and commendations in 1904, 1908 and 1912. He was also awarded a medal at the Universal Exhibition in Chicago in 1893, a bronze medal at the Paris exhibition of 1900 and a gold medal in Panama in 1916.

Fillol y Granel executed decorative pieces in Las Palmas, Valencia and other towns. He also provided illustrations for a number of magazines.

BIBLIOGRAPHY:

Arnáiz, José Manuel/López Jiménez, Javier/Merchán Díaz, Manuel (ed.), *Cien años de pintura en Espana y Portugal (1830-1930)*, Antiqvaria, Madrid, 1988 (One Hundred Years of Painting in Spain and Portugal (1830-1930)).

MUSEUMS AND GALLERIES:

CHICAGO: *The Second-Hand Clothes Dealer* - MADRID (Mus. Nacional Centro de Arte Reina Sofía): *The Glory of the People; Mr May; The Gossip of Foios; The Fiancée; Valencia Town Hall; La Bestia Humana* (*The Human Beast*) - VALENCIA: *El Primer Hijo* (*The First Son*); *The Glory of the People.*

FILLON, Arthur
French, 20th century.
Born 27 October 1900, in Loris (Loiret); died 14 December 1974, in Paris.
Painter (including gouache), watercolourist. Sporting subjects.

Arthur Fillon studied at the École des Beaux-Arts in Marseilles and later in Paris. He began to exhibit in 1924 at the Salon d'Automne then at the Salon des Indépendants.

He is best remembered for his circus scenes and sporting subjects. He is associated with Post-Impressionism.

AUCTION RECORDS:

PARIS, 4 June 1926, *Canal,* FRF 160; *Vase of Tulips,* FRF 85. PARIS, 16 Jan 1928, *Notre-Dame, Paris,* FRF 150. PARIS, 27 Feb 1936, *Acrobats,* FRF 170. PARIS, 22 Dec 1941, *Clowns,* FRF 1,600; *Circus,* FRF 1,100. PARIS, 9 July 1942, *Circus* (watercolour) FRF 300; *Head of a Clown* (watercolour) FRF 220. PARIS, 22 July 1942, *Nude Reclining,* FRF 300. PARIS, 11 Dec 1950, *Church of Notre-Dame, Paris. View from the Tour d'Argent,* FRF 45,000. PARIS, 22 June 1976, *Canal St-Martin* (1961, oil on canvas, 23 1/2 x 28 3/4 ins / 60 x 73 cm) FRF 1,700. PARIS,

23 May 1981, *Clown* (gouache, 11 x 9 ins / 27 x 22 cm) FRF 2,300. PARIS, 1 June 1983, *St-Germain-des-Prés* (1942, oil on canvas, 28 3/4 x 23 1/2 ins / 73 x 60 cm) FRF 6,300. NEW YORK, 10 April 1987, *Seine Embankments and the Passerelle des Arts* (oil on canvas, 25 1/2 x 32 3/4 ins / 65 x 83 cm) USD 6,000. RHEIMS, 3 March 1988, *Jardin des Tuileries; The Hunchback* (two oils on canvas, each 11 x 18 ins / 28 x 46 cm) FRF 14,600. VERSAILLES, 20 March 1988, *Merry-go-round at the Luxembourg* (oil on panel, 9 x 11 ins / 22 x 27 cm) FRF 8,500. VERSAILLES, 17 April 1988, *Barges at Anchor* (oil on panel, 7 1/4 x 9 3/4 ins / 18.5 x 25 cm) FRF 2,400. PARIS, 22 April 1988, *Music-Playing Clowns* (gouache, 14 1/4 x 19 1/4 ins / 36.5 x 49 cm) FRF 4,300. L'ISLE-ADAM, 11 June 1988, *Paris, le Pont-Neuf* (oil on canvas, 28 3/4 x 36 1/4 ins / 73 x 92 cm) FRF 28,000. PARIS, 14 Dec 1988, *Honfleur Harbour* (oil on canvas, 15 x 19 ins / 38 x 48 cm) FRF 8,500. PARIS, 3 March 1989, *Trawlers at Anchor* (oil/hardboard) FRF 7,500. PARIS, 26 May 1989, *Boat Trip* (gouache, 12 1/2 x 19 1/4 ins / 32 x 49 cm) FRF 3,500. PARIS, 22 Jan 1990, *Head of a Clown* (gouache, 10 1/4 x 7 3/4 ins / 26 x 20 cm) FRF 6,000. PARIS, 26 Oct 1990, *Notre-Dame, Paris* (1944, oil on canvas, 32 x 25 1/2 ins / 81 x 65 cm) FRF 23,000. PARIS, 14 Jan 1991, *The Church at Orsay* (1931, gouache, 12 1/4 x 18 1/2 ins / 31 x 47 cm) FRF 4,000. PARIS, 6 Feb 1991, *At the Cabaret* (gouache, 11 3/4 x 18 ins / 30 x 46 cm) FRF 6,500. PARIS, 10 June 1991, *Merry-go-round* (watercolour, 14 1/4 x 21 1/4 ins / 36 x 54 cm) FRF 7,500. NEW YORK, 27 Feb 1992, *Vase of Flowers* (oil on canvas, 18 x 15 ins / 46 x 38 cm) USD 1,320. CALAIS, 5 July 1992, *Vase of White Flowers* (oil on canvas, 18 x 15 ins / 46 x 38 cm) FRF 6,500. ST-JEAN CAP-FERRAT, 16 March 1993, *Still-life with a Bowl* (oil on canvas, 9 x 11 ins / 23 x 28 cm) FRF 7,000. PARIS, 26-27 Nov 1996, *Acrobats* (1929, oil on canvas, 36 1/4 x 26 ins / 92 x 66 cm) FRF 19,000. PARIS, 1 April 1998, *Country Outing* (oil on canvas remounted/panel, 17 1/4 x 21 1/4 ins / 44 x 54 cm) FRF 5,500. PARIS, 21 March 1999, *Public Garden, Village beyond* (oil on canvas on panel, 17 x 21 ins / 44 x 54 cm) FRF 11,000. CANNES, 15 Aug 2000, *Paris, the Seine, Notre-Dame* (oil on canvas, 31 x 24 ins / 78 x 60 cm) FRF 15,000. VERSAILLES, 21 Jan 2001, *Bank of the Seine* (oil on canvas, 18 x 24 ins / 46 x 61 cm) FRF 34,500. CALAIS, 11 Nov 2001, *Paris, the Seine at Pont Neuf* (oil on canvas, 15 x 18 ins / 38 x 46 cm) FRF 22,000. DIJON, 17 March 2002, *Quais de Notre-Dame, Paris* (oil on canvas, 24 x 29 ins / 60 x 73 cm) EUR 1,900. DETROIT, 18 Oct 2002, *Booksellers along the Seine in Paris* (oil on canvas, 32 x 25 ins / 81 x 64 cm) USD 3,000.

FILLON, Tony
French, 20th century.
Born in St-André de Cubzac (Gironde).
Sculptor.

Tony Fillon studied under Jean Coutan. He made his debut in Paris at the 1924 Salon des Artistes Français and was later asked to exhibit at the Salon des Tuileries.

FILLONIÈRE, Marianne (Mrs)
British, 18th century.
Active in London.
Painter. Flowers.

Marianne Fillonière exhibited with the Free Society of Artists from 1766 to 1776.

FILLOT, Emmanuel
French, 20th - 21st century.
Born 1 August 1957, in Tours.
Sculptor of assemblages.

Emmanuel Fillot's work is inspired by contemporary but primitive cultures. He assembles diverse elements to create objects imbued with traditional and ritual significance, which have a poetic quality.

He has exhibited at the Salon de la Jeune Peinture and the Salon des Réalités Nouvelles, both in Paris, but his work has mostly been displayed at the Galerie Lélia Mordoch since 1985, also in Paris. He also exhibited at the Galerie Bellint in 2000.

BIBLIOGRAPHY:
Plazy, G., '*Emmanuel Fillot*' in *Cimaise*, periodical, Paris, 2000.

FILLOZ, Claude Joseph
French, 18th century.
Born in Baume-les-Dames (Doubs); died 1759, in Besançon.
Engraver.

Claude Filloz is known to have executed an *ex libris* and a *View of Baume Abbey*.

FILLYON, Jules
French, 19th century.
Born 12 April 1824, in Compiègne (Oise); died 1883.
Painter.

Fillyon was a pupil of Brissot de Warville. He was a particularly good pastellist and charcoal draughtsman. He exhibited works at the Salon from 1868 to 1881. Works include *Reading*, a study, *Amateur Musician Facing a Difficult Passage, Dévideuse, Ponds in St-Pierre, Inside the Sheepfold, Farmyard, Han Gorge, Street in Quimper, Tourotte Church* and *Old Well*.

MUSEUMS AND GALLERIES:
COMPIÈGNE: *Portrait of Pierre-Charles-Marie Sauvage* (charcoal).

FILMENT-FAITDIEU, Pierre Germain
French, 18th century.
Died after 1768.
Sculptor.

Pierre Filment-Faitdieu was admitted to the Académie de St-Luc in Paris on 11 July 1748.

FILOCAMO, Antonio, Gaetano and Paolo
(brothers)
Italian, 18th century.
Born in Messina; died 1743, in Messina, of the plague.
Painters, fresco artists, draughtsmen. Allegorical subjects.

The Filocamo brothers each studied in Rome under Carlo Maratti before returning to their native Messina and establishing an academy of arts. Remarkably, the three worked together throughout their lives, working in both oils and fresco. Of the three, Antonio (born 1699) was perhaps the most accomplished; he was reputed to be a skilful painter in oils.

MUSEUMS AND GALLERIES:
MESSINA (Church of S Caterina di Valverde) - MESSINA (Church of S Gregorio).

AUCTION RECORDS:
LONDON, 3 July 1995, *Allegorical Scene* (ink and red chalk heightened with white, 9 x 8 3/4 ins / 22.9 x 22.4 cm) GBP 1,035.

FILODRORO, Stefano
Italian, 17th century.
Active in Rome.
Painter.

Stefano Filodroro painted frescoes for the walls and ceiling of the sacristy in the church of S Elisabeth dei Fornari, which no longer exists.

FILON, Théodorine (Mme)
French, 19th century.
Painter.

Filon exhibited at the Salon from 1831 to 1848.

FILONI, Charles
French, 20th century.
Born 21 June 1932, in Marseilles.
Painter.

Charles Filoni exhibits at the Salon des Artistes de Provence in Marseilles and in Paris at the Salon d'Automne, of which he was made an associate member in 1961.

FILONOV, Pavel Nikolaevich
Russian, 20th century.
Born 1883, in Moscow; died December 1941, in Leningrad (now St Petersburg).
Painter, draughtsman.
Symbolism.
Groups: Soiuz Molodezhi (Union of Youth), Collective of Masters of Analytical Art (MAI).

Orphaned at the age of 13 and from a modest family, Pavel Filonov went to live with his sister in St Petersburg in 1896 and attended private art workshops from 1901 onwards to try and gain entry to the art academy. He was admitted in 1908 and left in 1910. Then with Mikhail Vasilievich Matyushin's assistance he joined the group of artists led by Matyushin in St Petersburg and learned about the Futurist theories introduced into Russia by Marinetti himself. He also associated with many artists, including the poet Velimir Khlebnikov, whose ideas about the artist's mission he shared and with whom he put together the book-object *Wooden Idols*. A founder member of Union of Youth Soiuz Molodezhi, Filonov began exhibiting there. He met the Burlyuk brothers, Malevich and Maiakovsky. In 1911 he travelled to France and Italy, then in 1913 he designed the sets for Mayakovsky's play *Vladimir Mayakovsky, a Tragedy* and in 1914 he published *Paintings Worked through to Completion* where he outlined the principles of his 'organic analytical method', to which he conformed throughout his life.

Calling himself an 'artist-researcher-explorer', he demanded that the artist's expression of his own spirituality be completely dependent on the universal forces of the cosmos, in no way involving 'imitating the forms created by nature, but being inspired by the way in which nature creates them'. Work had to be produced in full awareness of the need for its tiniest details, 'atom by atom as organically and regularly as natural growth'. This rationality of plastic design demanded a perfectly controlled preliminary drawing, to which colour could then merely be subject, which explains the many drawings in his work, but contradicts the richness of the colour in his paintings.

From 1918, he formed a Collective of Analytical Art within the new art academy. In the 1920s, he made a vain attempt at clarifying the theory of the Analytical movement. Between 1923 and 1926, he continued the action of the Collective of Analytical Art with Matyushin and Malevich at the institute of art in Petrograd (now St Petersburg) where he managed the general ideology section. While his theorizing left a lot to be desired, his charisma among his students was highly effective since they took great care to imitate him. In 1925, he was the organiser of the Masters of Analytical Art, and he exhibited regularly between 1925 and 1929 with his students. In 1926 he opened a private school of art which closed two years later and in 1928, apparently, a solo exhibition was devoted to him. In 1929 or 1931, the Russian Museum in Leningrad (now St Petersburg) was preparing for a major retrospective; it was cancelled the day before opening, probably for reasons of 'bourgeois cosmopolitan formalism', even though the iconic, narrative content of Filonov's paintings was always consistent with the social ideas of the Revolution: obviously it was not in keeping with the formal sterility of Socialist Realism.

In 1932, however, he took part in the *Exhibition of Artists from the USSR in the 15 years between 1917 and 1932* at the Russian Museum in Leningrad. In 1936, he gave all his work 'to the Soviet people' with the aim of establishing a museum of analytical art, which did not materialise. The relative eclipse of his work continued long after his death from exhaustion in December 1941 during the siege of Leningrad. Only in 1967 his work was exhibited in Novosibirsk under the aegis of the Academy of Science in Siberia and in 1988 a complete retrospective was held in the Russian Museum in Leningrad and from there it travelled to Moscow, Paris and Düsseldorf.

Filonov's very early works, produced when he arrived at St Petersburg, were in the context of an Expressionism which was very widespread in Central Europe. In keeping with Mikhail Larionov and Natalia Gontcharova's theory of 'Neo-primitivism', Filonov's ambition initially, from 1910 onwards, was to establish a specifically Russian art. This brought him to the point of opposing the internationalism of modern Western art and violently attacking Post-Cézanne art, Cubism and Picasso in the *The Canon and the Law* (1912), denouncing their formalism, which conflicted with the organic way in which nature works. His own painting, however, had not escaped the analytical spirit of the pictorial event that founded Cubism and which, after Fauvism and Expressionism, was the only innovative proposal of the time.

Between 1911 and 1914, the shapes constituting his paintings consisted of an accumulation of small facets, exacerbating the Cubist breaking-up, which seem to grow by a labyrinthine development process, bringing both things and beings to life, proliferating like biological cells. It then creates a hallucinatory pictorial world, blending elements of reality with abstract, complex, but significant compounds in the way in which the central figure of the icon is surrounded by secondary extras and tokens. In 1910-1911, he painted a cycle of Utopian paintings inspired by popular art and Russian icons, representing people and animals living in total harmony with nature: *The Peasant Family, Three Figures Eating, The Magi, Flowers Blossoming Universally*. Between 1912 and 1916 on the other hand, he painted *The King's Feast*, illustrating Man being crushed by the city and machines. In 1916-1917, he executed the still relatively realistic series of *Officers* as well as still-lifes and landscapes.

After the Revolution in 1917 and enthusiastic about the plan for a new society, he started the series of *Formulas: The Formula of the Proletariat, The Formula of Spring* and so on, the formulas for him being 'atomic' analysis of each component of reality, being or thing. In 1923, he published the *Birth of the World*, birth taking place both through the historic Revolution and through the invention of the analytical method, the latter contributing to the glorification of the former, as a few titles between 1918 and 1921 show: *Formula of the Cosmos, Entering Universal Development, Formula of the Development of the Last Stage of Communism, Victory over Eternity*.

As it developed within the clear limits of his analytical theory, the principles he had been developing since 1914, Filonov's painting evolved along the lines of an increasing division of forms, the facets of which inextricably overlap into broken mosaics, the hand-crafted aspect sometimes being described as 'knitted'. From around 1930 onwards, this expansion of the decorative to the detriment of meaning seems to correspond to a decline in his messianic revolutionary, metaphysical, materialistic fervour, in favour of a more existential interest in human beings, for the human face and brain, as a container of all the phenomena that make up the universe. In the best and most numerous instances, this mosaic division resulting from a relatively static organic growth method, is subject to the development process of the great general rhythms of composition, a process that can be linked to Futurism and Orphism.

It seems futile to try and reduce Filonov's works to any kind of definition, since through their diversity they manage to avoid any reduction, including the unique principles of the analytical method devised by their author. His work stands almost alone in the international context of the times, in its curious unstable balance between a clear rigorous automatic reflex of his almost biological design method resulting from his materialistic (determinist, rationalist) concept of the universe, from the initial macrocosm to the microcosm of the pictorial act, and in its irrepressible exacerbated visionary Expressionism. The approach is similar to Chagall's pictures of the same period when he tinged his dreamlike expressionist imaginings with a Neo-Cubist formalism, only Filonov's is deeper and more violent. A visionary Slavonic, mystical ascetic, guardian of a mission, intolerant, his work suffered in his lifetime as a result of his haughty intransigence. His painting glorified the ambitions of the Revolution, a revolution that did not understand him. The result of a demanding, though vague theory, this work, eluding the rigours of its creator, overflows with a diversity rich in detail, in which an austere structure and oriental colour, discipline and refinement, messianism and sensuality, abstraction and folklore co-exist. Though he was over influenced by his times rather than by original concepts and in spite of a certain scientistic naivety and some mannerism, Filonov remains one of the major Russian artists of his period.

BIBLIOGRAPHY:
Filonov, exhibition catalogue, Éd. du Centre Georges-Pompidou, Paris, 1990. Kowalkov, Mikhaïl, '*Pavel Filonov ou le Matérialisme métaphysique en peinture*' in *Art Press*, periodical, Paris, winter 1990.

MUSEUMS AND GALLERIES:
COLOGNE (Mus. Ludwig) - ST PETERSBURG (Gosudarstvennyj Russkij Muz.): almost all of his works.

AUCTION RECORDS:
NEW YORK, 3 Nov 1978, *Flight into Egypt* (1918, oil on canvas, 28 x 35 ins / 71 x 89 cm) USD 33,000. MUNICH, 30 June 1982, *Man with a Mouth Organ* (chalk, 7 1/2 x 6 3/4 ins / 19 x 17 cm) DEM 2,500. LONDON, 3 Dec 1985, *Composition with Figures* (c. 1910, watercolour and pen, 7 1/2 x 5 1/2 ins / 19 x 14 cm) GBP 5,500. LONDON, 23 May 1990, *Three Faces with Horse* (pencil, pen and watercoloured ink, 13 1/2 x 12 1/2 ins / 34.4 x 31.7 cm) GBP 19,800. LONDON, 17 Oct 1990, *Magi* (1913, tempera/tinted paper/card, 18 1/4 x 13 3/4 ins / 46.5 x 35 cm) GBP 56,100. LONDON, 25 March 1992, *Eternal Revolution* (1926, ink, pencil, watercolour and gouache/card, 5 1/4 x 19 3/4 ins / 13.5 x 50.3 cm) GBP 13,750. LONDON, 1 July 1992, *Last Supper* (watercolour, 13 x 19 1/4 ins / 33 x 49 cm) GBP 28,600. LONDON, 1 July 1999, *Abstract Composition with Spheres* (c. 1930, oil on paper, 28 x 20 ins / 72 x 51 cm) GBP 40,000. LONDON, 10 May 2000, *Three Faces with a Horse* (watercolour, 13 x 12 ins / 34 x 31 cm) GBP 40,000.

FILOSA, Giovanni Battista

Italian, 19th - 20th century.
Born 1850, in Castellammare di Stabia (Campania); died 1935, in Resina (Campania).
Painter, watercolourist. Genre scenes.

Giovanni Battista Filosa studied under Domenico Morelli. He exhibited at the Paris Salon between 1875 and 1882, and subsequently in Turin in 1887, in Venice in 1895, and in Florence in 1896.

BIBLIOGRAPHY:
'*Giovanni Battista Filosa*' in *Allgemeines Lexikon der bildenden Künstler von der Antike bis zur Gegenwart..., herausgegeben von Dr Ulrich Thieme und Dr Felix Becker*, vol. XI, W. Engelmann, Leipzig, 1915.

MUSEUMS AND GALLERIES:
CLAMECY: *Young Girl Picking a Fruit* (watercolour) - GLASGOW: *The Love Letter*.

AUCTION RECORDS:
NEW YORK, 7 March 1981, *Young Woman Feeding a Parrot* (watercolour, 22 x 29 ins / 55 x 73.5 cm) USD 1,600. ROME, 1 June 1983, *Encounter in the Park* (watercolour, 20 1/2 x 27 1/2 ins / 52 x 70 cm) ITL 2,000,000. LONDON, 28 Nov 1985, *Gallant Conversation* (1873, watercolour and pencil, 21 x 29 ins / 53.5 x 73.5 cm) GBP 750. PARIS, 4 Dec 1985, *Return of the Fishermen near Naples* (1908, oil on canvas, 39 x 53 1/2 ins / 99 x 136 cm) FRF 60,000. NEW YORK, 25 Feb 1988, *Picking Flowers of the Forest* (1874, watercolour and gouache, 18 3/4 x 29 3/4 ins / 47.6 x 75.5 cm) USD 1,870. VERSAILLES, 18 March 1990, *Neapolitan Fishermen opposite Vesuvius* (1908, oil on canvas, 39 1/4 x 53 1/2 ins / 100 x 136 cm) FRF 68,000. ROME, 29 May 1990, *Coast near Sorrento* (watercolour, 24 3/4 x 24 3/4 ins / 63 x 63 cm) ITL 978,000. MILAN, 21 Nov 1990, *Young Shepherd in Profile* (watercolour/paper, 14 1/2 x 11 ins / 37 x 27 cm) ITL 1,500,000. ROME, 4 Dec 1990, *Confidences* (watercolour/paper/panel, 26 1/2 x 19 1/2 ins / 67.5 x 49.5 cm) ITL 8,000,000. NEW YORK, 17 Oct 1991, *Indolence* (oil on canvas, 25 1/2 x 19 3/4 ins / 64.8 x 50.2 cm) USD 10,450. LONDON, 25 Nov 1992, *The Love Letter* (watercolour, 27 x 21 ins / 68.5 x 53.5 cm) GBP 2,860. NEW YORK, 10 Jan 1996, *The Fortune Teller* (watercolour on board, 48x34ins / 121.9x86.4cm) USD 5,462. NEW YORK, 17 Jan 1996, *The Tame Cockatoo* (watercolour/pencil, 21 1/2 x 29 ins / 54.6 x 73.7 cm) USD 2,875. LONDON, 13 March 1996, *Nymphea Gardens in Italy* (watercolour, 48 x 30 ins / 122 x 76 cm) GBP 4,600. PARIS, 31 March 1998, *Confidence in the Woods* (oil on canvas, 38 3/4 x 24 3/4 ins / 98.5 x 63 cm) FRF 138,000. NEW YORK, 6 May 1999, *Springtime in the Meadow* (oil on canvas, 25 x 21 ins / 63 x 53 cm) USD 30,000. MILAN, 21 Dec 1999, *View of a Villa on the Roman Hills* (oil on canvas, 20 x 28 ins / 52 x 72 cm) ITL 5,000,000. LONDON, 12 Oct 2000, *Mounted Dromedaries* (1907, oil on canvas, 44 x 55 ins / 112 x 140 cm) GBP 9,000. MILAN, 7 Nov 2000, *In the Wood with the Herd* (watercolour on cardboard, 32 x 55 ins / 81 x 140 cm) ITL 7,000,000. LUCERNE, 15 May 2002, *Galleria Palatina* (watercolour, 36 x 28 ins / 91 x 71 cm) CHF 8,000. LONDON, 19 Nov 2002, *Visit to the Pitti Palace* (watercolour, 39 x 28 ins / 98 x 71 cm) GBP 7,000. LONDON, 26 March 2003, *Costume Ball* (watercolour, 18 x 28 ins / 45 x 72 cm) GBP 1,400.

FILOSI

Sculptor.

MUSEUMS AND GALLERIES:
METZ (La Cour D'or): *The Republic* (plaster bust).

FILOSI, Gioseffo

Italian, 18th century.
Active in Venice 1732-1744.
Engraver (burin).

Gioseffo Filosi engraved plates for a publication entitled *Vedute delle Ville et d'Altri Luoghi della Toscana* (*Views of Towns and Other Places of Interest in Tuscany*).

FILOSI, Giovanni Battista

Italian, 16th century.
Active in Italy c. 1560.
Engraver.

Giovanni Battista Filosi engraved plates for the *Philosophia generalis, sive Logica, Cosmologia generalis* published by Charles Wolff in Verona (1555-1562).

GB f.

FILOTESIO, Nicola or Niccolo or Cola di.

See **NICOLA DI FILOTESIO**

FILOTICO, Vincenzo

Italian, 17th century.
Active in Manduria.
Painter.

Four paintings by Vincenzo Filotico are housed in the college chapel of St Gregory the Great.

FILOV, Dimitri

Russian, 20th - 21st century.
Born 1952, in Simferopol (Crimea).
Painter.

Dimitri Filov studied in Simferopol in the Crimea and still works there. He is a founder member of the Crimean Avant-Garde group.

FILOZOF, Véronique, or Filosof, called Véronique
Swiss, 20th century.
Born 8 August 1904, in Basel; died 12 January 1977, in Mulhouse, France.
From 1923 active in France.
Painter, draughtswoman, illustrator. Religious subjects, rustic scenes, popular scenes. Stage sets.

Véronique Filozof arrived in Paris in 1923, but did not begin her career as a painter until the age of 44. She started her apprenticeship with traditional painting, attempting to portray a resemblance of the subject. However, allergic to any artifice such as perspective, and on the advice of the critic Georges Besson, she began to draw in other ways with only a pen and a bottle of Indian ink. Her main subject was, she stressed: 'Man: his life, his work, his joys, his sorrows'. She worked extensively in series, sometimes assembling drawings in volumes. The first of them was *Black Périgord* (1954), an illustration of peasant and village life in the Sarlat region. Others followed, including: *The Bible in Pictures, Spiritual Meadow, Easter Haggadah, Palais Royal, Life in Appenzell,* the *Fables* of La Fontaine, and *May 68*. She executed numerous drawings of Paris, a *Dance of the Dead,* a series on the *Hippies,* and another on the *Commune of 71*. Her work, without being naive, nevertheless evokes a spirit of the 'popular traditions'. Politically committed, she illustrated the wars in Algeria and Vietnam. Jean Cocteau used to say of her: 'Véronique's miracle consists in making herself seen by any eye, as a poet would make himself heard by any ear.' She exhibited from about 1949. From 1960 she took part in the Salon Comparaisons in Paris.

FILSER, Jakob
German, 19th century.
Born 1801, in Kaufbeuren (Bavaria); died 27 March 1880, near Munich.
Lithographer.

Some lithographs by Filser are known. He was an art teacher.

FILSJEAN, Roger Victor
French, 20th century.
Born in St-Mandé.
Sculptor.

Roger Filsjean studied under Paul François Niclausse. He exhibited a plaster *Nude* at the 1934 Salon and gained a honourable mention in 1936.

FILSSMOSSER, Daniel
Austrian, 18th century.
Died 1753.
Active in Fürstenfeld (Styria).
Sculptor.

FILTSCH, Christian
German, 17th century.
Died 18 June 1683.
Active in Brieg, Silesia (now Brzeg, Poland).
Painter.

FILTSCH, Christoph
German, 17th century.
Active in Brieg, Silesia (now Brzeg, Poland).
Painter.

FIMA, pseudonym of Roeytenberg Ephraim
Russian, 20th century.
Born 1916, in Harbin (Manchuria), to Russian parents.
From 1949 active and naturalised in Israel; from 1961 also active in France.
Painter, engraver. Stage costumes and sets.

Fima lived in Shanghai and Beijing until 1949, studying Chinese calligraphy and philosophy. He emigrated with his parents to Israel in 1949. He initially studied at a Chinese academy in 1935, where he started to learn about traditional calligraphy, and then at an academy of Russian painters. He produced stage sets and costumes for ballets and operas. He taught at the Izo academy in Beijing and then at the academy in Shanghai. From 1961 onwards, he lived in Israel and Paris. After preliminary works influenced by Cubism and Surrealism, Fima found his own style in an elegant synthesis of Far Eastern calligraphy.

He participated in several collective exhibitions in numerous countries including: *Pittsburgh International Exhibition* (1961, 1964 and 1967); Salon des Réalités Nouvelles, Paris and *La Forme de l'Impression,* five painters introduced by Jacques Lassaigne, Galerie Jacques Massol, Paris (1962); Premier Salon des Galeries Pilotes, cantonal museum, Lausanne (1963); *Art Israël* touring exhibition in several countries including the USA, Canada and Israel. Solo exhibitions include: Shanghai (1947); Jerusalem (1956, 1958, 1960, 1966, 1970 and 1978); Baltimore Museum of Art (1960); London (1962); Galerie Jacques Massol, Paris (1963, 1969 and 1970); Turku museum, Finland (1966); Jewish Museum, New York (1972); Tel Aviv (1974, 1976, 1987 and 1989); Geneva (1984); and Galerie Clivages, Paris (1995).

- Fima -

BIBLIOGRAPHY:
Ragon, Michel/Seuphor, Michel, *L'Art abstrait,* Maeght, Paris, 1974. Boudaille, Georges/Javault, Patrick, *Fima - Monographie,* Bineth Gall., Tel Aviv, 1990.
MUSEUMS AND GALLERIES:
HAIFA (MA) - HAIFA (MM) - JERUSALEM (Israel Mus.) - PARIS (MAMVP) - TEL AVIV (MA) - WINNIPEG (AG).
AUCTION RECORDS:
TEL AVIV, 3 Jan 1990, *Trees on a Street Corner* (oil on card, 17 3/4 x 12 1/2 ins / 45 x 31.5 cm) USD 990. TEL AVIV, 1 Jan 1991, *Environs of Jerusalem* (oil on canvas, 18 x 22 ins / 46 x 55 cm) USD 1,540. TEL AVIV, 6 Jan 1992, *Vase and Flowers* (oil on card, 11 1/4 x 14 1/2 ins / 28.5 x 37 cm) USD 660. TEL AVIV, 30 June 1994, *Chinese Actor* (1971, oil on canvas, 32 1/4 x 25 3/4 ins / 82 x 65.5 cm) USD 3,680. TEL AVIV, 5 Jan 1999, *Calligraphy* (1979, oil on canvas, 26 x 21 ins / 65 x 54 cm) USD 1,950. TEL AVIV, 15 Jan 2001, *Jewish Bride* (1970, oil on canvas, after a drawing by Rembrandt, 58 x 45 ins / 147 x 114 cm) USD 8,000. TEL AVIV, 12 June 2001, *Still-life with Bottles and Jars* (1960, oil on canvas, 26 x 39 ins / 67 x 100 cm) USD 4,000. TEL AVIV, 2 Oct 2003, *Composition* (oil on canvas, 25 x 36 ins / 64 x 92 cm) USD 3,000.

FIMBACHER, Ferdinand Sebastian
Austrian, 18th century.
Born 15 March 1714, in Vienna.
Painter. Stage sets.

Ferdinand Fimbacher was the son of Johann Fimbacher, and became a member of the Academy of St Luke in 1730. He followed in his father's footsteps as a theatre artist.

FIMBACHER, Franz Joseph
Austrian, 18th century.
Born 1710, in Vienna.
Painter.

Franz Joseph Fimbacher was the son of Johann Fimbacher, and became a member of the Academy of St Luke in 1728.

FIMBACHER, Johann
Austrian, 18th century.
Born 1680; died 13 May 1729.
Painter. Stage sets.

Born in Vienna, Johann Fimbacher worked at the court as a theatre artist. He was a close friend of Ferd. Galli Bibiena.

FIMMERS, Kallist
Belgian, 20th century.
Born 1906, in Antwerp; died 1969.
Draughtsman, engraver.
Fimmers specialised in woodcuts.

FIMOSA, P.
Italian, 17th century.
Painter.
C. Bloemert engraved a painting by P. Fimosa entitled *The Body of Christ in the Arms of God the Father.*

FÎN, pseudonym of Vilató Ruiz, José
Spanish, 20th century.
Born 4 January 1916, in Barcelona; died 8 March 1969, in Paris.
Active in France from 1946.
Painter, engraver. Figures, still-lifes.
José Vilató Ruiz, or 'Fìn' as he was known, was the son of Dr Ruan Vilató Gómez, a neuro-psychiatrist from Barcelona and Lola Ruiz Picasso, sister of Pablo. He was educated in Barcelona and for short periods he attended classes at the La Lonja school of fine arts and later at the San Jordi school. Called up in 1938, he fought in the Spanish Civil War, returning to Barcelona in 1939. In 1943 he became part of a very active group of four young painters with Alberto Fabra, Rámon Rogent and Javier Vilató. He returned to Paris in 1946 and settled there, exhibiting at the Salon de Mai and the Salon d'Automne. His first solo exhibition took place in Barcelona in 1935. He also exhibited regularly in Paris and Madrid. In September 1971 the city of Barcelona honoured him with a major retrospective at the Palacio de la Virreina, producing an illustrated catalogue to accompany the event.
BIBLIOGRAPHY:
Vélez, Pilar, *José Vilató Fín (1916-1969)*, catalogue raisonné, Omega, Barcelona, 1999.
AUCTION RECORDS:
MADRID, 20 March 1984, *Still-life* (oil on canvas, 25 1/2 x 36 1/4 ins / 65 x 92 cm) ESP 130,000. PARIS, 29 April 1991, *Still-life* (1954, oil on canvas, 28 3/4 x 36 1/4 ins / 73 x 92 cm) FRF 5,000. PARIS, 21 Dec 1992, *Still-life with Bunch of Flowers* (1954, oil on canvas, 28 3/4 x 36 1/4 ins / 73 x 92 cm) FRF 7,500. PARIS, 12 Dec 1996, *Cubist Figures* (oil on canvas, 28 1/4 x 36 1/2 ins / 72 x 93 cm) FRF 6,000. PARIS, 23 Nov 1997, *Still-life with Guitar* (1961, oil on canvas, 28 3/4 x 36 1/4 ins / 73 x 92 cm) FRF 10,000. STOCKHOLM, 6 Nov 2001, *Female Nude Model* (1956, oil on canvas, 36 x 28 ins / 91 x 72 cm) SEK 16,000.

FINA, Giovanni Antonio della
Italian, 15th century.
Born 15th century, in Lizzana (Trento).
Painter.
The church of St Florian contains a retable, dated 1481 and signed by Giovanni Antonio della Fina, representing *St Anthony, St Roch and St Blaise in a Flower Meadow.*

FINAAS, John
Norwegian, 18th century.
Sculptor.
The gallery in Bergen has a bust portrait of Rector Boaeth which John Finaas executed for the academy of music.

FINACER, José Antonio
Spanish, 18th - 19th century.
Active at the end of the 18th century and at the beginning of the 19th century.
Sculptor.

FINALDI, Filippo di Bartolo
Italian, 15th century.
Painter.
Florentine School.
Filippo di Bartolo Finaldi was made a member of the Accademia di San Luca in 1450.

FINALE, Cristoforo del
Italian, 16th century.
Painter.
Cristoforo del Finale paid his subscription as a member of the Accademia di San Luca in Rome on 27 April 1556.

FINALÉ, Moïse or Moisés
Cuban, 20th - 21st century.
Born 1957, in Cardenas (Matanzas).
Active in France from 1989.
Painter, engraver.
Moïse Finalé trained at the national fine arts institute near Havana. Although he comes from a cultured Hispanic family, he finds his inspiration in the history and popular culture of Cuba, in the meeting between Africa and Spain, between black and white, between the sacred and the profane, between the primitive and ancestral rites. His paintings are generally in muted tones, expressing mystery, sometimes with bright highlights associated with sex and drunkenness. His compositions with their iconic objects and forms - feet, hands, representations of animals, chalices - make reference to the syncretic cult of santeria. He is a member of the National Union of Writers, Painters and Engravers of Cuba.

He has taken part in group exhibitions, including: Havana (1981); *Trajectoire Cubaine* (*Cuban Trajectory*), alongside Humberto Castro and José Franco at the Pablo Neruda Art Centre in Corbeil-Essonnes (1989); Orvieto and Gibellina in Italy (1989); *Expressions Actuelles, 62 Artistes d'Amérique Latine* (*Contemporary Expressions, 62 Latin American Artists*) in Nanterre (1992).

He has also held solo exhibitions: Museo Nacional de Bellas Artes in Havana (1979 and 1988);, *Mitologicas* (*Mythologies*) - Gallery of Non-Aligned Countries, Belgrade (1985); *Formas Escondidas* (*Hidden Forms*) - Havana Arts Centre (1986); Museo Nacional de Bellas Artes in Havana (1988); *L'Imaginaire Merveilleux* (*The Marvellous Imagination*), Galerie Arichi, Paris (1990); *Cadeau d'Ange* (*Angel's Present*), Galerie Jacques de Vos, Paris (1990); Centre Culturel Albanville, Toulouse (1991); Espace Latino-Américain, Paris (1991); *Relations Occultes* (*Secret Relations*), Galerie Armand, Paris (1991); *Face-à-Face* (*Face to Face*), Galerie Artuel, Paris (1993).
BIBLIOGRAPHY:
Lassalle, Hélène, '*Moïse Finalé*' in *Artension* n° 28, periodical, Rouen, 1991.

FINALI, Giovanni Angelo
Italian, 18th century.
Born 1709, in Valsolda (Milan); died 1772.
Sculptor.
Giovanni Angelo Finali worked in Vienna alongside the sculptor Franz Blüml. His work includes a monumental sculpture entitled *Scipio Maffei* in Verona, a bust of *Vincent Pisani* for the latter's monument in the church of S Anastasia, and statues of *St Peter* and *St Paul* for the façade of the church of S Paolo on the Campo Marzio. Finali also produced statues of the *Twelve Apostles* and other saints for the church of S Prospero in Reggio nell'Emilia, and a statue of *St John Nepomuk* which now stands on a bridge in Mirandola. Finali died whilst travelling to Breslau (now Wroclaw, Poland).

FINARRO
Italian, 13th century.
Sculptor.

FINART, Noël Dieudonné, or Finert
French, 19th century.
Born 27 March 1797, in Condé; died 1852, in Paris.
Painter, watercolourist. Military subjects.
Finart was self-taught and developed his talent on his own by making close studies of nature and drawing inspiration

from the works of great painters. He first exhibited at the Paris Salon in 1817 with *Clignancourt Parade Ground* and continued to exhibit there until 1850, showing landscapes, genre scenes and military and other subjects. He received a third-class medal in 1840. His main works include *Exercise Ground for French Troops, Camp of Kalmucks, Fleeing Arab, Carrying his Wife, Lion Hunt in Africa, Louis XIV Walking at Rocher Canon, Marshall Ney during the Retreat of Russia, Portrait of Charles the First* and *Longchamp Promenade in Times of Louis XV.*

MUSEUMS AND GALLERIES:
CAMBRAI: *Arab Scene; Circassian Cavalry; Landscape at Dusk* - VERSAILLES (Trianon): *September Morning.*

AUCTION RECORDS:
PARIS, 19 March 1924, *Cossacks,* FRF 530. LONDON, 23 Feb 1925, *Allied Monarchs,* GBP 44. PARIS, 16-18 Nov 1925, *Military Subjects* (two watercolours) FRF 200. PARIS, 3 Dec 1925, *Scene from the Russian Campaign,* FRF 150. PARIS, 17 Dec 1928, *Scene from the Egypt Campaign,* FRF 555. PARIS, 9 Nov 1938, *Napoleon and His Staff* (watercolour) FRF 100. PARIS, 16 July 1942, *Two Horseriders and a Dog* (1840) FRF 360. PARIS, 23 Sept 1942, *Louis XIV and His Suite* (1844) FRF 1,700. PARIS, 16 April 1945, *Stagecoach in Sands* (watercolour) FRF 950. VERSAILLES, 24 Oct 1982, *Cossacks on Their Horses near Encampment* (1830, watercolour/graphite) FRF 15,000. PARIS, 12 March 1984, *Arab Cavalrymen at the Base of the Pyramids* (1831, watercolour heightened with gouache, 19 1/4 x 15 1/4 ins / 49 x 38.5 cm) FRF 19,200. LONDON, 4 Oct 1989, *Caravan Pausing in the Desert* (1838, oil on canvas, 6 x 8 1/4 ins / 15.5 x 21 cm) GBP 1,100. PARIS, 21 June 1990, *Skirmish between Circassian Cavalry and Russian Army in the Caucasus Mountains* (1840, oil on canvas, 21 1/4 x 33 3/4 ins / 54 x 86 cm) FRF 20,000. NEW YORK, 16 Feb 1995, *Napoleon at Aboukir* (oil on canvas, 15 x 22 ins / 38.1 x 55.9 cm) USD 12,650. PARIS, 18-19 March 1996, *Camp Scene* (oil on canvas, 20 1/2 x 26 ins / 52 x 66 cm) FRF 70,000. PARIS, 11 Dec 1996, *Russian Cavalrymen* (oil on canvas, 12 1/2 x 16 ins / 32 x 40.5 cm) FRF 18,000. PARIS, 3 June 1999, *Amazon* (oil on canvas, 10 x 14 ins / 26 x 35 cm) FRF 45,000. PARIS, 9 June 2000, *Arrival of Bonaparte in Alexandria* (oil on canvas) FRF 71,000. PARIS, 20 Oct 2000, *Cossack Charge against the Turks* (1830, black crayon/watercolour/gouache, 12 x 20 ins / 31 x 52 cm) FRF 18,000.

FINAUD-BOUNNAUD, Claire (Mme)
French, 20th century.
Born in Marseilles.
Painter.

Claire Finaud-Bounnaud studied under Marius Barret. She exhibited at the Salon des Artistes Français.

FINAZZI, Jean
French, 20th century.
Born 1920, in La Rochelle; died 1971, in Lyons.
Painter. Portraits, seascapes, landscapes.

Jean Finazzi studied at the École des Beaux-Arts in Lyons in 1944-45. From 1947 he took part in exhibitions in many French cities, in particular La Rochelle, Royan. He received several awards at the Salon des Beaux-Arts in Lyons, and also exhibited in Paris at the Salon des Artistes Indépendants on several occasions from 1952, as well as in Caracas.

He painted water, shores and harbours, registering atmospheric variations caused by time and the seasons.

FINCH, A. M.
British, 20th century.
Painter.

AUCTION RECORDS:
PARIS, 22 June 1945, *Boat Run Aground* (1915) FRF 500.

FINCH, Alfred William, called Willy
Belgian, 19th - 20th century.
Born 28 November 1854, in Brussels, of British origin; died 1930, in Helsinki.
From 1897 active in Finland.
Painter, ceramicist, decorative designer. Landscapes.
Septem Group.

Finch trained in 1878 and 1879 under the direction of Joseph Van Severdonck at the Académie des Beaux Arts in Brussels, where he met Ensor. He knew Seurat in 1887, when Seurat presented, at the Salon *A Sunday Afternoon on the Ile de la Grande-Jatte,* a picture which was to have a determining influence on Finch's painting. He studied with interest the divisionist principles of colour. In 1890 he was a practitioner of glazed earthenware painting in Belgium, and was initiated into ceramics. In 1897 he accepted Louis Sparre's request to manage a ceramics factory in Finland. Finch took up painting again in 1905, and became a lecturer at the School of Decorative Art in Helsinki. He was very interested in the ideas of William Morris and John Ruskin, who inspired the Arts and Crafts movement. In 1880 he exhibited at the Ghent Salon. He was a member of artistic societies such as Chrysalide and L'Essor, and was one of the founders of the Société des Vingt (Society of the Twenty) in 1884. In 1912 he founded, with Magnus Enckell and Sigurd Frosterus, a group of painters called Septem (Seven), seen as a renewal of Finnish painting.

Finch, who was an admirer of Monet, was the painter through whom Neo-Impressionism was introduced into Belgium and Finland. In that Pointillist method of working he produced some fine paintings of landscapes. He was also a pioneer in the field of design.

AW Finch

MUSEUMS AND GALLERIES:
HELSINKI (Ateneumin Taidemus.): *Horse Race at Ostend* (1888); *Orchard at La Louvière* (1890-1891); *The White Cliffs of Dover* (1891-1892) - IXELLES: *The Stacks* (1899) - OSTEND (Mus. voor Schone Kunsten) - TOURNAI: *Snow Effect; Boats Wrecked on the Sandbank.*

AUCTION RECORDS:
LONDON, 12 Oct 1970, *Country Road near the North Sea,* GBP 4,000. LONDON, 12 Nov 1970, *Country Road near the North Sea,* GBP 4,000. PARIS, 25 Nov 1977, *The Box at the Theatre* (pastel, 39 1/4 x 31 ins / 100 x 79 cm) FRF 17,000. NEW YORK, 19 May 1983, *The Breakwater at Heyst, Overcast Sky* (1889/1890, oil on canvas, 14 1/2 x 21 1/2 ins / 37 x 54.5 cm) USD 82,500. LONDON, 1 July 1987, *Harvesting* (1890, oil on canvas, 16 x 21 1/4 ins / 40.5 x 53.7 cm) GBP 24,000. LONDON, 19 Oct 1989, *Peasant in the Fields* (oil/palette, 20 1/4 x 12 3/4 ins / 51.5 x 32.4 cm) GBP 4,950. AMSTERDAM, 4 June 1997, *Boats on the Beach* (oil on canvas, 9 1/2 x 12 1/2 ins / 24 x 32 cm) NLG 23,064. AMSTERDAM, 2 Dec 1997, *The Nieuport Road* (1988, oil on canvas, 22 x 26 ins / 55 x 66 cm) NLG 530,472.

FINCH, Christopher
British, 18th century.
Active in London.
Painter. Portraits.

Christopher Finch exhibited with the Free Society of Artists from 1764 to 1765.

FINCH, E. H.
British, 20th century.
Born in London.
Watercolourist.

E.H. Finch studied under M.W. Egerton-Hine. He exhibited at the Salon des Artistes Français from 1926.

FINCH, Francis Oliver
British, 19th century.
Born 22 November 1802; died 27 August 1862.

Painter (gouache), watercolourist. Portraits, landscapes, landscapes with figures, waterscapes.

Early in his career, Francis Finch studied under John Varley and Henry Sass. In 1827 he became a member of the Society of Watercolourists, with whom he exhibited regularly for many years.

MUSEUMS AND GALLERIES:

CARDIFF: *Castle on a Wooded Hillside* - DUBLIN: *Classical Landscape* - LONDON (British Mus.): seven watercolours - LONDON (Victoria and Albert Mus.): *Fountains on a Palace Forecourt; Ruins; Morning; River by Moonlight; Ruined Temple; Cemetery, Evening; Classical Landscape; View of Mountains; Mountain Landscape with a Blasted Tree; Ruins and Fishermen; Calm Summer's Day; River and Castle; Moonlight; Landscape with a Tower; Ruins in a Forest; Ruins beside a Pond.*

AUCTION RECORDS:

LONDON, 1 May 1908, *On the River* (watercolour) GBP 9. LONDON, 28 May 1923, *Classical Landscape* (drawing) GBP 14. LONDON, 30 Nov 1923, *Landscape* (drawing) GBP 11. LONDON, 10 Dec 1923, *Solitude* (drawing) GBP 21. LONDON, 23 April 1928, *Classical Landscape,* GBP 11. LONDON, 6 July 1928, *Classical Landscape* (drawing) GBP 15. LONDON, 5 Dec 1930, *Classical Landscape* (drawing) GBP 6. LONDON, 6 March 1931, *Road along a River Bank* (drawing) GBP 16. LONDON, 8 March 1935, *Italian Lake,* GBP 5. LONDON, 24 May 1935, *Lake* (drawing) GBP 12. LONDON, 30 Oct-2 Nov 1936, *Classical Landscape* (drawing) GBP 7. LONDON, 30 Nov 1978, *The Dell of Comus* (watercolour heightened with gouache, 11 3/4 x 9 3/4 ins / 30 x 25 cm) GBP 520. LONDON, 17 Nov 1987, *Wooded Landscape with Setting Sun* (1835, watercolour, 5 x 7 1/4 ins / 12.5 x 18.1 cm) GBP 1,700. LONDON, 31 Jan 1990, *Classical Landscape with Figures Seated among Antique Ruins* (watercolour heightened with gouache, 14 1/2 x 18 1/2 ins / 37 x 47 cm) GBP 800. LONDON, 8 June 1999, *Figures and Horse beneath Ruined Castle* (pencil and watercolour heightened with gum arabic and scratching out, 15 x 22 ins / 38 x 56 cm) GBP 1,200. LONDON, 4 Dec 2002, *Dell of Comus* (watercolour and gouache, 11 x 13 ins / 29 x 34 cm) GBP 2,800.

FINCH, Heneage (Fourth Earl of Aylesford)
British, 18th - 19th century.
Born 4 July 1751, in London; died 20 October 1812.
Painter, engraver.

Finch met with equal success both as an amateur watercolour and oil painter and as an etcher and was an honorary exhibitor at the Royal Academy from 1786 to 1790. He specialised in architectural drawings and watercolours and rustic scenes.

MUSEUMS AND GALLERIES:

LONDON (Tate Collection): around 50 works/paper (watercolours, drawings, prints).

FINCH, R.
British, 18th century.
Active in London.
Miniaturist.

R. Finch is noted for a portrait of a man, at the Royal Academy of Art, London.

FINCH, Spencer
American, 20th - 21st century.
Born 1962, in New Haven.
Installation artist, sculptor, draughtsman.

Spencer Finch studied at Doshisha University in Kyoto, Japan (1983-1984) and then at Hamilton College where he obtained a BA in Comparative Literature. In 1989 he graduated from Rhode Island School of Design (RISD) with a Master's degree in Fine Art.

Finch produces installations such as *Sky*, an egg-shaped aluminium panel painted with dark grey acrylic paint and decorated with Rhinestones (2000) and *Blue (Sky over Los Alamos, New Mexico 5/5/00 Morning Effect)* made from light bulbs of varying sizes hanging from cables suspended in a mobile. In 2004 Finch presented *Sunlight in an Empty Room (Passing Cloud for Emily Dickinson, Amherst, MA, August 28, 2004)*, a cloud of cellophanes in different shades of blue incorporating fluorescent lights, filters and clothespins.

Finch's work has been the subject of annual solo exhibitions since 1994, including at the Postmasters Gallery in New York (2004), and at the Portikus Gallery in Frankfurt (2003). Finch also participates in group exhibitions such as the Whitney Museum of American Art Biennial, and the Scandinavian Cultural Centre in Berlin, both in 2004.

BIBLIOGRAPHY:

Camper, Fred, '*Focus on the Invisible*' in *The Chicago Reader*, 5 April 1996. Anton, Saul, '*Spencer Finch at Postmasters Gallery*' in *Art/Text*, May-July 1999. Anton, Saul, '*Colour Commentary: The Art of Spencer Finch*' in *Artforum*, April 2001. Volk, Gregory, '*Spencer Finch at Postmasters*' in *Art in America, p. 154*, New York, September 2001.

FINCK
German, 18th century.
Sculptor (wood).

Finck studied in Stuttgart.

FINCK, Adele von
German, 20th century.
Born 6 February 1879, in Berlin.
Painter. Genre scenes, landscapes.

Adele von Finck studied in Munich with Lenbach, in Brussels with Portaels and in Paris with G. Courtois, as well as in Italy. She exhibited in 1903 and 1904 in Prague, and from 1907 to 1913 in Berlin.

FINCK, Georg
German, 18th century.
Born 1721, in Augsburg; died 1757, in Kassel.
Engraver, architect.

Georg Finck worked with his father. In 1741 he went to Berlin, where he worked at the Opera. He produced several engravings.

FINCK, Hieronymus von der
Swiss, 18th century.
Died 1780, in Basel.
Engraver (wood).

Hieronymus von der Finck was probably a student of J.-B.M. Papillon. He supplied illustrations for literary works, including *Merkwürdigkeiten von Basel Land* (*Peculiarities of Basel Country*) by Bruckner, the *Balser Leichenpredigten* (*Funeral Sermons from Basel*) and 108 illustrations (1778) for *History of the Bible* by Jean Hubner.

FINCK, Jean
French, 20th century.
Painter.

Jean Fink featured at the Salon des Indépendants from 1941.

FINCK, Karl
German, 19th century.
Died 1890, in Kassel.
Painter.

FINCK, Ludwig
German, 19th century.
Born 22 November 1857, in Hanover.
Painter. Landscapes.

Ludwig Finck was the son and student of Karl Finck. In 1905 and 1906, in Frankfurt am Main, he exhibited landscapes of the Taunus region of Germany.

FINCKE, Hans
German, 19th century.
Born 5 May 1800, in Berlin; died 12 August 1849.
Engraver.

Fincke was a student of Buchhorn, and then of Linden, in London. He mostly engraved landscapes and architectural views.

FINCKE, Hermann

German, 19th century.

Born 25 November 1845, in Dresden.

Sculptor.

Hermann Fincke was a student of A. Gaber, and studied at Dresden with H. Bürkner.

FINCKE, L.

German, 19th century.

Engraver. Urban landscapes.

Fincke, who was active in the first half of the 19th century, is known to have produced nine views of Berlin, after drawings by Heinrich Hitze.

MUSEUMS AND GALLERIES:

BERLIN (Kupferstichkabinet): engravings.

FINCKEN, James Horsey

American, 19th century.

Born 9 May 1860, in Bristol (?); died before 1943, in Philadelphia.

Engraver (etching).

FINCKENZELLER, F. Felix

German, 17th century.

Born in Bavaria.

Active in Landshut (Bavaria) during the 17th century.

Painter.

Finckenzeller is known to have produced an altar painting for the Protestant church in Ergolding, representing the *Martyrdom of St Erasmus*, and another in the church at Gundihausen, representing *St Anthony*.

FIND, Ludvig

Danish, 19th century.

Born 16 May 1869, in Osterbygaard, near Vamdrup.

Painter. Portraits, genre scenes.

Ludvig Find was a pupil at the fine art school in Copenhagen and then at the Kr. Zahrtmann school. He participated in the Paris Exposition Universelle in 1900, where he won a bronze medal.

MUSEUMS AND GALLERIES:

COPENHAGEN (Den Hirschsprungske Samling): *Portrait of the Artist's Father* - COPENHAGEN (Statens Mus. for Kunst): *A Workshop*.

AUCTION RECORDS:

LONDON, 25 March 1987, *Children's Games* (oil on canvas, 20 x 27 1/4 ins / 50.5 x 69 cm) GBP 2,600. COPENHAGEN, 25 Oct 1989, *Little Girl Near a Piano* (1917, oil on canvas, 27 1/4 x 24 ins / 69 x 61 cm) DKK 7,000.

FINDEN, Dietrich

German, 18th century.

Born 1720, in Lauenburg (Schleswig-Holstein); died 1765.

Painter, engraver (etching).

Finden is mentioned by Nagler.

FINDEN, Edward Francis

British, 19th century.

Born 30 April 1791, in London; died 9 February 1857, in London.

Engraver.

Edward Finden was the younger brother of William Finden and, like him, a pupil of James Mitan. He produced a number of plates for the periodical *Literary Souvenir*. His other works include *Princess Victoria* after Westall, *Happy as a King* after Gainsborough, and *Othello Recounting his Exploits to Desdemona and Brabantio* after Douglas Cowper.

FINDEN, George C.

British, 19th century.

Engraver.

George C. Finden's first known engraving is his *Wellington as Rector of Oxford University*. He is also noted for portraits of *Lady Romney* after Reynolds, and *The Cooper Family* after E. Frère.

FINDEN, William

British, 19th century.

Born 1787; died 20 September 1852, in London.

Engraver.

A pupil of James Mitan, William Finden collaborated with his brother Edward and a number of assistants and pupils, on several series of engravings including: *The Gallery of the Graces* after Chalon, Landseer and others (1832-1834); *Portraits of Queen Victoria's Ladies-in-Waiting* after Chalon, Hayter and others; and *Portraits of Illustrious British Personalities*. The Finden brothers contributed illustrations to a number of works: *The Life and Works of Lord Byron, Artistic Journeys, Poetical Works of Campbell*. Finden also engraved *George IV* after Sir Thomas Lawrence, *The Interior of a Highlander's Home* after Edwin Landseer, a *Crucifixion* after Hilton, *Sickness and Health* after Webster and other works.

FINDENIGG, Franz Paul

Austrian, 18th century.

Born 1726 or 1727, in Villach; died 18 July 1771, in Vienna.

Painter.

Findenigg enrolled at the academy in Vienna on 7 December 1751.

FINDL, Johann Baptist

German, 19th century.

Active at the beginning of the 19th century in Munich.

Painter (porcelain).

A goblet on which Findl painted the *Oktoberfest* (October Festival) in Munich in 1801 is kept at the Bayerisches Nationalmuseum in Munich.

MUSEUMS AND GALLERIES:

MUNICH (Bayerisches Nationalmus.): goblet (1801).

FINDLATER, William

British, 18th - 19th century.

Active in London.

Painter. Battles.

William Findlater exhibited in London from 1800 to 1821, notably at the Royal Academy and the British Institution.

AUCTION RECORDS:

LONDON, 14 Dec 1927, *The Opening of Waterloo Bridge* (watercolour) GBP 18.

FINDLAV, J.

British, 19th century.

Draughtsman, watercolourist, engraver.

J. Findlav exhibited watercolours of London at the Royal Academy in 1827 and 1831. He also exhibited at the British Institution, and the Suffolk Street Gallery.

MUSEUMS AND GALLERIES:

LONDON (British Mus.): forty-one heightened drawings from the Grace collection.

FINDORFF, Dietrich

German, 18th century.

Born 23 March 1722, in Lauenburg (Schleswig-Holstein); died 3 May 1772, in Ludwigslust (Mecklenburg-Vorpommern).

Painter, engraver, sculptor.

Findorff's talent was discovered by Duke Christian Louis of Melseinburg, who sent him to practise sculpture with Naunheim and painting with Lehmann. He also worked with Dietrich in Dresden. He was principally an animal sculptor. Most of his paintings are housed at the gallery in Schwerin

(Mecklenburg-Vorpommern), including a self-portrait, other portraits and moral studies. His masterpiece is *Annunciation to the Shepherds*, which is in the church in Ludwigslust behind the altar. Findorff also made engravings.

FINE, Jud
American, 20th - 21st century.
Born 20 November 1944, in Los Angeles.
Sculptor.

Jud Fine obtained a BA in 1966 from the University of California at Santa Barbara, and an MFA from Cornell University in 1970. He has taught as visiting professor at Ohio University, Athens, and has been professor of art at the University of Southern California since 1979.

Fine is best known for his public artworks, many of them produced collaboratively with his wife Barbara McCarren, which are usually part of an organic whole with the environment they inhabit. His *Spine* (1993) in the Maguire Gardens of the Los Angeles Central Library is tied to the building it adjoins, and contains thematic references to books through a series of fountains with steps decorated by letters and numbers, the whole suggesting an open book laid on its spine. *Mark* (1999) is a series of 32 concrete and iron trail markers on the Ventura River Trail, San Buenaventura, CA. Each marker is made with an iron artefact from the Ventura oil fields, while carved messages on the bases refer to aspects of local history, biology, geology, archaeology and people. Fine's sense of offbeat humour can often be seen in works such as *Evolution*, a fountain sculpture designed for a garden of the Nestlé Company in Glendale, CA. It comprises an off-centre beam that pours water into a connecting stream, with the beam anchored by the figure of an egg-laying California newt.

Fine's exhibitions include: 1982 and 1989, solos at the Anderson Gallery, Virginia Commonwealth University, Richmond, and De Sassiet Museum, Santa Clara University, CA; 2004-2005, *Lost but Found: Assemblage, Collage and Sculpture, 1920-2002*, Norton Simon Museum, Pasadena; 2002, *Thai-American Art Exchange Project 2002*, Silpakorn University Art Gallery, Bangkok, Thailand; 1998, 1993, 1988 and 1987, San Diego Museum of Contemporary Art; 1987, University of California Art Gallery, Irvine; 1978, Santa Barbara Museum of Art; 1976, Indianapolis Museum of Art; 1974, Institute of Contemporary Art, Boston; 1974, *71st American Exhibition*, Art Institute of Chicago; 1973, the Paris Biennale; and 1972, *Documenta V*, Kassel. Fine has received a grant from the California State Arts Council (1983); a National Endowment for the Arts Fellowship (1982); the Laura Slobe Memorial Award, Art Institute of Chicago (1974); and a Contemporary Art Council New Talent Grant, Los Angeles County Art Museum (1972).

BIBLIOGRAPHY:
Fine, Jud, *Or, an Introduction*, Illustrated book, Dayton's Gallery 12, Minneapolis, 1974. *Jud Fine: Confessions and Related Work, 1970-1976*, Exhibition catalogue, Art Gallery, California State University Fullerton, Fullerton, 1976. *Jud Fine*, Exhibition catalogue, Los Angeles Municipal Art Gallery, Los Angeles, 1985. McDonald, Robert, '*Profile: Jud Fine*' in *Artscene*, Journal article, February 1987. Fine, Jud, *Red is Green*, Video, The Fellows of Contemporary Art, Los Angeles, 1988. *Jud Fine*, Exhibition catalogue, La Jolla Museum of Contemporary Art, La Jolla (CA), 1988. Pagel, David, '*Jud Fine*' in *ArtsMagazine*, Journal article, November 1988. Fine, Jud/Reese, Harry, *Spire: An Account of the Jud Fine Art Plan at the Maguire Gardens, Central Library, Los Angeles*, Illustrated book, Los Angeles Library Association, Los Angeles, 1993.

MUSEUMS AND GALLERIES:
CHICAGO (AI) - CHICAGO (MCA) - ŁÓDZ (Museum Stuki) - LOS ANGELES (Central Library): *Spine* (1993, sculpture) - LOS ANGELES (County MA) - LOS ANGELES (MCA) - MINNEAPOLIS (IA) - NEW HAVEN (AG, Yale University) - NEW YORK (Guggenheim Mus.) - PASADENA (Norton Simon Mus.): *Untitled* (1972, chicken wire sculpture) - PITTSBURGH (Carnegie MA): *Untitled* (pencil on paper) - SAN DIEGO (MCA): *Ayers' Analog* (1974-1988, sculpture) - SYDNEY (Power Institute of Fine Arts).

AUCTION RECORDS:
SAN FRANCISCO, 20 June 1985, *Removal No 1* (1978, mixed media/paper, 25 1/4 x 39 3/4 ins / 64 x 101 cm) USD 950. NEW YORK, 24 Feb 1995, *Pole* (1979, pencil and coloured inks/canvas with string wrapped around a copper tube, l. 104 3/4 ins / 266.1 cm) USD 805.

FINE, Perle
American, 20th century.
Born 1905, in Boston; died 1988.
Painter, engraver.

Perle Fine received advice from Hans Hoffmann. She was an abstract painter who took Mondrian's last American period as her starting point; her later work is freer in expression and almost monochrome, its attractiveness lying in its artistic haziness.

Fine exhibited in a number of group shows, including: 1950, Salon des Réalités Nouvelles, Paris; the Carnegie International Exhibition, Pittsburgh; the Witney Museum Annuals; 1960, the Mexico Biennale in Mexico City. She also held solo exhibitions in the USA. She received several awards, including the engraving prize of the Brooklyn Museum.

MUSEUMS AND GALLERIES:
LOS ANGELES (County MA) - NEW YORK (Brooklyn Mus.) - NEW YORK (Metropolitan Mus. of Art).

FINELLI, Carlo
Italian, 19th century.
Born 25 April 1785, in Carrara; died 6 September 1853, in Rome.
Sculptor.

Carlo Finelli is thought to have been a member of the same family as Giuliano Finelli. He studied in Rome with Canova, and worked at the Apostolic Palace in the Vatican and the Royal Palace in Turin. Siret refers to him as a history painter. He was elected to the Accademia di San Luca on 20 March 1814. In Novara Cathedral he sculpted the bronze *Caryatids* on the high altar; he is also known for busts of *Petrarch* and *Ariosto*; and the busts of *Masaccio* and *Ghiberti* in the Protomoteca hall at the Capitol in Rome; and finally, *Juno and the Young Mars*.

MUSEUMS AND GALLERIES:
FLORENCE (Uffizi): *Drawings* - MILAN (Pinacoteca di Brera): *Terracotta Low Relief in Memory of Alfieri*.

FINELLI, Giuliano
Italian, 17th century.
Born 13 December 1601, in Carrara; died 1657, in Rome.
Sculptor.
Neapolitan School.

Giuliano Finelli studied initially in Naples under his uncle Vitale Finelli the Elder, then under Naccarini. He moved to Rome to work under Bernini, then settled in Naples. He worked closely with Bernini's son Pietro. His body of work includes several statues in marble and bronze, such as a statue of *St Cecilia* for the church of S Maria di Loreto; monumental statues of the *Apostles Peter and Paul* for the Tesoro chapel in Naples Cathedral; 13 bronze statues of the saint-protectors of Naples; and two busts of members of the Filomarino family.

MUSEUMS AND GALLERIES:
MADRID (Prado): *Eight Monumental Lions* (bronze, used to support consoles).

FINELLI, Pietro
Italian, 18th - 19th century.
Born c. 1770, in Carrara; died 7 March 1812, in Rome.
Sculptor.
Pietro Finelli was the son of the sculptor Vitale Finelli the Younger and the brother of Carlo Finelli. He arrived in Rome around 1800. He was awarded a prize by the Accademia di San Luca on 15 November 1801 for his group sculpture of *Hercules and Deïaneira*, and was elected to membership of the academy on 19 April 1808.

FINELLI, Vitale, the Elder
Italian, 17th century.
Born 1583, in Carrara.
Sculptor, architect.
Vitale Finelli the Elder was the uncle and first teacher of Giuliano Finelli. He produced predominantly altar tables and decorative features for churches.

FINELLI, Vitale, the Younger
Italian, 18th century.
Born in Carrara.
Sculptor.
Vitale Finelli the Younger worked in Naples for seven years before being appointed to a professorship at the Nuova Accademia in Carrara.

FINERT, Noël Dieudonné. See **FINART**

FINES, C.
British, 19th century.
Active in London.
Sculptor.
C. Fines exhibited wax *bozzetti* at the Royal Academy in London from 1833 to 1846.

FINES, Eugène François
French, 19th century.
Born 19 July 1826, in Paris; died July 1901, in Bordeaux.
Painter. Genre scenes, landscapes with figures.
Fines attended the École des Beaux-Arts in Paris and was taught by Auguste Hesse and Léon Cogniet. He exhibited at the Paris Salon from 1859 to 1880. He produced many country scenes usually inspired by Breton landscape. Works include *Country Girl Spinning, Poussin at the Home of the Sculptor François Duquesnoy, Italian Countrywoman and Child, Grandfather, Sword*

EVG. FINES

BIBLIOGRAPHY:
Delouche, Denise/Michaud, Jean-Marc, et al., *Bretagne, terre des peintres*, exhibition catalogue, Musée des Beaux-Arts, Vannes, 2003.
MUSEUMS AND GALLERIES:
VANNES (Collection du conseil général du Morbihan): *Portrait of a Breton as bragou-braz* (oil on canvas).
AUCTION RECORDS:
NEW YORK, 25 Jan 1979, *Mother's Convalescence* (oil on canvas, 26 1/2 x 22 3/4 ins / 67 x 58 cm) USD 3,000. NEW YORK, 25 Jan 1980, *Mother's Convalescence* (oil on canvas, 26 1/2 x 23 ins / 67 x 58.5 cm) USD 1,700. ZURICH, 22 May 1987, *Preparations for the Ball* (oil on canvas, 28 3/4 x 23 1/4 ins / 73 x 59 cm) CHF 6,500. PARIS, 26 March 1995, *Young Children Being Reprimanded by the Sacristan as They Leave Church* (oil on canvas, 36 x 30 3/4 ins / 90.5 x 78 cm) FRF 25,500. BERN, 17 May 1999, *Church Interior with Women and Children* (oil on canvas, 22 x 26 ins / 56 x 67 cm) CHF 6,500. FAIRFIELD, 13 July 2001, *Genre Scene of Gypsy and Boy* (oil on canvas, 23 x 14 ins / 58 x 36 cm) USD 2,000. VEJLE, 4 Aug 2003, *Italian Scene with Monk Praying for Woman and Children* (oil on canvas, 22 x 27 ins / 56 x 69 cm) DKK 12,800. LONDON, 4 Dec 2003, *Family at Prayer* (oil on canvas, 22 x 27 ins / 55 x 69 cm) GBP 1,800.

FINES, L.
Flemish, 18th century.
Active in Liège during the first half of the 18th century.
Draughtsman, engraver.
Flemish School.
L. Fines is known to have produced approximately 30 engravings.

FINET, A A.
French, 19th century.
Sculptor.
Finet exhibited busts and statues at the Salon des Artistes Français from 1889 to 1902. Works include *Vengeance* and *Moses Saved from the Water.*

FINET, François I
French, 18th century.
Born 24 March 1719.
Painter. Religious subjects. Designs for tapestries.
François Finet I was appointed as a lecturer at the school of decorative arts called the Écoles d'Aubusson in 1758.
MUSEUMS AND GALLERIES:
MOUTIER-ROSEILLE (Church): *Assumption of the Virgin.*

FINET, François II
French, 17th - 18th century.
Born in Aubusson (Creuse).
Painter, draughtsman. History painting. Designs for tapestries.
François Finet II was the father of Gilbert and son of François Finet I, both also painters. He was the pupil of J. Jouvenet in Paris. From the age of 26 Finet was professor of drawing at the school of decorative arts called the Écoles d'Aubusson.
MUSEUMS AND GALLERIES:
GUÉRET: *Jesus Healing the Daughter of Jairus; Jesus Healing the Paralytic.*

FINET, Gilbert
French, 18th century.
Born 1685; died 1745, in Aubusson.
Painter, draughtsman. History painting. Designs for tapestries.
Gilbert Finet was the son of François Pinet II, whom he succeeded as Professor of drawing. He was appointed painter to the king. His works are little known.

FINET, Jean Robert
French, 20th century.
Died December 1947.
Painter.
Jean Finet came first in the Prix de Rome award.

FINETTI, Gino von (Cavaliere)
Italian, 20th century.
Born 9 May 1877, in Pisa.
Active in Germany.
Painter, draughtsman.
Gino von Finetti lived in Berlin, after attending the academy of fine arts in Munich. He worked as an advertising illustrator on the reviews *Die Jugend (Youth)* and *Ulk (Fun).* He exhibited his work in 1906, 1907 and 1912.

FINEZ, Grégoire Nicolas
French, 20th century.
Born 30 October 1884, in St-Saulve-les-Valenciennes (Nord); died 1 June 1975, in Menton.
Painter. Genre scenes, landscapes.
Grégoire Finez studied under Joseph Layraud in Valenciennes and, from 1908, under Fernand Cormon in Paris. He qualified to teach drawing in Paris and regularly exhibited at the Salon des Artistes Français, of which he was an associ-

ate member. He won a third class medal in 1910 and a gold medal in 1940, when he was declared hors concours. He made substantial donations of his works to his native town and to Valenciennes.

Museums and Galleries:
Tours: *Youth* - Valenciennes.

FINGER

German, 18th century.
Active in Berlin.
Painter. Landscapes.

One of Finger's known works is *View of the City of Kiel*, which he exhibited in Berlin in 1791.

FINGERHUTH, Johann Baptist

German, 18th - 19th century.
Born 1774; died 13 May 1836.
Active in Cologne (North Rhine-Westphalia).
Painter.

FINGHIUS, Mei

17th century.
Engraver (burin).

Almost certainly working in about 1660, he is referred to by Nagler as having engraved *The Temptation of St Anthony*.

FINI, Arone

Italian, 16th century.
Born 16th century, in Bornato near Brescia.
Sculptor.

Arone Fini worked on the Palazzo Municipale in Brescia.

FINI, Giuseppe

Italian, 19th century.
Active during the first half of the 19th century.
Painter. History painting.

Museums and Galleries:
Florence (Uffizi): drawing.

FINI, Leonor

Italian, 20th century.
Born 30 August 1908, in Buenos Aires, to Italian parents; died 18 January 1996, in Paris.
Active from 1933, then naturalised in France.
Painter (including gouache), watercolourist, pastellist, engraver, draughtswoman (including ink), illustrator.
Figure compositions, figures, portraits, animals. Stage costumes and sets, screens.
Surrealist group.

Leonor Fini began to paint at a very young age. Her early influences were the painters of the 15th century, and the 16th-century Mannerists, whose languid grace fascinated her as a child, as did the German Romantic painter Caspar David Friedrich. She studied in Trieste, then in Milan, where she was influenced by Carlo Carrà. She began taking part in activities organised by the Surrealist group as early as 1933, in Paris (where she was living) and London; then in New York, Zurich and Brussels, in 1938.

Fini had a penchant for satire and the written word, and was passionate about masks, and so was naturally drawn to the stage. Some of her best work was for the theatre and the ballet: *Leonor's Dream* for the Ballets des Champs-Élysées, in 1945; Wagner's *Tannhäuser*; *The Crystal Palace*, in 1947 at the Paris Opéra; *The Ladies of the Night* in 1948, at Roland Petit's Ballets de Paris; *Berenice* in 1955, for the Jean-Louis Barrault company; and *The Maids* by Jean Genêt, in 1961. She also worked on a film, Castellani's *Romeo and Juliet*, in 1953. She was also an illustrator, watercolourist and engraver. Among other works, she illustrated Shakespeare's *Sonnets* (1949) and *The Tempest* (1965); De Sade's *Juliette* (1944); poems by Edgar Allan Poe, Francis Ponge, Jean Cocteau and others for *Family Portraits* in 1950; *The Story of O* by Pauline Réage (the pseudonym of Dominique Aury) in 1962; and *Les Fleurs du Mal (The Flowers of Evil)*, by Charles Baudelaire, in 1964.

Physically, Fini's works tap into the classical tradition, which is often the case with the Surrealists: according to the precepts of André Breton, their aim was to present photographs of dreams. Her paintings successively featured silhouettes of adolescent girls, fantasy landscapes, bald women, germination (rendered in an almost abstract style), then back to figures again, which are still imbued with a strange atmosphere. When these works clearly and deliberately refer to the fantastic, her recourse to morbid eroticism can sometimes appeare forced. Perhaps the principal quality of her work is the truly disturbing atmosphere she creates, via the antiquated beauty of an age-old technique, and the ambiguous nature of her subjects. The strangely seductive sight of a young ephebe wrapped in fur is accentuated by the manner in which he is rendered: the use of ancient techniques gives him an almost religious quality, while the sumptuous furs and heavy fabrics heighten the stifling climate of the painting. Among her many works, some of the best known are: *The Shepherdess of the Sphinx* (1941); *Portrait of Jean Genêt* (1949-1950); *Spinners* (1954); *Portrait of Sylvia Monfort* (1955); and *The Secret Party* (1965). In the 1970s she produced a series of paintings entitled *Vertigo Games*, about which she wrote: 'In these games the important thing is the loss of consciousness, the happy collapse of the self. The back-and-forth motion of a swing starts with euphoria and laughter, and becomes absence and vertigo, which makes it difficult to stop: this is the attraction of the void.'

Fini took part in the 1936 exhibition *Surrealism* at the Burlington Gallery in London; and the exhibition *Fantastic Art, Dada, Surrealism* at the Museum of Modern Art in New York (also in 1936). Since her death, her work has appeared in various thematic group exhibitions, including: *La Révolution surréaliste* (*The Surrealist Revolution*) at the Pompidou Centre in Paris, in 2002; and *Phantom der Lust. Visionen des Masochismus in der Kunst* (*Phantom of Desire. Visions of Masochism in Art*), an exhibition dedicated to Sacher-Masoch, the originator of the term 'masochism', at the Neue Galerie am Ladesmuseum in Graz.

During her lifetime Fini staged a number of solo exhibitions of her work. After her first solo exhibition in Milan she held another in Paris, in 1932. Next she exhibited in New York, in 1936: Paul Éluard and Giorgio de Chirico wrote the preface to the catalogue. In 1986 there was a complete retospective of her work at the Musée du Luxembourg in Paris, comprising 80 paintings, along with gouaches, drawings, watercolours, books and masks. Since her death there have been several exhibitions devoted to her work: *Regards à la porte de l'insolite* (*Glances through the Door of the Unusual*), at La Malmaison in Cannes, in 2002; *Leonor fini et le portrait* (*Leonor Fini and the Portrait*) followed by *Le vide à l'envers. Peintures, dessins* (*The Upside-Down Void: Paintings and Drawings*), at the Galerie Minsky in Paris, also in 2002; and *Leonor Fini, Théâtre* (*Leonor Fini: Theatre*), at the Galerie Minsky again, in 2003.

Leonor Fini

Bibliography:

Audiberti, Jacques, *Léonor Fini*, Paris, 1950. Pieyre de Mandiargues, André, *Les Masques de Léonor Fini*, A. Bonne, Paris, 1951. Brion, Marcel, *Léonor Fini et son œuvre*, Éd. Jean-Jacques Pauvert, Paris, 1955. Bataille, G., *Les Larmes d'Éros*, Éd. Jean-Jacques Pauvert, Paris, 1961. Brion, Marcel, *L'Art fantastique*, Albin Michel, Paris, 1961. Gauthier, Xavière, *Léonor Fini*, Le Musée de Poche, Paris, 1979. Chadwick, Whitney, *Women Artists and the Surrealist Movement*, Thames and Hudson, London, 1985. Jelenski, C., *Léonor Fini*, exhibition catalogue, Musée d'Art Sogo, Yokohama, November-December 1985. *Léonor Fini*, exhibition catalogue, Editions Michèle Trinckvel, Paris, 1986. Godard, Jocelyne, *Léonor Fini ou les Métamorphoses d'une œuvre*, Le Sémaphore, Paris, 1996. Spies, Werner (ed.), *La Révolution surréaliste*, exhibition catalogue, Éd. du Centre Georges-Pompidou, Paris, 2002. Weibel, Peter (ed.), *'Phantom der Lust. Visionen des Masochismus in der Kunst'* in *2 vol.*, exhibition catalogue, Neue Galerie am Landesmuseum, Graz, Belleville Verlag, Munich, 2003.

Museums and Galleries:

Paris (MNAM-CCI): *Woman Dressed up* - Venice (Collezione Peggy Guggenheim): *The Shepherdess of the Sphinx.*

Auction records:

Paris, 21 June 1960, *Tree*, FRF 850. New York, 23 March 1961, *Roberto*, USD 425. Paris, 14 March 1974, *Portrait of Eddy Brofferio*, FRF 48,000; *Mandilia*, FRF 82,000. Versailles, 18 June 1974, *Swing No 2*, FRF 225,000. London, 4 Dec 1974, *Parcel*, GBP 17,000. Paris, 22 June 1976, *Face* (oil on card, 25 1/4 x 19 3/4 ins / 64 x 50 cm) FRF 19,000. Versailles, 27 Nov 1977, *Gathering of Women* (oil on panel, 63 3/4 x 45 ins / 162 x 114 cm) FRF 33,000. Toulouse, 5 Dec 1977, *Face* (watercolour, 13 1/2 x 9 3/4 ins / 34 x 25 cm) FRF 6,000. Antwerp, 8 May 1979, *Mourmour* (watercolour, 24 3/4 x 19 ins / 63 x 48 cm) BEF 140,000. Enghien-les-Bains, 27 May 1979, *Alice* (pen drawing, 11 3/4 x 15 1/4 ins / 30 x 38.5 cm) FRF 6,500. New York, 2 April 1981, *Head of a Woman* (1948, Indian ink and coloured inks/paper, 12 3/4 x 10 ins / 32.5 x 25.1 cm) USD 2,250. Milan, 24 Oct 1983, *Woman-Lion* (tempera/card, 30 x 22 ins / 76 x 56 cm) ITL 15,000,000. Zurich, 9 Nov 1984, *Head of a Woman* (Indian ink, 25 1/2 x 19 3/4 ins / 65 x 50 cm) CHF 6,000. Enghien-les-Bains, 25 Nov 1984, *Operation II* (1941, oil on canvas, 36 1/4 x 25 1/2 ins / 92 x 65 cm) FRF 235,000. Paris, 26 June 1986, *The Ladies of the Night* (gouache and watercolour/olive green paper, 12 1/2 x 10 ins / 32 x 25.3 cm) FRF 22,000. London, 30 June 1987, *Trying on* (c. 1958, oil on canvas, 46 x 35 ins / 116 x 89 cm) GBP 52,000. Lokeren, 28 May 1988, *Two Figures* (wash, 15 1/2 x 13 ins / 39.5 x 33 cm) BEF 38,000. Paris, 1 June 1988, *Couple* (brown ink, 16 1/2 x 13 3/4 ins / 42 x 35 cm) FRF 6,500. Paris, 12 June 1988, *Female Face* (1945, watercolour and Indian ink/paper, 13 x 9 ins / 33 x 23 cm) FRF 20,000. Paris, 23 June 1988, *Young Woman* (oil on canvas, 28 1/4 x 19 1/4 ins / 72 x 49 cm) FRF 140,000. London, 29 June 1988, *Capital Punishment* (1969, oil on canvas, 47 1/4 x 47 1/4 ins / 120 x 120 cm) GBP 44,000. New York, 6 Oct 1988, *Composition with Figures on a Terrace* (1938, oil on canvas, 39 1/4 x 32 ins / 99.5 x 81 cm) USD 154,000; *Pink Sphinx: Autumn* (watercolour and ink, 11 3/4 x 8 1/2 ins / 30 x 21.5 cm) USD 6,050. London, 19 Oct 1988, *Portrait of Mrs H* (1941, oil on canvas, 7 ins / 18 cm, 3/4 x 5 1/2 ins/2 x 14 cm, 1/2 ins/1 cm) GBP 2,970. London, 29 Nov 1988, *Young Girl in a Green Dress* (oil on canvas, 32 x 26 3/4 ins / 81.3 x 68 cm) GBP 38,500. Paris, 23 Jan 1989, *Portrait of a Young Woman* (watercolour and gouache/bistre-coloured paper, 17 3/4 x 12 1/4 ins / 45 x 31 cm) FRF 22,000. London, 22 Feb 1989, *Elective Antinomies* (1959, oil on canvas, 29 x 20 ins / 73.5 x 50.5 cm) GBP 8,800. Rome, 21 March 1989, *Portrait of a Young Girl* (oil on canvas, 10 1/4 x 9 ins / 26 x 22 cm) ITL 12,000,000. London, 5 April 1989, *Child's Bedroom* (1971, oil on canvas, 51 1/4 x 32 ins / 130 x 81 cm) GBP 49,500. New York, 17 May 1989, *Portrait of a Young Man* (oil on canvas, 16 1/2 x 13 ins / 42 x 33 cm) USD 11,000. Paris, 6 July 1989, *Actors: Hamlet Series* (1954, oil on canvas, 35 1/2 x 28 ins / 90 x 71 cm) FRF 820,000. Paris, 29 Sept 1989, *Three Figures* (pen drawing, 13 3/4 x 10 ins / 35 x 25.5 cm) FRF 12,000. London, 28 Nov 1989, *Owl* (oil on card, 9 1/4 x 6 1/4 ins / 23.7 x 16 cm) GBP 14,300. Milan, 19 Dec 1989, *Small Harbour* (1928, oil on panel, 23 x 25 1/4 ins / 57.5 x 64 cm) ITL 16,000,000. Paris, 22 Jan 1990, *Couple* (Indian ink drawing, 11 3/4 x 9 ins / 30 x 22 cm) FRF 10,500. London, 2 April 1990, *The Four Seasons* (oil on paper/canvas, four panels, each 53 1/4 x 16 ins / 135 x 40.5 cm) GBP 385,000. Paris, 26 April 1990, *Life and Death* (screen, 62 1/4 x 19 ins / 158 x 48 cm) FRF 75,000. Paris, 19 June 1990, *Asphodels* (1966-1967, oil on canvas, 39 1/4 x 25 1/2 ins / 100 x 65 cm) FRF 400,000. Paris, 6 Oct 1990, *Portrait of a Young Woman* (watercolour and pastel, 15 1/4 x 9 ins / 39 x 22 cm) FRF 30,000. Paris, 16 March 1991, *Madame X* (c. 1948-1949, oil on canvas, 36 1/2 x 25 1/2 ins / 93 x 65 cm) FRF 115,000. London, 19 March 1991, *Swing I* (1975, oil on canvas, diam. 46 1/2 ins / 118 cm) GBP 44,000. New York, 9 May 1992, *Ephebe* (watercolour/paper/card, 12 3/4 x 9 1/4 ins / 32.7 x 23.8 cm) USD 990. Lokeren, 5 Dec 1992, *Couple* (watercolour, 14 1/4 x 11 3/4 ins / 36 x 30 cm) BEF 100,000. Sceaux, 13 Dec 1992, *Feminine Dance* (watercolour and gouache, 13 3/4 x 9 1/2 ins / 35 x 24 cm) FRF 7,500. Paris, 28 May 1993, *Portrait of a Woman.* Paris, 28 June 1993, *Painting* (oil on canvas/wood, 67 1/4 x 27 1/2 ins / 171 x 70 cm) FRF 180,000. Lokeren, 9 Oct 1993, *Warrior and Woman* (gouache and pastel, 17 3/4 x 15 ins / 45 x 38 cm) BEF 240,000. Lokeren, 12 March 1994, *Two Figures* (mixed media/oil paint background, 17 1/4 x 14 1/2 ins / 44 x 37 cm) BEF 220,000. Paris, 24 June 1994, *Black Mass* (watercolour, 21 1/4 x 15 3/4 ins / 54 x 40 cm) FRF 11,000. Paris, 18 Oct 1994, *Two Women in Hats* (1960, oil on canvas, 22 x 15 1/2 ins / 55.7 x 39.4 cm) FRF 87,000. Le Touquet, 21 May 1995, *Two Friends* (Indian ink) FRF 5,000. London, 25 Oct 1995, *Portrait of André Pieyre de Mandiargues* (1942, oil on canvas, 13 x 9 ins / 33 x 22 cm) GBP 8,280; *Woman in a Big Hat* (1967, oil on card, 11 x 13 1/2 ins / 27 x 34 cm) GBP 12,075. Zurich, 14 Nov 1995, *Double Constancy* (oil on canvas, 39 1/4 x 25 1/2 ins / 100 x 65 cm) CHF 23,000. Calais, 24 March 1996, *Bird-Woman* (watercolour, 9 x 7 3/4 ins / 22 x 20 cm) FRF 19,000. Paris, 24 May 1996, *Three Faces* (ink and wash, 9 x 7 ins / 22 x 18 cm) FRF 8,000. Amsterdam, 4 June 1996, *Head* (oil/card, 7 3/4 x 6 ins / 20 x 15 cm) NLG 2,714. Paris, 30 Sept 1996, *La Belle Dorothée* (c. 1980, oil on paper/canvas, 15 x 11 ins / 38 x 28 cm) FRF 55,000. New York, 10 Oct 1996, *Portrait of a Woman* (1940, oil on canvas, 8 x 6 1/2 ins / 20.3 x 16.5 cm) USD 8,050. London, 23 Oct 1996, *Figure* (watercolour, pen and ink/paper, 11 x 7 ins / 28 x 18 cm) GBP 1,610. London, 3 Dec 1996, *Sphinx* (oil on paper, 12 1/4 x 16 1/4 ins / 31.1 x 41 cm) GBP 18,400. Lokeren, 8 March 1997, *Two Figures* (watercolour and pastel, 13 x 9 ins / 33 x 23 cm) BEF 65,000; *Romeo and Juliet* (1977, oil on canvas, 16 1/4 x 13 ins / 41 x 33 cm) BEF 240,000. Calais, 23 March 1997, *Dancer* (watercolour, 14 1/4 x 11 3/4 ins / 36 x 30 cm) FRF 11,000. Paris, 4 July 1997, *Fruits of Passion No 3* (gouache/mauve background, 16 1/2 x 13 ins / 42 x 33 cm) FRF 11,800. Paris, 9 March 1998, *Two Young Women* (pen, 11 1/2 x 8 1/4 ins / 29 x 21 cm) FRF 4,000. London, 29 June 1999, *Rasch, Rasch, Rasch* (1975, oil on canvas, 45 x 57 ins / 114 x 146 cm) GBP 60,000. Paris, 30 June 1999, *Comedians* (c. 1954, oil on canvas, 35 x 28 ins / 90 x 71 cm) FRF 250,000. Paris, 21 April 2000, *Cabinet Decorated with Female Birds, with Two Open Doors* (painted box, 87 x 55x14 ins / 220 x 140x36 cm) FRF 240,000. London, 29 June 2000, *Portrait of a Fairy* (oil on canvas, 41 x 21 ins / 103 x 54 cm) GBP 27,000. Paris, 5 Feb 2001, *Game of Truth* (oil on canvas, 35 x 50 ins / 88 x 128 cm) FRF 400,000. Paris, 18 Nov 2001, *Presumed Portrait of Marie-Laure de Noailles with Shellfish* (oil on canvas, 25 x 21 ins / 63 x 53 cm) FRF 300,000. London, 4 Feb 2002, *L'enroulement du silence* (1955, oil on canvas, 24 x 39 ins / 60 x 100 cm) GBP 100,000. London, 20 March 2002, *Black Cat. Pink Cat* (1948, gouache, a pair, 11 x 9 ins / 29 x 22 cm) GBP 9,500. Paris, 12 March 2003, *Self-portrait* (wax pastel, 22 x 21 ins / 57 x 53 cm) EUR 6,500. Paris, 27 Nov 2003, *Mutants* (oil on canvas, 37 x 58 ins / 95 x 147 cm) EUR 78,000. Trieste, 12 May 2004, *Shadows* (oil on canvas, 36 x 24 ins / 92 x 60 cm) EUR 31,000. London, 22 June 2004, *Margot Fonteyn and*

Friend (1948, oil on canvas, 22 x 18 ins / 55 x 46 cm) GBP 50,000.

FINI, Tommaso di Cristoforo. See **MASOLINO DA PANICALE**

FINIGUERRA, Maso or Tommaso

Italian, 15th century.
Born 1426; died 1464.
Goldsmith, sculptor, engraver, draughtsman, watercolourist.

Maso Finiguerra was born into an old and noble Florentine family, and was initially a goldsmith. Vasari in *Lives of the Painters* credits him with the invention of engraving in Italy, in that he was the first to produce proofs on paper of engravings on metal, although critics have challenged this assertion. What is undeniable, however, is that Finiguerra was an associate of Antonio Pollaiuolo and that Zibaldone refers to them about 1459 as master draughtsmen.

A number of important works, in particular the drawings of *St Zenobia between Two Deacons* and the *Virgin with an Angel*, provide evidence of Finiguerra's skill as a draughtsman, while engravings such as the *Crucifixion* and *Coronation of the Virgin* testify to his immense talent in this genre. The Cabinet des Estampes at the Bibliothèque Nationale in Paris has in its prints collection a proof of this extremely rare engraving, discovered there by scholarly biographer Abbé Zani.

Finiguerra's watercolours are reminiscent of the powerful execution and imaginative breadth of Albert Dürer, but are gentler. He also executed low reliefs and religious ornaments for various churches in Florence.

BIBLIOGRAPHY:

Currie, Stuart, *Drawing 1400-1600: Invention and Innovation*, Ashgate, Aldershot, 1998.

MUSEUMS AND GALLERIES:

CAMBRIDGE (Harvard University Art Museums): drawings, n° 1932.124, 1954-9-1, 1954-9-2 - FLORENCE (Uffizi): watercolours - PARIS (BNF, Prints Collection): *Coronation of the Virgin* (engraving).

AUCTION RECORDS:

VERSAILLES, 13 May 1964, *Portrait of a Young Roman*, FRF 10,500. MILAN, 9 April 1970, *Woman Tending Flowers*, ITL 5,200,000. LONDON, 12 Dec 1985, *Man, Seated* (pen and wash, 5¼ x 2½ ins / 13.4 x 6.4 cm) GBP 3,600.

FINK

Austrian, 18th century.
Died towards the middle of the 18th century, in Klausen.
Painter.

This artist was the brother of Bartholomae Fink. He painted animals and popular scenes.

FINK, Adolphe David

French, 19th century.
Born 5 April 1802, in Rouen.
Painter.

Adolphe Fink entered the École des Beaux-Arts on 6 July 1818 and was trained under Girodet Trioson. He exhibited a large number of watercolour and pastel portraits at the Paris Salon from 1833 to 1864.

FINK, Anton

Austrian, 19th century.
Born in Neustiff, near Brixen, South Tyrol (now Bressanone, Italy); died 10 February 1886, in Vienna.
Painter.

Fink worked in Meran, South Tyrol (now Merano, Trentino-Alto Adige, Italy).

MUSEUMS AND GALLERIES:

INNSBRUCK (Tiroler Landesmus. Ferdinandeum): *Portrait of Orientalist P. Pius Zinguerle* - MERANO: *Self-portrait*.

AUCTION RECORDS:

VIENNA, 11 March 1980, *Portrait of Child* (1873, oil on canvas, 17¾ x 14½ ins / 45 x 37 cm) ATS 25,000.

FINK, August

German, 19th century.
Born 30 April 1846, in Munich.
Painter. Landscapes with figures, landscapes.

Fink was a student of Stademann, Ed Schleich and, after 1872, Lier. He also worked with J. Wenglein. In 1889 he became a professor.

MUSEUMS AND GALLERIES:

MUNICH: *Winter Morning; Autumn Evening* - NUREMBERG: *Winter Night with Fox*.

AUCTION RECORDS:

COLOGNE, 27 June 1974, *Autumn Landscape*, DEM 5,500. COLOGNE, 1 June 1978, *Bavarian Landscape* (oil on canvas, 10 x 15¾ ins / 24.5 x 40 cm) DEM 6,500. NEW YORK, 1 March 1984, *Stags in a Winter Landscape* (oil on canvas, 20 x 32 ins / 50.8 x 81.2 cm) USD 1,600. NEW YORK, 24 Feb 1987, *Children Playing in a Winter Landscape* (oil on canvas, 33 x 56¾ ins / 83.8 x 144.1 cm) USD 12,000. HOUSTON, 29 Jan 1999, *Landscape at Dusk with Deer* (oil on canvas, 25 x 37 ins / 64 x 94 cm) USD 1,850. MUNICH, 27 Feb 1999, *Stagnant Water with Drake* (oil on canvas, 36 x 30 ins / 92 x 76 cm) DEM 6,500. HAMBURG, 1 April 2000, *Park of Nymphenburg Castle in the Winter* (oil on canvas, 47 x 67 ins / 120 x 170 cm) DEM 10,000. BERN, 10 May 2000, *Tranquil Winter River Landscape* (oil on canvas, 28 x 35 ins / 70 x 90 cm) CHF 2,600. MUNICH, 25 April 2001, *Wooded Landscape* (oil on canvas, 9 x 15 ins / 24 x 39 cm) DEM 4,200. MUNICH, 26 Sept 2001, *Deer by a Stream* (oil on canvas, 37 x 28 ins / 94 x 70 cm) DEM 3,800.

FINK, Bartholomae

Austrian, 17th - 18th century.
Born in the 17th century, in Innsbruck.
Painter.

Fink was a student of Franz Mez. He worked in Italy and settled in Klausen. He painted altar paintings - one of *St Joseph* in the Capuchin monastery at Klausen, and *Assumption of the Virgin* in the Augustinian monastery at Neustift. *Hercules' Battle with Lernean Hydra* is one of the paintings also owned by this monastery.

FINK, Carl W.E.

German, 19th century.
Born 22 September 1814, in Kassel.
Painter, draughtsman.

Fink was an art teacher in Cologne in 1885. He travelled to Italy and settled in Venice for five years.

FINK, Denman

American, 20th century.
Born 29 August 1880, in Springdale (Pennsylvania); died 1956.
Painter, illustrator.

Denman Fink's work includes illustrations to Mace's *History of the United States*.

FINK, Don

American, 20th century.
Born 1923, in Duluth (Minnesota).
Painter.

Don Fink was a pupil at the Walker Institute, Minneapolis, and the Art Students League, New York. An abstract painter, he was led by Jackson Pollock's example towards a gestural and calligraphic draughtmanship set against monochrome backgrounds.

While in Paris in 1953-1954 he held a solo show, with another in 1955. He took part in several group exhibitions in Paris, including the *Salon des Réalités Nouvelles* in 1957.

AUCTION RECORDS:
PARIS, 27 Oct 1993, *Composition* (1956, oil on canvas, 53 1/2 x 21 1/4 ins / 136 x 54 cm) FRF 3,400. PARIS, 3 April 1998, *Composition* (1961, oil on canvas, 38 1/4 x 51 1/4 ins / 97 x 130 cm) FRF 6,500.

FINK, Eduard
Austrian, 19th century.
Born 1844, in Vienna.
Engraver.
The print collection in Berlin has examples of four engravings known to be by Fink, two of which are small landscapes after Höger.

FINK, Frederick
American, 19th century.
Born 1817, in New York; died 1849.
Painter. Genre scenes.
Frederick Fink worked in New York with Morse. In 1840 he visited Europe, where he copied works by Murillo and Titian. Among his works are *An Artist's Studio* and *Shipwreck*.
AUCTION RECORDS:
NEW YORK, 20 Feb 1930, *Artist in his Studio*, USD 60.

FINK, Friedrich Wilhelm
Austrian, 19th century.
Born 10 October 1796, in Graz; died 22 April 1861, in Bertholdstein (Styria).
Lithographer, engraver.
Fink engraved the portrait of *Albert, Duke of Sachsen-Teschen* and two *Landscapes* after Isabey, *Frederick II on Horseback, Old Man at his Desk* (after C.W.E. Dietrich) and *Dog and Eagle Head* (after Friedrich Gauermann).

FINK, Hans
Austrian.
Sculptor.
An artist working at the court of Vienna, he received a salary for the commission of five heads of Jesus, which he produced for the church of the Capuchins.

FINK, Jakob
German, 19th century.
Born 23 November 1821, in Schwarzenberg (Saxony); died 6 September 1846, in Rome.
Painter.

FINK, Johann
German, 17th century.
Born 20 April 1628, in Freiberg (Saxony); died 10 December 1675, in Dresden.
Painter. History painting, portraits.
Fink travelled in Italy, especially to Naples. He became court painter to the Prince Elector in Dresden. His known works include the altar paintings in the churches at Obernhau and Dippoldiswalde, a picture above the altar in the chapel of the hunting lodge at Moritzberg, *Adam and Eve Driven out of Paradise, Escape to Egypt*, and some portraits of members of the Prince Elector's family.

FINK, Johann Nepomuk
German, 19th century.
Active in Munich during the first half of the 19th century.
Sculptor.
Fink produced crucifixes, statues of saints, and low reliefs of animals in wood and stone.

FINK, Lola
Polish, 20th century.
Born in Jaslo.
Painter.
Lola Fink exhibited at the Salon des Artistes Français in Paris.

FINK, Paul
French, 19th century.
Born in Louviers (Eure).
Draughtsman.
MUSEUMS AND GALLERIES:
LOUVIERS: drawing.

FINK, Tullan
Swedish, 20th century.
Born 1919, in Göteborg; died 4 January 2004, in Göteborg.
Painter.
Tullan Fink was a student at the Valand school of fine art in Göteborg and, during a study trip to Europe, at the Académie de la Grande Chaumière in Paris. She became director of an academy in Göteborg.

In 1962 Tullan Fink took part in an exhibition of work by young Swedish painters in Paris, devoted precisely to the Göteborg School. She held several solo exhibitions in Sweden.

FINK, Waldemar
Swiss, 20th century.
Born 1893, in Bern; died 1948, in Bern.
Painter. Landscapes, mountainscapes, village views.
Waldemar Fink exhibited in Munich in 1909, but resided at Adelboden in Switzerland. He is remembered in particular for one canvas: *Winter Evening in the Valley*.
AUCTION RECORDS:
BERN, 6 May 1981, *Adelboden in Autumn* (1922, oil on canvas, 23 1/2 x 31 1/2 ins / 60 x 80 cm) CHF 700. BERN, 21 Oct 1983, *Autumn Landscape* (1936, oil on canvas, 23 1/2 x 35 1/2 ins / 60 x 90 cm) CHF 1,400. BERN, 30 April 1988, *Mountain Landscape in Mist with a Woman Tending Goats* (oil on canvas, 31 1/2 x 27 1/2 ins / 80 x 70 cm) CHF 2,200. BERN, 26 Oct 1988, *Gsteig about Noon in Winter* (1922, oil on canvas, 24 3/4 x 28 3/4 ins / 63 x 73 cm) CHF 1,000. BERN, 7 May 1999, *View of Lake Champfersee, Silvaplana and Piz de la Margna* (1943, oil on canvas, 24 x 35 ins / 60 x 90 cm) CHF 6,200. BERN, 3 Nov 2000, *Mountain Landscape* (1916-1918, oil on canvas, 25 x 36 ins / 64 x 91 cm) CHF 2,600.

FINKE, Heinrich Jonathan
German, 19th century.
Born 9 April 1816, in Nuremberg; died 9 August 1868, in Altenburg (Saxony).
Painter.
Finke worked initially in Nuremberg, and then in Belgium and Holland. He became a professor in Altenburg.

FINKEL, Joseph
German, 18th century.
Born c. 1760, in Immenstadt (Bavaria).
Painter, engraver. Objets d'art.
Finkel travelled extensively, and mainly painted miniatures for rings, boxes and other decorative objects.

FINKELBURG, Augusta
American, 20th century.
Born in Fountain City (Wisconsin).
Painter. Landscapes.
Augusta Finkelburg was a pupil of the Chicago Art Institute and also studied in Paris, Italy, the Netherlands and England. She was a member of the Saint Louis Artists Guild.

FINKELSTEIN, Louis
American, 20th century.
Born 1923, in New York; died 2000.
Painter.
Louis Finkelstein was a pupil of the Cooper Union Art School, the Art Students League and the Brooklyn Museum Art School. In 1957-1958 he studied in Italy on a Fullbright Scholarship. He held several professorial posts and became

director of the art history department of the Philadelphia School of Art.

He took part in a number of group exhibitions in American museums and Rome, and also held solo shows in New York in 1950, 1953, 1956, 1960, and in Rome in 1958. A posthumous exhibition was held at the New York Studio School in 2002

FINKELSTEIN, Sacha
19th - 20th century.
Born 1895; died 1942.
Painter, draughtsman, illustrator. Landscapes.
School of Murols.

A friend of Victor Charreton, he belonged to the school of Murols, named after a village in the Auvergne where several painters worked between 1910 and 1925. He painted landscape compositions, and also illustrated *A travers le Quartier Latin* (*Through the Latin Quarter*) by Octave Charpentier.

BIBLIOGRAPHY:
Chabrol, Nicolas, *L'École de Murols. Peintres des paysages et des neiges d'Auvergne*, Un, Deux... Quatre Éditions, Clermont-Ferrand, 2001.

AUCTION RECORDS:
VIENNA, 6 Nov 1984, *Azaleas* (oil on canvas, 33 3/4 x 27 1/4 ins / 86 x 69 cm) ATS 13,000. PARIS, 19 March 1993, *Bateau Lavoir* (oil on canvas, 5 x 6 ins / 13 x 15 cm) FRF 5,500. CALAIS, 14 March 1999, *Profile Portrait of an Arab* (watercolour, 8x6 ins / 20x16 cm) FRF 4,000. PARIS, 29 Nov 1999, *Entry into the Mosque* (oil on canvas, 13x18 ins / 33x46 cm) FRF 28,000. BOLTON, 3 Feb 2000, *Middle Eastern Interior with Man and Figures Reading* (oil on canvas, 24x16 ins / 61x41 cm) USD 700.

FINKERNAGEL, E.
German, 19th century.
Active in Munich.
Painter.

Several engravings by Finkernagel are known, including *Shipwreck, Seascape, Torre del Greco near Vesuvius.*

FINKERNAGEL, F. Ph.
German, 19th century.
Born c. 1839, in Darmstadt.
Painter. Seascapes.

MUSEUMS AND GALLERIES:
GDANSK (Muz. Historyczne): *View of Sorrento.*

FINLAY, Ian Hamilton
British, 20th century.
Born 1925, in Nassau, Bahamas.
Sculptor. Artists' books.

Ian Finlay studied in Glasgow, and then moved to the Orkney Islands to work as a shepherd while also writing, mainly modern and concrete poetry. He collaborated on various publications including the *Poor Old Tired Horse*. Finlay's attraction to writing can also be seen in his sculptures: engraved stones, sundials, temples and plaques on which he inscribes wordplays, quotations, hermetic, ironic, violent, subversive and provocative texts, some of a tendentious nature. From 1967 he created a garden Little Sparta, at Stonypath (Dunsyre, Lanarkshire) in which to exhibit his work. He has exhibited widely in both solo and group shows, notably in Scotland. In 2002, he showed his work at Tate St Ives in Cornwall. In 2003, he took part in *Une Collection de 'Chefs-d'œuvre', Emprunts, Pastiches, Copies, Citations et Interprétrations* (*A Collection of 'Masterpieces', Borrowings, Pastiches, Copies, Quotations and Interpretations*), an exhibition exploring the practice of appropriation in art, mainly from the European viewpoint, held at the Fonds Régional d'Art Contemporain in Limoges.

BIBLIOGRAPHY:
Ian Hamilton Finlay, exhibition catalogue, Arts Council of Great Britain, London, 1977. Bann, S., *'A Description of Stonypath'* in *Journal of Gardening History*, vol 1 no. 2, 1981. Abrioux, Y., *Ian Hamilton Finlay: A Visual Primer*, Reaktion, Edinburgh, 1985. Jesse Sheele/Lawson, Andrew, *Little Sparta: The Garden of Ian Hamilton Finlay*, Frances Lincoln, London, 2003.

AUCTION RECORDS:
PARIS, 23 March 1998, *1794, Brevity Ran to Wit (with Richard Grasby)* (1987, engraved stone, 13 1/2 x 18 1/2 x 3 1/4 ins / 34.5 x 47 x 8 cm) FRF 27,000. ZURICH, 15 May 2001, *Pierrot* (metal, 9 x 5x2 ins / 22 x 13x5 cm) CHF 3,600. ZURICH, 15 May 2001, *Barque* (board, 11 x 15x4 ins / 28 x 38x10 cm) CHF 4,000.

FINLAY, Winifred
American, 20th century.
Born in South Orange.
Painter.

Winifred Finlay, a pupil of E. Chimot, exhibited at the Salon des Artistes Français from 1928.

FINLAYSON (Mrs)
British, 18th century.
Active in London.
Painter. Birds.

Mrs Finlayson was the wife of John Finlayson; she exhibited with the Society of Artists and the Free Society from 1762 to 1768.

FINLAYSON, Alfred
British, 19th century.
Painter. Genre scenes, still-lifes.

Alfred Finlayson was active in London, where he exhibited mainly at Suffolk Street and the Royal Academy, from 1857 to 1876.

FINLAYSON, John
British, 18th century.
Born c. 1730; died c. 1776.
Engraver, draughtsman.

John Finlayson was active in London, where he was awarded a prize by the Society of Arts. He produced a number of aquatint portraits and engravings of historical subjects, including: *The Duchess of Gloucester, Lady Charles Spencer* and *Count Buchau* after Sir Joshua Reynolds and *William Drummond* after C. Janssens. He also engraved his own drawing of *Candaules, King of Lydia, Allowing his Favourite Gyges to see the Queen Stepping out of her Bath*. He exhibited in London from 1762 to 1770, notably with the Royal Society of British Artists and the Free Society (of which he was a member). His works are highly sought after.

FINLEY, Chris
American, 20th - 21st century.
Born 1971, in Carmel (California).
Installation artist, draughtsman, painter.

Chris Finley studied at Art Center College of Design where he obtained a BFA in 1993. In 1991 he was the recipient of the Art Center 100 Scholarship, in 1999 he won the Society for the Encouragement of Contemporary Art (SECA) Award and in 2003 the Fleischhacker Award. Finley has taken up a position as Adjunct Professor at San Francisco Art Institute. Finley's first solo exhibition, *Principle Secret*, took place at FOOD HOUSE in Santa Monica in 1993, and was followed by *Double Click* in 1994, also at FOOD HOUSE. He exhibited at ACME in 2000, 2001 and 2003. In 2004 Finley exhibited *fluttersuckers* at the Rena Bransten Gallery in San Francisco. The title *fluttersuckers* referred to moths and ticks. The paintings appeared abstract and with a decorative quality. However their shapes were generated from nine portraits of members of President George W. Bush's cabinet including Colin Powell, Dick Cheney and Donald Rumsfeld. The portraits had been converted into lines with the help of a software program and transferred onto canvas and painted.

Finley has also taken part in numerous group exhibitions, including in 2003, in *Before and After Science* at the Marella Arte Contemporanea in Milan and *Beauty Stripped Bare: LA Black + White* at BGH Gallery in Los Angeles.

BIBLIOGRAPHY:

Duncan, Michael, *'Finley's Fun House'* in *Art in America*, February 1999.

MUSEUMS AND GALLERIES:

GREENSBORO (Weatherspoon AG) - LAGUNA BEACH (Laguna AM) - LOS ANGELES (California State University) - LOS ANGELES (County MA) - LOS ANGELES (MCA) - NEW YORK (MoMA) - NEWPORT BEACH (Orange County MA) - PARIS (MNAM-CCI) - SAN FRANCISCO (MoMA) - SANTA BARBARA (AM, University of California) - SEATTLE (Henry AG, University of Washington) - TEMPE, AZ (AM, Arizona State University).

FINLEY, Ella

American, 19th - 20th century.
Born 1868, in Philadelphia.
Painter.

Ella Finley was a pupil of the Pennsylvania Academy of Fine Arts.

FINLEY, Karen

American, 20th - 21st century.
Born 1964, in East Brunswick (New Jersey).
Installation and performance artist, painter, draughtswoman.

Karen Finley grew up in Chicago but went on to study at San Francisco Art Institute. Finley's work is known for its shocking qualities and its radical tackling of issues surrounded by taboos such as gender issues, women's rights, sexual abuse, AIDS, homelessness, and abuse of power.

In 1990, she produced and performed *We Keep Our Victims Ready*, a reaction to a real-life story of a young woman, Tawana Brawley, who was found, still alive, in a bag covered with faeces in upstate New York. When Brawley was accused of having done this herself, Finley reacted by addressing the issues of victimisation and the desperate situation behind this act. On stage Finley appeared naked but smeared in chocolate to resemble faeces. Finley discusses women's rights in *A Woman's Life isn't Worth Much* (1990), and explores the dynamics of a dysfunctional family in *The Theory of Total Blame* (1989).

Finley became famous in 1990 when she submitted her application for a grant from the National Endowment for the Arts (NEA) and her application, together with three others, was disqualified because it was deemed inappropriate. This prompted the artists to sue but although they won the court case their applications were eventually rejected. As a result part of Finley's work is concerned with the right to free speech and the oppression of certain groups by a political right wing. This brought her into to conflict with politicians such as Jesse Helms, Newt Gingrich, Bill Clinton and Orrie Hatch. Finley addressed this in *Shut Up and Love Me* (1999) performed at the New Conservatory Theater in San Francisco. The public was asked to give a $20 donation as the show was no longer receiving a grant from the NEA.

BIBLIOGRAPHY:

Finley, Karen, *Shock Treatment*, City Lights Books, 1990. Finley, Karen, *A Different Kind of Intimacy: The Collected Writings of Karen Finley*, Thunder's Mouth Press, 2000. Finley, Karen, *Aroused: A Collection of Erotic Writing*, Thunder's Mouth Press, 2001.

MUSEUMS AND GALLERIES:

LOS ANGELES (MOCA): *Black Sheep* (1990, two bronze plaques).

FINN, Herbert John

British, 19th century.
Born 1860.
Painter, watercolourist, engraver.

Herbert Finn studied in Antwerp and was active mainly in London and Folkestone.

MUSEUMS AND GALLERIES:

NOTTINGHAM: *View of Exeter Cathedral.*

AUCTION RECORDS:

LONDON, 13 March 1925, *Pond*, GBP 5. LONDON, 20 March 1925, *Durham Cathedral*, GBP 9. LONDON, 22 April 1927, *Boats in Harbour* (drawing) GBP 5. LONDON, 23 May 1929, *Gloucester Cathedral*, GBP 5; *Gloucester Cathedral*, GBP 4. LONDON, 1 April 1935, *York Minster* (drawing) GBP 4.

FINN, James Wall

American, 20th century.
Active in New York.
Painter.

James Wall Finn was awarded an honourable mention at the Salon de Paris in 1896 and a bronze medal at the Pan-American Exhibition of 1901.

FINNBERG, Gustaf Wilhelm

Finnish, 19th century.
Born 24 November 1784, in Parainen; died 28 June 1883, in Stockholm.
Painter. Portraits.

The museum in Helsinki possesses Gustaf Wilhelm Finnberg's *Portrait of Baron Gustaf Wredes, Portrait of Anton Tengstrom* and *Portrait of M. Lundgren.*

FINNE, Augusta

Norwegian, 19th century.
Born 11 March 1868, in Bergen.
Sculptor.

The museum in Copenhagen possesses two busts by Augusta Finne.

FINNEMORE, Joseph

British, 19th century.
Born 1860, in Birmingham; died 1839.
Painter, watercolourist. History painting, portraits, genre scenes.

Joseph Finnemore travelled and studied extensively in Russia, winning a prize for painting in Odessa. He was a member of the Royal Institute of Painters in Watercolours. He was a regular exhibitor with the Royal Academy in London, and was also active as a manuscript illuminator.

AUCTION RECORDS:

LONDON, 15 May 1984, *Doll* (watercolour, 14 x 19 1/4 ins / 35.5 x 48.8 cm) GBP 500. LONDON, 12 May 1993, *The Proclamation of King Edward VII at St James's Palace in 1901* (oil on panel, 9 x 12 3/4 ins / 23 x 32.5 cm) GBP 1,035.

FINNEY, J.

British, 19th century.
Engraver.

J. Finney is noted for his plates after Rubens and Correggio.

FINNEY, Samuel

British, 18th century.
Born 13 February 1721, in Winslow; died 1798, in Winslow.
Miniaturist.

Samuel Finney exhibited with the Royal Society of British Artists (of which he was a member) from 1761 to 1766, and became court painter to Queen Charlotte.

FINNIE, John

British, 19th - 20th century.
Born 1829, in Aberdeen; died 27 February 1907, in Aberdeen.
Painter, engraver. Genre scenes, landscapes.

John Finnie was an associate member of the Royal Society of Painter-Etchers and a member of the Society of British Artists. He exhibited from 1861 at the Royal Academy, the British Institution and the Suffolk Street Gallery. He also exhibited at the Salon des Artistes Français and received a commendation in 1896.

MUSEUMS AND GALLERIES:

LIVERPOOL: *View of Capel Curig; Welsh Landscape; Moel Siabod, Wales* - NORWICH (Castle Mus. and AG): *A Member of the Naval Reserve; In Tow* (watercolour); *Night Cometh On* (watercolour); *Llyn Idwal, North Wales* (watercolour); *The Lone, Lone Moon* (watercolour); *Off the South Coast* (watercolour).

AUCTION RECORDS:

CHESTER, 9 Dec 1982, *Children's Games* (oil on canvas, 39 1/4 x 27 1/4 ins / 100 x 69 cm) GBP 320. LONDON, 30 March 1994, *View over the Valley* (oil on canvas, 40 x 60 ins / 101.5 x 152.5 cm) GBP 6,670.

FINO DI SAVERIO

Italian, 13th century.
Active in Bologna in 1297.
Illuminator.

FINO DI TEDALDO

Italian, 13th century.
Active in Florence in 1292.
Painter.

FINOCCHIARO, Francesco Paolo

Italian, 19th - 20th century.
Born in Randazzo, near Messina (Sicily).
Painter.

Finocchiaro lived in Paris and in America, where he painted a portrait of *President Theodore Roosevelt.*

FINOGLIA, Paolo Domenico

Italian, 17th century.
Born 1590, in Orte; died probably in 1656, in Naples.
Painter, draughtsman. Religious subjects.

Paolo Domenico Finoglia studied under Massino Stanzioni and painted mainly in the manner of Spagnoletto. His draughtsmanship was held in some esteem in his day.

MUSEUMS AND GALLERIES:

NAPLES: *St Bruno* - NAPLES (Capitole): ten oil paintings - NAPLES (Convent of S Martino): *Life of St Martin* - STRASBOURG: *St Bruno.*

AUCTION RECORDS:

NEW YORK, 17 April 1986, *Tobias Curing his Father's Blindness* (oil on canvas, 51 1/2 x 63 1/2 ins / 131 x 161 cm) USD 45,000. LUGANO, 16 May 1992, *St John the Baptist* (oil on canvas, 24 3/4 x 30 1/4 ins / 63 x 77 cm) CHF 24,000. ROME, 29-30 Nov 1993, *Salome* (oil on canvas, 41 x 59 3/4 ins / 104 x 152 cm) ITL 20,035,000.

FINOT

French, 18th - 19th century.
Active in Paris.
Miniaturist.

Finot exhibited at the Salon in 1814.

FINOT

French, 18th - 19th century.
Active in Vic-en-Bigorre.
Painter.

Finot exhibited landscapes in pen and ink in Toulouse in 1835.

FINOT, Adèle (Mme)

French.
Painter. Urban landscapes.

MUSEUMS AND GALLERIES:

BAYONNE: *The Town Gates.*

FINOT, Alfred

French, 20th century.
Born 13 October 1876, in Nancy; died 11 January 1947, in Nancy.
Sculptor. Groups.

Alfred Finot studied under Louis Barrias. He exhibited in Paris at the Salon des Artistes Français, of which he was an associate member. In 1935, he showed *The Kiss,* a bronze group. He gained an honourable mention in 1908.

AUCTION RECORDS:

PARIS, 18 June 1981, *Dawn* (white marble, 35 3/4 x 13 1/2 x 9 ins / 91 x 34 x 23 cm) FRF 16,000.

FINOT, Jules (Baron)

French, 19th century.
Born 1826, in Guéret (Creuse); died 1906.
Painter, watercolourist. Hunting scenes, landscapes, landscapes with figures, animals.

Finot was a pupil of Auguste Delacroix and exhibited at the Paris Salon from 1857 to 1882. He produced many watercolours: landscapes, especially hunting scenes and racehorses, which demonstrate his knowledge of anatomy. Works include *Chantilly Races, Derby, Périgueux Racecourse* and *1859 Races at the Bois de Boulogne.* A retrospective exhibition of his work was held at the International Museum of Hunting at Gien in France in 2002.

AUCTION RECORDS:

PARIS, 6 May 1925, *In the Forest in Winter* (watercolour) FRF 90. PARIS, 25 May 1932, *Racehorse in his Box* (gouache) FRF 320; *Return of the Racehorses to the Stable,* FRF 430; *Ponds at Fay,* FRF 420; *Men and Women Riding in the Forest,* FRF 420. PARIS, 19 June 1933, *Flooded Meadows* (watercolour and gouache) FRF 50. PARIS, 4 April 1941, *Hunting Scenes* (five watercolours heightened with gouache) FRF 650. PARIS, July 1946, *At the Trainer's,* FRF 2,400. PARIS, 21 Jan 1947, *Hunting Scene* (watercolour) FRF 4,000. VERSAILLES, 21 Nov 1971, *Hunting Scenes* (1888, two watercolours) FRF 1,400. PARIS, 29 April 1981, *Return from Hunting* (oil on canvas, 20 x 32 1/2 ins / 51 x 82.5 cm) GBP 260. PARIS, 31 Jan 1983, *The Meet* (1897, oil on panel, 6 1/2 x 9 1/4 ins / 16.5 x 23.5 cm) FRF 9,000. PARIS, 20 June 1994, *Horses Warming up before the Race* (1894, watercolour) FRF 12,000. NEUILLY, 22 June 1999, *Hunting with Hounds* (1895, gouache, a pair, 4 x 6 ins / 9 x 15 cm) FRF 11,200. PARIS, 15 Oct 2001, *Huntsmen on Horses Dominating the Valley* (watercolour/gouache/grisaille, 2 x 4 ins / 5 x 9 cm) FRF 13,000. PARIS, 21 Oct 2001, *Valet de chiens* (watercolour/gouache, 12 x 8 ins / 30 x 21 cm) FRF 27,000. VERNOU EN SOLOGNE, 3 Feb 2002, *View* (gouache, 3 x 4 ins / 7 x 11 cm) EUR 5,900.

FINOTTI, Antonio Maria

Italian, 16th century.
Active in Ferrara in 1568.
Painter.

FINSINGER, Ehrenfried

German, 18th century.
Active in Plön (Schleswig-Holstein).
Painter.

FINSLER, Helias

Swiss, 16th century.
Died 1578, in Zurich.
Painter.

FINSLER, Konrad

Swiss, 16th century.
Active in Biel (Bern canton) towards the end of the 16th century.
Glass painter.

Konrad Finsler executed various works for buildings in Biel between 1589 and 1595.

FINSON

French, 16th century.
Painter. History painting.

Siret says that this artist painted the large painting of St-Trophime of Arles in Avignon. It is possible that he is the same person as Jacques Fynson.

FINSON, David
Dutch, 17th century.
Born c. 1597, in Amsterdam.
Painter. Figure compositions, portraits.

David Finson was apparently the nephew of Louis and the brother of Pieter Finson.

AUCTION RECORDS:
MONACO, 21 June 1991, *Scene of Life in Troy* (1642, oil on canvas, 55 1/4 x 88 1/4 ins / 140.5 x 224 cm) FRF 72,150.

FINSON, Jacques, or Fynson, Finsonius
Flemish School, 16th century.
Active in Bruges c. 1560.
Decorative artist.
Bruges School.

This artist was the father of Louis Finsonius. He was received as a master of the Bruges guild on 6 April 1560.

FINSON, Ludovicus or Louis, or Fynson, Finsonius
Flemish, 17th century.
Born between 1575 and 1580, in Bruges; died 1617, in Amsterdam.
Active in France.
Painter. Religious subjects, portraits.
Provencal School, Flemish School.

Ludovicus Finson visited Italy and worked in Naples under the guidance of Caravaggio, settling around 1609 in Aix-en-Provence, where he exhibited his works in the Peiresc gallery. His pupils included Mimault, Bigot and Fauchier. His monogram was *Ludovicus Finsonius Belga Brugensis* (*Ludovicus Finsonius Belgian of Bruges*). He painted portraits, such as *Portrait of Peiresc* (1613), which was reproduced as an engraving by Claude Mellan, and a portrait of *Du Vair* (another magistrate from Provence who entered the Church and died as Bishop of Lisieux). This painting was a gift from Du Vair to Peiresc and the latter inscribed the following line on the frame: 'Non alia melius pingetur magine virtus' (virtue cannot be better portrayed in any other guise). Finson also produced paintings for churches. His first work known in Aix is a *Resurrection* in the church of St-Jean-de-Malte, dated 1610, which evinces his emulation of the Venetians rather than Caravaggio, as is the case in his *Penitent Magdalene* (1613). Also noteworthy are *The Incredulity of St Thomas* for the cathedral of St-Saveur in Aix-en-Provence, *The Martyrdom of St Stephen*, and *The Adoration of the Magi* for St-Trophime in Arles. A remarkable painting in the still-life genre, *Flautist*, which had been wrongly attributed to Velázquez, has been ascribed to Ludovicus. He exerted a considerable influence on Provençal painting, infusing it with the realism which he had inherited from his master.

L. dla finso pin.

MUSEUMS AND GALLERIES:
AIX-EN-PROVENCE (Bibliothèque Méjanes): *Portrait of Du Vair* - AIX-EN-PROVENCE (Mus. Granet): *Portrait of Raymond d'Espagnet, Councillor in the Aix Parliament* - MARSEILLES (Mus. Longchamp): *Magdalene in Ecstasy* - NAPLES (Mus. di Capodimonte): *Annunciation*.

AUCTION RECORDS:
LONDON, 26 June 1930, *David and Goliath*, GBP 33. LONDON, 23 Oct 1941, *Susanna and the Elders*, GBP 63. PARIS, 23 June 1964, *The Annunciation*, FRF 18,000. BOURG-EN-BRESSE, 12 April 1987, *Magdalene in Ecstacy* (1613, oil on canvas, 44 x 34 1/4 ins / 112 x 87 cm) FRF 220,000. LONDON, 18 Oct 1995, *Cain Killing Abel* (oil on canvas, 54 1/4 x 41 1/4 ins / 138 x 104.5 cm) GBP 4,025. LONDON, 30 Oct 1996, *Cain Killing Abel* (oil on canvas, 54 1/4 x 41 1/4 ins / 138 x 104.5 cm) GBP 3,795. LONDON, 7 July 2004, *Triumph of David over Goliath* (oil on panel, 44 x 32 ins / 113 x 82 cm) GBP 25,000.

FINSON, Pieter
Dutch, 17th century.
Active in Delfshaven, c. 1632.
Painter.

Pieter Finson was the brother of David Finson and qualified as a free master in Delft on 12 November 1632.

FINSTER, Howard
American, 20th century.
Born 1916, in Alabama; died 2001, in Georgia.
Painter.

Howard Finster was a preacher until the age of 60, when he started to paint what he called 'sacred art'. By the time he died in 2001 he is reputed to have created some 50,000 original artworks. Executed in a naive, folk-art way, these range from wooden cut-out figures, including icons such as Elvis Presley, Billy Graham and Leonaro da Vinci, to record sleeves and book illustrations, some with brightly coloured written messages. He dated and numbered each one.

AUCTION RECORDS:
NEW YORK, 7 May 1991, *Stay Off the Cocaine* (1988, acrylic/panel, 17 1/4 x 17 ins / 43.8 x 43.1 cm; *Coca-Cola* (1988, acrylic/panel, 34 x 10 x 1/2 ins / 86.4 x 25.3 x 1 cm) USD 2,420. NEW YORK, 9 May 1992, *Informers* (1981, varnish/panel framed by the artist, 20 x 39 ins / 50.8 x 99 cm) USD 2,200. NEW YORK, 17 Nov 1992, *Angel* (1976, oil and felts/panel, 11 3/4 x 50 3/4 ins / 29.8 x 129 cm) USD 1,100. NEW YORK, 22 Feb 1993, *City of Salcona* (oil and felt pens/panel framed by the artist, 17 1/2 x 22 ins / 44.4 x 55.9 cm) USD 990. NEW YORK, 8 Nov 1993, *Howard's Hand* (lacquer/plaster, 7 1/2 x 5 3/4 x 1 ins / 19 x 14.5 x 2.5 cm) USD 1,265. NEW YORK, 23 Feb 1994, *Black Panther* (1976, oil and black felt/panel, 11 3/4 x 27 1/4 x 3 1/2 ins / 29.9 x 69.2 x 9.2 cm) USD 1,150. NEW YORK, 7 May 1996, *Without God They Lost it All* (1988, oil on cut panel, 11 1/2 x 26 1/2 ins / 29.2 x 67.3 cm) USD 2,070. NEW YORK, 20 Feb 2001, *Snakes of Orpichili and Happy People* (enamel on panel, 13 x 17 ins / 34 x 44 cm) USD 5,000. BUFORD, 15 Nov 2003, *A Small Corner of the World's Last War* (household paint on fibreboard, 19 x 36 ins / 48 x 91 cm) USD 4,600. BUFORD, 15 Nov 2003, *Jesus Take a Fig Tree* (oil on board, 16 x 13 ins / 41 x 33 cm) USD 6,500. BUFORD, 24 April 2004, *Little Town of Love and Peace* (painted wood and mirror, sculpture, 17 x 13 ins / 43 x 33 cm) USD 3,000. BUFORD, 24 April 2004, *Angels of the Sacred Clouds* (1981, oil on board, 43 x 43 ins / 109 x 109 cm) USD 16,000.

FINSTERWALDER, Johann Jakob
German, 19th century.
Born 1787, in Frankfurt am Main; died 1839.
Painter.

Finsterwalder worked for a long time in the studios of J.A.B. Reges and J.D. Scheel.

FINSTERWALDER, Mathias
German, 18th century.
Active in Frankfurt am Main c. 1760.
Painter.

FINTA, Alexander
Hungarian, 20th century.
Born 12 June 1881, in Túrkeve.
Sculptor.

A member of the American Federation of Arts, Alexandra Finta executed commemorative monuments in Czechoslovakia, Brooklyn and Rio de Janeiro.

FINTBONER, Hans
German, 15th century.
Active in Isny c. 1435.
Sculptor (wood).

FINZI, A.
Painter. Landscapes.
AUCTION RECORDS:
MILAN, 30 Nov 1933, *Roman Countryside*, ITL 2,200.

FIOCCHI, Alexandre
French, 19th century.
Born 1803, in Paris.
Miniaturist.
Fiocchi was of Italian origin.
MUSEUMS AND GALLERIES:
LONDON (Wallace Collection): *Portrait of Mlle Henriette Sontag* - ROCHEFORT: *Portrait of Empress Eugenie* (after Winterhalter).

FIODOROV, Aleksei
Russian, 20th century.
Born 1927, in Leningrad (now St Petersburg).
Painter. Figure compositions, figures.
Socialist Realism.
Aleksei Fiodorov began studying art at the Tavritcheskiy school in Leningrad (now St Petersburg), then worked under V.M. Orechnikov at the Ilya Repin Institute in Leningrad. He became a member of the Association of Painters in Leningrad.

He painted subjects in keeping with the glorification of the beneficial effects of the Soviet system extolled by the so-called authorities on the arts in the most academic tradition of the 19th century.
MUSEUMS AND GALLERIES:
MOSCOW (Ministry of Culture) - NOVGOROD (MFA) - ST PETERSBURG (Academy) - ST PETERSBURG (City History Museum).
AUCTION RECORDS:
PARIS, 18 Feb 1991, *Tugs on the Neva* (oil on canvas, 16 1/4 x 37 1/2 ins / 41 x 95 cm) FRF 8,500; *Technical Meeting* (1952, oil on canvas, 19 3/4 x 30 ins / 50 x 76 cm) FRF 13,500. PARIS, 26 April 1991, *The Turner* (1954, oil on canvas, 29 1/4 x 45 ins / 74.5 x 114 cm) FRF 5,200. PARIS, 29 Nov 1993, *White Nights* (1957, oil on canvas, 15 1/4 x 30 1/4 ins / 39 x 77 cm) FRF 6,100.

FIOL, Jan
Polish, 16th century.
Active in Cracow c. 1554.
Painter.

FIOLER, Adriaan
Dutch, 15th century.
Active in 's Hertogenbosch at the end of the 15th century.
Sculptor.

FIONDI, Francesco
Italian, 17th century.
Active in Naples in 1618.
Sculptor.

FIOR, Adam
French, 17th century.
Born c. 1648, in Valenciennes; died 1709, in Valenciennes.
Sculptor.
Adam Fior was the father of Jean Michel Fior.

FIOR, André Joseph
French, 18th century.
Active in Valenciennes.
Sculptor.
André Joseph Fior was the son and pupil of Jean Michel Fior.

FIOR, Jean Michel
French, 18th century.
Born 29 September 1678, in Valenciennes; died 20 May 1755.
Sculptor.
Jean Michel Fior worked for churches in Valenciennes.

FIOR, Joseph
French, 18th century.
Born 4 March 1696, in Valenciennes; died 23 March 1748.
Sculptor.
Joseph Fior was the brother and pupil of Jean Michel Fior. He collaborated with him.

FIOR, Philippe André
French, 18th century.
Born probably in 1711; died 27 March 1783, in Valenciennes.
Active in Valenciennes.
Sculptor.
Philippe André Fior was the son and pupil of Jean Michel Fior.

FIORANI, Illuminato
Italian, 18th century.
Born 1766, in San Severino; died 1790, in Lisbon.
Painter, sculptor.
A *Laocoön* by Illuminato Fiorani is preserved in the Palazzo Bellisomi in Pavia.

FIORAVANTE, Bolcioni
Italian, 20th century.
Born in Marseilles, France, to Italian parents.
Painter.
Fioravante exhibited at the Salon des Artistes Indépendants in Paris in 1925.

FIORAVANTE D'ANDREA
Italian, 15th century.
Active in Perugia in 1434.
Painter.

FIORAVANTI, Benedetto
Italian, 17th century.
Painter. Still-lifes (including flowers/fruit).
Benedetto Fioravanti painted still-lifes and inanimate objects. He excelled at exact and faithful representations of musical instruments, vases, flowers and fruit.
AUCTION RECORDS:
ROME, 22 March 1988, *Easter Repast in Rome: Vase of Flowers* (oil on canvas, 28 3/4 x 39 1/4 ins / 73 x 100 cm) ITL 16,000,000. PARIS, 10 April 1992, *Still-life with Fruit and Items of Jewellery* (oil on canvas, 25 1/4 x 46 3/4 ins / 64 x 119 cm) FRF 75,000.

FIORAVANTI, José
Argentinian, 20th century.
Born 1896, in Argentina; died 1977, in Buenos Aires.
Sculptor. Monuments.
José Fioravanti was awarded a gold medal at the international exhibition in Paris in 1937. He is responsible for producing some of Argentina's most important monuments.

FIORAVANTI, Neri
Italian, 14th century.
Active in Florence.
Architect, sculptor.
Neri Fioravanti is said on occasion to have decorated some of his own buildings.

FIORAVANTI, Ridolfo
Italian, 15th century.
Born 1415, in Bologna; died 1485 or 1486, in Moscow.
Architect, founder, medallist.
Rodolfo Fioravanti, a polymath, is known chiefly for having constructed, from 1475 to 1479, the Dormition cathedral inside the Kremlin, which despite its five gilded cupolas retains an essential simplicity.

FIORE, Angelo Agnello del
Italian, 15th century.
Born 15th century, in Naples.
Sculptor, architect.
Angelo Agnello del Fiore is noted for several remarkable works in Naples, in particular the tombs of Cardinal Rinaldo Piscinello in the cathedral and of Jean Cianello in the church of S Lorenzo, and various other mausoleums. His masterpiece is the tomb of Francesco Caraffa in the church of S Domenico Maggiore.

FIORE, Antonio del
Italian, 16th century.
Painter. Religious subjects.
Antonio del Fiore painted *St Charles Borromeo* for the cathedral in Lecce at the beginning of the 16th century.

FIORE, Christian
French, 20th century.
Born 1 October 1945, in Bodo-Diulasso, Upper Volta.
Painter.
Christian Fiore's canvases combine action painting with a relief style. He has taken part in exhibitions since 1972.

FIORE, Daniele del
Italian, 16th century.
Active in Venice in 1514.
Painter.

FIORE, Francesco del
Italian, 14th century.
Died c. 1400.
Active in Venice.
Painter.
The identity of Francesco del Fiore's master is unknown. None of his work survives in Venice; all that remains is his tomb in the church of SS Giovanni e Paulo. A diptych signed by him and dated 1412 was bought by a nobleman by the name of Strangt in London. He was the father of Jacobello and Niccolo del Fiore.

FIORE, Georga Eleanora
American, 20th century.
Born in Philadelphia.
Sculptor.
Georga Eleanora Fiore, a pupil of Frank B.A. Linton, exhibited a bronze bust in 1934 at the Salon des Artistes Français, Paris.

FIORE, Giovan Antonio del
Italian, 15th century.
Died c. 1506.
Active in Venice.
Painter.
Giovan Antonio del Fiore was the father of Lodovico Fiore.

FIORE, Jacobello del
Italian, 14th - 15th century.
Born c. 1370, in Venice; died 1439, in Venice.
Painter. Religious subjects.
Venetian School.
The son of Francesco del Fiore, Jacobello del Fiore served as senior master of the guild from 1415 to 1436, and was an important figure in Venice. In 1421, he was commissioned to paint *Justice between St Michael and St Gabriel* for the tribunal of Poprio.

Works painted during his youth in churches in Pisa have disappeared, and his earliest dated picture is the triptych *Madonna of Mercy* (1407). Jacobello del Fiore retained his rich Byzantine colouring while moving stylistically in the direction of the International Gothic in the manner of Gentile da Fabriano, who influenced his final works.

BIBLIOGRAPHY:
Muraro, Michelangelo, '*Affreschi di Nicolò di Pietro e di Jacobello del Fiore a Serravalle*' in *Rivista d'arte*, vol 30, 1955. Huter, Carl, '*Jacobello del Fiore, Giambono and the St. Benedict panels*' in *Arte Veneta, 32*, 1978. Lucco, M., '*Venetia 1400-1430*' in *La pittura nel Veneto: Il quattrocento*, Electa, Milan, 1989.
MUSEUMS AND GALLERIES:
AVIGNON (Mus. Calvet): *Virgin Suckling the Infant Jesus* - BERGAMO (Accademia Carrara, Pinacoteca d'Arte Antica): six religious paintings; *Virgin and Child* - CENEDA (Cathedral): *Coronation of the Virgin* (1438) - FERMO (Pinacoteca Civica): Scenes from the life of St Lucy - MILAN (Pinacoteca di Brera): *Madonna Adoring Jesus* - PESARO (Mus. Civico): polyptych, attributed - STOCKHOLM: triptych - STUTTGART: *Tiburtine Sibyl Revealing the Virgin to Augustus* - VENICE (Gal. Reale): *Justice; Virgin and Child* - VENICE (Mus. Correr): *Madonna* - VENICE (Palazzo Ducale): *Doge Loredano at the Feet of the Virgin; Paradise; Winged Lion of St Mark* (1415).
AUCTION RECORDS:
LONDON, 14 Dec 1907, *St Cyrus and St Paul*, GBP 17. BERLIN, 20 Sept 1930, *Virgin and Child*, DEM 5,500. LONDON, 8 July 1938, *Madonna Suckling the Infant Jesus*, GBP 63. LUCERNE, 21-27 Nov 1961, *Virgin and Child*, CHF 12,000. MILAN, 19 Nov 1963, *Crucifixion* (tempera/wood) ITL 4,200,000. MILAN, 6 April 1965, *Bishop Saint* (tempera/wood) ITL 2,200,000. LONDON, 25 March 1977, *Virgin and Child* (oil on panel, 21 1/2 x 17 ins / 54.5 x 43 cm) GBP 9,000. LONDON, 1 Nov 1978, *Virgin and Child* (oil on panel with gold ground, 11 3/4 x 18 1/2 ins / 30 x 47 cm) GBP 38,000. LONDON, 10 July 1981, *Virgin and Child* (oil and gold background/panel, curved façade, 21 1/2 x 17 ins / 54.6 x 43.2 cm) GBP 5,500. NEW YORK, 17 Jan 1985, *Madonna of Humility* (oil on panel with gold background, 22 1/4 x 18 ins / 56.5 x 46 cm) USD 13,000. NEW YORK, 21 May 1992, *Madonna of Humility* (tempera/paper with gold background, 25 x 17 1/4 ins / 63.3 x 43.9 cm) USD 77,000. LONDON, 3 July 1997, *Madonna of Humility with Two Saints and the Holy Trinity Above; Holy Bishop with St Mary Magdalene* (tempera/panel, gold ground, polyptych, 16 1/2 x 7 1/4 ins / 42 x 18.4 cm and 15 3/4 x 3 1/2 ins/40 x 8.6 cm) GBP 62,000. MILAN, 24 Nov 1999, *Madonna and Child* (tempera on panel, 25 x 18 ins / 63 x 45 cm) ITL 100,000,000. MILAN, 13 June 2001, *Crucifixion* (tempera on board, 19 x 13 ins / 48 x 34 cm) ITL 240,000,000.

FIORE, Lodovico
Italian, 16th century.
Active in Venice c. 1506.
Painter.
Lodovico Fiore was the son of Giovan Antonio del Fiore.

FIORE, Marzio. See **COLANTONIO Marzio de**

FIORE, Niccolo del
Italian, 13th - 14th century.
Active in Venice.
Painter.
Niccolo del Fiore was the brother of Jacobello del Fiore.

FIORELLI, Francesco
Italian, 17th century.
Born to a family originally from Fermo.
Active in Ascoli Piceno and Fermo.
Painter.
Francesco Fiorelli studied under Sacchi.

FIORELLI, Rodrigo
Italian, 19th century.
Born in Naples; died 1 October 1865, in Naples.
Painter. Landscapes.
Rodrigo Fiorelli worked in Rome, where he was friends with Morelli, Vertunni and Celentano. He also exhibited in Florence.

FIORENTINI, Aurelia
Italian, 17th century.
Born 1595, in Lucca.
Painter.
Aurelia Fiorentini took holy orders and became a Dominican nun, working in the convent of S Domenico in Lucca.

FIORENTINI, Domenico Antonio
Italian, 17th century.
Active in Rome.
Painter.
Domenico Antonio Fiorentini painted a *Life of St Francis* for the church of S Bartolomeo all'Isola.

FIORENTINI, Francesco
Italian, 18th century.
Active in Forlì c. 1700.
Painter. History painting.
Francesco Fiorentini was a priest and a pupil of C. Cignani.

FIORENTINI, Giacinto
Italian, 16th - 17th century.
Born 1564; died 1623.
Active in Piacenza.
Sculptor.
Giacinto Fiorentini sculpted the monumental statues of the *Tomb of Margaret of Austria,* aunt of Charles V.

FIORENTINI, Lorenzo
Italian, 17th century.
Born 1580, in Borgo Valsugana; died 4 July 1644.
Miniaturist.

FIORENTINI, Lorenzo
Austrian, 17th century.
Active in Innsbruck in 1666.
Miniaturist.
Fiorentini may have been related to the previous artist. Works attributed to him include portraits of Empress Marguerite of Austria and the archduke Sigismund Freund.

FIORENTINI, Orazio
Italian, 17th century.
Active in Carpi in 1615.
Painter.
Orazio Fiorentini is believed to have still been active as late as 1664.

FIORENTINI, Paola
Italian, 20th century.
Born in the 20th century, in Rome.
Active in France from 1956.
Painter. Still-lifes.
Paola Fiorentini studied at the academy of fine arts in Rome. She moved to France in 1956, and exhibited at the Salon des Artistes Indépendants in Paris.

FIORENTINO. See also first name

FIORENTINO, Jacopo
Italian, 16th century.
Active at the beginning of the 16th century.
Painter, engraver.
Jacopo Fiorentino engraved religious and genre subjects. He is associated with Francesco dell'Indaco.

FIORENTINO, Luca
Italian, 16th century.
Active at the beginning of the 16th century.
Engraver.
Luca Fiorentino, who as an engraver was also known as Luca A. De Giunta, adopted the style of Robetta. His best works include *Herod with the Head of St John the Baptist, Man with a Young Boy* and *Virgin, Child, St Anthony and St Francis.*

FIORENTINO, Pier Francesco. See **PIER FRANCESCO FIORENTINO**

FIORENTINO, Stefano. See **STEFANO FIORENTINO**

FIORENZA
Italian, 9th century.
Active in Florence.
Sculptor.

FIORENZO DI BARNABEO DI MAGIO
Italian, 15th century.
Died 1462, in Perugia.
Painter.
Fiorenzo di Barnabeo di Magio worked on the cathedral and Palazzo Pubblico in Perugia.

FIORENZO DI LORENZO
Italian, 15th - 16th century.
Born c. 1445, in Perugia; died c. 1525, in Perugia.
Painter, fresco artist. History painting, religious subjects.
Perugian School.
Nobody knows who taught Fiorenzo di Lorenzo the art of painting, but his name appears on the register of the guild of painters in Perugia. In addition, Mariotti tells us that in 1472 Fiorenzo was a member of the decemvirate there. In 1499, Bartolommeo Caporali and Fiorenzo were commissioned to value a fresco by Giannicola Manni, which is still in Perugia. In a legal instrument dated 9 December 1492 between the convent of St Sylvester in Perugia and Fiorenzo, he undertook to paint, for 225 ducats, a large picture consisting, on one side, of an *Assumption of the Virgin* with Saints Peter, Paul, Benedict and Sylvester, and, on the other, a *Madonna and Child* with Sts Jerome, Ambrose, Nicholas, Paulinus, the twelve apostles and a host of other figures. This work was executed, but its whereabouts is unknown. After 1488, Fiorenzo di Lorenzo is known to have painted, with Eusebio di San Giorgio, banners for the trumpets of Perugia, and in 1521 he was called upon to value the work of a painter named Giacomo di Guglielmo.

The Virgin in the museum in Perugia has a slender neck and small hands, and, in retrospect, the treatment of the angels foreshadows Perugino. As a result, it has been assumed in some quarters that Perugino was a pupil of Fiorenzo, thus elevating the latter to one of the great names in the Umbrian School; it is, however, difficult to arrive at a soundly based judgement of his style and talent, given the small number of authenticated works that survive.

The only known inscription mentioning Fiorenzo di Lorenzo is on one of the fragments of a large picture in the sacristy of the Franciscan church in Perugia; it appears on the border of the cloaks worn by the apostles St Peter and St Paul: *florentius laurenti pinxit mccccIxxxviii* (1488); the fabric is carefully draped and arranged in precise and regular folds. A fresco in the land registry in the Palazzo Pubblico in Perugia depicting a *Madonna and Two Angels* is attributed to Fiorenzo on the basis of its general style, as is another fresco, *Eternal Father between St Romanus and St Roch,* in San Francisco de Diruta.

BIBLIOGRAPHY:
Graham, J.C., *The Problem of Fiorenzo di Lorenzo,* Loescher and Co, Rome, 1903. Santi, F., *La Galleria Nazionale dell'Umbria: Dipinti, sculture ed oggetti dei secoli XV-XVI,* Istituto poligrafico e Zecca dello Stato, Libreria dello Stato, Rome, 1985. Todini, F., *La pittura umbra: Dal duecento al primo*

cinquecento, Longanesi, Milan, 1989. Bury, M., *'Bartolomeo Caporali: A New Document and its Implications'* in *Burlington Magazine*, vol 132, 1990.

Museums and Galleries:

Berlin: *Mary and the Infant Jesus* - Perugia: *Virgin; Saints* (painting /gold background); *Annunciation; St Sebastian; Eternal Father* - Perugia (Augustinian Church): *Virgin and Child in a Garland of Flowers* - Perugia (Palazzo Pubblico): *Madonna and Two Angels* (fresco) - Perugia (Sacristy of the Franciscan Church): *St Peter and St Paul.*

Auction records:

Paris, 19-20 April 1921, *St Sebastian* (school of Fiorenzo di Lorenzo) FRF 1,300. London, 16 March 1924, *Roman Warrior*, GBP 57. Paris, 16 May 1924, *Portrait of a Man* (attributed) FRF 380. Paris, 10-11 May 1926, *Two Warriors Leading a Martyr and Three Figures* (pen) FRF 1,550. London, 23 June 1934, *St Jerome in the Desert*, GBP 17. London, 10 Dec 1937, *Coronation of the Virgin*, GBP 483. New York, 15 Jan 1988, *Virgin and Child in a Garland of Seraphim* (oil on panel, 28 1/4 x 29 ins / 72 x 73.5 cm) USD 12,100. London, 7 July 1989, *Virgin and Child* (oil on panel, 11 x 9 ins / 28 x 22 cm) GBP 35,200.

FIORI, Carlo de'. See **VOGELAER Karel Van**

FIORI, Cesare

Italian, 17th century.
Born 1636, in Milan; died 1702, in Milan.
Painter, engraver, architect. Portraits.

Cesare Fiori was a pupil of Carlo Cane. He painted a *Portrait of Abbé Boisol*, founder of the library of Besançon.

Cesar fior.

Museums and Galleries:

Besançon: *Portrait of Abbé Boisol.*

FIORI, Ernesto de

Italian, 20th century.
Born 1884, in Rome, to an Austrian mother; died 1945, in São Paulo, Brazil.
Active and naturalised in Germany from 1914, then active in Italy and Brazil.
Sculptor. Statues, busts.

Ernesto de Fiori started out as a painter, and began taking lessons at the academy of fine arts in Munich in 1903, where he was influenced by Ferdinand Hodler. He then moved back to Rome. After this he went live in Paris, from 1911 to 1914. During this time, on the advice of the sculptor Hermann Haller, and because he was captivated by the works of Rodin, Degas and Maillol, he decided to work exclusively as a sculptor. He moved to Berlin in 1914, was naturalised as a German citizen, and remained there until 1936, when the Nazi regime forced him to emigrate to Brazil. There was a retrospective exhibition of his work at the Venice Biennale of 1950.

De Fiori's focus as an artist is essentially centred around the human figure. He said:

'I wish to sculpt man, undisturbed by events, in a perfect state of mental peace, in an Olympian attitude, far from the ephemeral agitation of daily life; it is not suffering that elevates man, but the way in which he deals with it.'

His sculptures are psychological, conspicuous in their technique, highly tactile and still Impressionist in style, whether in terracotta or bronze. De Fiori belonged to an intermediate generation that had abandoned the monumental aesthetic of the 1900s, but had yet to align itself with the Cubist or abstract movements. His works are imbued with a formal simplicity that nevertheless sometimes evokes a tempered form of Cubism. He depicts man on the move, in sculptures such as *Man Saluting, Man Walking* (1927) and *Woman Crouching* (1911-1922); he also sculpted statues of the boxers Jack Dempsey, in 1925, and Max Schmeling. The absence of effects in his works demonstrates his desire to render 'the interior movement of the human being' above all else, which is especially true of his busts.

Bibliography:

Laudanna, Mayra, *Ernesto de Fiori: Uma Retrospectiva. Pintura, desenho e escultura*, exhibition catalogue, Pinoteca do Estad de São Paulo, São Paulo, 1997.

Museums and Galleries:

São Paulo (Mus. of Brazilian Art): *The Dinner* (1942, oil on canvas); *Brazilian Man* (1938, bronze).

Auction records:

New York, 14 June 1985, *Englishwoman* (1925, golden-brown patinated bronze, h. 54 ins / 137 cm) USD 5,250. Cologne, 31 May 1986, *Young Man Standing* (1911, bronze, h. 69 3/4 ins / 177 cm) DEM 42,000. Paris, 13 Dec 1989, *Young Male Nude* (green-patinated bronze, h. 69 3/4 ins / 177 cm) FRF 300,000.

FIORI, Filippo

Italian, 18th century.
Born in Como.
Painter.

Filippo Fiori was first and foremost a fresco painter.

FIORI, Filippo, also known as Pietro Montalti

Italian, 18th century.
Born in Rome; died 15 March 1739, in Carpi.
Painter.

FIORI, Gasparo di. See **LOPEZ Gasparo**

FIORI, Mario de'. See **NUZZI Mario**

FIORI, Muzio di Paolo

Italian, 16th - 17th century.
Born to a family originally from Fratta (Umbria).
Painter.

Muzio di Paolo Fiori painted a *Last Supper* for a church in Fratta.

FIORI, Sebastiano

Italian, 16th century.
Born to a family originally from Arezzo (Tuscany).
Painter.

Sebastiano Fiori executed important decorative works in the Palazzo della Cancellaria in Rome about 1545.

FIORIDO, Osvaldo

Italian, 20th century.
Born 1 May 1870, in Verona.
Painter. Interior scenes, landscapes.

Osvaldo Fiorido studied art in Milan and Florence.

FIORILLO, Francesco or Domenico

Italian, 17th century.
Active in Naples at the beginning of the 17th century.
Painter.

Francesco Fiorillo was a pupil of Andrea Sabbatina. He was once (quite erroneously) credited with the major *Holy Virgin and Saints* dated 1521 and now in the museum in Naples.

FIORILLO, Johann Dominicus

German, 18th - 19th century.
Born 13 October 1748, in Hamburg; died 10 September 1821, in Göttingen (Lower Saxony).
Painter, scholar.

Fiorillo worked at the academy of Bayreuth in 1759, then in Rome in 1761 at the studio of P. Battoni, and finally, between 1765 and 1769, in Bologna under the direction of Vittorio Bigari. On his return to Germany, he went first to Hamburg, before becoming a curator in Göttingen in 1784, where he was appointed a professor at the university in 1799.

FIORILLO, Nicola
Italian, 18th century.
Active in Naples c. 1760.
Engraver.

FIORINI, Bernardino
Italian, 16th century.
Active in Ferrara.
Painter.

Bernardino Fiorini was the father of Girolamo Fiorini the Younger.

FIORINI, Costantino
Italian, 15th century.
Active in Ferrara at the end of the 15th century.
Painter.

FIORINI, Filippo Maria
Italian, 16th century.
Active in Ferrara c. 1528.
Painter.

FIORINI, Florio
Italian, 16th century.
Active in Ferrara in 1523.
Painter.

FIORINI, Gabriele, the Elder
Italian, 16th century.
Died c. 1576, in Bologna.
Active in Bologna in 1525.
Sculptor (wood).

FIORINI, Gabriele, the Younger
Italian, 16th - 17th century.
Sculptor.

Gabriele Fiorini, the son of Giovanni Battista the Younger, executed the tomb of Cardinal Agucchi in the church of S Giaccomo Maggiore in Bologna.

FIORINI, Gherardo
Italian, 15th century.
Died c. 1487.
Active in Ferrara.
Painter.

Gherardo Fiorini was the father of Costantino Fiorini.

FIORINI, Giacomo Filippo
Italian, 15th - 16th century.
Active in Ferrara.
Painter.

Giacomo Filippo Fiorini was the son of Giovanni Francesco Fiorini.

FIORINI, Giovanni Battista, the Elder
Italian, 16th century.
Active in Bologna.
Painter.

Giovanni Battista Fiorini the Elder was the uncle of Giovanni Battista the Younger.

FIORINI, Giovanni Battista, the Younger
Italian, 16th - 17th century.
Born c. 1540, in Bologna; died c. 1660, in Bologna.
Painter, architect.

Giovanni Battista Fiorini the Younger is known chiefly as the collaborator of Cesare Aretusi, with whom he executed several paintings in Bologna and Brescia. He distinguished himself as an excellent draughtsman and skilled innovator. His works include a *Christ Delivering the Keys to St Peter* in the cathedral in Bologna, a *Birth of the Virgin* in the church of S Afra in Brescia and a small painting in the Sala Regia in the Vatican.

FIORINI, Giovanni Francesco
Italian, 16th century.
Died probably c. 1528.
Active in Ferrara.
Painter.

FIORINI, Giovanni Maria
Italian, 16th century.
Active in Ferrara.
Painter.

Giovanni Maria Fiorini was the son of Bernardino Fiorini.

FIORINI, Girolamo, the Elder
Italian, 15th - 16th century.
Active in Ferrara.
Miniaturist, architect.

A Cistercian monk, Girolamo Fiorini worked for Cardinal Hippolyte d'Este. He is said to have been the master of Cosimo Tura.

FIORINI, Girolamo, the Younger
Italian, 16th century.
Active in Ferrara.
Painter.

FIORINI, Luigi
Italian, 19th century.
Born 1795, in Rome.
Painter. Genre scenes.

MUSEUMS AND GALLERIES:
MUNICH: *Easter in Rome*.

FIORINI, Marcel
French, 20th century.
Born 23 February 1922, in Guelma, Algeria.
Painter, engraver, sculptor.

Born in Algeria, Marcel Fiorini arrived in Paris in 1947, where he met Jean Fautrier, who introduced him to etching. He featured in numerous collective exhibitions, notably in Paris, at Galerie Jeanne Bucher (which also acted as his agency from 1951 to 1980) and in *École de Paris* (*Paris School*) at the Galerie Charpentier after the war. Some travelling exhibitions took his work to the USA and around Europe. His work was seen at the Salon d'Octobre and the Salon des Jeunes Peintres soon after the war, also at the Salon d'Automne, Salon de Mai, Salon des Réalités Nouvelles, Salon de la Jeune Gravure Contemporaine, and featured in Biennales including Tokyo, São Paulo and Vancouver. He also showed his paintings and engravings in solo shows in numerous countries.

Fiorini collaborated with Bissière on the illustration of the *Canticle of Brother Sun* in 1954, and with Jacques Villon from 1956 to 1960 on book illustrations. He also worked on Van Gogh's *Thatched Cottages at Cordeville* for the Chalcographie du Louvre. He designed a whole range of artefacts for the works at Sèvres and Coutances and for *Le Creuset*.

As an engraver, Fiorini has experimented with new techniques, applying intaglio techniques to wood engraving, also incorporating plaster, sand and glues into his plates. Some of his wood engravings are monumental. The combination of new processes with the deeply etched lines he favoured gives his output a wide interpretative range enhanced by a free use of colour. Abstract though his work is, it communicates animation and captures light.

FIORINI, Michele
Italian, 17th century.
Active in Bologna, during the second half of the 17th century.
Painter.

Michele Fiorini also worked in Venice.

FIORINI, Paolo, the Elder
Italian, 16th century.
Active in Bologna.
Sculptor, architect.

Paolo Fiorini the Elder is without doubt the sculptor known also as Maestro Polo, active during the early part of the 16th century.

FIORINI, Paolo, the Younger
Italian, 16th century.
Active in Bologna in the latter years of the 16th century.
Sculptor.
Paolo Fiorini the Younger worked on the decoration of the convent of St Gregory in Bologna.

FIORINI, Sebastiano
Italian, 17th century.
Active in Bologna.
Painter, architect.
Sebastiano Fiorini decorated several churches in Bologna around 1625.

FIORINI, Sigismondo, the Elder
Italian, 15th - 16th century.
Died c. 1512.
Active in Ferrara.
Painter.
Sigismondo Fiorini the Elder worked for the princes of the house of Este; he was the father of Girolamo the Elder and Bernardino Fiorini.

FIORINI, Sigismondo, the Younger
Italian, 16th century.
Active in Ferrara in 1528.
Painter.
Sigismondo Fiorini the Younger was the son of Bernardino Fiorini.

FIORINI, Sperandio
Italian, 16th century.
Active in Ferrara c. 1500.
Painter.

FIORINI, Stefano, called Stefano dei Ritratti
Italian, 17th century.
Active in Florence c. 1600.
Painter. Portraits.
A *St Francis* completed by Stefano Fiorini in 1620 was formerly on view in the church of S Maria della Torricella in Vicenza.

FIORINO, Jeremias Alexander
German, 19th century.
Born 3 May 1797, in Kassel; died 22 June 1847, in Dresden.
Painter.
Many portraits by Fiorino are at the museum in Dresden. After studying at the academy in Kassel, he became a teacher there. He also worked at the porcelain factory in the city.

FIORINO DI DOMENICO DA VERONA
Italian, 15th century.
Active in Ferrara c. 1460.
Sculptor.

FIORIO, Giovanni Battista
Italian, 18th century.
Born 1723, in Verona; died 24 May 1789, in Verona.
Painter.
Giovanni Battista Fiorio was a pupil of Michelangelo Prunati. He lived and worked in Rome and Naples before returning to his native Verona, where he painted portraits and a *St George* for the church of Rivoli.

FIORISELLO, Domenico
Italian, 16th century.
Active in Padua.
Painter.
Domenico Fiorisello executed a painting for the church of S Giovanni delle Navi in Padua.

FIORITI, Bernardino, also known as Focoso
Italian, 17th century.
Active in Rome.
Sculptor.
In 1673, Bernardino Fioriti sculpted several figures for the tomb of Salvator Rosa in the church of Sta Maria degli Angeli in Rome.

FIORONI, Ado
Italian, 19th century.
Born c. 1800.
Active in Milan.
Engraver.
Ado Fioroni was a pupil of Longhi. He engraved some beautifully executed plates in Milan, including: *Virgin and Child with St John*, after Raphael (1829); and *Virgin and Child*, after B Luini (1822).

FIORONI, Giosetta
Italian, 20th century.
Born 1933, in Rome.
Painter, assemblage sculptor, mixed media.
Giosetta Fioroni was one of the founder members of the Scuola di Piazza del Populo, a group of Rome-based artists who in the 1960s used unusual, 'low-grade' and industrial materials to create works of art.

BIBLIOGRAPHY:
Gualdoni, F., *Arte e Roma 1945-1980*, Giancarlo Politi, Milan, 1988. Boatto, Alberto/Sauzeau, Anne-Marie/Carancini, Andrea, *Giosetta Fioroni*, Edizioni Essegi, Ravenna, 1990.

AUCTION RECORDS:
ROME, 23 April 1985, *La Casetta* (light sculpture in painted wood and various materials, 69 1/4 x 22 x 25 1/2 ins / 176 x 55 x 65 cm) ITL 1,400,000. MILAN, 14 Dec 1988, *The Dimension of a Look* (1964, varnish/canvas, 46 x 35 ins / 117 x 89 cm) ITL 6,000,000. ROME, 9 Dec 1991, *House* (1982, oil on canvas, 47 1/4 x 39 1/4 ins / 120 x 100 cm) ITL 4,140,000. ROME, 28 March 1995, *James Joyce and the Castle Towers of Trieste* (silver varnish and pencil/paper, 38 1/2 x 26 1/2 ins / 98 x 67 cm) ITL 1,380,000. ROME, 13 June 1995, *Liberty* (1964, varnish/canvas, 47 1/4 x 39 1/4 ins / 120 x 100 cm) ITL 6,325,000. FLORENCE, 19 Nov 2001, *At Dawn* (1957, oil on canvas, 39 x 32 ins / 100 x 81 cm) ITL 5,000,000. MILAN, 20 Nov 2001, *Red Arrow* (1960, oil on canvas, 31 x 35 ins / 80 x 90 cm) ITL 7,000,000. VERCELLI, 12 Jan 2002, *Home Sweet Home* (2000, mixed media with collage, 39 x 28 ins / 100 x 70 cm) EUR 2,200. MILAN, 4 June 2002, *Woman* (1964, mixed media, 27 x 39 ins / 68 x 98 cm) EUR 2,600. ROME, 22 April 2004, *Sixties Girl* (1965, pencil and paint on canvas, 39 x 28 ins / 100 x 70 cm) EUR 4,200.

FIORONI, Luigi
Italian, 19th century.
Born 1795, in Santa Fiora (Tuscany); died c. 1864, in Rome.
Active in Rome.
Painter. History painting, genre scenes, landscapes.
Luigi Fioroni was the brother of the painter Enrica Fioroni-Narducci and the miniaturist Teresa Voigt.

MUSEUMS AND GALLERIES:
COPENHAGEN (Thorvaldsens Mus.) - MUNICH (Neue Pinakothek).

FIORONI-NARDUCCI, Enrica
Italian, 19th century.
Born 1806, in Santa Fiora (Tuscany); died 1892, in Rome.
Painter.
Enrica Fioroni-Narducci was the sister of Luigi Fioroni. She is chiefly remembered for her miniature portraits and copies of Old Masters.

FIORUZZI, Giovanni
Italian, 19th century.
Born in Piacenza; died c. 1884.
Painter. Genre scenes.

Giovanni Fioruzzi is known for a painting entitled *Return of the Zouave*.

FIOT, Jean Marie
French, 18th century.
Sculptor (wood).

Jean Fiot worked for the church of Notre-Dame in Bourg.

FIOT, Maximilien Louis
French, 20th century.
Born 22 January 1886, in Grand-Pressigny; died 19 September 1953, in Corbeil.
Sculptor. Animals.

Maximilien Fiot studied under Lecourtier. He regularly exhibited in Paris at the Salon des Artistes Français, of which he became an associate member. He gained a third medal in 1911 and a second medal in 1923.

AUCTION RECORDS:
NEW YORK, 21 Sept 1981, *Three Hounds Running* (bronze, l. 37 1/2 ins / 95 cm) USD 1,800. PARIS, 3 Dec 1984, *Great Stag* (bronze, h. 18 ins / 46 cm) FRF 7,100. PARIS, 9 Nov 1987, *Great Stag* (brown-green patinated bronze, h. 17 1/4 ins / 44 cm) FRF 8,000. NEW YORK, 23 Feb 1989, *Dogs' Heads* (bronze, a pair, each h. 8 ins / 20.3 cm) USD 2,420. LA VARENNE-ST-HILAIRE, 21 May 1989, *Panthers* (green-patinated bronze, h. 17 1/4 ins / 44 cm, l. 24 1/2 ins/62 cm) FRF 36,000. ST-DIÉ, 15 Oct 1989, *Albatross* (silvered bronze, 23 1/2 x 39 1/4 ins / 60 x 100 cm) FRF 18,500. MAYENNE, 18 Feb 1990, *Hounds Race* (bronze, l. 37 1/2 ins / 95 cm) FRF 51,000. PARIS, 19 March 1990, *Horse and Dog* (lost-wax bronze, h. 14 3/4 ins / 37.5 cm, l. 23 1/2 ins/60 cm) FRF 36,000. PARIS, 28 Oct 1990, *Eagle about to Take Wing* (plaster original, h. 31 1/2 ins / 80 cm, l. 39 1/4 ins/100 cm, w. 11 3/4 ins/30 cm) FRF 13,000. PARIS, 6 Nov 1992, *Two Lionesses Walking* (white marble, 11 1/2 x 8 1/4 x 25 1/4 ins / 29.5 x 21 x 64 cm) FRF 7,800. PERTH, 30 Aug 1994, *Two Swallows in a Nest* (lost-wax bronze, h. 4 3/4 ins / 12 cm) GBP 1,495. LOKEREN, 7 Oct 1995, *Dog Lying* (lost-wax bronze, h. 5 1/4 ins / 13.5 cm, w. 9 ins/22 cm) BEF 32,000. LONDON, 16 April 1999, *Standing Tiger* (brown patinated bronze, h. 11 ins / 29 cm, w. 19 ins/48 cm) GBP 4,000. LONDON, 5 Oct 2000, *Eagle Perched on a Rock* (brown patinated bronze, h. 13 ins / 33 cm, w. 14 ins/36 cm) GBP 3,200. PONTOISE, 16 Dec 2000, *Two Lions on the Prowl* (c. 1925, terracotta, 11 x 23x7 ins / 27 x 58x17 cm) FRF 20,000. LONDON, 2 Nov 2001, *Pair of Eagles in Combat* (dark brown patinated bronze, h. 28 ins / 72 cm, w. 18 ins/46 cm) GBP 3,000. BRUSSELS, 28 May 2002, *Eagle* (patinated bronze, 13 x 19x9 ins / 34 x 48x22 cm) EUR 4,800. PARIS, 21 June 2002, *Panther Lying on a Branch* (black patinated bronze, h. 20 ins / 52 cm) EUR 9,500. LONDON, 20 May 2003, *Pair of Lionesses* (green patinated bronze, h. 17 ins / 43 cm) GBP 3,800. PARIS, 24 June 2003, *Tiger Cleaning Itself* (black patinated bronze, 12 x 20x6 ins / 30 x 50x15 cm) EUR 10,000. LONDON, 21 April 2004, *Young Stag with Two Hinds* (brown patinated bronze, h. 15 ins / 38 cm, w. 24 ins/62 cm) GBP 4,800. PARIS, 12 May 2004, *Roe Deer* (brown and black patinated bronze, h. 16 ins / 41 cm) EUR 3,000. PARIS, 10 June 2004, *Pair of Panthers* (red and brown patinated bronze, h. 17 ins / 42 cm) EUR 6,000.

FIOT THIEBLEMONT, Yvonne Marie
French, 20th century.
Born in Authon.
Watercolourist.

Yvonne Fiot Thiéblemont studied under Barbier. Between 1929 and 1938, she exhibited in Paris at the Salon des Artistes Français, of which she became a member. She was awarded a silver medal in 1936.

FIQUEMONT, Marie
French, 20th century.
Born 10 May 1880, in Vouziers.
Painter.

Marie Fiquemeont made her debut in Paris at the Salon des Artistes Français in 1905.

FIQUENSCHER, Johann Adam
German, 18th century.
Active in the region of Bayreuth (Bavaria).
Painter (porcelain/glazed earthenware).

FIRDMANN, D.
British, 20th century.
Active in London.
Painter. Architectural views.

AUCTION RECORDS:
LONDON, 25 June 1931, *A Convent*, GBP 22.

FIRENS, César
French, 19th century.
Active in Paris at the beginning of the 19th century.
Engraver, print publisher.

FIRENS, Gaspard
French, 17th century.
Active in Paris at the beginning of the 17th century.
Engraver (burin), print publisher.

Gaspard Firens engraved religious subjects.

FIRENS, Jaques, or Fierens
Flemish, 17th century.
Died c. 1620.
Active in Antwerp.
Painter.
Flemish School.

After receiving instruction from Hans de Wael, Jaques Firens pursued his profession in Rome.

FIRENS, Jeronimus
Dutch, 17th century.
Draughtsman.

Noteworthy is an old work which contains landscapes reproduced after the drawings of Jeronimus Firens.

FIRENS, Jodocus, or Fierens
Dutch, 17th century.
Active in Middelburg.
Draughtsman.

Noteworthy are two prints engraved after Jodocus Firens's drawings by Houdius. He was also a landscape painter. Other painters of the same name and probably of the same family are mentioned in Middelburg: Isaac Fierens (in 1652), Jaques Fierens (died 9 December 1699), and Jan Fierens (in 1699).

FIRENS, Melchior
French, 17th century.
Born 25 December 1607, in Paris; died 1665, in Paris.
Painter, sculptor.

FIRENS, P.
French, 17th century.
Active in Beaumontel (Normandy) c. 1670.
Painter.

P. Firens is mentioned by E. Veuch in *Les Artistes Normands du XVIIe Siècle* (*Norman Artists of the 17th century*).

FIRENS, Pierre I
Flemish, 17th century.
Died c. 1636.
Active in Antwerp, and in Paris.
Engraver, printer.

Flemish School.

Pierre Firens I went to Paris at the beginning of the 17th century. He is known to have carried out various engravings, in particular a portrait of Louis XIII published as early as 1610. He also executed a portrait of Henri IV. His daughters married artists in Paris; Catherine married the engraver Charles David on 3 February 1619, Marie married the painter Jean Cars on 30 August 1620, and Jeanne married the painter François Ponfi in 1626. The copperplate sign of a printing house, which indicated the house of P. Firens in Rue St-Jacques, suggests that he was also a master printer.

FIRENS, Pierre II

French, 17th century.
Born 1637.
Active in Paris.
Painter.

Pierre Firens II was the son of Melchior Firens. He copied a portrait of the prince of Condé. He may be the same person as the P. Firens who executed a religious painting for the church in Beaumontel in 1668.

FIRENS, Pierre III

French, 17th century.
Born 1641, in Paris.
Engraver, print publisher.

Pierre Firens III was the son of Gaspard Firens.

FIRENZE, da. See first name

FIRESTONE, I. D.

American, 20th century.
Born 13 April 1894, in Austria-Hungary.
Painter, illustrator.

I.D. Firestone studied at the Carnegie Institute in Pittsburgh, the Evenong School of Industrial Art in New York, and the Art Students League. He was a member of the Pittsburgh Association and a teacher.

FIRLE, Walter, or Fierle

German, 19th - 20th century.
Born 22 August 1859, in Breslau (now Wroclaw, Poland); died 1929, in Munich.
Painter. Figures, portraits, genre scenes, landscapes.

Firle was a pupil of the landscape painter A. Dressler in Breslau, and then studied under Gabriel Max and Ludwig Lofftz at the Akademie in Munich. He worked in particular in Munich, Holland and Italy. He was awarded a medal in Munich in 1886, and at the Exposition Universelle in Paris in 1889.

MUSEUMS AND GALLERIES:

BREMEN: *The Divine Night* (triptych) - COLOGNE: *Forgive Us Our Sins* - DÜSSELDORF: *New Spring* - FRANKFURT AM MAIN: *Morning Meditation* - LEIPZIG: *Faith* (triptych) - MUNICH: *Our Father* (triptych) - WROCLAW: *In the Mortuary*.

AUCTION RECORDS:

ZURICH, 25 Nov 1977, *Two Little Girls with a Picture Book* (oil on canvas, 25 1/2 x 22 1/4 ins / 65 x 56.5 cm) CHF 4,000. BREMEN, 28 March 1981, *Festive Evening* (oil on canvas, 29 1/4 x 35 3/4 ins / 74 x 91 cm) DEM 3,000. NEW YORK, 25 May 1984, *The Reading of the Letter* (oil on canvas, 28 x 28 1/2 ins / 71.1 x 72.4 cm) USD 7,000. ZURICH, 29 Nov 1985, *Two Venetian Women* (oil on panel, 22 x 16 1/2 ins / 55 x 42 cm) CHF 5,000. VIENNA, 19 March 1986, *Portrait of a Girl* (oil on card, 19 1/4 x 16 ins / 49 x 40.5 cm) ATS 16,000. BERN, 26 Oct 1988, *Two Children Looking at a Picture Book* (oil on panel, 22 3/4 x 28 3/4 ins / 58 x 73 cm) CHF 9,000. LONDON, 6 Oct 1989, *An Absorbing Book* (oil on card, 19 1/2 x 25 ins / 49.5 x 63.5 cm) GBP 4,400. MUNICH, 12 Dec 1990, *Teatime* (oil on canvas, 24 x 33 ins / 61 x 84 cm) DEM 19,800.

FIRLER, Franz

Austrian, 18th century.
Born at the beginning of the 18th century, in Innsbruck; died 28 August 1784, in Innsbruck.
Painter.

Firler may have painted *Mary Magdalene at the Foot of the Cross*, which is kept at the castle in Ambras.

FIRMENICH, Joseph

German, 19th century.
Born 1820, in Cologne; died 18 January 1891, in Berlin.
Painter. Landscapes.

Firmenich was a student of Simon Meister. After a study trip to Italy, he settled in his native town in 1847. One of his works is *View over Naples and Vesuvius*.

AUCTION RECORDS:

LONDON, 17 Nov 1995, *Gulf of Palermo with Mount Pellegrino* (1887, oil on canvas, 53 x 74 1/4 ins / 134.6 x 188.8 cm) GBP 9,200. HAMBURG, 19 June 2004, *Island with Architectural Ruins* (1871, oil on canvas, 37 x 50 ins / 94 x 126 cm) EUR 2,600.

FIRMIAN, Carl Josef von (Count)

Italian, 18th century.
Born 6 August 1716, in Mezzocorona; died 20 July 1782.
Painter.

Carl Josef von Firmian was the brother of Franz Lactanz von Firmian and a fellow member of the Winckelmann group of artists who advocated a return to the principles of antiquity.

FIRMIAN, Franz Lactanz von (Count)

Italian, 18th century.
Born 28 January 1712, in Trento; died 6 March 1786, in Villa Lagarina.
Painter, engraver.

Franz Lactanz von Firmian was the brother of Carl Josef von Firmian. He painted portraits and nudes.

FIRMIN

French, 14th century.
Active in Cambrai.
Sculptor.

Firmin was working at Cambrai Cathedral in 1386.

FIRMIN

French, 18th century.
Active probably in Paris.
Painter. Portraits.

MUSEUMS AND GALLERIES:

RHEIMS: *Portrait of Antoine Hédouin de Pons-Ludon*.

FIRMIN, Claude

French, 19th - 20th century.
Born 18 February 1864, in Avignon; died 8 December 1944, in Avignon.
Painter. Portraits, genre scenes, local scenes, interiors with figures, landscapes.
Orientalism.

Claude Firmin studied under Léon Bonnat and at the École des Beaux-Arts in Avignon, where he later became a teacher, then the principal. He received an honourable mention in 1892.

He is best remembered for his portraits and interiors; the Avignon bourgeoisie and local scenery were his major sources of inspiration.

MUSEUMS AND GALLERIES:

AVIGNON (Mus. Calvet): *A Restorer of Objets d'Art: Interior*; *Noël Biret in his Studio*; *Rhone Sand Quarries near Villeneuve-lès-Avignon*.

AUCTION RECORDS:

LONDON, 13 June 1973, *Farm Scene*, GBP 1,000. NEW YORK, 22 May 1991, *In the Garden* (1899, oil on canvas, 21 3/4 x 18 1/4 ins / 55.2 x 46.4 cm) USD 13,750. PARIS, 12 Dec 1996, *Shepherds and Shepherdesses Talking under a Tree* (1904, oil on canvas, 28 3/4 x 36 1/4 ins / 73 x 92 cm) FRF 10,500.

FIRMIN, D.
British, 18th century.
Active in London at the beginning of the 18th century.
Painter. Portraits.

D. Firmin's work is known thanks to a number of engravings after his paintings.

FIRMIN, Hughe
Flemish School, 16th century.
Died c. 1547.
Active in Bruges.
Painter.

Hughe Firmin was the son of Jan Firmin the Elder and brother of Jan Firmin the Younger.

FIRMIN, Jan, the Elder, or Fremyn
Flemish School, 16th century.
Active in Bruges.
Painter.

Jan Firmin was the father of Jan the Younger and Hughe.

FIRMIN, Jan, the Younger
Flemish School, 16th century.
Died c. 1542.
Active in Bruges.
Painter.

Jan Firmin was the son of Jan the Elder.

FIRMIN, Thomas
French, 18th century.
Active in Paris in 1774.
Painter, sculptor.

FIRMIN-BADOIS, Jeanne (Mme)
French, 19th century.
Active in Verneuil-sur-Seine.
Pastellist, engraver. Flowers.

Firmin-Badois became a member of the Société des Artistes Français in 1895. She exhibited works depicting flowers at the Blanc et Noir Salon in 1892 under her maiden name.

FIRMIN-GIRARD, Firmin Marie François.
See **GIRARD Firmin**

FIRMINGER, T. A. C.
British, 19th century.
Painter.

T.A.C. Firminger exhibited regularly in London from 1834 to 1871, especially at the Royal Academy.

FIRNBACH, Jakob
Austrian, 18th century.
Born in Bamberg (Bavaria), Germany; died 23 February 1805, in Vienna.
Painter.

FIRNHABER, Élise (Mme)
French, 19th century.
Active in Asnières (Hauts-de-Seine).
Painter.

Firnhaber became a member of the Société des Artistes Français in 1890.

FIRPO, Walter
American, 20th century.
Born 1902, in San Juan, USA.
From 1914 active in France.
Painter.

Walter Firpo went to France in 1914 and settled in the South of France in 1930. A follower and friend of Albert Gleizes, his work thus developed out of Cubism. He held several exhibitions in Nice (with Albert Glaizes in 1930) and solo shows in Marseilles, Aix-en-Provence, Paris, Boulogne and Folkstone.

MUSEUMS AND GALLERIES:
MARSEILLES (Mus. Cantini): *Song for Spain.*

FIRQUET, Marcel Firmin
Belgian, 20th - 21st century.
Born 1947, in Verviers.
Also active in Canada.
Painter.

Firquet attended the Institut de St Luc in Liège. Meeting A. Blanck in 1968 and A. Courtois in 1974. He is a professor at the Université de Québec (Rimouski).

FIRSSOV, Dmitri Petrovich
Russian, 17th century.
Active in Moscow.
Painter.

Firssov decorated several churches as well as the private apartments of ths Tsars at the Kremlin.

FIRSSOV, Ivan
Russian, 18th century.
Active in St Petersburg.
Painter.

Firssov was a pupil of Valeriani's and of Peresinotti's. He was involved in the decoration of the imperial palaces of St Petersburg.

FIRSSOV, Mikhail Petrovich
Russian, 17th century.
Active in Moscow.
Painter.

Mikhail Firssov was the brother of Dmitri Petrovitch and a pupil of Bogdan Saltanov's at the same time as him.

FIRSSOV, Petr
Russian, 18th century.
Active in St Petersburg.
Painter.

Petr Firssov worked during the same period as Ivan on the decoration of the imperial palaces in St Petersburg.

FISAREK, Alois
Czech, 20th century.
Born 1906, in Prostejov.
Painter. Portraits, still-lifes.

Alois Fisarek preferred to paint still-lifes and portraits in a post-Cézannian vision and technique, even though he sometimes referred to late Cubism. After World War II he produced a series of monumental tapestries and paintings on folk themes. He showed at the Venice Biennale (1948) and at the exhibition *Fifty years of Czechoslovak Painting from the Collections of the Galleries, 1918-1958*, held in 1968 in several national museums to commemorate the 50th anniversary of the founding of the Republic.

FISCH, Fernand Alfred Antoine
Belgian, 20th century.
Born 1898, in St Joost-ten-Node.
Medallist.

Fernand Fisch produced effigies.

FISCH, Hans Balthasar
Swiss, 17th century.
Died 1656; buried 22 January in Ammerswil.
Active in Aarau.
Glass painter.

Hans Balthasar Fisch was the son of Hans Ulrich Fisch and was baptised on 20 or 30 August 1608. Between 1637 and 1652 he carried out work for the town of Biberstein, and the churches and other public buildings of Ammerswill, Birrwill, Kulm, Aunestein and Aarau. He also produced coats of arms.

FISCH, Hans Ulrich I, sometimes known as Fisch vom Stein
Swiss, 17th century.
Born 1583, in Aarau; died November 1647, in Aarau.
Painter, draughtsman. Designs for stained glass windows.

Hans Ulrich Fisch I lived at Aarau and held several official positions. He carried out work for his home town and also Lenzburg, Aarburg and Zöfingen. He produced many stained glass windows and coats of arms.

MUSEUMS AND GALLERIES:
AARAU (Gnadenthal Abbey): stained glass window (1620) - BASEL (Historisches Mus.): stained glass windows - BASEL (Öffentliche Bibliothek, Universität): book of coats of arms from Bern - BERN (Historisches Mus.): stained glass windows - WETTINGEN (Kloster): stained glass windows (1620).

AUCTION RECORDS:
LONDON, 2 July 1991, *Christian Virtues* (1641, ink and wash heightened with white, design for stained glass window, 7 1/4 x 11 3/4 ins / 18.7 x 29.9 cm) GBP 6,600.

FISCH, Hans Ulrich II
Swiss, 17th century.
Baptised in August 1613 in Aarau; died March 1686, in Aarau.
Glass painter.

The son of Hans Ulrich Zum Stein, Hans Ulrich Fisch II followed the same career as his father and worked at Zolfingen, Beromünster, Biberstein and Aarau. He was married in Aarau. Among his known works are a stained glass window representing Uly Flückiger and his wife (1646), and two stained glass windows of the coats of arms of Rudolf von Diesbach (1663) and Joh.-Georg Imhof (1665) at the church in Gränichen.

MUSEUMS AND GALLERIES:
BERN (Historisches Mus., Wyss Collection): stained glass windows.

FISCH, Hans Ulrich III
Swiss, 17th century.
Glass painter.

Hans Ulrich Fisch III was the son of Hans Ulrich Fisch II and was baptised in Aarau in March 1648. He worked for the provost of Biberstein around 1684-85.

FISCHACH, S.
German, 18th century.
Engraver, painter (?).

A painter by the name of Fischach produced two important portraits at Memmingen (Bavaria) in 1781.

FISCHBACH, August
Austrian, 19th century.
Born 7 March 1828, in Vienna; died 2 February 1860, in Munich.
Painter. Genre scenes.

August Fischbach was the son and pupil of Johann Fischbach.

FISCHBACH, Friedrich
German, 19th century.
Born 10 February 1839, in Aachen (North Rhine-Westphalia); died 12 September 1908, in Wiesbaden (Hesse).
Draughtsman, engraver, decorative designer.

Friedrich Fischbach was a student at the school of fine arts in Berlin. He then worked in Vienna. In 1870 he became a teacher at the academy of Hanau (Hesse), before travelling to Italy and Austria.

FISCHBACH, H.
German, 19th century.
Born 1833, in Unna (North Rhine-Westphalia).
Painter, art restorer.

FISCHBACH, Johann
Austrian, 19th century.
Born 5 April 1797, in Grafenegg; died 19 June 1871, in Munich.
Painter, draughtsman. Genre scenes, hunting scenes, landscapes.

Johann Fischbach studied at the academy in Vienna. He made his name with his 28 pencil drawings representing forests in Germany. In 2001 he was represented at the exhibition on the theme of *Still Lesen* (*Silent Reading*) at the Residenzgalerie in Salzburg.

BIBLIOGRAPHY:
Schaffer, Nikolaus, *Johann Fischbach, 1797-1871*, Salzburger Museum Carolino Augusteum, Salzburg, 1989.

MUSEUMS AND GALLERIES:
MUNICH (Gal.): *Salzburg Landscape* - VIENNA (Gal.): *Widow in Cemetery*.

AUCTION RECORDS:
VIENNA, 17 Sept 1974, *Hunter*, ATS 35,000. NEW YORK, 28 May 1981, *Gentle Conversation* (1868, oil on panel, 34 x 27 1/2 ins / 86.5 x 70 cm) USD 15,000. AMSTERDAM, 22 March 1983, *Family Beside a Mountain Lake* (1832, oil on canvas, 11 3/4 x 16 1/2 ins / 30 x 42 cm) NLG 3,500. VIENNA, 5 Nov 1986, *Patient Father* (oil on canvas, 23 1/2 x 17 3/4 ins / 60 x 45 cm) ATS 25,000. PARIS, 7 March 1989, *Hunting Scene in Pinzgau* (1842, oil on panel, 29 1/4 x 22 3/4 ins / 74.5 x 58 cm) FRF 260,000. MUNICH, 10 Dec 1992, *View of Mödling* (1820, pencil and ink/paper, 8 x 13 1/2 ins / 20.6 x 34.5 cm) DEM 2,486. MUNICH, 7 Dec 1993, *Young Woman Praying at Roadside Crucifix* (oil/copper, 12 1/4 x 9 3/4 ins / 31 x 25 cm) DEM 36,800. MUNICH, 3 Dec 1996, *Salzachtal near Salzburg* (oil on wood, 11 x 14 1/4 ins / 27 x 36 cm) DEM 4,800. MUNICH, 27 Feb 1999, *Mountain in Dachstein and Gosausee* (oil on canvas, 15 x 10 ins / 37 x 26 cm) DEM 8,000. VIENNA, 19 Nov 1999, *View of Steyr, Austria* (watercolour, 5 x 7 ins / 12 x 18 cm) ATS 60,000. VIENNA, 23 May 2000, *Landscape with Waterfall and Stag* (1840, oil on panel, 31 x 25 ins / 78 x 64 cm) ATS 55,000. VIENNA, 28 Nov 2002, *Smuggler* (1850, oil on canvas, 34 x 28 ins / 87 x 70 cm) EUR 6,500. VIENNA, 24 Nov 2003, *Riverside Town in the Pre-Alps* (oil on canvas, 18 x 22 ins / 45 x 55 cm) EUR 13,000.

FISCHBACH, Lucas
German, 15th century.
Active in Breslau (now Wroclaw, Poland) in 1482.
Painter.

FISCHBACHER, Franz
Austrian, 20th century.
Born 1925, in Vöcklabruck.
Sculptor.

Fischbacher studied at the state art school in Linz. His sculptures are created from assemblages of prefabricated components, and sometimes evoke the technique of Louise Nevelson.

FISCHBECK, Ludwig
German, 19th century.
Born 20 September 1866.
Painter, engraver. Landscapes.

Fischbeck worked in Oldenburg (Lower Saxony). He is best known for his landscapes and for producing ex-libris.

AUCTION RECORDS:
BREMEN, 30 June 1984, *Landscape at Dusk* (1936, oil on canvas, 12 1/2 x 18 ins / 31.8 x 46 cm) DEM 1,500. BREMEN, 23 Oct 1999, *Bookholzberg* (oil on panel, 28 x 39 ins / 70 x 99 cm) DEM 3,200.

FISCHE, Jakob
German, 18th century.
Active in Trier (Rhineland-Palatinate).
Sculptor.

In 1732 Fische worked on sculptures at the entrance of the Gangolf Church, Trier.

FISCHER
Austrian, 17th century.
Painter.
Fischer was active in Thunau around 1675. He produced three paintings to decorate the town's church.

FISCHER, A
Engraver.
This is the name of an artist who produced an engraving of *Quarrymen*, after Wouwermann.

FISCHER, A. L.
German, 19th century.
Miniaturist.
Fischer is said to have painted portraits.

FISCHER, Abraham Samuel
Swiss, 18th century.
Died 7 August 1809, in Bern.
Painter. Landscapes.
Fischer was baptised in Arch on 13 February 1744. He painted the picture *Bain Leuk*, which is kept at the municipal library in Bern. He exhibited a wash drawing and a genre painting in the exhibition of art and industry in Bern in 1804.

FISCHER, Adam
Czech, 18th century.
Born 1686, in Broumov.
Miniaturist.
Adam Fischer lived in Paris for many years.

FISCHER, Adam
Danish, 20th century.
Born 1888, in Denmark.
Also active in France.
Sculptor, potter.
Adam Fischer learned only drawing and painting at the school of fine art in Copenhagen, and yet he spent his working life as a sculptor. He specialised in executing ceramic sculptures, in which he remained faithful to popular traditions. He lived in Paris from 1913 to 1933, and was a member of the Salon d'Automne. He exhibited there regularly, and also at the Salon des Tuileries, from 1921 to 1931.

FISCHER, Adolf
Austrian, 19th century.
Born 18 May 1856, in Linz; died 2 February 1908, in Linz.
Painter, illustrator. Portraits, landscapes.
Adolf Fischer was the son of Michaël Fischer, and the father of Adolph Johannes Fischer. After studying in Vienna he came back and settled in Linz.
He is particularly known for landscapes and portraits.
MUSEUMS AND GALLERIES:
LINZ.
AUCTION RECORDS:
PARIS, 19 Jan 1992, *Portrait of Woman Wearing Turban* (1885, oil on canvas, 16 3/4 x 13 3/4 ins / 42.5 x 35 cm) FRF 12,000.

FISCHER, Adolf, pseudonym: Fischer Gurig
German, 19th century.
Born 2 June 1860, in Obergurig, near Bautzen (Saxony).
Active in Dresden.
Painter. Landscapes.
Adolf Fischer exhibited in Dresden, Berlin and Munich between 1884 and 1889. One of his works is *After the Rain*.

FISCHER, Adolphe Johannes
Austrian, 20th century.
Born 7 July 1885, in Gmunden.
Painter.
Adolphe Johannes Fischer was the son of the painter Adolf Fischer. He studied in Vienna before setting up in Linz.

FISCHER, Adrian
Austrian, 18th century.
Active in Altenburg (Saxony) at the end of the 18th century.
Painter.
Two watercolours signed by Fischer (who was a Dominican friar) are known.

FISCHER, Alexandre-Georges
French, 19th century.
Born 21 November 1820, in Paris; died 1890, in Paris.
Painter, lithographer. Figures, hunting scenes.
Georges Fischer entered the École des Beaux-Arts on 27 September 1841 and was taught by Paul Delaroche. He exhibited at the Salon from 1848 to 1870. Works include *Gaul Hunting in the Morning in the Marshes by the River*, *League Member* and *Youthful Pastimes*.
BIBLIOGRAPHY:
Delouche, Denise/Michaud, Jean-Marc, et al., *Bretagne, terre des peintres*, exhibition catalogue, Musée des Beaux-Arts, Vannes, 2003.
MUSEUMS AND GALLERIES:
NIORT: *Breton Storyteller.*

FISCHER, Andreas
German, 15th century.
Active in Breslau (now Wroclaw, Poland) at the end of the 15th century.
Painter.

FISCHER, Andreas
German, 16th century.
Active in Nuremberg (Bavaria) in 1589.
Illuminator.

FISCHER, Anna Katharina. See **BLOCK**

FISCHER, Anton
German, 18th century.
Died 22 March 1773, in Dillingen (Bavaria).
Sculptor.
There is a strong case for supposing that this artist may be identified with Johann Anton Fischer, who was working in the same region in 1756.

FISCHER, Anton
German, 18th century.
Active in Munich during the second half of the 18th century.
Engraver.

FISCHER, Anton Otto
German, 20th century.
Born 23 February 1882, in Munich; died 1962.
Painter, illustrator.
Anton Otto Fischer was the pupil of J.P. Laurens, and a student at the Académie Julian in Paris. He worked in the USA, where he was a member of the Society of Illustrators and of the American Federation of Arts.
AUCTION RECORDS:
NEW YORK, 29 April 1976, *Lynching Scene* (1911; *Workers in a Cabin* (1912, two oils on canvas, 30 x 21 ins / 76.2 x 53.3 cm) USD 1,100. NEW YORK, 11 March 1982, *The Arrival of the Boat* (1923, oil on canvas, 20 x 36 ins / 50.8 x 91.4 cm) USD 1,500. NEW YORK, 23 June 1987, *Abandoning Ship* (1935, oil on canvas, 22 x 36 1/4 ins / 56 x 92 cm) USD 7,500. NEW YORK, 17 March 1988, *The Coastguard Vessel* (oil on canvas, 17 1/4 x 25 ins / 43.7 x 63.7 cm) USD 2,090. NEW YORK, 7 April 1988, *Sailing Boats at Sunset* (oil on canvas, 25 1/2 x 27 1/2 ins / 65 x 70 cm) USD 1,650. NEW YORK, 14 Feb 1990, *Near to Capsizing* (1930, oil on canvas, 22 x 27 1/2 ins / 56 x 70 cm) USD 1,320. NEW YORK, 17 Dec 1990, *Clandestine Unloading of Merchan-*

dise (oil on canvas, 20 x 40 ins / 50.8 x 101.6 cm) USD 825. New York, 15 April 1992, *America Brings Reinforcements* (1942, oil on canvas, 26 x 36 ins / 66 x 91.4 cm) USD 6,325. New York, 31 March 1994, *The Sixth Day* (1948, oil on canvas, 24 x 36 ins / 61 x 91.4 cm) USD 5,175.

FISCHER, August
Danish, 19th - 20th century.
Born 11 March 1854, in Copenhagen; died 1921.
Painter. Genre scenes, urban landscapes, landscapes.
August Fischer was a student at the Kunstakademi in Copenhagen, and subsequently travelled extensively.

Auction records:
Copenhagen, 6 Dec 1973, *Street Scene in Lugano,* DKK 11,500. London, 11 Feb 1976, *The Pont-Neuf, Paris* (1883, oil on canvas, 11 x 18 ins / 28 x 46 cm) GBP 500. Cologne, 20 March 1981, *The Fruit Market in Nuremberg* (oil on canvas, 12¼ x 9½ ins / 31 x 24 cm) DEM 3,000. Copenhagen, 13 June 1984, *The Market Place in Nuremberg* (oil on canvas, 15¼ x 19¾ ins / 39 x 50 cm) DKK 15,000. London, 20 March 1985, *View of Nuremberg* (1891, oil on canvas, 24½ x 35¾ ins / 62.5 x 91 cm) GBP 3,000. London, 17 Feb 1989, *The River Ter* (1907, oil on canvas, 12 x 19¼ ins / 30.3 x 48.8 cm) GBP 1,760. London, 6 Oct 1989, *Street in Lugano* (1886, oil on card, 18¾ x 14½ ins / 47.5 x 37 cm) GBP 2,640. Copenhagen, 25 Oct 1989, *Canal at Trieste* (1890, oil on canvas, 19¾ x 16¼ ins / 50 x 41 cm) DKK 13,000. Stockholm, 15 Nov 1989, *A Farm at Gamle Lygtekro* (oil on canvas, 9¾ x 13 ins / 25 x 33 cm) SEK 7,000. Copenhagen, 21 Feb 1990, *Lake Geneva with a View of the Dents du Midi* (1888, oil on canvas, 19¾ x 31½ ins / 50 x 80 cm) DKK 7,500. New York, 15 Oct 1991, *The Piazza Erbe in Verona* (oil on canvas, 15 x 10½ ins / 38 x 26.8 cm) USD 1,980. Copenhagen, 5 Feb 1992, *An Italian Courtyard* (oil on canvas, 17¾ x 24½ ins / 45 x 62 cm) DKK 6,000. Lugano, 16 May 1992, *The Via Nassa Market in Lugano* (1886, oil on canvas, 18¾ x 14½ ins / 47.5 x 37 cm) CHF 22,000. Copenhagen, 2 Feb 1994, *Inn Yard near the Garden of the Presbytery in Kalundborg* (1880, oil on canvas, 18½ x 24 ins / 47 x 61 cm) DKK 14,000. Copenhagen, 16 Nov 1994, *Busy Street in an Italian Market Town* (oil on canvas, 29½ x 35½ ins / 75 x 90 cm) DKK 21,500. Amsterdam, 16 April 1996, *Vegetable Garden* (oil on canvas, 18 x 26 ins / 46 x 66 cm) NLG 2,360. Copenhagen, 21 May 1997, *Courtyard Seen from Gammel Mont 31, Copenhagen* (1907, 17 x 17¾ ins / 43 x 45 cm) DKK 16,500.

FISCHER, Benno Joachim Theodor
German, 19th century.
Born 11 April 1828, in Dresden; died 1865, in Dresden.
Painter. History painting, genre scenes.
Fischer was a student of Hübner. He painted mainly genre scenes.

FISCHER, Bertha
Swiss, 20th century.
Born 25 June 1864, in Bern.
Painter, watercolourist. Landscapes.
Bertha Fischer was a student at the art school in Bern under W. Benteli and Paul Volmar. She took part in Swiss exhibitions from 1900. She devoted herself particularly to watercolour painting.

FISCHER, Bruno
German, 19th century.
Born 30 April 1860, in Dresden.
Sculptor.
The son of Ernst Fischer, Bruno Fischer worked in Stuttgart, then in Dresden in Schilling's studio. He subsequently stayed for quite some time in Italy and then returned to Dresden, where he produced a number of monuments in a classical naturalist style.

FISCHER, Carl
German, 17th century.
Painter.
Carl Fischer was active in Magdeburg (Saxony-Anhalt) at the beginning of the 17th century. He carried out work for the town's cathedral.

FISCHER, Carl
German, 17th century.
Painter.
Fischer was active in Brunswick (Lower Saxony) at the beginning of the 17th century.

FISCHER, Carl
German, 18th century.
Painter.
This artist was active in Breslau (now Wroclaw, Poland) in the middle of the 18th century.

FISCHER, Carl
German, 19th century.
Draughtsman, lithographer.
Fischer was active in Berlin around 1840. He produced mainly portraits.

FISCHER, Carl
German, 19th century.
Born 8 December 1838, in Hüttenort (Rotehütte); died 22 February 1891, in Munich.
Sculptor.
Carl Fischer was a student of Josef Knabl in Munich. A particularly well-known work of his is *Christ on the Mount of Olives* in the church at Reichenhall.

FISCHER, Carl
Danish, 20th century.
Born 1887, in Copenhagen; died 1962.
Painter. Figures, scenes with figures, interiors, still-lifes, flowers.
Auction records:
London, 24 March 1988, *Cornflowers, Marguerites and Other Flowers in a Vase* (oil on canvas, 27½ x 39¼ ins / 70 x 100 cm) GBP 1,870. Cologne, 23 March 1990, *Still-life with Roses in a Copper Vase, Silverware, Crystals* (oil on canvas, 31½ x 45¼ ins / 80 x 115 cm) DEM 1,100. Copenhagen, 9 May 1990, *Still-life on a Table* (oil on canvas, 22 x 23½ ins / 55 x 60 cm) DKK 4,600. Copenhagen, 31 Oct 1990, *Young Woman Seated* (oil on canvas, 23¼ x 20 ins / 59 x 51 cm) DKK 6,000. Copenhagen, 12-14 Nov 1997, *Figures in front of a Kiosk in Rain* (oil on paper, 22 x 18 ins / 55 x 46 cm) DKK 12,500. Copenhagen, 3-5 Dec 1997, *Young Woman Seated, with Her Head Turned away, in an Interior* (1929, oil on canvas, 22 x 20 ins / 55 x 51 cm) DKK 32,000. Copenhagen, 31 Aug 1999, *Interior with Young Girl Seated by Table* (oil on canvas, 24 x 24 ins / 61 x 61 cm) DKK 12,000. Vejle, 29 Sept 1999, *Interior Scene with Woman Seen from behind Seated at Table* (oil on canvas, 28 x 23 ins / 70 x 59 cm) DKK 25,000. Copenhagen, 11 June 2001, *Coastal Landscape with Woman* (oil on canvas, 17 x 28 ins / 42 x 71 cm) DKK 17,000. Copenhagen, 3 Sept 2003, *Interior Scene with Woman Seated by Chest of Drawers* (1920, oil on canvas, 22 x 20 ins / 55 x 51 cm) DKK 16,000. Copenhagen, 9 June 2004, *Young Woman Seated Wearing Black Hat* (oil on canvas, 22 x 15 ins / 56 x 39 cm) DKK 12,000.

FISCHER, Carl Christian
German, 18th century.
Died 1794, in Hanau (Hesse).
Potter.

FISCHER, Caspar
German, 16th - 17th century.

Born at the end of the 16th century, in Rosenheim (Bavaria).
Active in Enns (Austria).
Painter.

FISCHER, Christian
Swiss, 19th century.
Baptised 30 May 1789 in Brienz; died 22 August 1848, in Brienz.
Sculptor (wood).

FISCHER, Christian Johann
German, 18th century.
Born in Hamburg; died 7 June 1802, in Hamburg.
Draughtsman.

FISCHER, Christian Nathanael
German, 18th - 19th century.
Born 1756; died 1817, in Leipzig.
Painter.
Fischer worked in Leipzig from 1791.

FISCHER, Clara Elisabet
German, 19th century.
Born 29 January 1856, in Berlin.
Painter, engraver. Genre scenes.
Clara Fischer exhibited in Berlin from 1886.

FISCHER, Daniel
Austrian, 18th century.
Born c. 1730, in Vienna.
Miniaturist.

FISCHER, Eduard
German, 19th - 20th century.
Born 6 November 1852, in Berlin; died 1905.
Painter. Genre scenes, landscapes.
Eduard Fischer made his debut in Berlin about 1874.
AUCTION RECORDS:
MUNICH, 14 May 1986, *Fishermen Drawing in their Nets on the Chiemsee* (oil on panel, 10 x 20 1/2 ins / 25.5 x 52 cm) DEM 3,000.

FISCHER, Egon
Danish, 20th century.
Born 1935, in Copenhagen.
Sculptor.
Egon Fischer is self-taught. He has been a member of the School of Experimental Art since 1961, and of the Den Frie (The Free) group since 1967. He has taken part in the following exhibitions: 1962 School of Experimental Art, Copenhagen; 1966 Biennale of Nordic Youth, Louisiana, for which he was awarded a prize; 1967 Göteborg and Stockholm; 1969 Warsaw and Paris; 1970 Venice Biennale, where he represented Denmark. His art has humour and an amusing irony.
BIBLIOGRAPHY:
Galy-Carles, Henry, *Art danois, 1945-1973*, exhibition catalogue, Gal. nationales du Grand Palais, Paris, 1973.
MUSEUMS AND GALLERIES:
AALBORG (Nordjyllands Kunstmus.) - ESBJERG - LOUISIANA - ODENSE - RANDERS.

FISCHER, Ellen
Danish, 20th century.
Born in Kornerup.
Painter.
Ellen Fischer exhibited in Paris at the Salon des Indépendants in 1925 and at the Salon des Tuileries in 1929.

FISCHER, Ernst
German, 19th century.
Born 6 November 1815, in Dresden; died 22 September 1874, in Dresden.
Painter, lithographer, engraver. Genre scenes.
Fischer established himself in Dresden in around 1861.

FISCHER, Ernst
German, 19th century.
Born 6 July 1850, in Dresden.
Landscape artist.
From 1877 to 1880 Ernst Fischer studied under Paul Mohn. He established himself as a painter in Dresden in 1875.

FISCHER, Ernst Albert, pseudonym of Fischer Corlin or Cornelin
German, 19th century.
Born 22 August 1853, in Körlin, Pomerania (now Korlino, Poland).
Illustrator, painter (gouache). History painting, genre scenes, interiors with figures.
Ernst Albert Fischer studied under Daege and Schrader in Berlin. He embarked on his career as a professional painter in Berlin in 1877, where he specialised in large historical paintings.
AUCTION RECORDS:
COPENHAGEN, 18 April 1978, *Couple in a Rococo Interior* (1890, oil on canvas, 39 1/4 x 28 ins / 100 x 71 cm) DKK 20,000. LONDON, 25 June 1987, *Romantic Conversation* (gouache, 29 1/2 x 41 1/4 ins / 75 x 105 cm) GBP 2,800. NEW YORK, 19 Jan 1995, *Green Vase* (1926, oil on canvas, 29 x 22 ins / 73.7 x 55.9 cm) USD 1,150. PHILADELPHIA, 12 Dec 1999, *Surprise Visitor* (1891, oil on canvas, 28 x 40 ins / 72 x 101 cm) USD 4,500. DÜSSELDORF, 31 Jan 2000, *Geisha Girls* (1890, oil on canvas, 39 x 28 ins / 100 x 70 cm) DEM 110,000. STOCKHOLM, 5 Dec 2000, *Teasing* (gouache, 30 x 42 ins / 77 x 106 cm) SEK 45,000.

FISCHER, Ferdinand Auguste
German, 19th century.
Born 17 February 1805, in Berlin; died 2 April 1866, in Berlin.
Sculptor, medallist.
Ferdinand Fischer studied at the academy in Berlin, of which he became a member in 1847. In 1848 he was appointed to the academic senate.

FISCHER, Franz
Bohemian School, 18th century.
Active in Prague.
Engraver.

FISCHER, Franz
Austrian, 19th century.
Active in Vienna.
Miniaturist.

FISCHER, Franz Josef
German, 17th century.
Active in Ravensburg (Baden-Württemberg).
Painter.

FISCHER, Franz Marcel
Czech, 20th century.
Born 28 November 1900, in Prague, to Russian parents; died 1980.
Active and naturalised in Switzerland.
Sculptor.
Franz Marcel Fischer studied in Zurich at the arts and crafts school, then worked as a stone-cutter in Lugano. He was in Rome between 1921 and 1923, then Paris between 1926 and 1928. In 1936, he settled in Zurich.

Fischer's work is divided into several periods. Archaistic to begin with, it developed into an expression close to abstraction. His mature sculptures were nevertheless characterised by a return to Realism, unrestricted and personal with a clear tendency towards Symbolism. His sculptures and bronze and stone reliefs were often designed in an architectural framework. He featured in the Venice Biennale (1948).
MUSEUMS AND GALLERIES:
LAUSANNE (Cantonal MFA): *Dying Dog* (1956).

AUCTION RECORDS:
ZURICH, 13 Nov 1976, *Pair of Lovers I* (1960, bronze relief, 34 1/4 x 33 1/2 ins / 87 x 85 cm) CHF 2,500. ZURICH, 30 May 1979, *Bull* (1960, bronze, h. 18 ins / 46 cm) CHF 7,500. ZURICH, 30 Oct 1980, *Zebu I* (bronze, h. 24 1/4 ins / 61.5 cm) CHF 4,600. ZURICH, 22 June 1985, *Dog Jumping* (1956, patinated bronze, h. 13 1/2 ins / 34 cm) CHF 8,500. ZURICH, 19 Nov 1997, *Thrower* (bronze, 7 1/2 x 7 3/4 x 3 1/4 ins / 19 x 20 x 8 cm) CHF 1,300.

FISCHER, Franz Xaver
German, 18th century.
Died 7 April 1809, in Dillingen (Bavaria).
Sculptor.

FISCHER, Georg
Bohemian School, 18th century.
Active in Prague.
Painter.

FISCHER, Georg
German, 18th century.
Active in Munich in 1700.
Painter.

FISCHER, Georg Peter
German, 17th century.
Active in Munich during the first half of the 17th century.
Draughtsman, illustrator.

FISCHER, Gottfried
Austrian, 17th century.
Died 1660.
Active in Vienna.
Painter.
Gottfried Fischer was the son of Thomas Fischer.

FISCHER, Gottlob
German, 19th century.
Born 17 June 1829, in Stuttgart; died 8 July 1905, in Stuttgart.
Painter. Portraits, genre scenes.
Gottlob Fischer studied in Holland and Paris with Ary Scheffer. From 1857 he lived in Stuttgart and Canstatt.
MUSEUMS AND GALLERIES:
STUTTGART: *Huguenot Sermon; Portrait of Woman.*
AUCTION RECORDS:
NEW YORK, 25 Feb 1986, *Gallant Trooper* (oil on panel, 16 x 12 1/2 ins / 40.7 x 31.7 cm) USD 2,700. HEIDELBERG, 14 Oct 1988, *Portrait of Young Girl* (1869, oil on canvas, 23 1/2 x 19 3/4 ins / 60 x 50 cm) DEM 1,300.

FISCHER, Gustaf Ericson
Swedish, 19th century.
Born 1846; died 1893.
Painter. Landscapes.
Gustaf Ericson Fischer was a pupil at the academy in Stockholm.
AUCTION RECORDS:
STOCKHOLM, 23 April 1980, *Summer Landscape* (1878, oil on canvas, 13 1/2 x 24 1/2 ins / 34.5 x 62.5 cm) SEK 5,500.

FISCHER, Hans
German, 16th century.
Active in Breslau (now Wroclaw, Poland) in 1575.
Painter.

FISCHER, Hans
German, 16th century.
Active in Wolfenbüttel (Lower Saxony) at the end of the 16th century.
Painter.

FISCHER, Hans
German, 17th century.
Active at the beginning of the 17th century.
Miniaturist.
In 1612 Hans Fischer painted a miniature of the *Crucifixion* for the Duke of Stettin's album.

FISCHER, Hans
Swiss, 20th century.
Born 1909, in Bern; died 19 April 1958, in Interlaken.
Painter, draughtsman, lithographer, illustrator. Stage sets, murals, advertising art.
Hans Fischer was a student at the École des Beaux-Arts in Geneva, and then a pupil of Otto Meyer-Amden at the Kunstgewerbeschule in Zurich from 1928 to 1930. As an advertising artist in Paris from 1931 to 1932 he attended the courses of the Académie Fernand Léger. Returning to Switzerland in 1932, he collaborated on satirical newspapers and specialised in executing theatre scenery. He illustrated numerous albums, including *The Musicians of the City of Bremen*, by the Grimm Brothers, and numerous others on his own subjects.

Hans Fischer had numerous solo exhibitions, from his first in Zurich in 1943, in Switzerland, Holland, Paris, London, the USA, among others. He executed 26 murals in different towns and cities in Switzerland. In 1955 he was awarded the prize for graphic work at the São Paulo Biennale.

FISCHER, Hans Christian
Danish, 19th century.
Died 3 April 1846.
Painter. Landscapes with figures.
Hans Christian Fischer was a pupil at the Kunstakademi in Copenhagen.
AUCTION RECORDS:
COPENHAGEN, 15 Jan 1986, *Little Girl in Undergrowth in Spring* (1878, oil on canvas, 49 1/4 x 43 1/4 ins / 125 x 110 cm) DKK 19,000.

FISCHER, Heinrich
Swiss, 17th century.
Born in Lauffenburg.
Active between 1605 and 1619.
Sculptor (wood/stone).
Heinrich Fischer worked with his brother Melchior in Massmünster (Alsace), Beromünster, at the Capuchin monastery in Sursee, at the monastery of Muri in Augsburg (Bavaria), and at Görmund. He is noted for his sculptures at Beromünster and his crucifixes at Sursee and Görmund.

FISCHER, Heinrich
Swiss, 19th century.
Born 20 April 1820, in Nänikon; died 26 October 1886, in Zurich.
Lithographer. Portraits, urban landscapes.
This artist studied in Munich and worked in Bern, Lucern, Vevey, Montreux, Nice and Zurich. In 1846 and 1848 he sent three portraits (one of them in stone) to the Swiss exhibition in Bern. Fischer's son Jakob Henri also pursued an artistic career. Some of his lithographic views of Bern are greatly admired.
AUCTION RECORDS:
AHLDEN, 23 April 1999, *Mill in a Mountain Valley* (oil on canvas, 33 x 42 ins / 84 x 107 cm) DEM 10,000. LONDON, 2 Dec 1999, *Watermill in Alpine River Landscape* (oil on canvas, 33 x 43 ins / 84 x 108 cm) GBP 2,500. VIENNA, 23 May 2000, *View of Castle Ouvo, Sorrento* (1885, oil on canvas, 16 x 24 ins / 40 x 62 cm) ATS 45,000. BERN, 8 Nov 2002, *View from Pilatus to Lake Vierwaldstat* (oil on paper/board, 16 x 22 ins / 41 x 55 cm) CHF 4,800. VIENNA, 24 Feb 2004, *Goats in the High Mountains* (oil on board, 11 x 15 ins / 27 x 37 cm) EUR 2,000.

FISCHER, Helene von
German, 19th century.
Born 20 April 1843, in Berlin.

Painter. Still-lifes, flowers.
Helene von Fischer established herself in Dresden in around 1880.

FISCHER, Henri or Heinrich, pseudonym:
Fischer Hinnen
Swiss, 19th century.
Born 20 April 1844, in Zurich; died 18 May 1898, in Bellegarde.
Painter, draughtsman, illustrator. Landscapes.
Henri Fischer spent time in Montreux, Nice, Zurich, London, Bern and Geneva, and lived for the last years of his life in Bellegarde in France. When in London he opened a gallery of paintings in 1880. He worked for the satirical magazine *Postheiri* in Lucerne. He painted numerous pictures of bears, six of which were commissioned by the Hotel Bären (Bear Hotel) in Bern. He is especially known for his landscapes and humorous paintings.
AUCTION RECORDS:
LUCERNE, 25 May 1982, *Lake of the Four Cantons* (oil on canvas, 22 1/2 x 29 1/2 ins / 57 x 75 cm) CHF 1,600. NEW YORK, 29 Oct 1986, *Walk in a Wood* (1878, oil on canvas, 48 3/4 x 43 1/2 ins / 123.8 x 110.5 cm) USD 4,200. BERN, 26 Oct 1988, *Rural Landscape with Old Oaks* (oil on card, 10 1/4 x 14 1/4 ins / 26 x 36 cm) CHF 850.

FISCHER, Hermann, or Vischer
German, 15th century.
Sculptor.
Franconian School.
Hermann Fischer may be the same person as Hermann Vischer the Elder. He may also be the author of some items attributed to Peter Flötner.

FISCHER, Hermann
German, 17th century.
Active in Neisse, Silesia (now Nysa, Poland) at the beginning of the 17th century.
Sculptor (wood).

FISCHER, Hermann
Swiss, 19th century.
Born 12 November 1855, in Lenzburg.
Engraver (wood).
Fischer studied and worked under the direction of J.R. Müller in Zurich, Stuttgart, Leipzig, Vienna and Berlin. From 1883 he ran a wood engraving studio in Zurich. His known works (some of which won awards in Geneva and Zurich between 1883 and 1896) include notably his illustrations for a work on botany and physics by Dr Keller (1901), and the portraits for *Swiss History* by the professor Dr Karl Dandliker.

FISCHER, Hervé
French, 20th century.
Born 1941, in Paris.
Painter, writer.
Art Sociologique (Sociological Art), Conceptual Art.
Hervé Fischer is university-educated, and began painting as an amateur. His early work is in a traditional style, but in 1968, influenced by the work of Jackson Pollock, he abandoned this in favour of an abstract style. Around 1972, within the context of what he called 'art hygiene' ('hygiène de l'art'), he attempted to demystify the idea of the 'work of art', and to analyse it as a sociological phenomenon. In doing so, he broke numerous artistic taboos, attacking, for example, the level of respect which artists receive, the manner in which their work is presented, the prizes they receive, and the way in which their art is distributed. Nevertheless, he sometimes played on words, as in the case of *Contraceptual Pills*.

In 1974, with Fred Forest and Jean-Paul Thénot, he founded the Collectif d'Art Sociologique (Sociological Art Collective), which he defines as follows: 'Sociological art is an existential experiment, testing the limits of an individual's lucidity within the context of society. As such, it is a philosophical practice.' Thus, all words bear an image, and are imbued with a strength, which should be used and never forgotten, in order both to understand and, if necessary, to denounce our socio-cultural environment, bound as it is by conventions.

Hervé Fischer has taken part in many group exhibitions, including: the Venice Biennale and São Paolo Biennales in 1976; the Atelier d'Art Politique, with Klaus Staeck, in 1976; and at Documenta 7 in Kassel. He has also staged a number of solo exhibitions, including the following: in 1974, when he exhibited *Déchirures* (*Scraps*) of other artists' works; a retrospective at the Musée d'Art Contemporain, in 1974; and *¿La Calle, Adonde Llega?* (*Where Does The Street Lead?*), at the Museo de Arte Moderno in Mexico City in 1983.
BIBLIOGRAPHY:
Fischer, Hervé, *Art et communication marginale*, Balland, Paris, 1974. Fischer, Hervé, *Théorie de l'Art sociologique*, Casterman, Paris, 1977. Fischer, Hervé, *Citoyens/Sculpteurs*, Segedo, Paris, 1981. *LHistoire de l'Art est terminée*, Balland, Paris, 1981. Fischer, Hervé, *L'Oiseau-chat*, Éd. La Presse, Montreal, 1983. *La Calle, adonde llega?*, exhibition catalogue, Arte y Edicion, Mexico, 1983. Fischer, Hervé, *La Mythanalyse*, Balland, Paris, 1984. *Écritures dans la peinture*, Centre National des Arts Plastiques, Villa Arson-Centre National des Arts Plastiques, Nice, 1984.

FISCHER, Ida
American, 20th century.
Painter.
Ida Fischer exhibited abstract works, well balanced and very thick in pigment, in Paris at the Salon des Réalités Nouvelles of 1950.

FISCHER, Ignaz
Austrian, 19th century.
Active in Vienna c. 1830.
Miniaturist.

FISCHER, Isaac
German, 17th century.
Died 1705.
Active in Augsburg (Bavaria).
Painter. History painting, portraits.
Isaac Fischer was working in Augsburg by 1677.

FF

FISCHER, J. H.
German, 18th century.
Active in Cologne at the end of the 18th century.
Painter. History painting, portraits.
Several religious paintings are attributed to this artist.

FISCHER, J. L.
German, 18th century.
Active in Nuremberg (Bavaria) at the end of the 18th century.
Engraver.
A great number of prints are known signed with the name J.L. Fischer.

FISCHER, Jacob
German, 17th century.
Active in Brieg, Silesia (now Brzeg, Poland) in 1664.
Painter.

FISCHER, Jacob Adolphe
German, 18th century.
Born 1755, in Magdeburg (Saxony-Anhalt).
Painter, miniaturist.
Jacob Adolphe Fischer studied at the academy in Berlin. He specialised in portraits in pastel and in miniature.

FISCHER, Jan
Dutch, 17th century.
Born c. 1636, in Amsterdam.
Painter. Animals.
According to Siret, Jan Fischer was an engraver who turned to painting at the age of 56.

FISCHER, Jocheim
German, 17th century.
Died 1633, in Lüben, near Liegnitz, Silesia (now Legnica, Poland).
Painter.

FISCHER, Joel
American, 20th - 21st century.
Born 1947, in Salem (Ohio).
Active in England.
Draughtsman, sculptor.
Without joining the Arte Povera movement, which sprang up primarily in Italy from 1968 onward, Joel Fischer nevertheless benefited from it, in that this movement looked at the coarsest materials through new eyes. However, the issue for Fischer is not one of expressivity, as it is for the Arte Povera artists, but rather a reflection on the ambitions of art. In his early career his work was above all intended to be a derisory activity. At this time he began to plait and spin hair, and make nails from old bits of metal or pieces of coarse paper from old clothes. By reaffirming ties with the artisan side of art, Fischer quickly found favour in the USA. Without losing interest in the materials, he began in the 1980s to explore meticulously the medium and subject of his future drawings: chiffon paper, which he makes entirely by hand. The imperfections are exaggerated with charcoal and, in a new space, come to signify a non-accidental form. In 1980 he declared:

'When the incident has been drawn, how many times can I redo it? Must we make do with the limits of the page alone or can we venture into other surfaces?'

Fischer has repeated the formal projection of his drawings, which came out of the initial imperfections, in three dimensions, with bronze sculptures over a metre high. They feature progressions in which the line dominates and the spatial volume is stretched elegantly open.

Fischer has been exhibited in the USA since 1970, and has also shown his works in Europe - particularly in London and Paris. He has taken part in various collective exhibitions, including: 1972, Documenta 5, Kassel; 1972, the Paris Biennale; and 1982, *Choix pour aujourd'hui. Regard sur 4 ans d'acquisitions d'art contemporain* (*Choices for Today: A Look at Four Years of Contemporary Art Acquisitions*) at the Musée National d'Art Moderne, Paris. He also holds solo exhibitions, for example from 1987-1988 at the Galerie Farideh Cadot, Paris.

BIBLIOGRAPHY:
Choix pour aujourd'hui, exhibition catalogue, Musée national d'Art moderne, Éd. du Centre Georges-Pompidou, Paris, 1982.

AUCTION RECORDS:
NEW YORK, 9 May 1990, '*Vas*' (1985, green-patinated bronze, h. 14 ins / 35.5 cm) USD 15,400. SAN FRANCISCO, 22 April 1999, *Sculpture* (verdigris-black patinated bronze, h. 30 ins / 76 cm) USD 2,500. PARIS, 25 June 2001, *Untitled* (bronze, sold with study in pencil, 6 x 6 ins / 16 x 16 cm) FRF 56,000. LONDON, 3 Feb 2003, *Untitled* (bronze, 25 x 46 ins / 64 x 116 cm) GBP 2,800. LUCERNE, 24 May 2003, *Untitled* (charcoal, 76 x 46 ins / 194 x 118 cm) CHF 3,400. NEW YORK, 12 Feb 2004, *Wanderer* (1985, brown patinated bronze, 48 x 40x26 ins / 122 x 101x66 cm) USD 6,500. NEW YORK, 12 Feb 2004, *Eggman* (1987, green patinated bronze, 39 x 29x22 ins / 100 x 74x56 cm) USD 12,000.

FISCHER, Johan
German, 17th century.
Active in Saxony at the beginning of the 17th century.
Engraver (wood).
Illustrations for a bible published in Strasbourg in 1606 are attributed to Johan Fischer.

FISCHER, Johann
German, 18th century.
Active in Berlin.
Painter. Architectural views.
Johann Fischer was a member of the academy in Berlin.

FISCHER, Johann
German, 18th century.
Born in Neuss, near Düsseldorf (North Rhine-Westphalia); died 19 January 1728, in Düsseldorf.
Painter.
Johann Fischer is best known for views of buildings.

FISCHER, Johann Baptist
Austrian, 17th century.
Born 1626, in Graz.
Sculptor.
Johann Baptist Fischer worked at the town hall in Graz and produced decorations to celebrate the triumphal entry of the emperor Leopold I into the town.

FISCHER, Johann Christian Richard
German, 19th century.
Born 1826, in Danzig (now Gdansk, Poland).
Painter. Landscapes.
J.C.R. Fischer studied under Sohn, Hildebrand and Schirmer. He travelled in Germany, Switzerland and the Tyrol, before settling in Berlin and, from 1862, in Danzig.

FISCHER, Johann Christoph
German, 18th century.
Active in Ansbach (Bavaria) c. 1700.
Sculptor.
There are firm grounds for believing that this artist is to be identified with a Johann Fischer who was working in Amberg in 1684

FISCHER, Johann Franz
Bohemian School, 18th century.
Died 4 November 1740, in Prague.
Engraver.
Johann Fischer produced mostly portraits and paintings of monuments.

FISCHER, Johann Friedrich
German, 18th century.
Active in Bayreuth (Bavaria) c. 1738.
Sculptor.

FISCHER, Johann Georg
German, 17th century.
Born 1580, in Augsburg; died 1643, in Munich.
Painter. History painting.
Johann Georg Fischer was painter to the court of Bavaria. He made copies of works by Albrecht Dürer.
MUSEUMS AND GALLERIES:
MUNICH: *Christ Taken Prisoner.*

FISCHER, Johann Georg
German, 17th century.
Died 1669.
Active in Erlau (now Eger, Hungary).
Sculptor (wood).
Bohemian School.
Johann Georg Fischer's relief in wood *Our Lady of the Angels* appeared in the exhibition *Lumière et Ténèbres, Art et Civilisation du Baroque en Bohême* (*Light and Darkness. Ba-*

roque Art and Civilisation in Bohemia) at the Palais des Beaux-Arts in Lille in 2002.

BIBLIOGRAPHY:
Vlnas, Vit (ed.), *Lumière et ténèbres, art et civilisation du Baroque en Bohême*, exhibition catalogue, Palais des Beaux-Arts, Lille, Réunion des musées nationaux, Paris, 2002.

FISCHER, Johann Heinrich
Swiss, 19th century.
Born 15 August 1811, in Aarau; died 7 August 1879, in Aarau.
Lithographer, draughtsman.
J.H. Fischer developed his skill at Bolliger's studio in Aarau and also worked in Zug and Zurich. He is best known for his two plates *Hoffnung* (*Hope*) and *Wiedersehen* (*Meeting*).

FISCHER, Johann Michael
Austrian, 17th - 18th century.
Active in Vienna.
Sculptor.
Johann Michael Fischer's widow married one of his students, Leopold Fischer, in 1714.

FISCHER, Johann Michael
German, 18th century.
Died 27 March 1801, in Dillingen (Bavaria).
Sculptor.
Among the works attributed to Johann Michael Fischer is the main altar in the church of St Catherine in Hall and part of the façade of the church in Neresheim.

FISCHER, Johann Thomas
German, 17th century.
Born 21 December 1603; died 16 October 1685.
Active in Nuremberg (Bavaria).
Watercolourist, illuminator.
Most of the works attributed to Johann Thomas Fischer are paintings of flowers.

FISCHER, Johann Wilhelm
German, 17th century.
Active in Cologne c. 1680.
Painter, draughtsman.
Johann Wilhelm Fischer appears to be the artist of that name who died in Hamburg on 2 December 1710.

FISCHER, Johannes
German, 16th - 17th century.
Active in Augsburg (Bavaria).
Painter.
This artist is often confused with Johann Georg and Georg Vischer of Munich.

FISCHER, Johannes Josef
German, 18th century.
Active in Bilin (now Bílina, Czech Republic) at the beginning of the 18th century.
Sculptor.

FISCHER, Johannes Sigismond
Austrian, 18th century.
Died May 1758, in Capodimonte, near Naples.
Painter (porcelain).
Johannes Fischer worked in Vienna in 1751.

FISCHER, Josef
Austrian, 18th century.
Born c. 1746; died 9 February 1779, in Vienna.
Painter.

FISCHER, Joseph
German, 18th century.
Born in Faulenbach (Bavaria).
Sculptor.
Fischer decorated churches in Ketterschwang, Jengen and Unterostendorf.

FISCHER, Joseph
German, 18th - 19th century.
Born 1761, in Munich; died perhaps in 1843, in Vienna.
Painter, painter (porcelain). Still-lifes (flowers/fruit).
Joseph Fischer studied in Augsburg, Vienna, Berlin and Antwerp and studied under J. Dorner in Munich. He also painted on porcelain.

AUCTION RECORDS:
VIENNA, 14 Sept 1983, *Bouquet of Flowers* (1806, watercolour and gouache, 35 1/2 x 25 1/4 ins / 90 x 64 cm) ATS 20,000.
PARIS, 15 Dec 1995, *Fruit and Flowers on an Entablature* (1788, oil on canvas, 16 1/4 x 12 1/4 ins / 41 x 31 cm) FRF 300,000.

FISCHER, Joseph
Austrian, 18th - 19th century.
Born 1769, in Vienna; died 5 September 1822, in Vienna.
Painter, engraver.
Joseph Fischer studied painting and engraving with Brand and Schmutzer at the academy in his native city. He then became a teacher there. His paintings at the gallery in Vienna include *View of Vienna* and *Landscape*. Some of his best engravings are considered to be *Christ in the Temple* after Ribera (1793); *Adulteress*, after Füger; *Portrait of Correggio*.

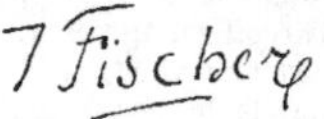

FISCHER, Joseph
German, 19th century.
Born 22 September 1853, in Stetten.
Painter.
A student of P. Deschwanden, this artist specialised in religious subjects.

FISCHER, Joseph Anton
German, 18th century.
Born in Augsburg; died 1750, in Vienna.
Miniaturist.
Fischer worked for most of his life in Vienna.

FISCHER, Joseph Anton
German, 19th century.
Born 28 February 1814, in Oberstdorf (Bavaria); died 20 March 1859, in Munich.
Painter.
Joseph Anton Fischer began life as a cowherd but was able, with the help of Ch. Schraudolf, to join the academy in Munich with Schlotthauer and visit Italy in 1832 and 1843. During this time, he produced some sketches of the Auerkirche for glass paintings, under the instruction of Hess, and also painted eight others for Cologne Cathedral between 1844 and 1848. Some very fine pen and ink drawings are to be found in various different collections, particularly in Munich.

MUSEUMS AND GALLERIES:
MUNICH (Gal.): *Flight into Egypt* (1841); *Adoration of the Magi* (1844); *The Visitation* (1845); *Burial* (1848).

FISCHER, Judas Thadeus
German, 18th century.
Active in Rosenheim (Bavaria) c. 1700.
Painter.

FISCHER, Karl, pseudonym: Fischer Köystrand
Austrian, 19th - 20th century.
Born 28 November 1861, in Vienna; died 1918.
Painter (gouache), watercolourist, pastellist, draughtsman, caricaturist. Genre scenes.
Karl Fischer, after having been the pupil of Christiann Griepenkerl at the Akademie der Bildenden Künste in Vien-

na, he was a leading figure in painting and caricature, collaborating with different Viennese newspapers.

AUCTION RECORDS:

LONDON, 25 March 1988, *After Woman* (watercolour and gouache, triptych, 19 x 63 1/2 ins / 48.3 x 161 cm) GBP 2,200. LONDON, 28 Nov 1990, *Portrait of the Singer Léonore Rellée* (pastel, 37 3/4 x 18 1/2 ins / 96 x 47 cm) GBP 9,900.

FISCHER, Karl von

German, 19th century.
Born 19 September 1782, in Mannheim (Baden-Württemberg); died 12 February 1820, in Munich.
Architect, watercolourist.

The architect Karl von Fischer produced some landscapes and views of buildings.

FISCHER, Konrad

Swiss, 18th century.
Born in Grosswangen.
Painter.

In 1731 Konrad Fischer restored the painting depicting the *Battle of Sempach* in a chapel in that town.

FISCHER, L.

British, 19th century.
Born 1814.
Painter, miniaturist. Portraits.

L. Fischer exhibited miniatures at the Royal Academy in London in 1854.

FISCHER, Leopold

Austrian, 19th century.
Born c. 1813, in Vienna; died 1860.
Painter, watercolourist, engraver.

Leopold Fischer was a student at the academy in Vienna and exhibited miniatures from 1844 onwards.

AUCTION RECORDS:

VIENNA, 17 May 1984, *Portrait of Young Woman in Lace Dress* (1844, watercolour, 9 x 6 3/4 ins / 23 x 17 cm) ATS 20,000. VIENNA, 28 March 2003, *Portrait of a Woman in Black Velvet Dress* (1839, watercolour, 8 x 6 ins / 20 x 15 cm) EUR 1,600.

FISCHER, Lothar

German, 20th century.
Born 1933, in Germersheim.
Painter, sculptor.
Spur Group.

Lothar Fischer was a student at the Akademie der Bildenden Künste in Munich. In 1961 he was awarded a scholarship by the Villa Massimo, in Rome. He has held exhibitions in Germany and other countries. In 1957 he and three other painters founded in Munich the *Trace* group, whose intentions are overtly expressionist and experimental, thus prolonging the activities of the CoBrA movement.

AUCTION RECORDS:

COLOGNE, 5 Dec 1981, *Figure Seated* (1974, terracotta, h. 67 ins / 170 cm) DEM 5,000. COLOGNE, 7 Dec 1984, *Reclining Nude* (1976, terracotta, h. 3 1/4 ins / 8 cm, w. 22 3/4 ins/58 cm) DEM 1,600. COLOGNE, 29 May 1987, *Large Clothed Woman Seated* (1975, terracotta, h. 49 1/4 ins / 125 cm) DEM 11,000. AMSTERDAM, 13 Dec 1989, *Gaia* (1962, terracotta, h. 27 1/2 ins / 70 cm) NLG 23,000. AMSTERDAM, 11 Dec 1991, *Torso* (1973, terracotta, h. 33 ins / 84 cm) NLG 4,830. COPENHAGEN, 1 Dec 1993, *The Competition Luge* (bronze, l. 15 3/4 ins / 40 cm, w. 6 1/4 ins/16 cm, h. 6 ins/15 cm) DKK 15,000. COPENHAGEN, 2 March 1994, *Untitled* (1964, ceramic, h. 11 3/4 ins / 30 cm, w. 18 ins/46 cm) DKK 16,000. MILAN, 24 May 1994, *Don Quixote* (painted terracotta, 21 1/4 x 13 3/4 x 5 1/2 ins / 54 x 35 x 14 cm) ITL 26,450,000. LUCERNE, 4 June 1994, *Standing Female Nude* (clay, h. 18 3/4 ins / 47.5 cm) CHF 2,600. COPENHAGEN, 8-9 March 1995, *Cupid and Psyche* (1960, bronze, h. 7 3/4 ins / 20 cm) DKK 25,000. AMSTERDAM, 10 Dec 1996, *Susanna Bathing* (1964, terracotta, h. 14 ins / 35.5 cm) NLG 7,495. COLOGNE, 12 Nov 1999, *Tower* (clay, h. 19 ins / 47 cm) DEM 9,000. MUNICH, 20 Nov 1999, *Footballer* (1970, painted clay and shoelace, 20 x 16x7 ins / 51 x 40x17 cm) DEM 8,000. COLOGNE, 6 June 2000, *Big Animal Head* (1922, patinated bronze, 22 x 47x5 ins / 55 x 120x12 cm) DEM 15,000. COLOGNE, 6 June 2000, *Tall Slim Man* (sculpture, h. 72 ins / 182 cm) DEM 17,000. COLOGNE, 30 May 2001, *Reclining Woman* (1969, patinated bronze, 15 x 22x13 ins / 38 x 57x32 cm) DEM 9,000. COLOGNE, 2 June 2001, *Rider* (clay, h. 18 ins / 46 cm) DEM 11,000. COLOGNE, 5 June 2002, *Norne* (1975, clay, h. 24 ins / 60 cm) EUR 9,000. HAMBURG, 24 Oct 2003, *Furniture Facade with Drawers* (clay with iron plinth, 20 x 10x3 ins / 51 x 25x7 cm) EUR 1,700. COLOGNE, 27 Nov 2003, *Small Kneeling Figure* (1979, brown and black patinated bronze, 7 x 5x5 ins / 18 x 13x12 cm) EUR 2,200. COLOGNE, 4 June 2004, *Kneeling Female Torso* (1985, clay, 24 x 13x15 ins / 62 x 34x38 cm) EUR 3,800. HAMBURG, 29 Oct 2004, *Europasiphee* (polished bronze, two parts, 10 x 10x4 ins / 25 x 25x10 cm) EUR 4,300.

FISCHER, Louis, real name: Louis-François Poisson de Marigny, (Marquis)

French, 19th century.
Born 25 August 1784, in Paris; died 15 February 1845, in Schwerin (Germany).
Painter, sculptor, engraver. Still-lifes.

Louis Fischer, formerly an officer in the French army, settled in Schwerin in 1815. He was the father of the painter Theodor Fischer Poisson. He produced lithographs.

MUSEUMS AND GALLERIES:

MAINZ: *Still-life*.

AUCTION RECORDS:

MUNICH, 18 April 1988, *Game of Chess in Schlosseichstätt* (oil on panel, 20 1/2 x 17 ins / 52 x 43 cm) DEM 9,900.

FISCHER, Ludwig

Austrian, 19th century.
Born 13 October 1825, in Vienna.
Painter. Landscapes, flowers.

Fischer studied under Steinfeld at the academy in Vienna.

AUCTION RECORDS:

VIENNA, 28 Nov 1967, *Mountain Landscape*, ATS 25,000. VIENNA, 30 Nov 2000, *Blacksmith* (1847, oil on canvas, 15 x 19 ins / 38 x 47 cm) ATS 50,000.

FISCHER, Ludwig Hans

German, 19th - 20th century.
Born 2 March 1848, in Salzburg; died 24 April 1915, in Vienna.
Painter (gouache), watercolourist. Landscapes, architectural views.

Hans Ludwig Fischer was the pupil of Lichtenfels, Jacoby and Unger. He travelled to Italy and Algeria, then set up in Vienna.

L·H·Fischer

MUSEUMS AND GALLERIES:

GRAZ: *Landscape* - VIENNA: *Beside the Sea*; *View of Jerusalem*; *Vajda Hunyad Castle in Hungary*.

AUCTION RECORDS:

VIENNA, 14 Nov 1978, *View of Vienna* (1912, watercolour, 3 3/4 x 5 3/4 ins / 9.5 x 14.5 cm) ATS 18,000. LONDON, 26 Nov 1981, *Panoramic View of Vienna* (1894, watercolour, 36 1/4 x 55 1/4 ins / 92 x 140.5 cm) GBP 1,400. LONDON, 22 March 1984, *View of the Souks, Cairo* (watercolour heightened with gouache, 13 1/4 x 10 1/4 ins / 33.5 x 26 cm) GBP 2,200. LONDON, 20 June 1984, *Reading a Letter in an Arab Market* (1890, oil on card, 39 x 28 1/2 ins / 99 x 72.5 cm) GBP 5,200. NEW YORK, 28 Oct 1986, *The Desert Wind* (oil on canvas, 69 x 46 1/2 ins / 175.3 x 118 cm) USD 23,000. LONDON, 27 Nov 1987, *Riva De-*

gli Schiavoni, Venice (1895, watercolour heightened with white, 11¾ x 18 ins / 30 x 45.8 cm) GBP 1,500. LONDON, 25 March 1988, *View of Constantinople* (oil on panel, 5 x 11 ins / 13 x 28 cm) GBP 2,860. LONDON, 16 June 1993, *The Mosque of the Vizier Khan in Lahore* (watercolour, 11¼ x 16¼ ins / 28.5 x 41 cm) GBP 5,520. ZURICH, 24 June 1993, *The Great Temple of Hampi* (watercolour, 9½ x 15 ins / 24.2 x 37.2 cm) CHF 2,200. PARIS, 30 June 1993, *View of an Interior* (watercolour and gouache, 12¼ x 19 ins / 31 x 48 cm) FRF 22,000. LONDON, 19 Nov 1993, *Caravan in the Desert at Dusk* (oil on canvas, 20 x 33 ins / 50.8 x 83.8 cm) GBP 6,325. LONDON, 10 Feb 1995, *Caravan in the Desert* (1903, oil on canvas/card, 26½ x 47½ ins / 67 x 120.7 cm) GBP 3,220.

FISCHER, Maria Anna, or Fisher
Maiden name: Felsenberg
German, 19th century.
Born 1785, in Vienna.
Engraver.
Maria Anna Fischer was the sister of Joseph Fischer. She engraved landscapes and battle scenes.

FISCHER, Mark. See **FISHER William Mark**

FISCHER, Martha
German, 19th century.
Active in Berlin.
Painter. Portraits, genre scenes.
Martha Fischer established herself as an artist in Hamburg around 1887.

FISCHER, Martin
Italian, 18th century.
Painter.
Martin Fischer painted a series of frescoes for the Palazzo Antonini in Udine in 1702.

FISCHER, Martin
German, 20th century.
Born 10 November 1879, in Kiel.
Active in the USA.
Painter, writer. Murals.
Martin Fischer was a member of the Duvenech Society of Painters and of the Cincinnati Art Club. He executed murals in Cincinnati. He was a lecturer and writer, being the author notably of *The Permanent Palette*, which has been translated into German.

FISCHER, Martin
British, 20th - 21st century.
Born 17 April 1946, in London.
Active in Switzerland.
Sculptor.
Martin Fischer lived in London until the age of 16 and had a musical training in jazz. He later moved to the canton of Argovia in Switzerland and has taken part in exhibitions of young Swiss artists. From 1972, he worked as a sculptor in a style close to Art Pauvre, constructing wind or string instruments which use the wind as their mechanical element.

FISCHER, Martin Johann
Austrian, 18th - 19th century.
Born 2 November 1741, in Bebele, near Hopfen; died 27 April 1820, in Vienna.
Sculptor.
Martin Johann Fischer studied under Tabota and J. Schletterer in Vienna and became a member of the academy of fine arts. In 1815 he was appointed as director of the school of art and sculpture. A great number of his works are to be found in Vienna, such as fountains entitled *Moses, Hygie, Leopold, Joseph, Vigilance*, a statue of *Mucius Scoevola* in the gardens at Schoenbrünn, four statues of the *Evangelists* on the high altar in the church of St Michael, and *Bust of Joseph II* at the university. He created the memorial to *Bishop H.J. Kerenz* in the cathedral of St Pölten, and the memorial to *General Zischkowitz and his Wife* in the cathedral in Prague. He carried out many decorative works and sculptures for distinguished clients, such as *The Three Graces* in the style of Eisgrub for the prince of Lichtenstein, *Mercury and Venus* for Countess Kinsky, *Apollo* for Count Althan, and the sculptures in the palace of the Duchess T.A.F. de Carignan, a princess of Lichtenstein by birth.

FISCHER, Marx
German, 16th century.
Sculptor.
Marx Fischer is mentioned in 1539 in Augsburg.

FISCHER, Mary Ellen Sigsbee
American, 20th century.
Born 26 February 1876, in New Orleans; died 1960, in Woodstock (New York).
Illustrator.
Mary Ellen Sigsbee Fischer, wife of Anton Otto Fischer, was a pupil of the Students League of Workington and New York, and from 1912 an associate member of the Society of Illustrators.

FISCHER, Melchior
Swiss, 17th century.
Born in Lauffenburg.
Active between 1605 and 1619.
Sculptor (stone/wood).
Melchior was the brother of Heinrich Fischer and worked with him in several towns in Alsace.

FISCHER, Michael, or Vischer
Austrian, 16th century.
Active in Vienna in 1587.
Painter.
This painter was employed by the ambassador Friedrich Kreskwitz to accompany him to Constantinople and make sketches of their visit.

FISCHER, Michael
German, 18th century.
Sculptor (marble), draughtsman.
Michael Fischer executed some works in marble in 1733 in the choir of the church in the castle at Bruchsal (Baden-Württemberg), above the bishop's seat and above that of the priest.

FISCHER, Michael
Austrian, 19th century.
Born 1826, in Aurolzmünster (Upper Austria); died 1887, in Linz.
Engraver, worker with precious stones. Seals.
This artist engraved metals, precious stones, gemstones and seals.

FISCHER, Niklaus von
Swiss, 19th century.
Born 1825, in Erlach.
Draughtsman, painter.
Niklaus von Fischer lived in the Riesbach district of Zurich and also in London. Dr Brun's dictionary notes a large panoramic drawing by him of the town of Zurich, entitled *View of Mount Jakob*, exhibited in Zurich in 1883. Fischer went to London in 1885.

FISCHER, Nikolaus
Swiss, 18th century.
Born 20 November 1768, in Triengen; died 1792, in Rome.
Painter. History painting, portraits, genre scenes.

Brother of Ulrich Fischer, the painter of Biblical history, and a student of Melchior Wyrsch, Nikolaus Fischer carried out work for Swiss churches and exhibited his portrait and other paintings in Lucerne in 1789. He is particularly known for his works *Annunciation* and *Noel* in the parish church in his home town, and an altar painting in the church in Eich (Lucerne canton) representing *St Lawrence*.

MUSEUMS AND GALLERIES:

MAINZ: *Portrait of Dr F. Werner*.

FISCHER, Oskar

Belgian, 20th century.
Born 1910, in Vienna.
Painter.

Oskar Fischer studied architecture, setting up definitively in Belgium in 1939. It was during World War II that he began to paint. Starting by treating his compositions in figurative terms, he was then won over by a form of Expressionism, before extending his investigations into the abstract mode of painting.

AUCTION RECORDS:

HAMBURG, 11 June 1982, *Crime of Passion* (1921, pen, 10 1/4 x 11 1/2 ins / 26 x 29.5 cm) DEM 1,200. COLOGNE, 4 June 1985, *Houses in the Trees* (1917, watercolour/Japanese paper, 16 3/4 x 11 1/2 ins / 42.5 x 29 cm) DEM 3,200. MUNICH, 3 June 1987, *The Dear Old Knife-grinder* (c. 1920, oil on canvas, 15 1/4 x 21 ins / 38.5 x 52.5 cm) DEM 15,000. MUNICH, 14 May 2004, *Illustration for Poem* (1920, watercolour and Indian ink, 8 x 5 ins / 20 x 13 cm) EUR 4,000.

FISCHER, Otto

German, 20th century.
Born 2 July 1870, in Leipzig.
Painter, engraver, lithographer. Portraits.

Otto Fischer was a student at the Hochschule für Bildende Künste in Dresden, and the pupil of Oehme, Preller and H. Preli. He lived in Loschwitz, near Dresden. He featured in most of the European exhibitions from 1894 to 1914. He was a member of the New Association of Artists in Munich. In 1912 he published *Das neue Bild* (*The New Image*), which caused the departure from the group of Jawlensky and Marianne von Werefkin.

MUSEUMS AND GALLERIES:

BREMEN: *Head of an Old Man* - SAN FRANCISCO (FAM): *Head of an Old Man* (drawing).

FISCHER, Paul

Danish, 19th - 20th century.
Born 22 July 1860, in Copenhagen; died 1934.
Painter, sculptor. History painting, portraits, genre scenes, market scenes.

Paul Fischer was a student at the Kunstakademi in Copenhagen. He painted some historical canvases, portraits and scenes from everyday life, in particular street and market scenes. He also produced a number of terracottas. He exhibited in Munich in 1891, and then occasionally in Paris.

PAUL
FISCHER

MUSEUMS AND GALLERIES:

HILLERØD (Frederiksbörg Slot): *Christian IX Receives a Deputation on the Occasion of the Election of Haakon VII as King of Norway*.

AUCTION RECORDS:

COPENHAGEN, 10 Feb 1966, *The Florist*, DKK 14,000. COPENHAGEN, 11 Feb 1969, *The Military Parade*, DKK 29,000. COPENHAGEN, 20 Sept 1972, *Market Scene*, DKK 20,000. COPENHAGEN, 26 March 1974, *The Florist*, DKK 38,000. COPENHAGEN, 5 May 1976, *The Fire* (1900, oil on canvas, 35 1/2 x 47 1/4 ins / 90 x 120 cm) DKK 20,000. COPENHAGEN, 16 March 1977, *Market Scene* (oil on canvas, 19 3/4 x 22 1/2 ins / 50 x 57 cm) DKK 27,000. COPENHAGEN, 29 Aug 1978, *Street Scene in Winter* (1904, oil on canvas, 20 1/2 x 13 1/2 ins / 52 x 34 cm) DKK 23,000. COPENHAGEN, 18 Aug 1981, *Street Scene in Winter, Nyhavn* (1924, oil on canvas, 25 1/2 x 35 1/2 ins / 65 x 90 cm) DKK 80,000. LONDON, 19 June 1984, *An Evening Performance at the Theatre Royal, Copenhagen* (1887-1888, oil on canvas, 86 1/2 x 67 3/4 ins / 220 x 172 cm) GBP 38,000. LONDON, 28 Nov 1984, *Street Scene, Copenhagen* (watercolour, pencil and Indian ink heightened with gouache, 7 1/2 x 15 ins / 19 x 38 cm) GBP 2,300. COPENHAGEN, 23 April 1987, *Street Scene* (1899, oil on canvas, 36 1/2 x 61 1/2 ins / 92.5 x 156.5 cm) DKK 1,000,000. LONDON, 23 March 1988, *The Flower Market at Amagertow* (1916, oil on canvas, 28 3/4 x 22 ins / 73 x 55 cm) GBP 39,600; *Gathering Spring Flowers* (1893, oil on canvas, 37 x 18 1/4 ins / 94 x 46.5 cm) GBP 41,800; *A Square in Copenhagen* (1923, oil on canvas, 12 1/4 x 15 ins / 31 x 38 cm) GBP 9,350; *University of Copenhagen* (oil on canvas, 10 x 12 1/2 ins / 24.5 x 32 cm) GBP 4,180; *The Royal Guard Parading in Ostergade in Copenhagen* (oil on canvas, 39 1/4 x 39 1/4 ins / 100 x 100 cm) GBP 30,800. STOCKHOLM, 15 Nov 1988, *Crossroads with Passers-by and a Car in Copenhagen* (oil on canvas, 12 1/2 x 9 3/4 ins / 32 x 25 cm) SEK 100,000. LONDON, 16 March 1989, *Changing the Guard at Amalienborg Palace* (1903, oil on canvas, 28 x 39 ins / 71 x 99 cm) GBP 26,400; *Hojbro Plads Flower Market in Copenhagen* (1902, oil on canvas, 26 1/2 x 35 3/4 ins / 67 x 91 cm) GBP 132,000. COPENHAGEN, 5 April 1989, *On the Road to Church* (oil on canvas, 4 3/4 x 9 3/4 ins / 12 x 25 cm) DKK 6,000. STOCKHOLM, 19 April 1989, *Scene from Everyday Life in a Street in Naples* (oil on canvas, 22 1/2 x 20 ins / 57 x 51 cm) SEK 90,000. GÖTEBORG, 18 May 1989, *The Coastline* (oil on canvas, 11 x 15 3/4 ins / 28 x 40 cm) SEK 25,000. LONDON, 20 June 1989, *Gammelstrand Fish Market in Copenhagen* (1919, oil on canvas, 35 x 47 1/2 ins / 89 x 120.5 cm) GBP 49,500. COPENHAGEN, 25 Oct 1989, *Hojbro Plads Market* (1916, oil on canvas, 19 x 27 1/4 ins / 48 x 69 cm) DKK 260,000. LONDON, 22 Nov 1989, *Copenhagen Flower Market* (oil on canvas, 22 x 28 3/4 ins / 56 x 73 cm) GBP 28,600. COPENHAGEN, 21 Feb 1990, *Promenade at the Hojbro Plads Flower Market* (oil on canvas, 15 1/4 x 12 1/2 ins / 39 x 32 cm) DKK 150,000. LONDON, 27-28 March 1990, *Kongens Nytorv in Copenhagen* (1908, oil on canvas, 29 x 39 ins / 73.5 x 99 cm) GBP 132,000. LONDON, 29 March 1990, *The Dancing Class at the Theatre Royal* (1889, oil on canvas, 20 3/4 x 40 1/2 ins / 52.6 x 102.9 cm) GBP 132,000. LONDON, 6 June 1990, *Sunbathing in the Dunes* (oil on canvas, 15 x 21 1/4 ins / 38 x 54 cm) GBP 15,400. COPENHAGEN, 29 Aug 1990, *Girl Reading in a Sitting-room* (1916, oil on canvas, 15 1/4 x 22 ins / 39 x 55 cm) DKK 80,000. STOCKHOLM, 14 Nov 1990, *Horse-drawn Carriages in a Snow Covered Street in Copenhagen* (oil on panel, 7 3/4 x 9 3/4 ins / 20 x 25 cm) SEK 36,000. LONDON, 28 Nov 1990, *Street in Copenhagen* (oil on panel, 14 1/2 x 11 ins / 37 x 28 cm) GBP 5,500. COPENHAGEN, 6 Dec 1990, *Mother and Her Little Girl Walking in Peblingesoen Park* (grisaille, 7 1/2 x 9 3/4 ins / 19 x 25 cm) DKK 19,000. COPENHAGEN, 1 May 1991, *Young Woman Standing* (oil on canvas, 16 1/4 x 11 ins / 41 x 27 cm) DKK 7,000. LONDON, 17 May 1991, *In the Tram* (oil on panel, 15 1/4 x 12 1/2 ins / 38.8 x 32 cm) GBP 8,800. LONDON, 19 June 1991, *Osterbro Street in Winter* (1918, oil on canvas, 14 1/2 x 21 ins / 37 x 53.5 cm) GBP 22,000. COPENHAGEN, 28 Aug 1991, *The Knife-grinder* (oil on canvas, 22 x 15 3/4 ins / 56 x 40 cm) DKK 36,000. COPENHAGEN, 6 May 1992, *Elegant Society Figures Promenading under the Trees in the Tivoli Gardens* (1901, oil on canvas, 19 x 37 1/2 ins / 48 x 95 cm) DKK 116,000. STOCKHOLM, 5 Sept 1992, *Hojbro Plads Flower Market in Copenhagen* (oil on canvas, 19 3/4 x 22 3/4 ins / 50 x 58 cm) SEK 190,000. LONDON, 16 June 1993, *Three Women Bathing* (oil on canvas, 21 3/4 x 29 ins / 55.5 x 73.5 cm) GBP 9,200. LONDON, 15 June 1994, *Kongens Nytorv in Copenhagen under Snow* (oil on canvas, 22 1/2 x 29 1/4 ins / 57 x 74.5 cm) GBP

18,975. PARIS, 26 Oct 1994, *Woman with a Parasol at the Seaside* (oil on canvas, 22 x 18 ins / 55 x 45.5 cm) FRF 15,000. COPENHAGEN, 16 Nov 1994, *View of Stengade in Helsingor* (oil on canvas, 14 1/4 x 18 ins / 36 x 46 cm) DKK 40,000. LONDON, 15 March 1996, *The Family of the Artist on the Veranda of Sofievej 23 in Hellerup* (1914, oil on canvas, 18 1/2 x 15 3/4 ins / 47 x 40 cm) GBP 20,700. LONDON, 12 June 1996, *The Fish Market, Copenhagen* (oil on canvas, 28 3/4 x 22 1/4 ins / 73 x 56.5 cm) GBP 5,175. NEW YORK, 12 Feb 1997, *Hvidsten* (1892, oil on canvas, 18 x 14 1/2 ins / 45.7 x 36.8 cm) USD 37,375. COPENHAGEN, 30 Nov 1999, *The Artist's Wife and Daughter Buying Red Roses at Hojbro Plads* (oil on canvas, 23 x 29 ins / 58 x 74 cm) DKK 680,000. COPENHAGEN, 30 Nov 1999, *From Hojbro Plads in April* (1890, oil on canvas, 67 x 87 ins / 171 x 220 cm) DKK 1,500,000. COPENHAGEN, 29 Feb 2000, *Spring Day by the National Scala with Two Young Ladies in foreground* (1893, oil on canvas, 30 x 22 ins / 75 x 56 cm) DKK 1,200,000. COPENHAGEN, 30 May 2000, *Ladies Buying Flowers at Amagertorv* (1924, oil on canvas, 22 x 29 ins / 57 x 74 cm) DKK 820,000. COPENHAGEN, 27 Nov 2001, *Winter's Day at Amalienborg Palace, Snow being Driven Away* (1933, oil on canvas, 30 x 39 ins / 75 x 100 cm) DKK 400,000. STOCKHOLM, 4 Dec 2001, *Shopping in the Market, Copenhagen* (oil on canvas, 30 x 23 ins / 76 x 59 cm) SEK 520,000. COPENHAGEN, 3 June 2002, *Mild Winter Weather - Street Scene from Kobmagergade with Figures* (1905, oil on canvas, 29 x 30 ins / 73 x 77 cm) DKK 1,200,000. COPENHAGEN, 2 Dec 2002, *Afternoon Tea at the Artist's Home at Sofievej* (oil on canvas, 24 x 29 ins / 62 x 74 cm) DKK 1,200,000. COPENHAGEN, 26 May 2003, *Artist's Wife Musse and Daughter Grethe in front of Palace Hotel with Elegant Cyclists* (print, 30 x 23 ins / 76 x 58 cm) DKK 1,100,000. COPENHAGEN, 9 Dec 2003, *By Peter Liep's House in Dyrehaven, Girls at Table* (1904, oil on canvas, 17 x 26 ins / 43 x 65 cm) DKK 600,000. COPENHAGEN, 2 March 2004, *Cyclists at Emilias Kilde - Evening at Strandvejen* (1899, oil on canvas, 26 x 23 ins / 65 x 58 cm) DKK 1,100,000. COPENHAGEN, 9 June 2004, *Artist's Wife Musse and Daughter Grethe Passing Girls on Bikes, Copenhagen* (1918, oil on canvas, 30 x 23 ins / 76 x 58 cm) DKK 1,000,000.

FISCHER, Paul, or Fisher

German, 19th - 20th century.

Born 1864, in Stuttgart; died 1931.

Active in Mexico.

Painter (gouache), watercolourist. Scenes with figures, landscapes.

Paul Fischer was a self-taught artist who worked as a painter in parallel to his profession as a doctor, practising from 1890 in the mines of the Durango Region. He tirelessly painted the landscapes of Mexico.

AUCTION RECORDS:

PARIS, 1 Feb 1980, *Girl at the Aquarium* (gouache, 11 3/4 x 17 1/2 ins / 30 x 44.5 cm) GBP 400. NEW YORK, 21 Nov 1989, *Mexican Garden* (watercolour and pencil/paper/card, 6 1/2 x 10 1/2 ins / 16.5 x 26.5 cm) USD 2,860. NEW YORK, 14-15 May 1996, *Mexican Landscape* (watercolour/reinforced paper, 11 3/4 x 19 1/4 ins / 29.8 x 48.9 cm) USD 9,200. NEW YORK, 25-26 Nov 1996, *The Hacienda* (c. 1865, watercolour/paper, 5 1/2 x 9 3/4 ins / 13.7 x 24.8 cm) USD 2,760.

FISCHER, Per

Swedish, 20th century.

Born 6 December 1877, in Lidköping.

Painter, draughtsman, engraver. Interiors, landscapes, flowers.

Per Fischer studied at the Chalmar Institute in Göteborg, then, in Norway, with Halfdan Strom and, finally, at the Akademie der Bildenden Künste in Munich. He exhibited his works in Stockholm and Malmö.

FISCHER, Peter. See **VISCHER**

FISCHER, Philip August

Danish, 19th century.

Born 1 April 1817, in Rudköbing.

Painter.

Philip August Fischer was the father of August Fischer.

FISCHER, Poisson. See **FISCHER Theodor**

FISCHER, R. M.

American, 20th - 21st century.

Born 1947.

Sculptor, installation artist.

R.M. Fischer grew up in Brooklyn. During the early part of his career, he created small sculptural pieces such as *Night Writer* (1986), a mixed media piece incorporating electric light, a characteristic element of Fischer's work. In 1985 Carl Solway commissioned Fischer's first large-scale work, *Empire Towers*, consisting of two stainless steel towers, cylindrical in shape and pierced with 4000 tiny holes. When the towers are illuminated at night, light radiates from within. Subsequently, Fischer was commissioned to carry out work for the Battery park in New York and completed *Rector Gate* in 1988. Made in stainless steel, bronze and granite it is a 50 feet (15 metre) high gateway to the park, green from the copper at day and illuminated at night. Visitors can rest on the incorporated seating. The design is light, skeletal columns topped by a cupola and spires. Fischer has also completed commissions for Massachusetts State House in Boston, MacArthur Park in Los Angeles, Union Square in San Francisco and Kansas City Convention Center.

Fischer's work has been the subject of exhibitions at the Whitney Museum of American Art, the Galerie Beaubourg in Paris, Boston's Contemporary Art Museum and Philadelphia's Institute of Contemporary Art. In 2002 Fischer exhibited *Polyluminators* at the Sandra Gering Gallery in New York, showing sculptures such as *Moondog*, again using electric light as a main feature. Made from polyethylene, brass, acrylic, chromed steel, wood, and electric lights, and hanging from the ceiling, Fischer presented several sculptures including *Heli* (2002), *Hydrog* (2001), *Carbo* (2001) and *Nitrog* (2001).

BIBLIOGRAPHY:

Marshall, Richard, *50 New York Artists*, 1986. Deitch, Jeffrey, *The Dakis Joannou Collection*, 1996.

MUSEUMS AND GALLERIES:

DALLAS (MA) - DENVER (AM) - KANSAS CITY (Nelson-Atkins MA) - NEW YORK (Jewish Mus.): *Adam's Rib* - NEW YORK (Whitney Mus. of American Art).

FISCHER, Romano

German, 17th century.

Active in Dormitz (Bavaria).

Painter.

Fischer painted a ciborium for the church in Dormitz in 1604.

FISCHER, Stefan

Austrian, 17th - 18th century.

Born 1660; died 26 December 1715, in Vienna.

Sculptor.

Stefan Fischer probably worked in the Graben district of Vienna on the Trinity Column, or Plague Column.

FISCHER, Susanna

German, 17th century.

Born 1600; died 1674.

Active in Augsburg (Bavaria).

Painter.

The daughter and student of Johannes Fischer, Susanna Fischer married a merchant, C.G. Mayr, with whom she had a son, Johann Ulrich Mayr.

MUSEUMS AND GALLERIES:
AUGSBURG (Maximilianmus.): *Portrait of Johann Ulrich Mayr, the Artist's Son.*

FISCHER, T.
German, 19th century.
Probably active in Leipzig (Saxony).
Pastellist.
Two pastels by this artist are known to be in a private collection in Leipzig.

FISCHER, T. Paul, or Paul Johann Georg
German, 19th century.
Born 16 September 1786, in Hanover; died 12 December 1875, in London.
Miniaturist, watercolourist, draughtsman.
T. Paul Fischer studied with Ramberg in his home town. In 1810 he went to London, where he exhibited at the Royal Academy from 1811 until 1871. He became miniaturist to King George IV.
MUSEUMS AND GALLERIES:
LONDON (British Mus.): *Queen Charlotte's Garden; Messenger; Seven Ages of Life.*
AUCTION RECORDS:
LONDON, 30 Nov 1978, *Military Uniforms of the Napoleonic Era* (1814-1816, twelve watercolours with pen, 8 x 11 1/2 ins / 20.5 x 29 cm) GBP 4,000. LONDON, 29 Nov 2000, *Duke of Cumberland's Hussars and Infantry of the Line of the Army of Hanover* (pen, ink and watercolour over pencil heightened with bodycolour, 8 x 11 ins / 20 x 29 cm) GBP 1,700. LONDON, 29 Nov 2000, *Italian Troops* (pen, ink and watercolour over pencil heightened with bodycolour and gum arabic, 8 x 11 ins / 20 x 29 cm) GBP 1,800. LONDON, 25 June 2003, *Possibly Augustus, 1st Duke of Cambridge, in Uniform* (1818, miniature, oval, h. 3 ins / 8 cm) GBP 1,700.

FISCHER, Theodor, pseudonym: Fischer Poisson
German, 19th century.
Born 13 June 1817, in Schwerin (Mecklenburg-Vorpommern); died 30 March 1873, in Schwerin.
Painter.
The son of Louis Fischer, Theodor Fischer studied under Schumacher, the court painter, then Bendemann at the academy in Dresden. His noted works include *Beautiful Melusine, Return of St Genevieve,* and portraits of the family of Count Maltzah. Many of his paintings are to be found at the grand duke's castle in Schwerin, including *Ruth and Boaz.* He is also known to have painted a picture representing a *Peasant Woman and Two Children* in a landscape and the portrait of his teacher *Schumacher,* and also numerous altar paintings in the churches of Mecklenburg.

FISCHER, Thomas or Thoman, or Vischer
Austrian, 16th - 17th century.
Active in Vienna.
Painter.
Thomas Fischer is mentioned between 1595 and 1616 as painting coats of arms.

FISCHER, Ulrich
Swiss, 18th - 19th century.
Born 1770, in Triengen; died 1859, in Triengen.
Painter. Religious subjects.
Ulrich Fischer specialised in painting religious subjects, studied under Xaver Hecht in Willisau, and produced paintings for the churches in his home town and for those in Eich and Willisau. Notable works of his include *God the Father* and *Saviour on the Cross,* formerly in Triengen, and *Christ Entombed* at the church in Willisau.

FISCHER, V. Hugo
Swiss, 19th century.
Born 1 July 1866, in Reinach (Aargau).
Painter, engraver, draughtsman.
V. Hugo Fischer studied in Zurich, Geneva and Munich. He also travelled to Italy and specialised in industrial art.

FISCHER, Valentin
German, 18th century.
Born 1722, in Nuremberg; died after 1797.
Engraver.

FISCHER, Vilhelm Theodor
Danish, 19th - 20th century.
Born 4 November 1857, in Holbæk; died 1928.
Active in Copenhagen.
Painter. Landscapes, animals.
Vilhelm Theodor Fischer studied at the Kunstakademi in Copenhagen. He worked at the porcelain factory, his works featuring at the Exposition Universelle in Paris in 1900. He favoured the depiction of birds and horses in his landscapes.
AUCTION RECORDS:
LONDON, 12 Oct 1984, *The Horse Market* (1886-1887, oil on canvas, 48 x 64 ins / 122 x 162.5 cm) GBP 4,200. NEW YORK, 4 June 1987, *The Horse Dealer* (1886-1887, oil on canvas, 48 3/4 x 65 1/2 ins / 123.7 x 166.4 cm) USD 40,000. LONDON, 16 March 1989, *Horses in a Meadow* (1887, oil on canvas, 32 1/4 x 46 ins / 82 x 116 cm) GBP 3,520. LONDON, 29 March 1990, *Basta* (1895, oil on canvas, 20 3/4 x 30 3/4 ins / 52.8 x 78.1 cm) GBP 1,540. COPENHAGEN, 8 Feb 1995, *Two Horses in a Meadow* (1892, oil on canvas, 29 1/2 x 39 1/4 ins / 75 x 100 cm) DKK 10,000.

FISCHER, Vincenz
Austrian, 18th - 19th century.
Born 1729, in Schmidham; died 1810, in Vienna.
Painter, architect. History painting.
Vincenz Fischer was a teacher of architecture at the academy in Vienna. The following works of his are noteworthy: *Raising of the Son of the Widow of Naim* (1763), and *Raising of Lazarus* (1763).
MUSEUMS AND GALLERIES:
GRAZ: *Suzanna Before the Judges; Moses Before the Throne of Pharoah* - VIENNA: *Allegory; Painting of Buildings; Same Subject* - VIENNA (Akademie der Bildenden Künste): *Moses Trampling on Pharoah's Crown.*

FISCHER GURIG. See **FISCHER Adolf**

FISCHER HINNEN. See **FISCHER Henri**

FISCHER KÖYSTRAND. See **FISCHER Karl**

FISCHER VON EHRENBACH, Johann Friedrich
German, 18th century.
Born c. 1680, in Eisenach (Thuringia); died c. 1759.
Painter.
After travelling for an extended period throughout Europe, Fischer von Ehrenbach settled in Vienna, where he painted portraits for the imperial court.

FISCHER-CORLIN. See **FISCHER Ernst Albert**

FISCHER-DIESKAU, Dietrich Albert
German, 20th century.
Born 28 May 1925, in Berlin.
Painter, draughtsman, watercolourist, musician.
Portraits.
After enlisting in the German Army in 1943 and being taken prisoner in Italy in 1945, Dietrich Albert Fischer-Dieskau, the lyrical bass-baritone, studied at the Berlin Conservatory for two years. As a self-taught painter, he has shown his works in solo and group exhibitions in Japan and Europe.

In a portrait of the pianist Sviatoslav Richter (1982), he built up the structure of the face by applying the paint with bold brush-strokes as though he were working on the surface of a photograph.

Bibliography:

Bellamy, Olivier, '*La double vie des musiciens*' in *Le Monde de la Musique*, periodical, Paris, November 2004.

FISCHER-ELPONS, Georg

German, 19th - 20th century.
Born 7 September 1866, in Berlin.
From 1890 active in Brazil.
Painter. Landscapes.

Georg Fischer-Elpons studied at the Akademie der Bildenden Künste in Munich. After living in Munich for 23 years he moved to São Paulo, where he directed an art school. He exhibited his works in Munich at the Glaspalast in 1904, 1907 and 1908, and in Berlin in 1906, 1908 and 1911.

Georg Fischer-Elpons is known to have executed *Lobsters and Crayfish*, which is in a private collection.

FISCHER-HANSEN, Else

Danish, 20th century.
Born 1905.
Painter. Figure compositions, landscapes.

Auction records:

Copenhagen, 3 March 1981, *Composition* (1973, oil on canvas, 26 3/4 x 21 1/4 ins / 68 x 54 cm) DKK 1,000. Copenhagen, 25 Feb 1987, *Composition* (1946, oil on canvas, 53 1/2 x 63 ins / 136 x 160 cm) DKK 36,000. Copenhagen, 30 Nov 1988, *Composition with Figures* (1933, oil on canvas, 20 1/2 x 24 ins / 52 x 61 cm) DKK 11,000. Copenhagen, 10 May 1989, *Composition* (1944, oil on canvas, 26 x 35 ins / 66 x 89 cm) DKK 40,000. Copenhagen, 20 Sept 1989, *Composition* (1983, oil on canvas, 59 x 39 1/4 ins / 150 x 100 cm) DKK 17,000. Copenhagen, 21-22 March 1990, *Composition* (1953, oil on canvas, 46 x 30 3/4 ins / 116 x 78 cm) DKK 16,000. Copenhagen, 30 May 1990, *Sun Setting on the Sea* (1966, oil on canvas, 28 3/4 x 21 1/4 ins / 73 x 54 cm) DKK 7,000. Copenhagen, 14-15 Nov 1990, *Composition* (1970, oil on canvas, 26 3/4 x 21 1/4 ins / 68 x 54 cm) DKK 6,500. Copenhagen, 30 May 1991, *Composition* (1965, oil on canvas, 20 3/4 x 16 1/4 ins / 53 x 41 cm) DKK 5,500. Copenhagen, 4 Dec 1991, *Composition* (1968, oil on canvas, 36 1/4 x 28 3/4 ins / 92 x 73 cm) DKK 8,000. Copenhagen, 10 March 1993, *Composition* (1965, oil on canvas, 28 3/4 x 36 1/4 ins / 73 x 92 cm) DKK 6,000. Copenhagen, 21 Sept 1994, *Composition* (1971, oil on canvas, 21 1/4 x 27 1/4 ins / 54 x 69 cm) DKK 4,400.

FISCHERN, Adolf von

German, 19th century.
Born 21 November 1838, in Meiningen (Thuringia); died 3 March 1902, in Emershausen.
Painter, draughtsman.

In 1894 Adolf von Fischern exhibited an oil painting entitled *View of Salzungen* and drawings entitled *Views of Gräfenthal* and *View of Römhild Castle* in an exhibition in Meiningen. In 1891 he published *Souvenir Illustrations for the Opening of the Casino in Meiningen*.

FISCHES, Isaac or Jesaias or Isaias, the Elder

German, 17th century.
Born 1638, in Augsburg; died 1706.
Painter, engraver. Religious subjects, portraits.

Father of Isaac Fisches the Younger, Fisches was a master in Augsburg. He produced several religious pictures housed in the churches in Augsburg, notably *Christ in the Garden of Gethsemane, Death on the Cross* and *Resurrection*. He also painted portraits, including those of famous people in the town, one of whom was *Goldsmith Christoph von Rad*.

Museums and Galleries:

Augsburg (Kunsthalle, Staatsgal.): *Goldsmith Christoph von Rad*.

Auction records:

London, 2 July 1997, *The Continence of Scipio* (1668, oil on canvas, 39 1/2 x 45 1/2 ins / 100.4 x 115.5 cm) GBP 7,475. Paris, 19 May 1999, *Old-fashioned Townspeople near a Waterfall* (oil on canvas, 36 x 44 ins / 91 x 113 cm) FRF 60,000.

FISCHES, Isaac, the Younger

German, 17th century.
Born 1677, in Augsburg; died 1705, in Augsburg.
Painter. Religious subjects, allegorical subjects, portraits.

Isaac Fisches the Younger was the son of Isaac or Jesaias Fisches. One of his known works is *Ecce Homo* in the St Anna-Kirche in Augsburg and noted among his religious paintings are *Birth of Christ*: *Martyrdom of St Peter, St Paul and St Sebastian*. He also painted allegories, including *Allegory of a Salutory Death*, history subjects, such as *Alexander at the Stripping of Darius*, and portraits. His painting *Minerva Protecting the Arts* was sold by auction in Paris with the Hautpoul collection in 1905. His works have often been printed by J.A. Corvinus, A. Geyer, J.W. and L. Heckenauer, J.D. Hertz, P.A. Kilian, B. Kilian, G.C. Kilian, and A.M. and J.G. Wolfgang.

Museums and Galleries:

Augsburg (Kunsthalle, Staatsgal.): *Allegory of a Salutory Death* (1688) - Ludwigsburg (Städtisches Mus.): *Alexander and the Wife of Darius* (c. 1685) - Nuremberg: *Alexander at the Stripping of Darius* (c. 1685).

Auction records:

Amsterdam, 2 Dec 1987, *Suzanna and the Elders* (oil on canvas, 57 x 48 1/2 ins / 145 x 123 cm) NLG 7,000. New York, 6 Oct 1995, *Minerva, Protector of the Arts* (oil on canvas, 28 3/4 x 20 3/4 ins / 73 x 52.7 cm) USD 3,450.

FISCHETTI, Fedele or Fidele

Italian, 18th century.
Born 1734, in Naples; died 1789 or 1809.
Painter, draughtsman. Religious subjects, allegorical subjects, mythological subjects.

Fedele Fischetti worked initially for the Naples court, then for various churches and assorted dignitaries. The bulk of his work is on view in the church of the Holy Spirit, including a *Virgin with Child Jesus, St Anne and St Jerome*, a *Conversion of St Paul*, and a *Virgin with St Anthony of Padua and a Bishop*. The church of S Eligio Maggiore houses his *Birth of Christ*, and a side-chapel in the church of S Domenico Maggiore has frescoes by Fischetti, together with a *Virgin of the Rosary*. Further altarpieces and frescoes are to be found in the church of S Caterina in Siena and the church of the Annunziata in Capua. Additionally, Fischetti painted allegorical and mythological subjects, including canvases of a *Story of Telemachus* and a *Four Seasons* for the Casa Mariano Carelli. Fischetti collaborated with Bonito at the Gobelin tapestry works.

Museums and Galleries:

Naples (Mus. Civico Gaetano Filangieri): *Reverie of a Young Prince*.

Auction records:

Paris, 24 June 1929, *Rectangular Ceiling with Three Panels* (pen) FRF 380; *Time* (pen) FRF 220; *Mythological Theme* (pen) FRF 110; *Spirit of Industry* (pen) FRF 100; *Ceres, Pomona and Vertumnus* (pen) FRF 115. Bari, 5 April 1981, *Holy Family* (oil on canvas, 48 3/4 x 28 ins / 124 x 71 cm) ITL 7,500,000. Rome, 28 May 1985, *Allegory of Summer* (oil on canvas, 22 1/2 x 40 1/4 ins / 57 x 102 cm) USD 7,000. London, 1 July 1986, *Bacchus and a Nymph Sitting on a Cloud and Surrounded by Putti* (black and red chalk, pen and wash, 23 1/4 x 17 1/4 ins / 58.9 x 44.1 cm) GBP 3,000. London, 8 Dec 1987, *Diana and Endymion* (black chalk, pen and wash, 17 1/2 x 12 1/4 ins / 44.4 x 31 cm) GBP 1,400. Rome, 11 May 1993, *Diana and Endymion* (oil on canvas, oval, 39 1/4 x 29 1/2 ins / 100 x 75 cm) ITL 28,000,000. Rome, 23 May 1996, *Allegory of Courage* (oil on canvas, 51 1/4 x 52 1/4 ins / 130 x 133 cm) ITL 57,500,000. London, 31 Oct 1997, *Cupid with Half-reclining Nymphs and a Landscape in the Background* (oil on canvas, 19 3/4 x 30 ins / 50.2 x 76.5 cm) GBP 13,800. NAPLES, 9 Nov 1999, *Mercury and Psyche* (oil on panel, 24 x 21 ins / 61 x 54 cm) ITL 38,000,000. VENICE, 14 Nov 1999, *Allegory of the Four Seasons* (oil on canvas, four, 28 x 23 ins / 72 x 59 cm) ITL 210,100,000. VENICE, 16 June 2000, *Spring. Summer. Autumn. Winter* (oil on canvas, four, 28 x 23 ins / 72 x 59 cm) ITL 160,000,000. PARIS, 23 Nov 2001, *Studies for Ceiling* (pen/ink wash, pair, 13 x 4 ins / 33 x 9 cm) FRF 12,000. LONDON, 13 Dec 2001, *Madonna and Child Adored by Saints* (pen/ink wash over black chalk, 15 x 10 ins / 39 x 25 cm) GBP 1,600. LONDON, 18 April 2002, *Hercules Returning Alcestis to Admetus. Hercules and Omphale* (oil on canvas, pair, 19 x 14 ins / 47 x 35 cm) GBP 28,000. MILAN, 27 Nov 2002, *St Anthony and the Infant* (oil on canvas, 30 x 24 ins / 76 x 62 cm) EUR 6,000. PARIS, 7 March 2003, *Royal Surrender in the Course of Battle* (pen/wash, 19 x 29 ins / 48 x 74 cm) EUR 4,500. VIENNA, 1 Oct 2003, *Death of Alexander the Great* (oil on canvas, 19 x 29 ins / 49 x 73 cm) EUR 9,000. LONDON, 20 April 2004, *Visitation* (pen/brown ink/grey wash/black chalk, oval, 19 x 15 ins / 47 x 37 cm) GBP 1,200.

FISCHETTI, Odoardo

Italian, 19th century.

Active in Naples.

Painter. History painting.

Fischetti worked in Rome and the surrounding area (Cardito, S Leucio and Fiatamone). His works include an oil painting entitled *Fable of Psyche*, and some studies for the Gobelins in the Palatine Chapel.

MUSEUMS AND GALLERIES:

NAPLES (Mus. di San Martino): *The Taking of Capri by Murat; The Same Subject.*

FISCHHOF, Georg

Austrian, 19th - 20th century.

Born 11 May 1859 or 1849, in Vienna; died after 1920.

Painter. Figures, portraits, landscapes.

Fischhof began his studies at the Hochschule für Angewandte Kunst in Vienna, continuing them in Munich. On returning to Vienna he specialised in copying Gobelins tapestries. Among his portraits he is remembered for *Archduke Rainer*, the *Duke and Duchess of Saxe-Coburg-Gotha* and *Princess Dora of Schleswig-Holstein*. The Wiener Club has a series of his decorative panels.

AUCTION RECORDS:

VIENNA, 18 May 1976, *The Small Fishing Port* (1903, oil on canvas, 29 1/4 x 39 3/4 ins / 74 x 101 cm) ATS 15,000. VIENNA, 15 April 1980, *The Return of the Fishermen* (1909, oil on canvas, 29 1/4 x 39 1/4 ins / 74 x 99.5 cm) ATS 18,000. VIENNA, 14 March 1984, *The Washerwomen* (1904, oil on canvas, 17 x 20 3/4 ins / 43 x 53 cm) ATS 30,000. LONDON, 18 June 1993, *On the Lagoon in Venice* (oil on canvas, 18 1/2 x 27 1/4 ins / 47 x 69 cm) GBP 2,530. AMSTERDAM, 19 April 1994, *Men Gathering Wood in a Forest* (1892, oil on panel, 24 3/4 x 17 3/4 ins / 63 x 45 cm) NLG 2,185. LONDON, 9 Oct 1997, *A Mediterranean Town in a Bay* (oil on canvas, 20 3/4 x 31 ins / 53 x 79 cm) GBP 632.

FISCHL, Eric

American, 20th - 21st century.

Born 1948, in New York.

Painter, engraver. Figure compositions.

Bad Painting.

Eric Fischl studied at the California Institute of the Arts in Valencia, where he met David Salle and Matt Mullican, artists of his generation who are now well known. He lives in New York.

Tempted by abstraction in his early career, Fischl then turned away from it and tackled pictorial figuration head on, as the appropriate means of expressing feelings and desire in a more illustrated manner. His first painting dates from 1979: entitled *Sleep-Walker*, it depicts a young adolescent boy masturbating in a small garden swimming pool. From that point on, Fischl applied himself to presenting, telling and illustrating 'scenarios'. This is a crisis induced by awareness of a form of social organisation which, wishing to absorb the fantastical lifestyle that is the American Way of Life, seeks above all to silence its contradictions and exaggerate the symbols which, for the most part, do not or no longer correspond to a living reality. And in this relationship with life, which, as Fischl emphasises, is too out of sync:

'... each new event is a crisis, and each crisis a confrontation that fills us with an anxiety very similar to that which we feel in dreams when we discover ourselves naked'.

His favourite themes are adolescence and family problems, and the intersecting relationships between father and daughter and mother and son, at the age when the desires and torments connected to adolescent sexuality are consumed by, but also separated from, Oedipal anxiety and its derivatives. Similarly, he treats relationships between black and white people as a sexual taboo. His favoured environments are the residential suburbs, swimming pools and cocoon-like bathrooms of middle-class America. Bathed in warm, sometimes dense, tones, executed with clumsy-artful brushstrokes and lines, these slices of life detach themselves in a pared-down atmosphere of existential necessity. The pervading slowness subtly clarifies and articulates the whole picture in a game of interpretations relating to the attitudes and body positions of these figures. The body, physical nudity and latent eroticism fill the space of representation, which is a receptacle for a moral and intellectual vacuity. Women, mothers, daughters and adolescent boys are frequently presented as objects of desire.

The painting *Bad Boy* (1981) is possibly Fischl's best known. It is an ambiguous scene in which an adolescent boy is gazing at a nude woman on a bed while he rifles through her purse.

Fischl claims to be amused by psychoanalysis, but knows full well that the ideas it brings to light are real, in parallel with the ideas that his juvenile, fictitious double - this shadow of himself - presents without indulgence. Other notable paintings by Fischl include: *The Old Man's Boat and the Old Man's Dog* (1982); *Vanity* (1984); *Birth of Love* (second version, 1987); *Portrait of an Artist as a Woman* (1988); and *Girl with Doll* (1987); he also makes numerous engravings of nudes. During the mid-1980s the Fischl seemed about to renounce his awareness - declared, then metabolised - of the conflicts of his own self; however, he went back to representing his initial themes, and thus revisiting them. Other sources for his figure compositions are portraits of celebrities like Joan Crawford, Ernest Hemingway and Truman Capote, and photographs he has taken himself, such as the series of paintings on India (*Kowdoolie*, 1990), which operate as an interrogation of the white man, the tourist - the 'exotic man' among the 'natives'.

Fischl took part in the 1984 Venice Biennale, the 1985 Paris Biennale, the 1986 Sydney Biennial and Documenta 8 in Kassel in 1987. He staged his first solo exhibitions in Canada, in 1979. He exhibits a great deal in New York and Toronto. In 1985 a major travelling exhibition was organised in Europe, which started at the Van Abbe Museum in Eindhoven and moved on to the USA, to the Chicago Museum of Contemporary Art and the Whitney Museum in New York. In 1990 a second retrospective of his work was held in Europe, in Lausanne (at the Musée Cantonal) and Vienna. The Galerie Daniel Templon in Paris has held regular exhibitions of his recent works, including one in 1999.

Fischl '94

Bibliography:
Fischl, Eric, *Tendances à New York*, Musée du Luxembourg, Paris, 1984. Marzorati, Gérard, *'Interview: I will think bad thoughts'* in *Parkett* n° 5, periodical, Zurich, 1985. Glenn, C.W./Barnes, L., *Eric Fischl: Scenes before the Eye*, exhibition catalogue, Art Museum, California State Univerity Long Beach; Art Museum, University of California, Berkeley; Contemporary Art Center, Honolulu; and elsewhere, 1986-1887. Schjeldahl, Peter/Whitney, David, *'Eric Fischl'* in *Art in America*, periodical, New York, 1988. Schjeldahl, P., *Eric Fischl*, New York, 1988.

Museums and Galleries:
Humlebæk (Louisiana Mus. for Moderne Kunst): *Birth of Love* (second edition).

Auction records:
New York, 11 Nov 1986, *Study for Father and Son Sleeping* (1980, charcoal and pastel/parchment, 38 x 36 ins / 96.5 x 91.5 cm) USD 8,250. New York, 5 May 1987, *Mother and Child* (1982, oil wash/paper, 20 x 51 1/2 ins / 50.8 x 130.8 cm) USD 36,000; *Untitled* (1978, gouache and brown ink/parchment, 16 3/4 x 31 1/2 ins / 42.7 x 80 cm) USD 8,500. New York, 5 Nov 1987, *Study for Tigers of Autumn* (1981, oil wash/paper, 24 x 57 1/4 ins / 61 x 145.4 cm) USD 29,000. New York, 3 April 1988, *Untitled* (1985, oil on paper, 16 x 12 ins / 40.8 x 30.7 cm) USD 24,200. New York, 10 Nov 1988, *Every Man for Himself* (1980, oil on paper, 24 1/4 x 57 1/2 ins / 61.5 x 145.8 cm) USD 49,500. New York, 3 May 1989, *Untitled* (oil on paper, 35 x 46 ins / 89 x 117 cm) USD 77,000. New York, 7 May 1990, *Champion* (1981, oil on canvas, 55 3/4 x 89 ins / 141.6 x 226 cm) USD 715,000. New York, 8 May 1990, *A Perfectly Fine Day* (1988, oil/material, 60 x 80 ins / 152.5 x 203.3 cm) USD 440,000. New York, 30 April 1991, *Untitled* (1989, oil on canvas in two panels, in all 95 x 113 ins / 241.3 x 287 cm) USD 187,000. New York, 13 Nov 1991, *Kid II* (1984, oil on canvas, 84 x 108 ins / 213.3 x 274.3 cm) USD 242,000. New York, 27 Feb 1992, *Untitled* (1986, charcoal/paper, 24 x 18 ins / 61 x 45.8 cm) USD 8,250. New York, 5 May 1992, *Cattle Market* (oil on canvas, 98 x 114 1/4 ins / 248.9 x 290.2 cm) USD 286,000. New York, 7 May 1992, *First Trip to Japan* (1988, oil/material, 58 x 54 ins / 147.3 x 137.2 cm) USD 77,000. New York, 18 Nov 1992, *The Beginning and the End* (1988, oil on canvas, 75 x 110 1/4 ins / 190.5 x 280 cm) USD 154,000. London, 3 Dec 1992, *Untitled* (1985, oil on paper, 22 x 35 ins / 55 x 88 cm) GBP 14,300. New York, 10 Nov 1993, *Untitled* (1990, oil on canvas, 18 x 14 ins / 45.7 x 35.6 cm) USD 32,200. New York, 3 May 1994, *Far from Rockaway* (1986, oil on canvas, two panels, 110 x 135 ins / 279.4 x 342.9 cm) USD 167,500. New York, 22 Feb 1996, *Untitled* (1985, oil on paper, 35 x 46 ins / 89 x 117 cm) USD 32,200. New York, 9 Nov 1996, *Beach* (1989, coloured aquatint, 35 1/2 x 54 1/4 ins / 90 x 137.5 cm) GBP 2,587. New York, 19 Nov 1996, *Untitled* (1986, oil on chromium paper, 12 3/4 x 10 3/4 ins / 32.4 x 27.3 cm) USD 5,175. New York, 20 Nov 1996, *First Sex* (1981, oil on canvas, 72 x 96 ins / 182.8 x 243.8 cm) USD 167,500. New York, 20 Nov 1996, *Untitled* (1983, charcoal and gouache/paper, 61 x 76 ins / 154.9 x 193 cm) USD 46,000. New York, 7 May 1997, *Untitled* (1983, oil/glassine, 47 3/4 x 57 1/2 ins / 121.3 x 146.1 cm) USD 28,750; *On the Temple Steps* (1989, oil on canvas, 115 x 140 ins / 292.2 x 355.6 cm) USD 178,500. New York, 19 May 1999, *Untitled* (1993, oil on linen, 50 x 65 ins / 127 x 165 cm) USD 65,000. New York, 17 Nov 1999, *Time for Bed* (1981, oil on canvas, 72 x 96 ins / 183 x 244 cm) USD 710,000. New York, 16 May 2000, *Noonwatch* (1983, oil on canvas, 65 x 100 ins / 165 x 254 cm) USD 900,000. New York, 17 May 2000, *Woman Surrounded by Dogs* (1979, oil on canvas, 65 x 96 ins / 165 x 244 cm) USD 300,000. New York, 18 May 2001, *Woman Bending* (1995, bronze, 56 x 39x24 ins / 141 x 98x61 cm) USD 120,000. New York, 15 Nov 2001, *Love* (1981, oil on canvas, 48 x 58 ins / 122 x 147 cm) USD 290,000. New York, 16 May 2002, *Untitled* (1993, oil on canvas, on four panels) USD 330,000. New York, 12 Nov 2002, *What There Is Between You and Me* (1992, oil on linen, 98 x 74 ins / 249 x 188 cm) USD 380,000. New York, 15 May 2003, *Artist* (1993, oil on chromecoat paper, 28 x 39 ins / 70 x 100 cm) USD 32,000. New York, 12 Nov 2003, *Japanese Bath* (1988, oil on canvas, 48 x 60 ins / 122 x 152 cm) USD 210,000. New York, 13 May 2004, *Father and Son Sleeping* (1980, oil on canvas, 74 x 74 ins / 188 x 188 cm) USD 170,000. Paris, 18 July 2004, *Collector and Family* (1991, oil on canvas, 107 x 75 ins / 272 x 190 cm) EUR 130,000.

FISCHLI, Hans

Swiss, 20th century.
Born 1909, in Zurich.
Sculptor, painter, architect.

Hans Fischli studied architectural drawing from 1925 to 1928. During a journey to Stuttgart he visited the Weissenhof estate, the first manifestation of modernity in architecture. From 1929 to 1930 he was a student of architecture and decoration at the Bauhaus, also attending courses in painting given by Kandinsky and Klee, and by Oskar Schlemmer in the wall painting department. At the Bauhaus he met Max Bill. On returning to Zurich in 1929, he worked as a design draughtsman and, in 1933, opened his own architect's office in Zurich. From 1933 he also resided in Meilen. In 1937 he built a studio for Oskar Schlemmer in Sehringen, near Badenweiler. In 1952 he travelled to Rome, Pompeii and Florence. From 1954 he was director of the Kunstgewerbeschule in Zurich, from which post he resigned in 1961, then dividing his time between painting, sculpture and architecture.

His abstract painting, executed with a full brush, pertains more particularly to lyrical abstraction. It was however to sculpture that he devoted the main part of his activity. By their style, his works have the constructional rigour of the Zurich Concrete School, tempered by a sensitive hand, which dresses and polishes the stones with an entirely Brancusian patience.

He took part in group exhibitions, including: 1950, Salon des Réalités Nouvelles, Paris; 1978, *Abstraction Creation 1931-1936*, Musée d'Art Moderne of the City of Paris.

Bibliography:
Hans Fischli als Maler und Zeichner, exhibition catalogue, Städtische Gal. Schwarzes Kloster, Freiburg, 1972.

FISCHLI AND WEISS, Peter and David

Swiss, 20th century.
Born in Zurich, Fischli born in 1952, Weiss born in 1946.
Sculptors, installation artists. Multimedia.
Neo-Conceptual Art.

Peter Fischli was a student at the Accademia di Belle Arti in Urbino (1975-1976), and then at the Accademia di Belle Arti in Bologna (1976-1977). David Weiss studied at the Kunstgewerbeschule in Zurich (1964-1965), then left for Basel.

Fischli and Weiss have worked together since 1979, producing a number of series of photographs, sculptures and three films. Their first joint work, *Series of Sausages*, made up of photographs, presents a road accident using slices of sausage, cigarette butts (members of the emergency services), a roll of lavatory paper (the motorway) and pieces of gruyere (the chalets). This work presaged the importance that trivial objects would have in works to come. This taste for collecting has led them to bring together on vast surfaces the diverse elements of everyday life. They also create sculptures in synthetic rubber. In 1980 they presented a work, *Suddenly, This Overall View*, made up of 250 objects in terracotta. The work *The Table*, 26 x 8 feet (8 x 2.5 metres), of 1992 plays with reality by bringing together more than 150 objects made of polyurethane, perfect imitations when seen at a distance, but viewed closely their counterfeit nature is obvious. Detergent, a Canigou box, a transistor, sponge, monkey wrench, can and glove are mixed up with humour and derision. Having lost their functions, they are there quite simply just to be seen.

Fischli and Weiss have taken part in group exhibitions, including: 1985, Paris Biennale; 1987, Documenta 8, Kassel; 1989, 20th Biennale, São Paulo; 1995, Venice Biennale Arts Festival (Swiss Pavilion); 1997, *Sculpture. Projects in Münster 1997*, Münster; 2001, exhibition on the unreal, the transreal and the reconstruction of reality, *Hypermental*, Kunsthalle, Hamburg; 2003, *L'état des choses* (*The State of Things*), a look at the status of everyday objects in contemporary art, an exhibition presented on the occasion of *Trésors publics, 20 ans de création dans les Fonds régionaux d'art contemporain (FRAC)* (*Public Treasury, 20 Years of Creation in the Regional Collection of Contemporary Art*), Musée des Beaux-Arts, Nantes. They had a first solo exhibition in Zurich in 1981, then: 1988, Musée de Grenoble; 1992-1993, Galeries Contemporaines, Musée National d'Art Moderne, Paris; 1996, Kunsthaus, Zurich; 2002-2003, *Moving Pictures*, an exhibition showing the use of photography, film and video in art since the end of the 1960s, Solomon R. Guggenheim Museum, New York.

BIBLIOGRAPHY:
Fischli et Weiss, exhibition catalogue, Musée national d'Art moderne, Paris, 1993. Sans, Jérôme, '*Interview: Peter Fischli, David Weiss*' in *Beaux-Arts Magazine*, periodical, Paris, January 1993. *Moving Pictures*, exhibition catalogue, Solomon R. Guggenheim, New York, 2002. Zahm, Olivier (preface), et al., *Trésors publics, 20 ans de création dans les Fonds régionaux d'art contemporain*, Flammarion, Paris, 2003 (text in French and English).

MUSEUMS AND GALLERIES:
BORDEAUX (FRAC Aquitaine): *The Outlaws* (1985); *Sans titre* (*Untitled*) (1985) - CARQUEFOU (FRAC Pays de la Loire) - DÔLE (FRAC Franche-Comté): *Curiosity* (1984) - NEW YORK (Solomon R. Guggenheim Mus.): *Untitled (Flowers)* (1997-1998, photos, portfolio).

AUCTION RECORDS:
NEW YORK, 7 May 1993, *Bungalow* (black rubber, 5 3/4 x 28 x 19 3/4 ins / 14.5 x 71.1 x 50.2 cm) USD 4,830. NEW YORK, 3 May 1994, *Cubic Pouf* (1987, black rubber, 15 x 21 1/4 x 21 1/4 ins / 38.2 x 54.2 x 54.2 cm) USD 8,050.

FISCHMANN, Charles

French, 20th century.
Born 17 October 1928, in Paris.
Painter.

Charles Fischman studied in Paris at the École des Arts Décoratifs under Desnoyer. Since 1918, he has exhibited in Paris at the Salon d'Automne and the Salon des Artistes Indépendants.

FISCHWEILER, Gustave

Belgian, 20th century.
Born 1911, in St-Servais-sur-Namur, France; died 1 May 1990, in Ohain.
Painter, sculptor, medallist.

Fischweiler was a very good technician.

FISÉ, Michael Johann. See **FISSÉ**

FISELIER, Jean, or Lefiselier

French, 15th century.
Active in Rouen.
Sculptor (wood).

In 1467, Jean Fiselier worked with a number of other artists under the direction of Philippot Viart on the carvings for the choir stalls in Rouen Cathedral. In 1459, he designed an episcopal throne, but the chapter rejected his design as being insufficiently elaborate. They chose instead a throne by Laurent Adam, which was destroyed during the French Revolution.

FISEN, Englebert or Engelbert

Flemish, 17th - 18th century.
Born 1655, in Liège; died 1733, in Liège.
Painter. Religious subjects, portraits.
Flemish School.

Englebert Fisen was a pupil of Berthol and Flemalle and he also worked in Italy with Carlo Maratti. On his return to Liège he executed religious paintings for various churches in that town.

E.FISEN FECIT A° J7J8

MUSEUMS AND GALLERIES:
LIÈGE: *Portrait of the Artist and his Family*.

AUCTION RECORDS:
AMSTERDAM, 20 June 1989, *Christ Healing the Lepers* (oil on canvas, 35 x 46 1/2 ins / 88.6 x 118.1 cm) NLG 10,925. AMSTERDAM, 12 May 1992, *Christ Giving the Keys of Paradise to St Peter* (oil on canvas, 32 x 44 ins / 81 x 112 cm) NLG 5,750. LILLE, 10 March 2002, *Adoration of the Shepherds* (1727, oil on canvas, 66 x 48 ins / 167 x 121 cm) EUR 3,500.

FISH, Janet

American, 20th century.
Born 18 May 1938, in Boston.
Painter, watercolourist, graphic artist, printmaker. Still-lifes, figures, landscapes.

Janet Fish's grandfather, Clark Voorhees, was an American Impressionist painter, her father was an art history teacher, and her mother, Florence Whistler Fish, was a sculptor and ceramicist. Fish studied sculpture and printmaking at Smith College, Northampton, MA, obtaining a BA in 1960; at Yale University School of Art and Architecture, New Haven (1961-1963), receiving a BFA and an MFA; and at Skowhegan School of Art, Maine (summer 1962). She has taught at the School of Visual Arts, New York; Skowhegan School of Art; Institute of Fine Arts, Santa Fe; Vermont Studio Center, Johnston; and has held the Albert Dorne visiting professorship at the University of Bridgeport, CT. Fish lives in New York City and near Rutland, Vermont.

Fish specialises in realistic still-life paintings, most often including glass items which allow for the depiction of chromatic and light effects. She always works from life, favours large-scale formats and explores formal issues of arrangement and shape. In the 1960s, Fish painted enlarged fruit and vegetables, and by 1969 began to paint them in boxes wrapped in supermarket cellophane, as the plastic supplied many reflections. An example of this type of work is *Box of Four Red Apples* (1969-1970). By the early 1970s, Fish focused on painting glass jars and bottles containing liquid, increasing the glassy reflections by placing the objects on mirrors. In the late 1970s and 1980s, she composed her still-lifes of many objects such as flowers in vases, curtains, fruit, stacked glass plates and tablecloths. In the 1980s, Fish also began to paint figurative works of people engaging in outdoor activities, such as *Sarah Swimming* (1986).

Fish has participated in group exhibitions, including: *The Liberation*, Corcoran Gallery of Art, Washington DC, 1976-1977; *New Viewpoints*, Seville World Exposition, Spain, 1992; *Selections from the Glen C. James Collection*, Spiva Art Museum, Joplin, OH, 1993; *Yale Collects Yale*, Yale University, New Haven, 1993; *Four Artists, Four Objects, Ten Years*, Oglethorpe University Museum, Atlanta, 2000; *Facing Reality: The Seavest Collection of Contemporary Realism*, Newberger Museum of Art, New York, 2003-2004.

She has had solo exhibitions: Delaware Art Museum, Wilmington, 1982; Columbia Museum of Art, SC, 1984; Smith College Museum of Art, Northampton, 1986; Marianne Friedland Gallery, Toronto, 1987, 1989, 1990, 1992; Orlando Museum of Art, FL, 1992; Museum of Arts and Sciences, Macon, GA, 1993; Aspen Art Museum, CO, 1993;

Janet Fish: Selected Works 1970s to 1990s, Museum of Art, Fort Lauderdale, FL, 1999; D.C. Moore Gallery, New York, 2000.

Her awards include: MacDowell Fellowships, 1968, 1969, 1972; the Harris Award, Chicago Biennial, 1974; an Australian Council for the Arts travel and lecturing grant, 1975; a Hubbard Museum Award, 1991; the Aspen Art Museum Women in Arts Award, 1993; and an American Academy of Arts and Letters Award, 1994.

BIBLIOGRAPHY:

Janet Fish, exhibition catalogue, Robert Miller Gallery, New York, 1980. Cottingham, Jane, '*Janet Fish: Perceptual Realist*' in *American Artist*, Journal article, October 1982. Henry, Gerrit, *Janet Fish*, illustrated book, Burton & Skira, Geneva, 1987. *Janet Fish: Recent Paintings and Watercolors*, exhibition catalogue, Robert Miller Gallery, New York, 1989. *Janet Fish, Recent Paintings*, exhibition catalogue, Grace Borgenicht Gallery, New York, 1994. Kramer, Linda Konheim, *The Prints of Janet Fish*, illustrated book, John Szoke Graphics, New York, 1997. *Janet Fish*, exhibition catalogue, D.C. Moore Gallery, New York, 2000. Katz, Vincent, *Janet Fish Paintings*, illustrated book, Harry N. Abrams, New York, 2002.

MUSEUMS AND GALLERIES:

BLOOMINGTON (AM, Indiana University): *Wine and Cheese Glasses* (1975) - BOSTON (MFA) - BUFFALO (Albright-Knox AG): *After Leslie Left* (1983-1984) - CHICAGO (AI) - CLEVELAND (MA) - DALLAS (MA): *Eight Vinegar Bottles* (1972-1973) - DETROIT (Institute of Arts): *Butterfly Wings* (1991, screenprint) - NEW YORK (Metropolitan Mus. of Art): *Raspberries and Goldfish* (1981, oil) - NEW YORK (Whitney Mus. of American Art) - NORTHAMPTON, MA (MA, Smith College) - SYDNEY (Powers Institute).

AUCTION RECORDS:

NEW YORK, 9 Nov 1982, *Campari bottles* (1973, oil on canvas, 48 x 42¼ ins / 122 x 107 cm) USD 7,500. NEW YORK, 1 Nov 1984, *Three glasses Skowhegan window* (1974, pastel/paper, 28½ x 28½ ins / 72.5 x 72.5 cm) USD 8,500. BARCELONA, 1 Oct 1985, *Tanqueray bottles* (1973, oil on canvas, 40 x 40 ins / 101.5 x 101.5 cm) USD 26,000. NEW YORK, 11 Nov 1986, *Six glasses of water* (1974, pastel/paper, 22 x 37¼ ins / 56 x 94.3 cm) USD 13,000. NEW YORK, 5 May 1987, *Pansies and tea* (1982, oil on canvas, 38 x 64 ins / 96.5 x 162.5 cm) USD 40,000. NEW YORK, 3 April 1988, *Seven Painted Glasses* (pastel, 29 x 24¼ ins / 73.7 x 61.7 cm) USD 11,500. NEW YORK, 8 Oct 1988, *Six Glasses of Water* (1974, pastel/paper, 22 x 37¼ ins / 56 x 94.3 cm) USD 19,800. NEW YORK, 5 Oct 1989, *Seven Painted Glasses in Skowhegen* (1974, pastel/tinted paper, 29 x 24¼ ins / 73.7 x 61.7 cm) USD 19,800. NEW YORK, 8 Nov 1989, *Carnations and Red Peppers* (1979, oil on canvas, 50 x 54 ins / 127.1 x 137.1 cm) USD 44,000. NEW YORK, 4 Oct 1990, *The Pink Jug* (1987, watercolour/paper, 39 x 29 ins / 99 x 73.6 cm) USD 8,800. NEW YORK, 14 Feb 1991, *Red Glass* (1977, coloured chalk/paper, 30¼ x 23¾ ins / 77 x 60.5 cm) USD 8,800. NEW YORK, 15 Feb 1991, *Painted Glasses* (1974, pastel/paper, 22 x 37 ins / 56 x 94 cm) USD 13,200. NEW YORK, 7 May 1992, *Glasses* (1976, oil on canvas, 64 x 40 ins / 162.6 x 101.6 cm) USD 44,000. NEW YORK, 3 May 1995, *Four Assorted Jars* (1972, acrylic/canvas, 50 x 56 ins / 127 x 142.2 cm) USD 32,200. NEW YORK, 9 May 1996, *Photos of Nan* (1984, oil on canvas, 36 x 58 ins / 91.4 x 147.3 cm) USD 28,750. NEW YORK, 10 Oct 1996, *Apples* (1972, pastel/paper, 18 x 23¾ ins / 45.7 x 60.3 cm) USD 6,325. NEW YORK, 20 Nov 1996, *Purple Pitcher, Cakes and Peonies* (1982, oil on canvas, 42¼ x 92 ins / 107.3 x 233.7 cm) USD 32,200. NEW YORK, 21 Nov 1996, *English Town* (1976, oil on canvas, 52 x 38 ins / 132.2 x 96.5 cm) USD 17,250. NEW YORK, 7 May 1997, *Bottles of Windex* (1971-1972, oil on canvas, 50 x 29¾ ins / 127 x 75.6 cm) USD 23,000. NEW YORK, 8 May 1997, *Seven Honey Jars* (1970, oil on canvas, 19¾ x 83¾ ins / 50.2 x 212.8 cm) USD 36,800. NEW YORK, 20 Nov 1997, *Vinegar Bottles* (1971-1972, oil on canvas, 50 x 60 ins / 127 x 152.4 cm) USD 14,950. NEW YORK, 20 May 1999, *Vinegar Bottles* (oil on canvas, 50 x 60 ins / 127 x 152 cm) USD 30,000. NEW YORK, 10 Nov 1999, *Skowhegan Glasses* (1974, oil on canvas, 54 x 66 ins / 138 x 168 cm) USD 35,000. NEW YORK, 15 Nov 2000, *Rain and Yellow Walls* (1976, oil on canvas, 60 x 40 ins / 152 x 102 cm) USD 25,000. NEW YORK, 20 Feb 2002, *Two Jars Hot Pepper Pickles* (oil on canvas, 54 x 52 ins / 138 x 133 cm) USD 38,000. NEW YORK, 7 Oct 2003, *Green Bananas* (1969, oil on canvas, 31 x 40 ins / 78 x 101 cm) USD 10,000. NEW YORK, 15 Sept 2004, *Pears* (1972, chalk, pastel and charcoal, 17 x 19 ins / 44 x 49 cm) USD 3,200.

FISHER

Italian, 18th century.
Active in Rome.
Portrait artist.

FISHER, A. Hugh

British, 19th century.
Born 1867, in London; died 1945.
Painter, engraver (etching).

A. Hugh Fisher was initially in trade, before studying art at the Lambeth School in London and, later, under Benjamin-Constant and Laurens in Paris. He painted landscapes in oils (*The Thames, Views of London and Paris*) and watercolour (*Paris under Snow*). His etchings include: *Mill on the Mersey, Stonehenge, The English Bridge in Canton, Grays Inn, St-Étienne du Mont* and *Rue Grenier on the Waterfront*. He exhibited at the Royal Academy, the Suffolk Street Gallery and the New Water-Colour Society in London, and with the Salon des Artistes Français in Paris.

FISHER, Alanson

American, 19th century.
Born 1807; died 1884.
Active in New York.
Painter. Portraits.

Alanson Fisher was an associate of the National Academy of Design in New York from 1843.

FISHER, Alexander

British, 19th - 20th century.
Born 1864; died 1936.
Painter, sculptor, worker in precious metals.

Alexander Fisher was a painter of flowers and mythological scenes. He also worked in gold, silver and enamels and founded his own studio in London. Fisher taught enamelling at the Central School of Arts and Crafts in London from 1896. He exhibited from 1886 at various venues in London.

MUSEUMS AND GALLERIES:

LONDON (Victoria and Albert Mus.): *Roses*.

FISHER, Alvan

American, 19th century.
Born 9 August 1792, in Needham; died 1863, in Dedham (Massachusetts).
Painter. Portraits, landscapes with figures, landscapes.

Alvan Fisher visited Europe in 1825 and studied for a while in Paris. His paintings are very similar to each other and not without merit, especially the portrait of Spurzheim.

AUCTION RECORDS:

NEW YORK, 17 June 1964, *Travellers' Halt*, USD 1,350. NEW YORK, 20 March 1969, *Travellers in a Landscape*, USD 2,250. NEW YORK, 20 Sept 1972, *Two Hunting Dogs*, USD 3,600. HYANNIS, 7 Aug 1973, *Cows Drinking*, USD 2,000. HYANNIS, 29 April 1976, *Hunter and his Dog in a Forest Interior* (oil on canvas, 30 x 25 ins / 76.2 x 63.5 cm) USD 1,500. HYANNIS, 24 Sept 1981, *Niagara Falls* (watercolour, 9¼ x 14¼ ins / 23.3 x 36.3 cm) USD 4,400. HYANNIS, 21 Oct 1983, *Children and a Dog in a Landscape* (oil on canvas, 22 x 27 ins / 55.9 x 68.6 cm) USD 1,200. HYANNIS, 20 March 1987, *Chieftain's Son*

(1834, oil on canvas, 30 x 25 1/4 ins / 76.2 x 64 cm) USD 4,000. HYANNIS, 6 Dec 1991, *After the Hunt* (1840, oil on canvas/aluminium, 30 x 25 1/4 ins / 76.5 x 64 cm) USD 17,600. NEW YORK, 26 Sept 1996, *Views of the Niagara Falls* (1822, oil on canvas, 33 x 47 ins / 83.8 x 119.4 cm) USD 35,650. HYANNIS, 4 Dec 1996, *By the Water* (1835, oil on canvas, 24 1/4 x 35 1/4 ins / 61.5 x 89.5 cm) USD 11,500. NEW YORK, 23 April 1997, *Discovery* (1846, oil on canvas, 22 x 27 ins / 55.9 x 68.6 cm) USD 5,750. MAINE, 1 May 1999, *View from East of Bear Island, Mt Desert Bay* (oil on canvas, 18 x 24 ins / 46 x 61 cm) USD 37,500. LOS ANGELES, 9 Dec 1999, *View of Tory Hill* (c. 1830, oil on board, 5 x 6 ins / 13 x 15 cm) USD 4,000. SAN FRANCISCO, 13 June 2001, *Leader of the Herd* (oil on canvas, 25 x 35 ins / 64 x 89 cm) USD 6,000. NEW YORK, 21 May 2002, *Coastal Scene, Nahant, Massachusetts* (oil on canvas, 14 x 18 ins / 36 x 46 cm) USD 9,200. NEW YORK, 5 March 2003, *Indians at Sunset* (oil on canvas, 14 x 20 ins / 36 x 51 cm) USD 10,000. PLAINFIELD, 6 Sept 2004, *Mt Chocorua with Figures and Animals* (oil on canvas, 28 x 40 ins / 71 x 102 cm) USD 60,000.

FISHER, Amy E. (Miss)
British, 19th century.
Painter. Genre scenes.

Amy Fisher exhibited at the Royal Academy, Suffolk Street and the Royal Institute from 1866 to 1890.

MUSEUMS AND GALLERIES:
LONDON (Victoria and Albert Mus.): *The Deanery, Westminster* (watercolour).

FISHER, Andrea
American, 20th century.
Born 1955, in New York; died 1997.
Active in England.
Installation artist.

Andrea Fisher studied at St Martin's School of Art in London, and at the University of Leeds. She took part in the exhibition *I, Myself and Others* held at Le Magasin, the national centre for contemporary arts in Grenoble, where she composed a decor conveying her sense of the world. Her solo shows included those at Gimpel Fils Gallery in London in 1992, 1994 and 1999, and *Andrea Fisher*, at the Museum voor Modern Kunst, Arnhem in 2000.

FISHER, Anna S.
American, 20th century.
Died 1942.
Painter.

Anna S. Fisher was a member of the American Watercolor Society, the New York Watercolor Club, the National Association of Women Painters and Sculptors, and the National Arts Club. She won the National Arts Club Prize from the National Association of Women Painters in 1919 and the Swift Prize in 1930.

MUSEUMS AND GALLERIES:
NEW YORK (National Arts Club).

AUCTION RECORDS:
NEW YORK, 3 Oct 1984, *Summer Morning* (watercolour, 17 x 20 1/2 ins / 43 x 52 cm) USD 900. MILFORD, 21 Oct 1999, *Fishing Boat at Dock* (oil on canvas, 30 x 25 ins / 76 x 64 cm) USD 5,000. WASHINGTON, 15 April 2000, *Tugboat Towing Sailboat down River* (oil on board, 11 x 11 ins / 29 x 29 cm) USD 4,500. PITTSFIELD, 12 May 2001, *Sunlit Barnyard, Fisher Farm* (oil on canvas, 20 x 16 ins / 51 x 41 cm) USD 1,950. PITTSFIELD, 12 May 2001, *Sunlit Garden Path* (oil on canvas, 38 x 27 ins / 97 x 69 cm) USD 15,000. MILFORD, 24 Oct 2002, *Path to the Harbour. Low Tide* (oil on canvas, a pair, 15 x 11 ins / 38 x 28 cm) USD 5,500.

FISHER, Brian
Canadian, 20th century.
Born in Uxbridge, England.
Painter, sculptor.
Kinetic Art.

Brian Fisher studied at the Regina School of Art in 1957 and then went to the USA where he worked under the direction of Roy Kiyooka in 1959. He graduated from the Vancouver School of Art in 1961 and went to Rome to continue his studies at the city's school of fine arts from 1962 to 1964. He has a similar approach to abstract art as Bloore, carefully painting series of straight lines which, where they intersect, create the effect of optical vibrations. He uses a wide range of materials including glass, metal and wire in the tradition of kinetic artists.

FISHER, Craig
American, 20th - 21st century.
Born 1951, in Cincinnati.
Painter, draughtsman.

Craig Fisher lives and works in New York. In 2002, he received distinctions from the Gottlieb Foundation and the Pollack-Krasner Foundation in New York. Closer to Supports Surfaces than to American Abstraction, he paints coloured shapes on raw cotton cloth. They repeat themselves, sometime broader, sometimes smaller, under the pressures the canvas is subjected to. His colours remain primary and the circles, blots, brush strokes thus generated answer to an organic, almost obsessive, rhythm. Fisher is essentially a Matterist, summoning to the white, free space of the canvas tensions and traces, like ghost images. He took part in the exhibitions *Exposition des collections* (*Show of the Collections*), Musée Picasso, Antibes, and *Art Frankurt*, Paal Gallery, Frankfurt. He has shown his works in solo exhibitions in New York, Munich and Paris galleries.

BIBLIOGRAPHY:
Cohen, David, '*Craig Fisher*' in *Art Press* n° 255, periodical, Paris, March 2000. Fréchuret, Maurice, *Craig Fisher*, exhibition catalogue, Gal. Corinne Caminade, Paris, 2001. Schwabsky, Barry, *Craig Fisher. Recent Paintings*, exhibition catalogue, Florence Lynch Gall., New York, 2002.

FISHER, Daniel
British, 19th century.
Active in London.
Painter. Landscapes.

Daniel Fisher exhibited in London at the Royal Academy and, particularly, Suffolk Street from 1875.

AUCTION RECORDS:
LONDON, 4 April 1910, *Mill-race*, GBP 1.

FISHER, E.J.
British, 19th century.
Painter. Portraits.

E.J. Fisher exhibited with the Royal Academy and the British Institution in London from 1836 to 1853. He is known for a *Portrait of the Lord Mayor, J. Kinnersly Hooper*. Davey engraved his *Portrait of a Cleric*.

AUCTION RECORDS:
LONDON, 6 Nov 1995, *Portraits of Mary and Emma Warrington in White and Blue Dresses* (oil on canvas, a pair, each 30 x 25 1/4 ins / 76 x 64 cm) GBP 8,625.

FISHER, Edward
Irish, 18th century.
Born 1722, in Dublin; died c. 1785, in London.
Engraver (mezzotint).

Of Irish descent, Edward Fisher settled in London where he engraved a large number of portraits after Sir Joshua Reynolds, including: *Garrick between Tragedy and Comedy* (1769), *Sir Thomas Harrison, The Marquis of Rockingham, Lady Elisabeth Lee, Lawrence Sterne, John Armstrong* and others. He also engraved *Mark Akenside* after Pond, and *George III* after Benjamin West.

FISHER, Flavius J.
American, 19th century.
Born 1832, in Wytheville (Virginia); died 9 May 1905, in Washington DC.
Painter. Portraits, landscapes.
Flavius J. Fisher studied in Philadelphia and then went to Europe. He was the first American to become a member of the Art Institute of Berlin. He settled in Washington DC, and painted portraits of a large number of notable Americans, as well as landscapes.

FISHER, George Bulteel (Major)
British, 18th - 19th century.
Painter, watercolourist, engraver. Landscapes.
George Fisher exhibited landscapes at the Royal Academy in London from 1780 to 1808.
AUCTION RECORDS:
LONDON, 13 March 1980, *View of Lisbon* (watercolour, 19 x 35 1/2 ins / 48 x 90 cm) GBP 950. LONDON, 1 June 1983, *Niagara Falls* (watercolour/pencil outlines, 8 1/2 x 12 1/4 ins / 21.5 x 31 cm) GBP 1,350. MONTREAL, 19 Nov 1991, *The Chaudière Falls* (engraving, 16 1/2 x 24 ins / 41.8 x 61 cm) CAD 950. LONDON, 2 June 1995, *Distant View of the Galtee Mountains in County Tipperary* (watercolour/pencil, 18 1/4 x 24 1/2 ins / 46.5 x 62 cm) GBP 575. LONDON, 21 March 2001, *Minto Hills from Teviot Valley, Scotland. Rubers Law from the Wells, Scotland* (watercolour over pencil, a pair, 11 x 16 ins / 28 x 40 cm) GBP 1,800.

FISHER, Harrison
American, 20th century.
Born 22 July 1875, in Brooklyn (New York City); died 19 January 1934.
Painter, draughtsman, illustrator.
Harrison Fisher was the son of a painter and spent his childhood on the east coast, in New York. He learned his craft quickly, studying at the Mark Hopkins Institute of Art, San Francisco, and at the age of sixteen drawing for some of the city's newspapers. He went to New York to further his career and worked for *Puck*. He was a member of the Society of Illustrators from 1911.

He became famous for drawing women of all periods, but especially 'modern' women living a life of action, such as his *Red Cross Nurse*. His *Fisher Girls* for a time appeared exclusively in the periodical *Cosmopolitan*. He also contributed to *Examiner, The Ladies' Home Journal, Life, McClure's, San Francisco Call, Saturday Evening Post*, and *Scribner's*. He also illustrated *The Market Place* by H. Frederics (1899), and Longfellow's *Hiawatha* (1906).
BIBLIOGRAPHY:
AUCTION RECORDS:
NEW YORK, 26 June 1981, *Charming Company* (1894, pen/paper, 27 1/4 x 20 ins / 69.1 x 50.4 cm) GBP 850. NEW YORK, 2 Oct 1985, *Shy Lovers* (1900, gouache and pen, 32 x 22 ins / 81.3 x 56 cm) USD 4,000. NEW YORK, 6 Nov 1999, *Young Woman Holding Riding Crop* (pastel, 17 x 14 ins / 43 x 36 cm) USD 6,000. LOS ANGELES, 9 Dec 1999, *Portrait of Lady with Dark Hair* (pastel on canvas, 30 x 22 ins / 76 x 56 cm) USD 8,500. NEW YORK, 4 Nov 2000, *Young Man with Monocle Eying Coquette* (1902, watercolour and gouache, 25 x 16 ins / 64 x 41 cm) USD 7,500. SAN FRANCISCO, 9 June 2002, *Evening Conversation* (1910, oil on canvas, 25 x 30 ins / 63 x 76 cm) USD 2,500. SAN FRANCISCO, 19 Nov 2002, *Portrait of a Lady in an Evening Gown* (1909, pencil and watercolour, 24 x 15 ins / 60 x 38 cm) USD 7,500. SAN FRANCISCO, 11 June 2003, *Portrait of a Young Woman in Profile* (pastel, 17 x 12 ins / 44 x 30 cm) USD 2,750. ALAMEDA, 10 Jan 2004, *Dutch Girl* (1909, watercolour and gouache on sketching board, 14 x 11 ins / 36 x 28 cm) USD 2,500. NEW ORLEANS, 3 April 2004, *Portrait of a Lady and her Suitor* (1909, watercolour, 24 x 19 ins / 61 x 48 cm) USD 9,000.

FISHER, Horace
British, 19th century.
Died 1893.
Painter. Genre scenes, landscapes.
Horace Fisher exhibited in London, notably at the Royal Academy and Suffolk Street, from 1882.
AUCTION RECORDS:
LONDON, 17 Nov 1933, *Terrace*, GBP 5. LONDON, 27 July 1984, *Woman Weaving* (oil on canvas, 41 1/4 x 27 1/4 ins / 104.7 x 69.2 cm) GBP 3,750. NEW YORK, 24 May 1989, *Young Peasant Girls Picking Wild Flowers* (oil on canvas, 50 x 35 ins / 127.1 x 89.1 cm) USD 6,600. NEW YORK, 19 July 1990, *On Bridge beside the Mill* (oil on canvas, 44 x 34 ins / 111.8 x 86.5 cm) USD 4,400. LONDON, 3 June 1992, *Terrace on Capri* (oil on canvas, 28 1/4 x 40 1/4 ins / 71.5 x 102 cm) GBP 3,520.

FISHER, Hugo Melville
American, 19th - 20th century.
Born 20 October 1876, in Brooklyn (New York City); died 1946.
Painter, watercolourist. Landscapes.
Hugo Melville Fisher, a pupil of Whistler and, in Paris, of Benjamin-Constant and J.P. Laurens, was a member of the American Art Association of Paris.
AUCTION RECORDS:
SAN FRANCISCO, 21 Jan 1981, *Stream in a Wood* (watercolour, 29 1/4 x 20 ins / 74 x 51 cm) USD 1,100. SAN FRANCISCO, 16 May 1985, *Falls of the Ausable, Adirondacks* (watercolour, 40 1/4 x 30 ins / 102 x 76 cm) USD 2,500. LOS ANGELES, 9 Dec 1999, *Rocky Shore with Sailboats and Island* (oil on canvas, 30 x 40 ins / 76 x 102 cm) USD 3,000. PORTLAND, 8 Aug 2003, *Esopus Creek* (oil on canvas, 26 x 42 ins / 65 x 107 cm) USD 3,500. SAN FRANCISCO, 8 June 2004, *Sailing Boats in an Inlet* (oil on canvas, 26 x 29 ins / 66 x 73 cm) USD 2,000.

FISHER, J.
British, 19th century.
Active in Bristol.
Miniaturist. Portraits.
J. Fisher exhibited miniatures at the Royal Academy in London from 1849 to 1858.
AUCTION RECORDS:
PARIS, 27 April 1910, *Portait of a Young Woman* (miniature) FRF 180.

FISHER, J. C.
American, 19th - 20th century.
Active in America.
Painter. Village views.
J.C. Fisher is referred to by Florence Levy.
AUCTION RECORDS:
NEW YORK, 15 Feb 1907, *Village Street*, USD 210.

FISHER, J.H. Vignoles
British, 19th century.
Active in London.
Painter, watercolourist. Landscapes.
J.H. Vignoles Fisher exhibited at the Royal Academy, Suffolk Street and with the New Water-Colour Society in London, from 1884.
AUCTION RECORDS:
LONDON, 29 June 1931, *Scene on the Norfolk Broads; Afternoon Light on the Sussex Downs* (collection) GBP 5.

FISHER, Janet
British, 20th century.
Born in Walton-upon-Trent (Derbyshire).
Painter, pastellist, engraver. Genre scenes.
Janet Fisher exhibited at the Salon of 1926 showing a piece entitled *Twilight*.
AUCTION RECORDS:
LONDON, 11 Nov 1981, *Young Girl Sewing* (pastel, 26 3/4 x 20 1/2 ins / 68 x 52 cm) GBP 1,700.

FISHER, Jonathan
Irish, 18th century.
Died 1809, in Dublin.
Painter. Landscapes.
Jonathan Fisher worked in the Stamp Office in Dublin, and was a protégé of Lord Portarlington.
MUSEUMS AND GALLERIES:
LONDON (Victoria and Albert Mus.): *The River Lymington; Distant View of the Isle of Wight* (watercolour).
AUCTION RECORDS:
LONDON, 17 March 1972, *Cork Harbour,* Gns 8,500. LONDON, 18 June 1976, *Irish Landscape* (oil on canvas, 21 1/2 x 40 1/2 ins / 54.7 x 103 cm) GBP 900. LONDON, 26 June 1981, *O'Sullivan's Cascade, Killarney* (oil on canvas, 40 x 50 ins / 101.6 x 127 cm) GBP 4,800. LONDON, 26 April 1985, *O'Sullivan's Cascade, Killarney* (oil on canvas, 40 x 50 ins / 101.6 x 127 cm) GBP 3,800. LONDON, 15 Nov 1989, *Landscape with a Distant View of a House* (oil on canvas, 42 1/2 x 57 3/4 ins / 108 x 147 cm) GBP 11,000. LONDON, 14 May 2004, *Views of Curraghmore House in 1768, Waterford* (pencil and grey and pale blue wash, album, 9 x 15 ins / 23 x 37 cm) GBP 9,000.

FISHER, M. J. (Miss)
British, 19th century.
Active in Wargrave.
Painter. Landscapes.
M.J. Fisher exhibited at the Royal Academy and Suffolk Street in London, from 1858 to 1866.

FISHER, Maria Anna. See **FISCHER**

FISHER, Mary
American, 19th - 20th century.
Born in Brooklyn.
Active in Boston.
Painter.
Mary Fisher was a pupil of Edmund C. Tarbell and Joseph de Camp.

FISHER, Melton Samuel
British, 19th - 20th century.
Born 2 January 1859 or 1861, in Herne Hill (London); died 2 September 1939, in Camberley.
Painter, watercolourist, draughtsman. History painting, genre scenes, portraits.
Melton Fisher studied at the Royal Academy from 1876 to 1881, receiving a gold medal and, in 1881, a travel bursary with which he went to Paris to study under Bonaffé. From 1878, he exhibited at the Royal Academy and at the Paris salons where he received a medal in 1896. He then spent ten years in Venice painting genre scenes. In 1895, he returned to London. He became an associate of the Royal Academy in 1917 and a member in 1924. He was also a member of the New Water-Colour Society. Fisher exhibited at the Suffolk Street Gallery.
MUSEUMS AND GALLERIES:
LIVERPOOL (Walker AG): *Chess Players* - LONDON (Guildhall AG): *John William Dodson, Second Baron Lord Monk Betton* (oil on canvas) - LONDON (Tate Collection): *In Realms of Fancy* (exhibited in 1898, oil on canvas) - SYDNEY: *Festa, Venetian Café.*
AUCTION RECORDS:
LONDON, 9 Dec 1907, *Southern Beauty,* GBP 6. LONDON, 3 April 1909, *David and Abiathar,* GBP 7. LONDON, 10 June 1909, *Olivia,* GBP 68. LONDON, 27 Nov 1922, *Rest* (drawing) GBP 17. LONDON, 11 Dec 1922, *Violetta,* GBP 7; *Catriona,* GBP 14. LONDON, 3 May 1935, *Slumber,* GBP 10. SAN FRANCISCO, 20 June 1985, *Portrait of a Lady* (oil on canvas, 60 x 32 ins / 152.5 x 81 cm) USD 2,500. NEW YORK, 24 Oct 1989, *The Mirror* (oil on canvas/synthetic resin, 52 1/2 x 40 1/2 ins / 133.3 x 102.8 cm) USD 15,400. LONDON, 5 June 1991, *Choosing a Necklace* (oil on canvas, 59 x 46 ins / 149 x 117 cm) GBP 7,150.

FISHER, Penelope
British, 20th century.
Painter.
Penelope Fisher exhibited *Broad Road, Fleggburgh* at the Paris Salon of 1933.

FISHER, Percy Harland
British, 19th - 20th century.
Born 1865; died 1944.
Painter. Genre scenes.
Percy Fisher exhibited at the Royal Academy in London from 1886.
AUCTION RECORDS:
LONDON, 23 Jan 1925, *The Goatherd,* GBP 21. LONDON, 20 April 1982, *The Goatherd* (oil on canvas, 15 x 12 ins / 38 x 30.5 cm) GBP 320. LONDON, 21 June 1983, *Two Sisters* (oil on canvas, 40 x 24 ins / 101.5 x 61 cm) GBP 5,000. LONDON, 1 Oct 1986, *The Goatherd, Capri* (oil on canvas, 24 x 36 ins / 61 x 91.5 cm) USD 2,500. LONDON, 13 June 1990, *Little Girl with a Straw Hat* (oil on canvas, 36 x 30 3/4 ins / 90.5 x 78 cm) GBP 4,620. LONDON, 26 Sept 1990, *Young Boy with a Terrier* (oil on canvas, 56 x 39 3/4 ins / 142 x 101 cm) GBP 7,040. LONDON, 13 Feb 1991, *Under a Tree in Blossom* (oil on canvas, 26 3/4 x 25 1/4 ins / 68 x 64 cm) GBP 4,400. LONDON, 3 June 1992, *His Canine Companion* (oil on canvas, 30 x 25 1/4 ins / 76 x 64 cm) GBP 2,420. LONDON, 3 June 1999, *The Sisters* (oil on canvas, 40 x 24 ins / 102 x 61 cm) GBP 25,000. LONDON, 8 June 2000, *Portrait of a Young Girl with a Cat on her Lap* (oil on board, 30 x 25 ins / 76 x 63 cm) GBP 2,000. SEVENOAKS, 11 July 2001, *Blue Veil* (oil on canvas, 30 x 26 ins / 76 x 65 cm) GBP 3,600. LONDON, 10 June 2003, *Charity* (1892, oil on canvas, 20 x 14 ins / 52 x 36 cm) GBP 9,000.

FISHER, Robert
British, 17th century.
Active in Oxford.
Painter. Portraits.
Robert Fisher is known for his signed and dated portrait of the Oxford musician *John Wilson.*
MUSEUMS AND GALLERIES:
OXFORD (Brasenose College): *Portrait de Thomas Yate* (attributed).

FISHER, S. Melton. See **FISHER Melton Samuel**

FISHER, Samuel
British, 19th century.
Reproductions engraver.
Samuel Fisher is noted for a plate after W.A. Bartlett: *Chamonix, the Mer de Glace.* He contributed to a number of collections of engravings including: *The Landscape Annual,* Finden's *Royal Gallery of British Art,* and Scott's *Lady of the Lake,* after designs by J.D. Harding, D. Roberts, C. Stanfield, and W.F. Witherington. He was a member of the Royal Academy, the Royal West of England Academy, and the Pastel Society.

FISHER, Thomas
British, 19th century.
Born 1782, in Rochester; died 1836, in Stoke Newington.
Painter, watercolourist, engraver, draughtsman. Landscapes.
An amateur artist and antiquarian, Thomas Fisher was an employee in the India Office. He made drawings of antique artefacts, which he subsequently engraved.
MUSEUMS AND GALLERIES:
LONDON (British Mus.): *View of Finsbury Square, London* (watercolour).
AUCTION RECORDS:
LONDON, 15 March 1984, *Chesham, Buckinghamshire* (watercolour/pencil outlines, 12 1/2 x 17 1/2 ins / 32 x 44.5 cm) GBP

620. LONDON, 11 July 1985, *Houghton Conquest, Bedfordshire* (watercolour and pencil outlines, 12 1/2 x 16 ins / 31.5 x 40.5 cm) GBP 900. LONDON, 29 Nov 2001, *Views of Bedfordshire* (watercolour over pencil heightened with gouache, folio, 12 x 19 ins / 30 x 47 cm) GBP 13,000.

FISHER, Vernon

American, 20th century.
Born 1943, in Fort Worth (Texas).
Painter (mixed media), sculptor of assemblages.
Conceptual Art.

Vernon Fisher studied at Hardin-Simmons University, where he received a BA in 1967, and at the University of Illinois, obtaining an MFA in 1969. He has taught as associate professor of art at Austin College, Sherman (1969(1978), and as professor of art at North Texas State University (1978(present). Fisher has received Visual Artist Award Grants, SECCA (1981, 1988), and Louis Comfort Tiffany Foundation Grants (1980, 1984).

As a graduate student, Fisher explored the concepts and techniques of Abstract Expressionism, before moving on to new approaches, such as narratives and language, the use of mechanisms and the concept of dysfunction. His work, which is tinged with humour, is associated with that of Paul Cézanne, Jackson Pollock and Donald Judd, and has also been influenced by Edward Ruscha's use of slang and colloquial language. Fisher began incorporating text into his art in the 1970s, his work functioning as visual stories, a practice which associates him with the Narrative Art Movement and traditional Texan storytelling. His work deliberately attempts to conceal meaning and confuse the viewer, posing questions concerning human progress and ambition, and the artificial construction of social symbols.

Fisher's exhibitions include: 1984, Bronx Museum of Arts, New York; 1984, Hirshhorn Museum and Sculpture Garden, Washington DC; 1986, Brooklyn Museum, New York;1990, Museum of Fine Arts, Houston; 1987, Lannan Museum, Lake Worth, FL; 1987, Institute of Contemporary Arts, London; 1987, Los Angeles County Museum of Art; 1987, Walker Art Center, Minneapolis.

BIBLIOGRAPHY:

Vernon Fisher, Exhibition catalogue, Gallerie 't Venster, Rotterdam, 1982 (text in Dutch and English). *Works 88: Vernon Fisher*, Exhibition catalogue, Hirshhorn Museum and Sculpture Garden, Washington DC, 1988. *Vernon Fisher: Lost for Words*, Exhibition catalogue, Dallas Museum of Art, Dallas, 1988. Fisher, Vernon, *Navigating by the Stars*, Book, Landfall Press, Chicago, 1989. Davies, Hugh Marlais, *Vernon Fisher*, La Jolla Museum of Contemporary Art, La Jolla (CA), 1989. *Vernon Fisher, Swimming Lessons*, Exhibition catalogue, Blue Star Art Space, San Antonio, 1994. *Vernon Fisher*, Exhibition catalogue, Board of Trustees, University of Illinois, Urbana-Champaign, 1994. *Vernon Fisher*, Exhibition catalogue, Gerald Peters Gallery, Dallas, 1997. Olsen, Valerie Loupe, *Vernon Fisher's File 00*, Exhibition catalogue, Glassell School of Art of the Museum of Fine Arts, Houston, 2000.

MUSEUMS AND GALLERIES:

BUFFALO (Albright-Knox AG) - FORT WORTH (MAM): *84 Sparrows* (1979, acrylic and graphite) - NEW YORK (Guggenheim Mus.) - NEW YORK (MoMA) - TEMPE, AZ (AM, Arizona State University): *Basutoland* (1986, installation) - WASHINGTON DC (Corcoran Gal. of Art): *Stick-Chart Navigation* (1983, acrylic, oil and shells) - WASHINGTON DC (Hirshhorn Mus. and Sculpture Garden).

AUCTION RECORDS:

NEW YORK, 4 Oct 1989, *Alignment* (acrylic/two sheets of paper mounted on a black painting, 25 3/4 x 54 3/4 ins / 65.7 x 139 cm) USD 6,820. NEW YORK, 9 Nov 1989, *Meditations on Cézanne* (1983, acrylic/laminated paper and canvas, 59 x 118 ins / 150 x 299.7 cm) USD 35,750. NEW YORK, 27 Feb 1990, *Renaissance Afternoon* (1976, acrylic/canvas, 129 1/2 x 129 1/2 ins / 328.7 x 328.7 cm) USD 17,600. NEW YORK, 4 Oct 1990, *Looking for Judd* (1976, acrylic/paper, 94 x 95 ins / 238.7 x 241.3 cm) USD 11,000. NEW YORK, 5 Oct 1990, *Pollock* (montage in three parts, acrylic on wood, acrylic on paper and urinal in porcelain and chrome, in all 75 x 140 x 13 3/4 ins / 190.5 x 355.6 x 35 cm) USD 15,400. NEW YORK, 4 May 1993, *Bridge* (acrylic/laminated paper and canvas, right part 66 x 66 ins / 167.6 x 167.6 cm, left part 72 x 72 ins/182.9 x 182.9 cm) USD 6,900. NEW YORK, 13 Nov 2001, *Twister Forms at Sea* (acrylic and oil on paper, 44 x 44 ins / 111 x 111 cm) USD 3,200.

FISHER, W.

British, 18th - 19th century.
Active in York.
Sculptor.

W. Fisher exhibited at the Royal Academy in London from 1800 to 1811.

FISHER, W. L. T.

British, 20th century.
Born in London.
Painter. Portraits, genre scenes.

W.L.T. Fisher exhibited *Little Lord* at the Paris Salon of 1929.

FISHER, William

Irish, 19th century.
Born 1817, in Cork; died 1895, in London.
Painter, watercolourist. Portraits.

William Fisher exhibited with the Royal Academy, the British Institution and the New Water-Colour Society from 1840 to 1886.

MUSEUMS AND GALLERIES:

CORK: *Portrait of Samuel Skillin* - LONDON (National Portrait Gal.): *Walter Savage Landor* (1839, oil on canvas).

AUCTION RECORDS:

LONDON, 21 Nov 1908, *Medora, The Favourite Dog by A. D. Wilde*, GBP 8. LONDON, 6 Sept 2001, *Artist's Wife Picking Flowers* (1884, oil on canvas, 16 x 19 ins / 41 x 48 cm) GBP 6,000.

FISHER, William Edgard

American, 20th century.
Born 24 October 1872, in Wellsville (New York).
Draughtsman, illustrator.

William Edgard Fisher studied at the Art Institute of Chicago. He belonged to the American Bookplate Society and the Salmagundi Club.

FISHER, William Mark

American, 19th - 20th century.
Born 1841, in Philadelphia, to Anglo-Irish parents; died 1923.
Painter. Genre scenes, landscapes with figures, landscapes.

William Mark Fisher studied initially at the Lowell Institute and then in Paris in Gleyre's studio. In 1879 he was elected a member of the Royal Institute. When he had finished his art education he returned to Boston, but having no succes there he went to England and settled in Newport. From then on he featured regularly in London exhibitions. He won a bronze medal at the Paris Exposition Universelle of 1889.

MUSEUMS AND GALLERIES:

BIRMINGHAM (Mus. and AG): *The Halt* (oil on canvas) - BRADFORD (Cartwright Hall AG): *Hill and Dale* (c. 1900, oil on canvas) - DUBLIN (Modern Art): *The Bath* - LEEDS (City AG): *Winter Pastures* (1888, oil on canvas); *In Algiers* (oil on canvas); several other paintings - MANCHESTER: *Landscape with Cattle* - MELBOURNE: *A Field in Antibes* - NORWICH (Castle Mus. and AG): *Near Sèvres* (watercolour).

AUCTION RECORDS:
LONDON, 30 Nov 1907, *Cows around a Fodder Cart*, GBP 14. LONDON, 4 June 1908, *Ferryboat*, GBP 15; *Cattle going to Graze*, GBP 18. LONDON, 6 March 1909, *Landscape*, GBP 18. LONDON, 19 March 1910, *Waiting for the Ferryboat*, GBP 37. LONDON, 30 April 1910, *Old Fountain in Algiers*, GBP 68; *Cattle near a Lake*, GBP 78. LONDON, 9 July 1920, *Castle near a Cottage* (oil on canvas, 15 1/2 x 20 ins / 39.5 x 51 cm) Gns 50. LONDON, 2 Feb 1923, *Farmyard Scene*, GBP 30. LONDON, 6 April 1923, *Cattle in a Landscape*, GBP 38. LONDON, 10 Dec 1923, *Cattle in a Landscape*, GBP 29. LONDON, 2 May 1924, *Coastal Village*, GBP 52. LONDON, 14 Nov 1924, *Hay Fields*, GBP 22; *Arabs and Camels*, GBP 10. LONDON, 3 April 1925, *Bay of Antibes* (drawing) GBP 31; *Village Scene*, GBP 88; *Sheep Shearing*, GBP 31. LONDON, 19 Feb 1926, *Shaded Pastures*, GBP 52. LONDON, 19 and 20 May 1926, *Fine Day in Antibes*, GBP 11. LONDON, 22 April 1927, *Shepherd*, GBP 23. LONDON, 30 March 1928, *Cattle Grazing*, GBP 29. LONDON, 13 April 1928, *Hazelnut Tree*, GBP 57. LONDON, 30 Nov 1928, *Cattle Grazing*, GBP 11. LONDON, 22 July 1929, *Pasture in Carton* (drawing) GBP 5. LONDON, 21 Nov 1929, *Village Scene* (watercolour) GBP 7. LONDON, 5 Dec 1930, *Cattle Grazing*, GBP 12. LONDON, 1 May 1931, *Family Fields*, GBP 30. LONDON, 27 Nov 1931, *Cattle Grazing*, GBP 5. LONDON, 1 Dec 1933, *Milking Time*, GBP 6. LONDON, 11 July 1934, *Pastures*, GBP 6; *Crossing the Ford*, GBP 11. LONDON, 11 March 1935, *Landscape*, GBP 7. LONDON, 19 July 1935, *Ploughed Field*, GBP 11. LONDON, 1 Aug 1935, *Change of Pasture*, GBP 21. LONDON, 21-24 Feb 1936, *Spring* (drawing) GBP 6; *Hampshire Meadows*, GBP 12; *Cattle Grazing* (drawing) GBP 23. LONDON, 1 May 1936, *Cattle Grazing*, GBP 10. LONDON, 30 and 31 July 1936, *Hampshire Meadows*, GBP 9. LONDON, 13 Feb 1937, *Sun and Shade*, GBP 27. LONDON, 25 June 1937, *Farm*, GBP 31. LONDON, 26 June 1940, *Pastures*, GBP 9. LONDON, 26 June 1941, *Margate Sands*, GBP 25. LONDON, 18 Sept 1942, *Margate Sands*, GBP 54. GLASGOW, 3 Nov 1944, *Pastures*, GBP 25. LONDON, 4 May 1945, *Road to a Farm*, GBP 42. LONDON, 9 May 1945, *Landscape*, GBP 35. LONDON, 9 and 10 April 1946, *Pastures*, GBP 33. LONDON, 20 Dec 1946, *Shady Pastures*, GBP 31. LONDON, 11 July 1947, *Sussex Downs*, GBP 31. LONDON, 8 July 1966, *Sussex Village*, Gns 280. LONDON, 12 April 1967, *River*, GBP 520. LONDON, 18 July 1969, *Garden in Flower*, Gns 950. LONDON, 12 June 1970, *Village*, Gns 2,200. LONDON, 13 July 1973, *By the Lea, Harlow, Essex*, Gns 1,800. LONDON, 14 May 1976, *Wooded Landscape* (1883, oil on canvas, 17 1/2 x 23 ins / 44.5 x 58.5 cm) GBP 400. LONDON, 25 Oct 1977, *Shepherd and Sheep in a Landscape* (oil on canvas, 20 3/4 x 28 1/4 ins / 53 x 72 cm) GBP 950. LONDON, 4 Feb 1981, *Figures in a Landscape* (watercolour, 14 1/2 x 19 1/4 ins / 37 x 49 cm) GBP 220. LONDON, 13 March 1981, *Castle near a Cottage* (oil on canvas, 15 1/2 x 20 ins / 39.5 x 51 cm) GBP 700. NEW YORK, 15 June 1984, *Flock in a Landscape* (oil on canvas, 34 1/2 x 48 1/2 ins / 87.5 x 123 cm) USD 2,800. LONDON, 15 May 1985, *Flock in a Pasture* (1875, oil on canvas, 30 x 50 ins / 76 x 127 cm) GBP 7,000. LONDON, 6 March 1986, *On the Cam* (1923, watercolour and gouache, 18 x 26 ins / 45.7 x 66 cm) GBP 1,300. LONDON, 29 July 1988, *Cows in a Field* (watercolour, 8 3/4 x 12 1/2 ins / 22.5 x 32 cm) GBP 462. BELFAST, 28 Oct 1988, *Cattle in a Wooded Meadow* (oil on canvas, 9 1/2 x 13 ins / 24.2 x 32.1 cm) GBP 495. LONDON, 2 March 1989, *Cattle Grazing near a River Borded by Trees* (oil on canvas, 23 1/2 x 31 1/2 ins / 60 x 80 cm) GBP 6,600. LONDON, 12 May 1989, *Summer Garden* (oil on canvas, 26 x 38 1/2 ins / 66.2 x 97.5 cm) GBP 1,870. STOCKHOLM, 16 May 1990, *Italian Holidays in Sorrento* (1869, oil on canvas, 41 x 51 1/2 ins / 104 x 131 cm) SEK 105,000. LONDON, 18 Oct 1990, *Sawbridgeworth Lock* (oil on canvas, 19 3/4 x 26 1/2 ins / 50 x 67 cm) GBP 1,870. LONDON, 25 Jan 1991, *Sheap Shearing in a Barn* (oil on canvas, 17 x 24 1/2 ins / 43 x 62.5 cm) GBP 1,980. NEW YORK, 15 May 1991, *Rustic Landscape* (oil on canvas, 13 1/2 x 20 ins / 34.3 x 50.8 cm) USD 1,320. NEW YORK, 21 May 1991, *Cows in a Meadow* (1883, oil on canvas, 30 1/2 x 46 1/2 ins / 77.5 x 118.1 cm) USD 4,400. NEW YORK, 28 May 1992, *Summer Day* (oil on canvas, 23 x 30 ins / 58.4 x 76.2 cm) USD 4,675. LONDON, 3 Feb 1993, *Grazing under Trees* (oil on canvas, 40 1/2 x 56 1/2 ins / 103 x 143.5 cm) GBP 3,220. NEW YORK, 24 Feb 1994, *Antibes* (oil on canvas, 21 x 25 ins / 53.3 x 63.5 cm) USD 1,035. EDINBURGH, 15 May 1997, *Sussex Village* (oil on canvas, 24 x 30 ins / 61 x 76.2 cm) GBP 2,875.

FISHER CLAY, Elizabeth Campbell.
See **CLAY Elizabeth Campbell Fisher**

FISHER-PROUT, Margaret. See **PROUT Margaret**

FISHWICK, Clifford

British, 20th century.

Born 21 June 1923, in Rising Bridge (Lancashire); died 1997.

Painter, printmaker. Landscapes, seascapes, sporting scenes.

Clifford Fishwick studied at Liverpool College of Art from 1940 to 1942, interrupting his studies for naval service in World War II from 1942 to 1946. He returned to Liverpool College in 1946, obtaining an art teacher's diploma in 1947. He taught at Exeter College of Art, was appointed principal there from 1958 to 1984, and lived in Topsham, Devon.

Fishwick's style changed throughout his career as he was influenced by different movements and painters, such as the Neo-Romantics, the Cornish painters, and painters from the second Paris School like Nicolas de Staël. His later work was darker, looser and more abstract than his early paintings. He was an avid rock climber and yachtsman and drew inspiration from the coast and landscape for his paintings, such as the seascape in oil *Dark Foreshore* (1957). He also painted and printed sports subjects, as in his 1953 lithograph *Goal*, and contributed to the 1953 *Football and the Fine Arts* exhibition, including his watercolour *Where Shall We Spend Eternity?*.

Fishwick had a solo show at St George's Gallery in 1957, and also exhibited at Dartington Hall (1959); Royal Albert Memorial Museum, Exeter (1960); Exeter University (1961); Plymouth City Art Gallery (1966); Essex University (1976); Spacex Gallery, Exeter (1982); Austin/Desmond Fine Art (1989, 1990); a two-man show with Michael Rees at Gordon Hepworth Fine Art, Exeter (1992); Bruton Street Gallery; the Royal Academy; the Royal Scottish Academy; and the Royal West of England Academy. He regularly exhibited with the Penwith Society in the 1950s and 1960s, and had a solo show there in 1983.

MUSEUMS AND GALLERIES:
BRADFORD (City Art Gallery) - EXETER (Public Gallery) - LONDON (UK Government Art Collection): *Potato Diggers* (1952, lithograph) - PLYMOUTH (Art Gallery).

AUCTION RECORDS:
LONDON, 16 April 2002, *Beach Ball* (1956, oil on board, 13 x 22 ins / 34 x 57 cm) GBP 1,300. LONDON, 13 June 2002, *At the Wheel of Boojum* (1956, oil on board, 30 x 13 ins / 77 x 34 cm) GBP 1,000. LONDON, 16 Oct 2003, *Still-life Abstract* (1956, oil on board, a pair, 24 x 30 ins / 61 x 77 cm) GBP 1,400. LONDON, 14 May 2004, *Totemic Abstract* (1959, wood, sacking, paint on panel, 30 x 6 ins / 77 x 16 cm) GBP 1,000.

FISK, William

British, 19th century.

Born 1796, in Thorpe-le-Soken (Essex); died 1872, in Danbury, near Chelmsford.

Painter. History painting, portraits.

William Fisk worked at first in trade, before devoting himself to art at the age of 31. He exhibited his early portraits with the Royal Academy from 1831 to 1835, after which he painted historical subjects including: *Leonardo da Vinci Dying in the Arms of François I* (submitted to the Royal Academy in 1838), and *The Pazzi Conspiracy* (*Attempted Assassination of Lorenzo de'Medici in Florence, in 1478*) (exhibited in 1839). The latter picture won a gold medal at the British Institution exhibition in Manchester, in 1840. His history paintings are well composed and feature authentic, carefully observed costumes. Fisk retired to his country property shortly after 1842, and ceased painting almost completely.

MUSEUMS AND GALLERIES:
CAPE TOWN: *Rivals; The Pazzi Conspiracy; Guardian Angel; Raising of Lazarus; Dutch Burgomaster and his Wife; Rajah Ram-Rey; Portrait of a Child; Charles I's Farewell to his Family; Cousins* - LIVERPOOL: *The Judgement of Count Strafford in Manchester.*

FISK, William Henry
British, 19th century.
Born c. 1827; died 13 November 1884, in Hampstead.
Painter, watercolourist, draughtsman. Religious subjects, genre scenes.

A pupil of William Fisk, W.H. Fisk studied at the Royal Academy and was appointed anatomical draughtsman to the Royal College of Surgeons. He was affiliated to University College School in London for 40 years. He continued to paint, and was a frequent exhibitor at the Royal Academy, the British Institution, the Suffolk Street Gallery and in Paris.

MUSEUMS AND GALLERIES:
LONDON (Victoria and Albert Mus.): *View of Ben Bevis from Navin* (watercolour).

AUCTION RECORDS:
LONDON, 18 March 1935, *The Demand,* GBP 12. DORDRECHT, 25 Nov 1969, *Lovers' Tryst,* NLG 3,800. LONDON, 13 June 1984, *Christ and the Woman of Samaria* (1870, oil on canvas, 38 1/2 x 73 ins / 98 x 185.5 cm) GBP 1,300. LONDON, 5 March 1993, *Troubled Days* (oil on canvas, 35 x 51 1/4 ins / 89 x 130 cm) GBP 3,450. GLASGOW, 14 Feb 1995, *Fugitives from the Massacre at Glencoe in 1692* (1859, oil on canvas, arched at the top, 40 1/4 x 26 ins / 102 x 66 cm) GBP 2,875.

FISKE, Chas. A.
American, 19th - 20th century.
Active in Greenwich (USA).
Painter.

Charles A. Fiske was a member of the National Academy of Design.

FISKE, Gertrude
American, 20th century.
Born 16 April 1879, in Philadelphia; died 1961.
Painter, engraver.

Gertrude Fiske was a member of several art societies, including the National Academy of Design, where in 1929 and 1931 she won prizes for portraits. She also exhibited and won awards in other salons.

AUCTION RECORDS:
NEW YORK, 23 Sept 1993, *Little Church* (oil on canvas, 24 1/4 x 30 1/4 ins / 61.6 x 76.8 cm) USD 2,875. NEW YORK, 28 Sept 1995, *Cool Waters* (oil on canvas, 24 x 28 ins / 61 x 71.1 cm) USD 2,875. NEW YORK, 7 June 1999, *Jade Bracelet* (oil on canvas, 17 x 21 ins / 43 x 53 cm) USD 2,600. MILFORD, 25 April 2002, *Study for Strollers* (1926, oil on canvas, 20 x 27 ins / 51 x 69 cm) USD 30,000.

FISOV, Ivan
Croat, 20th century.
Born in Zagreb.
Painter.

Student of Jean-Paul and Albert Laurens, Ivan showed the Salon des Artistes Français in Paris.

FISQUET, Théodore Auguste
French, 19th century.
Born 21 April 1813, in Toulon; died 11 January 1890, in Toulon.
Painter, watercolourist, draughtsman, lithographer.
Genre scenes, landscapes, landscapes with figures, flowers.

Fisquet entered the Navy as a lieutenant. He carried out many journeys, circumnavigating the world twice, thus fulfilling both his professional duties and his passion for painting. His ship's journal took the form of sketches and drawings and, later, lithographs. He was advised by a pupil of Baron Gros, Ferdinand Wachsmuth, and accentuated the effects of shade and light, particularly in his wash drawings. His style continued to develop until he retired in 1875 a rear admiral of the Navy. He then settled in Toulon and produced various watercolour and line drawings of flowers and plants.

MUSEUMS AND GALLERIES:
TOULON: *Chandernagor Monument; Ras-el-Tin Baths.*

FISSÉ, Michael Johann, or Fisé
Czech, 18th century.
Born to a family originally from Antwerp; died 1726, in Znojmo.
Painter.

Michael Fissé studied under Pozzo in Rome, and settled in Znojmo in Moravia, where he painted frescoes and several altarpieces for the church of the monastery of Hradec in 1710. He also worked on the Calvary of Olmütz (now Olomouc) and in Klosterbruck (now part of Znojmo).

FISSETTE, Leopold
German, 19th century.
Born 1814, in Dison.
Painter. Genre scenes.

Fissette was a student of F. de Brackeleer. The museum in Leipzig houses his work *Tavern Scene.*

FISSIER, Robert
French, 17th century.
Active in Montdidier.
Sculptor.

Robert Fissier executed the marble pulpit of the church of St-Sépulchre in Montdidier, where can be read on the first step: 'I was made by Robert Fissier, 1630.' With Pierre Blassel, a sculptor from Amiens, he decorated the high altar of the chapel of the Virgin in the church of St-Pierre in 1642.

FISTULATOR, Blasius or Plazy Pfeiffer
German, 17th century.
Died 1622, in Munich.
Sculptor, stucco artist.

Fistulator worked at the court in Munich from 1587 until his death and produced works in marble and stucco for the Residence and the Michaelskirche.

FISTULATOR, Wilhelm
German, 17th century.
Active in Munich.
Sculptor, stucco artist.

The son of Blasius Fistulator, Wilhelm Fistulator contributed to works in marble and stucco carried at the Royal Residence in Munich. One of his known works is *St Francis* in stucco.

FISZL, Hélène
Hungarian, 20th century.
Born 1912.
Active in France from c. 1930.
Painter.

Hélène Fiszl lived and worked near Fontainebleau. Her painting oscillates between a dreamlike representation, a Surrealist tendency and a temptation to Abstraction. In 1983 the Museum of Modern Art in Budapest devoted a retrospective exhibition to her.

AUCTION RECORDS:

PARIS, 14 May 1990, *Abstract Composition* (oil on canvas, 18 x 21 1/2 ins / 46 x 54.5 cm) FRF 20,000. PARIS, 29 June 1990, *Still-life* (oil on canvas, 18 x 22 ins / 46 x 55 cm) FRF 22,000.

FITA, Juan

Spanish, 18th century.
Died 1784, in Saragossa.
Active in Saragossa.
Sculptor.

Juan Fita was an honorary member of the Academia de San Fernando from 1760.

FITA Y ROVIRA, Magin

Spanish, 19th century.
Born c. 1850, in Barcelona.
Sculptor.

Magin Fita y Rovira studied at the school of fine arts in Barcelona. He was awarded medals in 1871 and 1875 and exhibited in Madrid in 1876.

FITCH, John L.

American, 19th century.
Born 1836, in Hartford (Connecticut); died 1895.
Painter. Genre scenes, landscapes.

John L. Fitch studied in Munich and Milan with Albert, Max and Richard Zimmermann. On returning to America he lived in New York and his home town, Hartford, and established a reputation with his scenes of forest life in the USA.

FITE, Pierre

French, 18th century.
Active in Paris.
Engraver (burin).

Pierre Fite engraved a plate depicting *La Rosière de Solence* after J.-B. Greuze.

FITE-WATERS, George. See **WATERS George Fite**

FITGER, Arthur Heinrich Wilhelm

German, 19th century.
Born 4 October 1840, in Delmenhorst (Lower Saxony); died 28 June 1909, in Bremen.
Painter. History painting, mythological subjects.

From 1858 to 1861 Fitger was a student at the academy in Munich. He then travelled to Belgium and Italy, where he stayed from 1863 to 1866. In 1870 he returned and settled in Bremen.

AUCTION RECORDS:

NEW YORK, 1 March 1990, *Diomedes Chasing Aphrodite as she Tries to Recover the Body of Aeneas* (1905, oil on canvas, 51 x 76 1/2 ins / 129.5 x 194.3 cm) USD 8,800. BREMEN, 29 Nov 2002, *Joseph and Potiphar in the Nude* (oil on canvas, 62 x 65 ins / 158 x 166 cm) EUR 7,500. BREMEN, 28 March 2003, *Bacchant Party* (oil on canvas, 37 x 59 ins / 95 x 151 cm) EUR 5,500.

FITLER, William Crothers

American, 19th - 20th century.
Born 1857, in Philadelphia; died 1915.
Active in New York.
Painter (gouache), draughtsman. Landscapes.

William Fitler studied art at the Pennsylvania Academy of Fine Arts. He was a member of the Salmagundi Club, New York Watercolor Club, Brooklyn Art Association, Artists Fund Society and New York Municipal Art Society.

MUSEUMS AND GALLERIES:

SYDNEY: drawings.

AUCTION RECORDS:

NEW YORK, 1 July 1982, *House beside Stream* (oil on canvas, 22 1/4 x 30 ins / 56.5 x 76.1 cm) USD 1,400. NEW YORK, 22 June 1984, *Morning Study, East Hampton* (oil on canvas, 12 1/2 x 21 1/2 ins / 31.7 x 54.6 cm) USD 2,600. NEW YORK, 26 June 1985, *Sunlight and Shadows* (oil on canvas, 14 x 20 ins / 35.5 x 50.8 cm) USD 650. NEW YORK, 30 Sept 1988, *Sunset* (gouache/paper, 9 1/4 x 12 3/4 ins / 23.5 x 32.5 cm) USD 1,760. NEW YORK, 30 May 1990, *Under the Willow; Twilight* (oil on canvas, a pair, each 8 x 10 ins / 20.3 x 25.4 cm) USD 1,870. NEW YORK, 15 May 1991, *Early Morning on Farm* (1892, watercolour/card/card, 9 3/4 x 15 ins / 24.8 x 38.1 cm) USD 1,100. NEW YORK, 4 May 1993, *Figures on a River Bank* (1882, oil on canvas, 11 x 15 1/2 ins / 28 x 39.4 cm) USD 3,680. NEW YORK, 21 May 1996, *Golden Autumn* (oil on canvas, 22 x 30 ins / 56 x 76 cm) USD 3,220.

FITOUSSI, Simon

French, 20th century.
Born 24 May 1940.
Painter, draughtsman, watercolourist.

Simon Fitoussi read art and literature at university in Paris. Among other collective exhibitions he featured at the Royal Academy, London in 1973 and in 1977 and 1978 at the Salon des Artistes Français in Paris. Since 1966, he has had solo exhibitions in North Africa, Paris and the USA.

Fitoussi is essentially an abstract landscape painter working on contrasting planes.

FITREMAN, Gérard

French, 20th century.
Engraver.

Gérard Fitreman mostly produces abstract engravings in which varying textures play a major part.

FITSCH, Eugene C.

American, 20th century.
Born 11 December 1892, in Alsace; died 1972.
Painter, engraver (etching).

Eugene C. Fitsch was a professor of graphic art at the Art Students League, New York.

FITSCHULKY, Benjamin Vertraugott

German, 18th century.
Painter.

Fitschulky was painter to the court and steward at the Castle of Ols in Silesia.

FITTLER, James

British, 18th - 19th century.
Born 1758, in London; died 1835, in Turnham Green.
Engraver.

James Fittler enrolled as a student at the Royal Academy in 1778, and became an affiliated engraver in 1800. His finest works include: *Lord Howe's Victory, The Battle of the Nile* after De Loutherbourg, a *Portrait of Benjamin West* (President of the Royal Academy from 1792 to 1805) and illustrations for *Bell's Theatre, Scotia Depicta* after Claude Nattes, and the *Illustrated Bible*. Fittler was an accomplished burin engraver; he excelled in the depiction of effects of light.

FITTON, Hedley

British, 19th century.
Born 1859, in Haslemere, near London.
Engraver (etching).

Hedley Fitton was an important English etcher, noted for his lively, sensitive depictions of sites visited during his travels. His work is highly sought after and includes a remarkable body of views of Florence, Venice and London. He exhibited at the Salon des Artistes Français in Paris. He won a jury commendation in 1906 and a third-class medal in 1907.

FITTON, James

British, 20th century.
Born 11 February 1899, in Oldham, near Manchester.
Painter, draughtsman, lithographer, designer.

At the age of 14, James Fitton worked with a designer and studied drawing at evening classes. In 1919, he went to London and studied at the Central School of Art. He did not begin exhibiting until 1929, at the Royal Academy and, in 1930 at the New English Art Club. In 1934 he became a member of the London Group. In 1954, he was made a member of the Royal Academy.
MUSEUMS AND GALLERIES:
LONDON (Tate Collection): *Frying Tonight* (1954, oil/panel).
AUCTION RECORDS:
LONDON, 17 Sept 1980, *Kent Landscape* (oil on panel, 25 x 32¾ ins / 63.5 x 83 cm) GBP 650. LONDON, 2 Nov 1983, *Petunias* (oil on card, 24 x 20 ins / 61 x 51 cm) GBP 1,000. LONDON, 4 March 1987, *Tree in Blossom* (oil on canvas, 22¾ x 30 ins / 58 x 76 cm) GBP 1,800. LONDON, 23 June 1999, *Private View* (1967, oil on canvas, 25 x 30 ins / 63 x 76 cm) GBP 6,800. LONDON, 22 March 2000, *London Landscape* (oil on paper, 20 x 24 ins / 51 x 61 cm) GBP 6,500. LONDON, 6 Dec 2000, *Down by the Quayside* (oil on board, 28 x 37 ins / 71 x 93 cm) GBP 13,000. LONDON, 17 July 2001, *London Landscape* (oil, pen, ink and gouache on card, 20 x 24 ins / 51 x 61 cm) GBP 8,800. LONDON, 12 March 2002, *Saloon Bar* (oil, ink and pastel over pencil on paper laid on board, 20 x 14 ins / 51 x 36 cm) GBP 5,000.

FITTS, Clara Atwood
American, 19th - 20th century.
Born 6 October 1874, in Worcester (Massachusetts).
Illustrator.
Clara Atwood Fitts, a pupil of the Boston Museum of Fine Arts School, was a member of the American Federation of Arts. She mainly illustrated children's books.

FITY, Jean René
French, 18th century.
Active in Paris in 1753.
Painter, sculptor.

FITZ, Benjamin Rutherford
American, 19th century.
Born 1855, in New York; died 1891, in New York.
Painter. Genre scenes.
MUSEUMS AND GALLERIES:
NEW YORK (Metropolitan Mus. of Art): *Portrait of a Woman* - WASHINGTON DC (NGA): *Pond in a Forest.*
AUCTION RECORDS:
NEW YORK, 31 Jan-1 Feb 1900, *Reflection,* USD 1,450.

FITZ, Georg, or Fritz
Czech, 16th century.
Died 28 March 1609, in Moravská Trebová.
Painter.
The Franzenmuseum in Brno owns a *Holy Trinity* by Georg Fitz. He also produced a *Pietà*, signed and dated 1582.

FITZ, Zbigniew
Polish, 20th century.
Born 17 April 1943, in Cracow.
Active in France from 1967.
Painter, engraver.
Zbigniew Fitz studied fine arts in Cracow before settling in France in 1967. His style has certain similarities with Surrealism and has erotic tendencies. He exhibited at the Salon des Artistes Français in Paris, winning an honourable mention in 1969.

FITZ RONDOLPH, Grace
American, 20th century.
Born in South Hadley (New York).
Sculptor.
Grace Fitz Rondolph was a pupil of Alden Weir and Augustus St-Gaudens in New York and of Benjamin-Constant, Girardot and Puech in Paris. She was a member of several art societies and won a bronze medal in Atlanta in 1896.

FITZ-GIBBON, Geraldine Dillen
American, 20th century.
Born in New York.
Painter.
Geraldine Dillen Fitz-Gibbon exhibited in Paris at the Salon des Artistes Français.

FITZ-HUGH, Elizabeth
American, 20th century.
Born in California.
Painter.
Elizabeth Fitz-Hugh exhibited at the Salon des Indépendants, Paris, in 1940.

FITZCOOK, Henry
British, 19th century.
Born 1824, in Pentonville.
Active in London.
Painter, illustrator. History painting, genre scenes.
A pupil of B.R. Haydon, Henry Fitzcook also studied at the Royal Academy. He was a contributor to the *Illustrated London News*, and illustrated numerous books. He is noted for his painting *Thalaba the Destroyer,* depicting a scene from the poem of the same name by Robert Southey (first published in 1801). He exhibited at the Royal Academy, Suffolk Street, the Society of British Artists and the British Institution.

FITZER, Karl H.
American, 20th century.
Born 4 May 1896, in Kansas City (Kansas).
Painter, pastellist, illustrator.
Karl H. Fitzer was a member of the Kansas City Society of Artists and was especially known for his pastels.

FITZGERALD, Florence (Miss)
British, 19th century.
Painter, sculptor. Flowers.
Florence Fitzgerald exhibited at the Royal Academy and Suffolk Street in London from 1887.
AUCTION RECORDS:
LONDON, 13 Feb 1991, *Garland of Daisies* (oil on canvas, 18 x 12 ins / 46 x 30.5 cm) GBP 1,980. LONDON, 7 Oct 1992, *The Rose Season* (oil on canvas, 20 x 30 ins / 51 x 76 cm) GBP 1,760.

FITZGERALD, G.
British.
Painter. Genre scenes.
MUSEUMS AND GALLERIES:
SYDNEY: *Where the Dew Falls Early; Path in the Hills.*

FITZGERALD, Gerald (Lord)
Irish, 19th century.
Born 6 January 1821; died 23 September 1886.
Draughtsman, engraver (etching).
Lord Fitzgerald was a member of the Dublin Etching Club and a contributor of two plates to the latter's published collection of *Passages from Modern English Poets.* He also engraved a series of ten views accompanying poems by Hood.

FITZGERALD, Harrington
American, 19th - 20th century.
Born 5 April 1847, in Philadelphia; died 1930.
Painter. Landscapes, seascapes.
Harrington Fitzgerald, a pupil of George W. Nicholson, won many distinctions in American exhibitions and was a member of the principal art groups in the Philadelphia area.
MUSEUMS AND GALLERIES:
PHILADELPHIA: *Remains of the Wreck.*
AUCTION RECORDS:
NEW YORK, 31 March 1994, *Smugglers' Cave* (oil on canvas, 16 x 26 ins / 40.6 x 66 cm) USD 2,415.

FITZGERALD, James

American, 20th century.

Born 8 March 1899, in Boston (Massachusetts); died 1971.

Watercolourist.

James Fitzgerald was a member of the California Watercolor Society, and won a first prize for watercolour at the Santa Cruz Statewide Exhibition of 1930.

In 1999, to coincide with the 100th anniversary of Fitzgerald's birth, the Portland Museum of Art held an exhibition devoted to the work he produced on Monhegan Island, his summer residence from 1940, towards the end of his career.

FITZGERALD, John Austen

British, 19th century.

Born 25 November 1832; died after 1906.

Watercolourist, painter (gouache/mixed media). Genre scenes, landscapes.

Symbolism.

Almost nothing is known of Fitzgerald's life, and the exact date of his death remains uncertain. He lived on Moore Park Road in Fulham, West London, in 1858, and was a member of the Maddox Street Sketching Club. He exhibited for the first time with the Royal Academy in 1845, and regularly after that until 1881. After a long spell of absence he began exhibiting with the academy once again in 1902. He also exhibited with the British Institution, the New Water-Colour Society, and at Suffolk Street. Fitzgerald is best known for his 'magical' subjects, treated in an almost Surrealist manner. Early in his career, he quickly eschewed the technique and ethos of the Pre-Raphaelite movement, embraced by many of his contemporaries.

Museums and Galleries:

Cardiff: *Heath* - Liverpool (Walker AG): *Ariel* (c. 1858-1868, oil on canvas).

Auction records:

London, 3 Feb 1976, *Phantasmagorical Landscape* (watercolour heightened with white, 11 x 14 3/4 ins / 28 x 37.5 cm) GBP 650. London, 14 May 1976, *The Captive Robin* (oil on canvas, 10 x 12 ins / 25.5 x 30.5 cm) GBP 4,800. London, 24 Oct 1978, *The Release of Ariel* (watercolour heightened with white, upper corners rounded, 19 x 11 1/2 ins / 48 x 29 cm) GBP 3,500. London, 23 March 1981, *The Enchanted Forest* (watercolour, 19 x 28 ins / 48 x 71 cm) GBP 10,800. London, 15 Feb 1983, *Creatures of the Night* (oil on canvas, 11 3/4 x 9 ins / 29.8 x 22.8 cm) GBP 1,000. London, 17 Oct 1984, *The Intruder* (gouache and watercolour/pencil outlines, 5 1/2 x 9 ins / 14 x 22.8 cm) GBP 650. London, 24 July 1985, *Woodland Scene with Nymph* (oil on canvas, 11 x 6 1/4 ins / 27 x 16 cm) GBP 700. London, 25 Jan 1988, *Fairytale Scene* (watercolour, 12 1/2 x 18 ins / 32 x 46 cm) GBP 2,640. London, 25 March 1988, *Concert* (mixed media/card, 10 x 7 1/2 ins / 25.5 x 19 cm) GBP 6,050. London, 21 Nov 1989, *Army of Phantasmagorical Insects Attacking a Bat* (watercolour and gouache, 14 x 21 1/4 ins / 35.5 x 54 cm) GBP 13,200. London, 9 Feb 1990, *Faery Banquet (recto); Alms* (oil on card, original sketch, 9 x 11 ins / 23 x 28 cm) GBP 30,800. London, 25-26 April 1990, *Intruders* (watercolour and gouache, 14 1/2 x 11 1/2 ins / 37 x 29 cm) GBP 7,150. London, 1 Nov 1990, *Christmas* (oil on canvas, 15 3/4 x 13 3/4 ins / 40 x 35 cm) GBP 5,500. London, 30 Jan 1991, *Faery Messengers* (ink and grisaille/parchment paper, 15 x 11 ins / 38 x 27 cm) GBP 990. London, 14 June 1991, *Faery Banquet (recto); Alms (verso)* (oil on card, original sketch, 9 x 15 ins / 23 x 38 cm) GBP 28,600. London, 30 March 1994, *Fledgling* (watercolour and gouache, 10 1/4 x 17 ins / 26 x 43 cm) GBP 36,700. London, 3 June 1999, *Woodcutter's Misfortune* (oil on canvas, 12 x 24 ins / 30 x 61 cm) GBP 32,000. Taunton, 31 Aug 2000, *Going to Mask Ball* (oil on board, 12 x 17 ins / 31 x 42 cm) GBP 88,000. London, 30 Nov 2000, *Death of the Fairy Queen* (oil on canvas, 8 x 10 ins / 20 x 25 cm) GBP 170,000. London, 14 June 2001, *Intruder* (watercolour over pencil with gouache and gum arabic, 15 x 11 ins / 38 x 29 cm) GBP 78,000. London, 28 Nov 2001, *Wounded Squirrel* (pencil, watercolour, gouache and gum arabic, 19 x 13 ins / 47 x 33 cm) GBP 110,000. London, 21 Nov 2002, *Fairies and Bird's Nest* (pencil, watercolour, gouache and gum arabic, arched, 10 x 8 ins / 26 x 20 cm) GBP 50,000. London, 4 Nov 2003, *Realms of Fairydom* (watercolour and gouache, 7 x 9 ins / 17 x 22 cm) GBP 9,000. London, 20 Nov 2003, *Fairies in the Snow* (pencil, watercolour, gouache, gum arabic and scratching out, 22 x 30 ins / 56 x 77 cm) GBP 60,000. Florida, 24 Jan 2004, *Five Scenes taken from 'A Midsummer Night's Dream'* (oil on board, five in one frame, 9 x 32 ins / 23 x 81 cm) USD 150,000.

FITZGERALD, Lionel Lemoine

Canadian, 20th century.

Born 1890, in Winnipeg (Manitoba); died 1956, in Winnipeg.

Painter, draughtsman. Landscapes.

Group of Seven.

Lionel Lemoine Fitzgerald was a pupil at Keszthelyi's School of Art, Winnipeg, about 1910, and then of K.H. Miller and B. Robinson at the Art Students League, New York. He travelled several times to the West Coast between 1942 and 1949, and to Mexico in 1951. Successively influenced by Impressionism, abstract art and Pointillism, he was primarily a landscape artist. He exhibited with The Group of Seven in 1930 and was a friend of Lawren Harris. A posthumous exhibition was held at the Winnipeg Art Gallery in 1963.

Bibliography:

Reid, Dennis, *A Concise History of Canadian Painting*, Oxford University Press, Toronto, 1973.

Auction records:

Toronto, 27 May 1980, *Nude* (1928, charcoal/paper, double-sided, 18 1/4 x 16 3/4 ins / 46.3 x 42.5 cm) CAD 1,100. Toronto, 26 May 1981, *Manitoba Landscape* (oil on canvas, 7 1/2 x 8 3/4 ins / 18.8 x 22.5 cm) CAD 6,000. Toronto, 3 May 1983, *Reclining Nude* (oil on canvas remounted on board, 10 x 12 ins / 25.6 x 30.6 cm) CAD 2,200. Toronto, 28 May 1985, *Autumn Leaves in a Bowl* (watercolour, 21 1/2 x 14 1/4 ins / 54.3 x 36.3 cm) CAD 2,200. Toronto, 18 Nov 1986, *Winter, the Banks of the Assiniboine River* (1921, oil on canvas, 10 1/4 x 13 1/4 ins / 26.3 x 33.8 cm) CAD 18,000. Toronto, 1 June 1999, *Figure in Woods* (1920, oil on canvas, 35 x 24 ins / 90 x 60 cm) CAD 15,000. Toronto, 7 Dec 1999, *Interior with Chair* (oil on canvas, 30 x 28 ins / 75 x 70 cm) CAD 17,000. Toronto, 23 May 2000, *Back Yard* (pencil, 10 x 13 ins / 25 x 32 cm) CAD 7,400. Vancouver, 9 Nov 2000, *Seated Nude* (watercolour and charcoal, 26 x 15 ins / 66 x 37 cm) CAD 6,000. Vancouver, 9 May 2001, *Still-life with Green Cup* (watercolour, 22 x 15 ins / 56 x 38 cm) CAD 11,000. Vancouver, 8 Nov 2001, *Bright Summer's Day* (1921, oil on panel, 10 x 12 ins / 25 x 30 cm) CAD 17,000. Toronto, 25 Feb 2002, *Winter Woodland* (oil on canvas, 16 x 20 ins / 41 x 51 cm) CAD 5,750. Vancouver, 2 May 2002, *Barn and Lane* (1920, oil on canvas, 22 x 20 ins / 56 x 51 cm) CAD 25,000. Toronto, 18 Nov 2003, *Prairie Scene* (1921, oil on canvas laid on board, 10 x 12 ins / 25 x 30 cm) CAD 30,000. Toronto, 2 Dec 2003, *Landscape with Setting Sun* (oil on canvas, 7 x 9 ins / 19 x 22 cm) CAD 15,000. Vancouver, 27 May 2004, *Figure in the Woods* (1920, oil on canvas, 36 x 24 ins / 91 x 61 cm) CAD 85,000. Toronto, 1 June 2004, *Prairies* (1929, oil on canvas, 11 x 14 ins / 29 x 36 cm) CAD 38,000.

FITZGERALD, Pitt Loofbourrow

American, 20th century.

Born 8 October 1893, in Washington DC; died 1971.

Painter, illustrator.

FITZGERALD, Tom

Irish, 20th century.

Born 1939, in Limerick.

Sculptor.

Tom Fitzgerald has exhibited regularly at all the major national exhibitions. He won a number of international prizes and in 1984 was one of 10 Irish artists selected to take part in the *Rosc'84* exhibition in Dublin.

FITZHUGH, William
British, 18th - 19th century.
Active in England.
Painter. Landscapes.
William Fitzhugh exhibited at the Royal Academy and Suffolk Street from 1799 to 1809.

FITZI, Johann Ulrich
Swiss, 19th century.
Born 1798, in Bühler (Appenzell); died 1855, in Speicher.
Painter, draughtsman. Landscapes, landscapes with figures, village views, natural history (animals/birds/botanical subjects).
Fitzi first drew and painted plants and animals for works on natural history, and then specialised in views of villages in the Appenzell canton of Switzerland and other landscapes.
AUCTION RECORDS:
BERN, 24 June 1983, *Castle Rhäzüns and Surrounding Area* (c. 1830, watercolour, 8 x 9 1/2 ins / 19.4 x 24.2 cm) CHF 2,200. ZURICH, 10 Dec 1996, *Jays* (1835, Indian ink and watercolour/paper, 10 1/4 x 17 1/2 ins / 26 x 44.5 cm) CHF 19,550. ST GALL, 2 Nov 1999, *View of Teuffen* (c. 1830, watercolour, ink and pen, 10 x 18 ins / 26 x 45 cm) CHF 9,500. ST GALL, 2 Nov 1999, *View of Speicher* (c. 1840, pen and watercolour, 7 x 11 ins / 19 x 28 cm) CHF 11,000. ST GALL, 15 Nov 2000, *View of Village* (pen and watercolour, 7 x 10 ins / 17 x 25 cm) CHF 11,500. ST GALL, 8 May 2001, *View of Speicher* (oil on panel, 12 x 19 ins / 30 x 49 cm) CHF 15,000. ZURICH, 23 June 2003, *Loft* (watercolour, 10 x 18 ins / 26 x 45 cm) CHF 3,300. ST GALL, 24 Oct 2003, *Trogen* (1851, watercolour and pen, 10 x 18 ins / 26 x 45 cm) CHF 22,000.

FITZIA
French, 20th century.
Born 1931, in La Baule.
Also active in Mexico.
Painter, collage artist.
Fitzia studied at the Grande Chaumière in Paris then in Mexico City, under Michel Baxte, working and living in Mexico from 1964 to 1967.

Her work has been seen in collective exhibitions at the Museums of Modern Art in New York, Mexico and Paris; various museums in Paris, including the Musée National d'Anthropologie; and in the Salon d'Automne, Salon Comparaisons, and Salon des Grands et Jeunes d'Aujourd'hui. She has had solo exhibitions in Mexico City since 1958 and has also shown in Tokyo, New York, Paris and Ciudad Juárez.

Her work is abstract and consists of waxed sheets of paper glued in layers to wood panels then polished to produce silky, transparent shifting shapes. She has also created frescoes, in Brazil in particular.
MUSEUMS AND GALLERIES:
ALLENTOWN (AM) - BILBAO (MBA) - CIUDAD JUÁREZ (MAH) - MEXICO CITY (MAC International Rufino Tamayo) - MEXICO CITY (MMA) - MEXICO CITY (Mus. del Palacio de Bellas Artes) - MORELIA (MCA) - PARIS (MAMVP) - STANFORD (Mus.).

FITZJAMES, Anna Maria (Miss)
British, 19th century.
Active in Bath.
Painter. Flowers.
Anna Maria Fitzjames exhibited in London at the Royal Academy and Suffolk Street from 1852 to 1876.

FITZPATRICK, Arthur
British, 19th century.
Painter. Genre scenes.
Arthur Fitzpatrick exhibited in London at the Royal Academy, the British Institution and Suffolk Street from 1862 to 1868.
AUCTION RECORDS:
LONDON, 25 June 1908, *The Chiropodist*, GBP 2. BELFAST, 30 May 1990, *Young Irishman Practising the Violin* (oil on canvas, 24 1/4 x 18 1/4 ins / 61.6 x 46.4 cm) GBP 2,200. NEW YORK, 17 Jan 1996, *Mother Arranging her Children's Hair* (oil on canvas/synthetic resin, 24 1/4 x 20 1/4 ins / 61.6 x 51.4 cm) USD 1,840.

FITZPATRICK, Edmond
Irish, 19th century.
Born in Ireland.
Painter. Genre scenes.
Edmond Fitzpatrick was an associate of the Royal Hibernian Academy, and took part in numerous exhibitions in Dublin. He exhibited in London at the British Institution and Suffolk Street from 1848 to 1870.

FITZPATRICK, Grace Marie
American, 20th century.
Born 25 July 1897, in Brooklyn.
Painter, teacher.
Grace Marie Fitzpatrick, a pupil of Benjamin Eggleston, was a member of the National Association of Women Painters and Sculptors. She was also a craftswoman.

FITZPATRICK, Helena
American, 20th century.
Born 1889, in New Jersey.
Painter, teacher.
Helena Fitzpatrick was a member of an art society in Philadelphia.

FITZPATRICK, John C.
American, 20th century.
Born 1876, in Washington; died 1940.
Painter, illustrator, writer.

FITZPATRICK, John Kelly
American, 20th century.
Born August 1888, in Alabama; died 1953.
Painter. Portraits, landscapes.
John Kelly Fitzpatrick, a pupil of the Chicago Art Institute, was a member of several art associations and won prizes in salons, where he exhibited mainly portraits. *Heart and Soul of the South* held at the Wiregrass Museum in Dotham, Alabama in 1999.

FITZPATRICK, Patrick
Irish, 18th century.
Active in Dublin.
Draughtsman, engraver.
Patrick Fitzpatrick was awarded a prize for landscape engraving by the Dublin Society in 1761 and 1763. He worked as a sign-painter, and designed friezes, maps and decorative ornamentation for books. His portrait of the statesman *Henry Grattan* was engraved by P. Roberts.

FITZPATRICK, Thomas
Irish, 19th - 20th century.
Born 27 March 1860, in Cork; died 16 July 1912.
Draughtsman.
Thomas Fitzpatrick was a lithographer and book illustrator who also worked as a political caricaturist. From 1905, his work was published in the comic monthly review *The Leprechaun*.

FITZPATRICK, Tony
American, 20th - 21st century.
Born 1958, in Chicago.

Illustrator, collage artist, printmaker.

Tony Fitzpatrick is also a poet, newspaper columnist, radio talk show host, occasional movie actor, founder of the World Tattoo Gallery in Chicago (1990) and owner of a tattoo parlour. His works are frequently accompanied by his own poetry.

He has spent the majority of his career in Chicago and much of his work is based on that city. Fitzpatrick's works combine drawing and etching with collage. In his recent collection, *The Wonder: Portraits of a Remembered City*, words and drawings on coloured fields are embellished with images taken from old matchbooks, postcards, gambling slips and ballgame stubs which evoke aspects of Chicago's grand history of hotels, clubs, restaurants and sports legends. This nostalgic aspect is emphasised by handwritten notes describing memories of Chicago by Fitzpatrick's father who taught him most of what he knows about the city. He tells visual stories that chronicle both the history of the city itself and of his own life as an inhabitant.

In Fitzpatrick's illustrations there is often a large central figure - a much-explored motif is a bird - which is surrounded by smaller supporting images, poems and collages. This theme is continued in Fitzpatrick's most recent exhibition, *Max & Gaby's Alphabet* (Museum of Contemporary Art, 2005), in which he collaborated with his two children to illustrate 24 letters of the alphabet. The main illustration for the letter R is a robot, which is surrounded by many other images of things and concepts beginning with the letter R, such as rocket and ruler.

Tony Fitzpatrick has taken part in many solo exhibitions, including: 2000, *Bum Town*, Bill Maynes Gallery, New York and Museum of Contemporary Art, Chicago; 2002, *The Secret Birds*, Big Cat Gallery (founded by Fitzpatrick), New York; 2003, *The Ruckus: New Drawings and Sketches*, Bill Maynes Gallery, New York; 2004, *The Wonder: Portraits of a Remembered City* (travelling). His group Exhibitions have included: 1996, *Comic Inspirations*, Adam Baumgold Fine Art, New York; 1997, Seattle ArtFair; 1999, *The Holy Slang*, Augen Gallery, Portland; and 1999, *Chicago Paper*, Fleisher/Ollman Gallery, Chicago.

BIBLIOGRAPHY:

Fitzpatrick, Tony, *Hard Angels: Tony Fitzpatrick, Drawings and Poems*, book, Janet Fleisher Gallery, Philadelphia, 1988. Fitzpatrick, Tony, *Dirty Boulevard*, Hard Press, West Stockbridge (MA), 1998. Fitzpatrick, Tony, *Max & Gaby's Alphabet*, exhibition catalogue, book, Museum of Contemporary Art, Chicago, 2001 (Contributors: Jonathan Demme, Lynne Warren, Mickey Cartin). Fitzpatrick, Tony, *The Wonder: Portraits of a Remembered City*, book, Last Gasp, San Francisco, 2004 (with an essay by Mickey Cartin).

MUSEUMS AND GALLERIES:

CHICAGO (AI) - CHICAGO (MCA) - MIAMI (MCA) - NEW YORK (MoMA) - PHILADELPHIA (MA) - PORTLAND, OR (AM) - WASHINGTON DC (Smithsonian American AM).

FITZSIMMONS, James

American, 20th century.
Born 1919, in Shanghai, China.
Photographer, painter.

James Fitzsimmons went to school in England and Switzerland and studied at Columbia University, New York. He researched photolithography after 1945 and produced coloured monotypes from photographic negatives. His paintings were influenced by Geometric Abstraction.

He exhibited his explorations in photography from 1947 to 1950 at the Museum of San Francisco, the Chicago Art Institute and the New York Art Gallery. He exhibited paintings in New York in 1951 and was also an art critic.

FIUMANA. See **ALBERTI Francesco**

FIUME, Laura

Italian, 20th - 21st century.
Born 10 August 1953, in Urbino (Marche).
Painter. Animals.

Laura Fiume paints dogs and fish floating in space. Her works, which are influenced by Cubism, are extremely simple, consisting of juxtaposed geometric planes with sharp contours. She uses a minimal chromatic palette, dominated by white, highlighting the thickness of the paint, which is worked and striated, and shimmers with light.

BIBLIOGRAPHY:

Munari, Carlo, *Laura Fiume*, Wichtig Ed., Milan.

FIUME, Salvatore

Italian, 20th century.
Born 23 October 1915, in Comiso (Sicily); died 3 June 1997, in Milan.
Painter (mixed media), sculptor, architect. Local figures, nudes, portraits, scenes with figures, interiors, landscapes.
Orientalism.

Salvatore Fiume enjoyed using contemporary technical materials. Among the many different themes he tackled, the large number of Orientalist subjects suggests that he spent some time in the Near East. He also painted groups of figures with horses.

FIUME
S. FIUME

BIBLIOGRAPHY:

Montalto, Domenico, *Salvatore Fiume*, exhibition catalogue, Centro Disegni, Téchne Editore, Milan, 2001. Fiertler, Gaia, *Salvatore Fiume: Catalogo generale delle opere 1930-1997, vol. I*, Téchne Editore, Milan, 2002.

AUCTION RECORDS:

MILAN, 9 March 1972, *Black Shawl*, ITL 2,000,000. MILAN, 13 June 1978, *Recumbent Woman* (oil/hardboard, 29 x 40 ins / 73.5 x 101.5 cm) ITL 4,600,000. MILAN, 14 April 1981, *Dance* (mixed media, 16 x 21 3/4 ins / 40.5 x 55.5 cm) ITL 1,100,000. MILAN, 14 June 1983, *Nude* (hardboard, 29 1/4 x 39 3/4 ins / 74 x 101 cm) ITL 9,000,000. MILAN, 4 April 1984, *Gentleman from Grenada* (1952, oil on paper, 13 1/2 x 9 1/2 ins / 34.5 x 24 cm) ITL 1,000,000. LONDON, 9 Dec 1986, *Il Porto della Statue* (1972, oil on canvas remounted on hardboard, 28 x 41 3/4 ins / 71 x 106 cm) ITL 24,000,000. MILAN, 1 Dec 1987, *Gladiators* (1946, watercolour, 13 3/4 x 13 ins / 35 x 33 cm) ITL 2,000,000. LONDON, 19 Oct 1988, *Landscape* (oil on card, 14 x 21 1/2 ins / 35.3 x 54.3 cm) GBP 6,380. ROME, 15 Nov 1988, *Sultan's Favourite* (1981, mixed media/card, 21 x 13 1/2 ins / 52.5 x 34.5 cm) ITL 12,000,000. MILAN, 14 Dec 1988, *Terrace in Harer* (1985, oil on card, 19 3/4 x 28 3/4 ins / 50 x 73 cm) ITL 24,000,000. ROME, 8 June 1989, *Model in the Studio* (oil on card/synthetic resin, 23 1/2 x 18 1/2 ins / 59.5 x 47 cm) ITL 15,000,000. LONDON, 25 Oct 1989, *Model Reclining* (oil on paper, 35 x 56 3/4 ins / 88 x 144 cm) GBP 17,600. ROME, 28 Nov 1989, *Stony Island* (oil/synthetic resin, 29 1/4 x 39 3/4 ins / 74 x 101 cm) ITL 26,000,000. MILAN, 27 March 1990, *Somali Women* (oil on card, 10 1/4 x 13 3/4 ins / 26 x 35 cm) ITL 11,000,000. LONDON, 17 Oct 1990, *Portrait of a Woman* (1958, oil on card, 66 1/4 x 28 ins / 168 x 70.2 cm) GBP 10,450. ROME, 30 Oct 1990, *Landscape with a Woman and a Horse* (oil/synthetic resin, 14 x 21 ins / 35.5 x 53.5 cm) ITL 13,000,000. MILAN, 13 Dec 1990, *Three People on Horseback* (oil/synthetic resin, 11 x 14 1/4 ins / 27 x 36 cm) ITL 9,000,000. MILAN, 20 June 1991, *Island* (1953, oil on canvas/panel, 18 1/2 x 53 1/4 ins / 47 x 135 cm) ITL 20,000,000. MILAN, 14 April 1992, *Stony Islands* (oil/synthetic resin, 30 3/4 x 20 ins / 78 x 51 cm) ITL 26,000,000. LONDON, 15

Oct 1992, *Portrait of a Woman* (1960, oil on card, 66 1/4 x 22 1/2 ins / 168 x 57 cm) GBP 6,050. MILAN, 9 Nov 1992, *Egyptian Figures* (1957, oil on canvas/synthetic resin, 28 3/4 x 43 1/4 ins / 73 x 110 cm) ITL 24,000,000. ROME, 25 March 1993, *Odalisque and Cavalrymen* (oil/synthetic resin, 14 1/2 x 21 1/4 ins / 37 x 54 cm) ITL 12,000,000. MILAN, 16 Nov 1993, *Sicilian Landscape* (oil/synthetic resin, 17 3/4 x 23 1/4 ins / 45 x 59 cm) ITL 12,650,000. ROME, 30 Nov 1993, *Blonde Odalisque* (oil on paper/synthetic resin, 35 1/2 x 67 ins / 90 x 170 cm) ITL 27,025,000. ROME, 28 March 1995, *Female Figures with a White Horse* (oil/synthetic resin, 14 1/4 x 21 1/4 ins / 36 x 54 cm) ITL 13,225,000. PARIS, 29 March 1995, *Nude in the Studio* (oil/hardboard, 9 x 15 ins / 23 x 38 cm) FRF 13,000. MILAN, 27 April 1995, *Female Nude* (oil/synthetic resin, 28 1/4 x 48 3/4 ins / 72 x 124 cm) ITL 29,325,000. MILAN, 19 March 1996, *Veiled Odalisque* (oil/synthetic resin, 14 x 21 ins / 35.5 x 53.5 cm) ITL 13,800,000. MILAN, 20 May 1996, *Odalisque* (oil/Masonite, 29 1/4 x 48 ins / 74 x 122 cm) ITL 27,600,000. MILAN, 25 Nov 1996, *Nude* (1988, oil/Plexiglas/aluminium, 31 x 41 ins / 78.5 x 104 cm) ITL 18,400,000. VENICE, 13 Nov 1999, *Cockerel* (1957, oil on panel, 96 x 134 ins / 245 x 340 cm) ITL 33,600,000. MILAN, 22 June 2000, *Female Nude* (oil on masonite, 28 x 39 ins / 72 x 100 cm) ITL 21,000,000. VERCELLI, 16 Dec 2000, *Mexican Men* (oil on board, 11 x 14 ins / 27 x 36 cm) ITL 21,000,000. PRATO, 8 June 2001, *Stone Statue* (oil on board, 29 x 40 ins / 74 x 102 cm) ITL 45,000,000. MILAN, 20 Nov 2001, *Battle between Statue Islands* (1950, oil on paper/masonite, 15 x 40 ins / 38 x 102 cm) ITL 40,000,000. FLORENCE, 20 Nov 2002, *Woman from Somalia* (oil on masonite, 63 x 33 ins / 160 x 85 cm) EUR 24,000. PRATO, 30 Nov 2002, *Odalisque* (oil on board, 21 x 28 ins / 54 x 72 cm) EUR 15,000. MILAN, 13 March 2003, *Model* (1994, oil on masonite, 21 x 28 ins / 54 x 72 cm) EUR 16,000. VERCELLI, 1 May 2003, *Island Lover* (oil on masonite, 31 x 43 ins / 80 x 110 cm) EUR 26,000. MILAN, 25 May 2004, *Stone Island* (oil on paper/board, 29 x 40 ins / 74 x 102 cm) EUR 15,000. VERCELLI, 30 May 2004, *Favourite* (oil on masonite, 28 x 21 ins / 72 x 54 cm) EUR 10,000.

FIUMI, Jean Napoléon

French, 20th century.
Born in Lourdes.
Painter.

Jean Fiumi exhibited at the Salon des Artistes Français in Paris.

FIVAZ, Émile

Swiss, 19th - 20th century.
Born 6 January 1858, in Ste-Croix; died 18 January 1912, in Lausanne.
Painter, watercolourist, illustrator.

Fivaz is known his caricatures and his views of Lausanne.

FIVET, Alphonse Émile

French, 20th century.
Born 27 December 1872, in Noyers Pont-Maugis; died 27 January 1946.
Sculptor. Rustic scenes.

Alphonse Fivet studied under Xavier-Mathieu. From 1921 he exhibited at the Salon des Artistes Français, of which he was an associate member.

AUCTION RECORDS:

PARIS, 8 Dec 1994, *Grape Harvest near Rome* (oil on canvas, 18 1/2 x 34 1/4 ins / 47 x 87 cm) FRF 4,000.

FIVIZZANI, Antonio

Italian, 18th century.
Active in Bologna.
Engraver.

Antonio Fivizzani engraved several portraits of saints, notably one portraying the *Death of St Joseph.*

FIVRONI, Luigi

Italian, 20th century.
Born in Italy.
Painter. Portraits.

AUCTION RECORDS:

LONDON, 25 March 1946, *Portrait of a Woman,* GBP 70.

FIX, Yvonne

French, 20th century.
Born in St-Mandé.
Sculptor.

Yvonne Fix was a member of the Société Nationale des Beaux-Arts in Paris and exhibited there from 1936.

FIX-ADAM, Lina

French, 19th century.
Born during the second half of the 19th century, in Kelbsteim (Haut-Rhin).
Miniaturist.

FIX-MASSEAU, Pierre

French, 20th century.
Born 7 June 1905, in Paris; died 2 October 1994.
Draughtsman, poster artist. Advertising art.

Pierre Fix-Masseau was the sculptor Pierre Félix's Fix-Masseau's son. In Paris he studied at the École Boule and the École des Arts Décoratifs, working from 1926 to 1928 with Cassandre.

His best-known posters, in particular *Punctuality,* were done for the SNCF, the French Railways, in 1932. He also worked for other French state monopolies such as the tobacco industry and the lottery.

BIBLIOGRAPHY:

Perec, Paulette/Weill, Alain, *Pierre Fix-Masseau. Affiches 1928-1983,* exhibition catalogue, Bibliothèque nationale de France, Paris, 1983.

AUCTION RECORDS:

PARIS, 22 June 1980, *For Renault Oils* (poster, 31 x 48 ins / 79 x 121 cm) FRF 2,400. NEW YORK, 13 March 1982, *Punctuality* (1929, gouache, 39 1/2 x 24 1/2 ins / 100.3 x 62.2 cm) USD 8,500. PARIS, 14 Dec 1987, *The Secret* (gilt-patinated bronze, h. 10 3/4 ins / 27.5 cm) FRF 9,500.

FIX-MASSEAU, Pierre Félix

French, 20th century.
Born 17 March 1869, in Lyons; died 1937, in Paris.
Sculptor. Figures, still-lifes, flowers. Busts.

Pierre Félix Fix-Massaud studied at the École des Beaux-Arts in Paris. He obtained a grant enabling him to visit Belgium, Holland, Switzerland, Italy and especially Florence. He was the principal of the École Nationale d'Art Décoratif in Limoges until 1935.

He took part in many collective exhibitions: in Paris, at the Salon des Artistes Français, and in 1890 at the Société Nationale des Beaux-Arts, of which he was an associate member. He was awarded the Légion d'Honneur.

A renowned sculptor and creator of many busts, among them *Anna de Noailles,* he was also an initiator of Art Nouveau and designed numerous artefacts in that style.

MUSEUMS AND GALLERIES:

LYONS: *The Secret* (wood and ivory) - PARIS (MAM): *Portrait of a Young Man* (marble, bust) - PARIS (Mus. d'Orsay): *The Secret* (1894) - PARIS (Mus. du Petit Palais, Dutuit Collection): *Bust of Eugène Dutuit.*

AUCTION RECORDS:

PARIS, 3 Dec 1927, *Still-life: Two Jays,* FRF 200. PARIS, 5 May 1928, *Still-life: Milk Can and Lemons,* FRF 1,500. PARIS, 4 June 1928, *Still-life,* FRF 705. PARIS, 31 Jan 1929, *Flowers and Fruit,* FRF 500. PARIS, July 1946, *Vase of Flowers with a Landscape in the Background,* FRF 9,200; *Flowers,* FRF 1,500. PARIS, 17 March 1975, *The Luxembourg* (oil on canvas, 7 1/2 x 9 1/2 ins / 19 x 24 cm) FRF 3,800. ENGHIEN-LES-BAINS, 8 July 1976, *The Secret* (gilded bronze) FRF 4,200. MONTE CARLO, 18 Nov 1978, *The Secret* (bronze, h. 14 ins / 35.5 cm) FRF

7,200. ENGHIEN-LES-BAINS, 8 April 1979, *The Secret* (bronze, h. 24 1/2 ins / 62 cm) FRF 20,000. PARIS, 27 Feb 1980, *The Secret* (gilded bronze, h. 11 ins / 28 cm) FRF 8,000. NEW YORK, 3 April 1982, *Head of a Woman* (bronze, h. 8 ins / 20.5 cm) USD 850. PARIS, 5 May 1987, *Bust of a Girl* (white glazed terracotta, h. 7 3/4 ins / 20 cm) FRF 13,000. NEUILLY, 1 March 1988, *Bust of Beethoven* (brown-patinated bronze, H.13 1/2 ins / 34 cm) FRF 2,400. PARIS, 27 June 1990, *Bunch of Flowers* (oil on canvas, 24 x 19 3/4 ins / 61 x 50 cm) FRF 5,500. PARIS, 3 Dec 1999, *Secret* (gilded bronze, h. 11 ins / 29 cm) FRF 18,000. LONDON, 20 April 2000, *Secret* (c. 1900, gilt bronze, h. 11 ins / 27 cm) GBP 3,500. LONDON, 22 Sept 2000, *Table with Flowers* (oil on canvas, 25 x 31 ins / 64 x 78 cm) GBP 7,500. LONDON, 11 July 2001, *L'emprise* (brown patinated bronze, h. 31 ins / 80 cm) GBP 20,000. PARIS, 1 July 2002, *Vers la joie* (brown patinated bronze, h. 19 ins / 48 cm) EUR 2,100. LONDON, 21 Jan 2004, *Still-life* (oil on canvas, 21 x 26 ins / 54 x 65 cm) GBP 4,200.

FIXON, Claude Pierre
French, 18th century.
Active in Paris.
Painter.

Claude Pierre Fixon was the son of Pierre Fixon. He was admitted to the Académie de St-Luc in Paris.

FIXON, Louis Pierre
French, 18th century.
Born c. 1748; died January 1792, in Paris.
Sculptor.

Louis Pierre Fixon was the son of Pierre Fixon. He was a member of the Académie de St-Luc in Paris and worked on the king's buildings.

AUCTION RECORDS:
PARIS, 7-8 May 1923, *View of a Port* (sepia wash) FRF 1,350. PARIS, 25 Feb 1929, *The Halt* (drawing) FRF 400. PARIS, 12 May 1937, *Rural Scenes* (sepia heightened with white, two pendants) FRF 330.

FIXON, Pierre
French, 18th century.
Died 8 April 1788.
Sculptor.

Pierre Fixon became a member of the Académie de St-Luc in Paris in 1748, and worked from 1756 to 1760 on Notre-Dame.

FIXON, Pierre François
French, 18th century.
Active in Paris.
Painter, gilder.

Pierre François Fixon was the son of Pierre Fixon.

FIZELIÈRE-RITTI, Marthe de La. See **LA FIZELIÈRE-RITTI**

FIZELLE, Rah
Austrian, 20th century.
Born in Sydney, Australia.
Painter, watercolourist. Landscapes.

AUCTION RECORDS:
SYDNEY, 20 Oct 1980, *View of a Port* (watercolour, 16 3/4 x 19 1/4 ins / 42.5 x 49 cm) AUD 750. SYDNEY, 29 June 1981, *Flannel Flowers* (watercolour, 15 x 22 1/2 ins / 38 x 57 cm) AUD 550.

FJAESTAD, Gustaf Edoff
Swedish, 19th - 20th century.
Born 1868, in Stockholm; died 1948.
Painter, engraver. Landscapes. Designs for tapestries.

Gustaf Edoff Fjaestad was the pupil of Karl Larsson and Bruno Liltefors in Stockholm. In 1905 he set up in Lake-Raecken. Gustaf Fjaestad specialised in the depiction of the Swedish winter, with water as his preferred subject, which he interpreted almost in an abstract way, with a very symbolist sensitivity. In 1929 he featured in the *Exposition de l'Art suédois* (*Exhibition of Swedish Art*) in Paris, where he displayed *Hoarfrost on the Ice*. He was awarded a bronze medal at the Exposition Universelle in Paris in 1900.

G Fjaestad

MUSEUMS AND GALLERIES:
COPENHAGEN: *First Ice on the Lake; Hoarfrost and Sun* - STOCKHOLM: *Winter Moonlight; Aurora Borealis.*

AUCTION RECORDS:
STOCKHOLM, 11 Oct 1956, *Landscapes of Hills,* SEK 2,900. STOCKHOLM, 26 Oct 1960, *Winter Landscape,* CHF 4,100. STOCKHOLM, 26-28 March 1969, *Winter Landscape,* SEK 12,300. GÖTEBORG, 24 March 1976, *Snow-covered Landscape* (1933, oil on panel, 30 3/4 x 48 ins / 78 x 122 cm) SEK 21,000. GÖTEBORG, 31 March 1977, *Snow-covered Landscape* (1923, oil on panel, 19 1/4 x 27 1/4 ins / 49 x 69 cm) SEK 20,000. STOCKHOLM, 22 April 1981, *Winter Landscape* (1912, oil on canvas, 59 x 72 ins / 150 x 182 cm) SEK 37,000. STOCKHOLM, 30 Oct 1984, *Winter Landscape* (1915, oil on canvas, 42 1/2 x 54 1/4 ins / 108 x 138 cm) SEK 66,000. STOCKHOLM, 20 Oct 1987, *Snow-covered Landscape in Sunlight* (1911, oil on canvas, 59 x 72 3/4 ins / 150 x 185 cm) SEK 760,000. STOCKHOLM, 15 Nov 1988, *Silent Evening Sailing Trip, Archipelago and Boats* (1909, oil, 18 x 26 ins / 46 x 66 cm) SEK 75,000. STOCKHOLM, 15 Nov 1989, *The Thaw, a Winter Landscape with a Lake Surrounded by Tree-covered Mountains* (oil, 24 x 34 1/4 ins / 61 x 87 cm) SEK 185,000. LONDON, 29 March 1990, *White Frost* (1920, oil on canvas, 36 x 43 3/4 ins / 90.5 x 111 cm) GBP 24,200. STOCKHOLM, 14 Nov 1990, *Study of Reflections on Water* (oil on panel, 6 3/4 x 9 ins / 17 x 22 cm) SEK 15,000. STOCKHOLM, 29 May 1991, *Sunlight Effects on a Snow-covered Lake in the Mountains* (oil on canvas, 35 1/2 x 40 1/2 ins / 90 x 103 cm) SEK 66,000. STOCKHOLM, 5 Sept 1992, *Birch Trees Covered in Hoarfrost* (oil on canvas, 48 x 57 ins / 122 x 145 cm) SEK 76,000. STOCKHOLM, 10-12 May 1993, *Birch Trees Covered in Hoarfrost* (oil on canvas, 48 x 57 ins / 122 x 145 cm) SEK 70,000. STOCKHOLM, 30 Nov 1993, *Landscape with a Brook and Oak Trees Covered in Hoarfrost under a Winter Sun* (oil on canvas, 26 1/2 x 33 3/4 ins / 67 x 86 cm) SEK 82,000. LONDON, 10 Feb 1995, *Reflections of Sunlight in Winter* (oil on canvas/card, 28 1/2 x 36 1/2 ins / 72.5 x 93 cm) GBP 3,680. SAN FRANCISCO, 26 May 1999, *Hoar Frost and Stars* (oil on card, 36 x 43 ins / 91 x 109 cm) USD 8,500. STOCKHOLM, 26 May 1999, *Early Spring Flood* (1910, oil on canvas, 59 x 33 ins / 150 x 84 cm) SEK 180,000. STOCKHOLM, 5 Dec 2000, *Winter Landscape, Fryksdalen* (1913, oil on canvas, 46 x 62 ins / 116 x 158 cm) SEK 90,000. STOCKHOLM, 5 Dec 2000, *Starlit Winter's Night* (1939, oil on canvas/panel, 51 x 44 ins / 130 x 111 cm) SEK 430,000. STOCKHOLM, 4 Dec 2001, *Hoar Frost on the Ice* (1932, oil on panel, 37 x 48 ins / 93 x 123 cm) SEK 320,000. STOCKHOLM, 4 Dec 2001, *Winter's Day, Glava* (1920, oil on canvas, 55 x 63 ins / 140 x 160 cm) SEK 390,000. STOCKHOLM, 28 May 2002, *Hoar Frost at Sunset* (1918, oil on panel, 37 x 51 ins / 95 x 130 cm) SEK 300,000. STOCKHOLM, 3 Dec 2002, *Twilight at Racken* (1905, oil on canvas, 47 x 58 ins / 120 x 147 cm) SEK 225,000. STOCKHOLM, 2 Dec 2003, *Hoare Frost on Frozen Lake, Varmland. Sketch of Winter Landscape* (1923, oil on canvas, double-sided, 39 x 49 ins / 99 x 125 cm) SEK 300,000. STOCKHOLM, 3 Dec 2003, *Winter Landscape from Varmland* (1932, oil on panel, 41 x 50 ins / 103 x 128 cm) SEK 260,000. STOCKHOLM, 26 May 2004, *Winter Landscape with Hoar Frost, Varmland* (1911, oil on canvas, 59 x 72 ins / 151 x 184 cm) SEK 175,000. UPPSALA, 28 May 2004, *Winter Landscape with Hoar Frost and Punt Frozen on Water* (1919, oil on canvas, 42 x 57 ins / 106 x 145 cm) SEK 250,000.

FJAESTAD, Kerstin Maria
Maiden name: Hallén

Swedish, 19th - 20th century.
Born 30 May 1873, in Hörby.
Painter. Portraits, landscapes.

FJELDE, Jakob
Norwegian, 19th century.
Born 10 April 1859, in Aalesund; died 5 May 1896, in Minneapolis.
Sculptor. Figures.

Jakob Fjelde was a pupil of B. Bergslien in Christiania (now Oslo), and then of C.G.V. Bissen in Copenhagen. After travelling to Rome he went to America, establishing himself there in 1887.

MUSEUMS AND GALLERIES:
MINNEAPOLIS (Public Library): *Woman Reading.*

FJELDE, Paul
American, 20th century.
Born 12 August 1892, in Minneapolis; died May 3 1984.
Sculptor. Monuments.

Paul Fjelde was the son of Jakob Fjelde, a Norweigen sculptor who emigrated to the USA in 1887. He studied in the academies of Minneapolis, New York, Copenhagen and Paris. He was also a teacher. He is best known for his *Lincoln* monument in Oslo, but he carved many other works in the USA.

FJELDSKOV, Niels Valdemar. See **FIELDSKOV**

FJELDSTED, S. See **FIELDSTED**

FJELL, Kai
Norwegian, 20th century.
Born 1907, in Sköger, near Drammen; died 1989.
Painter, illustrator, decorative designer. Figures, urban landscapes. Stage sets, advertising art.

Fjell began to draw when he was a child, encouraged by his teacher, Nils Schjelbred, a friend of Munch. In 1930 he worked in Oslo as a designer and painter of advertising material. He settled in the area around Telemark, so as to devote himself entirely to his art. In 1932 he attended for some time courses at the academy in Oslo. He subsequently left for Paris, but did not seek to come into contact with other artists, which was why he was not influenced by modern tendencies. His work is divided into two periods, the first being clearly Expressionist and revealing the tradition of Nordic Romanticism. From 1940 his work became brighter and returned to the fresh sources of popular art. He exhibited in 1937 and in 1952 took part in the Venice Biennale. He illustrated collections of poems and created stage sets for the national theatre in Oslo.

AUCTION RECORDS:
LONDON, 17 May 1991, *Figures in a Port* (1959, oil on canvas, 32 x 36 1/4 ins / 81.3 x 92.1 cm) GBP 27,500. LONDON, 15 June 1994, *The Virgin of Oslo* (1955, oil on canvas, 31 x 35 ins / 79 x 89 cm) GBP 36,700. LONDON, 28 June 1999, *Adorning the Bride* (1952, oil on canvas, 43 x 37 ins / 108 x 94 cm) GBP 50,000. LONDON, 28 June 1999, *The Party* (1950, oil on canvas, 46 x 54 ins / 118 x 138 cm) GBP 56,000. OSLO, 8 May 2000, *The Suitors* (c. 1948, oil on canvas, 43 x 47 ins / 110 x 120 cm) NOK 700,000. OSLO, 8 June 2000, *Reclining Female Nude* (1956, oil on canvas, 20 x 24 ins / 50 x 60 cm) NOK 300,000. OSLO, 3 April 2001, *Interior Scene with Seated Half Nude* (1941, oil on canvas, 15 x 19 ins / 39 x 47 cm) NOK 355,000. OSLO, 27 Nov 2001, *Seated Woman* (oil on panel, 18 x 22 ins / 46 x 55 cm) NOK 190,000. OSLO, 18 March 2002, *Young Girl* (c. 1948, oil on canvas, 43 x 47 ins / 110 x 120 cm) NOK 350,000. OSLO, 21 Nov 2002, *Reclining Nude on Bed* (1958, oil on canvas, 20 x 18 ins / 50 x 45 cm) NOK 80,000. OSLO, 13 Oct 2003, *Woman with Medallion* (1961, oil on panel, 14 x 11 ins / 35 x 27 cm) NOK 66,000. OSLO, 8 Dec 2003, *Young Girl* (c. 1948, oil on canvas, 43 x 47 ins / 110 x 120 cm) NOK 475,000. OSLO, 22 March 2004, *Two Women* (oil on canvas, 29 x 24 ins / 73 x 60 cm) NOK 450,000. OSLO, 6 Dec 2004, *Women Waiting II* (1955, oil on canvas, 32 x 36 ins / 81 x 91 cm) NOK 290,000.

FJERDINGSTAD, Carl Christian
Danish, 20th century.
Born 30 August 1891, on Christianso.
From 1917 active in France.
Goldsmith. Furniture, religious furnishings, designs (in gold and silver).

Fjerdingstad went to fight for France in 1914, but he was seriously wounded in May 1915, and discharged. As a goldsmith, he set up his workshop in the Paris area at the end of World War I, and made his mark on jewellery and secular as well as sacred art. He was an adviser to the Maison Christofle, and a member, in Paris, of the Salon d'Automne. He took part in the Exposition des Arts Décoratifs of 1925 in Paris. Several retrospectives of his work have been organised, including at the 1981 Pavillon Christofle and in 1982 Arthus Bertrand. He was awarded numerous military medals, as well as being made a Chevalier of the Légion d'Honneur and a Knight of the Order of the Danebrog.

BIBLIOGRAPHY:
Fjerdingstad, Carl Christian, *Escapade dans le passé ou la vie d'un Danois en France*, Éd. du Rocher, Paris, 1967.

FJETURSKY, Nikon. See **FIETURSKY**

FLACH, Charles
Brazilian, 19th century.
Born 22 February 1863, in Colonia Leopoldina.
Painter.

Charles Flach lived at various times in Bern, Dresden, Hanover and in England. He studied painting at Hubert Herkomer's art school near London and under Roll and Besnard in Paris. He travelled in Spain and Italy and exhibited from 1894 in Switzerland (in Turnus and Geneva) as well as in Paris.

FLACH, Johann Georg
German, 17th century.
Probably active in Leipzig (Saxony).
Painter, engraver. Frontispieces.

Johann Georg Flach produced engravings for the frontispieces for books in particular. One of his known works is a portrait of *Anna Elisabeth ab Enden*, printed by C. Romstedt.

FLACH, Kaspar
German, 17th century.
Sculptor.

In 1642 Kaspar Flach carved an altar depicting *The Passion of Christ* for the church of St Lawrence in Hof (Franconia).

FLACHAT, Antoine
French, 19th century.
Born in Lyons.
Painter.

Antoine Flachat was a pupil of Lepage and Chaine, in Lyons. He first painted insects and still-lifes in watercolour, which he exhibited at the Salon in Lyons from 1855 to 1865, and at the Paris Salon in 1864 and 1865. He went on to exhibit portraits, landscapes, still-lifes, religious subjects and genre scenes in Lyons until 1896.

FLACHAT, Jean Baptiste
French, 19th century.
Born 15 July 1828, in Lyons; died 19 January 1896, in Lyons.
Sculptor, decorative designer.

Jean Flachat was a pupil at the École de la Martinière in Lyons. He worked with a decorative sculptor in Lyons and from 1853 he headed, with various associates, a company providing decorations for interiors and, especially, furniture. He decorated the Cercle International in Vichy, the

Grand Cercle of the Villa des Fleurs in Aix-les-Bains, as well as the Préfecture du Rhône (police headquarters) and Foyer du Grand Théâtre both in Lyons. The pure style and the flawless execution of his furniture is remiscent of the sculptured wood of the Lyons Renaissance. Several of these pieces were exhibited in Paris at the Exposition Universelle from 1878 to 1889, when he received two gold medals, and at the Exposition des Arts Décoratifs in Paris in 1882, and in Lyons in 1884. Flachat was the teacher of the decorative art class at the École des Beaux-Arts in Lyons in 1894 to 1895. In 1895 he received the Légion d'Honneur. There is a Louis XIV credence table designed and executed in his workshops at the Musée des Tissus in Lyons.

Museums and Galleries:

Lyons (Mus. des Tissus): credence in Louis XIV style.

FLACHENECKER, Ferdinand Wolfgang

German, 19th century.

Born 1792, in Zirndorf, near Fürth (Bavaria).

Painter, lithographer.

Flachenecker studied at the Kunstakademi in Copenhagen, where he exhibited and won several awards. One of his moost notable works is *Elijah Raises the Widow's Son*. He went to Munich, Vienna and Rome. He produced lithographic copies of many paintings from the Pinakotek art gallery in Munich, including *Abduction of the Daughters of Leucippus*, by Rubens; *Emperor Charles V*, by Titian; *Portrait of the Duke of Neuburg*, by Van Dyck; and from his own works *Duke of Bavaria Refusing the Bohemian Crown in 1440*.

FLACHÉRON, Grégoire Isidore

French, 19th century.

Born 29 April 1806, in Lyons; died 1873, in Hyères (Var).

Painter, engraver. Religious subjects, landscapes, landscapes with figures, seascapes.

Grégoire was the son of L.C. Flachéron, the architect of the city of Lyons. He studied there at the École des Beaux-Arts from 1824 to 1827 and was the pupil of Pierre Révoil. He later studied with Ingres at the École des Beaux-Arts in Paris. In 1833 he went to Rome, where he remained for a long time.

He exhibited at the annual Salons in Paris and Lyons: first views of Italy, from 1833, and then from 1861, Provence, Nice and Algerian landscapes and seascapes. In Paris he received a third-class medal in 1841 for *Cain after the Murder of Abel*.

He engraved several etchings. His admiration for Poussin can be seen in his landscapes of Roman countryside which depict many characters, drawn from the Bible or from works by Virgil, in a grandiose natural setting.

Museums and Galleries:

Lyons (MBA): *View at Subiaco; Cain and Abel; Cain after the Murder of Abel*.

Auction records:

Paris, 17-18 Dec 1923, *Oriental Landscape*, FRF 230. Paris, 25 Nov 1925, *View of Subiaco*, FRF 250.

FLACHERON, Louis

French, 19th century.

Born in Rome, to French parents; died 1885.

Painter, watercolourist. Genre scenes.

Louis Flacheron was a pupil of Dumas and Cabanel. He was the son of Grégoire Isidore Flacheron. He first exhibited at the Salon in 1880.

FLACHET, Maurice

Belgian, 20th century.

Born 1872; died 1964.

Painter. Figures.

Auction records:

Copenhagen, 25-26 April 1990, *Man Reading a Letter* (oil on canvas, 53 1/4 x 73 1/4 ins / 135 x 186 cm) DKK 9,000.

FLACHNER, Lucas Anton

German, 18th century.

Born in Hammelburg; died 1769, in Würzburg (Bavaria).

Painter. Genre scenes, portraits.

The museum in Kassel houses a painting entitled *Village Tavern* by Flachner. Other known works by this artist include *St Anthony of Padua, St John the Evangelist*, and *St Christopher* in Würzburg.

FLACHOT, M.

French, 20th century.

Painter, pastellist. Urban landscapes.

Auction records:

Paris, 12 Feb 1945, *Market Square in Brussels* (1901, pastel) FRF 700.

FLACK, Audrey

American, 20th - 21st century.

Born 30 May 1931, in New York.

Painter, sculptor, graphic artist, printmaker, lithographer. Still-lifes, figures.

Audrey Flack studied at the Cooper Union, New York (1948-1951); Yale University, New Haven (BFA, 1952) with Jossef Albers; the Institute of Fine Arts, New York University (1953); and the Art Students League, New York, under Robert Beverly Hale. She has taught in New York at the Pratt Institute and New York University (1960-1968); the Riverside Museum Master Institute (1966-1967); the School of Visual Arts (1970-1974); and the National Academy of Design (from 1987). Flack has been Albert Dorne Professor at University of Bridgeport, CT (1975); Mellon Professor at the Cooper Union, New York (1982); C. & R. Smith Distinguished Visiting Professor, George Washington University (1992); and Visiting Professor, University of Pennsylvania Institute of Contemporary Art, Philadelphia (1994). She has served on the boards of directors of the College Art Association of America (1989-1994), the Wonder Woman Foundation, and Interns for Peace.

Although Flack painted in the Abstract Expressionist style in the 1950s, she moved to Realism in the 1960s because she believed that the purpose of art is to communicate. She was one of the first artists to use photographs as a basis for painting in the 1960s, using images of well-known monuments like Michelangelo's *David* or the cathedral of Amiens, or compositions of photographs of public figures like Roosevelt, Rockefeller, Hitler or Kennedy, as in *Kennedy Motorcade* (1964). In 1969, Flack first used the technique of using a slide projector to project an image onto a canvas, then applying paint onto the image, as in *Farb Family Portrait* (1969-1970). By the 1970s, her work had become Photo-Realist in style, as in the works *Crayola* (1972-1973) and *Energy Apples* (1980). Flack's style has evolved from abrupt and precise realism to a more subtle style. Flack began to sculpt in the early 1980s, favouring large bronze sculptures of heroic women and goddesses, which explore the role of women in society. Public commissions for sculptures include *Queen Catherine of Braganza*, placed opposite the United Nations building (early 1990s); and *Civitas: Four Visions*, Rock Hill City Gateway, South Carolina (1990-1991).

Flack has had solo exhibitions at: Roko Gallery, New York, 1959; Joseloff Gallery, University of Hartford, 1974; Carlson Gallery, University of Bridgeport, 1975; Fine Arts Gallery, University of South Florida, Tampa, 1981; Hewlett Art Gallery, Carnegie-Mellon University, Pittsburgh, 1984; *Saints and Other Angels*, Cooper Union (tour), 1986-1988; Belk Building, Town Center Mall, Rock Hill, SC, 1990; Parrish Art Museum, Southampton, NY, 1991; *Breaking the Rules: Au-*

drey Flack, A Retrospective 1950-1990, Frederick S. Wright Art Gallery, University of California, Los Angeles (tour), 1992-1993; *Audrey Flack - A 20-Year Survey,* Louis K. Meisel Gallery, New York, 1995; *Audrey Flack: Love Conquers All,* Art Museum of Western Virginia, Roanoke, 1996; *Audrey Flack: Daphne Speaks,* Guild Hall Museum, East Hampton, NY, 1996; *Audrey Flack: An Odyssey of Angels,* Joy Tash Gallery, Scottsdale, AZ, 1997; *Audrey Flack: Reflections in a Mirror,* Miami University Art Museum, Oxford, OH, 1997.

She has participated in other exhibitions, including: *22 Realists,* Whitney Museum of American Art, New York, 1970; and *Hyperréalismes USA 1965-75,* Musée d'Art Moderne et Contemporain, Strasbourg, 2003.

Flack has received an award of merit from the Butler Institute of American Art, Youngstown, 1974; an Honorary Doctorate, Cooper Union, 1977; the Saint-Gaudens Medal, Cooper Union, 1982; the Artist of the Year Award, New York City Teachers Association, 1985; and a Design for Transportation National Award, 1996.

BIBLIOGRAPHY:

The Gray Border Series/Audrey Flack, exhibition catalogue, Louis K. Meisel Gallery, New York, 1976. *Audrey Flack: Works on Paper, 1950-1980,* exhibition catalogue, USF Art Galleries, University of South Florida, Tampa, 1980 or 1981. *Audrey Flack on Painting,* Abrams, New York, 1981. *Audrey Flack, Light and Energy,* exhibition catalogue, Louis K. Meisel Gallery, New York, 1983. *Saints and Other Angels: The Religious Paintings of Audrey Flack,* exhibition catalogue, Cooper Union, New York, 1986. Gouma-Peterson, Thalia, et al., *Audrey Flack: Breaking the rules. A retrospective 1950-1990,* catalogue raisonné, Harry N. Abrams, New York, 1992. *Audrey Flack: Sketchbook, 1985-1989,* illustrated book, National Museum of Women in the Arts, Washington DC, 1992. Brigham, David R., *'The New Civic Art: an Interview with Audrey Flack'* in *American Art,* vol 9, journal article, Winter 1994. Lebensztejn, Jean-Claude, et al., *Hyperréalismes USA 1965-75,* group exhibition catalogue, Musée d'Art moderne et contemporain, Strasbourg, Hazan, Paris, 2003.

MUSEUMS AND GALLERIES:

BUFFALO (Albright-Knox AG): *Print from Presidential Portfolio; Fourth of July Still-life from Kent Bicentennial Portfolio* - CANBERRA (Nat. Gal. of Australia): *Jolie Madame* (1972, oil) - CHARLOTTE, NC (Mint Museum of Art) - CHICAGO (Smart MA): *Madonna* (lithograph); *Banana Split Sundae* (lithograph with embossing) - DALLAS (MA) - GAINESVILLE (Samuel P. Horn Museum of Art, University of Florida): *Islandia, Goddess of the Healing Waters* (1988, polychrome and gilded plaster) - HARTFORD (Wadsworth Atheneum) - HEMPSTEAD, NY (Hofstra Museum): *Lady Madonna* (c. 1972, lithograph with gold leaf) - LAFAYETTE, IN (Greater Lafayette Museum of Art) - LOS ANGELES (County MA) - LOUISVILLE, KY (J.B. Speed Art Museum) - MINNEAPOLIS (Walker Art Center) - NEW YORK (Metropolitan Mus. of Art) - NEW YORK (MoMA): *Leonardo's Lady* (1975, painting) - NEW YORK (Riverside Mus.) - NEW YORK (Solomon R. Guggenheim Mus.) - NEW YORK (Whitney Mus. of American Art) - OBERLIN, OH (Allen Memorial Art Museum) - OXFORD, OH (AM, Miami University): *Self-portrait* (1952); *Self-portrait: Dark Face* (1960); *Self-portrait in Underpants* (1958); *Anatomy Lesson* (1953) - SAN FRANCISCO (MoMA) - ST LOUIS (AM) - TUCSON (University of Arizona Art Museum): *Marilyn* (1977, painting) - WALTHAM, MA (Rose Art Museum, Brandeis University): *Farb Family Portrait* (1969-1970) - WASHINGTON DC (National Mus. of Women in the Arts): *Rolls Royce Lady* (1983, cibachrome print) - WASHINGTON DC (Smithsonian American AM): *(Presidential Portfolio) Banana Split Sundae* (1980, colour screenprint and inkless intaglio); *Tower of Pisa* (1971, oil) - WINTER PARK, FL (Cornell Fine Arts Museum, Rollins College): *Head of Civitas* (1993, bronze with patina).

AUCTION RECORDS:

NEW YORK, 4 May 1989, *Banana split sundae* (pencil and coloured chalk/paper, 22 1/2 x 30 ins / 57.1 x 76.2 cm) USD 5,500. NEW YORK, 8 May 1990, *Strawberry Tart* (oil and acrylic/canvas, 24 x 30 1/4 ins / 61 x 77 cm) USD 41,800. NEW YORK, 9 May 1990, *Blue Shiva* (1973, oil on canvas, 36 x 50 ins / 91.5 x 127 cm) USD 49,500. NEW YORK, 13 Nov 1991, *'Time to save'* (1979, oil on canvas, 80 x 64 ins / 203.2 x 162.6 cm) USD 253,000. NEW YORK, 7 Nov 2000, *Self-portrait* (1974, acrylic on linen, 80 x 64 ins / 203 x 163 cm) USD 15,000. PARIS, 12 Dec 2001, *Michelangelo's David* (oil on canvas, 66 x 46 ins / 167 x 117 cm) FRF 80,000.

FLACK, Thomas

British, 18th - 19th century.
Born 1771, in Garboldishom; died 1844, in Arras.
Painter, watercolourist. Landscapes.

MUSEUMS AND GALLERIES:

ARRAS: *Sandstone Bridge over the Scarpe* (watercolour).

FLACKER

Austrian, 18th century.
Born in the 18th century, in Vienna.
Sculptor.

Flacker may be the same artist as Carl Sebastian Plack, a sculptor in Graz. In 1720 he created altars and the pulpit in the church of the Pilgrimage in the town, and pieces entitled *St Francis* and *Crucifixion* in the chapel at Mount Thabor in 1733.

FLAD. See also **FLADT**

FLAD, Georg

German, 19th - 20th century.
Born 10 March 1853, in Heidelberg; died 2 June 1913, in Dachau.
Landscape artist.

Flad lived in Dachau, near Munich. He received honourable mention at the Expositions Universelles of 1889 and 1900, in Paris.

MUSEUMS AND GALLERIES:

MUNICH: *Spring Morning.*

FLAD, L. Alois

German, 19th century.
Active in Munich.
Lithographer.

Known works by Flad include lithographic views of Munich, Hohenschwangau Castle, the castle of Unterwittelsbach and other lithographs for the work *Mineral Springs in Bavaria* by V. Müller. Flad also painted watercolour views.

FLADAGER, Ole Henriksen

Norwegian, 19th century.
Born 1832, in Nordre Aurdal; died 1871, in Rome.
Sculptor.

The Oslo museum has Ole Henriksen Fladager's *Bust of P. A. Munch, Bust of Minister Jorgen Herman Vogi, David* and *Theseus.*

FLADE, Christian

German, 18th century.
Born c. 1680; died 23 March 1745.
Active in Lauban, Silesia (now Luban, Poland).
Painter.

In 1732 Christian Flade painted the galleries in the church in Herwigsdorf, near Löbau, only one of which remains: *Adoration of the Shepherds.*

FLADE, Georg Christoph

German, 18th century.

Born c. 1718; died 22 June 1759.
Active in Lauban, Silesia (now Luban, Poland).
Sculptor.

FLADE, Gottlob
German, 18th century.
Active in Dresden.
Sculptor.
The statue of an angel created for the church in Friedersdorf, near Zittau, in 1732 is attributed to Gottlob Flade.

FLADE, Johann Christian
German, 18th century.
Born 1712; died 1745.
Active in Liegnitz, Silesia (now Legnica, Poland).
Sculptor.

FLADT, or Flad or Fuldt
German, 18th century.
Born 1718; died 1780.
Painter. Architectural views.
MUSEUMS AND GALLERIES:
KASSEL: *Piece of Architecture* - MUNICH: *Thesaurus Palatinus.*

FLAESCHNER, Julius
German, 19th century.
Active in Berlin.
Sculptor.
Flaeschner took part in the exhibitions at the academy in Berlin in 1844, 1860 and 1862 with low reliefs entitled *Ariadne, Euterpe,* and others.

FLAGEL-CARRETTE, Henriette
French, 20th century.
Born 27 April 1883, in Paris.
Engraver.
Henriette Flagel-Carette studied under Édouard Léon. She exhibited at the Salon des Artistes Indépendants, the Société Nationale des Beaux-Arts in Paris and the Salon d'Automne, but she made her name at the Salon des Artistes Français.

She exhibited etchings since 1925 and obtained a bronze medal in 1937.

FLAGG, Charles Noel
American, 19th century.
Born 1848, in Brooklyn; died 1916.
Painter, teacher.
Charles Noel Flagg was the son and pupil of J. B. Flagg and from 1872 to 1882 a pupil of Louis Jacquesson de la Chevreuse in Paris. He became director of art education in Connecticut. There are several of his works in the museums of New Jersey, Northampton, Hartford, St Paul, and elsewhere.
MUSEUMS AND GALLERIES:
HARTFORD (Wadsworth Atheneum): *The Bather* (oil on canvas); other paintings.

FLAGG, George Whiting
American, 19th century.
Born 26 June 1816, in New Haven; died 1897.
Painter. History painting, genre scenes.
George Whiting Flagg was the brother of Jared Bradley Flagg and a nephew of the painter Washington Allston. He went to Boston at an early age to learn from his relative and his ability earned him the reputation of being an infant prodigy. He then went to Europe and worked for six years in London, where he was acclaimed by the art press. When he returned to America he was elected a member of the National Academy in 1851. Among his works are *Murder of the Princes, Columbus and the Egg,* and *Washington Receiving his Mother's Blessing.*
MUSEUMS AND GALLERIES:
NEW YORK (Historical Society): *Little Chimney Sweep; Little Match Seller; Woodchopper's Son.*

FLAGG, H. Peabody
American, 19th century.
Born 1859, in Somerville (Massachusetts); died 1937.
Painter.
H. Peabody Flagg was a pupil of Carolus Duran in Paris, and a member of the Boston Art Club and other American art societies.

FLAGG, James Montgomery
American, 20th century.
Born 18 June 1877, in New York; died 27 May 1960, in New York.
Painter, draughtsman, illustrator, poster artist.
James Montgomery Flagg studied art in New York, England and Paris. He exhibited in Paris at the Salon of 1900, in New York at the Watercolor Club and the National Academy of Design, and was a member of many art associations.

Talented and creative, he designed the famous recruitment poster for the American army in which Uncle Sam points his right index finger at the viewer with the words 'I want You for U.S. Army'. He wrote and illustrated many books: *Yankee Girls Abroad* (1900), *Tomfoolery* (1904), *If, A guide to Bad manners* (1905), *Why They Married* (1906), *The Adventures of Kitty Cobb* (1912), *All in the Same Boat, I Should Say So* (1914), *The Mystery of the Hated Man* (1916), *Boulevard* (1925). He contributed to a number of periodicals: *Cosmopolitan, Good Housekeeping, Liberty Weekly, Life, Judge, St Nicholas, Scribner's.*
BIBLIOGRAPHY:
Ingram, John H., *A Literary Tramp: Biographical Writings on the Zigzag Career of James M. Flagg, Author, Artist,* Rivington, London, 1917. Meyer, Susan E., *James Montgomery Flagg,* Watson-Guptill, New York, 1974.
AUCTION RECORDS:
NEW YORK, 18 Nov 1965, *Contemplation* (watercolour) USD 1,200. NEW YORK, 19 June 1981, *I Like it This Way* (oil on canvas, 48 x 28 ins / 121.9 x 71.1 cm) USD 3,200. NEW YORK, 1 July 1982, *Woman Reading on a Sofa* (1913, watercolour, 20 1/4 x 13 1/2 ins / 51.5 x 34.3 cm) USD 750. NEW YORK, 20 June 1985, *Golfer* (pen, 27 1/4 x 21 1/4 ins / 69.2 x 54 cm) USD 1,100. NEW YORK, 30 May 1986, *Self-portrait and Model* (oil on canvas, 24 1/4 x 18 ins / 61.4 x 46 cm) USD 2,000. NEW YORK, 30 Sept 1988, *Home, Sweet Home* (watercolour and gouache/paper, 15 x 22 ins / 38 x 56 cm) USD 1,320. NEW YORK, 24 Jan 1990, *Master Craftsman* (watercolour and pencil/card, 18 x 12 ins / 45.7 x 30.5 cm) USD 1,045. NEW YORK, 14 Feb 1990, *Policeman and the Mob* (watercolour and gouache/card, 24 x 22 ins / 61 x 56 cm) USD 2,200. NEW YORK, 31 May 1990, *Boca Raton Club* (1945, watercolour/card, 15 x 22 ins / 38.1 x 55.8 cm) USD 1,430. NEW YORK, 17 Dec 1990, *Ham Fisher with Three Nudes* (oil on canvas, 50 x 62 ins / 127 x 157.7 cm) USD 7,975. NEW YORK, 3 Dec 1992, *Study for a Boxing Mural* (1944, watercolour, gouache and pencil/reinforced paper, 9 1/4 x 29 1/4 ins / 23.5 x 74.3 cm) USD 7,150. NEW YORK, 8 May 1999, *Threesome in Costume, One Man Beseeching* (1923, pen and brush, 20 x 26 ins / 51 x 66 cm) USD 2,900. NEW YORK, 6 Nov 1999, *Masked Nude Woman Emerging from Pits of Hell* (watercolour, 22 x 11 ins / 56 x 28 cm) USD 6,000. NEW YORK, 6 May 2000, *Couple Embracing, He Kneeling on Floor* (pen and ink, 22 x 19 ins / 56 x 48 cm) USD 2,400. NEW YORK, 5 Dec 2000, *Alice in Wonderland* (oil on panel, 60 x 18 ins / 152 x 46 cm) USD 8,000. NEW YORK, 10 Nov 2001, *Goings on at a Victorian Wedding Reception* (pen and ink, 20 x 29 ins / 51 x 74 cm) USD 5,000. NEW YORK, 10 Nov 2001, *Model Kissing Artist* (c. 1941, watercolour and board, 41 x 26 ins / 104 x 66 cm) USD 9,500. CHEYENNE, 15 March 2002, *Untitled* (oil on canvas, 30 x 21 ins / 76 x 53 cm) USD 5,000. NEW YORK, 11 May 2002, *Couple at Elegant Club, with Woman Waving from Dance Floor* (oil on canvas, 24 x 46 ins / 61 x 117 cm) USD 9,500. NEW YORK, 10 May 2003, *Couple at Breakfast Table, Man Upset by Newspaper* (c. 1920,

watercolour and oil, 18 x 26 ins / 46 x 66 cm) USD 1,800. NEW YORK, 15 Nov 2003, *Man Carrying Woman into Room* (c. 1910, watercolour en grisaille, 27 x 15 ins / 69 x 38 cm) USD 2,000. NEW YORK, 31 March 2004, *By the Brook* (1930, watercolour, 15 x 22 ins / 38 x 56 cm) USD 7,000. BOSTON, 10 Sept 2004, *I Want You for U.S. Army* (colour lithograph, 40 x 30 ins / 102 x 76 cm) USD 6,000.

FLAGG, Jared Bradley
American, 19th century.
Born 16 June 1820, in New Haven; died 25 September 1899.
Painter. Genre scenes, portraits.

Jared Bradley Flagg was the younger brother of George Flagg and, like him, worked with their uncle Washington Allston. He was also a pupil of his brother. He first exhibited at the National Academy of New York with a portrait of his father. He became a member of the National Academy in 1849. Despite his success as a painter, he entered holy orders and became a Protestant minister in 1854. However, he continued to paint and exhibited a *Portrait of Commodore Vanderbilt* at the Philadelphia Exhibition, and his *Portrait of Charles L. Frost* and *Poet's Captive* at the National Academy in 1877.

MUSEUMS AND GALLERIES:
WASHINGTON DC: *Portrait of Alfred Vail* - WASHINGTON DC (Smithsonian American AM): *Alice Pike Barney, in Wedding Gown* (1876, oil on canvas).

FLAGG, Montague
American, 19th - 20th century.
Born 1842, in Hartford (Connecticut); died 24 December 1915, in New York.
Painter. Portraits, genre scenes.

Montague Flagg was the son of J.B. Flagg, and was a pupil of Jacquesson de la Chevreuse and the École des Beaux-Arts, Paris. He exhibited at the Salon de Paris from 1879 to 1882. He worked in New York, where he became a member of the National Academy of Design in 1910.

FLAHAUT, Léon Charles
French, 19th century.
Born 4 December 1831, in Paris.
Painter.

Flahaut was trained by Léon Fleury and Corot. He exhibited landscapes at the Salon from 1857 to 1880 and received medals in 1869 and 1878. He was awarded the Légion d'Honneur. Works include *Around Port-Royal, River Bank, Banks of the Lake of Geneva, Normandy Farm, Landscape at Magny-les-Hameaux, Mérantais Valley, Olive Grove in Beaulieu, St-Hubert Lake, Cliff, near Houlgate, Evening, Étang d'Or, Rambouillet Forest, St-Lambert Valley, In the Woods, Souvenir of Normandy Coast, Morning, Banks of the Loing at Montbouy, Briare Canal, Salles Sheepfold* and *Le Croisic*.

MUSEUMS AND GALLERIES:
ORLÉANS: *Pertuiseaux Farm at Sunset* - ROUEN (MBA): *Landscape*.

FLAHAUT, Lucien
French, 20th century.
Born in Arras.
Painter. Landscapes, still-lifes.

Lucien Flahaut exhibited at the Salon des Artistes Indépendants in 1937 and 1938.

FLAHAUT, René Louis Auber
French, 19th - 20th century.
Born in Paris.
Painter.

René Flahaut received a honourable mention in 1901.

FLAISSIÉRES, Joséphine (Mme)
French, 20th century.
Born in Constantine, Algeria.
Painter.

Joséphine Flaissiéres exhibited *Flowers* at the Salon des Artistes Français in 1932 and 1933.

FLAJOULOT, Charles Antoine
French, 19th century.
Born 1774, in Besançon; died 15 September 1840, in Besançon.
Painter, draughtsman. Religious subjects.

Flajoulot was a follower of Jacques-Louis David. He ran a studio at the École des Beaux-Arts in Besançon where Gustave Courbet was one of his pupils. He bequeathed his collection of works of art, including his collection of antique castings, to various establishments in his home town.

MUSEUMS AND GALLERIES:
BESANÇON: *St John, Chaplain*.

FLAKSTAD, Nels
Norwegian, 20th century.
Born 1908, in Hamar.
Sculptor, painter.

Flakstad was the pupil of Alvaskar and Revold at the academy of fine art in Oslo, from 1930 to 1932. He travelled to Italy and France. Between the two World Wars his painting was figurative, connected to the great Expressionist movement.

FLAMAËL, Bertholet I or Bartholomé.
See **FLÉMAL**

FLAMAND. See also **DUCERF**

FLAMAND, Albert. See **FLAMEN**

FLAMAND, Arthus
French, 16th century.
Painter. History painting, landscapes.

Flamand was a pupil of Dubreuil and lived during the reign of Henri IV of France (1589-1610).

FLAMAND, Hyacinthe
French, 19th century.
Sculptor (ivory).

MUSEUMS AND GALLERIES:
DIEPPE: egg cup (1814).

FLAMAND, Jacques
French, 18th century.
Active in Paris during the first half of the 18th century.
Sculptor.

FLAMAND, Obéline
French, 20th - 21st century.
Born 11 March 1952, in Heudicourt (Somme).
Painter, illustrator.

Obéline Flamand was a pupil of the American painter, Louise Janin. She works in an abstract style, employing curves, traces, and sometimes floral or streamer motifs, using colour in a distinctive way.

She has exhibited at a number of solo exhibitions in Paris: Galerie Christiane Vincent in 1976; Galerie le Fil d'Ariane in 1979 and 1981, and various other places and galleries. She has also taken part in various group exhibitions, including the following: International Contemporary Art Fair, in Paris in 1987, 1988 and 1989; Salon des Indépendants; Salon Comparaison; and the Salon des Femmes Peintres et Sculpteurs.

FLAMANT, Alexander
German, 19th century.
Born 28 March 1836, in Frankfurt am Main.
Painter. Portraits, landscapes.

Flamant studied under Hübner and Richter in Berlin and Dresden. He settled in Dresden and exhibited from 1867 onwards.

MUSEUMS AND GALLERIES:
DESSAU (Mus. für Stadtgeschichte): *Portrait of S.H. Schwabe the Astronomer*.

FLAMANT, Charles
French, 19th century.
Born 19th century, in Asnières (Hauts-de-Seine).
Painter.

Flamant was a pupil of André. He exhibited landscapes in watercolour at the Paris Salon in 1881 and 1882.

FLAMANT, Émile Marcel
French, 20th century.
Born 18 January 1896, in Bohain; died 12 September 1975, in Fresnoy-le-Grand.
Painter, fresco artist. Murals.

The son of a mill owner, Émile Flamant received grants from the towns of Caudry and Valenciennes in order to study at that city's École des Beaux-Arts and then in Paris. Notable among his collective exhibitions were: 1925, Exposition des Arts Décoratifs, Paris, when he was responsible for the frescoes adorning the Paris Salon des Beaux-Arts; 1931, Exposition Coloniale, Paris; 1937, Exposition des Arts et Techniques, Paris. He was a member of the Société des Artistes Français from 1922.

He created the frescoes for a number of town halls in the Nord region and for several public buildings in Lille, its administrative centre. His frescoes also adorn numerous local churches, notably in Boulogne-sur-Mer, some of which he copied from Romanesque churches. He also left some easel paintings.

BIBLIOGRAPHY:
'*Un grand artiste: Émile Flamant*' in *Bulletin municipal de Fresnoy-le-Grand* no. 7, Fresnoy-le-Grand, 1975.

FLAMANT-DUCANY-GIDE, Andrée
French, 20th century.
Born in Nîmes.
Painter.

Andrée Flamant-Ducany-Gide exhibited at the Salon des Artistes Français from 1923.

FLAMBART
French, 19th century.
Active c. 1870.
Draughtsman, caricaturist.

Ten plates of caricatures by Flambart dating from 1870 are known. These represent *Napoleon III and His Family* and *The King of Prussia*.

FLAMBERGE, Jean
French, 17th century.
Active in Moret-sur-Loing (Seine-et-Marne).
Sculptor.

Jean Flamberge executed the high altar of the church of St-Thugal in Château-Landon in 1651.

FLAMBERTI. See **FIAMBERTI**

FLAMEL, Guillaume
French, 16th century.
Active in Gy (Haute-Saône).
Painter.

FLAMEL, Jean
French, 15th century.
Active in Salins (Cantal).
Painter.

Jean Flamel is mentioned between 1480 and 1506 as a painter of coats of arms.

FLAMEL, Nicolas
French, 16th century.
Painter.

Nicolas Flamel is mentioned in 1585 in Salins (Cantal).

FLAMEL, Nicolaus
Flemish School, 16th century.
Illuminator.

Nicolaus Flamel worked in 1350 on miniatures for volumes of the work *The Wonders of the World*.

FLAMEN, Albert, or Flamand
Flemish, 17th century.
Born 1564 (?), to a family originally from Bruges; died perhaps 1648.
Active in Paris between 1646 and 1648.
Painter, pastellist, engraver, draughtsman. Figures, portraits, genre scenes, landscapes.
Flemish School.

A number of Albert Flamen's portraits were engraved by Poilly and Boulanger. As an engraver his style is reminiscent of that of Hollar.

MUSEUMS AND GALLERIES:
LONDON (British Mus.): 80 drawings.

AUCTION RECORDS:
PARIS, 16 Dec 1922, *Pier* (pen and Indian ink) FRF 55. LONDON, 4 June 1981, *Wedding Dance* (c. 1650, watercolour and pen, 6 3/4 x 12 1/2 ins / 17.2 x 31.7 cm) GBP 300. ENGHIEN-LES-BAINS, 21 March 1982, *Reading* (pastel, 35 1/2 x 28 ins / 90 x 71 cm) FRF 16,000. AMSTERDAM, 16 Nov 1993, *Village Scene* (ink and wash, 4 x 6 1/4 ins / 10.2 x 16 cm) NLG 3,910. NEW YORK, 23 Jan 2001, *View of Town on River with Figures Fishing and in Boats* (coloured ink/colour wash, 7 x 13 ins / 17 x 32 cm) USD 2,500. NEW YORK, 23 Jan 2001, *Farmhouses and their Surroundings* (1673, coloured ink, album of 21, 8 x 6 ins / 21 x 16 cm) USD 10,000.

FLAMEN, Anselme I (père)
French, 17th - 18th century.
Born 2 January 1647, in St-Omer; died 15 May 1717, in Paris.
Sculptor.

Anselme Flamen I père was the pupil of Marsy. He won his third prize for sculpture in 1673 and was sent to Rome in 1675. He was admitted to the Académie in 1681 with a low relief of *St Jerome*. Flamen became a lecturer at the Académie in 1701. He exhibited *Diana*, *Flora* (two bronze busts) and *Cupid* (marble statue) at the Salon of 1704.

MUSEUMS AND GALLERIES:
VERSAILLES (Mus.): several works.

AUCTION RECORDS:
PARIS, 3 June 1970, *Diana the Huntress* (white marble) FRF 60,000.

FLAMEN, Anselme II (fils)
French, 18th century.
Born 13 September 1680, in Paris; died 9 July 1730, in Paris.
Sculptor.

Anselme Flamen II fils was the son of Anselme Flamen I père. He was admitted to the Académie in 1708 with a marble statuette, *Plutus*, which is now in the Louvre.

FLAMEN, F.
Flemish, 17th century.
Born 17th century, in Flanders.
Active in Paris c. 1660.
Painter, engraver.
Flemish School.

F. Flamen was probably from the same family as Albert Flamen. He is known for his *Views of the Seine* after Israel Silvestre.

FLAMEN, Jules
French, 19th century.
Painter.
Flamen became a member of the Société des Artistes Français in 1888.

FLAMEN, Pierre
French, 18th century.
Born 27 November 1712, in Paris; died after 1793.
Sculptor.
Pierre Flamen was the son of Anselme Flamen II fils. He is remembered for a *Ganymede* and a *Leda*.

FLAMEN, Pieter
Flemish, 18th century.
Active in Bruges.
Painter.
Flemish School.
In 1767 Pieter Flamen was a governor of the guild.

FLAMENBAUM, Simon
Polish, 20th century.
Born in Radom.
Sculptor.
Simon Flamenbaum exhibited a *Portrait* and a *Female Nude* at the Salon des Artistes Indépendants, Paris.

FLAMENCO. See first name

FLAMENG, Élisa
French, 19th century.
Born in Brussels, to French parents.
Engraver.
Élisa Flameng exhibited at the Paris Salon in 1868 and 1869.

FLAMENG, François
French, 19th - 20th century.
Born 6 December 1856, in Paris; died 28 February 1923, in Paris.
Painter, draughtsman, engraver. History paintings, portraits, genre scenes, landscapes.
François Flameng, son of Leopold, studied under Alexandre Cabanel, Pierre Hédouin and Jean-Paul Laurens.

He exhibited at the Paris Salon from 1873, receiving several awards, notably the first prize on the occasion of the Exposition Universelle in 1889. He was made a Commandeur of the Légion d'Honneur. He was given a chair at the École des Beaux-Arts in 1905 and was made a member of the Institut and of the Comité des Artistes Français.

A rated artist, François Flameng undertook numerous commissions for historical paintings and portraits of public figures, among them *Victor Hugo on his Death Bed*, kept in the Comédie Française collection. He is best remembered for *A Lectern; The Girondins' Call; The Conciergerie Gaol; Capo di Monte in Naples; Banks of the Seine at Meudon; Undergrowth* and *Camille Desmoulins*.

MUSEUMS AND GALLERIES:
BEAUNE: *Frederick Barbarossa visits the Tomb of Charlemagne* - LIÈGE: *Portrait of Painter Florent Willems* - PARIS (MBA): *Music* - PARIS (Mus. d'Orsay): *Murat Leading a Charge of the French Cavalry; Portrait of Cartoonist Sem* - ROUEN (MBA): *The Conquerors of the Bastille* - SYDNEY: *Napoleon at Waterloo.*

AUCTION RECORDS:
PARIS, 13 May 1892, *Coquetterie,* FRF 2,050. PARIS, 22-23-24 April 1901, *The Novel,* FRF 205. NEW YORK, 19-20 March 1903, *Scouting,* USD 650. LONDON, 18 Jan 1908, *Constantinople, the Golden Horn,* GBP 50. NEW YORK, May 1910, *Hussar,* USD 626. LONDON, 17 May 1923, *Napoleonic Guard,* GBP 6. PARIS, 5 Dec 1923, *Isola Bella,* FRF 11,500. PARIS, 15 Feb 1926, *Nonchalant,* FRF 2,400. PARIS, 4 March 1926, *Ist Empire Hussar,* FRF 4,600. PARIS, 17-18 June 1927, *Postprandial Explanations, Walter Scott's Monastery* (drawing) FRF 200. PARIS, 17-19 Oct 1927, *Feuille d'éventail* (watercolour heightened) FRF 130. PARIS, 16 Feb 1928, *The Arrival of French Troops in Holland in 1795,* FRF 7,900. PARIS, 20 May 1935, *Portrait of a Young Woman in a Black Dress,* FRF 350. PARIS, 24 Dec 1942, *The Acropolis,* FRF 300; *Barracks,* FRF 130; *Crossing the Grand-St-Bernard Pass,* FRF 2,600. NEW YORK, 29 Jan 1944, *Inside a Palace,* USD 525. PARIS, 12 May 1944, *Dispatch Rider,* FRF 3,800. NEW YORK, 22-25 May 1946, *Returning from a Walk,* USD 450. PARIS, July 1946, *Study of a Man* (drawing heightened) FRF 3,000. NEW YORK, 11-14 Dec 1946, *Versailles,* USD 1,400. PARIS, 20 Feb 1947, *Gathering of Lords and Ladies in Court Dress on a Terrace before a Town Panorama,* FRF 500. PARIS, 6 June 1951, *Bonaparte in his Garret,* FRF 20,000. NEW YORK, 21 Oct 1959, *Julie,* USD 400. LONDON, 18 Dec 1963, *View of Dieppe,* GBP 600. LONDON, 1 March 1972, *Young Women Sitting in the Bois de Boulogne,* GBP 1,400. PARIS, 31 May 1972, *Portrait of the Duchesse de Villeroy* (1888, drawing) FRF 380. LONDON, 7 May 1976, *Arriving at Constantinople* (oil on panel, 11¾ ins / 30 cm, 2 x 15¾ ins/5 x 40 cm) GBP 2,000. SAN FRANCISCO, 21 June 1984, *Madame Simon, Florist* (oil on canvas, 28 x 20 ins / 71 x 51 cm) USD 7,500. LONDON, 21 June 1985, *Elegant Lady* (oil on canvas, 64½ x 33 ins / 164 x 84 cm) GBP 18,000. NEW YORK, 22 Feb 1989, *Ile Pointeaux* (oil on canvas, 28¾ x 36 ins / 73 x 91.6 cm) USD 49,500. VERSAILLES, 25 Nov 1990, *Ball Evening* (pastel, 48½ x 18½ ins / 123 x 47 cm) FRF 8,000. PARIS, 10 Dec 1990, *Portrait of Cléo de Mérode* (oil on canvas, 36¼ x 28¾ ins / 92 x 73 cm) FRF 55,000. NEW YORK, 20 Feb 1992, *Portrait of a Young Lady Sitting in a Landscape* (1907, oil on canvas, 32 x 25½ ins / 81.3 x 64.8 cm) USD 19,800. NEW YORK, 12 Oct 1993, *Autumn Beauty* (1901, oil on panel, 18 x 14¾ ins / 46 x 37.5 cm) USD 10,350. NEW YORK, 12 Oct 1994, *Reception for Napoleon I at Isola Bella during the Fifth Year of his Reign* (oil on panel, 41½ x 55½ ins / 105.4 x 141 cm) USD 156,500. LONDON, 18 Nov 1994, *Portrait of Jean Jacques Henner* (pencil/paper, 10¾ x 8½ ins / 27.3 x 21.3 cm) GBP 1,035. PARIS, 13 Oct 1995, *Young Woman Reading* (oil on panel, 35½ x 22 ins / 90 x 56 cm) FRF 25,000. LONDON, 22 Nov 1996, *Portrait of Marcelle Praince* (1913, oil on canvas, 39½ x 32 ins / 100.4 x 81.2 cm) GBP 3,450. PARIS, 1 April 1998, *Napoleon, Sitting in an Inn* (1892, oil on panel, 4½ x 7 ins / 11.5 x 18 cm) FRF 21,000.

FLAMENG, Léopold
French, 19th - 20th century.
Born 22 November 1831, in Brussels, to French parents; died September 1911, in Paris.
Painter, engraver.
Léopold Flameng studied under Calamatta and de Gigoux. He was awarded medals in 1864, 1866, 1867 and at the 1878 Exposition Universelle. He gained further distinctions in 1886 and 1900 (first prize). He was made a Chevalier of the Légion d'Honneur in 1870, rising to Officier in 1894. His skill with burin brought him to the attention of Charles Blanc, and his art reproductions for the Gazette des Beaux-Arts, which the noted art critic had founded, made the young engraver's name.

Léopold Flameng stands out among nineteenth-century French engravers for his artistic integrity, and his etchings after Eugène Delacroix, Ingres, Leonardo da Vinci and Rembrandt fully deserve the praise they received on publication, but he was more timid in his approach to nature and did not develop a full expressive range.

AUCTION RECORDS:
PARIS, 26 Feb 1943, *Normandy Farmyard*, FRF 1,000. PARIS, 29 Nov 1991, *Normandy Farmyard* (oil on canvas, 11 x 16 ins / 27 x 40.5 cm) FRF 4,000.

FLAMENG, Marie Auguste
French, 19th century.
Born 14 July 1843, in Metz; died 26 September 1893, in Paris.
Painter. Landscapes, seascapes.

Marie Flameng was a pupil of Palianti and Puvis de Chavannes. She exhibited at the Paris Salon from 1870 to 1882. Works include *Lorraine Village*, *Vaucotte Valley*, *Black Cows at Villers-sur-Mer*, *Ronceveaux*, *Low Tide at Cancale*, *Cliffs at Cancale*, *Mill at Malesherbes*, *Oyster Catchers in Mont St-Michel Bay*, *Chazelle Impasse in Paris*, *Sea at St-Vaast-la-Hougue* and *Shooner moored at Le Havre*.

MUSEUMS AND GALLERIES:
MULHOUSE: *Freight Slipway at Bordeaux* - NANCY: *Fishing Boats* - PARIS (MAMVP): *Fishing Boats in Dieppe* - PARIS (Mus. du Petit Palais): *Landing Oysters in Cancale*.

AUCTION RECORDS:
PARIS, 26 March 1896, *Quay in Bordeaux*, FRF 220; *Escaut river, Anvers*, FRF 205. PARIS, 17 June 1902, *Garonne River, Bordeaux*, FRF 115. PARIS, 3 Nov 1923, *Landscape*, FRF 390. PARIS, 28 Jan 1924, *Seascape: Fishing Boats and Steamer*, FRF 70. PARIS, 20 Nov 1925, *Port*, FRF 300. PARIS, 11 June 1926, *Port*, FRF 160; *Saltworks*, FRF 185. PARIS, 7-8 June 1927, *Seascape*, FRF 200. PARIS, 5 May 1928, *Flotilla of Fishing Boats*, FRF 105. PARIS, 23 May 1941, *Yachts at Sea*, FRF 320. PARIS, 9 and 10 June 1941, *Yachts*, FRF 480. PARIS, 4 Dec 1941, *Marshes*, FRF 3,000. PARIS, 8 Dec 1941, *Yachts*, FRF 600. PARIS, 15 Jan 1943, *Oyster Fishing*, FRF 1,450. PARIS, 8 March 1943, *Boats at Sea*, FRF 1,400. PARIS, 12 May 1944, *Port at Low Tide*, FRF 2,500. PARIS, 4 Dec 1944, *Port at Low Tide*, FRF 3,700. PARIS, 12 March 1945, *Port at Low Tide: Seascape*, FRF 750. PARIS, 20 July 1945, *Seascape*, FRF 1,050. PARIS, 11 Dec 1946, *Seascape*, FRF 620. PARIS, 26 Feb 1947, *Wave*, FRF 1,200. PARIS, 24 March 1947, *Dutch Landscape*, FRF 1,300. PARIS, 13 June 1947, *Grounded Boats*, FRF 450. VERSAILLES, 28 June 1981, *Normandy Coast* (oil on panel, 13 1/2 x 22 ins / 34 x 56 cm) FRF 5,500. LONDON, 28 June 1983, *The Seine* (oil on canvas, 20 1/2 x 32 1/4 ins / 52 x 82 cm) GBP 800. DETROIT, 21 March 1987, *Flotilla of Fishing Boats* (oil on panel, 17 1/2 x 22 ins / 44.5 x 56 cm) USD 1,600. VERSAILLES, 5 March 1989, *Port at Low Tide* (oil on panel, 11 1/4 x 15 1/4 ins / 28.5 x 39 cm) FRF 9,800. CALAIS, 4 July 1999, *Sailing Ships in the Harbour* (oil on panel, 18 x 22 ins / 45 x 55 cm) FRF 17,000. NEW YORK, 13 Sept 2000, *Coastal Landscape* (oil on canvas, 17 x 28 ins / 42 x 70 cm) USD 3,200.

FLAMENQ, Jean
French, 15th century.
Born in Toulon.
Sculptor (wood).

In 1426, Flamenq was commissioned to produce various pieces of work for the convent of St-Maximin (Var). It appears that he and another sculptor called Antonelle Gervaut carved the choir stalls that formerly embellished the church, along with other commissions.

FLAMENT (Mlle)
French, 19th century.
Painter, watercolourist.

Flament exhibited *Study of Dahlias* and *Study of Geraniums* at the Salon in 1835, and *Vase Filled with Flowers* in 1836.

FLAMENT, Édouard Casimir Arthur
French, 19th century.
Born during the second half of the 19th century, in Wavain.
Painter.

Édouard Flament first exhibited at the Salon des Artistes Français in 1903.

FLAMENT, Ernest Hippolyte
French, 19th century.
Born 19th century, in Paris.
Painter.

Ernest Flament was a pupil of Lucas and attended the École des Gobelins. He exhibited portraits and still-lifes at the Salon from 1870 to 1880.

FLAMENT, Guérard, or Flameng
French, 16th century.
Active in Cambrai in 1578.
Painter.

FLAMENT, Marc
French, 20th century.
Born 1929, in Bordeaux.
Painter.

Marc Flament was a photographer, writer and film director before turning to painting. He studied at the École des Beaux-Arts.

In colourful, bold strokes he aims to account for excess and 'permanent one-upmanship'.

AUCTION RECORDS:
PARIS, 15 Oct 1990, *Tall Blue Lavender* (acrylic/card, 48 x 35 3/4 ins / 121 x 91 cm) FRF 4,100; *Water Lilies: Homage to Monet* (acrylic/canvas, 39 1/4 x 32 ins / 100 x 81 cm) FRF 3,300.

FLAMENT, Pierre Joseph
French, 18th century.
Active in Arras.
Sculptor (wood).

Pierre Flament executed the stalls of the church of the abbey of Hénin-Liétard around 1785.

FLAMET, Eugène Jacques Marie
French, 19th century.
Born in Paris; died 1887, in Paris.
Engraver.

Flamet was a pupil of P. Delaroche and A. Martinet. He exhibited at the Paris Salon from 1842 to 1877.

FLAMINIO, Lucca
19th century.
Sculptor.

MUSEUMS AND GALLERIES:
MELBOURNE: *La Puberta* (*Puberty*).

AUCTION RECORDS:
MELBOURNE, 30 June 1987, *La Puberta* (*Puberty*) (1866, white marble, h. 26 1/2 ins / 67 cm) AUD 4,200.

FLAMM, Albert
German, 19th - 20th century.
Born 9 April 1823, in Cologne; died 28 March 1906, in Düsseldorf.
Painter, engraver. Landscapes.

Albert Flamm was a student at the Kunstakademie in Düsseldorf, and the pupil of Andreas Achenbach. He made study trips to Italy with Oswald Achenbach, then lived in Düsseldorf. He was awarded an honourable mention in 1863. He executed lithographs.

MUSEUMS AND GALLERIES:
DÜSSELDORF: *Italian Landscape*.

AUCTION RECORDS:
COLOGNE, 21 April 1967, *The Bay of Naples,* DEM 4,800. COLOGNE, 15 March 1968, *Landscape in Italy,* DEM 7,500. COLOGNE, 6 June 1973, *View of the Countryside around Rome,* DEM 7,500. COLOGNE, 26 March 1976, *Seaside* (oil on canvas, 29½ x 46 ins / 75 x 116 cm) DEM 28,000. COLOGNE, 23 Nov 1978, *Landscape in the Area around Rome* (oil on canvas, 26½ x 37¼ ins / 67.5 x 94.5 cm) DEM 13,000. LONDON, 25 March 1981, *Peasants beside the Sea* (1863, oil on canvas, 24 x 34¾ ins / 61 x 88.5 cm) GBP 2,800. LONDON, 11 May 1984, *Beside the Mediterranean* (oil on canvas, 31¼ x 41 ins / 79.4 x 104.2 cm) GBP 2,600. VIENNA, 22 Jan 1986, *Livestock beside a River* (oil on panel, 11½ x 28 ins / 29 x 71 cm) ATS 30,000. NEW YORK, 22 May 1990, *Figures on a Beach* (oil on canvas, 21¾ x 42¼ ins / 55.2 x 107.3 cm) USD 22,000. PARIS, 6 Dec 1990, *A Ship and an English Frigate Putting in to Naples* (lead pencil and chalk, 6 x 9 ins / 15 x 23 cm) FRF 3,800. MUNICH, 2 Dec 1997, *Landscape with a Roman Triumphal Arch* (oil on canvas, 25½ x 17¼ ins / 64.5 x 43.5 cm) DEM 13,800.

FLAMM, Carl
German, 20th century.
Born 14 May 1870, in Düsseldorf; died 9 September 1914, in Bonn.
Painter.

Carl Flamm was the son of Albert Flamm, and the pupil of F. Brütt in Düsseldorf. He is known to have painted the *Portrait of Emperor William II* at the Town Hall in Remscheid.

FLAMME, Jacques
French, 18th century.
Active in Paris c. 1730.
Painter (?), sculptor (?).

FLAMOND, Alexandre
French, 17th century.
Active in Paris in 1675.
Painter, sculptor.

FLANAGAN, Barry
British, 20th century.
Born 1941, in Prestatyn, Wales.
Sculptor, installation artist, draughtsman, engraver.
Animals. Monuments.
New Image (related to).

Barry Flanagan originally studied architecture at Birmingham College of Art before working in a variety of occupations. He then studied at St Martin's in London, where his teachers included Anthony Caro. He graduated in 1966. In 1973 he travelled in Italy. Flanagan lives in Daventry, Northamptonshire. He is a conceptual artist who works with materials such as canvas, sand, rope, glass and plaster, creating environments in galleries or using less confined outdoor spaces, such as beaches and the natural materials found there. In 1969, he created *Hole in the Sea* by placing a transparent, hollow cylinder on the sand at low tide. Other works dating from this period include: *Stand Muslin 2,* 1966; *Four Caps 2, Ring L1, Rope, gr 2 sp 606,* 1967; and *Pile 2' 68''*, 1968.

Commenting on his work of the 1970s Flanagan stated that one rarely succeeds in getting things to reveal themselves to the sculptural consciousness. It is the consciousness that reveals itself, not the agents of the sculptural phenomenon. In this sense, his work bears similarities with Arte Povera. From 1973, Flanagan began producing pieces in stone and bronze. It is the relationship between the intrinsic qualities of the matter and its forms that appears to interest him, more the object to be defined than the showing of it in a specially adapted space, as compared with his earlier work. He carves and chisels stone but takes care to leave part of it in its raw state, inscribing it with marks so that the whole suggests an animal's head or a body in convulsions. However, some of his pieces are formally different in origin. In these, Flanagan uses clay, which he shapes and squeezes between his hands to form a model for a stonecarver to produce on a larger scale. From 1978, he produced hares, moulding bronzes of varying sizes, some gigantic. Flanagan explored an analogy between the hare and human behaviour. This series includes pieces showing these animals as *The Cricketer, Boxers,* etc. As well as enormous hares standing up on their hind legs, Flanagan has produced other animals such as a baby elephant on an extraordinary scale. Multi-talented, he also draws delicate nudes and sculpts busts of his friends (Paul Potts, for example) in a highly classical technique and style. He has produced some monumental works, including one for the Rawlings School in Leicestershire entitled *Portoro 1,* as well as in Ghent, Venice, New York and in Victoria Plaza in London. He practised engraving in 1970 and has also made films and created choreographed performances (1973) and pottery (1974).

A pataphysician, Flanagan is a follower of Alfred Jarry and a friend of many poets. Unconstrained by any adherence to a particular kind of art, he has succeeded in producing work of varied form and substance which defies categorisation and which reflects his enjoyment in scoffing at manifest meaning in favour of a playful, imaginary and poetic sense.

He has taken part in major group exhibitions, including: in 1965, *Between Poetry and Painting* at the Institute of Contemporary Art (ICA), London; in 1966, *New Dimensions* at Camden Art Centre, London; in 1967, the Paris Biennale exhibition and the Tokyo Biennale; in 1967, *British Drawings: The New Generation,* at the Museum of Modern Art, New York; in 1968, *Young British Artists,* at the Museum of Modern Art, New York; in 1968, *Situaties en Cryptostructuren* at the Stedelijk Museum, Amsterdam; in 1968, *When Attitudes become Form* at the Kunsthalle, Bern; in 1968, *Nine Young Artists* at the Guggenheim Museum, New York; in 1970, the Tokyo Biennale; in 1970, *British Sculpture out of the Sixties* at the ICA, London; in 1971, *British Avant-garde,* New York; 1973, *11 Englische Zeichner* (*11 English Draughtsmen*) at the Staatliche Kunsthalle, Baden-Baden; in 1974, *Critics Choice* at Tooths Gallery, New York; in 1975, *From Britain '75* at the Taidhalli, Helsinki; in 1975, the Paris Biennale exhibition; in 1982, the Venice Biennale, at which he represented Britain; in 1991, *De Quelques Grands États de la Gravure Contemporaine (1945-1991)* at the Centre d'Art, Ivry; in 1996, *Un Siècle de Sculpture Anglaise* (*A century of English Sculpture*) at the Galerie Nationale du Jeu de Paume, Paris; in 2002, *Les Années 70: l'Art en Cause* (*The 1970s: Art in Question*) at the Capc-Musée d'Art Contemporain, Bordeaux; and in 2003, *Esprit des Lieux* (*The Spirit of Places*), on contemporary art and its exhibition space, an exhibition organised as part of the event *Trésors Publics, 20 Ans de Création dans les Fonds Régionaux d'Art Contemporain (FRAC)* (*Public Treasury, 20 Years of Creation in the Regional Collection of Contemporary Art (FRAC)*) event, at the Palais des Papes, Avignon.

Flanagan has also shown his work in numerous solo exhibitions: in 1966, 1968 and 1969-1974 at the Rowan Gallery, London; in 1974 at the Museum of Modern Art in New York and at the Museum of Modern Art in Oxford; in 1983 at the Musée National d'Art Modern, Paris; at the Pace Gallery, New York; at the Whitechapel Art Gallery, London; in 1983 at the Syracuse Centre for Contemporary Art; in 1986 at the Tate Gallery, London; in 1992 at the Galerie Durand-Dessert, Paris; in 1993 at the Musée des Beaux-Arts, Nantes; in 1996, a collection of engravings at the Bibliothèque Nationale, Paris; in 1997, drawings and engravings at the Tecla Sala, contemporary art centre, Barcelona; in 2002, *L'Oeuvre Gravé de Barry Flanagan* (*Engraved Works of Barry Flanagan*) at the Louis Nucéra Library, Nice, and *Barry Flanagan: Sculpture et Dessin* (*Barry Flanagan: Sculpture and Draw-*

ings) at the Musée d'Art Moderne et d'Art Contemporain, Nice.

BIBLIOGRAPHY:

'*Eye-Liner-Some Leaves from Barry's Flanagan Notebook*' in *Art and Artists*, periodical, Praeger, London, April, 1968. Harrison, Charles, '*Barry Flanagan's Sculpture*' in *Studio International*, periodical, London, May, 1968. Vaizey, Marina, '*Barry Flanagan*' in *Arts review*, periodical, London, April, 1971. Parent, Béatrice, '*Land Art*' in *Opus international*, periodical, Paris, April 1971. *IXe Biennale de Paris*, exhibition catalogue, Idea Books, Musée d'Art Moderne de la Ville de Paris, Paris, 1975. *Barry Flanagan*, Éd. du Centre Georges-Pompidou, Paris, 1983. Borer, Alain, '*Flanagan l'insaisissable*' in *Artstudio* n° 3, periodical, Gal. Templon, Paris, winter 1986-1987. *Barry Flanagan: a Visual Invitation: Sculpture 1967-1987*, Laing Art Gall., Newcastle, 1987. Barker, Barry, '*Réflexions sur les dernières sculptures de Barry Flanagan*' in *Artstudio* n° 10, periodical, Gal. Templon, Paris, autumn 1988. Zahm, Olivier (preface), et al., *Trésors publics, 20 ans de création dans les Fonds régionaux d'art contemporain*, Flammarion, Paris, 2003 (text in French and English).

MUSEUMS AND GALLERIES:

AMSTERDAM (Stedelijk Mus.) - LONDON (Arts Council Collection, Hayward Gal.) - LONDON (British Council): *Hole in the Sea* (1967-1970, two works); *Moon Thatch* (1978, steel); *Untitled* (1982, marble); *Cricketer* (1981, bronze); *Large Mirror Nijinski* (1992, bronze, in two parts) - LONDON (Contemporary Art Society) - LONDON (Tate Collection): *aaing j gni aa* (1965, mixed media); *Four Casb 2 '67* (1967, canvas and sand); *Sixties' Dish* (1970, mixed media); *A Nose in Repose* (1977, stone and wood); *Carving No. 2* (1981, marble); other sculptures, large collection of prints - LYONS (FRAC Rhône-Alpes): *Elephant* (1981) - NEW YORK (MoMA): *Vessel in Memoriam* (1980) - NÎMES (Carré d'Art, MAC) - OTTAWA (NG. of Canada) - PARIS (MNAM-CCI): *Casb* (1967) - ST-ÉTIENNE: *Pile 2'68''* (1968).

AUCTION RECORDS:

LONDON, 4 Dec 1984, *Acrobats* (1981, bronze, h. 66 1/4 ins / 168 cm) GBP 22,000. LONDON, 5 Dec 1986, *Large Leaping Hare* (1982, iron and bronze, green patina, 96 x 68 3/4 ins / 244 x 174.5 cm) GBP 45,000. NEW YORK, 3 May 1989, *Bolster* (jute sacking, straw and painted aluminium, 30 x 69 x 121 ins / 76.2 x 175.3 x 307.3 cm) USD 26,400. LONDON, 29 June 1989, *Founders' Tree* (bronze, h. 12 1/2 ins / 32 cm) GBP 3,080. PARIS, 8 Oct 1989, *Toothpick* (1988, acrylic/plates of glass, 4 x 7 3/4 ins / 10 x 20 cm) FRF 11,000. NEW YORK, 27 Feb 1992, *Elephant* (1981, bronze, 24 1/4 x 16 1/2 x 11 ins / 61.6 x 41.9 x 27.9 cm) USD 38,500. NEW YORK, 5 May 1992, *Acrobats* (1988, bronze, 120 x 37 x 25 3/4 ins / 304.8 x 94 x 65.4 cm) USD 93,500. LONDON, 2 July 1992, *Leaping Hare on Crescent and Bell* (1983, bronze, 45 3/4 x 23 1/2 ins / 116.5 x 60 cm) GBP 57,200. NEW YORK, 18 Nov 1992, *Plant 5* (1971, sacking, untreated wool, sand and resin, h. 50 ins / 127 cm) USD 7,150. NEW YORK, 19 Nov 1992, *Boxing Hare on Anvil* (bronze, 85 3/4 x 48 1/2 x 18 ins / 218 x 123.5 x 46 cm) USD 110,000. LONDON, 3 Dec 1992, *Hare with Drum* (1983, bronze, h. 33 1/4 ins / 84.5 cm) GBP 35,200. NEW YORK, 3 May 1993, *Hare on Pyramid* (bronze, 80 1/4 x 76 x 18 ins / 203.8 x 193 x 45.7 cm) USD 107,000. LONDON, 30 June 1994, *Hare and Vase* (bronze and ceramic, 34 3/4 x 18 3/4 x 9 1/2 ins / 88.3 x 47.9 x 24.1 cm) GBP 20,125. PARIS, 17 Oct 1994, *Untitled* (1986, earthenware, raku technique, 12 1/4 x 8 1/2 x 5 1/2 ins / 31 x 21.5 x 14 cm) FRF 7,500. LONDON, 27 June 1996, *Boxers* (1989, bronze, 110 x 43 1/2 x 100 ins / 279.5 x 110.8 x 254 cm) GBP 194,000. LONDON, 23 Oct 1996, *Hare and Bell* (1981, brown-patinated bronze, 51 1/2 x 37 1/2 x 24 ins / 130.8 x 95 x 61 cm) GBP 54,300. LONDON, 30 May 1997, *Hare on a Pyramid* (1988, black-patinated bronze, 80 1/4 x 74 1/2 x 18 ins / 204 x 189.2 x 45.7 cm) GBP 87,300. LONDON, 25 June 1997, *Nijinsky Hare* (1989, brown-patinated bronze, 94 1/2 x 45 1/4 x 29 1/2 ins / 240 x 115 x 75 cm) GBP 139,000. LONDON, 29 June 1999, *Hare Bell on Portland Stone Piers* (1983, bronze and stone, 96 x 112x75 ins / 243 x 284x191 cm) GBP 150,000. LONDON, 9 Dec 1999, *Gender I. Gender II* (bronze, a pair, 68 x 43x24 ins / 173 x 108x61 cm) GBP 200,000. NEW YORK, 16 May 2000, *Small Nijinski Hare* (1989-1990, bronze, 67 x 35x23 ins / 169 x 89x58 cm) USD 240,000. LONDON, 29 June 2000, *Drummer* (bronze, 96 x 68x36 ins / 244 x 173x91 cm) GBP 220,000. NEW YORK, 18 May 2001, *Hare on Curly Bell* (1980, bronze, 37 x 36x20 ins / 93 x 91x51 cm) USD 100,000. LONDON, 27 June 2001, *Elephant with Tusks and Nijinski Hare* (1996, bronze, 68 x 43x24 ins / 173 x 108x61 cm) GBP 90,000. NEW YORK, 15 May 2002, *Empire State with Bowler, Mirrored* (1997, bronze, two elements, 91 x 17x20 ins / 230 x 44x51 cm) USD 160,000. LONDON, 26 June 2002, *Large Boxing Hare on Anvil* (bronze, 86 x 48x19 ins / 219 x 123x47 cm) GBP 170,000. LONDON, 6 Feb 2003, *Boxing Hare on Anvil* (1989, bronze, 120 x 71x30 ins / 304 x 180x77 cm) GBP 260,000. LONDON, 26 June 2003, *Hare and Bell* (1981, brown patinated bronze, 52 x 37x24 ins / 131 x 95x61 cm) GBP 80,000. LONDON, 4 Feb 2004, *Nijinski Hares on Globe Form* (brown patinated bronze, two works, 65 x 20x21 ins / 164 x 51x53 cm) GBP 130,000. LONDON, 23 June 2004, *Drummer* (1989-1990, bronze, 96 x 68x36 ins / 244 x 173x91 cm) GBP 140,000.

FLANAGAN, John
American, 20th century.
Born 1865, in Newark (New Jersey); died 1952.
Sculptor, medallist.

John Flanagan was a pupil of Bartlett in Boston, St-Gaudens in New York and Falguière at the École des Beaux-Arts, Paris. Honoured in America, where he was a member of many art associations, he often exhibited in France. In addition to distinctions awarded him in the USA, he was made a Chevalier of the Légion d'Honneur in 1927 and won a silver medal at the Paris Exposition Universelle of 1900.

Apart from his sculptural works, such as *Aphrodite* for the Knickerbocker Hotel, New York, he became well-known as a sculptor of medals, many of which are to be found in European and American museums. He designed the Verdun medal that the USA donated to the town, and in 1932 the 'George Washington' silver quarter, the design still in circulation. Despite similarities, he does not seem to be the same artist as John Bernard Flannagan.

AUCTION RECORDS:

NEW YORK, 19 May 1966, *Negro Head* (black granite) USD 4,000.

FLANDEREISEN, Hans, real name: Schmid
German, 16th century.
Active in Leipzig (Saxony) c. 1580.
Sculptor (wood).

Flandereisen's works can be found in several churches in Leipzig.

FLANDERS, Dennis
British, 20th century.
Born 2 July 1915; died 1994.
Draughtsman.

After studying art, Dennis Flanders exhibited at the Royal Academy in London. His drawings were published in many English newspapers.

FLANDERS, Marguerite
British, 20th century.
Born in London.
Miniaturist.

Marguerite Flanders exhibited at the Salon des Artistes Français in Paris in 1932.

FLANDES, de. See first name

FLANDIN, Denise
French, 20th century.

Born in Paris.
Painter. Landscapes.
Denise Flandin exhibited at the Salon des Indépendants in 1935.

FLANDIN, Eugène Napoléon
French, 19th century.
Born 1809, in Naples, to French parents; died 1876, in Paris.
Painter, watercolourist, draughtsman. History painting, portraits, genre scenes, local scenes, landscapes with figures, urban landscapes.
Orientalism.

Flandin was a pupil of Horace Vernet. He accompanied the French army in its campaign in Algeria in 1837. In 1840, he was sent by the Institute on a mission to Persia. He was accompanied by the architect and painter Pascal Coste and together they produced an inventory of the ancient and modern monuments. They visited Hamadan, Kirmanshah and Esfahan and other further regions, such as Shiraz and Persepolis, finally travelling home through Mosul, Aleppo and Constantinople. Flandin returned to the Middle East in 1844, this time to Mesopotamia.

Flandin exhibited at the Paris Salon, receiving a second-class medal in 1837. He was awarded the Légion d'Honneur in 1842.

His early works depict the region of his birth. He painted views of monuments, landscapes, genre scenes and portraits, including *View of the Piazzetta and the Palazzo Ducale in Venice, Bridge of Sighs, Naples Beach, Portrait of Young Girl from Naples on a White Background.*

Flandin made various albums during his many journeys. On his return from his first trip to the Middle East, he produced a personal account of his travels in the form of a six-volume album, in collaboration with Pascal Coste; during his second journey, he drew sculptures and low reliefs discovered on the site of Kuyunjik in Nineveh. These drawings were published in 1850 in *Monument de Ninive* (*Nineveh Monument*). He also published *L'Orient* (*The East*) in 1856 in four volumes. He painted oils from some plates from this publication. In 1864 he published *Histoire des Chevaliers de Rhodes (History of the Knights of Rhodes)*. He was inspired by his numerous voyages and mainly painted pictures in an oriental style, as well as views of towns and architecture, in which he emphasised the documentary aspect over the anecdotal character. Works include *Esfahan, Entrance to the Grand Mosque in the Square of Shah Abbas, Constantine, Assault on 13 October 1837, Interior of Breach Battery, Interior of Tehran Bazaar, Around the Grand Mosque, Constantinople.*

BIBLIOGRAPHY:
Thornton, Lynne, *The Orientalists, Painter-Travellers,*, ACR, Paris, 1983.

MUSEUMS AND GALLERIES:
AUCH: *Bridge of Sighs, Venice* - CAEN: *Interior of Studio* - LA ROCHE-SUR-YON: *Entrance to Venetian Vaults* - LILLE: *View at Tripoli, Syria* - MARSEILLES: *View of Baghdad* - ROUEN: *View of Athens* - VERSAILLES: *French Army Entering Algiers on 5 July 1830.*

AUCTION RECORDS:
PARIS, 23 Feb 1891, *View of the East,* FRF 90. PARIS, 22 March 1924, *Prayer Time in the East* (watercolour) FRF 40. PARIS, 11-12 Dec 1924, *Arab Festival Attended by Many People,* FRF 400. PARIS, 17 Nov 1941, *View of Rhodes* (1843) FRF 1,150. PARIS, 15 Oct 1942, *View of the East* (1831) FRF 1,950. PARIS, 29-30 March 1943, *Eastern Town with Mosque* (watercolour heightened with gouache) FRF 1,200; *Dance for the Sultan* (watercolour and gouache) FRF 1,200. VERSAILLES, 15 Dec 1968, *Mosque* (oil on canvas, 18 x 15 1/4 ins / 46 x 39 cm) FRF 500. LONDON, 10 Feb 1977, *Royal Mosque in Esfahan* (c. 1840, oil on canvas, 49 1/2 x 78 3/4 ins / 126 x 200 cm) GBP 21,000. LONDON, 20 March 1981, *View of the Middle-East* (1837, oil on canvas, 35 3/4 x 52 3/4 ins / 90.7 x 134 cm) GBP 4,000. PARIS, 15 Feb 1983, *Caravan in the Desert* (gouache, 10 1/4 x 18 3/4 ins / 26 x 47.5 cm) FRF 22,500. COMPIÈGNE, 24 Feb 1985, *View of Constantinople* (oil on canvas, 9 x 15 ins / 22 x 38 cm) FRF 35,500. LONDON, 30 March 1990, *Ablutions* (1857, oil on canvas, 18 1/4 x 15 ins / 46.3 x 38.1 cm) GBP 13,200. AMSTERDAM, 24 April 1991, *Route of La Fa Kieh to Tripoli* (watercolour and gouache heightened with white/paper, 10 1/2 x 19 ins / 26.5 x 48 cm) NLG 4,600. PARIS, 21 Oct 1992, *Interior of Venetian Church* (watercolour, 10 1/4 x 8 ins / 26 x 20.5 cm) FRF 5,500. PARIS, 19 Nov 1992, *Mosque Entrance* (charcoal heightened with chalk/blue paper, 15 1/4 x 11 3/4 ins / 39 x 30 cm) FRF 4,000. PARIS, 27 May 1993, *Portrait of Young Neapolitan Girl against White Background* (1835, oil on canvas, 14 x 11 ins / 35.5 x 27 cm) FRF 17,000. LONDON, 11 Feb 1994, *Eastern Musicians in an Interior* (1852, pencil and watercolour/paper, 7 3/4 x 6 1/4 ins / 19.7 x 16 cm) GBP 1,150. PARIS, 22 May 1994, *View of Veracruz* (1839, graphite, black chalk heightened with white, 11 3/4 x 21 1/4 ins / 30 x 54 cm) FRF 6,800. LONDON, 16 Nov 1994, *View of Scutari from the Bosphorus* (watercolour, 20 x 14 1/2 ins / 50.5 x 37 cm) GBP 5,750. PARIS, 25 June 1996, *Tripoli Mosque, Syria* (1841, oil on panel, 7 3/4 x 11 1/2 ins / 20 x 29 cm) FRF 80,000. LONDON, 22 Sept 2000, *The Doge's Palace, Venice* (1836, oil on canvas, 20 x 32 ins / 51 x 82 cm) GBP 15,000. VERSAILLES, 19 Nov 2000, *Italian View, the Cathedral Square in Como* (1836, oil on canvas, 19 x 26 ins / 47 x 65 cm) FRF 126,000. LONDON, 17 Oct 2001, *Turks Smoking a Hookah* (watercolour over pencil/heightened bodycolour, 10 x 8 ins / 25 x 20 cm) GBP 1,700. PARIS, 23 Oct 2002, *Oriental Street Scene* (watercolour, 14 x 10 ins / 36 x 25 cm) EUR 2,200. NEW YORK, 29 Oct 2003, *Gondolas on the Grand Canal in front of the Doge's Palace, Venice* (1836, oil on canvas, 20 x 32 ins / 51 x 82 cm) USD 38,000.

FLANDIN, Hélène Charles
French, 20th century.
Born in Paris.
Sculptor. Busts.
Hélène Flandin exhibited at the Salon des Indépendants in Paris from 1935 to 1943. She specialised in busts and is remembered for *Marcel Bouteron, Member of the Institute,* heads of children and *Jules Cambon's Dog.*

FLANDIN, Roger
French, 20th century.
Born 21 August 1910, in St-Maur.
Painter. Landscapes, still-lifes.
Roger Flandin studied under Legeult at the École des Arts Décoratifs in Paris and under Dewambez at the École des Beaux-Arts.

FLANDIN, Violette, Mme Pierre Debray
French, 20th century.
Born in Paris.
Painter. Portraits, landscapes.
Violette Flandin showed a landscape and a portrait at the Salon des Indépendants in 1935.

FLANDRE, Charles
French, 20th century.
Painter. Landscapes.
Charles Flandre exhibited at the Salon des Indépendants in 1942 and 1943.

FLANDRIN, François Henri. See **FRANCK Henri**

FLANDRIN, Gilberte
French, 20th century.
Born in Bordeaux.
Painter. Flowers.

Gilberte Flandrin exhibited in Paris at the Salon de la Société Nationale des Beaux-Arts from 1933.

FLANDRIN, Hippolyte Jean
French, 19th century.
Born 23 March 1809, in Lyons; died 21 March 1864, in Rome.
Painter. Religious subjects, portraits.
Lyons School (French Nazarenes).

Hippolyte Jean Flandrin was born into an old Lyons family which had been involved in the textile trade in the 18th century. His own parents were of extremely modest means, however, not least because they had seven children. Three of the children went on to become painters, no doubt with the blessing of Flandrin's father, who had a taste for the arts and was a gifted miniaturist in his own right.

Hippolyte Flandrin's early ambition was to become a painter of military subjects. He studied drawing and painting initially under the sculptor Legendre Héral (a friend of Foyatier) and the animal painter Duclaux, who taught Flandrin how to paint from nature - chiefly horses and dogs. Flandrin went on to study at the École des Beaux-Arts in Lyons, where he received several commendations. At the age of 20, he travelled on foot to Paris in the company of his brother Paul in order to complete his studies. He secured a place in Ingres' atelier, where he was at first astonished by Ingres' teaching methods and style, then captivated by the approach to painting of his mentor and subsequent friend. Flandrin was awarded the Prix de Rome in 1832 and promptly attached himself to the Villa Medici school, in the company of Ambroise Thomas, Oudiné, Simart, the composer Boulanger and the architect Faminet. Flandrin was passionately fond of the Italian countryside and fascinated by the works of Raphael. He was receptive to the counsel of Ingres (who, by 1835, had been appointed principal of the Rome School) but nonetheless determined to develop his own personal style.

As a person, Flandrin emerges as a man of a gentle, not to say melancholy disposition, given to introspection. He was profoundly religious and spontaneously gravitated towards religious themes, as evidenced by two canvases submitted to the Salon, a *St Claire Restoring Sight to the Blind* (awarded a gold medal in 1837) and *Jesus Blessing the Children*. Flandrin returned to France in 1838 and was promptly commissioned to decorate the St John Chapel in the church of St Severinus and, soon afterwards, the sanctuary and Apostles' Chapel in the church of St-Germain-des-Prés. In the latter instance, he demonstrated not only his pronounced Christian sensitivity but also an accomplished mural technique and a remarkable compositional sense, allied to sober colours and clean, almost severe draughtsmanship (*Last Supper, Christ Entering Jerusalem, Ascent to Calvary*). Flandrin went on to paint two admirable series of saints for the two lateral friezes of the church of St-Vincent-de-Paul, subsequently described by Théophile Gautier as a 'Christian Panathenaea', which is to say a Christian version of the ritual procession held in Athens in celebration of the Greek goddess Athene: some 80 individual figures are portrayed on each side of the nave, grouped into twelve celestial choirs comprising the Apostles, martyrs, physicians, and so on. Flandrin was then invited to complete the decoration of St-Germain-des-Prés, where he opted to paint both sides of the nave with a series of 'matching' subjects drawn from the Old and New Testaments in order to illustrate the life of Christ as the fulfilment of an earlier prophesy; thus, *Adam's Transgression* is 'matched' by a *Nativity*, for example, with *Abraham's Sacrifice* juxtaposed with a *Calvary*, and *Jonah's Delivery* 'paired' with a *Resurrection*. This device echoes that of early Christian artists, who used religious illustrations in the service of dogma.

Fandrin was unquestionably France's leading religious painter of the 19th century. At the same time, however, he emerged as an extremely accomplished portraitist; here, too, his excellent draughtsmanship proved crucial, together with an ability to capture the essence of his subjects and translate their 'moral' physiognomy to canvas. He proved particularly adept at the portrayal of young girls and young women, when he invariably succeeded in rendering their ingenuity or their innate dignity. This talent is evidenced in Flandrin's *Portrait of Madame Vinet* and *Young Greek Girl* in the Louvre, or his celebrated *Portrait of Napoleon III* now in Versailles - a portrait that reportedly displeased his model on account of the vague and 'distant' expression on his face, yet faithfully recorded the subject's pensive air.

Flandrin's prolific output over a period of 25 years took its toll: he died at the age of 55 in Rome, where he had gone in a vain bid to find tranquillity. By this time, he had been awarded the Croix de Chevalier (1841) and become an officer of the Légion d'Honneur (1853), and had been elected to the Académie (also 1853). Flandrin attracted many young disciples, among them Elie Delaunay, Alexis Douillard, Blaise Desgoffe, Urbain Bourgeois and Eugène A. Guillon. He married Mlle Ancelot, a cousin of the sculptor Gatteaux, in 1843 and had several children, among them the painter Paul-Hippolyte Flandrin, born in 1856. Flandrin's collected *Letters and Thoughts* were edited by Delaborde and published by Plon in 1865. A biography of Hippolyte Jean Flandrin was written by one of his nephews, Louis Flandrin, and published initially by Laurens in 1902; a second edition was published by Perrin in 1909.

Flandrin exhibited widely and frequently. Among his vast and diverse output, mention should be made of major decorative works and portraits. The former category would include St John's Chapel in the church of St Severinus (1839-1841); Chateau Dampierre (1841); the sanctuary (1842-1846), Apostles' Chapel (1846-1848) and nave (1856-1861) of St-Germain-des-Prés; the church of St Paul, Nmes (1848-1849); the nave of St-Vincent-de-Paul (1849-1853); two figures of *Agriculture and Industry* at the Conservatoire des Arts et Métiers; and decorative work on the church of St-Martin-d'Ainay, in Lyons. Among Flandrin's portraits, major works include *Ambroise Thomas, Oudiné, Debay* (Villa Medici, 1837-1838); *Mlle Paule Baltard* (1839); *Mme Oudiné* (1840 Salon); *Mme Vinet* (1841 Salon, now in the Louvre); *Mlle Delessert* (1843 Salon); *Chaix d'Est Ange, M. Varcotier and Mme Féburier* (1845 Salon); *Mme Régnault; the Countess of Verdun* (1846 Salon); *Mme de Villiers du Terrage; Mme Auvray; Mme Hippolyte Flandrin; Mme de St-Didier* (1849); *Countess Marion* (1852); *M. Marc Séguin* (1855 Salon); *Baroness Fréteau de Pény* (1857); *M. and Mme Thiac; Mme Brolemann* (1855); *Mme Legentil* (1857 Salon); *Baron Fréteau du Pény* (1857); *M. Legentil; M. and Mme Sieyès; Mlle Maison (Baroness Mackau); Young Girl with Carnation* (1859 Salon); *Mlle Duchâtel (Duchess of Trémolle)* and *Prince Napoleon* (1861 Salon); *M. Gatteaux; Count Duchâtel; Count Walewski* (1863); *Casimir Périer; Mme Brame; Mme Anisson-Duperron; Duchess of Ayen; Emperor Napoleon III* (1863 Salon, now in the museum, Versailles), and *M. Say, Baron James de Rothschild* and *M. Marcotti-Genlis* (1863).

Several self-portraits are known, including one in profile painted in Rome in 1837 and now in the possession of the Flandrin family (with a copy preserved in the Villa Medici), a three-quarter length portrait in the Uffizi in Florence (a copy of which is in the possession of the Flandrin family), and a portrait of Flandrin at around 50, also in the family collection, together with a further portrait of Flandrin at his easel.

Among the rest of his work are *Shepherd* (1835); a *St Claire Restoring Sight to the Blind* (Nantes Cathedral, 1836); *Virgil's Shepherds* (1837); *St Louis Drafting the Ordinances* (Senate, 1842); *St Louis and the True Cross* (cartoon for stained glass window, Chapel of Dreux); *Mater Dolorosa* (church of St-Martory, near St-Gaudens, Haute-Garonne, 1845); *Napoleon I as a Legislator* (1847, burned in the Council of State fire); *Republic* (1848); four medallions for the *Cradle of the Prince Emperor* (1856); and a study of a *Young Woman* (1854).

Stamp of sale

Bibliography:

Bournand, F., *Trois artistes chrétiens: Michel-Ange, Raphael et Hippolyte Flandrin*, Paris, 1892. Masson, L., *Hippolyte Flandrin*, Paris, 1900. Foucart, J./Foucart, B., et al., *Hippolyte, Auguste et Paul Flandrin: Une Fraternité picturale au XIXe siècle*, exhibition catalogue, Musée Luxembourg, Paris, 1984-5.

Museums and Galleries:

Amiens: *Portrait of Napoleon III* (copy) - Angers: *St Claire Restoring Sight to the Blind* (sketch) - Bagnols: *St Peter and St Paul; St Paul on the Road to Damascus* - Calais: *Portrait of Napoleon III* - Florence (Uffizi): *Self-portrait* - Lille: *Diaspora; Samson in Judgement; Baruch the Prophet* - Lisieux: *Jesus Blessing the Little Children* - Lyons: *Dante and Virgil; Euripides* - Lyons (Church of St-Martin-d'Ainay) - Montauban: *Portrait of Ingres; Raphael and La Fornarina* - Nantes (MBA): *La Rêverie (Dreaming); Jeune Fille (Young Girl); Portrait de Napoléon III (Portrait of Napoleon III); Portrait de Mr Michot, directeur des octrois de Nantes (Portrait of Monsieur Michot, Director of Town Dues, Nantes)* - Nantes (MBA, Clarke-de-Feltre Collection): *Jeune Fille (Young Girl)* (1840); *Rêverie (Dreaming)* - Nîmes (Church of St-Paul) - Paris (Church of St-Germain-des-Prés) - Paris (Church of St-Severin) - Paris (Church of St-Vincent-de-Paul) - Paris (ENSBA): *Theseus Recognised by his Father; Copy of a Fragment of Raphael's School of Athens* - Paris (Louvre): *Young Male Nude Sitting beside the Sea; Young Greek Girl; Study; Portrait of a Young Girl; Portrait of Ambroise Thomas; Portrait of Mme Vinet* - Rouen: *Church Interior; Fra Angelico; Dead Christ; Last Supper; Twelve Dignitaries; Head of a Man; Nude Male Torso* - St-Étienne: *Polites Observing the Greeks* - Versailles: *Duchess of Vendome; Marchioness of Lavardin; Cardinal de Tournon; Diane de Poitiers; Emperor Napoleon III.*

Auction records:

Paris, 4-5 Dec 1918, *Penitent* (pencil study) FRF 40. Paris, 30 Nov-2 Dec 1920, *Man with Lance; St Francis of Assisi; Adam and Eve* (three drawings in red chalk) FRF 200; *Blesing of Christ; Study of Young Woman in Drapery; Apostle* (three drawings in red chalk) FRF 100; *Democritus and the Abderites* (pencil) FRF 180. Paris, 19 Feb 1921, *Landscape* (drawing) FRF 215. Paris, 29 April 1921, *Still-life*, FRF 380; *Village Scene in Noailly*, FRF 500. Paris, 26 Feb 1926, *Swing* (pencil) FRF 85. Paris, 19 May 1926, *Orchard*, FRF 1,000. Paris, 20 and 21 April 1932, *Profile Study of Woman in Drapery* (graphite) FRF 45. Paris, 8 March 1974, *Adoration of the Three Kings*, FRF 12,000. New York, 12 May 1978, *Young Woman with Red Shawl* (1834, oil on canvas, 22 x 18 ins / 55 x 46 cm) USD 2,000. Paris, 1 Dec 1983, *Prophet Hoseah* (oil on card, 12 3/4 x 5 ins / 32.5 x 12.5 cm) FRF 11,000. Cologne, 27 March 1987, *Portrait of Young Girl in a Landscape* (oil on canvas, 25 1/2 x 20 1/2 ins / 65 x 52 cm) DEM 5,500. Paris, 20 Jan 1988, *After the Combat* (watercolour, 9 x 12 1/2 ins / 22 x 31.5 cm) FRF 7,800. Paris, 10 Oct 1990, *Rome at Sunset* (watercolour, 3 1/2 x 7 3/4 ins / 9 x 20 cm) FRF 4,800. New York, 26 Oct 1990, *Study of Head of Young Man* (oil on paper/canvas, 16 x 12 ins / 40.6 x 30.5 cm) USD 4,675. Paris, 2 April 1993, *Venus and Psyche* (graphite, study, 10 3/4 x 7 3/4 ins / 27.5 x 20 cm) FRF 5,300. Paris, 4 June 1993, *Head of Pensive Young Woman* (oil on canvas, 15 x 11 1/4 ins / 38.4 x 28.4 cm) FRF 15,000. Paris, 18 Nov 1994, *Night View of Rome, seen from the Villa Medici* (1836, watercolour, 6 x 9 1/2 ins / 15 x 24 cm) FRF 108,000. Paris, 9 Dec 1994, *Dead Christ and an Angel Kneeling before the Instruments of the Passion* (lead pencil and grey wash, 11 1/2 x 9 3/4 ins / 29.5 x 25 cm) FRF 9,500. Paris, 22 Nov 1995, *Full-length Study of Male Nude* (oil on canvas, 32 x 23 1/2 ins / 81 x 60 cm) FRF 13,000. Paris, 28 Feb 1996, *Last Supper* (1852, oil on panel, 22 x 20 1/2 ins / 56 x 52 cm) FRF 61,000. New York, 23 May 1997, *Christ and the Little Children* (oil on canvas, 20 x 24 ins / 50.8 x 61 cm) USD 32,200. Paris, 8 Dec 1997, *Portrait of Saint John the Baptist and Réné d'Assy* (1850, oil on canvas, 52 1/4 x 36 1/2 ins / 133 x 93 cm) FRF 1,090,000. Paris, 23 March 2001, *Study for the Head of St John in 'The Calling of St John'* (1842, oil on paper, 9 x 7 ins / 24 x 18 cm) FRF 75,000. Paris, 16 Nov 2001, *Abraham and Melchizedek* (1859, oil on cardboard, 17 x 16 ins / 44 x 41 cm) FRF 155,000. Paris, 27 June 2002, *The Good Samaritan* (oil on canvas, 8 x 11 ins / 21 x 27 cm) EUR 1,800. Paris, 18 Nov 2002, *David. Jeremiah* (oil on cardboard, a pair, 13 x 5 ins / 32 x 12 cm) EUR 22,000. Paris, 10 Dec 2003, *Head of a Young Man* (oil on paper/canvas, 13 x 11 ins / 32 x 29 cm) EUR 8,500.

FLANDRIN, Jean

French, 17th century.
Active in Nantes.
Painter, glass painter.

FLANDRIN, Jean Baptiste Jacques

French, 18th - 19th century.
Born 1773; died 27 January 1838, in Lyons.
Active in Lyons.
Painter.

Jean Baptiste Jacques Flandrin first specialised in subjects from history and everyday life, then he painted miniature portraits. A double portrait on ivory of a man and a woman is known to be by him. It was exhibited in Berlin in 1906.

FLANDRIN, Jules Léon

French, 20th century.
Born 9 July 1871, in Corenc; died 25 or 27 May 1947, in Paris.
Painter, potter, draughtsman, pastellist, engraver.
Figure compositions, religious subjects, allegorical subjects, mythological subjects, portraits, genre scenes, still-lifes, flowers, landscapes. Designs for tapestries.

At the age of fifteen, Jules Flandrin started an apprenticeship as engraver-lithographer while still studying drawing. In 1893, he obtained a grant from Grenoble Town Council to study at the École des Arts Décoratifs in Paris. He studied under Gustave Moreau, whose studio at the École des Beaux-Arts he also attended. There he met Marquet, Matisse, Rouault and Guérin. He also had contacts with Puvis de Chavannes and became Maurice Denis' friend. In 1895, he met Jacqueline Marval, also a painter, whose life he would share for 35 years. He travelled to Italy at 38, exploring Venice, Florence and Rome. At 43, he saw action in the Somme and Champagne during World War I and drew the *Poilus*, his brothers in arms. In 1919, he opened a tapestry works, which he had to close in 1924. In 1931, he married a pupil, Henriette Deloras. From 1905 he worked on a mural composition, *St Peter; St Paul; Coronation of the Virgin*, for the church of his native Corenc, and in 1924 he painted two huge pieces commemorating the arrival of the Carthusians in the Dauphiné for the church of St Bruno in Grenoble.

In collective exhibitions he showed paintings and lithographs at the Salon du Champ de Mars, Paris, 1896; Salon de la Société Nationale des Beaux-Arts, of which he became an associate member, in 1897; Salon des Artistes Indépendants with the Fauves; Salon d'Automne; London, 1910; and thereafter in a number of cities in Europe and beyond, notably New York. A retrospective of his work was organised in Grenoble in 1972. In 1980, he featured in the exhibition *150 Ans de Peinture Dauphinoise* (*150 Years of Painting from the Dauphiné Region*), at the Château de la Condamine, Mairie de Corenc, and in 1995 in the exhibition *Girot, Marval, Flandrin, Mainssieux*, at the Musée Mainssieux, Vairon (Isère).

His landscapes of his native Dauphiné and Italy demonstrate Maurice Denis' touch. Though in contact with the Fauves he favoured a classical approach, taking his inspiration, he claimed, from nature alone.

JULES FLANDRIN

BIBLIOGRAPHY:

Marval, J., *Les Danseurs de Flandrin*, Paris, 1913. Klingsor, T.L., *Jules Flandrin*, Rue de l'Échelle, Paris, 1923. Wantellet, Maurice, *Deux siècles et plus de peinture dauphinoise*, M. Wantellet, Grenoble, 1987.

MUSEUMS AND GALLERIES:

CHAMBÉRY (MBA): *The Painter with the Chasseurs Alpins; Horsemen in the Woods* - PARIS (MNAM-CCI): *Road to the Grande Chartreuse; By the Fountain, Morning.*

AUCTION RECORDS:

PARIS, 12 Oct 1922, *Landscape*, FRF 1,000. PARIS, 7 April 1924, *Mount Blanc* (drawing) FRF 280; *Russian Dances* (three canvases) FRF 8,500. PARIS, 26 and 27 May 1924, *Mountain by the Lakeside*, FRF 155. PARIS, 4 June 1925, *View of the Dauphiné*, FRF 1,000. PARIS, 2 June 1926, *Vase of Flowers*, FRF 6,000. PARIS, 4 June 1926, *The Captains' House at Corenc*, FRF 525. PARIS, 12 June 1926, *Still-life*, FRF 1,400. PARIS, 27 Oct 1926, *Masked Pierrot*, FRF 150. PARIS, 20 and 21 Dec 1926, *Horseman*, FRF 3,000; *The Bench*, FRF 1,200. PARIS, 7 April 1927, *The Church of Notre-Dame in Paris seen from the Quai St-Michel, Sun Effects*, FRF 5,000. PARIS, 30 and 31 May 1927, *Drac Valley and Mount Aiguille*, FRF 820. PARIS, 26 Nov 1927, *Valley*, FRF 480; *Pasture*, FRF 380. PARIS, 17 May 1929, *The Church of Notre-Dame in Paris and Pont au Double*, FRF 1,610. PARIS, 10 Feb 1932, *Russian Student Sitting in a Café*, FRF 60. PARIS, 12 Feb 1932, *Stroll in the Woods*, FRF 750. PARIS, 13 Feb 1932, *Le golf sur la falaise* FRF 950. PARIS, 27 April 1932, *Pont St-Michel, Paris*, FRF 830. PARIS, 12 Dec 1932, *Ghost of the Rose: the Dream (Nijinsky et Karsavina)*, FRF 16,000. PARIS, 9 June 1933, *Ghost of the Rose*, FRF 1,520. PARIS, 9 June 1933, *Ghost of the Rose*, FRF 1,520. PARIS, 24 Feb 1934, *Taking the Stage*, FRF 105; *Fountain*, FRF 250. PARIS, 26 and 27 Feb 1934, *Cart on the Road on a Road into Town* (pencil drawing with watercolour wash) FRF 170. PARIS, 24 Feb 1936, *Cart with the White Horse, Vicinity of Grenoble, Summer*, FRF 380. PARIS, 8 May 1936, *Ancient Ruins at Taormina*, FRF 60. PARIS, 17 Feb 1937, *Three Dancers*, FRF 300. PARIS, 30 June 1937, *Anemones and Marigolds in a Vase*, FRF 750. PARIS, 1 July 1937, *Dauphiné Landscape*, FRF 220. PARIS, 9 Dec 1940, *Girl from Provence*, FRF 180. PARIS, 5 March 1941, *Girl Drawing*, FRF 820. PARIS, 27 June 1941, *Still-life with Binoculars*, FRF 650. PARIS, 2 March 1942, *Young Cowherd*, FRF 420. PARIS, 19 March 1942, *The River Seine in Paris*, FRF 2,800. PARIS, 1 April 1942, *Garden*, FRF 2,200. PARIS, 24 April 1942, *Mousquetaire*, FRF 320. PARIS, 9 July 1942, *Landscape* (1908, watercolour) FRF 400. PARIS, 15 April 1943, *Seamstress* (1912) FRF 700. PARIS, 16 June 1943, *Portrait* (Indian ink wash) FRF 120. PARIS, 10 Nov 1943, *The River Seine at the Quai des Orfèvres*, FRF 2,800. PARIS, 23 Feb 1945, *Flowers and Fruit on a Window* (1913) FRF 900. PARIS, 9 April 1945, *Dancing Dolls*, FRF 3,000. PARIS, 29 June 1945, *Dauphiné Landscape*, FRF 3,000. PARIS, Oct 1945-July 1946, *Dante and Beatrice in Paradise*, FRF 8,500. PARIS, 26 Dec 1946, *Dauphiné Landscape* (charcoal sketch) FRF 300. PARIS, 26 Feb 1947, *Flowers*, FRF 1,200. PARIS, 25 June 1947, *Dauphiné Landscape* (1918) FRF 5,000. PARIS, 2 July 1947, *Still-life* (flowers) FRF 1,000. VERSAILLES, 12 Dec 1976, *Rome: Piazza del Popolo* (1922, oil on canvas, 30 x 59 ins / 76 x 150 cm) FRF 7,100. GRENOBLE, 12 Dec 1977, *Civita Vecchia* (oil on card, $21\frac{3}{4}$ x $35\frac{1}{2}$ ins / 55.5 x 90 cm) FRF 5,000. GRENOBLE, 18 May 1981, *Rome* (1929, pastel, $14\frac{1}{4}$ x 18 ins / 36 x 46 cm) FRF 3,000. GRENOBLE, 12 Dec 1983, *Corenc: Meadows* (oil on canvas, $38\frac{1}{2}$ x $63\frac{3}{4}$ ins / 98 x 162 cm) FRF 29,500. PARIS, 10 Feb 1986, *Ballet Figure* (oil on canvas, $39\frac{1}{4}$ x $31\frac{1}{2}$ ins / 100 x 80 cm) FRF 24,000. PARIS, 7 Dec 1987, *Paris, the Pont Neuf* (oil on canvas, $23\frac{1}{2}$ x $36\frac{1}{4}$ ins / 60 x 92 cm) FRF 11,100. PARIS, 28 Jan 1988, *Still-life with Apples* (oil on canvas, $9\frac{1}{2}$ x $16\frac{1}{4}$ ins / 24 x 41 cm) FRF 5,000. PARIS, 6 May 1988, *Children on the Terasse* (1910, oil on canvas, 70 x $91\frac{3}{4}$ ins / 178 x 233 cm) FRF 75,000. PARIS, 18 Dec 1989, *Vase of Flowers* (oil on canvas, $25\frac{1}{2}$ x $21\frac{1}{4}$ ins / 65 x 54 cm) FRF 26,000. PARIS, 19 March 1990, *Grape Harvest* (1902, $51\frac{1}{2}$ x $64\frac{1}{4}$ ins / 131 x 163 cm) FRF 131,000. PARIS, 30 Jan 1995, *Orientals: Nijinsky* (oil on canvas, 32 x $25\frac{1}{2}$ ins / 81 x 65 cm) FRF 100,000. PARIS, 11 April 1996, *Vaslav Nijinski and Tamara Karsavina in the Ghost of the Rose* (oil on canvas, $32\frac{1}{4}$ x $39\frac{1}{4}$ ins / 82 x 100 cm) FRF 37,000. PARIS, 28 Nov 1999, *Interior of Notre-Dame de Paris* (oil on canvas, 35 x 46 ins / 89 x 116 cm) FRF 20,000. PARIS, 28 Nov 1999, *View of Florence* (oil on canvas, 30 x 59 ins / 75 x 151 cm) FRF 30,000. CALAIS, 1 July 2001, *Vase of Gladioli* (oil on canvas, 42 x 26 ins / 106 x 65 cm) FRF 33,000. PARIS, 14 Dec 2001, *Belladonna* (oil on canvas, 30 x 53 ins / 75 x 135 cm) FRF 23,000. PARIS, 9 Dec 2002, *Paris, pont St-Michel* (oil on canvas, 24 x 36 ins / 60 x 92 cm) EUR 11,800. PARIS, 23 May 2003, *St Michel Fountain, Paris* (oil on canvas, 38 x 57 ins / 97 x 146 cm) EUR 11,000. PARIS, 10 Dec 2003, *Bouquet in a Blue Vase* (oil on canvas, 26 x 20 ins / 65 x 50 cm) EUR 2,900. PARIS, 14 June 2004, *Country Jaunt* (1902, oil on canvas, 21 x 32 ins / 54 x 81 cm) EUR 3,000.

FLANDRIN, Madeleine Marie Noémie Marthe

French, 20th century.

Born 4 August 1904, in Montgeron.

Painter, sculptor.

Madeleine Flandrin studied under Pierre Laurens from 1926 to 1931 and under Grange. In Paris, she exhibited at the Salon des Artistes Français from 1929 and won numerous awards including the Irma Lukinovic Prize in 1934.

FLANDRIN, Paul Hippolyte

French, 19th - 20th century.

Born 1856, in Paris; died 1921.

Painter.

Paul Flandrin was the son of Jean Hippolyte Flandrin. He was an associate member of the Salon des Artistes Français and received an honourable mention in 1883, a third-class medal in 1890, a bronze medal in 1900 for the Exposition Universelle, second class in 1901, and was declared hors concours.

MUSEUMS AND GALLERIES:

NICE: *Statuette.*

FLANDRIN, Paul Jean

French, 19th century.

Born 28 May 1811, in Lyons; died 8 March 1902, in Paris.
Painter, draughtsman, caricaturist. Religious subjects, portraits.
Lyons School (French Nazarenes).

The younger brother of Hippolyte Flandrin, he first studied drawing and composition in Lyons under the sculptor Legendre Héral and the animal painter Duclaux, then went on to study at the École des Beaux-Arts during Artaud's time as principal there. From 1829 to 1838, Flandrin was in Paris, working alongside his brother in the atelier of Ingres, who regarded Paul Jean as one of his favourite pupils. He spent five years in Italy from 1833 to 1838 and painted a large number of landscapes and urban scenes during that period, chiefly of Rome and the surrounding region. His early work was in the manner of Poussin and showed a major preoccupation with form and style. His first appearance at the Salon (in 1839) saw him awarded a medal. He received the Knight's Cross in 1852, and in the same year married the daughter of his painter friend Alexandre Desgoffe; the couple had four children. He opened a drawing and painting studio for young women which was very popular for the better part of 50 years. He collaborated with his brother Hippolyte on a number of the latter's major works, notably in Nîmes.

Endowed with a singular talent for draughtsmanship, he produced many portraits; some of these were painted, but by far the greater number were drawn. He was also a gifted caricaturist, so much so that Ingres himself collected pieces of his pupil's work.

Paul Flandrin.

Paul Flandrin

BIBLIOGRAPHY:

Bodinier, G., *Un Ami angevin d'Hippolyte et Paul Flandrin: Correspondance de Victor Bodinier avec Hippolyte et Paul*, Angers, 1912. Foucart, J./Foucart, B., et al., *Hippolyte, Auguste et Paul Flandrin: Une Fraternité picturale au XIXe siècle*, exhibition catalogue, Musée Luxembourg, Paris, 1984-5.

MUSEUMS AND GALLERIES:

ANGERS: *Nymph in the Woods; Near Marseilles* - BAGNOLS: *Souvenir of Bas Bréau* - BORDEAUX: *By the Water* - COMPIÈGNE: *In the Woods* - LANGRES: *Gorges in the High Atlas* - LILLE: *Portrait of Fr Lacordaire* - LYONS: *Penitents; Banks of the Rhône; Indian Landscape* - MONTAUBAN: *Landscape; Landscape* - MONTPELLIER: *Hyères Valley; Near Vienna* - NANTES (MBA, Clarke-de-Feltre Collection): *Hippolyte and Paul Flandrin* (1842); *View of Montredon, near Marseilles* (1851); *Duke of Feltre* (drawing) - NICE: *Landscape* - ORLÉANS: *Landscape* - PARIS (Church of St-Severin): *Decorations for the Chapel of the Baptismal Fonts* (1844-1846) - PARIS (Louvre): *View of the Villa Medici* (drawing) - PARIS (MAM): *Portrait of Ambroise Thomas; Exile's Farewells* (1839); *Solitude* - PARIS (Palais de la Chancellerie): *Légion d'honneur Building in St-Denis* - ROUEN: *Statue; Landscape* - VERSAILLES: *Portrait of Hippolyte Flandrin*.

AUCTION RECORDS:

PARIS, 4-5 Dec 1918, *Democritus and the Abderites* (drawing, after the fable by La Fontaine) FRF 95. PARIS, 28 March 1919, *Balustrade with Flowers*, FRF 700; *Perseus of Florence*, FRF 2,000; *Flowers and Fruit*, FRF 1,050. PARIS, 4 and 5 March 1920, *Mist in the Valley*, FRF 740. PARIS, 3-4 June 1920, *Shepherds*, FRF 200. PARIS, 19 Nov 1931, *Portrait* (pencil) FRF 105. LONDON, 7 July 1939, *Brillet de Moncours* (drawing) GBP 11; *Louis Gueuria* (drawing) GBP 11; *Young Man* (drawing) GBP 18. LONDON, 15 May 1942, *Man*, GBP 29. PARIS, 27 Nov 1942, *Greek Shepherds in the Mountains*, FRF 3,800. PARIS, 18 April 1984, *Democritus and the Abderites* (1867, pencil, heightened with white, 10 1/2 x 8 1/2 ins / 26.5 x 21.5 cm) FRF 5,200. CHARTRES, 18 Oct 1987, *Portrait of Louis Jules Delon* (1860, oil on canvas, 38 1/2 x 31 1/2 ins / 98 x 80 cm) FRF 24,500. VERSAILLES, 5 March 1989, *Resting under the Trees by the Lake* (oil on canvas, 11 x 13 3/4 ins / 27 x 35 cm) FRF 29,000. PARIS, 30 June 1989, *Copse in the Grounds of the Villa Borghese, Rome* (oil on canvas, 11 1/2 x 8 1/4 ins / 29 x 21 cm) FRF 19,000. PARIS, 15 May 1992, *Young Woman Seated, Her Torso Nude* (oil on canvas, 13 3/4 x 7 3/4 ins / 35 x 19.5 cm) FRF 8,000. PARIS, 5 Nov 1993, *Caricature of Ingres in Rome* (pen, 9 x 14 ins / 22 x 35.5 cm) FRF 4,800. PARIS, 8 June 1994, *Male Portrait* (1833, lead pencil, 7 1/4 x 5 1/4 ins / 18.7 x 13.2 cm) FRF 12,800. PARIS, 28 June 1995, *Male Head in Profile* (oil on paper, 9 x 6 3/4 ins / 23 x 17 cm) FRF 32,000. LONDON, 21 Nov 1996, *Portrait of a Lady Seated and Holding a Daisy* (1871, pastel, 17 1/4 x 10 ins / 43.8 x 25.7 cm) GBP 4,025. PARIS, 24 March 1999, *Path through Undergrowth with a Young Walker Lying Down* (oil on canvas, 24 x 17 ins / 61 x 44 cm) FRF 30,000. PARIS, 29 March 2000, *La Gassaude* (1859, oil on paper, 10 x 14 ins / 26 x 36 cm) FRF 25,000. PARIS, 16 Dec 2002, *View of Montredon, near Marseilles* (oil on cardboard, 9 x 11 ins / 22 x 27 cm) EUR 3,900. PARIS, 18 Dec 2002, *Landscape, Shepherds Fighting* (1847, oil on canvas, 29 x 39 ins / 74 x 99 cm) EUR 40,500. PARIS, 30 March 2004, *Fontainebleau, the Bas-Breau* (oil/paper on canvas, 14 x 21 ins / 36 x 54 cm) EUR 5,100. PARIS, 1 April 2004, *Garden* (c. 1870, oil/paper on canvas, 9 x 9 ins / 24 x 24 cm) EUR 4,400.

FLANDRIN, Pierre
French, 17th century.
Active in Nantes.
Painter.

FLANDRIN, René Auguste
French, 19th century.
Born 1804, in Lyons; died August 1843, in Lyons.
Painter, lithographer.

The oldest in a family of seven children and brother of Hippolyte and Paul Flandrin, René Auguste Flandrin studied composition and painting at the École des Beaux-Arts in Lyons; he moved to Paris in 1833 to study under Ingres. He declined to travel with his mentor to Rome and remained instead in Lyons, where he began to make a name for himself as an accomplished artist. He died young - at the age of only 38. René Auguste Flandrin's atelier attracted a number of students who went on to make their mark, including Louis Lamothe, Joseph Pagnon, Cabuchet and Chancel. Flandrin was awarded a bronze medal in 1840.

MUSEUMS AND GALLERIES:

LYONS: *Savonarola Preaching in the Church of San Miniato*; several portraits.

FLANDRIN-LATRON, Simone (Mme)
French, 20th century.
Born in Vendôme.
Miniaturist.

Simone Flandrin-Latron studied under Jean-Paul Laurens and Darrois. In 1933 she exhibited at the Salon des Artistes Français, of which she is an associate member.

FLANGER, José. See **FLAUGÉ**

FLANIGEN, Jean Nevitt
American, 20th century.
Born 1898.
Painter.

Jean Nevitt Flanigen became a member of a number of painting associations after his studies.

FLANNAGAN, John Bernard
American, 20th century.

Born 1895, in Fargo (North Dakota); died 6 January 1942.

Sculptor. Figures, animals.

John Bernard Flannagan studied painting at the Minneapolis Institute of Arts 1914 to 1917. He was a friend of Arthur B. Davies, who organised the historic *Armory Show* in New York in 1913. Davies encouraged him to sculpt in wood, which he did from 1922. At this period he lived in extreme poverty, and it was not until 1929 that he was contracted by a New York gallery. After submitting to four trepanations, from 1939 he ceased to use metal, because his health did not allow him to carve directly. He committed suicide in 1942.

From wood-carving he moved to carving stone, a material in which he created a whole inventory of the animal world in an almost naive, even humorous, style. In what is considered his middle period, about 1938, he sculpted *Gold Prospector, White Horse, Lamb* and *Goat* in Alabama stone.

He was an unusual personality in the American artistic life of the inter-war period. His letters were published by the New York art dealer Curt Valentin. Despite similarities, he does not seem to be the same artist as John Flanagan.

BIBLIOGRAPHY:

Miller, Dorothy Canning, *The Sculpture of John B. Flannagan*, exhibition catalogue, Museum of Modern Art, New York, 1942.

MUSEUMS AND GALLERIES:

NEW YORK (Metropolitan Mus. of Art): *Figure of Dignity, Irish Mountain Goat*.

AUCTION RECORDS:

NEW YORK, 21 March 1974, *Snake*, USD 4,000. LOS ANGELES, 9 Nov 1977, *Mother and Child* (bronze, h. 18 1/4 ins / 46.3 cm) USD 2,600. NEW YORK, 21 April 1978, *Figures* (c. 1924-1925, wooden relief, 23 1/4 x 8 1/2 ins / 59 x 21.6 cm) USD 1,200. NEW YORK, 25 Sept 1980, *Colt* (watercolour, 13 1/2 x 6 3/4 ins / 34.2 x 17.4 cm) USD 650. NEW YORK, 4 June 1982, *Nun* (stone, h. 21 ins / 53.3 cm) USD 3,750. NEW YORK, 29 May 1987, *Negro Boy* (stone, h. 28 ins / 71.1 cm) USD 32,000. NEW YORK, 1 Oct 1987, *Nude* (brush and sepia ink, 18 3/4 x 12 1/2 ins / 47.5 x 31.5 cm) USD 2,400. NEW YORK, 17 Dec 1990, *Profile of Paul Wayland Bartlett* (round bronze with brown patina, diam. 12 ins / 30.5 cm) USD 6,600. NEW YORK, 22 May 1991, *Girl with Horse* (1938, Alabama stone) USD 22,000. NEW YORK, 31 March 1993, *Not Yet* (bronze, h. 13 ins / 33 cm) USD 6,325. NEW YORK, 21 Sept 1994, *Mother and Child* (beige stone, h. 15 ins / 38.1 cm) USD 6,900. NEW YORK, 30 Nov 1999, *Snake* (limestone, h. 26 ins / 65 cm) USD 38,000. NEW YORK, 15 June 2000, *Goat* (limestone, h. 9 ins / 23 cm) USD 22,000. NEW YORK, 29 Nov 2000, *Girl and Horse* (limestone, h. 16 ins / 41 cm) USD 22,000. NEW YORK, 21 May 2003, *Figure* (1942, stone, h. 35 ins / 89 cm) USD 19,000. NEW YORK, 21 May 2003, *Standing Child* (c. 1928, brown stone, h. 16 ins / 41 cm) USD 37,500.

FLANNEAU, Léon

French, 19th century.

Born 23 February 1837, in Paris.

Painter.

Exhibited *Bill of Fare* at the 1869 Salon and *Village Inn in Lower Picardy* at the Salon of the following year.

FLASCHNER, Alexander

Hungarian, 20th century.

Born 1903, in Hungary.

Active in France from 1924.

Painter. Landscapes, still-lifes.

In 1919, Alexander Flaschner discovered painting at an exhibition of works confiscated from private collections in Budapest. After attending the school of decorative arts in Vienna, he went to Paris in 1924 and became a student at the Othon Friesz workshop, at the Académie de la Grande Chaumière and the Lucien Simon workshop at the École des Beaux-Arts for four years.

Critics have emphasised the Cézanne connection of his paintings, mediated through Marquet and Friesz in particular. Through Marquet, his landscapes and still-lifes have retained Cézanne's overall simplification of large plans and the contour of volumes. Through Friesz he retained a feeling for wide, greasy brush trails.

Flaschner participated in the Salon d'Automne, Salon des Tuileries and Salon des Artistes Indépendants. Solo exhibitions include: Galerie Jeanne Castel (1937); at the Galerie Bassano (1973); Salon de la Rose-Croix with his sculptor wife and artist daughter (1988); and Galerie Rambaud (1990).

FLASCHNER, Madeleine

French, 20th century.

Painter, engraver, lithographer.

Madeleine Flaschner studied under Édouard Goerg before attending the École des Beaux-Arts in Paris, from 1952 to 1960. She has shown in collective exhibitions, including at the Salon des Artistes Français in Paris, when she won the 1988 Chassériau prize for engraving and a gold medal. She is also an associate member of the Salon d'Automne. She has taken part in the Bayeux Salon de Gravure, carrying off the prize in 1980. She had solo exhibitions in Paris in 1957, 1962 and 1991, and showed engravings and lithographs in Nordholm in 1973.

Expressionist in style, she favours reds lavishly applied against blacks, greens, browns and blues. Skilled in many subjects, she has often painted circus themes and situations, working-class and country scenes.

AUCTION RECORDS:

PARIS, 19 June 1989, *Old Ladies* (oil on canvas, 31 1/2 x 39 1/4 ins / 80 x 100 cm) FRF 4,000.

FLASCONARO, Antonio

Italian, 16th century.

Active in Palermo.

Painter.

FLASHAR, Max

German, 19th - 20th century.

Born 3 July 1855, in Berlin; died 8 June 1915, in Munich.

Painter, illustrator. Portraits, genre scenes.

Max Flashar was a student at the Kunstgewerbeschule in Weimar, where he was the pupil of Kalckreuth, then at the Akademie in Munich, and as a pupil of Knaus at the Akademie in Berlin. He adopted the humorous style in his works, and was a collaborator on the *Fliegende Blätter* in Munich. Amongst his portraits he is remembered for his depictions of the *Prince of Schönburg-Waldenburg* and the *Countess Lazar*

MUSEUMS AND GALLERIES:

HAMBURG (Kunsthalle): *Portrait of the Poet Freiligrath*.

FLASSCHOEN, Gustave

Belgian, 19th - 20th century.

Born 1868, in Brussels; died 1940.

Painter, watercolourist, draughtsman, engraver, illustrator.

Flasschoen was the pupil of Stroobant at the academy in Brussels. He made many trips abroad.

G. Flasschoen

AUCTION RECORDS:

BRUSSELS, 27 Oct 1982, *Return from Fishing, Holland* (watercolour, 37 1/2 x 50 1/2 ins / 95 x 128 cm) BEF 34,000. BRUSSELS, 13 Dec 1984, *Landscape with Mill* (oil on canvas, 30 3/4 x 46 3/4 ins / 78 x 119 cm) BEF 54,000. ANTWERP, 2 Dec 1986, *Before the Storm* (oil on canvas, 21 1/4 x 32 ins / 54 x 81 cm) BEF

260,000. LOKEREN, 5 March 1988, *The Port of Antwerp* (oil on panel, 9½ x 9¾ ins / 24 x 25 cm) BEF 36,000. PARIS, 8 Nov 1989, *The Dutch Women* (oil on panel, 13¾ x 22 ins / 35 x 55 cm) FRF 4,000. BRUSSELS, 19 Dec 1989, *Boats by Moonlight* (oil on canvas, 21¼ x 26 ins / 54 x 66 cm) BEF 58,000. PARIS, 22 June 1990, *Market at Biskra, Algeria* (oil on panel, 12¾ x 15¼ ins / 32.5 x 39 cm) FRF 30,000. PARIS, 16 Nov 1992, *Falconry* (oil on canvas, 43¼ x 39¼ ins / 110 x 100 cm) FRF 48,000. PARIS, 5 April 1993, *Algerian Caïd on Horseback* (oil on panel, 15¾ x 13 ins / 40 x 33 cm) FRF 9,500. AMSTERDAM, 20 April 1993, *View of Cap Ferrat* (oil on canvas, 43½ x 32¾ ins / 110.5 x 83 cm) NLG 5,750. LOKEREN, 15 May 1993, *View of a Port* (oil on canvas, 29¼ x 25½ ins / 74 x 65 cm) BEF 55,000. PARIS, 18 June 1993, *Les Cavaliers de la Fête* (oil on panel, 15¾ x 19¼ ins / 40 x 49 cm) FRF 8,500. PARIS, 8 Nov 1993, *Market at Sidi Okba* (oil on canvas, 23½ x 31½ ins / 60 x 80 cm) FRF 20,000. PARIS, 22 March 1994, *Camel Driver and Palanquin* (oil on canvas, 13¾ x 18 ins / 35 x 46 cm) FRF 15,000. LOKEREN, 10 Dec 1994, *Market at Biskra in Algeria* (oil on card, 8¾ x 9 ins / 22.5 x 23 cm) BEF 26,000. LONDON, 11 Oct 1995, *Arab Horsemen* (oil on panel, 11¾ x 15¾ ins / 30 x 40 cm) GBP 2,070. PARIS, 10-11 April 1997, *Camping Scene* (oil on panel, 14½ x 18 ins / 37 x 46 cm) FRF 8,000. AMSTERDAM, 1 Sept 1999, *Oriental Bazaar* (oil on canvas, 26 x 37 ins / 65 x 93 cm) NLG 6,500. BRUSSELS, 28 Sept 1999, *Fantasia* (oil on canvas, 24 x 31 ins / 60 x 80 cm) BEF 170,000. BRUSSELS, 15 May 2001, *Fantasia* (oil on canvas, 24 x 31 ins / 60 x 80 cm) BEF 310,000. PARIS, 17 Dec 2001, *Souika Street in Constantinople* (oil on canvas, 19 x 31 ins / 48 x 80 cm) FRF 29,000. VIENNA, 16 May 2002, *Cap Ferrat, Cote d'Azur* (oil on canvas, 45 x 34 ins / 114 x 86 cm) EUR 4,000. LOKEREN, 5 Oct 2002, *At the Dance* (oil on canvas, 11 x 15 ins / 29 x 37 cm) EUR 7,000. AMSTERDAM, 1 July 2003, *Old Port* (oil on canvas, 16 x 20 ins / 40 x 50 cm) EUR 4,500. BRUSSELS, 17 Feb 2004, *Fantasia in North Africa* (oil on canvas, 30 x 59 ins / 75 x 150 cm) EUR 9,500. BUENOS AIRES, 1 June 2004, *With the Troop* (oil on canvas, 32 x 39 ins / 81 x 100 cm) USD 37,000.

FLASSE, Edmond
Belgian, 20th century.
Born 23 November 1896; died 1968, in Ukkel.
Painter.

FLATAU, Joanna
Polish, 20th century.
Born in Warsaw.
Active in France from 1971.
Painter, pastel painter.

In 1969 Joanna Flatau graduated from the University and art academy in Warsaw in history of art. She has lived and worked in Paris since 1971.

Primarily a pastel painter, she does not use the medium for its delicacy but to express violence. A painter mainly of faces, she scrutinises their expressions and unceremoniously transcribes them between wild beauty and nasty laughter. She has featured in collective exhibitions including at the Galerie Idées d'artistes, Paris (2003). Solo exhibitions in France and abroad since 1982 include Galerie L'Œil de Bœuf, Paris; Centaur Gallery, London, St-Prex (Switzerland) (1995) and Galerie de l' Ancienne Douane

FLATEN, Arnold
American, 20th century.
Born in Minneapolis.
Sculptor.

Arnold Flaten, a pupil of M.J. Camus, exhibited in Paris at the Salon des Artistes Français in 1932.

FLATHE
German, 18th century.
Painter.

The chapel of the Calvary in Schöntal (Baden-Württemberg), built in 1716, contains frescoes by Flathe in the rotunda.

FLATMAN, Thomas
British, 17th century.
Born 1637, in London; died 1688, in London.
Painter, miniaturist.

Thomas Flatman attended Winchester School before going up to New College, Oxford, where he failed to obtain a degree. He studied for the Bar, but does not seem to have taken up the legal profession. He was a devotee of the arts, and established a reputation as a poet, miniaturist and portrait painter. His miniature self-portrait in the Victoria and Albert Museum, London, is intensely expressive.

MUSEUMS AND GALLERIES:
LONDON (Victoria and Albert Mus.): *Self-portrait* (miniature) - LONDON (Wallace Collection): *Portrait of Charles II*.

FLATTERS, Jean Jacques
French, 19th century.
Born 16 November 1786, in Crevelt; died 19 August 1845, in Paris.
Sculptor.

He enrolled at the École des Beaux-Arts on 15 February 1814 and studied under Houdon. A year previously, Flatters had been awarded a silver medal at the Prix de Rome. He went on to become a Chevalier of the Légion d'Honneur and a member of the Institute. He exhibited on a regular basis at salons between 1810 and 1839. Some of his work is quite remarkable, notably his *Ulysses and Neoptolemus Relieving Philoctetes of the Arms of Hercules*, *Bust of Haydn*, *Bust of Louis XVIII*, a small bronze statue entitled *Sleep*, a marble *Head*, a marble bust of *Duguay-Trouin*, a plaster *Awakening*, *Eve*, a marble bust of *Turenne*, and a bronze version of *Awakening*. Several of his works are housed in collections in London.

MUSEUMS AND GALLERIES:
ARRAS: *Bust of a Young Woman* (marble) - PARIS (Mus. de la Comédie-Française): *Mlle Rose Dupuis* (plaster, bust); *Mlle Duchesnois* (marble, bust); *Young Baptiste* (plaster, bust) - STRASBOURG: *Charles X* (marble, bust) - VALENCIENNES: *Mlle Duchesnois* - VERSAILLES: *Joseph Haydn*; *Marie-Joseph Lafayette*; *Pierre de France, Comte d'Alencon*; *Marshal Strozzi*; *Turenne*; *Count de Brueys of Aigalliers*; *Mazarin*.

FLATTERS, Richard Edmond
German, 19th century.
Born 1822, in Uerdingen (North Rhine-Westphalia); died October 1876, in Bremerhaven (Bremen).
Painter. Genre scenes.

Flatters made his début in the Salon in Paris in 1845, and settled there until 1860.

AUCTION RECORDS:
ROME, 6 June 1984, *Scene from the Revolution of 1848, Paris* (oil on canvas, 32¼ x 26 ins / 82 x 66 cm) ITL 6,000,000. NEW YORK, 19 Jan 1995, *Kittens Playing* (oil on canvas, 32½ x 25¾ ins / 82.6 x 65.4 cm) USD 5,750. COPENHAGEN, 25 Feb 2004, *Interior with Two Women and Cat* (1850, oil on canvas, 25 x 21 ins / 64 x 54 cm) DKK 12,000.

FLATTERY, Ivy Anne
British, 20th century.
Born in London.
Painter.

Ivy Flattery exhibited in Paris at the Salon des Artistes Français from 1928.

FLATTNER, Peter. See **FLOTNER**

FLATZ, Johann Gebhard
Austrian, 19th century.
Born 11 July 1800, in Wolfurt; died 1881, in Bregenz.

Painter, draughtsman. History painting, religious subjects.

Flatz studied under Caucig and Petter at the academy in Vienna. He worked for a long period in Rome.

MUSEUMS AND GALLERIES:

BREGENZ: *St Bonaventure* - INNSBRUCK (Tiroler Landesmus. Ferdinandeum): *Hector and Paris; Fra Angelico at Work Watched Over by St Luke* - VIENNA: *Virgin*.

AUCTION RECORDS:

VIENNA, 26 May 1982, *God the Father* (1880, pencil, 5 1/2 x 8 1/4 ins / 14 x 21 cm) ATS 11,000. LONDON, 22 Nov 1990, *Ecstasy of St Francis* (1864, oil on canvas, 54 x 38 ins / 137 x 96.5 cm) GBP 990.

FLAUBERT, Louis Eugène

French, 20th century.

Born 6 February 1885, in Paris.

Painter.

Louis Flaubert studied at the École des Arts Décoratifs. He showed his work from 1921 at the Salon des Artistes Français (honourable mention in 1926) and at the Salon des Artistes Indépendants.

FLAUBERT, Paul

French, 20th century.

Born 1928.

Painter. Scenes with figures, hunting scenes, landscapes, landscapes with figures, urban landscapes, waterscapes.

AUCTION RECORDS:

TOULOUSE, 14 June 1976, *River Seine in Normandy* (oil on panel, 11 x 15 1/4 ins / 28 x 39 cm) FRF 1,900. ST-BRIEUC, 12 Dec 1982, *The Stroll* (oil on panel, 7 3/4 x 9 1/2 ins / 19.5 x 24 cm) FRF 2,700. NANTERRE, 11 Oct 1987, *The Boulevards* (oil on panel, 20 1/2 x 14 1/2 ins / 52 x 37 cm) FRF 6,000. CALAIS, 3 July 1988, *The Bandstand* (oil on panel, 7 1/2 x 11 ins / 19 x 27 cm) FRF 7,800. PARIS, 19 Jan 1990, *Hunting on Horseback* (oil on panel, 7 x 9 1/2 ins / 18 x 24 cm) FRF 6,000. VERSAILLES, 8 July 1990, *Winter Landscape* (oil on panel, 15 x 18 ins / 38 x 46 cm) FRF 5,700. PARIS, 30 Oct 1990, *Venice, the Grand Canal* (oil on panel, 15 x 17 3/4 ins / 38 x 45 cm) FRF 12,000. RHEIMS, 21 April 1991, *Waterside Pursuits in Autumn* (oil on canvas, 18 x 22 ins / 46 x 55 cm) FRF 20,500. LE TOUQUET, 19 May 1991, *Peopled Beach* (oil on panel, 11 1/2 x 16 1/2 ins / 29 x 42 cm) FRF 13,500. LE TOUQUET, 8 June 1992, *Young Woman in a Garden full of Flowers* (oil on canvas, 18 x 22 ins / 46 x 55 cm) FRF 12,000. MADRID, 24 Jan 2000, *Boats near the Bank* (oil on panel, 9 x 14 ins / 24 x 35 cm) ESP 450,000.

FLAUD, Béatrice

French, 20th - 21st century.

Born 16 December 1946, in Boulogne-sur-Seine.

Painter, watercolourist, engraver, sculptor, art restorer. Figures, landscapes, still-lifes.

Symbolism.

Béatrice Flaud studied history of art at the École du Louvre in Paris, and received a broad artistic education, studying engraving, painting and art restoration.

She employs a classical figurative technique, representing her subjects in a fantastical or symbolist style. *The Pharaoh*, a face partially obscured by a golden mask, is one example of this, as is *Energies*. The latter is the panoramic landscape of a large metropolis, partially hidden by constructions, representing the factories which provide the city with energy.

She has participated in a number of group exhibitions in Paris, including the following: at the Salon des Artistes Français, the Salon des Indépendants (where she is an associate member), and the Salon d'Automne. She also staged a solo exhibition in Paris in 1980, and has taken part in various group exhibitions in the French exhibitions.

FLAUGÉ, José, or Flaugier or Flanger

Spanish, 18th - 19th century.

Born 1760; died 9 March 1812, in Barcelona.

Painter. Religious subjects, battles.

MUSEUMS AND GALLERIES:

BARCELONA (Mus. Nacional d'Art de Catalunya): *Holy Family; Adoration of the Shepherds*; two paintings.

AUCTION RECORDS:

NEW YORK, 28 May 1981, *Battle Scene* (oil on canvas, 28 1/4 x 44 ins / 72 x 112 cm) USD 3,000.

FLAUNET, Eugène Louis

French, 19th century.

Died 1885.

Painter.

Member of the Société des Artistes Français.

FLAUSCH, Fernand

Belgian, 20th - 21st century.

Born 1948, in Liège.

Painter, engraver, sculptor.

Fernand Flausch attended the Académie des Beaux-Arts in Liège. One of his aims is to incorporate art into the environment and notable among his works are the ceiling of the Opéra in Liege (1982), and the Ribaucourt station of the subway of Brussels (1988), where two 65-yard (60-metre)-long paintings face each other across the platforms.

MUSEUMS AND GALLERIES:

LIÈGE - NEW YORK (Metropolitan Mus. of Art).

FLAVELLE, William

Irish, 19th century.

Born c. 1786.

Active in Dublin.

Miniaturist.

An autograph drawing by William Flavelle was the basis for Basire's engraving of a view of Dublin in the *Public Records of Ireland*.

FLAVERI, Flavio de. See **FAVERI**

FLAVET, Claude

French, 20th century.

Born 1940, in Nantes.

Painter.

After 10 years living in Stockholm, Claude Flavet settled in the Savoy by Lake Aiguebellette.

He has had solo exhibitions in Paris in 1962; in Venice and Naples in 1965; in 1966 in Norrkoping and Stockholm; in 1968 at Helsingborgs, Östersunds and Landskrona museums; in 1973 in London; in 1981 and 1984 in Stockholm; in 1982 and 1996 in Grenoble; in 1992 in Los Angeles.

From abstract, his painting has evolved towards a sparse figuration, brightly coloured and lyrical.

FLAVIA, Antonio

Spanish, 17th century.

Born in Catalonia; died 1639, in Salsa.

Painter.

There are some biblical paintings by Antonio Flavia in the church of Salsa.

FLAVIGNY, Henri

Flemish School, 16th century.

Died before 1581.

Active in Antwerp.

Painter.

Henri Flavigny is probably the same person as Herry Flowyn, who in 1538 had J. Cleerbout as a pupil.

FLAVIGNY, Pierre

French, 16th century.

Active in Châlons-sur-Marne (Marne).

Painter.

Pierre was the son of Henri Flavigny and painter to Bishop Cosme-Clausse. It seems likely that the portrait of the bishop in the reception hall at the Commission des Hospices in Châlons-sur-Marne was painted by him.

FLAVIGNY, Robert Constant Jean
French, 20th century.
Born in Elbeuf.
Painter.

Robert Flavigny exhibited at the Salon des Artistes Français in 1924.

FLAVIN, Dan
American, 20th century.
Born 1 April 1933, in Jamaica (New York); died 29 December 1996, in New York.
Sculptor, installation artist, environmental artist, engraver.
Minimal Art.

Dan Flavin entered the Brooklyn Seminary in order to become a priest. He then trained as a meteorologist with the American army in Korea. He subsequently attended the New College of Social Research, New York, in 1956, and the painting classes of Hans Hoffmann (1955-1959), and followed this by art history studies at Columbia University, New York. He lived and worked in Garrison, New York.

Dan Flavin mastered drawing techniques, and began his painting career influenced by Abstract Expressionism and Pop Art. He then worked on his series of *Icons*, square-fronted constructions, dark in colour, the edges surrounded with tapered electric light bulbs - for example, *Icon V* (1962). He aimed to convey a 'plastic rigidity' that contrasted with the recent avatars of Abstract Expressionism. Although he used the term 'icon', it was certainly not in reference to a holy picture, but to the visible production of light. He soon joined the minimalist movement known as Geometric Abstraction. Historically, as he was to point out in some of his writings, Minimalism has its roots in the Constructivist movement of the 1920s in Europe. In the USA it followed, or was contemporary with - depending on which artists are grouped under the word - the abstract radicalism of Ad Rheinhardt, Barnett Newman and Frank Stella. This movement, at first pictorial and then oriented towards objects, eliminates anything that might lead to interpretative illusionism in favour of a single image arranged in accordance with a precise and carefully thought-out scheme. In sculpture, while adhering to formal principles, the elements are often manufactured and modular objects serially produced. It was the aim of the Minimalists to construct three-dimensional works in a search for radical simplicity, but Flavin, a powerful polemicist, rejected any association with ideas of sculpture or works in three dimensions. *Diagonal of May 25, 1963*, a fluorescent tube inclined at 45°, was Flavin's first installation, the point of departure for his future work and the manifesto for him of an art that had no explicit content and no definite subject. Flavin was to produce several versions of the same work, in different colours and different positions, comparing them with Constantin Bracusi's *Endless Column*. He was later to dedicate a series of *Monuments* to Vladimir Tatlin. Rooted in painting, recognising and benefiting from the influence of the work of other artists, Flavin's work can be understood through the many works he dedicated as *Memorials* to his contemporaries or predecessors: Newman, Lichtenstein, Brancusi, Mies van der Rohe, Mondrian, etc.

Flavin's composition is very rigorous. Usually the neon tube is articulated in rectangles with verticals and horizontals, cruciform plans sometimes, more rarely circular. The colour range is simple: blue, red, yellow..., with sometimes subtle variations: pink, greyish-white, gold...It is a 'light-colour'. The interior of the work is created by the beam of light that the neon tube makes in space, and which is repeated on the wall, the floor or the ceiling, as on the rigid shape of the tubes. Grouped in threes or fours and fixed on a wall or running along the skirting of a room, or simply placed in one of its corners, these fluorescent tubes sometimes bar access to the room - which undeniably adds subjective and associational elements to the formal rigour. It is, in fact, in a space that already has an architectural character - a real space as opposed to a pictorial space - that Flavin can best create 'situations' and frameworks of references: he does not reveal spaces, but constructs places. It is in the 'adaptation', as Flavin calls it, of his art to public places 'in an attentive or complementary way', that a number of his works show their power to emphasise lines, contours and spaces. The architecture of the work then becomes a determining factor in the meaning of the work. For a long time the universal symbol of many aspects of our material and spiritual life, light has a meaning in itself. The neon tube, an artificial light, often finds itself in confrontation with natural light of different hours of the day. It is dense, bright or dull, suggestive, a recreator of the surrounding space, but it is also an interactive force for the person it lights.

In 1964 Flavin exhibited *Diagonal* at one of the first exhibitions of Minimal Art, entitled *Black, White and Gray* and held at the Wadsworth Athenaeum. In 1966 he was represented in the exhibition *Primary Structures* at the Jewish Museum, together with Carl André, Sol Lewitt and Donald Judd. This was considered one of the founding acts of Minimal Art, as was *Kunst Licht Kunst* at the Stedelijk Museum, Eindhoven. Other group exhibitions in France included: 1989, Musée d'Art Contemporain, Lyons; 1989-1990, *L'Art conceptuel, une perspective* (*Conceptual Art: A Perspective*) at the Musée d'Art Moderne de la Ville de Paris; 1990, *Un choix d'art minimal dan la collection Panza* (*A Selection of Minimal Art from the Panza Collection*) at the Musée d'Art Moderne de la Ville de Paris; 2003, *Un tableau dans le décor. Peintures 1970-2000* (*A Painting in the Décor: Paintings 1970-2000*), an exhibition presented to mark the 20 years of existence of the FRAC, held at the Château des Ducs de Bretagne, Nantes.

His first solo show took place at the Judson Gallery, New York, in 1961. Among his many other personal exhibitions have been: 1969, a large retrospective shown in Ottawa and then at the Jewish Museum; 1974 and 1975, in Cologne, Rotterdam and Basel; 1982, the Guggenheim Museum, New York; 1985, *Monuments for V. Tatlin*, CAPC-Centre d'Art Contemporain, Bordeaux; 1985, the Kröller Müller Museum, Otterloo; 1985, 1987, Leo Castelli, New York; 1986, Harvard University, Boston; 1987, Stedjelijk Museum, Amsterdam. In 1979 the Dia Art Foundation set up the Dan Flavin Art Institute in a former Baptist church in Bridgehampton, New York State, to serve as a permanent gallery for his work.

BIBLIOGRAPHY:

Judd, Donald, '*Aspects de l'œuvre de Flavin*' in *Dan Flavin*, exhibition catalogue, National Gall. of Canada, Ottawa, 1969. Judd, D./Huber, C., *Dan Flavin, fünf Installationen in fluoreszierendem Licht*, exhibition catalogue, Kunsthalle, Basel, 1975. *Dan Flavin*, exhibition catalogue, Art Museum, Fort Worth, 1976. *Dan Flavin*, exhibition catalogue, Art Institute of Chicago, Chicago, 1977. *Dan Flavin*, exhibition catalogue, Kunsthalle, Baden Baden, 1989. *Dan Flavin: Untitled*, exhibition catalogue, Waddington Galleries, London, 1990. *Dan Flavin: the Architecture of Light*, exhibition catalogue, Solomon R. Guggenheim Foundation, New York, 1999. Govin, Michael, *Dan Flavin: the Complete Lights, 1961-1996*, exhibition catalogue, Dia Art Foundation/Yale University Press, New York, 2004. Feldman, Paula/Schubert, Karsten (ed.), *It Is What It Is: Writings on Dan Flavin since 1964*, Ridinghouse, London, 2004.

MUSEUMS AND GALLERIES:

BORDEAUX (CAPC-MAC): *Homage to Tatlin* (1964, fluorescent tubes) - BRIDGEHAMPTON, NY (Dan Flavin Art Institute) -

CAMBRIDGE, MA (Fogg AM, Harvard University): *Untitled in Respectful Homage to You, Nikki* - DUNKIRK (FRAC Nord-Pas de Calais): *Untitled* - NEW YORK (Dia Art Foundation): *Untitled* (1970) - NÎMES (Carré d'Art, MAC) - PARIS (MNAM-CCI).

AUCTION RECORDS:

NEW YORK, 17 Nov 1971, *The Alternate Diagonals of March 2* (five white neon tubes) USD 6,000. LOS ANGELES, 15 May 1972, *Untitled* (fluorescent tubes) USD 6,250. LONDON, 3 April 1974, *A Primary Picture* (five neon tubes) GBP 4,800. NEW YORK, 21 Oct 1976, *Puerto-Rican Light II, to Jeanie Blake* (1965, red, pink and yellow fluorescent lights, h. 96 ins / 244 cm) USD 5,500. NEW YORK, 13 May 1977, *Untitled, for Karin and Walther* (1966-1971, blue fluorescent light, 96 x 96 ins / 244 x 244 cm) USD 6,000. LONDON, 28 June 1978, *Untitled* (pink and green fluorescent tubes, h. 70 3/4 ins / 180 cm) GBP 2,200. LONDON, 28 June 1978, *Untitled* (red and blue fluorescent lights, 48 x 48 ins / 122 x 122 cm) GBP 1,000. LONDON, 5 Dec 1978, *Composition from August 5th 1964* (1966, white gouache/black paper, 11 3/4 x 11 3/4 ins / 30 x 30 cm) GBP 850. NEW YORK, 16 May 1980, *Untitled* (1971, pencil and ink/paper, 17 1/4 x 22 1/4 ins / 43.8 x 56.5 cm) USD 2,800. LONDON, 29 June 1982, *To Henri Matisse* (1965, fluorescent tubes, h. 104 ins / 264 cm) GBP 3,000. NEW YORK, 9 May 1984, *The Nominal Three, to William of Ockham* (1963, fluorescent light, 72 x 52 1/2 ins / 182.8 x 133.3 cm) USD 29,000. NEW YORK, 5 Nov 1985, *Untitled, for You Leo, in Long Respect and Affection* (1977, pink, red, blue and yellow fluorescent lights, 48 x 48 ins / 122 x 122 cm) USD 21,000. NEW YORK, 10 Nov 1988, *1969 in Red, Green and Light Yellow Fluorescent* (1972, colouring pencil and graphite/graph paper, 17 x 22 ins / 43.2 x 55.9 cm) USD 12,100. NEW YORK, 3 May 1989, *Untitled* (1966, four cold white fluorescent tubes, 96 x 10 1/4 ins / 244 x 26 cm) USD 66,000. NEW YORK, 5 Oct 1989, *Untitled* (yellow, green, blue and pink fluorescent tubes, h. 96 ins / 243.8 cm) USD 55,000. NEW YORK, 8 May 1990, *Barbara's Roses 3D* (flowers in an electric lightbulb in a vase and a plastic pot, h. 8 3/4 ins / 22.2 cm) USD 11,000; *Untitled, to Pat and Bob Rohm* (1969, red, green and yellow fluorescent tubes, 96 x 96 x 2 1/2 ins / 243.9 x 243.9 x 6.4 cm) USD 231,000. NEW YORK, 7 Nov 1990, *Untitled, to Barnett Newman* (yellow, red and blue fluorescent tubes, h. 96 ins / 243.8 cm) USD 66,000. NEW YORK, 30 April 1991, *The Diagonal of 25 May 1963, to Robert Rosenblum* (white fluorescent tube, l. 96 ins / 243.8 cm) USD 170,500. NEW YORK, 3 Oct 1991, *Untitled* (1964, montage of fluorescent tubes in daylight, cold and hot white in five sections, each section 60 ins / 152.5 cm, in all 300 1/4 ins/762.5 cm) USD 66,000. NEW YORK, 13 Nov 1991, *Monument to V. Tatlin* (1966, cold white fluorescent tubes, h. 122 ins / 309.6 cm) USD 99,000. NEW YORK, 14 Nov 1991, *The Diagonal of 25 May 1963 for Brancusi* (yellow fluorescent tube, l. 96 ins / 243.8 cm) USD 148,500. NEW YORK, 19 Nov 1992, *Untitled* (1970, blue and red fluorescent tubes, 7 1/4 x 48 x 3 ins / 18.4 x 121.9 x 6.7 cm) USD 19,800. NEW YORK, 10 Nov 1993, *Untitled, towards the Real Dan Hill* (1978, green, blue, yellow and pink fluorescent tubes, 96 x 5 x 8 1/4 ins / 243.8 x 12.8 x 21 cm) USD 27,600. LONDON, 29 June 1994, *To Bob and Pat Rohm* (1969, red, yellow and green fluorescent lights, 96 x 96 x 2 1/2 ins / 244 x 244 x 6.4 cm) GBP 34,500. NEW YORK, 3 Nov 1994, *Untitled, dedicated to Philip Johnson* (1964, pink, green, blue and red fluorescent tubes, 96 x 8 3/4 x 4 1/2 ins / 243.8 x 22.2 x 11.4 cm) USD 74,000. NEW YORK, 15 Nov 1995, *Untitled* (blue and red fluorescent tubes, 25 x 25 x 3 1/2 ins / 63.4 x 63.4 x 8.9 cm) USD 25,300. NEW YORK, 8 May 1996, *Untitled (to Don Judd, Colourist) I* (pink fluorescent tubes, 52 1/4 x 48 1/2 ins / 132.7 x 123.2 cm) USD 28,750. NEW YORK, 20 Nov 1996, *Untitled* (1984, red and blue fluorescent lights, 2 3/4 x 48 x 7 1/4 ins / 7 x 121.9 x 18.4 cm) USD 13,800. NEW YORK, 7 May 1997, *Untitled (For Margot)* (white fluorescent tubes, h. 96 ins / 243.8 cm) USD 23,000. NEW YORK, 8 May 1997, *Untitled (For You Leo in Long Respect and Affection) 2* (1977, pink, green, blue and yellow fluorescent lights, 104 3/4 x 104 3/4 ins / 266 x 266 cm) USD 51,750. NEW YORK, 18 May 1999, *Daylight and Cool White - to Sol Lewitt* (fluorescent light, 96 x 10x5 ins / 244 x 26x13 cm) USD 240,000. NEW YORK, 19 May 1999, *Untitled, to 'Buster' May* (1972, fluorescent lights in corridor, 96 x 96 ins / 244 x 244 cm) USD 130,000. NEW YORK, 17 May 2000, *Untitled* (flourescent light, h. 96 ins / 244 cm) USD 190,000. NEW YORK, 14 Nov 2000, *Alternate Diagonals of March* (red and gold fluorescent light, l. 144 ins / 366 cm) USD 300,000. NEW YORK, 15 May 2001, *Red and Green Alternatives, to Sonja* (red and green fluorescent light, h. 48 ins / 122 cm) USD 110,000. NEW YORK, 18 May 2001, *Untitled - to Janie Lee* (1971, coloured fluorescent light, l. 96 ins / 244 cm) USD 95,000. NEW YORK, 13 May 2002, *Monument for Tatlin* (1968, cool white fluorescent light, 96 x 32x5 ins / 244 x 82x13 cm) USD 230,000. NEW YORK, 13 Nov 2002, *Alternate Diagonals of March 2, 1964* (1964, daylight fluorescent light, l. 142 ins / 360 cm) USD 360,000. NEW YORK, 14 May 2003, *Untitled - Monument to V Tatlin* (1967, fluorescent light, 96 x 19x4 ins / 244 x 49x11 cm) USD 320,000. NEW YORK, 15 May 2003, *Untitled* (1976, blue, green and yellow fluorescent light, l. 96 ins / 244 cm) USD 155,000. NEW YORK, 11 May 2004, *Untitled* (1966, fluorescent light tubes, 73 x 217x45 ins / 185 x 550x114 cm) USD 420,000. NEW YORK, 11 May 2004, *Alternate Diagonals of March 2 1964* (1964, red and gold fluorescent light, l. 144 ins / 366 cm) USD 600,000.

FLAVITSKY, Konstantin Dmitrievich

Russian, 19th century.
Born 1830; died 1866, in St Petersburg.
Painter. History painting.

Flavitsky studied at the St Petersburg academy of fine arts where he then became a tutor. He produced a well-known painting: *The Death of Princess Tarakanova* in which she is shown trapped in her cell in the Petropavlovsk Fortress as the tide begins to flood it.

MUSEUMS AND GALLERIES:

MOSCOW (State Tretyakov Gal.): *The Princess Tarakanova in the Petropavlovsk Fortress During the St Petersburg Flood; Lord Savaaphe; Princess Tarakanova* (study) - SARATOV (Raditschev Gal.): *Portrait of Count Mussin-Pouchkin* - ST PETERSBURG (Gosudarstvennyj Russkij Muz.): *Princess Tarakanova* (study); *The Christian Martyrs in the Colisseum.*

FLAXIUS, Josef

Bohemian School, 18th century.
Died 1741.
Active in Prague.
Painter.

FLAXLAND, Joseph Frédéric

French, 19th century.
Born 1814, in Strasbourg; died 1884, in Paris.
Painter. History painting.

Worked on numerous churches in Alsace; also produced a large number of genre compositions and landscapes of the Alsace region.

AUCTION RECORDS:

PARIS, 6 March 1998, *Little Villagers* (oil on canvas, oval, 18 x 11 3/4 ins / 46 x 30 cm) FRF 8,000.

FLAXMAN, John I

British, 18th century.
Born in Buckinghamshire; died c. 1795, in London.
Sculptor, modeller.

John Flaxman I's family were staunch supporters of the Parliamentary cause during the English Civil War. He was employed as a modeller by the French-born English sculptor Roubiliac, and the Flemish sculptor Scheemakers. Flaxman ran his own plaster-cast shop in London, first in Covent Garden, and later on the Strand. He was the father of William Flaxman and John Flaxman II.

FLAXMAN, John II

British, 18th - 19th century.

Born 6 July 1755, in York; died 7 December 1826, in London.

Sculptor, watercolourist, draughtsman, illustrator.

Monuments, statues, low reliefs.

John Flaxman II enjoyed a reputation as one of the finest English sculptors of his age. The second son of the plaster-cast maker John Flaxman, he spent much of his childhood in his father's studio, drawing and modelling in wax or clay. He received a thorough grounding in Greek and Latin, and exhibited his first artistic work (a copy after an Antique original) with the Free Society of Artists in 1767, at the age of 12. He submitted a bust in 1768, and a representation of the *Assassination of Julius Caesar* in 1769. He enrolled at the Royal Academy Schools during this period, where his long experience of modelling enabled him to work alongside much older students. His failure to win a gold medal at the Academy in 1772 (and hence a travel bursary for studies in Italy) seemed undeserved. He befriended the visionary poet William Blake and the portrait painter George Romney, both of whom had a decisive influence on his work. During this period, he also produced numerous designs and models for the noted English ceramics manufacturer Josiah Wedgwood.

In 1782, he married Anne Denman, with whom he travelled to Italy five years later. He was fêted upon his arrival in Rome, and received numerous commissions, notably for an important marble group, the *Fury of Athamas*, based on an episode of Ovid's *Metamorphoses*. He also prouced interesting illustrations for Homer's *Iliad* and *Odyssey*, Dante's *Divine Comedy* and the *Tragedies* of Aeschylus, engraved in Rome by Piroli. He subsequently illustrated the poems of Hesiod. On the basis of this work, he became an academician in Florence and Verona.

His first work on his return to London in 1794 was the monument to William Murray, 1st Earl of Mansfield, in Westminster Abbey. He became an associate of the Royal Academy in 1797, and a full member in 1800. In 1810, his reputation firmly established, Flaxman became a professor at the Royal Academy Schools. His principal works include monuments to Sir Joshua Reynolds, the Earl of Bristol and Admiral Lord Nelson, statues of Washington and Reynolds and an important relief, the *Shield of Achilles*, executed in silver gilt by the silverware firm Rundle, Bridge & Rundle (now in the British Royal collection, at Windsor Castle). Flaxman was an important influence on the English art of his time, and played a central role in the revival of a taste for Greek statuary among contemporary sculptors and connoisseurs. Goethe admired his classicism, and his work also influenced Ingres and the Nazarenes. His status and influence may be compared to that of Louis David in France.

He exhibited with the Royal Academy for the first time in 1770, and regularly after that until 1787.

BIBLIOGRAPHY:

John Flaxman: 10th March-9th April 1976, presented by Christopher Powney and Heim Gallery (London) Ltd, exhibition catalogue, Heim Gallery, London, 1976. Irwin, David, *John Flaxman 1755-1826. Sculptor, illustrator, designer.*, Studio Vista, London, 1979. *The Poetic Circle: Fuseli and the British: Henry Fuseli and James Barry, William Blake, John Brown, John Flaxman, James Jefferys, John Hamilton Mortimer, George Romney, Alexander Runciman: Australia, New Zealand, April-November 1979*, Florence, 1979. Bassett, Mark, *John Flaxman Designs: at Roseville Pottery*, exhibition catalogue, Cleveland Public Library, 2001. Draper, James David/Scherf, Guilhem, et al., *L'esprit créateur de Pigalle à Canova. Terres cuites européennes 1740-1840*, exhibition catalogue, Musée du Louvre, Paris, 2003. Bindman, David (ed.), *John Flaxman, 1755-1826. Master of the purest line.*, Sir John Soane's Museum, London, 2003.

MUSEUMS AND GALLERIES:

BRISTOL: *Charity* (plaster) - CAMBRIDGE (Fitzwilliam Mus.): *Portrait of Woman Full Face* (black chalk/paper) - GLASGOW: *John Moore* (bronze, statue); *William Pitt* (bronze, statue) - LONDON (Sir John Soane's Mus.): *Britannia* (design); *Maternal Love* (design); *Bust of Hayley* (terracotta); *Bust of the Sculptor's Father* (terracotta) - LONDON (Victoria and Albert Mus.): *Self-portrait* (c. 1778, terracotta); *Orestes Pursued by the Furies; Ajax and Hector Separated by the Heralds; Man and Two Prostrate Women* (watercolour) - MANCHESTER: *Maternal Love* (watercolour) - NOTTINGHAM: drawings.

AUCTION RECORDS:

LONDON, 9 May 1910, *Various Studies*, GBP 1. LONDON, 22 Nov 1979, *The Adoration of the Magi* (pencil, pen and wash, drawing for a low relief, 11 x 17 1/4 ins / 27 x 44 cm) GBP 2,300. LONDON, 24 March 1981, *Pacification of Europe* (1821, pencil and pen/paper, sculpture design for Buckingham Palace, 2 x 15 ins / 5 x 38.3 cm) GBP 1,200. LONDON, 21 Nov 1984, *Dante and Beatrice* (1792, pen/pencil outlines, 12 1/2 x 14 1/2 ins / 32 x 37 cm) GBP 2,400. LONDON, 19 Feb 1987, *Design for a Vase with Hesiod and Victory* (pen, grey ink/pencil outlines and wash, 10 1/2 x 8 ins / 26.5 x 20.5 cm) GBP 1,300. LONDON, 25 Jan 1988, *Study of a Sleeping Child* (ink, 4 1/2 x 6 1/2 ins / 11.5 x 16.5 cm) GBP 385. LONDON, 7 July 1992, *Dante and Beatrice* (1792, black chalk and ink, 12 1/2 x 14 1/4 ins / 32 x 36.5 cm) GBP 7,150. LONDON, 8 June 1999, *Evil Spirits Cast Out, Em. Swedenborg's 'Arcania Coelestia'* (pencil and colour washes, 9 x 7 ins / 22 x 18 cm) GBP 4,500. LONDON, 25 Nov 1999, *Portrait of Harriet Mathew* (pencil stump, 7 x 6 ins / 19 x 15 cm) GBP 2,400. NEW YORK, 28 June 2000, *Ulysses Asleep, Placed on the Shore of Ithaca by the Phaecians* (black ink over pencil, 7 x 9 ins / 17 x 24 cm) USD 3,000. LONDON, 1 Nov 2001, *Head of Robert Burns* (pencil, 6 x 6 ins / 16 x 14 cm) GBP 4,800. HAMBURG, 13 June 2002, *Good and Angry Spirits* (wash and pen over pencil, 6 x 7 ins / 15 x 19 cm) EUR 3,000. LONDON, 4 July 2002, *Two Women with a Young Child* (pen, grey ink and wash over pencil, 6 x 7 ins / 15 x 18 cm) GBP 1,800. LONDON, 5 June 2003, *Study for Pandora Brought to Epimetheus* (pencil, 11 x 16 ins / 29 x 40 cm) GBP 1,300. HAMBURG, 11 June 2004, *Fall from Grace* (wash and brush over pencil, 5 x 8 ins / 13 x 20 cm) EUR 2,200. LONDON, 9 Nov 2004, *Ulysses Terrified by the Ghosts. Venus Presenting Helen to Paris* (pen and ink, a pair, 7 x 10 ins / 18 x 25 cm) GBP 2,400.

FLAXMAN, Mary Ann

British, 18th - 19th century.

Born 1768; died 1833, in London.

Painter, draughtswoman.

Mary Ann Flaxman was the sister of the celebrated sculptor John Flaxman II, with whom she lived for a time. She exhibited portraits, poetical subjects and domestic scenes at the Royal Academy from 1786 to 1819. Her works include: *Turkish Women* (1786), *Ferdinand and Miranda Playing Chess* (1789), *Sappho* (1810) and *Maternal Piety* (1819).

FLAXMAN, William

British, 18th century.

Born probably in York.

Sculptor, modeller.

Brother of John Flaxman II, William Flaxman seems to have been employed mostly as a workshop assistant, but exhibited an original *Venus* with the Free Society in 1768. He exhibited wax busts at the Royal Academy from 1781 to 1793, including one of his brother John (in 1781).

FLE, Jean Claude

Belgian, 20th - 21st century.

Born 1948, in Tilff.

Painter, draughtsman, watercolourist.

Fle attended the Institut de St Luc in Liège.

FLÈCHEMULLER, Jacques
French, 20th century.
Born 26 February 1945, in Monaco.
Also active in the USA.
Painter.

Jacques Flèchemuller studied at the École Nationale des Beaux-Arts and the École des Arts Appliqués in Paris. He has homes in Beaulieu, Ardèche, and New York.

First and foremost, Flèchemuller's paintings reflect the various supports which he uses, among others, canvas, tent canvas, mattress canvas, and wrapping paper on canvas, upon which he mixes colours. On the surfaces thus created, he draws, and subsequently paints, various motifs, often objects which he has gleaned on his travels (such as the *Texas Style* series), with which he creates a form of visual poetry.

His style is very broad, even eclectic. For example, in his 1997 painting, *Begognia*, he portrays a very young child, almost a baby, of indeterminate gender, made to look prematurely old by its bizarre clothes and its pose. Monique Daubigné writes that Flèchemuller 'loves Chaissac and Dubuffet, and, like them, keeps his inspiration free from all cultural prejudice.'

He has taken part in a number of group exhibitions, including the following: Salon des Réalités Nouvelles in Paris, in 1976; *Graphics from Paris*, at the Worpswede Museum, in 1985; and *Drawings and Sculptures*, at the Manhattan Art Museum in New York, in 1985.

He has also staged a number of solo exhibitions, including the following: Galerie Jeanne Bucher in Paris, from 1978 to 1983; at the Sag Harbor Art Museum in New York, in 1984; Anne Plumb Gallery in New York, in 1985, 1986 and 1988; *L'Étroit Séjour* (*The Narrow Visit*), at the Maison de Verre in Paris, in 1986; at the Linda Hodges Gallery, in Seattle, Washington, in 1987; at the Rena Bransten Gallery in 1988; at the Galerie Lavignes-Bastille in Paris, in 1989; at the Galerie Catherine Niederhauser in Lausanne, in 1997; and at the Jan Baum Gallery in Los Angeles, in 1997.

BIBLIOGRAPHY:
Daubigné, Monique, *Fonds National dArt Contemporain, Acquisitions 1989*, Ministère de la Culture, Paris, 1989.

MUSEUMS AND GALLERIES:
PARIS (FNAC): *Rita* (1988).

AUCTION RECORDS:
PARIS, 13 April 1988, *Untitled* (mixed media/canvas, 76 3/4 x 37 ins / 195 x 94 cm) FRF 10,000. PARIS, 12 Feb 1989, *Untitled* (1985, acrylic/canvas, 63 3/4 x 48 1/2 ins / 162 x 123 cm) FRF 10,000. NEW YORK, 7 May 1991, *Texas Style* (1986, acrylic/canvas, 81 3/4 x 55 ins / 207.7 x 139.7 cm) USD 1,650.

FLECHTNER, Jacob
German, 16th century.
Active in Zittau (Saxony).
Painter.

Flechtner was a citizen of Zittau and probably worked in Prague.

FLECK, Gabriel
Swiss, 17th century.
Active in Fribourg.
Sculptor (wood).

Gabriel Fleck carved the ancient pulpit at the church in Fribourg. He may also have built the stalls that date from the same period.

FLECK, Josef
German, 19th century.
Active in Düsseldorf (North Rhine-Westphalia).
Painter.

FLECK, Joseph Amadeus
Austrian, 20th century.
Born 25 August 1892.
Painter.

Fleck was a student at the Akademie der Bildenden Künste in Vienna. He worked in America, where he was a member of several art societies. He obtained numerous distinctions and awards, and his works can be seen in Virginia and Kansas.

AUCTION RECORDS:
SAN FRANCISCO, 3 Oct 1981, *Song of Mexico* (oil on canvas, 22 x 26 ins / 55 x 66 cm) USD 5,000. NEW YORK, 27 Jan 1984, *After the Storm* (1964, oil on canvas remounted on hardboard, 25 x 30 ins / 63.5 x 76.2 cm) USD 6,750. NEW YORK, 25 May 1989, *Taos Village in July* (oil/synthetic resin, 28 x 35 ins / 71.1 x 88.7 cm) USD 18,700. NEW YORK, 23 Sept 1992, *First Snow in a Taos Village* (oil/synthetic resin, 12 x 15 3/4 ins / 30.5 x 40.3 cm) USD 2,200.

FLECKEN, Otto Karl Leonard
German, 19th century.
Born 11 April 1860, in Düsseldorf.
Painter.

Flecken initially studied under Kaupert the sculptor in Frankfurt am Main, then with Hasselhorst at the Städel Institute in Frankfurt. He mainly painted northern landscapes, and was also an illustrator.

FLEDNER, Peter. See **FLOTNER**

FLEETWOOD-WALKER, Bernard.
See **WALKER**

FLEGEL, Georg
German, 16th - 17th century.
Born 1563, in Olmütz, Moravia (now Olomouc, Czech Republic); died 1638, in Frankfurt am Main.
Painter. Still-lifes (including flowers/fruit), vanitas.

Very little is known about this artist except that he lived in Frankfurt am Main. Since still-life painting was not part of the German tradition at that period, it is thought that Flegel learned his trade in the Netherlands, perhaps with Soreau. If that were the case, it would establish a link with Sebastian Stosskopff, the painter of still-lifes from Alsace.

While Flegel's work has a certain naivety not found in Français Baugin or the Italian Baschenis, his paintings of fruit, flowers, glassware, metal vessels and, after Abraham Mignon, brightly coloured birds and insects are executed with great care and attention to detail. Although he paid lip-service to the genre of the *vanitas*, a still-life where the choice of objects - say, a skull or crucifix - was intended to make the viewer meditate on the vanity of life, his work seems closer to the sensualism of the Dutch still-life painters, for whom the most important thing was the tactile realism of the material of the painted objects. Another characteristic of his work, when compared to other similar paintings of the period, is the importance of a sense of volume in space of the objects depicted and of the architecture of their arrangement.

The fruit and flowers in the paintings of Martin van Valckenborch are the work of Flegel.

BIBLIOGRAPHY:
Müller, Wolfgang J., *Der Maler Georg Flegel und die Anfänge des Stillebens*, Frankfurt, 1956. Bergström, Ingvar/Bott, Gerhard/Grimm, Claus/Heck, Michèle-Caroline/Seifertová, Hana, *Georg Flegel 1566-1638, Stilleben*, Hatje Cantz, Ostfildern, 1999.

MUSEUMS AND GALLERIES:
KARLSRUHE: *Still-life with Candle*.

AUCTION RECORDS:
LONDON, 28 Nov 1962, *Still-life with Fruit*, GBP 2,600. LONDON, 6 July 1966, *Still-life*, GBP 2,200. LONDON, 10 April 1970, *Still-life*, Gns 7,500. ZURICH, 1 June 1973, *Still-life*, CHF 60,000. ZURICH, 12 Nov 1976, *Still-life* (c. 1620-1625, oil on panel, 15 1/2 x 18 1/2 ins / 39.2 x 47 cm) CHF 60,000. LONDON, 12 July 1978, *Still-life* (oil on panel, 14 x 17 ins / 35.5 x 43 cm)

GBP 28,000. ZURICH, 15 May 1981, *Still-life* (c. 1620-1625, oil on panel, 15 1/2 x 18 1/2 ins / 39.2 x 47 cm) CHF 105,000. LONDON, 4 April 1984, *Still-life with Fruit* (1630, oil on panel, 12 x 19 1/2 ins / 30.5 x 49.5 cm) GBP 55,000. COLOGNE, 20 May 1985, *Still-life with Flowers, Fruit and a Lobster* (oil on canvas, 24 1/2 x 18 1/4 ins / 62 x 46.5 cm) DEM 360,000. NEW YORK, 10 Jan 1990, *Large Floral Composition in an Engraved Pewter Jug with a Glass of White Wine, a Slice of Bread, Cherries, a Knife and an Insect on an Entablature* (oil on canvas, 24 1/2 x 17 3/4 ins / 62.2 x 45 cm) USD 1,980,000. PARIS, 9 April 1990, *Basket of Peaches, Pears and Apples, Bowl of Strawberries, Kingfisher, Plates of Cherries and Chestnuts, Almonds, Peas and Red Peaches, and Bellflower on an Entablature* (oil on walnut panel, 11 x 16 1/2 ins / 28 x 42 cm) FRF 900,000. NEW YORK, 10 Jan 1991, *Floral Composition in a Silver-Gilt Vase. Fruit, Lobster on Pewter Plates, Bonbonniere and Loaf of Bread on a Marble Table* (oil on canvas, 24 1/2 x 18 1/4 ins / 62 x 46.5 cm) USD 253,000. LONDON, 3 July 1991, *Pinks in a Vase, White Wine in a Carafe and Cherries* (oil on birch panel, 9 1/2 x 6 1/4 ins / 24.4 x 16 cm) GBP 79,200. LONDON, 3 July 1997, *Still-life of Dried Fruit and Hazelnuts on a Porcelain Plate, Cherries in a Wanli Cup, Sigburg Kanne and Glass of Wine Arranged on an Entablature with Shells, Nuts and Other Sweetmeats* (oil on beech panel, 12 1/2 x 9 1/4 ins / 32 x 23.5 cm) GBP 265,500. LONDON, 11 July 2001, *Silver Tazza with Apples and Bunch of Grapes, Strawberries in a Pewter Dish* (oil on panel, 20 x 24 ins / 50 x 62 cm) GBP 200,000. LONDON, 11 July 2001, *Artichokes and Peas in the Pod in a Basket, Joint of Pork and Other Foods on a Table* (oil on canvas, 19 x 23 ins / 48 x 59 cm) GBP 380,000. COLOGNE, 16 Nov 2002, *Still-life with Fruit, Mouse and Bird* (oil on canvas, 11 x 17 ins / 28 x 42 cm) EUR 460,000.

FLEGEL, Georg
German, 17th century.
Painter.

Flegel was noted in 1671 for his work in the Friedenskirche (Church of Peace) in Jauer in Silesia (now Jawor, Poland).

FLEGEL, Johann Gottfried
German, 19th century.
Born 1815, in Leipzig; died in Leipzig.
Engraver (wood).

Flegel engraved prints for albums.

FLEGIER, Ange
French, 19th century.
Painter.

Also known as a musician and successful composer.

MUSEUMS AND GALLERIES:
DIEPPE (Château-Mus.): *View of Martigues* (watercolour).

FLEIGE
German, 19th century.
Active in Münster.
Sculptor.

Fleige is known to have created the bronze memorial to the *Minister of Furstenberg*, works entitled *Garden of Gethsemane* and *Pieta* for the churches, a fountain, and the monument to *Annette von Droste-Hülshoff*, all of which are in Münster.

FLEISCHBERGER, Johann Friedrich
German, 17th century.
Active in Nuremberg (Bavaria).
Engraver (burin).

Fleischberger is noted for engravings of ornaments and portraits.

FLEISCHER
Austrian, 18th century.
Painter (porcelain).

Fleischer worked initially for the porcelain factory in Meissen (Saxony), and later for the one in Vienna.

FLEISCHER, Alain
French, 20th century.
Born 1944, in Paris.
Installation artist, photographer, film maker, novelist. Multimedia.

Alain Fleischer studied French, linguistics and anthropology at university, and has taught at the University of Paris III, at the École d'Art de Cergy, at the Institut des Hautes Études Cinématographiques, and the École Nationale d'Art de Nice (the Villa Arson). He served as head of the École Expérimentale d'Art Contemporain du Fresnoy, in Tourcoing.

He has taken part in a number of group exhibitions, including the following: Galerie Ranelagh in Paris, in 1972; Musée National d'Art Moderne in Paris, in 1975 and 1982; and the Musée de l'Abbaye Ste-Croix in Les Sables d'Olonne, in 1985.

He has also put on a number of solo exhibitions, including the following: *Five Contemporary Artists*, at the Städtische Kunsthalle in Düsseldorf, and in the Hagen Museum, in 1975; *La Boîte* (*The Box*), part of the Art Recherche Confrontation event at the Musée d'Art Moderne de la Ville de Paris, in 1976; *Studio 81-82*, part of the same event at the same venue, in 1981; Salon de Montrouge in 1983; *Das Akstfoto*, in Munich Museum, as well as Vienna, Hamburg and Tokyo, in 1985; and *Machines affectées/affected machines*, at the Nexus Contemporary Art Center in Atlanta, in 1986. In addition, he has staged a number of solo exhibitions, including *Alain Fleischer, l'Image Traversée, Transportée* (*Alain Fleischer: the Image, Traversed and Transported*), in Espal, Le Mans.

BIBLIOGRAPHY:
Semin, D./Nuridsany, M./Baudry, J.L./Michaud, E., *Alain Fleischer: vanités*, Musée de l'Abbaye Sainte-Croix, Les Sables d'Olonne, 1985. *Fonds National dArt Contemporain, Acquisitions 1989*, Ministère de la Culture, Paris, 1989. Dagen, Philippe, '*Alain Fleischer, tous les coups de l'art*' in *Le Monde*, periodical, Paris, Thursday 31 January 2002. Arasse, Daniel/Bullot, Erik/Dagen, Philippe, *Alain Fleischer*, L. Scheer, Paris, 2003 (accompanied by a DVD-ROM).

MUSEUMS AND GALLERIES:
GENEVA (Mamco): *A Hand's Journey. Little Stories in Several Volumes* (1998, flipbook) - MARSEILLES (Mus. Cantini): *The Light Truck at the Musée des Plâtres* (1988) - PARIS (FNAC): *Triptych of a Bathroom* (1982).

FLEISCHER, Balthasar, or Flaischer
German, 17th century.
Active in Nuremberg (Bavaria).
Painter.

In 1603 Balthasar Fleischer gave up his citizenship rights.

FLEISCHER, Eduard Carl
German, 19th century.
Born 3 May 1815, in Dresden; died 17 June 1869, in Dresden.
Painter, draughtsman. Landscapes.

Eduard Fleischer was a student of C.A. Richter at the school of fine arts in Dresden. He entered in exhibitions in Dresden wash drawings, and pastel and pencil works inspired by the landscapes and surrounding areas of Dresden and the *Sächsische Schweiz* (an area of Saxony named after Switzerland, for its rocky outcrops). One of his known works is an oil painting entitled *Idyllic Landscape*.

FLEISCHER, Ernst Philipp
German, 19th century.
Born 1850, in Breslau (now Wroclaw, Poland).
Painter. History painting, portraits, genre scenes.

Ernst Fleischer studied under Schnorr and Carolsfeld in Dresden, and Piloty in Munich. He travelled for a long time in Italy. Fleischer established himself as an artist in Dresden in 1870.
MUSEUMS AND GALLERIES:
POZNAN (Muz. Narodowe): *Relief Team in the St Gothard Tunnel during Construction.*

FLEISCHER, Friedrich Martin or Fritz
German, 19th century.
Born 1 March 1861, in Breslau (now Wroclaw, Poland).
Painter. Portraits, genre scenes.
Friedrich Fleischer was active in Weimar (Thuringia). He was awarded a medal in Berlin in 1896.
MUSEUMS AND GALLERIES:
WEIMAR: *Old Man Reading.*
AUCTION RECORDS:
MUNICH, 2 July 1986, *Card Game* (oil on panel, 24 x 17 ins / 61 x 43 cm) DEM 4,500.

FLEISCHER, Georg
German, 16th century.
Born in Dresden.
Sculptor (wood).
Dresden School.
Georg Fleischer worked mainly at the court in Dresden. Two statues by him, representing the kneeling figures of Augustus, Elector of Saxony and his wife Anna, are in the museum in Freiberg. They were originally part of an altar that he made for the church in the castle of Freudenstein in Freiberg.

FLEISCHER, Georges
German, 16th - 17th century.
Active in Dresden from 1594 to 1613.
Sculptor.
This artist was the son of Georg Fleischer.

FLEISCHER, Josef
Austrian, 18th century.
Born 1676; died 19 November 1729.
Active in Vienna.
Painter.

FLEISCHER, Max
German, 19th century.
Born 4 July 1861, in Lipine.
Painter. Portraits, genre scenes, landscapes.
Max Fleischer studied at the art school in Breslau (now Wroclaw, Poland), the academies in Berlin and Munich (at the latter under the direction of the Ludwig Löfftz), and the Académie Julian in Paris. After spending some time in Zurich, he went to study in France, Italy and Tunisia, and settled in Rome in around 1894. He exhibited in Berlin, Bern and London, where he was awarded a gold medal. He received a distinction at the Exposition Universelle in 1889. His acknowledged works include *Accident Victim at the Carrare Quarries, Children Swimming, Breton Fishermen, First Communion.*
AUCTION RECORDS:
AMSTERDAM, 5 June 1996, *Mountain Landscape* (oil on canvas, 15¾ x 25½ ins / 40 x 65 cm) GBP 2,300.

FLEISCHER, Michael
Romanian, 19th - 20th century.
Born 8 July 1869, in Cincu.
Painter, draughtsman. Portraits, local scenes.
Michael Fleischer first studied sculpture in Kronstadt (now Brasov), then drawing at Budapest art school where he graduated. He travelled to Venice, Paris, Stuttgart, Munich and Vienna. In 1901 he exhibited a large painting *Wake in a Saxon Peasant's Home*, for which he won the Rath prize. He is also known for his painting *Buffalo at the River.* He painted many portraits.

FLEISCHHACKER, Leopold
German, 20th century.
Born 13 May 1882, in Felsberg (Hessen-Nassau).
Sculptor. Portraits, animals.
After studying at the Kunstgewerbeschule in Düsseldorf, he studied at the Akademie in Berlin with Herter and Breuer. In 1905 he was awarded the Prix de Rome. His works frequently featured in the exhibitions in Berlin, Düsseldorf and Munich: portraits in bronze, plaster or marble, such as *Judith* and *Old Trakehner Stallion.*

FLEISCHHAUER. See also **VLEESCHOUWERE**

FLEISCHHAUER, Hermann
German, 19th century.
Active c. 1850.
Painter, lithographer. Urban landscapes, horses.
Hermann Fleischhauer was an art teacher in Reutlingen, then in Stuttgart (Baden-Württemberg). He is known to have produced a lithograph published in 1856 in the *Album of Württemberg Artists: Out Falcon Hunting*, and a lithograph entitled *View of Aalen*

FLEISCHLIN, Jakob
Swiss, 17th century.
Painter. Religious subjects.
Fleischlin was a member of the brotherhood of St Luke, and, according to Brun, painted pictures for the churches in Lucerne around 1669.

FLEISCHMANN
Austrian, 19th century.
Active in Vienna.
Miniaturist.
This artist may be the same person as the Adolf Fleischman who is mentioned in London in 1851, and who exhibited the portrait of a prince at the Royal Academy.

FLEISCHMANN, Adolf Richard, pseudonym: Ado
German, 20th century.
Born 18 March 1892, in Esslingen; died 28 January 1968, in Stuttgart.
Active from 1938 in France, and from 1952 in the USA.
Painter (including gouache/mixed media), lithographer.
Groups: Espace, Réalités Nouvelles.
Fleischmann was a pupil of Adolf Hölzel at the Staatliche Akademie in Stuttgart from 1911 to 1913. He spent long periods abroad, first of all in Switzerland where he went to recover from severe war wounds, then from 1930 to 1933 in Ascona (Ticino), from 1933 to 1936 in Spain and from 1936 to 1938 in Italy. He then settled in France. He was one of the founders of the *Space* group, and a founder member of the Salon des Réalités Nouvelles. In 1952 he set up in the USA, in New York. He returned to Stuttgart in 1965.

During his French period Fleischmann executed extremely pure compositions, inspired by the work of Baumeister, making use first of all of lines curved into arabesques, then moving to the sole use of the straight line in horizontals and verticals, bringing to the Neo-Plasticism of Mondrian the shimmer of a range of rich and varied tones.

Fleischmann took part in group exhibitions, including: 1922, *New Secession*, Munich; in Berlin and in Stuttgart; 1932, 1945 and 1946, Salon des Surindépendants, Paris; at the Gallery of the City of Munich with a work called *Goldfish*; 1939, at the first exhibition of the Réalités Nouvelles, organised the Renaissance Plastique group, in Paris. He exhibited with the group of American Abstract Artists (AAA). Since his death, he has been represented in group or themed exhibitions, including: 2002, *Konkrete Kunst* (*Concrete Art*), Von der Heydt-Museum, Wuppertal. He staged several solo exhibitions, including: in Paris, 1948 (Galerie Raymond Creuse) and 1951 (Galerie Colette Allendy); 1952 in Stuttgart; 1955 in New York. A Tribute was paid to him at the Salon des Réalités Nouvelles in 1969. A retrospective of his work was organised at the Galerie der Stadt in Esslingen in 1992.

BIBLIOGRAPHY:

Alvard, Julien/Gindertael, R.V., *'Témoignages pour l'Art abstrait'* in *Art d'aujourd'hui*, periodical, Boulogne-sur-Seine, 1952. Damsch-Wiehager, Renate, *Adolf Fleischmann, Retrospektive zum 100. Geburtstag*, exhibition catalogue, Gal. der Stadt, Esslingen, 1992.

MUSEUMS AND GALLERIES:

GRENOBLE (Mus. de Grenoble): *Compositions No 43* - PARIS (MNAM-CCI) - PONTOISE: *Constructivist Composition* (1951).

AUCTION RECORDS:

HAMBURG, 3 June 1976, *Composition* (1957, gouache, 12 1/4 x 9 1/2 ins / 31.2 x 24 cm) DEM 2,000. MUNICH, 23 May 1977, *Composition No. 4* (1960-1961, oil and relief/card, 17 3/4 x 13 1/2 ins / 45 x 34.5 cm) DEM 5,600. HAMBURG, 12 June 1981, *Composition* (1959, gouache, 25 x 19 ins / 63.6 x 48 cm) DEM 4,800. MUNICH, 30 May 1983, *Composition* (1959, gouache, 23 1/2 x 19 ins / 59.5 x 48 cm) DEM 6,600. ZURICH, 28 Oct 1983, *Flowers in a Vase* (1928, oil on canvas, 29 1/4 x 24 1/2 ins / 74.5 x 62 cm) CHF 2,600. COLOGNE, 9 Dec 1986, *Geometric Composition* (gouache, 25 1/2 x 19 1/4 ins / 65 x 49 cm) DEM 4,800. LONDON, 29 June 1989, *Opus No. 123* (1959, oil on canvas, 36 x 29 1/4 ins / 91.7 x 74 cm) GBP 16,500. LONDON, 30 Nov 1989, *Composition No. 530* (1961, oil on canvas, 39 x 32 ins / 99.3 x 81.5 cm) GBP 24,200. LONDON, 28 June 1990, *Opus 301* (1962, oil on canvas, 40 1/4 x 30 ins / 102 x 76 cm) GBP 19,800. LONDON, 18 Oct 1990, *Composition No. 567* (1961, oil on canvas, 35 x 40 ins / 89 x 101.5 cm) GBP 24,200. LONDON, 21 March 1991, *C 110* (collage and gouache/paper, diam. 15 1/4 ins / 39 cm) GBP 6,050. MUNICH, 26-27 Nov 1991, *Composition* (gouache, 25 x 22 3/4 ins / 63.5 x 58 cm) DEM 35,650. LONDON, 15 Oct 1992, *Composition No. 12* (1960, watercolour and gouache/paper, 25 1/2 x 11 1/2 ins / 64.8 x 29.5 cm) GBP 7,700. ZURICH, 3 Dec 1993, *Couple* (oil on canvas, 30 3/4 x 24 3/4 ins / 78 x 63 cm) CHF 6,500. LONDON, 27 Oct 1994, *Composition in an Oval* (gouache/paper, 25 x 18 ins / 63.5 x 45.7 cm) GBP 10,350. LONDON, 23 May 1996, *Untitled* (gouache/paper, 25 1/2 x 19 3/4 ins / 65 x 50.2 cm) GBP 8,625. PARIS, 19 June 1996, *Composition on a Black Background* (gouache/paper, 9 1/2 x 12 1/2 ins / 24 x 31.5 cm) FRF 10,000. PARIS, 28 April 1997, *Bouquets of Flowers* (1931, gouache/paper/card, 24 3/4 x 18 3/4 ins / 63 x 47.5 cm) FRF 12,000. LONDON, 6 Oct 1999, *Composition No. 101* (1958, oil on paper, 30 x 38 ins / 76 x 96 cm) GBP 12,000. LONDON, 6 Oct 1999, *Untitled* (1950, oil on canvas, 46 x 35 ins / 116 x 89 cm) GBP 20,000. STUTTGART, 29 Jan 2000, *Composition Op 301 X* (1962, oil on canvas, 40 x 30 ins / 102 x 76 cm) DEM 37,000. HAMBURG, 1 Dec 2000, *Untitled* (1960, gouache on board, 25 x 20 ins / 64 x 50 cm) DEM 20,000. HAMBURG, 8 June 2001, *Composition* (gouache, 25 x 19 ins / 63 x 47 cm) DEM 28,000. COLOGNE, 8 Dec 2001, *Untitled* (gouache, 24 x 19 ins / 62 x 47 cm) DEM 22,000. BERLIN, 8 June 2002, *Opus No. 123* (1959, oil on canvas, 36 x 29 ins / 92 x 74 cm) EUR 23,000. LONDON, 27 June 2002, *Homage to Delaunay and Gleizes* (c. 1938, oil on canvas, 44 x 27 ins / 111 x 69 cm) GBP 13,000. COLOGNE, 29 May 2003, *Untitled* (1954, gouache over pencil, 18 x 12 ins / 45 x 31 cm) EUR 5,000. MUNICH, 5 Dec 2003, *Untitled* (oil on canvas, 32 x 26 ins / 81 x 65 cm) EUR 4,500. HAMBURG, 26 March 2004, *Cattle in Stable* (watercolour and Indian ink, 18 x 24 ins / 46 x 61 cm) EUR 3,000. HAMBURG, 3 Dec 2004, *Relief Painting* (oil on corrugated card/canvas, 40 x 17 ins / 101 x 43 cm) EUR 22,000.

FLEISCHMANN, Andreas Johann

German, 19th century.

Born 1811, in Nuremberg; died 7 June 1878, in Munich.

Engraver (burin).

One of Andreas Fleischmann's known works is *Shepherd Healer* (1839).

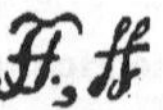

FLEISCHMANN, Arthur

Czech, 20th century.

Born 1896.

Also active in Australia.

Sculptor.

Arthur Fleischmann was a student at the art academy in Prague and then continued his training in Vienna. He worked in several European countries and was also active in the USA, South Africa and Australia. He featured in the Exposition Internationale de Sculpture, Musée Rodin, Paris (1961).

AUCTION RECORDS:

SYDNEY, 17 April 1988, *Seated Figure* (plastic, h. 15 3/4 ins / 40 cm) AUD 1,900. SINGAPORE, 1 Oct 2000, *Legong Dancer* (green patinated bronze, h. 14 ins / 36 cm) SGD 7,500.

FLEISCHMANN, Auguste Christian

German, 18th century.

Active in Nuremberg (Bavaria).

Engraver.

Auguste Fleischmann worked for publishers in Nuremberg, and produced portraits.

FLEISCHMANN, Carl

German, 19th century.

Born 11 December 1853, in Floss (Palatinate).

Active in Nuremberg (Bavaria).

Painter.

Carl Fleischmann studied at the school of arts and crafts in Nuremberg, and became a teacher there in 1873. He exhibited *Portraits of Women* in Nuremberg in 1891, *Monk Reading* in Leipzig in 1897, and *Still-lifes* in Munich in 1904 and 1909.

MUSEUMS AND GALLERIES:

NUREMBERG (City Art Collection): three portraits of men.

FLEISCHMANN, D.C.C.

German, 17th century.

Active in 1690 in Nuremberg (Bavaria).

Engraver (burin).

Together with Auguste Christian Fleischmann, D.C.C. Fleischmann worked for F. Rothscholz, a publisher in Nuremberg.

FLEISCHMANN, Friedrich

German, 19th century.

Born 1791, in Nuremberg; died 1834, in Munich.

Painter, engraver.

Friedrich Fleischmann studied under Ambrosius Gabler. His known works include portraits, miniatures and engravings of historical subjects.

FLEISCHMANN, Jacob

German, 19th century.

Born c. 1816, in Nuremberg; died 1866.

Engraver (including etching), draughtsman.

Jacob was the son of Friedrich Fleischmann. He studied under his brother Andreas, then under Henriquel-Dupont in Paris. He worked for booksellers in France and Germany.

FLEISCHMANN, Julius

German, 19th century.

Born 18 March 1813, in Meissen (Saxony).

Engraver, draughtsman.
Julius Fleischmann studied under A. Krüger and A. Richter in Dresden. His speciality was engraving landscapes.

FLEISHER, Samuel
American, 19th - 20th century.
Born 27 November 1871, in Philadelphia.
Painter.
Samuel Fleischer lived and worked in Philadelphia, where he set up a drawing course to give free artistic instruction to children from poor families.

FLEISSIG, Nicolae, or later Nicolas
Romanian, 20th - 21st century.
Born 24 March 1948, in Târgu Mures (Transylvania).
Active in France from 1982.
Sculptor. Monuments.
Nicolae Fleissig graduated from the N. Grigorescu Institute of flastic arts in Bucharest in 1973. In 1973 he won a major prize and in 1974 was awarded a scholarship. He has executed more than 10 monumental sculptures in marble, stone, granite or wood. Erected in public places, the most important are as follows: *Milestone* for the Magura Sculpture Park in Romania (1973); *Antiqua II* in Hoyerswerda in Germany (1977); *Milestone* in Burgas in Bulgaria (1980); and *Genesis* (1982) and *Loneliness* (1983) in New Hampshire in the USA.

Fleissig's work is characterised by a careful choice of material. The selection of the most appropriate material for the individual work and the most appropriate way of working it, constitute important phases in his creative process. He often sets the carefully polished primary elements of the work against an aggressive and scathing opposite.

He has taken part in group exhibitions in Romania, France, the USA, Luxembourg, Germany, Spain, Switzerland, Yugoslavia, Bulgaria and Russia, among others. His work has featured notably in the Salon Grands et Jeunes d'Aujourd'hui in Paris. He has taken part in some 10 sculpture symposia, primarily in Romania, Bulgaria, Yugoslavia, Germany and the USA. He has also had solo exhibitions in Romania, France and the USA, the first being in Bucharest in 1973.

BIBLIOGRAPHY:
Ionel Jianou, *Romanian Artists and the West*, American Romanian Academy of Arts and Sciences, Los Angeles, 1986.

FLÉMAL, Bertholet
German, 17th century.
Painter.
In 1687 Flémal won the right to practise his art freely in Cologne.

FLÉMAL, Bertholet or Bartholomé, or Flémalle or Flemaël or Flamaël
Flemish, 17th century.
Born 23 May 1614, in Liège; died 10 or 18 July 1675, in Liège.
Painter. Allegorical subjects, portraits.
Flemish School.
The son of the glass painter Renier Flémal, Bertholet Flémal trained under Hendrick Trippez and Geraert Douffet before leaving for Italy. He was in Rome in 1638, and was summoned to Florence by the grand duke of Tuscany, Ferdinand III, who commissioned him to decorate a gallery in his palace. Around 1644 he went to Paris where he was well received. In 1647 he stayed in Liège and after having executed major works in the churches of that town, he left for Brussels. In 1670 he was called back to Paris, where he was elected a member of the Académie Royale de Peinture (royal academy of painting). He was also a professor there. The desire to see his country again induced him to accept the prestigious projects which Maximilian von Bayern, Bishop-prince of Liège, offered him. Flémal painted the prelate's portrait, receiving as a reward a prebend in the collegiate church of St-Paul in Liège. He also executed the portrait of the Count of Monterey, governor of the Netherlands.

His reputation rests on the decoration of the ceiling of the royal chamber of audience in the Palais des Tuileries, executed in 1670 and today obliterated, the subject of which was *Religion Protecting France*.

MUSEUMS AND GALLERIES:
BAMBERG: *Angels Weeping over the Dead Christ*; *The Funeral of Hephaestus* - BRUSSELS: *Heliodorus Expelled from the Temple* - CAEN: *Adoration of the Shepherds* - DRESDEN: *Aeneas Bidding Farewell to Troy* - FONTAINEBLEAU: *Alexander at the Tomb of Achilles* - KASSEL: *The Farewell of Alexander the Great*; *The Dying Lucretia Surrounded by her Own* (no longer attributed) - LIÈGE (Mus. d'Art moderne et d'Art contemporain): *Self-portrait*; *The Flight into Egypt*; *The Martyrdom of St Catherine*; *Infanticide* - LILLE: *Episode from the Life of St Lambert* - NIORT: *St Lambert* - PARIS (cupola of the church of the Discalced Carmelites): *The Prophet Elijah Ascending into the Sky on a Chariot of Fire* - PARIS (Grands-Augustins, sacristy): *Adoration of the Three Magi* - PARIS (Louvre): *Mysteries of the Old and New Testaments* - PARIS (Mus. Marmottan-Monet): *Vision of St Bruno* - STOCKHOLM: *Achilles Wounded in the Heel by Paris* - WROCLAW: *The Magnanimity of Scipio*.

AUCTION RECORDS:
BRUSSELS, 18 June 1980, *Allegory of Victory* (oil on canvas, 38¼ x 52 ins / 97 x 132 cm) BEF 130,000. PARIS, 12 June 1986, *The Victories of Rome* (oil on canvas, 38½ x 52¼ ins / 97.5 x 132.5 cm) FRF 45,000.

FLÉMAL, Renier, the Elder, or Flémalle or Flemael
Flemish School, 16th - 17th century.
Active in Liège.
Glass painter.
Renier Flémal was the father of Bertholet, Willem, Renier the Younger and a fourth son, Hendrik, who was a goldsmith. Renier the Elder was responsible for the stained glass window in the church of St Paul in Liège depicting *The Adoration of the Magi*.

FLÉMAL, Renier, the Younger, or Flémalle
Flemish, 17th century.
Born 1610, in Liège.
Painter.
Flemish School.
Rénier Flémal the Younger was the son of Renier Flémal the Elder and it is surmised that he died in Spain. He is mentioned by Siret.

FLÉMAL, Willem, or Flémalle or Flemael
Flemish, 17th century.
Born in Liège; died 1676, in Liège.
Glass painter.
Liège School, Flemish School.
Willem Flémal was the brother of Bertholet Flémal. He was taught by his father Renier Flémal. He seems to have been primarily an artist in stained glass and probably took over from his father in this line of work.

MUSEUMS AND GALLERIES:
LIÈGE (Church of Ste-Madeleine): stained glass in grisaille.

FLÉMALLE, Master of. See **MASTERS** and **CAMPIN Robert**

FLEMING, Henry Stuart
American, 19th century.
Born 21 July 1863, in Philadelphia.

Active in New York.
Painter.
Henry Stuart Fleming was a pupil of Lefebvre and Benjamin-Constant in Paris.

FLEMING, Ian
British, 20th century.
Born 19 November 1906.
Painter, watercolourist, engraver (etching). Military subjects, landscapes, still-lifes.
Ian Fleming studied at the Glasgow School of Art and also trained in Paris. He took part in group exhibitions in Scotland and at the Royal Academy in London. Fleming was a member of several Scottish artists' associations.
AUCTION RECORDS:
EDINBURGH, 11 Nov 1980, *Green Gate* (1950, oil on canvas, 16¼ x 20 ins / 41 x 51 cm) GBP 380. LONDON, 4 March 1987, *Troops Disembarking* (1945, watercolour and pen, 16 x 20¾ ins / 40.5 x 53 cm) GBP 750. GLASGOW, 7 Feb 1989, *Still-life with Cactus, Bottle, Vase and Plate* (1946, oil on canvas, 18 x 24 ins / 46 x 61 cm) GBP 880. EDINBURGH, 14 Dec 1999, *Boulder Beach, Findon* (oil on board, 25 x 30 ins / 63 x 76 cm) GBP 1,500. EDINBURGH, 7 Dec 2001, *Brown Sail* (oil on canvas, 30 x 39 ins / 75 x 100 cm) GBP 2,400. EDINBURGH, 17 Oct 2002, *Sunset, St Monance* (oil on board, 17 x 25 ins / 44 x 64 cm) GBP 1,050. EDINBURGH, 8 April 2004, *Shetland Croft* (oil on canvas, 35 x 28 ins / 90 x 70 cm) GBP 2,100. SHREWSBURY, 28 April 2004, *Ben Lomond* (oil on canvas, double-sided, 20 x 24 ins / 51 x 61 cm) GBP 1,000.

FLEMING, Jean Robinson
American, 20th century.
Born 22 September 1874, in Charleston.
Painter.
Jean Robinson Fleming belonged to local artistic associations.

FLEMING, John
British, 19th century.
Born 1792; died 1845.
Painter, illustrator. Landscapes.
John Fleming is best known for a series of views painted for Swann's *Scottish Lochs*, published in 1834.
MUSEUMS AND GALLERIES:
GLASGOW (Corporation Gal.): *View of Greenock* (1827).
AUCTION RECORDS:
PERTH, 13 April 1981, *Landscape with Mill* (oil on canvas, 17 x 25 ins / 43 x 63.5 cm) GBP 450. SCOTLAND, 28 Aug 1984, *Duntreath Castle, Loch Fyne* (1869, oil on panel, 13¾ x 21¼ ins / 35 x 54 cm) GBP 1,650. EDINBURGH, 30 April 1985, *Cardwell, Bay, Gourock* (7 x 11 ins / 18 x 28 cm) GBP 1,600. LONDON, 26 Jan 2000, *Ladies and Children Bathing with a Merchant Ship and Other Vessels beyond* (1833, oil on panel, 20 x 29 ins / 51 x 74 cm) GBP 2,600. LONDON, 30 Aug 2000, *Clyde from Greenock toward Dumbarton* (1833, oil on panel, 20 x 30 ins / 52 x 76 cm) GBP 3,000. BILLINGSHURST, 18 July 2001, *Sailing Vessels in a Loch. Vessels at Anchor in a Loch* (1834, oil on panel, a pair, 5 x 7 ins / 13 x 17 cm) GBP 1,300. EDINBURGH, 24 Aug 2001, *Panoramic View of Dunbarton from the Northwest* (1832, oil on canvas, 20 x 31 ins / 52 x 80 cm) GBP 6,200.

FLEMING, Margaret
British.
Painter. Animals.
MUSEUMS AND GALLERIES:
SYDNEY: *The Parrot*.

FLEMING, Nicolas
French, 18th century.
Active in Paris in 1753.
Painter, sculptor.

FLEMING, Raoul P.
American, 20th century.
Born in Greenwich.
Painter. Landscapes.
Raoul P. Fleming was a pupil of Frank Vincent Du Mond and exhibited landscapes at the Salon des Artistes Français from 1933 to 1938.

FLEMING, William
British, 19th century.
Born 1804.
Painter. Interiors.
William Fleming was a pupil of Van den Broeek and C.-H. Hodges. He was active in Devon, and in France, from 1834 to 1837.

FLEMING, THE. See **LE ROY Guillaume**

FLEMMING, Ernst
German, 19th century.
Died 22 October 1865.
Active in Wolfenbüttel (Lower Saxony).
Painter (porcelain).
The ducal museum in Brunswick holds pieces of porcelain from the Fürstenberg factory painted by Flemming.

FLENSBORG, Valdemar
Danish, 19th century.
Born 31 July 1846, in Copenhagen; died 3 September 1876, in Copenhagen.
Painter.
After having studied at the Kunstakademi in Copenhagen, Valdemar Flensborg worked as a portrait painter in the city until his premature death in 1876.

FLENTJEN, Johann Auguste Ludwig
German, 19th century.
Born 25 August 1823, in Hitzacker (Hanover); died 10 May 1877, probably in Schaffhausen.
Engraver (wood).
Flentjen studied in Schaffhausen, where he became a citizen, in 1860. He exhibited illustrations for calendars, and other works, at the Swiss *Turnus* in 1865.

FLERDYN, Hans
Flemish School, 16th century.
Painter.
Antwerp School.
Flerdyn was received as a master in 1591.

FLERI, Joseph C.
American, 20th century.
Born 20 May 1889, in Brooklyn (New York City).
Sculptor. Religious subjects.
Joseph C. Fleri was a member of the National Society of Sculpture and the New York Architectural League. He carved religious works for Philadelphia and Bethlehem, Pennsylvania.

FLEROWSKY, Dionissi Nicolaiévitch
Russian, 19th century.
Born 26 September (7 October) 1791, in Tobolsk; died after 1862.
Sculptor (wood).
His sculptures, which represent religious subjects, such as *Mary on the Road from Bethlehem to Nazareth*, won awards at the Peasant Exhibition in St Petersburg in 1860, and in 1861 at the Great Exhibition in London.

FLERS, Camille
French, 19th century.
Born 15 February 1802, in Paris; died 27 June 1868, in Annet (Seine-et-Marne).

Painter (gouache), watercolourist, pastellist.
Landscapes, waterscapes.
Barbizon School.

Studied in Paris and was awarded bronze in 1840 and silver in 1847. Flers received the Chevalier of the Légion d'Honneur on 11 September 1849. He exhibited at Salons from 1831 to 1863, chiefly landscapes. His body of work includes *Watermill on the Marne; Courtyard at St-Leu-Taverny; View at Moulinal; Animals in a Landscape; Ruins of Arques Castle; Courtyard at Aumale; Chestnut Trees at Bercy after the Recent Floods; Moulin de la Louques; Country Road near Rivière-Thibouville; Moulin de Chelles; Village of St-Pierce on the Greater St Bernard; Côte des Deux Amants on the Seine; St-Ouen Island; Fishermen's Huts; Moulin des Cailloux; Floods at Charenton; Edge of a Wood at Montfermeil; Oyster Beds at Dieppe; Farmyard at Grand Bailly; Willows on the Beurronne; Harvest Time at Fresnes;* and *Henriette Island.*

Flers excelled at pastels and, in 1846, he published his theories on pastel work in the professional journal *Artist.* Flers was part of the pioneering phalanx of artists who stormed the bastion of classicism, opting to paint directly from nature; as such, he belonged to the School of 1830. While not having the visionary talents of a Théodore Rousseau, the expressive force of a Daubigny or, for that matter, the innate charm of Corot, Camille Flers nonetheless succeeded in translating nature to canvas with a notable degree of sincerity.

BIBLIOGRAPHY:

Miquel, Pierre, '*Le Paysage français au XIXe siècle 1800-1900. L'École de la nature*' in vol. II-III, Éd. de la Martinelle, Maurs-la-Jolie, 1985.

MUSEUMS AND GALLERIES:

AUTUN: *Hazel Trees on the Banks of the Bresle* - BÉZIERS: *Meadow at Aumale* - CHERBOURG: *Seascape* - LE HAVRE: *River in Brittany* - LE PUY-EN-VELAY: *Thatched Cottage in Normandy* - LILLE (MBA, Wicar Collection): Dessin - ORLÉANS: *Landscape* - PARIS (Louvre): *Landscape near Paris.*

AUCTION RECORDS:

PARIS, 1891, *Banks of the Oise,* FRF 970. PARIS, 24 Feb 1899, *View near Touques,* FRF 135. PARIS, 25 Feb 1901, *River Bank,* FRF 150. PARIS, 22-24 April 1901, *Bridge at Bois,* FRF 255. PARIS, 12 Feb 1909, *Banks of the Loire after a Storm,* FRF 550; *Spring Morning,* FRF 550. LONDON, 13 Feb 1909, *Washerwoman,* GBP 7. PARIS, 20 Nov 1918, *One in a Million (Robinson),* FRF 220; *Peasant Woman Driving Animals in the Mountains* (watercolour) FRF 155. PARIS, 4 and 5 Dec 1918, *Loaded Cart on a Country Road at Sunrise* (pastel) FRF 280; *Boat and Barge on a River* (watercolour) FRF 225. PARIS, 29 May 1919, *Landscape with Figures,* FRF 185; *Still-life,* FRF 260. PARIS, 14 Jan 1921, *Landscape with Mills and Watercourses,* FRF 470. PARIS, 18 April 1921, *Laundresses,* FRF 520. PARIS, 23-24 May 1921, *Fishing Boats on the Seine at St-Denis* (pencil) FRF 42; *Bridge at Charenton* (pencil) FRF 100; *River Bank* (pencil) FRF 37; *Dawn* (pastel) FRF 105. PARIS, 26 March 1923, *Normandy Landscape,* FRF 700. PARIS, 28 June 1923, *Evening Landscape* (watercolour) FRF 390. PARIS, 28 Jan 1924, *Floods at Charenton: Café under Water,* FRF 450; *Floods at Charenton: The Rescue Boat,* FRF 450. PARIS, 14 Nov 1924, *Landscape at Harvest Time,* FRF 1,050. PARIS, 4 Feb 1925, *Washhouse beside the River,* FRF 550. PARIS, 25 April 1926, *Little Fishermen* (pastel) FRF 680. PARIS, 10 Dec 1926, *Landscape* (pastel) FRF 550; *Seascape* (pastel) FRF 200. PARIS, 11 Dec 1926, *Sluice,* FRF 1,220. PARIS, 16 Feb 1927, *Evening View of a Pasture by a Stream in Normandy,* FRF 700. PARIS, 27 April 1928, *Landscape with Three Mills,* FRF 2,100. PARIS, 4 May 1928, *Pond* (pastel) FRF 220; *Before the Storm,* FRF 2,050. PARIS, 18 and 20 June 1928, *River Banks with Figures* (two panels) FRF 1,465. PARIS, 30 Oct 1928, *Landscape with Watercourse* (drawing) FRF 60. PARIS, 25 Jan 1929, *Thatched Cottage and Figures on the Banks of a River,* FRF 620. PARIS, 17 May 1929, *Footbridge over a River in Normandy,* FRF 1,150. PARIS, 27 March 1931, *Footbridge,* FRF 1,950. PARIS, 28 April 1937, *River Bank,* FRF 400. PARIS, 16 and 17 May 1939, *Boats on the River,* FRF 380. PARIS, 11 July 1941, *Landscape* (1855, pastel) FRF 600; *Banks of the River,* FRF 1,820. PARIS, 13 March 1942, *Country Road,* FRF 4,000. PARIS, 4 May 1942, *Bridge at Bois; Thatched Roofs; Sheds* (three drawings in pencil) FRF 400. PARIS, 22 June 1942, *Cattle Feeding by the River,* FRF 2,500. PARIS, 24 June 1942, *Clogmaker Family in the Woods* (1863) FRF 15,500. PARIS, 21 Dec 1942, *Landscape near Vichy* (pencil) FRF 750. PARIS, 3 Feb 1943, *Farmyard* (graphite, heightened with watercolour and white gouache) FRF 300. PARIS, 29 March 1943, *Cattle at Pasture* (watercolour) FRF 1,500. PARIS, 10 Dec 1943, *Cutting Reeds* (1835) FRF 11,000. PARIS, 14 June 1944, *Farmyard* (1849, pastel) FRF 8,800. PARIS, 20 Oct 1944, *Old Country Dwelling,* FRF 1,900. PARIS, 4 Dec 1944, *View near Soissons* (black chalk, heightened with white) FRF 320; *Marne at Vaires* (1852, black chalk, heightened with gouache) FRF 520. PARIS, 14 June 1945, *River Bank,* FRF 7,200. PARIS, 22 June 1945, *Country Road* (drawing in black pencil) FRF 500. PARIS, 27 Jan 1947, *Landscape,* FRF 4,000; *Landscape,* FRF 14,000. PARIS, 27 March 1947, *Landscape near Soissons* (1865, drawing) FRF 400. PARIS, 2 June 1947, *Farmers and Animals on the Road,* FRF 9,300. PARIS, 23 June 1954, *Cattle in a Meadow,* FRF 32,000. BORDEAUX, 31 May 1978, *Pastoral Scene* (oil on canvas, 21 1/4 x 16 1/2 ins / 54 x 42 cm) FRF 7,200. BERN, 6 May 1981, *Landscape with Stream* (pastel, 7 1/2 x 12 1/4 ins / 19 x 31 cm) CHF 1,900. PARIS, 3 Nov 1983, *Landscape* (1844, oil on canvas, 11 3/4 x 19 ins / 30 x 48 cm) FRF 20,000. VERSAILLES, 12 June 1985, *Kitchen Interior* (1863, oil on canvas, 39 1/2 x 32 ins / 100.5 x 81 cm) FRF 25,000. VERSAILLES, 19 Nov 1989, *Fording the River in the Autumn Mist* (oil on card, 11 1/2 x 17 1/4 ins / 29 x 44 cm) FRF 10,400. PARIS, 12 Dec 1990, *Washerwoman and Fisherman in a Boat near a Water Mill* (1850, oil on card, 15 x 21 1/4 ins / 38 x 54 cm) FRF 21,000. PARIS, 5 April 1992, *Landscape with Pond* (oil on panel, diam. 5 1/4 ins / 13.5 cm) FRF 6,400. LONDON, 16 June 1993, *River Flowing through Meadows* (1849, pastel, 10 1/4 x 16 ins / 25.8 x 40.5 cm) GBP 1,380. PARIS, 29 April 1994, *Landing Stage on the River Bank* (1847, pastel heightened with gouache, 6 3/4 x 9 ins / 17 x 23 cm) FRF 6,000. LYONS, 28 March 1999, *Lunch Beside the Seine* (oil on canvas, 14 x 24 ins / 35 x 61 cm) FRF 30,000. PARIS, 31 May 1999, *The Ferry* (1864, oil on canvas, 13 x 17 ins / 32 x 44 cm) FRF 31,000. CALAIS, 10 Dec 2000, *Collectors of Firewood* (oil on canvas, 14 x 22 ins / 36 x 57 cm) FRF 16,000. MELUN, 10 Dec 2000, *River with Fishermen and Sailing Boats* (1860, oil on panel, 8 x 12 ins / 21 x 30 cm) FRF 40,500. ZURICH, 21 March 2001, *Still-life of Vegetables* (1862, oil on canvas, 32 x 39 ins / 82 x 100 cm) CHF 8,000. PARIS, 23 Nov 2001, *Young Peasant in Countryside* (1846, oil on canvas, 26 x 41 ins / 67 x 104 cm) FRF 50,000. MELUN, 1 Dec 2002, *Voiliers au fild de l'eau* (oil on canvas, 18 x 26 ins / 45 x 67 cm) EUR 6,100. LILLE, 15 Dec 2002, *Bouquet of Flowers* (oil on canvas, 59 x 39 ins / 150 x 100 cm) EUR 3,500. NEW YORK, 7 Oct 2003, *End of the Day* (oil on canvas, 43 x 63 ins / 110 x 161 cm) USD 5,000. FONTAINEBLEAU, 7 Dec 2003, *Normandy Landscape* (oil on canvas, 13 x 18 ins / 32 x 46 cm) EUR 4,200.

FLES, Etha

Dutch, 19th - 20th century.
Born 1857, in Utrecht; died 1948.
Painter, engraver (etching). Genre scenes.

Etha Fles took part in group exhibitions, notably in Paris in 1900, where she was awarded a bronze medal at the Exposition Universelle. Her paintings consisted of picturesque and genre scenes.

AUCTION RECORDS:

AMSTERDAM, 17 Sept 1991, *Villagers Going to Church in Laren* (1887, oil on canvas, 23 1/4 x 34 1/4 ins / 59 x 87 cm) NLG 3,220.

FLESCH, Tivadar or Theodor. See **FELEDI**

FLESCH-BRUNNINGEN, Luma or Ludmilla,
later Frau von Csuzy
Austrian, 19th century.
Born 31 March 1856, in Brünn (now Brno, Czech Republic).
Painter. Portraits, genre scenes.

Flesch-Brunningen studied in Vienna, then Munich, where she settled. She was awarded a bronze medal in 1900 at the *World Fair*, and a third-class medal in 1902.

MUSEUMS AND GALLERIES:
BRNO (Academy of Moravia): *Lady in a Mask* - BRNO (Moravské zemské Muz.): *Self-portrait.*

AUCTION RECORDS:
VIENNA, 20 Sept 1977, *Love Token* (oil on canvas, 42 1/2 x 56 3/4 ins / 108 x 144 cm) USD 600.

FLESCHAUER. See **VLEESCHOUWERE**

FLESCHIÈRES, Fabien de, or Fléchières
French, 16th century.
Sculptor. Animals. Statues.

In 1573, Fabien de Fléschières repaired a statue of St John. In 1578, he executed statues of three lions in white stone for the law courts in the town of Cambrai.

FLESSELLES
French, 19th century.
Active in Paris c. 1800.
Miniaturist.

Studied under Bourgeois and Vincent and exhibited two portraits at the 1802 Paris Salon. A portrait of a man signed by Flesselles was shown at an exhibition of miniatures in Berlin in 1906.

FLESSHIER, B.
British, 17th century.
Painter.

B. Flesshier is mentioned by Walpole as a painter of seascapes, landscapes and still-lifes with fruit. His work was held in high esteem, as seen from the fact that several of his paintings featured in the collections of Charles I and Sir Peter Lely. He is probably identifiable as the painter also known as Benjamin Flessiers.

AUCTION RECORDS:
LONDON, 13 Feb 1925, *William Wood Yeare,* GBP 10.

FLESSIERS, Balthasar
Flemish, 17th century.
Born probably in Ghent; died before 29 June 1626, in The Hague, 1619 according to C. Wright.
Painter.
Flemish School.

Balthasar Flessiers was a member of the Guild of St Luke in The Hague. His portrait, *Eva Fliegen,* was engraved by A. Stock and auctioned in Amsterdam in 1886. Another of his paintings, *Georg Wilhelm von Brandenburg,* was also engraved by Stock.

FLESSIERS, Benjamin
Flemish, 17th century.
Painter.
Flemish School.

Benjamin Flessiers was the son of Balthasar Flessiers. He studied in Amsterdam around 1629 with Isaac Pietersz.

FLESSIERS, Claes
Dutch, 17th century.
Active in The Hague.
Painter.

FLESSIERS, Joris
Dutch, 17th century.
Born c. 1616, in The Hague.
Painter.

Joris Flessiers was the son of Balthasar Flessiers.

FLESSIERS, Tobias
Dutch, 17th century.
Painter.

Tobias Flessiers was the son of Balthasar Flessiers. He is mentioned in London between 1652 and 1653. He painted still-lifes and seascapes.

FLESSIERS, Willem
Dutch, 17th century.
Died 1614 according to C. Wright.
Active in The Hague.
Painter.

Willem Flessiers was the son of Balthasar Flessiers.

FLETCHER, Angus
British, 19th century.
Sculptor.

Angus Fletcher exhibited at the Royal Academy from 1831 to 1839. The National Portrait Gallery in London has a bust by Fletcher, of Felicia Dorothea Hemans.

FLETCHER, Anne
American, 20th century.
Born 18 June 1876, in Chicago.
Active in Richmond (Virginia).
Painter. Wall decorations.

Anne Fletcher studied in New York and Paris.

FLETCHER, Calvin
American, 20th century.
Born 24 June 1882, in Provo (Utah); died 1963.
Painter. Scenes with figures. Wall decorations.

Calvin Fletcher studied art in the USA and Europe and became the first president of the Utah Art Institute. He made his reputation painting murals in Logan, Utah.

FLETCHER, Edwin Henry Eugene or Edward
British, 19th - 20th century.
Born 1857; died 1945.
Painter. Urban landscapes, waterscapes, landscapes with figures, seascapes.

Edwin Fletcher painted views of the Thames and London, including the river estuary and ports.

E Fletcher

AUCTION RECORDS:
TORQUAY, 16 June 1981, *Port Scenes* (two oils on canvas, 20 x 30 ins / 51 x 76 cm) GBP 600. LONDON, 14 July 1983, *Sunset on the Thames and St Paul's Cathedral* (oil on canvas, 40 1/4 x 59 3/4 ins / 102 x 152 cm) GBP 1,700. LONDON, 3 June 1986, *The Thames at Nore* (oil on canvas, 30 x 50 ins / 76 x 127 cm) GBP 2,000. LONDON, 26 Sept 1990, *The Thames* (oil on canvas, 20 x 30 ins / 51 x 76 cm) GBP 1,210. LONDON, 18 Oct 1990, *Traffic at the Mouth of the Thames* (oil on canvas, 16 x 24 ins / 40.5 x 61 cm) GBP 495. NEW YORK, 19 Jan 1994, *Shipping on the Thames* (oil on canvas, 20 x 30 ins / 50.8 x 76.2 cm) USD 1,265. LONDON, 3 May 1995, *The Thames at Westminster* (oil on canvas, 24 x 16 ins / 61 x 40.5 cm) GBP 747. LONDON, 30 May 1996, *Tower Bridge* (oil on canvas, 16 1/4 x 24 ins / 41 x 61 cm) GBP 1,035.

FLETCHER, Flitcroft
British, 19th century.
Active in Croydon.
Painter. Landscapes.

Flitcroft Fletcher exhibited regularly at the Royal Academy in London, from 1882. His name also features in catalogues from the Suffolk Street Gallery.

FLETCHER, Frank Morley
British, 19th century.
Born 25 April 1866; died 1949, in Ojai (California), USA.
Painter, engraver (wood), draughtsman, illustrator.
Mountainscapes.
Japonisme.

Frank Fletcher studied at University College, London, as well as in Liverpool, and under Cormon in Paris. He was director of the Edinburgh College of Art from 1908 to 1923, and the first director of the newly founded Santa Barbara School of Art, in California, from 1923 to 1930. He was a member of several English artistic societies, and the winner of numerous honours at international salons, notably for his woodcuts. He is the author of a seminal work on colour woodblock printing (*Woodblock printing; A Description of the Craft of Woodcutting & Colourprinting Based on the Japanese Practice*), and played a central role in the dissemination of the Japonist movement and ethos in the USA.

His prints are strongly influenced by the clearly defined perspective planes characteristic of Japanese compositions. His works feature mainly mountainscapes, printed in softly textured tones of green and mauve. In 1896, he published two coloured woodcuts entitled *Eve and the Serpent* and *Harpies*, with J. D. Batten; in 1897, he published *Meadowsweet* (without Batten's collaboration). He also produced illustrations for the collected poems of Louise Mary Muller: *Blue-blossomed Garden; Poems of California* (published by the Shauer Printing Studio in Santa Barbara in 1927). In the early days of animated cartoons, a number of his Californian pupils went on to work for the Disney Studios.

He exhibited in London, Paris and Dresden in 1903, and at the Carnegie Institute in Pittsburgh, Pennsylvania, in the same year. In 2002, his work featured in the exhibition *Le Japonisme en Amérique: oeuvres sur papier, 1880-1930* (*Japonisme in America: Works on Paper, 1880-1930*) at the Museum of American Art/Terra Foundation in Giverny, northern France.

BIBLIOGRAPHY:

Arnold, Edwin, *Japonica*, C. Scribner's Sons, New York, 1891. Stevenson, Robert Louis/Osborne, Lloyd, *The Ebb-Tide: A Trio and Quartette*, Stone and Kimball, Chicago, 1894. Fletcher, Frank Morley, *Wood-block printing*, J. Hogg, London, 1916. Fletcher, Frank Morley, *Colour-control*, Faber and Faber, London, 1936. Green, Nancy E., '*Arthur Wesley Dow: American Arts/Crafts*' in *American Art Review*, periodical, December, 1999. *Le Japonisme en Amérique: œuvres sur papier, 1880-1930*, exhibition catalogue, Musée d'art américain, Giverny, Terra Foundation for the Arts, Evanston (IL), 2002.

MUSEUMS AND GALLERIES:

BOSTON (MFA) - BUDAPEST (Magyar Nemzeti Múz.) - CHICAGO (Terra Foundation for American Art Collection): *Ojai Valley* (c. 1930, woodcut) - DRESDEN (Prints Collection): engravings - LONDON (British Mus.) - LONDON (Victoria and Albert Mus.): engravings - SAN DIEGO (MA) - SAN FRANCISCO (San Francisco Museums of Art): *California (2) Mount Shasta* (c. 1930, woodcut); *California (1) Salinas River* (c. 1930, woodcut) - WASHINGTON DC (Smithsonian American AM).

FLETCHER, Geoffrey S.
British, 20th century.
Born 1923.
Draughtsman. Portraits, landscapes.

FLETCHER, Henry
British, 18th century.
Active c. 1729.
Engraver.

Henry Fletcher executed an engraving of *Bathsheba and her Companions, Bathing* after Sebastiano Conca, and a small number of portraits including *The Boston Minister Ebenezer Pemberton*, used as a frontispiece for a collection of the latter's sermons.

FLETCHER, Nicolas
18th century.
Engraver.

This artist is referred to by Basan, for having engraved, in about 1750, views of Rome, after Canaletto.

FLETCHER, Peter
American, 20th century.
Painter (mixed media).

Peter Fletcher works with composite products, such as marble dust and metal oxides, producing paintings that fall between abstraction and suggestions of New Figuration. In 1982, he produced a film in France, *Nostalgia for the Future*, for the Centre National d'Art et de Culture Beaubourg. He exhibited in 1979 at the California Institute of Art, where he may have been a pupil, in 1986 in New York, in 1987 in Houston, and in 1988 in Paris and at the Metropolitan Museum of Art, New York. He was short-listed at the Salon de Montrouge in 1985.

AUCTION RECORDS:

PARIS, 13 April 1988, *Interruption* (1987, mixed media/canvas, 76 3/4 x 57 ins / 195 x 145 cm) FRF 13,000.

FLETCHER, Thomas
British, 18th century.
Painter (porcelain).

Thomas Fletcher was active in Shelton (Shropshire) from 1786 to 1806.

FLETCHER, William
British, 17th century.
Painter. Portraits.

MUSEUMS AND GALLERIES:

OXFORD (Bodleian Library): *Portrait of Bishop James Ussher*.

FLETCHER, William Teulon Blandford
British, 19th - 20th century.
Born 1858; died 1936.
Painter. Genre scenes, landscapes, seascapes.

Blandford Fletcher exhibited at the Royal Academy in London from 1879.

BLANDFORD FLETCHER

AUCTION RECORDS:

NEW YORK, 24-26 Feb 1904, *English Cottage Garden*, USD 55. LONDON, 9 Dec 1907, *Truants*, GBP 5; *Wareham*, GBP 5. LONDON, 21 March 1910, *Seascape*, GBP 8. LONDON, 2 April 1910, *Winter Evening*, GBP 9. LONDON, 29 March 1982, *Evening in a Sussex Village* (oil on canvas, 16 x 11 1/2 ins / 40.5 x 29.5 cm) GBP 1,500. LONDON, 13 June 1984, *The Orchard* (1901, oil on canvas, 20 x 30 ins / 51 x 76 cm) GBP 2,300. LONDON, 13 Nov 1985, *Portrait of Dorothy, the Artist's Sister* (c. 1884, oil on canvas, 17 x 13 ins / 43 x 33 cm) GBP 6,500. LONDON, 12 March 1992, *The Walberswick Ferry* (oil on canvas, 17 x 24 ins / 43 x 61 cm) GBP 5,750. LONDON, 3 Nov 1993, *Old Culvert* (1899, oil on canvas, 20 x 30 ins / 51 x 76 cm) GBP 2,760. LONDON, 10 March 1995, *Summer Day* (oil on card, 9 3/4 x 7 1/2 ins / 25 x 18.8 cm) GBP 2,990. LONDON, 5 Nov 1997, *Disobedient Children* (oil on panel, 15 x 12 1/4 ins / 38 x 31 cm) GBP 9,200.

FLETCHER-WATSON, P. See **WATSON P. Fletcher**

FLETNER, Peter. See **FLÖTNER**

FLEUNER, Peter
Dutch, 16th century.
Engraver (wood).

One woodcut bearing the signature of this artist, and dated 1549, is known.

FLEUR, J. de
British, 18th century.
Painter.
J. de Fleur's portrait of *Lord G. Gordon* was engraved by Th. Trotter.

FLEUR, Jean
French, 17th century.
Died before 1656.
Active in Paris.
Painter.

FLEUR, Nicolas Guillaume de La.
See **DELAFLEUR**

FLEUR, Willy
French, 20th century.
Born 1888; died 1967.
Painter. Still-lifes, flowers.
AUCTION RECORDS:
AMSTERDAM, 30 Aug 1988, *Chrysanthemums in a Vase with Apples on a Pewter Dish and a Glass Bowl* (oil on canvas, 31 1/2 x 23 3/4 ins / 80 x 60.5 cm) NLG 1,092. AMSTERDAM, 17 Sept 1991, *Still-life with Chrysanthemums in a Vase and a Basket full of Apples and a Chinese Vase on a Table* (oil on canvas, 31 1/2 x 23 3/4 ins / 80 x 60.5 cm) NLG 1,610. AMSTERDAM, 18 Feb 1992, *Still-life with a Bunch of Asters in a Clay Vase, Pewter Pitcher and some Apples* (oil on canvas, 39 1/4 x 31 1/2 ins / 100 x 80 cm) NLG 1,265. AMSTERDAM, 19 April 1994, *Still-life of Fruit on a Table* (1920, oil on canvas, 23 1/4 x 31 ins / 59 x 79 cm) NLG 2,300. AMSTERDAM, 2 Sept 1997, *White Amaryllis in a Clay Vase* (oil on canvas, 23 1/2 x 20 ins / 60 x 51 cm) NLG 922.

FLEURAC, Louis Victor Marie de
French, 20th century.
Born in Paris.
Engraver.
Louis de Fleurac exhibited lithographs at the Salon des Artistes Français in 1928 and 1930.

FLEUREL, Jean
French, 16th century.
Active in Limoges c. 1570.
Enameller.

FLEURENT, Robert
French, 20th century.
Born 1904, in Bois-Colombes; died 1981.
Painter. Landscapes with figures.
Robert Fleurent exhibited at the Salon des Artistes Français in the 1930s.

He painted landscapes of many French regions.
AUCTION RECORDS:
HONFLEUR, 31 May 1987, *Barge on the River Seine* (oil on canvas, 19 3/4 x 25 1/2 ins / 50 x 65 cm) FRF 7,000.

FLEUREOT, René
French, 18th century.
Active in Paris in 1731.
Painter (?), sculptor (?).

FLEURET
19th century.
Painter, miniaturist. Portraits.
Worked from 1820 to 1850. A portrait of a man painted by him was sold in 1905 at auction in Cologne, at Heberle's, with the Jaffé collection.

FLEURET, Léon Louis
French, 19th century.
Born in Pacy-sur-Eure (Eure).
Engraver (wood).
Fleuret was a pupil of Hildebrand and the younger Pannemaker; he was a member of the Société des Artistes Français as of 1908. Fleuret received an honourable mention in 1882.

FLEURET, Pasquier
French, 16th century.
Engraver.
Fleuret worked at the Mint in Paris.

FLEURIAN, François Pierre
French, 18th - 19th century.
Born 21 October 1764, in Caen; died 17 September 1810, in Caen.
Painter. Figures.
François Pierre Fleurian was curator of the museum in Caen. In 1808 he sent *Head of a Child* to the Salon de Paris.
MUSEUMS AND GALLERIES:
CAEN: *Head of an Old Man*.

FLEURIAU DE BELLEMARE, Cécile
French, 19th century.
Born 1794.
Active in Nantes.
Watercolourist.
Pursued her studies under M. de Bellemare.

FLEURIET, René
French, 20th century.
Painter.
René Fleuriet exhibited at the Salon des Indépendants in 1941, 1942 and 1943, mainly *Snow Impressions*.

FLEURIOT, François
French, 17th century.
Active in Le Mans.
Painter.
François Fleuriot produced an *Adoration of the Magi* which hangs in the cathedral in Le Mans, and paintings of a *Rosary* which are in the church of Notre-Dame-du-Pré and the church in Sarcé.

FLEURIOT, Mathieu
French, 17th century.
Active in Angers.
Painter.

FLEURIVAL, Maurice
French, 20th century.
Born in Russia, of French origin.
Painter.
Maurice Fleurival exhibited at the 1931 Salon des Indépendants.

FLEURON, de
Painter. Portraits.
MUSEUMS AND GALLERIES:
VIENNA (Czernin'sche Gemäldegal.): *Portrait of a Woman*.

FLEUROT-MONNIER, Fernande
French, 20th century.
Born in Besançon.
Painter. Landscapes.
Fernande Fleurot-Monnier exhibited at the Salon de la Société Nationale des Beaux-Arts in Paris from 1923.

FLEURY
French, 19th century.
Born in Châtillon; died 1877.
Lithographer.
Worked on the review entitled *Vie Parisienne* (*Parisian Life*) and as a book illustrator.

FLEURY, Albert François
French, 19th century.
Born 2 February 1848, in Le Havre.
Painter. Landscapes, seascapes. Murals.
Studied under Lehmann and Renouf at the École des Beaux-Arts in Paris and made his début at the 1880 Paris Salon. Fleury chiefly painted murals. He settled in Chicago in 1888.

Auction records:
London, 17 May 1991, *By the Seaside* (1883, oil on card, 9 1/2 x 12 3/4 ins / 24 x 32.5 cm) GBP 3,080.

FLEURY, Andrée
French, 20th century.
Born in Paris.
Painter. Landscapes.
Andrée Fleury exhibited at the Salon d'Automne.
Auction records:
London, 29 March 1982, *Paris Snowed Under* (1900, oil on canvas, 12 1/4 x 18 ins / 31 x 45.5 cm) GBP 480.

FLEURY, Antoine
French, 17th - 18th century.
Active in Toulon.
Sculptor.
Antoine Fleury worked from 1691 to 1721 in the sculpture studio of the Arsenal de Toulon, and executed sculptures for the façade of the cathedral.

FLEURY, Antoine
French, 18th century.
Active in Hamburg from 1797 to 1799.
Painter.
The Germanisches Museum in Nuremberg has a miniature on ivory by Antoine Fleury depicting an *English Officer*. He may be the same artist as Antoine Claude Fleury.

FLEURY, Antoine Claude
French, 18th century.
Painter. Portraits, genre scenes.
Antoine Claude Fleury, who was the pupil of Regnault, exhibited at the Salon de Paris from 1795 to 1822.His most important works are *Two Young Lovers in front of a Tomb*, *Abduction by Moonlight* and *A Young Woman, Locked up by her Oppressors, is Released by her Lovers*.
Auction records:
Paris, 25 April 1990, *Two Young Lovers in front of a Tomb* (oil on canvas, 29 x 33 3/4 ins / 73.5 x 86 cm) FRF 23,000.

FLEURY, Auguste Antoine
French, 19th century.
Born in Châtillon-sur-Seine; died 1881, in Paris.
Painter.
Enrolled at the École des Beaux-Arts on 19 October 1848 and studied under Yvon; exhibited portraits and other work at Salons from 1849 to 1874. Remembered principally for his *A la Journée*, *Playing Truant*, a *Christ* and a *St Henry*.

FLEURY, Augustine
French, 19th century.
Painter. Portraits.
Showed examples of her work at the Paris Salons of 1839, 1841 and 1845.

FLEURY, Charles
French, 20th century.
Born in St-Satur.
Painter. Nudes, landscapes, still-lifes.
Charles Fleury exhibited in Paris at the Salon des Artistes Indépendants from 1931 to 1943.

FLEURY, Denise
French, 20th century.
Born in Courbevoie.
Painter, watercolourist.
Denise Fleury exhibited regularly in Paris at the Salon des Artistes Français from 1926. She received an honourable mention in 1936.

FLEURY, Édouard
French, 19th century.
Born 19th century, in Paris.
Painter.
Pupil of Couture and Monginot; exhibited at the Salon from 1863 to 1868. Examples of his work include *Game and Fruit*, *Two Friends*, *Dead Enemy*, *Bird and Flowers*, *Dog in the Vendée* and *Running Dogs*.

FLEURY, Fanny (Mme)
Maiden name: Laurent
French, 19th century.
Born 1848, in Paris.
Painter. Portraits, genre scenes, local scenes, still-lifes.
Studied under Henner and Carolus Duran and showed at the Salon from 1869 to 1882, chiefly portraits. She received an honourable mention at the Exposition Universelle of 1889.
Auction records:
Brussels, 1886, *Springtime* (study of a young girl) FRF 85. Paris, 1894, *Young Woman*, FRF 130. Paris, 28 April 1937, *Still-life*, FRF 90. London, 21 June 1989, *He Loves Me, He Loves Me Not...* (oil on canvas, 38 1/4 x 51 1/2 ins / 97 x 130.5 cm) GBP 11,000. London, 1 Oct 1993, *Dancing Class* (oil on canvas, 32 1/4 x 39 1/2 ins / 81.6 x 100.3 cm) GBP 2,070. London, 17 Nov 1993, *Young Parisienne under a Tree* (oil on panel, 8 1/2 x 16 1/4 ins / 21.5 x 41 cm) GBP 3,220. New York, 26 May 1994, *Bouquet* (oil on canvas, 24 x 17 3/4 ins / 61 x 45.4 cm) USD 21,850. Paris, 9 Dec 1996, *Portrait of a Young Kabyle (Berber)* (oil on panel, 13 3/4 x 10 1/2 ins / 35 x 26.5 cm) FRF 10,500. Paris, 27 March 1998, *Portrait of a Woman in Gloves Holding Roses* (oil on canvas, 50 1/2 x 35 ins / 128.5 x 89 cm) FRF 11,000. Paris, 8 Oct 1999, *Portrait of a Woman with Pink Ribbons* (oil on canvas, 10 x 7 ins / 25 x 19 cm) FRF 14,500. Cologne, 28 Oct 1999, *Reclining Young Woman in Landscape* (oil on panel, 9 x 16 ins / 22 x 41 cm) DEM 4,600. Paris, 22 June 2001, *Model with a Fan in the Studio* (oil on canvas, 24 x 13 ins / 60 x 33 cm) FRF 38,000. Watertown, 10 March 2002, *Ballerinas* (oil on canvas, 29 x 24 ins / 74 x 61 cm) USD 2,500. Paris, 7 Nov 2002, *Portrait of a Young Girl* (oil on panel, 11 x 9 ins / 27 x 22 cm) EUR 1,600. Cherbourg, 24 Nov 2003, *Young Woman Seated with a Blue Ribbon. Yvonne and Bobette* (oil on canvas, a pair, 51 x 38 ins / 130 x 97 cm) EUR 3,200. Paris, 12 Dec 2003, *Woman and Child* (oil on canvas, 26 x 18 ins / 65 x 46 cm) EUR 3,300.

FLEURY, Frédérique
French, 20th - 21st century.
Born 1957, in Grenoble.
Painter, installation artist.
Frédérique Fleury lives and works in Lyons, and studied at the Écoles des Beaux-Arts in Aix-en-Provence and Lyons. She has taken part in a number of group exhibitions since 1981, including: *Exposition de Noël* (*Christmas Exhibition*), at the Nouveau Musée de Villeurbanne, and in Lyons.

FLEURY, J. de
British, 18th - 19th century.
Painter. Landscapes.
J. de Fleury was active in London, where he exhibited with the Royal Academy from 1799 to 1823.

FLEURY, James V. de
British, 19th century.
Painter. Landscapes.
James de Fleury exhibited at the Royal Academy, the British Institution and Suffolk Street in London from 1842 to 1869.
Museums and Galleries:
Cape Town: *Bischofstein-am-Moselle*.
Auction records:
London, 5 March 1910, *Venice, the Grand Canal* (1865) GBP 15. London, 20 July 1923, *Gathering Seaweed*, GBP 9. Glasgow, 4 Sept 1946, *Hereford Market*, GBP 31. London, 21 Jan 1986, *Queen of the Hops* (1867, watercolour heightened with gouache, 21 x 29 1/2 ins / 53.5 x 75 cm) GBP 900. London, 14 Feb 1986, *The Pont de Treilles in Angers* (oil on canvas, 63 x

96 ins / 160 x 243 cm) GBP 18,000. LONDON, 3 Nov 1989, *The Cliffs at Etretat on the Normandy Coast* (1853, oil on canvas, 41 x 64 ins / 104 x 162.5 cm) GBP 4,620. LONDON, 9 Feb 1990, *Lake Maggiore* (1865, oil on canvas, 20 x 26 ins / 51 x 66 cm) GBP 1,760. ST ASAPH, 2 June 1994, *Continental European Town on the Banks of a River* (1865, oil on canvas, 31 x 46 ins / 79 x 117 cm) GBP 10,350. LONDON, 11 Nov 1999, *Across the Tyrol, Austria* (1870, oil on canvas, 20 x 30 ins / 51 x 76 cm) GBP 3,000. BRUSSELS, 15 Nov 1999, *River Landscape with Figures* (1860, oil on canvas, 24 x 38 ins / 61 x 97 cm) BEF 160,000. WELLINGTON, 12 April 2000, *Les Autelets, Sark, Early Morning* (oil on canvas, 18 x 32 ins / 45 x 81 cm) NZD 7,500. LONDON, 17 Jan 2001, *Les Autelets, Sark: Early Morning* (1866, oil on canvas, 18 x 32 ins / 45 x 81 cm) GBP 1,800. BURY ST EDMUNDS, 9 May 2001, *Figures and Houses in an Italianate Mountain and Lake Landscape* (1859, oil on canvas, 20 x 32 ins / 51 x 81 cm) GBP 1,750. LONDON, 19 Nov 2002, *Lago di Bolsena* (1870, oil on canvas, 24 x 43 ins / 61 x 109 cm) GBP 3,000. NANTWICH, 28 April 2004, *Italianate Landscape with Figures on a Path* (1863, oil on canvas, 17 x 28 ins / 43 x 70 cm) GBP 1,800.

FLEURY, Jean Baptiste

French, 18th century.
Active in Paris in 1788.
Painter, sculptor.

FLEURY, Jules Amédée Louis

French, 19th century.
Born 4 November 1845, in Cherbourg.
Painter.

Trained under Durand-Brager and exhibited landscapes at the Paris Salons of 1868, 1869 and 1870.

MUSEUMS AND GALLERIES:
CHERBOURG: *View of the Quincampoix Valley*.

AUCTION RECORDS:
PARIS, 3 April 1925, *Small Farm in Normandy*, FRF 360.

FLEURY, Léon François Antoine

French, 19th century.
Born 18 December 1804, in Paris; died October 1858, in Paris.
Painter. Religious subjects, portraits, genre scenes, landscapes, landscapes with figures.

Son and pupil of Antoine Claude Fleury; enrolled at the École des Beaux-Arts in Paris in 1821 and studied under Jean Victor Bertin and Louis Hersent. Léon Fleury spent time in Italy from 1827 to 1830.

Fleury exhibited at the Paris Salon between 1831 and 1855, receiving bronze in 1834, silver in 1837 and gold in 1845. Examples drawn from Léon Fleury's body of work include: *View of Ponte-Cotto, View of Watten, View of Ischia, Woods, View of Brussels, View near Maubeuge, View of the Château of Clisson, Path through the Rocks near Sassenage, View of Nice, Souvenir of Flanders, Copse, Village in Normandy, Pond and Mill at Contivert*. He also painted landscapes of the Auvergne region and views of the forest of Fontainebleau.

Fleury vacillated between neo-classicism (a style he adopted until around the middle of the 19th century) and the near-naturalism of the Barbizon School. He opted to people his landscapes with figures drawn with the same detail and precision as he lavished on their natural surroundings. Fleury also executed some large-scale religious compositions which can be seen in two Paris churches - St-Étienne du Mont and Ste-Marguerite.

Some examples of his work featured in *Un Paese incantato. Italia dipinta da Thomas Jones a Corot* (*An Enchanted Country. Italy Depicted by Artists from Thomas Jones to Corot*), an exhibition held in 2001 at the Centro Internazionale d'Arte e di Cultura di Palazzo Te in Mantua.

BIBLIOGRAPHY:
Ottani Cavina, Anna (ed.), *Un Paese incantato. Italia dipinta da Thomas Jones a Corot*, exhibition catalogue, Electa, Milan, 2001.

MUSEUMS AND GALLERIES:
AMIENS: *Road to Genoa, near Nice* - BAR-LE-DUC: *Lupold, Duke of Lorraine and Bar* (medallion); *Portrait in Three Crayons* (medallion); *Copse; King Louis XV of France* - BAYEUX: *View of Naples* - BLOIS (Château-MBA): *River Bank in Normandy* - COMPIÈGNE (Mus. national du Château): *Domino Costume; View of the Coast near Pouzzoles; Port Light at Ripetta Grande, Rome* (oil on canvas) - NANTES (MBA): *Landscape: River View* - ORLÉANS: *Landscape* - PARIS (Mus. d'Orsay): *Hen* (drawing) - ROCHEFORT: *View of Pompeii* - SAINTES: *Monk Seated beside the Sea* - SCEAUX (Mus. de l'Île-de-France): *St-Cloud* - VERSAILLES (Trianon): *Staircase of the Chateau de Blois*.

AUCTION RECORDS:
PARIS, 1895, *Countryside near Rome*, FRF 105; *Pond with Wooden Bridge*, FRF 120. PARIS, 31 Oct 1919, *Small Village*, FRF 180. PARIS, 18 March 1920, *Ruins of a Fortress*, FRF 170; *By an Alpine Lake*, FRF 155. PARIS, 5-6 March 1923, *Canal Barges*, FRF 400; *Windmills*, FRF 420. PARIS, 30 Jan 1929, *Mountainous Landscape*, FRF 620. PARIS, 13 Dec 1935, *View near Rome*, FRF 360. PARIS, 5 March 1945, *Old Manor House on a Hill*, FRF 7,000. PARIS, 2 Feb 1947, *Path near a Château*, FRF 4,000. PARIS, 3 Nov 1983, *Italian Countryside* (oil on canvas, 34 1/4 x 51 1/4 ins / 87 x 130 cm) FRF 60,000. PARIS, 5 Feb 1986, *Reading* (oil on canvas, 22 x 18 ins / 55 x 46 cm) FRF 13,500. TORONTO, 30 Nov 1988, *Gift* (oil on panel, 17 3/4 x 12 ins / 45 x 30.5 cm) CAD 3,000. NANCY, 19 March 1989, *Billet-Doux* (oil on canvas, 38 1/2 x 51 1/4 ins / 98 x 130 cm) FRF 79,000. RHEIMS, 17 June 1990, *Fishing Port* (oil on canvas, 11 1/2 x 16 3/4 ins / 29.5 x 42.5 cm) FRF 9,800. PARIS, 24 May 1991, *Farm* (oil on paper/canvas, 11 1/2 x 14 1/4 ins / 29 x 36.5 cm) FRF 10,000. PARIS, 18 Oct 2000, *River Landscape* (1846, oil on canvas, 21 x 30 ins / 53 x 75 cm) FRF 80,000. LONDON, 18 Jan 2001, *Figures on Mountain Track* (oil on canvas, 9 x 14 ins / 24 x 36 cm) GBP 1,400. NEW YORK, 29 May 2003, *Young Woman and a Girl in front of a House* (1834, oil on canvas, 23 x 27 ins / 59 x 69 cm) USD 7,000. PARIS, 7 April 2004, *The Wooden Bridge* (oil on panel, 11 x 16 ins / 27 x 41 cm) EUR 2,700.

FLEURY, Lucien

French, 20th century.
Born c. 1930; died 23 January 2004, in Ivry-sur-Seine.
Painter, screen printer. Figures, scenes with figures.
Nouvelle Figuration.
Groupe Coopérative des Malassis.

Lucien Fleury took part in collective exhibitions abroad and in annual Paris Salons, most notably the Salon de la Jeune Peinture. He was involved in the theoretical and practical activities of the Coopérative des Malassis (Malassis Co-operative), an offshoot of the Salon de la Jeune Peinture. The group's output consisted in collectively and anonymously produced works commenting on social and political issues. Though the group sought to expose the failures of capitalism, it was invited to the *Exhibition 72/72* or Expo Pompidou. However, *The Great Mechoui* - in which the sheep (some of which are spit-roasted at the *mechoui*) represent the duped electorate - was taken down at the private viewing. Works like his 1971 *The Other Side of the Note*, or *L'appartemensonge*, exploded the myths of consumer society. Lucien Fleury taught at the École des Beaux-Arts in Orléans. In his early individual work, post-Cubist influences are still perceptible, which would be rounded off through a range of encounters via the Salon de la Jeune Peinture. His *Trap-Pictures* are scathing about insipid suburban lifestyles, but also reveal a secret tenderness for their modest aspirations.

Bibliography:
Gaudibert, Pierre, *Images-pièges*, exhibition leaflet, Les loges de l'Odéon, Paris.
Auction records:
Calais, 28 Feb 1988, *Peopled Landscape* (oil on canvas, 13 x 18 1/2 ins / 33 x 47 cm) FRF 3,000.

FLEURY, Madeleine
French, 19th century.
Born in Constantinople, to French parents.
Painter.
Honourable mention in 1889.

FLEURY, Marcel Paul
French, 20th century.
Born 15 November 1883, in Le Logis-de-Nalliers; died 28 March 1955, in Fontenay-le-Comte.
Engraver, illustrator.
Marcel Fleury studied under Charles Coppier. He exhibited at the Salon des Artistes Français of which he was an associate member. He received an honourable mention in 1912 and a silver medal in 1937.

FLEURY, Marie Aimée Amélie
French, 19th century.
Born 7 May 1819, in Paris.
Miniaturist.
Exhibited at the Paris Salon between 1844 and 1849.

FLEURY, Marie Berthe
French, 19th century.
Painter.
She was made a life member of the Société des Artistes Français as of 1900 and received an honourable mention in 1902. Known to have been active in Paris in 1857.

FLEURY, Maurice
French, 20th century.
Born 29 November 1920, in Gisors.
Painter. Landscapes.
Maurice Fleury is self-taught. He exhibits at the Salon d'Automne, of which he is an associate member, and the Salon Comparaisons. He paints the landscapes of his native region in a naive style.

FLEURY, Nicolas
French, 16th century.
Active in Paris in 1586.
Painter.

FLEURY, Nicolas
French, 17th century.
Sculptor.
Under the direction of Gilles Guérin, Nicolas Fleury took part in the decoration of the Château de Fontainebleau in 1640.

FLEURY, Octavie
French, 19th century.
Born 19th century, in Paris.
Miniaturist.
Studied under Hussenot senior and J. Hussenot and exhibited at the Paris Salon from 1857 to 1861, chiefly anonymous portraits.

FLEURY, Pierre
French, 20th century.
Born 6 July 1900, in Boulogne-sur-Seine.
Painter. Seascapes.
Pierre Fleury studied under Paul Signac. In 1919, he exhibited in Paris at the Salon d'Automne. He exhibited from 1925 at the Salon des Artistes Indépendants and from 1927 at the Salon des Tuileries. After World War II he had regular solo exhibitions in Paris.

He was a fine observer of the multiple variations brought to sea and sky by changing weather conditions. He also knowledgeably painted all kinds of boats.

Auction records:
Paris, 31 Jan 1944, *Schooner with Topsails*, FRF 5,500. Paris, 8 Dec 1944, *Inshore Current*, FRF 7,000. Paris, 29 June 1945, *White Ketch in Heavy Weather*, FRF 3,400. Paris, July 1946, *Group Fishing in Fine Weather*, FRF 17,500. Paris, 16 Nov 1987, *Swell* (oil on canvas, 21 1/4 x 25 1/2 ins / 54 x 65 cm) FRF 5,200. Calais, 8 July 1990, *Paimpol Folk in the Mist* (1941, oil on canvas, 28 3/4 x 39 1/4 ins / 73 x 100 cm) FRF 7,500.

FLEURY, Richard François. See **RICHARD Fleury François**

FLEURY, Sylvie
Swiss, 20th - 21st century.
Born 1961, in Geneva.
Painter, assemblage artist.
Neo-Conceptual Art.
Fleury lives and works in Geneva. She borrows her objects, which she makes into assemblages; they are fashionable women's garments, haute couture, including shoes, designer accessories and cosmetics, and she enjoys portraying frivolity. In 1993 she exhibited a collection of shoes in fur-lined boxes, which were sold as multiples.

She has participated in group exhibitions: 1999, *Xn*, at the Espace des Arts, Chalon-sur-Saône; 2001, *L'Esprit de Famille* (*Family Spirit*), the Villa du Parc, Annemasse; 2003, *Mouth Open, Teeth Showing*, the Museum für Gegenwartskunst (contemporary art,), Siegen; 2003, *Phantom der Lust. Visionen des Masochismus in der Kunst* (*Phantom of Desire. Visions of Masochism in Art*) at the Neue Galerie am Landesmuseum, Graz; 2003, *L'État des Choses* (*The State of Things*), an exhibition which looked at the status of the everyday object in contemporary art held on the occasion of *Trésors Publics. 20 Ans de Création dans les Fonds Régionaux d'Art Contemporarin (FRAC)* (*Public Treasury, 20 Years of Creation in the Regional Collection of Contemporary Art (FRAC)*) at the Musée des Beaux-Arts, Nantes.

She has also held solo shows, including: 1995, Galerie Urbi et Orbi, Paris; 1995, Galerie Gilbert Brownstone, Paris; 2001, Le Magasin, Centre National d'Art Contemporain, Grenoble; 2002, *Oeuvres Récentes* (*Recent Works*), Galerie Thaddaeus Ropac, Paris.
Bibliography:
Ainardi, Dolène, '*Sylvie Fleury*' in *Art Press* n° 174, periodical, Paris, November 1992. Troncy, Éric/Brüderlin, Markus/Gillick, Liam/Nicol, Michelle, *Sylvie Fleury*, monograph, exhibition catalogue, Centre national d'Art contemporain, Grenoble, Réunion des musées nationaux, Presses du Réel, Paris, 2001 (text in French and English). Weibel, Peter (ed.), '*Phantom der Lust. Visionen des Masochismus in der Kunst*' in *2 vol.*, exhibition catalogue, Neue Galerie am Landesmuseum, Graz, Belleville Verlag, Munich, 2003. Zahm, Olivier (preface), et al., *Trésors publics, 20 ans de création dans les Fonds régionaux d'art contemporain*, Flammarion, Paris, 2003 (text in French and English).
Museums and Galleries:
Angoulême (FRAC Poitou-Charentes): *Slimt Fast* - Dunkirk (FRAC Nord-Pas de Calais) - Geneva (Mamco): *Pompilioblip (Felt Hats)* (1993, cardboard box with the Elvis Pompilio logo and shop stamp, mottled brown felt hat) - Paris (FNAC): *Current Issues, July-August 1995* (1995, colour video, sound).
Auction records:
London, 10 Dec 1999, *Sex, Money, Compromise* (1993, cibachrome print on aluminium, 61 x 47 ins / 155 x 120 cm)

GBP 4,200. NEW YORK, 28 Dec 1999, *Gucci Satellite* (mixed media) USD 5,000. LONDON, 30 June 2000, *New Woman's Free Diet 2000* (1995, cibachrome print on aluminium, 63 x 47 ins / 160 x 120 cm) GBP 3,000. LONDON, 8 Feb 2001, *Skin Crime 3 - Givenchy* (1997, compressed car enamel, 35 x 59 x 154 ins / 90 x 150 x 390 cm) GBP 26,000. NEW YORK, 15 May 2001, *Louis Vuitton 2000* (2000, solid bronze silver, 18 x 31 x 8 ins / 46 x 79 x 20 cm) USD 35,000. NEW YORK, 16 May 2002, *Chanel No 5* (2000, chromed bronze, 10 x 7 x 3 ins / 26 x 18 x 8 cm) USD 16,000. LONDON, 22 Oct 2003, *Harper's Bazaar* (1994, cibachrome print on aluminium, 64 x 49 ins / 163 x 124 cm) GBP 9,000. NEW YORK, 14 Nov 2003, *Crash teat 3-31* (2001, acrylic and steel, two parts, 70 x 40 x 4 ins / 179 x 102 x 9 cm) USD 10,500. PARIS, 29 March 2004, *Louis Vuitton Bag* (2000, bronze and silver, 13 x 18 x 8 ins / 34 x 46 x 20 cm) EUR 30,000. NEW YORK, 10 June 2004, *Be amazing* (neon, edition of three, 27 x 114 x 2 ins / 68 x 290 x 5 cm) USD 16,000.

FLEURY, Tony Robert. See **ROBERT-FLEURY**

FLEURY-BARABE, Marguerite

French, 20th century.
Born in Rouen.
Active in Rouen.
Painter. Flowers.

FLEURY-D'HERBEZ, Lucienne

French, 20th century.
Born in Marseilles.
Painter. Local figures.

Lucienne Fleury-d'Herbez studied under Fernand Sabatté and René Xavier Prinet. She exhibited in Paris at the Salon des Artistes Français from 1931, receiving an honourable mention in 1935, Prix T. Ralli in the same year, silver medal in 1938.

AUCTION RECORDS:

PARIS, 22 June 1992, *Moroccan Woman Sitting* (oil on canvas, 39¼ x 31½ ins / 100 x 80 cm) FRF 24,000. PARIS, 11 Dec 1995, *Portrait of a Berber Woman from Morocco* (oil on canvas, 17¾ x 14¾ ins / 45 x 37.5 cm) FRF 6,000.

FLEUSS, H.

German, 19th century.
Born c. 1800.
Lithographer.

Fleuss worked in Frankfurt am Main. He produced numerous portraits, both drawn and lithographed.

FLEUSS, Henry J.

British, 19th century.
Painter. Genre scenes.

Henry J. Fleuss taught at Marlborough College and exhibited with the Royal Academy in London from 1847 to 1874.

FLEUTTE, Michiel, or Verflute

Flemish School, 16th century.
Died after 1553.
Painter.
Bruges School.

Michiel Fleutte was received as a master in 1507.

FLEXNER, Roland

French, 20th century.
Born 1944, in Nice.
Active in the USA from 1983.
Draughtsman.
Hyperrealist.

A second-generation artist of the Nice School, Roland Flexner left Nice in 1983 to move to New York. In his painting and drawing, Flexner draws on art history themes. He has interpreted funerary sculpture of the 15th century, the 'weeping figures', in a series of diptychs combining monochromatic flatness and almost life-size figures. In the 1990s, he explored the representation of the soul in his drawings, so masterfully executed they neared photo-realism. This was particularly the case in his portraits, in which he represented half of the face in the midst of a laugh or a yawn, with the other half remaining static. His *vanitas*, with skulls and crystal balls, were executed in pencil or charcoal, and bespoke of solitude and absence. An exhibition presented at the Galerie Fernand Léger in Ivry in 2000 showed works created from crushed balls of glycerine mixed with ink, and produced by Flexner blowing through brushes like blow-pipes. These 'vocal gestures' are the result of chance and physical and human events. 'Born from the artist's breath', these drawings suggest a process of transformation, ephemeral creation from a part of reality - the bubble - with the drawing being its tangible result. In sum, it is a new *vanitas* genre.

Collective exhibitions include *Best of the Season*, Aldrich Museum of Contemporary Art, Ridgefield (1999). Solo exhibitions include: Galerie Météo, Paris (1994); Cleveland Center for Contemporary Art, Cleveland (1997); Centre Régional d'Art Contemporain, Sète (1997); Miller/Block Gallery, Boston (1999); Galerie Fernand Léger, Centre d'Art, Ivry-sur-Seine (2000).

BIBLIOGRAPHY:

Plazy, Gilles, *French Art 1979: An English Selection*, group exhibition catalogue, Association Francaise Artistique and Arts Council of Great Britain, Serpentine Gallery, 1979. *Figures and Vanitas*, exhibition catalogue, Cleveland Center for Contemporary Art, Cleveland, 1997. Réol, Jean-Marc/Tronche, Anne, *Roland Flexner*, Michel Baverey, Paris, 2002. Rubinstein, Raphael, ' *When Bubbles Burst*' in *Art in America, 2003,* vol 91, no. 2, periodical, February 2003.

MUSEUMS AND GALLERIES:

AMIENS (FRAC Picardie) - NICE (Mus. d'Art Moderne et d'Art Contemporain) - PARIS (FNAC) - ST-ÉTIENNE (MAM) - STRASBOURG (Mus. d'Art Moderne et Contemporain).

FLEXOR, Samson

Moldovan, 20th century.
Born 9 September 1907, in Soroca; died 1971.
Active and naturalised in France from 1927; active in Brazil from 1946.
Painter.

Originally a typical painter of the Paris School between the two World Wars, Samson Flexor first exhibited at the Salon d'Automne (1927 with a *Nude* and *Flowers*) then at the Salon des Artistes Indépendants (1928 to 1935) and the Salon des Tuileries (1936 to 1939). His work was interrupted by his engagement in the war, but he took up painting again at the end of it and produced numerous decorations for French churches, then left for Brazil in 1948. There the management of the brand new Museum of Modern Art in São Paulo had been entrusted to the Franco-Belgian critic Léon Degand. He opened it in 1949 with an exhibition of the main abstract European artists including Cicero Dias and Samson Flexor.

In his first period before World War II, Flexor painted various subjects, then moved on to landscapes, figures and still-lifes. In the few years he spent in Paris after the war, he produced works of a more systematic art form still based on real life, particularly in 1946. The influence of the critic Léon Degand made him move permanently towards abstraction. In his personal use of abstraction of a constructivist origin, he introduced a dynamic dimension obtained by a fragmentation of the surface of the painting as if it had exploded in a centrifugal direction into a multitude of arrow-like, sharp surfaces. At the end of his career in São Paulo, he went back to the allusive representations of humans and animals.

Flexor took part in many collective exhibitions the including Venice and São Paulo Biennales. In 1951 he opened an *Abstraction Workshop* in São Paulo, which contributed to the emancipation of native Brazilian art, all the more so given that at this time he was more involved in abstraction than

the pair who had also taken refuge in São Paulo, Szenès and Vieira da Silva. The Museum of Modern Art in São Paulo (1954) and in Rio de Janeiro (1955) devoted retrospective exhibitions to him.
MUSEUMS AND GALLERIES:
AGEN: *Table* - FÉCAMP: *Woman with a Cigarette* - PARIS (MNAM-CCI): *Still-life.*
AUCTION RECORDS:
PARIS, 24 April 1929, *House in the Trees,* FRF 165. PARIS, 2 March 1934, *Reclining Nude,* FRF 50. SÃO PAULO, 24 Oct 1980, *Biped* (oil on canvas, 74 x 46 1/4 ins / 188 x 117.5 cm) BRL 122,000.

FLEYSCHER, Michael, or Fleischer
German, 16th century.
Active in Breslau (now Wroclaw, Poland) in 1556.
Sculptor (wood).

FLICCIUS, Gerlach or Garlicke, or Flicke
British, 16th century.
Painter, engraver. Portraits.
The National Portrait Gallery in London has a *Portrait of Archbishop Cranmer,* dated 1546, by this artist. Other works by him include: *Portrait of Sir Peter Carew, Portrait of Jacques de Savoie, Duke of Nemours, Portrait of Queen Mary* and *Portrait of Garcilaso de la Vega* (the latter in the museum in Kassel).
AUCTION RECORDS:
LONDON, 17 and 18 May 1928, *Gentleman,* GBP 220. LONDON, 15 Feb 1929, *Bishop Cranmer,* GBP 12.

FLICK, Émile
French, 19th century.
Born c. 1845, in Metz.
Painter, watercolourist. Genre scenes, landscapes, landscapes with figures, seascapes, still-lifes.
Studied under Isidore Pils, Théodfore Devilly and Laurent Charles Maréchal; exhibited at the Paris Salon from 1870 to 1881 and awarded a gold medal at the 1889 Exposition Universelle. Examples of Flick's work include: *Banks of the Moselle, Cavalryman Standing Guard, Avenue in the Bois de Boulogne, Incoming Tide at Pornic with the Island of Noirmoutier in the Distance, On the Rocks.* His still-lifes are distinguished by their sweeping arabesques, a sensitive touch and a strong tactile sense. Flick's views of Paris and the banks of the Seine, together with his seascapes, reveal an ability to use colours imaginatively.
AUCTION RECORDS:
LONDON, 21 March 1908, *On the Seine, near Poissy,* GBP 8. PARIS, 22 Nov 1940, *Avenue of the Bois de Boulogne in 1886,* FRF 3,500. PARIS, 23 Feb 1979, *Fishermen on the Bank of the River* (1874, oil on panel, 7 1/2 x 11 ins / 19 x 27 cm) FRF 3,600. SAN FRANCISCO, 26 May 1999, *Avenue de Neuilly in the Snow* (1881, oil on canvas, 24 x 39 ins / 60 x 100 cm) USD 9,000.

FLICK, Félix Nicolas
French, 19th century.
Born c. 1852, in Metz.
Painter, watercolourist. Genre scenes, landscapes, landscapes with figures, seascapes.
Exhibited at the Paris Salon as of 1875. He is best known for his paintings of eastern France and Normandy, notably for early seascapes in bluish-greens and pearl greys and later work which took on a more diverse and contrasting colour palette.
AUCTION RECORDS:
PARIS, 17 May 1979, *Warriors on Horseback* (oil on canvas, 31 1/2 x 41 1/4 ins / 80 x 105 cm) FRF 1,500; *Curse* (oil on card) FRF 1,400.

FLICKEL, Paul Franz
German, 19th century.
Born 8 April 1852, in Berlin; died 1903, in Nervi.
Painter. Landscapes with figures, landscapes.
In 1871 Flickel enrolled at the art school in Weimar. From 1872 to 1873 he studied under Theodor Hagen. He then settled in Düsseldorf. In 1876 he went to Italy. Flickel was awarded a medal in Berlin in 1880.
MUSEUMS AND GALLERIES:
BERLIN: *Beech Forest* - ERFURT: *Villa Borghese in Rome.*
AUCTION RECORDS:
MUNICH, 11 March 1987, *Landscape with Mill* (1885, oil on canvas, 19 1/4 x 23 1/2 ins / 49 x 59.5 cm) DEM 3,300. LONDON, 29 Nov 1991, *Hunter on a Woodland Path beside a Lake* (1895, oil on canvas, 37 1/2 x 55 1/4 ins / 95.2 x 140.3 cm) GBP 11,000. CONSTANCE, 19 Nov 1999, *Couple Picnicking in Woods* (oil on canvas, 23 x 34 ins / 59 x 86 cm) DEM 7,500. DRESDEN, 4 March 2000, *Dune Landscape with Thatched Houses* (1884, oil on board, 14 x 17 ins / 36 x 44 cm) DEM 4,800. WARSAW, 9 March 2000, *Figures Walking in Shade* (oil on canvas, 26 x 41 ins / 66 x 105 cm) PLN 48,000. MUNICH, 21 March 2001, *Bordighera Street* (1882, oil on paper/board, 19 x 15 ins / 47 x 39 cm) DEM 7,500. BERLIN, 30 Nov 2001, *Birch Wood near Gravenstein on Ostsee* (1878, oil on board, 21 x 14 ins / 54 x 35 cm) DEM 4,800. TOESTORF, 10 May 2003, *Wild Garden at Dusk* (1889, oil on board, 21 x 15 ins / 53 x 37 cm) EUR 2,800. BOSTON, 16 May 2003, *Working in the Open Air* (oil on canvas, 23 x 33 ins / 58 x 84 cm) USD 6,000.

FLICKINGER, Paul
French, 20th century.
Born 11 August 1941, in Colmar.
Painter, sculptor. Scenes with figures, figures, animals. Sculpted groups.
Art Brut.
Paul Flickinger was born in Alsace, and lives and works in coal and iron country, in Marly, Lorraine. In 1974, he was one on of the twelve painters and sculptors who founded the Art Research group. In 1994, he constructed an imposing, anthropomorphic approximately 11 feet 6 in-high (3.4 metre) cast-iron totem, entitled *Summer of the Book,* in the Place d'Armes in Metz.

Initially a painter, later also a sculptor, Flickinger seems, in his works, to have something of a divided personality. His paintings reflect considerable knowledge of other artists, such as Picasso, Max Ernst and the Surrealists, and show considerable technical skill and flair. They portray people and fantastical creatures, and are extremely complex, replete with narrative details. His sculptures, however, are markedly different from his paintings, being raw and primitive in style. As such, his approach is reminiscent of Chaissac and Dubuffet: like Flickinger, Chaissac was very knowledgeable about his contemporaries, and Dubuffet, feeling stifled by his own cultural atmosphere, found inspiration in more primitive contemporary cultures. Flickinger employs two sculpting techniques: a very spontaneous approach, whereby he assembles pieces of wood to make figures of people and animals; or a more sophisticated technique of moulding and melting to produce the same sorts of models. Whichever technique he employs, his figures are strikingly polychrome. They are also comical and yet strangely affecting, rather like clowns.

Both Flickinger's sculptures and his paintings seem to have been produced by a number of different artists, such is the complexity of his œuvre, and of the personality which they reflect. This is quite marked in his paintings. His fantastical and very varied inspirations leave their viewers to make of them what they will; yet Flickinger has mastered a traditional narrative style, of the kind often evident in Surrealist and fantastical works, whose purpose is to make unreality recognisable.

He has taken part in a number of group exhibitions, including the following: Cercle d'Arts de Colmar in 1965; *The European Artists,* in Prüm, Germany, in 1972 and 1974; as a member of the Art Research group, in towns in Alsace, in 1974, 1977, 1980 and 1981; *Bilan de l'Art Contemporain* (*A Summing Up of Contemporary Art*), in Quebec in 1981; and in a number of Parisian exhibitions, including the Salon des Indépendants in 1974, the Salon des Artistes Français since 1975 (where he won a gold medal in 1981), and the Salon d'Automne in 1977.

He has also presented collections of his works in a number of solo exhibitions, including: Colmar in 1964 (his first); Metz in 1971; Nancy in 1973; *Les Personnages Fantastiques* (*Fantastic Characters*), at the Musée Bartholdi de Colmar in 1979; *Visions de l'Imaginaire* (*Visions of the Imaginary*), at the same venue in 1981; at the Galerie l'Arc-en-Ciel (the Rainbow Gallery) in Paris, in 1980 and 1981; at the Maison de la Culture de Metz in 1984; and at the Galerie Ars Gambetta, also in Metz.

BIBLIOGRAPHY:

Laporte, Gilles/Picard, Sam, *Flickinger*, Éd. Serpenoise, Metz, 1992 (extensive documentation). *Flickinger. Peintures, sculptures, bois polychrome*, exhibition catalogue, Gal. Arts Gambetta, Metz, 1993. Laporte, Gilles, *Paul Flickinger - Les Fontes aciérées polychromées*, Gal. Arts Gambetta, Metz, 1994. *Flickinger*, catalogue, Gal. Arts Gambetta, Metz, 1995. *Flickinger*, catalogue, Éd. P. Flickinger, Metz, 1996-1997.

AUCTION RECORDS:

PARIS, 18 March 1992, *Changes of Awareness* (1985, oil on canvas, 51 1/4 x 78 3/4 ins / 130 x 200 cm) FRF 82,000. PARIS, 21 Dec 1992, *Lion* (oil on canvas, 1/4 x 1/4 ins / 0.50 x 0.50 cm) FRF 18,000; *Sagittarius* (oil on canvas, 19 3/4 x 19 3/4 ins / 50 x 50 cm) FRF 18,000. PARIS, 5 July 1993, *Dragon* (oil on canvas, 36 1/4 x 28 3/4 ins / 92 x 73 cm) FRF 23,000. PARIS, 22 Dec 1993, *Gainsbourg II* (oil on canvas, 31 1/2 x 31 1/2 ins / 80 x 80 cm) FRF 20,000. PARIS, 15 Dec 1994, *The Races* (oil on canvas, 39 1/4 x 39 1/4 ins / 100 x 100 cm) FRF 30,000; *The Bird Ladies* (oil on canvas, 39 1/4 x 39 1/4 ins / 100 x 100 cm) FRF 25,000.

FLIEGAUF, Josef

Austrian, 18th century.
Born in the 18th century, in Vienna.
Sculptor.

Fliegauf was awarded citizenship in 1735.

FLIEHER, Anton

Italian, 19th century.
Born 20 June 1800, near Merano (Trentino-Alto Adige); died 25 January 1880.
Painter, sculptor (wood). Portraits, genre scenes, landscapes.

MUSEUMS AND GALLERIES:

MERANO (Mus.): three studies.

FLIER, Helmert Richard van der

Dutch, 19th century.
Born 26 March 1827, in Baarn; died 1899.
Painter. Landscapes with figures.

Helmert Richard van der Flier's master was James de Ryk.

MUSEUMS AND GALLERIES:

AMSTERDAM: *Sheep* - ROTTERDAM.

AUCTION RECORDS:

AMSTERDAM, 1881, *Sheep on Heath*, FRF 37. COLOGNE, 28 June 1991, *Horseman Resting near his Dog and Saddled Horse in a Landscape* (oil on canvas, 17 3/4 x 23 1/4 ins / 45 x 59 cm) DEM 5,000. COLOGNE, 5 April 2001, *Meadow with Sheep* (1881, oil on canvas, 21 x 31 ins / 53 x 80 cm) DEM 5,000. AMSTERDAM, 25 April 2001, *Shepherd with his Flock* (1833, oil on canvas, 16 x 12 ins / 41 x 30 cm) NLG 4,500. PARIS, 23 June 2003, *Cows and Sheep in a Landscape* (1853, oil on panel, 13 x 17 ins / 32 x 43 cm) EUR 1,700.

FLIES, Th.

German.
Active in Brunswick.
Painter (porcelain), decorative designer.

He worked at the Furstenburg porcelain factory as a painter of figures.

FLIESCHAUER. See **VLEESCHOUWERE**

FLIGHT, Claude

British, 20th century.
Born 1881, in London; died 1955.
Painter in oils and watercolours, linocut and woodcut artist; interior designer and illustrator. Figures, landscapes, townscapes.
7&5 Group; Grubb Group.

Claude Flight came to study art relatively late in life, at the age of 31, when he studied at Heatherley's School of Art (around 1912-1914). Here he became a friend of Christopher Nevinson who introduced him to the Futurist F.T. Marinetti. He served in France during World War I and was decorated as Chevalier du Mérite Agricole for his services to France. In 1918 he returned to Heatherley's and specialised in linocutting; he later became famous for his linocuts, particularly for his works of speed and movement. In the 1920s he exhibited widely on the continent, and in 1925 his linocuts were acquired by the British Museum and the Contemporary Art Society. In 1919 he became a founder member of the 7&5 Group, but left in 1928 following a row with Ben Nicholson, to found the Grubb Street Group. From 1925 to 1930 he ran the Grosvenor School of Modern Art with Iain McNab. In 1927 he established an interior decorating business with his second wife Edith Lawrence, producing wall hangings, ceramics and textiles, and from 1926 to 1927 he was also editor of the *Arts and Crafts Quarterly*. In 1929 he organised the first annual show of British Linocuts at the Redfern Gallery, followed by several other group shows in America, Canada, Australia and China. He held his own solo show at the Redfern Gallery in 1931 and a joint exhibition with his wife at the French Gallery in 1935.

Flight is considered one of the few, if not the only, British Futurist artists and is credited with having introduced Cyril Power, Sybil Andrews and Lill Tschudi to linocutting. Many of Flight's works and materials in his studio were destroyed by bombing in 1941.

BIBLIOGRAPHY:

Flight, Claude, *The Art and Craft of Linocutting and Printing*, Batsford, 1934. *Claude Flight and Edith Lawrence*, exhibition catalogue, London, 1973. '*Claude Flight and His Australian Pupils*' in *Print Quarterly*, exhibition catalogue, 1985 (vol. 2, no. 4; pp. 262-283). Parkin, M., '*Claude Flight and the Linocut*' in *Journal of Decorative and Propaganda Arts*, exhibition catalogue, Fall 1987 (no. 6; pp. 26-33). Coppel, S., '*British Colour Linocuts: The Critical Response Between the Wars*' in *Tamarind Papers*, 1991-1992 (vol. 14; pp. 21-30). Coppel, S., *Linocuts of the Machine Age: Claude Flight and the Grosvenor School*, Scolar Press, 1995. Gordon, Samuel, *The Cutting Edge of Modernity: Linocuts of the Grosvenor School*, Aldershot, Burlington, 2002.

MUSEUMS AND GALLERIES:

ADELAIDE (AG of South Australia): *Brooklands* (1929, linocut) - BIRMINGHAM (City Museum and Art Gallery): *Speed* (1922, linocut) - CANBERRA (Nat. Gal. of Australia): *Crossing the Road* (linocut); *Yachts* (1933, linocut); *Pigeon Bath* (1934, linocut); *The Estuary* (1935, linocut) - LONDON (British Mus.): *Women and Washing* (1925, linocut); *Descent from the Bus* (1927, linocut); *Singers* (1925, linocut) - LONDON (Victoria and Albert Mus.): *Spring* (1926, linocut); *Summer* (1926, linocut); *Autumn* (1926, linocut); *Winter* (1926, linocut); *Winter* (1926, linocut); *Mother and Child* (1929, linocut) - MIAMI (Wolfsonian Foundation): *Getting Up* (c. 1931, linocut) - NEW YORK (MoMA): *Paris Omnibus* (1923, linocut) - SYDNEY (AG of New South Wales): *Three Speeds* (1922, linocut).

Auction records:
London, 3 Nov 1981, *Dirt Track Racing* (linocut in colour, 9 3/4 x 12 ins / 25 x 30.3 cm) GBP 380. London, 14 Nov 1984, *Fishermen* (1928, oil on canvas, 28 x 32 1/2 ins / 71 x 82.5 cm) GBP 3,000. London, 13 Nov 1985, *Policeman in a Snowstorm* (1922, watercolour and black chalk, 11 3/4 x 15 3/4 ins / 30 x 40 cm) GBP 2,500. London, 13 Nov 1987, *Swimming: the Start of the Race* (oil on canvas, 18 x 24 ins / 45.7 x 61 cm) GBP 4,200. London, 28 April 1999, *Park* (1922, pencil, charcoal and watercolour, 18 x 24 ins / 46 x 61 cm) GBP 1,600. London, 16 June 1999, *Brooklands, Coppel 30* (1929, colour linocut, 13 x 11 ins / 33 x 28 cm) GBP 20,000. London, 8 Nov 2001, *Brooklands* (c. 1929, colour linocut, 12 x 10 ins / 31 x 26 cm) GBP 20,500. Nantwich, 28 Nov 2001, *Swinging Boats* (sepia ink, 8 x 11 ins / 21 x 28 cm) GBP 1,000. London, 1 July 2003, *Dirt Track* (c. 1928, colour linocut, 10 x 12 ins / 26 x 30 cm) GBP 8,000. London, 1 July 2003, *Paris Omnibus* (colour linocut, 9 x 11 ins / 22 x 28 cm) GBP 8,500. London, 10 March 2004, *Pont Voluntre, Cahors, Lot* (1925, linocut, 8 x 11 ins / 21 x 27 cm) GBP 1,800.

FLIGHT, J.
British, 18th - 19th century.
Miniaturist.

J. Flight exhibited with the Royal Academy in London from 1802 to 1806.

FLIN, John
Irish, 18th century.
Born c. 1690; died 23 September 1747, in Galway.
Painter.

FLINCH, Andreas Christian Ferdinand
Danish, 19th century.
Born 1813, in Copenhagen; died 1872, in Copenhagen.
Engraver (wood).

Andreas Flinch studied at the Kunstakademi in Copenhagen from 1832 to 1838. After having worked as a silversmith, he set himself up as a wood engraver. He introduced into Denmark the then-new method of putting only the principal lines on the block and then executing the details by hand. In 1840 he established himself as a lithographer and published the *Flinch Almanac*, with illustrations of engravings on wood.

FLINCH, Ingeborg
Danish, 20th century.
Born in Copenhagen.
Watercolourist.

Ingeborg Flinch exhibited in Paris at the Salon de la Nationale des Beaux-Arts.

FLINCK, Govaert
Flemish, 17th century.
Born December 1615 or 1616, in Cleves; died 2 December 1660, in Amsterdam.
Painter, draughtsman. Religious subjects, portraits, group portraits, genre scenes, landscapes.
Flemish School.

Govaert Flinck cultivated his own personal style as well as being an ambitious imitator, although it is to his ability in the latter field that he largely owes his reputation. After studying diligently under Lambert Jacob, he entered the studio of Rembrandt, whose portrait he painted. Flinck was so proficient in copying this master's style that until modern times some of his paintings were mistaken for authentic Rembrandts. But it was not only the Dutch master whom Flinck imitated. He also executed paintings after Murillo which reveal his excellent knowledge of the Spanish master's style. It is claimed that Flinck was so downcast at his failure to successfully imitate van Dyck and Rubens that he abandoned painting. However, he sometimes exhibited a very personal artistic touch, especially in his portraits. He carried out a number of commissions for Elector Friedrich Wilhelm of Brandenburg, Prince John Maurice of Nassau and the Duke of Cleves.

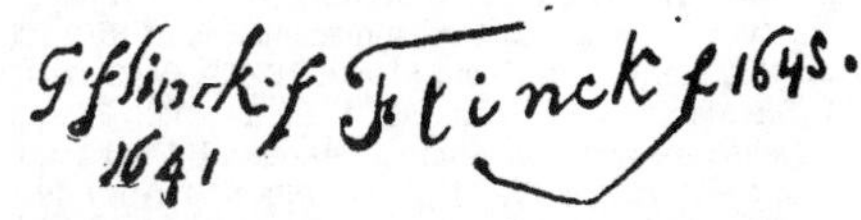

Bibliography:
Sumowski, Werner, '*Gemälde des Rembrandt-Schüler*' in *Paintings of the Rembrandt Pupils*, PVA, Landau, 1983.

Museums and Galleries:
Ajaccio: *Portrait of a Woman* - Amiens: *Portrait of a Man* - Amsterdam (Rijksmus.): *Portrait of Gozen Centen; Isaac Blessing Jacob; Joost van den Rondel; Amalia van Solms in Mourning for her Husband Prince Frédéric-Henri d'Orange; Gérard Pietter Hoelft; Four Governors of the Arquebusiers' Civic Guard, Amsterdam, 1642* (1642); *The Company of Captain Albert Bas and Lieutenant Conyn; The Amsterdam Civic Guard Celebrating the Signing of the Peace of Munster in 1648; Jonas Jacob Leeuwen Dircksz.* - Amsterdam (Six Collection): *Isaac Blessing Jacob* - Basel: *The Three Crosses at Golgotha* - Berlin: *Portrait of a Young Woman; Dismissal of Hagar* - Bern: *Portrait of a Young Man* - Besançon: *Dutchman Reading* - Bonn: *Sarah Leads Hagar to Abraham* - Boston: *Mythological Picture with Mercury* - Brunswick: *Shepherdess* - Brussels: *Portrait of a Woman* - Budapest: *Abraham Expelling Hagar; Manoah's Sacrifice* - Cherbourg: *St Jerome* - Copenhagen: *Group of Portraits* - Darmstadt: *Two Full-length Portraits* - Douai: *Portrait of the Duke of Brunswick* - Dresden: *Rest on the Flight into Egypt* - Dublin: *Head of a Rabbi; Bathsheba Appeals to David for the Crown for her Son Solomon* - Florence (Palazzo Pitti): *Portrait of a Man* - Hamburg: *Young Girl with Dog* - Kaliningrad: *Study of a Head* - Leiden: *Portrait of a Man* - London (Wallace Collection): *A Young Negro Archer* (c. 1640, oil/panel) - Munich: *Dutch Barrack Room; Isaac Blessing Jacob* - Nantes (MBA): *Young Girl with Flowers* - Nice: *Jacob Receiving Paternal Benediction* - Nuremberg: *Young Warrior* - Paris (Louvre): *An Angel Announcing the Birth of Christ to the Shepherds; Portrait of a Young Girl as a Shepherdess* - Rohrau (Schlossmuseum, Graf Harrach'sche Familiensammlung): *Portrait of a Man; Portrait of a Young Man* - Rotterdam: *Portrait of Dirck Graswinckel and his Wife* - Rouen: *Portrait of Andrea Doria* - St Petersburg (Hermitage): *Study of a Head; Bathsheba; Jacob Cats and William of Orange; Portrait of a Young Man* - Stuttgart: *Landscape* - Toulon: *Jacob's Blessing* - Vienna: *Christ among the Teachers; Old Man with Grey Beard* - Vienna (Liechtenstein Mus.): *Hagar in the Desert* - Wiesbaden: *Daedalus and Icarus*.

Auction records:
Paris, 9 March 1872, *Portrait of a Young Man*, FRF 1,110. Paris, 22 Feb 1893, *Portrait of a Woman*, FRF 1,872. New York, 9-11 March 1904, *Portrait of a Woman*, USD 1,300. New York, 6-7 April 1905, *A Rabbi*, USD 560. New York, 22-23 Feb 1907, *Portrait of a Noble Young Woman*, USD 750. London, 27 Feb 1909, *Portrait of a Young Boy*, GBP 89. New York, 1910, *Tobias and the Angel*, USD 1,100. Paris, 19 June 1910, *Portrait of a Man*, FRF 2,730. Paris, 4 June 1923, *Portrait of a Man*, FRF 9,500. Paris, 2 June 1924, *Portrait of a Young Man as a Shepherd*, FRF 11,000. Paris, 17-18 June 1924, *Portrait of a Young Woman*, FRF 1,300. Paris, 4 Dec 1924, *Portrait of a Nobleman*, FRF 6,000; *Portrait of a Woman*, FRF 1,350. Paris, 13-14 Dec 1926, *Young Woman and Two Sleeping Cupids*, FRF 360. Paris, 19 April 1928, *Portrait of a Young Man with a Black Cap*, FRF 5,200. Paris, 13 Nov 1933, *Portrait of a Woman*, FRF 7,900. London, 28 May 1936, *Gentleman*, GBP 180. London, 26 June 1936, *Tobias Heals his*

Father, GBP 168. LONDON, 24 May 1937, *Gentleman*, GBP 29. LONDON, 30 June 1937, *Sigismund*, GBP 18. NEW YORK, 4 March 1938, *Merchant*, USD 300. LONDON, 18 Nov 1938, *Young Man*, GBP 178. PARIS, 8 Dec 1938, *Jesus and the Samaritan Woman* (black chalk and Indian ink wash) FRF 2,100. LONDON, 12 April 1940, *Young Man*, GBP 609. PARIS, 1 Dec 1943, *The Man in the Turban*, FRF 1,150. LONDON, 26 June 1946, *Landscape with Tobias and an Angel*, GBP 105. PARIS, 30 June 1947, *Writer*, FRF 11,000. LONDON, 1 April 1960, *Manoah's Sacrifice*, GBP 682. LONDON, 17 May 1961, *Portrait of a Man*, GBP 320. NEW YORK, 1 May 1963, *Portrait of a Rabbi* (oil on panel, 24 1/2 x 20 1/2 ins / 62 x 52 cm) USD 65,000. PARIS, 27 June 1963, *Vertumnus and Pomona*, FRF 6,500. VIENNA, 1 and 4 Dec 1964, *Vertumnus and Pomona*, ATS 70,000. LONDON, 29 June 1966, *Portrait of Rembrandt*, GBP 800. AMSTERDAM, 10 Dec 1968, *Portrait of a Young Man*, NLG 7,200. COLOGNE, 8 May 1969, *Portrait of a Young Man*, DEM 10,000. LONDON, 25 Nov 1970, *Little Girl with Small Dog*, GBP 6,500. LONDON, 10 July 1974, *The Sacrifice*, GBP 5,200. ZURICH, 28 May 1976, *A Pair of Musicians* (1643, oil on canvas, 34 1/4 x 42 1/4 ins / 87 x 107.5 cm) CHF 60,000. COPENHAGEN, 9 Nov 1977, *Huntsman and his Dogs in a Wooded Landscape* (oil on canvas, 427 1/4 x 59 ins / 1085 x 150 cm) DKK 40,000. LONDON, 12 July 1978, *Portrait of a Gentleman* (1641, oil on panel, oval, 29 3/4 x 23 1/2 ins / 75.5 x 59.5 cm) GBP 7,000. AMSTERDAM, 29 Oct 1979, *Joseph Interpreting the Dreams* (pen, corners cut, 4 1/2 x 5 1/4 ins / 11.4 x 13.3 cm) NLG 4,800. NEW YORK, 8 Jan 1981, *Portrait of a Rabbi* (oil on panel, 24 1/2 x 20 1/2 ins / 62 x 52 cm) USD 75,000. LONDON, 9 March 1983, *Portrait of a Little Girl with Two Dogs* (oil on canvas, 45 x 35 3/4 ins / 114 x 91 cm) GBP 16,000. AMSTERDAM, 26 Nov 1984, *Study of a Young Girl in a Large Hat* (black and white chalk/blue paper, 15 x 7 1/2 ins / 37.7 x 19 cm) NLG 7,500. LONDON, 10 April 1985, *Diana, Seated Nude* (black and white chalk/blue paper, 15 x 9 1/2 ins / 38.4 x 24.4 cm) GBP 8,000. LONDON, 11 Dec 1985, *Self-portrait* (1643, oil on panel, 28 1/4 x 20 3/4 ins / 72 x 53 cm) GBP 140,000. NEW YORK, 14 Jan 1988, *Portrait of a Rabbi* (oil on panel, 24 1/2 x 20 1/2 ins / 62 x 52 cm) USD 341,000. AMSTERDAM, 29 Nov 1988, *Half-length Portrait of a Gentleman in Dark Attire with a Lace Collar* (1645, oil on panel, 27 3/4 x 23 1/2 ins / 70.8 x 60 cm) NLG 24,150. NEW YORK, 12 Jan 1989, *Portrait of a Young Man Carrying a Short Ornamental Sword* (1644, oil, 39 1/2 x 34 ins / 100.5 x 86.5 cm) USD 407,000. NEW YORK, 1 June 1989, *The Angel Disappearing before Manoah and his Wife* (oil on panel, 44 x 39 3/4 ins / 111.7 x 101 cm) USD 23,100. PARIS, 8 Dec 1989, *Negress* (oil on canvas, 35 x 26 3/4 ins / 88 x 68 cm) FRF 56,000. NEW YORK, 11 Jan 1990, *The Deposition* (oil on canvas, 35 x 28 1/4 ins / 89 x 71.5 cm) USD 209,000. LONDON, 6 July 1990, *Richly Dressed Little Girl with a Feather in her Hair and a Puppy in her Arms* (oil on canvas/panel, 28 x 22 3/4 ins / 71 x 57.8 cm) GBP 143,000. PARIS, 29 Nov 1991, *Portrait of a Young Man* (grey wash, 10 3/4 x 8 1/2 ins / 27.6 x 21.7 cm) FRF 10,000. LONDON, 11 Dec 1992, *Bust of Bearded Old Man Dressed in Black* (oil on panel, 22 1/4 x 18 1/4 ins / 56.6 x 46.5 cm) GBP 66,000. NEW YORK, 15 Jan 1993, *Landscape with Tower* (oil on panel, 16 x 22 1/2 ins / 40.6 x 57.2 cm) USD 112,500. NEW YORK, 14 Jan 1994, *Portrait of a Young Woman Holding an Orange* (oil on canvas, 29 1/4 x 23 3/4 ins / 74.6 x 60.3 cm) USD 96,000. NEW YORK, 11 Jan 1996, *Portrait of a Young Man Holding a Short Ottoman Sword in a Richly Embellished Sheath* (1644, oil on canvas, 39 1/2 x 34 ins / 100.3 x 86.4 cm) USD 360,000. AMSTERDAM, 12 Nov 1996, *Portrait of a Bearded Old Man* (pencil and brown ink, 4 x 5 ins / 10.3 x 12.8 cm) NLG 4,956. NEW YORK, 31 Jan 1997, *Suffer the Little Children to Come unto Me* (oil on canvas, 48 ins / 122 cm 69 1/4 ins/176 cm) USD 18,400. AMSTERDAM, 7 May 1997, *Half-length Portrait of Andries de Graeff* (oil on canvas, 17 3/4 x 14 1/2 ins / 45.1 x 37 cm) NLG 27,676. NEW YORK, 27 Jan 1999, *Study of Standing Woman* (black and white chalk, 17 x 11 ins / 42 x 29 cm) USD 16,000. LONDON, 14 Dec 1999, *Head of a Bearded Old Man* (oil on panel, 16 x 12 ins / 41 x 31 cm) GBP 2,800. LONDON, 19 April 2000, *Portrait of Lady in Black Dress with Ruff* (oil on canvas, 26 x 22 ins / 67 x 57 cm) GBP 34,000. LONDON, 7 July 2000, *Portrait of a Gentleman in Black Costume with a Lace Collar* (oil on panel, 20 x 15 ins / 52 x 39 cm) GBP 17,000. BRUSSELS, 18 June 2001, *Worthy* (oil on panel, 27 x 22 ins / 68 x 55 cm) BEF 145,000. LONDON, 10 Dec 2001, *Sleeping Cupid* (oil on canvas/panel, 28 x 21 ins / 70 x 54 cm) GBP 8,500. VIENNA, 2 Oct 2002, *Portrait of Saskia, Wife of Rembrandt* (oil on panel, 27 x 19 ins / 69 x 49 cm) EUR 115,000. LONDON, 9 July 2003, *Portrait of a Gentleman, Half-length* (1646, black chalk and wash heightened with white, 7 x 5 ins / 17 x 13 cm) GBP 6,500.

FLINCK, Nicolaes Anthoni
Dutch, 17th - 18th century.
Born 1646, in Amsterdam; died 1723; buried 8 January in Rotterdam.
Engraver (etching). Portraits.

Nicolaes Anthoni Flinck was the son of Govaert Flinck. He settled in Rotterdam. There is an signed etching by him, representing a young man with long hair, which may be a self-portrait.

MUSEUMS AND GALLERIES:
LONDON (British Mus.): two portraits (etching).

FLINDT, Eduard
German, 19th century.
Born 4 March 1861, in Altona (Hamburg).
Painter. Landscapes.

Eduard Flindt studied at the academy of fine art in Berlin. In 1892 he exhibited landscapes of the Harz region and northern Germany in the exhibition at the academy and also at the Grosse Kunstausstellung from 1893 to 1898.

FLINDT, Paul
German, 17th century.
Died after 1618, in Nuremberg.
Goldsmith, engraver (burin/wood).

Paul Flindt mostly engraved ornamental subjects. However, a mythological work is also attributed to him: *Orpheus Charming the Wild Animals* and *Months*, a sequence of thirteen prints.

FLINN, Doris K.
British, 20th century.
Born at the beginning of the 20th century, in Manchester.
Sculptor.

Doris Flinn exhibited at the Salon of the Société Nationale des Beaux-Arts in Paris in 1934.

FLINOIS, Arnould Joseph
French, 18th century.
Born 1709; died 11 December 1754, in Cambrai.
Painter.

Arnould Joseph Flinois moved to Cambrai before 1739.

FLINSCH, Alexander
German, 19th - 20th century.
Born 9 January 1834, in Leipzig; died 19 January 1912, in Berlin.
Watercolourist.

Flinsch was the pupil of A. Tissier and C. Flers in Paris. He spent time in Leipzig and Berlin, and paid numerous visits to Italy, Thuringia and the Baltic States, bringing back from them watercolour landscapes.
MUSEUMS AND GALLERIES:
LEIPZIG (Mus., Drawings Collection): two watercolours.

FLINT, Andreas
Danish, 18th - 19th century.
Born c. 1768, in Copenhagen; died 19 September 1824, in Copenhagen.
Engraver.
Andreas Flint was the son of Ole Nielsen Flint and a pupil at the Kunstakademi in Copenhagen, which awarded him silver medals in 1788 and 1791 for his landscape studies, and in 1792 and 1794 for his engravings after Poussin (*Moses Before the Burning Bush*) and Giordano (*The Death of Abel*). He engraved history paintings after C.A. Lorentzen (*The Goddess Hertha Abandoning her Sacred Wood* and *Sea Battle at Fhemarn*), Norwegian landscapes after Sigvard Schojdt, and views of Trondjem and its surroundings. He also executed numerous portraits of Danish kings and other figures of his time after his own drawings or those of other artists.

FLINT, F. Wighton
British, 19th century.
Painter. Landscapes.
F. Wighton Flint lived and worked in Edinburgh. He was the father of R. Purves and William Russell Flint.

FLINT, Francis Murray Russell
British, 20th century.
Born 3 June 1915.
Painter, watercolourist. Seascapes.
Francis Flint studied art in England and Paris. He became a member of the Royal Institute of Oil Painters, specialising in boats and the sea. He exhibited in various regional exhibitions and at the Royal Academy in London.
AUCTION RECORDS:
LONDON, 11 June 1982, *Above the Waves* (1955, watercolour, 15 x 22 ins / 38 x 56 cm) GBP 400. NEW YORK, 19 July 1990, *Lifeboat at Sea* (oil on canvas, 30 x 50 ins / 76.3 x 127 cm) USD 2,475. LONDON, 18 Dec 1991, *Shipyard* (watercolour and gouache, 21 1/2 x 30 ins / 54.5 x 76 cm) GBP 1,100. EDINBURGH, 13 May 1993, *The Abandoned Ardgour Jetty on Loch Linnhe* (gouache, 20 3/4 x 29 3/4 ins / 52.6 x 75.8 cm) GBP 1,870. LONDON, 11 May 1994, *The Lighthouse Boat in Heavy Weather* (oil on canvas, 28 x 36 ins / 71 x 91.5 cm) GBP 1,380. NEW YORK, 24 May 1995, *Conversation between Models* (tempera/paper, 26 1/2 x 36 ins / 67.3 x 91.4 cm) USD 37,375. VICTORIA, 4 April 2000, *Ardmair Point, Loch Broom* (watercolour, 14 x 21 ins / 36 x 53 cm) AUD 3,200. CREWKERNE, 16 Nov 2000, *St Tropez* (oil on canvas, 15 x 18 ins / 37 x 45 cm) GBP 1,050. NEW YORK, 30 Oct 2001, *Knighthood of Sir Francis Chichester at the Royal Navy* (oil on canvas, 48 x 72 ins / 122 x 183 cm) USD 3,000. LONDON, 21 Jan 2003, *MV Herdsman off Dover* (oil on board, 19 x 23 ins / 48 x 58 cm) GBP 1,500. LONDON, 21 Jan 2003, *MV Factor at Castries* (oil on canvas, 23 x 24 ins / 59 x 60 cm) GBP 2,200.

FLINT, Johannes
Danish, 19th century.
Baptised 15 August 1778; died 25 February 1823.
Active in Copenhagen.
Engraver.
Johannes Flint was the son of Ole Nielsen Flint. He received a medal from the Kunstakademi in Copenhagen in 1800. He is known for a view of Pisa Cathedral.

FLINT, Niels
Danish, 18th - 19th century.
Born 1776, in Copenhagen.
Painter.
Niels Flint was the son of the engraver Ole Nielsen Flint. He was a pupil at the academy of Copenhagen, where he received silver medals in 1793 and 1795, and a gold medal in 1797 for his painting *Abraham's Affliction at the Death of Sarah*. He received a grant which allowed him to travel to Kiel, Hamburg, Leipzig, Dresden, then on to Vienna and Italy, where he died after having apparently spent a dissipated 10 years.

In 1828 he showed at the exhibition in Milan as a history painter, with *Corinne Singing on the Shore before Lord Melville and his Italian Compatriots* and a scene from Mme de Staël's novel *Corinne or Italy*.

FLINT, Ole
Danish, 18th - 19th century.
Born 1785; died 1806.
Active in Copenhagen.
Engraver.
Ole Flint was the son of Ole Nielsen Flint.

FLINT, Ole Nielsen
Danish, 18th century.
Born 1739; died 8 January 1808, in Copenhagen.
Engraver.
Ole Nielsen Flint engraved mostly marine maps. He worked on a collection of Danish and Norwegian coats-of-arms with J. G. Friedrich of Nuremberg.

FLINT, R. Purves
British, 20th century.
Born 1883; died 1947.
Watercolourist, illustrator. Landscapes.
R. Purves Flint was the son of F. Wighton Flint. He lived and worked in Scotland. In the early 20th century he took part in exhibitions in Glasgow and Edinburgh. In 1913 an exhibition of his work was organised by the Walker Galleries in London.
AUCTION RECORDS:
EDINBURGH, 13 July 1929, *Donkeys at Margate* (watercolour) GBP 6.

FLINT, S.
British, 19th century.
Painter. Landscapes, animals.
S. Flint is mentioned in *Art Prices Current*.
AUCTION RECORDS:
LONDON, 23 March 1908, *Sheep on a Road* (1882) GBP 1.

FLINT, Saville Lumley William
British, 18th - 19th century.
Active in London.
Miniaturist.
Saville Flint exhibited at the Royal Academy from 1882 to 1895.

FLINT, William Russel (Sir)
British, 20th century.
Born 1880, in Edinburgh; died 1969.
Painter, watercolourist, illustrator. Figures, nudes, genre scenes, landscapes.
William Flint was the son of F. Wighton Flint. He studied with a lithographer in Edinburgh. From 1900, he worked as an illustrator in London before beginning to paint almost exclusively in watercolours. In 1917, he became a member of the Royal Society of Painters in Watercolours, of which he was president from 1936 to 1956. He was elected a member of the Royal Academy in 1933.

He is known in particular for the studies he brought back from trips to France and Italy, including: *Blue Riviera, the Garonne*; Scottish landscapes such as *Storm, Loch Earn*; female figures and nudes; genre scenes including *Sun, Sand and Conversation*; and Romantically inspired compositions such as *The Huntresses and the Knight* and mythological scenes such as *Andromeda, The Judgement of Paris*. He began to show his work at group exhibitions in 1905 and 1906 (Salon of the Société Nationale des Beaux-Arts in Paris). In 1906 and 1907, he showed at the Royal Academy in London; in 1909 and 1914 in Venice and in 1914 in Berlin. In 1912, he began working for the Riccardi Press in London providing watercolour designs for colour illustrations of M. Arnold's

Poems, Kingsley's *Heroes,* Malory's *Mort d'Arthur* and Chaucer's *Canterbury Tales.*

BIBLIOGRAPHY:

Palmer, A., *'More than Shadows. A Biography of W. Russel Flint'* in *The Studio,* periodical, London, New York, 1945. *Works by Sir William Russel Flint RA,* Royal Academy of Arts, London, 1962. Lewis, R., *Sir William Russel Flint. 1880-1969,* CH. Skilton, Edinburgh, London, 1980 (revised edn 1988).

AUCTION RECORDS:

LONDON, 23 July 1926, *Strawberries* (drawing) GBP 27. LONDON, 15 June 1932, *The Small Lagoon* (watercolour) GBP 28. LONDON, 21-24 Feb 1934, *Sun, Sand and Conversation,* GBP 79. LONDON, 19 Feb 1936, *Young Iberian* (watercolour) GBP 36. LONDON, 11 Dec 1936, *On the Sands* (drawing) GBP 86. LONDON, 14 June 1938, *Young Girls out Walking,* GBP 70. GLASGOW, 3 March 1943, *Pamela and Chloe* (watercolour) GBP 55; *Poitiers* (watercolour) GBP 23. LONDON, 26 Nov 1943, *Patience and Impertinence* (drawing) GBP 105. GLASGOW, 2 Feb 1945, *Rosneath on an Evening in June,* GBP 32. NEW YORK, 18-19 Oct 1946, *In a White Studio* (watercolour) USD 130. LONDON, 29 Jan 1947, *Young Girl on the Beach* (drawing) GBP 44. LONDON, 25 May 1960, *The Fountain of Echoes* (drawing) GBP 720. LONDON, 23 March 1962, *Danza Montana* (watercolour) Gns 1,100. LONDON, 15 Dec 1965, *Raquel, Leila and Cijita,* GBP 2,500. LONDON, 18 July 1969, *The Judgement of Paris,* Gns 3,800. LONDON, 19 May 1972, *Reclining Nude* (watercolour) Gns 3,000. LONDON, 11 Oct 1974, *The Swing,* Gns 3,600. LONDON, 12 Nov 1976, *Alycia* (1958, watercolour, 8 3/4 x 14 1/2 ins / 22.2 x 37 cm) GBP 2,600. LONDON, 4 March 1977, *Rosalind* (watercolour, 12 x 21 3/4 ins / 30.5 x 55.5 cm) GBP 6,500. LONDON, 17 June 1977, *Gypsy Dancers* (oil on canvas, 30 x 40 ins / 76.5 x 101.5 cm) GBP 2,600. LONDON, 15 Nov 1978, *The Toilette of Venus* (oil on canvas, 24 1/4 x 31 1/4 ins / 61.5 x 79.5 cm) GBP 2,100. NEW YORK, 26 Jan 1979, *Among Misty Isles* (watercolour, 20 3/4 x 30 1/4 ins / 53 x 77 cm) USD 7,000. LONDON, 14 Nov 1979, *Reclining Nude* (coloured chalk, 9 x 15 1/4 ins / 22 x 38.5 cm) GBP 2,100. NEW YORK, 9 June 1981, *The Three Graces* (black, brown and crimson chalks and watercolour/paper, 9 1/2 x 13 ins / 24.1 x 33 cm) USD 3,800. LONDON, 9 March 1984, *Ariadne* (black chalk/grey paper, 12 1/2 x 19 ins / 32 x 48.3 cm) GBP 1,500. LONDON, 9 Nov 1984, *Reclining Nude* (watercolour, 13 1/2 x 25 1/4 ins / 34.5 x 64.2 cm) GBP 18, 000. LONDON, 14 Nov 1984, *Kite Flyer* (oil on canvas, 45 1/2 x 68 1/2 ins / 115.5 x 174 cm) GBP 14,000. LONDON, 15 May 1985, *Ruth with Naomi and Orpah* (oil on canvas, 14 1/4 x 23 1/2 ins / 36 x 60 cm) GBP 11,000. LONDON, 12 June 1986, *Carlotta Verdi* (1954, red chalk, series of 10 drawings, 17 1/4 x 11 ins / 43.6 x 27.8 cm) GBP 10,000. LONDON, 12 June 1987, *Alexandrine and Josette* (watercolour, 19 1/4 x 26 1/2 ins / 49 x 67.5 cm) GBP 24,000. NEW YORK, 25 Feb 1988, *Reclining Female Nude* (red and brown chalks, 7 3/4 x 10 1/2 ins / 20 x 26.8 cm) USD 2,750; *Dawn Work* (oil on canvas, 37 x 39 ins / 94 x 99.1 cm) USD 9,900. NEW YORK, 25 May 1988, *Pontaix* (1962, watercolour, 11 1/4 x 15 1/2 ins / 28.5 x 39.2 cm) USD 2,750. LONDON, 9 June 1988, *Spring Comedy* (watercolour, 18 1/4 x 25 1/2 ins / 46.3 x 64.5 cm) GBP 23,100. LONDON, 29 July 1988, *Reclining Nude* (coloured chalk, 9 1/2 x 13 1/2 ins / 24.4 x 34.5 cm) GBP 2,750. EDINBURGH, 30 Aug 1988, *Highland Lake* (watercolour, 10 x 13 1/2 ins / 24.5 x 34.5 cm) GBP 1,650. EDINBURGH, 22 Nov 1988, *Sport on the Sands* (watercolour, 19 1/2 x 26 1/4 ins / 49.5 x 66.5 cm) GBP 32,000. NEW YORK, 23 Feb 1989, *Marble Columns* (1926, watercolour, 20 x 27 1/4 ins / 51 x 69.2 cm) USD 49,500. LONDON, 2 March 1989, *Argilliers Farm in Languedoc* (watercolour, 11 3/4 x 17 1/4 ins / 30 x 43.7 cm) GBP 10,450; *Germaines Beach* (watercolour, 19 3/4 x 25 1/2 ins / 50 x 65 cm) GBP 40,700. LONDON, 12 May 1989, *Maruja* (brown chalk/kraft paper, 12 3/4 x 8 1/2 ins / 32.5 x 21.8 cm) GBP 2,420. AMSTERDAM, 24 May 1989, *Lady Sitting on a Bench* (1919, oil on canvas, 56 1/4 x 33 3/4 ins / 143 x 86 cm) NLG 3,910. LONDON, 8 June 1989, *Gabrielle* (tempera, 16 1/2 x 26 1/4 ins / 41.8 x 66.7 cm) GBP 42,900. PERTH, 29 Aug 1989, *Sketch at Sandos* (watercolour, 14 1/2 x 22 ins / 37 x 56 cm) GBP 14,300. NEW YORK, 28 Feb 1990, *The Mallet* (watercolour/card, 12 3/4 x 19 1/4 ins / 32.7 x 48.6 cm) USD 25,300. LONDON, 8 March 1990, *Mario Schiavuta Street, Chioggia* (watercolour, 21 1/4 x 17 ins / 53.9 x 43.3 cm) GBP 19,800. NEW YORK, 23 May 1990, *The Diamond Necklace* (1961, watercolour/paper, 10 3/4 x 18 1/2 ins / 27.3 x 47 cm) USD 99,000. NEW YORK, 23 Oct 1990, *Chatting around the Well* (watercolour/card, 21 x 28 ins / 53.3 x 71.1 cm) USD 38,500. LONDON, 7 March 1991, *Vignette (Cécilmia)* (1956, watercolour, 9 1/2 x 13 ins / 24 x 33 cm) GBP 28,600. LONDON, 6 June 1991, *Silvery Shadows in the Languedoc* (watercolour, 19 x 26 3/4 ins / 48 x 68 cm) GBP 47,300. LONDON, 7 Nov 1991, *Gabrielle* (tempera, 16 1/2 x 26 1/2 ins / 42 x 67 cm) GBP 27,500. LONDON, 14 May 1992, *The Old Porch at Cordes* (watercolour and gouache, 22 x 14 ins / 56 x 35.5 cm) GBP 13,200. NEW YORK, 28 May 1992, *Ray* (1963, oil on canvas, 8 1/4 x 9 ins / 21 x 22.9 cm) USD 22,000. LONDON, 5 June 1992, *Scales* (1944, oil on canvas, 22 x 27 1/2 ins / 56 x 70 cm) GBP 22,000. LONDON, 6 Nov 1992, *Without any Bother* (watercolour, 22 1/4 x 32 ins / 56.5 x 81.5 cm) GBP 5,500. EDINBURGH, 19 Nov 1992, *Spanish Dancer* (red chalk/blue paper, 7 3/4 x 9 3/4 ins / 19.7 x 24.7 cm) GBP 2,640. LONDON, 12 March 1993, *Low Tide at St Malo* (oil on canvas, 30 x 40 1/4 ins / 76 x 102 cm) GBP 20,700; *Homage to Demeter in Provence* (oil on canvas, 36 1/4 x 62 1/4 ins / 92 x 158 cm) GBP 35,600. EDINBURGH, 13 May 1993, *Phyllis Alone* (watercolour, 19 1/4 x 26 1/4 ins / 48.9 x 66.6 cm) GBP 14,300. NEW YORK, 26 May 1993, *Abigail, the New Model* (1964, watercolour/card, 11 1/2 x 15 1/2 ins / 29.2 x 39.4 cm) USD 34,500. NEW YORK, 19 Jan 1995, *A Female Olympian* (watercolour/paper/card, 20 x 14 ins / 50.8 x 35.6 cm) USD 6,900. EDINBURGH, 23 May 1996, *The Pink Villa* (1948, watercolour, 9 3/4 x 13 1/4 ins / 24.8 x 33.7 cm) GBP 8,050. EDINBURGH, 26 Nov 1997, *Barbara among the Ruins* (1919, watercolour, 19 1/4 x 26 1/4 ins / 48.8 x 66.6 cm) GBP 11,500. NEW YORK, 6-7 March 1998, *Bagno della Marchesa; Shimmering Sand; The Shrimp Fisher* (1930-1933, three engravings, the largest, 13 1/2 x 8 1/2 ins / 34 x 21.9 cm) USD 2,070. LONDON, 20 Oct 1999, *The Silver Frock* (watercolour, 4 x 10 ins / 11 x 26 cm) GBP 42,000. LONDON, 5 Nov 1999, *Griselda* (1956, watercolour, 19 x 22 ins / 47 x 57 cm) GBP 58,000. LONDON, 6 June 2000, *Choice* (oil on canvas, 34 x 54 ins / 87 x 138 cm) GBP 50,000. LONDON, 6 June 2000, *Reading Play, Costume Group at Peel Cottage* (oil on canvas, 34 x 40 ins / 86 x 101 cm) GBP 80,000. LONDON, 7 June 2001, *Collection of Studies* (watercolour, 10 x 14 ins / 25 x 36 cm) GBP 52,000. LONDON, 26 June 2001, *Ladies of the Ensemble* (oil on canvas, 20 x 30 ins / 51 x 76 cm) GBP 130,000. ASHVILLE, 26 Oct 2002, *Venetian Canal Scene with Many Figures and Boats* (watercolour, 20 x 27 ins / 51 x 69 cm) USD 54,000. LONDON, 3 Dec 2002, *Gift of Gladioli* (pencil and watercolour, 12 x 16 ins / 30 x 40 cm) GBP 30,000. LONDON, 6 June 2003, *Dice Players* (oil on canvas, 20 x 30 ins / 51 x 76 cm) GBP 40,000. LONDON, 30 Oct 2003, *White Dress* (watercolour, 14 x 22 ins / 35 x 56 cm) GBP 26,000. LONDON, 4 March 2004, *Spanish Windows* (watercolour, 24 x 19 ins / 61 x 49 cm) GBP 17,000. SALISBURY, 7 April 2004, *Reclining Nude* (watercolour, 14 x 25 ins / 35 x 63 cm) GBP 76,000.

FLINTE, Fritz

German, 20th century.

Born 20 May 1876, in Hamburg; died 29 August 1963, in Hamburg.
Painter. Portraits, landscapes, still-lifes.
Hamburg Secession Group.

Fritz Flinte studied at the Hamburg college of arts and crafts and went on to work initially as a painter-decorator. He completed his art studies at the fine arts academy in Stuttgart between 1901 and 1905, and it was there that he first met and became friendly with Paul Bollmann. Flinte returned to Hamburg in 1905 and, in 1919, emerged as one of the founder members of the Hamburg Secession, the group of artists which set out to distance themselves from what they identified as sterile academism. He would remain a member of the Secession until it voluntarily disbanded in 1933 following pressure exerted by the Nazi authorities to exclude Jewish members from its ranks. Flinte spent extended periods in Paris in 1933, 1934 and 1936. Following World War II, he again joined the Hamburg Secession (1945-1953). He was appointed to a post at the free academy in Hamburg in 1950 and awarded the Edwin-Scharff Prize in 1962.

Examples of Flinte's work have featured in recent group exhibitions, most notably at *Malerei der Hamburgischen Sezession 1919-1933 aus der Sammlung Hermann-Josef Bunte* (*Paintings of the Hamburg Sezession 1919-1933 from the Hermann-Josef Bunte Collection*), an exhibition held in 2000 to highlight the importance and influence of the Secession during the Weimar Republic. The exhibition travelled to major venues throughout Germany, including the Fine Arts Museum in Hamburg. Since his death in 1963, solo exhibitions of Flinte's work have been few and far between, but a major retrospective was held in 2000 at the Haspa (Hamburger Sparkasse) Gallery in Hamburg, perhaps marking a rediscovery of his work. Overall, Cézanne appears to have been his greatest influence.

BIBLIOGRAPHY:

Ewers-Schultz, Ina, *Der Hamburger Maler Friz Flinte*, exhibition catalogue, Galerie der Haspa (Hamburger Sparkasse), Hamburg, 2000.

AUCTION RECORDS:

HAMBURG, 12 June 1981, *Apples* (oil on canvas, 21 3/4 x 31 1/2 ins / 55.5 x 80 cm) DEM 2,600. HAMBURG, 9 June 1983, *Still-life* (oil on canvas, 22 x 31 1/2 ins / 55 x 79.8 cm) DEM 3,400. HAMBURG, 4 Dec 1999, *Still-life* (oil on board, 15 x 19 ins / 39 x 48 cm) DEM 4,800. HAMBURG, 8 Dec 2001, *Still-life with Fruit* (oil on board, 13 x 22 ins / 33 x 56 cm) DEM 6,500. HAMBURG, 8 Dec 2001, *Workshop Still-life II* (oil on masonite, 17 x 19 ins / 43 x 49 cm) DEM 7,300.

FLINTOE, Johan or Johannes

Norwegian, 19th century.
Born 1786, in Copenhagen; died 27 January 1870, in Copenhagen.
Painter (including gouache). Landscapes, landscapes with figures.

Though Danish by birth, Johan Flintoe is considered a Norwegian artist because he was principally active in Norway and exerted a considerable influence on Norwegian art. He frequented the Kunstakademi in Copenhagen, receiving no medals for his work. He then settled in Christiania (now Oslo), where he was able to live from his portraits. He was also a teacher at the school of drawing, from which he resigned on 1 October 1851.

His Norwegian landscapes in paint and gouache enjoyed great success for a time.

AUCTION RECORDS:

COPENHAGEN, 8 Dec 1976, *Two Travellers on a Snow-covered Mountain Road* (1819-1825, gouache, 13 3/4 x 18 1/2 ins / 35 x 47 cm) DKK 9,000. COPENHAGEN, 2 Feb 1982, *The Valley* (gouache, 23 1/2 x 22 1/2 ins / 60 x 57 cm) DKK 23,000. COPENHAGEN, 7 Nov 1984, *The Trolhattan Lock* (gouache, 34 1/4 x 30 1/4 ins / 87 x 77 cm) DKK 50,000. COPENHAGEN, 18 Nov 1987, *View of a Village* (1822, gouache, 13 x 19 1/4 ins / 33 x 49 cm) DKK 46,000. OSLO, 22 March 1999, *View of Trondheim with Kristiansten Fort* (c. 1825, gouache, 24 x 38 ins / 62 x 97 cm) NOK 420,000. OSLO, 22 Nov 1999, *Norwegian Fjord Landscape with Figures in National Costume* (gouache, 26 x 33 ins / 67 x 83 cm) NOK 350,000. OSLO, 25 May 2000, *Landscape from Tollerud-Kleven in Hallingdal* (1819, oil on canvas, 17 x 20 ins / 43 x 50 cm) NOK 210,000. OSLO, 25 May 2000, *Landscape from Rukkedals river, Naes in Hallingdal with Figures* (1819, 20 x 16 ins / 51 x 41 cm) NOK 220,000. OSLO, 7 May 2001, *Genre Scene from Telemarken - Seated Girl Playing Norwegian Zither* (oil on tin plate, 13 x 10 ins / 32 x 25 cm) NOK 300,000. OSLO, 6 Nov 2001, *Landscape from Eggedal with Woman* (gouache, 14 x 19 ins / 35 x 47 cm) NOK 110,000.

FLINTOFF, T.

Australian, 19th century.
Painter. Portraits.

MUSEUMS AND GALLERIES:

MELBOURNE (Nat. Gal. of Victoria): *Portrait of Sir William John Clarke Bart, Member of the Legislative Council of Victoria; Portrait of Gordon August Thomson.*

FLINTZEP, Hugo

German, 19th century.
Born 4 May 1862, in Eisenach (Thuringia).
Painter. Landscapes.

The museum in Weimar has a painting by Flintzep entitled *Forest*

FLINZER, Fedor Alexis

German, 19th - 20th century.
Born 1832, in Reichenbach; died 1911, in Leipzig.
Painter, engraver. Animals.

Flinzer was the pupil of Julius Schnorr at the Kunstakademie in Dresden from 1849 to 1859, making his debut in Dresden around 1860. He illustrated numerous books for children.

FLIPART, Charles François

French, 18th century.
Born 1730, in Paris; died 1773.
Engraver.

Charles François Flipart was the son of Jean-Charles Flipart. He engraved after Fragonard and various other French masters of his time, such as Carème and Boucher.

FLIPART, Charles Joseph or Giuseppe

French, 18th century.
Born 1721, in Paris; died 1797, in Madrid.
Painter, engraver. Historical subjects, figures, portraits, genre scenes, interiors with figures.

Charles Joseph Flipart was the son of Jean Charles Flipart, from whom he received his first training. He went to Italy and, during his time in Venice, studied engraving under Tiepolo, Amiconi and Joseph Wagner. He also spent several years in Rome. It is probably from there that he was summoned to Spain in 1770 by King Ferdinand VI, and appointed painter and engraver to the Spanish court. There are works by him in two churches in Madrid, and he also engraved portraits of the king and queen of Spain.

AUCTION RECORDS:

PARIS, 29 April 1921, *The Drunken Cobbler* (black chalk, after Greuze) FRF 310. LONDON, 3 July 1985, *Interior of a Gaming House* (oil on canvas, 13 1/2 x 18 1/2 ins / 34 x 47 cm) GBP 6,000. NEW YORK, 9 Oct 1991, *Young Woman at a Harpsichord near a Man Playing the Viol in an Interior* (oil on canvas, 17 x 14 1/4 ins / 43.2 x 36.2 cm) USD 8,250. LYONS, 7 Feb 1999, *Portrait of Pietro Longhi* (oil on canvas, 28 x 23 ins / 72 x 59 cm) FRF 88,000. PARIS, 21 Oct 1999, *The Toilette of the Courtisan* (oil on canvas, 28 x 23 ins / 70 x 58 cm) FRF 110,000.

FLIPART, Jacques Nicolas
French, 18th century.
Born 1724, in Paris.
Active in the Netherlands.
Painter. Portraits.

Jacques Nicolas Flipart was the son of Jean Charles Flipart. He was present at his father's funeral in Paris in May 1750. He is the same person as the painter of portraits admitted as a freeman in The Hague in 1773, whom Siret calls N.-N. Flipart and Dr von Wurzbach calls John-Jac Flipart. There is no question of this being the painter Charles Joseph Flipart, who had been resident in Spain since 1770, nor Jean Jacques Flipart, who is not mentioned anywhere as a painter and whose admission to the corporation of The Hague would certainly have been related in the obituary which De la Blancherie devoted to him in *Les Nouvelles de la République des lettres et des arts* (*News from the Republic about Arts and Letters*) on 31 July 1782.

FLIPART, Jean Charles
French, 18th century.
Born 1684, in Abbeville; died 23 May 1751, in Paris.
Engraver (burin).

Jean Charles Flipart's master is not mentioned. He is remembered for religious subjects, notably *The Virgin and the Infant Jesus* and *Christ in the Garden of Gethsemane*, and prints after two paintings by Raphael from the Crozat collection. He also engraved after Le Brun and Houasse. He lived in the Rue St-Jacques. Four of his sons, Jean Jacques (engraver in burin), Jean Antoine (organist), Jacques Nicolas (painter) and Charles François (engraver), were present at his funeral. There is reason to believe that the painter and engraver Charles Joseph Flipart was also his son. Presumably he was a man of some substance, for his funeral was conducted with a certain style.

FLIPART, Jean Jacques
French, 18th century.
Born 1719, in Paris; died 10 July 1782, in Paris.
Engraver.

Jean Jacques Flipart was the eldest son of Jean Charles Flipart. Biographers do not agree on the date of his birth, some giving 1719, others 1723. Since his death certificate gives his age as 68, 1714 seems preferable. He was the pupil of his father, Peronneau, P. Aveline and Laurent Cars. He was by far the most well-known member of his family and holds a respected place amongst the French engravers of the 18th century. He was elected to the Académie on 28 June 1755 and continued to take part in its exhibitions until 1777. He collaborated on the *Dresden Gallery*. He specialised in engraving scenes from everyday life after the most famous painters of his period - Boucher, Chardin, Natoire, Vernet, Vien, Boullogne and Dietrich - but it was Greuze especially whose works he enjoyed reproducing, at great profit to himself. He is particularly remembered for his engravings of *A Girl Winding Cotton into a Ball, Portrait of Greuze, The Paralytic, Village Bride, Twelfth-night Cake, Dead Bird* and *Woman Knitting*.

FLIPSEN, Alfred Wilhelm Philippe and Victor Philippe. See **PHILIPSEN**

FLISCHER, Edith E.
American, 20th century.
Born 1890, in Cleveland (Ohio).
Painter. Portraits.

Edith E. Flischer was a pupil at the Pennsylvania Academy of Fine Arts, and a teacher.

FLISSIER. See **FLESSIERS**

FLOBERT-GRACIANSKY, Charlotte
French, 19th - 20th century.
Born in the second half of the 19th century, in Paris.
Painter.

Charlotte Flobert-Graciansky studied at the École des Beaux-Arts and worked with Humbert, Bilou and Roger. She became an associate member of the Salon des Artistes Français in 1929.

FLOC'H, M. J.
French, 16th century.
Sculptor.

The name of this Breton artist appears on one of the statues of the porch of the church at Landivisiau (Finistère). The construction dates from 1554.

FLOC'H, Yves
French, 20th century.
Born 24 May, in Carpont-en-Plouguerneau; died 1990.
Painter (gouache), watercolourist. Portraits, landscapes, landscapes with figures.

Yves Floc'h first studied art in the provincial town of Lesneven after his talent was spotted by the local priest. In 1930, he went to study at the École des Arts Décoratifs at the École des Beaux-Arts in Paris. He qualified to teach art and had a post first in St-Dié (Vosges) then in Dinan, Brittany. Dinan library showed his works in 2001.

Corot's art and all things Breton were the mainstay of his production, and his trips around the Mediterranean provided fresh inspiration for his landscapes.

BIBLIOGRAPHY:
Petit, Jacques, *Yves Floc'h*, monograph, 1992. *War roudou. Yves Floc'h*, 2000.

FLOCCI, Bernardino
Italian, 17th century.
Painter.

Bernardino Flocci is mentioned in 1630 in connection with stucco decorations for the principal church in Ciminna.

FLOCH, Jeanne
French, 20th century.
Born 6 June 1916, in Rotterdam, to French parents.
Painter.

Jeanne Floch trained at the Académies Libres of Montparnasse, hotbeds of modernity. She exhibited in Paris, especially at the Salon des Artistes Indépendants, and in Brussels.

An abstract painter, tachiste, she sought to break free from focal/central concepts. Her works are textured and have a descriptive brief, recognisable in their lines and identified in titles bound to reality.

FLOCH, Joseph
Austrian, 20th century.
Born 1894 or 1895, in Vienna; died 1977, in Paris.
Active in France, then in the USA.
Painter. Figures, interiors with figures, landscapes.

Floch exhibited in Paris, from 1926, at the Salon d'Automne and the Salon des Tuileries. After playing an important part in the Neo-Realist movement, supported in Paris between the Wars by the critic Waldemar-George, he took refuge in the USA, where he was somewhat influenced by the Surrealists.

Floch

MUSEUMS AND GALLERIES:
MULHOUSE: *Portrait of the Wife of the Artist*.

AUCTION RECORDS:
PARIS, 29 Oct 1926, *Landscape*, FRF 2,600. NEW YORK, 26-27 Jan 1944, *Portrait of a Young Boy*, USD 175. VIENNA, 17 March 1976, *Sailing Ships at Anchor* (oil on canvas, 19 1/4 x 25 1/4 ins / 49 x 64 cm) ATS 9,000. VIENNA, 4 Dec 1984, *The Roofs* (c. 1933, oil on canvas, 18 x 22 ins / 46 x 55 cm) ATS

50,000. VIENNA, 19 May 1987, *Portrait of a Bearded Man* (oil on canvas, 26 x 20 3/4 ins / 66 x 53 cm) ATS 80,000. NEW YORK, 18 Dec 1991, *In My Studio* (oil on canvas, 21 3/4 x 15 1/4 ins / 55.2 x 38.7 cm) USD 2,090. NEW YORK, 9 Sept 1993, *Repose* (oil on canvas, 39 1/2 x 35 1/2 ins / 100.3 x 90.2 cm) USD 3,450. NEW YORK, 21 Sept 1994, *Black Folding Screen with a Shawl* (oil on canvas, 48 1/2 x 38 ins / 123.2 x 96.5 cm) USD 7,187. PARIS, 3 April 1996, *Two Women in an Interior* (oil on canvas, 67 x 35 ins / 170 x 89 cm) FRF 130,000.

FLOCH, Lionel

French, 20th century.

Born 9 May 1905, in Quimper; died 7 December 1972, in Quimper.

Painter. Genre scenes.

Lionel Floch exhibited in Paris, regularly at the Salon des Artistes Français and in 1924 at the Salon d'Automne. He often painted circus subjects.

AUCTION RECORDS:

BREST, 3 March 1981, *Sailors on the Quayside* (oil on canvas, 18 x 24 ins / 46 x 61 cm) FRF 4,600. LORIENT, 3 Nov 1984, *Tuna Boat in Concarneau* (oil on canvas, 17 1/4 x 24 3/4 ins / 44 x 63 cm) FRF 9,700. DOUARNENEZ, 26 July 1987, *Fisherman's Wife Facing the Sea* (oil on canvas, 25 1/2 x 19 1/4 ins / 65 x 49 cm) FRF 10,000. PARIS, 17 Feb 1988, *In a Circus, Backstage* (oil on canvas, 22 x 18 ins / 55 x 46 cm) FRF 5,000; *Circus Encampment* (oil on card, 14 1/2 x 17 3/4 ins / 37 x 45 cm) FRF 5,500. PARIS, 26 Jan 1998, *Breton Women at Low Tide* (oil on canvas, 25 1/4 x 35 3/4 ins / 64 x 91 cm) FRF 10,500. BREST, 10 Dec 2000, *Pardon in the Pont-l'Abbé Region* (oil on canvas, 29 x 36 ins / 73 x 92 cm) FRF 27,000. BREST, 15 Dec 2002, *Roasting* (oil on canvas, 9 x 13 ins / 24 x 32 cm) EUR 1,580. BREST, 11 May 2003, *Port in Brittany* (oil on board, 9 x 13 ins / 24 x 32 cm) EUR 1,800. BREST, 21 Dec 2003, *Elegant Lady in a Flower Garden* (1925, oil on canvas, 24 x 29 ins / 60 x 73 cm) EUR 2,000. RENNES, 14 July 2004, *Wrack Collectors* (oil on canvas, 21 x 28 ins / 53 x 72 cm) EUR 3,500. BREST, 24 July 2004, *Fisherman with Basket* (oil on canvas, 39 x 31 ins / 100 x 80 cm) EUR 4,800.

FLOCKEMANN, August Christoph Friedrich

German, 19th - 20th century.

Born 6 April 1849, in Hiddersdorf (Hanover); died 17 July 1915, in Radebeul, near Dresden.

Active in Dresden.

Sculptor.

Flockemann was the pupil in Hanover of the sculptor H. Marten, and he took part in the restoration of the Cathedral of Güstrow (Mecklenburg-Schwerin). Thanks to a bursary he continued his study of sculpture with F. Eggers in Berlin, and then with J. Schilling in Dresden. He is known to have executed allegorical statues in marble such as *Lily of the Valley* (1899), busts, statuettes (of the *Emperor William I* (1880) and of *E.M. Dégremont*), as well as relief portraits as of the *Court Counsellor Dr E. Peschel*.

FLOCKENHAUS, Heinz

German, 19th - 20th century.

Born 1856, in Remscheid; died 1919, in Düsseldorf.

Painter. Landscapes, waterscapes.

AUCTION RECORDS:

COLOGNE, 22 Oct 1982, *Winter's Day* (oil on canvas, 25 1/4 x 38 1/2 ins / 64 x 98 cm) DEM 11,000. COLOGNE, 21 May 1984, *Winter Landscape with a Mill* (oil on card, 26 3/4 x 37 1/2 ins / 68 x 95 cm) DEM 18,000. LONDON, 9 Oct 1985, *A Winter's Evening* (1882, oil on canvas, 17 3/4 x 14 1/2 ins / 45 x 37 cm) GBP 1,100. COLOGNE, 20 Oct 1989, *Winter on the Lower Rhine* (oil on panel, 16 1/2 x 9 ins / 42 x 23 cm) DEM 6,000. COLOGNE, 23 March 1990, *Autumn on the Lower Rhine* (oil on panel, 7 x 11 ins / 18 x 27 cm) DEM 4,000. COLOGNE, 28 June 1991, *Canal in Holland in Autmun* (oil on panel, 15 1/4 x 19 3/4 ins / 39 x 50 cm) DEM 7,500. HAMBURG, 16 Oct 1999, *Riverside Village* (oil on panel, 13 x 19 ins / 32 x 48 cm) DEM 3,500. WARSAW, 5 Dec 1999, *Landscape with Stream at Sunset* (oil on panel, 9 x 7 ins / 24 x 18 cm) PLN 10,500. AHLDEN, 22 Sept 2000, *Winter Evening* (oil on panel, 17 x 13 ins / 44 x 33 cm) DEM 5,000. COLOGNE, 5 April 2001, *Winter Landscape* (oil on panel, 20 x 14 ins / 50 x 36 cm) DEM 3,400. ZURICH, 5 Sept 2001, *Lower Rhine Winter Landscape at Sunset* (oil on canvas, 27 x 39 ins / 69 x 99 cm) CHF 6,000. NEW YORK, 27 Feb 2002, *Winter Sunset, Dusseldorf* (oil on canvas, 23 x 18 ins / 58 x 46 cm) USD 1,900. COLOGNE, 21 Nov 2002, *Winter Landscape. Autumn Landscape* (oil on panel, two works, 9 x 6 ins / 24 x 16 cm) EUR 3,600. COLOGNE, 3 July 2003, *Winter Evening with Peasant Women Returning Home. Summer Stream* (oil on panel, two works, 7 x 10 ins / 18 x 26 cm) EUR 1,700. COLOGNE, 1 April 2004, *Stormy Weather over Northern Rhine Landscape* (1881, oil on canvas, 10 x 17 ins / 26 x 43 cm) EUR 2,000. STAUFEN, 23 Sept 2004, *Snowy Village Street* (oil on canvas, 27 x 39 ins / 68 x 98 cm) EUR 1,800.

FLOCKET. See **FLOQUET**

FLOCKHART, William

British, 19th century.

Painter. Landscapes.

William Flockhart was a regular exhibitor in London at the Royal Academy and Suffolk Street from 1880.

FLOCKTON, Margaret

British.

Painter. Genre scenes.

MUSEUMS AND GALLERIES:

SYDNEY: *Study of Waratahs*.

FLOCON, Albert, pseudonym of Mentzel

German, 20th century.

Born 1909, in Köpenick; died 12 October 1994, in Paris.

From 1933 active and from 1946 naturalised in France.

Painter, engraver, illustrator. Scenes with figures, perspectives.

Flocon was a student, and representative of the students, at the Bauhaus in Dessau from 1927 to 1930, receiving advice at the start from Albers, Kandinsky and Klee, before enrolling at the theatre workshop of Oskar Schlemmer. From 1931 to 1933 he worked in a graphics studio in Berlin and then in Frankfurt. In 1933, in the face of the rise of Nazism, he emigrated to Paris where he carried on the same activity as an independent operator, then in 1937, as the assistant to Vasarely. In 1939, with the declaration of war on Germany, he enlisted in the Foreign Legion and was posted to Algeria until demobilisation in 1941. After the occupation of France he set up in the Southern Zone, at that time unoccupied. In 1944 he was arrested in Toulouse with his wife and his elder daughter who were deported and killed at Auschwitz. In 1946 he obtained French citizenship. On his return to Paris, taking refuge in art, he began to engrave, practising in parallel painting and engraving, especially burin engraving, in works of personal expression, at the same time producing an important theoretical work on engraving, illustration and perspective. From 1950 to 1952 he directed, with Johnny Friedlaender, the *Hermitage Studio*, a free school for engraving and drawing, and founded the *Graphics* group. In 1954 he entered the École Estienne as a lecturer in drawing, the history of art and books, specialising in the trades and techniques of books. In 1964 he was appointed to the Chair of Perspective at the École des Beaux-Arts in Paris. In 1994 the Éditions Ides et Calendes published his book of recollections, *Vanishing Points*.

As an engraver, Flocon specialised in burin engraving. In 1948 he published his first collection of engravings, *Perspectives*, 'illustrated' by ten poems by Paul Éluard. In 1949 he was the project manager of the joint work of the *Graphics* group, *To the Glory of the Hand*, with a preface by Gaston

Bachelard. The collaboration between the philosopher and the engraver continued: in 1950 with *Landscapes*, for which Gaston Bachelard wrote his *Notes d'un philosophe pour un graveur* (*Notes by a Philosopher for an Engraver*); in 1953, when Bachelard wrote a preface to the *Traité du burin* (*Treatise on Burin Engraving*), written and illustrated by Flocon; in 1957, with the 18 burin engravings of *Châteaux en Espagne* (*Castles in Spain*), with a commentary by Bachelard. In 1954 Flocon illustrated *Notes d'un biologiste* (*Notes of a Biologist*) by Jean Rostand. He also illustrated his own theoretical and technical texts: in 1961 *Topo-Graphies* (*Topo-Graphics*), an essay on the use of space by an engraver; in 1975 *Entrelacs ou les divagations d'un buriniste* (*Interlacings or the Ramblings of a Burinist*); in 1980 *En corps* (*In Body*), 12 lithographs in two colours and 12 apologues; in 1984 *12 Caprices* (*12 Fantasy Views*); in 1987 *Scénographies au Bauhaus* (*Scenographies at the Bauhaus*), a text and 31 linocuts. As a specialist in perspective, he was particularly interested in non-Euclidian perspectives, notably curved perspectives, publishing in 1962 *La perspective, son histoire, ses méthodes* (*Perspective, Its History, Its Methods*), written in collaboration with René Taton, containing the first theoretical exposé of curvilinear perspective and in 1968 *La perspective curviligne, de l'espace visuel à l'image construite* (*Curvilinear Perspective, from the Visual Space to the Constructed Image*), in collaboration with André Barre. In its formal diversity and invention, the work of Albert Flocon very particularly adapted the science of perspectives to the rigour of burin engraving.

Exhibitions devoted to Flocon have been held in France and numerous other countries, notably in Montreal in 1987 and Metz in 1992.

BIBLIOGRAPHY:

Leymarie, Jean/Herzogenrath, Wulf/Grote, Ludwig/Gropius, Walter, *Le Bauhaus*, exhibition catalogue, Württembergischer Kunsteverein, Stuttgart, Musée national d'Art moderne, Paris, 1969. Flocon, Albert, *Scénographies au Bauhaus*, L'Atelier du Nombre d'Or, Paris, 1987. Monod, Luc, *Manuel de l'amateur de livres illustrés modernes 1875-1975*, Ides et Calendes, Neuchâtel, 1992. *Albert Flocon, une poétique de la vision*, exhibition catalogue, École des beaux-arts, Metz, 1992 (extensive documentation). Flocon, Albert, *Points de Fuite*, Ides et Calendes, Neuchâtel, 1994.

AUCTION RECORDS:

PARIS, 11 Feb 1987, *Composition* (1950, mixed media/paper, 19 3/4 x 16 1/2 ins / 50 x 42 cm) FRF 3,000.

FLOCQUET, Nicolas Claude

French, 18th century.
Active in Paris in 1761.
Painter, sculptor.

FLODIN-RISSANEN, Hilda Maria

Finnish, 20th century.
Born 16 March 1877, in Helsinki.
Also active in France.
Sculptor, engraver. Figures, landscapes.

Hilda Maria Flodin-Rissanen studied at the school of fine art at Helsinki, after which she moved to Paris, where she featured from 1901 in the Salon of the Société Nationale des Beaux-Arts, the Salon des Artistes Indépendants and the Salon d'Automne. She started by exhibiting sculptures, then exclusively etchings.

MUSEUMS AND GALLERIES:

HELSINKI: *Bust of an Old Man*; *Landscapes and Figures* (etchings).

FLODING, Per Gustaf

Swedish, 18th century.
Born 1731, in Stockholm; died 1791, in Stockholm.
Draughtsman, engraver.

A pupil of Charpentier, Per Gustaf Floding frequently stayed in Paris. He engraved a number of plates, among which are *Portrait of Alexandre Roslin, Painter* after Roslin; *Apollo and Daphne* after F. Boucher; *Gustav III, King of Sweden* after Pasch; *A Battle* after Casanova; and *The Wolf and the Fox* after Oudry.

FLODMAN, Carl or Karl Samuel

Swedish, 19th century.
Born 17 December 1863, in Stockholm; died 27 October 1888, in Stockholm.
Painter, engraver. Landscapes, seascapes.

Carl Flodman studied at the academy in Stockholm from 1883 to 1886 and painted landscapes. He also produced etchings with landscape motifs.

MUSEUMS AND GALLERIES:

STOCKHOLM (Kungliga Akademien): *Kungsor* - STOCKHOLM (Nationalmus.): *Seashore*.

AUCTION RECORDS:

STOCKHOLM, 15 Nov 1988, *Boats Near the Beach* (1885, oil, 10 1/4 x 13 3/4 ins / 26 x 35 cm) SEK 11,000. STOCKHOLM, 10-12 May 1993, *Boat Washed Ashore near a Shed* (oil on canvas, 14 1/4 x 19 ins / 36.5 x 48 cm) SEK 15,000. STOCKHOLM, 24 Nov 1999, *Landscape from Hvitemolle* (1885, oil on canvas, 10 x 16 ins / 26 x 41 cm) SEK 46,000. STOCKHOLM, 29 May 2000, *Danvikstull, Stockholm* (oil on canvas/cardboard, 9 x 11 ins / 23 x 27 cm) SEK 21,000. STOCKHOLM, 5 Dec 2000, *Farm by the Sea* (oil on canvas, 12 x 18 ins / 30 x 46 cm) SEK 20,000. STOCKHOLM, 3 Dec 2003, *Lake Landscape* (oil on canvas, 12 x 16 ins / 30 x 40 cm) SEK 27,000.

FLODNER. See **FLÖTNER Peter**

FLODT, Paul Ambroise

French, 18th century.
Active in Paris in 1739.
Sculptor.

FLOEGEL, Alfred E.

German, 20th century.
Born 4 September 1894, in Leipzig.
Active in the USA.
Painter. Figure compositions. Church decoration.

Floegel was originally German but he studied art entirely in the USA and at the American Academy in Rome. He was a member of the Architectural League of New York and of the Society of Mural Painters.

He produced numerous decorations for churches, notably in the States of Michigan and New Jersey. In Brooklyn, New York he painted the ceiling of the Church of the Redeemer.

FLOESSER, Chilian

German, 15th century.
Active during the second half of the 15th century.
Illuminator.

A breviary and an antiphonal, written in 1465 and 1468, were illuminated by Chilian Floesser. These manuscripts are in the royal library in Bamberg, Bavaria.

FLOETER, Kent

American, 20th century.
Born 1937, in Saginaw (Michigan).
Active in Hoboken (New Jersey).
Sculptor, draughtsman.

Kent Floeter studied at the University of Boston (Massachusetts) School of Fine and Applied Arts, graduating in 1961, and at Yale University School of Art and Architecture, from where he graduated in 1964. He has taken part in a number of international exhibitions of sculpture and drawing, and held regular solo exhibitions in the 1970s and 1980s in the USA and abroad.

MUSEUMS AND GALLERIES:

MÖNCHENGLADBACH (Mus. Abteiberg) - ROTTWEIL (Sculptor's Drawing Mus.).

FLÖTNER, Peter. See **FLÖTNER**

FLÖGEN, C.A. von
German, 18th century.
Active at the end of the 18th century.
Painter.
Flögen worked in the style of Vernet.

FLOGIL, Mertin
German, 14th century.
Active in Breslau (now Wroclaw, Poland).
Painter.
Mertin Flogil became a burgher of the town in 1398.

FLOGNY, Eugène Victor de
French, 19th century.
Born 7 May 1825, in Flogny (Yonne).
Painter. History painting, portraits, local scenes.
Pupil of Eugène Delacroix; exhibited at the Paris Salon from 1869 to 1876. As a military man who reached the rank of general, Flogny painted numerous studies of the campaigns in which he had been involved. Examples of his work include: *Spahi Cavalry on Watch; General Randon Chiding the O-Si-Yohia; Benthaleb; Dwelling of the Marabout Li-el-Hadi-M'barek;* and *Women Preparing Couscous.*
MUSEUMS AND GALLERIES:
ALGIERS: *Head of Berber Woman (Kabyle)* - AUXERRE: *Black Nurse and Child.*
AUCTION RECORDS:
LONDON, 26 Jan 1984, *Arab Horseman* (1865, oil on canvas, 29 1/4 x 20 3/4 ins / 74 x 53 cm) GBP 3,000. PARIS, 18 March 1992, *Livestock Drinking* (oil on canvas, 15 x 24 ins / 38 x 61 cm) FRF 5,900. MONACO, 14-15 Dec 1996, *Portrait of the Children of the Duke of Chartres* (1880, oil on canvas, 67 x 48 3/4 ins / 170 x 124 cm) FRF 52,650. AHLDEN, 24 Nov 2000, *Still-life of Fruit* (oil on canvas, 11 x 15 ins / 29 x 38 cm) DEM 9,500.

FLOH, A. W.
Dutch, 19th century.
Active in Enschede c. 1810.
Painter. Genre scenes, portraits.

FLOHR
German, 19th century.
Active c. 1839.
Painter. Genre scenes.

FLOIRAT, Marie, known as Floirette Bourbon
Maiden name: Bourbon
French, 20th century.
Born 28 August 1900, in Coussac-Bonneval (Haute-Vienne).
Painter, art restorer, enameller.
Marie Floirat exhibited from 1940 to 1967 at the Salon des Artistes Français, Salon des Artistes Indépendants, Salon de l'Académie Européenne des Arts and the Salons des Arts, Sciences et Lettres du Limousin and Salon des Artistes Marchois in Bellac. She was awarded the Paris silver medal for the arts in 1967.

She collaborated with the painter-restorer Vikke van den Bergh, sharing with him discovery and restoration work on many old masters, including the maquette of Veronese's *Marriage at Cana.*

FLOISTAD, Lisa
Norwegian, 20th century.
Active in the USA.
Installation artist, assemblage artist.
Lisa Floistad works on the depiction of woman in the Catholic imagination (the virgin, the courtesan...), selecting details from paintings which she enlarges using a photocopier and reveals desire and masculine sexuality. She has shown her works in solo exhibitions including 1996 at the Tecla Sala Centre of Contemporary Art in Barcelona.

FLONDOR-STRAINU, Constantin
Romanian, 20th century.
Born 1936, in Bucharest.
Painter.
Constantin Flondor-Strainu studied in Bucharest and lived and worked in Timisoara where he exhibited in 1968. In 1969, he took part in the exhibition *Constructive Art* in Nuremberg.

FLOOR, Laurens
Dutch, 17th century.
Born in Fredrikstad; died 1667; buried 17 September in Amsterdam.
Painter.

FLOORTEE. See **FLORTEN Jan**

FLOQUET, Bartholomy
Flemish, 17th century.
Died 1699 or 1690, in Antwerp.
Painter.
Flemish School.
Listed as the son of a master in 1665, Bartholomy Floquet was perhaps the son of Lucas Floquet the Elder.

FLOQUET, Gabriel I
French, 18th century.
Active in Paris at the beginning of the 18th century.
Painter.

FLOQUET, Gabriel II
French, 18th century.
Active in Paris at the beginning of the 18th century.
Painter.

FLOQUET, Jakob
German, 17th century.
Painter. History painting, portraits.
Reference is made to Floquet in Frankfurt am Main in 1660.

FLOQUET, Jean Paul
Painter.
He is mentioned by Marolles. N. Pitau engraved after this artist a *Portrait of H. L. Habert,* lord of Montmort. He may be the same person as Pauwel Floquet.

FLOQUET, Jeanne
French, 18th century.
Active in Paris in 1769.
Painter.

FLOQUET, Lucas, the Elder
Flemish, 16th - 17th century.
Born 1578, in Antwerp; died 1635, in Antwerp.
Active in Ghent and Antwerp.
Painter. History painting, religious subjects, portraits.
Flemish School.
Lucas Floquet the Elder became a member of the guild in Antwerp in 1598. In this town he had a number of pupils, including his nephew David Leeuwarts.
MUSEUMS AND GALLERIES:
BERGEN-ST-WINOX (church): altar painting.
AUCTION RECORDS:
LONDON, 29 Oct 1965, *Meeting of David and Abigail,* Gns 1,100. MADRID, 21 May 1985, *Noble Ladies Present their Petitions to a King* (oil on canvas, 32 x 44 1/4 ins / 81.5 x 112.5 cm) USD 13,000.

FLOQUET, Lucas, the Younger
Flemish, 17th century.
Died c. 1666.
Active in Antwerp.
Painter.
Flemish School.
Lucas Floquet the Younger was the son of Lucas Floquet the Elder and became a member of the guild in Antwerp in 1640.

FLOQUET, Pauwel
Flemish, 17th century.
Born in Antwerp; died 1667, in Antwerp.
Painter. History painting.
Flemish School.
Pauwel Floquet was the son of Lucas Floquet the Elder. He became a member of the Antwerp Guild of St Luke in 1631.

FLOQUET, Simon
Flemish, 17th century.
Painter, engraver. Religious subjects.
Flemish School.
Simon Floquet was the son of Lucas Floquet the Elder. He became a member of the guild in 1634.
MUSEUMS AND GALLERIES:
GÖTTINGEN (Kunstsammlung, Georg-August-Universität): *Death and the Miser* (after Parthey); *Esther and Ahasuerus* (after Parthey).
AUCTION RECORDS:
LONDON, 8 July 1992, *Rest on the Flight into Egypt* (oil/copper, 27 1/4 x 37 ins / 69 x 94 cm) GBP 7,150. PARIS, 21 Dec 2001, *Christ and the Woman Taken in Adultery* (oil on copper, 27 x 35 ins / 69 x 88 cm) FRF 85,000. VIENNA, 21 March 2002, *River Landscape with Mary Magdalene* (oil on copper, 7 x 9 ins / 17 x 23 cm) EUR 6,000.

FLOR. See also **FLUR** and **FLURER**

FLOR, Ferdinand
German, 19th century.
Born 22 January 1793, in Hamburg; died 5 April 1881, in Rome.
Painter.
Flor studied in Eutin, Dresden and Munich. In 1819 he went to Italy, visited Florence, then England and Paris. He finally settled in Rome in 1834. Notable works of his include *Christ Blessing the Little Children, Marriage of Mary and Joseph, Narcissus, Portrait of the King of Naples, Indian Dance, Italian Landscape,* in addition to various marine landscapes and moral paintings.
MUSEUMS AND GALLERIES:
COPENHAGEN (Thorvaldsens Mus.): *Portrait of Elise Thorvaldsen* - HAMBURG (Kunsthalle): *Portrait of the Actress Lina Fuhr.*

FLOR, Jan
German, 15th century.
Sculptor (wood).
Cologne School.
Flor is thought to have been responsible for carving the choir stalls in the Cologne church of St Mary, Schnurgasse.

FLOR, Johann. See **FLUR Johann Limpert**

FLOR-DAVID, pseudonym of David, Florence
French, 20th century.
Born 13 May 1891, in Paris; died 1958.
Painter, pastellist. Figures.
Flor-David studied under Désiré Lucas. She exhibited at the Salon des Artistes Français from 1923 and received a honourable mention and the Prix Léonie Dusseuil in 1934.
AUCTION RECORDS:
NEW YORK, 2 Nov 1993, *Woman with Green Shawl* (1937, oil on canvas, 46 x 32 ins / 117 x 81 cm) USD 863.

FLORA, Francesco
Italian, 19th century.
Born 30 June 1857, in Francavilla Fontana (Puglia).
Sculptor.
Francesco Flora was a student at the Accademia di Belle Arti in Venice. He worked in Venice and Naples, sculpting portraits, genre statues and funeral monuments.

FLORA, Paul
Austrian, 20th century.
Born 29 June 1922, in Glurns (Vinschgau, South Tyrol).
Draughtsman, engraver, illustrator.
Flora has lived since 1927 in Innsbruck. He was a student from 1942 to 1944 in Munich. By his graphic humour Flora is similar to Paul Klee, Calder and especially Steinberg. He reveals the enigmatic and comic reverse side of a civilisation which considers itself to be rationalist. Since 1945 he has exhibited in Europe and New York. In 1968 he took part in the Venice Biennale. In 2002 the Kunsthistorisches Museum in Vienna presented a retrospective exhibition of his drawings (1938-2001) at the Harrach Palace.

FLORA

BIBLIOGRAPHY:
Paul Flora: Zeichnungen 1972-1986, exhibition catalogue, Neue Gal., Linz, 1987. *Paul Flora: frühe Zeichnungen*, Verlagsanstalt Athesia, Bolzano, 1992.
MUSEUMS AND GALLERIES:
PARIS (MNAM-CCI).
AUCTION RECORDS:
VIENNA, 14 March 1980, *The Tramps* (1949, pen/paper, 10 1/2 x 14 1/4 ins / 26.5 x 36.5 cm) ATS 18,000. VIENNA, 16 March 1982, *Im ABC* (Indian ink, 16 3/4 x 23 3/4 ins / 42.5 x 60.5 cm) ATS 14,000. VIENNA, 4 Dec 1984, *Defeated Heroes* (pen and Indian ink, 14 1/4 x 20 ins / 36 x 50.5 cm) ATS 5,000. MUNICH, 26-27 Nov 1991, *Puppets* (ink and colouring pencil, 9 3/4 x 13 3/4 ins / 25 x 35 cm) DEM 2,185. VIENNA, 19 May 1999, *Ravens* (biro, 8 x 11 ins / 21 x 28 cm) ATS 25,000. VIENNA, 19 May 1999, *Cat* (1953, pen and ink, 14 x 14 ins / 35 x 36 cm) ATS 28,000. VIENNA, 25 May 2000, *Disabled General Pushed by Governess* (pen and ink, 14 x 19 ins / 35 x 47 cm) ATS 30,000. VIENNA, 25 May 2000, *Heros from Tyrol* (pen, ink and watercolour, 19 x 26 ins / 47 x 67 cm) ATS 40,000. VIENNA, 27 Nov 2001, *Firmly Rooted, Decaying Old Tyroler* (1980, pen and ink, 11 x 14 ins / 27 x 35 cm) ATS 28,000. VIENNA, 27 Nov 2001, *Priests* (1979, pencil, pen and ink, 11 x 15 ins / 27 x 37 cm) ATS 38,000. VIENNA, 23 April 2002, *Fat Harlequin and Thin Cat* (2001, colour pen, 9 x 11 ins / 24 x 29 cm) EUR 3,000. VIENNA, 23 April 2002, *In the Rain II* (2001, colour pen, 9 x 13 ins / 24 x 33 cm) EUR 3,000. VIENNA, 24 April 2003, *Cat* (1945, Indian ink, 11 x 7 ins / 28 x 18 cm) EUR 2,600. SALZBURG, 16 Oct 2003, *Rifle Club Formation* (Indian ink and watercolour, 22 x 29 ins / 55 x 74 cm) EUR 2,400. LINZ, 13 May 2004, *Flight Pioneers over Icebergs* (1979, pen, 13 x 20 ins / 34 x 50 cm) EUR 1,800. LINZ, 13 May 2004, *Soldiers* (1964, Indian ink, 17 x 25 ins / 44 x 63 cm) EUR 1,900.

FLORA, Thalia, later Mme Caravias
Greek, 20th century.
Born 1875, in Siatista.
Painter, pastellist. Genre scenes.
A student of Georges Jacobidès, Thalia Flora worked in Munich. She exhibited in Paris and was awarded an honourable mention at the 1900 Exposition Universelle.

FLORAE. See **DELAFLEUR Nicolas Guillaume**

FLORANCE, Eustache Lee
American, 20th century.
Born in Philadelphia.
Painter.
Eustache Lee Florance exhibited in Paris at the Salon de la Société Nationale.

FLORAND, Denise (Mme)
French, 20th century.
Born in Maisons-Laffitte.
Painter.

Denise Florand exhibited still-lifes and flowers at the Salon des Indépendants in 1938, 1939 and 1940.

FLORAT, Anne Élisabeth
French, 18th century.
Active in Paris in 1764.
Painter.

FLOREANI, Antonio
Italian, 16th century.
Born to a family originally from Udine.
Painter, architect.
Antonio Floreani worked in Friuli as an architect at the court of Maximilian II. None of his paintings survive.

FLOREANI, Floriano delle Cantinelle
Italian, 15th - 16th century.
Died 1511.
Active in Udine.
Painter.
Floriano delle Cantinelle Floreani was the son of Alberto da Tolmezzo Floreani.

FLOREANI, Francesco
Italian, 16th century.
Born in Udine; died 1593.
Painter, sculptor, architect.
Francesco Floreani was the pupil of Pellegrino and gained a reputation as a portrait painter. The emperor Maximilian II employed him and collected a large number of his works, including a *Judith* of extremely high quality.
MUSEUMS AND GALLERIES:
VIENNA: *Mary and the Infant Jesus.*

FLOREANI, Giovanni I
Italian, 16th century.
Born 1486, to a family originally from Udine; died 21 March 1540.
Painter, sculptor (wood).
Giovanni Floreani I was the son of Floriano delle Cantinelle.

FLOREANI, Giovanni II
Italian, 16th century.
Born to a family originally from Udine.
Painter.
Giovanni Florani I was the son of Pietro Floriani I.

FLOREANI, Giuseppe
Italian, 16th century.
Born to a family originally from Udine.
Painter.
Giuseppe Floreani was the son of Pietro Floreani I.

FLOREANI, Pietro I
Italian, 16th century.
Born to a family originally from Udine.
Painter.
Pietro Floreani I was the son of Giovanni Floreani I.

FLOREANI, Pietro II
Italian, 16th century.
Born to a family originally from Udine.
Painter.
Pietro Floreani II was the son of Pietro Floreani I.

FLOREN, Alonso
Spanish, 16th century.
Probably active in Seville c. 1554.
Painter.

FLORENCE, Lucette
French, 20th century.
Painter.
Lucette Florence exhibited portraits at the Salon des Indépendants in 1942.

FLORENCE, Mary
Maiden name: Sargent
British, 19th - 20th century.
Born 21 July 1857, in London; died 14 December 1954, in Twickenham (Middlesex).
Painter, fresco artist, watercolourist.
Mary Florence was the sister of the sculptor F. W. Sargant and studied in Paris with Luc-Olivier Merson and then at the Slade School with Legros. In 1888, she married the American musician Henry Smith Florence. She became a member of the New English Art Club in 1911.
MUSEUMS AND GALLERIES:
LONDON (Tate Collection): *Children at Chess* (c. 1903, tempera/wood); two drawings (gouache and pencil/paper).

FLORENCE, Prosper Joseph
French, 19th century.
Born 19th century, in Paris.
Painter.
Trained under Cabanel and exhibited at the Salon from 1875 to 1880 (notably portrait work).

FLORENCIA, Tomas de
Spanish, 16th century.
Of Italian origin.
Active in Valladolid.
Painter.
Tomas de Florencia was summoned to Valladolid by Pompeyo. He worked for the duke of Alba at the castle of Alba de Tormes.

FLORENS, Simon
Flemish, 17th century.
Active in Antwerp.
Sculptor.
Flemish School.
In 1666 Simon Florens qualified as a master of the guild.

FLORENSA Y ARNUS, Salvador
Spanish, 20th century.
Born in Barcelona.
Painter.
Salvador Florensa y Arnus exhibited in Paris at the Salon of the Société Nationale des Beaux-Arts.

FLORENT
French, 19th century.
Miniaturist.
MUSEUMS AND GALLERIES:
LILLE (MBA, Wicar Collection): miniature.

FLORENT, Alfred
French, 19th century.
Born in Boulogne-sur-Mer.
Painter.
Made his Salon début in 1880.

FLORENT, Maurice
French, 20th century.
Painter. Landscapes, still-lifes.
Maurice Florent exhibited at the Salon des Indépendants in Paris in 1943.

FLORENTI, FLORENTIA, FLORENTIN.
See first name

FLORENTIA, Bernardus de.
See **BERNARDUS DE FLORENTIA** and **DADDI Bernardo**

FLORENTIN
French, 19th century.
Painter.
AUCTION RECORDS:
PARIS, 23 March 1945, *Still-life: Bowl and Fruit,* FRF 1,400.

FLORENTIN, Dominique. See **DOMINIQUE FLORENTIN**

FLORENTINO, Jacobo or Jacopo. See **DELL'INDACO Jacopo**

FLORER, Ignaz Franz Joseph. See **FLURER**

FLORES, Alonso de
Spanish, 15th century.
Active in Seville at the end of the 15th century.
Painter.
A document records that Alonso de Flores bought a slave on 19 October 1492.

FLORES, Alonso de
Spanish, 17th century.
Active in Seville in 1642.
Painter.

FLORES, Antoine, or Florez
Flemish School, 16th century.
Died 1550.
Painter. History painting.
Siret says of this artist that he travelled to Spain with another Flemish painter, Pedro Campana or Pierre van Campen.

FLORES, Antonio
Spanish, 16th century.
Active in Cuenca.
Sculptor.
Antonio Flores constructed two altars in the Albornoz chapel for the cathedral of Cuenca. He embellished the wrought iron grille of the chapel railings with richly carved decorations representing heads of angels, trophies of war, skeletons and other symbols of life, death and battle.

FLORES, Felipe
Spanish, 19th century.
Born 19th century, in Benaguacil.
Painter. Religious subjects.
Felipe Flores trained at the academy in Valencia.
MUSEUMS AND GALLERIES:
VALENCIA: *Birth of Christ*.

FLORES, Francisco. See **FLOREZ**

FLORES, Frutos
Spanish, 16th century.
Painter.
Frutos Flores worked on the cathedral in Toledo and is perhaps the artist known also as Frutet (Frans) or Floris (Frans I).

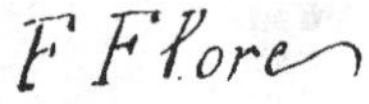

FLORES, Gonzalo de
Spanish, 16th century.
Active in Seville from 1518 to 1544.
Painter.

FLORES, José Joaquin
Spanish, 19th century.
Born in the 19th century, in Daimiel (Ciudad-Real).
Painter. Genre scenes.
José Joaquin Flores studied under Carlos Luis de Ribera and Carlos Mujica. He first exhibited at the national fine arts society in Madrid in 1866.

FLORES, Juan
Spanish, 16th century.
Active in Seville during the second half of the 16th century.
Engraver.
The name of Juan Flores appeared in connection with an inheritance in 1571.

FLORES, Juan de
Spanish, 16th century.
Active in Seville.
Painter.

FLORES, Lívia
Brazilian, 20th - 21st century.
Born 1959, in Rio de Janeiro.
Installation artist. Multimedia.
Flores studied at the Düsseldorf academy and lives and works in Rio de Janeiro. She uses a wide range of materials and objects and also creates multimedia installations. She works with signs, dream signs, signs of the passing of time and of experience. She began by working in carbon and plaster, making use of the effect of materials. In 1991 she attached a piece of yellow fabric with pockets containing coloured candles to a wall; with the effects of humidity and time the fabric turned orange. At the Capc (Museum of Contemporary Art) in Bordeaux she used mirrors and panes of glass to project infinitely repeating forms on to the walls, drawing the viewer into a virtual world. She studied at the Düsseldorf academy and lives and works in Rio de Janeiro.

She has taken part in group exhibitions, including: Salão Carioca de Arte Contemporânea in Rio de Janeiro (1983 and 1993); *Dialog/Experiências Alemãs* (*German Dialogue/Experiences*), Museu de Arte Moderna, Rio de Janeiro (1996); *Côte à Côte. Art Contemporain du Brésil* (*Coast to Coast. Contemporary Art of Brazil*), Capc-Musée d'Art Contemporain, Bordeaux (2001) She has also held solo exhibitions of her work: Kunsthaus, Mettmann (1989); Galerie im Kinderspielhaus, Düsseldorf (1991); Cultural Centre, São Paulo (1994); Marta Vidal gallery in Oporto (2001).

BIBLIOGRAPHY:
Cid Ferreira, Edemar/Fréchuret, Maurice/Aguilar, Nelson, *Côte à Côte. Art contemporain du Brésil*, exhibition catalogue, Capc musée d'Art contemporain, Bordeaux, 2001 (text in French, Portuguese and English).

FLORES, Luis Molinari
Ecuadorean, 20th century.
Born 1929.
Painter.
Luis Molinari Flores trained in Buenos Aires and Paris and also spent time in New York. He may have been influenced by Araceli Gilbert and adopted hard-line abstraction without concessions, following a course parallel to that of the Recherche d'Art Visuel group. His work takes a serial approach and is characterised by a violent use of colour.

FLORES, Pedro Victor
Spanish, 20th century.
Born 5 February 1897, in Murcia; died 1967, in Paris (?).
Also active in France.
Painter (including gouache), watercolourist, pastellist, engraver (etching), draughtsman, illustrator. Figure compositions, figures, bullfighting scenes, harbour views. Church decoration, stage sets, stage costumes.
Following the collapse of the family business, Pedro Flores was allowed to leave school and study drawing at the Friends of Murcia academy where he was awarded the Government of Murcia Prize for Painting at a very young age. He also appears to have studied at the Real Academia de Bellas Artes de San Fernando in Madrid. In 1924 he held his first exhibition and the following year he was well received by critics at an exhibition in Barcelona. In 1933 he took part in the exhibition of Spanish art in Paris and in the national Salon in Madrid. He cut short his time in Paris when he was appointed to teach drawing at the Balmes institute in Barcelona. Flores continued to play an active role in Spanish art though his permanent studio was in Paris and he was running two separate careers.

In 1937 he was awarded first national prize for engraving and second national prize for painting in 1938. In Paris he took part in various traditional Salons and also exhibited in Prague. In 1940 he settled permanently in Paris, holding solo exhibitions in Madrid, Barcelona, Santander and Murcia. Alongside his work as a painter, Flores also produced maquettes of sets and costumes for *La Zapatera Prodigiosa* (*The Shoemaker's Prodigious Wife*) by García Lorca (at the Théâtre Édouard VII), De Falla's *Three-Cornered Hat* (at the Opéra Comique) and Jacques Ibert's *Le Chevalier Errant* (*The Knight Errant*). He illustrated Jean Babelon's *Pieds Joints* (*Feet Together*) (a study on bullfighting), Molière's *Don Juan* (with coloured etchings) and J. Lancien's *Série Noire* (*Black Series*). He also produced mural paintings for the church of Nuestra Señora de la Fuensanta in Murcia.

Flores' painting displays a highly coloured Expressionism clearly influenced by his ethnicity; his depictions of Spain are in this vein. He often took on ambitious compositions requiring a large number of figures as in *Masters of Bullfighting*: in the foreground there are great figures from the history of bullfighting; in the middle ground a group of secondary figures such as picadors; and to the rear a vista showing a bullfight in progress, probably in the Madrid bullring, with buildings in the distance in a dusty haze of sunlight. He specialised mainly in familiar Spanish scenes such as Flamenco dancers and singers and women in traditional costume for which his Spanish companion provided the model.

Bibliography:

Campagne, Jean-Marc/Pantorba, B. de, *Pedro Florès*, Éd. Françaises, Paris, 1958. Arnáiz, José Manuel/López Jiménez, Javier/Merchán Díaz, Manuel (ed.), *Cien años de pintura en Espana y Portugal (1830-1930)*, Antiqvaria, Madrid, 1988 (One Hundred Years of Painting in Spain and Portugal (1830-1930)).

Museums and Galleries:

Paris (MAM).

Auction records:

Paris, 28 March 1955, *The Cottage*, FRF 37,000. Madrid, 27 June 1974, *Fishing Boat on the Beach*, ESP 250,000. Paris, 24 March 1976, *Lady with Fan* (oil on canvas, 22 x 15 ins / 55 x 38 cm) FRF 2,000. Madrid, 20 Dec 1976, *Don Quixote* (gouache, 12 1/4 x 9 1/2 ins / 31 x 24 cm) ESP 40,000. Madrid, 22 Nov 1977, *The Little Violin Player* (gouache, 25 1/4 x 19 3/4 ins / 64 x 50 cm) ESP 100,000. Madrid, 25 Nov 1980, *Armando a un Caballero* (*Arming a Gentleman*) (gouache, 19 3/4 x 35 1/2 ins / 50 x 90 cm) ESP 80,000. Madrid, 25 Jan 1983, *Dancer* (oil/hardboard, 29 1/4 x 23 1/2 ins / 74 x 60 cm) ESP 90,000. Paris, 6 May 1988, *Bullfighters* (oil on card, 14 3/4 x 23 3/4 ins / 37.5 x 60.5 cm) FRF 7,000. London, 22 Feb 1989, *The Cottage* (oil on canvas, 25 1/2 x 30 1/2 ins / 64.5 x 77.5 cm) GBP 3,080. Paris, 26 May 1989, *Portrait of a Woman* (oil on canvas, 22 x 18 ins / 56 x 46 cm) FRF 8,500; *Spanish Couple* (oil on canvas, 18 x 15 ins / 46 x 38 cm) FRF 18,000. Paris, 3 Dec 1992, *The Cockerel* (oil/hardboard, 9 1/2 x 7 1/2 ins / 24 x 19 cm) FRF 3,500. Paris, 15 Dec 1994, *The Lovers* (oil on canvas, 32 x 21 1/4 ins / 81 x 54 cm) FRF 15,000. Calais, 15 Dec 1996, *Harlequin with Guitar* (watercolour and pastel, 11 x 7 3/4 ins / 28 x 20 cm) FRF 3,200. Paris, 23 Feb 1997, *Harlequin with Guitar* (pastel and watercolour, 11 1/2 x 7 3/4 ins / 29 x 20 cm) FRF 7,000. Caen, 1 Jan 1999, *Circus Scene* (oil on canvas, 22 x 18 ins / 55 x 46 cm) FRF 23,500. Madrid, 27 April 1999, *Harlequin* (gouache, 24 x 19 ins / 62 x 49 cm) ESP 280,000. Calais, 7 May 2000, *Circus Folk* (oil on canvas, 18 x 22 ins / 46 x 55 cm) FRF 32,000. Madrid, 16 Jan 2001, *Carts in Village Square at Dawn* (oil on canvas, 15 x 18 ins / 38 x 46 cm) ESP 400,000. London, 20 Nov 2001, *Don Quixote and Sancho* (oil on canvas, 40 x 32 ins / 101 x 81 cm) GBP 1,600. Paris, 6 June 2002, *Homage to French Men of Letters* (oil on canvas, 46 x 32 ins / 116 x 81 cm) EUR 8,800. Houston, 16 Nov 2003, *Don Quixote and Sancho* (oil on canvas, 24 x 32 ins / 61 x 81 cm) USD 2,500. Madrid, 27 April 2004, *Calvary* (1962, gouache, 13 x 10 ins / 32 x 26 cm) EUR 2,750.

FLORES, Reinaldos de

Spanish, 16th century.
Active in Seville c. 1595.
Sculptor.

Reinaldos de Flores executed a sculpture representing the *Virgin* which was placed above one of the gates of the royal palace of Alcazar.

FLORÈS, Ricardo

French, 20th century.
Died 20 October 1918; on the battlefield.
Painter, watercolourist, newspaper cartoonist, humorist, illustrator. Figures, portraits, landscapes.

Ricardo Flores is best known for his contributions to the satirical papers *L'Assiette au Beurre* and *Le Rire*. He illustrated several books, including *The Beggars' Song*, and painted a few society portraits.

Auction records:

Paris, 26 Oct 1922, *Drawing* (pen) FRF 40; *Drawing* (pen) FRF 90. Paris, 29-30 May 1929, *Old Vagabond Sitting*; *Two Landscapes* (three sepias) FRF 270. Paris, 12 April 1943, *Tramp* (watercolour) FRF 110.

FLORES VALDEZ, Leopoldo

Mexican, 20th century.
Born 25 January 1935.
Painter. Murals.

Leopoldo Flores Valdes lives in Mexico City and studied at the city's school of fine arts. In 1965-1966 he went to France after being awarded a study bursary. When he returned to Mexico in 1967 he won a first prize in the national arts competition and has continued to exhibit since that date. His painting is abstract and brightly coloured. Flores Valdes has executed several mural and floor paintings.

FLORES-KNISTOFF, Freddy

Chilean, 20th - 21st century.
Born 1948, in Viña del Mar.
Active in the Netherlands since 1985.
Painter. Artists' books.
Visual Poetry.
Phases group.

Flores-Knistoff first studied science, philosophy and literature and then, from 1964 to 1968, studied at the Escuela de Artes y Oficios at Universidad Federico Santa Maria in Valparaíso. In his capacity as a painter he continues to experiment with automatism, of which he is one of the main proponents in Holland. His strongly coloured painting is as much of body movements as of people's faces, vibrantly brushed and with abstract tendencies. He produced artists' books such as *Die Wahre Geschichte, Warum Adolf Hitler Kein Künstler Wurde* (*The True Story of why Adolf Hitler did not become an Artist*), published by Hybriden Verlag in 1996. He is also a poet.

His work featured at group exhibitions on Surrealism, such as *Latin America and Surrealism* at Museum Bochum in 1993, and at several exhibitions on the Phases movement including *Le Mouvement Phases de 1952 à l'Horizon 2001* (*The Phases Movement from 1952 to the New Millennium*) at Kiosque Centre Culturel in Mayenne and at Centre Noroit in Arras, in 2000.

Museums and Galleries:

São Paulo (MAC, Universidade).

FLORET, Robert

French, 20th century.
Born 5 May 1931, in Lanobre.
Painter, engraver, illustrator.

Robert Floret studied in Clermont-Ferrand and Rabat, Morocco. He exhibits in provincial salons in Marseilles, Cannes and Vichy in particular.

FLOREZ, Antoine. See **FLORES**

FLOREZ, Francisco
Spanish, 15th - 16th century.
Painter.
Francisco Florez worked for Isabella of Spain and illuminated her prayer-book, now in the cathedral in Granada. He may also have been known as Fray Flores de Amberes, who worked for the cathedral in Toledo between 1500 and 1510, or alternatively as Frutos Flores.

FLOREZ-IBAÑEZ, Eduardo
Spanish, 19th - 20th century.
Born in Madrid.
Painter, watercolourist. Portraits, genre scenes, landscapes.
Eduardo Florez Ibáñez studied under Carlos de Haes at the Real Academia de Bellas Artes de San Fernando in Madrid. He began exhibiting in collective exhibitions in 1871. In 1873 he received a bronze medal at the national exhibition of the fine arts society of Madrid; in Paris he exhibited at the Salon of the Société Nationale des Beaux-Arts and received a commendation in 1889 at the Exposition Universelle. He was a member of the Madrid watercolourists' society and of the city's Círculo de Bellas Artes.

Eduardo Florez Ibáñez painted a wide range of subjects but he was primarily a painter of landscapes with figures. His effects of golden light seen through mist and blue-tinted fog over rivers clearly reveal Turner's influence.

FLORI. See **FIORI**

FLORIAN
Polish, 16th century.
Active in Cracow.
Sculptor, architect.
Florian was the son of Filippo da Fiesole.

FLORIAN
Austrian, 17th century.
Sculptor.
Florian may be the sculptor of the same name who produced the coats of arms for the abbot Johann in Admont. He also created the models for stucco decorations in the church of the Holy Trinity in Innsbruck.

FLORIAN, Antonio
Italian, 19th century.
Active in Venice.
Painter.
MUSEUMS AND GALLERIES:
VENICE (Church of S Maurizio) - VENICE (Church of S Pietro).

FLORIAN, Ernest
Swiss, 19th - 20th century.
Born 5 December 1863, in Chez-le-Bart; died 20 March 1914, in Paris.
Engraver (wood).
Ernest Florian was the pupil of his brother Frederic Florian. He was awarded an honourable mention in 1890 and a silver medal at the Exposition Universelle of 1900.

FLORIAN, Frédéric, pseudonym Rognon
Swiss, 19th century.
Born 20 February 1858, in Gorgier, near Neuchâtel.
Engraver (wood).
Florian created a very interesting niche for himself through the interpretation he gave to the works he reproduced. He did many illustrations for editions of works for book collectors. He was awarded a distinction in 1885 and a third-class medal in 1887.

FLORIAN, Georges
Romanian, 20th century.
Born in Jojib.
Also active in France.
Painter, draughtsman.
Georges Florian exhibited in Paris at the Salon des Artistes Français and at the Salon d'Automne (1926) as well as at the Salon des Artistes Indépendants (regularly from 1927).

FLORIAN, Walter
American, 20th century.
Born 1878, in New York; died 1 April 1909, in New York.
Painter, sculptor. Portraits, landscapes.
Walter Florian studied art at the Art Students League, New York, and at the Académie Julian in Paris. After spending two years in Spain, he visited the Netherlands, where he was advised by Joseph Israels, whose portrait he painted. He also painted many American personalities and was awarded a silver medal at the St Louis Exhibition of 1904.
MUSEUMS AND GALLERIES:
NEW YORK (Metropolitan Mus. of Art): *Portrait of Joseph Israels*.
AUCTION RECORDS:
NEW YORK, 7-8 Dec 1933, *Landscape at Twilight*, USD 50.
NEW YORK, 22 May 1980, *Portrait of a Young Woman* (1898, oil on canvas, 22 1/4 x 18 ins / 56.2 x 45.8 cm) USD 1,000.

FLORIAN-PARMENTIER, Ernest
French, 20th century.
Born in Valenciennes.
Painter. Landscapes, still-lifes.
Ernest Florian-Parmentier exhibited in Paris at the Salon des Artistes Indépendants between 1935 and 1943.

FLORIANE, pseudonym?
French, 20th century.
Born 26 October 1878, in Strasbourg.
Painter. Landscapes.
Floriane exhibited at the Salon des Artistes Français from 1921.

FLORIANI, Flaminio
Italian, 17th century.
Painter.
Venetian School.
Flaminio Floriani was a Venetian artist who is believed to have been a pupil of Tintoretto on the grounds that he copied and imitated the latter's work with considerable skill and success. Arguably his best work is a *St Lawrence* painted for the church of that name.

FLORIANI, Giuseppe, or Maffeotti
Italian, 17th century.
Born to a family originally from Rovereto, near Trento; died 1624.
Painter.

FLORIANO DELLE CANTINELLE.
See **FLOREANI**

FLORIAS, Tin
Greek, 20th century.
Born on Corfu.
Painter. Portraits, landscapes, still-lifes.
Tin Florias exhibited in Paris at the Salon des Artistes Indépendants (1935, 1937, 1938 and 1939).

FLORIDAN, Thomas
18th century.
Sculptor.

FLORIDI, Francesco
Italian, 19th century.
Active in Rome c. 1830.
Reproductions engraver.
Francesco Floridi worked for the Pitti Gallery, which was owned by L. Bardi, after Lorenzo Lotto and Andrea del Sar-

to; and for the *Calcografia Romana*, after Domenichino and Guido Reni.

FLORIGERIO, Sebastiano or Bastianello
Italian, 16th century.
Born 1500, in Udine; died c. 1545, in Udine.
Painter.

Sebastiano Florigerio was the pupil of Pelligrino and is believed to have married Pelligrino's daughter Aurelia. In 1525, he painted his first altarpiece for the church of Santa Maria di Villanuova, followed in 1529 by the altarpiece *St George and the Dragon* for the church of San Giorgio d'Udine. Shortly afterwards he went to Padua, where he painted the portal of the Palazzo del Capitaneo, and remained there until 1533. Having killed an adversary in a duel, he was obliged to flee and take refuge in Cividale until 1543. He is thought to have died in Udine soon afterwards.

Florigerio is noted for a *Descent from the Cross* in the church of S Bovo in Padua.

BIBLIOGRAPHY:
Marini, R., *Sebastiano Florigerio*, Udine, 1956.

MUSEUMS AND GALLERIES:
MUNICH: a painting - VENICE (Gal. dell'Accademia): *Madonna with Child, St Augustine and St Monica; St Francis, St Anthony and St Monica.*

FLORIMI, Giovanni, or Florini
Italian, 17th century.
Active in Siena in 1630.
Engraver.

Giovanni Florimi was a pupil of Cornelius Galle. He principally engraved portraits, including one by F. Vanni of Francesco Piccolomini.

FLORIMONT, C. T. B. de
Dutch, 19th century.
Born 29 August 1802, in Demerara (West Indies); died 1846, in Amsterdam.
Painter. Seascapes.

C. T. B. de Florimont was a pupil of Schotel in Dordrecht.

FLORIN, Jan
Belgian, 20th - 21st century.
Born 1955, in Zottegem.
Painter, graphic designer, poster artist.

Florin attended the St-Lucas Academie in Ghent and in Zottegem.

FLORINI, Matteo, or Florimi
Italian, 17th century.
Active in Siena.
Engraver (burin/wood), print publisher.

FLORIO, Christian
French, 20th - 21st century.
Born 1951.
Painter.

Christian Florio studied at the École des Beaux-Arts in Lyons, where he lives and works.

Though he was initially an abstract expressionist, Florio's exuberant compositions include figurative elements within an abstract framework, giving the impression of an old-fashioned mind expressing itself in a postmodern style. In contrast to these, he also creates works in a hyperrealist style, reproducing the folds in a piece of paper, or the metal blades of an awning. Reality, however, is always suggested rather than explicit; and serves as a point of departure for a simple architecture consisting of flat planes, occasionally broken by elusive markings.

He has taken part in a number of group exhibitions, including Octobre des Arts, in Lyons in 1984. He has also displayed his work in a number of solo exhibitions: in Lyons in 1978; in Avignon in 1980; in Nice in 1982; in Grenoble in 1985; and in Paris in 1987.

FLORIO, Giovanni Battista di Bernardo
Italian, 17th century.
Active in Treviso.
Sculptor (wood).

The Treviso church of S Margherita degli Eremitani houses wooden carvings by Giovanni Battista di Bernardo Florio, including statues of a *Misericordia* (*Compassionate Mother*), a *St Augustine* and a *St Monica*, together with a statue of the *Holy Virgin* under a *baldacchino* (canopy) supported by four angels. Florio also carved six statues for the S Stefano and S Benedetto altars in the Venice church of S Giorgio Maggiore in 1641 and, in 1644, *Four Fathers of the Church* which were placed above the principal entrance.

FLORION
French, 18th century.
Active in Paris.
Sculptor.

Florion was a student at the Académie Royale and in 1793 exhibited a bust of *Lepeletier de St-Fargeau* and some wax portraits.

FLORIS, Baptist, real name: Baptist de Vriendt
Flemish School, 16th century.
Born after 1547, in Antwerp.
Painter.

Baptist Floris was the son of Frans I Floris de Vriendt. He painted a portrait of the painter Frans Francken the Elder.

FLORIS, Claudius, real name: Claudius de Vriendt
Flemish School, 16th century.
Active in Antwerp in 1533.
Sculptor.

Claudius Floris was the son of Jan de Vriendt, known as Floris, and brother of Cornelis Floris the Elder.

FLORIS, Conrad
Dutch, 16th century.
Born to a family originally from Utrecht.
Sculptor. Bas-reliefs.

From 1563 to 1567, Conrad Floris worked in Schwerin (Mecklenburg-Vorpommern) on the castle chapel. The low reliefs on the throne at Güstrow have been attributed to him.

MUSEUMS AND GALLERIES:
SCHWERIN: *Story of Lot* (alabaster low relief).

FLORIS, Cornelis I, real name: Cornelis de Vriendt
Flemish School, 16th century.
Died 17 September 1538, in Antwerp.
Sculptor.

Cornelis Floris I was the son of Jan de Vriendt, known as Floris, and the father of Frans I Floris.

FLORIS, Cornelis II, real name: Cornelis de Vriendt
Flemish School, 16th century.
Born 1514, in Antwerp; died 20 February 1572; in 1575 according to some sources.
Sculptor, draughtsman, engraver, architect.

After a period working in Italy, Cornelis Floris II returned to Antwerp, where he married the sister of the painter Frans Pourbus. He is chiefly known as an architect, although he also painted decorative grotesques. He made the mausoleum of Jean de Mérode in Geel, the rood screen of Tournai Cathedral and the great tabernacle at the church of St Leonard in Léau that stands 59 feet (18 metres) high and has ten storeys.

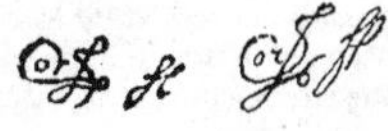

FLORIS, Cornelis III, real name: Cornelis de Vriendt
Flemish School, 16th - 17th century.
Born 1551, in Antwerp; died 12 May 1615, in Antwerp.
Painter, sculptor. Religious subjects, allegorical subjects.
Antwerp School.

Cornelis III was the son of Cornelis II and pupil of Hieronymus Francken in Paris. He became a master in Antwerp in 1577 and remained there for the rest of his life. In 1594 Hieronymus van Kessel was his pupil.

AUCTION RECORDS:

VIENNA, 30 Nov 1976, *Lot and his Daughters* (oil on panel, 30 x 42 ins / 76 x 106.5 cm) ATS 300,000. MONACO, 17 June 1988, *Man in a Straw Hat* (oil on panel, 9¾ x 7¼ ins / 25 x 18.3 cm) FRF 31,080. ROME, 13 April 1989, *Head of a Richly-Dressed Young Woman* (oil on panel, 19 x 13½ ins / 48 x 34 cm) ITL 6,500,000. NEW YORK, 31 May 1989, *Moses Suckled by his Mother* (oil on panel, 38¼ x 35½ ins / 97 x 90 cm) USD 33,000. NEW YORK, 31 May 1990, *Head of St John the Baptist* (oil on panel, 18¼ x 13½ ins / 46.6 x 34 cm) USD 71,500. AMSTERDAM, 25 Nov 1991, *Justice* (ink and wash heightened with white/paper, 11 x 6¼ ins / 28.2 x 15.6 cm) NLG 12,075. LONDON, 1 April 1992, *Virgin and Child with Angel* (oil on panel, 46½ x 38½ ins / 118 x 97.5 cm) GBP 6,600. PARIS, 8 April 1992, *Allegory of Profane Love with Ruins of the Colosseum in the Background* (oil on panel, 33¾ x 47¾ ins / 86 x 121.5 cm) FRF 280,000. NEW YORK, 22 May 1992, *Adam and Eve* (oil on panel, 69½ x 57 ins / 176.5 x 144.8 cm) USD 49,500. LONDON, 28 Oct 1992, *Holy Family* (oil on canvas, 44 x 52¾ ins / 111.5 x 134.2 cm) GBP 10,450. NEW YORK, 11 Jan 1995, *Arithmetica* (oil on canvas, 60 x 88¼ ins / 151.5 x 224.2 cm) USD 195,000.

FLORIS, Frans I, real name: Frans de Vriendt
Flemish School, 16th century.
Born 1516, in Antwerp; died 1570, in Antwerp.
Active also in Italy.
Painter, engraver (etching). History painting, portraits.
Antwerp School.

Like his father and grandfather, who were both sculptors - or stonecutters, as they were described at that time - Frans de Vriendt adopted the name Floris, a name already associated in the minds of art lovers with the fame of this family of artists and the esteem in which they were held. Frans Floris I studied sculpture in the studio of his uncle Claudius de Vriendt until he was about 20 years old. He had three brothers, who excelled respectively in the fields of architecture, painting on glass, and ceramics. The young Frans Floris, instinctively drawn towards painting, abandoned his work as a sculptor of statues and tombs and left Antwerp for Liège in order to study under Lambert Lombard, whose innovative teaching was fast becoming renowned. During a trip to Rome in 1538, Lombard had been greatly affected by the new discoveries of the great artists of the Renaissance, and was especially impressed by the works of Andrea del Sarto. Back in Liège he opened a school that quickly became famous. Floris, inspired by his master's enthusiasm, was soon able to imitate his work with great skill. However, he did not stop there. Returning home, he was first received as a master in the Guild of St Luke in 1540 and then immediately set out for Italy, the lure of which he could not longer resist. He stayed there for several years, although the exact dates of his time there are unknown. It seems that he was in Rome on Christmas Day 1541, when Michelangelo unveiled his great fresco of the *Last Judgement* after eight years of work. Whether or not he was there on that particular day, Frans must have been greatly impressed by Michelangelo's masterpiece, predisposed as he was to appreciate the power of the work both by the circumstances of his studies and his apprenticeship as a sculptor. From this time onwards, Michelangelo became almost his only model and inspiration, apart from Andrea del Sarto, whom Lombard's teaching had introduced to him. Consequently, the nickname 'the Flemish Raphael' that was given to him is in fact wholly inappropriate. Nevertheless, the name does testify to the enthusiasm that greeted Floris on his return to Flanders. He may be said to have been one of the first to introduce the Italian style into his country and his School. It is likely that the free and restless style and the powerful and violent nature of his first compositions must have initially caused some surprise, but it was not long before his fame spread throughout the Netherlands and into Spain. He soon acquired the admiration and patronage of the prince of Orange, and established even closer relations with the counts of Hoorn and Egmont. The town of Delft entrusted Floris with the commission for a *Crucifix* for one of principal churches. When Charles V entered Antwerp in 1549, Floris and Jean de Vries were commissioned to paint the triumphal arches erected in several parts of the town. Tradition has it that, in the course of a single day, he painted seven life-size figures. Again, a few years later, the decorations for the visit of Philip II were entrusted to Floris. In 1552, he engraved the composition, showing *Victory*, that he had produced for that occasion. In 1554, he painted the *Fall of the Rebel Angels* for the altar of St Michael, patron saint of swordsmen and fencers, a work considered by some to be his masterpiece. In this work, the painter presents a highly dramatic contrast between the celestial beings, depicted with a graceful and Italianate beauty and purity of line that does nothing, however, to diminish the force they have at their disposal in the terrible battle, and the rebel angels. The latter, portrayed with the heads of goats or boars, and with talons, claws and serpents' tails, present us with a fantastic vision worthy of the legends of the Middle Ages. In around 1559, Floris worked for the church of Our Lady in Antwerp, painting an *Assumption*, now lost, and a *Nativity* which is probably the same work as the *Adoration of the Shepherds* in the museum in Antwerp. This important work is remarkable particularly for its depth of expression. The artist seems here to be closer to the tenderness of an Andrea del Sarto, although he lacks the grace of the Italian master. On the other hand, from the point of view of the palette - which makes much use of greyish-reds and neutral tones, also seen in the *Last Judgement*, in Brussels - the painting shows far more the influence of Michelangelo's famous fresco. Having by now achieved great renown and admiration, Floris found it hard to keep working constantly at his demanding craft. An eccentric and a bon viveur, he spent all his wealth on his splendidly decorated house. He was extremely fond of drinking and entertained the most notorious drinkers of his day, competing with them in a manner worthy of Rabelais (and generally emerging the victor). Floris was highly literate and knowledgeable about mythology, and produced some very successful decorative works depicting various myths, particularly those for a wealthy citizen of Antwerp, Nicolas Jonghelingh, of *The Labours of Hercules* in ten large compositions. However, the execution of his protectors, the counts of Hoorn and Egmont, which he portrayed in *Beheading of the Counts of Hoorn and Egmont*, in 1568, marked the end of these happy times and this choice of subject. Returning to more sober themes, Floris was unable to complete the two works he had begun for the Grand Prior of Spain, *Christ on the Cross* and *The Resurrection*. He died in 1570, aged only around 50. His influence had been considerable and the importance of his school lasted into the early 17th century, until the time of Rubens, who arrived on the scene with all his genius to restore to the Flemish school its own original voice and its full autonomy of inspiration. Floris' pupils and followers included François Pourbus, Crispian van den Broecke, Martin de Vos, Lucas de Heere and Martin van Cleef. Floris left two sons, one of whom, Frans, worked for many years in Italy, where he was known particularly for his small paintings. Unfortunately, Floris' work fell victim of the religious upheaval of the 16th century and several important works were destroyed or lost. The engravings copied from these works often exaggerated the character and violence in his pictures, giving a false impression of his style, which could sometimes be passionate yet at other times very delicate.

HF. F. FLORIS;

BIBLIOGRAPHY:

Cuttler, Charles D., *Northern Painting: From Pucelle to Bruegel*, Holt, Rinehart and Winston, New York, 1968.

MUSEUMS AND GALLERIES:

ANTWERP: *The Fall of the Rebel Angels; St Luke; Adoration of the Shepherds* - AVIGNON: *Croesus Showing his Wealth to Solon* - BAMBERG: *Holy Family and St John as a Child* - BERLIN (Bodemus.): *Venus and Mars in Vulcan's Net* - BRUNSWICK: *Falconer* - BRUSSELS: *Last Judgement; Adoration of the Magi* - CAEN: *Portrait of an Old Woman* - COLOGNE: *Portrait of a Man* - COPENHAGEN (Statens Mus. for Kunst): *Cain and Abel* - DRESDEN: *Adoration of the Shepherds; Laughing Girl; Emperor Vitellius* - FLORENCE (Uffizi): *Adam and Eve* - GLASGOW: *Sts Catherine and Margaret* - GRAZ: *Allegory: Bent Old Age Raised up by Love and Hope* - HAMBURG: *Diana* - LANGRES: *Adoration of the Magi* - LIÈGE: *The Three Ages of Man* - LIERRE: *The Van Berchem Family* - LIVERPOOL: *Judgement of Paris* - MADRID (Prado): *Portrait of a Man; Portrait of a Woman; The Flood* - MOREZ: *A Tournament* - MUNICH (Alte Pinakothek): *Portrait of a Man; Judith* - MÜNSTER: *Vulcan's Forge* - PRAGUE (Nostitz Gal.): *The Wise Virgins and the Foolish Virgins; Woman's Head; Adoration of the Shepherds* - SCHWERIN: *Head of Christ; Adoration of the Shepherds* - ST PETERSBURG (Hermitage): *Allegory; Holy Family* - STOCKHOLM: *Banquet of the Sea Gods* - THE HAGUE (Mauritshuis): *Venus and Adonis* - TIRLEMONT: *St Francis* - TURIN: *Allegory: The Nine Muses Asleep in time of War* - VALENCIENNES: *Portrait of a Woman* - VIENNA: *Last Judgement* - VIENNA (Liechtenstein Mus.): *Adoration of the Shepherds* - WROCLAW (Muz. Narodowe): *Venus and Adonis.*

AUCTION RECORDS:

PARIS, 18 Dec 1893, *Bacchantes and Women*, FRF 335. PARIS, 10 and 11 May 1897, *Virgin and Child*, FRF 990. NEW YORK, 24 March 1905, *Virgin and Child*, USD 200. LONDON, 20 Dec 1922, *Deposition*, GBP 5. LONDON, 23 March 1923, *Holy Family*, GBP 12. LONDON, 27 July 1923, *Death of St Mary Magdalene; Jacob's Ladder* (group) GBP 5. LONDON, 4 Feb 1924, *Noah and the Animals Entering the Ark*, GBP 44. LONDON, 28 July 1924, *The Flagellation*, GBP 3. PARIS, 6 Nov 1924, *The Man of Sorrow*, FRF 330. LONDON, 13 Feb 1925, *The Trinity*, GBP 9. PARIS, 25 April 1925, *St Mary Magdalene*, FRF 1,000. LONDON, 1 Dec 1926, *Holy Family*, GBP 13. PARIS, 18 May 1927, *Judgement of Paris*, FRF 5,600. LONDON, 20 June 1927, *Peasants Driving their Flocks*, GBP 10. LONDON, 28 and 29 July 1927, *Judgement of Midas*, GBP 60. LONDON, 2 March 1928, *Road to Calvary*, GBP 25. LONDON, 16 Nov 1928, *Christ Mocked*, GBP 9. LONDON, 19 Dec 1928, *Mythological Composition*, GBP 30. LONDON, 18 Feb 1929, *Banquet of the Gods*, GBP 6. LONDON, 12 Dec 1930, *Mount of Olives*, GBP 16. LONDON, 17 April 1935, *Noli Me Tangere*, GBP 11; *Noblemen and Women at an Entertainment*, GBP 16; *Portrait of a Senator*, GBP 39. LONDON, 5 July 1935, *Noli Me Tangere*, GBP 5. LONDON, 13 March 1936, *Old Woman*, GBP 69. LONDON, 6 May 1938, *Charity*, GBP 8. LONDON, 8 July 1938, *Diana and Actaeon*, GBP 283. LONDON, 22 July 1938, *Harrowing of Hell; Ascension* (group) GBP 19. LONDON, 13 March 1939, *Paul Before Felix*, GBP 7. PARIS, 29 May 1941, *Family of the Virgin*, FRF 20,000. PARIS, 28 Nov 1941, *St Anne, Virgin and Child* (pen and wash) FRF 2,000. LONDON, 17 Dec 1941, *Mythological Subject*, GBP 7. LONDON, 19 June 1942, *Holy Family*, GBP 10. LONDON, 7 Aug 1942, *Last Judgement*, GBP 11. LONDON, 22 March 1944, *Mythological Scene*, GBP 62. LONDON, 1 Dec 1944, *Martyrdom of St Sebastian*, GBP 42. NEW YORK, 21 Feb 1945, *Charity*, USD 600. NEW YORK, 28 Feb and 1 March 1945, *River Nymphs*, USD 900. LONDON, 18 Jan 1946, *SS Peter and Mark*, GBP 89. LONDON, 1 Feb 1946, *Men and Woman*, GBP 57. VIENNA, 14 March 1967, *Head of a Bearded Man in a Red Cap*, ATS 40,000. VERSAILLES, 1 June 1969, *Mythological Scene*, FRF 12,500. VIENNA, 30 Nov 1971, *Venus, Satyr and Terpsichore*, ATS 70,000. PARIS, 23 Nov 1972, *Portrait of a Man*, FRF 14,000. LONDON, 20 Nov 1980, *David Playing the Harp Before Saul* (engraving on wood, 13 1/4 x 19 1/4 ins / 33.4 x 48.7 cm) GBP 300. LONDON, 19 Dec 1980, *Adam and Eve* (oil on panel, 69 1/2 x 57 ins / 176.5 x 145 cm) GBP 15,000. LONDON, 16 Feb 1983, *Jupiter's Command* (oil on panel, 48 x 66 1/2 ins / 121 x 169 cm) GBP 3,000. AMSTERDAM, 26 Nov 1984, *Woman Sitting at a Mirror* (red chalk, 6 3/4 x 9 ins / 17.3 x 23.1 cm) NLG 6,600. PARIS, 16 April 1986, *St Peter and Paul* (oil on panel, oval, 20 3/4 x 25 3/4 ins / 53 x 65.5 cm) FRF 68,000. PARIS, 11 Dec 1991, *Portrait of the Philosopher Diogenes* (oil on panel, 16 1/4 x 13 ins / 41 x 33 cm) FRF 49,000. MILAN, 18 Oct 1995, *The Family of Adam and Eve* (oil on canvas, 64 1/4 x 82 3/4 ins / 163 x 210 cm) ITL 69,000,000. NEW YORK, Jan 1998, *Head of a Bearded Man* (oil on panel, 18 1/4 x 13 1/2 ins / 46.4 x 34 cm) USD 12,650. LONDON, 9 July 1999, *'Suffer the little children to come unto me'* (oil on panel, 38 x 42 ins / 96 x 107 cm) GBP 35,000. AMSTERDAM, 8 Nov 1999, *The Continence of Scipio* (oil on panel, 30 x 74 ins / 75 x 188 cm) NLG 60,000. LONDON, 9 July 2002, *Head Study of a Woman* (oil on panel, 19 x 13 ins / 47 x 34 cm) GBP 5,000. BERLIN, 29 Nov 2002, *Victory Surrounded by Prisoners and Trophies* (etching, 12 x 17 ins / 31 x 43 cm) EUR 6,000. NEW YORK, 23 Jan 2004, *Christ Blessing the Children* (oil on canvas, 56 x 89 ins / 141 x 226 cm) USD 40,000.

FLORIS, Frans II, real name: Frans de Vriendt
Flemish School, 16th century.
Born 1545.
Painter.
Antwerp School.

The son of Frans Floris I, he was probably active in Antwerp. In 1604, he was working in Rome.

FLORIS, H. E.
Dutch, 16th century.
Active in Utrecht.
Painter (glass).

This artist is mentioned by Siret.

FLORIS, Jacob, the Elder,
real name: Jacob de Vriendt
Flemish School, 16th century.
Born 1524; died 8 June 1581.
Glass painter.
Antwerp School.

Brother of Frans Floris I, Jacob Floris was a master in Antwerp in 1551. For many years the stained glass windows in Tournai Cathedral were attributed to him. These are now attributed to Lucasi Adriaensz., but a number of the windows in the church of Ste-Gudule in Brussels and that of the Virgin in Antwerp are very likely to be the work of Floris.

FLORIS, Jacob, the Younger,
real name: Jacob de Vriendt
Flemish School, 15th - 16th century.
Glass painter.

Jacob Floris was probably the son of Jacob de Vriendt known as Floris the Elder. He decorated the windows of the church of the Great Carmelites in Antwerp with scenes from the story of *St Elias*. The church no longer exists.

FLORIS, Jan Baptista, real name: Jan Baptista de Vriendt
Flemish, 17th century.
Born c. 1617; died 10 January 1655, in Antwerp.
Painter.
Flemish School.
Jan Baptista Floris was the son of Frans Floris the Elder.

FLORIS, Jan I, real name: Jan de Vriendt
Flemish School, 16th century.
Born sometime before 1524.
Also active in Spain.
Potter.
Antwerp School.
Jan Floris I was the son of Cornelis Floris I. He was the first representative of his trade to be admitted to the Guild of St Luke, in 1550. He was later summoned to Spain by Philip II, where he worked at the royal palaces in Madrid, El Pardo and Segovia.

FLORIS, Jan II, real name: Jan de Vriendt
Flemish, 17th century.
Died 2 March 1650.
Active in Antwerp.
Painter.
Flemish School.
Jan Floris II received his artistic instruction from his father Cornelis Floris III and became a member of the guild in 1615.

FLORIS, Jan or Giovanni, real name: Jan de Vriendt
Flemish School, 16th century.
Also active in Italy.
Painter.
This artist is mentioned in Perugia (Umbria) in 1570 in connection with paintings for a triumphal arch based on designs by Galeazzo Alessi. He may be the same person as Jan Floris, the son of Claudius Floris.

FLORIS, Marcel
French, 20th century.
Born 11 September 1914, in France.
Active in Venezuela from c. 1950.
Sculptor.
Marcel Floris showed work at group exhibitions in South America from 1956: 1956, Caracas; 1958, 1970, Medellín Biennale; 1969 and 1971 (gold medal), São Paulo Biennale; 1972, Caracas (*Plastic Art in Venzuela*); 1979, Caracas (*Constructivism in Venezuela*). He also exhibited in Osaka, at the 1970 International Fair; in Paris, notably in 1989 at *In 3D*; 1991, Auxerre, 4th Sculpture Biennale.

He showed his work in numerous solo exhibitions in Paris, Venezuela, New York and many European cities.

He used card, wire mesh and metal tubing. These materials were folded and gathered in strictly geometric constructions in line with the platonic understanding of ideal beauty. Floris spices this up with anamorphosis, warning the public against 'spatial conjuring tricks'.

BIBLIOGRAPHY:
Diehl, Gaston (preface), *Floris*, exhibition catalogue, Gal. Franka Berndt, Paris, 1987. Diehl, Gaston (preface), *Floris*, exhibition catalogue, Gal. Lahumière, Paris, 1990.

MUSEUMS AND GALLERIES:
BOGOTÁ (MAC) - BOLIVAR (MAM Jesús Soto) - CARACAS (MAC Sofía Imber) - CARACAS (MBA) - IBIZA (MAC) - MARACAIBO (Casa de Cultura) - MEXICO CITY (Instituto Nacional de Bellas Artes) - MONTREAL (MAC) - NEW YORK (MoMA) - PARIS (BNF) - WASHINGTON DC (Smithsonian American AM).

FLORISELLO. See **FIORISELLO** and **FLORIGERIO**

FLORISZ. See also **BERCKENRODE**

FLORISZ., Jacob
Dutch, 17th century.
Active in Amsterdam in 1644.
Painter.
Jacob Florisz., cited by Obreen with no details, may be the same artist as the Flemish stained glass painter Jacob Floris.

FLORISZ., Willem
Dutch, 15th - 16th century.
Painter. Historical subjects. Ornaments.
Siret says that this artist established himself in Utrecht and was working there in 1479. He was still alive in 1502.

FLORIT, José Luis
Spanish, 20th century.
Born 25 April 1909, in Madrid.
Painter. Scenes with figures, local scenes.
José Luis Florit studied at the Real Academia de Bellas Artes de San Fernando in Madrid. In 1933 he began exhibiting at collective exhibitions in Madrid and Barcelona but was interrupted by the Spanish Civil War. He exhibited again in Barcelona in 1940, in Valencia in 1949 and in Barcelona in 1950. During this period he spent five years producing mural decorations. From 1956 onwards he exhibited in Spain, France and Italy.

Florit's work shows the carefree life of popular celebrations, the people behind the scenes in cabaret clubs and everyday street scenes, often with comical characters.

AUCTION RECORDS:
BARCELONA, 29 Oct 1986, *Mountain Village* (mixed media/canvas, 23 1/2 x 28 1/4 ins / 60 x 72 cm) ESP 95,000. MADRID, 15 Nov 1999, *View of Venice* (oil on canvas, 15 x 18 ins / 38 x 46 cm) ESP 270,000. MADRID, 19 June 2001, *Circus Scene* (1990, oil on canvas, 24 x 20 ins / 61 x 50 cm) ESP 675,000.

FLORIZOONE, Pieter
Belgian (?), 20th century.
Born 5 December 1937.
Sculptor.

FLORKIEWICZ, Witold
Polish, 19th - 20th century.
Born 1874, in Cracow.
Painter. Landscapes.
Witold Florkiewicz was a student at art school in Cracow and then in Paris. He worked in Cracow as a landscape painter.

FLORNICZER
Polish, 14th century.
Active in Cracow.
Painter.
Florniczer produced an altarpiece for the church of Corpus Christi in Kazimierz, near Cracow.

FLORNOY, Olivier
French, 20th century.
Born 4 March 1894, in Nantes.
Painter.
Olivier Flornoy studied under Ernest Laurent, Jules Adler and Louis Biloul at the École des Beaux-Arts in Paris. From 1922 he exhibited at the Salon des Artistes Français, where he won numerous awards (a silver medal in 1925, gold in 1931, hors concours in 1932). He was made Chevalier de la Légion d'Honneur in 1933.

FLORO, Serge
French, 20th century.
Born 11 October 1911, in Vallorbe, Switzerland.
Painter. Scenes with figures, landscapes.

Serge Floro took an interest in painting from an early age and was self-taught. He worked as a labourer, a photographer and, from 1947, a farmer. Gino Severini encouraged him to paint. He exhibited from 1959 and featured at the Salon Comparaisons in Paris.

His work is reminiscent of the Quattrocento, whilst remaining attuned to contemporary life. His landscapes are primitive and static. Floro's harmonious imaginary world remains bound to modern life.

FLOROT, Gustave
French, 20th century.
Born 1885; died 1965.
Painter. Genre scenes, local scenes.

Gustave Florot exhibited every year at the Salon d'Automne in Paris from 1921 until his death, also featuring at the Salon des Artistes Indépendants in 1925 and 1927. He was invited to the Salon des Tuileries in 1930.

His painting often touches on jazz and modern dance.

AUCTION RECORDS:
PARIS, 19 Dec 1984, *Street Acrobats* (oil on canvas, 46 x 34 3/4 ins / 116 x 88.5 cm) FRF 17,500. PARIS, 9 March 1987, *The Player* (oil on canvas, 45 1/4 x 33 1/2 ins / 115 x 85 cm) FRF 4,200.

FLOROV. See also **FROLOV**

FLOROV, Lavrenti
Russian, 18th century.
Active in Moscow.
Engraver.

Florov was an engraver book illustrations, particularly portraits, among which can be cited those of *Tsar Alexander I* and *Tsarina Elisabeth Alekseievna*.

FLOROV, M.
Russian, 18th century.
Painter.

This artist painted, some time before 1750, the portrait of *The Russian General G.V. de Hennin*, which was reproduced as an engraving by G.J. Heitman.

FLOROV, Mikhail Aleksandrovich
Russian, 19th century.
Born 1785, in St Petersburg.
Sculptor.

A pupil of J.P. Martoss at the St Petersburg academy of fine arts, Florov received a prize for his work *Venus in Vulcan's Forge*.

FLORSCHUETZ, Thomas
German, 20th - 21st century.
Born 1957, in Zwickau.
Photographer.

Florschuetz studied architecture and became an assistant photographer. He lives and works in Berlin. He has participated in group exhibitions in Dresden, Berlin and Essen; he has held solo shows in Berlin, Essen and Paris (at the Galerie du Jour in 1988) and Amsterdam.

FLORSHEIM, Lillian
American, 20th century.
Born in New Orleans.
Sculptor.
Neo-Constructivism, Op Art.

Lillian Florsheim assembles transparent Plexiglas tubes and discs in a Constructivist style, building up long and tall rhythmic columns. She exhibits mainly in the United Sates, but also in Tel Aviv and Paris, and has held shows of kinetic art in Germany.

FLORTE, Pieter, or Floorten
Dutch, 17th century.
Died 1662; buried 8 October in Haarlem.
Painter.

Pieter Florte was a master in Haarlem in 1639. He is almost certainly the artist Siret means when referring to the name Jean Florten.

FLORTEN, Jan, or Floortee
Dutch, 17th century.
Died after 1677.
Active in Haarlem.
Painter. Landscapes.

Jan Florten was a 'franc-maître' in Haarlem in 1639 and is mentioned by Siret who confuses him with Pieter Florte. However, there is another painter by the name of Jean Florten or Flortin, cited by Kramm, who is perhaps identical with the painter Floortie who was active in the university town of Leiden between 1650 and 1673.

FLORUS. See **FIORI** and **FLORIS**

FLOS. See **DUFLOS**

FLÖSCHAUER. See **VLEESCHOUWERE**

FLOSCHE, Daniel. See **FRÖSCHL**

FLOSER, Jorg
German, 16th century.
Painter.

The Kunsthalle in Karlsruhe has a painting signed by this artist and dated 1510. Originally in the monastery of Zwiefalten (Baden-Württemberg), it represents *The Virgin and Child*.

FLOSI
19th century.
Sculptor. Figures. Statuettes.

MUSEUMS AND GALLERIES:
COMPIÈGNE: *Antoine Vivenel* (statuette).

FLOSI, Monique
French, 20th century.
Born 18 April 1943, in Oran, Algeria.
Painter, engraver, illustrator. Figures, nudes, portraits, animals.

Monique Flosi studied engraving at the École des Beaux-Arts de Marseilles, obtaining her diploma in 1970. In 1984, using computer technology, she learned new techniques of image representation and graphic design. She has taken part in various exhibitions, not least in Marseilles and Provence. She has been a teacher since 1975, and has illustrated texts by Rabindranath Tagore and Salah Stétié.

FLOSSMANN, Joseph
German, 19th - 20th century.
Born 19 March 1862, in Munich; died 20 November 1914, in Munich.
Sculptor.

Flossmann was awarded an honourable mention in 1900 at the Exposition Universelle.

MUSEUMS AND GALLERIES:
MUNICH (Glyptothek): *Barbarian Mother Holding her Children Tight against her.*

FLOT, Louis
French, 19th - 20th century.
Painter. Local scenes.
Orientalism.

Louis Flot lived and worked in North Africa at the beginning of the twentieth century.

AUCTION RECORDS:
PARIS, 4 March 1988, *Orange Sellers in Tunis* (1908, oil on canvas) FRF 21,000. PARIS, 17 March 1989, *Mosque Courtyard at Sunset* (oil on panel, 13 3/4 x 10 1/2 ins / 35 x 26.5 cm)

FRF 3,100. PARIS, 11 Dec 1995, *Street Scene in Tunis* (1909, oil on panel, 13 3/4 x 10 1/2 ins / 35 x 26.6 cm) FRF 19,000.

FLOTATS, Juan
Spanish, 19th century.
Born in the 19th century, in Manresa.
Sculptor.

Juan Flotats studied under Vallmitjana. He first exhibited in Madrid in 1878.

FLÖTNER, Peter, or Flattner or Flodner or Floetner
German, 16th century.
Born c. 1485; died 23 October 1546, in Nuremberg.
Sculptor, engraver (wood).

Flötner's woodcuts are of ornamental subjects and genre scenes. Some work attributed to him may be by the sculptor Hermann Fischer. He was also a goldsmith and architect. After a visit to Italy between 1505 and 1510, he eventually came to settle in Nuremberg in 1522. His decorative work includes a number of Italian motifs. He made models for the Vischner foundry. Flötner was also known for his decorative carvings featuring shells and coconuts, as well as large ceremonial goblets.

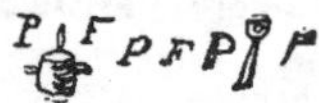

MUSEUMS AND GALLERIES:
BERLIN (Bodemus.): *Cupid Playing a Lute*; low relief - NUREMBERG (Germanisches Nationalmus.): *Dancing Cupids* (sculpted low relief) - VIENNA: *Adam* (sculpted wooden box, statuette).

FLOTOW, Mathilda von
Austrian, 19th century.
Born in Vienna.
Painter. Portraits.

Flotow was awarded a bronze medal in 1900 at the Exposition Universelle.

FLOTTE, de La (Miss). See **LA FLOTTE de**

FLOTTE DE SAINT JOSEPH
French, 18th century.
Born 1727.
Painter.

Flotte de Saint Joseph was an officer of the king's vessels and a member of the Académie de St-Luc. In 1753 he exhibited *Moonlight, Seascape, Sunrise in a Port in Italy* and *Sunset in a Roads in Africa*.

FLÖTTER, Hans Jorg
German, 17th century.
Active in Nuremberg (Bavaria).
Painter.

FLOTZ, Johannes, or Floz
Flemish, 17th century.
Born to a family originally from Antwerp.
Painter.
Flemish School.

Johannes Flotz worked in Klosterneuburg, where he executed two paintings of *St Francis*. He was also commissioned to execute a portrait of Ferdinand III at the court in Vienna.

FLOUEST
18th century.
Painter, draughtsman. History painting.

Nothing is known about this artist, except that he was at Versailles on 20 June 1789 and that he was present at the Tennis Court Oath, as he mentions on his drawing. He may be Marie Joseph Flouest (1747-1833).

AUCTION RECORDS:
NEW YORK, 15 Jan 1992, *Le Serment du Jeu de Paume à Versailles* (*The Tennis Court Oath at Versailles*) (black chalk, ink and wash, 14 x 5 1/4 ins / 35.6 x 13.1 cm) USD 35,200.

FLOUEST, Marie Joseph
French, 18th - 19th century.
Born 1747, in Dieppe; died 1833, in Dieppe.
Painter, sculptor. Portraits.

MUSEUMS AND GALLERIES:
DIEPPE: one portrait.

FLOUEST, S
German, 19th century.
Painter, miniaturist. Portraits.

A portrait of *Lola Montes* is known, signed by Flouest.

FLOUQUET, Pierre Louis
French, 20th century.
Born 1900, in Paris; died 1967, in Dilbeek (Brussels), Belgium.
From 1910 active in Belgium.
Painter, engraver, illustrator.
Assault Group.

From 1910, Pierre Flouquet lived in Brussels, where he studied under Montald at the Académie des Beaux-Arts. He worked with Magritte and exhibited with him at the Cercle d'Art in Brussels in 1919 and 1920 and in Berlin with the group Der Sturm in 1925, then in the USA. After 1930, he quit painting to write. He was in the thick of various avant-garde movements, organising exhibitions for the group Asaut (Attack) between 1925 and 1930. He contributed to the weekly *Sept Arts* (*Seven Arts*) from the outset; in Brussels he founded the *Journal des poètes* (*Poets' Journal*) and poetry biennials, and was the editor of the architecture review *La Maison* (*The House*), which also reviewed fine arts.

He tried his hand at many techniques such as etching on lino in stark blacks and whites, lithographs published by the Antwerp group *Ça ira* and stained glass for the ambitious urban project *Cité Moderne* at Berchem-Ste-Agathe in 1923. He illustrated poetry collections, continuing to draw after he stopped painting. His work bears the mark of Fernand Léger's Cubism, its planes invested by geometric objects, cylinders and angled tubing, sometimes inhabited by sketchy figures like distaff-shaped women. His colours are strong, modulating the pallor or darkness of volumes and underscoring the power of his constructions. He evolved toward pure abstraction after 1920, then, in 1928, converted to portraiture, fixing the faces of his artist and writer models in dramatic poses.

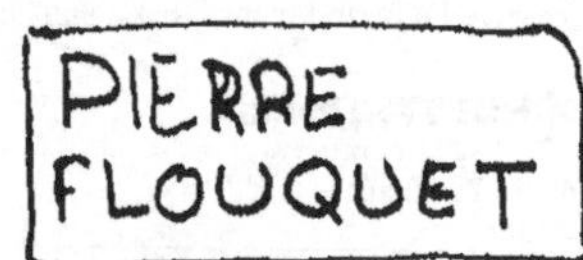

BIBLIOGRAPHY:
Eemans, Marc, *Moderne Kunst in België*, Heideland-Orbis, Deurne (BEL), 1975.

MUSEUMS AND GALLERIES:
BRUSSELS (Mus. royaux des Beaux-Arts de Belgique): *Composition* (1921); *Architecture-Forms* (1925, three drawings) - GRENOBLE (Mus. de Grenoble).

AUCTION RECORDS:
PARIS, 7 Nov 1982, *Meeting* (1919, Indian ink wash, 9 x 6 3/4 ins / 23 x 17 cm) FRF 5,000. PARIS, 8 Dec 1987, *For Icarus*

(1921, oil on canvas, 31 3/4 x 23 3/4 ins / 80.5 x 60.5 cm) FRF 39,000. LOKEREN, 8 Oct 1988, *Golgotha* (1931, oil on canvas, 31 1/2 x 39 1/2 ins / 80 x 100.5 cm) BEF 110,000. PARIS, 27 Oct 1988, *Madman* (gouache, 24 3/4 x 19 ins / 63 x 48 cm) FRF 16,500. PARIS, 16 Dec 1988, *Geometric Composition* (gouache, 10 x 14 ins / 25.5 x 35.5 cm) FRF 9,000. PARIS, 20 May 1992, *Eurika Shel Slange, Poet* (gouache, 24 3/4 x 19 ins / 63 x 48 cm) FRF 5,000. PARIS, 25 Nov 1993, *Motherhood* (1925, Indian ink, 14 1/4 x 10 1/2 ins / 36 x 26.5 cm) FRF 15,500. LOKEREN, 12 March 1994, *Portrait of Dichter a. Declercq* (1920, oil on canvas, 30 x 22 ins / 76 x 55 cm) BEF 750,000. PARIS, 4 Dec 1996, *Untitled* (1923, pencil, 9 x 13 1/2 ins / 22 x 34 cm) FRF 4,500.

FLOUR, François
French, 17th century.
Born to a family originally from Marseilles.
Painter.

François Flour is mentioned in Toulon from 1665 to 1694 as 'official painter' to the municipality.

FLOUR, Jules Adrien
French, 19th - 20th century.
Born 6 August 1864, in Avignon; died 10 February 1921, in Avignon.
Painter. Portraits, genre scenes, landscapes, landscapes with figures, still-lifes, flowers. Murals.
Groupe des Treize.

Jules Flour studied under Pierre Grivolas at the École des Beaux-Arts in Avignon from 1878, then went to Paris to study under Gérome. He settled first in Montparnasse, but after being appointed to teach at Avignon's École des Beaux-Arts in 1906, he worked with the Groupe des Treize (the Thirteen) to revive artistic activity in Avignon and Provence. He exhibited in Paris from 1887, at the Salon des Artistes Français.

In 1900 the city of Avignon commissioned him to undertake the decoration of two ceilings for the Town Hall's festival hall. His varied output showed special empathy with the Provençal landscape, of which he gave a realist account, using an understated palette deftly to capture its light.

MUSEUMS AND GALLERIES:
AVIGNON: *Spring of the River Vaucluse.*

AUCTION RECORDS:
PARIS, 20 Nov 1925, *Head of a Young Woman with a White Tie,* FRF 70. PARIS, 26 Feb 1926, *Autumn Landscape,* FRF 100. PARIS, 4 March 1926, *Grandfather's Lesson,* FRF 410; *After the Ball,* FRF 240. PARIS, 18 Dec 1981, *Japanese Cherry Tree* (oil on canvas, 36 1/2 x 28 3/4 ins / 93 x 73 cm) FRF 4,800.

FLOUR, Pierre
French, 17th - 18th century.
Active in Toulon.
Painter.

Pierre Flour was the son of François Flour. He worked for the French navy. In 1697 he executed a painting depicting *Angels Adoring the Host* for the cathedral in Toulon.

FLOURENS, Renée
French, 20th century.
Born in Paris.
Painter.

Renée Flourens exhibited from 1925 at the Salon des Indépendants.

FLOURET, Marthe
French, 20th century.
Born in Montivilliers.
Painter.

Marthe Flouret produced paintings for Parisian churches and showed at the Salon des Indépendants in 1931.

FLOURY, François Louis Lucien
French, 19th century.
Born 19th century, in Paris.
Painter.

Studied under Allongé and showed at the Salon from 1873 to 1882. Floury was first and foremost a watercolorist. Examples of his work include *Still-life with Ceramics and Sundry Objects, Clock Tower in Auxerre* and *Gorge-au-Loup in the Forest of Fontainebleau.*

FLOUTIER, Louis
French, 20th century.
Born in Toulouse.
Painter. Landscapes.

Louis Floutier studied under Fernand Cormon. He exhibited in the thirties at the Salon des Artistes Français.

AUCTION RECORDS:
PARIS, 23 April 1945, *Landscape,* FRF 920. PARIS, 9 Dec 1994, *Small Bridge over the River* (oil on canvas, 25 1/2 x 39 1/4 ins / 65 x 100 cm) FRF 22,000. PARIS, 29 Sept 2000, *Happy Family* (oil on canvas, oval, 24 x 28 ins / 62 x 70 cm) FRF 37,000. PARIS, 21 Dec 2000, *Pont de Socoa* (oil on canvas, 26 x 37 ins / 65 x 93 cm) FRF 30,500. PARIS, 1 July 2003, *Market Scene* (c. 1930, oil on panel, 17 x 21 ins / 44 x 54 cm) EUR 5,600. PARIS, 30 June 2004, *Basque Farm* (oil on panel, 16 x 13 ins / 40 x 32 cm) EUR 2,100. CALAIS, 4 July 2004, *Seascape with Setting Sun* (oil on canvas, 20 x 29 ins / 50 x 73 cm) EUR 4,500.

FLOWER, Bernard
British, 16th century.
Died c. 1513.
Glass painter.

Commissioned to provide painted windows for Henry VII's chapel at Westminster Abbey in London, Bernard Flower died before the work was finished. His designs were used by James Nicholson for the windows of King's College Chapel in Cambridge.

FLOWER, John
British, 19th century.
Born 1795, in Leicester; died 1861, in Leicester.
Painter. Architectural views.

John Flower received little formal artistic training, although he studied for a year in London under Peter de Wint.

MUSEUMS AND GALLERIES:
LEICESTER: *St Mary's Church; Leicester Castle.*

FLOWER, Marmaduke C. W.
Irish, 19th - 20th century.
Died 1 November 1910, in Ballycastle.
Painter. Genre scenes.

Marmaduke Flower worked in Leeds and, from 1878, frequently exhibited genre scenes at the Royal Academy.

FLOWER, Noël
British, 20th century.
Active in London.
Painter. History painting, genre scenes.

AUCTION RECORDS:
LONDON, 30 Jan 1909, *Between the Devil and the Deep Blue Sea,* GBP 5.

FLOWERS, J.
British, 18th - 19th century.
Painter. Portraits.

The British Museum holds an anonymous mezzotint after J. Flowers' portrait of the Baptist preacher *R. Hall,* and an engraving of *S. Freeman,* also after one of his works.

MUSEUMS AND GALLERIES:
LONDON (British Mus.).

FLOWERS, Peter
British, 20th century.
Born 2 January 1916; died 1950.
Painter, watercolourist. Landscapes.

Peter Flowers studied under Bertram Nicholls. He took part in various group exhibitions, notably at the Royal Academy in London. Flowers was a member of the Royal Society of British Artists.

FLOWYN, Herry. See **FLAVIGNY Henri**

FLOWYN, Marten
Flemish, 17th century.
Painter.
Flemish School.
Marten Flowyn qualified as a master in Antwerp in 1621.

FLOYD, Donald Harry
British, 19th - 20th century.
Born in London.
Also active in the USA.
Painter. Landscapes.
Donald Floyd studied in Paris with Bouguereau, Robert-Fleury and Humbert. He went to live and work in America.
AUCTION RECORDS:
AMSTERDAM, 8 Dec 1988, *View of Ash Grove Weir, Tintern* (1942, oil on canvas, 40¼ x 59¾ ins / 102 x 152 cm) NLG 6,900. AMSTERDAM, 18 Feb 1992, *Nedern Floods, Caldicot Castle* (1938, oil on canvas, 28¼ x 36¼ ins / 72 x 92 cm) NLG 1,265. NEWPORT, 11 Sept 2002, *Coastal Hamlet* (oil on canvas, 26 x 39 ins / 67 x 98 cm) GBP 1,250. NEWPORT, 11 Sept 2002, *Autumn Glitter, Tintern* (oil on canvas, 24 x 36 ins / 61 x 92 cm) GBP 1,550.

FLOYD, W.
British, 19th century.
Engraver.
W. Floyd was an engraver of views.

FLOYER, Ceal
British, 20th - 21st century.
Born 1948, in Karachi, Pakistan.
Active in England.
Installation artist, conceptual artist.
Ceal Floyer studied at Goldsmith's College (1991-1994). She is particularly known for her works using film and light projections that often play on meaning, function, inversion, dislocation and illusion. Her installation *Light Switch* (1992) projects the life-size image of a switch onto the wall by the door in trompe l'oeil fashion, while *Door* (1995) projects a band of light on the bottom of a closed door, thereby creating the illusion of light coming in from another room under the door. Floyer's installations play with the viewer's assumptions about the functions of everyday objects, and challenge and mislead despite their apparent simplicity.
BIBLIOGRAPHY:
Ceal Floyer, exhibition catalogue, Kunsthalle Bern, Bern, 1999 (essays by I. Blazwick and B. Fibicher). Torp, M./Rosenberg, A., *Ceal Floyer*, exhibition catalogue, X-Rummet Statens Museum for Kunst, Copenhagen, 2002.
MUSEUMS AND GALLERIES:
LONDON (Tate Collection): *Etching (at 45 rpm)* (2000, handmade etching); *Light Switch* (1992-1999, 35mm slide projection).

FLOZ, Johannes. See **FLOTZ**

FLU, Jilg von der, or Flue or Flueth
Austrian, 16th century.
Born to a family originally from Bern, Switzerland; died c. 26 January 1586, in Vienna.
Engraver, goldsmith.

FLÜCK, Johann
German, 19th century.
Born 1820, in Düsseldorf.
Painter. Genre scenes, portraits.

FLÜCK, Johann
Swiss, 19th century.
Born 13 November 1813, in Brienz; died 1 March 1897, in Brienz.
Sculptor (wood).
Johann Flück exhibited successfully from 1867. After working in Interlaken and Meiringen, he settled in his home town. He was also a statesman and was a member of the Great Council of Bern canton in Switzerland.

FLÜCK, Johann Peter, or Flueck
Swiss, 20th century.
Born 1902; died 1954.
Painter. Portraits, landscapes.
Flück specialised in painting mountains.
MUSEUMS AND GALLERIES:
BERN: *Mountainscape.*
AUCTION RECORDS:
BERN, 21 Oct 1976, *Livestock at Pasture* (1945, oil on canvas, 13 x 18 ins / 33 x 46 cm) CHF 1,100. BERN, 10 June 1978, *Portrait of Inge Rehberg* (1951, oil on canvas, 39¼ x 32 ins / 100 x 81 cm) CHF 4,200. BERN, 6 May 1983, *View of Lake Brienz near Interlaken* (1935, oil on canvas, 25¼ x 36¼ ins / 64 x 92 cm) CHF 3,200. BERN, 3 May 1985, *Harvest Scene, Brienz* (1934, oil on panel, 18 x 27½ ins / 46 x 70 cm) CHF 2,700. LUCERNE, 30 Sept 1988, *Bust Portrait of a Child* (oil on canvas, 19 x 15 ins / 48 x 38 cm) CHF 2,400. BERN, 12 May 2000, *Melting Snow in Mountain Landscape* (1947, oil on canvas, 39 x 29 ins / 100 x 73 cm) CHF 3,400. BERN, 9 Nov 2001, *Field Landscape with Farmer* (oil on panel, 20 x 24 ins / 50 x 60 cm) CHF 2,800.

FLUCK, Peter
British, 20th - 21st century.
Born 7 April 1941, in Cambridge.
Sculptor, multimedia artist. Puppets.
Peter Fluck is probably best known as the creator of the puppets for the satirical television series *Spitting Image* (1984-1996) co-founded with Roger Law. Fluck is, however, a man of many talents. He has produced a wide range of a work in a variety of media, including wind-driven sculptures for Milton Country Park in Cambridge (1993-1997), a sculpture design for the Landmark Piece at the Eden Project in Cornwall, and abstact digital transfer prints on canvas. He has worked as an artist-reporter and political cartoonist and taught at the Middlesex Polytechnic and Colchester Art School.

FLÜCK, Ulrich
Swiss, 19th century.
Born 1809, in Brienz; died 16 October 1881, in Interlaken.
Sculptor (wood).
Ulrich was the brother of Johann Flück. He opened a wood carving studio.

FLÜCK-SCHILD, Johann
Swiss, 19th - 20th century.
Sculptor (wood).
Flück-Schild directed the woodcarving studio at Fluhberg founded by his father Ulrich Flück.

FLÜCKIGER, Hans
Swiss, 17th century.
Baptised in August 1587 in Burgdorf; died 1629.
Glass painter.
Flückiger became a citizen of Burgdorf in 1611. According to Brun, he created the Aarberg coats of arms for the city of Bern in 1621.

FLUDER, Franz Jakob
Swiss, 18th century.
Sculptor.
Fluder was the grandson of the sculptor Urs Fluder. He became established in Lucerne in 1759.

FLUDER, Heinrich
Swiss, 17th century.
Born in the 17th century, in Lucerne.
Sculptor.
Heinrich Fluder was a member of the brotherhood of St Luke.

FLUDER, Urs Viktor
Swiss, 18th century.
Born in Lucerne.
Active c. the middle of the 18th century.
Sculptor.
Urs Fluder sculpted two altars in the church in the hospital in Lucerne.

FLUEHER
Austrian, 19th century.
Born to a family originally from Obermais, near Meran, South Tyrol (now Merano, Trentino-Alto Adige, Italy).
Painter.
Flueher painted landscapes and portraits. The altar painting of *St Sebastian* in the collegiate church in Stals (Upper Inn valley), Austria, is attributed to him.

FLÜGGE, B.
Danish, 18th century.
Active in Copenhagen.
Engraver.
B. Flügge engraved mostly landscapes and architectural views in small format. Nine plates of his are known.

FLÜGGE, Henny
German, 19th century.
Active in Munich.
Painter. Genre scenes, portraits.
Flügge exhibited in Berlin, Dresden and Munich from 1875 onwards.
AUCTION RECORDS:
LONDON, 29 Feb 1924, *Abandoned*, GBP 6.

FLÜGGEN, Gisbert
German, 19th century.
Born 9 February 1811, in Cologne; died 3 September 1859, in Munich.
Painter. Genre scenes.
Flüggen worked first in Düsseldorf and then in Munich, where he became a teacher at the academy in 1853. He first started to paint professionally in around 1840.
MUSEUMS AND GALLERIES:
MADRID: *Unlucky Gambler* - MAINZ: *Gambler* - MUNICH: *Anteroom of a Prince* - WROCLAW: *Gambler.*

FLÜGGEN, Joseph
German, 19th - 20th century.
Born 3 April 1842, in Munich; died 3 November 1906, in Bergen, near Traunstein.
Painter. Portraits, genre scenes, interiors.
Joseph Flüggen was the son and pupil of Gisbert Flüggen. He studied at the Akademie in Munich under the direction of Piloty, then travelled to France, England and Belgium. On returning to Munich he was appointed a lecturer at the Akademie. He made his debut exhibition in Munich in 1866 and took part in the Salons in Vienna, Berlin and Dresden.
MUSEUMS AND GALLERIES:
MUNICH: *Fugger's Fiancée Receiving her Wedding Presents.*
AUCTION RECORDS:
BERN, 2 May 1974, *Mother and Child*, CHF 2,400. BERN, 25 Nov 1982, *Mother and Child in an Interior* (1866, oil on canvas, 20 x 16 1/4 ins / 51 x 41.5 cm) DEM 2,400.

FLUHLER, Karl
German (?), 18th century.
Painter.
Fluhler is noted by Dr Brun as having been active in the Swiss canton of Nidwalden in 1708.

FLUMET, G. S. de
French, 18th century.
Active in Paris.
Engraver (burin).
G. S. de Flumet engraved subjects from everyday life.

FLUR, Johann Limpert, or Fluer or Flor
German, 18th century.
Born in Augsburg; died before 1755.
Painter.
Flur may be the artist Johann Flor, who entered the academy on 7 October 1730.

FLURER, Ignaz Franz Joseph, or Fluerer or Florer
Austrian, 18th century.
Died 25 June 1742, in Graz.
Painter.
In around 1730, Flurer painted a reredos and two pictures for the high altar in Graz cathedral, representing *Scenes from the Life of St Giles*. In 1732 he painted a ceiling fresco in the Kursaal in Tobelbad, near Graz. He is also known to have painted altar paintings in the churches in Semriach and Maletschnig, near Marburg (Hesse). The museum in Graz houses two of his landscapes.

FLURY, Paul
Swiss, 20th century.
Born 24 May 1878, in Santa Isabel (Brazil).
Also active in France.
Draughtsman, engraver.
Paul Flury lived at Conter (Grisons). He featured in some Swiss group exhibitions. From 1904 he travelled to Paris, where from 1907 he exhibited at the Salons of the Société Nationale des Beaux-Arts and of the Artistes Français.

FLURY, Urs
Swiss, 20th century.
Born 6 June 1937, in Solothurn.
Painter. Figures, landscapes.
Urs Flury travelled in Europe, especially Spain and Portugal. In Switzerland he set up in Aetingen where he took part in group exhibitions. His figurative painting shows influence of Matisse.

FLUYXENCH Y TRELL, Miguel
Spanish, 19th century.
Born 1820, in Tarragona; died 1874.
Painter. History painting, portraits.
Miguel Fluyxench y Trell studied at the school of fine arts in Barcelona. He spent some time in Rome, then returned to Spain where he was given a teaching post at the school of painting in Barcelona. He first exhibited around 1857 and went on exhibiting in Madrid, Barcelona and London until 1878. Also a talented illustrator, he provided the drawings for an 1862 edition of *Don Quixote.*

FLYE-SAINTE-MARIE, Pierre
French, 20th century.
Born in Avallon.
Painter. Local scenes.
Pierre Flye-Ste-Marie exhibited at the Salon des Artistes Indépendants from 1931 to 1943.
He painted mostly *Moroccan Scenes.*

FLYNT, Paul. See **FLINDT Paul**

FLYRI, Peter
Austrian, 19th century.
Born in Taufers (Tyrol).
Painter. Religious subjects.

Museums and Galleries:
Merano: *Holy Family*.

FO, G. R.
Swiss, 16th century.
Engraver.
This artist made engravings for Conrad Gesner's *L'Histoire des animaux* (*History of Animals*), published in 1551, and for the same author's *Médailles des Empereurs romains* (*Medals of the Roman Emperors*) published in 1559.

FOACHE, Arthur
French, 20th century.
Born in Janzé (Ille-et-Vilaine).
Painter. Landscapes.
Arthur Foache studied under Benjamin Constant, exhibiting at the Salon des Artistes Français in 1933.

FOACIER, Jacques
French, 17th - 18th century.
Died 14 March 1736, in Paris.
Painter. History painting.
Jacques Foacier won second prize at the Académie Royale in 1684 with *Enoch Beginning to Invoke the Name of the Lord*.

FOCARDI, Giovanni
Italian, 19th century.
Born 7 May 1842, in Florence; died end September 1903, in Florence.
Sculptor.
Giovanni Focardi lived in London from 1875 onwards, almost right up to his death. He created a large number of comic sculptures, on subjects inspired by the lives of the people of London. Among his other works, he is remembered for *Othello*, *Desdemona* and some busts. He exhibited several times at the Royal Academy.

FOCARDI, Piero, known as (the) Painter of Garda
Italian, 20th century.
Born c. 1889, in Settignano.
Painter. Landscapes.
Piero Focardi, the son of Ruggero Focardi, lived and worked in the Lake Garda region. In 1912 he showed a *View of Lake Garda* at the International Exhibition of Fine Arts in Amsterdam.

Focardi is also remembered for: *Scene from the Earthquake at Messina* and *Battle of Addua*.

Auction records:
Milan, 14 June 1989, *Landscape of the Garda Region* (oil on canvas, 7 1/4 x 11 3/4 ins / 18.5 x 30 cm) ITL 1,200,000. Milan, 6 June 1991, *Forest in Autumn* (oil on card/panel, 7 1/4 x 11 1/2 ins / 18.5 x 29 cm) ITL 1,900,000. Rome, 19 Nov 1992, *Salo Hill near Lake Garda* (1931, oil on panel, 7 3/4 x 16 1/4 ins / 20 x 41.5 cm) ITL 1,150,000. Monaco, 2 July 1993, *The Picturesque Corniche d'Or* (oil on canvas, 19 x 23 1/4 ins / 48 x 59 cm) FRF 8,880. Milan, 14 June 1995, *La Punta di Manerba* (1907, oil on canvas/card, 6 3/4 x 10 1/2 ins / 17 x 26.5 cm) ITL 2,300,000. Rome, 6 Dec 1999, *By the River* (oil on panel, 9 x 9 ins / 22 x 24 cm) ITL 3,600,000. Milan, 28 March 2000, *Bathers on a Rocky Beach* (oil on canvas, 33 x 56 ins / 84 x 142 cm) ITL 40,000,000. Milan, 15 June 2000, *View of Lake Garda* (1908, oil on canvas, 57 x 74 ins / 145 x 189 cm) ITL 58,000,000. Rome, 27 May 2002, *Winter Sun in Morgnaga* (oil on canvas, 24 x 17 ins / 62 x 44 cm) EUR 7,500. Paris, 5 Dec 2003, *Road by a Lake* (1908, oil on canvas, 18 x 28 ins / 46 x 70 cm) EUR 7,500.

FOCARDI, Ruggero
Italian, 19th - 20th century.
Born 1864, in Florence; died 1934, in Quercianella Sannino (near Livorno, Tuscany).
Painter. Portraits, genre scenes, landscapes with figures, seascapes.
At the beginning of his career, in 1881, Ruggero Focardi exhibited a number of sketches at the Royal Academy in London. In 1884, when he was 20 years old, he exhibited his first finished painting at the Florence Promotrice. In 1894 his street scenes earned him a distinction from the society of fine arts.

Focardi's landscapes demonstrate his interest in the effects of weather conditions: for example *Rainy Atmosphere* of 1884. He tackled a wide variety of themes, but constantly returned to painting landscapes with figures.

Museums and Galleries:
Florence (Palazzo Pitti): *Country Life*.

Auction records:
Milan, 14 Dec 1976, *Spinner in a Landscape* (oil on canvas, 59 x 47 1/4 ins / 150 x 120 cm) ITL 1,100,000. Milan, 19 March 1981, *Landscape* (1913, oil on canvas, 40 1/2 x 73 1/2 ins / 103 x 187 cm) ITL 5,500,000. London, 30 Nov 1984, *Game of Boules* (oil on canvas, 29 1/4 x 40 1/2 ins / 74.2 x 103 cm) GBP 11,000. Milan, 18 Dec 1986, *Self-portrait* (1906, oil on card, 22 3/4 x 15 3/4 ins / 58 x 40 cm) ITL 1,300,000. Milan, 6 June 1991, *Peeling Chestnuts* (1920, oil on panel, 15 1/4 x 20 ins / 38.5 x 51 cm) ITL 6,500,000. Milan, 12 Dec 1991, *The Countryside around Castigliocello with a Peasant Labouring with a Team of Oxen* (oil on panel, 11 3/4 x 15 3/4 ins / 30 x 40 cm) ITL 3,500,000. Bologna, 8-9 June 1992, *The Road to Castiglioncello* (1926, oil/plywood, 8 1/4 x 15 1/4 ins / 21 x 39 cm) ITL 2,990,000. Milan, 19 Dec 1995, *Lake Garda* (oil on panel, 9 1/4 x 13 1/4 ins / 23.5 x 33.5 cm) ITL 1,150,000. New Orleans, 3 June 2000, *Reading the Letter* (oil on canvas, 24 x 18 ins / 61 x 46 cm) USD 6,200. Rome, 21 Nov 2000, *Young Peasants* (oil on canvas, 26 x 35 ins / 65 x 90 cm) ITL 5,000,000. Venice, 16 Dec 2001, *Landscape in Tuscan Countryside* (oil on canvas, 15 x 21 ins / 37 x 53 cm) ITL 11,000,000. Venice, 16 Dec 2001, *Last Hours of the Day* (1920, oil on canvas, 40 x 35 ins / 101 x 89 cm) ITL 42,000,000. Milan, 23 Oct 2002, *Waiting* (oil on cardboard, 7 x 5 ins / 19 x 13 cm) EUR 7,500. Florence, 9 Dec 2003, *Autumnal Stroll* (oil on canvas, 22 x 29 ins / 57 x 74 cm) EUR 7,500.

FOCCORA. See **FOUQUET Jean**

FOCHI, Ferdinando
Italian, 17th century.
Painter.
Ferdinando Fochi executed frescoes in the Palazzo Magnani in Bologna and the Palazzo Bianchini in Lavino. He also painted the S Antonio library ceiling in Padua around the turn of the 18th century.

FOCHT, Frédéric
French, 20th century.
Born 17 July 1879, in Paris.
Sculptor. Monuments.
Frédéric Focht was an operatic tenor as well as a sculptor. He studied under Alexandre Falguiere. He exhibited at the Salon des Artistes Français, gaining a medal in 1900.

He executed the *War Memorial* in Lor (Aisne) and in Carcassone *Rise, Dead that You Are*.

Auction records:
London, 8 March 1976, *Winged Figure* (bronze, l. 31 ins / 79 cm) GBP 280. New York, 26 March 1983, *Force* (polychrome bronze, h. 20 1/4 ins / 51.2 cm) USD 3,000. Norwalk, 16 May 1999, *Flight* (bronze, h. 31 ins / 79 cm, w. 26 ins/66 cm) USD 7,200. London, 24 Feb 2000, *Young Female Skier Posed Downhill* (green patinated bronze, h. 24 ins / 60 cm) GBP 2,000. New York, 11 Dec 2003, *Man in Flight* (bronze, 39 x 34x14 ins / 98 x 86x35 cm) USD 32,500.

FOCILLON, Victor Louis
French, 19th - 20th century.
Born 1849, in Dijon; died 20 December 1918, in Paris.
Engraver.
Victor Focillon studied at the École des Beaux-Arts in Dijon. He made his debut at the Salon de Paris in 1876 (honourable

mention). He was awarded numerous medals, notably a gold in 1900 for the Exposition Universelle, and a médaille d'honneur in 1906.

FOCK, Harmanus
Dutch, 18th - 19th century.
Born 1 November 1766, in Amsterdam; died 1822.
Active in Franeker and Amsterdam.
Miniaturist, engraver.
MUSEUMS AND GALLERIES:
AMSTERDAM: *Self-portrait* (ivory).

FOCK, Johann
German, 17th century.
Sculptor (wood).
In 1644 Fock carved the organ gallery for the church in Hattstedt (Schleswig-Holstein).

FOCKE, C
German, 19th century.
Painter.
In 1805 Focke took part in the Dresden exhibition with a painting representing *Camp near Dresden* (picturing soldiers in front of the quartermaster's tent). Some of his portraits, dated between 1806 and 1810, were shown at exhibitions in Leipzig in 1912.

FOCKHEZER, Johann Georg
German.
Born to a family originally from Kissleg, near Lindau (Lake Constance).
Painter.
Painted mostly still-lifes (game).

FOCO, Paolo
Italian, 17th century.
Active in Casale c. 1660.
Landscape artist.

FOCOSI, Alessandro
Italian, 19th century.
Born 1839, in Milan; died 1869, in Milan.
Painter.
Alessandro Focosi worked as a history painter in Milan. His works include: *Catherine de Medici and Charles IX* (1867) and *Charles Emmanuel Giving the Spanish Ambassador the Insignia of the Golden Fleece*, which he painted for the Italian government.
MUSEUMS AND GALLERIES:
BOLOGNA (Pinacoteca Nazionale): *Tasso Fleeing to Sorrento* - MILAN (Pinacoteca Ambrosiana): *Portrait of Antonio Ronchette*.

FOCOSO. See **FIORITI Bernardino**

FOCQUER, Jacques. See **FOUQUIÈRES**

FOCUS, Georges. See **FAUCAS**

FODOR, Jakab
Hungarian, 17th century.
Painter.
Jakab Fodor painted ceiling decorations for the Unitary church of Moldovenesti, Romania. This ceiling, made of planks, was transferred to the Erdélyi Museum in Koloszvár at the beginning of the 20th century.

FODOR, Madeleine
Hungarian, 20th century.
Born in Budapest.
Sculptor.
Madeleine Fodor exhibited in Paris at the Salon d'Automne.

FODOROVICH, Stepan
Yugoslav, 19th century.
Painter.

FODRI, Lorenzo
Italian, 15th century.
Active in Cremona.
Miniaturist.
Lorenzo Fodri wrote and produced the miniatures for a *libro processionale* for the cathedral.

FOEDISCH, Carl
German, 19th century.
Miniaturist, painter (porcelain). Portraits, landscapes.
Carl Foedisch mainly painted portraits on porcelain and landscapes. His works were shown in the portrait exhibition in Leipzig in 1912.
MUSEUMS AND GALLERIES:
LEIPZIG (Stadtgeschichtliches Mus.): *Portrait of Woman* (painting/porcelain).

FOEDISCH, Heinrich Christian Friedrich
German, 19th century.
Active in Leipzig.
Painter (porcelain).
Heinrich was probably the son of Carl Foedisch.

FOELIX
German, 18th century.
Born c. 1736; died 1808, in Ehrenbreitstein (Rhineland-Palatinate).
Painter.
This artist was probably the father of Heinrich Foelix.

FOELIX, Heinrich
German, 18th - 19th century.
Born 28 January 1757; died 1821, in Ehrenbreitstein (Rhineland-Palatinate).
Painter.
Heinrich Foelix worked in Mainz and Trier.
MUSEUMS AND GALLERIES:
KOBLENZ: *Portrait of Peter and Clara Lang* - MAINZ: *Portrait of Sebastian Pfaff, Prince Elector of Mainz* (1786) - VERSAILLES: *Frederick Augustus I, King of Poland.*
AUCTION RECORDS:
LONDON, 11 Dec 1996, *Portrait of Clemens Wenceslas, Archbishop and Elector of Trier* (oil on canvas, 36 x 14 1/4 x 11 ins / 91.5 x 36 x 28 cm) GBP 4,600.

FOENARD
French, 18th century.
Painter.
Foenard painted a portrait, dated 1743, which hangs in the church of Bernay.

FOERSTER, Charles H.
Austrian, 19th - 20th century.
Born in the second half of the 19th century, in Lemberg (now Lviv, Ukraine).
Sculptor.
Foerster was the pupil of Coutan in Paris. He was awarded a third class medal at the Salon des Artistes Français in 1914.

FOERSTER-BOLLA, Mathilde
Hungarian, 20th century.
Born in Vienna, of Hungarian origin.
Painter.
Mathilde Foerster-Bolla exhibited *Hungarian Peasant Woman* in 1934 in Paris at the Salon de la Société Nationale des Beaux-Arts.

FOETSCH, Hermann
German, 19th century.
Born 5 January 1825; died 9 December 1883.
Active in Altenburg (Thuringia).
Painter.
Foetsch was a student of F. Döll. He executed portraits and reproductions.

FOGARTY, Thomas
American, 20th century.
Born 1873, in New York; died 11 August 1938.
Draughtsman, illustrator, painter. Genre scenes.

Thomas Fogarty was a pupil at the Art Students League, New York, later returning there as a teacher. From 1901, he was a member of the Society of Illustrators, and was also a member of the Salmagundi Club.

Fogarty was essentially an illustrator, creating images for periodicals, such as *Cosmopolitan* and *Scribners*, and for publications that include: 1896, Crockett's *Cleg Kelly*; Joshua Slocum's *Sailing Alone Around the World* (New York: century, 1900); 1913, D. Grayson's *Works, The Making of an American, The Road to Fortune*; Edmund Pearson's *The Voyage of the Hoppergrass* (New York: Macmillan, 1913); and Charles Dickens' *Dickens' People* (New York/London: Charles Scribner's Sons, 1935).

BIBLIOGRAPHY:
Baker, Ray Stannard, *The Friendly Road*, Doubleday, Page, Garden City (NY), 1913 (illustrated book). Osterwalder, Marcus (ed.), *Dictionnaire des illustrateurs 1800-1914*, Ides et Calendes, Neuchâtel, 1989.

AUCTION RECORDS:
SAN FRANCISCO, 24 June 1981, *Receiving the Post* (oil on card, 17 1/4 x 12 1/2 ins / 44 x 32 cm) USD 700. NEW YORK, 24 Jan 1990, *Indiscretion* (ink/paper, 14 x 26 ins / 35.6 x 66 cm) USD 715. NEW YORK, 14 March 1991, *Summer Picnic* (1937, oil on canvas, 48 x 76 1/2 ins / 122 x 194 cm) USD 13,200.

FOGEL, Fernand
French, 20th century.
Born 9 March 1889, in St-Aybert.
Painter. Landscapes.

Fernand Fogel taught art in Valenciennes and at the Académie des Beaux-Arts in Cambrai. He exhibited in Paris at the Salon des Artistes Français in 1933 and at the Société Nationale des Beaux-Arts in 1950.

FOGELBERG, Bengt Erland
Swedish, 19th century.
Born 1786, in Göteborg; died 1854, in Trieste.
Sculptor.

Bengt Erland Fogelberg was a pupil at the academy in Stockholm. In 1820 he went to Rome where his early work garnered some notice. He then returned to Sweden where he was named sculptor of the court. He mastered the treatment of historical subjects and groups borrowed both from antiquity and Scandinavian mythology. He enjoyed great reknown in Sweden. However, his failing health obliged him to depart for Italy and he died en route.

MUSEUMS AND GALLERIES:
GÖTEBORG: *Odin* - HELSINKI: *Bust of General A. F. Palmfelt* - STOCKHOLM: *Psyche*; *Venus*; *Paris*; *Cupid in a Shell*; *Gustav II Adolf*; *Charles XIV*; *K. F. von Breda*; *J. G. Sandberg*; *Apollo*; *Venus*; *Odin*; *Thor*; *Balder*; *Charles XIII*; *Helen*; 64 sketches.

FOGER, Stefan. See **FEGER**

FOGG, A.
British, 18th - 19th century.
Born to a family originally from Reading.
Painter.

A. Fogg exhibited a *View of Reading* at the Royal Academy in 1811.

FOGG, A.
British, 18th - 19th century.
Reproductions engraver.

A. Fogg engraved portraits after M. Bacciarelli, W. Beechey, J. Biedermann, J. S. Copley and Rubens. He is also known for his *Battle of Acre*, after Hamilton.

FOGGIA MORETTI, Mario. See **MORETTI-FOGGIA Mario**

FOGGIANO
Italian, 18th century.
Painter. Portraits.

Foggiano is probably identical with an artist called Vincenzo de Mita who used that soubriquet and worked in Naples around 1739. A *Portrait of Don Giovanni di Donato* by Foggiano featured in the 1911 Portrait Exhibition in Florence.

FOGGIE, David
British, 20th century.
Born 1878; died 1948.
Painter, watercolourist, pastellist. Landscapes with figures.

David Foggie studied in Antwerp, Paris and Florence. He exhibited at the Royal Academy in London, at the Glasgow Institute and in Munich. He was a member of the Royal Scottish Academy, the Royal Scottish Watercolour Society and the Scottish Arts Club.

AUCTION RECORDS:
GLASGOW, 12 Dec 1985, *Fatigue* (1923, oil on canvas, 24 x 20 ins / 61 x 50.8 cm) GBP 1,600. PERTH, 28 Aug 1989, *Working on the Shore* (1927, watercolour, 10 x 14 1/4 ins / 25.5 x 36.5 cm) GBP 682. LONDON, 1 Nov 2001, *Still-life with Red and White Roses* (1933, oil on canvas, 16 x 20 ins / 41 x 51 cm) GBP 2,000. LONDON, 28 Oct 2004, *Girl with Book* (1933, pastel, 27 x 21 ins / 68 x 53 cm) GBP 1,600.

FOGGINI, Giovanni Battista
Italian, 17th - 18th century.
Born 1652, in Florence; died 1725, in Florence.
Sculptor, draughtsman, architect. Religious subjects, mythological subjects. Groups, busts, statues, low reliefs, objets d'art.

Giovanni Battista Foggini studied initially in Florence and then moved to Rome to complete his studies at the request of Cosimo de' Medici III, Grand Duke of Tuscany. Foggini subsequently returned to work in Florence where, among other things, he produced a bust of *Galileo* for the church of S Croce.

BIBLIOGRAPHY:
Monaci, Lucia, *Disegni di Giovan Battista Foggini (1652-1725)*, exhibition catalogue, Gabinetto disegni e stampe degli Uffizi, Leo S. Olschki, Florence, 1977.

MUSEUMS AND GALLERIES:
FLORENCE (Uffizi): *Bust of Cardinal Leopoldo de' Medici* - LOS ANGELES (Getty Mus.) - PARIS (Louvre): *Scythian Animal Skinner in the Style of Antiquity* (marble) - PISA: drawings - VERSAILLES (Château, Parc): *Statue in the Style of Antiquity*.

AUCTION RECORDS:
LONDON, 28 Nov 1968, *Abduction of Persephone*; *Boreas Abducting Oreithyia* (two bronzes) GBP 4,200. MONTE CARLO, 27 May 1980, *Psyche and Eros* (bronze, l. 13 ins / 33 cm) FRF 140,000. LONDON, 7 July 1981, *Christ Insulted and Canopy (recto)*; *Betrayal of Christ and Kneeling Monk (verso)* (black chalk, pen and wash/paper, 11 1/2 x 8 1/4 ins / 29.5 x 21.2 cm) GBP 1,300. MONTE CARLO, 5 March 1984, *Cleopatra* (pen and wash/outlines in black chalk, 7 1/4 x 5 ins / 18.5 x 12.8 cm) FRF 5,500. LONDON, 13 Dec 1985, *Ajax Dying by his Own Hand* (bronze, h. 18 1/2 ins / 47 cm) GBP 24,000. NEW YORK, 11 Jan 1994, *Four Layers of Shells and a Sea Horse Surmounted by a Dolphin* (black chalk, ink and wash, sketch of a wall fountain, 7 3/4 x 7 ins / 20 x 18 cm) USD 4,370. NEW YORK, 12 Jan 1995, *Jupiter and Juno Supported by two Nudes on Rocks* (black chalk, ink and wash heightened with white, design for a group sculpture, 12 x 6 1/4 ins / 30.3 x 15.9 cm) USD 8,050. LONDON, 11 July 2001, *Beheading of St. Paul* (brown wax, h. 19ins / 48 cm) GBP 13,000.

FOGGINI, Jacopo Maria
Italian, 17th century.
Died 1683, in Florence.
Active in Florence.

Sculptor (including wood).

Jacopo Maria Foggini is recorded as having sculpted the funerary monument to *Baron von Starhemberg* which was placed in the secularised church of St Cecilia, together with a wooden *Ecce Homo* painted by B. Volterrano.

FOGGINI, Vicenzo

Italian, 18th century.

Sculptor.

Vicenzo Foggini was the son of Giovanni Battista Foggini. He sculpted the allegorical statue entitled *Astronomy* for the Galileo monument erected in Florence by his father. He also produced an equestrian statue of Emperor Francis I for the triumphal arch at the Porta San Gallo in Florence.

FOGGO, George

British, 19th century.

Born 1793; died 1869.

Painter, lithographer.

George Foggo collaborated with his older brother James on a series of lithographs after the Raphael cartoons in the Victoria and Albert Museum, London. He was also the author of a number of theoretical and campaigning essays on art.

FOGGO, James

British, 19th century.

Born 1790, in London; died 1860, in London.

Painter.

James Foggo was a pupil at the Académie Impériale in Paris. He returned to England with ambitious plans for an artistic career as a history painter in 1815, following Napoleon I's return from the island of Elba, and began work on the painting *Hagar and Ishmael*, in his confined lodgings. He was joined by his brother George in 1819, and for the next 40 years the pair laboured tirelessly on a large number of history paintings, most of which were never sold, despite public acclaim for their monumental work *The People of Parga Burying their Dead*, painted in 1821-1822. The *Entombment of Christ the Saviour* (the altarpiece of the French Protestant church of St-Martin-le-Grand in London) was painted subsequently. Their other works include: *Napoleon Signing the Death Warrant of the Duke of Enghien Despite his Mother's Supplications, General Williams among the Inhabitants of Kars* and *Christ at the Pool of Bethesda*.

FOGLIA, Celestino

Italian, 20th century.

Born 2 March 1905, in Trivero (Vercelli); died 1979.

Also active in Turkey.

Painter. Nudes, portraits, landscapes, flowers.

From 1934 to 1962 Celestino Foglia lived in Istanbul. He then went to live and work in Milan, and participated in a several regional group exhibitions. From 1946 to 1954 he showed his works in solo exhibitions in Istanbul, then from 1965 onward in various towns in Italy and abroad, including Montreal and Sao Paulo. His style of painting was Post-Impressionist in spirit, although he employed an impasto technique.

Foglia travelled extensively, to Mexico, Canada, Turkey, Africa, America, Australia, France, Spain, England, Belgium, Switzerland and Yugoslavia. From these trips he brought back views and sketches of local scenes. He also painted numerous portraits of women.

BIBLIOGRAPHY:

Celestino Foglia, Magalini Ed., Brescia, 1973.

FOGLIATI, Piero

Italian, 20th century.

Sculptor.

Piero Fogliati has shown his works in various solo exhibitions, including one in 1996 at the Museum of Electrical Energy in Mulhouse, in northeastern France.

He creates metal *Latomies* with engines and water, which he describes as being 'like Sicilian caves that transform and divert visual and auditory perception in space'.

FOGNONE. See **ANTONIO Vicentino**

FOGOLINO, Marcello

Italian, 15th - 16th century.

Born c. 1470, in San Vito; died after 1550.

Active in Venice and Marche from 1519 to 1548.

Painter, engraver. Religious subjects. Frescoes, miniatures.

Marcello Fogolino learned to paint in Vicenza. In 1523, he signed a contract with the Scuola di San Biagio in Pordenone, and settled in Trento in 1527.

One of his earliest works is a small picture of the *Epiphany*, formerly in the church of S Bartolomeo in Vicenza. He executed a *Virgin with Child, between St Blaise and St Apollonia* at Pordenone, followed by a *Glorification of St Francis, between Daniel and St John the Baptist*. Both these paintings are now in the cathedral in Pordenone.

From a letter written by Fogolino in 1536, we learn that he was a member of the group of painters engaged that year to decorate the city of Trento in honour of the visit by the king, Ferdinand; his altarpiece *St Anne* for the cathedral in Trento was painted on this occasion. On returning to his native region he executed a *Madonna Surrounded by Angels*, for S Corona, and a *Nativity*. Fogolino's works also include six signed engravings.

BIBLIOGRAPHY:

Puppi, L., *Marcello Fogolino pittore e incisore*, Collana Artisti Trentini, Trento, 1966. Barbieri, F., *Pittori di Vicenza, 1480-1520*, N Pozzi, Vicenza, 1981.

MUSEUMS AND GALLERIES:

AMSTERDAM (Rijksmus.) - BERGAMO (Accademia Carrara, Pinacoteca d'Arte Antica): *Choir of Monks* (miniature) - BERLIN (Bodemus.): *Madonna with Child and Six Saints* - CAMBRIDGE (Fogg Art Mus., Harvard University): *Adoration of the Magi* - MILAN (Mus. Poldi Pezzoli): *Virgin* - THE HAGUE (Mauritshuis): *Virgin with Child and Five Saints* - VENICE: *Virgin Enthroned* - VERONA (Mus. Civico): *Adoration of the Infant Jesus* - VICENZA (Mus. Civico): *Adoration of the Magi with Predella; Concert; Stigmatisation of St Francis* (predella).

FOGOLINO, Matteo

Italian, 16th century.

Active in Venice.

Painter.

FÖHL, Helga

German, 20th century.

Born 1935, in Berlin.

Sculptor.

Helga Föhl was a student from 1954 to 1958 at the Werkkunstschule in Darmstadt and the Hochschule für Bildenden Künste in Berlin. She specialises in using iron, which demands both rigour and decision, and she feels it to be a moderating element in her romantic dreams. Her sculptures are expressionist, often abstract, with massive shapes evoking organic elements. She has been represented in group exhibitions, including *Der andere Blick: Künstlerinnen des 20. Jahrhunderts* (*The Other View: Women Artists of the 20th century*), Diözesanmuseum, Trier, 1998.

BIBLIOGRAPHY:

Der andere Blick: Künstlerinnen des 20. Jahrhunderts, exhibition catalogue, Diözesanmuseum, Trier, 1998.

FOHN, Emanuel

Austrian, 20th century.

Born 26 March 1881, in Klagenfurt (Carinthia); died 14 December 1966, in Bozen (now Bolzano, Italy).

Painter. Portraits, landscapes.

Emanuel Fohn was a student at the Akademie der Bildenden Künste in Munich from 1907 to 1911. He made study and working trips to Sweden, Spain, Italy, France and elsewhere. He took part in group exhibitions and showed his paintings in solo exhibitions.

Em. Fohn

Auction records:
HEIDELBERG, 13 April 1982, *The Medici Villa in Rome* (1937, oil on canvas, 13 1/4 x 22 ins / 33.5 x 55 cm) DEM 1,200. MUNICH, 15 Sept 1983, *Vase of Flowers* (oil on card, 24 1/2 x 13 ins / 62 x 33 cm) DEM 2,700. MUNICH, 11 Nov 1999, *Peasants Harvesting Wheat* (oil on canvas, 17 x 20 ins / 42 x 51 cm) DEM 6,500. MUNICH, 15 Nov 2001, *Market Square in Bozen after Snowfall* (oil on panel, 24 x 20 ins / 60 x 50 cm) DEM 13,000. MUNICH, 15 Nov 2001, *Piazza San Marco* (oil on canvas, 38 x 53 ins / 97 x 135 cm) DEM 13,000. BERLIN, 30 Nov 2002, *Still-life of Flowers* (oil on card, 17 x 12 ins / 44 x 31 cm) EUR 4,000. VIENNA, 28 Jan 2003, *Church* (c. 1935, oil on canvas, 18 x 21 ins / 45 x 54 cm) EUR 5,000. VIENNA, 20 May 2003, *Over the Tree Line - Southern Tyrol* (oil on masonite, 27 x 34 ins / 68 x 87 cm) EUR 4,000.

FOHN, Germain
French, 20th century.
Born in Paris.
Painter.
Germain Fohn exhibited landscapes and figures at the Salon des Indépendants in 1931 and 1932.

FÖHN, Michael
Swiss, 19th century.
Born 26 July 1789, in Schwyz; died 1853, in Wallis.
Painter. History painting, portraits, landscapes.
Föhn ran an art school in Schwyz for some time and painted several landscapes in oils and watercolours.

FOHN, Sofie
Maiden name: Schneider
German, 20th century.
Born 2 August 1899, in Munich.
Active in Italy.
Painter, watercolourist. Portraits, scenes with figures, landscapes, still-lifes.
Sofie Fohn was the pupil of André Lhote in Paris. She was the wife of Emanuel Fohn. She took part in group exhibitions in South Tyrol.

FÖHR
German, 18th century.
Active in Berlin.
Sculptor.
Following plans by Daniel Chodowiecki, Föhr sculpted the statues and low reliefs on the gable of the French church (Franzosenkirche) in Berlin. He also worked at the castle there.

FOHR, Carl Philipp
German, 19th century.
Born 26 November 1795, in Heidelberg; died 29 June 1818, in Rome, by drowning.
Painter. Landscapes.
Nazarenes group (related to).
Carl Philipp Fohr was the brother of Daniel Fohr. He studied at the academy in Munich. The Grand Duchess of Baden-Baden, impressed by his artistic ability, gave him a bursary to go to Rome. While there, he painted two landscapes that attracted a lot of attention, but he then tragically drowned in the Tiber.

With Franz Pforr, who also died at the age of 24, Fohr represented the promise of great genius in German religious painting in the pivotal period between the 18th century and the Romantic Movement. In spite of his short career, he was one of many German artists who worked in association with the brotherhood of Nazarenes which was founded by Johann Friedrich Overbeck in the monastery of San Isodoro. Together with Koch, Fohr was one of the forerunners of German romantic landscape painting, which was to achieve its success through Friedrich, Carus and Oehme. In his portraits, he derived his technique and expression from the old German masters, such as Altdörfer, Cranach, and Dürer. This is particularly evident in the *Portrait of Wilhelm von Schadow*, which has been described as having a 'Faustian' look, in contrast to the superficiality of portraiture of the rococo period, which was just drawing to a close when Fohr began to paint.

Bibliography:
Brion, Marcel, *La Peinture allemande*, Éd. Pierre Tisné, Paris, 1959.

Museums and Galleries:
DARMSTADT (Schlossmus.): *Return from Hunting* - FRANKFURT AM MAIN: *Waterfalls at Tivoli; Heidelberg Castle* - HEIDELBERG (Kurpfälzisches Mus.): *Portrait of Wilhelm von Schadow*.

Auction records:
MUNICH, 6 and 8 Nov 1963, *The Four Castles at Steinach on the Neckar* (watercolour) DEM 12,000. MUNICH, 28 Nov 1979, *Portrait of the Artist Theodor Rehbenitz* (c. 1817-1818, pencil, 4 1/4 x 4 ins / 10.8 x 10 cm) DEM 17,000. MUNICH, 5 Dec 2000, *Four Drunken Students on the Way Home* (watercolour, bodycolour and Indian ink, 4 x 6 ins / 11 x 16 cm) DEM 34,000. MUNICH, 7 Nov 2001, *Martinswand in Tyrol, Zirl am Inn in the valley* (oil on canvas, 11 x 15 ins / 29 x 38 cm) DEM 10,000.

FOHR, Daniel
German, 19th century.
Born 1801, in Heidelberg; died 25 June 1862, in Baden-Baden (Baden-Württemberg).
Painter. Landscapes.
The brother of Carl Philipp Fohr, Daniel Fohr was painter to the court of Baden-Baden. He was a talented landscape painter who worked first in Munich, then in the Tyrol.

Museums and Galleries:
KARLSRUHE: *Eberstein Castle; Outskirts of Berchtesgaden; Rübezahl's Kingdom in the Giants' Mountain; Chiemsee; Kampenwand; Sacred Wood; St Boniface Felling an Oak* - MANNHEIM: *Eberstein Castle*.

Auction records:
LUCERNE, 23 May 1985, *Romantic Landscape* (1841, oil on canvas, 26 3/4 x 36 ins / 68 x 91.5 cm) CHF 19,000. FRANKFURT, 23 Nov 2002, *Coastal Landscape in the Evening with Figure* (oil on canvas, 32 x 44 ins / 81 x 112 cm) EUR 3,600.

FÖHRLEIN, Johann
German, 18th century.
Born c. 1701; died 1759.
Active in Frankfurt am Main.
Painter.

FOIDART, René
French, 20th century.
Born 30 April 1888, in Paris.
Painter.
René Foidart studied under G. Ferrier. In 1922 and thereafter, he exhibited drawings and pastels at the Salon des Artistes Français.

FOIN, Augustin Nicolas
French, 18th century.
Born 1726, in Paris; died after 1759.
Engraver (burin).

FOIN, Louis Joseph
French, 18th century.
Active in Paris in 1787.
Painter (?), sculptor (?).

FOIRESTIER, Laure Marie, later Mme Gozzoli
French, 19th century.
Born in Paris.
Painter. Figures, genre scenes, interiors with figures.
Educated under Le Poitevin; exhibited portraits and genre compositions at Salons between 1837 and 1864. Her body of work includes *Interior, At Prayer, Chit-Chat, Sleigh, Grandmother, Leisure Time, Despondency, Group of Children, Wooden Shoe, Woman Knitting* and *Beach Scene*.

FOIS, Giorgio
Italian, 17th century.
Of Sardinian origin.
Painter.
Giorgio Fois painted a *Virgin with Dominican Saints* for the church of S Maria in Tergo.

FOISSE, François, also called Brabant
French, 18th century.
Painter.
François Foisse was court painter to Duke Stanislas of Lorraine and is mentioned in Lunéville in 1746 and 1749. He is remembered for his portraits of Duke and Duchess Ossolensky, Louis XV, Marie Leczinska and the dauphin.

FOISSE, Jacques de
German, 18th century.
Active in Hamburg.
Draughtsman, engraver.
Jacques de Foisse's known works include views of *Avenues in Hamburg*: *In Front of the Dammtor and Steintor*.

FOISSY, Georges André
French, 20th century.
Born 26 September 1944, in Chambéry.
Engraver, painter.
Georges André Foissy studied at the École des Beaux-Arts de Grenoble, and then at the École des Beaux-Arts de Paris. He worked in Lucien Coutaud's engraving studio from 1964 to 1969. He has taken part in various group exhibitions, including the 1967 Biennale de Paris, as well as the Biennales de l'Estampe in Paris, and Biennale Engraving Exhibitions in Cracow, Poland, and Tokyo.

FOIT, Bernard
French, 18th century.
Born c. 1710, in Pau; died c. 1791, in Lisbon.
Painter.
Painter to the court of Joseph Emmanuel I of Portugal, Bernard Foit executed portraits and altar paintings for churches in Lisbon.

FOIT, Francis Wladimir
French, 20th century.
Sculptor.
Francis Foit exhibited at the Salon des Tuileries in 1928 with *Portrait* and *Centuries Gone by*.

FOIT, Franta
Czech, 20th century.
Born in Bohemia.
Sculptor.
Franta Foit exhibited a *Bust* at the Salon des Tuileries (1924) in Paris.

FOIX, Denis de
French, 16th century.
Sculptor.
Denis de Fois was invited to Auch (Gers) by the architect Jean de Beaujeu where, from 1560 to 1567, he worked on the sculptures for the façade of the Gothic cathedral (under construction there since 1489) and on the decoration on the inner side of the portal.

FOKAS, Odysseus
Greek, 19th - 20th century.
Born 1865, in Kalasteri; died 1946, in Athens.
Painter. Landscapes.
Odysseus Fokas went to Paris and Aix-en-Provence to complete his training.
MUSEUMS AND GALLERIES:
ATHENS (Ethnikí Pinakothíki).

FOKIN, Leonid Aleksandrovich
Russian, 20th century.
Born 1930, in Pavlograd; died 1985.
Painter. Portraits, genre scenes.
A graduate of the Ilya Repin institute of art in Leningrad (now St Petersburg), Leonid Aleksandrovich Fokin took part in collective exhibitions from 1956 onwards.

A painter of old-fashioned, sentimental genre scenes, portraitist and occasional landscape artist, his work is a compromise between the academic traditions of Realism of the 19th-century Peredvizhniki and the Socialist Realism of the years of Stalinist and post-Stalinist repression.
MUSEUMS AND GALLERIES:
KRASNODAR - LOANOV - MOSCOW - OREL - ST PETERSBURG.
AUCTION RECORDS:
PARIS, 5 Oct 1992, *Village Nursery School* (oil on canvas, 41 1/4 x 50 3/4 ins / 105 x 129 cm) FRF 10,000.

FOKIN, Nicolai Mikhailovich
Russian, 19th century.
Born 1869, in St Petersburg; died 1908, in St Petersburg.
Painter.
After studying for seven years at the St Petersburg academy of fine arts, the collection of which includes his work *The First Snow*, Fokin painted mostly scenes of Finland and snow covered landscapes, which were shown at St Petersburg exhibitions.
MUSEUMS AND GALLERIES:
ST PETERSBURG (Gosudarstvennyj Russkij Muz.): *Suburb; On the Lake*; study.

FOKINA, Elena
Russian, 20th - 21st century.
Born 1961.
Painter.
Elena Fokina studied at the polygraphic institute in Moscow where she was taught by Marina Topaz and Youri Bourdjelian. Her works have been shown at various exhibitions, including the Tokyo International Art Show (1991), *Mif Art* in Moscow (1991), and at the Gallery Art London in London (1991). She has also had solo exhibitions at private galleries in London, Dortmund and Moscow.

AUCTION RECORDS:
PARIS, 1 June 1994, *Cats from Tunis* (oil on canvas, 55 x 47 1/4 ins / 140 x 120 cm) FRF 5,500.

FOKKE, A. Willemsz.
Dutch, 18th century.
Active c. 1780.
Engraver.
Among A. Willemsz. Fokke's works the following two are notable: *The Stranding of a Fishing Boat Chased by Three Armed English Ships in Schevening, 1 January 1781* and *Shipwreck of the Frigate Woestduyn on her Return from the Indies, 24 July 1779*.

FOKKE, Arend Simonsz.
Dutch, 18th - 19th century.
Born 3 July 1755, in Amsterdam; died 15 November 1812, in Haarlem.
Engraver (etching), writer. Historical figures. Caricatures.
Arend Simonsz. Fokke was the son of Simon Fokke. The British Museum possesses two of his etchings with caricatures inspired by the history of England.
MUSEUMS AND GALLERIES:
LONDON (British Mus.).

FOKKE, Jan
Dutch, 18th - 19th century.
Born c. 1745, in Amsterdam; died 1812, in Amsterdam.
Engraver, writer.
Jan Fokke was the son of Simon Fokke.
MUSEUMS AND GALLERIES:
AMSTERDAM (Rijksprentenkabinet): several works.

FOKKE, Simon
Dutch, 18th century.
Born 1 September 1712, in Amsterdam; died 10 August 1784, in Amsterdam.
Painter, draughtsman, engraver. History painting, portraits.
Simon Fokke was a pupil of J.-C. Philips. He produced several portraits and a number of vignettes to illustrate various works.
AUCTION RECORDS:
PARIS, 23 May 1923, *Ferryman's Call* (pencil) FRF 135. MILAN, 1982, *Explosion of the Boat Alphen in the Port of Curaçao* (1778, pen and wash, 7 3/4 x 11 1/2 ins / 20 x 28.9 cm) NLG 2,000. LONDON, 18 April 1994, *Bombing of Bergen op Zoom, 1 August 1747* (1780, ink and wash/red chalk, 6 1/4 x 10 1/2 ins / 15.8 x 26.8 cm) GBP 1,840.

FOKKENS, Phocas
Dutch, 20th century.
Born 1888, in Amsterdam; died 1965.
Painter, draughtsman. Figures, genre scenes.
Fokkens exhibited regularly in Paris at the Salon de la Société Nationale from 1926.
AUCTION RECORDS:
AMSTERDAM, 7 Nov 1995, *Young Woman Playing the Violin* (1913, pastel, 32 1/4 x 28 3/4 ins / 82 x 73 cm) NLG 4,720.

FOL (Mme)
Swiss.
Painter. Portraits.
The Ariana Museum in Geneva has two portraits by Mme Fol: *J. Grandpierre of Geneva* and *Mlle Dimier.*

FOLARTON, Allart, or Follaton
French, 15th century.
Painter, illuminator.
This artist is mentioned in Tours (Indre-et-Loire) in about 1476. In 1478 he painted some coats of arms at the town hall there, while in 1479 he painted an *Annunciation* for the Great Hall and two portraits of the *Prince of Orange* to decorate the main portal. According to Siret, he worked for Louis XII.

FOLÂTRE, Catherine
French, 20th century.
Born 11 October 1944, in Pau.
Painter. Genre scenes.
Although Catherine Folâtre received a full artistic education, her painting is simple in style, and owes a lot to popular imagery, sometimes reflecting the influence of Pop Art. She broaches a number of varied subjects in her works, always treating them with humour: the boutiques and quartiers of Paris in 1966, the Far West in 1968, the circus in 1972, *In the Greenery* in 1974, and many more.
She has regularly exhibited her works at the Salon des Artistes Français in Paris, where she staged her first solo exhibition in 1966.

FOLAWN, Thomas Jefferson
American, 19th century.
Born in Youngstown (Ohio).
Painter.
Thomas Jefferson Folawn was a pupil of C. S. Niles at the Colorado School of Fine Arts, and of Van Waeyenberge in Paris. He was a member of the Denver Art Association, the Society of Independent Artists and the American Artists Professional League.

FOLCH Y AMICH, Mariano
Spanish, 19th century.
Born in the 19th century, in Manresa (Catalonia).
Painter.
Mariano Folch y Amich taught painting in his native town of Manresa around 1860; he painted landscapes of his local area, views of towns and battle scenes. He shows some similarity to Mariano Borrell y Folch.

FOLCH Y CARDONA, Francesco
Spanish, 18th century.
Painter.
Francesco Folch y Cardona taught at the academy in Valencia from 1752 and, in 1787, became director of the academy in Murcia. His portraits include that of *Count of Florida Blanca.*

FOLCH Y COSTA, Jaime
Spanish, 18th - 19th century.
Born c. 1760, in Barcelona; died 17 August 1816, in Barcelona.
Sculptor.
Jaime Folch y Costa trained at the school of fine arts in Barcelona, later at the Academia de San Fernando in Madrid, and then in Rome. He sent a low relief of the *Death of Seneca* from Rome for the academy exhibition in Madrid in 1784. He was appointed director of sculpture at the fine arts school of Granada and a number of his works are in this city, including *Adoration of the Shepherds* and *Adoration of the Magi* in the church of S José; the statues on the high altar of the church of S Pedro y S Pablo; a *Christ on the Cross* for the church of S Matias; and in Granada Cathedral, the funerary monument of Archbishop J.M. Moscoso y Peralta.

FOLCH Y COSTA, José
Spanish, 18th - 19th century.
Born 12 January 1768, in Barcelona; died 24 November 1814, in Madrid.
Sculptor.
José Folch y Costa studied drawing at the school of fine arts in Barcelona, and sculpture under the direction of the sculptor Raimondo Amedeu. He went to Madrid where he worked in the studio of Juan Adan and Manuel Alvárez. In 1797 he was made a member of the Academia de San Fernando and, in 1814, a few months before his death, he was appointed its director.

FOLCHART
Swiss, 9th century.
Active in St Gall.
Miniaturist.
The psalter decorated by this artist in St Gall is an excellent example of the painting and drawing of the Carolingian period.

FOLCHER, Jean Auguste Félix
French, 20th century.
Born in St-André-de-Sangonis (Hérault).
Painter (?), watercolourist.

Jean Folcher studied under the Laurenses and exhibited at the Salon des Artistes Français in 1931.

FOLCHETTI, Stefano
Italian, 15th - 16th century.
Born to a family originally from San Ginesio (Marche).
Painter.

The municipal museum in San Ginesio houses altarpieces by Stefano Folchetti. His other works include a triptych in the Urbisaglia collection, a triptych in the church of S Clemente in Genoa, a fresco of the *Virgin* in the church of the Rosary in Amendola and a *Crucifixion* in the municipal museum in Sarnano. This latter work, together with those in the museum in San Ginesio, were shown at a retrospective exhibition in Macerata in 1906.

FOLCHI, Ferdinand
Italian, 19th century.
Born 2 May 1822, in Florence; died 20 August 1883, in Florence.
Painter, draughtsman. Genre scenes.

Ferdinand Folchi studied under B. Sabatelli and Bezzuoli, and worked mainly in Florence..

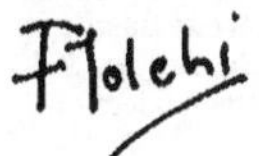

AUCTION RECORDS:
LONDON, 12 Feb 1993, *Bartering* (pencil and watercolour heightened with white/paper, 19 3/4 x 14 ins / 50.2 x 35.6 cm) GBP 6,160. LONDON, 17 Nov 1994, *Bartering* (pencil and watercolour heightened with white/paper, 19 3/4 x 14 ins / 50.2 x 35.6 cm) GBP 6,900. ST LOUIS, 18 Sept 1999, *Two Cardinals in an Interior* (watercolour, 21 x 29 ins / 53 x 74 cm) USD 2,500. LONDON, 1 May 2002, *Refreshment* (watercolour, 14 x 10 ins / 35 x 25 cm) GBP 1,400.

FOLCO, Giuseppe
Italian, 18th century.
Painter.

Giuseppe Folco studied in Genoa under P. L. Spoletti. He worked as a majolica ware decorative artist at the Savona manufacturing works.

FÖLDES, Lenke, or Helene
Maiden name: Sonnenfeld
Hungarian, 20th century.
Born 12 August 1896 or 1899, in Újpest.
Sculptor. Figures. Groups.

Lenke Földes trained in Budapest, Vienna and Paris. She exhibited a marble, *Motherhood* at the 1925 Salon des Tuileries and a group of direct-cut stone and marble sculptures in 1928.

FOLDES, Mihàly, also known as de Bische or de Bicske
Hungarian, 18th century.
Painter.

Mihàly Foldes painted ceiling decorations at the Reformist church of Vilonya, which were transferred to the National Museum of Budapest in 1910.

FOLDÈS, Peter
British, 20th century.
Born 1924, in Budapest, to English parents; died 29 March 1977, in Paris.
Also active in France.
Painter, draughtsman.
Nouvelle Figuration, Figuration Narrative.

Peter Foldès began his training at the school of fine arts in Budapest. From the age of 21, he also taught for a time at the school. In 1946, after a brief spell in Paris, where he discovered modern art, Foldès went to London, having received a travel bursary, and studied at the Slade School. Foldès's life was full of variety as was his career in terms of his artistic production. At the time of his early solo exhibitions he produced a strongly geometric style of abstraction. However, he soon returned to figurative art and in his own way contributed to the revival of the realism associated with the development of the Pop Art phenomenon in the 1960s. In a highly graphic style characterised by spontaneity of line, he often developed an action in time in a series of successive pictures juxtaposed on the same canvas. He worked in a kind of strip cartoon style, but also produced calligrammes, collage and 'motorised' works in which the various elements are in fact moved by mechanical means. His diverse writing, techniques, subjects and themes express humour, violence, sex and death or all these things and many others at once in a kind of inextricable.

He took part in international group exhibitions and in 1956 was awarded a Venice Biennale prize for an animated short film about an atomic explosion and the end of the world. In the 1960s, he participated in several group events in Paris, including the Salon de Mai, in 1961 the 2nd Paris Biennale, in 1963 the São Paulo Biennale, in 1964 the Venice Biennale, in 1964 *Mythologies Quotidiennes* (*Everyday Mythologies*) at the Musée d'Art Moderne de la Ville de Paris and in 1965 *La Figuration Narrative* (*Narrative Figuration*), brought together and organised by Gérald Gassiot-Talabot. His first solo exhibition was at the Hanover Gallery in London in 1948. It was followed by further exhibitions at the same gallery until 1955, in Paris in 1949, at the National Art Gallery of Sydney in 1954, at the Bussola Gallery in Turin in 1959, at the International Art Gallery in Washington DC in 1960 and in Paris at the Galerie Iris Clert.

BIBLIOGRAPHY:
Peter Foldès, exhibition catalogue, Gal. Y. Gastou, Paris, 1989.

AUCTION RECORDS:
PARIS, 5 Oct 1987, *Composition with Coins* (1962, oil on canvas, 63 x 50 3/4 ins / 160 x 129 cm) FRF 14,000. PARIS, 21 May 1990, *Rocket* (1958, oil on canvas, 46 3/4 x 40 1/4 ins / 119 x 102 cm) FRF 7,000. PARIS, 30 Jan 1995, *Composition with Figures* (1952, oil on canvas, 79 1/2 x 83 3/4 ins / 202 x 213 cm) FRF 4,200.

FOLDI, Peter
Hungarian, 20th - 21st century.
Born 1949, in Somoskoujfalu.
Painter. Scenes with figures.

Peter Foldi studied at the school of fine arts in Eger. Having grown up in the rural north of Hungary, he draws his inspiration from folklore and peasant life, using a very free illustrative graphic style and colours to narrate his work. He has taken part in national and international exhibitions, notably at the museum in Vác (1979) and in Hamburg (1983).

AUCTION RECORDS:
PARIS, 14 Oct 1991, *Arise, Sun* (1989, oil on panel, 17 3/4 x 22 3/4 ins / 45 x 58 cm) FRF 6,000.

FOLDSONE, John
British, 18th century.
Died c. 1784, in London.
Painter, miniaturist. Portraits.

John Foldsone exhibited with the Royal Academy until 1783, and died shortly after submitting his last work. He was the father of the miniaturist Mrs Mee.

FOLER, Antonio
Italian, 16th - 17th century.
Born 1528, in Venice; died 1616.
Painter.

Antonio Foler was a contemporary and friend of Paolo Veronese, whose style he successfully imitated. Rodolfi cites a number of works by Foler, including the *Assumption of the Virgin* and *Crucifixion* in the church of the abbey of S Gregorio, the *Birth of the Virgin* in S Barnaba, and *Christ in the Garden of Gethsemane* and *Resurrection* in S Caterina.

FOLETTI, Anton Yegorovich
Russian, 18th century.
Sculptor.

A pupil of G. Vitali at the St Petersburg academy, Foletti was awarded prizes for his busts of the architect *Ricard de Montferrand* and the sculptor *Vitali* and also for a statue *Adonis Resting*.

FOLEY, Charles Vandeleur
Irish, 19th century.
Born in Dublin; died after 1868, in Scotland.
Painter. Genre scenes, landscapes.

Charles Foley studied sculpture at the Royal Dublin Society School, but later devoted himself to painting, exhibiting genre scenes and a small number of landscapes with the Dublin Academy from 1846 to 1868. He exhibited with the Royal Academy in London from 1856 to 1860, and the British Institution from 1852 to 1860.

AUCTION RECORDS:
LONDON, 27 Jan 1986, *Village Street Scenes* (two oils on canvas, 10 x 14 ins / 25.5 x 35.5 cm) GBP 900. SOUTH QUEENSFERRY, 23 April 1991, *Edinburgh Castle* (oil on canvas, 18 x 10 ins / 46 x 25.5 cm) GBP 1,210. EDINBURGH, 28 April 1992, *Palace of Holyroodhouse, Edinburgh* (oil on card, 10¼ x 8¼ ins / 26 x 21 cm) GBP 990.

FOLEY, Edward N.
British, 19th century.
Born 1814, in Dublin; died 1874; committed suicide.
Sculptor.

Edward N. Foley exhibited with the Royal Academy and at Suffolk Street in London from 1834 to 1873.

MUSEUMS AND GALLERIES:
LONDON (National Portrait Gal.): *Samuel Lover* (1839, marble, bust).

FOLEY, Fiona
Australian, 20th - 21st century.
Born 1964, in Maryborough.
Painter, engraver, sculptor.

Fiona Foley is an Aboriginal and studied in Sydney and London, obtaining a master's degree in engraving. She has spent time living in Aboriginal communities, learning traditional art forms. Foley creates paintings consisting of representations of shells and fish bones or abstract signs in which bright colours stand out against dark backgrounds. In her engravings and sculptures, she pursues a policy of protest and recognition with regard to Aboriginal identity. She has taken part in exhibitions of 'urban' Aboriginal art. In 2003, she took part in *The American Effect, A Look at How America is Seen by Artists Around the World* at the Whitney Museum of American Art in New York. In this exhibition, some 30 foreign artists explored the way in which the USA is perceived as a superpower.

BIBLIOGRAPHY:
Murphy, Bernice, *Zeitgenössische Fotokunst aus Australien*, exhibition catalogue, Neuer Berliner Kunstverein, Berlin, 2000. Couderc, Sylvie, *Bonheurs des Antipodes, regards sur l'art contemporain australien*, exhibition catalogue, Musée de Picardie, Amiens, 2000 (text in French and English). Genocchio, Benjamin, *Fiona Foley: Solitaire*, Piper Press, Sydney, 2001. Rinder, Lawrence, et al., *The American Effect, A Look at How America is Seen by Artists Around the World*, exhibition catalogue, Whitney Museum of American Art, New York, 2003.

MUSEUMS AND GALLERIES:
CANBERRA (National Mus. of Australia): *Annihilation of the Blacks*.

FOLEY, J.B.
British, 19th century.
Active in London.
Painter. Seascapes.

J.B. Foley exhibited at the British Institution and Suffolk Street from 1863 to 1877.

FOLEY, John Henry
Irish, 19th century.
Born 1818, in Dublin; died 1874, in London.
Sculptor. Portraits, equestrian portraits. Busts.

John Henry Foley studied at the Royal Dublin Society Schools, and at the Royal Academy in London from 1834. He collaborated with Thomas Brock on a bust of Michael Faraday. He exhibited with the Royal Academy for the first time in 1837, and became an associate in 1859.

MUSEUMS AND GALLERIES:
BIRMINGHAM: *Oliver Goldsmith*; *Edmund Burke* - BRISTOL: *Edmund Burke* - LONDON (National Portrait Gal.): *Bryan Waller Procter* (marble, bust); *Helena Saville (née Faucit), Lady Martin* (1843, marble, bust) - LONDON (Royal Academy of Arts): *The Elder Brother* (c. 1858, marble, competition piece) - LONDON (Tate Collection): *Sir Joshua Reynolds, P.R.A.* (stone).

AUCTION RECORDS:
LONDON, 5 Nov 1980, *Equestrian Portrait of Queen Victoria* (c. 1865, bronze, h. 18½ ins / 47 cm) GBP 1,900. MADRID, 25 Oct 1983, *Warrior* (bronze, h. 24½ ins / 62 cm) ESP 140,000. PARIS, 9 Nov 1987, *Bath* (1846, patinated bronze medal, h. 21¼ ins / 54 cm) FRF 25,000. NEW YORK, 26 May 1993, *Gentlemen* (bronze, a pair, each 39½ ins / 100.3 cm) USD 6,900. PADDINGTON, 23 May 1999, *Caractacus* (c. 1860, bronze, h. 33 ins / 85 cm) AUD 2,800. NEW YORK, 9 Feb 2000, *Ducal Palace, Venice* (oil on canvas, 10 x 14 ins / 25 x 36 cm) USD 1,600. LONDON, 18 May 2000, *Youth at a Stream* (1846, dark brown patinated bronze, h. 21 ins / 54 cm) GBP 2,200. LICHFIELD, 27 Nov 2002, *Figure of Edmund Burke* (c. 1865, dark brown patinated bronze, h. 20 ins / 51 cm) GBP 2,000. LONDON, 21 July 2003, *John Julius* (1862, white marble, h. 26 ins / 56 cm) GBP 3,500.

FOLEY, Margaret F. (Miss)
British, 19th century.
Born in New Hampshire; died 7 December 1877, in Meran, South Tyrol (now Merano, Italy).
Sculptor. Figures, portraits.

Margaret Foley exhibited at the Royal Academy in London from 1870 to 1877.

AUCTION RECORDS:
LONDON, 14 May 1980, *Modest Bather* (1875, marble, h. 34¼ ins / 87 cm) GBP 1,400. NEW YORK, 30 Sept 1997, *Full-length Statue of Abram S. Hewitt, on a Base* (marble, h. 70 ins / 177.8 cm) USD 805.

FOLEY-RISLER, Amélie
French, 20th century.
Born in Baden-Baden, to French parents.
Painter (?).

Amélie Foley-Risler exhibited at the Société Nationale des Beaux-Arts in Paris.

FOLFI, Alessandro
Italian, 16th century.
Born 16th century, in Florence.
Sculptor (wood).

From 1576 to 1603, Alessandro Folfi produced sculptures in wood in the royal palace in Naples and in the churches of S Giacomo degli Spagnuoli, degli Incurabili, Croce di Luca and Gesu. He was the brother of Giacomo Folfi.

FOLFI, Giacomo
Italian, 16th - 17th century.
Sculptor (wood).
With his brother Alessandro, Giacomo Folfi executed sculptures in wood in numerous churches in Naples and in the chapel of the royal palace.

FOLGER, Michael
Austrian, 19th century.
Active in Vienna.
Miniaturist, lithographer.
From 1849 to 1851, Folger exhibited portraits in miniature and lithographs in the exhibition at the academy in Vienna.

FOLGUERAS Y DOIZTUA, Cipriano
Spanish, 19th century.
Born c. 1860, in Oviedo.
Active in Madrid.
Sculptor. Genre scenes.
Cipriano Folgueras y Doiztua was awarded a silver medal at the 1900 Exposition Universelle.
MUSEUMS AND GALLERIES:
MADRID (Mus. de Arte Moderno): *Tooth-pulling* (plaster).

FOLICHE, E.
Painter. Seascapes.
MUSEUMS AND GALLERIES:
BERN (musée): *At The Seaside.*

FOLIGNO, da. See first name

FOLIN. See **FOLLIN**

FOLINGSBY, Clara
Maiden name: Wagner
German, 19th century.
Painter. Landscapes.
Folingsby was the wife of the portrait painter Georges Folingsby. She exhibited her work in Vienna in 1868, Munich in 1869 and Breslau (now Wroclaw, Poland) in 1873.

FOLINGSBY, George Frederick
Irish, 19th century.
Born 23 August 1828, in Wicklow; died 4 January 1891, in Melbourne.
Painter. History painting, portraits, genre scenes.
A pupil of Piloty, George Folingsby settled in Munich from 1855.
MUSEUMS AND GALLERIES:
MELBOURNE: *Portrait of James Service; Portrait of Sir Charles Sladen; The First Meeting between Henry VIII and Anne Boleyn; Bunyan in Prison* - SYDNEY: *Sir Hercules Robinson.*
AUCTION RECORDS:
LONDON, 30 March 1990, *The First Piano Lesson* (oil on canvas, 32 3/4 x 25 ins / 83.2 x 63.5 cm) GBP 11,000. GLASGOW, 4 Dec 1991, *Anne of Denmark and James VI of Scotland* (1866, oil on canvas, 49 x 57 3/4 ins / 124.5 x 147 cm) GBP 7,150.

FOLINO. See **FOLLIN**

FOLINSBEE, John Fulton
American, 20th century.
Born 14 March 1892, in Buffalo (New York State); died 1972.
Painter. Figures, landscapes.
John Fulton Folinsbee was a pupil of Frank Vincent Du Mond and Thomas Alexander (?) Harrison. He was a member of the National Academy of Design, the Salmagundi Club and the National Art Club. Essentially a landscape painter, Folinsbee, like many Post-Impressionist artists, was particularly aware of the way light varies according to the time of day and season, and had a special predilection for winter landscapes. In 1917, he was awarded the Newport Art Association's Greenough Prize, in 1921, the Carnegie Prize, and, in 1931, the silver medal of the Pennsylvania Academy of Fine Arts.
MUSEUMS AND GALLERIES:
WASHINGTON DC (Corcoran Gal. of Art).
AUCTION RECORDS:
LOS ANGELES, 6 Nov 1978, *Towpath, Montrichard* (oil on canvas, 16 x 20 ins / 40.5 x 51 cm) USD 2,000. NEW YORK, 20 March 1984, *Cologan Outdoor Bar, Stockton* (1950, oil on mounted card, 16 x 23 1/2 ins / 40.5 x 59.7 cm) USD 1,400. NEW YORK, 24 April 1985, *The Outdoor Bar* (oil on card, 16 x 24 ins / 40.5 x 61 cm) USD 2,400. NEW YORK, 17 March 1988, *Winter Sunset* (oil on canvas, 15 3/4 x 19 3/4 ins / 40 x 50 cm) USD 8,250. NEW YORK, 27 Sept 1990, *Young Girl* (oil on card, 8 1/4 x 10 1/4 ins / 21 x 26 cm) USD 2,640. NEW YORK, 30 Nov 1990, *Winter Sun* (oil on canvas, 16 1/4 x 20 1/4 ins / 41 x 51.2 cm) USD 22,000. NEW YORK, 14 Nov 1991, *The River Delaware Frozen Over* (oil on canvas, 20 x 30 ins / 50.8 x 76.2 cm) USD 2,090. NEW YORK, 15 April 1992, *The West Bank* (oil on canvas, 24 x 30 ins / 61 x 76.2 cm) USD 17,600. NEW YORK, 28 May 1992, *Mill Dam* (oil on canvas, 16 1/4 x 20 ins / 41 x 50.8 cm) USD 4,400. NEW YORK, 31 March 1994, *View from Lopaus Point* (oil on canvas, 30 x 36 ins / 76.2 x 91.4 cm) USD 2,875. NEW YORK, 14 Sept 1995, *The Raritan* (oil on canvas, 32 x 40 ins / 81.3 x 101.6 cm) USD 27,600. NEW YORK, 30 Sept 1997, *Bridge* (oil on canvas, 24 x 30 1/4 ins / 61 x 76.8 cm) USD 19,550. NEW YORK, 5 May 1999, *Outdoor Bar* (oil on masonite, 16 x 24 ins / 41 x 61 cm) USD 14,000. DOWNINGTON, 19 June 1999, *Canal, Depicting New Hope* (oil on board, 10 x 14 ins / 25 x 36 cm) USD 5,250. SOUTH DEERFIELD, 2 June 2000, *Tenants Harbour* (oil on canvas, 19 x 29 ins / 48 x 74 cm) USD 6,000. NEW YORK, 13 June 2001, *New Hope Lane* (oil on canvas, 12 x 16 ins / 30 x 41 cm) USD 32,000. NEW YORK, 28 Nov 2001, *Mill Dam* (oil on canvas, 32 x 40 ins / 81 x 102 cm) USD 50,000. NEW YORK, 13 March 2002, *Hockamock Bay, Maine* (oil on canvas, 20 x 30 ins / 51 x 76 cm) USD 23,000. MILFORD, 25 April 2002, *Edward Redfield Painting* (1923, oil on panel, 10 x 8 ins / 25 x 20 cm) USD 15,000. MILFORD, 24 April 2003, *Grey Buildings* (oil on canvasboard, 16 x 20 ins / 41 x 51 cm) USD 14,000. PHILADELPHIA, 7 Dec 2003, *Beached Boat on the Maine Coastline* (oil on canvas, 26 x 40 ins / 66 x 102 cm) USD 16,000. PHILADELPHIA, 27 June 2004, *Maine Landscape* (oil on canvas, 16 x 24 ins / 41 x 61 cm) USD 19,000. MILFORD, 21 Oct 2004, *Bucks County Hills* (oil on canvas, 20 x 30 ins / 51 x 76 cm) USD 20,000.

FOLIO, A., or Foolio or Foly
Dutch, 17th century.
Active c. 1669.
Painter, miniaturist (?).
A. Folio was perhaps the same artist as Adriaen Foly, mentioned by Houbraken.

FOLIOT, François
French, 18th century.
Active in Paris in 1754.
Painter.

FOLIOT, Jean Baptiste Henry
French, 18th century.
Active in Paris in 1769.
Painter, sculptor.

FOLIOT, Julien
French, 18th century.
Active in Paris in 1766.
Painter, sculptor.

FOLIOT, Louis Pierre
French, 18th century.
Sculptor (wood).
Louis Pierre Foliot was a member of the Académie de St-Luc in Paris.

FOLIOT, Nicolas Quinibert
French, 18th century.
Died 20 May 1776, in Paris.

Sculptor (wood).
Nicolas Quinibert Foliot sculpted some armchairs which are in the Louvre.

FOLIOT, Toussaint François
French, 18th century.
Sculptor (wood).
Toussaint François Foliot was a member of the Académie de St-Luc in Paris, and was admitted as the master of a studio in 1773. He worked for the royal châteaux of Compiègne, Fontainebleau and Versailles.

FOLK, Charles
French, 20th century.
Born 15 October 1920, in Mulhouse.
Painter, engraver, fresco artist. Designs for stained glass.
Charles Folk studied from 1946 to 1950 in Strasbourg and at the Académie de la Grande Chaumière in Paris where he took part in the Salon de la Jeune Peinture, Salon d'Automne and Salon des Artistes Indépendants.

FOLKARD, Elisabeth F.
American, 19th century.
Active in London, England.
Painter, watercolourist. Genre scenes.
Elisabeth F. Folkard exhibited in London at the Royal Academy, Suffolk Street and the New Water-Colour Society between 1876 and 1884.

FOLKARD, Julia B. (Miss)
British, 19th century.
Active in London.
Painter. Genre scenes, figures.
Julia Folkard was a frequent exhibitor at the Royal Academy and Suffolk Street from 1872.

FOLKEMA, Anna
Dutch, 18th century.
Born 1695; died 1768, in Amsterdam.
Miniaturist, engraver.
Anna Folkema collaborated with her brother, the engraver Jakob Folkema, in Dokkum.

FOLKEMA, Fopje
Dutch, 18th century.
Active in Amsterdam.
Engraver (etching).
Fopje Folkema was perhaps the sister of Anna Folkema with whom she worked on the illustrations of *Il Callotto Resuscitato*.

FOLKEMA, J. C.
Dutch, 18th century.
Active in Amsterdam in 1716.
Draughtsman.
J. C. Folkema produced the drawings for *Il Callotto Resuscitato* which was engraved by Anna and Fopje Folkema.

FOLKEMA, Jakob
Dutch, 18th century.
Born 1692, in Dokkum; died 1767, in Amsterdam.
Draughtsman, engraver.
Jakob Folkema was a pupil of his father, the goldsmith Johann Jakobsz. Folkema, and then of Bernard Picard in Amsterdam. He was above all a fine mezzotint engraver.

FOLKEMA, Johannes Jakobsz.
Dutch, 17th century.
Engraver.
In 1680 two series of six plates by Johannes Jakobsz. Folkema were published at the house of C. Allard in Amsterdam. Another series of 12 plates are also known to be by him, entitled *Book of Leaf-work and Works of Gold Plate Invented by T. Le Juge*, which bears the signature *J. J. Folkema*.

FOLKEMA, R. Jakobsz.
Dutch, 15th century.
Engraver.
Jakobsz. Folkema was probably the brother of Johannes Folkema.
MUSEUMS AND GALLERIES:
LONDON (British Mus.): several plates.

FOLKERTS, Poppe
German, 19th - 20th century.
Born 9 April 1875, in Norderney.
Painter. Seascapes.
Folkerts was a student at the academies of fine art in Berlin and Königsberg (now Kaliningrad, Russia), also working in Düsseldorf, Kiel and Norderney. He painted subjects inspired by the coastlines of the North Sea, warships and scenes of rescue at sea. He featured at the Berlin Exhibition from 1889, the Dresden Exhibition from 1904, and at the Glaspalast in Munich in 1907.

Poppe Folkerts

FOLKESTAD, Berhard Dorotheus
Norwegian, 20th century.
Born 13 June 1879.
Painter. Still-lifes (flowers/fruit), interiors.
Folkestad spent a short time at the Laurits Tuxen and P.H. Kristian Zahrtmann School in Copenhagen. He received his training in particular in Norway. He travelled to Amsterdam and Paris. He exhibited in Oslo in 1907, at the Norwegian Exhibition in 1910, and in 1911 and 1914. He also exhibited in Brighton in 1914.
MUSEUMS AND GALLERIES:
OSLO (Nasjonalgal.).

FOLKMER, Johann Jacob
German, 18th century.
Active in Landeck, Silesia from 1712 to 1791.
Painter.

FOLLATON, Allart. See **FOLARTON Allart**

FOLLEN, Bishop Walter. See **BISHOP Walter Follen**

FOLLENWEIDER, Adolf
Swiss, 19th century.
Born 6 July 1823, in Basel; died 27 August 1895, in Basel.
Painter.
Adolf Follenweider was the son and student of the landscape painter Rudolf Follenweider. He also studied under the direction of H. Hess and Bernhardt and at the academy in Munich. He specialised in miniature watercolour portraits.

FOLLENWEIDER, Rudolf
Swiss, 18th - 19th century.
Born 29 December 1774, in Basel; died 3 November 1847, in Basel.
Painter, draughtsman, engraver. Portraits, urban landscapes, landscapes.
Rudolf Follenweider studied in Paris and in his home town, married Katharina Birmann, a member of the famous family of painters and dealers of objets d'art in Basel, and worked for a time as an art teacher in the school of industrial arts in Freiburg-im-Breisgau (Baden-Württemberg). Notable works of his include views of Switzerland, the cities of Heidelberg and Freiburg, and others. He wrote educational treatises on the art of drawing the landscape (published around 1819-1822), and painted some landscapes in the style of Peter Birmann.

FOLLER. See **FALLARO**

FOLLER, Antonio. See **FOLER**

FOLLET, Édouard
French, 19th century.
Born 19th century, in Sceaux.
Engraver.
Studied under Rouargue and Leroux and exhibited at the Paris Salon from 1859 to 1879.

FOLLEVILLE, Armand de
French, 17th century.
Sculptor.
Armand de Folleville appears from 1680 to 1688 on the list of sculptors in the king's household.

FOLLEVILLE, Léonce de
French, 19th century.
Active in Rouen.
Painter. Landscapes.
Exhibited at the Paris Salon from 1839 to 1842. Examples of his work include *Alpine View at Dusk, View at Lehon near Dinan,* and *View of Domfront (Orne).*

FOLLEVILLE, Marie Madeleine, wife of Delagardette, later widow
French, 18th century.
Active in Paris in 1782.
Painter (?), sculptor (?).

FOLLI, Sebastiano
Italian, 16th - 17th century.
Born c. 1568, in Siena; died 1621.
Painter, fresco artist. Religious subjects.
Sebastiano Folli, a pupil of Alessandro Casolani, established his reputation with several frescoes in churches in Siena, in particular the cupola of Santa Marta and various scenes from the *Life of St Sebastian* in the church dedicated to this saint which were painted in collaboration with Rutilio Manetti. Folli visited Rome and was commissioned to execute major works there by Cardinal de' Medici, later Leo XI.
AUCTION RECORDS:
MILAN, 5 Dec 1991, *Virgin and Child Enthroned, Surrounded by Saints* (oil on canvas, 32 x 24 ins / 81.5 x 61 cm) ITL 5,000,000. MILAN, 21 Nov 1996, *Mary Magdalene Listening to Christ's Sermon* (oil on canvas, 25 x 18 ins / 63.5 x 45.5 cm) ITL 9,320,000.

FOLLIA, Perino
Italian, 14th century.
Active in Vercelli at the end of the 14th century.
Painter.
Perino Follia was frequently commissioned to paint coats of arms for the Palazzo del Comune in Vercelli, and painted a *Blessed Virgin* for Chiavari.

FOLLIN, Bartolomeo, or Folin, Folino
Italian, 18th century.
Born 1730, in Venice; died in Warsaw.
Engraver (burin). Portraits.
Bartolomeo Follin studied under L. Zucchi.

FOLLIN DE LA FONTAINE, Octave de (Comte)
French, 19th century.
Born 19th century, in Le Lude (Sarthe).
Sculptor.
Exhibited a marble statue entitled *Drunkenness* at the 1880 Paris Salon, followed by *Woman Bathing* in 1882. Follin de la Fontaine was a member of the Société des Artistes Français as of 1885.

FOLLINI, Carlo
Italian, 19th - 20th century.
Born 24 August 1848, in Domodossola (Piedmont); died 1938, in Pegli (near Genoa, Liguria).
Painter. Figures, genre scenes, landscapes, landscapes with figures, urban landscapes, mountainscapes.
Carlo Follini was a pupil of Antonio Fontanesi at the Accademia Albertina in Turin, and also spent four years in Bologna. His work appeared in exhibitions in Turin, Florence, Venice and Rome.

He painted many different kinds of landscape, including views of mountains, Venice, the sea and the countryside.

Follini

MUSEUMS AND GALLERIES:
ROME: *Drinking Trough in the Alps* - TURIN (Gal. Civica d'Arte Moderna e Contemporanea): *Siesta.*
AUCTION RECORDS:
MILAN, 10 April 1969, *Landscape,* ITL 900,000. MILAN, 16 March 1972, *Farmyard,* ITL 1,200,000. MILAN, 28 March 1974, *Landscape,* ITL 2,400,000. MILAN, 28 Oct 1976, *Seashore with Figures* (oil on panel, 13 1/2 x 19 1/4 ins / 34 x 49 cm) ITL 1,100,000. MILAN, 5 Nov 1981, *Landscape* (watercolour, 9 x 13 1/2 ins / 23 x 34 cm) ITL 1,200,000. MILAN, 12 Dec 1983, *Road to Market* (oil on canvas, 34 1/2 x 55 ins / 87.5 x 139.5 cm) ITL 12,000,000. MILAN, 29 May 1986, *Landscape* (oil on canvas, 56 x 75 1/4 ins / 142 x 191 cm) ITL 13,000,000. MILAN, 23 March 1988, *Beach with Fishermen Drying Their Nets* (oil on panel, 10 1/4 x 17 1/4 ins / 26 x 44 cm) ITL 7,000,000. MILAN, 1 June 1988, *Rocks at Nervi* (oil on panel, 10 1/2 x 17 1/4 ins / 26.5 x 43.5 cm) ITL 6,000,000. MILAN, 14 March 1989, *Chapel in the Mountains* (oil on panel, 11 x 18 ins / 28 x 46 cm) ITL 10,000,000. MILAN, 19 Oct 1989, *Mountainscape with Figures* (1900, oil on panel, 11 x 17 1/4 ins / 27 x 44 cm) ITL 7,500,000. MILAN, 6 Dec 1989, *Autumn Landscape at Sunset* (oil on panel, 8 1/4 x 5 1/4 ins / 21 x 13.5 cm) ITL 4,500,000. MILAN, 8 March 1990, *Washerwomen on the Banks of the Po* (oil on canvas, 23 3/4 x 35 1/2 ins / 60.5 x 90 cm) ITL 24,000,000. MONACO, 21 April 1990, *At the Farm* (1898, oil on panel, 11 x 17 1/4 ins / 27 x 44 cm) FRF 44,400. MILAN, 5 Dec 1990, *Setting Sun* (oil on panel, 9 x 13 1/2 ins / 23 x 34.5 cm) ITL 11,000,000. MILAN, 7 Nov 1991, *The Piedmont Countryside* (oil on canvas, 23 1/4 x 36 1/4 ins / 59 x 92 cm) ITL 20,000,000. MILAN, 17 Dec 1992, *Pietrasanta Station* (1904, oil on panel, 10 3/4 x 17 1/4 ins / 27.5 x 44 cm) ITL 12,500,000; *Young Peasant Girl Reading* (oil on canvas, 21 1/2 x 13 1/2 ins / 54.5 x 34.5 cm) ITL 14,000,000. MILAN, 21 Dec 1993, *Country Landscape with Peasant Woman and Cows* (oil on canvas, 34 1/4 x 33 ins / 87 x 84 cm) ITL 22,425,000. MILAN, 22 March 1994, *Piedmont Countryside* (oil on canvas, 23 1/4 x 36 ins / 59 x 91.5 cm) ITL 20,125,000. ROME, 7 June 1995, *Landscape with Figures* (oil on canvas, 35 3/4 x 25 1/2 ins / 91 x 65 cm) ITL 15,525,000. MILAN, 26 March 1996, *Masked Ball* (oil on card, 10 x 7 3/4 ins / 24.5 x 19.5 cm) ITL 4,025,000. MILAN, 23 Oct 1996, *Viareggio Canal* (oil on canvas, 6 3/4 x 11 ins / 17 x 27 cm) ITL 13,980,000. LONDON, 21 Nov 1996, *Marina* (oil on canvas, 24 1/4 x 39 1/2 ins / 61.5 x 100.5 cm) GBP 4,140. ROME, 25 May 1999, *Landscape with Figures* (oil on panel, 7 x 11 ins / 18 x 28 cm) ITL 7,500,000. MILAN, 21 Dec 1999, *Old Canal at Viareggio* (oil on panel, 17 x 11 ins / 44 x 27 cm) ITL 18,000,000. TURIN, 4 Dec 2000, *Market Scene* (1892, oil on board, 10 x 17 ins / 26 x 44 cm) ITL 20,000,000. TURIN, 4 Dec 2000, *Coast in Liguria with View of Portofino* (1892, oil on board, 16 x 24 ins / 40 x 60 cm) ITL 27,000,000. VERCELLI, 24 Feb 2001, *Landscape with Figures* (oil on canvas, 18 x 24 ins / 46 x 60 cm) ITL 10,000,000. VERCELLI, 18 Nov 2001, *Afternoon at the Marina* (1910, oil on board, 10 x 17 ins / 26 x 44 cm) ITL 16,000,000. VERCELLI, 25 May 2002, *Countryside in Piedmonte* (oil on canvas, 26 x 35 ins / 66 x 90 cm) EUR 12,000. ROME, 27 May 2002, *Canal with Boats* (watercolour on card, 14 x 9 ins / 36 x 24 cm) EUR

2,800. TURIN, 26 June 2003, *Seascape* (1899, oil on board, 10 x 17 ins / 26 x 44 cm) EUR 10,000. VERCELLI, 1 Nov 2003, *Piedmontese Countryside* (oil on canvas, 26 x 35 ins / 65 x 90 cm) EUR 11,000. MILAN, 25 Feb 2004, *Landscape* (1880-1890, oil on canvas, 33 x 55 ins / 84 x 139 cm) EUR 18,000. TURIN, 22 March 2004, *Beach in Bordighera* (oil on canvas, 24 x 35 ins / 60 x 90 cm) EUR 13,000.

FOLLONG, Jules José
Belgian, 20th century.
Born in Moelenbech-St-Jean (Brabant).
Painter.

Follong exhibited a *Grisaille* at the Salon de la Nationale in 1930.

FOLLOT, Hélène
German, 20th century.
Born in Schleswig.
Active in France.
Painter. Landscapes with figures, flowers.

Hélène Follot came as a young woman to Paris where she married the interior decorator Paul Follot. She exhibited in Paris at the Salon des Artistes-Décorateurs, often embellishing with her decorative compositions the interiors shown by her husband.

FOLLOT, Paul
French, 20th century.
Born 17 July 1877, in Paris; died 1941, in Ste-Maxime.
Designer, architect.
Art Nouveau, Art Deco.

Paul Follot studied under Eugène Samuel Grasset, who was renowned as an interior decorator. He exhibited in Paris at the Salon de la Société Nationale des Beaux-Arts, Salon d'Automne and Salon des Artistes Décorateurs, in which he was very active.

He designed sets, furniture and rugs, including for his own home on Rue Schœlcher in Paris. Patterns for his tableware were purchased by English china manufacturers. He contributed to the classical approach to the decorative arts at the turn of the century.

FOLMER, Georges
French, 20th century.
Born 19 November 1895, in Nancy; died 1977, in Neumühl.
Painter, sculptor.
Groups: Vouloir, Réalités Nouvelles, Espace.

Georges Folmer studied at the École des Beaux-Arts in Nancy, then in Geneva. He later travelled to Algeria and Tunisia. After 1919, he lived in Paris, earning a living by doing odd jobs. He first exhibited in Nancy galleries. In 1926, he met Del Marle and exhibited with the group Vouloir (Will Power) in Lille, when Lempereur-Haut befriended him. From 1928 to 1934, he featured in Paris collective exhibitions: Salon d'Automne, Salon des Artistes Indépendants, Salon des Tuileries. In 1935 he exhibited at the 1st Salon d'Art Mural with Gleizes, Gorin and Kandinsky. In 1939 he was part of the group Frédo-Sidès that exhibited under the name of *Réalités Nouvelles*. After the war it became an association with its own salon, where Folmer regularly featured from 1947 to 1972, becoming its general secretary in 1956. In 1949 he became involved with the group Espace (Space), led by Del Marle, with Gorin, Beothy and Servanes, signing its manifesto in 1952. In 1960, he founded the group Mesure (Measure) with Gorin, exhibiting in France and Germany in 1964-1965. As a result of Espace and Mesure's research, he took a practical interest in an early collaboration between architects and artists at the planning stage. He retired to Alsace in 1968. Folmer had many solo shows in Paris and Strasbourg, notably in 1972 an *Hommage* at the Salon des Réalités Nouvelles. In 1985, Pontoise museum organised retrospective exhibitions of his paintings and sculptures, as did the Galerie Michèle Heyraud in Paris in 1988.

Initially a Cubist under Del Marle's guidance, as he got to know Herbin's work he became interested in abstraction. In 1942, he conceived a technique he called 'monotype', to which he returned in 1968. In 1950, he exhibited polychromed wood pieces. Thereafter, he produced an equal number of paintings and polychrome sculptures, his *structures spatiales*. In 1966, he turned his hand to Kinetic art and created a few *Roto-peintures* (*Roto-paintings*).

Between 1932 and 1943, he showed landscapes, portraits and still-lifes. His work is distinctive in its unconditional use of straight lines. This austere art is lightened by colour, toned down but often enlivened by a loud note. His abstract work, with colours set in aplats inside well-defined figures, achieves a high degree of purity through rigorously geometric form.

BIBLIOGRAPHY:
Lemoine, Serge/Mikaeloff, Yves, *Folmer*, exhibition catalogue, Yves Mikaeloff, Paris, 1990. Gelly-Saldias, Clara/Lemoine, Serge/Pétry, Claude, et al., *Folmer et l'abstraction géométrique*, exhibition catalogue, Musée des beaux-arts, Nancy, 1993 (with texts by the artist).

MUSEUMS AND GALLERIES:
NANTES (MBA): *J'ai troué dans le mur de toile une fenêtre* (*In the Canvas Wall, I Opened a Window*).

FOLO, Giovanni
Italian, 18th - 19th century.
Born 1764, in Bassano; died 1836, in Rome.
Engraver.

Giovanni Folo studied in his native Bassano under the painters Mengardi and Janotti before going on to study in Rome under Volpato. His early style is somewhat harsh, as exemplified to a degree in his engraving of Raphael's *Madonna de Candelabri*. That harshness is completely attenuated in his later engraving of Sassoferrato's *Mater Dolorosa*, in which he successfully captures the subtle shading of the original. His engraving of Annibale Carracci's *Christ Restoring the Widow's Son to Life* is rightly regarded as his masterpiece.

Folo was a member of the Accademia di San Luca in Rome. He was awarded a gold medal by the academy in Milan for his version of Nicolas Poussin's *Time Shielding Innocence against Evil and Jealousy*. Other examples of Folo's work include a *Last Supper* engraved after the Leonardo da Vinci original; Raphael's *Marriage of the Virgin*; Correggio's *Mystic Marriage of St Catherine*; Camuccini's *Death of Virginia*; and Michelangelo's *Christ on the Cross*.

FOLO, Pietro
Italian, 19th century.
Born 1790, in Rome; died 1867, in Rome.
Engraver (burin).

Pietro Folo studied under Valpoto, but he was also taught by his father, Giovanni Folo. He engraved effigies of saints.

FOLON, Jean-Michel
Belgian, 20th century.
Born 1 March 1934, in Brussels; died 20 October 2005, in Monaco.
Draughtsman, illustrator, engraver, watercolourist.

Folon was originally destined for architecture, started to study it but never practised, instead he very soon devoting himself to drawing. For a long time he was defined as a humorist draughtsman and he worked for various publications. Folon very early created a private world where an anonymous and undefined man, sometimes compared to the silent comic Buster Keaton, wanders in an absurd context, in general a ghost town. It was only later, about 1968, that his work took on a slightly pictorial aspect. In a short time his work was appeariang, on the front page of French and American weekly magazines, on the credits of television transmissions, and, during a period of keen interest, on the picture rails of art galleries. His style, which is often characterised by the use of subtle monochrome engravings, became familiar through the successful distribution of numerous screen prints. He has created designs for wallpapers, made animated films, and designed the poster for European Heritage Year in 1975. Denouncing the absurdities of contemporary life and of the human condition, Folon's work is often full of nostalgia. His watercolours are formally simple, reduced to a line drawing and two or three shaded colours. The anguish which they convey is the anguish of our time, where man, manipulated, channelled and guided by television, assumes his anonymity and alienation without realising it.

From 1970 the Musée des Arts Décoratifs in Paris organised a vast exhibition of a collection of his works. In 1972 he was invited to take part in the *Exposition 72/72* at the Grand-Palais in Paris. In 1965 he won the Grand Prix at the 3rd Triennale of Humour in Milan. In 1973 he was awarded the Grand Prix at the XII São Paulo Biennale. The Galerie Guy Pieters in St Paul-de-Vence staged a solo exhibition of his works in 2000 and 2002.

FOLON

FOLON

MUSEUMS AND GALLERIES:
MARSEILLES (Mus. Cantini).
AUCTION RECORDS:
ANTWERP, 28 April 1981, *The Dawn of Time* (1973, watercolour, 38 1/2 x 27 1/2 ins / 98 x 70 cm) BEF 70,000. NEW YORK, 11 May 1982, *Blue Man* (multiple, h. 73 1/2 ins / 186.5 cm) USD 1,100. MILAN, 4 April 1984, *Figure* (oil/tempera, 17 1/4 x 13 3/4 ins / 44 x 35 cm) ITL 3,300,000. PARIS, 11 Feb 1987, *Creating* (watercolour, 19 1/4 x 15 3/4 ins / 49 x 40 cm) FRF 48,000. PARIS, 16 Dec 1988, *Tomorrow* (1974, watercolour, 18 3/4 x 23 1/2 ins / 47.5 x 59.5 cm) FRF 8,500. PARIS, 3 March 1989, *The Observer* (1974, watercolour, 22 x 29 1/2 ins / 55 x 75 cm) FRF 23,000. PARIS, 26 Sept 1989, *Differences* (1981, 20 1/2 x 14 1/2 ins / 52 x 37 cm) FRF 16,000. PARIS, 8 Oct 1989, *Summer* (1984, watercolour/paper, 22 3/4 x 30 3/4 ins / 58 x 78 cm) FRF 60,000. PARIS, 15 Dec 1991, *Lunar Figure* (watercolour, 7 x 10 ins / 18 x 25.5 cm) FRF 11,000. AMSTERDAM, 19 May 1992, *A Dream* (1978, watercolour and collage/paper, 22 x 16 1/4 ins / 55 x 41 cm) NLG 3,450. LOKEREN, 15 May 1993, *Memory* (1973, watercolour, 17 x 22 ins / 43 x 55 cm) BEF 120,000. PARIS, 23 June 1993, *Man Alone* (watercolour, 15 1/4 x 20 1/2 ins / 39 x 52 cm) FRF 4,500. NEW YORK, 24 Feb 1994, *Morning Coffee* (1979, watercolour and pencil/paper, 13 x 10 ins / 33 x 25.4 cm) USD 2,875. PARIS, 29-30 June 1995, *The Snail* (watercolour, 26 3/4 x 40 1/4 ins / 68 x 102 cm) FRF 20,000. PARIS, 20 March 1998, *Brooklyn Bridge* (watercolour and collages, 23 3/4 x 18 ins / 60.5 x 45.5 cm) FRF 15,000. PARIS, 24 May 2000, *Birth or Non-existence* (watercolour and ink, 20 x 14 ins / 52 x 35 cm) FRF 25,000. PARIS, 19 Dec 2000, *Smoking* (1990, watercolour and collage, 22 x 15 ins / 56 x 38 cm) FRF 24,500. LOKEREN, 10 March 2001, *New York* (watercolour and collage, 24 x 18 ins / 60 x 45 cm) BEF 185,000. LONDON, 22 June 2001, *Man in the Town* (pen, ink and watercolour, 20 x 29 ins / 51 x 73 cm) GBP 1,700. LOKEREN, 9 March 2002, *Man Tree* (watercolour and ink, 25 x 17 ins / 63 x 44 cm) EUR 3,300. BRUSSELS, 26 Nov 2002, *Man and the Machine* (watercolour, 14 x 19 ins / 36 x 47 cm) EUR 2,800. BRUSSELS, 1 Dec 2003, *America* (1983, watercolour and gouache, 12 x 9 ins / 30 x 22 cm) EUR 3,800. BRUSSELS, 1 Dec 2003, *Bird and Hand* (bronze, h. 13 ins / 34 cm) EUR 7,000.

FOLQUES, Paul de
French, 16th century.
Active in Châlons-sur-Marne (Marne).
Painter.
A fresco in one of the chapels of the cathedral of Châlons-sur-Marne, showing *The Town of Châlons* has been attributed to Paul de Folques.

FOLSI, Alessandro and Giacomo. See **FOLFI**

FOLSON, E. A.
American, 19th - 20th century.
Born in the second half of the 19th century, in the USA.
Painter.
E. A. Folson exhibited in Paris at the Salon de la Société Nationale des Beaux-Arts in 1913.

FOLTMAR, Christian Ulrich
Danish, 18th century.
Active in Copenhagen.
Miniaturist, watercolourist.
Christian Ulrich Foltmar was court painter of miniatures. His brother was Christoffer Foltmar.

FOLTMAR, Christoffer
Danish, 18th century.
Born 17 October 1718, in Copenhagen; died 4 April 1759, in Copenhagen.
Painter, musician.
Christoffer Foltmar was a painter of miniatures and a drawing master to the Danish royal family.
MUSEUMS AND GALLERIES:
HILLERØD (Frederiksborg): portraits (miniatures).

FOLTYN, Frantisek
Czech, 20th century.
Born 1891, in Kralovske Stachy; died 1976.
Painter.
Groups: Cercle et Carré, Abstraction-Création.
After the arts college in Plzen, Frantisek Foltyn studied at the arts and crafts college in Prague in 1913. He then attended both the Académie Julian and the Académie de la Grande Chaumière in Paris. From 1921 onwards, he often exhibited in the cities in his native country. He started exhibiting in Paris in 1924. He became a member of the Cercle et Carré group in Paris in 1930 and the Abstraction-Création group in 1932.

Around 1922 he joined the Czech movement of poetic and social Realism for a time. Then, after he returned from Paris, he was influenced by Synthetic Cubism and around 1925, he painted in this style, combining elements from reality and abstract forms in his compositions. His style then resembled the Cubist style of Juan Gris, but he gave it an abstract tendency. He finally reached pure abstraction in the years he was involved in the Cercle et Carré and Abstraction-Création groups. After he returned to Czechoslovakia in 1934, he continued his work in the abstraction style for a few years. He gradually went back to the traditional landscape and still-life after 1940. In 1968 Foltyn was represented at the exhibition *Fifty years of Czechoslovak Painting from the Collections of the Galleries, 1918-1958* organised in the national museums to commemorate the 50th anniversary of the founding of the Republic.

Foltyn

Foltyn

FOLTYN

MUSEUMS AND GALLERIES:
BRNO (Moravská Gal.): collection of abstract works.
AUCTION RECORDS:
PARIS, 27 June 1983, *Spatial Composition* (1928, oil on canvas, 35¾ x 23¼ ins / 91 x 59 cm) FRF 8,000. PARIS, 29 Nov 1986, *Composition* (1924, oil on canvas, 25½ x 32 ins / 65 x 81 cm) FRF 7,500. LONDON, 5 April 1990, *Cubist Still-life* (1924, oil on canvas, 25¼ x 32 ins / 64 x 81 cm) GBP 60,500. LONDON, 4 Dec 1990, *Abstract Composition* (1926, oil on canvas, 36¼ x 23½ ins / 92 x 60 cm) GBP 19,800. PARIS, 9 Dec 1990, *Composition* (1927, oil on canvas, 36¼ x 25½ ins / 92 x 65 cm) FRF 90,000. PARIS, 16 April 1992, *Composition* (1927, oil on canvas, 28¾ x 36¼ ins / 73 x 92 cm) FRF 19,000. AMSTERDAM, 27-28 May 1993, *Cubist Still-life* (1926, oil on canvas, 25½ x 32 ins / 65 x 81 cm) NLG 23,000. PARIS, 16 June 1993, *Composition* (oil on canvas, 39¼ x 32 ins / 100 x 81 cm) FRF 52,000. LONDON, 19 March 1997, *Composition* (1934, oil on canvas, 24 x 19¾ ins / 61 x 50 cm) GBP 3,450. PARIS, 20 June 1997, *Untitled* (1927, oil on canvas, 32 x 25½ ins / 81 x 65 cm) FRF 58,000.

FOLTZ, Hans Christoph
German, 17th century.
Born to a family originally from Ulm (Baden-Württemberg).
Painter.
Hans Christoph Foltz was active in Nuremberg (Bavaria) from 1647 to 1683.

FOLTZ, Karoline
German, 19th century.
Born 1852, in Regensburg, Bavaria.
Painter. Landscapes.
Karoline Foltz was the daughter of Ludwig Foltz II.

FOLTZ, Lloyd Chester
American, 20th century.
Born 24 September 1897, in Brown (Kansas); died 1990, in Witchita (Kansas).
Painter, engraver.
Lloyd Chester Foltz studied at the Chicago Academy of Fine Arts and was a member of the Wichita Artists Guild and the Print Makers' Society of California.

FOLTZ, Ludwig I
German, 19th century.
Active in Bingen (Rhineland-Palatinate).
Painter, draughtsman, illustrator. Portraits.
Miniatures by Ludwig Foltz I include: *Portrait of a Young Girl, Portrait of the Linz Family*. The work *Costumes, Occupations and Feasts of the People of the Grand Duchy of Baden-Baden*, published by Herder in 1823, contained his illustrations.

FOLTZ, Ludwig II
German, 19th century.
Born 23 March 1809, in Bingen (Rhineland-Palatinate); died 10 November 1867, in Munich.
Architect, sculptor.
Ludwig Foltz II was the son of Ludwig I and studied under the sculptor Scholl in Mainz. He entered the academy in Munich in 1830, and joined the studio in Schwanthaler in 1832. At the latter he was part of a group of sculptors who created monumental statues for the throne room in the royal residence in Munich. His individual works include: a life-size statue of a *Mountain Hunter* erected in Berchtesgaden (Bavaria), small statuettes and ivory sculptures, humorous statues (only some 50 centimetres high) of a chess game in the Middle Ages, and monuments.

FOLTZ, Philipp von
German, 19th century.
Born 11 May 1805, in Bingen (Rhineland-Palatinate); died 5 August 1877, in Munich.
Painter. History painting, genre scenes.
Philipp von Foltz was the son and student of the artist Ludwig Foltz I. He then studied under Cornelius in Munich. From 1835 to 1838 he undertook a study trip in Italy. On his return to Germany, he became a professor, and later director of the academy in Munich. In 1855 he took part in the Exposition Universelle in Paris. Foltz painted many frescoes for the Munich Glyptothek, together with several important historical pictures for the Maximilianeum.
MUSEUMS AND GALLERIES:
COPENHAGEN (Thorvaldsens Mus.): *Blind Beggar at a Church Door in Rome; Plan for The Curse of the Singer* - DARMSTADT: *Scene on the Isar* - MUNICH (Glyptothek) - MUNICH (Maximilianeum): *Frederick Barbarossa Humbled Before Henry the Lion; The Age of Pericles* - MUNICH (Pinakothek): *The Curse of the Singer* - OBERSCHLEISSHEIM: *Entombment; Lorelei; Maternal Love; Pilgrimage in the Mountains; Otton von Wittelsbach in his Cell in Verona; Frauenlob the Troubadour* - VIENNA: *Götz von Berlichingen and the Monk.*
AUCTION RECORDS:
VIENNA, 12 Sept 1967, *Pilgrimage in the Bavarian Alps,* ATS 32,000. MUNICH, 8 Nov 2000, *Young Woman Leaning on a Tree* (oil on canvas, 48 x 38 ins / 121 x 97 cm) DEM 4,500. SWITZERLAND, 1 Dec 2000, *Sanger's Curse* (oil on canvas) CHF 5,000. VIENNA, 24 Nov 2003, *Fisherwoman on Italian Coast* (oil on canvas, 34 x 29 ins / 87 x 73 cm) EUR 6,500.

FOLTZER, Jean Baptiste
French, 19th century.
Born in Frenigen (Alsace).
Painter.
Exhibited watercolours at the Paris Salon: *Asparagus* in 1881, followed by *Alsace* in 1882.

FOLVESSE, Philbert
French, 18th century.
Active in Paris in 1766.
Painter, sculptor.

FOLWELL, Samuel
American, 18th - 19th century.
Born c. 1765; died 26 November 1813, in Philadelphia.
Engraver. Painted miniatures.
Among Samuel Folwell's known works are some engraved portraits in aquatint and stippling, including one of *George Washington*.
MUSEUMS AND GALLERIES:
NEW YORK (Historical Society): portrait (miniature).

FOLY, Adriaen. See **FOLIO A.**

FOMARI, A.
20th century.
Painter.
AUCTION RECORDS:
PARIS, 7 May 1943, *The Open Book* (1926) FRF 400.

FOMEZ, Antonio
Italian, 20th century.
Born 1938, in Naples.
Painter.
Antonio Fomez was a pupil at the school of fine arts in Naples. He staged his first exhibition in Milan in 1961, and has continued to show his works there, most memorably in 1971.
BIBLIOGRAPHY:
Prina, A., *Fomez*, monograph, Formaluce, Milan, 1971. Melloni, C., *Grafica Multipla di Fomez dal 1959 al 1965*, La Sfinge Malaspina, Ascoli Piceno, 1996.

FOMIN, Afanassi
Russian, 17th century.
Active in Moscow.
Painter.

Fomin produced,in about 1660, decorative paintings, icons and banners for the Tsar's Court and murals for Archangel Cathedral.

FOMIN, Ivan
Russian, 17th century.
Active in Moscow.
Painter.

A pupil of Ivan Besmin in Moscow, Fomin executed mural paintings at the Kremlin in 1686 and took part in producing an *Annunciation* and a *Crucifixion*, painted on canvas for the Tsar's Court.He decorated the appartments of Princess Tatiana Mikhailovna, with frescoes representing the *Legend of Melchizedek*

FOMIN, Ivan Aleksandrovich
Russian, 19th century.
Born 1840.
Painter, draughtsman. Genre scenes.

A student at the St Petersburg academy of fine arts, Fomin was one of the founders of the 'Old St Petersburg' Museum. He was also an architect and writer.

AUCTION RECORDS:
PARIS, 7 Nov 1988, *The Evening Party,* FRF 5,400.

FOMIN, Luca
Russian, 17th century.
Active in Moscow.
Painter.

Fomin Painted murals and icons in the Kremlin and in Moscow's Archangel Cathedral.

FOMIN, Nicolai Fadeevich
Russian, 18th century.
Active in St Petersburg.
Painter.

Fomin studied at the St Petersburg academy of fine arts, where he received several awards. W. Piadychev engraved after him in 1795, a portrait of *Count N.A. Tatishev*. Another known work by him is a miniature portrait of *M.V. Kachovsky*, which was exhibited in St Petersburg in 1905.

FOMIN, Terenti
Russian, 17th century.
Active in Moscow.
Painter.

Terenti Fomin is mentioned from 1660 to 1670 as an icon painter and for his mural paintings in Moscow's Archangel Cathedral and at the Kremlin.

FOMINE, Anatoli M.
Russian, 20th century.
Born 1925, in Aktubinsk, Kazakhstan.
Painter. Still-lifes.

Anatoli Fomine studied at the art studio in Dnepropetrovsk between 1950 and 1957. He became a member of the Association of Ukrainian Painters in 1970. In 1985 he took part in an exhibition of Ukrainian Painters in Poland and he had his own exhibition in Zaporojie in 1982.

AUCTION RECORDS:
PARIS, 5 April 1992, *Basket of Redcurrants* (oil on canvas, 25 x 32 3/4 ins / 63.5 x 83 cm) FRF 3,800. PARIS, 11 April 1992, *Zakorsk* (1965, oil on panel, 19 1/4 x 25 1/2 ins / 49 x 65 cm) FRF 5,000. PARIS, 5 Nov 1992, *Summer Evening* (oil on canvas, 25 1/4 x 46 3/4 ins / 64 x 119 cm) FRF 6,000. PARIS, 7 April 1993, *Flowers of the Fields* (1959, oil on canvas, 37 3/4 x 29 1/2 ins / 96 x 75 cm) FRF 8,000.

FOMINE, Piotr
Russian, 20th century.
Born 1919.
Painter. Urban landscapes, architectural views.

Piotr Fomine studied at the Ilya Repin Institute in St Petersburg and later taught there. A member of the Association of Artists of the USSR, he won the award 'Painter Emeritus'. He exhibited in Finland (1965 and 1969), Tokyo (1965), Madrid (1971), Paris and Cannes (1991).

MUSEUMS AND GALLERIES:
MOSCOW (State Tretyakov Gal.) - ST PETERSBURG (Gosudarstvennyj Russkij Muz.).

AUCTION RECORDS:
PARIS, 27 May 1992, *Nevski Prospect* (1979, oil on card, 16 1/4 x 19 ins / 41 x 48 cm) FRF 5,000. PARIS, 5 Oct 1992, *Volga Jetty* (1954, oil on canvas, 13 1/2 x 23 ins / 34.5 x 57.5 cm) FRF 5,200.

FOMISSON, Tony
New Zealander, 20th century.
Born 1939, in Christchurch.
Painter.

Tony Fomisson studied sculpture in Canterbury and also worked as a gallery assistant in 1962. In 1963, he was awarded a bursary that enabled him to travel in Europe. Fomisson paints harrowing subjects, often working from photographs. His painting is therefore realist but influenced by Surrealism and reveals, in particular, a psychoanalytical approach.

FOMSGAARD, Jes
Danish, 20th - 21st century.
Born 1948.
Painter, draughtsman, mixed media.

Examples of Jes Fomsgaard's work were submitted by the Copenhagen-based Asbaek Gallery to the 1995 FIAC (Foire Internationale d'Art Contemporain) in Paris. He works in a variety of techniques and frequently draws inspiration from anatomical drawings.

AUCTION RECORDS:
COPENHAGEN, 29 Nov 2000, *Table with Black Relief,* DKK 28,000. COPENHAGEN, 26 Nov 2003, *Building Fragment* (1988) DKK 4,200.

FONBONNE, Anne
French, 18th century.
Active in Paris.
Engraver.

Anne Fonbonne was the daughter of Quirijn Fonbonne.

FONBONNE, Quirijn
Dutch, 18th century.
Born c. 1680.
Also active in France.
Engraver.

Quirijn Fonbonne engraved genre subjects, views and history subjects. He worked in Amsterdam in about 1705 and in Paris from 1714 to 1734.

FONCE, Camille Arthur
French, 19th century.
Born 9 June 1867, in Briare (Loiret).
Engraver.

Studied under Lalanne, Allongé and Collier. A member of the Société des Artistes Français as of 1888, Fonce received an honourable mention in 1889 and was awarded a bronze in 1896, a silver in 1897 and a further silver at the Exposition Universelle of 1900. He was made a Chevalier of the Légion d'Honneur in 1906. Fonce's work found great favour with the British public and he engraved several major compositions for leading London publishers.

FONCIÈRES, Philippe de
French, 15th century.
Active in Paris.
Sculptor.

Between 1436 and 1440, working alongside Guillaume Jasse, Philippe de Foncières made the statues of *Charles VI* and *Charles VII* for the great portal of the Louvre.

FOND, Étienne Antoinette
French, 19th century.
Born during the second half of the 19th century, in Roanne (Loire).
Miniaturist.

FONDA, Enrico
Italian, 20th century.
Born 1892, in Fiume (now Rijeka, Croatia); died 1929, in Paris.
Painter. Portraits, landscapes.
Enrico Fonda exhibited in Paris, at the Salon d'Automne, of which he was a member.
Italian critics considered Cézanne to be Fonda's spiritual master.

FONDERIE, Henri
French, 19th century.
Born 1836, in The Hague.
Sculptor.
Studied in Paris under A. Toussaint and went on to sculpt pieces for the church in Lodelbach near Colmar. His marble statue entitled *Muse of Memory* was exhibited at the 1861 Paris Salon and was subsequently acquired by the king of Prussia. In subsequent salons, Fonderie exhibited bronze medallions and terracotta figures.

FONDESENDI, Hieronymus
Italian, 16th century.
Painter, engraver (wood).
Nagler makes reference to Hieronymus Fondesendi in Mechelen.

FONDET. See **RENOUST Jacques**

FONDEUR, Henry
French, 20th century.
Born in Paris.
Painter, watercolourist.
Henry Fondeur studied under Marcelle Fondeur-Cuby. He exhibited in Paris at the Salon des Artistes Indépendants and the Salon des Artistes Français, of which he was an associate member.

FONDEUR-CUBY, Marcelle
French, 20th century.
Born 2 March 1902, in Paris.
Painter.
Marcelle Fondeur-Cuby studied under Maguerite Martinet and Élisabeth Zabeth. She exhibited in Paris at the Salon des Artistes Français from 1928 to 1933.

FONDEVILA, Arturo. See **MAS Y FONDEVILA**

FONDIN, Evariste
French, 19th century.
Born in Paris.
Painter. Landscapes.
Made his Salon début in 1877; became a member of the Société des Artistes Français in 1883.
AUCTION RECORDS:
VERSAILLES, 5 March 1989, *Spring in the Village of Auvers-sur-Oise* (oil on canvas, 10 1/2 x 16 ins / 26.5 x 40.5 cm) FRF 7,000.

FONDULO, Giovanni Paolo
Italian, 16th century.
Active in Cremona.
Painter. History painting.
Giovanni Paolo Fondulo was a pupil of Antonio Campi.

FONDUTI, Agostino dei, called il Padovano
Italian, 15th century.
Born to a family originally from Crema.
Sculptor.
From 1483 onwards there are references to Agostino dei Fonduti in Milan and Piacenza, where he was commissioned to execute decorative works in various churches and palaces.

FONÈCHE, A.
French, 19th - 20th century.
Painter. Seascapes.
AUCTION RECORDS:
PARIS, 11 June 1942, *Seascape,* FRF 650. ORLÉANS, 14 Nov 1987, *Sailing Boats in a Storm* (oil on canvas, 22 1/2 x 40 1/4 ins / 57 x 102 cm) FRF 6,400. AMSTERDAM, 14 June 1994, *Brittany, Souvenir* (oil on canvas, 18 x 28 3/4 ins / 45.5 x 73 cm) NLG 1,840. LOKEREN, 8 Oct 1994, *Seascape with a Burning Ship* (oil on canvas, 17 3/4 x 28 3/4 ins / 45 x 73 cm) BEF 48,000. FONTAINEBLEAU, 2 Dec 2001, *Fishing Boat by a Village* (oil on canvas, 23 x 32 ins / 59 x 82 cm) FRF 34,000.

FONFREIDE, Victor
French, 20th century.
Born in Volvic.
Painter, sculptor, engraver.
Victor Fonfreide exhibited in Paris at the Salon of the Société Nationale des Beaux-Arts of which he was an associate member from 1922 to 1934.

FONFRIA-PEREDA, Malgorzata
Polish, 20th - 21st century.
Born 20 May 1947, in Gdansk.
Active in Germany.
Painter. Figures, nudes.
Malgorzata Fonfria-Pereda trained at the school of fine arts in Gdansk in 1972. In 1981 she published the thesis she had written for her doctorate exploring the Symbolism of Odilon Redon. The majority of her works depict the charms and eroticism of women. In 1974 her work featured in the exhibition of young Polish painters held in Sopot. In 1976 she won a prize at the eighth Festival of Modern Painting in Szczecin in Poland.
MUSEUMS AND GALLERIES:
BREMEN.

FONG LEE MAN
Chinese, 20th century.
Born 1913, in Guangdong; died 1988.
Painter. Landscapes, animals.
Fong Lee Man's family emigrated to Singapore when he was three years old. In 1932, he left for Indonesia and began his artistic career in an advertising agency in Jakarta. After 1940, he devoted himself entirely to painting. In 1949, he left for a scholarship to study in Holland for three years. On his return to Indonesia, his work was noticed and encouraged by President Soekarno.
AUCTION RECORDS:
AMSTERDAM, 23 April 1996, *Mount Wu-I in the Chosan Ling Mountains in Southern China* (1956, oil on card, 24 x 35 3/4 ins / 61 x 91 cm) NLG 68,440; *Cock and Hen* (1950, oil on card, 39 x 18 1/2 ins / 99 x 47 cm) NLG 165,200. SINGAPORE, 5 Oct 1996, *Goldfish* (oil on card, 48 x 96 ins / 122 x 244 cm) SGD 168,750. SINGAPORE, 29 March 1997, *Fighting Cock* (1946, oil on panel, 34 x 17 3/4 ins / 86.5 x 45 cm) SGD 63,250. SINGAPORE, 27 Sept 1997, *Satay Seller* (1958, oil on panel, 48 x 24 ins / 122 x 61 cm) SGD 57,500.

FONGUEUSE, Maurice
French, 20th century.
Born in Ry (Seine-Maritime).
Painter. Landscapes.
Maurice Fongueuse exhibited at the Salon des Indépendants from 1940 to 1943.

FONGUEUSE

FONGUS, Matthias. See **VANGUS**

FONIN, Aleksandr
Russian, 20th - 21st century.
Born 2 April 1948, in Moscow.
Active in Moscow.
Painter.

Aleksandr Fonin became a member of the Union of Soviet Artists. He showed his work in the following exhibitions, among others: *Christianity and Painting* in Moscow (1989); and with A. Djavid, A. Kitaikin and B. Otarov at the Galerie A. L. Expo in Paris (1990). He held solo exhibitions from 1978 onwards, notably in Tampere (1988) and Amsterdam and Hamburg (1989).

FONNER, F.
British, 20th century.
Painter. Genre scenes.

AUCTION RECORDS:
LONDON, 6 Dec 1926, *Group of Riders and Ladies,* GBP 58.

FONQUERGNE, Marcel
French, 20th century.
Born 23 September 1873, in Paris.
Sculptor.

Marcel Fonquergne studied under Falguière and Jacques Perrin. From 1923, he exhibited regularly at the Salon des Artistes Français, of which he was an associate member. He received an honourable mention in 1929, first medal in 1930 and silver medal in 1932.

FONQUERNIE, Jean-Paul
French, 20th century.
Born in Toulouse.
Sculptor.

Jean-Paul Fonquernie studied at the École des Beaux-Arts. He exhibited at the Paris Salon from 1922.

FONSAGA. See **FANSAGA**

FONSECA, Alfon de
Spanish, 15th - 16th century.
Painter.

Alfon de Fonseca had pupils, was married and is mentioned in various documents which show that he was in Seville from 1496 to 1511. He was possibly related to Alonso Perez de Fonseca.

FONSECA, Antonio Manuel da
Portuguese, 19th century.
Born 1796, in Lisbon; died 1890.
Painter. History painting, portraits.

Antonio Manuel da Fonseca was painter to the king in 1830; he was also appointed as a teacher at the fine arts academy in Lisbon. In 1852 he was made a corresponding member of the fine arts academy in Paris. Fonseca occupies a distinguished position in modern painting.

MUSEUMS AND GALLERIES:
BALTIMORE (Peabody Art Collection): *Old Cloister* (watercolour) - LISBON: *Transfiguration* (after Raphael).

FONSECA, Claudio
Brazilian, 20th - 21st century.
Born 1949, in Rio de Janeiro.
Painter.

Artistically speaking, Brazil did not really open up to the outside world until the 1980s. Various painters, Claudio Fonseca among them, soon took advantage of this rediscovered freedom. After being involved to a some extent in the coldness of the conceptual movement, he became totally absorbed in the materiality of painting. In technical terms, Fonseca's paintings are action based and make generous use of pigment, in keeping with Expressionism and Abstract Expressionism. They belong to both movements, being constructed on the plane of the canvas like abstract works, yet displaying an accumulation of high, mountainous peaks as if viewed from an aeroplane. With a pre-erosion sharpness these emerge from the magma with the violence of a world still being formed; for Fonseca this is a double metaphor expressing both the emergence of his own creative force and the explosion of a world opening up to existence. He has taken part in international group exhibitions, including the Nouvelle Biennale in Paris in 1985.

BIBLIOGRAPHY:
Pontual, Roberto, '*Claudio Fonseca*' in *Nouvelle Biennale de Paris,* exhibition catalogue, Electa, Le Moniteur, Paris, 1985.

FONSECA, Francisco de
Spanish, 17th century.
Painter.

Francisco de Fonseca is mentioned in Seville around 1631.

FONSECA, Gaspar Joaquin da
Spanish, 19th century.
Born c. 1796, in Viseu; died 1829, in Lisbon.
Sculptor (including wood).

Gaspar Joaquin da Fonseca studied under J.J. de Barros Laborao in Lisbon. In 1822 he was appointed to teach at the Lisbon academy.

FONSECA, Gaston de. See **SIMOES DE FONSECA**

FONSECA, Gonzalo
Uruguayan, 20th century.
Born 1922, in Montevideo; died 1997, in Italy.
Active in the USA.
Sculptor.
Atelier Torres García.

As a child Gonzalo Fonseca frequently visited Europe with his family. From 1939 to 1941 he studied architecture at the University of the Uruguayan Republic and from 1942 to 1949 studied under Joaquín Torres García in Montevideo. After 1950 he returned to live in Uruguay. From 1952 to 1957 he lived in Paris. Following a visit to New York in 1958, his work became known in the USA. Fonseca often divided his time between New York and Italy.

In the tradition of Torres García, Fonseca, together with other Uruguayan painters, including Julio Alpuy and José Gurvich, constituted a veritable school of art which in turn attracted new followers. In 1945 a visit to Peru and Bolivia awakened his interest in pre-Columbian history and art. His sculptures display geometric forms but are varied and executed in a variety of materials including wood, granite and marble, often combined in playful constructions. This proclivity towards the assemblage of forms and materials is also seen in creations Fonseca incorporated into architecture, notably in 1962 with monumental projects for the New School of Social Research in New York, in 1970 for the Alza Laboratory in Palo Alto, California, and also at Reston in Virginia.

He took part in a number of group exhibitions: in 1933 the *Latin-American Artists of the 20th century* exhibition at the Museum of Modern Art in New York and in 2001, *Abstraction: The Amerindian Paradigm* at the Julio González centre at the Valencia institute of modern art. In 1962 he held his first solo exhibition as part of the *Portland Art Exhibit.* In 1971, he mounted a second solo exhibition at the Jewish Museum of New York. In 1985, he was guest of honour at the Volkesund sculpture exhibition in Denmark. In 2003, the Julio González centre at the Valencia institute of modern art dedicated a retrospective to Fonseca and his son Caio.

BIBLIOGRAPHY:
Katz, Karl (ed.), *Gonzalo Fonseca: Recent Works,* exhibition catalogue, The Jewish Museum, New York, 1971. Kalenberg, A., *Uruguay: Gonzalo Fonseca,* exhibition catalogue, Museo Nacional de Artes Plásticas, Montevideo, 1990. Manley, M.

V., '*Gonzalo Fonseca*' in *Latin American Art*, vol 2 no 2, 1990. *Gonzalo Fonseca: XLIV Bienale di Venezia*, Montevideo, 1990. *Gonzalo Fonseca*, exhibition catalogue, Fundación César Manrique, Teguise, 1999. Paternosto, César/Frame, Mary/Lippard, Lucy R., et al., *Abstracción: El paradigma amerindio*, exhibition catalogue, Instituto Valenciano de Arte Moderno (IVAM), Valencia, 2001.

Museums and Galleries:

Austin (Jack S. Blanton MA, University of Texas): *Graneros III* (*Granaries III*) (1971-1975) - Caracas (MBA) - New York (Brooklyn Mus.).

Auction records:

Montevideo, 17 Nov 1982, *Dyke* (oil on canvas, 31 1/2 x 23 1/2 ins / 80 x 60 cm) UYU 40,000. Montevideo, 16 May 1984, *View of a Port* (1944, oil on card, 15 3/4 x 22 3/4 ins / 40 x 58 cm) UYU 170,000. Montevideo, 14 Aug 1986, *The By-road* (1949, oil on card, 15 x 19 3/4 ins / 38 x 50 cm) UYU 170,000. New York, 17 May 1989, *Concinnitas* (1970, marble, h. 34 1/2 ins / 87.5 cm) USD 47,300. New York, 20-21 Nov 1990, *Construction* (1971, pink marble, 20 3/4 x 24 1/2 x 5 ins / 53 x 62 x 13 cm) USD 55,000. New York, 15-16 May 1991, *Nivea Saturna Vacca* (1982, block of stone sawn with various objects, 11 x 12x12 ins / 28 x 30.5x30.5 cm) USD 30,800. New York, 18-19 May 1993, *Colombarium No. 1* (1966, construction of wood and objets, h. 86 ins / 218.4 cm) USD 107,000. New York, 22-23 Nov 1993, *Constructivist Furniture* (1950, painted panel incrusted with mother of pearl, 71 x 35 1/2 x 12 ins / 180.3 x 90 x 30.2 cm) USD 68,500. New York, 23-24 Nov 1993, *Untitled* (1971, pink marble, h. 22 1/2 ins / 57 cm, w. 26 ins/66 cm, depth 7 1/4 ins/18.5 cm) USD 79,500. New York, 18 May 1995, *The Tower of the Winds, Homage to Andronicus* (painted and engraved stone with wood and leather fasteners, 17 1/4 x 13 3/4 x 9 ins / 43.7 x 34.9 x 22.9 cm) USD 46,000. New York, 29-30 May 1997, *Nivea Saturna Vacca* (1982, painted and sculpted limestone with limestone, wood and leather accessories, 11 1/2 x 11 3/4 x 11 ins / 28.9 x 29.8 x 27.9 cm) USD 43,125. New York, 24-25 Nov 1997, *High Place I* (white Carrara marble, 19 3/4 x 29 x 22 1/2 ins / 50.2 x 72.8 x 57 cm) USD 63,000. Madrid, 22 Nov 1999, *Construction with Objects* (oil on panel, 22 x 21 ins / 55 x 54 cm) ESP 1,900,000. New York, 22 Nov 1999, *Construction* (1971, pink granite, 25 x 21x6 ins / 63 x 53x15 cm) USD 55,000. Montevideo, 5 Jan 2000, *Constructivist Couple in Black, Red and White* (oil on board, 12 x 9 ins / 31 x 24 cm) USD 9,000. Montevideo, 20 June 2000, *Old Town Landscape* (oil on canvas, 29 x 37 ins / 74 x 95 cm) USD 30,000. Los Angeles, 6 June 2001, *Stela with Baetylos* (1973-1976, Brazilian marble, 24 x 12x8 ins / 60 x 30x20 cm) USD 42,000. New York, 20 Nov 2001, *Tower* (c. 1974, white marble, 19 x 9x6 ins / 48 x 23x15 cm) USD 40,000. Montevideo, 30 July 2002, *Mediterranean Port* (oil on canvas, 20 x 24 ins / 50 x 60 cm) USD 10,000. Caracas, 23 Nov 2002, *Still-life* (oil on panel, 17 x 14 ins / 44 x 35 cm) USD 8,000. Montevideo, 3 June 2003, *Landscape seen from Bovedas* (1947, oil on canvas, 20 x 24 ins / 50 x 60 cm) USD 11,000. Montevideo, 25 Nov 2003, *Steam Boat* (1948, oil on card, 18 x 22 ins / 46 x 55 cm) USD 10,000. Montevideo, 5 Jan 2004, *Cart with Figures* (oil on card, 13 x 17 ins / 33 x 43 cm) USD 4,700. New York, 26 May 2004, *Composition with Figures* (1953, oil on board, 30 x 41 ins / 75 x 105 cm) USD 30,000.

FONSECA, Joao Thomaz da

Spanish, 18th - 19th century.
Born 1754, in Lisbon; died 1835.
Painter, illustrator.

Joao Thomaz da Fonseca was a pupil of Joao Grossi and J.M. da Rocha and father of the celebrated artist Antonio Manuel da Fonseca. He did mural paintings and decorative works of various kinds in the churches and palaces of Lisbon, and also illustrated prayer books.

FONSECA, José de

Spanish, 19th century.
Engraver.

José de Fonseca made engravings to illustrate a *Universal History* printed in Lisbon, with various portraits including *Portrait of Tsar Peter III*. He also engraved illustrations for the *Military Treatise* by Rojo de Flores.

FONSECA, Martinho Gomes da

Portuguese, 20th century.
Born 31 January 1890, in Lisbon; died 1972.
Painter, draughtsman. Figures, portraits. Wall decorations.

Martinho Gomes da Fonseca studied at the Lisbon fine arts academy and presented a painting of *Leda and the Swan* for his final examination. He became a teacher in vocational schools, taught drawing at the National Fine Arts Society and later became the Society's director. He made numerous trips to France and Spain. He took part in many collective exhibitions in Portugal and abroad and received a number of awards.

He executed a *Portrait of President Bernardino Machado* for the Belem Palace. He also executed paintings for the Portuguese pavilion at the Hispano-American Exhibition in Seville in 1929 and the decoration of the State Deposit Bank in Oporto. Fonseca was a figure painter and was influenced by Impressionism through the works of Degas and Renoir.

Bibliography:

Arnáiz, José Manuel/López Jiménez, Javier/Merchán Díaz, Manuel (ed.), *Cien años de pintura en Espana y Portugal (1830-1930)*, Antiqvaria, Madrid, 1988 (One Hundred Years of Painting in Spain and Portugal (1830-1930)).

Museums and Galleries:

Coimbra - Évora - Lisbon - Viseu.

FONSECA, Reynaldo, or Reynaldo Fonseca

Brazilian, 20th century.
Born 1925, in Recife.
Painter. Figure compositions.

Reynaldo Fonseca studied with Candido Portinari in Rio de Janeiro. In 1948 he spent a year in Europe and on his return to Rio began working with Henrique Oswald. In 1952 he had his first exhibition at Recife and taught at the school of fine arts at the Federal University of Pernambuco. In 1969 he moved to Rio where he continued to work. In 1970 he was a member of the jury of the national modern art exhibition, at which he also regularly exhibited. His paintings reveal the influence of Portinari: they are of ordinary people at their domestic tasks but he endows these people with hieratic, fixed attitudes and expressions as if they were posing for a photograph. Nevertheless, there are many elements of Fonseca's style that are personal to him: the painstaking accuracy of his realism with its careful, honest rendering of figures and other compositional elements; the geometricisation of the forms, somewhat reminiscent of 17th-century European Caravaggism, and above all his determination to limit himself to a sober palette of grey ochres and greyish browns as if internalising his message.

Auction records:

São Paulo, 11 Aug 1981, *Os Sentidos* (*The Senses*) (1969, oil on canvas, 28 1/4 x 20 3/4 ins / 72 x 53 cm) BRL 290,000. New York, 31 May 1984, *Supper* (1978, oil on canvas, 32 x 39 1/4 ins / 81 x 100 cm) USD 8,500. New York, 25 Nov 1992, *Young Girl Astride a Dog with a Woman* (1984, oil on canvas, 39 1/4 x 31 3/4 ins / 100 x 80.5 cm) USD 12,100. New York, 18 May 1993, *Meal, Mother and Daughter* (1978, oil on canvas, 32 x 39 1/2 ins / 81.3 x 100.4 cm) USD 13,800. New York, 18-19 May 1993, *Mother and Children Eating* (1976, oil on canvas, 29 x 39 1/2 ins / 73.7 x 100.6 cm) USD 13,800. New York, 22-23 Nov 1993, *The Red Book* (1985, oil on canvas, 31 3/4 x 39 1/4 ins / 80.6 x 99.4 cm) USD 6,900. New York, 23-24 Nov 1993, *Little*

Girl with Cat (1985, oil on canvas, 39 1/2 x 36 ins / 100.4 x 91.4 cm) USD 9,200. RIO DE JANEIRO, 1 April 2003, *Girl* (1972, oil on canvas, 18 x 15 ins / 46 x 38 cm) BRL 9,140. RIO DE JANEIRO, 17 June 2003, *Children* (1971, oil on canvas, 20 x 29 ins / 50 x 73 cm) BRL 25,730.

FONSECA Y FIGUEROA, Juan de
Spanish, 17th century.
Died 1627.
Painter.

Juan de Fonseca y Figueroa was canon and chancellor of Seville Cathedral and grand chamberlain at the court of Madrid. He produced some very fine portraits but was known mainly as a patron of artists, including Velázquez.

BIBLIOGRAPHY:
Muller, Joseph-Emile, *Velázquez*, Thames and Hudson, London, 1976.

FONSÈQUE, Maxime
French, 20th century.
Born in Bordeaux.
Binder.

Maxime Fonsèque exhibited in Paris at the Salon des Artistes Indépendants in 1931 and 1932 and at the Salon des Artistes Français from 1925 to 1933, receiving an honourable mention in 1932.

FONSON, Albert François
Flemish, 17th century.
Active in Mons.
Sculptor.
Flemish School.

In 1686 Albert François Fonson executed statues of *St Peter* and *St Paul* for the portal of the church of Ste-Élisabeth in Mons. In 1712 he produced an altar with statues of *St Roch, St Fabian* and *St Sebastian* for the weavers' guild. He also worked on the cathedral of Ste-Waudru.

FONSON, Charles Auguste
Flemish, 18th century.
Born 15 April 1706; died 13 March 1788.
Active in Mons.
Sculptor.
Flemish School.

Charles Auguste Fonson executed the statues of the apostles *James, Philip and John* in the cathedral of Ste-Waudru. He also executed a number of sculptures for the high altar and choir stalls of the church of St-Nicolas.

FONT, Constantin
French, 20th century.
Born 11 January 1890, in Auch (Gers).
Painter, engraver. Nudes, genre scenes, landscapes.

Constantin Font studied under Fernand Cormon. He won the Prix de Rome in 1921 when he was already exhibiting at the Salon des Artistes Français, gaining an honourable mention in 1910, silver medal in 1921, gold in 1922. He was made a Chevalier of the Légion d'Honneur in 1935.

AUCTION RECORDS:
PARIS, 17-18 Nov 1943, *The Garonne Riverbanks*, FRF 280. NEW YORK, 25 Oct 1984, *Odalisque* (oil on canvas, 57 x 112 ins / 144.8 x 284.5 cm) USD 20,000. LONDON, 10 July 1985, *Harem Interior* (oil on canvas, 38 1/4 x 51 1/4 ins / 97 x 130 cm) FRF 25,000. RHEIMS, 24 April 1988, *View of a Venice Canal* (oil on canvas, 19 3/4 x 39 1/4 ins / 50 x 100 cm) FRF 4,800. SCEAUX, 19 May 1988, *Nude Dozing* (oil on canvas, 21 1/4 x 25 1/2 ins / 54 x 65 cm) FRF 12,000. PARIS, 27 Oct 1988, *Reading* (oil on canvas, 19 3/4 x 24 ins / 50 x 61 cm) FRF 15,000. PARIS, 14 Dec 1988, *Woman at her Sewing* (1921, oil on canvas, 19 3/4 x 24 ins / 50 x 61 cm) FRF 13,500. VERSAILLES, 18 Dec 1988, *Nude Reclining* (oil on panel, 19 3/4 x 39 1/4 ins / 50 x 99.5 cm) FRF 10,500. NEW YORK, 23 Feb 1989, *Pastoral* (1919, oil on canvas, 57 x 44 1/2 ins / 144.8 x 113 cm) USD 6,050. PARIS, 3 March 1989, *Nude Reclining* (oil on canvas, 19 3/4 x 39 1/4 ins / 50 x 100 cm) FRF 12,000. PARIS, 4 April 1989, *Bullfight* (oil on canvas, 19 3/4 x 24 ins / 50 x 61 cm) FRF 8,000. PARIS, 19 Jan 1990, *Mediterranean Fishing Port* (oil on canvas, 18 1/4 x 22 ins / 46.5 x 55 cm) FRF 6,000. PARIS, 27 March 1990, *Fishing Port* (oil on canvas, 24 1/2 x 19 3/4 ins / 62 x 50 cm) FRF 10,000. NEW YORK, 20 Jan 1993, *Allegory of Youth* (1919, oil on canvas, 45 1/2 x 57 1/2 ins / 115.6 x 146.1 cm) USD 3,450. PARIS, 5 Dec 2003, *Harbour View at Rapallo* (oil on canvas, 20 x 24 ins / 50 x 61 cm) EUR 1,500.

FONT, Francisco
Spanish, 19th century.
Born in Barcelona.
Sculptor.

Francisco Font was a pupil of Domingo Talarn. He first exhibited at the exhibition of the national fine arts society of Madrid in 1856.

FONT Y BARRERA, Antonio
Spanish, 18th century.
Born 3 March 1778, in Cádiz; died 1800, in Cádiz.
Painter.

Antonio Font y Barrera studied at the school of fine arts in Cádiz and was awarded a bursary to complete his training in Rome. He is known for his portraits, including a number of self-portraits.

FONT Y VIDAL, Juan
Spanish, 19th century.
Born in the 19th century, in Port Mahon, Minorca.
Painter. Battles, harbour scenes.

Juan Font y Vidal painted views of the harbour at Port Mahon. He exhibited two battle paintings at the Madrid exhibition of 1864.

MUSEUMS AND GALLERIES:
MADRID (Mus. de Ingenieros): *Harbour of Port Mahon* (four views).

FONTAINAS, Andrée
French, 20th century.
Born in Paris.
Painter. Portraits, landscapes, flowers.

Andrée Fontainas exhibited at the Salon d'Automne from 1921 and at the Salon des Tuileries from 1924 to 1931.

Besides her usual subjects, she produced a *Judgement of Paris*.

FONTAINAS, Marguerite
French, 20th century.
Born in Paris.
Painter. Landscapes, flowers.

Marguerite Fontainas exhibited at the Salon d'Automne from 1930.

FONTAINE
French, 15th century.
Sculptor (wood).

Fontaine was one of the sculptors working under Philippot Viart on the choir stalls of Rouen Cathedral in 1467.

FONTAINE
French, 18th century.
Painter.

J. F. Feradiny engraved six plates of landscapes and seascapes after Fontaine, and De Fehrt engraved two views of Minorca in the Balearic Islands after him.

FONTAINE
French, 18th century.
Painter (?), draughtsman (?). Portraits.

Fontaine painted portraits of *Élisabeth de France* and her sister *Marie-Adélaïde*, engraved by P. A. Le Beau, and *Admiral P. A. de Suffren*, engraved by S. Goulet.

FONTAINE
French, 18th century.
Sculptor. Historical portraits. Medallions.
Fontaine was a student at the Académie Royale in Paris in 1747.
MUSEUMS AND GALLERIES:
ORLÉANS: *Portrait of Marie-Antoinette* (bronze, medallion).

FONTAINE (Mlle)
French, 19th century.
Painter.
She exhibited a female portrait at the 1819 Paris Salon and her *Scene from the Romance of Monsieur Desprez* and her *Marriage of Angelica and Medoro* at the Salon of 1822.

FONTAINE. See also **LAFONTAINE** and **DEFONTAINE**

FONTAINE, A. Victor
French, 19th century.
Born in St-Amour (Jura).
Sculptor. Statues.
Pupil of Prost; exhibited at the Paris Salon from 1867 to 1870, notably some medallions and a marble statue entitled *Regrets*.

FONTAINE, Alexandre Victor
French, 19th century.
Born 22 October 1815, in Paris.
Painter. Genre scenes.
Enrolled on 2 April 1836 at the École des Beaux-Arts, where he studied under Leroux and Guillemin. He exhibited work at the Salon on various occasions between 1844 and 1855. Fontaine is best remembered for his *Callot's Childhood, Down-Payment, Storm* and *Young Girls in the Woods*.
MUSEUMS AND GALLERIES:
CHANTILLY: *Bathers*.
AUCTION RECORDS:
LONDON, 6 Feb 1909, *Exhausted*, GBP 11.

FONTAINE, André
French, 19th century.
Born 21 January 1802, in Lyons.
Painter.
Studied under Révoil at the École des Beaux-Arts in Lyons and went on to exhibit in Lyons from 1831 to 1842-43, chiefly portraits, genre subjects and landscapes. An 1840 etched portrait of the librarian *J.-B. Poupar* is signed *Fontaine*.

FONTAINE, Andrée (Mlle)
French, 20th century.
Born in Lens.
Painter.
Andrée Fontaine studied under Alphonse and Stephane-Georges Debaene and exhibited figures at the Salon des Artistes Français in 1932 and 1933.

FONTAINE, Benoît
French, 19th century.
Born 1 November 1806, in Lyons; died August 1887, in Lyons.
Engraver.
Son of a Lyons librarian; studied theory and practice at the École des Beaux-Arts in that city in 1833 and went on to exhibit drawings and etchings of Lyons and the surrounding region from 1836 to 1840. A collection of Fontaine's engravings sold in Lyons between February and May 1888 totalled some 116 items, among them some of his best work - *Old Pont at Pierre* (1837), *View of the Pierre Scize Gardens, Waterfall at Glandieu, Château of Pierre Scize* and *Aquaducts at Ecully*.

FONTAINE, Charles
French, 19th century.
Painter.
AUCTION RECORDS:
NEW YORK, 3 Jan 1906, *Turning Point*, USD 375.

FONTAINE, Christian
Austrian, 18th century.
Born to a family originally from Zengg (now Senj, Croatia); died 12 December 1772, in Vienna.
Miniaturist.
Fontaine entered the academy in Vienna on 1 June 1766 to study engraving.

FONTAINE, E.
French, 17th century.
Active c. 1681.
Engraver (wood).
E. Fontaine engraved religious subjects.

FONTAINE, Edme Adolphe
French, 19th century.
Born 8 May 1814, in Noisy-le-Grand (Seine-St-Denis).
Painter, watercolourist. Military subjects, military portraits.
Enrolled at the École des Beaux-Arts on 7 April 1838 and studied under L. Cogniet; was awarded a bronze medal in 1852. His work was exhibited at salons between 1845 and 1878. Examples include *Ibrahim Pasha at the St-Cyr Military Academy, 22 May 1846; Jocelyn; Zouaves; Souvenir; Portrait of L. Mieroslawski; Supreme Court of Justice, Versailles; Portrait of General Alexandre; Letter; Mass at Pont-l'Abbé; Souvenir of Satory Encampment; Caesar's Fortune;* and *Portrait of a General: Baron Ameil*.
MUSEUMS AND GALLERIES:
TOUL: *Portrait of Captain Poirot of the 52nd* - VERSAILLES: *Attack on the Selinghins Stronghold; Portrait of the Duke of Massena*.

FONTAINE, Éloy
French, 17th century.
Painter.
Éloy Fontaine is only known to have painted a portrait of *Bishop J. L. de la Bourdonnaye* engraved by E. Gantrel and P. Drevet. He may be identical to the wood engraver E. Fontaine.

FONTAINE, Emmanuel
French, 19th - 20th century.
Born 8 December 1856, in Abbeville; died 21 September 1935, in Commercy (Meuse).
Sculptor. Busts.
Emmanuel Fontaine studied under Jouffroy and featured at the Paris Salon from 1877 to 1882, showing medallions and a few busts. An honourable mention in 1887, he was awarded numerous distinctions in 1893, 1896, 1900, including a first-class medal in 1904. He was made a Chevalier of the Légion d'Honneur in 1910. He was rated hors concours in 1922. Thematic group exhibitions include *Vénus et Caïn. Figures de la Préhistoire 1830-1930* (*Venus and Cain. Prehistoric Figures 1830-1930*), an exhibition tracing the emergence of archaeology as a scientific discipline and its artistic impact, Musée d'Aquitaine, Bordeaux, 2003.
BIBLIOGRAPHY:
Lafont-Couturier, Hélène/Dagen, Philippe/Loizeau, Ségolène, *Vénus et Caïn. Figures de la préhistoire 1830-1930*, exhibition catalogue, Musée d'Aquitaine, Bordeaux, 2003.
MUSEUMS AND GALLERIES:
ABBEVILLE: *Shipwrecked* - AMIENS: *Boucher de Crève-cœur de Perthes* - COMPIÈGNE: *A l'eau, Porthos!* - GRAY: *Fascination* - PARIS (Mus. du Petit Palais): *First Shiver*.
AUCTION RECORDS:
LOKEREN, 18 Oct 1986, *Into the River* (1910, dark-brown patinated bronze, h. 20 ins / 51 cm) BEF 90,000.

FONTAINE, François
French, 20th century.

Born 11 June 1938, in Boulogne-Billancourt.
Painter.
François Fontaine studied at the Académie de la Grande Chaumière in Paris. He exhibited at the Salon d'Automne, of which he was made an associate member, in 1968.

FONTAINE, Gabriel
Swiss, 18th century.
Born 9 May 1696, in Geneva; died 2 January 1767.
Painter.
Fontaine studied under J. Mussard. He may be the enamel painter of the same name who worked in Paris around 1727.

FONTAINE, Gaston
French, 20th century.
Born in Tours.
Painter.
Gaston Fontaine exhibited at the Salon des Indépendants from 1931 to 1932.

FONTAINE, Geneviève
French, 18th century.
Active in Paris in 1767.
Painter.

FONTAINE, Gustave Adolphe
Belgian, 20th century.
Born 1877, in Brussels; died 1952.
Sculptor. Portraits, busts.
Fontaine exhibited from 1921 at the Salon d'Automne in Paris, chiefly with busts and masks of women and children.
AUCTION RECORDS:
LOKEREN, 16 Feb 1985, *Female Bust* (lost-wax, bronze, h. 19 1/4 ins / 49 cm) BEF 28,000. AMSTERDAM, 2-3 June 1997, *Woman* (bronze, h. 11 ins / 27 cm) NLG 3,540.

FONTAINE, Hansequin
French, 15th century.
Active in Lille c. 1453.
Painter.

FONTAINE, Henri
French, 20th century.
Born in Lyons.
Painter, draughtsman.
Henri Fontaine exhibited at the Salon de la Société Nationale des Beaux-Arts from 1922 to 1935.

FONTAINE, Henriette Marie
French, 20th century.
Born in Bordeaux.
Sculptor. Groups.
Henriette Fontaine studied under Félix Févola. From 1930 she exhibited at the Salon des Artistes Français, of which she was an associate member. She received a mention in 1933.

FONTAINE, Jacques
French, 18th century.
Born 1735.
Painter (porcelain), decorative artist. Flowers. Ornaments, miniatures.
Jacques Fontaine worked from 1752 to 1793 at the Sèvres porcelain factory. The Musée de Céramique de Sèvres, the Wallace Collection and Buckingham Palace have examples of his work.

FONTAINE, Jacques de
Flemish, 17th century.
Painter.
Flemish School.
Jacques de Fontaine qualified as a master in the guild in Antwerp in 1648-1649.

FONTAINE, Jacques François José or Joseph. See **SWEBACH**

FONTAINE, Jacques Valentine
French, 19th century.
Active c. 1840.
Engraver.
Worked in Paris for the Gobelin factory; known to have published two compilations of engravings.

FONTAINE, Jean
Dutch, 17th century.
Died 1669.
Painter. Seascapes.

FONTAINE, Jean
Swiss, 17th - 18th century.
Born 22 December 1668, in Geneva; died 12 September 1716, in Geneva.
Enameller.
A student of Thomas Fontaine, Jean Fontaine went into partnership with him in 1695.

FONTAINE, Jean
French, 18th century.
Active in Paris in 1746.
Painter, sculptor.

FONTAINE, Jean Adolphe
French, 20th century.
Sculptor.
Jean Fontaine worked in Paris. He exhibited at the Salon des Artistes Français, of which he was an associate member, from 1901.

FONTAINE, Jean Joseph
French, 19th century.
Born 1802.
Painter (porcelain), watercolourist.
Exhibited a portrait of a man in 1835 and a still life with flowers in 1836.

FONTAINE, Jean Mathias
French, 19th century.
Born 1791, in Paris; died 10 October 1853, in Paris.
Engraver.
A salon exhibitor from 1827 to 1843, Fontaine was the first engraver in France to copy the 'English' method of engraving on steel plates.

FONTAINE, Jean Michel Denis La. See **LA FONTAINE**

FONTAINE, Jehan
Flemish School, 15th century.
Active in Tournai.
Sculptor.
Jehan Fontaine is mentioned in 1482 and 1487.

FONTAINE, Jenny Maria
French, 19th - 20th century.
Born 9 May 1862, in Arras; died 1938.
Painter, pastellist, draughtswoman. Portraits, genre scenes, flowers.
Jenny Fontaine studied under Gustave Boulanger, Jules Lefebvre, Jean-Paul Laurens and Benjamin-Constant. In Paris she featured at the Salon des Artistes Français, of which she was an associate member. She was awarded medals in 1892, 1896 and 1900, for the Exposition Universelle.

She treated flowers and genre scenes in a few paintings but concentrated almost exclusively on portraits, working in pastel or charcoal until 1890 and later turning to paint. She favoured female sitters, cleverly revealing their personality but hinting at their mysterious side. She worked mostly in ochre and muted greens.
MUSEUMS AND GALLERIES:
ARRAS: *Daydream; Portrait of a Girl, Shrimp-pickers at Villerville.*

FONTAINE, Johann Jakob. See **SWEBACH**

FONTAINE, Jules Léon
French, 19th century.
Born 12 April 1817, in Calais.
Painter.
Exhibited drawings in the manner of various Old Masters at Paris Salons from 1865 to 1870; a member of the Société des Artistes Français as of 1888.

FONTAINE, Léon
French, 19th century.
Born 13 October 1853, in Paris.
Painter.
Studied under W. Bouguereau and T.-R. Fleury; made his Salon des Artistes Français début in 1888.

FONTAINE, Lionel
French, 20th century.
Draughtsman, caricaturist.

FONTAINE, Lorraine
Canadian, 20th century.
Installation artist, environmental artist.
Lorraine Fontaine's work is concerned with the relationship between the natural world and the objects it contains, such as sticks of wood, and their placing by people - an exchange that evolves with the passage of time. Her first solo exhibition, held in France in 1997, was organised by the Cultural Department of the Canadian Embassy.

FONTAINE, Louis
French, 17th century.
Died 1664.
Sculptor (wood).
The sculptures on the stalls of the church of St-Maclou in Pontoise are attributed to Louis Fontaine.

FONTAINE, Louis de
French, 18th century.
Painter. Portraits.
Louis de Fontaine may be identical to a student at the Académie Royale who received a prize in 1704. In 1737 he became director of the Académie de St-Luc. A number of artists engraved works after De Fontaine: J. J. Pasquier engraved the portrait of the *Marquis of Cayla*, P. Fillieul engraved *King Stanislas Leczinski* and the *Marquis of Aubois*, G. F. Schmidt engraved *Adrienne Lecouvreur*, and N. Dupuis engraved *C. Rollin*.
MUSEUMS AND GALLERIES:
ORLÉANS: *Portrait of an Abbess*.

FONTAINE, Louis François
French, 18th century.
Active in Paris in 1753.
Painter, sculptor.

FONTAINE, Marcel Georges
French, 20th century.
Born 24 September 1889, in Paris.
Sculptor.
Marcel Fontaine studied under Marius Mercié, Jean Boucher and Ernest Dubois. He exhibited at the Salon des Artistes Français.

FONTAINE, Marie (Mme)
French, 19th century.
Born 1816, in Paris; died 1877, in Versailles.
Painter, pastellist. Portraits, still-lifes.
Studied under L. Cogniet and went on to marry Edme Adolphe Fontaine; exhibited some portraits and still-lifes at Salons between 1848 and 1866.

FONTAINE, Marie Antoinette (Mme)
French, 19th century.
Painter.
Wife of the painter André Fontaine; exhibited in Lyons in 1839 and again in 1842-1843, chiefly portraits and genre subjects.

FONTAINE, Marie Claire
French, 19th century.
Born in Versailles.
Painter. Portraits, flowers.
Daughter of Edme Adolphe Fontaine; exhibited at the Salon from 1875 to 1878, principally flower compositions and portraits.

FONTAINE, Mathurin
French, 16th century.
Sculptor.
Fontainebleau School.
Mathurin Fontaine was involved in decorative work for the palace of Fontainebleau between 1537 and 1540.

FONTAINE, N.
Flemish, 18th century.
Painter. Church interiors.
Flemish School.
According to Nagler, N. Fontaine worked in Courtrai in the manner of P. Neefs.

FONTAINE, Paul
French, 19th century.
Born 13 April 1833, in Paris; died 1897.
Painter.
Pupil of Couture; submitted several items to various Salons between 1865 and 1870. His body of work includes *Pond at Cernay*, *Souvenir of Vaux de Cernay*, *Evening on the Island of Capri*, *Garden on Capri* and *Beach*.

FONTAINE, Pierre François Léonard
French, 18th - 19th century.
Born 20 September 1762, in Pontoise; died 13 October 1853, in Paris.
Painter (gouache), watercolourist, draughtsman.
History painting, mythological subjects, architectural views.
Pierre François Léonard Fontaine was the pupil of Percier and later his collaborator. On 12 March 1812 he was appointed a member of the Institut and the following year the emperor made him his premier architect, a post which he retained under Louis-Philippe. Fontaine was a commander of the Légion d'Honneur and an honorary member of the academy in Munich. He exhibited at the Salon from 1791 to 1810, notably with architectural subjects.
MUSEUMS AND GALLERIES:
ORLÉANS: *Portrait of an Ursuline Abbess* - PONTOISE: *View of the Arch of Titus in Rome*.
AUCTION RECORDS:
PARIS, 1896, *View of the Ancient Church of St-Ambroise and the Fountain in the Rue Popincourt* (watercolour) FRF 360. PARIS, 4 Dec 1931, *View of the Château d'Eu, Taken from the Gardens in 1835* (watercolour) FRF 2,200. PARIS, 3 June 1935, *Strollers in the Ruins of an Ancient Roman Palace* (watercolour/pen outline, attributed) FRF 500. PARIS, 8 June 1982, *View of a Park and a Palace Portico* (1792, watercolour, 10¾ x 7½ ins / 27.5 x 19 cm) FRF 7,800. NEW YORK, 9 Jan 1991, *The Piazza della Signoria in Florence*; *The Caracalla Baths in Rome* (1792, black chalk, watercolour and gouache, a pair, each 25 x 37 ins / 63.5 x 94 cm) USD 18,700. PARIS, 22 March 1991, *View of the New Entrance to the Vatican Museum in 1790* (pen and wash, 10¼ x 13¼ ins / 25.9 x 33.5 cm) FRF 170,000; *Plan for a Tea Table* (black chalk and watercolour, 3¾ x 5 ins / 9.5 x 12.4 cm) FRF 50,000. PARIS, 19 Feb 1992, *Arrival of King Louis-Philippe at the Château d'Eu, Seen from the Gardens* (1835, watercolour, ink and wash, 11¼ x 18 ins / 28.4 x 46 cm) FRF 72,000. PARIS, 18 Nov 1994, *Plan for a Cornerstone* (black chalk and wash, 10¼ x 13 ins / 26 x 33.3 cm)

FRF 5,000. PARIS, 20 Nov 1994, *Plans for a Palace for Napoleon's Son, the King of Rome, to be Built on Chaillot Hill* (two drawings with watercolour) FRF 250,000. NEW YORK, 28 Jan 1999, *Roman Ruins with Tourists Guided by Cicerone* (1815, black chalk/bodycolour, 19 x 25 ins / 48 x 64 cm) USD 17,000. PARIS, 1 Dec 1999, *Study for a Tomb Monument* (1820, pen/wash, 24 x 35 ins / 61 x 90 cm) FRF 45,000. NEW YORK, 3 Feb 2000, *Italianate Landscape with Classical Ruins* (watercolour/gouache, 20 x 33 ins / 52 x 83 cm) USD 4,400. PARIS, 27 March 2001, *Ceremony of Magic in the Ruins* (watercolour/gouache, 20 x 29 ins / 52 x 73 cm) FRF 45,000. PARIS, 24 March 2003, *Collection of Ornaments* (pen/ink wash, 9 x 7 ins / 24 x 19 cm) EUR 3,500.

FONTAINE, René
French, 18th century.
Died 31 August 1787, in Paris.
Painter.
René Fontaine was the director of the Académie de St-Luc in Paris.

FONTAINE, Robin de
French, 14th - 15th century.
Active in Paris.
Illuminator.

FONTAINE, Thomas
Swiss, 17th century.
Born 5 October 1659, in Geneva; died 1 August 1703, in Geneva.
Painter (enamel), goldsmith.

FONTAINE, Victor
Belgian, 19th century.
Born 9 June 1837, in Cuesmes-lez-Mons; died 12 April 1884, in Ixelles.
Painter, pastellist. Nudes, portraits, still-lifes (flowers).
Victor Fontaine attended the Académie de Mons.

MUSEUMS AND GALLERIES:
MONS.
AUCTION RECORDS:
NEW YORK, 24 Feb 1987, *Still-life with Flowers of the Fields* (1877, oil on canvas, 26 x 32 1/4 ins / 66.3 x 82.2 cm) USD 3,750. SYDNEY, 16 Oct 1989, *Standing Nude* (pastel, 23 1/4 x 18 1/2 ins / 59 x 47 cm) AUD 1,100. SYDNEY, 26 March 1990, *Standing Nude* (pastel, 24 3/4 x 18 ins / 63 x 46 cm) AUD 750. LONDON, 5 Sept 2000, *Distant Thoughts* (oil on canvas, 40 x 33 ins / 101 x 85 cm) GBP 2,500. NEW YORK, 15 Dec 2000, *Sunny Day of Leisure* (oil on panel, 24 x 17 ins / 62 x 43 cm) USD 8,000. BRUSSELS, 10 June 2002, *Elegant Lady* (1878, oil on canvas, 27 x 17 ins / 68 x 42 cm) EUR 3,000.

FONTAINE-LAUGÉE, Jeanne
French, 20th century.
Born in Paris.
Painter.
Jeanne Fontaine-Laugée exhibited at the Salon des Artistes Français.

FONTAINE-LESREL, Jacques
French, 20th century.
Born in Octeville (Manche).
Painter.
Jacques Fontaine-Lesrel studied under Émile Renard and Louis Roger. He exhibits at the Salon des Artistes Français.

FONTAINES. See also first name

FONTAINES, Michelet de
French, 15th century.
Active in Nevers (Nièvre).
Sculptor.
In 1470, Michelet de Fontaines carried out sculptural work for the chapel of the corn market in Nevers. In 1471, he carved the arms of the duke of Brabant, the count of Nevers and the town of Nevers on the keystones of the vault.

FONTAINES, Pierre de
French, 15th century.
Painter, sculptor.
Pierre de Fontaines was one of the artists involved in the preparations made by Lyons in honour of the entry of Louis XII into the city.

FONTAINIÈRE. See **FONTANIÈRE Gaspard Moïse de**

FONTAINIEU, Prosper François Irénée Barrigues de. See **BARRIGUES**

FONTALLARD, Alexandre Henri
French, 19th century.
Born in Paris.
Painter, watercolourist. Portraits.
Studied under Rouget and exhibited at the miniatures Salon from 1831 to 1835; in all probability, the brother of Camille Fontallard.
MUSEUMS AND GALLERIES:
NOTTINGHAM: *Portraits of Major Sydenham and Mrs Sydenham.*

FONTALLARD, Camille
French, 19th century.
Born c. 1810.
Painter. Religious subjects, genre scenes, landscapes, landscapes with figures.
Exhibited at the Paris Salon from 1831 to 1850. Remembered for several compositions, among them *Poor Man's Offering to the Virgin, Commissary of the Grande Armée, Harvesters, Waterloo Plain, Little Fishermen, Burial of a Small Dog.*
AUCTION RECORDS:
PARIS, 31 May 1919, *Portrait of the Sculptor Clésinger,* FRF 150. ST ASAPH (WALES), 2 June 1994, *Bathers* (1847, oil on panel, 16 x 12 ins / 40.5 x 30.5 cm) GBP 2,645.

FONTALLARD, Henri-Gérard, or Gérard-Fontallard
French, 19th century.
Born c. 1798, in Paris.
Draughtsman, lithographer.
Son of Jean François Gérard Fontallard. Known chiefly as a caricaturist who worked variously on publications such as *Silhouette* (1830), *Aujourd'hui* (*Today*) (c. 1840) and the *Revue des Peintres* (*Artists' Review*). He is credited with creating the 16-plate *l'Histoire d'une épingle* (*History of a Pin*) and *Bluettes*, together with authorship of frontispieces for musical scores showing scenes from middle-class life.

FONTALLARD, Jean François Gérard
French, 19th century.
Born 1777; died 1858, in Paris.
Active in Mézières.
Painter, watercolourist.
Studied engineering and fine arts and worked in the ateliers of Paris and Augustin. He was an excellent miniaturist who exhibited at the Paris Salon from 1798 to 1858.
MUSEUMS AND GALLERIES:
CHÂTEAUROUX: *Portrait of Bourdillon.*
AUCTION RECORDS:
PARIS, 17 and 18 Nov 1920, *Portrait of a Fair-Haired Child,* FRF 1,100. PARIS, 20 June 1924, *Portrait of a Woman in a White Dress* (miniature) FRF 290. PARIS, 27-29 May 1929, *Portrait of General Jourdan as a Child,* FRF 10,000. LONDON, 22 Nov 1999, *Madame Henry Ochsenbein in Green Dress,*

White Underdress (1812, miniature, gilt mount, wood frame, oval, h. 3 ins / 7 cm) GBP 4,800. LONDON, 8 Oct 2002, *Lady Susan Reeve* (1821, miniature) GBP 2,900. LONDON, 10 Dec 2002, *Young Lady in a Maroon Dress* (1818, miniature, gilt, metal frame, h. 2 ins / 6 cm) GBP 2,200. LONDON, 18 Nov 2003, *Lady Leaning on Plinth* (miniature, gold frame, oval, 3 x ? ins / 7 x ? cm) GBP 5,800.

FONTAN, Arnaud
French, 17th century.
Sculptor (wood).
In 1619 Arnaud Fontan was commissioned to sculpt the church high altar, and the panelling and the lectern in the refectory, for the convent of St-Pantaléon in Toulouse.

FONTAN, Edmond J. Arnaud
French, 19th century.
Born in Bordeaux.
Painter. Urban landscapes.
MUSEUMS AND GALLERIES:
BORDEAUX: *Bordeaux: Place du Vieux-Marché (Old Marketplace).*

FONTAN, Guillaume
French, 17th century.
Sculptor (wood).
In 1642 Guillaume Fontan was commissioned to sculpt a retable for the chapel of St-Marie at the church of St-Sernin in Toulouse.

FONTAN, Joseph Augustin
French, 19th century.
Born in Crémens.
Painter. Genre scenes, portraits.
Made his Salon début in 1880.

FONTAN, Leo
French, 20th century.
Born 23 September 1884, in Douchery (Ardennes); died 26 June 1965, in Annecy (Savoy).
Painter (including gouache), watercolourist, pastellist, draughtsman, designer. Figures, portraits, scenes with figures, genre scenes, interiors with figures, urban landscapes. Decorative panels.
Leo Fontan studied under Luc-Olivier Merson, Léon Bonnat and Fernand Cormon. Established in Paris, he exhibited regularly at the Salon des Artistes Français, of which he was an associate member, and at the Humorists' Salon. He was awarded the Bonat former students' prize in 1936 and a silver medal in 1944, and was made a Chevalier of the Légion d'Honneur. He is known for the decorative panels he created for sea liners.
AUCTION RECORDS:
PARIS, 15-16 June 1923, *La réussite* (watercolour heightened with gouache) FRF 140; *Tango Dancing* (watercolour heightened with gouache) FRF 190. PARIS, 3 March 1947, *Garden Entrance with Gate,* FRF 100. MILWAUKEE, 26 Sept 1982, *Nude Reclining* (oil on canvas, 38 1/2 x 19 1/2 ins / 98 x 49.5 cm) USD 600. PARIS, 10 July 1983, *The Île-de-France Dining Room* (oil on canvas, 20 3/4 x 31 1/2 ins / 53 x 80 cm) FRF 12,500. PARIS, Jan 1984, *Elegant Lady with a Hat* (pastel, 15 1/4 x 14 1/4 ins / 39 x 36 cm) FRF 6,800. PARIS, 24 Oct 1986, *Girl in the Snow* (gouache, oval, h. 20 3/4 ins / 53 cm) FRF 9,000. PARIS, 16 Dec 1987, *The Flower Market at La Madeleine* (oil on canvas, 9 x 11 ins / 22 x 27 cm) FRF 4,000. PARIS, 12 June 1988, *The Île de France Lounge* (oil on canvas, 20 1/2 x 31 1/2 ins / 52 x 80 cm) FRF 27,000. PARIS, 24 June 1991, *Boccaccio's Decameron* (Indian ink and watercolour/beige paper, 15 3/4 x 19 1/4 ins / 40 x 49 cm) FRF 7,800. PARIS, 16 Oct 1992, *Venice* (oil on canvas, 23 1/2 x 28 1/2 ins / 60 x 72.5 cm) FRF 13,000. BERN, 5 May 1999, *Venetian Balconies Bedecked with Flowers* (oil on canvas, 18 x 22 ins / 46 x 55 cm) CHF 2,500.

FONTAN, Marie-Louise
French, 19th century.
Born 1 September 1863, in Paris.
Painter.
Exhibited examples of her work at the Salon des Artistes Français in Paris.

FONTAN, Victor
French, 19th century.
Sculptor. Figures.
MUSEUMS AND GALLERIES:
LYONS: *Ant. Coysevox; Sauzet; J.B. Say.*

FONTANA, Alberto
Italian, 16th century.
Born c. 1537, in Modena; died 1558.
Painter.
Alberto Fontana was the pupil of Antonio Begarelli and a friend of Niccolo dell'Abbate, with whom he collaborated on paintings in Modena executed mostly in the style of Begarelli. The styles of the two artists are largely similar, but although their skills in conveying emotion through facial expression are comparable, Fontana is less talented as a draughtsman, and there is something heavy and cold about his colouring. The Estense gallery in Modena has four frescoes by Fontana, representing *Vigilance, Prudence, Hope* and *Fidelity.*

FONTANA, Andrea di
Italian, 16th century.
Active in Genoa.
Painter.
Andrea di Fontana painted a retable for the village church of S Giulia in Lavagna.

FONTANA, Annibale
Italian, 16th century.
Died 1587, in Milan.
Sculptor, founder, medallist.
Annibale Fontana was a burgher of Palermo in 1570. He began working as a sculptor on his return to Milan, where he executed all the decorative sculptures, bronze garlands and low reliefs on the façade of the church of S Maria presso S Celso. For the interior of the church he sculpted a marble statue of the *Assumption,* a low relief of the *Death of Mary* and a statue of *St John the Baptist.*

FONTANA, Antonio
Italian, 18th century.
Active in Venice c. 1710.
Painter.
Antonio Fontana painted frescoes portraying episodes from the life of St Francis for the monastery of S Francesco di Paola.

FONTANA, Baldassare
Italian, 17th - 18th century.
Born c. 1658, in Chiasso (Ticino), Switzerland; died 1738.
Sculptor.
In 1679 Baldassare Fontana was commissioned to decorate the episcopal residence in Kromeriz (then Moravia). 1695 found him in Cracow, where he helped to decorate the church of St Anne and assumed responsibility for decorating the churches of St Andrew, the Dominicans, and St Mark, where he contributed a sculpture of the *Archangel Michael.* In 1702 he was again in Moravia, where he was commissioned to sculpt decorative components for castles, churches and monasteries. In Olomouc (Olmütz), he sculpted statues and altars for the church of the Calvary. A church in Chiasso (Ticino), Switzerland, also houses four stucco heads by Fontana.

FONTANA, Battista. See **FARINATI Giambattista**

FONTANA, Bill
American, 20th - 21st century.
Born 1947, in Cleveland (Ohio).
Installation artist.

Bill Fontana installs loudspeakers in different places so that the spectator can 'hear from further away than he can see'. Thus in Paris, at the Arc de Triomphe, you could look towards the Bourse, the Arche de la Défense or the Jardins de Bagatelle and hear the sounds in these places.

BIBLIOGRAPHY:
Amine, Patrick, *'Bill Fontana'* in *Art Press* n° 194, periodical, Paris, September 1994.

FONTANA, Camillo
Italian, 16th century.
Active in Urbino.
Painter.

FONTANA, Carlo
Italian, 19th century.
Born 20 October 1865, in Carrara; died 1956.
Sculptor.

Carlo Fontana won a prize in his home town, for a sculpture entitled *Destitute Man*, which enabled him to go to Rome, where he won another prize for his low relief of *Campanella the Philosopher Being Tortured in Prison*. He is best known for the *Monument to the Sculptor Pietro Tacca*; and monuments to *Shelley*, in S Terenzo; *Garibaldi*; and *Ugo Foscolo*, in the church of S Croce in Florence. He was also a draughtsman and aquafortist.

MUSEUMS AND GALLERIES:
PARIS (MAMVP): *Water Carrier* (bronze) - ROME (Gal. Nazionale d'Arte Moderna): *Eternal Dreamer*; *Farinata*.

FONTANA, Cesare
Italian, 17th century.
Died after 1660; according to Zani.
Active in 1620.
Engraver.

Cesare Fontana engraved a number of plates of funeral processions and cavalcades.

FONTANA, Corsin
Swiss, 20th century.
Born 19 April 1944, in Domat-Ems.
Sculptor, environmental artist.

Fontana produces small structures for manipulation, which have an obvious recreational nature.

FONTANA, Domenico Maria
Italian, 17th century.
Born c. 1607, in Parma.
Engraver.

Domenico Maria Fontana learned his craft in Bologna, where he engraved several plates from his own drawings and from originals by established artists. He is credited with many engravings, including a *Flight into Egypt with a Mountainous Landscape, The Sabine Women Re-establishing the Peace between Romans and Sabines, St John Preaching in the Wilderness* and *Christ Walking up to Calvary*.

It appears that there were two artists of this name in Parma. The second was still alive in 1644 and is believed to have left one solitary engraving of *Moses and the Tablets of the Law* from an original by Parmigiano.

FONTANA, Ernesto
Italian, 19th - 20th century.
Born 1837, in Milan; died 1918, in Curaglia (Switzerland).
Painter. Genre scenes, figures, portraits.

AUCTION RECORDS:
LUCERNE, 3 June 1981, *The Present* (1873, oil on canvas, 17 x 12 3/4 ins / 43 x 32.5 cm) CHF 6,500. LONDON, 27 March 1987, *Young Woman at Her Toilet* (oil on remounted canvas/panel, 10 1/2 x 6 3/4 ins / 26.5 x 17 cm) GBP 2,400. LONDON, 29 April 1988, *Portrait of a Pretty Woman* (oil on canvas, 18 1/2 x 14 1/4 ins / 47 x 36 cm) GBP 3,850. MONACO, 21 April 1990, *Portrait of an Italian Woman* (1887, oil on canvas, 23 1/4 x 18 1/4 ins / 59 x 46.5 cm) FRF 61,050. MILAN, 12 March 1991, *The Lovers' Signal* (1904, oil on canvas, 35 1/2 x 24 1/4 ins / 90 x 61.5 cm) ITL 20,000,000. LONDON, 22 June 2004, *The Awakening of the Daughter of Jaïris* (oil on canvas, 31 1/2x45 1/2ins / 80x116cms) EUR 4,182.50. AMSTERDAM, 22 June 2004, *Awakening of the Daughter of Jairus* (oil on canvas, 31 x 46 ins / 80 x 116 cm) EUR 3,500.

FONTANA, Ernesto
Italian, 20th century.
Born in Lugano (Ticino), Switzerland.
Painter. Landscapes with figures.

In 1900 Ernesto Fontana entered *At Sunrise* into the competition for the Prix de Rome.

FONTANA, Ferdinando
Italian, 19th century.
Born 1798, in Carrara; died 22 April 1847, in Carrara.
Sculptor.

Ferdinando Fontana studied under his brother, Pietro Fontana, and Desmarais. He won the Rome Prize at the academy of Carrara in 1810, and the following year won a prize for his low relief of *Achilles, Patroclus and Briseis* in Florence. He is also known for a statue entitled *Faith*.

MUSEUMS AND GALLERIES:
FLORENCE (Gal. dell'Accademia): *Achilles, Patroclus and Briseis*.

FONTANA, Flaminio
Italian, 16th century.
Active in Urbino c. 1556.
Miniaturist, painter (porcelain).

FONTANA, Francesco
Italian, 16th - 17th century.
Painter.

With his brother Baldassare Fontana, Francesco Fontana helped decorate the church of St Anne in Cracow.

FONTANA, Francesco, called Il Vecchio
Italian, 18th century.
Died c. 1750, in Mantua.
Active in Verona.
Painter. Landscapes, seascapes.

Francesco Fontana painted attractive landscapes, sea views and 'caprices' commissioned by private individuals to decorate their homes.

FONTANA, Francesco
Italian, 19th century.
Reproductions engraver.

Francesco Fontana was active in Rome in around 1824. He is remembered for an engraving after Raphael, of the *Madonna of the Chair*, and a portrait of *Gregory XVI*.

FONTANA, Francesco
Italian, 19th century.
Born 1843; died 1876, in Milan.
Painter, watercolourist, sculptor.

Many of Francesco Fontana's watercolours depict scenes from the Bible.

FONTANA, Gherardo
Italian.
Engraver (burin).

Worked in Rome and was mentioned by Nagler.

FONTANA, Giambattista or Giovanni Battista
Austrian, 16th century.
Born 1525, in Ala (Tyrol); died 1587.
Also active in Italy.
Painter, engraver. Religious subjects.

After studying as a pupil of Giovanni Carotto, Fontana was appointed a court painter to Archduke Ferdinand in Vienna. He also worked in Rome and Venice. His most important engravings are: *Christ Carrying the Cross*, *Crucifixion*, *St Martin*, *The Prophet Ezekiel* (1579), *Martyrdom of St Peter* (after Titian) and *St Agatha in Prison* (after Veronese).

His compositions are rich and majestic in style and his use of the burin is very skilful.

AUCTION RECORDS:
LONDON, 26 June 1985, *The Vision of Ezekiel* (copper, 15 x 16 3/4 ins / 38.1 x 42.5 cm) GBP 3,000.

FONTANA, Giovanni
Italian, 19th century.
Born 1795, in Genoa; died 16 December 1845, in Genoa.
Painter.

Giovanni Fontana was a pupil of Carlo Baratta at the academy in Genoa, where he later became a teacher himself. He painted a *Caritas Romana* and a *Joseph the Patriarch* for King Charles Albert; the *Panathenaea Festival* on the curtain at the Carlo Felice theatre; an allegorical fresco in the church of S Martino in Sampierdarena; a medallion depicting the *Miracle of St Martin*; and two altar paintings in Lavagna, of *The Martyrdom and Discovery of St Sebastian*.

FONTANA, Giovanni Domenico
Italian, 17th century.
Born to a family originally from Lucca.
Painter, engraver.

Giovanni Domenico Fontana is known to have engraved a battle scene from the war against the Turks.

FONTANA, Giovanni Giuseppe
Italian, 19th century.
Born 1821, in Carrara; died 1893, in London.
Active in London.
Sculptor, watercolourist.

Giovanni Fontana exhibited in London, from 1852 to 1886, notably at the Royal Academy, Suffolk Street and the New Water-Colour Society.

MUSEUMS AND GALLERIES:
LIVERPOOL: *Portrait of Charles Dickens*; *Statue of a Hero*; *Sleepwalker* (plaster); *Captive of Love* (group); *Antique Vase*; *Cupid Captivated by Venus* (group); *Jephthah and His Daughter*; *S.R. Graves*; *Juliet* - SYDNEY: *Sleepwalker*; *Patroclus and Achilles*.

FONTANA, Giovanni Pietro
Italian, 16th century.
Active in Venice.
Engraver (wood).

Giovanni Pietro Fontana produced the wood engravings for an *Officio della gloriosa Virgine* (*Office of the Blessed Virgin Mary*), published in 1536.

FONTANA, Girolamo
Italian, 16th century.
Of Veronese origin.
Painter.

Girolamo Fontana worked in Trento from 1545 to 1551. His works include the paintings on the triumphal arch to mark the visit of Maximilian, king of Bohemia, and his wife Maria.

FONTANA, Girolamo
Italian, 18th century.
Active in Verona.
Painter.

Girolamo Fontana was the son of Francesco Fontana (Il Vecchio).

FONTANA, Giulio
Italian, 16th century.
Born 16th century, in Verona.
Engraver.

Giulio Fontana is known for a plate dated 1569 depicting the *Venetians Fighting the Imperial Forces at Cadora*, after Titian, and a *Death of St Peter*, also after Titian.

FONTANA, Giuseppe
Italian, 19th century.
Born 1832; died 1881.
Active in Pisa.
Sculptor (wood).

The Museo Civico in Pisa has a sculpted wooden model made by Giuseppe Fontana for the reconstruction of the cathedral pulpit, which was carried out by Giovanni Pisano. Fontana also rebuilt certain sections of the choir stalls, which were designed by Girolamo Tacchi.

MUSEUMS AND GALLERIES:
PISA (Mus. Civico).

FONTANA, Guido
Italian, 16th century.
Died 9 July 1605.
Active in Urbino.
Painter.

Guido Fontana was the son of Camillo Fontana.

FONTANA, Lavinia, later Zappi
Italian, 16th - 17th century.
Born 1552, in Bologna; died 1614, in Rome.
Painter. History painting, religious subjects, portraits.

The daughter of Prospero Fontana, who was her master, Lavinia Fontana's history paintings were held in great esteem, but she achieved fame primarily as a result of the portraits she painted in Rome. She married Paolo Zappi, who painted the draperies in her works, including the *Portrait of Gregory XIII*, who became her patron.

BIBLIOGRAPHY:
Nochlin, L./ Sutherland Harris, A., *Women Artists, 1550-1950*, exhibition catalogue, County Museum of Art, Los Angeles; University of Texas Art Museum, Austin, Texas; Carnegie, Pittsburgh; Brooklyn Museum, New York, 1976-7. Tufts, E., '*Lavinia Fontana, Bolognese Humanist*' in *Le arti a Bologna e in Emilia dal XVI al XVII secole/Receuils d'actes des Congrès internationaux d'histoire de l'art, ed.* Andrea *Emiliani*, CLUEB, Bologna, 1982. *The Age of Correggio and the Carracci*, exhibition catalogue, National Gallery of Art, Washington D.C., Washington DC, 1986. Fortunati, V., *Lavinia Fontana (1552-1614)*, Electa, Milan, 1994. Murphy, C.P., '*Lavinia Fontana and le dame della città: Understanding Female Artistic Patronage in Late Sixteenth-century Bologna*' in *Renaissance Studies*, vol 10, 1996. Fortunati, V., *Lavinia Fontana of Bologna (1552-1614)*, exhibition catalogue, National Museum of Women in the Arts, Washington, D.C., 2002. Murphy, Caroline, *Lavinia Fontana: A Painter and her Patrons in Sixteenth-century Bologna*, Yale University Press, New Haven and London, 2002.

MUSEUMS AND GALLERIES:
BERLIN: *Venus and Cupid* - BESANÇON: *Self-portrait* - BOLOGNA (Pinacoteca Nazionale): *Louise of France before St Francis of Paola*; *Nativity of the Virgin* - BORDEAUX: *Portrait of Senator Orsini* - CHERBOURG: *Adoration of the Magi* - DRESDEN: *Holy Family with St Elizabeth and the Infant St John* -

DUBLIN: *Queen of Sheba Visiting King Solomon; Portrait of an Italian Warrior* - FLORENCE (Palazzo Pitti): *Portrait of a Woman* - FLORENCE (Uffizi): *Portrait of the Author*; two works; *Friar Panigarola; Jesus Appearing to Mary Magdalene* - MILAN (Ambrosiana): *Portrait of a Woman* - MILAN (Pinacoteca di Brera): *Family Portrait* - MODENA: *Portrait of a Franciscan Monk* - NAPLES: *Jesus and the Samaritan Woman* - PARMA: *Portrait of a Man* - ROME (Gal. dell'Accademia Nazionale di S Luca): *Self-portrait* - ROME (Mus. e Gal. Borghese): *Christ Sleeping* (copper); *Head of a Young Man* - SAN LORENZO DE EL ESCORIAL (Real Monasterio de San Lorenzo): *Holy Family and St John* - ST PETERSBURG (Hermitage): *Venus and Cupid; Marriage of St Catherine.*

AUCTION RECORDS:

LONDON, 4 May 1925, *Holy Family*, GBP 28. LONDON, 15 July 1927, *Woman in a Velvet Gown*, GBP 210. LONDON, 26 March 1928, *Venetian Men and Women*, GBP 16. NEW YORK, 22 Jan 1931, *Portrait of a Woman of the Isolani Family*, USD 1,000. NEW YORK, 14-16 Jan 1943, *Portrait of a Woman*, USD 410. VIENNA, 1-4 Dec 1964, *Holy Family*, ATS 80,000. LONDON, 16 July 1980, *Holy Family Surrounded by Holy Figures* (oil on canvas, 61 1/2 x 46 1/2 ins / 156 x 118 cm) GBP 5,000. MILAN, 26 Nov 1985, *Descent from the Cross* (oil on canvas, 47 1/4 x 35 ins / 120 x 89 cm) ITL 14,000,000. PARIS, 31 May 1988, *Portrait of a Patrician Woman* (oil/copper, 6 x 4 1/4 ins / 15.4 x 11 cm) FRF 150,000. ROME, 13 Dec 1988, *Portrait of the Young Antonia Ghino* (oil on canvas, 34 1/2 x 28 1/4 ins / 87.5 x 72 cm) ITL 10,000,000. NEW YORK, 11 Jan 1989, *Madonna with the Sleeping Infant Jesus, St Joseph and St Anne* (oil on canvas, 56 1/2 x 46 1/2 ins / 143.7 x 118.2 cm) USD 12,100. MONACO, 16 June 1989, *Nativity* (oil on canvas, 15 x 12 1/2 ins / 38 x 32 cm) FRF 166,500. LONDON, 12 Dec 1990, *Portrait of Pope Gregory XIII* (oil on canvas, 45 3/4 x 38 1/2 ins / 116.5 x 97.5 cm) GBP 22,000. NEW YORK, 9 Oct 1991, *Holy Family with the Infant St John and St Catherine* (oil on panel, 33 1/2 x 26 ins / 85.1 x 66 cm) USD 99,000. ROME, 28 April 1992, *St Jerome* (oil on canvas, 14 1/4 x 11 3/4 ins / 36.5 x 30 cm) ITL 35,000,000. MILAN, 13 May 1993, *Mystic Marriage of St Catherine* (oil/copper, 18 1/2 x 13 3/4 ins / 47 x 35 cm) ITL 22,000,000. MILAN, 19 Oct 1993, *Adoration of the Magi* (oil on panel, 29 x 24 ins / 73.5 x 61 cm) ITL 31,050,000. MILAN, 4 April 1995, *Holy Family with St John and St Anne* (oil/copper, 17 x 13 1/2 ins / 43 x 34 cm) ITL 39,100,000. NEW YORK, 12 Jan 1996, *Portrait of a Woman in a Green Gown with a White Lace Collar Wearing a Pearl Necklace and Medallion of Precious Stones* (oil on panel, 22 1/2 x 17 1/2 ins / 57.2 x 44.5 cm) USD 13,800. LONDON, 11-13 Dec 1996, *Judith and Holofernes* (oil on canvas, 69 1/4 x 52 1/2 ins / 175.6 x 133.4 cm) GBP 65,300; *Portrait of a Small Boy in a Red Embroidered Costume* (oil on canvas, 45 x 37 1/2 ins / 114.3 x 95.2 cm) GBP 14,950. NEW YORK, 29 Jan 1999, *Anna, Viscountess of Panigarola Beside Pillar with her Child* (1578, oil on canvas, 67 x 35 ins / 171 x 89 cm) USD 60,000. LONDON, 29 Oct 1999, *Portrait of Girl Wearing Yellow Silk Dress and Pearls* (oil on copper) GBP 20,000. NEW YORK, 24 Jan 2002, *Portrait of Costanza Alidosi Seated and Holding Small Dog* (oil on canvas, 62 x 48 ins / 157 x 121 cm) USD 70,000. NEW YORK, 24 Jan 2002, *Mystic Marriage of St Catherine with Sts Francis, Joseph and the Infant St John* (oil on copper, 10 x 8 ins / 26 x 20 cm) USD 115,000. VENICE, 21 Sept 2003, *Mystic Marriage of St Catherine* (oil on copper, 10 x 8 ins / 26 x 20 cm) EUR 140,000. NEW YORK, 27 May 2004, *Portrait of Girl in Pink Embroidered Dress* (oil on metal) USD 60,000.

FONTANA, Lorenzo

Italian, 18th century.
Active in Naples c. 1700.
Sculptor.

Lorenzo Fontana decorated a marble altar in the church of S Caterina in Formello.

FONTANA, Lucio

Argentinian, 20th century.
Born 19 February 1899, in Rosario de Santa Fé, to Italian parents; died 7 September 1968, in Comabbio (Varese).
Active in Italy from 1905, naturalised Italian.
Painter (including gouache/mixed media), watercolourist, sculptor, potter, draughtsman.
Spatialism.
Abstraction-Création group.

At the age of six, Lucio Fontana went to Italy with his parents, an Argentinian mother and his Italian father, Luigi Fontana, who was a funerary sculptor. It appears that he later went back to Argentina, only returning to Italy as a soldier during World War I. When the war was over he returned to Argentina and remained there from 1922 to 1927, working for a time in his father's business before devoting himself entirely to sculpture and returning to Italy in 1927. In Milan, Fontana enrolled as a student of sculpture with Adolfo Wildt at the Accademia di Belle Arti di Brera and received his diploma in 1930. In 1934, with other artists, he founded the Italian Abstract Artists group and in 1934-1935 joined the Abstraction-Création group in Paris. In 1936, again in Paris, he met Brancusi and Miró among other artists. Fontana returned to Argentina during World War II, from 1939 to 1946, where he founded the Academia de Altamira.

In Buenos Aires in 1946, with a group of students, he published the *White Manifesto*. On his return to Milan in 1947 he set out the content of the *White Manifesto* in the new manifesto *Spaziali* (*Spatialist Manifesto*). In this he declares that all systems are harmful and demands maximum freedom in the expressive and creative processes. The irrational must recover its value; the arbitrary and ineffable must be given form; the boundaries between nature and art, painting and sculpture must be abolished, and 'colour, sound, movement, and space' must be integrated into 'one unit that is both ideal and material'. In Milan Fontana was able to develop his ideas, particularly in the highly active artistic world centred around the Naviglio Gallery.

Despite belonging to a spatialist group that included a wide variety of artists (among them painters such as Morandi, Peverelli and others who continued to use very traditional techniques), Fontana radicalised the founding principles: 'The Spatialists go beyond this idea (futurist dynamism) with neither painting nor sculpture but forms, colours and sounds in and through space. Painted board and dressed stone no longer have any meaning.' Space is defined by the trajectory of action, whatever surrounds it is nothing, is the void. But a means of expressing the passage of this action was still needed. In 1951, after two further 'spatial' manifestos, Fontana published a *Technical Manifesto* to coincide with the Milan Triennale. In these various manifestos he advocated 'an art based on the unity of time and space'.

From 1931 to 1934, Fontana's work was sculptural - at first still of the traditionally figurative kind, modelled in plaster and clay, in the spirit of Maillol with reference to Archipenko, and then, or rather simultaneously, influenced by futurist dynamism. In 1933 and 1934, he began to produce more abstract sculptures, elegantly resolving the occupation of space with sheets stretched between curved metal or flat pieces of black cement carved with graffiti, which could perhaps be considered Fontana's first paintings. When he joined the Abstraction-Création group in 1934-1935 he became part of the abstract avant-garde, though not unambiguously so, as he continued working in sandstone in the same period and, in 1935, at Albisola, experimented with ceramics. In these media he pursued an Expressionist form of representation and continued to work in this way as late as 1949, in parallel with his abstract experimentation. In Paris in 1935, working in a figurative style, Fontana executed a series of sharp fire ceramics for the Sèvres porcelain works. When he returned to Argentina in 1939 he continued to work in an Expressionist style in his painting, taking part in various architectural projects and receiving official commendations for his work. On 5 February 1949, following the *Manifesto Blanco* (*White Manifesto*) of 1946 and the *Spatialist Manifesto* of 1947, he presented the exhibition *Space Perspective, with Spatial Form and Black Illumination*, also known as *Black Environment*, at the Naviglio Gallery in Milan. This exhibition, which was a first manifestation of the spirit of synthesis advocated by these manifestos, included the use of black light in an interestingly early foreshadowing of later experiments with habitable sculpture and other 'environments'.

After 1949, the figurative disappeared completely from Fontana's work. In 1951, for the Milan Triennale, Fontana created 200 metres (650 feet) of neon-tube arabesques for the ceiling of the grand staircase. This followed a varied assortment of other early experimental manifesto creations, including other 'environments' and preceded by some ten years the use of neon by artists of the Art Visuel (Visual Art) group and Lumino Kinetics. It also preceded its use by minimalist American artists. Fontana's paintings with embedded fragments of stones or glass - another means of escaping the flatness of the canvas - date from 1953 and also perhaps foreshadow his later torn canvases. Up to 1964, he continued to create assemblages of fluorescent tubes in simple geometric structures.

However, as early as 1949 he had begun to experiment with puncturing the canvas. From this time forward all his efforts were engaged by the notions of space and energy, the front in relation to the back, the exterior in relation to the interior, but also by the links between the perception of space and the perception of time - links to which he gives form in the marks left behind by the acts of aggression that caused the holes, slits and perforations that were to become a constant feature of his mature work and would come to be known by the term Spatial Concept. Fontana extended the materialisation of Spatial Concept to sculpture, creating crude spherical shapes, rustic globes (known as Nature) in ceramic and bronze on which he produced gashes. Thus, painting and sculpture were, by a very simple technique, connected with the spatial environment while retaining the mark of the moment of aggressive action. From 1952 until his death, Fontana pursued his investigation of spatial concepts with the 'hole' or ' *buchi* ' period and the incrustation or ' *pietre* ' period from 1949 to 1958, creating a constellation on the surface of the canvas suggestive of a star-filled sky. From 1959, he began producing the first gashes (' *atteste* ' and ' *inchiostri* ') in the canvas that would become the *Gashes* on plain or worked surfaces, sometimes on metal, first using plain, flat surfaces; later, in 1963 he produced the *Celestial Eggs* - perforated oval canvases, sometimes treated in sculptural form; from 1963-1966 Fontana produced *Theatres*, which consisted of two parallel planes placed side by side. Despite the diversity of his other earlier and simultaneous works, it is for his act - or action - pieces that Fontana is primarily known. These are characterised by two extreme actions, acts of aggression and therefore of the nullity of all that is not the act itself: the hole and the gash, the perforation and the slashing. He created these signs on media to which he was relatively indifferent.

In 1957, Fontana met Yves Klein at his Milan exhibition and was one of the first to purchase his work. Fontana now began to show a growing interest in colour. He allowed colour to give resonance to the aggressive act and eventually and rather strangely came to confer a synaesthetic value on it, identifying it with water, the sky, sand, and earth. He extended its meaning in a way far closer to the poetic than to metaphysical speculation about the relationship between space and time.

Some critics have identified a certain flamboyant Baroque quality in different periods of Fontana's work. Without going back as far as his figurative Expressionist period or his initial hesitant experiments with abstraction and neon-illuminated environments, it is possible to see this trend in his stone and glass-embedded works of the 1950s. It is there in the black fabric lining at the back of his gashed and perforated canvases placed there to enhance the aesthetic effect of the hole in the canvas space. It is there in his final years, in his *Spatial Concepts/Toy Theatres* with their carefully cut-out and painted figurative silhouettes placed in the foreground in front of a perforated canvas.

All of Fontana's work associated with the concept of spatialism appears to have developed along a dual path of spiritual demand and of provocation. Fontana, commenting on himself, said: 'As a painter working on one of my prepared canvases, I do not want to make a picture, I want to open the space, create a new dimension for art, connect it to the cosmos in all its infinite extent, going beyond the flat surface of the image.'

Lucio Fontana's work, with that of Malévitch, Marcel Duchamp and Yves Klein, is an example of the ambiguity of artistic approaches in which the evident desire to negate the possibility of art is contradicted by the final recourse to the aesthetic interpretation of the object, work or act whose very function appears to be to deny it. Marcel Duchamp's *Porte-Bouteilles*, Malévitch's *White Square on a White Background*, Yves Klein's painting *Monochrome* and César's *Compressions* must finally be seen in aesthetic and psychological terms - where the originating act itself denies its effect as a possible work of art, at least in terms of an aesthetic or psychological event. In the public perception Lucio Fontana was the artist who slashed monochrome canvases with a razor blade. Quite apart from all the possible variants associated with the mythology of the gash and the hole, the matter is not so simple, particularly since this was not all he did. Whether one interprets Fontana's work as a negative act of provocation or one rehearses the metaphysical implications or sees it as a challenge to the activity of representation, to the notion of the work of art, to the possibility of creation, the need for the artistic act, the need to be it, it seems increasingly clear that this austere and perhaps desperate work, executed always with great rigour and perfection, is a reflection of its time in its questioning of the reality of space and time.

In 1926, he exhibited for the first time, in Argentina, showing a plaster piece at the *Nexus* exhibition. Fontana exhibited at the Venice Biennale from 1930. In 1937, some of his sculptures were featured at the pavilion of fascist Italy at the Exposition Universelle in Paris. From 1939 to 1946, he took part in numerous exhibitions in Argentina. In 1948, 1950, 1954 and 1958 he had his own exhibition room at the Venice Biennale. He exhibited there again in 1964 and in 1966 - the year of the *White Room*, for which he was awarded the grand prix. He exhibited at the Rome Quadriennale in 1935, 1939, 1947 and 1955; at the Osaka Festival in 1958; at the São Paulo Biennale in 1959; at the *Arte Nuova* exhibition in Turin in 1959; at the Kassel Ducumenta II exhibition in 1959, and at the Salon des Réalités in Paris in 1963. In 2003, his work featured in the group exhibition at the Musée Ingres in Montauban entitled *Peindre en Trois Dimensions* (*Painting in Three Dimensions*).

He also mounted more than 120 solo exhibitions of his work all over the world. From 1930 to 1931, he held an exhibition of his work at the Galleria del Milione in Milan. Further solo exhibitions took place in Milan until his death. He had solo exhibitions in Rome in 1955 and 1957; in Turin in 1957; in Venice in 1957; in Zurich in 1959; at the Jeanne

Bucher Gallery in Paris in 1937; at the Zack Gallery in 1938, 1959, 1961 and 1963; in London in 1960, and in New York in 1961. In 1967 retrospectives of his work were held at the Museum of Modern Art in New York, the Stedelijk Museum in Amsterdam, the Louisiana Foundation in Copenhagen and the Moderne Museet in Stockholm. In 1970, retrospectives were held at the municipal museums of modern art in Turin and Paris and in 1996 at the Moderner Kunst Museum in Vienna.

BIBLIOGRAPHY:

Tapié, Michel, *Fontana*, Turin, 1967. *Lucio Fontana*, exhibition catalogue, Musée d'Art moderne de la Ville de Paris, Paris, 1970. Crispolti, Enrico, *Lucio Fontana*, exhibition catalogue, Istituto Italo-Latino Americano, Rome, 1972. Crispolti, Enrico/Van Der Marck, J., *Lucio Fontana, catalogue raisonné des peintures, sculptures et environnements spatiaux*, Éd. de la Connaissance, Brussels, 1974. *Lucio Fontana, rétrospective*, exhibition catalogue, Solomon R. Guggenheim Museum, New York, 1977. *Lucio Fontana, el espacio como exploracion*, exhibition catalogue, Palacio de Velázquez, Madrid, 1982. *Lucio Fontana, la cultura dell'ochio*, Castello di Rivoli, Turin, 1986 (extensive documentation). Crispolti, Enrico, '*Fontana, catalogo generale*' in *2 vol.*, catalogue raisonné, Electa, Milan, 1986. Hegewisch, K., *Lucio Fontana: 60 œuvres des années 1938 à 1966*, Gal. Neuendorf, Frankfurt am Main, 1987. *Lucio Fontana*, exhibition catalogue, Éd. du Centre Georges-Pompidou, Paris, 1987. Ceysson, Bernard/Hegyi, Lóránd/Messer, Thomas M./Martinez Sobrado, Ethel, *Lucio Fontana. Retrospektive*, Hatje Cantz, Ostfildern, 1996. Whitfield, Sarah/Ferleger Brades, Susan, *Lucio Fontana*, exhibition catalogue, Hayward Gall., London, 1999. Duchein, Paul/Vidal, Éric/Viguier, Florence, *Peindre en trois dimensions*, exhibition catalogue, Musée Ingres, Montauban, 2003.

MUSEUMS AND GALLERIES:

AMSTERDAM (Stedelijk Mus.) - BERLIN (Nationalgal.): *Spatial Concept/Nature* (1959) - BUENOS AIRES (MAM) - BUENOS AIRES (Municipal Mus.) - COLOGNE (Mus. Ludwig): *Spatial Concept/Laceration* (1961) - LONDON (Tate Collection): *Spatial Concept* (1949-1950, canvas); *Spatial Concept* (1958, pastel and canvas collage); *Nature* (1959-1960, bronze); *Spatial Concept `Waiting'* (1960, cut canvas) - MILAN (Civico Mus. d'Arte Contemporanea): *The Fisherman* (1931) - MILAN (Fontana Foundation): a collection of works; *Spatial Concept/Toy Theatre* (1965) - NEW YORK (MoMA) - PARIS (MNAM-CCI): *Abstract Sculpture* (1934, collection of paintings, sculptures, drawings, gift from Teresita Fontana) - ROME (Gal. Nazionale d'Arte Moderna).

AUCTION RECORDS:

MILAN, 26 March 1962, *Spatial Composition*, ITL 1,000,000. LONDON, 1 Dec 1965, *Spatial Concept of the Year 2000*, GBP 550. LONDON, 16 Oct 1969, *Spatial Concept* (1958, copper) GBP 933. MILAN, 4 Dec 1969, *Spatial Concept*, ITL 2,600,000. NEW YORK, 18 Nov 1970, *Spatial Concept*, USD 15,500. ROME, 28 Nov 1972, *Spatial Concept, the End of God* (holes/green canvas) ITL 15,500,000. LONDON, 3 April 1974, *Spatial Concept, the End of God*, GBP 28,000. PARIS, 29 Oct 1974, *The Couple* (painted ceramic, pair of eggs) FRF 18,000. ROME, 18 May 1976, *Concetto Spaziale* (*Spatial Concept*) (tempera and pencil, 26 x 17 3/4 ins / 66 x 45 cm) ITL 2,400,000. LONDON, 1 July 1976, *Spatial Concept, Gashes* (1966, oil on gashed canvas, 39 3/4 x 32 1/4 ins / 101 x 82 cm) GBP 9,500. ROME, 9 Dec 1976, *Spatial Concept* (1955, painted terracotta in black, 29 1/2 x 19 ins / 75 x 48 cm) ITL 3,400,000. MILAN, 25 Oct 1977, *Spatial Concept* (c. 1963, ceramic, 12 1/2 x 16 1/2 ins / 32 x 42 cm) ITL 1,400,000. ZURICH, 26 Nov 1977, *Spatial Concept* (1963, watercolour, 12 3/4 x 8 3/4 ins / 32.5 x 22.5 cm) CHF 4,700. MILAN, 13 Dec 1977, *Spatial Concept* (1958, crater/green canvas, 22 x 18 ins / 55 x 46 cm) ITL 5,000,000. MILAN, 18 April 1978, *Spatial Concept* (1958, holes, collage and aniline/canvas, 38 1/4 x 51 1/4 ins / 97 x 130 cm) ITL 15,000,000. MILAN, 14 April 1981, *Spatial Concept* (pencil and holes/paper, 12 1/4 x 18 ins / 31 x 46 cm) ITL 1,500,000. MILAN, 15 March 1983, *Spatial Concept, Gash* (1966, oil on canvas, 57 3/4 x 45 1/4 ins / 147 x 115 cm) ITL 22,000,000. MILAN, 4 April 1984, *Spatial Concept* (tempera/paper canvas, 26 1/2 x 17 3/4 ins / 67 x 45 cm) ITL 2,000,000. LONDON, 4 Dec 1984, *Spatial Concept, Nature* (1967, polished copper, h. 11 ins / 28 cm) GBP 2,500. MILAN, 18 Dec 1984, *Spatial Concept* (1954, charcoal and pencil, 9 1/2 x 13 1/2 ins / 24 x 34.2 cm) ITL 1,900,000. MILAN, 16 Oct 1986, *Spatial Concept* (1960, holes and pencil/untreated canvas, 25 1/2 x 33 ins / 65 x 84 cm) ITL 28,000,000. LONDON, 2 July 1987, *Spatial Concept, Baroque Venice* (1961, oil on canvas, 59 x 59 ins / 150 x 150 cm) GBP 140,000. PARIS, 24 Nov 1987, *Spatial Concept* (water paints/canvas, 28 1/4 x 31 ins / 72 x 79 cm) FRF 330,000. PARIS, 4 Dec 1987, *Spatial Concept, Nature* (1967, polished brass sculpture, no. 422/500, h. 9 3/4 ins / 25 cm, diam. 9 ins/22 cm) FRF 36,000. MILAN, 14 Dec 1987, *Spatial Concept* (1954, pastel and holes/grey and brown canvas, 32 1/4 x 25 1/2 ins / 82 x 65 cm) ITL 125,000,000. LONDON, 25 Feb 1988, *Spatial Concept* (1961, gold stitch, 2 1/4 x 1 1/2 ins / 5.8 x 3.5 cm) GBP 6,050; *Spatial Concept* (1966, water paints/canvas and wood, 29 1/2 x 37 ins / 75 x 94 cm) GBP 33,000. PARIS, 21 March 1988, *Spatial Concept* (1966-1967, oil on canvas, 22 x 18 ins / 55 x 46 cm) FRF 320,000. PARIS, 23 March 1988, *Spatial Concept* (1955, painted terracotta, 15 x 11 1/2 ins / 38 x 29 cm) FRF 125,000. MILAN, 24 March 1988, *Spatial Concept* (1956, oil and mixed media/canvas, bits of yellow, white and pink glass/red background, 31 1/2 x 25 1/2 ins / 80 x 64.5 cm) ITL 205,000,000; *Spatial Concept* (1963, oil, rips and graffiti/white canvas, 32 x 25 1/2 ins / 81 x 65 cm) ITL 77,000,000. NEW YORK, 2 May 1988, *Spatial Concept* (distemper/canvas, 36 1/2 x 54 1/4 ins / 93 x 138 cm) USD 132,000. LOKEREN, 28 May 1988, *Spatial Concept* (1957, gouache, 6 1/4 x 9 1/2 ins / 16 x 24 cm) BEF 90,000. MILAN, 8 June 1988, *Spatial Concept, Waiting* (1967, notches/canvas/blue background, 32 x 25 1/2 ins / 81 x 65 cm) ITL 115,000,000. LONDON, 30 June 1988, *Spatial Concept* (1955, mixed media, 31 1/2 x 25 1/2 ins / 80 x 65 cm) GBP 115,500. LONDON, 20 Oct 1988, *Spatial Concept* (water paints/canvas, 32 x 25 1/2 ins / 81 x 65 cm) GBP 53,900. STOCKHOLM, 21 Nov 1988, *Composition in Red* (sculpture, mixed media, 19 1/2 x 18 3/4 ins / 49.5 x 47.5 cm) SEK 9,000. LONDON, 1 Dec 1988, *Venice Lagoon* (1961, oil on canvas, 59 x 59 ins / 150 x 150 cm) GBP 396,000. MILAN, 14 Dec 1988, *Ascension* (polychrome painted ceramic, 28 x 13 3/4 ins / 71 x 35 cm) ITL 41,000,000. LONDON, 23 Feb 1989, *Spatial Concept* (1958, water paints, pencil and collage/canvas, 51 1/4 x 38 1/4 ins / 130 x 97 cm) GBP 88,000. ROME, 21 March 1989, *Spatial Concept* (1959, plastic matter, 37 x 37 ins / 94 x 94 cm) ITL 165,000,000. LONDON, 6 April 1989, *Spatial Concept* (1960, water paints/canvas, 37 x 45 3/4 ins / 93.7 x 116.2 cm) GBP 209,000. MILAN, 6 June 1989, *Spatial Concept* (1960, graffiti and oil on silver canvas, 24 x 18 ins / 61 x 46 cm) ITL 255,000,000. LONDON, 29 June 1989, *Spatial Concept* (1956, oil and scintillating mixed media on canvas, 53 x 39 1/4 ins / 134.5 x 100 cm) GBP 374,000. MILAN, 8 Nov 1989, *Spatial Concept* (1961, bits of bark and glass, oil and graffiti/gold canvas, 29 1/4 x 23 1/2 ins / 74 x 60 cm) ITL 570,000,000; *Spatial Concept, Form* (1958, iron sculpture, 17 1/4 x 5 3/4 x 5 1/2 ins / 44 x 14.5 x 14 cm) ITL 150,000,000. ROME, 6 Dec 1989, *Composition* (1952, mixed media/paper/glass, diam. 50 1/2 ins / 128 cm) ITL 27,600,000. MILAN, 19 Dec 1989, *Spatial Concept, Gash* (1967, water paints/blue canvas, 32 1/4 x 25 1/2 ins / 82 x 65 cm) ITL 480,000,000. PARIS, 15 Feb 1990, *Spatial Concept* (1952, perforated blotting paper, 18 x 22 3/4 ins / 45.5 x 58 cm) FRF 400,000. LONDON, 5 April 1990, *Spatial Concept* (1956, oil and mixed media/canvas, 39 1/4 x 31 1/2 ins / 100 x 80 cm) GBP 418,000. STOCKHOLM, 14 June 1990, *Spatial Concept, Gashes 1+1-ac34* (1962, mixed media/canvas, 24 x 19 3/4 ins / 61 x 50 cm) SEK 1,500,000. NEW YORK, 5 Oct 1990, *Spatial Concept* (1954, collage of canvas and water paints/canvas, 21 1/4 x 25 1/2 ins / 53.7 x 64.8 cm) USD 93,500. PARIS, 15 Oct 1990, *Spatial Concept* (green enamelled copper, 14 1/2 x 14 1/2 ins / 37 x 37 cm) FRF 55,000. NEW YORK, 7 Nov 1990, *Spatial Concept* (oil on canvas, 32 x 25 1/2 ins / 81.4 x 64.8 cm) USD 165,000. LONDON, 21 March 1991, *Fish* (1944, varnished polychrome ceramic, 9 1/2 x 10 x 6 ins / 24.1 x 25.4 x 15.3 cm) GBP 13,750. PARIS, 30 May 1991, *Composition* (glass painting, making a triangular table top, diam. 39 ins / 99 cm) FRF 100,000. LONDON, 27 June 1991, *Spatial Composition* (1962, oil on canvas, 57 3/4 x 45 ins / 146.5 x 114.5 cm) GBP 154,000. ZURICH, 16 Oct 1991, *Spatial Concept* (print, 25 x 19 1/2 ins / 63.7 x 49.7 cm) CHF 4,400. LUGANO, 28 March 1992, *Design for Spatial Environment* (1953, gouache/paper, 23 1/2 x 15 3/4 ins / 60 x 40 cm) CHF 41,000. MILAN, 14 April 1992, *Crucifix* (glazed ceramic, 13 3/4 x 9 1/4 ins / 35 x 23.5 cm) ITL 10,000,000. MILAN, 23 June 1992, *Figure on a Divan with a Dog* (Indian ink, 8 1/4 x 11 ins / 21 x 27 cm) ITL 3,900,000. LONDON, 2 July 1992, *Spatial Concept* (water paints/canvas, 32 x 39 1/4 ins / 81.2 x 100 cm) GBP 121,000; *The End of God* (1963, oil and glitter/canvas, 70 x 48 1/2 ins / 178 x 123 cm) GBP 319,000. PARIS, 1 Oct 1992, *Toy White/White Theatre, Spatial Concept* (1965, 61 3/4 x 64 1/2 ins / 157 x 164 cm) FRF 610,000. ROME, 14 Dec 1992, *The Tortoise* (1945, coloured ceramic, 3 1/2 x 5 x 4 3/4 ins / 9 x 13 x 12 cm) ITL 16,100,000. LONDON, 24-25 March 1993, *Spatial Concept* (two bronze balls, each h. 11 ins / 28 cm, w. 9 ins/22 cm) GBP 8,625. STOCKHOLM, 10-12 May 1993, *Spatial Concept, Gold Colour* (mixed media/canvas, 32 x 25 1/2 ins / 81 x 65 cm) SEK 450,000. LONDON, 24 June 1993, *Spatial Concept* (1958, oil on card, 26 3/4 x 34 ins / 68 x 86.5 cm) GBP 367,000. MILAN, 16 Nov 1993, *Spatial Concept, Gashes* (1965, water paints/canvas, 32 x 25 3/4 ins / 81.5 x 65.5 cm) ITL 241,500,000. LONDON, 2 Dec 1993, *The End of God, Series of Celestial Eggs* (1963, oil on canvas, 70 x 48 1/2 ins / 178 x 123 cm) GBP 320,500. MILAN, 24 May 1994, *Female Portrait* (painted ceramic, 5 3/4 x 5 x 2 1/2 ins / 14.5 x 12.5 x 6.5 cm) ITL 4,025,000. PARIS, 13 June 1994, *Spatial Concept* (stone and oil on canvas, 39 1/4 x 27 1/2 ins / 100 x 70 cm) FRF 700,000. LONDON, 1 Dec 1994, *Female Nude* (ink and watercolour/paper, 13 1/2 x 19 1/4 ins / 34 x 49 cm) GBP 6,325. LUCERNE, 20 May 1995, *Spatial Concept* (1959, ball-point pen/perforated sheet of silver in a gold frame, 7 1/2 x 6 1/4 ins / 19 x 16 cm) CHF 2,500. LONDON, 28 June 1995, *Spatial Concept, Gashes* (watercolour/canvas, 45 1/4 x 57 1/2 ins / 115 x 146 cm) GBP 430,500. MILAN, 19 March 1996, *Spatial Concept, Gashes* (1967, red watercolour/canvas with 4 notches, 23 1/2 x 23 1/2 ins / 60 x 60 cm) ITL 224,250,000; *Spatial Concept* (1963-1964, gouache and holes/paper, 18 1/2 x 12 1/2 ins / 47 x 32 cm) ITL 12,650,000. PARIS, 1 July 1996, *Spatial Concept* (1966-1967, ink/paper, 22 1/4 x 7 3/4 ins / 56.5 x 20 cm) FRF 13,000. MILAN, 25 Nov 1996, *Spatial Concept* (1947, terracotta, 10 x 12 1/4 ins / 25.5 x 31 cm) ITL 18,400, 000. LONDON, 4-5 Dec 1996, *Spatial Concept, the End of God* (1964, oil on canvas, 70 x 48 1/2 ins / 178 x 123 cm) GBP 397,500; *Spatial Concept, Waiting* (1964, watercolour/canvas, 24 x 18 ins / 61 x 46 cm) GBP 34,500. PARIS, 13 Dec 1996, *Composition* (1968, Indian ink/paper, 6 3/4 x 9 3/4 ins / 17 x 25 cm) FRF 8,100. PARIS, 28 April 1997, *Spatial Concept* (1949, Indian ink and lacerations/paper, 11 x 8 1/4 ins / 27 x 21 cm) FRF 9,500. MILAN, 19 May 1997, *Spatial Concept* (1957, mixed media/canvas, 22 x 22 ins / 55 x 55 cm) ITL 136,900,000. LONDON, 26 June 1997, *Spatial Concept* (gold paint and oil on canvas, 59 x 59 ins / 150 x 150 cm) GBP 529,000. LONDON, 27 June 1997, *Spatial Concept* (1952, oil on canvas, 15 3/4 x 19 3/4 ins / 40 x 50 cm) GBP 46,600. LONDON, 23 Oct 1997, *Spatial Concept, Waiting* (watercolour/canvas, 28 3/4 x 23 1/2 ins / 73 x 60 cm) GBP 56,500. LONDON, 21 Oct 1999, *Spatial Concept, Waiting* (1959, waterpaint on canvas, 47 x 65 ins / 120 x 165 cm) GBP 270,000. LONDON, 9 Dec 1999, *Spatial Concept* (1954, oil on canvas, 39 x 32 ins / 99 x 81 cm) GBP 220,000. LONDON, 28 June 2000, *Spatial Concept, At Dawn Venice was All in Silver* (silver paint and coloured glass on canvas, 59 x 59 ins / 150 x 150 cm) GBP 620,000. NEW YORK, 15 Nov 2000, *Spatial Concept, Waiting* (waterpaint on canvas, 39 x 54 ins / 100 x 136 cm) USD 650,000. LONDON, 7 Feb 2001, *Spatial Concept* (1954, glass pebbles, 57 x 39 ins / 145 x 100 cm) GBP 680,000. NEW YORK, 16 May 2001, *Coupure* (oil on canvas, 45 x 35 ins / 115 x 89 cm) USD 900,000. LONDON, 26 June 2002, *Spatial Concept, Second Sky of Venice* (1961, oil on canvas, 59 x 59 ins / 150 x 150 cm) GBP 1,250,000. LONDON, 21 Oct 2002, *Spatial Concept* (1957, glazed iron, 68 x 51 ins / 172 x 130 cm) GBP 560,000. LONDON, 6 Feb 2003, *Spatial Concept, God's End* (1963, oil and glitter on canvas, oval, 70 x 48 ins / 178 x 123 cm) GBP 700,000. LONDON, 25 June 2003, *Spatial Concept, The End of God* (1964, oil on canvas, 70 x 48 ins / 178 x 123 cm) GBP 1,225,000. LONDON, 5 Feb 2004, *Spatial Concept, Waiting* (1962, waterpaint on canvas, 35 x 46 ins / 89 x 116 cm) GBP 610,000. LONDON, 19 Oct 2004, *Spatial Concept, God's End* (1963, oil on canvas, 70 x 48 ins / 178 x 123 cm) GBP 1,100,000.

FONTANA, Luigi

Italian, 19th century.

Born in the 19th century, in Milan.

Sculptor.

After completing his studies at the academy in Milan, Luigi Fontana travelled to Buenos Aires and Rosario di Santa Fé. His best-known works include: the statue of the *Affliction* and an *Angel of Mercy* on the funeral monument of the Pinasco Family; a monument to Columbus in Rosario; and, in the city of Buenos Aires, a group inspired by the Buenos Aires revolution. Lesser-known works by Fontana include: a bust entitled *At the Church*; *The Orphans* (a group); and the *Monument to General S Martin*.

FONTANA, Luigi

Italian, 19th century.

Born 1827, in Monte San Petrangeli (Marche); died end December 1908, in Rome.

Painter, sculptor, architect.

Luigi Fontana began his studies with Palmaroli in Marcerata, and continued them in Rome with Minardi. He specialised in decorative painting. One of his best-known works is *Ezekiel's Vision*, after Raphael, in S Nicola da Tolentino. He painted frescoes in many churches in Rome, including: S Salvatore in Lauro *(The Four Prophets)*; S Lorenzo in Damaso, S Apostoli and S Maria in Trastevere. Fontana is also remembered for his paintings in the Palazzo Massini and the Palazzo Ricci, and for his sculptures: the marble funeral monument to his master, *Minardi*, in the Campo Santo cemetery; and busts of the archbishops *Minucci* and *De Angelis* in Fermo Cathedral.

FONTANA, Michele

Italian, 18th century.

Born to a family originally from Como; died 28 April 1729, in Brno.

Sculptor, stucco artist.

Michele Fontana was the son of Baldassare Fontana. He was granted citizenship of Brno in 1720. He worked on the monastery in Velehrad (Welehrad), Hradec (Hradisch), and at the Mount of Calvary in Olomouc.

FONTANA, Natale

Italian, 15th century.

Active in Venice in 1437.

Painter.

FONTANA, Orazio
Italian, 16th century.
Died after 1571.
Active in Urbino.
Miniaturist, painter (porcelain).

Museums and Galleries:
Berlin - London (British Mus.) - Paris (Louvre).

FONTANA, Pietro
Italian, 18th - 19th century.
Born 1762, in Bassano; died 1837, in Rome.
Engraver.

Pietro Fontana studied in Venice under the painter Mengardi, then travelled to Rome in 1785 and devoted himself exclusively to engraving, studying under Volpato and Morghen. He was a member of the Accademia di San Luca in both Rome and Venice. He engraved a vast number of plates, including Domenichino's *Sibyls*; Ludovico Carracci's *Christ Appearing before Pontius Pilate*; Guercino's *The Four Apostles*; Guido Reni's *Herod*; Camuccini's *Death of Caesar* and *Festival of the Gods*; and Thorvaldsen's *Apostles*.

FONTANA, Pietro
Italian, 19th century.
Born 1787, in Carrara; died 1858, in Carrara.
Sculptor.

Pietro Fontana was a pupil of Pizzi and Desmarais at the Accademia di Belle Arti in Carrara. He went to live in Milan, where he won the Rome Prize at the Accademia di Belle Arti di Brera in 1804. In 1806 he won the Academy of Florence Prize for his low relief of *Isaac and Sarah*. His key work was the monumental statue of *Duchess Maria Beatrice d'Este* in Carrara. Other well-known works include: the funeral monuments of two bishops in Reggio Cathedral; a low relief of *The Baptism of Christ*, in the church of Agnano, near Pisa; and marble busts of *Hector* and *Paris* in the ducal palace at Modena.

Museums and Galleries:
Carrara (Accademia di Belle Arti): *Theseus* (low relief) - Milan (Pinacoteca di Brera): *Bust of Raphael*.

FONTANA, Prospero
Italian, 16th century.
Born 1512, in Bologna; died 1597, in Bologna.
Painter, draughtsman. Religious subjects, portraits.
Fontainebleau School.

A pupil of Innocenzio da Imola, Prospero Fontana travelled to Rome, where he was employed by Pope Julius III, and was later engaged by Francesco Primaticcio, who was working at Fontainebleau at the time. From Fontainebleau he went to Genoa, where he worked for the Doria gallery. On returning to his native city he became the master of Lodovico, Annibale and Agostino Carracci, Dionysius Calvaert, Tiarini and Achille Calici, and was several times director of the guild of painters.

Fontana's most important works include the *Epiphany*, his masterpiece, but he was famed above all for his portraits. His best works in this genre are *Pope Julius III*, *Ulysse Aldrovandi* and *Achille Bocchi*.

Bibliography:
Gaston, Robert, '*Prospero Fontana's 'Holy Family with Saints*' in *Art Bulletin of Victoria*, vol 19, 1978. Pellicciari, Armanda, '*L'Intervento di Prospero Fontana nella sala di David di Palazzo Poggi a Bologna*' in *Bollettino d'arte, 5*, vol. a 70, periodical, Rome, 1985. Corrado, Rosini, *Dietro la moda delle grottesche Prospero Fontana e Paolo Vitelli*, Cassa di risparmio di Città di Castello, Città di Castello, 1986. *The Age of Correggio and the Carracci*, exhibition catalogue, National Gallery of Art, Washington, DC; Metropolitan Museum, New York; Pinacoteca, Bologna, 1986. Fortunati Pietrantonio, V., *La pittura bolognese del 500*, Bologna, 1986. Negri Arnoldi, Francesco, '*Un Trionfo di Galatea di Prospero Fontana*' in *Prospettiva, n°93-94*, periodical, Centro Di, Florence, 1999.

Museums and Galleries:
Berlin (Bodemus.): *Adoration of the Magi* - Bologna (Church of S Silvestro): *Epiphany* - Bologna (Pinacoteca Nazionale): *Entombment*; *Portrait of a Member of the House of Este* - Dresden: *Holy Family with St Catherine and St Cecilia* - Milan (Pinacoteca di Brera): *Annunciation*; *Virgin and Apostles* - Rome (Mus. e Gal. Borghese): *Holy Family* - Verona: *Holy Family* (attributed to B. India).

Auction records:
London, 22 Dec 1927, *Garland of Flowers*, GBP 21. London, 18 Dec 1936, *Virgin della Tenda* (after Raphael) GBP 10. London, 12 June 1968, *Portrait of a Cardinal*, GBP 2,800. Rome, 10 May 1988, *Portrait of a Woman with a Companion Carrying a Child* (oil on canvas, 46 x 37 3/4 ins / 117 x 96 cm) ITL 50,000,000. Rome, 13 Dec 1988, *Portrait of a Gentleman Wearing the Medal of St George* (oil on canvas, 24 3/4 x 17 1/4 ins / 63 x 44 cm) ITL 15,000,000. New York, 11 Oct 1990, *Virgin and Child with St John the Baptist and a Holy Bishop* (oil on panel, 31 x 27 ins / 79 x 68.5 cm) USD 46,200. New York, 14 Jan 1992, *Tightrope Walker and Pole Flanked by Two Panels Bearing a Greek Inscription: Endure and Be Abstinent, with Figures Watching from Below* (ink and wash/black chalk, 4 1/2 x 3 1/4 ins / 11.7 x 8.4 cm) USD 2,200. New York, 11 Jan 1996, *Virgin and Child with St John the Baptist* (oil on canvas, 11 x 9 3/4 ins / 27.9 x 24.8 cm) USD 60,250. London, 16-17 April 1997, *Madonna and Child with St Catherine* (pen and brown ink and wash, 7 x 8 1/4 ins / 17.7 x 21 cm) GBP 2,990. London, 10 July 2001, *Phaethon Receiving the Chariot of the Sun from his Father Apollo* (black chalk, pen and ink wash, 9 x 12 ins / 22 x 31 cm) GBP 7,000. London, 10 July 2002, *Battle of the Centaurs and Lapiths* (pen and brown ink wash, 7 x 11 ins / 18 x 29 cm) GBP 10,000. Venice, 11 July 2003, *Adoration of the Magi. Adoration of the Sheperds* (oil on copper, a pair, 20 x 9 ins / 52 x 24 cm) EUR 175,000. London, 7 July 2004, *Holy Family with St John* (oil on panel, 31 x 26 ins / 79 x 65 cm) GBP 85,000.

FONTANA, Roberto, or Fontano
Italian, 19th century.
Born 1844, in Milan; died 1907, in Milan.
Painter, watercolourist. Figures, portraits, genre scenes.

Roberto Fontana exhibited in Germany (notably in Munich) from 1888 onward. He won a medal in Philadelphia in 1876, and gained an honourable mention in Paris in 1889.

Museums and Galleries:
Göteborg: *Pierrot* - Milan (Gal. d'Arte Moderna): *Aesop Telling His Fables to His Children*.

Auction records:
London, 21 March 1908, *Italian Woman* (watercolour) GBP 4. Paris, 14-16 Jan 1926, *Young Woman Holding a Book*, FRF 220. Milan, 21 Oct 1969, *Village Street*, ITL 650,000. Milan, 17 Oct 1972, *Children in a Church*, ITL 500,000. Milan, 20 Dec 1977, *Portrait of a Little Girl* (oil on canvas, 17 1/4 x 12 1/2 ins / 44 x 32 cm) ITL 1,000,000. Milan, 6 Nov 1980, *Portrait of a Young Girl* (oil on canvas, 12 1/4 x 7 ins / 31 x 18 cm) ITL 4,000,000. London, 23 Feb 1983, *Young Girl with a Black Shawl* (oil on canvas, 20 1/2 x 17 1/2 ins / 52 x 44.5 cm) GBP 2,200. London, 21 June 1984, *Innocence* (watercolour heightened with white, 8 3/4 x 6 1/4 ins / 22.2 x 16 cm) GBP 500. Milan, 9 June 1987, *Standing Nude* (watercolour, 12 1/4 x 7 3/4 ins / 31 x 20 cm) ITL 1,800,000. Rome, 16 Dec 1987, *Ophelia* (oil on canvas, 48 3/4 x 44 ins / 124 x 112 cm) ITL 11,000,000. London, 29 April 1988, *In the Orchard* (oil, 7 3/4 x 11 ins / 19.5

x 28 cm) GBP 26,400. MILAN, 14 March 1989, *Reading* (oil on panel, 12¼ x 18 ins / 31 x 45.5 cm) ITL 9,000,000. MILAN, 14 June 1989, *Woman on a Balcony* (oil on panel, 7½ x 6 ins / 19 x 15.5 cm) ITL 7,000,000. MILAN, 5 Dec 1990, *Portrait of a Young Woman in the Studio of a Painter* (1883, oil on canvas/panel, 12½ x 5¼ ins / 32 x 13.5 cm) ITL 17,500,000. ROME, 16 April 1991, *Bust of a Young Girl* (oil on card, 5 x 3¼ ins / 12.5 x 8.5 cm) ITL 2,760,000. MILAN, 29 Oct 1992, *Model* (oil on panel, 4¼ x 7½ ins / 10.5 x 19 cm) ITL 7,500,000. NEW YORK, 30 April 2001, *Souvenirs from the East* (1888, oil on panel, 6 x 4 ins / 15 x 9 cm) USD 7,000. MILAN, 22 May 2002, *Gypsy Woman with a Tambourine* (1886, oil on canvas, 19 x 11 ins / 47 x 28 cm) EUR 2,500. MILAN, 8 April 2003, *Woman in Profile* (oil on canvas, 21 x 15 ins / 54 x 37 cm) EUR 1,500. LONDON, 16 June 2004, *Dante in the Underworld* (1873, oil on canvas, 73 x 97 ins / 186 x 247 cm) GBP 13,000.

FONTANA, Salvatore di Pietro

Italian, 16th century.
Died 26 July 1590, in Rome.
Active in Venice and in Rome.
Painter. History painting.

FONTANA, Veronica

Italian, 17th century.
Born 1651, in Bologna; died 1690.
Engraver.

Veronica Fontana studied under her father Domenico Maria Fontana. She produced engravings of scenes from the *Life of Mary* and a *Portrait of the Poet Andreini*, together with woodcut engravings for a Latin Bible and portraits for Malvasia's 1678 work *Felsina*.

FONTANA, Vincenzo

Italian, 17th century.
Active in Padua in 1615.
Painter.

FONTANA FREDO, Girardo

Italian, 16th century.
Engraver.

Girardo Fontano Fredo engraved an *Adoration of the Magi* after Polidoro da Caravaggio.

FONTANALS Y ROVIROSA, Francisco

Spanish, 19th century.
Born 1777, in Vilanova de Stiges; died 1827, in Vilanova de Stiges.
Painter, engraver, watercolourist. Religious subjects, historical subjects, figures.

Francisco Fontanals y Rovirosa received a bursary from Ferdinand VII to study in Rome. He was best known as an engraver.

MUSEUMS AND GALLERIES:

BARCELONA: *St Francis of Assisi* (copy) - VALENCIA (Real Academia de Bellas Artes de San Carlos): *Two Musicians* (watercolour); *St Isabel* (watercolour).

FONTANAROSA, Lucien Joseph

French, 20th century.
Born 19 December 1912, in Paris, to Italian parents; died 27 April 1975, in Paris.
Painter (gouache), watercolourist, engraver, lithographer, illustrator. Figure compositions, figures, genre scenes, still-lifes, flowers, landscapes.

Lucien Fontanarosa grew up in Paris and Padua in a modest family of Italian descent and qualified as a lithographer in 1931. In 1932, after taking evening classes at the École des Arts Appliqués, he was admitted to Lucien Simon's studio at the École des Beaux-Arts. In 1934 he made his debut with *Musicians* at the Salon de la Société Nationale des Beaux-Arts, and won a grant enabling him to tour Spain. In 1935 the Grand Prix de l'Afrique du Nord earned him a one-year stay in Morocco, and in 1936 he won the Grand Prix de Rome.

After returning from Italy in 1939 he settled in the Buttes-Chaumont, Paris, with his wife, Annette Faive, also a painter. In 1946 and 1952 he sat on the jury for the Prix de Rome, and in 1946 he taught at the American Summer Academy in Fontainebleau. Among other distinctions, he also won the Menton Biennale prize in 1951, became a member of the Institut in 1955 and was made a Chevalier of the Légion d'Honneur in 1957. In 1958 he was appointed to teach the handpicked students of the École Polytechnique, where he reorganised the teaching of art and drawing. In 1973, two years before his death, he was awarded the Prix des Peintres Témoins de leur Temps. In 1992 the city of Paris named a public garden after him.

He took part in the Salon de la Société Nationale des Beaux-Arts, on whose management committee he sat from 1941, and exhibited at the Salon des Peintres Témoins de leur Temps every year from 1953 onwards. From 1947 he had regular solo shows in Paris, the provinces and abroad (including Palm Beach, 1963). There have been many retrospectives of his work since his death, notably in 2002 at the Musée des Beaux-Arts in Menton.

He produced numerous lithographs, illustrated over 40 literary works by Gide, Mac Orlan and Montherlant and produced more than 120 *Livre de Poche* (*Paperback*) book covers between 1950 and 1974. He also executed wall paintings for a number of public buildings throughout France including the library of the Faculté des Sciences in Orsay. From 1964 to 1969 he was commissioned by the Banque de France to produce watercolour designs for the 10F, 50F, 100F and 500F notes.

In his formative years he learnt from the Cubists, who did not otherwise influence him, how to structure a piece, as his *Country Concert* shows. During the war he destroyed some of his early works as he strove for tighter control of his palette, settling on an ochre to brown range which would underpin all his work even after the period when he used no other colour. His children (who became well-known classical musicians) inspired his *Children* and *Musicians*. His move to Provence rekindled his Mediterranean sensitivities and inspired *Girls* and some still-lifes. His stays in Venice, from 1961, inspired his great Venetian landscapes, bathed in a light he loved.

Eschewing contemporary movements, Fontanarosa extolled simple joys in a universally accessible form.

FONTANAROSA

BIBLIOGRAPHY:

Ratier, Jacques, '*Lucien Fontanarosa*' in *coll. Les Cahiers d'Art-Documents*, Éd. Pierre Cailler, Geneva. Roger-Marx, Claude, *Fontanarosa. 150 œuvres: peintures, pastels, lithographies, illustrations de 1934 à 1973*, exhibition catalogue, Palais de la Méditerranée, Nice, 1973. Frontenac, Yves/Cesbron, Gilbert, *Fontanarosa ou le soleil sur la terre*, Éd. SNP-MD, Paris, 1977.

MUSEUMS AND GALLERIES:

FONTAINEBLEAU (Mus. d'Art Figuratif Contemporain) - PARIS (BNF): large collection of lithographs - PARIS (MAMVP) - PARIS (MNAM-CCI) - SCEAUX (Mus. de l'Île-de-France).

AUCTION RECORDS:

PARIS, 15 Dec 1943, *Old Street* (drawing in watercolour) FRF 420. PARIS, 20 June 1944, *Canal at La Villette, Snowed Under*, FRF 15,000. PARIS, 18 March 1969, *Church of S Maria della Salute in Venice*, FRF 6,500. PARIS, 20 May 1974, *Young Fishmonger*, FRF 10,000. PARIS, 25 Oct 1976, *Woman Musician* (pastel, 12¼ x 14¼ ins / 31 x 36 cm) FRF 3,000. LYONS, 24 March 1980, *Girl on a Deckchair* (oil on canvas, 9½ x 16¼ ins / 24 x 41 cm) FRF 3,300. PARIS, 15 June 1982, *Venice, Gon-*

doliers (oil on canvas, 19 3/4 x 39 1/4 ins / 50 x 100 cm) FRF 10,500. PARIS, 10 July 1983, *Grape Harvest* (oil on panel, 35 x 51 1/4 ins / 89 x 130 cm) FRF 100,000. PARIS, 30 June 1986, *Aïcha* (1936, oil on canvas, 20 x 17 ins / 51 x 43 cm) FRF 17,000. PARIS, 14 Dec 1988, *Brawl* (1933, oil on card, 20 1/2 x 23 1/2 ins / 52 x 60 cm) FRF 25,000. PARIS, 9 June 1989, *Nude Standing* (1937, 51 1/4 x 35 1/2 ins / 130 x 90 cm) FRF 92,000. PARIS, 11 May 1990, *Le Plateau* (oil on canvas, 6 3/4 x 13 1/2 ins / 17 x 34 cm) FRF 25,000. PARIS, 6 June 1990, *Odalisque Curled-up* (oil on panel, 7 1/2 x 9 1/2 ins / 19 x 24 cm) FRF 9,500. LYONS, 9 Oct 1990, *Child with Fruit* (oil on canvas, 18 x 29 1/2 ins / 46 x 75 cm) FRF 52,000. FONTAINEBLEAU, 18 Nov 1990, *Château at Fontainebleau* (1943, oil on paper, 7 x 13 3/4 ins / 17.5 x 35 cm) FRF 30,500. CALAIS, 9 Dec 1990, *Young Ballerinas* (oil on canvas, 28 3/4 x 19 3/4 ins / 73 x 50 cm) FRF 79,000. LYONS, 13 Dec 1990, *Child with an Apple* (oil on canvas) FRF 46,000. LE TOUQUET, 8 June 1992, *Canal at La Villette* (oil on panel, 20 3/4 x 26 ins / 53 x 66 cm) FRF 10,000. NEW YORK, 12 June 1992, *Still-life with Apples* (oil on canvas, 10 3/4 x 18 ins / 27.3 x 45.7 cm) USD 1,210. PARIS, 10 Feb 1993, *Pierrot and Harlequin* (1955, oil on canvas, 24 x 23 3/4 ins / 61 x 60.5 cm) FRF 45,000. LE TOUQUET, 22 May 1994, *Comedia dell'Arte or Guitarist and Small Monkey Musician* (1969, oil on canvas, 28 3/4 x 45 1/4 ins / 73 x 115 cm) FRF 82,000. PARIS, 5 April 1995, *Two Guitarists* (1962, oil on canvas, 23 1/2 x 47 1/4 ins / 60 x 120 cm) FRF 49,000. LE TOUQUET, 21 May 1995, *Venice, Church of S Maria della Salute* (1964, oil on canvas, 51 1/4 x 51 1/4 ins / 130 x 130 cm) FRF 111,000. CALAIS, 7 July 1996, *Portrait of Lucette Descaves* (oil on canvas, 13 x 9 1/2 ins / 33 x 24 cm) FRF 16,000. PARIS, 29 Nov 1996, *Woman at her Toilette* (oil on canvas, 23 1/2 x 28 3/4 ins / 60 x 73 cm) FRF 33,000. CALAIS, 23 March 1997, *Ballerinas* (1960, oil on canvas, 18 x 13 ins / 46 x 33 cm) FRF 31,000; *Venice, Church of S Maria della Salute* (1966, oil on panel, 7 1/2 x 13 ins / 19 x 33 cm) FRF 11,500. PARIS, 12 Dec 1997, *Still-life with Pitcher and Pears* (oil on canvas, 22 x 36 1/4 ins / 55 x 92 cm) FRF 8,000. PARIS, 22 March 1998, *Portrait of a Blonde Girl* (oil on canvas, 26 3/4 x 15 1/4 ins / 68 x 38.5 cm) FRF 15,000. PARIS, 5 March 1999, *Harlequin with Guitar* (oil on canvas, 22 x 18 ins / 55 x 46 cm) FRF 30,000. CALAIS, 4 July 1999, *Seated Nude* (pastel, 24 x 17 ins / 60 x 44 cm) FRF 11,000. PARIS, 20 Nov 2000, *Reclining Moroccan Woman* (oil on paper on board, 18 x 25 ins / 46 x 64 cm) FRF 50,000. LONDON, 1 Dec 2000, *Young Girl with Violin* (oil on canvas, 24 x 29 ins / 61 x 74 cm) GBP 3,800. CALAIS, 6 May 2001, *Trawler at the Harbour Entrance* (oil on canvas, 30 x 39 ins / 75 x 100 cm) FRF 31,000. PARIS, 7 Dec 2001, *Views of Paris* (gouache and watercolour, five in one frame, 5 x 7 ins / 13 x 17 cm) FRF 14,000. CHARTRES, 17 March 2002, *Success* (oil on canvas, 11 x 25 ins / 29 x 64 cm) EUR 2,600. PARIS, 24 May 2002, *Venice* (oil on canvas, 38 x 51 ins / 97 x 130 cm) EUR 10,000. PARIS, 6 June 2003, *Ballerina* (pastel, 25 x 19 ins / 63 x 49 cm) EUR 3,300. PARIS, 3 Dec 2003, *Young Man with Musical Instruments* (oil on canvas, 25 x 45 ins / 63 x 115 cm) EUR 5,000. PARIS, 27 April 2004, *Girl with Curtain* (c. 1964, oil on canvas, 20 x 39 ins / 50 x 100 cm) EUR 6,500.

FONTANE, Peter

German, 18th century.
Miniaturist.

Peter Fontane was art tutor to the royal children in Berlin. From 1787 to 1795 he submitted portraits and copies on ivory and in pastel to exhibitions at the academy.

FONTANELLA, Carlo

Italian, 18th century.
Painter.

Carlo Fontanella was probably a pupil of A. Zucchi. He exhibited a portrait at the Free Society in London in 1779 and another portrait the following year.

FONTANELLI, Giovanni Batista

Italian, 17th century.
Active in Bologna.
Engraver (burin).

Giovanni Batista Fontanelli engraved the frontispiece for *Ristrett Odella Vita*.

FONTANES, J.- J. Raymond, or Coignande de Fontanes

French, 19th - 20th century.
Born 27 July 1875, in Angers.
Painter. Landscapes.
Orientalism.

Raymond Fontaines studied under Marcel Baschet, François Schommer and Henri Royer. From 1906 he exhibited in Paris at the Salon des Artistes Français, of which he was an associate member. In 1913-1914 he showed work he had done in Egypt at the Salon des Peintres Orientalistes Français, among which were two views of the Cafr-el-Gamous cemetery near Cairo.

AUCTION RECORDS:

PARIS, 7 Dec 1992, *Ancient Tombs in Egypt* (oil on canvas, 22 3/4 x 28 1/4 ins / 58 x 72 cm) FRF 7,500.

FONTANES, Louise Méchin de (Mme)

French, 19th century.
Born in Caen.
Painter (porcelain).

Learned her craft at the Sèvres porcelain works; exhibited floral compositions at the Salon as of 1841.

FONTANESI, Antonio

Italian, 19th century.
Born 23 February 1818, in Reggio Emilia; died 17 April 1882, in Turin.
Painter. Mythological subjects, genre scenes, landscapes with figures, landscapes.
Macchiaioli group.

Antonio Fontanesi studied painting in Reggio Emilia, Turin and Rome, where he got to know Auguste Ravier. He stopped painting in 1847 to take part in Garibaldi's campaigns in 1848, and the second war of independence 11 years later. Between the wars he had to flee Italy: in 1850 he was living in exile in Geneva, where he became the pupil of the landscape artist Alexandre Calame. Fontanesi was resident in Paris in 1855, and London in 1866, before finally returning to Italy. He was appointed director of the academy in Lucca in 1868, then taught at the Accademia Albertina in Turin in 1869. He was summoned to Japan in 1875, to act as director of the academy in Tokyo for three years. However he was misunderstood there, and moved back to Turin in 1878, where he died a few years later.

Fontanesi painted almost exclusively landscapes. In his early years he was influenced by Auguste Ravier, which probably explains his affinity with the polychrome intensity of the Lyons School, which prefigured Pointillism and Fauvism. In Florence he was involved with the Macchiaioli Group, although he opposed their preoccupation with Symbolism. Following his return to Turin, he developed his own personal painting style, which may be regarded as similar to the Romanticism of Charles-François Daubigny.

Fontanesi exhibited in Geneva from 1845 to 1886, and then in Paris, at the 1855 Exposition Universelle, where he met Charles-François Daubigny and Corot.

BIBLIOGRAPHY:

Bernardi, M., *Antonio Fontanesi*, Turin, 1967. Farioli, Elisabetta/Poppi, Claudio, *Antonio Fontanesi e la Pittura di paesaggio in Italia 1861-1880*, Motta, 1999.

MUSEUMS AND GALLERIES:

BOLOGNA (Pinacoteca Nazionale): *Drinking Trough* - FLORENCE (Accademia di Belle Arti): *The Arno at Sunset, S Trinità Bridge* - PRATO: *View of the Arno at Sunset* - REGGIO

EMILIA: *Solitude; Storm at Sea; Entrance to a Japanese Temple* - ROME (Gal. Nazionale d'Arte Moderna): *Spring; Diana Bathing* - TURIN (Gal. Civica d'Arte Moderna e Contemporanea): *Pond; Morning; Evening Peace; April Landscape* - TURIN (Palazzo Reale): *November Landscape* - TURIN (Pinacoteca): *Pasture*.

AUCTION RECORDS:

MILAN, 16 March 1965, *Clouds*, ITL 22,000,000. MILAN, 11 Nov 1969, *Flock Drinking in a Landscape*, ITL 5,000,000. MILAN, 28 May 1974, *Flock in a Landscape*, ITL 3,300,000. MILAN, 10 June 1981, *Landscape* (charcoal/mounted paper, 15 1/4 x 23 1/2 ins / 39 x 60 cm) ITL 3,200,000. MILAN, 13 Oct 1987, *October: Shepherdess and Flock at Dusk* (oil on canvas, 36 1/2 x 52 ins / 93 x 132 cm) ITL 160,000,000. MILAN, 5 Dec 1990, *Lonely Valley* (oil on card, 12 1/2 x 10 1/4 ins / 32 x 26 cm) ITL 32,000,000. ROME, 16 April 1991, *Landscape with Figures* (oil on panel, 8 1/4 x 11 3/4 ins / 21 x 30 cm) ITL 23,000,000. MILAN, 19 March 1992, *In Savoy* (watercolour/paper, 7 x 10 ins / 18 x 25.5 cm) ITL 20,000,000. MILAN, 8 June 1993, *Trees and the Sea* (oil on panel, 6 1/4 x 11 3/4 ins / 16 x 30 cm) ITL 26,000,000. MILAN, 16 June 1999, *Landscape with Figures at Stream* (oil on panel, arched top, 17 x 12 ins / 44 x 31 cm) ITL 90,000,000. MILAN, 21 Dec 1999, *Lake Landscape* (charcoal on paper/board, 20 x 28 ins / 52 x 71 cm) ITL 8,000,000. VERCELLI, 18 Nov 2000, *Impression at Torrazza* (oil on cardboard, 11 x 7 ins / 28 x 19 cm) ITL 35,000,000. ROME, 21 Nov 2000, *Solitude* (oil on board, 20 x 28 ins / 52 x 70 cm) ITL 86,000,000. BOSTON, 22 March 2002, *Cows at Pasture* (oil on canvas, 9 x 13 ins / 23 x 33 cm) USD 4,000. MILAN, 10 Dec 2003, *At the Source* (1860, oil on canvas, 20 x 27 ins / 50 x 68 cm) EUR 70,000. MILAN, 25 Feb 2004, *Evening* (1862, oil on canvas, 31 x 28 ins / 80 x 70 cm) EUR 170,000. ROME, 10 June 2004, *Landscape in the Dauphine* (oil on canvas, 11 x 15 ins / 28 x 39 cm) EUR 27,000.

FONTANESI, Francesco

Italian, 18th century.
Born 4 October 1751, in Reggio nell'Emilia; died 9 October 1795.
Painter.

Francesco Fontanesi studied in Reggio nell'Emilia under G. Bazzani and P. Zannichelli. From 1780 he worked in theatres in Milan and Venice, designing stage sets, curtains and theatre interiors. He was solely responsible for the interior decoration of the Teatro della Fenice in Venice in 1790. Fontanesi was also a landscape painter and produced a notable oil painting entitled *Dawn*. The Chierici Museum in Reggio nell'Emilia has preserved his models and samples of his decorative work, and two of his stage set projects are on view in the Museo Teatrale alla Scala in Milan.

FONTANESI, Giovanni

Italian, 19th century.
Born 28 January 1813, in Reggio; died 14 February 1875, in Reggio.
Painter. Landscapes. Theatre decoration.

Giovanni Fontanesi was the grandson of Francesco Fontanesi, and regularly exhibited at the academy of fine arts in Modena. He painted theatre decorations, including the curtain for the Teatro Communale in Reggio, but was first and foremost a landscape painter.

FONTANET, Georges

French, 20th century.
Born in Le Mont-Doré.
Painter. Landscapes.

Georges Fontanet exhibited in Paris at the Salon from 1922.

FONTANET, Gil

Spanish, 15th century.
Glass painter.

Gil Fontanet executed the glass paintings designed by Bartolomé Bermejo for the windows of Barcelona cathedral in 1495.

FONTANET, Jaime

Spanish, 16th century.
Glass painter.

Jaime Fontanet, who was probably the son of Gil Fontanet, executed the *Window of Virtues* and other glass paintings for the city hall in Barcelona.

FONTANET, Juan

Spanish, 16th century.
Active in Barcelona in 1565.
Painter.

FONTANEY, Georges

French, 20th century.
Born 9 August 1935, in St-Étienne.
Painter.

Georges Fontaney studied in St-Étienne and exhibited in the provinces from 1966.

FONTANEZ, Jules

Swiss, 20th century.
Born 2 May 1875, in Geneva; died 1918, in Geneva.
Also active in France.
Painter, draughtsman, engraver, illustrator.

Fontanez studied woodcut engraving at the arts and crafts academy in Geneva, settled in Paris in 1900 and took part in numerous group exhibitions in Paris (Salon de la Société Nationale des Beaux-Arts), Geneva, Bern, Zurich, Stuttgart, Rome and elsewhere. He was a contributor to satirical reviews in Geneva (*Sapajou, Passe-Partout, Papillon*) and in Paris (*Courrier Français, Gil Blas*); he also worked as a book illustrator, notably for *Blood, Sensual Pleasure and Death* by Maurice Barrès, *Gaspard of the Night* by Aloysius Bertrand, and various children's books (*House of Birds; Tales of Jade and Yesteryear*). As a painter, he is best remembered for his views of Paris.

MUSEUMS AND GALLERIES:

SOLOTHURN: *Paris at Night*.

AUCTION RECORDS:

ZURICH, 1 June 1973, *Diabolo*, CHF 4,000. GENEVA, 29 Nov 1986, *Carnival* (oil on canvas, 28 1/4 x 38 1/2 ins / 72 x 98 cm) CHF 2,400. BERN, 26 Oct 1988, *Paris Street Scene at Night* (oil on canvas, 22 x 18 ins / 55 x 46 cm) CHF 1,400.

FONTANIÈRE, Gaspard Moïse de

French, 18th century.
Died 1784.
Draughtsman, engraver (etching).

FONTANIEU, Pierre Élisabeth de

French, 18th century.
Died 30 May 1784.
Draughtsman, engraver (etching).

Pierre Élisabeth de Fontanieu executed the drawings for the *Collections of Vases* (47 plates), engraved by Niodot, in 1770. De Fontanieu is also known to have made two series of engravings for the *Book of Thirteen Leaves Suitable for Sculptors* and others.

FONTANT, Antoine

French, 16th century.
Sculptor, architect.

Antoine Fontant worked for ten years at the chateau of La Rochefoucault in the Angoumois (Charente). He was responsible for the façade, decorated with 80 capitals, the great staircase, at the top of which he placed a bust of himself with the date 1538, the open gallery giving onto the courtyard and the chapel with its 16 vault keystones, each richly carved with escutcheons.

FONTANUS, E.
Flemish, 17th century.
Born at the beginning of the 17th century, in Flanders.
Active between 1625 and 1678.
Engraver (wood).
Flemish School.
E. Fontanus was primarily an engraver of religious subjects.

FONTAY, Jean de
French, 15th century.
Sculptor.
Jean de Fontay is thought to have been the sculptor of the tomb of Alain Chartier, which was formerly in the church of the canons of St Anthony in Avignon. This tomb had been commissioned by Guillaume Chartier, bishop of Paris and brother of the poet, in 1458.

FONTAYNE, de La. See **LA FONTAYNE de**

FONTAYNE, Juliette
French, 20th century.
Painter. Still-lifes.
Juliette Fontayne exhibited at the Salon des Indépendants in 1943.

FONTAYNE, René
French, 20th century.
Born 3 January 1891, in Vergèze; died 7 September 1952, in Paris.
Painter. Landscapes, seascapes.
René Fontayne exhibited at the Salon des Artistes Français from 1930, where he was awarded the Corot prize and a gold medal, also showing at the Salon d'Automne and the Salon des Artistes Indépendants.
AUCTION RECORDS:
PARIS, 20-21 Dec 1944, *Hovel in a Ravine*, FRF 420.

FONTEBASSO
Italian, 18th century.
Painter. History painting.
Fontebasso exhibited paintings of mythological subjects at the Lille Salon of 1779. Fontebasso is possibly Francesco Fontebasso's son Domenico, a member of the academy in Venice from 1770 to 1772.

FONTEBASSO, Francesco Salvator
Italian, 18th century.
Born 1709, in Venice; died 1769.
Painter, fresco artist, engraver, draughtsman. Religious subjects, mythological subjects, genre scenes.
Francesco Salvator Fontebasso's artistic aspirations were nurtured in Rome, but his formal studies were completed in Venice under Sebastiano Ricci. He settled in Trento until around 1761-1762, when he was appointed Tiepolo's successor as court painter in St Petersburg. He worked predominantly in Venice, however, where he served as president of the fine arts academy from 1768.

Little is known about his painting other than an *Assumption of the Virgin* in the Trento church of S Annunziata, and a painted ceiling in the Venice church of S Francesco della Vigna. As an engraver he is remembered for his version of Sebastiano Ricci's *Virgin Appearing to St Gregory Praying for the Deliverance of Souls from Purgatory*, and a suite of seven fantastical subjects based on his own drawings.
MUSEUMS AND GALLERIES:
STOCKHOLM: *Young Girl Eating from a Bowl* - UDINE (Mus. Civico): *Conversion of St Paul* (drawing) - VENICE (Athenaeum): *Meal in the House of the Pharisee* - VENICE (Palazzo Barbarigo): *Alexander and Diogenes* - VENICE (Pinacoteca Manfrediniana): *St Francis of Paola Healing a Blind Child*.
AUCTION RECORDS:
PARIS, 19 April 1895, *Virgin and Child with Saints*, FRF 650. MILAN, 12-13 March 1963, *Portrait of a Lady of Quality*, ITL 800,000. LONDON, 19 April 1967, *Adoration of the Magi*, GBP 2,100. MUNICH, 6 June 1968, *Virgin and Child with Two Saints*, DEM 11,500. LONDON, 28 June 1974, *The Continence of Scipio*, Gns 12,000. LONDON, 25 March 1977, *Judith with the Head of Holofernes* (oil on canvas, 27 1/4 x 35 ins / 69 x 89 cm) GBP 3,800. BERN, 9 June 1978, *Sophonisbe (or Artemisia)* (before 1760, etching) CHF 3,000. LONDON, 20 Nov 1980, *Pope Gregory I Praying for the Deliverance of Souls* (etching, 18 1/4 x 12 1/4 ins / 46.1 x 31.3 cm) GBP 780. LONDON, 9 March 1983, *Adoration of the Magi* (oil on canvas, 22 x 29 1/4 ins / 56 x 74 cm) GBP 14,000. LONDON, 21 April 1983, *Bacchanal* (etching, 10 3/4 x 15 1/4 ins / 27.3 x 38.7 cm) GBP 850. NEW YORK, 18 Jan 1984, *Holy Family with St John the Baptist and Putti* (pen and wash heightened with white/outline in black chalk, 18 1/4 x 13 1/4 ins / 46.5 x 33.5 cm) USD 19,000. NEW YORK, 15 Jan 1985, *Alexander the Great's Return to Rome* (oil on canvas, 18 1/2 x 24 ins / 47 x 61 cm) USD 15,000. LONDON, 1 July 1986, *Mary Magdalene at Christ's Feet* (pen and brown wash, 19 1/4 x 13 3/4 ins / 48.9 x 35.2 cm) GBP 18,000. ROME, 19 May 1987, *Assumption of the Virgin* (pen and brown ink, 9 x 6 ins / 22 x 15.5 cm) ITL 1,800,000. PARIS, 20 Oct 1988, *Apostles Peter and John Healing a Born Cripple* (pen and Indian ink, 13 x 10 ins / 32.8 x 25.5 cm) FRF 51,000. PARIS, 14 April 1989, *Charity* (oil on canvas, 26 x 33 ins / 66 x 84 cm) FRF 40,000. ROME, 23 May 1989, *Joseph Interpreting Pharaoh's Dream* (oil/vellum/canvas, 14 3/4 x 21 1/2 ins / 37.5 x 54.5 cm) ITL 7,000,000. PARIS, 22 June 1990, *Moses as a Child Trampling on Pharaoh's Crown* (oil on canvas, 32 1/4 x 48 ins / 82 x 121 cm) FRF 800,000. LONDON, 31 Oct 1990, *Meeting of Abraham and Melchizedek* (oil on canvas, 29 1/4 x 22 3/4 ins / 74 x 58 cm) GBP 15,400. LONDON, 19 April 1991, *Cloelia and her Companions Escaping from the Encampment of Lars Porsena* (oil on canvas, 17 1/4 x 21 1/2 ins / 43.5 x 54.8 cm) GBP 18,700. MONACO, 5-6 Dec 1991, *Moses as a Child Knocking the Crown from Pharaoh's Head* (oil on canvas, 13 1/2 x 17 3/4 ins / 34 x 45 cm) FRF 88,800. NEW YORK, 15 Jan 1993, *Family of Darius Appearing before Alexander* (oil on canvas, 36 1/2 x 49 3/4 ins / 92.7 x 126.4 cm) USD 90,500. LONDON, 23 April 1993, *Venus Visting Vulcan's Forge* (oil on canvas, 45 1/2 x 49 1/4 ins / 115.5 x 125 cm) GBP 166,500. PARIS, 5 Nov 1993, *Study of Two Women in Conversation* (Indian ink wash, white gouache and pen outlines, 17 1/4 x 11 1/2 ins / 44 x 29 cm) FRF 120,000. NEW YORK, 11 Jan 1994, *Martyrdom of a Saint* (black chalk and ink, 23 x 16 1/2 ins / 57.5 x 41.8 cm) USD 8,625. NEW YORK, 19 May 1994, *Mythological Scene (Alexander and Roxanne?)* (oil on canvas, 25 x 31 1/4 ins / 63.5 x 79.4 cm) USD 140,000. NEW YORK, 10 Jan 1995, *Young Man Standing and Holding a Vase beside an Old Man Sitting and Holding an Urn* (ink and wash/red chalk, 13 x 9 1/2 ins / 32.9 x 24.3 cm) USD 28,750. PARIS, 7 April 1995, *Moses Rescued from the Nile* (black ink, brown wash heightened with white/beige paper, 19 3/4 x 14 3/4 ins / 50 x 37.5 cm) FRF 85,000. PARIS, 26 Nov 1996, *St Helen Finding the True Cross* (pen and brown ink wash/sketch in black chalk, 20 1/4 x 10 ins / 51.5 x 25.5 cm) FRF 13,500. PARIS, 3 April 1998, *Holy Family with St Catherine of Alexandria and St Francis of Assisi* (pen and brown ink wash/black chalk, attributed, 8 3/4 x 4 1/2 ins / 22.5 x 11.3 cm) FRF 10,000. MUNICH, 1 Dec 1999, *Madonna Praying for Lost Souls* (oil on canvas, 37 x 19 ins / 95 x 49 cm) DEM 43,000. LONDON, 4 July 2000, *Three Male Nudes* (chalk/pen/ink wash, 13 x 9 ins / 32 x 24 cm) GBP 4,800. LONDON, 7 July 2000, *Diana and Endymion* (oil on canvas, 9 x 6 ins / 22 x 16 cm) GBP 12,000. NEW YORK, 24 Jan 2001, *Descent from the Cross* (black chalk/pen/red and brown ink/red and brown wash heightened with white, 18 x 13 ins / 46 x 33 cm) USD 140,000. LONDON, 25 April 2001, *Alexander Addressing his Soldiers. Family of Darius before Alexander* (oil on canvas, pair, 50 x 50 ins / 127 x 127 cm) GBP 55,000. LONDON, 11 April 2002, *Studies of a Girl's Head* (black chalk, 16 x 11 ins / 41 x 27 cm) GBP 19,000. PARIS, 26 June 2002, *Kneeling Man Looking Up* (pen/ink, 9 x 5 ins / 22 x 13 cm) EUR 7,200. LON-

DON, 8 July 2003, *St Jerome Seated in Profile* (black chalk/pen/brown ink, 15 x 10 ins / 38 x 25 cm) GBP 3,800. ZURICH, 19 Sept 2003, *Triumph of Peace* (oil on canvas, oval, 177 x 142 ins / 450 x 360 cm) CHF 210,000. NEW YORK, 22 Jan 2004, *Four Gesturing Hands* (black and white chalk, 17 x 11 ins / 42 x 28 cm) USD 10,000. PARIS, 18 March 2004, *Lamentation with Joseph of Arimathaea* (pen/brown ink, 11 x 7 ins / 27 x 19 cm) EUR 3,000.

FONTEBUONI, Anastasio
Italian, 16th - 17th century.
Born c. 1571, in Florence; died 1626.
Painter. History painting, religious subjects.

Anastasio Fontebuoni worked at Domenico Passignano's school and then visited Rome during the papacy of Paul V (1605-1621), painting several compositions for churches in the Italian capital. His best paintings are generally considered to be his *Birth of the Virgin* and *Death of the Virgin*.

MUSEUMS AND GALLERIES:
FLORENCE (Casa Buonarroti): *Michelangelo and Pope Julius II in Bologna* - FLORENCE (Church of S Giovanni de Fiorentini): *Birth of the Virgin; Death of the Virgin* - FLORENCE (Church of S Maria In Selci): *Annunciation* - FLORENCE (Mus. Mediceo): *Taking of Siena; Coronation of Cosimo I* - FLORENCE (Uffizi): *St John the Baptist.*

AUCTION RECORDS:
LONDON, 21 April 1993, *Queen Mother Catherine de' Medici Receiving Troilo Orsini, Who Pledges the Support of Cosimo de' Medici for King Charles IX in his Struggle against the Huguenots* (oil on canvas, 70½ x 97 ins / 179 x 245.5 cm) GBP 1,651,000.

FONTEBUONI, Bartolommeo
Italian, 17th century.
Died 1630, in Bengal, India.
Painter.

Bartolommeo Fontebuoni grew up in Florence and travelled to the Indies as a Jesuit missionary. During his time in Rome he painted various compositions for the church of S Silvestro at Monte Cavallo. In India he painted compositions for Jesuit churches in Goa.

FONTELLE, François
French, 17th century.
Died before 1696.
Sculptor, decorative artist.

François Fontelle was 'Sculptor of the Pleasures of the King' and worked with Gourville on the Hôtel Condé in Paris. He then worked particularly in the Parc de Versailles, where he restored statues and executed vases and trophies.

FONTENAY. See **BELIN**

FONTENAY, Alexis Léonard Dalige de.
See **DALIGE DE FONTENAY Alexis Léonard**

FONTENAY, André
French, 20th century.
Born 22 November 1913, in Compiègne.
Painter. Urban landscapes.

André Fontenay exhibited at the Salon d'Automne, of which he was an associate member. From 1966, he signed his works *Fontenay de St-Afrique*.

He painted scenes of Montmartre in a distinctive naive style.

AUCTION RECORDS:
NEW YORK, 24 Sept 1981, *Montmartre* (oil on canvas, 24 x 18 ins / 61 x 45.7 cm) USD 400. PARIS, 23 May 1990, *Montmartre Street Snowed Under* (oil on canvas, 22 x 18 ins / 55 x 46 cm) FRF 3,500.

FONTENAY, Belin or Blain, Blin de.
See **BELIN**

FONTENAY, Blain de. See **BELIN**

FONTENAY, Charles de
French, 20th century.
Died 10 January 1916, in La Main-de-Massiges.
Illustrator.

Charles de Fontenay illustrated books of poems. He died on the battlefield at La Main-de-Massigne.

FONTENAY, Claude
French, 17th century.
Active in Paris in 1682.
Painter, sculptor.

FONTENAY, Claude I de
French, 17th century.
Born 1619, in Fontainebleau; died 12 October 1694.
Painter.

Claude de Fontenay I is mentioned several times as a 'painter on enamel', but also as a 'painter and engraver'.

FONTENAY, Claude II de
French, 17th century.
Born 22 August 1653, in Fontainebleau; died 1673.
Painter.

Claude de Fontenay II was the son of Claude de Fontenay I.

FONTENAY, de
French, 20th - 21st century.
Born 1957.
Lithographer. Landscapes.

A professional lithographer, De Fontenay is inspired by the Greek countryside, in which the colour blue is particularly striking.

FONTENAY, Eugène
French, 19th century.
Born 1824, in Paris.
Painter, engraver, draughtsman. Landscapes with figures, landscapes.

Exhibited some landscapes and studies at the Salon from 1867 to 1870.

AUCTION RECORDS:
NEW YORK, 1 March 1984, *Figures on a Bridge Somewhere in the Colonies* (oil on canvas, 12¾ x 16 ins / 32.4 x 40.6 cm) USD 2,800.

FONTENAY, Henri François
French, 17th century.
Born 4 October 1657, in Fontainebleau.
Painter.

Henri François Fontenay was the son of Claude de Fontenay I. He is mentioned several times for his paintings in the 'outbuildings' of the Château de Fontainebleau.

FONTENAY, Jean de I
French, 17th century.
Died before 16 May 1642.
Active in Fontainebleau.
Painter.

Jean de Fontenay I was a 'royal sergeant' and is frequently mentioned from 1613.

FONTENAY, Jean de II
French, 17th century.
Baptised 28 May 1620 in Avon.
Painter.

Jean de Fontenay II was the son of Jean de Fontenay I and also worked in Fontainebleau.

FONTENAY, Louis Henri de
French, 19th century.
Born 15 May 1800, in Amsterdam, of French parents.
Painter, miniaturist. Historical subjects, genre scenes.

Pupil of Louis Autessier; exhibited miniatures at the Paris Salon from 1850 to 1852.

FONTENÉ, Robert
French, 20th century.
Born 6 January 1892, in Paris; died 4 June 1980, in Paris.
Painter.

Robert Fontené studied at the École des Beaux-Arts in Paris from 1910 to 1914 and attended the free Académies after 1918. In 1945 Auguste Herbin sponsored his participation at the first Salon des Réalités Nouvelles, to which he remained faithful, eventually becoming its chairman and holding the post until his death. He contributed to its selections in 1947 in Lille; 1948, Bordeaux; 1957, Nantes; 1958, Recklinghausen; 1964, Namur. He also exhibited at the Salon de Mai in Paris, in 1950 in *50 Years of Abstract Art*, in 1957 at the Milan Triennial and *80 Painters from the École de Paris*; in 1959 at Mannheim Museum; in 1963 and 1964 at the Salon Comparaisons in Paris; and at many collective exhibitions in France and abroad. He has shown his work in solo exhibitions in Paris (1953, 1955, 1958, 1962, 1969) and London (1958, 1974).

From 1921 to 1939 he exhibited figurative paintings of circus themes at the Salon des Artistes Indépendants, and also showed at the Salon d'Automne and Salon des Tuileries. He turned to non-figurative work under Herbin's influence, visible in his early abstract paintings. But Fontené soon developed a more flexible idiom, free from pre-arranged order, allowing the painting to unfold freely. This relaxed approach, edged with a taste for fine tuning, calls for a monitoring of the creative process to ensure a balance between sense and sensibility.

BIBLIOGRAPHY:
Grenier, Jean, *Entretiens avec dix-sept peintres non-figuratifs*, Calmann-Lévy, Paris, 1963.

FONTENEAU, Éric
French, 20th - 21st century.
Born 21 October 1954, in Cholet (Vendée).
Painter (mixed media), draughtsman.

Éric Fonteneau lives and works in Nantes, in Jules Verne country. His creative process is more typical of poetry than the visual arts. He deals with a very wide variety of themes, including, for example, imaginary maps. By making subtle graphical markings, he lends his themes a dream-like dimension.

He has taken part in a number of group exhibitions, including: *10 Grands Invitent 10 Jeunes*, where Gina Pane invited him to exhibit, at the Grand-Palais in Paris, in 1984; *Julien Gracq-Paysages*, at Nantes city library in 1986. He has also staged solo exhibitions since 1982, notably in Nantes and Paris, such as his 1990 exhibition at the Galerie Aline Vidal in Paris.

BIBLIOGRAPHY:
Première nuit d'été, exhibition catalogue, Bouchemaine, 1988. *Éric Fonteneau Comme dit si bien Kepler'*, exhibition catalogue, Centre Régional d'Art Contemporain Le 19, Montbéliard, 1991. Dary, Anne/Rausch, Alain/Obadia, Maurice, *Éric Fonteneau, La nuit porte conseil'*, exhibition catalogue, Musée Municipal, La Roche-sur-Yon, 1991.

FONTENEAU, Georges
French, 20th century.
Born in Douai.
Painter. Portraits.

George Fonteneau exhibited at the Salon des Indépendants.

FONTENEL, L.
French, 20th century.
Painter. Genre scenes, still-lifes.

AUCTION RECORDS:
PARIS, 8 Dec 1924, *Still-life*, FRF 2,310. PARIS, 25 May 1932, *A Village Open-air Auction Sale*, FRF 1,600. LONDON, 21 March 1941, *Milton and his Sisters*, GBP 6.

FONTENELLE, Charles Claude
French, 19th century.
Born 16 June 1815, in St-Marcel-de-Félines (Loire); died 29 May 1866, in Paris.
Sculptor.

Studied under David d'Angers; awarded a bronze medal in 1851. From 1843 to 1851, Charles Fontenelle exhibited low reliefs at the Salon, together with a stone statue of St Joachim. He is also credited with the inlaid tiles for the Ste-Chapelle.

FONTENELLE, Fr.
French, 18th century.
Sculptor.

Fr. Fontenelle executed a bust of the painter *A. P. Meusnier*, which is in Versailles. He may be identical to the sculptor Fontenelle mentioned in St-Marcel-de-Félines in 1784.

FONTENILLE
French, 18th century.
Active in Bordeaux.
Painter.

Fontenille executed some portraits of Schöffen for the city of Bordeaux in 1740.

FONTENILLE, Michel
French, 20th - 21st century.
Born 1947, in Dijon.
Potter. Scenes with figures.

On the evidence of his work, it would seem that Michel Fontenille was educated in the same way as the pupils of Jeanclos, at the École des Beaux-Arts de Paris. Fontenille creates earthenware low reliefs, showing a certain technical virtuosity in his work. Before firing the earth, he incorporates other elements into it, such as imprints, or moulds of figures.

He has taken part in a number of group earthenware and ceramics exhibitions since 1978, among other places, in Paris and its suburbs, Bordeaux, and the Eure region. He has also staged a number of solo exhibitions since 1981, in Paris and Poitiers, among other places.

FONTENILLE, Solange Marie Charlotte de
French, 20th century.
Born in Rennes.
Painter.

Solange Fontenille exhibited in Paris from 1926 at the Salon des Artistes Français.

FONTES
Portuguese, 18th century.
Active c. 1760.
Engraver (burin).

Fontes made portrait engravings.

FONTEYN, Adriaen Lucasz.
Dutch, 17th century.
Born in Ypres; died at the end of 1660, in Rotterdam.
Painter. Allegorical subjects, genre scenes, interiors with figures.

Adriaen Lucasz. Fonteyn settled in Rotterdam, where he married in 1645.

A. fonteyn 1657

MUSEUMS AND GALLERIES:
AMSTERDAM: *Mussel Market in Rotterdam*.

AUCTION RECORDS:
LONDON, 10 June 1932, *Livestock Market*, GBP 10. LONDON, 12 March 1937, *Interior*, GBP 8. LONDON, 26 May 1977, *Merry Group in an Interior* (oil on panel, 18 1/4 x 33 ins / 46.3 x 84 cm) GBP 1,300. PARIS, 13 Nov 1981, *Merry Gathering in a Tavern* (1650 (?), oil on wood, 22 x 29 1/4 ins / 55 x 74 cm) FRF 14,000. STOCKHOLM, 10-12 May 1993, *Musical Gathering: Allegory of the Five Senses* (oil on panel, 23 1/4 x 35 ins / 59 x 89 cm) SEK 50,000. AMSTERDAM, 4 Sept 2001, *Officers Smoking in a Guardroom* (oil on panel, 11 x 15 ins / 28 x 39 cm) EUR 1,900.

FONTEYN, Carel, or de Fontijni
Flemish, 17th century.
Painter.
Flemish School.
In 1656 Carel Fonteyn was a pupil of Simon van Dow and qualified as a master of the Guild of St Luke in Antwerp in 1664.

FONTEYN, Jan Anthonisz.
Dutch, 17th century.
Active in Amsterdam.
Painter.

FONTEYN, Pieter, or Fontyn, Fontijn
Dutch, 18th - 19th century.
Born 1773, in Dordrecht; died 1839.
Painter, draughtsman. Portraits, genre scenes, hunting scenes.
Pieter Fonteyn was a pupil of P. Hofman and W. van Leen. He also painted miniatures.
AUCTION RECORDS:
AMSTERDAM, 27 April 1976, *Fish Seller* (1812, oil on panel, 17 1/4 x 14 1/2 ins / 44 x 37 cm) NLG 15,000. LONDON, 10 July 1981, *Orphans at Shop Door* (1826, oil on panel, 33 x 26 ins / 83.8 x 66 cm) GBP 11,000. AMSTERDAM, 24 April 1991, *Return from the Hunt* (1832, oil on canvas, 24 1/2 x 19 1/4 ins / 62.5 x 49 cm) NLG 8,050.

FONTICELLI, Girolamo
Italian, 17th - 18th century.
Born 4 April 1662, in Perugia; died 5 May 1716, in Perugia.
Painter. Landscapes.
Girolamo Fonticelli studied under his uncle Pietro Montanini. Many of Fonticelli's landscapes were acquired for private collections in and near his native Perugia. Public examples of his work are to be found in the sacristy of the church of S Spirito in Perugia, in Corciano (near Perugia), and in the church of S Maria della Spina in Umbria.

FONTICOLI, Paola
Italian, 20th century.
Sculptor.
Paola Fonticoli lives and works in Milan. In her work, she cuts, engraves and scratches symbols into blocks of wood: although the symbols may appear insignificant, they are metaphorically charged with sensual and sexual connotations.
BIBLIOGRAPHY:
'*Paola Fonticoli*' in *Opus international* n° 119, periodical, Paris, May-June 1990.

FONTINELLE, Jean de La. See **LA FONTINELLE**

FONTYN, Jacobus
Dutch, 18th century.
Active in Haarlem.
Sculptor.
In 1724 Jacobus Fontyn was a member of the Guild of St Luke.

FONTYNE, G. van den
Belgian, 20th century.
Born in Brussels.
Painter.
Exhibited at the 1938 Salon des Indépendants.

FONVIELLE, Ulrich de
French, 19th century.
Born in Paris.
Painter.
Received honourable mentions in 1888 and at the 1889 Exposition Universelle. Ulrich de Fonvielle was a leading light in the scientific world, notably in aeronautics, where he was one of the pioneers of scientific navigation techniques.

FONVIELLES, Yvette
French, 20th century.
Born in Paris.
Painter.
In 1932, Yvette Fonvielles exhibited *My Favourite Corner* and *Impression* at the Salon de la Société Nationale des Beaux-Arts.

FONVILLE, Horace Antoine
French, 19th century.
Born 9 March 1832, in Lyons; died after 1905.
Painter, draughtsman, engraver. Genre scenes, landscapes, landscapes with figures.
Studied under his father Nicolas Victor Fonville and under Jacques Appian at the École des Beaux-Arts in Lyons (1847-1848). He settled first in Paris, then in Oyonnax in the Ain region, where he served as principal of a college of industrial drawing and design. He was named professor of drawing and composition at colleges in Bourg-en-Bresse and, later, Lyons (1881). He exhibited in Lyons in 1853 and 1854 and in Paris in 1860, showing principally oil and charcoal landscapes. In 1903, he was awarded a diploma of honour in Lyons for his charcoal sketch *Quarries at Ramasse*.

Horace Fonville produced large-scale religious compositions which can be seen today in the Paris churches of St-Étienne-du-Mont and Ste Marguerite. Examples of his other work include: *Mountain Path in the Haut-Bugey*; *River Ain at Neuville*; *Stream at Charabotte*; *The Suzan at Chatillonet*; *Estaque Mountain Scene*; *By the Sea at Saussel*; *Spa*; and *Daybreak at Montagnat*.

Horace Fonville painted directly from nature, seeking out some of the most remote corners of the countryside around Lyons and in the Bresse region. He worked neatly and precisely, notably in his depiction of cliffs and rocks. His draughtsmanship lent itself readily to subsequent etchings, of which he made twenty or so, including a ten-plate album published by Cadart around 1886. He also authored *Out and About in Bourg-en-Bresse* (1880).
MUSEUMS AND GALLERIES:
BESANÇON: *Mountain Path in Haut-Bugey* - BOURG-EN-BRESSE: *River Ain at Neuville* - ROANNE: *Swiss Chalet*.
AUCTION RECORDS:
PARIS, 29 Jan 1931, *Forest Glade*, FRF 100. MILAN, 20 March 1980, *Wooded Landscape at Dawn* (1849, oil on canvas, 25 3/4 x 39 ins / 65.5 x 99 cm) ITL 27,000,000. LYONS, 6 Dec 1983, *View of Lyons* (oil on card, 6 1/4 x 9 ins / 16 x 22 cm) FRF 14,600. PARIS, 13 Dec 1989, *Washerwomen* (oil on canvas, 39 1/4 x 53 1/4 ins / 100 x 135 cm) FRF 18,000. PARIS, 23 Oct 1992, *Provençal Landscape* (oil on paper/canvas, 11 x 14 3/4 ins / 28 x 37.5 cm) FRF 8,000. PARIS, 2 April 1993, *Landscape with Figures* (oil on panel, 11 3/4 x 16 1/4 ins / 30 x 41 cm) FRF 6,000. ZURICH, 22 Sept 2000, *Park Landscape* (oil on panel, 14 x 31 ins / 36 x 80 cm) CHF 15,000. LYONS, 10 Feb 2002, *Quai de Saone looking towards Vaise* (oil on canvas, 30 x 43 ins / 75 x 109 cm) EUR 15,000. LYONS, 28 March 2004, *Ferme aux environs de Bourge dans l'Ain* (oil on canvas, 26 x 32 ins / 65 x 81 cm) EUR 2,800. LYONS, 28 March 2004, *Farm near Bourge in the Ain region* (oil on canvas, 26 x 32 ins / 65 x 81 cm) EUR 2,800.

FONVILLE, Nicolas Victor
French, 19th century.
Born November 1805, in Thoissey (Ain); died 12 November 1856, in Thoissey (Ain).
Painter, engraver, lithographer. Landscapes, landscapes with figures.

He studied under the Lyons lithographer J. Brunet, subsequently becoming the latter's son-in-law and successor. He also took painting courses at the École des Beaux-Arts in Lyons as of 1820, studying under Augustin Thierriat and Jean Duclaux.

In 1830, Fonville travelled to Italy, where he remained for a year. On his return to France, he opened an atelier in Lyons which was frequented by, among others, François Gabillot and Louis Carrand; Fonville took his pupils on field excursions to the Bugey region, Savoy, Provence and Switzerland. He was subsequently appointed professor of drawing and composition at the college in Thoisset. He exhibited in Lyons as of 1821 and at the Paris Salon in 1833.

Fonville's body of work comprises mainly landscapes of Italy, the Ain Valley, Isère and the area around Lyons, rendered in oil, watercolour and charcoal. He made numerous drawings of Lyons and the surrounding region, including monuments and contemporary events; these were lithographed by himself and by others. Fonville also produced some etchings.

Museums and Galleries:
Lyons: *View of the Countryside near Lyons; View of Lyons from Vassieu.*

Auction records:
Versailles, 17 Nov 1985, *Fishermen and Their Boats on the Lake of Geneva* (1837, oil on canvas, 19 x 30 ins / 48.5 x 76 cm) FRF 18,500. Versailles, 6 Nov 1988, *Lake and Mountains* (1837, oil on canvas, 19¼ x 30 ins / 49 x 76 cm) FRF 18,000. Versailles, 19 Nov 1989, *Boats beside a Mountain Lake* (1837, 19 x 30 ins / 48.5 x 76 cm) FRF 12,500. Lyons, 5 Nov 1991, *Landscape in Bugey* (oil on canvas, 11¾ x 17 ins / 30 x 43 cm) FRF 9,000.

FONZO, Tiziana di
Italian, 20th century.
Painter.

Tiziana di Fonzo takes as her subject the death throes of Venice, rendered with thick, vigorously-applied paint, in deep green and purplish-blue tones enhanced with gold.

FOORT, Karel, called Karel or Charles d'Ypres
Flemish School, 16th century.
Born 1510, in Ypres; died 22 June 1562, in Courtrai.
Painter, engraver, sculptor, architect.

Foort first worked in Italy, where is believed to have been a pupil of Tintoretto. According to Van Mander, on his return to Flanders he left a wife and children behind in Italy, married again in Courtrai, and was subsequently accused of bigamy. Among his pupils were Pieter Vlerick and Nicolas Snallaert. Foort made many engravings from Dürer, Lucas van Leyden and the Italian masters.

FOOTE, Mary Hallock
American, 19th century.
Born in Millon.
Painter, illustrator.

Mary Hallock Foote initially studied at the Cooper Institute with Dr Rimmer and then became a pupil of Frost Jonston and, finally, of William J. Linton. She supplied many illustrations for Osgood & Co. and worked for *Scribner's Monthly* and the *St Nicholas.*

FOOTE, Will Howe
American, 20th century.
Born 29 June 1874 or 1878, in Grand Rapids (Michigan); died 1965.
Painter. Figures, landscapes with figures.

Will Howe Foote studied at the Chicago Art Institute, the Art Students League, New York, and with Jean-Paul Laurens and Benjamin-Constant at the Académie Julian in Paris. He exhibited with the National Academy of Design, of which he was an associate member, winning a prize in 1902. He also won a bronze medal at the St Louis Exhibition of 1904, a silver medal at Panama-Pacific Exhibition, San Francisco in 1915, and the Lyme Association's Eaton Prize in 1926. He was short-listed at the Carnegie International Exhibition of Pittsburgh in 1914.

Auction records:
New York, 19 June 1981, *Houses in a Spring Landscape and Portrait of Mrs Parrish* (oil on canvas, 24 x 29 ins / 61 x 73.7 cm) USD 2,500. New York, 1 Oct 1987, *Old Lyme Harbour from the Artist's Studio (recto); Sketch of a Café Scene (verso)* (1903, oil on panel, 5¾ x 8 ins / 14.6 x 20.3 cm) USD 6,000. New York, 17 March 1988, *Young Jamaican Woman in Blue* (oil on canvas, 29½ x 29½ ins / 75 x 75 cm) USD 5,500; *Statue and Poppy Urn in a Garden* (1909, oil on canvas, 13¼ x 8¾ ins / 33.5 x 22.5 cm) USD 1,760. New York, 23 Sept 1993, *Summer* (oil on canvas, 24¼ x 20 ins / 61.6 x 50.8 cm) USD 23,000. New York, 23 May 2000, *Industrial Harbour Scene* (oil on board, 6 x 8 ins / 15 x 20 cm) USD 4,500. New York, 20 June 2001, *Train Bridge* (oil on canvas, 11 x 6 ins / 28 x 15 cm) USD 2,200. Fairfield, 20 Aug 2003, *Hyrdangeas and Sunlight 1913* (oil on canvas, 30 x 30 ins / 76 x 76 cm) USD 7,000. Detroit, 13 Feb 2004, *Early Fall Landscape* (oil on canvas, 25 x 30 ins / 64 x 76 cm) USD 3,600.

FOOTTET, Frederick Francis, or Foot, Foottit
British, 19th - 20th century.
Born 1850, in Yorkshire; died 1935.
Painter, engraver, draughtsman. Figures, landscapes.

In 1873, Frederick Foottet exhibited a landscape entitled *December* at the Royal Academy. In 1890, he produced some etchings and in 1900 colour lithographs. From 1901, Foottet exhibited landscapes and figure paintings.

Auction records:
London, 8 June 1989, *Orchard in Normandy* (1892, oil on canvas, 29½ x 35½ ins / 75 x 90.4 cm) GBP 6,050. London, 21 Sept 1989, *Street Scene at Nightfall* (oil on canvas, 40 x 50 ins / 101.6 x 127 cm) GBP 3,850. London, 18 Nov 1992, *Buckfast Abbey on Banks of the River Dart in Devon* (1851, oil on canvas, 17¼ x 25½ ins / 44 x 64.5 cm) GBP 1,980.

FOOTTIT, Harrison
British, 18th century.
Miniaturist.

Harrison Foottit exhibited with the Royal Academy from 1772 to 1774.

FOPPA, Vincenzo de, also known as Vincenzo Bresciano
Italian, 15th - 16th century.
Born between 1425 and 1430, in Brescia; died between May 1515 and October 1516, in Brescia.
Painter, fresco artist. Religious subjects.
Lombard School (Milan)..

According to the latest research, Vincenzo de Foppa was the son of Giovanni de Bagnolo. L'Anonimo and others called him Vincenzo Vecchio, undoubtedly because of his great age. It is apparent from some of his works, very probably executed after 1492, that he must have been actively employed throughout the first decade of the 16th century. Despite the long period he spent in Brescia, no paintings there have been attributed to him.

Vincenzo de Foppa may have learned the fundamentals of art from Squarcione and become a disciple of Mantegna, though this is somewhat at odds with the style of painting that emerged in his early works, in which he seems to have been inspired by Stefano da Verona and Jacopo Bellini. Having completed his studies, it is likely that he returned in 1450 to Brescia, where he married Caylina, the daughter of a citizen. He moved with his wife and children to Pavia around 1456 and lived there for over 30 years, buying a house and acquiring citizen's rights between 1467 and 1468.

We have no record of Foppa's early works in Pavia, but it seems very likely that he was one of the painters employed between 1459 and 1460 by Francesco Sforza to decorate the Palazzo dell'Arengo in Milan. In 1461 he was in Genoa, working on frescoes for the Confraternity of St John the Baptist for its chapel in Genoa cathedral. When he had finished the ceiling of the chapel, he breached his contract by refusing to decorate the walls. He returned to Pavia, where the Carninel church possessed a painting signed and dated May 1462 (now lost). During this period he executed a great many works in Milan and the surrounding area, including *Episodes from the Life of Trajan* and decorative works in the Medici palace given by Francesco Sforza to Cosimo de' Medici. Other works include figures of prophets in a cloister in Pavia (1465) and an altarpiece of Santa Maria delle Grazie in Monza (1466). Having returned to Milan in 1468, Foppa executed frescoes for the Portinari chapel in the basilica of Sant'Eustorgio depicting the life of St Peter Martyr. These frescoes mark a revival in Lombard painting, using perspective to accentuate structures and light to emphasise solid forms.

These new developments were foreshadowed in Foppa's *Crucifixion* (1456). From 1470 onwards, he travelled to Genoa on many occasions, and as a result became more familiar with Flemish and Franco-Provençal paintings. In 1469, having failed to obtain work on the Campo Santo in Pisa, he returned to Genoa, where records show that he received payment for work on the chapel of St John the Baptist in 1471. After 1474, he was employed with other painters in Pavia on the composition of a large altarpiece for the chapel in the Castello. During this period he probably executed works for the city of Milan, none of which survives.

Of the vast body of work by Foppa in Genoa and Liguria as a whole, only two paintings have survived, a large altarpiece commissioned by Giuliano della Rovere for the cathedral in Savona (currently in the oratory of S Maria de Castello) and a badly damaged picture commissioned by Manfredo Fornani for the Certosa de Loreto, now in the gallery in Savona.

Foppa's artistic development was retraced in a solo exhibition featuring over 60 paintings by the artist at the Museo della Città Santa Giulia de Brescia in 2002.

BIBLIOGRAPHY:

Ffoulkes, C.J./Maiocchi, R., *Vincenzo Foppa of Brescia, Founder of the Lombard School: His Life and Works*, John Lane, London, 1909. Suida, W., *'Two Unknown Pictures by Vincenzo Foppa'* in *Burlington Magazine*, vol 45, 1924. Welch, E., *'New Documents for Vincenzo Foppa'* in *Burlington Magazine*, vol 127, 1985. Medica, M., *'Quattro tavole per un polittico di Vincenzo Foppa'* in *Paragone*, vol 431-3, 1986. Gregori, Mina, et al., *Pittura del cinquecento a Brescia*, Cassa di Risparmio delle Provincie Lombarde, Milan, 1986. Terraroli, V./Baini, L., *La pittura in Lombardia: Il Quattrocento*, Electa, Milan, 1993. Balzarini, Maria Grazia, *Vincenzo Foppa: la formazione e l'attivita giovanile*, La nuova Italia, Florence, 1995. Balzarini, Maria Grazia, *Vincenzo Foppa*, Grafo, Brescia, 1997. Balzarini, M.G., *Vincenzo Foppa*, Jaca, Milan, 1997. Mattioli Rossi, Laura (ed.), *Vincenzo Foppa, la chapelle Portinari*, Motta, Milano, Actes Sud, Paris, 1999. Agosti, G./Natale, M./Romano, G., *Vincenzo Foppa. un protagonista del Rinascimento*, exhibition catalogue, Museo di Santa Giulia, Brescia, 2002.

MUSEUMS AND GALLERIES:

BERGAMO (Accademia Carrara, Pinacoteca d'Arte Antica): *Crucifixion* - BERGAMO (Gal. Lochis): *St Jerome* - BERLIN (Bodemus.): *Virgin; Holy Women Weeping for Christ* - BRESCIA (Pinacoteca Tosio-Martinengo): *Standard of the Orzinuovi* - GLASGOW: *Adoration of the Magi* - LONDON (NG): *The Adoration of the Kings* (c. 1500, oil/wood) - LONDON (Wallace Collection): *Young Galeazze Sforza Reading Cicero* (fresco) - MILAN (Ambrosiana): triptych - MILAN (Castello Sforzesco): *St Benedict and St Ambrose; Martyrdom of St Sebastian; Virgin and Child;* two works; *St John the Baptist* (fresco); *St Francis Receiving the Stigmata* (fresco) - MILAN (Mus. Poldi Pezzoli): *Virgin and Child* - MILAN (Pinacoteca di Brera): *Madonna; St Clare and St Bonaventure; St Jerome and St Alexander; St Ludovic and St Bernardino; St Vincent and St Anthony of Padua; Redeemer; St Francis Receiving the Stigmata; Virgin, Jesus, St John the Evangelist and St John the Baptist; Martyrdom of St Sebastian; Dead Christ* - SAVONA (Palazzo Pubblico): *Altarpiece.*

AUCTION RECORDS:

LONDON, 12 May 1927, *Raising of Lazarus*, GBP 58. NEW YORK, 27 and 28 March 1930, *Madonna and Child*, USD 175. LONDON, 12 Dec 1930, *Adoration of the Magi*, GBP 441. LONDON, 4 June 1937, *Madonna and Child*, GBP 44. LONDON, 20 Aug 1941, *Christ Taken Prisoner; Christ before Pilate; Christ at Emmaüs* (collection) GBP 20. PARIS, 15 Dec 1958, *Pietà*, FRF 580,000. COLOGNE, 2 and 6 Nov 1961, *Virgin at Prayer before the Infant Jesus*, DEM 11,000. MILAN, 6 April 1965, *Virgin and Child* (tempera/wood) ITL 6,000,000. LONDON, 2 July 1965, *Portrait of a Gentleman, in Profile, from the Right*, Gns 2,200. LONDON, 19 April 1967, *St Jerome*, GBP 5,500. LONDON, 26 June 1970, *St Jerome in Cardinal's Robes*, Gns 6,000. MONACO, 16 June. 1989, *Angels Playing Music* (oil on panel, 5 1/2 x 7 3/4 ins / 14 x 20 cm) FRF 777,000. LUCERNE, 19 Nov 1998, *Madonna and Child* (oil on panel, 18 x 13 ins / 46 x 32 cm) CHF 5,800.

FOPPIANI, Gustavo, or Foppani
Italian, 20th century.
Born 1925, in Udine; died 1986, in Piacenza.
Painter (mixed media/gouache).

Foppiani's works have appeared in various group exhibitions, including: *Attraverso l'Immagine* (*Through the Image*), in 1995, at the Centro culturale in Cremona.

BIBLIOGRAPHY:

Attraverso l'immagine, exhibition catalogue, Centro culturale Santa Maria della Pietà, Cremona, 1995.

AUCTION RECORDS:

PARIS, 16 April 1992, *Citta Antica* (1955, mixed media/paper/canvas, 32 x 20 ins / 81 x 51 cm) FRF 21,000. ROME, 25 March 1993, *Street Poster in the Moonlight* (1962, oil/synthetic resin, 39 1/4 x 27 1/2 ins / 100 x 70 cm) ITL 4,000,000. NEW YORK, 24 Feb 1994, *Pig Snuffling for Truffles* (1957, oil on panel, 15 3/4 x 21 1/2 ins / 40 x 54.6 cm) USD 1,610. PARIS, 29 March 1995, *Da Salo sul Trono* (1974, gouache and ink/paper/panel, 13 3/4 x 9 1/2 ins / 35 x 24 cm) FRF 5,500. MILAN, 20 May 1996, *Cathedral and Tricycle* (oil on panel, 11 x 12 1/4 ins / 28 x 31 cm) ITL 4,600,000. MILAN, 29 May 2001, *Coliseum* (mixed media on board, 6 x 15 ins / 14 x 39 cm) ITL 3,500,000. ROME, 22 April 2004, *Artificial Satellite over Volterra* (1966, oil on board) EUR 6,400. MILAN, 25 May 2004, *Ancient Ttown* (1955, oil on canvas, 14 x 23 ins / 35 x 58 cm) EUR 4,000.

FORA, Gherardo di Giovanni di Miniato.
See **GHERARDO DEL FORA**

FORABOSCO, Girolamo. See **FERRABOSCO**

FORABOSCO, Michele
Italian, 18th century.

Active in Pavia.
Sculptor (wood).
Michele Forabosco sculpted allegorical statues of *Music* and *Poetry* for the Fraschini theatre in Pavia.

FORAIN, Jean Louis
French, 19th - 20th century.
Born 23 October 1852, in Rheims; died 11 July 1931, in Paris.
Painter (gouache), watercolourist, pastellist, engraver, lithographer, draughtsman, illustrator, caricaturist, poster artist. Figure compositions, figures.
Impressionist group.

Jean Forain was the son of a painter and decorator and was apprenticed to a visiting card engraver. He studied briefly under Gérôme and Carpeaux at the École des Beaux-Arts in Paris and regularly visited the Louvre, where he copied works by the masters. It is said that for a time he made a precarious living by selling small drawings in the style of Grévin. He went on to collaborate on various publications as a draughtsman and columnist, starting in 1876 on *La Cravache* and then collaborating on the newspapers *Le Journal Amusant, Le Figaro* and *L'Écho de Paris*. This introduced him to the diverse worlds of Paris society - the world of the theatre, of shows, and of literature - where he wryly noted the habits and shortcomings particular to each. This led him to follow a route very characteristic of this period, already seen in the work of Steinlen, Caran d'Ache and Toulouse-Lautrec in the journals *La Pléiade, La Vogue* and *La Revue Blanche*.

His work draws a picture of the society of the period, not in a strictly imitative fashion but in the form of the 'dessin-charge' or mild caricature. In 1880 he illustrated *Croquis Parisiens* (*Parisian Sketches*) by J.-K. Huysmans. The newspapers on which he collaborated did not allow him sufficient freedom to express the causticity he felt, but the creation of the *Courrier Français* and later the *Rire* allowed him to give free rein to his particular eloquence. The political and financial scandal of the bankruptcy proceedings against the *Compagnie Universelle du Canal Interocéanique* in 1892 provided him with rich ground from which to observe wheeler-dealers and shady politicians swimming in the troubled waters of the legal world. He decided to assemble his drawings in thematic albums which together provide a tableau of the society of his time; these were, in 1892 *L'Album Forain, La Comédie Parisienne*, in 1893 *Les Temps Difficiles, Nous, Vous, Eux* and in 1897 *Doux Pays*. In the Dreyfus affair Forain was on the side of those opposed to a retrial, and in 1898-1899 he and Caran d'Ache founded *Pss't!* which would become a vehicle of anti-Semitism - more ferocious than skilful - but one that would always find its market. Forain also founded the magazine *Le Fifre* and was one of the founder members of the *Société des Humoristes* (*Society of Humorists*). From 1914 to 1920 he produced a long series of illustrations on World War I for *Le Figaro*, in which he contrasted the heroism of the soldiers on the Front with the cowardice of those shirking in the background. He then underwent a religious conversion and devoted the final years of his life to pious subjects in which he was unable to employ the mainstay of his talent: his caustic wit and even a certain degree of spite. He was made a Chevalier of the Légion d'Honneur in 1893 and received numerous honours, including election to the Institut de France.

In addition to his many collaborations on magazines and journals of the period, Forain produced etchings and 99 lithographs, including some posters. Some of the albums of drawings he published contain series: *La Comédie Parisienne*, a series of 250 drawings, and *Les Temps Difficiles*, a series of 99 drawings. He also illustrated literary works, including: *Les Pantins de Paris* by Gustave Coquiot in 1920 and *Les Tribunaux* by Georges Courteline, 1931. He also collaborated on the illustration of *La Vraie Tentation du Grand Saint Antoine*, 1880, by Paul Arène, *Chansons Fin de Siècle*, 1891, by J. Oudot and *Montmartre Immortel*, 1922 by E. Bayard.

Early in his career Forain painted watercolours inspired by Japanese layouts. The somewhat neglected next stage of his career was as a painter and pastellist alongside his work as a caricaturist. It is thought that his admiration for Manet and the influence of Degas made their mark on his expansive technique, his incisive style and the choice of subjects in his pastel and gouache-heightened watercolours, his oil paintings and the clever, colourful studies that followed, such as those set in the wings of theatres, music cafés and bars.

He exhibited with his Impressionist friends Monet and Degas at the official Salon in 1884 and 1885 and, according to some sources, also in 1879, 1880 and 1881. Retrospective exhibitions of his work include: 1995 at the Fondation de l'Hermitage in Lausanne; 1996 an exhibition at the Galerie Hopkins-Thomas in Paris; 2003 at the Fondation Angladon-Dubrujeaud in Avignon; and 2003 at the Musée Yves Brayer at Les Baux-de-Provence.

forain
forain

BIBLIOGRAPHY:
Guérin, Marcel, *J.- L. Forain lithographe et aquafortiste, avec catalogue raisonné*, H. Floury, Paris, 1910-1912. Osterwalder, Marcus (ed.), *Dictionnaire des illustrateurs 1800-1914*, Ides et Calendes, Neuchâtel, 1989.

MUSEUMS AND GALLERIES:
MEMPHIS (Dixon Gal.): collection of over 50 works - PARIS (Mus. d'Orsay): *At the Nouvelle Athènes Café* (watercolour) - WASHINGTON DC (Georgetown University): *Backstage at the Opera Aida* (c. 1898, pastel/paper).

AUCTION RECORDS:
PARIS, 7 Feb 1901, *Privacy* (drawing) FRF 2,250. PARIS, 23 Feb 1910, *Dancer Tying her Ballet Shoe* (lithograph) FRF 470; *La Tonnelle* (lithograph, one of 10 copies) FRF 1,500; *Private Office*, FRF 630; *Breakfast*, FRF 750; *Scene in a Private Office* (touched up proof) FRF 300; *Dancer Leaning against a Flat* (one of six copies) FRF 380; *Female Nude Sitting on a Bed* (drawing) FRF 160; *Little Model on an Armchair*, FRF 320. PARIS, 24 April 1919, *In the Dancer's Dressing Room*, FRF 5,030; *The Art Dealer*, FRF 5,350. PARIS, 2 Nov 1920, *Before the Magistrate*, FRF 11,100. PARIS, 1-2 Dec 1920, *Dancers in the Wings* (watercolour) FRF 2,900. PARIS, 7 July 1921, *Woman at her Toilette* (watercolour) FRF 2,300. PARIS, 26 Oct 1922, *Buffet at a Soirée*, FRF 5,100. PARIS, 25 May 1923, *The Wings at the Opéra* (pastel) FRF 9,000; *A Serious Man*, FRF 13,100. LONDON, 1 June 1923, *Woman in Pink*, GBP 99. PARIS, 20 Oct 1926, *The Model at Rest* (pencil) FRF 2,450. PARIS, 30-31 May 1927, *In the Wings*, FRF 50,000. LONDON, 23 March 1928, *Preparing a Meal* (drawing) GBP 63. PARIS, 18-19 June 1928, *The Court*, FRF 153,000. PARIS, 3 May 1929, *A Man of Law* (drawing) FRF 4,750; *Dancers*, FRF 60,000; *Behold the Proof*, FRF 100,300. PARIS, 25 June 1931, *Privacy* (watercolour) FRF 4,050; *Evening Performance* (watercolour) FRF 7,000. PARIS, 12 Dec 1932, *Woman with Fan*, FRF 32,100; *Return of the Prodigal Son*, FRF 62,000; *Reclining Nude* (drawing in colouring pencil) FRF 1,100. PARIS, 17 Feb 1937, *Female Act* (pastel) FRF 3,000. PARIS, 10 June 1937, *Model - Standing Nude* (pastel) FRF 1, 800; *Wings of the Opéra in 1880*, FRF 31,200; *Dancer Standing Seen from Behind*, FRF 7,000. NEW YORK, 8-9 Jan 1942, *In the Courtyard*, USD 2,200; *The Outing*, USD 1,750. PARIS, 28 Jan 1942, *The Procuress and the Débutante*, FRF 23,000. PARIS, 11 Dec 1942, *Ballet*

Scene (fan-shaped drawing in watercolour) FRF 24,000; *Portrait Presumed to be of the Painter Courtois at his Easel*, FRF 106,000. NEW YORK, 20-21 Oct 1943, *After Bathing* (drawing) USD 270; *The Folies-Bergère* (pastel) USD 5,900. PARIS, 28 March 1945, *Un Soireux* (watercolour) FRF 10,000. LONDON, 10 July 1946, *Dancers*, GBP 180. PARIS, 30 May 1949, *In the Wings*, FRF 165,000. PARIS, 20 June 1951, *The Wings at the Opéra*, FRF 240,000. PARIS, 21 March 1958, *La Visite à la Loge* (1882, watercolour and gouache) FRF 920,000. PARIS, 15 June 1958, *Behind the Flat, the Season Ticket Holder* (oil on canvas) FRF 320,000. NEW YORK, 11 Nov 1959, *The Night Club* (oil on canvas) USD 3,200. PARIS, 10 Dec 1959, *Study Inspired by the Conquest of the Air* (gouache) FRF 1,000,000. LONDON, 20 May 1960, *Scene at the Opéra* (oil on canvas) GBP 3,990. NEW YORK, 16 April 1961, *The Idealist Painter* (pastel) USD 4,000. BERN, 9 June 1961, *Figures in the Foyer of a Theatre* (gouache and watercolour/pencil drawing) CHF 2,600. NEW YORK, 27 March 1963, *Little Girl Sitting Playing with a Dog* (pastel) USD 3,200. PARIS, 12 March 1964, *The Couple*, FRF 125,000. VERSAILLES, 8 June 1969, *Young Girl* (charcoal) FRF 4,200. PARIS, 10 March 1970, *In the Wings*, FRF 18,000. LONDON, 17 March 1970, *Season Ticket Holder and Dancer* (1892) GBP 3,200. GENEVA, 1 July 1971, *Privacy*, CHF 40,000. LONDON, 1 July 1971, *Study of a Woman with her Hands in a Muff* (1880) Gns 4,500. PARIS, 4 Dec 1972, *At the Café* (gouache) FRF 90,000. LONDON, 3 May 1973, *The Wings at the Paris Opéra* (1899) GBP 4,500. PARIS, 23 May 1973, *Wings at the Opéra* (1912) FRF 29,500. HAMBURG, 14 June 1973, *Barristers* (1908) DEM 16,000. GENEVA, 6 June 1974, *Dancer at the Opéra*, CHF 128,000. LONDON, 7 April 1976, *At the Theatre* (watercolour and gouache, 18 x 12 1/2 ins / 46 x 32 cm) GBP 2,600. PARIS, 25 May 1976, *Church Scene* (oil on canvas, 25 1/2 x 32 ins / 65 x 81 cm) FRF 5,300. LONDON, 29 June 1977, *In the Wings* (gouache, 16 3/4 x 11 ins / 42.5 x 27 cm) GBP 2,500. NEW YORK, 21 Oct 1977, *In the Wings at the Opéra in Paris* (1899, oil on canvas, 32 x 39 1/2 ins / 81.5 x 100.5 cm) USD 6,500. PARIS, 16 May 1979, *Mont Valérien seen from the Seine* (1877, watercolour, 6 x 10 1/2 ins / 15.2 x 26.4 cm) FRF 11,800. LONDON, 1 July 1980, *The Bal Mabille* (c. 1877, pen, wash and yellow chalk/paper, 7 x 9 1/2 ins / 18 x 24.4 cm) GBP 1,500. NEW YORK, 4 Nov 1982, *Strangers in Paris* (black ink and black chalk, 16 1/2 x 10 3/4 ins / 42 x 27.5 cm) USD 1,700. LONDON, 29 June 1983, *Romantic Gentleman* (c. 1890, watercolour and colouring pencil/pen outline, 11 x 4 1/4 ins / 27 x 11 cm) GBP 3,000. ENGHIEN-LES-BAINS, 27 May 1984, *A Fortunate Man* (oil on canvas, 23 1/2 x 28 3/4 ins / 60 x 73 cm) FRF 57,000. LONDON, 28 May 1986, *Two Dancers* (pen and pencil, 7 3/4 x 4 3/4 ins / 20 x 12.2 cm) GBP 1,200. LONDON, 3 Dec 1986, *Woman with Hat Veil* (oil on canvas, 30 x 23 3/4 ins / 76 x 60.3 cm) GBP 21,000. LONDON, 1 July 1987, *At the Folies-Bergère* (gouache, 13 1/2 x 9 3/4 ins / 34.5 x 25 cm) GBP 18,000. NEW YORK, 25 Feb 1988, *Le Buffet* (ink, 12 1/4 x 8 3/4 ins / 31 x 22.3 cm) USD 1,100. PARIS, 22 March 1988, *Theatre Scene* (oil on canvas, 23 1/2 x 29 1/4 ins / 60 x 74 cm) FRF 44,000. LONDON, 29 March 1988, *In the Wings* (1878, oil on panel, 10 x 8 1/4 ins / 25.5 x 21 cm) GBP 57,200. LOKEREN, 28 May 1988, *The Court* (dry-point, 18 3/4 x 23 3/4 ins / 47.5 x 60.3 cm) BEF 36,000. PARIS, 12 June 1988, *Ballerinas on Stage* (oil on canvas, 19 3/4 x 28 3/4 ins / 50 x 73 cm) FRF 260,000. PARIS, 14 June 1988, *At the Café* (Indian ink and watercolour, 5 1/4 x 4 ins / 13.5 x 10.4 cm) FRF 17,000. CALAIS, 3 July 1988, *Ballerina and her Patron* (Indian ink drawing, 11 1/2 x 9 ins / 29 x 23 cm) FRF 10,500. LOKEREN, 8 Oct 1988, *The Ballet* (black chalk and watercolour, 9 1/2 x 8 1/4 ins / 24 x 21 cm) BEF 40,000. LONDON, 19 Oct 1988, *Court Scene* (1924, watercolour, gouache and charcoal, 13 1/2 x 20 ins / 34.6 x 51 cm) GBP 6,820. PARIS, 28 Nov 1988, *At the Brothel* (oil on canvas, 23 1/2 x 28 3/4 ins / 60 x 73 cm) FRF 40,000. PARIS, 9 Dec 1988, *The Confession* (watercolour, 11 1/2 x 11 ins / 29.5 x 28 cm) FRF 6,500. LONDON, 22 Feb 1989, *Leaving the Theatre* (watercolour heightened with white gouache, 12 3/4 x 9 3/4 ins / 32.3 x 25 cm) GBP 11,550. PARIS, 11 April 1989, *Dancer at the Mirror* (pastel, 11 3/4 x 11 ins / 30 x 28 cm) FRF 118,000. NEW YORK, 23 May 1989, *Le Lever* (oil on canvas, 23 3/4 x 28 3/4 ins / 60.4 x 73 cm) USD 44,000. LONDON, 27 June 1989, *Circus Performers* (oil on canvas, 36 x 28 1/2 ins / 91.4 x 72.4 cm) GBP 16,500. PARIS, 3 July 1989, *Woman Rising* (oil on canvas, 31 1/2 x 27 1/4 ins / 80 x 69 cm) FRF 420,000. RHEIMS, 22 Oct 1989, *Sweet Country, the Député and the Légion d'Honneur* (Indian ink drawing with watercolour, 9 3/4 x 15 1/4 ins / 25 x 38.5 cm) FRF 3,500. NEW YORK, 24 Oct 1989, *At the Salon* (1921, oil on paper/canvas, 22 x 26 ins / 55 x 66 cm) USD 14,300. PARIS, 8 Nov 1989, *Ballerina's Dressing Room* (Indian ink heightened with blue pencil, 11 1/2 x 9 ins / 29 x 22 cm) FRF 9,000. PARIS, 26 Nov 1989, *Sullen Woman* (oil on canvas, 28 3/4 x 23 1/2 ins / 73 x 60 cm) FRF 100,000. PARIS, 24 Jan 1990, *A Family* (gouache, 19 3/4 x 24 ins / 50 x 61 cm) FRF 38,000. NEW YORK, 26 Feb 1990, *The Letter* (oil on canvas, 27 x 22 1/4 ins / 68.6 x 56.5 cm) USD 18,700. PARIS, 21 March 1990, *Society Reception* (oil on panel, 10 1/4 x 13 1/2 ins / 26 x 34 cm) FRF 78,000. GRANDVILLE, 29 April 1990, *At the Café* (painting/canvas) FRF 340,000. PARIS, 5 July 1990, *Profile View of Dancer* (charcoal, 16 3/4 x 12 3/4 ins / 42.5 x 32.5 cm) FRF 13,000. NEW YORK, 23 Oct 1990, *In the Wings* (oil on canvas, 24 x 29 ins / 61 x 73.7 cm) USD 12,100. LONDON, 4 Dec 1990, *At the Bar* (oil on canvas, 26 x 32 1/4 ins / 66 x 82 cm) GBP 22,000; *At the Milliner's* (pastel/paper/card, 21 1/2 x 18 ins / 54.6 x 46 cm) GBP 35,200. NEW YORK, 14 Feb 1991, *Chez Maxim in Paris* (oil on canvas, 23 1/2 ins / 60 cm, 1 1/4 x 29 ins/3 x 73.7 cm) USD 38,500. MONACO, 11 Oct 1991, *Gigolo and Gigolette* (ink and wash, 10 1/2 x 7 3/4 ins / 26.5 x 20 cm) FRF 28,860. LONDON, 2 Dec 1991, *Dancer* (gouache on silk, fan, l. 11 ins / 27 cm) GBP 17,600. NEW YORK, 26 Feb 1993, *The Singer* (ink and gouache/paper heightened with white, 10 3/4 x 7 ins / 27.3 x 17.8 cm) USD 4,600. PARIS, 28 May 1993, *Two Women on Bicycles* (gouache/brown paper, 28 1/2 x 59 ins / 72.5 x 150 cm) FRF 53,000. LONDON, 22 June 1993, *La Loge* (oil on panel, 9 1/2 x 7 1/2 ins / 24 x 19 cm) GBP 76,300. NEW YORK, 2 Nov 1993, *The Ballet Enthusiasts* (oil on canvas, 23 3/4 x 28 3/4 ins / 60.3 x 73 cm) USD 13,800. NEW YORK, 16 Feb 1994, *At the Dressing Table* (oil on paper/card, 15 1/4 x 18 ins / 38.7 x 45.7 cm) USD 23,000. AMSTERDAM, 19 April 1994, *Nymph of the Woods* (oil on canvas/panel, 113 1/2 x 7 ins / 288 x 18 cm) NLG 2,990. LONDON, 29 June 1994, *Portrait of Camille Pissaro* (watercolour, 8 1/4 x 5 1/2 ins / 21 x 14 cm) GBP 23,000. DEAUVILLE, 19 Aug 1994, *Le Lever* (pastel/paper/canvas, 22 x 25 1/2 ins / 55 x 65 cm) FRF 8,500. PARIS, 26 March 1995, *Study of Dancers* (pastel, 18 x 15 ins / 46 x 38 cm) FRF 10,200. ST-GERMAIN-EN-LAYE, 26 March 1995, *Brothel Scene* (oil on panel, 12 1/2 x 15 3/4 ins / 32 x 40 cm) FRF 85,000. NEW YORK, 24 May 1995, *The Dressing Room or Palace of Mirrors* (oil on canvas, 25 1/2 x 36 1/2 ins / 64.8 x 92.7 cm) USD 360,000. PARIS, 26 April 1996, *The Fitting Room* (ink and wash, 12 1/4 x 9 1/2 ins / 31 x 24 cm) FRF 4,900. PARIS, 22 May 1996, *Two Countries in the East* (watercolour, pen and black ink, 9 3/4 x 13 1/4 ins / 24.7 x 33.7 cm) FRF 6,200. NEW YORK, 12 Nov 1996, *The Court* (c. 1925, gouache, watercolour, brush, ink and black chalk/pencil/paper/card, 11 3/4 x 17 ins / 29.8 x 42.9 cm) USD 4,600. PARIS, 24 Nov 1996, *Woman and Child in the Street* (c. 1908, oil on canvas, 28 3/4 x 17 ins / 73 x 43 cm) FRF 13,000. PARIS, 16 March 1997, *Portrait of a Woman* (oil on monogram canvas, 18 x 15 ins / 46 x 38 cm) FRF 5,000. PARIS, 20 March 1997, *Marriage in the Winter Garden* (ink wash and watercolour, 12 1/2 x 9 ins / 31.5 x 22 cm) FRF 33,000. NEW YORK, 12 May 1997, *Dancer with Hoop* (1881, oil on panel, 13 x 9 1/4 ins / 33 x 23.5 cm) USD 387,500. AMSTERDAM, 2-3 June 1997, *Portrait of a Woman* (watercolour/paper, 14 1/2 x 10 1/4 ins / 37 x 26 cm) NLG 19,470. PARIS, 16 June 1997, *The Painter and his Model in the Studio* (watercolour and gouache, 16 x 19 1/4 ins / 40.5 x 49 cm) FRF 40,000. NEW YORK, 9 Oct 1997, *Court* (oil on canvas, 35¾ x 35 ins / 91 x 89 cm) USD 10,925. PARIS, 12 Dec 1997, *Society Lady on the Terrace of a Café* (ink and watercolour, 10 x 7¾ ins / 24.5 x 20 cm) FRF 122,000. NEW YORK, 18 March 1998, *Appeal for Clemency* (oil on canvas, 37½ x 39½ ins / 95.3 x 100.3 cm) USD 12,650. PARIS, 22 March 1998, *Model Posing* (watercolour and gouache, 13 x 17¾ ins / 33 x 45 cm) FRF 30,000. PARIS, 17 March 1999, *Backstage Corner at the Opera* (1883, watercolour and gouache, 12 x 9 ins / 30 x 24 cm) FRF 250,000. LONDON, 29 June 1999, *Standing Dancer* (c. 1890, oil on canvas, 25 x 21 ins / 64 x 53 cm) GBP 48,000. PARIS, 31 March 2000, *In the Wings* (oil on canvas, 24 x 29 ins / 60 x 73 cm) FRF 350,000. PARIS, 4 May 2000, *Rentree au pesage* (watercolour, pen and Indian ink, double-sided, 9 x 10 ins / 22 x 26 cm) FRF 88,000. NEW YORK, 9 May 2001, *Dancers Resting* (c. 1905, oil on canvas, 24 x 29 ins / 60 x 73 cm) USD 50,000. PARIS, 11 July 2001, *Couple* (ink and wash, 11 x 7 ins / 27 x 18 cm) FRF 70,000. LONDON, 9 April 2002, *Dancer* (1887, pastel, 20 x 16 ins / 51 x 41 cm) GBP 17,500. LONDON, 24 June 2002, *Jardin de Paris* (c. 1882, oil on panel, 17 x 22 ins / 42 x 57 cm) GBP 280,000. NEW YORK, 8 May 2003, *Dialogue* (oil on canvas, 28 x 22 ins / 70 x 55 cm) USD 105,000. NEUILLY, 27 June 2003, *In the Wings* (pastel, 15 x 12 ins / 38 x 30 cm) EUR 38,000. PARIS, 18 June 2004, *Races* (c. 1885-1890, oil on canvas, 26 x 36 ins / 65 x 92 cm) EUR 400,000. LONDON, 24 June 2004, *Nocturne* (c. 1890, pastel, 26 x 22 ins / 65 x 55 cm) GBP 22,000.

FORAIN, Jeanne
French, 20th century.
Painter, sculptor, pastellist, draughtswoman. Figures, nudes, portraits, flowers. Marionettes.

Jeanne Forain was the wife of Jean-Louis Forain and worked in his studio at Rue Spontini in Paris.

More a sculptor than a painter, she modelled marionette heads for the *Théatre des Nabots* which she created in 1905. Using a variety of techniques she produced nudes and, towards the end of her career, flowers, but mainly portraits, specialising in children's faces. Her works include: *Princess Caroline Murat; Jean-Loup as a Child; Little Girl in Blue* and *Young Woman with Rose.* She exhibited regularly at the Paris Salon.

AUCTION RECORDS:
PARIS, 13 Feb 1924, *Study for Bathing* (pastel) FRF 350. PARIS, 5 Nov 1936, *Study for Bathing* (heightened charcoal) FRF 100. PARIS, 20 June 1941, *Madame Trinité Sewing* (pastel) FRF 280. NEW YORK, 9 May 1989, *Old Woman* (bronze, h. 19½ ins / 49.5 cm) USD 1,100.

FORAND, Antony
French, 19th - 20th century.
Born in La Rochelle.
Sculptor. Figures.

Antony Forand studied at the École des Beaux-Arts in Paris.

MUSEUMS AND GALLERIES:
LA ROCHELLE: *Young Beggar* (plaster).

FORANI, Madeleine Christine
Belgian, 20th century.
Born 1916, in Arlon.
Sculptor. Monuments.

Forani studied archaeology before enrolling at the fine arts academy in Brussels in 1942. She was subsequently arrested and sent to the Dachau concentration camp. She survived and went on to become a pupil of Ossip Zadkine at the Académie de la Grande-Chaumière in Paris (1947-1948). She held her first solo exhibition in Naples in 1949 and featured in a further solo exhibition in Brussels in 1952. The following year, she was Belgium's prize-winning entry in an international competition for the *Tomb of the Unknown Political Prisoner.* That same year (1953), her work featured at the Salon de la Jeune Sculpture in Paris. Earlier - in 1945 - she had exhibited in Antwerp, a leading city in post-war sculpture, and had secured a travel scholarship to the Congo. She also took a long trip to America in 1958-1959.

Forani's technique involves enamels and coloured glass inserted into a metal infrastructure. Under the influence of Zadkine, her style evolved towards Abstract Symbolism. In the wake of her time spent in the Congo, however, she reverted to 'figurative allusion', a style she sustained until after her stay in New York.

FORASTIERI, Giovanni Battista, called lo Zoppo
Italian, 16th century.
Active in Ravenna.
Painter.

Giovanni Battista Forastieri painted armorial bearings. He may also have been known as Giovanni Battista Forastieri, companion of the painter Galeotto Corelli, who is mentioned in 1555.

FORBAT, Alfred
Hungarian, 20th century.
Born 1897; died 1972.
Active in Germany from 1918, and in Sweden from 1938.
Draughtsman.
Constructivism.

Alfred Forbat was mainly an architect. A student at the technical college in Munich, he worked in Walter Gropius' workshop at the Bauhaus between 1920 and 1922. He worked as an architect from 1924 to 1932, particularly in Berlin, and in 1932-33 he was a town planner in Moscow. He was back in Hungary as an architect from 1933 to 1938 and from 1938 onwards he settled in Sweden, still working as an architect. In 1959 was appointed professor of town planning in Stockholm.

He drew Abstract Constructivist compositions as projects for artistic insertions into an urban architectural environment, or simply as works in their own right.

BIBLIOGRAPHY:
Passuth, Krisztina/Szabó, Júlia, *L'Art en Hongrie 1905-1930. Art et révolution*, exhibition catalogue, Musée d'Art et d'Industrie, Saint-Étienne, musée d'Art moderne de la ville de Paris, Paris, 1980.

MUSEUMS AND GALLERIES:
BUDAPEST (Szépmuvészeti Múz.): *Abstract Composition* (1921).

AUCTION RECORDS:
PARIS, 19 Feb 1996, *Geometric Composition* (pastel, 11¾ x 9½ ins / 30 x 24 cm) FRF 4,700. ZURICH, 18 Nov 1997, *Composition* (1922, pencil, 7½ x 9½ ins / 19 x 24 cm) CHF 1,900.

FORBELL, Charles
American.
Illustrator.

He was a member of the Salmagundi Club and of the Artists Guild of the Authors League of America.

FORBERA, Antonio, or Fort-Bras
Italian, 17th century.
Born in Venice; died c. 1690, in Avignon, France

Antonio Forbera's most famous *trompe-l'oeil* is in the Calvet Museum in Avignon.

BIBLIOGRAPHY:
Morat, Florence, *La Question des limites dans l'œuvre d'Antoine Fort-Bras,* 1986 (thesis, Sorbonne, Paris). Mauriès, Patrick, *Le Trompe-l'œil,* Gallimard, Paris, 1996.

MUSEUMS AND GALLERIES:
AVIGNON (Mus. Calvet): *The Painter's Easel* (1686) - TARBES (Mus. Massey): *Three Ages of Life.*

FORBERG, Ernst Carl
German, 19th - 20th century.
Born 20 October 1844, in Düsseldorf; died 1915, in Düsseldorf.

Engraver (etching).
Forberg received an honourable mention in 1883 and a gold medal at the 1900 Exhibition Universelle.

FORBES, Alexander
British, 17th century.
Draughtsman.
The British Museum has a number of *Views* by Alexander Forbes signed and dated 1690 and 1691.
MUSEUMS AND GALLERIES:
LONDON (British Mus.): *Views*.

FORBES, Alexander
British, 19th century.
Died 1839.
Painter. Animals.
Alexander Forbes enjoyed a considerable reputation as a painter of horses and dogs.

FORBES, Anne
British, 18th - 19th century.
Born 1745; died 1834.
Painter.
Anne Forbes studied in Rome in around 1770, and exhibited portraits at the Royal Academy in London from 1772. She is noted for her portraits of Elizabeth Hamilton and Lord Polwarth.

FORBES, Charles Stuart
American, 19th - 20th century.
Born c. 1860, in Geneva, to American parents; died 1926.
Painter. Landscapes.
Charles Stuart Forbes was awarded a bronze medal at the Paris Exposition Universelle in 1889.
AUCTION RECORDS:
NEW YORK, 21 Sept 1984, *Pont des St-Pères* (1918, oil on panel, 7 1/4 x 11 ins / 18.7 x 27.1 cm) USD 700.

FORBES, Edwin
American, 19th century.
Born 1839, in New York; died 1895.
Painter, engraver. Military subjects, battles, animals.
Edwin Forbes began his studies as an animal painter around 1857 and worked under A.F. Tait in 1859. During the War of Secession he followed the military operations of 1862, 1863 and 1864. When he returned to New York he painted several military pictures, but soon went back to his original genre. He was made an honorary member of the London Etching Club in 1877. Among his works is an interesting series of etchings, *Studies from Life of the Army*, which was exhibited in Philadelphia, the prints of which were bought by General Sherman for the American government.
AUCTION RECORDS:
NEW YORK, 21 Nov 1980, *Union Supply Wagon* (oil on canvas, 12 x 18 ins / 30.5 x 45.8 cm) USD 3,000. NEW YORK, 15 March 1985, *Civil War Tune* (1867, oil on canvas, 16 x 20 1/4 ins / 40.7 x 51.4 cm) USD 32,000. NEW YORK, 21 May 2002, *Drummer Boy* (oil on canvas, 16 x 14 ins / 41 x 36 cm) USD 4,000. NEW YORK, 8 Oct 2004, *Civil War Scenes* (watercolour, three, 7 x 10 ins / 18 x 25 cm) USD 4,000. NEW YORK, 8 Oct 2004, *Civil War Scenes* (watercolour, three, 7 x 10 ins / 18 x 25 cm) USD 4,000.

FORBES, Elizabeth Adela (Mrs)
Maiden name: Armstrong
Canadian, 19th - 20th century.
Born 29 December 1859, in Ottawa; died 22 March 1912, in Newlyn (Cornwall), England.
Painter, watercolourist, engraver, draughtswoman, illustrator. Genre scenes, landscapes.
School of Newlyn.
Elizabeth Adela Forbes was the daughter of a Toronto civil servant and studied at the Art Students League, New York, with W. Chase. Subsequently, she went to Brittany, where she produced drypoint etchings, and to Cornwall, where she met Stanhope Forbes, who she married in 1890. She became a member of the Painter Etchers Society in London, and an associate of the Society of Painters in Watercolours. Her works include a set of illustrations for *King Arthur's Wood* and *The Poems of Herrick*.
She exhibited at the Royal Academy from 1890.
BIBLIOGRAPHY:
Cook, Judith, *Singing from the Walls: the Life and Art of Elizabeth Forbes*, exhibition catalogue, Sansom, Bristol, 2000.
MUSEUMS AND GALLERIES:
OTTAWA (Nat. Gal. of Canada): *A Woman and Child in a Hay Field* (c. 1910, watercolour over charcoal); *A May Evening* (c. 1910, watercolour over charcoal) - PLYMOUTH: *Imogen* - SYDNEY: *Mignon*.
AUCTION RECORDS:
LONDON, 4 June 1908, *Hammock*, GBP 5. LONDON, 7 March 1910, *Afternoon Fishing Party*, GBP 10. LONDON, 19 April 1926, *Take, Oh! Take Those Lips Away!*, GBP 31. LONDON, 22 Feb 1972, *The Gypsy*, GBP 320. LONDON, 13 May 1977, *The Ford* (oil on canvas, 43 x 31 1/2 ins / 109.3 x 80 cm) GBP 680. LONDON, 23 June 1981, *Spring Blossoms* (watercolour, 18 x 12 1/4 ins / 45.5 x 31 cm) GBP 6,500. LONDON, 23 Oct 1984, *Harvester in a Corn Field* (black chalk and wash heightened with white/grey paper, 16 3/4 x 12 ins / 42.5 x 30.5 cm) GBP 500. LONDON, 15 March 1985, *Haymaking* (oil on canvas, 18 x 25 ins / 45.7 x 63.5 cm) GBP 6,800. LONDON, 14 Nov 1987, *Fetching Water* (watercolour/outlines in black chalk heightened with white, 18 x 13 ins / 46 x 33 cm) GBP 7,500. LONDON, 2 March 1989, *Portrait of Marion Kerr* (oil on canvas, 17 3/4 x 10 3/4 ins / 45 x 27.5 cm) GBP 27,500. LONDON, 8 June 1989, *A Fairy Story* (oil on canvas, 46 3/4 x 37 1/2 ins / 118.8 x 95 cm) GBP 187,000.

FORBES, Helen K.
American, 20th century.
Born 3 February 1891, in San Francisco; died 1945.
Painter. Landscapes.
Helen K. Forbes was a member of the San Francisco Art Association, the Palo Alto Art Club and the San Francisco Society of Women Artists, where she was awarded first prize in 1930.
AUCTION RECORDS:
LOS ANGELES-SAN FRANCISCO, 12 July 1990, *Hillside* (oil on canvas, 33 x 33 ins / 84 x 84 cm) USD 1,540; *Storm over the Valley of Death* (1933, oil on canvas, 33 3/4 x 40 1/4 ins / 86 x 102 cm) USD 3,850. LOS ANGELES-SAN FRANCISCO, 10 Oct 1990, *The Valley of Death II* (oil on canvas, 36 1/4 x 32 1/4 ins / 92 x 82 cm) USD 1,320. SAN FRANCISCO, 14 June 2000, *Landscape, Hill, Road and Trees* (oil on canvas, 33 x 33 ins / 84 x 84 cm) USD 2,500. PASADENA, 15 June 2004, *Death Valley II* (oil on canvas, 36 x 32 ins / 91 x 81 cm) USD 4,250.

FORBES, James
British, 18th - 19th century.
Born 1749, in London; died 1819, in Aachen.
Draughtsman.
James Forbes was an explorer who made numerous sketches during the course of his travels. The drawings were engraved in aquatint by W. Stoker, for his *Memories of the Orient*.

FORBES, James G.
British, 19th century.
Born c. 1800, in Scotland.
Painter. Portraits, genre scenes.
James Forbes exhibited at the Royal Scottish Academy in Edinburgh from 1852 to 1854, and with the Royal Academy in London in 1853. He also exhibited with the British Institution, in 1852 and 1857. From 1860 to 1870, he lived in Chicago.

MUSEUMS AND GALLERIES:
CHICAGO (AI): *Portrait of A.N. Fullerton.*
AUCTION RECORDS:
LONDON, 29 Feb 1984, *Knife-grinder* (1859, oil on canvas, 20 x 16 1/4 ins / 51 x 41 cm) GBP 800.

FORBES, John Colin

Canadian, 19th - 20th century.
Born 23 January 1846, in Toronto; died 28 October 1925, in Toronto.
Painter. Portraits, still-lifes.

John Colin Forbes studied at the South Kensington Art School and the Royal Academy, London, before settling in New York as a portrait painter. He painted Gladstone, Campbell-Bannerman, Edward VII and Queen Alexandra, the last two of which were exhibited at the Royal Academy in 1906.

MUSEUMS AND GALLERIES:
OTTAWA (Parliament Building): *Portrait of King Edward VII; Portrait of Queen Alexandra* - TORONTO (Royal Canadian Academy of Arts): *Beware! I Know a Maiden Fair to See. Tale Care!* (c. 1873, oil).
AUCTION RECORDS:
TORONTO, 28 May 1980, *Still-life* (oil on board, 14 3/4 x 21 ins / 37.5 x 52.5 cm) CAD 850.

FORBES, Mary

British, 20th century.
Born in England.
Painter. Landscapes.

AUCTION RECORDS:
LONDON, 4 June 1923, *Landscape,* GBP 2.

FORBES, Pieter

Dutch, 17th century.
Born c. 1637.
Active in Amsterdam.
Painter. Still-lifes.

AUCTION RECORDS:
LONDON, 11 March 1983, *Still-life* (1663, oil on canvas, 51 1/2 x 43 ins / 130.8 x 109.2 cm) GBP 6,500.

FORBES, Stanhope Alexander

British, 19th - 20th century.
Born 18 November 1857, in Dublin; died 2 March 1947.
Painter. Portraits, genre scenes, landscapes with figures.
School of Newlyn.

Stanhope Forbes' father held an important position in the railway industry and married a French woman. Forbes studied at Dulwich College and then at Lambeth School of Art and the Royal Academy in London. He continued his studies in Berlin and with Léon Bonnat in Paris and spent several years in Brittany, where he painted prolifically before moving to Newlyn in Cornwall. He also visited and painted Venice. Forbes began exhibiting in 1874 in London at the Royal Academy. He became an associate of the Academy in 1892 and a full member in 1910. In 1905, he was made a corresponding member of the Institut de France. Forbes received a number of awards: in 1891 a medal in Berlin; in 1895 a gold medal in Munich; in 1900 a medal in Paris at the Exposition Universelle; and in 1910 a commendation in Pittsburgh. He painted an important decorative work entitled *The Fire of London* for the Stock Exchange in London. Portraiture was a less important aspect of his work but he did paint figures either alone or in everyday occupations and at work and in domestic genre scenes. He was a prolific landscape artist who specialised in painting Cornish scenes and fishing port scenes with figures.

Stanhope A Forbes

BIBLIOGRAPHY:
Birch, L., *Stanhope Forbes and Elizabeth S. Forbes,* London, 1906. Hind, C.L., *'The Art of Stanhope Forbes'* in *Art Journal, Christmas issue,* London, 1911. Fox, C./Greenacre, F., *Artists of the Newlyn School, 1800-1900,* exhibition catalogue, Plymouth City Museum and Art Gallery/Bristol Museum and Art Gallery, 1979. Fox, C./Greenacre, F., *Painting in Newlyn, 1800-1930,* exhibition catalogue, Barbican Art Gallery, London, 1985. Wood, Christopher, *Paradise Lost: Paintings of English Country Life and Landscape, 1850-1914,* Barrie & Jenkins, London, 1988.

MUSEUMS AND GALLERIES:
ABERDEEN (AG): *Self portrait* - BIRMINGHAM (Mus. and AG): *The Village Philharmonic* (1888, oil on canvas) - BRIGHTON (Mus. & AG): *Christmas Eve* (1897, oil on canvas); *Mousehole Harbour* (1910, oil on canvas) - BRISTOL (City Mus. & AG): *Beach Scene, St Ives* (1886); *Home-Along, Evening* (oil on canvas) - EXETER: *News of the Death of Queen Victoria, 29 January 1901* - HULL (Ferens Art Gallery): *Newlyn* (1906, oil on canvas); *At their Moorings* (1906, oil on canvas) - LIVERPOOL (Walker AG): *A Street in Brittany* (1881, oil on canvas); *By Order of the Court* (1881, oil on canvas); *Off to the Fishing Ground* (1886, oil on canvas) - LONDON (Royal Academy of Arts): *The Harbour Window* (1910, oil on canvas, competition piece) - LONDON (Tate Collection): *The Health of the Bride* (1889, oil on canvas) - MANCHESTER: *The Lighthouse* - NORWICH (Castle Mus. and AG): *Portrait of Sir Peter Eade, Mayor of Norwich* - OLDHAM: *Horses Drinking* - PLYMOUTH: *Post Office Worker* - SYDNEY: *Village Street* - WORCESTER: *Little Mount's Bay Fishermen.*
AUCTION RECORDS:
LONDON, 28 Nov 1908, *The Smithy,* GBP 105. LONDON, 30 April 1910, *Quimperlé Convent* (1882) GBP 63. LONDON, 27 Nov 1922, *Châteaudun* (drawing) GBP 4. LONDON, 3 April 1925, *The Convent,* GBP 54. LONDON, 17 Dec 1928, *End of the Day,* GBP 21. LONDON, 6 Dec 1935, *Cornish Village,* GBP 36. LONDON, 25 June 1941, *Cornish Fishermen,* GBP 16. LONDON, 15 Dec 1972, *Old Man Carrying Wood* (1904) Gns 320. LONDON, 14 July 1973, *Village Street,* GBP 320. LONDON, 10 June 1981, *The Saffron Cake* (1920, oil on canvas, 30 x 40 1/4 ins / 76 x 102 cm) GBP 7,000. LONDON, 14 Nov 1984, *Portrait of a Young Girl in Black* (1886, oil on mounted card, 15 x 10 3/4 ins / 38.1 x 27.3 cm) GBP 5,200. LONDON, 13 Nov 1986, *Horses Drinking* (1931, oil on canvas, 24 x 30 ins / 61 x 76.2 cm) GBP 22,000. NEW YORK, 25 May 1988, *Sta Maria della Salute* (oil on canvas, 30 1/4 x 24 1/4 ins / 76.8 x 61.5 cm) USD 9,350. LONDON, 9 June 1988, *Christmas Dinner* (1913, oil on canvas, 15 1/2 x 11 3/4 ins / 39.5 x 30 cm) GBP 8,250. LONDON, 2 March 1989, *Inn by the Fountain* (1939, oil on canvas, 20 x 25 ins / 50.6 x 63.7 cm) GBP 19,800. LONDON, 8 June 1989, *Village Street in Cornwall* (1909, oil on canvas, 23 1/4 x 17 1/4 ins / 58.8 x 43.8 cm) GBP 39,600. LONDON, 8 March 1990, *Daily Bread* (1886, oil on canvas, 21 1/2 x 15 1/2 ins / 54.9 x 39.5 cm) GBP 44,000. NEW YORK, 22 May 1990, *The Violinist* (oil on canvas, 36 1/2 x 33 1/2 ins / 92.8 x 85 cm) USD 16,500. LONDON, 7 March 1991, *A Quiet Street* (1921, oil on canvas, 30 x 24 ins / 76 x 61 cm) GBP 15,400. NEW YORK, 16 Oct 1991, *Sta Maria della Salute* (oil on canvas, 30 1/4 x 24 ins / 76.8 x 61.2 cm) USD 9,900. LONDON, 7 Nov 1991, *Cornish Village* (1925, oil on canvas, 23 1/2 x 29 1/2 ins / 60 x 75 cm) GBP 20,900. LONDON, 6 March 1992, *Old Newlyn Village* (1884, oil on canvas, 15 x 12 ins / 38 x 30.5 cm) GBP 50,600. LONDON, 6 Nov 1992, *The Old Weigh House, Penzance* (1922, oil on canvas, 24 1/4 x 30 ins / 61.5 x 76 cm) GBP 13,750. EDINBURGH, 13 May 1993, *Trungle Moor Spring* (1915, oil on canvas, 20 x 24 ins / 50.8 x 61 cm) GBP 6,600. PERPIGNAN, 3 Dec 1994, *Children on the Beach* (oil on canvas, 17 3/4 x 13 ins / 45 x 33 cm) FRF 82,000. LONDON, 27 March 1996, *A Schoolboy: Portrait of Thomas Ormsby* (oil on canvas, 13 3/4 x 11 3/4 ins / 35 x 30 cm) GBP 1,495.

FORBES-DALRYMPLE, Arthur Evan
British, 20th century.
Born 22 October 1912.
Painter.
Arthur Forbes-Dalrymple studied at Heatherley's Art School and Goldsmith's. He showed his work in group exhibitions at the Royal Academy, the Royal Institute of Oil Painters and the New English Art Club in London and also at the Paris Salon.

FORBES-ROBERTSON, Eric
British, 19th century.
Active in London.
Painter.
Eric Forbes-Robertson exhibited landscapes at the Royal Academy and Suffolk Street from 1885 to 1891. He was the brother of Sir Johnston Forbes-Robertson.

FORBES-ROBERTSON, Frances, later Mrs M. D. Harrod
British, 19th century.
Active in London.
Painter.
Frances Forbes-Robertson studied painting under Frank Brangwyn, but was chiefly a novelist.

FORBES-ROBERTSON, Johnston (Sir)
British, 19th century.
Born 16 January 1853, in London.
Painter, actor.
Johnston Forbes-Robertson was the son of the art writer John Forbes-Robertson. He was knighted in 1913. He was a pupil at the Royal Academy School in London, and exhibited portraits (especially actors) with the Royal Academy and at the Grosvenor Gallery. He devoted himself to the theatre in later years, but continued to paint as an amateur.

FORBES-ROBERTSON, Margaret
British, 19th century.
Active in London.
Painter.
Margaret Forbes-Robertson was the sister of Sir Johnston Forbes-Robertson. She exhibited portrait miniatures at the Royal Academy from 1892 to 1894.

FORBICINI, Eliodoro
Italian, 16th century.
Born c. 1532, in Verona; died after 1590.
Painter. History painting, portraits, decorative motifs (grotesques).
Eliodoro Forbicini decorated two rooms of the Palazzo Canossa which were much admired.

FORBIGLIO, Jio
Flemish, 17th century.
Painter.
Flemish School.
In 1695 Jio Forbiglio painted two ceilings in the palace of the governor, Elector Max Emmanuel von Bayern.

FORBIN (Comte)
French, 18th century.
Born c. 1721.
Engraver (etching).
Forbin is remembered for 11 engravings depicting landscapes. He was probably the uncle of Auguste Forbin.

FORBIN, Louis Nicolas Philippe Auguste de (Comte)
French, 19th century.
Born 19 August 1777, in La Roque d'Anthéron (Bouches-du-Rhône); died 23 February 1841, in Paris.
Painter, watercolourist, engraver, draughtsman. Historical subjects, figures, scenes with figures, architectural interiors, landscapes, urban landscapes, architectural views, ruins.
Count Louis Forbin worked in David's studio. At the time of the Directoire, he served for a period as chamberlain to Princess Pauline Bonaparte. He participated in the Portuguese, Spanish and Austrian campaigns and, when peace was declared in 1809, retired to private life with the rank of lieutenant-colonel. He settled in Rome and from that moment on devoted himself entirely to the arts and artistic pursuits. He was made a member of the Institute in 1816 and on 1 June that year was put in charge of the royal museums and galleries. He was responsible for reorganizing the Louvre, and it is thanks to him that Géricault's superb *Raft of the Medusa* remained in France. Count Forbin established the Charles X Museum and the Luxembourg Museum. During 1817 and 1818, he travelled throughout the Orient at the state's expense, acquiring a large number of antique items. Several of his own canvases were exhibited at salons between 1796 and 1840. He was awarded the Légion d'Honneur in 1809, being made an officer in 1817 and a commander in 1822.

His work is interesting for its light effects. The figures that appear in his landscapes were for the most part painted by Granet.

BIBLIOGRAPHY:
Angrand, P., *Le Comte de Forbin et le Louvre en 1819,* Lausanne, 1972.

MUSEUMS AND GALLERIES:
AIX: *Gonsalvez of Cordoba Capturing the Alhambra in Grenada on 2 January 1492; Assassination of King Albert of Hungary at Pausilippo* - BAYONNE: *Inquisition Scene; Coronation of the Dead Inès de Castro* - COMPIÈGNE: *View near Rome* - LILLE: *Friend* - MONTPELLIER: *Cloister Interior* - PARIS (Louvre): *Monastery Interior; Ruins of the Coliseum in Rome* - TOURS: *Ruins in Upper Egypt, at the Time of the Nile Flood; Ruins at Palmyra* - VERSAILLES (Grand Trianon): *View of Jerusalem.*

AUCTION RECORDS:
PARIS, 31 March-1 April 1924, *Ruins* (watercolour) FRF 200. PARIS, 21 Jan 1925, *Desert Scene* (heightened pen) FRF 120. PARIS, 14 Oct 1992, *Monk Amid Ruins* (pen and Indian ink wash, 23 x 19 1/2 ins / 57.5 x 49.5 cm) FRF 12,500. PARIS, 18 Nov 1994, *Stairway in Rome* (1826, wash, 5 3/4 x 4 ins / 14.5 x 10 cm) FRF 4,600. PARIS, 29 May 1996, *Tangiers: Moor Accused of Assisting in the Flight of a Nun* (oil on canvas, 18 x 14 3/4 ins / 46 x 37.5 cm) FRF 27,000.

FORCADE, Étienne de. See **DEFORCADE Jean Baptiste Étienne**

FORCADE, Raoul André Jacques
French, 19th century.
Born in Dieppe.
Painter, sculptor. Genre scenes, landscapes.
Pupil of Cabanel; exhibited at the Paris Salon from 1870 to 1883.

AUCTION RECORDS:
PARIS, 7 July 1943, *Venice,* FRF 800. VERSAILLES, 21 June 1981, *Gamekeeper in the Forest* (1884, oil on canvas, 28 3/4 x 23 1/4 ins / 73 x 59 cm) FRF 3,500.

FORCE, Clara G.
American, 19th century.
Born 30 October 1852, in Erie (Pennsylvania); died 1939, in Los Angeles.
Miniaturist.
Clara G. Force was a pupil of Mabel Welsh, Thayer and Du Mond, and a member of the California Art Club.

FORCELLA, Nicola
Italian, 19th century.
Painter. Local figures, local scenes.
Orientalism.

AUCTION RECORDS:
PARIS, 29 Nov 1986, *Dancer in the Harem* (oil on canvas, 23 1/2 x 36 1/4 ins / 60 x 92 cm) FRF 18,000. NEW YORK, 27 May 1993, *Hookah, or the Old Carpet Seller* (oil on canvas, 27 1/2 x 18 1/4 ins / 70 x 46.3 cm) USD 10,350. NEW YORK, 14 Oct 1993, *Portrait of an Arab* (oil on panel, 12 3/4 x 9 1/2 ins / 32.4 x 24.2 cm) USD 14,950. PARIS, 8 Nov 1993, *Koranic School* (oil on panel, 16 1/4 x 10 ins / 41 x 24.5 cm) FRF 15,000. PARIS, 6 Nov 1995, *Busy Lane in the Old Part of Cairo* (oil on canvas, 22 x 12 1/2 ins / 55 x 32 cm) FRF 12,000. LONDON, 15 March 1996, *At the Mosque* (oil on canvas, 20 x 28 ins / 51 x 71 cm) GBP 21,275. PARIS, 22 April 1996, *In the Cafe* (oil on canvas, 22 x 17 1/2 ins / 56 x 44.5 cm) FRF 52,000. NEW YORK, 5 May 1999, *Tambourine Player. Artisan* (oil on canvas, a pair, 15 x 10 ins / 39 x 26 cm) USD 15,000. PARIS, 3 April 2000, *Felucce on the Nile* (oil on panel, 11 x 20 ins / 27 x 50 cm) FRF 27,000. PARIS, 18 June 2001, *Meditation* (oil on canvas, 18 x 13 ins / 46 x 33 cm) FRF 30,000. PARIS, 24 March 2004, *Portriat of a Woman with a Ring* (oil on canvas, 20 x 13 ins / 51 x 34 cm) EUR 4,400. STOCKHOLM, 26 May 2004, *En Zouave* (oil on canvas, 15 x 9 ins / 39 x 23 cm) SEK 26,000.

FORCELLA, Paolo
Italian, 19th century.
Born 1868.
Painter. Figures, portraits, local scenes.
Orientalism.
The brother of the Orientalist painter Nicola Forcella, he painted a number of scenes inspired by several years' stay in Cairo.
AUCTION RECORDS:
PARIS, 26 March 1998, *Amina, Young Oriental Woman with a Green Headscarf* (pastel, 27 x 20 1/2 ins / 68.5 x 52 cm) FRF 7,000.

FORCELLINI, Simone
Italian, 17th century.
Born to a family originally from Treviso.
Active at the end of the 17th century.
Painter.
Simone Forcellini painted altarpieces for the churches of Maria Maddalena in Treviso and Padua

FORCESTER, family of artists
British, 17th century.
Active in England.
Painters (glass).

FORCEVILLE, Jacques de
French, 17th - 18th century.
Painter (?), sculptor (?).
Jacques de Forceville was admitted to the Académie de St-Luc in Paris in 1682 or 1782.

FORCEVILLE, M. J. Émilie
French, 19th century.
Born 4 August 1867, in Tonnerre (Yonne).
Miniaturist.

FORCEVILLE-DUVETTE, Gédéon Alphonse Casimir
French, 19th century.
Born 12 February 1799, in St-Maulvis (Somme); died 30 January 1886, in Amiens.
Sculptor. Statues, busts.
Exhibited at the Paris Salon from 1845 to 1880; awarded a bronze medal. Examples of his work include: *Celestial Venus; Marble Bust of the Astronomer Jean-Baptiste-Joseph Delambre; Monumental Bust of Nicolas Blasset* (for one of the large ornamental fountains in Amiens); *Young Girl; Happy Child; Young Neapolitan Fisherman*; busts of Dr Barbier (bronze) and the archaeologist Jacques Boucher de Crèvecoeur de Perthes (marble); an allegorical statue entitled *Night* (marble); a plaster *Odalisque*; and a bronze statuette of *St Cecilia*.
MUSEUMS AND GALLERIES:
AMIENS: *Gresset* (statuette in Sèvres biscuit-ware); *Barbier* (bronze); *Lagrénée* (marble) - AMIENS (Académie): *Grasset* (marble).
AUCTION RECORDS:
PARIS, 26 March 1980, *The Author Jean-Baptiste-Louis Gresset* (bronze, h. 17 ins / 43 cm) FRF 2,300.

FÖRCH, Adam Pankratz. See **FERG**

FORCHEM, Guillam, or Forchen
Flemish, 17th century.
Painter.
Flemish School.
Guillam Forchem became a member of the Antwerp Guild of St Luke in 1631-1632.

FÖRCHER, Joseph
German, 18th century.
Born in the 18th century, in Geisslingen, near Rottweil (Baden-Württemberg).
Sculptor.
After having worked in Weilheim, Türkheim, Dachau and Augsburg, Förcher became a resident of Munich, where several churches contain examples of his work, such as pulpits and statues of saints.

FORCHHAMMER, Émilie
Swiss, 19th - 20th century.
Born 13 January 1850, in St-Antonien; died 13 June 1912, in Coire.
Painter. Portraits.
Studied under Professor Weissbrod in Basel, then under Tony Robert-Fleury, Jean-Paul Laurens and Benjamin-Constant at the Académie Julian in Paris.

FORCHNER, Franz Xaver
German, 18th century.
Born to a family originally from Dietenheim (Swabia, Baden-Württemberg); died 19 September 1751, in Dietenheim.
Painter.
The church in Höselhurst contains ceiling frescoes by Franz Xaver Forchner depicting the *Adoration of the Magi* and *St Nicholas Entering Heaven*. The church in Muttensweiler has ceiling frescoes showing *Story of St Norbert and Saints of the Premonstratensian Order*, while the church in Dietenheim has a painting of *St Sepulcre*. The frescoes on the Stations of the Cross in the Monastery at Ochsenhausen are also attributed to him.

FORCHNER, J. Chrysostomus
German, 18th century.
Died 13 November 1791, in Dietenheim.
Active in Dietenheim (Baden-Württemberg).
Painter.
The three altar paintings in the church in Muttensweiler are by J. Chrysostomus Forchner.

FORCIER, Denis
Canadian, 20th century.
Born 1943, in Montreal.
Painter, screen printer.
Pop Art.

Denis Forcier was once a member of the Graff studio, which was run by Albert Dumouchel and Pierre Ayot and disseminated the spirit of a mass culture, inspired by Pop Art, in Quebec. Using the photographic transfer technique with silk screen printing, Denis Forcier has developed a personal imagery that includes cups of tea, bags of sweets, jukeboxes and group meetings. Though apparently objective, by representing these objects of consumption or their consumers, he is putting them on display, and therefore questioning them.

MUSEUMS AND GALLERIES:

MONTREAL (MAC): *Music Box* (1976, silk screen print).

FORCONI, Jacques Antoine Léonard

French, 20th century.
Born in Calais.
Painter. Urban landscapes.

Jacques Forconi exhibited in Paris at the Salon d'Automne from 1925. He painted views of Paris.

FORCROY

19th century.
Engraver (wood).

Mentioned by Nagler, he studied under Adam.

FORD (Miss)

British, 18th century.
Painter. Landscapes.

Ford exhibited at the Royal Academy from 1771 to 1783.

FORD, C.

British, 19th century.
Born to a family originally from Bath.
Painter.

C. Ford exhibited portrait miniatures at the Royal Academy in London from 1830 to 1856. His portrait of the surgeon *J.W. Howell* was engraved by J. Thomson.

FORD, Edward Onslow

British, 19th century.
Born 27 July 1852, in London; died 23 December 1901, in London.
Painter, sculptor. Figures, genre scenes. Statues, busts.

Edward Onslow Ford studied in Antwerp and Munich, and exhibited at the Royal Academy and Suffolk Street from 1875. He abandoned painting for sculpture. His works are notable for their powerful expressive qualities. He became an associate of the Royal Academy in 1888, and an academician in 1895.

MUSEUMS AND GALLERIES:

ANTWERP: *The Alma Tadema* - BIRMINGHAM: *Dr R.W. Dale* - BRADFORD (Cartwright Hall AG): *Head of a Girl* (bronze) - EDINBURGH (Scottish National Portrait Gallery): *Arthur James Balfour, 1st Earl of Balfour* (plaster) - LIVERPOOL: *Peace* (bronze, statuette) - LONDON (Guildhall AG): *George Swan Nottage, Lord Mayor* (c. 1884, marble); *Sir Henry Irving as Hamlet* (c. 1885, marble); *Sir James Whitehead Lord Mayor* (1888); *Queen Victoria* (1898, marble); *Sir Charles Read* (marble); *Lady Whitehead* - LONDON (National Portrait Gal.): *Sir Hubert von Herkomer* (1877, terracotta, bust); *Sir John Everett Millais, 1st Bt* (1923, bronze, bust) - LONDON (Natural History Mus.): *Thomas Henry Huxley* (1898, marble statue) - LONDON (Royal Academy of Arts): *Sir Lawrence Alma-Tadema* (1895, bronze bust, competition piece); *Bust of Sir John Everett Millais, Bt, P.R.A.* (1895, bronze, base in marble) - LONDON (Tate Collection): *Folly* (exhibited in 1886, bronze, statuette); *The Singer* (exhibited in 1889, bronze, coloured resin paste and semi-precious stones, statuette); *Sir W.Q. Orchardson, R.A.* (exhibited in 1895, bronze, bust) - MANCHESTER: *Charles Hallé* - PRESTON: *Peace* (bronze, statuette) - SYDNEY: *Head of a Young Girl* (bronze).

AUCTION RECORDS:

LONDON, 25 March 1981, *Peace* (bronze, h. 23 ins / 58.5 cm) GBP 980. LONDON, 14 Dec 1983, *Peace* (1890, patinated bronze, h. 22 ins / 56 cm) GBP 600. LONDON, 2 Oct 1985, *Frederick William Heilgers* (1879, marble, h. 31 ins / 79 cm) GBP 450. LONDON, 16 April 1986, *Folly* (dark-green and black patinated bronze, h. 19 3/4 ins / 50 cm) GBP 1,400. NEW YORK, 8 Oct 1988, *Bean Plant* (1961, mixed media/canvas, 120 1/4 x 36 ins / 305.2 x 91.5 cm) USD 13,200. NEW YORK, 25 Oct 1989, *Peace* (brown-patinated bronze, h. 21 3/4 ins / 55.2 cm) USD 3,300. PARIS, 10 June 1990, *Voyager with Blue Auras* (1989, oil on canvas, 37 1/2 x 32 ins / 95 x 81 cm) FRF 35,000. PARIS, 2 June 1991, *In Come* (acrylic/canvas, 62 1/4 x 38 1/2 ins / 158 x 98 cm) FRF 20,000. MONTREAL, 19 Nov 1991, *Head of a Young Girl* (1884, bronze, h. 14 1/2 ins / 36.8 cm) CAD 7,000. PARIS, 21 Oct 1992, *Alms; Sleeping Peasant Woman with her Child on her Knee* (1864, oil on canvas, a pair, 34 1/4 x 25 1/2 ins / 87 x 65 cm) FRF 16,000.

FORD, Elizabeth

American, 20th century.
Born in Arahi (Rhode Island).
Sculptor. Figures.

Elizabeth Ford exhibited in galleries in Paris, including the Salon d'Automne of 1924.

FORD, F.

British, 19th century.
Active in London.
Painter. Landscapes.

F. Ford exhibited at the Royal Academy and Suffolk Street from 1852 to 1860.

FORD, George Henry

British, 20th century.
Born 13 July 1912; died 1977.
Sculptor.

George Ford exhibited at the Royal Academy in London, at the Royal Scottish Academy and at the Walker Gallery in Liverpool.

FORD, Henry Chapman

American, 19th century.
Born 1828, in New York; died 1894.
Painter, draughtsman. Historical subjects, military subjects, landscapes with figures, animals.

Between 1857 and 1860, Henry Chapman Ford studied in Paris and Florence. He then returned to America to take part in the Civil War, of which he made sketches for the newspapers. After leaving the army he went to Chicago, where he opened his studio in 1863. He was one of the founder members of the Academy of Design and became its president in 1873.

AUCTION RECORDS:

SAN FRANCISCO, 6 Nov 1985, *Deer in a Landscape* (1874, oil on canvas, 25 x 42 1/4 ins / 63.5 x 107 cm) USD 3,000. NEW YORK, 15 May 1991, *Californian Landscape* (1879, oil on canvas, 23 x 17 ins / 58.4 x 43.2 cm) USD 1,870. NEW YORK, 25 May 1994, *Fairy Arch, Mackinac Island* (1874, oil on canvas, 30 x 50 1/2 ins / 76.2 x 128.3 cm) USD 32,200. NEW YORK, 28 Sept 1995, *Landscape in the West* (1874, oil on canvas, 30 1/4 x 50 ins / 76.8 x 127 cm) USD 3,910. LOS ANGELES, 30 Oct 2000, *Franciscan Missions of California, New York, Studio Press* (etchings, portfolio of 24, 7 x 13 ins / 17 x 32 cm) USD 17,000. LOS ANGELES, 13 Dec 2000, *View of a Western Homestead* (1878, oil on canvas, 15 x 30 ins / 39 x 75 cm) USD 25,000. CONNECTICUT, 21 June 2001, *Western Landscape* (1875, oil on canvas, 16 x 30 ins / 41 x 76 cm) USD 7,250. LOS ANGELES, 7 Nov 2001, *Wooded Interior* (1877, oil on canvas, 45 x 36 ins / 114 x 91 cm) USD 10,000. LOS ANGELES, 20 Nov 2002, *Water Lilies and Spanish Moss* (1874, oil on canvas, 30 x 48 ins / 76 x 122 cm) USD 9,500. CHICAGO, 23 May 2004, *Western Landscape* (oil on paper on canvas, 14 x 19 ins / 36 x 48 cm) USD 6,000.

FORD, Henry Justice
British, 19th - 20th century.
Born February 1860, in London; died 1941.
Painter (gouache), watercolourist, draughtsman, illustrator. Scenes with figures, religious subjects, mythological subjects.

Henry Ford studied at Cambridge, under Alphonse Legros, an engraver friend of Whistler and the Pre-Raphaelites, and under Hubert von Herkomer at the school he founded in Bushey. He associated with the Pre-Raphaelite artist Burne-Jones and was influenced by him. He was known mainly for the illustrations that he published between 1889 and 1913 to accompany the stories of Andrew Lang. He also illustrated many other literary works, generally short stories and legends. They included in 1888 Aesop's *Fables*; in 1890 *The Red Fairy Book*; in 1892 *The Green Fairy Book*; in 1894 *The Yellow Fairy Book*; in 1896 Lang's *Animal Stories*; in 1901 *The Violet Fairy Book*; in 1905 *The Tales of King Arthur*; in 1907 *Tales and Romances, Tales of Troy and Greece*; in 1912 *The Book of Saints and Heroes*; and in 1919 *The Thousand and One Nights*. Ford took part in group exhibitions at venues in London, including the Fine Art Society, the New Gallery, the Royal Academy and the Royal Institute of Oil Painters.

BIBLIOGRAPHY:
Osterwalder, Marcus (ed.), *Dictionnaire des illustrateurs 1800-1914*, Ides et Calendes, Neuchâtel, 1989.

AUCTION RECORDS:
LONDON, 27 April 1982, *St Francis Talking to the Birds* (watercolour, 12 3/4 x 8 ins / 32.5 x 20.5 cm) GBP 300. NEW YORK, 23 Feb 1983, *The Werewolf Carries Prince William Away* (gouache, 7 x 12 1/2 ins / 17.9 x 31.5 cm) USD 1,300. LONDON, 29 Oct 1991, *Psyche Losing Cupid* (pencil and watercolour, 11 x 6 1/2 ins / 28 x 16.5 cm) GBP 6,600. NEW YORK, 20 July 1994, *The Princess and the Wolves in the Forest* (1907, watercolour/card, 11 x 15 1/4 ins / 27 x 38.7 cm) USD 2,300. PARIS, 16 March 1997, *Indian Family* (oil on canvas, 24 1/2 x 17 1/4 ins / 62 x 44 cm) FRF 7,500. LONDON, 17 Jan 2001, *View of Lore Harbour* (oil on board, 13 x 9 ins / 32 x 24 cm) GBP 1,100. LONDON, 5 June 2003, *Princes and the Wolves in the Forest* (pencil and watercolour heightened with gouache, 9 x 15 ins / 22 x 37 cm) GBP 3,200. LONDON, 20 Nov 2003, *Escape* (pencil, pen, black ink and grey wash with scratching out, 11 x 7 ins / 27 x 19 cm) GBP 2,600.

FORD, James
Irish, 19th century.
Died after 1812.
Engraver.

James Ford studied at the Dublin Society School, and engraved a series of aquatint landscapes for the Society's *County Surveys*, as well as book illustrations and a portrait of the actor T. Ryder, after A. Shee.

FORD, John
British, 18th century.
Active in Bath.
Sculptor, enameller.

John Ford exhibited in London at the Royal Academy and the Free Society from 1764 to 1797.

FORD, L. W. Neilson
American, 20th century.
Painter.

L. W. Neilson Ford was initially a pupil of Hugh Newell in Philadelphia before studying in Paris, England and Berlin.

FORD, Laurens
American, 20th century.
Born 23 February 1891, in New York; died 1973.
Painter, watercolourist.

Laurens Ford was a pupil of Frederick Arthur Bridgman and Frank Vincent Du Mond, and a member of the American Watercolor Society.

AUCTION RECORDS:
NEW YORK, 25 March 1997, *Piazza S Pietro, Assisi* (c. 1930, oil on panel, 12 3/4 x 15 3/4 ins / 32.4 x 40.3 cm) USD 2,587.

FORD, Michael
Irish, 18th century.
Died 1765.
Engraver (mezzotint).

Michael Ford was probably a pupil of John Brooks, to whose print-dealing business in Dublin he succeeded in 1747. Ford is known for a number of engraved portraits, including some executed after his own original drawings. It is not known exactly how Ford died, but he is thought to have been lost at sea. His works include *William III*, after Kneller, *George II* after Hudson, and *Henry Singleton, Chief Justice of Ireland*, after his own drawing.

FORD, Michael
British, 20th century.
Born 28 July 1920.
Painter, draughtsman. Portraits.

Michael Ford exhibited in London at the Royal Academy, the New English Art Club, the Royal Society of Portrait Painters and the Royal Society of British Artists.

FORD, Richard
British, 19th century.
Born 1796, in London; died 1 September 1858, in Heavitree, near Exeter.
Engraver, watercolourist.

Richard Ford was the author of a *Guide for the Traveller in Spain*. An amateur engraver, he illustrated J.G. Lockhart's *Ancient Spanish Ballads*.

AUCTION RECORDS:
LONDON, 24 Nov 1926, *Continental Street Scene* (watercolour) GBP 50.

FORD, Rudolph or Wolfram Onslow, or Onslow Ford
British, 20th century.
Born c. 1880, in London.
Painter. Portraits, landscapes, still-lifes.

Rudolph Ford was the son of the sculptor Edward Onslow Ford. He studied at the Royal Academy in London. Ford painted numerous portraits, including one of his father, one of James McNeill Whistler and one of his young wife. His landscape subjects are familiar rustic themes such as *The Lock* and, in common with other artists of this period dominated by Impressionism, he revealed himself to be sensitive to the slightest nuances of light in terms of the weather, time and the seasons in works such as *February Morning*. He exhibited at the Royal Academy from 1897 to 1913. In 1910, he organised a solo exhibition of his portraits and landscapes at the Baillie Gallery in London.

AUCTION RECORDS:
LONDON, 31 March 1981, *Mrs Ralph Flower and her Children* (1905-1906, oil on canvas, 53 1/4 x 65 ins / 135 x 165 cm) GBP 750. LONDON, 11 June 1986, *Mr G. Warner* (1899, oil on panel, 23 1/2 x 18 1/2 ins / 59.5 x 47 cm) GBP 1,000. GLASGOW, 25 Aug 1997, *Wooded Landscape in Springtime* (1899, oil on panel, 10 1/2 x 18 ins / 26.6 x 45.7 cm) GBP 322.

FORD, Ruth van Sickle
American, 20th century.
Born 8 August 1898, in Aurora (Illinois); died 1980.
Painter.

Ruth van Sickle Ford was a member of the Painters and Sculptors of Chicago Institute. In 1931, she was awarded the fine arts prize at the city's Art Institute.

FORD, Samuel, or Forde
Irish, 19th century.
Born 8 April 1805, in Cork; died 29 July 1828, in Cork.
Painter. History painting.

Samuel Ford came from an impoverished family, but studied with success in Cork, where he became a Master of the Cork Institute of Mechanics in 1828. His works include *The Spirit of Tragedy* (1827) and *The Fall of the Angels*.

MUSEUMS AND GALLERIES:
LONDON (Victoria and Albert Mus.): *Tragic Vision* (watercolour).

FORD, Thomas
British, 18th century.
Died 29 August 1746, in Oxford.
Engraver. Portraits.

Thomas Ford was a cleric, and an engraver. He is noted for an oval self-portrait in mezzotint.

FORD, Walton
American, 20th - 21st century.
Born 1960, in New York.
Painter. Birds, animals, scenes with figures.

Walton Ford obtained a BFA in 1982 from the Rhode Island School of Design. He also studied in Rome in 1982, and has travelled in India. He began his career in New York, originally intending to become a filmmaker, but later changed to large-scale watercolour paintings. He now lives and works in Great Barrington, MA. Awards include: Guggenheim Fellowship (1992); National Endowment for the Arts Fellowship (1991); Mid-Atlantic Arts Foundation Grant (1990); New York Foundation for the Arts Fellowship (1989); Pollock-Krasner Foundation Grant (1989); Art Matters Inc. Fellowship (1988); and Penny McCall Foundation Grant (1989). Ford's works are held in the collections of the Whitney Museum of American Art; University Art Museum, California State University, Long Beach; and the Spencer Museum of Art, Kansas.

Ford's subjects, which focus on birds and animals, are in the tradition of the 19th-century bird artist John James Audubon, and concentrate in the early work on North American species, and later on the birds and fauna of India. His studies in natural history are combined with political commentary, layering together complex symbols, clues and jokes to satirise and draw attention to important contemporary issues, such as the environment, the history of colonialism and imperialism, the global economy and the impact of slavery and political oppression. *N.G.O. Wallahs* (1997), for example, depicts a European starling distributing Hershey's kisses to a local aviary, while *Dirty Dick Burton's Aide de Camp*, a 2002 watercolour, gouache and ink painting, uses the image of a monkey as mocking satire.

Ford's exhibitions include: 1990, *A Sense of Place*, Montgomery Museum of Fine Art, AL; 1993, the Contemporary Arts Center, Cincinnati, Ohio; 1994, *History 101: The Re-Search for Family*, Forum for Contemporary Art, St Louis, Missouri; 1995, *Next of Kin*, List Visual Arts Center, Massachusetts Institute of Technology, Cambridge, MA; 1997, *Animal Tales: Contemporary Bestiary and Animal Painting*, Whitney Museum of American Art at Champion, CT; 1997, Southeastern Center for Contemporary Art, North Carolina; 1999, the University Art Museum, California State University, Long Beach; 2000, *Brutal Beauty: The Paintings of Walton Ford*, Bowdoin College Museum of Art, Maine; 2004(2005, *Birdspace: A Post Audubon Artists Aviary*, Hudson River Museum, Yonkers, NY; 2004(2005, *Political Nature*, the Whitney Museum of American Art, New York.

BIBLIOGRAPHY:
Un regard autre, exhibition catalogue, Gal. Farideh Cadot, Paris, 1987. Durham, Jimmie, '*To Be a Pilgrim: Walton Ford*' in *Artforum*, Journal article, January 1993. *Walton Ford*, Exhibition catalogue, Southeastern Center for Contemporary Art, Winston-Salem (NC), 1997. Glenn, Constance W. (ed.), *Avatars: The Watercolors of Walton Ford*, Exhibition catalogue, University Art Museum, College of the Arts, California State University, Long Beach, 1998. *Tigers of Wrath, Horses of Instruction*, Illustrated book, Harry N. Abrams, New York, 2002.

MUSEUMS AND GALLERIES:
LAWRENCE (Spencer MA, University of Kansas) - LONG BEACH (University AM, California State University) - NEW YORK (Whitney Mus. of American Art).

FORD, William
British, 19th century.
Painter.

An enamel painter, William Ford exhibited at the Royal Academy and Suffolk Street from 1846 to 1858.

FORD, William B.
British, 19th century.
Painter.

A relative, possibly the son, of William Ford. William B. Ford's name appears frequently in the catalogues of the Royal Academy and Suffolk Street, from 1859. He was also active as an enamel painter.

FÖRDERREUTHER, Robert
German, 19th century.
Born 18 August 1859, in Nuremberg; died 13 September 1906, in Schwarzenbach an der Saale (Bavaria).
Painter. Landscapes.

Förderreuther was a student of Leon Pohle at the academy in Dresden. He initially concentrated on oil paintings (predominantly landscapes of northern Bavaria and the Isar region, and portrait studies), but later turned to watercolours.

FORDRAIN, Charles Antoine
French, 18th century.
Active in Paris in 1772.
Sculptor, painter.

FOREAU, Claude
French, 20th century.
Born 12 June 1903, in Paris.
Painter. Genre scenes.

Claude Foreau studied under Cormon. He exhibited regularly in Paris at the Salon des Artistes Français from 1924, receiving a silver medal in 1924, a gold medal in 1927 and various prizes and bursaries including the Prix National in 1932 and the Hemming Fry prize in 1944.

AUCTION RECORDS:
PARIS, 9 July 1942, *The Window*, FRF 200.

FOREAU, Henri-Louis
French, 19th - 20th century.
Born 19 February 1866, in Paris; died 1 April 1938, in Paris.
Painter, watercolourist. Genre scenes, landscapes with figures, landscapes.

Henri-Louis Foreau studied at the École des Beaux-Arts under Jules Lefebvre, Henry Lévy and Luc-Olivier Merson, and also received advice from Henri Harpignies.

His work is based around three main themes: the French countryside, parks and gardens, and Paris and the Paris region. He principally painted melancholic landscapes using a limited palette in a range of grey and bluish tones. He worked in a wide range of techniques but his talent is best displayed in his watercolours, in which sky and water play a dominant role.

He exhibited at group exhibitions in Paris and was a member of the Salon des Artistes Français from 1888. He received a commendation in 1891, a bronze medal in 1892, a silver medal in 1894 and a bronze medal at the Exposition

Universelle of 1900. Foreau was also president of the Association des Paysagistes Français (Association of French Landscape Artists) and was made a Chevalier of the Légion d'Honneur in 1911.

Bibliography:

Herment, Édith/Desmarest, Éric, *Henri Foreau, peintre de l'air et de l'eau*, Éd. de l'Amateur, Paris, 1992.

Museums and Galleries:

Niort: *Park in Winter* (watercolour) - Paris (Louvre): five watercolours - Paris (Mus. Carnavalet): *Evening (Fortifications of Paris)*; *Fortifications* (watercolour) - Paris (Mus. d'Histoire Contemporaine): *The Shepherd* (watercolour) - Paris (Mus. d'Orsay): *Autumn Landscape*; *Landscape or Lake Soubise* - Pau (MBA): *A Stagecoach in the Var* - Péronne (Historial de la Grande Guerre): *Prisoners at Work* - Rouen: *Pagan Procession* - Vienna: *The Grief of Orpheus*.

Auction records:

London, 21 March 1908, *The Soubise Ferry* (watercolour) GBP 7. Paris, 12 June 1926, *The Washing Place*, FRF 405. Paris, 17 May 1929, *A Path in the Tuileries Gardens* (watercolour) FRF 980. Paris, 19 Dec 1932, *The Lake*, FRF 400. Paris, 24 April 1942, *The Haywains*; *The Lake* (two watercolours) FRF 1,000. Paris, 23 June 1943, *The Pond*; *The Pergola* (two watercolours) FRF 3,600. Paris, 25 Sept 1944, *Animals on the Plain* (two watercolours) FRF 2,000. Paris, 28 June 1945, *The Ferryman*, FRF 1,700. Paris, 13 June 1947, *Sheep in a Valley*; *Birds of Passage* (two pendants) FRF 3,000. Paris, 2 March 1951, *River Bank*, FRF 9,000. Paris, 21 Dec 1953, *Landscape* (watercolour) FRF 2,000. Paris, 3 June 1970, *Animals by a Bridge*, FRF 6,000. Paris, 9 Feb 1979, *Shepherd and Sheep by the Sea* (watercolour, 11 x 15 1/4 ins / 28 x 39 cm) FRF 600. Versailles, 18 Feb 1979, *Shepherdess and Flock* (oil on canvas, 21 1/4 x 32 ins / 54 x 81 cm) FRF 2,000. New York, 30 June 1981, *Views of the Gardens of the Château of Versailles* (two watercolours, 16 1/4 x 24 ins / 41 x 61 cm) USD 1,300. Vienna, 20 April 1983, *On the Banks of the Seine* (oil on canvas, 10 1/4 x 14 1/2 ins / 26 x 37 cm) ATS 18,000. Lindau, 9 May 1984, *Harvesters in the Fields at Twilight* (oil on canvas, 25 1/2 x 39 1/4 ins / 65 x 100 cm) DEM 4,300. Vienna, 11 Sept 1985, *Normandy Beach* (oil on canvas, 41 1/4 x 35 ins / 105 x 88 cm) ATS 100,000. Paris, 10 Feb 1988, *Cows by a River* (watercolour, 11 x 15 1/4 ins / 28 x 38.5 cm) FRF 1,700. Paris, 3 June 1988, *Cottage in Winter* (oil on canvas, 18 x 25 1/2 ins / 46 x 65 cm) FRF 4,500. Montreal, 30 April 1990, *Figures by a River* (oil on canvas, 20 x 24 ins / 51 x 61 cm) CAD 1,430. Paris, 20 March 1991, *Sheep and Shepherds by a River* (watercolour and gouache, 10 1/2 x 14 1/4 ins / 26.5 x 36.5 cm) FRF 4,800. Paris, 18 May 1992, *Versailles* (watercolour, 9 1/2 x 14 1/4 ins / 24 x 36 cm) FRF 10,500; *Kelp Gatherers near Fouras* (watercolour, 10 1/4 x 12 3/4 ins / 26 x 32.5 cm) FRF 10,000. Paris, 22 March 1993, *Autumn* (watercolour, 14 1/4 x 22 ins / 36.5 x 55 cm) FRF 5,000. Paris, 22 March 1998, *Cows in a Meadow* (watercolour/paper, 12 1/2 x 19 ins / 31.5 x 48.5 cm) FRF 5,200. Newbury, 21 July 1999, *Wash Day on the Banks of the Seine* (oil on canvas, 24 x 30 ins / 62 x 76 cm) GBP 2,800. Paris, 4 July 2000, *Port at La Rochelle* (oil on canvas, 23 x 32 ins / 59 x 81 cm) FRF 11,000. Paris, 12 Dec 2001, *Poitevin Marsh* (watercolour, 15 x 21 ins / 37 x 54 cm) FRF 14,500. St-Germain-en-Laye, 19 Oct 2003, *Landscape with Figures at Twilight* (oil on canvas, 75 x 52 ins / 190 x 132 cm) EUR 1,500. Fontainebleau, 6 June 2004, *Landscape with Ferry* (oil on canvas) EUR 4,500.

FOREAU, Nicolas François

French, 18th century.
Active in Paris in 1763.
Painter.

FOREAU, Pierre Jacques

French, 18th century.
Active in Paris in 1758.
Painter, sculptor.

FOREIS, Pierre

French, 15th century.
Active in Chambéry (Savoy).
Illuminator.

In 1416 Pierre Foreis completed a missal for the chapel of the Château of Chambéry, which he had bound and illustrated with illuminated miniatures. He was a member of the Order of St Anthony.

FOREL, Alexis

Swiss, 19th century.
Born 5 May 1852, in Lully, near Morges; died 24 December 1922, in Morges.
Engraver (etching), collector. Urban landscapes, landscapes.

Alexis Forel was both an artist and a chemical engineer. After making a name for himself in science through his study of aniline paints, he moved to Paris and took up etching in 1881. He and his wife Emmeline, also an artist, set themselves up in the former studio and apartment of Delacroix, in Place Furstenberg. He formed a friendship with the engraver Félix Buhot. Being partially paralysed, he was not able to use his talent fully, and following further health problems he concentrated on art criticism. In 1913, he wrote *Voyage au pays des sculpteurs romans* (*Journey to the Land of the Romanesque Sculptors*). With Henry de Mandrot, he worked for the creation of a Musée Romand (Museum of French-speaking Switzerland) in La Sarraz, but resigned from the committee on account of a difference of opinion. His house in Morges became a museum in 1919, dedicated to engraving.

In Paris, he featured in the official Salons (1882-1890), and in 1889 participated in the Exposition Universelle (Swiss section) in Paris, and at the second exhibition of painters and engravers at the Galerie Durand-Ruel. In 1930, the engravings of Alexis and the pastels of his wife Emmeline were exhibited at the Galerie Simonson in Paris. The Musée Alexis Forel in Morges presented a retrospective of Forel's engravings in 2003.

The year 1885 was prolific: he produced no fewer than 36 plates on just one visit to Brittany. He aimed to reproduce the most picturesque 'corners of Paris'. It is evident that Forel was frequently inspired by Meryon. The eminent American publisher and writer on art Frederick Keppel has published one of his prints: *Lausanne Cathedral*.

Alexis Forel was also an astute collector, who assembled a collection of engravings from the 16th to the 19th century: Dürer, Rembrandt, Millet, Seymour Hayden, Félix Buhot. He collected or wrote when health problems prevented him from engraving or drawing. His collection, which has been progressively expanded, was presented to the Cabinet Cantonal des Estampes at the Musée Janisch in Vevey in 2003.

Bibliography:

Guex, Stéphanie/Sarto, Pietro/Tixhon, Thomas, *Alexis Forel, graveur et collectionneur (1852-1922)*, exhibition catalogue, Musée Jenisch, Vevey, 2003.

Museums and Galleries:

Morges (Mus. Alexis Forel) - Vevey (Musée Jenisch, Cabinet cantonal des estampes): on loan from the Prints Dept. of the Musée Alexis Forel.

FOREL, Emmeline

Swiss, 19th century.
Born 2 November 1860, in Morges; died 7 May 1957, in Morges.
Painter, pastellist. Landscapes.

Emmeline Forel studied in Paris at the Studios of Julian and Delécluzes, then with T. Bischoff in Lausanne. She was the wife of the etcher Alexis Forel.

She featured in Swiss exhibitions from 1895 to 1904. In 1930, her husband's engraving work and her own pastels were shown at the Galerie Simonson in Paris.

She illustrated her husband's monograph: *Voyage au pays des sculpteurs romans* (*Journey to the Land of the Romanesque Sculptors*) with coloured drawings and vignettes.

BIBLIOGRAPHY:
Guex, Stéphanie/Sarto, Pietro/Tixhon, Thomas, *Alexis Forel, graveur et collectionneur (1852-1922)*, exhibition catalogue, Musée Jenisch, Vevey, 2003.

MUSEUMS AND GALLERIES:
LAUSANNE: *Landscape*.

FORELL, Robert
German, 19th century.
Born 27 April 1858, in Bockenheim (Hesse).
Painter. History painting, genre scenes.

Forell was a student at the municipal institute in Frankfurt and the academy in Düsseldorf. He settled in Düsseldorf.

MUSEUMS AND GALLERIES:
KREFELD (Kaiser Wilhelm Mus.): *Death of the Count of Mansfeld*.

FORELLI, G.
French, 20th century.
Painter. Genre scenes.

AUCTION RECORDS:
PARIS, 16 April 1945, *Christ at Prayer*, FRF 1,250.

FOREMAN, Agnes Emily
British, 19th century.
Born in the second half of the 19th century, in London.
Miniaturist.

FORER, Rennwart
Swiss, 17th century.
Born in Lucerne.
Active 1606-1650.
Painter.

Forer lived in Lucerne. He painted several pictures for the churches and other public buildings in Lucerne, Wertenstein, Baden-Baden and Beromünster. Among his most notable works are *Birth of Christ* in the church of the Barefoot Carmelites in Lucerne, *Adoration of the Kings* (destroyed in a fire of 1633), and an *Assumption* in Baden-Baden.

FORES, Jozef
Lithuanian, 17th century.
Born in Vilnius; died 1661, in Warsaw.
Painter.

Jozef Fores was a member of a religious order when he died.

FORES, S.W.
British, 18th century.
Active in London.
Engraver.

S.W. Fores was active in London from 1785 to 1825, where he published numerous copies of caricatures by James Gillray, notably those of army chiefs and statesmen: *General Souvaroff*, *Catherine the Great*, the tsars *Paul* and *Alexander I*, *Napoleon*, the *Battle of Waterloo*, among others.

FORESMAN, Alice
American.
Born in Darien (Wisconsin).
Miniaturist.

A member of the California Society of Miniaturist Painters and the West Coast Arts Club, she was also a teacher.

FOREST, or Fourest
family of artists
French, 16th century.
Painters.

Working in Lyons, this family of artists consisted of Jean (known to be active 1515-1533), Laurent (active 1515-1554, and documented as being involved in preparations for the entries of royalty into the city in 1533 and 1540), and Sébastien (recorded in 1557).

FOREST
French, 18th century.
Born 18th century, in Soissons.
Sculptor.

Forest worked in 1736 on the façade of the town hall in Laon and in 1762 at the Château de Compiègne. He may be identical to the woodcarver Foret who executed the stalls of the cathedral in Soissons in 1770.

FOREST, Eugène Hippolyte
French, 19th century.
Born 24 October 1808, in Strasbourg.
Painter, engraver, caricaturist. Genre scenes, landscapes with figures, animals.

Pupil of Camille Roqueplan; exhibited at the Paris Salon from 1847 to 1866. His work includes *Old Bridge at Cahors*; *Poacher*; *View of the Valley of Cransac*; *Emouchet*; *Water Fowl*; *Bird Study*; *Pheasant and Partridge*; and *Drama in the Mountains*. As an engraver, he produced several albums of caricatures in the style of Henri Monnier.

AUCTION RECORDS:
PARIS, 25 May 1923, *At Pasture*, FRF 60. COLOGNE, 18 March 1983, *Shepherds and Flock Grazing in a Mountain Landscape* (oil on panel, 5 1/2 x 9 ins / 14 x 22 cm) DEM 3,500.

FOREST, Flavien
French, 20th century.
Born in Paris.
Painter.

Flavien Forest exhibited landscapes at the Salon des Indépendants in Paris.

FOREST, Fred
French, 20th century.
Born 6 July 1933, in Mascara, Algeria.
Draughtsman, painter, installation artist. Multimedia.
Art Sociologique (Sociological Art), Electronic Arts.
Collectif d'Art Sociologique.

Fred Forest lives and works in Paris and Anserville, and began exhibiting in the late 1960s.

At that time he painted in a style that derived from the French Nouvelle Figuration form of Pop Art and produced 'dessins-charges', or mild caricatures, for daily newspapers. He then abandoned traditional art media and since 1967 has worked in the open field of communication. He was the first French artist to use video. He co-founded the *Collectif d'Art Sociologique* and, in 1984, the *Groupe International de l'Esthétique et de la Communication* with Mario Costa at San Severino Mercato in Italy.

Sociological art explores the structural transformations of industrial society associated with its growth and development. It is an approach that seeks to get as close as possible to social reality - to analyse the dysfunctionality that results from a more complex form of social organisation, new social stratifications, methods of access to culture and, above all, the new audio and visual means of communication; all of which are important aspects of our lives together. Forest's artistic approach therefore incorporates the entire range of technological devices and tools borrowed from the world of telecommunications and information technology: video, telephone, television, radio, the written press and online data processing, but with particular focus on the image.

Around 1970 he created the 'picture-screen', which involved the use of collage and light synchronised with sound. His actions are of a sociological nature, often in the form of investigations and films which usually describe a moment of artistic life. He has filmed public auctions and, at the same auction, has filmed his own collector. He provokes some kind of disturbance at a given moment and films the resulting consequences in the chosen social environment.

At one event, which took place on 10 January 1986 at the École Nationale des Beaux-Arts in Paris as part of *Rencontres et Performances sur l'Esthétique de la Communication*, Forest broadcast by radio a series of messages he had previously recorded such as 'raise one arm' and 'take three steps forward', which he executed in public and in real time. During this action his own recorded voice asked him to move a vase standing on a television set; Forest executed the instruction but made the vase fall - the accident appeared genuine until the voice proceeded to order him to pick up the pieces of the broken vase and to turn on a video recorder. The television screen on which the vase had been standing then showed an image of the unbroken vase. This type of action draws our attention to the complexity of the media network, playing upon the mediatised physical presence and absence of the individual and of his senses, of reality and of the images of representation, of the concomitance and non-simultaneity of facts or events. Another of Forest's actions, the *Le Feu du Ciel ou la Danse des Électrons*, which took place during the 1990s, consisted of using the sun of Arizona to illuminate a summer's night on Lake Locarno in real time. The system he devised depended upon physical manipulation of a symbolic nature - fire and electrons - and computer technology with sophisticated light, images and sound, combined with the aesthetic principles of Land Art.

His first exhibition took place in 1967. After this he went on to produce *Family Portrait*, an urban event in the Paris suburbs. Other major events include: 1969, a video installation at the Galerie Ste-Croix, Tours; 1976, the *Sociological Art Collective* at the Venice Biennale; 1977, Documenta 6, Kassel; 1982, *Bourse de l'Imaginaire* at the Pompidou Centre, Paris; and in 1983 an event at the Musée d'Art Moderne de la Ville de Paris. In 1967 he was awarded the silver medal for Arts and Letters, in 1973 the communication prize at the 12th São Paulo Biennale and in 1990 the Laser d'Or video prize at the Festival of Locarno in Italy.

Bibliography:

Forest, Fred, '*Art sociologique*' in *coll. 10/18*, UGE, Paris, 1977. '*Fred Forest*' in *Revue d'art contemporain: + - 0* n° 43, periodical, October 1985 (published in Belgium). Forest, Fred/Virilio, Paul, '*Entretien*' in *Art Press*, periodical, Paris, 1989. '*Le Feu du ciel ou la danse des électrons*' in *Art Press special edition, 'Nouvelles Technologies un Art sans Modèle?'*, periodical, Paris, 1992. *Fred Forest 100 actions*, Z'Éditions, Nice, 1995. Hoog, Emmanuel (preface), *Fred Forest, pionnier expérimentateur: de lart vidéo... au Net art: art sociologique et esthétique de la communication*, L'Harmattan, Paris, 2004.

Museums and Galleries:

Épinal (Mus. départemental d'Art ancien et contemporain): *1 Mètre Carré artistique* (*1 Artistic Square Metre*).

Auction records:

Paris, 12 Feb 1990, *Ballad for Change in the Lenin-Gorbachev Régime* (1989, two photos, 12½ x 9½ ins / 32 x 24 cm) FRF 3,500.

FOREST, Jean Baptiste

French, 17th - 18th century.
Born 1635, in Paris; died 17 March 1712, in Paris.
Painter. Landscapes.

Jean Baptiste Forest is almost the prototype of those exceptionally gifted artists who, less by circumstances than by their own characters and even their originality, have not succeeded in giving full rein to their genius. He lacked for nothing in education and preparations for a brilliant career. Fully supported by his father, he was able to spend seven years in Italy. He had lessons from Pierre-François Mola, well known at the time as a painter of historical subjects and landscapes. On his return he sketched, with exquisite artistic feeling and a love of nature, some of the most beautiful sites in Provence and Franche-Comté. On 26 May 1674, at the age of 38, he was admitted to the Académie, subsequently excluded for being a Protestant, and re-admitted on 5 April 1699. He had married the daughter of Lafosse and later married off the daughter of that union to Largillière. In spite of his jealously independent character, which caused him to refuse two important commissions in the name of the king, he had no greater enemy than himself. He regularly lost patience with a sketch deemed admirable by his friends, covering it over with another rough outline or starting again from a completely different angle. Unfortunately, he persisted in inventing processes intended to make paintings more durable and more brilliant. The result was that most of his works have darkened with time to the point of becoming indecipherable. Luckily, Forest has left drawings which bear witness to a spirit and freedom of hand of rare quality, and which have such grandeur that they seem more like paintings. His successes indicate the excellence of his work. Fifteen of his landscapes, destroyed during a fire, were valued at 15,000 livres. It is said that Largillière, visiting his father-in-law on a stormy day, found him interpreting in his own unique way the effects of the stormy sky. Largillière, surprised and delighted by this sketch, stated that he was disposed to buy it. 'I'll give it to you', Forest replied, 'and to be sure you get it, put your name on the back of the canvas'. But the son-in-law, who didn't dare claim what had been promised, could only take possession of the canvas he had put his name on after the death of Forest, at which time he discovered, with some consternation, that Forest, unhappy with his sketch, had painted over the top of it.

Forest's biographer, d'Argenville, stated that 'his use of colour is dreadful, sometimes even a little exaggerated and too dark; but one is always sure to find something stimulating in his paintings, daring brush strokes which reveal the master and which painters call points of high colour... All the dark and muted areas only serve to emphasise a burst of light and a bold touch which the painter has handled with considerable skill'. The character of his landscapes is grandiose with a somewhat wild aspect. The human figures, minute in comparison to the whole, are normally penitents, monks at prayer or reformed prostitutes. The landscape, however enormous it may be, only ever seems to be an accompaniment to the tiny figure that it envelops. It is as if the feeling, always intense, is expressed both by the human attitude and the composition of the décor. The landscape must be considered a character in the drama, and not the least important one.

Forest, commissioned by M. de Seignelay to collect pictures and objets d'art in Italy to form a collection, carried out this task with considerable finesse and taste and brought back from his second stay numerous new studies. The Louvre does not possess a single painting by Forest, and only one drawing, *View of the Seaside*. Engravings compensate for the absence of canvases, notably a landscape engraved by Bernard, and the figure of a prostitute framed in a landscape engraved by Coelemans. There is also a portrait of the artist painted by Largillière in 1704 (and engraved by Pierre Drevet père), two versions of which are kept in the museums in Berlin and Lille.

Museums and Galleries:

Paris (Louvre): *View of the Seaside* (drawing); several engravings and drawings - Tours: *Young Bacchus Given to the Nymphs on the Island of Naxos*.

FOREST, Pierre

French, 17th century.
Born c. 1587; died 9 November 1675, in Paris.
Painter.

Pierre Forest was a Protestant and 'warden of the community of master painters and sculptors in Paris'.

FOREST, Pierre
French, 20th century.
Born 21 November 1881, in Nice; died 1971, in Paris.
Painter, pastellist. Landscapes, landscapes with figures, seascapes, still-lifes, flowers.

Pierre Forest was the nephew of the Lyons engraver Tony Forest-Fleury. He painted many views of his native town of Nice. His contact with the landscapes of the Île-de-France subdued his palette and he began to work in pastels, becoming a specialist in this medium. He exhibited from 1931 to 1943 at the Salon des Indépendants in Paris, of which he was a member. He held solo exhibitions in a number of cities in France, including Paris, and also in South America, Switzerland and Morocco. A retrospective exhibition of his work was held by the town of Nice in 1981.

AUCTION RECORDS:
PARIS, 11 May 1977, *The Rabat Medina* (pastel/paper, 12 1/2 x 10 ins / 32 x 25 cm) FRF 800. PARIS, 28 Nov 1978, *Le Sichon, Allier* (pastel/paper, 13 1/2 x 10 ins / 34 x 25 cm) FRF 1,600. PARIS, 12 June 1985, *Basket of Roses* (oil on panel, 22 x 18 ins / 55 x 46 cm) FRF 5,500.

FOREST, Roy de
American, 20th century.
Born 11 February 1930, in North Platte (Nebraska).
Active in California.
Painter.
Funk Art.

Roy de Forest studied in California, including San Francisco, from 1950 to 1953. His painting was influenced by Allan Davie and combines figuration and abstract motifs, drawn with a very free line that sometimes suggests the manner of a child.

He has taken part in several group exhibitions, including the Whitney Museum, New York, in 1962, and *Confrontations* at Galerie Darthea Speyer, Paris, in 2001. Solo shows in the USA and Canada include: 1974, Museum of Modern Art, San Francisco and the Art Museum, Fort Worth; 1975, Whitney Museum, New York, and Utah Museum of Fine Arts, Salt Lake City.

MUSEUMS AND GALLERIES:
BOSTON (MFA) - CHICAGO (AI) - PARIS (MNAM-CCI).

AUCTION RECORDS:
NEW YORK, 2 Nov 1984, *Untitled* (coloured chalk and graphite/paper mounted/card, 28 x 33 3/4 ins / 71 x 85.6 cm) USD 2,800. NEW YORK, 20 Feb 1988, *The Good Swiss Gentledog* (1973, acrylic/canvas, 66 x 72 ins / 167.9 x 182.8 cm) USD 12,100. NEW YORK, 4 May 1989, *Life on the Bull* (acrylic/canvas, 66 1/4 x 72 1/4 ins / 168.3 x 183.5 cm) USD 23,100. NEW YORK, 23 Feb 1990, *Untitled* (1985, watercolour, spray-on varnish, chalk and coloured wax crayon and charcoal/paper, 34 3/4 x 43 ins / 88.2 x 109.1 cm) USD 4,950. NEW YORK, 6 Nov 1990, *Untitled* (1976, acrylic/canvas, 21 x 16 1/2 ins / 53.3 x 41.6 cm) USD 4,180. LOS ANGELES, 14 Dec 1999, *Untitled* (1977, colour crayon, charcoal and pencil on paper, 22 x 30 ins / 55 x 75 cm) USD 2,200. LOS ANGELES, 14 Dec 1999, *Untitled* (colour crayon, charcoal and ink on paper, 28 x 40 ins / 71 x 102 cm) USD 2,600. LOS ANGELES, 5 Dec 2000, *Brothers Beneath the Skin* (oil on canvas, 68 x 68 ins / 172 x 172 cm) USD 12,000. SAN FRANCISCO, 8 May 2001, *Untitled* (mixed media on paper, 74 x 69 ins / 187 x 176 cm) USD 15,000. SAN FRANCISCO, 22 April 2003, *Dog's View of Egypt* (1995, colour lithograph, 37 x 57 ins / 94 x 145 cm) USD 2,750. PARIS, 9 June 2004, *The Taylor Brothers in the Great North Woods* (1973, mixed media on canvas, 66 x 72 ins / 168 x 183 cm) EUR 10,950. NEW YORK, 29 Sept 2004, *In Search of Allan Q* (1976, polymer paint on canvas, 66 x 72 ins / 168 x 183 cm) USD 15,000.

FOREST-BRUSH, George de. See **BRUSH**

FOREST-FLEURY, Tony, or Forest de Lemps Fleury
French, 19th century.
Engraver.

Lived in Lyons in the second half of the 19th century and exhibited an *Approach to Lyons by the Narrows* in 1866. Forest-Fleury produced a large number of etchings of Lyons and environs, most of which were published in a series of portfolios for which he also supplied the accompanying text, notably *Lyons Old and New* (1875, 105 plates); *Lyons in History, Arts and Painting* (40 etchings); *Monument to the Children of the Rhône* (1887); *Disappearing Lyons* and *Lyons: The Grolée District* (1890); and *Lyons: Ancient and Modern* (1891). The various collections of engravings also contain several portraits.

FORESTIER
French, 18th - 19th century.
Born c. 1755, in Néhou (Manche); died 1828.
Painter. Figures, portraits, landscapes, seascapes.

Forestier invented a new method of figure drawing.

MUSEUMS AND GALLERIES:
SAINTES: *Portrait of General Chasseloup de Laubat.*

FORESTIER, Adolphe
French, 19th century.
Born 1801, in Paris; died 1885, in Paris.
Painter, engraver. Mythological subjects, portraits, genre scenes, landscapes.

Studied under his father until the latter's death in 1828, then under Valenciennes and Thibault. Adolphe Forestier was commissioned by the French government to provide a number of compositions.

MUSEUMS AND GALLERIES:
NEUCHÂTEL: *Urania the Muse.*

FORESTIER, Alice de
French, 19th century.
Born 19th century, in Paris.
Painter.

Sent a number of watercolours to the Salon between 1863 and 1882. Examples of her work include *Old Oaks by the Sea, Grassland on the Banks of the Toucques* (Calvados), *Oberville Cliff at Low Tide* and *Grassland in Normandy*. Alice de Forestier was a member of the Société des Artistes Français as of 1883.

FORESTIER, Antonin Clair
French, 19th - 20th century.
Born 18 October 1865, in Cannes; died January 1912.
Sculptor. Statues, busts.

Antonin Forestier studied under Gauthier and Charpentier at the École des Arts Décoratifs. He was awarded a bronze medal in 1890 and a silver medal in 1897. He is known for *Study of a Head* (1885), busts and medallions (1895), *Old Seadog* (1890), a plaster *Bacchante* (1891), a decorative bust (1893), *First Desire*, plaster (1894), *Desert*, a stone statue (1895) and *The Storm and the Leaf* (1897). He also executed busts of the governor of Australia and of Melbourne's most notable figures.

MUSEUMS AND GALLERIES:
CANNES: *First Desire* (plaster).

AUCTION RECORDS:
NEW YORK, 19 June 1981, *The Storm and the Leaf* (bronze, h. 38 ins / 96.5 cm) USD 4,250. PARIS, 7 July 1983, *Victory* (bronze, h. 15 3/4 ins / 40 cm) FRF 6,800.

FORESTIER, Auguste
French, 19th century.
Born 1780, in Paris; died 1850, in Paris.
Painter. Landscapes.

Studied predominantly in Rome.

Museums and Galleries:
Fribourg: *Study of the Roman Countryside; Study of the Roman Countryside.*

FORESTIER, Auguste
French, 19th - 20th century.
Painter. Toys.
Art Brut.

Auguste Forestier was the son of farmers from Lozère and was confined to a mental institution for life in 1914 after derailing a train. He devoted his life to drawing and making toys and other objects. Picasso is believed to have owned some pieces by him.

Bibliography:
Monnin, Françoise, *Tableaux choisis. L'Art brut*, Éd. Scala, Paris, 1997.

FORESTIER, Charles
French, 19th century.
Born 19th century, in Paris.
Painter.

Studied under Lepic; exhibited a *Beach at Berck* at the 1880 Salon and *Disused Boats* in 1882.

FORESTIER, Charles Aimé
French, 19th century.
Born 1789, in Paris.
Engraver.

Lived and worked in Paris around 1824; painted portraits and vignettes.

FORESTIER, Étienne
French, 20th century.
Born in Paris.
Sculptor. Figures. Statues.

Étienne Forestier exhibited in Paris at the Salon of the Société Nationale des Beaux-Arts.

Auction records:
London, 29 Oct 1981, *Dancer at Play* (1914, bronze, h. 12 1/2 ins / 32 cm) GBP 400. Melbourne, 30 June 1987, *Dancers* (1914, two bronzes, h. 15 1/4 ins / 38.5 cm) AUD 2,600. Paris, 30 Jan 1995, *After Isadora Duncan* (lost-wax bronze, h. 15 3/4 ins / 40 cm) FRF 29,000.

FORESTIER, Gabriel
French, 20th century.
Born in the second half of the 20th century, in Eymet.
Sculptor.

Gabriel Forestier exhibited in Paris at the Salon des Artistes Français in 1922, 1924, 1925, 1934 and 1935. He received a commendation in 1913, a travel bursary in 1922, a silver medal in 1925 and a gold medal in 1934.

FORESTIER, Henri, or Fortier
French, 17th century.
Active in Lyons in 1640.
Painter.

Henri Forestier was a master in his professional guild in 1648.

FORESTIER, Henri Claude
Swiss, 19th - 20th century.
Born 25 February 1875, in Geneva; died 1922.
Painter, watercolourist, engraver (wood), draughtsman, humorist, illustrator. Sporting subjects, scenes with figures, hunting scenes, still-lifes, flowers.

Forestier studied woodcut engraving under A. Martin at the arts and crafts academy in Geneva and went on to work in Paris as a book illustrator. He returned to Geneva in 1896 to illustrate humorous periodicals (*Sapajou* (*Monkey Business*), *Passe-Partout* and *Album Genevois*). In 1903, Sajot Editions in Paris published a series of his colour engravings featuring hunting scenes and a further series on boxing. From 1906 he devoted himself to painting exclusively still-lifes of flowers.

Auction records:
Bern, 21 Oct 1976, *Still-life* (oil on canvas, 16 1/4 x 13 ins / 41 x 33 cm) CHF 1,100. Bern, 6 May 1981, *Still-life with Flowers* (oil on canvas, 24 x 19 3/4 ins / 61 x 50 cm) CHF 1,500. Geneva, 8 Dec 1983, *Market Day* (two watercolours, 12 1/2 x 37 ins / 32 x 94 cm and 12 1/2 x 44 ins/32 x 112 cm) CHF 1,500. Geneva, 29 Nov 1986, *Bouquet of Flowers* (oil on canvas, 35 1/2 x 42 1/2 ins / 90 x 108 cm) CHF 4,000. Bern, 11 May 2001, *Still-life of Flowers* (oil on canvas, 24 x 20 ins / 60 x 50 cm) CHF 2,600.

FORESTIER, Henri Joseph de
French, 19th century.
Born 1787, in Santo Domingo; died 1872, in Paris.
Painter. History painting, religious subjects, mythological subjects.

Studied under François Vincent and Jacques-Louis David; awarded silver at the Prix de Rome of 1812 and gold the following year for his *Death of Jacob*. Awarded the Légion d'Honneur in 1832. After the 1848 revolution, he gave up his artistic career in favour of politics, and he became a colonel of the 6th legion of the National Guard. On 13 June 1849, he took part in a demonstration and was arrested, only to be exonerated by the Supreme Court in Versailles. Forestier exhibited at the Paris Salon from 1819 to 1855, painting chiefly biblical or historical subject matter such as: *Ecce Homo, St Peter Delivered from Prison by an Angel, St Front Invoking the Holy Ghost in Preparation for Spreading the Christian Gospel, Good Samaritan, Jesus Casting Out Demons, Funeral of William the Conqueror.*

Museums and Galleries:
Caen: *Funeral of William the Conqueror* - Paris (ENSBA): *Venus and Anacreon* - Paris (Mus. d'Orsay): *Jesus Curing a Young Man.*

Auction records:
Paris, 6 Dec 1982, *Saul in his Fury Ready to Kill David?* (pen and wash, 6 1/2 x 10 ins / 16.4 x 24.5 cm) FRF 3,000. Paris, 5 April 1991, *Ulysses Slaughtering Penelope's Suitors* (oil on canvas, 45 x 58 1/4 ins / 114 x 148 cm) FRF 130,000. New York, 29 Oct 1992, *Ulysses Slaughtering Penelope's Suitors* (oil on canvas, 45 x 58 1/4 ins / 114.3 x 148 cm) USD 44,000.

FORESTIER, Jean Baptiste
French, 18th century.
Active in Paris.
Sculptor.

Jean Baptiste Forestier was a student at the Académie and is mentioned as having sculpted a bust of the *Abbé de Mably.*

FORESTIER, Jeanne J. G. (Mme)
French, 20th century.
Active in Paris.
Painter.

Jeanne Forestier became a member of the Société des Artistes Français in 1901.

FORESTIER, Marie Anne Julie
French, 19th century.
Born 1789, in Paris.
Painter. Portraits.

Studied under David and Debret and exhibited examples of her work at the Salon between 1804 and 1819.

Museums and Galleries:
Chartres: *Portrait of the Chartres Poet Gaillard.*

Auction records:
Paris, 9 June 1993, *Portrait of the Duchess of Angoulême* (1814, oil on canvas, 23 1/2 x 20 ins / 60 x 51 cm) FRF 7,000.

FORESTIER, Paul Raymond
French, 20th century.
Born in Gottenhausen.
Watercolourist.

Paul Forestier exhibited in Paris at the Salon d'Hiver and at the Salon des Artistes Français from 1927.

FORESTIER, Pierre Jacques
French, 18th century.
Died 28 July 1771.
Active in Paris.
Painter.
Pierre Jacques Forestier was a member of the Guild of St Luke.

FORESTIER, Rodolphe
Swiss, 20th century.
Born in Geneva.
Painter. Landscapes.
Forestier exhibited at the 1930 Salon d'Automne in Paris.

FORESTIER, Roland
French, 19th century.
Born 15 May 1806, in Moirans; died 14 June 1885, in Lons-le-Saunier (Jura).
Sculptor (including wood).
Studied under J.J.C. Bourgeois at Lons-le-Saunier; sculpted statues for churches and gardens.

FORESTIER-BARBE, Andrée (Mme)
French, 19th century.
Born in Liverdun.
Sculptor.
Honourable mention in 1899.

FORESTO, C.
Italian, 20th century.
Born 15 April 1931, in Foresto-Sparso (Bergamo).
Active in Switzerland.
Painter, fresco artist. Landscapes, urban landscapes, still-lifes.
Foresto was a pupil at the Accademia Carrara di Belle Arti in Bergamo. He lives in Geneva. He has been regularly exhibiting since 1963, particularly in Switzerland (in Geneva) and Italy, but also in France, the USA and Canada. In 1971 he won the silver medal in the *Italia 1971* Grand Prize, awarded by the San Marco academy in Rome. He was admitted as a member of the academy of science, arts and literature in Milan in 1973.

In 1953 Foresto decorated the church of the military hospital in Verona with his paintings; and in 1958, painted frescoes in the church of S Fermo (Bergamo).

In his works, Foresto mixes together several different traditional pictorial styles. Painting for him is more of a means of expression than a discipline. He favours compositions with figures and misty landscapes, in which a white light sometimes gives a metaphysical totality to the ensemble.

BIBLIOGRAPHY:
Caldini, Giancarlo, *Foresto, immagini da Ginevra*, exhibition catalogue, Gall. Arte, Florence. Werpen, R.M., *C. Foresto*, Les Presses de l'Arquebuse, Geneva, 1979.

FORET, Paul
French, 19th century.
Born in Paris.
Painter. Still-lifes (flowers/fruit/sea shells).
Pupil of Goupil and Vollon; exhibited still lifes at the Salon from 1870 to 1882. Examples include: *Musical Instruments, Objets d'Art, Ewer and Violets, Peacock, Plate of Oysters, Flower Stall, Hare and Plate of Oysters, Tide,* and *Memory of my Thirteen Days.*

AUCTION RECORDS:
PARIS, 4 May 1928, *Flowers in a Vase,* FRF 120. NÎMES, 15 Oct 1981, *Ewer and Platter* (oil on canvas, 26 x 31½ ins / 66 x 80 cm) FRF 4,000. BERN, 1 May 2002, *Still-life with Apples and Copper Kettle* (oil on canvas, 26 x 31 ins / 65 x 80 cm) CHF 3,300.

FORETAY, Alfred Jean
Swiss, 19th - 20th century.
Born 12 January 1861, in Morges; died 1944, in Geneva.
Active in France.
Painter, sculptor. Figures, portraits, scenes with figures.
Foretay studied sculpture under Alexandre Falguière at the École des Beaux-Arts in Paris from 1877. He took up painting after returning to his native Switzerland in about 1910. He moved to France in 1918 and remained there until 1935, spending extended periods in Haute Savoie, Brittany and southern France and also travelling in Italy. He exhibited at the Salon des Artistes Français in Paris, securing an honourable mention in 1891 and a bronze medal in 1904. He exhibited solo in Morges in 1977. He is also remembered for having sculpted several public monuments in Geneva.

AUCTION RECORDS:
PARIS, 16 May 1979, *Dancer with Scarf* (bronze, h. 24¾ ins / 63 cm) FRF 6,000. ZURICH, 3 June 1983, *Subset* (oil on canvas, 19¾ x 28¼ ins / 50 x 72 cm) CHF 1,600. PARIS, 23 March 1987, *Flower of Womanhood* (brown-patinated bronze, h. 13¾ ins / 35 cm) FRF 4,500. BERN, 12 May 1990, *Bathers* (oil on canvas, 14½ x 22 ins / 37 x 55 cm) CHF 1,500.

FOREY, Jules Jean Baptiste
French, 19th century.
Born 1807, in Dijon; died 1854, in Paris.
Painter. History painting, genre scenes.
Exhibited at the Salon from 1843 to 1846, chiefly portraits and genre subjects. Examples include *Jesus and Martha, Portrait of Baron de Breteniѐre, Cimabue Meeting Giotto Drawing His Goats.*

MUSEUMS AND GALLERIES:
DIJON: *Susannah Bathing.*

FOREY, Perrier de
French, 14th century.
Active in Dijon.
Sculptor.
Perrier de Forey is known to have worked, in 1391, on the decoration of the Carthusian church of Champmol, Dijon, under the direction of Claus Sluter.

FÖRG, Günther
German, 20th - 21st century.
Born 1952, in Füssen.
From c. 1980 active in Switzerland.
Painter, sculptor, installation artist. Murals, multimedia.
From 1973 to 1979, Günther Förg studied painting under Karl Fred Dahmen at the art school in Munich. He lives and works in Areuse (Switzerland). Studying the work of artists linked to the history of abstract art (Russian Constructivism, the Bauhaus), then contemporary art (Newman, Rothko, Ad Reinhardt), has to a large extent influenced Förg's objectives. Setting himself the problem of repeating an image to infinity in painting, he endeavours to enlarge the pictorial field outside the strict conventions of the frame in order to encompass and dominate the walls and occupy a new space. Later, he would add photographic elements to the painted surface.

Between 1983 and 1986 he preferred architectural photography, generally with large formats, and from 1986 he continued to combine photographs and murals, whilst also working fully on his painting. Later, he produced works in bronze, notably the *Stations of the Cross* series of 1989, which aimed at sculpture whilst having the characteristics of a painting.

He has participated in group exhibitions, notably in France: 1985, Nouvelle Biennale de Paris, Paris; 1989, *Une Autre Objectivité* (*A Different Objectivity*), the Centre National d'Art Contemporain, Paris; 1990, *Un Art de la Distinction* (*An Art of Distinction*), the Centre d'Art Contemporain, Meymac; 2002, *Painting on the Move,* featuring a century of contemporary art, simultaneously held at the Kunstmuseum, the Kunsthalle and the Museum für Gegenwarts Kunst (contemporary art), Basel. He has held solo shows, including: 1980, Munich; 1981, Amsterdam; 1983, Cologne Fair, presented by the Galerie Max Hetlzer; 1984, Kunstraum, Munich; 1986, Kunsthalle, Bern; Westfälischer Kunstverein, Münster; 1987, Museum Hans Lange, Krefeld; 1987, Maison de la Culture et de la Communication, St-Étienne; 1988, Gemeentemuseum, The Hague; 1989, Newport Harbour Art Museum, Newport Beach; 1989, Museum of Modern Art, San Francisco; 1989, Art Museum, Milwaukee; 1989-1900, *Günther Förg: the Complete Editions*, Museum Boymans van Beuningen, Rotterdam, then the Neue Galerie am Landesmuseum Joanneum, Graz; 1990-1991, a travelling exhibition: the Museum Fridericianum, Kassel; the Museum Hedendaagse Kunst, Ghent; the Museum der Bildenden Künste, Leipzig; the Kunsthalle, Tübingen; the Kunstraum, Munich; 1991, Museum of Contemporary Art, Tokyo; 1991, Galerie Grässlin-Ehrhardt, Frankfurt; 1991, Galerie Rüdiger Schöttle, Paris; 1991, the Galerie Crousel Robelin Bama, Paris; 1991, the Musée d'Art Moderne de la Ville de Paris; 1996, the Galerie Samia Saouma, Paris; 1997, the Galerie Lelong, Paris.

BIBLIOGRAPHY:

Parent, Béatrice/Fuchs, Rudi/Diacono, Mario/Quéloz, Catherine, *Günther Forg*, exhibition catalogue, Musée d'Art moderne de la Ville de Paris, Paris, 1991. *Günther Förg*, exhibition catalogue, Stedelijk Museum, Amsterdam, 1995. Bürgi, Bernhard Mendes, et al., *Painting on the Move*, exhibition catalogue, Kunstmuseum, Kunsthalle, Museum für Gegenwartskunst, Basel, 2002.

MUSEUMS AND GALLERIES:

DUNKIRK (FRAC Nord-Pas de Calais): *Untitled* (1987) - NEW YORK (MoMA) - NÎMES (Carré d'Art, MAC) - ROCHECHOUART (Mus. Départemental d'Art Contemporain): *Mailand Triennial II* (1986) - ST-ÉTIENNE: *MCC Installation*.

AUCTION RECORDS:

NEW YORK, 8 May 1990, *Copper Painting* (1987, oil/copper/wood, 75 x 35 1/2 ins / 190.2 x 90.2 cm) USD 38,500. NEW YORK, 9 May 1990, *Untitled* (1986, paint/lead, 21 1/2 x 20 1/2 ins / 54.5 x 52 cm) USD 16,500. NEW YORK, 7 Nov 1990, *Lead Screen* (1987, acrylic/lead on two wooden panels, 71 x 98 1/2 ins / 180.5 x 250 cm) USD 26,400. NEW YORK, 2 May 1991, *Untitled* (1989, six panels of acrylic/wood, each 23 1/2 x 19 3/4 ins / 60 x 50 cm) USD 35,200. NEW YORK, 13 Nov 1991, *Lead Painting* (1988, acrylic/lead mounted on card, 94 1/2 x 63 ins / 240 x 160.3 cm) USD 8,800. NEW YORK, 25-26 Feb 1992, *Untitled* (1988, bronze, 47 1/4 x 31 1/2 x 2 1/4 ins / 120 x 80 x 6 cm) USD 8,800. NEW YORK, 27 Feb 1992, *Untitled* (oil on panel, collection of three panels, each, 27 1/2 x 21 3/4 ins / 69.8 x 55.2 cm) USD 19,800. NEW YORK, 6 May 1992, *Untitled* (1988, acrylic and lead/panel, 94 1/2 x 63 ins / 240 x 160.3 cm) USD 20,900. NEW YORK, 19 Nov 1992, *Untitled* (1987, cast bronze, 38 1/2 x 23 1/4 ins / 97.8 x 59 cm) USD 9,900. NEW YORK, 19 Nov 1992, *Rome* (1987, photograph framed by the artist, 111 x 51 1/4 ins / 282 x 130 cm) USD 11,000; *Untitled* (1987, acrylic and lead/panel, 48 x 27 1/4 ins / 122.2 x 69.5 cm) USD 12,650. NEW YORK, 24 Feb 1993, *Untitled* (1987, 12 watercolour panels and metallic pigments/paper, each 12 1/4 x 9 1/4 ins / 31.4 x 23.8 cm) USD 14,850. LONDON, 25 March 1993, *Untitled* (1987, bronze, 47 1/4 x 27 3/4 x 2 1/2 ins / 120 x 70.5 x 6.5 cm) GBP 5,750. NEW YORK, 5 May 1993, *Untitled* (acrylic and lead/wood, 94 3/4 x 63 1/4 ins / 240.7 x 160.6 cm) USD 18,400. NEW YORK, 3 May 1994, *Window I* (oil on panel, 63 x 55 ins / 160 x 139.7 cm) USD 11,500. LONDON, 27 Oct 1994, *Lead Image* (1987, acrylic/lead, 35 1/2 x 98 1/2 ins / 90 x 250 cm) GBP 8,050. AMSTERDAM, 7 Dec 1994, *Untitled* (black and white photograph, 106 1/4 x 47 1/4 ins / 270 x 120 cm) NLG 16,100. LONDON, 26 Oct 1995, *'Canto'* (1989, acrylic/paper, 84 1/2 x 62 1/2 ins / 214.5 x 159 cm) GBP 8,280. NEW YORK, 16 Nov 1995, *Untitled* (1989, acrylic/Canson paper, 103 1/4 x 58 3/4 ins / 262.3 x 149.2 cm) USD 8,050. NEW YORK, 19 Nov 1996, *Bronze Relief* (1987, bronze, 102 1/4 x 55 1/2 ins / 260 x 141 cm) USD 10,925. NEW YORK, 21 Nov 1996, *Lead Painting* (oil on lead panel, triptych, 83 x 100 1/2 ins / 210.8 x 255.3 cm) USD 23,000. LONDON, 6 Dec 1996, *Untitled* (1989, pencil and acrylic/paper, 102 1/4 x 59 ins / 260 x 150 cm) GBP 8,050. NEW YORK, 6-7 May 1997, *Untitled (49/87)* (1987, oil/lead/wood, 23 x 15 1/4 ins / 58.7 x 38.7 cm) USD 50,600. NEW YORK, 20 Nov 1997, *Untitled* (acrylic/lead/wood, 118 x 79 ins / 299.7 x 200.7 cm) USD 19,550. LONDON, 29 June 1999, *Untitled* (1988, acrylic on lead on wood, 63 x 94 ins / 160 x 240 cm) GBP 18,000. NEW YORK, 18 Nov 1999, *32 Lead Paintings* (1987, acrylic on panel, in 32 parts, 24 x 16 ins / 61 x 41 cm) USD 290,000. NEW YORK, 17 May 2000, *Villa Wittgenstein, Vienna* (gelatin silver print photograph, 111 x 52 ins / 282 x 132 cm) USD 33,000. HAMBURG, 1 Dec 2000, *Untitled* (1990, tempera, in 26 parts, 22 x 15 ins / 56 x 38 cm) DEM 65,000. LONDON, 29 June 2001, *Untitled - 1-4* (1988, acrylic on lead on board, set of four, 31 x 24 ins / 80 x 61 cm) GBP 12,000. LONDON, 23 Oct 2001, *Homage to Le Corbusier* (2000, watercolour, in 23 parts, 20 x 15 ins / 50 x 37 cm) GBP 16,000. COLOGNE, 3 Dec 2002, *Untitled* (1987, acrylic on lead on panel, two, 35 x 98 ins / 90 x 250 cm) EUR 18,000. BERLIN, 31 May 2003, *Window I* (1989, acrylic on panel, 63 x 55 ins / 160 x 140 cm) EUR 14,000. LONDON, 22 Oct 2003, *Eur, Roma* (gelatin silver print photograph, 111 x 52 ins / 282 x 131 cm) GBP 17,000. NEW YORK, 8 Nov 2004, *Bauhaus* (gelatin silver print photograph, two, 70 x 46 ins / 178 x 118 cm) USD 52,000. NEW YORK, 12 Nov 2004, *Untitled* (1987, oil on lead mounted on wooden panel, 23 x 15 ins / 59 x 39 cm) USD 52,000.

FORG, Hans Oswald

German, 17th century.

Born to a family originally from Aichach (Bavaria).

Painter.

Forg was a member of the Munich Guild. His known works include drawings of animals' heads bearing his monogram and dated from 1615 to 1618.

AUCTION RECORDS:

PARIS, 20 June 1938, *Children's Games; Goat* (two canvases painted in grisaille, overdoor decorations) FRF 200.

FORGACH, Elisabeth

Hungarian, 20th century.

Born in Budapest.

Sculptor.

A student of Sicard, Elisabeth Forgach exhibited a (plaster) *Bust Portrait* at the 1928 Salon.

FORGAS, Robert

French, 20th century.

Born 1929, in Vincennes.

Painter.

Robert Forgas is known for his scenes with children which are painted in a populist style. He exhibited in Paris at the Salon des Peintres Témoins de leur Temps and went on to exhibit with Groupe 109.

FORGE, de La. See **LA FORGE**

FORGE, F. de

French, 18th century.

Painter.

F. de Forge painted a *Meeting of Peasants* after Brouwers which is in the gallery in Bamberg.

FORGELOT, Charles Albert

French, 20th century.

Born 19 October 1876, in Paris; died 21 February 1975.

Painter. Landscapes.

Charles Forgelot studied under Georges Moteley. He exhibited in Paris at the Salon des Artistes Français from 1926, becoming a member of the Salon in 1928 and receiving a commendation in 1953.

FORGEOIS, Michèle
French, 20th century.
Born 16 May 1929, in Bois-Colombes.
Sculptor, illustrator.

Michèle Forgeois studied mainly at independent studios and at the École des Arts Décoratifs in Paris in 1945. Her sculptures are abstract. She works in lead, creating an esoteric, sensual and mystic universe. She also exhibits illustrations at book exhibitions.

FORGEOT
French, 18th century.
Painter. Portraits.

MUSEUMS AND GALLERIES:
ST-LÔ: *Portrait of Geoffroy de Baudot, Knight* (1711).

FORGEOT
French, 18th century.
Sculptor.

Forgeot executed models for bisque groups for the royal porcelain factory in Sèvres from 1779 to 1819, including *Republic, Nymph with Swan, When Love Speaks, Temptation* and *Jesus*.

FORGEOT, Claude Édouard
French, 19th century.
Born 1826, in Moule (Saône-et-Loire) according to some sources, in Lays-sur-le-Doubs according to others.
Sculptor. Figures, historical figures. Busts.

Pupil of Rude; exhibited several times at the Salon between 1853 and 1877 and received an honourable mention in 1891.

MUSEUMS AND GALLERIES:
GRAY: *Bust of MacMahon; Bust of a Gypsy; Bust of the Artist's Father* - ST-LÔ: *Personages in Armour from the Reign of Louis XIV.*

FORGERON, Alfred Armand
French, 19th century.
Born 3 April 1842, in Paris.
Painter. Portraits, genre scenes.

Enrolled at the École des Beaux-Arts on 8 April 1858 and studied under Aug. Hesse and Gérôme; exhibited portrait work at the Salon from 1861 to 1882. Examples of his work include *The Virtuous Susannah; Louis XVII at the Temple Prison; Portrait of M. de Beauplan; Virgin Mary at the Age of Fifteen Years; Lesson*; and *Portrait of Madame Halanzier.*

FORGES, René de
French, 20th century.
Born in Quimperlé.
Painter.

René de Forges exhibited at the Salon des Indépendants in Paris in 1931.

FORGET
French, 18th century.
Painter, engraver (burin).

Forget exhibited landscapes at the Salon in 1791 and 1793.

FORGET, Charles Gabriel
French, 19th century.
Born 4 August 1807, in Paris; died 1873.
Painter.

Pupil of Isabey and Th. Rousseau; exhibited watercolours at the Salon from 1846 to 1970. Examples of his work include *Rue St-Lubin, Blois* and *Chemin des Vaux-Verts.*

MUSEUMS AND GALLERIES:
ORLÉANS: two landscapes.

FORGET, Charles Jean
French, 20th century.
Born 25 January 1886.
Engraver, draughtsman. Scenes with figures.

Charles Forget exhibited in Paris at the Salon des Artistes Français from 1922.

Ch Forget

AUCTION RECORDS:
LONDON, 18 May 1988, *The 14 July Celebrations at the Madeleine* (1938, oil on canvas, $19\frac{3}{4}$ x $25\frac{1}{2}$ ins / 50 x 65 cm) GBP 3,300.

FORGET, E.
French, 19th century.
Active in Paris.
Reproductions engraver.

His body of engraving work includes a *Holy Virgin* (after Batoni), *Adoration of the Magi* (Blaisot), *Foligno Madonna* (Raphael), plates for Cuvier's *Animal Kingdom*, portraits of *King Frederick VI of Denmark* and *Marshal Kellermann*, and, taken from the book by L. Freycinet, *Voyage Around the World: Chinese Women on Timor Island*, after Arago.

FORGET, Louise
Canadian, 20th century.
Born 1931, in St-Agathe-des-Monts (Quebec).
Painter, watercolourist.

Louise Forget studied at the Montreal School of Fine Arts from 1951 to 1956. After travelling in Mexico, where she learned engraving and mural art, she undertook further study in Montreal before going to Paris, where she worked with Stanley Hayter at Atelier 17. Her colours are highly transparent, conveying light with minimum pigment, while her watercolours have the spontaneity of Lyrical Abstraction.

FORGET, Marie Thérèse
French, 19th century.
Born 19th century, in Blois.
Painter.

Studied under Henner and Carolus Duran; exhibited portraits and studies of heads at the Paris Salon from 1878 to 1882 and received an honourable mention in 1888.

FORGEUR, Ernest
Belgian, 20th century.
Born 1897, in Liège; died 1961.
Painter, draughtsman.

Forgeur studied at Liège academy and worked as a caricaturist in the 1930s before going on to paint female nudes.

FORGEVSKY, Marina
Russian, 19th century.
Born 1824, in St Petersburg; died 1855, in Vienna.
Watercolourist.

On her return from studying archeological sites in Italy, Marina Forgevsky was taught by Adalbert de Krüss. Her watercolours were popular with tourists visiting St Petersburg and can be found in many collections. She was known for a painting of *Count Schloezer's Library.*

FORGIOLI, Attilio
Italian, 20th century.
Born 1933, in Salò (Lombardy).
Painter, pastellist. Portraits, landscapes.

AUCTION RECORDS:
MILAN, 8 June 1982, *Landscape* (1962, oil on canvas, $27\frac{1}{2}$ x $39\frac{1}{4}$ ins / 70 x 100 cm) ITL 550,000. MILAN, 19 Dec 1985, *Landscape* (oil on canvas, 67 x 68 ins / 170 x 173 cm) ITL 2,700,000. MILAN, 7 Nov 1989, *Tales* (1982, oil on canvas, 14 x $31\frac{3}{4}$ ins / 35.5 x 80.5 cm) ITL 1,900,000. MILAN, 27 March 1990, *Landscape* (mixed media, $37\frac{3}{4}$ x $27\frac{1}{2}$ ins / 96 x 70 cm) ITL 1,800,000. MILAN, 27 Sept 1990, *Landscape* (1967, oil on canvas, $23\frac{1}{2}$ x $26\frac{3}{4}$ ins / 60 x 68 cm) ITL 2,000,000. MILAN, 20 June 1991, *Island* (1972, oil on canvas, $39\frac{1}{4}$ x $35\frac{1}{2}$ ins / 100 x 90 cm) ITL 4,600,000. MILAN, 15 Dec 1992, *Landscape* (oil on

canvas, 13 1/4 x 16 1/4 ins / 33.5 x 41 cm) ITL 2,200,000. MILAN, 22 Nov 1993, *Landscape* (pastel/canvas, 23 1/2 x 23 1/2 ins / 60 x 60 cm) ITL 2,357,000. MILAN, 26 Oct 1995, *Portrait* (1986, oil on canvas, 37 3/4 x 27 1/2 ins / 96 x 70 cm) ITL 2,645,000. ROME, 13 May 2000, *Sicily* (1978, oil on canvas, 31 x 39 ins / 80 x 100 cm) ITL 4,200,000. ROME, 22 April 2004, *Shoe* (oil on canvas, 15 x 13 ins / 38 x 33 cm) EUR 1,800. VERCELLI, 12 June 2004, *Landscape* (oil on canvas, 28 x 31 ins / 70 x 80 cm) EUR 1,950.

FORGUES
French, 19th century.
Engraver.
Béraldi refers to his *Distribution of Standards, 10 May 1852.*

FORI, Luciano. See **FOTI**

FORICHON, F.
French.
Painter. Portraits.
A drawing teacher at the Nimes Lycée.
MUSEUMS AND GALLERIES:
ALÈS: *Portrait of a Woman.*

FORINGER, Alonzo Earl
American, 20th century.
Born 1 February 1878, in Kaylor (Pennsylvania); died 1948.
Painter, illustrator. Murals.
Alonzo Earl Foringer was a pupil of Stevenson in Pittsburgh and of Mowbray in New York, and was a member of the Association of Mural Painters and the New York Architectural League.

FORINO. See **FURINI**

FORIOLLI, Marcantonio
Italian, 17th century.
Active in Rome.
Painter.
Marcantonio Foriolli is on record as having worked in the Quirinal Gallery in 1657.

FORISSIER, Roger
French, 20th century.
Born 26 June 1924, in Feurs.
Painter, watercolourist, engraver, lithographer, illustrator. Figure compositions, figures, portraits, landscapes, urban landscapes, seascapes, still-lifes. Murals.
Roger Forissier studied at the École des Beaux-Arts in Lyons from 1942 and at the École des Beaux-Arts in Paris in 1947. He was awarded a bursary by the government of the Netherlands in 1951, by the Descartes house in Amsterdam in 1952 and the Casa Velázquez in Madrid in 1953. He lived in Lyons until 1947 and then in Paris.

He was awarded a number of prizes: in 1965 the Prix du Conseil Général de Seine-et-Oise; in 1973 the Prix du Conseil Général de Seine-et-Marne; in 1973 the Prix Paul-Louis Weiller; and in 1980 the Grand Prix de la Peinture awarded by the Ville de Corbeil-Essonnes. He was president of the École de Moret (Moret School) art association in Seine-et-Marne. He produced 16 lithographs to illustrate *Le Diable au Corps* by Raymond Radiguet. He also executed a mural for the new Mont-Dore thermal baths in 1975. His work was purchased by the State and the Ville de Paris and he was made a Chevalier des Arts et Lettres.

He has exhibited at group exhibitions, including: the Salon de la Jeune Peinture, Paris; the Salon Comparaisons, Paris; the Salon de la Société Nationale des Beaux-Arts; and also at the *Peintres Lyonnais Contemporains* (*Contemporary Painters from Lyons*) exhibition at the Musée d'Art Moderne in Lyons; the *Artistes Figuratifs* (*Figurative Artists*) exhibition at the Musée du Mans; the *Artistes Français en Hollande* (*French Artists in Holland*) exhibition at the Dutch Institute; and the *En bateau sur la Seine* (*In a Boat on the Seine*) and *Peintre de la Banlieue* (*Local Painter*) exhibition at the Musée de Courbevoie.

He has held numerous solo exhibitions: regularly from 1949 to 1984 in Paris; in 1952 and 1975 in Amsterdam; from 1961 to 1996 in Geneva; from 1962 to 1987 in Lyons; 1966 and 1982 in Zurich; 1970, a retrospective at the Centre Culturel Pablo Neruda in Corbeil-Essonnes; 1992, a quadruple exhibition in Paris - in May landscapes, in June still-lifes, in July portraits and in November watercolours and engravings; in 1977 at Coulommiers; and in 2001 at Avallon.
BIBLIOGRAPHY:
Kohler, Arnold, *Roger Forissier ou le Plaisir de peindre*. Forissier, Roger, *Propos d'Artiste*. Duplessis, Bertrand, *L'Enracinement de Forissier*. Cogniat, Raymond, *Pour Forissier*, Éd. Pierre Cailler, Geneva, 1961. *Forissier*, exhibition catalogue, Palais de la Méditerranée, Nice, 1970. Gorter, Sadi de, *Roger Forissier*, Librairie de la Bibliothèque des Arts, Paris, 1986.
MUSEUMS AND GALLERIES:
FONTAINEBLEAU (Mus. d'Art Figuratif Contemporain) - PARIS (MAMVP) - PARIS (MNAM-CCI) - SCEAUX (Mus. de l'Île-de-France).
AUCTION RECORDS:
PARIS, 3 May 1985, *Ile St-Louis, Paris* (1958, oil on canvas, 39 1/4 x 28 3/4 ins / 100 x 73 cm) FRF 9,000.

FORKNER, Edgar J.
American, 19th - 20th century.
Born 1867, in Richmond (Virginia); died 1945.
Painter.
Edgar Forkner studied with Du Mond and at the Art Students League, New York. He was a member of the Chicago Gallery Association and won the Hoosier Salon's first prize in 1916, the Owsley Prize in 1917, and first prize at the Seattle F.A.S. in 1918 and 1923.

FORKUM, Roy
American, 20th century.
Born in Kane.
Painter.
Roy Forkum exhibited at the Salon in 1928.

FORLANI. See **FURLANI**

FORLEO-BRAYDA, Francesca
Italian, 19th century.
Born 1779, in Francavilla (Puglia); died 3 June 1820.
Painter.
A pupil of the painter Lodovico delle Guanti, Francesca Forleo-Brayda chiefly painted religious pictures, such as a *Baptism of Christ* and *Beheading of St John the Baptist* for the church of S Maria della Fontana. She was also a history painter, taking scenes from Torquato Tasso's *Gerusalemme Liberata*; and she painted rustic subjects, like *Tarentella* and *Rest of the Reapers*, as well as some small-scale genre paintings.
MUSEUMS AND GALLERIES:
FRANCAVILLA (Palazzo Forleo): several works.

FORLI, da. See first name

FORLI, Giovanni Vincenzo. See **VINCENZO DA FORLI**

FORMAINO, Andrea
Italian, 16th century.
Born to a family originally from Ravenna.
Sculptor.
Andrea Formaino erected the funeral monument of Brunoro Zampeschi at Forlìmpopoli, near Forlì.

FORMAL
20th century.
Engraver.
Mentioned in *Art Prices Current.*

FORMAN, Emil
Brazilian, 20th - 21st century.
Born 1954, in Rio de Janeiro.
Installation artist. Multimedia.
Emil Forman studied at the C.P.A. (Centre for Art Research) with Ivan Serpa in Rio de Janeiro between 1971 and 1973. He lives in Rio de Janeiro.

Forman has taken part in collective exhibitions. At the 9th Paris Biennale in 1975, Forman exhibited an audio-visual installation reminiscent of Boltanski which consisted of a series of slides showing a collection of personal effects such as a ball of wool, a toothbrush and scissors, which had belonged a woman who had hoarded objects of this sort all her life. He has also held solo exhibitions in Rio de Janeiro at the C.P.A. (1973) and at the Buarque-Bittencourt gallery (1974).

BIBLIOGRAPHY:
IXe Biennale de Paris, exhibition catalogue, Idea Books, Musée d'Art moderne de la Ville de Paris, Paris, 1975.

FORMAN, Helen
American.
Born in London.
Engraver (etching).
Studied at the Chicago Institute of Art. A member of the Chicago Society of Etchers.

FORMAN, L.. See **FOSMAN Gregorio**

FORMAN, Vera Smith
American, 20th century.
Born 26 October 1889, in Jacksonville (Illinois).
Painter, illustrator.
Vera Smith Forman was a pupil of John Douglas Patrick and a member of the Illinois Academy of Fine Arts. She was awarded prizes at the Des Moines Women's Club in 1925, 1927, 1929 and 1931.

FORMARINI
Czech, 17th century.
Painter.
In 1647, Formarini produced paintings for the castle of Náchod.

FORMELLO, Donato da, called Donatello
Italian, 16th century.
Born in Formello (duchy of Bracciano); died c. 1580.
Painter. Religious subjects. Murals.
A pupil of Giorgio Vasari, Donato da Formello visited Rome (according to Baglione) at the beginning of the reign of Gregory XIII. He painted frescoes representing scenes from the life of St Peter on the walls of a staircase in the Vatican.

FORMENOY, Niclaes
Flemish, 18th century.
Active in Antwerp.
Miniaturist.
Flemish School.
Niclaes Formenoy qualified as a master on 10 September 1760.

FORMENT, Damián, or Formente
Spanish, 16th century.
Born c. 1480, in Valencia; died c. 1543, in Santo Domingo de la Calzada.
Active in Saragossa.
Sculptor.
Damián Forment, one of the foremost Spanish sculptors, shows in his development the transformation from Gothic art to Renaissance art, art that was less reliant on the evolution of religious ideas in the mind of the artist and owed more to the new methods beginning to be disseminated. It is interesting to speculate whether his attempt to subordinate the Christian ethos of the Middle Ages to the study of nature, the correction of forms and the elegant majesty of antique draperies was instinctive or conscious.

Forment's earliest surviving work, the altarpiece of the high altar in Nuestra Señora del Pilar, in Saragossa, provides a glimpse of the Renaissance; the design and the arrangement of the altarpiece and its ornamentation are, however, deliberately Gothic, despite the shell placed above the base - a motif of which Berruguete was to make frequent use a little later. In the S Pablo altarpiece, which is very similar, featuring the same rectangular form and curved Gothic lines, the gradual transformation in Forment's style is no less apparent. In this great work there are fragments to rival the work of the greatest Renaissance sculptors. In his next altarpiece, at Huesca, the evolution is even clearer; the design is the same, but with more curved lines and less angularity the impression is one of gracefulness.

The altarpiece of the cathedral in Santo Domingo de la Calzada bears witness to the increasing momentum of the Renaissance movement in which Forment was caught up. With its total absence of discordant notes and its brilliant harmony, this is Forment's climactic achievement; in it, he adapted the Christian ethos of the Middle Ages to the forms of beauty found in nature, and was so elated by the expression of his religious feelings that he proclaimed himself 'a rival of Phidias and Apelles'.

BIBLIOGRAPHY:
Abizanda Broto, M., *Damián Forment, el escultor de la corona de Aragón*, Barcelona, 1942. Souto Silva, I.A., *El retablo de San Miguel de los Navarros*, Saragossa, 1983.

FORMENTE
Spanish, 16th century.
Active in Valladolid.
Sculptor.
The similarity in their names has often led to Formente being confused with Damián Forment, but their work is very different. Formente was also a great artist, but remained resistant to new ideas and was one of the last representatives of pure Gothic art.

FORMENTE, Lucas
Spanish, 16th century.
Born c. 1526.
Active in Valladolid.
Sculptor.
A close friend of Berruguete, Lucas Formente collaborated with him on a number of works, yet does not appear to have been affected in any way by the Renaissance ideals which transformed art. Martí y Monzó notes that many talented sculptors bore the name of Formente, but that Damián was the only one to have embraced the Renaissance.

FORMENTI, Lazzaro
Italian, 16th century.
Born to a family originally from Carrara.
Sculptor.
There is a reference to Lazzaro Formenti in 1563 in Messina.

FORMENTI, Tommaso, or Formentino
Italian, 18th century.
Active in Milan c. 1720.
Painter.
Tommaso Formenti painted altarpieces in Milan, Como and Pavia, and executed landscapes in Brescia.

FORMENTINI, L.
Italian, 18th century.
Active in Venice.
Painter. Landscapes.
Marchesini collaborated with L. Formentini to 'flesh out' the latter's compositions.

FORMENTROU, Jacob de
Flemish, 17th century.
Active in Antwerp.
Painter.
Flemish School.

Jacob de Formentrou qualified as a master in 1659.

FORMICA, Jean Pierre
French, 20th century.
Painter.

Jean Formica exhibited at FIAC (Foire Internationale d'Art Contemporain) in Paris in 1993. He has also shown his work in solo exhibitions, including in 2003 at the Galerie Lavignes Bastille, Paris.

FORMIGÉ, Jean Camille
French, 19th - 20th century.
Born 24 July 1845, in Bouscat-lez-Bordeaux; died 28 August 1926, in Paris.
Painter, architect.

Jean Formigé exhibited at the Paris Salon from 1868, showing views of monuments and watercolours.

FORMIGÉ, Marie Emma
French, 19th century.
Born 19th century, in Bordeaux.
Painter.

Studied under Laurens and Carolus-Duran; exhibited flower watercolours at Paris salons between 1876 and 1882.

FORMIGINE, Andrea da. See **MARCHESE Andrea di Pietro**

FORMILLI, Attilio
Italian, 19th - 20th century.
Born 8 June 1866, in Alexandria; died 1933.
Sculptor. Figures. Busts.

Attilio Formilli worked in Florence, where he was a pupil at the academy, along with Rivalta. His best-known works are a *Christ on the Cross*, shown in Florence in 1896, and a bronze bust of *Schopenhauer*, shown in Berlin in 1899.

MUSEUMS AND GALLERIES:
PISA (Mus. Civico): *Bust of Mosè Supino, Founder of the Museum*.

FORMIS BEFANI, Achille
Italian, 19th century.
Born 1832, in Naples; died 1906, in Milan.
Painter. Genre scenes, landscapes, urban landscapes, waterscapes, mountainscapes.

Achille Formis Befani regularly exhibited in Milan, Turin and Venice. He also exhibited at the Salon of the Société des Artistes Français, in 1880; in Berlin, in 1896; and in Munich, in 1901 and 1906. He painted Eastern scenes, Alpine landscapes, Italian lakes, views of Venice and lagoons. The best-known of his works are: *All Going Fishing, Como, Peasant Women at Work* and *Pallestrina Lagoon*.

MUSEUMS AND GALLERIES:
ROME (Gal. Nazionale d'Arte Moderna): *Torrent*.

AUCTION RECORDS:
MILAN, 26 Nov 1968, *Lake Maggiore*, ITL 650,000. LONDON, 12 May 1972, *Mountainscape*, Gns 1,200. MILAN, 28 Oct 1976, *Seashore* (oil on remounted canvas/panel, 11 3/4 x 23 1/2 ins / 30 x 60 cm) ITL 1,000,000. MILAN, 14 March 1978, *Alpine Landscape* (oil on canvas, 26 1/2 x 48 1/2 ins / 67 x 123 cm) ITL 1,200,000. MILAN, 17 June 1981, *Venice* (oil on panel, 23 x 9 3/4 ins / 58.5 x 25 cm) ITL 4,400,000. MILAN, 21 April 1983, *Landscape* (oil on canvas, 22 1/2 x 14 1/4 ins / 57 x 36.5 cm) ITL 5,000,000. MILAN, 21 April 1983, *Sailing Ships at Chioggia* (oil on panel, 10 x 22 3/4 ins / 24.5 x 58 cm) ITL 6,600,000. NEW YORK, 1 March 1984, *Street in Venice* (oil on panel, 24 x 12 1/4 ins / 61 x 30.8 cm) USD 5,000. LONDON, 20 June 1986, *Fountain of Sultan Ahmed, Constantinople* (oil on canvas, 29 1/2 x 30 3/4 ins / 75 x 78 cm) GBP 400,000. LONDON, 27 March 1987, *Water Duty* (oil on canvas, 9 x 23 ins / 23 x 57.5 cm) GBP 8,000. MILAN, 31 March 1987, *Cascinale* (1900, oil on panel, 10 1/4 x 17 1/4 ins / 26 x 43.5 cm) ITL 2,600,000. MILAN, 23 March 1988, *Corni di Conzo Mountains* (oil on canvas, 28 x 21 ins / 71 x 53.5 cm) ITL 10,000,000. LONDON, 29 April 1988, *Farmyard and Poultry* (oil on canvas, 12 1/2 x 7 1/2 ins / 31.5 x 19 cm) GBP 1,650. MILAN, 1 June 1988, *Village Street and Peasant Woman* (oil on panel, 23 x 9 1/2 ins / 57.5 x 24 cm) ITL 3,200,000. MILAN, 14 June 1989, *Sunlight Effect* (oil on panel, 12 1/2 x 7 1/4 ins / 31.5 x 18.5 cm) ITL 6,000,000. NEW YORK, 23 May 1990, *Farmyard* (oil on canvas/card, 12 1/2 x 7 1/2 ins / 31.7 x 19 cm) USD 4,950. NEW YORK, 16 Oct 1991, *On the Banks of the Bosphorous* (oil on canvas, 25 1/4 x 49 ins / 64.2 x 124.5 cm) USD 44,000. MILAN, 19 March 1992, *Courtyard of a Rustic House in Valtellina* (oil on panel, 22 3/4 x 9 ins / 58 x 23 cm) ITL 3,000,000. MILAN, 29 Oct 1992, *End of the Village* (oil on panel, 11 1/2 x 23 3/4 ins / 29.5 x 60.5 cm) ITL 6,000,000. MILAN, 26 March 1996, *Mountainscape with Hut and Peasant Woman* (oil on panel, 22 3/4 x 10 ins / 58 x 24.5 cm) ITL 11,500,000. MILAN, 23 Oct 1996, *Ships Anchored at Tremezzo* (oil on canvas, 10 x 15 1/4 ins / 25.5 x 38.5 cm) ITL 22,135,000; *Boats at Chioggia* (1897, oil on panel, 11 1/2 x 23 1/2 ins / 29 x 60 cm) ITL 16,892,000. MILAN, 18 Dec 1996, *Landscape with Boats and Figures* (oil on canvas, 14 1/2 x 26 1/4 ins / 37 x 66.5 cm) ITL 33, 785,000. MILAN, 25 March 1997, *Washerwomen on the Riverbank* (oil on canvas, 19 1/4 x 31 1/2 ins / 49 x 80 cm) ITL 40,775,000. MILAN, 29 March 1999, *Clearing in Lombardy* (1887, oil on canvas, 14 x 22 ins / 36 x 57 cm) ITL 4,000,000. MILAN, 29 March 1999, *Valmadrera and Corni di Canzo* (1871, oil on canvas, 24 x 18 ins / 60 x 45 cm) ITL 10,000,000. VENICE, 13 May 2000, *Fishermen on Lake* (oil on canvas, 16 x 31 ins / 40 x 80 cm) ITL 8,200,000. MILAN, 4 Dec 2000, *On the Lake* (oil on canvas, 28 x 20 ins / 70 x 50 cm) ITL 16,000,000. MILAN, 5 June 2001, *Young Women by Lake* (oil on canvas, 31 x 16 ins / 80 x 40 cm) ITL 36,000,000. LONDON, 26 Sept 2001, *Crossing a Bridge* (oil on canvas, 49 x 25 ins / 124 x 64 cm) GBP 21,000. LONDON, 28 Nov 2001, *Idle Afternoon on the Venetian Lagoon* (oil on canvas, 19 x 16 ins / 47 x 41 cm) GBP 1,400. TURIN, 18 June 2002, *Marine* (1867, oil on canvas, 20 x 39 ins / 52 x 100 cm) EUR 13,000. MILAN, 23 Oct 2002, *Lake with Boats* (oil on canvas, 15 x 27 ins / 39 x 68 cm) EUR 14,000. MILAN, 18 March 2003, *Peasant Girl with Goat* (oil on canvas, 26 x 13 ins / 67 x 34 cm) EUR 6,000. MILAN, 19 May 2004, *Washerwomen* (oil on canvas, 30 x 20 ins / 76 x 51 cm) EUR 20,000.

FORMOSA, Romualdo
Italian, 18th century.
Active in Naples c. 1755.
Painter.

Romualdo Formosa is on record as having worked on the Palazzo Gravina.

FORMOZOV, Valerian Mikhailovich
Russian, 20th century.
Born 1921, in Tepelevo.
Painter. Figure compositions, landscapes.

In 1937, Valerian Mikhailovich Formozov was admitted to the art school in Gorki, but his studies were interrupted by the war. Demobilized in 1946, he entered the art academy in Latvia and trained with E. Kalnins and J. Tiberg. At the same time he completed art classes in Gorki without taking an exam. He obtained his degrees in 1952 and was appointed to teach painting and design at the art academy and school of applied art in Riga, where he worked from 1953 to 1964. From 1964 onwards, he lived and worked in Moscow. Formozov participated in many national exhibitions, obtaining awards on many occasions from the Federation of Painters in Moscow. His works can be found in several museums in Russia. He executed cycles of pictures with the theme of war, the life of country women, portraits of rural workers and landscapes.

MUSEUMS AND GALLERIES:

RIGA (Mus. of Latvian Art) - RIGA (Russian Mus.).

AUCTION RECORDS:

PARIS, 3 Oct 1990, *Girls' Conversation* (1957, oil on card, 23 1/2 x 27 1/2 ins / 60 x 70 cm) FRF 17,500; *Open Air* (1968, oil on card, 39 1/4 x 22 3/4 ins / 100 x 58 cm) FRF 17,000. PARIS, 9 Dec 1991, *Garden of Flowers* (1973, oil on card, 22 1/2 x 27 1/4 ins / 57 x 69 cm) FRF 3,800. PARIS, 19 April 1993, *Goriatchy Klioutch* (oil on canvas, 42 1/4 x 40 1/2 ins / 107 x 103 cm) FRF 3,500. PARIS, 24 Oct 1993, *Lady in Grey* (1957, oil on canvas, 31 x 23 1/2 ins / 79 x 60 cm) FRF 6,000.

FORMSTECHER. See also **MOSES**

FORMSTECHER, Alfred Wolf

French, 19th century.

Engraver.

FORMSTECHER, Anna

French, 19th century.

Born 7 August 1848, in Paris.

Painter.

Studied under Frère; exhibited portraits at the salons of 1869, 1870 and 1879, together with a genre composition entitled *Artistic Recreation*.

FORMSTECHER, Bertha (Mme)

French, 19th century.

Born 19th century, in Paris.

Painter.

Studied under L. Cogniet and Chaplin; sent portraits to the Salon from 1868 to 1881.

FORMSTECHER, Emma

French, 19th century.

Painter.

Pupil of Chaplin and Léon Cogniet.

MUSEUMS AND GALLERIES:

CLAMECY: *Head of an Alsatian Woman*.

FORMSTECHER, Hélène

French, 19th century.

Born 25 February 1852, in Paris.

Engraver.

Studied under her father, Frère and Louis Lucas; made her Salon début in 1880 and received honourable mentions in 1885 and at the Exposition Universelle of 1900. Formstecher (listed incorrectly in the Nice Museum catalogue as 'Formstecker') engraved from originals by Frère, Terbury, Greuze, Salmson and Bacon.

FORMSTER, Alfred

French, 19th century.

Engraver.

Exhibited at the Paris Salon from 1841 to 1844.

FORNACI, Luca

Italian, 16th century.

Active in Chieti.

Painter.

There is a fresco of the *Virgin* by Luca Fornaci in the church of S Domenico in Chieti. He is also known for his *Genealogical Tree of the Franciscan Order*, dated 1590.

FORNANDER, Andreas

Swedish, 19th century.

Born 1820; died 1903.

Sculptor.

The museum in Stockholm possesses a plaster sculpture by Andreas Fornander entitled *Deer*.

FORNARA, Carlo

Italian, 19th - 20th century.

Born 27 October 1871, in Prestinone (Novara province, Piedmont); died 1968, in Prestinone.

Painter. Portraits, landscapes with figures, landscapes.

Carlo Fornara was a student of Enrico Cavalli at the Santa-Maria Maggiore School of Art, and was an enthusiastic supporter of the Italian painter Giovanni Segantini. He spent time in France and South America, and returned for good to the village where he was born in 1922. His work was shown in Paris, at the Divisionist exhibition in 1907, and at the Salon d'Automne in 1909.

In 1916 Fornara painted *Conquest of the Earth* for the chamber of the parliament building in Buenos Aires. In his early years he was influenced by the Barbizon School; later in his career he began to share many of Claude Monet's ideas about painting, and was something of a spokesman for him in Italy. He applied his paint with the palette knife, scoring his canvases with long strokes. Favouring pure tones, and disassociating form and colour, he leaves it to the viewer to put them together. Fornara's most famous works are: *The Last Pasturelands, Winter Sadness, Small White Church, Prelude to Spring, October on the Mountain, Winter Afternoon, Portrait of the Artist,* and *In the Open Air*.

C. FORNARA

AUCTION RECORDS:

MILAN, 11 Nov 1969, *Shepherdess and Flock in a Landscape*, ITL 4,000,000. MILAN, 25 Nov 1971, *Peasants in a Landscape*, ITL 20,000,000. MILAN, 28 March 1974, *Pastureland*, ITL 10,500,000. MILAN, 28 Oct 1976, *Landscape* (oil on panel, 6 3/4 x 7 ins / 17 x 18 cm) ITL 950,000. MILAN, 26 May 1977, *October in Arvonio* (1930, oil on canvas, 27 1/2 x 39 1/4 ins / 70 x 100 cm) ITL 20,000,000. MILAN, 19 March 1981, *Melancholy Spring* (oil on canvas, 15 x 19 3/4 ins / 38 x 50 cm) ITL 15,000,000. MILAN, 30 Oct 1984, *Portrait of a Man* (1889, charcoal, 27 1/2 x 22 1/4 ins / 70 x 56.5 cm) ITL 1,800,000. MILAN, 9 June 1987, *Summer Afternoon* (1898, oil on canvas, 19 x 23 1/4 ins / 48.5 x 59 cm) ITL 112,000,000. PARIS, 22 March 1989, *Springtime in the Alps* (oil on canvas, 21 x 25 3/4 ins / 52.5 x 65.5 cm) FRF 440,000. MONACO, 21 April 1990, *View of a Church at the Top of a Hill* (oil on panel, 11 3/4 x 15 1/2 ins / 30 x 39.5 cm) FRF 199,800. MILAN, 5 Dec 1990, *Small Garden with Cherry Trees in Bloom* (oil on panel, 19 3/4 x 15 3/4 ins / 50 x 40 cm) ITL 99,000,000. MILAN, 12 March 1991, *Roses in a White Vase* (1962, oil on panel, 14 1/2 x 11 ins / 37 x 28 cm) ITL 20,000,000. MILAN, 7 Nov 1991, *Garden of the Painter's House in Prestinone* (1943, oil on canvas/card, 19 3/4 x 15 3/4 ins / 50 x 40 cm) ITL 82,000,000. MILAN, 8 June 1993, *A Corner of My Garden* (oil on panel, 15 3/4 x 11 3/4 ins / 40 x 30 cm) ITL 35,000,000. MILAN, 22 March 1994, *Last Pasturelands* (1950, oil on panel, 15 3/4 x 19 3/4 ins / 40 x 50 cm) ITL 64,400,000. MILAN, 29 March 1995, *The Painter's House in Prestinone* (oil on canvas, 25 3/4 x 31 3/4 ins / 65.5 x 80.5 cm) ITL 115,000,000. ROME, 23 May 1996, *Vigezzo Valley* (c. 1900, oil on paper, 13 3/4 x 19 ins / 35 x 48.5 cm) ITL 26,450,000. MILAN, 18 Dec 1996, *Silence* (lead pencil/paper/card, 18 x 24 3/4 ins / 46 x 63 cm) ITL 4,194,000. ROME, 27 May 1997, *High Pasturelands* (1934, oil on card, 15 1/2 x 13 1/2 ins / 39.5 x 34.5 cm) ITL 46,000,000. MILAN, 21 Dec 1999, *Still-life with Fruit* (1958, oil on panel, 12 x 16 ins / 30 x 40 cm) ITL 30,000,000. VENICE, 13 May 2000, *April Evening* (oil on canvas, 11 x 16 ins / 29 x 40 cm) ITL 40,000,000. ROME, 21 Nov 2000, *At the Fountain* (pastel on cardboard, 20 x 24 ins / 50 x 62 cm) ITL 28,000,000. TURIN, 10 Dec 2002, *April* (oil on board, 2 x 10 ins / 6 x 25 cm) EUR 20,000. ROME, 24 June 2003, *Mountain Flowers* (oil on canvas, 30 x 25 ins / 76 x 63 cm) EUR 22,000. ROME, 24 June 2003, *Spring Night Dream* (pastel on card, 19 x 19 ins / 47 x 48 cm) EUR 25,000. VERCELLI, 1 May 2004, *Landscape* (oil on cardboard, 16 x 12 ins / 40 x 30 cm) EUR 20,000. LONDON, 16 June 2004, *Village in the Valle Vigezzo* (oil on panel, 15 x 11 1/2ins / 38x29cms) GBP 23,900.

FORNARA, Sallustio
Italian, 19th - 20th century.
Born 1852, in Milan; died 1922, in Cernobbio.
Painter. Local figures, scenes with figures, landscapes with figures.
Orientalism.

Sallustio Fornara was a student of Giovan Battista Lelli at Brera Ginnasio (Secondary School) in Milan, then attended the studio of Eleuterio Pagliano. He was a friend of Umberto Dell'Orto and went with him to Liguria in 1879. He visited Capri and Morocco in 1881, and travelled with Pompeo Mariani to Egypt.

A specialist in open air painting, his *Boats on the Beach*, 1879, is well known. This canvas, with its dull coloration, is strongly structured around the dark shapes of the boats. The realism is a little cold, but it is softened by the thickly painted vegetation on the nearby hill. In the 1880s, following these travels to North Africa, he chose mainly orientalist themes, before turning his attention to the landscapes of Lombardy in the next decade.

Group exhibitions at which his paintings have been shown include: 1879, *Esposizione nazionale di Belle Arti* (*National Exhibition of Fine Arts*), Accademia di Brera, Milan (with *On the Road to Bordighera*); 1879, Società Promotrice di Belle Arti, Genoa (with *Surroundings of Teutan*); 1999, *Scoperta del Mare. Pittori lombardi in Liguria tra 1800 e 1900* (*Discovering the Sea: Lombard Painters in Liguria between 1800 and 1900*), Palazzo Ducale, Genoa.

BIBLIOGRAPHY:
Grandi, Dunia, *Pittori orientalisti lombardi del secondo Ottocento: Umberto Dell'Orto, Sallustio Fornara, Pompeo Mariani*, Università degli studi, Pavia, 1995. Ginex, Giovanna/Rebora, Sergio, *Scoperta del Mare. Pittori lombardi in Liguria tra 1800 e 1900*, group exhibition catalogue, Palazzo Ducale, Genoa, Mazzetta, Milan, 1999.

AUCTION RECORDS:
MILAN, 21 April 1983, *Street in Cairo* (1881, oil on canvas, 14 1/4 x 11 ins / 36 x 28 cm) ITL 3,000,000. MILAN, 28 Oct 1986, *Pair of Peasants in a Mountain Landscape* (oil on canvas, 39 1/4 x 27 1/2 ins / 100 x 70 cm) ITL 6,500,000. MILAN, 30 May 1990, *Young Peasant Girls Carrying Hay on Their Heads in Capri* (oil on canvas, 47 1/4 x 33 1/2 ins / 120 x 85 cm) ITL 26,000,000. MILAN, 5 Dec 1990, *Houses in the Sunlight in Venice* (oil on panel, 9 1/4 x 15 1/4 ins / 23.5 x 39 cm) ITL 10,500,000. MILAN, 16 June 1992, *Arab Camp outside the Walls of a Town* (oil on panel, 6 1/2 x 12 1/2 ins / 16.5 x 32 cm) ITL 7,500,000. ROME, 26 May 1993, *Mountain Farm* (oil on canvas, 17 3/4 x 13 3/4 ins / 45 x 35 cm) ITL 12,500,000. ROME, 29-30 Nov 1993, *Snake Charmers* (1882, oil on canvas, 30 x 23 ins / 76 x 58.5 cm) ITL 20,035,000.

FORNARI, Anselmo de
Italian, 15th - 16th century.
Born c. 1470, in Castelnuovo di Scrivia; died between 1521 and 1529, in Genoa.
Sculptor (wood). Religious furnishings.

The choir stalls in the cathedral in Savona are the most important work by Anselmo de Fornari. In 1514 he began work on the choir stalls in Genoa cathedral, which were completed by other artists after his death.

AUCTION RECORDS:
PARIS, 27 Feb 1930, *Composition*, FRF 530. PARIS, 30 May 1945, *Head of a Woman*, FRF 400.

FORNARI, Benvenuto
Italian, 13th century.
Painter.

This artist was active in Genoa.

FORNARI, Giovanni Battista
Italian, 16th century.
Sculptor.

Giovanni Battista Fornari cannot have been the son of the sculptor Fornari Piccapietro, born in 1491. From 1520 to 1586 he was employed as a sculptor in Parma by Duke Ottavio Farnese, for whom he executed a statue of Neptune for a fountain.

FORNARI, Simone, also known as Moresini
Italian, 16th century.
Active in Reggio.
Painter. History painting.

Siret refers to Simone Fornari.

FORNARI PICCAPIETRO, or PICCAPIETRA, real name: Giovanni Battista Ferrari
Italian, 16th century.
Born 1491; died 1542.
Sculptor.

A statue in the church of St John the Baptist in Parma (above the sacristy door) is attributed to Fornari Piccapietro.

FORNARINO. See **ROMANI Tommaso**

FORNARO, Elisa, later Mme Fr-Jos Büeler
Swiss, 18th century.
Born 15 September 1724, probably in Rapperswil; died 19 January 1796.
Painter.

Notable works by Elisa Fornaro include the miniature portraits of Maria-Theresa and Francis I from the collection at Einsiedeln.

FORNARO, Marie Louise
Swiss, 19th century.
Born 26 June 1812, in Rapperswil; died 4 December 1840, in Munich.
Painter.

Marie Louise Fornaro worked in Munich. She is mentioned in letters written by the painter Gottfried Keller.

FORNASIERO, Giuliano
Italian, 16th century.
Active in Padua.
Sculptor.

FORNAVERT, P. P.
Engraver.

According to Strutt, he produced the cover of a book of devotion, representing *Moses and Aaron and the Four Evangelists*.

FORNAZERIS, Jacques de
French, 16th - 17th century.
Draughtsman, engraver.

Little is known about this artist, who is thought to have been born in either Turin or Lyons. A painter of this name worked for the king of France from 1570 until the early years of the 17th century. He is not, however, as has sometimes been claimed, the same person as Isaïe Fournier. His engravings are signed in a variety of different ways, with the first name appearing as *I. Iacomo, Jacobus* or *Jacques* and the family name, with or without the particle, *de Fournazeri, Fornazeris, Fornazerii, Fournazeri*. His real name was probably *Fournasayre*, which is how he signed his name on the baptismal roll at the christening of his daughter, who was born in Lyons in July 1608. He was living in Lyons in 1601 and 1619 and worked for Horace Cardon. He engraved portraits and numerous title pages or frontispieces, including portraits of *Henri IV on Horseback, Marie de' Medici, James I, King of England, Carlo Emmanuele of Savoy*, of the botanist *Bauderon*, the Jesuit *Favro* and well as depictions of *The Marriage of Henri IV* and *Henri IV and Marie de' Medici Listening to the Dauphin's Lesson* (1605).

FORNÈ, Tomaso

Italian, 16th century.
Of Genoese origin.
Sculptor.

Tomaso Fornè worked in Carrara from 1519 to 1521 with Adamo Wibaldo, under the supervision of the Spaniard B. Ordóñez, on the funeral monument of *Cardinal Ximénez de Cisneros* for the church of Alcalá university in Spain.

FORNENBERG, Alexander van

Flemish, 17th century.
Active in Antwerp, in the middle of the 17th century.
Painter.
Flemish School.

Alexander van Fornenberg was established in Antwerp, where he published a work on Quentin Metsys in 1658.

FORNENBURGH, Jan Baptist van, the Elder

Flemish, 17th century.
Born c. 1600, in Delft; died 1649, in The Hague.
Painter (including gouache). Still-lifes (flowers/fruit), insects.
Flemish School.

AUCTION RECORDS:

NEW YORK, 5 June 1980, *Vase of Flowers* (oil on panel, 15 x 11 ins / 38 x 28 cm) USD 110,000. ZURICH, 7 June 1984, *Still-life with Fruit* (oil on panel, 28 1/4 x 35 1/2 ins / 72 x 90 cm) CHF 22,000. NEW YORK, 15 Jan 1985, *Vase of Flowers and Shells on an Entablature* (oil on canvas, 15 x 11 1/2 ins / 38 x 29 cm) USD 55,000. MONACO, 17 June 1988, *Still-life with Fruit on an Entablature* (oil on canvas, 28 1/4 x 35 3/4 ins / 71.5 x 91 cm) FRF 222,000. LONDON, 14 Dec 1990, *Still-life with a Tulip, Rose, Lizard, Fly and Mouse on an Entablature* (oil on panel, 14 1/4 x 11 1/2 ins / 36 x 29.2 cm) GBP 82,500. LONDON, 30 Nov 1993, *Flowers in an Ornamental Vase with a Lizard on the Table* (gouache/vellum, 13 1/4 x 9 1/2 ins / 33.5 x 24 cm) GBP 24,150. AMSTERDAM, 13 Nov 1995, *Apples, Quince and Walnuts on a Stone Entablature* (oil on panel, 9 1/2 x 16 ins / 24.3 x 40.5 cm) NLG 34,500. NEW YORK, 16 May 1996, *Still-life of Flowers in a Glass Vase in a Stone Niche with Lizards, Insects and Flower Petals on the Entablature* (1626, oil on panel, 42 1/4 x 30 ins / 107.3 x 76.2 cm) USD 519,500. LONDON, 11 Dec 1996, *Still-life with Peaches, Walnuts, Grapes and Butterfly on a Stone Entablature* (oil on panel, 12 1/4 x 15 3/4 ins / 31.3 x 40.1 cm) GBP 13,225. NEW YORK, 28 Jan 2000, *Flowers in a Glass Vase with a Frog and Lizard on a Ledge* (oil on panel, 13 x 10 ins / 34 x 26 cm) USD 100,000. PARIS, 31 March 2000, *Vase of Flowers with Insects on a Ledge* (oil on copper, 7 x 5 ins / 17 x 13 cm) FRF 142,000. PARIS, 26 June 2002, *Roses and Lilies in a Glass* (oil on panel, 15 x 12 ins / 37 x 30 cm) EUR 60,000.

FORNER, Raquel

Argentinian, 20th century.
Born 1902, in Buenos Aires; died 1987, in Buenos Aires.
Painter. Scenes with figures.

Raquel Forner studied at the national academy of fine arts in Buenos Aires. She also studied in Paris under Friesz from 1929 to 1930.

Forner is considered one of Argentina's major mid-20th century artists. Although displaying a talent for large-scale compositions, she was never afforded the opportunity to show her skills as a mural artist. Inspired by the Spanish Civil War, her work expresses a tragic personal nature and, from the 1950s onwards, the fantastical thread in her work began to develop into a fully visionary art.

In Paris she exhibited at the Salon des Tuileries in 1930, showing a painting entitled *Arab Women* and five watercolours. She also exhibited at the Pittsburgh international exhibition in 1933, at the exhibition of Argentinian painting at the National Gallery of Art in Washington in 1956, at the Biennale exhibitions in Mexico and Venice in 1958 and at the *150 Years of Argentinian Art* exhibition held in Buenos Aires in 1961. She was awarded the Palanza prize in Buenos Aires in 1955 and the grand prix d'honneur at the Buenos Aires national fine arts exhibition.

BIBLIOGRAPHY:

Raquel Forner, exhibition catalogue, UNESCO, Paris, 1977 (essay by P. Restany). Whitelow, G., *Raquel Forner*, Buenos Aires, 1980.

AUCTION RECORDS:

NEW YORK, 7 Nov 1980, *El Recuerdo (Memory)* (1954, oil on canvas, 22 x 15 ins / 55 x 38 cm) USD 2,900. NEW YORK, 14-15 May 1996, *Icarus* (1943, gouache/paper, 13 3/4 x 10 3/4 ins / 34.9 x 27.3 cm) USD 2,645. BUENOS AIRES, 4 May 2004, *Fight* (1973, mixed media, 15 x 20 ins / 38 x 51 cm) USD 6,000. BUENOS AIRES, 1 June 2004, *Compromised* (oil on canvas, 29 x 39 ins / 73 x 100 cm) USD 34,000.

FORNERI, Biago

Italian, 15th century.
Born to a family originally from Caresana (Piedmont).
Active c. 1459.
Painter.

A citizen of the town of Ivrea, Biago Forneri also worked in Rome.

FORNERI, Giovanni

Italian, 14th century.
Born to a family originally from Pinerolo (Piedmont).
Painter.

Giovanni Forneri worked for the duke of Savoy at the castle of Gentilly, near Paris, in 1316, and in 1342 for the prince of Achaja in the chapel of the castle at Vigone, near Pinerolo.

FORNEROD, Rodolphe

Swiss, 19th - 20th century.
Born 22 June 1877, in Lausanne; died 1953.
Active in France.
Painter, illustrator. Portraits, landscapes, landscapes with figures, still-lifes, flowers.

Fornerod settled in Paris, where he studied under Jules Lefebvre and Tony Robert-Fleury at the École Nationale des Beaux-Arts (1898-1904) before going on to complete his formal education at the Académie Julian. He exhibited in Paris (Salon des Artistes Indépendants, Salon d'Automne, Salon de la Société Nationale des Beaux-Arts), in Brussels (at the Salon de la Libre Esthétique) and at various exhibitions in Geneva and Zurich. His time spent living in a number of small Spanish villages is reflected in a large number of canvases painted in a limpid yet vigorous style. He also worked as a book illustrator.

AUCTION RECORDS:

PARIS, 27 Feb 1936, *Female Head; Montmartre Street-Singer* (collection) FRF 100. PARIS, 10 Nov 1943, *Woman with Cat*, FRF 1,250. PARIS, 23 Feb 1945, *Bouquet of Flowers*, FRF 1,000. VERSAILLES, 2 Dec 1973, *Young Girl with a Grey Hat* (c. 1925) FRF 2,300. ZURICH, 7 Nov 1981, *Church* (oil on card, 23 x 30 3/4 ins / 58.5 x 78 cm) CHF 1,000. ZURICH, 13 June 1986, *View of Montmartre* (oil on canvas, 36 1/4 x 28 3/4 ins / 92 x 73 cm) CHF 2,500. VERSAILLES, 29 Oct 1989, *Young Girl with a Hat* (oil on paper, 16 1/4 x 14 1/2 ins / 41.5 x 37 cm) FRF 8,500. VERSAILLES, 25 March 1990, *Apples* (oil on card, 27 1/4 x 22 ins / 69.5 x 55 cm) FRF 12,500. PARIS, 10 April 1996, *Young Girl with Braided Hair* (oil on canvas, 36 1/2 x 28 3/4 ins / 92.5 x 73 cm) FRF 16,000.

FORNET, Eugène Alexandre
French, 19th century.
Born in Paris.
Engraver.
Pupil of Louis Lucas; received an honourable mention in 1885 and bronze medals in 1888 and at the Exposition Universelle of 1900.

FORNEY, Clarisse
French, 19th century.
Born 19th century, in Paris.
Sculptor.
Pupil of Madame Léon Bertaux; exhibited at the Salon in 1881 and 1882. She is remembered for a bronze bust of *A. Dantier*.

FORNIER, Cristofano, or Fornieri
Italian, 17th century.
Of French origin.
Active in Perugia c. 1650.
Sculptor.
Cristofano Fornier is known to have carved a large wooden crucifix for the choir section of Perugia Cathedral and a similar crucifix for the church of St Elisabeth.

FORNIER, Kitty, Mme Tollin-Fornier from 1892
French, 19th century.
Born in Geneva; died c. 1908.
Painter, pastellist. Figures, portraits, genre scenes.
Pupil of Loubet and Cesbron; exhibited chiefly portraits and figures in Lyons as of 1885 and, as of 1888, in Paris. Notable among her body of work is *Mary of Nazareth*, shown in Paris in 1892, *Diabolical Beauty* (Paris, 1892), *Smile* (Paris, 1901) and *Portrait of Sylvia* (Paris, 1903). She was awarded a gold medal in Lyons in 1891.
MUSEUMS AND GALLERIES:
LYONS (Préfecture): *Louise Labé; Mme Récamier* (1893, decorative rings).
AUCTION RECORDS:
LONDON, 11 Feb 1994, *Small Slave* (1901, oil on canvas, 40¼ x 25¾ ins / 102.5 x 65.6 cm) GBP 5,290.

FORNIER DE VIOLET, Clotilde
French, 19th century.
Painter.
Exhibited examples of her work at Paris salons from 1840 to 1847, chiefly portraits and studies of heads.

FORNO, Giovanni del
Italian, 16th century.
Active in Amalfi.
Painter.
From 1500 to 1525, Giovanni del Forno painted the frescoes in a chapel in Amalfi cathedral.

FORNONI, Giulio
Italian, 19th century.
Born 1866, in Venice.
Active in Venice.
Painter.
Giulio Fornoni exhibited from 1890 onwards in Turin, Florence, Munich and Venice. His works were chiefly inspired by the canals of Venice.

FORNS BADA, Carlos
Spanish, 20th - 21st century.
Born 1955, in Madrid.
Painter.
Carlos Forns Bada's painting displays a Cubist influence and, above all, a Surrealist influence, and also recalls certain works by Dalí and Chirico. He has taken part in numerous group exhibitions, including: in 1977, the *28th Salon de Jeune Peinture* at the Musée du Luxembourg, Paris; in 1982, the *Salón de los 16* at the museum of contemporary art in Madrid, at the 2nd Internationale Jugentrienale in Nuremberg, and at the cantonal fine arts museum in Lausanne.

FORRÈCHE, A.
Painter. Seascapes.
AUCTION RECORDS:
PARIS, 29 June 1988, *A Rowing Boat* (oil on canvas, 21¼ x 28¾ ins / 54 x 73 cm) FRF 7,800.

FORRER, Daniel
Swiss, 16th century.
Born 26 September 1540, in Schaffhausen; died 6 October 1604, in Schaffhausen.
Glass painter.
Schaffhausen School.
A number of armorial windows with the initials *D. F.* in the Historical Association in Schaffhausen and in Zurich are attributed to Forrer. He was a member of a confraternity of decorative and glass painters founded in 1588 and of the Grand Council of Schaffhausen.

FORRER, Georg
Swiss, 18th century.
Active in Winterthur in the middle of the 18th century.
Glass painter.

FORRER, Jakob
Swiss, 17th - 18th century.
Born 1 January 1661, in Winterthur; died 21 July 1719, in Winterthur.
Glass painter, decorative artist.
Jakob Forrer produced stained glass windows for the church in Belp (Bern canton) and for his home town.

FORRER, Johann Gustav
Swiss, 19th century.
Born 1830, in Winterthur; died 1880, in Winterthur.
Draughtsman.
Johann Gustav Forrer work mainly as a draughtsman in factories producing oriental fabrics.

FORRER, Karl Gustav
Swiss, 19th century.
Born 31 December 1852, in Winterthur.
Draughtsman.
Karl Gustav Forrer followed the same career as his father Johann Gustav, who was his teacher. He also worked in Paris from 1879 and spent some time as an art teacher at the school of industrial arts in Leipzig (Saxony).

FORRER, Rennwart. See **FORER**

FORRES, Agnes Freda
British, 20th century.
Born in Weybridge, near London.
Sculptor.
Agnes Forres studied under Charles Jagger. She exhibited a bronze *Bust Portrait* in Paris at the Salon des Artistes Français in 1926 and a plaster *Bust Portrait* in 1927.

FORREST
British, 18th century.
Painter (including glass).
A pupil and collaborator of Jarvis, Forrest worked in St George's Chapel at Windsor Castle, and executed a number of works in Birmingham, with Eguiton.

FORREST, Charles
Irish, 18th century.
Painter. Portraits.
Charles Forrest exhibited in London, notably seven portraits at the Free Society in 1776.

FORREST, Charles Ramus
British, 18th - 19th century.
Painter, watercolourist, draughtsman. Landscapes.

Charles Ramus Forrest was active from 1802 to 1827; he also worked in Quebec.

AUCTION RECORDS:

LONDON, 3 Nov 1976, *Wolsfield* (watercolour, 13 1/2 x 20 ins / 34 x 51 cm) GBP 2,500. LONDON, 1 June 1977, *On the Jacques Cartier River* (1821, watercolour, 17 1/2 x 26 ins / 44.5 x 66 cm) GBP 3,400. LONDON, 22 Oct 1986, *Cape Diamond and Point Levi, Québec* (1823, watercolour/traces of pencil, 12 3/4 x 16 3/4 ins / 32.5 x 42.5 cm) GBP 7,200.

FORREST, Grace Banker

American, 20th century.

Born 5 January 1897.

Painter, illustrator. Portraits.

Grace Banker Forrest was a pupil of J.W. Gies, J.P. Wicker and F.P. Paulus, and worked in Grosse Pointe City, Michigan. She was a member of the Detroit Society of Women Painters and Sculptors, the New York Society of Independents and the Arts Club of Chicago.

FORREST, John B.

British, 19th century.

Born c. 1814, in Aberdeenshire, Scotland; died 1870, in Hudson (New York), USA.

Engraver.

A pupil of Thomas Fry in London, John B. Forrest travelled to Philadelphia in 1837, where he worked for the National Portrait Gallery, and subsequently to New York, where he painted portrait miniatures. He is noted for his engraved portrait of the painter *R.A. Stothard*, after a bust by E H. Baily.

FORREST, Robert

British, 19th century.

Born 1789, in Carluke (Lanarkshire); died 29 December 1852, in Edinburgh.

Sculptor.

Robert Forrest is noted for a statue of *Wallace* (1817).

FORREST, Theodosius Thomas

British, 18th century.

Born 1728; died 5 November 1784.

Painter, draughtsman. Architectural views.

A pupil of Lambert, Theodosius Forrest was a regular exhibitor with the Royal Academy from 1769 to 1775.

AUCTION RECORDS:

LONDON, 26 Nov 1930, *St Botolph's Priory* (watercolour) GBP 4.

FORREST, W.S.

British, 19th century.

Active in Greenhithe.

Painter. Sporting subjects.

W.S. Forrest exhibited at the Royal Academy, the British Institution and Suffolk Street from 1840 to 1866.

FORREST, William

British, 19th century.

Born 1805; died 1889.

Active in London.

Engraver.

William Forrest is known for his landscape engravings after N. Chevalier, F.E. Church, Claude Lorraine and A. Waterloo, and for his *Gathering of the Clans* after W. Allan.

FORRESTALL, Thomas de Vany, or Tom

Canadian, 20th century.

Born 1936.

Painter. Landscapes.

Magic Realism.

Thomas de Vany Forrestall painted the desolate landscapes and weather of New Brunswick in a highly realistic style, similar to what, in 1955, was called Magic Realism.

AUCTION RECORDS:

TORONTO, 19 Oct 1976, *To me, a strange room* (1963, oil on plastered card, 15 3/4 x 35 1/2 ins / 40 x 90 cm) CAD 2,000. TORONTO, 26 May 1981, *View from Cellar Window* (1963, oil on card, 23 1/2 x 35 1/2 ins / 60 x 90 cm) CAD 2,400. TORONTO, 3 June 1986, *Summer Rain* (1964, acrylic/card, 16 x 11 1/2 ins / 40.6 x 29.2 cm) CAD 1,500. MONTREAL, 13 Dec 1999, *Family Trade, Parker's Cove, Nova Scotia* (1972, oil on canvas, 28 x 36 ins / 71 x 91 cm) CAD 5,500. TORONTO, 13 June 2000, *Burning Field* (oil on canvas, 14 x 15 ins / 36 x 38 cm) CAD 2,800. TORONTO, 25 Feb 2002, *Leaving the Lake* (1975, oil on canvas, 13 x 19 ins / 33 x 48 cm) CAD 6,000. TORONTO, 27 May 2003, *Midsummer* (1964, oil on masonite, 18 x 40 ins / 46 x 102 cm) CAD 5,500. TORONTO, 27 May 2003, *Culvert* (1965, acrylic on gesso on masonite, 23 x 44 ins / 58 x 112 cm) CAD 7,000.

FORRESTER, Alfred Henry, pseudonym: Alfred Crowquill

British, 19th century.

Born 1804, in London; died May 1872, in London.

Caricaturist.

'Crowquill' contributed to a number of periodicals, including *Beutley's Miscellany*, the *Illustrated London News* and *The Humorist*. He is best-known for his *Eccentric Tales*.

MUSEUMS AND GALLERIES:

NORWICH (Castle Mus. and AG): *Very Animated Nature* (drawing); *St George and the Dragon* (drawing).

FORRESTER, James

Irish, 18th century.

Born 1729, in Dublin; died 1775, in Rome.

Painter, engraver. Landscapes with figures, landscapes.

James Forrester lived in Italy for a number of years, where he painted landscapes.

AUCTION RECORDS:

LONDON, 19 July 1985, *Wooded Landscape in Stormy Weather with Figures beside a Stream* (1766, oil on canvas, 52 x 76 1/2 ins / 132 x 194.3 cm) GBP 2,800. LONDON, 9 Feb 1990, *Stormy Night: Italian Landscape with Figures beside an Aqueduct* (oil on canvas, 38 1/2 x 53 1/2 ins / 97.9 x 136 cm) GBP 3,520. LONDON, 8 April 1992, *Italian Landscape by Moonlight, with an Aqueduct in the Background* (oil on canvas, 37 3/4 x 52 3/4 ins / 96 x 134 cm) GBP 6,050. LONDON, 20 May 1999, *Italianate Wooded River Landscape with Figures by a Tomb* (oil on canvas, 27 x 44 ins / 68 x 111 cm) GBP 5,200.

FORRESTER, John

New Zealander, 20th century.

Born 1922, in Wellington.

Active in France from 1960.

Painter.

Nouvelle Figuration.

John Forrester began painting in 1938 but was called up to serve in the forces during World War II, which he spent in the Pacific and in Africa. He lived in England from 1953 to 1958 and was employed on the Sheffield reconstruction project. From 1958 to 1960, he lived in Siena and then in Paris from 1960. Attracted for a time by the approach of the Nouveaux Réalistes, supported by Restany who believed in appropriating contemporary reality into their work, Forrester took inspiration from the graffiti and torn wall posters of French city streets. In Paris, Forrester took part in various group events including the Salon Comparaisons, the Donner à Voir group and the Figuration Narrative group organised in 1965 by G. Gassiot-Talabot. He also held several solo exhibitions including: in 1946 at the National Library in Wellington; in 1955 in London; in 1960 in Pistoia; in 1962 in London; and in 1963 in Paris.

BIBLIOGRAPHY:

Dictionnaire des artistes contemporains, Libraires Associés, Paris, 1964.

Auction records:
Paris, 22 Nov 1987, *Out of Nowhere* (1973, oil on canvas, 59 x 59 ins / 150 x 150 cm) FRF 13,000. Paris, 20 March 1988, *A Room with a View* (acrylic/canvas, 35 1/2 x 35 1/2 ins / 90 x 90 cm) FRF 3,000. Victoria, 9 Nov 1999, *Vessels off Rocky Coast* (oil on canvas, 19 x 30 ins / 49 x 75 cm) AUD 2,600. London, 14 May 2004, *Mark Black Two* (1961, oil on canvas, 36 x 29 ins / 91 x 73 cm) GBP 1,700. London, 14 May 2004, *Aldila Mark* (1962, oil on canvas, 36 x 32 ins / 91 x 81 cm) GBP 2,000.

FORRESTER, Joseph James (Baron)
British, 19th century.
Born 1809, in Kingston-upon-Hull; died 1861.
Painter, watercolourist, cartographer. Landscapes.

The son of a merchant, Joseph James Forrester exported goods to Portugal, but was also a cartographer, photographer and accomplished amateur artist, notably in watercolour. He is known for a series of seven Portugese landscapes, painted on zinc.

Auction records:
London, 15 Dec 1993, *View of the Douro, with the Tagus (recto); Portugese Riverscape with a Ferry (verso)* (oil/zinc, 16 3/4 x 23 1/2 ins / 42.5 x 59.7 cm) GBP 9,775.

FORS, Claix and Guillaume, (brothers)
Flemish School, 15th century.
Born to a family originally from Brussels.
Sculptors.

In 1461 these brothers made the statues of *St Philip* and *St Elizabeth* for the palace of Philip the Good in Brussels.

FORS, Curt
Swedish, 20th century.
Born 1935, in Malmö.
Also active in France.
Painter, collage artist, engraver, draughtsman.

Since 1965 Curt Fors has shown his work in numerous solo exhibitions in Malmö, Stockholm (most notably at the Erik Höglund Gallery in 1995), Helsingborg and Halmstadt, Vienna (1968), Vetlanda (1976), Ystad (1980), Paris (1983 at the Swedish Cultural Centre and 1990 at the K'Art Gallery) and in Lund (1988, retrospective).

He takes everyday objects - bowls, vases, packaging, ashtrays - and reduces them to their most basic form, the objective being not so much to paint the objects themselves as to present them in relationship with the space that surrounds them. He achieves a sense of depth by working virtually in monochrome.

Museums and Galleries:
Paris (BNF, Prints Collection) - Stockholm (Nationalmus.) - Vienna (Albertina Mus.) - Ystad (Konstmus.).

FORSBERG, Anders Vilhelm
Swedish, 19th - 20th century.
Born 30 June 1871, in Karlstad; died 16 May 1914, in Stockholm.
Draughtsman, illustrator.

Forsberg studied at the arts and crafts college in Stockholm and was appointed that institution's first professor of drawing and composition (1896). He illustrated various satirical publications.

Museums and Galleries:
Stockholm (Nationalmus.).

FORSBERG, Carl Johan
Swedish, 19th - 20th century.
Born 1868, in Sweden; died 1938, in Sonderho.
Painter, watercolourist.

Forsberg studied at the Stockholm college of arts and crafts and at Stockholm academy and spent many years outside his native country. He organised an exhibition of his watercolours in Stockholm in 1904, showing chiefly Italian and Swiss landscapes, together with other less conventional subjects (notably *Death Seated in an Alpine Landscape*). He exhibited again in 1913, showing diverse subjects but predominantly views of Stockholm, Göteborg, Copenhagen and the Danish coast.

Museums and Galleries:
Stockholm (Nationalmus.).

Auction records:
London, 25 March 1987, *Beach Scene* (1903, watercolour and gouache, 13 3/4 x 10 ins / 35 x 25.5 cm) GBP 3,200. London, 16 March 1989, *Lake Aegeri* (pencil and watercolour, 10 1/4 x 28 1/4 ins / 26 x 72 cm) GBP 4,950. London, 29 March 1990, *Reflections on the Water* (1930, oil and watercolour/paper, 25 1/4 x 19 1/2 ins / 64 x 49.5 cm) GBP 3,080. Copenhagen, 29 Aug 1990, *Vesuvius Erupting* (1899, watercolour, 15 1/4 x 14 1/4 ins / 39 x 36 cm) DKK 10,500.

FORSBERG, Elmer A.
Finnish, 20th century.
Born 16 July 1883, in Gamalakarleby; died 3 August 1950, in Chicago.
Painter.

Elmer Forsberg studied at the Art Institute in Chicago and was a member of the Chicago Painters and Sculptors Association. He lectured extensively on art.

FORSBERG, Jan
Swedish, 20th century.
Born 1932, in Stockholm.
Engraver.

Studied at the fine arts academy in Stockholm and exhibited his engravings at various Biennales, including Ljubljana and Cracow.

FORSBERG, Nils, the Elder
Swedish, 19th - 20th century.
Born 17 December 1842, in Riseberga; died 1934.
Painter. Portraits, genre scenes, landscapes.

Forsberg was a pupil of Bonnat. He lived and worked in France and exhibited at the Salon des Artistes Français, where he was awarded a gold medal in 1888, followed by a silver medal; and at the 1889 and 1900 Exhibition Universelle, being awarded a gold medal in 1900. He was made a Chevalier of the Légion d'Honneur in 1901.

Nils Forsberg

Museums and Galleries:
Göteborg: *Acrobat Family*; *Gustavus Adolphus at the Battle of Lützen* - Helsingborg: *Stenbock Mail Coach* - Stockholm: *Death of a Hero*.

Auction records:
Paris, 25 May 1951, *Harvest*, FRF 30,000. Stockholm, 10 Nov 1982, *Gustav II Adolf (Gustavus Adolphus)* (1889, oil on canvas, 45 1/4 x 31 ins / 115 x 79 cm) SEK 14,000. Stockholm, 14 Nov 1990, *Watercourse and Balustrade, Versailles* (oil on panel, 11 3/4 x 15 3/4 ins / 30 x 40 cm) SEK 6,500. London, 17 March 1995, *Belly-dancer* (oil on canvas, 82 3/4 x 48 3/4 ins / 210 x 124 cm) GBP 25,300. Stockholm, 24 Nov 1999, *Cavalry Attacking* (1886, oil on canvas, 46 x 35 ins / 116 x 89 cm) SEK 30,000. Stockholm, 23 May 2000, *The Acrobat Family* (1879, oil on canvas, 23 x 18 ins / 58 x 46 cm) SEK 20,000.

FORSBERG, Nils, the Younger
French, 19th - 20th century.
Born 15 November 1870, in Paris; died 1961.
Painter. Genre scenes, landscapes with figures, urban landscapes.

Nils Forsberg the Younger studied under Fernand Cormon and Fernand Humbert. He exhibited in Paris at the Salon des Artistes Français, of which he became a member in 1901. He received a commendation in 1907 and a bronze medal in

1909. He also exhibited at the Salon des Indépendants in 1891, 1901 and 1907. He painted mainly craftsmen and Paris gardens.

Museums and Galleries:

Toledo (MA): *The Potter of St-Amand.*

Auction records:

Paris, 9 May 1977, *Cavalryman and Nanny in the Parc Monceau* (oil on canvas, 18½ x 13½ ins / 47 x 34 cm) FRF 5,000; *Miss Jessie* (watercolour and gouache/paper, 55 x 40¼ ins / 140 x 102 cm) FRF 1,000. Stockholm, 13 April 1992, *Young Girl with Sunshade in a Park in France* (1895, oil on canvas, 20¾ x 17¼ ins / 53 x 44 cm) SEK 7,500.

FORSBERG, P. William

Swedish, 20th century.
Born in Sweden.
Sculptor.

Forsberg was a pupil of M.E. Fernand-Dubois and exhibited in Paris at the Salon des Artistes Français every year from 1927 to 1932.

FORSELLES, Sigrid Maria Rosina af

Finnish, 19th century.
Born 4 May 1860; died 1935.
Active in Paris.
Sculptor.

Sigrid af Forselles spent most of her career in France and Italy, and was the pupil and assistant of Auguste Rodin. In the Helsinki museum is a bronze by her, *Youth*, and a low relief, *The Fight*.

FORSHALL, Catherine

British, 20th - 21st century.
Born 1958, in Scotland.
Active in France from 1985.
Painter. Interiors, landscapes, still-lifes.

Catherine Forshall studied art and draughtsmanship in Florence in 1976. In 1979, she moved to London where she worked as a ceramics restorer. Later, she worked at a museum in Germany before settling in the Lot region of France. She enjoys painting everyday life, using warm colours and adopting a free technique. Forshall has taken part in group exhibitions and has exhibited regularly at the Salon d'Automne in Paris since 1988.

FORSMAN, Alina

Finnish, 19th century.
Born 1845, in Lohja.
Sculptor.

Alina Forsman's marble medallion of *Sculptor Runeberg* and her plaster busts of *The Singer Signe Hebbe* and *The Musician Dornnstrom* are in the museum of Helsinki.

FORSMAN, Chuck

American, 20th - 21st century.
Born 1944, in Nampa, Idaho.
Painter. Landscapes.

Chuck Forsman studied at the University of California, Davis and at the Skowhegan School of Painting and Sculpture. He later taught at the Fine Arts Department of the University of Colorado.

Forsman's landscapes and cityscapes are often produced in black and white, and in great detail, as seen in *Across the Wide Missouri, Fort Bertold Indian Reservation, North Dakota* and *City of Commerce, with the Denver Skyline, Colorado*. Both of these works see the subject through a car window, a recurring feature in Forsman's work. In 2003 Forsman produced a series of photographs taken from behind the wheel of his car, which were published as a collection in *Western Rider: Views from a Car Window*.

Forsman's first solo exhibition took place in 1971, and since then his work has been the subject of over 40 exhibitions. Venues have included the Art Museum of South Texas, Yellowstone Art Center, the Nevada Museum of Art, National Academy of Sciences, Tuscon Art Museum, Denver Art Museum, and Wichita Art Museum. Forsman has also received several grants during his career, namely the National Endowment Fellowship (1979, 1985 and 1995), the University of Colorado Faculty Fellowship (1979 and 1986), the Ucross Foundation (1986), the American Academy of Arts and Letters Purchase Award (1979), the West Publishing: 'Arts & The Like' Purchase Award (1988, 1993 and 1996), and the Colorado Council on the Arts Covisions Recognition Award (1995).

Bibliography:

Wooden, Howard E., *Collected Essays on 101 Art Works*, Wichita Art Museum, 1988. Harrison, Helen A., et al., *Arrested Rivers. Paintings by Chuck Forsman*, University Press of Colorado, 1994. Hurwitz, Laurie, *'Making Miracles in the Southwest'* in *American Artist*, October 1994. Sims Lowery/Rewald, Sabine, *Still Life. the Object in American Art, 1915-1995*, 1996. Melrod, George, *'Openings'* in *Art & Antiques*, 1996. Hagerty, Donald J., *Leading the West. One Hundred Contemporary Painters and Sculptors*, 1997. Forsman, Chuck, *Western Rider: Views From a Car Window*, Center for American Places, 2003.

Museums and Galleries:

Billings (Yellowstone AM) - Denver (AM) - Knoxville (Knoxville Museum of Art) - New York (Metropolitan Mus. of Art) - Phoenix (AM) - Wichita (AM).

FORSMANN, Abel Margaretha Sophia

Maiden name: Meyer
German, 18th - 19th century.
Born 1753, in Rendsburg; died 28 February 1836, in Hamburg.
Active in Hamburg.
Sculptor (ivory).

Forsmann married the engraver G. A. Forsmann. She sculpted portraits in relief on ivory, bowls and bunches of flowers. Some of her works are held by the Museum für Kunst und Gewerbe in Hamburg.

FORSMANN, Gustav Andreas

German, 18th - 19th century.
Born 1773, in Hamburg; died 26 April 1830, in Hamburg.
Engraver.

Gustav Forsmann engraved portraits, among which were those of Lessing and of Lord Nelson. His works include his engraving *American Aloes in Flower* and his engravings on mother-of-pearl, an example of which is in the Museum für Kunst und Gewerbe in Hamburg.

FORSSELL, Christian Didrik

Swedish, 19th century.
Born 1777, in Helsingborg; died 19 October 1852, in Stockholm.
Engraver (burin), draughtsman.

After having studied at the Kunstakademi in Copenhagen, Christian Didrik Forssell became a teacher at the academy of Stockholm and engraver to the court. Among his best works are *Coronation of the Virgin* after a drawing by Ternite, *The Camocus* after Gérard, and *Louis XVIII* after Augustin.

FORSSELL, Eugénie

Swedish, 19th century.
Born 1808; died 1833.
Draughtswoman.

Eugénie Forssell was the daughter of Christian Forssell. She executed pencil drawings.

FORSSELL, Juho, also known as George

Swedish, 20th century.
Born 1853, in Halino; died 1939.
Painter.

Exhibited his *After the Bath* at the 1921 Salon d'Automne in Paris.

FORSSELL, Viktor Reinhold, or Forsell
Swedish, 19th - 20th century.
Born 1846, in Sala; died 1931.
Painter. Landscapes with figures, landscapes.

MUSEUMS AND GALLERIES:
STOCKHOLM: *Springtime at the Zoo.*
AUCTION RECORDS:
STOCKHOLM, 31 March 1971, *Narrow Country Road*, SEK 10,500. STOCKHOLM, 19 April 1972, *Cattle Slaking Their Thirst*, SEK 5,000. GÖTEBORG, 5 April 1978, *Landscape* (1871, oil on canvas, 23 1/2 x 35 ins / 60 x 88 cm) SEK 10,500. STOCKHOLM, 8 April 1981, *Woodcutter in a Snow-Covered Landscape* (oil on canvas, 15 1/4 x 24 3/4 ins / 39 x 63 cm) SEK 49,000. STOCKHOLM, 30 Oct 1984, *Village Street in Winter* (1879, oil on panel, 12 1/4 x 15 ins / 31 x 38 cm) SEK 80,000. STOCKHOLM, 19 Oct 1987, *Landscape with Lake* (oil on panel, 16 1/2 x 13 ins / 42 x 33 cm) SEK 220,000. STOCKHOLM, 19 April 1989, *Young Girl Tending her Animals in a Clearing by a Lake* (oil on canvas, 20 1/2 x 35 ins / 52 x 88 cm) SEK 7,500. STOCKHOLM, 19 May 1992, *Gotland Coast Landscape with Children Playing in a Boat* (oil on panel, 23 1/2 x 19 3/4 ins / 60 x 50 cm) SEK 47,000.

FORSSLUND, Jonas
Swedish, 18th century.
Born 1754, in Fors (Jämtland); died 1809, in Stockholm.
Painter, sculptor.
MUSEUMS AND GALLERIES:
STOCKHOLM: a medallion in plaster and several portraits in pastel.
AUCTION RECORDS:
STOCKHOLM, 30 Oct 1984, *Portrait of Gustaf Erik Ruth; Portrait of Hedda Eleonora Ruth* (pastel, two, 24 3/4 x 20 ins / 63 x 51 cm) SEK 16,000. STOCKHOLM, 5 Dec 2000, *Countess Anna Charlotta Ulfsparre of Broxvik* (1792, pastel, oval, 24 x 19 ins / 60 x 47 cm) SEK 16,000. STOCKHOLM, 5 Dec 2000, *Portrait of Eva Ulrica Morner of Marlanda* (1797, pastel, oval, 23 x 18 ins / 58 x 45 cm) SEK 22,000. HELSINKI, 1 Dec 2002, *Young Woman* (pastel, oval, 24 x 16 ins / 60 x 40 cm) EUR 3,000. STOCKHOLM, 4 June 2003, *Portraits of Pehr Alexander Rudbeck and his Wife Anna Elisabeth* (1789, pastel, oval, a pair, 22 x 18 ins / 56 x 46 cm) SEK 17,000. STOCKHOLM, 3 Dec 2003, *Portrait of Baroness Catharina Margareta Cederhielm* (oil on canvas, 53 x 43 ins / 135 x 110 cm) SEK 24,000.

FORSSTROM, Karl Wilhelm
Swedish, 19th century.
Born 18 September 1854, in Hedemora.
Draughtsman.
Karl Wilhelm Forsstrom studied at the academy of Stockholm from 1876 to 1883 and was exclusively a humoristic draughtsman. He collaborated on several cartoon projects such as *Puck*. He published a series of drawings in 1900 called *Boströms Bilderbok: En Statsministers Saga.*

FORST, Johann Hubert Anton
German, 18th century.
Born 1756, in Berlin.
Miniaturist, painter (including porcelain). Portraits, landscapes.
Johann Forst was a pupil of C. W. Boehme. In 1771 he joined the Royal Workshop in Berlin where he took up the post of Director of Painting from 1796 to 1815. At the Berlin academy he exhibited painted plates and vases as well as oil paintings and views of the castles of Berlin.

FORST, Johann Victor von der
German, 19th century.
Born 1864, in Münster; died 30 March 1901, in Herten (Westphalia).
Painter. History painting.
Johann Victor Forst studied at the academies in Düsseldorf and Munich and worked mainly for churches.

FORST, Miles
American, 20th century.
Born 1923, in Brooklyn (New York City).
Painter.
Miles Forst was a pupil of M. Kantor at the Art Students League, and, from 1950, of Hans Hofmann in New York. He has taken part in many group exhibitions, including: 1954, *Young American Painters*, Guggenheim Museum, New York; 1957, *New York Painters, Second Generation*, Jewish Museum, New York; and 1958 and 1959, Carnegie Institute, Pittsburgh. He held solo exhibitions in New York in 1953, 1954, 1955 and 1958.

FORST, Ullrich van
Dutch, 17th century.
Born to a family originally from Oldenzaal; died 1677, in Vienna.
Glass painter.
Ullrich van Forst resided in Vienna where he was granted citizenship. His paintings were bought by Prince Karl Eusebius von Liechtenstein.

FORSTEN, Berndt Lennart
Finnish, 19th century.
Born 1817, in Kuopio; died 1886.
Painter. Landscapes.
Berndt Lennart Forsten was also a poet. One of his landscapes is in the Helsinki museum.

FORSTER (Mrs)
British, 19th century.
Painter. Portraits.
Mrs Forster exhibited at the Royal Academy in London from 1800 to 1814.

FORSTER. See also **FOERSTER**

FORSTER, A.
Czech, 18th century.
Sculptor.
A. Forster is known for works Viskov and Paclavice (statues of the *Immaculate Conception*) and in Mohelnice.

FORSTER, Antonius
German, 16th century.
Born in the 16th century, in Frankfurt am Main.
Engraver (wood).
Four woodcuts by this artist are mentioned by Nagler: *Christ Before Pilate, Christ on the Cross with Luther and a Saxon Prince*, both kneeling, *Christ on the Cross with St John and the Virgin* and the decoration of the frontispiece of the third volume of *Luther* published in Jena.

FORSTER, Asmus
Italian, 15th century.
Sculptor.
Asmus Forster worked in Gardolo, near Trento, from 1494 to 1495.

FORSTER, Berthold Paul
German, 19th century.
Born 2 November 1851, in Westerau.
Painter. Landscapes.
Berthold Paul Forster worked in Weimar then in Dresden. He exhibited in Berlin and then in Düsseldorf. The museum in Weimar has his *Footpath in the Fields* in its collection.

FORSTER, C.
British, 19th century.
Born 1824 or 1825 in Islington (London).
Active in London.
Painter. Portraits.
C. Forster exhibited at the Royal Academy from 1828 to 1847.

FORSTER, Cajetan
Austrian, 18th century.
Born to a family originally from Merano.
Painter.
Cajetan Forster studied at the academy in Vienna. He is probably the painter of the same name who died in Burghausen in Upper Bavaria; the hospital at that town's church has a picture signed C. Forster: *Virgin with Saint John of Thaddeus and Saint Bartholomew*.

FORSTER, Charles (Jr.)
British, 19th century.
Painter. Rustic scenes.
Charles Forster was probably a relative of C. Forster. He exhibited at the Royal Academy, the British Institution and Suffolk Street in London from 1835 to 1876.

FORSTER, Christian
German, 19th century.
Born c. 1826; died 6 August 1902, in Hamburg.
Active in Hamburg.
Draughtsman, illustrator.
Christian Forster's many wood engravings were inspired by Hamburg street scenes: *Water Carrier, Washerwoman*. He also worked for the journal *Reform*, which earned him the name 'Reform Förster', and drew various caricatures, among which is *Civic Guard 1840*. These drawings are also preserved as lithographs and copper engravings.

FORSTER, Christoph, or Vorster
Austrian, 16th century.
Died 1597, in Vienna.
Painter. Playing cards.
This artist is probably related to Georg or Hans Forster. He specialised in painting playing cards.

FORSTER, Conrad
German, 16th century.
Sculptor. Armorials, bas-reliefs.
Conrad Forster is mentioned between 1545 and 1552 as working at the castle of Heidelberg, where he was responsible for a fireplace and some low reliefs of coats of arms. A fireplace at the castle of Neumarkt, the remains of which are now in the Bayerisches Nationalmuseum in Munich, is also attributed to him.
MUSEUMS AND GALLERIES:
MUNICH (Bayerisches Nationalmus.).

FORSTER, Cornelia
Swiss, 20th century.
Born 1906, in Zurich; died 1990.
Draughtsman.
Cornelia Forster exhibited two drawings at the Salon d'Automne in Paris.

FORSTER, Ernst Joachim
German, 19th century.
Born 8 April 1800, in Munchergasserstadt; died 29 April 1885, in Munich.
Painter, art critic.
Ernst Forster began working at the University of Iena then under the direction of Schadow in Berlin and finally of Cornelius in Munich. After marrying the sister of Johann-Paul (Jean-Paul) Richter, he began to work on literature on art. In 1832 he undertook a trip to Italy on behalf of Prince Max of Bavaria, during the course of which he produced many drawings in the antique style. He carried out some of the decorations at the palace in Munich. He was a prolific author of art criticism.

FORSTER, François
French, 19th century.
Born 22 August 1790, in Le Locle, Switzerland; died 1872, in Paris.
Engraver.
Enrolled at the École des Beaux-Arts in 1805 and went on to be awarded a silver at the 1809 Prix de Rome and a gold at the 1814 Prix de Rome. He was elevated to the Légion d'Honneur on 23 April 1838. Forster was awarded a silver medal at 1824 and a gold in 1831. He was elected to membership of the institute in 1844 and, on 14 August 1863, was promoted to officer rank in the Legion. Forster became a French citizen in 1828. He is regarded as one of the most accomplished engravers of his day.
AUCTION RECORDS:
PARIS, 1898, *Harvesters* (watercolour) FRF 6,425. LONDON, 1899, *Ships in a Gust of Wind* (watercolour) FRF 7,875; *Lake Stratfort* (watercolour) FRF 10,500; *Collecting Seaweed* (watercolour) FRF 1,825.

FORSTER, G.
British, 19th century.
Painter. Genre scenes.
G. Forster exhibited with the Royal Academy, the British Institution and at Suffolk Street from 1816 to 1830.

FORSTER, Georg or Hans, or Vorster
Austrian, 16th century.
Died 6 September 1584, in Vienna.
Painter, engraver, illustrator.
Georg Forster was active in Krumau (Bohemia). Some playing cards painted by him are preserved in the state library in Vienna. He also provided engraved illustrations for a bible printed in Prague in 1570.

FORSTER, George
American, 19th century.
Active 1844-1890.
Painter. Still-lifes (flowers/fruit).
George Forster sometimes added insects, birds or small animals to his still-lifes.
AUCTION RECORDS:
NEW YORK, 10 June 1976, *Still-life* (1866, oil on panel, 14 x 10 3/4 ins / 35.5 x 27.5 cm) USD 800. SAN FRANCISCO, 8 Nov 1984, *Still-life with Fruit and Flowers* (1870, oil on canvas, 27 1/2 x 22 ins / 70 x 56 cm) USD 22,500. NEW YORK, 4 Dec 1987, *Grapes and Currants* (1869, oil on canvas, 8 x 10 ins / 20.6 x 25.7 cm) USD 12,000. NEW YORK, 30 Sept 1988, *Still-life with Grapes and a Glass of Wine* (1878, oil on canvas, 8 1/4 x 10 ins / 21 x 25.5 cm) USD 6,050. NEW YORK, 14 March 1991, *Still-life with Currant Bush, a Mouse, Grasshopper and Ladybird* (1869, oil on canvas, 10 x 8 ins / 25.5 x 20.5 cm) USD 12,100. NEW YORK, 21 May 1991, *Grapes and Peaches*; *Grapes and Plums* (1853, oils on panel, a pair, each 5 3/4 x 7 1/4 ins / 14.6 x 18.5 cm) USD 6,050. NEW YORK, 27 May 1993, *Still-life with Fruit* (1886, oil on canvas, 25 x 30 ins / 63.5 x 76.2 cm) USD 32,200. NEW YORK, 29 Nov 1995, *Still-life with Fruit* (1840, oil on canvas, 8 x 10 ins / 20.3 x 25.4 cm) USD 9,200. NEW YORK, 9 March 1996, *Still-life with Fruit, a Butterfly and a Nest* (1882, oil on canvas, 14 x 17 1/2 ins / 35.5 x 44.5 cm) USD 34,500. NEW YORK, 27 Sept 1996, *Still-life with Chinaware and Cakes* (1872, oil on panel, 14 x 17 ins / 35.5 x 43.2 cm) USD 40,250. NEW YORK, 12 Jan 1999, *Grapes and Plums. Grapes and Peaches* (1853, oil on panel, a pair, 6 x 7 ins / 15

x 18 cm) USD 12,000. NEW YORK, 1 Dec 1999, *Still-life with Fruit* (1862, oil on canvas, 17 x 15 ins / 44 x 37 cm) USD 25,000. DOWNINGTON, 25 Feb 2000, *Portrait of a Mother and Child Carrying a Basket of Fruit* (oil on canvas, 27 x 23 ins / 69 x 58 cm) USD 3,500. EAST DENNIS, 22 Nov 2002, *Still-life with Grapes and Plums in a Bowl* (1866, oil on canvas, 8 x 10 ins / 20 x 25 cm) USD 16,000. NEW YORK, 4 Dec 2003, *Still-life with Fruit, Nest of Eggs and Insects* (1862, oil on canvas, 17 x 15 ins / 44 x 37 cm) USD 40,000. MILFORD, 6 May 2004, *Still-life with Bird's Nest, Figs, Peaches and Grapes* (oil on canvas, 17 x 21 ins / 43 x 53 cm) USD 26,000.

FORSTER, Gottfried
German, 18th century.
Painter. Religious subjects.

Gottfried Forster was a member of the order of St Francis. In 1758 he painted a *Last Supper* for his monastery in Randerath near Gelsenkirchen.

MUSEUMS AND GALLERIES:
RANDERATH (Parish Church): *The Last Supper.*

FORSTER, Gustav
German, 19th century.
Died c. 1887, in Budapest.
Painter. Historical subjects, battles, portraits, animals.

Gustav Forster lived in Vienna until 1875 and then near Budapest. He painted portraits and animals as well as battle scenes such as the *Battle of Solferino* and scenes from the history of Hungary.

AUCTION RECORDS:
MUNICH, 22 June 1993, *Margarethe, Curt, Adolphine and Gerhart von Werne* (1850, oil on canvas, 41¼ x 48½ ins / 105 x 123 cm) DEM 9,200.

FORSTER, Hans
German, 20th century.
Born 8 February 1885.
Draughtsman.

Hans Forster studied at the college of arts and crafts in Hamburg and under Orlik in Berlin. His drawings focus on costumes, customs and landscapes from the area around Hanover. He lived and worked in Hamburg.

MUSEUMS AND GALLERIES:
DRESDEN (Prints Collection) - HAMBURG (Mus. für Hamburgische Geschichte) - HAMBURG (Mus. für Kunst und Gewerbe).

FORSTER, Hans Werner or Werni, or Foster
Swiss, 17th century.
Born in Oberkirch (Baden-Württemberg), Germany.
Glass painter.

Hans Werner Forster worked for Beromünster at the beginning of the 17th century. He is mentioned in 1600.

FORSTER, Heinrich Gottfried, or Forshter or Forschter
Moravian School, 18th century.
Died 23 November 1760, in Brno.
Engraver.

Heinrich Forster's known works include two series of six or seven decorative engravings.

FORSTER, Hieronymus
Austrian, 17th century.
Born to a family originally from Merano.
Sculptor.

FORSTER, Jean
American, 20th century.
Born in the USA.
Draughtsman.

Jean Forster exhibited a *Still-life* (drawing) in Paris at the Salon d'Automne in 1931.

FORSTER, Joachim
German, 16th century.
Born soon after 1500, in Augsburg; died 1579, in Augsburg.
Sculptor, goldsmith.

After studying with the sculptor Jakob Murmann, Joachim Forster lived abroad for many years, often working at the courts of princes and nobles. The collection in Berlin contains a medal (showing portraits of the artist's parents) dated from 1521 to 1527 that is certainly his work.

FORSTER, Johann Jobst, or Vorster
German, 17th century.
Active in Augsburg.
Painter. Playing cards.

The Germanic Museum in Nuremberg holds copies of Johann Jobst Forster's playing cards.

FORSTER, Johann Ludwig Wilhelm
German, 18th - 19th century.
Born 12 May 1769, in Lübeck; died 22 June 1833, in Lübeck.
Painter.

After studying at the Kunstakademi in Copenhagen, Johann Ludwig Forster worked in Lübeck as a genre and portrait painter and design teacher. The Lübeck museum has two oil paintings by him in the form of a frieze portraying the pleasure of wine and hunting in groups of Cupids.

FORSTER, John
Irish, 18th century.
Painter.

John Forster studied in Dublin and Paris. He exhibited landscapes and portraits in pastel and crayon from 1773 to 1780.

FORSTER, John Wycliffe Lowes
Canadian, 19th - 20th century.
Born in Norval.
Painter.

John Wycliffe Lowes Forster was a pupil of Boulanger, Lefebvre, Tony Robert-Fleury, Bouguereau and Carolus-Duran in Paris, and was a member of the Royal Academy of Canada.

FORSTER, Jorg or Georg
German, 16th - 17th century.
Born in Württemberg.
Active in Switzerland c. 1584-1606.
Sculptor (wood).
Lucerne School.

Jorg Forster was a member of the confraternity of St Luke in Lucerne, the town of which he became a citizen and where he worked until about 1606. Among his works are the wooden sculptures on the town hall (c. 1602) and various items in the old church.

FORSTER, Joseph Simon
French, 18th century.
Engraver (burin).

Joseph Simon Forster is mentioned by Nagler. He engraved portraits of saints, including a *St George*, and a portrait of *Pope Benedict XIII.*

FORSTER, Klaus
Swiss, 15th century.
Active c. 1470.
Painter.

This artist is mentioned by Brun.

FORSTER, Lorenz Joseph
German, 18th century.
Painter.

Lorenz Forster painted the ceiling frescoes in the Chapel of Pilgrimage of the Heart of Jesus in Velburg.

FORSTER, Mary (Miss)
later Mrs Lofthouse
British, 19th century.
Born 1853, in Holt (Wiltshire); died 1885, in Halliford.
Active in Trowbridge.
Painter, watercolourist. Landscapes.

The daughter of T.W.B. Forster, Mary Forster was an associate of the Royal Watercolours Society, where she exhibited. She also exhibited with the Royal Academy from 1873 to 1884.

AUCTION RECORDS:
LONDON, 30 May 1985, *Near Holt, Norfolk* (watercolour, 5 1/2 x 11 ins / 14 x 28 cm) GBP 600. GLASGOW, 7 Feb 1989, *View of Ayr, in Scotland, from Newark Hill* (watercolour, 12 x 22 3/4 ins / 30.5 x 58 cm) GBP 770.

FORSTER, Michael
Canadian, 20th century.
Born 4 May 1907, in Calcutta, India; died 4 July 2002, in Porthcurno, Cornwall.
Painter (gouache), draughtsman.

Michael Forster settled in Canada in 1928. He painted a series of works In France after the arrival of the Allies and the Liberation, which are in the National Gallery of Canada, Ontario.

MUSEUMS AND GALLERIES:
OTTAWA (Nat. Gal. of Canada): *Spring in the Bush* (1949, lithograph crayon); *Swamp* (1949, oil and black ink) - OTTAWA (NG. of Canada): *North Shore* (1964, oil).

FORSTER, Richard
German, 20th century.
Born 25 September 1873, in St Petersburg.
Sculptor, medallist. Figures. Busts.

Richard Forster studied at the Städel Institute in Frankfurt am Main. He exhibited at the Winterpalast and the Secession from 1904 and on a number of occasions showed his bronze and marble statuary at the Paris Salon: *Remorse, Christ, Funeral Cortège of Bacchus,* and various busts and bronze and silver medallions.

FORSTER, Robert E.
British, 19th century.
Active in London.
Painter. Portraits.

Robert E. Forster exhibited frequently with the Royal Academy from 1838 to 1855.

FORSTER, Rolf
Swiss, 20th century.
Born 1938, in Dussnang.
Painter.

Rolf Forster studied at the Stuttgart academy between 1959 and 1961, then at the Académie Julian in Paris; between 1961 and 1964 he completed his studies in Spain, Greece and Italy. He has lived in the Swiss canton of Schaffhausen since 1964.

He has been involved in group exhibitions at the All Saints' Museum in Schaffhausen (1968, 1970, 1981, 1985, 1987, 1989); at the Singen Art Centre in Germany (1969-1972); at the Suzanne Bollag Gallery in Zurich (1983-1993); in The Hague (1987-1990); and elsewhere. He has had solo exhibitions since 1965, predominantly in Switzerland (notably from 1983 at the Suzanne Bollag Gallery) and in Germany.

His work is characterised by rigid Geometric Abstraction - 'concrete' in the Van Doesburg sense of the term - and his compositions are built up from straight horizontal and vertical lines and bright colours, dissected by diagonals traced over a grey or black back ground.

FORSTER, Rose
French, 20th century.
Born in Boulogne-Billancourt.
Painter, watercolourist. Flowers.

Rose Forster exhibited in Paris at the Salon des Artistes Français from 1922.

FORSTER, T.B.W.
British, 19th century.
Active in Chippenham.
Painter. Landscapes.

T.B.W. Forster exhibited with the Royal Academy and the Suffolk Street Gallery from 1859 to 1886.

FORSTER, Thomas
British, 18th century.
Miniaturist. Portraits. Miniatures.

Thomas Forster specialised in miniatures painted on parchment.

MUSEUMS AND GALLERIES:
LONDON (British Mus.): *Portrait of the Maritime Commissioner, George St Lo; Portrait of an Unknown Subject; Portrait of Margaret Harcourt* - LONDON (Victoria and Albert Mus.): *Portrait of the Duke of Marlborough; Portrait of Sarah Jennings.*

AUCTION RECORDS:
NEW YORK, 19 Jan 1982, *Portrait of John Blackstone* (1707, pencil, 4 1/2 x 3 1/2 ins / 11.7 x 8.8 cm) USD 1,100. LONDON, 24 May 2000, *James Denew in a Cloak and Cravat* (1690, graphite on vellum, oval miniature, h. 4 ins / 11 cm) GBP 1,800. LONDON, 24 May 2000, *Young Boy in Coat and White Cravat* (1707, graphite on vellum, oval miniature, h. 4 ins / 11 cm) GBP 3,200. LONDON, 6 March 2001, *Gentleman in Full Wig, Lace Jabot and Robes* (c. 1695, graphite, oval miniature, h. 4 ins / 9 cm) GBP 1,100. LONDON, 9 April 2001, *Mrs Thomas Hay in Loose Fitting Robes* (graphite, oval miniature, h. 4 ins / 10 cm) GBP 1,100. LONDON, 10 April 2002, *Charles, 2nd Earl of Berkeley* (1699, graphite, oval miniature, h. 4 ins / 9 cm) GBP 2,400. LEYBURN, 21 April 2004, *Portrait of a Bewigged Gentleman, reputed to be Richard Steele* (1700, oval miniature, 4 x 3 ins / 10 x 8 cm) GBP 2,800.

FORSTER, William C.
Irish, 19th - 20th century.
Born in Dublin; died 1911, in Canada.
Painter, engraver, draughtsman.

In 1844, 1845 and 1846, William Forster received prizes for his hand-engraved stones. He moved to Canada in 1872. Forster also produced chromolithographs such as *Dogs,* copied after Armstrong and a number of views taken from his own drawings.

FORSTERLING, Otto
German, 19th century.
Born 18 June 1843, in Berlin.
Painter, engraver. Religious subjects, mythological subjects, landscapes with figures, landscapes.

Forsterling was a pupil at the Berlin academy and of Julius Schrader. From 1867 he travelled in Germany, Austria and Italy. He specialised in painting landscapes with mythological and biblical scenes. From 1890 he settled in Leipzig. He exhibited in Dresden and in Berlin.

FORSTL, Christian
German, 17th century.
Active in Passau.
Sculptor.

In 1597 Forstl built a fountain on the Cathedral Square featuring the coats of arms of the Cathedral canons.

FORSTMAN, Gregorio. See **FOSMAN**

FORSTMOSER, Alois
Austrian, 19th century.
Born 10 May 1866, in Uttendorf; died 3 November 1905, in Uttendorf.
Painter, illustrator.

Alois Forstmoser was a pupil of Defregger in Munich and worked as an illustrator for the Francisco Carolinum Museum in Linz and for the collection, in several volumes, of works by Austrian poets. His most important work was his *Portrait by Himself* completed shortly before his death.
MUSEUMS AND GALLERIES:
LINZ: drawings.

FORSTNER, Leopold
Austrian, 20th century.
Born 2 November 1878, in Bad Leonfelden; died 1936.
Painter (glass), mosaicist, draughtsman.
Forstner studied at the Akademie für Angewandte Kunst in Vienna and at the Akademie der Bildenden Künste in Vienna. Before embarking on a professional career in Vienna, he went on study trips to Germany, Holland, Belgium and (most importantly) Italy. He focused almost exclusively on stained glass and mosaics. In 1908 he founded the Vienna Mosaic Studios.

His most important works include his mosaics for the high altar in the *Am Steinhof* church in Vienna, the apse of Ebelsberg church in Upper Austria, and the Hotel Wiesler in Graz.
AUCTION RECORDS:
VIENNA, 16 Nov 1982, *Poster Project for Austrian Lloyd/Trieste Lines* (mixed media, 40$1/2$ x 29$1/4$ ins / 103 x 74 cm) ATS 20,000. VIENNA, 11 June 2002, *Man Taking a Walk* (watercolour and Indian ink, 18 x 11 ins / 45 x 28 cm) EUR 3,000.

FORSTNER, S
German, 19th century.
Active in Laufen an der Salzach (Bavaria) c. 1850.
Painter.
One painting signed by Forstner is known: *View of Laufen*.

FORSYTH, Constance
American, 20th century.
Born 18 August 1903, in Indianapolis (Indiana); died 22 January 1987, in Austin (Texas).
Painter, engraver, etcher.
Constance Forsyth was a pupil of William Forsyth and of Harding and Carter, and was a member of the Indianapolis Art Association. She was awarded the Hoosier Prize at the Chicago salon in 1928.

FORSYTH, James
British, 19th - 20th century.
Born 1826; died 1910, in London.
Sculptor.
James Forsyth exhibited at the Royal Academy in London from 1864 to 1889.
MUSEUMS AND GALLERIES:
SYDNEY: *Andromeda*.

FORSYTH, James Nesfield
British, 19th - 20th century.
Sculptor.
James Nesfield Forsyth was the son of James Forsyth. From 1885, he frequently exhibited at the Royal Academy in London.

FORSYTH, Lilian
British, 20th century.
Born in Hornsey.
Painter, watercolourist.
Lilian Forsyth exhibited a watercolour entitled *Sweet Peas* at the Salon des Artistes Français in Paris in 1938.

FORSYTH, William
American, 20th century.
Born 1854, in Hamilton (Ohio); died 1935.
Painter.
William Forsyth was a pupil at the Royal Academy, Munich, and a member of the American Watercolor Society. He was awarded a medal in Munich in 1885, a silver (watercolour) and a bronze (painting) at the St Louis Exhibition of 1904, and won the Holcomb Prize in 1904.
AUCTION RECORDS:
NEW YORK, 24 Jan 1990, *Woman Walking in a Park* (1885, watercolour and gouache/card, 11 x 12$1/2$ ins / 28.2 x 32 cm) USD 2,860.

FORSYTHE, Victor Clyde Elyre
American, 20th century.
Born 24 August 1885, in Orange (California); died 1962.
Painter.
Victor Clyde Elyre Forsythe was a pupil of L.E. Garden Macleod and F.V. Du Mond, and was a member of the Salmagundi Club and the California Art Club. He was awarded a bronze medal by the Society of Painters of the West in 1927.
AUCTION RECORDS:
NEW YORK, 21 Nov 1980, *The Wolf Attack* (1920, oil on canvas, 24$1/4$ x 34$1/4$ ins / 61.5 x 86.7 cm) USD 700. NEW YORK, 28 May 1987, *Old Prospector with Donkeys* (1928, oil on canvas, 30 x 40 ins / 76.2 x 101.6 cm) USD 5,000. NEW YORK, 24 June 1988, *Silence* (oil/synthetic resin, 11$3/4$ x 16$3/4$ ins / 30 x 42.5 cm) USD 1,210. LOS ANGELES, 29 April 1999, *Desolation Canyon, Death Valley* (1950, oil on canvas, 25 x 34 ins / 63 x 86 cm) USD 7,500. LOS ANGELES, 9 Dec 1999, *Desert Wanderers* (oil on canvas, 30 x 42 ins / 77 x 107 cm) USD 6,000. PASADENA, 15 Feb 2000, *Landscape* (oil on canvasboard, 12 x 16 ins / 30 x 41 cm) USD 1,600. LOS ANGELES, 30 Oct 2000, *Desert Landscape* (oil on canvas on board, 5 x 6 ins / 13 x 15 cm) USD 1,500. MAINE, 26 Jan 2001, *The Thorn* (1924, oil on canvas) USD 7,400. LOS ANGELES, 2 May 2001, *Golden Hills* (1953, oil on canvas, 20 x 28 ins / 51 x 71 cm) USD 4,000. CHEYENNE, 15 March 2002, *Smoke Trees* (oil on canvas on board, 12 x 16 ins / 30 x 41 cm) USD 1,500. PASADENA, 11 June 2002, *Blue Mountain, South of Victorville* (oil on canvasboard, 12 x 16 ins / 30 x 41 cm) USD 2,000. PASADENA, 17 June 2003, *Atmospheric Landscape* (oil on board, 12 x 16 ins / 30 x 41 cm) USD 1,900. PASADENA, 15 June 2004, *Panoramic Landscape* (1949, oil on masonite, 24 x 34 ins / 61 x 86 cm) USD 3,250.

FORT, Elisabeth
French, 20th century.
Born 1815.
Painter. Landscapes.

FORT, François
French, 20th century.
Born 22 October 1942, in Paris.
Painter.
François Fort studied at the École Nationale des Beaux-Arts de Paris, and has displayed his work in various exhibitions since 1966. His painting style is abstract.

FORT, Léon
French, 19th - 20th century.
Born 1870, in L'Isle-Adam; died 1965, in L'Isle-Adam.
Painter. Landscapes. Murals.
The Musée Senlecq at L'Isle-Adam held a retrospective exhibition of the work of Léon Fort in 1970. He collaborated on various decorative panels commissioned by the Ville de Paris, some of which were destined for the Collège de France and the Palais de Justice.

FORT, Louis Pierre Gustave
French, 19th century.
Born in Bordeaux.
Sculptor.
Made his Salon début in 1868.

FORT, Martha
American, 19th - 20th century.
Born in the second half of the 19th century, in the USA.
Draughtswoman.

Martha Fort exhibited at the Salon des Artistes Français in 1914.

FORT, Martin
French, 16th century.
Active in Paris in 1585.
Painter.

FORT, Siméon Jean Antoine
French, 19th century.
Born 28 August 1793, in Valence; died 24 December 1861, in Paris.
Painter, watercolourist, draughtsman. History painting, landscapes.

A gifted artist who studied under Christian Brune, Siméon Fort was awarded a silver medal in 1831 and a gold in 1836; he was also made a member of the Légion d'Honneur on 4 June 1842. Fort exhibited at the Salon from 1824 to 1847.

Siméon Fort was commissioned by the state to record the principal events of the Revolution and the Empire, to be used as decorative elements for Versailles. To this end, he travelled extensively in Germany, Italy, Spain and Belgium, devoting ten years of his life to complete the project with which he had been entrusted.

Museums and Galleries:

Bourges: *Swiss Lake* - Rouen: *Horse in Harness; Horse; Cavalry Charge; Horsemen; Court Attire* - Valence: *Sunset near Meaux* - Versailles: *View of the Château de St-Cloud; View of Compiègne Castle; View of the Palais-Royal; View of Pau Castle; View of the Château d'Eu; View of Chateau de Randau; Battle of Guenzburg; Surrender of Memmingen; Battle of Wagram, Day One; Battle of Wagram, Day Two; French Army Arriving at the Gates of Constantina; Second Attack on Constantina; General View of the Biban Valleys or Iron Gates; Battle of Lemdiyya; Siege of Antwerp; Oran; Tlemcen, Algeria; First Assault on Constantina; Battle of Lig; Army Arriving at Mascara; Plan of the Siege of Antwerp; View of Constantina Province as far as Algiers; View of Smalah d'Abdel-Kader; Overview of the Battle of Isly; Siege of Namur; Siege of Toulon; View from Genoa to Nice seen from the Appennines across the Alpes Maritimes; View of Part of Italy; Siege of Mantua; Battle of Abu Qir; Siege of Gdansk (Danzig), 12 March 1807; Siege of Tarragona, 29 June 1811; Plan of the Siege of Antwerp* (1832); *French Army Marching on Mascara in 1835; Battle of Saalfeld; Battle of Jena; Battle of Thamm; Battle of Ebersberg; Surrender of Glogau; Battle of Eylau; Battle of Wertingen; French Army Entering Munich; Capture of Braunau; Crossing the Tramm at Lambach; Battle of Elchingen; Battle of Hollabrunn; Assault and Capture of Asturica Augusta (Astorga); Battle of Krasnoye; Crossing the Suna at Dietikov; Crossing the Inn; Capture of Königsberg; Siege of Grandeutz; Siege of the Imperial Fortress, Algiers; Battle of Téniah; Taking of Mons; Battle of Heilsberg; Battle of Friedland; Battle of Steyer; Battle of Armstetten; French Army Advancing on Vienna through the Molk Pass; Surrender of Erfurt; French Army Entering Leipzig; Battle of Valjonau and Villeneuve-le-Comte; Battle of Montereau; Battle of Berry-au-Bac; Battle of Eylau; Capture of Dirschau; Battle of Champaubert; Battle of Montmirail; Battle of Eckmühl; Siege of Gdansk (Danzig); Crossing the Vistula at Thorn; Battle of Chateau-Thierry; Battle of Mormant; French Army Entering Poznan; Capitulation of Magdeburg; Battle of Austerlitz; Battle of Durnstein; Crossing the Danube at Vienna; Battle of Wesen; Battle of Zurich; Crossing the Lunth at Bilten; Battle of Noeffels Bridge; Battle of Anzin near Valenciennes; Battle of Glaris; Battle of Brienne.*

Auction records:

Paris, 1868, *Landscape and River at Sunset,* FRF 90. Paris, 22-23 Feb 1929, *Torrent* (watercolour) FRF 400. Paris, 4 Dec 1931, *Staging Post in the Forest of Eu* (1843) FRF 4,100; *House in Twickenham,* FRF 2,800. Paris, 13 June 1947, *Landscapes* (two sepia washes) FRF 1,050. Lille, 11 Dec 1983, *Children Playing in Castle Grounds* (oil on canvas, 20 x 34¼ ins / 51 x 87 cm) FRF 8,000. Rheims, 24 Oct 1994, *Italian Scene* (oil on canvas/panel, 11 x 14¼ ins / 28 x 36 cm) FRF 7,500. Monaco, 14-15 Dec 1996, *Château de Randan, Puy-de-Dome* (1843, oil on canvas, 17¾ x 12 ins / 45 x 30.5 cm) FRF 84,240. Paris, 19 April 2002, *Old Tower in Countryside* (1839, oil on canvas, 14 x 20 ins / 35 x 51 cm) EUR 1,800. Paris, 17 Dec 2003, *Mediterranean Landscape with Setting Sun* (oil on canvas, 9 x 13 ins / 23 x 34 cm) EUR 1,500.

FORT, Théodore
French, 19th century.
Born c. 1810.
Painter, watercolourist. Military subjects.

Son of the painter Simon Fort, he made his Salon début in 1842. He painted a large number of watercolours, mainly of military subjects where horses play an important role.

Museums and Galleries:

Louviers: *Study of Horses* - Mulhouse: *Carriage of the Cardinal* - Pontoise: *Study of Horses* (two watercolours).

Auction records:

Bordeaux, 1889, *Horse and Groom in Louis XV Attire* (watercolour) FRF 40. Paris, 27 Feb 1929, *Hussars at the Gallop* (watercolour) FRF 170. Paris, 19 June 1933, *Chasseur Pursuing an Arab Horseman* (watercolour) FRF 260. Paris, 9 Nov 1938, *Coaches,* FRF 240. Paris, 4 Jan 1945, *Landscape* (watercolour) FRF 2,800; *Landscape* (gouache) FRF 3,000. Paris, July 1946, *Workhorses* (watercolour) FRF 2,800; *Heavy Cart* (watercolour) FRF 2,000. Paris, 2 Dec 1946, *Cavalrymen, Field Artillerymen and Lancers* (six watercolours) FRF 6,250. Nice, 27 May 1970, *Promenade in a Barouche* (oil on canvas, 17¾ x 23½ ins / 45 x 60 cm) FRF 500. Versailles, 4 Oct 1981, *Coachman and Team* (watercolour, 11 x 18¼ ins / 27 x 46.5 cm) FRF 2,400. Paris, 24 Oct 1983, *Stabled Horse, Horses and Ostler* (oil on canvas, pair, 6¼ x 9 ins / 16 x 23 cm) FRF 17,000. Paris, 23 June 1988, *Drays* (oil on paper/canvas, 32¼ x 39¾ ins / 82 x 101 cm) FRF 8,000. Rheims, 20 June 1993, *Stabled Horses* (oil on canvas, 19¾ x 24 ins / 50 x 61 cm) FRF 13,500. Lyons, 18 May 1994, *Stable Lad and Two Horses at the Manger; Groom Leading Two Horses Back to the Stables* (oil on canvas, a pair, each 5¼ x 8½ ins / 13.5 x 21.5 cm) FRF 10,500. Milan, 28 March 2001, *Battle Scenes* (watercolour, 6 x 9 ins / 14 x 23 cm) ITL 3,200,000. Fontainebleau, 7 Dec 2003, *At the Blacksmith's* (oil on canvas, 14 x 26 ins / 35 x 65 cm) EUR 2,000.

FORT-BRAS, Antoine. See **FORBERA Antonio**

FORT-SIMÉON, Élisabeth
Maiden name: Collin
French, 19th century.
Born in Paris.
Painter, watercolourist. Landscapes.

Pupil of Rémond and wife of the painter Siméon Fort; exhibited at the Salon in her maiden name from 1835 to 1848 and in her married name from 1851 to 1865. Among her accomplished landscape work, mention may be made of: *Mahogany Sawmill at Montataire, Watermill at Montataire, View of Cramoisi, View of Château-Gaillard, View of Port Morin, Andelys, Birse Waterfall at Moutiers, Near Fribourg, Factory Building at Serrières on the Lake of Neuchâtel.*

Museums and Galleries:

Dieppe: landscape - Montpellier: *Mountain Gorge; View of Lake Como.*

Auction records:
Paris, 10 April 1924, *Torrent* (watercolour) FRF 250. Bern, 6 May 1981, *Landscape with Château* (oil on canvas, 7 1/2 x 11 ins / 19 x 28 cm) CHF 3,000.

FORTAN, Joseph Lambert
French, 18th century.
Active in Paris.
Sculptor.

FORTAN, Nicolas
French, 18th century.
Active in Paris in 1745.
Painter, sculptor.

FORTAN, Toussaint
French, 17th century.
Active in Paris.
Painter.
Toussaint Fortan was admitted to the Guild of St Luke in Paris in 1663.

FORTANER DE USESQUE. See **USESQUE**

FORTE, Angelo
Italian, 16th century.
Active in Treviso (Venezia).
Painter.
In 1560, Angelo Forte painted an altarpiece for the church of S Niccolo in Treviso.

FORTE, Gaetano
Italian, 19th century.
Born 1790, in Salerno (Campania); died 1871, in Naples.
Painter, architect.
Two of Gaetano Forte's portraits appeared in the Florence portrait exhibition of 1911.

FORTE, Luca or Lucas
Italian, 17th century.
Born between 1600 and 1605, in Naples; died c. 1670.
Active 1640-1670.
Painter. Landscapes, still-lifes (flowers/fruit).
Museums and Galleries:
Naples: *Still-life with Fruit* (two works).
Auction records:
London, 3 Dec 1969, *Still-life with Fruit,* GBP 2,000. Paris, 25 June 1973, *Village in the Valley,* FRF 2,000. London, 14 April 1978, *Still-life with Fruit* (oil on canvas, 29 x 38 1/2 ins / 73.7 x 97.8 cm) GBP 4,800. Milan, 3 Nov 1982, *Still-life with a Garland of Flowers* (oil on canvas, 67 x 48 ins / 170 x 122 cm) ITL 45,000,000. London, 12 Dec 1984, *Still-life with Grapes* (metal, 12 1/4 x 9 3/4 ins / 31 x 25 cm) GBP 40,000. Milan, 4 April 1989, *Still-life with Grapes and Peaches; Still-life with Grapes and Apples* (oil on canvas, a pair, each 13 1/2 x 17 ins / 34 x 43 cm) ITL 32,000,000. Amsterdam, 20 June 1989, *Still-life with a Vine Stock in a Pot, an Apple, a Fig and a Pomegranate* (oil/copper, 12 x 10 1/4 ins / 30.7 x 25.8 cm) NLG 184,000. New York, 11 Jan 1990, *Pomegranates and Melon on a Stone Entablature* (oil on canvas, 19 1/4 x 28 ins / 49 x 71 cm) USD 88,000. Rome, 19 Nov 1991, *Figs, Plums and Strawberries* (oil on canvas, 12 1/2 x 22 3/4 ins / 32 x 58 cm) ITL 40,000,000. Paris, 17 June 1997, *Still-life with Grapes, Apples, Figs and Flowers* (canvas, a pair, 25 1/2 x 30 3/4 ins / 65 x 78 cm) FRF 420,000. New York, 30 Jan 1998, *Still-life with Three Apples, Bunches of Grapes and a Dragonfly on an Entablature* (oil on canvas, 6 1/4 x 8 ins / 15.6 x 20.6 cm) USD 200,500. London, 11 July 2002, *Still-life with Fisherman* (oil on canvas, 57 x 38 ins / 145 x 96 cm) GBP 18,000.

FORTE, Tommaso
Italian, 17th century.
Sculptor (wood).
Tommaso Forte was involved in carving stalls in the church of Bagnoli Irpino (Calabria) in 1652.

FORTE, Vicente
Argentinian, 20th century.
Born 1912, in Lanus (Buenos Aires).
Painter.
Vicente Forte travelled in Spain, Portugal and France. From 1945 onwards he exhibited at numerous art exhibitions in Argentina and other countries in the West, including the USA. His work appeared in the *150 Years of Argentinian Art* exhibition in 1961. He was awarded first prize at the national exhibition in 1952 as well as other official honours. His work is displayed in Buenos Aires and in provincial museums.
Museums and Galleries:
Buenos Aires: collection of works - San Francisco (AI).
Auction records:
New York, 8 May 1981, *Boats* (1953, oil on canvas, 17 3/4 x 21 3/4 ins / 45.2 x 55.2 cm) USD 3,750. New York, 21 May 1986, *Still-life with Lamp* (1961, oil on canvas, 71 x 23 ins / 180.3 x 58.7 cm) USD 1,600. New York, 17 May 1989, *Old Instrument* (1968, oil on canvas, 27 1/2 x 39 1/4 ins / 70 x 100 cm) USD 4,620. Montevideo, 14 June 1999, *Ships* (oil on canvas, 20 x 28 ins / 51 x 71 cm) USD 2,400. Buenos Aires, 1 June 2004, *Bird and Fruit* (oil on canvas, 24 x 47 ins / 60 x 120 cm) USD 9,000. Buenos Aires, 5 Oct 2004, *Blue Boat* (1973, oil on canvas, 22 x 39 ins / 55 x 100 cm) USD 11,000.

FORTEA, José
Spanish, 18th century.
Born c. 1700; died in 1751, in Valencia.
Active in Aragon.
Painter, engraver.
José Fortea was a pupil of Apolinario Larraga of Valencia.

FORTES, Victor
Portuguese, 20th century.
Born 1943, in Madeira.
Engraver.
Victor Fortes was invited to exhibit at the São Paulo Biennale and the Paris Biennale.

FORTESCUE, William B.
British, 19th century.
Died 1924.
Painter. Landscapes, seascapes, architectural views, architectural interiors.
William Blackstone Fortescue was active at St Ives in Cornwall. He exhibited in London from 1880, and submitted landscapes and interiors to the Royal Academy from 1887.
Auction records:
London, 11 Nov 1981, *Good Day's Catch* (oil on canvas, 34 x 50 ins / 86.5 x 127 cm) GBP 550. London, 9 March 1984, *Porthminster Beach in the Bathing Season* (1902, oil on canvas, 14 x 18 ins / 35.5 x 45.7 cm) GBP 850. London, 12 June 1987, *Village Gossip* (oil on canvas, 24 x 18 ins / 61 x 45.7 cm) GBP 14,000. Montreal, 23-24 Nov 1993, *Courtyard of S Gregorio, Venice* (oil on canvas, 26 3/4 x 19 1/2 ins / 68 x 49.5 cm) CAD 1,800. London, 4 Nov 1994, *Courtyard of S Gregorio, Venice* (oil on canvas, 26 3/4 x 19 1/2 ins / 68 x 49.5 cm) GBP 1,725. Penzance, 14 Oct 1999, *Feeding Time, Cottage Interior* (oil on canvas, 14 x 18 ins / 36 x 46 cm) GBP 3,300. Newmarket, 17 Nov 1999, *Across Downs at Trelyon. Higher Tregenna St Ives* (oil on canvas, a pair, 18 x 14 ins / 46 x 36 cm) GBP 3,300. London, 29 June 2000, *Watering Stop* (oil on canvas, 18 x 14 ins / 46 x 35 cm) GBP 2,200. Taunton, 30 Nov 2000, *Old Quarry* (oil on canvas, 36 x 28 ins / 91 x 71 cm) GBP 2,400. London, 8 March 2001, *Mending the Nets. Collecting Water* (oil on canvas, a pair, 12 x 9 ins / 30 x 23 cm) GBP 7,500. Chester, 7 Nov 2001, *Gleaners in a Field before a Coastal Landscape* (oil on canvas, 18 x 27 ins / 46 x 69 cm) GBP 4,000. Penzance, 26 Sept 2002, *Cornish Pasty* (oil on canvas, 36 x 46 ins / 91 x 117 cm) GBP 9,500. Toronto, 3 Dec 2002, *Young Angler* (oil on canvas, 8 x 12 ins / 21 x 30 cm) CAD 19,000. Penzance, 19 June 2003, *Fetching Water, Back Lane Newlyn*

(oil on canvas) GBP 8,200. PENZANCE, 2 Oct 2003, *Mending Nets, Young Woman in a Newlyn Cottage Doorway* (oil on canvas, 11 x 8 ins / 29 x 21 cm) GBP 9,400. LONDON, 4 March 2004, *Noonday Shade* (oil on canvas, 17 x 14 ins / 43 x 35 cm) GBP 1,500. LONDON, 4 March 2004, *Fisherman's Dwelling* (oil on canvas, 18 x 14 ins / 46 x 36 cm) GBP 4,000.

FORTESCUE-BRICKDALE, Eleanor

British, 19th - 20th century.
Born 1871; died 1945.
Painter, watercolourist, illustrator, designer. Genre scenes.

Fortescue-Brickdale studied at the Crystal Palace School of Art, at the Royal Academy Schools and under the direction of Byam Shaw. She was a member of the Royal Society of Painters in Watercolours of London and exhibited at the Royal Academy in London from 1896. She won a prize for best furniture decoration and designed stained glass windows for Bristol Cathedral. She produced several illustrations for books of old English songs, including the *Golden Treasury of the Best Songs and Lyrical Poetry in the English Language* by Palgrave in 1925, and also *Ivanhoe* by Walter Scott, and *Idylls of the King* by Tennyson. Her decorative style stems from the final stages of the Pre-Raphaelite movement.

E.F BRICKDALE

BIBLIOGRAPHY:

Osterwalder, Marcus (ed.), *Dictionnaire des illustrateurs (1800-1914)*, Éd. Hubschmid & Bouret, Paris, 1983.

MUSEUMS AND GALLERIES:

BRISTOL (City Mus. & AG): *The Lover's World; Labour and the Broken Heart.*

AUCTION RECORDS:

LONDON, 26 April 1909, *Little Footman*, GBP 157. LONDON, 23 April 1923, *Gareth and Lynette*, GBP 3. LONDON, 25 Nov 1927, *Scandal* (drawing) GBP 16. LONDON, 11 June 1934, *Adoration of the Kings*, GBP 6. LONDON, 14 Feb 1978, *Five Wise Virgins* (1901, watercolour heightened with gouache, 4 3/4 x 12 ins / 12 x 30.5 cm) GBP 1,200. LONDON, 25 Sept 1979, *Fairyland* (watercolour, 20 3/4 x 14 1/4 ins / 53 x 36 cm) GBP 1,500. LONDON, 27 Oct 1983, *But When the Heart Suffers a Blow* (watercolour, 18 x 11 ins / 46 x 28 cm) GBP 1,700. LONDON, 5 June 1984, *Gareth and Lynette* (watercolour, 14 x 11 1/4 ins / 35.5 x 28.5 cm) GBP 2,800. LONDON, 30 May 1985, *O Love! Has She Done This to Thee?* (watercolour/pencil outlines, 14 1/4 x 9 1/4 ins / 36.5 x 23.5 cm) GBP 3,200. LONDON, 31 Oct 1986, *Picking Primroses* (1890, oil on canvas, 36 1/4 x 48 1/4 ins / 92 x 122.5 cm) GBP 7,000. LONDON, 16 Dec 1986, *Guardian Angel, Memorial Dedicated to the Honourable Charles Stewart Rolls* (1910, watercolour and pencil/mounted paper/canvas, 30 x 19 1/2 ins / 76.2 x 49.5 cm) GBP 6,500. LONDON, 26 Jan 1987, *Annunciation* (watercolour heightened with gouache, 14 1/2 x 10 1/4 ins / 37 x 26 cm) GBP 1,500. LONDON, 25 Jan 1988, *Poet* (1904, watercolour, 18 3/4 x 11 ins / 47.5 x 28 cm) GBP 1,100. NEW YORK, 24 May 1988, *Fair Enid, Illustration for Idylls of the King* (watercolour and gouache/paper, 19 3/4 x 10 1/2 ins / 50.2 x 26.6 cm) USD 13,200. LONDON, 25 Jan 1989, *The Wise and Foolish Virgins* (watercolour, 15 x 40 ins / 38 x 101.5 cm) GBP 9,900. LONDON, 30 Jan 1991, *Tournament* (watercolour and gouache, 26 1/2 x 54 1/2 ins / 67.5 x 138.5 cm) GBP 2,970. LONDON, 12 June 1992, *Magic Nature* (watercolour, 21 1/4 x 14 ins / 54 x 35.5 cm) GBP 5,500. LONDON, 13 Nov 1992, *St Michael and a Prisoner* (1904, coloured chalks, 32 1/2 x 17 1/2 ins / 82.6 x 44.5 cm) GBP 1,100. LONDON, 8-9 June 1993, *Surprise Guest* (oil on canvas, 35 x 50 ins / 89 x 127 cm) GBP 51,000. NEW YORK, 12 Oct 1994, *Romance* (watercolour and gouache, 18 x 25 ins / 45.7 x 63.5 cm) USD 17,250. LONDON, 6 Nov 1995, *Spring and Autumn* (watercolour and gouache/paper, diam. 24 3/4 ins / 63 cm) GBP 10, 120. LONDON, 5 June 1996, *Haro on Cupid* (watercolour, 15 3/4 ins / 40 cm, 2 x 12 1/4 ins/5 x 31 cm) GBP 6,900. LONDON, 8 Nov 1996, *Love and its Imitations* (oil on canvas) GBP 95,000. LONDON, 8 Nov 1996, *Love and its Simulations* (pencil and watercolour with scratches/paper/linen, 26 x 52 1/4 ins / 66 x 133 cm) GBP 85,000. LONDON, 12 March 1997, *For, What are the Voices of Birds...* (watercolour heightened with gouache, 13 1/4 x 9 ins / 33.5 x 23 cm) GBP 5,280. LONDON, 3 June 1999, *Mary for All Generations* (oil on canvas, 30 x 76 ins / 76 x 193 cm) GBP 15,000. LONDON, 8 June 1999, *Rosamond* (oil on canvas, 48 x 29 ins / 122 x 74 cm) GBP 85,000. LONDON, 6 June 2001, *Today for Me* (1901, watercolour heightened with gouache over pencil, 20 x 14 ins / 51 x 35 cm) GBP 5,000. LONDON, 6 June 2001, *Gift Better Than Rubies* (1899, watercolour heightened with gouache, 13 x 19 ins / 34 x 47 cm) GBP 12,000. LONDON, 17 July 2002, *Illusions Burial* (watercolour on canvas, 30 x 14 ins / 76 x 35 cm) GBP 2,800. LONDON, 17 July 2002, *Today for Me* (1901, watercolour heightened with gouache, 20 x 14 ins / 51 x 35 cm) GBP 3,200. LONDON, 25 Nov 2004, *The Rose* (watercolour over pencil heightened with gouache, 14 x 10 ins / 36 x 26 cm) GBP 6,500.

FORTESS, Karl Eugene

American, 20th century.
Born 1907; died 1993.
Painter. Genre scenes.
Woodstock Artists' Colony.

Karl Eugene Fortess worked in Woodstock in the 1930s when the American government was subsidising art, where he painted examples of 'American scenes'.

AUCTION RECORDS:

NEW YORK, 28 Nov 1995, *Pipeline Hill* (oil on canvas, 22 x 32 ins / 55.8 x 81.3 cm) USD 863.

FORTEZA, Rafa

Spanish, 20th - 21st century.
Born 18 August 1955, in Palma (Majorca).
Painter (mixed media), engraver.

Rafa Forteza forms part of the same generation of post-Franco artists as Barceló and Sicilia, which is well known on the international scene. His work seems to be an intimist quest for origins expressed through a re-composition of space into filamentous or even scriptural disorder with hints of the molecular suggested through solids and voids.

He has exhibited in solo exhibitions, including: in 1982 and 1985, at the 4 Gats gallery in Palma de Mallorca; in 1987, at the Angel Romero gallery, Madrid; in 1989 and 1992, at the Ferran Cano gallery, Barcelona; in 1991, at the Laurens A. Daane gallery, Amsterdam, and at the Musée d'Art Moderne, Collioure; in 1994, at the Salon Découvertes, Paris, and a solo exhibition hosted by the Oniris gallery, Rennes.

Forteza has taken part in group exhibitions, including: in 1982, the 4th Barcelona Biennale; in 1984, *Thirteen Neo-Figurative Painters in Majorca* at Sa Llotja, Palma de Mallorca; in 1985, Arco '85, Madrid; in 1987, at the Tossan-Tossan Gallery, New York, and *Seven Majorcan Artists* at the Palau Moja, Barcelona; in 1988, at the Sebastià Petit gallery, Lleida; in 1989, at the Mainz museum, Frankfurt; and, in 1992, at the engraving Biennale, Sarcelles. Forteza was a finalist at the 4th Barcelona Biennale in 1982.

BIBLIOGRAPHY:

Matamoros, Joséphine, *Rafa Forteza*, exhibition catalogue, Musée d'Art moderne, Colioure, 1991.

FORTEZZA

Italian, 16th century.
Born c. 1530; died c. 14 May 1596.
Active in Sebenico (now Sibenik, Croatia).
Illuminator, goldsmith.

In 1578 Fortezza also worked on the restoration of paintings.

FORTI, Carlo Antonio
Italian, 17th - 18th century.
Born 1657, in Parma; died 1732.
Active in Modena.
Engraver (etching).
Carlo Antonio Forti made etchings of religious allegories.

FORTI, Ettore or (in error) Eduardo
Italian, 19th century.
Painter. History painting, genre scenes.
Ettore Forti was active in Rome. It is surprising that there is so little information about him, given that his name appears in auction records from as far back as the early 19th century, and that his work was so highly specialised (comprising anecdotal paintings illustrating life in ancient Rome).

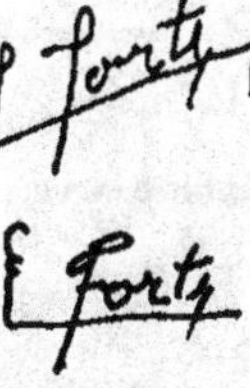

MUSEUMS AND GALLERIES:
ALBANY: *Street Scene in Pompeii.*
AUCTION RECORDS:
NEW YORK, April 1903, *Singers in Pompeii,* USD 475. NEW YORK, 12 Nov 1908, *Ablutions in Pompeii,* USD 95. LONDON, 16 Dec 1935, *Fountain of Diana,* GBP 19. PARIS, 25 May 1951, *Street in Pompeii,* FRF 35,000. LOS ANGELES, 28 Feb 1972, *Roman Chariot Race,* USD 3,600. LOS ANGELES, 9 April 1973, *Romans on a Terrace in Pompeii,* USD 3,250. NEW YORK, 7 Oct 1977, *Pottery Seller* (oil on canvas, 19 1/2 x 31 ins / 49.5 x 79 cm) USD 4,000. NEW YORK, 12 May 1978, *Gossip* (oil on canvas, 19 1/2 x 30 3/4 ins / 49.5 x 78 cm) USD 4,000. ROME, 1 Dec 1982, *Two Women on a Couch* (oil on panel, 9 x 16 ins / 22 x 40.5 cm) ITL 3,600,000. LONDON, 28 Nov 1984, *Chariot Race* (oil on canvas, 23 1/2 x 39 1/4 ins / 59.5 x 100 cm) GBP 2,000. NEW YORK, 23 May 1985, *Merchants of Pompeii* (oil on canvas, 21 1/2 x 34 ins / 54.5 x 85.5 cm) USD 7,500. STOCKHOLM, 21 Oct 1987, *Interior of a Roman Palace* (oil on canvas, 24 1/2 x 39 1/4 ins / 62 x 100 cm) SEK 170,000. NEW YORK, 25 Feb 1988, *Figures on a Veranda with Vesuvius in the Background* (oil on canvas, 23 3/4 x 39 1/2 ins / 60.3 x 100.3 cm) USD 12,100. NEW YORK, 23 Feb 1989, *Roman Empress Boarding a Boat* (oil on canvas, 31 1/2 x 55 ins / 80 x 139.7 cm) USD 49,500. NEW YORK, 24 May 1989, *Carpet Seller* (oil on canvas, 20 3/4 x 33 ins / 52.7 x 83.8 cm) USD 19,800. NEW YORK, 24 Oct 1989, *Young Pompeian Woman with a Swan* (oil on canvas, 39 1/2 x 24 ins / 100.3 x 61 cm) USD 14,300. NEW YORK, 28 Feb 1990, *Hadrian's Cortege Leaving the Villa Tivoli* (oil on canvas, 31 1/2 x 55 1/4 ins / 80 x 140.5 cm) USD 22,000. MONACO, 21 April 1990, *Spring Celebration* (oil on canvas, 36 1/4 x 56 1/4 ins / 92 x 143 cm) FRF 255,300. ROME, 10 Dec 1991, *Courtyard of a Palace in Pompeii* (oil on canvas, 21 1/2 x 37 3/4 ins / 54.5 x 96 cm) ITL 29,000,000. LONDON, 19 March 1993, *Sandal Sellers in Pompeii* (oil on canvas, 19 1/2 x 30 1/2 ins / 49.5 x 77.5 cm) GBP 11,500. NEW YORK, 27 May 1993, *Departure of the Master of the House* (oil on canvas, 23 1/4 x 39 1/4 ins / 59 x 100 cm) USD 20,700. LONDON, 18 June 1993, *Interesting Discussion* (oil on canvas, 24 x 39 1/2 ins / 61 x 100.5 cm) GBP 16,100. ROME, 31 May 1994, *Chariot Race* (oil on canvas, 27 1/2 x 45 ins / 70 x 114 cm) ITL 64,817,000. NEW YORK, 24 May 1995, *Roman Chariot* (oil on canvas, 23 3/4 x 39 1/2 ins / 60.3 x 100.3 cm) USD 18,400. LONDON, 14 June 1995, *Antique Shop* (oil on canvas, 20 1/2 x 32 3/4 ins / 52 x 83 cm) GBP 17,250. NEW YORK, 1 Nov 1995, *Pompeians Meeting around a Well* (oil on canvas, 39 1/2 x 23 3/4 ins / 100.3 x 60.3 cm) USD 63,000. NEW YORK, 17 Jan 1996, *A New Friend* (oil on canvas, 25 3/4 x 11 3/4 ins / 65.4 x 29.8 cm) USD 10,350. LONDON, 14 June 1996, *Dangerous Distraction* (oil on canvas, 23 3/4 x 39 1/2 ins / 60.4 x 100.3 cm) GBP 14,950. NEW YORK, 24 Oct 1996, *Roman Greeting* (oil on canvas, 24 x 39 1/2 ins / 61 x 100.3 cm) USD 46,000. LONDON, 20 Nov 1996, *Flower Seller* (oil on canvas, 20 1/2 x 32 3/4 ins / 52 x 83 cm) GBP 38,900. VENICE, 11 Dec 1999, *Oriental Court Scene with Entertainers* (oil on canvas, 24 x 39 ins / 60 x 100 cm) ITL 127,000,000. VENICE, 11 Dec 1999, *Celebrating the Coming of Spring* (oil on canvas, 37 x 56 ins / 93 x 142 cm) ITL 152,000,000. NEW YORK, 3 May 2000, *Rug Seller* (oil on canvas, 24 x 39 ins / 60 x 100 cm) USD 50,000. NEW YORK, 5 April 2001, *Performance on the Balcony* (oil on canvas, 24 x 39 ins / 62 x 99 cm) USD 40,000. NICE, 26 June 2001, *Family Scene at Pompeii* (oil on canvas, 24 x 39 ins / 60 x 100 cm) FRF 490,000. LONDON, 19 Nov 2002, *Merchant of Pompeii* (oil on canvas, 21 x 33 ins / 54 x 85 cm) GBP 25,000. NEW YORK, 21 Nov 2002, *Pottery Seller* (oil on canvas, 19 x 31 ins / 49 x 78 cm) USD 23,000. NEW YORK, 29 Oct 2003, *Afternoon at the Jeweller's* (oil on canvas, 21 x 33 ins / 53 x 83 cm) USD 45,000. NEW YORK, 29 Oct 2003, *At the Fruit Seller's* (oil on canvas, 19 x 30 ins / 49 x 77 cm) USD 45,000. NEW YORK, 23 April 2004, *Art Lesson* (oil on canvas, 19 x 30 ins / 49 x 77 cm) USD 75,000.

FORTI, Francesco Cipriano
Italian, 18th century.
Born 23 March 1713, in Correggio; died 11 June 1779, in Correggio.
Painter, architect, poet.
Francesco Cipriano Forti studied in Modena under Giorgio Magnanini. He worked for theatres and churches in Modena (Court Theatre), Corregio and Vescovado, as well as in the church of S Barnaba and the Palazzo Bellaria in S Martino di Mugnano.

FORTI, Giacomo
Italian, 15th century.
Active in 1483.
Painter.
Giacomo Forti, a pupil of Zoppo, helped his master with frescoes. A fresco of the Virgin in the church of S Tommaso al Mercato in Bologna is attributed to him.

FORTIER. See also **FORESTIER**

FORTIER, Claude François
French, 19th century.
Born 10 April 1775, in Paris; died 21 June 1835, in Paris.
Engraver.
Salon exhibitor as of 1819.

FORTIER, Jean
French, 16th century.
Painter.
Fontainebleau School.
Fortier worked at the palace of Fontainebleau from 1536 to 1550. From 1556 to 1565, he lived in Troyes.

FORTIER, Marie Louise
French, 20th century.
Born in Paris.
Painter.
Marie Fortier studied under Adler, Berges and Sabatté. She exhibited at the Paris Salon in 1934, 1935 and 1936 and received a commendation in 1935.

FORTIER, Natalie
Canadian, 20th - 21st century.
Born 1959, in Canada.
Since 1980 active in France.
Painter, draughtswoman, illustrator.
Natalie Fortier is involved in several collective exhibitions in Brive and Paris, where she has been holding solo exhibitions of her works since 1989. She has also illustrated a short story

by Herman Melville: *Me and My Chimney* (published in French by L'Ampoule, 2003).
Auction records:
Paris, 24 May 1992, *Air Pocket* (1992, mixed media/wood) FRF 7,000.

FORTIER, Pierre
French, 17th century.
Active in Dreux.
Sculptor.

Pierre Fortier sculpted the casing of the organs in the church of St-Pierre in Dreux in 1614. He also executed this church's rood-screen in 1620, which was destroyed during the French Revolution.

FORTIMANY, Mattia
Spanish, 15th century.
Born to a family originally from Majorca (Balearic Islands).
Sculptor, architect.

From 1469 to 1474, Mattia Fortimany worked in Naples on the construction of the Castel Nuovo. His sculptures cannot be identified with any certainty.

FORTIN
French, 18th century.
Active in La Rochelle.
Sculptor.

Fortin executed decorative sculptures for gardens.

FORTIN, Augustin Félix
French, 18th - 19th century.
Born 1763, in Paris; died 4 July 1832, in Paris.
Painter, sculptor, lithographer.

Augustin Félix Fortin was the nephew and pupil of the sculptor Lecomte. He won second prize for sculpture in the Prix de Rome in 1782, and first prize the following year with *Dead Man Resuscitated by the Touch of the Bones of the Prophet Elijah.* On 25 April 1789 he was elected to the Académie. He took part in the exhibitions at the Louvre from 1789 to 1824. Amongst his sculptures, the most notable are *A Hunter Resting* (plaster statue), *Reconciliation* (plaster low relief), *Phocion* (plaster statue), *The Bird of Lesbos* (terracotta), *Charity* (low relief, executed for the fountain in Popincourt), *The Fallen Woman* (marble low relief), and *Paris* (terracotta low relief). His best paintings are *Socrates Teaching Wisdom, Shem, Cursed by Noah, Retires into the Wilderness* and *Aristophanes Writing the Comedy 'The Clouds'*.
Museums and Galleries:
Angers: *Philippe de Champaigne* (marble, bust) - Nîmes: *Visconti* - Paris (Mus. de la Comédie-Française): *Michel Bayron; J. B. L. Gresset.*

FORTIN, Charles
French, 19th century.
Born 12 June 1815, in Paris; died 19 October 1865, in Paris.
Painter. Religious subjects, genre scenes, local figures, interiors, church interiors.

Son of Augustin Félix Fortin and pupil of Joseph Beaume and Camille Roqueplan; exhibited at the Paris Salon from 1835 to 1865 and at the Nantes Salon from 1842 to 1854. He was awarded several medals, notably in 1849, 1857 and 1859, and was made a Chevalier of the Légion d'Honneur in 1861.

Charles Fortin painted genre compositions, drawing on peasant life in Normandy and Brittany; his attics, cellars and interiors are more often than not rendered in chiaroscuro. Examples of his work include *Interior with Carousing Sailors, Cellar, Attic Interior in Normandy, Rag and Bone Merchant,* and *Breton Peasants in Morbihan Dress.*

C. Fortin

Museums and Galleries:
Grenoble: *During Vespers* - Lille (MBA): *Chouans* - Nantes (MBA): *Intérieur breton pris à Port-Nichet* (*Breton Interior at Pornichet*); *Portrait de femme* (*Portrait of a Woman*) - Paris (Mus. d'Orsay): *Benediction* - Szczecin: *Breton Peasants' House.*
Auction records:
Paris, 2 May 1894, *Lost,* FRF 420. Paris, 25 June 1937, *Secondhand Dealer,* FRF 100. Bern, 30 April 1980, *Rustic Scene* (oil on canvas, 16 1/2 x 21 1/4 ins / 42 x 54 cm) CHF 4,300. London, 28 Oct 1992, *Breton Couple beside a Fountain* (oil on canvas, 15 3/4 x 12 1/2 ins / 40 x 32 cm) GBP 770. Monaco, 2 July 1993, *Breton Children Playing with a Bird* (1854, oil on panel, 14 x 11 ins / 35.5 x 28 cm) FRF 16,650. London, 1 May 2002, *Patient* (oil on panel, 18 x 15 ins / 45 x 37 cm) GBP 4,200.

FORTIN, Henry
French, 18th century.
Active in Paris in 1711.
Sculptor.

FORTIN, Joséphine (Mme)
Maiden name: Thierry
French, 19th century.
Born 19th century, in Caen.
Sculptor.

Exhibited examples of her work at Paris salons between 1864 and 1873, chiefly busts - including that of *Mme Elisabeth* - and a marble statuette of *Charlotte Corday.*

FORTIN, Marc-Aurèle
Canadian, 20th century.
Born 1888, in Montreal; died 1970.
Painter, watercolourist.

Marc-Aurèle Fortin studied at the Monument National from 1903 to 1906, and, from 1906 to 1908, under Ludger Larose. He travelled in the USA for three years and finished his studies at the Chicago Art Institute.

MA Fortin

Museums and Galleries:
Ottawa (Nat. Gal. of Canada): *Autumn Landscape in Sun Valley* (1935, oil); *Fire in the Port of Montreal* (c. 1928, oil) - Quebec (Mus. du Quebec): *Landscape, Hochelaga.*
Auction records:
Toronto, 17 May 1976, *Quebec Landscape* (oil on card, 11 3/4 x 16 1/4 ins / 30 x 41 cm) CAD 1,800. Toronto, 15 May 1978, *Hochelaga* (oil on panel, 21 1/4 x 17 1/4 ins / 54 x 43.5 cm) CAD 6,000. Toronto, 26 May 1981, *French Canadian Village* (watercolour and pencil, 9 1/2 x 11 3/4 ins / 24.4 x 30 cm) CAD 6,000. Toronto, 3 May 1983, *Start of a Storm in Hochelaga* (oil on board, 38 x 45 3/4 ins / 96.3 x 116.3 cm) CAD 22,000. Montreal, 13 Nov 1984, *Untitled* (watercolour) CAD 2,100. Toronto, 18 Nov 1986, *Autumn Shadows* (oil on board, 37 x 46 3/4 ins / 93.8 x 118.8 cm) CAD 43,000. Montreal, 25 Nov 1986, *Village* (watercolour, 14 1/2 x 19 1/4 ins / 37 x 49 cm) CAD 5,000. Montreal, 25 April 1988, *For Jacques Cartier* (watercolour, 14 1/4 x 20 ins / 36 x 51 cm) CAD 5,000. Montreal, 17 Oct 1988, *Landscape in Sainte Scholastique, Quebec* (oil on panel, 20 x 24 ins / 51 x 61 cm) CAD 42,000. Montreal, 1 May 1989, *Washing-line in a Backyard* (oil on panel, 7 x 7 3/4 ins / 18 x 20 cm) CAD 3,600. Montreal, 30 Oct 1989, *Hochelaga in Winter* (oil on panel, 33 3/4 x 41 ins / 86 x 104 cm) CAD 154,000. Montreal, 30 April 1990, *Landscape with Houses* (oil on panel, 24 x 48 ins / 61 x 122 cm) CAD 37,400. Montreal, 5 Nov 1990, *Boats on the Shore in Perce* (1944, watercolour, 15 x 22 ins / 38 x 56 cm) CAD 8,250. Montreal, 4 June 1991, *Dark Clouds over Hochelaga* (oil on panel, 16 3/4 x 25 1/2 ins / 42.5 x 64.7 cm) CAD 30,000. Montreal, 19 Nov

1991, *Scene in Ste-Rose* (watercolour, 21 x 27½ ins / 53.2 x 69.8 cm) CAD 12,000. MONTREAL, 1 Dec 1992, *Autumn Colours* (oil on panel, 8¼ x 7 ins / 21 x 17.8 cm) CAD 3,800. MONTREAL, 23-24 Nov 1993, *Boats* (watercolour, 10¼ x 13½ ins / 26 x 34.2 cm) CAD 1,700. MONTREAL, 3 Dec 1996, *Landscape near Montreal* (pencil, 8¾ x 12 ins / 22.2 x 30.5 cm) CAD 1,700. TORONTO, 1 June 1999, *Rivière des Prairies, Ste Rose, 1923* (watercolour on paper, 22 x 30 ins / 56 x 75 cm) CAD 17,000. TORONTO, 17 Nov 1999, *Landscape near Ste Rose* (c. 1937, oil on board, 23 x 30 ins / 59 x 76 cm) CAD 50,000. TORONTO, 24 May 2000, *The Red House* (oil on panel, 39 x 30 ins / 99 x 75 cm) CAD 25,000. TORONTO, 21 Nov 2000, *Winter Landscape* (oil on board, 13 x 14 ins / 34 x 35 cm) CAD 20,000. TORONTO, 29 May 2001, *Hochelaga* (oil on canvas, 14 x 16 ins / 35 x 40 cm) CAD 60,000. TORONTO, 4 Dec 2001, *House* (oil on board, 8 x 13 ins / 21 x 32 cm) CAD 20,000. TORONTO, 14 May 2002, *Farm at Ste Rose* (c. 1926, watercolour on paper, 19 x 26 ins / 47 x 67 cm) CAD 17,000. TORONTO, 14 May 2002, *Landscape* (oil on canvas, 22 x 26 ins / 55 x 65 cm) CAD 34,000. TORONTO, 27 May 2003, *Autumn Landscape* (oil on board, 22 x 28 ins / 56 x 71 cm) CAD 30,000. TORONTO, 3 June 2003, *Homestead in Winter* (c. 1919-1920, oil on board, 8 x 9 ins / 20 x 22 cm) CAD 22,000. TORONTO, 1 June 2004, *Hiver Laurentien* (c. 1925, oil on canvas, 33 x 28 ins / 85 x 70 cm) CAD 130,000. TORONTO, 1 June 2004, *View of Montreal, the St Lawrence in Winter* (c. 1915, oil on canvas, 30 x 36 ins / 76 x 91 cm) CAD 135,000.

FORTIN, Maurice, or Fortin-Locquirec
French, 20th century.
Born 10 April 1911, in Laval.
Painter, watercolourist, engraver, lithographer.
Portraits, landscapes, still-lifes.

Maurice Fortin attended classes in painting and modelling run by the Ville de Laval. He had a long career as a model maker in Nice and a graphic designer for the printing industry. From the 1980s he devoted himself to painting and engraving. He sees himself as following in the Cubist tradition -with a certain sense of humour - and also in the Surrealist tradition with clear references to René Magritte, the two artists sharing a similar sense of humour. In fact, Fortin is primarily a painter of still-lifes which he executes using the technique of the old masters, sometimes taken to the point of trompe-l'œil.

He exhibited in Paris at the Salon des Artistes Français, of which he was a member, and at the Salon d'Automne. He was awarded a silver medal in 1958 at the Exposition Universelle in Brussels. He shows his work mainly in group exhibitions in Brittany where he has won regional prizes.

FORTIN, Philippe
French, 16th century.
Active in Gisors (Eure).
Sculptor (wood).

Fortin made two doors (which still exist) featuring the twelve apostles for the great portal of the church of St-Gervais and St-Protais in Gisors. In 1578, he carved the organ case for the same church.

FORTIN, R.
French, 18th century.
Born in Paris.
Miniaturist.

R. Fortin exhibited at the Royal Academy from 1790 to 1794.

FORTINELLI
British, 18th century.
Painter.

Fortinelli exhibited landscapes with ruins with the Free Society in 1783.

FORTINI, Benedetto
Italian, 17th - 18th century.
Born 1675, in Settignano; died 1732, in Settignano.
Painter. Fruit.

Benedetto Fortini studied under B. Bimbi and J. Chiavistelli.

FORTINI, Carlo
Italian, 17th century.
Active in Ferrara.
Painter.

Carlo Fortini worked on the church of S Bartolomeo Fuori della Mure in 1648.

FORTINI, Eduardo
Italian, 20th century.
Born in Florence.
Sculptor.

Eduardo Fortini exhibited at the Salon of the Société des Artistes Français in Paris in 1914.

FORTINI, Giovacchino
Italian, 17th - 18th century.
Born 1671, in Settignano; died 12 December 1736, in Florence.
Sculptor, medallist, architect.

The church of the Annunziata in Florence houses some of Giovacchino Fortini's statues. Fortini was responsible for completing work on the façade of the church of S Firenze started by A. Maria Ferri. He also completed a tomb for the physician *G. Neri* in the church of S Giuseppe. Other examples of his work include statues in the Florence church of SS Michele e Gaetano. Cologne Cathedral houses his funerary monument in honour of *Marshal von Hochkirchen*.

FORTINI, Raffaelo
Italian, 17th century.
Active in Pisa in 1600.
Sculptor.

Raffaelo Fortini was commissioned to prepare models for a low relief and four statues of the Apostles for the doors of Pisa Cathedral. The projects themselves were never carried out.

FORTINO, Giuseppe
Italian, 18th century.
Painter.

Giuseppe Fortino painted a *Virgin* for the Naples church of S Maria dell'Ajuto in 1781.

FORTINY
French, 20th century.
Active in Paris.
Sculptor.

The Simu museum in Bucharest has a *Bust of a Woman* in marble by Fortiny.

FORTIS, Tommaso de
Italian, 16th century.
Of Veronese origin.
Painter.

Tommaso de Fortis is mentioned in 1589 in Rome.

FORTLING, Christian Edvard
Danish, 19th century.
Born 10 April 1809, in Copenhagen; died 12 August 1875, in Copenhagen.
Lithographer.

Christian Edvard Fortling was a pupil at the Kunstakademi in Copenhagen and exhibited his drawings and lithographs there from 1838 to 1873. He made numerous lithographic portraits, among which were those of the kings and queens of Denmark and that of the cleric *N. F. S. Grundtvig*.

FORTLING, Jakob
Danish, 18th century.
Born 23 December 1711, of German origin; died 16 July 1761, in Kastrup.
Sculptor, potter, architect.

Jakob Fortling was a court sculptor in Copenhagen, where he founded a porcelain factory in 1760.

FORTNER, Andreas
Austrian, 19th century.
Born 16 June 1809, in Prague; died 14 March 1862, in Munich.
Painter, sculptor, engraver. Historical subjects.
Andreas Fortner settled in Munich from 1840.

FORTNER, Georg
German, 19th century.
Born 20 October 1814, in Munich; died 27 July 1879, in Munich.
Painter. History painting.
Georg Fortner was a pupil of Schlotthauer and of Heinrich Hess. He made frescoes for the National Museum of Bavaria and decorations for various churches.

FORTON, Louis
French, 20th century.
Born 14 March 1879, in Sées; died 1934.
Draughtsman, illustrator. Comic strips.
Louis Forton was the son of a horse dealer and worked as a stable boy and jockey. In 1907 his drawings for *Les Aventures de Séraphin Laricot* (*The Adventures of Séraphin Laricot*) were published, followed the next year by *Les Exploits d'Isidore MacAron* (*The Exploits of Isidore MacAron*). He is the creator of the celebrated cartoon strip *Les Pieds Nickelés* (*The Nickel-plated Feet*). Forton also wrote *La Carrière militaire d'Onésime Baluchon* (*The Military Career of Onésime Baluchon*), 1900, *Les 126 métiers de Caramel* (*The 126 jobs of Caramel*), 1920 and *Bibi Fricotin*, 1929.
BIBLIOGRAPHY:
Osterwalder, Marcus (ed.), *Dictionnaire des illustrateurs 1800-1914*, Ides et Calendes, Neuchâtel, 1989.

FORTORI, Alessandro
Italian, 16th century.
Active in Arezzo c. 1568.
Painter. History painting.
The churches and palaces of Arezzo contain works by Alessandro Fortori.

FORTSCH, Sebastian
German, 18th century.
Born c. 1753, to a family originally from Pottenstein (Franconia); died 22 August 1803.
Painter. Religious subjects, portraits.
MUSEUMS AND GALLERIES:
BAMBERG (Municipal Collection): *Solomon Receives the Queen of Sheba* - MUNICH (Bayerisches Nationalmus.): *Portrait of the Duchess Franziska von Zweibrücken* - NUREMBERG (Germanisches Nationalmus.): *Portrait; Same Subject.*

FORTSMAN, Gregorio. See **FOSMAN**

FORTT, Frederick
British, 19th century.
Painter. Genre scenes, architectural views.
Frederick Fortt was a member of the Society of British Artists. Active in Bath, he exhibited in London, notably at the Royal Academy, the British Institution and Suffolk Street.
AUCTION RECORDS:
NEW YORK, 20 July 1995, *Fortune-teller* (1884, oil on canvas, 50 x 40 ins / 127 x 101.6 cm) USD 6,900.

FORTUNA, Alessandro
Italian, 17th century.
Born c. 1596; died 6 August 1623, in Rome.
Painter. History painting.
Alessandro Fortuna was a pupil of Domenichino.

FORTUNA, Giovanni
Italian, 16th - 17th century.
Born 1535; died 1611.
Active in Siena.
Goldsmith, draughtsman.
In 1588, A. Andreani engraved an allegorical plate, *Triumph of Death*, from a design by Giovanni Fortuna.

FORTUNATO
Italian, 16th century.
Died 1579, in Rome.
Active in S Angelo in Vado, near Urbino.
Painter.

FORTUNATO, Domenico
Italian, 17th century.
Active in Naples.
Painter.
Domenico Fortunato is on record in 1665 as a member of the guild of St Luke.

FORTUNATUS
Austrian, 19th century.
Miniaturist.

FORTUNÉ, L.
French, 19th century.
Active c. 1830.
Lithographer.
Published several lithographs, including an *Indiscretions of the Age*.

FORTUNEY
French, 20th century.
Born 1878; died 1950.
Painter, pastellist. Genre scenes, landscapes with figures, urban landscapes, seascapes.
Fortuney was essentially a pastellist. He produced some seascapes but mainly pieces showing life in Paris, brightly coloured street and café scenes, drawn from life.
AUCTION RECORDS:
PARIS, 26 Feb 1926, *Dancer behind a Flat* (pastel) FRF 100. PARIS, 24 April 1942, *The Fishing Port* (pastel) FRF 420. PARIS, 3 Nov 1944, *Evening Performance; Private Dining Room; On the Deck of the Yacht; At the Weigh-in* (four pastels) FRF 3,500. PARIS, 4 Nov 1946, *View of the Mediterranean Coast* (pastel) FRF 650. PARIS, 8 Dec 1976, *The Outing* (pastel, 45 1/4 x 63 3/4 ins / 115 x 162 cm) FRF 16,000. PARIS, 3 Dec 1982, *Café Scene* (pastel, 18 1/2 x 11 3/4 ins / 47 x 30 cm) FRF 4,200. PARIS, 14 Dec 1984, *The Port of Cassis* (pastel, 25 1/4 x 31 1/2 ins / 64 x 80 cm) FRF 8,900. PARIS, 23 March 1987, *A Walk in the Woods* (pastel, 45 x 64 1/4 ins / 114 x 163 cm) FRF 160,000. PARIS, 6 May 1988, *An Easterly Wind at Le Trayas* (pastel, 19 1/4 x 23 1/4 ins / 49 x 59 cm) FRF 7,500. PARIS, 7 Oct 1988, *Society Lady in a Park* (oil on canvas, 22 x 15 ins / 55 x 38 cm) FRF 22,000. CALAIS, 13 Nov 1988, *Society Lady in a Wood* (pastel, 19 1/4 x 12 1/2 ins / 49 x 32 cm) FRF 70,000. PARIS, 8 Nov 1989, *Couple in an Arbour* (1906, oil on canvas, 19 x 24 ins / 48 x 61 cm) FRF 18,000. VERSAILLES, 19 Nov 1989, *Parisian Woman* (pastel, 19 x 11 3/4 ins / 48.5 x 30 cm) FRF 9,000. PARIS, 21 Nov 1989, *At a Restaurant; The Box* (two pastels, each 18 1/2 x 12 1/2 ins / 47 x 31.5 cm) FRF 46,000. PARIS, 25 June 1990, *Society Lady* (pastel, 20 1/2 x 13 3/4 ins / 52 x 35 cm) FRF 13,500. NEUILLY, 26 June 1990, *Provençal Landscape* (oil on card, 16 3/4 x 19 3/4 ins / 42.5 x 50 cm) FRF 13,000. CALAIS, 10 March 1991, *Society Lady with an Ermine Muff* (pastel, 19 x 12 1/4 ins / 48 x 31 cm) FRF 11,500. NEUILLY, 23 Feb 1992, *The Creek* (pastel, 9 1/2 x 12 1/4 ins / 24 x 31 cm) FRF 7,500. NEW YORK, 16 Feb 1994, *In Full Sail* (pastel/paper, 19 1/2 x 26 ins / 49.8 x 65.1 cm) USD 3,450. PARIS, 12 July 1994, *Oriental Nude Seated at a Mirror* (pastel, 12 1/4 x 9 1/2 ins / 31 x 24 cm) FRF 15,500. CALAIS, 24 March 1996, *Society Lady with Hat* (pastel, 13 3/4 x 9 1/2 ins / 35 x 24 cm) FRF 5,000. NEW YORK, 15 June 1999, *Tea Time* (pastel, 19 x 12 ins / 48 x 30 cm) USD 4,000. PARIS, 5 Aug 1999, *Embarcations on the River* (1909, oil on canvas, 21 x 26 ins / 54 x 65 cm) FRF 30,000. AMSTERDAM,

7 June 2000, *Moulin Rouge* (1908, pastel, 19 x 12 ins / 48 x 31 cm) NLG 8,500. VERSAILLES, 21 Jan 2001, *Fisherman Breaking Bread* (pastel, 18 x 12 ins / 46 x 30 cm) FRF 31,500. VERSAILLES, 7 April 2002, *Red Rocks* (1941, pastel, 28 x 39 ins / 70 x 100 cm) EUR 1,800. PARIS, 12 March 2003, *Two Women and a Man in a Theatre Box* (pastel, 19 x 12 ins / 48 x 31 cm) EUR 1,450. PARIS, 12 March 2003, *Boat* (1906, oil on canvas, 16 x 13 ins / 41 x 32 cm) EUR 1,700.

FORTUNIO
Italian, 17th century.
Born to a family originally from Parma.
Painter.

Two altarpieces by Fortunio are to be found in the church of Zittelle. His allegorical *Hope* is housed in the Palazzo del S Monte de Pietà.

FORTUNY Y CARBO MARSAL, Mariano.
See **FORTUNY Y MARSAL Mariano**

FORTUNY Y DE MADRAZO, Mariano
Spanish, 19th - 20th century.
Born 1871, in Granada; died 1949.
Painter. Portraits.

Mariano Fortuny y de Madrazo was almost certainly the son of Fortuny y Marsal. He exhibited at the Exposition Universelle of 1900 where he was awarded a silver medal.

BIBLIOGRAPHY:
Deschodt, Anne-Marie, *Mariano Fortuny: un magicien de Venise*, Éd. du Regard, Paris, 2000 (Mariano Fortuny: A Magician of Venice).

AUCTION RECORDS:
LONDON, 16 May 1903, *Innomanita* (1896, oil on panel, 34 1/4 x 28 3/4 ins / 87 x 73 cm) GBP 735. LONDON, 23 June 1981, *Innomanita* (1896, oil on panel, 34 1/4 x 28 3/4 ins / 87 x 73 cm) GBP 7,500. MADRID, 27 Oct 1987, *The Valkyrie* (1893, tempera/card, 11 3/4 x 9 3/4 ins / 30 x 25 cm) ESP 1,000,000. MILAN, 23 March 1988, *Venice Carnival* (oil on canvas, 22 x 30 1/2 ins / 56 x 77.5 cm) ITL 10,000,000. PARIS, 10 Dec 1996, *Young Woman with Blue Blouse* (1889, oil on wood, 3 3/4 x 3 ins / 9.7 x 7.7 cm) FRF 21,000. LONDON, 7 April 2000, *El Darro, Granada* (tempera on panel, 7 x 5 ins / 17 x 13 cm) GBP 3,360. LONDON, 22 Sept 2000, *Scene from the Spanish Civil War* (oil on canvas, 9 x 11 ins / 23 x 28 cm) GBP 13,000. ROME, 11 June 2003, *Portrait of Teenage Boy* (oil on canvas, 18 x 15 ins / 46 x 37 cm) EUR 6,500. PRATO, 14 Nov 2003, *Village* (oil on canvas, 12 x 22 ins / 30 x 55 cm) EUR 12,000. MADRID, 22 March 2004, *Viewing a Work of Art* (oil on board, 12 x 8 ins / 30 x 20 cm) EUR 2,000. MADRID, 22 March 2004, *Musketeer* (oil on board, 12 x 8 ins / 30 x 20 cm) EUR 2,250.

FORTUNY Y MARSAL, Mariano, or Fortuny y Carbo Marsal
Spanish, 19th century.
Born 11 June 1838, in Reus (Catalonia); died 21 November 1874, in Rome.
Also active in Italy.
Painter, watercolourist, draughtsman, engraver.
History painting, religious subjects, portraits, genre scenes, local scenes, landscapes with figures, urban landscapes.
Orientalism.

Mariano Fortuny y Marsal studied under Claudio Lorenzale at the school of fine arts in Barcelona. In 1857 he was awarded a bursary to study in Rome. He first visited Morocco in 1860, sent by the city of Barcelona as a war artist to commemorate the Spanish victory at Tetouan with a painting. In 1863 he visited Naples, where he met the painter of historical subjects, Domenico Morelli. In 1866 he went to Paris and became friends with French academic painters such as Jean Léon Gérome and Ernest Meissonier. In 1867 he returned to Rome where he became friends with Henri Regnault. By 1869 he was back in Madrid and began to study Goya's technique in earnest. In 1871, in the company of the French orientalist painter Georges Clairin, he visited Tangier and Tetouan. He went to Granada and Seville to study the legacy of the Moors and also visited England. In 1873 he moved to Portici in Italy, but caught malaria there and had to return to Rome, where he died shortly after.

On his visits to Morocco Fortuny made many pencil and watercolour sketches of Arab soldiers and of the country's landscape, habitat, population and animals. When he returned from his travels he used these studies as the basis for paintings and engravings of 'oriental' daily life. He freely copied the weapons, fabrics, wall hangings, carpets, bronzeware and pottery that he brought back from his journeys abroad and kept in his studio; he became famous as a designer of fashionable fabrics and is mentioned by Proust in *Un amour de Swann* (*Swann in Love*).

The luminosity and intense colours of North Africa brought a freshness to his palette and freed him from the classicism of his early style. Goya's influence is also apparent in his work, particularly in *La Vicaria*. The French poet and critic Théophile Gautier said of this painting that it was like a 'sketch by Goya reworked by Meissonier'. Indeed, Fortuny does share something of Goya's freedom of technique and his palette is closer to that of Goya than Meissonier. What makes Fortuny special is his attention to detail, which he carried to an extreme in the latter half of his career with his fashionable fabric designs. He may sometimes have forgotten that overall composition must take priority over meticulousness of execution but he was an outstanding exponent of the intense and vivid qualities of light. His 'oriental' works include: *Arabian Fantasia*; *On the Hills of Algiers*; *Fantasia in Granada*; *Travellers' Halt*; *Battle of Tetouan in Morocco*; and *Indian Snake Charmer*.

Fortuny's last studies show that he had begun to turn his attention more to the internal structure of landscapes, creating wider, more open skies and concentrating less on superficial detail. Other works include: *Penitent Hermit*; *The Gallant Abbot*; *Luncheon in the Courtyard of an Old Convent*; *The Antique Dealer*; and *Alhambra Courtyard*.

Fortuny exhibited at the Barcelona Salon and at various exhibitions organised by the Parisian art dealer Adolphe Goupil, who, from 1870, had exclusive rights to handle Fortuny's work. In 2003 a major retrospective of Fortuny's work was staged by the Museu Nacional d'Art de Catalunya in Barcelona.

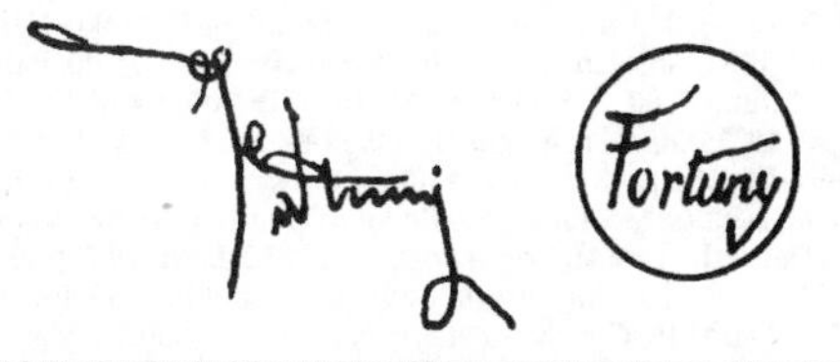

Stamps of sale

M Fortuny

BIBLIOGRAPHY:
Osborne, Harold (ed.), *The Oxford Companion to Art*, Oxford University Press, Oxford, 1970. *18 acuarelas y dibujos, Mariano Fortuny 1838-1874: Expuestos en Sala Parés*, exhibition catalogue, Barcelona, 1972. Russel, P. E. (ed.), *Spain, a Companion to Spanish Studies*, Methuen, Suffolk, 1973. De

Osma, Guillermo, *Mariano Fortuny: His Life and Work,* Aurum, 1980. Janés, Clara, *Fortuny,* Sarpe, Barcelona, 1990. Navascués, Pedro/Quesada Martín, María Jesús, *El Siglo XIX: Bajo el signo del Romanticismo,* SILEX, Madrid, 1992. Hamilton, George Heard, *Painting and Sculpture in Europe 1880-1940,* Yale University Press, Pelican History of Art, Singapore, 1993. Juler, Caroline, *Les Orientalistes de l'école italienne,* ACR Édition, Paris, 1994. Desvaux, Delphine, *Fortuny (Fashion Memoir),* Thames and Hudson, 1998. Moffitt, John F., *The Arts in Spain,* Thames and Hudson, London, 1999. Deschodt, Anne-Marie/Poli Doretta, Daranzo, *Fortuny,* Harry N. Abrams, 2001. *Mariano Fortuny,* exhibition catalogue, Museu Nacional d'Art de Catalunya, Barcelona, 2003.

MUSEUMS AND GALLERIES:

BALTIMORE (Walters AM): *Indian Snake Charmer; Arabian Fantasia; Swiss Guard* - BARCELONA: *Art Lover in his Room; Slave; Moorish Sentry: Moroccan Blacksmith; Moorish Sentry: Battle of Tetouan* - BARCELONA (MAM del Mus. Nacional d'Art de Catalunya): *Battle of Tetouan; Military Officer* - BUCHAREST: *Darro Stream* - BUENOS AIRES: *Return from the Procession in the Rain* - CASTRES: *Bull-running in Spain; Windows* - CHICAGO: *Warrior* - CINCINNATI (Taft MA): *Arab Guard* - COPENHAGEN (Ny Carlsberg Glyptotek): *Head Study of Young Roman Woman* - DALLAS (Meadows Mus.): *Playa en Portici (Beach at Portici)* - LONDON (British Mus.) - LONDON (NG): *The Bull-Fighter's Salute* (1869?, oil on canvas) - MADRID: *Battle of Wad-Ras; Queen Maria Cristina of Spain Reviewing the Troops* - MADRID (Prado) - MADRID (Prado, Casón del Buen Retiro): *The Artist's Children in the Japanese Salon; Landscape; Moroccan* - MANNHEIM: *Head Study of Young Roman Woman* - MILAN (Mus. Poldi Pezzoli): *Tangier* (watercolour) - MOSCOW (State Tretyakov Gal.): *Art Lover in his Room; Moroccan Snake Charmers* - MUNICH: *Duet* - NEW YORK (Hispanic Society of America): *Tangiers* (after 1862?); *Arabs Ascending a Hill* (1862-1863); *Portico, Church of San Ginés* (1868) - NEW YORK (Metropolitan Mus. of Art): *Madame Gaye* (1865, oil on canvas) - PARIS (Mus. d'Orsay) - ST PETERSBURG (Hermitage) - THE HAGUE (Mus. Mesdag): *Anchorite* - VENICE (Mus. Fortuny): important collection of works - WASHINGTON DC (Corcoran Gal. of Art).

AUCTION RECORDS:

PARIS, 9 May 1874, *Two Gendarmes,* FRF 7,300. NEW YORK, 1887, *Snake Charmer,* FRF 65,000. LONDON, 1891, *Interior of a Bazaar,* FRF 25,000. PARIS, 1892, *Arab Sentry,* FRF 4,300. NEW YORK, 1898, *Court at the Alhambra,* FRF 10,750; *Luncheon in the Courtyard of an Old Convent,* FRF 34,500; *Antique Dealer,* FRF 76,000. ANTWERP, 1898, *Armenian,* FRF 3,400. PARIS, 1898, *Man Seated* (drawing) FRF 125. PARIS, 20-21 May 1898, *Landscape outside Rome,* FRF 1,000. NEW YORK, 1899, *Arabian Fantasia* (watercolour) FRF 37,500. PARIS, 21 June 1900, *The Gallant Abbot,* FRF 400. PARIS, 22-24 April 1901, *Knife Grinder,* FRF 360. LONDON, 22 May 1908, *At the Door,* GBP 43. PARIS, 4 June 1909, *Arab Seated,* FRF 1,000. LONDON, 15 July 1910, *Bedouin Guard,* GBP 37. PARIS, 4-5 Dec 1918, *Crossroads in Spain,* FRF 230; *Battle of Tetouan in Morocco* (drawing heightened with white) FRF 50. PARIS, 27-28 Feb 1919, *Courtyard in Spain,* FRF 130. PARIS, 7 March 1923, *Moorish Patio,* FRF 2,300. PARIS, 17 March 1923, *Old Philosopher,* FRF 260; *Antechamber* (in collaboration with F. Roybet) FRF 3,250. PARIS, 12 June 1923, *Woman Standing* (watercolour) FRF 115. LONDON, 9 May 1924, *Sentry* (drawing) GBP 63; *Arab Horseman* (drawing) GBP 346. LONDON, 5 June 1924, *Mistral Blowing near Agay* (pastel) GBP 5. PARIS, 10-11 June 1925, *Bust of a Young Woman,* FRF 2,400. PARIS, 21-22 Dec 1925, *Moorish Fountain,* FRF 9,500. PARIS, 19 June 1926, *Roman Woman at a Fountain* (watercolour) FRF 850. LONDON, 25 Feb 1927, *Hazelnut Seller* (drawing) GBP 10. LONDON, 13 May 1927, *Picador* (drawing) GBP 86. LONDON, 22 July 1927, *Arab Chieftain* (drawing) GBP 78. PARIS, 3 Feb 1928, *Study of a Man* (pencil) FRF 200. LONDON, 30 March 1928, *Rocky Landscape,* GBP 68; *Slave,* GBP 220. PARIS, 3 and 4 June 1929, *Young Italian Woman at a Well* (watercolour) FRF 8,500. PARIS, 12 June 1929, *Pomegranate Tree,* FRF 1,850; *Fantasy Head,* FRF 1,850. PARIS, 26 June 1929, *Arab Crouching* (watercolour) FRF 5,300. PARIS, 18 June 1930, *Moor's Head,* FRF 2,950. NEW YORK, 4 and 5 Feb 1931, *Marriage Contract,* USD 220. PARIS, 20 June 1932, *After the Execution,* FRF 3,300. NEW YORK, 7-8 Dec 1933, *Country Beauty,* USD 225. PARIS, 14 Dec 1933, *Knife Grinder,* FRF 45,100. PARIS, 14 Dec 1933, *Young Venetian Gentleman in the Middle Ages* (watercolour) FRF 1,650; *Knife Grinder,* FRF 45,100. PARIS, 8 March 1934, *Woman Seated, Front View,* FRF 100. PARIS, 8 and 9 May 1934, *Brigand* (watercolour) FRF 2,000; *Old Bridge over a Stream in a Spanish Town,* FRF 450; *Lunch in the Courtyard of a Spanish Inn,* FRF 1,420. NEW YORK, 17-18 May 1934, *Visitor,* USD 450. NEW YORK, 4 Jan 1935, *Mandolin Player* (watercolour) USD 160. NEW YORK, 4 Jan 1935, *Mandolin Player* (watercolour) USD 160. NEW YORK, 8 Feb 1935, *Visitor,* USD 625. LONDON, 15 Feb 1935, *Woman with Fan,* GBP 7. LONDON, 13 Feb 1936, *Queen of Spain,* GBP 7. PARIS, 17 Dec 1936, *Chariot of Venus* (after original by Tiepolo in the Prado) FRF 4,200. PARIS, 16 and 17 May 1939, *Moorish Warrior* (watercolour) FRF 1,120. PARIS, 29 Dec 1941, *Elegant Supper, Illustration for Rolla* (gouache) FRF 700. PARIS, 13 May 1942, *Ceiling Design* (after Tiepolo) FRF 700. PARIS, 8 March 1943, *Seville Bullring,* FRF 41,000. PARIS, 27 June 1944, *Tapestry* (watercolour) FRF 4,200. PARIS, 24 Jan 1945, *Figure in Drapery* (pencil drawing) FRF 3,000. NEW YORK, 18-19 April 1945, *Court Jester,* USD 1,050; *Arabian Fantasia,* USD 2,900. NEW YORK, 31 Jan 1946, *Breakfast at the Alhambra,* USD 5,200. NEW YORK, 12 Oct 1946, *L'hôte,* USD 875. PARIS, 8 June 1949, *Two Arabs,* FRF 62,000. PARIS, 20 June 1951, *Arab Scene,* FRF 50,000. PARIS, 18 March 1955, *White Houses,* FRF 108,000. PARIS, 12 June 1969, *Portrait of an Actor,* FRF 14,500. MILAN, 16 March 1972, *Reading,* ITL 3,700,000. NEW YORK, 10 Oct 1973, *Auction Sale,* USD 3,250. NEW YORK, 9 Oct 1974, *Pan Pipes* (watercolour) USD 3,000. LONDON, 7 May 1976, *Art Lover* (oil on panel, 11 1/2 x 7 3/4 ins / 29.5 x 19.5 cm) GBP 620. MADRID, 25 May 1977, *Woman with Fan* (watercolour, 19 x 12 3/4 ins / 48 x 32.5 cm) ESP 330,000. MILAN, 10 Nov 1977, *Painter's Studio* (1897, oil on canvas, 21 1/4 x 32 ins / 54 x 81 cm) ITL 4,800,000. LONDON, 30 Sept 1981, *Egg Seller* (watercolour and pencil, 9 1/2 x 11 3/4 ins / 24.4 x 30 cm) GBP 1,700. BARCELONA, 26 May 1982, *Aqueduct* (oil on canvas, 20 3/4 x 15 ins / 53 x 38 cm) ESP 300,000. NEW YORK, 25 Feb 1983, *Sentry* (1862, oil on canvas, 25 1/2 x 15 1/4 ins / 64.7 x 38.7 cm) USD 7,000. LONDON, 24 Nov 1983, *Young Woman in a Blue Dress* (1866, watercolour heightened with white, 14 1/4 x 9 3/4 ins / 36.2 x 24.7 cm) GBP 3,200. LONDON, 19 June 1984, *Battle of Wad-Ras* (oil on canvas, study) GBP 32,000. MADRID, 24 Oct 1984, *Portrait of a Gentleman* (pen, 10 1/4 x 10 ins / 26 x 25 cm) ESP 250,000. MADRID, 27 Feb 1985, *Portrait of José Aixala* (1873, oil on canvas, 23 1/2 x 19 1/4 ins / 60 x 49 cm) ESP 2,070,000. NEW YORK, 21 May 1987, *Arabian Fantasia in Tangier* (1866, oil on canvas, 20 x 24 1/2 ins / 50.8 x 62.2 cm) USD 200,000. MONTEVIDEO, 2 Dec 1987, *Carpet Seller* (watercolour, 7 3/4 x 11 ins / 20 x 28 cm) UYU 4,027,000. PARIS, 6 May 1988, *Male Nude* (pencil heightened with gouache, 15 x 7 3/4 ins / 38.4 x 20 cm) FRF 61,000. LONDON, 22 June 1988, *Young Donkey Boy* (oil on panel, 6 3/4 x 9 ins / 17 x 23 cm) GBP 48,400. LONDON, 21 June 1989, *Fairy Flower* (1868, watercolour and gouache, 9 1/4 x 5 3/4 ins / 23.5 x 14.5 cm) GBP 8,580. NEW YORK, 24 Oct 1989, *Exit from the Church of San Ginés in Madrid* (watercolour/paper, 5 x 8 1/4 ins / 12.7 x 21 cm) USD 14,300. ROME, 4 Dec 1990, *Portrait of Francis of Bourbon* (pencil and chalk/paper, 23 1/2 x 18 ins / 60 x 46 cm) ITL 3,500,000. PARIS, 4 March 1992, *Boat* (1860, watercolour, 2 1/4 x 4 1/2 ins / 5.5 x 11.5 cm) FRF 7,500. NEW YORK, 16 Feb 1993, *Tune on the Mandolin* (1869, watercolour/card, 11 1/4 x 7 3/4 ins / 28.5 x 19.7 cm) USD 3,520. MONAco, 2 July 1993, *Study of Male Nude Standing* (charcoal heightened in colour, 17 x 11 ins / 43 x 28.2 cm) FRF 66,600. PARIS, 4 March 1994, *Side View of a Young Woman in a Blue Blouse* (1889, oil on panel, 3¾ x 3 ins / 9.8 x 7.8 cm) FRF 7,100. MILAN, 8 June 1994, *Convalescence* (1871, oil on panel, 8½ x 5 ins / 21.5 x 13 cm) ITL 16,675,000. NEW YORK, 23 May 1997, *Contemplation of a Portrait* (1874, oil on panel, 16 x 12½ ins / 40.6 x 31.8 cm) USD 28,750. LONDON, 18 June 1998, *Marroqui* (c. 1862, oil on canvas, 16 x 13 ins / 40 x 34 cm) GBP 36,000. NEW YORK, 16 July 1998, *Going to the Well* (1865, oil on panel, 18 x 13 ins / 46 x 32 cm) USD 19,000. EDINBURGH, 14 Dec 1999, *Figure Study* (oil on canvas, 26 x 17 ins / 65 x 43 cm) GBP 3,000. LONDON, 22 June 2000, *Arab Fantasia at Tangiers* (1866, oil on canvas, 20 x 24 ins / 51 x 62 cm) GBP 320,000. MADRID, 6 June 2000, *Man with Mandoline* (1869, watercolour, 11 x 7 ins / 28 x 18 cm) ESP 8,000,000. NEW YORK, 1 May 2001, *Summer Day, Morocco* (oil on canvas, 10 x 26 ins / 25 x 66 cm) USD 40,000. MADRID, 19 June 2001, *Summer Day in Morocco* (oil on canvas, 9 x 25 ins / 24 x 64 cm) ESP 13,000,000. NEW YORK, 30 Oct 2002, *Council House, Granada* (1873, oil on canvas, 14 x 19 ins / 35 x 48 cm) USD 240,000. MADRID, 17 Dec 2002, *Arab Outpost* (c. 1860, watercolour, 11 x 17 ins / 28 x 44 cm) EUR 37,500. MADRID, 4 March 2003, *Tangiers Street* (pen and ink wash, 9 x 7 ins / 23 x 17 cm) EUR 17,000. MADRID, 16 Sept 2003, *Balcony* (oil on panel, 7 x 4 ins / 18 x 11 cm) EUR 13,000. BERN, 12 May 2004, *At the Butchers* (1874, watercolour, 9 x 7 ins / 24 x 17 cm) CHF 32,000. PARIS, 24 June 2004, *Passer-by Along a Wall in a Roman Park* (oil on panel, 5 x 7 ins / 13 x 19 cm) EUR 42,000.

FORTUYN, Willem
Dutch, 18th century.
Active between 1757 and 1762.
Engraver.
Willem Fortuyn is perhaps identical with the engraver Gugliemo Fortuyn, who was active in Italy a little later.

FORTUYN AND O'BRIEN, group
Dutch and British, 20th century.
Active in the Netherlands and in the USA.
Sculptors.
Dutch artist Irene Broogleever Fortuyn (born 1959) and Robert O'Brien (born 1951 in England) live and work in Amsterdam and New York and have worked in tandem since 1984. They produce sculptures, generally in the form of arcades, fashioned from supporting steel or wooden rods and which act as semi-transparent elements (they can be standalone or viewed through Plexiglas or a grille) that mark off and impart greater spatial depth to a building interior or exterior.
BIBLIOGRAPHY:
Hefting, Paul, *De eigen ruimte: beeldhouwkunst in Nederland na 1945*, Elsevier, Amsterdam, Brussels, 1986. *Fortuyn-Obrien. Have a nice day*, exhibition catalogue, Centrum Sztuki Wspó, Warsaw, 1992.

FORTY, Jean François
French, 18th century.
Active in Paris.
Draughtsman, engraver.
Jean François Forty published a series of designs for gold work and especially wrought-iron work, including *Bronze Sculptures, Gold Objets d'Art for Churches,* and the three handbooks *Ironwork Pieces*. His drawings were used for executing the staircase and main gate of the École Militaire, and for railings at the Palais Royal and St-Germain-l'Auxerrois in Paris, in the church of the Augustines and at the monastery of the Bernardins in Marseilles.
AUCTION RECORDS:
PARIS, 1896, *Bronze Wall Bracket* (pen and Indian ink) FRF 360; *Chimneypiece* (pen heightened with sepia and Indian ink) FRF 100; *Organ Casing* (pen and watercolour) FRF 159. PARIS, 10-11 April 1929, *Ciborium* (drawing, attributed) FRF 350; *Carved Bronze Frame* (drawing, attributed) FRF 80.

FORTY, Jean Jacques
French, 18th century.
Born 1743, in Marseilles; died December 1800, in Aix-en-Provence.
Painter, draughtsman. History painting.
Jean Jacques Forty was the pupil of Vien and was admitted as an academician on 25 June 1791. In the same year he sent to the Salon de Paris *Impartiality of Epaminondas, Portrait of an Old Hermit* and *Jacob Recognising the Bloodstained Coat of his Son Joseph*. He exhibited there again in 1793 and 1795.
MUSEUMS AND GALLERIES:
AIX: decorative painting.
AUCTION RECORDS:
PARIS, 3 Oct 1991, *Hercules and Hebe* (oil on paper, 9 x 6½ ins / 22 x 16.5 cm) FRF 4,200.

FORTY DE LAMAR, Pierre Denis
French, 18th century.
Active in Paris in 1771.
Painter, sculptor.

FORTY YEARS, Master of the.
See **MASTERS**

FORVETU, Joseph
French, 19th century.
Painter.
Exhibited landscapes at the Paris Salon from 1833 to 1839.

FORZONI-ACCOLTI, Giovanna Gastona
Italian, 19th century.
Active in Volterra (Tuscany).
Painter.
There is a *Madonna of Arezzo* and a *Christ in the Garden of Gethsemane* by Forzoni-Accolti in the Chapel of Mercy in Volterra Cathedral. His signature can also be seen on a large oil painting entitled *St William of Aquitaine in the Church of S Agostino in San Gimignano*.

FORZORI, Alessandro. See **FORTORI**

FOS, Johann Dietrich
German, 18th century.
Active in Hamburg.
Engraver.
Fos's works include the engraved portrait *Pastor J. Chr. Wolf*.

FOSBERY, Ernest George
Canadian, 20th century.
Born 29 December 1874, in Ottawa (Ontario).
Painter, illustrator.
Ernest George Fosbery studied at the Ottowa Art School, the Royal College of Arts from 1890 to 1897, of which he became a member, and, from 1897 to 1898, with Fernand Cormon. He exhibited in Boston, Buffalo, Chicago, St Louis, New York and a number of other cities in Canada and the USA, winning several prizes and medals.

FOSBROOKE, Leonard
British, 19th century.
Active in Ashby-de-la-Zouche.
Painter, watercolourist. Landscapes.
Leonard Fosbrooke was a fairly regular exhibitor with the Royal Academy, Suffolk Street and the New Water-Colour Society, from 1884.

FOSCARDI, Ambrogio. See **TAGLIAPIETRA**

FOSCARI, Orfeo
Italian, 16th century.
Active in Rome in 1578.
Painter.

FOSCATO, S
Italian, 20th century.
Born in Bologna.
Painter.

In 1938 Foscato exhibited two paintings - *Montmartre* and *Nude* - at the Salon des Artistes Indépendants in Paris.

FOSCHI, Andrea
Italian, 16th century.
Born to a family originally from Faenza.
Sculptor (wood).

Andrea Foschi worked in Venice and sculpted a retable and a crucifix for the church of S Giovanni in Latisana (Venezia). The Brera museum in Milan has a medal with a portrait of him.

FOSCHI, Antonio
Italian, 16th century.
Died c. 1602.
Active in Faenza from 1566 onwards.
Painter.

FOSCHI, Antonio
Italian, 16th century.
Active in Faenza.
Painter, goldsmith.

In 1516, Antonio Foschi executed an altarpiece for the Confraternity of S Antonio.

FOSCHI, Apollonio
Italian, 16th century.
Died before 1531.
Active in Massa (Carrara).
Painter.

FOSCHI, Ascanio
Italian, 17th century.
Born to a family originally from Cesena.
Painter.

Ascanio Foschi's *Proclamazione del Perdono d'Assisi*, painted in 1612, is kept in the church of S Apollinare Nuova in Ravenna.

FOSCHI, Carlo
Italian, 18th century.
Born to a family originally from Macerata.
Painter.

Carlo Foschi is on record as having been a landscape painter of some repute.

FOSCHI, Francesco
Italian, 18th century.
Born in Ancona; died 1780, in Rome.
Active in Bologna.
Painter. Landscapes with figures, landscapes.

MUSEUMS AND GALLERIES:

CAMBRAI: *Impression of Snow* - DARMSTADT: *Winter Scene* - GRENOBLE: *Impression of Snow* - LILLE: *Landscape* - TOULOUSE: *Winter*.

AUCTION RECORDS:

PARIS, 21 May 1927, *Travellers in the Snow,* FRF 520. PARIS, 8 May 1940, *Winter Landscape,* FRF 520. LONDON, 24 March 1976, *Winter Landscape* (oil on canvas, 11 3/4 x 19 1/4 ins / 30 x 49 cm) GBP 2,200. LONDON, 9 March 1983, *Winter Landscapes* (two oils on canvas, 9 1/2 x 11 1/2 ins / 24 x 29 cm) GBP 8,000. MILAN, 25 Feb 1986, *Winter Landscape* (oil on canvas, 25 1/2 x 35 ins / 65 x 89 cm) ITL 9,000,000. PARIS, 16 June 1987, *Winter Landscapes* (two oils on canvas, 28 x 39 3/4 ins / 71 x 101 cm) FRF 250,000. NEW YORK, 7 April 1988, *Snow-covered Landscape with a Person on a Path and Houses on a Hill* (oil on canvas, 18 1/4 x 23 1/2 ins / 46.5 x 59.5 cm) USD 7,700. MONACO, 17 June 1988, *Winter Landscape* (oil on canvas, 12 1/2 x 17 1/4 ins / 32 x 44 cm) FRF 61,050. ROME, 13 Dec 1988, *Mountainous Landscape in Winter with Travellers; Mountainous Landscape in Winter with Shepherds and their Animals in a Grotto* (1776, oil on canvas, two pendants, each 48 3/4 x 67 1/4 ins / 124 x 171 cm) ITL 120,000,000. ROME, 23 May 1989, *Winter Landscape* (oil on panel, 9 1/2 x 12 3/4 ins / 24 x 32.5 cm) ITL 8,000,000. NEW YORK, 10 Jan 1990, *Winter Landscape with Travellers on a Snow-covered Path by a River* (oil on canvas, 47 x 67 ins / 119.3 x 170.2 cm) USD 60,500. ROME, 8 March 1990, *Winter Landscape with Travellers* (oil on canvas, 29 1/2 x 39 1/4 ins / 75 x 100 cm) ITL 25,000,000. ROME, 8 April 1991, *Winter Landscape* (oil on canvas, a pair, 38 1/2 x 53 1/2 ins / 97.5 x 136 cm and 39 1/4 x 53 1/2 ins/100 x 136 cm) ITL 17,250,000. BRIVE-LA-GAILLARDE, 28 April 1991, *Winter Landscape* (oil on canvas, 35 1/4 x 38 ins / 89.5 x 96.5 cm) FRF 200,000. MONACO, 5-6 Dec 1991, *Alpine Landscape* (oil on canvas, 33 3/4 x 37 ins / 86 x 94 cm) FRF 244,200. ROME, 26 Nov 1992, *View of Loreto with Peasants Dancing in the Foreground* (oil on canvas, 17 1/2 x 23 ins / 44.5 x 57.5 cm) ITL 25,000,000. LONDON, 7 July 1993, *Winter Landscape with a Duck Hunter and Travellers on a Path by the River* (oil on canvas/panel, 18 1/2 x 29 1/4 ins / 47.2 x 74.3 cm) GBP 9,200. PARIS, 29 March 1994, *Winter Landscape with Figures* (oil on canvas, 28 x 39 ins / 71 x 99 cm) FRF 300,000. PARIS, 12 Dec 1995, *Winter Landscape with Waterfall and Peasants* (oil on canvas, 28 x 39 ins / 71 x 99 cm) FRF 230,000. PARIS, 27 March 1996, *Setting Off in a Snow-covered Landscape* (oil on canvas, 39 1/2 x 52 1/4 ins / 100.5 x 132.5 cm) FRF 70,000. PARIS, 17 July 1996, *Winter Landscape with Peasant Figures* (oil on canvas, 28 1/4 x 37 ins / 72 x 94 cm) FRF 92,000. NEW YORK, 30 Jan 1997, *Winter Landscape* (1779, oil on canvas, 12 3/4 x 18 1/2 ins / 32.7 x 46.7 cm) USD 32,200. PARIS, 17 Dec 1997, *Snow-covered Landscape near a River with People Walking* (canvas, 19 x 29 1/4 ins / 48 x 74 cm) FRF 125,000. LONDON, 17 Dec 1999, *Winter Mountain Landscape with Peasants on Barge* (oil on canvas, 39 x 53 ins / 98 x 135 cm) GBP 17,000. LONDON, 14 Dec 2000, *Winter Landscape with Travellers Crossing a Bridge* (oil on canvas, 19 x 24 ins / 47 x 61 cm) GBP 20,000. NEW YORK, 23 May 2001, *Winter Landscape* (oil on canvas, 19 x 25 ins / 48 x 63 cm) USD 7,000. NEW YORK, 24 Jan 2002, *Winter Landscape* (oil on canvas, 25 x 30 ins / 63 x 76 cm) USD 30,000. LONDON, 10 July 2002, *Winter Landscape with Waterfall and Peasants Chopping Wood* (1778, oil on canvas, 38 x 53 ins / 97 x 134 cm) GBP 60,000. LONDON, 10 Dec 2003, *Mountainous Winter Landscape with Peasants by a Farmhouse* (oil on canvas, 49 x 70 ins / 125 x 179 cm) GBP 24,000. MILAN, 12 May 2004, *Winter Landscape with Figures* (oil on canvas, 13 x 18 ins / 34 x 45 cm) EUR 5,500. PARIS, 25 June 2004, *Winter Landscape* (oil on canvas, 17 x 24 ins / 43 x 60 cm) EUR 17,000.

FOSCHI, Giambattista
Italian, 17th century.
Active in Ancona.
Painter.

Giambattista Foschi painted two major compositions in 1629 for the church of S Niccolo de Tolentino depicting the life of that saint.

FOSCHI, Giuseppe
Italian, 18th century.
Active in Bologna.
Engraver.

Giuseppe Foschi engraved a *St Anne Teaching Mary to Read* in 1743 and a portrait of *The Surgeon L. F. Anderlani* in 1763.

FOSCHI, Nicola
Italian, 16th century.
Active in Faenza.
Painter, goldsmith.

With his brother Antonio, Nicola Foschi collaborated on an altarpiece for the Confraternity of S Antonio.

FOSCHI, Pier Francesco di Jacopo. See **TOSCHI Pier Francesco di Jacopo di Domenico**

FOSCHI, Salvadore (Fra)
Italian, 16th century.
Active in Arezzo (Tuscany).
Painter. History painting.
The Uffizi Gallery in Florence has four drawings of the Virgin by Salvadore Foschi in its collection.

FOSCHI, Sigismondo
Italian, 16th century.
Born in Faenza; died after 13 September 1532.
Painter.
The Brera museum in Milan has a *Madonna and Child* painted by Sigismondo Foschi in the church of S Bartolommeo in his native Arezzo. A *Virgin with Saints* in the Pinacoteca in Faenza is also attributed to him.
AUCTION RECORDS:
NICE, 18 and 19 Feb 1946, *Crown of Thorns*, FRF 30,000; *Virgin, Holy Infant, St John*, FRF 32,000.

FOSCHINI, Arcangelo, or Fosquini
Portuguese, 18th - 19th century.
Born 1771, in Lisbon; died 4 April 1834, in Lisbon.
Painter.
Arcangelo Foschini was the son of the Italian painter Francesco Foschini; he studied under J.M. da Rocha at the academy in Lisbon and completed his studies in Rome and Florence. When he returned to Lisbon he became painting teacher to the Infante Don Pedro Carlo, and from 1803 to 1823 he collaborated on the decoration of three rooms at the royal palace of Paço d'Ajuda near Lisbon. There is an altarpiece dated 1829 by Foschini in a church in Santarem near Lisbon.

FOSCHINI, Francesco
Italian, 18th century.
Born c. 1745, in Faenza; died 1805, in Lisbon.
Painter.
Francesco Foschini copied Guido Reni's *Virgin with St Francis and St Christina* for the church of the Capuchin monastery in Faenza. In 1771 he was invited by the marquis of Pombal to work as a painter in the porcelain manufactory in Lisbon.

FOSCHINI, Michele
Italian, 18th century.
Born 1711, in Guardia Sanframondi; died 1770.
Painter.
Michele Foschini studied under N. M. Rossi and Fr. Solimera. He painted an altarpiece for Nusco Cathedral and altarpieces and frescoes for the Naples convent of S Gaudioso. He also painted a fresco for the vault of the church of S Maria della Pace in that city.

FOSCHINI, Pedro Maria, or Fosquini
Portuguese, 19th century.
Active in Lisbon.
Sculptor.
Pedro Maria Foschini was the son of the painter Arcangelo Foschini and studied with the court sculptor J.J. de Aguiar. In 1822 he made a statue of *Ceres* for the royal palace of Paço d'Ajuda.

FOSCO, Antonio and Nicola di. See **FOSCHI**

FOSDICK, Gertrude Christiane
American, 19th century.
Born 19 April 1862, in Middlesex (Virginia).
Painter, sculptor.
Gertrude Christiane Fosdick was a pupil of William Bouguereau and Jules Lefebvre at the Académie Julian in Paris, and a member of the Allied Artists of America.

FOSDICK, James William
American, 19th - 20th century.
Born 13 February 1858, in Charlestown (Massachusetts); died 1937.
Painter, fresco painter. Figure compositions, religious subjects, mythological subjects.
James William Fosdick was both a painter and writer, who studied at the Boston Museum of Fine Arts School and at the Académie Julian in Paris under Gustave Boulanger, Jules Lebebvre and Raphael Collin. He specialised in frescoes and painted the subject of *Joan of Arc* several times.
AUCTION RECORDS:
NEW YORK, 31 March 1994, *Nymphs Playing near Waterfalls* (oil on canvas, 30 x 24 ins / 76.2 x 61 cm) USD 1,380.

FOSELLA, Giovanni
Italian.
Born in Sargana (Punjab), Pakistan.
Engraver.
He was a pupil of Granara.

FOSIE, Elisabeth
Danish, 18th century.
Active in Copenhagen.
Engraver (etching).
Elisabeth Fosie was the sister of Johanne Marie Fosie and the daughter of Jacob Fosie.

FOSIE, Jacob
Danish, 18th century.
Died 1 December 1763, in Copenhagen.
Active in Copenhagen.
Painter, engraver (etching), musician.
Jacob Fosie was a pupil of the Copenhagen painter Hendrik Krock. Upon finishing his studies in Italy he became a drawing master at the junior school. He produced watercolours of landscapes, fruit and flowers, among which were copies of works by Wouwerman and other Dutch artists. As an etcher Fosie published a collection of his landscapes in 1746, and in 1747 a collection of works depicting his pupils, among whom were his son and two daughters.

FOSIE, Johanne Marie, later Mrs Westengaard
Danish, 18th century.
Born 24 March 1726, in Copenhagen; died 23 August 1764.
Painter, engraver (etching).
Johanne Marie Fosie was the daughter and pupil of Jacob Fosie. Like her father, she painted landscapes, fruit and flowers in watercolour, many of which were copies after Dutch masters. Her etchings include *Christ before Pilate, Two Views of the Castle of Christianborg, Illuminations for the Arrival of Princess Louise in Copenhagen, 11 December 1743*, various landscapes, and subjects by the sea.

FOSIE, Michael
Danish, 18th century.
Born 20 January 1724; died 22 May 1794.
Engraver (etching).
Michael Fosie, a cleric in Randers, was the son of Jacob Fosie.

FOSKHO, Josef
Russian, 20th century.
Born in Russia.
Sculptor.
Joseph Foskho exhibited in Paris in a show organised by Rodin, and at the Worcester Art Museum in 1933.

FOSMAN, Gregorio, or Forstman or Vosman
Spanish, 17th century.
Engraver.
The works of Gregorio Fosman include: *Title Page for a Life of Sto Domingo de Silos* (1653); *Auto-da-Fé Held in the Main*

Square in Madrid on 30 June 1860; St Francis Xavier; and *Portrait of Archbishop F. Manso de Zúñiga.*

FOSMAN Y MEDINA, Gregorio
Spanish, 17th century.
Born in 1653; died in 1715.
Engraver.

Gregorio Fosman y Medina was probably the son of Gregorio Fosman and, like him, a highly regarded engraver. His works include *Portrait of Cardinal Enrique Noris* and illustrations for a *Life of St Julian*, after A. Palomino y Velasco.

BIBLIOGRAPHY:
Aterido Fernández, Ángel, *El grabador madrileño Gregorio Fosman y Medin*, Consejo Superior de Investigaciones Científicas, Madrid, 1997.

FOSQUINI, Arcangelo and Pedro Maria.
See **FOSCHINI**

FOSS, Harald Frederick, or Voss
Danish, 19th - 20th century.
Born August 1843, in Fredericia; died 1922.
Painter. Landscapes.

Son of Hans Vilhelm Voss.

MUSEUMS AND GALLERIES:
COPENHAGEN: three paintings.

AUCTION RECORDS:
COPENHAGEN, 18 March 1980, *Rainy Weather* (1889, oil on canvas, 13 1/2 x 22 ins / 34 x 56 cm) DKK 4,500. STOCKHOLM, 19 April 1989, *Coastline* (1900, oil on canvas, 15 3/4 x 22 3/4 ins / 40 x 58 cm) SEK 12,500.

FOSS, Harriet Campbell
American, 19th century.
Born c. 1860, in Middleton (Wisconsin); died 1938, in Darien (Connecticut).
Active in New York.
Painter.

Harriet Campbell Foss was a pupil of Alden Weir in New York and of Alfred Stevens and Courtois in Paris. She took part in the exhibitions of the Société Nationale des Beaux-Arts in Paris.

FOSS, Olivier
French, 20th century.
Born 1920.
Painter. Urban landscapes, seascapes.

Olivier Foss painted mainly traditional views of Paris.

AUCTION RECORDS:
LOS ANGELES, 18 March 1980, *View of a Village* (oil on canvas, 24 x 29 ins / 61 x 73.6 cm) USD 625. LUCERNE, 7 Nov 1985, *St-Martin Canal, Paris* (1965, oil on canvas, 18 x 22 ins / 46 x 55 cm) CHF 2,200. PARIS, 16 Dec 1987, *Place de la Concorde* (oil on canvas, 15 1/4 x 21 1/2 ins / 38.5 x 54.5 cm) FRF 3,200. PARIS, 4 July 1990, *Return from Fishing* (oil on canvas, 21 1/4 x 25 1/2 ins / 54 x 65 cm) FRF 5,000. LE TOUQUET, 21 May 1995, *Street in Ménilmontant* (oil on canvas, 22 x 18 ins / 55 x 46 cm) FRF 8,000. NEW YORK, 7 Nov 1995, *On the Seine* (oil/synthetic resin, 18 x 21 1/2 ins / 45.7 x 54.5 cm) USD 920. ST GALL, 2 Nov 1999, *View of Restaurant Mariaberg in Rorschach* (oil on canvas, 18 x 22 ins / 46 x 55 cm) CHF 3,900. ST GALL, 8 May 2001, *Old Village* (oil on canvas, 26 x 32 ins / 65 x 81 cm) CHF 6,500. ST GALL, 21 Nov 2001, *Viviani Square* (oil on canvas, 18 x 22 ins / 46 x 55 cm) CHF 4,000.

FOSSA, Franco
Italian, 20th century.
Born in Milan.
Painter, engraver.

Franco Fossa frequented the Accademia di Belle Arti di Brera in Milan. He participated in various Biennales in Italy (including Verona and Milan), and exhibited at the Mostra di Carrara.

Fossa's works, which contain highly visible graphic elements, evoke the confinement and anguish of the human condition.

FOSSA, François de (Vicomte)
French, 19th century.
Born 3 April 1861, in Paris.
Watercolourist, writer.

A pupil of Vignal, under the pseudonym of 'Yvan d'Assofil' he showed views of Fontainebleau and Marseilles at a number of exhibitions. His work, *A History of the Château of Vincennes*, contains several of his sketches.

FOSSA-CALDERÓN, Julio Eduardo
Chilean, 20th century.
Born in Valparaíso.
Painter.

Julio Fossa-Calderón studied under Cormon, Laurens and Biloul. He exhibited regularly at the Salon des Artistes Français from 1922 to 1938 and was awarded a silver medal in 1930, a gold medal in 1936 and was declared hors-concours.

AUCTION RECORDS:
PARIS, 1 July 1992, *The Swing* (oil on panel, 16 1/4 x 13 ins / 41 x 33 cm) FRF 20,000.

FOSSAERT, Mainnaert
Flemish, 17th century.
Active in Antwerp.
Painter.
Flemish School.

In 1605 Mainnaert Fossaert was a pupil of Thomas Franken and in 1611 became a master of the guild.

FOSSANO, da. See also first name

FOSSANO, Stefano da. See **BORGOGNONE Ambrogio**

FOSSAT, Vincent
French, 19th century.
Born 1822, in Nice; died 1891, in Nice.
Painter, draughtsman, watercolourist, illustrator.
Natural history (botanical subjects/fish), seascapes.

Vincent Fossat's work appeared in the exhibitions *Paysages de Nice au XIXe siècle* (*Nice Landscapes in the 19th century*) at the Musée des Beaux-Arts in 1999. He executed more than 4,000 botanical plates on the flora of Nice, mushrooms, 360 models of Mediterranean fish and many coloured moulds. He illustrated Jean-Baptiste Barla's *Flore illustrée de Nice et des Alpes-Maritimes. Iconographie des Orchidées* (*Illustrated Flora of Nice and the Alpes-Maritimes. Iconography of Orchids.*) As a painter his favourite subject was the beach at Nice.

BIBLIOGRAPHY:
Bauchot, M.L., '*Poissons de la Mer de Nice peints par Vincent Fossat*' in *Annales du Muséum d'Histoire Naturelle de Nice* vol. 11, Muséum d'Histoire Naturelle, Nice, 1996. *Paysages de Nice au XIXe siècle*, exhibition catalogue, Musée des Beaux-Arts, Nice, 1999.

MUSEUMS AND GALLERIES:
NICE (Mus. d'Histoire Naturelle): 7,000 moulded mushrooms painted in watercolour.

FOSSAT, Yvonne
French, 20th century.
Born 3 March 1894, in Le Havre.
Painter.

Yvonne Fossat originally studied at the École des Beaux-Arts in Le Havre in the studio of the engraver Alphonse Lamotte and then in Paris at the École des Beaux-Arts and the Académie Colarossi. She exhibited in Paris at the Salon d'Automne and the Salon des Artistes Français.

FOSSATI
French, 18th century.
Active in Marseilles.
Sculptor.
Fossati sculpted a marble altar in the church of the Grands-Augustins in Marseilles. He received a first prize from the Académie in 1763.

FOSSATI, Andrea
Italian, 19th century.
Born 1844, in Toscolano (Lake Garda, Lombardy).
Painter.
Andrea Fossati studied and worked in Milan, painting genre scenes and portraits. He presented a painting of the *Ballroom in the Old Palace of Delai in Toscolano* in 1900 at the annual exhibition in Milan.

FOSSATI, Bernardino
Italian, 16th century.
Active in Arzo near Mendrisio.
Sculptor (stone).
There is a reference to Bernardino Fossati in 1589.

FOSSATI, Carlo Francesco
Italian, 18th century.
Sculptor, architect.
Carlo Francesco Fossati is on record as having worked in St Petersburg around 1740. He is possibly identical with an artist of the same name reported to have sculpted stucco trophies for the Nevsky Prospect.

FOSSATI, Davide Antonio
Italian, 18th century.
Born 1708, in Morcote, near Lugano; died 1780, in Vienna.
Painter, engraver.
Davide Antonio Fossati studied under Mariotti and Daniel Gran. He was responsible for decorating the refectory of the monastery of St Martinsberg in Pressburg (now Bratislava) in 1728. He is also credited with paintings in a villa in Torre (near d'Este) and in the S Margaretta cloister near Lugano. His best engraving work includes Solimena's *Diana and Callisto*; Bellucci's *Darius and Family Appearing before Alexander* and *Rebecca and the Servant of Abraham*; and a sequence of 24 views of Venice and the surrounding countryside based on work by Marco Ricci.

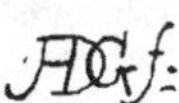

FOSSATI, Domenico
Italian, 18th century.
Born 1743, in Venice; died 1784, in Venice.
Painter, architect.
Domenico Fossati was the son and pupil of Giorgio Fossati. He studied at the academy in his native Venice and built a reputation based on his decorative and architectural work. Examples of his work are to be seen in theatres and *palazzi* in Venice, Padua, Vicenza, Verona, Udine, Monza, Graz, and at La Scala in Milan.

FOSSATI, Gaetano
Swiss, 19th - 20th century.
Born 1862, in Meride, near Mendrisio.
Painter. Religious subjects, genre scenes.
Educated at the Accademia di Belle Arti di Brera in Milan and at the Accademia Albertina in Turin, Fossati exhibited in Geneva, Bern, Lugano, Turin and Milan, and received several awards and distinctions, notably in Turin and Milan. Examples of his work include *Christ Crucified; Idyll; Returning from the Fields*.

FOSSATI, Giorgio
Italian, 18th century.
Born 1706, in Morcote; died 1778.
Engraver, architect.
Giorgio Fossati engraved plates for *Raccolta di Varie Tavole* published in Venice in 1744. He also contributed drawings and sculptures to the Scuola di San Rocco in Venice.

FOSSATI, Giorgio
Italian, 19th century.
Born c. 1800, in Piacenza.
Sculptor.
A marble altar and two angels, which Giorgio Fossati sculpted around 1840, can be seen in the Capella del Santissimo in the church of S Antonio in Piacenza.

FOSSATI, Giovanni Maria
Swiss, 18th century.
Born to a family originally from Morcote (Lake Lugano, Switzerland).
Sculptor, architect.
Fossati may be the brother of David Antonio Fossati. He worked in Dresden where he created the old baroque style marble altar for the St-Thomas church in Leipzig, which was transferred to St John's Church. The marble altar of the Catholic section of the Bautzen Cathedral is attributed to him and the one in the church of Grossröhrsdorf near Bautzen is also likely to be Fossati's work.

FOSSATI, Guiseppe Luigi
Italian, 18th - 19th century.
Born 1759, in Venice; died 6 October 1811, in Venice.
Painter.
Giuseppe Luigi Fossati was the son of Davide Antonio Fossati. He studied at the academy in Venice around 1775 and went on to devote himself to art and literary history.

FOSSATI, Pierre
French, 18th century.
Active in Grenoble.
Painter.

FOSSÉ, Athanase
French, 19th - 20th century.
Born 7 January 1851, in Allonville; died 18 June 1923.
Sculptor. Figures, historical figures. Statues.
Athanase Fossé studied under Cavelier and exhibited at the Paris Salon from 1876. He produced a bronze statue of *Joan of Arc Imprisoned* for the town of Crotoy. He was a member of the Société des Artistes Français and received a bronze medal in 1882, a bronze again in 1889 at the Exposition Universelle and a silver medal in 1900.
MUSEUMS AND GALLERIES:
AMIENS: *Th. Caudron; Jules Barnt; Woodcutter; The Wave; Joan of Arc Imprisoned; The Night of 4 December 1851* - ARRAS: *Dancer*.

FOSSE, Charles de La. See **LAFOSSE Charles de**

FOSSE, de La. See **DELAFOSSE** and **LAFOSSE de**

FOSSE, Désiré
French, 19th - 20th century.
Born 10 January 1862, in Nantillois; died December 1913, in Nantillois.
Active in Paris.
Sculptor.
Désiré Fosse was a member of the Société des Artistes Français. He was awarded a bronze medal in 1890 and a travel bursary the same year.

FOSSÉ, Jacques
French, 17th century.
Sculptor.

Jacques Fossé worked in 1659 with Pierre Pavillon and Jean Rombaud on the decoration of the façade of the town hall of Aix-en-Provence.

FOSSE, Louis
French, 18th century.
Active in Paris.
Painter.

Louis Fosse painted a *Baptism of Christ* which is in the possession of the church of St-Médard in Paris.

FOSSES-MENGELLE, Pierre Émile
French, 19th - 20th century.
Born in the second half of the 19th century, in Bagnères-de-Bigorre.
Sculptor.

Pierre Fosses-Mengelle first exhibited in Paris at the Salon des Artistes Français in 1903.

FOSSEY, André
French, 19th - 20th century.
Active in Paris.
Painter.

André Fossey became a member of the Société des Artistes Français in 1884.

FOSSEY, Félix
French, 19th century.
Born 12 August 1826, in Paris.
Painter, draughtsman, watercolourist, pastellist.

He enrolled at the École des Beaux-Arts on 2 October 1844 and studied under Blondel and L. Cogniet. Fossey was awarded silver at the 1852 Prix de Rome for his *Raising of Jairus' Daughter from the Dead*. He exhibited on a fairly regular basis at the Salon between 1847 and 1869 and was one of twenty artists shortlisted in a competition to design the emblem of the Second Republic. Examples of Fossey's work include a *St Sebastian*, an *Instruction of the Virgin, Four Seasons, Truth and Fabrication, Love and Madness,* and a *St Helen* for the church of Fère-en-Tardennois.

AUCTION RECORDS:
NEW YORK, 18 March 1998, *Allegory of The Republic* (oil on canvas, 25 3/4 x 17 ins / 65.4 x 43.2 cm) USD 10,350.

FOSSEY, Jean
French, 18th century.
Active in Bayeux.
Painter.

FOSSEYEUX, Jean Baptiste
French, 18th - 19th century.
Born 1752, in Paris; died 1824, in Paris.
Engraver.

Jean Baptiste Fosseyeux was the pupil of Moreau the Younger and engraved after Velázquez and Domenichino. He exhibited at the Salon from 1793 to 1822.

FOSSIER
French, 18th century.
Active c. 1775.
Draughtsman, designer of ornamental architectural features.

Fossier is remembered for a series of *Trophies* engraved by Berthault, two plates of *Goldsmith's Work* engraved by Bénard, and two plates for *Happy Misfortunes* by Ingouf. Patas engraved several plates of his drawings for the *Historical Iconology of the Sovereigns of France*.

FOSSIER, Christian
French, 20th century.
Born 9 September 1943, in Paris.
Engraver, draughtsman.

Fossier's engravings are very distinctive. They are in an abstract style, and are suggest a hybrid universe, a cross between the animal and the mechanical. They invent a world of strange encounters between iron and flesh, and between breath and silence. Always in black and white, and often considerable in size, Fossier's engravings are striking for their purity, both in the materials he uses and in the techniques he applies.

Christian Fossier exhibited his work at the Jeune Gravure Contemporaine (exhibition of young engravers' work), in 1963, 1964 and 1965. He has also taken part in the Salon des Réalités Nouvelles and the Salon de Mai. He was also twice invited to the Biennale de Paris, in 1965 and 1967, also exhibiting at the Tokyo Biennale, in 1966, and the Ljubljana Biennale (in Slovenia) in 1967. In 1977, he took part in *Papier sur Nature* (*Paper on Nature*), part of the Festival d'Automne in Paris. This exhibition was conceived by Jean Clair, calling for a revival of drawing and figuration. He was also represented in the *Major Developments in Contemporary Engraving (1945-1991)* exhibition, at the Centre d'Art d'Ivry in 1991. The Musée de Grenoble staged an exhibition of his work in 1972.

FOSSIER, Matthis
Dutch, 17th century.
Painter.

In 1685 Matthis Fossier became a member of the guild.

FOSSIN, Jean Baptiste (father)
French, 19th century.
Born 1786, in Paris.
Painter, sculptor.

Salon exhibitor in 1846 and 1847 with *Triumph of Christ, Act of Prayer* (marble), *Virgin and Child with Passion Flowers,* and a marble statue entitled *Mirror*. Fossin was awarded a bronze medal in 1847.

FOSSIN, Jules Jean Baptiste (son)
French, 19th century.
Born 1808, in Paris.
Sculptor.

Studied under his father and exhibited at the Salon from 1852 to 1861.

FOSSLAND, Toroff
Norwegian, 20th century.
Born 20th century.
Painter.

A restrained abstract painter whose primary interest is the interplay of form and colour, Toroff Fossland's overall style is can best be described as gently geometric, softened by scraps of cloth incorporated into the painted surface.

FOSSOUX, Claude
French, 20th - 21st century.
Born 1946.
Painter, lithographer. Figures, landscapes with figures.

Claude Fossoux has regularly displayed his work in Paris, and has also exhibited in New York and Chicago. He mostly paints elegant young women, striking informal poses, or in fields full of flowers.

AUCTION RECORDS:
PARIS, 29 Nov 1982, *The Conversation in the Garden* (oil on canvas, 24 x 19 3/4 ins / 61 x 50 cm) FRF 7,800. MEGÈVE, 10 March 1984, *Sleeping Village* (oil on canvas, 21 1/4 x 25 1/2 ins / 54 x 65 cm) FRF 8,000. LA VARENNE-ST-HILAIRE, 6 March 1988, *Young Woman on a Bicycle* (oil on canvas, 21 1/4 x 25 1/2 ins / 54 x 65 cm) FRF 8,500. PARIS, 30 May 1988, *Young Girls Applying Their Make-up in a Garden* (oil on canvas, 24 x 19 3/4 ins / 61 x 50 cm) FRF 16,000. LA VARENNE-ST-HILAIRE, 23 Oct 1988, *Young Woman Picking Flowers* (oil on canvas, 25 1/2 x 32 ins / 65 x 81 cm) FRF 14,000. PARIS, 16 Dec 1988, *In St-Paul de Vence* (oil on canvas, 24 x 19 3/4 ins / 61 x 50 cm) FRF 42,500. PARIS, 15 Feb 1989, *Outside the Café* (oil on canvas, 18 1/4 x 22 ins / 46.5 x 55 cm) FRF 8,300. LA VARENNE-ST-HILAIRE, 3 Dec 1989, *The Poppy Picking* (oil on canvas, 19 3/4 x

24 ins / 50 x 61 cm) FRF 15,200. PARIS, 11 March 1990, *Afternoon in a Garden* (oil on canvas, 25½ x 32 ins / 65 x 81 cm) FRF 41,000. PARIS, 9 Dec 1991, *Open-Air Restaurant* (oil on canvas, 19¾ x 25½ ins / 50 x 65 cm) FRF 10,000. PARIS, 3 June 1992, *Le Café de Flore* (oil on canvas, 19¼ x 25¼ ins / 49 x 64 cm) FRF 8,500. CALAIS, 6 May 2001, *Young Girls in a Poppy Field* (oil on canvas, 24 x 18 ins / 61 x 46 cm) FRF 12,000. CALAIS, 30 May 2004, *Young Girl in a Flower Meadow* (oil on canvas, 16 x 13 ins / 41 x 33 cm) EUR 2,700.

FOSTÉ, Théodore
Flemish, 18th century.
Active in Mechelen.
Sculptor (wood).
Flemish School.
In 1730 Théodore Fosté worked with Verhaegen on the stalls of the church of St-Jean.

FOSTER, A.J.
British, 19th century.
Born 1834, in Westminster; died 1897.
Painter. Portraits.
A.J. Foster came to England from Australia as an infant, and became a Supreme Court Judge in 1876. He does not appear to be identifiable as the artist Arthur Joseph Foster.
MUSEUMS AND GALLERIES:
SYDNEY: *Judge Sir William Windeyn.*

FOSTER, Alan
American, 20th century.
Born 2 November 1892, in Fulton (New York); died 1934.
Painter.
Alan Foster designed covers for reviews and magazines.
AUCTION RECORDS:
NEW YORK, 14 Dec 1973, *The Other Side,* USD 1,600. NEW YORK, 26 June 1981, *A Disputed Call* (1930, oil on canvas, 30 x 24¼ ins / 76.2 x 61.5 cm) USD 3,750.

FOSTER, Arthur Bell
British, 20th century.
Born 5 March 1900.
Painter, illustrator. Landscapes.
Arthur Foster studied at Sheffield School of Arts. He exhibited at the Royal Academy, the Royal Institute of Painters in Watercolours, the Glasgow Institute, the Paris Salon and in various English towns and cities. He was a member of the United Society of Artists.

FOSTER, Arthur Joseph
British, 19th - 20th century.
Painter. Portraits, landscapes.
Arthur Foster exhibited fairly regularly at the Royal Academy and at the Suffolk Street Gallery from 1880 to 1904.
AUCTION RECORDS:
LONDON, 21 July 1981, *View of Lake Como* (1874, oil on canvas, 24 x 42¼ ins / 61 x 107 cm) GBP 230.

FOSTER, Arthur Turner
American, 20th century.
Born 1867, in Brooklyn (New York City); died 1947.
Painter.
Arthur Turner Foster was a self-taught artist and a member of the Artland Club, the Los Angeles P.S.C. and the Californian Watercolor Society.

FOSTER, Benjamin or Ben
American, 19th - 20th century.
Born 31 July 1852, in North Anson; died 1926.
Active in New York.
Painter, art writer. Landscapes.
Benjamin Foster was a pupil of Abbott H. Thayer in New York and of Aimé Morot and Olivier Merson in Paris. He was a member of the National Academy and was awarded the second Cleveland prize in 1895, the Chicago gold medal in 1893, a bronze medal in Paris in 1900, a silver medal in St Louis in 1904 and the Webb Prize in 1901.
MUSEUMS AND GALLERIES:
MONTREAL: *Misty Moonlight* - PARIS (MAM): *Soothed by the Murmur of a Stream.*
AUCTION RECORDS:
NEW YORK, 31 Jan- 2 Feb 1898, *In the Cold and Silence,* USD 210; *Lonely Road,* USD 500. LONDON, 5 May 1899, *Lake Stafford,* FRF 10,500. NEW YORK, 9 March 1906, *Herd Returning,* USD 115. NEW YORK, 11 March 1909, *Light Effect,* USD 185. NEW YORK, 4 March 1937, *Evening Star,* USD 75. NEW YORK, 14 Oct 1943, *Under a Cloudy Sky,* USD 200. NEW YORK, 29 Jan 1981, *House by Stream* (oil on canvas, 30 x 24¼ ins / 76.2 x 61.5 cm) USD 3,500. NEW YORK, 23 June 1983, *Brook through the Woods* (oil on canvas, 36 x 30 ins / 91.4 x 76.2 cm) USD 3,000. NEW YORK, 30 Sept 1985, *Hazy Moonrise* (oil on canvas, 11½ x 42¼ ins / 29 x 107.4 cm) USD 1,500. NEW YORK, 1 Oct 1986, *Waning Days and Hills* (oil on canvas, 18 x 22 ins / 45.7 x 56 cm) USD 1,500. NEW YORK, 7 April 1988, *Reflecting Pond* (oil on canvas, 19¾ x 35 ins / 50 x 88.9 cm) USD 1,210. NEW YORK, 30 May 1990, *Moonrise in October* (oil on canvas, 42 x 48 ins / 106.7 x 122 cm) USD 3,300. NEW YORK, 31 May 1990, *Meeting House and Stream* (oil on canvas, 30 x 30 ins / 76.2 x 76.2 cm) USD 3,300. NEW YORK, 21 May 1991, *Evening* (oil on canvas, 34 x 26 ins / 86.3 x 66 cm) USD 990. NEW YORK, 10 June 1992, *Waning Day* (oil on canvas, 30 x 30 ins / 76.4 x 76 cm) USD 3,300. NEW YORK, 23 Sept 1993, *The Litchfield Hills* (oil on canvas, 42¼ x 36¼ ins / 107 x 91.8 cm) USD 9,200. NEW YORK, 31 March 1994, *Morning, Late Autumn* (oil on canvas, 42 x 48 ins / 106.7 x 121.9 cm) USD 4,888.

FOSTER, Bertha Knox
American, 20th century.
Born 25 May 1896, in Hymer (Kansas).
Painter.
Bertha Knox Foster was a pupil of Clark, Schaeffer and Wright Poor, and a member of the California Art Club and the Society of Women Painters of the West.

FOSTER, Catherine
British, 20th century.
Born in England.
Engraver.
Catherine Foster exhibited two drypoint engravings at the 1930 Paris Salon.

FOSTER, Charles B.
American, 19th century.
Born 4 July 1850, in North Anson; died 1931.
Active in Formington (Missouri).
Painter.
Charles Foster studied with Cabanel at the École des Beaux-Arts in Paris, and also worked with Jacquesson de la Chevreuse.

FOSTER, Edward Ward
British, 18th - 19th century.
Born 1761; died 1864.
Painter. Landscapes.
Edward Foster was active in London, where he exhibited with the Royal Academy from 1809 to 1828. He also made silhouettes.

FOSTER, Enid
American, 20th century.
Born 28 October 1896, in San Francisco.
Sculptor.
Enid Foster was a pupil of Chester Beach.

FOSTER, F.E. (Miss)
British, 19th century.
Active in Hitchin.

Painter. Fruit.
F.E. Foster was a regular exhibitor at Suffolk Street from 1871 to 1879.

FOSTER, Frederick
British, 19th century.
Active in London.
Painter. Landscapes.
Frederick Foster exhibited at Suffolk Street from 1867 to 1876.

FOSTER, Grace
American, 20th century.
Born 9 March 1879, in Wolfe City (Texas); died 1941.
Painter. Genre scenes, landscapes with figures.
Grace Foster was a pupil of Elia. J. Hobbs, Zella Web and Frank Reaugh, and was a member of the Southern States Art League.
AUCTION RECORDS:
NEW YORK, 10 June 1992, *Young Boy with Cattle by a Stream* (oil on canvas, 16 x 22 ins / 40.7 x 55.9 cm) USD 1,430.

FOSTER, Herbert Wilson
British, 19th century.
Painter, watercolourist. Figures.
Herbert Wilson Foster exhibited regularly at the Royal Academy from 1870, and less frequently at Suffolk Street and the New Water-Colour Society.

FOSTER, J. Ernest
British, 20th century.
Born 1877, in Hull; died c. 1965.
Engraver.
Ernest Foster studied at the Royal College of Art in London. He exhibited two engravings, *The Old Barn* and *Old Squeezed Hops* at the 1924 Salon.

FOSTER, John
American, 17th century.
Born 1648, in Dorchester (Massachusetts); died 9 September 1681, in Boston.
Engraver (wood).
John Foster was a student at Harvard College and in 1675 founded Boston's first printing works. Two engravings that he printed himself are attributed to him; a portrait of the churchman *R. Mather* and a *Map of New England*.

FOSTER, Leonida Adelaide
American, 20th century.
Born in Boston (Massachusetts).
Painter. Landscapes.
Leonida Adelaide Foster was a pupil of Victor Charreton. She exhibited *Spring Flowers* in 1923 and *Autumn on the Farm* in 1925.

FOSTER, Maria Jane
British, 20th century.
Engraver.
Maria Foster exhibited two wood engravings at the 1927 Paris Salon.

FOSTER, Marianne. See **BARRETT**

FOSTER, Miles, or Myles Birket, known as Birket
British, 19th century.
Born 4 February 1825, in North Shields; died 27 March 1899, in Weybridge.
Painter, watercolourist, engraver, draughtsman, illustrator. Portraits, genre scenes, landscapes, seascapes.
The youngest of seven children, Myles Birket Foster was born into an old Quaker family. His grandfather was a friend of the engraver and draughtsman Thomas Bewick (1753-1828), the illustrator of numerous books, and credited with the revival of woodcut printing in England. The family settled in London when Myles was five years old. He studied drawing in Tottenham and Hitchin, and under Parry, and was apprenticed to the engraver Stone at the age of 16. Stone committed suicide on the day the apprenticeship was due to begin, and Birket Foster subsequently joined the workshop of the woodcut-printer Ebenezer Landells (1808-1860), a friend of Bewick's from their youth. Landells worked for numerous publications and periodicals; during his five-year apprenticeship, Birket Foster perfected the technique of woodcut engraving and produced innumerable drawings published in *Punch, Punch's Almanack*, the *Illustrated London News* and the *Annual Almanack*, among others.

In 1846, aged 21, he left Landells and found a publisher (Vigetelly). His illustrations for *Évangeline* were an early success, after which he travelled to the Rhineland. The journey inspired Birket Foster's illustrations to Longfellow's poem *Hyperion*, and provided material for his own album, *The Rhine and its Picturesque Journey*, published in 1856. From 1846 to 1859, he devoted himself to book illustration, and produced a large number of woodcuts for celebrated works of the period. He began painting in watercolours at the age of 34, in 1859, and exhibited a view of Arundel Castle at the New Water-Colour Society in 1859. He became an associate of the Royal Society of Painters in Watercolours the following year, together with the celebrated figure painter Frederick K. Smallfield. He became a full member in 1861, the year in which his father died. A confusion of names led to the announcement of Birket Foster's own death, an error which he discreetly corrected.

He left London and settled in Surrey where he built a country house, The Hill in Witley, decorated by his friends Rossetti (the dining-room), Burne-Jones, William Morris, Hunt, Walker, Pinwell and Houghton (the staircases). Birket Foster continued to paint the simple, now often unrecognisable, landscapes of rural Surrey - village churches, small streams - until his death at the age of 74. His conventional compositions, almost always drawn from rural life, are usually small in size with careful, highly detailed drawing beneath transparent dabs of fresh, closely juxtaposed colour, reminiscent of the Neo-Impressionists. From 1861 to 1899, when Impressionism was little-known in England, Birket Foster's work was categorised as Realist: he sought to present a realistic rendering of the (admittedly) most appealing aspects of the rural scene. His bucolic watercolours reflect his illustrations for the works of the elegiac poets, and were perfectly in keeping with the English mood of the time.

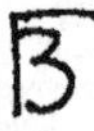

BIBLIOGRAPHY:
Reynolds, J., *Birket Foster*, London, 1984.
MUSEUMS AND GALLERIES:
ABERDEEN (AG): *Self-portrait* - BLACKBURN: *Landscape with Cottage; Apenheim* - GLASGOW: *The Rock of the Lorelei* - LIVERPOOL: *Seascape with Ships* - LONDON (Victoria and Albert Mus.): *Seascape with Ships* - SYDNEY: *Spring*.
AUCTION RECORDS:
MANCHESTER, 1861, *Resting Post Beside a Gate* (watercolour) FRF 3,300. LONDON, 1874, *Egg Stealers* (drawing) FRF 4,050. LONDON, 1874, *Seashore* (drawing) FRF 4,725. LONDON, 1877, *Former Home of Robert Bruce* (watercolour) FRF 8,250. LONDON, 1887, *Dog Training* (drawing) FRF 7,230. LONDON, 1891, *The Meeting* (drawing) FRF 13,385. LONDON, 1898, *Spring* (drawing) FRF 6,025; *Harvesters* (drawing) FRF 6,425. LONDON, 1899, *Stradfort Lake* (watercolour) FRF 10,500. LONDON, 1899, *Pack of Hounds Breaking Cover* (drawing) FRF 4,050; *Market in Seville* (watercolour) FRF 5,250. LONDON, 30 Nov 1907, *Chair Mender* (watercolour) GBP 204. LONDON, 15 Feb

1908, *Landscape* (watercolour) GBP 105; *Young Girl Gathering Water Lilies* (watercolour) GBP 94; *Rialto, Venice* (watercolour) GBP 105. London, 29 May 1908, *Koblenz* (watercolour) GBP 94. London, 19 June 1908, *Drawing Water from a Stream* (watercolour) GBP 105. London, 26 June 1908, *Wood-cart* (watercolour) GBP 462; *Fruiterer's Shop* (watercolour) GBP 210. London, 10 July 1908, *Rustic Fishermen* (watercolour) GBP 199. London, 6 Feb 1909, *Edinburgh* (watercolour) GBP 75. London, 13 Feb 1909, *Lake Maggiore* (watercolour) GBP 136. London, 27 March 1909, *St Andrew* (watercolour) GBP 131. London, 11 June 1909, *On the Way to Market* (watercolour) GBP 252. London, 25 June 1909, *Dance Lesson* (watercolour) GBP 315. London, 16 April 1910, *Ford*, GBP 131. London, 23 April 1910, *Greta Bridge* (watercolour) GBP 126. London, 27 May 1910, *Animals Drinking from a Trough* (watercolour) GBP 126. London, 13 June 1910, *Dead Gull* (watercolour) GBP 147. London, 24 June 1910, *Hexham* (watercolour) GBP 210. London, 2 Feb 1923, *The Abbey of San Gregorio* (drawing) GBP 157; *Stream* (drawing) GBP 215; *Rocky Coastline* (drawing) GBP 183. London, 23 Nov 1923, *Mother and Daughter* (drawing) GBP 31; *Butterfly Hunting* (drawing) GBP 30; *Beside the Farm* (drawing) GBP 86. London, 15 Feb 1924, *Bradgate Castle* (drawing) GBP 42; *In the Meadow*, GBP 152. London, 21 March 1924, *In Hambledon* (drawing) GBP 89; *Farm Beside a Road* (drawing) GBP 35. London, 2 May 1924, *Hunter* (drawing) GBP 420; *Garden* (drawing) GBP 178; *Highland Loch* (drawing) GBP 136. London, 13 June 1924, *Children's Teatime* (drawing) GBP 110; *Chartres* (drawing) GBP 89; *Ferry Boat* (drawing) GBP 81. London, 14 Nov 1924, *Sheep and Ducks* (drawing) GBP 157. London, 23 Feb 1925, *Dover* (drawing) GBP 54. London, 15 March 1925, *The Tyne Valley* (drawing) GBP 105; *Granada* (drawing) GBP 71; *On Lake Como* (drawing) GBP 65; *Island of San Giorgio Maggiore, Venice* (drawing) GBP 48; *River; Italian Lake* (two drawings) GBP 22. London, 19 June 1925, *Threshers* (drawing) GBP 651. London, 2 Dec 1927, *Arundel* (drawing) GBP 367; *Haymaking* (drawing) GBP 388; *Going to Market* (drawing) GBP 367; *Roquebrune* (drawing) GBP 241; *Gypsies* (drawing) GBP 225; *Seville* (drawing) GBP 141; *Pisa* (drawing) GBP 162. London, 28 Feb-3 March 1930, *Meeting* (watercolour) GBP 945; *Red Lion Inn* (watercolour) GBP 525; *Burying the Favourite* (watercolour) GBP 378; *Venice* (watercolour) GBP 892; *Cattle Returning to the Fold* (watercolour) GBP 210; *Gathering Blackberries* (watercolour) GBP 42; *Overtaking the Flock* (watercolour) GBP 756; *Beside the Thames* (watercolour) GBP 241. Birmingham, 15 Nov 1933, *Aberdeen* (watercolour) GBP 60; *Witley* (watercolour) GBP 52; *Cattle Returning Home* (watercolour) GBP 210; *Butterflies* (watercolour) GBP 32. London, 13 April 1934, *At the Well* (drawing) GBP 48. New York, 17-18 May 1934, *Meadow* (watercolour) USD 150. London, 30 Oct-2 Nov 1936, *Milan* (drawing) GBP 29; *The Lido, Venice* (drawing) GBP 71; *On the Rhine; Rio Ognissanti* (two drawings) GBP 88; *Rhenish Town; On the Canals; Fishing Village* (three drawings) GBP 162; *Italian Lake* (drawing) GBP 102. London, 22 June 1938, *Wooded Landscape* (drawing) GBP 28. London, 23 June 1939, *Three Children* (drawing) GBP 81. London, 21 June 1940, *Lake Como* (drawing) GBP 31; *Young Country Folk* (drawing) GBP 68. London, 26 June 1941, *Rustic Bridge* (drawing) GBP 98; *Fribourg* (drawing) GBP 29. London, 31 March 1943, *Landscape* (watercolour) GBP 220; *On the Coast* (watercolour) GBP 250. London, 23 June 1943, *Florence* (watercolour) GBP 48; *In Holland; In Venice* (two watercolours) GBP 96. London, 17 Sept 1943, *Near Dalmally* (drawing) GBP 714; *Windsor Lock* (drawing) GBP 819; *Summer Landscape* (drawing) GBP 945; *Forest Scene* (drawing) GBP 441; *Feeding the Cat* (drawing) GBP 52; *Loch Awe* (drawing) GBP 294; *Old, Old Story* (drawing) GBP 336; *Spring* (drawing) GBP 168; *Shoreline* (drawing) GBP 47; *Harbour at Marseilles* (drawing) GBP 94; *York* (drawing) GBP 126. London, 10 May 1944, *Meadow* (watercolour) GBP 820; *Clovelly* (watercolour) GBP 280; *Ferry Boat* (watercolour) GBP 460; *Harvest* (watercolour) GBP 270. London, 22 Nov 1946, *Spring* (drawing) GBP 120; *Lagoon, Venice* (drawing) GBP 50. London, 24 Jan 1947, *Gathering Primroses* (drawing) GBP 315. London, 2 April 1947, *On the Back of a Donkey* (drawing) GBP 94; *Lake Como* (drawing) GBP 131; *Terrified* (drawing) GBP 57; *Gleaners* (drawing) GBP 63; *Skylark* (drawing) GBP 52. London, 25 April 1947, *Italian Lake* (drawing) GBP 36. London, 25 April 1947, *Gleaners Returning Home* (drawing) GBP 157. London, 25 July 1947, *St Goarhausen* (drawing) GBP 52; *At Work* (drawing) GBP 68. London, 22 July 1959, *Village Inn* (watercolour) GBP 550. London, 11 March 1960, *Wooded Landscape in Surrey* (drawing) GBP 945. London, 16 June 1961, *Wooded Landscape in Surrey* (drawing) GBP 577. London, 22 April 1966, *Eton Chapel seen from the River* (watercolour) Gns 550. London, 19 Nov 1968, *Wood-cart* (watercolour and gouache) Gns 1,100. London, 15 June 1971, *Surrey Landscape* (watercolour heightened with white) Gns 3,000. London, 7 March 1972, *Alfresco Dance* (watercolour) Gns 750. London, 20 June 1972, *View of Bellagio on Lake Como*, GBP 900. London, 20 June 1972, *View of Bellagio on Lake Como*, GBP 900. London, 28 Nov 1972, *Sailing-Boat in a Tub* (gouache and watercolour) GBP 800. London, 27 March 1973, *Alpine Landscape*, GBP 500. London, 5 Nov 1974, *Market Scene, Falaise* (watercolour) Gns 1,500. London, 9 Nov 1976, *Picnic* (watercolour heightened with white, 8¼ x 12¾ ins / 21 x 32.5 cm) GBP 850. London, 3 April 1977, *Estuary at Sunset* (watercolour heightened with white, 5 x 7 ins / 12.5 x 17.8 cm) GBP 550. London, 26 April 1977, *Estuary at Sunset* (watercolour heightened with white, 5 x 7 ins / 12.5 x 17.8 cm) GBP 550. London, 3 July 1979, *Harvest Scene* (watercolour heightened with gouache, 8½ x 13½ ins / 21.5 x 34 cm) GBP 3,200. London, 6 May 1981, *Village Tree* (watercolour, 8¼ x 10¾ ins / 21 x 27.3 cm) GBP 2,600. London, 19 Oct 1983, *Ford* (oil on canvas, 39 x 59 ins / 99 x 150 cm) GBP 7,500. London, 15 May 1984, *Country Inn* (watercolour, gouache and pencil, 31 x 26½ ins / 79 x 67.5 cm) GBP 21,000. London, 26 Jan 1987, *Oxford from Christchurch Meadows* (watercolour heightened with gouache, 13 x 28 ins / 33 x 71 cm) GBP 23,000. London, 29 Jan 1988, *Leith Hill in Surrey* (oil on canvas, 9 x 12 ins / 22.9 x 30.5 cm) GBP 825. Edinburgh, 30 Aug 1988, *Tummel Falls* (watercolour and gouache, 12½ x 17½ ins / 32 x 44.5 cm) GBP 1,705. London, 25 Jan 1989, *Glasgow Cathedral* (watercolour and gouache, 6 x 7¾ ins / 15 x 20 cm) GBP 3,300; *Returning Home* (watercolour and gouache, 7¾ x 5¾ ins / 19.5 x 14.5 cm) GBP 7,150. Chester, 20 July 1989, *Thatched Cottage near Braemar* (watercolour and gouache, 7¾ x 11 ins / 19.5 x 27 cm) GBP 12,650. London, 31 Jan 1990, *Swing* (watercolour heightened with gouache, 11 x 16½ ins / 28 x 42 cm) GBP 41,800; *Nightfall* (watercolour/pencil and gouache, 8¼ x 13 ins / 21 x 33 cm) GBP 9,240. Glasgow, 6 Feb 1990, *Ben Cruachan* (watercolour and gouache, 8¼ x 10¼ ins / 21 x 26 cm) GBP 8,800. London, 25-26 April 1990, *Crossing the Ford* (1882, watercolour and gouache, 30¼ x 26½ ins / 77 x 67 cm) GBP 25,300. London, 26 Sept 1990, *Young Cowgirl* (watercolour heightened with gouache, 14 x 23½ ins / 35.5 x 60 cm) GBP 13,200. London, 30 Jan 1991, *Thatched Cottage in the Trossachs* (watercolour and gouache, 11 x 15 ins / 28 x 38 cm) GBP 11,000. London, 8 Feb 1991, *Bridge of Sighs in Venice* (watercolour heightened with white, 11½ x 9 ins / 29.5 x 22.7 cm) GBP 13,200. London, 5 June 1991, *Young Girl Feeding a Branch to a Donkey in Front of a Little Girl Sitting on the Grass* (watercolour heightened with white, 6¼ x 5 ins / 16 x 13 cm) GBP 5,280. London, 29 Oct 1991, *Beside the Duckpond* (pencil, watercolour and gouache, 9¼ x 13½ ins / 23.5 x 34.4 cm) GBP 10, 450. London, 19 Dec 1991, *Ships on the Basin near the Salute in Venice* (watercolour and gouache, 14 x 21 ins /

35.6 x 53.3 cm) GBP 19,800. LONDON, 3 June 1992, *Venetian Canal seen from a Balcony* (watercolour and gouache, 5 1/2 x 4 ins / 14 x 10 cm) GBP 1,760. LONDON, 13 Nov 1992, *View of Holmwood Common, Surrey* (watercolour and gouache, 15 x 30 ins / 38.2 x 76.2 cm) GBP 15,400. EDINBURGH, 13 May 1993, *Cottage near Bannavie* (watercolour and gouache, 6 3/4 x 10 1/4 ins / 17.2 x 26 cm) GBP 3,300. LONDON, 8-9 June 1993, *Venice* (oil on canvas, 64 1/2 x 111 ins / 164 x 282 cm) GBP 29,900. LONDON, 5 Nov 1993, *Fishermen's Children* (pencil and watercolour, 11 x 15 1/2 ins / 27 x 39.2 cm) GBP 24,150. LONDON, 30 March 1994, *Feeding the Chickens* (watercolour and gouache, 13 3/4 x 23 1/2 ins / 35 x 60 cm) GBP 20,700. MILAN, 20 Dec 1994, *Children at the top of a Cliff* (watercolour/paper, 11 3/4 x 18 ins / 30 x 45.5 cm) ITL 3,910,000. LONDON, 29 March 1995, *Doge's Palace in Venice; Island of San Giorgio* (watercolour and gouache, each 6 x 7 3/4 ins / 15 x 20 cm) GBP 16,100. NEW YORK, 18-19 July 1996, *Young Peasant Boy Trying to Reach a Waterlily* (watercolour/card, 8 1/4 x 11 1/4 ins / 21 x 28.6 cm) USD 19,550. LONDON, 8 Nov 1996, *Anderlecht, on the Rhine* (pencil and watercolour heightened with white, 6 x 8 3/4 ins / 15.2 x 22.2 cm) GBP 5,000. LONDON, 14 March 1997, *Sailing Boats on the Basin near the Salute, Venice* (pencil and watercolour heightened with white, 14 x 21 ins / 35.6 x 53.3 cm) GBP 32,200. LONDON, 4 June 1997, *Kite Stuck in a Tree* (watercolour heightened with gouache, 6 x 8 ins / 15 x 20.5 cm) GBP 11,500. LONDON, 5 Nov 1997, *Flower-Market, Toulon* (watercolour heightened with gouache, 18 1/2 x 28 1/4 ins / 47 x 72 cm) GBP 20,700; *On the Footbridge* (watercolour heightened with gouache, 10 1/4 x 15 1/4 ins / 26 x 38.5 cm) GBP 20,700. LONDON, 7 Nov 1997, *Henley-on-Thames* (pencil and watercolour heightened with white, 4 1/4 x 5 3/4 ins / 10.5 x 14.6 cm) GBP 9,430. LONDON, 10 June 1999, *Market Day on Giudecca, Venice* (pencil and watercolour heightened with gouache, gum arabic and scratching out, 24 x 36 ins / 61 x 91 cm) GBP 62,000. BILLINGSHURST, 26 Oct 1999, *Surrey Landscape* (watercolour heightened with gouache, 35 x 30 ins / 90 x 77 cm) GBP 25,000. LONDON, 28 Nov 2000, *Old Curiosity Shop* (pencil, watercolour and gum arabic heightened with gouache, 22 x 31 ins / 56 x 79 cm) GBP 15,000. LONDON, 29 Nov 2000, *Preparing Dinner* (watercolour over pencil heightened with gouache, 8 x 11 ins / 21 x 28 cm) GBP 19,000. LONDON, 7 June 2001, *To Gather King-cups in the Yellow Mead and Prink Their Hair with Daisies* (pencil and watercolour heightened with gouache, 31 x 27 ins / 79 x 69 cm) GBP 85,000. LONDON, 28 Nov 2001, *Meet* (pencil, watercolour, gouache and gum arabic, 28 x 60 ins / 71 x 152 cm) GBP 215,000. LONDON, 1 May 2002, *Donkey Ride* (watercolour, 13 x 28 ins / 33 x 70 cm) GBP 31,000. LONDON, 21 Nov 2002, *Picking Blackberries* (pencil, watercolour and gouache, 14 x 24 ins / 36 x 61 cm) GBP 22,500. LONDON, 4 Nov 2003, *Cottage in Surrey* (watercolour and gouache, 8 x 13 ins / 21 x 33 cm) GBP 17,000. LONDON, 3 Dec 2003, *Errant Harvesters* (pencil, watercolour and gouache, 6 x 7 ins / 14 x 18 cm) GBP 13,000. PARIS, 17 March 2004, *Rheims* (watercolour and gouache, 31 x 26 ins / 78 x 67 cm) EUR 45,000. LONDON, 18 Nov 2004, *Children Gathering Primroses* (pencil, watercolour, goauche and gum arabic with scratching out, 17 x 25 ins / 42 x 64 cm) GBP 60,000.

FOSTER, Nicolas

French, 20th - 21st century.
Born 1960, in Paris.
Painter, draughtsman, engraver. Figures, nudes, landscapes.
Point 4 Group.

Nicholas Foster attended the École des Beaux-Arts de Paris from 1980 to 1982. From 1983 to 1987, he was a member of the Point 4 group, along with P. Goemaere, V. Teneze and L. Zunino. He lives and works in Paris.

Foster's paintings represent nude women, whether on their own or in couples, captured in suggestive or lascivious poses, on a background of vivid colour. They convey a sense of constant visual interaction between the curves of the female form. He is also an engraver. He has taken part in various group exhibitions, most notably the following: the Point 4 exhibitions, from 1983 to 1987, at the Ranelagh Theatre, at the Galerie Le Point Nommé, at the Cloître des Billettes, and at the Cercle Charles Péguy; at the Salon des Réalités Nouvelles, from 1989-1992, in Paris; and *De Bonnard à Baselitz - Dix ans d'enrichissements du Cabinet des estampes 1978-1988* (*From Bonnard to Baselitz: A Decade of Acquisitions by the Prints Collection 1978-1988*) in 1993, at the National Library in Paris. He has also staged a number of solo exhibitions: at the Galerie J. Debaigts in Paris, 1997; an open exhibition at the 204 in Paris, from 1992-2001; and at the 2001 Foire de Gand, staged by the Parisian gallery, La Capitale.

BIBLIOGRAPHY:

Beaumont-Maillet, Laure/Woimant, Françoise/Pernoud, Emmanuel, *De Bonnard à Baselitz - Dix ans d'enrichissements du Cabinet des estampes*, exhibition catalogue, Bibliothèque nationale de France, Paris, 1992.

MUSEUMS AND GALLERIES:

PARIS (BNF): *Paysage* (1981, engraving).

FOSTER, O. L.

American, 20th century.
Born 12 May 1878, in Ogden (Indiana).
Painter.

O. L. Foster was a pupil of Laura A. Fry and Harry Leith-Ross.

FOSTER, Ralph L.

American, 20th century.
Born 20 May 1887, in Providence (Rhode Island).
Draughtsman, illustrator.

FOSTER, Thomas

Irish, 19th century.
Born 1798, in Dublin; died 1826, in London.
Portrait artist.

Thomas Foster travelled to England from Ireland at a young age and enrolled at the Royal Academy Schools. He subsequently exhibited with the Royal Academy from 1819 to 1825. He committed suicide. His works include: *Miss Tree, Right Hon. John Wilson Croker, Sir Henry Bishop.*

FOSTER, Walter H. Wallis

British, 19th century.
Painter. Landscapes.

Walter H. Wallis Foster was active in Kingsland and Haslemere. He was a regular exhibitor at Suffolk Street and occasionally at the Royal Academy, from 1861 to 1881.

FOSTER, Willet S.

American, 20th century.
Born 11 March 1885, in Gouverneur (New York); died 1940.
Painter.

Willet S. Foster was a pupil of K. Yens and N.W. Warner, and a member of the California Watercolor Society.

FOSTER, William

British, 19th century.
Died 1812.
Active in London.
Painter. Portraits.

William Foster exhibited quite regularly with the Society of Artists, the Royal Academy and the British Institution.

FOSTER, William

British, 19th century.
Born 1853, in London; died 1924, in London.
Painter, watercolourist. Genre scenes.

William Foster exhibited with the Royal Academy, the Suffolk Street Gallery, and the New Water-Colour Society, from 1870. He was active mainly in Witley, and was the son of Myles Birket Foster.

FOSTER, William Friederich
American, 20th century.
Born 13 August 1882, in Cincinnati (Ohio); died 1953.
Illustrator, watercolourist. Figures, scenes with figures.
William Friederich Foster won the Clarke Prize in 1926.
AUCTION RECORDS:
SAN FRANCISCO, 24 June 1981, *Escorted Ladies* (1930, oil on canvas, 33 3/4 x 40 ins / 86 x 101.5 cm) USD 700. LONDON, 11 Oct 1995, *Small Boy Feeding his Favourite Bird* (watercolour, 22 x 17 1/4 ins / 55 x 43.5 cm) GBP 2,300. NEW ORLEANS, 29 July 2000, *Woman Playing Spanish Guitar* (oil on canvas, 36 x 42 ins / 91 x 107 cm) USD 3,600. CINCINNATI, 10 Sept 2000, *Hat Shop* (oil on canvas, 36 x 24 ins / 91 x 61 cm) USD 3,250. SAN FRANCISCO, 12 Dec 2001, *Seated Nude with a Cockatoo* (oil on canvas, 40 x 30 ins / 102 x 76 cm) USD 2,750. SAN FRANCISCO, 12 Dec 2001, *Seated Woman* (oil on canvas, 27 x 27 ins / 69 x 69 cm) USD 3,250. SAN FRANCISCO, 9 June 2002, *Portrait of a Young Lady in Yellow Dress, Umbrella on her Lap* (1922, oil on canvas, 50 x 42 ins / 127 x 107 cm) USD 4,250. PASADENA, 18 Nov 2003, *Seated Nude* (oil on canvas, 32 x 25 ins / 81 x 64 cm) USD 2,250.

FOSTER, William Gilbert
British, 19th century.
Born 1855, in Manchester; died 1906.
Painter. Portraits, genre scenes, landscapes.
William Foster exhibited at the Royal Academy and Suffolk Street from 1876.
MUSEUMS AND GALLERIES:
BRADFORD (Cartwright Hall AG): *The Hush of Night* - LEEDS (City AG): *A Life of Shadows* (1895, oil on canvas).
AUCTION RECORDS:
LONDON, 8 June 1973, *Shadows and Light*, Gns 600. LONDON, 28 April 1987, *A Mother and Child at the Gate of a Cottage* (watercolour heightened with white, 21 1/2 x 14 3/4 ins / 54.7 x 37.5 cm) GBP 800. LONDON, 30 March 1994, *Hop Garden at Rolvenden in Kent* (1884, oil on canvas, 22 x 35 3/4 ins / 56 x 91 cm) GBP 2,530. LONDON, 29 March 1995, *Endless View of the Other Side* (1894, oil on canvas, 42 1/4 x 72 ins / 107.5 x 183 cm) GBP 4,025. LONDON, 7 Nov 1997, *Harvesters' Return* (1898, oil on canvas, 42 x 72 ins / 106.7 x 182.9 cm) GBP 16,100. LONDON, 11 March 1999, *Children Resting by a Bridge in a Wooded Landscape* (1877, oil on canvas, 22 x 36 ins / 56 x 91 cm) GBP 1,400. LEYBURN, 13 April 2000, *Cabbage Garden* (1891, oil on canvas, 22 x 36 ins / 55 x 91 cm) GBP 7,500. PENZANCE, 12 July 2001, *Quiet Moments: Woman and Children in a Cottage Garden* (1902, oil on canvas, 36 x 48 ins / 91 x 121 cm) GBP 9,000. MUNICH, 19 March 2003, *Young Girl Carrying a Pail of Water along a Field Path* (oil on canvas, 36 x 22 ins / 91 x 56 cm) EUR 2,200. SCARBOROUGH, 9 Sept 2003, *Lady Palmer's Cottage in Runswick Bay, Children Playing* (oil on canvas, 9 x 18 ins / 22 x 45 cm) GBP 1,700. BATH, 16 Feb 2004, *Children in a Field overlooking the Sea* (oil on canvas, 6 x 11 ins / 16 x 28 cm) GBP 1,450. SCARBOROUGH, 30 March 2004, *Be the Day Weary or Be the Day Long, at Last It Ryngeth to Evensong* (1906, watercolour, 21 x 35 ins / 54 x 89 cm) GBP 5,100.

FOTHERGILL, J.
British, 20th century.
Painter. Figures.
AUCTION RECORDS:
LONDON, 6 Nov 1935, *Mrs Dudgeon*, GBP 15.

FOTI, Eileen M.
American, 20th - 21st century.
Born 1963, in Brooklyn (New York City).
Engraver, lithographer.
Eileen M. Foti was one of the American artists invited to exhibit at the 1995 Jeune Gravure Contemporaine (Young Contemporary Engraving) exhibition in Paris. All her engraved work evokes the materiality of skin, starting with the paper itself.

FOTI, Luciano, or Fori
Italian, 18th century.
Born 1694, in Messina; died 1779.
Painter, copyist, art restorer. History painting.
Luciano Foti was a pupil of Placido Celi. He was a skilled restorer of paintings. He made copies of the work of Polidoro Carravagio in particular, but also imitated the latter artist in his own work. Foti's copies were of sufficiently high quality as to be mistaken by subsequent generations for originals.

FOTINSKY, Serge
Ukrainian, 20th century.
Born 3 February 1887, in Odessa; died 1 September 1971, in Paris.
Active in France from 1908.
Painter, watercolourist, engraver, illustrator.
In 1903 Serge Fotinsky completed his art studies in Odessa. In 1904 he was admitted to the art academy in St Petersburg. After the repression of the Winter Palace demonstrations in 1905, Fotinsky went into exile, first to Berlin, then Munich, where he worked at the academy. In 1908 he reached Paris where he settled.

A wood engraver, he illustrated Georges Duhamel's *Ballads* (1926) and collaborated on numerous magazines: *Montparnasse* (1922 to 1924), *Clarté* (1923), *Monde* (1928) and *Europe* (1950, 1964 and 1975). As a painter he enjoyed the friendship of André Derain who on several occasions revealed in writing the admiration he felt for his work, linking it to the Paris School of the interwar period and the Fauvism and Cubism of the past, while acknowledging a debt to Cézanne.

Fotinsky appeared in many collective exhibitions, particularly in France, including: Salon des Indépendants (between 1912 and 1965); Salon d'Automne (from 1920); Limoges and Bordeaux (1927); Rheims (1928); Grenoble and Périgeux. Exhibitions abroad include: Vienna (1927); Moscow (1928); Prague, Zagreb and Ljubljana (1930); Warsaw and Budapest (1931). He held solo exhibitions in the Billiet-Vorms gallery, Paris (1926, 1927 and 1932). He was one of the organisers of the Exhibition of Contemporary French Painting at the Museum of Modern Western Art in Moscow (1928).
AUCTION RECORDS:
PARIS, 15 March 1943, *Sailing Boat in the Harbour* (1927, watercolour) FRF 210. PARIS, 21 May 1986, *Tulips in the Window Facing the Harbour* (1928, oil on canvas, 39 1/4 x 32 ins / 100 x 81 cm) FRF 7,200. PARIS, 29 Nov 1989, *Tugs in Marseilles* (oil on canvas, 26 x 32 ins / 66 x 81 cm) FRF 9,000. PARIS, 18 Dec 2000, *Women Bathing* (oil on canvas, 26 x 20 ins / 65 x 50 cm) FRF 35,000. PARIS, 18 Dec 2000, *Oriental Woman* (oil on canvas, 19 x 13 ins / 48 x 33 cm) FRF 52,000. PARIS, 25 Nov 2001, *At the Races* (oil on canvas, 29 x 24 ins / 73 x 60 cm) FRF 26,000. PARIS, 13 March 2002, *Spanish Dancer* (oil on canvas, 32 x 26 ins / 81 x 65 cm) EUR 4,400. LONDON, 25 Nov 2003, *Still-life* (oil on board, 15 x 18 ins / 38 x 46 cm) GBP 2,000. PARIS, 15 March 2004, *Chapel Amongst the Trees* (oil on canvas, 29 x 21 ins / 73 x 54 cm) EUR 4,300. PARIS, 16 June 2004, *The Grand Boulevards* (gouache, 59 x 43 ins / 150 x 110 cm) EUR 12,000.

FOTIOU, Haziklia
Greek, 20th century.
Also active in France.
Painter, engraver.
Haziklia Fotiou studied at art school in Athens and continued her training in Paris at the Académie de la Grande

Chaumière and the Académie André Lhote. Her painting is expressive and her composition shows a deft touch.

She featured in several collective exhibitions including: *Peintres et sculpteurs grecs de Paris* (*Greek Painters and Sculptors of Paris*), Musée d'Art Moderne de la Ville de Paris (1961), Salon des Terres Latines, Salon d'Autome, Salon des Femmes Peintres (where she was selected for a prize) and Salon des Indépendants; Greece and Germany (since 1952); and Galerie St-Placide, Paris (1965).

Fotiou was selected for the Othon Friesz prize, New York (1961) and the Gemmail international prize in Tours (1961 1970 and 1972) and chaired the association of Greek art exchanges in France.

Museums and Galleries:

Athens (Gal.) - Frankfurt am Main (Städel) - Paris (FMAC).

FOTUH

Spanish, 10th century.
Active c. 976.
Sculptor.

In Cordova a façade capital on a house in the Carrera del Puente that has Moorish decoration carries the signature of this artist and the year 366 of the Hejira (976-977).

FOU, E.

French, 20th century.
Engraver.

E. Fou produced etchings. There is an original etching by him entitled *Outskirts of Montereau* in the collection at the Victoria and Albert Museum in London.

FOUACE

French, 18th century.
Active in Caen.
Painter.

Fouace is mentioned from 1775 to 1783.

FOUACE, Guillaume Romain

French, 19th century.
Born May 1827, in Réville (Manche); died 1895, in Paris.
Painter. Portraits, rustic scenes, animals, still-lifes (flowers/fruit/sea shells).

A pupil of Yvon, he exhibited at the Paris Salon as of 1870. His still-lifes of fish and shellfish are more richly coloured than are his portraits. Fouace was awarded medals in 1884 and in 1891. Examples of his work include *Portrait of Admiral Ducrest de Villeneuve, Apples, Pot-au-feu, Portrait of Dr Le Petit, Tame Rabbits, Béatrix* and *Fish and Shellfish*. An exhibition of his work was held in 1995 at the Thomas Henry Museum in Cherbourg. Overall, Fouace emerges as a somewhat 'naïve' artist preoccupied with painting everyday subjects drawn from his immediate experience and region.

G Fouace

Museums and Galleries:

Bourges: *Time Off* - Cherbourg: *Portrait of Vauban; Portrait of Jean Bart* - Paris (Mus. du Petit Palais): *Double Hit* - St-Brieuc: *Oysters and Chablis* - Stuttgart: *Still-life on Sideboard.*

Auction records:

Paris, 18 May 1900, *Bottle of Sauternes,* FRF 270. Paris, 15 June 1900, *Still-life,* FRF 105. Paris, 12 Dec 1904, *Sideboard,* FRF 660; *Hare, Pheasant, Woodcock, Small Game Birds and Large Copper Pan,* FRF 600. Paris, 23 March 1910, *Duck and Kitchen Utensils,* FRF 115. Paris, 16 May 1923, *Plate of Oysters,* FRF 45. Paris, 8 May 1924, *Ham,* FRF 650. Paris, 16 May 1924, *Still-life,* FRF 95. Paris, 4 March 1925, *Still-life,* FRF 1,000; *Still-life,* FRF 650; *Still-life,* FRF 720; *Still-life,* FRF 450. London, 3 April 1925, *Still-life,* GBP 9. Paris, 6 May 1925, *Still-life with Brioche,* FRF 350. Paris, 30 Dec 1925, *Still-life with Lobster, Oysters, Paté, Wine and Flowers,* FRF 850. Paris, 15 Feb 1926, *Rough Weather near Cherbourg,* FRF 1,950; *Radishes and Eggs,* FRF 800. Paris, 20 Feb 1926, *Partridge,* FRF 310; *Artichokes,* FRF 310. Paris, 10 March 1926, *Branch of Apple-Tree in Blossom,* FRF 195; *Hen Pheasant,* FRF 350. Paris, 3 May 1926, *Still-life,* FRF 1,080; *Pot-au-feu,* FRF 1,200. Paris, 16-17 May 1927, *Still-life with Hare and Partridge beside a Copper Pot,* FRF 1,250. Paris, 17 May 1929, *Still-life,* FRF 1,900. Paris, 10 Feb 1932, *Still-life,* FRF 380. Paris, 8 May 1941, *Prawns,* FRF 180. Paris, 19 April 1943, *Still-life,* FRF 8,100. Paris, 5 May 1944, *Still-life,* FRF 1,750. Paris, 14 June 1944, *Grapes* (1882) FRF 1,600. Paris, 8 Dec 1944, *Partridge,* FRF 1,510. Paris, 20 April 1945, *Still-life with Fruit and Vegetables,* FRF 4,500. Paris, 30 May 1945, *Fruit Bowl,* FRF 300. Paris, Oct 1945-July 1946, *Still-life with Soup Tureen,* FRF 4,000. Paris, 18 Nov 1946, *Figs and Pumpkin,* FRF 3,200. Paris, 26 Feb 1947, *Plate of Oysters* (1891) FRF 6,000. Amsterdam, 15-18 and 21 April 1947, *Still-life,* NLG 1,350. Amsterdam, 26 May 1970, *Still-life with Peaches,* NLG 6,600. Cologne, 15 Nov 1972, *Still-life with Fruit* (1884) DEM 2,500. Amsterdam, 21 Nov 1973, *Still-life,* NLG 2,100. Versailles, 22 Feb 1976, *Still-life with Plums* (oil on canvas, 25 1/2 x 32 ins / 65 x 81 cm) FRF 3,300. Nantes, 25 Nov 1981, *Still-life with Shellfish; Still-life with Game* (two oils on canvas, 31 1/2 x 51 1/4 ins / 80 x 130 cm) FRF 36,000. Vernon, 13 Dec 1987, *Still-life* (oil on canvas, 52 3/4 x 68 ins / 134 x 173 cm) FRF 50,000. Amsterdam, 3 May 1988, *Still-life with Apples* (oil on canvas, 18 1/4 x 24 ins / 46.5 x 61 cm) NLG 6,325. Rome, 14 Dec 1988, *Still-life with Turkey* (oil on canvas, 28 1/2 x 39 1/4 ins / 72.5 x 100 cm) ITL 5,500,000. Paris, 18 Dec 1989, *Still-life with Oysters* (oil on canvas, 15 x 18 ins / 38 x 46 cm) FRF 46,000. Paris, 9 March 1990, *Still-life with Pears* (oil on canvas, 18 x 25 1/2 ins / 46 x 65 cm) FRF 65,000. Amsterdam, 11 Sept 1990, *Still-life with Pumpkin* (oil on canvas, 18 1/2 x 25 1/2 ins / 47 x 65 cm) NLG 6,900. Amsterdam, 6 Nov 1990, *Still-life with a Basket of Peaches* (1875, oil on canvas, 20 3/4 x 25 1/4 ins / 53 x 64 cm) NLG 9,200. Cherbourg, 24 March 1991, *Pears* (1872, oil on canvas, 17 1/4 x 25 1/2 ins / 43.5 x 65 cm) FRF 73,000. Cherbourg, 24 March 1991, *Pears* (1872, oil on canvas, 17 1/4 x 25 1/2 ins / 43.5 x 65 cm) FRF 73,000. Amsterdam, 18 Feb 1992, *Landscape with Horse Resting* (oil on canvas, 19 1/2 x 25 3/4 ins / 49.5 x 65.5 cm) NLG 1,265. New York, 30 Oct 1992, *Still-life* (1890, oil on canvas, 21 3/4 x 27 1/2 ins / 55.2 x 69.8 cm) USD 8,800. New York, 16 Feb 1995, *Still-life with Fish and Oysters* (1875, oil on canvas, 25 3/4 x 32 ins / 65.4 x 81.3 cm) USD 7,475. Amsterdam, 11 April 1995, *Still-life with Ham* (1892, oil on canvas, 19 1/4 x 28 3/4 ins / 49 x 73 cm) NLG 17,110. Paris, 22 Dec 1996, *Roses in a Garden* (oil on canvas, 44 x 28 1/4 ins / 112 x 71.5 cm) FRF 27,500. Paris, 16 March 1998, *Reclining Male Nude* (oil on canvas, 45 x 74 ins / 114 x 188 cm) FRF 200,000. New York, 9 Feb 1999, *In Pursuit of a Meal* (1890, oil on canvas, 22 x 28 ins / 55 x 70 cm) USD 6,500. Amsterdam, 27 April 1999, *Still-life with Apples* (oil on canvas, 11 x 16 ins / 27 x 41 cm) NLG 11,000. Calais, 12 March 2000, *Vase of Flowers* (oil on canvas, 14 x 9 ins / 35 x 24 cm) FRF 46,000. Turin, 21 March 2000, *Vase of Flowers* (oil on canvas, 35 x 26 ins / 90 x 65 cm) ITL 8,000,000. Amsterdam, 15 April 2003, *Still-life with a Lobster* (1885, oil on canvas, 26 x 37 ins / 65 x 94 cm) EUR 9,500. Cherbourg, 24 Nov 2003, *Still-life with Oysters and Mussels* (1892, oil on canvas, 23 x 29 ins / 58 x 73 cm) EUR 15,000. Antwerp, 26 April 2004, *Still-life with Sugarpot and Strawberries* (oil on canvas, 14 x 21 ins / 35 x 54 cm) EUR 2,500.

FOUARD, Ernest

French, 20th century.
Born 27 April 1883, in Montpellier; died 14 September 1951, in Montpellier.
Painter.

Ernest Fouard studied under Cormon and exhibited in Paris at the Salon des Artistes Français from 1913, receiving his first medal the same year. He was awarded a silver medal in 1914, a gold medal in 1921 and the Prix Thirion in 1921.

FOUARD, Moïse Jean Baptiste
French, 17th - 18th century.
Born 1653, in Paris; died 16 March 1726, in Paris.
Engraver.

Moïse Jean Baptiste Fouard was the pupil of Adolphe Perrelle.

FOUASSIER, Jacques
French, 17th century.
Active in Paris in 1692.
Painter, sculptor.

FOUAT, Michel
Belgian, 20th century.
Born 1939, in Rocourt (Liège).
Painter.

Michel Fouat studied at the fine arts academy in Liège and went on to teach there; his fantasy landscapes betray the influence of Paul Klee.

FOUBARD, Abel
French, 20th century.
Born 8 July 1879, in Drivyes-les-Belles-Fontaines; died 1 February 1957, in Auxerre.
Painter. Landscapes.

Abel Foubard studied under Henri Harpignies and Gosselin. He is known for his sensitive landscapes of the Yonne region where he was born and the banks of the Loing. He exhibited in Paris at the Salon des Artistes Français, of which he became a member, receiving a commendation in 1926, a silver medal in 1935, a gold medal in 1942 and the Corot prize the same year.

FOUBERT, Claude Alain
Belgian, 20th century.
Born 1945, in Bois-d'Haine.
Painter, draughtsman.

Foubert attended the Institut St Luc in Brussels.

FOUBERT, Émile Louis
French, 19th - 20th century.
Born 1848, in Paris; died 1911, in Paris.
Painter. Religious subjects, allegorical subjects, mythological subjects, portraits, genre scenes, landscapes with figures, landscapes.

Émile Foubert studied painting at the École Muncipale de Bayonne and then under Léon Bonnat, Charles Busson and Henri Lévy. His works include: *The Chastisement of Caiaphas, Hesiod and the Muse, Christ at the Column* and *Nymphs and Faun.* He exhibited in Paris at the Paris Salon from 1875 to 1879 and at the Salon des Artistes Français, of which he was a member, from 1884. He received a commendation in 1879, a bronze medal in 1889, a silver medal in 1885, a bronze medal in 1889 and a silver medal in 1900.

EMILE FOUBERT

MUSEUMS AND GALLERIES:
BAYEUX: *Corot; Millet* - COMPIÈGNE: *An Arm of the Seine* - ST-ÉTIENNE: *St John in the Wilderness.*

AUCTION RECORDS:
PARIS, 27 Jan 1923, *Market in Brittany,* FRF 230. PARIS, 30 Nov 1923, *Rebecca at the Fountain,* FRF 850. PARIS, 5 Dec 1923, *Vétheuil,* FRF 125. PARIS, 16 March 1925, *Small Village,* FRF 155. PARIS, 4 March 1926, *The Lock,* FRF 260. PARIS, 16 Jan 1928, *Landscape,* FRF 210; *The Little Port,* FRF 120. PARIS, 25 Nov 1942, *Women by the Side of a Shady Stream,* FRF 1,800. PARIS, 8 Dec 1944, *Woman Bathing and her Child beside a Lake in front of a Château,* FRF 1,300. PARIS, 9 March 1945, *Washerwomen,* FRF 1,500. PARIS, 14 Feb 1947, *Boat,* FRF 900. PARIS, 27 March 1947, *River Banks,* FRF 400. PARIS, 29 Nov 1950, *Village Scenes* (two pendants) FRF 22,600. LONDON, 21 July 1976, *The Lonely Angler* (1898, oil on canvas, 25 1/2 x 32 ins / 65 x 81 cm) GBP 600. PARIS, 31 Oct 1980, *Odalisque and Slave* (1879, oil on canvas, 28 3/4 x 18 1/4 ins / 73 x 46.5 cm) FRF 3,300. NEW YORK, 22 May 1986, *The Spring* (1881, oil on canvas, 78 3/4 x 37 3/4 ins / 200 x 96 cm) USD 6,500. PARIS, 13 Dec 1989, *Glade* (oil on canvas, 15 x 22 ins / 38 x 55 cm) FRF 3,500. ROME, 26 May 1993, *Portrait of a Child* (oil on canvas, 19 1/4 x 15 1/4 ins / 49 x 39 cm) ITL 1,800,000. NEW YORK, 17 Feb 1994, *Painting in the Open Air* (oil on canvas, 15 x 18 1/4 ins / 38 x 46.5 cm) USD 1,495. NEW YORK, 1 Nov 1995, *Game of 'La Main Chaude'* (1902, oil on canvas, 36 1/2 x 28 3/4 ins / 92.7 x 73 cm) USD 16,100.

FOUBERT, Hugues
French, 15th century.
Active in Paris.
Painter.

In 1401, Hugues Foubert painted the illuminated miniatures and made the costly binding for two books for the children of the Duchess of Orléans.

FOUBERT, Jean Antoine
French, 18th century.
Active in Paris in 1767.
Painter.

FOUBERT, Jean Joseph
French, 18th century.
Active in Paris in 1770.
Painter, sculptor.

FOUBERT, Pierre
French, 17th century.
Active in Paris in 1675.
Painter, sculptor.

FOUBERT, Rolland
French, 16th century.
Sculptor (wood).

In 1545, Rolland Foubert undertook to carve the organ case for Chartres Cathedral.

FOUCART, Jean Georges
French, 19th - 20th century.
Born in Valenciennes.
Engraver (etching).

Jean Foucart studied under L. Lucas. He exhibited in Paris at the Salon des Artistes Français, receiving a commendation in 1887 and a bronze medal in 1900 at the Exposition Universelle.

FOUCAUCOURT, Gaston de
French, 19th century.
Born 1835, in Paris; died 1891.
Painter.

Son and pupil of Louis-Édouard de Foucaucourt; also studied under Haroignies.

MUSEUMS AND GALLERIES:
AMIENS: *Banks of the Somme.*

FOUCAUCOURT, Gustave de
French, 19th century.
Born 19th century, in Paris.
Painter. Landscapes.

Salon exhibitor from 1865 to 1888. Examples of his work include *Ponds at St-Pierre, Mont Blanc and Chamonix Valley, Evening in the Water Meadows, Pont du Souverain,* and *Mill near Boulogne-sur-Mer.* This artist is often confused with Gaston de Foucaucourt.

Auction records:
Paris, 12 Nov 1946, *Hunting Scene* (under the direction of G. de Foucaucourt) FRF 10,000.

FOUCAUCOURT, Louis Édouard de (Baron)
French, 19th century.
Born 1800, in Foucaucourt.
Painter.
Paris Salon exhibitor from 1839 to 1859; awarded a bronze medal in 1846. His body of work includes *View of the Valley of Llangollen, Countryside in Wales, Castle of the Counts of Tyrol, Stand of Palm Trees in Bordighera on the Genoan Riviera, Farewells of Charles-Edouard* and *Near Lake Como.*

FOUCAUD, Auguste
French, 19th century.
Born 1786, in Périgueux; died c. 1844.
Painter, lithographer.
Studied in Bordeaux under Lacour and exhibited at the Paris Salon in 1827, 1837 and 1838. His work includes an *Adoration of the Magi* (lithograph after a German original) and *Secrets* (watercolour).

FOUCAULT, Foucault Pautard
French, 20th century.
Born 1 December 1945, in Cairo.
Painter.
Foucault studied at the Institut d'Arts Plastiques de Tournai, in Belgium, and has participated in group exhibitions in Paris, in particular, at the Salon Figuration Critique, and at the Grands et Jeunes d'Aujourd'hui.

FOUCAULT, Denis
French, 17th century.
Active in Paris in 1680.
Painter, sculptor.

FOUCAULT, Georges
French, 20th century.
Born in Montereau.
Painter. Landscapes, still-lifes.
Georges Foucault exhibited in Paris at the Salon d'Automne from 1921 to 1931.

FOUCAULT, Gustave Louis
French, 19th century.
Painter. Portraits.
Exhibited portraits at the 1837 and 1848 Paris salons.

FOUCAULT, Hélène
French, 20th century.
Born 6 March 1886, in Paris.
Painter.
Hélène Foucault studied under F. Humbert. She exhibited in Paris at the Salon des Artistes Français.

FOUCAULT, Henri
French, 20th century.
Sculptor, collage artist.
Henri Foucault has specialised in photograms since 1991, using metal filament to draw white figures on to photographic paper exposed to the light, necessarily working within a very short time frame. He assembles his forms and arranges his volumes on large panels or uses them as models for some of his sculptures. To produce these, he explores a range of materials including carpeting, blotting paper and vinyl. He showed his work in solo exhibitions in 1994 in Paris at the Salon Découvertes, presented by the Galerie Michèle Chomette, and at the Espace St-Eustache.
Bibliography:
Genty, Gilles, *'Henri Foucault'* in *Beaux-Arts Magazine* n° 121, periodical, Paris, March 1994. Païni, Dominique, *'Henri Foucault'* in *Art Press* n° 193, periodical, Paris, July-August 1994.

FOUCAULT, Pierre
French, 16th century.
Active in Troyes.
Sculptor (wood).
Between 1508 and 1509, Foucault worked on a throne for the church of St-Jean in Troyes. In 1525, he made the designs for the choir stalls in Troyes Cathedral.

FOUCAULT, Simon C.
French, 20th century.
Born 3 May 1884, in Nantes.
Sculptor.
Simon Foucault studied under Coutan. He was awarded the Grand Prix de Rome in 1912.

FOUCEEL
French, 17th century.
Engraver (etching). Landscapes.
Fouceel engraved *Landscapes.*

FOUCHÉ, Hugues
French, 14th century.
Sculptor.
Fouché was one of the artists working in 1386 on the decoration of the castle of Riom (Puy-de-Dôme) for the Duke of Berry.

FOUCHÉ, Nicolas, or Foucher
French, 17th - 18th century.
Born January 1653, in Troyes; died 1733, in Paris.
Painter, engraver. Mythological subjects, portraits, genre scenes, landscapes.
Nicolas Fouché was the pupil of Mignard.
Museums and Galleries:
Amiens: *View of the Banks of the Somme* - Rennes: *Mother and Child* (drawing) - St-Lô: *Portrait of Marie de Lorraine, Duchess of Valentinois.*
Auction records:
Monaco, 2 Dec 1989, *Marie-Thérèse de Bourbon, Princess of Conti* (oil on canvas, 46½ x 35 ins / 118 x 88 cm) FRF 61,050. Paris, 28 June 1993, *The Judgement of Paris; Pan and Syrinx* (oil on canvas, a pair, each 17 x 32 ins / 43 x 81 cm) FRF 98,000. New York, 21 Oct 1997, *Portrait of Marie de Lorraine, Duchess of Valentinois, and her Sister Charlotte de Lorraine, Mademoiselle d'Armagnac, in front of a Parapet, a Landscape in the Distance* (oil on canvas, 38½ x 51½ ins / 97.8 x 130.8 cm) USD 90,500. London, 26 April 2001, *Portrait of Lady as Flora, Accompanied by Zephyr* (oil on canvas, 34 x 27 ins / 87 x 68 cm) GBP 21,000.

FOUCHER, Alphonse Charles
French, 19th century.
Born 19th century, in Paris.
Engraver (wood).
Exhibited at the Salon des Artistes Français, where he received an honourable mention in 1899.

FOUCHER, Dominique
French, 20th century.
Born 9 December 1936, in Boulogne-sur-Mer.
Painter. Designs for mosaics.
Dominique Foucher studied in Brianchon's studio at the École des Beaux-Arts in Paris. Her painting is non-figurative. She produces mainly mosaics. She exhibited at the Salon d'Automne and in 1963 at the Paris Biennale.

FOUCHER, Jean François
French, 18th century.
Born 1761, in Paris.
Painter. Seascapes.
Auction records:
Auch, 19 June 1982, *Port Scene* (1806, oil on canvas) FRF 4,600.

FOUCHER, Luc Antoine
French, 19th century.
Born 30 July 1851, in Melle (Deux-Sèvres).
Active in Paris.
Painter.
Member of the Société des Artistes Français as of 1904. Painted mainly miniatures.

FOUCHIER, Bertram de, or Fouquier
Dutch, 17th century.
Born 14 February 1609, in Bergen op Zoom; died 25 August 1673, in Bergen op Zoom.
Painter. Portraits, genre scenes.
Bertram de Fouchier was taught by van Dyck in Antwerp from 1634 to 1636. He then became the pupil of Jan Bylert in Utrecht. After practising painting in Venice, Rome, Florence, Paris and Antwerp, he returned to his native town. He copied the works of Jacopo, Tintoretto and Adrien Brouwer, and was also a glass painter.
MUSEUMS AND GALLERIES:
VIENNA (Albertina Mus.): *Vulcan, Mars and Venus.*

FOUCHIER, N. and Robert. See **FAUCHIER**

FOUCHIER, Paulus de, or Fouquier
Dutch, 17th - 18th century.
Born 1643, in Bergen op Zoom; died 1717, in Haarlem.
Painter.
Paulus de Fouchier was the son of Bertram de Fouchier. He had a son who was also called Paulus and who was possibly also a painter.

FOUCHIER, Willem de
Dutch, 17th - 18th century.
Born after 1674; died before 1739, in Amsterdam.
Painter.
Willem de Fouchier was the son of Paulus Fouchier. He initially executed ornamental life-size paintings, then small paintings representing shops, inns, and masquerades in the manner of Janssen, Metsu and Biset, then flowers, and finally murals with hunting or battle scenes.

FOUCOU, Jean Joseph or Louis
French, 18th - 19th century.
Born 7 June 1739, in Riez; died 1815, in Paris.
Sculptor. Mythological subjects, historical figures. Statues, busts.
Jean Joseph Foucou was made an academician on 30 July 1785 for his work *A River*, in marble. He exhibited from 1779 to 1812 at the Salon.

His most notable works include *The Bailiff of Suffren* (marble statue for the town of Salon); *Ariadne Abandoned*; *Puget* (stone statue); *Bust of Cardinal Maury*; *Erigone* (marble statue); *Lancer* (marble statue for the triumphal arch at the Place du Carrousel); *Glory* (marble statue); and *Bust of Jean Goujon*.
MUSEUMS AND GALLERIES:
AIX: *Love* (terracotta, figurine) - MARSEILLES: *Faun* (statuette); *Bacchante* (marble, statuette); *Venus* (marble, statuette); *Bust of Puget*; *Plan for a Monument to Pierre Puget* - PARIS (Louvre): *A River* (marble, statuette); *Bacchante Carrying a Small Satyr* (marble) - PARIS (Mus. de la Comédie-Française): *Regnard-Dancourt* (marble, bust); *Bust of Regnard* (marble) - VERSAILLES: *Bust of General Auguste Dampierre*; *Duguesclin*; *Bust of the Comic Poet Florent Dumont.*
AUCTION RECORDS:
PARIS, 21-22 March 1935, *Bacchante Dancing* (white marble) FRF 5,100. PARIS, 25 Jan 1937, *Profile of a Child* (plaster, low relief) FRF 500. MONTE CARLO, 6 Feb 1978, *Bust of a Woman* (1776, white marble, h. 25 1/2 ins / 65 cm) FRF 6,000. MONTE CARLO, 25 Nov 1979, *Women in Classical Clothing* (white marble, pair of candelabrum, h. 52 3/4 ins / 134 cm, diam. 9 1/2 ins/24 cm) FRF 320,000. PARIS, 18 March 1981, *Women Draped in Classical Clothing Holding Torches* (terracotta, h. with base 41 3/4 ins / 106 cm) FRF 250,000.

FOUCQUART, Lottard
Flemish School, 15th century.
Active in Tournai.
Sculptor.

FOUCQUET. See also **FOUQUET**

FOUCQUET, Lambert
French, 17th century.
Active in Paris in 1683.
Painter, sculptor.

FOUCQUIER. See **FOUQUIÈRES**

FOUCQUIÈRE. See **FOUQUIÈRES**

FOUERE-MARTIN, Yves Charles
French, 20th century.
Born 16 October 1891, in Rennes.
Painter, potter.
Yves Fouere-Martin was a member of the Salon des Artistes Décorateurs and exhibited in Paris at the Salon d'Automne.

FOUET, Jacques
French, 17th century.
Painter.
Jacques Fouet is said by Siret to have been admitted to the Académie in 1664 but expelled almost immediately.

FOUET, Louise Berthe
French, 19th century.
Born 19th century, in Paris.
Painter, pastellist. Flowers, fruit.
Studied under Mme Mallou; exhibited at the salons of 1878, 1879 and 1880.

FOUET, Robert
Swiss, 20th century.
Born in Geneva.
Painter.
Fouet exhibits landscapes painted in the course of his travels.

FOUGEAU, family of artists
French, 16th - 17th century.
Active in Saumur (Maine-et-Loire).
Sculptors, architects.

FOUGEIROL, Jacques
French, 20th century.
Born 30 June 1929, in St-Laurent-du-Pape (Ardèche).
Painter, engraver.
Jacques Fougeirol was self-taught and it was only after working in various professions that he decided to devote himself to his true vocation. His assemblages of structured volumes, which follow the fissures of minerals and rocks, are more often perceived as dream-like developments based on themes such as the human face than as purely abstract pieces. He handles his materials with great gentleness but an extremely assured technique, and uses a muted chromatic range. His first solo exhibitions, in Marseilles and then Paris, were in 1968. In 1969 he exhibited at the *Exposition d'Art Fantastique* (*Exhibition of Fantastic Art*) at the Château de Culan (Cher).
MUSEUMS AND GALLERIES:
MULHOUSE (MBA, Prints Collection) - PARIS (MAMVP).

FOUGEIROL, Thomas
French, 20th - 21st century.
Born 1965.
Painter, draughtsman. Figures, animals.
Thomas Fougeirol graduated from the École des Beaux-Arts in Paris in 1992. He won the first prize of the Fondation Coprim in 1998.

He started by drawing sketchbook pictures of various subjects, landscapes, objects or faces, which came to him almost by instinct and which he sometimes picked up again in his paintings. The same applied to the series of *Cages* standing on the ground, *Dresses* simply hanging up in front of a neutral background, or the series featuring birds, partridges or cocks hung as for still-lifes. The subject is only important to him to the extent that it gives him the freedom to develop the chosen shape through the colour and the material, which is sometimes dripping with moisture, on the surface of the canvas.

He has shown his work in solo exhibitions including: 1995, Galerie de l'Equerre, Paris; 1997, Cloître des Arts, Avignon; 2001 and 2002, Galerie Guigon, Paris.

BIBLIOGRAPHY:
Céna, Olivier, *'Rencontre avec Thomas Fougeirol'* in *Télérama,* n° 2699, periodical, Paris, 2001. *Thomas Fougeirol,* exhibition catalogue, Galerie Guigon, Paris, 2002.

FOUGERAT, Emmanuel
French, 20th century.
Born 25 December 1869, in Rennes; died 3 September 1958, in Paris.
Painter. Figures, nudes, portraits, landscapes, local scenes.

Emmanuel Fougerat studied under Albert Maignan and Jean-Paul Laurens. He became director of the École des Beaux-Arts in Nantes and founding curator of the museum. He remained loyal to his native Brittany, painting landscapes and genre scenes of the region.

He continued to exhibit regularly up to 1945 in Paris at the Salon des Artistes Français, receiving a number of awards from 1899. He was made a Chevalier of the Légion d'Honneur in 1912.

FOUGERAT

MUSEUMS AND GALLERIES:
NANTES (MBA): *Jeune Ouvrier* (*Young Worker*); *Emile Sarradin, maire de Nantes* (*Emile Sarradin, Mayor of Nantes*); *Portrait d'Eugène Livet* (*Portrait of Eugène Livet*) - PARIS (MAMVP): *Portrait of Madame Fougerat* - ST-NAZAIRE: *Child* - VITRÉ: *The Painter and his Wife.*

AUCTION RECORDS:
PARIS, 12 May 1923, *The Toilette,* FRF 450. LONDON, 27 July 1973, *Nude at a Mirror,* Gns 300. VERSAILLES, 14 Dec 1980, *Young Seated Female Nude* (oil on canvas, 9 x 6¼ ins / 22 x 16 cm) FRF 2,000. VERSAILLES, 22 April 1990, *Seated Nude* (oil on canvas, 18 x 15 ins / 46 x 38 cm) FRF 10,000. PARIS, 23 Oct 1991, *Bust View of a Languid Young Woman* (oil on canvas, oval, 9½ x 12 ins / 24 x 30.5 cm) FRF 7,000.

FOUGÈRE, Amanda
French, 19th century.
Born 1821, in Coutances (Manche).
Painter. Religious subjects, figures, genre scenes, local scenes, portraits, flowers, fruit.

Studied under Steuben and Monvoisin; she exhibited at the Salon from 1844 to 1870 and was a medal-winner in 1847. Her body of work includes *St Paul, Spanish Beggar, Woman Weaving, St Cecilia, Solitaire, Portrait of Mgr Deperg, Bishop of Gap, Two Orphan Boys, Hermit's Repast, Little Village Girl* and *Young Moorish Girl.*

AUCTION RECORDS:
PARIS, 22 June 1992, *Basket of Cherries* (oil on canvas, 46 x 35 ins / 116 x 89 cm) FRF 21,000.

FOUGÈRE, Germaine
French, 20th century.
Sculptor.

Germaine Fougère exhibited in Paris at the Salon des Artistes Français in 1939.

FOUGEREZ, F.
French, 20th century.
Painter.

AUCTION RECORDS:
LONDON, 9 July 1926, *Seated Woman,* GBP 42. LONDON, 28 and 29 July 1926, *Seated Woman,* GBP 14.

FOUGERON, André
French, 20th century.
Born 1 October 1913, in Paris; died 10 September 1998.
Painter (including gouache), watercolourist, engraver, designer. Figure compositions, figures, harbour views, still-lifes, flowers. Designs for mosaics, stage sets, church decoration, wall decorations.
Nouvelle Figuration.

André Fougeron came from a family of peasant labourers originally from the Creuse area. In his biography he describes his working life: after completing his basic education he began working as an apprentice draughtsman and then as a metalworker at one of the Renault plants before being made unemployed; he also married and had three children. As an artist he was largely self taught and attended evening classes. In 1939 he joined the Communist Party and during the French Occupation was active in the Resistance. In 1942 he worked for the Front National des Arts and then became secretary of the Union des Arts Plastiques. In 1947 he went to Italy and visited Milan, Venice, Ravenna, Padua, Arezzo and Naples and lived in Rome for several months studying art. It was there that he became close friends with Renato Guttuso, Gina and Nino Franchina and Ewa Garztecka.

He decorated the church of Romainville and executed numerous decorations for public buildings. In 1946 he was awarded the Prix National de la Direction des Arts et Lettres, in 1968 the Grand Prix des Peintres Témoins de leur Temps and in 1976 the prize for painting at the second international triennale of realist art in Sofia. He was a corresponding member (of the painting division) of the Accademia Delle Arti Del Disegno in Florence in 1980.

Before the war he had associated with artists such as Gischia, Pignon, Robin and Tal-Coat when researching into arabesque ornamentation. He was also part of the Art Cruel group brought together by J. Cassou at the Billiet-Worms gallery. An intellectual Marxist, he engaged in a virulent Expressionism, illustrating political events such as the Spanish Civil War with *Homage to Franco!!!* (1937) and the resistance to Nazism in *Death to the Beast* (1944). The 11th Congress of the Communist Party had a determining influence on Fougeron's style of painting; with *Parisian Women at the Market* (1947-1948) he began developing an aesthetic that could be described as social realist, the international and expansionist expression of the cultural policy of the Soviet Union, officially declared in 1934.

Fougeron then became part of the 'Querelle du Réalisme' when the Communists of western Europe named this art 'New Realism'. His paintings, with their strictly defined iconography, became political acts at the service of the Marxist-Leninist dialectic: a 'correct' reflection of reality seen through a revolutionary perspective. True to his political beliefs, in 1950-1951, while living in Lens, Fougeron produced the series *Mining Country,* showing workers treated in a uniquely realist manner as in *Dead Worker.* Outspokenly political, he protested against the North Atlantic Treaty Organisation (NATO) in *French Peasants Defending their Lands* (1953) and against the Vietnam War in *Vietnam 67* (1967). During the 1970s his approach lost its 'historical' nature and developed into a more flexible and perhaps more fertile stylisation.

Though he is known primarily for his social realist period, Fougeron's work was not monolithic. It slid in the direction of Narrative Figuration - which he had broadly hinted at 20 years earlier - which places importance on recounting a story in space and time. Certain retrospective thematic exhibitions serve to remind that he also tackled more traditional subjects. Examples include the series of works exhibited in 1989 at the Galerie Jean-Jacques Dutko in Paris, entitled *Women of Italy*, which presented female figures strikingly coloured in a chromatic range of red, yellow, orange and green, applied in flat tints or with rapid brushstrokes. His composition highlights the rounded forms and elegant arabesques of his figures. Other gouache watercolours, mosaics and oil paintings (*Women of Italy*, 1947) reveal the influence of the spatial projection of Cubism and the Fauvist aesthetic, without, however, abandoning realism of attitude and form. Another theme close to Fougeron's heart is rugby. In the artist's own words, *Leaving the Scrum* (1965-1966), *Line-out* (1967-1968), *Catch* (1970) and *Rugby Spectacle* (1973) depend on the 'inextricable intermingling of forms' with players captured in the scrummage, in a tackle or in a catch. These works are brought to life by the cutting and entanglements of arms, heads, torsos and other body parts and by the contrast of colours - red and white splashed with black.

He first exhibited at the Salon des Surindépendants in 1937 and held numerous solo exhibitions in France and abroad, the main ones being: in 1946 at the Galerie Billiet-Caputo in Paris; in 1951 at the Galerie Bernheim-Jeune in Paris; from 1952 to 1955, at the Galerie Raymond Creuze in Paris; in 1953 at the La Colona gallery in Milan; in 1956 at the Musée des Beaux-Arts in Tours; in 1956 at the Galerie Sagot-le Garrec in Paris; in 1958 at the Galerie La Proue in Brussels; in 1960 at the Galerie Montmorency in Paris; from 1964 to 1969 at the Galerie Katia Granoff in Paris; in 1967 at the Neue Berliner Galerie, Berlin (in the German Democratic Republic); in 1968 at the Kunsthalle, Weimar (GDR); in 1968 at the Albertinum (*Neue Meister*) exhibition in Dresden (GDR); in 1968 at the Pushkin museum in Moscow; at the Hermitage museum in Leningrad; in 1972 at the Centre International d'Art Contemporain in Paris; in 1973 at the Chapelle des Cordeliers in Châteauroux; in 1974 at the Centre d'Art Dramatique in Tours; in 1975 at the Galerie Jeanette Laverrière in Paris; in 1977 at the Maison de la Culture in Châteauroux; in 1976-1977 at the Toninelli gallery, Rome, Bologna, Milan and Palermo; in 1978 at the Städtische Kunsthalle, Recklinghausen, (Federal Republic of Germany); and in 1987, 1989 and 1993 at the Galerie Jean-Jacques Dutko in Paris.

BIBLIOGRAPHY:

Aragon, Louis, *Album de dessins*, Éd. Les 13 Épis, Paris, 1946. *Nouveau dessin, nouvelle peinture*, Librairie Médicis, Paris, 1946. Fréville, J., *Le Pays des Mines*, Éd. Cercle d'Art, Paris, 1951. Uhlitzsch, J., *André Fougeron*, E. A. Seemann, Leipzig, 1970. Rollin, Jean, *André Fougeron*, Éd. Hentschel, Berlin, 1972. *L'Art en Europe, les années décisives 1945-1953*, Skira, Geneva, 1987. *Pièces détachées 1937-1987*, catalogue, Gal. Jean-Jacques Dutko, Paris, 1987.

MUSEUMS AND GALLERIES:

PARIS (MAMVP): *Young Girl with Mirror*; *People of the Sea* - PARIS (Mus. du Petit Palais): *The Pebble Sorter*.

AUCTION RECORDS:

PARIS, 25 Oct 1987, *Pensive Young Woman* (1945, oil on canvas, 24 x 18 ins / 61 x 46 cm) FRF 22,000. VERSAILLES, 21 Feb 1988, *Orange Seller in Rome* (1947, gouache, 25 3/4 x 19 1/2 ins / 65.5 x 49.5 cm) FRF 6,500. LE TOUQUET, 12 Nov 1989, *Rugby Scrum* (oil on canvas, 9 x 13 ins / 22 x 33 cm) FRF 42,000. PARIS, 22 Jan 1990, *Portrait of a Woman* (1944, pastel, 17 3/4 x 24 1/2 ins / 45 x 62 cm) FRF 14,000. NEUILLY, 7 Feb 1990, *Young Poultry Seller* (1946, watercolour, 24 x 18 1/2 ins / 61 x 47 cm) FRF 43,000. MILAN, 27 Sept 1990, *Couple Decried* (oil on canvas, 39 1/4 x 28 1/4 ins / 100 x 72 cm) ITL 2,000,000. PARIS, 29 April 1991, *Face of a Woman* (charcoal, 19 x 24 3/4 ins / 48 x 63 cm) FRF 4,200. CALAIS, 5 April 1992, *Vase of Flowers* (1946, oil on canvas, 22 x 15 ins / 55 x 38 cm) FRF 7,500. PARIS, 4 March 1994, *Still-life* (1944, oil on canvas, 22 x 17 3/4 ins / 55 x 45 cm) FRF 4,500. PARIS, 28 June 1999, *Woman at Her Toilette* (1946, oil on canvas, 32 x 24 ins / 81 x 60 cm) FRF 11,000. CALAIS, 4 July 1999, *Young Girl Reading* (1944, oil on canvas, 21 x 28 ins / 54 x 72 cm) FRF 15,000.

FOUGERON, Ignace

British, 18th century.
Active in London.
Engraver.

Ignace Fougeron exhibited with the Society of Artists and the Free Society.

FOUGEROUSSE, Jean Louis

French, 20th century.
Born 10 December 1870, in Paris.
Painter. Genre scenes.

Jean Fougerousse was a member of the Salon des Artistes Français in Paris. He received a commendation there in 1909.

FOUGEROUX, Georges

French, 20th century.
Born 13 May 1902, in Paris.
Painter.

Georges Fougeroux worked with Lapoujade. He exhibited at the Salon des Artistes Français, the Salon d'Automne and the Salon des Indépendants in Paris.

FOUGERT, Huguette

French, 20th century.
Born 1 November 1928, in St-Cyr-sur-Morin.
Painter. Landscapes, flowers.

Huguette Fougert studied under Charles Bischoff. Her painting is figurative, though sometimes comes close to abstraction, using transparency in a rather Expressionist spirit. She is principally a landcape artist but also tackles themes from modern life. She also paints flowers. She exhibited in Paris at the Salon d'Automne and the Salon de la Société Nationale des Beaux-Arts.

FOUGERY, Anny

French, 20th century.
Born 14 September 1915, in Paris.
Painter.

Anny Fougery exhibited in Paris at the Salon des Réalités Nouvelles and was a member of the Salon d'Automne.

FOUGET, Simonet

French, 14th century.
Sculptor.

In 1386, Simonet Fouget worked together with other artists on the decorations for the castle of Riom in the Auvergne region (Puy-de-Dôme) for the duke of Berry.

FOUGSTEDT, Arvid

Swedish, 20th century.
Born 1888, in Sweden.
Painter.

Fougstedt studied in 1909 and 1910 under Henri Matisse at his academy in Paris. Examples of his work (three portraits and a composition entitled *Balcony*) were shown at a 1929 exhibition of Swedish art in Paris.

AUCTION RECORDS:

STOCKHOLM, 16 May 1984, *Portrait of a Man* (1932, oil on canvas, 36 1/4 x 32 3/4 ins / 92 x 83 cm) SEK 12,000. STOCKHOLM, 20 April 1985, *Self-portrait* (oil on paper, 9 1/2 x 7 1/4 ins / 24 x 18.5 cm) SEK 4,900. STOCKHOLM, 27 April 1999, *The Picador* (1917, oil and egg tempera, 9 x 9 ins / 22 x 22 cm) SEK 74,000. STOCKHOLM, 2 May 2000, *Woman in Deep Thought* (1937, oil on canvas, 36 x 29 ins / 91 x 73 cm) SEK 40,000. STOCKHOLM, 2 May 2000, *Erik* (1893, oil on canvas, 32 x 21 ins / 82 x 54 cm) SEK 50,000. STOCKHOLM, 2 May 2001, *Self-portrait* (oil on canvas, 26 x 22 ins / 65 x 55 cm) SEK 55,000. UPPSALA, 9 Dec

2001, *The Violinist* (oil on canvas, 24 x 20 ins / 60 x 50 cm) SEK 32,000. STOCKHOLM, 23 April 2002, *Still-life* (1920, oil on canvas, 17 x 18 ins / 42 x 46 cm) SEK 62,000. STOCKHOLM, 6 Nov 2002, *Spanish Street Musicians* (1918, oil on canvas, 21 x 26 ins / 54 x 65 cm) SEK 90,000. STOCKHOLM, 27 April 2004, *French Cafe* (1928, watercolour and gouache, 15 x 18 ins / 37 x 45 cm) SEK 56,000. STOCKHOLM, 2 Nov 2004, *Erik in the Doorway - In and Out* (1926, oil on canvas, 46 x 34 ins / 116 x 86 cm) SEK 95,000.

FOUILHOUZE, Félix
French, 19th century.
Born 19th century, in St-Dié (Vosges); died 1885.
Painter.

Studied under Bellel and Ouvrié; exhibited at the Paris Salon from 1836 to 1882. Examples of his work include *Lake of Brientz, View of Oberwesel, Valley of Meyringen, Rocheson Valley, Landscape in the Vosges* and *Souvenir of Switzerland.*

FOUILLEUL, Georges René
French, 20th century.
Born in Paris.
Painter, watercolourist.

Georges Fouilleul exhibited in Paris at the Salon de la Société Nationale des Beaux-Arts from 1923.

FOUINET, Ernest (Mme)
French, 19th century.
Painter.

MUSEUMS AND GALLERIES:
PONTOISE: *Church at Eaubonne.*

FOULAIN, Jean
French, 15th century.
Illuminator, illustrator.

Between 1456 and 1457, Jean Foulain worked for the bishop of Troyes.

FOULARD
French.
Miniaturist. Portraits.

MUSEUMS AND GALLERIES:
ROUEN: *Portrait of a Woman.*

FOULD, Consuelo. See **CONSUELO-FOULD**

FOULHOUZE, de La. See **LA FOULHOUZE Amable Gabriel de**

FOULIS, Andrew and Robert
British, 18th century.
Andrew died 15 September 1775, Robert died in 1776.
Active in Glasgow.
Printers, art lovers.

The Foulis brothers founded an academy of painting and sculpture in Glasgow, financed through loans from local merchants. Students at the Foulis Academy, housed in the University, could apply for grants to study in Italy. The scheme foundered on the death of one of its major supporters, however, and both brothers were ruined. Their work was influential on the subsequent development of Scottish art.

FOULKES, Llynn
American, 20th century.
Born 1934, in Yakima (Washington).
Painter.

Llynn Foulkes, who settled in California, paints fantastic landscapes of volcanic rock in a painstakingly detailed style, in which dull, monochrome colour heightens the atmosphere of uunreality.

He has exhibited since 1961 and, in 1992, took part in *Art in the 1990s* at the Museum of Contemporary Art, Los Angeles. He also exhibits regularly in Paris, notably at the Galerie Darthea Speyer in 1997, and, in 1967, won prizes at the Paris and São Paulo Biennales.

AUCTION RECORDS:
NEW YORK, 13 May 1981, *Union 76* (oil and paper under glass in a copper frame, 22 1/4 x 19 ins / 56.5 x 48.5 cm) USD 1,500. NEW YORK, 2 Nov 1984, *Exercises Series* (c. 1964, Indian ink and oil on canvas, 11 x 14 ins / 28 x 35.5 cm; 12 1/4 x 16 ins/31 x 40.6 cm; 9 3/4 x 11 1/2 ins/24.8 x 29.5 cm) USD 2,800. NEW YORK, 23 Feb 1985, *Holley's Rock* (1965, oil on canvas, 65 1/2 x 65 ins / 166.3 x 165 cm) USD 1,100. NEW YORK, 21 Feb 1990, *In der Fuhrer's Face* (1976, mixed media and collage/synthetic resin, 8 1/2 x 10 3/4 ins / 21.6 x 27.3 cm) USD 990. NEW YORK, 23 Feb 1994, *The Hill is Blue* (1984, oil, acrylic and chalk/board/panel, 49 3/4 x 41 ins / 126.3 x 104.2 cm) USD 5,175.

FOULKS, Elisa
Russian, 19th century.
Born 27 March 1864, in Piatigorsk (Caucasia).
Painter. Genre scenes, portraits.

Elisa Foulks studied at the Institute of Fine Arts in Naples with Autorielli and Mancinella. She painted in oil, watercolour and pastel and exhibited her work in Naples, Palermo and London.

FOULLIOUX, Fernand
French, 20th century.
Born in Egletons.
Painter.

Fernand Foullioux exhibited at the Salon des Indépendants from 1931.

FOULLON, Benjamin, or Foulon
French, 16th - 17th century.
Born c. 1553, in Paris; died after 1623, in Paris.
Painter, draughtsman. Portraits.

Benjamin Foullon was the nephew of François Clouet. He was painter and valet to Henry III and Henry IV of France. In 1925, at the Bibliothèque Nationale in Paris, Louis Dimier grouped 36 of Foullon's portraits around the portrait of César, Duke of Vencôme (natural son of Henry IV and Gabrielle d'Estrée).

BIBLIOGRAPHY:
Salmon, Xavier/Malgouyres, Philippe: *Catalogue raisonné des dessins anciens du musée centre des Arts de Fécamp. XVIe siècle-1825*, Fécamp, 1994.

MUSEUMS AND GALLERIES:
CHANTILLY: *Portrait de Gabrielle d'Estrées* (*Portrait of Gabrielle d'Estrée*) (drawing, attributed) - FÉCAMP (Mus. des Arts et de l'Enfance): *Gabrielle d'Estrée, duchesse de Beaufort* (*Gabrielle d'Estrée, Duchess of Beaufort*) (drawing, attributed) - PARIS (BNF): *Portrait de Rachel de Cochefilet, Madame de Béthune, duchesse de Sully* (*Portrait of Rachel de Cochefilet, Madame de Béthune, Duchess of Sully*) (drawing); *Portrait de Jacqueline de Bueil, comtesse de Moret* (*Portrait of Jacqueline de Bueil, Countess of Moret*) (drawing); *Portrait de César, duc de Vendôme* (*Portrait of César, Duke of Vendôme*) (drawing) - ST PETERSBURG (Hermitage): *Portrait de Scipion Sardini* (*Portrait of Scipion Sardini*) (drawing); *Ronsard* (drawing) - VERSAILLES (Mus. national des châteaux de Versailles et de Trianon): *Guy de Montmorency-Laval, marquis de Nesles* (*Guy de Montmorency-Laval, Marquis of Nesles*) (oil on wood, attributed); *Gabrielle d'Estrée.*

FOULLON, César
French, 17th century.
Born c. 1580, in Neuves-Maisons (Meurthe-et-Moselle); died c. 1644, in Nancy.
Active in Nancy.
Sculptor.
School of Lorraine.

In 1621 César Foullon sculpted some wooden figures to decorate the coach of the Duchess of Lorraine.

FOULLON, Pierre
French, 16th century.
Born in the 16th century, in Antwerp.
Painter.
With Monsieur de Boisy as his patron, Pierre Foullon received his letters of naturalisation from King Francis I in 1538. This artist is not the father of Benjamin Foulon.

FOULLON-VACHOT, Lucille Louise
French, 18th - 19th century.
Born c. 1775, in Le Havre; died 1865, in Antibes.
Painter, miniaturist. Portraits.
Lucille Louise Foullon-Vachot was the pupil of Robert Lefèvre. She exhibited at the Salon de Paris from 1793 to 1822 and occasionally at the Royal Academy in London. The city of Lille commissioned from her the *Full-length Portrait of Louis XVIII*. She painted ceremonial portraits in which her figures are often set against Romantic landscapes.
AUCTION RECORDS:
VERSAILLES, 18 July 1979, *Mme du Blézel and her Daughter* (oil on canvas, 83 1/2 x 53 1/4 ins / 212 x 135 cm) FRF 18,000. PARIS, 28-29 June 1980, *Portrait of the Count of Thermes in the Uniform of a Colonel of Hussars* (oil on canvas, 50 1/2 x 37 3/4 ins / 128 x 96 cm) FRF 14,000. VERSAILLES, 2 March 1986, *Girl Offering her Mother a Rose* (1819, oil on canvas, 80 3/4 x 52 3/4 ins / 205 x 134 cm) FRF 18,500. NEW YORK, 9 Oct 1991, *Portrait of a Lady Wearing a Black Dress Decorated with White Lace, and a Red Shawl, Seated in a Landscape* (1807, oil on canvas, 39 1/4 x 32 ins / 99.9 x 81.3 cm) USD 7,150.

FOULLONGNE, Alfred Charles, or Foulongne
French, 19th century.
Born 26 March 1821, in Rouen; died 1897, in Paris.
Painter, watercolourist. Religious subjects, genre scenes, landscapes.
Enrolled at the École des Beaux-Arts in Paris in 1855 and studied under Paul Delaroche and Marc Gleyre; exhibited at the Paris Salon from 1848 to 1882 and was awarded a medal in 1869. Foullongne painted landscapes, genre compositions and some religious subjects, among them *Daydream*, *St John as a Child*, *Spring*, *Trappist Burial*.
AUCTION RECORDS:
LONDON, 23 March 1987, *Reclining Male Nude* (oil on canvas, 10 1/4 x 18 1/2 ins / 26 x 47 cm) GBP 1,300.

FOULON, Balthasar or Baltazin, or Foullon
French, 16th century.
Glass painter.
Between 1515 and 1544, Balthasar Foulon worked on various buildings in Cambrai, including the 'praetorium' at the town hall, the cathedral and the abbey church of the St-Sépulchre.

FOULON, François
French, 18th century.
Active in Paris in 1771.
Painter, sculptor.

FOULON, Jean
French, 17th century.
Active in Nancy.
Sculptor (wood).
Jean Foulon was the son and pupil of Nicolas François Foulon I. He was admitted to the Guild in Nancy in 1682.

FOULON, Jeanne
French, 19th century.
Born 19th century, in La Rochelle.
Painter.
Pupil of Lequin and Haquette. At the 1879 Paris Salon she exhibited *Market Scene* and *Readying for Departure*.

FOULON, Nicolas François I
French, 17th century.
Born 19 May 1628, in Nancy; died 26 April 1698, in Nancy.
Sculptor (wood).
Nicolas François Foulon I was the son and pupil of César Foulon. He was admitted as a member of the Guild in Nancy in 1667. He participated in the works executed by the woodcarver César Bégard for Duke Charles IV of Lorraine and for Louis XIV.

FOULON, Nicolas François II
French, 17th - 18th century.
Born 30 October 1658, in Nancy; died 10 June 1740, in Paris.
Sculptor (wood).
Nicolas François Foulon II was the son and pupil of Nicolas François Foulon I.

FOULON, Pierre
French, 17th century.
Ivory worker.
Pierre Foulon married in Dieppe in 1686.

FOULON, Serge
French, 20th century.
Born 5 January 1923, in Le Mans.
Painter. Landscapes, waterscapes.
After attending the École des Beaux-Arts in Le Mans, Serge Foulon studied under the landscape painter Merio Ameglio. His aim as a painter is to capture at close hand the 'poetic reality' of the French landscape. He has exhibited at numerous group and solo exhibitions in France and abroad.

FOULONNEAU, Charles
French, 19th century.
Active in Quintin.
Sculptor. Busts.
MUSEUMS AND GALLERIES:
ST-BRIEUC: *Glais-Bizoin* (marble bust).

FOULQUES
Flemish School, 11th century.
Active in Liège c. 1081.
Sculptor, illuminator.
This artist was a monk at the abbey of St-Hubert in the Ardennes.

FOULQUET, Pierre
French, 15th century.
Sculptor.
In 1484, Pierre Foulquet agreed with the canons of the church of St-Sauveur to make, in the space of one year, a tomb for Charles II, the last Count of Provence and nephew of King René, who had died three years previously. The figure of the count lay on a slab of black marble, with two angels at the head and two lions at the feet. The monument was destroyed in 1793, although a drawing of it by Millir survives.

FOULQUIER, François Joseph
French, 18th century.
Born 1744, in Toulouse; died 1789, in Martinique (French Caribbean).
Engraver.
François Joseph Foulquier was a councillor in the Toulouse parliament, and died as the administrator of Martinique. He possessed a fortune and moved as a very young man to Paris, where he was the pupil of Loutherbourg and the miniaturist Hall. M. H. Vienne has catalogued 26 prints by him.

FOULQUIER, Jean Antoine Valentin
French, 19th century.

Born October 1822, in Paris; died 1896, in L'Isle-Adam (Val-d'Oise).
Painter, watercolourist, pastellist, engraver, draughtsman, illustrator. Landscapes, landscapes with figures, still-lifes.

A pupil of Abdel de Pujol, he exhibited at the Paris Salon as of 1848. His body of work comprises a small number of still-lifes, but is mainly made up of landscapes created using a variety of techniques - drawing, watercolour, pastel, etching, and so on. He was known above all as an able illustrator.

Museums and Galleries:
Montauban: *Seascape* (two canvases).

Auction records:
Paris, 11 July 1941, *Cliffs at Sunset,* FRF 150. Paris, 26 Feb 1943, *Green Apple,* FRF 160.

FOUNARI, Sho
Japanese, 20th century.
Born in Tokyo.
Painter. Landscapes.

Sho Founari exhibited at the Salon d'Automne in 1931.

FOUNEV, Ivan
Bulgarian, 20th century.
Born in Bulgaria.
Sculptor.

Founev lived for a year in Paris during the war where he studied the works of Despiau, Bouchard and Wierick. He strove towards a proletarian art form.

FOUNTAIN. See LAFONTAINE Georg Wilhelm

FOUQUÉ, Charles
French, 19th - 20th century.
Born in Avranches.
Painter. Portraits, genre scenes.

Exhibited portraits and genre compositions at the Paris Salon from 1865 to 1882. Among his genre work, mention might be made of *Fantasy for Oboe, Melody* and *Woman Weaving.* He became a member of the Société des Artistes Français as of 1883.

Museums and Galleries:
Auxerre: *Mother Jacqueline* - Avranches: *M. Le Héricher.*

Auction records:
Nantes, 17 June 1992, *Le Guignol* (1874, oil on canvas, 46 x 35 ins / 116 x 89 cm) FRF 13,900.

FOUQUE, Jean Marius
French, 19th century.
Born 20 July 1822, in Arles.
Painter.

He enrolled at the École des Beaux-Arts on 7 October 1846 and studied principally under de Lestang-Parade. He visited the Far East and found favour with the king of Siam, who retained him as official court painter. Fouque exhibited at Paris salons from 1846 to 1879. His principal works include *Joséphine de la Pagerie, accompanied by Two Friends, consults a Fortune-Teller who predicts that Josephine will one day be Empress; Diana and Endymion; Phylax and Juliana* and *Portrait of the Sculptor James Pradier.*

FOUQUE, Marie-Rose
French, 20th century.
Born 27 January 1907, in Paris; died 21 January 1993, in Clamart, near Paris.
Painter (including gouache), illustrator. Religious subjects, figures, nudes, interiors, flowers, landscapes, still-lifes.

Marie-Rose Fouque studied at the Atelier d'Art Sacré in Paris, under the direction of Georges Desvallière and Maurice Denis. She painted landscapes of Brittany, the Midi region, the Yvelines in Andrésy, working in her studio from her sketches. She illustrated Giraudoux's *Le Choix des Élus* (*The Choice of the Elect*), Claudel's *Le Chemin de Croix* (*The Station of the Cross*), as well as *La Liturgie de la messe* (*The Liturgy of the Mass*) and *Le Mystère du rosaire* (*The Mystery of the Rosary*).

She exhibited at the Salon d'Automne in Paris for the first time in 1934, and then regularly until 1938. She participated in the 1937 Exposition Universelle, Paris.

Bibliography:
M. R. Fouque, leaflet, Rémi Gaultier, Paris.

FOUQUERAY, Dominique Charles
French, 19th - 20th century.
Born 23 April 1869 or 1872, in Le Mans; died 1956, in Paris.
Painter (gouache), watercolourist, engraver, illustrator, poster artist, designer. History painting, scenes with figures, landscapes, landscapes with figures, seascapes.

Dominique Fouqueray studied in the studios of Alexandre Cabanel and Fernand Cormon at the École des Beaux-Arts in Paris. He was familiar with a wide range of techniques and soon received various awards and honours, including the Rosa Bonheur prize in 1909 and a gold medal for engraving in 1920. He was a member of the jury of the École des Beaux-Arts in Paris and a member of the Institut and was made an Officier de la Légion d'Honneur.

Fouqueray decorated the town halls of Niort, Le Bourget and Fouras. He also produced numerous war posters. He painted decorative panels for the Exposition Coloniale of 1922 in Marseilles, and there is a panel showing the capture of the Douaumont fort by him in the Musée de la Guerre in Versailles. He also illustrated numerous works of literature, including: *Chez les Anthropophages* by E. Salgari in 1904; *Un Sauvetage* by L. Daudet in 1907; *Les Croix de Bois* by Dorgelès in 1925; *Heart of Darkness* by Joseph Conrad in 1928; *Kim* by Rudyard Kipling in 1931; *Mutiny of the Elsinore* by Jack London and *Œuvres diverses* by Baudelaire in 1934; *Roman d'un Spahi* by Pierre Loti; *Around the World in 80 Days* by Jules Verne and *Jonques et Sampans* by Farrère in 1945; *La Bataille* by Claude Farrère in 1947 and *Escale d'Asie* also by Farrère in 1947, as well as *En Mer.* Fouqueray also collaborated on various magazines and journals including: *L'Illustration, Univers Illustré, Revue Mame* and the *Monde Illustré;* he also worked on periodicals published by the French naval ministry. He illustrated his publication *Les Uniformes de la Marine Française* (*The Uniforms of the French Navy*). He was always attracted by travel and the colonies and was known as one of the outstanding official artists of the colonial war of the first half of the 20th century.

He was a committee member of the Salon des Artistes Français in Paris and exhibited there from 1890 to 1955; he also exhibited at the Exposition Universelle of 1900.

CHARLES FOUQUERAY

D CHARLES FOUQUERAY

Bibliography:
Osterwalder, Marcus (ed.), *Dictionnaire des illustrateurs 1800-1914,* Ides et Calendes, Neuchâtel, 1989. Beguin Billecocq, Xavier, *Charles Fouqueray, un peintre français en Arabie saoudite, 1917-1924,* Beguin Billecocq, Paris, 1998.

Museums and Galleries:
Bordeaux: *Le 1er Prairial, an III* (*First Prairial, Year III (9 May 1795)*) - La Rochelle: *Roll Call on the Deck of the Cruiser Jean-Bart* - Paris (MAMVP): *Barbarossa's Sailors; Palermo; Death in the Leissèques Camp* - Rochefort: *Algeciras* - Versailles (Mus. de la Guerre): *Capture of Douaumont Fort.*

AUCTION RECORDS:
PARIS, 20 Nov 1925, *On the Front* (1916, watercolour) FRF 140. PARIS, 17 and 18 June 1927, *The English Enter Contalmaison in the Somme* (1916, watercolour) FRF 160. PARIS, 28 June 1929, *Street in Amsterdam at Evening* (watercolour) FRF 190. PARIS, July 1946, *Ships at Sea; Naval Combat* (two watercolours) FRF 1,200. PARIS, 19 March 1947, *Eastern Port* (watercolour) FRF 1,000. PARIS, 18 Feb 1980, *Disembarking at a Port in Arabia* (oil on canvas, 39 1/4 x 32 ins / 100 x 81 cm) FRF 6,500. NEW YORK, 28 Oct 1986, *Society Ladies and Officers on the Deck of a Warship* (oil on canvas, 18 1/4 x 21 3/4 ins / 46.5 x 55.3 cm) USD 14,000. PARIS, 7 Nov 1988, *Slaves* (oil on canvas, 59 x 42 1/2 ins / 149 x 108 cm) FRF 35,000. PARIS, 10 April 1989, *Naval Combat* (1911, oil on canvas, 25 1/2 x 21 1/4 ins / 65 x 54 cm) FRF 6,500. PARIS, 9 Nov 1990, *Palmyra* (1919, oil on canvas, 21 1/4 x 25 3/4 ins / 54 x 65.5 cm) FRF 10,500. PARIS, 22 June 1992, *The Port of Akaba on the Red Sea* (1917, gouache, 17 1/2 x 12 1/2 ins / 44.5 x 32 cm) FRF 6,200. PARIS, 5 April 1993, *The Port of Yambo Em-Bahr* (oil on canvas, 21 1/4 x 25 1/2 ins / 54 x 65 cm) FRF 20,000. PARIS, 3 June 1994, *Breton Peasant Women* (oil on canvas, 21 1/4 x 25 1/2 ins / 54 x 64.5 cm) FRF 4,700. PARIS, 9 Dec 1996, *At the Town Gates, Morocco* (oil on canvas, 18 x 15 ins / 45.6 x 38 cm) FRF 8,000. PARIS, 8 March 1999, *Jerusalem* (1919, gouache, 20 x 26 ins / 50 x 65 cm) FRF 10,000. PARIS, 29 June 1999, *Halt at Palmyre* (1919, oil on canvas, 21 x 26 ins / 54 x 65 cm) FRF 50,000. PARIS, 12 May 2000, *Al Quads Fountain in Jerusalem* (1919, oil on canvas, 29 x 21 ins / 73 x 54 cm) FRF 30,000. PARIS, 17 Dec 2001, *Street Scene* (oil on canvas, 26 x 21 ins / 65 x 54 cm) FRF 12,000. PARIS, 24 June 2002, *Feast at Akala* (1918, mixed media on paper on canvas, 39 x 24 ins / 99 x 61 cm) EUR 2,000. NEUILLY, 19 Dec 2002, *Aboard the Steamer La Couronne* (1895, oil on canvas, 25 x 26 ins / 64 x 65 cm) EUR 15,000. LONDON, 10 March 2004, *Rowing Ashore* (oil on canvas, 46 x 35 ins / 116 x 90 cm) GBP 1,500. ST-GERMAIN-EN-LAYE, 21 March 2004, *Sacred Baths at Madura* (1921, watercolour, 15 x 11 ins / 37 x 28 cm) EUR 3,100.

FOUQUEREAU, Robert
French, 20th century.
Born in Elbeuf.
Painter.
Robert Fouquereau exhibited landscapes in Paris at the Salon des Artistes Français from 1933.

FOUQUEREL, Jean
French, 15th century.
Died 1454, in Dijon.
Sculptor.
Burgundy School.
Jean Fouquerel was involved in the construction of the hospital in Beaune (Côte-d'Or) in 1447.

FOUQUES, Henri Amédée, called Fouques de Saint-Leu
French, 19th century.
Born 1857, in Paris; died 1903, in Paris.
Sculptor. Animals. Statues.
Made his Salon début in 1881.
MUSEUMS AND GALLERIES:
GRAY: *Siesta* - PARIS (Mus. du Petit Palais): *Gun Dog* (marble) - PARIS (Mus. Galliera): *Five O'clock*.
AUCTION RECORDS:
NEW YORK, 1 March 1980, *Cat and Dog* (bronze, h. 11 3/4 ins / 30.1 cm) USD 1,600.

FOUQUES, Robert Henry
French, 20th century.
Born 28 February 1892, in New Caledonia.
Painter. Landscapes, seascapes.
Robert Fouques was a member of the Salon des Artistes Français in Paris.

AUCTION RECORDS:
PARIS, 10 July 1983, *Landscape with River* (oil on panel, 12 3/4 x 18 ins / 32.5 x 45.5 cm) FRF 5,800.

FOUQUES-DUPARC, René
French, 19th century.
Died 1889.
Painter.

FOUQUET, Anatole
French, 19th century.
Born 1793.
Watercolourist.
Studied under Pernot and exhibited at the Paris Salon from 1833 to 1837, chiefly with views of Normandy and Savoy. His *View of the Lake of Bourget near Aix in Savoy* was submitted to the 1833 Salon, followed by a watercolour *View of Orbe (Switzerland)*, together with a *View of Bourget* in 1834, a *View of Dieppe from the High Ground behind the Castle* and some watercolours in 1835, and a watercolour *View of Normandy* in 1837.
AUCTION RECORDS:
LONDON, 29 May 1908, *Portrait of Mrs Margaret Strachey* (1838) GBP 7.

FOUQUET, Bernard
French, 17th - 18th century.
Sculptor (wood).
Bernard Fouquet was the younger brother of Jacques Fouquet and, like him, worked for the King of Sweden.

FOUQUET, Émile
French, 20th century.
Painter. Landscapes.
Émile Fouquet exhibited at the Salon des Indépendants from 1935, showing landscapes.

FOUQUET, Émile François
French, 19th century.
Born 13 June 1817, in Paris.
Sculptor.
A pupil of Foyatier, he exhibited at the Salon from 1865 to 1879, chiefly busts of private individuals, a stone low relief entitled *Virgin and Child*, and a number of wax medallions.

FOUQUET, Félicie
French, 19th century.
Born 7 September 1845, in Paris.
Painter (including porcelain), watercolourist.
Landscapes, flowers.
A pupil of Madame Mery, she exhibited her painted porcelain of *Flowers* (from a Van Dael original) at the Salon of 1869, followed by another *Flowers* (also from Van Dael), together with a canvas entitled *View at Boigueville (Loiret)* at the 1870 Salon.

FOUQUET, François. See **FOUQUET Louis and François**

FOUQUET, Henri
Belgian, 19th century.
Born 1826, in Limburg.
Reproductions engraver.
In 1869 Henri Fouquet exhibited a painting in Brussels entitled *The Farm in Les Sables*.

FOUQUET, Jacques
Flemish, 17th century.
Active in Tournai.
Sculptor, draughtsman. Designs for tapestries.
Flemish School.
In 1699 Jacques Fouquet worked at the cathedral in Tournai, where he decorated the belfry with sculptures and sculpted the arms of the town on the large cathedral clock. These are still visible.

FOUQUET, Jacques
French, 17th - 18th century.
Painter. History painting.
Jacques Fouquet won second prize at the Académie in 1691. He worked in Stockholm for the King of Sweden.

FOUQUET, Jacques Henri
French, 20th century.
Painter.
Jacques Fouquet worked in Paris. In his work, forms produced by the randomness of techniques comparable to that of monotype are skilfully developed into what could be described as Abstract Landscapism with a marked fantastic colouring. From 1949 to 1956 he exhibited at the Salon des Réalités Nouvelles, showing compositions that were abstract in appearance.

FOUQUET, Jean
French, 17th century.
Painter.
Jean Fouquet was a member of the Académie de St-Luc in Paris in 1678.

FOUQUET, Jean
French, 18th century.
Painter, draughtsman. Portraits, genre scenes, landscapes.
From 1793 to 1798 Jean Fouquet exhibited hundreds of portraits in pencil at the Louvre (which were subsequently engraved by Chrétien), as well as some landscapes with figures. In 1781 he sent the Salon de la Correspondance a small painting with an interesting composition entitled *Women Drinking*.

FOUQUET, Jean, or Jehan, or Foucquet
French, 15th century.
Born c. 1420, in Tours; died between 1477 and 1481, in Tours.
Painter, miniaturist, illuminator. Religious subjects, portraits.
Once considered to be one of the most famous painters of his time, Fouquet was forgotten so completely that when two of his paintings were acquired by the Louvre in the 19th century, one was listed as a 'Greek work', while the other was described as a work of the German school. His resurrection is due mainly to the intuition of a collector who anticipated by a long way the work of scholars. In 1806, George Brantano-Laroche, the half-brother of the German Romantic poet, Clemens Brentano, discovered 40 miniatures from *Hours of Étienne Chevalier*, then in the possession of an antiquarian. A few years later, in Munich, he found a work showing *Étienne Chevalier Presented by St Stephen*, which he immediately realised was connected with his miniatures. Thus the first group of Jean Fouquet's works was assembled, presenting scholars with the basis for their research. However, the very small amount of certain or plausible information that has been retrieved from documents or from contemporary accounts has meant that modern scholars have had to more or less invent a personality for Fouquet. The only works that can be considered as definitely authentic are a few miniatures from the historian Flavius Josephus' *Judaic Antiquities*, now in the Bibliothèque Nationale in Paris. These were vouched for by François Robertet, librarian to Pierre II, the duke of Bourbon. Yet even this guarantee, made some 20 or 30 years after the execution of the miniatures, can only be seen as relatively secure, since Robertet does not seem to have counted very exactly the miniatures in the first volume of the manuscript. The same problem arises with a passage from Filarete's *Trattato di architettura (Treatise on Architecture)*, usually cited to prove that Fouquet, while in Rome, painted the portrait of the pope, Eugenius IV, with two of his entourage. The artist was a certain 'Grachetto' or 'Giachetto Francioso' who might well not be the same artist as the 'Givanni Fochetta or 'Foccora' mentioned at a later date by Vasari. On the other hand, a letter written by Francesco Florio in 1477 certainly mentions a portrait of Eugenius IV, but also refers to some religious works produced for the church of Notre-Dame-la-Riche in Tours, and of these works there is no trace. It is not possible within the confines of this current work to sift all the often contradictory facts and shaky hypotheses. Nevertheless, when taken together, we have enough to allow us to form some kind of an idea about Fouquet the man.Fouquet was born in Tours, the son of a priest and an unmarried woman (according to K. Perls) and was an apprentice in Paris from 1440 to 1445. Perls also believes that Fouquet worked in the studio of Haincelin de Haguenau, the latter being the 'Master of the Duke of Bedford', but there is little to support this thesis. Attempts made to date to identify Fouquet's first illuminations, which are likely to have been influenced by the Limbourg brothers, have met with little success. Whatever the facts, it is hard to understand how simply the influence of the Touraine landscape, the contemplation of sculpture and the example of Italy could have been enough to stimulate this miniaturist to break away from the 'analytical' discipline of the Van Eycks to achieve the monumental breadth - even and particularly in his illuminations - that we now associate with him. It should not be forgotten that Fouquet was a contemporary of the Flemish artist Dirck Bouts and the Italian Piero della Francesca. Bearing this in mind, it becomes easier to locate him within the international movement to which he belongs and then to analyse his style. Even before 1450, a first reaction away from the Gothic style was evident all over Europe. The reasons for this reaction can be seen as essentially mystical. In Italy, Piero della Francesca sided with Siena against the tradition of Giotto, while in the north Dirck Bouts was countering the work of Jan van Eyck, who had just died, with his own plain and more hermetic vision. The contorted expressions and gestures perpetuated by Rogier van der Weyden began to be rejected and replaced by impassive figures whose inner light came 'from the soul'. This revolution is often explained as no more than a new stage in the development of technique, yet it has been observed that the technique used by Fouquet in his painting - controlled and minutely detailed - is scarcely different from that of other northern painters. As for the 'feeling of life' so often admired in his figures (and the naturalism of Piero della Francesca has often been commented on), it is clearly of a very different order to the realism of Van Eyck. In the earliest painting attributed to Fouquet, the *Charles VII* in the Louvre, the model has the appearance of a rather unattractive relative of Van Eyck's Arnolfini, and we are conscious of the barrier separating the curious spectator from the monarch. This 'victorious' king is less concerned to express his glory than to keep himself at a distance in the attitude of prayer in which Fouquet, in order to be even more explicit, so frequently shows his subjects. On balance, the view that this painting was done before Fouquet's journey to Italy, which took place possibly as early as 1444 seems the most plausible explanation. Certainly, by 1446 Fouquet was in Rome and did not return to Tours until 1448. At this date Italy had not yet been visited by Rogier van der Weyden and did not yet know the northern style of painting as translated by Antonello da Messina. As a result, Fouquet was received with the sympathetic curiosity reserved for visitors from the north. The fact that Pope Eugenius IV should commission a portrait from this young foreigner shows an extraordinarily rapid appreciation of the talents of an unknown artist. While it is true that the portrait of *Charles VII* shows no sign of Italian influence, all the other works grouped under the name of Fouquet were obviously painted by an artist for whom the craft of the early 15th-century painters of the Italian Renais-

sance held no secrets. While his lengthy stay in Paris is demonstrated by the faithfulness with which he painted Parisian views and landscapes, we need no clues from ancient documents to be convinced that he travelled to Italy. We have only to look at the style of his ornamentation, his use of perspective, his vision freed of all pettiness, and the legendary aspect with which he endows many scenes inspired by subjects that might otherwise appear prosaic. It has been commented that his miniatures might owe something to Fra Angelico, yet Fouquet never descends into the sweet or the picturesque. His preferences seem to have been drawn rather towards the broader. It seems unlikely that he met Piero della Francesca, but he nevertheless breathed the same atmosphere and Piero painted a portrait of *Charles VII* for what was to be the Chamber of Heliodorus, that might conceivably have been taken from the work by Fouquet. Finally, it is worth noting the strange resemblance between Domenico Veneziano's *St Dominic* in the National Gallery in London and Fouquet's portrait of *Étienne Chevalier*.

On his return to France, it seems likely that Fouquet continued to combine the two activities of portrait painter and illuminator under Charles VII and Louis XI. There is a disturbing difference detectable, however, between the style used by the artist for the miniatures and that in the portraits. A document of 1475 refers to Fouquet as the King's Painter. In 1461 and 1476, he is mentioned as overseer of ceremonies in Tours. In 1461, the death mask of Charles VII was brought to him from Paris. In 1469, he received payment for a piece of work carried out for the Order of St Michael. In 1472, he travelled from Tours to Blois to discuss a project for an illuminated book with Marie de Clèves, duchess of Orléans. In 1474 his name appears in connection with a plan for a tomb for Louis XI. The same year, he was involved in a dispute with Commines over payment for one or two books of hours. In 1477, Francesco Florio refers to Fouquet in a letter in a way that makes it clear he is still alive. By 8 December 1481 we know that Fouquet's wife was a widow. These are the few details about his life that are known.

Central to Fouquet's work as a miniaturist is the group of eleven illuminated illustrations in the first volume of *Judaic Antiquities* and a single illustration, apparently authentic, in the second volume. All these were painted for the duke of Nemours, Jacques d'Armagnac, whose execution in 1477 allows us to date the miniatures to somewhere between 1470 and 1476. The similarity of these illustrations to those in *Hours of Étienne Chevalier* led to the latter being attributed to Fouquet, though it is generally agreed, however, that the *Hours of Étienne Chevalier* date from considerably earlier (1452-1460). Originally bound together in a single volume, they were split up and some pages have been lost. The largest group consists of 40 illuminated pages acquired from the son of George Brentano in 1891 by the duke of Aumale. They are now at Chantilly in the Musée Condé. Two other pages are in the Louvre. The Bibliothèque Nationale in Paris, the British Museum in London and Viscount Bearsted each possess one page. Finally, two hitherto unknown pages from the collection of Louis Fenoulhet were sold at Sotheby's in London in 1946, bringing the total number of identified miniatures to 47. Other manuscripts that very probably contain illustrations by Fouquet include *The Statutes of the Order of St Michael* (Bibliothèque Nationale), a miniature (frontispiece c. 1470), *Ancient History up to Caesar and the Deeds of the Romans* (Musée du Louvre), four miniatures, two of which come from the Yates-Thompson collection, late works (c. 1475?). A number of other works exist which are likely to be the product of the school of Fouquet, particularly the *Boccaccio* in the library in Munich, the *Chronicles of France* (Bibliothèque Nationale), the *Book of Hours of Charles of France* (Bibliothèque Mazarine), the *Livy* (Bibliothèque Nationale), the *Hours of Diane de Croy* (Ruskin Art Museum, Sheffield).

Fouquet's authenticated paintings are as follows: 1. *Portrait of Charles VII* (Louvre) c. 1444, already described above; 2. *Étienne Chevalier Presented by St Stephen* (Berlin), acquired in 1896 from the son of George Brentano; 3. *Virgin and Child with Red Angels* (Antwerp). The Virgin may be a portrait of Agnes Sorel, mistress of Charles VII. The two latter works seem to have been arranged as a diptych in Melun Cathedral between 1461 and 1475. The date of the work is c. 1450; 4. *Portrait of Guillaume Jouvenel des Ursins* (Louvre) from the Gaignières, painted c. 1455; 5. *Portrait of Guillaume Jouvenel des Ursins* (Berlin),a preparatory study for the previous portrait, a head in three-quarters profile and almost life-size. The drawing, in black chalk and coloured pencil on grey paper, was formerly attributed to Holbein but claimed for Fouquet by M.J. Friedländer in 1910. It should be remembered that the painted version in the Louvre was attributed first to Dürer and then Wolgemuth. To these works can be added two small enamels that may come from the frame of the Melun diptych; 6. *Portrait Thought to be of the Artist* (Louvre); 7. *Believers and Unbelievers* (Berlin, Schlossmuseum). The latter was destroyed in 1945. Another two paintings and a drawing that are generally accepted as being by Fouquet, although not by all scholars are: 8. *Pietà* (in the church at Nouans), discovered by Paul Vitry in 1931. This large composition that may be one of the religious paintings mentioned by Francesco Florio seems certainly to have been designed by Fouquet, but the actual painting does not seem to be entirely in his hand; 9. *Portrait of a Monk* (Tours Museum), part of a larger painting; 10. *Portrait of a Papal Legate* (Metropolitan Museum, New York). This drawing in silverpoint from the collections once owned by Heseltine, Oppenheimer and Duveen is, according to C. Schaeffer (1967), a portrait of Cardinal d'Estoutville. In the present state of knowledge about Fouquet, these ten works represent the firm basis for critical studies of Fouquet's art.Further attributions remain in the realm of hypothesis. The Loches *Triptych*, dated 1485, could be attributed to Fouquet's two sons, Louis and François. A *Portrait of a Man of 1465* (Liechtenstein Collection) and a *Man with Glass of Wine* (Louvre), both exhibited in 1904 as works by Fouquet, are no longer accepted as such today, but are still associated with him in the minds of critics. Finally, there are three drawings that have, from time to time, been attributed to Fouquet: a *Portrait of a Man* (Louvre), exhibited in 1904 and Flemish in origin, a *Head of a Young Man* (Hermitage, St Petersburg), probably French but only distantly related to Fouquet's work, as is also true for the third drawing, a *Standing Figure of a Young Man* in the Liechtenstein Collection. An excellent bibliography relating to Fouquet was brought out by Charles Sterling in the *Art Bulletin* for 1946. More recent studies, including those of Laborde, have provided new theories and a number of specific details but major difficulties remain. Robert Fiot (1970) has attributed the designs and perhaps even the execution of a number of stained glass windows in the church of Notre-Dame-la-Riche in Tours to Fouquet. These windows would be, according to Fiot, the 'religious images' mentioned by Florio in 1477. That Fouquet worked as a glass painter and goldsmith is beginning to seem more and more probable.

Exhibitions that have featured Fouquet's work include: *L'Art du Val de Loire de Jean Fouquet à Jean Clouet* (Art of the Loire Valley from Jean Fouquet to Jean Clouet), Musée des Beaux-Arts, Tours, 1952; *The Age of Jan Van Eyck: the Mediterranean world of early Netherlandish painting, 1430-1530*, Groeningmuseum, Bruges, 2002. Exhibitions devoted to Fouquet alone: 1981, Musée du Louvre, Paris; 2003, *Jean Fouquet. Peintre et enlumineur du XVe siècle* (Jean Fouquet: Painter and Illuminator of the 15th century), Bibliothèque

Nationale, Paris, an exhibition illustrating the many aspects of the artist's activities from illumination to panel painting; 2003 *L'Enluminure en France au temps de Jean Fouquet* (Manuscript Illumination at the Time of Jean Fouquet), Cabinet des Livres, Musée Condé, Chantilly.

BIBLIOGRAPHY:

Wescher, Paul Reinhold, *Jean Fouquet and his time*, Pleiades Books, London, 1947. Alazard, Jean, *Fouquet*, monograph, Electa, Florence, 1952. Cuttler, Charles D., *Northern Painting: From Pucelle to Bruegel*, Holt, Rinehart and Winston, New York, 1968. Castelnuovo, Enrico, *Jean Fouquet*, Fabbri, Milan, 1979. Reynaud, Nicole, *Jean Fouquet*, exhibition catalogue, Musée du Louvre, Réunion des musées nationaux, Paris, 1981. Gousset, Marie-Thérèse/Avril, François/ Guenée, Bernard, *Les Grandes Chroniques de France. Reproduction en fac-similé des miniatures de Fouquet, manuscrit français 4665 de la Bibliothèque nationale de France*, P. Lebaud, Paris, 1987. Bazin, Germain, *Jean Fouquet, le livre d'heures d'Étienne Chevalier*, Somogy, Paris, 1990. Schaefer, Claude, *Jean Fouquet*, Verlag der Kunst, Dresden, 1994. Schaefer, Claude, *'Lart et l'histoire: Étienne Chevalier commande au peintre Jean Fouquet le diptyque de Melun'* in *Art et architecture à Melun au moyen âge*, Picard, Paris, 2000. Brochert, T., *The Age of Jan Van Eyck: the Mediterranean world of early Netherlandish painting*, exhibition catalogue, Groeningemuseum, Bruges, Thames & Hudson, London, 2002. Avril, François (ed.), *Jean Fouquet. Peintre et enlumineur du XVe siècle*, exhibition catalogue, Bibliothèque nationale de France, Hazan, Paris, 2003.

MUSEUMS AND GALLERIES:

ANTWERP: *Virgin and Child with Red Angels* - BERLIN (Gemäldegal.): *Étienne Chevalier with his Patron Saint St Stephen* - BERLIN (Kupferstichkabinet): *Portrait of Guillaume Juvénal or Jouvenel des Ursins* - BERLIN (Palace Mus.): *Believers and Disbelievers* (destroyed in 1945) - CHANTILLY (Mus. Condé): *Day of the Dead; All Hallows Day; Job and his Councellors; St Thomas Aquinas Teaching in a Dominican Convent; St Hilarius Presiding over a Council; Enthronement of St Nicholas, Bishop of Myra; Martyrdom of St Catherine of Alexandria; St John on the Island of Patmos; Martyrdom of St Apollonia; Martyrdom of St Andrew; Martyrdom of St Peter; St Paul on the Road to Damascus; Martyrdom of St James the Major; Coronation of the Virgin; Martyrdom of St Stephen; Assumption of the Virgin; Enthronement of the Virgin; Death of the Virgin; Funeral of the Virgin; The Angel Announces to the Virgin that She Will Enter into the Kingdom of Heaven; The Mission of the Apostles and the Unity of the Apostolic Ministry; The Ascension; Pentecost; Entombment; Virgin Holding the Dead Christ in her Lap; Crucified Christ; Deposition; Christ Carrying the Cross; Christ before Pilate; The Betrayal; Last Supper; Mary Magdalene Anoints the Lord's Feet with Perfumes; Adoration of the Magi; Shepherds Adoring the Newly-Born Christ Child; Birth of St John the Baptist; Annunciation; Visitation; Virgin and Child in the Celestial Court with Étienne Chevalier and his Patron Saint St Stephen; Marriage of the Virgin; Étienne Chevalier and St Stephen Pay Homage to the Virgin* - LONDON (British Mus.) - MUNICH (Bayerische Staatsbibliothek): *Boccaccio* - NEW YORK (Metropolitan Mus. of Art): *Portrait of a Papal Legat* - PARIS (Bibliothèque Mazarine): *Book of Hours of Charles of France* - PARIS (BNF): *Livy; Chronicles of France; Statues of the Order of St Michael; Judaic Antiquities* - PARIS (Louvre): *Portrait of Charles VII, King of France; Portrait of Guillaume Juvénal or Jouvenel des Ursins; Portrait of Pope Eugenius IV; Portrait of Louis XI; Portrait Thought to be of the Artist; Ancient History up to Caesar and the Deeds of the Romans* - SHEFFIELD (Ruskin Gal.): *Missal Album of Lady Diana de Croy (Horae)* (1450-1500) - TOURS: *Portrait of a Monk* (part of a larger painting) - VIENNA (Liechtenstein Mus.): *Portrait of a Man* (attributed).

AUCTION RECORDS:

PARIS, 1884, *Portrait of Anne of Brittany*, FRF 1,800; *Portrait Thought to be of Anne of Brittany*, FRF 600. PARIS, 1889, *Cavalry and the Return of the Escort*, FRF 540. PARIS, 10 and 11 May 1926, *Virgin and Child in a Frame of Gothic Niches with Statuettes* (miniature heightened with gold on parchment) FRF 15,000. LONDON, 10-13-14 July 1936, *Portrait of an Ecclesiastic*, GBP 107. NEW YORK, 15 Nov 1945, *Charles VII* (after J. F.) USD 225.

FOUQUET, Louis and François, or Foucquet

French, 15th century.

Painters, miniaturists.

These two sons of Jean Fouquet are mentioned by J. Brèche in *Ad titulum Pandectarum de verborum significatione Commentarii* (Lyons 1556), but no other documentary proof of their existence has been found. In the document of 8 November 1481 from Tours mentioned above, it merely says 'the widow and heirs of the late Jehan Foucquet, painter'. Attempts have been made to associate François Fouquet with 'Master François', a miniaturist in Paris in the second half of the 15th century. It is likely that Fouquet's sons would have been his pupils and that, having collaborated with their father during his lifetime, they continued to paint in his style after his death. The triptych of the *Passion of Christ* (church of St-Antine, Loches, and today in the chateau), dating from 1485 cannot be attributed to Bourdichon, despite the initials F. I. B. This is a work that must have been executed directly under the influence of Fouquet, and most likely by his sons, or by one of them whose identity could be defined on the basis of this work.

Laborde also attributes to Fouquet's pupils the large miniatures of the book of hours of Anne of Brittany, and believes that these same painters were responsible for the book of hours of Marie de' Medici (Dome Collection, no. 112, Oxford, Bodleian Library). 'The best miniatures in the hours of Anne of Brittany were, I believe, painted by a French artist of the school of Jean Fouquet. These are *Christ* and the marginalia of Fol. 1, *Pentecost, Virgin and Child*, a painting where the Flemish influence is more marked than usual although the clarity of Fouquet is there too and *Original Sin* (with a chateau reminiscent of Chambord in the background of a charm and elegance that is clearly French)'. Canon Fochem, whose name appears several times in this manuscript has written the following list: 'This book contains as well as many other ornaments: Human Figures, 585; Birds, 64; Insects, 314; Flowers, 1503; Fruit, 309; Leaves, 1259-4031. The Munich *Boccaccio*, and that of Geneva and many other manuscripts once attributed to Jean Fouquet are now recognised as having been executed by his pupils'.

FOUQUET, Louis Socrate

French, 19th century.

Born 13 May 1795, in Paris; died after 1831, in Paris.

Painter. Portraits.

He spent many years of his life in Germany, where, as of 1815, he served as painter at the royal porcelain factory in Berlin. He went on to occupy a similar post in Nymphenburg until his appointment in 1821 as enamel painter to the prince of Saxony-Gotha. He went on to work successively for the king of Prussia, King Maximilian, and Eugène de Beauharnais, prince of Hoerdenborg. Ultimately, he returned to teach in Paris. Fouquet was also an accomplished miniaturist.

It is probable that this artist is the animal painter Fouquet cited by Siret.

MUSEUMS AND GALLERIES:

GOTHA: *Portrait of a Woman on Enamel*.

AUCTION RECORDS:

PARIS, 22 Oct 1982, *Portrait of a Lady of Standing* (oil on canvas, 25 1/2 x 21 1/4 ins / 65 x 54 cm) FRF 3,800.

FOUQUET, Louis Vincent
French, 19th century.
Born 1803, in Orléans; died 1869.
Painter (including gouache), watercolourist. Figures, scenes with figures, genre scenes, interiors with figures, landscapes.

He studied draughtsmanship at college in Orléans, then went on to work in the Decamps' atelier, exhibiting at the Salon from 1827 to 1868; he was a medal-winner in 1833. Examples of his work include *Township of Batz, Brittany, Street Sweeper, Wise Monkeys, Nail Factory Interior, Scene during Cholera Outbreak, Widow, Antique Dealer, Children Clustered around the Rabbit Hutch, Kitchen Interior at Franchard* and *Breton Notable and his Train.*

Museums and Galleries:
Bourges: *Beggar* - Orléans: *Studio Interior; Child with Marionettes.*

Auction records:
Paris, 15 Oct 1990, *Couple Caught in a Storm* (oil on panel, 27¼ x 20 ins / 69 x 51 cm) FRF 18,000. Paris, 10-11 June 1997, *Turkish Bath and Massage* (watercolour and gouache, a pair, 7 x 4¾ ins / 17.5 x 12 cm) FRF 55,000. Calais, 10 May 1998, *Figures in Street in Oriental Town* (watercolour/gouache, 11 x 7 ins / 27 x 18 cm) FRF 11,800.

FOUQUET, Michel, or Fouqué
French, 18th century.
Died 1782, in Angers.
Sculptor (wood).

Michel Fouquet was working in 1780 in the cathedral in Angers with Jacques Gaultier.

FOUQUET, Valentin
Flemish, 18th century.
Died 1744.
Active in Tournai.
Sculptor.
Flemish School.

Valentin Fouquet was the son of Jacques Fouquet. Noteworthy amongst his works are a frame for a portrait of Charles VI which he executed in 1721 and a tabernacle for the Dominican boys' school, executed in 1728.

FOUQUET-DORVAL, Georges
French, 20th century.
Engraver.

Georges Fouquet-Dorval worked in Paris. He studied under Gérome and Waltner and became a member of the Salon des Artistes Français in Paris in 1903; he received a bronze medal and travel bursary in 1902, a silver medal in 1907 and a gold medal in 1910. He was declared hors concours and was made a member of the jury.

FOUQUEUR, Jean Louis
French, 19th century.
Born 1786, in Tierceville; died 20 April 1866, in Villeneuve-les-Genêts.
Painter, draughtsman. Religious subjects.

He studied under David and Regnault, but soon turned to political activism. A staunch admirer of Napoleon, Fouqueur signed up for army service, and it was not until 1831 that he started to exhibit at the Salon, initially with a composition entitled *Battle of Borodino*. Other works by Fouqueur include three *Portraits of Louis XVIII* (now housed in Auray, Ploërmel and Lorient respectively); a portrait of *Charles X* (in Vannes); a composition entitled *St Vincent de Paul Confiding the Statutes of the Order to his Missionaries* (painted for the Vannes seminary); and an *Assumption* and stations of the cross for Vannes Cathedral. The church of Bernières houses a *Nativity* altarpiece by him, together with two interesting frescoes, of the *Assumption* and the *Last Supper*. Fouqueur also produced a number of pen-and-ink drawings.

FOUQUIER, Bertram and Paulus de.
See **FOUCHIER**

FOUQUIER, Victor
French, 14th century.
Active in Marseilles.
Painter.

FOUQUIÈRES, Jacques, or Foucquière or Foucquier
French, 17th century.
Born c. 1580, in Antwerp; died 1659, in Paris.
Painter, engraver. Landscapes.

Jacques Fouquières had very modest origins, even though he wished it to be believed that he belonged to the well-to-do Fuggers family, called Fokkiers in Flanders. According to Juste d'Egmont, his father was a carter. He was the pupil of Velvet Brueghel, as is evidenced by his first works, executed in the style of that master. He may also have been the pupil of Losse de Momper, a well-known landscape painter, the 'pictor montium' (painter of hills) of the 100 portraits by Van Dyck. Fouquières was certainly a gifted artist who at the start of his career had an excellent style, basing himself on the faithful observation of nature. His talent caused him to be considered by certain critics as the 'Flemish Titian'. He painted and drew with ease and was also skilful with pen and ink.

However, Fouquières did not persevere in his initial style, sometimes considered naive, seeing in it nothing but 'a copy of nature'. He sought instead to idealise the natural world, bringing together in compositions of his own invention those elements which he had observed directly, aiming for the majestic aspects, the imposing masses, with everything inclined to be on a grand scale. This preoccupation, which tended to make him lose the essence of his origins, has been attributed to the influence of Rubens. It is a fact that the latter knew Fouquières and appreciated his talent, entrusting him with the execution of a number of landscape backgrounds in history paintings which he did not have time to complete himself.

In 1621 Fouquières went to Paris, in the same year as Rubens who had been summoned by Maria de' Medici to paint the gallery at the Palais du Luxembourg. Although he probably did not have him in his retinue, it is likely that Rubens at least caused Fouquières to go to France. Success came rapidly to Fouquières, all the more so in that landscape at the time was still not a genre in its own right. He knew very well how to adjust to the taste of the day and to adapt his style to the concepts of the period, adopting the Italianist form used by Forest, for example. At first he executed numerous paintings for the decoration of the large town houses, but none of these works survive. Louis XIII became captivated by his landscapes to the point of granting him not only French citizenship, but also letters patent of nobility, with the title of baron. Unfortunately for Fouquières, the baron's coronet proved fatal, for he became arrogant and proud in the extreme. He would only paint for the most important noblemen and always with a long rapier at his side, affecting to condescend to oblige them but requiring nonetheless to be paid handsomely.

On the orders of the king he was commissioned to paint views of the main cities in France between the windows of the main gallery in the Louvre. For this purpose he made a journey to Marseilles and Provence, during which he surrendered to the easy life, notably in the form of idleness and good wine. However, on the arrival in Paris of Nicolas Poussin, the commission was transferred to him, and Fouquières, in high dudgeon, was left to harry Poussin and try to restore his own authority. Poussin made merry with his friends at the expense of Fouquières who, furious and discomfited, departed to work for a time for the Elector Palatine. Prodigality, drunkenness and disorderly conduct led to his ruin. He was taken in by a virtually unknown painter called Sylvain who lived in St-Jacques in Paris, where he died in reduced circumstances.

Fouquières' friend Nicolas Montagne drew his portrait when, in old age, he was on the point of death, but Mariette, who had seen this portrait, did not know what had become of it. There were four of his landscapes, in medallions, in the palace at the Tuileries (Salle du Conseil des Ministres), which also had seven others painted on panels in the Bibliothèque and three in the Salon des Dames. Engravings by him do not exist, but a certain number of his landscapes were engraved by Arnould de Jode, Alexandre Voet, Michel Montagne, Perelle and especially Jean Morin. Some of his drawings have appeared at auction.

Whilst adopting the style in vogue, Fouquières did not entirely abandon his original inclinations. His wild settings, free of mythological figures, are not unworthy of the success they received and his pursuit of grandeur did not exclude rustic charm, especially in the scenes which depict or evoke hunting.

Museums and Galleries:
Besançon: *Landscape* - Bordeaux: *Landscape with Figures* - Cologne: *Landscape* - Grenoble: *Landscape with Horsemen* - Heidelberg: *Landscape* - Nantes (MBA): *Large Landscape with Whips* - Toulouse: *Forest Edge*.

Auction records:
Paris, 1753, *Winter Landscape,* FRF 129. Cologne, 1862, *Landscape with Figures,* FRF 150. Paris, 1873, *Landscape,* FRF 400. Paris, 14 May 1935, *The Inn on the Hill* (attributed) FRF 4,000. London, 31 July 1939, *Wooded Landscape,* GBP 7. Paris, 7 March 1955, *Landscape with Tower* (bistre wash) FRF 26,000. London, 27 March 1963, *A Stag Hunt,* GBP 800. Brussels, 13 May 1969, *Riverscape with Figures,* BEF 2,000,000. Vienna, 4 Dec 1973, *Landscapes with Figures* (two panels) ATS 500,000. Paris, 7 June 1974, *Scene from the Life of Christ,* FRF 16,000. Paris, 28 Nov 1978, *Scene from the Life of Christ* (oil on wood, 19 1/4 x 37 ins / 49 x 94 cm) FRF 24,000. New York, 17 Jan 1985, *Peasants in a Wooded Landscape* (oil on canvas, 23 x 33 1/4 ins / 57.5 x 84.5 cm) USD 32,000. Amsterdam, 18 Nov 1985, *Steep Wooded Landscape with a View of a Château in the Background* (black and red chalk, 9 1/4 x 15 ins / 23.6 x 38 cm) NLG 26,000. Zürich, 20 Nov 1987, *Travellers in a Wooded Landscape* (oil on panel, 23 x 33 1/4 ins / 57.5 x 84.5 cm) CHF 44,000. New York, 5 April 1990, *Vast Landscape with Animals and Figures Walking on a Path* (oil/copper, 6 1/2 x 9 ins / 16.5 x 22 cm) USD 4,400. London, 8 July 1992, *Town in Winter with a Frozen Canal and a Hog Fair on a Quay in the Foreground* (oil on panel, 22 x 33 1/2 ins / 56 x 85 cm) GBP 121,000. Paris, 5 Feb 1998, *The Joys of Winter* (oil on canvas, attributed, 32 1/4 x 44 ins / 82 x 112 cm) FRF 125,000.

FOUR, Amélie. See **FRUCHARD**

FOUR, du. See **DUFOUR**

FOUR, Michel
French, 20th century.
Born 15 February 1945, in Aurillac (Cantal).
Painter, lithographer, poster artist, mixed media.
Figures, nudes. Designs for tapestries.

Michel Four studied at the École des Beaux-Arts de Paris from 1964 to 1967, and produced many mural decorations. His early work is in an abstract yet materialist style, drawing on the volcanic Auvergne region, the colours of its stones and the physical sensations which it induces. Later, in 1980, he began painting women, often in the nude, initially in dark surroundings but later in lighter environments. In these, he conveys a peculiar impression, somewhere between desire and eroticism. His paintings are distinctive in their ambivalent figuration, which is abstract yet recognisably representative. They are sketches of tormented, precise yet violent, body language, deriving from the conflicts and contrasts between masculinity and femininity, and within femininity itself.

He has taken part in group exhibitions since 1969, including the Salon d'Automne (of which he is an associate), the Salon Comparaisons, the Salon Grands et Jeunes d'Aujourd'hui, and the Salon de la Jeune Peinture. He has also displayed his works in group exhibitions outside Paris: at the Biennale Japanese Exhibition of Young Painters, in Tokyo in 1972; at the Warsaw Museum of Modern Art in 1973; at the Nuremberg Kunsthalle, also in 1973; in Tehran in 1974; and at the Musée d'Art Moderne de Vevey in 1975.

He has also staged a number of solo exhibitions, including the following: Musée d'Aurillac in 1967; Galerie Knoll International, in 1971; Orangerie du Sénat, in 1973; École Polytechnique in 1975; Galerie St-Merri in 1979 (all in Paris); Galerie Jardin des Arts in Montreal, also in 1979; Galerie Grey in Cannes, also in 1982; Meridian Gallery in Boston, in 1984; Galerie 10 in Paris, also in 1984; Galerie Pascal Gabert, also in Paris, in 1984 and 1989; a retrospective exhibition, entitled *Quinze Ans de Peinture* (*Fifeen Years of Painting*), at the Centre Culturel d'Aurillac, in 1987; and at the Galerie le Cadre Noir, in St-Denis-de-la-Réunion, in 1988.

Bibliography:
Persin, Patrick-Gilles (preface), *Michel Four*, exhibition catalogue, Gal. Pascal Gabert, Paris, 1989.

Museums and Galleries:
Aurillac - Paris (MAMVP) - Paris (MNAM-CCI) - Rio de Janeiro (MAM).

FOUR, Pieter de. See **FURNIUS Pieter Jalhea**

FOURAU, Hugues, or Foureau
French, 19th century.
Born 9 May 1803, in Paris; died 1 December 1873, in Paris.
Painter. History painting, mythological subjects, portraits, genre scenes.

He enrolled at the École des Beaux-Arts in Paris in 1828, where he studied under Pierre Guérin and Antoine Gros. Fourau exhibited at the Paris Salon from 1827 to 1864. His body of work comprised historical canvases, genre compositions and portrait work; it was as a portraitist that he was in greatest demand. Examples of his work include *Death of the Greek Patriarch Gregory, Death of Adonis, A Mother's Tenderness, Madwoman, Ulysses and Nausicaa, General Ferrand at the Defence of Valenciennes in 1793* and *Ambroise Paré*.

Museums and Galleries:
Moulins: *Woman Breastfeeding her Child*.

Auction records:
Paris, 1-2 March 1869, *Battle of Palestro,* FRF 200; *Mirabeau and the Marquis of Dreux-Brézé,* FRF 255; *Luncheon* (pastel/paper) FRF 110. London, 30 May 1932, *Last Moments of Chatterton,* GBP 8. Paris, 15 May 1933, *Ambroise Paré Held Prisoner in Spain,* FRF 1,405. Paris, 30 May 1980, *Portrait of a Young Girl with a Dog* (pastel/paper, 25 1/4 x 20 1/2 ins / 64 x 52 cm) FRF 4,500. Paris, 27 June 1994, *Achilles Pursued by the Xanthi* (oil on canvas, 44 x 57 ins / 112 x 145 cm) FRF 102,000.

FOURAU, Laure (Mrs). See **COUSSIN Laure**

FOURAUT, Célénie (Mme)
French, 19th century.
Active in Paris.
Sculptor.

Member of the Société de Artistes Français as of 1889.

FOURBAULT, Yvon
French, 15th century.
Painter.

Yvon Fourbault was Louis XI's court painter. In 1464 he painted two banners with images of *Our Lady of Aix* and *St Denis with two Martyrs.*

FOURCADE
French, 19th century.
Active in the south of France c. 1830.
Miniaturist.

Portrait miniatures by this artist are to be found in the Bordeaux and Toulouse regions.

FOURCADE, Dominique Philippe Jean
French, 20th century.
Born 1871, in Le Plan.
Sculptor, engraver, medallist.

Dominique Fourcade became a member of the Salon des Artistes Français in Paris in 1903. He received a commendation in 1899 and a silver medal in 1908.

FOURCADE, F. de
French, 19th century.
Sculptor. Portraits.

MUSEUMS AND GALLERIES:
DIEPPE (Château-Mus.): *Portrait of Charles-Camille Saint-Saëns.*

FOURCADE-CANCELLE, Jeanne
French, 20th century.
Born 20th century, in Paris.
Painter, potter.

Jeanne Fourcade-Cancelle exhibited in Paris at the Salon of the Société Nationale des Beaux-Arts in 1933.

FOURCAUD, Adolphe
Flemish, 19th century.
Died 1849.
Active in Liège.
Painter (porcelain), watercolourist.
Flemish School.

FOURCHE, Étienne
French, 17th century.
Active in Troyes from 1634 to 1644.
Painter.

FOURCHEY, Étienne, or Fourché
French, 17th - 18th century.
Active in Troyes in 1692 and 1707.
Painter.

FOURCROY, Nicole. See **PUCE**

FOURCY, Jacques Charles
French, 20th century.
Born 1906, in Paris.
Watercolourist.

Jacques Fourcy exhibited at the Paris Salon.

FOURDIN, H.
French, 19th century.
Sculptor. Figures. Medallions.

MUSEUMS AND GALLERIES:
NICE: *Salvator Olivette* (medallion).

FOURDINOIS, Henri
French, 19th century.
Active in Paris.
Sculptor (wood), cabinet maker.

Henri Fourdinois retained artists such as J.J. Perraud and J. Taballon to design and carve the ornamentation for his pieces, subsequently shown at Great Exhibitions in London (1851), Paris (1867, 1878) and Vienna (1873).

FOURDRIN, Adrien
French, 19th century.
Sculptor.

He submitted to the 1849 Paris Salon a bronze study of a head entitled *Childhood Recollection,* followed at the 1850 Salon by a bronze medallion entitled *Study of a Head with Flowers* and a large bronze medallion, *Study of a Head.*

FOURDRIN, Camille (Mme)
Maiden name: Lemaire
French, 19th century.
Painter.

She exhibited examples of her watercolours at Paris Salons from 1831 to 1848. Examples of her work include *Butterflies; Flycatcher; Bouquet of Peonies; Primulas, Primroses and Crown Imperials; Roses, Tulips and Stocks;* and *Camellias and Roses.*

FOURDRINIER, Pierre, or Fourdrinière
French.
Born in France; died in London.
Engraver.

He worked mainly in London, engraving mostly portraits and plates for illustrations. His architectural engravings are also referred to.

FOURÉ (Abbé)
French, 19th - 20th century.
Born 1819 or 1839, in Rothéneuf, near St-Malo; died 1910.
Sculptor.

Fouré devoted 30 years of his life to sculpting naive monumental figures on the rocks of the cliff at Rothéneuf. These illustrate the epic poem of the Rothéneufs, a family of pirates whose actions and deeds were not always edifying. He was influenced by the popular statuary that decorates church walls, altars and stations of the cross in Brittany.

FOURÉ, Antoine
French, 18th century.
Painter, architect.

Antoine Fouré was a student at the Académie Royale. He later worked as a painter for the count of Clermont, and as an architect for the prince of Conti, before setting up in 1770 in Strasbourg. He is probably identical to the painter of the same name who executed paintings at the theatre in Nancy in 1770.

FOURÉ, Jacques
French, 18th century.
Active in Paris in 1748.
Painter, sculptor.

FOURÉ, Louis Ernest
French, 19th century.
Born 19th century, in Paris.
Painter.

He sent *Near Mussidan* to the Salon of 1878 and *Banks of the Seine, Moulineaux* to the Salon of the following year.

FOURE, Mathieu, or Fourée
French, 18th century.
Painter.

Mathieu Foure was a painter of flowers at the Sèvres porcelain factory from 1748 to 1778. A dish of a service belonging to Catherine II has his mark, as well as certain parts of a table service at Buckingham Palace.

FOUREAU
French, 18th century.
Active in Versailles in 1768.
Sculptor (wood).

Foureau worked with Pajou on the theatre of the Château de Versailles.

FOUREAU. See also **FOURAU**

FOUREST, Suzanne
French, 20th century.

Born in Paris.
Painter.

Suzanne Fourest studied under Sabatté. She exhibited in Paris at the Salon des Artistes Français from 1930. She received a commendation in 1934 and a silver medal in 1938.

FOURESTIER, Jacques. See **FABRÈGE**

FOURIÉ, Albert Auguste

French, 19th century.
Born 1854, in Paris; died 17 December 1937, in L'Isle-Adam (Val-d'Oise).
Painter, sculptor, engraver, illustrator. Religious subjects, genre scenes, landscapes, landscapes with figures.

He enrolled at the École des Beaux-Arts in Paris, where he studied sculpture under Jean Gautherin; he subsequently turned to painting and studied under Jean-Paul Laurens. Fourié exhibited for the first time at the Paris Salon in 1877, when he showed a *Bust of a Young Girl*. As of 1879, he exhibited canvases, securing an honourable mention in 1883, a bronze in 1884, a silver in 1887 and a gold at the 1889 Exposition Universelle. He was appointed to the rank of Chevalier of the Légion d'Honneur. Fourié's body of work includes *Recreation in the Cloister, Judith, Numismatist, First Communion* and *Eve's Daughter*.

MUSEUMS AND GALLERIES:

NÎMES: *Through the Woods* - PARIS (Mus. d'Orsay): *Under the Branches* - ROUEN (MBA): *Wedding Feast at Yport; Death Chamber of Mme Bovary* - SAINTES: *Memory of Versailles* - SÈTE: *Betrothal; Betrothal; Golden Wedding* - ST-ÉTIENNE: *Etienne Marcel and the Dauphin* - TOURCOING: *Mourning*.

AUCTION RECORDS:

PARIS, 15 June 1900, *After the Bath*, FRF 220. PARIS, 4-5 Dec 1918, *Leda and the Swan* (drawing) FRF 240. PARIS, 15 April 1921, *Female Nude*, FRF 800. PARIS, 18-19 May 1925, *Swan*, FRF 115. LONDON, 22 Dec 1926, *End of a Dream*, GBP 31. PARIS, 18 April 1928, *Young Woman Bathing*, FRF 175. PARIS, 13 June 1941, *Female Reaper*, FRF 100. PARIS, 18 Feb 1942, *Woman Bathing* (pastel/paper) FRF 300. PARIS, 24 April 1942, *Footbridge*, FRF 320. PARIS, 14 March 1945, *Male Nude among Flowers*, FRF 850. LOS ANGELES, 13 Nov 1972, *Young Girl with Lizard*, USD 1,100. NEW YORK, 23 Feb 1989, *Young Woman Seated by a Forest Path* (1908, oil on canvas, 37 1/4 x 29 1/2 ins / 94.7 x 75 cm) USD 8,800. DOUAI, 2 July 1989, *Child with Basket* (oil on canvas, 18 1/2 x 13 3/4 ins / 47 x 35 cm) FRF 8,100. VERSAILLES, 19 Nov 1989, *Reflection in the Water* (1910, oil on canvas, 32 x 39 1/4 ins / 81 x 100 cm) FRF 52,000. PARIS, 12 Dec 1990, *Young Women Bathing in a Parkland Setting* (pastel, 9 x 12 1/4 ins / 23 x 31 cm) FRF 6,000. NEW YORK, 29 Nov 1999, *Haymaking in Criquebeuf, Normandy* (1888, oil on canvas, 57 x 89 ins / 145 x 225 cm) USD 14,000. PARIS, 25 March 2001, *Women Bathing in the Spring* (oil on canvas, 32 x 39 ins / 82 x 100 cm) FRF 120,000. NEW YORK, 30 April 2001, *Aurora* (oil on canvas, oval, 36 x 29 ins / 92 x 73 cm) USD 6,500.

FOURIER, Anthoine

French, 17th century.
Active in Paris in 1614.
Painter (?), sculptor (?).

FOURMAINTRAUX-WINSLOW, Rachel

French, 20th century.
Born 1880, in London.
Watercolourist.

Rachel Fourmaintraux-Winslow studied under Walter Sickert. She exhibited in Paris at the Salon des Artistes Français from 1922.

FOURMALS, J. M.

French, 20th century.
Born 1905, in Paris.
Painter.

J.M. Fourmals studied under Guirand de Scévola. She exhibited landscapes and flower paintings, notably at the Salon des Artistes Français in Paris in 1928, and received a gold medal at the International Exhibition of 1937.

FOURMANOIR, Cleto

Flemish School, 16th century.
Sculptor.

Cleto worked with his father Jean Fourmanoir for the church of St Waudru in Mons.

FOURMANOIR, Jacques

Flemish School, 16th century.
Sculptor.

Jacques was probably the son of the sculptor Jean Fourmanoir. He carved the coats of arms of Philip II on the mint in Antwerp.

FOURMANOIR, Jean

Flemish School, 16th century.
Active in Mons.
Sculptor (wood).

Between 1535 and 1549, Jean Fourmanoir was engaged on carving the choir stalls in the church of St Waudru in Mons, following the designs of J. Dubroeucq. The stalls were destroyed in 1797.

FOURMAUX, Luce

French, 20th century.
Painter.

Luce Fourmaux paints memories of her childhood in Lubéron region in southern France, in addition to timeless subjects, such as bouquets, gardens in bloom, and tranquil scenes with figures. She exhibited in Paris at the Salon d'Automne (1987-1992), the Salon des Artistes Français, of which she has been a member since 1989, as well as in 1984 at the Biennale d'Art Naïf in Quinsac, where she received a prize. She has also had solo exhibitions, including: Galerie Protée, Toulouse (1980); Galerie Racine, Nice (1997).

MUSEUMS AND GALLERIES:

CÉRET (Mus. municipal d'Art moderne) - PARIS (Mus. d'Art Naïf-Max Fourny) - SHERBROOK, CAN - VICQ (Musée d'Art Naïf de l'Île-de-France).

FOURMENTIN, Michel. See **FROUMENTIN**

FOURMOIS, Théodore

Belgian, 19th century.
Born 14 October 1814, in Presles; died 16 October 1871, in Ixelles.
Painter, watercolourist, engraver, draughtsman, lithographer. History painting, landscapes, landscapes with figures.
Tervuren School.

Self-taught, Théodore Fourmois was initally a draughtsman, later evolving as a painter of scenes of the 1830 Belgian Revolution. From 1836 onwards he devoted himself to landscape painting. He painted from nature in Brussels and the surrounding countryside, and in France in the Ardennes as well as in Barbizon, out of admiration for Théodore Rousseau, Jules Dupré and Charles Daubigny. He numbered among the forerunners of the École de Tervuren (Tervuren School) and was the initiator of the realism of the painting of the Belgian countryside.

T fourmois

T. fourmois
1854

MUSEUMS AND GALLERIES:
BRUSSELS (MBA): *The Mill of Éprave; View Taken in Campine.*
AUCTION RECORDS:
PARIS, 7-8 Dec 1891, *Landscape,* FRF 540. PARIS, 28 April 1900, *View of the Dauphiné,* FRF 725. LONDON, 4 May 1908, *Twilight,* GBP 1. PARIS, 30 March 1925, *A Corner of a Forest,* FRF 105. BRUSSELS, 24-25 Oct 1938, *Old Mill,* BEF 1,600. NICE, 2 June 1945, *Landscape,* FRF 11,200. PARIS, 18 March 1955, *Ardennes Landscape,* FRF 44,000. PARIS, 17 Feb 1971, *Oak* (oil on panel, 9 1/2 x 12 1/2 ins / 24 x 32 cm) FRF 1,300. LONDON, 13 April 1972, *Farm,* GBP 400. LONDON, 6 Dec 1973, *Wheat Harvest* (1841) GBP 620. BRUSSELS, 28 Oct 1981, *Landscape with Figures and Watermill* (1871, oil on canvas, 31 1/2 x 43 1/4 ins / 80 x 110 cm) BEF 275,000. LONDON, 23 Feb 1983, *Livestock by a River* (oil on canvas, 18 x 24 ins / 46 x 61 cm) GBP 850. BRUSSELS, 27 March 1985, *Landscape with Figures and Watermill* (1871, oil on canvas, 31 x 42 1/2 ins / 79 x 108 cm) BEF 260,000. BERN, 30 April 1988, *Untitled* (oil on canvas, 17 x 21 1/2 ins / 43 x 54.5 cm) CHF 8,000. LOKEREN, 21 March 1992, *Undergrowth* (oil on card, 13 1/2 x 18 1/2 ins / 34 x 47 cm) BEF 38,000. AMSTERDAM, 2-3 Nov 1992, *Undulating Landscape with Figures on a Path Promenading along a Creek* (oil on panel, 19 1/4 x 27 1/4 ins / 49 x 69 cm) NLG 11,500. LONDON, 7 April 1993, *Figures in a Landscape* (1845, oil on panel, 7 3/4 x 11 ins / 20 x 27 cm) GBP 517. LOKEREN, 4 Dec 1993, *Watermill* (oil on canvas, 39 1/4 x 55 ins / 100 x 140 cm) BEF 380,000. LOKEREN, 12 March 1994, *Cows at the Drinking Trough* (oil on panel, 25 1/2 x 17 3/4 ins / 65 x 45 cm) BEF 60,000. LOKEREN, 7 Oct 1995, *Extensive Landscape with Cows being Watered, near the Sea* (oil on canvas, 29 1/2 x 39 1/4 ins / 75 x 99.5 cm) BEF 220,000. AMSTERDAM, 22 April 1997, *Peasant Woman and Cows near a Farm* (1866, oil on canvas, 31 x 40 1/4 ins / 79 x 102 cm) NLG 21,240. BRUSSELS, 17 May 1999, *La Hulpe in August* (1871, oil on canvas, 20 x 25 ins / 50 x 64 cm) BEF 100,000. ANTWERP, 11 Oct 1999, *La Hulpe* (1815, oil on canvas, 19 x 24 ins / 48 x 61 cm) BEF 180,000. BRUSSELS, 15 Feb 2000, *Farmer and his Animals by the River* (oil on canvas, 22 x 29 ins / 55 x 73 cm) BEF 188,000. LONDON, 28 Nov 2000, *Figures before a Mill in a Rocky Landscape. Fishing before a Mill* (1869, oil on canvas, two, 20 x 27 ins / 52 x 69 cm) GBP 3,000. ANTWERP, 30 April 2001, *Landscape in the Ardennes* (oil on canvas, 29 x 42 ins / 74 x 107 cm) BEF 260,000. BRUSSELS, 15 May 2001, *Water Mill* (oil on mahogany panel, 9 x 13 ins / 23 x 32 cm) BEF 102,000. BRUSSELS, 26 Nov 2002, *Landscape with Travellers* (1867, oil on canvas, 39 x 57 ins / 98 x 145 cm) EUR 7,400. PARIS, 20 Dec 2002, *Study of a Felled Tree* (oil on canvas, 7 x 14 ins / 18 x 36 cm) EUR 2,400. LOKEREN, 15 May 2004, *Landscape with Cows and Herdsman* (watercolour, 13 x 19 ins / 33 x 48 cm) EUR 1,500.

FOURMOIS, William
French, 20th century.
Painter. Genre scenes, landscapes.
AUCTION RECORDS:
PARIS, 14 May 1945, *A Country Outing,* FRF 5,000.

FOURMOND, Coraly de
French, 19th century.
Born 1803; died 1853.
Painter.
She exhibited portraits and miniatures at Paris salons from 1831 to 1850. Her work includes a *Portrait of Sidi Mohamed Machsen, Governor of Tripoli; The Virtuous Susannah; Portrait of Eugène Janvier; Fredegond and Gregory of Tours.*

FOURNASAYRE, Jacques. See **FORNAZERIS Jacques de**

FOURNEAU, Daniel
Belgian, 20th - 21st century.
Born 1953, in Liège.
Painter.
Fourneau was the son of Charles Félix Fourneau, and attended the Académie des Beaux-Arts de Liège until 1978. He exhibits in Liège and New York. He uses a 'free-style' in his painting.

FOURNEAU, Louis
French, 20th century.
Born in Trouville-sur-Mer.
Painter.
Louis Fourneau exhibited in Paris at the Salon des Artistes Français from 1920.

FOURNEL, Eugénie (Miss). See **PELLETIER Laurent, Mrs**

FOURNEL, Jean-Baptiste
French, 19th century.
Born c. 1835, in Lyons.
Painter, watercolourist. Animals, landscapes, seascapes, flowers, fruit.
Fournel lived and worked in Pierre-Bénite in the Rhône valley and exhibited at the Lyons Salon from 1857 to 1892. He was first and foremost a still-life painter (flowers, fruit and birds), although he very occasionally painted oil or watercolour landscapes and seascapes.
AUCTION RECORDS:
ARLES, 10 Nov 1985, *Still-life with Fruit Bowl and Stoneware Pitchers on a White Tablecloth* (oil on canvas, 23 1/2 x 28 3/4 ins / 60 x 73 cm) FRF 14,000.

FOURNEL, Pierre
French, 20th century.
Born 27 May 1924, in Rodez.
Painter (mixed media), engraver, lithographer, medallist. Landscapes.
After studying at the École Nationale des Beaux-Arts in Paris, Pierre Fournel qualified as a teacher of drawing in 1949. In 1950 he was appointed to teach in Montpellier and settled in the village of Castelnau. He produced medals of Joseph Delteil and Jean Hugo for the Paris Mint as well as commemorative medals of the Marquis Jean Pierre and Gabriel Couderc, founder of the Musée Paul Valery in Sète.

He uses a traditional technique, painting the countryside around Montpellier and the villages of the Languedoc region. Attracted by space and the distant horizon, in 1959 he turned to ponds and the sea as his subject. In 1960 he painted the landscape of Spain and Brittany and then of the Venice Lagoon and the open spaces of the Sahara. Around 1970 he began using sand and crumpled paper, applying this to large expanses of his landscapes. This process imbued his work with a warm tonality and brought structure to his compositions through a discreet use of relief. During the 1990s, Fournel, who was born in the region, took the *Chemins Cathares* (*The Roads of Cathar*) as his subject, often bringing an element of ornamental abstraction to his work. He also produced engravings, at first using the traditional methods of etching, dry point and lithography but soon replacing engraved plates with a substrate of synthetic resin.

He exhibited at many Paris Salons including the Salon d'Automne, the Salon Comparaisons and the Salon des Peintres Témoins de leur Temps, and also in the provinces. There have been regular solo exhibitions in Montpellier, Toulouse, Aix, Paris (at the Galerie Vendôme, notably in 1998 and 2002) and in Geneva. Several retrospectives of his work have been held: in 1966 at the Musée de Narbonne; in 1980, *10 Ans de Peinture* (*10 Years of Painting*) at the Musée de Pau; in 1984 at the Musée Paul Valery in Sète; and in 1999, *Pierre Fournel. Grains de Sable* (*Pierre Fournel - Grains of Sand*) at the Musée Denys, Rodez.
BIBLIOGRAPHY:
Paire, Alain, *Pierre Fournel, peintures 1970-1980,* exhibition catalogue, Musée des Beaux-Arts, Pau, 1980. Comte, Phil-

ippe, *Pierre Fournel*, exhibition catalogue, Musée Paul-Valéry, Sète, 1984. Imbernon, Laurence/Loubière, Mireille/Laboucarié, Sophie, *Pierre Fournel. Grains de sable*, exhibition catalogue, Musée des Beaux-Arts Denys-Puech, Rodez, 1999.

MUSEUMS AND GALLERIES:

AVIGNON - LUXEMBOURG - LYONS - MONTPELLIER (Mus. Fabre): *The Castelnau Crossroads*; *Causses Landscape* - NARBONNE (MAH): *Cadaquès* (1961, oil on canvas) - NICE - PARIS (MAMVP) - PAU: *Salt Works Roads* - RODEZ - SÈTE: *Espiguette Beach*.

AUCTION RECORDS:

PARIS, 1 July 1986, *Saharan Triptych* (three oils and sand/canvas, 39¼ x 39¼ ins / 100 x 100 cm; 44½ x 57½ ins/113 x 146 cm; 39¼ x 39¼ ins/100 x 100 cm) FRF 8,100.

FOURNEREAU, Jean François Mathieu, called Mathéus
French, 19th century.
Born 29 December 1829, in Mornant (Rhône); died 13 December 1901, in Lyons.
Painter.

An occasional painter who studied under H. Flandrin, he exhibited landscapes and studies of heads in oil, charcoal and crayon in Lyons in 1858-1859 and 1861 and, in 1888, a *Samson Burning the Corn of the Philistines*. He painted decorations for the choir in the church at Couzon (Rhône) and for the baptistery of the church at St-Didier-sous-Riveria.

FOURNERY, Félix
French, 19th century.
Born in the 19th century, in Paris.
Painter, illustrator.

Félix Fournery was a member of the Société des Artistes Français from 1887 onwards. He travelled extensively in northern Europe before returning to Paris to work as an unusually stylish illustrator.

FOURNETS, Marie
Maiden name: Vernaud
French, 19th century.
Born 1865, in Paris.
Active in Paris.
Painter.

Marie Fournets studied under D. Mailart. She painted historical subjects and genre compositions, together with portraits. Fournets exhibited at the Salon des Artistes Français in 1885, 1893 and 1900.

FOURNIALS, J. Marguerite
French, 20th century.
Born in Paris.
Painter. Landscapes.

J. Marguerite Fournials studied under Guirand de Scévola and was awarded a travel bursary in 1931. From 1928, she exhibited at the Salon of the Société Nationale des Beaux-Arts in Paris, showing landscapes. She later became a member of the Société. She was awarded a gold medal at the International Exhibition of 1937 and the Charles Cottet prize in 1941.

FOURNIALS, Roger
French, 20th century.
Born 1910, in Paris.
Painter.

Roger Fournials exhibited in Paris at the Salon des Indépendants, the Salon d'Automne, the Salon of the Société Nationale des Beaux-Arts and the Salon Populiste. He was awarded the Intersalon gold medal in 1957.

FOURNIÉ
French, 18th century.
Active in Bordeaux.
Sculptor (wood).

Fournié sculpted the statues of *St Michael* and *St William* for the church of St-Michael in Bordeaux in 1720.

FOURNIER
French, 18th century.
Died 19 October 1739, in Rome.
Painter.

Fournier was a student at the Académie de Paris and won first prize for painting in the Prix de Rome in 1737 with *Samson, with Delilah, Surprised by the Philistines*. He has often been confused with Jean Fournier, the pupil of Troy.

FOURNIER
French, 18th century.
Painter.

Fournier painted an *Ascension* which hangs in the church in Contres. He is designated a 'painter at the Académie'.

FOURNIER (Dom)
French, 18th century.
Painter.

Dom Fournier belonged to the order of St Benedict. The Abbaye-aux-Hommes in Caen possesses some paintings by him depicting subjects from the Old and New Testaments.

MUSEUMS AND GALLERIES:

CAEN (Abbaye-aux-Hommes): subjects from the Old and New Testaments.

FOURNIER, Alain A.
French, 20th century.
Born 1 April 1931, in Coutances; died 19 May 1983, in Le Plessis-Robinson.
Painter, watercolourist, engraver. Landscapes, seascapes, flowers. Murals.
Poetic Reality.

Alain Fournier studied in Paris under Édouard Goerg and Maurice Brianchon, at the École des Beaux-Arts. He was awarded the Prix de Rome in 1957. He learned rigorous composition from Goerg and a delicate sense of light from Brianchon. He produced many flower paintings and landscapes of Normandy, Brittany and Venice. During his early period he tended to display a certain Expressionism in his technique which later became more serene.

He exhibited at group exhibitions in Paris, including: in 1959 the Biennale des Jeunes; the Salon d'Automne; the Salon de la Jeune Peinture; the Salon des Artistes Français; the Salon Comparaisons; the Salon de la Marine for the first time in 1947; and the 1968 Biennale in Cherbourg. His work has also been shown in solo exhibitions: from 1959 to 1968 at the Galerie Dauphine in Paris; from 1969 to 1980 at the Galerie Emmanuel David in Paris; in 1991 a retrospective exhibition in St-Lô; in 1994, paintings and watercolours at the Galerie des Orfèvres in Paris.

ALAIN A FOURNIER

ALAIN FOURNIER

BIBLIOGRAPHY:

Alain A. Fournier, Les Cahiers de l'ODAC, St-Lô, 1991.

AUCTION RECORDS:

VERSAILLES, 23 March 1986, *Large Bunch of Flowers* (oil on canvas, 46 x 35 ins / 116 x 89 cm) FRF 7,800. VERSAILLES, 13 Dec 1987, *The Salute, Venice* (oil on canvas, 32 x 39¼ ins / 81 x 100 cm) FRF 9,500. VERSAILLES, 21 Feb 1988, *Young Woman and Child by a Large Canal in the Gardens of Versailles* (oil on canvas, 32 x 39¼ ins / 81 x 100 cm) FRF 6,000. VERSAILLES, 23 March 1988, *Fishing Boat near a Lighthouse* (oil on canvas, 38¼ x 51½ ins / 97 x 131 cm) FRF 5,500. VERSAILLES, 17 April 1988, *Landscape with Flowers* (oil on canvas, 39 1/4 x 32 ins / 100 x 81 cm) FRF 2,800. LE TOUQUET, 21 May 1995, *Port in Brittany* (oil on canvas, 51 1/4 x 63 3/4 ins / 130 x 162 cm) FRF 13,000. CALAIS, 25 June 1995, *Breton Port* (oil on canvas, 35 1/2 x 46 ins / 90 x 116 cm) FRF 6,500. CALAIS, 7 July 1996, *Brittany, Boats by a Sea Wall* (oil on canvas, 51 1/4 x 38 1/4 ins / 130 x 97 cm) FRF 5,500.

FOURNIER, Albert
French, 19th century.
Born 1843, in Bordeaux.
Painter.

Albert Fournier studied under Léon Cogniet and S. Cornu; he exhibited *Shepherd and Sea* at the 1869 Paris Salon and, in 1870, a canvas entitled *Child on a Terrace* together with a further *Study*.

FOURNIER, Alexandre
French, 19th century.
Born 5 December 1831, in Gannat (Allier).
Painter.

Alexandre Fournier was admitted to the École des Beaux-Arts on 5 April 1849, where he studied under Léon Cogniet and Corot. He exhibited at Paris Salons from 1864 to 1870. Examples of his work include *Forest of Francheville, Vagabond, Neapolitan Shepherd* and *Pride of Lions*.

FOURNIER, Alexis Jean Joseph
French, 19th - 20th century.
Born 1865; died 1948.
From 1903 active in the USA.
Painter. Landscapes.

In 1903, Alexis Fournier moved to a property known as East Aurora near New York to pursue a career as an artist. With his artist friends and students he created the Paint and Varnish Club, making numerous boat trips with the group to find attractive spots to paint.

He was a painter of the outdoors who enjoyed painting from nature. He also painted his house and garden, particularly in summer.

BIBLIOGRAPHY:
Cohen, R.N., *L'Art d'Alexis Jean Fournier*, St-Cloud, 1985.

AUCTION RECORDS:
SAN FRANCISCO, 24 June 1981, *Sunny Landscape* (oil on canvas, 19 1/2 x 23 3/4 ins / 49.5 x 60.5 cm) USD 1,600. PORTLAND, 28 Sept 1985, *Spring Landscape* (oil on panel, 14 x 18 ins / 35.5 x 45.7 cm) USD 1,800. NEW YORK, 30 May 1990, *The Old House* (oil on canvas, 18 x 24 ins / 45.5 x 61 cm) USD 3,850. NEW YORK, 27 Sept 1990, *Niagara Falls by Moonlight* (oil on canvas, 28 x 38 1/4 ins / 71 x 97 cm) USD 7,700. NEW YORK, 23 Sept 1992, *Hollyhocks in the Garden of Bungle House* (oil on canvas, 26 1/4 x 40 1/4 ins / 66.5 x 102 cm) USD 41,800. NEW YORK, 11 March 1993, *Venice* (1913, oil on canvas, 15 x 22 ins / 38 x 55 cm) USD 6,325. NEW YORK, 22 Sept 1993, *Landscape at the End of Summer* (1892, oil on reinforced canvas, 12 x 20 ins / 30.5 x 50.9 cm) USD 2,875. NEW YORK, 17 March 1994, *Morning on the Banks of the Mississippi* (1891, oil on canvas, 28 x 60 ins / 71.1 x 152.4 cm) USD 14,950. NEW YORK, 28 Nov 1995, *Field of Squashes* (1892, oil on card, 12 x 18 1/2 ins / 30.5 x 47 cm) USD 3,450.

FOURNIER, Amable Nicolas
French, 19th century.
Born 1789, in Cayeux (Somme); died 22 June 1854, in Paris.
Engraver.

This artist exhibited at the Salon from 1835 to 1850.

FOURNIER, Anatole
French, 20th century.
Active in Sèvres.
Painter.

Anatole Fournier became a member of the Société des Artistes Français in 1907.

FOURNIER, André Désiré Jules Louis
French, 19th century.
Born in Orléans (Loiret).
Sculptor.

André Fournier was a member of the Société des Artistes Français from 1904 onwards; he received an honourable mention in 1907.

FOURNIER, André Georges
French, 20th century.
Born 1882, in Paris.
Painter.

It does not seem appropriate to suggest a link between André Georges Fournier and Georges Fournier. André Georges Fournier studied under Forget and Quenioux.

MUSEUMS AND GALLERIES:
LIMOGES: three sketches.

FOURNIER, Antoine
French, 17th century.
Sculptor (wood).

Antoine Fournier worked with his son Noël in Troyes. No doubt related to Innocent Fournier, they executed stalls for the churches of Ste-Madeleine, St-Étienne, St-Nicolas and St-Rémi in Troyes, and sculpted the case of the organ in the church of St-Jean. In 1626 at the church of Ste-Savine they executed the pulpit which still exists today, but which is unfortunately now covered with paint.

FOURNIER, Antoine
French, 17th century.
Died 6 April 1679.
Sculptor.

Antoine Fournier sculpted confessionals for the church of St-Pantaléon in 1671 and 1672.

FOURNIER, Armand
French, 19th century.
Painter.

Armand Fournier exhibited at the 1839 Paris Salon with *Forest Glade* and at the 1848 Salon with *View near Montauban*.

FOURNIER, Brigitte
French, 20th - 21st century.
Born 1958.
Sculptor, painter.

Brigitte Fournier obtained a master's degree in the visual arts from the Sorbonne, and studied sculpture under Étienne-Martin at the École des Beaux-Arts de Paris. The subject of Fournier's work is the human figure, which she represents in a style somewhere between Expressionism and a more stylised figuration.

She has taken part in a number of group exhibitions, including the Salon d'Antony in 1996, and the Salon Figuration Critique in Paris in 1998 and 2000. She has also staged solo exhibitions, such as those at the Adac-Galerie Atelier in Paris in 1996 and 2001.

FOURNIER, Charles
French, 19th century.
Born 30 January 1803, in Salmaise (Côte-d'Or); died 16 January 1854, in Birkenhead (England).
Painter. Portraits, genre scenes, landscapes with figures.

Charles Fournier was a pupil of Prud'hon. He enrolled at the École des Beaux-Arts on 4 March 1825 and went on to exhibit at the Paris Salon from 1833 to 1850. Examples of his work include: *Scene from Alfred de Vigny's novel 'Cinq-Mars'; Triumph of Relgion over Love; Scene drawn from 'Paul et Virginie' by Bernardin de Saint Pierre; Don Juan and Haydée; Tempest; Beautiful Spirits; Widow's Mite; Portrait of Dr. Rattier; Hagar Arriving in the Wilderness;* and *Poor Woman with Grand-Daughter*.

MUSEUMS AND GALLERIES:
DIJON: *Death of Abel; Full-length Portrait of Pierre-Paul Prud'hon* - SEMUR-EN-AUXOIS: *Roman Woman.*
AUCTION RECORDS:
LONDON, 14 May 1976, *Landscape with Mother and Child* (1843, oil on canvas, 46 1/2 x 37 ins / 118.2 x 94 cm) GBP 650. MILAN, 25 Feb 1986, *Portrait of the Marchioness del Carretto* (1839, oil on canvas, 36 1/4 x 28 1/4 ins / 92 x 72 cm) ITL 11,000,000. PARIS, 18 April 1991, *Portrait of the Countess of Solancy and her Son* (oil on canvas, 46 1/4 x 35 ins / 117.5 x 89 cm) FRF 50,000. PARIS, 6 Dec 1995, *Rustic Festival* (1838, oil on canvas, 32 1/4 x 26 ins / 82 x 66 cm) FRF 29,000. PARIS, 2 June 1997, *Young Girls of the Légion d'honneur* (1838, canvas, 32 1/4 x 25 1/2 ins / 82 x 65 cm) FRF 48,000.

FOURNIER, Charles Louis
Flemish, 18th century.
Born 21 February 1730, in Ypres; died 28 August 1803.
Painter, poet. Genre scenes.
Flemish School.
The museum in Ypres holds Charles Louis Fournier's *Portrait* and four supra-portas representing the *Four Seasons.*

FOURNIER, Claude, the Elder
French, 17th century.
Painter.
Claude Fournier the Elder was one of the founders of the Académie de Bordeaux in 1691 and was a lecturer there at the same time as Mar. Fournier the Younger.

FOURNIER, Claude
French, 18th century.
Active in Troyes.
Sculptor (wood).
Claude Fournier was the son of Antoine Fournier II. He took part in the carving of the panelling at the church of St-Pantaléon in Troyes.

FOURNIER, Clotilde Marie Geneviève
French, 20th century.
Born in Guadeloupe.
Painter, pastellist.
Clotilde Fournier studied at the École des Beaux-Arts in Paris. She exhibited at the Salon from 1922.

FOURNIER, Daniel
French, 18th century.
Born c. 1710; died c. 1766, in Wild Court.
Draughtsman, engraver.
Daniel Fournier was a shoemaker and caterer. In 1764 he published a work on perspective. He executed engravings in mezzotint.

FOURNIER, Edmond Charles
French, 19th - 20th century.
Active in Paris.
Painter. Landscapes.
Edmond Fournier became a member of the Société des Artistes Français in 1904 and received a commendation in 1905.
AUCTION RECORDS:
PARIS, 5 June 1985, *Garden in Autumn* (oil on canvas, 50 1/2 x 63 ins / 128 x 160 cm) FRF 13,000.

FOURNIER, Édouard. See **ÉDOUARD-FOURNIER Paul Joseph Albert**

FOURNIER, Édouard
French, 19th century.
Born 1857, in Orléans or Dijon.
Sculptor.
Édouard Fournier was a pupil of Georges Lemaire. He was a member of the Société des Artistes Français, and was awarded a bronze medal in 1889.

FOURNIER, Élise (Mme)
Maiden name: Bernard
French, 19th century.
Born in the 19th century, in Paris.
Painter.
Élise Fournier exhibited portraits and pastels at the Salon between 1848 and 1852. She is often confused with the pastel painter Elisabeth Bernard.

FOURNIER, Émile
French, 19th century.
Painter.
Émile Fournier exhibited views of the Seine at the Paris Salons of 1848 and 1849.

FOURNIER, Félicie (Miss). See also **SCHNEIDER**

FOURNIER, Félicie (Mme)
Maiden name: Monsaldy
French, 19th century.
Born 1797; died 1879.
Engraver.
Félicie Fournier was the daughter of the engraver Monsaldy and the wife of Anatole Nicolas Fournier. She exhibited at the Paris Salon from 1837 to 1847.

FOURNIER, Gabriel
French, 17th century.
Active in Bordeaux.
Painter.
Gabriel Fournier was associated with François de Laprérie. He visited Holland and is mentioned in Amsterdam in 1641.

FOURNIER, Gabriel Francisque Alexis, also called Gabriel-Fournier
French, 20th century.
Born 26 May 1893, in Grenoble; died 13 April 1963, in Fontainebleau.
Painter, watercolourist, draughtsman, illustrator.
Figures, nudes, landscapes, still-lifes, flowers. Designs for tapestries.
Gabriel Fournier learned to paint with Lucien Mainssieux. He attended the École des Beaux-Arts in Lyons from 1910 and then the École des Arts Décoratifs in Paris in 1912. He studied under Aubert. Keen to perfect his skills, he made numerous copies of works by Fra Angelico and Delacroix at the Louvre and of Veronese, Sisley and Delacroix again at the Musée de Grenoble; he then worked for four years in the studio of Raoul Dufy until he was called up in 1918.

In Montparnasse he got to know Soutine, Kisling, Max Jacob, Picasso, Modigliani, Cendrars and Satie and met Léopold Zborowski who, when he became a dealer, offered Fournier a contract. In 1917 he exhibited at a group exhibition at the Salle Huyghens where recitals of works by Satie, Poulenc, Auric and Honegger took place. Zborowski sent him to paint at St-Paul-de Vence, where he spent time with Matisse, Dufy, Jean Renoir, Signac and Gimond. Élie Faure, André Salmon, Louis Vauxcelles and other critics began to take an interest in him. From 1926 to 1940 he lived at La Murette near Voiron in the Dauphiné region and also painted in Provence and at Fontainebleau. From 1943 he illustrated various literary works including Virgile's *La Fille d'Auberge* in 1945 and Nerval's *Les Chimères* in 1948. He also produced tapestry cartoons, notably the *Baptism of Christ* commissioned by the Gobelins works in 1943. In 1956 he had a collection of his memories of fellow artists published by Pierre Cailler in Geneva. His numerous still-lifes, landscapes and figures reveal him to be a sensitive artist with a meticulous touch.

He exhibited in Paris, starting at the Salon des Indépendants, and became a member of the Salon d'Automne. In 1933 he was elected to the Galerie Druet's premier group of artists, alongside Signac, Luce, Bonnard, Vuillard, Maurice

Denis and Roussel. In 1939 his work featured in an exhibition at the Kunsthalle in Basel, together with that of Marquet, Laprade, Bouche and Mainssieux. In 1959 the Galerie Katia Granoff in Paris held a major solo exhibition of Fournier's work.

Bibliography:

Ferrotin, Balthazar, *Gabriel Fournier*, Imprimerie Legrand, Paris, 1956. Duplessis, Bertrand, *Gabriel Fournier*, Éd. SNP-MD, Paris, 1973. Wantellet, Maurice, *Deux siècles et plus de peinture dauphinoise*, M. Wantellet, Grenoble, 1987.

Museums and Galleries:

Chambéry (MBA): *Vase of Flowers* - Moscow (Mus. of Western Art) - Paris (Mus. du Petit Palais).

Auction records:

Paris, 9 Feb 1925, *Landscape*, FRF 750. Paris, 22 March 1926, *Flowers*, FRF 1,100. Paris, 16 Feb 1929, *The Road*, FRF 980; *Seated Woman*, FRF 800. Paris, 13 July 1942, *Bandol* FRF 800. Paris, 22 Oct 1946, *Landscape* (watercolour) FRF 310; *View of the South of France* (watercolour) FRF 400. Paris, 22 May 1981, *Street in Paris* (oil on canvas, 28 3/4 x 23 1/2 ins / 73 x 60 cm) FRF 2,650. Paris, 25 May 1983, *The Artist's House and Garden near Fontainebleau* (oil on canvas, 22 x 18 ins / 55 x 46 cm) FRF 5,500. Rheims, 22 Dec 1985, *The Village of Villiers-sous-Grez* (1957, oil on canvas, 18 x 22 ins / 46 x 55 cm) FRF 13,500. Rheims, 21 Dec 1986, *Mist Lifting over the Village of Larchant* (oil on canvas, 15 x 22 ins / 38 x 55 cm) FRF 5,500. Paris, 7 June 1988, *St-Gervais Church* (oil on canvas, 28 3/4 x 36 1/4 ins / 73 x 92 cm) FRF 14,000; *The White Window* (oil on canvas, 46 x 35 ins / 116 x 89 cm) FRF 11,000; *St-Étienne du Mont Church* (oil on canvas, 32 x 39 1/4 ins / 81 x 100 cm) FRF 13,500. Paris, 7 Dec 1990, *Town Walls, Antibes* (oil on canvas, 25 1/2 x 39 1/4 ins / 64.5 x 100 cm) FRF 5,500. Paris, 5 Feb 1992, *Nude Seen from the Rear* (1939, graphite, 15 x 9 ins / 38 x 23 cm) FRF 6,000. Paris, 28 June 1995, *Avenue of Trees Leading to a Village* (oil on canvas, 23 1/2 x 28 3/4 ins / 60 x 73 cm) FRF 4,000. Neuilly, 9 May 1996, *Still-life with Flowers in an Apothecary's Vase* (oil on canvas, 32 3/4 x 21 1/4 ins / 83 x 54 cm) FRF 5,500.

FOURNIER, Georges

French, 20th century.
Born in Paris.
Painter.

It does not seem appropriate to suggest a link between Georges Fournier and André Georges Fournier. Georges Fournier exhibited landscapes at the Salon des Indépendants in Paris from 1903.

FOURNIER, Guillaume

French, 18th century.
Active in Marchéville (Eure-et-Loir).
Sculptor (wood).

Guillaume Fournier executed a pulpit, panelling and other works for the church in Marchéville in 1732 and 1737.

FOURNIER, Hippolyte

French, 19th century.
Born 4 June 1799, in Coutances (Manche); died 30 December 1863.
Painter.

Hippolyte Fournier initially studied music before turning to painting. He received a pension from his native city of Coutances, which enabled him to travel to Paris, where he studied under Bertin.

Museums and Galleries:

Coutances: *Landscape*.

FOURNIER, Hippolyte

French, 19th - 20th century.
Born 1852, in Rablay; died 1926.
Painter, watercolourist. Nudes, genre scenes.

Hippolyte Fournier studied under Jean-Paul Laurens and exhibited at the Salon des Artistes Français.

Fournier painted a variety of genre scenes, including: *Reading to Grandfather; The Last Communion; Evening by a Cradle*, all of which are homages to family life. He produced another series of scenes of peasant life in the Anjou region. He also painted some nudes, treated in a diaphanous manner in which he approaches Symbolism. In Paris he was awarded a bronze medal at the Exposition Universelle of 1889, a silver medal in 1890 and a bronze medal at the Exposition Universelle of 1900. He became a member of the Société in 1903.

Museums and Galleries:

Angers: *The First Meal*.

Auction records:

Paris, 5 March 1997, *The Young Mother* (1893, oil on canvas, 53 x 65 3/4 ins / 134.9 x 167 cm) FRF 50,000.

FOURNIER, Innocent

French, 16th century.
Active in Troyes.
Sculptor (wood).

Innocent Fournier was involved in work on the choir stalls in Troyes Cathedral between 1525 and 1526.

FOURNIER, Isaïe

French, 17th century.
Engraver, architect.

In 1600 Isaïe Fournier worked on the construction of the main gallery of the Louvre. Most biographers erroneously identify him with Fornazeris.

FOURNIER, Jean

French, 16th century.
Active in Paris in 1526.
Carver.

This artist may be the same person as Jean Fournier the sculptor.

FOURNIER, Jean

French, 16th century.
Sculptor, founder.

In 1519, Jean Fournier made a lectern of copper in the form of an eagle and decorated with the figures of Sts Andrew, Peter and Paul for the church of St-André in Châteaudun (Eure-et-Loir). He also made a copper cross for the high altar. That same year he made three bells for the church of St-Médard.

FOURNIER, Jean

French, 18th century.
Born c. 1700; died 1765, in The Hague.
Painter. History painting, portraits.

Jean Fournier was the pupil of Fr. de Troy. He left France for unknown reasons and established himself in Holland, where he was admitted as a member of the Confrérie Pictura guild in The Hague. One of his best paintings was in the premises of this guild, *The Citizen Officers of the Blue Flag*, but he was primarily known as a portrait painter.

Museums and Galleries:

Amsterdam: two portraits - Haarlem: *Portrait of Dr Pieter Steyn; Portrait of Cornelia Schellinger, Wife of Dr Steyn; Portrait of Dr Elias Schellinger; Portrait of Elizabeth Buys, Wife of Dr Schellinger*.

Auction records:

Paris, 1891, *Nymph; Young Faun* (two pendants) FRF 650.

FOURNIER, Jean

French, 20th century.
Painter. Interiors, landscapes, still-lifes.

Jean Fournier studied at the École des Beaux-Arts in Paris. He lived in Delhi for seven years and in 1961, continuing with his travels, moved to Ouessant.

Fournier's painting shows a great sensitivity to subtle harmonies that suggest a landscape and an atmosphere. His work shows the influence of the Nabis.

FOURNIER, Jean Auguste

French, 19th century.

Born 1 September 1790, in Vincennes (Val-de-Marne); died 1835, in Paris.

Painter, miniaturist.

Jean Auguste Fournier was admitted to the École des Beaux-Arts on 6 September 1816, where he studied under Gros. He exhibited portraits at the Salons of 1831, 1833 and 1835.

FOURNIER, Jean Baptiste

French, 18th century.

Active in Paris in 1764.

Painter.

FOURNIER, Jean Simon

French, 18th century.

Born in Paris.

Painter. Figures, genre scenes, interiors with figures.

Jean Simon Fournier was the pupil of Regnault and exhibited at the Louvre from 1791 to 1799. His most notable works include *A Girl Adorning Herself with Flowers in front of a Mirror, A Girl Sitting down at her Harpsichord* and *The Dangerous Rose Bush*.

AUCTION RECORDS:

PARIS, 6 June 1928, *The Longed-for Letter; A Girl Adorning Herself with Flowers in front of a Mirror* (two) FRF 62,400. PARIS, 1-2 April 1954, *The Appointed Hour*, FRF 210,000. VERSAILLES, 23 May 1978, *Two Young Women in an Interior* (1795, oil on canvas, 22 x 18 1/2 ins / 56 x 47 cm) FRF 20,000. PARIS, 31 Oct 1991, *The Confidence* (oil on canvas, 22 x 18 1/4 ins / 56 x 46.5 cm) FRF 38,000. NEW YORK, 27 Jan 2000, *Interior Scene with a Young Woman Being Offered Flowers by a Suitor* (oil on canvas, a pair, 16 x 13 ins / 41 x 33 cm) USD 35,000. NEW YORK, 1 May 2000, *The Time of Meeting* (1836, oil on canvas, 20 x 24 ins / 51 x 61 cm) USD 95,000. NEW YORK, 5 Oct 2001, *Interior Scene with Young Couple* (oil on canvas, 18 x 15 ins / 46 x 38 cm) USD 4,700. PARIS, 27 March 2003, *Three Young Girls in an Interior* (graphite/chalk, 20 x 16 ins / 51 x 41 cm) EUR 4,800.

FOURNIER, Jean-Baptiste Fortuné de

French, 19th century.

Born 1795 or 1798, in Ajaccio (Corsica); died 17 February 1864, in Paris.

Painter, watercolourist, engraver. Portraits, interiors with figures, architectural interiors. Murals.

Jean-Baptiste Fournier studied at the Naples Polytechnic and exhibited at the Paris Salon from 1843 to 1864. He was made a Chevalier of the Légion d'Honneur in 1855. Fournier was first and foremost a watercolorist whose speciality was interiors, specifically salons, galleries and palatial chambers, the furnishings and decoration of which he rendered faithfully and precisely. Typical examples of his work include: *Interior of the Salle de' Medici, Florence, Interior of the Niobe Chamber of the Uffizi in Florence, Interior of the St Louis XV Chamber in the Tuileries*, and *Eight Interiors of the Tuileries Palace* (commissioned by the Emperor). Fournier also produced engravings for the Pitti de Bardi Gallery, painted various decorative panels, and executed a number of portraits, among them *Full-length Portrait of Napoleon III in Imperial Dress* and *Full-length Portrait of Napoleon III in General's Dress Uniform*.

AUCTION RECORDS:

LONDON, 18 June 1926, *Bath Scene*, GBP 27. PARIS, 10-11 April 1929, *Chamber of Marshals, Tuileries Palace* (watercolour) FRF 4,100. NEW YORK, 3 June 1980, *Portrait of a Young Woman* (graphite/paper, 14 1/4 x 9 ins / 36.3 x 22.6 cm) USD 1,900. MONACO, 8 Dec 1990, *Interior of the Medici Chamber, Florence* (watercolour, 18 x 23 1/2 ins / 46 x 59.5 cm) FRF 44,400. PARIS, 20 Oct 1997, *Medallions and Chatelaines* (watercolour/paper, 11 x 8 1/4 ins / 28 x 21 cm) FRF 2,000.

FOURNIER, Louis

French, 18th century.

Sculptor.

Louis Fournier was an adviser at the Académie de St-Luc where, on 25 August 1774, he exhibited *Portrait*, painted in Copenhagen. He was also a manufacturer of porcelain.

FOURNIER, Louis

French, 19th century.

Born in the 19th century, in St-Donat (Drôme).

Sculptor.

Louis Fournier exhibited busts and medallions at Paris Salons between 1864 and 1872. Examples of his work include a marble bust of *Canon Ouin-la-Croix*, secretary general of the chaplaincy of France, a bust of *Monsieur Germain* and a statue of *Monseigneur Darboy*.

MUSEUMS AND GALLERIES:

ROUEN: *Bust of Abbot Ouin-la-Croix*.

FOURNIER, Louis Antoine

French, 18th century.

Active in Paris in 1771.

Painter, sculptor.

FOURNIER, Louis Édouard Paul

French, 19th century.

Born 1857, in Paris.

Painter, watercolourist, decorative artist, draughtsman, illustrator. History painting, portraits.

Louis Édouard Fournier was a pupil of Cabanel. He was awarded the Grand Prix de Rome in 1881, together with a bronze medal in 1885 and a further bronze at the Exposition Universelle of 1900. He was made a Chevalier of the Légion d'Honneur. Louis Fournier was entrusted with various decorative projects, including one for the École Normale at the Institute itself. He also drew the design for the *History of Art* glass mosaic mural which runs the length of the corniche of the Grand Palais des Beaux-Arts on the Champs-Elysées, and decorated several monuments in Lyons. He illustrated several publications, among them Lucien's *Dialogue des Courtisanes* (*Dialogue of the Courtesans*), the *La Matrone d'Éphèse* (*Widow of Ephesus*) by Petronius, and Albert Samain's *Contes* (*Tales*). First and foremost, however, Fournier was a portraitist.

MUSEUMS AND GALLERIES:

AIX: *OrestesTaking Refuge at the Altar of Apollo* - BELFORT: *Son of Gaul* - LIVERPOOL: *Cremation of Shelley's Corpse* - MORLAIX: *Velleda, Prophetess of Gaul* - PARIS (Mus. de la Comédie-Française): *Monsieur Buloz* - PÉRIGUEUX: *Science; Snake-Charmer* - SENS: *Suleka, Woman of Cairo* - ST-BRIEUC: *Marauder*.

AUCTION RECORDS:

PARIS, 1894, *Scenes from Molière* (watercolour, set of thirty-eight) FRF 151. NEW YORK, 17 May 1984, *Flowers from the Garden* (oil on canvas, 19 1/2 x 25 1/2 ins / 49.5 x 65 cm) USD 3,000. NEW YORK, 28 Oct 1986, *Harem Beauty* (1885, oil on canvas, 18 3/4 x 24 3/4 ins / 47.5 x 63 cm) USD 9,000. NEW YORK, 25 Feb 1988, *Portrait of a Young Woman wearing a Hat* (black chalk, 21 1/2 x 16 ins / 54.6 x 39.7 cm) USD 1,320. LONDON, 11 Oct 1995, *Mounet Sully on Stage, Attired as a Roman* (oil on card, 5 1/2 x 9 1/2 ins / 14 x 24 cm) GBP 1,725. LONDON,

26 May 2004, *Beside a River* (oil on canvas, 29 x 39 ins / 73 x 100 cm) GBP 3,500.

FOURNIER, Luc
French, 20th - 21st century.
Born 1956.
Painter. Figures, landscapes.
Luc Fournier is a former student of Zao Wou-Ki. He paints his canvases in a rather stylised manner, trimming the edges in various ways to suit the subject.

FOURNIER, Mar., the Younger
French, 17th - 18th century.
Painter. Vignettes.
Mar. Fournier the Younger was assistant professor at the Académie de Bordeaux in 1691 at the same time as Claude Fournier the Elder.
AUCTION RECORDS:
PARIS, 18 Jan 1945, 1781, black chalk, three vignettes) FRF 600.

FOURNIER, Marcel
French, 19th - 20th century.
Born 1869; died 1917; on active service.
Painter. Landscapes.
Marcel Fournier exhibited in Paris at the Salon des Artistes Indépendants from 1922.
AUCTION RECORDS:
PARIS, 29 and 30 Dec 1919, *The Last Rays*, FRF 115. PARIS, 15 June 1945, *The Harvest*, FRF 450. PARIS, 14 Feb 1947, *River in the Gorges*, FRF 320.

FOURNIER, Nicolas
French, 17th century.
Active in Troyes.
Sculptor (wood).
Nicolas Fournier was the brother of Antoine and Noël Fournier. He executed the pulpit of the church of St-Nicolas in Troyes from 1623 to 1632.

FOURNIER, Nicolas
French, 18th century.
Active in Paris in 1750.
Painter, sculptor.

FOURNIER, Noël
French, 17th century.
Born c. 1580; died after 1630.
Active in Troyes.
Sculptor (wood).
Noël Fournier was the son of Antoine Fournier.

FOURNIER, Paul
French, 19th century.
Born 1859, in Paris.
Sculptor, dramatist. Figures. Statues.
Paul Fournier's statue of *Shakespeare* was unveiled on the Boulevard Haussmann in Paris in 1888, while his *Balzac* inaugurated in Tours (Indre-et-Loire) in 1891.
MUSEUMS AND GALLERIES:
NICE: *Ophelia*.

FOURNIER, Paul Albert
French, 19th century.
Born 6 December 1847, in Paris.
Engraver.
This artist is possibly the same person as Paul Joseph Albert Edouard-Fournier. He engraved in the style of Meissonier and exhibited at the Salon for the first time in 1870, gaining an honourable mention in 1896.

FOURNIER, Philippe Joseph
French, 18th century.
Active in Paris in 1755.
Painter.

FOURNIER, Pierre
French, 18th century.
Active in Paris.
Sculptor.
Pierre Fournier was a member of the Académie de St-Luc as 'sculptor to the king'. At Versailles he worked in 1705 on the Bains d'Apollon, and in 1740 executed the decorative parts of the portal of Notre-Dames-des-Victoires in Paris.

FOURNIER, Pierre
French, 19th century.
Born in Lyons.
Painter.
Pierre Fournier was a pupil of Sigalon. He settled in Levallois-Perret and exhibited at the Paris Salon from 1872 onwards, chiefly with paintings of fruit.

FOURNIER, Pierre Charles
French, 18th century.
Active in Paris in 1759.
Painter.

FOURNIER, Pierre Émile
French, 19th century.
Born 20 May 1829, in Paris.
Sculptor, painter. Animals, anatomical subjects.
Pierre Émile Fournier studied sculpture initially under Frémiet and Barye and completed his studies under Couture and Emile Lecomte. He exhibited at the Salon from 1866 to 1878. Among his work, mention may be made of a lost-wax bronze *Gazelle*, and wax groups entitled *Catching a Dragonfly, Death of the Fawn; Stags of Cochin China, Stag Attacked by a Bear* and *Bull and Mastiff*. Pierre Émile Fournier provided zoological and anatomical cartoons for a number of institutions.

FOURNIER, Pierre Simon
French, 18th century.
Born 16 September 1712, in Paris; died 8 October 1768, in Paris.
Engraver (wood), sculptor.
Pierre Simon Fournier was the pupil of Colson at the Académie de St-Luc. He is known to have produced some woodcuts depicting flowers and some vignettes. He was also a type founder.

FOURNIER, Ulysse
French, 19th century.
Born in the 19th century, in Ville-St-Jacques; died 1895.
Engraver.
Ulysse Fournier studied under Coste and first exhibited at the Salon in 1865.

FOURNIER, Victor Alfred
French, 20th century.
Born 1872, in Paris; died 1924, in Paris.
Painter. Seascapes, landscapes.
Victor Fournier studied under Albert Maignan. He exhibited at the Salon des Artistes Français in Paris and became a member in 1901. He received a commendation in 1902 and a bronze medal in 1906.
AUCTION RECORDS:
VERSAILLES, 7 June 1990, *Afternoon on a Beach in Brittany* (1907, oil on canvas, 39 1/4 x 52 1/2 ins / 100 x 133.5 cm) FRF 90,000. PARIS, 14 Jan 1991, *Breton Market* (1921, oil on canvas, 19 3/4 x 24 ins / 50 x 61 cm) FRF 8,000. CALAIS, 5 April 1992, *View of Le Tréport* (1903, oil on canvas, 17 x 22 ins / 43 x 55 cm) FRF 10,000. CALAIS, 12 March 2000, *Breton Woman on the Path by the River* (oil on canvas, 20 x 24 ins / 50 x 61 cm) FRF 11,000. LE HAVRE, 21 April 2002, *Sweet Nothings* (oil on canvas, 20 x 26 ins / 51 x 66 cm) EUR 6,000. BREST, 11 May 2003, *Young Breton Women outside Concarneau* (oil on canvas, 20 x 28 ins / 50 x 72 cm) EUR 4,200. LONDON, 1 Oct 2003, *Concarneau* (1915, oil on canvas, 15 x 18 ins / 38 x 46 cm) GBP 1,900.

FOURNIER DE BERVILLE, C. V.
French, 19th century.
Died June 1848, in Paris.
Painter. Figures, portraits.

Fournier de Berville was a Paris Salon exhibitor from 1831 to 1847. Examples of his work include *Count d'Aranda at the feet of the Duc de Lerme*; *D'Alembert with Madame de Tencin*; *Two Chimney Sweeps*; *Birds of Prey*; and an enigmatic *Superstition of King Charles II of Spain*.

MUSEUMS AND GALLERIES:
NARBONNE: *Charles II Opening the Coffin of Philippe IV*.

AUCTION RECORDS:
PARIS, 30 June 1989, *Portrait of Viscount Alexandre de Beauharnais* (25 1/2 x 21 1/4 ins / 64.5 x 54 cm) FRF 12,000.

FOURNIER DES CORATS, Marie-Antoinette.
See **BOULLARD-DEVÉ**

FOURNIER DES CORATS, Pierre
French, 20th century.
Born 1884, in Moulins.
Sculptor.

Pierre Fournier des Corats studied under Coutan and was a member of the Salon des Artistes Français in Paris. He received various awards including a bronze medal in 1928, a silver medal in 1929 and a gold medal in 1933. He was made a Chevalier of the Légion d'Honneur in 1934.

FOURNIER DES ORMES, Charles
French, 19th century.
Born 6 March 1777, in Paris; died 18 January 1850, in Paris.
Painter, draughtsman. Landscapes with figures.

Fournier des Ormes was a pupil of Hubert Robert. He exhibited at the Paris Salon from 1817 to 1849, and painted landscapes from the Eure and Perche region in the style of his mentor. Among Fournier des Ormes' many canvases are: *Retreat near a Rushing Torrent*; *Prince of Brunswick Rescuing one of his Subjects from the Waves*; *Spring*; *Thatched Cottage in Beauce*; *Ruins of Rabetan Castle*; *View of the Town of Chartres*; *Forest Interior*; and *View of Longsuaux Valley*.

MUSEUMS AND GALLERIES:
CHARTRES: *View of the Three Ancient Bridges near Chartres*.

AUCTION RECORDS:
PARIS, 21 June 1926, *Farm in a Forest Clearing*, FRF 105. PARIS, 22 Jan 1947, *Chartres*, FRF 1,200. PARIS, 12 April 1996, *Hunter and Dog in a Rocky Landscape* (oil on canvas, 15 x 18 1/4 ins / 38 x 46.5 cm) FRF 9,500.

FOURNIER-SARLOVÈZE, M. (Mme)
French, 19th century.
Born 1845, in Paris.
Sculptor, painter.

This artist was a pupil of Mathieu-Meusnier. She exhibited a marble medallion at the 1868 Salon, followed by a still-life in 1870 and four watercolour portraits in 1880.

FOURNIER-SARLOVÈZE, Raymond Joseph de
French, 19th century.
Born 9 January 1836, in Moulins (Allier).
Active in Paris.
Painter, sculptor.

Raymond Fournier-Sarlovèze was a member of the Société des Artistes Français from 1883 onwards and a Chevalier of the Légion d'Honneur.

FOURNIÈRES, R.
Painter. Portraits.

Mentioned by Mireur.

AUCTION RECORDS:
PARIS, 1890, *Portrait of a Man*, FRF 510.

FOURNIQUET, Pierre
French, 18th century.
Active in Paris in 1759.
Painter.

FOURQUES
French, 14th century.
Born to a family originally from Meaux (Seine-et-Marne).
Illuminator.

Two manuscripts decorated with miniatures in the Royal Library in Brussels were copied by Fourques in 1359.

MUSEUMS AND GALLERIES:
BRUSSELS (Bibliothèque royale Albert Ier): *Le Roman de la Rose* (illuminated manuscript); *Testament of Master Jehan of Meung* (illuminated manuscript).

FOURQUET, Georges Émile
Madagascan, 20th century.
Born 10 December 1945, in Mahajanga.
Naturalised in France.
Painter.

Self-taught, he frequented the École des Beaux-Arts and private studios in Paris from 1959 to 1965. He took part in group exhibitions in Paris (1965), Rheims (1965), in the Salon des Surindépendants (1966, 1968, 1981, 1982), the Salon des Indépendants (1986, 1987, 1988, 1989), and the Madagascan Artists Salon (1990). He has had solo exhibitions in Paris (1966, 1967, 1968) and in Caen (1985, 1987).

His painting is figurative and uses warm colours.

FOURQUET, Léon Charles
French, 19th century.
Born 20 December 1841, in St-Forget.
Sculptor.

Léon Fourquet studied under Jouffroy and exhibited at the Paris Salon from 1866 to 1880. His body of work includes a marble statue of *Triptolemy Teaching the Principles of Agriculture*, a plaster statue entitled *Source of the Yvette*, a marble statuette of *Psyche Swooning* and a wood-carved statuette of *Flora*. Fourquet was awarded bronze medals in 1873 and 1874, together with a bronze at the 1889 Exposition Universelle in Paris.

MUSEUMS AND GALLERIES:
NIORT: *Triptolemy*.

FOURQUET, Napoléon
French, 19th century.
Born 15 August 1807, in Dôle.
Sculptor.

Napoléon Fourquet enrolled at the École des Beaux-Arts on 2 April 1834 and studied under David d'Angers. He exhibited at the Salon from 1842 to 1857, and is remembered for his bust of *Albert de Luynes*.

FOURRÉ, Hugues
French, 16th century.
Active in Senlis (Oise).
Sculptor.

This artist was working in 1524 with Pierre Bezault at the church of Notre-Dame in Senlis.

FOURREAU, Jacques François
French, 18th century.
Born c. 1736; died 1795.
Sculptor.

In 1791, Jacques François Fourreau sent a bronze low relief depicting *The Taking of the Bastille* and a plan of a tomb for Mirabeau to the Salon de Paris.

FOURRIER, Odette
French, 20th century.
Born in Paris.
Painter, sculptor.

Odette Fourrier studied at the École des Beaux-Arts and exhibited at the Salon from 1932.

FOURTINA, Anny
French, 20th century.
Born c. 1915, in Bordeaux; died c. 1965, in Paris.
Painter.

Anny Fourtina is the pseudonym used by the wife of the draughtsman Chaval. Like her husband she studied at the École des Beaux-Arts in Bordeaux. She came to use abstract language, with a tendency to the geometric, early in her career. She was encouraged by Sonia Delaunay with whom she sometimes exhibited in group exhibitions. She exhibited at the Salon de Mai and at the Salon des Réalités Nouvelles in 1949, 1953 and 1956.

Museums and Galleries:
Bordeaux: *Composition*.

FOURY, Germaine
French, 20th century.
Born 19 March 1902, in Paris.
Painter, designer, illustrator. Murals.

Germaine Foury studied under Humbert at the École Nationale des Beaux-Arts. She was awarded a travel bursary by the Ville de Paris authorities in 1930. Her works include a portrait of *The Princess of Asturias*; *West Indian Woman with Hibiscus*; and *Sakalave Motherhood*. She produced mural paintings and decorative pieces, notably for the Guadeloupe pavilion at the Exposition Universelle of 1937, and also illustrated M.A. Leblond's *Belles et fières Antilles* (*Beautiful and Proud West Indies*).

She exhibited from 1925 to 1937 at the Salon d'Automne, the Salon des Artistes Français, the Salon of the Société Coloniale and the Exposition Universelle. She travelled with her husband, the painter A. Gianelli, visiting the West Indies and Africa; she also exhibited in Guadeloupe, Antananarivo, Nossi-Bé, Diego Suárez (now Antsirana), Johannesburg, Pretoria (at the *French Week* organised by the cultural centre) and Cape Town. She took part in the Universal Exhibitions in Brussels and Rome and was awarded the Guadeloupe prize in 1932.

Museums and Galleries:
Marseilles (Mus. Cantini): *Modernity*.

FOUS, Alain
French, 20th century.
Born 28 September 1928, in Perpignan.
Sculptor. Portraits. Monuments, busts, statuettes.

Alain Fous was the son of the naive painter Jean Fous. He studied in Paris, and later went to Madagascar, where he executed the monument to Alfred Grandidier at Antananarivo and the bust of the first president of the republic of Madagascar, Philibert Tsiranana. He also sculpted busts of smiling children, nymphs and fauns and some busts of men.

FOUS, Jean
French, 20th century.
Born 9 April 1901, in Paris; died 1970.
Painter.

The widespread reputation of Jean Fous dates from the 1940s when he exhibited in Paris at the Salon d'Automne and in private galleries. His work often featured popular fairs and village weddings. However, his favourite subject - and the one for which he is best known - was the Paris Flea Market, where he himself dealt in secondhand goods, selling all manner of things including postcards and decorated frames that he made himself. Not wishing to follow in his father's footsteps, he left for the South of France and began working as a secondhand dealer near the church of St-Sernin in Toulouse.

He exhibited at the major international exhibitions of naive painting, notably: *Naive Painting* at Knokke-le-Zoute in 1958; *La Peinture Naïve* (*Naive Painting*) at the Maison de la Pensée Française in Paris in 1960; *Primitives to Picasso* in London in 1962; and *Naive Painters* in Rome in 1964. In 1944 he held his first solo exhibition in the Rue du Dragon where his father had a framing shop; this was followed by further solo exhibitions in 1945, 1948 and 1954, all of which were prefaced by Anatole Jakovsky.

Jean Fous

Bibliography:
Jakovsky, Anatole, *La Peinture naïve*, Jacques Damase, Paris, 1947. Bihalji-Merin, Oto, *Les Peintres naïfs*, Delpire, Paris, 1960.

Museums and Galleries:
Paris (MAM): *Place Denfert-Rochereau* - Paris (Mus. National des Arts et Traditions Populaires): *Circus*.

Auction records:
Versailles, 3 June 1970, *Synthesis on Paris and the Latin Quarter*, FRF 14,000. Paris, 12 June 1972, *Joyful Sunday*, FRF 4,300. Paris, 4 April 1974, *Winter Wedding*, FRF 3,100. New York, 28 May 1976, *Notre-Dame de la Mouise in the Old District* (1938, 21 3/4 x 18 1/4 ins / 55.5 x 46.5 cm) USD 1,200. Versailles, 20 Dec 1981, *Large Sailing Ship, Cannes* (oil on canvas, 19 3/4 x 25 1/2 ins / 50 x 65 cm) FRF 3,000. Versailles, 23 March 1986, *Arrival of the Travellers* (oil on canvas, 19 3/4 x 25 1/2 ins / 50 x 65 cm) FRF 6,600. Paris, 6 March 1988, *The Flea Market* (oil on canvas, 13 x 16 1/4 ins / 33 x 41 cm) FRF 1,800. Paris, 17 April 1988, *Rue St-Vincent in Montmartre in Winter* (oil on canvas, 19 3/4 x 25 1/2 ins / 50 x 65 cm) FRF 2,900. Paris, 18 May 1988, *The Luxembourg Gardens* (oil on canvas, 15 x 22 ins / 38 x 55 cm) FRF 4,100. Versailles, 18 Dec 1988, *Retreat by Torchlight* (oil on canvas, 19 3/4 x 25 1/2 ins / 50 x 64.5 cm) FRF 7,500. Sceaux, 18 Nov 1990, *Return from the Hunt* (oil on canvas, 10 3/4 x 13 3/4 ins / 27.5 x 35 cm) FRF 7,500. Paris, 22 Nov 1990, *The Bottemens Camp* (oil on canvas, 21 1/4 x 25 1/2 ins / 54 x 65 cm) FRF 23,000. Paris, 22 March 1993, *Lion Hunting* (oil on canvas, 15 x 22 ins / 38 x 55 cm) FRF 3,800. Calais, 3 July 1994, *Long Live the Bride* (oil on panel, 16 1/4 x 12 1/2 ins / 41 x 32 cm) FRF 4,000. Paris, 28 Oct 1996, *Campagne d'Hiver* (oil on canvas, 19 3/4 x 25 1/2 ins / 50 x 65 cm) FRF 3,800. Paris, 8 Dec 2003, *Village Scenes* (gouache, six, 9 x 11 ins / 22 x 27 cm) EUR 3,000.

FOUSSARD, Pierre
French, 16th century.
Active in Gray (Haute-Saône).
Painter.

In 1506, Foussard painted some coats of arms for the funeral of Philip the Handsome.

FOUSSEDOIRE, Émile J.
French, 19th century.
Active in Pierrelage.
Sculptor.

Foussedoire was a member of the Société des Artistes Français from 1888 onwards.

FOUSSEREAU, Joseph Marie
French, 19th century.
Born 5 December 1809, in Paris.
Painter, watercolourist.

Foussereau was admitted to the École des Beaux-Arts on 17 November 1827, where he studied under Guillon Lethière. He exhibited at the Salon from 1831 to 1853. Foussereau is remembered for a number of works, including: *Murat Saved by a Dragon*; *Ligurian Monk Standing Watch on the Banks of the Seine*; *Ostlers Watering their Horses*; *Escapee*; *Gathering for the Hunt*; *Imperial Carabineer*; *Imperial Cuirassier*; *Hunter from the Reign of Louis XIII*; *Postilion and Team*; *Breton*

Hunters Pausing at an Ancient Druid Site; Trumpeter from the Reign of Louis XIII; and *Cavalry Charge.*

AUCTION RECORDS:

PARIS, 20 and 21 Feb 1899, *French Hussars Engaging their Austrian Counterparts; Charge of the French Cavalry* (1842; *Guardsman* (1853, graphite and pen, three drawings) FRF 190.

FOUSSIER, Ernest
French, 19th - 20th century.
Born 1859; died 1917.
Architect, designer.

Ernest Foussier decorated many private houses in Paris. There are albums which show these decorations.

FOUSSIER, Jean
French, 20th century.
Born 29 August 1886, in Paris; died 7 October 1950, in Loudun.
Painter, pastellist, designer, illustrator. Portraits, scenes with figures, landscapes, ruins. Murals, stage sets.

Jean Foussier was the son of the architect and designer Ernest Foussier. He began studying drawing at the École Bernard Palissy before joining the studio of Luc-Olivier Merson and Raphaël Collin at the École des Beaux-Arts.

He was called up in 1914 but taken prisoner at Bischoot on 14 November that year. For the next four years he continued with his art, painting portraits of his comrades, scenes of life in the camp and the countryside. After returning to France on 22 January 1929, he spent a considerable time painting the ruins found in the Soissons region in works such as *A Section of Soissons Cathedral.* Some of his paintings were reproduced as engravings. After this he returned to a wider range of subjects including landscapes of various regions, portraits in oils and pastels and illustrations for publications. He illustrated works on animal and plant physiology and lectured on art in Belgium.

He exhibited at numerous group exhibitions, including the Salon des Artistes Français (for the first time in 1919) and the Salon of the École Française, as well as exhibitions in Poitiers, Troyes and Nantes. He produced publicity panels for various exhibitions, notably the Exposition Coloniale of 1931; he also created stage sets and decorations for the Mission de la Salette at Fourqueux near Paris.

MUSEUMS AND GALLERIES:

PARIS (Mus. Carnavalet): *St-Étienne-du-Mont Church.*

FOUTE, Michael
German, 17th century.
Active c. 1620.
Engraver.

This artist may be M. Faulte, known for the work *Assumption.*

FOUTELLE, François
French, 17th century.
Sculptor.

In 1679, François Foutelle worked at Versailles restoring statues in the park. He executed vases, consoles and ornaments in the entrance hall of the Château facing the Parterre d'Eau in 1680 and sculpted some trophies for the Swiss Guard. He then worked in 1681 and 1682 on the Chapelle de la Reine in the parish church of Versailles, and was commissioned in 1683 to decorate the catafalque of Queen Marie-Thérèse. He also collaborated on the Labyrinthe de Versailles in 1682 and on the Bains d'Apollon in 1686.

FOUTIN, J.
French, 17th century.
Active in Châteaudun at the beginning of the 17th century.
Engraver.

J. Foutin was also a goldsmith.

FOUTREL-GAUGY, Clément
French, 18th century.
Active in Nantes.
Painter.

Clément Foutrel-Gaugy was the son of Nicolas Foutrel-Gaugy I.

FOUTREL-GAUGY, Nicolas I
French, 18th century.
Born c. 1693; died 20 January 1755.
Active in Nantes.
Painter.

FOUTREL-GAUGY, Nicolas II
French, 18th century.
Baptised 29 August 1720.
Active in Nantes.
Painter.

Nicolas Foutrel-Gaugy II was the son of Nicolas Foutrel-Gaugy I and is mentioned in 1755 and 1756. To him is attributed a *Portrait of J. B. Gellée de Prémion,* signed *N. Gaugy.*

MUSEUMS AND GALLERIES:

NANTES (Mus. Archéologique): *Portrait of J. B. Gellée de Prémion* (attributed).

FOUYER, Pierre, sometimes known as Jehan
French, 16th century.
Active in Doué (Maine-et-Loire).
Painter.

This artist went to court to demand payment for a planned funerary monument that he apparently made for Louis Buget, the lord of Les Landes.

FOVEAU DE COURMELLES, Mme A. Wegl
French, 19th century.
Died 1903.
Sculptor.

FOVELIN, Aleksandra Ivanovna
Russian, 19th century.
Born c. 1850.
Painter.

Pupil of A.G. Goravsky in St Petersburg, Aleksandra Fovelin painted mostly scenes with chidren, such as *Peasant Children on the Feast of the Holy Trinity,* for which she received a prize at the St Petersburg academy Exhibition of 1872. Another work to be mentioned is *Little Street Sellers.*

FOWERAKER, A. Moulton
British, 19th - 20th century.
Born 1873; died 1942.
Painter (including gouache), watercolourist. Scenes with figures, urban landscapes, landscapes with figures, figures, portraits, landscapes.

AUCTION RECORDS:

LONDON, 4 March 1980, *The Palais des Papes by Moonlight* (watercolour, 13 1/2 x 20 ins / 34 x 51 cm) GBP 280. LONDON, 17 Oct 1984, *A Spanish Town* (watercolour, 20 3/4 x 30 ins / 53 x 76 cm) GBP 1,600. LONDON, 29 April 1987, *Street Scene at Night* (watercolour heightened with gouache, 11 x 9 ins / 28 x 23 cm) GBP 650. LONDON, 25 Jan 1989, *Winter Evening* (watercolour, 8 1/2 x 11 ins / 21.5 x 27 cm) GBP 990. LONDON, 12 May 1989, *After Hot Weather in the Sierras near Segovia* (oil on canvas, 17 3/4 x 9 3/4 ins / 45.3 x 24.6 cm) GBP 1,100. CHESTER, 20 July 1989, *Transhumance; Haymaking* (oil on canvas, a pair, each 8 1/2 x 11 1/2 ins / 21.5 x 29 cm) USD 1,760. LONDON, 13 Dec 1989, *Albi* (oil on canvas, 44 x 54 ins / 112 x 137 cm) GBP 2,860. LONDON, 31 Jan 1990, *Moonlight on Antequera* (watercolour, 9 3/4 x 13 3/4 ins / 25 x 35 cm) GBP 1,320. LONDON, 25-26 April 1990, *Newton St Cyres in Devon, by Moonlight* (watercolour, 10 1/4 x 13 3/4 ins / 26 x 35 cm) GBP 1,100. LONDON, 26 Sept 1990, *Mediterranean Fishing Village* (watercolour, 9 3/4 x 13 3/4 ins / 25 x 35 cm) GBP 935. LONDON, 30 Jan 1991, *Driven by the Wind* (watercolour, 13 x 17 ins / 33 x 43 cm) GBP 1,540. LONDON, 9 June 1994, *Portrait of a Man in a Boater* (oil on card, 6 1/4 x 6 1/4 ins / 16 x 16 cm) GBP 575. KNOWLE, 7 July 1999, *Spanish Street Scene by Moonlight with Figures and Horse and Cart* (pencil and watercolour heightened with white, 14 x 20 ins / 35 x 52 cm) GBP 2,400. LONDON, 21 Oct 1999, *Spanish Mountainous Village by Moonlight* (watercolour and pencil, 14 x 20 ins / 35 x 52 cm) GBP 3,200. AMERSHAM, 2 Nov 2000, *Spanish Market in a Small Town Square* (watercolour, 8 x 10 ins / 20 x 25 cm) GBP 1,950. LONDON, 14 March 2001, *Moonlight, Granada, Spain* (watercolour, 14 x 21 ins / 36 x 53 cm) GBP 2,800. PENZANCE, 12 July 2001, *Moonlight - the Mill Pond, Swanage* (watercolour, 13 x 20 ins / 34 x 52 cm) GBP 2,500. TORONTO, 27 May 2002, *Evening in Spanish Hillside Village* (watercolour, 15 x 21 ins / 37 x 54 cm) CAD 4,750. LONDON, 25 June 2002, *Figures in a Continental Village at Night* (watercolour, 10 x 14 ins / 25 x 35 cm) GBP 3,000. LONDON, 11 March 2003, *Devon Village* (1930, watercolour, 9 x 11 ins / 23 x 28 cm) GBP 1,900. PENZANCE, 26 Feb 2004, *Sheep in a Meadow before a Church and Distant Town* (oil on board, 9 x 13 ins / 23 x 32 cm) GBP 1,800.

FOWKE, Thomas
British, 19th century.
Sculptor. Figures. Busts.

Thomas Fowke was active in London, where he exhibited regularly with the Royal Academy from 1851 to 1877.

AUCTION RECORDS:
LONDON, 24 Sept 1987, *The Young Prince of Wales* (1864, bronze, h. 33 ins / 84 cm) GBP 8,500.

FOWLE, Bertha
British, 20th century.
Born 2 March 1894; died 1964.
Miniaturist, watercolourist.

Bertha Fowle studied at the Gravesend School of Arts. She exhibited at the Royal Academy, the Royal Institute of Painters in Watercolours and at the Walker Art Gallery. She was a member of the Royal Society of Teachers.

FOWLER, Daniel
Canadian, 19th century.
Born 1810; died 1894.
Painter, draughtsman. Genre scenes, landscapes, landscapes with figures, flowers, fruit.

Daniel Fowler was a member of the Royal Canadian Academy in Toronto.

MUSEUMS AND GALLERIES:
MONTREAL (MBA): *Hollyhocks*.

AUCTION RECORDS:
LONDON, 11 June 1923, *Lake Garda* (drawing) GBP 26. TORONTO, 27 May 1981, *Landscape with Bridge* (1886, watercolour, 7 1/2 x 10 1/2 ins / 18.8 x 26.9 cm) CAD 2,400.

FOWLER, Evangeline
American, 20th century.
Born 1885, in Ohio; died 1934.
Painter.

Evangeline Fowler, who studied in America and France, devoted much of her time to teaching. She was a member of the Southern States Art League and won a number of awards, including a gold medal in 1885 in New Orleans and a first prize in 1930.

FOWLER, Frank
American, 19th - 20th century.
Born 12 July 1852, in Brooklyn; died 18 August 1910, in Canaan (Connecticut).
Painter, illustrator. Portraits, genre scenes.

Frank Fowler studied with Edwin White and Carolus-Duran and at the École des Beaux-Arts in Paris. He became a member of the National Academy in 1899, and won a bronze medal at the Paris Exposition Universelle of 1889 and many awards at American exhibitions.

AUCTION RECORDS:
NEW YORK, 25-26 Feb 1904, *Feeding her Favourites*, USD 130. NEW YORK, 31 May 1943, *John Bigelow*, USD 150. NEW YORK, 30 Sept 1988, *Two Friends* (oil on canvas, 15 x 12 ins / 38 x 30.5 cm) USD 2,860.

FOWLER, George
British, 19th - 20th century.
Painter. Landscapes, waterscapes, seascapes.

AUCTION RECORDS:
LONDON, 13 July 1934, *Cliffs and Seagulls*, GBP 35. TORONTO, 29 July 1981, *Landscape* (oil on canvas, 28 x 35 1/2 ins / 71.3 x 90 cm) CAD 700. GLASGOW, 25 Aug 1997, *Waves Breaking* (1898, oil on canvas, 40 x 30 ins / 101.6 x 76.2 cm) GBP 592.

FOWLER, John
British, 20th century.
Born 1943.
Sculptor.

John Fowler studied at St Martin's College and the Royal College of Art. He participated in group exhibitions from 1962, particularly at exhibitions of young, contemporary sculptors.

FOWLER, Robert
British, 19th century.
Born c. 1853, in Anstruther, Scotland; died 1926.
Painter, watercolourist, draughtsman. Mythological subjects, figures, landscapes with figures.

Robert Fowler studied at the Heatherley School of Art in London before settling in Liverpool, where he remained until 1903. His studio in Castle Street became a focal point for the city's artistic life. His work was influenced by Leighton and Albert Moore, whose Japonist tastes he shared. He was an associate of the Royal Cambrian Academy, and a member of the Royal Institute of Painters in Watercolours. He exhibited regularly with the Royal Academy, Suffolk Street and the Royal Institute from 1876 to 1903, as well as in Paris and Munich.

MUSEUMS AND GALLERIES:
BOOTLE: *Head Study* - LIVERPOOL: *Eve and the Voices*; *Ariel*; *Sleeping Nymphs Surprised by Shepherds* - MAGDEBURG (Kulturhistorisches Mus.): *Frightened Nymph*.

AUCTION RECORDS:
WASHINGTON DC, 22 May 1982, *The Nymph and the Tortoise* (oil on canvas, 48 x 37 ins / 121 x 94 cm) USD 1,000. LONDON, 29 March 1983, *Young Women Feeding Swans* (oil on canvas, 41 1/2 x 90 1/4 ins / 105.5 x 229 cm) GBP 1,600. LONDON, 11 Oct 1983, *Michal Watches with Contempt the Dancing of David* (1886, watercolour, 48 x 27 1/4 ins / 122 x 69 cm) GBP 650. CHESTER, 12 July 1985, *Daffodils* (watercolour, 19 x 29 ins / 48 x 73.5 cm) GBP 580. LONDON, 31 Oct 1986, *The Nymph* (oil on canvas, 30 x 24 1/2 ins / 76 x 62 cm) GBP 4,500. LONDON, 15 June 1988, *Sheep in the Meadows on the Banks of the Dee* (oil on canvas, 47 1/4 x 83 1/4 ins / 120 x 211.5 cm) GBP 1,430. LONDON, 23 Sept 1988, *A World of Colours* (1887, oil on canvas, 48 1/2 x 24 ins / 123 x 61 cm) GBP 12,650. NEW YORK, 1 March 1990, *The Birth of Venus* (oil on canvas, 69 1/4 x 29 1/2 ins / 175.8 x 74.9 cm) USD 6,600. NEW YORK, 21 May 1991, *Classical Female Figure on a Beach* (oil on canvas, 28 x 36 1/2 ins / 71 x 92.8 cm) USD 6,050. LONDON, 5 March 1993, *Eunoe* (1883, oil on canvas, 50 1/4 x 30 1/4 ins / 127.7 x 76.6 cm) GBP 6,900. LONDON, 5 Nov 1993, *Young Greek Woman* (pencil and watercolour, 9 1/4 x 13 1/2 ins / 23.8 x 34.3 cm) GBP 977. LONDON, 6 Nov 1995, *Classical Figures with Masks* (1885, watercolour, 27 3/4 x 47 1/2 ins / 70.5 x 120.5 cm) GBP 3,450.

FOWLER, Trevor Thomas
Irish, 19th century.
Born c. 1800, in Dublin.

Painter. Portraits, genre scenes.
In 1829, Trevor Fowler exhibited a *Portrait of a Man* at the Royal Academy in London. He exhibited 35 portraits with the Royal Hibernian Academy in Dublin from 1830 to 1835, and genre scenes at the Royal Irish Art Union in 1843 and 1844.

FOWLER, Walter
British, 19th century.
Active in Richmond.
Painter. Landscapes.
Walter Fowler exhibited from 1887 at London's Royal Academy and Suffolk Street Gallery.

FOWLER, William
British, 18th - 19th century.
Born 12 March 1761, in Winterton (Lincolnshire); died 22 September 1832, in Winterton.
Engraver, draughtsman.

FOWLER, William
British, 19th century.
Born 1796; died c. 1880, in London.
Painter. Portraits, landscapes.
William Fowler's best-known work is arguably a portrait of Queen Victoria, subsequently engraved by J.B. Jackson.
AUCTION RECORDS:
NEW YORK, 17-18 May 1934, *Portrait of a Young Man,* USD 70. LONDON, 8 March 1977, *Village by a Pond* (1841, oil on canvas, 39 x 55 ins / 99 x 140 cm) GBP 2,800. LONDON, 24 March 1981, *Spring in Windsor Great Park* (1859, oil on canvas, 30 x 48 ins / 76 x 122 cm) GBP 900. NEW YORK, 19 Jan 1995, *View of Windsor* (1840, oil on canvas, 20 1/2 x 27 1/2 ins / 52.1 x 69.9 cm) USD 2,645.

FOWLER, William
British, 19th century.
Active in London.
Painter, watercolourist. Landscapes.
William Fowler was a member of the Royal Society of Artists and a regular exhibitor in London at the Royal Academy, the British Institution, the Suffolk Street Gallery and the New Water-Colour Society where he had exhibitions between 1825 and 1867.
AUCTION RECORDS:
LONDON, 27 March 1973, *Village by a River* (1841) GBP 6,000. COPENHAGEN, 11 June 2001, *Rue de la Grosse Horloge, Rouen* (1830, oil on canvas, 19 x 15 ins / 48 x 39 cm) DKK 16,000.

FOWLES, Arthur Wellington
British, 19th century.
Painter. Seascapes.
MUSEUMS AND GALLERIES:
ORLÉANS: *Seascape.*
AUCTION RECORDS:
LONDON, 15 June 1925, *Regatta on the Thames; Fleet Review; Spithead Review* (one of three) GBP 36. LONDON, 30 Jan 1970, *Seascape,* Gns 1,200. LONDON, 17 March 1982, *Regatta off the Isle of Wight* (oil on canvas, 8 x 12 ins / 20.5 x 30.5 cm) GBP 420. LONDON, 6 June 1984, *Regatta off the Isle of Wight* (1864, oil on canvas, 32 x 54 ins / 81 x 137 cm) GBP 16,000. GÖTEBORG, 18 May 1989, *Seascape with Yacht in a Heavy Swell* (1858, oil on canvas, 7 3/4 x 11 3/4 ins / 20 x 30 cm) SEK 10,800. LONDON, 31 May 1989, *Schooner Cambria (188 tons) Racing Offshore at Ryde* (1868, oil on canvas, 24 x 42 1/4 ins / 61 x 107 cm) GBP 16,500. LONDON, 22 May 1991, *Royal Yacht Victoria and Albert II, Cowes* (1867, oil on canvas, 30 x 54 ins / 76 x 137 cm) GBP 8,800. LONDON, 20 May 1992, *Schooner Diana at Sea off Norris* (1860, oil on canvas, 15 3/4 x 24 ins / 40 x 61 cm) GBP 6,380. LONDON, 18 Nov 1992, *Queen Victoria Arriving at Cowes, Isle of Wight* (oil on canvas, 20 x 33 3/4 ins / 51 x 86 cm) GBP 5,500. LONDON, 20 Jan 1993, *Yacht under Full Canvas* (oil on canvas, 20 x 30 ins / 51 x 76 cm) GBP 4,600. LONDON, 28 April 1999, *Cutter Yachts Racing in the Thames Estuary* (oil on canvas, 12 x 16 ins / 31 x 41 cm) GBP 3,000. LONDON, 28 April 1999, *Cutter off the Isle of Wight* (1853, oil on canvas, 16 x 20 ins / 40 x 52 cm) GBP 3,500. LONDON, 9 Nov 2000, *Indian Troopship Serapis Arriving at Portsmouth* (1876, oil on canvas, 34 x 59 ins / 86 x 149 cm) GBP 19,000. LONDON, 30 Nov 2000, *Ryde, Isle of Wight* (1862, oil on canvas, 26 x 39 ins / 66 x 99 cm) GBP 15,000. LONDON, 24 May 2001, *Racing Yachts, One Dismasted and in Distress, a Port beyond* (1853, oil on canvas, 11 x 14 ins / 28 x 36 cm) GBP 3,000. LONDON, 24 May 2001, *Schooner Yacht America Racing to Windward in the Channel* (1855, oil on canvas, 14 x 21 ins / 36 x 53 cm) GBP 16,000. LONDON, 16 Jan 2002, *Racing Yawl off the Needles* (1874, oil on canvas, 12 x 20 ins / 30 x 51 cm) GBP 1,900. LONDON, 22 Jan 2003, *Cambria Winning the International Race, Cowes* (1859, oil on canvas, 28 x 39 ins / 71 x 99 cm) GBP 30,000. LONDON, 22 Jan 2003, *Cambria Winning at Cowes, 1868* (1869, oil on canvas, arched top, 28 x 39 ins / 71 x 99 cm) GBP 30,000.

FOX, Augustus H.
British, 19th century.
Active in London.
Painter.
Augustus Fox exhibited portraits and genre compositions in London at the Royal Academy and at the Society of British Artists between 1841 and 1849.

FOX, Charles
British, 18th - 19th century.
Born 1749, in Falmouth; died 1809, in Bath.
Painter. Portraits, landscapes.
Charles Fox began his career as a librarian before turning to portrait and landscape painting. He was also a poet and an occasional translator of Persian texts.
MUSEUMS AND GALLERIES:
LONDON (British Mus.): *Park.*

FOX, Charles
British, 19th century.
Born 17 March 1794, in Cossey Hall; died 28 February 1849, in Leyton.
Painter, engraver, reproductions engraver.
Charles Fox studied engraving at Bungay under William Camden Edwards, then moved to London where he entered John Burnet's studio. His work includes various illustrations for contemporary periodicals, notably a series of plates engraved from originals by Sir David Wilkie for the Cadell edition of the works of Sir Walter Scott. His major engravings include a *Full-length Portrait of Sir George Murray* (from an original by Pickersgill), together with Wilkie's *Royal Privy Councillor* and *Village Recruits.*

FOX, Charles
British, 19th century.
Died 1854, in Brighton.
Modeller.
Charles Fox exhibited at London's Suffolk Street Gallery in 1850 and 1852. His *Group of Children* earned him a Royal Society of British Artists medal in 1847.

FOX, Charles James
British, 19th century.
Born 1822, in Leeds; died 1904.
Painter, watercolourist. Figures, landscapes with figures, landscapes.
Fox exhibited at the Royal Academy, the Suffolk Street Gallery and the New Water-Colour Society in London from 1883 until his death in 1904.

AUCTION RECORDS:
LONDON, 13 Dec 1989, *Children by the River Feeding the Swans* (oil on canvas, 31 x 48 ins / 79 x 122 cm) GBP 9,350. LONDON, 26 Sept 1990, *Breeze on the River* (oil on canvas, 31 x 49 1/4 ins / 79 x 125 cm) GBP 2,200. MONTREAL, 4 June 1991, *Dignitary* (oil on canvas, 44 x 34 ins / 111.7 x 86.4 cm) CAD 2,000. LONDON, 3 June 1992, *Wilton, Somerset* (oil on canvas, 19 x 27 ins / 48 x 68.5 cm) GBP 2,145. LONDON, 3 Feb 1993, *Making Hay* (oil on canvas, 31 x 48 ins / 79 x 122 cm) GBP 1,035.

FOX, Edward
British, 19th century.
Active in London.
Painter, watercolourist. Landscapes.
Between 1813 and 1854, Edward Fox exhibited a large number of works in London at the Royal Academy, the British Institution, the Suffolk Street Gallery and the Society of Painters in Watercolours.
MUSEUMS AND GALLERIES:
BRIGHTON (Mus. & AG): views of Brighton.

FOX, Edwin M.
American, 19th century.
Born c. 1830; died 1870.
Active in the USA.
Painter. Genre scenes, animals.
AUCTION RECORDS:
NEW YORK, 11 April 1929, *Pink Pearl; Dark Regan* (two) USD 125. LONDON, 26 May 1989, *Mr Faulkner on a Bay Hunter with Two Dogs in Foxrock* (1869, oil on canvas, 25 x 30 ins / 63.2 x 76.2 cm) GBP 3,740. LONDON, 9 Feb 1990, *Grey Carriage Horse in a Stable with a Dog* (1861, oil on canvas, 25 x 30 ins / 63.5 x 76 cm) GBP 1,320. LONDON, 14 July 1993, *Bay Hunter in a Stable with a Fox Terrier* (1850, oil on canvas, 19 1/2 x 23 1/2 ins / 49.5 x 60 cm) GBP 3,680. LONDON, 25 March 1994, *Maltese Terrier, White English Terrier and Two Dwarf Terriers with a Grey African Parrot in a Living Room* (1868, oil on canvas, 15 3/4 x 20 ins / 40 x 50.8 cm) GBP 4,370.

FOX, Eliza Florence. See **BRIDELL**

FOX, Emmanuel Philips
Australian, 19th - 20th century.
Born 1865, in Melbourne; died 1915, in Paris.
Active in France.
Painter. Figures, portraits, scenes with figures, genre scenes.
Emmanuel Fox studied painting at the École des Beaux-Arts in Paris and in London before eventually settling in Paris. Fox's painting is directly influenced by that of Manet and by Monet's early period. His subjects are domestic and intimate. His real subject is not so much narrative as the light he uses to enliven colours and create shadow and reflections on water. He exhibited at the Salon of the Société Nationale des Beaux-Arts and received a bronze medal in 1894.

E-P-FOX

BIBLIOGRAPHY:
Creating Australia: 200 Years of Art 1788-1988, exhibition catalogue, Art Gall. Board of South Australia, Adelaide, 1988.
MUSEUMS AND GALLERIES:
MELBOURNE: *Captain Cook Comes Ashore at Botany Bay; Love Story; Portrait of Robert L. J.; L. J. Elleret; Portrait of Sir Frederick Sargood* - SYDNEY: *Adelaide; Autumn Showers; Lady in Black.*
AUCTION RECORDS:
MELBOURNE, 11-12 March 1971, *Landscape with Stormy Sky*, AUD 800. LONDON, 17 May 1974, *Wooded Landscape*, Gns 1,600. SYDNEY, 6 Oct 1976, *Sorrento, Victoria* (1915, oil on canvas, 14 3/4 x 17 3/4 ins / 37.5 x 45.2 cm) AUD 600. MELBOURNE, 11 March 1977, *Garden Path* (oil on canvas, 15 x 18 ins / 38 x 46 cm) AUD 2,600. SYDNEY, 10 March 1980, *Blush Track* (oil on canvas, 23 1/2 x 13 1/2 ins / 60 x 34 cm) AUD 2,600. LONDON, 23 May 1984, *Cremorne Point, Sydney Harbour* (1913, oil on card, 6 x 7 3/4 ins / 15 x 20 cm) GBP 1,600. SYDNEY, 29 Oct 1987, *Nude Study* (1910, oil on canvas, 23 1/2 x 36 1/4 ins / 60 x 92 cm) AUD 165,000.

FOX, Ernest R.
British, 19th century.
Born c. 1860.
Painter. Landscapes.
Ernest Fox was active in Strood (Kent) and exhibited from 1886 at London's Royal Academy and Suffolk Street Gallery.
AUCTION RECORDS:
LONDON, 25 May 1983, *St Michael's Mount, Evening* (oil on canvas, 36 x 60 ins / 91.5 x 152.5 cm) GBP 650. LONDON, 22 July 1986, *Twickenham Ferry* (1885, oil on canvas, 14 x 24 ins / 35.5 x 61 cm) GBP 1,450.

FOX, Ethel Carrick. See **CARRICK-FOX Ethel**

FOX, George
British, 19th century.
Painter. Genre scenes.
George Fox exhibited from 1873, notably at the Royal Academy and the Suffolk Street Gallery in London.
AUCTION RECORDS:
LONDON, 30 Nov 1908, *Card Players*, GBP 3. LONDON, 27 Feb 1925, *Unpleasant Letter*, GBP 12. LONDON, 16 Nov 1928, *Amusing Anecdote*, GBP 5. LONDON, 29 Feb 1980, *Devil's Own Luck* (oil on canvas, 11 1/2 x 15 1/2 ins / 29.2 x 39.3 cm) GBP 380. LONDON, 27 Sept 1989, *Cheating* (oil on panel, 9 x 12 ins / 23 x 30.5 cm) GBP 1,320. GUILDFORD, 29 June 1999, *Lawyer Seated in a Study* (oil on board, 8 x 12 ins / 20 x 30 cm) GBP 1,000. BILLINGSHURST, 26 Oct 1999, *Hunting Song. Chess Players* (oil on board, a pair, 10 x 13 ins / 26 x 34 cm) GBP 1,750. BISHOPS STORTFORD, 17 Oct 2000, *Three Gentlemen Discussing a Voyage* (oil on board, 9 x 11 ins / 24 x 28 cm) GBP 1,600. BATH, 21 July 2003, *Good Vintage. Good Tale* (oil on canvas, a pair, 10 x 13 ins / 25 x 34 cm) GBP 1,900. LYMINGTON, 1 Oct 2003, *English Gossip. French Intrigue.* (oil on canvas, oil on board, a pair, 4 x 6 ins / 10 x 14 cm) GBP 1,400.

FOX, Gilbert
British, 19th century.
Born c. 1776, probably in London.
Engraver.
Gilbert Fox studied in around 1793 in London under T. Medland and later worked as an engraver in Philadelphia.

FOX, Henry Charles
British, 19th - 20th century.
Born c. 1860; died c. 1930.
Painter, watercolourist. Landscapes with figures, waterscapes, landscapes.
Henry Fox was a member of the Society of British Artists. He exhibited at the Royal Academy and the Suffolk Street Gallery from 1879.
MUSEUMS AND GALLERIES:
MONTREAL (MBA): *At Oatlands in Surrey* - SYDNEY: *Landscape.*
AUCTION RECORDS:
LONDON, 20 March 1909, *The Old Manor*, GBP 7. LONDON, 20 March 1909, *On the River* (1893, watercolour) GBP 5. LONDON, 17 May 1923, *Bindon* (drawing) GBP 5. LONDON, 28 Nov 1924, *Duck Pond; Blackberry Time* (both) GBP 10. LONDON, 10 Nov 1926, *Landscape* (watercolour) GBP 2. LONDON, 19 Dec 1928, *Hunting Scenes*, GBP 70. LONDON, 15 May 1984, *A Sussex Village* (1915, watercolour and gouache, 27 1/4 x 39 1/4 ins / 69 x 100 cm) GBP 700. LONDON, 26 Jan 1987, *Sonning on*

Thames (1904, watercolour heightened with gouache, 14 x 20 ins / 35.5 x 51 cm) GBP 650. CHESTER, 20 July 1989, *Woodcutters in the Woods; Returning to the Village* (1920, watercolour and gouache, a pair, 19 1/2 x 29 1/2 ins / 49.5 x 75 cm) GBP 3,740. LONDON, 1 Nov 1990, *Near Cookham on Thames, House by the River with Ducks Swimming* (watercolour heightened with white, 14 1/2 x 21 1/2 ins / 36.9 x 54.9 cm) GBP 825. LONDON, 30 Jan 1991, *On the Way Home* (1900, watercolour, 10 x 14 ins / 25.5 x 35.5 cm) GBP 880; *Horses Pulling a Cart on a Farm Road; Cattle Drinking outside a Farm surrounded by Trees* (1911, watercolour heightened with white, a pair, 14 1/4 x 21 1/4 ins / 36.5 x 54 cm) GBP 2,640. LONDON, 12 June 1992, *Evening, Milkmaid Bringing her Cows in along the Road* (1905, watercolour heightened with white, 15 1/4 x 22 ins / 38.8 x 56 cm) GBP 605. LONDON, 9 May 1996, *River Landscape* (1899, watercolour heightened with white, 13 3/4 x 20 ins / 35 x 51 cm) GBP 862. LEWES, 9 March 1999, *Changing Pastures. Arundel, Sussex* (1920, watercolour, a pair, 14 x 21 ins / 36 x 53 cm) GBP 1,600. LEOMINSTER, 15 March 2000, *In the Springtime, Country Lane with Horses, Cart and Figure* (watercolour, 25 x 39 ins / 64 x 99 cm) GBP 2,400. BILLINGSHURST, 23 Oct 2000, *Hemingford Grey, Huntingdonshire* (1899, watercolour and gouache, 19 x 30 ins / 49 x 75 cm) GBP 2,000. CRANBROOK, 24 Sept 2001, *Cattle Watering by Stream* (watercolour, a pair, 21 x 14 ins / 53 x 36 cm) GBP 1,600. CHESTER, 7 Nov 2001, *Farm Horses at a Village Pond. Boy and Farm Horses on a Lane* (1906, watercolour, a pair, 20 x 15 ins / 52 x 37 cm) GBP 1,800. CASTLECOMER, 5 March 2002, *Shades of Autumn* (watercolour, 15 x 11 ins / 37 x 27 cm) EUR 3,500. PARTRIDGE GREEN, 8 Oct 2003, *Frosty Morning, Landscape with Cattle* (watercolour heightened with white, 24 x 39 ins / 62 x 98 cm) GBP 1,500. GODALMING, 24 March 2004, *Watering Place. Cattle on a Track* (1909, watercolour, a pair, 15 x 22 ins / 38 x 56 cm) GBP 1,350.

FOX, J.

British, 19th century.
Active in London.
Miniaturist.

J. Fox exhibited at the Royal Academy in London from 1830 to 1846.

FOX, John Richard

Canadian, 20th century.
Born 1927, in Montreal.
Painter. Still-lifes.

John Richard Fox was influenced by Matisse and possibly Picasso, but he probably learned more from the Canadian painter Morrice. He was an assistant to John Lyman.

AUCTION RECORDS:

TORONTO, 27 May 1980, *Figure* (oil on canvas, 23 1/2 x 29 1/2 ins / 60 x 75 cm) CAD 2,500. MONTREAL, 25 April 1988, *Dresser* (oil on canvas, 22 x 27 1/4 ins / 56 x 69 cm) CAD 1,900. MONTREAL, 5 Nov 1990, *Still-life with Books and a Vase of Flowers* (oil on canvas, 24 x 20 ins / 61 x 51 cm) CAD 2,420. TORONTO, 3 June 2003, *Boats at Mooring* (oil on canvas, 31 x 22 ins / 80 x 55 cm) CAD 2,800.

FOX, John Shirley

British, 19th - 20th century.
Born c. 1867; died 1939.
Painter. Portraits, genre scenes, hunting scenes, landscapes with figures.

John Fox trained in Paris before moving to London in 1890. His many portraits include *Portrait of Miss Evelyn Gayer* now in a private royal collection and *Portrait of the King and Queen of England* which was exhibited at the Royal Academy in 1914. In Paris, he exhibited portraits at the Salon des Artistes Français in 1887 and 1889. In London, he exhibited at the Royal Academy, the Society of British Artists and the New Gallery.

AUCTION RECORDS:

LONDON, 30 Jan 1946, *Hunting*, GBP 82. NEW YORK, 16 Feb 1994, *The Lilac Season* (1896, oil on canvas, 36 x 24 1/4 ins / 91.4 x 61.6 cm) USD 17,250. LONDON, 9 June 1994, *The Engagement Ring* (1898, oil on canvas, 24 x 18 ins / 61 x 46 cm) GBP 2,990.

FOX, Margaret Taylor

American, 19th century.
Born 26 July 1857, in Philadelphia.
Painter, illustrator.

FOX, R.

British, 19th century.
Painter. Flowers, fruit.

R. Fox exhibited at London's Royal Academy in 1867.

AUCTION RECORDS:

LONDON, 4 May 1908, *Fruit*, GBP 1.

FOX, Robert

Irish, 19th century.
Born c. 1810, in Dublin.
Painter. Genre scenes.

Robert Fox exhibited from 1846 to 1868 on a regular basis in London, notably at the Royal Academy, the British Institution and the Suffolk Street Gallery.

FOX, Robert Atkinson

Canadian or American, 19th - 20th century.
Born 1860; died 1927.
Painter. Local figures, landscapes.

Robert Atkinson Fox is a different artist to Robert Atkinson.

AUCTION RECORDS:

CHICAGO, 4 June 1981, *Yosemite* (oil on canvas, 36 x 23 ins / 91.5 x 58.5 cm) USD 1,300. NEW YORK, 15 May 1991, *Rushing Stream in Mountains* (oil on canvas, 28 x 36 ins / 71.1 x 91.4 cm) USD 2,200. LONDON, 7 Oct 1992, *Portrait of a High-Caste Hindu* (oil on canvas/panel, 22 1/4 x 17 1/2 ins / 56.5 x 44.5 cm) GBP 3,080. NEW YORK, 15 Oct 1993, *Arab Huntsman on a White Horse* (oil on canvas, 20 x 15 3/4 ins / 50.8 x 40.2 cm) USD 1,725. NEW YORK, 17 Feb 1994, *Coastal Landscape at Twilight* (oil on canvas, 16 x 26 ins / 40.5 x 66 cm) USD 1,265. NEW YORK, 20 March 1996, *Western Summit, said to be Mount Rainier* (oil on canvas, 26 x 35 3/4 ins / 66 x 90.8 cm) USD 5,750. NEW YORK, 30 Oct 1996, *Harvest Time* (c. 1895, oil on paper/card, 24 1/4 x 30 ins / 61.6 x 76.2 cm) USD 3,450. NEW YORK, 25 March 1997, *Old Faithful* (oil on canvas, 34 1/2 x 25 1/2 ins / 87.6 x 64.8 cm) USD 2,185. MILFORD, 22 April 1999, *Cows Watering* (oil on canvas, 24 x 36 ins / 61 x 91 cm) USD 2,600. HAYDEN, 31 July 1999, *Bighorn Rams* (oil on canvas, 30 x 20 ins / 76 x 51 cm) USD 3,000. PHILADELPHIA, 24 June 2001, *Cattle by a River* (oil on canvas) USD 2,500. NEW ORLEANS, 8 Dec 2001, *Western Landscape with a Hunter on Horseback and his Burro* (oil on canvas, 12 x 9 ins / 30 x 22 cm) USD 2,150. NEW YORK, 12 Feb 2002, *Open Season* (oil on canvas, 18 x 24 ins / 46 x 60 cm) USD 2,500.

FOX, T.M.

British, 19th century.
Active in London.
Miniaturist.

T.M. Fox exhibited at the Royal Academy in London from 1843 to 1846.

FOX, Terry

American, 20th - 21st century.
Born 1943, in Seattle.
Installation artist, performance artist, mixed media.

Terry Fox attended the Accademia di Belle Arti in Rome between 1962 and 1963. He is known for his mixed media and sound installations and for his performances such as *White Bread* (Minneapolis, 1984), *Swallowing the century* (Venice, 1985), *Segreto* (Florence, 1986), *La Trota* (Leeuwarden, 1987),

Tisch Koncert (Berlin, 1988), and *Process Vol. 2 - Reflection Punkt und Linie Berlin* (Berlin, 2003).

Fox began his career with four performances in 1967 in Europe and the USA. His work has, since 1969, been the subject of numerous solo exhibitions including *Terry Fox* (2000), *Cornered and Articulated* (2001), *Terry Fox: Vocale vocale* (2002) and *(RE/DE) Constructions* (2003).

BIBLIOGRAPHY:

Fox, Terry, *Ocular Language. 30 Years of Speaking and Writing About Art*, Gesellschaft für Aktuelle Kunst, Bremen. Plagens, Peter, *Sunshine Muse*, Praeger, New York, 1974. Lippard, Lucy, *Overlay*, Pantheon, New York, 1983. Hoptman, Laura (Ed.), *Primary Documents: A Sourcebook for Eastern and Central European Art since the 1950s*, MoMA, New York, 1983. Albright, Thomas, *Art in the San Francisco Bay Area: 1945-1980*, University of California, Berkeley, 1985. Nash, Steven A., *Facing Eden: 100 Years of Landscape Art in Bay Area*, 1995. Fox, Terry, *Works with Sound*, exhibition catalogue, Kehrer Verlag, Heidelberg, 1998.

MUSEUMS AND GALLERIES:

OTTAWA (Nat. Gal. of Canada) - ROSKILDE (Museet for Samtidskunst) - SAN FRANCISCO (MoMA).

FOX TALBOT, William Henry
British, 19th century.
Born 1800, at Lacock Abbey; died 1877, at Lacock Abbey.
Draughtsman, photographer.

William Fox Talbot was a scientist and one of the earliest and most significant a pioneers of photography.

FOXEL, Maurice Frederick
British, 20th century.
Born 15 August 1888; died 1981.
Painter, engraver.

Maurice Foxel made wood engravings. He exhibited at the Society of Parson Painters and held the degree of Master of Arts. He was a member of the Royal Victorian Order.

FOXKIRCH
German, 17th century.
Active in Stolp.
Painter.

By 1632 Foxkirch had completed 150 biblical paintings of which 49 have been preserved for the Church of Schmolsin near Stolp.

FOY, André
French, 20th century.
Born 14 April 1886 or 1892, in Paris; died April 1953.
Painter, watercolourist, draughtsman, humorist, illustrator. Religious subjects, portraits, genre scenes, landscapes with figures, landscapes, still-lifes, flowers. Stage sets, stage costumes.

André Foy began his career by producing drawings for various humorous French newspapers and the London *Bystander* magazine. He illustrated several books for children, including: *La Veillée des Petits Soldats de Plomb; Bib et Bop; Faut pas s'en faire*; the tales of R. Bizet; *Cinéma* by A. Arnoux; and *Les Gaietés de l'Escadron* by G. Courteline. He published a work on musical cafés and *Sauvegarde de la Méditation*, a satire on modern furnishings. Foy produced stage sets and costumes for *La Mort de Socrate* (*The Death of Socrates*) at the Théâtre de l'Atelier; for a review by Rip; and for *Angélique* by Jacques Ibert at the Opéra-Comique. As a painter he produced portraits, still-lifes in the classical style, flower studies and landscapes of Brittany. His paintings include: *The Female Clown*, 1927, *Portrait of the Actor Pauley*, *Cloakroom at the Masked Ball*, *The Masked Court* and *The Temptation of St Anthony*.

He exhibited at numerous group exhibitions in Paris, including: the Salon des Artistes Indépendants, of which he became a member in 1914; the Salon de l'Araignée, which he founded in 1920 with his friends Jean-Gabriel Daragnès and Gus Bofa, and which had a considerable influence on French illustrators; at the Salon d'Automne in 1935; at an exhibition at the Musée du Petit-Palais in 1938; and at the Salon des Humoristes. He became vice president of the Salon de l'Imagerie. He also held numerous solo exhibitions.

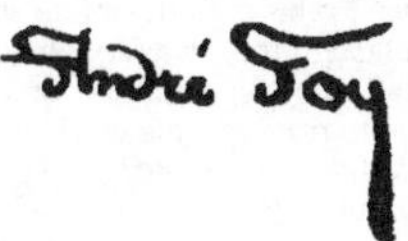

MUSEUMS AND GALLERIES:

HELSINKI - PARIS (MAMVP).

AUCTION RECORDS:

PARIS, 1 April 1920, *In a Paradise of Flowers* (drawing) FRF 300; *Virgins of the Nihil* (drawing) FRF 290; *Desert Idyll* (drawing) FRF 280. PARIS, 24 March 1930, *White Mask* (watercolour) FRF 125; *Flowers* (watercolour) FRF 105; *Masks and White Tureen*, FRF 100; *Clock*, FRF 305.

FOY, Edith Gellenbeck
American, 20th century.
Born 1893, in Cincinnati (Ohio); died 1982.
Painter.

FOY, Francis M.
American, 20th century.
Born 1890, in Chicago; died 1963.
Painter, illustrator.

FOY, Michael
Irish, 18th century.
Active in Dublin.
Sculptor.

Michael Foy studied at the Society School in Dublin and exhibited mythological group sculptures at the Society of Artists in Dublin from 1767 to 1770.

FOY, William
British, 19th century.
Born 1791, in Londonderry; died after 1861.
Active in London.
Painter. Portraits.

William Foy exhibited from 1828 to 1861 at the Royal Academy, the British Institution and the Suffolk Street Gallery in London.

FOY DE VALLOIS, Gaspard
French, 18th century.
Engraver.

M. Jal erroneously asserts that this artist was born on 27 November 1748; this is in fact the date of birth of one of his brothers. The daughter of Gaspard Foy de Vallois was Anne-Louise Foy de Vallois, also an engraver, who worked under the name Anne-Louise Chéreau.

FOYA, Philippe
French, 18th century.
Active in Grenoble.
Sculptor.

FOYATIER, Denis
French, 19th century.
Born 22 September 1793, in Bussières (Loire); died 19 November 1863, in Paris.
Sculptor. Religious subjects, historical subjects. Groups, equestrian groups, busts.

Denis Foyatier first studied under Chinard at the École des Beaux-Arts, Lyons, then, on the death of Chinard, under Marin. On 3 August 1817, he entered the École des Beaux-Arts in Paris.

On his first appearance at the Salon, in 1819, he showed several busts (the actor *Joanny*, and *Doctor Gall*), some figures (*Soldier Ploughman*, and *Young Shepherd*) and *Young Faun Composing Music*, which won him a gold medal and the commission for a statue of *St Mark* for Arras cathedral. Today it stands outside the cathedral.

The young artist left for Italy in 1822, and when in Rome conceived the idea for his famous statue: *Spartacus Breaking his Chains*. The plaster model was shown in 1827, and established the reputation of the young sculptor. He received a State commission to produce this work in marble. Together with Pradier and Rude, he also sculpted part of the frieze of the Arc de Triomphe in Paris.

Foyatier is an elegant artist, fluid and expressive. He left 118 works. His chief works in the Loire region are a bronze bust at Bussières, *St Christopher and the Infant Jesus* in the Chapel of Notre-Dame, *Néronde* and *Colonel Michel Combe* (bronze) at Feurs.

BIBLIOGRAPHY:

Cornand, René, *Foyatier: statuaire*, Roanne, 1993.

MUSEUMS AND GALLERIES:

BAGNÈRES-DE-BIGORRE: *Bust of Louise Labbé* - FEURS: *Colonel Combes* (bronze statue) - LANGRES: *Mongin de Montrol* - LYONS: *Bacchante couchée* (*Bacchante Reclining*) (1839, marble, statue); *Jeune fille au chevreau* (*Girl with Kid*) (marble, group); *Louise Labbé*; *Baron Lemot* - ORLÉANS: *Joan of Arc* (inaugurated 8 May 1855, equestrian statue) - PARIS (Church of Notre-Dame-de-Lorette): *La Foi* (*Faith*) - PARIS (Church of St-Étienne du Mont): *Virgin and Child* - PARIS (Church of St-Vincent-de-Paul, façade): *St Matthew* - PARIS (Church of the Madeleine): four pendants - PARIS (Jardin des Tuileries): *Germanicus*; *Cincinnatus* - PARIS (Louvre): *Sully*; *L'Amour* (*Love*) (1825, marble, statuette); *Spartacus brisant ses chaînes* (*Spartacus Breaking his Chains*) (1830, marble, statue); *La Sieste* (*Siesta*) (marble); *Andrea del Sarto* (*Andrea del Sarto*) (1826, marble, bust); *La Siesta (dit aussi La Sieste)* (*Siesta*) (1848, marble, statue) - PARIS (Mus. de l'Arc de Triomphe): frise - PARIS (Palais-Royal): *The Regent* (marble statue) - PARIS (Sénat, cour d'honneur): statue*Étienne Pasquier* - ROANNE: *The Artist* - ST-ÉTIENNE (Mus. d'Art et d'Industrie): *'Spartacus brisant ses chaînes'* (*Spartacus Breaking his Chains*) (plaster) - TOURNUS: low relief - VERSAILLES: *Suger, abbé de St-Denis* (*Suger, Priest of St-Denis*); *Maréchal de La Palice*; *Olivier de Clisson*.

AUCTION RECORDS:

NEW YORK, 25 May 1988, *Joan of Arc* (1852, bronze, equestrian group, h. 17 3/4 ins / 45.1 cm) USD 1,100.

FOYOT-D'ALVAR, Madeleine (Mme)

French, 19th - 20th century.
Active in Paris.
Painter.

Madeleine Foyot-d'Alvar became a member of the Société des Artistes Français in 1895.

AUCTION RECORDS:

PARIS, 20 and 21 April 1928, *The Vase*, FRF 210. LONDON, 27 May 1999, *Lemons, Passion Fruit, Melons and Grapes on a Table* (oil on canvas, 35 x 43 ins / 89 x 108 cm) GBP 2,000. NEW YORK, 29 Nov 1999, *Elegant Breakfast* (oil on canvas, 32 x 39 ins / 81 x 100 cm) USD 10,000. NORTH BETHESDA, 10 Sept 2001, *Azalias* (oil on canvas, 26 x 32 ins / 66 x 81 cm) USD 4,500.

FOZEMBRAS, Charles Émile

French, 19th century.
Born in Bordeaux.
Painter, watercolourist. Landscapes.

Fozembras made his Salon début in 1880. He may possibly be the same artist as Fozembas Etienne-Charles, who died in 1893.

FRAASS, Gustave

French, 20th century.
Born 4 September 1920, in Mulhouse.
Painter.

Gustave Fraass studied at the school of drawing and engraving in Mulhouse. From 1949 he exhibited at the Salon d'Automne in Paris and at various group exhibitions. He was awarded numerous prizes and honours and received a commendation at the Salon des Artistes Français. He also exhibited in many galleries in France and abroad.

G Fraass

FRAAY-KARTE, Klasina

Dutch, 20th century.
Born 1892, in Zaandijk.
Painter. Landscapes.

Fraay-Karte was a housewife who painted lyrical garden views distinguished by their meticulous and naive attention to detail.

BIBLIOGRAPHY:

Gans, Louis, *Meesters der Europese naïven*, exhibition catalogue, Centraal Museum, Utrecht, 1970.

FRABONI, Alain

French, 20th century.
Painter.

Alain Fraboni exhibited at the Paliss'art public painting exhibition in May 1987 in Paris and in July 1988 exhibited at *Art Rythmic* at the Art Jonction International exhibition at the Palais des Expositions in Nice.

AUCTION RECORDS:

PARIS, 16 June 1988, *The Laughing Man* (1987, oil on canvas, 57 1/2 x 45 ins / 146 x 114 cm) FRF 5,000. PARIS, 12 Feb 1989, *The Dreamer* (1987, oil on canvas, 57 1/2 x 45 ins / 146 x 114 cm) FRF 4,200.

FRACALANZA, Nicolo

Italian, 16th century.
Active in Verona.
Painter, sculptor.

The works of Nicolo Fracalanza include a painting of the *Virgin* for the church of S Giovanni della Beverara, which is no longer in existence.

FRACANZANO, Alessandro, or Fracanzani

Italian, 16th - 17th century.
Born c. 1576.
Active in Naples.
Painter.

FRACANZANO, Carlo Antonio, or Fracanzani

Italian, 17th century.
Born 1640, in Naples.
Painter.

Carlo Antonio Fracanzano was the son of Cesare Fracanzano.

FRACANZANO, Cesare

Italian, 17th century.
Born c. 1605, in Bisceglia; died before 1653.
Painter.

Cesare Fracanzano was the father of Carlo Antonio and Michelagnolo Fracanzano. He studied under José Ribera. Although his roots were in the Naples of Caravaggio, his own work tended more towards the Baroque, presaging the likes of Preti and Giordano.

MUSEUMS AND GALLERIES:

NAPLES: *Three Heads of Apostles*.

AUCTION RECORDS:

NEW YORK, 13-15 March 1947, *Landing of Columbus*, USD 220. ROME, 28 May 1985, *Philosopher* (oil on canvas, oval, 33 x 24 1/2 ins / 84 x 62 cm) ITL 7,000,000. LONDON, 15 Dec 2000, *St Andrew* (oil on canvas, 50 x 39 ins / 127 x 100 cm) GBP 3,800.

FRACANZANO, Francesco, or Francanzano
Italian, 17th century.
Born 1612, in Monopoli; died 1656, in Naples, sentenced to death.
Painter. Religious subjects.

Like his brother Cesare Fracanzano, Francesco Fracanzano studied under José Ribera and subsequently taught his own brother-in-law Salvator Rosa. He also had roots in the Naples of Caravaggio but, unlike his brother Cesare, he did not turn his back on the luminist Naturalism of the Neapolitan style of the 1630s. Instead, he and others - including Guarino, Do, Bassante and, not least, Ribera himself - continued that tradition, paving the way for its spread into other parts of Europe, notably Spain.

BIBLIOGRAPHY:
Salmi, Mario/Bazin, Germain, *Le Caravage et la Peinture italienne du XVIIe siècle*, exhibition catalogue, Musée du Louvre, Paris, 1965. Spinosa, Nicolà, et al., *Les Mystères de Naples. Sublime et triviale: la peinture napolitaine*, collective exhibition catalogue, Musée Fesch, Ajaccio, 2003.

MUSEUMS AND GALLERIES:
BÉZIERS: *Spanish Woman Weaving* - COMPIÈGNE: *Child* - FLORENCE (Uffizi): drawings - MADRID (Prado): *Two Wrestlers* - NAPLES (Church of S Gregorio Armeno): paintings (c. 1635) - NAPLES (Mus. di Capodimonte): *Head of Apostle* (c. 1640, oil on canvas, formerly attributed to Lanfranco) - VIRE: *Love at Rest*.

AUCTION RECORDS:
LONDON, 22 July 1983, *Prophet Elijah* (oil on canvas, 39 x 29 ins / 99 x 73.6 cm) GBP 6,500. NEW YORK, 5 Nov 1986, *Joseph Sold by his Brothers* (oil on canvas, 39 1/4 x 49 ins / 100 x 124.5 cm) USD 23,000. NEW YORK, 3 June 1988, *St Peter* (oil on canvas, 36 1/4 x 28 3/4 ins / 92 x 73 cm) USD 35,750. MILAN, 12 Dec 1988, *St Anthony* (oil on canvas, 35 1/2 x 27 1/2 ins / 90 x 70 cm) ITL 5,000,000. MILAN, 13 Dec 1989, *Saint at Prayer* (oil on canvas, 30 1/4 x 25 1/2 ins / 77 x 65 cm) ITL 12,000,000. NEW YORK, 30 Jan 1997, *Head of St Peter* (oil on canvas, 24 3/4 x 19 1/4 ins / 62.9 x 48.9 cm) USD 34,500. NEW YORK, 25 May 1999, *Male Saint Holding Staff* (oil on canvas, 30 x 24 ins / 77 x 62 cm) USD 15,000. LONDON, 18 April 2000, *St Bartholomew* (oil on canvas, 19 x 14 ins / 47 x 36 cm) GBP 4,000. LONDON, 25 April 2001, *St John the Baptist Preaching to the Multitude* (oil on canvas, 28 x 24 ins / 72 x 61 cm) GBP 10,000. LONDON, 12 Dec 2002, *Executioner with Head of St John the Baptist* (c. 1630, oil on canvas, 25 x 20 ins / 63 x 50 cm) GBP 10,000.

FRACANZANO, Michelagnolo
Italian, 17th century.
Born c. 1644; died c. 1685, in France.
Painter.

Michelagnolo Fracanzano was the son of Cesare Fracanzano.

FRACAO, Francesco
Italian, 16th - 17th century.
Active in Treviso (Venezia).
Sculptor.

Francesco Fracao made the St Thomas Aquinas altar in the church of S Nicolo in Treviso in 1590.

FRACARO, Domenico
Italian, 17th century.
Active in Padua.
Painter.

Paintings on the ceiling of the Scuola de Battuti in Monselice are signed by Domenico Fracaro and dated 1682.

FRACASSA, Giovanni Antonio. See **DUNESIO**

FRACASSI, Cesare, or Fracassini
Italian, 19th century.
Born 1838; died 1868, in Rome.
Painter, fresco artist. Religious subjects.

Cesare Fracassi studied painting in Rome, and produced several frescoes for the church of S Lorenzo. One of his most important works is *The Martyrs of Gorkum*. He is probably the same artist that Siret lists as Charles Fracassi.

MUSEUMS AND GALLERIES:
ORVIETO: *Belisarius Saving Orvieto* (study) - ROME (Gal. Nazionale d'Arte Moderna): *Judgement of St Stephen* (drawing) - VATICAN (Mus. Vaticani): *The Martyrs of Gorkum*; *Petrus Canisius before the Emperor Ferdinand*.

AUCTION RECORDS:
NEW YORK, 18 Sept 1981, *Declaration of Love* (1860, oil on canvas, 24 3/4 x 19 1/2 ins / 63 x 49.5 cm) CAD 1,600.

FRACASSI, Girolamo
Italian, 17th century.
Active in Perugia c. 1678.
Painter.

FRACASSI, Patrizio
Italian, 19th century.
Died at the beginning of 1904, in Siena.
Active in Siena.
Sculptor.

The academy of Siena awarded Patrizio Fracassi a prize for his painting of *Christ Driving the Merchants from the Temple*. Other key works include *Work* and *Humanity*.

FRACASSO, G
Italian, 19th century.
Active in Verona.
Painter.

Fracasso's painting of *Mary in the Temple* is in the church of the Holy Apostles in Verona. He may have been the Fracasso who painted a *St Anthony* in 1808 for the church of S Lorenzo in the same town.

FRACCARI, Pier Cesare
Italian, 20th century.
Born 1920, in Vicenza.
Painter.

Fraccari exhibits mostly in Italy, and regularly in Milan. His abstract, brightly-coloured paintings seem to be constructed according to a dynamic of form directly descended from Futurism.

FRACCAROLI, Innocenzo, also known as Innocenzo da Imola
Italian, 19th century.
Born 1805, in Castelrotto, near Bolzano (Trentino-Alto Adige); died 1882, in Milan.
Sculptor.

After studying in Venice, Milan and Rome, Fraccaroli became a teacher at the academy of Florence in 1842. He was later admitted as a member of the academies of Milan and of Venice.

MUSEUMS AND GALLERIES:
LIVERPOOL (Walker AG): *Venus de Milo* (plaster) - MILAN (Gal. d'Arte Moderna): *Achilles Wounded*; *Cyparissus Lamenting the Death of His Stag* - MILAN (Pinacoteca di Brera): *Pietro Verri* - VENICE (Gal. dell'Accademia): *The Painter Matteini* - VIENNA (Österreichische Gal. Belvedere): *Massacre of the Innocents*.

FRACHET, Odile
French, 20th - 21st century.
Born 17 May 1947, in Paris.
Painter, collage artist, sculptor of assemblages, mixed media, potter.

Odile Frachet was originally a decorator of crockery and porcelain, and has taught in a number of different workshops. She creates ceramic panels and collages, in a solidly structured, naturalistic yet abstract style. She also made a fountain for the water treatment factory in Toulouse.

She has taken part in numerous group exhibitions, including: Salon d'Hiver in Paris in 1967; Annual Salon of Ceramics in Caracas, Venezuela, in 1974; and the Salon des Artistes Décorateurs in Paris, in 1979 and 1981. She has shown her work in solo exhibitions, including: Marcos Costillo Gallery in Caracas in 1967; Alliance Française in San Pedro Sula, Honduras; Maison des Métiers d'Art Français in Paris in 1977; in Le Buisson Richard, Mesnil-le-Roi, in 1978; *Contemporary Ceramics*, at the Forney Library in 1978; Galerie Ikébana in Paris in 1982; Atelier Celadon, Courbevoie, in 1982, 1983, 1984, 1986 and 1988; and the Manifestation d'art Contemporain 2000 Paris in 1988.

FRACHISSE
French, 18th century.
Active in Tain (Drôme).
Sculptor (wood).

Franchisse's works include the panelling that he sculpted for the sacristy of the cathedral in Valence.

FRACHON-SPAZIN, Julie Christiane (Mme)
Maiden name: Spazin
French, 19th - 20th century.
Born in Lyons.
Painter.

Julie Frachon-Spazin studied under Perrachon. From 1898 she signed herself *J.- C. Frachon-Spazin*. She exhibited in Lyons from 1845 and in Paris from 1909, showing flower paintings.

FRADEL, Denis
French, 18th century.
Active in Paris.
Sculptor.

Denis Fradel was accepted as a member of the Académie St-Luc in 1735.

FRADELLE, Henri Jean-Baptiste Victoire, or Fradel or Fredel
French, 19th century.
Born 15 June 1778, in Lille; died 14 March 1865, in London.
Active in England.
Painter, draughtsman. Historical subjects, portraits. Miniatures.

For many years, Henri Jean-Baptiste Victoire Fradelle was confused with his son Henri Joseph. He has been cited using the spelling Fredel (without Christian name). He studied in Paris, travelled to Italy, and in 1816 settled in London, where he died. In 1834, he was awarded a third class medal at the Salon de Paris.

He exhibited chiefly at the Royal Academy in London, from 1817 to 1839; at the Society of British Artists in London, from 1817 to 1854; and in Paris from 1827 to 1855.

Dates of exhibitions may vary, owing to the confusion of identity between father and son, which often makes them appear to be the same person. Caution is also necessary when attributing works for sale at auction, especially since Fradelle sometimes gave his son the task of making copies of his works.

Several of his works were engraved, in particular by William Say. Works that we know to be by him include: *Milton Dictating Paradise Lost to his Daughter*, 1817; *Belinda at her Toilet*; *Queen Elizabeth and Lady Paget*; *Lady Jane Grey*. In particular, he painted 36 pictures illustrating the works of Shakespeare and Sir Walter Scott.

MUSEUMS AND GALLERIES:
BORDEAUX (MBA): *Deux amours musiciens* (*Two Cupids Playing Musical Instruments*); *Tête de jeune fille* (*Head of Girl*); *Le joyeux frère dans 'Richard CŒur de Lion'* (*The Joyful Brother in 'Richard the Lionheart'*) - LONDON (British Mus.): preparatory study*The Earl of Leicester's Visit to Amy Robsart at Cumnor Place* (black chalk) - PARIS (Mus. de la Comédie-Française): *Portrait de Pierre Ligier* - STRATFORD-UPON-AVON (Royal Shakespeare Theatre Collection): *Othello Relating the Story of his Life to Brabantio and Desdemona* (1824, oil on canvas).

AUCTION RECORDS:
LONDON, 15 Feb 1928, *Jane Grey*, GBP 11. LONDON, 15 Feb 1935, *Queen Elisabeth and Lady Paget*, GBP 10. NEW YORK, 3 Dec 1936, *Molière*, USD 90. VIENNA, 16 Jan 1985, *Monastery Interior* (1855, oil on canvas, 24 3/4 x 21 1/4 ins / 63 x 54 cm) ATS 11,000. LONDON, 7 April 1993, *Queen Elisabeth and Lady Paget* (oil on panel, 14 1/4 x 17 3/4 ins / 36 x 45 cm) GBP 977. MILAN, 22 March 1994, *Origin of Painting* (1834, oil on panel, 30 3/4 x 41 ins / 78 x 104 cm) ITL 19,550,000. LONDON, 6 Sept 2001, *Dance in the Campagna* (1847, oil on canvas, 28 x 36 ins / 71 x 91 cm) GBP 3,000. NEW ORLEANS, 16 Nov 2002, *Interior Scene depicting a Shakespearean Man Reciting Poetry to a Lady* (1810, oil on canvas, 25 x 21 ins / 64 x 53 cm) USD 4,600. MADRID, 22 March 2004, *Moliere and Servant* (oil on board, 26 x 21 ins / 65 x 54 cm) EUR 3,500.

FRADELLE, Henri Joseph, or Fradel
French, 19th century.
Born 1805, in France; died 21 December 1872, in St Pancras (Middlesex).
Active in England.
Painter. Portraits.

For many years, Henri Joseph Fradelle was confused with his father, Henri Jean-Baptiste Victoire, and was known only as Henri Joseph. In 1816, he came to England with his father and he made a career as a portraitist, although his reputation never matched that of his father.

It is important to distinguish carefully between the two bodies of work, as they are very often assimilated under the name of the son.

FRADIN
French, 16th century.
Active c. 1580.
Engraver (wood).

FRADIN, Corneille C.
French, 19th century.
Died 1900.
Painter.

FRADIN, Jacques
French, 17th century.
Active in Paris.
Painter.

Jacques Fradin is said to have been a godfather of Estienne Moreau (son of the sculptor of the same name, who was baptised on 18 October 1668 in Paris).

FRAEK, Freddy
Danish, 20th century.
Born 1935, in Copenhagen.
Also active in France.
Sculptor, draughtsman.

Studied from 1960 to 1966 at the Kongelige Danske Kunstakademi in Copenhagen and went on to teach metalwork there between 1967 and 1979. Fraek divides his time between Paris and Copenhagen and has participated in various group events in Sweden, Germany, France and Italy. He has exhibited solo on numerous occasions since 1964.

He works with elementary forms and uniform colours to produce monumental, airy sculptures that are essentially exercises in equilibrium (*Discrepant Planes; Open Planes; Four Planes*). His playful 'assemblies' are usually constructed in lightweight or perforated steel and appear as fragile as a house of cards on the point of collapsing. He also produces sculptural elements intended to be integrated into architectural designs.

Bibliography:

Gordillo - Fraek, exhibition catalogue, Gal. Denise René, Paris, 1991.

FRAENCKEL, Liepmann

German, 18th - 19th century.
Born 1772, in Parchim (Mecklenburg); died 1857, in Copenhagen.
Miniaturist. Portraits.

Fraenckel spent 10 years in Sweden.

Museums and Galleries:

Hillerød (Frederiksborg): *Portrait of Captain F. Monck* - Stockholm: *Portrait of Marshall Baron K. F. Bennet*.

FRAENKEL, Theodore Oscar

American, 19th century.
Born 17 March 1857, in Chicago.
Active in New Orleans.
Watercolourist.

Theodore Oscar Fraenkel studied in Chicago, where he initially worked. He later moved to New Orleans, where he was awarded a gold medal for watercolours at the exhibition of 1900.

FRAENKEL, Walter

German, 20th century.
Born 12 March 1879, in Breslau (now Wroclaw, Poland).
Active in Austria.
Painter. Religious subjects, figures.

Walter Fraenkel studied under A. Kaufmann in Munich before enrolling at the Munich academy of fine arts and later working in H. Knirr's painting academy. He travelled in Italy and visited Paris. He started exhibiting his work in 1902. His themes are primarily religious (*Salome; Annunciation; Three Wise Men*) but occasionally allegorical, as in *Vanity*.

FRAENKEL-HAHN, Louise

Austrian, 20th century.
Born 12 August 1878, in Vienna.
Painter. Religious subjects, portraits, flowers.

The wife of the painter Walter Fraenkel, Louise Fraenkel-Hahn studied at the arts and crafts college in Vienna and at H. Knirr's painting academy in Munich. She travelled extensively in Italy and Greece and spent some time in Paris in 1907. She started exhibiting in Vienna in 1902. Examples of her work include various religious subjects (*David; Suffer the Little Children to Come unto Me; Virgin*) and portraits (including a self-portrait).

FRAERMANN, Theophil

Ukrainian, 20th century.
Born 1884, in Odessa.
Active in France.
Painter. Portraits, genre scenes. Murals.

After studying at the art school in Odessa, Theophil Fraermann went to Paris in 1905 where he continued his studies at the École des Beaux-Arts with Gabriel Ferrier. He first exhibited at the Salon d'Automne (1908 to 1910 becoming a member in 1909). He also exhibited at the Salon des Humoristes at the Salon des Artistes Indépendants.

FRAET, Alexandre or Sanders

Flemish School, 15th century.
Active in Bruges.
Painter.

Alexandre Fraet drew the designs for embroidery work executed for the Palais du Franc in Bruges by Pierre Van Messene in 1445.

FRAET, Jan

Flemish School, 15th century.
Active in Antwerp.
Painter.

FRAET, Joris

Flemish School, 15th century.
Active in Antwerp.
Painter.

FRAGA, Rodrigo da

Spanish, 16th century.
Sculptor.

Rodrigo da Fraga worked in Santiago de Compostela, where in 1532 he sculpted for the church of the Franciscan monastery a high altar presided over by Christ and two angels collecting his blood in goblets.

FRAGGI, Alain

French, 20th century.
Painter. Scenes with figures.

Alain Fraggi exhibited at numerous exhibitions.

Bibliography:

'*Alain Fraggi*' in *Art Press* n° 165, periodical, Paris, January 1992.

FRAGGI, Raymond Michel

French, 20th century.
Born 1902, in Marseilles.
Painter.

Raymond Fraggi exhibited at the Salon des Artistes Français in Paris before World War II. He was a member of the Salon.

FRAGIACOMO, Antonietta

Italian, 19th - 20th century.
Painter. Landscapes.

Antonietta was the sister of Pietro Fragiacomo. Her work appeared in several exhibitions in Venice and Turin.

FRAGIACOMO, Pietro

Italian, 19th - 20th century.
Born 14 August 1856, in Trieste; died 1922, in Venice.
Active in Venice.
Painter, watercolourist. Genre scenes, landscapes.

Pietro Fragiacomo was a student at the Accademia di Belle Arti in Venice. He won a bronze medal at the 1889 Exposition Universelle in Paris and a silver medal at the same event in 1900.

Museums and Galleries:

Berlin: *Sadness* - Florence (Gal. d'Arte Moderna): *Traghetto; Armonic del Silenzio* - Paris (MAM): *Gondola* - Rome (Gal. Nazionale d'Arte Moderna): *Rest; Winter* - Trieste (Civico Mus. Revoltella): *Evening Bell* - Venice (Gal. d'Arte Moderna): *In the Wind; St Mark's Square; Sad Sunset; Swallows*.

Auction records:

London, 12 July 1968, *Riverbanks,* Gns 900. Milan, 21 Oct 1969, *Canal in Venice,* ITL 1,300,000. Milan, 24 March 1970, *Fishing Boat,* ITL 1,700,000. Milan, 18 May 1971, *Boat on the Lagoon,* ITL 2,400,000. Milan, 20 Nov 1973, *Boats on the Lagoon,* ITL 700,000. Milan, 12 Dec 1974, *The Lagoon,* ITL 3,800,000. Milan, 20 Dec 1977, *Confidences* (oil on canvas, 16 1/4 x 26 3/4 ins / 41 x 68 cm) ITL 2,400,000. Milan, 10 June 1981, *Fishing Boats off the Coast* (oil on canvas, 22 3/4 x 39 3/4 ins / 58 x 101 cm) ITL 18,000,000. Milan, 15 June 1983, *Le Zattere, Venezia* (oil on canvas, 19 1/4 x 38 1/4 ins / 49 x 97 cm)

ITL 12,000,000. ROME, 16 May 1985, *Gondola on the Lagoon* (watercolour, 6¼ x 11¾ ins / 16 x 30 cm) ITL 2,000,000. MILAN, 28 Oct 1986, *Riva degli Schiavoni* (oil on canvas, 28 x 51¼ ins / 71 x 130 cm) ITL 70,000,000. NEW YORK, 25 Feb 1988, *Green Harmonies* (oil on card, 31 x 46¼ ins / 78.7 x 117.5 cm) USD 10,450. LOKEREN, 28 May 1988, *The Grand Canal and S Maria della Salute in Venice* (oil on panel, 4 x 5 ins / 10 x 13 cm) BEF 160,000. MILAN, 1 June 1988, *Villa la Malcontenta* (oil on card, 8¼ x 12½ ins / 21 x 31.5 cm) ITL 5,400,000; *Dawn* (oil on canvas, 34¾ x 74½ ins / 88.5 x 189 cm) ITL 62,000,000. LONDON, 24 June 1988, *La Giudecca in Venice* (oil on panel, 18¾ x 30¼ ins / 47.5 x 77 cm) GBP 12,100. MILAN, 14 March 1989, *Morning on the Lagoon* (oil on canvas, 18¼ x 27¼ ins / 46.5 x 69.5 cm) ITL 120,000,000. MILAN, 19 Oct 1989, *Fishing Boats on the Lagoon* (oil on canvas, 14¾ x 23 ins / 37.5 x 58.5 cm) ITL 44,000,000. LONDON, 30 March 1990, *Chioggia* (oil on canvas, 19¼ x 31½ ins / 49 x 80 cm) GBP 13,200. MONACO, 21 April 1990, *Fishermen in Venice* (oil on canvas, 23¼ x 39 ins / 59 x 99 cm) FRF 444,000. BERN, 12 May 1990, *Lake Garda* (watercolour, 6 x 9¾ ins / 15 x 25 cm) CHF 1,500. ROME, 31 May 1990, *Landscape with a Canal* (oil on canvas, 21¼ x 27½ ins / 54 x 70 cm) ITL 24,000,000. MILAN, 18 Oct 1990, *Venice from the Lagoon* (oil on canvas, 14½ x 23½ ins / 37 x 60 cm) ITL 75,000,000. ROME, 11 Dec 1990, *The Venice of the Poor* (oil on panel, 13¾ x 22 ins / 35 x 55 cm) ITL 63,250,000. MILAN, 6 June 1991, *Seascape* (1913, oil on card, 6¼ x 8¾ ins / 16 x 22.5 cm) ITL 4,500,000. LONDON, 19 June 1991, *Boats on the Lagoon in Venice* (oil on canvas, 14¼ x 25½ ins / 36 x 65 cm) GBP 14,300. NEW YORK, 15 Oct 1991, *Bridge over a Canal* (oil on panel, 15¼ x 7½ ins / 38.9 x 19 cm) USD 4,950. MILAN, 12 Dec 1991, *Boat in the Wind* (oil on canvas, 15¾ x 25½ ins / 40 x 65 cm) ITL 18,000,000. LONDON, 20 March 1992, *On the Lagoon* (1882, oil on canvas, 21¾ x 39½ ins / 55.2 x 100.3 cm) GBP 50,600. MILAN, 29 Oct 1992, *The Lagoon in Venice* (oil on panel, 19 x 30¾ ins / 48 x 78 cm) ITL 40,000,000. ROME, 6 Dec 1994, *Reflections of the Moon* (oil on canvas, 10¾ x 14 ins / 27.5 x 35.5 cm) ITL 7,660,000. MILAN, 25 Oct 1995, *Willow* (oil on card, 13½ x 9¾ ins / 34 x 25 cm) ITL 5,750,000. ROME, 5 Dec 1995, *Fishermen on the Lagoon* (oil on canvas, 18 x 32¼ ins / 46 x 82 cm) ITL 82,495,000. ROME, 23 May 1996, *Hut in a Landscape* (oil on paper, 5¾ x 7½ ins / 14.5 x 19 cm) ITL 2,990,000. ROME, 28 Nov 1996, *Boat on the Sand* (oil on card, 6½ x 12½ ins / 16.5 x 32 cm) ITL 12,000,000. NEW YORK, 9 Feb 1999, *Venice* (oil on canvas, 7 x 19 ins / 19 x 49 cm) USD 15,000. MILAN, 16 June 1999, *Evening on the Canal, Chioggia* (oil on panel, 17 x 34 ins / 42 x 86 cm) ITL 50,000,000. MILAN, 7 Nov 2000, *Fishermen at Rest* (oil on canvas, 9 x 12 ins / 24 x 31 cm) ITL 20,000,000. MILAN, 4 Dec 2000, *Fishing* (oil on board, 11 x 18 ins / 29 x 45 cm) ITL 22,000,000. MILAN, 5 June 2001, *Landscape with Figures* (oil on canvas, 38 x 61 ins / 97 x 155 cm) ITL 40,000,000. MILAN, 27 Nov 2001, *Boat and Fishermen* (oil on canvas, 12 x 21 ins / 31 x 54 cm) ITL 31,000,000. LONDON, 17 Jan 2002, *Bustling Venetian Backwater* (oil on canvas, 24 x 16 ins / 60 x 40 cm) GBP 11,000. MILAN, 22 May 2002, *Seascape* (oil on canvas, 14 x 26 ins / 36 x 66 cm) EUR 51,000. MILAN, 27 May 2003, *Venice* (oil on canvas, 26 x 41 ins / 65 x 103 cm) EUR 49,000. MILAN, 27 May 2003, *Venezia, il Gamalo di S Marco* (oil on canvas, 26 x 41 ins / 65 x 103 cm) EUR 49,000. MILAN, 25 Feb 2004, *Venice* (oil on board, 19 x 38 ins / 49 x 97 cm) EUR 42,000. NEW YORK, 27 Oct 2004, *Quiet Pond* (1902, oil on canvas, 22 x 39 ins / 55 x 100 cm) USD 22,000.

FRAGNAY, François

French, 19th century.
Born 5 July 1824, in Pérouges (Ain).
Painter.

Fragnay studied at the École des Beaux-Arts in Lyons from 1839 to 1843 and exhibited in that city from 1844-1845 to 1862, chiefly portraits and rustic interiors. Examples of his work include *Child Jesus Asleep* (1846-1847) and *Young Peasant Woman Threshing Straw* (1858-1859). In 1861-1862, Fragnay went on to paint four figures for the audience chamber of the Lyons Tribunal of Commerce: *Eloquence, Meditation, Authority* and *Modesty*. He signed his work *F. Fragnay*.

FRAGONARD, Alexandre Evariste

French, 19th century.
Born October 1780, in Grasse; died 10 November 1850, in Paris.
Painter, sculptor, illustrator, lithographer. History painting, religious subjects, mythological subjects. Murals.

Alexandre Evariste studied under his father Jean-Honoré Fragonard and under Jacques-Louis David. He exhibited at the Paris Salon from 1799 to 1842.

Fragonard began painting mythological subjects, before turning to religious, monarchist and Napoleonic themes. He was also an illustrator, many of whose drawings appeared in publications during the revolutionary years. As a stamp designer, some of his work (*Freedom, Truth,* and *Republic*) was subsequently engraved by Jean-Alexandre Allais, Louis-François Mariage and Jacques-Louis Copia. Under the restoration, Fragonard turned to lithography. As a painter, he established his credentials to the point where a number of major commissions came his way, notably for the decoration of the Louvre, where he produced among others *Francis I in Knight's Armour, Francis I Accepting the Paintings Brought Back from Italy by Primaticcio,* and *Science and the Fine Arts Honouring their Respective Patrons*. Fragonard also worked on the decoration of the palace of Versailles.

BIBLIOGRAPHY:

Simons, K., '*Vivant Denon et le Romantisme: À propos d'un tableau d'Alexandre Evariste Fragonard*' in *Rev. Inst. Napoléon* vol 132, 1976 (pp. 55-65). Chaudonneret, Marie-Claude, '*Le Concours de 1830 pour la Chambre des Députés: Deux Esquisses d'Alexandre Evariste Fragonard au Louvre*' in *Rev. Louvre* vol 2, 1987 (pp.128-135).

MUSEUMS AND GALLERIES:

ARRAS: *The Burghers of Calais before Edward III* - MONTPELLIER: *Portrait of J.J.B. de Joly* - MOREZ: *Leonarda da Vinci and Francis I* - ORLÉANS: *Joan of Arc Entering Orléans* - PARIS (Louvre): decorative paintings - ST-ÉTIENNE (Mus. d'Art et d'Industrie): *Jean Le Hennuyer* - VERSAILLES: *Battle of Marignan; Isabel of Aragon Entreating Charles VIII; Frances I in Knight's Armour; Portrait of Bayard.*

AUCTION RECORDS:

PARIS, 9 June 1975, *Armed Soldiers Inspecting a Church* (oil on canvas, 17 x 25½ ins / 43 x 65 cm) FRF 3,500. MONTE CARLO, 8 Feb 1981, *Death of Condorcet* (black chalk/paper, 7½ x 9½ ins / 19 x 24 cm) FRF 8,000. LYONS, 18 Dec 1983, *Lucretia* (oil on canvas, 48 x 54¼ ins / 121 x 138 cm) FRF 50,000. NEW YORK, 17 Jan 1985, *Psyche Displaying her Gifts to her Sisters; Judgment of Psyche* (two oils on canvas, 16 x 26 ins / 40.5 x 66 cm) USD 125,000. MONTE CARLO, 22 Feb 1986, *Anger of Oedipus* (pen and brown ink, brown wash and gouache heightened with white, 30¼ x 21 ins / 77 x 52.5 cm) FRF 280,000. NEW YORK, 24 May 1989, *Sorcerer* (oil on canvas, 24 x 28½ ins / 61 x 72.5 cm) USD 33,000. PARIS, 12 Dec 1989, *Henry IV, Sully and Gabrielle d'Estrées* (canvas, 20 x 16½ ins / 50.5 x 42 cm) FRF 850,000. PARIS, 12 June 1990, *Spendthrift* (pen and wash/paper, 5½ x 3¼ ins / 13.9 x 8.4 cm) FRF 42,000. NEW YORK, 12 Oct 1994, *Anger of Oedipus* (ink and gouache heightened with white, 30½ x 21 ins / 77.5 x 53.3 cm) USD 47,150. PARIS, 7 Nov 1997, *Pastoral Scene at the foot of a Statue of Jupiter* (pen and gouache, 16¼ x 25½ ins / 41 x 65 cm) FRF 15,500. PARIS, 3 April 1998, *Joan of Arc Led to the Stake* (watercolour, 17¾ x 14½ ins / 45 x 36.7 cm) FRF 32,000. NEW YORK, 3 Nov 1999, *The Dismissal of a Suitor* (oil on canvas/sketch, 16 x 13 ins / 41 x 33 cm) USD 2,200.

VERSAILLES, 3 Dec 2000, *The Doctor's Visit* (oil on canvas, 15 x 19 ins / 39 x 48 cm) FRF 62,000. PARIS, 21 Nov 2001, *Reason. Equality* (crayon, a pair, 15 x 10 ins / 39 x 26 cm) FRF 14,000. PARIS, 28 June 2002, *Mythological Scenes* (black chalk/pen/wash, set of three drawings, 5 x 31 ins / 13 x 79 cm) EUR 2,000. PARIS, 25 June 2003, *Francois 1er recevant les œuvres rapportees d'Italie* (oil on canvas, 26 x 32 ins / 65 x 82 cm) EUR 27,000. MARSEILLES, 25 Oct 2003, *Homer Reciting the 'Odyssey' to Shepherds* (1823, drawing, Chinese ink/wash, 21 x 34 ins / 53 x 86 cm) EUR 32,000. PARIS, 19 March 2004, *Christopher Colombus Presenting his Discoveries to Ferdinand and Isabella* (pen/brown ink/wash/heightened/gouache black pencil, 7 x 10 ins / 17 x 25 cm) EUR 2,500.

FRAGONARD, Antonin

French, 19th century.
Died 1887.
Sculptor.

Antonin was the grandson of Honoré Fragonard. He exhibited a statue of a ballerina and a statuette entitled *Aurora* at the 1882 Salon de la Société des Artistes Français. He died insane in Charenton Asylum.

FRAGONARD, Jean Honoré (Mme)

Maiden name: Marie-Anne Gérard
French, 18th - 19th century.
Born 1745, in Grasse; died 1823.
Painter, miniaturist.

Mme Fragonard, née Marie-Anne Gérard, was the eldest of a family of 17 children and moved to Paris to live with an uncle. The young girl demonstrated exceptional aptitudes and so was given a place as a student with Honoré Fragonard. She was a charming person; intelligent, lively, friendly and very cheerful: the couple fell in love and married. They had two children: a girl who showed extraordinary artistic talent but who died too young to be able to develop them and a son, Alexandre-Evariste, who was also a painter.

Marie-Anne was principally a miniaturist and showed remarkable qualities in this genre. It is likely, if not certain, that she also produced some works with genre themes. She exhibited at the Salon de la Correspondance in 1779.

MUSEUMS AND GALLERIES:

BESANÇON: *Portrait of L.-A. Trouard, the Architect* (miniature) - PARIS (Mus. Jacquemart-André): *Child Dressed as a Valet in Comedy* (miniature on ivory); *Child in a Bonnet with a White Feather* (miniature on ivory).

AUCTION RECORDS:

PARIS, 1783, *Bust of a Young Boy; Bust of a Young Girl* (two miniatures) FRF 137. PARIS, 1787, *Head of a Child* (miniature) FRF 17. PARIS, 1846, *Malvina* (drawing) FRF 17.

FRAGONARD, Jean-Honoré

French, 18th century.
Born 5 January or April 1732, in Grasse; died 22 August 1806, in Paris.
Painter. History painting, genre scenes, landscapes.

Jean Honoré Fragonard came from a fairly rich family but, after his father died, his financial situation changed significantly. He then had to travel to Paris with his mother, who was dealing with a major law-suit. Honoré Fragonard, or 'Frago' as he was called and often liked to sign his name, first worked as a junior clerk to a lawyer, then, showing a definite interest in painting, joined François Boucher's studio where he was placed under the direction of Chardin. The young Southerner made rapid progress and in 1752 won the Grand Prix de Rome.

When Fragonard went to say goodbye before his trip to Italy, Boucher reportedly replied in a casual way: 'You are leaving for Italy, my son; if you study Michelangelo and Raphael, you will be... lost'. Fragonard took Boucher's advice. Among the thousands of small sketches that he produced there - pictures or fragments outlined in a few pen-strokes sketched on washes - there are many more subjects drawn from Barocci, Pietro da Cortona, Tiepolo and other 17th- and 18-century masters than from the great artists of the Italian Renaissance. I

In Rome, Fragonard was on intimate terms with Hubert Robert. The abbot of St Non took them as travelling companions to Naples and Sicily. During the trip, this distinguished art lover engraved a number of Fragonard's drawings with an admirable faithfulness to the originals.

Two years after his return to Paris (1765), Fragonard sent *Coresus Sacrificing Himself to Save Callirhoe* to the Salon where it became a success. It was eventually bought by the king to be reproduced as a tapestry at the Gobelins factory. However, the difficulties experienced by Fragonard in obtaining payment for his work seem to have discouraged him from undertaking further official works and he showed little desire for academic honours. He exhibited once more at the Salon in 1767. Fragonard preferred the charming whimsical pieces and graceful decorative works that he was asked to produce in financial and theatrical circles to those of history painting.

Fragonard's disputes with 'la Guimard' about the decoration of the famous dancer's house were the talk of Paris and are reported in detail in Bachaumont's *Secret Memoirs*. The painter and the dancer were friends but after a financial dispute Fragonard abandoned the work. It was completed by David and by Taraval, who painted the ceilings. Fragonard made a second visit to Italy in 1773, accompanied by the financier Bergeret, who then had the nerve to appropriate the sketches made by the artist on the journey. A trial followed which Fragonard won.

The revolution of 1789 was a serious blow to Fragonard's career. David's protection helped him to obtain a post as curator at the museum of painting that had recently been established by the Assemblée Nationale, but Fragonard did not feel safe in Paris and he left for Grasse. He took with him four major compositions that he had started in 1772 for Mme du Barry's pavilion at Louveciennes: *Love and the Young Girl, The Surprise, Offer of the Rose* and *The Love Letter*, with which he decorated the drawing-room of the house in which he was living, completing the series with a fifth composition, *Crowning of Love*. These paintings constituted one of the notable features of the town of Grasse for many years. Finally the owners accepted an offer of FRF 1, 250, 000 and sold the works on 8 February 1898.

Fragonard returned to Paris, but his work did not regain popularity. He could not adapt to the rigid forms in fashion. Fragonard died very poor in the lodgings that he had found at the Louvre. In 1769, he had married his student and relative, Marie-Anne Gérard. They had a son, who also became a painter.

Frago. Fragonard.

BIBLIOGRAPHY:

Molotiu, Andrei, *'The progress of love and the magic garden: Jean Honoré Fragonard's decorative ensemble for the villa Maubert in Grasse'* in *La Gazette des Beaux-arts*, exhibition catalogue, periodical, 2001, v.137, no.1585, February, p. 91-114. Sheriff, M.D., *Fragonard. Art and Eroticism*, University of Chicago Press, Chicago, 1900. Nolhac, Pierre de, *J.H. Fragonard*, Manzi, Joyant et Cie, Paris, 1906. Wildenstein, Georges, *Les Peintures de J.H. Fragonard*, Phaidon, London, 1960 (French edition 1960). Ananoff, Alexandre, *L'Œuvre dessiné de Jean-Honoré Fragonard, catalogue raisonné 4 vol.*, Nobele, Paris, 1961-1970. Wildenstein, George, *Fragonard*, Phaidon, London, 1976. *Diderot et l'Art de Boucher à David*, exhibition catalogue, Hôtel de la Monnaie, Paris,

1984. Cuzin, Pierre, *Jean-Honoré Fragonard. Vie et Oeuvre. Catalogue Complet des Peintures*, catalogue, Paris, 1987. Cabanne, Pierre, *Fragonard*, exhibition catalogue, Somogy, Paris, 1987. Rosenberg, Pierre/Dupuy, M., *Jean-Honoré Fragonard, 1732-1806*, exhibition catalogue, periodical, Réunion des musées nationaux, Paris, 1987. Cabanne, P., *Fragonard*, exhibition catalogue, periodical, Paris, 1987. Ashton, Dore, in *Fragonard in the Universe of Painting*, Smithsonian Institution Press, Washington, London, 1988. Rosenberg, P., *Fragonard*, exhibition catalogue, periodical, Metropolitan Museum, New York, 1988. Rosenberg, Pierre, *Tout l'Oeuvre Peint de Fragonard*, annotated catalogue, Flammarion, Paris, 1989. Bailey, Colin, et al., *Les Amours des Dieux: La Peinture Mythologique de Watteau à David*, exhibition catalogue, RMN, Paris, 1991. Kavanagh, Thomas M., '*The libertine moment*' in *Yale French Studies*, exhibition catalogue, periodical, 1998, no.94, p.79-100. Rosenberg, Pierre, *From drawing to painting: Poussin, Watteau, Fragonard, Davis & Ingres*, exhibition catalogue, periodical, Princeton University Press, 2000. Milam, Jennifer, '*Playful constructions and Fragonard's swinging scenes*' in *Eighteenth-century studies*, exhibition catalogue, periodical, 2000, v.33, no. 4, summer, p.543-559. *Fragonard et le voyage en Italie, 1773-1774: les Bergeret, une famille de mécènes*, exhibition catalogue, periodical, Musée Louis-Senlecq, L'Isle-Adam, Somogy, Paris, 2001. Schroder, Anne L., '*Reassessing Fragonard's later years: the artist's nineteenth-century biographers, the Rococo and the French Revolution*' in *Art and Culture in the eighteenth century: new dimensions and multiple perspectives*, exhibition catalogue, periodical, London, 2001. Bailey, Colin B., *The age of Watteau, Chardin and Fragonard: masterpieces of French genre painting*, exhibition catalogue, periodical, Yale University Press, 2003.

MUSEUMS AND GALLERIES:

AMIENS (Mus. de Picardie): *Cradle* (c. 1762-1765) - ANGERS (MBA): *Coresus Sacrificing Himself to Save Callirhoe* (sketch); *Jupiter and Calisto* (c. 1755, oil on canvas); *Cephale and Procris* (c. 1755, oil on canvas); *Jupiter and Io* (c. 1763-1765, oil on canvas) - BALTIMORE (The Baltimore Museum of Art): *The Rest during the Flight into Egypt* - BARCELONA (Museo de Arte de Cataluna): *A Horseman in Spanish Costume Sitting next to a Fountain* - BESANÇON (MBA et d'Archéologie): *Young Couple* (oil on canvas); *Young Mother Holding her Child* (oil on canvas); *The Triumph of Venus* (1765-1770) - CHARTRES (MBA): *The Ford* (oil/paper/panel) - DETROIT (IA): *Harvester; Grape Harvester; Shepherdess; Gardener* - GRASSE (Cathédrale): *Washing the Feet* (1755, oil on canvas) - GRASSE (Mus. Jean-Honoré-Fragonard): *Landscape with Washerwomen near a Pond where a Donkey stopped* (c. 1768, oil on canvas); *The Three Graces* (c. 1780-1785, oil on canvas); *Portrait of a Small Blond Boy* (c. 1780-1785, oil on canvas); *The Stair of Grasse* (oil on canvas) - HAMBURG (Kunsthalle): *The Philosopher* (c. 1767, oil on canvas) - LISBON (Museu Calouste Gulbenkian): *The Feast at Rambouillet* (c. 1768-1770, oil on canvas) - LONDON (NG): *Psyche showing her Sisters her Gifts from Cupid* (1753, oil on canvas) - LONDON (Wallace Collection): *Le Petit Parc* (c. 1762-1765, oil on canvas); *The Souvenir* (oil/panel); *The Fountain of Love* (c. 1784, oil on canvas); *Say Please* (c. 1780, oil on canvas); *A Boy as Pierrot* (c. 1785, oil on canvas); *The Swing* (1767, oil on canvas); *A Young Scholar* (c. 1775-1778, oil on canvas); *The Musical Contest* (c. 1754-1755, oil on canvas) - LOS ANGELES (County MA): *The Winter* (1755, oil on canvas) - LOS ANGELES (Getty Mus.): *The Fountain of Love* (c. 1785, oil on canvas) - LOS ANGELES (The Armand Hammer Foundation): *The Education of the Virgin* (c. 1775, oil/wood) - LUGANO (Collection Thyssen-Bornemosza): *The Bascule* - MUNICH (Alte Pinakothek): *Young Girl Making Her Dog Dance on Her Bed* (c. 1768, oil on canvas) - NEW HAVEN (AG, Yale University): *The Rest during the Flight to Egypt* (c. 1775, oil on canvas) - NEW YORK (Frick Collection): *The Pursuit; The Meeting; The Lover Crowned; Love Letters* (1773, four panels showing 'The Progress of Love'); *The Abandoned* (c. 1790, oil on canvas) - NEW YORK (Metropolitan Mus. of Art): *The Lost Forfeit - The Stolen Kiss* (1756-1761, oil on canvas); *The Cascade* (c. 1773, oil on canvas); *A Shaded Avenue* (c. 1773); *Italian Interior* (1761-1765, oil on canvas); *The Love Letter* (c. 1778, oil on canvas); *Young Woman Reading; The Two Sisters* (1770-1772, oil on canvas) - NEW YORK (Pierpont Morgan Library): *Young Woman Seated in a Garden* (study drawing) - NICE (Musée Chéret): *Old Man with White Hair* (c. 1769, oil on canvas) - PARIS (Banque de France): *The Party at St-Cloud* (1774, oil on canvas) - PARIS (École des Beaux-Arts): *Jeroboam Sacrificing for the Idols* (1752, oil on canvas, Prix de Rome) - PARIS (Hôtel Matignon): *Springtime* (1755, oil on canvas); *Summer* (1755, oil on canvas); *Autumn* (1755, oil on canvas) - PARIS (Louvre): *Grand Fountain in Tivoli* (1760-1761, oil on canvas); *The Cart Stuck in the Mud* (1759, oil on canvas); *A Man, a Young Woman, and a Child Sitting in front of the Fire, and an Old Man Sleeping* (c. 1765, oil on canvas); *The White Bull in the Stables* (1760-1765, oil on canvas); *Bevy of Lovers* (1765-1767); *M. de la Breteche* (1769, oil on canvas); *Portrait of Diderot* (c. 1769); *Le Feu aux Poudres* (c. 1763-1764, oil on canvas); *Portrait of a Singer Looking at her Music Book* (c. 1769, oil on canvas); *Coresus and Callirhoe* (1765, oil on canvas, entry piece for the Academie); *Portrait of the Abbot of St Non* (1769, oil on canvas); *Portrait of Presumed Jacques-André Naigeon* (1769, oil on canvas); *Portrait of Anne François Harcourt Duke of Beuvron* (c. 1769, oil on canvas); *Young Girls Throwing Roses (said: 'Les Petits Curieuses')* (c. 1775, oil on canvas); *The Adoration of the Shepherds* (c. 1776, oil on canvas); *The Bolt* (c. 1776, oil on canvas); *Cupboard* (etching); *Don Quixote* (pencil); *Reading* (wash); *The Music Lesson* (oil on canvas); *Bathers; The Stolen Shirt* (c. 1770, oil on canvas); *Inspiration; The Declaration of Love* (c. 1780-1785); *Child with Flowers* (c. 1780, oil on board); *The Sleeping Warrior* (c. 1780) - PARIS (Mus. du Petit Palais): *Shady Path* (1773-1774, wash); *Portrait of Jerome Lalande* (c. 1769, oil on canvas); *Vindicated Servant* (c. 1780, wash); *People from Rheims* (wash) - PARIS (Mus. Jacquemart-André): *Head of an Old Man with a Hat* (c. 1769, oil on canvas); *Model's Debut* (c. 1771); *Blonde Young Girl; Anacreon Crowned by Venus* - RICHMOND (Virginia MFA): *Landscape with Washerwomen* (c. 1765, oil on canvas) - ROCHEFORT: *Landscape* (watercolour) - ROUEN (MBA): *The Dream of Plutarch* (around 1780, oil on board) - ST LOUIS (The St Louis Art Museum): *The Washerwomen* (c. 1760) - ST PETERSBURG (Hermitage): *Farmer's Family* (1765, oil on canvas); *The Stolen Kiss* (c. 1785-1788, oil on canvas) - TOLDEO (Toledo Museum of Art): *Blind Mans Bluff* - TROYES (MBA): *Holy Family at Rest* (c. 1775, oil on canvas) - WASHINGTON DC (NGA): *Diana and Endymion* (c. 1753-1755, oil on canvas); *A Young Girl Reading* (c. 1776, oil on canvas); *Love as Folly* (c. 1775, oil on canvas, two oval paintings); *The Visit to the Nursery* (before 1784, oil on canvas); *A Game of Horse and Rider* (1767-1773, oil on canvas); *A Game of Hot Cockles* (1767-1773, oil on canvas); *The Swing* (oil on canvas); *Blindman's Buff* (probably c. 1765, oil on canvas) - WILLIAMSTOWN (Sterling and Francine Clarck Institute): *Le Guerrier* (*Portrait of a Man*) (c. 1769, oil on canvas).

AUCTION RECORDS:

Flautist, GBP 52. PARIS, 20 June 1826, *Don Quixote* (nineteen drawings) FRF 305. PARIS, 1-3 June 1865, *The Swing*, FRF 30,200; *The Souvenir*, FRF 35,000. PARIS, 6 - 9 March 1872, *A Game of Hot Cockles; Cast of a Horse* (collection) FRF 10,400. PARIS, 1876, *Torrent* (oil on paper, 10 x 14 ins / 25.5 x 35.5 cm) FRF 420. PARIS, 12-16 April 1880, *Don Quixote* (set of drawings) FRF 1,045. PARIS, 1881, *Nature Awakening*, FRF 15,900; *Visiting the Foster-Mother*, FRF 9,000; *Wooden Bridge*, FRF 6,600. PARIS, 1886, *Maternal Kisses*, FRF 8,600. PARIS, 14 June 1891, *Performers*, FRF 19,000. PARIS, 16-17 May 1892, *Spring*,

FRF 22,000; *Nature Awakening,* FRF 20,000; *Sacrifice of the Rose,* FRF 60,000; *Portrait of Diderot,* FRF 16,000. PARIS, 6-7 April 1893, *Reconciliation,* FRF 16,200. PARIS, 20 - 22 June 1898, *The Declaration of Love,* FRF 18,510; *Triumphant Love and Madness of Love,* FRF 12,200. PARIS, 1899, *The Letter,* FRF 44,500; *Love,* FRF 15,000. PARIS, 10-12 May 1900, *Sleeping Vigilance,* FRF 17,500. PARIS, 4 June 1903, *Winter,* FRF 8,900. PARIS, 4-5 Dec 1905, *Love Letter,* FRF 420,000; *Woman Reading,* FRF 182,000; *Portrait of a Little Girl,* FRF 3,800. NEW YORK, 23-24 Feb 1906, *Attempted Kiss,* USD 13,500. PARIS, 13 May 1907, *Happy Mother,* FRF 29,000. PARIS, 13-15 May 1907, *Useless Resistance,* FRF 62,100. LONDON, 23 Nov 1907, *Pastoral,* GBP 6. LONDON, 15 May 1908, *Portrait of a Woman,* GBP 89. LONDON, 28 May 1908, *Landscape* (sepia) GBP 200; *Park Entrance* (sepia) GBP 660. LONDON, 2 July 1909, *Lovers,* GBP 136. LONDON, 18 July 1910, *Dancer in a Garden,* GBP 378. PARIS, 25 Nov 1918, *Head of a Young Woman,* FRF 29,000. PARIS, 12-13 May 1919, *Suitor Surprised* (red chalk/pencil) FRF 27,000; *Futile Resistance* (bistre wash and watercolour) FRF 33,100. PARIS, 13 March 1920, *Happy Family* (wash) FRF 25,000. PARIS, 20 March 1920, *Landscape,* FRF 10,500. PARIS, 6-7 May 1920, *Annette and Lubin,* FRF 24,000. PARIS, 10-11 May 1920, *Shady Path* (pen and sepia wash) FRF 143,600. PARIS, 31 May 1920, *Collection* (including 125 of Fragonard's counterproof etchings heightened with sepia) FRF 29,500. PARIS, 8-10 June 1920, *Coquette* (red chalk) FRF 32,100. PARIS, 21-22 June 1920, *Umbrella Pines at the Villa Pamphila in Rome* (sepia wash) FRF 20,000; *Portrait of a Woman* (wash) FRF 21,000; *Ferryboat* (wash) FRF 4,550; *Man Reading* (red chalk) FRF 3,600; *Conversation* (wash) FRF 1,800; *Ruins and Figures* (wash) FRF 13,100; *Study* (wash, after Lucas Giordano) FRF 1,810. PARIS, 3 July 1920, *Travelling on the Road from Savona to Genoa* (wash) FRF 34,050. LONDON, 24 Nov 1922, *Virtue* (drawing) GBP 283; *Child Playing with a Dog* (gouache) GBP 388; *Love Letter* (drawing) GBP 273. PARIS, 14-15 Dec 1922, *Lovers Surprised* (sepia wash) FRF 22,600. PARIS, 22 Nov 1923, *Nativity or Adoration of the Shepherds,* FRF 85,000; *Love Triumphant,* FRF 20,000. PARIS, 10 Dec 1923, *Cupboard* (chalk and bistre wash) FRF 8,100; *Scene from the Life of Jesus* (wash and pencil) FRF 3,100. LONDON, 14 Dec 1923, *Venus Sleeping,* GBP 997. PARIS, 22 Dec 1923, *Head of a Man* (graphite) FRF 1,100. PARIS, 28-29 Dec 1923, *Composition for 'Mad Roland'* (pencil and sepia) FRF 305. LONDON, 14 March 1924, *Old Woman,* GBP 50. PARIS, 19 March 1924, *Antique Arch* (red chalk) FRF 17,200. PARIS, 26 June 1924, *Night,* FRF 86,000; *Terrace of a Roman Villa, with Figures* (red chalk) FRF 36,500. LONDON, 30 June 1924, *Press; Lover* (two) GBP 31. PARIS, 17-18 Nov 1924, *Illustration for a Fable by La Fontaine* (drawing with sepia wash) FRF 3,000. PARIS, 25 Nov 1924, *Broken Strap* (black chalk and sepia wash) FRF 40,000; *Shepherd and Sheep* (sepia wash) FRF 42,000. PARIS, 22 Dec 1924, *Group of Women and Children* (graphite, black chalk, red chalk and watercolour wash) FRF 5,100. PARIS, 24 Dec 1924, *Wall in Ruins* (red chalk) FRF 2,500; *Crowning of Franklin* (bistre wash) FRF 38,000. LONDON, 16 Jan 1925, *Venus and Adonis,* GBP 25. PARIS, 26 Feb 1925, *Small Temple* (black chalk and wash, heightened with watercolour, attributed) FRF 2,300. PARIS, 7 March 1925, *Italian Peasant* (attributed) FRF 850. PARIS, 25 March 1925, *Portrait Presumed to Be of Aunt Rosalie* (red chalk) FRF 40,000. PARIS, 22 May 1925, *Happy Family,* FRF 721,000. LONDON, 22 May 1925, *Lover* (sepia) GBP 147. PARIS, 8 June 1925, *Confessional Husband* (sepia wash) FRF 19,100; *Old Woman Fanchon,* FRF 680,000; *Portrait of Suzanne Griois,* FRF 326,500. PARIS, 17-18 June 1925, *Terrace of the Villa Reale, in Naples* (sepia wash) FRF 275,000; *Shepherd* (drawing in gouache and pastel) FRF 27,200; *Surprise* (red chalk) FRF 39,200; *Farm* (pencil, black chalk, pen and wash) FRF 115,000; *The Sultana* (sepia wash) FRF 65,100; *Head of a Woman* (red chalk) FRF 7,700; *Young Italian Woman, Standing* (sepia wash) FRF 72,000; *Sancho Panza* (red chalk) FRF 13,000; *Pan and Syrinx,* FRF 218,000; *Philosopher,* FRF 415,000; *Approaching Storm,* FRF 70,000; *The Toilette of Venus,* FRF 40,500. PARIS, 26 June 1925, *Roman Countryside and Aqueduct* (black chalk) FRF 800. LONDON, 10 Dec 1925, *Vine; Shepherds* (two) GBP 42. PARIS, 11-12 Dec 1925, *Sketch of a Vase* (wash and pen) FRF 3,250. PARIS, 12 Dec 1925, *Virgin at the Crib* (study) FRF 2,000. LONDON, 18 Dec 1925, *Woman in Pink,* GBP 42. LONDON, 26 Feb 1926, *Two Women Sewing,* GBP 17. PARIS, 10-11 May 1926, *Stopping-Place in a Wood* (wash) FRF 21,000; *Shepherds and Animals on the Mountain* (wash and watercolour) FRF 7,400; *Consultation* (wash, attributed) FRF 16,300. PARIS, 27-28 May 1926, *Head of an Old Man,* FRF 67,000. LONDON, 3 June 1926, *Italian Landscape* (drawing) GBP 26. PARIS, 3-4 June 1926, *Sacrifice to the Rose,* FRF 200,000. PARIS, 29 Jan 1927, *Italian Landscape with Waterfall* (red chalk) FRF 12,550. PARIS, 11 May 1927, *Park Entrance* (red chalk) FRF 2,900. PARIS, 16 May 1927, *Visiting the Grandfather,* FRF 57,000. PARIS, 20 May 1927, *Ford* (red chalk) FRF 22,000. PARIS, 22-24 June 1927, *Bust of a Young Girl,* FRF 200,000. LONDON, 16 Dec 1927, *Holy Family and St John,* GBP 35; *Woman,* GBP 52. LONDON, 24 Feb 1928, *Boy,* GBP 63. PARIS, 17 May 1928, *Death of the Hermit* (drawing) FRF 31,000. PARIS, 21-22 May 1928, *Maternal Kisses, or Childhood Jealousies,* FRF 315,000. PARIS, 23 May 1928, *Footbridge* (black chalk) FRF 15,200; *Horse Riding* (black chalk) FRF 33,850. PARIS, 1 June 1928, *Visitation of the Virgin,* FRF 205,000. PARIS, 7-8 June 1928, *Ferryboat,* FRF 21,000. PARIS, 9 June 1928, *Jeroboam Making a Sacrifice to the Idols* (red chalk) FRF 6,500. LONDON, 15 June 1928, *Young Student,* GBP 1,470. LONDON, 22 March 1929, *Old Man,* GBP 94. PARIS, 13-15 May 1929, *Muse Crowning Bust of Franklin* (drawing) FRF 103,000; *Children at a Cage* (drawing) FRF 55,000; *Antique Statue* (drawing) FRF 28,000; *Main Path in the Parc St-Cloud* (drawing) FRF 340,000; *Staircase in the Park of an Italian Villa* (drawing) FRF 195,000; *Fountains* (drawing) FRF 295,000; *Poet's Inspiration* (drawing) FRF 160,000; *Park of an Italian Villa* (drawing) FRF 105,000; *Villa d'Este, in Tivoli, near Rome, Water Terrace* (drawing) FRF 64,000; *Portrait of Hubert Robert in Rome* (drawing) FRF 21,000; *Portrait of Mlle Gérard, Standing* (drawing) FRF 185,000; *Confidence, Portraits of Mme Fragonard and of Her Sister Marguerite Gérard* (drawing with sepia wash) FRF 560,000; *Consultation* (drawing) FRF 60,000; *Column of Marcus Aurelius and Colonna Square in Rome* (drawing with sepia wash) FRF 48,000; *Avaricious Woman - Gallant Swindler* (drawing with sepia wash) FRF 260,000; *Misunderstandings* (drawing with sepia wash) FRF 18,000; *Return of the Herd* (drawing with sepia wash) FRF 250,000. PARIS, 3-4 June 1929, *Danaë* (drawing) FRF 500,000. PARIS, 12 June 1929, *Cave of the Nymph Egeria,* FRF 8,500. LONDON, 14 June 1929, *Bathers,* GBP 577. LONDON, 26 June 1929, *Head of an Old Man,* GBP 60. PARIS, 26 June 1929, *Staircase in a Park,* FRF 25,000. NEW YORK, 27-28 March 1930, *Diana's Nymphs,* USD 1,600; *Venus and Cupid,* USD 425. NEW YORK, 11 Dec 1930, *Desired Moment; Family Scene* (drawing) USD 120. LONDON, 27 Feb 1931, *Venus, Cupid and a Satyr,* GBP 42. PARIS, 1 Dec 1932, *Adoration of the Shepherds* (sepia) FRF 107,000; *Visiting the Doctor* (sepia) FRF 136,000; *Donkey's Stable,* FRF 300,000. PARIS, 12 Dec 1932, *Venus and Psyche; Psyche and Her Sisters* (two drawings) FRF 9,800. PARIS, 27 March 1933, *Rising,* FRF 120,000. PARIS, 26 May 1933, *The Bolt* (attributed) FRF 67,500. LONDON, 7 Dec 1933, *Despatched Kiss,* GBP 34. PARIS, 8-9 May 1934, *Coquette* (red chalk) FRF 36,000; *Young Maid,* FRF 15,200. PARIS, 15 June 1934, *Happy Family,* FRF 600,000. LONDON, 29 June 1934, *Glass of Water,* GBP 168. LONDON, 6 July 1934, *Young Girl in Blue,* GBP 11. LONDON, 23 Nov 1934, *Woman in Black,* GBP 16. PARIS, 3 Dec 1934, *Rape of the Sabines* (sepia wash) FRF 15,000. LONDON, 12 Dec 1934, *Diana; Venus* (two) GBP 250. LONDON, 1 March 1935, *Head of a Young Girl,* GBP 178. PAR-

IS, 15 March 1935, *Settled Coquette,* FRF 28,000. LONDON, 8 April 1935, *The Toilette of Venus,* GBP 81. STOCKHOLM, 11-12 April 1935, *Composition,* SEK 6,000. LONDON, 27-29 May 1935, *Interior, with Woman Seated* (red chalk) GBP 265. LONDON, 5 July 1935, *Lovers,* GBP 13. LONDON, 4 Dec 1935, *Bull,* GBP 1,100; *Beggar's Dream,* GBP 540; *The Sultana,* GBP 780; *My Shirt is Burning,* GBP 440; *Park in Italy,* GBP 260; *Children in a Cowshed,* GBP 95; *Wooded Landscape,* GBP 98. PARIS, 14 Dec 1935, *Blind Man's Buff* (drawing in black chalk and sepia wash) FRF 171,000; *Orange Tree Overturned* (pen drawing and bistre wash with watercolour) FRF 90,000. PARIS, 17 Dec 1935, *Misunderstandings* (sepia wash, fairytale by La Fontaine) FRF 12,000. PARIS, 14 May 1936, *Useless Resistance* (sepia wash) FRF 40,000; *Old Oak Tree* (red chalk) FRF 15,500; *Caprarola, Palace and Terraces* (black chalk) FRF 3,300. PARIS, 23 June 1936, *Waterfall* (red chalk) FRF 5,000; *Fountain,* FRF 18,000. LONDON, 11 Nov 1936, *Classical Subject,* GBP 11. PARIS, 17 Nov 1936, *Two Women Captured by Robbers are Led into Their Underground Den* (sepia wash) FRF 4,500; *Woman Captured by Brigands and Taken to the Chief of the Band* (sepia wash) FRF 4,500. PARIS, 30 Nov 1936, *Stone Basin* (sepia wash) FRF 20,000; *Dawn,* FRF 91,000. PARIS, 5 Dec 1936, *Italian Park* (red chalk) FRF 15,000. PARIS, 14 Dec 1936, *Study of Trees* (red chalk) FRF 11,100. LONDON, 15 Jan 1937, *Impetuous Lover,* GBP 350. LONDON, 28 May 1937, *Cradle,* GBP 299. PARIS, 25 June 1937, *Italian Park* (black chalk) FRF 5,100. LONDON, 2 July 1937, *Fortune Teller,* GBP 388. LONDON, 22 July 1937, *Corner of the Tivoli Gardens,* GBP 2,900. LONDON, 25 Feb 1938, *Venus Sleeping,* GBP 18. LONDON, 2 March 1938, *Gabrielle de Vergy,* GBP 90. LONDON, 18 May 1938, *Head of a Woman,* GBP 460. PARIS, 15 June 1938, *The Bolt* (red chalk and sepia wash) FRF 350,000; *Hubert Robert* (black chalk and sepia wash) FRF 11,100; *Footbridge* (pen and sepia wash) FRF 5,100. PARIS, 22 June 1938, *Beggar's Dream* (sepia wash) FRF 205,000. LONDON, 24 June 1938, *Gardens at the Villa d'Este,* GBP 399. PARIS, 26 Sept 1941, *Reward or He Won the Prize* (black chalk and Indian ink wash) FRF 215,000. PARIS, 20 Nov 1941, *Cake* (black chalk and bistre wash) FRF 180,000; *Death of Marie de Gonzague* (black chalk and bistre wash) FRF 123,000; *Staircase and Fountain of the Amphitheatre in the Villa d'Este Gardens in Tivoli* (red chalk, pen and bistre wash) FRF 415,000; *Young Woman Standing* (red chalk) FRF 32,000; *Portrait of a Man* (black chalk) FRF 125,000. PARIS, 19 Dec 1941, *Cavalcade* (black chalk and Indian ink wash, lightly heightened with watercolour) FRF 180,000. LONDON, 2 Oct 1942, *Inspiration* (drawing) GBP 78. PARIS, 12-13 Oct 1942, *Christ Appearing to the Apostles, in the Style of Ludovico Carracci* (black chalk) FRF 160,000. LONDON, 8 March 1944, *Portrait of a Woman,* GBP 78. LONDON, 31 March 1944, *Sleeping Nymph,* GBP 630. PARIS, 15 April 1944, *The Kiss,* FRF 9,800. LONDON, 9 June 1944, *Cinderella* (drawing) GBP 577. NEW YORK, 22 Nov 1944, *Farm Interior* (drawing) USD 85; *Noah's Family Going into the Ark* (drawing) USD 225. LONDON, 24-25 Nov 1944, *Mlle Marie Madeleine Guimard,* GBP 17,000; *Chevalier de Billaut,* GBP 12,000. PARIS, 20 Dec 1944, *Doughnuts* (sepia) FRF 400,000. PARIS, 8 Feb 1945, *La cuisine* (sepia wash) FRF 310,000; *Reward or He Won the Prize* (black chalk and Indian ink wash) FRF 350,000. PARIS, 12 Feb 1945, *Temple* (black chalk and bistre wash, attributed) FRF 19,500. PARIS, 16 March 1945, *Family Scene,* FRF 21,000. PARIS, 11 May 1945, *Young Brunette,* FRF 3,250,000; *Antiochus and Stratonicus,* FRF 220,000. PARIS, Oct 1945-July 1946, *Small Valley,* FRF 610,000; *Sacrifice of the Rose,* FRF 1,200,000; *Travelling on the Road from Savona to Genoa* (sepia) FRF 340,000. LONDON, 6 March 1946, *Cupid,* GBP 640. PARIS, 18 Dec 1946, *Gardens of the Villa d'Este* (red chalk) FRF 160,000. PARIS, 13 Jan 1947, *Purposeful Flight,* FRF 16,500. LONDON, 14 Feb 1947, *Vulcan's Forge,* GBP 168. PARIS, 19 March 1947, *View of the Gardens of the Villa Falconieri at Frascati* (black chalk) FRF 152,000. PARIS, 4 June 1947, *Pan and Syrinx* (sepia wash, attributed) FRF 13,500. PARIS, 21 March 1952, *Don Quixote* (series of drawings) FRF 2,050,000. PARIS, 14 May 1952, *Young Girl with Dogs,* FRF 10,600,000. PARIS, 6 April 1957, *Clélie's Flight* (drawing) FRF 320,000. LONDON, 26 June 1957, *Bed,* GBP 2,400. LONDON, 20 Nov 1957, *Villa Aldobrandini* (red chalk) GBP 220. LONDON, 26 Feb 1958, *Park Landscape,* GBP 3,500. PARIS, 21 March 1958, *View of the Gardens at the Trianon* (red chalk) FRF 1,000,000. PARIS, 26 March 1958, *Somersault* (drawing in wash) FRF 800,000. PARIS, 16 May 1958, *Fountain* (sepia wash) FRF 170,000. NEW YORK, 6 Dec 1958, *Bull in the Roman Countryside,* USD 4,500. NEW YORK, 23 May 1959, *Two Loves,* USD 4,000. LONDON, 10 June 1959, *Philosopher,* GBP 13,000. PARIS, 23 June 1959, *Resting in the Forest* (red chalk) FRF 2,500,000. PARIS, 10 Dec 1959, *The Vow of Love* (pencil and bistre wash) FRF 2,800,000. LONDON, 27 April 1960, *Love Triumphant,* GBP 2,600. PARIS, 14 June 1960, *Hide-and-Seek,* FRF 150,000. LONDON, 22 June 1960, *Donkey's Stable,* GBP 5,500. PARIS, 4 March 1961, *Fragonard's Servant* (bistre wash on chalk) FRF 52,000. LONDON, 10 May 1961, *Sacrifice to the Minotaur* (black chalk, wash and watercolour) GBP 5,500. NEW YORK, 15 Nov 1961, *Woman Reading,* USD 875,000. LONDON, 27 Nov 1963, *La jardinière,* GBP 36,000. LONDON, 6 Dec 1967, *Venus Fastening Cupid's Wings,* GBP 34,500. VERSAILLES, 26 June 1968, *Inquisitive Child,* FRF 100, 000. LONDON, 9 July 1968, *Good Mother* (watercolour and gouache) GBP 5,000. LONDON, 26 March 1969, *Woman Reading,* GBP 33,000. PARIS, 25 Nov 1971, *Venus Awakening or Dawn,* FRF 550,000. LONDON, 8 Dec 1971, *Anne-François d'Harcourt, Duc de Beuvron,* GBP 340,000. LONDON, 7 July 1972, *Wooden Bridge,* Gns 65,000. NEW YORK, 6 Dec 1973, *Diana Resting,* USD 25,000. PARIS, 7 Dec 1973, *Portrait of Madame Griois,* FRF 332,000. LONDON, 12 Dec 1973, *Watering Place,* GBP 10,500. PARIS, 25 May 1976, *Beggar's Dream* (oil on canvas, 28 3/4 x 35 3/4 ins / 73 x 91 cm) FRF 2,300,000. PARIS, 23 June 1976, *Walk* (pencil and bistre wash, 6 3/4 x 9 1/4 ins / 17 x 23.2 cm) FRF 15,000. PARIS, 11 May 1977, *Cupboard* (etching) FRF 11,000. NEW YORK, 28 Oct 1977, *Happiness of the First Kiss* (oil on panel, 13 x 9 1/2 ins / 33 x 24 cm) USD 85,000. BERN, 9 June 1978, *Park* (c. 1765) CHF 3,000. LONDON, 1 Nov 1978, *Wooden Bridge* (oil on canvas, 24 1/2 x 33 ins / 62 x 84 cm) GBP 150,000. LONDON, 24 June 1980, *Cinderella, Fragonard's Servant* (1774, red chalk/paper, 9 1/2 x 8 1/4 ins / 24.1 x 20.9 cm) GBP 28,000. NEW YORK, 11 June 1981, *Torrent* (oil on paper, 10 x 14 ins / 25.5 x 35.5 cm) USD 20,000. MONTE CARLO, 14 Feb 1983, *Lock* (oil on panel, 10 1/4 x 12 3/4 ins / 26 x 32.5 cm) FRF 2,500,000. LONDON, 13 Dec 1984, *Bull Returning to the Cowshed* (black chalk, brown and grey wash, 10 x 16 ins / 25.6 x 40.4 cm) GBP 105,000. PARIS, 29 Nov 1985, *Portrait Presumed to be of Marguerite Gerard, Young Woman Seated, Supporting Her Forehead with Her Left Arm, Leaning on a Table* (1773-1780, red chalk, 12 3/4 x 9 ins / 32.2 x 23 cm) FRF 1,950,000. NEW YORK, 14 Jan 1987, *Gardens at the Villa d'Este* (gouache/parchment, 7 3/4 x 9 1/2 ins / 19.9 x 24.4 cm) USD 185,000. MONTE CARLO, 20 June 1987, *Watering Place* (oil on canvas, 20 1/4 x 24 3/4 ins / 51.5 x 63 cm) FRF 4,400,000. MONACO, 20 Feb 1988, *Canal* (ink and watercolour, 11 ins / 27 cm, 2 1/4 x 16 ins/6 x 39.7 cm) FRF 1,087,800; *Figures in a Landscape at Velletri* (black chalk, 14 1/4 x 11 ins / 36.5 x 28 cm) FRF 399,600. PARIS, 9 March 1988, *Waterfall* (with Faucigny-Lussinge stamp, 11 1/4 x 8 1/4 ins / 28.5 x 21 cm) FRF 105, 000. PARIS, 14 April 1988, *Old Oak Tree* (oil on panel, 9 x 6 3/4 ins / 22 x 17 cm) FRF 850,000. PARIS, 30 May 1988, *Happy Fecundity* (oil on canvas) FRF 8,000,000. PARIS, 31 May 1988, *Young Girl with Small Dogs* (oil on canvas, oval, 24 1/2 x 19 3/4 ins / 62 x 50.2 cm) FRF 2,400,000. STOCKHOLM, 15 Nov 1988, *Venus Witnessing the Death of Adonis* (oil, 62 1/2 x 38 1/2 ins / 159 x 98 cm) SEK 200,000. NEW YORK, 1 June 1989, *Holy Family Resting on the Course of the Flight to Egypt* (oil on canvas, oval, 75 x 87 ins / 190.5 x 221 cm) USD 352,000. LONDON, 5 July 1989, *Sapgo*

Inspired by Cupid (oil on canvas, oval, 24 1/4 x 21 ins / 61.5 x 52.5 cm) GBP 264,000. NEW YORK, 12 Jan 1990, *Coquette* (red chalk, 14 1/4 x 8 1/4 ins / 36.5 x 21 cm) USD 297,000. LONDON, 2 July 1990, *Bireno Leaves the Islands* (black chalk and wash, taken from Orlando Furioso, 15 1/2 x 10 1/2 ins / 39.5 x 26.8 cm) GBP 41,800. MONACO, 7 Dec 1990, *Reward* (oil on paper/panel, 10 1/4 x 13 1/2 ins / 26 x 34 cm) FRF 333,000; *Landscape with Cornfield and Hitched Wagon or the Harvesters Resting* (oil on canvas, 22 x 25 1/2 ins / 55 x 64.8 cm) FRF 1,276,500. PARIS, 12 Dec 1990, *Renaud in the Gardens of Armide* (black chalk and bistre wash, 13 3/4 x 18 ins / 35 x 46 cm) FRF 3,200,000. PARIS, 12 Dec 1990, *Renaud in the Gardens of Armide* (black chalk and bistre wash, 14 x 18 ins / 35.5 x 46 cm) FRF 3,200,000. NEW YORK, 8 Jan 1991, *Study of a Young Girl on a Donkey* (red chalk, 6 1/2 x 9 1/2 ins / 16.5 x 24 cm) USD 2,750. NEW YORK, 9 Jan 1991, *Departure of the Herd* (black chalk and brown wash, 5 x 7 1/2 ins / 11.8 x 19.3 cm) USD 20,900. NEW YORK, 22-23 March 1991, *Tower of Cards or Burnt Wig* (black chalk and wash, 8 1/2 x 12 1/4 ins / 21.6 x 31.2 cm) USD 35,200. NEW YORK, 31 May 1991, *Number* (oil on card, 11 1/2 x 15 1/4 ins / 29 x 39 cm) USD 93,500. MONACO, 21 June 1991, *Portrait of Young Girl Seated* (red chalk, 13 3/4 x 9 ins / 34.8 x 22.7 cm) FRF 555,000. PARIS, 28 Nov 1991, *Virgin with Child* (black chalk, 11 1/2 x 8 ins / 29.5 x 20.4 cm) FRF 18,000. NEW YORK, 15 Jan 1992, *Waterfall at the Villa Aldobrandi at Frascati* (red chalk, 14 x 18 1/2 ins / 35.4 x 47 cm) USD 110,000. LONDON, 15 April 1992, *Rest on the Flight into Egypt* (oil on canvas, oval, 75 x 87 ins / 190.5 x 221 cm) GBP 170,000. MONACO, 18-19 June 1992, *Visitation of the Virgin* (oil on canvas, 9 1/2 x 12 3/4 ins / 24.3 x 32.4 cm) FRF 888,000. LONDON, 6 July 1992, *Romulus Drawing the Boundaries of Rome* (black chalk, 7 3/4 x 11 ins / 19.7 x 27 cm) GBP 2,530. NEW YORK, 13 Jan 1993, *Garden of an Italian Villa with Gardener and Two Children* (brown wash on black chalk, 13 1/4 x 17 3/4 ins / 33.8 x 45.1 cm) USD 343,500. PARIS, 29 March 1994, *Temple in a Park* (red chalk, 12 3/4 x 14 1/2 ins / 32.4 x 37 cm) FRF 240,000. LONDON, 10 June 1994, *Shepherdess Sitting under a Tree with Sheep and Holding a Basket of Flowers near Ruins* (oil on canvas, 28 1/4 x 36 1/2 ins / 71.8 x 92.5 cm) GBP 287,500. PARIS, 14 Dec 1994, *Children Playing with a Cat* (oil/copper, diam. 7 1/4 ins / 18.6 cm) FRF 2,280,000. NEW YORK, 12 Jan 1995, *Brigands Discovering Orlando with Isabelle and Gabrina in Their Cave* (black chalk, brown and grey wash, extract from Orlando Furioso, 15 1/2 x 9 3/4 ins / 39.4 x 24.8 cm) USD 57,500. PARIS, 12 Dec 1995, *Two Young Women on a Bed Playing with a Small Dog: Rising* (oil on canvas, 29 1/4 x 23 1/4 ins / 74 x 59 cm) FRF 8,200,000. LONDON, 2 July 1996, *View of an Italian Garden with a Villa, Antique Statues, Fountain and Sarcophagus* (red and black chalk, 9 1/4 x 13 1/4 ins / 23.8 x 33.4 cm) GBP 54,300. PARIS, 25 April 1997, *Agar Consoled by an Angel in the Style of Castiglioni and Three Heads of Old Men in the Style of Sebastiano Ricci* (black chalk, 11 1/2 x 7 3/4 ins / 29 x 20 cm) FRF 70,000. PARIS, 2 June 1997, *Medallion with a Portrait of Mme de la Girennerie* (black chalk and red chalk, diam. 5 ins / 12.5 cm) FRF 27,000. PARIS, 18 June 1997, *Group on a Hillock with a Figure Climbing on to a Ladder in the Foreground* (black chalk and brown wash, 17 3/4 ins / 45 cm, 1 1/2 x 11 1/2 ins/4 x 29 cm) FRF 25,000. LONDON, 2 July 1997, *Atalanta is Conquered by Bradamanta ('Orlando Furioso' [Mad Roland'], Ariosto, IV, 25-26)* (black chalk and brown wash, 14 1/4 x 9 1/2 ins / 36.4 x 23.9 cm) GBP 17,250. PARIS, 16 Dec 1997, *Don Quixote's Meal at the Inn; Don Quixote Imploring the Hotelier to Arm Him as a Knight; Don Quixote is Armed as a Knight by the Hotelier and Two Prostitutes; Don Quixote's Annoying Incident with the Yang Muleteers; Ladies from the Coach Pleading with Don Quixote to Spare the Man from Vizcaya; Don Quixote Carried Home Bruised by Blows following his Adventure with the White Penitents; La cuisine* (black chalk, wash, bistre, seven preparatory drawings for the illustrations of Don Quixote, 16 1/2 x 11 ins / 42 x 28 cm env.) FRF 1,380,000. NEW YORK, 28 Jan 1998, *Coquette, Study of a Young Woman, Standing, Almost in Profile, with Head Raised* (red chalk/notes in black chalk, 14 3/4 x 9 3/4 ins / 37.5 x 24.7 cm) USD 310,500. PARIS, 4 March 1998, *St Peter, prostrate* (c. 1768-1770, oil on canvas) FRF 8,000,000. NEW YORK, 29 Jan 1999, *The Fountain of Love* (oil on canvas, 24 x 20 ins / 62 x 51 cm) USD 2,000,000. LONDON, 17 Dec 1999, *The Bolt* (oil on panel, 10 x 13 ins / 26 x 32 cm) GBP 4,800,000. LONDON, 13 Dec 2000, *Girl Playing with a Dog and a Cat, said to be Marie Madeleine Colombe* (oil on canvas) GBP 2,300,000. LONDON, 13 Dec 2000, *Girl Holding a Dove, said to be a Portrait of Marie Catherine Colombe* (oil on canvas) GBP 3,200,000. NEW YORK, 24 Jan 2001, *Le Montreur de marionnettes (Puppeteer)* (black chalk and brown wash, 11 x 15 ins / 27 x 39 cm) USD 130,000. NEW YORK, 24 Jan 2001, *Visitation* (oil on panel, 9 x 13 ins / 24 x 33 cm) USD 280,000. PARIS, 21 March 2002, *The Dwarf Bajocco between Two Posts* (1774, chalk, brush, ink wash, 14 x 11 ins / 36 x 28 cm) EUR 120,000. LONDON, 9 July 2002, *Study of Trees at the Edge of Wood, with Figures Resting in the Shade* (red chalk, 12 x 18 ins / 31 x 46 cm) GBP 110,000. NEW YORK, 24 Jan 2003, *Venus Crowning Cupid* (oil on canvas, 29 x 50 ins / 73 x 127 cm) USD 240,000. PARIS, 30 Sept 2003, *Plutarch's Dream* (chalk, brush, ink wash, 14 x 19 ins / 35 x 49 cm) EUR 160,000. NEW YORK, 27 May 2004, *Watering Place* (oil on canvas, 20 x 25 ins / 51 x 63 cm) USD 900,000. PARIS, 23 June 2004, *Etude d'Amours* (oil on canvas, oval, 18 x 11 ins / 46 x 27 cm) EUR 32,000.

FRAGONARD, Théophile Évariste Hippolyte
French, 19th century.
Born 2 February 1806, in Paris; died 1876, in Neuilly-sur-Seine.
Painter, lithographer, draughtsman, illustrator. History painting, portraits, genre scenes, landscapes.

Théophile was the son and pupil of Alexandre Évariste Fragonard and grandson of Jean-Honoré Fragonard. He was attached for many years to the Royal Porcelain Works at Sèvres. Fragonard was awarded a gold medal in 1850 and was made a Chevalier of the Légion d'Honneur in 1869. He was a leading illustrator for the journal *L'Illustration (Illustration)* and also illustrated several literary works, including *1001 Nights, Contes et Nouvelles de La Fontaine (La Fontaine's Fables)*, Sir Walter Scott's *Quentin Durward* and Chateaubriand's *Le Génie du Christianisme (Genius of Christianity)*. He also produced a large number of lithographs.

MUSEUMS AND GALLERIES:
AMIENS: *Undulating Landscape* - BAGNÈRES-DE-BIGORRE: *Angelo, Tyrant of Padua* - ROUEN (MBA): *Portraits of the Artist's Mother and Father; Plutarch's Dream* - VERSAILLES: *Ptolemy's Seat.*

AUCTION RECORDS:
PARIS, 1875, *Rendezvous* (fan) FRF 320; *Serenade* (fan) FRF 1,160; *Life at the Chateau* (fan) FRF 1,200. PARIS, 27 April 1921, *Cupids Readying their Arrows; Tarnished Cupids* (two watercolours) FRF 810. PARIS, 29 April 1921, *Rustic Embrace; Dancing to the Guitar* (two watercolours) FRF 300. PARIS, 18 Nov 1926, *Corpus Christi* (watercolour) FRF 730. PARIS, 3 Dec 1927, *Courtly Scene,* FRF 700. PARIS, 20 March 1941, *Four Books of Notes and Sketches,* FRF 650. PARIS, 30 May 1941, *Sketchbook* (studies in pencil and wash) FRF 300. PARIS, 22 July 1942, *Clemency of Louis XI* (watercolour) FRF 500. PARIS, 26 Feb 1943, *Fear* (pencil and sepia wash/paper) FRF 680. PARIS, 6 June 1945, *Impassioned Pleading* (watercolour) FRF 7,700. VERSAILLES, 16 June 1982, *Children at Play* (watercolour and black chalk, 11 1/2 x 38 1/2 ins / 29 x 98 cm) FRF 3,400. MONTE CARLO, 5 March 1984, *Scene from the Life of Henry IV* (oil on canvas, 21 x 14 1/4 ins / 52.5 x 36.5 cm) FRF 100,000. VERSAILLES, 22 June 1986, *Portrait of a Young Man* (oil on canvas, 16 1/4 x 13 ins / 41 x 33 cm) FRF 4,800. PARIS, 22 March 1991, *Unrequited Love* (watercolour and lead pencil, 9 1/2 x 7 1/4 ins / 24 x 18.5 cm) FRF 16,000. LOKEREN, 10 Oct

1992, *Drum* (1833, oil on canvas, 35 1/2 x 46 ins / 90 x 116 cm) BEF 300,000. PARIS, 24 March 1997, *Riot* (oil on canvas, 23 1/4 x 19 1/4 ins / 59 x 49 cm) FRF 9,000. PARIS, 15 Dec 1997, *Courtly Scene* (oil on canvas, 9 1/4 x 12 1/2 ins / 23.8 x 32 cm) FRF 9,500. LOKEREN, 8 Dec 2001, *The Drum* (1833, oil on canvas, 35 x 46 ins / 90 x 116 cm) BEF 330,000.

FRAGOSO, João
Portuguese, 20th century.
Born 1913, in Caldas da Rainha.
Painter.
João Fragoso taught at the fine arts academy in Lisbon and received many awards. His classical, traditional style of painting is characteristic of a certain kind of official art in Portugal. He exhibited at the Musée Rodin in Paris in 1966.

FRAGOVSKY, Nole
Macedonian, 20th century.
Born 1939, in Galicnik.
Painter.
Fragovski studied at the art school in Belgrade and has been exhibiting since 1968 in the former Yugoslavia, notably in Skopje and Belgrade. His paintings have an Expressionist resonance and are often laden with a distinctly committed symbolism.

FRAGUIER, Gabriel Auguste Claire Armand de (Comte)
French, 19th century.
Born 18 November 1803, in Besançon; died 31 July 1873, in Besançon.
Painter.
Fraguier studied under Camille Roqueplan and exhibited at the Paris Salon from 1833 to 1859. Known for his *Kitchen Interior, Merchant of Syra* and *Memento of Syra*.
MUSEUMS AND GALLERIES:
BESANÇON: *Fruit and Flowers.*

FRAHIER, Thérèse
French, 20th century.
Born in the Aube.
Painter.
Thérèse Frahier exhibited in Paris from 1933 at the Salon des Artistes Français. From 1944 she exhibited at the Salon of the Société Nationale des Beaux-Arts.

FRAHM, Christian Daniel
German, 18th century.
Born in Wismar; died 1778, in Rome.
Painter. Religious subjects.
Frahm was stabbed in Rome.
MUSEUMS AND GALLERIES:
KASSEL: *Holy Family.*

FRAÏCHE DE BRENEST, Guillaume
French, 18th century.
Born to a family originally from Tarbes.
Painter.
Guillaume Fraïche was reportedly in Angers in 1784 and 1785. He may be the same artist as the painter Fraiche de Brenet who visited La Rochelle in 1788 as 'painter to the court of Spain' and produced some works there.

FRAICHOT, Claude
French, 18th century.
Born 18th century, in Morteau.
Painter.
Claude Fraichot was the brother of Pierre Fraichot.

FRAICHOT, Claude Joseph I
French, 18th century.
Active in Besançon.
Sculptor.
Claude Fraichot was the brother of Jean Fraichot.

FRAICHOT, Claude Joseph II
French, 18th century.
Born 22 March 1732, in Besançon; died c. 1803, in Besançon.
Painter, draughtsman. Portraits, genre scenes, still-lifes.
Member of a family of artists from Besançon and Morteau, Claude Joseph Fraichot was the son of Jean Fraichot. He taught drawing at the École de Peinture in Besançon. He is known principally for his still-lifes.
AUCTION RECORDS:
VERSAILLES, 26 June 1985, *Still-life with Fish* (oil on canvas, 26 1/2 x 36 1/4 ins / 67 x 92 cm) FRF 34,000. PARIS, 27 June 1989, *Kitchen Table; Meal* (oil on canvas, 29 x 40 1/2 ins / 73.5 x 103 cm) FRF 60,000. MILAN, 13 Dec 1989, *Cuisine* (oil on canvas, 32 3/4 x 42 1/4 ins / 83.5 x 107 cm) ITL 40,000,000. PARIS, 14 Feb 1990, *Still-life with a Bottle of Wine, Cheese and Cherries* (oil on canvas, 17 3/4 x 21 ins / 45 x 52.5 cm) FRF 38,000. NEW YORK, Jan 1998, *Still-life with Artichokes and Crayfish on a Porcelain Plate* (oil on canvas, 22 x 41 3/4 ins / 55.9 x 106.1 cm) USD 9,200. NEW YORK, 28 Jan 1999, *Still-life, Bowl of Salad, Bread, Cherries, Poultry* (oil on canvas, 22 x 28 ins / 56 x 70 cm) USD 20,000. LONDON, 16 Dec 1999, *Still-life of Ham with Pie, Radishes, Pewter Salver and Fruit* (oil on canvas, 37 x 44 ins / 95 x 111 cm) GBP 12,500. NEW YORK, 26 Oct 2001, *Pears and Bread on Plates, with Bottle of Wine and Glasses on a Stone Ledge* (oil on canvas, 26 x 32 ins / 65 x 82 cm) USD 12,000. PARIS, 10 June 2003, *Still-life with Brioches, Raspberries and Bottle of Wine* (oil on canvas, 22 x 27 ins / 55 x 69 cm) EUR 16,500. VIENNA, 1 Oct 2003, *Still-life with Vegetables and Jar* (oil on canvas, 26 x 32 ins / 65 x 81 cm) EUR 4,000.

FRAICHOT, Jean
French, 18th century.
Born in Morteau (Doubs); died before 1758.
Painter.
Jean Fraichot became a burgher of Besançon in 1747.

FRAICHOT, Jean Baptiste
French, 18th century.
Born 17 October 1727, in Besançon.
Painter.
Jean Fraichot was the son of Pierre Antoine Fraichot.

FRAICHOT, Jean Pierre
French, 18th century.
Active in Besançon.
Painter.
In 1769, Jean Fraichot started work on a contract to produce a picture of *Our Lady of the Rosary* for the church at Nancray (Doubs).

FRAICHOT, Pierre
French, 18th century.
Born in Morteau (Doubs); died 14 January 1713, in Besançon.
Painter. Portraits.
A portrait by Pierre Fraichot, dated 1675, is preserved in Besançon (Doubs). There are also some of his paintings at the Hospital of the Holy Spirit in Besançon.
MUSEUMS AND GALLERIES:
BESANÇON: *Portrait* (1675).

FRAICHOT, Pierre Antoine
French, 18th century.
Born 1690, in Besançon; died c. 1763.
Painter. Still-lifes.
AUCTION RECORDS:
PARIS, 20 April 1988, *Still-life with Ham; Still-life with Fish* (oil on canvas, a pair, 23 1/2 x 29 1/4 ins / 60 x 74 cm) FRF 148,500. PARIS, 26 Oct 1992, *Still-life with Vegetables* (oil on canvas, 22 1/2 x 29 1/4 ins / 57 x 74 cm) FRF 34,000.

FRAIDEL, Alois
German, 19th century.
Fresco artist.

Fraidel painted ceiling frescoes in the churches of Obersulmetingen, Demmingen, Ummendorf and Grundsheim. He settled in Söflingen and occasionally designed lithographs.

FRAIKIN, Charles Auguste
Belgian, 19th century.
Born 14 June 1817, in Herenthals; died 1893, in Schaerbeek.
Sculptor. Statues, busts.

Charles Auguste Fraikin attended the academy in Antwerp and exhibited from 1846 onwards. He was a knight of the Ordre de Léopold (Order of Leopold) in 1848, officer in 1858, member of the royal academy of Belgium in 1847, a full member of the academic board in 1882, and a Chevalier de la Légion d'Honneur in 1878. A year later he exhibited at the Royal Academy, London.

MUSEUMS AND GALLERIES:
ANTWERP: *Mother of Moses* - BRUSSELS: *Venus and Amor* - YPRES: *Marie-Henriette, Queen of the Belgians* (two busts); *Léopold II* (two busts).

AUCTION RECORDS:
LOKEREN, 19 Oct 1985, *Woman with Dove* (brown-patinated bronze, h. 11 1/2 ins / 29.5 cm) BEF 45,000. BRUSSELS, 25 Jan 1999, *Young Girl* (white Carrara marble, h. 20 ins / 51 cm) BEF 63,000. STAUFEN, 4 May 2001, *Sculptress* (patinated bronze, h. 25 ins / 63 cm) DEM 3,500. LONDON, 2 Nov 2001, *Venus with a Dove* (1841, dark brown patinated bronze, h. 12 ins / 30 cm) GBP 2,800. LONDON, 21 April 2004, *Bust of the Water Fairy* (white marble, h. 24 ins / 62 cm) GBP 6,000.

FRAILE, Alfonso
Spanish, 20th century.
Born 1930, in Marchena (Andalusia); died 1988, in Madrid.
Painter. Figures.

Alfonso Fraile studied at the school of fine arts in Madrid and first exhibited in Madrid in 1957. From 1963 he received a number of awards: first prize for painting at the Exposición Nacional in Madrid (1963); Critics' first prize at the *Ateneo* in Madrid (1966); a gold medal at the national exhibition of the fine arts society of Madrid (1968); first national prize for fine arts (Madrid, 1988). He has exhibited regularly in Madrid and also abroad: in 1978 at FIAC (Foire Internationale d'Art Contemporain) in Paris; in 1980 at the Naviglio gallery in Milan; 1985-1986 at the national museum of contemporary art in Madrid, and also in Washington.

Fraile came under the influence of Tachisme and until the end of the 1960s; his work is in the tradition of the Paris School but also reveals a concern with composition. In 1975 he broke completely with this approach and began working on the human figure. He skilfully deconstructs his figures, as in the *Great Triptych* of 1977 which includes 143 figures. Mixing humour and irony he presents us with a universe tinged with the fantastical in which biomorphic and anthropomorphic forms develop often in the manner of Kandinsky or Miró.

BIBLIOGRAPHY:
Catálogo nacional de arte contemporáneo 1990-1991, Ibérico 2Mil, Barcelona, 1990-1991 (National Catalogue of Contemporary Art 1990-1991).

MUSEUMS AND GALLERIES:
BILBAO (MBA) - MADRID (Mus. Nacional Centro de Arte Reina Sofía) - SEVILLE (Centro Andaluz de Arte Contemporáneo) - TOLEDO (MAC).

AUCTION RECORDS:
MADRID, 13 Dec 1990, *Authorised Assembly* (1976, oil on canvas, 47 1/4 x 43 1/4 ins / 120 x 110 cm) ESP 2,240,000. MADRID, 28 Nov 1991, *120 Figures No. 7* (1978, mixed media/paper/panel, 51 1/4 x 43 1/4 ins / 130 x 110 cm) ESP 2,464,000. MADRID, 22 April 1999, *Portrait* (1985, acrylic and mixed media on paper, 79 x 51 ins / 200 x 130 cm) ESP 1,600,000. MADRID, 20 Dec 1999, *Two Dogs* (1979, mixed media on paper, 43 x 51 ins / 110 x 130 cm) ESP 1,400,000. MADRID, 28 Nov 2000, *323 figures, number 0* (1978, mixed media on board, 71 x 79 ins / 180 x 200 cm) ESP 3,000,000. MADRID, 19 Dec 2000, *Twenty-Five* (1986, mixed media on canvas, 79 x 61 ins / 200 x 155 cm) ESP 1,900,000. NORTH BETHESDA, 22 May 2001, *Composition - Mother Child* (oil on canvas, 35 x 28 ins / 90 x 70 cm) USD 4,200. MADRID, 17 Dec 2001, *Solitary* (1976, oil on canvas, 51 x 43 ins / 130 x 110 cm) EUR 16,530. MADRID, 21 May 2002, *P/A 2* (1986, mixed media on paper, 52 x 74 ins / 133 x 189 cm) EUR 12,000. MADRID, 17 Dec 2002, *Pinta Punto* (1980, mixed media on paper laid on board, 60 x 51 ins / 152 x 130 cm) EUR 10,000. MADRID, 27 May 2003, *In the Kitchen* (oil on canvas, 32 x 39 ins / 81 x 100 cm) EUR 14,000. MADRID, 16 Dec 2003, *Figures* (1981, mixed media on paper laid on board, 59 x 51 ins / 150 x 130 cm) EUR 14,000. MADRID, 6 Oct 2004, *Composition* (1987, mixed media and collage on paper laid on board, 87 x 68 ins / 220 x 172 cm) EUR 16,000.

FRAILE, María Julia
Spanish, 20th century.
Born in Cartagena.
Painter. Scenes with figures.

María Fraile paints pleasant scenes, attractive places with gardens, palm trees and boats on the sea and with people bustling about: children playing, parents and nannies, garden attendants and the like. She has taken part in many group exhibitions including the Salon International d'Art Naïf in Paris in 1989.

FRAILLION, Paul
French, 19th century.
Active in Paris.
Painter.

Fraillion was a member of the Société des Artistes Français from 1891.

FRAILONG, Pierre Jean Charles
French, 20th century.
Born 1886, in Châteauneuf; died 1961, in El-Biar (in Algiers).
Painter. Landscapes with figures.
Orientalism.
School of Algiers.

From 1923, Pierre Frailong exhibited in Paris at the Salon des Artistes Français, showing compositions inspired by Algeria. In 2003, as part of the 'Djazaïr, a Year of Algeria in France' event, his work was exhibited at the *Les Peintres de l'autre rive. Alger 1830-1930* (*Painters from the Other Shore. Algiers 1830-1930*) exhibition at the Musée de la Castre in Cannes. Also in 2003, his work was shown in the *L'École d'Alger* (*The School of Algiers*) exhibition at the Musée des Beaux-Arts in Bordeaux.

BIBLIOGRAPHY:
Barrucand, Victor, *L'Algérie et les Peintres orientalistes*, B. Arthaud éditeur, Grenoble, 1930. Vidal-Bué, Marion, *Les Peintres de l'autre rive. Alger 1830-1930*, exhibition catalogue, Musée de la Castre, Cannes, 2003. Cazenave, Elisabeth/Dalia, Mahammed-Orfali/Vidal-Bué, Marion, *L'École d'Alger*, exhibition catalogue, Musée des Beaux-Arts, Bordeaux, 2003.

MUSEUMS AND GALLERIES:
ALGIERS (Mus. National des Beaux-Arts): *Un hiver dans le Sahel* (*Winter in the Sahel*); *Place d'El-Biar* (*El-Biar Square*).

FRAIMAN, Philippe, or Freyman
Flemish, 17th century.
Active in Tournai.
Sculptor.

Flemish School.

In 1651 Philippe Fraiman carved the altar of Notre-Dame-du-Bon-Secours for the church of St-Brice in Tournai.

FRAIN DE LA GAULAYRIE, Christian

French, 20th century.

Born 6 November 1916, in St-Pol-de-Léon.

Painter (gouache), watercolourist, draughtsman, engraver, illustrator. Landscapes with figures, seascapes.

Christian Frain de la Gaulayrie studied at the École des Beaux-Arts in Rennes and at the École Nationale Supérieure des Arts Décoratifs in Paris. His preferred media are gouache and watercolour and his work is strongly influenced by the Impressionists, his preferred subjects being skies, seas and boats. He exhibited regularly in France, notably at the Salon de la Marine.

FRAINAIS D'ALBERT, Jacques Nicolas

French, 18th - 19th century.

Born 9 December 1763, in Alençon; died 28 December 1816, in Alençon.

Painter. Genre scenes, still-lifes, flowers.

Jacques Frainais d'Albert painted mainly still-lifes and his style is slightly reminiscent of Chardin.

MUSEUMS AND GALLERIES:

ALENÇON: *Last Day of Carnival; Dog Knocking Down a Cat; Bacchus.*

AUCTION RECORDS:

PARIS, 7 March 1923, *Vase of Flowers,* FRF 750. PARIS, 18 Dec 1981, *Little Boy on a Swing; Château in the Countryside* (two gouaches) FRF 12,000.

FRAINCRY, Anthoine de

French, 16th century.

Born to a family originally from Boulogne (Pas-de-Calais).

Painter.

Fraincry and R. le Carpentier executed some decorative paintings in the abbey of Notre-Dame in 1532 and 1533.

FRAINET, Jean David

Swiss, 18th century.

Born 3 November 1752, in Geneva; died 7 July 1788.

Enameller.

Frainet was a pupil of F. J. Malignon.

FRAIPONT, Georges

French, 19th - 20th century.

Born c. 1873, in Paris; died 24 November 1912.

Painter, engraver, illustrator.

Georges Fraipont was the son of the artist Gustave Fraipont and studied under Gérôme and L.-O. Merson. He produced some interesting drypoint pieces as well as numerous illustrations for works such as *La Seine à travers Paris* (*The Seine through Paris*) by Saint Juirs. He exhibited at the Salon des Artistes Français from 1901 and was made a member in 1905.

g. FRAIPONT

AUCTION RECORDS:

PARIS, 14 May 1943, *Woman with Wheelbarrow* (drawing and chalk) FRF 100. LONDON, 8 June 1983, *Place de la Concorde, Paris* (oil on canvas, 17 3/4 x 21 ins / 45 x 53.5 cm) GBP 2,000. DOUARNENEZ, 12 Aug 1983, *Market, Guimiliau Parish Enclosure* (watercolour and gouache, 14 1/2 x 20 3/4 ins / 37 x 53 cm) FRF 6,200. PARIS, 22 March 1993, *Paris - The Republic* (watercolour, 10 x 14 1/4 ins / 25.5 x 36.5 cm) FRF 19,000. PARIS, 4 June 1993, *Square at Lisieux* (oil on canvas, 29 1/2 x 23 1/2 ins / 75 x 60 cm) FRF 10,500.

FRAIPONT, Gustave

Belgian, 19th - 20th century.

Born 1849, in Brussels.

Active and naturalised in France.

Painter, watercolourist, engraver, illustrator, poster artist. Genre scenes, landscapes, landscapes with figures.

Gustave Fraipont was a pupil of Henri Hendrick and Henri de Hem. Resident in Paris, he exhibited in the Salon des Artistes Français in 1882 and subsequently from 1896 to 1910. In 1896 he was made a Chevalier de la Légion d'Honneur.

He painted views of Paris, Brittany, Belgium and Holland and executed a number of watercolour paintings, as well as several posters illustrating his own articles in newspapers and his works, such as *Paris Illustrated, The Art of Painting Animals* and *The Art of Sketching.*

MUSEUMS AND GALLERIES:

MONT-DE-MARSAN: *Storm in Bas-Sennois.*

AUCTION RECORDS:

PARIS, 29 Feb 1895, *Loft* (watercolour) FRF 56. LONDON, 23 April 1910, *Mont St-Michel* (watercolour) GBP 6. PARIS, 13 May 1976, *Church in Paris* (oil on canvas, 19 3/4 x 28 3/4 ins / 50 x 73 cm) FRF 4,000.

FRAISINGER, Caspar

German, 16th century.

Active in Ingolstadt (Bavaria) at the end of the 16th century.

Painter, engraver. History painting.

Fraisinger's works featured allegorical religious subjects.

AUCTION RECORDS:

PARIS, 1856, *Valley of the Aqueducts near Tivoli,* FRF 160.

FRAISSE, Édouard

French, 20th century.

Born 14 May 1880, in Beaune; died 13 July 1945, in Paris.

Sculptor, medallist. Sporting subjects.

Édouard Fraisse is known mainly for his compositions inspired by sport. He was a member of the Société des Artistes Français and the Société Nationale des Beaux-Arts; he also exhibited at the Salon d'Automne. He was made a Chevalier of the Légion d'Honneur in 1929 and was awarded a gold medal in 1937.

FRAISSE, J.

French.

Sculptor.

MUSEUMS AND GALLERIES:

PERPIGNAN: *A Branch of Laurel.*

FRAISSE, Jean Antoine

French, 18th century.

Active in Chantilly at the beginning of the 18th century.

Engraver (burin), painter.

FRALEY, Laurence K.

American, 20th century.

Born 17 May 1897, in Portland (Oregon).

Sculptor.

FRAMA, pseudonym of Maryan, Henrich

French (?), 20th century.

Draughtsman.

AUCTION RECORDS:

PARIS, 28 Oct 1990, *Untitled* (drawing heightened with colour, 24 x 18 1/2 ins / 61 x 47 cm) FRF 115,000. PARIS, 31 Oct 1990, *Homage* (1989, drawing in colouring pencil, 18 3/4 x 24 1/4 ins / 47.5 x 61.5 cm) FRF 110,000. PARIS, 14 Nov 1990, *Homage to Arthur Rimbaud* (1989, ink, 24 1/2 x 19 ins / 62 x 48 cm) FRF 40,000. PARIS, 18 Dec 1991, *Energy* (oil on canvas, 24 x 19 3/4 ins / 61 x 50 cm) FRF 59,000.

FRAMBOLUTI. See **FROMBOLUTI**

FRAMEGAUDUS
French, 9th century.
Miniaturist.

In Munich this artist painted a Carolingian Gospel Book that is now in the national library of the city. The Bibliothèque Nationale, Paris, possesses a Gospel Book of about 900 bearing his name.

MUSEUMS AND GALLERIES:
PARIS (BNF).

FRAMERY
Flemish School, 16th century.
Active in Tournai in 1541.
Painter.

This artist was the son and pupil of Loïs de Framery.

FRAMERY, Loïs de
Flemish School, 16th century.
Died before 1563.
Active in Tournai.
Painter.

According to Siret, Loïs de Framery was the pupil of Jean du Jonquoit and of Bernard (?) in Milan.

FRAMERY, Robin de
Flemish School, 16th century.
Active in Tournai from 1528 to 1546.
Painter.

Robin was a son and pupil of Loïs de Framery.

FRAMONT, Gilian
Dutch, 17th century.
Born 17th century, in Hoorn.
Painter.

Gilian Framont was a member of the Guild of St Luke in Dordrecht.

FRAMPTON, Christabel A. (Lady).
See **COCKERELL**

FRAMPTON, Edward
British, 19th century.
Born c. 1850.
Painter.

Edward Frampton studied and worked in London and exhibited at the Royal Academy from 1877 to 1895, showing chiefly sketches for paintings on glass for churches in London and abroad.

MUSEUMS AND GALLERIES:
CHESTER (Catholic Church of St John): three windows - DENVER (St John's Cathedral): ten windows - LONDON (St Margaret's Church): *Memory* (commemorative window for Admiral Blake).

FRAMPTON, Edward Reginald
British, 19th - 20th century.
Born 1872; died 1923, in Paris.
Painter (gouache), watercolourist. Figure compositions, religious subjects, landscapes.
Symbolism.

Edward Frampton was the son of a stained-glass artist and attended Brighton Grammar School, where he was a contemporary of Aubrey Beardsley. They continued their studies together at the Westminster School of Art. Frampton then began working with his father while making study trips to Italy and France. In his early career he painted mainly decorative murals and also decorated war memorials but was chiefly known for the easel paintings he exhibited regularly from 1894. Frampton's paintings took as their themes literary, religious and symbolist subjects. He later concentrated on landscapes of Sussex, Cumberland, the Channel Isles, Brittany and the Bernese Oberland. He died suddenly in Paris while on one of his trips to Austria and was buried at St-Germain. Frampton's knowledge of stained-glass work, the influence of the early Italian masters and of Puvis de Chavannes and Burne-Jones combined to give him a very personal style similar to that of the Pre-Raphaelites.

C Reginald Frampton

BIBLIOGRAPHY:
auction catalogue, Christie's, London, March 13, 1992.

MUSEUMS AND GALLERIES:
BRADFORD (Cartwright Hall AG): *A Madonna of Britanny* (1913, oil on canvas) - LIVERPOOL (Walker AG): *Our Lady of the Snows*.

AUCTION RECORDS:
LONDON, 18 June 1909, *St Cecilia*, GBP 31. PARIS, 15 Dec 1972, *The Annunciation*, Gns 4,500. LONDON, 14 June 1977, *Young Girl with Flowers* (1906, gouache heightened with gold, 12 1/4 x 8 1/4 ins / 31 x 21 cm) GBP 800. LONDON, 12 Dec 1978, *Bishopstone* (oil on canvas, 23 1/4 x 23 1/2 ins / 59 x 60 cm) GBP 3,800. LONDON, 15 June 1982, *Flora of the Fields* (tempera, 12 x 12 ins / 30.5 x 30.5 cm) GBP 2,000. LONDON, 21 June 1983, *A Maid of Bruges* (tempera, 21 x 17 3/4 ins / 53.5 x 45 cm) GBP 8,200. LONDON, 4 Nov 1983, *Love in the Alps* (oil on canvas, 30 x 36 ins / 76.2 x 91.5 cm) GBP 6,500. LONDON, 26 Nov 1985, *The Birth of Neptune* (oil on canvas, 46 x 65 3/4 ins / 117 x 167 cm) GBP 30,000. LONDON, 26 Nov 1986, *A Maid of Bruges* (tempera/card, 21 x 17 3/4 ins / 53.5 x 45 cm) GBP 15,000. LONDON, 13 March 1992, *'Stone Walls do Not a Prison Make, Nor Iron Bars a Cage'* (oil on canvas, 35 1/2 x 21 3/4 ins / 90.1 x 55.2 cm) GBP 33,000. LONDON, 5 March 1993, *Spring* (1911, watercolour and gouache, 13 1/2 x 15 1/2 ins / 34.3 x 39.4 cm) GBP 3,450. LONDON, 8-9 June 1993, *St Cecilia* (1905, oil on canvas, 45 1/4 x 49 1/2 ins / 115 x 125.5 cm) GBP 76,300. LONDON, 25 March 1994, *Study in Blue and Pink* (oil on card, 12 3/4 x 9 1/2 ins / 32.4 x 24.2 cm) GBP 1,840. LONDON, 10 March 1995, *Gothic Tower* (watercolour and gouache, 36 1/2 x 15 1/2 ins / 92.7 x 39.4 cm) GBP 10,350. LONDON, 6 June 1997, *Spring* (1911, watercolour and gouache heightened with gold, 13 1/2 x 15 1/2 ins / 34.3 x 39.4 cm) GBP 6,900. LONDON, 3 April 2001, *'Stone walls do not a prison make, nor iron bars a cage'* (oil on canvas, 35 x 22 ins / 90 x 55 cm) GBP 38,000. LONDON, 20 Feb 2003, *Maiden Holding Book and Flowers* (1901, oil on canvas, 23 x 8 ins / 58 x 21 cm) GBP 16,000. LONDON, 26 Nov 2003, *Angel of the Sea* (1906, oil on canvas, 48 x 27 ins / 122 x 69 cm) GBP 45,000.

FRAMPTON, George James (Sir)
British, 19th - 20th century.
Born 1860, in London; died 1928.
Sculptor. Busts, low reliefs.

George Frampton was an associate member of the Royal Academy and took part in its exhibitions from 1884. He received a commendation and the Grand Prix at the Expositions Universelles of 1889 and 1900.

MUSEUMS AND GALLERIES:
GLASGOW: *Sir J. D. Marwick* (marble bust); *Queen Victoria* (marble bust) - LIVERPOOL: *Mysteriarche* (bust, high relief) - LIVERPOOL (Walker AG): *My Thoughts are my Children* (1894, bronze) - LONDON (Guildhall AG): bust*Chaucer* (1902-1903, marble); *King George V* (1914, marble); *Queen Mary* (1914, marble) - LONDON (Kensington Gardens): *Peter Pan* - LONDON (National Portrait Gal.): *Sir George Frampton* (1894, pencil); casting, death mask*Sir Herbert Beerbohm Tree* (1918, plaster) - LONDON (Royal Academy of Arts): bust*Lamia* (1899-1900, bronze, ivory, opals, glass); competition piece-*Bust of the Marchioness of Granby* (1902, marble) - LONDON (Tate Collection): relief, with preparatory casting in plaster-

Charles Keene (1896, bronze) - VENICE (Mus. d'Arte Moderna): *The Belle Dame sans Merci* (bronze).

AUCTION RECORDS:

LONDON, 28 April 1982, *Enid the Fair* (c. 1907, bronze, h. 14 1/2 ins / 37 cm) GBP 600. LONDON, 30 Nov 1983, *Peter Pan* (1918, bronze, h. 18 1/4 ins / 46.5 cm) GBP 2,300. LONDON, 29 Jan 1987, *Peter Pan* (1915, bronze, h. 19 ins / 48 cm) GBP 9,000. LONDON, 21 Nov 1989, *Peter Pan* (1915, brown-patinated bronze/marble plinth, total height 20 3/4 ins / 53 cm) GBP 13,200. NEW YORK, 5 May 1999, *Peter Pan* (1913, green patinated bronze, h. 23 ins / 58 cm) USD 52,500. LONDON, 5 July 2000, *Bust of Enid the Fair* (1907, dark brown patinated bronze, h. 20 ins / 52 cm) GBP 9,000. LONDON, 14 Dec 2001, *Peter Pan* (1916, dark brown patinated bronze, h. 19 ins / 48 cm) GBP 48,000. LONDON, 9 July 2002, *Peter Pan* (1921, brown patinated bronze, h. 19 ins / 48 cm) GBP 36,000. OXFORD, 30 April 2003, *Bust of a Girl* (1907, dark brown patinated bronze, h. 21 ins / 53 cm) GBP 3,700. LONDON, 21 April 2004, *Peter Pan* (1915, brown-green patinated bronze, h. 20 ins / 52 cm) GBP 28,000.

FRAMPTON, Lola (Mrs)
Maiden name: Clark
British, 19th century.
Draughtswoman.

Lola Frampton was the wife of Edward Reginald Frampton.

FRAMPTON, Meredith George Vernon
British, 20th century.
Born 17 March 1894, in London; died 16 September 1984, in Mere, Wiltshire.
Painter. Portraits.

Son of the sculptor Sir George Frampton. Meredith Frampton attended Westminster School until 1910 and then studied at St John's Wood Art School. Between 1912 and 1915 he studied at the Royal Academy Schools, winning first prize and a silver medal for his painting *A Harvest Procession*. He was elected a member of the Art Worker's Guild in 1915, and between 1915 and 1918 he served in the Army. Frampton is known for his portraits which are consistently described as having been executed meticulously, with great precision and realism, but also variously as having an 'enigmatic' (Spalding), 'surreal' or even 'sinister' (Buckman) quality to them. By the time of World War II Frampton's eyesight began to fail him and he produced virtually no more paintings. He was associated in 1934 and elected as a member of the Royal Academy in 1942. In 1982 the Tate Gallery in London held a major retrospective of his work.

BIBLIOGRAPHY:

Chamot, Mary/Farr, Dennis/Butlin, Martin, *The Modern British Paintings, Drawings and Sculpture*, London, 1964. Morphet, Richard, *Meredith Frampton*, exhibition catalogue, Tate, London, 1982. Spalding, F., *20th century Painters and Sculptors*, Antique Collectors' Club, Woodbridge, 1990. Buckman, D., *The Dictionary of Artists in Britain Since 1945*, Art Dictionaries Ltd, Bristol, 1998.

MUSEUMS AND GALLERIES:

EDINBURGH (Scottish National Portrait Gallery): *Sir Charles Grant Robertson* (1941, oil on canvas) - LONDON (Art Worker's Guild): *C.F.A. Voysey* (1924, oil on canvas); *Gilbert Bayes* (1930, oil on canvas); *Sir Edwin Lutyens* (1935, oil on canvas) - LONDON (Imperial War Mus.): *Sir Ernest Gowers* (1943, oil on canvas) - LONDON (National Portrait Gal.): *Sir George Frampton* (1919, oil on canvas); other portraits - LONDON (Royal Academy of Arts): *Still-life* (1932, oil on canvas, competition piece) - LONDON (Tate Collection): *Nude with Flying Swans* (1919, tempera/wood); *Portrait of a Young Woman* (1935, oil on canvas); *Marguerite Kelsey* (1928, oil on canvas).

AUCTION RECORDS:

LONDON, 13 Nov 1985, *Portrait of Joseph Ivimey* (1924, oil on canvas, 47 1/4 x 37 ins / 120 x 94 cm) GBP 5,000. CONSTANCE, 23 June 2000, *Portrait of a Young Woman* (1938, oil on canvas, 25 x 17 ins / 63 x 43 cm) DEM 3,200.

FRAMPTON, Richard
British, 15th century.
Illuminator.

Frampton illuminated a book of official deeds relating to the duchy of Lancaster for King Henry V. He was probably also the artist who painted the illuminations in two volumes in the Record Office in London. Several of the initials contain portraits of Henry, Duke of Lancaster.

FRAMTON, Thomas
British, 15th century.
Painter.

FRAN-BARO, pseudonym of Baro Francisco
Spanish, 20th century.
Born 4 October 1926, in Valencia; died March 2000, in Paris.
Active in France from 1961.
Painter. Genre scenes, scenes with figures, seascapes, waterscapes, urban landscapes, harbour scenes, gardens. Murals.

Francisco Baro graduated from the Valencia school of fine arts. He painted genre and dance scenes but he is known primarily as a seascape painter and his work shows views of ports on the coasts of France. As a waterscape artist he also painted views of the Paris quays.

He participated in collective exhibitions including in France, Spain and the USA, receiving many awards. From 1975 to 1980 he was president of the Association of Spanish artists in France.

AUCTION RECORDS:

VERSAILLES, 28 March 1976, *Second-Hand Booksellers at Notre Dame* (oil on canvas, 21 1/4 x 25 1/2 ins / 54 x 65 cm) FRF 2,200. VERSAILLES, 28 June 1981, *Rehearsal* (oil on canvas, 23 1/2 x 28 3/4 ins / 60 x 73 cm) FRF 3,600. VERSAILLES, 18 March 1984, *First Dance Steps* (oil on canvas, 25 1/2 x 32 ins / 65 x 81 cm) FRF 5,100. VERSAILLES, 13 Dec 1987, *Honfleur, La Lieutenance* (oil on canvas, 23 1/2 x 28 3/4 ins / 60 x 73 cm) FRF 13,000. PARIS, 23 June 1988, *Paris - The Seine and Notre Dame* (1979, oil on canvas, 21 1/4 x 25 1/2 ins / 54 x 65 cm) FRF 16,000. VERSAILLES, 25 Sept 1988, *Boats in Port, Lesconil* (oil on canvas, 23 1/2 x 28 3/4 ins / 60 x 73 cm) FRF 16,000. VERSAILLES, 6 Nov 1988, *Paris, the Seine, Notre Dame and the Quays* (oil on canvas, 23 1/2 x 28 3/4 ins / 60 x 73 cm) FRF 25,000. VERSAILLES, 18 Dec 1988, *The Seine at Issy-les-Moulineaux* (oil on canvas, 23 1/2 x 28 3/4 ins / 60 x 73 cm) FRF 16,000. VERSAILLES, 29 Jan 1989, *Haliguen Port, Quiberon Peninsula* (21 1/4 x 25 1/2 ins / 54 x 65 cm) FRF 13,600. PARIS, 19 March 1989, *Sailing Ships at Menton* (oil on canvas, 23 1/2 x 28 3/4 ins / 60 x 73 cm) FRF 23,000. PARIS, 19 June 1989, *Notre Dame Quays* (oil on canvas, 19 3/4 x 24 ins / 50 x 61 cm) FRF 16,500. PARIS, 11 Oct 1989, *Barges at the Pont Neuf* (oil on canvas, 18 x 22 ins / 46 x 55 cm) FRF 16,000. LE TOUQUET, 12 Nov 1989, *Banks of the Seine in the Cité* (oil on canvas, 18 x 22 ins / 46 x 55 cm) FRF 10,000. PARIS, 20 June 1990, *Terrace in Honfleur* (oil on panel, 13 x 16 1/4 ins / 33 x 41 cm) FRF 18,500. VERSAILLES, 8 July 1990, *Paris - Pont St Michel* (oil on canvas, 15 x 18 ins / 38 x 46 cm) FRF 10,500. METZ, 14 Oct 1990, *La Lieutenance and the Honfleur Basin* (oil on canvas, 19 3/4 x 25 1/2 ins / 50 x 65 cm) FRF 22,500. CALAIS, 20 Oct 1991, *The Grand Canal in Venice* (oil on canvas, 19 3/4 x 25 1/2 ins / 50 x 65 cm) FRF 20,000. NEUILLY, 23 Feb 1992, *The Outer Harbour, Honfleur* (oil on canvas, 23 1/2 x 28 3/4 ins / 60 x 73 cm) FRF

28,000. LE TOUQUET, 8 Nov 1992, *Rue Mouffetard Market* (oil on canvas, 23½ x 28¾ ins / 60 x 73 cm) FRF 12,000. PARIS, 26 Oct 1993, *Autumn on the St Martin Canal* (oil on canvas, 23½ x 28¾ ins / 60 x 73 cm) FRF 23,000. PARIS, 20 Nov 1994, *The Marie Bridge* (oil on canvas, 23½ x 28¾ ins / 60 x 73 cm) FRF 17,000. LE TOUQUET, 21 May 1995, *Venice* (oil on canvas, 19¾ x 25½ ins / 50 x 65 cm) FRF 14,000. NEUILLY, 27 Nov 1997, *Luxembourg Gardens*.

FRANA, Franciscus
Bohemian School, 15th century.
Active in Prague.
Illuminator.

Franciscus Frana may be the same artist as Frana de Brunna, who is recorded as living in Prague in 1370, or Franciscus Franek, who is recorded as being a painter in Prague from 1378 to 1414.

FRANC, Désiré Fleury
French, 20th century.
Born 3 July 1888, in Marseilles.
Painter.

Désiré Franc exhibited in Paris at the Salon des Artistes Français. He enjoyed a certain regional fame.

FRANC, Jhérosme
French, 16th century.
Active in Paris in 1593.
Painter, sculptor.

FRANC, Léo
French, 20th century.
Active in Marseilles.
Painter.

FRANC, Pierre
French, 20th century.
Born in Fontenay-aux-Roses.
Painter. Flowers.

Pierre Franc exhibited at the Salon des Indépendants from 1909.

FRANC-BELT
Flemish, 17th century.
Painter.
Flemish School.

A tabernacle sculpted in painted wood and signed *Franc-Belt* is to be found in the church of Ettelgheim, as well as an oil painting representing the *Assumption* in the church of Schoore (near Ostend).

FRANC-LAMY. See **LAMY Pierre Désiré Eugène Franc**

FRANCA
French, 20th century.
Painter. Landscapes.

Franca painted landscapes of Italy and Morocco, where she also exhibited.

FRANCA, Antonio della. See **ANTONIO DELLA FRANCA**

FRANÇAIS, Anne
French, 20th century.
Born 30 May 1909, in Châtenois; died 1995, in Paris.
Painter, watercolourist, pastellist, illustrator. Nudes, portraits, interiors, landscapes, architectural views, seascapes. Posters, stage sets.

Anne Français was self-trained, notably in the free studios of the Grande Chaumière academy in Paris. She lived in Paris, in the Lyons region and on the Côte d'Azur. After 1950 she created what she called 'ionist' painting, which was characterised by hatching. She also published an illustrated book on the stately houses of the Blois region and became involved in numerous architectural projects. Several of her works were purchased by the State, and by the Ville de Paris.

In 1933 she exhibited a pastel *Nude* at the Salon des Artistes Français in Paris and in 1946 she exhibited at the Salon des Tuileries, also in Paris. She held solo exhibitions of her work in Lyons in 1943 and in Paris in 1945, where she showed female nudes and portraits of actors, notably of Fernandel and François Périer. She went on to exhibit at other exhibitions, including: the Galerie La Boétie, Paris in 1951; the Galerie St-Placide, Paris in 1967 and 1968; and the Galerie Jean-Paul Villain, Paris in 1987, 1990 and 1991.

BIBLIOGRAPHY:
Français, Anne, *Un beau jour à Menars*, Hachette, Paris, 1964. Perreau, Jean, *Anne Français*, catalogue, Gal. Jean-Paul Villain, Paris, 2000.

MUSEUMS AND GALLERIES:
CANNES (Mus. de la Castre) - ÉPINAL (Mus. départemental d'Art ancien et contemporain): *Le Petit Gouffre de Castelmeur* (1964) - MONACO (Mus.) - PARIS (MAMVP) - PARIS (MNAM-CCI) - TOULON (MA).

AUCTION RECORDS:
PARIS, 7-8 Dec 1987, *La Danse des Voiles sur planche* (oil on canvas, 15 x 18 ins / 38 x 46 cm) FRF 4,800; *The White Moulin Rouge through the Poplars; Village Belltower* (two oils on canvas, 19¾ x 25½ ins / 50 x 65 cm) FRF 12,000. PARIS, 30 May 1988, *Two Boats with White Sails for Pyrotechnics* (1970, oil on paper remounted/canvas) FRF 6,500. PARIS, 31 Jan 1990, *Calvados* (oil on canvas, 24 x 19¾ ins / 61 x 50 cm) FRF 14,800. VERSAILLES, 10 June 2001, *Hello to the Old Port* (oil on canvas, 26 x 20 ins / 65 x 50 cm) FRF 11,000. LE HAVRE, 25 Nov 2001, *People in the Sea, Cannes* (oil on canvas, 29 x 24 ins / 73 x 60 cm) FRF 14,000. LE HAVRE, 21 April 2002, *Paris, Place Joffrin* (oil on paper on canvas, 24 x 29 ins / 60 x 73 cm) EUR 3,500. LE HAVRE, 24 Nov 2002, *Cannes* (oil on canvas, 26 x 20 ins / 65 x 50 cm) EUR 1,900. LE HAVRE, 23 Feb 2003, *Le Triomphe at the Cafe des Champs Elysees* (oil on canvas, 21 x 26 ins / 54 x 65 cm) EUR 2,700. LE HAVRE, 11 Nov 2003, *Douarnenez* (oil on canvas, 51 x 39 ins / 130 x 98 cm) EUR 5,000. LE HAVRE, 7 March 2004, *Sunbathing* (oil on canvas, 24 x 36 ins / 60 x 91 cm) EUR 3,000.

FRANÇAIS, François Louis
French, 19th century.
Born 17 November 1814, in Plombières (Vosges); died 1897, in Paris.
Painter (gouache), watercolourist, pastellist, draughtsman. Portraits, landscapes with figures.

François Français came to Paris at the age of fifteen years and trained initially as a librarian. He took up drawing and produced a number of woodcut engravings and lithographs. He requested advice from Corot, who - typically - welcomed the young man and encouraged him, subsequently arranging for him to visit Italy. Français also pursued his studies under the eye of Jean Gigoux. He made his Paris Salon début in 1837 with a composition entitled *Willow Song*, a landscape with figures painted in by Baron. In 1846, he asked Meissonier to help him with his landscape entitled *Park of St-Cloud*. He continued to exhibit, submitting work which was on a par with that produced by many who had enjoyed formal (classical) training. His enthusiasm found favour with the juries, which awarded him a bronze medal in 1841 and Exposition Universelle gold medals in 1848, 1855 and 1867, together with a medal of honour in 1878. Français was made a Chevalier of the Légion d'Honneur in July 1853 and promoted to officer grade on 29 June 1867. He was ultimately elected to membership of the Institute in 1890.

Français is particularly remembered for his decorative work on the baptismal fonts on the Paris church of the Trinity. As an artist, he was constantly alert to, and profited from, the experience and skill of those around him.

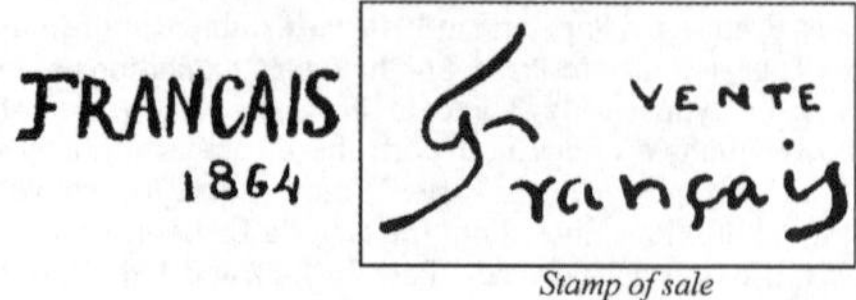

Stamp of sale

BIBLIOGRAPHY:

Miquel, Pierre, *Le paysage français au XIXe siècle, 1824-1874: L'École de la Nature iii*, Édition de la Martinelle, Maurs-la-Jolie, 1975 (pp. 608-645). in *Aquarelles, dessins et gravures de François-Louis Français*, exhibition catalogue, Région Lorraine, 1982-1983. in *Tradition and Revolution in French Art 1700-1800: Paintings and Drawings from Lille*, exhibition catalogue, National Gallery, London, 1993.

MUSEUMS AND GALLERIES:

ALENÇON: *Sunset* - AMIENS: *Twilight in the Woods* - AVIGNON: *Mont Cervin* - BAYONNE (Mus. Bonnat): *Landscape with River* - BESANÇON: *The Miroir de Scey; Sheltering under the Rock at Cléron* - BORDEAUX: *Beeches on the Côte de Grâce* - CHANTILLY: *Hamlet of Chantilly* - ÉPINAL: *Landscape; Portrait* - FLORENCE (Uffizi): *Self-portrait* - GRENOBLE: *Pré-Cabri at Plombières* - LA ROCHELLE: *Sèvre River at Moulin-Neuf; Wood Nymphs; View of Clisson Castle* (watercolour) - LILLE: *Hallowed Wood* - LYONS: *Two Landscapes* - MONTPELLIER: *Sunset Scene* - MULHOUSE: *Idyll; Landscape; Grisaille* - NANCY: *Puits Noir Ravine; Spring; Sunken Path; Dam* - NANTES (MBA): *By the Water near Paris; Portrait of Mademoiselle Housset; Self-portrait; Church at Clisson; Portrait of Madame Cresty* - PARIS (Louvre): *Winter's End* - PARIS (Mus. du Petit Palais): *Adam and Eve Banished from the Garden; View of Bougival* - PLOMBIÈRES-LES-BAINS: *View of the Paris Countryside; Antic Garden* - POITIERS: *Landscape* - RHEIMS: *Vale of the Eugronne near Plombières; Lower Seine View* - ROUEN: *Landscape* - STRASBOURG: *View of Antibes* - TOURS: *Under the Willows.*

AUCTION RECORDS:

PARIS, 1897, *Forty-One Paintings,* FRF from 105 to 5,200; *Fifty-Five Watercolours,* FRF from 35 to 1,400. PARIS, 1899, *The Cascatelles of Tivoli,* FRF 3,650; *Washerwomen at Vaux-de-Cernay,* FRF 900; *Olive Tree in Antibes,* FRF 2,550; *View of Lake Geneva and Mont Blanc,* FRF 6,500; *View of Clisson,* FRF 460; *Bas-Meudon,* FRF 2,250; *Lemon Trees and Palm Trees in the Garden of the Villa Frémy, Nice,* FRF 320; *Ravine* (drawing) FRF 225; *Early Spring at Vaux-de-Cernay* (drawing) FRF 620; *Ground Floor of the Villa Gentil at Beaulieu* (drawing) FRF 3,100; *View of Clisson* (drawing) FRF 480; *St. John's Bay between Beaulieu and Monaco* (drawing) FRF 950. PARIS, 1900, *Sunset in the Rome Countryside,* FRF 510; *Angler,* FRF 1,320. PARIS, 11 Feb 1901, *Dusk by the Water,* FRF 2,000. PARIS, 26-27 May 1902, *Country Road, Combes-la-Ville,* FRF 4,000. NEW YORK, 10 Feb 1903, *Sunset in the Rome Countryside,* USD 1,200. PARIS, 20 Nov 1918, *Beasts at Pasture* (pastel) FRF 610. PARIS, 21 June 1919, *Fishermen on the Juyne near Étampes,* FRF 360. PARIS, 26 Nov 1919, *Watercourse in the Vosges,* FRF 480. PARIS, 28 Jan 1920, *Anastasy the Painter on the Île de Croissy,* FRF 585. PARIS, 29 May 1920, *Part of the Villa Borghese, Rome,* FRF 320. PARIS, 3-4 June 1920, *Villa in the Green,* FRF 190. PARIS, 19 June 1920, *Villa by the Sea* (watercolour) FRF 400. PARIS, 1-2 Dec 1920, *The Seine at Bougival,* FRF 280. PARIS, 7 March 1921, *Spring,* FRF 420. PARIS, 29 April 1921, *Landscape at Sunset,* FRF 280. PARIS, 30 Dec 1922, *River Banks at Sunset,* FRF 300. PARIS, 27 Jan 1923, *First Leaves in the Neufpré Gorge near Plombières,* FRF 900. PARIS, 30 and 31 May 1923, *Sunset,* FRF 270. PARIS, 27 June 1923, *Floral Display in Nice,* FRF 500. PARIS, 26 and 27 Oct 1923, *Portrait of Count de Fersen* (pastel) FRF 600. PARIS, 21 Jan 1924, *Resting in the Countryside,* FRF 720. PARIS, 3 March 1924, *River Banks at Sunset,* FRF 250. PARIS, 26-27 May 1924, *Stone Bridge,* FRF 130. PARIS, 10 May 1926, *Tall Trees by a Pool in a Park,* FRF 750. PARIS, 12 June 1926, *Hayfields near Plombières,* FRF 910. PARIS, 3 July 1926, *By the Pond,* FRF 910. PARIS, 11 Dec 1926, *Path in the Forest of Fontainebleau* (heightened drawing) FRF 150. PARIS, 16 and 17 May 1927, *Villa in a Garden of Flowers,* FRF 300. PARIS, 29 June 1927, *Fisherman under the Trees,* FRF 500. LONDON, 1 July 1927, *Cattle and Sheep by the River,* GBP 26. PARIS, 9 Feb 1928, *River Bank,* FRF 2,130. PARIS, 9 Feb 1928, *River Bank* (watercolour) FRF 280. PARIS, 2 July 1928, *Harbour View,* FRF 405. PARIS, 10 June 1932, *Banks of the Seine at Bougival,* FRF 920. PARIS, 13 Oct 1933, *River,* FRF 310. PARIS, 23 June 1936, *Antic Scene: Women Gathering Flowers in a Meadow,* FRF 510. PARIS, 9 Dec 1940, *Portrait of Seated Woman* (lead pencil heightened with gouache and red chalk) FRF 140. PARIS, 7 Feb 1941, *Valley of the Yvette* (1880, watercolour) FRF 600. PARIS, 9 Feb 1942, *Path* (watercolour) FRF 300. PARIS, 3 March 1942, *Offering,* FRF 4,100; *Fishing by the River,* FRF 4,800. PARIS, 24 April 1942, *Montsoreau Fair* (pen and wash) FRF 330. PARIS, 22 July 1942, *Landscape at Sunset* (1878) FRF 3,000. PARIS, 29 March 1943, *River Bank,* FRF 2,400. PARIS, 26 Nov 1943, *Tree-Lined Road* (pen and wash) FRF 1,000; *Lake* (pen and wash) FRF 800; *Sawmill* (pen and wash) FRF 1,850; *Forest of Fontainebleau* (pen and wash) FRF 750; *Among the Ruins* (1848, watercolour and gouache) FRF 380; *The Seine at Bas-Meudon* (lead pencil) FRF 275; *Reading* (charcoal and red chalk) FRF 550; *Clisson Castle* (pen and wash) FRF 1,850; *Small River and Pasture Land in Normandy* (graphite) FRF 500; *Peasant in a Meadow* (pen and wash) FRF 750; *The Old Castle at Clisson* (1882, watercolour) FRF 7,100; *Woman Gathering Grass* (1882) FRF 4,000; *Undergrowth in the Ajol Valley* (1881) FRF 3,400; *Thatched Cottages at Dusk,* FRF 3,000; *Near Poncin* (1878) FRF 3,600; *Washerwomen in a Meadow* (1872) FRF 4,100; *Road Beside the Stream* (1889) FRF 11,100. PARIS, 7 Feb 1944, *Le Pouliguen* (1867, watercolour) FRF 1,800. PARIS, 12 May 1944, *River Bank,* FRF 700; *Landscape,* FRF 280; *Artist by the Torrent* (wash) FRF 480. PARIS, Oct 1945-July 1946, *Terrace of the Babel Spa in Plombières* (1895) FRF 8,000; *Three canvases,* FRF from 2,100 to 2,800; *Two drawings,* FRF 800 et 1,100. PARIS, 21 Oct 1946, *Bucolic Landscape* (1878) FRF 3,800. PARIS, 18 Nov 1946, *Profil of Harpignies* (drawing) FRF 520. PARIS, 27 Nov 1946, *Reclining Female Nude,* FRF 6,500. PARIS, 20 Jan 1947, *Standing Timber* (charcoal) FRF 320. PARIS, 20 June 1947, *Landscape* (heightened drawing) FRF 400. PARIS, 14 June 1960, *Loire River and Amboise Castle,* FRF 4,500. PARIS, 16 March 1970, *Dusk by the Water* (1890) FRF 3,500. PARIS, 19 May 1971, *Shepherds by a Lake,* FRF 4,000. PARIS, 27 May 1972, *Reading in the Forest,* FRF 5,500. PARIS, 16 March 1973, *River Bank,* FRF 7,500. BERN, 6 May 1976, *Banks of the Rhône* (1856, oil on canvas, $31\frac{1}{2}$ x $47\frac{1}{4}$ ins / 80 x 120 cm) CHF 9,000. VERSAILLES, 4 Oct 1981, *Pine Trees by the Sea* (1880, watercolour wash and Indian ink, $14\frac{3}{4}$ x $21\frac{1}{2}$ ins / 37.5 x 54.5 cm) FRF 4,200. LILLE, 19 June 1983, *Sailing on a Pond* (oil on canvas, $10\frac{1}{4}$ x $2\frac{1}{4}$ ins / 26 x 6 cm) FRF 20,000. PARIS, 23 March 1984, *Garden at St-Jean* (1882, watercolour, 15 x $12\frac{1}{2}$ ins / 38 x 32 cm) FRF 23,000. BAYEUX, 6 Oct 1985, *Undergrowth in the Morning* (watercolour, $11\frac{3}{4}$ x $15\frac{1}{4}$ ins / 30 x 39 cm) FRF 12,000. NEW YORK, 25 May 1987, *Road near Rome* (1848, oil on canvas, oval, 29 x 26 ins / 73.5 x 66 cm) USD 8,500. VERSAILLES, 25 Sept 1988, *River Bank* (1858, oil on panel, $11\frac{1}{4}$ x 18 ins / 28.5 x 46 cm) FRF

16,500. PARIS, 21 Nov 1989, *Two Italian Peasant Women* (watercolour, 11 x 7 3/4 ins / 27 x 19.5 cm) FRF 5,500. PARIS, 15 June 1990, *View of a Garden by the Sea with a Young Woman Watering Flowers* (watercolour, 14 3/4 x 12 1/2 ins / 37.5 x 32 cm) FRF 38,000. PARIS, 27 June 1990, *Lake in the Vosges* (watercolour, 19 x 25 1/2 ins / 48 x 65 cm) FRF 110,000. PARIS, 19 June 1991, *Twilight at Auvers* (1855, oil on panel, 11 1/2 x 15 1/4 ins / 29.5 x 39 cm) FRF 8,000. PARIS, 13 April 1992, *Roman House, Capri* (1864, watercolour and gouache/paper, 11 1/4 x 12 3/4 ins / 28.5 x 32.5 cm) FRF 34,000. NEW YORK, 16 Feb 1993, *Dense Forest* (1882, oil on canvas, 21 1/4 x 18 1/2 ins / 54 x 47 cm) USD 1,100. CALAIS, 14 March 1993, *Fisherman and Elegant Lady on the River* (oil on panel, 13 x 9 1/2 ins / 33 x 24 cm) FRF 19,500. PARIS, 31 March 1993, *Cryptoporticus in a Park* (oil on canvas, 28 1/4 x 24 ins / 72 x 61 cm) FRF 35,000. PARIS, 11 June 1993, *Landscape* (oil on canvas, 11 1/4 x 18 ins / 28.5 x 46 cm) FRF 20,000. AMSTERDAM, 19 Oct 1993, *In the Countryside* (oil on canvas, 18 x 22 ins / 46 x 55 cm) NLG 14,950. LONDON, 27 Oct 1993, *Morning Mist* (1866, oil on canvas, 28 x 37 ins / 71 x 94 cm) GBP 2,415. PARIS, 18 April 1994, *Woman under a Tree* (1879, oil on canvas, 9 1/2 x 13 1/2 ins / 24 x 34 cm, 2 ins/5 cm) FRF 23,000. PARIS, 29 April 1994, *Excavations at Pompeii* (1886, watercolour, 12 x 16 1/4 ins / 30.5 x 41 cm) FRF 50,000. PARIS, 31 March 1995, *Italian Landscape* (oil on canvas, 5 1/2 x 14 1/2 ins / 14 x 37 cm) FRF 23,000. NEW YORK, 18-19 July 1996, *Homage to Flora* (oil on canvas, 40 x 30 ins / 101.6 x 76.2 cm) USD 6,900. PARIS, 4 March 1998, *Sunset in the Country* (oil on canvas, 15 3/4 x 23 1/4 ins / 40.3 x 59.3 cm) FRF 7,500. NEW YORK, 2 Nov 1999, *Road to Rome* (1848, oil on canvas, 29 x 26 ins / 74 x 66 cm) USD 9,500. FONTAINEBLEAU, 5 Dec 1999, *Beside the River* (oil on canvas, 13 x 18 ins / 32 x 46 cm) FRF 20,000. NEW YORK, 8 March 2000, *Gardens of the Villa Fremy's* (1881, oil on canvas, 18 x 22 ins / 45 x 55 cm) USD 7,000. NEW YORK, 1 May 2001, *Female Camaraderie at Dusk* (1845, oil on canvas) USD 11,000. PARIS, 21 Nov 2001, *Corner of a Garden* (1881, watercolour/gouache, 19 x 15 ins / 47 x 38 cm) FRF 52,000. PARIS, 21 March 2002, *Beside a Stream* (1872, gouache) EUR 3,000. PARIS, 25 March 2002, *Cernay la Ville* (1860, oil on panel, 11 x 18 ins / 28 x 45 cm) EUR 5,000. PARIS, 26 Sept 2003, *Winter Landscape* (oil on canvas, 40 x 53 ins / 101 x 135 cm) EUR 28,000. FONTAINEBLEAU, 7 Dec 2003, *Interior of a Forest* (c. 1850, oil on panel, 15 x 22 ins / 39 x 56 cm) EUR 4,000. PARIS, 30 March 2004, *Women Bathers in Undergrowth* (oil on panel, 13 x 9 ins / 33 x 24 cm) EUR 2,200. PARIS, 30 March 2004, *Valley of Rossillon* (1873, oil on canvas, 24 x 18 ins / 61 x 46 cm) EUR 5,500.

FRANCALANCIA, Riccardo
Italian, 20th century.
Born 1886, in Assisi; died 1965, in Rome.
Painter. Landscapes with figures, landscapes, still-lifes.
Francalancia only painted Italian landscapes, but chose a wide variety of picturesque locations.
AUCTION RECORDS:
ROME, 20 May 1986, *Woman at the Foot of a Mountain* (1934, oil on canvas, 25 1/2 x 33 3/4 ins / 65 x 86 cm) ITL 13,500,000. ROME, 15 Nov 1988, *Country Road* (1949, oil on canvas, 15 3/4 x 19 3/4 ins / 40 x 50 cm) ITL 9,500,000. MILAN, 20 March 1989, *Window in the Studio* (1933, oil on canvas, 23 1/2 x 19 3/4 ins / 60 x 50 cm) ITL 16,000,000. ROME, 21 March 1989, *Beach with Bathers and a Boat* (1922, oil on canvas, 11 3/4 x 15 3/4 ins / 30 x 40 cm) ITL 18,000,000. ROME, 28 Nov 1989, *Tiberina Valley* (1923, oil on canvas, 15 x 18 1/2 ins / 38 x 47 cm) ITL 19,000,000. ROME, 10 April 1990, *Amphora and Shell* (1960, oil on canvas, 25 1/2 x 19 3/4 ins / 65 x 50 cm) ITL 15,000,000. ROME, 3 Dec 1991, *Village Lane* (oil on panel, 15 3/4 x 11 3/4 ins / 40 x 30 cm) ITL 13,000,000. ROME, 19 Nov 1992, *San Rufino, No 16* (1935, oil on canvas, 18 x 22 3/4 ins / 45.5 x 58 cm) ITL 14,500,000. ROME, 30 Nov 1993, *Still-life with Pears on a White Cloth* (1960, oil on canvas, 14 x 18 1/4 ins / 35.5 x 46.5 cm) ITL 5,750,000. MILAN, 19 May 1997, *Mountain Road* (1959, oil on canvas, 23 1/2 x 31 1/2 ins / 60 x 80 cm) ITL 23,000,000. PRATO, 10 Nov 2000, *Landscape* (1963, oil on canvas, 24 x 20 ins / 60 x 51 cm) ITL 12,000,000. ROME, 23 Nov 2000, *View of Gallicano* (1926, oil on canvas, 14 x 18 ins / 36 x 46 cm) ITL 7,500,000. VERCELLI, 21 April 2001, *La Maddalena, Italy* (1939, oil on canvas, 15 x 18 ins / 38 x 45 cm) ITL 10,000,000. ROME, 18 April 2002, *Still-life by the Window* (1960, oil on canvas, 18 x 14 ins / 45 x 36 cm) EUR 3,600. ROME, 10 April 2003, *Jug and Shell* (oil on canvas, 26 x 20 ins / 65 x 50 cm) EUR 4,600. FLORENCE, 10 June 2003, *Villages. Landscape* (1927, oil on canvas, a pair, 26 x 32 ins / 67 x 82 cm) EUR 16,000. MILAN, 24 May 2004, *Street in Wales I* (1928, oil on board, 17 x 13 ins / 42 x 34 cm) EUR 9,000.

FRANCART, François
French, 17th century.
Born 1622; died 1672.
Painter, decorative designer.
François Francart was an ordinary painter to the king. On 15 July 1669, he married Anne-Élisabeth Le Geret, daughter of Jean Le Geret, a sculptor.

FRANCART, François
French, 17th century.
Baptised the 22 January 1663.
Painter, draughtsman.
François Francart was the son of Gilbert Francart. He was in the service of Vauban and in 1683 worked on the château at Bazoches. He was designated 'ordinary painter to the king in the house of Gobelins'. He may be the same as the painter Francart who worked in 1690 at the château in Chantilly.

FRANCART, Gilbert
French, 17th century.
Painter. History painting.
Gilbert Francart was the Brother of François Francart. He is known for his picture of *St Sebastian*, signed and dated 1661, which is in the church at Bazoches-du-Moran.

FRANCART, Laurent, or Francard
French, 17th century.
Born 17th century, in Paris.
Painter, draughtsman, architect.
Laurent Francart was the son of Gilbert Francart. In some 1681 documents he is described as 'draughtsman for M. de Vauban, marshal of the king's encampments and armies' and in 1686 as 'the king's engineer'. He worked for Vauban at the château in Bazoches and contributed to the decorative work on the portal for the dome at Invalides. Other known works by him are two engraved sketches for the door and fireplace.

FRANCAVILLA. See also **FRANCHEVILLE**

FRANCAVILLA, Liliana
Italian, 20th century.
Born 18 April 1918, in Florence.
Active in France from 1949.
Painter. Urban landscapes.
Liliana Francavilla exhibited in Florence, Paris and Milan. She settled in Paris and specialised in Parisian landscapes.

FRANCE, Alexandre de. See **DEFRANCE Alexandre**

FRANCE, Eurilda (Mrs)
American, 20th century.
Born 1865, in Pittsburg; died 1931.
Painter, watercolourist.
Eurilda France was a pupil of A. Morot, J. Lefebvre and Benjamin-Constant in Paris, and the wife of M.H. France.
AUCTION RECORDS:
PORTLAND, 17 July 1982, *Tiger Lilies* (watercolour, 17 x 22 ins / 43 x 56 cm) USD 2,000. NEW YORK, 3 Oct 1984, *In the Garden* (watercolour, 12 1/4 x 20 ins / 31 x 50.8 cm) USD 850. CON-

NECTICUT, 24 May 1999, *Still-life* (oil on canvas, 26 x 20 ins / 66 x 51 cm) USD 1,800.

FRANCE, Henri de
French.
Painter.

AUCTION RECORDS:
PLESSIS-BELLIÈRE, 10-11 May 1879, *Ruined Castle*, FRF 95.

FRANCE, Jacques. See **LECREUX Paul**

FRANCE, Jean Baptiste Félix
French, 19th century.
Born 22 February 1844, in Dijon; died 1903.
Painter.

France studied initially at the Dijon College of Drawing and Composition, then under Cabanel; exhibited at the Paris Salon from 1870 to 1880, chiefly portraits - including those of J. Cornu and M. Garraud - and a genre composition entitled *Danae*.

MUSEUMS AND GALLERIES:
DIJON: *Portrait of the Painter J.J. Cornu.*

FRANCE, Jean de, also called Jean du Cateau
French, 16th century.
Active in Cambrai.
Sculptor.

Jean de France provided a model for the decoration of the *bretique* (the balcony from which legal announcements were made) for the town hall in Cambrai in 1533.

FRANCE, Jean Pierre de. See **DEFRANCE**

FRANCE, Jessie Leach
American, 19th century.
Born 8 October 1862, in Cincinnati.
Active in Buffalo.
Painter, illustrator.

Jessie Leach France was a pupil of H. W. Mesdag, Carolus Duran and Benjamin-Constant, and himself later taught painting.

FRANCE, Jules
French, 20th century.
Born 22 October 1920, in Anzin.
Sculptor, medallist, designer. Monuments, designs for stained glass.

Jules France studied at the École des Beaux-Arts in Valenciennes, at the École Nationale Supérieure des Beaux-Arts in Paris and the École Nationale Supérieure des Arts Décoratifs in Paris. He received numerous prizes and awards including the Premier Grand Prix de Rome for medals in 1948. From 1957 to 1983 he was director of the École des Beaux-Arts in Valenciennes.

He decorated numerous public buildings such as museums, libraries and schools. He also constructed various memorials and produced medals, often emblematic medals of towns; he also restored numerous stained glass windows.

FRANCE, Milos
Czechoslovak, 20th century.
Born 11 August 1928, in Plzen.
Painter, ceramicist.

Graduate of the ceramic school in Prague, Milos France was a frequent exhibitor in Prague (1984 to 1992) and in Plzen (1985 to 1988). He painted compositions on ceramics that were inspired by a decorative post-Cubism.

FRANCE, Pierre de
French, 17th century.
Parisian, active during the 17th century.
Sculptor.

Pierre de France went to Albi with another sculptor called Bastien Gayon. In 1603 they created a new pillar of Justice there. On it were sculpted the town's coat-of-arms and those of the monsignor of Albi. It was to be placed in the centre of the town square.

FRANCE RAPHAËL. See **RAPHAËL France**

FRANCE-WAGNER. See **WAGNER France**

FRANCELET, Jean Max
French, 20th century.
Born in Paris.
Watercolourist, pastellist.

Jean Francelet exhibited at the Salon des Artistes Français from 1926.

FRANCELLI, Pietro
Italian, 18th - 19th century.
Born 1764, in Bologna; died 1850.
Painter.

Pietro Francelli painted in the Venetian manner, providing numerous decorative compositions for churches, castles and theatres.

FRANCEN, Aper. See **HOEVEN Aper Fransz. Van**

FRANCEQUIN, Jean, or Francisquin
French, 16th - 17th century.
Sculptor, architect.

Born in Lorraine, Francequin worked with the sculptor Jean de Trémont on various sculptural and architectural projects in the church of the Minims in Nancy (Meurthe-et-Moselle) in 1613.

FRANCÉS
French, 19th century.
Of Spanish origin.
Active in Paris.
Sculptor. Figures. Busts.

MUSEUMS AND GALLERIES:
DIEPPE (Château-Mus.): *Bust of Sarasat* - PARIS (Hôpital du Val-de-Grâce): *Bust of the Surgeon Michel Lévy.*

FRANCÉS. See also first name

FRANCÉS, Antonio
Spanish, 16th century.
Active in Seville.
Sculptor.

Antonio Francés is mentioned in 1533 as having collaborated with others on the decoration of the friezes and windows of the chapter houses.

FRANCÉS, Didier
Spanish, 16th century.
Active in Seville in 1534.
Sculptor.

Didier Francés carved the ribs of the vaulted ceiling of the vestibule in the chapter house in Seville.

FRANCES, Esteban
Spanish, 20th century.
Born 1914, in Port Bou (Catalonia); died 1976, in Barcelona.
Active in France from 1937, then in the USA.
Painter (mixed media).
Paris Surrealist group.

Soon after arriving in Paris, Esteban Frances was involved with the Surrealists. During World War II he took refuge in the USA and eventually settled there.

His most important contribution to Surrealist techniques was the invention of the automatic 'grattage' or 'scraping' process, described by André Breton thus: 'After distributing colours randomly on a wooden block, Esteban Frances scrapes at this prepared surface in an equally random way using a razor blade. He limits himself to identifying light and shade. An invisible hand then takes his and helps him to reveal the large, hallucinatory figures that were latent in this amalgam'. Combining this process with distortions inspired by Picasso's work, Esteban Frances overturns space completely, creating a dialogue between contradictory perspectives, geometric rigour and dishevelled forms.

AUCTION RECORDS:

LONDON, 3 July 1987, *Trompe l'Oeil* (watercolour and oil on paper, 18 1/4 x 13 1/2 ins / 46.5 x 34 cm) GBP 1,400. LONDON, 29 March 1988, *Fantastical Masks on a Blue Background* (watercolour and oil à l'essence/paper, 22 x 28 ins / 55.9 x 71.1 cm) GBP 2,860. LONDON, 29 Nov 1989, *Trompe l'Oeil* (watercolour and diluted oil/paper, 18 1/4 x 13 1/2 ins / 46.5 x 34 cm) GBP 6,050. NEW YORK, 2 Nov 1993, *Surrealist Figure* (colouring pencil and ink/paper, 23 1/4 x 14 1/2 ins / 59 x 37 cm) USD 5,750.

FRANCÉS, Gil

Spanish, 16th century.
Active in Seville.
Sculptor.

Gil Francés worked on the cathedral in Seville.

FRANCÉS, Gusman

Spanish, 16th century.
Active in Seville towards the middle of the 16th century.
Sculptor.

Gusman Francés worked on the chapter house in 1534, in particular on the ribs of the vaulted ceiling.

FRANCES, H.E.

British, 19th century.
Active in London.
Painter. Genre scenes.

H.E. Frances exhibited in London from 1851 to 1875 at the Royal Academy, the British Institution and the Suffolk Street Gallery.

FRANCES, Juana

Spanish, 20th century.
Born 1926, in Alicante.
Painter (mixed media).

Juana Frances lived and studied in Madrid. She began exhibiting in Spain in 1953 and has also exhibited in Switzerland. In 1968 an exhibition of her work toured various museums in Northern Europe. She took part in the Venice Biennale in 1964 and 1966. Her work is an abstract and mysterious blend of composition and painting.

FRANCES, Mathilde

French, 20th century.
Born 23 December 1879, in St-Pons; died 12 August 1964, in Montpellier.
Painter. Portraits, landscapes.

After studying at the École des Beaux-Arts in Montpellier, Mathilde Francis completed her studies in Paris under the direction of J.-P. Laurens and H. Royer. She exhibited in Paris at the Salon des Artistes Français, of which she became a member in 1922.

FRANCÈS, Nicolas. See **NICOLAS Francès**

FRANCÉS, Tomás

Spanish, 16th century.
Active in Seville.
Sculptor.

Tomás Francés was employed to work on the cathedral in Seville.

FRANCÉS Y AGRAMUNT, José

Spanish, 19th century.
Born c. 1860, in Valencia.
Painter.

José Francés y Agramunt was the son of Plácido Francés y Pascual and a pupil of J. Capuz in Valencia. He exhibited landscape paintings at Madrid exhibitions until 1912.

FRANCÉS Y ARRIBAS DE VALLCORBA, Fernanda

Spanish, 19th century.
Born c. 1860, in Valencia.
Painter.

Fernanda Francés y Arribas de Vallcorba was the daughter and pupil of Plácido Francés y Pascual and worked in Madrid. From 1881 she exhibited flower paintings and still-lifes, including *Branches of Almond in Blossom*, in Madrid. She also exhibited from time to time in Munich and Berlin.

MUSEUMS AND GALLERIES:

MADRID (Mus. de Arte Moderno): *Oysters and Fowl.*

FRANCÉS Y MEXIA, Juan

Spanish, 19th - 20th century.
Born c. 1870, in Madrid.
Painter. Portraits, genre scenes.

Juan Francés y Mexia was the son of Plácido Francés y Pascual and studied with his father and E. Sala y Francés. He worked in Madrid and regularly exhibited there. In 1913 some of his work was shown in Munich, including *Love that Passes*. He was awarded a number of medals for his paintings.

FRANCÉS Y MEXIA, Luis

Spanish, 20th century.
Born c. 1880, in Madrid.
Painter. Landscapes.

Luis Francés y Mexia was the son of the painter Plácido Francés y Pascual. He exhibited landscape paintings at Madrid exhibitions up to 1912.

FRANCÉS Y PASCUAL, Plácido

Spanish, 19th century.
Born c. 1840, in Alcoy; died 1901.
Painter. Genre scenes, local scenes.

Plácido Francés y Pascual studied under Carlos Mujica at the Academia de San Fernando. He first exhibited at the exhibition of the national fine arts society of Madrid in 1862 and continued to exhibit regularly up to 1882. He was awarded medals in 1868 and 1871 and received the Order of Charles III in 1882.

MUSEUMS AND GALLERIES:

MADRID (Mus. de Arte Moderno): *Spanish Woman, 1800.*

AUCTION RECORDS:

LONDON, 24 Nov 1976, *Arabs Feeding Pink Flamingos* (1880, oil on panel, 11 1/2 x 18 ins / 29 x 46 cm) GBP 800. LONDON, 30 Nov 1977, *Romance in the Patio* (1873, oil on canvas, 17 1/4 x 23 ins / 44 x 58.5 cm) GBP 3,000. LONDON, 17 Feb 1989, *Spanish Wedding in a Village Street* (1873, oil on canvas, 25 1/2 x 32 ins / 64.7 x 81.3 cm) GBP 33,000. LONDON, 21 June 1989, *Tax Collection* (1879, oil on panel, 17 1/2 x 25 1/2 ins / 44.5 x 65 cm) GBP 11,000. PARIS, 12 April 1991, *Farandole* (1878, oil on canvas, 35 1/2 x 49 1/4 ins / 90 x 125 cm) FRF 41,000. LONDON, 15 June 1994, *Five Young Spanish Beauties* (oil on canvas, 20 x 57 1/2 ins / 51 x 146 cm) GBP 8,050. MADRID, 11 July 2000, *Offering to Venus* (1880, oil on canvas, a pair, 67 x 48 ins / 169x123 cm) ESP 3,250,000.

FRANCES-LLAMAZARES, Agapito

Spanish, 19th century.
Born in Palencia; died 28 November 1869, in Rome.
Painter. History painting.

Agapito Frances-Llamazares studied in Rome under the direction of Coghetti and Podesti. He first exhibited at the exhibition of the national fine arts society of Madrid in 1864.

FRANCESC (Mestre). See **FRANCISCO DE CERVERA**

FRANCESCA, Piero della. See **PIERO DELLA FRANCESCA**

FRANCESCA DA FIRENZE
Italian, 16th century.
Active in Florence c. 1528.
Miniaturist.

FRANCESCHELLI, Ferdinando
Italian, 18th century.
Active in Rome c. 1700.
Engraver (etching).

FRANCESCHETTI, Giovanni
Italian, 19th century.
Born 1816, in Brescia; died 1845, in Milan.
Sculptor.
Franceschetti executed the decorative sculptures on the Appiani monument and the Arco del Sempione in Milan.

FRANCESCHI, Alessandro
Italian, 19th century.
Born 1789; died 1834.
Active in Bologna.
Sculptor.
Originally a pupil of G. di Maria, Alessandro Franceschi sculpted numerous funeral monuments for Bologna cemetery. He also sculpted the *Bevilacqua* funeral monument in Ferrara cemetery. He is remembered for a *Venus*, in Holland, and a *Birth of Christ*, in Spain.

FRANCESCHI, Domenico dei
Italian, 16th century.
Active in Venice at the end of the 16th century.
Engraver.
As well as working as an engraver, Domenico dei Franceschi was also a typographer and print seller. There are two engravings by Franceschi dated 1565, one depicting *Corpus Christi Procession in Venice*, the other the *Parade of the Emperor Sulaiman II in Constantinople*.

FRANCESCHI, Emilio
Italian, 19th century.
Born 1839, in Florence; died 1890, in Naples.
Sculptor. Statues.
Emilio Franceschi started out as a wood sculptor, then moved on to marble and bronze.
MUSEUMS AND GALLERIES:
ROME (Capodimonte Palace): *Opimia* (marble) - ROME (Gal. Nazionale d'Arte Moderna): *Eulalia Christiania* (bronze); *Fossor* (bronze); *The Poet Parini* (marble).
AUCTION RECORDS:
MILAN, 14 June 1995, *Peasant Taking a Break* (marble, h. 13¾ ins / 35 cm) ITL 2,760,000.

FRANCESCHI, Francesco dei
Italian, 15th century.
Active in Venice.
Painter.
Francesco dei Franceschi is noted for three altarpieces depicting the saints of the churches of S Giobbe, S Giorgio d'Alega and S Samuele in Venice. The museum in Padua has in its collection an altarpiece by Franceschi in 12 parts, originally in the church of S Pietro in Padua.

FRANCESCHI, Giovanni dei
Italian, 16th century.
Born in Venice; died 23 April 1595, in Rome.
Painter.
Giovanni dei Franceschi was admitted as a member of the guild of St Luke in 1575.

FRANCESCHI, Giovanni dei
Italian, 18th century.
Active c. 1743.
Engraver.
Giovanni dei Franceschi engraved originals by David (*Portrait of Pope Clement XII*), Parmigianino and C. Giaquinto.

FRANCESCHI, Jean Paul Paschal
French, 19th century.
Born 26 March 1826, in Bar-sur-Aube; died 18 March 1894, in Besançon.
Sculptor.
Jean Paul was the brother of Jules Franceschi. After being awarded the first prize for drawing and sculpture in Besançon in 1839, 1840 and 1841, Jean Paul Franceschi attended the École des Beaux-Arts in Paris, where he studied under François Rude and Carpeaux. He returned to Besançon, where he sculpted statues and low reliefs for various churches. His body of work includes statues of *Sts Francis Xavier, Vincent de Paul and Joseph* for the chapel of the Catholic College, a statue of the missionary *Parrenin* for the latter's tomb in Roussey (Doubs), medallions for tombs in Besançon Cemetery, and a number of busts.

FRANCESCHI, Lazzaro dei
Italian, 15th century.
Died before 6 June 1483.
Active in Venice.
Painter, sculptor (wood).

FRANCESCHI, Louis Julien, called Jules
French, 19th century.
Born 11 January 1825, in Bar-sur-Aube; died 1 September 1893, in Paris.
Sculptor (bronze/marble/stone). Religious subjects, figures, portraits. Statues, groups, busts, low reliefs, funerary monuments (recumbent statues).
Louis Franceschi studied under François Rude and was a medal winner in 1861, 1864 and 1869. He was made a Chevalier of the Légion d'Honneur in 1874. Franceschi exhibited several works at Paris Salons from 1848 onwards. Examples from his body of works include: *Young Shepherd Bleeding his Sick Dog*; *Roses* (statue); *Neapolitan Playing Mora*; *Princess Solovoy* (bronze bust); *Young Huntress Teasing a Fox*; *Countess Charles Tascher de la Pagerie* (marble bust); *Marchioness de Pastoret* (marble bust); *Andromeda* (stone statue); a bronze cast of *Mieczyslaw Kamienski* (1833-1859; killed at the battle of Magenta) destined for his tomb in Montmartre Cemetery, Paris; *Danaide* (marble statue); *St Sulpice*, stone statue for the Paris church of St-Sulpice; *Death of Commander Baroche* (low relief for the chapel of Le Bourget); *Madame Carvalho* (marble bust); and *Albert Wolf* (bronze bust).
MUSEUMS AND GALLERIES:
AMIENS: *Madame Worms-Baretta*; *Head of Christ* - BESANÇON: *Awakening* - CLAMECY: *Monsieur Bigée*; *Madame Collard* - NÎMES: *Awakening* - PARIS (MAM): *Fortuna* - PARIS (Mus. de la Comédie-Française): *Régnier*; *François Ponsard* - RHEIMS: *Sleep* - TROYES: *Religion*; *Awakening* (two versions); *Group for Funerary Monument*; *War and Art*; *Fortuna*; *Painting*; *Mademoiselle Croizette*; *Mademoiselle Reichenberg*; *Mademoiselle Krauss*; *Madame Miolan-Carvalho*; *Marie-Amélie of Orléans, Queen of Portugal*; *Head of Christ*; *Redemption*; *Hebe*; *Andromeda*; *Flautist*; *Poesy*; *Émile Augier*; *Gounod*; *Commander Rivière*; *Régnier*; *Abbot Poiré*; *Monsieur Séguier*; *Monsieur Bouchot*; *Monsieur Seligman*; *Madame X*; *Madame Judic*; *Pierre Franceschi*; *Paul Franceschi*; *Portrait of a Child*.
AUCTION RECORDS:
PARIS, 20 Nov 1979, *Seated Woman with two Birds* (bronze, h. 25¼ ins / 64 cm) FRF 7,500. NEW YORK, 20 July 1995, *Seated Woman* (bronze, h. 14¾ ins / 37.5 cm) USD 3,450. PARIS, 5 March 1999, *Bust of a Woman* (1874, sculpture, white marble, h. 33 ins / 85 cm) FRF 19,000. LOKEREN, 9 Dec 2000, *Huntresses* (sculpture, brown patinated bronze, h. 21 ins / 53 cm) BEF 180,000. NORTH BETHESDA, 10 Sept 2001, *Hebe* (sculpture, brown patinated bronze, h. 24 ins / 61 cm) USD 5,000. LONDON, 12 Feb 2002, *Young Huntress Teasing a Fox* (1857,

sculpture, bronze, h. 22 ins / 55 cm) GBP 1,500. NEW YORK, 21 May 2003, *Egyptian Beauty* (sculpture, brown patinated bronze, h. 38 ins / 97 cm) USD 6,500. AMSTERDAM, 11 June 2003, *Seated Nude, Flanked by a Couple of Pigeons* (sculpture, brown patinated bronze, h. 25 ins / 63 cm) EUR 1,800.

FRANCESCHI, Marguerite, Mme Poiré
French, 19th century.
Active in Paris.
Sculptor.

Marguerite was the daughter of Jules Franceschi; she exhibited busts at the Salon between 1883 and 1885.

FRANCESCHI, Mariano de
Italian, 19th century.
Born 1849, in Rome; died 1896.
Painter, watercolourist, draughtsman. Genre scenes, landscapes.

Mariano de Franceschi studied at the Accademia di S Luca before perfecting his skills in the studio of the Spanish painter Baldomero Gelofre. He exhibited a canvas entitled *Love Leads us to Death* (from a poem by Dante), and a watercolour of *The Pantheon*, in 1884 in Turin. Other famous works by him include *May He Soon Return*; *Riva degli Schiavoni*; and *Squero di San Trovaso*.

MUSEUMS AND GALLERIES:

ROME (Gal. Nazionale d'Arte Moderna): *Village Lunatic*.

AUCTION RECORDS:

LONDON, 7 Dec 1907, *In the Monastery Garden* (drawing) GBP 5. LONDON, 13 Dec 1909, *View of Venice*, GBP 12. NEW YORK, 25 Oct 1977, *Venetian Marriage* (oil on canvas, 27 x 18 ins / 68.5 x 46 cm) USD 2,400. NEW YORK, 27 Feb 1982, *View of Ancient Rome* (watercolour, 25 1/2 x 18 1/2 ins / 64.8 x 47 cm) USD 1,200. ENGHIEN-LES-BAINS, 4 March 1984, *Travelling Salesmen in an Arab Town* (watercolour, 20 3/4 x 29 1/2 ins / 53 x 75 cm) FRF 40,000. NEW YORK, 31 Oct 1985, *Marriage Scene, Tangiers* (oil on canvas, 22 x 30 1/4 ins / 56 x 76.9 cm) USD 4,500. ROME, 14 Dec 1988, *Fishing Boats on the Beach* (distemper/paper, 20 1/4 x 27 ins / 51.5 x 68.5 cm) ITL 3,800,000. NEW YORK, 17 Jan 1990, *Market in the Middle East* (oil on canvas, 19 1/2 x 29 1/2 ins / 49.3 x 75 cm) USD 6,600. NEW YORK, 19 July 1990, *Street in an Arab Village* (oil on canvas, 19 1/2 x 29 1/4 ins / 49.4 x 74.3 cm) USD 4,675. NEW YORK, 29 Oct 1992, *Arab Caravan* (watercolour/paper, 13 1/2 x 20 1/4 ins / 34.2 x 51.4 cm) USD 715. ROME, 26 May 1993, *Alley in an Oriental Village* (oil on panel, 15 3/4 x 9 ins / 40 x 23 cm) ITL 2,000,000. LONDON, 17 Nov 1994, *Arab Marketplace* (pencil and watercolour/paper, 20 x 28 1/2 ins / 50.8 x 72.5 cm) GBP 5,980. NEW YORK, 13 Sept 2000, *Carnival* (watercolour, 13 x 21 ins / 34 x 53 cm) USD 1,700. BATH, 26 March 2001, *Figure with an Ox Cart beside a Roman Portico* (watercolour over pencil, 25 x 18 ins / 64 x 45 cm) GBP 1,600. BOSTON, 16 Nov 2001, *Marketplace* (oil on canvas, 20 x 30 ins / 51 x 76 cm) USD 7,000. LONDON, 21 March 2002, *Market Scene. Driving the Ducks to Market* (oil on panel, a pair, 15 x 9 ins / 38 x 23 cm) GBP 2,000. FLORIDA, 16 July 2002, *Peasant Woman and Boy Watching a Baby near an Archway* (watercolour, 29 x 21 ins / 74 x 53 cm) USD 1,600. LONDON, 21 July 2003, *Young Girls of Capri. Washerwomen of Capri* (oil on panel, a pair, 6 x 4 ins / 16 x 10 cm) GBP 1,500.

FRANCESCHI, Marthe
French, 20th century.
Born 18 January 1899, in Besançon.
Painter. Portraits.

Marthe Franceschi studied under Fernand Sabatté. She exhibited in Paris at the Salon des Artistes Indépendants. She was a member of the Salon des Artistes Français and received a commendation in 1923 and a bronze medal in 1926.

FRANCESCHI, Paolo dei, or Franchoys, Francken, real name: Franck Pauwels or Paul, also known as Paolo Fiammingo
Flemish School, 16th century.
Born c. 1540, in Antwerp; died 1596, in Venice.
Painter. History painting, religious subjects, mythological subjects, hunting scenes, landscapes.
Prague School.

When still a young man, this artist went to Italy, where he became the pupil of Tintoretto. He spent the rest of his life in Italy, and excelled particularly in the painting of landscapes, although he also occasionally painted historical subjects. He was employed by Emperor Rudolph II.

P Francefchi.

MUSEUMS AND GALLERIES:

NANTES (MBA): *Bust of an Unknown Man* - OBERSCHLEISSHEIM: *Pietà* - VENICE (Gal. dell'Accademia): *St John the Baptist in the Wilderness; Prodigal Son; Deposition; St John Preaching in the Wilderness* - VIENNA (Akademie der Bildenden Künste): *Pietà*.

AUCTION RECORDS:

VIENNA, 14 June 1966, *Orpheus Charming the Animals*, ATS 45,000. NEW YORK, 9 Jan 1981, *Baptism of Christ* (oil on canvas, 40 x 59 ins / 101.5 x 150 cm) USD 9,500. NEW YORK, 9 June 1983, *Hunting Scene* (oil on canvas, 46 1/2 x 59 3/4 ins / 118 x 152 cm) USD 15,000. LONDON, 15 June 1983, *Mercury and a Wounded Girl in a Landscape overlooked by Venus* (pen and black ink, 14 3/4 x 21 1/2 ins / 37.5 x 54.5 cm) GBP 1,050. MILAN, 21 April 1988, *St John the Baptist Preaching* (oil on canvas, 68 x 86 1/2 ins / 173 x 220 cm) ITL 36,000,000. MILAN, 12 Dec 1988, *St John the Baptist Preaching* (oil on canvas, 68 x 86 1/2 ins / 173 x 220 cm) ITL 34,000,000. NEW YORK, 11 Jan 1995, *The Baths at Bethesda* (oil on canvas, 43 1/2 x 59 1/2 ins / 110.5 x 151 cm) USD 21,850. VENICE, 7-8 Oct 1996, *Venus* (oil on canvas, 11 1/4 x 35 ins / 28.5 x 89 cm) ITL 27,850,000. VIENNA, 29-30 Oct 1996, *St Dominic Directing Building Work on a Church* (oil on canvas, 38 1/2 x 54 1/4 ins / 98 x 138 cm) ATS 184,000.

FRANCESCHI, Pietro. See **PIERO DELLA FRANCESCA**

FRANCESCHIELLO. See **MURA Francesco de**

FRANCESCHINI, Baldassare, called Il Volterrano Giuniore
Italian, 17th century.
Born 1611, in Volterra; died 1689, in Florence.
Painter, fresco artist, draughtsman. History painting, religious subjects, mythological subjects.
Florentine School.

Baldassare Franceschini was the son of the sculptor Gasparo Franceschini. He was known as Il Volterrano Giuniore (the young one from Volterra) to set him apart from Daniele Ricciarelli da Volterra. He studied initially under Matteo Rosselli, then under Giovanni da San Giovanni. There is a degree of speculation to the effect that the latter was jealous of Franceschini and, having taken him on as a collaborator for certain projects at the Palazzo Pitti, promptly parted company with him once Franceschini's talent had been made obvious. Major examples of Franceschini's work are on show at the ducal palace in Florence, including the four large paintings portraying scenes from the Medici dynasty. Franceschini was one of the most accomplished fresco painters of his day.

MUSEUMS AND GALLERIES:

BORDEAUX: *Moses before Pharaoh; Apotheosis of Ovid; Apollo and Marsyas* - FLORENCE (Palazzo Pitti): *Venal Cupid; Cupid Asleep* - FLORENCE (S Mus. Maggiore): *Ascension of Elijah* - FLORENCE (Uffizi): *St Catherine of Siena; Brother of the Augustinian Order; St Peter; Portrait of the Artist; Curé*

Arlotto's Joviality; Suffering Christ (drawing) - LILLE (MBA, Wicar Collection): *Gods and Cupids* (red chalk) - LUCCA: *Head of an Angel* - MONTPELLIER: *Eternal Father* - NEW YORK (Metropolitan Mus. of Art): *Head of an Angel* - VENICE (Pinacoteca Manfrediniana): *St John the Baptist* - VOLTERRA (S Agostino): *St Roch; Purification of the Virgin.*

AUCTION RECORDS:

PARIS, 1775, *St Stanislas Kostcka; Allegorical Subect* (two drawings) FRF 27; *Pope on a Cloud with St Francis de Sales; Venus Whipping Eros* (two drawings) FRF 200. PARIS, 8 Nov 1922, *Anthology* (410 drawings) FRF 3,811. LONDON, 3 July 1980, *Study for 'Rest during the Flight into Egypt'* (black chalk/paper, 11 1/2 x 8 1/2 ins / 29.2 x 21.4 cm) GBP 3,700. LONDON, 23 March 1982, *View of a Farm in Tuscany* (red chalk and wash, 10 1/2 x 16 3/4 ins / 26.9 x 42.4 cm) GBP 1,650. LONDON, 22 Oct 1984, *Studies for a Virgin and Child* (pen and brown ink/outlines in red and black chalk, 10 1/4 x 6 3/4 ins / 26 x 17.1 cm) GBP 850. MONTE CARLO, 29 Nov 1986, *Study of a Young Man Wearing a Cape* (red chalk heightened with white, 14 x 7 1/4 ins / 35.5 x 18.5 cm) FRF 155,000. NEW YORK, 14 Jan 1987, *Aurora on her Chariot* (black and white chalk, 10 x 16 1/4 ins / 25.4 x 41.1 cm) USD 4,250. BERN, 30 April 1988, *Coronation of Mary* (oil on canvas, 43 1/4 x 43 1/4 ins / 110 x 110 cm) CHF 11,000. MILAN, 25 Oct 1988, *Judith and the Head of Holofernes* (oil on canvas, 46 1/2 x 36 1/4 ins / 118 x 92 cm) ITL 22,000,000. LONDON, 14 Dec 1990, *St George* (oil on canvas, 53 1/4 x 38 3/4 ins / 135.5 x 98.7 cm) GBP 22,000. LONDON, 6 July 1992, *Study of a Saint and of Clasped Hands* (chalk heightened with white, 8 3/4 x 5 1/2 ins / 22.1 x 14 cm) GBP 770. NEW YORK, 20 May 1993, *Bacchus with Putti* (oil on canvas, 57 x 90 3/4 ins / 144.8 x 230.5 cm) USD 4,888. LONDON, 4 July 1994, *Wine Game* (red chalk and red wash squared for remounting, 9 1/2 x 14 1/2 ins / 24.2 x 36.7 cm) GBP 91,700. PARIS, 18 Nov 1994, *St John the Evangelist* (red chalk, 13 x 8 3/4 ins / 33.2 x 22.4 cm) FRF 16,000. NEW YORK, 12 Jan 1995, *Virgin and Child with St John the Baptist* (black chalk and ink, study recto and verso, 9 3/4 x 14 ins / 24.7 x 35.7 cm) USD 5,175. LONDON, 24 Feb 1995, *St Dorothy* (oil on canvas, 47 1/2 x 38 ins / 120.7 x 96.5 cm) GBP 24,150. LONDON, 2 July 1996, *Rest during the Flight into Egypt* (black chalk, 11 1/2 x 8 1/2 ins / 29.3 x 21.6 cm) GBP 20,700. NEW YORK, 27 Jan 1999, *St Filippo Benizzi in Glory, Kneeling Mother and Child below* (chalk, 15 x 10 ins / 39 x 26 cm) USD 23,000. NEW YORK, 28 Jan 1999, *Farmhouse in Tuscany with Woman at Well* (red chalk/wash, 11 x 17 ins / 27 x 42 cm) USD 28,000. ROME, 12 Dec 2001, *Moses and the Miracle of the Water from the Rock* (pencil, 10 x 7 ins / 26 x 18 cm) ITL 3,200,000. LONDON, 13 Dec 2001, *Studies of Two Hands* (black chalk heightened with white, 7 x 7 ins / 17 x 17 cm) GBP 1,100. NEW YORK, 25 Jan 2002, *Study of a Soldier in Profile* (red chalk heightened with white chalk, 15 x 10 ins / 38 x 25 cm) USD 95,000. PARIS, 21 March 2002, *Studies for Altar. Study of Head* (red chalk, double-sided, 10 x 7 ins / 26 x 17 cm) EUR 3,800. PARIS, 27 March 2003, *Studies of Hands* (chalk, 11 x 15 ins / 27 x 38 cm) EUR 6,000. LONDON, 11 Dec 2003, *Diana and Callisto* (oil on canvas, 79 x 102 ins / 200 x 258 cm) GBP 320,000. CLEVELAND, 16 Jan 2004, *Seated Woman with Three Small Children Asleep on her Lap* (red chalk heightened with white, 31 x 44 ins / 79 x 112 cm) USD 3,500.

FRANCESCHINI, Domenico Mariano

Italian, 18th century.
Born in Verona.
Active in Rome.
Engraver.

Domenico Mariano Franceschini is known only for a small engraving dated 1725 and entitled *Amphitheatre of Flavius.*

FRANCESCHINI, Filippo Antonio

Italian, 18th century.
Active in Turin.
Painter.

Filippo Antonio Franceschini was the son of Mattia Franceschini. He worked on the decoration of the church of the Pazzarelli hospital in Turin.

FRANCESCHINI, Gasparo or Gaspero

Italian, 17th century.
Active in Volterra 1610-1630.
Sculptor.

Gasparo Franceschini executed the statue of *St Francis* on the Leonori Chapel altar in the Volterra church of S Francesco. He also carved wooden crucifixes and alabaster statuettes.

FRANCESCHINI, Giacomo

Italian, 17th - 18th century.
Born 1672, in Bologna; died 1745, in Bologna.
Painter.

Giacomo Franceschini was the son and pupil of Marco Antonio Franceschini. He was appointed canon of the church of S Maria Maggiore. He painted historical subjects in the manner of his father. Many of his compositions may be seen in his native Bologna: *Saints Usnaldo, Marguerite, Lucia and Cecilia* in the church of S Maria Incoronata; *Crucifixion* in the church of S Simone; and *St Anne* in the church of S Martino.

FRANCESCHINI, Girolamo

Austrian, 19th century.
Born 12 May 1820, in Trento; died 7 January 1859, in Vienna.
Draughtsman, lithographer.

Franceschini was costume director of the two theatres at the court of Vienna and produced many costume designs of which he himself lithographed a few plates. Among these works are: *Militiaman from Vienna 1848,* costume designs for balls and for the theatre. In Bäuerle he occasionally collaborated on the *Illustrated Theatre Journal,* for which he did the *Satirical Images.*

FRANCESCHINI, Marco Antonio

Italian, 17th - 18th century.
Born 1648, in Bologna; died 1729, in Bologna.
Painter, draughtsman, fresco artist. History painting, religious subjects, mythological subjects, portraits.
Designs for mosaics.
Bolognese School.

Marco Antonio Franceschini studied under Giovanni Maria Galli before going on to become one of Carlo Cigani's most diligent disciples. Some of his early work is to be found in Imola, Ozzano and Piacenza. Under Cigani's direction and with his encouragement, Franceschini painted several oils and frescoes in Bologna, Piacenza, Modena and Reggio nell'Emilia. 1702 saw him working on the palace of the council of Genoa, where he painted subjects relating to the history of that republic. By 1711 he was in Rome, commissioned by Pope Clement XI to provide several cartoons for mosaics in St Peter's. This commission would earn him the papal Order of Christ. He went on to decorate the chapel of the Madonna dei Carmine in Cremona in 1716, before returning to Bologna and continuing to work there until the age of 80. His later works show no deterioration in quality, as may be seen in his *Founders of the Order* for the Padri Servi in Bologna, and his *Pietà* for the Augustinian order in Imola.

MUSEUMS AND GALLERIES:

AUCH: *Lot and his Daughters* - BOLOGNA (Church of Corpus Domini): *Death of St Joseph* - BOLOGNA (Church of S Maria della Carità): *St John on the Island of Patmos* - BOLOGNA (Church of S Maria di Galliera): *St Francis de Sales Kneeling before the Virgin and Child* - BOLOGNA (Pinacoteca Nazionale): *Annunciation; Virgin and Child; Holy Family; Fama; St Thomas*

Aquinas - BUDAPEST: *Moses Rescued from the Waters* - CHAMBÉRY: *St Praxedes* - COPENHAGEN (Statens Mus. for Kunst): *Diana Hunting* - DRESDEN: *Birth of Adonis* (engraving on copper); *Atonement of St Mary Magdalene* - FLORENCE (Uffizi): *Cupid Firing an Arrow; Self-portrait* - MILAN (Pinacoteca di Brera): *St Catherine Vigri* (red chalk) - RAVENNA (Pinacoteca): *St Bartholomew and St Severus* - RIMINI: *St Thomas of Villeneuve Giving Alms to the Poor* - ROME: *Death of Adonis* - ST PETERSBURG (Hermitage): *Judgement of Paris* (drawing) - VIENNA: *Charity; Penitent Mary Magdalene* - VIENNA (Czernin): *Venus and Eros* - VIENNA (Liechtenstein Mus.): *Jacob and Rachel; Joseph and Potiphar's Wife; St Sebastian and St Irene; The Child Jesus Sleeping; Lucretia; Narcissus; Diana, Venus and Adonis; Bacchus, Ariadne and Apollo.*

AUCTION RECORDS:

LONDON, 5 Dec 1908, *Virgin and the Child Jesus*, GBP 11. LUCERNE, 28 Nov 1964, *Landscape with Cupid Preparing to Launch an Arrow*, CHF 5,500. ROME, 24 May 1973, *Mercury Waking Aeneas*, ITL 7,500,000. PARIS, 16 March 1981, *Mars and Venus* (oil on canvas, 53 1/4 x 48 ins / 135 x 121 cm) FRF 26,500. LONDON, 12 April 1983, *Tancredi and Erminia* (black chalk, pen and wash, 9 3/4 x 13 1/2 ins / 24.7 x 34.4 cm) GBP 1,600. LOKEREN, 20 Oct 1984, *St Jerome in the Wilderness* (oil on canvas, 24 3/4 x 19 ins / 63 x 48 cm) BEF 220,000. MILAN, 26 Nov 1985, *Sibylla* (oil on canvas, 77 1/2 x 68 ins / 197 x 173 cm) ITL 18,000,000. ROME, 22 March 1988, *Portrait of an Adolescent Girl* (oil on canvas, 22 x 17 3/4 ins / 56 x 45 cm) ITL 15,000,000. MILAN, 27 March 1990, *Joshua Arresting the Sun in its Course; Story of the Prophet Elijah* (oil on canvas, 41 3/4 x 59 ins / 106 x 149 cm) ITL 58,000,000. LONDON, 24 May 1991, *Abduction of Europa* (oil on canvas, 45 3/4 x 59 3/4 ins / 116.5 x 152 cm) GBP 26,400. NEW YORK, 30 May 1991, *Intoxication of Pan* (oil on canvas, 44 1/2 x 57 3/4 ins / 113 x 147 cm) USD 121,000. ROME, 4 Dec 1991, *Diana and Actaeon* (oil on canvas, 22 x 32 1/4 ins / 56 x 82 cm) ITL 17,250,000. NEW YORK, 15 Oct 1992, *Penitent Magdalene with an Angel Bringing her the Crown of Thorns* (oil on canvas, 49 x 37 1/2 ins / 124.5 x 95.3 cm) USD 33,000. LONDON, 6 Dec 1995, *Tarquin and Lucretia* (oil on canvas, 73 x 73 ins / 184.5 x 184.5 cm) GBP 78,500. NEW YORK, 10 Jan 1996, *St Zosimus the Hermit Giving the Last Rites to St Mary the Egyptian* (oil/copper, 16 3/4 x 21 1/2 ins / 42.6 x 54.3 cm) USD 112,500. MILAN, 3 April 1996, *Biblical Scene; Jacob and Rachel* (oil on canvas, 59 3/4 x 45 1/4 ins / 152 x 115 cm) ITL 92,000,000. LONDON, 11 Dec 1996, *Hagar and the Angel* (oil on canvas, 86 x 85 ins / 217.5 x 215 cm) GBP 54,300. NEW YORK, 31 Jan 1997, *Intoxication of Pan* (oil on canvas, 44 1/2 x 57 3/4 ins / 113 x 147 cm) USD 34,500. LONDON, 4 July 1997, *Mercury Capturing Birds, Cupid Capturing Hearts* (oil on canvas, 34 1/4 x 98 1/2 ins / 87 x 250 cm) GBP 84,000. LONDON, 15 April 1999, *The Penitent Magdalene with an Angel* (oil on canvas, 47 x 58 ins / 119 x 147 cm) GBP 6,000. NEW YORK, 28 Jan 2000, *Ariadne on the Island of Naxos, Theseus at Sea Beyond* (oil on copper, 18 x 25 ins / 46 x 63 cm) USD 150,000. LONDON, 6 July 2000, *Armida Discovers the Sleeping Rinaldo. Erminia and the Shepherds* (oil on canvas, a pair, 37 x 51 ins / 95 x 129 cm) GBP 75,000. NEW YORK, 23 May 2001, *Triumph of Venus* (oil on canvas, oval, 35 x 46 ins / 90 x 117 cm) USD 120,000. LONDON, 11 July 2001, *Liberality. Maternal Charity* (oil on copper, a pair, 17 x 22 ins / 42 x 57 cm) GBP 220,000. PARIS, 26 June 2002, *Study of Young Man, Hands and Foot* (chalk, 12 x 9 ins / 30 x 22 cm) EUR 2,200. LONDON, 10 Dec 2003, *Holy Family with St Anne* (oil on canvas, 27 x 22 ins / 69 x 55 cm) GBP 26,000. PARIS, 18 March 2004, *Thetis Entrusts the Young Achilles to Chiron the Centaur* (pen/brown ink/brown wash heightened with white, 13 x 16 ins / 34 x 41 cm) EUR 5,500.

FRANCESCHINI, Mattia

Italian, 18th century.
Active in Turin c. 1745.
Painter. History painting.

FRANCESCHINI, Vincenzo

Italian, 18th century.
Born 1680, in Rome.
Active in Florence 1700-1740.
Engraver (burin), painter.
Florentine School.

Vincenzo Franceschini was probably related to Domenico Franceschini. He engraved some of the illustrations for the *Museo Fiorentino* published in 1748.

FRANCESCHINI, Vincenzo

Italian, 19th century.
Born 1812, in Cassandrino; died 1885, in Naples.
Painter. Religious subjects, landscapes with figures, landscapes.

Franceschini was a pupil of Pitloo and Marsigli in Naples, where he won a gold medal at an exhibition. Thereafter, he spent many years in Rome, mainly painting landscapes.

MUSEUMS AND GALLERIES:

NAPLES (Mus. di San Martino): *Temptation of Christ in the Desert.*

AUCTION RECORDS:

ROME, 25 May 1988, *Landscape with Washerwomen* (oil on canvas, 20 3/4 x 29 1/4 ins / 53 x 74.5 cm) ITL 4,000,000. BOLOGNA, 8-9 June 1992, *Visitors inside the Coliseum* (oil on canvas, 20 x 14 ins / 50.5 x 35.5 cm) ITL 2,990,000.

FRANCESCHINI, Vittorio

Italian, 18th century.
Active in Florence in 1744.
Engraver.

Vittorio Franceschini engraved illustrations for *Twenty-four Selected Views of the City of Florence.*

FRANCESCHINO DA CASTELNUOVO-SCRIVIA

Italian.
Painter. Religious subjects.

He worked in Piedmont at the beginning of the 16th century, in 1507 producing an altar painting in the church of the Holy Trinity in Pozzuolo-Formigaro.

AUCTION RECORDS:

MILAN, 3 April 1996, *Virgin and Child* (tempera/panel, 15 3/4 x 11 ins / 40 x 27 cm) ITL 21,850,000.

FRANCESCHINO DA PADOVA

Italian, 14th century.
Miniaturist.

Among the treasures of the cathedral in Gemona (Friuli) is an antiphonary which Franceschino da Padova decorated with historical and allegorical images. He may perhaps be the same artist as a 'Frate Francesco miniatore' (miniaturist) mentioned in Padua in 1344.

FRANCESCHINO DA VENEZIA

Italian, 14th century.
Active in Verona.
Sculptor.

Franceschino da Venezia sculpted the armorial bearings of Prior Pietro degli Specchi in the chancel of the church of S Anastasia in Verona.

FRANCESCHITTO, or Francisquito

Spanish, 17th century.
Born 1681, in Valladolid; died 1705, in Naples.
Painter.

Franceschitto was a pupil of Luca Giordano and accompanied his teacher to Italy. In Naples he executed a superb painting of *St Pascal Surrounded by Angels* for the church of Sta Maria del Monte. Unfortunately his promising career was cut short by his early death.

AUCTION RECORDS:
PARIS, 1843, *Landscape with Three Figures,* FRF 700; *Landscape with Animals,* FRF 155. LONDON, 10 June 1932, *Young Man,* GBP 9.

FRANCESCO
Italian, 14th century.
Active in Venice c. 1300.
Painter.
The school of St John the Evangelist in Venice has a painting of the Virgin signed by Francesco.

FRANCESCO
Italian, 14th century.
Active in Siena c. 1361-1388.
Painter, fresco artist. Religious subjects.
Sienese School.
A *Christ on the Cross* painted in tempera by Francesco, a primitive artist, is in the museum in Berlin.

AUCTION RECORDS:
LONDON, 31 March 1944, *Annunciation; Assumption* (group) GBP 997.

FRANCESCO, called Franciscus Italus
Italian, 16th century.
Active in Poland.
Sculptor, architect.
Francesco, the first Renaissance artist in Poland, worked from 1502 to 1509 for the prince Sigismund Jagiello, later Sigismund I, king of Poland. The *Funeral Monument of King Jan Albert of Poland* in the cathedral in Cracow is attributed to him. He is not to be confused with Francesco della Lora of Florence, also called Franciscus Italus, who was the architect at the court of King Sigismund.

FRANCESCO (Father)
Italian, 17th century.
Active in Perugia, c. 1600.
Painter (including glass). History painting.
Francesco was a priest from Monte Cassino.

FRANCESCO. See also first name

FRANCESCO, Benjamino de
Italian, 19th century.
Born in Naples; died 1869, in Dinard, France.
Painter, engraver. Genre scenes.
Benjamino de Francesco's work was shown at exhibitions in Naples and Florence.
MUSEUMS AND GALLERIES:
ANGERS: *Petrarch and Laura* - COPENHAGEN (Thorvaldsens Mus.): *Aeneas with the Sibyl; Landscape.*
AUCTION RECORDS:
PARIS, 1870, *Port of Annunziatella,* FRF 1,800; *View of the Tower at Chiaja,* FRF 630; *Study of Plants,* FRF 810; *Study of Poppies,* FRF 510. PARIS, 1 May 1900, *The Four Seasons* (four decorative panels) FRF 140.

FRANCESCO, Betto di. See **BETTO DI FRANCESCO FIORENTINO**

FRANCESCO, Francese. See **PERRIER François**

FRANCESCO, Giovanni Battista de
Italian, 18th century.
Born to a family originally from Predazzo; died c. 1720, in Turin.
Painter. Portraits.

FRANCESCO, Raffaello di. See **BOTTICINI Raffaelo di Francesco**

FRANCESCO D'ALESSANDRO. See **ALESSANDRO Francesco d'**

FRANCESCO D'ANDREAS
Italian, 15th century.
Active in Siena.
Painter.
Francesco d'Andreas painted the fresco of the *Battle of Poggio Imperiale* in the Mappamondi room in the city hall in 1480.

FRANCESCO D'ANTONIO
Italian, 15th century.
Born 1394; died after 1433.
Painter. Religious subjects.
Francesco d'Antonio may have been related to Francesco d'Antonio da Viterbo.
AUCTION RECORDS:
MILAN, 3 March 1987, *Virgin and Child* (oil on panel with gold ground, arched altarpiece, 37 3/4 x 18 1/2 ins / 96 x 47 cm) ITL 59,000,000. LONDON, 8 July 1987, *Virgin and Child Surrounded by Angels* (tempera/panel with gilt ground, rounded altarpiece, 37 x 22 1/2 ins / 94 x 57 cm) GBP 72,000.

FRANCESCO D'ANTONIO DA VITERBO, called Balletta
Italian, 15th century.
Painter. Religious subjects.
A number of works by Francesco d'Antonio da Viterbo are still in Viterbo, including his principal work, a triptych in the church of S Rosa. Remnants of frescoes dating from 1449 can be found in the church of S Maria della Verità.
MUSEUMS AND GALLERIES:
VITERBO (Mus. Civico): *Virgin with Angels* (fresco).

FRANCESCO D'AREZZO
Italian, 14th century.
Sculptor.
Francesco d'Arezzo, a pupil of d'Oredigna, collaborated with Betto di Francesco on the altar of Arezzo cathedral. He is linked with Giovanni di Francesco d'Arezzo, who may have been his son and collaborator.

FRANCESCO D'AREZZO
Italian, 15th century.
Born in Tuscany.
Active during the 15th century in Tuscany.
Painter.
Francesco d'Arezzo painted the votive image in the church of S Caterina at Galatina.

FRANCESCO D'OBERTO DA MONEGLIA
Italian, 14th century.
Painter. Religious subjects. Miniatures.
Francesco d'Oberto da Moneglia worked in Ferrara in 1368, was a member of the team working on the civic hall in Fassolo, and later worked in Genoa. The academy in Genoa has his small painting of the *Virgin between St Dominic and St John the Evangelist* in its collection.

FRANCESCO DA BERGAMO
Italian, 16th century.
Sculptor.
With his son, Bartolomeo di Francesco da Bergamo, Francesco da Bergamo sculpted a statue of *St Mary Magdalene* for the church of S Maria de'Servi in Venice.

FRANCESCO DA CARONA. See **CASELLA Francesco**

FRANCESCO DA CASTELLO
Italian, 15th century.
Active in Milan.
Miniaturist.
Francesco da Castello decorated a breviary, now in the monastery at Lambach (Upper Austria), with miniatures.

FRANCESCO DA CITTÀ DELLA PIEVE
Italian, 15th century.
Painter.
A fresco of the *Crucifixion* in the church of S Giuseppe in Paciano bears the signature of Francesco da Città della Pieve.

FRANCESCO DA CITTA DI CASTELLO
Italian.
Born to a family originally from Città di Castello (Arezzo).
Painter.
We know of a small number of his works, which reveal the influence of Perugino (of whom he was perhaps a pupil), Signorelli and Raphael.
MUSEUMS AND GALLERIES:
CITTÀ DI CASTELLO: *Virgin with Child, Surrounded by St Catherine, St Nicholas of Tolentino and Two Other Saints; Virgin with Child between St Jerome and Another Saint; Annunciation.*

FRANCESCO DA CODIGORO. See **CODIGORO Francesco de**

FRANCESCO DA FABRIANO. See **GHISSI Francescuccio** or **Francesco**

FRANCESCO DA FIRENZE. See **MICHELI Francesco**

FRANCESCO DA LUGANO
Italian, 17th century.
Sculptor.
Francesco da Lugano collaborated with Bernardo da Lugano on statues for the monastery of S Pietro in Reggio nell'Emilia.

FRANCESCO DA MILANO
Italian, 15th century.
Of Lombard origin; died before 12 November 1505.
Sculptor.
Francesco da Milano worked in Rome and later in Naples and the surrounding area, where he executed numerous sculptural works for the nobility. Only the armorial bearings of Jacopo Rocco in the church of S Lorenzo in Naples survive.

FRANCESCO DA MILANO
Italian, 16th century.
Active in Bologna.
Sculptor.
Francesco da Milano worked with Alfonso Lombardi on the church of S Petronio in Bologna.

FRANCESCO DA MILANO, or Francesco Pagani
Italian, 16th century.
Active in Milan c. 1540.
Painter. History painting.
Francesco da Milano imitated Titian and Pordenone. His *St Roch, St Sebastian and St Nicholas* is in the church in Caneva di Sacile, and an *Assumption* in the church at Soligo. Other works attributed to him include a *St Anthony, St Lucia and St Apollonia* at Porcia, near Pordenone, the remains of a polyptych at Sedico and an *Adoration of the Shepherds*, now destroyed, in the church of S Martino in Conegliano.
MUSEUMS AND GALLERIES:
CANEVA (Church of S. Tomaso): *S. Sebastiano, S. Rocco e S. Nicolo* (*St Roch, St Sebastian, St Nicholas*) (1512, triptych) - PIEVE DI SOLIGO (Church of S Maria Assunta): *Assunzione di Maria* (*Assumption*) (1540, altar painting) - PORCIA (Church of S Giorgio): *S. Lucia tra S. Antonio di Padova e S. Apollonia, Annunciazione, il Padreterno tra angeli* (*St Anthony, St Lucy and St Apollonia*) (c. 1518, altar painting) - TREVISO: *Virgin with Angels* - VENICE (Gal. dell'Accademia): *Virgin with Angels; Pietà* (attributed).

FRANCESCO DA MILANO
Italian, 17th century.
Active in Reggio nell'Emilia.
Sculptor.
Francesco da Milano worked alongside Giacomo da Milano in 1622 to produce statues and low reliefs for an altar in the church of the Madonna della Chiara.

FRANCESCO DA MONTEREALE
Italian, 16th century.
Active in L'Aquila (Abruzzi).
Painter.
Francesco da Montereale was the son of Paolo da Montereale, and a member of the Accademia di San Luca in Rome in 1535. A fresco of the *Virgin with St Sebastian and St Roch* can be found in the church of S Silvestro in L'Aquila.

FRANCESCO DA NAPOLI. See **PAGANO Francesco**

FRANCESCO DA PARMA
Italian, 15th century.
Active in Padua from 1467 to 1477.
Sculptor (wood).
Francesco da Parma worked with Domenico da Piacenza on the restoration of the church of St Justina in Padua.

FRANCESCO DA PAVIA. See **FERRARI Francesco de**

FRANCESCO DA PERUGIA. See **BARONI Francesco**

FRANCESCO DA RAGUSA
Italian, 17th century.
Born c. 1591, in Rome or Ragusa; died 20 February 1665, in Rome.
Painter.
Francesco da Ragusa painted compositions for churches in Rome and for the Brescia church of S Francesco dei Monaci.

FRANCESCO DA RIMINI
Italian, 14th century.
Painter.
Francesco da Rimini painted the frescoes in the Franciscan monastery in Bologna, which was destroyed in 1882. His work is strongly influenced by Giotto, and he is sometimes confounded with the master of Verrucchio.

FRANCESCO DA SAN SIMONE
Italian, 13th century.
Mosaicist.
This artist worked in Pisa Cathedral in 1301 and was replaced by Cimabue.

FRANCESCO DA SIENA
Italian, 14th century.
Active in Pistoia.
Painter.
In 1346, Francesco da Siena collaborated with Bartolommo di Vanni on a retable for the church of S Giovanni Fuorcivitas.

FRANCESCO DA SIENA
Italian, 16th century.
Active in Siena.
Painter. Historical subjects, portraits. Ornaments.
Francesco da Siena was the pupil of Baldassare Peruzzi.

FRANCESCO DA SIENA
Italian, 17th century.
Painter.
Francesco da Siena studied under Mascagni and worked under the latter's direction on Salzburg Cathedral and Heilbrunn Castle. Two altarpieces in the Franciscan church in Salzburg are attributed to him, namely a *Martyrdom and Ascent of St Sebastian* and an *Adoration of the Shepherds* in the

Capuchin monastery. Salzburg Cathedral houses a copy of his *Transfiguration*.

FRANCESCO DA TERRANOVA (Fra)
Italian, 15th century.
Painter. Religious subjects.
There is a reference to Francesco da Terranova's paintings in the church of S Francesco in 1476 in Assisi.

FRANCESCO DA TOLENTINO
Italian, 15th century.
Miniaturist.
Francesco da Tolentino's signature appears on a manuscript in the Vatican library, originally in the library of Federigo da Montefeltro. The frontispiece depicts *Duke Federigo da Montefeltro on Horseback before Cyrus on a Throne*.

FRANCESCO DA TOLENTINO
Italian, 16th century.
Painter.
A chapel in the church of the monastery in Liveri, near Nola, contains altarpieces by Francesco da Tolentino in the style of Pinturricchio, entitled *Pietà, Adoration of the Magi* and *Christ with Saints*. A number of frescoes in S Maria Nuova in Naples are attributed to him including the *Coronation of the Virgin Mary, Adoration of the Magi with Saints of the Franciscan Order, Annunciation* and *Birth of Christ*.

FRANCESCO DA URBINO, or Francesco da Urbina, or Francisco de Urbino or Urbina
Italian, 16th century.
Painter, designer of ornamental architectural features. Grotesques.
The father of Diego da Urbina, Francesco da Urbino was appointed court painter in Spain and worked on the Escorial and in Madrid and Segovia. He worked in Urbino around 1575.

FRANCESCO DA URBINO (Fra)
Italian, 16th century.
Architectural draughtsman.
The work of Francesco da Urbino includes a book of sketches for altars, confessionals and chests for churches in Jesi, Cagli and other towns.

FRANCESCO DA VENEZIA
Italian, 14th century.
Active in Aquilèia.
Painter.
Francesco da Venezia painted two small altarpieces in Aquilèia, the *Coronation of Mary* and *Mary with the Infant Jesus*.

FRANCESCO DA VERONA. See **BONSIGNORI Francesco**

FRANCESCO DA VICENZA. See **COZZI Francesco di Giampietro**

FRANCESCO DA VOLTERRA, or also known as Francesco di Neri da Volterra
Italian, 14th century.
Active in Pisa.
Painter.
In 1344, Francesco da Volterra executed a painting for the cathedral in Pisa and was one of the artists to work on the Campo Santo. He is known also as Francesco Neri da Volterra, to whom a picture of the *Virgin* in the Galerie Estense in Modena is attributed.

FRANCESCO DA VOLTERRA. See also **CAPRIANI Francesco**

FRANCESCO DE ALESIIS
Italian, 15th century.
Active in Udine during the second half of the 15th century.
Painter.
Francesco de Alesiis is noted for the decorative fresco above the door of the Confraternita di S Giromano in Udine. This work, signed by the master, is dated 1494 and depicts *St Jerome Surrounded by Monks*. The frescoes in a chapel in Contovello, near Trieste, are also attributed to him.

FRANCESCO DE ALIENZA. See **ALIENZA Francesco de**

FRANCESCO DE AMOROTTO. See **AMOROTTO Francesco de**

FRANCESCO DE FERRARI. See **FERRARI Francesco**

FRANCESCO DE GIOVANNELLI. See **GIOVANNELLI Francesco de'**

FRANCESCO DE MURA. See **MURA Francesco de**

FRANCESCO DE VICO
Italian, 15th century.
Painter. History painting, portraits.
Lombard School.
Francesco de Vico painted the portraits of *Francesco Sforza, Duke of Milan and Bianca Maria, his Wife, Kneeling before Pope Pius II* for the chapel of the Ospedale in Milan. This painting is thought to have been destroyed in the 17th century and is known as a result of an old copy kept in the council chamber at the Ospedale.

FRANCESCO DEI FRANCESCHI. See **FRANCESCHI Francesco dei**

FRANCESCO DEI GABRIELLI
Italian, 15th century.
Active in Florence c. 1425.
Painter.
Francesco dei Gabrielli painted a retable for the hospice of St Andrew in Percusina.

FRANCESCO DEL FIORE. See **FIORE Francesco del**

FRANCESCO DEL TINTORE. See **TINTORE Francesco del**

FRANCESCO DELLA BIAVA
Italian, 15th century.
Born 15th century, in Verona.
Painter.
Francesco della Biava worked in Ferrara about 1470 for Duke Borso.

FRANCESCO DI AGOSTINO ERICELLO. See **ERICELLO Francesco di Agostino**

FRANCESCO DI ANTONIO DEL VALENTE. See **VALENTE Francesco di Antonio del**

FRANCESCO DI BONAJUTO
Italian, 16th century.
Painter.
There is a reference to Francesco di Bonajuto in Venetico, a province of Messina, in 1533.

FRANCESCO DI BORGO
Italian, 15th century.
Active in Borgo San Sepolcro, c. 1446.
Painter. History painting.
Siret points out that the style of Francesco di Borgo bears such a strong resemblance to that of Piero della Francesca that he might well have been confused with the latter, were it not for the fact that he was his pupil.

FRANCESCO DI CECCO. See **GHISSI Francescuccio** or **Francesco**

FRANCESCO DI COLA. See **COLA Francesco**

FRANCESCO DI DOMENICO. See **MONCIATTO** and **VALDAMBRINO**

FRANCESCO DI FILIPPO
Italian, 16th century.
Sculptor.

Francesco di Filippo was a pupil of Peruzzi. In 1534, he sculpted the travertine sarcophagus of *Celia Petrucci* in the church of l'Osservanza in Siena.

FRANCESCO DI FRANCESCO. See **BARCKE**

FRANCESCO DI GENTILE DA FABRIANO
Italian, 15th century.
Born to a family originally from Fabriano.
Painter.

Francesco di Gentile da Fabriano may have been the son of Gentile da Fabriano. Works held in private collections include a triptych representing the *Virgin, St John the Baptist and Christ*, a *Virgin with Angels* and two *Annunciations*, in Florence, and an *Ecce Homo* in London.

MUSEUMS AND GALLERIES:
ROME (Gal. Colonna): *Portrait of the Infant Jesus* - VATICAN (Pinacoteca Vaticana): *Virgin and the Infant Jesus* - WASHINGTON DC (Melchett Court): *Ecce Homo*.

AUCTION RECORDS:
LONDON, 16 Jan 1925, *Madonna and Child Enthroned*, GBP 210. LONDON, 9 May 1934, *Madonna and Child*, GBP 105. LONDON, 18 March 1935, *Madonna and Child*, GBP 52. LONDON, 28 May 1936, *Madonna and Child*, GBP 55. LONDON, 31 May 1946, *Madonna Adoring the Infant Redeemer*, GBP 120.

FRANCESCO DI GIORGIO MARTINI
Italian, 15th century.
Born September 1439, in Siena; died January 1502, in Siena.
Painter, sculptor, architect.
Sienese School.

A universal artist par excellence, Francesco di Giorgio Martini worked as a sculptor and painter and above all as an architect. He loved arabesque and delicate lines, and admired Donatello, whose style is echoed in particular in the broken low reliefs of the *Deposition* in Venice and in the architectural structure of the *Flagellation* in Perugia.

Francesco di Giorgio Martini artist was a pupil of Lorenzo di Pietro, called Vecchietta, and his early sculptures and paintings were inspired by the style of his master, apparent from one of the two angels flanking Lorenzo di Pietro's candelabra door in the cathedral in Siena as well as from his paintings *Annunciation* and *Coronation of the Virgin* (1472) in Siena. Bringing together the genius of Florence and Siena, he staged his *Nativity* (1490) in front of a Roman triumphal arch. He had been summoned to Urbino in 1477, where he must have noted the research into perspective in inlaid work which was in progress there around 1475. 'Manuscript 148' in Turin, consisting of imaginary architectural compositions, is also attributed to him. An interest in military architecture led him to design defensive walls and fortresses and to write a *Treatise on Civil and Military Architecture*. He was attracted by the symbolism of astrology and fascinated by the geometrical relationships between the human figure and architecture, on one occasion incorporating a diagram of a man's body within the architectural plans for a church. This work was to be pursued by Leonardo da Vinci and later by Dürer. The finest architectural work by Martini is the little church of the Madona del Calcinaio (1485), in Cortona; the design is based on a Latin cross, and its structural features are emphasised by the use of pietra serena (Fiorenzuola stone) in a manner which would later be taken up by Michelangelo and Brunelleschi in Florence.

BIBLIOGRAPHY:
Betts, R.J., '*On the Chronology of Francesco di Giorgio's Treatises: New Evidence from an Unpublished Manuscript*' in *Journal of the Society of Architectural Historians*, vol 36, 1977. Vertova, Luisa, '*Cupid and Psyche in Renaissance Painting before Raphael*' in *Journal of the Warburg & Courtauld Institute*, vol 42, 1979. Ericsson, C.H., *Roman Architecture Expressed in Sketches by Francesco di Giorgio Martini: Studies in Imperial Roman and Early Christian Architecture*, Societas Scientiarum Fennica, Helsinki, 1980. Lowic, L., '*The Meaning and Significance of the Human Analogy in Francesco di Giorgio's Trattato*' in *Journal of the Society of Architectural Historians*, vol 42, 1983. Christiansen, Keith/Kanter, L./Strehlke, C., *Renaissance Painting in Siena*, exhibition catalogue, Metropolitan Musuem of Art, New York, 1988. Kolb, C., '*The Francesco di Giorgio Material in the Zichy Codex*' in *Journal of the Society of Architectural Historians*, vol 47, 1988. Dechert, M.S.A., '*The Military Architecture of Francesco di Giorgio in Southern Italy*' in *Journal of the Society of Architectural Historians*, vol 49, 1990. Bellosi, Luciano, *Francesco di Giorgio e il rinascimento a Siena, 1450-1500*, exhibition catalogue, S. Agostino, Siena, 1993. Fiore, F.P./Tafuri, M., et al., *Francesco di Giorgio, architetto*, Milan, 1993-1994.

MUSEUMS AND GALLERIES:
DRESDEN (Gemäldegal. Alte Meister): *Aesculapius* (bronze) - FLORENCE (Uffizi): *Life of St Benedict*; *Nativity* - FRANKFURT AM MAIN: *Virgin* - LONDON (NG): *Virgin and the Infant Jesus* - MUNICH (Alte Pinakothek): *St Anthony* (predella) - PARIS (Louvre): *Rape of Europa* - SIENA (Accademia): *Annunciation*; *Story of St Joseph*; *Virgin*.

AUCTION RECORDS:
NEW YORK, 20 Nov 1931, *Triumph of Chastity*, USD 3,100. NEW YORK, 18 and 19 April 1934, *Triumph of Chastity*, USD 550. LONDON, 7 July 2000, *Archery Tournament with Maidens Drawn in Chariots* (oil on panel, 13 x 50 ins / 34 x 128 cm) GBP 70,000.

FRANCESCO DI GIOVANNI
Italian, 15th century.
Active in Ascoli Piceno.
Sculptor (wood).

Francesco di Giovanni carved the Lamusa door for a portal in Ascoli cathedral; a number of the stalls there are also attributed to him.

FRANCESCO DI GIOVANNI. See also **FERRUCCI Francesco**

FRANCESCO DI GIULIANO
Italian, 15th - 16th century.
Active in Verona c. 1500.
Sculptor.
Veronese School.

The museum in Berlin has a low relief in wood of two cupids carrying the head of St John the Baptist on a platter, the base of which bears the signature of Francesco di Giuliano. He may be the painter Franciscus Juliani pictor, born in Verona in 1462 and recorded there until 1502.

FRANCESCO DI MAESTRO GIOTTO
Italian, 14th century.
Painter. History painting.

Francesco di Maestro Giotto was a pupil of Giotto.

FRANCESCO DI MANTOVANA
Italian, 17th century.
Active c. 1663.
Painter. Flowers, fruit.

FRANCESCO DI MICHELE, Francesco da Firenze
Italian, 14th century.
Active in Florence in 1385.
Painter.

A *Virgin with Saints* in the Louvre is attributed to Francesco di Michele, who was also known as Francesco da Firenze.

FRANCESCO DI NERI DA VOLTERRA. See **FRANCESCO DA VOLTERRA**

FRANCESCO DI NERI DI UBALDO (Fra), called Sellaio
Italian, 14th century.
Born 14th century, in Florence.
Sculptor.
In 1366, Francesco di Neri di Ubaldo was a member of the committee of experts whose remit was the construction of the cathedral. He sculpted the statues of apostles and evangelists on the cathedral façade.

FRANCESCO DI PELLEGRINO. See **PELLEGRINO**

FRANCESCO DI PIERO. See **GIOVANNELLI Francesco de'**

FRANCESCO DI PIETRO D'ASSISI
Italian, 14th century.
Of Sienese origin.
Active in Cortona.
Sculptor.
Francesco di Pietro d'Assisi worked with Angelo di Pietro d'Assisi on the tomb of Bishop Ranieri Ubertoni in the church of St Francis and on the funeral monument to St Margaret in the church dedicated to her in Cortona.

FRANCESCO DI PIETRO DA VENEZIA
Italian, 16th century.
Active in San Severino.
Sculptor.
Francesco di Pietro da Venezia worked with his brother, Antonio di Pietro da Venezia.

FRANCESCO DI SIMONE
Italian, 14th century.
Painter. History painting.
According to Siret, Francesco di Simone was the pupil of master Simone.

FRANCESCO DI STEFANO. See **PESELLINO**

FRANCESCO DI STEFANO
Italian, 15th century.
Sculptor.
Sienese School.
In 1444, Francesco di Stefano collaborated with Antonio Federighi on the funeral monument of the bishop *Carlo Bartoli* in the cathedral in Siena. He also worked in Rome and Orvieto.

FRANCESCO DI VANNI, called Il Chiancianese
Italian, 14th century.
Active in Siena.
Painter.
Francesco di Vanni worked on the cathedral in Siena in 1385.

FRANCESCO DI VANNI
Italian, 14th century.
Died 6 November 1394.
Active in Siena.
Painter.
With his brother, Andrea di Vanni, Francesco di Vanni executed the paintings for three chapels in Siena Cathedral in 1370.

FRANCESCO FIAMMINGO. See **BARCKE Francesco di Francesco**

FRANCESCO FIORENTINO, known as Zucca
Italian, 16th century.
Active in Naples.
Sculptor (wood).
In 1536, Francesco Fiorentino made the stalls, now destroyed, in the church of Carmine Maggiore in Naples.

FRANCESCO FIORENTINO
Italian, 16th century.
Active in Venice.
Sculptor (wood).
Francesco Fiorentino did the carvings for the organ in the church of S Sebastiano in Venice about 1559.

FRANCESCO MIRANDA. See **MIRANDA Francesco**

FRANCESCO NAPOLETANO
Italian, 15th - 16th century.
Of Neapolitan origin.
Active in Milan c. 1500.
Painter. Religious subjects.
Francesco Napoletano was influenced by Ambrogio da Predis, who was undoubtedly his master, and by Leonardo da Vinci, and had a keen eye for detail.
Museums and Galleries:
Milan (Pinacoteca di Brera): *Virgin with the Infant Jesus* - Zurich: *Virgin Enthroned between St John the Baptist and St Sebastian; Virgin, Half-length Portrait.*

FRANCESCO NAPOLETANO
Italian, 16th century.
Painter.
There are references to Francesco Napoletano as a member of the Accademia di San Luca in Rome between 1534 and 1561.

FRANCESCO PADUANO
Italian, 16th century.
Born 16th century, in Padua.
Active in Trento between 1548 and 1550.
Painter.
Francesco Paduano may be the 'maestro Francesco depentor' whose paintings at the Porta dell'Aquila are mentioned in Trento in 1549.

FRANCESCO PAGANO. See **PAGANO Francesco**

FRANCESCO PAPPALETTERE
Italian, 15th century.
Painter.
Francesco Pappalettere painted murals and ceiling frescoes in Naples and Capua in 1492 and 1498.

FRANCESCO PLACIDO DI GIACOMO. See **POLAZITO DI GIACOMO**

FRANCESCONI, Gasparo
Italian, 19th century.
Of Venetian origin.
Painter.
Around 1800, Francesconi painted a *Virgin Seated, Surrounded by Four Saints* for Treviso Cathedral.

FRANCESCUCCIO DI CECCO. See **GHISSI**

FRANCESE. See also first name

FRANCESE, Franco
Italian, 20th century.
Born 1920, in Milan.
Painter.
Francese studied sculpture with Manzu at the Accademia di Belle Arti di Brera in Milan, then took up painting immediately afterwards. Early on in his career his style of painting was Realist, and influenced by the widely-adopted Neo-Cubism of the day. It then evolved in an Abstract Expressionist direction, although a few evocations of reality still remained.

Francese participated in the Venice Biennale in 1952, and then again in 1960, when an entire room was devoted to his work. Other key exhibitions include the Rome Quadriennale in 1955 and 1959; the third and fourth Marzotto prize, in 1954 and 1960; and the São Paulo Biennale in 1961. A large number of his works were also shown in solo exhibitions in Milan in 1954, 1955 and 1956.

AUCTION RECORDS:

MILAN, 9 Nov 1976, *Landscape No 1* (1953, oil on canvas, 36 1/4 x 28 3/4 ins / 92 x 73 cm) ITL 700,000. MILAN, 7 Nov 1978, *Elegy for Kronstadt* (1970, oil on canvas, 32 x 51 1/4 ins / 81 x 130 cm) ITL 1,300,000. MILAN, 12 March 1980, *Motherhood* (1956, charcoal/paper, 27 1/2 x 22 ins / 70 x 56 cm) ITL 850,000. ROME, 20 April 1982, *Guitarist* (1961, mixed media, 15 x 19 ins / 38 x 48.5 cm) ITL 800,000. MILAN, 5 April 1984, *Le Malinconia del Dürer No 1* (*Dürer's Melancholia I*) (1962, oil on canvas, 48 1/2 x 39 ins / 123 x 99 cm) ITL 5,000,000. MILAN, 19 June 1986, *Sunday* (1966, oil on remounted canvas, 8 1/4 x 17 3/4 ins / 21 x 45 cm) ITL 1,500,000. LONDON, 8 July 1987, *A Quelli di Kronstadt* (1966, oil on canvas, 21 1/4 x 29 1/4 ins / 54 x 74 cm) ITL 4,500,000. MILAN, 20 March 1989, *Study of the Studio* (1987, oil on canvas, 18 1/2 x 30 3/4 ins / 47 x 78 cm) ITL 5,500,000. MILAN, 7 June 1989, *Starry Night* (1973, oil on canvas, 28 3/4 x 23 1/2 ins / 73 x 60 cm) ITL 6,000,000. MILAN, 19 Dec 1989, *Bird Tapping on the Glass* (oil on canvas, 32 x 25 1/2 ins / 81.5 x 65 cm) ITL 7,000,000. MILAN, 27 March 1990, *Starry Night* (1973, oil on canvas, 18 x 15 ins / 46 x 38 cm) ITL 4,000,000. MILAN, 19 June 1991, *Study for Cinemascope* (1958, oil on canvas, 25 1/2 x 20 3/4 ins / 64.5 x 53 cm) ITL 5,500,000. MILAN, 14 April 1992, *Boarding* (1982, oil on canvas, 25 3/4 x 21 1/4 ins / 65.5 x 54 cm) ITL 5,500,000. MILAN, 16 Nov 1993, *Night of Love* (1960, oil on canvas, 59 3/4 x 62 1/4 ins / 152 x 158 cm) ITL 21,850,000. MILAN, 15 March 1994, *Striptease* (1961, oil on canvas, 85 x 78 3/4 ins / 215 x 200 cm) ITL 14,605,000. MILAN, 22 June 1995, *Study for the Studio* (1985, oil on canvas, 17 1/4 x 28 3/4 ins / 44 x 73 cm) ITL 7,475,000. MILAN, 23 May 1996, *La Bestia Addosso* (1961, mixed media/paper, 19 3/4 x 13 1/2 ins / 50 x 34 cm) ITL 2,530,000. MILAN, 11 April 2000, *Siesta* (1964, tempera on paper, 21 x 16 ins / 53 x 40 cm) ITL 4,000,000. MILAN, 15 Nov 2000, *Elegy for Kronstadt* (oil on canvas, 17 x 32 ins / 42 x 81 cm) ITL 6,500,000. MILAN, 27 March 2001, *Beast Selection Two* (1968, oil on canvas, 22 x 18 ins / 57 x 45 cm) ITL 4,500,000. PRATO, 1 Dec 2001, *Figures* (1957, oil on canvas, 32 x 26 ins / 81 x 65 cm) ITL 6,000,000. VERCELLI, 2 March 2002, *Boarding* (1974, oil on canvas, 26 x 22 ins / 65 x 57 cm) EUR 3,000. MILAN, 14 May 2002, *Pregnant Woman* (1956, oil on canvas, 36 x 28 ins / 91 x 72 cm) EUR 7,200. VERCELLI, 1 May 2003, *Starry Night* (1973, oil on canvas, 23 x 13 ins / 58 x 34 cm) EUR 2,000. MILAN, 10 June 2003, *Gallo* (1954, mixed media, 47 x 31 ins / 120 x 80 cm) EUR 1,800. ROME, 22 April 2004, *Love Night* (1959, oil on canvas/board, 26 x 28 ins / 67 x 70 cm) EUR 4,500.

FRANCESI, Alessandro

Italian, 18th century.
Of Neapolitan origin.
Painter.

Alessandro Francesi worked on the Rome churches of S Andrea della Valle, S Maria in Traspontina and S Agata. His only extant work, however, is an altarpiece entitled *Mary with the Child Jesus* for the church of S Andrea della Valle.

FRANCESINO, Il. See GIUSTAMMANI Giovanni Battista

FRANCET, E.

French, 19th century.
Painter.

MUSEUMS AND GALLERIES:

VIRE: *Crossroads at Episy.*

FRANCEY, Achille Adolphe

French, 19th century.
Born in the 19th century, in Paris.
Landscape painter.

Francey studied under X. Leprince and exhibited landscapes at the Salon from 1835 to 1859. Examples of his work include *Edge of the Wood, View of the Ruins of the Former Château de Viviers* and *Near Montpellier.*

FRANCH, Juan

Spanish, 19th century.
Active in Madrid in 1860.
Painter.

Juan Franch worked in Cuba as well as Madrid.

FRANCH Y MIRA, Ricardo

Spanish, 19th century.
Born 1839, in Valencia; died before 1897.
Engraver.

Ricardo Franch y Mira studied at the Academia de San Fernando under Domingo Martínez. He first exhibited in Madrid in 1862 and also exhibited regularly in Valencia and Paris. He produced engravings after Titian, Murillo, Zurbaran and Carducho.

FRANCHECOURT, Marin

French, 18th century.
Active in Paris in 1751.
Painter, sculptor.

FRANCHEQUIN

French, 16th century.
Active in Cambrai.
Sculptor.

In 1507, the builders of Cambrai Cathedral engaged Gilles Titre and Charlot Canonne to decorate the St-Gangolph portal of the cathedral. Their work was not considered satisfactory and was entirely removed, and the task was commissioned from Franchequin instead.

FRANCHÈRE, Joseph-Charles

Canadian, 19th - 20th century.
Born 1866; died 1921.
Painter. Portraits, genre scenes, landscapes with figures, landscapes.

Joseph-Charles Franchère painted Quebec landscapes and, occasionally, family scenes.

MUSEUMS AND GALLERIES:

OTTAWA (Nat. Gal. of Canada): *Sylphide* (1916, oil); *The End of the Day* (1913, oil).

AUCTION RECORDS:

TORONTO, 2 March 1982, *Seascape* (oil on card, 7 1/2 x 12 3/4 ins / 18.8 x 32.5 cm) CAD 950. MONTREAL, 27 Aug 1985, *Portrait of an Old Man with a Pipe* (oil on panel, 13 x 9 ins / 33 x 23 cm) CAD 1,000. MONTREAL, 27 April 1986, *Wooded Landscape with Lake* (watercolour, 10 x 14 ins / 25.3 x 35.5 cm) CAD 1,000. MONTREAL, 25 April 1988, *The Waterfalls of Lake Marios* (oil on panel, 9 1/2 x 13 1/2 ins / 24 x 34 cm) CAD 900. MONTREAL, 1 May 1989, *Perrot Island* (oil on canvas, 14 1/4 x 22 ins / 36 x 56 cm) CAD 1,000. MONTREAL, 30 Oct 1989, *Powder Store* (oil on canvas, 29 1/4 x 39 ins / 74 x 99 cm) CAD 23,100. MONTREAL, 30 April 1990, *After Supper* (1906, oil on canvas, 33 x 42 1/4 ins / 84 x 107 cm) CAD 11,000. MONTREAL, 5 Nov 1990, *Forest Scene with Lake and Waterfall* (oil on canvas, 16 1/4 x 22 ins / 41 x 56 cm) CAD 770. MONTREAL, 6 Dec 1994, *Young Woman Seated in front of a Fire* (oil on panel, 12 1/4 x 10 ins / 31 x 25.3 cm) CAD 2,100. MONTREAL, 22 Feb 1999, *Portrait of Firmin Hudon and of his wife Azelie d'Orsonnance* (oil on canvas, a pair, 27 x 21 ins / 68 x 54 cm) CAD 3,500. TORONTO, 7 Dec 1999, *La Sylphide* (oil on canvas, 35 x 30 ins / 88 x 76 cm) CAD 5,000. MONTREAL, 18 Sept 2000, *Place Jacques Cartier* (oil on canvas, 10 x 15 ins / 25 x 38 cm) CAD 10,500. MONTREAL, 16 Oct 2000, *La Nonchalante* (oil on canvas, 34 x 26 ins / 87 x 65 cm) CAD 9,500. MONTREAL, 11 Dec 2001, *Snowshoer* (oil on canvas, 11 x 16 ins / 29 x 40 cm) CAD 5,200. MONTREAL, 11 Dec 2001, *Rue de la Gauchetière* (oil on canvas, 24 x 36 ins / 62 x 91 cm) CAD 36,000. MONTREAL, 15 April 2002, *Romantic Scene* (oil on canvas, 22 x 30 ins / 56 x 76 cm) CAD 40,000. TORONTO, 3 Dec 2002, *Rue de la Gauchetière* (oil on canvas, 24 x 35 ins / 61 x 90 cm) CAD 70,000. MONTREAL, 12 Feb 2003, *Encampment* (oil on canvas on board, 23 x 31 ins / 59 x 80 cm) CAD 29,000. TORONTO, 2 Dec 2003, *Lady with Parasol* (oil on canvas, 16 x 22 ins / 40 x 55 cm) CAD 9,500. OTTAWA, 9 June 2004, *Afternoon Glow, Laurentians* (oil on panel, 9 x 13 ins / 22 x 33 cm) CAD 3,000. BRUSSELS, 7 Sept 2004, *Portrait of a Young Girl at Work* (1914, oil on canvas, 42 x 25 ins / 106 x 63 cm) EUR 3,400.

FRANCHES, Rinaldo. See **FRANCK Aernout**

FRANCHESQUINI, Christofle
French, 16th century.
Potter.

Also known as 'Francisquyn', Franchesquini is mentioned in Lyons between 1557 and 1559 as a 'painter of earthenware vessels'.

FRANCHET, Augustin
French, 19th century.
Painter. Portraits.

Franchet exhibited portrait work at the Paris Salon between 1834 and 1847. Examples of his work include *Portrait of Ad. Galin, Portrait of Casimir Noël, Apennine Hunter* and *Raising of the Daughter of Jairus*.

FRANCHEVILLE, Guillaume de.
See **GUILLAUME DE FRANCHEVILLE**

FRANCHEVILLE, Pierre de, or Franqueville or Francavilla
French, 16th - 17th century.
Born between 1548 and 1553, in Cambrai; died 25 August 1615, in Paris.
Sculptor, painter, architect.
Second School of Fontainebleau.

After a five-year period of study with a woodcarver in Innsbruck - where he was singled out by Archduke Ferdinand - Pierre de Francheville was sent to Florence by Ferdinand to study with Giambologna (1574) and then to work as his collaborator. Together, the two sculptors made the groups representing the Centaur and the Rape of the Sabine Women. In 1585, in Genoa, Francheville made the colossal figures of Juno and Jupiter. In Florence, he made five statues for the church of Santa Croce: *Prudence, Humility, Virginity, Moses and Aaron*. In Pisa, he made a statue of *Cosimo I*. Summoned to Paris by Henri IV, he was granted lodgings at the Louvre and given numerous commissions. The two most famous of these are *Time Capturing Truth* and *The Rape of Cybele by Saturn* in the Tuileries Gardens. Louis XIII made him his official sculptor and commissioned an equestrian statue of Henri IV, destroyed in 1792.

BIBLIOGRAPHY:

Francqueville, R. de, *Pierre de Francqueville, sculpteur des Médicis et du roi Henri IV*, A. et J. Picard, Paris, 1968. Avery, Charles, '*Pietro Francavilla's drawings of Giambologna's models*' in *Apollo* n° 463 p. 22, periodical, London, september 2000.

MUSEUMS AND GALLERIES:

BERLIN (Bodemus.): *Ferdinand I* (wax, model); *Head of Christ* (marble) - FLORENCE (Palazzo Pitti): *Seven Scenes from the Passion* (bronze, bas-relief) - FLORENCE (Uffizi): *Louis XIII on Horseback* (bronze) - FONTAINEBLEAU: *Strength and Peace* - GENOA (Palazzo Bianco): *Jupiter* (marble); *Janus* (marble) - PARIS (Louvre): *Mercury* (marble, statue); *Orpheus* (marble); *David* (marble); *Capture of Psyche; Four Slaves* (bronze, from the statue of Henri IV); *Giambologna* (bronze and alabaster); *Bust of Martin Fréminet; Battle of Ivry* (bas-relief) - VALENCIENNES: *Henri d'Oultreman* (marble, bust) - VERSAILLES: *Henri IV* - VIENNA: *Capture of Psyche*.

AUCTION RECORDS:

PARIS, 1 Dec 1965, *Female Figure* (bronze) FRF 8,500.

FRANCHI. See also **FRANCO**

FRANCHI, Alessandro
Italian, 19th - 20th century.
Born 15 March 1838, in Prato; died 29 April 1914, in Siena.
Painter.

Alessandro Franchi was a pupil of Mussini at the academy of Siena, and eventually succeeded him in 1888. His first works - *St Louis of France* and *St Elizabeth of Hungary* - won prizes in 1861 in Florence. His key works in Siena are the restoration of the marble floor of the cathedral, which made him famous; the ceiling paintings in the chapel of the Istituto S Teresa and the murals of the *Life of St Teresa*; the altar painting in the church of S Maria dei Servi; a painting of *The Visitation* in the church of the Visitation; *The Baptism of Christ* for the high altar in the baptistery of the cathedral; and frescoes in several chapels at the cemetery. Beside these works, Franchi is also famous for his frescoes and altar paintings in the Arcivescovile seminary in Genoa, and the fresco in the chapel of the Crucifix in Prato Cathedral. His best-known secular works in Siena include his frescoes in the Palazzo Bichi-Ruspoli; and *Italy Triumphant, Venice* and *Lombardy* in Victor Emmanuel's room in the Palazzo Pubblico.

FRANCHI, Antonio, called Il Lucchese
Italian, 17th century.
Born 1634, in Lucca; died 1709, in Florence.
Painter. History painting, religious subjects, portraits.

Antonio Franchi studied under Baldassare Franceschini (called Il Volterrano), but was greatly influenced by the work of Pietro da Cortona. Franchi was retained by the Grand Duke of Tuscany and produced several paintings for his and other private collections. His *St Joseph of Calasanzio* in the church of the Padri Scolopi is distinguished by its remarkable draughtsmanship and bold use of colour.

MUSEUMS AND GALLERIES:

CAPORGNANO (Church): *Christ Entrusting the Keys to St Peter* - CHAMBÉRY (MBA): *Portrait of a Woman* - FLORENCE (Gal. Corsini): *Flora* - FLORENCE (Uffizi): *Self-portrait*.

AUCTION RECORDS:

PARIS, 20 June 1994, *Flora* (oil on canvas, 50 1/2 x 40 1/4 ins / 128 x 102 cm) FRF 70,000. LONDON, 5 July 1995, *Temple of Venus* (oil on canvas, 102 1/4 x 126 1/2 ins / 260 x 321 cm) GBP 1,156,500.

FRANCHI, Antonio Maria
Italian, 18th century.
Painter.

FRANCHI, Cesare
Italian, 16th - 17th century.
Born c. 1580, in Perugia; died 1615.
Painter.

FRANCHI, Domenico, called Il Lucchese
Italian, 17th century.
Active in Siena.
Painter.

A *Visitation* in the monastery of Le Trafisse in Siena has been attributed to Domenico Franchi. The work is probably that of Antonio Franchi.

FRANCHI, Francesco
Italian, 17th century.
Born c. 1600, in Rome; died 13 September 1653, in Rome.
Painter.

AUCTION RECORDS:
MILAN, 14 Nov 1990, *Trompe-l'oeil with Engravings Representing Antiquity* (watercolour/paper, page with a dedication to Marquis Giuseppe Beccadelli of Bologna and a map of the two hemispheres, 14 1/2 x 21 ins / 37 x 53.5 cm) ITL 4,800,000. MILAN, 31 May 1994, *Trompe-l'oeil* (1778, tempera/canvas, 15 x 20 3/4 ins / 38 x 53 cm) ITL 8,050,000.

FRANCHI, Gaetano Maria
Italian, 18th century.
Active in Pisa.
Painter.
Gaetano Maria Franchi painted two compositions for the church of S Antonio in 1766 and, in 1776, an altarpiece for the church of S Bartolomeo in Bagni di San Giuliano (near Pisa).

FRANCHI, Giulio
Italian, 19th century.
Active in Ravenna.
Sculptor.
Giulio Franchi sculpted a large number of busts for funeral monuments in Ravenna cemetery, and the monument to Garibaldi in the Piazza Byron.
MUSEUMS AND GALLERIES:
ROME (Gal. Nazionale d'Arte Moderna): *Elderly Woman* (terracotta).

FRANCHI, Giunta di Jacopo
Italian, 15th century.
Born c. 1379.
Painter.
The brother of Rossello di Jacopo Franchi, Giunta di Jacopo Franchi was a member of the Accademia di San Luca.

FRANCHI, Giuseppe
Italian, 17th century.
Born 28 March 1634, in Rome.
Painter.
Giuseppe Franchi was the son of Francesco Franchi.

FRANCHI, Giuseppe
Italian, 18th century.
Born 1731, in Carrara; died 11 February 1806, in Milan.
Sculptor.
Giuseppe Franchi studied initially in Carrara and then in Rome. He was appointed to an academy professorship in Milan, where he taught Grand Dukes Ferdinand and Maximilian. He was elected to membership of the Accademia di San Luca in 1791. His body of work in Milan includes statues of deities for the Caryatid Chamber in the royal palace; sirens and dolphins sculpted for the Fountain of the Sirens in the Piazza Fontana; the tomb of Count Firmian in the church of S Bartolomeo; a bust of *Parini* in the Brera; the tomb of *Emperor Leopold*; a bust of *G. B. Branca*; and a bust of *Maria Gaetana Agnesi* for the Ambrosiana library. Franchi also produced two *Cherubs* for Monza castle; a bust of *P. Sacchi* for the Bologna Institute of Sciences; a relief of *Abbé Carli* for Siena; a monument to *Princess Grillo Pamfili* in the Assisi church of S Maria degli Angeli; and a statue of the *Virgin* for Sarzana Cathedral.

FRANCHI, Giuseppe and Margherita
Italian, 17th century.
Active in Lucca.
Painters.
Giuseppe and Margherita Franchi were the son and daughter of Antonio Franchi.

FRANCHI, Lorenzo
Italian, 16th century.
Died before 1539, in Bologna.
Painter.
Franchi is mentioned by Zani.

FRANCHI, Lorenzo
Italian, 16th - 17th century.
Born c. 1563, in Bologna; died c. 1630, in Reggio nell'Emilia.
Painter.
Lorenzo Franchi was a pupil of Camillo Procaccini and imitated the style of Annibale Carracci.

FRANCHI, Pietro
Italian, 18th century.
Active in Carrara.
Sculptor.
Pietro Franchi worked with his father Pompeo Franchi in the studio of Diego Jori, producing decorative sculptures for the Carthusian monastery in Calci (near Pisa).

FRANCHI, Pietro
Italian, 19th century.
Active in Carrara.
Sculptor.
Around 1870 Pietro Franchi sculpted some marble statues in his own studio, copied after models by other artists, as well as some genre statues of his own design.

FRANCHI, Pompeo
Italian, 18th century.
Active in Carrara.
Sculptor.
Pompeo Franchi was a pupil of Diego Jori. He worked in the latter's studio and produced numerous decorative pieces in marble for the Carthusian monastery of Calci near Pisa. He collaborated with Jori to sculpt marble statues for the monastery façade, including an *Assumption*, a *St John the Evangelist* and other saints, allegorical statues of *Faith* and *Charity*, and the armorial bearings of the Carthusian order.

FRANCHI, René
French, 20th century.
Born 31 May 1912, in Paris, to Italian parents; died 1991.
Painter, illustrator.
René Franchi demonstrated particular expertise in trompe-l'œil effects. He illustrated Dostoevsky's *The Gambler* (1946). He exhibited in Paris at the Salon Comparaisons, the Salon des Artistes Indépendants and the Salon des Artistes Français.

FRANCHI, Romuald
Italian, 19th century.
Painter. History painting.

FRANCHI, Rossello di Jacopo
Italian, 15th century.
Born c. 1377; died 10 August 1456.
Painter. Religious subjects.
MUSEUMS AND GALLERIES:
EMPOLI (Dominican church of S Miniato al Tedesco): frescoes - EMPOLI (Mus. della Collegiata di Sant'Andrea): *Virgin Mary* - FLORENCE (Church of S Miniato al Monte): frescoes - FLORENCE (Gal. dell'Accademia): *Coronation of the Virgin* - FLORENCE (Mus. di S Marco, library): *Resurrection* (painting adorning a missal); *The Ascension* (painting adorning a missal) - FLORENCE (Uffizi): *Virgin and Four Saints*; *Virgin with Saints and Donors*; *St Zenobia* - NEW YORK (Metropolitan Mus. of Art): *Virgin Mary* - PISA (Mus. Civico): *Virgin Mary* - PRATO (Cathedral of S Stefano): *St Stephen between Angels* (painting adorning an antiphonary) - VALDEMA (Charterhouse): *Virgin Mary*.
AUCTION RECORDS:
NEW YORK, 24-28 Sept 1946, *Madonna and Child,* USD 250. LONDON, 5 April 1963, *Virgin and Child with Four Saints,* Gns 500. LONDON, 1 July 1966, *Virgin and Child,* Gns 3,200. LONDON, 27 June 1969, *Virgin and Child with St Stephen and St Jerome,* Gns 6,000. LONDON, 10 July 1974, *Virgin and Child,*

GBP 14,000. LONDON, 14 April 1978, *Virgin and Child* (oil on panel/gold background, arched pediment, 24 3/4 x 14 3/4 ins / 63 x 37.5 cm) GBP 13,000. NEW YORK, 5 June 1980, *Virgin Surrounded by St Peter, St John the Baptist and Other Saints* (oil on panel/gold background, 35 1/2 x 19 3/4 ins / 90.2 x 50.2 cm) USD 30,000. NEW YORK, 17 Jan 1985, *St Francis and St John the Evangelist* (tempera/panel, 27 1/2 x 16 1/2 ins / 70 x 42 cm) USD 9,000. LONDON, 4 July 1986, *The Prophet Jeremiah* (oil on panel, gold background, curved pediment, 13 3/4 x 7 1/4 ins / 34.9 x 18.1 cm) GBP 15,000. VENICE, 29 Nov 1987, *Saints Christopher, Paul, Bernardino of Siena and Lawrence in Apex of Archway Occupied by Virgin of the Annunciation* (tempera/panel, gold background, arched at the top, 74 3/4 x 27 1/4 ins / 190 x 69 cm) ITL 100,000,000. LONDON, 8 July 1988, *Saints James the Great and James the Less with Woman Donor in Bottom Corner* (tempera/panel with gilt ground, 33 x 16 1/2 ins / 84 x 42 cm) GBP 22,000. ROME, 8 May 1990, *Annunciation* (tempera/panel, 10 1/4 x 16 ins / 26 x 40.5 cm) ITL 52,000,000. LONDON, 11 Dec 1991, *Virgin and Child* (oil and tempera/panel with gilt ground, ogive arch at top, 25 1/4 x 17 ins / 64.3 x 43.2 cm) GBP 35,200. LONDON, 19 April 1996, *St Francis Receiving the Stigmata* (oil on panel, 26 3/4 x 7 3/4 ins / 68 x 20 cm) GBP 36,700. LONDON, 9 July 1998, *Madonna and Child* (oil and tempera on panel, 25 x 17 ins / 64 x 43 cm) GBP 32,000. MILAN, 25 Nov 1998, *Madonna and Child Enthroned with Sts James and John the Baptist* (tempera on panel, 35 x 20 ins / 88 x 50 cm) ITL 120,000,000.

FRANCHI, Veronica
Italian, 17th century.
Active in Bologna c. 1670.
Painter.

Veronica Franchi was a pupil of Sirani. Among her portraits and historical compositions are the notable *Cleopatra*, *Lucretia* and *Abduction of Helen*.

FRANCHINA, Nino
Italian, 20th century.
Born 1912, in Palmanova-di-Udine (Friuli-Venezia Giulia); died 1987, in Rome.
Sculptor. Monuments.

Nino Franchina spent his childhood in Palermo, then lived in Milan between 1936 and 1937 before moving to Rome. After World War II, he joined the Fronte Nuovo delle Arti (New Arts Front), and exhibited as a member of this group at the Venice Biennale of 1948. He went to live in Paris until 1950, staging a solo exhibition of his complete works there in 1949, and participating in the Salon des Réalités Nouvelles in 1949 and 1950. He was given an entire room to himself at the 1958 Venice Biennale. In 1959 his works featured at the São Paulo Biennale; then in 1962 he participated in an exhibition in Spoleto entitled *Sculptures in the City*. An entire room was once again devoted to his work at the Venice Biennales of 1966 and 1972. In 1973 he took part in the Antwerp Middelheim sculpture Biennale.

Before the war, Franchina was a figurative sculptor, but his time in Paris stimulated a move towards abstraction. At the Salon des Réalités Nouvelles he exhibited some monumental works with extremely simplified forms, in the tradition of Brancusi, or the functional art of the Bauhaus. At this time he was using metallic materials and industrial techniques for his sculptures, which include *Metallurgy* and *Aerodynamics* of 1953: both are made of sheet metal, and *Aerodynamics* is polychromed. He then began to produce sculptures with fragile forms, highlighting their almost animate fragility in space, evoking trembling plants or winged animals - for example, *Trinacria* of 1955. Beside these slender creations, which echo the delicate craft of a goldsmith, Franchina also produced some monumental works in Cornigliano in 1960 and Lausanne in 1970.

BIBLIOGRAPHY:
Carandente, Giovanni, *Nino Franchina*, Officina Ed., Rome, 1968.

AUCTION RECORDS:
MILAN, 22 April 1982, *Caccia Preferita* (oil on panel, 11 x 17 3/4 ins / 28 x 45 cm) ITL 550,000. ROME, 7 April 1988, *Heraldry* (ink/paper, 18 3/4 x 13 1/2 ins / 47.5 x 34 cm) ITL 2,600,000. MILAN, 22 Nov 1993, *Nike* (brass, h. 13 ins / 33 cm) ITL 1,340,000. MILAN, 2 April 1996, *Untitled* (1959, sculpture, h. 24 3/4 ins / 63 cm) ITL 3,450,000. ROME, 18 Dec 2002, *Untitled* (painted steel, h. 24 ins / 60 cm) EUR 2,000. ROME, 13 Nov 2003, *Red Wing* (metal, wood and enamel, h. 19 ins / 47 cm) EUR 2,000.

FRANCHINI
French, 19th century.
Sculptor. Figures. Statuettes.

Franchini is known to have been active in Troyes (Aube) around 1847.

MUSEUMS AND GALLERIES:
TROYES: *Henri, Count of Champagne* (statuette).

FRANCHINI, Antonio
Italian, 19th century.
Painter, sculptor. Genre scenes.

MUSEUMS AND GALLERIES:
ARRAS: *Sacrificer.*

AUCTION RECORDS:
NEW YORK, 17 Jan 1990, *People Conversing in a Square* (oil on canvas, 20 1/2 x 27 ins / 52.1 x 68.6 cm) USD 1,760. NEW YORK, 23 May 1990, *Cupid's Little Emissary* (marble, h. 29 ins / 73.7 cm) USD 121,000. DENMARK, 3 Nov 1999, *Biblical Scene* (oil on canvas, 50 x 64 ins / 128 x 163 cm) DKK 31,000. JOHANNESBURG, 17 Oct 2000, *Europa and the Bull* (oil on canvas, 16 x 19 ins / 40 x 48 cm) ZAR 15,000. STOCKHOLM, 21 May 2001, *David Preaching for Saul* (oil on canvas, 50 x 64 ins / 128 x 162 cm) SEK 42,000. LONDON, 19 July 2001, *Heralding the Dawn* (1887, oil on canvas, 12 x 10 ins / 31 x 26 cm) GBP 1,600.

FRANCHINI, Giralomo
Italian, 18th century.
Active in Este.
Engraver, potter.

Giralomo Franchini engraved illustrations for *Ricerche Stor.-Crit. delle Antichita di Este* published by Alessi in 1776.

FRANCHINI, Jacopo
Italian, 17th - 18th century.
Born 1665; died 1736.
Active in Siena.
Sculptor, architect.

Jacopo Franchini built the Oratorio della Visitazione della Madonna in Siena and sculpted statues for the churches of S Concezione and S Gaetano.

FRANCHINI, Niccolo
Italian, 18th century.
Born 1704, in Siena; died 1783.
Painter.

Niccolo Franchini was the son of the sculptor Giacomo Fanchini. Examples of his work include *St Francis de Sales* for the baptistery of S Giovanni, *St Christopher* for the church of S Agostino, and *Death of the Virgin* for the church of S Giorgio.

FRANCHINI, Umberto
Italian, 20th century.
Painter.

Using blues and purplish reds, Umberto Franchini expresses human pain, with pessimism, anguish and sadness. Haunted faces peer out from the nebulous atmosphere of his paintings, which are particularly reminiscent of certain Abstract Expressionists.

FRANCHINO, Giovanni Battista
Swiss, 17th century.
Active in Mendrisio (Ticino).
Painter.
In 1669 Franchino painted a *Pietà* for the Maria Sonnenberg chapel.

FRANCHOYS, Lucas, the Elder
Flemish School, 16th - 17th century.
Born 25 January 1574, in Mechelen; died 16 September 1643, in Mechelen.
Painter. Religious subjects, portraits.
Lucas Franchoys was the father of the painters Lucas the Younger and Peeter Franchoys.
MUSEUMS AND GALLERIES:
ANTWERP: *Education of the Virgin; Apparition of the Virgin and Child to St Simon Stock.*
AUCTION RECORDS:
PARIS, 1746, *Elevation of the Cross,* FRF 294. BRUSSELS, 1797, *Sacrifice to the God Therm* (three other drawings, group) FRF 23. LONDON, 15 Dec 1998, *Peeter Franchoys in black tunic and white lace collar* (oil on copper, oval, 3 x 3 ins / 8 x 7 cm) GBP 9,200.

FRANCHOYS, Lucas, the Younger
Flemish, 17th century.
Born 28 June 1616, in Mechelen; died 3 April 1681, in Mechelen.
Painter. History painting, religious subjects, portraits.
Flemish School.
Lucas Franchoys the Younger studied under his father Lucas Franchoys, and was subsequently a pupil of Rubens. After the death of the latter he remained in Antwerp, but failed to find work in that town and went to France. On his return to Mechelen he entered the guild in 1655.

He painted pictures for various churches in his native town. He was on familiar terms with Jordaens, van Dyck and J. Boeckhurst, and allowed his personality to be somewhat swamped by these masters.
MUSEUMS AND GALLERIES:
AMSTERDAM: *François Vilain de Tournai* - MECHELEN - TOULOUSE: *Christ Persecuted.*
AUCTION RECORDS:
PARIS, 6 May 1925, *Presumed Portrait of the Artist,* FRF 3,200. LONDON, 29 March 1974, *Portrait of a Gentleman,* Gns 6,500. AMSTERDAM, 24 March 1980, *Portrait of a Man* (oil on canvas, 23 1/4 x 19 3/4 ins / 59 x 50 cm) NLG 3,500. AMSTERDAM, 14 Nov 1991, *Bust Portrait of a Gentleman in Black Garb* (oil on canvas, 30 3/4 x 25 1/2 ins / 78.3 x 64.8 cm) NLG 3,220.

FRANCHOYS, Lucas Elias
Flemish, 17th century.
Born c. 1670.
Painter.
Flemish School.
Lucas Elias Franchoys was trained by his father Lucas Franchoys the Younger. Unfortunately, very little is known about him, although it is known that he travelled to Rome.

FRANCHOYS, Paul. See **FRANCESCHI Paolo dei**

FRANCHOYS, Peter
Flemish, 17th century.
Born 20 October 1606, in Mechelen; died 1654 or 1681, in Mechelen.
Active in Antwerp and Mechelen.
Painter. History painting, portraits, landscapes.
Flemish School.
Peter Franchoys was the son of Lucas Franchoys and a pupil of his father and G. Seghers.

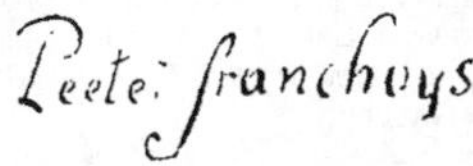

MUSEUMS AND GALLERIES:
BERLIN: *Portrait of a Young Man* - COLOGNE: *Portrait of an Old Man* - DRESDEN: *Portrait of a Knight* - FRANKFURT AM MAIN: *Portrait of a Man* - HAMBURG: *Portrait of a Young Man* - LILLE: *Portrait of Gisbert Mutzarto.*
AUCTION RECORDS:
NEW YORK, 12 Jan 1989, *Portrait of an Architect* (oil on panel, 28 x 22 ins / 71 x 56 cm) USD 6,600.

FRANCI, Agostino
Italian, 19th century.
Active in Spain.
Sculptor.
Franci was a pupil at the academy of Milan in 1860, and worked in Seville and Regla (near Cádiz) in Spain from 1865 to 1867.

FRANCI, Francesco
Italian, 17th - 18th century.
Born 1658, in Siena; died 1721, in Siena.
Painter.
A relatively large number of Francesco Franci's paintings are preserved in his native Siena, including a *St Jerome* in the church of Fonte Giusla, and a *Last Supper* in the Osservanti refectory.

FRANCIA (Mme)
French, 19th century.
Painter.
This artist was the wife of Louis Francia. She exhibited landscapes at the Royal Academy in London in 1801 and 1803.

FRANCIA, pseudonym of Tobacman, Francia
American, 20th - 21st century.
Born 10 September 1950, in New York.
Painter, collage artist, assemblage artist, installation artist. Landscapes.
Francia studied at the Art Students League in New York from 1967-1969 and graduated from New York City College in 1971. Although she started out painting realist landscapes, she went on to create architectural forms from painted wood, in vibrant colours (with pink as the dominant hue), onto which she glued photographs and other items, to evoke the Holocaust. All her art is related to Jewish history and ritual.

In 1972 she began participating in collective exhibitions, notably: 1972 and 1986 in New York; 1973 in Evansville; 1975 in Brooklyn; 1984 at the Indianapolis Biennial and the Élancourt Festival; 1985 and 1989 in Chicago; 1993 in a travelling exhibition that went from Nashua to Portland, New Haven and Meridan; and 1995 in San Antonio, Texas.

Solo exhibitions of her work have been held in 1973 at the Owensboro Museum of Fine Art, in 1974 in Louisville, in 1979 at New York University, and in 1989 at the J. Dauphin Gallery in Wilmington.
MUSEUMS AND GALLERIES:
EVANSVILLE - OSWEGO (Tyler AG, State University of New York) - OWENSBORO (MFA) - PARIS (BNF).

FRANCIA, Alexandre T.
French, 19th century.
Born 1815 or 1820, in Calais; died 1884, in Brussels.
Painter (gouache), watercolourist. Genre scenes, landscapes with figures, seascapes.

Alexandre Francia studied under his father Louis Francia and exhibited at the Paris Salon from 1841 to 1866. His body of work includes *The Veloce Running Aground* (commissioned by the town of Calais), *View of the Guines Canal*, and *St Pierre of Dieppe Foundering off Calais on 18 October 1791*.

MUSEUMS AND GALLERIES:

CALAIS: four seascapes.

AUCTION RECORDS:

PARIS, 19 Nov 1919, *View of Venice*, FRF 235. PARIS, 27 April 1927, *Fishermen on the Jetty* (watercolour) FRF 520. PARIS, 22 March 1928, *Houseboat on a Dutch Canal* (watercolour) FRF 450. PARIS, 17 Feb 1937, *Farm near the Water*, FRF 450. LONDON, 14 June 1972, *Harbour Scene at Sunset*, GBP 600. LONDON, 15 March 1974, *Canal Scene near Amsterdam*, Gns 900. BRUSSELS, 10 Dec 1976, *View of Quimperlé* (watercolour, 11 3/4 x 9 ins / 30 x 23 cm) BEF 32,000. LONDON, 17 Feb 1984, *Fishermen and Boats on the Beach* (oil on canvas, 9 1/4 x 12 1/4 ins / 23.5 x 31 cm) GBP 700. LONDON, 15 March 1984, *Venice* (watercolour/pencil outlines, 14 x 22 ins / 35.5 x 56 cm) GBP 850. LONDON, 16 July 1987, *Boats on a River in a French Town* (watercolour, 7 1/4 x 12 1/4 ins / 18.5 x 31 cm) GBP 2,400. LONDON, 19 June 1991, *S. Maria della Salute, Venice* (watercolour, 20 1/2 x 36 1/2 ins / 52 x 93 cm) GBP 2,145. NEW YORK, 15 Oct 1991, *Midday Break* (watercolour and gouache/paper, 16 1/2 x 27 ins / 42 x 68.5 cm) USD 880. PARIS, 14 March 1997, *Bringing Home the Catch* (watercolour, 16 1/4 x 27 1/4 ins / 41 x 69 cm) FRF 24,000. CALAIS, 7 Nov 1999, *Beach with Figures at Low Tide* (oil on canvas, 16 x 24 ins / 40 x 60 cm) FRF 23,000. LONDON, 9 Nov 1999, *Fishing Boats in Harbour* (pencil/watercolour, 9 x 15 ins / 24 x 37 cm) GBP 2,400. NEW ORLEANS, 17 March 2001, *Cove of the Fishermen, with Natural Bridge* (1866, oil on canvas, 21 x 33 ins / 53 x 84 cm) USD 4,000. PARIS, 5 Oct 2001, *Venice, Church of S Maria della Salute* (watercolour/gouache, 22 x 30 ins / 55 x 75 cm) FRF 48,000. CALAIS, 10 March 2002, *Seascape* (oil on canvas, 29 x 48 ins / 74 x 123 cm) EUR 9,500. LONDON, 15 Aug 2002, *Congested Shipping Lanes Offshore* (oil on canvas, 39 x 63 ins / 100 x 160 cm) GBP 4,000. DORCHESTER, 3 July 2003, *River Scene with Burning City to the Far Bank* (watercolour/bodycolour, 18 x 27 ins / 46 x 69 cm) GBP 1,300. PARIS, 6 Nov 2003, *View of the Surroundings of Venice* (oil on canvas, 16 x 25 ins / 41 x 64 cm) EUR 4,000. LONDON, 26 May 2004, *City Ablaze* (pencil/watercolour, 17 x 27 ins / 44 x 68 cm) GBP 1,200. BRUSSELS, 15 June 2004, *Departure of the Fishermen* (oil on panel, 8 x 12 ins / 21 x 30 cm) EUR 1,900.

FRANCIA, Angelo

French, 20th century.

Born in Rodez.

Sculptor. Figures. Busts, medallions.

Angelo Francia exhibited at the Paris Salon from 1867 to 1882. His works include a bust of *Théophile de Marcol*, a medallion of *Darolle*, a bust of *Monsignor Bauer*, a bronze bust of the *Marquise de Blocqueville* and a bronze bust of *Aurélien Scholl*.

AUCTION RECORDS:

PARIS, 25 Sept 1997, *Bust of a Woman in a 16th-Century Style Dress* (silver-plated bronze, h. 15 1/4 ins / 39 cm) FRF 17,000.

FRANCIA, de. See first name

FRANCIA, Domenico

Italian, 18th century.

Born 1702, in Bologna; died 1758, in Bologna.

Painter.

Domenico Francia was the son of the engraver Francesco Maria Domenico Francia. He studied under Ferdinand Galli (called Bibiena) and was appointed court architect by the King of Sweden.

FRANCIA, Francesco, real name: Francesco di Marco Raibolini

Italian, 15th - 16th century.

Born 1450, in Bologna; died 5 January 1517, in Bologna.

Painter, engraver, medallist. History painting.

Bolognese School.

Francesco Francia belonged to a distinguished Bolognese family, though at the time of his birth the family fortunes were at a low ebb. His father, Marco Raibolini, a wood engraver or carver, apprenticed him to the jeweller Duc, known as Francia, whose nickname Francesco later adopted. Francia became a highly reputed jeweller in his native town, and his works were acquired by men of power and influence. In a letter dated 1546, he is mentioned as the foremost jeweller in Bologna. He also made medals, designed the Bolognese coinage, and cut the first characters used in printing. He is thought to have produced the first Italic fonts, which he supplied to Aldus Manutius. As a goldsmith, he was particularly noted for his niello work. He is generally thought to have been taught by Marco Zoppo and Squarcione.It is believed that Francia's decision to become a painter was determined by Lorenzo Costa's arrival in Bologna in 1483. It does not seem likely that Francia was Costa's pupil, as Francia's fame as an artist excludes the possibility that he would make himself subordinate to a younger man. But a close friendship was established between the two artists, who lived in the same house. They worked together, in particular on an altarpiece for the church of the Misericordia. The central panel was painted by Francia, the remainder by Lorenzo Costa. The first fruits of this collaboration, or at least the works produced by Francia and Lorenzo at the beginning of their acquaintance, are so similar in style and technique that they could be ascribed to either artist. But, in the long run, Francia's superiority became evident.The first painting known to be by Francia, dated 1494, is a *Madonna and Child with Six Saints*, kept at the Pinacoteca Nazionale in Bologna. The technical skill displayed in the painting gives the lie to the idea that this was his first work, as Vasari affirms. Dated from the following year is a *Virgin and Child with St Joseph*, which Count Jean Palffy acquired at the Dudley Sale in 1892. In 1499, Raibolini painted an altarpiece for Giovanni Benlevoglio for the chapel the latter had built in the church of S Giacomo Maggiore. This work earned Francia a commission to paint a *Nativity* for the church of the Misericordia; the work is now in the Pinacoteca Nazionale in Bologna. For the same church, Raibolini also painted the small predella, depicting the birth and death of Christ (also now in the Bologna Pinacoteca). As well as these works, the Gallery houses the famous *Masignoli Madonna*, which, according to Vasari, Francia painted for the same church. In 1500, Francia painted an *Annunciation* for the outside walls of the church of the Annunziata. Dated from 1502 are a *Virgin in Glory with the Child Jesus and Saints* and two *Annunciations*, one kept in the Bologna Pinacoteca, the other produced for the duke of Mantua and now in Milan. Vasari also mentions a *Birth of Christ*, made for Paolo Zambeccaro, now in the Farli Gallery. From the same period date a *Madonna and Two Saints*, in the Vienna Museum; a *St Francis*, in the collection of Dr Frizzoni; a *Madonna in the Rose Garden*, kept in Munich; a *Head of the Man of Sorrows Bearing his Cross*, kept in Bergamo; a *Figure of St Sebastian*, belonging to the Duke of Ferman Nuñez, in Madrid; and a *Presentation in the Temple*, in Cesena. Special mention is due to the major work conserved in the church of S Martino Maggiore in Bologna, which can still be admired in the chapel where the artist placed it, and the *Annunciation* in the Chantilly collections. In 1505, Francia painted the *Madonna of the Earthquake*, for the Town Hall in Bologna. From 1506 date the frescoes he painted in the Chapel of St Cecilia, depicting the *Marriage of St Celilia* and the *Burial of St Cecilia*. Continuing in chronological order, the *Dead Christ*, in the Dresden Museum, dates from 1509, and there are references to further works produced in 1512 and 1514, and two in 1515, one in Parma, the other in Turin.

Apart from these works that can be accurately dated, Francia's corpus of work includes many other paintings, in particular his admirable Madonnas. Vasari reports that, in his lifetime, Francia was regarded by the people of Bologna as a god. Some more modern critics have seen him as an imitator, however.

francia aurifaber bonon.

BIBLIOGRAPHY:

Negro, Emilio/Roio, Nicosetta, *Francesco Francia e la sua scuola*, Artioli, Modena, 1998.

MUSEUMS AND GALLERIES:

BERGAMO: *Head of the Man of Sorrows Bearing his Cross* - BERGAMO (Accademia Carrara): *Christ Crucified* - BERLIN: *Virgin in Glory with Saints; Holy Family* - BÉZIERS: *Virgin and Child; St Francis in Ecstasy* - BOLOGNA (Pinacoteca Nazionale): *Virgin and Saints; Madonna and Child with Six Saints* (1494); *Nativity; Masignoli Madonna* (Birth and Death of Christ, predella); *Annunciation* - BORDEAUX: *Christ Crucified* - BUDAPEST: *Virgin and Child with Two Angels; Virgin and Child with the Infant St John* - CESENA: *Presentation in the Temple* - CHANTILLY: *Annunciation* - COLOGNE: *Madonna* - DIJON: *Virgin and Child* - DRESDEN: *Baptism of Christ; Adoration of the Magi; Dead Christ* - DUBLIN: *Lucretia Killing Herself with a Sword* - FLORENCE (NG): *Evangelist* - FLORENCE (Palazzo Pitti): *Two Men's Portraits; Virgin and Child* - GENOA: *Portrait of a Man* - GLASGOW: *Nativity* - LA FÈRE: *Holy Family* - LONDON (NG): *The Virgin and Child with an Angel* (1480-1490, oil/wood); *The Virgin and Child with Two Saints* (1500-1510, oil/wood); *The Virgin and Child with St Anne and other Saints; Pietà* (1511-1517, oil/wood, lentille); altarpiece formerly in chiesa de S. Frediano in Lucques; *Mourning over the Dead Christ* (1510-1517, oil/wood) - MADRID: *Figure of St Sebastian* - MILAN (Pinacoteca di Brera): *Annunciation* - MUNICH: *Madonna in a Rose Bush; Virgin and Child* - NICE: *Virgin and Child with St John the Baptist and St Catherine* - PARIS (Louvre): *Nativity; Christ Crucified; Virgin and Child with Saints* (three versions) - PARMA: *Deposition; Virgin and Child with St John; Virgin and Child with Saints* - ROME (Mus. e Gal. Borghese): *Virgin and Child; St Stephen* - ST PETERSBURG (Hermitage): *Virgin and Child* - TURIN: *Entombment* - VATICAN: *Virgin and Child with St Jerome* - VERONA: *Virgin and Child with Saints* - VIENNA: *Madonna and Two Saints* - WASHINGTON DC (Georgetown University): *Christ Bearing the Cross* (oil/wood).

AUCTION RECORDS:

PARIS, 1793, *Holy Family with St Peter and St Paul*, FRF 2,500. PARIS, 1847, *Holy Family*, FRF 1,080. PARIS, 1859, *Annunciation*, FRF 2,080; *Virgin and Child*, FRF 3,432. PARIS, 1863, *Portrait of a Man*, FRF 1,200; *St Joseph and the Virgin Mary Adoring the Christ Child*, FRF 2,050. PARIS, 6 Feb 1865, *The Virgin Bearing the Infant Jesus on her Knees*, FRF 21,500; *Virgin and Child*, FRF 14,000. PARIS, 1867, *Holy Family*, FRF 18,000. PARIS, 1870, *Virgin and Child*, FRF 3,000. LONDON, 1874, *Virgin and Child with St John and Two Angels*, FRF 17,050. LONDON, 1898, *Virgin and Child*, FRF 12,600. LONDON, 24 March 1899, *Madonna and Child*, FRF 3,800. LONDON, 4 and 5 June 1907, *Virgin with Donor*, FRF 8,000; *Virgin and Child with St Lawrence and a Pope*, FRF 11,000. LONDON, 12 June 1919, *Virgin and Child*, FRF 16,000. LONDON, 19 and 20 April 1921, *Virgin and Child with a Female Saint*, FRF 1,610. LONDON, 25 Feb 1924, *St Michael* (pen and wash, heightened) FRF 1,000. LONDON, 26 Oct 1925, *Virgin and Child with Two saints, in a Landscape*, FRF 1,500. LONDON, 13 Dec 1926, *Virgin and Child with St John, St Joseph and a Donor* (school of Francia) FRF 10,100. LONDON, 19 Dec 1928, *Virgin and Child with St John*, FRF 5,000. LONDON, 24 April 1929, *Virgin and Child*, FRF 4,000. NEW YORK, 10 April 1930, *Virgin and Child with St John, Surrounded by Saints*, USD 1,700. NEW YORK, 4 Jan 1935, *Virgin and Child with St John and St Francis*, USD 500. NEW YORK, 6 May 1937, *Virgin and Child with St John and Other Saints*, USD 350. PARIS, 28 Feb 1938, *St Sebastian* (pen and bistre wash, heightened with gouache) FRF 1,000. PARIS, 18 June 1943, *Virgin and Child* (in the style of R.) FRF 6,300. PARIS, 20 Dec 1943, *Virgin and Child* (in the style of R.) FRF 18,000. NEW YORK, 15 Jan 1944, *Virgin and Child, Surrounded by Saints*, USD 12,000. NEW YORK, 4 May 1944, *Marriage of St Catherine*, USD 2,900. NEW YORK, 2 Dec 1944, *Virgin and Child with St Francis*, USD 2,000. NEW YORK, 31 Jan 1946, *St Mary Magdalene*, USD 425; *Head of Nicodemus*, USD 425. LONDON, 28 May 1965, *Holy Family*, Gns 1,100. PARIS, 20 June 1966, *Virgin and Child Surrounded by Saints*, FRF 21,000. ENGHIEN-LES-BAINS, 27 Feb 1983, *Madonna au parapet* (oil on panel, 23 1/2 x 19 ins / 60 x 48 cm) FRF 140,000. LONDON, 21 April 1989, *Lamentations* (oil on panel, 12 1/2 x 15 1/2 ins / 31.8 x 39.5 cm) GBP 41,800. NEW YORK, 1 June 1989, *Virgin and Child with an Angel and St John* (oil on panel, 22 3/4 x 19 1/4 ins / 58 x 48.9 cm) USD 407,000. NEW YORK, 28 Jan 1999, *Madonna with Christ Child Holding a Bird* (oil on panel, 15 x 11 ins / 37 x 29 cm) USD 120,000. FLORENCE, 11 June 2003, *St Francis Receiving the Stigmata* (oil on board, 11 x 22 ins / 29 x 55 cm) EUR 436,000.

FRANCIA, Francesco Domenico Maria
Italian, 17th - 18th century.
Born 1657, in Bologna; died 1735, in Bologna.
Engraver (etching/burin).

Francesco Domenico Maria Francia was the father of the painter Domenico Francia. He produced an extensive body of engravings.

AUCTION RECORDS:

LONDON, 24 May 1963, *Virgin and Child*, Gns 900.

FRANCIA, Francesco Maria
Italian, 18th century.
Active in Florence in 1752.
Engraver.

FRANCIA, Giacomo, real name: Giacomo Raibolini
Italian, 16th century.
Born before 1486; died 1557, in Bologna.
Painter, engraver. Religious subjects.

Giacomo was the son of Francesco Francia. Most of his works were painted jointly with his brother Giulio. He also worked as a goldsmith.

MUSEUMS AND GALLERIES:

BOLOGNA (Accademia): *The Virgin Mary, St John and Four Saints* (from the chiesa of S Francesco) - BOLOGNA (Basilica di S Stefano): *Crucifixion with St Jerome and St Francis* - BOLOGNA (Church of S Cristina): *Birth of Christ; Adoration of the Magi* - MADRID (Prado): *St Margaret between St Jerome and St John* - MILAN (Pinacoteca di Brera): *Virgin with Angels, Four Saints and Four Nuns* (from the Chiesa of Saints Gervasio and Protasio, Bologna) - MODENA (Gal.): *Assumption with Apostles* (from Mirandola Cathedral) - PARMA (Church of S Giovanni Evangelista): *Birth of Christ*.

AUCTION RECORDS:

LONDON, 1 Feb 1924, *Madonna*, GBP 25. LONDON, 24 Nov 1924, *Mystic Marriage of St Catherine*, GBP 16. LONDON, 11 June 1926, *Head of Donor; Head of Woman* (one of a pair) GBP 73. LONDON, 28 and 29 July 1926, *Pietà*, GBP 21. LONDON, 15 July 1927, *Madonna and Child*, GBP 220. LONDON, 8 Feb 1928, *Pietà*, GBP 23. LONDON, 27 April 1934, *Madonna and Child*, GBP 33. LONDON, 21 May 1935, *Holy Family*, GBP

15. LONDON, 9 July 1936, *Adoration of the Magi*, GBP 38. LONDON, 14 Dec 1938, *Madonna and Child*, GBP 88. LONDON, 6 March 1940, *Madonna and Child*, GBP 36. LONDON, 3 May 1940, *Madonna and Child*, GBP 6. LONDON, 18 Dec 1940, *Madonna and Child*, GBP 11. LONDON, 20 Aug 1941, *Madonna and Child*, GBP 30. LONDON, 5 Dec 1941, *Holy Family and St Anthony of Padua*, GBP 157. LONDON, 14 Aug 1942, *Madonna and Child*, GBP 31. NEW YORK, 4 Nov 1944, *Madonna and Child*, USD 3,000. MILAN, 12 and 13 March 1963, *Virgin and Child with St Peter and St Sebastian*, ITL 2,700,000. LONDON, 2 July 1965, *Virgin and Child*, Gns 600. FLORENCE, 10 April 1974, *Virgin and Child with the Young St John the Baptist*, ITL 6,400,000. LONDON, 14 June 1984, *Venus and Cupid in Clouds* (engraving/card, 12 x 8 1/2 ins / 30.7 x 21.5 cm) GBP 2,200. FLORENCE, 27 May 1985, *Holy Family with Female Saint* (oil on panel, 23 1/2 x 18 1/4 ins / 60 x 46.5 cm) ITL 15,000,000. LONDON, 5 Dec 1985, *Venus and Cupid* (c. 1528-31, engraving/card, 12 x 8 1/2 ins / 30.6 x 21.7 cm) GBP 6,000. NEW YORK, 31 May 1989, *Virgin and Child with the Young St John the Baptist* (oil on canvas, 24 x 19 3/4 ins / 61 x 50 cm) USD 49,500. NEW YORK, 10 Jan 1990, *Holy Family and St Francis* (oil on panel, 26 3/4 x 20 1/2 ins / 67.9 x 52.2 cm) USD 24,200. LONDON, 9 April 1990, *Virgin and Child* (oil on panel, 23 1/2 x 17 1/4 ins / 59.5 x 44 cm) GBP 33,000. PARIS, 9 April 1991, *Virgin and Child with St Catherine* (oil on panel, 23 x 19 1/2 ins / 57.5 x 49.5 cm) FRF 180,000. NEW YORK, 16 Jan 1992, *Mystic Marriage of St Catherine* (oil on panel, 25 1/2 x 21 ins / 64.7 x 53.3 cm) USD 104,500. LONDON, 23 April 1993, *Virgin and Child with St John the Baptist* (oil on panel, 24 x 19 ins / 61 x 48.2 cm) GBP 29,900. MILAN, 28 Nov 1995, *Virgin and Child with Two Saints* (oil on panel, 29 1/4 x 22 ins / 74 x 56 cm) ITL 69,000,000. LONDON, 19 April 1996, *Virgin and Child with Shepherd in a Landscape* (oil on panel, 22 x 16 1/2 ins / 55.9 x 42.2 cm) GBP 21,850. VENICE, 20 Feb 2000, *Madonna and Child and Infant St John the Baptist with Saints* (oil on panel, 70 x 58 ins / 179 x 147 cm) ITL 75,000,000. LONDON, 6 July 2000, *Sacra Conversazione, Madonna and Child Flanked by Sts John the Baptist and Jerome* (oil on canvas, 28 x 28 ins / 72 x 72 cm) GBP 26,000. LONDON, 11 Dec 2001, *Mystic Marriage of St Catherine* (oil on panel, 24 x 20 ins / 60 x 50 cm) GBP 26,000. LONDON, 23 April 2004, *Mystic Marriage of St Catherine* (oil on panel, 30 x 24 ins / 76 x 62 cm) GBP 6,500.

FRANCIA, Giovanni Battista

Italian, 16th century.

Born 27 June 1533; died 13 May 1575, in Bologna.

Painter. Religious subjects.

The son of Giulio Francia, Francia painted a number of works for churches in Bologna.

AUCTION RECORDS:

MILAN, 31 May 1966, *Virgin and Child with Two Saints* (tempera/wood) ITL 7,000,000. NEW YORK, 18 Jan 1983, *Virgin and Child with St Joseph and St Christopher* (oil on panel, gold background, 24 1/2 x 20 1/4 ins / 62 x 51.5 cm) USD 6,500.

FRANCIA, Giulio

Italian, 16th century.

Born 20 August 1487; died 1540.

Active in Bologna.

Painter, goldsmith.

The son of Francesco Francia, Giulio Francia worked with his brother Giacomo. He is mentioned as having painted some saints for the pillars of the church of S Giovanni in Monte, Bologna, an altarpiece for the church of S Margarita and two works for the church of S Sigismondo.

FRANCIA, Juan Bautista

Spanish, 17th century.

Engraver.

Juan Bautista Francia was a pupil of F. Quesadez. He engraved portraits, including those of *Fray Marcelo Marona; Sister Josefa Maria de Santa Inés de Beniganim*; and the *Grand Master of Malta, Don Ramón Rabaza de Perellos*. His engravings on religious subjects include the bull of indulgence granted by the archbishop of Valencia, Fray J.T. Rocaberti.

FRANCIA, Louis François Thomas

French, 18th - 19th century.

Born 21 December 1772, in Calais; died 6 February 1839, in Calais.

Painter, watercolourist. Landscapes, seascapes.

Louis Francia was an artist whose works were highly sought after. He settled in London, where he became permanent secretary of the Society of Water Colourists and painter to the Duke of York. He became the master of Bonington.

Returning to France in the last few years of his life, he took part in the Salons at the Louvre, in 1835 with *Seascape, Beach at Low Tide, Following Heavy Weather*, in 1836 with *Smugglers*, in 1838 with *Family of Fishermen, View of Pont-Avenue in Lower Brittany, View of Treport in Normany, Evening Light, Interior of the Port in Brittany in the Morning, Beach in Picardy, Low Tide* and in 1839 with *Shipwreck of Amphitrite, View of the Seine near Marly, Red Fort in Calais, in the Evening, View of Amsterdam, in the Morning, Dieppe, at Low Tide* and *Canal in Rotterdam*. His style bears certain similarities to Turner.

BIBLIOGRAPHY:

Bauer, Gérald, *L'Éloquence de la couleur ou le génie des émules de Bonnington*, Clem arts, Levallois-Perret, 2003.

MUSEUMS AND GALLERIES:

CALAIS: *Seascapes* (five watercolours) - CARDIFF: *Houses along the Road; Landscape with Cottage* - CLAMECY: watercolours - DUBLIN: *Calais* (watercolour) - LONDON (Victoria and Albert Mus.): watercolours - MANCHESTER: watercolours - NORWICH (Castle Mus. and AG): *Saving the Crew of the brig 'Leipzig' wrecked on Yarmouth bar; Saving the crew and passengers from the brig 'Providence', wrecked off Winterton* - PÉRIGUEUX: watercolours.

AUCTION RECORDS:

LONDON, 30 Nov 1923, *Boats Run Aground* (drawing) GBP 14. LONDON, 30 July 1924, *High Tide*, GBP 19. LONDON, 10 Nov 1933, *Road through Woods*, GBP 44. LONDON, 27 July 1938, *Mousehold Heath*, GBP 14. LONDON, 4 March 1943, *Wooded Landscape* (watercolour) GBP 25. LONDON, 11 March 1969, *Boats off Dunkirk* (watercolour) Gns 360. LONDON, 6 June 1972, *Port of Calais at Low Tide*, Gns 1,600. LONDON, 24 Nov 1977, *Greenwich Observatory, with the Artist Seated, Drawing* (1828, watercolour, 10 3/4 x 17 ins / 27.5 x 43 cm) GBP 850. LONDON, 20 March 1979, *Quays at Calais* (watercolour, 5 x 7 3/4 ins / 12.5 x 20 cm) GBP 2,200. LONDON, 16 July 1981, *Fisherman on the Beach* (watercolour, 6 1/2 x 12 1/4 ins / 16.5 x 31 cm) GBP 2,100. LONDON, 30 March 1983, *Portsmouth Harbour from Portsdown Hill* (1808, watercolour/pencil outlines, 7 1/4 x 12 1/4 ins / 18.5 x 31 cm) GBP 3,700. LONDON, 9 July 1985, *Yachts in a Strong Sea* (1835, watercolour, 6 1/2 x 10 ins / 16.2 x 25.5 cm) GBP 7,500. PARIS, 21 March 1990, *River's Edge* (watercolour, 13 1/2 x 21 1/4 ins / 34 x 54 cm) FRF 9,000. CALAIS, 9 Dec 1990, *Seascape* (c. 1830, 34 1/4 x 38 1/2 ins / 87 x 98 cm) FRF 63,000. LONDON, 30 Jan 1991, *Yachts Run Aground near a Chateau with Mountains in the Background* (1831, watercolour, 18 3/4 x 25 1/4 ins / 47.5 x 64 cm) GBP 385. LE TOUQUET, 19 May 1991, *Boats Leaving Port* (oil on canvas, 14 1/2 x 22 ins / 37 x 56 cm) FRF 47,000. PARIS, 5 July 1993, *Dunkirk - Outer Harbour* (watercolour, 3 3/4 x 7 ins / 9.5 x 18 cm) FRF 8,000. PARIS, 29 Nov 1995, *Ships in a Strong Sea* (1834, watercolour, 16 1/4 x 22 ins / 41 x 55 cm) FRF 15,000.

FRANCIABIGIO, also known as Francesco di Cristofano or Francesco Bigi, or Bigio
Italian, 16th century.
Born 1482, in Florence; died 1525, in Florence.
Painter. History painting, portraits.
Florentine School.

Franciabigio was renowned for his portraits, examples of which can be seen in several European museums. He received guidance from Albertinelli and also studied in the Brancacci Chapel (Church of the Carmine, in Florence, famous for its frescoes by Masaccio). Some of his frescoes, still interesting despite the ravages of time, can be seen in the churches of S Giovanni Battista della Calza and S Maria della Candele in Florence. Franciabigio was the son of Christofano di Francesco d'Antonio, a Milanese painter. He was a close friend and associate of Andrea del Sarto and his first major works were produced in collaboration with the Florentine master for the Convent of the Servites and the Convent of the Annunziata, where he painted a *Marriage of the Virgin*. It is said that, when one of the monks discovered one of Franciabigio's frescoes before he had finished it, the painter flew into a rage, took a hammer to some of the heads in the composition and would never touch it again. During Andrea del Sarto's stay in France, Bigio continued his work. He painted a *Triumph of Cicero* for the hall of the Medici villa at Poggio a Caiano. Two influences are clearly apparent in his work: that of Leonardo, as in the *Triumph of Hercules* or *Job* (Florence), and that of Raphael, evident in his *Portrait of a Young Man* (Louvre) or *Holy Family* (Vienna).

MUSEUMS AND GALLERIES:
BARNARD CASTLE (Bowes Mus.): *Portrait of a Man* - BERLIN: *Portrait* - BRUSSELS: *Leda* - DRESDEN: *The Story of Bathsheba* - FLORENCE (Palazzo Pitti): *Portrait; The Calumny of Apelles* - FLORENCE (Uffizi): *Glorification of Hercules; Virgin at the Well; Virgin with St John the Baptist and Job* - LONDON (NG): *Portrait of a Knight of Rhodes* (1514, oil/wood) - PARIS (Louvre): *Portrait of a Man; Portrait of a Young Man* - PARIS (Mus. Jacquemart-André): *St Mary the Egyptian Receiving her Final Communion from Zozimus* - TURIN: *Annunciation* - VIENNA: *Holy Family* - VIENNA (Liechtenstein Mus.): *Portrait* - WIESBADEN: *The Story of Lucretia*.
AUCTION RECORDS:
PARIS, April 1920, *Virgin, Child and St Joseph* (attributed) FRF 5,100. LONDON, 12 Feb 1932, *Holy Family*, GBP 23. LONDON, 20 April 1932, *Virgin and Child*, GBP 18. LONDON, 27-29 May 1935, *Portrait of a Man* (chalk drawing) GBP 300. LONDON, 16 April 1937, *Nobleman*, GBP 29. NEW YORK, 24 May 1944, *Portrait of a Man*, USD 300. LONDON, 2 March 1945, *Portrait of a Bearded Man*, GBP 31. LONDON, 11 Oct 1946, *Samson Killing the Lion*, GBP 115. VERSAILLES, 20 May 1965, *Portrait of a Young Woman with the Attributes of St Catherine*, FRF 22,000. NEW YORK, 5 Feb 2003, *Portrait of a Gentleman in a Black Coat and Hat* (oil on panel, 22 x 19 ins / 57 x 49 cm) USD 10,000.

FRANCIÈRE, Jean de
French, 16th century.
Sculptor.

Probably related to Gérard de Francières, Jean de Francière lived in Beauvais (Oise) between 1579 and 1580, where he executed various pieces in carved wood for the enclosure to the choir at the church of St-Vivien in Rouen. He then went to Amiens where, in 1594, he made a retable for the church of St-Pierre in Roye (Somme). He carved the king's coat of arms on the new town hall in Amiens in 1595.

FRANCIÈRES, Gérard de, or Franssières
French, 16th century.
Sculptor.

In 1545, together with Firmin Cadot, this artist made two statues of prophets for the great hall at Amiens town hall (Somme). François Louvel, lord of Glisy, commissioned a group from him in 1549 showing *The Woman of Samaria Giving Water to Christ*. Now destroyed, this group was formerly in the old cemetery of the church of St-Denis.

FRANCIÈRES, Jacques de.
See **FRANSSIÈRES**

FRANCILLON, Anny. See **LIEROW Anny**

FRANCILLON, René
Swiss, 20th century.
Born 28 December 1876, in Lausanne or in Geneva; died 1973.
Painter, sculptor, engraver. Landscapes, village views.

Francillon studied at the college of applied arts in Geneva. *Autumn*, a composition by him, is listed in a 1909 Munich exhibition catalogue. His work is believed to have been well received in Switzerland.
AUCTION RECORDS:
LUCERNE, 30 Sept 1988, *Village Street* (oil on canvas, 18 x 22 ins / 46 x 56 cm) CHF 750.

FRANCIN, pseudonym of Mme Marie Bouasse Francine
French, 19th century.
Active in Paris.
Engraver.

Marie Francin became a lifelong member of the Société des Artistes Français in 1887, and received an honourable mention in 1889.

FRANCIN, Claude
French, 18th century.
Born 1702, in Strasbourg; died 19 March 1773, in Paris.
Sculptor. Religious subjects, figures. Busts.

On 31 January 1767, Claude Francin was made a member of the French academy for *Christ Tied to the Pillar*, which can now be seen in the Louvre. On 29 August 1767, he became a professor. His work appeared in the Louvre exhibitions from 1737 to 1745.

His major works are: *Child Sleeping on a Pillow* (terracotta), *Daniel Saving Suzanne as She is Being Led to Her Death, Two Angels*, (at the pediment of the church of St Roch), *Two Priests from the Roman Church*, (group for the portal of St Roch), *Ganymede* (statue for the king). He won a second prize in 1729 and a first prize in 1730.
MUSEUMS AND GALLERIES:
VERSAILLES: *Bust of d'Alembert*.

FRANCIN, François Alexis. See **FRANSIN**

FRANCIN, Guillaume
French, 18th - 19th century.
Born 1741, in Paris; died 1830.
Sculptor.

Guillaume Francin was the son of Claude Francin. He first studied with his father, then entered the studio of Coustou. In 1793, he sent to the Louvre: *Love Crowning Friendship* (marble statue) and in 1800: *Jacques Angot, Bishop of Auxerre* (bust).
MUSEUMS AND GALLERIES:
LANGRES: *Bust of Marivetz* - PARIS (Louvre): *Gluck* (marble, bust copied after Houdon); *Peiresc* - PARIS (Mus. des Monuments Français): *D'Alembert* (marble, bust) - VERSAILLES: *Jean Goujon*.

FRANCINI, Alexandre
French, 17th century.
Died 1648.
Sculptor.

Under the reign of Henri II, Alexandre Francini, who was certainly of Italian origin, worked at the château of Fontainebleau. He created the fountain of *Perseus*, in the fountain courtyard, and decorated the water-fountains in the park and the fountain of Diana. These works were partly demolished under Louis XIV.

AUCTION RECORDS:

PARIS, 10-11 April 1929, *Moulded Entablature. Triumph of Neptune* (drawing) FRF 180.

FRANCINI, Filippo, or Franchini or Franzini
Italian, 17th century.
Of Florentine origin.
Painter.

Filippo Francini was a pupil and assistant of Agostino Tasso. After working with the latter in Livorno and Genoa, he moved in 1610 to Rome, where he and Tasso collaborated on paintings for the Sala Regia in the Quirinal and paintings for the Palazzo Altemps. The two painters also worked together in Bagnaja.

FRANCINO
Italian, 17th century.
Born to a family originally from Fivizzano.
Sculptor.

Francino's *Risen Christ* is housed in the church of S Antonio in Fivizzano.

FRANCINO, Giovanni
Italian, 15th century.
Born to a family originally from Pinerolo.
Painter.

In 1410, Francino painted an altarpiece for the church of the Brothers Minor in Nice.

FRANCIOLI, Enrico
Italian, 19th century.
Probably born in Milan.
Painter.

Francioli is mentioned in St Petersburg from 1855 to 1858. He exhibited an *Annunciation* at the academy of St Petersburg, which earned him a diploma. He was then charged with renovating a ceiling painting in the ballroom of the Tsarskoye Selo palace. Later in his career Francioli painted a fresco in the chapel of the Rosary in the church of S Simpliciano in Milan.

FRANCIONE, Pedro, called Pedro Espanol, Pietro Hispano, Pietro Spagnuolo, lo Spagnuolo
Spanish, 16th century.
Painter. History painting.

Francione's works can be seen in Naples.

FRANCIOTTI, Brigida
Italian, 16th century.
Active in Lucca.
Painter, sculptor.

Brigada was a nun at the convent of S Giorgio in Lucca.

FRANCIS. See also **CONSCIENCE Francis Antoine**

FRANCIS, F.L.
British, 18th - 19th century.
Painter, watercolourist. Landscapes.

F.L. Francis is cited in *Art Prices Current*.

AUCTION RECORDS:

LONDON, 28 May 1908, *Mountain Stream* (1801, watercolour) GBP 3.

FRANCIS, Filip
Belgian, 20th century.
Born 10 April 1944, in Duffel.
Installation artist, performance artist, painter, draughtsman.
Conceptual Art.

Filip Francis initially used traditional graphic schemes, but then saw that film and video were better suited to his performances. As his methods of experimentation are different in every case, they can only be interpreted during the course of his personal journey; Francis himself considers that they constitute his diary. His fundamental aim is to highlight the concept of space-time. According to some commentators, his performances contain a certain humour: for example, either during live action, or recalled through film or video, he wrote the same number, the same word or the same insult in different languages, over a predetermined space of time; *Infinite Limitation* of 1973 is a more specific example, and is the result of writing two words, rigorously repeated with determination for nine days and nine nights. The time element is present in all of Francis' work as a subjective and objective reality, both for the artist and the spectator.

Since 1965, Francis has participated in many shows and group exhibitions, primarily in the galleries of the main towns and principal museums of Belgium, notably Antwerp, including: 1968, Brussels, *Prix de la Jeune Peinture Belge* (*Young Belgian Painting Prize*), at the Palais des Beaux-Arts; also in other countries, including: 1972, the Eindhoven Triennial, at the Van Abbemuseum; 1974, Paris, *15 Jeune Artistes Belges* (*15 Young Belgian Artists*), the Galerie de Varenne; and *Tendances de l'Art Actuel en Belgique* (*Trends in Contemporary Belgian Art*), Stuttgart; 1976, *Vidéo International* (*International Video*), the Kunstmuseum, Aarhus.

Francis also has held solo shows, including: 1970, Berchem; 1973, Maastricht; 1975, Antwerp; 1976, Maastricht; and 1981, 1993 and 2001 Brussels. In addition, since 1966, he has developed his ideas at many performance-acts in Belgian cities including Brussels, Antwerp and Ghent.

BIBLIOGRAPHY:

Bex, Florent, *Filip Francis*, exhibition catalogue, Internationaal Cultureel Centrum, Antwerp, 1977 (extensive documentation).

MUSEUMS AND GALLERIES:

AMIENS (FRAC Picardie): *Whilst Looking Left with the Right Hand and Looking Right with the Left Hand* (1993, pastel) - MARSEILLES (FRAC Provence-Alpes-Côte d'Azur): *Peripheral Field of Vision whilst Looking Left and Looking Right* (1993) - MONTPELLIER (FRAC Languedoc-Roussillon): *Copy of 'The Meeting' by Courbet in the Peripheral Field of Vision* (1994).

FRANCIS, James
Canadian, 20th - 21st century.
Born 1949.
Sculptor.

James Francis exhibited in Paris at the Salon des Réalités Nouvelles in the 1980s. His work is essentially abstract, but frequently evokes specific ideas and forms, such as flames, or maybe a kiss.

FRANCIS, John
British, 19th century.
Born 3 September 1780, in Lincolnshire; died 30 August 1861.
Sculptor. Busts.

John Francis exhibited from 1820 to 1857 at the Royal Academy, the British Institution and the Suffolk Street Gallery in London.

MUSEUMS AND GALLERIES:

LONDON (National Portrait Gal.): *John Russell, 1st Earl Russell* (1832, marble, bust); *Prince Albert of Saxe-Coburg-Gotha* (1844, plaster bust, now painted black); *Arthur Wellesley, 1st Duke of Wellington* (1852, marble, bust) - MELBOURNE: *Lord Melbourne*.

FRANCIS, John Deffett
British, 19th century.

Born 1815, in Swansea; died 21 February 1901, in Swansea.

Painter. Genre scenes.

John Deffett Francis exhibited from 1837 to 1860 at the Royal Academy, the British Institution and the Suffolk Street Gallery in London.

AUCTION RECORDS:

LONDON, 4 June 1908, *Young Girl of Forborn,* GBP 3. LONDON, 12 Nov 1992, *Little Red Riding Hood* (1859, oil on canvas, 47 1/2 x 32 ins / 120.5 x 81.5 cm) GBP 2,750. NEW YORK, 26 Feb 1997, *Little Red Riding Hood* (oil on canvas, 47 1/2 x 32 ins / 120.6 x 81.3 cm) USD 7,475. LEEDS, 20 Nov 2001, *Two Yorkshire Bairns* (1865, oil on canvas, 28 x 36 ins / 70 x 92 cm) GBP 2,500.

FRANCIS, John F.

American, 19th century.

Born 1808, in Philadelphia; died 1886.

Painter. Portraits, still-lifes (fruit).

In the 1830s and 1840s John F. Francis painted portraits in Pennsylvania, Ohio and Tennessee, but in the 1850s he became a painter of still-lifes. His art, meticulous in its observation and treatment, is in the 18th-century, especially Dutch, tradition of flower and fruit painting. He exhibited in the annual Salons of the Pennsylvania Academy of Fine Arts in 1847, 1855 and 1859, and seems to have stopped working in 1879.

J Francis 1866

AUCTION RECORDS:

NEW YORK, 22 March 1978, *Fruit and Wine* (1858, oil on canvas, 25 x 30 ins / 63.5 x 76.2 cm) USD 65,000. NEW YORK, 11 Dec 1981, *Cakes, Wine and Fruit* (1852, oil on canvas, 20 x 24 ins / 50.8 x 61 cm) USD 20,000. NEW YORK, 1 June 1984, *Desserts on a Table* (oil on canvas, 15 x 19 ins / 38.4 x 48.5 cm) USD 24,000. NEW YORK, 29 May 1987, *Basket of Cherries* (1868, oil on canvas, 10 1/2 x 13 1/2 ins / 26.7 x 34.5 cm) USD 65,000. NEW YORK, 26 May 1988, *Apples and Hazelnuts* (oil on canvas, 10 1/2 x 13 1/2 ins / 26.5 x 34.3 cm) USD 13,200. NEW YORK, 1 Dec 1988, *Still-life with Pineapple, Oranges and Walnuts* (1865, oil on panel, 10 x 11 3/4 ins / 25.4 x 29.8 cm) USD 9,900. NEW YORK, 25 May 1989, *Wine Tasters' Table* (1858, oil on canvas, 25 1/4 x 30 ins / 64.1 x 76.4 cm) USD 264,000. NEW YORK, 24 May 1990, *Still-life with Peaches and Pears* (oil on canvas, 15 x 19 ins / 38.1 x 48.2 cm) USD 12,100. NEW YORK, 22 May 1991, *Still-life with Apples and Chestnuts* (oil on card, 11 x 14 1/4 ins / 28 x 36 cm) USD 10,450. NEW YORK, 28 May 1992, *Still-life with Apples and Chestnuts* (oil on canvas, 25 x 30 ins / 63.5 x 76.2 cm) USD 22,000. NEW YORK, 3 Dec 1992, *Still-life with a Basket of Currants* (1866, oil on canvas, 10 1/2 x 13 1/4 ins / 26.7 x 33.7 cm) USD 26,400. MONACO, 2 July 1993, *Still-life with Apples and Chestnuts* (1867, oil on panel, 7 1/4 x 9 ins / 18.5 x 22 cm) FRF 25,530. NEW YORK, 23 Sept 1993, *Still-life with Cherries and Currants round a Glass* (oil on card, 11 1/4 x 13 1/2 ins / 28.6 x 34.3 cm) USD 4,313. NEW YORK, 25 May 1995, *Basket of Cherries* (1863, oil on panel, 14 3/4 x 19 ins / 37.5 x 48.3 cm) USD 76,750. NEW YORK, 1996, *Basket of Fruit* (oil on canvas, 25 x 30 ins / 63.5 x 76.2 cm) USD 36,800. NEW YORK, 26 Sept 1996, *Oranges and Grapefruit* (1866, oil on canvas, 10 1/2 x 13 1/2 ins / 26.7 x 34.3 cm) USD 9,200. MILFORD, 22 April 1999, *Currants in Compote* (1865, oil on canvas, oval, 10 x 12 ins / 25 x 30 cm) USD 21,000. CLEVELAND, 29 July 1999, *Portrait of Juliet Campbell* (oil on canvas, 30 x 24 ins / 76 x 61 cm) USD 5,000. NEW YORK, 15 June 2000, *Portrait of a Man* (1846, oil on canvas, 36 x 29 ins / 91 x 74 cm) USD 2,200. NEW YORK, 30 Nov 2000, *Strawberries and Cream* (c. 1875, oil on canvas, 15 x 19 ins / 39 x 49 cm) USD 200,000. NEW YORK, 28 Nov 2001, *Still-life with Nuts and Apples in a Basket* (1865, oil on board, 10 x 12 ins / 25 x 30 cm) USD 37,500. NEW YORK, 28 Nov 2001, *Still-life with Cherries* (oil on canvas, 13 x 15 ins / 32 x 38 cm) USD 45,000. NEW ORLEANS, 12 Oct 2002, *Portrait of a Young Girl in White* (1836, oil on canvas, 30 x 25 ins / 76 x 64 cm) USD 7,000. NEW YORK, 4 Dec 2002, *Red and Yellow Apples in a Basket* (1862, oil on panel, 15 x 19 ins / 37 x 48 cm) USD 40,000. DOWNINGTON, 17 May 2003, *Still-life with Bottles of Cognac and Wine Surrounded by Goblets and Glasses, Cheese and Biscuits* (oil on canvas, 19 x 23 ins / 48 x 58 cm) USD 37,500. MILFORD, 23 Oct 2003, *Apples, Oranges and Grapes* (1869, oil on panel, 6 x 9 ins / 15 x 23 cm) USD 4,750. NEW YORK, 19 May 2004, *Still-life with Fruit and Wine Glass* (1856, oil on canvas, 15 x 19 ins / 38 x 48 cm) USD 32,500.

FRANCIS, Mark

Irish, 20th century.

Painter.

Mark Francis studied at St Martin's School of Art in London. He has a strong interest in human anatomy and paints enlargements of cellular structures. Impeccably polished, the aesthetic of his work with its strong optical effects also conveys a sense of the threat of invasion and mutation in the biological order. He took part in *New British Painting in the 1990s* in 1997 at the Museum of Modern Art in Oxford. He has also shown his work in solo exhibitions, notably in 1996 and 1998 at the Galerie Anne de Villepoix in Paris.

FRANCIS, Mike

British, 20th century.

Born 1938, in London.

Painter.

Mike Francis is a self-taught artist. He exhibited for the first time in London in 1962. Francis has exhibited his work in Belgium, France and Italy.

AUCTION RECORDS:

PARIS, 12-13 Oct 1987, *Frustration* (mixed media/panel, 4 1/4 x 32 ins / 11 x 81 cm) FRF 20,000; *Connivance* (mixed media, 72 1/2 x 48 ins / 184 x 122 cm) FRF 18,000. LUCERNE, 20 Nov 1993, *I've Put my Red Skirt On* (1974, oil and acrylic/canvas, 24 1/4 x 29 1/2 ins / 61.5 x 75 cm) CHF 3,400. LONDON, 27 June 2002, *Vertical forms - S.B.L* (1998, oil on canvas, 60 x 48 ins / 153 x 122 cm) GBP 5,000. LONDON, 3 July 2003, *Hide and Sneak* (acrylic and collage on canvas, 19 x 24 ins / 48 x 60 cm) GBP 1,600.

FRANCIS, Sam

American, 20th century.

Born 25 June 1923, in San Mateo (California); died 4 November 1994, in Santa Monica (California).

Painter (including gouache), watercolourist, lithographer, sculptor.

Post-painterly Abstraction.

Sam Francis studied medicine and psychology at the University of California, Berkeley. Called up during the war, he served in the USA Army Air Corps from 1943 to 1945. In 1943, his plane crashed during manoeuvres in the Arizona Desert, injuring his spine, and it was during the four years that he was immobilised in hospital that he began to paint. He said of this period, 'I painted to stay alive'. Francis then entered the California School of Fine Arts, San Francisco, where he worked under Clyfford Still, graduating in 1950. The same year he went for the first time to Paris, staying there, with occasional breaks, until 1960. These years were enriched by the discovery of European art that, until then, he had only seen in reproductions. He worked for a short while in Léger's private academy and met the Canadian painter Jean-Paul Riopelle and American artists living in Paris. He was soon invited to exhibit at the Salon de Mai and in various group shows organised by Nina Dausset and Georges Duthuit, and, in 1952, in Michel Tapié's *Signifiants de l'informel* (*Signifiers of Informal Art*). Francis also made long journeys, including a tour of the world in 1957 with stops in

New York, Mexico, and stays in Japan, Thailand and India, which were an important influence on his development. On one of his frequent return visits to Japan he painted a large mural for the Sogestsu School, Sofu Teshigahara. This was followed, in 1956-58, by a triptych for the staircase of the Kunsthalle, Bern, at the request of the director, Arnold Rudlinger, who remained a constant supporter, and, in 1959, by a mural for the Chase Manhattan Bank, New York. In 1961, Francis became seriously ill and was hospitalised in Bern. When he returned to the USA, he bought a house in Santa Monica, California, where he set up huge studios in disused factory premises.

Sam Francis is one of the most important painters of the post-war American School, though he stands apart from other artists. His paintings of 1946 demonstrate his relationship with Monet and Bonnard: 'I do pure late Monet,' he said at the time, referring to the *Lilies* that were a foreshadowing of the American future. From 1947, his painting tended towards abstraction, but retained a Bonnard-like character. 1960 marked the start of the *Blue Balls* series, in which balloon-shaped blue stains were projected on to the canvas, partly by chance, but with some degree of decision. In 1960, before his hospitalisation in Bern, and in 1963 in Santa Monica, he returned to this medium on a larger scale of production. In 1965, between his painting activities and while in Japan, he constructed a large ceramic sculpture.

In the usually large paintings of his first abstract period, Francis sought both subtlety and sumptuousness. The paint is brushed lightly, almost as if watercolour, and consists of regular, monochrome cells that let the white surface of the canvas occasionally show through. *For Fred* and *Opposites*, painted at the beginning of 1950, prefigure the Paris works of 1950-1952 known as the *White Paintings*, which may be interpreted as a desire for purification, to return to the springs of painting. For Francis, to paint was to recreate 'the very substance of which light is made'. However, this series is defined less by the monochrome of the white than by the diversity and intensity of the colour, which is evoked in titles such as *Pale Green* (1951) or *Yellowish Green* (1952), in which colour intensifies towards the edge of the picture, illuminating a central void. In canvases such as *Blue Black* (1952), *Around Black* (1954), *Around Orange and Black* (1954-1955), on the other hand, white is replaced by black as the revelatory colour. In *In the Adorable Colour Blue* (1955-1957), he undertook the first of a number of vast murals, a change of format made possible by the move to a larger studio. In these large compositions, the colour blue increases in importance, while the coloured cells break down into small fragments characteristic of the Byzantine mosaics he discovered in Italy. Throughout Francis's work the large paintings were accompanied by small works on paper.

While not totally apart from it, Francis was little influenced by Action Painting, or by Pop and Op Art, adhering to his own style. On the other hand, the development of his work in 1967 reveals that he was strongly attracted to Minimalism. In the works painted after 1967, Francis aimed again to convey 'the substance of light', but this time in large canvases that are entirely white apart from a thin border along the outer edge, executed in his characteristic flowing stroke.

Abandoning his monochrome whites in the 1980s, Francis returned to colour paintings in which white once again plays a contrasting role, and, at the same time, introduced some occasional rough sketches of faces. In what was to be the last period of his work, the concern with size, which, until then, had affected only his paintings, took on new aspects. In workshops in California and Japan, Francis entered into a compulsive phase of activity with collaborators, printers and publishers, producing engravings, lithographs, posters and books. He continued to paint, but in enormous formats, using brooms on immense canvases stretched on the ground, on which, he said 'I literally rolled in the paint, just as I rolled on the canvases'.

Until his Minimalist period, Francis's achievement lay in reconciling the European preoccupation with light with the American appetite for scale and space, combining the preciosity of a diamond-sparkling palette with the monumental canvas, large studio size, production capacity and 'body engagement' of American art.

Francis took part in many group exhibitions, including: 1959, Musée National d'Art Moderne, Paris, and 1964, Documenta, Kassel; but he mainly presented his work in solo shows - 124 by 1983, that included: 1948, San Francisco and Paris; 1952, Galerie Nina Dausset; 1955 and 1956, Galerie Rive Droite; 1956, Galerie Martha Jackson, New York; 1960, Kunsthalle, Bern; 1967, Houston; 1968, Centre National d'Art Contemporain, Paris; from 1971, many at the Galerie Jean Fournier, Paris; 1972, travelling exhibition in Buffalo, Washington, New York and Dallas; 1978, retrospective, Centre Pompidou, Paris; 1986, paintings from the Idemitsu Museum, Tokyo, at Pavillon des Arts, Paris; 1988, Modern Art Museum, Toyama, Japan; 1991, Kornfeld Gallery, Bern; and 1996, *Sam Francis, les années parisiennes, 1950-1961* (*Sam Francis, the Paris Years, 1950-1961*) Galerie Nationale du Jeu de Paume, Paris.

Bibliography:

Tapié, Michel (preface), *Sam Francis*, exhibition catalogue, Gal. Rive Droite, Paris, 1956. Meyer, Franz (preface), *Sam Francis*, exhibition catalogue, Kunsthalle, Bern, 1960. Sweeney, James J. (preface), *Sam Francis*, exhibition catalogue, University Art Museum, University of California, Berkeley, Museum of Fine Arts, Houston, 1967. *Sam Francis: the Fifties*, exhibition catalogue, Phillips Collection, Washington DC, 1980. Seltz, Peter Howard, *Sam Francis*, H.N. Abrams, New York, 1982. Hulten, Pontus, *Sam Francis: monotypes*, Gal. de Séoul, Seoul, 1988. Michaud, Yves, *Sam Francis: introduction à l'œuvre peint sur papier 1947-1988*, Gal. Jean Fournier, Paris, 1988. Lembark, Connie W., *The Prints of Sam Francis: a Catalogue Raisonné, 1960-1990*, Hudson Hills Press, New York, 1992. *Sam Francis, les années parisiennes, 1950-1961*, exhibition catalogue, Éd. du Jeu de Paume, Réunion des musées nationaux, Paris, 1995. Mössinger, Ingrid (ed.), *Sam Francis: the Shadow of Colors*, Editions Stemmle, Zurich, 1995. Francis, Sam, *Saturated Blue: Writings from the Notebook*, Lapis Press, Santa Monica, 1995. *Sam Francis: Color is the Essence of It All*, exhibition catalogue, Martin Sosin, Santa Monica, 2003.

Museums and Galleries:

Amsterdam (Stedelijk Mus.): *Basel Mural II* (1956-1958) - Basel (Kunsthalle) - Bern (Kunstmus.) - Buffalo (Albright-Knox AG): *The Whiteness of the Whale* (1957) - Dayton (AI) - Houston (The Menil Collection): a drawing - Humlebæk (Louisiana Mus. for Moderne Kunst): *Untitled* (1956) - Kurashiki (Ohara MA): *Mexico* (1957) - London (Tate Collection): *Around the Blues* (1957-1962, oil and acrylic/canvas); *Painting* (1957, watercolour/paper) - Marseilles (Mus. Cantini): *Untitled* (1971, ink/paper) - Montreal (MBA): *Untitled* (c. 1947) - New York (MoMA): a large collection - New York (Solomon R. Guggenheim Mus.): *Red and Black* (1954); *Shining Back* (1958) - Paris (MNAM-CCI): *In the Adorable Colour Blue* (1955-1957); *Another white* (1952) - Rennes (MBA): *Blue Composition on a White Background* (1960) - Stockholm (Moderna Mus.): *The Yellow Above II* (1958-1960) - Stuttgart (Staatsgal.): *The Yellow Above* (1957-1958) - Tokyo (Idemitsu MA): *Opposites* (1948); *Opposites* (1950); *For Fred* (1949); *Deep Black* - Zurich (Kunsthalle).

Auction records:

London, 6 July 1960, *Painting in Blue and Yellow* (1956) GBP 2,800. London, 6 July 1961, *Red, Blue and Yellow Composition* (watercolour) GBP 550. Bern, 25 May 1962, *Untitled* (gouache/paper) CHF 15,500; *Blue and Red* (oil on canvas)

CHF 35,000. NEW YORK, 21 Oct 1964, *Red no. 2,* USD 16,500. GENEVA, 7 Nov 1969, *Blue,* CHF 83,000. NEW YORK, 4 March 1970, *Pale Violet* (watercolour) USD 5,000. LONDON, 22 April 1971, *Untitled* (gouache) GBP 1,450. NEW YORK, 26 Oct 1972, *Blue no. 3* (1952) USD 19,000. GENEVA, 8 Dec 1973, *Composition,* CHF 23,000. NEW YORK, 1 May 1974, *Violet, Yellow and White,* USD 45,000. BERN, 13 June 1974, *Blue* (watercolour) CHF 10,800. BERN, 9 June 1976, *Dark Blue* (1954, oil on canvas, 25 1/2 x 21 1/4 ins / 64.5 x 54 cm) CHF 60,000. LONDON, 1 July 1976, *Painting* (1957, gouache and watercolour, 21 1/4 x 28 3/4 ins / 54 x 73 cm) GBP 2,600. BERN, 8 June 1977, *Foot Print* (1960, coloured lithograph, 25 x 33 3/4 ins / 63.3 x 86 cm) CHF 3,200. LONDON, 29 June 1977, *Untitled* (1971, oil on canvas, 31 1/2 x 31 1/2 ins / 80 x 80 cm) GBP 5,500. LONDON, 7 Dec 1977, *Untitled* (c. 1959, gouache, 15 x 11 ins / 38 x 28 cm) GBP 1,600. BERN, 7 June 1978, *Flying Love* (1963, coloured lithograph, 24 x 18 3/4 ins / 60.7 x 47.7 cm) CHF 2,600. LONDON, 6 Dec 1978, *Red and Black* (oil on canvas, 77 1/4 x 38 1/4 ins / 196 x 97 cm) GBP 22,000. BERN, 20 June 1979, *Upper Left Red* (1961, watercolour, 15 x 12 1/2 ins / 38.1 x 32 cm) CHF 11,500; *Heart of Stone* (coloured lithograph, 24 1/2 x 36 ins / 62.5 x 90.5 cm) CHF 4,000. NEW YORK, 19 Nov 1981, *Untitled* (1960, gouache/paper, 20 x 26 ins / 50.5 x 66 cm) USD 9,000. NEW YORK, 9 May 1984, *Blue Balls* (1967, gouache/paper, 29 1/2 x 41 ins / 75 x 104.2 cm) USD 45,000. BERN, 20 June 1984, *White Line* (coloured lithograph, 33 1/2 x 25 ins / 85.2 x 63.3 cm) CHF 16,500. NEW YORK, 1 Nov 1984, *Towards Disappearance* (1957-1958, oil on canvas, 116 1/2 x 126 ins / 296 x 320 cm) USD 700,000. NEW YORK, 2 May 1985, *Black* (1950, oil on canvas, 77 3/4 x 51 1/2 ins / 197.5 x 130.5 cm) USD 180,000. NEW YORK, 19 Nov 1985, *The White Line* (1960, coloured lithograph, 35 1/2 x 25 ins / 90.2 x 63.5 cm) USD 10,000. BERN, 17 June 1987, *White Line* (1959, watercolour and gouache, 40 x 27 ins / 101.5 x 68.5 cm) CHF 209,000. PARIS, 21 Dec 1987, *Composition* (watercolour and gouache, 14 3/4 x 11 ins / 37.5 x 28 cm) FRF 98,000. PARIS, 20 March 1988, *Composition* (1970, watercolour, 17 3/4 x 23 1/2 ins / 45 x 60 cm) FRF 130,000. NEW YORK, 3 May 1988, *Untitled* (acrylic/paper/Japanese paper, 40 3/4 x 28 3/4 ins / 103.5 x 73 cm) USD 46,750; *Passing Through* (acrylic/paper mounted/canvas, 30 1/4 x 22 ins / 77 x 56 cm) USD 60,500; *Untitled* (1953, watercolour/paper, 25 3/4 x 19 3/4 ins / 65.5 x 50 cm) USD 77,000. LONDON, 30 June 1988, *Untitled* (watercolour/paper, 22 3/4 x 30 3/4 ins / 58 x 78 cm) GBP 39,600. NEW YORK, 8 Oct 1988, *Untitled* (1962, oil and gouache/paper, 17 x 20 ins / 43.2 x 50.5 cm) USD 60,500. PARIS, 26 Oct 1988, *Blue Composition* (1960, watercolour, 19 3/4 x 25 1/2 ins / 50 x 65 cm) FRF 190,000. NEW YORK, 9 Nov 1988, *Towards Disappearance I* (oil on canvas, 108 x 126 ins / 274.6 x 320.3 cm) USD 1,320,000. LONDON, 1 Dec 1988, *Untitled* (1974, acrylic/paper, 36 1/2 x 72 ins / 93 x 182 cm) GBP 66,000. PARIS, 12 Feb 1989, *Composition* (1970, 19 3/4 x 24 ins / 50 x 61 cm) FRF 150,000. NEW YORK, 14 Feb 1989, *Untitled* (1970, acrylic/paper, 22 x 29 1/2 ins / 56.1 x 74.9 cm) USD 30,800; *Untitled* (1986, acrylic/canvas, 35 1/2 x 139 ins / 90.2 x 353.2 cm) USD 198,000. PARIS, 6 March 1989, *Untitled* (lithograph/paper, 24 3/4 x 28 1/4 ins / 63 x 72 cm) FRF 6,000. PARIS, 23 March 1989, *Composition* (1972, acrylic/paper, 30 x 21 3/4 ins / 76.5 x 55.5 cm) FRF 280,000. NEW YORK, 2 May 1989, *Untitled* (1958, oil on canvas, 40 x 29 ins / 101.6 x 73.7 cm) USD 484,000; *Untitled* (1962, oil on canvas, 51 x 77 ins / 129.5 x 195.5 cm) USD 605,000. NEW YORK, 5 Oct 1989, *Untitled* (1984, acrylic/canvas, 72 x 36 ins / 182.8 x 91.5 cm) USD 264,000. PARIS, 7 Oct 1989, *Untitled* (1960, watercolour/paper, 17 x 12 3/4 ins / 43 x 32.5 cm) FRF 175,000. PARIS, 8 Oct 1989, *Untitled* (1960, gouache and watercolour, 19 1/2 x 27 1/4 ins / 49.5 x 69.5 cm) FRF 350,000. PARIS, 9 Oct 1989, *Composition.* NEW YORK, 7 Nov 1989, *Untitled* (1957, watercolour/paper, 26 1/2 x 40 ins / 67.2 x 101.6 cm) USD 352,000. NEW YORK, 8 Nov 1989, *Silvio Set One* (1963, oil on canvas, 47 1/2 x 40 ins / 120.7 x 101.7 cm) USD 990,000. PARIS, 22 Nov 1989, *Blue and Yellow Composition* (gouache, 5 1/2 x 3 3/4 ins / 14 x 9.5 cm) FRF 115,000. PARIS, 9 Dec 1989, *Composition* (2 nov. 1960, watercolour/paper, 9 1/4 x 12 3/4 ins / 23.5 x 32.5 cm) FRF 250,000. PARIS, 18 Feb 1990, *Dripping* (acrylic and gouache/paper, 30 x 22 ins / 76 x 56 cm) FRF 280,000. LONDON, 22 Feb 1990, *Untitled* (1988, acrylic/paper, 14 3/4 x 11 ins / 37.5 x 27 cm) GBP 24,200. PARIS, 29 March 1990, *Dripping* (1973, acrylic/canvas, 83 3/4 x 120 ins / 213 x 305 cm) FRF 3,100,000. PARIS, 8 April 1990, *Tokyo* (1973, acrylic/paper, 22 x 29 1/2 ins / 55 x 75 cm) FRF 480,000. NEW YORK, 7 May 1990, *Around the World* (1959, oil on canvas, 108 x 126 1/2 ins / 274.3 x 321.3 cm) USD 1,870,000. NEW YORK, 8 May 1990, *Blue Center III* (1959, oil on canvas, 72 x 96 ins / 182.8 x 243.8 cm) USD 1,650,000. LONDON, 28 June 1990, *Untitled* (1956, gouache/paper, 30 x 22 1/2 ins / 76.5 x 57.1 cm) GBP 99,000. NEW YORK, 4 Oct 1990, *Untitled* (1977, acrylic/canvas, 78 x 54 ins / 198 x 137 cm) USD 192,500. PARIS, 28 Oct 1990, *Untitled* (1979, acrylic/paper/canvas, 42 1/4 x 137 3/4 ins / 107 x 350 cm) FRF 1,500,000. NEW YORK, 7 Nov 1990, *Untitled* (1956, oil on canvas, 72 3/4 x 77 3/4 ins / 184.6 x 197.5 cm) USD 935,000. MILAN, 13 Dec 1990, *From Tokyo I* (1970, acrylic/mounted paper, 27 1/2 x 40 1/2 ins / 70 x 103 cm) ITL 35,000,000. NEW YORK, 15 Feb 1991, *Untitled* (1958, watercolour and acrylic/paper/board, 20 x 27 ins / 50.8 x 68.5 cm) USD 93,500. LONDON, 21 March 1991, *Untitled* (gouache and oil on paper, 12 1/4 x 9 1/2 ins / 31 x 24 cm) GBP 30,800. NEW YORK, 2 May 1991, *Untitled* (1971, acrylic/canvas, 51 1/2 x 64 ins / 130.8 x 162.6 cm) USD 99,000. AMSTERDAM, 23 May 1991, *Untitled* (1960, watercolour/paper, 18 1/2 x 12 1/4 ins / 47 x 31 cm) NLG 12,650. LONDON, 27 June 1991, *Composition no. 6* (1973, acrylic/canvas, 72 x 59 3/4 ins / 182 x 152 cm) GBP 105,600. LONDON, 17 Oct 1991, *Red, Green and Blue* (1959, gouache/paper, 6 x 3 ins / 15 x 7.5 cm) GBP 6,050. VERSAILLES, 15 Dec 1991, *Composition* (1984, acrylic/canvas, 32 x 25 1/2 ins / 81 x 65 cm) FRF 460,000. NEW YORK, 25-26 Feb 1992, *Untitled* (1982, acrylic/canvas, 36 x 71 3/4 ins / 91.4 x 182.2 cm) USD 115,500. NEW YORK, 6 May 1992, oil on canvas, 36 1/4 x 24 1/4 ins / 92.1 x 61.3 cm) USD 148,500. AMSTERDAM, 21 May 1992, *Composition* (1960, watercolour/paper, 17 x 13 ins / 43 x 33 cm) NLG 17,250. PARIS, 13 June 1992, *Untitled* (1987, acrylic/paper, 22 x 30 ins / 56 x 76 cm) FRF 115,000. LONDON, 2 July 1992, *Composition no. 4* (1973, acrylic/canvas, 83 3/4 x 72 ins / 213 x 183 cm) GBP 74,800. NEW YORK, 18 Nov 1992, *Untitled* (1977, acrylic/canvas, 72 1/4 x 84 1/4 ins / 183.5 x 213.7 cm) USD 176,000. MUNICH, 1-2 Dec 1992, *Pasadena Box* (object painted in gouache, h. 19 3/4 ins / 50 cm) DEM 46,000. ZURICH, 21 April 1993, *For the Blue Threads of Air* (1990, coloured lithograph, 53 1/2 x 32 ins / 136 x 81 cm) CHF 5,000. NEW YORK, 3 May 1993, *Silvio, first state* (1963, oil on canvas, 47 3/4 x 40 ins / 121.3 x 101.6 cm) USD 288,500. LONDON, 24 June 1993, *Blue Bubbles* (1961, gouache/paper/canvas, 40 1/4 x 24 1/2 ins / 102.5 x 62.5 cm) GBP 29,900. NEW YORK, 10 Nov 1993, *Mid-Blue III* (1959, oil on canvas, 72 x 96 ins / 182.9 x 243.8 cm) USD 1,047,500. ZURICH, 3 Dec 1993, *Composition* (1973, acrylic/paper, 20 x 14 1/4 ins / 50.5 x 36 cm) CHF 55,000. NEW YORK, 3 May 1994, *Blue Tokyo* (1961, acrylic/paper, 51 1/2 x 32 ins / 130.8 x 81.3 cm) USD 145,500. NEW YORK, 4 May 1994, *red chalk* (1956, oil on canvas, 122 x 75 ins / 309.9 x 190.5 cm) USD 1,267,500. LONDON, 30 June 1994, *Untitled* (1964, acrylic/canvas, 48 x 60 1/4 ins / 122 x 153 cm) GBP 133,500. PARIS, 23 Nov 1994, *Composition* (acrylic/paper, 17 3/4 x 23 1/2 ins / 45 x 60 cm) FRF 100,000. HEIDELBERG, 8 April 1995, *Untitled* (1974, coloured lithograph, 30 x 22 ins / 76 x 56 cm) DEM 4,400. ZURICH, 14 Nov 1995, *Untitled* (1974, acrylic/rice paper, 36 1/2 x 71 1/4 ins / 93 x 181 cm) CHF 110,000. AMSTERDAM, 15 Nov 1995, *Untitled* (gouache/paper, 59 1/2 x 44 ins / 151.1 x 111.8 cm) NLG 365,500. PARIS, 22 Nov 1995, *Untitled* (1986, acrylic/canvas, 61 x 35 3/4 ins / 154 x 91 cm) FRF 555,000. NEW YORK, 22 Feb 1996, *Untitled* (1987, acrylic on canvas) USD

85,000. NEW YORK, 8 May 1996, *Untitled* (1955, watercolour on paper, 22¼ x 17¾ ins / 56.5 x 45.1 cm) USD 123,500. LONDON, 23 May 1996, *Untitled* (1974, acrylic and watercolour on paper, 36¼ x 72 ins / 92 x 182 cm) GBP 54,300. NEW YORK, 9 Nov 1996, *Meteorite* (1986, colour lithograph, 71¾ x 42 ins / 182.5 x 106.5 cm) USD 9,200. NEW YORK, 19 Nov 1996, *Composition* (1957, oil on canvas, 51½ x 25¼ ins / 130.8 x 64.3 cm) USD 200,500. NEW YORK, 20 Nov 1996, *Untitled* (acrylic/canvas, 48 x 60 ins / 121.9 x 152.4 cm) USD 90,500. MILAN, 25 Nov 1996, *Pale Blue and Deep Blue* (watercolour, 11¾ x 7¾ ins / 30 x 20 cm) ITL 8,050,000. ZURICH, 8 April 1997, *San-Zurich, 8 April 1997: Untitled* (1990, acrylic/paper, h. 18 x 12¾ ins / 45.5 x 32.7 cm) CHF 24,000. NEW YORK, 7 May 1997, *Untitled* (1958, watercolour/paper, 40 x 25½ ins / 101.9 x 64.8 cm) USD 96,000. NEW YORK, 8 May 1997, *Red, Yellow, Blue* (1960, oil on canvas, 32¼ x 21¼ ins / 81.6 x 53.7 cm) USD 151,000. PARIS, 20 June 1997, *Untitled* (1974, acrylic/paper, 24 x 22¼ ins / 61 x 56.5 cm) FRF 71,000. LONDON, 27 June 1997, *Untitled* (1969, gouache/paper, 48 x 63¾ ins / 122 x 162 cm) GBP 20,700. NEW YORK, 19 Nov 1998, *Untitled* (1980, acrylic/rice paper, 72 x 36½ ins / 182.9 x 92.7 cm) USD 57,500. NEW YORK, 18 May 1999, *Abstract Composition* (oil on canvas, 35 x 51 ins / 89 x 130 cm) USD 625,000. NEW YORK, 17 Nov 1999, *Towards Disappearance I* (oil on canvas, 108 x 126 ins / 274 x 321 cm) USD 3,100,000. NEW YORK, 9 May 2000, *Untitled* (oil on canvas, 91 x 79 ins / 230 x 200 cm) USD 2,000,000. NEW YORK, 15 Nov 2000, *Untitled* (oil on canvas, 71 x 94 ins / 180 x 239 cm) USD 750,000. NEW YORK, 16 May 2001, *Black* (oil on canvas, 74 x 63 ins / 189 x 161 cm) USD 2,200,000. NEW YORK, 13 Nov 2001, *Yellow* (1953, oil on canvas, 76 x 62 ins / 194 x 158 cm) USD 1,000,000. NEW YORK, 14 May 2002, *White 5* (1951, oil on canvas, 76 x 51 ins / 194 x 129 cm) USD 240,000. NEW YORK, 14 May 2002, *Untitled* (1989, acrylic on canvas, 89 x 179 ins / 226 x 455 cm) USD 260,000. NEW YORK, 14 May 2003, *Big Orange* (1954-1955, oil on canvas, 118 x 76 ins / 300 x 193 cm) USD 2,400,000. BERN, 20 June 2003, *Yellow Green* (1955, gouache and watercolour, 40 x 27 ins / 102 x 69 cm) CHF 200,000. NEW YORK, 11 May 2004, *White* (1952, oil on canvas, 97 x 59 ins / 246 x 150 cm) USD 750,000. NEW YORK, 15 Sept 2004, *Untitled* (1974, acrylic on canvas, 83 x 191 ins / 210 x 484 cm) USD 220,000.

FRANCIS, Sidney
French, 20th century.
Born 22 October 1945, in Paris.
Painter (mixed media).

Sidney Francis has developed a very distinctive technique. He uses images, which he arranges in photographic montages, as the inspiration for his work, and creates a strangely hallucinatory, poetic atmosphere. He calls his finished products Chronographismes, as they are intended to express the passing of time.

He has exhibited in Paris since 1969 at various Salons, including: Salon Comparaisons, and the Salon Grands et Jeunes d'Aujourd'hui. He has also staged a number of solo exhibitions since 1971.

FRANCIS, Yoseph, also known as Alimazi, Yoseph
Mozambican, 20th century.
Born 1930.
Active in Tanzania from 1955.
Sculptor.

Yoseph Francis was the brother of Matayo; he moved to Dar-es-Salaam with his brother in 1955 and they worked together. He made Makonde carvings and had many followers.

BIBLIOGRAPHY:
Stöter-Bender, Jutta, *L'Art contemporain dans les pays du tiers-monde*, L'Harmattan, Paris, 1995 (Contemporary Art in the Countries of the Third World).

FRANCIS-BERNARD. See **BERNARD Francis**

FRANCISCI, Anthony de
Italian, 20th century.
Born 13 June 1887, in Italy; died 1964.
Active in the USA.
Sculptor, medallist. Figures, nudes.

Anthony de Francisci was a teacher at the Institute of Fine Arts in New York. He sculpted statuettes and nudes, and his work as a medallist included designing the 'Maine Centannial' silver half dollar.

AUCTION RECORDS:
NEW YORK, 29 Sept 1977, *Cup of Basil* (1940, gold patinated bronze, h. 11¾ ins / 30 cm) USD 1,100. NEW YORK, 30 May 1990, *Female Nude* (golden-brown patinated bronze, h. 20¼ ins / 51.4 cm) USD 2,200. NEW YORK, 28 Nov 1995, *Woman* (bronze, h. 16¾ ins / 42.5 cm) USD 2,530.

FRANCISCO
Spanish, 15th century.
Engraver.

Francisco was a Dominican monk in Valencia.

MUSEUMS AND GALLERIES:
MADRID (Prints Collection): *Virgin of the Rosary with Dominican Saints; Scenes from the Life of Mary and of Christ.*

FRANCISCO, also known as Francesco Florentin
Italian, 16th century.
Of Florentine origin.
Active in Spain.
Sculptor.

From 1520 to 1522, working with Martin Milanes, Francisco sculpted the marble baptismal fonts for Granada Cathedral in the Italian Renaissance style. These fonts are now in the 'Sagrario' parish church.

FRANCISCO
Spanish, 18th century.
Active in Seville.
Painter.

FRANCISCO, Antonio. See **ANTONIO Francisco**

FRANCISCO, Carlos V.
Filipino, 20th century.
Born 1913, in the Philippines.
Painter.

Together with Edades and Ocampo, Francisco was one of the founding and leading figures in modern art in the Philippines. His painting is greatly influenced by Gauguin.

FRANCISCO, John Bond
American, 19th - 20th century.
Born 14 December 1863, in Cincinnati (Ohio); died 1931.
Painter. Landscapes.

John Bond Francisco studied with Feichner in Berlin, in Munich and in Paris with Bouguereau and Courtois.

AUCTION RECORDS:
LOS ANGELES, 17 March 1980, *Sacramento River* (oil on canvas, 22 x 28 ins / 56 x 71.1 cm) USD 1,600. LOS ANGELES-SAN FRANCISCO, 7 Feb 1990, *Landscape at Twilight* (oil on card, 7¾ x 11 ins / 20 x 27 cm) USD 2,750. LOS ANGELES-SAN FRANCISCO, 10 Oct 1990, *Sunset in Sierras* (oil on board, 7 x 10 ins / 18 x 25.5 cm) USD 2,200. LOS ANGELES, 28 Oct 1999, *Still-life with Canteen and Spurs* (oil on canvas, 35 x 24 ins / 88 x 61 cm) USD 4,200. PASADENA, 14 Nov 2000, *California Hillside* (oil on canvas, 6 x 8 ins / 16 x 20 cm) USD 3,750. SAN FRANCISCO, 13 June 2001, *Still-life with a Wine Flask* (1892, oil on canvas, 18 x 24 ins / 46 x 61 cm) USD 7,000. SAN FRANCISCO, 12 Dec 2001, *Scrub Oak in a Canyon* (oil on canvas, 26 x 34 ins / 66 x 86 cm) USD 10,000. PASADENA, 18 Feb 2003, *Mountain River Landscape* (oil on canvas, 28 x 32 ins / 71 x 81 cm) USD 2,750. PASADENA, 17 Feb 2004, *View of San Francisco Harbour* (oil on canvas, 22 x 26 ins / 56 x 66 cm) USD

9,500. PHILADELPHIA, 27 June 2004, *Sunlit Trees in a Mountain Landscape* (oil on canvas, 16 x 20 ins / 41 x 51 cm) USD 4,000.

FRANCISCO, José
Portuguese, 19th century.
Painter.

José Francisco taught landscape painting at the Lisbon academy and exhibited paintings of the gardens of stately homes and palaces. He may be identical with the painter of the same name who drew up a plan for the gardens of the 'Quinta das Virtudes' in Oporto, which earned him the name 'José Francisco das Quintas'.

FRANCISCO, Juan
Spanish, 16th century.
Active in Valladolid.
Sculptor.

Very little is known about this artist. He must have been talented, however, as he was one of Berruguete's most favoured assistants.

FRANCISCO, Pascual
Spanish, 16th century.
Active in Seville in 1575.
Painter.

FRANCISCO, Pietro de
Italian, 20th century.
Born in Palermo (Sicily).
Painter. Scenes with figures, genre scenes, local scenes, landscapes.
Orientalism.

In 1926 Pietro de Francisco showed *Vision of Provence* at the Salon of the Société des Artistes Français in Paris. He also exhibited popular scenes, 'expressions of movement' and some Orientalist studies at the Salon of the Société Nationale des Beaux-Arts.

AUCTION RECORDS:
PARIS, 24 March 1930, *Market in Spain*, FRF 60. MILAN, 16 June 1980, *Via Appia* (oil on canvas, 23 1/2 x 48 ins / 60 x 122 cm) ITL 750,000. NEW YORK, 29 Nov 1984, *The Races at St-Cloud* (oil on panel, 16 1/2 x 29 3/4 ins / 42 x 75.5 cm) USD 2,800.

FRANCISCO D'AVILA
Spanish, 17th century.
Active in Seville.
Painter. Portraits.

Francisco d'Avila was renowned for the colour and life-like qualities of his portraits. He painted some remarkable ones from memory. D'Avila worked in the service of archbishop Don Pedro de Castro.

FRANCISCO DA REGGIO (Fra)
Italian, 16th century.
Miniaturist.

FRANCISCO DE BURGOS
Spanish, 15th century.
Active in Seville c. 1450.
Painter.

FRANCISCO DE CERVERA, called mestre Francesco
Spanish, 15th century.
Painter.

Francisco de Cervera is first mentioned in 1479 as being in Barcelona, and was working on a chapel in the cathedral in 1486.

FRANCISCO DE HOLLANDA, or Francisco d'Ollanda or Dolanda
Portuguese, 16th century.
Born c. 1517, probably in Lisbon; died 19 June 1584, in Lisbon.
Miniaturist, draughtsman.

The pupil and biographer of his father, Antonio, Francisco de Hollanda was an excellent draughtsman and architect, as well as an illuminator. According to Taborda, he illuminated the choir books of the royal monastery at Thomar, and his biographer, the abbé de Castro, says that he also worked on those of the monastery at Belém, which were destroyed in the Lisbon earthquake. He visited Rome twice, first in his youth, when he accompanied the two royal princes Don Fernando and Don Alfonso, and later on the orders of King John III. On this latter occasion, he also visited other parts of Italy, Spain and France. In Venice he made friends with Serlio and, in Rome, with Michelangelo, Clovio, Lattansio and Claudio Tolomei. He travelled as the king's accredited messenger and spent nine or ten years in Italy, and is reported as being in Rome in 1539. He returned to Portugal in 1548, where he compiled his treatise on painting. During his final years, Francisco de Hollanda worked incessantly on his memoires, which were never published. His work as an illuminator includes John III's breviary. The British Museum owns a missal produced for John III, which was begun while Francisco was in his service. His sketchbook is conserved in the Escorial Library; it contains sketches of Roman buildings, costume studies, Italian and French landscapes (Vesuvius, Mont Cenis), and miniature portraits of *Pope Paul III*, *Doge Pietro Lando of Venice* and *Michelangelo*. For Donna Maria, daughter of King John III of Portugal, he painted a portrait of her father.

MUSEUMS AND GALLERIES:
SAN LORENZO DE EL ESCORIAL (Real Monasterio de San Lorenzo, Biblioteca): *Imperial Villa* (c. 1538-1540, pen, black ink and watercolour).

FRANCISCO FIAMMINGO. See **DUQUESNOY François**

FRANCISCUS
German, 15th century.
Illuminator.

Franciscus is mentioned in Basel in 1485.

FRANCISCUS, Juliani. See **FRANCESCO DI GIULIANO**

FRANCISCUS ITALUS. See **FRANCESCO**

FRANCISQUE
French, 20th century.
Born in Marseilles.
Sculptor.

Francisque exhibited in Paris at the Salon des Artistes Français from 1929.

AUCTION RECORDS:
LONDON, 8 March 1976, *Pierrot and Colombine* (bronze, w. 24 3/4 ins / 63 cm) GBP 280.

FRANCISQUIN, Geronimo
Spanish, 16th century.
Painter, sculptor.

Probably of Italian origin, Francisquin is mentioned as being in Seville around 1554.

FRANCISQUIN, Jean. See **FRANCEQUIN**

FRANCISQUITO. See **FRANCESCHITTO**

FRANCISY-ECKERT, pseudonym of Eckert, Marie-France
French, 20th century.
Born 24 May 1915, in Marseilles.
Painter.

Francisy-Eckert studied at the École des Beaux-Arts in Marseilles and the École Internationale de Dessin et Peinture in Monte Carlo. Working in a Post-Impressionist style, she tackled a variety of genres, including landscapes (often of the outskirts of Marseilles), seascapes, portraits and still-lifes.

She was awarded several medals, notably the gold medal at the Grand Prix de Paris, and other medals in Geneva, Lyons and Mexico City. She was awarded several regional prizes including those of Deauville, Provinces Françaises, Montpellier and Fontaine-de-Vaucluse. A number of her works were purchased by local institutions in Marseilles and the Bouches-du-Rhône region.

She took part in numerous group exhibitions in all the major towns of southern France (at the Musée de Marseilles in 1962) and at the Salon des Artistes Indépendants in Paris as well as abroad - in England, Luxembourg, Belgium, Germany, Spain, Algeria, Italy and New York and Washington in the USA. She was a member of the Salon des Artistes Français, the Salon des Indépendants, the Salon de l'Art Libre and the Société des Arts Graphiques et Plastiques. She also held solo exhibitions of her work, notably at the Galerie Marcel Bernheim in Paris in 1961.

MUSEUMS AND GALLERIES:

MARSEILLES.

FRANCISZEK

Polish, 18th century.

Active in Lemberg (now Lviv, Ukraine).

Sculptor (wood).

In 1775 Franciszek was working on Lemberg cathedral.

FRANCK

German, 18th century.

Engraver.

Franck was active in Mainz.

FRANCK

Belgian, 19th century.

Engraver.

Franck was part of the Brussels school around 1850.

FRANCK. See also **FRANCKE, FRANCKEN, FRANK, FRANKE, FRANKEN, VRANCK, VRANCX...**

FRANCK, Adolf Theodor

German, 19th century.

Born 11 July 1841, in Billwärder, near Hamburg.

Painter. Genre scenes, landscapes.

Adolf Franck was a pupil of G. and M. Gensler in Hamburg and then studied at the Munich academy. In 1863 he went to Florence and in 1865 to Rome. He made many study trips to the Tyrol where he painted pictures which were engraved on wood by his friend T. Knesing and appeared in many reviews. His works include: *Sermon on the Mountain in the Tyrol, Struggle with Poachers, Cabaret in Botzen*. He also made etchings of Tyrolean landscapes.

FRANCK, Aernout

Flemish School, 16th century.

Died 1592, in Rome.

Painter, engraver.

This Flemish painter is documented in Rome from 1582 onwards, where he was known as Rinaldo Franches.

FRANCK, Albert Jacques

Canadian, 20th century.

Born 1899; died 1973.

Painter, watercolourist. Urban landscapes.

Albert Jacques Franck painted, often in watercolour, the streets and local scenes of Canadian towns that look British.

AUCTION RECORDS:

GÖTEBORG, 31 March 1977, *Shuter Street* (1963, oil on card, 11 3/4 x 15 3/4 ins / 30 x 40 cm) CAD 2,100. TORONTO, 15 May 1978, *Ontario Street* (1969, oil on board, 20 x 16 ins / 51 x 40.5 cm) CAD 7,400. TORONTO, 30 Oct 1978, *Howard Street* (watercolour, 11 x 9 1/2 ins / 28 x 24.3 cm) CAD 2,600. TORONTO, 14 May 1979, *Grenville Street* (1963, watercolour, 19 1/2 x 24 1/4 ins / 49.5 x 61.5 cm) CAD 4,000. TORONTO, 28 May 1980, *Campus Arch* (pen/paper, 4 1/2 x 3 3/4 ins / 11.3 x 9.4 cm) CAD 1,100. TORONTO, 1 June 1982, *Wellesley East at Parliament* (1968, watercolour, 23 3/4 x 19 3/4 ins / 60.6 x 50 cm) CAD 9,000. TORONTO, 3 May 1983, *Berryman Street in Snow* (1966, oil on board, 22 x 25 1/2 ins / 55 x 65 cm) CAD 5,500; *Lane behind Spruce* (1965, watercolour, 5 1/2 x 5 ins / 13.8 x 12.5 cm) CAD 2,000. TORONTO, 28 May 1985, *Ontario Street* (1970, watercolour, 7 1/4 x 5 1/2 ins / 18.1 x 13.8 cm) CAD 1,400; *Behind Henry Street* (1966, oil on board, 19 3/4 x 15 3/4 ins / 50 x 40 cm) CAD 4,200. TORONTO, 12 June 1989, *Lane turning off Isabella Street* (watercolour, 5 x 6 3/4 ins / 12.7 x 17.1 cm) CAD 1,700. TORONTO, 2 June 1999, *House on Bleecker Street* (1962, oil on board, 24 x 20 ins / 61 x 51 cm) CAD 5,000. TORONTO, 7 Dec 1999, *Farm near Haliburton* (oil on canvasboard, 20 x 24 ins / 50 x 60 cm) CAD 3,000. TORONTO, 23 May 2000, *Backyards on Massey Street, Toronto* (oil on canvas, 24 x 35 ins / 60 x 90 cm) CAD 9,500. TORONTO, 13 June 2000, *Twenty Five Homewood Ave* (oil on board, 16 x 12 ins / 41 x 30 cm) CAD 5,500. TORONTO, 26 Nov 2001, *Old House, McCaul Street* (oil on canvasboard, 24 x 20 ins / 61 x 51 cm) CAD 13,500. TORONTO, 3 Dec 2002, *Bellair Street* (oil on canvas on board, 16 x 20 ins / 40 x 50 cm) CAD 7,500. TORONTO, 3 Dec 2002, *Back of Berkeley St* (oil on board, 12 x 10 ins / 30 x 25 cm) CAD 26,000. TORONTO, 27 May 2003, *Behind Euclid Avenue* (oil on masonite, 30 x 24 ins / 76 x 61 cm) CAD 13,000. TORONTO, 3 June 2003, *House on Isabella Street* (oil on board, 30 x 24 ins / 75 x 60 cm) CAD 15,000. TORONTO, 31 May 2004, *Backyard on Belmont Street* (oil on canvas, 10 x 16 ins / 25 x 40 cm) CAD 7,000. TORONTO, 1 June 2004, *Behind Ross Street* (watercolour on paper, 7 x 5 ins / 17 x 13 cm) CAD 2,600. TORONTO, 1 June 2004, *Richmond Street, West* (oil on board, 12 x 10 ins / 30 x 25 cm) CAD 5,750.

FRANCK, Alfred von

Austrian, 19th century.

Born 3 March 1808, in Vienna; died 4 December 1884, in Graz.

Painter, engraver (etching), lithographer.

Alfred von Franck studied initially at the Engineering School in Vienna and, from 1849 to 1856, he taught at the design academy in Vienna-Neustadt, which came about as a result of having the Emperor Franz-Joseph as a pupil. He drew and painted landscapes in oils and painted watercolours of wild plants. His etchings and lithographs were of landscapes, genre scenes and plant and animal studies. His lithographs also include portraits and copies of drawings.

FRANCK, Antoine Pierre

Flemish, 18th century.

Born 1723; died 24 December 1796.

Active in Liège.

Sculptor.

Flemish School.

Antoine Pierre Franck was a pupil of G. Evrard. Among his numerous works in the churches of Liège, the most notable are the monumental statues of the four church fathers at the choir entrance and four low reliefs in the choir in St-Martin; the sculptures on the main doors in St-André and the church of the Augustinians; the statue of St Roch in St-Nicolas-au-Trez; the statue of an angel in St-Thomas; two wooden statues and a tabernacle in Ste-Agatha; a statue of the prophet Elijah in the Carmelite convent; and two statues of saints in the Franciscan monastery.

FRANCK, Arnold, or Franken

Flemish School, 16th - 17th century.

Active in Antwerp.

Painter.

Siret states that this artist was taken on as a pupil by the sculptor Cardon in 1611.

FRANCK, Arthur
American, 20th century.
Painter.
Arthur Franck exhibited in Paris at the Salon de la Société Nationale des Beaux-Arts, the Salon d'Automne and the Salon des Artistes Indépendants from 1922.

FRANCK, Christoffel Frederik
Dutch, 18th - 19th century.
Born May 1758, in Zwolle; died 1816, in Bennebroek, near Haarlem.
Active in Louvain and then Haarlem.
Painter. Portraits, landscapes with figures, landscapes.

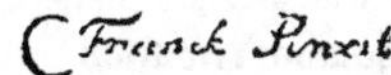

Museums and Galleries:
Amsterdam: *Self-portrait.*
Auction records:
Amsterdam, 28 Oct 1980, *Wooded Landscape* (oil on canvas, 12 1/4 x 18 ins / 31 x 46 cm) NLG 5,200. Monaco, 17 June 1989, *Bringing in the Hay* (oil on canvas, 33 1/2 x 38 3/4 ins / 85 x 98.5 cm) FRF 35,520. London, 31 Oct 1990, *Figures in front of a House by a River* (oil on canvas, 15 x 21 1/4 ins / 38 x 54 cm) GBP 3,300. Amsterdam, 10 Nov 1997, *Huntsman and Travellers Resting in a Forest Inn* (oil on canvas, 34 1/4 x 39 3/4 ins / 87 x 101 cm) NLG 40,362.

FRANCK, Franz Friedrich
German, 17th century.
Born 1627, in Kaufbeuren; died 1687, in Augsburg.
Painter. History painting, portraits, still-lifes.
Franz Friedrich Franck was the son of Hans Ulrich Franck. He was influenced by his father, by the art of Rembrandt and by Italian still-life painters.

Museums and Galleries:
Vienna: *Portrait of a Man.*
Auction records:
London, 31 May 1932, *Dives and Lazarus,* GBP 42.

FRANCK, Friedrich Carl
German, 19th century.
Born 29 May 1799, in Annaberg (Saxony); died 21 August 1872, in Dresden.
Painter, draughtsman. Landscapes.
Friedrich Franck was 30 years old by the time he did his studies at the Dresden academy. He travelled in Poland and in Galicia and exhibited oil paintings with views of these countries in 1864 and 1865. Almost without exception, his other paintings represent landscapes of Swiss Saxony.
Museums and Galleries:
Dresden (Prints Collection): *Track with Pine Trees; Boat Hauler* - Dresden (Stadtmus.): *The Loschwitzgrund near Dresden* (oil painting).

FRANCK, Friedrich Wilhelm
German, 17th century.
Born to a family originally from Kahla (Saxony-Altenbourg).
Painter.
In the church in Strasbourg near Plauen are murals by Friedrich Wilhelm Franck portraying *The Birth of Christ* and *The Ascension* with biblical inscriptions. These paintings are signed by the artist.

FRANCK, Frigyes
Hungarian, 20th century.
Born 1890.
Painter. Scenes with figures, landscapes.
Frigyes Franck was a student at art school in Budapest between 1908 and 1911. He exhibited from 1911 onwards and is probably the same person who exhibited at the Salon de Paris from 1925 onwards as Frédéric Franck.
Museums and Galleries:
Budapest (Magyar Nemzeti Gal.).

FRANCK, Hans, or Frangk
German, 16th century.
Painter.
Hans Franck entered the service of Duke O. Heinrich of Pfalz in 1555, painting a number of portraits for him.

FRANCK, Hans or Jan
German, 16th century.
Engraver (wood).
Augsburg School.
Mentioned between 1514 and 1522 in Augsburg (Bavaria), Hans Franck is almost certainly the same person as Hans Lützlburger, who worked in Basel from 1522 to 1526.

FRANCK, Hans Ulrich
German, 17th century.
Born between 1590 and 1595 or 1603, in Kaufbeuren; died 1675 or 1680, in Augsburg.
Painter, engraver. Religious subjects.
Hans Ulrich Franck was the father of Franz Friedrich. He settled in Augsburg in 1637. He is mainly known for his engravings of scenes of the Thirty Years War portraying massacres, pillages, rapes and other atrocities.

Auction records:
New York, 17 March 1945, *Crucifixion,* USD 225. London, 6 July 1982, *Moses Saved from the Waters* (black chalk, pen and wash, 4 3/4 x 7 1/2 ins / 12.2 x 19.2 cm) GBP 300.

FRANCK, Helene (Miss)
later Mrs A. Fairlie
British, 19th century.
Painter. Genre scenes.
Helene Franck was a frequent exhibitor in London between 1883 and 1911, notably at the Royal Academy and the Suffolk Street Gallery.

FRANCK, Henri, pseudonym of Flandrin, François Henri
French, 20th century.
Born 7 May 1877, in Grenoble; died 10 October 1957, in Corenc.
Painter, draughtsman, watercolourist. Interiors, landscapes.
Henri Franck was the brother of the celebrated painter Jules Flandrin. In order to differentiate himself, Franck signed using the initials F.F. and his two forenames - Henri François (transformed into Franck). After studying at the Lycée de Grenoble he worked as a pharmacist. In 1912 he abandoned this profession to devote himself to music and painting. In 1939 he retired to Corenc where he painted his village until his failing sight made it impossible for him to continue. His painting, which is very different from that of his brother, is dominated by pastel tones and particularly by mauves and pale blue-greens; he also characteristically uses the pointillist technique.

He exhibited in Paris in numerous Salons: the Salon des Artistes Indépendants from 1908 to 1922; the Salon des Tuileries from 1919 to 1922; the Salon of the Société Nationale des Beaux-Arts from 1920 to 1922; and also in Grenoble at the Galerie Feneglio. In 1933 the Musée Mainssieux at Voiron (in Isère) held an exhibition of his work.

BIBLIOGRAPHY:
Wantellet, Maurice, *Deux siècles et plus de peinture dauphinoise*, M. Wantellet, Grenoble, 1987.

FRANCK, Isaac, or Francken
Flemish, 17th century.
Active in Antwerp.
Painter.
Flemish School.
A pupil of Jan Franssen (?) in 1608, Isaac Franck is mentioned by Siret.

FRANCK, J. F.
German, 18th century.
Painter. Portraits.
J. F. Franck probably worked in Ratisbonne. Attributed to him are the portraits of the chaplain of Ratisbonne, *J. J. Gassner*, and the superintendent *H. Chr. Schäffer* which was engraved following his style by G. P. Nussbiegel.

FRANCK, Jacob
Swiss, 16th century.
Active in Fribourg in Switzerland c. 1539.
Miniaturist.
Jacob Franck was an Augustinian monk. The cantonal library in Fribourg owns an antiphonal from the former Augustinian monastery in Fribourg written by this artist, which is richly decorated with miniatures including depictions of religious figures, humorous scenes and dances of death. One is a self-portrait of the artist as a young monk.
MUSEUMS AND GALLERIES:
FRIBOURG (Bibl. Cantonale): antiphonal with miniatures.

FRANCK, Jean François
Belgian, 19th century.
Born 30 November 1804, in Ghent.
Sculptor.
After having studied under his father, who was a decorative sculptor, in 1831, Jean François Franck was a pupil of David d'Angers. Thereafter he became a professor in Louvain.

FRANCK, Jean-Michel
French, 20th century.
Born 1893; died 1941.
Sculptor, designer, decorative artist. Furniture.
Art Deco.
Jean-Michel Franck was one of the great decorators in France in the 1940s. The inlay work of his furniture established his fame. His work as a sculptor, however, is little documented.

FRANCK, Jeremias
Austrian, 16th century.
Active in Graz.
Sculptor.
Jeremias Franck is probably the author of the funerary monument to Georg Schafmann in the church of St Bartholomew in Friesach (Carinthia). He also made models for four low reliefs for the casting of the large bell, known as 'Liesel' in Graz. In 1590, he made the important funerary monument to the Freiherr von Racknitz and his wife in the church at Bernegg.

FRANCK, Johan Willem, or Frank
Dutch, 18th century.
Born probably in 1720; died 1761, in The Hague.
Painter. History painting, birds, still-lifes (including flowers/fruit).
Johan Willem Franck was a member of the guild in The Hague in 1745. He imitated Berchem, Potter, van de Velde and other Flemish and Dutch masters.
AUCTION RECORDS:
AMSTERDAM, 18 May 1981, *Still-life* (oil on panel, 27 x 20 1/4 ins / 68.7 x 51.5 cm) NLG 36,000.

FRANCK, Johann
German, 15th century.
Illuminator.
Johann Franck was a monk at the abbey of St Ulrich and St Afra in Augsburg. He worked on choir books and a number of manuscripts for his monastery.

FRANCK, Johann
German, 17th century.
Born in Kaufbeuren.
Engraver.
Johann Franck was the son of the painter Hans Ulrich. He was mainly occupied engraving for booksellers. He worked together Susanna Sandrart and J. Mayer.

FRANCK, Johann Friedrich
German, 19th century.
Active in Berlin.
Painter.
This artist exhibited his portraits at the Berlin academy from 1880 to 1889.

FRANCK, Johannes, or Franch
Danish, 17th century.
Died c. 1687, in Copenhagen.
Active in Copenhagen.
Sculptor.
Johannes Franck is thought to have produced the base of the equestrian statue of Christian V in Copenhagen. He is also thought to have produced a bust of the same king, and statues of *Fear of God* and *Justice* at the 'North Gate' in Copenhagen.

FRANCK, Joseph
German, 18th century.
Born c. 1745; died 19 October 1790.
Active in Namslau (Silesia).
Sculptor.

FRANCK, Joseph
Belgian, 19th century.
Born 1825, in Brussels; died 1883.
Engraver.
Joseph Franck was a pupil of Calamatta. He executed engravings after the old and modern masters, especially Rubens, Leonardo da Vinci, van Dyck, Portaels, Gérome and Metsys. In 1854 he was elected a member of the royal academy of Belgium. A number of his works, such as *Prisoner* after Gérome, were highly successful. He worked for the Goupil house.

FRANCK, Lucien. See **FRANK Lucien**

FRANCK, Maximilian, or Frans or France
Flemish School, 16th century.
Born 1490, in Bruges; died 1547.
Painter.
Bruges School.
Maximilian Franck was a pupil of Jean Prévost, and may have been the master of Johannes Stradanus. He became mayor of Bruges in 1524.

FRANCK, Maximilian
German, 19th century.
Born c. 1780, in Düsseldorf.
Painter, lithographer.
Maximilian Franck settled in Munich in 1806 where he painted biblical themes and portraits and worked for the lithography studio of A. Senefelder. He published lithographs of eighty small bust portraits of German artists, with the title: *Gallery of German Artists*, and 20 portraits of the Regents of Bavaria, Wittelsbach. In 1830 he made a lithograph portrait of *King William I* painted by Albrecht Adam in Stuttgart.

FRANCK, Maximilien. See **FRANCKEN**

FRANCK, Melchior
Swiss, 17th century.
Born 6 January 1577; died 23 December 1625.
Active in St Gall.
Engraver, goldsmith.

Melchior Franck is the author of a bird's eye town plan of St Gall, which he also engraved.

FRANCK, Michael
German, 16th century.
Active in Hanau (Hesse).
Sculptor.

FRANCK, Myriam
French, 20th - 21st century.
Born 1948.
Sculptor.

AUCTION RECORDS:
PARIS, 5 Feb 1990, *Aleph* (1985, black-patinated bronze, 7 3/4 x 6 1/4 x 6 1/4 ins / 20 x 16 x 16 cm) FRF 11,000. PARIS, 21 May 1990, *In the Beginning* (1989, light-brown-patinated bronze) FRF 20,000. PARIS, 7 Oct 1991, *Aleph* (1985, bronze, 7 3/4 x 6 1/4 x 6 1/4 ins / 20 x 16 x 16 cm) FRF 10,000. PARIS, 5 Oct 1992, *Aleph* (1985, bronze, 7 3/4 x 6 1/4 x 6 1/4 ins / 20 x 16 x 16 cm) FRF 9,500.

FRANCK, P. J.
Bohemian School, 18th century.
Active in Prague c. 1700.
Engraver. Religious subjects. Frontispieces.

P.J. Franck engraved images of saints, and several frontispieces.

FRANCK, Paul
Swiss, 20th century.
Born 4 July 1918, in Gryon.
Active in Belgium, and from 1956 in France.
Painter, engraver, sculptor.
Haute Nuit Group.

Paul Franck studied in Tournai and Liège, then in Antwerp, and then at the fine arts academy in Liège. He was admitted to the Young Belgian Painting (Jeune Peintre Belge) group in 1945 and in 1947 in Mons co-launched a Surrealist group known as Deepest Night (Haute Nuit). He joined the CoBrA group in 1950. In 1954 he moved to Paris to work at William S. Hayter's Atelier 17. He settled in Colombes, France, in 1956.

He started out as an Impressionist, developed as a Surrealist and finally turned towards abstraction, where (as author and art historian Jean Rousselot has pointed out) 'from one canvas to the next, the artist becomes progressively divorced both in physical and conceptual terms from the canvas, as paint is applied more thinly and colours become colder, with greys, blues and greens substituted for warm colours. Brushstrokes become increasingly thread-like and the whole reduces more and more to become an exercise in geometric composition'. He was also an accomplished musician and a feeling for formal rigour and tonal harmony permeates his work.

He was been involved in various group exhibitions in Belgium from 1942, at the Museum of Modern Art in Liège (as part of the Walloon Artistic Association) and at the Brussels museum of modern art. He has also exhibited in Paris, notably at the Salon de la Jeune Peinture, Salon des Réalités Nouvelles and Salon Comparaisons, and in England, Yugoslavia and Brazil. He exhibited solo in Belgium, Switzerland and France and was awarded an engraving medal in Liège.

BIBLIOGRAPHY:
Courthion, Pierre, *Franck, gravures, dessins, sculptures*, exhibition catalogue, Musée de la Boverie, Cabinet des Estampes, Liège, 1981. Rousselot, Jean, *P. Franck. Œuvres abstraites 1949-1955*, exhibition catalogue, Paris, 1988.

MUSEUMS AND GALLERIES:
AMSTERDAM (Stedelijk Mus.) - BRUSSELS (Bibliothèque royale Albert Ier, Prints Collection) - PARIS (Prints Collection).

FRANCK, Paul or Pauwels.
See **FRANCESCHI Paolo dei**

FRANCK, Philipp
German, 17th century.
Born to a family originally from Giessen (Hessen).
Sculptor.

In Butzbach there is a stone epitaph on the tomb of the landgrave Philip III of Hesse executed by Philipp Franck in 1622.

FRANCK, Philipp
German, 19th - 20th century.
Born 9 April 1860, in Frankfurt am Main; died 1944.
Painter, engraver (etching), illustrator. Figures, portraits, interiors with figures, landscapes with figures, waterscapes, gardens.

Franck studied at the Städel Institute in Frankfurt, and from 1881 under K. F. Eduard von Gebhardt and E.G. Drücker at the fine arts academy in Düsseldorf. He lived successively in Potsdam, Würzburg, Halle and Berlin, and from 1903 exhibited at the Berlin Secession. He taught at the Berlin fine arts academy from 1903 and went on to become its principal.

While in Frankfurt, he illustrated romantic tales in the manner of Edward Steinle. His watercolour portraits and landscapes were painted in a style typical of the 19th century; this is particularly true of his landscapes, notably his views of the rococo gardens in Potsdam and the views of the River Havel, which feature canoes and bathers. He was especially skilled at painting landscapes reflected in large stretches of water. His interiors offer an insight into *petit bourgeois* life of the period.

MUSEUMS AND GALLERIES:
ROSTOCK: several works.

AUCTION RECORDS:
MUNICH, 15 Sept 1983, *Tree-Lined Avenue* (c. 1920, oil on canvas, 28 x 39 1/4 ins / 71 x 100 cm) DEM 3,300. MUNICH, 10 June 1985, *Sailboats on the Wannsee near Berlin* (oil on canvas, 36 x 39 1/4 ins / 90.5 x 100 cm) DEM 9,500. AMSTERDAM, 16 Nov 1988, *Patch of Flowers in a Wood near a Stream* (oil on canvas, 5 x 8 1/4 ins / 12.5 x 21 cm) NLG 1,265. NEW YORK, 24 Feb 1994, *Corner of the Garden* (1906, oil on canvas, 34 x 29 ins / 86.4 x 73.7 cm) USD 9,488. LONDON, 13 March 1996, *Summer Landscape* (oil on canvas, 33 x 43 3/4 ins / 84 x 111 cm) GBP 3,565. FRANKFURT, 6 March 1999, *Summer Taunus Landscape* (oil on canvas, 11 x 23 ins / 29 x 58 cm) DEM 4,200. BERLIN, 5 June 1999, *Sailing Boats before Schwanenwerder* (1918, oil on canvas, 27 x 31 ins / 69 x 80 cm) DEM 33,000. BERLIN, 30 June 2001, *Wooded Landscape with Canal* (1909, oil on canvas, 30 x 33 ins / 75 x 85 cm) DEM 18,000. BERLIN, 1 Dec 2001, *Rose Hedge near Wannsee* (1927, oil on canvas, 29 x 39 ins / 74 x 100 cm) DEM 18,000. KÖNIGSTEIN, 24 May 2002, *Poplar Avenue in Park Landscape* (1927, watercolour on card, 21 x 28 ins / 53 x 71 cm) EUR 2,600. BERLIN, 8 June 2002, *Schloss Sanssouci in Potsdam* (1933, oil on canvas, 33 x 39 ins / 85 x 100 cm) EUR 15,000. BERLIN, 29 Nov 2003, *Boots on the Havel in Potsdam* (1936, oil on canvas, 35 x 45 ins / 90 x 115 cm) EUR 18,000.

FRANCK, Philippe
French, 19th century.
Born c. 1780, in Stettin (now Szczecin, Poland).
Painter. Mythological subjects.

Franck was a pupil of David. He exhibited at the Salon from 1812 to 1837. He exhibited his *Hylas Abducted by the Ascanius River Nymphs* at the Salon of 1824.

MUSEUMS AND GALLERIES:
LOUVIERS: *Hylas Abducted by the Ascanius River Nymphs*.

FRANCK, Tobias, or Francken or Vranck
British, 16th - 17th century.
Born 1574, in London.
Painter.
This painter married in Amsterdam and became a burgher of the town on 28 December 1598.

FRANCK-KOHLER, Pierre Victor
French, 20th century.
Born in Sarrebourg.
Watercolourist.
Pierre Franck-Kohler exhibited from 1927 at the Salon des Artistes Français in Paris.

FRANCKE (Meister)
German, 15th century.
Painter. History painting.
Hamburg School.
This artist, who was active between 1380 and 1430, was a follower of Bertram and may even have been his pupil, the influence of the master being very evident. Francke can be seen as one of the most important colourists of the German School, and he marks a high point in Hanseatic painting, which, after him, was to come under the influence of the Dutch and Westphalian Schools. His work was hardly known until the 18th century, and even now many paintings attributed to him by contemporaries have not come to light. It is known that he painted a large altarpiece, and several other works depicting the life of the Virgin and the lives of the saints, particularly St Thomas à Becket of Canterbury. Very few of these paintings have come down to us, but those that do survive seem to represent the best of his work. The earliest seems to be *Christ as the Man of Sorrows* in the museum in Hamburg. The museum in Leipzig has a small replica of this work. Although much debated in the past, the authenticity of this piece seems incontestable. This work, *Christ as the Man of Sorrows*, can arguably be said to be one of the most remarkable works of the German School at this period.

An exhibition was devoted to the work of Francke in 1969 at the Kunsthalle in Hamburg. His work was also shown in the section devoted to precursors, contemporaries and followers of *Hans Memling* in the exhibition at the Groeningemuseum in Bruges in 1994.

BIBLIOGRAPHY:
Puttfarken, Thomas/Bruchhausen, Heilwig, *Meister Francke und die Kunst um 1400*, exhibition catalogue, Hamburger Kunsthalle, Hamburg, 1969. Leppien, Helmut R., *Der Thomas-Altar von Meister Francke in der Hamburger Kunsthalle*, Gerd Hatje, Stuttgart, 1992.

MUSEUMS AND GALLERIES:
HAMBURG: *Christ as the Man of Sorrows (or The Man of Sorrows)* (1415 or 1420); *Crucifixion*; *Flagellation*; *Flight of Thomas of Canterbury* - LEIPZIG (Mus. der Bildenden Künste): *Christ as the Man of Sorrows (The Man of Sorrows)* (copy of the work in Hamburg).

FRANCKE, or Franco
German, 16th century.
Active in Deventer.
Painter.
Francke was a lay brother. Some of his works are in Münster Cathedral.

FRANCKE. See also **FRANCK**

FRANCKE, Bernhard Christoph, or Franck, or Frank, or Francken, or Franken
German, 18th century.
Died 1729; buried 28 January in Brunswick.
Active in Brunswick.
Painter.
Bernhard Francke was painter to Rudolphe Augustus of Brunswick. Francke painted a portrait of him hunting wild boar, which is to be found in the Kestner Museum in Hanover. It has also been engraved by Heckenauer. Also attributed to him are portraits of the dukes Anthony-Ulrich, Ludwig-Rudolph and Ferdinand-Albert II and his wife Antoinette Amalie, in the castles of Brunswick and Königsberg. Other portraits by him can be found in the Brunswick Museum.

FRANCKE, Carl Ludwig
German, 19th century.
Born 12 August 1797, in Neusalz (now Nowa Sól, Poland); died 3 August 1846, in Berlin.
Painter. Religious subjects, genre scenes, portraits, landscapes.
Carl Ludwig Francke was a pupil at the Berlin academy and was represented in the exhibitions of the academy from 1826 to 1844 with many historical and genre paintings, portraits and landscapes. He was also a writer of scientific works, poetry and a *History of the Bible in Verse*.

AUCTION RECORDS:
ZURICH, 16 May 1980, *Adoration of the Shepherds* (1842, oil on panel, 11 x 13½ ins / 28 x 34 cm) CHF 2,100.

FRANCKE, Heinrich Christian
German, 19th century.
Active in Hamburg c. 1830.
Miniaturist, painter. Enamel, ivory, porcelain.
Heinrich Francke concentrated on enamel and ivory and only later devoted himself to painting on porcelain.

FRANCKE, Rudolf, or Francke-Nautschutz
German, 19th century.
Born 6 August 1860, in Nautschutz (Thuringia).
Sculptor, illustrator.
Rudolph Francke studied at the Berlin academy. He also worked in Berlin and travelled in the German colonies. He exhibited busts and bronzes from 1881. His sculptures *Indian and Nubian* and his memorial of *G. Hagenbeck* are located in the zoological garden of Hagenbeck in Hamburg. He also produced drawings of the German colonies.

FRANCKEN. See also **FRANCK**

FRANCKEN, Ambrosius I, the Elder, or Franck
Flemish School, 16th - 17th century.
Born 1544; died 16 October 1618, in Antwerp.
Painter. Religious subjects, portraits, landscapes.
Antwerp School.
Ambrosius the Elder was of the second generation of artists of the Francken family which was to number five generations of artists in total. He was the third of four sons born to Nicolas (1520-1596), the founder of a dynasty that has long presented problems for historians of art. Like his two elder brothers, Hieronymus, born in 1540 and Frans, born in 1542, Ambrosius has had the title 'the Elder' added to his name, or more recently 'the First', in order to distinguish him from Ambrosius II, the son of his brother Frans I.

Ambrosius I seems to have had a more active career than his elder brothers and was successful for longer. His training was the same as theirs: all three were pupils of Frans Floris, who was of the same age as their father Nicolas. Van Mander relates how he was summoned to Tournai when still young by the bishop of Tournai. He appears also to have travelled to Italy, although we have no details. Whether or not he made that journey, he was in Flanders in 1569. The following year, at the age of 26, he went to Fontainebleau (Seine-et-Marne), as we know from evidence from the records from the church at Avon, dated 27 May 1570, where the artist is named as a godfather for a baptism. It is not known whether he worked on the decorations being carried out just then by François I. His name does not appear in the royal accounts, which would seem to indicate that he did not. It is possible that he came to Fontainebleau to continue his studies. Whatever his reasons, even without having first-hand contact with Italy, he had the opportunity to see the great frescoes painted by Rosso and Primaticcio for Fontainebleau. He clearly admired them greatly, to judge from the influence they left on his own work. Back in Antwerp, Ambrosius was received as a master in the Guild of St Luke in 1573 when he was 29. In 1577, he was made a citizen of Antwerp and, in 1581, he became dean of the guild. He was not to leave Flanders again; he died in Antwerp on 16 October 1618, aged 74. He married twice, in 1577 and 1583, but left no children. He took on as pupil one of the sons of his brother Frans the Elder, Hieronymus II (who lived from 1578 to 1623).

Ambrosius's work includes quite a large number of paintings, still mainly to be found in Antwerp in the museum or the church of St James. Broadly speaking, he continues the tradition of Frans Floris and his 'Italianising' school although his style differs in a number of ways. In particular, he abandons Floris' palette - somewhat grey and gloomy - in favour of brighter and lighter colours. This could be seen as a return to the natural style of the Antwerp School. One influence that seems to have been important as far as his draughtsmanship was concerned was that of Martin de Vos, another of Floris' pupils but older than Ambrosius by fourteen years and much admired by the younger man. Other influences may include that of Otto Vénius. These influences combined with Ambrosius' memories of the great works he had seen at Fontainebleau. These recollections are evident in works such as the *Martyrdom of Sts Crispin and Crispinian* (in the museum) and the two wings in the church of St James: *The Woman Taken in Adultery* and the *Raising of the Daughter of Jairus*. His *Martyrdom of St Crispin* has been criticised for a certain monotony, resulting from the absence of well-contrasted shadows. On the other hand, some details of the painting give evidence of a Flemish realism and an appreciation of the familiar very different from the entirely Italianate figures in the foreground. Similarly, in a painting that survives as an engraving by Gérard de Jose, *Jesus in the House of Martha and Mary*, the artist has depicted a kitchen interior that owes nothing to the influence of his masters. A number of portraits by Ambrosius the Elder survive in the church of St James, including those of Nicolas Mertens and his wife Jeanne Brandt. In addition to the two wings mentioned above, there is also a triptych of 1608 depicting the *Holy Trinity*, as well as a *Christ on the Cross*. Like Otto Vénius, Ambrosius painted a number of compositions of allegorical and moral subjects. One of these is a large engraving in the Italian style of 1578, showing *Man Sustained by Grace and Illuminated by Truth*. The two women's figures are robustly rendered, but not without a certain elegance. Other similar works include *The Struggle between Virtues and Vices*, a series of eight engraved plates dating from 1579, and six illustrations after Poggio of the fable of the *Miller and his Son*, later immortalised by La Fontaine.

MUSEUMS AND GALLERIES:
AIX: *Landscape; The Abduction of Deianira* - ANTWERP: *Miracle of the Loaves and Fishes* (triptych); *Martyrdom of SS Crispin and Crispinian; Charity of SS Cosmas and Damian; St Cosmas Doctor and Martyr; Martyrdom of SS Cosmas and Damian; St Damian Doctor and Martyr; Martyrdom of St Catherine of Alexandria; St Sebastian in Prison; Miraculous Healing of Zoë; Beating of St Sebastian; Life of St George* - BRUSSELS: *Daniel Frees Suzannah* - CALAIS: *Finding of Moses* - LA FÈRE: *Wedding at Cana* - OSLO: *Esther and Ahasuerus* - ST-OMER: *Jephtha's Daughter; Triumph of David* - VALENCIENNES: *Entrance into the Ark.*

AUCTION RECORDS:
PARIS, 20 May 1925, *Crossing of the Red Sea*, FRF 520. PARIS, 18 Feb 1926, *Christ Carrying the Cross*, FRF 2,520. LONDON, 24 Feb 1984, *Adoration of the Shepherds* (oil on panel, 44 1/2 x 63 ins / 113 x 160 cm) GBP 9,000. PARIS, 19 Dec 1994, *Dormition of the Virgin* (oil on panel, 44 x 36 1/4 ins / 112 x 92 cm) FRF 20,000. NEW YORK, Jan 1998, *Man Brought before a Judge (recto); Artisan Working Metal* (oil on panel on recto and brown tone on verso, triptych, attributed, 83 3/4 x 28 3/4 ins / 212.7 x 73 cm) USD 17,250. PARIS, 18 March 2001, *Preaching of St John the Baptist* (oil on panel, 14 x 18 ins / 35 x 46 cm) FRF 35,000. MADRID, 26 Jan 2004, *Wedding at Cana* (oil on copper, 13 x 17 ins / 34 x 43 cm) EUR 10,000.

FRANCKEN, Ambrosius II, the Younger, or perhaps Francken, Amman
Flemish, 17th century.
Born probably, in Antwerp; died 1632.
Painter. History painting, religious subjects.
Antwerp School, Flemish School.

Ambrosius Francken II or the Younger was the son and pupil of Frans Francken III or the Elder. He qualified as a master in Antwerp in 1624. Little is known about him. He is cited by Siret as Amman Francken. It may be surmised that he resided in Louvain where he assisted Mathieu van Negre, a pupil of Martin de Vos, in the completion of a number of paintings for the church there.

FRANCKEN, Ambrosius III, or Franck
Flemish, 17th century.
Painter.
Antwerp School, Flemish School.

Ambrosius Francken III was the son of Frans Francken II or the Younger. He is probably the Ambrosius Francken who qualified as a master in Antwerp in 1644-1645, as the son of a master.

FRANCKEN, Amman. See **FRANCKEN Ambrosius II, the Younger**

FRANCKEN, C. A. V.
Dutch, 18th century.
Active in The Hague c. 1754.
Miniaturist. Portraits.

C. A. V. Francken is listed in *Pictura*.

FRANCKEN, Constantinus or Constantijn, or Franck
Flemish, 17th - 18th century.
Born 1661, in Antwerp; died 1717, in Antwerp.
Painter. History painting, battles.
Antwerp School, Flemish School.

Constantinus Francken was the son of Hieronymous Francken III and in 1694 became a member of the Guild of St Luke. His masterpiece is considered to be *The Siege of Namur*.

MUSEUMS AND GALLERIES:
ANTWERP: *The Battle of Eckeren; Martin van Rossum after the Attack of Antwerp.*

AUCTION RECORDS:
LONDON, 6 April 1977, *William III at the Siege of Namur* (1695, oil on canvas, 56 1/4 x 75 1/2 ins / 143 x 192 cm) USD 5,500.

FRANCKEN, Cornelis, or Franck
Flemish School, 16th century.
Born c. 1545, in Antwerp.
Painter.
Antwerp School.

Cornelis was the fourth son of Nicolas Francken and father of Hans Francken. Little is known about him.

FRANCKEN, Frans, the Elder, or Frank
Flemish School, 16th - 17th century.

Born 1542, in Herenthals (Antwerp); died 3 October 1616, in Antwerp.
Painter. Mythological subjects, religious subjects, battles, portraits.
Antwerp School.

This artist was the second son of Nicolas Francken (1520-1596), the founder of the famous family of artists that was to continue for five generations. Frans the Elder, or Frans I, was the father of the next three generations, apart from one son born to his brother Cornelis of whom no more is heard. Not much is known about Frans' early years, except that he came when still young to study in Antwerp. Like his brothers, he became a pupil of Frans Floris, then at the peak of his fame, and endeavoured to continue the style of his master - to a greater extent than his brother Ambrosius I. Nevertheless, both artists were dedicated propagators of the 'Italianising' movement, the initial success of which was due to Floris. Frans I became a citizen and burgher of Antwerp in 1567 and was received, either that year or two years later, as a master in the Guild of St Luke. He was dean of the guild in 1588, a few years after his younger brother Ambrosius, who had been dean in 1581. Frans is even more unlikely to have travelled to Italy than Ambrosius. He married Elizabeth Mertens in 1573 (or possibly 1575) and the couple had four children: Thomas, Hieronymus (known as II), Frans II and Ambrosius II. They were all painters, but their careers followed somewhat different paths, Frans II, still called Frans the Younger, being the only one to have enjoyed a renown comparable to that of his father and uncles. The name of Frans I appears in a number of contemporary documents: as a godfather on the act of baptism of a child born to David Ryckaert the Elder in 1594; later, in 1607, as a witness at his son Frans II's wedding. A much respected artist, Frans the Elder taught many good artists in addition to his own sons including Goltzius, Jean de Waal and Herman Van der Maest. He never left Antwerp and died there on 3 (or 5) October 1616 in his 74th year. He was buried in the church of St Andrew.

Notable among his works from his best period is a vast triptych in Antwerp Cathedral. Its central panel shows *Jesus with the Doctors*, while the wings depict the *Miracle of Elijah at Sarepta* and *St Ambrose Baptising St Augustine*. Dated 1587, this work was closely studied by Reynolds when he travelled to Flanders. It is an accomplished work that successfully continues along the path laid down by Floris. Its Italianism is principally apparent in the concern with facial expression and the correction of contours. Frans Francken's work generally, and these paintings in particular, has been criticised for lacking in daring and accent, suppressing individuality in the search for mere imitation and careful study rather than artistic inspiration. And yet the smooth technique, created by carefully superimposed glazes, is of an irreproachable perfection. The work of his brother, Ambrosius the Elder, shows more independence and confidence - if not a truly personal originality, then at least a properly Flemish temperament. These artists were, on the whole, diligent and hard-working, remaining resolutely within the bounds laid down by their master like well-behaved schoolboys. A painting of *Eteocles and Polynices* in the museum in Antwerp, originally from the Serment de l'Escrime (fencing club), is a carefully arranged composition in grisaille with a crowd of warriors grouped around the two main figures who are about to start fighting. The background, painted with a similar care, shows a pyre ready for the cremation of the corpse of the loser. The painting is somewhat lacking in character. Other works of interest include, in the chapel of St John the Baptist in the church of St James in Antwerp, a diptych showing, on the inner sides, *The Entombment* and *The Appearance of Christ to Mary Magdalene*. The other sides are painted in grisaille and show *St Severius Bishop* and *St Ambrose*. A painting in the Louvre depicting the *Story of Esther*, attributed by M. Villot in the catalogue to Frans I, is in fact by his son Frans the Younger.

Frans Francken the Elder also painted portraits of some of the most important figures of his time, including William of Orange. A small painting, *The Destruction of Pharaoh's Army in the Red Sea* (Blenheim, England) has been described by M. Waagen as being of 'an extraordinary delicacy'.

Do ffranck inventor et fecit A° 1587:

MUSEUMS AND GALLERIES:
ABBEVILLE: *Virgin and Child* - ANTWERP: *Eteocles and Polynices* - AUXERRE: *The Crossing of the Red Sea* - CHARTRES: *St John the Baptist Preaching* - DRESDEN: *Christ on the Road to Golgotha* - FLORENCE (Uffizi): *Triumph of Neptune and Amphitrite* - GENEVA (MAH): *Hangings Carried out on the Order of the Duke of Alba in Flanders* - GLASGOW: *Road to Calvary* - MADRID (Prado): *Christ Sentenced and Brought before the People; St John Preaching; Ecce Homo; Arrest of Christ; Neptune and Amphitrite; Interior of a Church* - MOSCOW (Rumiantsev Mus.): *Adoration of the Golden Calf; Recognition of Achilles; Crucifixion* - NANTES (MBA): *Jesus on the Cross between the Two Thieves* - PARIS (Louvre): *Story of Esther* - POITIERS: *Belshazzar's Feast* - RHEIMS: *Adoration of the Magi* - ST PETERSBURG (Hermitage): *Marriage at Cana* - STOCKHOLM: *Lazarus and the Rich Man* - STUTTGART: *Adoration of the Magi.*

AUCTION RECORDS:
PARIS, 25 June 1892, *Virgin and Child,* FRF 13,000. PARIS, 15-16 March 1897, *Death of the Virgin,* FRF 120; *Political Celebrations,* FRF 1,200. PARIS, 4 May 1900, *Christ, Virgin and Twelve Apostles,* FRF 300. PARIS, 16 Feb 1920, *Belshazzar's Feast,* FRF 260. LONDON, 5 July 1920, *Queen of Sheba before Solomon,* GBP 35. PARIS, 15 Feb 1923, *Esther and Ahasuerus,* FRF 1,750. LONDON, 2 March 1923, *Recognition of Achilles,* GBP 110. PARIS, 23 March 1923, *Holy Family Resting,* FRF 1,520. LONDON, 26 March 1923, *Adoration of the Magi,* GBP 39. PARIS, 14 June 1923, *Jesus Led to Calvary,* FRF 1,150. LONDON, 25 June 1923, *Esther and Ahasuerus,* GBP 14. LONDON, 21 Nov 1924, *Road to Calvary; Crucifixion* (both) GBP 63. LONDON, 3 Dec 1924, *Bishop Baptising Children,* GBP 12. LONDON, 9 July 1926, *Coriolanus, Volumnia and Virgil,* GBP 52. PARIS, 19 April 1928, *Adoration of the Shepherds,* FRF 4,000; *Christ on the Cross with Three Saints,* FRF 2,000. LONDON, 27 July 1928, *Marriage of the Virgin,* GBP 23; *Virgin Lamenting over the Dead Christ,* GBP 52. PARIS, 19 Nov 1928, *Feast of Lazarus,* FRF 8,500. LONDON, 8 March 1929, *Work and Rest,* GBP 44. LONDON, 11 April 1929, *Wedding at Cana,* GBP 27. LONDON, 19-22 June 1931, *Love Song,* GBP 13. LONDON, 2 Aug 1934, *Crucifixion,* GBP 13. LONDON, 16 April 1937, *Interior of an Artist's Studio,* GBP 19. LONDON, 29 April 1938, *Wise and Foolish Virgins,* GBP 28. LONDON, 16 June 1938, *Esther Before Ahasuerus,* GBP 18. LONDON, 6 March 1940, *Moses Striking the Rock,* GBP 15. PARIS, 10 and 11 March 1941, *Adoration of the Magi,* FRF 2,750. PARIS, 26 and 27 May 1941, *Orpheus Charming the Animals; Roman Scene in the Peristyle of a Palace* (group) FRF 3,400. LONDON, 4 Sept 1941, *Adoration of the Magi,* GBP 16. PARIS, 4 Dec 1941, *Road to Calvary* (school of Francken) FRF 5,200. PARIS, 19 Dec 1941, *Belshazzar's Feast* (attributed) FRF 4,300. LONDON, 5 June 1942, *Banquet in a Garden,* GBP 21. LONDON, 30 Oct 1942, *Rape of the Sabine Women,* GBP 21. PARIS, 30 Oct 1942, *Calvary* (school of Francken) FRF 26,500. PARIS, 25 June 1943, *Wedding at Cana* (school of Francken) FRF 15,500; *Christ Before Pilate* (school of Francken) FRF 10,500. LONDON, 30 July 1943, *Feast of Esther and Ahasuerus,* GBP 31. PARIS, 13 Dec 1943, *The Five Senses* (in collaboration with J. 'Velvet' Breughel) FRF 81,000. LONDON, 18 Feb 1944, *Herod's Feast,* GBP 42. PARIS, 24 April 1944, *Christ before Pilate* (school of

Francken) FRF 15,600. PARIS, 14 May 1945, *Adoration of the Magi* (attributed) FRF 10,100. LONDON, 13 Feb 1946, *Feast of Bacchus,* GBP 62. PARIS, July 1946, *The Rich Man's Feast* (1606) FRF 43,000. LONDON, 15 Nov 1946, *Wedding at Cana,* GBP 36. PARIS, 17 Feb 1947, *Battle Scene* (school of Francken) FRF 26,100. PARIS, 13 March 1947, *Wedding at Cana,* FRF 35,000. LONDON, 19 March 1947, *Interior,* GBP 35. PARIS, 5 May 1947, *Adoration of the Magi* (attributed) FRF 15,000. LONDON, 20 June 1947, *Minerva and Other Figures,* GBP 68. LONDON, 15 Nov 1961, *The Collector,* GBP 950. PARIS, 1 June 1967, *Wedding at Cana,* FRF 19,100. BRUSSELS, 26-28 March 1968, *Golgotha,* BEF 100,000. VERSAILLES, 4 June 1970, *Golgotha.* PARIS, 12 April 1973, *Scene from the Life of Lot,* FRF 2,000. PARIS, 26 March 1974, *The Hebrews Fleeing to the Promised Land,* FRF 46,000. PARIS, 26 March 1977, *Ball at Court* (oil on panel, 20½ x 29½ ins / 52 x 75 cm) FRF 82,000. COPENHAGEN, 28 April 1981, *Crucifixion* (oil on panel, 38½ x 61 ins / 98 x 154 cm) DKK 13,000. PARIS, 3 July 1987, *Belshazzar's Feast* (oil on panel, 21 x 31½ ins / 52.5 x 80 cm) FRF 82,000. LONDON, 3 July 1996, *Doubting Thomas* (oil on panel, 30¼ x 40¼ ins / 77 x 102.2 cm) GBP 12,650. VENICE, 8 July 2000, *The Last Supper* (oil on board, 10 x 8 ins / 26 x 20 cm) ITL 76,000,000. VENICE, 17 Nov 2000, *The Virgin and Saint Anne* (oil on copper, 4 x 4 ins / 11 x 9 cm) ITL 7,500,000. STUTTGART, 21 June 2001, *The Transfiguration of Christ* (oil on copper/panel, 14 x 18 ins / 35 x 45 cm) DEM 7,500. LONDON, 11 Dec 2001, *Adoration of the Magi* (oil on copper, 7 x 10 ins / 17 x 26 cm) GBP 19,000. VIENNA, 2 Oct 2002, *The Visitation. The Annunciation* (oil on copper, two, 27 x 22 ins / 69 x 55 cm) EUR 24,000. MADRID, 7 Oct 2002, *Ecce Homo* (oil on copper, 14 x 11 ins / 35 x 28 cm) EUR 9,000.

FRANCKEN, Frans II, the Younger, or known as Francken de Jonge
Flemish, 17th century.
Born 6 May 1581, in Antwerp; died 6 May 1642, in Antwerp.
Painter, engraver. Religious subjects, allegorical subjects, mythological subjects, genre scenes, village scenes.
Antwerp School, Flemish School.

Frans Francken II or the Younger is the third in order of descent in the Francken family tree. Born in 1581, the son of Frans Francken I or the Elder, he was the brother of Thomas, born in 1574, of Hieronymous II, born in 1578 and died in 1623, and of Ambrosius II, the last in line, who died in 1632. Hieronymous II, who died at the age of 56, is only known for his painting *Horatius Cocles at Sublicius Bridge*. Frans the Younger was initially a pupil of his father, who was then at the height of his career. In his father's studio he imbibed all the teaching of the tradition of Frans Floris. He also spent long periods in Italy, where he familiarised himself in particular with the masters of the Venetian school. Such study in situ enabled him to break away from the well-worn methods of Flemish Italianism, as practised by his father and uncles. It is conceivable that the young artist met Rubens, who was in Italy at the time.

In 1605, at the age of 24, on his return to Antwerp, Frans the Younger became a master in the Antwerp Guild of St Luke. In 1607 he married Elisabeth Placquet in Antwerp. Three sons and eight daughters resulted from this marriage. His children made up the fourth generation in the dynasty. Better known are Frans III (1607-1667) and Hieronymus, born in 1611. The latter had a son, Constantinus (1661-1717), who marks the end of the line. The family of Francken painters runs from 1520 to 1717.

As one of the most active masters in Antwerp, Frans II was appointed dean of the guild in 1614. He was also a member of the Violette, a major literary association, for which he painted an award-winning symbolic coat of arms. He was intimate with the most celebrated artists, in particular van Dyck, who executed a very fine portrait of him, judging by the engraving by Willem Hondius and Pieter de Jode. It is also likely that he was on familiar terms with Rubens who was his near contemporary. He died in Antwerp on 6 May 1642 at the age of 61, outlived by both Rubens and van Dyck.

The first securely dated work of Frans the Younger is *Christ on the Cross* from the gallery in Vienna, painted in 1606. *Witches' Sabbath* (Vienna) and *The Works of Mercy* (Antwerp) are dated 1607 and 1608 respectively. In these two latter works the painter proves himself adept at painting figures and allegorical scenes. *The Works of Mercy* represents various groups of figures, symbolising the different activities inspired by Christian charity. Paupers and beggars occupy the foreground, the ensemble being dominated by the figure of the glorious Christ.

While Frans the Younger cannot be compared with the masters of this great first generation of Antwerp, which was illuminated and steered by the genius of Rubens, he does nevertheless merit attention. He succeeded in developing and bringing into fashion an anecdotal genre on a more modest scale, elements of which were to inform the last representatives of the Francken family for over a century. Frans the Younger was undoubtedly the most talented draughtsman in the family. While his art may be criticised for its lack of grandeur and solemnity, the execution shows great talent. His brush stroke was vigorous and his imagination, albeit restrained, was brilliant. His interest in tonal values was highlighted by his study and appreciation of his remarkable contemporaries. This enabled him to carry out landscapes and also fleshy figures, which made him altogether worthy of the brilliant period to which he belonged. While detail certainly preoccupied him, he treated it with intelligence and even esprit, as witnessed in *The Parable of the Prodigal Son* and *A Prince's Visit to the Treasury of a Church* (both in the Louvre). The scenes painted in grisaille, which surround the principal motif of the *Prodigal Son,* are characteristic of his style. He excelled in painting jewellery, ornaments, and textiles with shot silk effects. A large number of his figures inhabit the neutral backgrounds of the interiors of apartments and galleries. He carried out such work not only under his own auspices, but also for other artists, such as Peeter Neeffs, van Bassen, Josse de Momper, and Breughel.

Den·f·ffranck

BIBLIOGRAPHY:

Härting, Ursula Alice, *Studien zur Kabinettbildmalerei des Frans Francken II, 1581-1642. Ein Repräsentativer Werkkatalog,* G. Olms, Hildesheim, 1983. Härting, Ursula Alice, *Frans Francken der Jüngere (1581-1642): die Gemälde mit Kritischen Oeuvrekatalog,* catalogue raisonné, Luca Verlag, Freren, 1989 (with a summary in English).

MUSEUMS AND GALLERIES:

AIX: *Arrival of the Hebrews in the Promised Land* - AMIENS: *Adoration of the Magi* (sketch) - AMSTERDAM: *Abdication of Charles V of Spain; Adoration of the Magi; The Prodigal Son; Same Subject; Scenes from the Old Testament* - ANTWERP: *A Collector's Cabinet; Miracles at the Tomb of St Bruno; The Works of Mercy; The Four Crowned Martyrs Condemned; Flagellation of the Four Crowned Martyrs; Stoning; The Four Crowned Martyrs at Work* - ARRAS: *The Passion* - AUGSBURG: *Moses Striking Water from the Rock* - BAMBERG: *The Festival of Dancing* - BESANÇON: *The Crossing of the Red Sea; Crossing the Jordan; Christ Delivered to the Insults of the Jews; Christ Carrying the Cross* - BORDEAUX: *Christ at Calvary; Same Subject* - BRUSSELS: *Croesus Showing Solon his Treasures* - BUDAPEST: *Esther and Ahasuerus* - CAEN: *The Slaves of the Furies of Love* - CHAMBÉRY (MBA): *Adoration of the Magi* - CHERBOURG: *The Woman Taken in Adultery* - COLOGNE: *Adoration of the*

Magi - COMPIÈGNE: *Allegory* - DRESDEN: *The Calumny of Apelles; The Flight into Egypt; The Queen of the Heavens Crowned with Flowers; The Adultress before Christ; The Creation of Eve* - DUNKIRK: *The Feast of Herod* - FLORENCE (Palazzo Pitti): *Christ Led to Calvary* - FLORENCE (Uffizi): *The Flight into Egypt* - HAMBURG: *Drowning of Pharoah's Army* - HANOVER: *The Prodigal Son* - KASSEL: *The Kiss of Judas* (copper) - KASSEL (Gemäldegal. Alte Meister): *Apelles and the Cobbler* (copper) - LILLE: *Christ on the Way to Calvary* - MAINZ: *David, Conqueror of Goliath* - MUNICH: room decorated with pictures and objets d'art; *The Seven Works of Mercy; A Tournament* - NANCY: *The Virgin and Child Served by Angels; Christ in the Desert Served by the Angels* - NANTES (MBA): *The Embarkation of Cleopatra; The Death of Adonis* - NICE: *Christ in the Garden of Gethsemane* - OBERSCHLEISSHEIM: *The Temptation of St Anthony* - OLDENBURG (Augusteum): *Apollo and the Muses* - ORLÉANS: *Christ before Caiaphus* - OSLO: *Gathering of Men and Women in front of an Inn* - PARIS (Louvre): *The Parable of the Prodigal Son; The Passion; Ulysses Recognises Achilles amongst the Daughters of Lycomedes; Croesus and Solon* - PARIS (Mus. Marmottan-Monet): *Christ Preaching on the Sea of Tiberias* - RENNES: *Christ in the House of Simon the Pharisee* - ROHRAU (Schlossmuseum, Graf Harrach'sche Familiensammlung): *Studio* (allegorical subject) - ROME (Mus. e Gal. Borghese): *Picture Dealer* - ST PETERSBURG (Hermitage): *Crossing the Red Sea; The Seven Acts of Christian Mercy; Entry of David into Jerusalem* - STOCKHOLM: six paintings - STUTTGART: *Adoration of the Magi; Last Judgement; The Four Elements; Jupiter and Juno* - THE HAGUE: *A Ball at the Court of Albert and Isabelle* - TOURS: *The Abduction of Helen* - VIENNA: *Witches' Sabbath; Croesus and Solon; The Dance; The Crucifixion; Christ and Nicodemus; A Cabinet of Art and Curiosities* (1636); *Gathering of Witches.*

AUCTION RECORDS:

PARIS, 1847, *Belshazzar's Feast,* FRF 310. PARIS, 1861, *Interior of a Museum,* FRF 980. PARIS, 1872, *The Works of Mercy,* FRF 2,300. PARIS, 1899, *Visit to a Gallery,* FRF 2,100. PARIS, 8 May 1900, *Belshazzar's Feast,* FRF 880; *Jacob's Children,* FRF 100. PARIS, 17 Nov 1919, *Marriage of the Virgin,* FRF 300. PARIS, 19 Dec 1919, *Young Woman Imploring the Clemency of a King,* FRF 900. PARIS, 29-30 April 1920, *Allegory of Christianity,* FRF 2,600. PARIS, 26 May 1920, *Dido and Aeneas,* FRF 440. PARIS, 28 Feb 1921, *The Return of Jacob,* FRF 3,600. PARIS, 9-10 June 1926, *Subject Taken from Ancient History,* FRF 3,400. PARIS, 9 May 1927, *Adoration of the Three Magi,* FRF 1,600. PARIS, 7 July 1927, *St John the Baptist Preaching,* FRF 860. PARIS, 25 Nov 1927, *Helen Abducted by Paris,* FRF 1,055. PARIS, 25 March 1935, *Solomon Sacrificing to the Idols,* FRF 850. PARIS, 16 Feb 1939, *Scenes from the New Testament: The Nativity, The Adoration of the Magi, The Circumcision, The Crowning with Thorns, The Crucifixion, The Resurrection, Christ appearing to the Apostles and The Assumption of the Virgin* (set of eight compositions) FRF 2,700. PARIS, 11 Jan 1943, *Belshazzar's Feast,* FRF 90,000. PARIS, 25-26 June 1945, *The Wicked Rich Man,* FRF 21,400. PARIS, 21 Oct 1946, *Christ and the Paralytic* (attributed) FRF 11,000. PARIS, 9 Dec 1961, *Solomon and the Queen of Sheba* (panel) FRF 4,000. LONDON, 27 June 1962, *Interior of a Picture Gallery,* GBP 1,900. COLOGNE, 11 Nov 1964, *Adoration of the Kings,* DEM 7,500. LONDON, 8 Dec 1965, *The Banquet,* GBP 1,200. COPENHAGEN, 12 May 1969, *St Anthony,* DKK 13,000. VIENNA, 16 March 1971, *The Way of the Cross,* ATS 35,000. LONDON, 12 Dec 1973, *The Worship of the Golden Calf,* GBP 5,500; *Feast of the Gods,* GBP 29,000. BRUSSELS, 26 March 1974, *Elegant Gathering in an Interior,* BEF 400,000. VERSAILLES, 23 May 1976, *The Crucifixion* (copper, 16 1/4 x 13 1/2 ins / 41.5 x 34 cm) FRF 9,500. LONDON, 6 July 1976, *Village Scene* (1634, watercolour and pen, 8 x 12 1/4 ins / 20.6 x 31.3 cm) GBP 1,600. VERSAILLES, 5 March 1978, *The Way to Golgotha* (oil on wood, 20 1/2 x 28 3/4 ins / 52 x 73 cm) FRF 38,000. PARIS, 18 March 1981, *A Ball at the Court* (oil on wood, 19 3/4 x 28 ins / 50 x 71 cm) FRF 125,000. VERSAILLES, 27 Nov 1983, *The Crucifixion before Numerous Spectators* (oil on panel, 28 3/4 x 48 ins / 73 x 121 cm) FRF 55,000. NEW YORK, 7 June 1984, *The Triumph of Neptune* (oil on panel, 21 x 29 3/4 ins / 53.5 x 75.5 cm) USD 42,000. LONDON, 19 April 1985, *The Parable of the Wise and Foolish Virgins* (1616, oil on panel, 26 1/2 x 43 1/2 ins / 67.3 x 110.5 cm) GBP 28,000. NEW YORK, 7 April 1988, *Belshazzar's Feast* (oil/copper, 26 x 32 1/2 ins / 66 x 82.5 cm) USD 6,325. PARIS, 14 April 1988, *The Banquet* (oil on panel, 29 1/4 x 41 1/2 ins / 74 x 105.5 cm) FRF 110,000. MILAN, 10 June 1988, *The Adoration of the Magi* (oil on panel, 39 3/4 x 25 1/4 ins / 101 x 64 cm) ITL 34,000,000; *An Antiquary's Shop* (oil on panel, 19 3/4 x 28 1/4 ins / 50 x 72 cm) ITL 73,000,000. LONDON, 17 June 1988, *The Virgin and Child with St John the Baptist as a Child* (oil/copper, 12 x 9 1/2 ins / 30.5 x 24.1 cm) GBP 5,500. NEW YORK, 21 Oct 1988, *The Crossing of the Red Sea* (oil on panel, 16 x 22 1/4 ins / 40.5 x 56.5 cm) USD 8,800. PARIS, 12 Dec 1988, *Solomon and the Queen of Sheba* (oil on panel, 32 x 46 1/4 ins / 81 x 117.5 cm) FRF 620,000. NEW YORK, 11 Jan 1989, *Fancy-Dress Ball* (1608, oil on panel, 18 1/2 x 27 1/2 ins / 47 x 70 cm) USD 38,500. LONDON, 31 March 1989, *The Last Supper with the Four Evangelists and God the Father* (oil/copper, oval painting on rectangular background, 21 1/4 x 15 3/4 ins / 54 x 40 cm) GBP 5,500. PARIS, 12 April 1989, *Christ Presented to the Crowd* (oil on panel, 14 x 18 1/2 ins / 35.5 x 47.3 cm) FRF 16,000. PARIS, 14 April 1989, *The Feast* (oil on inlaid wood, 13 3/4 x 15 ins / 35 x 38 cm) FRF 130,000. STOCKHOLM, 19 April 1989, *Battle between the Jews and Egyptians* (oil on panel, 39 x 59 ins / 99 x 150 cm) SEK 92,000. NEW YORK, 12 Oct 1989, *Death and the Miser* (oil/copper, 9 x 6 3/4 ins / 23 x 17.2 cm) USD 26,400. LONDON, 18 Oct 1989, *The Meeting between Antony and Cleopatra* (oil on panel, 27 1/2 x 41 1/2 ins / 70 x 105.5 cm) GBP 33,000. LONDON, 11 April 1990, *The Triumph of Bacchus* (oil/copper, 21 x 29 3/4 ins / 53.5 x 75.6 cm) GBP 115,500. STOCKHOLM, 14 Nov 1990, *Lazarus and the Rich Man* (oil on panel, 17 1/4 x 24 3/4 ins / 44 x 63 cm) SEK 40,000. ROME, 19 Nov 1990, *Duel between Minerva and Mars in the Presence of Mercury during the War of Troy* (oil on panel, 22 x 33 1/2 ins / 56 x 85 cm) ITL 10,350,000. PARIS, 30 Nov 1990, *Adoration of the Magi* (oil on panel/canvas, 22 x 31 1/2 ins / 55 x 80 cm) FRF 230,000. LONDON, 12 Dec 1990, *Floral Composition in a Painted Metal Vase Representing the Rape of Dejanira* (oil on panel, 23 3/4 x 19 ins / 60.5 x 48.5 cm) GBP 462,000. NEW YORK, 11 April 1991, *Rest on the Flight into Egypt with a Stag in the Distance* (oil on panel, 15 1/4 x 16 1/4 ins / 38.5 x 41 cm) USD 38,500. AMSTERDAM, 2 May 1991, *Christ Preaching on the Sea of Galilee* (oil on panel, 16 x 25 1/4 ins / 40.7 x 64.3 cm) NLG 28,750. MILAN, 30 May 1991, *The Work of Mercy* (oil on panel, 19 3/4 x 30 ins / 50 x 76 cm) ITL 28,000,000. MONACO, 22 June 1991, *The Legend of Virgil and the Emperor's Daughter* (oil on panel, 23 1/4 x 31 1/2 ins / 58.8 x 80 cm) FRF 188,700. COLOGNE, 28 June 1991, *Christ and Pontius Pilate* (oil/copper, 22 1/2 x 28 3/4 ins / 57 x 73 cm) DEM 3,300. PARIS, 6 Nov 1991, *The Creation of Adam and Eve* (three oil paintings/copper, each 4 3/4 x 11 1/4 ins / 12 x 28.5 cm) FRF 30,000. MONACO, 5-6 Dec 1991, *Belshazzar's Feast* (oil/copper, 14 1/4 x 21 ins / 36 x 52.5 cm) FRF 133,200. NEW YORK, 16 Jan 1992, *Daniel Taming the Dragon of Babylon* (oil on panel, 9 1/2 x 13 1/4 ins / 24.3 x 33.7 cm) USD 12,100. PARIS, 26 June 1992, *Solomon Welcoming the Queen of Sheba* (copper, 14 1/2 x 20 ins / 37 x 50.5 cm) FRF 60,000. LONDON, 10 July 1992, *The Crossing of the Red Sea* (oil on canvas, 50 1/2 x 66 ins / 128.3 x 166.8 cm) GBP 12,100. NEW YORK, 14 Jan 1993, *The Different Ways to Achieve Immortality* (1610, oil on panel, 30 3/4 ins / 78 cm, 1/2 x 57 1/2 ins/1 x 146 cm) USD 20,900. NEW YORK, 15 Jan 1993, *The Building of the Tower of Babel* (oil/copper, 27 1/4 x 34 ins / 69.2 x 86.4 cm) USD 34,500. PARIS, 6 July 1993, *Christ on the Lake of Gennesareth* (oil on oak panel, 33 1/4 x 64 1/2 ins / 84.5 x 164 cm) FRF

360,000. London, 6 July 1994, *The Parable of the Rich Man and Lazarus* (1608, oil on panel, 18 x 30 1/4 ins / 46 x 77 cm) GBP 16,675. New York, 12 Jan 1995, *The Israelites on the Red Sea with the Relics of Joseph* (oil on panel, 25 x 32 ins / 63.5 x 81.3 cm) USD 68,500. La Flèche, 2 April 1995, *The Virgin and Child in a Landscape* (oil/copper, 16 1/2 x 22 ins / 42 x 55 cm) FRF 66,000. Paris, 12 Dec 1995, *The Meal in the House of Simon* (oil on oak panel, octagonal, 11 3/4 x 26 ins / 30 x 66 cm) FRF 60,000. New York, 11 Jan 1996, *Elegant Company Dancing in an Inn* (oil/copper, 19 3/4 x 29 ins / 50.2 x 73.7 cm) USD 37,950. L'Isle-Adam, 28 Jan 1996, *The Crossing of the Red Sea* (oil on panel, 20 x 28 3/4 ins / 51 x 73 cm) FRF 80,000. New York, 3 Oct 1996, *The Golden Age* (oil/copper, 13 1/4 x 16 ins / 33.7 x 40.6 cm) USD 13,800. New York, 4 Oct 1996, *Belshazzar's Feast* (c. 1610, oil on panel, 21 1/2 x 30 1/4 ins / 54.5 x 76.7 cm) USD 28,750. London, 30 Oct 1996, *Presentation to Emperor Charles V* (oil on panel, border in grisaille, 20 3/4 x 16 1/2 ins / 53 x 42 cm) GBP 17,825. Paris, 17 June 1997, *Christ Entering Jerusalem* (oak panel, 20 1/2 x 32 1/4 ins / 52 x 82 cm) FRF 110,000. Amsterdam, 11 Nov 1997, *The Idolatry of Solomon* (c. 1640, oil on panel, 15 x 26 ins / 38.3 x 65.2 cm) NLG 29,983. London, 3-4 Dec 1997, *The Feast of Herod* (oil on panel, 21 1/4 x 29 1/2 ins / 53.8 x 74.7 cm) GBP 19,550. New York, Jan 1998, *The Adoration of Solomon* (oil/panel, in collaboration with C. de Baellieur, 18 3/4 x 25 ins / 47.6 x 62.6 cm) USD 21,850. Amsterdam, 8 Nov 1999, *Collector's Cabinet with Abraham Ortelius and Justus Lipsius* (1618, oil on canvas, 20 x 29 ins / 52 x 73 cm) NLG 520,000. London, 17 Dec 1999, *Picture Gallery with Man of Science Making Measurements with Globe* (1612, oil on panel, 35 x 43 ins / 89 x 109 cm) GBP 750,000. Paris, 31 March 2000, *Triumph of Neptune and Amphitrite* (oil on panel, 20 x 29 ins / 52 x 74 cm) FRF 1,400,000. London, 13 Dec 2000, *Interior of a Collector's Cabinet with Justus Lipsius* (oil on panel, 21 x 29 ins / 53 x 74 cm) GBP 120,000. London, 11 July 2001, *Solomon in his Treasury* (oil on panel, 41 x 53 ins / 103 x 135 cm) GBP 38,000. Madrid, 14 Nov 2001, *Solomon Showing his Wealth* (oil on board, 41 x 53 ins / 103 x 135 cm) ESP 20,000,000. Amsterdam, 5 Nov 2002, *Parable of the Royal Wedding Feast* (oil on panel, 19 x 18 ins / 49 x 46 cm) EUR 68,000. London, 12 Dec 2002, *Belshazzar's Feast* (1614, oil on canvas, 59 x 89 ins / 150 x 227 cm) GBP 40,000. Madrid, 30 Sept 2003, *Charity* (oil on canvas, 45 x 44 ins / 115 x 112 cm) EUR 35,000. London, 10 Dec 2003, *Interior Scenes* (painted ebony cabinet, 32 x 35x16 ins / 82 x 89x41 cm) GBP 75,000. New York, 23 Jan 2004, *Nimrod Supervising the Construction of the Tower of Babel* (oil on copper, 22 x 17 ins / 57 x 44 cm) USD 65,000. Paris, 25 June 2004, *Two Collectors Having Lunch in an Art Gallery* (oil on panel, 22 x 34 ins / 57 x 87 cm) EUR 245,000.

FRANCKEN, Frans III, the Elder,

pseudonym: Francken, Rubens
Flemish, 17th century.
Born 1607, in Antwerp; died 4 September 1667, in Antwerp.
Painter. Religious subjects, figures, portraits, church interiors.
Antwerp School, Flemish School.

Frans Francken III or the Elder was the older son of Frans Francken II or the Younger. His pseudonym Rubens Francken has yet to be explained. In about 1655 he became dean of the Guild of St Luke. He was mainly commissioned to paint figures, for the most part in the interiors of churches by Pieter Neefs.

Museums and Galleries:

Antwerp: *Family Portraits* - Augsburg: *St John Preaching; Moses Striking the Rock* - Douai: *Adoration of the Magi* - Dresden: *Interior of the Cathedral of Antwerp* - Hanover: *Belshazzar's Feast* - The Hague: *Interior of Cathedral.*

Auction records:

Paris, 23 Jan 1928, *King Solomon*, FRF 2,000. Paris, 6 Dec 1984, *The Battle between the Centaurs and Lapiths* (oil on panel, 20 x 30 ins / 50.5 x 76 cm) FRF 15,000. New York, 21 Oct 1988, *Adoration of the Magi* (oil on panel, 21 x 26 ins / 53.5 x 66 cm) USD 10,450. Strasbourg, 11 March 1989, *Nativity* (oil on canvas, 25 1/2 x 19 1/2 ins / 65 x 49.5 cm) FRF 66,000. Le Touquet, 19 May 1991, *Merry Feast* (oil/copper, 9 x 11 1/2 ins / 22 x 29 cm) FRF 40,000. Lokeren, 23 May 1992, *The Battle* (oil on panel, 18 1/4 x 23 ins / 46.5 x 58.5 cm) BEF 300,000. Amsterdam, 13 Nov 1995, *Belshazzar's Feast* (oil on panel, 25 1/2 x 38 ins / 65 x 96.5 cm) NLG 43,700. Paris, 18 Dec 1996, *Golgotha* (oil on panel, 18 x 22 3/4 ins / 45.5 x 58 cm) FRF 48,000. London, 11 July 2001, *Elegant Company Banqueting at a Table with Musicians* (oil on copper, 17 x 14 ins / 43 x 35 cm) GBP 26,000. Paris, 19 Dec 2001, *Shop of Art Dealer* (oil on canvas, 23 x 29 ins / 59 x 73 cm) FRF 78,000. London, 9 July 2003, *Sense of Sight* (oil on panel, 7 x 6 ins / 19 x 16 cm) GBP 5,000. Brussels, 3 Dec 2003, *Scenes from the Life of Abraham* (oil on copper, eight, 5 x 11 ins / 12 x 29 cm) EUR 12,000.

FRANCKEN, Gabriel, or Franck or Vrancken

Flemish, 17th century.
Died 1639.
Active in Antwerp.
Painter.
Antwerp School, Flemish School.

In 1605 Gabriel Francken was a pupil of Geert Schoofs. In 1620 he qualified as a master and in 1634 he became a member of the Guild of St Luke.

Museums and Galleries:

Karlsruhe: *A Ball* - La Fère: *The Death of Adonis* - Lisbon: *Autumn.*

FRANCKEN, Hans, or Franck

Flemish, 17th century.
Born 1581, in Antwerp; died 24 December 1624, in Antwerp.
Painter. Religious subjects.
Antwerp School, Flemish School.

Hans Francken was the son of Cornelis Francken and a pupil of his uncle Ambrosius I or the Elder. In 1607 he went to Paris, returning in 1608 to Antwerp where he qualified as a master in 1611.

Museums and Galleries:

Bruges: *Christ among the Teachers; Descent of the Holy Spirit* - Brussels: *The Beheading of St John the Baptist.*

FRANCKEN, Hieronymus I, the Elder, or Franck

Flemish School, 16th - 17th century.
Born 1540, in Herenthals; died 1610, in Paris.
Painter. History painting, religious subjects, portraits, genre scenes.
Antwerp School.

Hieronymus was the eldest son of Nicolas Francken, the painter from Herenthals who founded a dynasty of well-known artists. Little is known about Nicolas. He is believed to have lived from 1520 to 1596, and his portrait, which he painted himself, could still be seen on his tomb in the church at Herenthals in the mid-18th century. Nicolas had four sons of whom the first three, Hieronymus, Frans and Ambrosius (each with 'the Elder' added to their names to distinguish them from their sons or nephews) were successful painters.

Neither the fourth son, Cornelis, born in 1545, nor his son Hans (1581-1624) were to achieve the same fame.

Hieronymus I, or the Elder, was a pupil of Frans Floris, as were his brothers. It is likely that their father Nicolas Francken worked in the Italianising style popularised particularly by Frans Floris. Unlike his younger brothers, who either did not go to Italy or, if they did, made a very fleeting visit, Hieronymus stayed there for a significant period. Leaving Italy, he went to Paris where he won fame at court; King Henri III apparently demonstrated his confidence in the painter by commissioning a portrait of himself. There is no trace of this portrait, but an inscription added below a portrait of the artist, taken from a now-lost self-portrait and preserved as an engraving by Jean Morin, confirms that Hieronymus was 'painter to the king'. One thing is known for certain: Christophe de Thou, the first president of the parliament, took the Flemish artist under his wing commissioning a painting of the *Adoration of the Shepherds* that Francken completed in 1585 when he was 45 years old, including representations of de Thou with his family. Now disappeared without trace, before the French Revolution this work adorned the altar in the church of the Cordeliers. Mariette knew the painting well, and says of it: 'Jérôme Francken seems to have wished to imitate the manner of drawing and composing of Frans Floris whose work, although quite crude, was much appreciated at that time'. In around 1590, Hieronymus returned to Antwerp but subsequently (and again, unlike his brothers, who remained in Antwerp all their lives) returned to Paris in 1595, probably summoned by the king or his patrons. He remained in Paris during the reign of Henri IV and died there in 1610, shortly after the accession of Louis XIII. A contemporary document mentions a sum of 120 ecus received by a certain 'Jérôme Francan', as payment for a painting depicting the provost of the merchants and the échevins together with other municipal officers. Hung in the town hall, this painting too no longer survives. Hieronymus, described as living in the Faubourg St-Germain in 1604, died there at about the age of 70. (Some scholars have given the date of his death as c. 1620, or ten years later.) He married a French woman and had two sons, who died young, and three daughters.

The greater part of Hieronymus Francken I's output has been lost. One of his best known surviving works is *The Abdication of Charles V* in the museum in Amsterdam. This vast composition shows, in the central group, the figures of the emperor on his throne, his brother Ferdinand I and Philip II. They are surrounded by a crowd of courtiers while the foreground is occupied by allegorical figures representing the four corners of the earth. The painting in the Lille museum of *Charles V Taking Religious Orders*, attributed to Frans Francken I, has been seen by some scholars as more likely to be by his brother Hieronymus. It is also possible that some of the portraits attributed to François Pourbus, whose wife was called Elizabeth Francken, may be by Hieronymus. If that were the case, these portraits would have been made during one of his periods in Paris.

Hieronymus the elder and his brothers Frans and Ambrosius can be seen as hardworking propagators of the style begun and 'launched' by Frans Floris. As such, they enjoyed considerable fame. When they were still young, they were active at the time of the death of Floris, the master of Italianism; by the end of their careers, Rubens had arrived. By then, their work was beginning to seem formulaic and old-fashioned and they were ill-prepared to confront the whirlwind of change that Rubens ushered in.

HF HF

MUSEUMS AND GALLERIES:

AACHEN: *Venetian Carnival; Portrait of Hieronymus Francken* - AMSTERDAM: *Abdication of Charles V* - AVIGNON: *Adoration of the Magi* - BRUSSELS: *Adoration of the Magi* - DRESDEN: *Beheading of St John the Baptist* - LILLE: *Emperor Charles V Taking Religious Orders* (attributed?) - OSLO: *Acts of Charity* - ROHRAU (Schlossmuseum, Graf Harrach'sche Familiensammlung): religious subject - STOCKHOLM (Universitet konstsamling): *Reunion* - TROYES: *Institution of the Feast of the Holy Redeemer by Pope Urban IV*.

AUCTION RECORDS:

PARIS, 8 Jan 1945, *Belshazzar's Feast* (attributed) FRF 26,100. BRUSSELS, 2-4 June 1965, *Christ Falling with the Cross*, BEF 100,000. NEW YORK, 27 Nov 1968, *Huguenots at Table*, USD 1,600. NEW YORK, 8 Jan 1981, *Adoration of the Magi* (oil/copper, 14 x 11 ins / 35.5 x 28 cm) USD 6,250. MONTE CARLO, 25 June 1984, *Adoration of the Magi* (oil on panel, 45 1/4 x 34 3/4 ins / 115 x 88.5 cm) FRF 55,000. NEW YORK, 7 April 1989, *Abigail Giving Food to David and his Soldiers* (oil/copper, 20 x 27 1/2 ins / 51 x 70 cm) USD 8,250. MADRID, 25 April 2001, *Biblical Scene* (oil on board, 22 x 30 ins / 57 x 75 cm) ESP 2,400,000. MADRID, 25 Feb 2002, *Courtesan Scene* (oil on board, 21 x 26 ins / 54 x 66 cm) EUR 24,000. MADRID, 15 Dec 2003, *Dice Players* (oil on copper, 10 x 7 ins / 26 x 19 cm) EUR 3,800.

FRANCKEN, Hieronymus II, or Franck, called the Younger

Flemish, 17th century.

Born 1578, in Antwerp; died 17 March 1628, in Antwerp.

Painter. History painting, portraits.

Antwerp School, Flemish School.

Hieronymus Francken II was called the Younger because he was the son of Frans Francken the Elder and a pupil of his uncle Ambrosius Francken. In 1607 he qualified as a master in the Guild of St Luke. He primarily painted portraits, and Gaspard van Bergen figured among his pupils.

2 JERONIMVS. FRANCKEN. INVET. FECIT ANNO 1620 3 sy 14 Aygusti

MUSEUMS AND GALLERIES:

ANTWERP: *Horatius Cocles* - BRUSSELS: *Interior of Studio* - DOUAI: *Interior* - THE HAGUE: *The Studio of Apelles* - VALENCIENNES: *The Abdication of Charles V*.

AUCTION RECORDS:

LONDON, 17 April 1996, *The Visitation; The Annunciation* (oil/copper, a pair, 27 1/4 x 21 1/4 ins / 69.4 x 54.1 cm) GBP 18,400. PARIS, 6 July 1999, *Scene de Collation* (oil on panel, 20 x 26 ins / 50 x 65 cm) FRF 160,000. LONDON, 14 Dec 1999, *Lazarus in the House of the Rich Man* (oil on panel, 28 x 63 ins / 72 x 159 cm) GBP 15,000. MADRID, 29 May 2000, *Exodus of the Israelites* (oil on copper, 21 x 21 ins / 54 x 54 cm) ESP 4,200,000. LONDON, 6 July 2000, *Elegant Young Man and Woman Looking in a Mirror* (oil on panel, 7 x 6 ins / 19 x 16 cm) GBP 5,000. MADRID, 25 April 2001, *The Seven Works of Charity* (1621, oil on copper, 27 x 34 ins / 69 x 87 cm) ESP 7,500,000. MADRID, 7 Oct 2002, *Jesus before Pilate* (oil on copper, 22 x 28 ins / 56 x 72 cm) EUR 13,000. MADRID, 21 Jan 2003, *Jesus before Pilate* (oil on copper, 22 x 28 ins / 56 x 72 cm) EUR 11,000. MADRID, 30 Sept 2003, *Jesus before Pilate* (oil on copper, 22 x 28 ins / 56 x 72 cm) EUR 8,000. MADRID, 26 Jan 2004, *Peter's Denial* (oil on board, 16 x 21 ins / 40 x 53 cm) EUR 7,000. AMSTERDAM, 17 May 2004, *Poor Mans Meal, Loaf of Bread, Porridge, Buns and a Herring on a Table* (1599, oil on panel, 14 x 18 ins / 36 x 46 cm) EUR 18,000.

FRANCKEN, Hieronymus III

Flemish, 17th century.

Born 1611, in Bruges.

Painter. Religious subjects.

Antwerp School, Flemish School.

Hieronymus Francken III was the son of Frans Francken II or the Younger. He received his artistic instruction from his father and Jacob van der Lamen. He worked in Antwerp, where he became a member of the guild in 1645.

FRANCKEN, Jan Baptist, or Vrancx
Flemish, 17th century.
Born 1599, in Antwerp; died 1653.
Painter.
Flemish School.

Jan Baptist Francken was the son and pupil of Sebastian Francken. He applied himself to the study of Rubens and van Dyck. After having devoted himself to painting historical subjects, he turned his attention to the execution of pictures of interiors. He regularly collaborated with Pieter Neeffs.

MUSEUMS AND GALLERIES:
BRUGES: *Christ among the Teachers; The Assumption; The Visitation; Descent of the Holy Spirit on the Apostles; Adoration of the Shepherds* (four copies after Rubens) - BRUSSELS: *The Beheading of St John* - CHARTRES: *The Wedding at Cana; The Miracle of the Loaves and Fishes* - MULHOUSE: *Taste; Hearing; Smell; Touch* - YPRES: *Abigail Attempting to Weaken David*.

AUCTION RECORDS:
PARIS, 18 Nov 1920, *Scene from the Story of Esther* (attributed) FRF 480. LONDON, 26 March 1923, *Convoy Attack*, GBP 31. LONDON, 28 March 1923, *Dutch Festivities*, GBP 33. PARIS, 18 Feb 1926, *St John Preaching*, FRF 900. PARIS, 22 March 1926, *The Tower of Babel*, FRF 1,030. LONDON, 2 Feb 1927, *Sermon on the Mount*, GBP 31. LONDON, 25 May 1927, *Interior*, GBP 16. LONDON, 13 June 1927, *The Passing of Time*, GBP 14. PARIS, 14 April 1937, *The Adoration of the Kings* (attributed) FRF 1,750.

FRANCKEN, Laurens or Laureys, or Franck
Flemish, 17th century.
Painter. History painting, landscapes.
Flemish School.

Laurens Francken was the pupil and nephew of Gabriel Francken, and the master of Francisque Millet. He settled in Paris in 1660.

FRANCKEN, Maximilien, or Franck or Vrancx
Flemish, 17th century.
Died 1651.
Painter. History painting, genre scenes.
Flemish School.

Maximilien Francken was the brother of Laurens Francken and perhaps the son of Jan Baptist Francken.

MF.

FRANCKEN, Nicolas, or Franck
Flemish School, 16th century.
Born c. 1520, in Herenthals; died 12 March 1596, in Antwerp.
Painter.
Antwerp School.

Nicolas Francken lived in Antwerp, and was the founder of the Francken dynasty of artists that continued with his four sons Hieronymus I, Frans I, Ambrosius I and Cornelis.

FRANCKEN, P. H. or H. P.
Flemish, 17th century.
Active in Antwerp, c. 1652.
Painter. History painting.
Antwerp School, Flemish School.

P. H. Francken was a pupil of the Rubens school.

MUSEUMS AND GALLERIES:
ANTWERP: *The Poisoned Cup; St Louis as a Crusader; St Anthony of Padua.*

FRANCKEN, Ruth
Czech, 20th century.
Born 8 August 1924, in Prague.
Active in France from 1952.
Painter, sculptor of assemblages.

Ruth Francken was a student of A. Segal in England before studying at the Art Students' League in New York. She finally settled in Paris in 1952.

Up to 1964, a pivotal date in her work, Francken was affiliated with Abstract Expressionism. Since then, her work has diversified: her *Heads* series comprises small heads expurgated to a non-representative degree drawn on paper; she also produces object-sculpture as in her *Telephones*, which probably owe a great deal to Surrealism and Pop Art. Between 1977 and 1986, she undertook a new series based on the portrait, or rather the anti-portrait, once again depicting the problem of non-communication, a theme already present in her former works. Accumulating techniques, assembling photographs, collages and drawings, she submits the faces of famous people, like Sartre, Monory or the philosopher Lyotard, to numerous modifications and distortions, dissolving their image, only to record the person's vacillating identity. Since 1987 she has continued her research into object-sculpture with the *Wittgenstein Variations*. She featured in collective exhibitions including the Paris Salons and the Venice Biennale (1952). Solo exhibitions include: Paris (1950); Metz museum (1991) and Eric Dupont gallery (1997). She has also shown work in most cities in Europe and in the USA.

BIBLIOGRAPHY:
Francken, R./Lyotard, Jean François, *L'Histoire de Ruth*, Le Castor Astral, Paris, 1983. '*Ruth Francken*' in *Art Press* n° 165, periodical, Paris, January 1991.

AUCTION RECORDS:
PARIS, 17 Dec 1985, *Telephone 5* (1967, steel, 11 3/4 x 11 3/4 x 11 3/4 ins / 30 x 30 x 30 cm) FRF 5,000. PARIS, 20 March 1988, *Blake's Little Valley* (1957, oil on canvas, 28 3/4 x 39 1/4 ins / 73 x 100 cm) FRF 7,000. PARIS, 10 April 1992, *Composition* (1950, oil on canvas, 42 1/4 x 37 1/2 ins / 107 x 95 cm) FRF 6,000. ZURICH, 8 April 1997, *Composition* (1959, oil on canvas, 31 1/2 x 63 ins / 80 x 160 cm) CHF 1,900.

FRANCKEN, Sebastien. See **VRANCX**

FRANCKEN, Thomas, or Franck
Flemish School, 16th - 17th century.
Born 1574, in Antwerp.
Painter.

Thomas was the eldest son of Frans Francken I, known as the Elder. Little is known about this artist.

FRANCKX. See also **FRANCK**

FRANCKY BOY, Sevehon
French, 20th - 21st century.
Born 1954, in Paris.
Painter, sculptor of assemblages, mixed media. Stage sets.
Figuration Libre.

A self-taught artist, Francky Boy was one of the founder members of the 'Musulmans Fumants' group. The style of his paintings lies somewhere between children's drawings and comic strips, while his sculptures are inspired by arrangements of toys.

Since 1983, he has taken part in a number of group exhibitions, notably in 1984 at the International Contemporary Art Fair in Paris in 1984. Since 1984, he has also staged solo exhibitions in St-Étienne, Paris in 1989, Mulhouse and Belgrade.

AUCTION RECORDS:

PARIS, 13 April 1988, *Warm up* (1987, 61 x 88 1/2 ins / 155 x 225 cm) FRF 6,500. PARIS, 12 Feb 1989, *Jojo's Pal* (1987, acrylic/canvas, 59 x 66 1/2 ins / 150 x 169 cm) FRF 16,500. PARIS, 9 April 1989, *Yet Another Shipwreck* (acrylic/canvas, 38 1/4 x 57 1/2 ins / 97 x 146 cm) FRF 13,000. PARIS, 8 Oct 1989, *The Very Pleasant Weekend* (acrylic/canvas, 28 3/4 x 36 1/4 ins / 73 x 92 cm) FRF 20,300. PARIS, 15 Feb 1990, *Weekend in the Countryside* (1989, acrylic/canvas, 59 x 78 3/4 ins / 150 x 200 cm) FRF 105,000. PARIS, 21 June 1990, *'Francky plane'* (1988, polyester sculpture covered in tarlatan, painted in acrylic, 33 1/2 x 44 x 44 ins / 85 x 112 x 112 cm) FRF 35,000. PARIS, 29 June 1990, *Jane* (acrylic/canvas, 46 x 35 1/2 ins / 116 x 90 cm) FRF 23,000. PARIS, 7 Feb 1991, *Charlie Bravo* (acrylic/canvas, 57 1/2 x 45 ins / 146 x 114 cm) FRF 29,000. PARIS, 16 April 1992, *Adieu Valérie* (1987, acrylic/canvas, 48 1/2 x 61 3/4 ins / 123 x 157 cm) FRF 6,500. PARIS, 29 Nov 1992, *La Belle Lulu* (mixed media/canvas, 59 x 78 3/4 ins / 150 x 200 cm) FRF 15,500. PARIS, 22 April 1994, *Proute, Proute* (1992, acrylic/canvas, 39 1/4 x 32 ins / 100 x 81 cm) FRF 7,500.

FRANCO
Flemish School, 10th century.
Almost certainly active in the region of Liège.
Miniaturist.

The Bibliothèque Nationale, Paris, owns a manuscript catalogued as 15176 that must be by this artist.

FRANCO. See also **FRANCKE**

FRANCO, Agnolo or Angiolo
Italian, 15th century.
Died c. 1455.
Active in Naples.
Painter.

To him are attributed the frescoes in the Brancaccio Chapel of S Domenico Maggiore, Naples, representing the *Crucifixion* and scenes from the lives of saints and martyrs. He was a pupil of N.A. del Fiore and an imitator of Giotto.

FRANCO, Andrea
Italian, 16th century.
Active in 1594.
Engraver.

The only known work by Andrea Franco is a print representing a mythological subject, dated 1594 and signed with his name.

FRANCO, Antonio
Spanish, 16th century.
Active in Cádiz in 1587.
Painter.

Antonio Franco, who may have been of Dutch origin, spent time in Rome, then came to Cádiz to work on the cathedral.

FRANCO, Barthélemy
French, 20th century.
Born 22 August 1923, in Nice.
Painter.

Barthélemy Franco exhibited mainly in Nice, showing landscapes of the Côte d'Azur as well as portraits of gypsies and flower paintings.

FRANCO, Battista
Spanish, 20th century.
Born in Spain.
Ceramicist.

FRANCO, Cesare
Italian, 16th century.
Born in Padua.
Sculptor, architect.

Towards the end of his life, Franco seems to have worked in Naples, where he carved statues for churches of which he had overseen the construction.

FRANCO, Francesco
Italian, 17th century.
Active in Cremona c. 1600.
Painter.

Francesco Franco painted a retable for the church of St Apollinaire in Cremona.

FRANCO, Francisco
Spanish, 17th century.
Died 23 March 1694, in Saragossa.
Sculptor.

Francisco Franco worked on the decoration of Saragossa Cathedral.

BIBLIOGRAPHY:

Ponz, Antonio, *Viaje de España, 4*, Aguilar, Madrid, 1988.

FRANCO, Giacomo
Italian, 16th - 17th century.
Born 1556, in Venice; died 28 June 1620, in Venice.
Draughtsman, engraver.

A relative of Giovanni-Battista Franco, Giacomo was a pupil of Agostino Carracci. Most of his works are signed with his name, sometimes with a monogram. They include: *Clothing Worn by Venetian Women*, published in 1626, *The Crucifixion*, and *Hercules between Virtue and Pleasure*, based on a classical low relief.

FRANCO, Giovanni
Italian, 18th century.
Active in Naples.
Painter.

Giovanni Franco was a pupil of Giuseppe Sammartino.

FRANCO, Giovanni Battista, called Il Semolei
Italian, 16th century.
Born 1498 or 1510, in Udine; died 1580, in Venice.
Painter, fresco artist, draughtsman (including sanguine/ink), engraver (including etching/burin), decorative designer. Mythological subjects, religious subjects, historical subjects, battles, portraits, figures. Ornaments, designs (majolica), theatre decoration, murals.

Some scholars believe that Giovanni Battista Franco was born in 1498, others in 1510. If he was born in Udine, as the former maintain, it would not exclude him from Venetian citizenship, as Udine had come under Venetian domination in 1445. At a very young age, he travelled to Rome, where he conceived a boundless admiration for Michelangelo, who was then at the height of his powers. According to Vasari, there was not a subject or sketch by Michelangelo that Franco did not religiously draw; and it is said that Giovanni Battista Franco was the best draughtsman of his era.

His application to drawing seems to have led him to neglect colour. When he was commissioned in 1536 to paint four large frescoes at the Capuan Gate, through which the Emperor Charles V was due to enter the city, his inexperience with the brush was revealed by comparison with the work of some Dutch painters, who were skilled in chiaroscuro effects and had been engaged on the same task.

In the same year - 1536 - Vasari employed him as his assistant in decorating the residence of Ottaviano de' Medici in Florence. At around this time, he also painted a canvas of the *Rape of Lucretia by Tarquinius Sextus*. After the assassination of Duke Alessandro de' Medici in early 1537, Vasari left Florence, leaving Franco to complete the commissions he had accepted: a portrait of Alessandro's father, Pope Clement VII, and another of Ippolito de' Medici. He also painted an enlarged version of a cartoon by Michelangelo: *Noli me tangere*.

At the end of the same year, he was required to depict the battle won by Duke Cosimo I against the Florentine exiles. A curious feature of the painting is his introduction of Ganymede being carried off by Jupiter as an eagle, an idea borrowed from Michelangelo. When Cosimo married Eleanora de Toledo, Giovanni Battista was commissioned to paint a triumphal arch depicting the exploits of Giovanni delle Bande Nere, the duke's brother. Another work he painted, for the courtyard of Palazzo Medici, depicts Cosimo receiving the ducal insignia. Ridolfo Ghirlandaio (not to be confused with Domenico, who had died in 1498), with whom he had already collaborated, then took him to paint some frescoes of the life of Joseph for the cloister of a Camaldolese convent.

In 1541, he returned to Rome. Michelangelo had just completed his immense fresco of the *Last Judgement* and Franco was unable to rest until he had copied every last figure. His fellow Venetian, Cardinal Grimano, then asked him to decorate a loggia of his palazzo, close to St Peter's, with grotesques and arabesques. At the same time, he began a fresco painting of *St John the Baptist Thrown into Prison*. Vasari reports that spatial perspective was completely sacrificed to the details of musculature, arms, legs and torsos; seen individually, these features were perfectly drawn and modelled, but they did not hang together as a whole.

As a result of this failure, Franco decided to accept the invitation of Guidobaldo II to come to Urbino, where he was required to paint the main vault of the palace church with a scene of the *Assumption of the Virgin*. He set about drawing angels, saints, prophets, apostles and sibyls, inspired by his admiration for the ceiling of the Sistine Chapel, but the result was another failed masterpiece. However, his skill in drawing gave the duke the idea of seconding the painter to his majolica factories of Urbino, Pesaro and Castel Durante. Majolica ware was then the height of fashion, recently introduced into Italy by Arab or Spanish craftsmen from Majorca. By replacing the lead glaze with a tin glaze, which gave a pure white background, it was possible to decorate earthenware in a more varied and artistically satisfying manner. The factories multiplied: as well as those already mentioned, majolica works were established in Faenza (1425), Gubbio (1480), Rovezzano, Rovigo, Bologna and Cetto di Castello. The most brilliant period lasted from 1520 to 1560, when Franco was active. The most celebrated ceramic artist, Georgio Andreoli (1498-1552) owned a factory at Gubbio. Franco supplied a large number of drawings to the duke's factories. He taught a number of pupils, including Orazio Fontana of Urbino (1520-1582) (by whom the Louvre owns a goblet depicting the *Rape of Europa*) and Raffaele del Colle. In the meanwhile, Franco was commissioned, in the place of Vasari, who was ill, to decorate the triumphal arches for the duke's marriage with Vittoria Farnese.

On returning to Rome in 1579, Franco began drawing antiquities with all his usual enthusiasm, intending to compile a collection (he was not unskilled as an engraver), when Andrea dell'Anguillea asked him to decorate the theatre he was founding in Rome. During the same period, he also painted the frescoes that can be seen in the church of S Maria sopra Minerva.

Returning to Venice, he executed many commissions, including a *Diana and Acteon* for the ceiling of St Mark's library. He was working on the Grimani Chapel, where a *Baptism of Christ* still survives, when he died in 1580.

Although his paintings are few, his drawings are legion. The Louvre alone owns 93 of them, but not a single painting.

AUCTION RECORDS:
PARIS, 17 and 18 May 1920, *Jesus among the Teachers* (pen) FRF 205. PARIS, 22 Dec 1923, *Jesus among the Teachers* (pen and sepia) FRF 750. PARIS, 21 Jan 1924, *Religious Composition* (pen) FRF 1,300. PARIS, 28 and 29 June 1926, *Virgin and Child with St John* (pen and sepia) FRF 600. LONDON, 4 June 1937, *Baptism of Christ*, GBP 33. PARIS, 28 Feb 1938, *Holy Family* (pen, red chalk and bistre) FRF 350. PARIS, 18 Jan 1945, *Warrior* (pen) FRF 800. LONDON, 7 April 1981, *Man Leaning Forward, Touching the Ground with his Right Hand* (black chalk and pen/blue paper, 6 1/2 x 4 1/2 ins / 16.2 x 11.5 cm) GBP 1,500. LONDON, 25 March 1982, *Twelve Attitudes of Men in Distress* (pen, 9 x 13 1/2 ins / 23.1 x 34.4 cm) GBP 3,800. LONDON, 17 June 1983, *Christ among the Teachers* (etching, 14 3/4 x 18 1/2 ins / 37.3 x 47.2 cm) GBP 700. LONDON, 5 Dec 1985, *Flagellation* (etching and burin, 16 1/4 x 22 ins / 41.4 x 55 cm) GBP 2,800. LONDON, 1 July 1986, *Jupiter Carried by an Eagle* (black and red chalks, 15 x 12 ins / 38.2 x 30.2 cm) GBP 8,500. LONDON, 7 Dec 1987, *Battle Scene* (pen and brown ink, 6 1/2 x 11 1/4 ins / 16.5 x 28.3 cm) GBP 1,100. ROME, 13 April 1989, *Lamentation over the Dead Christ* (oil on panel, 31 1/2 x 25 1/4 ins / 80 x 64 cm) ITL 7,500,000. MONACO, 15 June 1990, *Scene from Classical History* (ink, 10 x 8 1/4 ins / 25.5 x 21.2 cm) FRF 9,990. NEW YORK, 9 Jan 1991, *Battle of Lapiths and Centaurs* (ink and wash, 5 1/2 x 16 3/4 ins / 13.7 x 42.8 cm) USD 6,600. MONACO, 2 July 1993, *Nude Man Lying Down Holding a Mask; Two Other Silhouettes* (red chalk and ink, 6 1/2 x 11 1/4 ins / 16.2 x 28.5 cm) FRF 31,080. LONDON, 18 April 1994, *Parnassus* (ink, diam. 4 1/2 ins / 11.7 cm) GBP 2,530. NEW YORK, 10 Jan 1996, *Couple with Child Followed by an Old Woman* (black chalk and ink, 9 1/4 x 6 1/4 ins / 23.5 x 16 cm) USD 10,350. LONDON, 3 July 1996, *Study of Four People* (ink, 10 x 9 1/4 ins / 25.5 x 23.2 cm) GBP 1,840. LONDON, 2 July 1997, *Profile of a Crouching Male Nude* (c. 1552, black chalk/blue paper, study, 13 x 8 3/4 ins / 33.1 x 22.4 cm) GBP 5,175. NEW YORK, 28 Jan 1999, *Mucius Scaevola* (colour ink, 11 x 14 ins / 28 x 35 cm) USD 12,000. NEW YORK, 28 Jan 1999, *Bearded Man Sitting on Globe, Allegories of Day and Night* (colour ink with stylus, 10 x 7 ins / 26 x 17 cm) USD 15,000. NEW YORK, 26 Jan 2000, *Three Flying Angels* (pen, brown ink wash and black chalk, 6 x 6 ins / 14 x 16 cm) USD 2,800. NEW YORK, 28 Jan 2000, *Figures Fishing in Bay* (black chalk, pen, brown ink, brown wash heightened with white, 11 x 17 ins / 27 x 44 cm) USD 22,000. NEW YORK, 22 Jan 2003, *Studies* (chalk, pen and ink, 9 x 14 ins / 24 x 35 cm) USD 10,000. NEW YORK, 22 Jan 2003, *Ideal Female Head* (pen, chalk and ink, 14 x 10 ins / 36 x 25 cm) USD 28,000. PARIS, 18 March 2004, *Flight of Cloelia* (pen and brown ink wash, 7 x 9 ins / 18 x 24 cm) EUR 12,000.

FRANCO, Giuseppe, called dalle Lodole or de Monti
Italian, 16th - 17th century.
Born c. 1550, in Rome; died c. 1627, in Rome.
Painter. History painting.

Giuseppe Franco worked at the Vatican under Sixtus V. Siret says that his nickname derives from the skylark (*allodola*) he included in his compositions.

FRANCO, Giuseppe del
Italian, 20th century.
Artist.
Body Art.

Since 1966, Giuseppe del Franco has exhibited on several occasions in Italy and France. He studied architecture in

Paris in 1968, and became interested in problems with art and communication. Del Franco belongs to the movement known as 'Body Art', which uses the human body as the canvas, in an attempt to lessen the distance between the artist and his work.

FRANCO, José
Cuban, 20th - 21st century.
Born 1958, in Cuba.
Active in France.
Painter.

José Franco studied in Havana at the Academia Nacional de Bellas Artes San Alejandro and then at the Escuela de Bellas Artes. His work is brightly coloured. He places dreamlike fauna against backgrounds of geometric motifs that suggest the coats of certain animals, or finely-veined butterfly wings enlarged under a microscope. He lives in Paris.

Since 1974 he has taken part in collective exhibitions in Cuba and abroad, including: Tokyo (1984); Buenos Aires and Barcelona (1986); *Trajectoires Cubaines* (*Cuban Trajectory*) exhibition, Pablo Neruda Art Centre, Corbeil-Essonnes (1989). He has held solo exhibitions since 1977, notably at the Galerie Artuel, Paris (1989).

AUCTION RECORDS:
PARIS, 9 April 1989, *Filbert* (mixed media/paper, 27 3/4 x 19 3/4 ins / 70.5 x 50 cm) FRF 7,000.

FRANCO, José Maria
Spanish, 19th century.
Active at the beginning of the 19th century.
Painter. History painting.

FRANCO, Joseph Napoléon
French, 19th century.
Born 18 August 1811, in Paris.
Painter, painter (porcelain). Still-lifes (flowers/fruit).

Franco exhibited at the Paris Salon from 1840 to 1859; he also painted on porcelain and alabaster.

AUCTION RECORDS:
NEW YORK, 24 May 1995, *Flowers and Fruit on a Marble Slab* (1850, oil/marble, oval painting/rectangular background, 15 x 21 ins / 38.4 x 52.4 cm) USD 8,050.

FRANCO, Manuel
Portuguese, 17th century.
Active in Lisbon in 1650.
Painter.

FRANCO, Pedro, the Elder
Spanish, 16th century.
Born in Seville.
Active in Seville.
Sculptor.

In 1550, Pedro Franco the Elder was working on the cathedral of his native city.

FRANCO, Pedro, the Younger
Spanish, 17th century.
Died 24 October 1694, in Saragossa.
Sculptor.

Pedro Franco the Younger was the son and pupil of Francisco Franco.

FRANCO, Salvatore
Italian, 18th century.
Active in Naples.
Sculptor.

Salvatore Franco was a pupil of Giuseppe Sammartino.

FRANCO, Siron
Brazilian, 20th - 21st century.
Born 1947, in Goiás Velho.
Painter, installation artist. Figures.

Siron Franco lives and works in Goiâna in Brazil. During the 1970s he depicted man's anguish, painting him nude, doubled up, mutilated and deformed against ochre-coloured backgrounds. His work is violent: he paints then corrects; he makes an assault on representation in order to purge it in an expression of intimate revolt. In his installation pieces Franco depicted with humour the indifference of the Brazilian people; he engaged in the struggle against infant mortality with a piece entitled *Bandeira Brasileira* which brings together 1020 children's coffins for the International Week of the Child organised by UNICEF. During the 1990s he again began to paint works blending primitive culture with a phantasmagorical universe, making use of signs, the abstract and figuration. Siron Franco has shown his work in solo exhibitions: São Paulo (1987); London (1992 and 1994); Paris (1993) and Florence (1997).

BIBLIOGRAPHY:
Ades, Dawn, *Siron Franco: figures and likenesses; paintings 1968-1995*, Editora index, Rio de Janeiro, 1995. Jimenez, Marc, '*Siron Franco de la chute à la révolte*' in *Art Press* n° 221, periodical, Paris, February 1997.

AUCTION RECORDS:
NEW YORK, 17 May 1989, *Indefinite Figure* (1986, oil on canvas, 27 1/2 x 23 1/2 ins / 70 x 59.6 cm) USD 5,280. NEW YORK, 21 Nov 1989, *Driven out of Paradise* (1976, oil on compressed card, 35 1/2 x 47 1/4 ins / 90 x 120 cm) USD 8,250. NEW YORK, 2 May 1990, *Best Friends* (1980, oil on canvas, 60 1/2 x 53 ins / 153.7 x 134.5 cm) USD 7,150. NEW YORK, 18-19 May 1992, *Glass - Take Care* (1990, oil on canvas, 53 1/4 x 53 1/4 ins / 135 x 135 cm) USD 12,100. NEW YORK, 18 May 1993, *International Debt* (1991, oil on canvas, 70 3/4 x 74 1/2 ins / 179.7 x 189.3 cm) USD 17,250. NEW YORK, 16 Nov 1994, *Badly Told Story* (oil on canvas, 63 x 78 1/4 ins / 160 x 198.8 cm) USD 16,100. NEW YORK, 14-15 May 1996, *Ancient Decline* (1990, oil on canvas, 53 1/2 x 60 3/4 ins / 135.6 x 154.6 cm) USD 10,350. NEW YORK, 25-26 Nov 1996, *Furs II* (1990, oil on canvas, 63 x 78 3/4 ins / 160 x 200 cm) USD 29,900. NEW YORK, 21 Nov 2000, *Flagrante* (1990, oil on canvas, 78 x 63 ins / 199 x 159 cm) USD 12,000. NEW YORK, 21 Nov 2000, *Pieles, tenda cuidado, vidrio* (oil on canvas, 53 x 61 ins / 135 x 155 cm) USD 14,000. RIO DE JANEIRO, 1 April 2003, *All Blue* (oil on canvas, 53 x 61 ins / 135 x 155 cm) BRL 57,750. RIO DE JANEIRO, 17 June 2003, *Caught* (1990-1991, oil on canvas, 78 x 62 ins / 198 x 158 cm) BRL 68,250. RIO DE JANEIRO, 27 April 2004, *Horror Stories* (1975, oil on canvas, 79 x 71 ins / 200 x 180 cm) BRL 82,000. RIO DE JANEIRO, 6 July 2004, *Untitled* (1980, oil on canvas, 61 x 54 ins / 156 x 137 cm) BRL 50,000.

FRANCO BOLOGNESE, also known as Franco da Bologna
Italian, 14th century.
Active at the beginning of the 14th century.
Painter, miniaturist.

Franco founded a school of painting in Bologna that was attended by painters such as Vitale, Lorenzo, Simone Jacopo, Cristoforo and possibly also Simone da Bologna. He was a miniaturist and worked with Oderigi da Gubbio (whose pupil he is said to have been) and Giotto in illustrating some books commissioned by Pope Boniface VIII. These works are now kept in the Vatican Library. Dante mentions him in his *Purgatory* and seems to place him higher even than Giotto. There are references to a *Virgin Enthroned* by Franco, dating from 1313.

FRANCO DE SOUZA, Francisco
Portuguese, 20th century.
Born in Madeira.
Sculptor.

Francisco Franco de Souza was a member of the Salon d'Automne in Paris.

FRANCO DI ARGENTERE, Alfonso
Italian, 15th - 16th century.
Born 1466, in Messina; died 1524, in Messina.
Painter.

Alfonso Franco di Argentere painted a *Pietà*, dated 1524, which can be seen in the church of S Francesco de Paola in Mesina. He died of the plague.

FRANCO DI PIERO
Italian, 15th century.
Active in Florence in 1406.
Painter.

FRANCO Y CORDERO, José
Spanish, 19th century.
Born in Jerez de la Frontera (Andalusia).
Painter. Landscapes.
José Franco y Cordero was a pupil of José Jiménez Aranda. He first exhibited in Madrid in 1878.

FRANCO Y SALINAS, Luis
Spanish, 19th century.
Born 19 March 1850, in Valencia; died c. 1897 or 1899, in Barcelona.
Painter. History painting, portraits, genre scenes.
Luis Franco y Salinas was a pupil of Bernardo Ferrandiz. He first exhibited in Valencia in 1867 and went on to exhibit regularly in exhibitions in Valencia and Madrid.
MUSEUMS AND GALLERIES:
MADRID: *Office*; *In the Dressing Room*.
AUCTION RECORDS:
LONDON, 25 March 1987, *Young Woman at the Piano* (oil on panel, 10 3/4 x 9 ins / 27.5 x 22 cm) GBP 11,500. MADRID, 18 Dec 2000, *The Violinist* (oil on board, 14x10 ins / 36x25 cm) ESP 1,900,000. MADRID, 19 Nov 2002, *Looking at the Sea* (oil on canvas, 24x17 ins / 60x44 cm) EUR 8,500. MADRID, 27 May 2003, *Portrait of the Mother of the Painter Dna* (oil on panel, 7x6 ins / 17x14 cm) EUR 400.

FRANÇOIS (Maître)
French, 15th century.
Active between 1460 and 1480.
Miniaturist, illuminator.
This artist has sometimes been identified with François Fouquet, the son of Jean Fouquet.

Quite a large number of manuscripts illustrated by this artist have survived. He was considered to be the best Parisian illuminator of his day and was known as 'Maître François'. He was the successor to Maître Jean Rolin as the head of his workshop. Of his work, one of the best-known series of illustrations is that for Raoul de Presle's translation into French of St Augustine's *City of God*.
MUSEUMS AND GALLERIES:
MELBOURNE (NG of Victoria): *Book of Hours* (c. 1475) - PARIS (Bibliothèque Ste-Geneviève) - PARIS (BNF).

FRANÇOIS, called Le Jeune Cœur ('the Young Heart')
French, 16th century.
Painter, carver.
François was living in Lyons in 1535 and 1574. He was a master in the painters' guild in 1569 and worked for the entries into the town of 1558 and 1574. He was also working in Dijon in this same period, particularly on the occasions of the solemn entry into Dijon of Henri II in 1548 and of Henri III in 1574.

FRANÇOIS
French, 17th century.
Active in Paris in 1683.
Painter, sculptor, engraver, illuminator.

FRANÇOIS
French, 18th century.
Active in Paris.
Sculptor.
François was a student of Gois.

FRANÇOIS
19th century.
Painter. History painting.
Siret referred to a painter by this name as having worked with Étienne Dubois on the painting *Louis-Philippe Giving the Flag to the National Guard in 1830* (Museum of Versailles). However, his first name has been mistaken for his surname; the artist with whom Étienne Dubois collaborated was none other than his brother, François Dubois.

FRANÇOIS, Alexandre
Belgian, 19th - 20th century.
Born 1824, in Brussels; died 1 March 1912, in Albany, USA.
From 1849 active in the USA.
Painter. Portraits, genre scenes, landscapes with figures, landscapes.
Alexandre François studied at the Brussels academy under his uncle Pierre Joseph François; settled first in Paris, then moved to the USA in 1849, living in New York City, Rochester, and finally in Albany, state capital of New York State. He painted some landscapes and genre compositions but is primarily known for his portraits painted in dark and sombre tones.

FRANÇOIS, Alphonse
French, 19th century.
Born 25 August 1814, in Paris; died 7 July 1888, in Paris.
Engraver.
Alphonse François was a pupil of Henriquel-Dupont. He was awarded medals in 1851 and 1857, together with a gold medal of the 1867 Exposition Universelle. He exhibited at the Salon from 1842 to 1880. A talented artist, François was elected to membership of the Institute in 1873 and made an officer of the Légion d'Honneur in 1857.

FRANÇOIS, André. See **FARKAS André**

FRANÇOIS, Ange
Flemish, 19th century.
Born 2 January 1800, in Brussels.
Painter. Religious subjects, genre scenes, portraits.
Flemish School.
Ange François was the son and pupil of Pierre Joseph Célestin François. Noteworthy is his *Louis XIV and Mme de Maintenon*.
AUCTION RECORDS:
PARIS, 1844, *Interiors with figures*, FRF 690. PARIS, 1894, *The Little Woman*, FRF 170. MONTE CARLO, 26 May 1980, *A Kiss on the Hand* (oil on panel, 18 x 14 1/4 ins / 46 x 36.5 cm) FRF 11,000. LONDON, 8 Oct 1986, *St Sebastian* (1823, oil on canvas, 32 x 23 ins / 81 x 57.5 cm) GBP 1,100. NEW YORK, 25 May 1988, *Games in the Loft* (oil on panel, 12 1/4 x 14 1/2 ins / 31.4 x 36.8 cm) USD 5,500. MONACO, 3 Dec 1989, *The Poet Charles of Orléans* (1845, oil on panel, 18 1/4 x 15 1/4 ins / 46.5 x 39 cm) FRF 72,150. MICHIGAN, 30 Jan 2001, *Annunciation* (oil on panel, 26 x 20 ins / 66 x 51 cm) USD 5,000. VLAAMSE KAAI, 18 March 2003, *Woman with Bunch of Grapes* (oil on panel, 16 x 13 ins / 41 x 32 cm) EUR 5,000. PARIS, 1 Dec 2003, *Anthony and Cleopatra* (oil on canvas, 44 x 57 ins / 113 x 145 cm) EUR 28,000.

FRANÇOIS, Auguste
French, 19th century.
Born in Neuville-sur-Ornain (Meuse).
Sculptor.
Auguste François' mentors were David d'Angers and François Rude. He submitted his plaster statue entitled *Last of the Maccabees* to the 1848 Paris Salon. This was followed by a *Christ Dying on the Cross* (1849 Salon) and an allegorical *France Protecting its Standard by the Sword* (Salon of 1874).

FRANÇOIS, Barthélemy
French, 17th - 18th century.
Born April 1640, in Le Puy; died 6 February 1713, in Le Puy.
Painter.
Barthélemy François was a nephew and student of Guy François. He worked in Le Puy. No work has been attributed with certainty to this painter.

FRANÇOIS, Bastien or Sébastien
French, 15th - 16th century.
Died c. 1523.
Active in Tours.
Sculptor, architect.
Bastien François married Marie Regnault, the daughter of the sculptor Guillaume Regnault, who was a nephew by marriage of Michel Colombe. He was the master of works at Tours Cathedral in 1500. Between 1504 and 1507, with his brother Martin, he built the bell tower on the north tower of the cathedral. The brothers' initials can still be seen beneath the dome of the lantern. In 1509, they built the now-ruined cloister at the church of St-Martin. In 1508, Bastien worked in the studio of Michel Colombe. In 1510, again in collaboration with his brother Martin, he made his masterpiece, the beautiful fountain at Beaune-Semblançay. Damaged by Protestant reformers in 1562, it was reconstructed in 1820 in the marketplace where it still stands. A cast of the fountain can also be seen in the Trocadéro Museum. In 1513, Bastien was nominated master of works for the town of Tours.

FRANÇOIS, Célestin
Belgian, 19th century.
Active in Brussels.
Painter. Genre scenes.
Célestin François was the son of Jacob François and a pupil of his uncle Joseph.
AUCTION RECORDS:
LONDON, 22 March 1985, *The Visit to the Doctor* (1823, oil on panel, 14 1/2 x 17 3/4 ins / 36.8 x 45 cm) GBP 3,000. AMSTERDAM, 24 April 1991, *The Eavesdroppers* (oil on panel, 13 1/2 x 11 ins / 34 x 27 cm) NLG 4,600. BURY ST EDMUNDS, 24 March 1999, *Lover's Gift* (1839, oil on panel, 13 x 10 ins / 34 x 25 cm) GBP 1,800. LONDON, 15 Dec 1999, *Exchange of Outfits* (oil on canvas, 19 x 15 ins / 48 x 37 cm) GBP 1,000. BRUSSELS, 12 Dec 2000, *Temple of the Sibyl at Tivoli* (oil on canvas, 30 x 24 ins / 77 x 62 cm) BEF 160,000. BURY ST EDMUNDS, 6 May 2002, *Last Note, Family Musicians in a Parlour* (1825, oil on panel, 11 x 9 ins / 29 x 23 cm) GBP 5,600.

FRANÇOIS, Ch. A., called Fontenay
French, 19th century.
Active in Viroflay (Seine-et-Oise).
Engraver (wood). Urban landscapes, hunting scenes.
This artist was a member of the Société des Artistes Français from 1894 onwards. He received an honourable mention in 1898.
AUCTION RECORDS:
PARIS, 11 May 1897, *St-Jean-de-Luz*, FRF 95; *Bear Hunt*, FRF 65.

FRANÇOIS, Charles
French, 20th century.
Born in Nice.
Painter.
Charles François exhibited in Paris at the Salon des Indépendants from 1939.

FRANÇOIS, Charles-Émile
French, 19th century.
Born 23 October 1821, in Paris.
Painter.
Charles-Émile François studied under Durand-Duclos and Georges Rouget. He exhibited at the Salon from 1848 to 1880. Notable paintings in his body of work are: *Interior of a Drawing Studio, Chemist, Nun of the Order of the Sisters of Mercy, Orientalist, Monks at Study, Nun of the St Elizabeth Order, Pierre Corneille at the Cobbler's, Portrait of Monseigneur Darboy, Archbishop of Paris*, and *Portrait of Baron Taylor* (University of Uppsala). Charles-Emile François also painted a *Disciples of Emmaus* commissioned by the king of Portugal and a *Lady-in-Waiting* for the Bey of Tunis.

FRANÇOIS, Claude, called frère Luc
French, 17th century.
Born 1615, in Amiens; died 17 May 1685.
Painter.
A student of Vouet and Le Brun, Claude François is better known by his monastic name, 'frère Luc' or 'frère Lucas' de La Haye, because he entered the order of the Recollets at the age of 26. He painted a picture over the altar in the chapel of St Étienne at Amiens Cathedral.

FRANÇOIS, Claude
French, 17th century.
Born in Toul.
Painter, engraver.
Claude François was working in Nancy in around 1615.

FRANÇOIS, Edme
French, 17th century.
Active in Auxerre.
Sculptor.
Edme François worked with Lambert.

FRANÇOIS, Édouard
French, 19th - 20th century.
Born 1866, in Paris; died 1924.
Painter, watercolourist.
Édouard François exhibited regularly at the Salon des Artistes Français in Paris.

FRANÇOIS, Félix Léon
French, 20th century.
Born in Joinville-le-Pont.
Painter.
Félix François studied under Cormon and became a member of the Salon des Artistes Français in 1929.

FRANÇOIS, Ferdinand or François
French, 18th century.
Active in Paris in 1777.
Painter (?), sculptor (?).

FRANÇOIS, Georges
French, 20th century.
Born 25 June 1880, in St-Gourgon (Loir-et-Cher).
Engraver.
Georges François studied under J.-P. Laurens. He exhibited line engravings in Paris at the Salon des Artistes Français, receiving a medal in 1914.

FRANÇOIS, Gustave, pseudonym of Barraud, Gustave
Swiss, 20th century.
Born 4 May 1883, in Geneva; died 1968, in Geneva.
Painter, engraver, illustrator. Figure compositions, nudes, landscapes.
Brother of the painter Maurice Barraud, with whom he collaborated for a time. Gustave studied at the fine arts academy in Geneva. In addition to his nudes and landscapes of the region around Geneva, he is remembered for his illustrations for Rachilde's *Discovery of America*.
MUSEUMS AND GALLERIES:
GENEVA: *Leda* - SCHAFFHAUSEN: *Woman in Pink* - WINTERTHUR: *Trayas Landscape* - ZURICH: *Toilette*.
AUCTION RECORDS:
ZURICH, 29 May 1976, *Nude* (1925-1930, pastel, 24 x 18 1/2 ins / 61 x 47 cm) CHF 3,700. ZURICH, 12 May 1977, *Nude with*

Turban (pastel, 24 1/2 x 21 ins / 62 x 52.5 cm) CHF 1,900. ZURICH, 23 Nov 1977, *Pink and Black* (oil on canvas, 28 3/4 x 23 1/2 ins / 73 x 60 cm) CHF 1,900. ZURICH, 11 May 1978, *Uncovered* (oil on canvas, 28 3/4 x 39 1/4 ins / 73 x 100 cm) CHF 2,800. BERN, 2 May 1979, *Reclining Nude* (pastel, 21 1/4 x 30 3/4 ins / 54 x 78 cm) CHF 1,300. ZURICH, 4 June 1983, *Seated Woman* (pastel, 14 x 11 1/4 ins / 35.5 x 28.7 cm) CHF 3,300. ZURICH, 9 Nov 1984, *Carnival* (oil on canvas, 32 x 25 1/4 ins / 81 x 64 cm) CHF 1,600. CHESTER, 4 Oct 1985, *Public Auction, Paris* (1911, watercolour/ivory, 6 1/4 x 8 ins / 16 x 20.5 cm) GBP 6,100. ZURICH, 14 Nov 1986, *Young Female Nude beside a Bathtub* (pastel, 17 x 21 1/2 ins / 43 x 54.5 cm) CHF 1,900. BERN, 8 May 1987, *Sunbathing* (oil on panel, 39 x 27 1/2 ins / 99 x 70 cm) CHF 3,400. BERN, 26 Oct 1988, *Landscape with Trees in Blossom* (oil on panel, 6 1/2 x 9 ins / 16.5 x 22 cm) CHF 600. PARIS, 22 Nov 1988, *Café Scene* (oil on canvas, 22 x 18 ins / 55 x 46 cm) FRF 30,000. ZURICH, 25 Oct 1989, *Youth* (oil on canvas, 39 1/4 x 25 1/2 ins / 100 x 65 cm) CHF 7,500. BERN, 12 May 1990, *Summer Landscape* (oil on canvas, 18 x 25 1/2 ins / 46 x 65 cm) CHF 2,200. ZURICH, 18 Oct 1990, *Reclining Nude* (charcoal, 11 1/2 x 19 ins / 29.2 x 48.1 cm) CHF 1,300. ZURICH, 4 June 1992, *Reclining Nude* (oil on canvas, 25 1/2 x 39 1/4 ins / 65 x 100 cm) CHF 6,780.

FRANÇOIS, Guy, known as Guido Francisco, called le Grand François
French, 17th century.
Born 20 November 1580, in Le Puy-en-Velay; died after 5 October 1650.
Painter. Religious subjects.

Guy François signed his name *Guido Francisco*. This may have caused confusion with Guido Reni, the only painter of those associated with Caravaggio whom he greatly admired. He was held in such high regard by his contemporaries to be called 'Le Grand François' (the Great François). Contrary to Félibien's account, he did not work with Simon Vouet. After a brief stay in Italy, he settled in Le Puy before 1614. He set up a studio there that enjoyed a considerable reputation throughout the Languedoc and Auvergne regions.

His signed and dated works are: *Christ on the Cross*, 1619, at the church of the secondary school at Le Puy-en-Velay, *Our Lady of the Rosary with St Louis and St Dominic*, 1619, at the church of St Laurent at Le Puy-en-Velay, *St Peter of Alcantara*, 1625, at the church of Montferrand (Puy-de-Dôme), *Adoration of the Shepherds*, 1630, at the church at the secondary school in Le Puy, *Adoration of the Shepherds* at the church in Gannat (Allier), of the same date, as well as *Virgin Mary, Christ Child and St Ignatius*, at the church of the secondary school in Le Puy-en-Velay, *Adoration of the Shepherds*, 1631, at the church of St Bonnet near Riom (Puy-de-Dôme), *Pieta* (*Compassion*), 1635, at the church of St Laurent in Le Puy-en-Velay, *St Hyacinth and the Lady of Coubladeur*, 1635, at the church of St Laurent in Le Puy-en-Velay, *Descent from the Cross*, 1640, at the church of the Penitents in Craponne (Haute-Loire).

The following works are also attributed to him: a picture in the church of St Julian in Tournon (Ardèche), a picture in the church at Montpezat (Tarn-et-Garonne), a *Virgin and Child*, *Marriage of St Catherine and Purification* at the museum in Toulouse, *St Ignatius* (church of the Carmelites in Le Puy), *Incredulity of St Thomas* (church of St Laurent in Le Puy) and the ceiling in the church of the Penitents in Le Puy (an *Assumption* and 56 angels).

In his composition he pursues chiaroscuro effects, while his execution aims at realism. He often uses rich colour.

BIBLIOGRAPHY:

Gautheron, E., *Études sur l'histoire de l'art dans la Haute-Loire. Peintres et sculpteurs du Velay*, Imprimerie la Haute-Loire, Le Puy-en-Velay, 1927. Sterling, Charles/Jamot, Paul, *Les Peintres de la réalité en France au XVIIe siècle*, exhibition catalogue, Musée de l'Orangerie, Paris, 1934.

MUSEUMS AND GALLERIES:

TOULOUSE (MBA, Mus. des Augustins): *Marriage of St Catherine and Purification* (attributed).

AUCTION RECORDS:

NEW YORK, 31 May 1991, *St John the Baptist* (oil on canvas, 38 1/4 x 29 1/4 ins / 97.2 x 74.3 cm) USD 38,500. LONDON, 11 Dec 1996, *Adoration of the Magi* (oil on canvas, 74 3/4 x 57 1/2 ins / 190 x 146 cm) GBP 67,500.

FRANÇOIS, Henri J.
French, 18th century.
Born 18th century.
Painter. Portraits.

Henri François was a student of Brenet. In 1785 and 1786, he exhibited work at the Salon de la Correspondance; he then featured in the Louvre exhibitions from 1791 to 1806. He was also a poet.

AUCTION RECORDS:

PARIS, 1 July 1987, *Portrait of a Painter* (1779, oil on canvas, 40 1/4 x 32 1/2 ins / 102 x 82.5 cm) FRF 230,000.

FRANÇOIS, Henri Louis
French, 19th century.
Born 1841, in Vert-le-Petit (Essonne); died 5 September 1896, in Paris.
Sculptor, engraver. Cameos.

Henri François studied under Bonnat and Chapu and exhibited at the Paris Salon from 1867 onwards. He is remembered for his cameo work, including *Venus Disarming Cupid* (oriental onyx), an allegorical *Freedom* (cornelian), *Prometheus* and *St George* (ruby), *Venus Playing with Cupid* (onyx), *Love Gone Cold* (cornelian), *Eve* (onyx), *Egyptian Woman* (red jasper with a beaten and enamelled gold and lapis lazuli setting), *Venus Leaving her Bath* (agate) and others, including an *Andromeda* and a cameo entitled *Filial Piety*.

FRANÇOIS, Jacob
Flemish, 19th century.
Active in Antwerp, c. 1800.
Painter. History painting.
Flemish School.

Jacob François was perhaps the father of Célestin François.

FRANÇOIS, Jacques
French, 17th century.
Active in Senlis.
Sculptor.

Jacques François sculpted several tombstones in the churches of Villiers-le-Sec, Villeron and Marly-la-Ville in the region of Seine-et-Oise.

FRANÇOIS, Jacques
Flemish, 17th century.
Active in Antwerp, in 1600.
Sculptor.
Flemish School.

FRANÇOIS, Jacques
French, 17th century.
Active in Paris in 1602.
Painter, sculptor.

FRANÇOIS, Jacquet
French, 15th century.
Active in Tours.
Sculptor (wood).

Jacquet François lived in Tours from 1478 to 1483. In 1478 he made a wooden statue of St Martin on horseback for Louis XI. It was painted by Jean Bourdichon and erected in the chapel of the chateau of Plessis-lès-Tours. Jacquet François is likely to have been related to Bastien and Martin François, both sculptors like him.

FRANÇOIS, Jean Charles
French, 18th century.
Born 4 May 1717, in Nancy; died 21 March 1769, in Paris.
Engraver.

Jean François was an engraver of drawings to the king's cabinet and ordinary engraver to the king of Poland. He made many discoveries in the art of engraving, imitating drawing and even water-colour in an extraordinary way. These procedures were taken up by Demarteau and helped to establish the fame of this famous engraver.

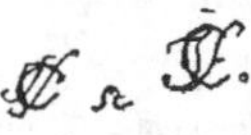

BIBLIOGRAPHY:
Hérold, Jacques, *Jean-Charles François, catalogue de l'œuvre gravé*, Société pour l'étude de la gravure française, Paris, 1931.

FRANÇOIS, Jean I
French, 17th century.
Born 20 November 1580, in Le Puy-en-Velay; died c. 1650, in Paris.
Painter.

The twin brother of Guy François, Jean François began to paint in Le Puy-en-Velay and seems to have settled in Paris in around 1622. His works are sometimes confused with those of his nephew, Jean II François. There is a lack of certainty attributing works to either one of them. However, it is certainly him whom Marolles refers to as 'Jean François père' (the father) and some of his portraits were engraved by Cossin.

MUSEUMS AND GALLERIES:
LE PUY-EN-VELAY: *Portrait of a Man*.

FRANÇOIS, Jean II
French, 17th century.
Born in Le Puy-en-Velay; died 1684, in Le Puy.
Painter.

The son and student of Guy François, Jean François II painted many religious pictures and seems to have had most success as a portrait painter. His signed and dated works are as follows: 1653, thanksgiving plaque said to be for *Vow for the Plague*, representing the consuls of Le Puy, *St Sebastian and St Roch* (at the cathedral in Le Puy-en-Velay); 1663, *Christ on the Cross* (church of the Carmelites in Le Puy-en-Velay); 1669, *Consuls of Puy with St Ignatius and St Francis Regis* (church at the secondary school in Le Puy-en-Velay); 1679, *Birth of the Virgin* (church of the Carmelites in Le Puy-en-Velay); 1649 and *Disciples from Emmaus* (museum in Toulouse). Various other religious paintings are attributed to him. However they are just as likely to be the work of his uncle Jean I and not of any interest.

MUSEUMS AND GALLERIES:
TOULOUSE: *Disciples from Emmaus* (1649).

FRANÇOIS, Jean III
French, 17th - 18th century.
Sculptor.

Jean François III was the brother of Louis François, known as 'François l'Aîné' (François the Elder). Like him, he worked at Versailles, St-Germain-en-Laye, Chantilly and the church at Invalides.

FRANÇOIS, Jean-Michel
Belgian, 20th - 21st century.
Born 1955, in Namur.
Painter.

François studied in Namur and attended the Académie des Beaux-Arts in Brussels.

FRANÇOIS, Joseph. See **FRANCOIS Pierre Joseph Celestin**

FRANÇOIS, Joseph Charles
Belgian, 19th - 20th century.
Born 1851, in Brussels; died 1949.
Painter. Landscapes, landscapes with figures.

Joseph François exhibited in Brussels and Paris, securing a silver medal at the 1913 Salon des Artistes Français.

AUCTION RECORDS:
LOKEREN, 28 May 1988, *Summer Landscape* (oil on canvas, 14 1/4 x 19 3/4 ins / 36.5 x 50 cm) BEF 33,000. BRUSSELS, 19 Dec 1989, *Gathering Wood* (oil on canvas) BEF 50,000. COPENHAGEN, 6 Dec 1990, *Stream Snaking through the Undergrowth* (oil on canvas, 20 x 29 1/2 ins / 51 x 75 cm) DKK 7,000. LOKEREN, 15 May 1993, *Wooded Landscape* (oil on canvas, 35 1/2 x 43 1/4 ins / 90 x 110 cm) BEF 110,000. LOKEREN, 20 May 1995, *Flooding at Cureghem, 27 January 1891* (oil on canvas, 28 x 39 1/4 ins / 71 x 100 cm) BEF 44,000. BRUSSELS, 11 May 1999, *Mounting the Landing Stage* (oil on canvas, 24 x 31 ins / 60 x 78 cm) BEF 350,000. BRUSSELS, 9 Nov 1999, *Walking in the Dunes* (oil on canvas, 46 x 79 ins / 116 x 200 cm) BEF 480,000. BRUSSELS, 9 May 2000, *Walk on the Landing Stage* (oil on canvas, 20 x 31 ins / 50 x 80 cm) BEF 460,000. BRUSSELS, 9 May 2000, *Beach Scene* (oil on canvas, 16 x 30 ins / 40 x 75 cm) BEF 460,000. BRUSSELS, 12 Feb 2001, *Fashionable People and Children on the Beach* (oil on canvas, 22 x 26 ins / 55 x 65 cm) BEF 155,000. BRUSSELS, 20 March 2001, *In Wallonie* (oil on canvas, 67 x 91 ins / 170 x 230 cm) BEF 160,000. BRUSSELS, 12 June 2002, *Village of Gaume* (oil on canvas, 36 x 28 ins / 92 x 72 cm) EUR 1,700. BRUSSELS, 12 June 2002, *Small Farm in Autumn* (oil on canvas, 25 x 32 ins / 64 x 81 cm) EUR 1,900. BRUSSELS, 13 May 2003, *Ardennes Landscape under Autumn Mist* (oil on canvas, 66 x 92 ins / 168 x 233 cm) EUR 3,000. LOKEREN, 17 May 2003, *On the Beach* (oil on canvas, 17 x 30 ins / 42 x 75 cm) EUR 9,000. BRUSSELS, 23 Nov 2004, *Valley of Flavion* (oil on canvas, 31 x 43 ins / 80 x 110 cm) EUR 3,200. BRUSSELS, 6 Dec 2004, *Walk by the Lighthouse of Ostende* (oil on canvas, 18 x 26 ins / 45 x 65 cm) EUR 10,000.

FRANÇOIS, Jules Charles Rémy
French, 19th century.
Born 24 December 1809, in Paris; died 16 October 1861, in Neuilly-sur-Seine.
Engraver.

Jules was the brother of Alphonse François. He studied under Henriquel-Dupont and engraved almost without exception in the manner of Paul Delaroche. He was awarded medals in 1847, 1851, 1853 and 1859 and was made a Chevalier of the Légion d'Honneur in 1859.

FRANÇOIS, Lambert
French, 17th century.
Active in Auxerre.
Sculptor.

Lambert François worked for the church in Beine.

FRANÇOIS, Léon
French, 20th century.
Painter. Landscapes.

Léon François exhibited at the Salon des Indépendants from 1925.

FRANÇOIS, Louis
French, 16th century.
Portrait artist.
Fontainebleau School.

Louis François was working at Fontainebleau in 1548.

FRANÇOIS, Louis
French, 17th century.
Active in Paris c. 1680.
Painter, sculptor, engraver, illuminator.

FRANÇOIS, Louis, called François the Elder
French, 17th - 18th century.
Sculptor.
From 1671 to 1711, Louis François produced a series of works for Versailles, Clagny, Marly, Chantilly and the church at Invalides.

FRANÇOIS, Louis Charles
French, 18th century.
Active in Paris in 1756.
Painter, sculptor.

FRANÇOIS, Louise Jeanne
French, 20th century.
Born in the Somme.
Painter.
Louise François studied under Sabatté. She became a member of the Salon des Artistes Français in 1927.

FRANÇOIS, Luc
French, 20th century.
Born 1936, in St-Laurent-du-Maroni, French Guiana.
Painter. Landscapes.
Luc François studied at the École des Arts Appliquées in Paris and then at the École Blot in Rheims. He painted landscapes of Provence. He exhibited in Paris at the many Salons of which he was a member.
Museums and Galleries:
Narbonne (MAH): *The Road and Pines at Grambois in the Vaucluse; Landscape at Ménerbes, Vaucluse.*

FRANÇOIS, Lucas Elias. See **FRANCHOYS**

FRANÇOIS, Marcel
French, 20th century.
Born 18 March 1908, in Paris; died 1987.
Painter. Landscapes, seascapes, still-lifes, flowers.
Marcel François studied at the École des Arts Décoratifs in Paris. He painted various regions of France including Finistère, Morbihan and the Gironde. He exhibited at most of the annual Paris Salons.
Auction records:
Paris, 10 Feb 1988, *Arcachon* (oil on canvas, 18 x 24 ins / 46 x 61 cm) FRF 2,000. Paris, 17 June 1988, *Doëlan* (oil on canvas, 15 x 18 ins / 38 x 46 cm) FRF 1,600; *Fruit Bowl* (oil on canvas, 18 x 22 ins / 46 x 55 cm) FRF 1,600.

FRANÇOIS, Marie Catherine
Maiden name: Frédou
French, 18th century.
Born c. 1712; died 10 April 1773, in Paris.
Painter. Portraits.
Marie François was the wife of Jean-Charles.

FRANÇOIS, Martin
French, 15th - 16th century.
Born to a family originally from Tours; died c. 1527.
Sculptor, architect.
Martin François was the brother of Bastien and Jacquet François. In 1490, he was summoned to Amboise to repair the bridge over the Loire and to build a new one over the Amasse. He worked with his brother Bastien, building the following structures: the north bell tower of Tours Cathedral (1507); the cloister of the church of St-Martin (1509); the fountain at Beaune-Semblançay (1510). In 1519, with the master of works, Gatien François (perhaps another brother), he worked on the church of the Minims at Plessis-lès-Tours. Finally, in 1524 and on his own, he built the church of Marchenoir.

FRANÇOIS, Michel
Belgian, 20th - 21st century.
Born 1956, in St-Trond (Limburg).
Sculptor, installation artist.
Michel François is primarily concerned with creating an emotional experience; in his initial works *Apartment to Let* and *Spider*, he presented two situations and put the emphasis on the paradox and inherent contradictions in each situation by keeping some everyday objects rather than others. Since then, he has continued his work, subjecting his creations to a game of division, either by presenting them separately, as autonomous objects, or by integrating them into a pre-existing installation. Thus, the installation *Plums II* comprises different pieces fixed to the wall that can be bought individually, including a hat, a ball of intertwined rubber bands and a pullover hanging from a cement sphere.

Each installation, which relies on walls and floors for its structure, aims to suggest that forms are primarily forces, but are also a movement which carries and touches. He also produces black and white photographs, which, as in the sculptures, retain everyday objects and forms.

He has participated in many group exhibitions, including: the museum of Brussels; the Espace Nord, Liège; the MUKHA (museum of modern art), Antwerp; the Galerie Maeght, Paris; Salon de Montrouge; Documenta, Kassel; the Palais des Beaux-Arts, Brussels; 2002, *Coconut Tour*, the Centre Régional d'Art Contemporain, Sète, Languedoc-Roussillon. He also exhibits his sculpture-performances in many solo shows: since 1986, regularly at the Galerie Isy Brachot, Brussels; 1996: the Fonds Régional d'Art Contemporain (regional contemporary art collection), Limoges; the Musée d'Art Moderne, Brussels; the Museum Voor Hendendaagse, Ghent; 1997, Tecla Sala, the contemporary art centre, Barcelona; 1998, the Espace Départemental d'Art Contemporain Cimaise et Portique, Albi; 1999, the Venice Biennale, where he represented Belgium; the Palais des Beaux-Arts, Charleroi.
Bibliography:
Marcelis, Bernard, '*Michel François*' in *Art Press* n° 178, periodical, Paris, March 1993.
Museums and Galleries:
Limoges (FRAC Limousin): *Casablanca* (1993, video); *Untitled* (1995) - Rheims (FRAC Champagne-Ardenne).

FRANÇOIS, Nicolas
French, 18th century.
Active in Paris in 1766.
Painter, sculptor.

FRANÇOIS, Nicolas Le. See **LE FRANCOIS**

FRANÇOIS, Pierre
French, 18th century.
Active in Paris in 1765.
Sculptor.

FRANÇOIS, Pierre Joseph Célestin
Belgian, 18th - 19th century.
Born 1759, in Namur; died 1851.
Painter, miniaturist, decorative artist. History painting, mythological subjects, portraits, genre scenes, landscapes. Murals.
Pierre Joseph Célestin François was a pupil of Andreas Cornelis Lens. He worked in France, Italy and Germany before settling in Belgium. He was successively a professor in the academies of Brussels, Charleroi and Antwerp.

He chiefly executed large-format paintings of historical and mythological subjects, and he also had a hand in the embellishment of churches in Ghent, Brussels, Mons and Charleroi.
Museums and Galleries:
Nancy: *Portrait of Abbé Grégoire.*
Auction records:
Versailles, 19 May 1974, *The Judgement of Paris; Venus Presenting Arms to Aeneas; Venus and Aeneas* (three oils on canvas, 110 x 110¼ ins / 279 x 280 cm) FRF 20,400. Brus-

SELS, 25 Nov 1981, *Track in the Forest of Soignes* (oil on canvas, 36 1/4 x 28 3/4 ins / 92 x 73 cm) BEF 20,000. BRUSSELS, 28 March 1984, *Young Women on the Pier* (oil on canvas, 35 1/2 x 47 1/4 ins / 90 x 120 cm) BEF 160,000. LOKEREN, 21 Feb 1987, *Narcissus* (oil on panel, 19 3/4 x 15 ins / 50 x 38 cm) BEF 120,000. BRUSSELS, 28 Oct 1987, *Young Women and Little Girls on a Break-water* (oil on canvas, 66 1/4 x 91 ins / 168 x 231 cm) BEF 450,000. NEW YORK, 24 May 1988, *Coriolanus* (oil on panel, 28 1/2 x 22 1/4 ins / 72.4 x 56.5 cm) USD 25,300. LONDON, 21 June 1991, *The Death of Marcus Curtius* (oil on panel, 26 x 20 ins / 66 x 51 cm) GBP 7,150. LOKEREN, 7 Oct 1995, *Brawl* (1842, oil on panel, 24 1/2 x 31 ins / 62.5 x 78.5 cm) BEF 440,000. NEW YORK, 3 Nov 1999, *Death of Marcus Curtius* (oil on panel, 26 x 20 ins / 67 x 51 cm) USD 12,000. BRUSSELS, 8 May 2001, *Teverone Landscape* (oil on panel, 19 x 26 ins / 49 x 66 cm) BEF 260,000. PARIS, 26 June 2002, *Jupiter and the Goat Amalthea* (oil on canvas, 41 x 31 ins / 103 x 80 cm) EUR 4,300.

FRANÇOIS, Raymond
French, 20th century.
Born in Charleville.
Painter. Genre scenes.

Raymond François exhibited from 1932, showing café and dancehall scenes at the Salon des Artistes Indépendants in Paris.

AUCTION RECORDS:
LYONS, 1 Dec 1987, *The Champs Élysées* (oil on canvas, 18 x 22 ins / 46 x 55 cm) FRF 9,000. PARIS, 20 Nov 1994, *Night Club in Montmartre* (oil on canvas, 18 x 22 ins / 46 x 55 cm) FRF 15,500.

FRANÇOIS, Simon, called le Petit François
French, 17th century.
Born 3 December 1606, in Tours; died 22 May 1671, in Paris.
Painter, engraver.

We know that Simon François was under the patronage of the queen and cardinal Richelieu. He travelled to Italy, to Rome from 1632 to 1636, and became a friend of Guido Reni, who did his portrait. He was court painter and accepted as a member of the academy on 7 August 1653.One of his works is the *Portrait of the Dauphin, Louis XIV*. His signature was a monogram formed from the letters 'F' and 'S', intertwined.Thematic collective exhibitions have included: in 2002, *Les Mystérieux du XVIIe siècle. Une enquête au cabinet d'art graphique* (*Mysteries of the 17th century: An Exploration of the Graphic Art Collection*), held at the Musée des Beaux-Arts in Nancy. This was an exhibition of forgotten artists of the 17th century, whose work was known or indicated only by their prints or by prints in their style.

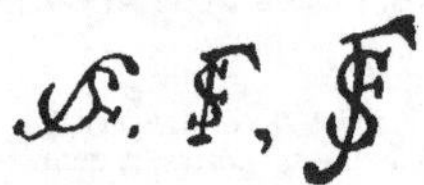

BIBLIOGRAPHY:
Paul, Céline/Harent, Sophie, '*Les Mystérieux du XVIIe siècle. Une enquête au cabinet d'art graphique*' *coll. Lire en filigrane*, Musée des Beaux-Arts, Nancy, 2002.

FRANÇOIS, Solange
Belgian, 20th century.
Born 1938.
Painter.

Solange François studied at the Leonardo da Vinci art school at the American University of Cairo and under Paul Delvaux at the College of La Cambre, and was awarded the Godecharle Prize in 1961.

FRANÇOIS, Théodore
French, 19th century.
Born 1837, in Paris.
Painter.

Théodore François was a pupil of Cornu. He submitted a *Chailly Plain* and a *Corner of the Atelier* to the 1868 Salon, followed by a *Entraigues Stream* in 1869.

FRANÇOIS, Thierry
French, 20th century.
Sculptor. Masks.

Between 1978 and 1982, Thierry François studied sculpture and mask work with Cyrilles Dives. He runs a sculpture and theatrical mask studio for the Ville de Paris. He is also a performer and director. He creates spirit-like, wood-fibre masks in many different forms.

FRANÇOIS ALLEMAND, or the German
French, 15th century.
Active in Toul (Meurthe-et-Moselle).
Glass painter.

In 1470, this artist worked at Mirecourt in the Vosges on a window in the church of the convent of St Francis. In 1485, in Nancy, he painted a reading desk for the duchess of Lorraine.

FRANÇOIS D'ORLEANS. See **ORLÉANS François**

FRANÇOIS DE HÉDINCOURT
French, 14th century.
Active at the beginning of the 14th century.
Sculptor.

François de Hédincourt worked with his brother Raoul on the tomb of Robert of Artois at the abbey of St-Denis.

FRANÇOIS-AUBERT, Marcel
French, 20th century.
Born in Paris.
Painter. Landscapes, portraits.

Marcel François-Aubert studied under Montézin. From 1924 he exhibited in Paris at the Salon des Artistes Français, receiving the silver medal and the Prix de la Savoie in 1928.

FRANÇOIS-CURILLON
French, 19th century.
Born in Tournus (Saône-et-Loire).
Sculptor.

François-Curillon received an honourable mention in 1902.

FRANÇOIS-DEDIEU, Marie
French, 20th century.
Born in Auma, Algeria.
Painter. Still-lifes, flowers.

Marie François-Dedieu exhibited at the Salon des Artistes Indépendants in Paris from 1935.

FRANÇOIS-LOUBENS, Emma
French, 20th century.
Painter.

Emma François-Loubens exhibited in Paris at the Salon des Artistes Français and became a member of the Society in 1919.

FRANÇOIS-MOREAU, Hippolyte.
See **MOREAU François**

FRANCOLIN, Robert
French, 20th century.
Painter.

Robert Francolin exhibited in Paris at the Salon des Tuileries and the Salon d'Automne from 1926.

FRANCON DE KEMPE
Flemish School, 14th century.
Painter.

This artist is probably the same person as Francon of Endout, mentioned by Siret as being in Mechelen in around 1386.

FRANCONI, Paolo
Italian, 18th century.
Active in Naples.
Painter.
Paolo Franconi was a pupil of Solimena.

FRANCONIO, Juan Bautista
Spanish, 17th century.
Active in Seville c. 1600.
Sculptor, goldsmith.

FRANCONVILLE, Jeanne
French, 20th century.
Painter.
Jeanne Franconville exhibited in Paris at the Salon des Artistes Français, of which she became a member in 1909.

FRANCONVILLE, Moricaud
French, 18th century.
Engraver.
Moricaud Franconville produced some caricatures.

FRANCOS, L.
French, 19th century.
Active in Paris c. 1879.
Painter. Genre scenes.
MUSEUMS AND GALLERIES:
STRASBOURG: *Spanish Horseman.*

FRANCOVICH, A.
French, 19th - 20th century.
Active in Paris.
Painter.
A. Francovich was awarded a major prize at the Exposition Universelle in Paris in 1900.

FRANCQUART, Gilbert
French, 17th century.
Active in Paris in 1657.
Painter, sculptor.

FRANCQUART, Jacques
Flemish, 17th century.
Born 1577, in Brussels; died 1651, in Brussels.
Painter. History painting, portraits.
Flemish School.
After having travelled to Italy, Jacques Francquart returned to Brussels where he was appointed painter and architect to the governor of Flanders. He executed paintings and drawings for the church of the Jesuits in Brussels.

FRANCQUEVILLE, Jean de
French, 20th century.
Painter.
Jean de Francqueville lived in Amiens. He exhibited in Paris at the Salon des Artistes Français and became a member of the Société in 1909.

FRANCQUIN
French, 18th century.
Active in Toulon c. 1700.
Painter.
Francquin went to Rome in 1699.

FRANCUCCI, Francesco
Italian, 17th century.
Active in San Severino, Madrid and Rome.
Sculptor.

FRANCUCCI, Innocenzo di Pietro, called Innocenzo da Imola
Italian, 16th century.
Born c. 1494, in Imola; died c. 1550, in Bologna.
Painter. Religious subjects, allegorical subjects.
Bolognese School.
Francucci lived mainly in Bologna. In 1508, he joined the school run by Francesco Francia but, according to Malvasia, he then went off to work in Florence under Mariotto Albertinelli. According to Vasari, he died of a pestilential fever.

He seems to have made a very careful study of the works of Andrea del Sarto, because his style is very close to that of this artist (and also to that of Fra Bartolommeo). Many works by Francucci are owned by the churches of Bologna. Some of them are so similar to the work of Raphael in their simplicity and beauty that they could have been based on Raphael's drawings. His works include a *Christ Crucified with Saints* (1549), kept in the church of S Salvatore.

MUSEUMS AND GALLERIES:
AVIGNON: *Holy Family* - BERGAMO: *Mystical Marriage of St Catherine* - BERLIN: *Virgin and Child with Two Saints* - BOLOGNA (Pinacoteca Nazionale): *The Madonna in Glory with Saints* - CHAMBÉRY (MBA): *The Virgin Appearing to a Carthusian Monk* - GENEVA: *Angel Playing a Tambourine; Angel Playing a Flageolet; Faith; Hope* - KARLSRUHE: *Virgin and Child* - LISBON: *Lot; Baptism of the Queen of Ethiopia* - MOSCOW (Rumiantsev Mus.): *Betrothal of St Catherine* - MUNICH: *The Virgin and Infant Jesus in a Cloud of Angels* - ROME (Gal. Colonna): *Holy Family with St Francis* - ROME (Mus. e Gal. Borghese): *The Virgin Mary, Jesus, St Jerome and St Anthony; The Marriage of St Catherine to Jesus* - ST PETERSBURG: *Virgin and Child with Saints.*

AUCTION RECORDS:
PARIS, 1852, *Holy Family,* FRF 1,950. PARIS, 1870, *Mystical Marriage of St Catherine,* FRF 1,520; *The Virgin Mary and Jesus,* FRF 1,500. PARIS, 2 Feb 1874, *St Catherine Receiving Jesus from the Hands of the Virgin Mary,* FRF 7,100. LONDON, 1 Feb 1924, *Holy Family,* GBP 15. LONDON, 23 May 1924, *Adoration of the Shepherds,* GBP 50. LONDON, 16 Jan 1925, *Mystical Marriage of St Catherine,* GBP 8. LONDON, 21 Oct 1925, *St Veronica,* GBP 10. LONDON, 12 Feb 1926, *Holy Family,* GBP 33. LONDON, 26 March 1926, *Madonna and Child,* GBP 42. LONDON, 22 Dec 1927, *The Virgin and Child,* GBP 73. LONDON, 15 June 1928, *Madonna and Child,* GBP 33. LONDON, 12 July 1929, *The Virgin and Child,* GBP 63. NEW YORK, 25 and 26 March 1931, *The Virgin and Child,* USD 550. LUCERNE, 28 Nov 1964, *Birth of the Virgin,* CHF 11,500. LONDON, 10 July 1979, *The Magi* (red heightened with white gouache, 10 1/4 x 17 ins / 26 x 42.3 cm) GBP 3,000. MILAN, 18 March 1982, *Head of Churchman* (black chalk, 11 1/2 x 9 ins / 29.5 x 22 cm) ITL 5,500,000. LONDON, 4 April 1984, *Portrait of a Young Woman* (oil on panel, 23 3/4 x 17 1/2 ins / 60.2 x 44.5 cm) GBP 10,500. ZURICH, 29 Nov 1985, *Mystical Marriage of St Catherine* (tempera/panel, 34 3/4 x 27 ins / 88.5 x 68.5 cm) CHF 34,000. NEW YORK, 13 Oct 1989, *Holy Family with St John the Baptist and St Elizabeth* (oil on panel, 24 1/2 x 19 ins / 62.5 x 48 cm) USD 19,800. NEW YORK, 1 June 1990, *Holy Family with St John the Baptist and St Elizabeth* (oil on panel, 36 1/2 x 28 1/2 ins / 92.5 x 72.5 cm) USD 18,700. MILAN, 3 Dec 1992, *Holy Family with St John* (oil on panel, 29 1/2 x 22 3/4 ins / 75 x 58 cm) ITL 22,600,000. NEW YORK, 19 May 1993, *Virgin and Child with St John the Baptist, St Jerome and St Francis* (oil on panel, 37 3/4 x 29 1/2 ins / 95.9 x 75 cm) USD 81,700. NEW YORK, 12 Jan 1994, *St John the Evangelist* (part of fresco, 27 x 19 1/4 ins / 68.5 x 49 cm, 2 ins/5 cm) USD 27,600. LONDON, 7 Dec 1994, *Marriage of the Virgin* (oil on panel, 87 1/2 x 46 1/2 ins / 222 x 118 cm) GBP 20,700. CASTLECOMER, 14 Oct 1999, *Circumcision* (oil on panel, 5 x 12 ins / 12 x 31 cm) IEP 5,000. MILAN, 31 May 2000, *Madonna and Child, Sts Anna, Jerome and Francis* (oil on panel, 35 x 28 ins / 90 x 71 cm) ITL 48,000,000. LONDON, 1 Nov 2001, *Madonna and Child with the Infant St John the Baptist and Sts Jerome and Francis* (oil

on panel, 38 x 30 ins / 96 x 75 cm) GBP 20,000. DUBLIN, 26 Nov 2003, *Circumcision* (oil on panel, predella, 5 x 12 ins / 12 x 31 cm) EUR 2,000.

FRANDSEN DE SCHOMBERG, Théodore Émile (Baron)
French, 20th century.
Born 14 June 1902, in Hénin-Liétard (Pas-de-Calais), now Hénin-Beaumont; died 11 April 1969, in Valbonne (Alpes-Maritime).
Painter, sculptor, potter. Religious subjects, figures, nudes, scenes with figures, still-lifes, flowers.

Of Franco-Danish parentage, Théodore Émile Frandsen de Schomberg was self-taught in the fine arts, and saw active service during World War II. He developed the concept of 'tensism' as a way of approaching artistic creation through 'introspective psychology'. He left an eclectic body of work, alternating religious subjects with a celebration of woman. He exhibited at the Chapelle des Pénitents Noirs in Valbonne.

FRANGEPAN, Torquat Aleksandr Julius
Croat, 17th century.
Painter, draughtsman, engraver.

Was of Croatian origin.

FRANGES-MIKHANOVIC, Robert
Serb, 19th - 20th century.
Born 2 October 1872, in Sremska Mitrovica.
Sculptor.

Robert Franges lived and worked in Zagreb. In 1900 he won the gold medal at the Exposition Universelle in Paris.

FRANGIAMORE, Salvatore
British, 19th century.
Born 1853; died 1915.
Painter. Genre scenes.

Salvatore Frangiamore lived and worked in London and painted genre compositions typical of the turn of the century.

AUCTION RECORDS:
LONDON, 18 May 1925, *Favourite Page,* GBP 16. LONDON, 16 March 1945, *Love Song,* GBP 35. PARIS, 28 Feb 1951, *Stubborn Chambermaid,* FRF 40,000. LONDON, 30 July 1982, *The Presentation* (1897, oil on canvas, 22 x 33 1/2 ins / 55.9 x 85 cm) GBP 1,500. LONDON, 12 Oct 1984, *Rebuff* (oil on canvas, 24 1/4 x 19 3/4 ins / 61.5 x 50.2 cm) GBP 2,200. LONDON, 27 Nov 1985, *Recital for a Cardinal* (1908, oil on canvas, 20 1/2 x 28 1/2 ins / 52 x 72.5 cm) GBP 4,500. NEW YORK, 25 Feb 1988, *Flowers for the Cardinal* (oil on canvas, 22 x 29 1/2 ins / 55 x 75.2 cm) USD 18,700. NEW YORK, 25 May 1988, *Isabelle Orsini Listening to Tasso's Sons* (oil on canvas, 24 1/4 x 19 3/4 ins / 61.9 x 50.2 cm) USD 15,400. LONDON, 6 Oct 1989, *A Good Book* (oil on canvas, 27 x 21 1/2 ins / 68.5 x 54.5 cm) GBP 4,620. NEW YORK, 23 May 1991, *Unveiling in the Atelier* (oil on canvas/card, 24 1/2 x 19 3/4 ins / 62.2 x 50.2 cm) USD 13,200. NEW YORK, 19 Feb 1992, *Unveiling in the Atelier* (oil on canvas/card, 24 1/2 x 19 3/4 ins / 62.2 x 50.2 cm) USD 14,300. MILAN, 9 Nov 1993, *Children in Traditional Costume at the Trevi Fountain, Rome* (oil on canvas, 32 1/2 x 22 ins / 82.5 x 55 cm) ITL 19,550,000. LONDON, 22 Feb 1995, *Arab Fiddler* (watercolour, 26 3/4 x 19 1/4 ins / 68 x 49 cm) GBP 1,782.

FRANGIPANE, Niccolo
Italian, 16th century.
Born 1550 or 1555, in Tarcento; died 1600, in Tarcento.
Painter. Religious subjects, mythological subjects, genre scenes.

Frangipane painted a very large number of altar paintings, but was more successful with mythological subjects. There is an *Assumption* by him in the Church of the Conventuals in Rimini, while the church of S Bartolommeo in Padua owns an attractive *St Francis,* dated 1588, and S Stefano in Pesaro has an altarpiece. It would seem that a second painter of the same name who was also active at this time was undoubtedly this artist's father.

MUSEUMS AND GALLERIES:
ANGERS: *Four Heads Laughing at the Sight of a Cat* - ROME (Palazzo Doria Pamphili): *Jesus and Veronica.*

AUCTION RECORDS:
ROME, 21 Nov 1989, *Shepherd with a Flute* (oil on canvas, 21 3/4 x 18 1/2 ins / 55.5 x 47 cm) ITL 18,500,000. LONDON, 8 July 1992, *Ecce Homo* (oil on canvas, 38 1/4 x 47 ins / 97.2 x 119.2 cm) GBP 6,600. NEW YORK, 16 May 1996, *Christ Bearing the Cross* (1574, oil on panel, 21 x 17 3/4 ins / 53.3 x 45.1 cm) USD 14,950. MILAN, 19 May 1999, *Judgement of Solomon. Massacre of the Innocents* (1596/1595, oil on canvas, a pair, 36 x 50 ins / 91 x 126 cm) ITL 56,000,000. MADRID, 5 June 2000, *Ecce Homo* (1574, oil on canvas, 16 x 16 ins / 40 x 40 cm) ESP 3,800,000.

FRANK. See also **FRANCK**

FRANK, A. C.
German, 19th century.
Active in Hamburg c. 1826.
Lithographer.

A. C. Frank's works include a portrait of the Dane *Urban Jürgensen* in the style of C. Homeman, the frontispiece of the *Astronomical News* by Schumacher and an *Ecce Homo* in the style of Dolci.

FRANK, Bena V.
American, 20th century.
Born 31 May 1900, in Norfolk; died 1984.
Painter, teacher.

Bena V. Frank was a pupil at the Art Students League, New York.

FRANK, Bernhard
German, 18th - 19th century.
Born 1770, in Eltingen; died 29 November 1836, in Stuttgart.
Sculptor.

Bernhard Frank was a pupil of the Karlsschule in Stuttgart and was given the title of court sculptor. He is mainly known for a medallion portrait of Schiller in Weimar in 1884. Also attributed to him is a high relief in lead on the tomb of Count F. L. von Sponeck and his wife in the sacristy of the parish church of Winterbach.

FRANK, Caroline
German, 18th century.
Active in Berlin.
Painter.

Caroline Frank exhibited portraits at the Berlin academy from 1787 to 1791.

FRANK, Caspar
Polish, 16th century.
Active in Cracow in 1599.
Painter.

FRANK, Christoph
German, 17th century.
Sculptor. Wood.

Christoph Frank was active in Spire from 1621 to 1635, where two richly carved church cupboards by him can be found in the town's history museum.

FRANK, Christoph
German, 17th century.
Active in Kaufbeuren.
Painter.

Paintings depicting the *Apostles* and a *Salvator Mundi* are in the evangelical church of Kaufbeuren.

MUSEUMS AND GALLERIES:
NUREMBERG (Ebner): *Death in the Rich Man's Home.*

FRANK, Christoph
Austrian, 19th century.
Born c. 1787, in Eger; died 1822, in Vienna.
Painter, miniaturist. Portraits.

Christoph Frank studied at the Prague academy from the age of 17 and worked in Vienna. Attributed to him are the portraits of the occulist *G. J. Beer* and the actor *F. Raimund* engraved by J. Passira. His output also includes two miniature portraits of women in a Viennese collection.

FRANK, Daniel
Swiss, 16th - 17th century.
Born 1573, in St Gall.
Painter.

Daniel Frank is known for a large *Portrait of Klaus Gugger* in the town museum in St Gall. He seems to have left his home town some time after 1615.

FRANK, Franciscus
German, 16th century.
Painter. History painting.

In the period around 1563, when we know that this artist was living, the influence of Dutch art was particularly evident. The museum in Hamburg has one of his paintings, showing *Christ Carrying the Cross*, a work reminiscent of a painting of the same subject by Pieter Aertsen, now in Berlin. The main difference is that Frank's palette is richer.

FRANK, Franz
German, 20th century.
Born 7 April 1897, in Kirchheim; died 1 April 1986, in Marburg.
Painter, draughtsman, engraver, lithographer, illustrator. Landscapes, still-lifes.

Franz Frank graduated with a degree in art history and went on to study under Arnold Waldschmidt and Robert Breyer at the fine arts academy in Stuttgart. He forged a close friendship with Eduard Reinacher. In 1933, he refused a post as a lecturer offered him by the Nazi authorities. He served in the army during World War II, surviving the conflict despite being seriously wounded. From 1945 he travelled extensively, visiting Italy, Switzerland, Greece and Ibiza.

Frank belongs to the generation of painters that emerged in the 1920s and is only now being rediscovered. Collectively, their style has been described by one critic (Dr Rainer Zimmermann) as 'Realist-Expressionist', a term which alludes to their attempts to deploy Expressionist techniques to develop a more realistic and picturesque post-Cézanne approach to their work. Not surprisingly, Frank's body of work betrays the influence of Emil Nolde and, even more, of Lovis Corinth. Before fully espousing this new aesthetic, however, Frank painted from 1926 in a more gritty, Realist style, influenced by the time he lived in a working-class district in Dresden. Some of his work from around this period was specifically noted by Otto Dix. Frank also painted an 'apocalypse' series which evoked the rising tide of Nazism. His later work is more abstract. In total, Frank produced something approaching 1,500 paintings. He also illustrated a number of popular works of fiction, including *Malli die Gärtnerin* (*Mali the Gardener*); *Kater Jaule* (*Jaule the Tomcat*); and *Die Hofkirchweih* (*The Court Chapel*).

Frank exhibited within the framework of the Stuttgart New Secession in the 1920s. His final exhibition under the Nazi regime was in 1936. After the war, however, his work again began to appear at solo exhibitions and in retrospectives, notably in 1982 and 1987 at the University Museum in Marburg, in Berlin (1988), and in 1997, when an exhibition of his engravings was held in his native Kirchheim.

Bibliography:

Zimmermann, Rainer, *Franz Frank: Leben und Werk des Malers*, Klinkhardt & Biermann, Munich, 1985. Zimmermann, Rainer, *Franz Frank, Druckgraphik: Werkverzeichnis der Radierungen und Lithographien*, catalogue raisonné, Hirmer, Munich, 1994. Friederich, Matthias, *Franz Frank, das malerische Werk*, Marburger Universitätsmuseum für Kunst und Kulturgeschichte, Marburg, 1997.

Museums and Galleries:

Böblingen (Städtische Galerie) - Darmstadt (Hessisches Landesmus.) - Dresden (Staatliche Kunstsammlungen) - Hausen ob Verena (Kunststiftung Hohenkarpfen) - Kisslegg (Mus. Expressiver Realismus, Neues Shloss) - Marburg (Universitäts-Museum für Bildende Kunst).

Auction records:

Cologne, 27 March 1987, *Garden in Bloom* (1950, oil on canvas, 31 x 25 1/2 ins / 78.5 x 65 cm) DEM 11,000.

FRANK, Franz Friedrich. See **FRANCK**

FRANK, Frigyes. See **FRANCK**

FRANK, Gerald A.
American, 20th century.
Born 1888, in Chicago.
Painter.

Gerald A. Frank belonged to many art societies.

Auction records:

New York, 2 June 1982, *Revelry Reflected in a Pool* (1925, oil on board, 40 1/4 x 59 3/4 ins / 102 x 152 cm) USD 700.

FRANK, Gustav
Czech, 19th century.
Born 14 September 1859, in Vlasim.
Painter, draughtsman.

Gustav Frank studied painting at the Akademie der Bildenden Künste in Vienna, and trained under J. Sonnenleiter. He worked mostly as a portrait painter and as an illustrator for the *Art Treasures of Italy* by C. Von Lützow, and for *The Austro-Hungarian Monarchy in Words and Pictures*, and other works. He engraved and etched many portraits. In 1890 he was invited to work for the state publishers in St Petersburg, and he became its director. Also in St Petersburg, he produced etched portraits, including those of President Felix Faure, the writer Leo Tolstoy and the actress Eleonora Duse. The last two portraits were from works by Ilya Repin.

FRANK, Gustav
German, 19th century.
Active in Oldenburg c. 1860.
Lithographer.

Gustav Frank executed a series of views of German towns: Breslau, Dessau, Hamburg, Leipzig and Oldenburg.

FRANK, Hans and Leo
Austrian, 20th century.
Born 13 May 1884, in Vienna; Leo died in 1959.
Painters, engravers (wood), draughtsmen. Portraits, landscapes, still-lifes, animals, birds, flowers.

Hans and Leo Frank were twin brothers who both studied at the Akademie für Angewandte Kunst in Vienna and went on to complete their formal education at the Vienna Akademie der Bildenden Künste. They produced numerous drawings and paintings, but Hans Frank is noted also for his coloured woodcut engravings of birds and animals of the forest and, in particular, for his *Portrait of a Young Girl*.

Auction records:

Vienna, 16 Sept 1981, *Portrait of a Young Girl* (oil on card, 22 x 18 3/4 ins / 55 x 47.5 cm) ATS 6,000. Vienna, 10 April 1984, *Vase of Flowers* (oil on panel, 30 1/4 x 20 ins / 77 x 51 cm) ATS 20,000. London, 11 Feb 1994, *Rabbit in the Dandelion Patch* (1910, oil on card, diam. 13 1/2 ins / 34.3 cm) GBP 2,875. Vienna, 1 March 2000, *View of Maria Worth, Karnten* (1943, tempera on paper/board, 19 x 25 ins / 48 x 63 cm) ATS 32,000. Vienna, 20 Sept 2000, *Gars am Kamp* (1941, oil on card, 28 x 35 ins / 71 x 90 cm) ATS 45,000. Vienna, 5 March 2002, *Lady's Slipper and Woodruff* (oil on paper/board, 13 x 9 ins / 33 x 24 cm) EUR 1,900. Vienna, 21 April 2004, *Landscape* (oil on card, 11 x 14 ins / 29 x 35 cm) EUR 1,900. MUNICH, 25 June 2004, *Vienna* (1940, oil on canvas, 39 x 51 ins / 100 x 130 cm) EUR 10,500.

FRANK, Hans Heinrich
German, 18th century.
Born 1738.
Painter. Portraits.
Cited by Siret.

FRANK, Heinrich Friedrich
German, 17th century.
Sculptor.
Heinrich Friedrich Frank worked on the interior decoration of the great hall of Bayreuth Castle around 1626.

FRANK, Hémery
Flemish School, 16th century.
Active in Antwerp.
Painter, illuminator.
Hémery Frank is mentioned in Tours in 1522 in relation to a contract for the painting of several pictures.

FRANK, Henri. See **FRANCK**

FRANK, Jane
American, 20th century.
Painter.
Jane Frank's painting is abstract, but conveys something of landscape seen from the air. She has exhibited in the USA, Paris and London since 1958.

FRANK, Johann, or Franck de Langraffen
Austrian, 17th century.
Active in Vienna.
Engraver.
Johann Frank's output includes the frontispiece of a work by J. Ch. Frölich von Frölichsburg, *Nemesis Romano-Austriaco-Tirolensis* and nine allegorical engravings on the subject of the marriage of the Emperor Francis I of Austria to Amalia of Brunswick. Copies are held in the engravings exhibition room in Munich.
MUSEUMS AND GALLERIES:
MUNICH (Staatliche Graphische Sammlung).

FRANK, Johann Andreas Joseph, or Franke, or Francke
German, 18th century.
Born 24 March 1756, in Dresden; died 25 September 1804, in Dresden.
Miniaturist.
Johann Frank studied in Dresden and was represented, mainly with miniature portraits, in the exhibitions of its academy from 1773 to 1791. During one period he made copies of paintings in the Dresden Gallery such as *Mary Magdalene Repents* by Batoni and *Chaste Joseph* by Cignani. He also copied paintings by A. Kauffmann, Hutin, Rubens and van Dyck.

FRANK, Johann Jakob
German, 18th century.
Active in Nuremberg.
Miniaturist.

FRANK, Johann Willem. See **FRANCK**

FRANK, Julius
German, 19th - 20th century.
Born 11 April 1826, in Munich; died 1912.
Painter. History painting, genre scenes.
Julius Frank was the son of Michael Sigismond Frank and a pupil of Schraudolph. He lived and worked in Munich.
AUCTION RECORDS:
LONDON, 12 Jan 1942, *Masterstroke*, GBP 6. ENGHIEN-LES-BAINS, 16 Oct 1983, *Oriental Dancer Performing for the Sultan* (oil on canvas, 20 3/4 x 30 1/4 ins / 53 x 77 cm) FRF 41,000.

FRANK, Junko
Japanese, 20th century.
Born 1 August 1930, in Wakayama.
Active in France from 1957.
Painter.
Junko Frank studied at the Tokyo University of Fine Arts and went to France in 1957. She exhibited in Paris at the Salon d'Automne, of which she became a member in 1961. In her paintings, she creates an imaginary world with plant-like overtones, sometimes incorporating stones, fruit and vegetables.

FRANK, Leo. See **FRANK Hans** and **Leo**

FRANK, Lorenz
Austrian, 18th century.
Born to a family originally from Burgeis (the Tyrol).
Sculptor.
Lorenz Frank entered the academy in Vienna in 1771 and gained a prize there in 1787.

FRANK, Lucien
Belgian, 19th century.
Born 1857, in Brussels; died 1920, in Ohain.
Painter, pastellist. Landscapes, landscapes with figures, urban landscapes, village views, still-lifes.
Lucien Frank probably studied in Paris, and worked in Brussels and Paris where from 1886 onwards he exhibited small Impressionist landscapes and views of French and Flemish towns.

L. Frank

MUSEUMS AND GALLERIES:
BRUSSELS: *April* - PARIS (MAM): two paintings.
AUCTION RECORDS:
PARIS, 27-28 June 1927, *Vase of Flowers and an Orange*, FRF 100. PARIS, 10 May 1944, *Sunset on the Sea*, FRF 5,000. BRUSSELS, 4 May 1976, *Spring Landscape* (oil on canvas, 17 3/4 x 25 1/2 ins / 45 x 65 cm) BEF 22,000. BRUSSELS, 28 Oct 1981, *April Evening on the Pond* (oil on canvas, 24 3/4 x 17 1/4 ins / 63 x 44 cm) BEF 42,000. ANTWERP, 27 April 1982, *Fisherman near the Pond* (1905, pastel, 35 3/4 x 44 ins / 91 x 112 cm) BEF 45,000. ANTWERP, 26 April 1983, *October in Tervuren* (oil on canvas, 48 x 66 1/2 ins / 121 x 169 cm) BEF 55,000. BRUSSELS, 1 March 1984, *Champs-Elysées* (gouache, 12 1/4 x 15 1/4 ins / 31 x 39 cm) BEF 60,000. BRUSSELS, 8 May 1985, *The Town, Evening* (pastel, 21 1/4 x 15 ins / 54 x 38 cm) BEF 56,000. ANTWERP, 2 Dec 1986, *Sunday in the Woods* (oil on panel, 11 x 14 1/4 ins / 27 x 36 cm) BEF 160,000. BRUSSELS, 25 Nov 1987, *Nocturnal Landscape* (oil on canvas, 29 1/4 x 40 1/2 ins / 74 x 103 cm) BEF 100,000. PARIS, 20 Jan 1988, *Landscape with Figures* (oil on panel, 11 x 14 1/4 ins / 27 x 36 cm) FRF 27,000. LOKEREN, 28 May 1988, *Setting Sun on the Meadows* (oil on panel, 13 x 20 3/4 ins / 33 x 53 cm) BEF 90,000. LOKEREN, 8 Oct 1988, *Twilight* (oil on canvas, 15 3/4 x 12 1/2 ins / 40 x 32 cm) BEF 44,000. BRUSSELS, 27 March 1990, *In the Barcelona Park* (oil on panel, 9 x 12 1/4 ins / 23 x 31 cm) BEF 425,000. BRUSSELS, 12 June 1990, *Flower Market in Barcelona* (oil on panel, 9 x 13 ins / 23 x 33 cm) BEF 260,000. BRUSSELS, 9 Oct 1990, *Itinerant Musicians* (oil on panel, 12 1/4 x 9 ins / 31 x 23 cm) BEF 175,000. AMSTERDAM, 30 Oct 1990, *Figures on the Wharves in Dordrecht* (oil on panel, 14 1/4 x 11 ins / 36 x 27 cm) NLG 3,220. BRUSSELS, 13 Dec 1990, *Promenade* (oil on panel, 12 1/2 x 15 3/4 ins / 32 x 40 cm) BEF 250,800. LOKEREN, 21 March 1992, *Corner of the Main Square of Furnes* (oil on panel, 6 1/4 x 10 ins / 16 x 24.5 cm) BEF 48,000. LOKEREN, 23 May 1992, *Snowy Landscape with a Walker* (oil on panel, 11 x 14 1/4 ins / 27 x 36 cm) BEF 200,000. LOKEREN, 10 Oct 1992, *Entrance of the Beguine Convent of Bruges in the Evening* (mixed media/card, 15 x 18 ins / 38 x 46 cm) BEF 130,000.

AMSTERDAM, 2-3 Nov 1992, *Walk in a Park* (oil on card, 17 3/4 x 14 1/2 ins / 45 x 37 cm) NLG 2,990. LOKEREN, 5 Dec 1992, *Pond* (oil on canvas, 30 x 41 1/2 ins / 76 x 105.5 cm) BEF 140,000. AMSTERDAM, 10 Dec 1992, *On the Quays* (oil on panel, 15 x 18 ins / 38 x 46 cm) NLG 8,625. PARIS, 6 April 1993, *Landscape, Rising Sun* (oil on panel, 5 1/2 x 9 1/4 ins / 14 x 23.5 cm) FRF 4,200. LOKEREN, 9 Oct 1993, *Walkers* (oil on paper, 23 1/2 x 17 1/4 ins / 60 x 44 cm) BEF 80,000. AMSTERDAM, 31 May 1995, *Village* (oil on canvas, 17 1/4 x 22 ins / 44 x 55 cm) NLG 8,024. LOKEREN, 9 Dec 1995, *Boulevard* (gouache, 25 1/4 x 18 1/2 ins / 64 x 47 cm) BEF 130,000. PARIS, 2 June 1997, *Mill, Blue Light* (oil on panel, 8 1/4 x 6 1/4 ins / 21 x 16 cm) FRF 9,500. LOKEREN, 6 Dec 1997, *Pond in the Evening* (oil on canvas, 30 x 41 3/4 ins / 76 x 106 cm) BEF 750,000. LOKEREN, 6 March 1999, *Orchard in Bloom* (oil on canvas, 30 x 52 ins / 77 x 131 cm) BEF 180,000. BRUSSELS, 23 Nov 1999, *Flower Market* (oil on panel, 10 x 14 ins / 26 x 36 cm) BEF 250,000. BRUSSELS, 11 Sept 2000, *Avenue de la Toison d'Or in Winter* (oil on canvas, 34 x 44 ins / 86 x 113 cm) BEF 1,450,000. BRUSSELS, 11 Dec 2000, *Fisherman at Dusk* (oil on canvas, 24 x 33 ins / 61 x 84 cm) BEF 430,000. LOKEREN, 10 March 2001, *Summer Landscape* (oil on canvas, 24 x 33 ins / 60 x 84 cm) BEF 440,000. BRUSSELS, 10 Dec 2001, *Boulevard in the Snow* (oil on canvas, 25 x 33 ins / 63 x 84 cm) BEF 650,000. BRUSSELS, 13 May 2002, *Ships in Harbour* (oil on panel, 27 x 33 ins / 68 x 83 cm) EUR 11,000. BRUSSELS, 13 May 2002, *St Germain des Pres in the Snow with Figures* (oil on canvas, 63 x 102 ins / 160 x 260 cm) EUR 53,000. LOKEREN, 15 March 2003, *Lisiere a Vossem* (oil on canvas, 30 x 41 ins / 75 x 105 cm) EUR 11,000. ANTWERP, 17 March 2003, *Fisherman in a River Landscape before a Village* (oil on canvas, 24 x 33 ins / 60 x 84 cm) EUR 9,000.

FRANK, Magda
Hungarian, 20th century.
Born 20 July 1914, in Cluj.
Active and naturalised in Argentina, also active in France.
Sculptor.

Magda Frank studied at the school of art in Budapest before going to Paris where she was Marcel Gimond's student. She then went to Argentina, where she was naturalised and pursued a dual career as sculptor and teacher. Her abstract sculpture conjures up three-dimensional symbols of totem poles. She took part in the São Paulo Biennale and since she settled in France she featured at numerous exhibitions in Paris including: Salon Comparaisons, Salon des Réalités Nouvelles and Salon de la Jeune Sculpture. She has also been invited to the International Sculpture Exhibitions at the Rodin Museum.

AUCTION RECORDS:
NEW YORK, 27 Feb 1985, *Head* (ceramic, 17 1/4 x 17 x 9 1/4 ins / 43.9 x 43.2 x 23.5 cm) USD 2,600.

FRANK, Mary
British, 20th century.
Born 1933, in London.
Active in the USA.
Sculptor, painter, draughtsman, mixed media. Figures, landscapes.

Mary Frank went to live in New York as a child and during her youth took lessons there under Alfred Van Loeb, Max Beckmann and Hans Hoffmann. In 1940, she graduated from the Children's Professional School. She spent two years in Europe with her first husband, the celebrated photographer Robert Frank. Early in her career Frank began specialising in drawing, making plaster casts and, particularly around 1953, in wood sculpture, often representing imaginary landscapes. Her first sculptures, which were primitive in style, were strongly influenced by Brancusi, Raoul Hague and African art. However, through producing small wax sculptures she came to work in plaster and then, in 1969, in clay, which soon became her medium of choice. Her sculptures, in the Cubist tradition, consist of several pieces placed side by side and extending up to 10 feet (3 metres) in length. She has also made prints of leaves and ferns on damp slabs and, using stamps she produced herself, printed series of small animals and figurines. Frank also makes charcoal drawings, often taking ceramic sculptures as her models as well as little known Expressionist narrative paintings. Frank's work shows an astonishing unity with regard to motifs and themes but is given new life by her own personal experiences. Her figures, whether full bodies or mere sketches, have a powerful sensuality, are essentially feminine and expressive of psychological states. From 1958, she exhibited regularly in New York and from 1968 at the Galerie Zabriskie in Paris.

BIBLIOGRAPHY:
'Mary Frank' in *Zabriskie Gazette* vol. IV n° 2, periodical, Gal. Zabriskie, Paris, spring 1981. Hayden, Herrera, *Mary Frank*, Adams, New York, 1990. Morgan, Robert C., *'Trois stratégies personnelles: Michael Goldberg, Lang, Mary Frank'* in *Art Press* n° 213, periodical, Paris, May 1996.

MUSEUMS AND GALLERIES:
CHICAGO (AI) - NEW HAVEN (AG, Yale University) - NEW YORK (Metropolitan Mus. of Art) - NEW YORK (Whitney Mus. of American Art).

AUCTION RECORDS:
NEW YORK, 19 Oct 1979, *Ghost Dancer* (1972-1973, ceramic, 24 x 12 1/2 x 18 1/2 ins / 61 x 32 x 47 cm) USD 3,000. NEW YORK, 16 Oct 1981, *Untitled* (watercolour, 25 1/2 x 20 ins / 64.7 x 50.7 cm) USD 550. NEW YORK, 12 Nov 1982, *Untitled* (black ink, 17 1/2 x 23 ins / 44.5 x 58.5 cm) USD 400. NEW YORK, 5 May 1987, *Untitled, Woman with Petal Arms* (1981, ceramic in six parts, 8 3/4 x 48 x 31 ins / 22.5 x 122 x 79 cm) USD 9,000. NEW YORK, 5 Oct 1989, *Daphnis* (1979, ceramic in eight parts, 39 x 38 x 5 1/2 ins / 99 x 96.5 x 14 cm) USD 7,150. NEW YORK, 23 Feb 1990, *Series of Head Sections* (1974, oxidised stone, 12 x 10 x 9 ins / 30.5 x 25.4 x 22.9 cm) USD 7,150. NEW YORK, 10 Oct 1990, *Untitled* (terracotta in two parts, en tout 10 x 15 x 13 ins / 25.4 x 38.2 x 33.1 cm) USD 3,850. NEW YORK, 13 Feb 1991, *Valley* (1973, terracotta, 18 x 18 1/2 ins / 45.7 x 47 cm, 2 1/4 x 15 1/2 ins/6 x 39.4 cm) USD 2,200. NEW YORK, 9 May 1992, *Woman-Flower* (1982, terracotta in two parts, 26 1/2 x 17 1/4 x 22 1/2 ins / 67.3 x 43.5 x 57.1 cm) USD 7,150. NEW YORK, 24 Feb 1995, *Woman Walking* (1981, charcoal and black chalk/paper, 25 1/2 x 19 3/4 ins / 64.8 x 50.2 cm) USD 1,495.

FRANK, Melchior
Swiss, 18th century.
Sculptor. Wood.

Melchior Frank collaborated in carving the stalls of the Cistercian Church of St Urban in the canton of Lucerne.

FRANK, Michael Sigismund
German, 18th - 19th century.
Born 1769, in Nuremberg; died 18 January 1847, in Munich.
Painter (including porcelain), glass painter.

Michael Frank worked for the Bavarian court and the Prince of Wallenstein. His works include the stained glass windows of Ratisbonne Cathedral.

FRANK, Peter
Polish, 16th century.
Engraver.

Peter Frank worked as a surveyor to King Stephen Bathory of Poland. In 1579 he published engravings of the siege of Plock and Sokol. He was a Knight of the order of Jelita.

FRANK, Raoul
Austrian, 19th - 20th century.
Born 1 May 1867, in Linz; died 1939.
Painter. Landscapes, seascapes.

Raoul Frank worked successively in Munich, Graz, Berlin, London and Karlsruhe.

Museums and Galleries:
Munich (Pinakothek): *Passing Clouds; Korean Coastline.*
Auction records:
London, 19 March 1980, *Boats on the Danube* (1904, oil on canvas, 26 1/2 x 30 3/4 ins / 67 x 78 cm) GBP 1,000. Vienna, 17 March 1987, *Harbour Scene* (oil on canvas remounted on board, 17 x 21 1/4 ins / 43 x 54 cm) ATS 13,000. Vienna, 15 June 1999, *Angelus, Sailing Ship* (1894, oil on canvas, 24 x 31 ins / 61 x 79 cm) ATS 30,000.

FRANK, Theresia
Swiss, 18th - 19th century.
Born 18th century, in Lucerne; died 18 August 1810, in Lucerne.
Sculptor.

Theresia Frank was the wife and assistant of the sculptor Friedrich Schäfer. She also collaborated with his son (Schäfer Junior). Attributed to her are *William Tell* and *Milkmaid* exhibited in at the Artistic Association in Lucerne in 1889.

FRANK-BOGGS, pseudonym of Boggs, Frank Myers
American, 19th - 20th century.
Born 6 December 1855, in Springfield (Ohio); died 6 August 1926, in Meudon (Hauts-de-Seine), France.
Active and naturalised in France.
Painter, watercolourist, engraver, draughtsman. Urban landscapes, seascapes.

Frank-Boggs was a pupil of Jean-Léon Gérôme at the École des Beaux-Arts in Paris. His generally small drawings are spontaneous and lively, while his many watercolours, which form an important part of his work, are highly nuanced. A lover of Paris, he painted its many views - quays, buildings and the banks of the Seine - as well as French and foreign ports, the lively markets of small towns in La Rochelle, the Netherlands, Belgium and Venice, in pictures with an identifiable style that were attractive to the public. Between 1906 and 1907, he also made etchings.

Frank-Boggs exhibited until the end of his life at the Salon des Artistes Français, where he received several distinctions, including being placed out-of-competition, and was awarded a silver medal at the Exposition Universelle of 1998. In 1885, he exhibited *Rough Sea in Honfleur* in New York, which won him a prize of 2,500 dollars.

Museums and Galleries:
Boston (MFA): *Rough Sea in Honfleur* (c. 1885) - Montreal (MBA): *Morning Seascape* - Mulhouse: *View of Paris* (watercolour) - Nantes (MBA): *Fishing Boats in Trouville* - New York: *On the Thames* (1883) - Niort: *Isigny Harbour.*
Auction records:
Boston, 1883, *Place St-Germain,* FRF 1,500. Paris, 1897, *Isigny,* FRF 200; *Market,* FRF 245. Paris, 1900, *The Thames,* FRF 620. Paris, 13-14 March 1900, *The Thames,* FRF 620. Paris, 1-2 Dec 1902, *The Pont-Marie* (watercolour) FRF 1,800. London, 24 April 1909, *On the River,* GBP 5. London, 14 May 1909, *Fishing Boats at Anchor* (drawing) GBP 8; *In Rotterdam* (drawing) GBP 19. Paris, 1 Dec 1920, *The Pont-Marie* (watercolour) FRF 1,800. Paris, 20 Nov 1922, *The Seine, the Pont des Arts and the Institute, from the Quai Voltaire,* FRF 3,010. Paris, 4 June 1928, *The Écluse de la Monnaie,* FRF 4,000. Paris, 15 Feb 1929, *St-Étienne-du-Mont, Paris* (watercolour) FRF 1,000. Paris, 28 June 1929, *View of Paris,* FRF 3,000. Paris, 16-17 May 1939, *The Place St-Germain-des-Prés,* FRF 1,700. Paris, 5 Nov 1941, *Boats Grounded at the Foot of Cliffs* (watercolour) FRF 700. Paris, 24 Nov 1941, *Sunset at Low Tide* (watercolour) FRF 2,000. Paris, 4 Dec 1941, *Village by the Sea,* FRF 7,800. Paris, 9 March 1942, *Boats at Low Tide, Dieppe,* FRF 12,500. Paris, 20-21 July 1942, *The Tour St-Jacques,* FRF 18,000. Paris, 22 Jan 1943, *The Place de la Concorde,* FRF 26,200. Dordrecht, 27 Jan 1943, *Road* (watercolour) FRF 9,200. Paris, 22 Feb 1943, *Sailing Boats in Harbour,* FRF 27,100. New York, 1 Oct 1943, *The Seine and the Institute* (watercolour) FRF 5,800. New York, 14 Oct 1943, *The Pont-Marie* (1905) USD 450. New York, 14 Oct 1943, *The Pont-Marie* (1905) USD 450. Paris, 20 March 1944, *Caudebac* (watercolour) FRF 4,100; *The Pont-Marie,* FRF 10,500. Paris, 10 May 1950, *Seascape,* FRF 31,000. Paris, 28 June 1951, *The Seine at the Pont-Marie,* FRF 48,000. Paris, 9 June 1954, *The Seine at the Quai St-Nicholas, Quai du Louvre,* FRF 72,000. Paris, 26 June 1957, *The Quays of the Seine, Paris* (oil on canvas) FRF 155,000. New York, 14 Jan 1959, *View from the Pont des Arts,* USD 800. London, 27 Nov 1964, *Porte St-Denis, Paris* (pastel and watercolour) Gns 280. Paris, 23 Feb 1965, *The Seine at the Louvre,* FRF 20,000. Paris, 3 May 1967, *The Pont-Neuf* (watercolour) FRF 4,300. Versailles, 15 Dec 1968, *Rouen Harbour,* FRF 34,000. Geneva, 8 Nov 1969, *View of Malines* (watercolour) CHF 8,000. Paris, 1 Dec 1969, *The Seine at the Institute,* FRF 50,600. London, 19 March 1973, *Low Tide in Grandchamp,* GBP 2,000. Paris, 30 March 1973, *The Seine and Notre-Dame,* FRF 38,000. Paris, 30 March 1973, *The Seine and Notre-Dame,* FRF 38,000. Paris, 13 June 1974, *The Seine in Paris,* FRF 23,000. Le Havre, 26 March 1976, *The Seine at the Louvre* (oil on canvas, 23 1/2 x 28 3/4 ins / 60 x 73 cm) FRF 20,500. Paris, 22 Nov 1977, *Church of St-Wulfrun, Abbeville* (1912, watercolour, 22 x 18 ins / 55 x 46 cm) FRF 6,000. Versailles, 7 June 1978, *Keep Overlooking a Port* (oil on canvas, 35 x 51 1/2 ins / 89 x 131 cm) FRF 33,000. London, 6 Dec 1978, *The Seine in Paris, Pont Henri IV* (watercolour and charcoal, 10 1/4 x 15 3/4 ins / 26 x 40 cm) GBP 850. Enghien-les-Bains, 9 Dec 1979, *Reims Cathedral* (1914, watercolour, 17 1/2 x 14 1/4 ins / 44.5 x 36.5 cm) FRF 11,500. Brest, 12 Nov 1982, *Notre-Dame in Snow* (watercolour, 13 3/4 x 17 ins / 35 x 43 cm) FRF 7,050. Versailles, 18 March 1984, *Windmills near Dordrecht* (1902, watercolour, 10 1/4 x 15 3/4 ins / 26 x 40 cm) FRF 16,000. New York, 1 June 1984, *View of the Seine in Paris* (oil on canvas, 24 x 29 ins / 61 x 73.7 cm) USD 7,000. London, 25 June 1985, *The Quais des Grands-Augustins, Paris* (oil on canvas, 25 3/4 x 31 3/4 ins / 65.4 x 80.6 cm) GBP 18,000. Enghien-les-Bains, 24 Nov 1985, *The Port of Le Havre in Snow* (watercolour, 12 1/2 x 15 3/4 ins / 32 x 40 cm) FRF 30,000. Calais, 8 Nov 1987, *Market Square* (1906, watercolour, 19 1/4 x 11 1/2 ins / 49 x 29 cm) FRF 21,000; *View of Notre-Dame and the Île de la Cité* (oil on canvas) FRF 100,000. Paris, 11 Dec 1987, *Sailing Boats in the Harbour of Honfleur* (oil on canvas, 21 1/4 x 25 1/2 ins / 54 x 65 cm) FRF 25,000. Paris, 17 Feb 1988, *The Moulin de la Galette; The Flower Market at the Conciergerie* (oil on canvas, pendants, each 47 1/4 x 22 ins / 120 x 55 cm) FRF 78,000. Paris, 26 Feb 1988, *Landscape with Church* (watercolour and charcoal, 10 x 15 1/2 ins / 25.5 x 39.5 cm) FRF 7,000. Calais, 28 Feb 1988, *Rouen Harbour* (oil on canvas, 13 x 22 ins / 33 x 55 cm) FRF 45,000. Neuilly, 9 March 1988, *Sailing Boats in a Light Breeze* (oil on canvas, 21 1/4 x 32 1/4 ins / 54 x 82 cm) FRF 30,000. Paris, 18 March 1988, *The Pont-Neuf, Paris* (oil on canvas, 23 1/2 x 28 3/4 ins / 60 x 73 cm) FRF 165,000. Paris, 15 April 1988, *Marseilles, Entrance to the Port, with the Cathedral and St John's Castle on the Right* (oil on canvas, 28 1/4 x 35 3/4 ins / 72 x 91 cm) FRF 140,000. London, 18 May 1988, *View of Martigues* (1921, watercolour and charcoal, 10 1/4 x 15 1/4 ins / 26 x 39 cm) GBP 2,860. New York, 26 May 1988, *The Louvre and the Arc du Caroussel* (oil on canvas, 24 x 29 ins / 60.9 x 73.7 cm) USD 11,000. Versailles, 15 June 1988, *The Pont-Neuf and the Cité, Paris* (watercolour, 19 3/4 x 31 1/2 ins / 50 x 80 cm) FRF 57,000. Calais, 3 July 1988, *Ancient Street in Lisieux* (oil on canvas, 18 1/2 x 22 ins / 47 x 56 cm) FRF 52,000. New York, 30

Sept 1988, *Honfleur* (1898, oil on canvas, 12½ x 18 ins / 31.8 x 45.5 cm) USD 5,500. Versailles, 23 Oct 1988, *Sailing Boats in Dordrecht* (watercolour, 11¾ x 15¾ ins / 30 x 40 cm) FRF 25,200. Calais, 13 Nov 1988, *Sailing Boats at Sea* (oil on canvas, 15¼ x 22 ins / 39 x 55 cm) FRF 52,000. Paris, 12 Feb 1989, *The Seine and Notre-Dame, Paris* (oil on canvas, 21¼ x 28¾ ins / 54 x 73 cm) FRF 150,000. Paris, 15 Feb 1989, *The Pont de Notre-Dame, Paris* (watercolour and charcoal, 10 x 15½ ins / 25.5 x 39.5 cm) FRF 22,500. Paris, 22 March 1989, *The Cathedral and the Rue St-Leu, Amiens* (watercolour, 15¾ x 12½ ins / 40 x 32 cm) FRF 25,000. Paris, 7 April 1989, *Returning from Fishing* (oil on canvas, 19¾ x 25½ ins / 50 x 65 cm) FRF 95,000. Lyons, 27 April 1989, *Church in Paris* (oil on canvas, 12½ x 15¾ ins / 32 x 40 cm) FRF 50,000. New York, 3 May 1989, *Low Tide in Grandcamp* (1882, oil on canvas, 15 x 22 ins / 38.4 x 55 cm, ¾ ins/2 cm) USD 33,300. La Varenne-St-Hilaire, 21 May 1989, *Sailing Boats at Sea, Grandcamp* (1899, watercolour, 15¾ x 22¾ ins / 40 x 58 cm) FRF 19,500. Paris, 11 Oct 1989, *Beaumont-le-Roger* (1904, graphite and watercolour, 16¼ x 9¾ ins / 41 x 25 cm) FRF 15,000. New York, 18 Oct 1989, *The Pont St-Michel* (1922, oil on canvas, 29 x 36 ins / 73.6 x 91.4 cm) USD 49,500. Paris, 9 Dec 1989, *Port of Marseilles* (oil on canvas, 19 x 25½ ins / 48.5 x 65 cm) FRF 120,000. Calais, 4 March 1990, *Bank of the Seine, Paris* (oil on canvas, 13 x 18 ins / 33 x 46 cm) FRF 63,000. Paris, 3 April 1990, *The Pont-Neuf* (watercolour, 12½ x 18 ins / 32 x 46 cm) FRF 25,100. Paris, 5 July 1990, *Beach in Trouville* (watercolour, 11 x 15¾ ins / 27 x 40 cm) FRF 15,000. New York, 27 Sept 1990, *The Pont-Royal* (oil on canvas, 15¼ x 22 ins / 38.5 x 55 cm) USD 7,700. New York, 29 Nov 1990, *Dieppe* (1881, oil on canvas, 23 x 32 ins / 58.4 x 81.3 cm) USD 12,100. Paris, 25 March 1991, *The Seine and the Hôtel de Ville, Paris* (oil on canvas, 15 x 22 ins / 38 x 56 cm) FRF 65,000. Paris, 15 April 1991, *Honfleur* (1921, watercolour, 19 x 22 ins / 48 x 55 cm) FRF 56,000. London, 3 Dec 1991, *The Port of Marseilles* (oil on canvas, 22 x 44 ins / 55 x 112 cm) GBP 17,600. Le Touquet, 8 Nov 1992, *The Pont-Neuf, Paris* (watercolour, 12½ x 18 ins / 32 x 46 cm) FRF 18,000. New York, 27 May 1993, *Banks of the Seine* (oil on canvas, 25½ x 32 ins / 64.8 x 81.3 cm) USD 17,250. Paris, 14 June 1993, *Sailing Boat off Honfleur* (1884, oil on canvas, 32 x 21 ins / 81 x 53.5 cm) FRF 50,000. Paris, 29 April 1994, *The Seine in Paris* (1915, watercolour, 11 x 14¼ ins / 28 x 36.5 cm) FRF 11,000. New York, 25 May 1994, *Paris Street Scene* (1878, oil on canvas, 38 x 59 ins / 96.5 x 149.9 cm) USD 37,375. Royan, 16 July 1994, *The Seine at the Hôtel de Ville, Paris* (1884, oil on canvas, 52¾ x 72¾ ins / 134 x 185 cm) FRF 470,000. Paris, 19 Feb 1996, *Rotterdam* (watercolour and charcoal, 11 x 13¾ ins / 27 x 35 cm) FRF 5,300. Calais, 24 March 1996, *The Seine and the Louvre, Paris* (watercolour, 10¼ x 15¾ ins / 26 x 40 cm) FRF 14,000. New York, 23 May 1996, *Boats in the Harbour of Dordrecht with the Cathedral in the Background* (oil on canvas, 15¼ x 22 ins / 38.5 x 56 cm) USD 19,550. Paris, 5 June 1996, *View of Paris, Second-hand Booksellers* (1904, oil on canvas, 21¼ x 32 ins / 54 x 81 cm) FRF 47,000. New York, 26 Sept 1996, *View of the Seine, Paris* (1898, oil on canvas, 22 x 32 ins / 55.9 x 81.3 cm) USD 17,250. Paris, 16 Oct 1996, *Tugs on the Seine, the Pont-Royal and the Pavillon de Flore, Paris* (watercolour, 10¾ x 18 ins / 27.5 x 46 cm) FRF 15,000. London, 23 Oct 1996, *Street Scene* (watercolour and charcoal/paper, 15¾ x 11 ins / 40 x 27 cm) GBP 977. Paris, 12 Dec 1996, *View of the Square, Bruges* (watercolour, 12½ x 15¾ ins / 32 x 40 cm) FRF 6,800. Paris, 20 Jan 1997, *The Pont St-Benezet, Avignon* (wash, 9 x 13½ ins / 22 x 34 cm) FRF 3,500; *Three-master in Le Havre* (oil on canvas, 32 x 21¼ ins / 81 x 54 cm) FRF 120,000. Paris, 26 May 1997, *The Seine at Conflans Ste-Honorine* (watercolour/paper, 10¼ x 15¾ ins / 26 x 40 cm) FRF 6,800. Paris, 17 Oct 1997, *Returning from Fishing in Normandy* (oil on canvas, 17¾ x 25½ ins / 45 x 65 cm) FRF 20,100. Paris, 19 Dec 1997, *View of the Seine at the Pont-Neuf with the Île de la Cité and the Louvre* (1898, oil on canvas, 19¾ x 25½ ins / 50 x 64.5 cm) FRF 55,000. Paris, 16 March 1998, *The Seine and Notre-Dame, Quai de la Rapée* (watercolour, 5¼ x 9¾ ins / 13.5 x 25 cm) FRF 9,000. Paris, 22 June 1999, *Quays on the Seine, Paris* (oil on canvas, 24 x 29 ins / 60 x 74 cm) FRF 80,000. New York, 1 Dec 1999, *Ship at Harbour* (1882, oil on canvas, 22 x 15 ins / 56 x 38 cm) USD 17,000. New York, 15 June 2000, *Port* (oil on canvas, 19 x 26 ins / 49 x 65 cm) USD 24,000. New York, 15 Dec 2000, *Paris, le Moulin de la Galette* (oil on canvas, 22 x 15 ins / 55 x 38 cm) USD 45,000. New York, 24 May 2001, *The Seine, Paris* (oil on canvas, 21 x 26 ins / 54 x 65 cm) USD 21,000. New York, 13 June 2001, *Port of Marseilles* (oil on canvas, 19 x 24 ins / 49 x 60 cm) USD 17,000. London, 21 March 2002, *The Seine, Quai Henri IV, Paris* (oil on canvas, 13 x 18 ins / 32 x 45 cm) GBP 12,000. Paris, 15 Nov 2002, *The Seine and the Pont Neuf, Paris* (oil on canvas, 26 x 32 ins / 65 x 81 cm) EUR 13,000. Paris, 9 Dec 2003, *Église St-Medard, Paris* (oil on canvas, 28 x 38 ins / 72 x 96 cm) EUR 10,000. Paris, 9 Dec 2003, *Quai Henri IV, Paris* (oil on canvas, 24 x 32 ins / 60 x 81 cm) EUR 17,000. Versailles, 29 Feb 2004, *Notre-Dame, Paris* (oil on canvas, 28 x 35 ins / 70 x 90 cm) EUR 14,000. New York, 11 March 2004, *The Seine and Notre-Dame* (1899, oil on board, 13 x 16 ins / 33 x 41 cm) USD 12,000.

FRANK-WILL, pseudonym of Boggs, Frank William
French, 20th century.
Born 13 March 1900, in Nanterre; died 29 December 1950.

Painter, watercolourist. Urban landscapes, seascapes. Frank-Will was the son of the painter Frank Myers Boggs, known as Frank-Boggs, and was taught by his father. He abandoned his architectural studies to become a painter. Frank-Will was a typical Montmartre figure and was particularly associated with Gen-Paul and Leprin. In 1922 he made his first visit to the Normandy coast. Other trips included La Rochelle in 1926-1927, Amiens in 1929 and Barfleur in 1930. With Leprin, he visited Moret-sur-Loing, Auxerre and Avallon. In 1943 he exhibited *La Chignole* (*The Jalopy*) at the event created by Gen-Paul. He was a heavy drinker and failed to recover from an operation on a pulmonary abcess.

He repeatedly changed his signature: in 1916 he signed himself both Frank and Franque; in 1918 William Franck; in 1920 Franck-Will and later Frank-Will; and from 1936 to 1939 he used the pseudonym Naudin. He is principally known for his Parisian watercolours. Though more intense in style, he painted exactly the same subjects and in the same technique and manner as his father, which had enjoyed such popular appeal. His work is over-prolific, repetitive and uneven in quality. His approach was a blend of populist Post-Impressionism typical of Montmartre with flashes of violent Expressionism that lean towards the tragic. From 1929 his work was on permanent exhibition at the Galerie Georges Petit. He also exhibited with Hector Brame, his father's art dealer, and then under contract with Henri Bureau.

Bibliography:

Coisne, Denis, *Frank-Will (1900-1950), sa vie, son œuvre, son époque*, ABC Décor, Paris, 1988.

Auction records:

Paris, 23 Dec 1927, *The Little Bridge* (watercolour) FRF 125. Paris, 10 May 1935, *The Port and Quays, La Rochelle* (watercolour) FRF 190. Paris, July 1943, *Reflections*, FRF 7,500; *Les Manèges* FRF 1,500. Paris, 28 Jan 1955, *Rue Lepic*, FRF 35,000. Versailles, 26 Nov 1967, *The Seine at Rouen*, FRF

6,500. NICE, 24 April 1974, *Houses in the Snow,* FRF 10,000. PARIS, 23 March 1976, *The Moulin de la Galette* (watercolour, 17 1/4 x 21 1/4 ins / 44 x 54 cm) FRF 4,500. VERSAILLES, 25 Oct 1976, *Street with Figures, Paris* (oil on canvas, 20 x 24 ins / 50.5 x 61 cm) FRF 6,000. VERSAILLES, 13 Nov 1977, *Tug Boats on the Seine, Paris* (1927, watercolour, 18 x 24 ins / 46 x 61 cm) FRF 4,400. ST-BRIEUC, 13 Nov 1977, *The Seine and Quays, Paris* (oil on canvas, 23 1/2 x 28 3/4 ins / 60 x 73 cm) FRF 8,500. PARIS, 4 April 1978, *Honfleur* (watercolour, 18 x 23 1/2 ins / 46 x 60 cm) FRF 3,000. GRENOBLE, 20 Nov 1978, *Notre-Dame de Paris and the Seine* (oil on canvas, 25 1/2 x 21 1/4 ins / 65 x 54 cm) FRF 13,500. VERSAILLES, 18 Feb 1979, *Fortified Gate at Chartres* (oil on canvas, 22 x 25 1/2 ins / 55 x 65 cm) FRF 14,800. VERSAILLES, 18 March 1979, *Rue de Montmartre and the Sacré-Cœur under Snow* (oil on canvas, 18 x 14 3/4 ins / 46 x 37.5 cm) FRF 8,800. PARIS, 28 Nov 1979, *Factory at Issy-Plaine* (watercolour, 17 1/4 x 20 3/4 ins / 44 x 53 cm) FRF 3,500. PARIS, 6 June 1980, *The Port* (oil on canvas, 21 1/4 x 31 1/2 ins / 54 x 80 cm) FRF 4,000. VERSAILLES, 30 Nov 1980, *The Seine and Ile de la Cité, Paris* (watercolour, 19 x 39 ins / 48.5 x 99 cm) FRF 19,500. VERSAILLES, 10 Oct 1981, *Self-portrait* (oil on canvas, 25 1/2 x 21 1/4 ins / 65 x 54 cm) FRF 1,900. ENGHIEN-LES-BAINS, 13 Dec 1981, *Rue de Montmartre* (watercolour, 23 1/2 x 17 3/4 ins / 60 x 45 cm) FRF 7,000. ROUEN, 28 Nov 1982, *The Seine at Paris* (watercolour, 9 3/4 x 15 ins / 25 x 38 cm) FRF 2,400. BREST, 12 Dec 1982, *Porte St-Martin* (oil on canvas, 17 3/4 x 25 1/2 ins / 45 x 65 cm) FRF 10,800. HONFLEUR, 3 April 1983, *The Seine at Paris* (1928, watercolour, 19 1/4 x 24 3/4 ins / 49 x 63 cm) FRF 9,000. NEW YORK, 14 April 1983, *Notre-Dame, Paris* (oil on canvas, 27 3/4 x 35 1/2 ins / 70.5 x 90 cm) USD 1,600. PARIS, 22 Nov 1984, *Entrance to the Port of La Rochelle* (1926, oil on canvas, 21 1/4 x 25 1/2 ins / 54 x 65 cm) FRF 32,000. PARIS, 14 Dec 1984, *Place du Tertre, Paris, under Snow* (watercolour, 38 1/4 x 41 1/4 ins / 97 x 105 cm) FRF 35,000. PARIS, 9 Dec 1985, *Mont St-Michel* (watercolour, 19 1/4 x 23 1/2 ins / 49 x 60 cm) FRF 11,000. PARIS, 13 Dec 1985, *Le Loing at Montargis* (oil on canvas, 25 1/2 x 21 1/4 ins / 65 x 54 cm) FRF 16,000. PARIS, 16 June 1986, *The Seine by the Conciergerie, Paris* (1923, watercolour, 11 3/4 x 18 ins / 30 x 46 cm) FRF 4,200. VERSAILLES, 18 June 1986, *Notre-Dame and the Seine under Snow, Paris* (oil on canvas, 24 x 19 3/4 ins / 61 x 50 cm) FRF 13,000. ST-GERMAIN-EN-LAYE, 5 July 1987, *Market Square, Dieppe* (watercolour, 22 x 16 1/2 ins / 56 x 42 cm) FRF 25,500. CALAIS, 8 Nov 1987, *View of Notre-Dame Chancel* (oil on canvas, 21 1/4 x 25 1/2 ins / 54 x 65 cm) FRF 33,000. L'ISLE-ADAM, 20 Dec 1987, *View of Paris with the Quays and Boats* (watercolour, 17 1/4 x 20 1/2 ins / 44 x 52 cm) FRF 17,000. PARIS, 10 Feb 1988, *The Port, Rouen* (watercolour, 24 1/2 x 62 1/2 ins / 62.5 x 159 cm) FRF 57,000. PARIS, 17 Feb 1988, *The Port of Marseilles* (oil on canvas, 23 1/2 x 35 3/4 ins / 60 x 91 cm) FRF 36,000. PARIS, 7 March 1988, *The Port of La Rochelle* (watercolour, 19 x 25 1/4 ins / 48 x 64 cm) FRF 13,000. PARIS, 19 March 1988, *The Sacré-Cœur, Montmartre* (watercolour, 12 1/2 x 17 3/4 ins / 32 x 45 cm) FRF 11,500. PARIS, 4 May 1988, *View over the Ile de la Cité* (watercolour, 17 3/4 x 19 3/4 ins / 45 x 50 cm) FRF 45,000. VERSAILLES, 15 May 1988, *Boats Unloading, Rouen* (1929, watercolour, 17 1/2 x 23 1/2 ins / 44.5 x 59.5 cm) FRF 17,000. LA VARENNE-ST-HILAIRE, 29 May 1988, *View of Moret* (oil on canvas, 23 1/2 x 32 ins / 60 x 81 cm) FRF 51,000. PARIS, 23 June 1988, *Place de la Concorde and Rue Royale, Paris* (watercolour, 11 x 19 ins / 27 x 48 cm) FRF 32,500. VERSAILLES, 6 Nov 1988, *Tug Boat on the Seine by Notre-Dame* (oil on canvas, 28 3/4 x 39 1/4 ins / 73 x 100 cm) FRF 31,500. CALAIS, 13 Nov 1988, *The Market, Honfleur* (watercolour, 11 3/4 x 9 ins / 30 x 22 cm) FRF 20,500; *The Quays of the Seine and Notre-Dame* (watercolour, 17 3/4 x 23 1/2 ins / 45 x 60 cm) FRF 31,100. PARIS, 9 Dec 1988, *Trawler Returning to Port* (watercolour, 16 1/2 x 21 1/4 ins / 42 x 54 cm) FRF 21,000. PARIS, 1 Feb 1989, *Flower Market* (watercolour, 14 x 10 ins / 35.4 x 24.5 cm) FRF 14,000. PARIS, 12 Feb 1989, *The Place Blanche* (1938, watercolour, 10 x 12 3/4 ins / 24.5 x 32.5 cm) FRF 26,000. PARIS, 19 March 1989, *Tug Boats on the Seine at Pont-Neuf, Paris* (oil on canvas, 23 1/2 x 28 3/4 ins / 60 x 73 cm) FRF 50,500. PARIS, 9 June 1989, *Boats Alongside the Quay* (oil on canvas, 23 1/2 x 32 ins / 60 x 81 cm) FRF 100,000. PARIS, 22 Oct 1989, *Market at Louviers* (watercolour, 11 1/2 x 15 1/4 ins / 29 x 39 cm) FRF 27,000. LE TOUQUET, 12 Nov 1989, *Port of Barfleur at Low Tide* (watercolour, 19 1/4 x 25 1/2 ins / 49 x 65 cm) FRF 45,000. PARIS, 20 Feb 1990, *Notre-Dame* (watercolour in blue monochrome paint, 17 1/4 x 21 1/4 ins / 44 x 54 cm) FRF 28,000. NEW YORK, 21 Feb 1990, *View of Notre-Dame* (watercolour and charcoal/paper, 18 x 21 1/2 ins / 44.8 x 54.6 cm) USD 7,700. PARIS, 4 March 1990, *Sailing Boats in the Bay of St-Tropez* (oil on canvas, 17 1/4 x 23 1/2 ins / 44 x 60 cm) FRF 900,000. PARIS, 27 March 1990, *Port of Rouen* (watercolour, 12 1/4 x 17 3/4 ins / 31 x 45 cm) FRF 23,000. PARIS, 3 April 1990, *Notre-Dame and the Seine* (watercolour, 19 1/2 x 26 ins / 49.5 x 66 cm) FRF 35,000. PARIS, 10 April 1990, *The Pont du Carrousel* (watercolour, 11 x 18 1/2 ins / 28 x 47 cm) FRF 28,000. NANTERRE, 24 April 1990, *Old Houses at Montargis* (watercolour, 16 1/2 x 11 ins / 42 x 28 cm) FRF 15,000. CALAIS, 8 July 1990, *The Pont-Neuf* (oil on canvas, 17 3/4 x 25 1/2 ins / 45 x 65 cm) FRF 61,000. SOISSONS, 4 Nov 1990, *Sunshine over Notre-Dame and the Ile de la Cité* (oil on canvas, 28 3/4 x 39 1/4 ins / 73 x 100 cm) FRF 135,100. PARIS, 7 June 1991, *The Mère Catherine under Snow* (oil on canvas, 27 1/2 x 35 1/2 ins / 70 x 90 cm) FRF 190,000. NEW YORK, 5 Nov 1991, *View of Honfleur* (oil on canvas, 15 x 18 ins / 38 x 45.7 cm) USD 4,400. PARIS, 9 Dec 1991, *Place du Tertre* (watercolour, 17 3/4 x 21 1/4 ins / 45 x 54 cm) FRF 30,000. PARIS, 19 June 1992, *Fécamp* (watercolour, 17 x 20 3/4 ins / 43 x 53 cm) FRF 8,000. PARIS, 15 March 1993, *The Seine* (watercolour, 17 3/4 x 21 1/4 ins / 45 x 54 cm) FRF 26,000. PARIS, 25 June 1993, *The Conciergerie, Paris* (watercolour, 12 x 15 1/4 ins / 30.5 x 39 cm) FRF 14,500. NEW YORK, 2 Nov 1993, *The Opéra, Paris* (oil on canvas, 23 1/2 x 32 ins / 60 x 81 cm) USD 4,600. PARIS, 6 Feb 1994, *The Opéra, Paris* (oil on canvas, 23 1/2 x 32 ins / 60 x 81 cm) FRF 45,000. AMSTERDAM, 19 April 1994, *The Port of Honfleur, France* (1927, watercolour, 14 1/4 x 20 ins / 36 x 51 cm) NLG 3,335. PARIS, 12 July 1995, *Notre-Dame de Paris* (watercolour and gouache, 17 3/4 x 21 1/4 ins / 45 x 54 cm) FRF 12,000. CALAIS, 24 March 1996, *Market in Normandy* (oil on canvas, 24 x 20 ins / 61 x 51 cm) FRF 36,000. CALAIS, 7 July 1996, *The Seine and Notre-Dame, Paris* (oil on canvas, 25 1/2 x 32 ins / 65 x 81 cm) FRF 24,000. PARIS, 28 Oct 1996, *Notre-Dame de Paris* (watercolour, 11 1/2 x 15 1/4 ins / 29 x 38.5 cm) FRF 7,000. PARIS, 24 Nov 1996, *Galleons Fighting* (watercolour, 22 3/4 x 27 1/2 ins / 58 x 70 cm) FRF 18,500. PARIS, 20 Jan 1997, *Village under Snow, Winter* (oil on canvas, 25 1/2 x 32 1/4 ins / 65 x 82 cm) FRF 8,500. PARIS, 10 March 1997, *Meaux Cathedral* (drawing with watercolour, 22 x 17 ins / 55 x 43 cm) FRF 4,500. PARIS, 21 April 1997, *Market at Dreux* (pen and watercolour, 22 1/2 x 28 1/2 ins / 57 x 72.5 cm) FRF 9,000. PARIS, 28 May 1997, *Fécamp* (watercolour, 17 x 20 1/2 ins / 43 x 52 cm) FRF 9,000. PARIS, 6 June 1997, *Market at Rouen* (oil on canvas, 25 1/2 x 21 1/4 ins / 65 x 54 cm) FRF 15,000. PARIS, 16 June 1997, *Semur* (1929, watercolour and charcoal, 19 3/4 x 25 1/2 ins / 50 x 65 cm) FRF 15,000. PARIS, 25 June 1997, *The Seine at the Vert-Galant* (charcoal and watercolour, 13 x 19 3/4 ins / 33 x 50 cm) FRF 4,200. PARIS, 27 Oct 1997, *Le Tréport* (watercolour, 15 3/4 x 20 1/2 ins / 40 x 52 cm) FRF 11,000. PARIS, 22 March 1998, *The Quays* (watercolour, 15 1/4 x 10 1/2 ins / 39 x 26.5 cm) FRF 5,000. PARIS, 26 March 1998, *Duquesne's Bombardment of Algiers* (watercolour and gouache, 28 1/4 x 39 1/4 ins / 72 x 100 cm) FRF 27,000. PARIS, 5 March 1999, *Paris, Place du Tertre* (watercolour, 25 x 32 ins / 64 x 81 cm) FRF 30,000. PARIS, 19 Nov 1999, *Montmartre in the Snow* (oil on canvas, 29 x 36 ins / 73 x 92 cm) FRF 32,000. VERSAILLES, 18 June 2000, *Paris, Quai de l'Horloge* (oil on canvas, 24 x 29 ins / 60 x 73 cm) FRF 50,000. CALAIS, 10 Dec 2000, *Paris, Pont Neuf and the City* (oil on canvas, 24 x 29 ins / 60 x 73 cm) FRF 38,000. PARIS, 29 Jan 2001, *Sailors and Boats in the Port at Dunkirk* (watercolour, 26 x 39 ins / 65 x 100 cm) FRF 42,000. CALAIS, 11 Nov 2001, *Paris, the Seine and*

Notre-Dame (oil on canvas, 16 x 42 ins / 41 x 106 cm) FRF 46,000. NEUILLY, 14 March 2002, *Honfleur, la Lieutenance* (watercolour, 33 x 46 ins / 83 x 116 cm) EUR 7,000. CALAIS, 19 May 2002, *Paris, Grands Boulevards* (oil on canvas, 26 x 32 ins / 65 x 81 cm) EUR 7,800. NEUILLY, 28 March 2003, *Naval Battle* (watercolour, 12 x 18 ins / 31 x 46 cm) EUR 4,500. NEUILLY, 28 March 2003, *Port at Fecamps* (watercolour over crayon, 37 x 20 ins / 93 x 52 cm) EUR 7,000. PARIS, 26 April 2004, *Paris, the Seine at the Pont Louis-Philippe* (watercolour, 24 x 35 ins / 60 x 90 cm) EUR 7,000. PARIS, 17 June 2004, *Market at Honfleur* (oil on canvas, 25 x 30 ins / 63 x 76 cm) EUR 3,600.

FRANKE. See also **FRANCK**

FRANKE, Albert Joseph

German, 19th - 20th century.

Born 1860, in Breslau (now Wroclaw, Poland); died 1924.

Painter. Genre scenes.

Orientalism.

Albert Josef Franke studied at the academies in Breslau and Munich. He travelled extensively in North Africa in 1887 and painted some lively compositions, capturing the architecture, costumes and everyday objects of the region in meticulous detail.

MUSEUMS AND GALLERIES:

BUCHAREST (Muz. National de Arta al României): *Albanian Sitting in a Café.*

AUCTION RECORDS:

LONDON, 10 Nov 1971, *Art Lovers*, GBP 480. LONDON, 3 Nov 1977, *Two Arabs Conversing* (1886, oil on panel, 13 x 10 ins / 33 x 25.3 cm) GBP 800. VIENNA, 15 Sept 1981, *Visit* (oil on panel, 13 x 10 ins / 32.8 x 25.5 cm) ATS 75,000. NEW YORK, 31 Oct 1985, *Nubian Guard* (1889, oil on canvas, 25 1/4 x 20 1/4 ins / 64.1 x 51.5 cm) USD 28,000. NEW YORK, 25 Feb 1988, *Chess Players* (oil on panel, 9 1/2 x 7 ins / 24.1 x 18 cm) USD 6,050. NEW YORK, 23 Feb 1989, *After-Dinner Conversation* (oil on panel, 12 1/4 x 8 ins / 31.1 x 20.6 cm) USD 4,400. LONDON, 7 June 1989, *Meeting the Cardinal* (oil on panel, 12 1/4 x 16 1/4 ins / 31 x 41 cm) GBP 990. MUNICH, 7 Dec 1993, *Art Experts* (oil on panel, 12 1/4 x 16 ins / 31 x 40.5 cm) DEM 12,650. LONDON, 17 Nov 1994, *Palace Guard* (1889, oil on canvas, 25 1/4 x 20 ins / 64 x 51 cm) GBP 34,500. LONDON, 15 March 1996, *Arab Street Market at the City Gates* (oil on panel, 9 1/2 x 14 1/4 ins / 24 x 36.2 cm) GBP 18,400. COLOGNE, 25 March 1999, *Gentleman Reading in Castle Interior* (oil on panel, 8 x 6 ins / 21 x 16 cm) DEM 3,000. NORTH BETHESDA, 29 Nov 2001, *Arab Street Scene* (1890, oil on canvas, 27 x 18 ins / 68 x 45 cm) USD 5,000. MUNICH, 5 Dec 2001, *Collector with Friends* (oil on panel, 10 x 8 ins / 25 x 20 cm) DEM 4,400. AMSTERDAM, 24 April 2002, *Diversions of Gentlemen* (oil on panel, 15 x 11 ins / 37 x 29 cm) EUR 3,800. NEW YORK, 4 June 2003, *Admiring Giambologna's Rape of the Sabine Woman* (oil on panel, 12 x 16 ins / 31 x 40 cm) USD 6,000. WARSAW, 19 Oct 2003, *Street Scene in Tunisia* (1886, oil on card, 13 x 17 ins / 32 x 44 cm) PLN 45,000.

FRANKE, Chrétien J.

French, 19th century.

Painter, watercolourist.

Franke exhibited his *Felis Caracal from the Barbary Coast* to the 1836 Paris Salon, followed by *African Gazelles* in 1839.

FRANKE, Heinrich

German, 19th century.

Active in Berlin.

Painter. History painting, religious subjects, portraits.

As a student, Heinrich Franke exhibited at the Berlin academy from 1820 to 1824 and then in 1832 with historical paintings, paintings of saints and portraits.

FRANKE, Tobias, or Francke

German, 18th century.

Active in Militsch (now Milicz, Poland).

Painter.

FRANKEL, Clemens

German, 19th - 20th century.

Born 11 June 1872, in Frankfurt am Main; died 1944, in Munich.

Painter. Landscapes.

Frankel attended private art school under Knirr in Munich, then went on to study under Löfftz at Munich academy. He spent some time in Italy, returning in 1906 to set up a school for landscape painters at Leoni on the Starnbergersee.

AUCTION RECORDS:

MUNICH, 1 June 1981, *Tempest* (1923, oil on card, 8 3/4 x 11 ins / 22.5 x 27 cm) DEM 900. COLOGNE, 23 March 1990, *Autumn near Amper* (oil on canvas, 19 3/4 x 23 1/2 ins / 50 x 60 cm) DEM 1,100.

FRÄNKEL, Friedrich

German, 19th century.

Born 6 April 1832, in Nuremberg; died 8 October 1891, in Nuremberg.

Engraver.

Fränkel studied at the school of fine arts in Stuttgart and then in Nuremberg. Among his engravings are *Old Woman with Wallflowers* in the style of G. Dou, *Portrait of the Prince Bishop Dalberg, Erwin von Steinbach* and plates in the style of Defregger, Grützner and Waldmüller.

FRANKEN. See also **FRANCK** and **FRANCKEN**

FRANKEN, Hélène von

Maiden name: Köber

German, 19th century.

Born 19 March 1825.

Painter.

Hélène von Franken studied in Mitau (now Jelgava, Latvia) and in Dresden where she was a pupil of Paul von Franken whom she married. She lived with him in Mitau, St Petersburg and Tiflis (now Tbilisi, Georgia). She painted portraits and some genre paintings.

FRANKEN, Paul von

German, 19th century.

Born 1818, in Bad Godesberg; died 1884, in Düsseldorf.

Painter. Genre scenes, landscapes.

Paul von Franken studied at the Kunstakademie in Düsseldorf and in 1852 he went to Mitau (now Jelgava, Latvia), then to Tiflis (now Tbilisi, Georgia) from where he travelled to the Caucasus which became the subject of his painting. His works include a series of paintings of this region, for example *Kurds Hunting Birds*.

AUCTION RECORDS:

LUCERNE, 15 May 1986, *View of a Russian Town* (1854, oil on canvas, 25 1/2 x 33 1/2 ins / 65 x 85 cm) CHF 6,000. LONDON, 26 March 1997, *Turkish Village Scene near a River* (1864, oil on canvas, 20 x 27 ins / 51 x 68.5 cm) GBP 11,500; *Gate of an Oriental Town* (1860, oil on canvas, 34 x 26 3/4 ins / 85.5 x 68 cm) GBP 11,500. COLOGNE, 15 May 1999, *Caucasian Landscape* (1871, oil on canvas, 42 x 75 ins / 106 x 190 cm) DEM 24,000. VIENNA, 16 Nov 1999, *Caucasian Landscape* (1871, oil on canvas, 42 x 75 ins / 106 x 190 cm) ATS 280,000. LONDON, 7 April 2000, *Oriental Travellers* (1878, oil on canvas, 42 x 35 ins / 107 x 90 cm) GBP 5,400. AMSTERDAM, 4 Sept 2001, *Mountainous Landscape with Oriental Travellers by an Inn* (1875, oil on canvas, 30 x 44 ins / 75 x 112 cm) EUR 4,000. MUNICH, 20 March 2002, *Ambush* (1872, oil on canvas, 22 x 30 ins / 55 x 75 cm) EUR 3,300. LONDON, 19 Nov 2003, *Travellers Resting by the Lake, Georgia* (1854, oil on canvas, 25 x 32 ins / 64 x 82 cm) GBP 40,000. LONDON, 19 Nov 2003, *View of Tiflis* (1866, oil on canvas, 28 x 40 ins / 72 x 102 cm) GBP 55,000. CO-

LOGNE, 1 April 2004, *Kura Shore in Evening with Tiflis* (1865, oil on canvas, 33 x 46 ins / 84 x 116 cm) EUR 55,000. LONDON, 26 May 2004, *Caucasian Scene* (oil on canvas, 38 x 61 ins / 97 x 156 cm) GBP 30,000.

FRANKEN, Petrus Johannes Cornelis or Piet
Dutch, 19th - 20th century.
Born 7 January 1866, in Tilburg; died 1911, in The Hague.
Painter. Landscapes, animals.

Franken lived and worked in The Hague and exhibited in The Hague, at the Ice Palace in Munich and at the Salon de la Société Nationale des Beaux-Arts in Paris.

AUCTION RECORDS:
AMSTERDAM, 22 April 1992, *Cattle on a Country Road* (oil on canvas, 14¼ x 19¼ ins / 36 x 49 cm) NLG 1,035. THE HAGUE, 24 April 2002, *View of Sea and Dunes* (oil on canvas, 17 x 25 ins / 44 x 64 cm) EUR 2,200.

FRANKEN, Pierre Antoine
French, 20th century.
Born in Paris; died 1928.
Painter. Landscapes.

Pierre Franken exhibited in Paris at the Salon des Indépendants.

AUCTION RECORDS:
PARIS, 12 Dec 1990, *Rue du Moulin de Beurre in Paris on a Rainy Evening* (1924, oil on canvas, 24 x 17 ins / 61 x 43 cm) FRF 8,000.

FRANKEN, Theodore
German, 19th century.
Born 1811, in Geilenkirchen, near Aachen; died 28 March 1876, in Düsseldorf.
Painter. Genre scenes.

Theodore Franken was a pupil of Schadow at the Kunstakademie in Düsseldorf.

FRANKENBACH, Carl Jacob
German, 19th century.
Born 17 October 1861, in Idstein.
Active in Wiesbaden.
Painter. Portraits.

Carl Frankenbach studied in Munich

FRANKENBERG EN PROSCHLITZ, Désiré Oscar Léopold van
Belgian, 19th century.
Born 16 January 1822, in Ghent; died December 1907, in The Hague.
Active in The Hague.
Painter. Portraits, interiors with figures.

Désiré van Frankenberg en Proschlitz was a pupil of W.-H. Schmidt in Delft.

MUSEUMS AND GALLERIES:
AMSTERDAM: *Visit to the Studio of Paul Potter.*

AUCTION RECORDS:
BONN, 19 May 1971, *Portrait of a Woman,* DEM 2,600.

FRANKENBERG LUDWIGSDORFF, Margareta Sylvie von
German, 19th century.
Born 14 January 1857, in Ratibor (now Racibórz, Poland).
Painter. Landscapes, flowers.

Margareta Sylvie von Frankenberg Ludwigsdorff exhibited her works in Berlin and Munich.

FRANKENBERGER, Johann
German, 19th century.
Born 3 April 1807, in Hadamar; died 30 April 1874, in Vienna.
Painter. Portraits, genre scenes.

Johann Frankenberger studied at the academy in Vienna. He was court painter to the Prince of Braunfels.

MUSEUMS AND GALLERIES:
MAINZ: *Portrait of Duke Ferdinand of Wurtemberg, Governor of Mainz.*

FRANKENDAAL, Nicolaas van
Dutch, 18th century.
Active in Amsterdam in 1765.
Engraver.

Nicolaas van Frankendaal was a pupil of Hendrick de Peth and collaborated with him.

FRANKENDORFER, Konrad
German, 15th century.
Active in Nuremberg (Bavaria) c. 1498.
Illuminator.

Frankendorfer made a copy of the *Evangelia Anniversaria cum Epistolis festivalibus,* now in the public library in Nuremberg. The book is wonderfully illuminated with remarkably beautiful initials.

FRANKENSTEIN, John
American, 19th century.
Died 16 April 1881, in New York.
Painter, sculptor.

German by birth, John Frankenstein lived in Cincinnati, Philadelphia and New York.

FRANKENTHALER, Helen
American, 20th century.
Born 12 December 1928, in New York.
Painter, lithographer.
Action Painting, Colour Field Painting, Post-painterly Abstraction.
Second School of New York.

Helen Frankenthaler was a pupil of Rufino Tamayo at the Dalton School, New York, and of Paul Feeley at Bennington College. In 1949, she attended Meyer Shapiro's courses at Columbia University and, in 1950, Hans Hofmann's summer school in Provincetown. In 1958, she married Robert Motherwell.

While with Tamayo, Frankenthaler learned how to control spontaneity by technique and developed a taste for colour. However, her real training began with Paul Feeley, who helped her to understand Cubism, while with Hofmann she was encouraged to eliminate the subject. She also responded to the influences of Wassily Kandinsky, Jackson Pollock and Arshile Gorky - particularly the latter's expressionist *Mountains and Sea* of 1952-1953 - though it was Pollock's work that proved the most decisive influence. A meeting with him at his Long Island studio in 1951 persuaded her to abandon the traditional use of materials and to work on canvases stretched on the floor. Rejecting both drawing and gestural painting, she developed a technique for soaking or staining canvas, in which liquid colours were thrown or poured on to the surface and allowed to spread naturally. Staining gives colour an autonomy of form, often blurred, free from the intervention of the artist and, indeed, for certain American artists, any forethought about the work was associated with academicism.

This procedure, which identifies Frankenthaler with Action Painting, placed her at the centre of pre-war American abstract painting and was later adopted by Morris Louis, Kenneth Noland and Jules Olitski. What distinguished her method from Pollock's was the use of very liquid colours applied over white, unprimed canvas, which became deeply absorbed, eliminating effects of depth or transparency. For Louis, this technique, which later became known as Chromatic Abstraction, provided the bridge 'between Pollock and what is possible'. After 1960, Frankenthaler began to use it a more masterly manner, projecting acrylic paint on to the canvas by different methods and creating shapes with firmer outlines. She also exploited increasingly fluid monochrome colour, pushing the other colours to the edges and achieving an effect sometimes similar to Rothko's Colour Field painting. From time to time, Frankenthaler would change her work by adding new elements, such as calligraphy or impasto, or even incorporating famous paintings, as in *Portrait of Margherita Trip*, after Rembrandt, of 1980. In 1975, she started to make painted ceramics. Although differences between the various techniques of dripping have become less significant with time, Frankenthaler's importance in American painting is largely due to her development of a new form of automatism for a generation of artists inspired by Surrealism.

Frankenthaler has taken part in many group exhibitions, including: 1955, 1958, 1961, Carnegie International, Pittsburgh; 1958, *Nature in Abstraction*, Whitney Museum, New York; 1959, Documenta II, Kassel and the Paris Biennale des Jeunes Artistes; 2002, *The Big Americans*, National Gallery of Australia, Canberra. Solo shows include: 1961, Paris; 1962, Milan; 1969 and 1989, retrospectives, Museum of Modern Art, New York; 1984, graphic works, Solomon Guggenheim Museum, New York; 2003, *Frankenthaler: Paintings on Paper (1949-2002)*, Museum of Contemporary Art, Miami.

Frankenthaler

BIBLIOGRAPHY:

Carmean, E.A. Jr., *Helen Frankenthaler: a Painting Retrospective*, exhibition catalogue, Museum of Modern Art, New York, 1989. Elderfield, John, *Helen Frankenthaler*, Abrams, New York, 1989. *Frankenthaler: Santa Fe Series, Pastels and Other Works on Paper*, exhibition catalogue, Gerald Peters Gallery, Santa Fe, 1990. *Frankenthaler: A Selection of Paintings from the Collection of the Artist 1951-1992*, exhibition catalogue, Neuberger Museum of Art, Purchase (NY), 1992. Fine, Ruth, *Helen Frankenthaler: Prints*, exhibition catalogue, National Gallery of Art, Washington DC, 1993. Pegram, Harrison, *Frankenthaler: a catalogue raisonné, Prints 1961-1994*, Abrams, New York, 1996. Goldman, Judith, *Frankenthaler: the Woodcuts*, exhibition catalogue, Naples Museum of Art, Naples (FL), 2002.

MUSEUMS AND GALLERIES:

BUFFALO (Albright-Knox AG) - GENEVA (MAH): *Passport* (1953) - LOS ANGELES (County MA) - NEW YORK (MoMA): *Jacob's Ladder* (1957); *Mauve District* (1966) - NEW YORK (Whitney Mus. of American Art) - PARIS (MNAM-CCI): *Spring Bank* (1974) - PITTSBURGH (Carnegie MA): *The Facade* (1954, oil on canvas) - RICHMOND (Virginia MFA): *Mother Goose Melody* (1959, oil on canvas) - SYRACUSE (Everson MA): *The Human Edge* (1967, acrylic); *Mattress I* (1975, earthenware) - VIENNA (Mus. Moderner Kunst Stiftung Ludwig): *Salome* (1978) - WASHINGTON DC (Hirshhorn Mus. and Sculpture Garden) - WASHINGTON DC (NGA): *Wales* (1966, acrylic/canvas); *Nature Abhors a Vacuum* (1973, acrylic/canvas).

AUCTION RECORDS:

China (acrylic/canvas, 105 1/2 x 81 ins / 267.8 x 205.8 cm) USD 187,000. NEW YORK, 26 Oct 1972, *Hanging Garden*, USD 15,000. LOS ANGELES, 22 Jan 1973, *Yellow Canon* (1968) USD 6,500. LONDON, 3 April 1974, *Carnival Overture*, GBP 7,800. NEW YORK, 6 May 1976, *Yellow Span* (aquatint, 14 x 18 1/2 ins / 35.5 x 47.3 cm) USD 1,000. NEW YORK, 27 May 1976, *Ridge* (1973, acrylic/canvas, 85 3/4 x 133 ins / 218 x 338 cm) USD 14,000. NEW YORK, 17 Nov 1977, *Swan Lake no. 2* (1961, acrylic/canvas, 93 x 93 1/2 ins / 236 x 237.5 cm) USD 41,000. NEW YORK, 31 March 1978, *Lot's Wife* (1971, coloured lithograph, triptych, 130 x 36 1/2 ins / 330.2 x 92.7 cm) USD 3,300. NEW YORK, 16 May 1980, *Untitled* (1965, mixed media, 18 x 23 3/4 ins / 45.7 x 60.3 cm) USD 4,750. NEW YORK, 8 Nov 1983, *Arriving in Africa* (1970, acrylic/canvas, 82 x 117 3/4 ins / 208.5 x 299 cm) USD 60,000. NEW YORK, 3 May 1984, *Mulberry Essence* (1977, woodcut in colour, 39 1/4 x 18 3/4 ins / 100 x 47.5 cm) USD 12,000. NEW YORK, 2 May 1985, *Boulevard* (1973, acrylic/canvas, 79 1/4 x 257 ins / 201.2 x 652.8 cm) USD 65,000. NEW YORK, 14 Nov 1987, *White Portal* (1967, coloured lithograph, 19 x 14 1/2 ins / 48.5 x 37 cm) USD 4,000. NEW YORK, 3 May 1988, *Face of a Landscape* (acrylic/paper, 22 3/4 x 15 3/4 ins / 57.8 x 40 cm) USD 20,900. NEW YORK, 8 Oct 1988, *Green and Beyond* (1979, acrylic/canvas, 51 1/2 x 61 1/2 ins / 130.8 x 156.2 cm) USD 40,700. NEW YORK, 9 Nov 1988, *Reunion* (1969, acrylic/canvas, 67 x 35 1/2 ins / 170.2 x 90.3 cm) USD 99,000. LONDON, 1 Dec 1988, *Recumbent in a Square* (1961, oil on canvas, 36 x 48 ins / 91.5 x 122 cm) GBP 57,200. NEW YORK, 14 Feb 1989, *Mars* (1963, acrylic/canvas, 89 x 47 1/2 ins / 226.2 x 120.7 cm) USD 71,500. NEW YORK, 3 May 1989, *Cravat* (1973, acrylic/canvas, 62 3/4 x 58 3/4 ins / 159.4 x 149.2 cm) USD 220,000. NEW YORK, 5 Oct 1989, *Deepest August* (1978, acrylic/canvas, 94 1/2 x 167 ins / 240 x 424.2 cm) USD 60,500. NEW YORK, 7 Nov 1989, *Orange Shapes in a Frame* (acrylic/canvas, 93 x 74 1/4 ins / 236.5 x 188.3 cm) USD 649,000. NEW YORK, 8 May 1990, *Yellow Chenille* (oil on canvas, 93 1/2 x 120 ins / 237.5 x 304.8 cm) USD 715,000. NEW YORK, 4 Oct 1990, *Aladdin* (1979, acrylic/canvas, 50 3/4 x 46 1/4 ins / 129 x 117.5 cm) USD 82,500. NEW YORK, 14 Feb 1991, *Golden Day* (1967, acrylic/canvas, 93 x 81 1/2 ins / 236.2 x 207 cm) USD 93,500. NEW YORK, 25-26 Feb 1992, *Yellow Crater* (oil on canvas, 80 3/4 x 68 3/4 ins / 205.1 x 174.6 cm) USD 159,500. NEW YORK, 6 Oct 1992, *April I* (1963, oil on paper, 17 x 14 ins / 43.2 x 35.6 cm) USD 8,250. NEW YORK, 19 Nov 1992, *Emerson Series III* (1965, acrylic/paper, 18 x 23 3/4 ins / 45.7 x 60.3 cm) USD 7,150. NEW YORK, 3 May 1993, *Yellow Lightning* (1963, oil on canvas, 53 1/2 x 69 1/2 ins / 135.9 x 176.5 cm) USD 200,500. NEW YORK, 9 Nov 1993, *Swan Lake II* (1961, oil on canvas, 93 x 93 1/2 ins / 236.2 x 237.5 cm) USD 244,500. NEW YORK, 3 May 1994, *Blue Chenille* (oil on canvas, 117 1/4 x 68 3/4 ins / 297.5 x 174.9 cm) USD 189,500. LONDON, 27 Oct 1994, *Untitled* (1976, acrylic/paper, 28 x 23 1/2 ins / 71 x 60 cm) GBP 5,750. NEW YORK, 5 May 1996, *Nepenthe* (1972, etching and aquatint, 15 3/4 x 24 1/4 ins / 40 x 61.5 cm) USD 2,300. NEW YORK, 9 May 1996, *Blue Right-Angle* (1969, acrylic/canvas, 106 x 88 1/2 ins / 269.2 x 224.8 cm) USD 104,250. NEW YORK, 20 Nov 1996, *Mist* (1984, acrylic/canvas, 61 1/2 x 72 1/4 ins / 156.2 x 183.5 cm) USD 46,000. NEW YORK, 21 Nov 1996, *Untitled* (1973, acrylic/canvas, 28 1/2 x 27 ins / 72.4 x 68.5 cm) USD 28,750. NEW YORK, 7 May 1997, *High Frequency* (1970, acrylic/canvas, 71 1/4 x 60 1/4 ins / 181 x 153 cm) USD 46,000. NEW YORK, 8 May 1997, *Cats Green* (1967, acrylic/canvas, 44 1/2 x 25 1/2 ins / 113.3 x 64.8 cm) USD 34,500. NEW YORK, 17 Feb 1999, *Tantric* (1977, acrylic on canvas, 70 x 67 ins / 177 x 171 cm) USD 40,000. NEW YORK, 17 Feb 1999, *Untitled* (acrylic on canvas, 96 x 78 ins / 244 x 198 cm) USD 88,000. NEW YORK, 10 May 2000, *Arcadia* (1962, oil on canvas, 89 x 81 ins / 225 x 205 cm) USD 115,000. NEW YORK, 16 Nov 2000, *Winter Blue* (1983, acrylic on canvas, 52 x 89 ins / 131 x 226 cm) USD 75,000. NEW YORK, 16 May 2001, *Summer View* (1963, oil on canvas, 60 x 46 ins / 153 x 116 cm) USD 105,000. NEW YORK, 17 May 2001, *Dusk* (acrylic on canvas, 34 x 27 ins / 86 x 69 cm) USD 155,000. NEW YORK, 16 May 2002, *Harbinger* (acrylic on canvas, 54 x 95 ins / 136 x 241 cm) USD 42,500. NEW YORK, 14 Nov 2002, *Devil's Mist* (acrylic on canvas, 79 x 76 ins / 201 x 192 cm) USD 140,000. NEW YORK, 11 Nov 2003, *Mountain Storm* (1955, oil on canvas, 72 x 48 ins / 183 x 122 cm) USD 450,000. NEW YORK, 12 Nov 2003, *Courtyard of El Greco's House* (1959, oil on canvas, 46 x 61 ins / 116 x 154 cm) USD 200,000. NEW YORK, 13 May 2004, *Big Dipper* (acrylic on canvas, 82 x 52 ins / 208 x 131 cm) USD 120,000. NEW YORK, 15

Sept 2004, *Sea Strip* (1965, acrylic on canvas, 52 x 39 ins / 133 x 99 cm) USD 170,000.

FRANKFORT, Eduard
Dutch, 19th century.
Born 21 June 1864, in Meppel.
Painter.

AUCTION RECORDS:
LONDON, 6 Feb 1925, *Frugal Meal*, GBP 6.

FRANKFURT, Master of. See **MASTERS**

FRANKFURTER, Max
German, 19th century.
Active in Düsseldorf.
Painter.

FRANKHART, P.
German, 18th century.
Born c. 1710, in Hamburg; died 1743.
Painter. Portraits.
Frankhart was a pupil of J. Rundt.

FRANKL, Gyulia
Slovak, 19th century.
Born 1840, in Cadca.
Painter.
Gyulia Frankl worked in Munich and Paris.

FRANKLIN, Dwight
American, 20th century.
Born 28 January 1888, in New York.
Painter, sculptor.

FRANKLIN, George
British, 19th century.
Painter. Religious subjects.
George Franklin was a frequent exhibitor in London between 1825 and 1847, notably at the Royal Academy and the British Institution.

FRANKLIN, John
British, 19th century.
Born c. 1800.
Painter. History painting, architectural views.
John Franklin exhibited between 1830 and 1868 at London's Royal Academy, British Institution and Suffolk Street Gallery.

MUSEUMS AND GALLERIES:
LONDON (Victoria and Albert Mus.): *Council Chamber, Doge's Palace, Venice.*

FRANKLIN, Mary
American, 19th century.
Born in Athens (Ohio).
Active in Paris.
Painter, engraver.
Mary Franklin was a pupil of Geoffroy and Louis Deschamps. She exhibited mainly portraits and genre paintings, including *Toilette* and *Slice of Bread.*

FRANKLIN-GROUT, Caroline (Mme)
French, 19th century.
Active in Antibes.
Painter.
Franklin-Grout was a member of the Société des Artistes Français from 1889.

FRANKO, François Caspar
Austrian, 18th century.
Active in Vienna in 1701.
Sculptor.

FRANKOT, Roel
Dutch, 20th century.
Born 1911, in Meppel.
Painter (mixed media).
Roel Frankot received no formal artistic training. He started out as a photographer and started painting around 1935. He took part in numerous group exhibitions featuring the work of contemporary Dutch artists. His first solo exhibition was in Amsterdam in 1950.

Influenced by the Paris School, he typically re-arranged everyday objects, applying post-Cubist precepts to generate compositions that were abstract in form if not in content. His work, which often features inconsequential scraps of material mixed into the paint, became progressively abstract over time.

AUCTION RECORDS:
AMSTERDAM, 27-28 May 1993, *Untitled* (1961, oil on canvas, 51 1/4 x 76 3/4 ins / 130 x 195 cm) NLG 5,060.

FRANKS, Frederick
British, 19th century.
Died 1844.
Painter, watercolourist.

MUSEUMS AND GALLERIES:
LONDON (British Mus.): 22 watercolours.

FRANKY BOY, Sevehon
French, 20th century.
Painter, sculptor.
Figuration Libre.
In 1980 with Tristam and Waty, Sevehon Franky Boy founded the painters' group known as Les Musulmans Fumants (The Smoking Muslims) which exhibited in 1982-1983 at the Palace in Paris and in 1984 at the FIAC (Foire Internationale d'Art Contemporain). In addition to their paintings, sometimes executed jointly, they also produced record covers and videos. Franky Boy held solo exhibitions of his work in Paris in 1986 and 1987 and in London in 1988.

AUCTION RECORDS:
PARIS, 13 April 1988, *Setting Out to Sea* (mixed media, 27 1/2 x 12 1/4 x 7 3/4 ins / 70 x 31 x 20 cm) FRF 4,500. PARIS, 18 Oct 1990, *Untitled* (1987, acrylic/canvas, diptych, each panel 25 1/2 x 18 ins / 64.5 x 46 cm) FRF 20,000. PARIS, 4 Oct 1994, *Hot Air Balloon with Giraffe* (1989, mixed media/canvas, 35 x 46 ins / 89 x 116 cm) FRF 7,500. PARIS, 20 Nov 1994, *Giraffe in a Blue Car* (polystyrene sculpture, h. 11 3/4 ins / 30 cm) FRF 4,800.

FRANOZ, François Charles de
French, 19th century.
Born c. 1850, in Paris; died 1908.
Sculptor.
Franoz exhibited at the Salon des Artistes Français from 1889 to 1904.

FRANQUE, Jean-Pierre
French, 19th century.
Born 1774, in Le Buis (Drôme); died 1860, in Paris.
Painter. History painting, religious subjects, mythological subjects, portraits.
Groupe des Penseurs (or the Primitifs).
Jean-Pierre Franque studied under Jacques-Louis David and exhibited at the Paris Salon from 1806 to 1853, securing a silver medal in 1812. He was made a Chevalier of the Légion d'Honneur in 1836. Franque painted predominantly historical portraits and a range of mythological and biblicval themes. In 1828, he painted a composition entitled *St John the Baptist Rebuking Herod for his Adultery* for the Paris church of St-Jean-François-de-Assisi. His *Virgin Crushing a Serpent's Head* hangs in the church of Moissac in the Tarne-et-Garonne region. Other examples of his work include *Battle of Zurich, Hercules Freeing Alceste, Archangel Michael Slaying the Dragon, Shepherd in Terror of the Storm, A New Life, Virgin and Child, Portrait of Monsignor de Quélen, Archbishop of Paris,* together with a composition for the

Elysée Palace entitled *Dream of Love Induced by the Power of Harmony*.

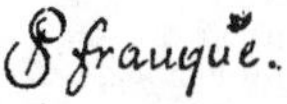

Bibliography:
Rosenthal, D., *'Joseph Franque's Scene During the Eruption of Vesuvius'* in *Bull. Philadelphia Mus. A.*, vol lxxv/324, 1976 (pp. 2-15). Levitine, G., *The Dawn of Bohemianism: The Barbu Rebellion and Primitivism in Neoclassical France*, University Park (PA), 1978.

Museums and Galleries:
ANGERS: *Angélique and Médor* - BESANÇON: *Charles Nodier* - DIJON: *Conversion of St Paul* - MONTAUBAN: *Jupiter Lying Asleep in the Arms of Juno on Mount Ida* - NÎMES: *Josabeth Protecting Joash from the Fury of Athaliah* - VALENCE: *Dream of Love* - VALENCIENNES: *Mademoiselle de Condé* - VERSAILLES: *Battle of Lens; Marchioness de Montespan; Eleonor of Austria, Queen of Poland; Princes de Baden-Baden; Cardinal de Talleyrand-Périgord; Begum Somrou, Mongolian Princess; Villars; Charles Henri d'Estaing; Henry IV; Louis XVIII.*

Auction records:
MONACO, 17 June 1988, *Portrait of the Duc de Barry* (oil on canvas, 48 1/2 x 37 3/4 ins / 123 x 96 cm) FRF 88,800.

FRANQUE, Jérôme
17th century.
Painter.

Mentioned by Marolles, this artist seems to have been one of the Hieronymus Francken.

FRANQUE, Joseph
French, 18th - 19th century.
Born 1774, in Le Buis; died 14 November 1833, in Naples.
Painter. History painting, allegorical subjects, mythological subjects, portraits.
Groupe des Penseurs (or the Primitifs).

Joseph Franque was a student of David like his twin brother Jean-Pierre. Towards the end of the Empire, he left France and settled in Naples, where he became a professor of the academy. He sent various works to the Salon, from 1806 to 1827, of which the following are mentioned: *Hercules Snatching Alcestis from Hell, Daphnis Showing Chloë How To Play the Flute, Allegory of the State of France before the Return from Egypt* and *Portrait of Asker-Kan, Persian Ambassador*.

Museums and Galleries:
VERSAILLES: *Empress Marie-Louise Watching the King of Rome Sleeping.*

Auction records:
PARIS, 30 March 1987, *Empress Marie-Louise Watching the King of Rome Sleeping* (oil on canvas, 22 x 18 ins / 55 x 46 cm) FRF 52,000.

FRANQUE, Lucile
Maiden name: Messageot
French, 18th century.
Born 1780; died 1802.
Active in Lons-le-Saulnier (Jura).
Painter.
Groupe des Penseurs (or the Primitifs).

Lucile Franque was the wife of Jean-Pierre Franque.

FRANQUEBALME, Henriette
Maiden name: Cousin
French, 19th century.
Painter.

Franquebalme exhibited at the Paris Salon from 1842 to 1845 under her maiden name of Henriette Cousin and subsequently, from 1847 to 1849, under her married name of Franquebalme. Examples of her work include *Taking the Veil, Young Girl with a Daisy, Odalisque, Sick Child* and *Gamekeeper's Hut*.

FRANQUELIN, Ève
French, 20th century.
Born in Paris.
Painter.

Ève Franquelin exhibited in Paris at the Salon d'Automne in 1929 and also at the Salon des Indépendants.

FRANQUELIN, Jean-Augustin
French, 19th century.
Born 1 September 1798, in Paris; died 4 January 1839, in Paris.
Painter, miniaturist. Religious subjects, portraits, genre scenes.

Franquelin studied at the École des Beaux-Arts in Paris in 1812 under Jean-Baptiste Regnault. He exhibited at the Paris Salon from 1819 to 1839 and was awarded silver in 1827. The town of Douai also acknowledged his work with the award of a silver medal in 1821 and gold medals in 1823 and 1827. Franquelin's body of work alternates from portraits to genre compositions and to scenes from the life of Christ. Examples include *Jesus Leaving the Temple* (Tours Cathedral), *Death of Malvina* (Fontainebleau Palace) and *Baptism of Christ* (church of St-Philippe du Roule), together with *Prison Interior, Shipwreck, Sailor's Widow, Letter of Reply, Wedding Day, Catalan Woman Praying for her Sick Son, Regrets*, and *Jealousy*.

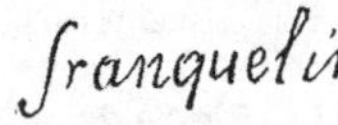

Museums and Galleries:
AMIENS: *Christ Bringing Jairus' Daughter Back to Life* - DOUAI: *Young Cook Learning of the Death of her Fiancé*; two studies - GRENOBLE: *Young Woman with Child Asleep in her Arms and a Dog by her Side* - KALININGRAD: *Waiting; Roman Woman Praying to the Madonna to Protect her Son* - LEIPZIG: *Bragella* - VERSAILLES: *View of Brisach.*

Auction records:
PARIS, 1863, *Token of Love*, FRF 250. PARIS, 1873, *Memory and Regrets*, FRF 2,000. PARIS, 11 March 1925, *Henry IV and the Young Shepherd*, FRF 1,210. PARIS, 6 Dec 1946, *Box of Mementoes*, FRF 56,000. NEW YORK, 7 Oct 1977, *Reading the Palm* (oil on canvas, 21 3/4 x 18 ins / 55.5 x 46 cm) USD 1,700. VERSAILLES, 16 Nov 1980, *Reading Lesson* (oil on wood, 19 3/4 x 15 1/2 ins / 50 x 39.5 cm) FRF 10,500. LONDON, 21 May 1982, *Young Chimney Sweep* (oil on canvas, 12 1/4 x 15 3/4 ins / 31 x 40 cm) GBP 2,000. LONDON, 9 Oct 1985, *Pain of Love* (oil on canvas, 28 3/4 x 24 1/2 ins / 73 x 62 cm) GBP 3,000. BERN, 26 Oct 1988, *Sicilian Fisherman's Family* (oil on canvas, 19 x 14 3/4 ins / 48 x 37.5 cm) CHF 2,600. NEW YORK, 22 Feb 1989, *Small Bedroom* (oil on canvas, 18 x 15 ins / 45.7 x 38.1 cm) USD 93,500. EDINBURGH, 22 Nov 1989, *Favourite Doll* (oil on canvas, 8 3/4 x 7 1/4 ins / 22.3 x 18.4 cm) GBP 4,620. PARIS, 9 April 1990, *Before the Masked Ball* (oil on canvas, 18 x 15 1/2 ins / 45.5 x 39.5 cm) FRF 190,000. PARIS, 11 Dec 1991, *Pensive Young Woman Leaning against a Rock* (oil on canvas, 18 1/4 x 15 1/4 ins / 46.5 x 38.5 cm) FRF 20,000. NEUILLY, 19 March 1994, *Returning to the Valley* (oil on canvas, 28 3/4 x 23 1/2 ins / 73 x 60 cm) FRF 16,000. LONDON, 6 July 1999, *Sleeping Child* (chalk, 4 x 7 ins / 11 x 19 cm) GBP 4,000. NEW YORK, 2 May 2000, *Mother and Child* (oil on canvas, 22 x 18 ins / 55 x 46 cm) USD 13,000. NEW YORK, 3 May 2000, *The Attendant* (oil on canvas, 18 x 15 ins / 46 x 38 cm) USD 35,000. PARIS, 25 Oct 2001, *Preparations for the Ball* (oil on canvas, 18 x 15 ins / 46 x 38 cm) FRF 30,000. LONDON, 8 July 2003, *At the Milliners* (1829, oil on canvas, 7 x 9 ins / 18 x 24 cm) GBP 2,000.

FRANQUESA, Francesc
Spanish, 20th century.

Born 1899, in Barcelona.
Painter. Landscapes.

Francesc Franquesa moved to Madrid while still young and studied at the Real Academia de Bellas Artes de San Fernando. He exhibited at collective and solo exhibitions in Madrid and Barcelona, notably at the Modern Art Salon in Madrid in 1925. Although he produced work other than landscape painting, he is primarily known for his views of the Aran Valley.

FRANQUET, José
Spanish, 17th century.
Active in Cornudella, c. 1650.
Painter.

José Franquet was a pupil of Juan Juncosa and is mentioned by Siret. He collaborated with Joachim Juncosa, his teacher's son, on paintings for the hermitage of Nuestra Señora de la Misericordia near Reus.

FRANQUETTE, Jacques
French, 14th century.
Active in Dijon.
Sculptor. Monuments.

Franquette worked on the tomb of Philip the Bold in 1398 and 1399.

FRANQUEVILLE, Jacques Adouldan de
French, 18th century.
Active in Paris.
Engraver.

Jacques Franqueville's plates after Lemoine or Rosalba Carriera are mentioned.

FRANQUEVILLE, Pierre de.
See **FRANCHEVILLE**

FRANQUINET, Willem Hendrik
Dutch, 19th century.
Born 25 December 1785, in Maastricht; died 12 December 1854, in New York.
Painter, lithographer. History painting.

Willem Hendrik Franquinet was a pupil of Herreyns in Antwerp. He was a professor in Maastricht from 1804 to 1815. He subsequently travelled to Germany, Holland and France, and between 1822 and 1834 he published *The Painters' Gallery* in collaboration with J. Chabert.

FRANS (Master), or Franz
Dutch, 15th century.
Glass painter.

In 1436, this artist was working on the cathedral in Florence.

FRANS, Adriaen
Flemish School, 17th century.
Died 1706, in Bruges.
Painter.

A work by this artist is in the English Jesuit college in Bruges.

FRANS, Hans or Johannes, erroneously known as Frank
Flemish School, 17th century.
Active at the beginning of the 17th century.
Painter.

Hans Frans was the son of Gillis Frans and probably the nephew of Ambrosius Francken. He is almost certainly the Hans Frans recorded as a pupil of Lambrecht de Jode. He taught painting in Antwerp in 1603, and became a member of the Guild of St Luke in the same city in 1606.

FRANS, Maximilian. See **FRANCK**

FRANS, Nicolaus
Flemish School, 16th century.
Born 1539, in Mechelen.
Painter. History painting.

It is not known with whom this Franciscan monk studied. Three of his works have been identified, two in the church at Hanswyck near Mechelen and the other, *The Flight into Egypt*, in the church of Our Lady in Mechelen.

AUCTION RECORDS:
ANTWERP, 1853, *Interior of an Inn*, FRF 150; *The Fortune Teller*, FRF 32. LONDON, 18 March 1932, *Christ in the House of Simon*, GBP 7. LONDON, 10 June 1932, *Christ in the House of Simon*, GBP 5.

FRANSE, Jacques Jos.
Flemish School, 18th century.
Painter.

Franse was a pupil at the Antwerp academy in 1782.

FRANSEN, Isaacq
Dutch, 17th century.
Active in Amsterdam, c. 1645.
Painter.

FRANSEN, Jan
Dutch, 17th century.
Born c. 1605, in Amsterdam; died c. 1646.
Painter.

Most of Fransen's works are landscapes and still-lifes.

FRANSIN, François Alexis
French, 17th century.
Sculptor.

François Fransin was the king's sculptor in Paris. On 12 January 1693, he married Eléonore Coustou. At the wedding were Antoine Coysevox, ordinary sculptor to the king, from the royal house of Gobelins, and Nicolas Coustou and Guillaume Hulot, also sculptors to the king.

FRANSKIN, Louis
French, 17th - 18th century.
Born in Rochefort.
Sculptor.

Louis Franskin worked for the abbey of St Rémi and the church at Marche.

FRANSOLET-CARLIER, Cécile
Belgian, 20th century.
Died 1968.
Painter. Landscapes, seascapes.

Lived and worked in Huy in the Belgian province of Liège.

FRANSONIO, Luigi
Italian, 17th century.
Active in Naples at the beginning of the 17th century.
Painter.

FRANSSEN
British, 20th century.
Painter. Portraits, genre scenes.

Franssen worked in London.
AUCTION RECORDS:
LONDON, 25 June 1930, *A Meal*, GBP 35.

FRANSSIÈRES, Jacques de
French, 18th century.
Active in Beauvais.
Engraver.

Jacques Franssières produced some plates for a book about Turkish costumes published in Paris in 1714.

FRANTA, pseudonym of Merte Frantisek

Czechoslovak, 20th century.
Born 16 March 1930, in Trebíc.
Active from 1959 and naturalised in France.
Painter, sculptor, draughtsman. Figure compositions.
Franta studied at the school of art in Prague, then lived in Perugia in Italy where he continued his studies before settling in Paris. He has lived and worked in Nice and St-Paul-de-Vence since 1959.

Whatever technique he used, Franta carried out the same research into the human condition. The will to do this is already apparent in his first works, as in the portrait of his wife *Jacqueline* (1965), in which he sets out to examine the human face based on sweeping, impulsive movements inherited from Expressionism and to cross-examine the face until its subjectivity and ambivalent feelings are understood. In the 1970s, new concerns appear. From then on Franta portrays bodies, their integrity threatened, in forms defying definition, piles of bruised flesh, clashing with a garishly coloured totalitarian world composed of hostile machines or threatening geometric forms. Wash or Indian ink drawings from the same period take up these themes, as do the series of *Traps*, which again show a disabled man confronted with the modern world, as well as sculptures. However (a result no doubt of his numerous trips to Africa), his painting becomes more objective from 1980 onwards: the bodies of men and women with black skin no longer clash but share in an exuberant, multicoloured vegetation, the light becomes warmer, the colours more vibrant. Franta seems to lose himself in these images full of exoticism in order to relinquish for once his tragic view of existence. A harmony emerges, but Franta is not fooled by it: he is aware of its vulnerability.

Franta featured in many collective exhibitions and in the Paris Salons including: Salon de la Jeune Peinture, Salon Comparaisons, Salon de Mai, Salon Grands et Jeunes d'Aujourd'hui. He was also invited to the Paris Biennale (1963 and 1965). His first solo exhibition took place in Paris in 1960, followed by many others in France and abroad, including: Galliera Museum, Paris (1984); Bronx Museum of the Arts, New York (1989); Kunstmuseum, Bochum (1990);, Musée d'Art Moderne et Contemporain, Nice (1996); and *L'Afrique*, Espace St-Jean, Melun (2001).

BIBLIOGRAPHY:
Richthofen, Alice von, '*Franta, Musée de Bochum*' in *Opus international* n° 118, periodical, Paris, March-April 1990. Artaud, Evelyne, et al., *Franta. Monographie*, Éd. Cercle d'Art, Paris, 2001.

MUSEUMS AND GALLERIES:
ÉPINAL (Mus. départemental d'Art ancien et contemporain): *Metro* (1967).

AUCTION RECORDS:
PARIS, 20 May 1989, *Free and Equal* (1989, acrylic and pastel/paper, 57 1/2 x 45 ins / 146 x 114 cm) FRF 26,000. PARIS, 21 June 1990, *Woman crouching 2* (1989, oil on canvas, 57 1/2 x 45 ins / 146 x 114 cm) FRF 65,000.

FRANTSOUSOV, Youri, or Iuri
Russian, 20th - 21st century.
Born 1946.
Painter. Figures.
Youri Frantsousov was a student at the Repin Institute in Leningrad (now St Petersburg), where he was a pupil of E. Moisseinko.

AUCTION RECORDS:
PARIS, 9 Dec 1991, *Little Ballerinas* (1969, oil on canvas, 13 x 24 1/2 ins / 33 x 62 cm) FRF 6,500.

FRANTZ
Swiss, 16th century.
Active in Lucerne c. 1590.
Glass painter.
This artist may be the same person as Franz Fallenter.

FRANTZ, F.
French, 19th century.
Painter, watercolourist. Seascapes.

MUSEUMS AND GALLERIES:
PERPIGNAN: *Rough Seas* (watercolour).

AUCTION RECORDS:
LONDON, 4 June 1908, *Two Seascapes* (watercolour) GBP 2. PARIS, 10 April 1924, *Grand Canal, Venice*; *Turkish Merchants in Istanbul* (two watercolours) FRF 700. PARIS, 15 May 1931, *Landscape by the Sea* (watercolour) FRF 20. PARIS, 13 June 1934, *View of Venice; View of Naples* (two watercolours) FRF 280. PARIS, 27 Dec 1940, *Oriental Scenes; Seascapes* (watercolour, forming a pair) FRF 440. PARIS, 17 and 18 Dec 1941, *Fishing Boats* (watercolour) FRF 280. PARIS, 29 Jan 1945, *Fishermen and Boats Run Aground* (watercolour) FRF 610. PARIS, 27 June 1945, *Boats Aground on a Rocky Shore* (watercolour) FRF 400. PARIS, Oct 1945-July 1946, *Yachts on Shore* (watercolour) FRF 4,100. PARIS, 2 Dec 1946, *Boats Aground; Low Tide* (two watercolours) FRF 1,550.

FRANTZ, Johann Martin
German, 18th century.
Active in Künersberg.
Potter.
Johann Martin Franz worked on decorating in the regions of Amstadt and Eichstaat.

FRANTZ, Johann Wentzel
German, 18th century.
Active in Striegau.
Sculptor.
Johann Frantz married the daughter of the sculptor J. B. Scholtz.

FRANTZ, Marshall
Ukrainian, 20th century.
Born 26 December 1890, in Kiev.
Active in the USA.
Illustrator.
Frantz illustrated many works and magazines.

FRANTZEN, Christian
Danish, 17th century.
Died 1630, in Næstved.
Painter. Portraits.

FRANTZEN, Conrad
Danish, 17th century.
Active in Copenhagen.
Painter. Portraits.

FRANTZEN, Franz
German, 19th century.
Died 25 July 1873, in Cologne.
Painter.

FRANTZEN, Gustave
French, 19th - 20th century.
Born 1873, in Paris.
Painter, engraver.
Gustave Frantzen produced paintings and wood engravings copied after the old masters. He was awarded a gold medal at the Salon des Artistes Français in Paris.

FRANTZEN, Heinrich
Swedish, 18th century.
Active in Marielberg.
Potter.
Heinrich Frantzen was the father of Johann Otto Frantzen.

FRANTZEN, Johann Carl
German, 18th century.
Active in Augsburg.
Painter.
The *Portrait of J. J. Holzapfel* is attributed to Johann Frantzen.

FRANTZEN, Johann Otto
Danish, 18th century.
Painter (porcelain).
Johann Otto Frantzen was the son of Heinrich Frantzen.

FRANTZEN, Thomas
Dutch, 16th century.
Born in Utrecht; died before 5 August 1597.
Sculptor.
Frantzen worked particularly in Danzig (now Gdansk).

FRANTZEN, Tom
Belgian, 20th - 21st century.
Born 1954, in Watermaal-Bosvoorde.
Sculptor. Figures, animals. Monuments.
Tom Frantzen attended the École Nationale Supérieure des Arts Visuels in La Cambre, the Rijkhoger Kunstonderwijs in Etterbeek and the Académie des Beaux-Arts in Watermael-Boitsfort.

He was appointed to the post of professor at the art academy in Overijse. He won the Prix Godecharle in 1981. As he is a bronze specialist, he built his own bronze foundry in 1978. He has produced several monuments: *Ernest Claes* at the Grote Markt (large square) in Zichem; *André Demedts*, at the Demedtshuis in Sint-Baafs-Vivje; *Vaartkapoen* at the Sainctelettteplein (square) in Brussels. He has participated in many group exhibitions, including: 1982, 1st Triennale de Sculpture, Galerie Delta, Brussels; 1985, Antwerp-Middelheim Biennale; 1986, *The Automobile in Art*, Haus der Kunst, Munich; 1987, *Lineart*, Ghent. He has had solo shows, including: 1982, Palais des Beaux-Arts, Charleroi; 1984, Centre Culturel Mutualiste, Brussels; 1987, Maison de la Belgique, Cologne.

BIBLIOGRAPHY:
Piet Peere, Tom Frantzen, exhibition catalogue, Gal. Amaryllis, Brussels, 1989.

FRANZ
Polish, 16th century.
Born in Wislica.
Active in Cracow.
Painter.
Franz worked for King Sigismund I.

FRANZ, pseudonym of Franz Dappier
Belgian, 20th century.
Born 11 June 1948, in Charleroi; died 8 January 2003, in France.
Active in France.
Draughtsman. Comic strips.
Franz Dappier studied art at St Luke's Academy in Brussels and at the Academy in Mons. As a contributor to *Spirou* and *Tintin*, he is regarded as one of the last representatives of classic 1970s Belgian bandes dessinés (comic strip) art. He is perhaps best known as the creator of characters such as Kaurigan and, above all, Lester Cockney, an Irish rebel and adventurer serving in the British Army. Franz, as Dappier liked to be known, also collaborated with Frédéric Dard, the creator of the novel character San Antonio.

FRANZ, Adam
Austrian, 16th century.
Active in Linz.
Sculptor.
Adam Franz undertook work at the church of St Florian.

FRANZ, Andreas
German, 18th century.
Born in Grün; died c. 1783.
Sculptor.
Andreas Franz was a pupil of Mutschelle in Bamberg.

FRANZ, Bernhard
Austrian, 16th century.
Born c. 1550, in Vienna.
Sculptor.
Bernhard Franz was the nephew and pupil of Caspar Woller.

FRANZ, Carl Joseph
German, 19th century.
Born 9 September 1829, in Dresden; died 8 December 1875, in Dresden.
Painter. History painting, genre scenes.
Carl Joseph Franz studied at the Dresden academy and with the painter Schwind in Munich. He exhibited fairly regularly in Dresden from 1852.

FRANZ, Ettore Roesler. See **ROESLER FRANZ Ettore**

FRANZ, Gottfried
German, 19th century.
Born 1846, in Mainz; died 14 June 1905, in Munich Pullack.
Painter, illustrator.
This artist was a pupil of Diez in Munich.

FRANZ, Johann Michael
German, 18th century.
Active in Eichstätt.
Painter.
Johann Franz came originally from Souabe. He was painter to the prince bishop of Eischstatt and carried out the decoration of his residence. He also worked for the Church of Kemnathen.

FRANZ, Julius
German, 19th century.
Born 1824, in Berlin; died 16 December 1887, in Berlin.
Sculptor.
Julius Franz studied at the Berlin academy under the tutelage of Wichmann the Younger and Ferdinand August Fischer. He completed his studies in the studios of Wredow and Rauch.

MUSEUMS AND GALLERIES:
LEIPZIG (Leipzig Mus.): *Shepherd Attacked by a Panther.*

FRANZ, Wilhelm
German, 19th century.
Born 1863, in Cologne.
Painter. Portraits.
Wilhelm Franz worked mainly in Chemnitz. A portrait of the king Albert of Saxony is attributed to him.

FRANZ OF ANTWERP. See **AMBERES Francisco de**

FRANZ-DREBER, Heinrich. See **DREBER Heinrich**

FRANZ-NAMUR. See **NAMUR Paul Franz**

FRÄNZEL, Wilhelm
Austrian, 19th century.
Born 1826, in Vienna.
Sculptor (ivory). Portraits, historical figures. Busts, medallions, low reliefs.
Wilhelm Fränzel studied at the Bongiovanni modelling school in Vienna, and then at the academy in Vienna. He went to Venice, Paris, England and St Petersburg. He specialised in portraits. His works include *Bust of the Emperor Nicholas of Russia*, a medallion of *Francis I, Bust of Metternich*, and a low relief with *Ajax*.

MUSEUMS AND GALLERIES:
VIENNA: *Bust in Ivory of Marshall Radetzky; Bust of Francis Joseph II.*

FRANZEN, August
Swedish, 19th - 20th century.
Born 1868, in Norrköping; died 1938.
Painter. Genre scenes.

August Franzen was a pupil of Dagnan Bouveret and settled in New York. He was awarded a medal at the Chicago Exhibition of 1893, a bronze medal in Paris in 1900 and a silver medal in Buffalo in 1901.

MUSEUMS AND GALLERIES:

BROOKLYN, NY.

AUCTION RECORDS:

VERSAILLES, 18 June 1981, *Charity* (oil on canvas, 28 x 36 ins / 71 x 91.5 cm) FRF 26,500. NEW YORK, 27 Jan 1984, *A Backyard* (oil on panel, 16 x 11 3/4 ins / 40.5 x 29.9 cm) USD 6,250.

FRANZÉN, John Erik

Swedish, 20th century.

Born 1942, in Stockholm.

Painter.

Franzén made many trips to the USA. In 1971 he participated in a Parisian exhibition of the work of eight young Swedish artists. Since 1962 he has used prefabricated, everyday images including magazine photographs, labels and adverts to establish the facts about the contemporary myths of our society. His painting, which verges on Hyperrealism in technique, differs from it in spirit: he has no wish to draw up a 'neutral' inventory of post-industrial civilisation, but prefers to use the images which make their presence felt, as a source of inspiration and poetry.

AUCTION RECORDS:

STOCKHOLM, 26 April 1982, *Self-portrait Sitting in an Interior* (oil on canvas, 69 x 53 1/4 ins / 175 x 135 cm) DKK 60,000. STOCKHOLM, 16 May 1984, *Portrait of a Man* (1979, watercolour, 19 3/4 x 17 1/4 ins / 50 x 44 cm) SEK 10,700. STOCKHOLM, 13 April 1992, *Ulrika - Nude Model Standing* (1961, oil on canvas, 35 x 22 ins / 88 x 56 cm) SEK 11,000. STOCKHOLM, 13 March 2000, *Harley Davidson* (1986, gouache, 11 x 18 ins / 29 x 46 cm) SEK 14,000. STOCKHOLM, 2 May 2001, *Venice California* (1995-1999, oil on canvas, 30 x 30 ins / 77 x 76 cm) SEK 210,000. STOCKHOLM, 6 Nov 2001, *Fylleskog - Landscape with Lake* (1975-1977, oil on canvas, 20 x 16 ins / 50 x 40 cm) SEK 39,000.

FRANZESE, Gennaro

Italian, 18th century.

Active in Monte Cassino in 1750.

Sculptor (wood).

Gennaro Franzese worked for the abbey of Monte Cassino.

FRANZESE, Guglielmo

Italian, 17th century.

Active in Naples in 1603.

Sculptor.

Guglielmo Franzese sculpted several statues for the church of Christ in Naples.

FRANZETTI, A.

Italian, 18th century.

Engraver.

A. Franzetti predominantly engraved views of ancient ruins.

FRANZETTO, G. B.

Italian, 17th century.

Active in Milan.

Painter.

G. B. Franzetto is on record as living in Rome in 1671.

FRANZHEIM, Élizabeth

American, 20th century.

Born 1923, in Chicago; died 2 April 1990, in Paris.

From 1959 active in France.

Painter, collage artist, sculptor, draughtsman. Murals.

When she was still a child, Elizabeth Franzheim's drawings were noticed by the portrait painter William Adam, who invited her to join his adult classes, and, in 1940, she enrolled at the Fine Arts School of Yale University. While pursuing her painting she also made murals in Houston and, from 1956, undertook theatre research, designing stage sets that employed video.

Franzheim's early work was figurative, but in Paris she explored Surrealism, abstraction and Hyperrealism and, in the 1950s, moved towards abstract signs, producing huge calligraphic drawings in black, white and grey that recall American Lyrical Abstraction. She also made mineral-coloured collages using blotting paper, boxes, X-rays and algae, combined with figures and signs, set against a luminous and transparent background, which create a world bathed in mysticism reminiscent of certain Eastern painting.

Franzheim took part in group exhibitions in the USA, Europe and Japan, and, from 1949, held solo shows, including large retrospectives in Paris, Milan and Chicago. She received many prizes and distinctions.

E Franzhein

BIBLIOGRAPHY:

Elizabeth Franzheim, exhibition catalogue, Galerie d'Art International, Paris, 1979 (text in English and French). Bouyeure, Claude, '*Élizabeth Franzheim, une façon de recevoir les signes*' in *Cimaise* n° 147, periodical, Paris, summer 1980. *Élizabeth Franzheim - L'Œuvre 1965-1985*, exhibition catalogue, Art Center, Paris, 1985.

FRANZINI D'ISSONCOURT, Charles Henri

French, 19th - 20th century.

Born 1872, in Virieu.

Painter. Portraits.

Charles Franzini d'Issoncourt studied under Cabanel and Cormon. He was awarded hors concours at the Salon des Artistes Français in Paris, where he received a number of medals. He was also awarded a silver medal at the Exposition Universelle in Paris in 1900.

AUCTION RECORDS:

BERN, 30 April 1980, *Landscape with Flock of Sheep* (oil on canvas, 21 1/4 x 25 1/2 ins / 54 x 65 cm) CHF 1,400. LONDON, 25 Nov 1992, *Portrait of Two Children* (1896, oil on canvas, 57 x 38 1/4 ins / 145 x 97 cm) GBP 4,620. LONDON, 7 April 1993, *Portrait of a Lady* (1901, oil on canvas, 46 x 34 1/4 ins / 116 x 87 cm) GBP 483.

FRANZKO

German, 14th century.

Active in Schweidnitz, Silesia (now Swidnica, Poland) at the end of the 14th century.

Painter.

FRANZONI, Albert

Swiss, 19th century.

Born 25 December 1857, in Geneva.

Painter, engraver (wood).

Albert Franzoni studied at the Brera in Milan and under the direction of B. Menn. He exhibited in Switzerland and in Paris, where he gained a bronze medal in 1900. Among his works are canvases (*The Midday Angelus in the Mountains* and *Portrait of a Lady*), watercolours (*Corn in Emen, Emen in Springtime, Haute-Valais*) and others. The Rath Museum in Geneva has his *Summer in Valais*.

FRANZONI, Bartolomeo

Italian, 18th - 19th century.

Active in Carrara.

Sculptor.

Bartolomeo Franzoni sculpted copies of works by Chaudet and Canova.

FRANZONI, Carlo

Italian, 18th - 19th century.

Active in Carrara.

Sculptor.

Carlo Franzoni studied under his father Bartolomeo Franzoni.

FRANZONI, Emanuele
Italian, 19th century.
Born 15 July 1788, in Carrara.
Sculptor.
Emanuele Franzoni worked with his brother Carlo in Bologna.

FRANZONI, Enrico
Italian, 19th century.
Born in Carrara; died 11 November 1852, in Port-au-Prince, Haiti.
Sculptor.
For many years, Enrico Franzoni was a soldier.

FRANZONI, Filippo
Swiss, 19th - 20th century.
Born 1857, in Locarno (Ticino); died 23 March 1911, in Mendrisio.
Active in Italy.
Painter. Portraits, landscapes.
Franzoni studied painting in Milan, Florence and Rome and spent several periods living in France. He also worked in Austria and in the Munich area and participated in various exhibitions in Paris. He was preoccupied by light and its effects and would not start a painting without first studying photographs and producing several preliminary studies.
MUSEUMS AND GALLERIES:
NEUCHÂTEL: *Maggia River Delta.*
AUCTION RECORDS:
BERN, 8 May 1987, *View of Locarno* (oil on panel, 121/4 x 7 ins / 31 x 17.5 cm) CHF 11,500.

FRANZONI, Francesco Antonio
Italian, 18th - 19th century.
Born 23 January 1734, in Carrara; died 3 March 1818, in Rome.
Sculptor.
Francesco Antonio Franzoni found favour with Pope Pius VI, who commissioned him, among other things, to restore a large number of works of antiquity.

FRANZONI, Giuseppe
Italian, 18th century.
Born c. 1752, in Carrara.
Sculptor.
Giuseppe Franzoni was almost certainly the brother of Francesco Antonio Franzoni.

FRANZONI, Giuseppe Antonio
Italian, 19th century.
Born c. 1778, in Carrara; died 1814, in Washington DC.
Sculptor.
Giuseppe Franzoni was the son of Bartolomeo Franzoni. He emigrated to America in 1806.

FRANZONI, Thérèse Agnes
Maiden name: Patron
Swiss, 19th century.
Born 8 March 1856, in Geneva.
Painter. Landscapes.
This artist was the wife of Albert Franzoni.
MUSEUMS AND GALLERIES:
LUGANO: *Landscape.*

FRAPIER, André
French, 20th century.
Born 20th century.
Potter.

FRAPOLLI, Giuseppe
Italian, 19th century.
Active in Seville c. 1858.
Sculptor.
Frapolli worked for the cathedrals of Cádiz, Cordova and Malaga.

FRAPPA, José, or Frapa
French, 19th century.
Born 18 April 1854, in St-Étienne; died 16 February 1904, in Paris.
Painter. Religious subjects, genre scenes, portraits.
Frappa studied first under Pierre Charles Comte at the École des Beaux-Arts in Lyons, and then at the Beaux-Arts in Paris under Isidore Pils. He exhibited widely in Paris, showing at the Paris Salon for the first time in 1876. Frappa was first and foremost a portraitist who painted ecclesiastical dignitaries (often in the course of their work) with meticulous attention to detail. Among his better work are his *Vicar's Song* and *Celebration of His Eminence.*

José FRAPPA

MUSEUMS AND GALLERIES:
LYONS: *Blond Woman* - MULHOUSE: *Dozing* - PARIS (Mus. d'Orsay) - ST-ÉTIENNE (Mus. d'Art et d'Industrie): *Final Moments of St Francis of Assisi* - STRASBOURG: *Lamb Among the Wolves.*
AUCTION RECORDS:
PARIS, 12 Dec 1877, *In Flagrante Delicto,* FRF 950. PARIS, 6 May 1895, *Obsession,* FRF 2,000. NEW YORK, 10 Feb 1903, *Art Gallery,* USD 700. PARIS, 21-22 Nov 1920, *Young Woman with Oranges,* FRF 420; *Fine Wine,* FRF 580. PARIS, 6 Feb 1930, *Feast Day,* FRF 1,700. LONDON, 11 Dec 1936, *Conferring,* GBP 14. NEW YORK, 27-28 May 1943, *Priest at Breakfast,* USD 170. PARIS, 11 June 1945, *Two Monks in the Monastery Garden,* FRF 200. NEW YORK, 6 Oct 1966, *Hail to his Eminence,* USD 1,800. VIENNA, 18 Sept 1973, *La Prise,* ATS 35,000. NEW YORK, 10 Oct 1973, *Dancer,* USD 1,400. NEW YORK, 14 May 1976, *Gentleman's Pastime* (oil on panel, 24 x 193/4 ins / 61 x 50 cm) USD 3,500. VERSAILLES, 19 July 1981, *Portrait of a Young Woman* (1882, pastel, 353/4 x 281/4 ins / 91 x 72 cm) FRF 5,500. NEW YORK, 26 Feb 1986, *Cardinal Playing the Harp* (oil on panel, 181/4 x 133/4 ins / 46.3 x 35 cm) USD 4,500. NEW YORK, 29 Oct 1992, *Young Woman with Oranges* (oil on canvas, 323/4 x 21 ins / 83.2 x 53.3 cm) USD 3,960. CALAIS, 25 June 1995, *Street Talk* (oil on panel, 133/4 x 101/4 ins / 35 x 26 cm) FRF 13,000. PARIS, 10 Dec 1996, *Acrobat with Mandolin* (oil on canvas, 32 x 26 ins / 81 x 66 cm) FRF 7,000. PARIS, 5 Feb 1999, *Le pas de danse chez Monseigneur* (oil on panel, 35 x 46 ins / 88 x 116 cm) FRF 22,000. NEW YORK, 2 Nov 1999, *Cardinal's Birthday* (oil on canvas, 26 x 35 ins / 66 x 90 cm) USD 82,500. LONDON, 6 April 2000, *On the Way to a Ball* (oil on canvas, 46 x 32 ins / 117 x 82 cm) GBP 4,000. MILFORD, 11 May 2000, *Flautist* (1875, oil on panel, 13 x 10 ins / 33 x 25 cm) USD 1,800. PARIS, 25 June 2001, *Two Clergymen in a Museum* (oil on panel, 22 x 18 ins / 55 x 46 cm) FRF 38,000. LONDON, 18 June 2003, *Recital* (oil on panel, 18 x 15 ins / 46 x 37 cm) GBP 2,500. LONDON, 21 Jan 2004, *Surprised* (oil on panel, 24 x 18 ins / 61 x 45 cm) GBP 2,000. NEW YORK, 22 April 2004, *L'intrus* (oil on panel, 26 x 30 ins / 66 x 76 cm) USD 10,000.

FRAPPANTI, Bartolomeo
Italian, 15th century.
Active in Bologna in 1474.
Painter.

FRAPPART, Félicie (Mme)
French, 19th century.
Painter.
Frappart exhibited at the Paris Salon from 1831 to 1836. Examples of her work include *Duke, Lst Farewells of Louis XIV*

to Henrietta of England on her Deathbed, Louis XV and Madame du Barry and *Margaret of Scotland with Alain Chartier.*

FRAPPART, Jean
French, 14th century.
Active in Dijon.
Sculptor.

In 1398, Frappart worked under the direction of Claus Sluter on the decoration of the *Well of Moses* in the cloister of the Carthusian church at Champmol, Dijon.

FRAPPAZ, Jules Marc François
French, 19th century.
Born 12 October 1813, in Dunkirk.
Painter.

Frappaz enrolled at the École des Beaux-Arts on 4 October 1834 and studied under Ingres and Paul Delaroche. He exhibited at the Paris Salon from 1840 to 1855, submitting chiefly portraits and watercolours, together with some genre compositions such as his *Peasant from near Rome Listening to a Capuchin Monk.*

FRAQUAIR-LANG, Annie. See **LANG Annie Fraquair**

FRARI, Il. See **BIANCHI-FERRARI Francesco de '**

FRARY, Mathieu Florent, or Flament
French, 17th century.
Died 1697; buried the 28 October in Paris.
Sculptor, painter.

Mathieu Frary worked in Lyons around 1685 and in Paris in 1689.

FRASCÀ, Nato
Italian, 20th century.
Born 1931, in Rome.
Painter, sculptor, engraver.

After studying architecture in Italy, Nato Frascà worked in Paris in Stanley Hayter's print workshop, *Atelier 17*. He participated in numerous exhibitions and was awarded various prizes and distinctions in Italy. Initially influenced by Expressionism, Frascà's work grew more abstract between 1955 and 1956. Influenced by Hayter, he developed the line, according it an autonomy of its own in his canvases and his relief constructions, which share certain similarities with Op Art. The colours used are very soft - a rarity in this form of abstract art.

FRASCARI, Giuseppe
Italian, 18th century.
Active in Rome during the first half of the 18th century.
Painter, sculptor.

Giuseppe Frascari sculpted a monumental statue of *St Gregory Thaumaturgus* for the façade of the basilica of S Giovanni in Laterano.

FRASCHERI, Giuseppe
Italian, 19th century.
Born 1808; died 1886, in Genoa.
Painter. History painting, portraits, genre scenes.

Frascheri was active in Savona in 1809.

MUSEUMS AND GALLERIES:
FLORENCE (NG): *Self-portrait.*

AUCTION RECORDS:
MILAN, 11 Dec 1978, *Francesca da Rimini* (oil on canvas, 23 x 14¼ ins / 57.5 x 36 cm) ITL 1,900,000.

FRASER, Alec
British, 20th century.
Painter. Landscapes.

Alec Fraser was active between 1903 and 1912.

AUCTION RECORDS:
GLASGOW, 22 Nov 1990, *Fishing Village in Scotland* (oil on canvas, 14 x 21 ins / 35.3 x 53.3 cm) GBP 1,100. EDINBURGH, 11 May 2000, *Still-life of Vase of Flowers, a Book and Bowl of Fruit* (oil on board, 27 x 23 ins / 69 x 58 cm) GBP 1,850. MONTREAL, 22 Oct 2002, *River in Autumn* (oil on canvas, 47 x 59 ins / 119 x 150 cm) CAD 3,500. EDINBURGH, 18 Aug 2004, *Boys Guddling on the Shore* (pastel, 14 x 22 ins / 36 x 55 cm) GBP 1,250.

FRASER, Alexander, the Younger
British, 19th century.
Born 12 January 1828, in Woodcockdale, near Linlithgow, Scotland; died 24 May 1899, in Musselburgh.
Painter. Genre scenes, landscapes.

Alexander Fraser was sent by his father to study in Edinburgh. His first submission to the Royal Academy of Scotland exhibition was a genre composition. He was elected to associate membership of the Academy in 1858 and to full membership in 1862. His best work includes *Hills of Surrey, Spring Sun, Forest Glade* and *Highland Torrent.* His most accomplished landscapes were painted in Surrey and in Cadzow Forest. He proved particularly adept at rendering changing light on the hills and heather. His warm and vibrant palette, which perfectly captures nuances of late summer and autumn, his excellent compositional sense and his choice of subject matter ensured him a prominent place among the ranks of British landscape painters of his day.

MUSEUMS AND GALLERIES:
EDINBURGH: *Barnelinth* - GLASGOW: *Scene; Landscape; Country Path; Highland Clearance; View of Cadzow Forest; Autumn in Cadzow Forest; Spring in Cadzow Forest; Woodcutters in Cadzow Forest; Autumn Scene in Cadzow Forest; Castle Campbell in Spring; Waterfall; Scottish Highlands; Sunshine at North Berwick; Bass Rock seen from Canty Bay* - LONDON (Victoria and Albert Mus.): *Forest Scene; Young Fishermen on a Rock; Shepherd Playing the Bagpipes; Favourite; Fisherman's Son; Barnelinth Gardens.*

AUCTION RECORDS:
LONDON, 25 Jan 1908, *Robinson Crusoe,* GBP 2. LONDON, 14 March 1908, *Mary Stuart at Holyrood Palace,* GBP 18. LONDON, 10 July 1908, *River Styx,* GBP 22. LONDON, 12 Feb 1910, *Walter Scott as a Young Man,* GBP 98. LONDON, 19 March 1910, *Bothwell Castle,* GBP 57. LONDON, 3 June 1910, *Ben Alan; Ben Venue,* GBP 110; *Landscape,* GBP 68. PERTH, 13 April 1976, *Stealing Beer* (oil on canvas, 28½ x 35½ ins / 72.5 x 90 cm) GBP 320. LONDON, 21 Oct 1977, *Kilchurn Castle, Argyll* (oil on canvas, 29 x 40½ ins / 73.6 x 102.8 cm) USD 800. LONDON, 28 April 1981, *Cardington Mill, Bedford* (1886, watercolour heightened with gouache, 17 x 22¾ ins / 43 x 58 cm) GBP 400. EDINBURGH, 12 April 1983, *Woodcutting in Cadzow Forest* (oil on canvas, 47¼ x 50 ins / 120 x 127 cm) GBP 5,000. LONDON, 30 Jan 1987, *Hunting Hare* (oil on panel, 25 x 30 ins / 63.2 x 76 cm) GBP 4,500. EDINBURGH, 30 Aug 1988, *Craigneathan Castle* (oil on canvas, 12¼ x 18 ins / 31 x 46 cm) GBP 1,760. LONDON, 27 Sept 1989, *Morning Catch* (oil on panel, 14 x 19½ ins / 35.5 x 49.5 cm) GBP 4,180. SOUTH QUEENSFERRY, 1 May 1990, *Hot Drink* (oil on canvas, 28 x 36 ins / 71 x 91.5 cm) GBP 2,530. SOUTH QUEENSFERRY, 23 April 1991, *Autumn in the Surrey Hills* (1867, oil on canvas, 30 x 42¼ ins / 76 x 107 cm) GBP 3,300. PERTH, 26 Aug 1991, *Resting in the Meadow* (oil on canvas, 11½ x 19½ ins / 29.5 x 49.5 cm) GBP 1,100. LONDON, 3 June 1992, *Church of St Nicholas' Hospital, Harbledown, Kent* (oil on card, 13 x 18¾ ins / 33 x 47.5 cm) GBP 1,045. PERTH, 1 Sept 1992, *Major Discovery* (oil on canvas, 10 x 14¼ ins / 25.5 x 36 cm) GBP 3,300. NEW YORK, 29 Oct 1992, *Evening Meal* (oil on canvas, 19¾ x 24 ins / 50.2 x 61 cm) USD 1,540. EDINBURGH, 23 March 1993,

Unloading the Catch (1869, oil on canvas, 15 x 24 3/4 ins / 38 x 63 cm) GBP 1,725. GLASGOW, 1 Feb 1994, *Ducks on a Pond* (oil on reinforced canvas, 9 3/4 x 7 3/4 ins / 25 x 20 cm) GBP 1,092. MONTREAL, 21 June 1994, *Interior of a Fisherman's Cottage at Newtonhill, Kincardineshire* (oil on canvas, 25 x 30 ins / 63.5 x 76.2 cm) CAD 1,700. PERTH, 29 Aug 1995, *Ducks* (oil on canvas, 18 1/2 x 25 1/2 ins / 47 x 64.5 cm) GBP 1,380; *Village Street* (oil on canvas, 36 x 28 ins / 91.5 x 71 cm) GBP 1,610. GLASGOW, 16 April 1996, *A Peep of the Gareloch* (oil on canvas, 18 x 26 1/4 ins / 45.5 x 66.5 cm) GBP 2,875. PERTH, 20 Aug 1996, *Cottage in the Sun* (oil on canvas, 19 x 29 ins / 48.5 x 73.5 cm) GBP 2,185. LONDON, 6 June 1997, *Uddingston on the River Clyde with Bothwell Castle in the Distance* (1872, oil on canvas, 26 x 37 ins / 66 x 94 cm) GBP 21,275. GLASGOW, 25 Aug 1997, *Moss Hag at Dalmally on Loch Awe* (oil on panel, 11 1/4 x 18 ins / 28.5 x 45.7 cm) GBP 690. GLASGOW, 25 Feb 1999, *Vicar's Bridge on the Devon, Perthshire* (oil on canvas, 24 x 34 ins / 61 x 87 cm) GBP 3,000. BILLINGSHURST, 26 Oct 1999, *Rest by the Stream* (oil on canvas, 27 x 35 ins / 69 x 89 cm) GBP 5,000. EDINBURGH, 12 May 2000, *Feeding the Hens* (oil on canvas, 30 x 42 ins / 75 x 106 cm) GBP 3,800. EDINBURGH, 25 Aug 2000, *Thrush's Nest* (oil on board, 8 x 13 ins / 21 x 34 cm) GBP 1,600. LONDON, 8 March 2001, *On Loch Falloch* (1882, oil on canvas, 16 x 24 ins / 41 x 61 cm) GBP 1,800. LONDON, 7 March 2002, *Highland River Landscape* (oil on canvas, 29 x 41 ins / 74 x 104 cm) GBP 1,900. LONDON, 14 April 2003, *Old Watermill, North Wales* (oil on canvas, 33 x 26 ins / 85 x 67 cm) GBP 2,000. OTTAWA, 21 Nov 2003, *Fishing at Puneugh Point, Dairy, Ayshire* (oil on canvas, 12 x 19 ins / 30 x 47 cm) CAD 4,500. EDINBURGH, 19 Feb 2004, *Prince Charlie's Bedroom, Holyrood* (oil on panel, 13 x 20 ins / 34 x 50 cm) GBP 1,700. EDINBURGH, 18 Aug 2004, *Glen Falloch* (oil on canvas, 17 x 28 ins / 44 x 72 cm) GBP 2,200.

FRASER, Alexander George, the Elder

British, 19th century.
Born 7 April 1786, in Edinburgh; died 15 February 1865, in Wood Green (Middlesex).
Painter, illustrator. Figure compositions, genre scenes, landscapes, seascapes, animals.

Alexander Fraser began his career in Edinburgh before moving to London in 1812, where he exhibited until 1848. He was a member of the Royal Academy of Scotland from 1840. The vast majority of his early work was seascapes. He later provided illustrations for Scott's *Waverley Novels*, several of which were subsequently engraved. His major works include *Scene from Sir Walter Scott's Heart of Midlothian, Robinson Crusoe Reading the Bible, Final Moments of Mary Stuart* and *Tun of Ale*.

MUSEUMS AND GALLERIES:

LONDON (Tate Collection): *Interior of a Cottage in the Hebrides* (c. 1835?, oil on canvas); *Figures Outside an Inn: Scene from 'Peveril of the Peak'* (oil on canvas).

AUCTION RECORDS:

PARIS, 1859, *Village View*, FRF 4,940. PARIS, 1861, *Village Sign Painter* (watercolour) FRF 3,700. PARIS, 20 March 1874, *Fisherman's Rest*, FRF 4,250. LONDON, 20 Dec 1922, *Fish Merchant* (drawing) GBP 50. LONDON, 21 Dec 1923, *Woodcutter's Cottage*, GBP 10. LONDON, 30 May 1924, *Highland Landscape*, GBP 39. LONDON, 14 July 1924, *Glen Falloch*, GBP 13. LONDON, 23 March 1925, *Sunshine after the Rain*, GBP 25. LONDON, 17 June 1927, *Pastures New*, GBP 19. LONDON, 2 Dec 1927, *Sheepshearing*, GBP 9. LONDON, 23 May 1928, *Boglehill Girl Herding Geese*, GBP 10. EDINBURGH, 27 Oct 1928, *Tarbert*, GBP 9. EDINBURGH, 15 Dec 1928, *Edge of the Wood*, GBP 29. EDINBURGH, 26 March 1929, *Dalmally*, GBP 22. EDINBURGH, 13 July 1929, *Landscape*, GBP 9; *Lanercost Abbey*, GBP 92. LONDON, 16 Dec 1929, *Home is the Hunter*, GBP 27. LONDON, 4 April 1930, *Returning Flock*, GBP 13. LONDON, 16 May 1930, *Cottage Door*, GBP 11. LONDON, 27 Nov 1930, *Ben Lawers*, GBP 8. EDINBURGH, 29 Nov 1930, *Cadzow Forest*, GBP 16. EDINBURGH, 25 April 1931, *Bridge at Inverstruan*, GBP 7. LONDON, 18 June 1931, *Landscape*, GBP 40. EDINBURGH, 7 May 1932, *Robinson Crusoe*, GBP 4. GLASGOW, 2 Nov 1933, *Autumn in Surrey*, GBP 220; *Glen Falloch*, GBP 135; *Dalmally*, GBP 75; *Glen Falloch*, GBP 30; *Trossachs*, GBP 13; *Conway Valley*, GBP 14. EDINBURGH, 11 Nov 1933, *Grey Day*, GBP 8. LONDON, 8 June 1934, *Kilchurn Castle*, GBP 11. LONDON, 3 May 1935, *Tinsmith*, GBP 17. EDINBURGH, 22 June 1935, *Perthshire Landscape*, GBP 19. EDINBURGH, 13 July 1935, *Dunblane*, GBP 4. GLASGOW, 4 June 1936, *Glen Falloch*, GBP 10. LONDON, 2 April 1937, *Burns Night Supper*, GBP 11. LONDON, 26 July 1937, *Burns Night Supper*, GBP 13. NEW YORK, 4 March 1938, *Wayside Halt*, USD 90. PARIS, 7 June 1943, *Welsh Cottage*, FRF 3,900. GLASGOW, 14 Dec 1944, *Landscape*, GBP 23. LONDON, 22 Feb 1946, *Three Generations*, GBP 31. LONDON, 19 June 1946, *Ardconnall Castle*, GBP 37. LONDON, 14 July 1972, *Banks of the Avon*, Gns 1,700. GLASGOW, 4 Dec 1991, *Old Copperware* (oil on card, 9 3/4 x 8 ins / 25 x 20.5 cm) GBP 935. GLASGOW, 1 Feb 1994, *Ducks by the River* (oil on canvas, 18 1/2 x 25 1/2 ins / 47 x 65 cm) GBP 1,265. EDINBURGH, 25 Nov 1997, *Game of Draughts* (1850, oil on panel, 11 3/4 x 16 ins / 29.9 x 40.4 cm) GBP 3,450. AUGSBURG, 10 Nov 2000, *Interior with Mother, Daughter and Man* (oil on cloth, 35 x 46 ins / 88 x 118 cm) DEM 12,000. MERE, 12 June 2004, *Children at the Village Pump* (1829, oil on canvas, 18 x 14 ins / 46 x 36 cm) GBP 1,500. BATH, 26 July 2004, *Robinson Crusoe* (oil on board, 12 x 16 ins / 30 x 40 cm) GBP 1,800.

FRASER, Andrea

American, 20th - 21st century.
Born 27 September 1965, in Billings (Montana).
Installation artist, performance artist, video artist, writer. Multimedia.

Andrea Fraser studied at the School for Visual Arts (1982(1983) and at the Whitney Museum of American Art Independent Study Program, New York (1984(1985). She has taught as a guest artist in sculpture at the Cooper Union (1990, 1996), and in performance at the Tyler School of Art in 1992. She works in New York City and Brazil. Fraser has received awards from the New York Foundation for Arts (1991); the National Endowment for the Arts (1991); and Art Matters Inc. Fellowships (1987, 1989).

Since the late 1980s, Fraser has been best known for her performances as a 'museum docent', giving staged tours of museums in which she raises institutional criticism to the level of art. She addresses issues of art publications and sponsorship, gender and class relations in institutions, the history of art organisations and cultural transfer. Her first tour was conceived as part of the *Damaged Goods: Desire and the Economy of Object* exhibition at the New Museum of Contemporary Art, New York, in 1986, in which Fraser adopted the fictional persona of Jane Castleton who appeared to give an improvised tour, although her performance was carefully researched and scripted. She aims to further the public's awareness of what large art establishments expect from their visitors, and to relate the aesthetic values of museums to economic and social values. Fraser has used 'Jane Castleton' in performances at other venues, including Artists Space, New York (1986), Philadelphia Museum of Art (1989) and Wadsworth Atheneum, Hartford, CT (1991), and has also used audio tours, educational videos and wall labels as media for her critiques. More recently, Fraser has worked in video installations such as *Exhibition*, in which she performs as a scantily clad Samba dancer in order to show the importance of popular culture in the context of art, and *Soldadero*, where she plays a horse-riding revolutionary, evoking the Mexican revolution in order to address US Mexican relations.

Fraser's exhibitions include: 1992, *Aren't They Lovely?*, University Art Museum, Berkeley; 1993, *A Society of Taste*,

Kunstverein, Munich; 1993, the Whitney Biennial; 1993, the Venice Biennale; 1995, *A Project in Two Phases*, EA-Generali Foundation, Vienna; 1996, *Temporarily Possessed*, New Museum of Contemporary Art, New York; 1997, *Collected*, The Photographers' Gallery/The Wallace Collection, London; 1999, *The Museum as Muse: Artists Reflect*, Museum of Modern Art, New York; 2001, *Antagonisms*, Museum of Contemporary Art, Barcelona; 2002, *Exhibition*, Belkin Art Gallery, University of British Columbia, Vancouver; 2003, *Works: 1984 to 2003*, Kunstverein, Hamburg.

BIBLIOGRAPHY:

Fraser, Andrea, *Woman 1: Madonna and Child, 1506-1967*, Illustrated book, A. Fraser, New York, 1984. Fraser, Andrea, *May I Help You? January 12-February 2, 1991*, Video, 1987. Fraser, Andrea, *Welcome to Wadsworth: A Tour Conducted at the Wadsworth Atheneum, Hartford, Connecticut...*, Video, 1991. *Andrea Fraser: Works, 1984 to 2003*, Exhibition catalogue, Dumont, Cologne, 2003 (text in German and English). *Exhibition: Andrea Fraser*, Exhibition catalogue, Morris and Helen Belkin Art Gallery, Vancouver, 2004.

MUSEUMS AND GALLERIES:

ANTWERP (Mus. Van Hedendaagse Kunst Antwerpen): *Museum Highlights* (video) - BARCELONA (Antoni Tapiès Foundation) - HANOVER (Sprengel Mus.) - HARTFORD (Wadsworth Atheneum) - LONDON (Royal Academy of Arts) - NEW YORK (MoMA) - PARIS (École des Beaux Arts) - PARIS (MNAM-CCI) - PHILADELPHIA (MA): *Museum Highlights: A Gallery Talk* (1989, betacam video) - ROTTERDAM (Mus. Boijmans Van Beuningen).

FRASER, Arthur Anderson

British, 19th - 20th century.

Born 1861, in Bedford; died 1904, in Holywell.

Watercolourist.

Arthur Anderson Fraser was one of nine brothers. He left Bedford School in 1880 and became an accomplished watercolourist and cartoonist. He exhibited his work mainly between the years of 1884 and 1904. His compositions generally concentrated on the Bedfordshire landscape (most especially the River Ouse and surrounding streams), showing a heightened sensitivity towards both light and colour in the depiction of water.

AUCTION RECORDS:

LONDON, 3 July 2001, *Spring Floods* (1885, watercolour heightened with white, 12 x 18 ins / 30 x 45 cm) GBP 2,400.

FRASER, Calum

British, 20th - 21st century.

Born 1956, in Edinburgh.

Active in France.

Painter, watercolourist. Figures, scenes with figures, landscapes.

Nouvelle Figuration.

Calum Fraser studied at the Slade School of Fine Arts in London from 1974 to 1978 and then at the École des Beaux-Arts in Paris from 1978 to 1980. In 1983, he received a bursary from the British Art Council and in 1981 a Scottish Young Contemporaries prize. He settled in Paris, where he works with warm, dark colours applied in light touches in subtle gradations of tone, painting figures that are stilted but evolving. A disturbing atmosphere fills his vague yet menacing scenes in which plots - both contemporary and from the past - are being hatched. He transports the viewer into another time, 'the other side of the mirror', a fictional universe that is erotic, aggressive and rich in mystery and irony. Fraser took part in 1987 in the exhibitions *Figuration d'Aujourd'hui* (*Representative Art Today*) at the MJC, Hauts-de-Belleville, Paris; in 1987 in *Art LA 87* in Los Angeles; and in 1988 in the Armory Show in New York. He showed his work regularly in solo exhibitions from 1979 in Paris: in 1979 at the Galerie Peinture Fraîche; in 1984 at the Galerie Philippe Frégnac; and in 1987 at the Galerie Lavignes-Bastille.

BIBLIOGRAPHY:

Calum Fraser, exhibition catalogue, Gal. Lavignes-Bastille, Paris, 1987. *Calum Fraser*, exhibition catalogue, Gal. Lavignes-Bastille, Paris, 1989.

AUCTION RECORDS:

PARIS, 18 Feb 1990, *Tokyo Scene* (1985, 65 x 45 ins / 165 x 114 cm) FRF 15,000. PARIS, 23 April 1990, *Man with Umbrella* (1986, acrylic/canvas, 47 1/4 x 15 ins / 120 x 38 cm) FRF 14,000. PARIS, 8 Nov 2004, *James Joyce* (1991, oil on canvas, 79 x 83 ins / 200 x 210 cm) EUR 1, 500.

FRASER, Charles

American, 19th century.

Born 20 August 1782, in Charleston; died 1860, in Charleston.

Painter, miniaturist. Portraits, genre scenes, landscapes.

Charles Fraser studied law before becoming an artist. In 1825 he painted a portrait of Lafayette. In 1857 an exhibition of his works was held in his home town, Charleston; it included 313 miniatures and 130 landscapes and other paintings. Fraser's works were included in *Love and Loss: American Portrait and Mourning Miniatures* at the Gibbes Museum of Art in Charleston in 1983.

BIBLIOGRAPHY:

Severns, Martha R./Wyrick, Charles L. Jr., *Charles Fraser of Charleston: Essays on the Man, his Art and his Times*, Gibbes Museum of Art, Charleston, 1983.

MUSEUMS AND GALLERIES:

CHARLESTON (Gibbes MA): *James Reid Pringle (1782-1840)* (1845, watercolour on ivory).

AUCTION RECORDS:

LONDON, 11 April 1967, *View of the Hudson River* (watercolour) GBP 400. LONDON, 18 June 1972, *Collecting for the Regiment*, Gns 220. NEW YORK, 14 Nov 1991, *Trenton Falls, West Canada Creek, New York State* (oil on canvas, 23 x 31 ins / 58.4 x 78.7 cm) USD 4,400. COLUMBIA, 24 March 2001, *Portrait of Thomas Gilman Fletcher in a Black Coat with a White Shirt* (miniature, 3 x 3 ins / 8 x 8 cm) USD 8,500.

FRASER, Claud Lovat, or Lovat Claud

British, 20th century.

Born 15 May 1890, in London; died 18 June 1921, in Folkestone.

Theatre designer, woodcut artist, illustrator, draughtsman.

Claud Lovat Fraser was a largely self-taught artist. He briefly attended Westminster School of Art, where he studied under Sickert, but left after a year to take up his own studio in London. His preferred media are known to have been reed and steel pens, watercolour and ink. In a short career, he produced an astonishing number of illustrations and designs for books, broadsides and greeting cards; from 1917 he also worked designing textiles for theatre. Some of the books he illustrated include H. Beerbohm Tree's *Thoughts and Afterthoughts* (Cassel, 1913) and several chapbooks and rhyme sheets produced in partnership with Ralph Hodgson. Between 1914 and 1919 he served in the Army and suffered in a gas attack at Ypres, Flanders, after which he worked in the War Office on visual propaganda. His designs for theatre include designs for the costumes of *As You Like It* (performed at Stratford upon Avon in 1919); for the sets and dresses of Beaumont and Fletcher's *The Captain*, and for *The Maid Turned Mistress* and *La Serva Padrona*; the last two were performed at the Opera House, Hammersmith, in 1919. Fraser also designed the costumes for Holst's *Savitri* which played at the Lyric Hammersmith (1921). He held his first solo exhibition at his own studio at Roland Gardens, London, in 1913 and again at the Leicester Galleries in 1921. He died young, aged 31, after an operation.

Bibliography:

Millard, C., *The Printed Work of Claud Lovat Fraser*, H. Danielson, London, 1923. Fraser, C.L., *Sixty-three Unpublished Designs*, First Edition Club, London, 1924 (Introduction by Holbrook Jackson). *Claud Lovat Fraser*, exhibition catalogue, Victoria and Albert Museum, London, 1969 (Includes essay by artist's widow Grace Lovat Fraser). Driver, C.E., *The Art of Claud Lovat Fraser: Book Illustrator, Theatrical Designer and Commercial Artist; An Exhibition*, exhibition catalogue, Rosenbach Foundation, Philadelphia, 1971. Rogerson, Ian, *Claud Lovat Fraser: An Exhibition of His Illustrations*, exhibition catalogue, Manchester Polytechnic Library, Manchester, 1984. Lee, B.N., *The Bookplate Designs of Claud Lovat Fraser*, exhibition catalogue, H. Berliner, Nevada City (CA), c. 1985. *A Catalogue of the Illustrated Books, Broadsides etc.*, exhibition catalogue, Manchester Metropolitan University Library, Manchester, 1993.

Museums and Galleries:

London (Tate Collection): *The Slave Market* (1912-1913, gouache, watercolour and drawing on canvas); *Seated Female Nude* (1919, watercolour and drawing on paper); *Nude Study: Two Seated Women* (c. 1919, ink, pencil and wash on paper) - London (Victoria and Albert Mus.).

Auction records:

London, 16 March 1934, *Morana alias Mac Heath*, GBP 8. London, 22 Feb 1980, *Filch (Mr Alfred Heather) in 'The Beggar's Opera'* (1920, watercolour and pen, 16 1/4 x 10 ins / 41 x 25.3 cm) GBP 300. London, 3-4 March 1988, *Lieutenant Tom Boisling* (1737, watercolour, black ink, 10 1/4 x 7 1/4 ins / 26.2 x 18.3 cm) GBP 572. London, 21 Sept 1989, *Equestrienne Anglaise* (watercolour and ink, 13 x 8 1/2 ins / 33.1 x 21.6 cm) GBP 825. London, 5 April 2001, *Costume Design for Uberto in La Serve Padrona* (1919, pen, ink, watercolour and silver paint, 13 x 9 ins / 32 x 24 cm) GBP 2,800.

FRASER, Donald Hamilton, or Hamilton-Fraser
British, 20th century.
Born 1929, in London.
Painter (including mixed media). Still-lifes, landscapes, seascapes.

After studying at St Martin's School of Art in London, Donald Fraser was awarded a bursary by the French government to study in Paris from 1953 to 1954. He taught at the Royal College of Art in London from 1965 to 1983. He was elected a member of the Royal Academy in 1985. Fraser's earliest works display a technique which evolved very little: he makes strong arrangements of broad flat tints - dense yellows, reds and blacks harmonised by greys - applied with a knife and using textural effects. He also works in collage, using brightly coloured paper - blues, reds and yellows, harmonised with greys - which he integrates with each other through layering. His approach, notably in his landscapes, is in the tradition of Nicolas de Staël's late period.

Fraser's work has also been included in many group exhibitions, including *Six British Painters*, in Chicago, Buffalo and Ottawa, 1957-1958; *British Art Today*, in Dallas, Santa Barbara and San Francisco, 1963; *25 Years of British Painting*, at the Royal Academy, London, 1977; and *British Landscape Painting*, in Hong Kong, 1995. He has held numerous solo exhibitions in London, Zurich, Paris and New York since his first one-man show in 1953 at Gimpel Fils, London.

Bibliography:

Six Young Painters: Donald Hamilton Fraser, Anthoney Fry, Peter Kinley, Edward Middleditch, Jack Smith, Michael Wishart, Midland Group of Artists Gallery, Nottingham, 1957. *Young British Painters October 18-November 15, 1964*, exhibition catalogue, North Carolina Museum of Art, Raleigh, 1965.

Auction records:

London, 3 Dec 1976, *Landscape* (1967, polymer/canvas, 48 x 36 ins / 122 x 91.5 cm) GBP 250. London, 12 June 1981, *Blue Sea Coast with Distress Rocket* (1953, oil on canvas, 36 x 28 ins / 91.5 x 71.2 cm) GBP 400. London, 9 March 1984, *Jetty, Capernaum* (oil on paper, 22 x 16 ins / 56 x 40.5 cm) GBP 700. New York, 2 May 1985, *The Beach* (1957, oil on canvas, 48 x 36 ins / 122 x 91.5 cm) USD 2,400. London, 12 May 1989, *Flowers and Chair* (oil on canvas, 28 x 19 1/2 ins / 71.2 x 49.4 cm) GBP 1,980. London, 2 May 1991, *Blue Seascape* (oil on paper/panel, 9 x 7 ins / 23 x 18 cm) GBP 550. London, 7 June 1991, *Landscape* (1967, oil on canvas, 48 x 35 ins / 121 x 89 cm) GBP 4,070. London, 14 May 1992, *Bowl of Fruit* (1959, oil on canvas, 13 1/2 x 17 1/2 ins / 34.5 x 44.5 cm) GBP 1,980. London, 11 June 1992, *Evening Landscape* (1957, oil on canvas, 36 x 28 ins / 90.5 x 71 cm) GBP 3,080. London, 23 Oct 1996, *Yellow and Green Landscape* (1953, oil on canvas, 36 x 24 ins / 91.5 x 61 cm) GBP 2,070. London, 27 Jan 1999, *Landscape II Rond Point* (1965, oil on canvas, 30 x 30 ins / 76 x 76 cm) GBP 3,000. London, 11 Nov 1999, *Seascape Storm* (oil on paper, 24 x 20 ins / 61 x 51 cm) GBP 3,200. London, 6 June 2000, *Coastal Landscape* (oil on canvas, 40 x 30 ins / 102 x 76 cm) GBP 5,500. London, 9 June 2000, *Seascape, Beach and Rocks* (1966, oil on canvas, 30 x 40 ins / 77 x 102 cm) GBP 9,500. London, 1 March 2001, *Beachscape* (1976, oil on canvas, 40 x 40 ins / 102 x 102 cm) GBP 8,000. London, 13 June 2001, *Porte St Sauveur* (1959, oil on canvas, 48 x 36 ins / 122 x 91 cm) GBP 2,800. Cirencester, 1 Nov 2002, *Blue Seascape* (1957, oil on canvas, 28 x 36 ins / 72 x 92 cm) GBP 5,200. London, 3 Dec 2002, *Horizontal Composition - Blue* (oil on canvas, 17 x 21 ins / 42 x 54 cm) GBP 5,000. London, 25 March 2003, *Vertical Landscape with Eiffel Tower, Oct 53* (oil on paper, 15 x 11 ins / 37 x 29 cm) GBP 3,000. London, 14 April 2003, *Painting Towards Childhood* (oil on panel, 15 x 13 ins / 38 x 32 cm) GBP 3,400. London, 19 April 2004, *Blue and Orange Still-life* (oil on canvas, 36 x 48 ins / 91 x 122 cm) GBP 7,000. London, 1 July 2004, *Evening Landscape* (1957, oil on canvas, 36 x 28 ins / 91 x 71 cm) GBP 11,000.

FRASER, Eric George
British, 20th century.
Born 1902; died 1984.
Painter.

FRASER, Francis Arthur
British, 19th century.
Born 1846, in Corfu.
Active in London.
Painter. Figures.

Francis Arthur Fraser was a frequent exhibitor in London between 1867 and 1883.

FRASER, Garden William. See **GARDEN William Fraser**

FRASER, George Gordon
British, 19th century.
Born 1859, in Scotland; died 1895, in Hemingford Abbots (Bedfordshire).
Painter, watercolourist. Portraits, landscapes.

George Gordon Fraser was a frequent exhibitor at London's Royal Academy between 1880 and 1893.

Auction records:

London, 17 Oct 1984, *Riverbank at Nightfall* (watercolour heightened with white, 10 1/2 x 15 ins / 26.6 x 38 cm) GBP 1,600. London, 22 May 1986, *House at Hemingford Grey* (watercolour heightened with gouache, 14 1/2 x 11 ins / 37 x 27 cm) GBP 1,600. London, 2 June 1987, *Portrait of a Lady* (1899, oil on canvas, 84 x 57 1/4 ins / 213.3 x 145.5 cm) GBP 2,800. London, 19 Dec 1991, *River Landscape* (watercolour, 6 1/2 x 6 1/4 ins / 16.5 x 15.9 cm) USD 605. London, 4 June 1997, *Hemingford Abbots from the Meadows* (watercolour heightened with gouache, 10 1/2 x 15 ins / 26.5 x 38 cm) GBP 1,265. BILLINGSHURST, 18 May 1999, *River Landscape* (watercolour heightened with gouache, 7 x 13 ins / 18 x 34 cm) GBP 1,150. BILLINGSHURST, 18 May 1999, *Riverside Walk, Thames Lock* (1884, watercolour heightened with gouache, 13 x 19 ins / 34 x 47 cm) GBP 1,900. LONDON, 27 June 2001, *Larne, Northern Ireland* (1886, watercolour heightened with white, 12 x 22 ins / 30 x 55 cm) GBP 1,200.

FRASER, Gilbert Baird

British, 19th - 20th century.
Born 1866, in Bedford; died 1947.
Watercolourist.

Gilbert Baird Frasers was the brother of Arthur Anderson Fraser (1861-1904).

FRASER, James Baillie

British, 19th century.
Born 11 June 1783, in Reelick; died January 1856, in Reelick.
Painter. Landscapes.

James Baillie Fraser exhibited in London between 1827 and 1831.

FRASER, James Earle

American, 20th century.
Born 4 November 1876, in Winona (Minnesota); died 11 October 1953, in Westport (Connecticut).
Sculptor, medallist. Figures, portraits, sporting subjects.

James Earle Fraser studied art at the Art Institute of Chicago under Richard W. Bock, at the École des Beaux-Arts in Paris under Alexandre Falguere, and at the Académie Julian and Académie Colarossi in Paris. He was assistant to Augustus St-Gaudens at his Paris studio in 1900, where he worked on the *Sherman Monument*, and was later in charge of St-Gaudens' studio in Cornish, New Hampshire, for a period. Fraser set up his own studio in New York City in 1902, but continued to do finishing work such as patination on some of St-Gaudens' work. Fraser married the sculptor Laura Gardin. He was the first recipient of the Saltus Medal, American Numismatic Society (1919), and also received a Gold Medal, National Institute of Arts and Letters (1951), the century Association Medal of Honor (1952), and the National Sculpture Society Medal of Honor (1952).

Fraser was a prolific creator of medallion reliefs, allegorical sculptures and statues of prominent Americans. His best known sculpture is *End of the Trail*, originally executed as a small bronze in 1894, when he was only 17; it won him an award from the American Art Association in Paris in 1898. In 1915 Fraser created a monumental plaster version of this piece for the Panama-Pacific Exposition, San Francisco, where it became a popular subject often reproduced in small statues, pictures and other forms. After the exposition, the sculpture was put in the scrap heap, as the scarcity of metal during World War I meant that the work could not be cast in bronze at that time. The sculpture was salvaged by Tulare County, California, and placed in Mooney Grove Park, later being moved to the National Cowboy and Western Heritage Museum, Norman, Oklahoma. Fraser's public sculptures and commissioned memorials include *Thomas A. Edison*, Edison Institute, Dearborn, Michigan; *Journey through Life*, Rock Creek Cemetery; *Peaceful Arts*, Lincoln Memorial Plaze; *Pioneers and Discovers*, Michigan Avenue Bridge, Chicago; *John Jay Memorial*, Cleveland, Ohio; General *George S. Patton*, West Point; and *Bishop Potter*, cathedral of St John the Divine, New York. Fraser's papers are held at Donald C. and Elizabeth M. Dickinson Research Center, National Cowboy and Western Heritage Museum.

BIBLIOGRAPHY:

James Earle Fraser: American Sculpture, exhibition catalogue, Kennedy Galleries, New York, 1969. Krakel, Dean Fenton, *End of the Trail: the Odyssey of a Statue*, illustrated book, University of Oklahoma Press, Norman, 1973. *James Earle Fraser: The American Heritage in Sculpture*, illustrated book, Gilcrease Institute of American History and Art, Tulsa, 1985.

MUSEUMS AND GALLERIES:

BUFFALO (Fine Arts Academy) - DETROIT (Institute of Arts): *End of the Trail* (1918, bronze) - GHENT (Ghent Mus.): (medals) - NEW YORK (Metropolitan Mus. of Art): (medals) - OKLAHOMA CITY (National Cowboy and Western Heritage Mus.): *End of the Trail* (1915, plaster); *Theodore Roosevelt* (1920); *Abraham Lincoln* (sculpture) - READING, PA (Reading Public Mus.): *End of the Trail* (bronze) - SAN FRANCISCO (FAM): *End of the Trail* (bronze) - WASHINGTON DC (Smithsonian American AM): *Elihu Root* (1926, bronze); *Pony Express* (1952, bronze medal); *The Arts of Peace* (cast plaster) - WASHINGTON DC (US Senate): *Theodore Roosevelt* (1910, marble); *John Nance Garner* (1943, marble).

AUCTION RECORDS:

NEW YORK, 27 Oct 1971, *Rider* (green-patinated bronze) USD 3,252. NEW YORK, 29 April 1976, *End of the Trail* (brown-patinated bronze, h. 11 3/4 ins / 29.8 cm) USD 4,000. NEW YORK, 29 Sept 1977, *End of the Trail* (1918, dark-green-patinated bronze, h. 33 1/2 ins / 85.1 cm) USD 22,000. NEW YORK, 25 April 1980, *End of the Trail* (1918, bronze, h. 31 3/4 ins / 80.6 cm) USD 47,000. LOS ANGELES, 3 May 1982, *End of the Trail* (1918, bronze, h. 45 ins / 114 cm) USD 52,500. NEW YORK, 9 Dec 1983, *End of the Trail* (1918, bronze, h. 33 1/2 ins / 85 cm) USD 75,000. SAN FRANCISCO, 28 Feb 1985, *End of the Trail* (1918, gilt-patinated bronze, h. 33 1/2 ins / 85 cm) USD 45,000. BRUSSELS, 20 Jan 1986, *Indian on Horseback* (bronze, h. 32 1/4 ins / 82 cm) BEF 380,000. NEW YORK, 23 May 1990, *End of the Trail* (bronze, h. 11 3/4 ins / 29.8 cm) USD 9,900. NEW YORK, 14 Nov 1991, *Bust Portrait of Elihu Root* (1926, bronze, h. 19 ins / 48.2 cm) USD 1,100. NEW YORK, 6 Dec 1991, *End of the Trail* (bronze equestrian group, h. 12 1/2 ins / 31.9 cm) USD 6,600. NEW YORK, 25 Sept 1992, *Low Relief of Dr William Nye Swift at the Helm* (brown-patinated bronze, 21 1/4 x 25 ins / 54 x 63.5 cm) USD 1,430. NEW YORK, 2 Dec 1993, *End of the Trail* (1918, bronze, h. 34 1/2 ins / 87.6 cm) USD 167,500. NEW YORK, 23 May 1996, *Horses in a Storm* (1918, bronze, h. 15 3/4 ins / 40 cm) USD 25,300. NEW YORK, 15 June 2000, *Wind Swept* (brown patinated bronze, h. 5 ins / 13 cm) USD 9,500. LOS ANGELES, 13 Dec 2000, *Roosevelt* (1920, green patinated bronze relief, 13 x 10 ins / 33 x 25 cm) USD 2,250. SANTA FE, 19 May 2001, *End of the Trail* (bronze, h. 38 ins / 97 cm) USD 510,000. NORTH BETHESDA, 9 Feb 2002, *End of the Trail* (brown patinated bronze, 21 x 25 ins / 53 x 63 cm) USD 38,500. SANTA FE, 18 May 2002, *The Roosevelt Bas-relief* (bronze plaque, 13 x 10 ins / 33 x 25 cm) USD 4,800. SANTA FE, 23 May 2003, *Roosevelt Bas-relief* (bronze, 13 x 10 ins / 33 x 25 cm) USD 3,000. SANTA FE, 15 May 2004, *Roosevelt Bas-relief* (bronze and iron, 12 x 9 ins / 30 x 23 cm) USD 4,000. SANTA FE, 23 Oct 2004, *The Roosevelt Bas-relief* (bronze and iron, 13 x 10 ins / 33 x 25 cm) USD 4,000.

FRASER, James P.

British, 19th century.
Active in London.
Painter. Figures.

James P. Fraser was a regular exhibitor in London between 1864 and 1884.

FRASER, Jessie

British, 19th century.
Active in England.
Painter. Figures.

Jessie Fraser is cited in *Art Prices Current*.

AUCTION RECORDS:

LONDON, 28 Nov 1908, *Head of a Young Peasant Girl*, GBP 1.

FRASER, John Arthur
British, 19th century.
Born 1838 or 1839, in London; died 1 January 1898, in New York.
Painter, watercolourist. Figures, landscapes.

John Arthur Fraser made his mark in the USA and Canada. He was one of the founders, with the Marquis of Lorne of the Royal Canadian Academy of Arts. He exhibited a watercolour at the Paris Salon of 1890 and received an honourable mention in 1893 and a bronze medal in 1897.

AUCTION RECORDS:
LONDON, 3 Nov 1993, *Young Lad with a Cricket Bat* (1868, watercolour and gouache, 19 x 16 ins / 48 x 40.5 cm) GBP 1,380.

FRASER, John P.
British, 19th century.
Painter. Genre scenes.

John P. Fraser was active in London and, from 1872, in Birmingham.

AUCTION RECORDS:
LONDON, 31 July 1987, *A Peep at Baby* (1871, oil on canvas, 14 x 12 ins / 35.5 x 30.5 cm) GBP 3,600.

FRASER, John S.
British, 19th century.
Born 1858; died 1957.
Painter, watercolourist. Historical subjects, harbour scenes, seascapes, boats.

John S. Fraser was a member of the Royal Society of British Artists and a regular exhibitor in London from 1879, notably at the Royal Academy, the Suffolk Street Gallery and the New Water-Colour Society.

MUSEUMS AND GALLERIES:
BRISTOL: *Summer Gust of Wind; Royal Yacht Britannia; America off the Needles* - CAPE TOWN: *Episode from the Voyage of Vasco de Gama* - LIVERPOOL: *Murray Straits.*

AUCTION RECORDS:
LONDON, 22 Feb 1908, *Bristol Channel* (1890, watercolour) GBP 3. LONDON, 18 June 1909, *Rounding the Cape* (watercolour) GBP 15. LONDON, 20 Feb 1931, *Yacht Race,* GBP 4. TORQUAY, 16 June 1981, *Hove-To for a Pilot* (1885, oil/hardboard, 17 1/4 x 35 1/2 ins / 44 x 90 cm) GBP 1,100. LONDON, 6 May 1983, *Magellan in the Straits* (oil on canvas, 38 1/4 x 66 1/4 ins / 97.1 x 168.3 cm) GBP 3,200. LONDON, 30 Sept 1987, *Whitstable Harbour at Low Tide* (1885, oil on canvas, 20 x 40 ins / 51 x 101.5 cm) GBP 2,800. LONDON, 30 May 1990, *Frigate Amphion off Spithead* (watercolour, 15 1/2 x 24 3/4 ins / 39.5 x 63 cm) GBP 1,760. LONDON, 7 Oct 1992, *Rocky Headland* (watercolour, 20 x 30 ins / 51 x 76 cm) GBP 1,045. LONDON, 11 May 1994, *Magellan in the Straits* (oil on canvas, 38 1/4 x 66 1/4 ins / 97 x 168 cm) GBP 10,120. PARIS, 28 June 1996, *Fishing Boat Entering an Estuary* (watercolour, 21 1/4 x 30 3/4 ins / 54 x 78 cm) FRF 5,000. EXETER, 3 March 1999, *In Bressay Sound, Shetland* (1881, oil on canvas, 26 x 39 ins / 65 x 100 cm) GBP 4,600. LONDON, 28 April 1999, *Frigate Amphion off Spithead* (watercolour over pencil, 15 x 25 ins / 39 x 63 cm) GBP 1,750.

FRASER, Laura Gardin
American, 20th century.
Born 14 September 1889, in Chicago; died 1966.
Sculptor, medallist. Portraits, sporting subjects.

Laura Gardin Fraser became a member of the National Academy of Design in 1916. She won a number of prizes and was commissioned to design the George Washington commemorative medallion.

AUCTION RECORDS:
NEW YORK, 23 May 1979, *Racehorse with Jockey* (bronze, h. 16 1/2 ins / 42 cm) USD 2,200. NEW YORK, 15 April 1992, *Horse and Jockey* (1930, brown-patinated bronze, h. 16 3/4 ins / 42.5 cm) USD 1,100.

FRASER, Malcolm
Canadian, 19th century.
Born 19 April 1858, in Montreal.
Active in New York.
Painter. Animals, landscapes.

Malcolm Fraser was a pupil of Wyatt Eaton at the Art Students League in New York, and of Boulanger and Jules Lefebvre in Paris.

AUCTION RECORDS:
SCOTLAND, 30 Aug 1983, *Sheep in a Snow-covered Landscape* (oil on canvas, 30 x 40 ins / 76 x 101.5 cm) GBP 880. LONDON, 12 April 1985, *Sheep in a Winter Landscape at Twilight* (oil on canvas, 29 1/4 x 39 ins / 74 x 99 cm) GBP 2,200. EDINBURGH, 30 Aug 1988, *Sheep in the Snow* (oil on canvas, 20 x 30 ins / 51 x 76 cm) GBP 770.

FRASER, Patrick Allan
British, 19th century.
Died 17 September 1890, in Arbroath, Scotland.
Painter.

Patrick Allan Fraser made his debut in Paris and went on to exhibit in London from 1841 to 1878.

FRASER, Robert Winchester or Winter
British, 19th - 20th century.
Born 1848, in Scotland; died 1906, in Gibraltar.
Painter, watercolourist. Landscapes.

Robert Fraser worked in Bedford and regularly took part in exhibitions at the Royal Academy, the Suffolk Street Gallery and the New Water-Colour Society in London from 1874.

AUCTION RECORDS:
LONDON, 9 Dec 1907, *Windsor* (watercolour) GBP 2. LONDON, 27 April 1908, *On the Lake* (1899, watercolour) GBP 3; *Near Weybridge* (1893, watercolour) GBP 3. LONDON, 14 May 1923, *Bell Wein; Iffley Mill* (both) GBP 4. NEW YORK, 27 Feb 1982, *Autumn Landscape* (watercolour, 17 1/2 x 28 3/4 ins / 44.2 x 73 cm) USD 650. LONDON, 26 May 1983, *River Banks* (1886, watercolour, 16 1/2 x 29 ins / 42 x 73.5 cm) GBP 520. LONDON, 30 May 1985, *Anglers by a River* (watercolour heightened with gouache, 9 1/2 x 13 1/2 ins / 24 x 34.5 cm) GBP 1,050. LONDON, 25 Jan 1988, *Near Ely* (1892, watercolour, 10 x 21 1/2 ins / 25.5 x 54.5 cm) GBP 880; *By the River* (1886, watercolour, 16 1/4 x 28 ins / 41 x 71 cm) GBP 2,750. LONDON, 25-26 April 1990, *Hurley Mill* (1887, watercolour, 11 1/2 x 21 ins / 29 x 53.5 cm) GBP 770. LONDON, 3 June 1992, *Biddenham* (1890, watercolour, 9 3/4 x 19 ins / 25 x 48 cm) GBP 660. LONDON, 11 June 1993, *Vast River Landscape with Figures on a Path* (pencil and watercolour, 6 1/2 x 13 3/4 ins / 16.5 x 35.1 cm) GBP 874.

FRASER, Thomas
British, 19th century.
Died 1851, in Edinburgh.
Painter. Portraits.

MUSEUMS AND GALLERIES:
EDINBURGH (Scottish National Portrait Gallery): *Charles Kirkpatrick Sharpe* (1829, oil on canvas, on loan from the National Museums of Scotland).

FRASER, Thomas Douglas
American, 20th century.
Born 1883, in California; died 1955.
Painter.

FRASER, William
British, 19th century.
Painter. History painting, portraits.

William Fraser exhibited at London's Royal Academy at the beginning of the 19th century.

AUCTION RECORDS:
PARIS, 19 June 1992, *Portrait of an Officer* (oil on canvas, 96 1/2 x 74 1/2 ins / 245 x 189 cm) FRF 26,000.

FRASER, William Lewis
American, 19th century.
Born 5 November 1841, in London; died 23 October 1905, in New York.
Draughtsman, illustrator, art writer.

William Lewis Fraser went to America in 1856 and made a name among the illustrators of the New World. He edited *Century Magazine* and spent the last years of his life writing books and giving lectures on art. He belonged to many American art groups.

FRASER, William Miller. See **FRAZER**

FRASER COMFORT, Charles. See **COMFORT Charles Fraser**

FRASEZ, Gabrielle
French, 20th century.
Born 6 September 1882, in Roubaix; died 6 December 1970.
Painter. Scenes with figures, landscapes.

Gabrielle Frasez particularly favoured Breton subjects. She studied under P. de Winter and exhibited in Paris at the Salon des Artistes Français, becoming a member of the Salon in 1908.

FRASQUERO, Luis
Spanish, 19th century.
Born in the 19th century, in Granada.
Painter. Landscapes, architectural views.

Luis Frasquero first exhibited in Granada in 1835.

FRASS, Leo
German, 15th century.
Died 1502, in Augsburg (Bavaria).
Painter.

This artist sometimes signed his name *Maurer*.

MUSEUMS AND GALLERIES:
AUGSBURG: one painting.

FRASSATI, Dominique
French, 20th century.
Born 29 March 1896, in Corte, Corsica; died 10 July 1947, in Corte, Corsica.
Painter, designer. Religious subjects, scenes with figures, landscapes, seascapes. Murals, church decoration.

Dominique Frassati's uncle wanted to make him a rich landowner in Argentina but he preferred to be a painter. In 1923 he left for Algeria where he began painting. In 1929 he settled in Paris and attended the studio of the painter Albert Laurens, but found the teaching style too classical. He then joined the Académie Julian, studying there for two years. In 1931 he returned to Corsica where he executed various works to earn a living, including shopfronts, the processional banner of Saint Théophile, the decoration of private houses and of the Hôtel du Nord at Corte. In 1936 he was appointed curator of the town hall museum in Ajaccio. In 1939 he was commissioned to provide paintings for the church of St-Michel at Bastelica, and the Ajaccio authorities commissioned him to paint the ceiling of the great Napoleon room.

Frassati exhibited at exhibitions in Algeria from 1923 and in Paris in 1937 at the Exposition Internationale, where he was awarded a silver medal. He also exhibited in Ajaccio, Bastia and on the Côte d'Azur. In 1992 some of his paintings were shown at the *Peintres d'Ajaccio et de la Corse* (*Painters of Ajaccio and Corsica*) exhibition at the Musée Fesch in Ajaccio.

BIBLIOGRAPHY:
Peintres d'Ajaccio et de la Corse, exhibition catalogue, Musée Fesch, Ajaccio, 1992.

FRASSI, Pietro
Italian, 18th century.
Born 1706, in Cremona; died 1778, in Rome.
Painter.

Pietro Frassi was a pupil of Angiolo Massarotti. He worked initially in Florence and then in Rome. He was elected to membership of the Accademia di San Luca on the strength of his *Miracle of St Vincent Ferrer*, painted for the Dominican order in Cremona.

FRASSINELLI
Italian, 17th century.
Active in Pistoia.
Painter.

Frassinelli worked on the convent of S Domenico.

FRASSINELLI, Guglielmo
Italian, 16th century.
Active in Rome in 1579.
Sculptor.

Frassinelli was still alive in 1600.

FRASSO, Michele
Italian, 14th century.
Born 14th century, in Sassari (Sardinia).
Painter.

FRATACCI, Antonio
Italian, 18th century.
Born at the beginning of the 18th century, in Parma.
Painter.

Antonio Fratacci studied first under Ilario Spolverini and then in Bologna under Carlo Cignagni, whose style he subsequently imitated. A *St John* and *Epiphany* by him are to be seen in the Milan church of S Eustorgio.

FRATE, Cecchino del
16th century.
Active in Italy.
Painter.

Was a follower of Fra Bartolommeo. No works can be attributed to him with certainty.

FRATE, Domenico del
Italian, 18th - 19th century.
Born c. 1765, in Lucca; died 12 November 1821, in Rome.
Painter, draughtsman.

Domenico del Frate studied in Florence prior to joining Nocchi's studio in Rome. He produced large frescoes, portraits and historical compositions. He worked on the Vatican Palace.

FRATE, Giovambattista del
Italian, 18th century.
Active in Milan.
Sculptor (wood).

Giovambattista del Frate worked for the abbey of S Spirito in Sulmona.

FRATE, Mateo
Spanish, 19th century.
Born 1788, in Madrid.
Sculptor.

FRATELLINI, Giovanna
Maiden name: Marmochini Cortesi
Italian, 17th - 18th century.
Born 1666, in Florence; died 18 April 1731, in Florence.
Painter, pastellist. History painting, portraits.

Giovanna Fratellini's considerable potential was evident from a very early age. Ippolito Galantini introduced her to the technique of miniatures and she went on to complete her studies under Antonio Domenico Gabbiani.

Her body of work comprises chiefly portraits and historical subjects painted in oils, pastels and pen, and on enamel.

She excelled in the latter technique and may be said to be at least equal to the celebrated Rosalba. Fratellini's reputation quickly spread throughout Italy and she was commissioned to paint portraits of *Cosimo III* and other court dignitaries and prominent men of the age. The ducal gallery in Florence houses what is undoubtedly one of her best works, a self-portrait showing her painting a portrait of her son.

AUCTION RECORDS:

ROME, 28 May 1985, *Portrait of a Child* (pastel, 15 3/4 x 12 1/2 ins / 40 x 32 cm) ITL 3,000,000.

FRATELLINI, Lorenzo Maria

Italian, 18th century.

Born 1690, in Florence; died 1729.

Painter.

Lorenzo Maria Fratellini was the son of Giovanna Fratellini, who taught him the rudiments of painting before he went to study under Antonio Domenico Gabbiani, who had also been his mother's mentor. He died at the early age of 39.

FRATI, Leonardo

Italian, 19th century.

Died c. 1810.

Active in Florence.

Draughtsman.

Frati lived in France for a while and may also have been a painter, sculptor and engraver.

FRATIN, Christophe

French, 19th century.

Born 1801, in Metz; died 16 August 1864, in Le Raincy (Seine-St-Denis).

Sculptor. Animals. Equestrian groups.

Fratin was a pupil of Géricault. He exhibited at the Paris Salo from 1831 to 1863. Notable paintings from his considerable body of work include: *Wild Horse Attacked by a Tiger* (group for the Petit-Montrouge Square); *Canadian Stag Held at Bay by a Pack of Dogs* (group); *Panther Seizing a Gazelle* (group); *Vulture Devouring a Gazelle* (bronze group); *Tiger Bringing Down a Young Camel* (bronze group); *Lion Devouring a Zebra* (bronze group); *Elephant Seizing a Tiger* (bronze group); *Lioness Carring her Prey to her Cubs* (bronze group); *Recumbent Stag Licking its Wounds* (bronze figure); *Dead Horse* (bronze figure); *Lion Carrying Off its Prey* (bronze group); *Eagle and Vulture Fighting over their Prey* (bronze group); *Two Dogs* (bronze); *Horse* (bronze); *Stag at Bay* (bronze); and *Two Eagles* (bronze).

BIBLIOGRAPHY:

Mackay, J., *The Animaliers: A Collector's Guide to the Animal Sculpture of the 19th and 20th Centuries*, New York, 1973. Bougon, Jacqueline J.A., *Christophe Fratin: le sculpteur animalier. Essai sur sa vie et sur son œuvre*, J. A. Bougon, Le Raincy, 1983. Poletti, Michel, *Fratin: objets décoratifs & sculptures romantiques*, exhibition catalogue, Univers du bronze, Paris, 2000.

MUSEUMS AND GALLERIES:

CHÂLONS-EN-CHAMPAGNE: *Dog* - COMPIÈGNE: *Lioness and Cubs; Horse (Tony)* - METZ: *Amphitheatre*.

AUCTION RECORDS:

LONDON, 30 Oct 1970, *Equestrian Group* (patinated bronze) GBP 1,000. LONDON, 6 May 1971, *Mare and Young Horse* (bronze) Gns 380. LONDON, 2 Dec 1976, *Mare and Young Horse* (bronze, l. 16 3/4 ins / 42.5 cm) GBP 600. ENGHIEN-LES-BAINS, 13 March 1977, *Mare and Foal* (brown-patinated bronze) FRF 10,500. ENGHIEN-LES-BAINS, 18 Dec 1978, *Horses in Combat* (bronze, 13 1/2 x 14 1/4 ins / 34 x 36 cm) FRF 9,000. ENGHIEN-LES-BAINS, 2 March 1980, *Mare and Foal* (bronze, h. 11 ins / 28 cm) FRF 12,200. ENGHIEN-LES-BAINS, 22 Feb 1981, *Labrador Running* (bronze, l. 15 3/4 ins / 40 cm) FRF 2,800. LONDON, 23 June 1983, *Mare and Foal* (c. 1860, bronze, h. 14 1/2 ins / 37 cm) GBP 3,100. LONDON, 5 July 1985, *Arab Stallion* (c. 1850, brown-patinated bronze, h. 11 ins / 27 cm) GBP 3,500. PARIS, 24 April 1988, *Self-portrait* (brown-patinated bronze, h. 7 3/4 ins / 19.5 cm) FRF 38,000. NEW YORK, 9 June 1988, *Elephant Attacking a Tiger* (1834, silvered bronze, h. 8 1/2 ins / 21.6 cm) USD 3,300. PARIS, 24 June 1988, *Two Dogs Attacking a Stag* (h. 15 3/4 ins / 40 cm) FRF 20,000. NEW YORK, 24 May 1989, *Stallion and Trainer* (bronze, h. 12 3/4 ins / 32.4 cm) USD 7,150. PARIS, 6 July 1989, *Two Dogs Resting* (bronze, l. 20 ins / 51 cm) FRF 11,500. FONTAINEBLEAU, 25 Feb 1990, *Lioness Feeding her Cubs* (brown-patinated bronze, H.11 ins / 28 cm) FRF 15,000. NEW YORK, 1 March 1990, *Stallion* (brown-patinated bronze, h. 15 1/2 ins / 39.3 cm, l. 18 ins/45.8 cm) USD 2,640. COMPIÈGNE, 9 June 1991, *Rhinoceros Attacked by a Snake* (brown-patinated bronze, h. 12 1/4 ins / 31 cm, l. 17 1/4 ins/44 cm, depth 9 ins/22 cm) FRF 75,000. NEW YORK, 4 June 1993, *Rhinoceros Attacked by a Snake* (bronze, h. 12 1/2 ins / 31.8 cm, l. 18 ins/45.7 cm) USD 16,100. PARIS, 23 June 1993, *Bear Washing Itself* (bronze, h. 6 1/2 ins / 16.5 cm) FRF 38,000. LOKEREN, 28 May 1994, *Mare and Foal* (bronze, h. 10 1/4 ins / 26 cm, w. 14 1/2 ins/37 cm) BEF 85,000. PERTH, 30 Aug 1994, *Lion and Prey* (bronze, h. 8 1/4 ins / 21 cm) GBP 2,185. NEW YORK, 20 July 1995, *Tiger and Antelope* (bronze, h. 10 1/2 ins / 26.7 cm, l. 16 1/4 ins/41.3 cm) USD 2,300. PARIS, 8 Nov 1995, *Stud Farm Scene* (bronze, h. 30 ins / 76 cm) FRF 297,000. NEW YORK, 18-19 July 1996, *Bear Sitting and Smoking a Pipe* (bronze, h. 6 3/4 ins / 17.1 cm) USD 6,900. PERTH, 26 Aug 1996, *Lion Devouring a Zebra* (1834, bronze, 6 3/4 x 12 ins / 17 x 30.5 cm) GBP 1,265. PARIS, 18 Dec 1996, *Wolf Caught in a Trap* (patinated bronze, H.7 3/4 ins / 19.5. cm l.9 1/2 ins/24 cm) FRF 6,000. NEW YORK, 9 Jan 1997, *Bear as a Dentist* (brown-patinated bronze, h. 6 ins / 15.2 cm) USD 6,037. PARIS, 13 May 1997, *Mare and Foal* (patinated bronze, h. 8 1/4 ins / 21 cm) FRF 26,000. LONDON, 12 Nov 1997, *Arab Stallion* (dark-brown patinated bronze, 15 x 16 3/4 ins / 38 x 42.5 cm) GBP 5,750. PARIS, 26 March 1998, *Jewel Box in Silver-Plated bronze with a Relief of a Cow, a Calf and Bulls* (h. 5 ins / 12.5 cm) FRF 3,200. NEW YORK, 9 April 1999, *Mare and Foal* (sculpture, brown patinated bronze, h. 17 ins / 42 cm) USD 4,800. PARIS, 14 April 1999, *Horse at the Fence* (sculpture, brown patinated bronze, h. 16 ins / 40 cm) FRF 31,000. AMSTERDAM, 23 May 2000, *Two Bears, One Seated on a Chair and One Standing* (sculpture, gold brown patinated bronze/oval base, h. 6 ins / 15 cm) NLG 16,000. PARIS, 1 Dec 2000, *Mare and Foal* (sculpture, patinated bronze, 15 x 17x6 ins / 37 x 42x15 cm) FRF 45,000. LONDON, 27 April 2001, *Whippet Seated on Stool* (sculpture, brown patinated bronze, 7 x 4x? ins / 19 x 9x? cm) GBP 3,000. NEW YORK, 6 June 2001, *Figure of a Greyhound with Hare* (sculpture, golden brown patinated bronze, h. 34 ins / 87 cm) USD 9,500. LYONS, 17 March 2002, *Etalon* (sculpture, bronze, 33 x 33x? ins / 84 x 84x? cm) EUR 5,000. LONDON, 16 April 2002, *Le Père Odry - Bear Playing the Violin, a Container* (sculpture, dark brown patinated bronze, two, h. 7 ins / 18 cm) GBP 3,000. LONDON, 9 April 2003, *Rainbow, a Standing Stallion* (sculpture, brown patinated bronze, 12 x 15x? ins / 31 x 37x? cm) GBP 2,500. PARIS, 21 Nov 2003, *Singerie* (sculpture, patinated bronze, h. 20 ins / 52 cm) EUR 6,000. LONDON, 17 Feb 2004, *Horse Protecting its Foal from a Dog* (sculpture, brown patinated bronze/marble base) GBP 2,200.

FRATINO, Giovanni

Italian, 16th century.

Born c. 1510; died 1570.

Active in Vicenza.

Painter, mosaicist.

Fratino also seems to have worked in Pisa, Orvieto, Padua, Rome and, in 1560, in Venice.

AUCTION RECORDS:

MILAN, 4 Dec 1980, *St Jerome* (pencil heightened with white, 15 1/2 x 9 3/4 ins / 39.2 x 24.7 cm) ITL 2,000,000.

FRATREL, Joseph, the Elder
French, 18th century.
Born 1730, in Épinal (Vosges); died 15 May 1783, in Mannheim.
Painter, engraver.

On 5 January 1759, Joseph Fratrel obtained a law qualification in Besançon and became a lawyer; he then gave it up to pursue a career in the arts. After becoming professor of painting at the academy in Metz, he was made ordinary painter to the king of Poland in 1754, then to the Palatine Elector Karl-Theodor. As a result, he was made professor at the academy in Düsseldorf.

In 1782, he exhibited *Christ and the Woman Taken in Adultery* at the Salon de la Correspondance. A beautiful canvas, *Cornélie*, can be seen in Munich. His other works include: *Cora* and *Vestal*.

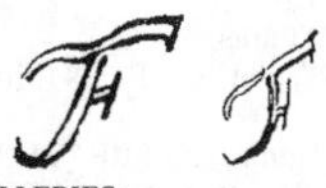

MUSEUMS AND GALLERIES:
MUNICH (Gal.): *Cornélie*.

FRATREL, Joseph, the Younger
German, 19th century.
Born in Mannheim; died 19th century, in Heidelberg.
Painter.

This artist was the son of Joseph the Elder.

FRATTA, Antonio Cola della
Italian, 16th century.
Active at the beginning of the 16th century.
Miniaturist.

Around 1509, Fratta illuminated choir books for the abbey of Monte Cassino.

FRATTA, Domenico Maria
Italian, 18th century.
Born 18 March 1696, in Bologna; died 10 August 1763, in Bologna.
Painter, draughtsman. Religious subjects, architectural views.

Domenico Maria Fratta studied under Giovanni Viviani, Carlo Rambaldi and Donato Creti. Early in his career Fratta discarded the brush in favour of pen-and-ink, a medium in which he subsequently excelled and achieved Europe-wide recognition.

AUCTION RECORDS:
PARIS, 6 Dec 1943, *Ruins with Figures* (1732, two pendants) FRF 1,900. LONDON, 26 March 1969, *Tomb of the Marchioness of Wharton and the Count of Dorset* (two grisailles) GBP 1,800. PARIS, 30 March 1984, *Mystic Marriage of St Catherine* (pen, 15 x 11 ins / 37.7 x 28 cm) FRF 5,500. NEW YORK, 14 Jan 1987, *Lakeside Landscape with Figures* (pen and brown ink, 12 1/4 x 20 ins / 31 x 49.9 cm) USD 2,750. PARIS, 15 April 1996, *Tobias and the Angel* (brown ink, 11 1/2 x 7 1/2 ins / 29 x 19 cm) FRF 5,000. PARIS, 27 March 2003, *River Landscape* (pen/ink, 10 x 7 ins / 26 x 18 cm) EUR 1,600.

FRATTA, Flori dell
Italian, 16th century.
Active in Fratta.
Painter.

A *Last Supper* in the church of S Bernardino de Fratta is believed to be by this artist.

FRATTINI, Gaetano
Italian, 18th century.
Active in Ravenna.
Painter. History painting.

Gaetano Frattini was a pupil of M. A. Franceschini.

FRATZ, Mary
American, 19th - 20th century.
Born in Philadelphia.
Active in Philadelphia.
Painter.

Mary Fratz was a pupil of Robert W. Vonnoh and Cecilia Beaux. She won the Topan first prize.

FRAU, José
Spanish, 20th century.
Born 1898, in Vigo; died 24 March 1976, in Madrid.
Painter. Scenes with figures, landscapes.

José Frau studied at the Real Academia de Bellas Artes de San Fernando in Madrid. In 1925 he took part in the first Exhibition of Iberian Artists alongside Dalí, Borès, Ferrant and Palencia. He went on to take part in many other exhibitions in Madrid, Pittsburgh, Mexico City and Montevideo among others. He received numerous awards and prizes and in 1943 was given a gold medal for his piece entitled *Nature*. After his death a major retrospective of his work was held in Spain.

BIBLIOGRAPHY:
Arnáiz, José Manuel/López Jiménez, Javier/Merchán Díaz, Manuel (ed.), *'Cien años de pintura en Espana y Portugal (1830-1930)'*, vol. II, Antiqvaria, Madrid, 1988 (One Hundred Years of Painting in Spain and Portugal (1830-1930)).

AUCTION RECORDS:
MADRID, 15 June 1976, *Landscape* (1969, oil on canvas, 31 1/2 x 25 1/2 ins / 80 x 65 cm) ESP 85,000. MADRID, 23 May 1984, *Romance en el Puerto* (oil on canvas, 17 1/4 x 22 ins / 44 x 55 cm) ESP 110,000. MADRID, 24 Jan 1985, *Springtime* (oil on canvas, 32 x 25 1/2 ins / 81 x 65 cm) ESP 180,000. MADRID, 18 May 1999, *Sunset Over the Village* (oil on panel, 17 x 26 ins / 42 x 65 cm) ESP 450,000. MADRID, 13 Oct 1999, *Landscape with Figures* (oil on panel, 17 x 26 ins / 42 x 65 cm) ESP 800,000. CONNECTICUT, 17 Jan 2000, *Spanish Village* (1922, oil on canvas, 33 x 33 ins / 84 x 84 cm) USD 6,000. MADRID, 10 July 2000, *El Papaluapán* (1951, oil on canvas, 34 x 40 ins / 86 x 102 cm) ESP 2,200,000. MADRID, 15 March 2001, *Angelus* (oil on canvas, 26 x 31 ins / 65 x 80 cm) ESP 900,000. MADRID, 8 May 2001, *Bearded Face* (oil on canvas, 29 x 24 ins / 73 x 60 cm) ESP 320,000. MADRID, 12 March 2002, *Dry Land* (1970, oil on board, 35 x 48 ins / 89 x 123 cm) EUR 8,000. MADRID, 18 June 2002, *Water in the Field* (1974, oil on canvas, 29 x 36 ins / 73 x 92 cm) EUR 4,750. MADRID, 20 May 2003, *Landscape* (oil on canvas, 35 x 46 ins / 90 x 116 cm) EUR 6,000. MADRID, 23 June 2003, *Landscape* (oil on panel, 19 x 28 ins / 49 x 70 cm) EUR 3,800. MADRID, 26 Jan 2004, *Landscapes* (1913, oil on canvas, a pair, 14 x 20 ins / 36 x 50 cm) EUR 1,800.

FRAU, Josep
Spanish, 20th century.
Born 1887, in Barcelona.
Painter. Landscapes.

Josep Frau studied at the school of fine arts in Barcelona and then at the Real Academia de Bellas Artes de San Fernando in Madrid. He was awarded a bursary by the Spanish government to study at the Paular landscape school. He began exhibiting in 1918 in both collective and solo exhibitions. Frau took part in many artistic events including the Barcelona fine arts exhibition of 1921.

BIBLIOGRAPHY:
Arnáiz, José Manuel/López Jiménez, Javier/Merchán Díaz, Manuel (ed.), *'Cien años de pintura en Espana y Portugal (1830-1930)'*, vol. I, Antiqvaria, Madrid, 1988 (One Hundred Years of Painting in Spain and Portugal (1830-1930)).

FRAUEN, A.. See **TRAUEN Asmus**

FRAUENDORFER, Johannes
German, 15th century.
Born in Dürrenstein.
Miniaturist.

A manuscript dated 1454 and dedicated to Duke Albert of Bavaria was illuminated by Johannes Frauendorfer.

FRAUENDORFER-MÜHLTHALER, Helene von. See **MÜHLTHALER**

FRAUENFELDER, Hans Konrad
Swiss, 19th century.
Born 26 November 1822, in Zurich; died 20 December 1896, in Zurich.
Painter. Landscapes.

Frauenfelder was a pupil of the Kummer brothers in Hofacker. He painted gouaches of Swiss landscapes.

FRAUENSTADT, Caspar
German, 15th century.
Active in Breslau (now Wroclaw, Poland) during the second half of the 15th century.
Painter.

FRAUGHTON, Edward J.
American, 20th century.
Born 1939.
Sculptor. Figures.

Edward J. Fraughton's sculptures evoke the American West. In 1987, he exhibited in *À la découverte de l'Ouest américain* (*Discovering the American West*), organised by the Salon d'Automne and the National Cowboy and Western Heritage Museum.

MUSEUMS AND GALLERIES:
OKLAHOMA CITY (National Cowboy and Western Heritage Mus.): *At the End of the Trail* (1973).

FRAUSTADT, Friedrich Auguste
German, 19th century.
Born 9 April 1821, in Lauchstadt.
Painter. History painting, figures.

Fraustadt exhibited in Belgium, Austria and Germany. He was a pupil of Neher in Leipzig.

AUCTION RECORDS:
LOKEREN, 28 May 1988, *Young Egyptian Woman* (oil on panel, 19 1/2 x 10 ins / 49.5 x 25.5 cm) BEF 33,000. PARIS, 17 Nov 2003, *Oriental Dance in an Ancient Roman Palace* (oil on panel, 42 x 73 ins / 106 x 185 cm) EUR 11,000.

FRAUTSCHOLD
Painter.

A name given by mistake in Siret's dictionary to the painter Trautschold.

FRAUY, Jacques
French, 18th century.
Active in Paris in 1732.
Painter.

Jacques Frauy's father was also a painter.

FRAVEGA, Giovanni, called Giovanni da Nervi
Italian, 14th - 15th century.
Born in Nervi.
Painter.

Giovanni Fravega worked in Genoa.

FRAYE, André
French, 20th century.
Born 18 October 1887, in Nantes; died 1963, in Paris.
Painter, watercolourist, engraver, draughtsman, illustrator. Military subjects, portraits, landscapes, seascapes, still-lifes.

André Fraye moved to Paris in 1909 and studied under M. Maufra; he also attended the Académie Julian. He was a friend of Albert Gleizes but was only influenced by Cubism to a limited extent. During World War I he executed numerous drawings and watercolours, some slightly Cubist in style, depicting the spectacle of daily life on the Front. He was principally an outdoor painter and is known mainly for his visually astute seascapes. He also illustrated numerous works of literature, including Mérimée's *La Vénus d'Ille* and *Les Croix de bois* by Dorgelès. His use of colour was lively and attractive and he enjoyed making colour appear to vibrate. Although he did not belong to any school, Fraye has been compared with Van Dongen, Bonnard and Marquet and also with the Neo-Realist Dunoyer de Ségonzac.

He exhibited for the first time in 1911 in Paris at the Salon d'Automne, of which he became a member. He also exhibited in Paris at the Salon des Tuileries and the Salon des Indépendants and took part in various group exhibitions, notably in the USA, Europe and Japan. In 1921 he was awarded the Blumenthal prize, the first to be awarded for painting.

MUSEUMS AND GALLERIES:
PARIS (MAM): *The Black Vest* - PARIS (Mus. de l'Armée).

AUCTION RECORDS:
PARIS, 30 May 1923, *Landscape*, FRF 750. PARIS, 2 March 1929, *Red Sail, Honfleur*, FRF 2,000. PARIS, 1 June 1933, *The Port of Nice* (watercolour) FRF 200. PARIS, 5 May 1937, *The Coast Road, Marseilles* (watercolour) FRF 85. PARIS, 6 March 1940, *Boats on the Charente*, FRF 160. PARIS, 9 March 1942, *Regatta*, FRF 2,600. PARIS, 10 May 1944, *Port at Low Tide*, FRF 10,000. PARIS, 14 June 1944, *Sailing Ship at Sea* (watercolour) FRF 380. PARIS, 24 Jan 1947, *Fishing Boats at Low Tide* (watercolour) FRF 2,200. PARIS, 24 Feb 1950, *Ile d'Yeu Seascape*, FRF 30,000. PARIS, 20 June 1973, *The Bridge*, FRF 1,000. PARIS, 17 Nov 1980, *The Little Port* (oil on canvas, 19 3/4 x 25 1/2 ins / 50 x 65 cm) FRF 2,700. ZURICH, 13 May 1983, *Boats* (oil on canvas, 23 1/2 x 28 3/4 ins / 60 x 73 cm) CHF 1,800. PARIS, 25 Nov 1986, *Entrance to the Port of Honfleur* (oil on canvas, 25 1/2 x 32 ins / 65 x 81 cm) FRF 5,000. PARIS, 30 May 1988, *The Seine at Triel* (1923, oil on canvas, 23 1/2 x 28 3/4 ins / 60 x 73 cm) FRF 4,000. PARIS, 14 Dec 1988, *The Yacht at Goulphar, Belle-Île-en-Mer* (oil on canvas, 32 x 39 1/4 ins / 81 x 100 cm) FRF 16,000. LYONS, 21 March 1990, *The Port* (oil on canvas, 21 1/4 x 28 3/4 ins / 54 x 73 cm) FRF 18,500. PARIS, 26 March 1990, *Ste-Maxime* (1922, oil on canvas, 23 1/2 x 28 3/4 ins / 60 x 73 cm) FRF 8,500. NEW YORK, 12 June 1992, *View of Sanary-sur-Mer Port, Côte d'Azur* (oil on canvas, 25 3/4 x 31 3/4 ins / 65.4 x 80.6 cm) USD 1,650. LONDON, 27 June 2002, *Sailing Boats* (oil on canvas, 24 x 29 ins / 60 x 73 cm) GBP 3,600.

FRAYER, J. B. Jules
British, 19th - 20th century.
Painter.

AUCTION RECORDS:
LONDON, 10 Dec 1923, *Breakfast Time*, GBP 18.

FRAYSSE, Michel
French, 20th - 21st century.
Born 9 November 1947, in Agen.
Painter.

Michels Fraysse's painting style, of pure and free expression, is in a lyrically abstract vein. He exhibited in 1973 in Paris.

FRAYSSEIX-BONNIN, Étienne de (Marquis). See **BONNIN DE FRAYSSEIX**

FRAZEE, John
American, 19th century.
Born 18 July 1790, in Rahway; died 1852, in New York.
Sculptor.

John Frazee, a self-taught artist, was one of the initiators of a specifically American school of sculptors. He carved a large number of busts, including *Jurist Wells* in New York and others in the Boston Athenaeum.

FRAZER, Alexander George. See **FRASER**

FRAZER, Alexandre R.
19th - 20th century.
Sculptor.

FRAZER, Harland
American, 20th century.
Painter. Portraits.
Harland Frazer exhibited and received many prizes in the 1920s.

FRAZER, Hugh
Irish, 19th century.
Born in Dromore.
Painter. Portraits, genre scenes, landscapes.
Hugh Frazer exhibited in Dublin from 1826 to 1861.

FRAZER, Mabel Pearl
American, 20th century.
Born 28 August 1887, in Utah; died 1981.
Painter.
Mabel Pearl Frazer worked as a teacher as well as a painter. She was a member of the Art Students League in New York.

FRAZER, William Miller
British, 19th - 20th century.
Born 1864 or 1865, in Scone (Perthshire), Scotland; died 1961.
Painter. Landscapes with figures, landscapes, waterscapes.
William Frazer lived in Edinburgh and exhibited principally in London. He specialised in typical landscape views of the north of Britain and sought to render a sense of nature as affected by the time of day or the season.

W M Frazer

AUCTION RECORDS:
LONDON, 28 May 1926, *The Tay near Newburgh,* GBP 7. LONDON, 29 Nov 1930, *On the Banks of the Tay,* GBP 11. EDINBURGH, 18 May 1935, *Landscape,* GBP 12. PERTH, 13 April 1976, *Summer Landscape* (oil on canvas, 15 1/4 x 23 1/2 ins / 39 x 59.5 cm) GBP 280. SCOTLAND, 1 Sept 1981, *Animals in a Clearing* (1906, oil on canvas, 28 x 36 ins / 71 x 91.5 cm) GBP 550. SCOTLAND, 30 Aug 1983, *Womack Broad, Norfolk* (1916, oil on canvas, 12 x 20 ins / 30.5 x 51 cm) GBP 780. PERTH, 26 Aug 1986, *St Ives on the Ouse* (1909, oil on canvas, 28 x 36 ins / 71 x 91.5 cm) GBP 4,800. EDINBURGH, 30 Aug 1988, *In the Ogle Valley in Perthshire* (oil on canvas, 10 x 14 ins / 25.5 x 35.5 cm) GBP 1,265. GLASGOW, 7 Feb 1989, *Holywell at St Ives* (oil on canvas/card, 9 3/4 x 13 3/4 ins / 25 x 35 cm) GBP 770. LONDON, 12 May 1989, *Sheep in a Meadow at the Foot of a Windmill* (oil on canvas, 24 1/2 x 29 3/4 ins / 62.5 x 75.6 cm) GBP 1,760. PERTH, 28 Aug 1989, *The White Peak: Ben Lawers* (1912, oil on canvas, 30 1/4 x 50 ins / 77 x 127 cm) GBP 6,050. EDINBURGH, 22 Nov 1989, *A Farm in the Fens* (oil on canvas, 20 1/4 x 24 1/4 ins / 51.4 x 61.6 cm) GBP 1,760. GLASGOW, 6 Feb 1990, *A Farm in East Lothian* (oil on canvas, 14 1/4 x 18 ins / 36 x 46 cm) GBP 2,200. EDINBURGH, 26 April 1990, *Animals in a Side Street in East Lothian* (oil on canvas, 10 x 14 ins / 25.4 x 35.6 cm) GBP 990. PERTH, 27 Aug 1990, *Whitekirk* (oil on canvas, 24 1/2 x 29 1/2 ins / 62 x 75 cm) GBP 1,760. SOUTH QUEENSFERRY, 23 April 1991, *Children Playing on a Beach* (1933, oil on reinforced canvas, 10 x 14 ins / 25.5 x 35.5 cm) GBP 1,870. PERTH, 26 Aug 1991, *Near East Linton in Haddingtonshire* (oil on canvas, 24 x 20 ins / 61 x 51 cm) GBP 3,850. GLASGOW, 4 Dec 1991, *Evening at Struan* (oil on canvas, 24 1/2 x 29 1/2 ins / 62 x 75 cm) GBP 1,870. EDINBURGH, 28 April 1992, *Boats Pulled up on the Shore* (oil on canvas, 12 x 14 ins / 30.5 x 35.5 cm) GBP 770. PERTH, 1 Sept 1992, *Fishing in the Marshes* (oil on canvas, 15 1/4 x 22 ins / 38.5 x 56 cm) GBP 1,320. PERTH, 31 Aug 1993, *Summer Morning at Sannox Bay, Arran; On the Arran Coast* (oil on card, a pair, each 10 x 14 ins / 25.5 x 35.5 cm) GBP 2,990. PERTH, 30 Aug 1994, *Landscape with Windmill.* PERTH, 29 Aug 1995, *September* (oil on canvas, 30 x 25 ins / 76 x 63.5 cm) USD 6,210. GLASGOW, 16 April 1996, *On the Beach* (oil on canvas, 15 3/4 x 24 ins / 40 x 61 cm) GBP 3,910. GLASGOW, 11 Dec 1996, *The Stream* (oil on canvas, 18 x 14 1/4 ins / 46 x 36.5 cm) GBP 437. EDINBURGH, 15 May 1997, *The Last Coal Boat for Tarbet at Blackwaterfoot, Arran* (oil on canvas, 18 x 24 ins / 45.7 x 61 cm) GBP 4,830. GLASGOW, 25 Feb 1999, *Boats in Calm, Norfolk* (oil on canvas, 20 x 30 ins / 51 x 76 cm) GBP 3,800. LONDON, 28 Oct 1999, *Hills of Atholl* (oil on canvas, 25 x 30 ins / 63 x 76 cm) GBP 3,200. LONDON, 30 Aug 2000, *Winds in the Trees* (oil on canvas, 24 x 36 ins / 61 x 91 cm) GBP 6,000. EDINBURGH, 16 Dec 2000, *Bringing Home the Harvest near East Linton* (oil on canvas, 11 x 19 ins / 29 x 49 cm) GBP 4,200. EDINBURGH, 25 May 2001, *In Kilbrannon Sound* (oil on canvas, 18 x 30 ins / 45 x 75 cm) GBP 5,800. LONDON, 1 Nov 2001, *Beached Boats, Machrihanish, Kintyre* (oil on canvas, 12 x 20 ins / 30 x 51 cm) GBP 5,000. LONDON, 15 April 2002, *Drumadoon Bay, Arran, with Kintyre in the Distance* (oil on canvas, 12 x 20 ins / 30 x 50 cm) GBP 5,200. CASTLECOMER, 2 July 2002, *Salmon Leap on the Garry, near Clunes* (1890, oil on canvas, 33 x 50 ins / 84 x 127 cm) EUR 7,700. EDINBURGH, 11 Dec 2003, *Harvest Landscape, Summer Skies* (oil on canvas, 20 x 30 ins / 51 x 75 cm) GBP 3,800. EDINBURGH, 11 Dec 2003, *Wooded River Landscape with Punt* (oil on canvas, 24 x 20 ins / 61 x 51 cm) GBP 3,800. LEYBURN, 22 July 2004, *Summer River Landscape with Young Boy Fishing from a Punt* (oil on canvas, 30 x 25 ins / 76 x 63 cm) GBP 6,000. LONDON, 1 Sept 2004, *Near Crail, Fife. Near Ludham, Norfolk* (oil on panel, a pair, 14 x 19 ins / 36 x 47 cm) GBP 6,000.

FRAZIER
American, 18th century.
Active in Norfolk (Virginia), in 1763.
Painter.

FRAZIER, John R.
American, 20th century.
Born 29 July 1889, in Stonington (Connecticut); died 1966.
Painter, watercolourist.
John R. Frazier belonged to many art societies and was mainly known for his watercolours. He won a number of awards in 1921 and 1922.

FRAZIER, Kenneth
American, 19th - 20th century.
Born 14 June 1867, in Paris, to American parents; died 1949.
Painter. Figures, portraits, landscapes.
Kenneth Frazier lived initially in Paris, where he was a pupil of Sir Hubert von Herkomer, Benjamin-Constant, Jules Lefebvre and Henri Lucien Doucet, and exhibited there at the Salon de la Société Nationale des Beaux-Arts. Subsequently, he moved to New York, where he showed in a number of group exhibitions: 1977, Amarillo Art Center, Texas; Westmoreland County Art Museum, Greensburg, Pennsylvania; and 1980-1981, San José Museum of Art, California. In 1979, *Kenneth Frazier (1867-1949): An American Impressionist* was held at the Southern Alleghenies Art Museum.

AUCTION RECORDS:
NEW YORK, 5 Dec 1980, *Portrait of the Parthema Passano* (oil on canvas) USD 9,000. NEW YORK, 25 May 1989, *Uplands in the Hudson* (oil on canvas, 25 x 30 ins / 63.5 x 76.3 cm) USD 19,800. NEW YORK, 14 Sept 1995, *Souvenir of the 1890s* (oil on canvas, 36 x 50 ins / 91.4 x 127 cm) USD 8,050. NEW YORK, 26 Sept 1996, *Woman with a Rose* (c. 1891-1892, oil on canvas, 51 x 38 ins / 129.5 x 96.5 cm) USD 29,900. BOLTON, 9 Aug 2002, *West Point from Garrison-on-Hudson* (oil on canvas) USD 2,400.

FRAZIOLE, Laurent
French, 17th century.
Active in Paris.
Sculptor.
On 19 June 1664, Laurent Fraziole married Anne Bitouzé.

FREARSON, John
British, 18th - 19th century.
Active in London.
Painter. Religious subjects.
John Frearson was a frequent exhibitor in London between 1797 and 1831.

FRECCIA, Pietro
Italian, 19th century.
Born 24 July 1814, in Castelnuovo di Magra, near La Spezia (Liguria); died 22 July 1856, in Florence.
Sculptor.
MUSEUMS AND GALLERIES:
PRATO (Mus. Civico): *Cupid*.
AUCTION RECORDS:
LONDON, 16 July 1979, *Putti* (1855, two figures in white marble, h. 31½ ins / 80 cm) GBP 2,400. LONDON, 28 April 1982, *Summer; Winter* (1855, two in Carrara marble, h. including pedestal 37¾ ins / 96 cm) GBP 2,800.

FRECH, Hans
Austrian, 17th century.
Died 1632.
Active in Vienna.
Sculptor, cabinet maker.
Frech came from the Tyrol and worked for the emperors Matthias and Ferdinand.

FRECHA, Francisco
Spanish, 16th century.
Active in Seville in 1503.
Sculptor.
Frecha was a wood carver, probably of choir stalls.

FRECHER, Daniel
Polish, 17th century.
Active in Cracow.
Painter.
The Franciscan convent in Warsaw owns works by Daniel Frecher.

FRÉCHET, André
French, 20th century.
Born 14 January 1875, in Châlons-sur-Marne.
Painter, draughtsman, designer, pastellist.
André Fréchet studied at the École des Beaux-Arts in Nantes from 1905 to 1911 and went on to teach history of art in Paris at the École Boulle, of which he was director from 1919 to 1934. From 1935 to 1939 he taught art and history of art at the Académie Julian in Paris. He was made a Chevalier of the Légion d'Honneur in 1924 and was promoted to Officier in 1937. He was also a Chevalier of Arts et Lettres.

Although he worked mainly as a decorative artist, Fréchet also produced easel paintings. His simplified use of colour brings great evocative power to his canvases and in particular to his Indian ink drawings and pastels. In Paris he exhibited at the Salons of the Société des Artistes Décorateurs and at the decorative arts exhibitions and the Expositions Universelles of 1889 and 1900.

FRÉCHET, Annie
French, 20th century.
Born 27 October 1880, in Paris; died 1973, in St-Thibault (?).
Painter. Portraits, landscapes, flowers.
Annie Fréchet studied in Paris at the École des Arts Décoratifs and then at Humbert's studio at the École Supérieure des Beaux-Arts. She taught art in Toulouse and later Paris and married the decorative artist André Fréchet, with whom she shared the same artistic concerns. She exhibited at numerous exhibitions in Paris, Bourges, Cosne and Sancerre.

FRÉCHET-TRÉMENTIN, Léa
French, 20th century.
Born in Lyons.
Painter. Landscapes, flowers.
Léa Fréchet-Trémentin exhibited in Paris at the Salon des Artistes Indépendants from 1937 onwards.

FRECHEVILLE, Raymond
French, 20th century.
Born in Carcassonne.
Painter.
Raymond Frecheville studied under J.P. Laurens and exhibited at the Salon des Artistes Français from 1922.

FRECHKOP, Leonid
Russian, 20th century.
Born 1897, in Moscow; died 1982, in Brussels.
Active in France and in Belgium from 1922.
Painter, draughtsman, engraver. Landscapes, figures, nudes, portraits, flowers. Stage sets.
After studying drawing and painting in Moscow, Leonid Frechkop left his native country for Paris and Brussels.

His taste for mystery tinged with Romanticism can be seen in his figures, dancers, young girls and nudes full of tenderness.

MUSEUMS AND GALLERIES:
BRUSSELS (Bibliothèque royale Albert Ier) - DINANT - IXELLES.
AUCTION RECORDS:
BRUSSELS, 16 Dec 1982, *Old Woman in a Blue Shawl* (oil on panel, 23½ x 19¼ ins / 60 x 49 cm) BEF 5,000. PARIS, 22 Oct 1986, *Young Woman in Black Velours* (oil on canvas, 29½ x 19¾ ins / 75 x 50 cm) FRF 23,000. AMSTERDAM, 10 Dec 1992, *Reclining Nude in a Landscape* (1926, oil on canvas, 35¾ x 23½ ins / 91 x 60 cm) NLG 11,500. AMSTERDAM, 8 Dec 1993, *Seated Nude* (1944, oil on canvas, 36¼ x 27½ ins / 92 x 70 cm) NLG 4,600. LOKEREN, 8 Oct 1994, *Nude with Greyhound* (1935, oil on canvas, 27½ x 31½ ins / 70 x 80 cm) BEF 44,000. AMSTERDAM, 7 Dec 1994, *Three Nudes in an Interior* (oil on canvas, 51½ x 72 ins / 131 x 182 cm) NLG 18,400.

FRÉCHON, Charles
French, 19th - 20th century.
Born 1856, in Blangy-sur-Bresle; died 1929.
Painter. Portraits, rustic scenes, landscapes with figures, landscapes, waterscapes, architectural views, still-lifes.
School of Rouen.
Charles Fréchon joined the Académie de Peinture et de Dessin in Rouen in 1879 and met Joseph Delattre and Charles Angrand. He then went to Paris and in 1881 enrolled at the Académie Colorossi. When he returned to Rouen he painted mainly from life.Fréchon painted landscapes in an Impressionist style and was one of the instigators of the so-called School of Rouen. The School took its name from the fact that painters such as Joseph Delattre, Léon Jules Lemaître and Charles Angrand painted the region, working outdoors in opposition to the official aesthetic and sometimes adopting the Divisionist technique. Fréchon's banks of the Seine, fields under snow and orchards in blossom are executed in pale tones applied with small brushstrokes.

In 1887 the piece he sent to the Paris Salon was accepted. He began exhibiting in 1894 at the Salon des Indépendants and showed work at the Salon d'Automne from 1903. He also exhibited regularly in Normandy. His first solo exhibition was held in Paris by the Galerie Durand-Ruel in 1901. His work featured posthumously in 2003 at the group exhibition *Autour de l'Impressionnisme: Dix-neuf Peintres de l'École Normande* (*Around Impressionism: Nineteen Painters from the School of Normandy*) at the Maison des Arts in Antony.

BIBLIOGRAPHY:

Dubosc, Georges, *L'École de Rouen, ses peintres et ses ferronniers*, Lecerf fils, Rouen, 1914. Fournier, Philippe, *Atelier de Marcel Couchaux (1877-1939), dessins, pastels, gouaches, aquarelles, tableaux modernes de lécole rouennaise*, auction catalogue, Rouen, 1968. *L'École de Rouen*, BDS, Rouen, 1972. *École normande, École de Rouen 1870-1930*, exhibition catalogue, Centre culturel du Palais Bénédictine, Fécamp, 1989. Lespinasse, François, *L'École de Rouen*, Lecerf, Rouen, 1995. *L'École de Rouen, de l'impressionnisme à Marcel Duchamp 1878-1914*, exhibition catalogue, Musée des Beaux-Arts, Rouen, 1996. *Autour de l'Impressionnisme: dix-neuf peintres de l'école normande*, exhibition catalogue, La Maison des Arts, Antony, 2003.

MUSEUMS AND GALLERIES:

LOUVIERS: *The Pré aux Loups; Hillside in Beauvoisin; Boulevard Cauchoise; Forest Corner at St-Aignan* - ROUEN: *Landscape; Spring Foliage.*

AUCTION RECORDS:

PARIS, 25 April 1901, *Watering Place at Pré au Loup*, FRF 400. ROUEN, 17 Dec 1972, *House in the Trees*, FRF 6,800. LONDON, 4 May 1973, *Harvesters around a Cart* (1853) Gns 750. ROUEN, 7 June 1973, *Path through the Woods*, FRF 6,300. ROUEN, 22 March 1981, *The Harvest* (oil on canvas, 23 1/2 x 28 3/4 ins / 60 x 73 cm) FRF 15,000. ROUEN, 27 March 1983, *View of Rouen Port and Cathedral* (oil on canvas, 7 1/2 x 13 3/4 ins / 19 x 35 cm) FRF 15,000. PARIS, 19 June 1985, *Rouen Cathedral and the Quays* (oil on canvas, 21 1/4 x 25 1/2 ins / 54 x 65 cm) FRF 138,000. GRANDVILLE, 16-17 July 1988, *River Bank* (oil on canvas, 11 1/4 x 14 1/4 ins / 28.5 x 36.5 cm) FRF 22,500. NEW YORK, 3 May 1989, *River Bank in Forest Interior* (oil on canvas, 22 x 18 ins / 56 x 46 cm) USD 42,180. PARIS, 19 June 1989, *Normandy Belltower* (oil on canvas, 18 1/4 x 18 ins / 46.5 x 45.5 cm) FRF 11,000. PARIS, 30 Nov 1992, *The Artist's Garden at Mont-St-Aignan* (oil on canvas, 25 1/2 x 32 ins / 65 x 81 cm) FRF 255,000. LE TOUQUET, 14 Nov 1993, *House in a Snow-covered Garden* (oil on canvas, 23 1/2 x 28 3/4 ins / 60 x 73 cm) FRF 80,000. PARIS, 19 Nov 1995, *Church in the Snow* (oil on panel, 12 1/4 x 16 1/4 ins / 31 x 41 cm) FRF 27,000.

FRÉCON, Jan

French, 16th century.

Painter.

Jan Frécon worked in Lyons in 1548 on preparations for the entry of Henri II into the town.

FRECOURT, Maurice

French, 20th century.

Born 1890, in Charenton.

Sculptor. Animals.

Maurice Frecourt studied under Valton and Jean Boucher. He exhibited in Paris at the Salon des Artistes Français from 1920 and was a member of the Salon.

FRECSKAY, Endre

Hungarian, 20th century.

Born 15 July 1875, in Sighet.

Painter. Landscapes.

Endre Frecskay studied in Munich and lived mainly in Budapest.

FRECSKAY, Laszlo von

Hungarian, 19th - 20th century.

Born 25 June 1844, in Budapest; died 1916.

Painter, illustrator. Genre scenes.

Laszlo von Frecskay studied in Vienna where he collaborated on various journals. He finally returned to his native city in 1911.

AUCTION RECORDS:

NEW YORK, 29 Feb 1984, *End of Dinner* (1908, oil on canvas, 16 3/4 x 23 3/4 ins / 42.5 x 60.5 cm) USD 2,800.

FRED-MONEY. See **MONEY Fred**

FREDDIE, Wilhelm, pseudonym of Carlsen, Frederik Wilhelm

Danish, 20th century.

Born 7 November 1909, in Copenhagen; died 24 November 1995, in Copenhagen.

Painter, collage artist. Scenes with figures, nudes, portraits, landscapes.

Wilhelm Freddie was self-taught and made his debut at the 1909 autumn salon in Copenhagen. After meeting Salvador Dalí in 1929, he was instrumental in introducing Surrealism to Denmark - to the consternation of art critics and the public alike. From then on, he never ceased to shock. In 1937 one of his shows was banned by the Danish police and three of his paintings, deemed pornographic, were confiscated and consigned to the Museum of Criminology (to be returned only in 1961), and Freddie was sent to prison. A determined opponent of the Nazi occupation, he was forced to flee to Sweden in 1944. He remained there until 1950. In 1953, after spending a couple of years in France, he aligned himself with the group that had formed around the French review Phases and emerged as one of its most active protagonists. In 1970 he was commissioned by the Danish State to decorate a school at Vallensbaek and in 1973 he was appointed to a teaching post at the college of fine arts in Copenhagen. He was awarded the Thorvaldsen Medal in 1970 in acknowledgement of his body of work.

He occupies an important position in the history of Scandinavian painting. His bold (and frequently proscribed) images are highly original in that they do not adhere strictly to the conventions of Pop, Abstract or Surrealist art. After painting some early and resolutely naturalist canvases, when he was only eighteen Freddie started producing what he called 'abstract reliefs', which juxtaposed textures and structures. When he discovered Surrealism in 1929, however, he took the lead in Denmark by integrating real, everyday objects into his compositions (as opposed to the collages favoured by the Dadaists and Cubists). His canvases and collages (*Meditations on Anti-Nazi Love*, 1937) and 'object-sculptures' (*Sex-Paralysappeal*) are aggressively erotic.

His work took a new turn during his exile in Sweden, when he used more traditional means and themes to express his anguish and despair. He soon recognised the limits of this more conventional approach, however, and his work evolved in a different direction immediately after he returned to his native Denmark. He started introducing geometric forms into his compositions (triangles, circles, arrows), combining them with figurative elements such as flames, masks and mirrors and with photographs and everyday objects. In this way he created a new and totally disruptive universe, a space where interior and exterior are superimposed, where flowers, women, infernal machines, endless staircases, ruined buildings and starry nights exist side by side. The titles of his late compositions are evocative (*Women of the Grands Boulevards I Have Blinded; The Next Couple after Us*) and the works themselves are innovative, often featuring photographic blow-ups. Eroticism is still the watchword, however: his distorted, trance-like figures, painted boldly and not without humour, reveal the world as an existence dominated by baser passions.

He participated in numerous group exhibitions at home and abroad, including every major Surrealist exhibition organised in Scandinavia, France, Switzerland and Italy and, in particular, those of the Phases group - in London (1936), New York (Museum of Modern Art, 1936, 1960, 1964), Paris (1938 and at the Galerie Maeght in 1947), Amsterdam (Stedelijk Museum, 1957), Milan (1959 and at the Palazzo Reale in 1989), Rio de Janeiro (Museum of Modern Art, 1964), Humlebaek (Museum Louisiana, 1966), Hanover (Kunstverein, 1966), Bern (Kunsthalle, 1966), Stockholm (Moderna Museet, 1970), Copenhagen (Statens Museum for Kunst, 1986), Lausanne (Cantonal Fine Arts Museum, 1987), Helsinki (Amos Andersons Konstmuseum, 1988), Le Havre (Musée des Beaux-Arts André Malraux, 1988), Marseilles (Centre de la Vieille Charité, 1989), and again in Paris (Jacquemart-André Museum, 1989). He featured posthumously in group exhibitions, including *La Révolution Surréaliste* (*The Surrealist Revolution*) at the Georges Pompidou Centre in Paris in 2002. He also had a number of solo exhibitions, both in Denmark and abroad, including: Göteborg (Kunstmuseum, 1967), a Danish retrospective (1989), Lund (Kunsthall, 1968) and Paris (Galerie 1900-2000). A posthumous one-man show was held in 2002 at the Kunstmuseum in Bayreuth.

freddie

Bibliography:

Jean, Marcel, *Histoire de la peinture surréaliste*, Éd. du Seuil, Paris, 1962. Jaguer, Édouard, *Wilhelm Freddie*, Gal. de l'Université, Paris, December 1964. Jaguer, Édouard, *Wilhelm Freddie. Pilene fra den elektriske bue*, Svend Hansen, Copenhagen, 1969. Thorsen, Jens Jorgen, *Freddie, 1909-1972: 28 September-10 November 1972*, exhibition catalogue, Surrealist Art Centre, London, Monte Carlo, 1972. Galy-Carles, Henry, *Art danois, 1945-1973*, exhibition catalogue, Gal. nationales du Grand Palais, Paris, 1973. Matthews, J.H., *Eight Painters: The Surrealist Context*, Syracuse University Press, New York, 1982 (chapter on Wilhelm Freddie). Jaguer, Édouard, *Wilhelm Freddie*, Gal. 1900-2000, Paris, 1990. Freddie, Wilhelm/Mossin, Per, *A Mental State*, video, Roland Collection, Northbrook (IL), 1990 (49 minutes). Spies, Werner (ed.), *La Révolution surréaliste*, exhibition catalogue, Éd. du Centre Georges-Pompidou, Paris, 2002.

Museums and Galleries:

Aalborg (Nordjyllands Kunstmus.) - Copenhagen (Statens Mus. for Kunst) - Göteborg (Konstmus.) - Humlebæk (Louisiana Mus. for Moderne Kunst) - New York (MoMA) - Stockholm (Moderna Mus.).

Auction records:

Copenhagen, 14 March 1972, *Portrait of C.W.T. Jr set in a Landscape*, DKK 7,100. London, 5 Dec 1974, *Reclining Model*, GBP 4,600. Copenhagen, 6 April 1976, *Composition* (1934-1961, oil on canvas, 51 1/2 x 39 1/4 ins / 131 x 100 cm) DKK 12,000. Copenhagen, 8 March 1977, *Cubist Composition* (1929-1937, oil on canvas, 39 1/4 x 49 1/4 ins / 100 x 125 cm) DKK 16,000. Copenhagen, 31 March 1981, *Composition* (1953, oil on canvas, 4 3/4 x 11 ins / 12 x 27 cm) DKK 3,000. London, 23 Feb 1983, *Female Head* (1940, wax and wood, h. 8 1/4 ins / 21 cm) GBP 600. Copenhagen, 3 April 1984, *Two Roses* (1975, mixed media, 25 1/2 x 22 ins / 65 x 55 cm) DKK 8,500. New York, 12 Nov 1984, *Mysterious Dances* (1945, pencil and black chalk, 10 3/4 x 9 ins / 27.3 x 22 cm) USD 950. Stockholm, 26 May 1987, *Composition* (1943, oil on canvas, 26 3/4 x 37 1/2 ins / 68 x 95 cm) SEK 145,000. Copenhagen, 2 March 1988, *Landscape near Jaegerspis* (13 3/4 x 15 3/4 ins / 35 x 40 cm) DKK 14,000. Stockholm, 6 June 1988, *Woman, Lion, Whueel and Cup of Soup* (1954, oil, 22 x 17 ins / 56 x 43 cm) SEK 26,000. Copenhagen, 8 Feb 1989, *Interior* (1946, oil on canvas, 13 x 16 1/4 ins / 33 x 41 cm) DKK 69,000. Copenhagen, 22 Nov 1989, *Surrealist Composition* (1940, pastel, 19 3/4 x 27 1/4 ins / 50 x 69 cm) DKK 87,000. Copenhagen, 30 May 1990, *Self-portrait* (1939, oil on canvas, 11 1/2 x 11 1/2 ins / 29 x 29 cm) DKK 280,000. Stockholm, 14 June 1990, *Somnambulist in a Surrealist Setting* (oil on panel, 16 1/4 x 13 ins / 41 x 33 cm) SEK 75,000. Copenhagen, 14-15 Nov 1990, *Composition* (1981, collage and coloured chalks, 24 1/2 x 19 1/4 ins / 62 x 49 cm) DKK 25,000. Copenhagen, 13-14 Feb 1991, *Death of Trotsky* (1960, oil on canvas, 25 1/4 x 39 1/4 ins / 64 x 100 cm) DKK 50,000. Copenhagen, 4 March 1992, *Madame Boucher in the Bath* (1974, collage, 22 x 16 1/4 ins / 56 x 41 cm) DKK 5,000. Copenhagen, 20 May 1992, *Head* (1953, brass, h. 14 1/4 ins / 36 cm) DKK 30,000. Copenhagen, 6 Sept 1993, *Surrealist Composition* (1943, painting/plywood, 12 1/4 x 20 ins / 31 x 51 cm) DKK 26,000. Amsterdam, 9 Dec 1993, *Untitled* (1947, oil on card, 25 1/4 x 20 3/4 ins / 64 x 53 cm) NLG 13,800. Copenhagen, 21 Sept 1994, *Surrealist Composition* (1947, painting/synthetic resin, 25 1/2 x 21 1/4 ins / 65 x 54 cm) DKK 50,000. Copenhagen, 12 March 1996, *Surrealist Composition* (1941, collage, 13 x 17 ins / 33 x 43 cm) DKK 22,000. Copenhagen, 15 March 1997, *Composition* (1981, coloured lithograph) DKK 3,000. Copenhagen, 22-24 Oct 1997, *My Beautiful Baby* (1958, oil on canvas, 32 x 25 1/2 ins / 81 x 65 cm) DKK 28,000. Copenhagen, 29 Sept 1999, *Woman of the Night* (1947, oil on masonite, 14 x 11 ins / 35 x 27 cm) DKK 75,000. Copenhagen, 17 Nov 1999, *Love's Metamorphosis* (1938-1939, oil on canvas, 39 x 32 ins / 100 x 81 cm) DKK 240,000. Copenhagen, 28 March 2000, *Self-portrait with Pipe* (oil on canvas, 17 x 17 ins / 42 x 42 cm) DKK 105,000. Copenhagen, 3 Oct 2000, *Young Girl* (1927, oil on masonite, 18 x 13 ins / 45 x 32 cm) DKK 260,000. Copenhagen, 2 Oct 2001, *Satanic Love - Surrealistic Figure Composition* (1934-1935, oil veneer on canvas, 32 x 28 ins / 81 x 71 cm) DKK 150,000. Copenhagen, 2 Oct 2001, *Freedom, Likeness and Brotherhood* (1929-1930, oil and tempera, 34 x 33 ins / 86 x 85 cm) DKK 360,000. Copenhagen, 10 April 2002, *Surrealistic Figure Composition* (1946, oil on canvas, 26 x 29 ins / 65 x 73 cm) DKK 75,000. Stockholm, 5 Nov 2002, *Surrealistic Composition* (1942, oil on canvas, 15 x 18 ins / 38 x 46 cm) SEK 90,000. Copenhagen, 1 April 2003, *Front Promenade - Surrealist Composition* (1943-1946, oil on canvas, 39 x 35 ins / 100 x 89 cm) DKK 140,000. Copenhagen, 17 Sept 2003, *I'm Certainly Going to Have a Better Shirt* (1937, oil on canvas, 39 x 31 ins / 100 x 80 cm) DKK 140,000. Copenhagen, 29 March 2004, *Bathers* (1947, oil on canvas, 14 x 10 ins / 35 x 26 cm) DKK 58,000. Copenhagen, 29 March 2004, *Forward and Backward* (1980, oil on canvas, 45 x 64 ins / 114 x 163 cm) DKK 85,000.

FREDEAU, Ambroise

French, 17th century.

Born 1589, in Paris; died 1673, in Toulouse.

Painter, sculptor. Religious subjects.

Ambroise Fredeau was a monk from the order of the hermits of St Augustin. He was a student of Simon Vouet and his works are in the museum in Toulouse.

Museums and Galleries:

Toulouse: several works.

Auction records:

Paris, 18 Nov 1987, *Elijah and Rebecca* (oil on canvas, 44 3/4 x 52 1/4 ins / 113.5 x 133 cm) FRF 70,000.

FREDEAU, Michel

French, 17th century.

Painter.

Michel Fredeau's *Descent from the Cross* can be seen at the church of Senlis.

FREDER, Frederick C.

American, 20th century.

Born 4 June 1895, in Monroe (New York); died 1954.

Painter.

Frederick C. Freder studied in the USA, Germany and Paris. He was a member of the Salmagundi Club and, in 1920, was awarded the Pulitzer Prize by the University of Colombia.

FRÉDÉRIC, Georges
Belgian, 20th century.
Born 1900, in Brussels; died 1981.
Painter, decorative designer. Landscapes, seascapes.
Georges Frédéric was educated at the fine arts academy in Brussels and was influenced by his painter father Léon Frédéric. He was noted for his decorations for the packet boats *Prince Philippe, Dover-Ostend* and *Queen Astrid*.
MUSEUMS AND GALLERIES:
MONS (MBA).
AUCTION RECORDS:
BRUSSELS, 24 March 1976, *Flood* (oil on panel, 15 3/4 x 21 1/4 ins / 40 x 54 cm) BEF 36,000. BRUSSELS, 23 Nov 1977, *Village Square Fairground Scene* (oil on canvas, 26 3/4 x 35 1/2 ins / 68 x 90 cm) BEF 75,000. ANTWERP, 29 April 1981, *Flemish Festival* (1937, oil on canvas, 27 1/2 x 36 1/2 ins / 70 x 93 cm) BEF 36,000. BRUSSELS, 27 Feb 1985, *Old Mill at Lisseweghe* (1944, oil on panel, triptych, 18 x 36 1/4 ins / 46 x 92 cm) BEF 36,000. BRUSSELS, 27 March 1990, *Notre-Dame-des Champs* (1946, triptych, 23 1/2 x 46 ins / 60 x 117 cm) BEF 50,000. LOKEREN, 23 May 1992, *Nieuport* (1963, oil on canvas, 23 1/2 x 31 1/2 ins / 60 x 80 cm) BEF 24,000. LOKEREN, 9 Oct 1993, *Winter* (1944, oil on canvas, 28 3/4 x 37 ins / 73 x 94 cm) BEF 280,000. LOKEREN, 9 March 1996, *Winter* (1944, oil on canvas, 28 3/4 x 37 ins / 73 x 94 cm) BEF 180,000. BRUSSELS, 15 Nov 1999, *The Life of a Fishing Boat* (1935, oil on canvas, triptych, 45 x 31 ins / 115 x 80 cm) BEF 100,000.

FREDERIC, Gérard
Flemish School, 15th century.
Active in Louvain.
Miniaturist.
Gérard Frederic was involved in the preparations for a banquet in Bruges in 1468. He appears under the name of Vridric in the account books of the dukes of Burgundy.

FREDERIC, Heynderic
Flemish School, 15th - 16th century.
Active in Ghent.
Sculptor.
This sculptor worked on the church of Our Lady in Sint-Pieter near Ghent.

FRÉDÉRIC, Léon Henri Marie (Baron)
Belgian, 19th - 20th century.
Born 26 August 1856, in Brussels; died 1940, in Brussels.
Painter.
Symbolism.
Baron Léon Frédéric studied under Jules van Kersblick and Jean François Portaels at the fine arts academy in Brussels. After failing to secure the Prix de Rome in 1876, he travelled to Italy where he lived and worked for two years - in Venice, Florence, Rome and Naples. He returned to Belgium and, in 1878, exhibited at the Brussels Salon and subsequently at the Essor Art Circle. He went on to exhibit regularly in Brussels, Ghent, Liège, Munich, Nice and Paris, receiving bronze and gold medals at the Paris Exhibitions Universelles of 1889 and 1900 respectively. He was also awarded a medal in Berlin in 1891. He was made a Knight of the Order of Leopold.

He started painting landscapes and cityscapes during his time in Italy, but in 1883 he discovered the beauty of the Ardennes and this was to become his principal source of inspiration. In addition to his large naturalist compositions, Frédéric also produced numerous religious and symbolic paintings, notably in the 1880s, and it was not until the following decade that he turned to 'idealist' art, particularly to English Pre-Raphaelite models and Symbolism proper. From the 1890s, his work is suffused with pantheism. He painted floral compositions, landscapes and portraits, but it is his religious work, in which he allies social comment with Christian mysticism, that is particularly significant. He particularly favoured the triptych format (*Chalk Sellers; Moonlight*).

MUSEUMS AND GALLERIES:
BRUSSELS (Mus. royaux des Beaux-Arts de Belgique): *Chalk Sellers* - IXELLES (MBA): *Studio Interior* (1882) - PARIS (Mus. d'Orsay): *Golden Age; Age of the Workers.*
AUCTION RECORDS:
PARIS, 23 Dec 1935, *Road Leading to a Village*, FRF 300. PARIS, 17 Feb 1937, *Scenes from the Life of St Francis of Assisi* (triptych) FRF 850. ANTWERP, 10 Oct 1972, *Landscape with Girl*, BEF 30,000. ANTWERP, 24 Oct 1973, *Grandfather* (1883) BEF 80,000. ANTWERP, 19 Oct 1976, *Convalescent* (1883, oil on canvas, 44 x 37 1/2 ins / 112 x 95 cm) BEF 85,000. BRUSSELS, 25 Oct 1978, *Holy Family* (1922, triptych, central panel 36 1/4 x 27 1/2 ins / 92 x 70 cm; two wings: 33 x 25 1/4 ins/84 x 64 cm) BEF 280,000. LOKEREN, 25 April 1981, *Weaver* (1898, charcoal/paper, 38 1/2 x 25 1/2 ins / 98 x 65 cm) BEF 36,000. BRUSSELS, 23 March 1983, *Chalk Seller* (1887, oil on canvas, 32 x 22 ins / 81 x 55 cm) BEF 130,000. ANTWERP, 19 May 1987, *Dinner* (oil on canvas, 39 x 51 1/4 ins / 99 x 130 cm) BEF 400,000. LOKEREN, 28 May 1988, *Annunciation* (oil on canvas, 33 3/4 x 25 1/2 ins / 86 x 65 cm) BEF 140,000. LOKEREN, 8 Oct 1988, *Forest* (1887, pastel, 20 1/2 x 13 3/4 ins / 52 x 35 cm) BEF 40,000. LOKEREN, 23 May 1992, *Self-portrait* (pastel, 16 3/4 x 14 1/2 ins / 42.5 x 37 cm) BEF 28,000. LOKEREN, 10 Oct 1992, *Street Market, La Roche* (1929, oil on canvas, 29 1/2 x 39 1/4 ins / 75 x 100 cm) BEF 60,000. LOKEREN, 5 Dec 1992, *Garden in Flower* (oil on canvas, 11 3/4 x 15 1/4 ins / 30 x 38.5 cm) BEF 26,000. LOKEREN, 9 Oct 1993, *Self-portrait* (pastel, 16 3/4 x 14 1/2 ins / 42.5 x 37 cm) BEF 48,000. LOKEREN, 10 Dec 1994, *Solitude* (1921, oil on panel, triptych, each 11 1/2 x 17 1/2 ins / 29.5 x 44.5 cm) BEF 100,000. LOKEREN, 9 Dec 1995, *Frost* (1896, oil on canvas/panel, 16 x 44 ins / 39.7 x 112 cm) BEF 110,000. LOKEREN, 8 March 1997, *Mariamaand* (1913, oil on canvas, triptych, 63 x 73 3/4 ins / 160 x 187.5 cm; 63 x 37 ins/160 x 94 cm) BEF 500,000.

FRÉDÉRIC-TOURTE, Pierre Marc.
See **TOURTE Frédéric Pierre Marc**

FREDERICH, Eduard
German, 19th century.
Born 2 March 1811, in Hanover; died 5 February 1864, in Hanover.
Painter. Military subjects.
Frederich was a court painter in Hanover.
MUSEUMS AND GALLERIES:
HANOVER: *The Skirmishers; Attack; Ceremonial March; Transporting French Prisoners of War.*

FREDERICH, Johann
German, 15th - 16th century.
Active in Barcelona.
Sculptor (wood).
Of German origin, this artist was also known as Juan de Alemania.

FREDERICK, Edmund
American, 19th century.
Born 1870, in Philadelphia.
Illustrator.

FREDERICK, Frank Forrest
American, 19th - 20th century.
Born 21 October 1866, in Methuen.
Painter.

Frank Forrest Frederick studied at the Massachusetts Normal Art School, the Royal College of Art, London, with Stanhope Forbes and Newlin, and with T. Robertson in Venice. He taught art history and drawing at the University of Illinois.

FREDERICK, John L.
American, 19th century.
Died c. 1880, in Philadelphia.
Engraver.

Among John L. Frederick's works are views of the *White House in Washington* and *Capitol in Harrisburg*.

FREDERICK, Lois
British (?), 20th century.
Painter.

Lois Frederick exhibited on a number of occasions at the Salon des Réalités Nouvelles in Paris from 1956 to 1964.

FREDERICKSZ., Glysbert
Dutch, 16th century.
Active in Amsterdam in 1528.
Painter.

FREDERIKSEN, Stinius
Norwegian, 20th century.
Born 1902, in Stavanger.
Sculptor.

Frederiksen studied in Paris under Bourdelle and Despiau and went on to participate in several international exhibitions, including the 1952 Venice Biennale and the São Paulo Biennale of 1953. He also worked on the restoration of Trondheim Cathedral.

FREDET, Denise Claudia
French, 20th century.
Born 1888, in Paris; died 1971.
Engraver.

Denise Fredet studied under Édouard Léon. She exhibited in Paris at the Salon des Artistes Français, of which she was a member. She received a commendation from the Salon in 1910.

FREDET, Pierre
French, 16th century.
Active in Pont-à-Mousson (Meurthe-et-Moselle) between 1542 and 1545.
Painter.

Pierre Fredet may be the same painter as one called 'de Fredet' who was working at the convent of Ste-Claire for the duchess of Gueldre in 1541.

FREDI, Bartolo di. See **BARTOLO DI FREDI**

FREDIANI, Alessandro
Italian, 17th century.
Active in Cagliari in 1648.
Painter.

FREDIANI, Pellegrino
Italian, 18th century.
Born in Carrara.
Sculptor.

Pellegrino Frediani worked for Empress Catherine in St Petersburg.

FREDIANI, Vincenzo. See **PEINTRE DE PAOLO BUONVISI**

FRÉDIC, S.
French, 20th century.
Born in Paris.
Sculptor.

S. Frédic exhibited at the Paris Salon from 1922 onwards.

FRÉDO-SIDÈS
French, 19th - 20th century.
Born at the end of the 19th century; died before 1955.
Artist (?).

Frédo-Sidès is mentioned as president and founder of the Salon des Réalités Nouvelles in Paris in 1946. His name does not appear in any catalogues, nor is it found in any of the works on abstract art consulted. It is not known whether he was in fact a practising artist.

FRÉDOU, Jean Martial
French, 18th century.
Born c. 1711, in Fontenay-le-Père; died 1795, in Versailles.
Painter, pastellist.

Jean Frédou's work contains many of the most attractive qualities of the 18th century. He continues to command a great deal of attention from art lovers. He was the first painter of Monsieur, the king's eldest brother.

MUSEUMS AND GALLERIES:
VERSAILLES (Mus.): *Portrait de Louis XVIII* (*Portrait of Louis XVIII*); *Portrait du duc de Bourgogne* (*Portrait of the Duc de Bourgogne*).

AUCTION RECORDS:
PARIS, 1885, *Portrait of Woman and Nymph*, FRF 2,800. PARIS, 5-6 May 1898, *Portrait of the Artist* (drawing in red chalk) FRF 220; *Portrait of a Young Woman* (drawing) FRF 195; *Portrait of J. A. Portail* (pastel) FRF 195. PARIS, 10 March 1899, *Portrait of a Woman Awaking*, FRF 280. PARIS, 22 Feb 1901, *Portrait of Mme de Bragelonne*, FRF 1,400. PARIS, 23 April 1910, *Allegorical Portrait of a Young Woman* (pastel) FRF 340. PARIS, 22 and 23 May 1919, *Portrait of a Young Woman*, FRF 8,100. PARIS, 22-25 April 1921, *Happy Family*, FRF 10,000. PARIS, 4 May 1921, *Portrait of a Woman* (pastel) FRF 4,000. PARIS, 13-15 Nov 1922, *Young Woman, Leaning Her Head* (red chalk) FRF 360. PARIS, 16 June 1923, *Portrait of Bust of a Man, in a Grey Costume, with Three-Cornered Hat under His Arm* (pastel) FRF 1,600. PARIS, 24 Dec 1924, *Small Portrait of Marie Antoinette as a Young Girl*, FRF 800. LONDON, 13 April 1927, *Duc de Berry as a Child*, GBP 17. LONDON, 27 June 1930, *Portrait of Jacqueline*, GBP 546. PARIS, 22-23 March 1933, *Portrait of a Young Boy*, FRF 3,700. PARIS, 14 Dec 1935, *Portrait of the Duc de Bourgogne* (pastel) FRF 13,300. PARIS, 14 May 1936, *Portrait of a Young Girl, with a Rose in Her Hair* (pastel) FRF 1,950. PARIS, 8 May 1944, *Portrait Presumed To Be of D'Alembert* (1762, black chalk and red chalk) FRF 6,100. PARIS, 23 Feb 1968, *Portrait of Marie-Antoinette*, FRF 10,200. VERSAILLES, 16 May 1971, *Grand Dauphin* (pastel) FRF 12,000. MONTE CARLO, 8 Feb 1981, *Portrait of a Man* (pastel, 26 3/4 x 19 3/4 ins / 68 x 50 cm) FRF 12,000. PARIS, 22 Oct 1982, *Portrait of a Young Woman* (black chalk, 12 1/2 x 9 ins / 31.5 x 22 cm) FRF 7,500. MONTE CARLO, 22 Feb 1986, *Portrait of a Young Woman* (1760, pastel, 15 1/2 x 12 ins / 39.5 x 30.5 cm) FRF 32,000. MONACO, 20 Feb 1988, *Portrait of Jean-François; Marie Anne Julie Baucheron de Lavauverte* (pencil, a pair, each 8 3/4 x 6 3/4 ins / 22.5 x 17 cm) FRF 13,320. PARIS, 25 Nov 1993, *Portrait of a Man* (1789, pastel, 15 1/2 x 12 1/2 ins / 39.5 x 31.5 cm) FRF 4,000. PARIS, 22 March 1995, *Portrait of Bust of a Young Man* (black chalk, red chalk and pastel, 15 1/4 x 11 ins / 39 x 28 cm) FRF 15,000. PARIS, 5 July 1996, *Portrait Presumed To Be of a Daughter of King Louis XV* (1764, pastel, 17 1/4 x 14 1/2 ins / 44 x 36.8 cm) USD 4,500. PARIS, 24 March 1998, *Three-Quarter Bust of Young Boy in Green Jacket Facing Right* (oil on canvas, 18 x 15 ins / 46 x 38 cm) FRF 13,800. PARIS, 24 March 1999, *Portrait of Mlle. Silvestre, Wife of Monsieur de la Vigne* (1730, black chalk heightened with white, 13 x 9 ins / 32 x 22 cm) FRF 20,500. PARIS, 31 March 2000, *Head-and-Shoulder Portrait of a Man* (1748, pastel, 14 x 11 ins / 36 x 28 cm) FRF 50,000. LONDON, 5 July 2000, *Portrait of Young Woman, Head and Shoulders* (chalk, 11 x 9

ins / 27 x 23 cm) GBP 3,500. NEW YORK, 7 June 2002, *Portrait of a Man, said to be the Artist* (oil on canvas, 26 x 22 ins / 65 x 55 cm) USD 8,000. PARIS, 27 March 2003, *Portrait of a Young Draughtsman* (chalk and wash, 14 x 11 ins / 36 x 27 cm) EUR 7,500.

FRÉDOU, Marie Catherine. See **FRANÇOIS**

FRÉDOUILLE, Félix Maurice
French, 20th century.
Born 1896, in Oran, Algeria.
Painter.
Orientalism.

Félix Frédouille exhibited in Paris at the Salon des Artistes Français, of which he was a member. In 1925 he was awarded a silver medal and the Th. Ralli prize.

FREDRIKS, Johannes Hendrik
Dutch, 19th century.
Born 1751, in Breda (North Brabant); died 1822, in Breda.
Active in Breda, Haarlem and The Hague.
Painter. Still-lifes (flowers/game), insects.

AUCTION RECORDS:
LONDON, 21 June 1940, *Fruit on a Marble Slab*, GBP 16. LONDON, 3 July 1946, *Flowers*, GBP 30. LONDON, 1 Oct 1980, *Still-life with Fruit* (1794, oil on panel, 15 1/2 x 11 3/4in/39.5 x 30cm) GBP 1,900. PARIS, 27 March 1987, *Autumn* (1786, oil on canvas, 42 1/2 x 41in/108 x 104cm) FRF 55,000. PARIS, 17 March 1989, *Bouquet of Flowers on a Stone Entablature* (1774, oil on panel, 22 3/4 x 18in/58 x 45.8cm) FRF 440,000. LONDON, 5 July 1991, *Large Composition with Flowers and Fruit, with a Mouse and Insects on a Stone Entablature* (oil on panel, 27 1/2 x 23 1/2in/70 x 59.5cm) GBP 46,200. NEW YORK, 21 May 1992, *Large Floral Composition with Baby Birds in a Nest on a Marble Entablature* (1774, oil on panel, 22 3/4 x 18in/58 x 45.8cm) USD 88,000. LONDON, 27 Oct 1993, *Still-life of Roses, Tulips, Lilacs and other Flowers with Peaches, Prunes, Apricots on a Marble Entablature* (1797, oil on panel, 27 1/2 x 23 1/4in/70 x 59cm) GBP 18,400. LONDON, 8 Dec 1993, *Still-life with Fruit and a Woodcock beside a Copper Wine-cooler, with Game Hanging above a Gun; Still-life with Fruit on a Draped Table-top, with a Hare and a Goldfish Bowl* (1788, oil on canvas, a pair, each 39 3/4 x 32 1/4in/101 x 82cm) GBP 25,300. PARIS, 31 Jan 1994, *Still-life with Fruit, a Wine-cooler, Rohmer and Game Hanging beside a Gun, against a Green Backcloth* (1788, oil on canvas, 39 3/4 x 32 1/4in/101 x 82cm) FRF 570,000. LONDON, 31 Oct 1997, *Roses, a Tulip, a Peony, Marigolds, Hollyhocks, Anemones, Forget-me-nots and Peaches on a Marble Pedestal* (1785, oil on metal, 29 1/4 x 23 1/2in/74.3 x 59.7cm) GBP 32,200. AMSTERDAM, 9 May 2000, *Melons, Grapes and Other Fruit with Flowers and Songbird Draped on a Ledge* (oil on panel, 30 x 23 ins / 76 x 59 cm) NLG 330,000. DONCASTER, 28 Sept 2003, *Still-life with a Lavish Display of Various Fruits and Flowers on Marble Ledge* (oil on canvas, 30 x 24 ins / 77 x 60 cm) GBP 9,400. NEW YORK, 17 June 2004, *Irises, Peonies, Roses and Other Flowers Surrounding a Terracotta Urn, with Bird's Nest* (1774, oil on panel, 23 x 18 ins / 58 x 46 cm) USD 70,000.

FREDRIKSEN, Raymond
French, 20th century.
Born in Bécon-les Bruyères.
Painter.

Raymond Fredriksen studied under A. Laurens; he exhibited at the Salon des Artistes Français from 1933.

FREDRIKSEN, Stinius. See **FREDERIKSEN**

FREDRIKSON, Lars
Swedish, 20th century.
Born 1926, in Stockholm.
Active in France since 1965.
Sculptor.
Kinetic Art.

Lars Frederikson studied at the fine arts academy in Stockholm from 1940 and travelled extensively in Africa, New Zealand and the USA. He showed his work at several exhibitions in Stockholm, Copenhagen, Milan and Paris (notably at the Salon Comparaisons). His first solo exhibition was in Stockholm in 1964. He taught at the École Internationale d'Art in Nice from 1970.

Initially influenced by the Expressionists and Constructivists, he also drew inspiration from Kasimir Malevich and Piet Mondrian. He was intrigued by the potential of acoustic and visual electronics and his body of work reflects this, particularly his wood frame and mechanical compositions, in which a motor drive is concealed behind white plastic: intermittent pulses disturb the perfect surface slowly, then in sudden and unexpected bursts, creating fascinating and disturbing effects similar to stop-motion film of plants growing.

BIBLIOGRAPHY:
L'Art moderne à Marseille. La Collection du Musée Cantini, Musée Cantini, Marseilles, 1988.

MUSEUMS AND GALLERIES:
MARSEILLES (Mus. Cantini): *Dynamic Structures* (1968).

FREDRIKSSON, Carl Einar Figge
20th century.
Born 1887; died 1951.
Painter. Still-lifes, flowers.

AUCTION RECORDS:
GÖTEBORG, 18 Oct 1988, *Still-life with Flowers* (1945, oil on canvas, 13 x 9 3/4 ins / 33 x 25 cm) SEK 2,500. STOCKHOLM, 28 Oct 1991, *Still-life of an Autumn Bouquet in a Vase* (1938, oil on canvas, 21 1/4 x 17 3/4 ins / 54 x 45 cm) SEK 3,500. STOCKHOLM, 27 May 1999, *Slussen from the South* (1934, oil on canvas, 16x12 ins / 40x30 cm) SEK 9,000. LONDON, 8 Sept 1999, *Waiting on the Jetty* (1966, oil on board, 20x28 ins / 51x70 cm) GBP 300. STOCKHOLM, 27 Nov 2001, *Roof-tops in Stockholm* (1930, oil on canvas, 16x12 ins / 41x30 cm) SEK 17,000. STOCKHOLM, 14 June 2004, *View of the Town Hall in Stockholm* (1922, oil on canvas, 33x26 ins / 85x66 cm) SEK 6,000. LONDON, 24 Oct 2004, *Boat on the River* (oil on board, 12x19 ins / 31x48 cm) GBP 350.

FREDSBERG, Olof
Swedish, 18th century.
Born 1728; died 24 May 1795, in Stockholm.
Painter.

Olof Fredsberg produced a series of portraits of Swedish monarchs, from St Eric to Queen Christina.

FREDSLUNG ANDERSEN, Age
Danish, 20th century.
Born in Denmark.
Painter.

FREDUREAU, Paul
French, 19th - 20th century.
Died 1927.
Painter.

Paul Fredureau exhibited at the Salon des Indépendants in Paris.

FREE, Karl
American, 20th century.
Born in Iowa.
Active in Europe in 1928.
Painter.

FREEBAIRN, Alfred Robert
British, 19th century.
Born 1794, in London; died 21 August 1846, in London.
Engraver.

Alfred Robert Freebairn was the son of Robert Freebairn. He produced engravings of a large number of his father's landscapes.

FREEBAIRN, R.G.

British, 19th century.
Sculptor.

R.G. Freebairn worked in London and was a frequent exhibitor at the Royal Academy between 1818 and 1825.

FREEBAIRN, Robert

British, 18th century.
Born 1765; died 23 January 1808, in London.
Painter, engraver. Landscapes.

Robert Freebairn studied under Richard Wilson immediately prior to the latter's death. He then settled for ten years in Italy, producing some 40 engravings of Italian and English landscapes.

Auction records:

London, 6 Nov 1959, *Powis Catle, Montgomeryshire,* GBP 630. New York, 21 April 1961, *Ludlow Castle, Shropshire,* USD 300. London, 13 Dec 1972, *Landscape with Lake,* GBP 450. London, 16 July 1981, *Italian, Swiss and English Landscapes* (series of 26 watercolours) GBP 6,200. London, 22 March 2000, *Italianate Landscape with View of a Lake* (oil on canvas, 33 x 50 ins / 85 x 126 cm) GBP 4,000. London, 4 July 2000, *View of Lake Albano and Castel Gastel Gandolfo* (oil on canvas, 16 x 24 ins / 40 x 60 cm) GBP 11,000.

FREEBAIRN, Robert

British, 18th - 19th century.
Born 1764, in London; died 23 January 1808, in London.
Painter, watercolourist, printmaker. Landscapes.

Robert Freebairn was renowned for his oils and watercolours of Italian landscapes. He studied initially under Richard Wilson, thereafter moving to Italy in the mid 1780s. Images such as *Promontory of Prosilipio* typify Freebairn's style in its dramatic treatment of light, shade and colour. Freebairn returned to Britain in 1792 and was one of the first artists to be elected to the Society of Painters in Watercolours in 1805. He first exhibited at the Royal Academy in 1782, and continued to show work depicting the Italian countryside throughout the 1790s.

Bibliography:

Freebairn, Robert, *Six Select Views in Italy,* R. Freebairn, London, 1806.

Museums and Galleries:

Cambridge (Fitzwilliam Museum): *Landscape with a Bridge* (etching).

Auction records:

London, 22 March 2000, *Italianate Landscape with View of a Lake* (oil on canvas, 33 x 50 ins / 85 x 126 cm) GBP 4,000. London, 4 July 2000, *View of Lake Albano and Castel Gastel Gandolfo* (oil on canvas, 16 x 24 ins / 40 x 60 cm) GBP 11,000.

FREEBORNE, Zara Malcolm

American, 19th century.
Born c. 1861, in Allentown (Pennsylvania); died 31 May 1906, in Boston.
Painter, sculptor. Portraits.

Zara Malcolm Freeborne was a pupil of Willian Rimmer in Boston and initially painted portraits. A long stay in Italy, mainly in Florence, led her to take up sculpture, and she built up a considerable reputation.

Auction records:

New York, 21 Sept 1981, *Faun Catching the Sound of a Waterfall* (bronze, h. 29 ins / 73.6 cm) USD 1,200.

FREEDE

German, 19th century.
Died 1871.
Painter. Animals.

Freede was of Prussian origin and is cited by Siret. He is known to have drowned accidentally.

FREEDLANDER, Arthur B.

American, 20th century.
Born 1875, in New York; died 1940.
Active in New York.
Painter.

Arthur B. Freedlander was a pupil of Chase in New York and of Cormon in Paris.

FREEDLEY, Durr

American, 20th century.
Born 1888, in Indianapolis; died 1918.
Painter. Portraits.

Durr Freedley exhibited at the Salon d'Automne, Paris, from 1924.

FREEDMAN, Barnett

British, 20th century.
Born 1901; died 1958.
Painter. Military subjects, portraits, landscapes.

Barnett Freedman was an official war artist in France.

FREELON, Allan

American, 20th century.
Born 2 September 1895, in Philadelphia; died 1960.
Painter, engraver, lithographer. Portraits, landscapes, animated scenes, harbour scenes.

Allan Freelon studied at the Pennsylvania Museum School of Industrial Art at the University of Pennsylvania under Earl Horter, and then he went to Temple University. He was a pupil of Hugh Breckenridge and Allan Gruppe. He fought during World War I.

Whilst pursuing painting he taught at public high schools in Philadelphia and was the director of an educational art programme. He was member of numerous art groups and editor of the afro-American magazine *Black Opals* (1927-1928) during the New Negro Movement that came before the Harlem Renaissance. In the 1930s he participated in the Work Progress Administration for the Public Art Project. He painted scenes of Philadelphia and of the port of Gloucester (Massachusetts) where he spent his summers in an artist colony directed by Allan Gruppe. He was essentially interested in the experimentation of colour, organizing his compositions in solid blocks, ofetn using orange and dark blue for his paintings of port Gloucester.

He took part in group exhibitions such as 1928-1931, Harmon Foundation, New York; 1934, *Regoinal Exhibition of Oil Painting and Sculpture,* Whitney Mus. of American Art, New York; 1999 *To Conserve a Legacy. American Art from Historically Black Colleges and Universities,* Addison Gallery of Art, Phillips Academy, Andover (Massachusetts). His solo exhibitions include 1934, Atlanta University, (Georgia); 1935, Warwick Gallery, Philadelphia; 1940, Temple University, Philadelphia. Retrospectives of his work include: 2000, *The Rediscovery of Allan Freelon,* Martin Art Gallery, Muhlenberg College, Allentown (Pennsylvania); 2004, *Allan Freelon: Pioneer African American Impressionist,* North Carolina Central University Art Museum, Durham (North Carolina).

Bibliography:

Dover, Cedric, *American Negro Art,* New York Graphic Society, Greenwich (CT), 1960. Porter, James A., *Modern Negro Art,* Howard University Press, Washington DC, 1992 (1st edition 1943). *To Conserve a Legacy. American Art from Historically Black Colleges and Universities,* collective exhibition catalogue, Addison Gall. of Art, Phillips Academy, Andover (MA), 1999. Verderame, Lori, *'The Rediscovery of Allan R. Freelon'* in *American Art Review,* periodical, January-February 2000.

Museums and Galleries:
New York (Whitney Mus. of American Art) - Philadelphia (Institute of Contemporary Art, University of Pennsylvania) - Philadelphia (MA) - Washington DC (GA, Howard University): *Number One Broad Street* (engraving).

FREEMAN, Augusta
British, 19th century.
Active in Rome c. 1845.
Sculptor.

Augusta Freeman was the wife of James Edward Freeman.

FREEMAN, Edith Demogene
American, 20th century.
Born 16 June 1876, in Chicago.
Painter.

Edith Demogene Freeman was a pupil of Lorado Taft and worked as a painter and teacher.

FREEMAN, Florence
American, 19th century.
Born 1836, in Boston; died c. 1876, in Rome.
Sculptor.

Florence Freeman was a niece of James Edward Freeman and a pupil of Greenough and Hiram Power.

FREEMAN, G.
British, 19th century.
Active in Bath.
Painter. Portraits.

G. Freeman was an exhibitor at London's Royal Academy from 1828 to 1830.

FREEMAN, George
American, 19th century.
Died February 1906, in Birmingham (Alabama).
Active in Boston.
Miniaturist.

George Freeman was mysteriously killed by a gunshot.

FREEMAN, James Edward
American, 19th century.
Born 1808, in Grand Passage (Nova Scotia); died 22 November 1884, in Rome.
Painter.

James Edward Freeman studied at the Academy in New York and then settled in Rome, where he painted genre subjects depicting mainly Italian scenes.

FREEMAN, Jane
American, 20th century.
Born 11 February 1883; died 1963.
Painter, watercolourist.

Jane Freeman was a member of the Association of Women Painters, which awarded her the watercolours prize in 1928.

FREEMAN, John
British, 17th century.
Active in London.
Painter. History painting.

John Freeman painted stage sets for London's Covent Garden theatre.

Museums and Galleries:
Paris (Louvre): five paintings (attributed).

FREEMAN, Joseph
British, 18th century.
Died 1799, in Cambridge.
Active from 1775.
Draughtsman, painter, copyist. Still-lifes, animals, portraits.

Joseph Freeman was a surveyor and land agent by profession. As an artist he was self-taught. He lived in Cambridge and was much employed by the colleges as a copyist and a restorer of portraits. His activity is well documented in the accounts of Emmanuel College. He copied most of the portraits of the palace at Ely.

He featured in the 1775 exhibition at the Society of Artists of Great Britain in London with a *Rabbit, from Nature* and showed a couple of chalks at the Free Society of Artists in London: a *Drawing after G.B. Piazzetta* in 1775 and *A Frost Piece* in 1776.

Bibliography:
Owst, G.R., *'Iconomania in 18th century Cambridge'* in *Proceedings of the Cambridge Antiquarian Society*, vol 42, 1949.

FREEMAN, Lou Blackstone
American, 19th century.
Born in America; died 2 November 1906, in Paris.
Painter.

Lou Blackstone Freeman settled in Paris and frequently exhibited at the Salon.

FREEMAN, Mary Winifride
British, 19th - 20th century.
Painter, watercolourist.

Mary Freeman worked in London and exhibited watercolours there at the Royal Academy from 1895 to 1912.

FREEMAN, Samuel
British, 18th - 19th century.
Born 1773; died 27 February 1857.
Active in London.
Engraver.

Works by Samuel Freeman include a *Holy Family* (engraved from an original by Correggio), a *Madonna* (Raphael), and a *St Ambrose Refusing Thoedorus Entry to the Church* (Van Dyck).

FREEMAN, T.
British, 18th century.
Active in London at the end of the 18th century.
Painter.

T. Freeman exhibited at London's Royal Academy, notably with paintings inspired by John Milton's *Paradise Lost*.

FREEMAN, William Henry
French, 19th century.
Born in the 19th century, in Paris.
Painter. Portraits.

Freeman exhibited anonymous (untitled) portraits at the Paris Salon from 1839 to 1875. He also showed a *View of the Parthenon* from the northeast.

FREER, Cora F.
American, 19th - 20th century.
Born in Chicago.
Active in New York.
Painter.

Cora F. Freer studied in Paris with Courtois, Neerson and Colin.

FREER, Frederick Warren
American, 19th century.
Born 16 June 1849, in Chicago; died 7 March 1908, in Chicago.
Painter, engraver. Figures, genre scenes, flowers.

Frederick Warren Freer initially studied in Chicago and then became a pupil at the Munich academy. When he returned to America in 1880 he settled in New York, where he was an active member of the artistic community. In 1890 he went back to Chicago to become a professor at the Art Institute. He was awarded many medals at the main American exhibitions.

Auction Records:
New York, 31 Jan-2 Feb 1898, *Morning*, USD 350. New York, 11 and 12 April 1907, *Model*, USD 45. New York, 23 and 24 Nov 1945, *Spring Flowers*, USD 120. New York, 26 and 27 Feb 1947, *Bouquet*, USD 260. San Francisco, 28 Feb

1985, *Young Woman in the Artist's Studio* (oil on canvas, 43 1/2 x 26 ins / 110.5 x 66 cm) USD 2,500. NEW YORK, 10 March 1993, *Old Letter* (oil on canvas, 24 1/4 x 19 1/4 ins / 61.6 x 48.9 cm) USD 5,175. PORTSMOUTH, 2 Nov 2002, *Last Look* (oil on panel, 14 x 10 ins / 36 x 25 cm) USD 4,800.

FREER, Harry
British.
Painter. Genre scenes.
MUSEUMS AND GALLERIES:
WARRINGTON: *A Private Examination.*

FREER, John (Mrs). See **EDWARDS Mary Ellen**

FREESE, Albertus I
Dutch, 18th century.
Died 18 March 1756, in The Hague.
Painter. History painting.
He was the father and master of Albertus Freese II.

FREESE, Albertus II
Dutch, 18th century.
Baptised in 1714 at the Lutheran church in The Hague (South Holland), Netherlands; died before 1788, in The Hague.
Painter.
He was a pupil of his father Albertus Freese I, and of Theodorus Justinus. He is recorded as a member of the 'Pictura' confraternity in 1753. Among the small number of his works to survive is a portrait of *Henri Nelse* in the city museum at The Hague. One of his portraits was engraved by Coster.

FREESE, Albertus III
Dutch, 18th century.
Active in The Hague, in 1759.
Draughtsman.
He was the son of Albertus Freese II, for whom he subsequently produced studies and working drawings.

FREESE, Anton Günter
German, 17th century.
Active in Broel in 1686.
Sculptor.
Anton Freese worked for the churches in Ulderup and Satrup.

FREESE, Ernst
German, 19th century.
Born 24 January 1865, in Nauen.
Sculptor.
Ernst Freese studied at the Berlin academy under Alb. Wolff, Fr. Schapper and E. Herter between 1885 and 1994. Between 1895 and 1896 he travelled in Italy. He worked in Berlin. He received an honourable mention at the Exposition Universelle of 1900 in Paris.
MUSEUMS AND GALLERIES:
BERLIN: *Girls Taking a Bath; Bust of the Councillor Professor de Hinzpeter.*

FREESE, Hans
German, 17th - 18th century.
Active in Lübeck.
Sculptor.
Hans Freese's output includes works for the church of St Mary in Lübeck and busts for the cathedral in Schleswig.

FREESE, Heinrich
German, 19th century.
Born in Dollrott; died 8 May 1837, in Hamburg.
Painter, miniaturist. Landscapes.
The museum in Kiel has several miniatures by Heinrich Freese in its collection.

FREESE, J.
British, 18th century.
Active at the end of the 18th century.
Miniaturist. Portraits.
J. Freese exhibited at the Royal Academy in London from 1794 to 1814.

FREESE, Jakob
German, 18th century.
Born in Stralsund.
Sculptor (wood).
Jakob Freese worked for different churches in Greifswald.

FREESE, Johann Carl
German, 18th century.
Died 14 November 1766, in Neukirchen.
Painter.
Johann Carl Freese repainted a Renaissance retable in the church in Neukirchen.

FREESE, Johann Georg von, or Freezen
German, 18th century.
Born 15 March 1701, in Palts, near Heidelberg; died 1775, in Kassel.
Painter. Portraits.
This artist was a pupil of Jan Van Nikkelen and then of Philip van Dyck. Under the patronage of the Duke of Hesseil he was appointed historical painter and portraitist at the court of Kassel.

FREESE, Johann Oscar Hermann
German, 19th century.
Born 14 May 1819, in Pomerania; died 25 July 1871, in Hasenfelds.
Painter. Hunting scenes, animals.
It was only at the age of 34 that Freese began to devote himself to art. He was a pupil of Brucke, then of Steffeck in Berlin. Three of his paintings are in the Berlin Alte Nationalgalerie.

FREESE, Theophilus Wilhelm
German, 18th century.
Died 1763, in Bremen.
Sculptor.
Theophilus Freese worked for the Bremen town hall among others.

FREESTONE, Anthony
British, 20th century.
Also active in France.
Painter.
Conceptual Art, Appropriation Art.
Anthony Freestone has an English father and a French mother. He showed his work in a solo exhibition in 1994 at the Musée des Beaux-Arts in Le Havre. Freestone has described his work thus: 'My pictures are like a game of dominos in which the pieces are dispersed at the start of the game and gradually joined together in various combinations.' He blends historical, everyday and personal references, not actually creating any of the images used but reproducing them with a copyist's care. Examples include medieval miniatures, classical paintings, naive illustrations, Scottish tartans, advertising logos, photographs yellowed with age and geographical maps, all of which are brought into correlation by serving as pieces representing landmarks in his own personal history.
BIBLIOGRAPHY:
Cohen, Françoise/Freestone, Anthony, *Anthony Freestone*, exhibition catalogue, Musée des Beaux-Arts André-Malraux, Le Havre, 1994.

FREETH, H. Andrew
British, 20th century.
Born 29 December 1912; died 1986.
Painter, engraver. Portraits.

H. Andrew Freeth worked at the British School in Rome. He took part in numerous exhibitions mounted abroad by the British Council.

FREEZOR, George Augustus
British, 19th century.
Painter. Genre scenes, figures.
George Augustus Freezor exhibited at London's Royal Academy between 1861 and 1879.
AUCTION RECORDS:
LONDON, 22 March 1946, *Saying Grace,* GBP 39. GLASGOW, 28 Aug 1985, *Interior with Children at Play* (1871, oil on canvas, 15 x 20¾ ins / 38 x 53 cm) GBP 3,200. LONDON, 27 Sept 1989, *Good Friends* (1886, oil on canvas, 20¾ x 16¼ ins / 53 x 41 cm) GBP 4,180. LONDON, 7 Oct 1992, *Family Gathering* (oil on canvas, 13¾ x 21 ins / 35 x 53.5 cm) GBP 1,320.

FREGERE, Claude
French, 20th century.
Born 1921.
Painter. Figures, still-lifes.
Claude Fregere exhibited regularly at the Salon d'Automne in Paris.
AUCTION RECORDS:
ST-DIÉ, 10 Feb 1990, *The Cellist* (oil on canvas, 28¾ x 23½ ins / 73 x 60 cm) FRF 5,600. NEUILLY, 3 Feb 1991, *Guitar and Trumpet* (oil on canvas, 28¾ x 21¼ ins / 73 x 54 cm) FRF 6,000.

FRÉGEVIZE, Edouard
Swiss, 19th century.
Born 1804, in Berlin; died c. 1860, in London.
Painter, lithographer.
The son of Frédéric Frégevize, Edouard lived mainly in Geneva. He exhibited a historical painting of Berlin in 1826. His works consist mainly of portraits and landscapes.

FRÉGEVIZE, Frédéric
Swiss, 18th - 19th century.
Born 1770, in Geneva; died 9 October 1849, in Geneva.
Active in Germany.
Painter (including enamel). Landscapes, landscapes with figures.
Frédéric Frégevize came from a family of French Huguenots who settled in Berlin, where he worked for many years before moving permanently to Geneva in 1829. He was appointed to membership of the Berlin academy in 1820. He painted many idyllic landscapes - mountains, lakes of his own country, the Rhône Valley. The detail in these paintings is reminiscent of the precision needed for painting on enamel, a technique he had used early in his career.
MUSEUMS AND GALLERIES:
BERLIN (Nationalgal.): *Lake Geneva; Rhône Valley.*
AUCTION RECORDS:
BERLIN, 7 July 1971, *Swiss Landscape,* DEM 4,000. BERN, 21 Oct 1977, *Country Festival* (oil on canvas, 17 x 22¾ ins / 43 x 58 cm) CHF 4,000. ZURICH, 27 May 1982, *The Shipwreck* (1807, oil on canvas, 30¼ x 36½ ins / 77 x 93 cm) CHF 6,000. BERN, 26 Oct 1984, *The Wine Growers' Festival* (oil on canvas, 32¼ x 40¼ ins / 82 x 102 cm) CHF 7,000. NEW YORK, 13 Feb 1985, *The River Aar near Thoune* (1830, oil on canvas, 28 x 37¼ ins / 71 x 94.5 cm) USD 14,000. LUCERNE, 2 May 2001, *Country Party near Geneva with Mont Blanc Beyond* (1849, oil on canvas, 16 x 20 ins / 41 x 52 cm) CHF 20,000. AHLDEN, 20 Sept 2002, *Fredericke A. Frick with Son* (1812, oil on canvas, 31 x 24 ins / 79 x 62 cm) EUR 4,000.

FREGIER
French, 20th century.
Painter. Still-lifes.
AUCTION RECORDS:
MARSEILLES, 5-6 Dec 1946, *Lemons,* FRF 9,950.

FRÉGIER, Louis
French, 20th century.
Draughtsman, illustrator.
Louis Frégier was a military painter and specialised in historical depictions of soldiers' uniforms and costume of the Napoleonic period. He also illustrated various books, including *Huit Siècles de Gendarmerie* (*Eight Centuries of the Gendarmerie*) and *Honneurs et Fidélité. C'est la Légion* by Louis Gaultier and Charles Jacquot (1963).

FRÉGONNIÈRE, Jacques de la. See **LA FRÉGONNIÈRE**

FRÉHAUT, Jean
French, 19th - 20th century.
Painter. Seascapes.
AUCTION RECORDS:
PARIS, 23 May 1923, *The Port,* FRF 1,150.

FREHEH, M.
German, 16th - 17th century.
Born 1565; died 1614.
Active in Augsburg (Bavaria).
Painter.
Freheh was also an historian.

FREI, Emil
Swiss, 20th century.
Born 20 September 1882, in Andelfingen.
Painter.
Frequent exhibitor in Zurich, predominantly of portraits.

FREI, Hans
Swiss, 17th century.
Active in Aarau c. 1606.
Glass painter.

FREI, Hans
Swiss, 19th century.
Born 30 April 1868, in Basel.
Sculptor, metal worker.
Frei was a pupil at the school of industrial arts under Jos. Hollubetz in Basel, and studied in Vienna, Berlin, Cologne, Geneva and Paris. He gained a bronze medal at the Exposition Universelle in Paris in 1900.

FREI, Hans Friedrich
Swiss, 16th century.
Born in Mellingen.
Active in Basel from the beginning of 1504.
Glass painter.
Hans Frei presented his home town with a stained glass window decorated with his own coat of arms.

FREI, Konrad
Swiss, 17th century.
Active in Winterthur c. 1654.
Sculptor (stone).
Konrad Frei created a stone statue for a fountain in Winterthur in 1654.

FREI, Urs
Swiss, 20th - 21st century.
Born 1958, in Zurich.
Sculptor, assemblage artist. Consumer society, daily life.
Exhibited solo in 1994 at the Kunsthalle in Zurich. His assemblies comprise recycled everyday objects, such as empty plastic bottles, and his sculptures are vividly coloured.

FREIBACH, Carl. See **FABRICE Ilka Freiin von**

FREIBURG, Georg
German, 16th - 17th century.
Born c. 1557, in Schweidnitz, Silesia (now Swidnica, Poland); died 3 September 1619.
Painter.

Georg Freiburg worked chiefly in Breslau (now Wroclaw, Poland), at the churches of St Mary Magdalene and St Martin, among others.

FREIBURG, von. See first name

FREIDA, Raphaël
French, 20th century.
Born 26 May 1877, in Digne.
Painter, illustrator, designer. Designs for stained glass.
Raphaël Freida was a member of the Société des Artistes Français in Paris. He illustrated numerous works of literature with original etchings, including: *Les Poèmes Barbares* by Leconte de Lisle; *Thaïs* by Anatole France; *Hérodias* by Flaubert and *Le Jardin des Supplices* by Octave Mirbeau. He was awarded a silver medal in 1923 and a gold medal in 1928.

FREIDHOFF, Johann Joseph
German, 18th - 19th century.
Born 1768, in Heggen; died 1818, in Berlin.
Engraver (burin).
Freidhoff engraved mainly mythological and religious subjects. He was a pupil of J. G. Huck and worked in Holland, France and Germany. In 1783 he was a member of the Haarlem Guild. Works attributed to him include reproductions in the style of Poussin or Ruisdael and his *Portrait of Prince Leopold of Dessau* in the style of Pesne.

FREIDING, Jorg
German, 16th century.
Active in Rattenberg in 1505.
Painter.

FREIESLEBEN, Ernst
German, 19th century.
Died 1883, in Weimar.
Painter. Genre scenes.
Freiesleben exhibited his works in Dresden, Berlin, Munich and Hanover from 1869.
AUCTION RECORDS:
LONDON, 26 Nov 1986, *A Love Letter* (oil on canvas, 23 x 17 1/4 ins / 58.5 x 44 cm) GBP 1,500. MUNICH, 24 March 1999, *Two Children at the Window of an Old Farmhouse* (1872, oil on canvas, 32 x 25 ins / 81 x 64 cm) DEM 7,500. LONDON, 9 April 2002, *Das kleine eichhornchen - The Little Squirrel* (oil on canvas, 37 x 28 ins / 94 x 72 cm) GBP 3,000.

FREIHARDT, Wolf Christian
German, 18th century.
Active in 1717 in Weiler Dettenroden.
Painter.
Freihardt worked for the Church of St Sebastian in Weiler-Dettenroden.

FREIHEIT, Ludwig
Austrian, 20th century.
Born 4 February 1876, in Vienna.
Painter. Portraits.
Studied at the fine arts academy in Vienna; noted for his portraits of *Princess Anna* and the *Heir Apparent François Ferdinand d'Este*.

FREIHOFF. See **FREYHOFF**

FREILE DE GUEVARA, Pedro
Spanish, 17th century.
Born c. 1582, in Guadix, near Granada.
Sculptor.
Pedro Freile de Guevara worked for Cordova Cathedral.

FREILES, Antonio
Italian, 20th century.
Painter.
Antonio Freiles teaches at the school of fine arts in Catania, Sicily. He has taken part in many group exhibitions and international salons, and also shows his works in solo exhibitions.

Since the 1980s Freiles has been working on his *Chartae*, using ancient craft techniques and preparing his own paper. He uses home-made vegetable-based paints (often in primary colours) both to dye the paper and to create abstract, ephemeral images that can suggest landscapes, familiar forms or fantasy universes.
BIBLIOGRAPHY:
Pic, Rafael, '*Antonio Freiles*' in *Art Press* n° 173, periodical, Paris, October 1992.

FREILICHER, Jane
American, 20th century.
Born 1924, in Brooklyn.
Painter. Landscapes.
Jane Freilicher studied at Brooklyn College and the University of Columbia, where she was advised by the painter Hans Hofmann. She has taken part in many group exhibitions, including the Whitney Annuals in New York and the Carnegie International shows in Pittsburgh. She has held solo shows in New York from 1953, and, in 1987, exhibited at the Marion Koogler McNay Art Museum, San Antonio.
MUSEUMS AND GALLERIES:
NEW YORK (Brooklyn Mus.) - PROVIDENCE (Rhode Island School of Design).
AUCTION RECORDS:
NEW YORK, 27 Feb 1992, *Blue Horizon* (1984, oil on canvas, 80 x 70 ins / 203.2 x 177.8 cm) USD 15,400. NEW YORK, 10 Oct 1996, *Still-life with Teacup and Spoon on a Table* (1954, pastel/paper, 23 1/2 x 18 1/2 ins / 59.7 x 47.3 cm) USD 1,495. NEW YORK, 17 Feb 1999, *Studio Interior* (1982, oil on canvas, 50 x 60 ins / 127 x 152 cm) USD 14,000. NEW YORK, 19 Dec 2003, *Study for Autumnal Landscape* (pastel on paper, 26 x 20 ins / 65 x 50 cm) USD 3,500. NEW YORK, 29 June 2004, *Cabana Days* (1958, oil on canvas, 40 x 30 ins / 102 x 76 cm) USD 6,000.

FREIMAN, Lillian
Canadian, 20th century.
Born 1908, in Guelph; died 1986.
Painter.
Lillian Freiman exhibited in Paris at the Salon d'Automne in 1929 and 1930.
MUSEUMS AND GALLERIES:
OTTAWA (Nat. Gal. of Canada): *Rehearsal* (1959, watercolour and pastel); *The Bird Market* (1930, oil); *Girl in Plum Hat* (1946, graphite, pastel amd enamel paint).

FREINDT, Anton
Austrian, 17th - 18th century.
Born 1664, in Olmütz (now Olomouc, Czech Republic); died 9 January 1727.
Engraver.
Anton Freindt mainly illustrated holy subjects for the Jesuits.

FREINDT, Johann, the Elder
Austrian, 18th century.
Active in Olmütz (now Olomouc, Czech Republic).
Painter, sculptor, engraver.
Johann Freindt's works include a *St Thomas Aquinas*.

FREINDT, Johann, the Younger
Austrian, 18th century.
Born 1752, in Olmütz (now Olomouc, Czech Republic).
Engraver, painter.
Johann Freindt settled in Vienna.

FREINDT, Johann Anton
Austrian, 18th century.
Died c. 1778.

Active in Olmütz (now Olomouc, Czech Republic).
Engraver.

FREINDT, Joseph
Austrian, 18th century.
Active in Olmütz (now Olomouc, Czech Republic).
Engraver.
Joseph was the son of Johann Anton Freindt.

FREIRE, Ignacio Tiburcio
Spanish, 18th century.
Born 1699, in Noya.
Painter.
In 1732, Ignacio Freire worked in Santiago de Compostela.

FREIRE, Luciano
Portuguese, 19th - 20th century.
Born 1864, in Lisbon; died January 1935.
Painter. History painting, figures, portraits, landscapes.
From 1878 to 1886, Luciano Freire studied at the Lisbon school of fine arts and in 1888 exhibited at the Universal Exhibition in Lisbon when two of his works were purchased by city's authorities, one of which was his portrait of *Don Sebastiao*. In 1896 he was appointed to teach at the Lisbon fine arts academy. In 1933 he began working on the restoration of 15th century paintings. He held the chair in life drawing at the fine arts academy. In 1911 he was appointed curator of the Lisbon vintage vehicle museum, which he reorganised.

In addition to his history paintings he painted many landscapes, having become particularly interested in the genre during his visit to France and England. In the late 1890s his work began to show the influence of the modern and Symbolist movements.

BIBLIOGRAPHY:
Arnáiz, José Manuel/López Jiménez, Javier/Merchán Díaz, Manuel (ed.), *'Cien años de pintura en Espana y Portugal (1830-1930)'*, vol. II, Antiqvaria, Madrid, 1988 (One Hundred Years of Painting in Spain and Portugal (1830-1930)).

FREISINGER, Lienhart
German, 15th century.
Active in Bozen, South Tyrol (now Bolzano, Italy) in 1499.
Painter.

FREIST, Greta
Austrian, 20th century.
Born 21 July 1904, in Vienna; died 1993.
From 1937 active in France.
Painter.
Freist studied at a fine arts college in Vienna, then moved to Paris, where she exhibited at the Salon des Artistes Indépendants from 1938. Between 1953 and 1956 she also exhibited at the Salon des Réalités Nouvelles in Paris. She belonged to the movement Der Kreis (The Circle). Her early work is figurative, albeit betraying Surrealist tendencies, but from around 1949 her painting (typically large compositions in heavy tonalities) became progressively abstract.

AUCTION RECORDS:
BOULOGNE-SUR-SEINE, 27 Nov 1994, *Portrait of Madame Worms* (oil on canvas, 39 1/4 x 32 ins / 100 x 81 cm) FRF 9,000. VIENNA, 9 March 1999, *Wall with Multi-coloured Shapes* (1957, oil on canvas, 39 x 35 ins / 99 x 89 cm) ATS 45,000. MUNICH, 11 Nov 1999, *Murmauer, Abstract Composition* (oil on canvas, 24 x 33 ins / 60 x 85 cm) DEM 5,000. MUNICH, 13 May 2004, *Birds in Tree* (watercolour, 18 x 15 ins / 46 x 38 cm) EUR 1,500.

FREITAG, Andreas
Swiss, 18th century.
Died 1771.
Active in Zurich.
Painter.
Andreas Freitag was mentioned in 1716 as a member of the brotherhood of *Meise*.

FREITAG, Benjamin
German, 18th century.
Died 1748, in Breslau (now Wroclaw, Poland).
Painter.
This artist's works include a *Crucifixion*.

FREITAG, Johann Conrad. See **FREYTAG Johann Konrad**

FREITAG, Johann Jakob
Austrian, 18th century.
Born in Rheinfelden; died 1730, in Vienna.
Painter.
Johann Jakob was the father of Anton and Mathias Freitag.

FREITAG, Mathias
Austrian, 18th century.
Active in Vienna in 1738.
Painter.
Mathias was the son of Johann Jakob Freitag.

FREITAG, Rudolf
German, 19th century.
Born 5 February 1805, in Breslau (now Wroclaw, Poland); died May 1890, in Danzig (now Gdansk, Poland).
Sculptor.
Rudolf Freitag was a pupil of Schaller and Kasaamann. He lived in Rome for many years as a collaborator of Thorvaldsen. His works include the busts of *Prince Albert of Prussia, Frederick-William IV* and *King William*.

FREITAG-LORINGHOVEN, Mathilde von
German, 19th century.
Born 30 October 1860, in Copenhagen; died 1941, in Weimar.
Painter. Landscapes.
This artist may be M. Freytag. Her *Forest of Sivland* is in the Weimar Museum collection.

FREITAS, Ignacio José de
Portuguese, 19th century.
Died 1817, in Lisbon.
Engraver.
Ignacio José de Freitas was a pupil of Carneiro da Silva.

FREIWIRTH-LUTZOW, Oskar
Russian, 19th century.
Born 12 May 1862, in Moscow.
Painter. Genre scenes.
Freiwirth first studied in Geneva and Düsseldorf, the went to perfect his technique in Paris, with Tony Robert-Fleury and Bouguereau and at Toby Edward Rosenthal's studio in Munich. Was a member of the Munich and St Petersburg artistic associations.

FREIXANES, José
Spanish, 20th - 21st century.
Born 1953, in Pontevedra (Galicia).
Painter (mixed media).
José Freixanes lives and works in Madrid and has exhibited at the Juana Mordo gallery in Madrid, as well as in Vigo and at the Pierre Birtchansky gallery in Paris.

Influenced in his early career by Expressionism, Freixanes soon distanced himself from this approach and began to create a universe of his own, with multiple references, which seeks to capture the objects of this world by forging fortuitous relationships. Drawing from a variety of sources, he displays objects and weaves emotional links around them, seeking to achieve a balance with the background, but also producing figures that merge with the landscape. Freixanes has a keen interest in ethnology and anthropology and, from prehistoric art borrows an iconography of signs and totems that are there to be decrypted. He also draws inspiration from ancient maps and, like the cartographers of the past, gives his vision of the world, scattering it as they did, with lacunae and unexplored territories. Working in series (*The Hunters; The Negroes; The Maps; The Mistress of the Château* [a series that makes reference to the Gulf War of 1991]), he explores the unknown and reverts to the completely primitive in order to take possession of images and to construct a macrocosm. Against diluted backgrounds, or backgrounds doomed to disappear because of the use of unstable materials such as chalk or talc, he addresses the question of mystery and also that of time - the work no longer being designed to last, but destined to be remembered.

BIBLIOGRAPHY:

Castro, Anton, *'Interview: José Freixanes'* in *Artension* n° 30, periodical, Rouen, 1991-1992.

AUCTION RECORDS:

PARIS, 17 Dec 1989, *Sacrolusitania* (1988, oil on canvas, 78 3/4 x 55 ins / 200 x 140 cm) FRF 28,000. PARIS, 8 April 1990, *Mareante* (1989, oil on canvas, 78 3/4 x 78 3/4 ins / 200 x 200 cm) FRF 32,000. PARIS, 26 Oct 1990, *Faro Mareante* (oil on canvas, 55 x 55 ins / 140 x 140 cm) FRF 15,000. MADRID, 21 Feb 2000, *Map of the Lost Continent* (1990, oil on canvas, 55 x 79 ins / 140 x 200 cm) ESP 650,000. MADRID, 12 June 2001, *Map of an Island with Two Towers* (1990, oil and pigment on canvas, 55 x 55 ins / 140 x 140 cm) ESP 400,000. MADRID, 16 Dec 2003, *Map of Lost Continents* (1990, oil on canvas, 55 x 79 ins / 140 x 200 cm) EUR 1,600. MADRID, 29 June 2004, *Figura adoecida* (1986, oil on fabric, 39 x 32 ins / 100 x 81 cm) EUR 2,600.

FRÉLAUT, Jean

French, 20th century.
Born 17 July 1879, in Grenoble; died 22 December 1954, in Vannes.
Painter, engraver, illustrator, draughtsman.
Landscapes, seascapes.

Jean Frélaut studied at Cormon's studio at the École des Beaux-Arts in Paris and also studied engraving with Marcel Beltrand and Donald Shaw. He visited London, Holland and Belgium and returned with numerous sketchbooks from his trips to Algeria in 1911 and the Menton region in 1952 and 1953. In 1927 he was elected as a regular member of the Société des Peintres Graveurs Français. He was awarded the prize for engraving at the Venice Biennale in 1934. In 1937 he was appointed curator of the Musée de Vannes.

He was mainly known as an illustrator, having illustrated La Fontaine's *Fables*, *Monsieur des Lourdines* by Chateaubriand, *Le Grand Meaulnes* by Alain-Fournier and *Le Roman de Renart.* He worked with a delicate yet sure and accurate touch, depicting to perfection and in depth the melancholic life of the Morbihan countryside, which he knew well, its villages, farms, heathland, processions and ships. The sketches he made on his travels, often heightened with watercolour, studied form, gestures and attitudes: the silhouettes of women in colourful costumes, shepherds in burnouses exuding exoticism in brown monochrome, mountain villages and the narrow, winding side streets of southern France in harmonious colours illuminated by the bright light of the south.

He exhibited at the main Paris Salons and held his first solo exhibition in 1912. In 2001 the Musée de Vannes showed two major collections of his watercolour drawings relating to two of his trips; the exhibition was entitled *Jean Frélaut et la Méditerranée* (*Jean Frélaut and the Mediterranean*).

J Frelaut 1924

BIBLIOGRAPHY:

Delteil, Jean, *'Jean Frélaut'* in *Le Peintre-graveur illustré,* vol. XXXI, Chez l'auteur, Paris, 1921 (Collectors Da Capo Press, New York, 1969). Frélaut, Bertrand, *Catalogue raisonné de l'œuvre gravé de Jean Frélaut 1947-1954*, La Bibliothèque des Arts, Lausanne, 1999. Le Saux, Marie-Françoise, *Jean Frélaut - La Méditerranée*, exhibition catalogue, Musée des Beaux-Arts, Vannes, 2001.

MUSEUMS AND GALLERIES:

VANNES (MBA La Cohue): *Vue de Cherchell* (*View of Cherchell*) (1911, drawing with watercolour).

AUCTION RECORDS:

PARIS, 23 May 1923, *The Port,* FRF 1,150. PARIS, 4 March 1977, *La Grenouillère* (1937, etching) FRF 4,000. PARIS, 6 Dec 1978, *Country Wedding* (1936, etching and dry-point) FRF 6,800. LONDON, 27 Feb 1980, *The Customs Officers' Room* (1920, oil on canvas, 21 1/4 x 29 ins / 54 x 73.5 cm) GBP 230. PARIS, 24 Oct 1984, *La Grenouillère* (1937, etching and dry-point) FRF 6,000. PARIS, 11 Feb 1987, *Recollection of Berehis* (1929, oil on panel, 13 x 15 3/4 ins / 33 x 40 cm) FRF 6,800.

FRÉLAUT, Monique

French, 20th century.
Born in Nice.
Painter, engraver.

In 1938, Monique Frélaut was awarded a travel bursary by the Salon des Artistes Français.

FRELENS, Gui de

German, 15th century.
Painter.

Gui de Frelens is mentioned by Siret. He was in the service of the duke of Burgundy in 1419-1420.

FRELET, Ferjeux

French, 18th century.
Active in Pontarlier.
Sculptor (wood).

In 1749, Ferjeux Frelet was working for the church in La Cluse.

FRELEZEAU, Jean

French, 20th century.
Born in Dijon.
Painter. Scenes with figures, landscapes.

Jean Frelezeau exhibited in Paris at the Salon d'Automne and the Salon des Artistes Indépendants from 1928.

AUCTION RECORDS:

PARIS, 15 Jan 1943, *Little Girl with Daisy,* FRF 1,000. PARIS, 7 April 1943, *St-Cyr-sur-Morin,* FRF 2,000.

FRELIN, Pierre

French, 17th century.
Active in Paris in 1615.
Painter, sculptor.

FRELINGHUYSEN, Suzy

American, 20th century.
Born 1912, in New Jersey; died 1988.
Painter.
American Abstract Artists (AAA).

Suzy Frelinghuysen was a self-taught artist, who initially painted in her leisure time while pursuing a career as an opera singer. She lived in New York and was married to the painter L. K. Morris. At first a realist, in about 1936, she moved to abstraction and exhibited with the *American Abstract Artists*. She also took part in other group exhibitions in the USA, Rome and Amsterdam, and at the Salon des Réalités Nouvelles in Paris in 1949 and 1950.

AUCTION RECORDS:

NEW YORK, 20 March 1987, *Abstract Variations of Purple* (1942, oil on card, 16 1/4 x 12 1/4 ins / 41 x 31 cm) USD 4,500. NEW YORK, 14 Nov 2000, *Untitled* (oil on canvas) USD 32,000.

FRELON, Joseph

French, 19th century.
Lithographer.

Frelon exhibited at the Paris Salon in 1850.

FREMANTLE, Christopher
American, 20th century.
Born 17 December 1906, in the United Kingdom.
Active in France, also active in the USA and naturalised American.
Painter.

FREMD, Adolf
German, 19th century.
Born 18 May 1853, in Vaihingen.
Sculptor.

Adolf Fremd worked mainly in Stuttgart where his *Uhland* is in the town hall.

FREMERS, Folkhard
German, 17th century.
Died 3 September 1638.
Active in Jever.
Sculptor (wood).

Folkhard Fremers worked for the town hall in Jever and other towns.

FRÉMERY, Martin
French, 17th century.
Sculptor (wood).

Martin Frémery worked on the decoration of the Dauphin's apartments in the Tuileries, from 1666 to 1678, and at the château in Clagny in 1678.

MUSEUMS AND GALLERIES:
VERSAILLES (Mus.): copies of antique statues.

FRÉMIET, C.
French, 19th century.
Active at the end of the 19th century.
Engraver.

MUSEUMS AND GALLERIES:
DIEPPE: aquatint, 1894.

FRÉMIET, Emmanuel
French, 19th century.
Born 6 December 1824, in Paris; died 10 September 1910, in Paris.
Sculptor, engraver, draughtsman. History painting, religious subjects, allegorical subjects, mythological subjects, natural history (animals). Busts, equestrian statues, equestrian groups.

Emmanuel Frémiet was the nephew and pupil of François Rude. He apprenticed as a lithographer and initially drew studies from nature for the Paris School of Medicine, prepared anatomical moulds for the Orfila Museum, and collaborated with the painter Jacques Christophe Werner on behalf of the zoological and myological (muscle anatomy) departments of the Musée National d'Histoire Naturelle to produce osteological (bone science) studies. Frémiet went on to be appointed in 1892 as Antoine Barye's successor as professor of drawing and composition at the Musée National d'Histoire Naturelle. He was made a Chevalier of the Légion d'Honneur in 1860, an officer of that institution in 1878, a commander in 1878 and, ultimately, grand officier of the Légion in 1900.

Frémiet exhibited at the Paris Salon from 1843 onwards and received awards on several occasions, including a bronze medal at the Salon of 1849 and the 1855 Exposition Universelle, a silver in 1851 and 1867, a medal of honour in 1887 and the Grand Prix in 1900.

Emmanuel Frémiet achieved celebrity primarily on account of his sculpture; his drawings went largely ignored. He produced numerous plaster or bronze studies of prehistoric animals, hominoids and Early Man, inspired in no small degree by Darwinian research; examples include an 1852 *Plesiosaurus* and an *Orang-Utan and Malay Savage* from 1895. Even his *Female Gorilla Carrying Off a Negress*, largely rejected as a 'tasteless juxtaposition', was nonetheless found 'acceptable' as an artistic parallel to the scientific positivism of the day.

Frémiet was commissioned to sculpt a wide variety of compositions, including a collection of statuettes ordered by Napoleon III to illustrate the diverse equipment and weaponry employed by the French army (*Light Cavalry, Mounted Police, Bombardier, Republican Guard, Artilleryman, Zouave, Sapper, Horse Trooper*, etc.). Among his other work, mention should be made of *Napoleon I*, a model for the eponymous statue in Grenoble; a *Louis d'Orléans, Brother of Charles VI* (for the Château de Pierrefonds); a *St Michael* for the spire of Mont-St-Michel; a *Monument to Ferdinand de Lesseps* in Suez; a *Bear Cub Tracker* for the Jardin des Plantes; allegorical equestrian groups entitled *Famous Artists* and *Famous Scientists* for the pylons of the Pont Alexandre III bridge in Paris; *Sea Horses* for the Observatoire fountain; an equestrian statue of *Joan of Arc* for the Place des Pyramides (1880); a *Lantern-Holder* for the Paris Hôtel de Ville; and much more besides.According to one contemporary observer, Emmanuel Frémiet was a diligent product of the École des Beaux-Arts, preoccupied with capturing minute details in his equestrian groups. That said, while his horses are most lifelike, the same can hardly be said of those sitting astride them: his human figures are stilted and, at best, academic. His work reveals an eye for minutiae which can be traced to his preoccupation with the sciences. As a result, Frémiet was perhaps more successful at developing a closely-observed typology - of saints, medieval citizens or large primates, for example - than in conveying any sense of individuality. His work is deliberately static - calm and detached, not to say clinical. As a result, there is some justification in criticism of his work as a whole as being too cold and impersonal. Frémiet's work has featured in several thematic exhibitions, most recently in *Vénus et Caïn. Figures de la préhistoire 1830-1930* (*Venus and Cain. Prehistoric Figures 1830-1930*), an exhibition at the Musée d'Aquitaine in Bordeaux designed to demonstrate the emergence of prehistory as both a scientific discipline and as a source of artistic inspiration. His work has also featured in solo exhibitions, including notably a 1989 retrospective at the Musée des Beaux-Arts in Dijon entitled *Emmanuel Frémiet, la main et le multiple* (*Emmanuel Frémiet: The Sculptor's Hand and his Many Sculptures*).

BIBLIOGRAPHY:
Biez, Jacques de, *Un Maître imagier: Emmanuel Frémiet*, Paris, 1896. Masson, Frédéric/Biez, Jacques de, *Emmanuel Frémiet*, Jouve, Paris, 1910. Faure-Frémiet, Philippe, *Frémiet*, Plon, Paris, 1934. Fusco, P./Janson, H.W. (ed.), *The Romantics to Rodin: French Nineteenth-century Sculpture from North American Collections*, exhibition catalogue, 1980-1981. Chevillot, Catherine (ed.), *Emmanuel Frémiet: Le Main et le multiple*, exhibition catalogue, Musée des Beaux Arts, Dijon, 1988-1989. Lafont-Couturier, Hélène/Dagen, Philippe/Loizeau, Sigolène, *Vénus et Caïn. Figures de la préhistoire 1830-1930*, exhibition catalogue, Musée d'Aquitaine, Bordeaux, 2003.

MUSEUMS AND GALLERIES:
BAYONNE: *Louis d'Orléans; Centaur Slaying a Bear* - BUCHAREST: *St Michael; Spanish Singer; St George* - DIJON (MBA): *Soldiers; Gorilla Carrying Off a Negress* - GRAY: *Monkey* - HAMBURG: *Injured Dog; St George* - LE PUY-EN-VELAY: *St Michael Slaying the Dragon* - LIMOGES: *Cleopatra* - MELBOURNE: *Gorilla Abducting a Woman; Joan of Arc; St George and the Dragon* - MONTPELLIER (Mus. Fabre): *St George Slaying the Dragon* - MOULINS: *Condé the Great* - NANTES (MBA): *Horses in Harness; Gorilla Abducting a Woman* - NIORT: *Dog Resting; Cat Suckling her Kittens* - PARIS (Mus. d'Orsay): *Injured Dog; Pan and Bear Cubs* - PARIS (Mus. des Arts décoratifs): *Étienne Marcel* - PARIS (Mus. National d'Histoire Naturelle): *Plesiosaurus; Orang-Utan and Malay Savage* - PHILADELPHIA (Fairmount Park/International Sculpture Garden): *Joan of Arc* (1890) - RENNES (MBA): *Horse Artilleryman;*

Mounted Cavalryman; Carabiniere on Horseback - SEMUR-EN-AUXOIS: *Picket Horse; Zouave; Guard Artilleryman; Cat; Heron; Griffon* - ST-GERMAIN-EN-LAYE (Mus. des Antiquités Nationales): *Gaulish Chieftain.*

AUCTION RECORDS:

PARIS, 23 Nov 1894, *Equestrian Statue of Joan of Arc* (drawing) FRF 155. PARIS, 27 March 1931, *Monkey* (bronze) FRF 230. PARIS, 4 Dec 1941, *Gun Dog* (graphite) FRF 200. LONDON, 1 Nov 1972, *Circus Horse* (patinated bronze) GBP 560. LONDON, 21 April 1976, *Two Mounted Racehorses* (green-brown-patinated bronze, h. 18 ins / 45.5 cm) GBP 3,000. PARIS, 14 June 1977, *St George Slaying the Dragon* (gilt bronze, h. 23 1/2 ins / 60 cm) FRF 4,000. NANCY, 22 Oct 1978, *Auriga* (gilt bronze) FRF 16,000. PARIS, 8 Dec 1980, *Dromedary* (bronze, h. 12 1/4 ins / 31 cm) FRF 21,000. ENGHIEN-LES-BAINS, 10 Oct 1982, *Two Basset Hounds* (bronze, h. 6 ins / 15 cm) FRF 5,950. MONTE CARLO, 6 March 1984, *Monkeys Playing with Soap Bubbles* (1899-1900, gilt bronze decorated with six glass balls, height of the bronze 37 1/2 ins / 95 cm, total height 67 3/4 ins/172 cm) FRF 150,000. LONDON, 7 Nov 1985, *Two Mounted Jockeys* (c. 1860, brown-patinated bronze, h. 18 1/2 ins / 47 cm) GBP 12,500. PARIS, 20 Dec 1987, *Horseman* (silvered bronze) FRF 15,000. PARIS, 24 April 1988, *Two Tethered Dogs* (brown-patinated bronze, h. 9 3/4 ins / 25 cm) FRF 7,800; *Man Attacked by a Bear* (brown-green-patinated lost-wax bronze, h. 11 1/4 ins / 28.5 cm) FRF 7,500. NEW YORK, 9 June 1988, *Cavalry Regiment Mount* (bronze, h. 12 ins / 30.5 cm) USD 2,750. TROYES, 16 Oct 1988, *St Michael Slaying the Dragon* (brown-patinated bronze, h. 23 1/2 ins / 60 cm) FRF 8,500. PARIS, 24 Oct 1988, *Francis I on Horseback* (patinated gilt bronze, h. 19 1/4 ins / 49 cm) FRF 24,000. NEW YORK, 24 May 1989, *Thoroughbred and Jockey* (bronze, h. 17 3/4 ins / 45 cm) USD 6,600. PARIS, 19 June 1989, *Berber Warrior on Horseback* (bronze repatinated in gold) FRF 10,000. PARIS, 6 July 1989, *Two Basset Hounds from the Artois* (bronze, h. 6 1/4 ins / 16 cm, l. 7 ins/18 cm) FRF 9,500. NEW YORK, 1 March 1990, *Gaulish Chieftain on Horseback* (brown-patinated bronze, h. 16 1/4 ins / 41.2 cm) USD 1,540. NEW YORK, 24 Oct 1990, *Roman Chariot Race* (green-patinated bronze, equestrian group, h. 15 3/4 ins / 40 cm) USD 3,080. PARIS, 26 Jan 1991, *Dray* (bronze, h. 9 1/2 ins / 24 cm) FRF 19,000. MAYENNE, 16 June 1991, *Pack Hounds* (brown-patinated bronze, h. 9 3/4 ins / 25 cm) FRF 53,000. MAYENNE, 13 July 1991, *Gorilla Abducting a Woman* (1877, brown-patinated bronze, h. 17 1/4 ins / 44 cm) FRF 150,000. NEW YORK, 27 May 1992, *Horse and Jockey* (bronze, h. 17 3/4 ins / 45.1 cm) USD 6,050. JOIGNY, 28 March 1993, *Bear* (bronze, h. 25 1/2 ins / 65 cm) FRF 98,000. LOKEREN, 4 Dec 1993, *Joan of Arc* (bronze, h. 29 1/4 ins / 74 cm, w. 17 3/4 ins/45 cm) BEF 48,000. PERTH, 30 Aug 1994, *St Michael and the Dragon* (bronze, h. 22 1/2 ins / 57 cm) GBP 1,725. NEW YORK, 12 Oct 1994, *Muse Crowning Pierre Corneille* (1879, bronze, h. 26 ins / 66 cm) USD 23,000. RAMBOUILLET, 22 Oct 1995, *Joan of Arc* (bronze, h. 28 3/4 ins / 73 cm) FRF 56,000. LOKEREN, 9 March 1996, *Roman Charioteer* (bronze) BEF 65,000. PARIS, 3 July 1996, *St Michael* (gilt bronze, h. 12 1/2 ins / 31.5 cm) FRF 4,000. CALAIS, 15 Dec 1996, *Monkey Sitting on Haunches* (c. 1890, brown-patinated bronze, H.7 ins / 18 cm, w. 11 1/2 ins/29 cm) FRF 12,000. PARIS, 20 March 1998, *Two Basset Hounds: Ravageot and Ravageole* (patinated bronze, h. 6 ins / 15 cm) FRF 12,000. LONDON, 14 May 1999, *The Muse Crowning Pierre Corneille* (1879, sculpture, green brown patinated bronze, h. 26 ins / 67 cm) GBP 3,600. PARIS, 16 June 1999, *Joan of Arc* (c. 1872, sculpture, black wax study, h. 30 ins / 75 cm) FRF 200,000. BRUSSELS, 9 May 2000, *Two Jockeys* (sculpture, patinated bronze, 18 x 21x8 ins / 46 x 53x20 cm) BEF 920,000. PARIS, 23 June 2000, *Equestrian Statue* (sculpture, brown patinated bronze/wood base) FRF 190,000. LONDON, 27 April 2001, *Louis d'Orleans* (sculpture, silvered bronze, 29 x 13x? ins / 74 x 34x? cm) GBP 6,200. LONDON, 27 April 2001, *St George and the Dragon* (sculpture, gilt bronze, 21 x 9x? ins / 53 x 22x? cm) GBP 8,000. LONDON, 16 April 2002, *Cocher Romaine - Roman Charioteer* (sculpture, brown patinated bronze/veined green marble socle, 16 x 14x? ins / 40 x 36x? cm) GBP 4,000. LONDON, 5 Nov 2002, *St Michael* (1876, sculpture, gilt bronze, h. 22 ins / 55 cm) GBP 4,000. LONDON, 8 July 2003, *Cheval prime* (sculpture, dark brown patinated bronze/green marble base, 17 x 14x? ins / 43 x 36x? cm) GBP 5,500. LONDON, 28 Oct 2003, *Duguesclin* (sculpture, patinated bronze, 26 x 15x? ins / 65 x 38x? cm) GBP 4,000. PARIS, 23 March 2004, *Pelicans* (sculpture, patinated bronze, a pair, sold with pencil drawing, h. 9 ins / 23 cm) EUR 7,800. LONDON, 21 April 2004, *Cat Feeding her Kittens* (1849, sculpture, white marble, 10 x 24x? ins / 25 x 62x? cm) GBP 25,000.

FRÉMIET, Marie

French, 19th century.
Born in Paris.
Painter. Animals.

Marie, the daughter and pupil of Emmanuel Frémier, exhibited drawings at the Paris Salons of 1876 and 1877.

FRÉMIET, Sophie. See **RUDE**

FRÉMIN, René

French, 17th - 18th century.
Born 1 October 1672, in Paris; died 17 February 1744.
Sculptor.

René Frémin was a student of Girardon and Coysevox. He won the Prix de Rome in 1694. He was accepted by the academy in 1701, for a low relief in marble: *Time Reveals Truth.*

He spent some time in Spain, where he was director of the academy in Madrid. As first sculptor to Philip V, he made busts of the king, the queen, their son Louis I and his wife. In France, he produced a low- relief, in the chapel of Noailles at Notre Dame Cathedral: *Prudence* and *Temperance.* In the gardens at Versailles are copies of antique statues by him.

AUCTION RECORDS:

ARGENTEUIL, 22 Oct 1991, *Diana, the Huntress* (1717, reformed stone, h. 72 ins / 182 cm, l. 31 1/2 ins/80 cm) FRF 85,000.

FREMIN DE REVELLE. See **REVELLE Fremin de**

FRÉMINET, Jean. See **AILLET**

FRÉMINET, Louis

French, 17th century.
Born probably in Paris; died c. 1651.
Painter. History painting.

Louis Fréminet was the son of Martin Fréminet. According to *(Moreri's Supplement)*, he was a fairly accomplished painter. He must have benefited from his father's reputation because he received an allowance of 2000 pounds and had the title of gentleman of the court.

After Martin Fréminet died, Louis' mother married Ambroise Dubois, with whom she had two sons. One of them, Louis Dubois, received the rest of his half-brother's allowance. The Fréminet and Dubois families appear to have occupied a position of some importance in the royal household.

FRÉMINET, Martin, or Fréminel

French, 16th - 17th century.
Born 29 September 1567, in Paris; died 18 June 1619, in Paris.
Painter, engraver (etching).
Second School of Fontainebleau.

Martin Fréminet's first teacher was his father Médéric. Even at an early age, Martin showed remarkable talent. By the time he left for Italy, in about 1592, he had already produced several paintings. When he arrived in Italy, he found the artists there divided into two camps, those who supported

Michelangelo Merisi, better known as Caravaggio, and those who supported Arpino. Although the Frenchman Fréminet was naturally attracted to the powerful realism of Caravaggio, circumstances arose that made him the friend of Arpino. Perhaps this apparent contradiction can be explained by Fréminet's desire for success. It should be remembered that Caravaggio was regarded with suspicion by many employers; his disdain for tradition, which produced, for example, his masterpiece *The Death of the Virgin* led to its rejection by the religious community that had commissioned it. Fréminet remained in Italy for several years, studying particularly Michelangelo and Parmigianino and working mainly in Rome. On his journey home, he passed through Venice, Lombardy and Turin, where the duke of Savoy detained him in his palace to paint several compositions. He was very well received on his return to France, and on the death of Pierre du Moustier in 1603 Henri IV named him his chief painter. The king also authorised him to purchase the post of *valet de chambre* and commissioned him to paint decorations in the chapel of the Holy Trinity at Fontainebleau. Begun in 1608 and surviving to this day, the work was completed under Louis XIII in 1615, earning the painter the title of 'Knight of St Michael'. Fréminet painted several pictures for the abbey of Barbeaux near Fontainebleau where, at his request, he was buried. The abbey was destroyed in 1793. Fréminet's works are rare, although a few more are known through engravings made by Philippe Thomassin and Crispin de Passe. A number of his beautiful drawings, with hints of mannerism, are preserved in the Louvre.

Museums and Galleries:

Orléans: *St Matthew; St Mark; St Luke; St John; St Augustine; St Jerome; St Gregory; St Ambrose* - Paris (Louvre): *Mercury Orders Aeneas to Abandon Dido.*

Auction records:

Paris, 1809, *Venus Hunting a Boar,* FRF 51; *Judith,* FRF 15. Paris, 1859, *Christ Presented in the Temple* (pen drawing with bistre wash) FRF 18. Paris, 1894, *The Titans Assaulting Heaven,* FRF 22. Paris, 19 June 1925, *Adoration of the Shepherds,* FRF 70. Paris, 10 Feb 1943, *Wine Harvest* (attributed) FRF 35,500. New York, 30 Jan 1998, *Seated Cupid Holding Bow and Looking at Two Birds* (black chalk, pen, brown ink, 8 x 7 ins / 20 x 17 cm) USD 24,000. London, 6 July 1999, *Annunciation, with God the Father Flanked by Four Allegorical Figures* (chalk, pen, ink wash heightened with white, 7 x 11 ins / 19 x 29 cm) GBP 55,000. London, 9 July 2003, *Penitent Attended by an Angel and Another Figure* (pen/brown ink wash, 17 x 13 ins / 44 x 32 cm) GBP 17,000.

FRÉMINET, Médéric, or Fréminel
French, 16th century.
Active in Paris at the end of the 16th century.
Painter.

Médéric was the father and teacher of Martin Fréminet. He seems to have worked chiefly at producing designs for tapestries.

FRÉMINVILLE, de
French.
Watercolourist. Figures.

Museums and Galleries:

St-Brieuc: *Fisherwomen* (watercolour).

FRÉMIOT, Joël
French, 20th - 21st century.
Born 25 September 1947, in Paris.
Painter.
Minimal Art.

Joël Frémiot studied at the École des Beaux-Arts de Bourges, where he teaches drawing. Frémiot's paintings revive the abstract style of American artists like Newman, Reinhart and Ryman. Like them, he regards the painted surface as a blank to fill in, rather than a page on which to write in a language. Using simple and repetitive elements, but showing sensitivity in his use of colour, Frémiot 'brings painting back' to the surface of the canvas, and eschews any psychological, narrative or metaphysical purpose beyond that.

He has taken part in numerous group exhibitions, including the Salon d'Art Sacré in 1966, the Salon Comparaisons in 1969, and various avant-garde art events from 1970 onwards. In 1973, he was invited to take part in the Biennale de Paris, and his first solo exhibition took place in Bourges in 1971.

FRÉMIOT, Nicolas François
French, 18th century.
Active in Paris in 1735.
Painter, sculptor.

FREMLIN, Arbogast
Swiss, 17th century.
Active in Basel.
Painter.

Arbogast Fremlin was admitted into the corporation of painters of Basel in 1653. He is cited by Brun.

FRÉMOND, André, or Frémont
French, 20th century.
Born in Le Havre; died 1965, in Montreuil.
Painter. Battles, hunting scenes.

André Frémond studied under Luc-Olivier Merson. He exhibited in Paris at the Salon des Artistes Français from 1928.

Auction records:

Paris, 19 Jan 1992, *Crossing the Village* (oil on panel, 13 1/2 x 27 1/2 ins / 34.5 x 70 cm) FRF 9,000. Paris, 24 April 1992, *Huntsman on Horseback* (oil on canvas, 32 x 39 1/4 ins / 81 x 100 cm) FRF 10,500. Paris, 5 June 1996, *Stag Hunting Scene* (oil on canvas, 32 x 39 1/4 ins / 81 x 100 cm) FRF 12,000.

FRÉMONT, Caroline Céline Gabrielle
French, 19th century.
Born c. 1850, in Lille.
Painter.

Caroline Frémont studied under Cassmann and Dessart. She exhibited numerous paintings on ceramic and porcelain before starting to submit painted ivory miniatures to the Paris Salon from 1881 onwards.

FRÉMONT, Charles
French, 17th century.
Born c. 1655.
Active in Paris.
Painter.

FRÉMONT, L. Charles
French, 19th century.
Active in Paris.
Sculptor.

This artist was a member of the Société des Artistes Français from 1895.

FRÉMONT, P.R.
British, 18th century.
Active in London.
Draughtsman, engraver.

P.R. Frémont was a parliamentary lawyer who painted in his free time.

FREMONT, Pierre
French, 20th century.
Born 20 October 1886, in Paris; died 12 March 1974.
Painter (gouache), watercolourist. Landscapes.

Pierre Fremont studied at the École des Arts Décoratifs and under Jules Adler. He exhibited at the major Paris Salons and enjoyed rapid success with his views of the Seine.

Auction records:

Paris, 15 Jan 1943, *Moroccan Courtyard* (gouache) FRF 160. Paris, 30 April 1945, *The Seine at Triel,* FRF 750. Paris, 23

May 1945, *Landscape* (watercolour gouache) FRF 150. VERSAILLES, 5 Nov 1989, *View of Beirut* (oil on card, 9 1/2 x 13 1/4 ins / 24 x 33.5 cm) FRF 19,500; *Large Waterfall in the Lebanese Mountains* (oil on card, 13 1/4 x 9 1/2 ins / 33.5 x 24 cm) FRF 16,000. LYONS, 13 Nov 1989, *Black Panther* (1923, pastel, 13 1/2 x 20 3/4 ins / 34 x 53 cm) FRF 5,500. PARIS, 22 April 1994, *The Galata Bridge, Constantinople* (oil on card, 9 1/2 x 13 ins / 24 x 33 cm) FRF 5,200.

FRÉMONT, Suzanne Camille Désirée
French, 20th century.
Born 10 April 1876, in Châtillon-sous-Bagneux; died 12 March 1962, in Bormes.
Painter (gouache), watercolourist. Portraits, nudes, figures, landscapes, scenes with figures.

Suzanne Frémont studied at the studios of Maximilien Luce, Eugène Carrière, G. Jeanniot and Rame. During World War I she took a break from painting to devote herself to public service. In 1921 she founded the École des Beaux-Arts in Antananarivo, Madagascar.

Having been trained by some of the Impressionist masters she produced many landscapes imbued with a poetic, serene atmosphere, seeking to reconstruct the moment at which the painting was conceived. She also produced large figure paintings. After World War I she began to favour the light and sun of the Orient and her colours grew warmer and her draughtsmanship firmer.

She exhibited in Paris at the Salon des Artistes Français, the Salon of the Société Nationale des Beaux-Arts and at the Salon d'Automne, of which she became a member in 1907. She also showed her work in numerous solo exhibitions from 1913 onwards. She received a number of awards at colonial Salons and exhibitions.

MUSEUMS AND GALLERIES:
MARSEILLES: *Flava-Vénus-Nu* - PARIS (Mus. Carnavalet) - ROCHEFORT.

AUCTION RECORDS:
SAUMUR, 25 June 1989, *Reclining Female Nude* (oil on canvas, 11 x 13 3/4 ins / 27 x 35 cm) FRF 9,000; *The Port* (oil on canvas, 32 x 39 1/4 ins / 81 x 100 cm) FRF 18,000; *Woman of the Aurès Mountains* (watercolour, 18 1/2 x 12 1/4 ins / 47 x 31 cm) FRF 3,500; *Djara* (mars 1921, watercolour, 11 1/2 x 16 1/2 ins / 29 x 42 cm) FRF 1,500; *White Town* (gouache, 5 1/2 x 8 1/4 ins / 14 x 21 cm) FRF 2,100.

FRÉMONT-CHERVIER, Suzanne
French, 20th century.
Born 16 March 1895, in Lyons.
Painter.

Suzanne Frémont-Chervier exhibited in Paris at the Salon d'Automne and became a member of the Salon in 1934.

FRÉMONT-GEORGE, Janine Sylvie
French, 20th century.
Born in Paris.
Painter.

Janine Frémont-George studied under Fouqueray. She exhibited at the Salon des Artistes Français from 1932.

FREMOUT, Gilliam or Willem. See **FERMOUT**

FRÉMY
French, 16th century.
Active in Lorraine during the 16th century.
Sculptor.

Frémy carved the coat of arms of the duke of Lorraine on the walls of the convent of St Claire in Pont-à-Mousson (Meurthe-et-Moselle) in 1542.

FRÉMY (Mlle)
French, 18th century.
Active in Paris.
Miniaturist, pastellist.

Mlle Frémy was a student of Mme Labille-Guyard.

FRÉMY, Antoine Alexandre Auguste
French, 19th century.
Born 14 December 1816, in Toulon; died 28 November 1885, in St-Jean-de-Luz.
Painter, watercolourist, draughtsman. Genre scenes, landscapes, seascapes.

Antoine Frémy studied in Toulon under Bernard Sénéquier and the Marquis of Clinchamp. In around 1860, Frémy left with a party of explorers to investigate the coasts of South America, his role being to create a pictorial record of the expedition. He went on to work in Rio de Janeiro for the Brazilian emperor. Frémy set off on his travels once again in 1852 as an envoy of the Marquis de la Valette to Constantinople, Smyrna (Izmir) and Athens. On his return to France, he lived for a while in the Toulon region before finally settling in St-Jean-de-Luz in the Basque country. Antoine Frémy produced numerous landscapes and seascapes in watercolour, pen-and-ink and charcoal heightened with gouache. His work is scrupulously detailed and particularly interesting in his rendering of different light effects.

MUSEUMS AND GALLERIES:
TOULON: *Fishermen Preparing to Put to Sea; Drawings.*

FRÉMY, Édouard Pierre Désiré
French, 19th century.
Born 17 January 1829, in Paris; died 15 July 1888.
Sculptor.

Édouard Frémy exhibited at the Paris Salon from 1865 to 1879. His body of work included a bronze medallion of *Pasquier*, a plaster bust of *Madame Frémy*, a bronze medallion of *Madame Gastat*, a terracotta medallion of *Irmond Libre Bardin*, a bronze medallion of *Gruet*, a terracotta medallion of *Doctor Dereins*, and bronze medals of *Madame Ricard* and *Babinet of the Institute*.

FRÉMY, Jacques Noël Marie
French, 19th century.
Born 25 December 1782, in Paris; died 1867, in Paris.
Painter, miniaturist, engraver, illustrator. History painting, mythological subjects, allegorical subjects, genre scenes, portraits.

Jacques Frémy studied painting under Jean-Baptiste Regnault and Jacques-Louis David. He made the rounds of the various salons of the Restoration period, finding a patron in the Countess of Neeserold, in whose company he travelled to St. Petersburg around 1830. On his return to France, he worked in Versailles as a painter and restorer at the court of Louis-Philippe. Frémy exhibited at the Paris Salon between 1808 and 1866, winning a silver medal in 1817.

Frémy's body of work comprises principally historical subjects drawn from the Napoleonic era and the subsequently reinstated monarchy, together with allegorical and mythological compositions, genre subjects and portraits; as an engraver, he worked in conjunction with Jean-Dominique Ingres. Examples of Frémy's work include: *Modesty and Love, Portrait of the Duke of Aumale, Self-portrait in the Artist's Studio, Turenne Asleep on a Gun Carriage, Condé Sleeping, Echo Mourning, Narcissus Transformed into a Flower, National Guard on Horseback, Counterfeiters, Captive Cavalry, Basket Handle, Amphitrite Asleep* and *Returning from the Woods*. Frémy also illustrated the works of Jack London. His miniature work taught him how to render details with extreme precision, notably in his genre compositions.

FRÉMY, Zoé
French, 19th century.
Painter.

This artist exhibited her portrait of two children at the 1848 Paris Salon, followed by *Prayer* in 1849 and *Reward and Punishment* in 1850.

FRENA, Abraham
Dutch, 18th century.
Active in Amsterdam,in 1711.
Painter.

FRENAIS D'ALBERT, Jacques Nicolas.
See **FRAINAIS d'ALBERT**

FRENCH, Alice Helm
American, 19th - 20th century.
Born 17 March 1864, in Lake Forest (Illinois); died after 1953.
Painter.

Alice Helm French studied at the Chicago Art Institute and was a member of the American Federation of Arts.

FRENCH, Annie
British, 19th - 20th century.
Born 1873; died 1965.
Painter, watercolourist, draughtsman, illustrator.
Scenes with figures, genre scenes.

Annie French studied at the Glasgow School of Art. She exhibited from 1906 at the Royal Academy in London and went on to exhibit at many other venues. She transforms a simple line with grace and elegance into landscapes and delicate figures.

ANNIE FRENCH

BIBLIOGRAPHY:
Osterwalder, Marcus (ed.), *Dictionnaire des illustrateurs 1800-1914*, Ides et Calendes, Neuchâtel, 1989.

AUCTION RECORDS:
SCOTLAND, 29 Aug 1978, *Young Woman in a Ball Gown* (1902, watercolour heightened with gouache and gold, 9 1/2 x 6 ins / 24 x 15 cm) GBP 550. PERTH, 13 April 1981, *Moon Gazing* (black ink/paper, 9 x 7 1/2 ins / 23 x 19 cm) GBP 1,600. SCOTLAND, 31 Aug 1982, *Greetings* (pen and wash, 9 x 8 ins / 23 x 20.5 cm) GBP 750. EDINBURGH, 27 March 1984, *Fairy Abundance* (pen and colour wash heightened with gouache and gold, 10 x 14 ins / 25.5 x 35.5 cm) GBP 1,400. LONDON, 5 June 1984, *The Toy Vendor* (watercolour and pen heightened with gouache and gold, 7 3/4 x 11 3/4 ins / 20 x 30 cm) GBP 2,400. NEW YORK, 24 May 1985, *Rose* (watercolour, gouache, pencil, pen and gold, 7 3/4 x 11 1/2 ins / 20 x 29.4 cm) USD 5,000. SISSINGHURST (KENT), 16 July 1985, *At the Sign of the Spellbound Lodge* (pencil and pen heightened with watercolour, gouache and gold, 12 1/2 x 19 3/4 ins / 31.6 x 50 cm) GBP 3,300. EDINBURGH, 30 Aug 1988, *O Bessie Bell and Mary Gray (Old Scottish Ballad)* (ink and gouache, 12 1/4 x 9 1/2 ins / 31 x 24 cm) GBP 2,090. GLASGOW, 6 Feb 1990, *Allegory of Autumn* (ink and watercolour heightened with gouache, 9 3/4 x 6 3/4 ins / 25 x 17 cm) GBP 2,750. SOUTH QUEENSFERRY, 1 May 1990, *Picking Roses* (ink and watercolour heightened with gouache, 9 1/2 x 17 1/4 ins / 24 x 44 cm) GBP 2,860. PERTH, 27 Aug 1990, *Courtly Love* (ink and watercolour, 9 3/4 x 11 1/4 ins / 25 x 28.5 cm) GBP 4,180. PERTH, 30 Aug 1994, *The Sleeping Princess* (watercolour and ink, 11 1/2 x 16 ins / 29.5 x 40.5 cm) GBP 2,760. GLASGOW, 14 Feb 1995, *Conversation in the Garden* (watercolour and ink, 11 1/2 x 15 1/4 ins / 29 x 38.5 cm) GBP 1,150. PERTH, 26 Aug 1996, *Rose* (watercolour and ink, 7 1/2 x 11 1/4 ins / 19 x 28.5 cm) GBP 6,900. GLASGOW, 11 Dec 1996, *Three Young Girls Picking Flowers* (1917, pen, ink, watercolour, gouache, 9 1/2 x 14 1/4 ins / 24 x 36.5 cm) GBP 2,300. LONDON, 29 Nov 1999, *Homage to a Bride* (pen, ink and watercolour heightened with gold gouache, 9 x 15 ins / 24 x 37 cm) GBP 5,800. LONDON, 10 April 2000, *Dreaming* (pen, ink and watercolour, 10 x 15 ins / 26 x 39 cm) GBP 6,800. LONDON, 10 April 2000, *Family Album of Verse for Robert and Agnes Muir* (pen, ink and watercolour) GBP 16,000. LONDON, 6 Dec 2001, *Reading Amongst the Foxgloves* (pencil, pen and ink, 7 x 11 ins / 18 x 27 cm) GBP 2,400. LONDON, 13 June 2002, *Regal Embrace* (pencil, pen, ink, watercolour and scratching out heightened with white) GBP 2,200. LONDON, 27 Aug 2003, *Flowers for Mother* (pen, ink and watercolour, 4 x 5 ins / 10 x 13 cm) GBP 3,800. LONDON, 19 April 2004, *Peacock and the Roses* (watercolour and pen, 9 x 8 ins / 22 x 20 cm) GBP 7,000. LONDON, 1 Sept 2004, *Homage to a Bride* (pen, ink and watercolour, 9 x 15 ins / 24 x 38 cm) GBP 7,000.

FRENCH, Daniel Chester
American, 19th - 20th century.
Born 20 April 1850, in Exeter (New Hampshire); died 1931.
Active in New York.
Sculptor. Figures. Monuments.

Daniel Chester French was a pupil of Thomas Bell. He carved several monuments that were erected in the USA. He was awarded a third-class medal at the Salon de Paris in 1892 and the Grand Prix at the Exposition Universelle of 1900. He became a member of the National Academy in 1901 and of the Accademia di San Luca in Rome.

AUCTION RECORDS:
NEW YORK, 29 Sept 1977, *The Concord Minute Man of 1775* (bronze, h. 32 1/4 ins / 82 cm) USD 26,000. NEW YORK, 5 Dec 1980, *Architecture* (1898, bronze, h. 12 1/4 ins / 31.1 cm) USD 2,400. NEW YORK, 30 May 1984, *The Concord Minute Man of 1775* (bronze, h. 32 1/4 ins / 82 cm) USD 27,000. WASHINGTON DC, 3 March 1985, *Bust of Ralph Waldo Emerson* (brown-patinated bronze, h. 23 ins / 58.5 cm) USD 1,900. NEW YORK, 31 May 1990, *Lincoln Seated* (1915, bronze, h. 9 3/4 ins / 24.8 cm) USD 3,520. NEW YORK, 14 March 1991, *Rip van Winkle* (1925, bronze, h. 18 1/2 ins / 46.7 cm) USD 4,950. NEW YORK, 27 Sept 1996, *George Washington* (1900, brown-patinated bronze, h. 32 1/4 ins / 81.9 cm) USD 34,500. NEW YORK, 4 Dec 1996, *Narcissus* (1901, brown-patinated bronze, h. 12 1/2 ins / 31.5 cm) USD 5,750. SAN FRANCISCO, 13 June 2001, *Seated Lincoln* (brown patinated bronze, h. 11 ins / 28 cm, w. 7 ins/19 cm) USD 6,500. NEW YORK, 28 Nov 2001, *Victory: Model for the First Division Memorial, Washington DC* (c. 1922, gilded bronze, h. 75 ins / 190 cm) USD 250,000. DALLAS, 25 Feb 2004, *Lincoln* (bronze, h. 9 ins / 23 cm) USD 9,000. WASHINGTON, 18 Sept 2004, *Daybreak* (1876, marble, h. 11 ins / 29 cm, w. 11 ins/29 cm) USD 3,600.

FRENCH, David M.
American, 19th - 20th century.
Born c. 1827, in New Market; died 19 April 1910, in Newburyport.
Active in Boston.
Sculptor.

FRENCH, Edwin Davis
American, 19th century.
Born 19 June 1851, in North Attleboro; died 18 December 1906, in New York.
Engraver.

Edwin Davis French was a pupil of Sartrain in New York and mainly illustrated books.

FRENCH, Elizabeth
American, 20th century.
Born 1878, in Pennsylvania; died 1943.
Painter, sculptor, decorative designer.

Elizabeth French was known mainly for her decoration of churches.

FRENCH, Frank
American, 19th century.
Born 1850, in Loudon (New Hampshire); died 1933.

Active in New York.

Painter, engraver (wood).

Frank French was a pupil of Henry Herrik. He was awarded many medals at American exhibitions, mainly for wood engravings, and was a member of the American Society of Wood Engravers.

MUSEUMS AND GALLERIES:

CLEVELAND (MA): *Lacing the Sandal* (1886); *In the Enemy's Country* (1887).

FRENCH, Henry

Irish, 17th - 18th century.

Born towards the end of the 17th century; died 1726.

Painter. History painting.

Henry French studied in Rome, where he was awarded a medal at the Accademia di San Luca. He subsequently moved to London but failed to make a name for himself there.

FRENCH, Howard Barclay

American, 20th century.

Born 1906, in Kentucky.

Painter.

Howard B. French was a member of the National Arts Club.

FRENCH, Jared Blandford

American, 20th century.

Born 1905; died 1987.

Painter, photographer. Compositions with figures.

PaJaMa group.

Jared French studied at Amherst College in Massachusetts, where he met Paul Cadmus, who was to become a lifelong friend and collaborator, in 1926. He travelled to Europe with Cadmus in 1931-1933. During the 1930s and 1940s he was a prominent figure in the gay artistic and literary circle that developed around Cadmus, though in 1937 he married the artist Margaret Hoening. With Cadmus and Hoening he formed the PaJaMa group (taking its name from the first two letters of each member's first name) which worked in photography, although he is better known for his painting.

French's works in oil and tempera typically depict realistically rendered, somewhat vacant figures in unreal or dreamlike settings. He uses these subjects to discuss human sexuality and often incorporates the kind of erotic and psychological symbolism employed by a great many 20th century painters and writers, for example the sea to represent the unconscious. He was heavily influenced by Jung's writing on psychoanalysis and the idea of a collective consciousness and inherited cultural memory, and said himself that the meanings of his paintings were to be deciphered with reference to Jung. In *Face to Face* (1949) a young nude male figure with his back to the viewer sees his reflection in a mirror, perhaps symbolising the confrontation with one's own sexuality. The reflected figure appears to be in an interior, and the mirror is the kind one might find in a bedroom, yet the scene appears to be in a grassy outdoor space and two other naked figures look on in the background. The exact meaning of the work is not immediately clear, but issues of voyeurism, dreams and the self are clearly raised. The technique, influenced by pointillism, adds to the hazy, dreamlike atmosphere. Other works, such as *Evasion* (1947) and *Business* (1961), explore similar themes.

Although it did influence his later output, French's photographic work with the PaJaMa group is far less ambiguous. It predominantly shows him and friends such as Glenway Westcott, Monroe Wheeler and the other members of the group in natural, carefree poses on Fire Island, where the gay artistic community congregated in the 1930s and 1940s. Late in his career, in the 1960s, his painting style changed to depict strange rock formations resembling fantastic creatures or parts of the human body.

His photographs were shown at *PaJaMa: The Photographs of Paul Cadmus, Jared French and Margaret French* at the D.C. Moore Gallery in New York in 1997.

BIBLIOGRAPHY:

Wechsler, Jeffrey, *The Rediscovery of Jared French*, Midtown Payson Galleries, Inc, New York, 1992. Cadmus, Paul/French, Margaret/French, Jared, *Collaboration*, Twelvetrees Press, Santa Fe, 1992. Grimes, Nancy, *Jared French's Myths*, Pomegranate Artbooks, San Francisco, 1993. Haggerty, George E. (ed.), *Gay Histories and Cultures: An Encyclopedia*, Garland, New York, 2000.

MUSEUMS AND GALLERIES:

MINNEAPOLIS (Frederick R. Weisman AM, University of Minnesota): *Business* (1961, egg tempera on canvas) - NEW YORK (D.C. Moore Gallery): *Coupla Girls* (1954); *Face to Face* (1949); *George Platt-Lynes & Jonathan Tichenor, Fire Island* (1945, photo).

AUCTION RECORDS:

NEW YORK, 7 June 1999, *Back View Nude Leaning on Pole, Couple in landscape* (pen, ink and wash heightened with white, a pair) USD 1,800. NEW YORK, 21 Sept 2001, *Portrait Head of Ted* (1954, pen, ink and gouache, 6 x 5 ins / 14 x 12 cm) USD 3,000. LONDON, 28 Sept 2001, *Three Male Nudes* (pencil and gouache, 5 x 8 ins / 13 x 20 cm) GBP 1,200. NEW YORK, 17 July 2002, *Study for the Double* (pencil, 15 x 20 ins / 39 x 50 cm) USD 12,000. NEW YORK, 4 Dec 2002, *Three Women and a Lifeguard* (oil on canvas, 24 x 28 ins / 62 x 71 cm) USD 55,000. NEW YORK, 19 Dec 2003, *Syzygy* (pencil, crayon and ink, 26 x 39 ins / 67 x 100 cm) USD 4,250. NEW YORK, 27 Sept 2004, *Man* (tempera on canvas on masonite, 24 x 9 ins / 62 x 23 cm) USD 9,500.

FRENCH, Leonard

Australian, 20th century.

Born 1928, in Brunswick, near Melbourne.

Painter (mixed media), murals, and stained glass.

Leonard French is largely a self-taught artist. He worked his way through London, Ireland, and Belgium between 1949 to 1951, studying as he went. In 1959, he won a scholarship to visit Asia where he became interested in Byzantine Art. He began exhibiting in Melbourne in 1951, and has held many solo shows since then. His first retrospective was held at the Art Gallery of South Australia in 1970.

AUCTION RECORDS:

LONDON, 25 June 1980, *Street* (1969, mixed media, 52 1/4 x 46 1/2 ins / 133 x 118 cm) GBP 2,200. SYDNEY, 29 Oct 1987, *The Grand Performance* (c. 1957, enamel/card, 30 x 47 3/4 ins / 75.3 x 121.3 cm) AUD 20,000. SYDNEY, 16 Oct 1989, *Double Cruciform* (varnish, 10 1/4 x 8 1/4 ins / 26 x 21 cm) AUD 1,600. SYDNEY, 26 March 1990, *Rain and Fire* (mixed media, 20 3/4 x 19 1/4 ins / 53 x 49 cm) AUD 2,600. LONDON, 28 Nov 1991, *The Merry-go-round* (varnish/card, 53 1/2 x 47 1/4 ins / 135.9 x 120 cm) GBP 11,000. MELBOURNE, 26 April 1999, *Fourth Chant* (1965-1968, gold leaf and enamel on board, 53 x 48 ins / 135 x 122 cm) AUD 14,000. MELBOURNE, 22 Nov 1999, *Sixth Chant* (enamel on composition board, 54 x 47 ins / 136 x 120 cm) AUD 24,000. MELBOURNE, 28 June 2000, *Cruciform* (enamel and gold leaf on hessian on board, 54 x 48 ins / 138 x 122 cm) AUD 75,000. MELBOURNE, 28 June 2000, *Death Full of Wounds* (enamel on hessian on board, 72 x 60 ins / 183 x 152 cm) AUD 75,000. MELBOURNE, 8 May 2001, *Rainbow Dragonfly* (enamel on hardboard, 54 x 48 ins / 136 x 121 cm) AUD 22,500. SYDNEY, 28 Aug 2001, *Assault* (enamel on board, 72 x 144 ins / 183 x 366 cm) AUD 50,000. PADDINGTON, 26 Aug 2002, *Song for Morning* (c. 1980, mixed media on paper, 23 x 26 ins / 59 x 65 cm) AUD 12,000. MELBOURNE, 27 Aug 2002, *Flight* (enamel on board, 26 x 23 ins / 67 x 59 cm) AUD 11,500. MELBOURNE, 5 May 2003, *Night Fisherman* (enamel and gold leaf on hessian, 60 x 72 ins / 152 x 183 cm) AUD 34,000. SYD-

NEY, 30 July 2003, *The Tower* (1961, enamel and gold leaf on hessian on board, 90 x 48 ins / 229 x 122 cm) AUD 53,000. MELBOURNE, 15 March 2004, *Storm* (1987-1989, enamel and gold leaf on hessian on hardboard, 60 x 72 ins / 152 x 183 cm) AUD 85,000. MELBOURNE, 8 Sept 2004, *From the Fire* (1974-1976, enamel on hessian on board, 54 x 48 ins / 137 x 121 cm) AUD 18,000.

FRENCH, Nathanael
British, 18th century.
Active in 1747.
Painter.

MUSEUMS AND GALLERIES:
SIBIU (Muz. National Brukenthal): two large landscapes.

FRENCH, Thomas
British, 18th century.
Died September 1803, in Bath.
Painter, draughtsman, decorative designer. Stage sets.

Thomas French worked extensively for the theatre in Bath.

FRENCH, Wallace
Canadian, 20th century.
Born 1940, in Bay Roberts.
Sculptor.

Wallace French studied at the Ontario College from 1959 to 1963, where he now teaches. He makes abstract, geometric, polychrome sculptures, characterised by a purity of form that makes them sometimes seem almost minimalist.

FRENCH, William
British, 19th century.
Born c. 1815; died 8 January 1898, in East Grinstead.
Engraver.

William French engraved a large number of paintings by his contemporaries.

FRENCH, William Percy (known as Percy)
British, 19th century.
Born 1854, in Cloonyquin; died 1920.
Painter, watercolourist. Landscapes.

Percy French is best known as a singer and comic songwriter, but he also painted watercolour landscapes.

AUCTION RECORDS:
COUNTY MEATH, 12 May 1981, *Landscape* (1904, watercolour and gouache, 10 x 13 3/4 ins / 25.5 x 35 cm) GBP 600. LONDON, 28 April 1983, *Landscape at Twilight* (1916, watercolour, 7 3/4 x 12 1/4 ins / 19.5 x 31 cm) GBP 500. LONDON, 27 May 1987, *Windsor Castle* (1905, watercolour heightened with white, 10 x 14 ins / 25.4 x 35.5 cm) GBP 580. DUBLIN, 24 Oct 1988, *Sunset over the Marshes* (watercolour, 6 1/2 x 9 1/2 ins / 16.2 x 24.2 cm) IEP 770. BELFAST, 30 May 1990, *Twilight on the Meadows of Western Ireland* (watercolour, 7 1/4 x 11 ins / 18.4 x 27 cm) GBP 1,210. LONDON, 14 June 1991, *Connemara* (watercolour, 7 x 10 ins / 17.5 x 25.3 cm) GBP 825. DUBLIN, 26 May 1993, *Irish Marshland* (watercolour and gouache, 9 1/4 x 14 1/4 ins / 23.5 x 36.2 cm) IEP 2,420. LONDON, 2 June 1995, *Lake View* (watercolour, 5 1/2 x 9 1/4 ins / 14 x 23.5 cm) GBP 1,092. DUBLIN, 8 Dec 1999, *Purple Moor* (watercolour, 15 x 23 ins / 38 x 58 cm) IEP 13,000. DUBLIN, 8 Dec 1999, *Adventurers* (1916, watercolour, 10 x 14 ins / 25 x 36 cm) IEP 20,000. LONDON, 19 May 2000, *Paintbrush and Pen, Impressions for Pictures and Snatches of Song* (watercolour, 5 x 7 ins / 13 x 18 cm) GBP 50,000. DUBLIN, 31 May 2000, *Bundoran* (watercolour, 6 x 9 ins / 15 x 23 cm) IEP 23,000. LONDON, 17 May 2001, *Cottage in a Landscape* (gouache and gum arabic, 10 x 14 ins / 25 x 36 cm) GBP 7,000. LONDON, 17 May 2001, *Portrush, Co. Antrim* (1910, pencil and watercolour with scratching out, 8 x 14 ins / 20 x 35 cm) GBP 9,200. DUBLIN, 27 March 2002, *Sheep in a Winter Wooded Landscape* (1905, watercolour, 11 x 8 ins / 28 x 20 cm) EUR 13,000. DUBLIN, 19 Nov 2002, *Garden That I Love* (1896, watercolour, 11 x 17 ins / 29 x 44 cm) EUR 14,000. AYLSHAM, 17 Oct 2003, *Moorland Landscapes* (1909, watercolour, a pair, 6 x 9 ins / 15 x 23 cm) GBP 6,200. DUBLIN, 10 Dec 2003, *Donegal Bog, Sunset* (watercolour, 11 x 15 ins / 27 x 38 cm) EUR 9,000. DUBLIN, 26 May 2004, *River Fall. Moonlight on the Water. Geese on a Country Track* (watercolour, three in one frame, 5 x 7 ins / 13 x 18 cm) EUR 15,000. DUBLIN, 29 Sept 2004, *Alpine Chalet* (1915, watercolour, 19 x 25 ins / 48 x 63 cm) EUR 15,000.

FRENDER, Helge
Swedish, 20th century.
Born 1906; died 1976.
Painter. Figures, nudes, interiors with figures, landscapes, flowers.

AUCTION RECORDS:
GÖTEBORG, 18 May 1989, *Coastal Landscape* (oil on canvas, 19 3/4 x 24 1/2 ins / 50 x 62 cm) SEK 4,600. STOCKHOLM, 22 May 1989, *Interior with Female Nude on a Red Chair* (oil on canvas, 19 1/4 x 23 1/2 ins / 49 x 60 cm) SEK 10,500. STOCKHOLM, 14 June 1990, *Flowers in a Vase* (1946, oil on canvas, 22 x 18 ins / 55 x 46 cm) SEK 11,500. STOCKHOLM, 28 Oct 1991, *Orchard in Spring with Flowering Cherry* (oil on canvas, 19 1/4 x 23 1/2 ins / 49 x 60 cm) SEK 4,600.

FRENEL, Yitzhak, or Isaac, Alexandre, real name Isaac Frenel-Fraenkel
Ukrainian, 20th century.
Born 1899, in Odessa; died 1981, in Tel Aviv.
Active in Israel and France.
Painter (including gouache). Figures, local figures, nudes, interiors with figures, local scenes, still-lifes, landscapes, landscapes with figures. Stage sets, stained glass designs.
Safed Artists Colony.

Yitzhak Frenel was the great-grandson of Rabbi Levi Yitzhak of Berdichev. He studied at the Art Academy in Odessa under the painter Alexandra Ekster in 1917, and emigrated to Palestine in 1919. In 1920, he established the artists' cooperative Ha-Tomer in Jaffa and an art studio in Herzliya. He then went to Paris, where he completed his training at the École des Beaux-Arts and the Académie de la Grande Chaumière, studying sculpture with Bourdelle and painting with Matisse, and frequenting the Jewish artists of the École de Paris. On his return to Palestine in 1925, he founded the studio of painting arts of the Histradut in Tel Aviv, which would later attract and influence many students. He returned to Paris from 1929 to 1934, and once more to Palestine, settling in Safed. He would later be one of the cofounders of the Safed Artists Colony.

Frenel's career resembles that of Chagall, except in matters of success. Like Chagall, Frenel was at first caught up in the Constructivist movement in Russia, and like Chagall he moved on, representing scenes from Jewish folklore, with its strange stories and rich tradition.

Frenel exhibited in Israel before and after independence, at the Salon des Indépendants in 1925, and the 1950 and 1952 Venice Biennale. In 1973, the Yitzhak Frenel Museum was officially opened in his house in Safed, which contains works spanning the sixty years between 1920 and 1981. In 1979, a retrospective of his work was held at the Orangerie. Between 1936 and 1949, he designed sets and costumes for the Ha-ohel and Ha-bimah theatre.

BIBLIOGRAPHY:
Frenel, exhibition catalogue, Gal. d'art la Contrescarpe, Paris, 1974. Nieszawer, Nadine/Boyé, Marie/Lanzmann, Claude (preface), *Peintres juifs de l'école de Paris 1905-1939*, Denoël, Paris, 2001.

MUSEUMS AND GALLERIES:
SAFED (Frenel-Frenkel Museum).

AUCTION RECORDS:
TEL AVIV, 21 Nov 1981, *Nude in Interior* (oil on canvas, 11 1/2 x 9 1/2 ins / 29.5 x 24 cm) ILS 9,000. ZURICH, 23 Sept 1982,

Seated Nude (oil on canvas, 36¼ x 23½ ins / 92 x 60 cm) CHF 2,800. ZURICH, 8 June 1983, *Still-life with Pheasant* (oil on canvas, 28¾ x 36¼ ins / 73 x 92 cm) CHF 4,500. TEL AVIV, 4 June 1984, *Nathalia* (oil on canvas, 15 x 18 ins / 38 x 45.5 cm) USD 1,400. TEL AVIV, 17 June 1985, *Praying Hasid* (oil on canvas, 21 x 17½ ins / 53.5 x 44.5 cm) ILS 1,400,000. PARIS, 20 March 1988, *Landscape* (oil on canvas, 23½ x 39¼ ins / 60 x 100 cm) FRF 5,500. TEL AVIV, 25 May 1988, *Landscape with Figures* (gouache, 19 x 24¼ ins / 48 x 61.5 cm) USD 990. TEL AVIV, 2 Jan 1989, *Jewish Musicians* (oil on canvas, 7½ x 18¾ ins / 19 x 47.5 cm) USD 880. TEL AVIV, 3 Jan 1990, *Still-life with Violin* (oil on card mounted on canvas, 21 x 16½ ins / 53.5 x 42 cm) USD 2,530. TEL AVIV, 19 June 1990, *Road at Safed* (oil on canvas, 16¼ x 13 ins / 41 x 33 cm) USD 1,320. TEL AVIV, 6 Jan 1992, *Jerusalem* (1935, oil on synthetic resin, 13½ x 19¾ ins / 34.5 x 50 cm) USD 1,210.

FRENER, Johann Baptist
Swiss, 19th century.
Born 10 December 1821, in Lucerne; died 1 May 1892, in Guatemala.
Engraver, modeller, medallist.

Frener began by studying drawing and sculpture with Franz Schlatt in Lucerne and then in Paris with Antoine Bovy, Pradier and at the École des Beaux-Arts. His output consisted mainly of medallions and he also produced busts of dramatic poets and, in 1841, a funeral monument. He travelled in Germany and in Italy where he gained the patronage of the Duke of Tuscany and formed a friendship with Giuseppe Verdi. Around 1854 Frener left for Guatemala. He exhibited in Paris in 1878 and received a gold medal.

FRÉNET, Jean-Baptiste
French, 19th century.
Born 31 January 1814, in Lyons; died 12 August 1889, in Charly (Rhône).
Painter, sculptor, engraver. Religious subjects, allegorical subjects, portraits, genre scenes, landscapes. Murals.

Jean-Baptiste Frénet studied under Claude Bonnefond at the École des Beaux-Arts in Lyons from 1827 to 1833, then enrolled at the Beaux-Arts in Paris in 1834. He travelled to Rome before returning to settle for good in his native Lyons. He exhibited in both Lyons and Paris from 1837 onwards.

Frénet painted religious and allegorical themes, genre subjects, portraits and landscapes, and sculpted some groups and statuettes. His painted work includes: *Man's Quest for Truth, Hope, Humanity, Masonic Scene, Consequences of the Fall from Innocence, Saint Jean de Dieu, Notre-Dame de Bon Conseil* (for the Lyons church of Fourvière), *Virtue in Heaven, Virtue on Earth Struggling with Human Passions, Muse of the Odyssee, Golden Age, Roman Night,* and *Peasant Farandole in Valence*. He painted murals for the church at Charly, together with cartoons and sketches for frescoes in the Lyons church of Ainay (on which he subsequently based a series of fourteen engravings). He is also remembered for his engraved portrait of *Sister Marguerite Deville*, the abbess of the convent of St-Charles in Brignais. Jean-Baptist Frénet emerges as a something of a mystic obsessed by metaphysical issues and egalitarian ideology, both of which are mirrored in work that is often unusual and invariably displays a complex amalgam of techniques.

MUSEUMS AND GALLERIES:
BERLIN: *Herd among the Dunes; Bull in the Water* - KALININGRAD: *Elbe March* - LYONS (MBA): *Self-portrait* - MUNICH: *Favourite*.

FRENGERL, Franz
German, 17th century.
Born in Augsburg.
Sculptor.

Frengerl also worked in Vienna.

FRENGUELLI, Giuseppe
Italian, 19th - 20th century.
Active in Perugia.
Sculptor.

Giuseppe Frenguelli was a pupil, and then a teacher, at the academy of Perugia. He sculpted a monument to *Garibaldi* in Todi, Umbria.

FRENGUELLI, Pasquale
Italian, 19th - 20th century.
Born in Perugia.
Painter.

Pasquale Frenguelli made a retable for the church of S Vivaldo in Castelfiorentino.

FRENJEK, Isaac. See **FRENELYitzhak**

FRENKEL, Boris Borvine
Polish, 20th century.
Born c. 1895, near Kalisz; died 1 May 1984, near Évreux, France.
Active in France from 1929.
Painter. Scenes with figures.

An anarcho-socialist, Boris Borvine Frenkel left Poland at the beginning of the 1920s, having been imprisoned for his revolutionary ideas. He spent time in Berlin and Paris and toured the world as a sailor. He was deported from Belgium and Luxembourg and he settled in Paris in 1929. He was also an actor, appeared in films and was a theatre and literary critic.

In painting he regarded himself as a 'non-believing Yiddish painter'. He painted the rites and ceremonies of small world of Polish Jews he yearned for, the familiar subjects of Chagall and Mané-Katz. His style fell within an expressionist Realism occasionally tinged with post-Cubism, particularly in his set design for *My Town*.

Solo exhibition include: Brussels (1927); Palais des Beaux-Arts, Brussels, (1938); Vidal gallery, Paris (1962); Aleph gallery, Paris (1977) and retrospective, Maison de la Culture, Grenoble (1980-1981). Solo posthumous exhibitions: retrospective, Musée d'Art Juif, Paris (1988); retrospective, Cloitre des Cordeliers, Tarascon (1989); retrospective, Schiltigheim (1991). posthumous collective exhibitions include: *Kikoïne et ses amis*, Couvent des Cordeliers, Paris; and *The Town*, Centre Georges Pompidou, Paris (1994).

BIBLIOGRAPHY:
Borvine Frenkel, exhibition leaflet, Cloître des Cordeliers, Tarascon, 1989. *Borvine Frenkel*, exhibition catalogue, Biennale littéraire Mitteleuropa, Schiltigheim, 1991. Nieszawer, Nadine/Boyé, Marie/Lanzmann, Claude (preface), *Peintres juifs de l'école de Paris 1905-1939*, Denoël, Paris, 2001.

AUCTION RECORDS:
PARIS, 8 April 1990, *Le Chemin* (oil on canvas, 15 x 18 ins / 38 x 46 cm) FRF 10,000. PARIS, 14 April 1991, *Lighting the Candles* (oil on card, 13¾ x 9½ ins / 35 x 24 cm) FRF 6,000. PARIS, 17 June 1991, *Study* (oil on wood, 13¾ x 10¼ ins / 35 x 26 cm) FRF 6,000. PARIS, 17 May 1992, *Jew with a Rooster* (oil on canvas, 18 x 15¼ ins / 46 x 38.5 cm) FRF 5,500. PARIS, 27 March 1994, *Jerusalem* (oil on card, 11¼ x 16¼ ins / 28.5 x 41 cm) FRF 4,000. PARIS, 5 Oct 2001, *The Demonstration* (1929-1930, oil and gouache on canvas, 31 x 43 ins / 78 x 108 cm) FRF 46,000. PARIS, 5 Oct 2001, *Jewish Marriage* (oil on canvas, 53 x 39 ins / 135 x 100 cm) FRF 170,000. PARIS, 16 April 2002, *Prostitute* (watercolour, ink wash and crayon, 8 x 6 ins / 20 x 15 cm) EUR 2,410. PARIS, 16 April 2002, *Café Scene* (c. 1930, oil on canvas, 20 x 26 ins / 50 x 65 cm) EUR 6,020.

FRENKEN, Jaak
Dutch, 20th century.
Born 1929, in 's Hertogenbosch.

Sculptor of assemblages.

Frenken was educated in Amsterdam and participated in numerous group exhibitions, notably at Amsterdam's Stedelijk (Municipal) Museum. He has had solo exhibitions in Amsterdam and Eindhoven. His work is very much akin to Pop Art and New Realism. He assembles *utensilia* and 'dematerialises' them by applying a coat of white paint.

FRENSCH, Jakob
German, 19th century.
Born 25 July 1832, in Hesselbach; died 1864, in Berlin.
Sculptor.

Jakob Frensch was a pupil of Launitz in Frankfurt- am-Main. He sculpted a *Virgin* for the church in Wied.

FRENTZ, Rudolf
German, 19th century.
Born 2 October 1831, in Berlin.
Painter. Genre scenes.

Frentz was a member of the academy of St Petersburg. He was awarded a gold medal in Berlin in 1886. He worked mainly in Russia.

FRENTZEL, Christian
German, 18th century.
Died 23 December 1721, in Breslau (now Wroclaw, Poland).
Painter.

Christian Frentzel painted a *Crucifixion* among others.

FRENTZEL, Georg Friedrich Jonas
German, 18th century.
Born 1754, in Leipzig; died 22 April 1799, in Leipzig.
Engraver.

Georg Frentzel was a pupil of Oeser. Some of his works can be found in the Leipzig Museum.

FRENTZEL, Johann
German, 17th century.
Active in Saxony.
Draughtsman.

FRENZ, Alexander
German, 19th century.
Born 13 October 1861, in Rheydt.
Painter, engraver. Mythological subjects, portraits, genre scenes, interiors, landscapes.

Frenz lived mainly in Bonn and Düsseldorf after spending some time travelling in Italy.

AUCTION RECORDS:
ST-BRIEUC, 8 May 1983, *The Lady and the Unicorn* (oil on panel, 26 x 21 ins / 66 x 53.5 cm) FRF 12,500.

FRENZEL, Friedrich August
German, 19th century.
Born 10 September 1814, in Dresden; died probably in 1898.
Painter, lithographer. History painting.

Friedrich August Frenzel was the son of Johann Gottfried Abraham. His subjects were connected with the theatre or military reviews.

FRENZEL, Georg, or Frenthel
German, 16th - 17th century.
Engraver.
Nuremberg School.

Frenzel was working in Nuremberg (Bavaria) between 1595 and 1650.

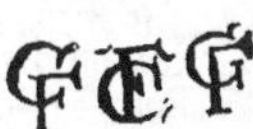

FRENZEL, Johann Gottfried Abraham
German, 19th century.
Born 1 January 1782, in Dresden; died 6 November 1855, in Dresden.
Engraver.

This artist was a pupil of Darnstedt. He mainly engraved landscapes. He was the curator of the engravings collection in Dresden.

FRENZEL, Oskar
German, 19th century.
Born 12 November 1855, in Berlin.
Painter. Genre scenes, landscapes.

Oskar Frenzel was a pupil of Megerheim and E. Bracht of the naturalist school at the Berlin academy. He gained medals in Berlin in 1891 and at the Exposition Universelle in Paris in 1900. He also exhibited his works in Munich.

FRENZEL, Paul
German, 19th century.
Born 8 June 1824, in Dresden; died 3 July 1872, in Dresden.
Painter. Animals, landscapes.

Paul Frenzel was the son of Johann Gottfried Abraham. The Berlin Museum has one of his works.

FREOUR, Jean
Sculptor. Nudes.

AUCTION RECORDS:
LONDON, 4 Dec 1984, *Nude Standing* (bronze, h. 23 ins / 58.4 cm) GBP 650.

FREQUENEZ, Paul Léon
French, 20th century.
Born 18 August 1876, in Mouzon.
Painter, engraver, watercolourist. Landscapes.

Paul Frequenez exhibited at the Salon des Artistes Français in Paris; he received various awards including a gold medal in 1924.

AUCTION RECORDS:
NEW YORK, 25 Oct 1989, *Parc de St Cloud in the Snow* (oil on canvas, 60 3/4 x 78 3/4 ins / 154.3 x 200 cm) USD 22,000. NEW YORK, 28 June 2001, *Parc de St Cloud in the Snow* (oil on canvas, 61 x 79 ins / 154 x 201 cm) USD 12,000.

FRERARTS, Gillis
Dutch, 17th century.
Born 1607; died 1664.
Painter.

Frerarts was probably resident in Amsterdam.

FRÈRE, Charles Édouard
French, 19th century.
Born 10 July 1837, in Paris; died 3 November 1894, in Paris.
Painter. Genre scenes, landscapes, landscapes with figures, animals.

Charles was the son of Pierre-Edouard Frère and nephew of Théodore Frère. He studied initially under his father, and then under Thomas Couture and Alexandre Defaux, before going on to exhibit at the Paris Salon from 1861 to 1893.

From an early age, Frère ostensibly painted landscapes; in fact, they were only there as a background against which to portray horses in various postures. Examples of his work include *Horse Grooming, Farrier, Demolition Work in Paris, Leading, Mule-Driver in the Alpes-Maritimes, Cart Race* and *Horse Dealers*.

MUSEUMS AND GALLERIES:
BORDEAUX: *Lime Quarry at St-Brice* - LOUVIERS: *Stabled Horses* - SHEFFIELD: *Blacksmith's Forge*.

AUCTION RECORDS:
LONDON, 10 June 1910, *Hanging Out Clothes*, GBP 8. PARIS, 19 Nov 1924, *Child with Wooden Horse*, FRF 200; *Young Boy Drawing on a Wall*, FRF 250. PARIS, 2 March 1925, *Village Scene*, FRF 110. PARIS, 26 April 1944, *Near Pontoise* (1880) FRF 650. LONDON, 12 May 1972, *Youth and Old Age*, Gns

1,300. LONDON, 19 Oct 1978, *Cutting Turf* (1874, oil on canvas, 27 x 51 1/4 ins / 68.5 x 130.2 cm) GBP 1,600. LONDON, 16-17 March 1983, *Young Peasant Woman Peeling Carrots* (oil on panel, 16 1/4 x 12 3/4 ins / 41 x 32.5 cm) GBP 1,800; *School is Out* (1877, watercolour and black chalk heightened with white, 22 1/2 x 18 ins / 57.2 x 45.7 cm) GBP 1,400. DETROIT, 31 Jan 1985, *Children on Parade* (c. 1882, oil on canvas, 26 x 32 ins / 66 x 81.5 cm) USD 27,500. PARIS, 1 March 1989, *Stable with Peasant Women and She-Asses* (1881, oil on canvas, 49 1/2 x 75 1/2 ins / 126 x 192 cm) FRF 32,000. NEW YORK, 1 March 1990, *Troop of Children* (1889, oil on panel, 24 x 32 ins / 61 x 81.3 cm) USD 23,100. MONTREAL, 30 April 1990, *Young Musician* (oil on panel, 16 1/2 x 12 1/2 ins / 42 x 32 cm) CAD 3,300. LONDON, 22 Nov 1990, *Young Woman Selling Fish* (1872, oil on panel, 13 1/2 x 17 1/2 ins / 34.3 x 44.5 cm) GBP 1,210. LONDON, 25 Nov 1992, *First Communion* (1867, oil on panel, 22 3/4 x 28 1/4 ins / 58 x 72 cm) GBP 7,150. LONDON, 31 Oct 1996, *Children with a Model Yacht* (oil on panel, 16 1/4 x 12 3/4 ins / 41.5 x 32.5 cm) GBP 2,875. TORONTO, 1 June 1999, *Preparing the Meal* (1880, oil on panel, 13 x 10 ins / 34 x 26 cm) CAD 19,000. NEW YORK, 13 Sept 2000, *Tomb of Mehemet Ali, Cairo* (oil on panel, 9 x 14 ins / 24 x 35 cm) USD 12,000. BERN, 1 May 2002, *Spring* (1878, oil on canvas, 17 x 22 ins / 43 x 55 cm) CHF 6,500. TORONTO, 3 June 2002, *Three Girls in a Summer Pasture* (oil on panel, 14 x 11 ins / 36 x 27 cm) CAD 4,200.

FRÈRE, Charles Théodore

French, 19th century.

Born 21 June 1814, in Paris; died 24 March 1888, in Paris.

Painter, watercolourist, draughtsman. History painting, genre scenes, local scenes, landscapes, landscapes with figures, seascapes.

Orientalism.

Charles Théodore Frère was a pupil of Camille Roqueplan and Léon Cogniet. He travelled in Normandy, Alsace and the Auvergne before visiting Algeria in 1837 (where he witnessed the fall of the city of Constantine to the French, in their victory over Abd el-Kader's rebellion). He visited Algeria a second time the following year, stopping en route in Malta, Greece and Smyrna. Frère also stayed for a time in Egypt (around 1853), setting up a studio in Cairo and being formally accorded the courtesy title of *bey* by the government of the day. He continued on to Syria, Palestine and Nubia, returning to France with a full sketchbook and laden down with oriental objets d'art.

Frère exhibited at the Paris Salon from 1834 to 1887, participated at the Paris Expositions Universelle of 1855, 1867 and 1878 and, up to and including 1887, at the Salon des Artistes Français. He was awarded medals in 1848 and in 1865.

His body of work comprises almost exclusively oriental subject matter; indeed, he was one of the few French artists to have painted Beirut, Jerusalem, Damascus and Palmyra. He also produced a series of thirteen watercolours recording the inauguration of the Suez Canal in 1869, some of which he subsequently redid in oil. Examples of his work include a *View of the Sidi Abder Rhaman Mosque near Algiers, View of the Baba-Zounn Suburb, Garden inside the Casbah, Algiers* and *Mitidja Plain near Algiers*. Frère's strong point was an ability to inject a sense of atmosphere into his landscapes, not least by painting them at different times of the day in order to capture the soft light at sunset or the pale golden yellows of dawn, with Bedouin tents and minarets appearing through a heat haze. As a rule, he eschewed 'decorative' elements, preferring to paint in a flat yet cleanly-contoured style. His lesser-known French landscapes exhibit a heavier, fleshier style, oddly reminiscent of Dutch masters of the 17th century.

TH.FRERE BEY

TH.FRÈRE

BIBLIOGRAPHY:

L'Orient en question, group exhibition catalogue, Musée Cantini, Marseilles, 1975. Thornton, Lynne, *Les Orientalistes, peintres voyageurs, 1828-1908*, ACR Édition, Paris, 1993.

MUSEUMS AND GALLERIES:

AUTUN (Mus. Rolin): *Simoom; Ruins of Palmyra* - BAGNÈRES-DE-BIGORRE: *Caravan* - BOURGES: *Evening on the Nile* - CHICAGO - LAVAL: *Vue of Karnak; Ruins at Luxor* - MINNEAPOLIS - MULHOUSE: *Camel-Drivers in Cairo; Cairo Street* - NANCY: *Arabs at Rest* - NEW YORK (Metropolitan Mus. of Art) - PARIS (Mus. de la Marine): thirteen watercolours - PERPIGNAN: *Museum, Rome* - RHEIMS: *Caravan Traversing the Arabian Desert; Arabs at Rest* - ROCHEFORT: *Washing the Gramigna, Naples* - SOISSONS: *Water Trough* - STRASBOURG: *Ass.*

AUCTION RECORDS:

PARIS, 1872, *Sunset in Cairo*, FRF 420. PARIS, 1886, *Prayer*, FRF 12,750. NEW YORK, 15-16 March 1906, *Persian Encampment near Mecca*, USD 110. PARIS, 31 Jan 1929, *Cairo Street Scene*, FRF 1,400. PARIS, 30 June-1 July 1941, *Algerian Courtyard* (watercolour/paper) FRF 200. PARIS, 23 Dec 1942, *Oriental Sea*, FRF 6,200. PARIS, 29-30 March 1943, *Coffee House at Baléasse*, FRF 7,000; *Upper Nile Landscape* (watercolour) FRF 900. PARIS, 24 April 1944, *Oriental Street* (heightened drawing) FRF 750. PARIS, 17 May 1945, *Halt in the Desert*, FRF 8,000. PARIS, 26 Feb 1947, *Caravan near Minieh*, FRF 10,800. NEW YORK, 8 March 1947, *Halt in the Desert*, USD 175. LONDON, 8 Nov 1972, *Street Scene in the Snow*, GBP 450. NEW YORK, 15 Oct 1976, *Iskenderun (Alexandretta)* (oil on canvas, 12 1/2 x 24 1/2 ins / 32 x 62 cm) USD 1,600. NEW YORK, 15 Dec 1978, *View of Jerusalem from the Josaphat Valley* (oil on canvas, 15 3/4 x 24 1/2 ins / 40 x 62 cm) USD 6,600. NEW YORK, 7 Jan 1981, *Coal Market in Constantinople* (pencil and black chalk/paper, 9 x 15 1/2 ins / 22.8 x 39.5 cm) USD 1,100. ENGHIEN-LES-BAINS, 21 Oct 1984, *Caravan in the Desert* (pencil and charcoal/paper, 22 3/4 x 39 1/4 ins / 58 x 100 cm) FRF 35,000. LONDON, 30 Nov 1984, *Arabs at the Entrance to Damascus* (oil on canvas, 25 1/2 x 21 1/4 ins / 65 x 54 cm) GBP 15,000. LONDON, 25 Nov 1987, *Nile at Sunset* (1877, oil on canvas, 43 1/4 x 71 ins / 110 x 179.5 cm) GBP 16,000. LONDON, 26 Feb 1988, *On the Nile* (oil on panel, 8 x 16 1/2 ins / 20.3 x 42 cm) GBP 3,520. PARIS, 26 Feb 1988, *Oriental Landscape* (watercolour, 8 x 15 ins / 20.5 x 38 cm) FRF 6,800. PARIS, 7 March 1988, *Fellah near Bridge in Old Section of Cairo* (oil on canvas, 6 x 7 1/4 ins / 15 x 18.5 cm) FRF 7,000. PARIS, 6 May 1988, *Arab Village* (oil on panel, 6 3/4 x 5 ins / 17 x 12.5 cm) FRF 9,500. NEW YORK, 25 May 1988, *Caravan at Dusk* (oil on panel, 9 3/4 x 16 ins / 24.8 x 40.7 cm) USD 7,150. PARIS, 17 June 1988, *Caravan by the Nile* (watercolour, 4 3/4 x 6 3/4 ins / 12 x 17 cm) FRF 3,800. PARIS, 7 July 1988, *Fountain at Bab-el-Oued* (oil on panel, 14 1/4 x 21 1/4 ins / 36 x 54 cm) FRF 46,000. PARIS, 16 Dec 1988, *Damascus Street Scene* (oil on panel, 16 1/4 x 10 ins / 41 x 25.5 cm) FRF 28,000. NEW YORK, 23 May 1989, *Oasis Halt* (oil on canvas, 17 1/4 x 28 1/4 ins / 44 x 72 cm) USD 29,700. NEW YORK, 24 Oct 1989, *Caravan Bound for Jerusalem* (oil on canvas, 13 3/4 x 24 ins / 35 x 61 cm) USD 33,000. VERSAILLES, 19 Nov 1989, *Balta Liman on the Bosphorus* (drawing, 11 1/2 x 18 1/4 ins / 29 x 46.5 cm) FRF 5,000. COMPIÈGNE, 28 Jan 1990, *Cairo* (oil on canvas/panel, 35 1/2 x 28 ins / 90 x 71 cm) FRF 102,000. LONDON, 14 Feb 1990, *Arabs Halting at an Oasis* (oil on panel, 10 x 17 ins / 25.5 x 43 cm) GBP 2,200. TROYES, 20 May 1990, *North African Street Scene* (oil on panel, 9 x 6 ins / 22 x 15 cm) FRF 13,200. NEW YORK, 24 Oct 1990, *Caravan Approaching a River* (1857, oil on canvas, 12 x 22 1/2 ins / 30.5 x 57.2 cm) USD 11,000. PARIS, 20 Nov 1990, *Caravan near Minieh* (oil on panel, 12 1/2 x 19 3/4 ins / 32 x 50 cm) FRF 150,000. LONDON, 4 Oct 1991, *Beirut Street*

Scene (oil on canvas, 24 x 19 1/4 ins / 61 x 49.2 cm) GBP 6,160. NEW YORK, 17 Oct 1991, *Sunset at the Oasis* (oil on panel, 9 1/2 x 13 3/4 ins / 24.1 x 34.9 cm) USD 6,600. PARIS, 3 April 1992, *View of Yport* (1873, watercolour, 3 1/4 x 6 1/4 ins / 8.3 x 16 cm) FRF 8,200. PARIS, 2 June 1992, *Great Caravan passing through Upper Egypt* (oil on panel, 6 1/2 x 11 1/2 ins / 16.5 x 29 cm) FRF 58,000. NEW YORK, 29 Oct 1992, *Outskirts of the Town* (oil on panel, 12 1/2 x 18 3/4 ins / 31.8 x 47.6 cm) USD 8,800. PARIS, 5 April 1993, *Water-Carriers in Cairo* (charcoal, 9 1/4 x 18 1/4 ins / 23.5 x 46.5 cm) FRF 6,000. TEL AVIV, 14 April 1993, *Jerusalem* (oil on canvas, 18 x 23 1/2 ins / 46 x 60 cm) USD 29,900. PARIS, 22 April 1994, *By the Nile at Manfalut in Upper Egypt* (oil on panel, 16 1/4 x 12 1/2 ins / 41 x 32 cm) FRF 50,000. NEW YORK, 26 May 1994, *Caravan* (1871, oil on canvas, 16 x 24 ins / 40.6 x 61 cm) USD 10,925. LONDON, 17 Nov 1994, *Pilgrims Prostrating Themselves at their First Sight of Jerusalem* (oil on canvas, 56 x 80 1/4 ins / 142.2 x 203.8 cm) GBP 133,500. NEW YORK, 1 Nov 1995, *By the Nile at Gizeh* (oil on canvas, 38 x 51 ins / 96.5 x 129.5 cm) USD 57,500. PARIS, 6 Nov 1995, *Great Caravan arriving at Baalbek from the Southeast* (oil on panel, 9 1/4 x 15 ins / 23.5 x 38 cm) FRF 180,000. LONDON, 11 Oct 1996, *Shores of the Bosphorus* (oil on panel, 8 1/2 x 6 1/4 ins / 21.5 x 16 cm) GBP 8,970. PARIS, 5-7 Nov 1996, *Pilgrim Caravan Bound for Mecca* (oil on canvas, 21 1/4 x 25 1/2 ins / 54 x 65 cm) FRF 130,000. PARIS, 9 Dec 1996, *Encampment at Sunset* (oil on canvas, 9 1/2 x 13 1/2 ins / 24 x 34 cm) FRF 30,000. NEW YORK, 26 Feb 1997, *Caravan at an Oasis at Sunset* (oil on panel, 5 1/2 x 8 3/4 ins / 14 x 22.2 cm) USD 4,600. PARIS, 14 March 1997, *Pyramids of Giza* (oil on panel, 6 3/4 x 14 1/4 ins / 17 x 36 cm) FRF 29,000. LONDON, 21 March 1997, *Oasis* (1855, oil on panel, 10 1/2 x 16 1/4 ins / 26.5 x 41.2 cm) GBP 4,600. LONDON, 13 June 1997, *Caravenserai near Beirut* (oil on canvas, 12 1/2 x 25 ins / 31.7 x 63.2 cm) GBP 37,800. LONDON, 21 Nov 1997, *Arabs at the Edge of a Town* (oil on panel, 8 x 12 3/4 ins / 20.6 x 32.4 cm) GBP 9,775. PARIS, 26-27 March 1998, *Encampment below the Citadel, Cairo* (oil on canvas, 31 x 49 1/2 ins / 79 x 126 cm) FRF 300,000. NEW YORK, 5 May 1999, *Twilight near Cairo* (c. 1875, oil on canvas, 33 x 55 ins / 84 x 140 cm) USD 72,500. PARIS, 16 Nov 1999, *Game of Backgammon in a Caravanserai* (oil on canvas, 36 x 29 ins / 92 x 73 cm) FRF 400,000. NEW YORK, 28 March 2000, *Sunrise and Sunset, Cairo* (oil on panel, a pair, 5 x 7 ins / 12 x 17 cm) USD 24,000. LONDON, 12 Oct 2000, *Ruines de Palmyre* (oil on canvas, 39 x 67 ins / 98 x 169 cm) GBP 17,000. PARIS, 14 May 2001, *Washerwomen and Mosque near Cairo* (1855, oil on canvas, 26 x 21 ins / 65 x 54 cm) FRF 430,000. PARIS, 17 Dec 2001, *Upper and Lower Egypt* (watercolour, 12 works) FRF 130,000. NEW YORK, 29 Oct 2002, *Sunset on the Nile* (oil on canvas, 18 x 26 ins / 46 x 65 cm) USD 13,000. PARIS, 16 Dec 2002, *Halt on the Banks of the Nile* (oil on panel, 8 x 15 ins / 21 x 37 cm) EUR 14,000. PARIS, 16 June 2003, *Caravan in the Middle East* (oil on canvas, 15 x 24 ins / 39 x 61 cm) EUR 22,000. PARIS, 19 Oct 2003, *Market Scene in Cairo* (oil on canvas, 25 x 16 ins / 63 x 41 cm) EUR 15,000. PARIS, 3 June 2004, *Evening, Banks of the Nile* (oil on panel, 8 x 15 ins / 21 x 37 cm) EUR 11,000. PARIS, 3 June 2004, *Cairo* (1853, oil on canvas, 15 x 27 ins / 38 x 68 cm) EUR 12,000.

FRÈRE, Élisabeth F. T.

French, 20th century.
Born in London.
Engraver (etching).

Élisabeth Frère studied under Miss C. Smilt. She exhibited at the Salon des Artistes Français in Paris from 1925.

FRÈRE, Jean Jules

French, 19th century.
Born 1 October 1851, in Cambrai; died 1906, in Paris.
Sculptor.

Jean Jules Frère studied under Cavelier and Cordier. He exhibited at the Paris Salon from 1874 to 1880, and was awarded a bronze medal in 1878, a silver in 1883 and a further bronze in 1889, together with a bronze at the Exposition Universelle in Paris in 1900. Examples of his work include *Bust of General d'Aigremont*, *Cinderella* and *Oriental Singer*.

MUSEUMS AND GALLERIES:

CAMBRAI: *Oriental Singer*.

FRÈRE, Marcel

Belgian, 20th century.
Born 1931, in Jumet.
Painter.
Symbolism.

Frère studied at the fine arts academy in Charleroi and went on to paint numerous compositions featuring flowers and/or skeletons. His work symbolises his deeply held religious beliefs.

FRÈRE, Michel

Belgian, 20th - 21st century.
Born 1961, in Brussels.
Painter. Landscapes with figures.

Frère lives and works in Brussels. His work is traditional in style, and in particular draws its inspiration from late-19th century Belgian painting. Frère reinforces this effect by framing his paintings and covering them with a pane of glass, for the sheen effect. He aims to make colour sing - not excluding, for all that, the motif - by successively painting several layers of different colours of various intensities; he most frequently uses briefly manipulated impasto.He has participated in many group exhibitions since 1984 in Brussels. He also exhibited at the Salon de Montrouge in 1988. He has held various solo shows in Belgium, notably at the Galerie Baronian, Brussels, in 1988; Palais des Beaux-Arts de Charleroi in 1995, but also in cities including Amsterdam, Munich and New York.

BIBLIOGRAPHY:

Busine, L., *Catalogue de l'exposition Michel Frère*, Gal. A. Baronian, Brussels, 1988.

FRÈRE, Pierre

French, 17th century.
Active in Paris in 1684.
Painter, sculptor.

Pierre Frère is without doubt the same as the following artist.

FRÈRE, Pierre

French, 18th century.
Active in Paris.
Sculptor.

Pierre Frère is said to have attended the wedding of Alexandre Gremont and Marguerite Aveline, on 9 September 1723.

FRÈRE, Pierre Édouard

French, 19th century.
Born 10 January 1819, in Paris; died 1886, in Écouen.
Painter, lithographer. Genre scenes, landscapes with figures.

Pierre was the younger brother of the orientalist painter Charles Théodore Frère. He enrolled at the École des Beaux-Arts in Paris in 1836 and studied under Paul Delaroche. Pierre Frère exhibited at the Paris Salon and at the Salon des Artistes Français between 1842 and 1886, and at the Royal Academy in London from 1868 to 1885. He was awarded medals on several occasions and was made a Chevalier of the Légion d'Honneur in 1855. Frère's body of work principally comprises genre compositions featuring scenes from everyday village life: washerwomen, housewives, children playing, and so on. He is noted for his accomplished rendering of sunlit landscapes. Examples of his work include: *Laundry, Hen that laid the Golden Eggs, Woodcut Engraver, Young Woman Combing, Interior with Women and Children Shelling Peas, Children Throwing Snowballs, Lully as a Child,*

Good Friday, Old Lady Sewing, Beggars in Dunkirk, Tea Party and *Mother and Child*. Frère personally lithographed some of his work.

E. Frere

BIBLIOGRAPHY:

Bailly-Herzberg, Janine, *L'Eau-forte de peintre au XIXe siècle*, Librairie Léonce Laget, Paris, 1972.

MUSEUMS AND GALLERIES:

BERNAY: *Arrival at the Oasis* - CARDIFF: *Child in a Meadow* - CHARTRES: *Kitchen Interior; Laundress; Reading Lesson* - GLASGOW: *Mother and Children* - HAMBURG: *Stamp Merchant; Crucifix* - MELBOURNE: *Interior of Thatched Cottage* - PARIS (BNF, Prints Collection): *Collected Engravings* - SHEFFIELD: *Opposite the School*.

AUCTION RECORDS:

PARIS, 1-2 June 1865, *Luncheon*, FRF 4,150. PARIS, 25 April 1891, *Gruel*, FRF 3,940. NEW YORK, 18-20 April 1906, *Young Boys after School*, USD 1,000. LONDON, 29 June 1908, *Saying Grace*, GBP 451; *Sewing Lesson* (1868) GBP 241. LONDON, 3 June 1910, *Seamstress*, GBP 68; *Bird-Catcher* (winter scene) GBP 120. LONDON, 11 May 1923, *Sheltering from the Rain*, GBP 48. LONDON, 2 Dec 1927, *Evening Prayer*, GBP 63. PARIS, 18 June 1930, *Young Cook*, FRF 1,600. LONDON, 19 Feb 1937, *Saying Grace*, GBP 94. NEW YORK, 5 Nov 1943, *Washerwoman*, USD 90. NEW YORK, 18-19 April 1945, *Young Washerwoman*, USD 225. PARIS, 16 Feb 1950, *Bosom of the Family*, FRF 32,700. LONDON, 14 Nov 1969, *Soup*, Gns 460. LONDON, 19 Oct 1976, *School is Over* (1869, watercolour heightened with white, 36 x 27 1/4 ins / 91.5 x 69.5 cm) GBP 500. LONDON, 29 Oct 1976, *Harvest Dance* (1850, oil on canvas, 9 3/4 x 12 3/4 ins / 25 x 32.5 cm) GBP 300. BERN, 6 May 1977, *Old People's Home* (1851, oil on canvas, 20 1/2 x 28 3/4 ins / 52 x 73 cm) CHF 3,300. LONDON, 18 Oct 1978, *Snowball Attack* (1866, oil on panel, 16 x 12 1/2 ins / 40.5 x 32 cm) GBP 3,400. NEW YORK, 28 May 1981, *Country Kitchen* (1886, oil on panel, 16 x 12 1/2 ins / 40.5 x 32 cm) USD 3,250. NEW YORK, 27 May 1983, *Little Drum* (1858, oil on panel, 11 1/4 x 9 ins / 28.5 x 22.8 cm) USD 14,000. LONDON, 18 June 1986, *Children at their Homework* (1881, oil on panel, 15 3/4 x 13 ins / 40 x 33 cm) GBP 11,500. PARIS, 18 June 1989, *Interior of Thatched Cottage* (oil on canvas, 9 x 12 1/2 ins / 22 x 32 cm) FRF 15,000. LONDON, 28 Nov 1990, *Children Gathering Wood on a Snow-Covered Forest Path* (1883, oil on panel, 12 1/2 x 9 1/2 ins / 32 x 24 cm) GBP 4,180. LONDON, 19 June 1991, *Straw Hat Decorated with Wild Flowers* (oil on canvas, 21 1/4 x 17 1/4 ins / 54 x 44 cm) GBP 4,180. LONDON, 4 Oct 1991, *At the Grandmother's* (oil on canvas, 25 3/4 x 21 1/4 ins / 65.5 x 54 cm) GBP 3,960. LONDON, 22 May 1992, *Worn Thin* (1882, oil on panel, 18 1/2 x 15 ins / 47 x 38 cm) GBP 6,820. LONDON, 17 March 1993, *Family at Home* (1880, oil on panel, 22 x 17 3/4 ins / 56 x 45 cm) GBP 9,430. LE TOUQUET, 14 Nov 1993, *Resting in the Meadow* (oil on canvas, 9 1/2 x 12 1/2 ins / 24 x 32 cm) FRF 12,500. LONDON, 16 March 1994, *Children's Games* (1864, oil on panel, 13 x 16 1/4 ins / 33 x 41 cm) GBP 16,675. PARIS, 7 April 1995, *Miners Coming to the Surface after an Explosion* (oil on canvas, 8 1/2 x 16 1/4 ins / 21.5 x 41.5 cm) FRF 5,000. NEW YORK, 17 Jan 1996, *Hour of Prayer* (1878, oil on panel, 14 3/4 x 11 1/2 ins / 37.5 x 29.5 cm) USD 8,625. NEW YORK, 23 May 1997, *Knitting Lesson* (1883, oil on panel, 22 x 18 1/4 ins / 55.9 x 46.4 cm) USD 26,450. NEW YORK, 23 Oct 1997, *Playing Mother* (1865, oil on panel, 9 3/4 x 7 3/4 ins / 24.8 x 19.7 cm) USD 9,775. LONDON, 22 June 1999, *Family Album* (1869, oil on panel, 17 x 13 ins / 42 x 33 cm) GBP 23,000. LONDON, 21 Oct 1999, *Getting Up* (1878, oil on panel, 10 x 8 ins / 26 x 21 cm) GBP 11,000. LONDON, 4 April 2000, *Little Bit of Fun* (1860, oil on panel, 13 x 16 ins / 32 x 40 cm) GBP 20,000. BILLINGSHURST, 25 May 2000, *La glisade* (oil on panel, 23 x 30 ins / 58 x 77 cm) GBP 22,000. LONDON, 19 June 2001, *Lighting the Stove* (1886, oil on panel, 18 x 15 ins / 46 x 38 cm) GBP 16,000. UPPSALA, 9 Dec 2001, *Tasting the Soup - Kitchen Interior with Children* (oil on canvas, 15 x 12 ins / 39 x 31 cm) SEK 190,000. KNOWLE, 24 April 2002, *The Reprimand* (1859, oil on panel, 16 x 13 ins / 41 x 32 cm) GBP 7,100. LONDON, 30 May 2002, *Feeding the Children* (1873, oil on panel, 17 x 22 ins / 43 x 56 cm) GBP 13,000. LONDON, 20 March 2003, *Special Bath* (oil on panel, 10 x 7 ins / 25 x 19 cm) GBP 5,500. LONDON, 19 Nov 2003, *First Steps in Life* (1867, oil on panel, 25 x 30 ins / 63 x 76 cm) GBP 15,000.

FRÈRE, Samuel

French, 19th - 20th century.

Painter. Landscapes.

Samuel Frère was active in Rouen. He became a member of the Société des Artistes Français in 1909.

MUSEUMS AND GALLERIES:

ROUEN: *Cap Hernu*.

AUCTION RECORDS:

PARIS, 28 March 1985, *Village in Brittany* (1905, oil on canvas, 32 x 45 1/4 ins / 81 x 115 cm) FRF 15,600.

FRÈRE, Théodore. See **FRÈRE Charles Théodore**

FRÈRE DE MONTIZON, Flore

French, 19th century.

Born 1794, in Paris.

Painter.

Like her sister Thérèse, Flore Frère de Montizon painted landscapes, historical subjects and genre compositions.

FRÈRE DE MONTIZON, Thérèse Justine

French, 19th century.

Born 1792, in Paris.

Painter.

Thérèse Frère de Montizon taught and served as principal at the Royal Free College of Drawing for young persons. Examples of her work include a *Portraits of France's Children* (commissioned by the Duchess de Berry), a *St Theresa*, an *Abraham at Prayer Before Preparing to Sacrifice his Son*, and a *St Andrew on the Cross*.

FRÈREBEAU, Maurice Georges

French, 20th century.

Born 1879, in Paris.

Painter, engraver. Landscapes.

Maurice Frèrebeau studied under Gérome. He was awarded a bronze medal at the Paris Exposition Universelle of 1900.

FRÈREDOUX, André

French, 14th century.

Active in Tours.

Sculptor, architect.

André Frèredoux was responsible for sculpting the tomb of the canon Jean Gervaise in Tours Cathedral and also the altar of the chapel endowed by the canon in his will. Frèredoux was still alive in 1398. In the 15th century, Tours Cathedral had two cathedral architects, Aimery and Olivier Frèredoux, probably André's sons.

FRÈRES, Theodorus or Dirk, or Ferraris

Dutch, 17th century.

Born 1643, in Enkhuizen; died 1693, in Enkhuizen.

Painter. History painting.

Frères studied art in Rome before returning to Holland, where he enjoyed great popularity. Many of his paintings and drawings were acquired by the Prince of Orange, and he also worked briefly in England, at the invitation of Sir Peter Lely. His drawing is technically and artistically quite accomplished.

FRÉRET, Alexandre

Flemish School, 15th century.

Painter.

Bruges School.
Mentioned in Siret, this painter was a member of the confraternity of St Luke in Bruges in 1450.

FRÉRET, Armand
French, 18th century.
Active in Cherbourg.
Sculptor.
Armand Fréret was the brother of Pierre.

FRÉRET, Armand Auguste
French, 19th century.
Born in the 19th century, in Cherbourg.
Painter. Landscapes, seascapes.
Armand Fréret studied under Yvon and exhibited at the Paris Salon from 1865 to 1874. Examples of his work include *Beach near Cherbourg, Sunset at Low Tide on Vauville Bay* and *View of the Coast near Cherbourg.*
MUSEUMS AND GALLERIES:
CHERBOURG: *Laying the Foundation Stone at the Hospice in Cherbourg* - ST-LÔ: *Beach in Holland.*

FRÉRET, Louis
French, 19th century.
Active c. 1800.
Draughtsman. Seascapes.
Aubertin engraved originals by Louis Fréret.

FRÉRET, Pierre
French, 18th century.
Died before 1787.
Active in Cherbourg.
Sculptor.
Pierre Fréret worked for the church of the Trinity in Cherbourg. He is also known to have been a draughtsman.

FRERICHS, William or Wilhelm Charles Anthony
Belgian, 19th century.
Born 1829, in Ghent; died 16 March 1905, in Tottenville, Staten Island NY.
Painter. Portraits, landscapes with figures, landscapes.
After studying in Belgium under van Hove, Frerichs settled in America, where he became a renowned teacher.
BIBLIOGRAPHY:
Berko, P./Berko, V., *Dictionary of Belgian Painters Born between 1750 and 1875*, Brussels, 1981.
AUCTION RECORDS:
HYANNIS, MA, 7 Aug 1973, *Autumn Landscape,* USD 1,600. NEW YORK, 30 Sept 1982, *Mountain Stream* (oil on canvas, 36 x 60 1/4in/91.7 x 152.8cm) USD 1,900. WASHINGTON DC, 9 Dec 1984, *Skaters on a Frozen River* (oil on canvas, 30 x 46in/76.2 x 117cm) USD 4,100. RALEIGH, NC, 5 Nov 1985, *Mountain Falls* (oil on canvas, 53 x 69in/134.5 x 175.2 cm) USD 20,000. NEW YORK, 26 May 1988, *Coming Alongside* (oil on canvas, 35 3/4 x 60in/91 x 152.1cm) USD 6,600. NEW YORK, 30 Sept 1988, *Lake in Autumn* (oil on canvas, 22 x 36in/56 x 91.5cm) USD 8,800. NEW YORK, 31 May 1990, *Fishermen beside a Stream* (oil on canvas, 22 x 35in/55.8 x 88.9cm) USD 2,200. NEW YORK, 28 May 1992, *Portrait of a Naval Officer* (oil on canvas, 35 1/2 x 28 3/4in/90.3 x 73.2cm) USD 9,900. NEW YORK, 4 Dec 1992, *Skating in Winter* (oil on canvas, 30 x 46in/76.2 x 116.9cm) USD 15,400. NEW YORK, 27 May 1993, *Huntsmen Shooting Birds beside a Stream at the Bottom of a Gorge* (1878, oil on canvas, 29 1/2 x 49 3/4in/74.9 x 126.4cm) USD 13,800. NEW YORK, 31 March 1994, *Bear Crossing a Stream near a Waterfall* (oil on canvas, 25 x 33in/63.5 x 83.8cm) USD 2,875. NEW YORK, 14 March 1996, *Skaters* (oil on canvas, 30 x 46in/76.2 x 116.8cm) USD 21,850.

FRERING, Élisabeth
French, 20th - 21st century.
Born 25 December 1955, in Argenteuil.
Painter.
Élisabeth Frering studied at the Escuela de Arte y Oficios in Valencia, Spain, where she taught drawing from 1979 to 1981. She then moved to Alsace, not far from Strasbourg, where she works.

Frering's works are influenced by the Spanish artists, Tapiès, Clavé and Goya. She paints interior landscapes, which resemble old sepia-tinted photographs, and also recall autumn leaves faded by the wind and the rain. On cardboard, which she soaks, smooths or otherwise treats, then puts on canvas, she paints wide beaches in mineral colours. Upon these, she superimposes enigmatic signs, such as a cross, a twig or a cane. In her paintings, she subtly achieves a very fragile state of equilibrium, suspending time in order to perpetuate an ephemeral image.

She has staged a number of solo exhibitions in French and Spanish galleries since 1977.
BIBLIOGRAPHY:
Souchaud, Pierre, *'Élizabeth Frering'* in *Artension* n° 31, periodical, Rouen, February-March 1992.

FRÉROT, Marie (Mme)
French, 19th century.
Born in the 19th century, in Paris.
Painter.
Marie Frérot studied under Jospeh G. Tourny and exhibited her work at Salons between 1874 and 1882, chiefly comprising watercolour copies of compositions by Veronese, Titian and Rubens.

FRESCHI, Andrea
Italian, 18th - 19th century.
Born 1774, in Bassano.
Engraver.
Andrea Freschi was a pupil of Schiavonetti. He engraved numerous portraits, including one of *King George III of England* produced during the course of Freschi's many years spent in London.

FRESCHI, Paolo di Cristoforo dei
Italian, 16th century.
Died at the beginning of the 17th century, in Venice.
Active in Venice in 1578.
Painter.
Freschi worked for the seminary of S Maria della Salute in Venice.

FRESE, Albert. See **FREESE Albertus**

FRESE, Daniel
German, 16th - 17th century.
Born 1540, in Dithmarschen (Schleswig-Holstein); died 1611, in Lüneburg (Lower Saxony).
Painter.
Hamburg School.
Daniel Frese lived and worked principally in Hamburg, but also executed some works for churches in Dithmarschen and Lüneburg. One of his works is a *Judgement of Solomon,* painted in 1568 for the church of St Catherine in Hamburg.

FRESE, Heinrich
German, 19th century.
Born 27 May 1794, in Bremen; died 20 July 1869, in Bremen.
Sculptor.
Heinrich Frese was a pupil of Andreas Steinhäuser.

FRESE, Samuel
German, 17th century.
Died 4 February 1620, in Hamburg.
Painter.
Samuel Frese was related to Daniel Fresez.

FRESEN, Jean Baptiste
French, 19th century.
Born 1800; died 1867.

Active in Longwy (Meurthe-et-Moselle).
Painter. Portraits.
Fresen studied under Pierre Maisonnet and at the Brussels academy.

FRESENIUS, Hermann Julius Richard
German, 19th century.
Born 18 June 1844, in Frankfurt am Main; died 7 January 1903, in Monaco.
Painter. Seascapes.
Fresenius studied at the Munich academy and with Gude in Karlsruhe. He travelled in Germany and Norway. He exhibited his works in Vienna and Munich from 1869.
AUCTION RECORDS:
COLOGNE, 18 March 1989, *Sunset on the Coast* (oil on canvas, 9 x 15 1/4 ins / 22 x 38.5 cm) DEM 2,000.

FRESET, Georges Eugène
French, 20th century.
Born 22 July 1894, in Luxeuil-les-Bains; died 25 July 1975, in Bourbonne-les-Bains.
Painter, engraver, lithographer, draughtsman, illustrator. Landscapes, flowers.
Georges Freset studied under Jules Adler. He became a primary school teacher in 1919, but managed to combine art with teaching and painted from nature whenever he had the time.

His painting is full of minute detail, generosity and freshness. Around 1940, when he was finally able to devote himself exclusively to painting, he abandoned large landscapes and developed an original approach: he began to paint things as he perceived them as a child, at ground level, concentrating on the foreground. With great sensitivity and rigorous observation he constructed an entire universe from a few twigs, a flower and a bit of moss.

From 1923 to 1939 he exhibited at numerous Salons, notably in Paris at the Salon des Artistes Français from 1928, becoming a member of the Salon in 1930. In 1935 he was awarded a gold medal by the Société Artistique de la Haute-Marne. He went on to take part in various group exhibitions and also showed his work in solo exhibitions, the first being in Luxeuil in 1921. In 1984 the Musée de Vesoul held the first retrospective of his work.
BIBLIOGRAPHY:
Georges Freset: peintre et graveur: 1894-1975, exhibition catalogue, Musée de Vesoul, Vesoul, 1984.
MUSEUMS AND GALLERIES:
BELFORT - BESANÇON - BOURBONNE-LES-BAINS - ÉPINAL - LUXEUIL-LES-BAINS - PARIS (MAMVP) - PARIS (Mus. National).

FRESEZ, Daniel, or Fressez
Luxembourg, 19th century.
Active in Luxembourg.
Painter, draughtsman.
Fresez is known to have been active around 1828; he was decorated with the 'Order of the Oak Wreath'.

FRESLON, Gobert
French, 16th century.
Active in Paris.
Painter.

FRESLON, Jean
French, 16th century.
Active in Paris in 1528.
Painter.

FRESLON, Martin
French, 16th century.
Active in Paris c. 1550.
Painter.

FRESNAYE, Marie Alphonsine
French, 19th century.
Born in the 19th century, in Marenta.
Sculptor.
Fresnaye exhibited a number of medallions and genre compositions at the Paris Salon from 1874 to 1882, including *Slumber* (plaster high-relief), *Apollodorus' Daughter* (statuette), *Sibyl* (statue), *Little Owner* (group), *Little Thief* (marble statuette), *Slumber of the Christ Child*, and *Cherubim* (Arras Museum). She received an honourable mention in 1884 and was a bronze medal winner at the 1900 Exposition Universelle in Paris.
MUSEUMS AND GALLERIES:
ARRAS: *Cherubim*.

FRESNAYE, Roger de. See **LA FRESNAYE Roger de**

FRESNEY-TOUVENAINT, Marie (Mme)
French, 19th century.
Active in Paris.
Painter.
Fresney-Touvenaint was a member of the Société des Artistes Français from 1883.

FRESNIEL, Jean
French, 14th century.
Born in Le Mans.
Sculptor.
In 1356 and 1357, Fresniel worked at the castle of Escaudoeuvres near Cambrai (Nord).

FRESON, Florence
Belgian, 20th - 21st century.
Born 1951, in Liège.
Sculptor.
Freson studied the history of art, and also sculpture, under Jaques Moeschal and M. Guyaux at the Académie des Beaux-Arts in Brussels. She explores the numerous structural uses of stone, which is her favourite material. Above all, her approach is synthetic. She has exhibited regularly in Belgium since the early, notably in 2002 in Liège in Bonjour - 24 artistes vous rencontrent.

FRESSEL, Pietrequin
French, 15th century.
Born in Paris.
Active during the 15th century.
Sculptor (wood).
Fressel went to work in Rouen (Seine-Maritime) in 1461 at the request of Philippot Viart. Under the direction of Viart, he assisted in the carving of the choir stalls in Rouen Cathedral.

FRESSINIAT, Jules de
French, 19th century.
Born 1820, in Limoges; died after 1876.
Painter. Portraits.
According to Fressiniat's own testimony, he was a pupil of Michel M. Drolling. He exhibited portraits at the Paris Salon in 1846, 1848 and 1869 and, according to some accounts, was still active in 1876.

FRESSON, François Charles
French, 18th century.
Active in Paris in 1749.
Painter, sculptor.

FRESTEL, Charles
French, 20th century.
Born in St-Lô.
Sculptor.
Charles Frestel studied under Navellier. He exhibited in Paris at the Salon des Artistes Français from 1923 and also at the Salon d'Automne.

FRETAY, de. See **DUFRETAY**

FRETEAU

Engraver. Portraits.

MUSEUMS AND GALLERIES:

DOUAI: *Portrait of a Man* (print).

FRETON, Jeannie

20th century.

Painter.

Freton shows her work in solo exhibitions, including the one held at the Le Navire gallery, Brest, in 1996. She takes certain motifs from the great masters, such as Velázquez and Piero della Francesca, which she reworks in her own way.

FRETTE, Auguste A.

French, 19th - 20th century.

Born at the end of the 19th century, in Grenoble.

Sculptor.

FRETZ, Rudolf

Swiss, 19th century.

Born 17 April 1863, in Zurich.

Engraver (wood).

Rudolf Fretz was a pupil of the engraver H. Bachmann and completed his studies in Munich, Freiburg and Brisgau. He worked for a house in Zurich and used a technique which enabled him to imitate etching exactly.

FRETZER, Klaus

Swiss, 15th century.

Active in Basel in 1473.

Painter.

FREUD, Lucian

British, 20th century.

Born 1922, in Berlin.

Active moved to England 1933 and naturalised 1939.

Painter, sculptor, draughtsman, engraver. Portraits, nudes, landscapes, still-lifes.

London School.

A grandson of the father of psychoanalysis Sigmund Freud, Lucian Freud lived in London from the age of 11. He studied sculpture at London's School of Arts and Crafts, but never worked as a sculptor. Between 1939 and 1942, he attended courses in painting at the East Anglian School of Painting and Drawing in Dedham, an institution directed by the innovative landscape painter C. Morris, and at Goldsmiths' College in London. Freud did not start painting until after the start of World War II. He spent some time in Paris in 1946, where he discovered French painting and the work of Ingres in particular; the latter was to prove a major influence on his work. He visited Greece in 1947. In 1951 he was awarded the Arts Council Prize at the Festival of Britain. He taught at London's Slade School of Art from 1949 and was awarded the Order of Merit in 1993.

His early work was clearly influenced by the Surrealist movement that was so much in vogue in London at the time (all the more so, perhaps, because of the links between Surrealism and Sigmund Freud's psychoanalytical theories), but he was soon attracted to the 'Neue Sachlichkeit' (New Objectivity) exemplified by, among others, Otto Dix and Georg Grosz. His work was figurative inasmuch as it comprised human figures portrayed in isolation or in groups (following the tradition of English portraiture). He opted for a Classical style - 'Ingresque', as he once termed it - to create portraits that were linear, angular, limpid and unaccented. These included a chiaroscuro series of young girls with bulging eyes and sloping foreheads, painted in a style reminiscent of the Expressionists yet strangely devoid of sentiment and seduction. His impassive style gave priority to every element in the composition rather than simply focusing on the human subject. In the 1960s his chill grey tones and minute attention to interior details gradually gave way to warmer colours - yellows, oranges, ochres and reds. At the same time, his pigments thickened to the point of becoming tactile, in contrast to his earlier work, in which the paint appeared merely to draw a veil over the subject matter. Over time, his figures began to shed their clothing, becoming increasingly voluptuous, fleshly creatures. He was concerned to express not only the face but every part of the human body - hair, pores, muscles, and so on. As he explained: 'Normally I underplay facial expression when painting the figure because I want expression to emerge through the body. I used to do only heads, but came to feel that I relied too much on the face. I want the head, as it were, to be more like another limb.'

In his *Nude Reflection* of 1980, a fleshy reclining nude exposes herself to the viewer but also to the fully-dressed male whose foot is visible in the background. The intention behind this painting, as behind so many others by Freud, is not to exalt Beauty or the nude female form but to capture an instance of humanity at its most intense. He does so by portraying white, pink, orange-tinted, violet, bruised flesh, over-exposed in all its multiple imperfections. This desire to bring out every pore and show human flesh at its least seductive is intensified by his use of a gritty, 'lumpy' white paint reserved exclusively for painting the human form. By the 1990s, Freud's quest for realism and *Neue Sachlichkeit* had gone even further: by then, his models were deliberately selected for their intrinsic ugliness.

Freud's body of work - its academic elements apart - lies outside other contemporary art movements (although it may be said to run in parallel with the work of Francis Bacon). What he offers is a finite universe bounded by his own studio and his models who, for the most part and with the notable exception of his introspective Self-portraits, are drawn from his immediate family and his circle of friends, including his wife and his mother Lucie, whose ageing he has pitilessly documented on canvas. These contorted, emaciated or bloated nudes hint at an underlying and brutal psychological truth at which we can only guess. Freud's is a solitary and intensely personal quest. 'I want my painting to be as flesh', he once said. 'For me, the painting is the person and I want its effect on me to be the same as the effect of flesh.'

He participated in numerous exhibitions of work by young English painters, showing not only in the United Kingdom but also in Tokyo, New York and Venice (1954 Biennale). His work later featured at exhibitions in London (Tate Gallery, 1963), Tokyo (National Museum of Western Art, 1975 and Tokyo Metropolitan Art Museum, 1982), London again (National Gallery, 1987), and New York (Museum of Modern Art, 1991). Solo exhibitions were held in 1944 at the Alex Reid and Lefevre Gallery in London; in 1950 and 1952 at London's Hanover Gallery; in 1958, 1963 and 1968 at the Marlborough Fine Art Gallery in London; in 1974 at a travelling retrospective held first at the Hayward Gallery in London, then at Bristol City Art Gallery, Birmingham City Museum and Art Gallery, Leeds City Museum and the Anthony d'Offay Gallery in London. In 1988, the British Museum organised a Freud retrospective at the Hayward Gallery; this was subsequently repeated in a number of countries, including the USA (Hirschhorn Museum, Washington DC), France (Musée National d'Art Moderne, Paris), and Germany (Neue Nationalgalerie, Berlin).

Other major exhibitions of Freud's work have since included those at the Galerie Berggruen in Paris and the Saatchi Collection in London in 1990. A 1993 retrospective moved from the Whitechapel Art Gallery in London to the Museum of Modern Art in New York and then to the Museo Nacional Reina Sofia in Madrid. In 1995, the St Paul-de-Vence-based Fondation Maeght mounted an exhibition entitled *Francis Bacon-Lucian Freud* and, in 2002, some 140 paintings, drawings and engravings by Freud were exhibited at London's Tate Gallery, then at the La Caixa Foundation in Barcelona and at the Museum of Contemporary Art in Los Angeles. Since then, art shows in Basel, Chicago, New York and Miami Beach, as well as the 16th London Contemporary Art Fair, have included Freud's work.

BIBLIOGRAPHY:

Gowing, Lawrence, *Lucian Freud*, Thames & Hudson, New York, 1982. Clair, Jean, '*Lucian Freud: Restoring the Paint-flesh Ritual*' in *Art International* n° 1, periodical, Paris, autumn 1987. Hughes, Robert, *Lucian Freud, Paintings*, Thames & Hudson, London, 1987 (French edition, Thames & Hudson, Londres, 1987). Hartley, Craig, *The Etchings of Lucian Freud: a catalogue raisonné 1946-1995*, Marlborough Graphics, London, 1995. *Francis Bacon - Lucian Freud*, exhibition catalogue, Fondation Maeght, St-Paul-de-Vence-de-Vence, 1995. Bernard, Bruce, *Lucian Freud*, Random House, New York, 1996. Willcox, Scott/Freud, Lucian, *Lucian Freud Etchings from the Painewebber Art*, 1999. Ammann, Jean-Christophe/Hartley, Craig/Lauter, Rolf, *Lucian Freud. Naked Portraits: Werke der 40er bis 90er Jahre*, Hatje Cantz, Ostfildern-Ruit, 2001 (text in German and English). Feaver, William/Auerbach, Frank, *Lucian Freud*, travelling exhibition catalogue, Fundació La Caixa, Barcelona, Los Angeles Museum of Contemporary Art, Tate Britain, London, 2002. Hughes, Robert, *Lucian Freud*, Thames & Hudson, Paris, 2002. *Lucian Freud: After Cézanne*, catalogue, National Gall. of Australia, 2002.

MUSEUMS AND GALLERIES:

CANBERRA (Nat. Gal. of Australia): *After Cézanne* (1999-2000, oil on canvas) - LIVERPOOL (Walker AG): *Interior near Paddington* (1951) - LONDON (British Council): *Girl with Roses* (1947-1948, oil on canvas); *Naked Girl with Egg* (1980-1981, oil on canvas) - LONDON (National Portrait Gal.): *Lucian Freud* (1963, oil on canvas); *Arnold Abraham Goodman, Baron Goodman* (1985, charcoal); *Nathaniel Charles Jacob Rothschild, 4th Baron Rothschild (Man in a Chair)* (1989, oil on canvas) - LONDON (Tate Collection): *Girl with a White Dog* (1950-1951, oil on canvas); *Man with a Thistle (Self-portrait)* (1946, oil on canvas); *Francis Bacon* (1952, oil/metal, portrait); *Naked Portrait* (1972-1973, oil on canvas); *Two Plants* (1977-1980, oil on canvas); *Standing by the Rags* (1988-1989, oil on canvas); *Leigh Bowery* (1991, oil on canvas, portrait); other paintings, drawings, prints including etchings - NEW YORK (MoMA) - PARIS (FNAC): *Man Posing* - WASHINGTON DC (Hirshhorn Mus. and Sculpture Garden): *Night Portrait* (1985-1986, oil/linen).

AUCTION RECORDS:

LONDON, 12 April 1967, *Nude with Black Hair*, GBP 800. LONDON, 4 June 1971, *Sleeping Head*, Gns 1,200. LONDON, 26 April 1972, *Self-portrait* (watercolour) GBP 800. LONDON, 22 Nov 1972, *Self-portrait*, GBP 4,400. LONDON, 13 July 1973, *Smiling Woman* (1958-1960) Gns 4,800. LONDON, 14 Dec 1973, *Portrait of a Young Girl* (1967) Gns 12,000. LONDON, 10 May 1974, *Portrait of Billy*, Gns 16,000. LONDON, 7 June 1978, *Seated Nude* (watercolour and pencil, 12 3/4 x 9 1/4 ins / 32.5 x 23.5 cm) GBP 1,200. LONDON, 10 June 1981, *Head of a Young Girl* (pen/paper, 17 1/2 x 14 1/2 ins / 44.5 x 37 cm) GBP 850. LONDON, 25 May 1983, *Nude with Dark Hair (Pregnant Girl)* (1960-1961, oil on canvas, 34 1/2 x 27 1/2 ins / 87.5 x 70 cm) GBP 40,000. LONDON, 4 Nov 1983, *Boy Posing* (watercolour and pen, 14 1/2 x 9 1/2 ins / 37 x 24 cm) GBP 750. LONDON, 23 May 1984, *Startled Man* (pencil, 9 x 5 1/2 ins / 22 x 14 cm) GBP 6,800. LONDON, 7 June 1985, *Fish Head* (watercolour, 6 1/2 x 9 ins / 16.2 x 22 cm) GBP 1,700. LONDON, 8 Nov 1985, *Dead Monkey (illustration for 'The Ruin and the Sun')* (1944, pen, 8 x 13 ins / 20.3 x 33 cm) GBP 7,000. LONDON, 2 July 1987, *Adventure Playground* (1974, oil on canvas, 9 x 13 ins / 22 x 33 cm) GBP 58,000. LONDON, 22 July 1987, *A Peculiar Gull* (pen and Indian ink, 5 x 7 ins / 12.5 x 18 cm) GBP 4,000. LONDON, 9 June 1988, *Model Resting* (ink, 14 1/4 x 9 1/4 ins / 36.3 x 23.8 cm) GBP 5,280. LONDON, 30 June 1988, *Male Head* (1966, oil on canvas, 18 1/4 x 15 1/4 ins / 46.5 x 39 cm) GBP 275,000. LONDON, 23 Feb 1989, *Man in the Train* (pencil/paper, 7 x 4 3/4 ins / 18 x 12 cm) GBP 7,700. LONDON, 29 June 1989, *Young Girl in a White Dress* (1947, pencil and pastel/kraft paper, 22 1/2 x 19 ins / 57 x 48 cm) GBP 308,000. LONDON, 10 Nov 1989, *Portrait of Lincoln Kirstein* (1950, oil on canvas, 20 x 16 ins / 50.8 x 40.7 cm) GBP 143,000. LONDON, 5 April 1990, *Seated Female Nude* (oil on canvas, 13 3/4 x 8 3/4 ins / 35 x 22.3 cm) GBP 357,500. LONDON, 28 June 1990, *Man Smoking* (oil on canvas, 22 3/4 x 22 3/4 ins / 58 x 58 cm) GBP 660,000. LONDON, 18 Oct 1990, *Rabbit on a Chair* (1944, pencil/paper, 17 3/4 x 11 1/2 ins / 45 x 29 cm) GBP 93,500. PARIS, 28 March 1991, *Portrait of Christian Bérard* (1948, pencil heightened with white on grey paper, 16 1/4 x 12 1/4 ins / 41 x 31 cm) FRF 200,000. LONDON, 27 June 1991, *Garden by the Sea* (pencil and pencil/paper, 5 x 7 ins / 12.7 x 17.7 cm) GBP 15,400; *Woman with Exposed Breast* (oil on canvas, 25 x 19 1/2 ins / 63.5 x 49.5 cm) GBP 374,000. MONACO, 11 Oct 1991, *Portrait of Christian Bérard* (1948, lead pencil and white pencil/grey paper, 16 x 16 3/4 ins / 40.5 x 42.5 cm) FRF 1,831,500. LONDON, 8 Nov 1991, *Portrait of a Man* (oil on canvas, 9 1/2 x 7 1/2 ins / 24 x 19 cm) GBP 126,500. LONDON, 26 March 1992, *Self-portrait* (1952, oil on card, 4 1/2 x 3 1/2 ins / 11.5 x 8.8 cm) GBP 88,000. LONDON, 2 July 1992, *Man in a Sport's Shirt* (oil on canvas, 20 x 16 ins / 50.9 x 40.7 cm) GBP 275,000; *Loch Ness seen from Drumnadrochit* (1943, ink/paper, 14 3/4 x 17 3/4 ins / 37.5 x 45 cm) GBP 55,000. LONDON, 3 Dec 1992, *Annabel* (1990, oil on canvas, 10 x 6 1/2 ins / 24.5 x 16.2 cm) GBP 126,500. MILAN, 21 June 1994, *Head of a Woman* (pencil, 9 x 6 1/2 ins / 22 x 16.5 cm) ITL 1,955,000. LONDON, 29 June 1994, *Painter's Room* (1943, oil on canvas, 24 1/2 x 30 ins / 62 x 76 cm) GBP 416,000. LONDON, 29 Nov 1995, *Man with a Moustache* (oil on canvas, 9 1/2 x 7 1/2 ins / 24 x 19 cm) GBP 155,500. LONDON, 30 Nov 1995, *Rose and Pea* (oil on canvas, 12 x 7 3/4 ins / 30.5 x 20 cm) GBP 52,100. NEW YORK, 1 May 1996, *Male Model Posing* (1985, etching, 35 x 29 ins / 89 x 73.7 cm) USD 13,800. LONDON, 26 June 1996, *Young Girl in a White Dress* (Conté pencil and pastel/buff-coloured paper, 22 1/2 x 19 ins / 57 x 48 cm) GBP 364,500. LONDON, 24 Oct 1996, *Self-portrait* (1943, ink and pencil/paper, 10 x 8 1/2 ins / 25.1 x 21.3 cm) GBP 17,250. NEW YORK, 9 Nov 1996, *IB (Hartley 22)* (1984, aquatint, 11 1/2 x 11 1/2 ins / 29.5 x 29.5 cm) GBP 5,175. LONDON, 25 June 1997, *John Deakin* (1963-1964, oil on canvas, 12 x 9 3/4 ins / 30.2 x 24.8 cm) GBP 892,500. NEW YORK, 18 May 1999, *The Artist's Mother* (1982-1984, oil on canvas, 41 x 50 ins / 105 x 128 cm) USD 3,000,000. LONDON, 1 July 1999, *Reclining Woman* (1989, charcoal, 20 x 18 ins / 51 x 46 cm) GBP 32,000. LONDON, 20 June 2000, *Pluto* (dry-point etching, 13 x 24 ins / 32 x 60 cm) GBP 20,000. LONDON, 29 June 2000, *Filly* (1970, oil on canvas, 7 x 11 ins / 19 x 27 cm) GBP 240,000. NEW YORK, 8 May 2001, *Seaside Garden* (1944, colour crayon and pencil, 5 x 7 ins / 13 x 18 cm) USD 140,000. LONDON, 23 Oct 2001, *Strawberries* (c. 1950, oil on copper, 4 x 5 ins / 10 x 12 cm) GBP 60,000. LONDON, 26 June 2002, *Annabel* (1972, oil on canvas, 13 x 9 ins / 32 x 23 cm) GBP 420,000. LONDON, 27 June 2002, *Two Fragments* (1977, bush and sepia, two parts, 13 x 9 ins / 33 x 23 cm) GBP 32,000. LONDON, 5 Feb 2003, *Head of a Child* (c. 1954, oil on canvas, 10 x 7 ins / 25 x 17 cm) GBP 300,000. NEW YORK, 12 Nov 2003, *Self-portrait* (1980, charcoal and pastel, 13 x 9 ins / 34 x 24 cm) USD 90,000. LONDON, 4 Feb 2004, *Factory in North London* (1972, oil on canvas, 28 x 28 ins / 71 x 71 cm) GBP 1,850,000. LONDON, 2 July 2004, *Head and Shoulders of a Girl* (etching, 27 x 21 ins / 69 x 54 cm) GBP 16,000. LONDON, 9 Feb 2005, *Naked Portrait* (2002, oil/canvas) GBP 3,928,000.

FREUDEBERG, Sigmund.
See **FREUDENBERGER**

FREUDEMANN, Victor
German, 19th century.
Born 25 February 1857, in Berlin.
Painter. Landscapes.

Freudemann began his career in Berlin around 1881. He was awarded a medal in Berlin in 1891 and an honourable mention at the Exposition Universelle in Paris in 1900.

AUCTION RECORDS:
COLOGNE, 21 May 1981, *November Morning* (1894, oil on canvas, 32 3/4 x 52 1/4 ins / 83 x 133 cm) DEM 2,400.

FREUDENBERG, Eduard
German, 19th century.
Born 1808, in Neuwied; died 1855.
Painter. Genre scenes.

Freudenberg studied at the Dresden academy. He began his career around 1831 in Munich.

AUCTION RECORDS:
VIENNA, 14 March 1984, *Joy of Motherhood* (1843, oil on canvas, 33 x 25 1/4 ins / 84 x 64 cm) ATS 220,000.

FREUDENBERG, Jacobus
Dutch, 19th century.
Born 1818; died 1873.
Painter. Landscapes with figures.

Freudenberg was a painter of picturesque landscapes typical of the Dutch School.

AUCTION RECORDS:
LONDON, 6 May 1977, *Winter Landscape with Skaters* (oil on canvas, 22 x 28 1/2in/56 x 72.5cm) GBP 2,200. COLOGNE, 21 May 1981, *November Morning* (oil on canvas, 32 3/4 x 52 1/4in/83 x 133cm) DEM 2,400. AMSTERDAM, 3 May 1988, *Riverscape with Peasants in Boats and a Sailing Boat, near a Windmill* (oil on canvas, 13 1/4 x 19 1/4in/33.5 x 49cm) NLG 7,475. LONDON, 24 June 1988, *River Scene in Winter with Skaters* (oil on panel, 22 x 31 1/2in/56 x 80cm) GBP 11,000. LINDAU, 3 Dec 1999, *Winter Ice Pleasures with Windmill, Church, Houses* (oil on panel, 12 x 16 ins / 31 x 41 cm) DEM 6,500. LINDAU, 7 Dec 2001, *Figures on Frozen Canal with Windmill and Church* (oil on panel, 12 x 16 ins / 31 x 41 cm) DEM 6,000.

FREUDENBERGER, Franz Friedrich
Swiss, 19th century.
Born 8 November 1804, in Bern; died 1 March 1862, in Bern.
Painter, draughtsman.

Franz Freudenberger was a pupil of Nicolas König and also studied in Zurich and Munich. He worked in Geneva and in Lyons, travelled a great deal in Italy and settled for a time in Constantinople. He exhibited in Bern in 1824.

FREUDENBERGER, Sigmund, or Freudeberg
Swiss, 18th century.
Born 16 June 1745, in Bern; died 15 November 1801, in Bern.
Painter, watercolourist, draughtsman, engraver.
Portraits, genre scenes.

After working with Emmanuel Handmann in Basel, Sigmund Freudenberger went to Paris, where he spent eight years studying Parisian life and manners and taking advice from the German engraver J.-G. Willie, de Greuze, Boucher and Roslin. Political events at the end of the 18th century led him to return to Switzerland in 1773.

He specialised in portraying intimate genre scenes in the manner of Lancret and Boucher, as well as Swiss peasants in oil and pastel. His works include a series of plates depicting the history of the manners and customs of the French in the 18th century: *Le bon père, La jeune fille à la fontaine, La gaieté conjugale, Les adieux du laboureur, Lison dormait.* The Ariana Museum in Geneva has in its collection *Fêtes galantes* and the museum in Neuchâtel has sepias and drawings.

MUSEUMS AND GALLERIES:
BERN: *Portrait de Louis XVIII; Horoscope réalisé.*

AUCTION RECORDS:
PARIS, 26 April 1873, *Jeune femme dans un parc,* FRF 6,000. PARIS, 1881, *La visite inattendue* (sepia drawing heightened with white) FRF 4,550; *La soirée d'hiver* (sepia drawing heightened with white) FRF 2,220. PARIS, 1894, *Le bain* (sepia drawing) FRF 5,400; *L'occupation* (bistre drawing, outlines in pen) FRF 5,100. PARIS, 1899, *Les époux curieux,* FRF 4,300; *Le coucher* (bistre drawing/pen outlines) FRF 8,200; *L'heureux ménage* (watercolour) FRF 2,700. NEW YORK, 26-28 Feb 1902, *Interruption* (sepia) USD 100. PARIS, 17 March 1910, *La Cabaretière caressée* (drawing) FRF 77. PARIS, 16-19 June 1919, *Le marchand de chansons; L'heureuse famille* (watercolour wash, two drawings) FRF 14,350. PARIS, 10-11 May 1920, *La Toilette* (watercolour and gouache) FRF 36,100. PARIS, 23-24 May 1921, *Le Boudoir* (attributed) FRF 1,100. PARIS, 8 Dec 1922, *La Propreté villageoise; La Toilette champêtre* (watercolour, a pair) FRF 9,500. PARIS, 7-8 May 1923, *Le Malin* (watercolour) FRF 10,000. PARIS, 18 May 1923, *Zemire et Azor, ou l'Heureuse Union* (watercolour) FRF 16,200. PARIS, 2 June 1923, *L'Heureuse famille,* FRF 1,600. PARIS, 6 Dec 1923, *Le Cabaret suisse,* FRF 2,700. PARIS, 19 March 1924, *La Toilette* (wash and watercolour) FRF 1,500. PARIS, 25 March 1925, *Paysan debout* (red chalk) FRF 2,400. PARIS, 10 and 11 May 1926, *Hangar de ferme,* FRF 3,700. PARIS, 3 and 4 June 1926, *Le retour du fermier* (watercolour/outlines in pen, attributed) FRF 3,000. LONDON, 17 Dec 1926, *Dans un parc; Forêt de Deer* (both) GBP 110. PARIS, 12 June 1931, *La Toilette* (attributed) FRF 4,110. PARIS, 10 June 1932, *Le Repentir; La Toilette* (pen and watercolour wash, two drawings) FRF 6,800. PARIS, 23 April 1937, *Scene familiale dans une chaumière* (pen and watercolour wash) FRF 8,600. LONDON, 22 July 1937, *Le soldat en Semestre,* GBP 85. LONDON, 4 May 1938, *Le marché,* GBP 25. PARIS, 18-19 Dec 1940, *L'heureux ménage* (pen and watercolour wash, attributed) FRF 1,850. PARIS, 19 March 1947, *L'Occupation* (pen and Indian ink wash) FRF 25,000. PARIS, 11 and 12 June 1947, *La lecture* (watercolour) FRF 11,200. LONDON, 20 Nov 1957, *La lettre interrompue* (pastel) GBP 600. LONDON, 21 Jan 1959, *Le retour du chasseur,* GBP 500. LUCERNE, 25 June 1960, *Le retour du soldat,* CHF 6,000. LUCERNE, 7 Dec 1965, *Jeunes filles et fillettes jouant devant une chaumière* (watercolour) CHF 4,800. PARIS, 18 Dec 1967, *L'heureuse fermière* (watercolour) FRF 7,500. BERN, 11 June 1976, *Retour du soldat suisse dans le pays* (1780, etching, 11 1/4 x 12 1/4 ins / 28.4 x 31 cm) CHF 5,600. NEW YORK, 2 Dec 1976, *Scène familiale dans un intérieur* (1771, watercolour and ink, 8 1/4 x 11 ins / 21 x 28 cm) USD 8,000. LONDON, 27 April 1977, *Le départ du soldat suisse; Le retour du soldat suisse* (two etchings in colour, each 11 1/4 x 12 1/4 ins / 28.5 x 31 cm) GBP 3,300. BERN, 27 Nov 1979, *La leçon de guitare; La leçon de clavecin* (two colour engravings, 9 x 7 1/4 ins / 22.8 x 18.1 cm) CHF 18,000. LONDON, 11 Dec 1980, *La complaisance maternelle* (watercolour and pen, 10 x 7 1/4 ins / 24.5 x 18.4 cm) GBP 5,000. LONDON, 5 July 1983, *Ne cherche point à calmer mes alarmes* (black chalk, pen and watercolour, 7 1/2 x 8 3/4 ins / 18.8 x 22.4 cm) GBP 2,400. LONDON, 8 March 1984, *Le retour du faucheur; La balançoire* (two etchings, colour, 8 1/2 x 6 1/4 ins / 21.3 x 15.6 cm) GBP 4,000. PARIS, 13 Nov 1985, *L'heureux ménage* (drawing in watercolour, 12 1/2 x 9 1/2 ins / 32 x 24 cm) FRF 46,000. LUCERNE, 13 Nov 1986, *Depart du soldat suisse; Retour du soldat suisse* (two engravings, 8 3/4 x 11 ins / 22.5 x 27 cm) CHF 9,000. PARIS, 6 May 1987, *La confiance enfantine* (1771, watercolour and pen, 9 x 7 ins / 23 x 17.5 cm) FRF 60,000. LONDON, 4 Dec 1987, *Depart du soldat suisse; Retour du soldat suisse* (two etchings, colour, 8 3/4 x 11 ins / 22.5 x 27 cm) USD 2,800. LONDON, 28 March 1990, *Souhaits de bienvenue à la porte de la ville* (ink and watercolour, 7 1/2 x 10 1/4 ins / 19 x 26 cm) GBP 5,500. ZURICH, 4 June 1992, *Le bon père; La*

balançoire (coloured etching, a pair, each 7 1/2 x 5 3/4 ins / 19 x 14.5 cm) CHF 7,910. ZURICH, 24 Nov 1993, *Paysan assis* (pencil/paper, 6 x 4 1/4 ins / 15 x 11 cm) CHF 920. ZURICH, 12 June 1995, *Les soins maternels; Le villageois content* (colour engraving, a pair, each 6 3/4 x 8 3/4 ins / 17 x 22.5 cm) CHF 1,725. NEW YORK, 9 Jan 1996, *Tête de jeune femme* (1773, red chalk, 12 1/4 x 9 1/2 ins / 31.4 x 24.3 cm) USD 1,725. NEW YORK, 28 Jan 1998, *Femmes préparant la fiancée pour le mariage* (pen, black ink, grey-brown wash/black chalk, heightened with white, 15 x 18 1/4 ins / 38.2 x 46.5 cm) USD 5,175. BERN, 10 May 2000, *Departure of Swiss Soldier* (engraving, 9 x 11 ins / 22 x 27 cm) CHF 6,500. BERN, 10 May 2000, *Return of the Swiss Soldier* (engraving, 9 x 11 ins / 22 x 27 cm) CHF 6,500. BERLIN, 18 May 2001, *Girl Reading* (pen/watercolour, 7 x 5 ins / 17 x 12 cm) DEM 5,300. SION, 21 June 2003, *First Steps* (crayon/ink/watercolour, 17 x 13 ins / 43 x 32 cm) CHF 6,900. SION, 21 June 2003, *The Visit* (crayon/ink/watercolour, 17 x 13 ins / 43 x 32 cm) CHF 7,000. BERN, 13 May 2004, *Untitled* (Indian ink/pen/brush, four, 4 x 6 ins / 11 x 16 cm) CHF 2,400. BERN, 13 May 2004, *Departure of Swiss Soldier. Return of Swiss Soldier* (etching, two, 9 x 10 ins / 22 x 26 cm) CHF 5,500.

FREUDENREICH, Marie Pierrette Amélie von
Maiden name: de Mestral d'Aruffens
Swiss, 19th century.
Born 1786; died 1 October 1831, in Freudheim-am-Gerzensee.
Painter.

Freudenreich exhibited watercolour drawings and charcoal in Bern in 1804 and 1810.

FREUDENTHAL, Peter
Swedish, 20th century.
Born 1938.
Painter.

Peter Freudenthal's abstract paintings closely resemble those of the American 'hard-edge' school.

AUCTION RECORDS:
STOCKHOLM, 21 Nov 1988, *Composition* (1967, gouache, 7 1/2 x 3 1/2 ins / 19 x 9 cm) SEK 3,500. STOCKHOLM, 14 June 1990, *Noon in the Square* (1985, acrylic/canvas, 39 1/4 x 19 3/4 ins / 100 x 50 cm) SEK 25,000. STOCKHOLM, 5-6 Dec 1990, *Perspective* (1966, acrylic/canvas, 22 x 26 1/2 ins / 55 x 67 cm) SEK 7,500. STOCKHOLM, 21 May 1992, *Souvenir of Neuchâtel* (oil on canvas, 17 3/4 x 25 1/2 ins / 45 x 65 cm) SEK 6,200. STOCKHOLM, 30 Nov 1993, *Empty Square II* (oil on canvas, 25 1/2 x 39 1/4 ins / 65 x 100 cm) SEK 20,000. STOCKHOLM, 26 Oct 1999, *Untitled Composition* (1973, oil on canvas, 39 x 63 ins / 100 x 160 cm) SEK 15,000. STOCKHOLM, 2 May 2000, *Encounter in New York* (1987, oil on canvas, 39 x 25 ins / 100 x 64 cm) SEK 16,000. STOCKHOLM, 6 Nov 2001, *We Were in Gurre* (1983-1984, oil on canvas, 79 x 102 ins / 200 x 260 cm) SEK 37,000. STOCKHOLM, 5 Nov 2002, *Untitled Composition* (mixed media, 79 x 14 ins / 200 x 36 cm) SEK 22,000. STOCKHOLM, 2 Nov 2004, *Adam* (1983, oil on canvas, 47 x 60 ins / 120 x 152 cm) SEK 14,000. STOCKHOLM, 2 Nov 2004, *Shir - Composition* (1977, oil on canvas, 35 x 51 ins / 89 x 129 cm) SEK 21,000. STOCKHOLM, 3 Nov 2004, *Memnon* (1988-1989, oil on canvas, 39 x 47 ins / 100 x 120 cm) SEK 16,000.

FREUDWEILER, Daniel Albert
Swiss, 19th century.
Born 18 December 1793, in Felsberg, near Coire; died 30 April 1827, in Zurich.
Painter, lithographer. Genre scenes.

This artist was a pupil of Johann Pfenniger in Zurich.and spent five years in Italy. He copied old masters and perfected his drawing technique. When he returned to Switzerland he became very involved in teaching and portrait painting in watercolour and in miniatures. He was responsible for the artistic education of Hitz Gonzenbach and Balder. The Zurich artistic association has his self-portrait in its collection.

AUCTION RECORDS:
ZURICH, 16 May 1981, *Mother and Child in an Interior* (1812, tempera, 20 x 16 1/2 ins / 51 x 42 cm) CHF 3,200.

FREUDWEILER, Heinrich
Swiss, 18th century.
Born 16 October 1755, in Zurich; died 1 December 1795, in Zurich.
Painter, watercolourist, decorative designer. History painting, genre scenes, landscapes.

Heinrich Freudweiler was a pupil of H. Wuest and studied in Düsseldorf, Dresden and Berlin and also formed a friendship with Chodwiecky. Specialising in genre he painted scenes of contemporary social life. Among his works are historical paintings in the collection of the artistic association of Zurich of which he was one of the founder members.

AUCTION RECORDS:
LONDON, 20 Nov 1931, *Courtyard filled with Soldiers*, GBP 6. PARIS, 3 June 1935, *Swiss Woman Holding a Book and Flowers* (watercolour) FRF 310. BERN, 24 June 1983, *View of the Town and the Lake of Zoug* (c. 1785, coloured etching, 9 1/2 x 13 3/4 ins / 24 x 35.2 cm) CHF 6,000. ZURICH, 12 June 1995, *View of the Town and the Area around Zurich* (etching in colour, 8 1/4 x 13 1/2 ins / 21 x 34.5 cm) CHF 3,450. ZURICH, 29 May 2000, *Women from Zurich in Wood Landscape* (oil on panel, 28 x 22 ins / 70 x 55 cm) CHF 35,000. ZURICH, 22 Sept 2000, *The Game* (1790, oil on canvas, 19 x 22 ins / 47 x 57 cm) CHF 27,000. VIENNA, 24 March 2004, *Portrait of Johann Georg Sulzer with Grandson Carl Anton Graff* (oil on panel, 9 x 8 ins / 23 x 20 cm) EUR 9,000.

FREULER, Bernhard
Swiss, 19th century.
Born 23 August 1796, to a family originally from Schaffhaus; died 18 March 1858, in Schaffhausen.
Painter. Landscapes.

Bernhard Freuler studied in his home town and in Vienna and travelled in Austria. He painted sepia and watercolours and held the post of head of design at the German school of Schaffhausen.

FREULER, Fridolin
Swiss, 19th century.
Born 24 May 1842, in Glarus; died 9 May 1868.
Draughtsman.

Fridolin Freuler studied in Glarus and in Paris and died at the age of 26.

FREULER, Kaspar
Swiss, 19th century.
Born 1837, in Glarus; died 1899, on the Bachistock Mountain.
Painter, draughtsman.

Kaspar Freuler studied in Paris and in Lyons where he lived for ten years. The Glarus Collection contains flower paintings by him.

FREUND, Anton
Austrian, 18th century.
Born c. 1773, in Eschenbach; died 6 November 1808, in Vienna.
Sculptor.

This artist married the daughter of the sculptor from Lyons, Privet.

FREUND, Anton
German, 19th century.
Born 17 January 1827, in Langwalde; died 22 May 1856, in Berlin.
Sculptor, painter.

After studying at the Königsberg academy, Freund lived in Dresden and in Berlin.

FREUND, Chr.
Danish, 19th - 20th century.
Sculptor.
MUSEUMS AND GALLERIES:
COPENHAGEN: *Gathering Flowers; Playing Boccia; Thirsty Horse.*

FREUND, Christoph
German, 18th century.
Active in Dessau.
Painter.
Christoph Freund mainly produced portraits including some in miniature.

FREUND, Ernst
German, 18th century.
Active in Berlin in 1701.
Sculptor.
Ernst Freund worked on decorations created for the occasion of the coronation of Frederick I of Prussia.

FREUND, Franz
German, 18th century.
Born to a family originally from Bernkastel.
Painter.

FREUND, Fritz
German, 19th - 20th century.
Born 13 April 1859, in Darmstadt; died 1942.
Painter. Genre scenes, landscapes.
Freund studied at the academy in Munich.
AUCTION RECORDS:
PARIS, 18 May 1897, *Bavarian Shepherd,* FRF 625. MUNICH, 26 Nov 1981, *Children Gathering Flowers* (oil on canvas, 28¾ x 23½ ins / 73 x 59.5 cm) DEM 4,600. NEW YORK, 26 Oct 1983, *Sunlit Clearing* (oil on canvas, 37 x 59 ins / 94 x 150 cm) USD 4,250. BREMEN, 19 April 1986, *Bench in the Woods* (1896, oil on canvas, 37½ x 31 ins / 95 x 79 cm) DEM 7,500. LONDON, 22 May 1992, *Beautiful View* (oil on canvas, 31½ x 23½ ins / 80 x 59.7 cm) GBP 2,200. NEW YORK, 23 Oct 1997, *Snowball Fight* (oil on canvas, 39½ x 63 ins / 100.3 x 160 cm) USD 57,500.

FREUND, Georg Christian
Danish, 19th century.
Born 7 February 1821, in Altona; died 6 April 1900, in Copenhagen.
Sculptor.
Georg Christian Freund was the nephew and pupil of Hermann Ernst Freund. He then studied with Bissen at the Kunstakademi in Copenhagen.
MUSEUMS AND GALLERIES:
COPENHAGEN: several works.

FREUND, Henry Lewis
American, 20th century.
Born 16 September 1905, in Clinton; died 1979.
Painter, illustrator.

FREUND, Hermann Ernst
Danish, 19th century.
Born 15 October 1786, in Uthlede; died 13 June 1840, in Copenhagen.
Sculptor.
Several of Hermann Ernst Freund's works are in the Copenhagen museum. He worked for several churches in Copenhagen and engraved many medals bearing the effigies of Danish sovereigns.

FREUND, Johann
Austrian, 18th century.
Active in Vienna during the first half of the 18th century.
Sculptor.

FREUND, Johann Nikolaus
German, 17th - 18th century.
Born at the end of the 17th century, in Römhild.
Sculptor, architect.
After completing his studies in Rome and Venice he returned to settle in Augsburg.

FREUND, Josef
Austrian, 18th century.
Born c. 1708, in Vienna; died 2 January 1746.
Sculptor.
Josef Freund was the brother of Johann.

FREUND, Karl
Austrian, 18th century.
Born c. 1720, in Vienna; died 31 March 1773, in Vienna.
Painter (porcelain).

FREUND, N.
German, 19th century.
Active c. 1800.
Miniaturist.
A portrait of Louis XVIII is attributed to this artist.

FREUND, Philipp
German, 19th century.
Active in Paris in 1803.
Painter. Landscapes, seascapes.

FREUND, Theodor
German, 17th century.
Born to a family originally from Waldsassen.
Painter.
The church at Waldsassen has a work by Theodor Freund.

FREUND, Wilhelm
German, 19th century.
Born 23 June 1860, in Schönbach.
Painter.
Wilhelm Freund settled in Berlin around 1883. Most of his paintings were landscapes.

FREUNDECKE, Brunck de. See **BRUNCK-FREUNDECKE Richard de**

FREUNDLICH, Otto
German, 20th century.
Born 10 July 1878, in Stolp (Pomerania); died 9 March 1943, in Lublin-Maidanek, Poland.
From 1909 to 1914 and from 1924 active in France.
Painter, sculptor, engraver, draughtsman, pastellist.
Groups: Novembergruppe, Gruppe Progressiver Künstler (Progressive Art Group), Abstraction-Création.
Otto Freundlich may not rank among the greatest artists of the first half of the 20th century, but he was undoubtedly one of the heroes of the age, not so much because he was arrested by the Germans in Paris, banned as a 'degenerate' artist and deported to Maidanek concentration camp, but rather because he belonged to that cosmopolitan group of artists who, although literally dying of hunger, continued to uphold and practise the creed of Abstraction.

Freundlich originally worked in trade and studied art in his free time; he took courses in Berlin and then in Munich, under Heinrich Wölfflin (1903), before spending time in Florence (1904-1905). He did not start painting until he was 27, but he very quickly assimilated the principal artistic movements of the day, from Munich-style Jugendstil to the Secession group and Die Brücke and, not least, the nascent Abstract movement spearheaded by Der Blaue Reiter.

He settled in Paris in 1909 and moved in avant-garde circles, meeting Picasso, Gris, Braque, Kandinsky, Delaunay, Herbin and others. His first sculptures date from this time. He was also involved with Cubist groups in Paris, Amsterdam and Cologne, albeit without fully espousing that movement's formal credo. He was called up for military service at the outbreak of the World War I and duly returned to Germany. There, he worked on the periodical *Die Aktion* and joined the Novembergruppe (an association of Berlin artists) in 1918. In 1919 he produced his first genuinely abstract composition. He was involved with the Dadaists in Cologne and, during his stay there, received a number of commissions that enabled him to experiment with new techniques such as stained glass and mosaics. He returned to Paris in 1924 and joined the Cercle et Carré (Circle and Square) group founded at the instigation of Michel Seuphor, then in 1925 became involved in another group, Abstraction-Création, alongside Georges Vantongerloo. Freundlich's work was seized and destroyed in Germany in 1937, and in 1939 one of his sculptures had the distinction of appearing on the cover of the catalogue of the Nazi-organised *Entartete Kunst* (*Degenerate Art*) exhibition. He was arrested in 1943 and deported to Poland; he died there, probably on the day he arrived in Maidanek.

From about 1911, his painting still betrayed traces of Expressionism but was in the process of becoming progressively abstract. By 1924 he had evolved a highly personal pictorial style and language, using a system of irregular geometric shapes, notably triangles and quadrilaterals. He was influenced by both Cezanne and Van Gogh, borrowing a sense of architectural form from the former and a feeling for vivid colour from the latter. Before embarking on a composition, he would 'pre-construct' it on squared paper, much as he would have done a mosaic or a stained glass window (of which he had considerable experience, having worked on the restoration of the stained glass in Chartres before the war). Then, like a stained glass artist, he would proceed to mark out on paper fragments of subtly shaded areas and light. In effect, he sacrificed three-dimensionality in favour of chromatic exactitude. He used colour to build up his compositions and achieve balance. In his *Composition No. 6*, for example, the various surface areas are broken down by a series of 'force lines', then further reduced into progressively smaller units, each area being given a dominant colour and the surface being modulated by different shades of that colour. From 1937 he began to use more often an element that had appeared in embryonic form in his earlier work: a diagonal half-rib or arch comprised of a straight line and a curved line. This element was repeated time and again, up to and including one of his final compositions, *Rosace II* (1941).

Freundlich's sculpture evolved in tandem with his painting, becoming increasingly abstract from 1929. He produced two monumental sculptures in 1929 and 1933, both on the theme of the cosmos, and in 1934 he sculpted a low relief and a 'sculpture-mountain', which he intended one day to be reproduced on a gigantic scale and integrated into a natural landscape. When not sculpting or painting, he engraved on wood, linoleum and zinc and produced pen and Indian ink drawings.

Freundlich took part in the first Neue Sezession exhibition in Berlin in 1911 and went on to exhibit in Paris at the Salon des Artistes Indépendants and the Salon des Surindépendants. A tribute to him and his work was organised within the framework of the inaugural Salon des Réalités Nouvelles in 1947. He had exhibited solo from 1924 in Germany, France, Belgium and Israel. An exhibition commemorating his sixtieth birthday was held at the Galerie Jeanne Bucher in Paris in 1938, and a posthumous retrospective was organised in Paris in 1954. In 1960 the Wallraf-Richartz Gallery in Cologne mounted an exhibition of his work; this was followed in 1968 by an exhibition at the Goethe Institute in Paris (in conjunction with Jeanne Kosnick-Kloss); in 1969 and 1982 at the Musée de Pontoise (which had been the recipient of the Freundlich Bequest in 1967); in 1978 at the Israel Museum in Jerusalem; in 1979 at the Rhineland Regional Museum in Bonn, the Kunstverein in Brunswick and the Kunstverein in Berlin; in 1982 at the Regional Museum of Art and Cultural History of Westphalia in Münster; in 1985 at the Goethe Institute in Brussels and the Municipal Gallery in Böblingen; in 1988 at the Contemporary Art Museum in Rochechouart; and in 1990 at the Franka Berndt Gallery in Paris.

BIBLIOGRAPHY:

Seuphor, Michel, *L'Art abstrait, ses origines, ses premiers maîtres*, Maeght, Paris, 1949. Hahn, Otto, *Aspects historiques du constructivisme et de l'art concret*, exhibition catalogue, Musée d'Art moderne de la Ville de Paris, Paris, 1977. Fabre, Gladys C., *Abstraction-Création 1931-1936*, exhibition catalogue, Westfälisches Landesmuseum für Kunst und Kulturgeschichte, Münster, Musée d'Art moderne de la ville de Paris, Paris, 1978. *La Collection*, catalogue, Musée national d'Art moderne, Paris, 1986. *Otto Freundlich*, exhibition catalogue, Gal. Franka Berndt, Paris, 1990. Mettay, Joël, *Le Pas perdu, à la recherche d'Otto Freundlich*, L'Aphélie, Céret, 1993. *Art in the Holocaust: A Documentary*, video, Hollywood's Attic, Burbank (CA), 1996 (30 minutes). *Otto Freundlich: Sculpture*, exhibition catalogue, Michael Werner Gallery, New York, 2001. Kuspit, Donald B., '*Otto Freundlich*' in *Artforum (USA)*, vol. 40, no. 5, Jan 2002.

MUSEUMS AND GALLERIES:

BERLIN (Berlinische Gal.) - PARIS (MNAM-CCI): *Ascension* (1929); *My Heaven is Red* (1933) - PONTOISE (Mus. Tavet-Delacour): major bequest - ST-ÉTIENNE (Mus. d'Art et d'Industrie).

AUCTION RECORDS:

LONDON, 6 Dec 1961, *Mother*, GBP 800. NEW YORK, 12 June 1968, *Abstract Composition*, CHF 12,400. PARIS, 15 Nov 1972, *Mother*, FRF 58,000. GENEVA, 1 June 1973, *Composition* (1936) CHF 29,600. PARIS, 17 March 1974, *Springtime*, FRF 18,100. HAMBURG, 6 June 1974, *Composition* (gouache) DEM 17,000. PARIS, 22 June 1981, *Personage* (Indian ink/paper, 5 3/4 x 5 1/4 ins / 14.5 x 13.5 cm) FRF 16,500. VERSAILLES, 20 March 1983, *Composition* (1942, monogrammed mosaic, 11 1/2 x 9 ins / 29 x 23 cm) FRF 17,000. PARIS, 31 May 1983, *Untitled* (1928, pastel/canvas, 16 x 13 ins / 40.5 x 33 cm) FRF 170,000. PARIS, 8 Dec 1986, *Geometric Composition* (pastel, 14 1/2 x 11 1/2 ins / 37 x 29 cm) FRF 85,000. LONDON, 6 Dec 1990, *Composition* (1932, oil on canvas, 25 1/2 x 20 ins / 65 x 50.5 cm) GBP 110,000. BERLIN, 27 Nov 1992, *Composition* (1930, oil on canvas, 45 3/4 x 34 3/4 ins / 116.5 x 88.5 cm) DEM 361,600. LONDON, 20 May 1993, *Composition* (pastel/paper, 21 x 14 3/4 ins / 53.2 x 37.5 cm) GBP 18,400. AMSTERDAM, 7 Dec 1994, *Untitled* (oil on canvas, 6 1/2 x 7 ins / 16.5 x 18 cm) NLG 16,100. PARIS, 16 Oct 1996, *Composition* (1938, enamel/mortar, 13 3/4 x 9 3/4 ins / 35 x 25 cm) FRF 19,500. AMSTERDAM, 10 Dec 1996, *Untitled* (c. 1928, oil on canvas, 6 1/2 x 7 ins / 16.5 x 18 cm) NLG 10,378. PARIS, 14 Dec 1999, *Composition* (1936, gouache, 12 x 7 ins / 30 x 18 cm) FRF 45,000. PARIS, 14 Dec 1999, *Composition* (1931, gouache, 12 x 12 ins / 30 x 30 cm) FRF 115,000. BERLIN, 24 Nov 2000, *Composition* (gouache, 13 x 10 ins / 33 x 25 cm) DEM 58,000. BERLIN, 24 Nov 2000, *Composition* (1936, oil on panel, 15 x 13 ins / 39 x 32 cm) DEM 92,000. LONDON, 27 June 2001, *Composition* (c. 1938, pastel, 24 x 19 ins / 61 x 48 cm) GBP 42,000. BERLIN, 1 Dec 2001, *Untitled* (c. 1934, gouache, 8 x 7 ins / 21 x 17 cm) DEM 75,000. COLOGNE, 4 June 2002, *Composition* (gouache, five, 5 x 4 ins / 12 x 9 cm) EUR 32,000. BERLIN, 7 June 2002, *Cosmic Eye* (1922, pastel on cardboard, 32 x 26 ins / 81 x 65 cm) EUR 52,000. LONDON, 21 Oct 2003, *Abstract Composition* (gouache on board, 19 x 14 ins / 47 x 35 cm) GBP 23,000. PARIS, 8 Dec 2003, *Red Tree* (1933, gouache, 16 x 30 ins / 40 x 75 cm) EUR 47,000. HAMBURG, 26 March 2004, *Composition in Black and White* (Indian ink, 12 x 8 ins / 30 x 21 cm) EUR 5,600. AHLDEN, 26 Nov 2004, *Mother with Child* (dark brown terracotta, h. 14 ins / 36 cm) EUR 9,200.

FREUNDT, Johann Christian
German, 19th century.
Died 5 April 1822, in Hamburg.
Painter, miniaturist. Portraits.

FRÉVILLE, Félix
French, 19th century.
Active in Paris c. 1870.
Caricaturist.

FRÉVILLE, Jacques François
French, 18th century.
Active in Paris in 1749.
Painter, sculptor.

FREW, Alexander
British, 19th century.
Died 1908.
Active in Glasgow.
Painter. Landscapes.

Alexander Frew exhibited from 1898 at London's Royal Academy.

FREY, Adam, or Fry or Frei
Swiss, 17th century.
Born in Willisau.
Glass painter.

Adam Frey was accepted as a member of the brotherhood of St Luke in Lucerne in 1641.

FREY, Adam
Polish, 19th century.
Born 1794, in Pulawy.
Painter. History painting.

Adam Frey was a student at the Akademie der Bildenden Künste in Vienna from 1815 to 1824.

FREY, Albert
Swiss, 19th - 20th century.
Born 13 July 1870, in Zurich.
Painter, lithographer. Landscapes.

Frey studied at Winterthur polytechnic and learned the basics of lithography in his father's workshop. He completed his studies at various art schools in Paris. He showed his *Alpine Chalets at St-Antonien* at the Turnus Suisse exhibition of 1902.

AUCTION RECORDS:
ZURICH, 14 May 1982, *Still-life with Flowers and Fruit* (oil/hardboard, 20 3/4 x 16 1/2 ins / 53 x 42 cm) CHF 950.

FREY, Alice
Belgian, 20th century.
Born 25 June 1895, in Antwerp; died 1981.
Painter, watercolourist. Figure compositions, mythological subjects, figures, nudes, portraits, genre scenes, circus scenes, local scenes, interiors.

Educated at the fine arts academy in Antwerp, where she studied under F. Gogo and J. de Vriendt, Alice Frey was a founder member of the Lumière (Light) and Ça ira groups. She was awarded the City of Ostend Prize in 1949.

Her earliest work was influenced by her friend, the painter James Ensor. She began as something of an Expressionist but went on to paint quasi-genre compositions (circuses, balls, beach scenes, family groups, and so on). She also painted mythological subjects in a fresh and almost naive style.

Alice Frey

MUSEUMS AND GALLERIES:
ANTWERP - BRUGES - BRUSSELS - OSTEND.

AUCTION RECORDS:
LOKEREN, 13 March 1976, *Young Woman with a Cat* (oil on canvas, 23 1/2 x 19 3/4 ins / 60 x 50 cm) BEF 90,000. LOKEREN, 5 Nov 1977, *Young Woman with a Puppy* (oil on canvas, 11 3/4 x 9 1/2 ins / 30 x 24 cm) BEF 55,000. LOKEREN, 11 March 1978, *Nymphs* (watercolour, 18 1/2 x 24 1/2 ins / 47 x 62 cm) BEF 40,000. LOKEREN, 14 Oct 1978, *Painting from the Heart* (oil on canvas, 39 1/4 x 31 1/2 ins / 100 x 80 cm) BEF 300,000. LOKEREN, 17 Oct 1981, *Young Girls* (watercolour, 14 1/4 x 20 1/2 ins / 36 x 52 cm) BEF 50,000. ANTWERP, 3 April 1984, *Rough Sea* (oil on canvas, 24 1/2 x 28 3/4 ins / 62 x 73 cm) BEF 75,000. LOKEREN, 21 Feb 1987, *Picking Flowers* (1940, oil on canvas, 22 x 26 ins / 55 x 66 cm) BEF 130,000. LOKEREN, 28 May 1988, *Homage to Botticelli's 'Birth of Venus'* (1938, oil on canvas, 31 1/2 x 39 1/4 ins / 80 x 100 cm) BEF 140,000. LOKEREN, 23 May 1992, *Dancers* (oil on canvas, 19 3/4 x 24 ins / 50 x 61 cm) BEF 44,000. LOKEREN, 15 May 1993, *Self-portrait* (1937, oil on canvas, 18 x 15 1/4 ins / 45.5 x 38.5 cm) BEF 36,000. LOKEREN, 9 Oct 1993, *Cheerful Extravagance* (1956, oil on canvas, 26 x 21 1/4 ins / 66 x 54 cm) BEF 190,000. LOKEREN, 4 Dec 1993, *Seated Nude* (oil on canvas, 17 3/4 x 15 ins / 45 x 38 cm) BEF 44,000; *Garden of Love* (oil on canvas, 39 1/4 x 78 3/4 ins / 100 x 200 cm) BEF 120,000. LOKEREN, 12 March 1994, *Young Girl in a White Frock* (oil on canvas, 18 x 15 ins / 46 x 38 cm) BEF 44,000. LOKEREN, 11 March 1995, *Child Playing in a Park* (oil on canvas, 19 3/4 x 24 ins / 50 x 61 cm) BEF 85,000. LOKEREN, 13 May 2000, *The Acrobats* (oil on canvas, 24 x 20 ins / 60 x 50 cm) BEF 95,000. LOKEREN, 9 Dec 2000, *Venus with Flowers* (oil on canvas, 59 x 31 ins / 150 x 78 cm) BEF 170,000. BRUSSELS, 10 Oct 2001, *Tea-time for Geishas* (oil on canvas, 51 x 59 ins / 130 x 150 cm) BEF 200,000. VLAAMSE KAAI, 23 Oct 2001, *Funanbule* (1963, oil on canvas, 31 x 28 ins / 80 x 70 cm) BEF 70,000. LOKEREN, 11 May 2002, *Couple of Dancing Clowns* (1930, oil on canvas, 47 x 28 ins / 120 x 70 cm) EUR 9,500. ANTWERP, 23 Sept 2002, *Gypsies on the Beach* (oil on canvas, 15 x 19 ins / 38 x 47 cm) EUR 1,600. LOKEREN, 11 Oct 2003, *At the Opera* (1935, oil on canvas, 28 x 25 ins / 70 x 63 cm) EUR 2,800. BRUSSELS, 1 Dec 2003, *Children and Dog on the Beach* (oil on canvas, 24 x 29 ins / 62 x 73 cm) EUR 4,000.

FREY, Anton Melchior
Austrian, 18th century.
Born 1732, in Vienna; died 1764, in Ludwigsburg.
Painter (porcelain).

FREY, Christian
German, 18th century.
Born in Augsburg.
Painter.

Christian Frey settled in Vienna possibly around 1720 and worked for porcelain manufacturers among others.

FREY, Eduard
Swiss, 19th century.
Born 27 August 1821, in Como; died 28 June 1873, in Munich.
Landscape artist.

Eduard Frey settled in Munich and concentrated on landscapes. He travelled in Italy and exhibited views of Verona and Venice, at the Turnus in Venice and in Basel.

FREY, Erwin F.
American, 20th century.
Born 21 April 1892, in Lima (Ohio); died 1967.
Sculptor.

Erwin F. Frey was a pupil of Landowsky in Paris and a member of the National Sculpture Society.

FREY, Eugène H.
Belgian, 19th - 20th century.
Born 16 October 1864, in Brussels; died 1930.

Painter. Landscapes, waterscapes, boats, flowers. Stage sets.

Having abandoned science studies to pursue an artistic career, Eugène Frey exhibited at the Salon de la Société Nationale d'Horticulture. He is remembered for his experimental lighting sets for the Paris Opera, where he projected a painting on glass against a back canvas. He started painting landscapes in about 1918.

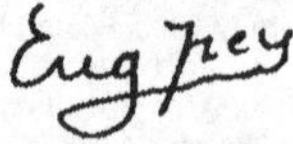

AUCTION RECORDS:

BARBIZON, 22 April 1979, *Houseboats on the River* (1894, oil on canvas, 26 1/2 x 35 3/4 ins / 67 x 91 cm) FRF 1,500. GRENOBLE, 18 Feb 1980, *Thatched Roofs* (oil on canvas, 13 x 16 1/4 ins / 33 x 41 cm) FRF 1,800; *By the River* (oil on canvas, 15 x 19 3/4 ins / 38 x 50 cm) FRF 2,700. GRENOBLE, 13 Oct 1980, *Thatched Cottage* (oil on canvas, 13 x 15 3/4 ins / 33 x 40 cm) FRF 2,500. BRUSSELS, 7 Oct 1991, *Landscape* (oil on canvas, 19 3/4 x 25 1/2 ins / 50 x 65 cm) BEF 30,000.

FREY, Franz Bernhard
German, 18th century.
Born 1716, in Guebwiller, France; died 1806, in Guebwiller, France.
Portrait artist.

MUSEUMS AND GALLERIES:

STRASBOURG: *Portrait of Andreas Silbermann; Portrait of Anna-Salomea Silbermann.*

FREY, Frederike
Swiss, 19th century.
Active in Fribourg in Breisgau at the end of the 19th century.
Painter. Still-lifes.

FREY, Hans Heinrich
Swiss, 17th century.
Born in Hochdorf.
Active in Lucerne from 1650 to 1680.
Engraver (wood).

FREY, Hans Konrad
Swiss, 20th century.
Born 14 August 1877, in Ward.
Sculptor.

Hans Frey studied at the Berlin academy, then travelled extensively before settling in Zurich.

FREY, Heinrich Johann or Hans
Swiss, 18th century.
Active in Lucerne at the end of the 18th century.
Sculptor (wood/stone).

FREY, Hugo
Swiss, 20th century.
Born 30 December 1878, in Zurich.
Painter.

Studied in Stuttgart, Paris and England.

FREY, Ignatz
German, 18th century.
Born 1727, in Iglau (now Jihlava, Czech Republic); died 1790, in Brno.
Engraver, painter.

Ignatz Frey seems to have worked in Prague.

FREY, Ignatz Alois
German, 18th - 19th century.
Born 1752, in Eichstätt; died 1835.
Painter.

This artist worked in Freising and in Munich and executed paintings for the cathedral of the capital city among others.

FREY, Jakob, the Younger
Swiss, 18th century.
Born 25 January 1757, in Rome; died c. 1806, in Paris.
Engraver.

This artist was the son of Philipp and the grandson of Jakob the Elder.

FREY, Jakob, Jacobus, Johann, the Elder
Swiss, 18th century.
Born 17 February 1681, in Hochdorf; died 11 January 1752, in Rome.
Draughtsman, engraver.

Jakob Frey was the son of the wood carver Hans Heinrich Frey. He left for Rome in 1702, where he received tuition from Arnold Van Westerhout and Carlo Maratti and it was in this field that he attained the height of his talent and of his reputation. In 1726, Frey returned to Switzerland but quickly returned to Rome where he then remained. His many works include a *Portrait of the Marquis of Châtelet* in pastel.

FREY, Johann Daniel
German, 18th century.
Active in Frankfurt am Main at the end of the 18th century.
Draughtsman, engraver.

Johann Frey's output includes an engraving portraying the coronation of the emperor Francis.

FREY, Johann Evangelist
German, 19th century.
Born 17 October 1840, in Hundham; died 8 March 1909, in Munich.
Sculptor.

Johann Frey worked mainly in Munich.

FREY, Johann Jakob
Swiss, 19th century.
Born 27 January 1813, in Basel; died 30 September 1865, in Frascati.
Painter. Landscapes with figures, landscapes.

Johann Jakob Frey was the son and pupil of Samuel Frey. He continued his studies under H. Hess in Basel, then in Paris, Munich, Rome and Naples. After visiting Sicily and Spain Frey joined an Egyptian archaeological expedition led by R. Lepsius then settled permanently in Rome where he married and had two daughters. Frey enjoyed the patronage of persons of note such as King Louis I of Bavaria and the king of Prussia for whom he painted landscapes of Italy can now be found in Potsdam.

MUSEUMS AND GALLERIES:

BASEL: *Italian Landscape; Caudine Forks; Caravan surprised by the Simoon; Landscape near Monreale, Sicily; View of the Outskirts of Rome; Landscape near Granada; Landscape in the Mountains of Rome* (unfinished) - GDANSK: *Sicilian landscape; Sunset in Rome; Pyramids near Giza* - LEIPZIG: *Columns of Memnon near Thebes; Sphinx near Memphis during the Simoon* - MUNICH (Neue Pinakothek): *Columns of Memnon near Thebes; Storm in the Desert* - POTSDAM: *Italian Landscape* (several).

AUCTION RECORDS:

ZURICH, 12 Nov 1976, *Water Carriers* (1846, oil on canvas, 24 3/4 x 17 3/4 ins / 63 x 45 cm) CHF 3,000. BERN, 21 Oct 1977, *Sicilian Landscape* (1862, oil on canvas, 41 x 50 ins / 104 x 127 cm) CHF 6,000. COLOGNE, 21 May 1981, *Roman Forum* (1859, oil on canvas, 23 1/4 x 31 1/2 ins / 59 x 80 cm) DEM 23,000. LUCERNE, 8 Nov 1984, *Sandstorm in the Desert* (1845, oil on canvas, 39 1/4 x 54 ins / 100 x 137 cm) CHF 13,000. ZURICH, 5 June 1986, *View of Capri* (oil on canvas, 29 1/4 x 39 ins / 74.5 x 99 cm) CHF 20,000. ROME, 25 May 1988, *View of a Village* (oil on canvas, 18 1/2 x 26 1/2 ins / 47 x 67 cm) ITL 4,000,000. LONDON, 19 June 1991, *Mountainous Landscape with Ruins and Figures; Wooded Landscape with Figures* (1859, oil on canvas, a pair, each 38 x 53 ins / 96.5 x 134.5 cm) GBP 26,400. NEW YORK, 17 Oct 1991, *On the Banks of the Nile* (1856, oil on canvas, 25 x 32 1/2 ins / 63.5 x 82.6 cm) USD 24,200. LONDON, 17 Nov 1993, *Ruins of Philae in Egypt* (oil on canvas, 29 1/2 x 44 ins / 75 x 112 cm) GBP 10,350. ROME, 29-30 Nov 1993, *View of Castel dell'Ovo with the Hill of Piazza Falcone* (1861, oil on canvas, 9 3/4 x 14 1/2 ins / 25 x 37 cm) ITL 18,856,000. ROME, 5 Dec 1995, *Ariccia Landscape* (1852, oil on card, 11 x 16 1/2 ins / 28 x 42 cm) ITL 2,828,000. LONDON, 13 March 1996, *Figures in an Andalousian Landscape* (oil on canvas, 39 x 54 ins / 99 x 137 cm) GBP 15,525. LONDON, 26 March 1997, *View of Granada* (1859, oil on canvas, 38 1/4 x 53 1/4 ins / 97 x 135 cm) GBP 16,675. BERN, 17 May 1999, *Campagna Landscape* (oil on canvas, 24 x 36 ins / 61 x 92 cm) CHF 17,500. ROME, 25 May 1999, *Sunset over the Colosseum* (1846, oil on canvas, 20 x 25 ins / 50 x 64 cm) ITL 10,000,000. MUNICH, 22 March 2000, *Bay of Naples* (1841, oil on canvas, 14 x 21 ins / 35 x 54 cm) DEM 18,500. HAMBURG, 6 Sept 2000, *Extensive Landscape* (oil on canvas, 11 x 16 ins / 29 x 40 cm) DEM 14,000. SWITZERLAND, 30 Nov 2001, *Arcadian Landscape* (1859, oil on canvas, 17 x 25 ins / 44 x 63 cm) CHF 5,800. ZURICH, 3 Oct 2002, *Southern Landscape with Goatherder* (1854, oil on canvas, 13 x 17 ins / 33 x 44 cm) CHF 9,500. HEIDELBERG, 11 Oct 2002, *Italian Landscape with Cattle by Stream* (oil on paper/canvas, 17 x 23 ins / 44 x 58 cm) EUR 2,800. LONDON, 18 June 2003, *Ruins at Philae, Egypt* (oil on canvas, 30 x 44 ins / 76 x 113 cm) GBP 9,500. LONDON, 3 Dec 2003, *Mountainous Landscape* (1859, oil on canvas, 40 x 54 ins / 101 x 138 cm) GBP 11,000. MUNICH, 17 March 2004, *Bay of Naples* (1842, oil on canvas, 17 x 24 ins / 42 x 60 cm) EUR 15,000. ZURICH, 14 June 2004, *Shepherd with Flock Resting by Stream* (oil on canvas, 24 x 29 ins / 62 x 73 cm) CHF 9,500.

FREY, Johann Michael
German, 18th - 19th century.
Born 30 April 1750, in Biberach; died 1813, in Augsburg.
Painter, engraver. Landscapes, battles, animals.

Johann Frey worked in Augsburg between 1768 and 1789. He made engravings in the style of Bega.

FREY, Johann Wilhelm
Austrian, 19th century.
Born 24 December 1830, in Rastatt.
Painter, watercolourist. Landscapes.

Johann Frey lived in Vienna, after studying in Amsterdam.

AUCTION RECORDS:

NEW YORK, 16 Feb 1993, *View of Vienna* (watercolour and ink with traces of pencil/paper) USD 1,100. VIENNA, 2 Dec 1999, *Old Town Theatre* (watercolour, 11 x 8 ins / 28 x 21 cm) ATS 28,000. VIENNA, 20 March 2001, *River Landscape in Vienna* (1880, pen/ink/watercolour, 13 x 19 ins / 34 x 48 cm) ATS 40,000.

FREY, Johann Zacharias
Polish, 18th - 19th century.
Born 3 June 1769, in Vienna; died August 1829, in Warsaw.
Painter, watercolourist, engraver.

Johann Frey studied at the Akademie der Bildenden Künste in Vienna, and then went to London, where he worked with the painter West. In 1804, he went to Poland and worked at the court of Duke Czartoryski, before settling in Warsaw, where he taught engraving and painting.

FREY, Johannes
German, 18th century.
Active in Braunsberg.
Sculptor (wood).

Johannes Frey worked for St Mary's church in Braunsberg; the museum there holds some of his works.

FREY, Konrad
Swiss, 17th century.
Active in Winterthur in 1654.
Sculptor.

FREY, Marguerite, wife of Surbeck
Swiss, 20th century.
Born 23 February 1886, in Delsberg.
Painter.

Frey was a pupil of Paul Klee. She exhibited in Switzerland, the USA and Paris (notably at the Salon d'Automne and the Salon des Indépendants).

AUCTION RECORDS:

PARIS, 2 Dec 1976, *Woman Reading in a Garden* (oil on panel, 25 3/4 x 22 ins / 65.5 x 55 cm) CHF 2,000. BERN, 6 May 1981, *Tunisian Landscape* (oil on canvas, 31 1/2 x 45 1/4 ins / 80 x 115 cm) CHF 5,300. BERN, 17 Nov 1983, *Spring Landscape* (oil on canvas, 24 x 15 ins / 61 x 38 cm) CHF 1,500. BERN, 11 May 1984, *Window with Flowers* (oil on canvas, 19 3/4 x 24 ins / 50 x 61 cm) CHF 2,800.

FREY, Martin
Austrian, 18th - 19th century.
Born 11 November 1769, in Wurzach; died 7 April 1831, in Vienna.
Painter, engraver.

Martin Frey was a pupil of John Gottfried Muller. He worked in Vienna.

FREY, Max
German, 19th - 20th century.
Born 16 April 1874, in Karlsruhe.
Painter, decorative designer. Stage sets.

Worked as a stage set designer in Mannheim and Berlin.

FREY, Melchior
Swiss, 17th century.
Sculptor (wood).

Melchior Frey lived in Bade, Eschenbach and Hochdorf and sculpted, among other works, figures of angels for the altars of Hochdorf, Rotenburg and others.

FREY, Michael
18th century.
Active in Rome in 1743.
Engraver (burin).

FREY, Nikolaus
German, 15th century.
Active in Nuremberg (Bavaria) in 1407.
Painter.

FREY, Philipp
Swiss, 18th century.
Born 25 March 1729, in Lucerne; died 15 October 1793, in Rome.
Engraver.

Philipp Frey helped his father in his engraving studio, touching up his plates and doing some himself, among which is *Sacrifice de Myriel*

FREY, Samuel
Swiss, 19th century.
Born 1785, in Sissach; died 1836, in Basel.
Painter, watercolourist, draughtsman, engraver, lithographer. Landscapes, animals.

Samuel Frey studied in Basel and Constance under J. J. Biedermann and Gabriel Lory the Elder. After travelling in the Netherlands and Paris, he settled in Basel and worked as a design teacher at the art school founded by the state-approved association where he remained for five years. Among his coloured engravings and lithographies, Brun

cites: *Entry of the Grand Duke John into the Fortress of Huningue (Hüningen)* (1815), a *View of Bonfontaine* and a series of animal drawings in the style of Ridinger. He produced a large number of landscapes and watercolours.
Auction records:
London, 27 Feb 1979, *The Chamonix Valley* (c. 1810, coloured etching, 16 x 24 ins / 40.5 x 61 cm) GBP 1,500. Bern, 24 June 1983, *View of the town of Soleure on the River Aar* (c. 1810, coloured etching, 9 1/4 x 14 1/4 ins / 23.8 x 36.2 cm) CHF 1,900.

FREY, Sebastian
Swiss, 17th century.
Sculptor (wood).

FREY, Stephan Joseph
German, 18th century.
Active in Frankfurt am Main in 1744.
Painter.

FREY, Wilhelm Frederick
German, 19th - 20th century.
Born 24 June 1826, in Karlsruhe; died 4 February 1911, in Mannheim.
Painter. Landscapes, seascapes, animals.
Frey was a pupil of Koopmann and studied under Heinlein in Munich. He exhibited his landscapes and seascapes regularly in Munich and Berlin. He was later appointed curator of Mannheim Museum.
Auction records:
Munich, 13 March 1974, *Landscape with Flock*, DEM 10,000. Bern, 25 Nov 1976, *Summer Landscape* (1898, oil on canvas, 12 1/4 x 20 1/2 ins / 31 x 52 cm) CHF 1,200. San Francisco, 3 Oct 1981, *At the Trough* (oil on canvas, 16 1/4 x 23 ins / 41 x 58.5 cm) USD 1,500. Heidelberg, 15-16 Oct 1993, *Young Peasant with a Black Cow* (1868, oil on canvas, 14 1/4 x 18 1/2 ins / 36.5 x 47 cm) DEM 3,400. London, 22 Feb 1995, *Horses Grazing in a Meadow* (1887, oil on canvas, 16 1/4 x 22 1/2 ins / 41 x 57 cm) GBP 1,265.

FREY, or FREIJ, Anna de, or Alida de, Aletta de
Dutch, 18th century.
Born in Amsterdam; died 1808, in Mannheim.
Painter, draughtswoman.
She was the sister of Johannes de Frey and a pupil of her brother-in-law Johannes Jacobus Lauwers. She produced mainly copies of the old masters.
Auction records:
London, 30 Jan 1909, *Portrait of a Woman* (pastel) GBP 7.

FREY, or FREIJ, Johannes Pieter de
Dutch, 18th - 19th century.
Born 1 February 1770, in Amsterdam; died 1834, in Paris.
Engraver.
He was a pupil of his brother-in-law Jacobus Johannes Lauwers. After losing the use of his right hand in an accident, he learned to engrave with his left, and produced accomplished prints after Rembrandt, Gerrit Dou and Finck. He was resident in Paris from 1806.

Stamp of sale

Auction records:
Paris, 1880, *Two Views of Royal Castles from the Time of Louis XIV*, FRF 830. Paris, 1892, *Portrait, thought to be the Marquise du Châtelet* (pastel) FRF 580.

FREY-SURBECK, Marguerite. See **FREY Marguerite**

FREYBECHKE, Johann
German, 15th century.
Miniaturist.
Freybechke was a monk at the convent of Königsbrück (Alsace), and was active in around 1428.

FREYBERG, Conrad
German, 19th century.
Born 14 March 1842, in Stettin (now Szczecin, Poland); died 1915, in Stettin.
Painter, sculptor. Historical subjects, battles, figures, genre scenes, animals.
Freyberg studied in Steffeck. He was appointed to the position of teacher at the Berlin court from 1866.
Museums and Galleries:
Gravelotte (Mus. départemental de la Guerre de 1870): *Battle of the 5th Corps of Armed in Wissenburg, the 4th August 1870* (1880, oil on canvas).
Auction records:
New York, 28 Oct 1982, *Surrender at Metz* (1876, oil on canvas, 48 1/2 x 104 1/2 ins / 123 x 265.5 cm) USD 18,500. New York, 15 Feb 1985, *Surrender at Metz* (1876, oil on canvas, 48 1/2 x 104 1/2 ins / 123 x 265.5 cm) USD 12,000. New York, 1 March 1990, *Little Girl with a Basket of Flowers* (1884, oil on canvas, 41 1/4 x 31 1/2 ins / 104.8 x 80 cm) USD 12,100. New York, 3 June 1994, *Old Games* (1861, oil on canvas, 17 x 23 ins / 43.2 x 58.4 cm) USD 7,475. Amsterdam, 24 March 1999, *Equestrian Portrait of Friedrich Franz III* (1885, oil on canvas, 27 x 35 ins / 68 x 88 cm) NLG 26,000. Erlangen, 27 Nov 1999, *Battle Scene with Cavalry in Extensive Landscape* (1872, oil on canvas, 25 x 41 ins / 63 x 103 cm) DEM 6,000. Bremen, 1 April 2000, *Prinz Friedrich Karl in der Schlacht von Vionville* (1872, oil on canvas, 25 x 40 ins / 63 x 102 cm) DEM 13,000. New York, 4 Sept 2002, *Ubergabe von Metz* (1876, oil on canvas, 48 x 104 ins / 123 x 265 cm) USD 20,000. Amsterdam, 10 Dec 2003, *Elegant Ladies on Horseback* (1871, oil on canvas, 50 x 42 ins / 126 x 107 cm) EUR 10,000.

FREYBERG, Maria Electrina von
Maiden name: Stuntz
German, 19th century.
Born 14 March 1797, in Strasbourg; died 1 January 1847, in Munich.
Painter. History painting, genre scenes.
Maria Freyberg worked in France, Italy and Munich. She was a pupil of her father and of the painter and lithographer Johann Baptiste Stuntz. She travelled in France and Italy. In 1821-1822 she was in Rome where she became a member of the Acccademia di San Luca. She settled in Munich in 1822.

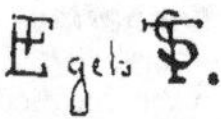

Museums and Galleries:
Munich: *Madonna and Child; Baptism of Saint John; Portrait Study; Boy Playing the Flute.*

FREYBERG-EISENBERG, Charlotte
German, 19th century.
Active in Karlsruhe.
Painter. Landscapes.
Charlotte Freyberg-Eisenberg exhibited in Berlin, Dresden, Düsseldorf and Munich.

FREYBERGER, Johann
German, 16th - 17th century.

Born 1571, in Wolfsberg (Carinthia, Austria); died 1631, in Augsburg (Bavaria).
Painter.
There are some paintings by this artist in the town hall in Augsburg.

Joan Freyb.

FREYBURG, Karl Bogislaw
German, 19th century.
Born in Stralsund.
Painter.
This artist settled in Rome around 1822.

FREYDENFUSS, Wolfgang
Austrian, 16th century.
Active in Salzburg c. 1500.
Painter.

FREYDER, G.
French, 17th century.
Active in Strasbourg.
Painter.
There is an engraving by P. Aubry after G. Freyder.

FREYE, Georg Hermann
German, 19th century.
Born 14 October 1844, in Dresden.
Painter. History painting.
Freye studied at the Dresden academy and with the painter F. Gonne. He exhibited works in Dresden from 1866.

FREYENFELD, Ignaz Maximilian von
Austrian, 18th century.
Born c. 1762, in Vienna.
Painter.
Freyenfeld studied at the academy in Vienna.

FREYER, Achim
German, 20th century.
Born 1934, in Berlin.
Painter, director, scenographer. Stage costumes and sets.
Freyer studied at the fine arts academy in Berlin between 1954 and 1956 and taught at the Karlsruhe College of Arts from 1976. He had a solo exhibition at the Berlin fine arts academy in 1994. He is particularly noted for his stage sets, not least his designs for the transposition of Bach's *Mass in B Minor* into operatic form for performance by the Los Angeles Opera.

BIBLIOGRAPHY:
Achim Freyer Taggespinste Nachtgesichte, exhibition catalogue, Académie des Beaux-Arts, Berlin, 1994.

FREYHART, Matthys
German, 16th century.
Active in Nordlingen (Bavaria) at the beginning of the 16th century.
Painter, glass painter.

FREYHAUSER
German, 18th century.
Active in Mahr-Schönberg.
Painter.
Freyhauser is known to have worked for various churches.

FREYHOFF, Eduard
German, 19th century.
Born c. 1810, in Potsdam; died c. 1843.
Painter.
Freyhoff exhibited views of Potsdam in Berlin between 1832 and 1842.

FREYHOLD, Karl von
Swiss, 20th century.
Born 8 July 1878, in Freiburg im Breisgau.
Painter, illustrator.
Freyhold studied at the academy in Karlsruhe, later moving to France and then to England.

FREYMANN, Ivan Petrovich
Russian, 19th century.
Active in St Petersburg.
Painter.
Freymann studied at the St Petersburg academy of fine arts and won an award in 1870.

FREYMANN, Joseph Anton
German, 19th century.
Born 1810, in Weil der Stadt.
Painter, draughtsman.
Freymann lived in Munich, where he established a reputation as a lithographer.

FREYMUTH, Alfons, or Freijmuth
Dutch, 20th century.
Born 1940.
Painter (gouache), watercolourist, pastellist. Scenes with figures, figures, nudes, portraits, interiors with figures.

AUCTION RECORDS:
AMSTERDAM, 16 June 1980, *Portrait of the Painter Hubert van Hille* (1973, oil on canvas, 31 1/2 x 39 1/4 ins / 80 x 100 cm) NLG 4,500. AMSTERDAM, 24 Oct 1983, *Mariska* (1976-1978, acrylic/canvas, 79 1/2 x 59 3/4 ins / 202 x 152 cm) NLG 8,600. AMSTERDAM, 8 Dec 1987, *Reclining Nude* (1972, calyl./canvas, 55 x 69 1/4 ins / 140 x 176 cm) NLG 4,000. AMSTERDAM, 9 Dec 1988, *Three People-Shaped Clouds* (1987, oil on canvas, 22 3/4 x 26 1/2 ins / 58 x 67.5 cm) NLG 2,990. AMSTERDAM, 22 May 1990, *Woman Carrying a Little Black Dog* (1974, acrylic/canvas, 15 3/4 x 43 1/4 ins / 40 x 110 cm) NLG 5,720. AMSTERDAM, 11 Dec 1991, *Young Girl* (1976, pastel/paper, 18 x 16 1/2 ins / 45.5 x 42 cm) NLG 1,840. AMSTERDAM, 21 May 1992, *Wedding* (1979, acrylic/canvas, 47 1/4 x 47 1/4 ins / 120 x 120 cm) NLG 5,750. AMSTERDAM, 27-28 May 1993, *Still-life with P.M. II* (1979, coloured chalks/paper, 25 1/2 x 21 ins / 64.5 x 52.5 cm) USD 1,725. AMSTERDAM, 31 May 1994, *Three Figures* (1985, gouache and watercolour/paper, 22 x 29 1/4 ins / 56 x 74 cm) NLG 1,495. AMSTERDAM, 5 June 1996, *Three Figures* (oil on canvas, 55 x 31 1/2 ins / 140 x 80 cm) NLG 6,900. AMSTERDAM, 2-3 June 1997, *Young Girl before a Mirror* (1974, oil on canvas, 47 1/4 x 31 1/2 ins / 120 x 80 cm) NLG 6,136. AMSTERDAM, 1 Dec 1999, *Kriskras* (1986, bronze, h. 14 ins / 35 cm) NLG 6,000. LOKEREN, 7 Oct 2000, *Portrait* (1972-1974, acrylic on canvas, 55 x 71 ins / 140 x 180 cm) BEF 110,000. AMSTERDAM, 3 Dec 2002, *Red Table* (1967, acrylic, 45 x 37 ins / 115 x 95 cm) EUR 4,000. AMSTERDAM, 9 June 2004, *Untitled* (1971, acrylic on canvas, 55 x 47 ins / 140 x 120 cm) EUR 2,000. AMSTERDAM, 30 Nov 2004, *Still-life with Flowers in a Vase* (1973-1977, oil on canvas, 24 x 31 ins / 60 x 80 cm) EUR 2,000.

FREYSE, Albert
German, 17th century.
Born 17th century, in Behringen (Thuringia).
Painter, draughtsman.
Freyse's known works consist mainly of portraits, some of which are engraved.

FREYSE, Johann Friedrich, the Elder
German, 18th century.
Born 18 April 1753, in Hamburg; died 18 November 1808, in Hamburg.
Painter. Portraits.
Among Freyse's works are oil paintings and miniatures.

FREYSE, Johann Friedrich, the Younger
German, 19th century.
Born 23 April 1788.

Painter, lithographer.
Freyse was the son of Johann Friedrich the Elder.

FREYSINGER, F. J.
German, 18th century.
Active in Hall at the beginning of the 18th century.
Sculptor.

FREYSINGER, Johann
German, 18th century.
Born at the beginning of the 18th century, in Albertshausen (Bavaria).
Miniaturist.
Johann Freysinger worked mainly in Vienna around 1730.

FREYSS, Simone
French, 20th century.
Born in Strasbourg.
Sculptor.
Simone Freyss exhibited in Paris at the Salon des Artistes Français.

FREYSTEIN, Johanna Mariane
German, 18th century.
Born 1 May 1760, in Leipzig; died 21 June 1807, in Leipzig.
Painter.
The Museum in Oslo has a *German Landscape* by Freystein.

FREYTAG, Albert
German, 19th century.
Born 12 January 1851, in Nuremberg.
Painter.
Albert Freytag taught at the school of industrial arts in Zurich from 1882. He studied in his home town and exhibited his works in Switzerland. Among his works is an *Amphitrite*, which he sent to Zurich in 1883.

FREYTAG, Heinrich
German, 20th century.
Born 13 June 1876, in Duisburg.
Painter, engraver.
Freytag studied at the fine arts academy in Karlsruhe and subsequently settled there.

FREYTAG, Johann
German, 18th century.
Active in Rheinfelden in 1721.
Sculptor.

FREYTAG, Johann Heinrich
Swiss, 18th century.
Born 1702, in Hombrechtikon; died 3 May 1781, in Zurich.
Engraver, illustrator. Landscapes, topographical views.
Freytag is recorded for a few landscapes and almanac illustrations.

FREYTAG, Johann Konrad, the Elder, or Freitag
Swiss, 18th - 19th century.
Born 19 November 1770, in Riesbach near Zurich; died 2 May 1837, in Riesbach near Zurich.
Painter, engraver. Landscapes.
According to Nagler, Freytag was still working in 1822. Some Swiss landscapes by Freytag were engraved by Stegi and Billwiller in aquatint. The museum in Soleure has several of his works in its collection.

FREYTAG, Johann Konrad, the Younger, or Freitag
Swiss, 19th century.
Born 15 June 1802, in Riesbach near Zurich; died 20 December 1834, in Riesbach near Zurich.
Painter, watercolourist, engraver. Genre scenes, landscapes.
The son of Johann Konrad the Elder, he specialised, like his father, in landscape painting.
AUCTION RECORDS:
NEW YORK, 30 Sept 1982, *Seaweed Collectors* (oil on canvas, 24 x 36 ins / 61 x 91.2 cm) USD 850.

FREYTAG, Mathilde
German, 19th century.
Active in Munich.
Painter. Landscapes.
Mathilde Freytag exhibited in Munich, Dresden and Magdeburg from 1880.

FREYTAG, Otto
German, 20th century.
Born 1888, in Duisburg; died 1980, in Berlin.
Painter. Figures, scenes with figures.
Otto Freytag studied in Düsseldorf, Munich, Paris and Berlin (under Lovis Corinth). His style is often recognised by his use of sweeping colours outlined in black.

An exhibition commemorating the centenary of his birth was held in Berlin in 1988.
BIBLIOGRAPHY:
Corazolla, Paul/Herrmann, Sabine, *Otto Freytag: Leben und Werk*, exhibition catalogue, Kunstamt Tiergarten, Berlin, 1988.
AUCTION RECORDS:
HAMBURG, 7 June 1985, *Festival at Vorpommern* (1921, watercolour and pencil, 17 3/4 x 23 1/2 ins / 45.1 x 59.8 cm) DEM 4,000.

FREYTAG, Richard
German, 19th century.
Born 16 February 1820, in Gotha; died 22 May 1894, in Gotha.
Painter.
Richard Freytag studied in Düsseldorf, Munich, Anvers and Paris. He spent a long time in Italy before returning to his native town where he devoted himself mainly to landscape painting. His works also include portraits.
MUSEUMS AND GALLERIES:
GOTHA.

FREYTAG, Viktor
German, 19th - 20th century.
Born 18 November 1870, in Berlin.
Painter. Portraits.
Freytag studied in Paris and Karlsruhe, and exhibited from 1906, chiefly in Munich and Berlin.

FREYTAG-LORINGHOVEN, Elsa von
(Baroness)
German, 19th - 20th century.
Born 1874, in Swinemünde (now Swinoujscie, Poland); died 14 December 1927, in Paris.
From 1910 active in the USA.
Sculptor of assemblages, poet.
Dadaism.
Baroness Elsa von Freytag-Loringhoven returned to Berlin in 1923, having spent the years from 1910 in New York, where she cut an improbable Bohemian-cum-Dadaist figure instantly recognisable in Greenwich Village by her outrageous clothes and her equally outrageous escapades and tantrums. She was a model for various painters, including Marcel Duchamp, and was one of those female Dadists that art historians appear to have forgotten, despite the fact that she featured at *Making Mischief: Dada Invades New York*, an exhibition at the Whitney Museum of American Art in New York in 1996. In 2001, Francis Naumann Fine Art mounted the first ever exhibition devoted to her and her work.

In 1918, Freytag-Loringhofen used a brush, pebbles, some metal objects and other detritus to produce a 'portrait' of the photographer Berenice Abbott; in 1920 she produced a portrait of Marcel Duchamp using feathers, metal utensils and a stemmed glass; and it is now generally agreed that she was responsible for the celebrated 'ready-made' sculpture *God* of 1918, a sculpture made from metal tubing twisted into a knot and mounted on a wooden chopping-block. In some quarters, she is also credited with having anticipated 'junk sculpture'.

Bibliography:
Hjartarson, Paul/Spettigue, Douglas O., *Baroness Elsa: The Autobiography of the Baroness Elsa von Freytag-Loringhoven*, Oberon Press, Ottawa, 1992. Sawelson-Gorse, Naomi (ed.), *Women in Dada. Essays on sex, gender and Identity*, MIT Press, Cambridge (MA), 1998.

Museums and Galleries:
New York (MoMA) - Philadelphia (MA): *God* (1918, wood and metal assembly, attributed).

FREYTAG-LORINGHOVEN, Mathilde von

Danish, 19th century.
Born 30 October 1860, in Copenhagen.
Painter, engraver. Landscapes.

Mathilde von Freytag-Loringhoven studied in Danzig (now Gdansk) and Weimar. She exhibited regularly in Berlin from 1887.

FREYTAS, Francisco Pereira

Spanish, 19th century.
Active c. 1843.
Painter. Landscapes.

FRÉZALS, Maurice

French, 20th century.
Born in Figeac.
Painter. Landscapes.

Maurice Frézals exhibited in Paris at the Salon des Indépendants from 1939.

FREZANO, Claire

American, 20th century.
Active in New York.
Sculptor. Religious subjects.

Claire Frezano specialised in traditional religious sculpture.

FREZEL

French, 19th century.
Born in the 19th century.
Engraver. Historical portraits.

Museums and Galleries:
Rouen: *Portrait of Louis XVIII* (copied from a painting by Gros).

FREZIER, Amédée François

French, 18th century.
Born 1682, in Chambéry; died 1773, in Brittany.
Architect, painter.

Amédée Frezier decorated the church of St Louis in Brest.

FREZIN, Julia

Belgian, 19th - 20th century.
Born 1870, in Lessines (Hainaut); died 1950.
Painter, sculptor.

Frezin was a pupil of Portaels at the fine arts academy in Brussels.

FRÉZIN, Roger

French, 20th century.
Born 5 June 1927, in Lille.
Painter, sculptor, draughtsman. Frescoes.
Phases group.

Roger Frézin's father and grandfather were engravers. He studied at the École des Beaux-Arts in Lille. In 1958 he founded the *Atelier de la Monnaie*, an exhibition and events centre which became known as the *Atelier* in 1992. He taught at the École des Beaux-Arts in Lille from 1972 to 1989.

Until 1965, Frézin took a rich, free abstract approach based on collage and allowed himself allusions to reality. Between 1965 and 1970 he abandoned collage in favour of a stricter approach using oils, charcoal, pastels and ink to depict impressive, complex machines. While continuing to paint in oils he increasingly used purely graphic techniques in drawings of unusual dimension, often more than two metres across. His drawings appear to be divided into two categories: the first consists of disparate elements difficult to identify, from which parts of a human body sometimes emerge; the second consists of an accumulation of small details, like small spare parts intended to repair creatures that are somewhere between man and machine. He also produced monumental works, including frescoes, notably for the Fâches-Thusmesnil Conservatoire and Lille Town Hall (1990).

In addition to the works he showed in his Atelier, Frézin also exhibited at numerous group exhibitions, including: from 1963 to 1965 at the Salon des Réalités Nouvelles in Paris; from 1967 to 1975 he took part in the activities of E. Jaguer's Phases group; in 1968 at the Melbourne museum; in 1970 in Lille; in 1972 at the Honfleur Festival; in 1980 at the Salon de Mai; in 1988 at the *30ème Anniversaire de l'Atelier de la Monnaie* (*30th Anniversary of the Atelier de la Monnaie*) at the Hospice Comtess, Lille; in 1990 and 1992 at the Salon Comparaisons; in 1997 at the *Les Vaches de...* exhibition at the Musée de Bailleul; in 2000 at *Le Mouvement Phases de 1952 à l'Horizon 2001* (*The Phases Movement from 1952 to the New Millennium*) at the Kiosque Centre Culturel in Mayenne and the Centre Noroit in Arras.

Frézin has also shown his work in numerous solo exhibitions, including: in 1960 at the Galerie La Chèvre Folle, Ostend; in 1967 at the Galerie Régis Langlois, Paris; in 1971 at the Musée de Calais; in 1973 *Le Mouvement Phases Présente Roger Frézin* (*The Phases Movement Presents Roger Frézin*) exhibition at the Galerie Lucien Duriez, Paris; 1986 at the Musée d'Art Moderne, Villeneuve d'Asq; in 1933 at the Galerie Jacqueline Storme, Lille; in 1994 at the Musée du Touquet; in 1997, *Roma - Fragments d'un Séjour Romain* (*Roma - Fragments of a Stay in Rome*) at the Fondation Wicar-Ville de Lille, Rome; and in 1998, *Hommage du Nord-Pas de Calais à Roger Frézin, 1958-1998, 40 ans de peinture* (*The Nord-Pas de Calais Pays Homage to Roger Frézin, 1958-1998, 40 Years of Painting*) at the Centre Culturel Noroit, Arras.

Bibliography:
Reyrolle, Michel, *Roger Frézin*, exhibition catalogue, Nouveau Musée, Calais, 1971. Jaguer, Édouard, *Le mouvement Phases présente Roger Frézin*, exhibition catalogue, Gal. Lucien Duriez, Paris, 1973. Bonnier, Alexandre, *Roger Frézin*, exhibition catalogue, Musée de Villeneuve d'Asq, Villeneuve d'Ascq, 1986. *Hommage du Nord-Pas-de-Calais à Roger Frézin. 40 ans de peinture*, exhibition catalogue, Centre culturel Noroit, Arras, 1988.

Museums and Galleries:
Ostend: *Painting* (1960) - Paris (MAMVP): *Painting* (1965).

Auction records:
Paris, 14 April 1991, *Chaplin's Boots* (mixed media/paper/canvas, 59 x 55 ins / 150 x 140 cm) FRF 13,000. Paris, 24 April 1991, *Homage to Carpeaux* (1991, oil and acrylic/canvas, 25 1/2 x 19 3/4 ins / 65 x 50 cm) FRF 7,000.

FRÉZOULS, Frédéric

French, 19th century.
Painter.

This artist exhibited a number of portraits and still-lifes at the Paris Salon between 1834 and 1848.

FREZZA, Giovanni Girolamo

Italian, 17th - 18th century.
Born 1659, in Canemorto; died c. 1741.
Engraver.

Giovanni Girolamo Frezza learned his craft in Rome as a pupil of Arnold van Westerhout. His work is distinguished by care and attention to detail. Examples include Ludovico Carracci's *Virgin Breastfeeding her Child*; Carlo Maratti's *Twelve Months of the Year* and *Judgement of Paris*; and *Venus* and *Pallas (Athene)*, two works drawn from antiquity.

FREZZA, Isodoro
Italian, 18th century.
Active in Naples c. 1775.
Painter, engraver.

FREZZA, Orazio
Italian, 17th century.
Born 17th century, in Naples.
Painter.

Orazio Frezza was a pupil of G. B. Banaschi. He closely studied the work of Lanfranco and Domenichino, and imitated those two artists with some degree of success.

FRIANI, Giacomo
Italian, 17th century.
Active mostly in Bologna and Parma.
Painter. History painting. Decorative schemes.

Giacomo Friani was a pupil of A. Metelli.

FRIANT, Émile
French, 19th - 20th century.
Born 16 April 1863, in Dieuze; died 1932, in Nancy, in Paris according to other sources.
Painter, sculptor, draughtsman. Portraits, genre scenes, local scenes, landscapes, still-lifes. Murals.
Orientalism.
School of Nancy.

Émile Friant went to Paris as a young man and joined the École des Beaux-Arts, studying in Cabanel's studio.

He painted some Orientalist subjects, including *Street in Tunis* and *The Arab Souk in Tunis*, but mainly painted genre scenes that were very well received by the general public, such as: *The Condemned Man's Mass*, *The Orphan*, *Fever* and *The Old Horse*. He is also known for *The Prodigal Son*, *The Painter's Studio*, *Studio Corner* and *All Saints' Day*. In the latter, the crowd of relatives in mourning hurrying to the entrance of the snow-covered cemetery was reproduced often and for many years, notably in calendars issued by the French postal service. He also decorated a ceiling for the police headquarters of Meurthe-et-Moselle and produced numerous sculptures and some drawings.

From 1882 he exhibited at the Salon des Artistes Français, receiving a commendation in 1882, second place in the Grand Prix de Rome in 1883, a bronze medal in 1884, a silver medal in 1885, a travel bursary in 1886, the Prix du Salon in 1889 and a gold medal at the Exposition Universelle in Paris in 1900. Friant was also decorated with the Légion d'Honneur and elected as a member of the Institut.

Thematic exhibitions featuring his work include: in 2003, *Vénus et Caïn. Figures de la Préhistoire 1830-1930* (*Venus and Cain. Prehistoric Figures 1830-1930*), an exhibition showing the emergence of prehistory as a scientific discipline and source of artistic inspiration, held at the Musée d'Aquitaine, Bordeaux.

BIBLIOGRAPHY:
Lafont-Couturier, Hélène/Dagen, Philippe/Loizeau, Sigolène, *Vénus et Caïn. Figures de la préhistoire 1830-1930*, exhibition catalogue, Musée d'Aquitaine, Bordeaux, 2003.

MUSEUMS AND GALLERIES:
ÉPINAL (Mus. départemental d'Art ancien et contemporain): *Still-life* - MONTPELLIER (Mus. Fabre): *The Struggle* - NANCY (MBA): *Pain*; *Capital Punishment*; *Women's Baths at Twilight*; *Idyll on the Footbridge*; *Sculptor in his Studio*; *The Artist*; *View of a Port*; *Faith* (plaster) - PARIS (MAMVP): *All Saints' Day* - TOUL: *Bread*.

AUCTION RECORDS:
PARIS, 1893, *Political Debate*, FRF 10,600; *The Fighters*, FRF 4,000; *Monaco*, FRF 9,000; *Street in Tunis*, FRF 3,000; *Slumber* (pastel) FRF 620; *A Quay* (watercolour) FRF 600. PARIS, 1899, *Hope* (charcoal) FRF 190. PARIS, 13 June 1906, *The Arab Souk in Tunis*, FRF 2,100. NEW YORK, 2 April 1909, *Landscape*, USD 270. PARIS, 12 May 1923, *The Evil Eye* (graphite) FRF 1,220. PARIS, 16 Dec 1927, *Meditation*, FRF 4,000; *Mandolin Lesson*, FRF 4,100; *Motherly Affection*, FRF 5,200. PARIS, 20 April 1928, *A Short Rest* (ink) FRF 420. PARIS, 30 Nov 1942, *Concarneau*, FRF 1,800. PARIS, 19 Jan 1945, *Portrait of the Painter Lhermitte* (graphite) FRF 1,500. PARIS, 2 Dec 1976, *Capital Punishment or Atonement* (1908, oil on canvas, 65 x 69 ins / 165 x 175 cm) FRF 20,500. VERSAILLES, 21 March 1982, *Don Quixote and Sancho Panza* (1889, oil on canvas, 16 x 21 1/2 ins / 40.5 x 54.5 cm) FRF 3,900. LONDON, 26 June 1987, *The Artist's Studio* (1885, oil on panel, 10 1/2 x 8 1/4 ins / 26.5 x 21 cm) GBP 5,200. PARIS, 26 Jan 1990, *Head of a Man* (oil on panel, 11 x 7 3/4 ins / 28 x 20 cm) FRF 6,200. PARIS, 22 March 1990, *Young Girl by a Fountain* (oil on panel, 17 3/4 x 19 3/4 ins / 45 x 50 cm) FRF 42,000. LONDON, 6 June 1990, *Unloading Fish on the Shore* (1893, oil on panel, 11 1/2 x 18 ins / 29 x 45.5 cm) GBP 5,500. NANCY, 24 June 1990, *Portrait of a Young Girl with a White Lily* (1911, oil on canvas, diam. 26 1/2 ins / 67 cm) FRF 34,000. PARIS, 25 March 1993, *Portrait Presumed to be of Gambetta* (oil on panel, 9 1/2 x 7 1/4 ins / 24 x 18.5 cm) FRF 5,000. PARIS, 24 Jan 1996, *Session with Nude Model* (oil on canvas, 18 x 13 1/2 ins / 46 x 34 cm) FRF 6,500. PARIS, 19 Oct 1997, *Portrait of the Sculptor Eugène Gatlet* (1924, pencil/paper, 20 x 13 1/2 ins / 51 x 34 cm) FRF 3,700. PARIS, 9 Dec 1998, *Young Soldier Seated with his Dog* (oil on canvas, 25 x 18 ins / 63 x 46 cm) FRF 9,500.

FRIAS, Antonio de
Dutch, 16th century.
Active in Toledo c. 1500.
Sculptor (wood).

Antonio de Frias worked at Toledo Cathedral.

FRIAS, Eugenio de
Portuguese, 17th century.
Active in Lisbon in 1609.
Painter.

Eugenio de Frias is known for a number of miniatures.

FRIAS, Oscar
Mexican, 20th century.
Born 1920, in Monterrey (Nuevo León).
Lithographer.

FRIAS Y ESCALANTE, Juan Antonio de.
See **ESCALANTE Juan Antonio de Frías y**

FRIBERT, Charles Wilhelm
Swedish, 19th century.
Born 15 April 1868, in Malmö.
Active in Philadelphia.
Sculptor.

Charles Wilhelm Fribert was a pupil at the academy in Stockholm and also studied under Falguière at the École des Beaux-Arts in Paris. He produced a silver statue which was presented to King Oscar II.

FRIBORG, Jørgen
Danish, 17th century.
Died c. 1620.
Sculptor, architect.

Jørgen Friborg worked for King Christian IV.

FRIBOULET, Jef E.
French, 20th century.
Born 1919, in Fécamp.
Painter. Landscapes, scenes with figures, still-lifes.
After working for some time in an Impressionist vein, Jef Friboulet moved towards a rather traditional figurative Expressionism. His draughtsmanship is bold, his colour vigorous and rustic. The forms he paints are imprisoned within black lines and appear to be flattened, as if existing only in his own gaze. His first solo exhibition took place in Paris in 1955. He went on to exhibit in Munich, Frankfurt, New York, Moscow, London, Tokyo and in 1994 at the Galerie Katia Granoff in Honfleur.

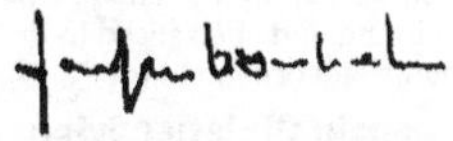

AUCTION RECORDS:
ROUEN, 6 Nov 1976, *Reapers* (oil on canvas, 17 x 13 ins / 43 x 33 cm) FRF 1,700. CALAIS, 13 Nov 1988, *Musicians* (oil on canvas, 23 1/2 x 29 1/4 ins / 60 x 74 cm) FRF 7,000. CALAIS, 4 March 1990, *Still-life with Apples* (oil on canvas, 13 x 16 1/4 ins / 33 x 41 cm) FRF 7,500. SCEAUX, 11 March 1990, *Man with a Red Jacket* (oil on canvas, 16 1/4 x 13 ins / 41 x 33 cm) FRF 7,200. VERSAILLES, 8 July 1990, *Composition with Mirror* (oil on canvas, 39 1/2 x 28 3/4 ins / 100.5 x 73 cm) FRF 11,000. SCEAUX, 13 Dec 1992, *Young Girl with Fan* (oil on canvas, 22 x 18 ins / 55 x 46 cm) FRF 9,000. PARIS, 5 July 1993, *The Gardener* (oil on canvas, 28 3/4 x 21 1/4 ins / 73 x 54 cm) FRF 5,800. PARIS, 25 May 1994, *Composition* (1959, oil on canvas, 39 1/4 x 39 1/4 ins / 100 x 100 cm) FRF 8,000. CALAIS, 11 Dec 1994, *Still-life with Siphon* (oil on canvas, 22 x 25 1/2 ins / 55 x 65 cm) FRF 12,000. LE HAVRE, 25 March 2001, *Still-life on a Blue Background* (oil on canvas, 22 x 18 ins / 55 x 46 cm) FRF 15,500. LE HAVRE, 25 Nov 2001, *Still-life with Fruit and Teapot* (oil on canvas, 21 x 26 ins / 54 x 65 cm) FRF 15,000. LE HAVRE, 21 April 2002, *Still-life* (oil on canvas, 36 x 26 ins / 92 x 65 cm) EUR 2,800. LE HAVRE, 11 Nov 2003, *Family* (oil on canvas, 24 x 29 ins / 60 x 73 cm) EUR 4,500. LE HAVRE, 11 Nov 2003, *Boat at Yport* (oil on canvas, 21 x 32 ins / 54 x 81 cm) EUR 4,900. LE HAVRE, 7 March 2004, *Still-life with Corn* (oil on canvas, 24 x 29 ins / 60 x 73 cm) EUR 1,500. LE HAVRE, 7 March 2004, *Pebble Collector* (oil on canvas, 29 x 36 ins / 73 x 92 cm) EUR 2,100. LE HAVRE, 7 March 2004, *Two Friends* (1999, gilt patinated bronze) EUR 2,500.

FRIBOURG
French, 19th century.
Born in the 19th century, in Paris.
Painter.
Fribourg, who studied under Suvée, submitted a portrait drawing and a portrait miniature to the Salon of 1799.

FRIBOURG, Broquart de. See **BROQUART DE FRIBOURG**

FRIBOURG, de. See also first name

FRICANT, Luce
French, 20th century.
Born 1889.
Painter, watercolourist.
Luce Fricant exhibited in Paris from 1924 at the Salon des Artistes Français; she was awarded a silver medal in 1934.

FRICERO, Joseph
French, 19th century.
Born in Nice.
Painter, watercolourist.
Fricero is on record as having been active between 1830 and 1865.
MUSEUMS AND GALLERIES:
NICE: watercolours, sepias.

FRICH, Joachim Christian
Norwegian, 19th century.
Born 1810, in Bergen; died 1858, in Christiania (now Oslo).
Painter. Figures, landscapes, architectural views, local scenes.
Joachim Christian Frich learned the art of drawing with the portrait artist Carle Lehmann in Bergen. He studied theology for a time and then attended the Kunstakademi in Copenhagen. Attracted to landscapes, he joined Johan Christian Dahl in Dresden in order to study with him. He was in Munich from 1837 to 1839 and went to Paris in 1885. He often travelled to Norway, and he was named dean of the royal school of drawing and an executive member of the Nasjonalgalleriet in Christiania.

From his numerous study trips to Norway he brought back paintings of churches and landscapes, and figures in regional costume. He increasingly retreated from Naturalism to adopt a more decorative approach.

In 2001 he was included in the exhibition *Da Dahl a Munch: Romanticismo, Realismo e Simbolismo nella Pittura di Paesaggio Norvegese* (*From Dahl to Munch: Romanticism, Realism and Symbolism in Norwegian Landscape Painting*) at the Palazzo dei Diamanti in Ferrara.
BIBLIOGRAPHY:
Noss, Aagot, '*Joachim Frichs draktakvarellar*' in *coll. Norske folkedrakter*, Norske samlaget, Oslo, 1973 (With an English summary). *Da Dahl a Munch. Romanticismo, realismo e simbolismo nella pittura di paesaggio norvegese*, exhibition catalogue, Palazzo dei Diamanti, Ferrara Arte editore, Ferrara, 2001.
MUSEUMS AND GALLERIES:
OSLO (Nasjonalgal.): *Landscape of the Telemark Region* (1852, oil on canvas).

FRICK, Adolf
German, 19th century.
Born 25 December 1870, in Weilburg.
Sculptor.
Frick was a pupil of S. Eberle in Munich where he also worked.
MUSEUMS AND GALLERIES:
LEIPZIG: *Echo*.

FRICK, Christian Georg
German, 19th century.
Died 4 July 1848, in Berlin.
Glass painter.
Christian Frick did much of his work for the royal porcelain factory in Prussia.

FRICK, Ferdinand
German, 19th century.
Active in Berlin.
Painter.
Frick was a pupil of Ternite.

FRICK, Frigk Ulrich
Swiss, 16th century.
Active in Zurich during the second half of the 16th century.
Glass painter.
One of Frick's works was a stained glass window that was sent to Adlischwil in 1566. Other works of his exist, dated 1577. Frick's name appears again in documents of 1601 in Zurich.

FRICK, Gottlieb
Swiss, 20th century.
Born 16 July 1877, in Obfelden.
Painter. Portraits, landscapes.
Educated at the industrial arts college in Zurich and at the École des Arts Decoratifs in Paris, Frick also attended the

École Supérieure des Beaux-Arts in Paris, where he studied under Benjamin-Constant and Jean-Paul Laurens. He exhibited a portrait of his father in 1902 and is also remembered for numerous views of Bern.

FRICK, Henri Émile
French, 19th century.
Born in Paris.
Engraver.

Frick was a pupil of J. Jacquet. He received an honourable mention at the 1900 Exposition Universelle in Paris and again at the same event in 1901.

FRICK, Jacques François
French, 18th century.
Born c. 1720, in Besançon.
Painter.

Jacques Frick was still working in 1782.

FRICK, Johann Friedrich
German, 18th - 19th century.
Born 31 October 1774, in Berlin; died 21 September 1850, in Bad Kreuznach.
Engraver.

Frick's main work is the series of 19 aquatints representing the *Marienburg Castle*

FRICK, Paul de
French, 19th - 20th century.
Born 1864, in Paris; died 1935, in Paris.
Painter. Genre scenes, landscapes, urban landscapes, still-lifes.

Paul de Frick studied under Gustave Boulanger and later under Luc Olivier-Merson. He often idealised his subjects and the portraits he was commissioned to paint, as can be seen in his *Jésus chez les Bretons* (*Jesus Among the Bretons*). He exhibited in Paris at the Salon des Artistes Français and received a commendation in 1914.

AUCTION RECORDS:
CHARTRES, 27 Jan 1980, *Garden Interior* (oil on panel, 6 1/4 x 9 ins / 16 x 22 cm) FRF 2,300. VIENNA, 16 Feb 1982, *Evening in Venice* (oil on panel, 9 3/4 x 13 1/2 ins / 25 x 34 cm) ATS 11,000. NEW YORK, 25 Oct 1984, *Young Women and Doves in a Garden* (1895, oil on canvas, 57 3/4 x 35 1/4 ins / 146.6 x 89.5 cm) USD 3,000. DOUARNENEZ, 25 July 1987, *A Walk on the Shore at Sunset* (oil on card, 11 3/4 x 19 3/4 ins / 30 x 50 cm) FRF 4,000. PARIS, 9 Dec 1988, *The Shore* (oil on card, 7 1/2 x 9 1/4 ins / 19 x 23.5 cm) FRF 4,800. PARIS, 5 June 1989, *The Pont des Arts* (oil on canvas, 21 1/4 x 32 ins / 54 x 81 cm) FRF 12,000. PARIS, 13 Dec 1989, *River* (oil on canvas, 10 1/4 x 14 1/2 ins / 26 x 37 cm) FRF 3,500. PARIS, 12 Oct 1990, *Vines with Well* (oil on canvas, 4 x 39 1/4 ins / 10 x 100 cm) FRF 12,500. LE TOUQUET, 8 Nov 1992, *Paris - Street Scene with Figures* (oil on canvas, 16 1/4 x 11 ins / 41 x 27 cm) FRF 8,500. PARIS, 23 April 1993, *Still-life with Fruit* (oil on canvas, 18 x 22 ins / 46 x 55 cm) FRF 4,200. PARIS, 9 April 1999, *Luxembourg in Summer* (oil on canvas, 16 x 22 ins / 40 x 55 cm) FRF 13,500. ROME, 11 Dec 2003, *Life in the Lagoon* (1899, oil on canvas, 35 x 57 ins / 90 x 145 cm) EUR 2,800. PARIS, 9 June 2004, *Woman Playing with Kittens* (1896, oil on canvas, 18 x 22 ins / 46 x 55 cm) EUR 3,000.

FRICKE, August
German, 19th century.
Born 24 March 1829, in Brunswick; died 27 June 1894, in Berlin.
Painter. Landscapes.

August Fricke was a member of the Berlin academy and a court painter.

FRICKE, August
German, 20th century.
Born 16 January 1875, in Grüningfeld.
Painter. Seascapes, landscapes.

Fricke lived and worked in Munich from 1906.

A-FRICKE

AUCTION RECORDS:
MUNICH, 29 May 1980, *Landscape with Lake* (1871, oil on canvas, 10 1/2 x 16 1/2 ins / 26.5 x 42 cm) DEM 1,300. AMSTERDAM, 22 April 1992, *Paddle-Steamer in the Sea off Hamburg* (oil on canvas, 32 3/4 x 53 1/4 ins / 83 x 135 cm) NLG 36,800.

FRICKE, Friedrich August
German, 19th century.
Died 1858, in Leipzig.
Painter, lithographer, draughtsman. Portraits.

Fricke taught painting and specialised in drawings of landscapes, monuments and ornaments.

FRICKE, Longin Christianovich
Russian, 19th century.
Born 1816, in St Petersburg; died 1893, in St Petersburg.
Painter. Landscapes.

Fricke was a pupil of Vorob'ev and later specialized in painting Alpine landscapes.

AUCTION RECORDS:
NEW YORK, 12 May 1978, *The Country House* (1850, oil on canvas, freehand oval shape, 18 x 26 ins / 45.5 x 66 cm) USD 2,300.

FRICKEL, Peter
German, 18th century.
Active in Hanau in 1706.
Potter.

Peter Frickel worked for the earthenware factory in Hanau.

FRICKER, Bernhard
Swiss, 18th century.
Active in Basel c. 1751.
Sculptor (stone).

Fricker worked on the restoration of Basel Cathedral.

FRICKER, Henri
French, 20th century.
Born 20 May 1881, in Besançon; died 18 June 1952, in La Planée.
Painter.

Henri Fricker exhibited at the Salon des Artistes Indépendants in Paris.

FRICOTEAU
French, 19th century.
Born in Rheims; died 1859.
Painter.

Fricoteau painted views of the city ramparts, towers, fortifications and churches of Rheims.

MUSEUMS AND GALLERIES:
RHEIMS: 80 views of Rheims.

FRICQUEGNON, Suzanne
French, 20th century.
Born 1897.
Painter, miniaturist.

Suzanne Fricquegnon exhibited in Paris at the Salon des Artistes Français from 1923.

FRID, Ludwig
French, 19th century.
Born 26 January 1855, in Skede; died 29 January 1909.
Painter.

Ludwig Frid studied at the Stockholm academy and went on to paint landscapes and, above all, genre compositions.

FRIDEL, Christof
German, 17th century.
Active in Brisach in 1600.

Draughtsman.
There is only one work known by Fridel, who was an imitator of Stimmer.

FRIDEMANN, David
German, 16th century.
Died 1607.
Active in Erfurt (Thuringia).
Painter.

FRIDEMANN, Hans, the Elder
German, 16th century.
Died c. 1600.
Active in Erfurt (Thuringia).
Sculptor, architect.
Hans was the brother of David Fridemann.

FRIDEMANN, Hans, the Younger
German, 17th century.
Died c. 1628, in Erfurt.
Sculptor, architect.
Fridemann was the son of Hans the Elder.

FRIDEMANN, Heinrich
German, 17th century.
Born 10 October 1601, in Erfurt; died 1668, in Erfurt.
Sculptor.
Heinrich was the son of Hans the Younger.

FRIDEMANN, Paul
German, 17th century.
Died 1632, in Erfurt.
Sculptor, architect.
Paul was the brother of Hans the Younger.

FRIDERICH, Jacob Andreas. See **FRIDRICH the Elder and the Younger**

FRIDERICI, Julius
German, 19th century.
Born in Trier; died 1833, in Trier.
Painter. History painting.
Friderici studied at the Kunstakademie in Düsseldorf, which has his *Adam and Eve* and *Flight into Egypt* in its collections.

FRIDERICI, Walter
German, 19th - 20th century.
Born 26 September 1874, in Chemnitz.
Painter. Genre scenes, interiors.
Friderici lived and worked in Dresden and exhibited there regularly from 1897; he also exhibited in Munich and Berlin.

FRIDERICUS
German, 13th century.
Active in Mainz c. 1200.
Miniaturist.
The Bibliothèque Nationale, Paris, owns a manuscript illustrated by this artist.

FRIDLI, Martin
Swiss, 17th century.
Painter, decorative designer.
Fridli worked on the altars of the church in Giswi in 1641.

FRIDLIN (Meister)
Swiss, 15th century.
Painter.
Basel School.
Fridlin was received as a member of the guild of painters in Basel in 1450.

FRIDLIN, or Fridolin de Zug
Swiss, 18th century.
Died c. 1730.
Painter.
Fridlin may well be Brother Fridolin of Mariastein.

FRIDMAN, Leonid
Egyptian, 20th century.
Born 1908, in Ismailia; died 5 January 1979, in Paris.
Active and naturalised in France.
Painter, sculptor.
Leonid Fridman started his career in Belgium where his family had taken refuge. From 1936 onwards, he devoted himself entirely to painting. He settled in Paris just after 1950 and exhibited there at the Salon d'Automne and Salon des Artistes Indépendants in Paris.

FRIDOLIN
German, 14th century.
Died 1393, in Meran, South Tyrol, Austria (now Merano, Trentino-Alto Adige, Italy).
Painter, fresco artist.
Fridolin painted several frescoes in Meran between 1369 and 1371.

FRIDRICH, Bernhard Gottlieb
German, 18th century.
Born 1710, in Augsburg.
Painter, engraver. Portraits.
Bernhard Fridrich was the son of Jacob Andreas the Elder. His works include *Charles Albert of Bavaria as Emperor of Germany*
AUCTION RECORDS:
STOCKHOLM, 15 Nov 1989, *Portraits of a Man and a Woman* (oil on canvas, a pair, each 35 3/4 x 27 1/2 ins / 91 x 70 cm) SEK 26,000.

FRIDRICH, Jacob Andreas, the Elder
German, 18th century.
Born 19 February 1684, in Nuremberg; died 1751, in Augsburg.
Engraver.
Jacob Andreas Fridrich, the father of Bernhard Gottlieb and Jakob Andreas the Younger, was a pupil of Christoph Weigel. He engraved military subjects in the style of Rugendas.

FRIDRICH, Jacob Andreas, the Younger
German, 18th century.
Born 1714, in Nuremberg; died 1779, in Nuremberg.
Engraver.
The son of Jakob Andreas the Elder, Fridrich was a court engraver in Stuttgart.

FRIDRITZ, Ivan Pavlovich
Russian, 19th century.
Born c. 1803, in St Petersburg; died c. 1860.
Engraver, draughtsman, painter.
In 1815 Fridritz was a pupil of Utkin at the St Petersburg academy. He then specialised in portraits.

FRIECH, Joachim
Norwegian, 19th century.
Born 24 July 1810, in Bergen; died 29 January 1858, in Christiania (now Oslo).
Painter.
Joachim Friech began his studies at the Kunstakademi in Copenhagen but soon left to go to Dresden and follow Dahl. From there he went to Munich where he continued his studies with Carl Rottmann, but he soon returned to his own country. At the time of the construction of the castle of Oscarhal near Christiania, Friech was entrusted with the decoration of the dining room.

FRIED, Georg
German.
Active in Hanau.
Earthenware maker.
Worked in the Hanau earthenware factory.
MUSEUMS AND GALLERIES:
KASSEL (Hessisches Landesmus.): a work.

FRIED, Heinrich Jacob
German, 19th century.
Born 11 March 1802, in Queichheim; died 2 November 1870, in Munich.
Painter, lithographer. History painting, landscapes.
Fried studied art in Augsburg and at the Munich academy under the tutelage of Langer and Cornelius. He visited Rome and Naples and subsequently settled in Munich where he became keeper of the art circle in 1845.
MUSEUMS AND GALLERIES:
MUNICH: *The Azure Cave in Capri.*

FRIED, Otto
German, 20th century.
Born 13 December 1922, in Koblenz.
From 1936 active in the USA and since 1962 also active in France.
Painter (mixed media).
Otto Fried graduated in art and architecture from the University of Portland, Oregon; in 1949 he was awarded a travel scholarship, which enabled him to go to France to study under Fernand Léger. He returned to Portland in 1951 but finally settled in Paris in 1962. He showed his work at numerous group exhibitions in both the USA and France, notably in Paris at the 1950 Salon d'Automne and the 1951 Salon de Mai. Since 1955, Fried has had solo exhibitions in New York, Tübingen, Paris, Tokyo and Washington, D.C.

His early abstract compositions are based on permutations of the circle: discs, spheres, globes, ellipses. Each circular form is filled with waves of greys, ochre or coral punctuated by touches of blue suggesting landscapes or views of the land as seen from an aircraft - vast tracts of forest, extinct volcanic craters and mountain ranges.

He created a personal universe with its own order. In his later work, he abandoned circles and spheres in favour of tiny squares of equal size in alternating colours on a canvas coated in black pigment with tiny scraps of paper glued onto it. The whole suggests instability and evanescence. The circles reappear, now within the confines of the individual squares and accompanied with other forms - symbols, curves, letters, all threatening to burst out of the constraints of the canvas. The underlying theme is communication and the conduit that is language (*Mysterious Communication; Metaphysical Conversation; Heretical Tongues*) - a dialectic that alternates between the finite and the infinite.
BIBLIOGRAPHY:
Margolis, Larry/Fried, Otto, *We 3,* Somagy, Paris, 1950. Witham, Vernon, *Folio of Individially Autographed Serigraph Reproductions of Paintings by 12 New Painters,* Eugene Witham, Oregon, 1953. Bouyeure, Claude, '*Otto Fried, les iliades du cercle*' in *Cimaise,* periodical, Paris, summer 1990. Fried, Otto/West, Thomas, *Otto Fried,* Foundation of Fine Art of the century, Geneva, 1995.
MUSEUMS AND GALLERIES:
EUGENE - KOBLENZ (Mittelrhein Mus.) - NEW YORK (Metropolitan Mus. of Art) - PARIS (MNAM-CCI) - PORTLAND (MA).

FRIED, Pal
Hungarian, 20th century.
Born 1893.
Painter, pastellist.
Pal Fried only painted female figures, mainly ballerinas relaxing.
AUCTION RECORDS:
LINDAU, 6 May 1981, *Back view of Two Nudes* (charcoal/paper, 20 1/2 x 17 1/4 ins / 52 x 44 cm) DEM 1,600. LYONS, 21 Oct 1987, *Young Woman with Bare Breasts* (oil on canvas, 25 1/2 x 19 ins / 65 x 48 cm) FRF 11,000. AMSTERDAM, 19 Sept 1989, *Young Girl in a Pink Tutu Untying Her Ballet Shoes* (pastel/paper, 31 1/2 x 23 1/4 ins / 80 x 59 cm) NLG 1,035. LONDON, 4 Oct 1989, *Three Ballerinas* (oil on canvas, 29 3/4 x 23 1/2 ins / 75.5 x 60 cm) GBP 1,320. LONDON, 14 Feb 1990, *Portrait of Monique* (oil on canvas, 23 1/4 x 29 1/2 ins / 59 x 75 cm) GBP 2,420. LONDON, 6 June 1990, *During the Interval* (oil on canvas, 29 1/2 x 23 1/2 ins / 75 x 60 cm) GBP 2,420. LONDON, 28 Oct 1992, *Ballerina* (oil on canvas, 30 1/4 x 22 3/4 ins / 77 x 58 cm) GBP 1,650. LONDON, 7 April 1993, *Lizette* (oil on canvas, 29 1/4 x 23 1/4 ins / 74 x 59 cm) GBP 1,840. MONTREAL, 23-24 Nov 1993, *Mona* (oil on canvas, 30 x 24 ins / 76.1 x 61 cm) CAD 850. LONDON, 22 Feb 1995, *Nude* (pastel, 26 3/4 x 19 ins / 68 x 48 cm) USD 690. LONDON, 9 Oct 1997, *Ballerinas* (oil on canvas, 23 x 30 3/4 ins / 58.5 x 78 cm) GBP 632.

FRIED, Theodore
Hungarian, 20th century.
Born in Budapest.
Painter.
Theodore Fried exhibited in Paris at the Salon d'Automne from 1925 and then at the Salon des Artistes Indépendants from 1928.
AUCTION RECORDS:
PARIS, 28 Nov 1985, *The Merry-go-round* (1928, oil on canvas, 29 1/4 x 35 1/2 ins / 74 x 90 cm) FRF 13,000.

FRIEDBICHLER
British, 20th century.
Born in Scotland.
Painter. Local scenes.
AUCTION RECORDS:
EDINBURGH, 15 Dec 1928, *A Country Fair,* GBP 12.

FRIEDEL, P.
German, 19th century.
Born in Wetzlar; died c. 1814, in Berlin.
Painter.
Friedel exhibited portraits and compositions at the Berlin academy from 1800 to 1814.

FRIEDEMANN, L.
German, 18th century.
Died September 1802, in St Petersburg.
Sculptor.
Friedemann studied in Berlin and in Vienna before settling in Russia. Busts of the tsar, Alexander I, and his wife are attributed to him.

FRIEDENBERG, Wilhelm
German, 19th - 20th century.
Born 30 June 1845, in Frankfurt am Main; died 1911, in Kronberg.
Painter.
Pupil of Lindenschmidt; known for genre compositions and portraits.

FRIEDENSON, Arthur A.
British, 19th - 20th century.
Born 1872; died 1955.
Painter. Landscapes, seascapes.
Arthur Friedenson studied in Leeds, Paris and Antwerp. He exhibited at the Royal Academy from 1889.
MUSEUMS AND GALLERIES:
LEEDS (City AG): *October Sunshine* (oil on canvas); *The Flowing Tide* (1900, oil on canvas).
AUCTION RECORDS:
LONDON, 23 May 1910, *Summer Breeze,* GBP 18. LONDON, 27 Nov 1922, *October Afternoon,* GBP 9. LONDON, 16 Feb 1923, *Gravel Pit,* GBP 8. LONDON, 2 May 1924, *Sunset after Storm,* GBP 44. PARIS, 1 March 1926, *Firewood Gatherers,* FRF 190. LONDON, 19 and 20 May 1926, *Evening,* GBP 13. LONDON, 23 March 1928, *The Storm Clears,* GBP 9. CHESTER, 17 March 1983, *Brunswick Bay, Yorkshire* (oil on canvas, 17 1/4 x 22 3/4 ins / 44 x 58 cm) GBP 1,000. LONDON, 5 March 1987, *Seaside Scene* (oil on canvas, 13 1/2 x 20 1/2 ins / 34.5 x 52 cm) GBP 2,500. LONDON, 12 May 1989, *The Gravel Quarry* (1918, oil on canvas, 27 1/2 x 35 1/2 ins / 70 x 90 cm) GBP 3,520. LONDON, 11

Oct 1991, *The Artist's Admirers* (1881, oil on canvas, 22 x 16 ins / 56 x 40.7 cm) GBP 3,080. ILKLEY, 28 April 1999, *Country Crossroads with Figures in Foreground* (oil on board, 9 x 12 ins / 23 x 30 cm) GBP 1,450. LEEDS, 14 Nov 2000, *Village Street* (1893, oil on canvas, 15 x 10 ins / 37 x 25 cm) GBP 1,800. LEEDS, 22 June 2001, *River at Wareham, Evening* (1916, oil on canvas, 20 x 26 ins / 50 x 65 cm) GBP 3,200. LEEDS, 20 Nov 2001, *A Dartmoor Road* (1926, oil on canvas, 76 x 56 ins / 193 x 141 cm) GBP 3,300. NEWBURY, 18 Sept 2002, *River Landscape with Bridge and Figures* (1910, oil on panel, 13 x 16 ins / 33 x 40 cm) GBP 1,950. LEEDS, 18 Nov 2003, *River Landscape* (oil on board, 12 x 15 ins / 31 x 39 cm) GBP 2,900. SALISBURY, 7 April 2004, *Thruxton, Hampshire* (oil on board, 10 x 14 ins / 26 x 35 cm) GBP 2,000. SALISBURY, 7 April 2004, *Winter Sketch, Wensleydale, Yorkshire* (oil on board, 8 x 11 ins / 21 x 27 cm) GBP 2,600.

FRIEDERICHSEN, Stephan Dietrich
German, 18th century.
Born 4 August 1784, in Lübeck; died 19 August 1805, in Lübeck.
Miniaturist.
Friederichsen was a pupil of Groger. The Lübeck Museum has six of his portraits in its collection.

FRIEDERSDORFF, Gertrud
German, 20th century.
Born 3 December 1882, in Wirsitz.
Painter.
Lived and worked mainly in Düsseldorf.

FRIEDERSDORFF, Robert
German, 20th century.
Born 1 August 1885, in Wirsitz.
Painter. Portraits, landscapes.
A pupil of Spatz and Claus Meyer, Friedersdorff lived and worked in Düsseldorf.

FRIEDGES, Georges
French, 20th century.
Born in Paris.
Painter. Urban landscapes.
Georges Friedges exhibited in Paris from 1923 at the Société Nationale des Beaux-Arts and the Salon d'Automne, showing views of Paris.

FRIEDHEIM, Christian Ludwig
German, 19th century.
Born 1781, in Taubenheim; died 16 May 1810, in Leipzig.
Painter. History painting, portraits.
Friedheim studied under Schenau at the Dresden academy and also lived there as well as in Leipzig.

FRIEDL, Maximilian Joseph
German, 19th century.
Born 11 September 1815, in Munich; died 23 December 1838, in Munich.
Painter.
Friedl was a pupil of Quaglio and specialised in paintings of landscapes and monuments.

FRIEDL, Theodor
Austrian, 19th century.
Born 13 February 1842, in Vienna; died 1899, in Vienna.
Sculptor.
Theodor Friedl executed a large number of monumental and ornamental sculptures in Hamburg, Budapest, Augsburg and Vienna.

FRIEDLAENDER, Adolph, or Friedlander
German, 19th century.
Painter, lithographer. Genre scenes.
Friedlaender was active in Hamburg.
AUCTION RECORDS:
LONDON, 27 Feb 1985, *Siesta* (oil on panel, 8 x 12 1/4 ins / 20.5 x 31 cm) GBP 1,000.

FRIEDLAENDER, August M., or Friedlander
German, 19th century.
Born 1856; died 25 April 1897, in Colorado Springs, USA.
Painter. Portraits, genre scenes.
Friedlaender mainly worked in America.
AUCTION RECORDS:
NEW YORK, 21 May 1991, *Encampment* (oil on panel, 8 x 12 1/2 ins / 20.3 x 31.7 cm) USD 660.

FRIEDLAENDER, Hedwig.
See **FRIEDLAENDER VON MALHEIM Hedwig**

FRIEDLAENDER, Johnny Gotthard
German, 20th century.
Born 21 June 1912, in Pless, Upper Silesia (now Pszczyna, Poland); died 18 June 1992, in Paris.
From 1937 active and from 1952 naturalised in France.
Painter, engraver, illustrator, watercolourist. Figures, bestiaries.
Johnny Friedlaender studied at the school of fine arts in Breslau (now Wroclaw, Poland) under Otto Müller (a former member of Die Brücke) and Carlo Mense. He moved to Dresden in 1930 and lived there until 1933, apart from short stays in Berlin and Paris. In 1933, Friedlaender was interned in the first of the Nazi concentration camps, but was released in 1935. He sought refuge in Czechoslovakia before moving to Holland. He moved to Paris in 1937 and earned a living by contributing to various periodicals. At the outbreak of World War II he was arrested in Paris along with other foreign nationals, but made good his escape and enlisted in the British Army. He was captured again but once more somehow contrived to escape. At the end of the war, he returned to live in Paris where, in 1949, he set up an engraving workshop (*L'Atelier de l'Ermitage*), together with another refugee, the engraver Albert Flocon. That same year, he met and made friends with Jacques Villon. In 1959 he opened an engraving workshop annexed to the Modern Art Museum in Rio de Janeiro. In 1966-1967 he taught at the Salzburg summer school and it was during this period that he started painting again for the first time since the 1940s.

Friedlaender's earliest work dates from 1928 and comprises black-and-white figurative engravings in the Expressionist manner. Over time, however, he worked in etching and aquatint to develop his own pictorial language which, as Bernard Gheerbrandt has pointed out, used 'progressively abstract symbols to conduct a magic dialogue with the cosmos' (*White Birds; Evening Landscape; Frost*).

His backgrounds are built up from delicate points, dots, tracings and mysterious forms that evoke complex landscapes. His later engravings are equally subtle, with all the point and counterpoint of a musical fugure.

Parallel to his work as a painter and engraver, he was an accomplished illustrator of poetry, including Jerôme and Jean Tharaud's *A Kingdom of God* (1947), thirteen etchings for Paul Eluard's *Season of Loves* (1949), Jean Cassou's *Little Bestiary* (1963), Victor Segalen's *Steles* (1968); Arthur Rimbaud's *Illuminations* (1979), and Paul Eluard's *Twelve Cosmic Dreams*.

He was a highly accomplished engraver, able to evoke emotion with a single line or graceful curve. His work stands apart from the purist engravings of a Flocon, the multiple-inking technique of a Hayter or the incised monochrome of a Courtin: Friedlaender's work is complex and baroque. As Nesto Jacometti has remarked: 'His engravings reinvent and reinstate an ancient and long-forgotten alchemy.'

Friedlaender started exhibiting in 1930, notably in group exhibitions in Dresden. He went on to participate in numerous group exhibitions elsewhere, including the 1946 Salon de Mai in Paris, the Museum of Modern Art in Tokyo in 1951, the first engraving Biennale in Ljubliana in 1955 (where he was awarded the Jakopic Prize), the 1957 Tokyo Biennale (Kamakura Prize), the 1958 and 1991 Venice Biennale (as a representative of French engraving), and the 7th International Biennale in Norway in 1984, where he was awarded a gold medal.

He had his first solo exhibition in 1949 at La Hune Gallery in Paris; he would continue to exhibit there until his death in 1992. His work found favour with Christian Zervos, who wrote an enthusiastic review for the *Cahiers d'Art*. Subsequently, he exhibited internationally, notably at the Musée Rath in Geneva (1951); Kunstmuseum in Lucerne (1951); Neuchâtel Museum (1951); Museum of Modern Art in São Paulo (1953, 1959); Museum of Art and History in Geneva (1954); Staatliches Museum in Berlin (1957); Museum of Modern Art in Rio de Janeiro (1959); Museum of Art in Cincinnati (1961); Jerusalem Museum of Art (1965); University of Rochester Memorial Art Gallery (1973); municipal libraries in Strasbourg, Mulhouse and Colmar (1974); Museum of Modern Art in Tel-Aviv (1976); Musée de l'Art Moderne de la Ville de Paris (1978); Dresden (first retrospective, 1980); Finland (six museums, 1983); Musée du Luxembourg (1984); Kunsthalle in Bremen (1987); Chancellery in Bonn (1992); Couvent des Cordeliers and Goethe Institute in Paris (1994); at *Homage*, an exhibition of painting, sculpture and the graphic arts held at the 14th arrondissement town hall in Paris (1994); and in 2001 at the Musée d'Unterlinden in Colmar as part of the Brigitte Coudrain Bequest.

Friedlaender was awarded the Cross of Merit of the Federal German Republic in 1969 and made an Officier des Arts et Lettres in France in 1978; he was also elected to membership of the Belgian Académie Royale des Beaux Arts in 1990. In 1974, French television released a film on his life (*Le Graveur Friedlaender* (*Friedlaender the Engraver*) and he featured in two major radio programmes, *Johnny Friedlaender: Twilight Reality* (made in 1987) and *Friedlaender: A century of Memories* (1991).

Bibliography:

Fouchet, Max-Pol, *Johnny Friedlaender - Œuvre 1961-1965*, Touchstone, New York, 1965. Schmücking, Rolf, *Johnny Friedlaender: Radierungen 1930-1972*, catalogue raisonné, Gal. Schmücking, Braunschweig, 1973. Schmücking, Rolf, *Friedlaender: Werkverzeichnis der Radierungen 1973 - 1976*, catalogue raisonné, Gal. Schmücking, Braunschweig, 1977. Lassaigne, Jacques, *Friedlaender, rétrospective de l'œuvre gravé 1948-1978*, exhibition catalogue, Musée d'Art moderne de la Ville de Paris, Paris, 1978. Friedlaender, Johnny/Schmidt, Werner, *Johnny Friedlaender*, exhibition catalogue, Albertinum, Dresden, 1980. *Friedlaender, Zeichnungen, Radierungen, Aquarelle, Gemälde, Alben und Mappenwerke*, exhibition catalogue, Kunsthalle, Bremen, 1987. Berthold, Roland, *Johnny Friedlaender*, travelling exhibition catalogue, Bundeskanzleramt, Bonn, Landesmuseum, Mainz, 1992. *Johnny Friedleander - De Dresde à Paris - Du noir à la couleur*, exhibition catalogue, Couvent des Cordeliers, Goethe Institut, Gal. de Condé, Paris, 1994. Lecoq-Ramond, Sylvie, *La donation Johnny Friedlaender (1912-1992)*, catalogue raisonné, Musée d'Unterlinden, Colmar, 1996. Bouret, Claude/Lecoq-Ramond, Sylvie/Coudrain, Brigitte, '*Johnny Friedlaender. Donation Brigitte Coudrain*' in *coll. reConnaître*, Musée d'Unterlinden, Colmar, Réunion des musées nationaux, Paris, 2001.

Museums and Galleries:

Colmar (Mus. d'Unterlinden): *Woman at the Mirror* (1930-1939, zinc etching on paper, eleven (Dresden, The Hague, Paris)); *Truth* (1934, aquatint and copper etching on vellum); *Nude* (1936, copper etching on vellum); *Fish and Eel* (c. 1938, etching and aquatint on paper); *Dogs* (1939, aquatint and copper etching on Rives paper); *Firing Squad* (1945, aquatint and etching on Japanese paper, ten from album 'Images of Misfortune'); *L'exil* (*Exile*) (c. 1947, copper etching on vellum, nine from 'The Shadow of the Cross' by Jérôme and Jean Tharaud); *Rabbi Reading* (1947, etching and copper aquatint on paper, 15 from 'A Kingdom of God' by Jérôme and Jean Tharaud); *Nausikaa* (1953, eight engravings (Bibliofila Klubben, Lund, Sweden)) - Dresden (Prints Collection): bequest - Mainz: bequest.

Auction records:

Milan, 13 May 1971, *Composition* (tempera) ITL 600,000. Munich, 23 May 1977, *Composition* (1959, watercolour, 12 1/2 x 9 1/2 ins / 32 x 24 cm) DEM 4,200. Hamburg, 2 June 1978, *Composition* (1961, gouache, 18 3/4 x 13 1/4 ins / 47.8 x 33.9 cm) DEM 7,000. Cologne, 3 Dec 1980, *Birds* (1973, oil on canvas, 23 1/2 x 36 1/4 ins / 60 x 92 cm) DEM 20,000. London, 30 Nov 1982, *Untitled* (1977, watercolour, 26 1/2 x 18 1/2 ins / 67.5 x 47 cm) GBP 2,200. Cologne, 6 Dec 1983, *Forms II* (1977, oil on canvas, 36 1/4 x 28 3/4 ins / 92 x 73 cm) DEM 24,000. Cologne, 7 Dec 1984, *Golden November* (1967, etching and coloured aquatint, 30 1/2 x 22 1/2 ins / 77.7 x 57 cm) DEM 1,800. Cologne, 3 Dec 1985, *Birds* (bronze relief, 15 1/2 x 12 1/2 ins / 39.2 x 32 cm) DEM 4,800. London, 29 June 1989, *Untitled* (1980, oil on canvas, 32 3/4 x 25 1/2 ins / 83.5 x 65 cm) GBP 14,850. Montreal, 30 April 1990, *Untitled* (aquatint, 20 3/4 x 16 1/2 ins / 53 x 42 cm) CAD 770. Rome, 9 April 1991, *Untitled* (aquatint, 22 3/4 x 15 3/4 ins / 58 x 40 cm) ITL 850,000. Paris, 4 Dec 1991, *Solar* (colour etching, 30 x 22 ins / 76 x 56 cm) FRF 3,700. Munich, 26 May 1992, *Composition* (aquatint, 30 x 22 ins / 76 x 55 cm) DEM 3,105. Heidelberg, 9 Oct 1992, *Madrigal* (colour etching, 20 3/4 x 15 ins / 53 x 38 cm) DEM 1,100. Heidelberg, 3 April 1993, *Composition 4-85* (1985, watercolour, 8 x 7 1/2 ins / 20.5 x 18.8 cm) DEM 8,200. Amsterdam, 8 Dec 1993, *Composition* (1958, watercolour/paper, 10 3/4 x 9 ins / 27.5 x 22 cm) NLG 3,680. Paris, 28 Jan 1994, *Couple* (etching, aquatint and dry-point, 23 x 30 3/4 ins / 58.5 x 78.4 cm) FRF 4,700. Heidelberg, 15 Oct 1994, *Evening Landscape* (1964, colour etching, 23 x 16 ins / 57.5 x 40.5 cm) DEM 1,400. Paris, 27 Nov 1997, *Abstraction Composition on a Grey Ground* (etching and aquatint). Paris, 17 March 1998, *Dominant Red* (1967, aquatint) FRF 3,100. Munich, 30 Nov 1998, *Poppies* (1985, pencil, brown chalk/cardboard, 17 x 14 ins / 44 x 36 cm) DEM 4,500. Hamburg, 2 Oct 1999, *Untitled* (1964, watercolour/Indian ink/pencil, 20 x 15 ins / 50 x 38 cm) DEM 6,500. Milan, 21 June 2001, *Untitled* (1960, watercolour and Indian ink, 11 x 8 ins / 27 x 21 cm) ITL 4,200,000. Hamburg, 13 June 2003, *Landscape 7. 1982* (1982, oil on canvas, 32 x 39 ins / 81 x 100 cm) EUR 6,000.

FRIEDLAENDER, Julius, or Friedlander

Danish, 19th century.

Born 29 January 1810, in Copenhagen; died 18 September 1861, in Copenhagen.

Painter. Genre scenes.

Julius Friedlaender entered the Kunstakademi in Copenhagen in 1824. From 1843 to 1844 he visited Paris and Italy. Among his works may be cited *Doctor beside a Sick Man*, *Young Boys Playing in Capri* and *Scene from a Nursery*.

Auction records:

Copenhagen, 19 Aug 1980, *Mouse Chase* (1852, oil on canvas, 24 3/4 x 31 1/2 ins / 63 x 80 cm) DKK 13,000. Copenhagen, 23 April 1982, *Russian Soldier Buying Fruit* (1851, oil on canvas, 15 1/4 x 14 1/4 ins / 39 x 36 cm) DKK 11,000. Stockholm, 25 April 1984, *Children's Games* (1858, oil on canvas, 22 1/2 x 29 1/2 ins / 57 x 75 cm) SEK 60,000. Copenhagen, 12 Aug

1985, *Young Boy with Fruit Basket* (1856, oil on canvas, 13 1/2 x 9 1/2 ins / 34 x 24 cm) DKK 17,000. LONDON, 17 Nov 1993, *Sick Child* (1852, oil on canvas, 21 1/4 x 20 ins / 54 x 51 cm) GBP 12,075. COPENHAGEN, 2 March 1999, *Three Generations by Ruins* (1847, oil on canvas, 11 x 9 ins / 29 x 24 cm) DKK 14,000. VEJLE, 11 Aug 1999, *Shipwreck off the Coast, with Figures on Shore* (1837, oil on panel, 10 x 11 ins / 25 x 29 cm) DKK 12,000. VEJLE, 15 March 2000, *Fisherman and Family by Coast in Evening Landscape* (1857, oil on canvas, 11 x 12 ins / 29 x 31 cm) DKK 30,000. COPENHAGEN, 21 March 2001, *Figures on the Spanish Steps, Rome* (oil on canvas, 11 x 13 ins / 29 x 34 cm) DKK 90,000. COPENHAGEN, 27 Aug 2002, *Fishermen and Families by Fishing Place* (oil on canvas, 9 x 11 ins / 23 x 27 cm) DKK 16,000. COPENHAGEN, 2 Sept 2003, *The Young Hornblower Saying Goodbye to his Family* (1850, oil on canvas, 24 x 29 ins / 62 x 73 cm) DKK 28,000. COPENHAGEN, 2 March 2004, *Figures by Fishing Village on the Coast of North Sjaelland* (oil on canvas, 26 x 37 ins / 66 x 95 cm) DKK 20,000. VEJLE, 10 May 2004, *Fisherboy from Aalsgaard who has been Collecting Worms* (1859, oil on canvas, 20 x 16 ins / 52 x 41 cm) DKK 16,500.

FRIEDLAENDER, Leo

American, 20th century.

Born 1889, in New York; died 1966, in White Plains (New York).

Sculptor.

Leo Friedlaender studied art in Paris, New York and Brussels. He was a member of many art societies and received a variety of awards.

FRIEDLAENDER, R. J.

German, 19th century.

Active in Hamburg c. 1850.

Lithographer.

FRIEDLAENDER VON MALHEIM, Alfred, or Friedlander, also known as Chevalier von Malheim

Austrian, 19th - 20th century.

Born 21 September 1860, in Vienna; died 1927.

Painter. Genre scenes.

Studied at the Akademie der Bildenden Künste in Vienna and under W. Diez in Munich; lived and worked in Vienna.

MUSEUMS AND GALLERIES:

GRAZ: *Wine-Taster*.

AUCTION RECORDS:

VIENNA, 16 Jan 1973, *Travellers on the Attack*, ATS 13,000. LONDON, 12 Oct 1977, *Military Encampment* (oil on panel, 14 1/2 x 22 1/2 ins / 37 x 57 cm) GBP 2,400. VIENNA, 7 April 1981, *Riders at Rest* (oil on canvas, 8 1/4 x 12 1/2 ins / 21 x 32 cm) ATS 11,000. NEW YORK, 27 Oct 1983, *Courtly Discourse* (oil on panel, 11 3/4 x 8 ins / 29.8 x 20.3 cm) USD 2,800. VIENNA, 10 Dec 1987, *Horsemen Departing* (oil on canvas, 14 3/4 x 19 ins / 37.5 x 48 cm) DEM 3,500. AMSTERDAM, 9 Nov 1994, *Field of Battle* (oil on panel, 8 x 12 1/2 ins / 20.5 x 32 cm) NLG 2,070. VIENNA, 29-30 Oct 1996, *Arrival of the Cavalry* (22 x 35 1/2 ins / 55 x 90 cm) ATS 161,000. LONDON, 5 April 2001, *The Retreat* (oil on canvas, 22 x 35 ins / 55 x 90 cm) GBP 4,000. LONDON, 5 April 2001, *Approaching Cavalry* (oil on canvas, 22 x 35 ins / 55 x 90 cm) GBP 4,200. COLOGNE, 21 Nov 2002, *Filling the Pipe. Enjoying the Pipe* (oil on panel, two works, 9 x 6 ins / 24 x 15 cm) EUR 4,800. BERN, 13 May 2004, *Lively Military Camp on Beach* (oil on canvas, 24 x 35 ins / 60 x 90 cm) CHF 2,500.

FRIEDLAENDER VON MALHEIM, Camilla, or Friedlander

Austrian, 19th - 20th century.

Born 10 December 1856, in Vienna; died 1928.

Painter. Still-lifes.

Studied under her father and made her debut in Vienna around 1864.

AUCTION RECORDS:

LONDON, 17 Oct 1973, *Still-life*, GBP 360. NEW YORK, 25 Oct 1977, *Roses in a Vase* (oil on panel, 6 1/2 x 9 ins / 16.5 x 23 cm) USD 2,100. NEW YORK, 27 May 1982, *Oriental Still-life* (oil on panel, 6 1/2 x 9 ins / 16.5 x 23 cm) USD 2,200. ANGERS, 8 Dec 1984, *Still-life with Oriental Items* (oil on panel, 6 3/4 x 9 ins / 17 x 23 cm) FRF 23,500. BERN, 2 May 1986, *Still-life* (oil on panel, 6 1/2 x 9 ins / 16.6 x 23 cm) CHF 14,000. NEW YORK, 15 Oct 1993, *Still-life with a Book, a Rose and an Item of Jewellery on a Table* (oil on panel, 7 1/4 x 5 ins / 18.4 x 12.5 cm) USD 863.

FRIEDLAENDER VON MALHEIM, Friedrich

(Ritter), or Friedlander

Austrian, 19th century.

Born 10 January 1825, in Kohljanowitz; died 13 June 1901, in Vienna.

Painter. Genre scenes.

Friedlaender von Malheim was a pupil of Waldmuller at the academy in Vienna. After visiting Paris and Italy he returned to settle in Vienna in 1866 and was elected a member of the academy in 1889.

MUSEUMS AND GALLERIES:

VIENNA: *Invalids in the canteen*.

AUCTION RECORDS:

MUNICH, 26 June 1907, *Rustic Interior*, FRF 800. COLOGNE, 26 Nov 1970, *Return from the Market*, DEM 8,200. VIENNA, 21 March 1972, *The Prodigal Sons*, ATS 65,000. VIENNA, 17 Sept 1974, *The Two Invalids*, ATS 60,000. COLOGNE, 25 Nov 1976, *Old Soldiers at the Inn* (oil on panel, 12 1/2 x 17 3/4 ins / 32 x 45 cm) DEM 12,000. VIENNA, 29 Nov 1977, *Preparations for the Festival* (oil on canvas, 21 1/2 x 27 ins / 54.5 x 68.5 cm) ATS 80,000. VIENNA, 17 Nov 1981, *The Reaper's Family* (1860, oil on panel, 22 x 17 3/4 ins / 55 x 45 cm) ATS 100,000. MUNICH, 24 Nov 1983, *The Four Humours* (c. 1889, oil on panel, 9 3/4 x 11 3/4 ins / 25 x 30 cm) DEM 26,000. VIENNA, 20 March 1986, *Peasants around the Table* (watercolour, 7 1/2 x 5 ins / 19 x 13 cm) ATS 25,000. VIENNA, 10 Dec 1987, *The Billet* (1871, oil on canvas, 32 3/4 x 41 3/4 ins / 83 x 106 cm) ATS 320,000. LONDON, 5 May 1989, *Two Old Men Seated at a Table in the Inn* (1879, oil on panel, 7 1/4 x 6 ins / 18.5 x 15.2 cm) GBP 1,540. PARIS, 26 March 1990, *At the Ironware Merchant's* (oil on panel, 13 3/4 x 11 ins / 35 x 27 cm) FRF 15,500. LONDON, 4 Oct 1991, *A Good Drink* (oil on panel, 15 1/2 x 12 1/2 ins / 39.5 x 31.6 cm) GBP 3,740. STOCKHOLM, 30 Nov 1993, *A Host of Customers in the Garden of an Inn in the Evening* (1881, oil on canvas, 22 x 27 1/4 ins / 56 x 69 cm) SEK 67,000. LONDON, 22 Feb 1995, *Two Friends Together around a Bottle* (oil on panel, 9 x 7 1/2 ins / 23 x 19 cm) GBP 2,070. AHLDEN, 23 April 1999, *The Untimely Billeting* (1871, oil on canvas, 32 x 41 ins / 82 x 105 cm) DEM 95,000. COLOGNE, 15 May 1999, *The Village Politicians* (oil on panel, 13 x 9 ins / 32 x 24 cm) DEM 9,000. VIENNA, 23 May 2000, *Memories* (oil on panel, 11 x 15 ins / 29 x 37 cm) ATS 60,000. VIENNA, 23 May 2000, *Before the Lottery House* (1868, oil on canvas, 22 x 27 ins / 55 x 69 cm) ATS 150,000. SAN FRANCISCO, 16 May 2001, *Kitchen Interior with Man Peeling Vegetables* (oil on canvas, 27 x 21 ins / 69 x 53 cm) USD 4,000. VIENNA, 16 May 2002, *At the Blacksmith's* (oil on panel, 26 x 22 ins / 65 x 56 cm) EUR 6,000. VIENNA, 22 Oct 2002, *Two Invalids* (oil on panel, 21 x 16 ins / 53 x 41 cm) EUR 6,500. VIENNA, 22 May 2003, *Two Veterans in Friendly Chat* (oil on panel, 10 x 8 ins / 26 x 20 cm) EUR 3,200. LUCERNE, 19 Nov 2003, *Celebrating the New Wine* (1863, oil on canvas, 27 x 22 ins / 69 x 57 cm) CHF 11,000. LUCERNE, 16 June 2004, *In the Local Inn* (oil on panel, 11 x 8 ins / 29 x 21 cm) CHF 4,500.

FRIEDLAENDER VON MALHEIM, Hedwig

Austrian, 19th century.

Born 13 February 1863, in Vienna.

Painter. Genre scenes, flowers.

Hedwig was the daughter of Friedrich Friedlaender von Malheim. She was a pupil of Laufberger and Jul. Berger and began her career in Vienna in 1888.

AUCTION RECORDS:

LONDON, 20 March 1985, *Young Woman Knitting* (oil on canvas, 22 3/4 x 18 ins / 58 x 46 cm) GBP 6,000. COPENHAGEN, 16 Nov 1994, *Two Children Lying Down* (paint/mahogany, 7 1/2 x 9 ins / 19 x 22 cm) DKK 5,500. VIENNA, 23 May 2000, *Knitting Lesson* (oil on panel, 15 x 11 ins / 37 x 27 cm) ATS 120,000. VIENNA, 16 May 2002, *My All* (oil on panel, 8 x 6 ins / 21 x 16 cm) EUR 3,000. ST LOUIS, 13 Sept 2003, *Interior Scene of a Mother Bathing her Children* (oil on canvas, 19 x 15 ins / 48 x 38 cm) USD 1,800.

FRIEDLANDER, Adolph. See **FRIEDLAENDER Adolph**

FRIEDLANDER, Alfred. See **FRIEDLAENDER von Malheim Alfred**

FRIEDLANDER, August M.. See **FRIEDLAENDER August M.**

FRIEDLANDER, Johnny. See **FRIEDLAENDER Johnny**

FRIEDLANDER, Julius. See **FRIEDLAENDER Julius**

FRIEDLANDER VON MALHEIM. See **FRIEDLAENDER VON MALHEIM**

FRIEDLEIN, Johann

German, 17th century.
Active in Hamburg c. 1685.
Engraver.

Johann Friedlein worked in Kiel and in Copenhagen at the end of the 17th century.

FRIEDMAN, Arnold

American, 20th century.
Born 1879; died 1946.
Painter. Figures, nudes, portraits, landscapes.

AUCTION RECORDS:

NEW YORK, 3 June 1983, *Dutchess Country Landscape* (oil on canvas, 20 x 24 ins / 50.8 x 61 cm) USD 7,500. NEW YORK, 20 June 1985, *Landscape* (oil on canvas, 30 x 25 ins / 76.2 x 63.5 cm) USD 5,500. NEW YORK, 7 April 1988, *Portrait of his Son* (oil on canvas, 21 1/4 x 15 1/2 ins / 53.8 x 39.4 cm) USD 4,180. NEW YORK, 30 May 1990, *Nude in a Landscape* (oil on panel, 6 x 9 1/4 ins / 15.5 x 23.2 cm) USD 2,310. NEW YORK, 27 May 1992, *Abstraction* (oil on canvas, 17 x 21 ins / 43.2 x 53.3 cm) USD 18,700. NEW YORK, 24 May 2000, *Fresh Mounts* (oil on canvasboard, 9 x 13 ins / 23 x 34 cm) USD 15,000. NEW YORK, 4 Oct 2000, *Country Road, Vermont* (oil on board, 13 x 34 ins / 34 x 86 cm) USD 5,000. NEW YORK, 24 May 2001, *Sleeping Female Nude - Betty* (oil on canvas, 29 x 46 ins / 74 x 117 cm) USD 25,000. NEW YORK, 24 May 2001, *Three Flowers in a Vase* (oil on canvas, 15 x 19 ins / 38 x 47 cm) USD 42,500. NEW YORK, 13 March 2002, *Venus* (oil on canvas, 29 x 46 ins / 74 x 117 cm) USD 20,000. NEW YORK, 26 May 2004, *Floral Still-life on a Table* (oil on canvas, 20 x 24 ins / 51 x 61 cm) USD 25,000. NEW YORK, 29 June 2004, *Untitled - Leaf Abstraction* (1923, oil on canvas, 16 x 21 ins / 41 x 53 cm) USD 23,000.

FRIEDMAN, Mark

American, 20th century.
Born in New York.
Sculptor.

Mark Friedman was a pupil of Niclausse and exhibited in Paris at the Salon des Artistes Français in 1932.

FRIEDMAN, Terri

American, 20th century.
Installation artist.

Terri Friedman makes mechanical and kinetic installations activated by water - either uncoloured or yellow, pink or red, which circulates in tubes and runs into bowls - that have a humorous dimension. She held a solo show at Special K Exhibitions, Los Angeles in 1997.

FRIEDMAN, Tom

American, 20th - 21st century.
Born 1965, in St Louis.
Sculptor.
Neo-Conceptual Art.

Tom Friedman is an art graduate of Washington University with a master's degree in sculpture from the University of Illinois, Chicago. He is based in Massachusetts. Heir to Surrealism, Pop Art, Minimalism, and Process Art, he uses unusual materials (tooth-picks, pencils, spaghetti, hair), to develop elaborate constructions that demand outstanding dexterity and technical expertise. He constantly challenges perception by putting forward a new perspective on everyday matters and things, for instance by carving his head in an aspirin tablet displayed at eye level. He has worked on tiny scales, challenging the eye all the way down to the disappearing act of *One Thousand Hours of Staring* (1992-1997), a blank sheet the artist looked at for a thousand hours. Implicated in his own works, he has offered a self-portrait (*Untitled*, 2000), which through the use of cut-out and shredded coloured paper shows him laying in his own blood, the victim of a horrendous motorbike accident. His colours are bright and varied, opening on multiple possibilities and sensations. The spectator must adjust his perception to deal with changes in scale, space and function. Friedman's world is teasing, misleading, both there and not there, said one critic. In a show in Tokyo, he displayed a Plasticine recreation in miniature of his complete works. He began taking part in collective exhibitions in 1994. These have included *Critical Mass* at Gallery A&A, Yale University School of Art, New Haven, *Oltre la Normalità Concentrica* (*Beyond Concentric Normality*), Palazzo da Zara, Padua, and *Affinities: Chuck Close and Tom Friedman*, Art Institute of Chicago. He has shown his works in solo exhibitions since 1987, in galleries and museums in St Louis, New York, Chicago, San Francisco, Naples, Geneva, Tokyo and Milan.

BIBLIOGRAPHY:

Celant, Germano, '*Tom Friedman*' in *Interni*, periodical, December, 2000. Cooper, Dennis/Hainley, Bruce/Searle, Adrian, *Tom Friedman*, Phaidon, New York, 2001. *Tom Friedman*, exhibition catalogue, Fondazione Prada, Milan, 2002. Gisbourne, Mark, *Face/Off: a portrait of the artist*, group exhibition catalogue, Kettle's Yard, Cambridge, 2002 (exhibition on self-portrait). Eskin, Blake, '*Still life with garbage and bee*' in *Art News*, periodical, New York, May, 2002.

FRIEDMANN, Gloria

German, 20th - 21st century.
Born 1950, in Kronach (Bavaria).
Since 1977 active in France.
Sculptor, assemblage artist, environmental artist, mixed media.
Arte Povera.

Friedmann is self-taught and settled in Aignay-Le-Duc in Burgundy in 1977, where she lives and works. In the early 1980s, she started photography, focusing on disused locations. Since 1982, she has worked on the countryside, producing kinds of relief-paintings, in which she sets out to recreate nature with practically worthless products from everyday life and from industry, such as pipes, windscreens and rusty iron plates. In this way, she uses dustbin bags, emphasizing their plastic qualities in her work *Cloudy Sky over Westschleswig*. Then she turned to sculpture, and henceforth favoured minimal forms and natural materials including wood, bone, horsehair, granite and earth, in order to create a vision of original life but also of its destruction. Effectively, a large number of the materials she uses in her works are dead. They have been subjected to transformations, like coal, resulting from the slow decomposition of organic matter, or stuffed animals; thus she produced a white stag with superb antlers on a pile of dead leaves opposite a sphere made of monumental moss and a cone made of bark in her 1992 work *Representatives*; or the cock with gleaming colours perched on a pile of charred wood.

Alongside these almost baroque environments, Friedmann produces works which can be compared to Arte Povera: she produced an oak log called *Satellite*, as well as two large rectangles of granite and skin - the first placed against the wall whilst the second is fixed to the wall in *Lascaux*; but there is also a memorial to nature, *From the Land*, comprising a wooden box, hollowed out in its centre, which stands 9 feet (3 metres) high on a mound of freshly turned earth, and in which leaves, skulls, pieces of wood, feathers, and all these fragments of nature chosen by her are visible through railings. She is not advocating a return to nature in the Rousseau sense, but instead sets out to produce the decay of a doomed world. She draws the strength but also the materials in her works from the universe, without ever plagiarizing it. Thus, she shows that by borrowing from nature, she can only portray a still-life: 'I don't imitate nature, I recreate it by evoking it and by contrasting it'.

Since 1980, she has participated in many group exhibitions in France - Villeurbanne, Strasbourg, Dijon and mainly Paris: 1980, 11th Biennale; 1981, Musée National d'Art Moderne; 1985, Salon de la Jeune Sculpture; 1995, *Décrochages (Disengagements)*, and 1997, *Made in France*, at the Musée National d'Art Moderne; 2000, *Voilà, Un Monde dans la Tête (Voilà, a World in the Head)*, Musée d'Art Moderne de la Ville de Paris; and abroad: 1986, Berlin, Rome; 1987, Zagreb and Documenta 8 in Kassel; 1988, Hamburg, New York; 1991, Essen, Padua, Los Angeles; 1999, 2000, *La Casa, il Corpo, il Cuore (House, Body, Heart)*, Museum Moderner Kunst in Vienna and the modern art museum, Prague; 2003, *Paysages (Landscapes)*, an exhibition confronting the new experience of man in the countryside seen through contemporary art, and organised within the context of *Trésors Publics. 20 Ans de Création dans les Fonds Régionaux d'Art Contemporain (FRAC) (Public Treasury, 20 Years of Creation in the Regional Collection of Contemporary Art (FRAC))*, at the Centre Européen d'Actions Artistiques Contemporaines, Strasbourg.

Friedmann also has held solo shows, in Paris: 1980, Musée d'Art Moderne de la Ville de Paris; 1986, 1988, 1991, Galerie Montenay; 1987, Musée de Grenoble; 1992, Museum Moderner Kunst, Vienna and Kunstmuseum, Ittigen; 1993, Le Consortium, Dijon, and Kunsthaus, Nuremberg; 1994, Centre d'Art Contemporain, Vassivière, Limousin; 1995, *Pour qui? Contre qui? (For whom? Against whom?)*, Villa Arson, Nice; 1998, 2001, Galerie Cent 8, Paris; 2001, *Rose c'est la Vie (Life is Pink)*, Musée Château d'Annecy. In addition to museums and galleries, Friedmann has exhibited in more original places such as the church of the Jesuits of Sion, the church of Val-de-Vesle, the 17th-century court of the Liechtenstein Palace in Vienna, but also in nature, in the Bar-Le-Duc forest.

BIBLIOGRAPHY:

Douroux, Xavier/Gautherot, Frank, *Gloria Friedmann*, Le Coin du miroir, Dijon, 1983. Gourmelon, Mo, *Gloria Friedmann, des évidences telles..*, La Criée, Rennes, 1986. Soutif, Daniel, *Gloria Friedmann, un hommage au beau naturel*, exhibition catalogue, Musée de Bar-le-Duc, Bar-le-Duc, 1986. Marcadé, Bernard, *Gloria Friedmann*, exhibition catalogue, Église des Jésuites, Sion, 1987. *Gloria Friedmann*, exhibition catalogue, Stiftung Ludwig, Vienna, 1992. Lebovici, Elisabeth/Cuvelier, P., *Gloria Friedmann*, Centre d'Art contemporain de Vassivière en Limousin, Beaumont-du-Lac, Annely Juda Fine Art, London, 1994. Bouisset, Maïten, '*Gloria Friedmann - De la nature des êtres et des choses*' in *Art Press* n° 200, periodical, Paris, March 1995. Troncy, Éric/Restany, Pierre, *Gloria Friedmann. Rose c'est la vie*, exhibition catalogue, Éd. du Regard, Paris, 2001 (Exhibition at the Musée-Château d'Annecy. text in French and German). Zahm, Olivier (preface), et al., *Trésors publics, 20 ans de création dans les Fonds régionaux d'art contemporain*, Flammarion, Paris, 2003 (text in French and English).

MUSEUMS AND GALLERIES:

DIJON (FRAC Bourgogne): *Hautes herbes agitées par le vent* (1983) - GRENOBLE (Mus. de Grenoble) - PARIS (FNAC).

FRIEDMANN, Nicolaï
German, 19th century.
Born 1842, in Mannheim; died in Frankfurt am Main.
Painter. Portraits.

There are a large number of Friedmann's portraits in Frankfurt.

FRIEDRICH
German, 13th - 14th century.
Glass painter.

This artist was working at Klosterneuburg (Lower Austria) in around 1280 and again in the early years of the 14th century, with his son Walther as his assistant.

FRIEDRICH
German, 15th century.
Painter.

Friedrich was active in Villach (Carinthia, Austria) in 1415. He decorated the church at Millstätt.

FRIEDRICH
German, 15th century.
Painter.

It appears that this artist worked both at Ansbach (Bavaria) in 1438 and in Nuremberg twenty years later.

FRIEDRICH, A. C.
German, 19th century.
Born c. 1815, in Bremen; died 1855, in Bremen.
Painter. Animals.

Many of Friedrich's works were exhibited in Vienna in 1854.

FRIEDRICH, Adolf (Duke of Ostrogoth)
Swedish, 18th century.
Born 18 July 1750, in Drottningholm; died 12 December 1803, in Montpellier.
Painter, engraver.

Adolf Friedrich was a marshal and the son of King Adolf Friedrich of Sweden. He worked under the direction of the engraver J. E. Rehn in Stockholm.

FRIEDRICH, Alexander
German, 18th century.
Born 27 March 1744, in Friedrichstadt (Holstein); died 14 May 1793, in Dresden.
Painter. History painting.

Alexander was the son of the painter David Friedrich. His works include *Meleager and Atalanta*.

FRIEDRICH, André, or Friedrick
French, 19th century.
Born 17 January 1798, in Rappoltsweiler (now Ribeauvillé, Haut-Rhin); died 9 March 1877, in Strasbourg.
Sculptor, draughtsman, lithographer.

André Friedrich enrolled at the École des Beaux-Arts on 2 January 1821 and studied under Bosio and Schadow; went on to live for a time in Stuttgart, Munich and Berlin, and then in Strasbourg. Friedrich exhibited at the Paris Salon from 1835 to 1842. His principal work includes: *Young Woman Weeping* (marble low relief); *Night* (marble group); *Statue of the Poet Pfeffel* (erected in Colmar on 5 June 1859); *Bishop Werner* (statue for Strasbourg Cathedral); *Statue of the Architect Erwin* (erected in Strasbourg on 29 August 1844);

Archbishop Boll (statue for Fribourg Cathedral); *Monument to the Archbishop of Poznan*; *Francis Drake* (statue); *Gravedigger* (statue in Baden cemetery); *Monument to Turenne* (Sasvach); and *Monument to Grand-Duke Leopold*.
MUSEUMS AND GALLERIES:
COLMAR: *Statuette of the Sculptor* - STRASBOURG: *Slumber*.

FRIEDRICH, Andres
German, 16th - 17th century.
Born c. 1560, in Leipzig; died c. 1617.
Painter, engraver.
Around one hundred engravings can be attributed to this artist.

FRIEDRICH, August (Duke of Brunschwick)
German, 18th century.
Born 29 October 1740; died 8 October 1805.
Engraver.
Two caricatures by August Friedrich are known: *The Misunderstood* and *The Marvellous Effects of Music*.

FRIEDRICH, Bernhard
German, 16th century.
Active in the region of Kissingen (Bavaria) between 1525 and 1550.
Sculptor.
Bernhard Friedrich worked at the church at Münnerstadt.

FRIEDRICH, Bernhard Gottlieb.
See **FRIDRICH**

FRIEDRICH, Carl
German, 19th century.
Born 3 October 1787, in Dresden; died 19 March 1840, in Dresden.
Painter, miniaturist. Flowers.
Carl Friedrich was the son of Jakob Friedrich. On the death of his father, Carl replaced him as botanical painter to the king at the court of Frederick August II, king of Saxony.

FRIEDRICH, Caroline
German, 19th - 20th century.
Born 20 October 1828, in Dresden; died 29 July 1914, in Dresden.
Painter. Still-lifes, flowers.
Caroline Friedrich was the wife of Gustav Adolf Friedrich and the mother of Harald Friedrich.

FRIEDRICH, Caroline Friederike
German, 18th - 19th century.
Born 4 March 1749, in Dresden; died 20 January 1815, in Dresden.
Painter. Still-lifes, flowers.
Caroline was the daughter and pupil of the painter David Friedrich. In 1774, she was accepted as a member of the Dresden academy. She was quite an outstanding painter of flowers.
AUCTION RECORDS:
MUNICH, 29 Nov 1989, *A Moss Rose and a Branch of Mallow* (1807, gouache, two flower studies, a pair, 9 3/4 x 7 3/4 ins / 25 x 20 cm and 11 x 7 ins/27 x 18 cm) DEM 6,600.

FRIEDRICH, Caspar David
German, 18th - 19th century.
Born 5 September 1774, in Greifswald; died 7 May 1840, in Dresden.
Painter, engraver, draughtsman. Figure compositions, landscapes.
Friedrich was born in the Pomerania province on the North Sea, where his protestant family, originally from Silesia, had taken refuge from the disputes between Prussia, Austria and Catholic Poland during the 18th century. Friedrich was brought up in a puritan atmosphere. Having been introduced to drawing by Gottfried Quistorp in Greifswald, he entered the Kunstakademi in Copenhagen in 1794 at the age of 20. To the traditional education which he received there he added the discovery of Nordic poetry, of Ossian, Klopstock, and Kosegarten. In 1798, he settled in Dresden. With its fascinating museum and lively intellectual and artistic atmosphere Friedrich became acquainted with the Romantics: Novalis, Tieck, Schelling, Fichte and Kleist. He also made the acquaintance of the Romantic painter Philipp Otto Runge, who seems to have been the first painter whom he got to know after 1801. Friedrich divided his life between Dresden and his native land. He went from the edges of the Baltic to the Riesengebirge (Mountains of Giants) and to the Hartz Mountains. One of his preferred themes was the deserted landscapes of the island of Rügen and the shores of Pomerania, and the ever-expanding sea and sky.

Friedrich's drawings and watercolours show an emotional depth that anticipates his future work. He drew his Romantic inspiration from a meticulous and passionate observation of reality reminiscent of Flemish painting and of Dürer. Friedrich quickly removed himself from outside influences and adopted a personal and original style, a style which spurred the debate regarding form and content that engaged German artists towards the end of the 18th century. Some of his paintings, especially *The Altar of Tetschen* and *Monk on the Sea Shore* were the subjects of lively debates.

When discussing Friedrich, it is important to distinguish the Nazarenes from the creators of Romantic landscapes. The Nazarenes were part of the *Lukasbund* in the Convent of St Isidoro in Rome under the auspices of Johann Friedrich Overbeck. The Lukasbund brought together Cornelius, Ramboux, Schnorr von Carolsfeld, Schadow and others who promoted the aesthetic ideals of the Italian Renaissance combined with Roman Catholic religious sentiments. The Romantic landscape painters based their work on observations of nature and their religious beliefs were distinctly pantheistic and animistic. Karl Philipp Fohr, the Olivier brothers and Joseph Anton Koch in particular, were active forerunners of German Romantic landscape painters. However although Friedrich's work had a decisive influence on the Olivier brothers, on Georg Friedrich Kersting, Gerhard von Kügelgen, Ferdinand Hartmann, the Riepenhausen brothers, Ernst Ferdinand Oehme, Carl Gustav Carus and on those painters who evolved towards a more realist technique stripped of all allegorical content, such as Christian Friedrich Gille and especially Johann Christian Clausen Dahl, Friedrich himself led a life which was quite withdrawn from the world.

During his long walks in the countryside, Friedrich made very precise sketches, which he used in his studio (and also during his later years) when composing landscapes. Friedrich wrote: 'Close your physical eye, all the more to see your painting with the spiritual eye. Then bring forth into the daylight that which you have seen in the darkness of your night.' For him, 'the artist's law is feeling. Pure feeling can never contradict nature but is always in harmony with her'. Subjectivity is the absolute point of departure through which the artist, haunted by a secret and mysterious longing, can hope to regain the lost unity of nature and the spirit beyond the tragic dualism.

Friedrich was undoubtedly the most Romantic of all the German painters.

While German Romanticism has been seen as rationalist and materialist, in fact it partly arose as the antithesis of a materialist conception of the world. Friedrich was a religious and mystical painter whose vision opened onto another world. The activity of painting is the tangible expression of an invisible reality; man's experience of metaphysical anguish at his own destiny when exposed to the grandiose spectacle of nature. In Friedrich's paintings, space takes on spiritual dimensions. Seen through his eyes and painted by his brush everything becomes something of the spirit or rather of the soul.

Despite the great variety of landscapes painted by Friedrich, a similar atmosphere of melancholy, of pensive stillness. The same silence and the same anguish can be found in the limitless horizons, some of sea, some of strange, high mountains. This is Friedrich's contemplation on the fragility of temporal things and the certainty of a life in eternity. His paintings, usually small, are painted meticulously with a seemingly photographic realism and finished off with a glaze giving overall uniformity and a feeling of impersonality as if the artist wished to efface himself when confronted with the spectacle of nature. It was this modesty that led to Friedrich only rarely signing or dating his paintings.

In Friedrich's paintings, nature is seen as she is and not idealised in a system of mythological references or aesthetic criteria. As a counterpoint to his main theme of endless space, Friedrich, haunted by the idea of death, added emotional overtones that obscure his motives: the ruined monastery of Eldena very near his home town Greifswald; a crucifix overhanging the wild escarpments of mountain heights where rocks amass in indescribable and menacing chaos; a funeral garden through the arbour of which can be seen across the river, bathed in moonlit clarity, the celestial town with the gothic spires of cathedrals in ruins; impenetrable forests where a soldier of the Great Army loses his way; the wreck of a ship called *Hope* in the icy waters of the Arctic; more rarely figures come to a halt in a forest of tormented trees to gaze on the moonlight shining through the clouds; or others are seated on a rock lost in the spectacle of an immense seascape where two great sailing ships are returning to port or even perhaps are sailing away for ever. The mist, the effects of dusk, the twilight, this blurring which annoints the simplest things with a sense of grandeur, the everyday with a feeling of the sublime, these are his preferred themes, embodying also the thought of Novalis: 'Everything becomes poetry in distance: distant mountains, distant men, distant events... Everything becomes Romantic. And from there our primitive poetic nature. Poetry of the night and of the dusk'.

The mysterious character of Friedrich's work prompted admiration but also contributed to a misunderstanding of his work. The allegorical dimension of Friedrich's work remained unrecognised. Friedrich attempted to express his religious and patriotic vision of a world where pines and fir trees represent Christians whose faith never falters, whilst the oak which is depicted dead, uprooted, its branches twisted in a sort of indescribable suffering, represents paganism, ignorant of the hope of resurrection. However some of Friedrich's paintings express a more serene state where humankind is at peace, sure of its own immortality, such as the *Woman in the Sunset*. Human figures, which appear only rarely in his landscapes, are invariably seen from behind, the subject being not the figures who are gazing but what they are gazing at.

During his lifetime, Friedrich was also a solitary being, in spite of honorary rewards bestowed upon him rather too late, and his election to the academy of fine arts in Dresden in 1816 where he was appointed professor in 1817. He became less and less tolerant of his contemporaries, only hastening the decline of his mental faculties that dominated his later years. When he died in Dresden in 1840, Friedrich was unknown and no longer influential as an artist.

He would not be rediscovered until the 20th century. when he eventually gained recognition among the expressionists of Central, Eastern and Northern Europe, notably by Edvard Munch, and also among the surrealists, and by Max Ernst in particular. Sadly some of Friedrich's major works were consumed in the terrible fire which destroyed the Glaspalast in Munich in 1931 while it was holding the exhibition which finally did justice to German Romantic painting.

Friedrich has been represented in many themed collective exhibitions including: 2002, *Expedition Kunst. Die Entdeckung der Natur von C. D. Friedrich bis Humboldt* (*Dispatching Art. Discovering Nature from C. D. Friedrich to Humboldt*) at the Kunsthalle in Hamburg in 2002, an exhibition which portrayed the links btween the natural sciences and the painted landscape. Thanks to loans from Russian museums, a very important exhibition of all his works, *The Romantic Vision of Caspar David Friedrich* was presented at the Art Institute in Chicago and in the Metropolitan Museum in New York in the 1990s. In 1996, the Van Gogh Museum in Amsterdam compared the works of Caspar David Friedrich with those of Philipp Otto Runge. And, in 2001, the state museum of Schwerin and then the museum of Fine Arts in Rouen put on a parallel exhibition of about one hundred drawings, water colours and sepias by Caspar Friedrich and Johan Christian Dahl which emphasised the ideas which they had in common as well as the differences in their temperaments.

Bibliography:

Caspar David Friedrich: His Life and Work, German Library of Information, New York, 1940. Sumowski, Werner, *Caspar-David Friedrich: Studien*, F. Steiner, Wiesbaden, 1970. Vaughan, William/Börsch-Supan, Helmut/Neidhardt, Hans Joachim, *Caspar David Friedrich, 1774-1840: Romantic Landscape Painting in Dresden*, Tate Gallery, London, 1972. Börsch-Supan, Helmut/Jähnig, Karl Wilhelm, *Caspar-David Friedrich: Gemälde, Druckgraphik und bildmässige Zeichnungen*, Prestel, Munich, 1973. Hofstätter, Hans Helmut, *Caspar-David Friedrich, Das gesamte graphische Werk*, Rogner & Bernhard, Munich, 1974. Börsch-Supan, Helmut, *Caspar David Friedrich*, London, 1974. Finke, U., *German Painting from Romanticism to Expressionism*, London, 1974. Guillard, Jacqueline/Guillard, Maurice, *Caspar David Friedrich: Line and Transparency*, Centre Cultural du Marais, 1984. Koerner, Joseph Leo, *Caspar David Friedrich and the Subject of Landscape*, London, 1990. Rewald, Sabine (ed.), *The Romantic Visions of Caspar David Friedrich: Paintings and Drawings from the U.S.S.R.*, Metropolitan Museum of Art, New York, 1990. Hohl, Hanna/Runge, Philipp Otto, *Caspar David Friedrich: The Passage of Time*, Van Gogh Museum, Amsterdam, 1996. Jensen, Christian, *Caspar David Friedrich: Leben und Werk*, DuMont, Cologne, 1999. Hofmann, Werner, *Caspar David Friedrich: Naturwirklichkeit und Kunstwahrheit*, Beck, Munich, 2000. Hofmann, Werner, *Caspar David Friedrich*, Thames & Hudson, London, 2000 (translated by Mary Whittall).

Museums and Galleries:

Berlin (Nationalgal.): *Moonlight on the Sea; Oak Tree in the Snow* - Berlin (Schloss Charlottenburg): *Monk on the Sea Shore; Abbey in the Oak Forest; Morning in the Riesengebirge; Cross on the Baltic Sea* - Berlin (Schloss Charlottenburg, Gal. der Romantik): *Der einsame Baum* (*Solitary Tree*) (1822); *Frau am Fenster* (*Woman at the Window*) (1822); *The Watzmann* - Bremen: *The Tomb of Ammonius* - Cologne (Wallraf-Richartz Mus.): *Cross on the Shores of the Baltic Sea* - Dresden: *The Altar of Tetschen; Two Men Contemplating the Moon; Boats in Port, Evening Time; Tombs of Huns in Autumn* - Essen (Folkwang Mus.): *Landscape of Mountains with a Rainbow; Woman in the Sunset* - Fort Worth (Kimbell AM): *A Mountain Peak with Drifting Clouds* (c. 1835, oil on canvas) - Gotha: *Girls Summoning a Boat* - Hamburg (Kunsthalle): *Shipwreck of Hope in the Icy Waters; First Snows; Sunrise over Neubrandenburg; Meadows near Greifswald; Racing Clouds; Tombs of the Heroes of the War of Liberation* - Kaliningrad: *Landscape of the Mountains of Bohemia* - Leipzig (Mus. der Bildenden Künste): *Periods of Life* (1830-32) - Los Angeles (Getty Mus.): *A Walk at Dusk* (c. 1832-1835, oil on canvas) - Munich (Neue Pinakothek): *Summer; Landscape of the Riesengebirge with Mist; Ruins of a Church in a Forest* - Nuremberg (Germanisches Nationalmus.) - Oslo: *In the Moonlight* - Prague (Národní Gal. V Praze): *The North Sea in the Moonlight* - Riga: *On the Sea Shore* - Stralsund: *Landscape* - Vienna (Kunsthistorisches Mus.): *Seashore with Fisherman; Mist; Rocky Gorge* - Weimar: *Hutten's Tomb*.

AUCTION RECORDS:
LONDON, 22 June 1925, *Vase of Flowers,* GBP 28. LONDON, 1 Aug 1935, *Still-lifes,* GBP 11. MUNICH, 3 Nov 1958, *Village Street* (watercolour) DEM 6,200. LONDON, 4 May 1973, *Three Women Seen from behind on a Road at Dawn,* Gns 55,000. DÜSSELDORF, 20 June 1973, *Night,* DEM 35,000. BERN, 8 June 1977, *The Town of Neudorf on Fire* (1802, etching) CHF 7,200. COLOGNE, 23 Nov 1978, *Alpine Lake at Dawn* (oil on canvas, 28 3/4 x 37 ins / 73 x 94 cm) DEM 2,300. MUNICH, 30 May 1979, *Boy Asleep on a Tomb* (c. 1802-1803, engraving/wood) DEM 5,200. MUNICH, 27 Nov 1980, *Plan for a Tomb and Three Urns* (pen/paper, 5 1/2 x 5 ins / 14 x 13 cm) DEM 6,200. LONDON, 25 Nov 1981, *Mountain Peak in Clouds* (c. 1835, oil on canvas, 9 1/4 x 11 1/2 ins / 23.5 x 29.5 cm) GBP 170,000. BERLIN, 5 Dec 1986, *Ruins of the Holy Cross Monastery near Meissen* (1880, pen and brown wash, 4 x 4 1/2 ins / 10.2 x 11.7 cm) DEM 38,000. HAMBURG, 10 June 1987, *Couple in a Wooded Landscape* (1799, etching, 3 1/2 x 4 1/2 ins / 9 x 11.5 cm) DEM 2,800. MONTE CARLO, 7 Dec 1987, *Winter Landscape with Church* (oil on canvas, 13 x 17 1/4 ins / 33 x 44 cm) FRF 14,000,000. MUNICH, 18 May 1988, *Little Gaus* (1826, watercolour, 10 1/2 x 8 3/4 ins / 26.5 x 22.5 cm) DEM 371,000. MUNICH, 10 May 1989, *Fir tree* (1898, pencil, 10 1/2 x 8 1/2 ins / 26.5 x 21.5 cm) DEM 115,500. MUNICH, 29 Nov 1989, *Priessnitz on the Elbe* (1800, pencil and brown ink, 9 1/4 x 15 ins / 23.5 x 38 cm) DEM 77,000. MUNICH, 31 May 1990, *Study of Boats Fishing nets and a Bush* (1884, pencil, 7 1/4 x 5 3/4 ins / 18.5 x 14.5 cm) DEM 74,800. LONDON, 20 May 1993, *Walk at Dusk* (oil on canvas, 13 x 17 ins / 33 x 43 cm) GBP 2,311,500. LONDON, 13 Oct 1994, *Sailing Ship Finding its Way between Two Rocks on the East Coast* (oil on canvas, 9 x 12 1/4 ins / 22 x 31.2 cm) GBP 639,500. LONDON, 9 Oct 1996, *Caroline at the Top of the Staircase* (oil on canvas) GBP 375,500. LONDON, 1 July 1999, *Fichtenbau. Waldchen* (1798 and 1840, pencil, double-sided, 11 x 8 ins / 27 x 21 cm) GBP 30,000. LONDON, 7 Oct 1999, *Zwei Manner in Betrachtung des Mondes - Two Men Looking at the Moon* (c. 1830, oil on canvas, 14 x 17 ins / 35 x 44 cm) GBP 700,000. LONDON, 9 Nov 2001, *Figures Contemplating the Moon* (1794-1798, watercolour/pen/ink, 4 x 5 ins / 9 x 13 cm) GBP 30,000. HAMBURG, 8 Dec 2001, *View of Arcona with Moon and Fishing Nets* (pencil/brush/sepia, 16 x 27 ins / 41 x 69 cm) DEM 1,300,000. NEW YORK, 23 Jan 2002, *Landscape Study. Clouds and Hills* (black lead, double-sided, 5 x 8 ins / 13 x 20 cm) USD 10,000. COLOGNE, 16 Nov 2002, *Studies of a Young Man* (1798, pencil, 10 x 8 ins / 26 x 21 cm) EUR 40,000. BERLIN, 11 June 2004, *Two Sailboats at Sea* (Indian ink/wash/sepia, 10 x 8 ins / 26 x 20 cm) EUR 82,000. LONDON, 15 June 2004, *A Nordic Landscape, Spring* (c. 1825, oil on canvas, 14 x 19 ins / 35 x 49 cm) GBP 920,000.

FRIEDRICH, Christian
German, 18th century.
Born 1770, in Greifswald.
Sculptor (wood).
Christian was the son of Caspar David Friedrich and worked mainly for the Church of St Nicholas in Greifswald.

FRIEDRICH, David
Swiss, 17th century.
Born 8 January 1637, in St Gall; died 18 December 1695, in St Gall.
Sculptor (wood).
David was the father of Johannes Friedrich.

FRIEDRICH, David
German, 18th century.
Born 2 October 1719, in Grosschönau; died 21 May 1766, in Dresden.
Painter, engraver.
David Friedrich was the father of Alexander, Caroline Fr. and Johann C. J. Friedrich. He specialised in wallpaper.

FRIEDRICH, Eustach
German, 18th century.
Born 1768, in Ebermannstadt.
Engraver.
Eustach Friedrich was living in Bamberg in 1843.

FRIEDRICH, Franz
German, 16th century.
Active in Frankfurt-an-der-Oder (Brandenburg) between 1550 and 1580.
Draughtsman, engraver (wood/burin).
Franz Friedrich engraved portraits and worked for the painter Eichhorn.

FRIEDRICH, Gustav Adolf
German, 19th century.
Born 23 December 1824, in Dresden; died 4 January 1889, in Dresden.
Painter. Genre scenes, animals.
Gustav Adolf Friedrich was the son of Caspar David Friedrich. He studied at the Dresden academy and exhibited his works in Dresden from 1856.

AUCTION RECORDS:
LONDON, 20 May 1993, *The Horse Show* (1863, oil on canvas) GBP 23,000. HAMBURG, 6 June 1969, *Threshing,* DEM 6,500. LUCERNE, 25 May 1982, *Forge in a Mountainous Landscape* (oil on canvas, 18 1/4 x 22 1/4 ins / 46.5 x 56.5 cm) CHF 10,000. LONDON, 20 March 1985, *Farmyard Scene* (1872, oil on canvas, 30 1/4 x 4 1/2 ins / 77 x 11.5 cm) GBP 6,500. MUNICH, 18 May 1988, *Village Street in the 19th century* (1956, oil on canvas, 16 1/2 x 21 ins / 42 x 52.5 cm) DEM 19,800. AMSTERDAM, 14-15 April 1992, *Horse Fair* (1863, oil on canvas, 26 1/4 x 43 ins / 66.5 x 109.5 cm) NLG 25,300. NEW YORK, 21 May 2002, *Painting the Horse Fair in the Artist's Studio* (oil on canvas, 16 x 14 ins / 41 x 36 cm) USD 3,750. ZURICH, 28 March 2003, *Winter Market* (1871, oil on canvas, 29 x 39 ins / 74 x 100 cm) CHF 18,000. BREMEN, 26 March 2004, *Sachsen, Switzerland* (oil on board, 9 x 12 ins / 22 x 30 cm) EUR 2,700. AMSTERDAM, 1 Sept 2004, *Tending to the Horses* (oil on canvas, 16 x 21 ins / 41 x 54 cm) EUR 4,000.

FRIEDRICH, Hans Konrad Heinrich
Swiss, 17th century.
Active at the end of the 17th century.
Painter.
Among Friedrich's works are the painitngs in the cathedral and in the town hall in Bern. He also carried out the decorations for the house of Daniel Engele in Schaffis am Bielersee.

FRIEDRICH, Harald
German, 19th century.
Born 14 April 1858, in Dresden.
Painter. Portraits, genre scenes, still-lifes.
Harald was the son of Gustav Adolf and Caroline Friedrich. He was a pupil of Pohle and of Pauwel in Dresden. He became a teacher at the Hanover academy. He made his debut around 1880 and exhibited his works mainly in Dresden.

AUCTION RECORDS:
MUNICH, 29 June 1982, *Berchtesgaden* (oil on canvas, 37 x 29 1/4 ins / 94 x 74 cm) DEM 6,700.

FRIEDRICH, Jacob Andreas. See **FRIDRICH**

FRIEDRICH, Johann Christian Jacob, called Jacob
German, 18th - 19th century.
Born 13 October 1746, in Friedrichstadt (Holstein); died 3 June 1813.
Watercolourist, painter (gouache), engraver. Genre scenes, flowers, landscapes.
Johann Friedrich was the second son of the painter David Friedrich.

AUCTION RECORDS:
LONDON, 15 July 1980, *Flowers* (four watercolour and gouaches, 13 1/2 x 6 ins / 34.6 x 15.4 cm) GBP 650. NEW YORK, 25 May 1984, *Flowers* (three gouaches/brown paper, 13 1/2 x 6 3/4 ins / 34.6 x 17.2 cm; 11 1/2 x 7 3/4 ins/29.2 x 20 cm; 15 x 8 1/4 ins/37.2 x 21 cm) USD 6,500. STOCKHOLM, 29 May 1991, *The Greasy Pole* (oil on canvas, 17 1/4 x 23 1/2 ins / 44 x 60 cm) SEK 58,000.

FRIEDRICH, Johann Gottlieb
German, 18th century.
Born 1742, in Nuremberg; died 13 November 1809, in Copenhagen.
Engraver.
Johann Gottlieb Friedrich was the son of Bernhardt Gottlieb Friedrich. He worked initially in Regensburg where he painted a large number of portraits.

FRIEDRICH, Johann Heinrich August
German, 19th century.
Born 1 July 1789, in Dresden; died 2 June 1843, in Dresden.
Painter. Flowers.
Tthe son of Johann C. J. Friedrich, Johann Heinrich August was a pupil of his aunt, Caroline Friederike Friedrich.
AUCTION RECORDS:
NEW YORK, 30 Oct 1985, *Tulip and Other Flower* (1817, gouache, 11 x 8 1/2 ins / 28 x 21.3 cm) USD 1,200.

FRIEDRICH, Johann Josef
German, 18th century.
Active in Liebenthal.
Sculptor.
Johann Josef Friedrich worked for the Cistercian Church of Liebenthal.

FRIEDRICH, Johann Josef
Bohemian School, 18th century.
Active in Bohemia.
Painter.
Johann Friedrich was a student at the Akademie der Bildenden Künste in Vienna in 1737. He may be the same artist as a man enrolled at the academy at the same time, whose first name is also listed as Joseph.

FRIEDRICH, Johann Nepomuk
Austrian, 19th century.
Born 24 April 1817, in Mahr-Neustadt; died 24 September 1895, in Vienna.
Painter.
This artist was a pupil of Gsellhofer at the academy in Vienna and specialised mainly in portraits and historical paintings.

FRIEDRICH, Johannes
Swiss, 17th - 18th century.
Born 6 May 1663, in St Gall; died 15 October 1731, in St Gall.
Sculptor (wood/stone).
Johannes Friedrich was a pupil of his father, the sculptor David Friedrich. His output included sandstone figures for public fountains and he also worked for the cathedral in Bern in 1717.

FRIEDRICH, Ludwig
German, 19th - 20th century.
Born 22 June 1827, in Dresden; died 1 June 1916, in Dresden.
Engraver. Landscapes.
The son of Johann Heinrich-August Friedrich, Ludwig studied in Dresden under L. Richter. He engraved in the style of Calame, Meissonier, Schwind, A. Richter and other modern masters. He died by his own hand.

FRIEDRICH, Nicolaus
German, 19th century.
Born 17 July 1865, in Cologne.
Sculptor.
Nicolaus Friedrich studied at the Berlin academy from 1893 to 1897 and was a pupil of Karl Begas from 1897 to 1901. From 1891 to 1893, he worked for the Universal Exhibition in Chicago, after which he travelled in Italy, England, Belgium and France. In 1896, he received the Rome prize (Prix de Rome). He also worked in Berlin and in 1900 received an honourable mention at the Exposition Universelle in Paris.
MUSEUMS AND GALLERIES:
BERLIN: *Man Fastening his Sandal*; *The Archer.*

FRIEDRICH, Otto
Austrian, 19th - 20th century.
Born 2 July 1862, in Raab; died 1937.
Painter. History painting, nudes, portraits, genre scenes.
Otto Friedrich won a gold medal in Berlin in 1887. He settled in Munich and exhibited in this city in particular.
AUCTION RECORDS:
VIENNA, 16 March 1982, *Andante* (1913, oil on canvas, 78 1/4 x 78 1/4 ins / 199 x 199 cm) ATS 300,000. VIENNA, 19 May 1987, *Portrait of a Violinist* (oil on card, 15 3/4 x 11 ins / 40 x 28 cm) ATS 38,000. LONDON, 10 Feb 1988, *Green Nude* (oil on canvas, 58 x 42 1/4 ins / 147.5 x 107 cm) GBP 3,300.

FRIEDRICH, Peter
German, 17th century.
Died 26 September 1616, in Görlitz.
Painter.

FRIEDRICH, Thalia
German, 19th century.
Born 13 May 1815, in Dresden; died 19 September 1840, in Dresden.
Painter.
Thalia Friedrich was the daughter and pupil of Karl. Her works consist mainly of flower paintings, often watercolours.

FRIEDRICH, Theodor
German, 19th century.
Born 16 February 1820, in Dresden; died 7 November 1840, in Dresden.
Painter. Portraits.
Theodor was the son of Karl Friedrich. He was a pupil of Vogel at the Dresden academy.

FRIEDRICH, Waldemar
German, 19th - 20th century.
Born 20 August 1846, in Gnadau (Saxony Anhalt); died 16 October 1910, in Berlin.
Painter, watercolourist. Historical subjects, genre scenes, still-lifes.
Waldemar Friedrich studied under Steffeck at the Berlin academy and under Ramberg in Weimar and went on to teach at both academies. He was awarded a medal in Berlin in 1886 and elected to Academy membership in 1889. He travelled to the Indies with the Grand Duke of Schleswig-Holstein.

FRIEDRICH, Wilhelm I (King of Prussia)
German, 18th century.
Born 14 August 1688; died 31 May 1740.
Painter.
Wilhelm I painted and drew some military scenes.

FRIEDRICH, Wilhelm IV (King of Prussia)
German, 19th century.
Born 15 October 1795; died 2 January 1861.
Painter.

Wilhelm IV was the most assiduous painter among the amateur artists of the Prussian dynasty. He painted and drew in a very classical style.

FRIEDRICH I OF ANHALT (Duke)
German, 19th century.
Born 29 April 1831, in Dessau; died 24 January 1904, in Ballenstedt.
Engraver.

In his youth, this prince did a few engravings under the tutelage of the landscape artist Wilhelm Krause.

FRIEDRICH II DER GROSSE (King of Prussia), or Frederic the Great
German, 18th century.
Born 24 January 1712; died 17 August 1786.
Painter.

Frederick the Great took an amateur interest in painting and drawing.

FRIEDRICH VON ASCHAFFENBURG
German, 15th century.
Active in Frankfurt am Main in 1448.
Painter.

Friedrich von Aschaffenburg was commissioned by the confraternity of St Sebastian to paint an altar for the Dominican church in Frankfurt.

FRIEDRICHS
German, 18th century.
Active c. 1700.
Painter.

Friedrichs decorated a church in Erfurt.

FRIEDRICHS, Fritz
German, 20th century.
Born 17 May 1882, in Hamburg.
Painter, engraver. Portraits, landscapes.

Friedrichs was a pupil of Siebelist.

FRIEDRICHSEN, Ernestine
German, 19th century.
Born 29 June 1824, in Danzig (now Gdansk, Poland); died 21 July 1892, in Düsseldorf.
Painter. Genre scenes.

This artist was a pupil of Marie Wiegmann and Son in Düsseldorf. She travelled in Germany, Holland, Belgium, England and Italy. She exhibited her works mainly in Dresden.

AUCTION RECORDS:
NEW YORK, 13 Feb 1985, *Praying in front of Calvary* (1869, oil on canvas, 37 x 43 1/2 ins / 94 x 110.5 cm) USD 3,000. STAUFEN, 23 May 2003, *Interior with Grandmother and Children* (1864, oil on canvas, 22 x 20 ins / 56 x 50 cm) EUR 3,000.

FRIEMAN, J.
British, 18th century.
Active in London in 1799.
Miniaturist.

FRIEND, Donald Stuart Leslie
Australian, 20th century.
Born 1915, in Sydney; died 1989.
Painter (gouache), watercolourist. Scenes with figures, nudes, portraits.

Donald Friend is known for his picturesque scenes of military life and for paintings inspired by jazz music. He studied at the Royal School of Art in Sydney. He lived in London for a number of years and in 1940 returned to live in Australia. During World War II, he made his first trip to Indonesia, returning there in 1966 and moving to Sanur in 1980. He first exhibited in London in 1936 and took part in many group exhibitions, notably the *Art in Bali* exhibition in Honolulu in 1988. Also in 1988 he was awarded a prize for his life's work by the University of Sydney.

BIBLIOGRAPHY:
Hughes, R., *Donald Friend*, Sydney, 1970. Fry, G./Fry C., *Donald Friend: Australian War Artist, 1945*, Melbourne, 1981.

MUSEUMS AND GALLERIES:
LONDON (British Mus.).

AUCTION RECORDS:
LONDON, 5 July 1972, *Guitarist* (watercolour and pen) GBP 850. LONDON, 17 March 1976, *The Apparition* (watercolour and pen, 27 1/2 x 40 3/4 ins / 70 x 103.5 cm) GBP 500. ROSEBERY, 29 June 1976, *Jazz* (collage, 19 1/2 x 25 ins / 49.5 x 63.5 cm) AUD 700. LONDON, 31 March 1978, *Girl - Woolloomooloo* (1950, oil on canvas, 19 1/2 x 23 1/4 ins / 49.5 x 59 cm) GBP 1,400. MELBOURNE, 19 June 1978, *The Sculptor* (1945, mixed media/paper, 23 3/4 x 19 1/2 ins / 60.4 x 49.5 cm) AUD 1,500. LONDON, 12 June 1981, *Standing Nude* (1948, oil on canvas, 14 3/4 x 10 3/4 ins / 37.5 x 27.5 cm) GBP 300. LONDON, 1 March 1984, *Young Black Girl on a Divan* (watercolour) Gns 900. LONDON, 9 Nov 1984, *Sant'Angelo* (1952, coloured chalk, pen and wash, 12 3/4 x 18 1/2 ins / 32.5 x 47 cm) GBP 650. MELBOURNE, 30 July 1986, *Self-portrait with a Guitarist* (oil on card, 15 1/4 x 19 ins / 39 x 48.5 cm) AUD 7,000. SYDNEY, 29 Oct 1987, *The Celestial Music* (mixed media, 22 1/2 x 30 3/4 ins / 57 x 78 cm) AUD 8,000. LONDON, 1 Dec 1988, *A Market in Ceylon* (ink and gouache, 13 x 19 3/4 ins / 33.3 x 50.2 cm) GBP 4,950. SYDNEY, 20 March 1989, *Three Shy Nudes* (ink, 30 x 22 ins / 76 x 56 cm) AUD 7,500. SYDNEY, 3 July 1989, *Mr Cosmic and Miss Rocket* (oil on card, 11 3/4 x 15 3/4 ins / 30 x 40 cm) AUD 6,000. LONDON, 30 Nov 1989, *Sofa on the Verandah* (ink, watercolour and coloured chalks, 28 1/4 x 41 1/2 ins / 71.7 x 105.4 cm) GBP 9,900. SYDNEY, 15 Oct 1990, *Young Native Girl* (gouache, 13 x 16 1/4 ins / 33 x 41 cm) AUD 3,000. MELBOURNE, 20-21 Aug 1996, *Hill End* (1956, oil on canvas, 29 1/2 x 39 1/4 ins / 75 x 100 cm) AUD 36,800. SINGAPORE, 5 Oct 1996, *Two Young Boys* (watercolour/paper/card, 30 x 22 ins / 76 x 55 cm) SGD 43,700. NEW YORK, 10 Oct 1996, *Seated Models* (1952, Indian ink and ink wash/paper, 12 1/2 x 19 ins / 31.8 x 48.3 cm) USD 6,325. MELBOURNE, 29 April 1997, *Roof Thatchers in Bali* (ink and gouache/paper/panel, 30 1/2 x 53 1/4 ins / 77.5 x 135 cm) AUD 34,500. MELBOURNE, 27 April 1999, *Acts of John the Baptist* (1951, oil on canvas, 20 x 24 ins / 51 x 61 cm) AUD 35,000. SYDNEY, 3 Aug 1999, *Market* (1940, oil ink on canvas, 30 x 40 ins / 76 x 101 cm) AUD 40,000. MELBOURNE, 1 May 2000, *Window, Townsville* (1955, oil on canvas, 15 x 11 ins / 37 x 29 cm) AUD 38,000. MELBOURNE, 27 Nov 2000, *Port Douglas* (1955, oil on canvas, 15 x 19 ins / 39 x 49 cm) AUD 55,000. MELBOURNE, 9 May 2001, *Boy with a Ddog* (1949, oil on board, 15 x 10 ins / 38 x 26 cm) AUD 32,000. SYDNEY, 28 Aug 2001, *Hasten Edward, the Troopers are Upon us* (oil on board, 11 x 15 ins / 29 x 39 cm) AUD 38,000. MELBOURNE, 27 Aug 2002, *Fishermen* (oil and gold leaf on board, 11 x 15 ins / 27 x 37 cm) AUD 20,000. SYDNEY, 26 Aug 2003, *Cairns Harbour* (1942, oil on board, Oil Painting, 15 x 20 ins / 37 x 50 cm) AUD 50,000. SYDNEY, 26 Aug 2003, *Motley Jacket, Ischia* (1950, oil on canvas, 23 x 19 ins / 58 x 48 cm) AUD 70,000. HONG KONG, 25 April 2004, *Ketjak* (watercolour, 59 x 43 ins / 149 x 109 cm) HKD 200,000. MELBOURNE, 16 June 2004, *Girl, London* (1950, oil on canvas, 20 x 24 ins / 51 x 60 cm) AUD 40,000.

FRIEND, J.S.
British, 19th century.
Active in London.
Painter. Figures.

J.S. Friend exhibited in London at the Royal Academy from 1839 to 1841.

FRIEND, Washington
Canadian, 19th century.
Born 1820; died 1886.
Painter, watercolourist, draughtsman. Landscapes.

Washington Friend was very probably the same artist as W. F. Friend, who is known from London auctions of 1923 and 1934.

Auction records:

London, 23 April 1923, *Views of Quebec, Montreal, and Victoria Bridge* (three drawings) GBP 84. London, 30 Nov 1934, *Niagara Falls* (drawing) GBP 4. Toronto, 2 Nov 1982, *Torrents* (watercolour, 10¼ x 14¾ ins / 26.3 x 37.5 cm) CAD 600. London, 19 Nov 1985, *Quebec, View from Levi Bridge* (watercolour heightened with white, oval, 13¾ x 21¾ ins / 35 x 55.5 cm) GBP 3,600. Montreal, 4 June 1991, *Panoramic View of the Île d'Orléans* (watercolour, 10 x 20½ ins / 25.5 x 52 cm) CAD 2,400.

FRIES

Russian, 18th century.

Draughtsman.

We can cite a *Portrait of General Suvarov* by Fries, who was an officer in the Russian army and active at the end of the 18th century.

FRIES, Adam Philipp

German, 18th century.

Born 1768, in Bamberg.

Sculptor.

Adam Fries was the son of Pankraz Fries.

FRIES, Adolf

German, 19th century.

Born in Hanau (Hesse).

Engraver, lithographer.

Adolf Fries worked in Geneva in 1830 and in Paris around 1840.

FRIES, Aloys

German, 19th century.

Born 18 December 1831, in Giesing.

Painter, draughtsman.

Museums and Galleries:

Munich (Museum): a drawing.

FRIES, Andreas

German, 18th century.

Active in Nuremberg.

Sculptor.

Andreas was the son of Pankraz Fries.

FRIES, Anna Susanna

Swiss, 19th century.

Born 30 January 1827, in Zurich; died 11 July 1901, in Sestri.

Painter. Portraits, landscapes.

Anna Fries was a pupil of the art schools in Paris and in Munich and completed her studies under the tutelage of J. C. Zeller in Zurich. She visited Italy, Holland and the Orient, which inspired several landscapes. She was mainly a portrait painter and worked for the Dutch court. Anna Fries also ran a design school for ladies in Florence where she settled. She took part in Swiss exhibitions, notably in Zurich in 1883 where she showed two canvases: *Cairo* and *Paestum*.

Museums and Galleries:

Berlin: *Landscape*; *Town of Heidelberg* - Frankfurt am Main: *Mountain Landscape* - Hamburg: *Mountains* - Leipzig: *Roman Landscape* - Munich: *Waterfall* - St Gall: *Oriental Seascape* (gift from the artist).

Auction records:

Zurich, 26 April 1973, *The Four Seasons*, CHF 8,000. Zurich, 20 Sept 1985, *Portrait of a Young Italian Woman* (1850, oil on canvas, 37¾ x 30½ ins / 96 x 77.5 cm) CHF 3,000. Paris, 17 Dec 2001, *The Island of Philae, Sunset* (oil on canvas, 16 x 23 ins / 40 x 58 cm) FRF 17,000. London, 21 June 2002, *Young Girl in Italian Festive Dress* (oil on canvas, 37 x 30 ins / 94 x 75 cm) GBP 2,200.

FRIES, Anton

German, 18th - 19th century.

Born c. 1764, in Kronach; died 1834, in Detmold near Lippe.

Sculptor.

Anton Fries was the son of Pankraz Fries and worked mainly in Nuremberg.

FRIES, Benedikt

German, 15th century.

Active in Nuremberg (Bavaria) in 1469.

Painter.

FRIES, Bernhardt

German, 19th century.

Born 16 May 1820, in Heidelberg; died 21 May 1879, in Munich.

Painter. Landscapes.

Bernhardt Fries was the youngest son of the landscape artist Ernst Fries and was a pupil of Professor Koopmann in Karlsruhe and at the Munich academy, where he worked with Rottmann. From 1838 to 1845, he was in Rome and Geneva, in Heidelberg in 1848 and in Munich in 1850.

Museums and Galleries:

Munich: *Environs of the Tiber near Rome* - Stuttgart: *Landscape at Mount Serone.*

Auction records:

Munich, 27 May 1977, *Mountainous Landscape* (oil on panel, 9¾ x 13½ ins / 25 x 34 cm) DEM 4,000. Zurich, 15 May 1981, *Walk in the Woods* (oil on canvas, 11 x 14¼ ins / 27 x 36 cm) CHF 2,400. Heidelberg, 20 April 1985, *Banks of the Neckar with View of Heidelberg Castle* (oil on canvas, 28 x 37 ins / 71 x 94 cm) DEM 16,500. Munich, 28 Nov 1985, *Landscape of Palermo* (c. 1850, watercolour, 10¾ x 14¼ ins / 27.5 x 36 cm) DEM 3,500. Munich, 26 May 1992, *Two Hunters on a Forest Track* (oil on canvas, 13½ x 17 ins / 34 x 43 cm) DEM 16,100. Heidelberg, 15 Oct 1994, *Sacred Wood near Rome* (oil on canvas, 13¾ x 18¼ ins / 35 x 46.5 cm) DEM 7,000. Stuttgart, 25 June 1999, *Landscape with Castle Runkelstein near Bozen, Etschtal* (oil on canvas, 38 x 51 ins / 97 x 130 cm) DEM 12,000. Munich, 1 Dec 1999, *Evening Scene with Shipwreck at Rocky Coast* (1842, oil on board, 13 x 17 ins / 34 x 44 cm) DEM 16,000. Düsseldorf, 31 Jan 2000, *Umbrian Landscape with Lake* (oil on canvas, 37 x 54 ins / 95 x 137 cm) DEM 32,000. Ahlden, 12 May 2001, *Extensive Landscape* (oil on canvas, 39 x 52 ins / 100 x 133 cm) DEM 16,000. Berlin, 25 July 2003, *Italian Mountain Landscape with Two Figures by Stream* (oil on panel, 17 x 24 ins / 44 x 60 cm) EUR 2,400. Stuttgart, 25 Sept 2003, *Italian Coast Landscape in Evening* (oil on canvas, 56 x 82 ins / 142 x 209 cm) EUR 3,300. Stuttgart, 24 June 2004, *Southern Italian Coastline in Morning Light* (oil on canvas, 38 x 51 ins / 97 x 130 cm) EUR 4,500.

FRIES, Charles Arthur

American, 19th century.

Born 14 August 1854, in Hillsboro (Ohio); died 15 December 1940, in San Diego (California).

Painter, illustrator. Landscapes.

Museums and Galleries:

New Orléans: *Landscape* - San Diego (MA): *Desert from Vallecitos Point, Laguna Mountain Resort* (1928, oil on canvas); *Point Loma from Logan Heights* (oil on canvas).

Auction records:

San Francisco, 19 March 1981, *Afternoon Light in Laguna Hills* (oil on canvas, 19 x 27 ins / 48 x 68.5 cm) USD 600. San Francisco, 17 June 1999, *Gold King Mountain, Evening* (oil on canvas, 18 x 24 ins / 46 x 61 cm) USD 5,000. Pasadena, 19 Oct 1999, *Edge of a Grove* (oil on canvas, 16 x 20 ins / 41 x 51 cm) USD 4,000. Pasadena, 15 Feb 2000, *Game of Croquet* (1936, oil on canvas, 28 x 36 ins / 71 x 91 cm) USD 11,000. Los Angeles, 3 May 2000, *Water Source* (oil on canvas, 18 x 24 ins / 46 x 61 cm) USD 6,000. San Francisco, 12 Dec 2001,

Roundup (oil on canvas, 32 x 46 ins / 81 x 117 cm) USD 8,500. PASADENA, 12 Feb 2002, *Cajon Mountain from Alpine* (oil on canvas, 20 x 30 ins / 51 x 76 cm) USD 13,000. PASADENA, 29 Oct 2002, *Ocean Front* (oil on canvas, 12 x 18 ins / 30 x 46 cm) USD 8,000. SAN FRANCISCO, 11 June 2003, *View of San Diego from Point Loma* (1898, oil on canvas, 14 x 28 ins / 36 x 71 cm) USD 16,000. PASADENA, 17 June 2003, *Landscape, Rocky Arroyo* (oil on canvas, 18 x 24 ins / 46 x 61 cm) USD 6,000. PASADENA, 17 Feb 2004, *Evening Light on Morongo Mts at Palm Springs* (oil on canvasboard, 24 x 30 ins / 61 x 76 cm) USD 9,000. OAKLAND, 6 March 2004, *Hills near San Diego Gorge* (oil on canvasboard, 15 x 20 ins / 38 x 51 cm) USD 6,500.

FRIES, Christoph
German, 19th century.
Died c. 1810, in Stuttgart.
Sculptor.

Christoph was the son of Pankraz Fries.

FRIES, Emmanuel
French, 19th century.
Born 17 July 1778, in Mulhouse; died 21 January 1852, in Mulhouse.
Painter. Still-lifes (flowers/fruit).

Fries studied in Paris under Jean-Baptiste Regnault; painted fruit and flowers and also dabbled in industrial design.

AUCTION RECORDS:
PARIS, 9 June 1954, *Basket of Fruit and Flowers with Background Landscape,* FRF 50,000. VERSAILLES, 16 May 1971, *Still Life with Grapes,* FRF 6,200. PARIS, 27 April 1976, *Basket of Fruit with Landscape in the Background* (1829, oil on canvas, 56 3/4 x 44 1/2 ins / 144 x 113 cm) FRF 20,000. LONDON, 17 Nov 1993, *Still Life with Grapes and Peaches on a Marble Relief, with an Italian Landscape in the Background* (1839, oil on canvas, 56 1/4 x 43 3/4 ins / 143 x 111 cm) GBP 23,000.

FRIES, Ernst
German, 19th century.
Born 22 June 1801, in Heidelberg; died 12 October 1833, in Karlsruhe.
Painter, engraver. Portraits, landscapes.

Ernst Fries was the brother of Bernhard Fries and a pupil of Kuntz in Karlsruhe. He was a disciple of the English painter Wallis, whom he met in Heidelberg, and then of Moller in Darmstadt. In 1821, he returned to Munich. From 1823 to 1827, he worked in Italy then returned to Germany, where he lived first in Munich and then in Karlsruhe. Several of his landscapes were displayed in the exhibition *Un Paese incantato. Italia dipinta da Thomas Jones a Corot* held in 2001 at the international centre of Arts and Culture of the Palazzo Te in Mantua.

He died young, his promise unfulfilled and leaving the impression that, along with Reinhold, Rottman, Wöchter, Wässmann, Heinrich-Maria von Hess and Franz Horny, he might have been one of the successors of Josef Anton Koch who, as a product of the Nazarenes in Rome, was, if not the best, at least the creator of the German Romantic landscape to which Caspar David Friedrich would later bring the full force of his creativity.

BIBLIOGRAPHY:
Bott, Elisabeth, *Ernst Fries, 1801-1833: studien zu seinen Landschaftszeichnungen*, dissertation, Universität, Heidelberg, 1978. Wechssler, Sigrid, *Ernst Fries*, catalogue raisonné, Kehrer, Heidelberg, 2000. Ottani Cavina, Anna (ed.), *Un Paese incantato. Italia dipinta da Thomas Jones a Corot*, exhibition catalogue, Electa, Milan, 2001.

MUSEUMS AND GALLERIES:
HEIDELBERG (Kurpfälzisches Mus.): *The Grotto Azzurra in Capri* (oil on canvas); *Nomentano Bridge in Rome* (oil/card); *Hadrian Villa in Tivoli* (watercolour) - NUREMBERG (Germanisches Nationalmus.): *Tivoli* (oil on canvas).

AUCTION RECORDS:
LUCERNE, 18 Nov 1978, *Italian Landscape* (oil on canvas, 9 1/2 x 7 1/2 ins / 24 x 19 cm) CHF 4,500. WASHINGTON D.C., 23 Feb 1979, *Sicilian Landscape* (watercolour sepia /pencil outlines, 11 3/4 x 18 3/4 ins / 30 x 47.5 cm) DEM 12,500. MUNICH, 27 Nov 1980, *Roman Forum* (1824, pencil/paper, 9 1/2 x 20 1/4 ins / 24 x 51.5 cm) DEM 8,200. VIENNA, 22 May 1982, *View of Salzburg; View of Königsee* (two drawings, 7 x 11 ins / 17.5 x 27 cm) ATS 70,000. COLOGNE, 21 Nov 1985, *Italian Landscape* (oil on canvas, 11 1/2 x 16 3/4 ins / 29 x 42.5 cm) DEM 35,000. HEIDELBERG, 14 Oct 1988, *Neuburg Convent near Heidelberg* (1825, lithograph, 5 1/2 x 7 3/4 ins / 14.2 x 19.6 cm) DEM 3,200. MUNICH, 10 Dec 1992, *Louisa the Artisit's Sister* (1828, pencil/paper, 9 1/4 x 7 1/4 ins / 23.8 x 18.4 cm) DEM 10,735. HEIDELBERG, 15 Oct 1994, *Heidelberg Castle* (1820, lithograph) DEM 1,550. COLOGNE, 25 March 2000, *Bernese Alps with View of Hadliberg* (watercolour over pencil, 11 x 15 ins / 28 x 37 cm) DEM 6,500. MUNICH, 7 Nov 2000, *Ponte Maggio presso Casoli* (Indian ink/brush over pencil, 10 x 14 ins / 25 x 36 cm) DEM 5,800. ZURICH, 17 June 2002, *Italian Study* (oil on paper/board, 10 x 15 ins / 26 x 37 cm) CHF 13,000. COLOGNE, 13 Dec 2003, *Landscape near Massa* (oil on panel, 9 x 7 ins / 23 x 17 cm) EUR 20,000.

FRIES, Franz
German, 18th - 19th century.
Born c. 1764, in Bamberg; died c. 1821.
Painter.

Franz was the son of Pankraz Fries.

FRIES, Friedrich
German, 19th century.
Died c. 1810, in Fürth.
Sculptor.

Friedrich was the son of Pankraz Fries.

FRIES, Georg, or Friess
Austrian, 18th century.
Active in Salzburg.
Sculptor.

Georg Fries worked for the Church of St Sebastian in Salzburg.

FRIES, Georg Fritz
German, 17th century.
Active in Mainz c. 1670.
Sculptor.

Georg Fritz may have been the son of Johann Fries.

FRIES, Hans
Swiss, 15th - 16th century.
Born between 1460 and 1465, in Fribourg; died c. 1520.
Painter. History painting.
Bern School.

Hans Fries was a pupil of Heinrich Bichler of Bern, but later came under the influence of the Augsburg school and Hans Burckmair. Fries worked in Basel and Bern. He was a member of the Grand Council of Fribourg, where he was engaged as town painter between 1501 and 1510. By 1517, he is recorded as being in Basel again, where he produced six paintings depicting scenes from *The Life of the Virgin*. The museum in Fribourg held an exhibition of his works in 2001.

Fries' paintings are expressive of sincerity and religious feeling. They include: *St John the Baptist Preaching before Herod and his Court, St John the Evangelist, St Joachim and St Anne Choosing Sacrificial Lambs, St Joachim with St Anne before the Temple, The Birth of the Virgin, The Visitation* and *The Return from Egypt* (Basel Museum). He had been a member of the guild of painters in 1488 in Basel. His early works seem to have been full of detail and a more original expression of violence, as, for example, in *St Barbara, St Christopher* and two panels showing *The Apocalypse*

BIBLIOGRAPHY:

Villiger, Verena, *Hans Fries*, exhibition catalogue, Musée d'Art et d'Histoire, Fribourg, 2001.

MUSEUMS AND GALLERIES:

BASEL: *The Twelve-Year-Old Jesus in the Temple* - MUNICH (Alte Pinakothek): *St Francis Receiving the Stigmata* - ZURICH: *Vision of St John the Evangelist; St John Before Domitian.*

FRIES, Hans
German, 19th - 20th century.
Born 8 April 1872, in Heidelberg.
Sculptor. Religious subjects.

After studying at the fine arts academy in Berlin, Hans Fries returned to his native Heidelberg, where he was in demand as a sculptor, working mainly in churches.

FRIES, Hans Rudolf
Swiss, 17th century.
Died 1661, in Schaffhausen.
Active in Schaffhausen in the middle of the 17th century.
Painter, glass painter, decorative designer.

Hans Rudolf Fries was made a bourgeois of Scaffhouse in 1633.

FRIES, J. D.
Dutch, 17th century.
Active in Groningen.
Engraver.

Fries is known only for a portrait of *Professor Eyssonius.*

FRIES, Johann, or Friess
German, 17th century.
Active in Mainz at the beginning of the 17th century.
Sculptor.

FRIES, Johann Balthasar
German, 17th century.
Active in Mainz in the middle of the 17th century.
Sculptor.

Johann Balthasar Fries was the son of Johann Fries.

FRIES, Johann Conrad, or Friess
Swiss, 17th century.
Born 1617, in Zurich; died 31 March 1693, in Zurich.
Painter. Portraits.

Johann Conrad Fries was a pupil of Samuel Hoffman around 1631 and carried out different functions for the corporation of artists in his home town. Several of his portraits were engraved by Johannes Meyer, J. Schweizer and Konrad Meyer.

FRIES, Johann Georg
German, 18th century.
Born c. 1764, in Bamberg; died 1784.
Sculptor.

Johann Georg was the son of Pankraz Fries.

FRIES, Johann Georg
German, 19th century.
Born c. 1786, in Nuremberg.
Painter.

Johann Georg was the son of Anton Fries.

FRIES, Johann Georg Christoph
German, 19th century.
Born 1787, in Nuremberg; died c. 1860.
Painter, miniaturist. Architectural views.

The son of Anton Fries, Johann Georg Christoph Fries was also a singer and an actor.

FRIES, Karl Friedrich
German, 19th century.
Born 20 November 1831, in Winnweiler; died 23 December 1871, in St Gall.
Painter.

Karl Fries studied at the Munich academy and was then a pupil of Berdellé. He also worked in Vienna under the direction of Rahl. He later visited Venice, Florence and Calabria. His style is reminiscent of the Venetian Masters.

FRIES, Mathes
German, 17th century.
Active in Augsburg in 1639.
Painter.

FRIES, Pankraz
German, 18th century.
Born in Baunach; died c. 1781, in Bamberg.
Sculptor.

Pankraz Fries worked for Birkenfekd Castle in 1758.

FRIES, Samuel
Swiss, 17th century.
Died 1696 or 1596 according to Leu, in Mahren according to Nagler.
Active in Zurich.
Painter, sculptor.

FRIES, Simon
Austrian, 17th - 18th century.
Active in Salzburg.
Sculptor (wood).

Simon Fries worked for the churches in Salzburg.

FRIES, Wilhelm
German, 19th century.
Born 1819, in Heidelberg; died 29 March 1878, in Constance.
Painter. Landscapes.

Wilhelm Fries was the brother of Bernhard and Ernst Fries. He was curator of the museum in Wessenberg.

AUCTION RECORDS:

HEIDELBERG, 15 Oct 1994, *Schoenberg Castle* (1870, oil on canvas, 12 1/4 x 18 ins / 31 x 46 cm) DEM 1,350. CONSTANCE, 22 June 2001, *Lake Landscape* (1873, oil on canvas, 9 x 26 ins / 24 x 65 cm) DEM 3,600. STUTTGART, 25 March 2004, *Tree-lined Stream in Valley* (1874, oil on canvas, 19 x 24 ins / 47 x 62 cm) EUR 3,300.

FRIES, Willy
Swiss, 20th century.
Born 25 February 1881, in Zurich; died 1965, in Zurich.
Painter. Landscapes.

Willy Fries studied under Loefftz in Munich and was influenced by Leibl and Welti.

AUCTION RECORDS:

ZURICH, 8 Nov 1980, *Bahnhofbrücke, Zurich* (1916, oil on canvas, 23 1/2 x 31 1/2 ins / 60 x 80 cm) CHF 2,000. ZURICH, 8 Nov 1985, *Child's Bedroom* (oil on panel, 31 1/2 x 24 3/4 ins / 80 x 63 cm) CHF 28,000. ZURICH, 30 Nov 1995, *Terrace of the Waldhaus Dolder Hotel, Zurich* (oil on card, 15 3/4 x 22 ins / 40 x 55 cm) CHF 4,370. ZURICH, 19 Nov 1997, *Nude (rear view)* (oil on panel, 46 x 28 1/2 ins / 117 x 72.5 cm) CHF 850. ST GALL, 2 Nov 1999, *Landscape in Toggenburg with View of Santis* (1938, mixed media on panel, 27 x 31 ins / 69 x 79 cm) CHF 3,200. BERN, 8 Nov 2002, *Village in the Dunes* (1930, oil on canvas, 17 x 21 ins / 43 x 54 cm) CHF 3,000. BERN, 14 May 2004, *Reverence with Flowers* (1972, oil on panel, 16 x 21 ins / 40 x 54 cm) CHF 3,000.

FRIESE, Leopold August
Czech, 19th century.
Born 27 January 1793, in Nové Krecany; died 1842.
Painter.

Leopold Friese studied in Prague and worked on an important series of drawings depicting the history of Bohemia.

FRIESE, Richard Bernhardt Louis

German, 19th - 20th century.

Born 15 December 1854, in Gumbinnen; died 1918.

Painter, watercolourist, draughtsman. Battles, landscapes, animals.

Friese studied at the Berlin academy until 1880, then travelled in Syria and Norway before settling in Berlin, where he was awarded a medal in 1886. He was a bronze medal winner in 1885 and received an honourable mention at the Exhibition Universelle in Paris in 1900.

MUSEUMS AND GALLERIES:

BERLIN: *On the Field of Battle* - BREMEN: *Lions and Zebras* - KALININGRAD: *Elche in the Snow; Bresdzuller Moor.*

AUCTION RECORDS:

LONDON, 8-18 July 1940, *Brigands*, GBP 10. COLOGNE, 26 March 1976, *Landscape with Reindeer* (1886, watercolour, 24 x 38 1/2 ins / 61 x 98 cm) DEM 3,500. COLOGNE, 11 May 1977, *Landscape with Stag* (oil on canvas, 35 3/4 x 64 ins / 91 x 162.5 cm) DEM 14,000. COLOGNE, 21 March 1980, *Landscape at Sunset with Reindeer* (oil on canvas, 29 3/4 x 42 1/2 ins / 75.5 x 108 cm) DEM 6,000. LONDON, 22 June 1990, *Lion and Lioness Stalking Prey* (1886, oil on canvas, 19 1/2 x 31 1/4 ins / 49.5 x 79.4 cm) GBP 23,100. LONDON, 21 June 1991, *Polar Bear in an Arctic Landscape* (1899, oil on canvas, 35 x 64 ins / 89 x 162.5 cm) GBP 6,600. AMSTERDAM, 21 April 1993, *Stag in a Snow-Covered Forest* (1893, oil on panel, 11 1/4 x 8 1/4 ins / 28.5 x 21 cm) NLG 3,220. LONDON, 17 June 1994, *Lion's Head* (1910, pencil, watercolour and gouache/paper, 14 1/2 x 15 1/2 ins / 36.9 x 39.4 cm) GBP 8,280.

FRIESEKE, Frederick Carl

American, 19th - 20th century.

Born 1874, in Owosso (Michigan); died 1939, in Le Mesnil-sur-Blangy (Calvados), France.

Active in France from 1898 to 1939.

Painter (gouache and oil), pastellist, watercolourist, draughtsman. Figures, nudes, portraits, genre scenes, interiors with figures, still-lifes, flowers, landscapes with figures.

Frederick Carl Frieseke studied at the Chicago School of Fine Arts from 1884, and at the Art Students League, New York. In 1888, he went to the Académie Julian in Paris, where he worked under Benjamin-Constant and Jean-Paul Laurens, also receiving advice from Whistler. In Paris, he also became acquainted with the work of contemporary artists, particularly Fantin-Latour and Renoir, and discovered Giverny, which he visited frequently during the summer months. In 1906, having achieved a degree of financial and artistic success, Frieseke was able to buy Théodore Robinson's former house in Giverny, which was next door to Monet's. In 1919, he moved to the Normandy village, Le Mesnil-sur-Blangy, where, after a brief return to the USA in 1937, he died.

Frieseke primarily painted female figures and nudes, such as *Woman with a Mirror, Young Girl Playing the Piano* or *Model in front of a Screen*, gradually progressing to intimate scenes of women and, like Renoir, voluptuous nudes posed in the open air, their bodies lit by sunlight filtered through foliage. His methods ranged from a strictly Impressionist technique of separate brushstrokes, to one approaching divisionism, as in *Mrs Whitman's Garden* of about 1912, to a broader application of colour, as in *Ladies in a Boat in Giverny* of 1910. At times, he even went beyond Impressionism to a manner inspired by Fauvism, heightening the colours - mauves, blues and pinks - to 'exaggerate the effect'. At the same time, Frieseke was also concerned, like Degas, with traditional figure painting, despite often setting them in an Impressionist-style landscape, as in *Hollyhocks* of 1912-1913.

Frieseke took part in many group exhibitions in Paris, including the Salon des Artistes Français and the Société Nationale des Beaux-Arts, of which he became an associate member in 1901 and a permanent member in 1907. He held a solo show at the Venice Biennale in 1909, followed by another in Rome in 1911, and a show in New York in 1912. He received a number of distinctions: 1909, a gold medal at the Munich International Exhibition; 1913, the Temple Prize from the Pennsylvania Academy of the Fine Arts, Philadelphia; 1915, the Grand Prix at the Panama-Pacific International Exhibition, San Francisco; 1915, a gold medal at the Philadelphia Art Club; and was made a Chevalier de la Légion d'Honneur. In 1982, he was included in *Impressionnistes Américains (American Impressionists)* at the Musée du Petit Palais, Paris, and, in 2002, in *L'Impressionnisme américain 1880-1915 (American Impressionism 1880-1915)* at the Fondation de l'Hermitage, Lausanne.

F-C-Frieseke

BIBLIOGRAPHY:

Frederick Frieseke, exhibition catalogue, Telfair Academy of Arts and Sciences, Savannah (GA), 1974. *Impressionnistes américains*, exhibition catalogue, Smithsonian Institution, Washington DC, musée du Petit Palais, Paris, 1982. Hélène Ahrweiler, Roger Mandle, D. Scott Atkinson, William H. Gerdts, Carole L. Shelby, Jochen Wierich, *Lasting Impressions: American Painters in France 1865-1915*, exhibition catalogue, Musée d'Art américain, Giverny, Terra Foundation for the Arts, Evanston (IL), 1992. Mac-Donald, Margaret F., *James McNeill Whistler: Drawings, Pastels and Watercolours, a Catalogue Raisonné*, Published for the Paul Mellon Centre for Studies in British Art by Yale University Press, New Haven and London, 1995. Kilmer, Nicholas et al., *Frederick Carl Frieske. The Evolution of an American Impressionist*, exhibition catalogue, Telfair Museum of Art, Savannah, 2001. Cikovski, Nicolai/Hauptman, William, *L'Impressionnisme américain 1880-1915*, Fondation de l'Hermitage, Lausanne, 2002.

MUSEUMS AND GALLERIES:

CHICAGO (Terra Foundation for American Art Collection): *The Green Belt* (1904); *Woman in a Garden* (c. 1912); *Lilies; Tea-time in Giverny; Skein of Silk* (c. 1915) - LUGANO (Thyssen-Bornemisza Collection): *Hollyhocks* (1912-1913) - RICHMOND (Virginia MFA): *Blue Interior: Giverny (The Red Ribbon)* (c. 1912-1913, oil on canvas) - ST LOUIS (AM) - WASHINGTON DC (Corcoran Gal. of Art): *Peace* (1917) - YOUNGSTOWN (Butler Institute of American Art): *Good Day* (c. 1910).

AUCTION RECORDS:

PARIS, 14 May 1925, *Young Woman with Fruit*, FRF 2,020. NEW YORK, 29 Oct 1926, *Basket of Flowers*, USD 800. NEW YORK, 4-5 Feb 1932, *In the Garden*, USD 180. PARIS, 23 Dec 1942, *Portrait of a Woman*, FRF 1,050. NEW YORK, 2 March 1944, *Young Girl in Pink*, USD 125. PALM BEACH, 3 Feb 1970, *Young Woman in front of a Mirror*, USD 6,400. NEW YORK, 21 March 1974, *Young Girl at the Piano*, USD 4,000. NEW YORK, 28 Oct 1976, *Young Woman on the Beach* (oil on panel, 14 1/2 x 18 ins / 37 x 45.7 cm) USD 3,900. NEW YORK, 21 April 1977, *Model in front of a Screen* (oil on canvas, 24 x 19 3/4 ins / 61 x 50 cm) USD 3,600. LOS ANGELES, 12 March 1979, *Model Resting* (1929, watercolour and charcoal, 9 x 11 3/4 ins / 22.8 x 30 cm) USD 900. NEW YORK, 19 June 1981, *Still-life with Flowers* (gouache, 9 x 11 1/2 ins / 22.9 x 29.2 cm) USD 3,250. NEW YORK, 1 June 1984, *Woman Sewing in a Garden* (c. 1920, oil on canvas, 28 1/4 x 36 ins / 72 x 91.7 cm) USD 85,000. NEW YORK, 29 May 1987, *The Open Window* (oil on canvas, 51 1/2 x 40 1/2 ins / 130.9 x 102.9 cm) USD 750,000. NEW YORK, 3 Dec

1987, *The Pink Parasol* (oil on canvas, 32 x 26 ins / 81.3 x 66 cm) USD 400,000. FONTAINEBLEAU, 28 Feb 1988, *Young Woman Seated and Wearing a Shawl* (1902, oil on panel, 18 x 14 1/4 ins / 46 x 36 cm) FRF 530,000. NEW YORK, 26 May 1988, *Woman Sewing in a Garden* (oil on canvas, 32 x 32 ins / 81.2 x 81.2 cm) USD 88,000. NEW YORK, 24 June 1988, *Bowl of Flowers* (1928, watercolour/paper, 11 3/4 x 16 ins / 29.7 x 40.6 cm) USD 4,400. NEW YORK, 1 Dec 1988, *The Tree of Judea* (oil on canvas, 32 x 25 1/2 ins / 81.2 x 64.7 cm) USD 407,000. PARIS, 14 Dec 1988, *Young Woman with a Bouquet* (oil on panel, 13 3/4 x 11 ins / 35 x 27 cm) FRF 480,000. NEW YORK, 24 May 1989, *Flowers in a Garden* (oil on canvas, 32 1/4 x 32 1/4 ins / 82 x 82 cm) USD 440,000. NEW YORK, 30 Nov 1989, *Woman in front of a Mirror* (oil on canvas, 32 x 25 3/4 ins / 81.3 x 65.4 cm) USD 82,500. NEW YORK, 14 Feb 1990, *House by the Sea* (watercolour/paper, 10 1/4 x 13 3/4 ins / 25.8 x 35 cm) USD 6,050. NEW YORK, 24 May 1990, *Nude in a Blue Interior* (1925, oil on canvas, 36 1/4 x 28 3/4 ins / 92 x 73 cm) USD 85,250. NEW YORK, 23 May 1991, *Mirror* (1912, oil on canvas, 32 ins / 81 cm, 1 1/4 x 32 ins/3 x 81.3 cm) USD 181,500. NEW YORK, 27 May 1992, *Woman Trying on Shoes* (oil on panel, 13 3/4 x 10 1/2 ins / 34.9 x 26.7 cm) USD 44,000. NEW YORK, 4 Dec 1992, *On the Beach* (oil on canvas, 32 1/4 x 32 1/4 ins / 82.2 x 82.2 cm) USD 396,000. NEW YORK, 22 Sept 1993, *Cup of Tea* (watercolour and charcoal/paper, 15 1/2 x 20 ins / 39.5 x 50.5 cm) USD 16,100. NEW YORK, 1 Dec 1994, *On the River* (oil on canvas, 27 1/2 x 34 ins / 69.9 x 86.4 cm) USD 470,000. LYONS, 4 Dec 1994, *On the River* (oil on canvas, 25 1/4 x 31 1/2 ins / 64 x 80 cm) FRF 2,100,000. NEW YORK, 25 May 1995, *The End of October* (oil on canvas, 25 3/4 x 32 ins / 65.4 x 81.3 cm) USD 299,500. NEW YORK, 29 Nov 1995, *In the Garden, Giverny* (oil on canvas, 32 x 32 ins / 81.3 x 81.3 cm) USD 1,020,000. NEW YORK, 22 May 1996, *At a Laid Table* (1918, oil on canvas, 32 x 32 ins / 81.3 x 81.3 cm) USD 162,000. NEW YORK, 4 Dec 1996, *Blue Curtains* (1924, oil on canvas, 36 1/4 x 36 1/4 ins / 92 x 92 cm) USD 85,000. NEW YORK, 4 Dec 1997, *Near a River* (oil on canvas, 25 1/2 x 31 3/4 ins / 64.7 x 80.6 cm) USD 233,500. NEW YORK, 27 May 1999, *Japanese Parasol* (c. 1908, oil on canvas, 32 x 26 ins / 81 x 65 cm) USD 575,000. NEW YORK, 30 Nov 1999, *In the Nursery* (oil on board, 20 x 25 ins / 52 x 64 cm) USD 260,000. NEW YORK, 24 May 2000, *On the River* (oil on canvas, 26 x 32 ins / 65 x 81 cm) USD 1,100,000. NEW YORK, 30 Nov 2000, *Woman before a Mirror* (c. 1912, oil on canvas, 37 x 29 ins / 93 x 73 cm) USD 310,000. NEW YORK, 28 Nov 2001, *Repose at Noonday* (c. 1911, oil on canvas, 26 x 32 ins / 66 x 81 cm) USD 290,000. NEW YORK, 28 Nov 2001, *Nude in Sunlight* (1910, oil on canvas, 30 x 30 ins / 76 x 76 cm) USD 300,000. NEW YORK, 25 April 2002, *Breakfast Room* (oil on canvas, 32 x 32 ins / 81 x 81 cm) USD 350,000. NEW YORK, 5 Dec 2002, *Garden Path* (oil on canvas, 26 x 32 ins / 65 x 81 cm) USD 780,000. NEW YORK, 21 May 2003, *Silhouette* (oil on canvas, 36 x 29 ins / 92 x 74 cm) USD 90,000. NEW YORK, 4 Dec 2003, *Woman Seated in Park with Basket* (1921, oil on canvas, 29 x 36 ins / 73 x 92 cm) USD 320,000. NEW YORK, 19 May 2004, *Luxembourg Gardens* (1901, oil on canvas, 26 x 32 ins / 66 x 81 cm) USD 130,000.

FRIESELHEM, P.

German, 18th century.
Painter, engraver.

Among this artist's works are *Portrait of the Count of Estaing* and that of the *Duke of Sully* in the style of Pourbus.

FRIESENBERG, Marx

Swiss, 16th century.
Died before 1607.
Active in Solothurn.
Painter.
Solothurn School.

Friesenberg became a burgher of the town of Solothurn in 1570 and a member of the confraternity of St Luke in 1587.

FRIESNER, Karoline

German, 19th century.
Died 1830.
Active in Breslau (now Wroclaw).
Painter.

Oil paintings of fruit and flowers are attributed to Karoline Friesner.

FRIESS, Franz Heinrich

German, 17th century.
Active in Cologne c. 1680.
Painter.

FRIESS, Johann of

German, 17th century.
Active in Cologne c. 1625.
Painter.

FRIESS, Ludwig

German, 15th century.
Active in Ulm (Baden-Württemberg) at the end of the 15th century.
Painter.

This artist has sometimes been confused with Ludwig Schongauer.

FRIESZ, Achille Émile Othon

French, 20th century.
Born 6 February 1879, in Le Havre; died 10 January 1949, in Paris.
Painter, watercolourist, engraver, illustrator. Figure compositions, figures, portraits, military portraits, landscapes, still-lifes, flowers.
School of Honfleur (or of St-Siméon).

Achille Friesz was the son of a family of sailors from Le Havre. From 1885 he often spent time in Marseilles visiting his maternal uncles. As a child he dreamed of going to sea, but from the age of 12 he developed a passion for art, and after secondary school he attended the École des Beaux-Arts in Le Havre. There, from 1896 to 1898, he studied under Charles-Marie Lhullier who had been a friend of Jongkind and whom, like Dufy and Braque, he remembered fondly throughout his life. Lhullier introduced his students to the work of Chardin, Corot, Géricault and Delacroix.

After receiving a bursary from the local authorities in 1898, he went to Paris and, while his friends Matisse, Rouault and Marquet studied under Gustave Moreau, enrolled at the École des Beaux-Arts at the studio of Léon Bonnat, where he was joined by Dufy. However, he scarcely attended the studio, preferring to go to the Louvre and make copies of the works of Clouet, Veronese, Rubens, Claude Lorraine and Delacroix. He did his military service in Paris in 1902 but continued with his art. Around this time he met Camille Pissarro and sought his advice.

As a young man he began to make frequent trips away, not necessarily travelling very far, but looking for subjects for his work, usually landscapes. Among the places he visited were the Creuse region around 1903, Antwerp in 1905, returning there with Braque in 1906, and La Ciotat, Cassis and L'Estaque in 1906-1907, again in the company of Braque. In Paris he frequently moved lodgings until 1914. He moved in with Henri Matisse at the Couvent des Oiseaux from 1905-1910, that is to say at the period when Fauvism was at its height. In 1908 he returned to his native Normandy to reimmerse himself in his early environment; he would return to the region throughout his life. He made a trip to Munich with Dufy in 1909, and visited Portugal in 1911-1912 and Belgium in 1912. In 1914 he was called up and assigned to technical services, not being demobilised until March 1919, although he did manage to maintain a certain independence. From 1914 until his death he lived in Paris at 73 Rue Notre-Dame-des-Champs, where he occupied Bouguereau's old studio. He made frequent trips to Cap-Brun near Toulon where, in 1923, he acquired a property called *Les Jarres*, as well as making numerous visits to Normandy and Le Havre.

In 1925 he received the highest commendation at the Carnegie Prize in Pittsburgh for *Portrait of the Decorative Artist Paul Paquereau*. Also in 1925, at the same time as Matisse, he was made a Chevalier of the Légion d'Honneur, rising to in Officier in 1933 and Commandeur in 1937. He was also made Commander of the Swedish order of Vasa in 1934. Throughout his life, Friesz was a teacher: from 1913 at the Académie Moderne; from 1929 at the Académie Scandinave; and from 1941 until his death at the Académie de la Grande-Chaumière.

Alongside his activity as a painter, he illustrated several works of literature, including: in 1920 *Le Pacte de l'Écolier Juan* by Jules Tellier; in 1924 *Échelles de Soie* by Jean Pédron; in 1926 *Le Jardin sur l'Oronte* by Maurice Barrès; in 1926 *En Suivant la Seine* by Gustave Coquiot; in 1929 *Rouen* by André Maurois; in 1931 *The Song of Songs*; in 1934 *Poésies* by Pierre de Ronsard; in 1945 *Le Bouquet de la Mariée* by Gabriel-Joseph Gros; in 1947 *Paul et Virginie* by Bernardin de St-Pierre; in 1949 *Le Livre de Job* by Pierre Poussard; in 1949 Petronius's *Satyricon*, and in 1949 a collection of 12 unpublished lithographs for *Le Désert de l'Amour* by François Mauriac. He also designed several pieces of decorative art: from 1906 to 1909 ceramics executed by Metthey among others; a façade for a private house in Le Havre; a china service for two for the Le Havre writer J.-G. Aubry; vases, dishes and plates; in 1912 four sets for *La Lumière* by Georges Duhamel, performed at the Odéon; in 1916 a screen for the Le Havre collector Léon Pédron; in 1918 panels for Pédron's dining room; in 1920 a mural entitled *Enfants Dansant* (*Children Dancing*); in 1920 *Les Volières* for the apartment of Vicomte Amédée de Flers; in 1935 *La Paix* (*Peace*), a Gobelins tapestry presented by France to the Palais des Nations in Geneva; in 1937 *La Seine* in collaboration with Dufy for the Palais de Chaillot, with each artist taking half of the river's course - *From the Source to Paris* by Friesz and *From Paris to the Estuary* by Dufy.

The Fauves were producing Fauve paintings before they knew it: it was not until the critic Louis Vauxcelles saw their work at the Salon des Indépendants in 1905 and mockingly used the word Fauve to describe it that the term was born. It is known that Vlaminck and Derain worked together and that the École de Chatou was composed of just these two artists. Friesz was living with Matisse and after his first trip to Antwerp in 1905, he returned in 1906 with Braque. In 1906-1907 Friesz and Braque went to La Ciotat to paint and there they met up with Matisse. The paintings Friesz produced in Antwerp are Fauve inasmuch as they are painted in pure colours and are more or less free of the divisionism of the Impressionists, although the draughtsmanship is fairly standard; these works include *The Port, The Escaut, The Canals, The Dock with Sailing Ships* and *The Red Slipway*. Those of Braque the following year, in particular *Terrace on the Escaut*, show great similarities with those Friesz painted of the same subject. Friesz was already avoiding the hardness of pure flat tints by graduating them in thin glazes, allowing the whiteness of the canvas to penetrate the transparency, a technique that came to characterise his entire Fauve period.

At La Ciotat Friesz and Braque adopted completely different Fauve styles, with Braque composing his paintings on horizontal and vertical orthogonals painted in small, regular, spaced-out touches, whereas Friesz developed his own personal rhythmical style of wide arabesques of colour in works such as *The Bec-de-l'Aigle, Women Bathing* and *L'Estaque*. Many of Friesz's Fauve works were produced in the south of France, and his *Portrait of Fernand Fleuret* also dates from this period.

When he returned to Normandy in 1908 the period that he described as his 'return to form' began; with compromise paintings such as *Entrance to the Port of Honfleur, Côte de Grâce Landscape, The 'Bains Marie-Christine' in Le Havre* and the great compositions characteristic of this period - *Autumn Labours, Spring, Fisherman on a Rock* and *Women Bathing*. His draughtsmanship retains something of the rhythm of the Fauve period, his figures following the lines of the landscape and the colour remaining clear and resonant. In 1909 he painted the Cirque Médrano series: *The Trapeze Artist, The Clown* and *The Horsewoman*. In the south of France he also painted the *Olive Trees* series. He made a trip to Munich with Raoul Dufy resulting in *Winter in Munich*. This was also the year of his first trip to Italy. *Boat in a Rocky Inlet* of 1910 marks one of the pivotal points between a totally rhythmic drawing style of sensual curves typical of his Fauve period and a reduced palette of muted ochres, browns and blues. From 1910 onwards, the final traces of Fauvism become less and less apparent in his work. His use of colour follows the same course, towards the transcription of reality, with broken tones, ochres and browns.

After his demobilisation, as well as in his studio in Paris, Friesz spent time in his house in Toulon, returned to Normandy and Le Havre and continued to make frequent, often local, forays in search of new subjects: in 1919 to Jura, producing the series *Forests, Pine Trees, Road in the Snow* and *Invitation to Skate*; in 1920 to Italy producing *Piedmont Village, Florence Grape Pickers*; in 1920 to Le Havre, producing *The Étretat Cliffs, People Bathing at Étretat*; in 1923 to his house in Toulon, producing *View of Coudon, Women Bathing, Grape Harvesting, Jars*; in 1924 he painted the *Large Nude* (which he exhibited at the Salon d'Automne the same year) and landscapes of Toulon; in 1928 he made a trip to Algiers, producing *The Algiers Kasbah and its Phantoms*; in 1931 to Annecy, producing *Women Bathers by a Lake*; in 1934-1935 to Dinan and St-Malo producing *The Great Dinan Viaduct, The Dock with the Terre-Neuvas, After Bathing*; in 1936 to Honfleur; in 1941-1944, remaining in Paris because of the war, he painted mainly still-lifes, including *Studio Corner, Earthenware*. In 1946 he returned to Honfleur; and in 1947 to La Rochelle producing *The Port Tower, Tuna Boats, The Red Sail*.

Numerically Friesz's work is dominated by landscapes but it should be remembered that throughout his career he tackled more ambitious compositions and appeared to do so with great ease. These include *Boat in a Rocky Inlet* of 1910 with its frolicking women bathers, *Allegory of War* of 1915 executed in 24 hours, *Invitation to Skate* of 1919, numerous paintings of *Women Bathing* over several periods and much later *Women beside a Pond* of 1944, which clearly demonstrates his attachment to Cézanne.

He exhibited at the Salon des Artistes Français from 1901 to 1903 and then at the Salon des Artistes Indépendants. From 1906 he exhibited annually at the Salon d'Automne, of which he later became a committee and jury member. In 1923 he took part in the founding of the Salon des Tuileries and became head of two of the Salon's sections. His work has been exhibited at countless group exhibitions all over the world. Among the most recent thematic exhibitions is *Le Fauvisme en Noir et Blanc. De Gauguin à Vlaminck, l'Estampe des Fauves et son Environnement* (*Fauvism in Black and White. From Gauguin to Vlaminck, Fauvist Engraving and its Setting*) at the Musée d'Art Moderne in Villeneuve d'Ascq in 2001.

He also showed his work in numerous solo exhibitions in Paris: his first in 1904 at the Galerie des Collectionneurs and another the same year at the Société des Peintres du Paris Moderne; in 1905 at the Galerie Berthe Weill; under contract at the Galerie Druet from 1907; with the Galerie Katia Granoff from 1924; and from December 1939 until his death with the Galerie Pétridès. He exhibited in Paris in other galleries than those with which he was contracted, and outside Paris he held solo exhibitions in 1913 at the Cassirer gallery, Berlin; in 1921, 1928, 1936 and 1958 in London; in 1921 and 1950 in Le Havre; in 1925 and 1929 in Brussels; in 1929 and 1938 in New York; in 1930 in Chicago; in 1938 in Zurich; and in 1948 in Lucerne and Geneva. His posthumous exhibitions and retrospectives include: a tribute in 1949 at the Salon d'Automne in Paris; a retrospective in 1950 at the Galerie Charpentier in Paris; an exhibition in 1950 in Geneva and again in 1953 at the Musée d'Art et d'Histoire; in 1950 at the Musée de Toulon; in 1950 in Marseilles; in 1951 at the Algiers museum; in 1951 at the Musée d'Honfleur; in 1956 at the Musée de Dieppe; in 1979 at the Musée de la Rochelle and the Musée de La Roche-sur-Yon; in 1989 the *E. Othon Friesz, Rétrospective* at the Galerie Katia Granoff, Paris; 1995, *Émile Othon Friesz. Périodes Fauve et Cézannienne (1906-1920)* at the Galerie Larock-Granoff in Paris.

E. Othon Friesz

E. Othon Friesz

E. Othon Friesz

BIBLIOGRAPHY:

Burgess, G., '*The Wild Men of Paris*' in *Archit. Rec. xxviii, 5*, 1910 (pp. 401-414). Fleuret, F./Vildrac, Ch./Salmon, A., *Friesz, œuvres 1901-1927*, Chroniques du Jour, Paris, 1927. George, Waldemar/Richter, Ch. de, *Friesz*, exhibition catalogue, Gal. Motte, Geneva, 1950. Vildrac, Charles/Bersier/Gauthier, M., *Friesz*, exhibition catalogue, Gal. Charpentier, Paris, 1950. Gauthier, M., *Othon Friesz*, Éd. Pierre Cailler, Geneva, 1957. Busse, Jacques, *Othon Friesz, notices diverses*, Éd. Pierre Cailler, Geneva, 1958 (extensive documentation). Larock, Marc, et al., *E. Othon Friesz, rétrospective*, exhibition catalogue, Gal. Katia Granoff, Paris, 1989. Aittouarès, Odile/Martin, Robert, '*Émile Othon Friesz: l'œuvre peint*' in *2 vol.*, catalogue raisonné, Éd. Aittouarès, Paris, 1995. *Braque, Friesz*, exhibition catalogue; Musée de Lodève, Mazzotta, 2005 (bilingual edition in French and English).

MUSEUMS AND GALLERIES:

ALBI: drawings - ARLES: drawings - BALTIMORE: *Women Bathing* (1926) - COPENHAGEN: *Madame and Jacqueline F.* - COPENHAGEN (Statens Mus. for Kunst): *Motherhood* (1914) - GENEVA (MAH): *St-Cirq-Lapopie* (1946) - GENEVA (Petit Palais): *Corvette Entering Port* (1906); *Women Bathing* (1907) - GRENOBLE: *Allegory of War* (1915); *Grape Harvesting* (1923); *Le Coudon* (1923) - LE HAVRE: *Landscape* - LEEDS (City AG): *Honfleur* (1937, oil on canvas) - LILLE (Mus. de Picardie) - MOSCOW: *Rouen Cathedral* (1908) - NEW YORK (MoMA) - OSLO: *Autumn Labours* (1908); *The Red Street* (1905) - PARIS (MNAM-CCI): *La Ciotat* (1906); *L'Estaque* (1906); *Portrait of Fernand Fleuret* (1906); *Portrait of Madame Andrée Othon Friesz* (1923); *Landscape of Méounes, Var* (1925); *Port of Dieppe* (1930) - PARIS (Mus. de l'Armée): *The French Enter Strasbourg* (1918); *Maréchal Joffre on Horseback* (drawings) - PARIS (Mus. de l'Aviation): *Air Force Camps during the 1914-1918 War* (studies) - POITIERS: drawings and lithographs - ST-MALO: *Women Bathers by the Sea; The Old Town of St-Malo before the Destruction Caused by the 1939-1945 War* (drawings) - STOCKHOLM: *Port of Honfleur* - TOULON: *The Artist's House at Toulon* (1919); *Nude* (drawings) - TROYES (MAM, Pierre and Denise Lévy donation): *L'Estaque* (1906) - ZURICH: *Cassis Landscape* (1909).

AUCTION RECORDS:

PARIS, 28 March 1919, *Port of Antwerp*, FRF 1,830. PARIS, 9 June 1920, *The Escaut at Antwerp*, FRF 1,900; *Canal in Holland*, FRF 4,200. PARIS, 3 March 1924, *Women at a Fountain*, FRF 2,000. PARIS, 18 June 1925, *Skaters*, FRF 2,005; *Snow*, FRF 5,100. PARIS, 26 April 1926, *Nude Reclining on a Blue Couch*, FRF 11,000. PARIS, 2 June 1926, *Table of Fruit*, FRF 17,000; *Méounes Landscape*, FRF 15,000; *Women Bathing*, FRF 30,000. PARIS, 16 Feb 1927, *Women Bathing*, FRF 7,200; *The Great Jar*, FRF 9,000; *Fauve Landscape*, FRF 1,400. PARIS, 2 April 1928, *Flowers*, FRF 13,100; *Women at a Fountain*, FRF 25,000. PARIS, 11 Oct 1928, *Toulon Quay*, FRF 16,500. PARIS, 16 Feb 1929, *Women Bathing* (watercolour) FRF 36,000; *Entrance to the Port of Le Havre*, FRF 16,000. PARIS, 6 June 1929, *Seated Nude seen from the Back*, FRF 8,720. PARIS, 14 June 1929, *Women on a Terrace*, FRF 8,000; *Cap-Brun*, FRF 10,010. PARIS, 20 June 1941, *Corner of the Gardens*, FRF 3,000. PARIS, 24 Nov 1941, *Port* (1927) FRF 14,000; *Honfleur* (1939) FRF 13,500. PARIS, 14 Oct 1942, *Garden Entrance*, FRF 6,200; *The Artist's House* (1924) FRF 12,500; *Fruit*, FRF 43,000; *Canals in Antwerp* (1906) FRF 28,000; *Port of Le Havre* (1921) FRF 40,000; *Fountain and Gardener* (1922) FRF 23,500. PARIS, 25-26 Jan 1943, *Nude in a Landscape*, FRF 25,000; *Harvesting* (1929) FRF 40,000; *Grape Harvesting* (1920) FRF 23,000. PARIS, 31 Jan 1944, *Nude on a Chaise Longue* (1927) FRF 20,200. PARIS, 23 Feb 1945, *Reclining Nude* (1933, drawing) FRF 3,100. PARIS, 26 Feb 1945, *The Terre-Neuvas Heading out to Sea, St-Malo* (1935) FRF 35,000. PARIS, 12 Nov 1946, *Seascape*, FRF 51,000. PARIS, 14 Feb 1947, *Landscape with Aeroplanes* (1917) FRF 20,000; *The Seine at the Institut de France*, FRF 31,000. PARIS, 31 Jan 1949, *Garden in Toulon*, FRF 80,000. PARIS, 10 May 1950, *Women Bathing*, FRF 130,000. PARIS, 20 Dec 1950, *Rodin's Gardens*, FRF 150,000. PARIS, 3 June 1954, *Port of Antwerp*, FRF 1,000,000. NEW YORK, 8 Nov 1957, *Bridge over the Seine, Paris*, USD 2,400. LONDON, 11 Dec 1957, *Table with a Copper Kettle*, GBP 140. PARIS, 11 June 1958, *Port of Toulon*, FRF 1,000,000. LONDON, 23 Nov 1960, *Honfleur*, GBP 850. PARIS, 10 June 1963, *Port*, FRF 80,000. NEW YORK, 10 Oct 1968, *Barges, Port of Antwerp*, USD 33,000. GENEVA, 14 June 1970, *Cassis* (gouache) CHF 20,500. GENEVA, 2 July 1971, *La Côte de Grâce* CHF 130,000. LONDON, 29 Nov 1972, *Regatta in Antwerp*, GBP 26,000. GENEVA, 7 Dec 1973, *Port* (1906) CHF 245,000. PARIS, 21 March 1974, *Barges in Antwerp*, FRF 200,000. GENEVA, 6 June 1974, *Landscape at Cassis*, CHF 450,000. NEW YORK, 28 May 1976, *Le Pavois, Honfleur* (1945, oil on canvas, 25 1/2 x 32 ins / 65 x 81 cm) USD 4,300. ZURICH, 12 Nov 1976, *Sailing Ships* (1921, watercolour, 17 1/2 x 25 1/4 ins / 44.4 x 64 cm) CHF 4,200. ZURICH, 20 May 1977, *Aups* (1925, oil on canvas, 19 3/4 x 24 ins / 50 x 61 cm) CHF 13,000. LOS ANGELES, 9 Nov 1977, *Port of Toulon* (watercolour/paper, 19 3/4 x 25 ins / 50.2 x 63.5 cm) USD 2,500. PARIS, 16 May 1979, *Port of St-Tropez* (1930, watercolour, 18 1/2 x 23 1/4 ins / 47 x 59 cm) FRF 10,800. ENGHIEN-LES-BAINS, 10 July 1980, *Nude with Drapery by a Lake* (charcoal heightened with pastels/paper, 24 3/4 x 19 ins / 63 x 48.5 cm) FRF 20,000. PARIS, 19 March 1984, *Ovoid Vase* (polychrome enamelled ceramic with medallion decorations, h. 11 ins / 28 cm) FRF 7,500. LONDON, 28 March 1984, *Landscape at La Ciotat* (c. 1905-1907, watercolour/pencil outlines, 15 1/4 x 12 1/4 ins / 39 x 31 cm) GBP 2,500. NEW YORK, 16 May 1984, *Trees in Autumn* (1907, oil on canvas, 42 1/4 x 27 1/2 ins / 107 x 70 cm) USD 105,000. PARIS, 22 Nov 1984, *Port of Toulon* (watercolour wash/tracing paper remounted/canvas, 13 3/4 x 18 1/2 ins / 35 x 47 cm) FRF 15,000. LONDON, 23 June 1986, *Road to La Ciotat* (1905-1907, oil on canvas, 25 1/2 x 32 ins / 65 x 81 cm) GBP 100,000. LYONS, 3 Dec 1986, *Fauve Landscape* (watercolour gouache and pencil, 10 1/4 x 16 1/2 ins / 26 x 42 cm) GBP 7,500. PARIS, 22 June 1987, *Siesta Time* (oil on canvas, 35 x 46 ins / 89 x 116 cm) FRF 120,000. VERSAILLES, 13 Dec 1987, *Landscape in the Jura* (1919, oil on canvas, 36 1/2 x 49 1/2 ins / 93 x 126 cm) FRF 84,000. VERSAILLES, 7 Feb 1988, *Morning in the Park, New York* (watercolour, 11½ x 11½ ins / 29.5 x 29.5 cm) FRF 6,000. CALAIS, 28 Feb 1988, *Sea Shore* (1919, oil on canvas, 28¾ x 36¼ ins / 73 x 92 cm) FRF 125,000. PARIS, 18 March 1988, *Port of La Rochelle* (oil on canvas, 21¼ x 25½ ins / 54 x 65 cm) FRF 150,000. PARIS, 19 March 1988, *Landscape at Niermont* (watercolour, 9 x 12¼ ins / 23 x 31 cm) FRF 15,000. PARIS, 15 April 1988, *Port* (1905-1906, watercolour, 12¼ x 17¾ ins / 31 x 45 cm) FRF 18,000. TROYES, 24 April 1988, *Village View* (1942, oil on canvas, 25½ x 32 ins / 65 x 81.5 cm) FRF 61,000. VERSAILLES, 15 May 1988, *Female Nude in a Landscape* (oil on panel, 11¾ x 9¼ ins / 30 x 23.5 cm) FRF 19,000. PARIS, 6 June 1988, *Seated Model* (1928, oil on canvas, 18 x 11 ins / 46 x 27 cm) FRF 10,000. PARIS, 12 June 1988, *Vase of Anemones* (1921, oil on canvas, 18 x 22 ins / 46 x 55 cm) FRF 75,000. PARIS, 23 June 1988, *Interior* (oil on canvas, 18 x 15 ins / 46 x 38 cm) FRF 25,000. LONDON, 29 June 1988, *Antwerp Canals* (oil on canvas, 24 x 19¾ ins / 61 x 50 cm) GBP 49,500. GRANDVILLE, 16-17 July 1988, *Landscape* (pencil drawing, 12¼ x 17¼ ins / 31 x 44 cm) FRF 27,100. LONDON, 21 Oct 1988, *Landscape in Provence* (oil on canvas, 12¾ x 16½ ins / 32.2 x 42.2 cm) GBP 7,150. LA VARENNE-ST-HILAIRE, 23 Oct 1988, *Bathing* (oil on canvas, 25¾ x 32 ins / 65.5 x 81.5 cm) FRF 120,000. VERSAILLES, 6 Nov 1988, *The Val d'Ante Road at Falaise* (1897, oil on canvas, 11¾ x 15½ ins / 30 x 39.5 cm) FRF 30,000. PARIS, 20 Nov 1988, *Rocky Coast* (1914, oil on canvas, 11 x 18 ins / 28 x 46 cm) FRF 150,000. PARIS, 22 Nov 1988, *Entrance to the Port of Honfleur* (oil on canvas, 19¾ x 24 ins / 50 x 61 cm) FRF 132,000. LUCERNE, 3 Dec 1988, *Still-life with Fruit and a Cat* (oil on canvas, 39¼ x 27½ ins / 100 x 70 cm) CHF 32,000. PARIS, 16 Dec 1988, *Port of Honfleur* (oil on canvas, 20 x 24 ins / 50.5 x 61 cm) FRF 191,000. LONDON, 22 Feb 1989, *Port of Le Havre* (1921, oil on canvas, 32 x 39¼ ins / 81 x 100 cm) GBP 26,400. PARIS, 22 March 1989, *Landscape with Fortified House* (1926, oil on canvas) FRF 120,000. PARIS, 7 April 1989, *A Meal in the Islands* (oil on canvas, 25½ x 31¾ ins / 65 x 80.5 cm) FRF 130,000. NEW YORK, 3 May 1989, *Port of Honfleur* (oil on canvas, 23½ x 28¾ ins / 59.7 x 73 cm) USD 277,500. NEW YORK, 10 May 1989, *Trees in Autumn* (1907, oil on canvas, 42¼ x 27½ ins / 107 x 70 cm) USD 440,000. STOCKHOLM, 22 May 1989, *The Aviary* (oil on paper/canvas, 17¾ x 12¼ ins / 45 x 31 cm) SEK 45,000. LONDON, 27 June 1989, *Landscape* (1905, oil on canvas, 28¾ x 23½ ins / 73 x 60 cm) GBP 68,200. PARIS, 29 Sept 1989, *Study of Roofs* (watercolour and pencil, 9½ x 12¼ ins / 24 x 31 cm) FRF 3,500. PARIS, 11 Oct 1989, *Village Street* (oil on canvas, 31½ x 23½ ins / 80 x 60 cm) FRF 356,000. PARIS, 22 Nov 1989, *Port of Toulon on a Sunny Morning* (oil on canvas, 23¾ x 28¾ ins / 60.5 x 73 cm) FRF 320,000. PARIS, 23 Nov 1989, *Village* (oil on canvas, 7¾ x 9¾ ins / 20 x 25 cm) FRF 100,000. NEW YORK, 21 Feb 1990, *Port of Antwerp* (1906, oil on canvas, 12 x 17¾ ins / 30.5 x 45.2 cm) USD 96,250. NEW YORK, 26 Feb 1990, *Landscape* (oil on canvas, 19¾ x 25½ ins / 50.3 x 64.7 cm) USD 418,000. PARIS, 14 March 1990, *Still-life* (1943, oil on canvas, 15 x 18¼ ins / 38 x 46.5 cm) FRF 115,000. PARIS, 2 April 1990, *Sailing Ships Leaving the Port of Honfleur* (1907, oil on canvas, 18 x 23½ ins / 46 x 60 cm) FRF 4,350,000. PARIS, 30 May 1990, *Sunny Street* (1904, oil on canvas, 18½ x 15¼ ins / 47 x 39 cm) FRF 330,000. PARIS, 16 June 1990, *On the Beach* (oil on canvas, 28¾ x 36¼ ins / 73 x 92 cm) FRF 340,000. PARIS, 19 June 1990, *Village in a Valley* (1942, oil on canvas, 25½ x 32¼ ins / 65 x 82 cm) FRF 141,000. LONDON, 17 Oct 1990, *Port of Toulon* (oil on canvas, 21¼ x 26 ins / 54 x 66 cm) GBP 11,000. PARIS, 23 Nov 1990, *Port of Antwerp* (1906, oil on canvas, 23½ x 31½ ins / 60 x 80 cm) FRF 1, 620,000. NEW YORK, 15 Feb 1991, *Government Square, Algiers* (1928, oil on canvas, 21¼ x 25½ ins / 54 x 65 cm) USD 33,000. BOURG-EN-BRESSE, 14 April 1991, *Landscape in the South of France* (watercolour and gouache, 16¼ x 12¼ ins / 41 x 31 cm) FRF 525,000. PARIS, 17 April 1991, *Outside L'Estaque* (1907, oil on canvas, 32¼ x 23½ ins / 82 x 60 cm) FRF 1,200,000. AMSTERDAM, 23 May 1991, *Seated Nude* (oil on canvas, 21¼ x 14½ ins / 54 x 37 cm) NLG 13,800. BOURG-EN-BRESSE, 9 June 1991, *Mediterranean Landscape* (1907, oil on canvas, 36½ x 23¾ ins / 92.5 x 60.5 cm) FRF 1,470,000. LONDON, 16 Oct 1991, *Landscape* (1911, oil on canvas, 19 x 15 ins / 48 x 38 cm) GBP 11,770. NEW YORK, 14 May 1992, *Port of Toulon* (1927, oil on canvas, 23¾ x 28¾ ins / 60.3 x 73 cm) USD 28,600. MUNICH, 26 May 1992, *Female Nude Standing* (oil on card, 18 x 8½ ins / 46 x 21.5 cm) DEM 3,680. PARIS, 14 Dec 1992, *Le Havre Dock* (1906, oil on canvas, 24¾ x 32 ins / 63 x 81 cm) FRF 500,000. NEW YORK, 12 May 1993, *The Figuerolles Inlet* (1907, oil on canvas, 25½ x 32 ins / 65 x 81 cm) USD 244,500. LONDON, 21 June 1993, *Belle-Isle-en-Mer* (oil on canvas, 23½ x 28½ ins / 59.5 x 72.5 cm) GBP 45,500. PARIS, 21 Oct 1993, *Sailing Ships Leaving the Port of Honfleur* (1907, oil on canvas, 18 x 23½ ins / 46 x 60 cm) FRF 1,300,000. STOCKHOLM, 30 Nov 1993, *Forest* (oil on canvas, 23¼ x 28¾ ins / 59 x 73 cm) SEK 72,000. PARIS, 10 March 1994, *Sailing Ships in the Port of Toulon* (1936, oil on canvas, 28½ x 36 ins / 72.5 x 91.5 cm) FRF 200,000. LONDON, 23-24 March 1994, *Port of Toulon* (watercolour, 12¼ x 17¼ ins / 31 x 43.5 cm) GBP 2,530. LE TOUQUET, 13 Nov 1994, *Woman by a Fountain in Guardia* (1911, oil on canvas, 32 x 25½ ins / 81 x 65 cm) FRF 93,000. PARIS, 21 June 1995, *Port of Antwerp* (1905, oil on canvas, 23½ x 28¾ ins / 60 x 73 cm) FRF 1,000,000. LONDON, 28 June 1995, *Port of Antwerp* (1906, oil on canvas, 19¾ x 24 ins / 50.2 x 61 cm) GBP 78,500. PARIS, 13 Dec 1995, *Le Havre Dock* (1906, oil on canvas, 24¾ x 32 ins / 63 x 81 cm) FRF 650,000. PARIS, 1 April 1996, *Bec de l'Aigle, Fauve Landscape* (1907, oil on canvas, 18 x 22 ins / 46 x 55 cm) FRF 610,000. PARIS, 15 May 1996, *Woman Bathing* (oil on canvas, 18 x 15 ins / 46 x 38 cm) FRF 25,000. LONDON, 25 June 1996, *Autumn in Honfleur* (1939, oil on canvas, 23½ x 28¾ ins / 60 x 73 cm) GBP 10,350. CALAIS, 7 July 1996, *Portrait of a Woman* (1910, oil on canvas, 16½ x 13½ ins / 42 x 34 cm) FRF 13,500. TEL AVIV, 30 Sept 1996, *Bunch of Flowers* (c. 1930, oil on panel, 22 x 15 ins / 55 x 37.8 cm) USD 9,200. NEW YORK, 9 Oct 1996, *Seated Woman* (charcoal, pencil and watercolour/paper, 16¾ x 10½ ins / 42.5 x 26.4 cm) USD 2,875. NEW YORK, 12 Nov 1996, *Port* (1935, oil on canvas, 19¾ x 25½ ins / 50 x 65 cm) USD 10,925. CALAIS, 24 Nov 1996, *Map of the World* (oil on canvas, 48¾ x 37¾ ins / 124 x 96 cm) FRF 29,000. LONDON, 4 Dec 1996, *Summer Afternoon* (oil on canvas, 28¾ x 23½ ins / 73 x 60 cm) GBP 11,500. PARIS, 8 Dec 1996, *Horse Fair at Falaise* (1904, oil on canvas, 15 x 18 ins / 38 x 46 cm) FRF 60,000. PARIS, 12 Dec 1996, *St-Malo* (13 x 16¼ ins / 33 x 41 cm) FRF 19,500. PARIS, 23 May 1997, *Women Bathing* (monotype, 13 x 11½ ins / 33 x 29 cm) FRF 10,000; *Bunch of Anemones and Bottle* (1942, oil on canvas, 25¾ x 31¾ ins / 65.5 x 80.5 cm) FRF 36,000. PARIS, 20 June 1997, *La Clairière* (1919, oil on canvas, 28¾ x 36½ ins / 73 x 93 cm) FRF 60,000. LONDON, 22 Oct 1997, *Côte de Grâce, Honfleur* (1938, oil on canvas, 21¼ x 25½ ins / 54 x 65 cm) GBP 5,520. PARIS, 21 Nov 1997, *Women Bathing* (1930, oil on canvas, 25½ x 32 ins / 65 x 81 cm) FRF 30,000. PARIS, 13 March 1998, *Ste-Victoire Mountain* (oil on canvas, c. 1930) FRF 36,500. PARIS, 11 March 1999, *Honfleur from above* (oil on canvas, 26 x 32 ins / 65 x 81 cm) FRF 116,000. LONDON, 29 June 1999, *Seaside at Cassis* (1907, oil on canvas, 13 x 16 ins / 33 x 41 cm) GBP 65,000. NEW YORK, 9 May 2000, *Port at Rouen* (oil on canvas, 15 x 18 ins / 38 x 46 cm) USD 150,000. LONDON, 28 June 2000, *Ciotat* (1907, oil on canvas, 26 x 32 ins / 66 x 81 cm) GBP 190,000. NEW YORK, 10 May 2001, *Port* (1906, oil on canvas, 18 x 12 ins / 45 x 30 cm) USD 85,000. LONDON, 23 Oct 2001, *Repairing the Boats* (1909, oil on canvas, 35 x 46 ins / 89 x 116 cm) GBP 25,000. LONDON, 5 Feb 2002, *Honfleur Bay* (1905, oil on canvas, 17 x 21 ins / 43 x 53 cm) GBP 170,000. NEW YORK, 8 May 2002, *Bay at Bec d'Aigle* (1907, oil on canvas, 18 x 22 ins / 46 x 55 cm) USD 200,000. NEW YORK, 8 May 2003, *L'Estaque* (1907, oil on canvas, 22 x 26 ins / 55 x 65 cm) USD 340,000. PARIS, 4 June 2003, *Midi Landscape* (watercolour and gouache, 17 x 12 ins / 43 x 31 cm) EUR 33,000. LONDON, 3 Feb 2004, *Antwerp* (c. 1906, oil on canvas, 15 x 18 ins / 38 x 46 cm) GBP 32,000. PARIS, 9 June 2004, *Port at Antwerp* (oil on canvas, 13 x 16 ins / 33 x 41 cm) EUR 63,000.

FRIG, Hélias
Swiss, 16th century.

Born 1565, in Zurich; died 3 June 1608, in Zurich.
Engraver (wood), painter.
Zurich School.
Hélias was the son of Ludwig Frig the Elder.

FRIG, Ludwig, the Elder, or Fryg
Swiss, 16th century.
Engraver.
Ludwig Frig the Elder made woodcuts at the end of the 16th century.

FRIG, Ludwig, the Younger
Swiss, 16th - 17th century.
Active in Zurich.
Engraver (wood).
This artist was the son of Ludwig the Elder.

FRIGARA, Bernard
French, 20th - 21st century.
Born 1948, in Paris.
Active in Belgium.
Painter, sculptor, draughtsman, watercolourist.

FRIGERO, Joseph
French, 19th century.
Born 1807, in Nice; died 1870.
Painter.
After a period in Ingres' studio, Joseph Frigero travelled extensively, maintaining a painted record of his travels in the form of landscapes, portraits and assorted watercolours.

FRIGIMELICA, Francesco
Italian, 17th century.
Born in Padua; died probably in 1621, in Belluno.
Painter.
Francesco Frigimelica produced a large number of religious paintings to be found in the region of Friuli.

FRIGIMELICA, Pompeo
Italian, 17th century.
Active in Belluno.
Painter.
Pompeo Frigimelica was the son of Francesco Frigimelica.

FRIGINISCO, Bartolomeo
Italian, 15th century.
Active in San Severino.
Painter.
There is a fresco signed by Friginisco and dated 1466 in the little church of S Maria delle Vergini in San Severino.

FRIGIOLINI, Carlo
Italian, 19th century.
Born 1814, in Varallo (Piedmont); died 12 July 1880, in Varallo.
Painter.
Frigiolini studied under Avondo and Geniani.

FRIGIOTTI, Filippo
Italian, 18th century.
Active in Rome.
Painter. History painting.
Filippo Frigiotti painted large compositions for several churches in Rome.

FRIGOLA, Louis Jean Jacques
French, 19th century.
Born in the 19th century, in St-Laurent-de-la-Salanque (Pyrénées-Orientales).
Painter.
Frigola studied under Cabanel and submitted a self-portrait to the 1878 Paris Salon.

FRIIS, Achton
Danish, 20th century.
Born 1871; died 1939.
Painter.
Lived and worked in Copenhagen and began exhibiting in 1908.

A Friis

FRIIS, Frederick Trap
Swedish, 19th - 20th century.
Born 1865; died 1909.
From 1890 active in the USA.
Painter. Scenes with figures, interiors with figures, landscapes, urban landscapes, architectural views.
Friis emigrated to New York in 1890 and moved to New Bedford in Massachusetts two years later. He and his family later spent two years living near Florence.

AUCTION RECORDS:
NEW YORK, 14 March 1991, *Backyard* (oil on canvas, 29¼ x 29 ins / 74 x 73.5 cm) USD 14,300. NEW YORK, 26 Sept 1991, *Santa Croce, Florence* (oil on canvas, 20¾ x 20¾ ins / 53 x 53 cm) USD 6,050. NEW YORK, 12 March 1992, *Nude Class at the Art Students' League* (1890, oil on canvas, 17¾ x 17¼ ins / 45.1 x 43.8 cm) USD 5,500. NEW YORK, 23 Sept 1992, *Piazza San Lorenzo, Florence* (oil on canvas, 25½ x 23½ ins / 65 x 60 cm) USD 4,400.

FRIIS, Hans Gabriel
Danish, 19th century.
Born 7 September 1838, in Habro; died 20 July 1892, in Roskilde.
Painter. Landscapes with figures, landscapes, animals.

MUSEUMS AND GALLERIES:
COPENHAGEN (Statens Mus. for Kunst): three works.

AUCTION RECORDS:
LONDON, 27 Nov 1981, *Deer in a Wooded Landscape* (1877, oil on canvas, 37½ x 56 ins / 95 x 142 cm) GBP 3,800. NEW YORK, 29 Feb 1984, *Deer in a Wooded Landscape: Spring* (1877, oil on canvas, 37¾ x 57 ins / 96 x 145 cm) USD 7,500. LONDON, 23 June 1987, *Children Gathering Flowers in a Forest in Spring* (1875, oil on canvas, 41¼ x 32¼ ins / 105 x 82 cm) GBP 12,000. COPENHAGEN, 25 Oct 1989, *Son of a Fisherman in Summer at Sorup* (1874, oil on canvas, 11¾ x 15 ins / 30 x 38 cm) DKK 8,000. COPENHAGEN, 21 Feb 1990, *Daybreak in Kjaerstrup, near Lolland* (1868, oil on canvas, 24½ x 31½ ins / 62 x 80 cm) DKK 17,800. CONNECTICUT, 17 Jan 2000, *Snow Scene* (oil on canvas, 12 x 21 ins / 30 x 53 cm) USD 2,600. HELSINKI, 12 May 2001, *Shepherdess in the Mountains* (1869, oil on canvas, 33 x 50 ins / 83 x 128 cm) FIM 25,000. COPENHAGEN, 3 Sept 2001, *Winter Scene from the Outskirts of a Wood at Sunset* (1887, oil on canvas, 21 x 33 ins / 54 x 85 cm) DKK 24,000. COPENHAGEN, 2 Dec 2002, *Landscape from Handeck, Switzerland* (1873, oil on canvas, 26 x 39 ins / 67 x 100 cm) DKK 20,000. VEJLE, 10 March 2003, *Twilight in Winter* (1891, oil on canvas, 31 x 50 ins / 79 x 126 cm) DKK 46,000. COPENHAGEN, 25 Feb 2004, *Landscape from Kjaerstrup, Morning Fog, Late Summer* (1871, oil on canvas, 43 x 63 ins / 108 x 160 cm) DKK 66,000.

FRIKKE, Loggin Khristyanovich
Russian, 19th century.
Born 1820; died 1893.
Landscape painter. Landscapes.
Frikke's works can be seen in Russian art institutions: in The Alexander III Museum: *View of the Fall Estate, near Revel*; in the Rumanziev Museum: the same subject and in the Tretyakov Gallery: *View of Switzerland*.

FRILAY, Pierre
French, 20th - 21st century.
Born 11 January 1946, in Paris.
Painter.

Pierre Frilay studied under Arpad Szénès, and paints in an abstract style similar to the 'nuagistes', rather like a Laubiès or a Benrath.

FRILET DE CHATEAUNEUF, Marie Augustine
French, 19th century.
Born 2 July 1807, in Cadia; died 27 September 1874, in Angers.
Painter.

Frilet de Chateauneuf exhibited examples of her studies and portraits at the Paris Salon between 1835 and 1839.
MUSEUMS AND GALLERIES:
ANGERS: *Blind Man and Young Girl; Odalisque.*

FRILING, Hermann
German, 19th - 20th century.
Born 23 August 1867, in Cologne.
Painter.

Friling experimented with a variety of techniques and media. He exhibited in Berlin.

FRILLEY, Jean Jacques
French, 19th century.
Born 18 July 1797, in Paris.
Engraver, draughtsman. Portraits.

Frilley enrolled at the École des Beaux-Arts on 13 February 1815 and studied under Pauquet. He exhibited at the Salon from 1824 to 1850.
AUCTION RECORDS:
PARIS, 1879, *Portrait of Béranger Sitting in a Garden* (drawing in charcoal) FRF 180.

FRILLIÉ, Félix Nicolas
French, 19th century.
Born 26 January 1821, in Dijon; died 6 September 1863, in Is-sur-Tille.
Painter. Allegorical subjects, mythological subjects, figures, genre scenes.

Frillié was a Paris Salon exhibitor from 1841 to 1859. Examples of his work include *Madness Pursuing Inspiration, Gipsy Children, Artistes, Chaldean Shepherds Gazing at the Stars, Bunch of Grapes* and *Child Washing.*
MUSEUMS AND GALLERIES:
AIX: *Kiss of the Muse* - DIJON: *René Telling his Life Story.*

FRIMBERGER, Marianne
Austrian, 20th century.
Born 14 June 1877, in Mahr Ostrau (now Ostrava).
Painter, draughtsman, lithographer.

Marianne Frimberger lived, studied and worked in Vienna for most of her life.

FRIMODT, Charlotte
Danish, 19th century.
Born 23 June 1862, in Copenhagen.
Painter.

Charlotte Frimodt was a pupil of Ch. Sode. She mostly exhibited paintings of landscapes and flowers.

FRIMODT, Johanne Nicoline Louise
Danish, 19th - 20th century.
Born 1861; died 1920.
Painter. Portraits, seascapes, landscapes, still-lifes.

Frimodt studied under Stevens in Paris and went on to live and work in Copenhagen; her work mostly comprises landscapes, seascapes and child portraits.
AUCTION RECORDS:
LONDON, 25 March 1987, *Field of Flowers near the Sea* (1902, oil on canvas, 33 1/4 x 47 3/4 ins / 84.5 x 121.5 cm) GBP 4,800. COPENHAGEN, 28 Aug 1991, *Still-life* (oil on canvas, 21 1/4 x 28 1/4 ins / 54 x 72 cm) DKK 11,000. LONDON, 18 Nov 2004, *Field of Buttercups by the Coast* (1902, oil on canvas, 33 x 47 ins / 84 x 120 cm) GBP 6,500.

FRIMOUT, Cyr César Clovis
Belgian, 20th century.
Born 1938, in Properinge.
Painter, draughtsman. Figures, nudes.

Frimout was a professor of fine arts. He won the Berthe Art Prize in 1971 and the West Flanders Prize in 1972. His work is influenced by Cubism and comprises disjointed planes painted and lightly shaded, and pallid greens and yellows.
AUCTION RECORDS:
BRUSSELS, 27 Oct 1976, *Nude and Red Light* (oil on canvas, 27 1/4 x 23 1/4 ins / 69 x 59 cm) BEF 14,000. LOKEREN, 23 May 1992, *Reclining Nude* (1970, oil on canvas, 39 x 50 ins / 99 x 127 cm) BEF 40,000.

FRIND, August
Austrian, 19th century.
Born 21 November 1852, in Schönlinde.
Painter. History painting, genre scenes.

Frind was a pupil of Pauwels at the Dresden academy. He was awarded the gold medal in Dresden in 1886. He exhibited his works in Dresden and in Munich.

FRINK, Elisabeth (Dame)
British, 20th century.
Born 14 November, in Thurlow (Suffolk); died 18 April 1993, in Blandford Forum, Dorset.
Active in France 1967-1973.
Sculptor, printmaker. Figures, animals.

Elisabeth Frink studied at Guildford School of Art (1947-1949) and at Chelsea School of Art (1949-1953) under Bernard Meadows and Willi Soukop; here she also met Henry Moore, whom she acknowledged as having a deep influence on her. She met with almost immediate success, winning the prize for a competition organised by the Institute of Contemporary Arts for *Monument to the Unknown Political Prisoner*, exhibited at the Tate Gallery the same year. She taught at the Chelsea School of Art from 1953 to 1961 and at St Martin's from 1954 to 1962; between 1956 and 1967 she was a visiting instructor at the Royal College of Art. Frink is known for her powerful images of men, heads, horses and birds, and for her preference and inclination to express emotion and spirit though her forms at the cost of anatomical accuracy. She has had a number of public commissions: the first major one was from Harlow New Town for her *Boar* (1957), followed in 1958 by *Birdman* for London County Council. In 1959 she joined Waddington Galleries, remaining with them for the next 27 years. Other well-known commissions include: *Eagle*, a lectern for Coventry Cathedral (1962); *Eagle* as the J.F. Kennedy Memorial in Dallas, Texas (1964); and *Walking Madonna* (1981) for Salisbury Cathedral. She is also noted for her illustrations which exude a similar force to her sculpture: these include illustrations for *The Canterbury Tales* (Leslie Waddington, 1972), *The Odyssey* (Folio Society, 1974) and *The Iliad* (Folio Society, 1975). She was elected Royal Academician in 1977 and made a Dame in 1982. Her solo exhibitions include: St George's Gallery, London (1955); Waddington Galleries, London (regularly between 1959 and 1981); Bertha Schaefer Gallery, New York (1964); Kettle's Yard, Cambridge (1973); and Beaux Arts Gallery, Bath (1982).

Frink

BIBLIOGRAPHY:
Mullins, Edwin, *The Art of Elisabeth Frink*, Lund Humphries, London, 1972. *Elisabeth Frink: Sculpture and Drawings*, exhibition catalogue, Dorset Natural History and Archaeological Society, Dorchester, 1982. *Elisabeth Frink; Sculpture*, catalogue raisonné, Harpvale Books, Salisbury, 1984 (Introduction by Bryan Robertson). Lucie-Smith, Edward, *Elisabeth*

Frink: Sculpture Since 1984 and Drawings, Art Books Internatiional, London, 1984. *Elisabeth Frink: Sculpture and Drawing: 1952-1984*, exhibition catalogue, Royal Academy, London, 1985. *Elisabeth Frink: Recent Sculpture and Drawings*, exhibition catalogue, Fischer Fine Arts, London, 1989. Gardiner, S., *Frink: The Official Biography of Elisabeth Frink*, Harper Collins, London, 1998. *Elisabeth Frink*, exhibition catalogue, Djanogly Art Gallery, Nottingham, 2001.

Museums and Galleries:

Birmingham (City Museums and Art Gallery) - Bolton (Museum and Art Gallery) - Brisbane (Art Gallery) - Cambridge (Fitzwilliam Museum) - Cape Town (South African NG) - Dorchester (Dorset County Museum) - Edinburgh (Scottish Gallery of Modern Art) - Ipswich (Museums and Galleries) - Liverpool (Walker AG) - London (British Mus.) - London (Royal Academy of Arts) - London (Tate Collection): *Torso* (1958, bronze); *Bird* (1952, bronze); *Dead Hen* (1957, bronze); *Dying King* (1963, bronze); *Spinning Man I* (1965, lithograph on paper); *Guillemot* (1967, lithograph on paper) - Manchester (Whitworth Gallery) - Melbourne (Nat. Gal. of Victoria) - Middlesbrough (Art Gallery) - New York (MoMA) - Oldham (Art Gallery) - Pittsburgh (Carnegie Institute Museum of Art) - Portsmouth (City Museum and Art Gallery) - Provincetown (Chrysler AM) - Salford (Art Gallery) - Salisbury (Salisbury and South Wiltshire Museum) - Sheffield (City Art Galleries) - Southport (Atkinson Gallery) - Washington DC (Joseph Hirshhorn Collection).

Auction records:

London, 23 April 1969, *Sentinel* (bronze) GBP 900. New York, 29 Oct 1970, *Dog* (bronze) USD 2,200; *Warrior* (bronze) USD 1,100. London, 11 June 1976, *Reclining Horse* (1974, gold, w. 9 1/4 ins / 23.5 cm) GBP 5,000. London, 16 Nov 1977, *Boar* (1966, bronze, h. 6 1/4 ins / 16 cm) GBP 650. London, 8 March 1978, *New Bird I* (1965, bronze, h. 21 1/2 ins / 54.6 cm) GBP 680. London, 13 March 1981, *Crucifixion* (1951, watercolour and pen, 29 1/4 x 22 ins / 74 x 55 cm) GBP 260. London, 18 April 1984, *Boar* (1969, watercolour/pencil outlines, 30 x 40 ins / 76 x 101.5 cm) GBP 400. London, 23 May 1984, *Soldier's Head* (bronze, h. 16 ins / 40.5 cm) GBP 2,900. London, 18 July 1984, *Horse and Rider* (1974, pencil, 33 x 23 ins / 84 x 58.5 cm) GBP 380. London, 26 Sept 1985, *Horse with Seated Rider* (1969, pencil and colour wash, 30 x 40 1/4 ins / 76 x 102 cm) GBP 1,000. London, 14 Nov 1986, *Judas* (1963, bronze, h. 75 ins / 190.5 cm) GBP 18,000. London, 22 July 1987, *Reclining Horse* (1973, watercolour, 22 3/4 x 32 1/2 ins / 58 x 82.5 cm) GBP 1,700. London, 13 Nov 1987, *Horse in the Rain III* (1981, brown-patinated bronze, Length. 12 1/2 ins / 32 cm) GBP 8,000. London, 3-4 March 1988, *Winged Figure* (bronze, h. 20 1/4 ins / 51.2 cm) GBP 4,400. London, 9 June 1988, *Seagull* (watercolour, 23 x 29 1/2 ins / 57.5 x 75 cm) GBP 1,430. London, 29 July 1988, *Bird Man* (1960, wash and watercolour, 29 1/2 x 22 ins / 75 x 55 cm) GBP 550. London, 9 June 1989, *Torso* (1958, bronze, l. 38 ins / 96.3 cm) GBP 11,000. London, 21 Sept 1989, *Figure and Bird* (ink and wash, 29 1/4 x 21 ins / 74.3 x 53.3 cm) GBP 770. London, 10 Nov 1989, *Diving Eagle* (1969, watercolour and pencil, 26 1/2 x 36 ins / 67.4 x 91.6 cm) GBP 880. London, 9 March 1990, *Man Walking* (brown-patinated bronze, h. 15 ins / 38.2 cm) GBP 8,250. London, 24 May 1990, *The First Man* (bronze, h. 80 ins / 203 cm) GBP 44,000; *Horse* (bronze, h. 86 1/2 ins / 220 cm, l. 101 1/4 ins/257 cm) GBP 110,000. London, 8 June 1990, *Man Walking with Goggles* (bronze, h. 19 ins / 48 cm) GBP 12,650. London, 9 Nov 1990, *Head of Christ* (black-patinated bronze, h. 31 ins / 79 cm) GBP 28,600. London, 8 March 1991, *Sleeping Horse* (1972, dark-grey-patinated bronze, l. 80 ins / 203.5 cm) GBP 110,000. London, 2 May 1991, *Two Eagles* (1956, watercolour, gouache and ink, 29 x 19 1/2 ins / 73.5 x 49.5 cm) GBP 2,200. London, 7 June 1991, *Fox* (1968, pencil and watercolour, 26 1/2 x 39 1/2 ins / 67.5 x 100.5 cm) GBP 5,060. London, 8 Nov 1991, *Water Buffalo* (green-patinated bronze, l. 13 ins / 33 cm) GBP 8,800. London, 11 June 1992, *Chinese Horse I* (bronze, l. 19 ins / 48.3 cm) GBP 10,450. London, 2 July 1992, *Goggled Head* (1969, bronze, h. 25 1/2 ins / 64.8 cm) GBP 14,300. New York, 22 Feb 1993, *Male Nude* (1962, watercolour/paper, 30 x 22 ins / 76.2 x 56 cm) USD 1,100. London, 26 March 1993, *Front Runner* (greyish-blue patinated bronze, h. 75 1/4 ins / 191 cm) GBP 31,050. London, 25 Nov 1993, *Horse Lying Down* (bronze, l. 15 ins / 38 cm) GBP 17,250; *Horse Lying Down* (1980, pencil and watercolour, 22 1/4 x 29 3/4 ins / 56.5 x 75.6 cm) GBP 4,600. London, 25 May 1994, *Barking Dog* (bronze, l. 40 1/4 ins / 102 cm) GBP 23,000. London, 25 Oct 1995, *Horse* (1978, bronze, l. 98 ins / 249 cm) GBP 144,500. London, 23 Oct 1996, *Horse* (1980, green-brown patinated bronze, 90 1/4 x 99 1/4 ins / 229 x 252 cm) GBP 155,500; *Seated Horse* (1977, pencil and watercolour, 30 3/4 x 22 ins / 78.1 x 55.9 cm) GBP 7,130. London, 30 May 1997, *Goggled Head II (Teeth)* (1969, brown-patinated gilded bronze, h. 25 3/4 ins / 65.5 cm) GBP 28,750. London, 12 Nov 1997, *Horse* (bronze, l. 13 ins / 33 cm) GBP 14,950. London, 11 Dec 1997, *Maquette of a Vulture* (plaster and rope, 19 x 11 1/2 x 8 1/2 ins / 48.2 x 29.2 x 21.6 cm) GBP 747. London, 8 June 1999, *Man* (1872, brown patinated bronze, h. 74 ins / 188 cm) GBP 34,000. London, 9 June 2000, *Eagle* (brown patinated bronze, h. 58 ins / 147 cm, w. 46 ins/117 cm) GBP 78,000. London, 21 June 2000, *Tribute II* (brown patinated bronze, h. 35 ins / 89 cm) GBP 46,000. London, 8 June 2001, *General* (1980, dark brown patinated bronze, h. 16 ins / 41 cm) GBP 44,000. London, 23 Nov 2001, *Standing Dog* (1980, brown patinated bronze, w. 49 ins / 124 cm) GBP 55,000. London, 7 June 2002, *Walking Madonna* (dark brown patinated bronze, h. 81 ins / 206 cm) GBP 160,000. London, 3 July 2002, *First Man* (dark brown patinated bronze, h. 76 ins / 193 cm) GBP 75,000. London, 21 Nov 2003, *In Memoriam II* (1981, green patinated bronze, h. 50 ins / 127 cm) GBP 110,000. London, 3 Dec 2003, *Easter Head I* (1989, patinated bronze, h. 19 ins / 49 cm) GBP 92,000. London, 17 Nov 2004, *In Memoriam III* (1983, bronze, h. 51 ins / 129 cm) GBP 120,000. London, 17 Nov 2004, *Boar* (1969, grey-green patinated bronze, h. 44 ins / 112 cm) GBP 130,000.

FRIOLI, Liguorio

Italian, 19th century.
Active in Rimini c. 1850.
Sculptor.

Museums and Galleries:

Rimini (Town Hall): *Bust of Cavour*; *Bust of Luigi Pani*.

FRION, Louis

French, 17th century.
Born 1644; died 1699; buried the 26 December in Paris.
Sculptor.

FRIONNET, Charles

French, 20th century.
Engraver (etching).

Charles Frionnet exhibited in Paris at the Salon des Artistes Français from 1922.

FRIPP, Alfred Downing

British, 19th century.
Born 1822, in Bristol; died 13 March 1895, in London.
Painter, watercolourist, draughtsman. Genre scenes, landscapes.

Alfred Downing Fripp was influenced by W.J. Muller early in his career. In 1840 he followed his brother to London to study sculpture at the British Museum and the Royal Academy. He then turned to watercolours, submitting three works to exhibitions in 1842. He was elected to associate membership of the Society of Painters in Watercolours in 1844, and became a full member two years later. From that point on, his reputation grew. He visited Ireland on three occasions and painted some charming subjects there. He also painted scenes from Italian life, including a *Pompeii, City of Death* dating from 1853. He returned home and reverted to English themes, painting an *Early England* and an *Irish Mother*, two works which enjoyed widespread popularity.

MUSEUMS AND GALLERIES:

BRISTOL: *Irish Landscape* - DUBLIN: *Cloumarnoise* - LIVERPOOL: *Dinner Time* - MANCHESTER: *Springtime in Sulworth, Dorset* - SYDNEY: *Community*.

AUCTION RECORDS:

LONDON, 6 May 1899, *Quarry Road* (watercolour) FRF 1,595. PARIS, 17 Feb 1908, *Fisherman's Children*, FRF 184. LONDON, 28 Jan 1924, *Shepherd*, GBP 4. LONDON, 25 June 1926, *Grand Canal, Venice*; *Venitian Palazzo* (drawing, two) GBP 14; *San Rocco* (drawing) GBP 7; *In a Foreign City*, GBP 7. LONDON, 28 Nov 1930, *On the Cliffs*, GBP 4. LONDON, 14 Dec 1979, *Hedgehogs* (1865, watercolour heightened with white, 21 x 25 ins / 52.5 x 63.5 cm) GBP 1,300. RHEIMS, 23 Oct 1983, *Maternal Scene* (oil on canvas, 12 x 12 ins / 30.5 x 30.5 cm) FRF 6,000. LONDON, 22 May 1986, *Gleaners* (watercolour heightened with gouache, 16 1/4 x 20 ins / 41 x 51 cm) GBP 4,000. LONDON, 25 Jan 1988, *Family in the Country* (watercolour, 15 1/2 x 11 1/2 ins / 39.4 x 29.2 cm) GBP 1,320. LONDON, 14 June 1991, *Durdle Door, Dorset* (1890, pencil and watercolour heightened with white, 19 1/4 x 30 ins / 48.8 x 75.3 cm) GBP 2,090. LONDON, 8 Feb 2000, *Every Little Helps* (watercolour, 12 x 17 ins / 30 x 43 cm) GBP 4,000. EXETER, 18 Oct 2000, *Crofters' Girls* (1880, watercolour, 24 x 19 ins / 60 x 47 cm) GBP 1,300. LONDON, 3 May 2001, *Bather* (1843, pencil, watercolour and scratching out, arched, 27 x 21 ins / 68 x 53 cm) GBP 1,100. LONDON, 6 Dec 2001, *Figures before an Irish Post Office* (pencil and watercolour heightened with white and gum arabic, 16 x 12 ins / 41 x 31 cm) GBP 1,000. LONDON, 28 Aug 2002, *Leaving Arran* (watercolour heightened with gouache, 21 x 27 ins / 54 x 69 cm) GBP 3,000. LONDON, 5 Nov 2002, *Traghetto, Ferry on the Grand Canal, Venice* (13 x 24 ins / 33 x 60 cm) GBP 1,600. LONDON, 20 Nov 2003, *Pompeii* (pencil and watercolour, 135 x 94 ins / 344 x 240 cm) GBP 2,400. CREWKERNE, 14 Jan 2004, *Hallowed Relic* (1847, oil on canvas, 13 x 19 ins / 33 x 48 cm) GBP 2,400.

FRIPP, Charles Edwin

British, 19th century.

Born 1854, in London; died 1906, in Montreal.

Watercolourist.

Charles Edwin Fripp was the son of George Arthur Fripp. He was active in Munich and London.

FRIPP, Constance L.

British, 19th century.

Active in Southampton at the end of the 19th century.

Painter. Landscapes.

FRIPP, George Arthur

British, 19th century.

Born 1813, in Bristol; died 17 October 1896, in London.

Painter, watercolourist. Portraits, genre scenes, landscapes, landscapes with figures.

George Arthur Fripp was a pupil of J.B. Pyne and Samuel Jackson. He spent several years as a portrait painter in his native Bristol before moving to London in 1841. He was acclaimed for a landscape in oils entitled *Mont Blanc from above Cormayeur*. Thereafter, he limited himself to watercolours. In 1872 or 1873 he was elected to membership of the Belgian society of watercolourists.

He was a prolific exhibitor, sending some 600 paintings to London exhibitions over 50 years. He ranks as an accomplished landscape painter, particularly of English subjects, and is noted above all for his delicate, virtually translucent palette. His work was admired by Queen Victoria, and in 1864 he stayed at Balmoral Castle in Scotland and produced a number of local scenes there.

MUSEUMS AND GALLERIES:

BLACKBURN: *Thames Bridge at Caversham* - BRISTOL (City Mus. & AG): *River Thames at Streatley Mill* (oil on canvas); *Lake Wallenstadt* (oil on canvas); *View of the Avon Gorge* (oil on canvas); *Tivoli* (oil on canvas) - DUBLIN: *Vale of Leith, Surrey*; *Fountains Abbey* (watercolour) - EDINBURGH (Nat. Gal. of Scotland, Print Room): *River Scene* (watercolour) - LIVERPOOL: *Mont Blanc* - LONDON (Victoria and Albert Mus.): *Country Church*; *Landscape*; *White Cliffs of Dover*; *Landscape*; *Bolton Abbey, Yorkshire*; *River Thames at Cookham*; *Landscape*; *Old Windmill*; *Children of the Mist*; *Landscape with Herd of Deer*; *Dunstaffnage Castle*; *Bolton Abbey, Yorkshire* - TORBAY (Torre Abbey): *Mont Blanc from above Cormayeur*.

AUCTION RECORDS:

LONDON, 26 Feb 1894, *Braemar* (watercolour) FRF 790. NEW YORK, 23 Jan 1903, *On the River* (watercolour) USD 300. LONDON, 7 Dec 1907, *River Thames at Marlow* (watercolour) GBP 6. LONDON, 15 Feb 1908, *Scottish Landscape* (watercolour) GBP 14; *Farm* (1866, watercolour) GBP 12. LONDON, 13 April 1908, *Beachy Head* (1860, watercolour) GBP 18. LONDON, 13 Feb 1909, *Stream in Devon*, GBP 6. LONDON, 23 May 1910, *Lochnagar* (watercolour) GBP 47. LONDON, 27 Nov 1922, *Glen Rosa* (drawing) GBP 22; *Harvest*; *Haymaking (E. Duncan)* (two drawings) GBP 9. LONDON, 16 Feb 1923, *Haymaking* (drawing) GBP 7. LONDON, 9 March 1923, *Durham* (drawing) GBP 21. LONDON, 28 Jan 1924, *Near Ullswater* (drawing) GBP 6. LONDON, 7 March 1924, *Tintagel* (drawing) GBP 6; *Murk Sœ* (drawing) GBP 3. LONDON, 14 April 1924, *Close of Day* (drawing) GBP 4. LONDON, 3 May 1924, *Ordeal* (drawing) GBP 7. LONDON, 28 Nov 1924, *Near Dolgelly* (drawing) GBP 4. LONDON, 29 Jan 1926, *Autumn in the Highlands* (drawing) GBP 8. LONDON, 28 May 1926, *Ullswater*, GBP 35. LONDON, 21 Nov 1927, *Haymaking*, GBP 5. LONDON, 8 June 1928, *Pangbourne* (watercolour) GBP 13. LONDON, 3 Dec 1928, *Kilchurn Castle*, GBP 4. LONDON, 17 Dec 1928, *October Twilight*, GBP 7; *Burton Pond*, GBP 4. LONDON, 25 Feb 1929, *Kilchurn Castle*, GBP 5. LONDON, 26 June 1931, *Windy Day* (drawing) GBP 7; *View of the Thames*, GBP 7. LONDON, 18 May 1932, *Caerphilly Castle*, GBP 6. LONDON, 6 Dec 1935, *Near Leamington* (drawing) GBP 5. LONDON, 30 Oct-2 Nov 1936, *Mapledurham*, GBP 11. LONDON, 30 April 1937, *River*, GBP 13. LEEDS, 15 and 16 April 1942, *Landscape*, GBP 12. LONDON, 8 Oct 1943, *Saltwood Castle* (drawing) GBP 28. LONDON, 21 Nov 1945, *Kinlochaline*, GBP 17. LONDON, 8 March 1946, *River*, GBP 18. LONDON, 21 Dec 1982, *Market Scene, Rome* (watercolour and gouache, 10 3/4 x 18 ins / 27.3 x 45.5 cm) GBP 800. LONDON, 10 July 1984, *Durham Cathedral* (1846, watercolour and pencil with touches of gouache, 13 1/4 x 24 1/4 ins / 33.5 x 61.5 cm) GBP 1,900. LONDON, 26 April 1985, *Lake Maggiore* (oil on panel, 21 1/2 x 38 ins / 54.6 x 96.5 cm) GBP 6,500. LONDON, 12 March 1987, *Goring-on-Thames, Oxfordshire* (watercolour and pencil heightened with gouache, 12 1/4 x 19 1/2 ins / 31 x 49.5 cm) GBP 1,800. LONDON, 2 Nov 1989, *Figures near a Sluice* (1837, oil on canvas, 20 x 30 ins / 50.8 x 76.2 cm) GBP 2,860. LONDON, 31 Jan 1990, *Landscape with Figures* (watercolour and pencil, 9 x 14 1/4 ins / 23 x 36 cm) GBP 1,375. LONDON, 25-26 April 1990, *Sheep Drovers by a River* (1858, watercolour, ink and gouache, 9 1/2 x 13 1/2 ins / 24 x 34 cm) GBP 1,045. GLASGOW, 22 Nov 1990, *Glen Sligachan, Isle of Skye* (watercolour, 13 3/4 x 22 ins / 35 x 55.8 cm) GBP 935. LONDON, 10 April 1992, *Ponte Lucano, Tivoli* (1835, oil on canvas, 14 1/2 x 22 1/2 ins / 36.8 x 57.2 cm) GBP 2,860. AMSTERDAM, 20 April 1993, *Landscape with River* (1861, watercolour, 13 x 19 ins / 33 x 48 cm) NLG 1,150. LONDON, 11 June 1993, *Gossip among Milkmaids* (oil on canvas, 9 1/4 x 12 1/2 ins / 23.7 x 31.5 cm) GBP 1,265. LONDON, 3 June 1994, *Richmond, Yorkshire seen from the South* (1882, pencil and watercolour, 6 3/4 x 10 ins / 17.2 x 25.2 cm) GBP 805. BILLINGSHURST, 18 May 1999, *Southend* (watercolour heightened with white, 13 x 19 ins / 33 x 49 cm) GBP 2,200. LONDON, 17 Nov 1999, *Thames at Wargrave, Berks* (1865, watercolour, 10 x 14 ins / 25 x 36 cm) GBP 2,800. LONDON, 8 June 2000, *Isola Bella, Lake Como, Italy* (1857, oil on panel, 22 x 38 ins / 55 x 97 cm) GBP 6,500. LONDON, 30 Nov 2000, *St Vincent's Rock, Clifton, Bristol* (watercolour over pencil heightened with gouache, gum arabic, stopping out and scratching, 15 x 24 ins / 37 x 62 cm) GBP 5,000. LONDON, 4 July 2001, *Cricket on the Green* (1843, watercolour over pencil heightened with gouache, 10 x 16 ins / 25 x 41 cm) GBP 1,800. LONDON, 29 Nov 2001, *Ducks on a River with Cattle Grazing on the Banks beyond* (watercolour over pencil heightened with scratching out, 14 x 20 ins / 35 x 50 cm) GBP 3,600. LONDON, 21 March 2002, *Bolton Abbey on the Wharf, Yorkshire* (watercolour over pencil heightened with gouache scratching out and stopping out, 22 x 37 ins / 57 x 93 cm) GBP 7,800. LONDON, 21 March 2002, *Lago Maggiore* (oil on panel, 21 x 37 ins / 53 x 95 cm) GBP 10,500. LONDON, 22 Jan 2003, *Trees on the Banks of a Lake at Dusk* (1837, pencil and watercolour with scratching out, 11 x 8 ins / 29 x 21 cm) GBP 4,200. LEYBURN, 17 July 2003, *Figures beside a Stone Bridge near a Cottage* (1840, oil on canvas, 13 x 17 ins / 34 x 44 cm) GBP 1,500. LEYBURN, 21 April 2004, *Loch Awe with Kilchurn Castle* (1853, pencil and watercolour, 13 x 23 ins / 33 x 59 cm) GBP 4,500. LONDON, 18 Nov 2004, *At Southend, Essex* (1851, pencil and watercolour with scratching out, 14 x 20 ins / 35 x 50 cm) GBP 7,500.

FRIQUET, Louise

French, 19th century.

Painter. Landscapes with figures, architectural views.

Friquet is on record as having been active in France at the beginning of the 19th century.

AUCTION RECORDS:

PARIS, 13 Dec 1996, *Goatherd and Goats near Antic Ruins* (1824, oil on canvas, 10 x 13 ins / 24.5 x 33 cm) FRF 12,500.

FRIQUET, Paul-Henri

French, 20th century.

Born 11 December 1933, in Nice.

Sculptor.

Paul-Henri Friquet's teachers included Henri Georges Adam; he attended courses run by the Ville de Paris from 1954 to 1956 and studied at the École des Beaux-Arts in Paris from 1957 to 1961. He was awarded the Prix de la Fondation de la Vocation in 1961 and the Prix Fénéon in 1968. He showed a collection of his sculptures in a solo exhibition at the Galerie AA in Paris in 1990. His sculptures have been purchased by the Affaires Culturelles department, notably a marble entitled *Cité Flottante* (*Floating City*) in 1976, and the Ville de Paris commissioned a medal from him.

He has exhibited at various of the annual Paris Salons, including: from 1963 to 1967 the Salon de la Jeune Sculpture; in 1965 the Salon Comparaisons; from 1982 to 1987 the Salon de Mai; in 1981 at the Salon du Petit Bronze; and regularly at the Salon des Réalités Nouvelles, of which he became a committee member in 1976. He also took part in numerous group exhibitions, notably at Gravelines in 1964, at the Fondation du Mécénat exhibition at the Musée des Arts Décoratifs in Paris in 1969, in Luxembourg in 1973, in the first European Sculpture Biennale at the Centre National d'Art Contemporain in Jouy-sur-Eure in 1982 and in *Matières et Lumières - Trois Peintres, Trois Sculpteurs* at the Galerie St-Rémy in Meaux in 1991.

AUCTION RECORDS:

PARIS, 22 May 1989, *Urban Window* (1988, Carrara white marble, 8 1/4 x 7 x 3 1/2 ins / 21 x 18 x 9 cm) FRF 6,200.

FRIQUET DE VAUROZE, Jacques Antoine

French, 17th - 18th century.

Born 1648, in Troyes; died 25 June 1716, in Paris.

Painter.

Jacques Friquet de Vauroze was a student of Bourdon. On 16 October 1670, he was made a member of the academy. He also became a professor of anatomy on 5 July 1670.

His work appeared in Louvre exhibitions from 1673 to 1704 and includes the following: *Moses Carried by Two Men to the Pharaoh's Daughter, Jethro's Daughters, Martha and Magdalene at the Feet of Jesus* and *Triumph of Thetis over the Waters*. The Louvre museum owns a work by him entitled *The King Bringing Peace to Europe*.

FRIRY, Charles

French, 19th century.

Born 1802; died 1881.

Engraver.

Charles Friry was an erudite man and a collector. He engraved in the style of his collection. His participation in *Les Mystérieux du XVIIe siècle. Une enquête au cabinet d'art graphique* (*The Mysteries of the 17th century. An Enquiry into the Graphic Art Collection*) organised by the Musée des Beaux-Arts in Nancy in 2002 was to illustrate the process of rediscovery of Georges de la Tour with his engraved reproduction of *Hurdy Gurdy Player with his Bag*.

BIBLIOGRAPHY:

Paul, Céline/Harent, Sophie, *'Les Mystérieux du XVIIe siècle. Une enquête au cabinet d'art graphique'* in coll. *Lire en filigrane*, Musée des Beaux-Arts, Nancy, 2002.

FRIS, Jacques

Belgian, 18th - 19th century.

Born 1774, in Geraardsbergen (East Flanders); died 1852, in Mechelen.

Painter. History painting.

He was a professor at the academy in Mechelen from 1812 to 1834.

FRIS, Jan or Johannes

Dutch, 17th century.

Born c. 1627, in Amsterdam; died c. 1672.

Painter. Still-lifes.

He was married in Amsterdam in 1649, and became a burgher of the city in 1651.

AUCTION RECORDS:

PARIS, 1888, *Still-life*, FRF 537. PARIS, 3 Dec 1959, *Still-life with a Stoneware Pot*, FRF 1,000,000. LONDON, 17 Feb 1960, *Still-life*, GBP 400. LONDON, 29 June 1966, *Still-life with a Wineglass*, GBP 2,000. LONDON, 30 Nov 1973, *Still-life*, Gns 2,000. COLOGNE, 14 Nov 1974, *Still-life*, DEM 38,000. LONDON, 15 April 1983, *Still-life* (1665, oil on panel, 19 1/4 x 16 1/2in/49 x 42cm) GBP 22,000. NEW YORK, 20 May 1993, *Still-life with an Upturned Stone Pitcher, a Metal Plate with a Pipe and Egg-shells, a Broken Glass and Bread on a Table* (oil on panel, 18 1/2 x 24 3/4in/47 x 62.9cm) USD 21,850. LONDON, 7 July 2004, *Vanitas* (1670, oil on canvas, 54 x 45 ins / 138 x 115 cm) GBP 17,000.

FRIS, Pieter, or Frits, Fritz

Dutch, 17th century.

Born c. 1620, in Amsterdam; died before 1708, in Delft.

Painter.

He was a member of the Guild of St Luke in Haarlem and, from 1660 to 1682, in Rotterdam.

MUSEUMS AND GALLERIES:

MADRID (Prado): *Descent of Orpheus into the Underworld* - THE HAGUE (Ministry of Fine Arts): *Murder of the Witt Brothers*.

FRISA, Pedro

Spanish, 16th century.

Active in Valladolid.

Painter.

A little-known artist, Pedro Frisa borrowed both from the Florentine school and from the style of Martens, with whom he often worked.

FRISCH, F.
German, 19th century.
Active in Augsburg at the beginning of the 19th century.
Engraver (aquatint).
This artist's output was mainly landscapes.

FRISCH, Ferdinand Helfreich
German, 18th century.
Born 7 February 1707, in Berlin; died 1758, in Berlin.
Engraver.
Ferdinand Frisch was the son of Johann Leohard. He was a pupil of Hanrich and Busch and is best known for his portraits.

FRISCH, Friedrich
German, 19th century.
Born 13 February 1813, in Darmstadt; died 9 December 1886, in Darmstadt.
Painter, lithographer.
Friedrich Frisch was a pupil of Adam and von Hess in Munich before working for the king of Wurtemburg and the court of Baden.

FRISCH, Heinrich
German, 17th century.
Born 1644, in Hamburg; died 1693, in Meran (now Merano, Italy).
Painter.
After having been a prisoner of the barbarians in Tripoli, Heinrich Frisch spent some time in Rome and then worked in the Tyrol where he decorated churches.

FRISCH, Johann Christoph
German, 18th - 19th century.
Born 9 February 1738, in Berlin; died 28 February 1815, in Berlin.
Painter, engraver. History painting, mythological subjects, local scenes.
Johann Christoph Frisch was a pupil of Bernhard Rode in Berlin. Some of his works are contained in the palace of Sans-Souci. He painted imaginary caves in the winter garden of Paretz Castle.

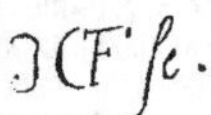

MUSEUMS AND GALLERIES:
BERLIN: *Spirits Playing.*
AUCTION RECORDS:
NEW YORK, 25 Feb 1983, *On the banks of the Nile* (oil on canvas, 18 x 30 ins / 45.7 x 76.2 cm) USD 3,500. MONACO, 17 June 1988, *Daphne and Apollo* (oil on canvas, 18 1/4 x 14 1/4 ins / 46.5 x 36.5 cm) FRF 16,650. NEW YORK, 16 Feb 1993, *Arab Caravan* (oil on canvas, 18 x 30 ins / 45.5 x 76.2 cm) USD 1,540. NEW YORK, 13 March 2001, *Cairo, Egypt* (oil on canvas, 12 x 18 ins / 30 x 46 cm) USD 3,000.

FRISCH, Johann Gottfried
German, 17th - 18th century.
Active in Straubing.
Sculptor.

FRISCH, Johann Leonhard
German, 17th - 18th century.
Born 19 March 1666, in Sulzbach; died 21 March 1743, in Berlin.
Draughtsman.
Frisch was better known as a zoologist and used drawings mainly to illustrate his work.

FRISCH, John Didrik
Norwegian, 19th century.
Born 4 May 1835, in Charlottedal; died 23 November 1867, in Florence.
Painter. Portraits, genre scenes, landscapes.
John Didrik Frisch studied with Harder at the academy in Sorø. He then went on to Copenhagen to perfect his art. He left for Italy in 1867 but died there during that same year.
AUCTION RECORDS:
COPENHAGEN, 3 June 1980, *Two Neighbours in Conversation* (1866, oil on canvas, 37 x 32 ins / 94 x 81 cm) DKK 9,000. COPENHAGEN, 8 June 1982, *Self-portrait* (1859, oil on canvas, oval, 23 1/2 x 19 3/4 ins / 60 x 50 cm) DKK 2,200. COPENHAGEN, 27 March 1985, *Laundry in the Courtyard of a Farm* (1865, oil on canvas, 15 3/4 x 15 3/4 ins / 40 x 40 cm) DKK 37,000.

FRISCH, Philipp Jacob
German, 18th century.
Born 1702, in Berlin; died 4 December 1753, in Grünberg (Silesia).
Painter, engraver.
The son of Johann Leonhard, Jacob Frisch was a pupil of Hanrich and de Buschs.

FRISCHAUFF, Gottlieb Theodor
German, 18th century.
Active in Oschatz (Saxony).
Painter.
Frischauff decorated Stösitz Castle near Oschatz.

FRISCHBIER, Balthasar
German, 15th century.
Active in Schweidnitz, Silesia (now Swidnica, Poland) at the end of the 15th century.
Painter.

FRISCHE, Arnold
German, 19th - 20th century.
Born 18 December 1869, in Düsseldorf.
Sculptor.
Arnold Frische was the son of the painter Heinrich Ludwig. He worked in the Rhineland, Westphalia, Alsace and Bremen.

FRISCHE, Emil
German, 19th - 20th century.
Born 6 February 1872, in Düsseldorf.
Painter.
Emil Frische was the son of Heinrich Ludwig. He studied with Claus Meyer and spent much of his time in Florence.

FRISCHE, Heinrich Ludwig
German (?), 19th century.
Born 9 January 1831, in Altenbruch; died 5 December 1901, in Düsseldorf.
Painter. Landscapes.
Frische studied in Düsseldorf between 1858 and 1862 under Gude. After undertaking study trips he settled in Düsseldorf.
MUSEUMS AND GALLERIES:
COLOGNE: *Harz Landscape* - HANOVER: *Outing in the Oder Valley.*
AUCTION RECORDS:
LONDON, 2 Nov 1973, *Marshy Landscape,* Gns 650. MUNICH, 22 March 2000, *Harz Landscape* (oil on canvas, 31 x 39 ins / 80 x 100 cm) DEM 4,400. COLOGNE, 29 June 2000, *Landscape with Figures, Collecting Brushwood* (oil on canvas, 41 x 56 ins / 104 x 141 cm) DEM 10,000. COLOGNE, 20 Nov 2003, *Near Cuxhafen in the Evening* (oil on canvas, 27 x 42 ins / 69 x 107 cm) EUR 7,500.

FRISCHE, Rudolf
German, 19th - 20th century.
Born in Osnabrück (Lower Saxony).
Painter.

Rudolf Frische studied at the Bavarian royal academy in Munich. He exhibited for the first time at the Munich International Exhibition in 1890 and again the following year. He also won a prize at the 1894 exhibition in London for his painting *One Morning*. He entered *Madonna with Iris* in the Alinari competition in 1900.

FRISCHER
German, 19th century.
Active c. 1837.
Painter (glass).

Frischer is cited by Siret.

FRISCHHEINTZ, Hans
German, 16th century.
Active in Dresden at the end of the 16th century.
Painter.

Hans Frischheintz worked on the painted decoration of the castle of Moritzburg.

FRISCHHEINZ, Barthel
German, 16th - 17th century.
Active in Königsberg, East Prussia (now Kaliningrad, Russia).
Painter.

Barthel Frischheinz is known to have painted an *Equestrian Portrait of Margrave Joachim Ernst of Brandenburg-Ansbach*.

FRISCHHERZ, David, or Frischhertz
Swiss, 16th century.
Active in Schlettstadt (now Sélestat, France).
Sculptor.
Zurich School.

David Frischherz was a burgher of Zurich in 1519 and a member of the 'Lux et Loyen' confraternity there. He is probably the same person as the artist D. Frichherz, mentioned in the Basel archives in 1517 and 1518.

FRISCHING, Friedrich Rudolf von
Swiss, 19th century.
Born 26 March 1833, in Bern; died 26 October 1906, in Bern.
Painter. Landscapes.

Von Frisching worked in Bern and Geneva, having completed his studies in Düsseldorf where his mentor was K. Jungheim. Frisching took part in exhibitions in Bern, Geneva and St Gall between 1859 and 1876. The museum in Bern has his landscape *Iseltwald on Lake Brientz* (morning scene) in its collection.

FRISCHKE, Arthur
American, 20th century.
Born 25 June 1893, in New York.
Painter.

FRISE, Laurent
French, 18th century.
Active in Paris in 1759.
Painter.

FRISENDAHL, Carl
Swedish, 20th century.
Born 14 August 1886, in Adalsliden; died 18 March 1948, in France.
From 1907 active in France.
Painter, sculptor, draughtsman. Figures, nudes, animals.

Carl Friesendahl studied with Antoine Bourdelle in Paris and settled there in 1907. He exhibited at the Salon d'Automne, of which he became a member, Salon de la Société Nationale des Beaux-Arts and Salon des Tuileries. He also exhibited in Rome, Edinburgh and Helsinki. He exhibited in Sweden for the first time in 1929, together with the painter Lennart, and had solo exhibitions in Göteborg, Lund and Paris. The Swedish academy of fine arts awarded him the Jenny Lind prize during World War I. In 1940 he received an important commission from Sweden for a fountain in the inner court of the historical museum in Stockholm.

His painting shares the same themes as his sculpture, transposing the three-dimensional forms of his favourite animals, bears, bison and horses, into colour.

BIBLIOGRAPHY:
Trois artistes suédois contemporains, exhibition catalogue, Musée Galliera, Paris, 1957.

MUSEUMS AND GALLERIES:
STOCKHOLM (Nationalmus.).

AUCTION RECORDS:
STOCKHOLM, 15 Nov 1988, *Wild Boar Sitting* (terracotta, h. 24 ins / 61 cm) SEK 17,500. STOCKHOLM, 7 Nov 2000, *Neckan* (dark patinated bronze, h. 13 ins / 33 cm) SEK 16,000.

FRISERI, Bastien
Italian, 15th - 16th century.
Born at the end of the 15th century, in Fossano (Piedmont).
Painter.

Friseri painted the altarpiece of *Our Lady of the Snows* for the church of La Brigue (Alpes-Maritimes), for Pierre Lascaris 'the Magnificent'.

FRISHMUTH, Harriet Whitney, or Frismuth
American, 20th century.
Born 17 September 1880, in Philadelphia; died 1 January 1980, in Waterbury (Connecticut).
Sculptor, draughtsman, medallist. Allegorical subjects, figures, nudes.
Philadelphia Ten.

Harriet Frishmuth studied sculpture briefly with Rodin in Paris, and also studied at the Académie Colarossi under Jean-Antoine Injalbert, and possibly under Henri Gauquié. She worked for two years with Cuno von Euchtriz in Berlin. After returning to the USA, Frishmuth studied at the Art Students League, New York, under Gutzon Borglum and Hermon A. MacNeil, then worked as assistant to the sculptor Karl Bitter, and performed dissections at the College of Physicians and Surgeons in New York to learn about anatomy. Frishmuth received awards at the National Academy of Design (the Helen Foster Barnett Prize, 1915), the Elizabeth N. Watrous Gold Medal (1922), and the Julia A. Shaw Memorial Prize (1923); and also received the Augustus St-Gaudens Prize, Art Students League. Frishmuth was a member of the Philadelphia Ten, a group of women painters and sculptors, which also included Isabel Branson Cartwright, Constance Cochrane, Mary Russell Fernell Colton and Edith Lucile Howard. This group exhibited together from 1917 to 1945.

Frishmuth initially made small decorative objects such as the bronzes *Girl and Frog Ashtray* (1910), and *Pushing Men Bookends* (1912). She moved to making life-size figures and playful fountains, such as *Joy of the Waters* (three versions in different sizes, 1917, 1920). Frishmuth is well known for her lyrical sculptures of nude female figures in motion, most often using the dancer Desha as a model, such as *Sweet Grapes* (1922), and *The Vine* (1927). She also did busts and memorials, such as *President Woodrow Wilson* (1924) for the Virginia State Capitol in Richmond, and *Dill Memorial* (1929) for Bridgewater, Massachusetts.

Frishmuth's exhibitions include the Paris Salon (1903); the National Academy of Design (1908-1949); Pennsylvania Academy of Fine Arts, Philadelphia (1908-1939); the Art Institute of Chicago (1912-1935); a show of women sculptors, Gorham Galleries, New York (1912); Panama-Pacific Exposition, San Francisco (1915); *American Sculpture*, National Sculpture Society, New York (1923); *Woman's World Fair*, Chicago (1925); *Famous Small Bronzes*, Gorham Galleries

(1928); Grand Central Art Galleries, New York (1928); the National Sculpture Society, California Palace of the Legion of Honor (1929); a solo at Black, Starr and Gorham, New York (1946); and *The Philadelphia Ten: A Women's Artist Group 1917-1945*, Westmoreland Museum of American Art, Greensburg, Pennsylvania (1998).

BIBLIOGRAPHY:

Brookgreen Gardens: Sculpture by Harriet Whitney Frismuth, Brookgreen Gardens (SC), 1937. Talcott, Ruth (ed.), *'Harriet Whitney Frismuth, 1880-1980'* in *National Sculpture Review, 29*, Summer 1980. Proske, Beatrice Gilman, *'Harriet Whitney Frismuth, Lyric Sculptor'* in *Aristos: Journal of Esthetics, 2*, June 1984.

MUSEUMS AND GALLERIES:

COLUMBIA, SC (MA): *The Hunt* (c. 1921, bronze) - DALLAS (MA): *Play Days* (1925) - DAYTON (Art Institute): *Joy of the Waters* (1917, bronze) - HARTFORD (Wadsworth Atheneum): *Joy of the Waters, Ecstasy* (1920); *Slavonic Dancer* (1921, bronze) - JACKSON HOLE (National Mus. of Wildlife Art): *Rupert Eagle* (1912, bronze) - LOS ANGELES (County MA) - MONTCLAIR (AM): *Joy of the Waters* (1920, bronze) - NEW YORK (Metropolitan Mus. of Art): *The Vine* (1927, bronze) - NEW YORK (National Academy of Design Mus.): *Joy of the Waters* (1920, bronze) - READING, PA (Reading Public Museum and Art Gallery): *Crest of the Wave* (1925) - SAN FRANCISCO (FAM): *Temptation (Fantasy)* (1922, bronze) - TELFAIR, GA (Museum of Art): *Play Days* (1925, bronze).

AUCTION RECORDS:

NEW YORK, 29 April 1976, *Crest of the Wave* (1925, brown and green patinated bronze, h. 20 3/4 ins / 53 cm) USD 2,750. NEW YORK, 21 April 1977, *Water Nymph* (1925, bronze, h. 53 1/2 ins / 136 cm) USD 10,000. NEW YORK, 21 April 1978, *Play Days* (bronze, h. 52 1/2 ins / 133.4 cm) USD 10,500. NEW YORK, 25 April 1980, *The Dance* (bronze, h. 16 1/2 ins / 41.9 cm) USD 9,500. NEW YORK, 3 Dec 1982, *Joy of the Waters* (1920, bronze, h. 39 1/2 ins / 100.3 cm) USD 17,000. NEW YORK, 2 June 1983, *Joy of the Waters* (1920, bronze, h. 43 1/4 ins / 109.9 cm) USD 16,000. NEW YORK, 4 Dec 1987, *Joy of the Waters* (1920, greenish-brown patinated bronze, h. 18 1/4 ins / 46.3 cm) USD 210,000. NEW YORK, 17 March 1988, *Crest of the Wave* (1925, bronze, h. 20 1/2 ins / 52.2 cm) USD 14,300. LOS ANGELES, 9 June 1988, *Joy of the Waters* (1920, bronze, h. 43 1/4 ins / 110 cm) USD 33,000. NEW YORK, 24 June 1988, *The Star* (1918, bronze, h. 19 3/4 ins / 50 cm) USD 9,900. PARIS, 22 May 1989, *Exultation* (1920, greenish-brown patinated bronze, h. 16 1/2 ins / 42 cm) FRF 35,000. NEW YORK, 24 May 1989, *Globe Sundial* (1921, bronze, h. 43 ins / 109.2 cm) USD 19,800. NEW YORK, 28 Sept 1989, *Nymph Standing on the Crest of the Wave* (bronze, h. 21 ins / 53.3 cm) USD 13,200. NEW YORK, 30 Nov 1989, *Bubble Dance* (1923, brown-patinated bronze, h. 19 1/2 ins / 49.5 cm) USD 36,300. NEW YORK, 1 Dec 1989, *Desire* (dark-green-patinated bronze on marble plinth, h. 26 ins / 66.3 cm) USD 44,000. NEW YORK, 24 May 1990, *Playdays* (patinated bronze brownish-green, h. 53 ins / 134.6 cm) USD 143,000. NEW YORK, 14 March 1991, *Vine - Figure of Nymph* (greenish-brown-patinated bronze, h. 11 3/4 ins / 29.9 cm) USD 6,050. NEW YORK, 12 April 1991, *Crest of the Wave* (1925, brown-patinated bronze, h. 21 1/2 ins / 54.6 cm) USD 8,800. NEW YORK, 22 May 1991, *Joy of the Waters* (bronze fountain, h. 62 ins / 157.5 cm) USD 77,000. NEW YORK, 23 May 1991, *Playdays* (green-patinated bronze, h. 51 1/2 ins / 130.8 cm) USD 88,000. NEW YORK, 25 Sept 1991, *Crest of the Wave* (bronze, h. 67 ins / 170.2 cm) USD 82,500. NEW YORK, 26 Sept 1991, *Pas de Deux* (bronze, group of two dansers, h. 15 ins / 38 cm, l. 27 1/2 ins/69.8 cm) USD 15,400. NEW YORK, 6 Dec 1991, *Meditation* (1930, bronze, fountain, h. 57 1/2 ins / 146.1 cm) USD 49,500. NEW YORK, 4 Dec 1992, *Amusements or Nymph with Frogs* (bronze, h. 50 1/4 ins / 127.5 cm) USD 71,500. NEW YORK, 23 Sept 1993, *Joy of the Waters* (1920, bronze, h. 63 1/2 ins / 161.3 cm) USD 63,000. NEW YORK, 17 March 1994, *The Vine* (1921, bronze/black marble plinth, h. 12 ins / 30.5 cm) USD 5,750. NEW YORK, 20 March 1996, *The Vine* (bronze, h. 11 3/4 ins / 29.8 cm) USD 7,475. NEW YORK, 22 May 1996, *Joy of the Waters* (1912, green-patinated bronze, h. 61 1/2 ins / 156.2 cm) USD 173,000. NEW YORK, 27 Sept 1996, *The Star, Nymph* (1918, greenish-brown patinated bronze, h. 18 1/2 ins / 47.3 cm) USD 6,900. NEW YORK, 3 Dec 1996, *Woman with Frog* (bronze, ash-tray, h. 4 3/4 ins / 12 cm) USD 7,130. NEW YORK, 23 April 1997, *Head of Jester* (1910, reddish-brown patinated bronze, h. 6 ins / 15.2 cm) USD 1,150. NEW YORK, 5 June 1997, *Pas de Deux* (brown-patinated bronze, group, h. 17 ins / 43.1 cm) USD 25,300. NEW YORK, 6 June 1997, *Ruppert Eagle* (1912, green-patinated bronze, h. 42 ins / 106.7 cm) USD 54,625. NEW YORK, 27 May 1999, *Fantaisie* (1922, patinated bronze, h. 10 ins / 25 cm) USD 35,000. NEW YORK, 27 May 1999, *Bubble Dance* (1929, green-brown patinated bronze, h. 90 ins / 229 cm) USD 525,000. BOSTON, 12 May 2000, *Fisherman Sundial* (1912, green-brown patinated bronze, h. 15 ins / 38 cm) USD 33,000. NEW YORK, 30 Nov 2000, *Fisherman, Bird Bath* (weathered green patinated bronze, 17 x 11 ins / 42 x 28 cm) USD 65,000. BOSTON, 9 March 2001, *Crest of the Wave* (1925, brown patinated bronze, h. 21 ins / 53 cm) USD 35,000. NEW YORK, 29 Nov 2001, *Joy of the Waters* (bluish-green patinated bronze, h. 43 ins / 109 cm) USD 35,000. BOSTON, 10 May 2002, *Crest of the Wave* (1925, gold patinated bronze, h. 21 ins / 53 cm) USD 23,000. NEW YORK, 5 Dec 2002, *Vine* (reddish brown patinated bronze, h. 11 ins / 29 cm) USD 30,000. NEW YORK, 22 May 2003, *Joy of the Waters* (verdigris patinated bronze, h. 61 ins / 156 cm) USD 150,000. NEW YORK, 4 Dec 2003, *Joy of the Waters* (1917, patinated bronze, h. 63 ins / 160 cm) USD 150,000. NEW YORK, 19 May 2004, *Dancers* (1921, dark brown patinated bronze, 16 x 27 ins / 41 x 69 cm) USD 47,500. NEW YORK, 19 May 2004, *Playdays - a Fountain* (1925, weathered green patinated bronze, h. 53 ins / 132 cm) USD 130,000.

FRISIA, Donato

Italian, 20th century.

Born 30 August 1883, in Merate; died 13 December 1953, in Merate.

Painter. Portraits, self-portraits, landscapes, urban landscapes, waterscapes, seascapes, still-lifes.

Donato Frisia, whose father was a decorative artist, studied at the Accademia di Brera, Milan, where he was taught by Cesare Tallone, Enrico Butti and Camillo Boito. From 1919, he frequently travelled to Paris, where he formed an association with Modigliani. Indeed, he painted five portraits of him. In Paris, he shared a studio with Anselmo Bucci. He also travelled in Europe and North Africa. He received a number of awards, including the Prix Mylius in Milan in 1921, the Prix Principe Umberto in 1922 for *Portrait of Signora Cavallotti*.

In the tradition of Lombard Naturalism, he painted with a lively and sensuous touch, with a restrained range of colours that testified to poetic humanism and a lyrical approach to nature. He portrayed the landscapes he had observed in the course of his numerous travels, as well as, from the 1930s, the Ligurian coast and views of Venice.

Group exhibitions at which his paintings have been shown include: 1911, Palazzo della Permanente, Milan; 1920-1952, Venice Biennale; 1915, then at regular intervals, Amatori e Cultori di Arte, Rome; 1922, Milan Triennale; 1927 and 1929, *Esposizione nazionale del Paesaggio* (*National Landscape Exhibition*), Bologna (gold medal in 1929); 1937, Exposition Universelle Paris (silver medal); 1939, *Mostra Pittura Antica* (*Exhibition of Ancient Painting*), Bergame; 1999, *Scoperta del Mare. Pittori lombardi in Liguria tra 1800 e 1900* (*Discovering the Sea: Lombard Painters in Liguria between 1800 and 1900*), Palazzo Ducale, Genoa.

Solo exhibitions have included: 1932 and 1933, Galleria Pesaro, Milan; 1941, Palazzo della Permanente, Milan; 1942, Solo Room at Venice Biennale; 1978 and 1993, Galleria Ponte Rosso, Milan; 1983, to celebrate the centenary of his birth, Merate.

BIBLIOGRAPHY:

Donato Frisia nel centenario della nascita, 1883-1983, exhibition catalogue, Commune di Merate, Bertoni e figli, Merate, 1983. Pizziolo, Marina/Passoni, Franco (preface), *Donato Frisia: l'invenzione del vero*, Bolis, Bergamo, 1991. De Grada, Raffaele, *Donato Frisia*, exhibition catalogue, Galleria Ponte Rosso, Consonni, Milan, 1993. Ginex, Giovanna/Rebora, Sergio, *Scoperta del Mare. Pittori lombardi in Liguria tra 1800 e 1900*, group exhibition catalogue, Palazzo Ducale, Genoa, Mazzetta, Milan, 1999.

MUSEUMS AND GALLERIES:

MILAN (Gal. d'Arte Moderna) - MILAN (Pinacoteca di Brera) - MONZA (Galleria Civica) - ROME (Gal. Nazionale d'Arte Moderna) - VALLETTA (National Musem of Fine Arts).

AUCTION RECORDS:

MILAN, 21 April 1983, *Snowscape* (oil on card, 13 x 17 ins / 33 x 43 cm) ITL 950,000. MILAN, 16 Oct 1986, *Canale a Venezia* (1938, oil on canvas, 25½ x 31½ ins / 65 x 80 cm) ITL 3,600,000. MILAN, 6 June 1991, *Bridge under Construction in Paris* (oil on canvas/card, 13½ x 18½ ins / 34 x 47 cm) ITL 3,400,000. MILAN, 25 Oct 1994, *Venice: the Cannareggio Canal, the Ponte delle Guglie and the church of S Geremia* (1936, oil on canvas, 31¾ x 49¼ ins / 80.5 x 125 cm) ITL 18,400,000. MILAN, 26 Oct 1995, *Village* (1953, oil on canvas, 10¾ x 14 ins / 27.5 x 35.5 cm) ITL 1,725,000. MILAN, 29 March 1999, *Still-life with Fruit* (1949, oil on canvas, 20 x 24 ins / 50 x 60 cm) ITL 5,500,000. MILAN, 21 Dec 1999, *House beyond the Olive Trees* (1947, oil on canvas, 41 x 30 ins / 104 x 75 cm) ITL 7,000,000. MILAN, 22 March 2000, *Venice* (oil on panel, 11 x 20 ins / 27 x 50 cm) ITL 4,000,000. MILAN, 5 Dec 2001, *Houses by the Sea* (1924, oil on canvas, 14 x 19 ins / 35 x 48 cm) ITL 5,200,000. MILAN, 15 Sept 2004, *Milan, Largo Augusto* (1948, oil on board, 28 x 20 ins / 70 x 50 cm) EUR 6,700.

FRISING, Marc
Luxembourg, 20th - 21st century.
Born 15 January 1960, in Luxembourg.
Engraver.

Frising trained as an engraver at the École des Arts Décoratifs in M. Alfred Edel's studio in Strasbourg. In 1986, he stayed in Paris and attended the Cité Internationale des Arts. He teaches regularly at the summer academy in Weinviertel (Lower Austria). He lives and works in Sandweiler.

Marc Frising's engravings of still-lifes are distinguished by their rigorous composition. Rope knots, pieces of material, a violin, tree branches, a cross and a wing are meticulously distributed within the area of the plate, suggesting different planes of perception, supported by a play of light and colours.

Frising has participated in group exhibitions, including 1984, 1986, 1988, 1991, the international engraving Biennale, Cracow; 1988, the Biennale Internationale de la Gravure, Menton, where he won a prize; 1991, the international engraving Biennale 'Mezzotinta 91', Sopot (Gdansk), where he won First Prize. He has held solo shows, including 1988, the Galerie du Luxembourg, Luxembourg; 1991, Le Carré des Arts, Stavelot (Liège); 1993, the Galerie Schwitzer, Mondorf-les-Bains.

FRISIUS. See **EILLARTS Joannes**

FRISIUS, Simon Weynouts, called Simon de Vries
Flemish School, 17th century.
Born c. 1580, probably in Louvain; died before 1628, in The Hague.
Engraver.

He was probably a relative of Joannes Eillart Frisius. He settled in The Hague from 1614, and is recorded in Prague in 1620.

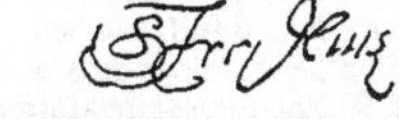

FRISMUTH, Harriet. See **FRISHMUTH Harriet Whitney**

FRISON, Barthélemy
Belgian, 19th century.
Born 21 September 1816, in Tournai; died 3 May 1877, in Paris.
Active in France, naturalised French citizen.
Sculptor.

Frison was admitted to the École des Beaux-Arts in Paris on 19 September 1842, where he became a pupil of Ramey and A. Dumont. He became a naturalised French citizen on 5 June 1848, and exhibited at the Paris Salon from 1847 to 1877, winning a second-class medal in 1851 and 1863. His works include *A Marble-player* (statue), a marble bust of *Braquenié the Elder*, a bronze bust of *M. Depré*, a granite group depicting *Art and Science Weeping on a Tomb*, a marble bust of *William Mackenzie*, and a marble group entitled *A Memory*. He executed two stone statues for the belfry in Tournai: *The Gunners' Oath* and a *Fighter with a Broadsword*. Low reliefs by Frison are to be found in the church of St-Eustache, in Paris.

MUSEUMS AND GALLERIES:

BRUSSELS: *Naïs* (marble statue) - CHÂLONS-EN-CHAMPAGNE: *Bacchante* - CHARTRES: *Libation to Bacchus* - COMPIÈGNE: *Venus genetrix* (marble, statue) - TOURNAI: *Innocence* - VERSAILLES: *General Breton* (marble bust).

FRISON, Gualbert
French, 19th - 20th century.
Born in Nantua.
Painter.

Gualbert Frison exhibited in Paris at the Salon des Artistes Français, becoming a member of the Salon in 1906.

FRISON, Gustave
French, 19th century.
Born 21 March 1850, in Valenciennes.
Draughtsman, caricaturist.

Frison studied at the École des Beaux-Arts in Paris, then went on to work as an illustrator and caricaturist for some of the leading satirical reviews published in the latter half of the 19th century.

FRISON, Jehan
Belgian, 20th century.
Born 1882, in Brussels; died 1961.
Painter, sculptor (wood), engraver. Figure compositions, landscapes, landscapes with figures, seascapes, still-lifes, flowers.

Jehan Frison studied with Auguste Oleffe. He exhibited on various occasions with the Fauves Brabançons (Brabant Fauves), who met at the Demeure du Rouge-Cloître owned by Auguste Oleffe. This movement was closer to Post-Impressionism than to French Fauvism.

He painted landscapes, seascapes and still-lifes using pure, light colours applied in thick layers with rough surfaces that hint at his other activities of wood-engraving and woodcarving. He is best known for *Skaters, The Bridge at Malines, Girl with a Sunshade* and *Landscape near Linkebeek.*

JFRISON.

Auction records:
Lokeren, 10 Oct 1987, *Young Woman with a Parasol* (1916, oil on canvas, 47 1/4 x 39 1/4 ins / 120 x 100 cm) BEF 260,000. Lokeren, 5 Feb 1988, *Girl with a Sunshade* (oil on canvas, 23 1/2 x 23 1/2 ins / 60 x 60 cm) BEF 140,000. Lokeren, 8 Oct 1988, *Still-life with Sunflowers* (oil on canvas, 39 1/4 x 31 1/2 ins / 99.5 x 80 cm) BEF 90,000. Brussels, 19 Dec 1989, *Interior* (oil on canvas, 23 1/2 x 19 3/4 ins / 60 x 50 cm) BEF 100,000. Brussels, 27 March 1990, *Bridge at Malines* (oil on canvas, 19 3/4 x 23 1/2 ins / 50 x 60 cm) BEF 120,000. Lokeren, 10 Oct 1992, *Still-life* (1942, oil on canvas, 23 1/2 x 23 1/2 ins / 60 x 60 cm) BEF 110,000. New York, 10 Nov 1992, *Poppies and Lamp* (1941, oil on canvas, 28 x 24 ins / 71 x 61 cm) USD 2,750. Lokeren, 4 Dec 1993, *Still-life with Flowers and a Fan* (1935, oil on canvas, 39 1/4 x 31 1/2 ins / 100 x 80 cm) BEF 140,000. Paris, 5 July 1994, *Bunches of Flowers* (1941, oil on canvas, 28 x 24 ins / 71 x 61 cm) FRF 5,600. Lokeren, 20 May 1995, *Landscape at Linkebeek* (1927, oil on canvas, 23 1/2 x 23 1/2 ins / 60 x 60 cm) BEF 74,000. Lokeren, 8 March 1997, *Still-life* (oil on canvas, 23 1/2 x 31 1/2 ins / 60 x 80 cm) BEF 44,000. Lokeren, 6 Dec 1997, *Ham* (1959, oil on canvas, 23 1/2 x 27 1/2 ins / 60 x 70 cm) BEF 120,000. Brussels, 13 June 2000, *Street Scene at Bou-Saada* (1926, oil on canvas, 24 x 28 ins / 60 x 70 cm) BEF 120,000. Paris, 20 Nov 2000, *Koubba at Waters Edge* (1927, oil on canvas, 26 x 30 ins / 65 x 75 cm) FRF 25,000. Brussels, 12 June 2001, *Ray of Sunlight* (1911, oil on canvas, 58 x 51 ins / 147 x 130 cm) BEF 550,000. Paris, 18 June 2001, *Street Scene* (1927, oil on canvas, 30 x 26 ins / 75 x 65 cm) FRF 30,000. Lokeren, 9 March 2002, *White Peonies* (oil on canvas, 28 x 31 ins / 70 x 80 cm) EUR 4,400. Lokeren, 7 Dec 2002, *Woman with Mirror* (1913, oil on canvas, 23 x 17 ins / 58 x 42 cm) EUR 4,000. Lokeren, 9 Oct 2004, *Bird-catcher* (1909, oil on canvas, 37 x 26 ins / 94 x 67 cm) EUR 8,500. Brussels, 8 Nov 2004, *Young Girls at the Seaside* (oil on canvas, 24 x 31 ins / 62 x 78 cm) EUR 4,400.

FRISON, Pelegrin
French, 16th century.
Active in Toulouse in 1504.
Painter.

FRISON-FABRICE, Lucienne
French, 20th century.
Born 1889, in Paris.
Miniaturist.

Lucienne Frison-Fabrice studied under Madame Oudin-Petit. She exhibited in Paris at the Salon des Artistes Français, becoming a member of the Salon in 1914.

FRISONI, Luigi
Italian, 18th - 19th century.
Born 1760, in Verona; died 10 January 1811, in Verona.
Painter.

Luigi Frisoni was a pupil of A. Pacheco. He painted several frescoes for the church of S Maria Rocca Maggiore in Verona.

FRISONI, Pasquino
Italian, 17th century.
Active in Urbino at the beginning of the 17th century.
Painter.

FRISQUET, Jean
French, 15th century.
Active in Bar-le-Duc (Meuse) in 1473.
Painter.

FRISSA, Pedro de
Dutch, 16th century.
Active in Valladolid.
Painter.

Dutch in origin and possibly called Vries, this artist worked in Spain.

FRISSON, Madeleine
French, 20th century.
Born 1884, in Paris.
Painter.

Madeleine Frisson exhibited at the Salon des Artistes Français in Paris.

FRISTER, Christian
German, 18th century.
Born 1700, in Zwickau; died 25 January 1772, in Vienna.
Painter.

Christian Frister married the daughter of the painter J. B. Marsch and settled in Vienna. His four sons devoted themselves to the arts.

FRISTER, Eduard
Austrian, 18th - 19th century.
Active in Vienna.
Painter.

FRISTER, Johann Christian
Austrian, 18th - 19th century.
Born 10 January 1749, in Vienna; died 8 March 1831, in Vienna.
Painter, engraver. Portraits.

The son of Christian Frister, Joahann Christian succeeded his father and his brother Karl as Instructor at the academy in Vienna in 1783.

FRISTER, Johann Michael
Austrian, 18th - 19th century.
Born 24 March 1764, in Vienna; died 15 March 1819, in Rabb.
Painter (?).

Johann Michael was the son of Christian Frister and was a painter like his father.

FRISTER, Josef
Austrian, 18th - 19th century.
Born 19 July 1758, in Vienna; died after 1822.
Engraver.

Josef Frister was the son of Christian. During the latter part of his life he became a seller of prints.

FRISTER, Karl
Austrian, 18th century.
Born 7 May 1742, in Vienna; died 27 July 1783, in Vienna.
Painter.

Karl was the son of Christian Frister and is known for his frescoes in Wieselburg Church.

FRISTON, David Henry
British, 19th century.
Painter. Genre scenes, figures.

David Henry Friston exhibited at London's Royal Academy from 1853 to 1869.

Auction records:
London, 1 Oct 1986, *Newborn Child* (oil on canvas, 14 x 18 ins / 35.5 x 46 cm) GBP 1,400.

FRISTRUP, Niklaus or Niels
Danish, 19th century.
Born 24 September 1837; died 15 June 1909, in Copenhagen.
Painter. Landscapes, urban landscapes, animals.

Niklaus Fristrup studied at the Kunstakademi in Copenhagen after having stayed in Italy. He specialised in the painting of landscapes and animals.

Auction records:
Copenhagen, 24 Aug 1982, *Birds in a Landscape* (oil on canvas, 24 3/4 x 36 1/2 ins / 63 x 93 cm) DKK 17,000. London, 28 Nov 1984, *Venice: Shipbuilder's Yard with a View of S Maria della Salute in the Background* (1875, oil on canvas, 11 3/4 x 12 1/4 ins / 30 x 31 cm) GBP 4,500. Copenhagen, 2 Oct 1985,

Sunflowers (oil on canvas, 26 x 19 1/4 ins / 66 x 49 cm) DKK 24,000. LONDON, 4 Oct 1989, *Courtyard behind S Gregorio in Venice* (oil on canvas, 12 x 12 1/4 ins / 30.5 x 31 cm) GBP 6,600. NEW YORK, 28 Feb 1990, *The Piazzetta in Venice* (oil on canvas, 15 x 24 1/4 ins / 38.1 x 61.6 cm) USD 13,750. COPENHAGEN, 1 Dec 1998, *Landscape with Cattle Grazing by Circle of Stones* (1861, oil on canvas, 36 x 50 ins / 91 x 127 cm) DKK 20,000. NEW YORK, 9 Feb 1999, *Lily Pond* (oil on canvas, 31 x 25 ins / 79 x 63 cm) USD 8,000. VEJLE, 19 Nov 1999, *View through a Pergola to Town, Sea and Mountains, Italy* (1891, oil on canvas, 48 x 37 ins / 121 x 94 cm) DKK 31,000. HAVNEN, 6 April 2002, *View of Venice in the Moonlight* (1878, oil on canvas, 42 x 31 ins / 106 x 80 cm) DKK 38,000. COPENHAGEN, 2 Dec 2002, *La Piazetta, Venice with Figures at Sunset* (1878, oil on canvas, 43 x 31 ins / 108 x 80 cm) DKK 44,000. LONDON, 18 Sept 2003, *S Giorgio Maggiore seen from the Piazzetta, Venice* (1878, oil on canvas, 42 x 31 ins / 106 x 79 cm) GBP 4,500.

FRISWELL, Harry P. Hain

British, 19th century.
Born 1857, in London.
Painter, art critic.

Harry P. Hain Friswell was the son of the essayist James Hain. He exhibited in London between 1882 and 1892.

FRITEL, Paul Honoré

French, 19th century.
Born in Évreux.
Engraver (burin).

Paul Fritel received an honourable mention in 1897.

FRITEL, Pierre

French, 19th century.
Born 5 July 1853, in Paris.
Painter, sculptor, engraver.

Pierre Fritel studied under Millet and Cabanel and exhibited at the Salon from 1876 to 1879. He was awarded a silver medal in 1879, a travel scholarship in 1885, and a bronze at the Exposition Universelle of 1889, together with the Prix Bellin-Dollet in 1909 for his body of engraved work. He was awarded a gold medal in 1920. Examples of his work include *St John the Baptist, Oedipus in Despair, Electra*, and a *Mater Dolorosa* for the church at Batignolles. His *Conquerors* is housed in Lucerne Museum.

FRITH, F.

British, 19th century.
Active in Scotland and in Ireland c. 1835.
Caricaturist.

F. Frith was noted for a lithograph of the Duke of Wellington.

FRITH, William Powell

British, 19th century.
Born 9 January 1819, in Aldfield (Yorkshire); died 2 November 1909, in London.
Painter, watercolourist. Historical subjects, figure compositions, figures, genre scenes, horse racing scenes.

A leading representative of Victorian painting in England, William Powell Frith studied at Henry Sass's academy in Bloomsbury from 1835 to 1837 before gaining a place at the Royal Academy schools. He first exhibited in 1838 at the British Institution, where he met with considerable success. He was made an associate of the Royal Academy in 1845 and a member in 1853. He exhibited at every major London exhibition, including the Royal Academy, the British Institution and the Suffolk Street Gallery. He also exhibited with equal success at the Brussels and Vienna Academies, and he was especially attracted to the exhibition scene in Paris. He was a medal-winner in 1855 and a silver medal winner at the Exposition Universelle of 1889. He was made a Chevalier of the Légion d'Honneur in 1878.

Frith was particularly noted for his genre scenes depicting large crowds, which he painted with a delicate and precise touch. The most successful of his paintings were probably *Derby Day*, subsequently engraved in France by Auguste Blanchard, and *Railway Station*. His work reached the height of its popularity in or around 1900, when it consistently attracted high prices. Towards the end of his life he published articles attacking modern trends in art.

BIBLIOGRAPHY:

Frith, William Powell, '*My Autobiography and Reminiscences*' in *2 vols*, London, 1887. Lister, Raymond, *Victorian Narrative Paintings*, Museum Press, London, 1966. Noakes, Aubrey, *William Frith, Extraordinary Victorian Painter: a Biographical & Critical Essay*, Jupiter, London, 1978. *Great Victorian Pictures*, exhibition catalogue, Arts Council of Great Britain, 1978. Cowling, Mary, *The Artist as Anthropologist: The Representation of Type and Character in Victorian Art*, Cambridge University Press, Cambridge, 1989.

MUSEUMS AND GALLERIES:

BRUSSELS: *Epsom Derby* - LEICESTER: *Railway Station* - LONDON (National Portrait Gal.): *Mary Elizabeth Maxwell (née Braddon)* (exhibited in 1865, oil on canvas); two self-portraits (1838 and 1867, oil on canvas) - LONDON (Royal Academy of Arts): *Portrait of Thomas Creswick* (c. 1862, oil on canvas); *The Sleeping Model* (1853, oil on canvas, competition piece) - LONDON (Tate Collection): *Dolly Varden* (c. 1842-1849, oil/wood); *The Derby Day* (1856-1858, oil on canvas); *Uncle Toby and the Widow Wadman* (1865, oil on canvas, scene from 'Tristram Shandy' by Laurence Sterne) - LONDON (Victoria and Albert Mus.): *Charles Dickens* (1859, oil on canvas, portrait); *Dolly Varden* (1842, oil on canvas, scene from 'Barnaby Rudge' by Dickens) - SHEFFIELD: *John Knox Rebuking Mary, Queen of Scots*.

AUCTION RECORDS:

LONDON, 1855, *Monsieur Jourdain and the Marchioness*, FRF 23,000. LONDON, 24 April 1875, *Sterne's Maria*, FRF 23,625; *Before Dinner at Boswell's Lodgings in Bond Street*, FRF 114,237; *Before Dinner*, FRF 43,000; *Vicar of Wakefield*, FRF 11,025; *Doge's Palace, Venice*, FRF 6,550. LONDON, June 1888, *Dolly Varden*, FRF 19,420. LONDON, July 1890, *Dolly Varden*, FRF 26,250. LONDON, June 1892, *Merrymaking in the Olden Times*, FRF 11,290. LONDON, 1898, *Halt (Daughter of the Guard)*, FRF 4,575; *In the Forest*, FRF 2,750. LONDON, 1899, *Taking Measurements*, FRF 6,025. PARIS, 1899, *Nell Gwyn*, FRF 2,750. LONDON, 30 Nov 1907, *Chimney-Sweep*, GBP 13. LONDON, 7 Dec 1907, *Widow Waldman Offering a Chair to Uncle Toby*, GBP 17. LONDON, Feb 1908, *Scene from The Vicar of Wakefield*, GBP 178. LONDON, Feb 1908, *Sterne and the Grisette*, GBP 35. LONDON, 12 June 1908, *Sterne and the French Innkeeper's Daughter*, GBP 110; *Charles II and Lady Castlemaine* (watercolour) GBP 30. LONDON, 19 June 1908, *Favourite Falcon*, GBP 152; *Claude Duval* (1886) GBP 110. NEW YORK, 7 May 1909, *New Model*, USD 110. LONDON, 24 June 1909, *Dolly Varden*, GBP 99. LONDON, 6 May 1910, *Scene from Sterne's Sentimental Journey*, GBP 89. LONDON, 27 May 1910, *Claude Duval*, GBP 651. LONDON, 17 June 1910, *Amy Robsart*, GBP 81. LONDON, 30 April-3 May 1926, *Sir Roger de Coverley*, GBP 33. LONDON, 16 July 1926, *Motherly Kiss*, GBP 35. LONDON, 29 March 1927, *Intercepted Letter*, GBP 10. LONDON, 12 May 1927, *At My Window*, GBP 15. LONDON, 24 June 1927, *Witch* (drawing) GBP 14. LONDON, 4 July 1928, *New Model*. LONDON, 23 July 1928, *Sketch for Derby Day*, GBP 105. LONDON, 15 Feb 1929, *Charles II and Lady Castlemaine*, GBP 11. LONDON, 28 Feb and 3 March 1930, *Charles II and Lady Castlemaine*, GBP 29. LONDON, 25 July 1930, *Charles II and Lady Castlemaine*, GBP 11. LONDON, 13 Feb 1931, *Request*, GBP 22. LONDON, 24 March 1931, *Queen Elisabeth and Amy Robsart*, GBP 7. LONDON, 22 Dec 1931,

Gleaner, GBP 8. LONDON, 4 March 1932, *Katherine; Bianca* (both) GBP 12. LONDON, 17 June 1932, *Mary Stuart's Farewell,* GBP 6. LONDON, 17 Nov 1933, *Gleaner* (drawing) GBP 25. LONDON, 1 Dec 1933, *Flirt* (drawing) GBP 8. LONDON, 2 July 1934, *Archer,* GBP 8. LONDON, 17 Dec 1934, *Henry VIII and Anne Boleyn,* GBP 23; *Alexander Pope Rejected by Lady Montague,* GBP 30. LONDON, 21-24 Feb 1936, *Pope and Lady Montague,* GBP 28. LONDON, 24 April 1936, *Card Game,* GBP 15. LONDON, 1 May 1936, *Charles II and Lady Castlemaine,* GBP 48. LONDON, 8 March 1937, *Village Festivities,* GBP 77. LONDON, 24 May 1937, *Sir Roger de Coverley,* GBP 24. LONDON, 26 July 1937, *Fair,* GBP 11. LONDON, 17 Dec 1937, *Malvolio,* GBP 22. LONDON, 22 Dec 1937, *Gleaner; Le Bourgeois Gentilhomme* (both) GBP 11. LONDON, 18 July 1938, *Juliette and the Children's Maid,* GBP 9. LONDON, 10 June 1942, *Sisters,* GBP 19. LONDON, 16 April 1943, *Gabrielle,* GBP 89. LONDON, 23 Dec 1943, *Fortune-Teller,* GBP 48. LONDON, 23 June 1944, *Gleaner,* GBP 31. PARIS, 19 March 1945, *Two Young Women* (1864) FRF 20,000. LONDON, 17 April 1946, *Claude Duval,* GBP 160. LONDON, 26 April 1946, *Old Woman Accused of Bewitching a Girl,* GBP 54; *Lovers,* GBP 189; *Ramsgate Sands,* GBP 336. LONDON, 29 Nov 1946, *Mother and Daughter,* GBP 31. LONDON, 24 Jan 1947, *Monsieur Jourdain,* GBP 42. LONDON, 11 July 1947, *Mr Honeywood,* GBP 63. LONDON, 14 Nov 1962, *Road to Ruin: College, Ascot, Arrest, Struggles, The End,* GBP 7,200. LONDON, 22 Nov 1967, *King Charles II at Whitehall,* GBP 1,600. NEW YORK, 23 Feb 1968, *Departure of the Newly-Weds,* USD 5,250. NEW YORK, 3 June 1971, *Castle Courtyard with Several Figures,* USD 6,750. LONDON, 20 June 1972, *Sick Doll,* GBP 1,400. LONDON, 5 Oct 1973, *Coming of Age in Days of Old,* Gns 5,500. LONDON, 18 Oct 1974, *Milady or her First Cigarette,* Gns 3,400. LONDON, 16 July 1976, *Fish-Seller* (1880, oil on canvas, 32 x 23 ins / 81.5 x 58.5 cm) GBP 1,300. LONDON, 14 June 1977, *Claude Duval* (1860, oil on canvas, 30 x 40 ins / 76 x 101.5 cm) GBP 6,200. LONDON, 19 May 1978, *Village Pastor* (oil on canvas, 22 x 31 1/2 ins / 56 x 80 cm) GBP 5,500. LONDON, 10 Nov 1981, *Incident on Stage, 1750; Bagshot Heath* (c. 1890, oil on canvas, 14 1/4 x 12 1/2 ins / 36 x 32 cm) GBP 7,000. LONDON, 16 Feb 1984, *Village Pastor* (pencil and black chalk heightened with white, 25 x 34 ins / 63.5 x 86.5 cm) GBP 950. LONDON, 19 June 1984, *Gabrielle d'Estrée* (1869, oil on canvas, 30 x 25 1/4 ins / 76.2 x 64 cm) GBP 15,000. NEW YORK, 30 Oct 1985, *Coming of Age in Days of Old* (1849, oil on canvas, 50 x 79 ins / 127 x 200.7 cm) USD 110,000. LONDON, 3 June 1988, *Hope and Fear* (1869, oil on canvas, two pendants, 15 1/2 x 14 ins / 39.5 x 35.6 cm) GBP 5,720. LONDON, 30 March 1990, *Portrait of Mary Freer sitting under the Trees in a Garden Chair* (oil on canvas, 31 x 25 ins / 79 x 63.5 cm) GBP 7,150. LONDON, 15 June 1990, *Back-to-Back* (1867, oil on canvas, 13 1/2 x 9 3/4 ins / 34 x 25 cm) GBP 4,950. NEW YORK, 24 Oct 1990, *At My Window in Boulogne* (1872, oil on canvas, 36 x 28 ins / 91.4 x 71.1 cm) USD 24,200. LONDON, 8 Feb 1991, *Sketch for Many Happy Returns of the Day* (oil on card, 15 3/4 x 29 3/4 ins / 40.3 x 75.5 cm) GBP 13,200. LONDON, 5 June 1991, *Awkward Reply* (1891, oil on canvas, 13 1/2 x 10 1/2 ins / 34 x 26.5 cm) GBP 3,520. LONDON, 14 June 1991, *Norah Creina* (1846, oil on canvas, 13 x 10 1/4 ins / 33 x 26 cm) GBP 3,850. LONDON, 3 June 1992, *The Crossing Sweeper* (1858, oil on canvas, 9 x 7 1/2 ins / 23 x 19 cm) GBP 10,450. NEW YORK, 29 Oct 1992, *Hogarth and the Governor of Calais* (1850, oil on canvas, 12 1/2 x 16 1/4 ins / 31.8 x 41.3 cm) USD 6,600. LONDON, 3 Nov 1993, *Evening Prayers ('When We Devote our Youth to God...')* (1852, oil on canvas, 36 1/2 x 28 3/4 ins / 93 x 73 cm) GBP 23,000. NEW YORK, 16 Feb 1994, *The Trysting Place* (1875, oil on canvas, 27 1/2 x 21 3/4 ins / 69.9 x 55.2 cm) USD 4,140. LONDON, 2 Nov 1994, *The Crossing Sweeper* (1858, oil on canvas, 9 x 7 1/2 ins / 23 x 19 cm) GBP 16,675. LONDON, 6 Nov 1995, *Incident in the Life of Lady Mary Wortley Montague* (1872, oil on canvas, 45 1/4 x 57 1/4 ins / 115 x 145.5 cm) GBP 14,375. LONDON, 8 Nov 1996, *Little Dorrit* (1859, oil on canvas, 23 x 19 ins / 58.4 x 48.2 cm) GBP 4,500. NEW YORK, 12 Feb 1997, *Scene from Molière's L'Avare* (1876, oil on canvas, 35 x 55 ins / 88.9 x 139.7 cm) USD 68,500. LONDON, 12 March 1997, *Lovers* (1855, oil on panel, 15 x 12 1/4 ins / 38 x 31 cm) GBP 38,900. LONDON, 6 June 1997, *John Knox Rebuking Mary, Queen of Scots* (1861, oil on canvas, 23 x 30 1/4 ins / 57.5 x 77 cm) GBP 10,350. LONDON, 7 Nov 1997, *Street-Sweeper* (1858, oil on canvas, 17 x 14 ins / 43.1 x 35.5 cm) GBP 34,500. LONDON, 4 Nov 1999, *Henry VIII and Anne Boleyn Deer Shooting in Windsor Forest* (oil on canvas, 48 x 40 ins / 123 x 101 cm) GBP 22,000. LONDON, 14 Dec 1999, *Scene from The Merry Wives of Windsor* (1843, oil on canvas, 46 x 67 ins / 117 x 170 cm) GBP 18,000. NEWCASTLE, 14 March 2000, *Lady Seated in Her Library Writing a Letter* (1874, oil on canvas, 24 x 17 ins / 60 x 44 cm) GBP 19,500. DUBLIN, 15 Nov 2000, *Nell Gwynne at Drury Lane* (1869, oil on canvas, 23 x 20 ins / 59 x 50 cm) IEP 24,000. KNOWLE, 10 Jan 2001, *The Gloves, Paris: Scene from Sterne's Sentimental Journey* (1843, oil on canvas, 25 x 21 ins / 63 x 53 cm) GBP 23,000. LONDON, 3 April 2001, *Sherry, Sir. Did You Ring, Sir?* (1853, oil on canvas, a pair, 11 x 9 ins / 28 x 24 cm) GBP 13,000. LONDON, 13 Feb 2002, *Henry VIII and Anne Boleyn Deer Shooting in Windsor Forest* (1903, oil on canvas, 18 x 15 ins / 46 x 38 cm) GBP 6,500. LONDON, 11 June 2002, *Keepsake* (1865, oil on canvas, 16 x 12 ins / 41 x 31 cm) GBP 6,000. LONDON, 19 Feb 2003, *For Fetter, For Worse* (1881, oil on canvas, 61 x 50 ins / 155 x 126 cm) GBP 230,000. LONDON, 12 June 2003, *Crossing Sweeper* (1858, oil on canvas, 17 x 14 ins / 43 x 35 cm) GBP 34,000. LONDON, 11 June 2004, *Hope* (oil on canvas, 33 x 30 ins / 84 x 76 cm) GBP 35,000. LONDON, 16 June 2004, *Green Parrot* (oil on canvas, 24 x 20 ins / 61 x 51 cm) GBP 13,500.

FRITH, William S.
British, 19th century.
Born c. 1850.
Active in London.
Sculptor.

William S. Frith was educated at Lambeth Art School. He went on to work for the churches of St Andrew and St Bartholomew in Kensington, London. He was an exhibitor at the Royal Academy in London from 1884 to 1892.

FRITSCH
French, 15th - 16th century.
Born at the end of the 15th century, in Zeinheim.
Sculptor.

After working in Alsace, Fritsch spent some time in the German Rhineland and Basel.

FRITSCH, C. C.
Danish, 20th century.
Painter. Flowers.

MUSEUMS AND GALLERIES:
COPENHAGEN.

FRITSCH, Daniel
German, 16th century.
Active in Torgau (Saxony) during the second half of the 16th century.
Painter, copyist.

Daniel Fritsch was an imitator and copyist of Lucas Cranach.

FRITSCH, Elizabeth
British, 20th - 21st century.
Born 1940, in Whitchurch (Shropshire), England.
Ceramicist (clay).

Elizabeth Fritsch studied at the Royal College of Art in London under Hans Coper, who had himself worked with Lucie Rie. She worked at the Bing and Grondahl porcelain factory in Copenhagen (1972-1973). Among one of Britain's most famous studio potters today, Fritsch is known for her non-utilitarian pots, jars, bottles and urns. Her pots are built up from

coils of clay, none are thrown on a potter's wheel, and they are decorated with slip in geometrical designs. She held her first solo exhibition in 1974, organised jointly by the Crafts Advisory Council and the British Council.
MUSEUMS AND GALLERIES:
LONDON (Victoria and Albert Mus.): *Optical Pot* (1980).

FRITSCH, Émile
French, 20th century.
Born in Brunstatt (Upper Rhine).
Painter. Landscapes.
Émile Fritsch exhibited views of Paris at the Salon des Artistes Indépendants in Paris from 1928.

FRITSCH, Ernst
German, 20th century.
Born 1892, in Berlin; died 1962 or 1965, in Berlin.
Painter, draughtsman. Portraits, genre scenes, landscapes with figures.
Novembergruppe.
Ernst Fritsch was a member of the Novembergruppe in 1918. From 1828 to 1929 he lived in Paris and Rome. When he returned to Germany, he suffered under the rise of Nazism and was declared a 'degenerate artist'. After the war, he taught at the Berlin academy.
AUCTION RECORDS:
MUNICH, 27 May 1974, *Sleeping Woman,* DEM 9,000. HAMBURG, 8 June 1979, *House in the Mountains* (1922, watercolour/pencil outlines, 15 1/4 x 12 ins / 39 x 30.7 cm) DEM 3,200. HAMBURG, 5 June 1980, *Standing Nude* (1926, oil on canvas, 30 3/4 x 18 3/4 ins / 78 x 47.5 cm) DEM 8,000. MUNICH, 28 Nov 1983, *Man seated at a Table* (1920, oil on canvas, 47 1/4 x 38 1/4 ins / 120 x 97 cm) DEM 28,000. MUNICH, 26 Nov 1984, *Village Street* (1920, watercolour and gouache/pencil outlines heightened with white, 13 1/4 x 10 ins / 33.9 x 25.7 cm) DEM 3,600. LONDON, 20 May 1993, *The Schumachers' Son* (1922, oil on canvas, 46 x 31 ins / 117 x 79 cm) GBP 23,000. BERLIN, 27 May 2000, *Girl on Bench* (Indian ink and watercolour, 19 x 13 ins / 48 x 34 cm) DEM 6,000. COLOGNE, 7 June 2000, *Evening Mood on the Wannsee* (1935, oil on canvas, 29 x 39 ins / 73 x 100 cm) DEM 15,000. BERLIN, 1 Dec 2001, *House in Roman Countryside* (1929, oil on canvas, 26 x 32 ins / 65 x 81 cm) DEM 17,000. COLOGNE, 4 Dec 2004, *Man and Woman infront of Houses* (1922, oil on canvas, 32 x 36 ins / 81 x 92 cm) EUR 15,000.

FRITSCH, Hans
German, 19th - 20th century.
Born 2 May 1870, in Dresden; died 1945.
Painter.
Hans Fritsch studied with Kuehl. He exhibited in Dresden, Berlin, Munich and Leipzig.

FRITSCH, Johann Kaspar
German, 18th - 19th century.
Born in Freudenthal.
Painter.

FRITSCH, Josef
Austrian, 19th century.
Born 1840, in Setzdorf.
Sculptor.
Josef Fritsch studied in Vienna and worked mainly in Ulm.

FRITSCH, Josef Anton
German, 18th century.
Born 1714, in Holleschau; died 1770, in Tobitschau.
Sculptor.
Josef Anton Fritsch was a pupil of Donner at the academy in Vienna. He spent a considerable time travelling before returning to settle in his native province of Moravia.

FRITSCH, Katharina
German, 20th - 21st century.
Born 1956, in Essen.
Assemblage artist, installation artist, performance artist.
From 1977, Fritsch attended the Kunstakademie in Düsseldorf, graduating in 1981. She lives and works in Düsseldorf. From the early stages of her career, Fritsch has developed sculptures, installations and performances, painting directly onto the walls of an exhibition venue (1991, Berlin) and simultaneously adding a soundtrack. Drawing her inspiration and materials from the consumer society and collective memory in 1984, she produced a standardized reproduction of the Madonna of Lourdes, which she painted in yellow and exhibited in a shop window, as if it were a private individual. Exploring this concept of the 'removal of the sacred aura', she exhibited the Madonna again in 1987; this time it was life-size and placed in the street between a church and a supermarket. At the same time, Fritsch produced a tower 8.85 feet (2.7 metres) high with 240 copies of this same Madonna, each level being separated by aluminium sheets, which emphasized the sense of infinity by reflecting the figures. Similarly, the 32 life-size figures of men sitting along a table, entitled *Company at Table* (1988), evoke both the infinity of existence and the loss of identity. Ranging from the colossal to the miniature, and inspired by mythology, literature or religion, her works are developed to a high degree of perfection. There are some who think her sculptures-assemblages are similar to ready-mades. However, the objects and the materials presented have not been selected at random; the experience and memory of the artist gives them meaning, and she endeavours to create a new context for them, so that they can be understood.

Since 1982 Fritsch has participated in group exhibitions: 1982, the Museum für Kunst und Gewerbe, Hamburg; 1986, the New Museum of Contemporary Art, New York; 1988, the Capc-Musée d'Art Contemporain, Bordeaux; 1992, the Hayward Gallery, London; 1995, the Venice Biennale, where she was selected to represent Germany; 1996, the Museum of Modern Art, San Francisco; 1997, the Biennale d'Art Contemporain, Lyons; 2001, *Hypermental,* which was an exhibition about the unreal, the transreal and the reconstruction of reality, held at the Kunsthalle, Hamburg; 2003, *Un Tableau dans le Décor. Peintures 1970-2000* (*A Painting in the Décor: Paintings 1970-2000*), held at the Château des Ducs de Bretagne, Nantes, and *L'État des Choses* (*The State of Things*), an examination of the status of the everyday object in contemporary art, held at the Musée des Beaux-Arts, Nantes, which were two group exhibitions presented on the occasion of *Trésors Publics. 20 Ans de Création dans les Fonds Régionaux d'Art Contemporain (FRAC)* (*Public Treasury, 20 Years of Creation in the Regional Collection of Contemporary Art (FRAC)*); 2003, *C'est Arrivé Demain* (*It Happened Tomorrow*), the Lyons Biennale. Fritsch has held solo shows in Germany, notably at the Galerie Rüdiger Schöttle, as well as abroad: 2001, the Tate Modern, London.
BIBLIOGRAPHY:
Katharina Fritsch, exhibition catalogue, Kunsthalle, Basel, 1988. Barak, Ami, '*Katharina Fritsch*' in *Art Press* no. 159, periodical, Paris, June 1991. *Doubletake*, group exhibition catalogue, Hayward Gall., London, 1992. *Sammlung Ackermans im Museum Kurhaus, Kleve*, Salon Verlag, Cologne, 1997. Blazwick, Iwona, *Katharina Fritsch,* exhibition catalogue, Whitechapel Gall., London, Tate Modern, London, 2001. Suchin, Peter, '*Katarina Fritsch*' in *Art Press* no. 274 p. 70, periodical, Paris, December 2001. Zahm, Olivier (preface), et al., *Trésors publics, 20 ans de création dans les Fonds régionaux d'art contemporain,* Flammarion, Paris, 2003 (text in French and English).
MUSEUMS AND GALLERIES:
BORDEAUX (FRAC Aquitaine): *Madonna* (1987); *Bilder* (*Pictures*) (1990) - CLEVES (Mus. Kurhaus): *Mann und Maus* (*Man and Mouse*) (1991-1992, polyester, paint); *Doktor* (*Doctor*)

(1999, polyester, paint); *Mönch* (*Monk*) (1999, polyester, paint) - KREFELD (Kaiser Wilhelm Mus.): *Warengestell* (*Display Stand*) (1979-1984, glass, aluminium, objects dating from 1979-84) - SAN FRANCISCO (MoMA): *Child (or Baby) with Poodles* (1995-1996, plaster of paris, foil, polyurethane, and paint) - STUTTGART (Staatsgal.): *Warengestell mit Madonna* (*Display Stand with Madonna Figures*) (1987-1989, aluminium, plaster cast, paint).

AUCTION RECORDS:

PARIS, 18 March 1992, *Sequences* (acrylic/canvas, 28³/₄ x 39¹/₄ ins / 73 x 100 cm) FRF 12,000. NEW YORK, 10 Nov 1993, *Display* (1989, 60 printed silk scarfs and acrylic on steel, 36 x 35¹/₂ x 35¹/₂ ins / 91.5 x 90 x 90 cm) USD 18,400. FRANKFURT AM MAIN, 14 June 1994, *Multiples: Cat, Brain, Madonna* (synthetic resin, plaster, vase, cloth, coins, 6³/₄ x 6³/₄ x 2¹/₄ ins / 17 x 17 x 6 cm and 11³/₄ x 3¹/₄ x 2¹/₄ ins/30 x 8 x 6 cm) DEM 5,200.

FRITSCH, Melchior
Austrian, 19th century.
Born 2 January 1825, in Vienna; died 5 May 1889, in Vienna.
Painter. Hunting scenes, landscapes.

Melchior Fritsch studied at the academy in Vienna of fine arts. He went on study trips to Bavaria, Dresden, Paris and Constantinople.

MUSEUMS AND GALLERIES:

MULHOUSE: *Landscape after the Rain* - VIENNA: *Dachstein and Lake Gosau.*

AUCTION RECORDS:

COLOGNE, 26 March 1971, *Mountainous countryside and wooden bridge,* DEM 2,600. VIENNA, 10 June 1980, *Hunting scene* (1866, oil on canvas, 39¹/₂ x 56 ins / 100.5 x 142.5 cm) ATS 35,000. VIENNA, 26 June 1986, *Hunting scene* (1866, oil on canvas, 39¹/₂ x 56 ins / 100.5 x 142.5 cm) ATS 100,000. LONDON, 12 June 1997, *Mountainous countryside with a shepherd (dairy farmer?) and his animals in front of a chalet* (1873, oil on canvas, 44¹/₂ x 59³/₄ ins / 113 x 152 cm) GBP 3,450. VIENNA, 20 May 1999, *Figures on Hill Path, the Mountain Group 'Three Brothers' Beyond* (oil on canvas, 31 x 25 ins / 78 x 63 cm) ATS 25,000. VIENNA, 15 June 1999, *Ruined Tower in Southern Tyrolean Landscape* (oil on canvas, 29 x 39 ins / 73 x 100 cm) ATS 30,000. VIENNA, 30 Nov 2000, *Landscape with Path and Couple* (oil on canvas, 16 x 20 ins / 40 x 50 cm) ATS 60,000. VIENNA, 10 April 2001, *Mountain Landscape* (oil on canvas, 11 x 14 ins / 29 x 35 cm) ATS 25,000. VIENNA, 28 May 2001, *Rocky Terrain in Pinzgau* (1880, oil on canvas, 39 x 32 ins / 100 x 81 cm) ATS 45,000. SALZBURG, 16 April 2003, *Mountain Landscape with View of Dachstein* (1871, oil on canvas, 43 x 60 ins / 110 x 152 cm) EUR 7,000.

FRITSCH, Norbert
German, 20th - 21st century.
Born 20 February 1952, in Riesa.
Painter, watercolourist. Scenes with figures, landscapes.

From 1974 to 1980, Fritsch attended the art academy in Berlin. In 1979, he worked alongside Professor Opperman. In 1983, he obtained a grant from the Bundesverband der Deutschen Industrie (BDI). Fritsch lives and works in Berlin and Montvicq (Allier). He paints oppressive landscapes with passion and sensuality. Since 1980, he has participated in many group exhibitions in Berlin and Munich, as well as in France, notably at Billom (Puy-de-Dôme) with Hans Hartung in 1980. He has also held solo shows in Germany and France.

FRITSCH, Sigmund Anton
Austrian, 18th century.
Born c. 1693; died 5 November 1749.
Active in Vienna.
Painter.

FRITSCH, Willibald
German, 20th century.
Born 16 May 1876, in Berlin.
Sculptor. Animals.

Willibald Fritsch was a pupil of Manzel.

AUCTION RECORDS:

LONDON, 10 Nov 1983, *Racehorse* (c. 1930, bronze, h. 20 ins / 51 cm) GBP 2,700.

FRITSCHE, Adolphe
French, 18th century.
Active in Paris in 1772.
Painter, sculptor.

FRITSCHE, Bartolomaus
German, 16th - 17th century.
Active in Königsberg, East Prussia (now Kaliningrad, Russia).
Painter. Portraits.

Bartolomaus Fritsche was employed by the dukes of Prussia.

FRITSCHE, George Christian
German, 17th century.
Active in Dresden at the end of the 17th century.
Painter.

FRITSCHÉ, Jean Jules Charles
Swiss, 19th century.
Born 11 December 1839, in Lausanne.
Painter. Landscapes.

This amateur artist exhibited his works in Geneva several times.

FRITSCHE, Pierre
French, 18th century.
Painter.

In 1774, Pierre Fritsche sent two miniatures to the exhibition at the Académie St-Luc: *Interior of Peasants' Bedroom, Showing Two Women and a Child* and *Woman Spinning and Two Children Playing with a Cat.*

FRITSCHMANN
German, 15th century.
Born in Ulm (Baden-Württemberg); died c. 1429, in Basel.
Painter, architect.

FRITTE, Dieudonné
French, 18th century.
Born c. 1722, in Nancy.
Sculptor (wood).

FRITTELLI, Gino
Italian, 20th century.
Born 1879, in Florence.
Painter. Landscapes.

Frittelli was a student at the academy of Florence. In 1900 he took part in the Alinari competition, presenting a painting entitled *View from a Hill in Florence.*

FRITZ
Swiss, 15th century.
Sculptor.

Fritz is mentioned in the Basel town archives in 1485.

FRITZ, Andreas
Danish, 19th century.
Born 2 November 1828, in Mou, near Aalborg; died 22 February 1906.
Painter. Portraits, landscapes.

Andreas Fritz was a pupil of Marstrand in Copenhagen. He regularly showed landscapes of Jutland and portraits in Copenhagen and Lübeck.

AUCTION RECORDS:

LONDON, 5 May 1989, *Wooded Slope with a Sheep* (1877, oil on canvas, 41³/₄ x 35¹/₄ ins / 106 x 89.5 cm) GBP 1,320. LON-

DON, 14 Feb 1990, *Landscape with a Lake* (1881, oil on canvas, 36½ x 33 ins / 93 x 84 cm) GBP 2,090. VEJLE, 10 Nov 2003, *The Garden of Hvirring Vicarage with the Artist's Sister Sewing* (1867, oil on canvas, 22 x 30 ins / 55 x 75 cm) DKK 23,000.

FRITZ, Anton
German, 18th century.
Active in Rome during the first half of the 18th century.
Engraver.

This artist is known to have produced engravings after Berettini and Rosalba Salvioni.

FRITZ, August
German, 19th century.
Born 1843, in Oberamstadt.
Watercolourist. Landscapes.

August Fritz was a pupil of Segers in Darmstadt and at the Karlsruhe and Munich academies.

FRITZ, Georg
Bohemian School, 18th century.
Active in Prague c. 1711.
Painter.

FRITZ, Georges. See **FITZ**

FRITZ, Heinz
German, 19th - 20th century.
Born 12 June 1873, in Cologne.
Sculptor.

Heinz Fritz studied with Karl Janssen at the Dresden academy.

FRITZ, Henry E.
German, 19th - 20th century.
Born 12 October 1875, in Germany.
Active in the USA.
Painter.

Henry Fritz was a teacher as well as a painter.

FRITZ, Johann
Austrian, 18th century.
Born c. 1736, in Vienna; died 26 February 1789, in Vienna.
Painter.

Johann Fritz was a pupil at the academy in Vienna.

FRITZ, Johann Friedrich
German, 19th century.
Born 31 July 1798, in Wandsbek; died 1 March 1870, in Altona (Hamburg).
Painter, lithographer.

This artist studied in Hamburg and specialised in genre painting.

FRITZ, Johann Ludwig
Russian, 19th century.
Born 28 April 1811, in Riga; died 26 May 1848, in Rome.
Painter.

Fritz was a pupil of Roessler at the Dresden Academy and lived mostly in Rome. The Riga Museum has paintings by this artist.

FRITZ, Marcus Beck
Danish, 19th - 20th century.
Born 22 May 1868, in Aarhus.
Painter. Landscapes.

Marcus Beck Fritz was the son of Andreas Fritz. He studied at the Dresden academy. His favourite subject was forest landscapes.

FRITZ, Max
German, 19th century.
Born 14 July 1849, in Berlin.
Painter, watercolourist. Landscapes.

A pupil of Alexius Geyer in Berlin, Max Fritz's training focused mainly on the study of nature. He started quite late in around 1881 and later exhibited in Dresden, Berlin, Munich, Vienna and Paris, where he gained an honourable mention in 1900 at the Exposition Universelle.

AUCTION RECORDS:

ZURICH, 12 Nov 1982, *River Bank* (1889, watercolour, 23½ x 38¾ ins / 60 x 98.5 cm) CHF 2,000. NEW YORK, 28 March 2000, *River Reflections* (1904, oil on canvas, 28 x 36 ins / 71 x 92 cm) USD 3,500. MUNICH, 27 Sept 2000, *Mill near Bautzen am Spreeufer* (oil on canvas) DEM 6,500. STUTTGART, 19 Sept 2002, *Lower Rhine Landscape* (oil on canvas, 25 x 39 ins / 63 x 99 cm) EUR 1,800.

FRITZ, Max Hermann
German, 19th - 20th century.
Born 13 July 1873, in Neuhaus; died 1948, in Dresden.
Sculptor, medallist. Religious subjects, figures, animals.
Funerary monuments, designs (porcelain).
Art Deco.

Max Hermann Fritz was a student of Lorenz Hutschenreuther, and was active in Dresden from 1898. He carried out numerous sculptures for Hartau Church (including a *Statue of Christ*) and a significant number of monuments for the city of Dresden, including a sculpture *Four Cherubs* for the Rose Garden. He worked for the porcelain factories of Meissen (KPM) and Fraureuth. He created funerary monuments for the cities of Dresden, Zittau and Liegnitz (now Legnica, Poland).

MUSEUMS AND GALLERIES:

DRESDEN (Albertinum, Skulpturensammlung): *Junge spielende Bären* (*Bear Cubs at Play*) - DRESDEN (Kunstgewerbemus.): *Medaille für Verdienste um das Kunstgewerbe* (*Medal for Services to Arts and Crafts*) - LEIPZIG (Mus. der Bildenden Künste): *Bison mit Bär kämpfend* (*Bison Fighting with a Bear*) (bronze); *Bärin mit jungen* (*She-Bear with Young*) (bronze); *Stier* (*Bull*) (bronze) - ZWICKAU (König-Albert-Museum): *Mädchenbüste* (*Bust of Girl*).

FRITZ, Otto
German, 19th century.
Died 1903.
Painter. Landscapes.

Otto Fritz exhibited in Vienna and Munich.

AUCTION RECORDS:

BREMEN, 31 March 1984, *Game of Draughts* (1890, oil on canvas, 36½ x 28 ins / 93 x 71 cm) DEM 10,500.

FRITZE, Margarete Augusta
German, 19th century.
Born 28 October 1845, in Dreileben.
Portrait artist.

Margarete Fritze was a pupil of Grutzner in Munich and then of Canon in Vienna. After settling in Berlin, she exhibited both there and in the city of Bremen.

FRITZEL, Wilhelm
German, 19th - 20th century.
Born 16 October 1870, in Hamburg; died 1943, in Orense.
Painter. Landscapes.

Wilhelm Fritzel lived in the Düsseldorf area, which provided the subject-matter for his paintings.

AUCTION RECORDS:

COLOGNE, 26 March 1976, *Harvest Scene* (oil on canvas, 27½ x 39¼ ins / 70 x 100 cm) DEM 3,300. COLOGNE, 28 Oct 1983, *Lake Shore in Summer* (oil on canvas, 35 x 45½ ins / 88 x 115.5 cm) DEM 15,000. COLOGNE, 21 Nov 1985, *Autumn Landscape* (oil on canvas remounted/panel, 9 x 11½ ins / 22 x 29.5 cm) DEM 3,000. COLOGNE, 20 Oct 1989, *Summer in Niederrhein* (oil on canvas, 38½ x 53¼ ins / 98 x 135 cm) DEM 4,000. NEW YORK, 17 Jan 1990, *Rocky Coast* (oil on canvas, 34½ x 45 ins / 87.8 x 114.3 cm) USD 4,400. COLOGNE, 23 March 1990, *Harvest* (oil on canvas, 31½ x 47¼ ins / 80 x

120 cm) DEM 2,500. COLOGNE, 28 Oct 1999, *Corn Harvest in Rhine Landscape* (oil on canvas, 28 x 35 ins / 70 x 90 cm) DEM 4,800. AMSTERDAM, 4 July 2000, *Summer Landscape with Blossoming Poppies* (oil on canvas, 36 x 43 ins / 91 x 108 cm) NLG 4,000.

FRITZIUS
Dutch, 18th century.
Draughtsman, engraver.

Fritzius illustrated an edition of Louis-Sébastian Mercier's *Complete Plays*.

FRITZSCH, Christian F.
Dutch, 18th century.
Born 3 April 1695, in Saxony; died 1747, in Schifbeck, near Hamburg.
Engraver.

He was active in Amsterdam.

FRITZSCH, Christian Friedrich
German, 18th century.
Born c. 1719, in Hamburg; died before 1774.
Draughtsman, engraver.

Christian Friedrich was the son and pupil of Christian Fritzsch, whose style he imitated.

FRITZSCH, Claudius Ditlev
Danish, 18th - 19th century.
Born 1763, in Kiel; died 27 November 1841, in Copenhagen.
Painter. Still-lifes, flowers.

Claudius Ditlev Fritzsch became a member of the academy in 1806. He lived in Copenhagen and had a house in Charlottenborg.

MUSEUMS AND GALLERIES:
COPENHAGEN - OSLO: *A Painting of Flowers*.

AUCTION RECORDS:
COPENHAGEN, 2 Oct 1984, *Still-life with Flower Vase* (1797, gouache, 22 3/4 x 17 3/4 ins / 58 x 45 cm) DKK 15,000. COPENHAGEN, 29 Feb 2000, *Still-life with Melon, Peaches, Grapes and Cherries in Basket on Ledge* (1819, oil on canvas, 51 x 39 ins / 130 x 100 cm) DKK 260,000. COPENHAGEN, 4 Dec 2000, *Still-life with Tulips, Roses and Lilac* (oil on canvas, 28 x 24 ins / 71 x 60 cm) DKK 58,000.

FRITZSCH, Johann Christian Gottfried
German, 18th century.
Born c. 1720, in Hamburg; died 1802, in Hamburg.
Engraver.

Johann was the brother of Christian Friedrich and the son of Christian Fritzsch. His father was also his master.

FRITZSCHE, F. G.
German, 17th - 18th century.
Active in Saxony.
Painter.

This artist is noted for a *Portrait of the Count of Bunau*.

FRITZSCHE, Hans
German, 17th century.
Active in Freiberg (Saxony) at the beginning of the 17th century.
Sculptor.

Hans Fritzsche worked at Freiberg cathedral.

FRITZSCHE, Julius Otto
German, 19th - 20th century.
Born 28 March 1872, in Dresden.
Painter.

Julius Otto Fritzsche studied with Prell in Dresden. He stayed in Paris, where he exhibited at the Salon de la Société Nationale, and then in Rome, before returning to settle in the town where he was born.

FRITZSCHE, Theobald Otto Wilhelm
German, 19th century.
Born 1 March 1832, in Altenburg (Saxony); died 9 September 1899, in Dresden.
Sculptor.

Theobald Fritzsche studied in Dresden. His most significant work is *Monument to the Dead of the Town of Altenburg*.

FRIZE, Bernard
French, 20th - 21st century.
Born 1949, in St-Mandé (Val-de-Marne).
Painter (mixed media), collage artist, engraver.

Bernard Frize lives and works in Paris. In 1976, he became known for his subversive approach: he produced a series of paintings, entitled *All Over*, which he painted using a small brush called a 'traînard', usually used to paint rigging in nautical scenes, then a roller and, finally, broad brushes. He wanted to focus attention on the procedures which he had followed, and the techniques and material which he used. In this vein, he focused attention on colour itself by leaving paint pots open, and letting discs of paint form on the canvas, and he suspended reservoirs of acrylic colours more than (200 metres) off the ground (at the Musée d'Art Moderne de la Ville de Paris in 1988).

He also produces works using techniques intended for other purposes. For example, he used varnish normally used by potters to paint a bowl in his 1986 work, *Japanese Item*, and he has used the same technique to portray vases and other receptacles. In addition, he uses other artists' paintings as points of departure for his own material. For example, in *Still-life with a Hunting Scene No.3*, painted in 1984, he uses the zones of bright colour in another artist's still-life as a starting point for his own work, but does not emulate the original composition in any other way.

In all of his series, whether abstract or figurative, Bernard Frize seems to provide the viewer with clues to make his work understood. As he switches from technique to technique, and from style to style, the artist himself disappears, his works accumulate, and he creates an infinite world of images. The theme common to all of them is the act of painting itself.

He has taken part in a number of group exhibitions, including: Musée d'Art Moderne de la Ville de Paris in 1977 and 1981; Villa Arson in Nice in 1986; the Shanghai Biennale in 2000; *Painting on the Move* in 2002, which presented a century of contemporary painting, with exhibitions in the Basel Kunstmuseum, Kunsthalle and Museum für Gegenwartskunst; and, in 2003, *Un Tableau dans le Décor. Peintures 1970-2000* (*A Painting in the Décor: Paintings 1970-2000*), at the Château des Ducs de Bretagne, and *Esprit des Lieux* (*The Spirit of Places*), at the Palais des Papes in Avignon.

He has also staged a number of solo exhibitions in France, notably: Galerie Lucien Durand in Paris; Musée d'Art Moderne de la Ville de Paris; Musée du Havre in 1988; Musée de Rochechouart in 1991; Centre Culturel Pomel in Issoire, in 1997; Musée d'Art Contemporain de Nîmes, in 1999; Galerie Emmanuel Perrotin in Paris in 2000; Patric Painter Gallery in Santa Monica, Los Angeles, in 2002; Gemeentemuseum in The Hague in 2002; and the Musée d'Art Moderne de la Ville de Paris in 2003.

BIBLIOGRAPHY:
Lamarche-Vadel, Bernard/Frize, Bernard, '*Entretien*' in *Artistes* n° 6, periodical, Paris, October-November 1980. Martin, J.H./Aupetitallot, Y., *Bernard Frize*, St-Étienne, 1986. Cohen, F./Sans, J., *Bernard Frize*, exhibition catalogue, Musée des Beaux-Arts, Le Havre, 1988. *Bernard Frize: tableaux d'une exposition*, exhibition catalogue, Musée départemental, Rochechouart, 1991. Barak, Ami, '*Bernard Frize*' in *Art Press* n° 159, periodical, Paris, June 1991. Falguières, Patricia, *Bernard Frize*, Hazan, Paris, 1997. Tosatto, Guy/Hegyi, Lóránd/Fuchs, Reiner, *Bernard Frize. Size Matters*, exhibition catalogue, Carré d'art-musée d'art contemporain,

Nîmes, 1999 (text in French and English). Mendes Bürgi, Bernhard Mendes, et al., *Painting on the Move*, exhibition catalogue, Kunstmuseum, Kunsthalle, Museum für Gegenwartskunst, Basel, 2002. *Aplat*, exhibition catalogue, Musée d'Art moderne de la Ville de Paris, Paris-Musées, Paris, 2003 (texts in French and English). Zahm, Olivier (preface), et al., *Trésors publics, 20 ans de création dans les Fonds régionaux d'art contemporain*, Flammarion, Paris, 2003 (text in French and English).

MUSEUMS AND GALLERIES:

CARQUEFOU (FRAC Pays de la Loire): *Suite Segond* (1980); *Oreiller* (1991) - CHÂTEAUGIRON (FRAC Bretagne): *Standard and Poors* (1987); *Vony* (1993) - CLERMONT-FERRAND (FRAC Auvergne): , 1992) - METZ (FRAC Lorraine): *Sans titre* (1980); *Sans titre B4* (1990) - NÎMES (Carré d'Art, MAC): *Untitled* (1986, acrylic and primer/canvas) - PARIS (FNAC): *Lime* (1998) - ROCHECHOUART (Mus. Départemental d'Art Contemporain): *La Pile* (1980); *Untitled* (1984); *The Large Vase* (1985) - ST-ÉTIENNE (MAM).

AUCTION RECORDS:

PARIS, 20 March 1988, *Campo Formio* (1983, oil on canvas, 31 1/2 x 39 1/4 ins / 80 x 100 cm) FRF 22,000. PARIS, 15 June 1988, *Painting* (1980, oil on canvas, 19 3/4 x 26 ins / 50 x 66 cm) FRF 15,000. PARIS, 23 Jan 1989, *Circles* (1981, acrylic/canvas, 51 1/4 x 76 ins / 130 x 193 cm) FRF 29,500. PARIS, 13 Dec 1989, *The Military Exploits* (collage) FRF 10,500. PARIS, 5 Feb 1991, *Still-life in Broken Pots* (acrylic/canvas, 63 x 78 3/4 ins / 160 x 200 cm) FRF 16,000. PARIS, 3 July 1991, *Untitled* (acrylic/canvas, 57 1/2 x 45 ins / 146 x 114 cm) FRF 39,000. PARIS, 24 March 1996, *Volunteers* (1982, acrylic/canvas, 68 x 102 1/4 ins / 173 x 260 cm) FRF 50,000. PARIS, 29 Nov 1996, *Well-Loved* (1986, acrylic and resin/canvas, 55 x 63 ins / 140 x 160 cm) FRF 19,000. PARIS, 8 April 1997, *Untitled* (1990, paint and lacquer/canvas, 35 1/2 x 37 ins / 90 x 94 cm) FRF 12,000. PARIS, 27 Oct 2000, *Le Devin* (1982, watercolour and collage, 22 x 30 ins / 55 x 75 cm) FRF 11,500. MELBOURNE, 2 Sept 2003, *Untitled, Detail No. 1* (synthetic polymer on paper, 63 x 55 ins / 160 x 140 cm) AUD 13,000. NEW YORK, 14 May 2004, *Darche* (2003, acrylic resin on canvas, 64 x 58 ins / 162 x 148 cm) USD 38,000. NEW YORK, 10 June 2004, *Oreiller III, Pillow III* (acrylic resin, ink and mother of pearl on canvas, 93 x 93 ins / 237 x 237 cm) USD 26,000.

FRIZERI, Bastiano

Italian, 15th - 16th century.
Born in Fossano.
Painter.

This artist lived in Nice.

MUSEUMS AND GALLERIES:

LA BRIGUE (Collégiale St-Martin): *Virgin Mary*.

FRIZON, Auguste Joseph Xavier

French, 19th century.
Born 12 November 1839, in Crest (Drôme).
Sculptor.

Frizon enrolled at the École des Beaux-Arts on 8 October 1857 and exhibited busts at Salons between 1959 and 1882, together with some genre compositions including *The Dove and the Ant, Fife Player, Widow* and *Remorse*. Frizon received an honourable mention in 1881.

MUSEUMS AND GALLERIES:

AJACCIO: *Hercules and Anteia* - LOUVIERS: *Louis Delahaye*.

FRIZZI, Federigo

Italian, 15th century.
Born 1470, in Florence.
Sculptor.

Frizzi is known to have been in Rome around 1520.

FRIZZLE, O.

Dutch, 18th century.
Active in London in 1773.
Engraver.

Known for his engraving of *The Content Dutchman*, after Jan Steen.

FRIZZONI, Thomas

Swiss, 18th - 19th century.
Born 1760, in Celerina (Upper Engadine); died 1845, in Bergamo (Lombardy, Italy).
Painter.

Frizzoni was born deaf and dumb, but thanks to his father's perseverance and encouragement he developed a passion for drawing. He attended courses at the academy in Florence and studied painting in Rome. Works for which he is noted include landscapes, seascapes, portraits (including two self-portraits), which are held in private collections in Zurich, Winterthur, Bergamo, and other locations.

FRÖBE, Johann

French, 17th century.
Painter. Religious subjects.

Johann Fröbe was active in Strasbourg at the beginning of the 17th century. One of his known works is a *Crucifixion*.

FROBEL, Balthasar

German, 17th century.
Born in Königsberg (now Kaliningrad, Russia); died 18 January 1688, in Brünn (now Brno, Czech Republic).
Sculptor.

FROBEL, Hans

German, 17th century.
Born in Königsberg (now Kaliningrad, Russia); died 17 February 1695, in Brünn (now Brno, Czech Republic).
Sculptor.

FRÖBEL, Johann

German, 17th century.
Sculptor.

Fröbel was active in Schömberg in Silesia (now Chelmsko Slaskje, Poland).

FROBENIUS, B.

German, 16th century.
Active in Crailsheim (Baden-Württemberg) c. 1590.
Sculptor.

FROBENIUS, Hermann

German, 19th - 20th century.
Born 30 April 1871, in Erfurt; died in Bad Reichenhall.
Painter. Mythological subjects, landscapes.

Hermann Frobenius lived in Dresden and Berlin, and also in Italy.

AUCTION RECORDS:

MUNICH, 12 Dec 1990, *The Abandoned Ariadne* (1934, oil on canvas, 40 1/4 x 37 1/4 ins / 102.5 x 94.5 cm) DEM 16,500.

FROBISCHER, Marguerite

French, 20th century.
Painter.

Marguerite Frobischer was a member of the Royal College of Art. She exhibited at the Paris Salon from 1923.

FROBÖSE, Georg

German, 18th century.
Born in Hornburg.
Sculptor (wood).

Froböse worked for various churches in the region of Halberstadt (Saxony- Anhalt).

FROC-ROBERT, Désiré

French, 19th century.
Sculptor.

Ths artist is on record as having worked on the church of St-Samson in Clermont (Oise).

FROCOURT, Lucien

French, 20th century.

Born in Paris.
Painter. Nudes, genre scenes.
Lucien Frocourt exhibited at the Salon des Artistes Indépendants in Paris from 1935.

FRODMAN-CLUZEL, Boris
Russian, 20th century.
Born in St Petersburg.
Sculptor.
Boris Frodman-Cluzel participated in the Salon des Artistes Indépendants from 1927.
AUCTION RECORDS:
MONTE CARLO, 26 June 1976, *Gorschkova, the Dancer* (1910, lost-wax bronze, h. 11 ins / 28 cm) FRF 5,500. LONDON, 23 Oct 1980, *Anna Pavlova* (c. 1907-1908, bronze, h. 8 1/4 ins / 21 cm) GBP 900. PARIS, 30 Jan 1995, *Jeanne Schwarz* (1910, lost-wax bronze, h. 11 ins / 28 cm) FRF 44,000. PARIS, 9 Oct 1997, *Dancer* (1909, patinated bronze, proof, h. 9 3/4 ins / 25 cm) FRF 6,800.

FROEBE, Ludovika
Maiden name: Stohl
Austrian, 19th century.
Born 27 January 1847, in Vienna.
Painter. Genre scenes.
Ludovika Froebe was the pupil of Tina Blau.

FROEHLICH. See **FRÖHLICH**

FROER, Veit
German, 19th century.
Born 1 July 1828, in Nuremberg.
Engraver.
Froer was a pupil of Petersen and later of Dertinger in Stuttgart.

FROEY, Jean de La. See **LA FROEY Jean de**

FROGER, Albert
French, 19th century.
Born in the 19th century, in Paris.
Sculptor.
Froger made his début at the 1881 Salon and received an honourable mention in 1889.

FROGET, Pierre Marie
French, 19th century.
Born 4 February 1814, in Pannissières (Loire).
Sculptor.
Froget enrolled at the École des Beaux-Arts on 9 October 1839 and studied under Ramey and A. Dumont. He exhibited at the Paris Salon between 1847 and 1855. He worked extensively in churches; examples of his work include a statue of *St Cecilia* for the church of St-Eustache, a statue of *St Michael* for the Tour St-Jacques, statues of the *Virgin* for the church of Foreign Missions and for Beauvais Cathedral, and a statue of *St Joseph* for the church of St-Maur in Lunéville.

FROGHERI, Gino
Italian, 20th century.
Born 1937, in Nuoro (Sardinia).
Painter.
Frogheri's first exhibition was in his home town of Nuoro in 1955. He also took part in an exhibition of figurative art in Palermo the same year. He showed his work mostly in Italy, and particularly in Milan.

In Frogheri's paintings, which rapidly evolved towards abstraction, the texture of the paper plays a major role, as does the texture of the drawing, which stands out against coloured backgrounds.

FRÖHLICH, Anton
German, 19th century.
Born 1776, in Tölz (Bavaria); died 1841, in Tölz.
Sculptor, painter.
Anton Fröhlich worked in Munich, where he was a pupil of Schwanthaler. He is particularly noted for his religious subjects.

FRÖHLICH, Bernhard, or Frohlich
German, 19th century.
Born 1823, in Munich; died 7 March 1885, in Munich.
Painter, engraver. Genre scenes.
Bernhard Fröhlich was a pupil of Sagstatter at the academy in Munich.

AUCTION RECORDS:
NEW YORK, 12 Oct 1994, *Leaving School* (1884, oil on canvas, 22 x 35 ins / 55.9 x 88.9 cm) USD 5,750. CONNECTICUT, 22 Feb 1999, *Children Playing with Their Boats* (1884, oil on canvas, 12 x 20 ins / 30 x 51 cm) USD 2,750. MIAMI, 25 Jan 2000, *Barnyard Scene with Two Children* (1884, oil on canvas, 13 x 17 ins / 33 x 43 cm) USD 1,700.

FRÖHLICH, Betty
Maiden name: Bogner
Austrian, 19th century.
Born 1798, in Vienna; died 30 June 1878, in Vienna.
Painter.
Betty Fröhlich was a pupil of Daffinger, and exhibited at the academy in Vienna from 1822.

FRÖHLICH, Caspar
German, 18th century.
Active in Neustadt an der Weinstrasse (Rhineland-Palatinate).
Painter.
Caspar Fröhlich executed two altarpieces for the church of Engelbrechtsmünster.

FRÖHLICH, Christoph
German, 18th century.
Active in Mühldorf (Bavaria).
Sculptor.

FRÖHLICH, Emil
German, 19th century.
Born 3 May 1862, in Leipzig.
Painter. Landscapes.
Emil Fröhlich was a pupil of H. and W. van Diez at the academy in Munich and exhibited mainly in Berlin.

FRÖHLICH, Ernst
German, 19th century.
Born 1810, in Kempten (Bavaria); died 19 February 1882, in Munich.
Painter, engraver. Genre scenes.
A pupil at the academy in Munich, Ernst Fröhlich exhibited in Dresden and Munich. He collaborated on *Falling Leaves*.
AUCTION RECORDS:
HAMBURG, 4 June 1980, *Mending Nets* (oil on panel, 8 3/4 x 11 1/2 ins / 22.3 x 29.3 cm) DEM 10,000.

FRÖHLICH, Ernst
German, 19th century.
Born 1808, in Coburg (Bavaria); died 30 September 1869, in Erlangen (Bavaria).
Painter, illustrator.
Ernst Fröhlich was active in Munich between 1830 and 1840.

FRÖHLICH, Franz
German, 18th century.

Active in Tölz (Bavaria) at the beginning of the 18th century.
Sculptor.
This is undoubtedly the same artist as the one working in Innsbruck during the same period.

FRÖHLICH, Fritz
Austrian, 20th century.
Born 1910, in Linz.
Painter.
From 1929 to 1937, Fritz Fröhlich studied at the Akademie in Vienna. After 1953, he took part in many group exhibitions in Austria.
AUCTION RECORDS:
VIENNA, 25 June 1986, *Person seated at a Table in an Inn* (1958, oil on canvas, 38½ x 44 ins / 98 x 112 cm) ATS 30,000. VIENNA, 15 June 1999, *Advice in ZK* (1999, oil on canvas, 43 x 40 ins / 108 x 102 cm) ATS 190,000. VIENNA, 13 Oct 1999, *The Second Face* (1980, oil on canvas, 43 x 40 ins / 110 x 102 cm) ATS 350,000. VIENNA, 29 Nov 2000, *What's Behind Your Mask* (1980, oil on canvas, 28 x 33 ins / 72 x 84 cm) ATS 100,000. VIENNA, 21 Nov 2001, *Architecture* (oil on canvas, 20 x 26 ins / 50 x 66 cm) ATS 55,000. LINZ, 18 Nov 2002, *Yes, What Are You Looking For Then?* (1997, oil on canvas, 15 x 19 ins / 37 x 49 cm) EUR 2,800. LINZ, 14 May 2003, *At Night* (1978, acrylic, 16 x 31 ins / 40 x 78 cm) EUR 2,200. LINZ, 13 May 2004, *Composition* (1978, oil on canvas, 43 x 39 ins / 110 x 100 cm) EUR 6,500. LINZ, 29 Nov 2004, *Composition with Figure* (1894, oil on canvas, 46 x 40 ins / 118 x 101 cm) EUR 2,000.

FRÖHLICH, Hans, or Frollich
Swiss, 15th century.
Painter. Religious subjects.
Hans Fröhlich is mentioned in Basel in around 1480.

FRÖHLICH, Nicolaus
German, 14th century.
Active in Breslau (now Wroclaw, Poland) at the end of the 14th century.
Painter.

FRÖHLICH, Otto
German, 19th century.
Born 15 March 1869, in Schleiz (Thuringia).
Painter, engraver.
Otto Fröhlich lived in Weimar (Thuringia), where he mainly executed a large number of portraits.
MUSEUMS AND GALLERIES:
WEIMAR: *Portrait of the Artist.*

FRÖHLICH, Wolfgang
German, 16th century.
Active in Olmütz, Moravia (now Olomouc, Czech Republic).
Miniaturist.
Wolfgang Fröhlich decorated the accounts book of the town of Znaïm (now Znojmo, Czech Republic) with illuminations.

FRÖHLICHER, Otto. See **FRÖLICHER Otto**

FRÖHLICHER, Wolfgang
Swiss, 16th century.
Painter.
Solothurn School.
Wolfgang Fröhlicher's name and coat of arms were recorded in the book of the confraternity of St Luke at Solothurn in 1587. He became a burgher of the town in 1559.

FROHNER, Adolf
Austrian, 20th century.
Born 1937, in Gross-Inzersdorf.
Painter. Scenes with figures.
Adolf Frohner studied at the Akademie in Vienna from 1954 to 1958. He took part in many group exhibitions, notably the Paris Biennale of 1967 and the Ljubljana Biennale on two occasions. His first solo exhibition was in Vienna in 1961.

His painting is figurative, or perhaps allusive would be a better word. He plays on distortions and layouts that are sometimes reminiscent of children's drawings in order to create the often tragic world of anguished humanity.
AUCTION RECORDS:
VIENNA, 4 Dec 1984, *Untersicht* (*Underside*) (1966-1967, tempera and graphite, 55 x 24¾ ins / 140 x 63 cm) ATS 28,000. VIENNA, 7 April 1987, *Figur und der Mauer* (*Figure and the Wall*) (1966, mixed media, 23½ x 21¾ ins / 60 x 55.5 cm) ATS 35,000. VIENNA, 9 March 1999, *Skull* (mixed media on canvas/board, 39 x 28 ins / 100 x 70 cm) ATS 22,000. VIENNA, 11 April 2000, *red chalk* (1996, oil on board, 27 x 17 ins / 69 x 43 cm) ATS 30,000. VIENNA, 11 April 2000, *One of Lot's Daughters* (1991, oil on canvas, 47 x 37 ins / 120 x 95 cm) ATS 85,000. VIENNA, 30 May 2001, *Provocation* (1968, graphite, 51 x 35 ins / 130 x 90 cm) ATS 160,000. VIENNA, 27 Nov 2001, *Untitled* (1961, oil canvas/board, 24 x 20 ins / 60 x 50 cm) ATS 35,000. VIENNA, 14 May 2002, *Flanders Princess* (oil on canvas, 59 x 39 ins / 150 x 100 cm) EUR 7,000. VIENNA, 24 Sept 2002, *Man Showing His Wounds* (1979, tempera and graphite on paper/panel, 76 x 30 ins / 192 x 76 cm) EUR 28,000. VIENNA, 28 Oct 2003, *Crucifixion* (1977, mixed media on canvas, 79 x 118 ins / 200 x 300 cm) EUR 25,000. VIENNA, 26 Nov 2003, *The Three Graces* (oil on canvas, 39 x 31 ins / 99 x 80 cm) EUR 9,000. VIENNA, 6 Oct 2004, *The Heart of Mankind* (1993, mixed media, 24 x 17 ins / 61 x 43 cm) EUR 2,200. PARIS, 17 Oct 2004, *Female Nude* (1978, oil and acrylic on canvas, 51 x 35 ins / 130 x 90 cm) EUR 5,000.

FROIDE-MONTAGNE. See **KOUVENBERG Willem de**

FROIDEVAUX, Georges
Swiss, 20th century.
Born 27 November 1911, in La Chaux-de-Fonds (Neuchâtel).
Painter. Landscapes.
Georges Froidevaux was invited to take part in the São Pãolo Biennale. He mostly painted his native region. The harsh landscape of the Jura is evident, even in his most abstract canvases.

FROIDEVAUX, Paul
Swiss, 20th century.
Born in Geneva.
Painter. Landscapes.
Paul Froidevaux exhibited landscapes at the Salon des Artistes Indépendants in Paris from 1935.
AUCTION RECORDS:
PARIS, 27 June 1945, *Snow Scene*, FRF 200.

FROIDURE, Jaquemart
French, 15th century.
Painter.
Active in Tournai (Belgium), Froidure was the pupil of Jacques Le Fèvre.

FROIDURE DE PELLEPORT, Ernestine (Mme)
French, 19th century.
Born in the 19th century, in Paris.
Painter. Figures, portraits.
Froidure de Pelleport studied under J. Gigoux and submitted examples of her work to the Paris Salon between 1845 and 1868, including a *Peasant Woman Carrying Fruit* (1866), a female portrait and a head of young girl (1868).

FROISSART, Philippe
French, 16th century.
Sculptor.
Philippe Froissart added sculptural decorations to the Hotoie Gate in Amiens (Somme). These were listed as two sala-

manders, six crowned 'F's, six crowned fleur-de-lis and an escutcheon bearing the arms of Amiens.

FROISSÉ, Élisabeth
French, 18th century.
Active in Paris in 1781.
Painter (?), sculptor (?).

FROISSÉ, Raoul Toussaint
French, 18th century.
Active in Paris c. 1773.
Painter.

FROITZHEIM, Heinrich
German, 19th - 20th century.
Born 21 December 1866, in Cologne; died 29 February 1904, in Munich.
Painter.

Heinrich Froitzheim exhibited in Cologne from 1902.

FROLICH, Charles
Swiss, 20th century.
Painter. Landscapes, flowers.

Charles Frohlich exhibited in Paris at the Salon of the Société Nationale des Beaux-Arts in 1922, and from then on at the Salon des Artistes Indépendants.

AUCTION RECORDS:
PARIS, 14 Feb 1990, *Cottage* (1927, oil on panel, 8 1/2 x 10 3/4 ins / 21.5 x 27.5 cm) FRF 46,000.

FRÖLICH, Edma Vilhelmine Cornelia
Danish, 19th century.
Born 14 August 1859, in Fontainebleau.
Painter, pastellist. Portraits, interiors with figures, still-lifes.

Edma Frölich was the daughter of Lorens Frölich and was also his pupil. She mostly produced portraits in pastel.

AUCTION RECORDS:
COPENHAGEN, 15 Nov 1993, *Interior with Books and a Rose on a Table* (oil on canvas, 19 1/4 x 16 1/4 ins / 49 x 41 cm) DKK 6,500.

FROLICH, Finn Haakon
American, 19th century.
Born 13 May 1869, in Christiania (now Oslo), Norway; died 1947, in Carnel (California).
Active in New York.
Sculptor.

Finn Haakon Frolich was a pupil of D.C. French in New York and Barrias in Paris. He was awarded a silver medal at the Paris Exposition Universelle of 1900.

FRÖLICH, Johann
Flemish School, 17th century.
Born in Antwerp.
Active in Salzburg.
Sculptor.

FRÖLICH, Lorens or Lorenz
Danish, 19th century.
Born 25 October 1820, in Copenhagen; died 25 October 1908, in Copenhagen.
Painter, engraver, illustrator. Mythological subjects, genre scenes, landscapes with figures, animals.

Lorens Frölich received lessons in drawing from A. Bissen and studied under Körbye, Hetch and Eckersberg in Denmark. He perfected his art in Munich and Dresden, and visited Rome and Paris. From 1877 Frölich was a teacher at the Kunstakademi in Copenhagen. He won a medal in 1873 for his engravings, and received an honourable mention at the Exposition Universelle in Paris in 1900.

Noted among his works are *Cupid and the Naiad, Capture of the Naiads, Idylls of Theocritus,* nine illustrated plates for the *Zwei Kirchtusme* by Oehlenschlager, illustrations for English children's stories, illustrations for *Danish Legends,* nine plates for *Götter des Nordens* (*Gods of the North*), and nine plates for *Vater Unser.*

MUSEUMS AND GALLERIES:
DRESDEN: *Capture of the Naiads* - LEIPZIG: *Cupid and the Naiad.*

AUCTION RECORDS:
COPENHAGEN, 30 April 1981, *Children in a Landscape with Snow* (1880, oil on panel, 7 3/4 x 10 1/4 ins / 20 x 26 cm) DKK 7,000. LONDON, 23 March 1988, *Herd of Deer in a Park* (oil on canvas, 35 x 41 1/4 ins / 88 x 105 cm) GBP 3,300. LONDON, 29 March 1990, *Storyteller* (1843, oil on canvas, 21 1/2 x 29 ins / 54.9 x 73.7 cm) GBP 8,800. COPENHAGEN, 18 Nov 1992, *Diana Killing a Centaur* (oil on canvas, 8 1/4 x 12 1/4 ins / 21 x 31 cm) DKK 5,500. COPENHAGEN, 10 Feb 1993, *Nymph and Putti* (oil on canvas, 6 x 8 1/4 ins / 15 x 21 cm) DKK 5,800. COPENHAGEN, 15 Nov 1993, *Pan Singing for Guderne* (oil on canvas, 14 1/2 x 24 1/2 ins / 37 x 62 cm) DKK 13,000. COPENHAGEN, 16 Nov 1994, *Child Playing with a Dog* (oil on paper/panel, 4 1/4 x 6 ins / 11 x 15 cm) DKK 8,800. COPENHAGEN, 8 Feb 1995, *Thor with Hymer* (oil on canvas, 14 1/4 x 22 ins / 36 x 55 cm) DKK 10,500. COPENHAGEN, 30 May 2000, *Italian Landscape with Figures and Donkey* (1830, oil on canvas, 16 x 21 ins / 40 x 53 cm) DKK 60,000. HAVNEN, 26 Aug 2000, *Interior Scene with Figures Playing Cards* (oil on canvas, 24 x 29 ins / 61 x 74 cm) DKK 40,000. COPENHAGEN, 5 March 2001, *Thor and Hymer* (1855, oil on canvas, 14 x 21 ins / 36 x 54 cm) DKK 19,000. COPENHAGEN, 4 March 2002, *Female Nude Model in the Artist Thomas Couture's Studio* (oil on canvas, 22 x 18 ins / 56 x 46 cm) DKK 33,000. COPENHAGEN, 3 June 2002, *Peasants from Sabine Mountains Preparing Dinner in Grotto* (1850, oil on canvas, 24 x 31 ins / 62 x 78 cm) DKK 35,000. COPENHAGEN, 3 Sept 2003, *Self-portrait* (c. 1860, oil on cardboard, 18 x 13 ins / 46 x 34 cm) DKK 26,000. COPENHAGEN, 3 Sept 2003, *Portrait of the Artist's Second Wife Benedicte Frolich* (c. 1878, oil on canvas, 24 x 17 ins / 60 x 44 cm) DKK 35,000.

FRÖLICH, Lucas
German, 15th century.
Painter.

Mentioned in Augsburg on 24 September 1490, Lucas Frölich was still working there in 1511.

FRÖLICHER, Johann Joseph
Swiss, 18th - 19th century.
Born 26 September 1772, in Solothurn; died 3 August 1841, in Kriegstetten.
Painter.

Johann Joseph Frölicher was a priest. He settled in Egerkingen and in Aesch, Switzerland, and painted for the chapel of St Michael in Hüniken (in the parish of Aesch) a *Coronation of the Virgin.* He may also be responsible for two historical paintings of the choir at the church of Aesch.

FRÖLICHER, Johann Peter
Swiss, 17th - 18th century.
Born 11 November 1662, probably in Solothurn; died 26 August 1725.
Sculptor (wood).

Johann was the brother of Wolfgang Frölicher.

FRÖLICHER, Otto, or Fröhlicher
Swiss, 19th century.
Born 5 June 1840, in Solothurn (Bern); died 2 November 1890, in Munich.
Active in Germany.
Painter, engraver. Landscapes with figures, landscapes.

The grandson and pupil of Joseph Anton Koch, Otto Frölicher started his studies at the cantonal school of Solothurn, joined the academy in Munich in 1859 and worked under the guidance of Steffan in 1860. By 1863 he was living in Munich, where Oswald Achenbach completed his artistic education. Frölicher visited Paris in 1876 and Barbizon during the following year, and thereafter spent the rest of his life in Munich. He exhibited in Solothurn, Bern, Zurich, Basel, Munich, Dresden, Vienna, Bremen, Hanover, and other cities. He began his career by painting views of the Alps, then chose to concentrate on intimist landscapes, justifying this choice by claiming: 'Art should seek interest in pictorial beauty and not seek beauty in the interest of the subject.' Canvases for which he is noted include *High Valley in Switzerland, Moonlit Landscape, Haslital, Woodland Landscape, Area around Barbizon.*

The Barbizon School had a tremendous influence on the development of this painter, who managed to break with tradition and create an original style for himself. He also produced engravings on wood for a number of Swiss construction works, notably the *Schweizerhaus* (1879).

MUSEUMS AND GALLERIES:

BASEL: *Autumn Landscape on the Outskirts of Munich; Summer Landscape with a Storm in the Distance* - BERN: *Landscape in Upper Bavaria; Area around Handeck; Stormy Weather in Bavaria; Landscape Study* - MUNICH: *Landscape* - SOLOTHURN: *Alpine Landscape* - ZURICH: *Forest in Upper Bavaria.*

AUCTION RECORDS:

LONDON, 25 March 1942, *Landscape,* GBP 5. PARIS, 12 May 1947, *Swiss Landscape with Fishermen,* FRF 2,800. LUCERNE, 21 June 1963, *Alpine Landscape,* CHF 6,000. LUCERNE, 3 Dec 1966, *Landscape in Stormy Weather,* CHF 15,000. BERN, 18 Nov 1972, *Landscape of Barbizon,* CHF 30,000. BERN, 27 Nov 1974, *Stormy Landscape,* CHF 13,500. BERN, 7 May 1976, *Flock in a Landscape* (1865, oil on canvas, 17 1/4 x 27 1/2 ins / 44 x 70 cm) CHF 5,500. BERN, 21 Oct 1977, *Alpine Landscape* (oil on canvas, 18 1/4 x 23 1/4 ins / 46.5 x 59 cm) CHF 7,000. ZURICH, 29 Nov 1978, *Stormy Landscape* (oil on canvas, 28 x 43 3/4 ins / 71 x 111 cm) CHF 18,500. BERN, 6 May 1981, *Stormy Landscape on Lake Starnberg* (oil on canvas, 12 x 18 ins / 30.5 x 45.5 cm) CHF 10,000. LUCERNE, 7 June 1984, *Moon Rising* (oil on canvas, 15 1/4 x 22 3/4 ins / 39 x 58 cm) CHF 11,000. BERN, 25 Oct 1985, *Alpine Landscape at the Lake* (oil on canvas in grisaille, 16 1/2 x 23 1/4 ins / 42 x 59 cm) CHF 3,600. BERN, 30 April 1988, *Area around Barbizon* (oil on canvas, 35 x 46 ins / 88 x 116 cm) CHF 4,800. ZURICH, 4 June 1992, *Landscape of the Outskirts of Sitten* (1861, oil on canvas/card, 11 x 17 3/4 ins / 27 x 45 cm) CHF 7,345. ZURICH, 9 June 1993, *Marshland* (oil on canvas, 17 1/2 x 25 ins / 44.5 x 63.5 cm) CHF 8,050. ZURICH, 2 June 1994, *View of Solothurn* (oil on canvas, 23 1/4 x 35 ins / 59 x 88 cm) CHF 32,200. ZURICH, 10 Dec 1996, *Sheep Grazing in a Wooded Landscape* (c. 1879, 23 1/2 x 35 1/2 ins / 60 x 90 cm) CHF 23,000. ZURICH, 8 Dec 1999, *Cows at River's Edge* (oil on canvas, 21 x 29 ins / 53 x 73 cm) CHF 15,000. DÜSSELDORF, 31 Jan 2000, *Figures in Mountainous Landscape* (oil on canvas, 53 x 74 ins / 134 x 188 cm) DEM 18,000. ZURICH, 6 July 2000, *Landscape with Figure* (1878, oil on canvas, 30 x 43 ins / 76 x 110 cm) CHF 6,000. SWITZERLAND, 8 June 2001, *Trees in Autumn* (oil on canvas, l, 20 x 24 ins / 50 x 62 cm) CHF 10,000. ZURICH, 11 Dec 2001, *Mountain Landscape with Small Lake and Cows* (oil on canvas, 24 x 16 ins / 60 x 41 cm) CHF 14,000. ZURICH, 26 May 2003, *Riverside Mill* (oil on canvas, 29 x 43 ins / 74 x 110 cm) CHF 45,000. ZURICH, 16 Sept 2003, *Storm Gathering over Wooded Landscape* (oil on canvas, 25 x 21 ins / 64 x 53 cm) CHF 4,500. BERN, 14 May 2004, *Landscape with Shepherdess* (1878, oil on canvas, 30 x 39 ins / 75 x 100 cm) CHF 8,200. ZURICH, 17 May 2004, *Gathering Storm* (oil on canvas, 29 x 41 ins / 73 x 104 cm) CHF 45,000.

FRÖLICHER, Wolfgang

Swiss, 17th century.
Born 24 June 1652, in Solothurn; died 26 June 1700, in Trier (Rhineland-Palatinate, Germany).
Sculptor.

Wolfgang Frölicher may have been a freeman of Frankfurt am Main, where he worked; he was also active in Trier. His statues of the *Emperor Constantine* and *St Helen* are still kept at Trier. Frölicher completed a number of works for the church of St Catherine, the cemetery of St Peter in Frankfurt and also the German church of Cordeliers in Sachsenhausen.

FRÖLING, J. G.

German, 18th century.
Painter.

There is a known portrait engraved after a work by this artist.

FROLING, M. W.

German, 18th century.
Active in Helmstedt (Lower Saxony) c. 1720.
Painter.

Many portraits were engraved after this artist.

FROLKA, Anton

Slovak, 20th century.
Born 1877, in Knezdub.
Painter.

Anton Frolka was a student of Uprka before studying in Munich and Vienna.

FROLOFF. See also **FLOROV**

FROLOFF, Alexander P.

German, 19th century.
Active in Munich.
Landscapist.

Froloff exhibited in Vienna, Munich and Dresden.

FROLOV, Sergei

Russian, 20th century.
Born 1924, in Leningrad (now St Petersburg).
Painter. Figure compositions, landscapes.

Frolov studied at the Ilya Repin Institute in Leningrad under Sergei Vasilevich Gerasimov and Anna Petrovna Ostrumova-Lebedeva. In the barren artistic context of the Stalinist era and reduced to painting various insignificant subjects, Frolov fulfilled his futile task in a perfectly innocuous technique. He has featured in national exhibitions from 1955 and in exhibitions abroad from 1975. Between 1975 and 1984 he took part eight times in *Soviet Art,* Tokyo; he also showed in Prague (1978), Osaka (1982), Madrid, Brussels and Helsinki (1990). Two solo exhibitions were devoted to him, one in Ouglitch (1976) and a retrospective in Leningrad (1986). He was a member of Leningrad's Association of Painters.

BIBLIOGRAPHY:

L'École de Léningrad, auction catalogue, Drouot, Paris, 19 November 1990.

MUSEUMS AND GALLERIES:

MOSCOW (Ministry of Culture) - MOSCOW (State Tretyakov Gal.) - OSAKA (Gal. of Soviet Art) - ST PETERSBURG (Gosudarstvennyj Russkij Muz.) - ST PETERSBURG (Mukhina School of Arts and Industry).

AUCTION RECORDS:

PARIS, 19 Nov 1990, *Summer Evening* (oil on card, 19 3/4 x 31 ins / 50 x 79 cm) FRF 9,800. PARIS, 18 Feb 1991, *Pleasure Harbour* (oil on card, 19 3/4 x 27 1/2 ins / 50 x 70 cm) FRF 4,500. PARIS, 25 March 1991, *St Isaac's Square in Leningrad* (1986, oil on canvas, 25 1/2 x 35 ins / 65 x 89 cm) FRF 7,500. PARIS, 6 Dec 1991, *Children of Chukotka* (1969, tempera/canvas, 59 x 98 1/2 ins / 150 x 250 cm) FRF 49,000. PARIS, 27 Jan 1992, *Kostroma's Countryside* (oil on card, 16 x 20 ins / 40.5 x 50.5 cm) FRF 4,000. PARIS, 5 April 1992, *Oranienbaum Park* (watercolour, 18 1/2 x 25 1/4 ins / 47 x 64 cm) FRF 4,100. PARIS, 20 May 1992, *Tea-time* (1946, oil on canvas, 27 1/2 x 39 1/4 ins / 70 x 100 cm) FRF 5,000. PARIS, 23 Nov 1992, *The Town of Pskov* (oil on card, 19 1/2 x 31 ins / 49.8 x 79 cm) FRF 4,500.

FROLOV, Yakob
Russian, 19th century.
Active in Moscow then in St Petersburg.
Sculptor.

FROM, Henrik Christian
Danish, 19th century.
Born 6 September 1811, in Copenhagen; died 18 July 1879, in Copenhagen.
Painter, architect.

Henrik Christian From produced mostly landscapes and decorative projects.

FROMAGE, Jean Baptiste Pierre
French, 18th century.
Active in Paris in 1756.
Painter, sculptor.

FROMAGER, Martin
French, 17th century.
Active in Paris in 1682.
Painter, sculptor.

FROMAIGE, Jean
French, 16th century.
Sculptor (wood).

Jean Fromaige assisted in the preparations for the festivities organised in 1577 by the town on Tours (Indre-et-Loire) in honour of the solemn entry into the town of the Duke of Anjou and Touraine.

FROMAN, Ann
American, 20th century.
Born 1942, in New York.
Sculptor, draughtswoman. Figures, nudes.
Monuments, groups.

Ann Froman studied at the Fine Arts School, New York, and in Fontainebleau; she was taught painting by Henri Goetz and architecture by Le Corbusier. Her subjects are mainly inspired by the Bible or the dance world, and she also carves sculptures based on observation of popular American culture, which are characterised by humour and fantasy.

She is a member of the Salmagundi Club, exhibits in many group and solo exhibitions, and won a first prize for sculpture in 1980.

BIBLIOGRAPHY:
Poroner, P., '*Sculpture and Poetry Unite in Ann Froman's Art*' in *Art Speaks*, periodical, February, 1994.

MUSEUMS AND GALLERIES:
NEW YORK (Metropolitan Mus. of Art).

FROMANGER, Alexis Hippolyte
French, 19th century.
Born 20 June 1805, in Paris; died 1892, in Paris.
Sculptor.

Fromanger enrolled at the École des Beaux-Arts on 1 October 1828 and studied under Lemaire; exhibited at the Salon between 1835 and 1870. Examples of his work include *St Dominic, Perseus Freeing Andromeda* (group), *Religion* (marble statue for the chapel of the Duke de Luynes at Dampierre), *St Stephen* (for the church of St-Étienne-du-Mont), plus a *St Maur* and *St Rémy*, two stone statues for the church of St-Clotilde.

FROMANGER, Gérard
French, 20th century.
Born 6 September 1939, in Pontchartrain.
Also active in Italy.
Painter, lithographer, collage artist, environmental artist.
Nouvelle Figuration, Figuration Narrative.

Gérard Fromanger only studied art briefly at the studio of Busse and Gillet at the Grande-Chaumière academy in Paris and at evening classes in the city. He spent only 18 days at the École des Beaux-Arts. Nevertheless he found success as a painter, as well as a designer of sets and costumes for Stockhausen's ballet *Hymnen* in Grenoble in 1970 and the backcloth for *La Farce de Burgos* at the Théâtre d'Annecy in 1971. In 1964 he was awarded the Premier Grand Prix of the Festival d'Avignon and in 1970 the Governor's Prize at the 7th International Engraving Biennale in Tokyo.

In common with his fellow artists at the Grande Chaumière academy, Fromanger's early period was one of figurative compositions painted in a range of chiaroscuro greys and earth colours and of drawings and lithographs in a style related to that of Giacometti. However, he then went on to paint *The Prince of Hamburg* using contrasting flat tints. In the series of works that followed, he explored the whys and the hows of painting with: *Le Tableau en Question* in 1966; *Mon Tableau Fuit* and the relief pictures *Paysages Découpés* in 1967 - *Paysage Découpé en Dix* (*Landscape Cut in Ten*) consists of wooden panels, cut up, painted and assembled. In 1968, in response to both the social and political events of the time and the prevailing situation in the world of art he produced 'environmental' sculptures consisting of 'bubbles'; known as *Souffles* or *Sculptures Soufflées*; these were transparent red hemispheres that reflected whatever was happening in the street where they were placed, reducing it to the scale of a bubble through the effect of concavity.

The figurative element of his earliest period and then the capturing of everyday reality in his bubbles characterised Fromanger's initial direction from an ethical and strategic point of view and conditioned some of his later activities, or at least the important period that immediately followed. In his serigraphies of 1970, and in his paintings of 1971 and after, he faithfully reproduced Paris street scenes using a monochrome photo-reportage technique inspired by Jacques Monory. These were mainly of the Boulevard des Italiens filled with people painted as red silhouettes without any further explanation, symbolically communicating the sensation of oppression exerted by the backdrop of the consumer society on its willing and dehumanised victims. The product of a way of thinking that may later have seemed puerile, at the time it reflected the social questioning of the student generation of that period. Other series followed: firstly, in 1972, *Vie et Mort d'un Mineur* (*Life and Death of a Miner*). In the series of paintings exhibited in 1973-1974 under the title *Annoncez la Couleur* (*Announce Colour*) and in the *Le Peintre et le Modèle* (*Painter and Model*) lithographs of 1972-1973, Fromanger diversified the colouring of the silhouette figures, including his own standing back and observing, adopting a similar colour coding to that used to differentiate areas on geographical, geological, human and economic maps which show cereal or mineral production or the alcoholism rate of a population, generally with directional markings and differentiated colouring.

Fromanger can be described as one of the principal representatives of Narrative Figuration, the French Pop Art movement. However, he did not take part in the Narrative Figuration exhibition organised by Gérald Gassiot-Talabot. Taking a similar analytical approach to sociological phenomena as he had applied in his photo-reportage work and colour coding technique, Fromanger moved on to the series entitled *Le Désir est Partout* (*Desire is Everywhere*) in 1975 and *Questions et Hommage à Topino-Lebrun* (*Questions and Homage to Topino-Lebrun*) in 1976-1977. When, in 1978, he painted the picture-poem *Je suis dans l'atelier en train de peindre...* (*I am in the Studio Painting*) - in which the linearly-written text consitutes almost the entire pictorial element - it was clear that he was inspired by a questioning of both the act of painting and the action of the painting. In 1979, for his exhibition at the Pompidou Centre, he painted the series *Tout Est Allumé* (*Everything is Lit*), the final painting of which - *À Mon Seul Désir* - presents a hotchpotch of coloured marks and signs but ordered, or rather disordered, exclusively in accordance with the pleasure principle. After moving to Italy, near Siena, he departed from the sociological foundation on which his artistic activity had been based for so long in favour of a specifically art-based approach, or one he at least intended to be so. From an artistic activity that had been collective and militant he turned to an individual, hedonistic concept of art based on the pleasure of line, form and colour in their own right in a succession of series: in 1982 *Allegro*, in 1984 *Trente et une peintures* (*Thirty-one Paintings*), in 1985 *Chimères, 105 Petits Formats* (*Chimera, 105 Small Format Pieces*) and in 1986 *Cythère Ville Nouvelle* (*Cythera New Town*). His production became considerable, arising out of a kind of inexhaustible automatism. One theme succeeded another; themes that were no longer intentions but rather inexplicit images often bordering on the non-figurative but remaining just allusive and repetitive: in the *Chimera* series two schematised eyes are repeated in the 100 or so paintings in the series; in the *Cythera New Town* series there are hundreds of sketchy silhouettes of human bodies.

He has exhibited in Paris, at the Salon de Mai since 1964, at the Salon de la Jeune Peinture from 1965 to 1976, at the Salon Grands et Jeunes d'Aujourd'hui in 1972, 1973 and 1974 and in various group exhibitions, including: in 1966 *Climat 66* at the Musée de Grenoble; in 1968 *Art Vivant 1965-68* at the Fondation Maeght; 1969, *Police et Culture I* at the Musée d'Art Moderne de la Ville de Paris; 1971, *Kunst und Politik* at Karlsruhe, Wuppertal and Frankfurt; and in 1991, *Rencontres - Cinquante Ans de Collages* (*Encounters - Fifty Years of Collage*), an exhibition organised by Françoise Monin at the Galerie Claudine Lustman in Paris.

He has shown collections of his work, usually in series, in numerous solo exhibitions, including: in 1966 in Grenoble; in 1971, *Boulevard des Italiens*, at the ARC (Art, Research, Confrontation) at the Musée d'Art Moderne de la Ville de Paris; in 1973, *Le Peintre et le Modèle* at Galerie 9 in Paris and Brussels; 1973, *Annoncez la Couleur* at the Galerie Jeanne Bucher, Paris; 1974 at the Maison de la Culture in Namur; 1975 at the museum of modern art in Hertogenbosch; 1979 at the Pompidou Centre in Paris; in 1983 at the Musée des Beaux-Arts in Caen and the Palazzo Pubblico in Siena; in 1984 at the French cultural centre in Beijing; in 1986 at the Galerie Isy Brachot in Brussels; in 1990 at the Maison de la Culture in Bourges; in 1991 in Paris; in 1993 at FIAC (Foire Internationale d'Art Contemporain) in Paris, presented by the Galerie Claudine Lustman; in 2002, *Série Noire* at the Espace Ernst Hilger in Paris; and in 2003 at the Galerie Rive Gauche in Paris.

Bibliography:

Prévert, Jacques/Jouffroy, Alain, '*Fromanger, boulevard des Italiens*' in *coll. Bibli-Opus*, Georges Fall, Paris, 1971. Deleuze, Gilles, '*Le Froid et le Chaud*' in *Fromanger, le peintre et le modèle*, exhibition catalogue, Gal. 9, Paris, 1973. Tronche, Anne/Cloagen, Hervé, *L'Art actuel en France*, Balland, Paris, 1973. Foucault, Michel, '*La Peinture photogénique*' in *Fromanger, le désir est partout*, exhibition catalogue, Gal. Jeanne Bucher, Paris, 1975. *Gérard Fromanger 1978-79*, exhibition catalogue, Musée national d'Art moderne, Paris, 1979. *Gérard Fromanger: chimères*, exhibition catalogue, Gal. Isy Brachot, Paris, 1985 (extensive documentation). Guattari, Félix, '*Nouvelle Donne*' in *Fromanger, Cythère ville nouvelle*, exhibition catalogue, Gal. Isy Brachot, Paris, Foire internationale d'Art contemporain, Paris, 1986 (extensive documentation). *Gérard Fromanger. Last Spring in New York*, exhibition catalogue, Gal. Claude Lustman, Paris, 1990. July, Serge, *Gérard Fromanger*, Éd. Cercle d'Art, Paris, 2002.

Museums and Galleries:

Rotterdam (Mus. Boijmans Van Beuningen): *At the Opéra, Versailles, Portrait of Michel Bulteau, the World's Greatest Poet* (1975).

Auction records:

Paris, 27 Nov 1973, *Absent-minded Man* (1971) FRF 5,000. Paris, 28 April 1981, *Boulevard des Italiens* (1971, acrylic, 39¼ x 39¼ ins / 100 x 100 cm) FRF 5,500. Versailles, 19 June 1983, *Cash* (1971, oil on canvas, 39¼ x 39¼ ins / 100 x 100 cm) FRF 9,500. Paris, 6 Dec 1986, *Boulevard des Italiens, 'The Isle of Lost Loves'* (1971, oil on canvas, 39¼ x 39¼ ins / 100 x 100 cm) FRF 17,000. Paris, 3 Dec 1987, *Colours* (1982, oil on canvas, 51¼ x 38¼ ins / 130 x 97 cm) FRF 29,000. Paris, 23 June 1988, *Il Campo* (1988, pastel, 40¼ x 28¼ ins / 102 x 72 cm) FRF 7,500. Paris, 6 April 1989, *Everyday Life, Midnight* (1984, oil on canvas, 59 x 39¼ ins / 150 x 100 cm) FRF 38,000. Paris, 13 Oct 1989, *Boulevard des Italiens* (1939, oil on canvas, 39¼ x 39¼ ins / 100 x 100 cm) FRF 44,000. Paris, 13 Dec 1989, *Broken and Calm Landscape* (1967, mixed media, 48 x 23½ ins / 122 x 60 cm) FRF 28,000. Paris, 23 April 1990, *People Walking* (1987, pastel/canvas, 28 x 39¼ ins / 71 x 100 cm) FRF 33,000. Paris, 3 May 1990, *Daily Life* (1984, oil on canvas, 39¼ x 59 ins / 100 x 150 cm) FRF 65,000. Paris, 20 Nov 1991, *Violet de Bayeux, the Painter and his Model* (1972, oil on canvas, 59 x 78¾ ins / 150 x 200 cm) FRF 60,000. Paris, 26 June 1992, *Boulevard des Italiens, Red* (1971, oil on canvas, 39¼ x 39¼ ins / 100 x 100 cm) FRF 26,000. Paris, 22 Dec 1992, *Existe, Série des Questions* (1976, oil on canvas, 51¼ x 76¾ ins / 130 x 195 cm) FRF 41,000. Paris, 10 June 1993, *The Triumph of Belle-Ile en Mer* (1964, collage, 9¼ x 11¾ ins / 23.6 x 29.7 cm) FRF 4,000. Paris, 10 Feb 1994, *Salto di gatto, Allegro Series* (1982, oil on canvas, 78¾ x 59 ins / 200 x 150 cm) FRF 27,000. Paris, 19 June 1995, *Meeting, Allegro Series* (1982, oil on canvas, 78¾ x 59 ins / 200 x 150 cm) FRF 23,000. Paris, 24 Nov 1995, *Midday* (1984, oil on canvas, 86½ x 59 ins / 220 x 150 cm) FRF 18,000. Paris, 29 April 1997, *Single Snapshot* (oil on canvas, 28¾ x 23½ ins / 73 x 60 cm) FRF 15,000. Paris, 7 Dec 1997, *They Are on the Moon* (1972, screen print/Plexiglas, numbered 16/60, 24½ x 32 ins / 62 x 81 cm) FRF 3,800. Paris, 11 Dec 1997, *Couple Embracing* (1965, oil on canvas, 63¾ x 45 ins / 162 x 114 cm) FRF 8,600. Paris, 21 March 1999, *Exist, Questions Series* (1976, oil on canvas, 51 x 77 ins / 130 x 195 cm) FRF 59,000. Paris, 29 Oct 1999, *Boulevard des Italiens* (1971, oil on canvas, 39 x 39 ins / 100 x 100 cm) FRF 80,000. Paris, 23 May 2000, *Fleury Villandry or New Society 2* (acrylic on canvas, 79 x 59 ins / 200 x 150 cm) FRF 130,000. Paris, 23 Nov 2000, *Violet of Egypt, Painter and Model* (oil on canvas, 59 x 79 ins / 150 x 200 cm) FRF 140,000. Paris, 22 May 2001, *Artist's Life, 1797/1997 Homage to Topino Lebrun* (1975, mixed media on canvas, 79 x 118 ins / 200 x 300 cm) FRF 140,000. Versailles, 24 June 2001, *Red Circle* (1971, oil on canvas, 51 x 38 ins / 130 x 97 cm) FRF 71,000. Paris, 4 Feb 2002, *Prince of Hombourg* (1965, oil on canvas, 79 x 98 ins / 200 x 250 cm) EUR 61,000. Paris, 11 Dec 2002, *Circulate* (1977, oil on canvas, 51 x 77 ins / 130 x 195 cm) EUR 25,500. Paris, 18 May 2004, *Orange* (1989, acrylic on canvas, 79 x 98 ins / 200 x 250 cm) EUR 7,000.

FROMANT, Marin

French, 18th century.

Active in Paris in 1752.

Painter.

FROMANTIOU, Hendrik de, pseudonym: Fernandeau

Dutch, 17th century.

Born c. 1633, in Maastricht; died c. 1694, in Berlin.

Painter. Still-lifes, flowers, animals.

According to Kramm, Fromantiou was a pupil of Rembrandt. He was summoned to Berlin in 1670 by Count

Friedrich Wilhelm, where he became both court painter and picture-restorer, as well as advising the family on the decoration of their castles. Returning to Amsterdam in 1672, he married Ludovica Wouwerman, the sister of the painter Philip Wouwerman. He is recorded in London in 1682, and as a member of the Pictura confraternity in The Hague in 1683. The silvery tonalities of his still-lifes show the influence of Willem van Aelst.

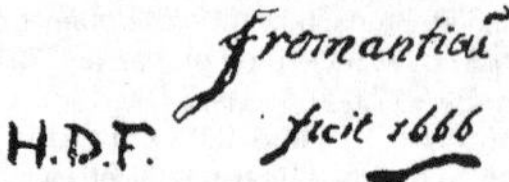

BIBLIOGRAPHY:
Bernt, W., *Netherlandish Painters of the Seventeenth century*, Oxford, 1969. *Old Master Paintings*, auction catalogue, Sotheby's Publications, London, 11 December 1996.
MUSEUMS AND GALLERIES:
BRUNSWICK (Herzog Anton Ulrich-Mus.): *Still-life with Flowers in a Vase on a Marble Base*.
AUCTION RECORDS:
NEW YORK, 18 Jan 1984, *Dead Game and Hunting Trophies on an Entablature* (1665, oil on canvas, 38 1/2 x 33in/98 x 84cm) USD 13,000. PARIS, 14 April 1989, *Bouquet of Flowers in a Glass Vase* (oil on copper, 11 x 7 1/2in/27 x 19cm) FRF 3,450,000. NEW YORK, 31 May 1989, *Game and Hunting Equipment on an Entablature* (oil on canvas, 23 1/2 x 18 1/2in/59.5 x 47cm) USD 22,000. AMSTERDAM, 14 Nov 1991, *Partridge, Falcon, Kingfishers and other Small Birds Hanging in a Niche above a Marble Entablature* (oil on canvas, 25 3/4 x 22 1/2in/65.4 x 57.2cm) NLG 55,200. LONDON, 11 Dec 1996, *Still-life with Flowers in a Vase on a Marble Base* (1667, oil on canvas, 29 x 22 3/4in/73.5 x 58cm) GBP 62,000.

FROMBECK, Carl F.
Austrian, 19th century.
Born 6 December 1821, in Mährisch-Weisskirchen, Moravia (now Hranice, Czech Republic); died 20 October 1851, in Vienna.
Engraver.
Carl Frombeck was a pupil of Rahl in Vienna. He is credited with copies after the old masters, as well as contemporary portraits and subjects.

FROMBOLUTI, Sideo
American, 20th century.
Born 3 October 1921, in Hersey (Pennsylvania).
Active in New York.
Painter.
Sideo Fromboluti graduated from the Tyler School of Art, Philadelphia in 1943. A figurative painter, he takes his cue from nature - a flower, a garden chair under a tree, a woman's body in dancing posture - though light is his true subject. His canvases are virtually monochrome, painted in thick pigment often in pink, orange or mauve, enlivened by the play of light and shade.

He has taken part in many group exhibitions, including: 1954 and subsequently, Stable Annuals; 1958, Whitney Annual, New York. He held solo exhibitions regularly through the 1950s and 1960s in New York, and, from 1969 to 1999, at the Galerie Darthea Speyer in Paris.
BIBLIOGRAPHY:
Kingsley, April, *Sideo Fromboluti. Femmes endormies*, exhibition catalogue, Gal. Darthea Speyer, Paris, 1984. *Sideo Fromboluti: Landscapes*, exhibition catalogue, Gross McLeaf Gallery, Philadelphia, 1984. Scott, Bill/Poncet, Florence, *Fromboluti*, exhibition catalogue, Gal. Darthea Speyer, Paris, 1993.
MUSEUMS AND GALLERIES:
PHILADELPHIA (MA) - PITTSBURGH (Carnegie MA): *Moonrise on Higgins Pond* (1983, oil on canvas).

FROMEL, Marx
German, 16th century.
Miniaturist.
Fromel painted some illuminated miniatures at the court of Bavaria in around 1587.

FROMELL, Johann Tobias
Dutch, 17th century.
Active in Amsterdam, in the middle of the 17th century.
Painter.

FROMEN, Agnes Valborg
American, 19th century.
Born 27 December 1868, in Sweden.
Sculptor.
Agnes Valborg Fromen was a member of the Chicago Society of Artists, where she won a number of awards.

FROMENT, Augustin
Swiss, 18th century.
Active in Geneva in 1789.
Enameller.

FROMENT, Émile Alphonse
French, 19th century.
Born in Paris.
Engraver (wood).
Émile Froment received an honourable mention in 1892.

FROMENT, Eugène
French, 19th century.
Born 2 December 1844, in Sens; died 1900, in Paris.
Painter, engraver, illustrator. Genre scenes, landscapes.
Eugène Froment studied under Alphonse Tauxier and at the College of Decorative Arts. He exhibited at the Paris Salon from 1866 onwards and subsequently at the Salon des Artistes Français, where he was awarded a bronze medal in 1875 and a silver in 1884; he was also the recipient of a gold medal at the 1900 Exposition Universelle in Paris.

Froment painted some landscape and genre compositions, but he was primarily a woodcut engraver, whose *Episode from the American War of Independence* in particular proved highly popular at the time. Froment also illustrated several poems, most notably by Alphonse de Lamartine and by Victor Hugo.
AUCTION RECORDS:
PARIS, 31 Oct 1975, *On the Beach* (oil on canvas, 21 1/4 x 27 1/2 ins / 54 x 70 cm) FRF 4,100.

FROMENT, Ferdinand Florentin
French, 19th century.
Active in Paris.
Engraver (wood).
Ferdinand Froment was a pupil of Linton and a member of the Société des Artistes Français from 1887. He received an honourable mention in 1889.

FROMENT, François
French, 17th century.
Active in Paris in 1690.
Painter, sculptor.

FROMENT, Georges
French, 18th century.
Active in Paris in 1753.
Painter, sculptor.

FROMENT, Jeanne
French, 20th century.
Painter. Landscapes with figures.
Jeanne Froment exhibited in Paris at the Salon des Artistes Indépendants from 1925.

FROMENT, Joël
French, 20th century.
Born 1938, in Versailles.
Sculptor, painter.
Neo-Constructivism.

Joël Froment exhibited in Paris, where he lives and works, notably during the 1980s and 1990s at the Salon des Réalités Nouvelles and in 1997 at the *Abstraction-Intégration* touring exhibition in Essonne.

FROMENT, Louis-Pierre
French, 19th century.
Active in Paris c. 1830.
Painter. History painting, portraits.

He was a pupil of Regnault.

FROMENT, Marie Émilie
French, 20th century.
Born 1891, in the Oise.
Painter, draughtswoman.

Marie Froment exhibited in Paris at the Salon des Artistes Français from 1922.

FROMENT, Nicolas
French, 15th century.
Born c. 1425, in Uzès (Gard); died between 1483 and 1486, in Avignon.
Painter.
Provençal School.

This important artist was painter to King René of Anjou in around 1461. He was known particularly for his two portraits showing King René and his wife, which now hang in the Louvre. Although now seen as a major figure in the school of early French painters, Nicolas Forment's works were unfortunately so little appreciated when Italian art became all the rage that many fine paintings were destroyed. Yet it was Nicolas Froment and Enguerrand Quarton (or Charonton) who introduced the new Flemish style with its raw realism, so different from the soft elegance of Italian art, into the artistic milieu created, thanks to the wealth of the merchant classes, around the papal court in Avignon. It should be remembered that the only French School existing at the time when the papacy left Avignon in 1417, and one that was entirely dominated by the influence of the Sienese School, was based in Provence, in towns like Avignon, Marseilles and Nice, the latter town belonging to the Duke of Savoy.

Little is known about Froment's life. He is recorded as being in Florence in 1461, where he may have painted *The Raising of Lazarus*, still in Florence, in the Uffizi. From 1468, he had the tenancy of a house in Avignon and he seems not to have moved from there. The triptych of the *Burning Bush* was commissioned by King René of Anjou in 1476 for the Carmelite church in Aix. The account books appear to indicate that he also designed some stained glass windows for the church. The triptych of the *Burning Bush* is full of symbolic details requiring detailed decoding. It is the Virgin, for example, and not God who appears to Moses, the bush that burns without being consumed being a symbol of Mary's virginity. The figures depicted are true portraits while the very specific landscape has a new sense of real nature, here imbued with the gentle air of the Mediterranean. In the period around 1450, Quarton and Froment gathered many followers around them, providing the basis of the realist tendency in the early Provençal School. Much appreciated at the time, these works were subsequently neglected until relatively recently. Quarton's retention of some of the decorative elements of Sienese art meant that he suffered a less harsh fate, but Nicolas Froment's work was considered crude, the draughtsmanship clumsy and the colours lacking in subtlety. What is interesting is that the art lovers of the time, the rich merchants and the prelates, fully understood the revolution brought about by Froment. Casting aside the amiability of Sienese art, he introduced the macabre, and in the place of a refined celestial world he substituted a sordid realism. This so-called 'crudeness' attributed to Froment can be seen in his very fine *Pietà* in Avignon and would be seen again in the work of Fouquet. It seems clear that, in order to paint his *Resurrection of Lazarus*, Froment painted a real corpse. A face like that given to Lazarus, the closed eyes seeming to see all the horrors of the next world, is not something an artist could invent. Those art historians who for so long declared that the few known works by Froment were inferior both in terms of composition and colour were applying criteria inherited from the most obscurantist academism that has always misunderstood genius, even that of the 15th century. It is true that his figures no longer smile and that the fabrics, once bright, are now dull and faded, but the figure of Lazarus still expresses all the terror of death and burial in the earth. This clumsiness of line and poverty of colour mayin fact be a first manifestation of what was to become, and remains today, the French style - profoundly attached to reality and full of anxiety about the human condition.

Two exhibitions, one at the Petit Palais in Paris in 1900 and the other an exhibition devoted to works by early medieval painters, helped promote a greater appreciation of Froment's remarkable qualities of realism and power of expression. Works by Froment shown at this second exhibition included his *Portrait of St Siffrein Bishop of Carpentras*, now in Avignon. Painted in egg tempera, it was for many years used as a lid to a chest in the church of Mazan. Also shown were *The Burning Bush Triptych*, *The Marteron Diptych* and *The Resurrection of Lazarus*. His work has been shown subsequently in other thematic exhibitions including, in 2002, *The Age of Jan Van Eyck: the Mediterranean world of early Netherlandish painting, 1430-1530* at the Groeningemuseum in Bruges.

BIBLIOGRAPHY:

Chamson, Lucie/Froment, Nicolas, *Nicolas Froment et l'école avignonnaise au XVe siècle*, Éd. Rieder, Paris, 1931. Marignane, M., *Nicolas Froment*, Éd. Albert Morancé, Paris, 1936. Vaudoyer, Jean-Louis, *Les peintres provençaux de Nicolas Froment à Paul Cézanne*, La Jeune Parque, Paris, 1947. *Les Primitifs français du XVe siècle*, Éd. du Chêne, Paris, 1950. Spears Grayson, M., '*The Northern Origin of Nicolas Froment's 'Resurrection of Lazarus' Altarpiece in the Uffizi Gallery*' in *Art Bulletin*, vol 58, 1976. Grayson, Marion Lou, *The documentary history of Nicolas Froment, French artist of the fifteenth century*, dissertation, Columbia University, New York, 1979. Nishino, Y., '*Le Triptyque du buison ardent de Nicolas Froment et son programme iconographique*' in *Artibus et Historiae*, vol 12, no. 24, 1991. Borchert, T., *The Age of Jan Van Eyck: the Mediterranean world of early Netherlandish painting, 1430 - 1530*, exhibition catalogue, Groeningemuseum, Bruges, Thames & Hudson, London, 2002.

MUSEUMS AND GALLERIES:

AIX-EN-PROVENCE (Cathédrale St-Sauveur): *Triptych of the Burning Bush* - AVIGNON: *Portrait of St Siffrein Bishop of Carpentras* - FLORENCE (Uffizi): *Raising of Lazarus* - PARIS (Louvre): *Portrait of King René of Anjou; Portrait of Queen Jeanne of Laval.*

AUCTION RECORDS:

PARIS, 1 July 1942, *Christ Blessing* (attributed) FRF 60,000. LONDON, 21 April 1967, *Portrait of a Man and his Wife*, Gns 7,000.

FROMENT, Simone Suzanne Marie
French, 20th century.
Born 1904, in Granville; died 1986.
Painter, lithographer. Religious subjects. Wall decorations, church decoration.

Simone Froment studied at the École des Beaux-Arts in Angers and in Paris. She studied under Maurice Denis and Georges Desvallière, probably at their Atelier d'Art Sacré (sacred art studio) and was awarded the Blumenthal prize in 1930.

Froment executed mural decorations in France for the Hôpital Broussais chapel (kept at the Musée de l'Assistance Publique) as well as in Switzerland, Great Britain, Germany and Papua.

FROMENT-DELORMEL, Jacques Victor Eugène
French, 19th century.
Born 17 June 1820, in Paris; died 1 March 1900, in Paris.
Painter, draughtsman, illustrator. Religious subjects, allegorical subjects, mythological subjects, genre scenes.

Jacques Froment-Delormel studied under Pierre Jules Jollivet, Paul Lecomte and Amaury-Duval. He settled in Autun (Saône-et-Loire) in 1846, but returned to Paris and set up his studio, together with Alfred Gobert and Philibert Mariller, in Boulevard Montparnasse. He was subsequently retained by the Sèvres Porcelain Factory from 1855 to 1886. Froment-Delormel exhibited at the Paris Salon from 1842 to 1880 and was made a Chevalier of the Légion d'Honneur in 1883.

Much of Froment-Delormel's work comprises mythological allegories, such as *Love Disarmed, Captive Love, The Graces, The Seasons, Almoner of Love, Dance of the Muses, Distress follows Pleasure, Art Consoles*, and so on. He was thus firmly anchored in the favourite themes of the Neoclassicists, although, thanks to a light and deft touch, he was able to avoid undue mawkishness. Mention should be made of other compositions by Froment-Delormel such as *Daisy, Nest, Farewell, Angel Intercessor, St Peter Curing a Cripple at the Gates of the Temple, Red Indians Preparing a Surprise Attack on an Enemy Camp* and *Pawnee Indians Encamped on the Banks of the Platte River*. Froment-Delormel also worked as an illustrator for Hetzel (alongside the engraver Eugène Froment, with whom Froment-Delormel is often confused).

BIBLIOGRAPHY:
Vuillemot, G. (ed.), *La Tradition d'Ingres à Autun*, exhibition catalogue, Musée Rolin, Autun, 1971.

MUSEUMS AND GALLERIES:
AUTUN (Mus. Rolin): *Angel Intercessor; Love Nourished by the Muse* - BOURGES: *Young Girl at the Well* (from a theme in Goethe's 'Faust') - DIEPPE: *Amicitia (Friendship); Captive Love* - LYONS (MBA): *Omphale*.

AUCTION RECORDS:
NEW YORK, 23 Jan 1903, *Cupids*, USD 250. NEW YORK, 12 Oct 1994, *Young Red Indian Children Playing on the Banks of the Platte River* (oil on canvas, 16 1/2 x 61 ins / 41.9 x 154.9 cm) USD 33,350.

FROMENT-MEURICE, Jacques Charles François Marie
French, 19th - 20th century.
Born 1864; died January 1948.
Sculptor. Animals. Monuments, busts.

Jacques Froment-Meurice came from a family of goldsmiths. He studied sculpture under Chapu and travelled in Europe and Africa, exhibiting regularly at the Paris Salon and receiving a commendation in 1892.

Froment-Meurice is best known as an animal sculptor and as part of the Art Nouveau movement. He produced a series of sculptures of donkeys known as *Les Gestes des Anes*. His work ranges from studies for monuments to busts, medallions and animals. He donated works to several museums, including Poitiers, Rouen and Chantilly. The Hébrard foundry produced *La Courbette* and *La Ruade* from his *Gestes des Anes* series.

MUSEUMS AND GALLERIES:
BAYONNE: *The Montargis Dog; Meissonier on his Horse, Rivoli* - CHANTILLY - POITIERS - ROUEN.

AUCTION RECORDS:
LYONS, 7 March 1983, *Amphitrite, Queen of the Sea* (sculpture in solid silver, h. 23 1/2 ins / 60 cm) FRF 28,000. PARIS, 27 March 1987, *Virgin with Lily* (gold and silver, h. 11 1/4 ins / 28.5 cm) FRF 128,000. PERTH, 30 Aug 1994, *Donkey Rearing Up* (bronze, h. 6 ins / 15.2 cm) GBP 1,035. PARIS, 22 March 2000, *Donkey Rearing Up* (brown patinated bronze, h. 7 ins / 18 cm) FRF 22,000. LONDON, 19 April 2000, *Bust of Chopin* (brown patinated bronze, h. 16 ins / 41 cm) GBP 1,500. LOKEREN, 11 May 2002, *Group of Four Ships* (silver, 9 x 11 ins / 22 x 28 cm) EUR 2,800.

FROMENTAL, Benoît
French, 19th century.
Active in Paris.
Painter.

Benoît Fromental was a member of the Société des Artistes Français from 1883.

FROMENTAL, Maximilien
French, 19th century.
Born in Paris.
Sculptor.

Maximilien Fromental received an honourable mention in 1899.

FROMENTAN, Jean
French, 17th century.
Sculptor.

Under the direction of Gilles Guérin, Jean Fromentan worked on the decorations at the château in Fontainebleau in 1640.

FROMENTEAU, Jacqueline
Swiss, 20th century.
Painter.

Patrick Waldberg featured the work of Jacqueline Fromenteau in the exhibition *Signs of a Surrealist Revival*, which he organised in Brussels in 1969.

FROMENTI
French, 20th century.
Born c. 1886, in Fontvieille; died January 1970.
Painter, potter.

FROMENTIN, Christine
French, 20th century.
Active in the USA.
Painter. Figures.

Christine Fromentin exhibited at group exhibitions including one at The Arnot Art Museum in New York in 1974-1975. She has also shown her work in solo exhibitions in Paris: in 1979 at the Galerie Liliane François; and in 1982 at the Galerie Jean Pierre Lavignes. Since 1978 she has exhibited in New York.

FROMENTIN, Eugène, or Fromentin-Dupeux
French, 19th century.
Born 24 October 1820, in La Rochelle; died 27 August 1876, in La Rochelle, in an accident.
Painter, draughtsman. Local scenes.
Orientalism.

Eugène Fromentin spent his early childhood years in La Rochelle, where his grandfather had served as a parliamentary advocate and his father - an occasional landscape painter - had worked as a doctor. Eugène's brother was destined for medical studies, whereas Eugène himself was earmarked to study law. During his studies at the *lycée*, Fromentin published poetry in local periodicals. At around the age of 20, he moved to Paris to commence his law studies; these he duly completed, graduating with a diploma and subsequently serving an internship as a solicitor's clerk.

Fromentin continued to be fascinated by literature, however, and contributed regular articles on that subject - and on poetry in particular - to various journals published in and around La Rochelle. He also wrote a critique of the 1845 Salon. Over time, he had developed a passion for painting, so much so that he decided to pursue it as a career - subject, that is, to his family (crucially, his father) giving consent. His father did agree, stipulating only that Eugène would be granted leave to break off his doctoral studies in order to become an artist - providing that he did so strictly by the book and submit to formal training. Accordingly, the would-be painter took courses with Rémond, only to leave the latter's studio less than a year later to study under Cabat, a teacher whose influence on him would subsequently be negligible, although Fromentin repeatedly expressed his gratitude to Cabat throughout his later life.

In 1844, Fromentin visited an exhibition of oriental paintings by Prosper Marilhat that left such an indelible impression on him that he decided to travel not to Rome, as he had originally intended, but (albeit briefly) to Algeria in the company of his close friend Armand du Mesnil, whose niece he was destined to wed soon after. In 1852, he travelled once again to Algeria, this time in the company of his young wife, and spent time successively in Mustafa, Biskra, and as far afield as Laghouat. At the time, orientalism was in full swing, with Belly, Dehodencq, Ziem, Tournemine, Guillaumet and others very much in the public eye.

Fromentin's Salon début would roughly coincide with the advent of the Second Empire, namely during a period of profound social change ushered in by the revolutionary upheavals of 1848. As it happened, Fromentin exhibited at the Salon for the very first time one year earlier, in 1847, when he was twenty-seven years old and between his two voyages to Algeria: he showed a *Landscape near La Rochelle* and two 'Algerian' studies: *Mosque near Algiers* and *Gorges of the Chiffa*. Two years later, he was awarded a silver medal. His submission to the 1850 Salon comprised eleven paintings of the countryside around Biskra. A third stay in Algeria lasted two full years and resulted in Fromentin bringing back not only countless sketches and drafts which he would later transpose to canvas but also two compositions which are beyond doubt among his finest work - *Summer in the Sahara* and a *Year in the Sahel*, which were shown in 1856 and 1858 respectively. These were followed by *Dominique* several years later. Fromentin was awarded a gold medal and made a Chevalier of the Légion d'Honneur in 1859; he received a further gold at the 1867 Exposition Universelle and was elevated to officer rank in the Légion in 1869. His celebrated *Falcon Hunt* was shown at the 1873 Salon and now hangs in the Louvre.

Fromentin's development following his schooling under Rémond And Cabat, both late classicists, may be compared with that of Corot (born in 1796 and Fromentin's senior by twenty-four years), whose studies under Bertin - a man very much in the Rémond mould - also started comparatively late. In the event, Corot painted figures and portraits and even historical subjects before establishing himself as a landscape artist. There, however, the analogy ends. As an orientalist, Fromentin followed in the footsteps of Decamps and Delacroix and did not hesitate to borrow from both. It should be recalled that his initial contacts with the East had been vicarious, namely as a result of the Marilhat exhibition, following which he immediately decided to experience for himself the Orient and what he himself termed its 'fascinating permasun'. That said, the manner in which he transposed the Orient to canvas was muted and temperate. What is more, this moderate vision of the East - which came naturally to him - would emerge as a principal reason for the public appeal of his work and as the touchstone for his success.

In a sense, it is true to claim that Fromentin painted only one painting, but a painting that was nevertheless constantly renewed, amended and perfected. His intention was never to shock or deceive; accordingly, his subject matter was rendered clearly and succinctly with, as it were, no 'rough edges'. An accomplished technician, Fromentin used his influences well, borrowing from the Dutch School, notably from Philips Wouwerman and even more so from the brilliant colours and careful proportions of Van der Meulen, and from Delacroix in order to develop a 'literary' narrative that is as effective as it is inoffensive. In later life, he painted from memory for the better part of twenty years, emerging, one might even suggest, as an illustrator of his own body of work.

Eug. Fromentin 1850

Stamp of sale

BIBLIOGRAPHY:

Fromentin: Le peintre et l'écrivain, 1820-1876, exhibition catalogue, Musée des Beaux-Arts, La Rochelle, 1970. Wright, B., *Eugène Fromentin: A Bibliography*, London, 1973. Fromentin, Eugène / Sagnes, Guy (ed.), *Œuvres complètes: Eugène Fromentin*, Coll. Bibliothèque de la Pléiade, Gallimard, Paris, 1984. Thompson, James, *Eugène Fromentin, Painter and Writer*, dissertation, University of North Carolina, Chapel Hill (NC), 1985 (doctorat). Thompson, J./Wright, B., *La Vie et l'Œuvre d'Eugène Fromentin*, ACR Édition, Paris, 1987. Wright, Barbara, *Eugène Fromentin: a life in art and letters*, Lang, Bern, 2000.

MUSEUMS AND GALLERIES:

BAYEUX: *River Nile* - BRUSSELS: *Land of Thirst* - CHANTILLY: *Arab Falconers* - DOUAI: *View of El Laghouat* - GENEVA (MAH): *Evening Prayer* - GRAZ: *Two Nocturnal Combats* - LA ROCHELLE: *Arab Horsemen; Fording a Stream; Hunting Gazelle; Attack on a Caravan; Arab on a Wall* (c. 1854-1857, oil on canvas) - MONTPELLIER: *Smala de Si Hamed Ben-Hadj* - MOSCOW (State Tretyakov Gal.): *Banks of the Nile* - NANTES (MBA): *Gazelle Hunt in the Chott el-Hodna* - PARIS (Louvre): *Falcon Hunt, Algeria; Arab Camp; Arab Women on the Banks of the Nile; Falcon Hunt; Horsemen's Halt; Moorish Burial; Fantasia; Arab Horsemen at the Halt* - RHEIMS: *Falcon Hunt* - RHEIMS (MBA) - ROUEN: *Three Seated Arabs; Bird; Woman Holding a Pruning Knife; Three Figures Seen from the Rear; Young Man Seated; Man Beating a Drum; Young Arab Girl; Seated Arab; Harvest-Time in Provence; Arab Standing.*

AUCTION RECORDS:

PARIS, 13 Feb 1891, *Alert*, FRF 30,000. PARIS, 6 May 1891, *Arab Horsemen*, FRF 13,000. PARIS, 28 Jan 1892, *Lion Hunt*, FRF 15,000. PARIS, 8-13 May 1892, *Centaurs*, FRF 17,500. PARIS, 16-17 June 1892, *Battle in a Mountain Gorge*, FRF 26,000. PARIS, 2 May 1894, *Arabs at the Fountain*, FRF 10,500. PARIS, 4 May 1896, *Arab Horsemen*, FRF 8,900. PARIS, 18-19 May 1897, *Chiffa Gorge*, FRF 56,000. NEW YORK, 10 April 1900, *Algiers*, USD 500. PARIS, 8 May 1900, *Halt*, FRF 3,500. PARIS, 11 June 1900, *Hunt*, FRF 23,000. PARIS, 26-27 May 1902, *Caravan*, FRF 31,000. NEW YORK, 9-11 March 1904, *Centaurs*, USD 4,500. NEW YORK, 27 Jan 1905, *Arabs on the Move*, USD 3,500. NEW YORK, 22-23 Feb 1907, *Caravan Encampment*, USD 8,500. LONDON, 21 May 1909, *Return from the Hunt*, GBP 651. PARIS, 4-5 Dec 1918, *Return of the Wounded*, FRF 2,800. PARIS, 18 Dec 1918, *Arab Camp* (pencil) FRF 105. PARIS, 3 Feb 1919, *Pasture Land near a Mosque,* FRF 3,300. PARIS, 22 May 1919, *Horsemen's Halt,* FRF 5,100; *Arab Horsemen Nearing a Town,* FRF 3,600. PARIS, 16-19 June 1919, *Smokers,* FRF 13,050; *Arabs at the Fountain,* FRF 6,000. PARIS, 8-9 Dec 1919, *Douar (Arab Village),* FRF 200. PARIS, 16-17 Dec 1919, *Clear Night,* FRF 7,400. PARIS, 4-5 March 1920, *Camels Lying Down,* FRF 310. PARIS, 14 May 1920, *Palazzo on a Canal in Venice,* FRF 7,350. PARIS, 27 May 1920, *Horse Trader,* FRF 16,100; *Caravan Halt,* FRF 42,200; *Nymphs and Faun,* FRF 5,300. PARIS, 3-4 June 1920, *Oued el-Akounn* (charcoal) FRF 125. PARIS, 20-30 Nov 1920, *Rocky Beach and Cliff* (watercolour) FRF 470. PARIS, 12 Feb 1921, *Family Scene on a Terrace above the Sea,* FRF 1,380. PARIS, 7 April 1921, *Camels at Rest,* FRF 220. PARIS, 3 and 4 Dec 1923, *Nomads,* FRF 15,600. PARIS, 7-9 April 1924, *Figures by the Sea,* FRF 6,200. PARIS, 19 May 1924, *Ford,* FRF 20,100. PARIS, 22 May 1924, *Falcon Hunt,* FRF 25,000. PARIS, 11 June 1924, *Arab Study; Standing and Sitting* (graphite, heightened with watercolour) FRF 320. LONDON, 11 July 1924, *Arab Camp,* GBP 5. PARIS, 17 Dec 1924, *Arab Camp* (pencil) FRF 175. PARIS, 6 March 1925, *Horses at the Trough,* FRF 4,000. PARIS, 5 Nov 1926, *Palazzo on a Canal in Venice,* FRF 2,000. PARIS, 29-30 Nov 1926, *Two Women Lying on the Ground* (pencil) FRF 650. PARIS, 9 Feb 1927, *Falconers,* FRF 410. PARIS, 3 Feb 1928, *Camp at Rocher de Sel (Salt Rock)* (heightened drawing) FRF 120. PARIS, 16 Feb 1928, *Old Shepherd,* FRF 260. PARIS, 26 June 1928, *Arab at the Fountain,* FRF 18,500. PARIS, 16 Nov 1928, *Arab Types* (drawing, study) FRF 410. PARIS, 5 Dec 1928, *Palm Trees at El-Laghouat,* FRF 430. LONDON, 21 June 1929, *Halt by the Nile,* GBP 131. PARIS, 2-3 July 1929, *Arab Horseman,* FRF 6,000. NEW YORK, 1 May 1930, *Arabs Watering their Horses,* USD 250. NEW YORK, 1 May 1930, *Arabs Watering their Horses,* USD 250. PARIS, 17 May 1930, *Souvenir of Algeria; Horses Presented to the Caid,* FRF 10,100. PARIS, 20 April 1932, *Odalisque* (graphite) FRF 105. NEW YORK, 5 May 1932, *Arab Camp,* USD 375. PARIS, 3 April 1933, *Arab Horsemen at Halt,* FRF 8,800. NEW YORK, 7-8 Dec 1933, *Alert,* USD 500. PARIS, 26-27 Feb 1934, *Stream in the Dale; Landscape Study at Sunset,* FRF 660. PARIS, 18 May 1934, *Grand Canal, Venice,* FRF 900. NEW YORK, 23 Nov 1934, *Falcon Hunt,* USD 1,125; *Desert Cavalcade,* USD 650. NEW YORK, 4 Jan 1935, *Hunt,* USD 700. PARIS, 28 May 1935, *Watering Trough,* FRF 7,600. LONDON, 6 March 1936, *Oasis,* GBP 40. PARIS, 14 April 1937, *Study of an Oriental Figure* (study) FRF 600. LONDON, 23 June 1937, *Landscape,* GBP 28. LONDON, 20 Feb 1942, *Arab Horseman* (graphite) FRF 380. LONDON, 15-16 June 1942, *Horse* (graphite, study) FRF 200. LONDON, 29 July 1942, *Landscape,* GBP 34. PARIS, 3 Feb 1943, *Turco on Horseback* (pen and graphite) FRF 810. PARIS, 12 March 1943, *Caid* (1874) FRF 12,500; *Horse Bath,* FRF 73,000; *Arab Types* (1874) FRF 28,000. PARIS, 12 April 1943, *Camel Drivers; Oasis* (forming a pair) FRF 3,000. PARIS, 2 June 1943, *Riders, Horses and Dogs* (six watercolours and drawings) FRF 8,100. PARIS, 5 July 1943, *Arab Restraining Two Greyhounds,* FRF 2,000. PARIS, 26 Nov 1943, *Landscape with Minaret* (lead pencil) FRF 550; *Shepherdess* (lead pencil) FRF 500; *Seated Arab* (charcoal drawing) FRF 350. NEW YORK, 2 March 1944, *Young Arab Boys Playing,* USD 300. PARIS, 20 March 1944, *Arab Horse* (graphite) FRF 750. NEW YORK, 4 May 1944, *Arab Combat,* USD 425. PARIS, 12 May 1944, *Sacred Wood (Blidah)* (graphite) FRF 250. PARIS, 17 May 1944, *Ambush* (1860) FRF 113,000. PARIS, 6 March 1945, *Pheasant* (attributed) FRF 650. NEW YORK, 18-19 April 1945, *Arabs Watering their Horses,* USD 7,700. PARIS, 16-17 May 1945, *Kabyles Leading Mules* (charcoal heightened with white) FRF 1,050. PARIS, 24 May 1945, *Shepherd and Flock* (lead pencil) FRF 800; *Valley of the Arcades* (1840, wash) FRF 420. NEW YORK, 20-21 Feb 1946, *Arabs,* USD 375. PARIS, July 1946, *Men and Dromedaries in front of a Tent, Algeria,* FRF 37,500; *Caravan Attack,* FRF 3,600; *Arab Horses Drinking,* FRF 37,100. PARIS, 4 Nov 1946, *Palm Trees* (attributed) FRF 1,500. PARIS, 7 Nov 1946, *Seated Arab* (lead pencil, heightened with chalk) FRF 1,050. PARIS, 20 June 1947, *Caravan at Halt in the Dunes,* FRF 90,000. PARIS, 4 July 1947, *Indigenous African (head study)* (pencil) FRF 1,400. PARIS, 9 July 1947, *Lion Hunt,* FRF 68,000. PARIS, 30 May 1949, *Slaves,* FRF 85,000. PARIS, 15 June 1954, *Egyptian Countryside,* FRF 220,000. LONDON, 5 July 1961, *Arabs Attacked by a Lioness,* GBP 450. VERSAILLES, 2 June 1965, *Arab Scene,* FRF 7,000. PARIS, 2 June 1971, *Arab Horsemen at Halt,* FRF 12,500. VERSAILLES, 17 Dec 1972, *Meeting of Arab Tribal Chiefs,* FRF 21,200. LONDON, 29 March 1973, *Arab Horsemen Attacked by a Lion,* GBP 2,500. LOS ANGELES, 9 April 1973, *Artist's Tent, Algeria,* USD 5,500. LONDON, 6 March 1974, *Arab Warriors at Rest,* GBP 1,600. ENGHIEN-LES-BAINS, 25 April 1976, *Arab Halt* (oil on panel, 24 3/4 x 19 3/4 ins / 63 x 50 cm) FRF 20,000. LONDON, 3 Nov 1977, *Horse Thieves at Night* (1865, oil on canvas, 51 3/4 x 80 ins / 131.5 x 203.5 cm) GBP 13,000. LONDON, 31 March 1978, *Landscape with Arab Horseman* (watercolour, 13 1/2 x 9 1/2 ins / 34 x 24 cm) GBP 1,800. ST-BRIEUC, 29 March 1981, *Arab Horseman* (1845, oil on panel, 14 1/4 x 11 ins / 36 x 27 cm) FRF 20,000. PARIS, 27 April 1983, *Horse (study)* (black chalk heightened with white/blue paper, 11 x 15 1/4 ins / 28 x 39 cm) FRF 7,800. MONTE CARLO, 5 March 1984, *Africa* (watercolour and wash, with rounded edges, 8 x 8 ins / 20.5 x 20.5 cm) FRF 7,000. NEW YORK, 25 Oct 1984, *Arab Horsemen Attacked by a Lion* (1872, oil on panel, 23 3/4 x 19 1/2 ins / 60.3 x 49.5 cm) USD 24,000. NEW YORK, 22 May 1985, *Gust of Wind in the Alfa Plains in the Sahara* (1864, oil on canvas, 46 x 64 ins / 116.8 x 162.8 cm) USD 115,000. PARIS, 10 Dec 1987, *Shepherd and Flock in the Shade of a Wall* (1857, watercolour, 4 1/4 x 5 1/4 ins / 10.5 x 13.5 cm) FRF 5,800. PARIS, 11 March 1988, *Two Young Arabs seen from the Rear* (watercolour/pencil outlines, 7 x 3 3/4 ins / 17.5 x 9.7 cm) FRF 7,500. NEW YORK, 25 May 1988, *Centaurs Practising Archery* (oil on canvas, 79 x 54 ins / 200.8 x 137.2 cm) USD 15,400. PARIS, 12 May 1989, *Oriental* (graphite drawing, 7 3/4 x 4 1/4 ins / 20 x 11 cm) FRF 4,000. NEW YORK, 24 May 1989, *Shimoom* (oil on canvas, 21 3/4 ins / 55.2 cm x 25 3/4 ins/65.4 cm) USD 99,000. NEW YORK, 24 Oct 1989, *Caravan on the Move Escorted by Arab Horsemen* (1875, oil on panel, 13 x 16 ins / 33 x 40.7 cm) USD 55,000. NEW YORK, 28 Feb 1990, *Arabs Leading their Horses to Water* (1873, oil on panel, 15 3/4 x 12 1/4 ins / 40 x 31.1 cm) USD 22,000. PARIS, 21 March 1990, *Arab (study)* (lead pencil/paper, 8 x 4 1/2 ins / 20.5 x 11.5 cm) FRF 12,000. NEW YORK, 22 May 1990, *Arab Horsemen* (oil on panel, 14 1/4 x 17 3/4 ins / 36.2 x 45 cm) USD 22,000. PARIS, 15 June 1990, *Falcon Hunt* (lead pencil and stump/outlines in red chalk, study, 15 1/4 x 11 1/2 ins / 39 x 29 cm) FRF 14,500. NEW YORK, 24 Oct 1990, *Arab Horsemen on Falcon Hunt* (oil on panel, 16 x 10 1/4 ins / 40.6 x 26 cm) USD 16,500. PARIS, 7 Nov 1990, *Ambush* (1868, oil on panel, 25 1/2 x 18 ins / 65 x 46 cm) FRF 160,000. NEW YORK, 22 May 1991, *Arab Horsemen in a Sudden Gust of Wind* (1857, oil on panel, 9 1/4 x 15 1/4 ins / 23.2 x 38.7 cm) USD 35,750. MONACO, 21 June 1991, *Landscape with Two Horsemen and a Bedouin and his Flock* (1873, oil on canvas, 18 x 25 3/4 ins / 45.5 x 65.5 cm) FRF 66,600. NEW YORK, 17 Oct 1991, *Audience at a Sahara Caliphate* (oil on panel, 13 1/2 x 20 1/2 ins / 34.3 x 52 cm, 2 3/4 ins/7 cm) USD 27,500. PARIS, 15 May 1992, *Woman* (black chalk, study, 10 1/2 x 14 3/4 ins / 26.9 x 37.6 cm) FRF 24,000. NEW YORK, 28 May 1992, *Horseman by the Banks of the Nile* (oil on panel, 10 3/4 x 15 ins / 27.3 x 38.1 cm) USD 20,900. MONACO, 20 June 1992, *Arab Horseman* (black and white chalk/beige paper, 8 3/4 x 6 ins / 22.5 x 15.5 cm) FRF 19,980. PARIS, 25 March 1993, *Seated Arab* (charcoal and white chalk, 10 3/4 x 9 ins / 27.5 x 23 cm) FRF 10,000. LONDON, 16 June 1993, *Arab Caravan in a Palm Grove* (1857, oil on panel, 19 3/4 x 39 1/4 ins / 50 x 100 cm) GBP 27,600. NEW YORK, 16 Feb 1994, *Falcon Hunt* (1872, oil on panel, 23 1/2 x 29 ins / 59.7 x 73.7 cm) USD 107,000. LON-

DON, 18 March 1994, *Horsemen Halt near El-Aghouat* (1857, oil on panel, 27 1/2 x 39 1/4 ins / 70 x 100 cm) GBP 67,500. PARIS, 22 April 1994, *Oasis during the Sirocco* (oil on canvas, 28 1/4 x 43 ins / 72 x 109 cm) FRF 400,000. NEW YORK, 16 Feb 1995, *Night Thieves, Algeria* (1865, oil on canvas, 52 x 80 1/4 ins / 131.8 x 203.8 cm) USD 277,500. PARIS, 12 May 1995, *Château de Lavardin* (1864, oil on panel, 11 x 15 1/4 ins / 27 x 39 cm) FRF 35,500. NEW YORK, 23-24 May 1996, *Arabs Attacked by a Lioness* (1868, oil on canvas, 56 x 40 1/2 ins / 142.2 x 102.9 cm) USD 167,500. LONDON, 13 June 1997, *Falcon Hunt in Algeria: The Quarry* (1863, oil on canvas, 32 1/4 x 23 ins / 81.6 x 58.6 cm) GBP 53,200. LONDON, 17 June 1999, *The Tombs of the Caliphs in Cairo* (oil on canvas, studio of Eugène Fromentin, 28 x 44 ins / 70 x 111 cm) GBP 45,000. LONDON, 13 Oct 1999, *Une alerte* (oil on canvas, 24 x 17 ins / 60 x 42 cm) GBP 22,000. PARIS, 20 Nov 2000, *Arab Horsemen Passing a Ford* (oil on panel, 11 x 14 ins / 27 x 35 cm) FRF 150,000. COLOGNE, 25 Nov 2000, *Bedouin Camp* (1871, oil on panel, 15 x 18 ins / 39 x 46 cm) DEM 56,000. LONDON, 21 June 2001, *River Crossing* (oil on canvas, 41 x 56 ins / 103 x 142 cm) GBP 30,000. NEW YORK, 31 Oct 2001, *The Horse Merchant* (1875, oil on canvas, 26 x 32 ins / 66 x 81 cm) USD 180,000. PARIS, 16 Dec 2002, *Horsemen and Horses Drinking at a River* (oil on canvas, 28 x 43 ins / 72 x 109 cm) EUR 37,000. NEUILLY, 19 Dec 2002, *Horsemen* (oil on canvas, 12 x 20 ins / 31 x 52 cm) EUR 27,000. PARIS, 16 June 2003, *Desert Encampment* (oil on canvas, 19 x 37 ins / 48 x 95 cm) EUR 21,000. NEW YORK, 29 Oct 2003, *Halt of Mule-drivers, Algeria* (1869, oil on panel, 18 x 22 ins / 46 x 55 cm) USD 24,000. PARIS, 3 June 2004, *Horsemen beside the Sea* (1873, oil on panel, 16 x 12 ins / 40 x 31 cm) EUR 25,000.

FROMENTIN, Gustave-Achille
French, 19th century.
Born 1818; died 1878.
Painter, draughtsman, watercolourist.

AUCTION RECORDS:
PARIS, 10 Dec 1919, *Courtyard behind some Old Houses* (watercolour) FRF 32. PARIS, 2-4 June 1921, *Camel Halt at Aïn Mahdi* (drawing) FRF 900.

FROMENTIN-DUPEUX, Pierre Samuel Toussaint
French, 19th century.
Born 3 June 1786, in Mauzé; died 19 December 1867, in La Rochelle.
Painter. Landscapes.

Fromentin-Dupeux was the father of Eugène Fromentin, and the pupil of Bertin.

MUSEUMS AND GALLERIES:
LA ROCHELLE: *Landscape*.

FROMILLER, Benedikt
German, 18th century.
Died 4 April 1726, in Klagenfurt (Carinthia, Austria).
Painter.

Benedikt was the father of Josef Ferdinand Fromiller.

FROMILLER, Johann Benedikt
German, 18th century.
Born 1696; died 1762.
Active in Klagenfurt (Carinthia).
Painter.

Johann Benedikt was the brother of Josef Ferdinand Fromiller.

FROMILLER, Josef Ferdinand
German, 18th century.
Born 1693; died 9 December 1760, in Klagenfurt (Carinthia, Austria).
Painter, engraver.

This artist, who was responsible for a large number of portraits and religious paintings, executed some important frescoes in Baroque style imitating the Carracci. He enjoyed a great reputation in his day, though this has receded in modern times. The museum at Klagenfurt holds some of his works.

FROMKNEHGT, Gottlieb Christian
German, 17th - 18th century.
Born in Breslau (now Wroclaw, Poland).
Painter.

Fromknehgt spent most of his life working in Prague.

FROMM, Friedrich Gustav Johann
German, 19th century.
Born in Breslau (now Wroclaw, Poland).
Painter. Landscapes.

Friedrich Gustav Fromm lived in Italy and France for a long time.

FROMM, Friedrich Joseph
German, 19th century.
Born 17 June 1795, in Cologne; died 4 August 1840, in Cologne.
Painter.

This artist, who studied in Cologne and Berlin, is known mainly as a collector.

FROMM, Kaspar
German, 19th century.
Active in Wiesentheid.
Sculptor.

Kaspar Fromm worked for the church in Grosslangheim in 1821.

FROMMANN, Alwine
German, 19th century.
Born 16 March 1800, in Jena (Thuringia); died 2 August 1875, in Jena.
Painter.

Alwine Frommann was reader to the Empress Augusta. She is mainly credited with flower paintings and book illustrations.

FROMMANN, Johanna Charlotte
Maiden name: Wesselhoeft
German, 18th - 19th century.
Born 17 June 1765, in Hamburg; died 9 September 1831, in Jena (Thuringia).
Draughtswoman, miniaturist.

The Goethe Museum in Weimar has a miniature by this artist. She was the mother of Alwine Frommann.

FROMMEL, Carl Ludwig
German, 19th century.
Born 29 April 1789, in Birkenfeld (Baden-Württemberg); died 6 February 1863, in Ispringen.
Painter, engraver. Landscapes.

Carl Frommel learned painting under Philipp Jacob Becker and engraving under Haldenwang. Having visited Paris and Italy, he settled in Germany and became a teacher of painting and engraving in Karlsruhe (Baden-Württemberg). In 1824 Frommel travelled to England and, along with H. Winckles, set up a steel engraving studio. In 1829 he was appointed director of the gallery in Karlsruhe.

His landscapes are pleasant and discerning. Notable works of his include *Vesuvius Erupting, Salzburg Cemetery, View of Rome, The Tasso House in Sorrento, View of Vesuvius, View of Mount Etna.*

AUCTION RECORDS:
LONDON, 20 June 1980, *Villa Maecenas, Tivoli* (oil on panel, 13 x 17 ins / 33 x 43.2 cm) GBP 500. STUTTGART, 10 Dec 1999, *Sawmill in Hollental near Freiburg* (watercolour and pencil, 17 x 22 ins / 44 x 57 cm) DEM 3,500. STUTTGART, 22 March 2001, *Wooded Landscape* (1854, oil on board, 14 x 18 ins / 35 x 46 cm) DEM 5,000. HEIDELBERG, 19 April 2002, *Pinie. Mon-*

astery on Gulf of Naples (Indian ink over pencil, a pair, 17 x 11 ins / 42 x 28 cm) EUR 3,600. COLOGNE, 22 May 2004, *Como* (1846, pencil heightened with white on paper/board, 11 x 15 ins / 28 x 38 cm) EUR 2,100.

FRÖMMEL, Johann Georg
German, 18th - 19th century.
Born in Fulnek.
Painter.

Johann Frömmel was a pupil of Sattler in Olmütz, Moravia (now Olomouc, Czech Republic). He is noted for an altarpiece executed for the church at Mankendorf.

FROMMEL, Otto
German, 19th century.
Born 9 January 1835, in Karlsruhe (Baden-Württemberg); died 21 July 1861, in Lichtenthal (Baden-Württemberg).
Painter, lithographer. Landscapes.

Otto was the son and pupil of Carl Ludwig Frommel. He completed his studies in Düsseldorf, France and Holland.

FROMMER, Esther Maria
German, 17th - 18th century.
Miniaturist, watercolourist.

Esther was the daughter of Wilhelm Frommer, and married the engraver W. Ph. Kilian.

FROMMER, Wilhelm
German, 17th century.
Active in Augsburg (Bavaria).
Draughtsman, engraver, miniaturist.

Wilhelm Frommer is known only for some engravings.

FROMONT, Claude
French, 18th century.
Active in Paris in 1759.
Painter, sculptor.

FROMONT, Jean Baptiste Michel
French, 18th century.
Active in Paris in 1785.
Painter, sculptor.

FROMONT, Pierre de. See **DEFROMONT Pierre**

FROMUND
German, 10th century.
Draughtsman, miniaturist.

This calligrapher, who worked at Tegernsee, illustrated a number of manuscripts with drawings and miniatures in the Byzantine style.

FROMUTH, Charles Henry
American, 19th - 20th century.
Born 1861, in Philadelphia; died 1937, in Concarneau (Finistère), France.
From 1889 active in France.
Painter, pastellist, draughtsman. Genre scenes, landscapes, seascapes.

Charles Henry Fromuth, who was the son of German immigrants, studied at the Philadelphia School of Fine Arts under Thomas Eakins. In 1889, he went to Paris to become a pupil of Tony Robert-Fleury and William Bouguereau at the Académie Julian. In 1890 he settled permanently in Concarneau.

While in Concarneau, Fromuth abandoned oils for charcoal heightened with colours, and, later, pastels, which he found more suitable for conveying the restless activity of the port. In 1930 he said, 'Movement is the keystone of my work, but without structure and strength movement is nothing. You cannot achieve it by technique, nor by simply painting what you see; you have to introduce it to your work by constant thought and application; in fact, by living it; there is no other way.'

He exhibited in Munich in 1897, where he received a second-class medal, and, in 1900, at the Paris Exposition Universelle, where he won a silver medal. He was a member of the Society of Pastellists, London, the Berlin Secession and the Société des Peintres de marine, Paris.

BIBLIOGRAPHY:
Hélène Ahrweiler, Roger Mandle, D. Scott Atkinson, William H. Gerdts, Carole L. Shelby, Jochen Wierich, *Lasting Impressions: American Painters in France 1865-1915*, exhibition catalogue, Musée d'Art américain, Giverny, Terra Foundation for the Arts, Evanston (IL), 1992.

MUSEUMS AND GALLERIES:
CHICAGO (Terra Foundation for American Art Collection): *Winter Morning Mist in Concarneau* (1892) - QUIMPER (MBA): *Boats Laid Up in Snow* (1897).

AUCTION RECORDS:
BREST, 13 Dec 1981, *Concarneau in Snow* (pastel and gouache, 29 1/2 x 26 3/4 ins / 75 x 68 cm) FRF 5,000. BREST, 18 Dec 1983, *Tuna Boats in Concarneau* (Oct. 1919, pastel, 15 3/4 x 13 3/4 ins / 40 x 35 cm) FRF 4,000. BREST, 17 May 1987, *Boats in Snow* (1909, pastel heightened with gouache, 17 3/4 x 13 1/2 ins / 45 x 34 cm) FRF 26,500. PARIS, 14 Dec 1988, *Tuna Boat in Concarneau* (Oct. 1919, pastel, 19 1/4 x 17 3/4 ins / 49 x 45 cm) FRF 22,000. BREST, 22 July 2000, *Boats under Sail* (1924, pastel, 12 x 10 ins / 30 x 26 cm) FRF 23,000. PARIS, 1 Dec 2000, *Fishing Boats* (pastel, 18 x 13 ins / 46 x 33 cm) FRF 21,500. BREST, 20 May 2001, *Concarneau, Enclosed Town and Sardine Boats* (1918, pastel, 18 x 16 ins / 45 x 41 cm) FRF 20,000. BREST, 20 May 2001, *The Red Sail* (pastel, 18 x 13 ins / 46 x 34 cm) FRF 28,000. BREST, 20 July 2002, *Sailing to Concarneau* (1904, pastel, 18 x 13 ins / 45 x 32 cm) EUR 4,000. BREST, 19 July 2003, *Wave Effect* (pastel, 8 x 12 ins / 21 x 31 cm) EUR 1,500. BREST, 21 Dec 2003, *Sails* (pastel, 29 x 18 ins / 73 x 45 cm) EUR 5,800. BOSTON, 2 May 2004, *Sailboats at Rest* (1906, pastel, 14 x 12 ins / 36 x 30 cm) USD 1,800.

FRONDAT, Napoléon-Charles-Louis
French, 19th century.
Born February 1846, in Paris.
Caricaturist.

He founded *La Puce en colère* (*The Furious Flea*) and contributed to *Grelot* (*The Bell*) and *Sifflet* (*The Whistle*).

FRONDAT, Th. de
French, 19th century.
Painter.

He exhibited at the Paris Salon in 1835 and 1837, and is remembered particularly for his genre composition entitled *Curé Visiting the Farm*.

FRONEN, Abraham
Flemish School, 17th century.
Active in Antwerp in 1610.
Watercolourist.

FRONHAUSEN, Lorenz
German, 16th century.
Active in Nordhausen (Thuringia).
Sculptor (wood).

As well as working in Nordhausen, Fronhausen was also active in Bleicherode (Thuringia).

FRONHOFER, Ludwig
German, 18th century.
Born 24 August 1746, in Ingolstadt (Bavaria); died 9 November 1800, in Munich.
Engraver.

Ludwig Fronhofer produced a dissertation on the study of engraving.

FRONIUS, Hans
Austrian, 20th century.
Born 1903.
Draughtsman, engraver, illustrator.

Hans Fronius illustrated or recounted in pictures fantasies of his own invention, usually characterised by Kafkaesque black humour.

AUCTION RECORDS:

VIENNA, 16 March 1982, *Harbour Scene* (1950, charcoal and chalk, 11 1/2 x 8 1/4 ins / 29.5 x 21 cm) ATS 8,000. VIENNA, 13 Sept 1983, *Circus Horses* (1967-1968, oil on canvas, 28 x 19 ins / 71 x 48 cm) ATS 50,000. VIENNA, 3 Dec 1986, *Istanbul* (1985, oil/hardboard, 20 1/2 x 22 1/2 ins / 52 x 57 cm) ATS 80,000. VIENNA, 22 Sept 1999, *Prostitutes* (1982, oil on canvas, 27 x 22 ins / 68 x 55 cm) ATS 150,000. VIENNA, 1 Dec 1999, *Meadow Landscape* (1966, oil on panel, 14 x 19 ins / 36 x 47 cm) ATS 100,000. VIENNA, 29 Nov 2000, *Harbour* (1964, oil on canvas, 23 x 30 ins / 58 x 76 cm) ATS 130,000. MUNICH, 1 Dec 2001, *My Mother* (1986, oil on board, 25 x 14 ins / 63 x 36 cm) DEM 15,000. MUNICH, 1 Dec 2001, *Tower Bridge* (1982, oil on board, 25 x 14 ins / 63 x 36 cm) DEM 26,000. VIENNA, 27 Nov 2002, *Poor Lazarus* (1979, oil on panel, 18 x 24 ins / 46 x 60 cm) EUR 7,000. VIENNA, 25 March 2003, *Evening Landscape* (1983, oil on panel, 22 x 27 ins / 55 x 68 cm) EUR 10,000. COLOGNE, 24 May 2003, *Still-life of Flowers* (1972, oil on masonite, 27 x 19 ins / 69 x 49 cm) EUR 8,000. VIENNA, 28 April 2004, *St Denis* (1982, oil on panel, 24 x 21 ins / 60 x 54 cm) EUR 16,000. VIENNA, 25 May 2004, *Toledo* (1978, oil on canvas, 20 x 28 ins / 51 x 70 cm) EUR 15,000.

FRONT, Henri
French, 20th century.
Born 8 June 1940, in Chalon-sur-Saône.
Painter.

Henri Front painted in a style similar to lyrical abstraction.

AUCTION RECORDS:

PARIS, 23 March 1988, *The Kassapiau Carpet* (1987, oil on paper, 19 3/4 x 25 1/2 ins / 50 x 65 cm) FRF 2,000.

FRONTEAU, François
French, 18th century.
Active in Paris in 1750.
Painter, sculptor.

FRONTI, Michel
French, 19th - 20th century.
Born 1 November 1862, in Marseilles.
Painter, pastellist.

Michel Fronti studied under Benjamin Constant and Jules Lefebvre after attending the École des Beaux-Arts in Marseilles. He exhibited at the Salon des Artistes Français, of which he was a member, and was awarded a silver medal in 1922.

FRONTIER, Jean Charles
French, 18th century.
Born 22 August 1701, in Paris; died 2 September 1763, in Lyons.
Painter.

A student of Claude-Guy Hallé, Jean Frontier painted mythological and religious subjects and exhibited work in Paris from 1743 to 1750, in particular *Moses and the Bronze Serpent* (1743, for the church of St Cross in Lyons, today at the church of St Peter in Lyons), *The Nativity* (1745, museum of Grenoble) and *St John's Sermon in the Desert.*

He was made an academician on 30 July 1744, for his *Prometheus Bound to the Caucasus* (now at the Louvre). He settled in Lyons in 1756 and was professor of drawing and then professor of painting at the École gratuite de dessin. In Lyons, he painted *Rebecca Giving a Drink to Abraham's Servant* (for the church of the Carthusians) and *David Playing the Harp* (for the church of St Anthony). He had the title of painter-in-ordinary to the king.

Froutier.

MUSEUMS AND GALLERIES:

GRENOBLE (Mus. de Grenoble): *The Nativity* (1745) - PARIS (Louvre).

FRÖR, Ch.
German, 18th - 19th century.
Born c. 1770, in Nuremberg; died 1832.
Painter, watercolourist. Landscapes.

FRORIEP, Berta
German, 19th century.
Born 16 May 1833, in Berlin.
Painter. Portraits, genre scenes.

Berta Froriep exhibited in Dresden and Berlin from 1870. She lived for the greater part of her life in Weimar (Thuringia).

FROSCH, Carl
German, 18th - 19th century.
Born 1771, in Halle (Saxony-Anhalt).
Engraver.

Carl Frosch lived most of his life in Leipzig and was predominantly a book illustrator and drawer of vignettes.

FROSCH, Moritz
German, 16th century.
Active in Feldkirch, Austria c. 1550.
Painter.

Moritz was probably the son of Sebastian Frosch. He painted religious works for the churches in his native Feldkirch area. He also worked in Innsbruck.

FROSCH, Sebastian
German, 16th century.
Active in Feldkirch, Austria c. 1510.
Painter.

Sebastian Frosch painted some works for the parish house in Hall.

FROSCHI, Giovanni de
Italian, 16th century.
Painter.

Froschi is thought to have been active in Brescia around 1500.

FRÖSCHL, Carl
Austrian, 19th century.
Born 23 August 1848, in Vienna; died 1934.
Painter, pastellist. Portraits, genre scenes.

Carl Fröschl studied at the academy in Vienna and was also a pupil of W. Diez in Munich. He was awarded two medals in Vienna in 1887 and 1889 and a bronze medal in Paris in 1900 at the Exposition Universelle.

AUCTION RECORDS:

VIENNA, 16 Sept 1969, *Siesta*, ATS 30,000. LONDON, 29 Nov 1984, *Group of Four Children* (pastel, 55 1/4 x 41 1/4 ins / 140.5 x 104.5 cm) GBP 5,300. LONDON, 18 March 1992, *Young Girl with a Bunch of Flowers* (pastel, 29 1/2 x 23 1/4 ins / 75 x 59 cm) GBP 9,900. MUNICH, 7 Dec 1993, *Young Girl with a Rabbit* (1883, pastel and gouache/paper, 24 1/4 x 18 3/4 ins / 61.5 x 47.5 cm) DEM 14,950. MUNICH, 27 Feb 1999, *Young Girl Seated at Table Sewing* (1879, oil on canvas, 37 x 22 ins / 93 x 57 cm) DEM 6,000. BERN, 3 Nov 1999, *Girl in Red Dress before Screen* (pastel, 46 x 31 ins / 118 x 79 cm) CHF 7,000. CEDAR FALLS, 1 Dec 2001, *Madonna and Child* (oil on board, 8 x 12 ins / 20 x 30 cm) USD 1,700. CEDAR FALLS, 1 Dec 2001, *Madonna and Child* (oil on board, 6 x 5 ins / 15 x 13 cm) USD 5,400. MUNICH, 4 Dec 2002, *Girl with Bouquet of White Flowers* (pastel, 35 x 22 ins / 89 x 56 cm) EUR 1,800.

FRÖSCHL, Daniel, or Froeschl
German, 16th - 17th century.
Born 1563; died 15 October 1613, in Prague.

Miniaturist, painter. Botanical subjects.
Prague School.

Between 1597 and 1604, Fröschl worked in the service of the Grand Duke of Tuscany, Ferdinand I de' Medici. A passionate botanist, Ferdinand had his extensive collection of plants illustrated by a number of different artists; Daniel Fröschl painted two views of a *Sunflower* for him, showing this plant, only recently introduced into Tuscany from Peru, from the front and from behind. Fröschl also worked as a miniaturist for Emperor Rudolph II in Prague, receiving, from 1603 onwards, a salary of 15 florins a month. He was subsequently appointed 'Guardian of His Majesty's Antiquities' (according to Doppelmayer). Between 1607 and 1611, he carried out an inventory of the *Kunstkammer* (Art Chamber) that housed Rudolph's collection of art and curiosities. He painted reduced versions of some of the items in the collection.

The work of this artist has appeared in several group or thematic exhibitions, including: *The Flowering of Florence: Botanical Art for the Medici,* National Gallery of Art, Washington, 2002; *Praga Magica. L'Art à Prague au temps de Rodolphe II* (*Praga Magica. Art in Prague under Rudolph II*), Musée Magnin, Dijon, 2002.

BIBLIOGRAPHY:

DaCosta Kaufmann, Thomas, *L'École de Prague,* Flammarion, Paris, 1985. Trnek, Helmut, '*Daniel Fröschl. Kaiserlicher Miniatormahler und Antiquarius*' in *Exotica. Jahrbuch des Kunsthistorischen Museums Wien,* Vienna, 2001. Tongiorgi Tomasi, Lucia/Hirschauer, Gretchen A., *The Flowering of Florence: Botanical Art for the Medici,* exhibition catalogue, National Gall. of Art, Washington DC, 2002. *Praga Magica. L'Art à Prague au temps de Rodolphe II,* exhibition catalogue, Musée Magnin, Dijon, Réunion des musées nationaux, Paris, 2002.

FRÖSCHLE, Jakob

German, 18th century.
Born 20 February 1742, in Krumbach (Swabia, Baden-Württemberg); died 26 April 1782, in Krumbach.
Fresco artist.

Jakob Fröschle executed ceilings for several churches in Swabia, such as Bad Wörishofen, Haupeltshofen, Tussenhausen, Ursberg.

FROSINO, Battista di. See **GIOVANNI BATTISTA DI FROSINO**

FROSNE, Jean

French, 17th century.
Born c. 1630, in Paris; died after 1676.
Engraver.

Jean Frosne engraved portraits and plates illustrating ornaments and landscapes. As his prints bear only his name, it is likely that the engravings were produced from his own drawings.

FROSSARD, Émilien

French, 19th century.
Born 1802; died 1881.
Painter, watercolourist, draughtsman. Landscapes.

He worked from 1848 as a pastor in Bagnères-de-Bigorre (Hautes-Pyrénées), leaving in 1855 to coordinate the Protestant chaplaincy in the East at the time of the Crimean War. He participated in the *Les Pyrénées romantiques* (*Romantic Pyrenées*) exhibition of 1879. Emilien Frossard was a passionate geologist with a particular fascination for natural phenomena in the mountain regions of France. He produced numerous watercolour and crayon views of the Pyrenées, which are distinguished by their accuracy and attention to detail.

FROSSARD, G.

French, 19th century.
Born in Marseilles.
Painter. Portraits.

MUSEUMS AND GALLERIES:

SÈTE: *Portrait of Carlotta Patti.*

FROST, Anna

American, 20th century.
Born 1873, in Brooklyn; died 1955.
Painter, teacher.

Anna Frost was a member of several societies.

FROST, Arthur

American, 20th century.
Born probably between 1880 and 1885.
Also active in France.
Painter.

Arthur Frost was probably not the Arthur Burdett Frost born in 1851, but very little record of the artist exists. René Huyghe, in *Les Contemporains* (*The Contemporaries*), recalls that, from 1913, Frost exhibited in Paris at the Salon des Indépendants with Patrick Henry Bruce and Kupka among the Orphists surrounding Delaunay. And Michel Seuphor, in *Le Style et le Cri* (*The Style and the Cry*), also remembers this colleague and disciple of both Bruce and Delaunay, who may have died young and who left practically nothing but a reproduction in the 1914 review *Montjoie* of a painting that looks similar to Delaunay's *Simultaneous Discs.* With Macdonald-Wright, Morgan Russell and a few others, Bruce and Frost were among the first generation of abstract American painters, who only achieved recognition after World War II.

AUCTION RECORDS:

NEW YORK, 10 June 1976, *Study for Sorcery* (watercolour, 11 1/2 x 16 1/2 ins / 29.5 x 42 cm) USD 650.

FROST, Arthur Burdett

American, 19th - 20th century.
Born 17 January 1851, in Philadelphia; died 1928.
Painter (gouache), watercolourist, draughtsman, illustrator, cartoonist. Sporting subjects.

Arthur Burdett Frost painted mainly hunting scenes and worked as an illustrator for, among others, Lewis Carroll.

BIBLIOGRAPHY:

Smolderen, Thierry (preface), *L'Anthologie A. B. Frost,* Éd. de l'An 2, Angoulême, 2003 (bilingual French-English edition).

AUCTION RECORDS:

NEW YORK, 7-8 Jan 1947, *Breaking the Ice* (watercolour/paper) USD 1,550. NEW YORK, 28 Jan 1970, *Still-life,* USD 1,100. NEW YORK, 28 April 1978, *The Circus* (gouache, 14 1/2 x 20 ins / 37 x 51 cm) USD 2,200. NEW YORK, 19 June 1981, *West Village* (1880, pencil and gouache/paper, 10 x 13 ins / 25.4 x 33 cm) USD 750. NEW YORK, 8 June 1984, *Cautious Approach* (watercolour heightened with white, 11 x 14 ins / 28 x 35.5 cm) USD 17,000. NEW YORK, 1 Nov 1984, *Point of Honor* (pencil and charcoal, 16 x 20 1/2 ins / 40.8 x 52 cm) USD 850. NEW YORK, 30 Sept 1985, *Words of Wisdom* (pen and wash/mounted paper/card, 19 3/4 x 14 ins / 50 x 35.5 cm) USD 5,500. NEW YORK, 30 May 1986, *The Rural Pest* (watercolour and grisaille gouache/board, 19 x 26 ins / 48 x 65.2 cm) USD 8,000. NEW YORK, 18 Oct 1989, *Quail Shooting* (wash and gouache/paper, 11 1/2 x 14 1/2 ins / 29.2 x 36.8 cm) USD 60,500; *Fall of a Wounded Woodcock* (watercolour and gouache/paper, 13 1/2 x 21 1/2 ins / 34.2 x 54.6 cm) USD 85,250. NEW YORK, 23 May 1990, *Quail Shooting* (watercolour, gouache and pencil in grisaille/tinted paper, 15 1/2 x 19 ins / 39.2 x 48.2 cm) USD 19,800. NEW YORK, 10 March 1993, *Shot at Pheasant* (1901, watercolour and grisaille gouache/board, 25 3/4 x 17 ins / 65.4 x 43.2 cm) USD 17,250. NEW YORK, 26 May 1993, *Political Talk* (watercolour, gouache and pencil in grisaille/paper/board, 18 1/4 x 25 3/4 ins / 46.3 x 65.3 cm) USD 7,475. NEW YORK, 22 Sept 1993, *Shoot, Shoot, man - Why don't you shoot* (ink and grisaille gouache/board, 19 1/4 x 21 1/2 ins / 48.7 x

54.7 cm) USD 15,525. NEW YORK, 31 March 1994, *A Strategic Movement* (ink and pencil/paper, 20 1/2 x 16 1/2 ins / 51.8 x 41.6 cm) USD 1,380. NEW YORK, 25 May 1995, *Circus in a Town* (gouache/paper, 17 1/2 x 26 1/2 ins / 44.5 x 67.3 cm) USD 5,750. NEW YORK, 14 Sept 1995, *On a Point* (gouache/paper, 16 x 24 1/2 ins / 40.6 x 62.2 cm) USD 36,800. NEW YORK, 3 Dec 1997, *Elk Ahead* (gouache/board, 12 x 15 ins / 30.5 x 38.1 cm) USD 27,600.

FROST, Cyril James
British.
Painter. Portraits.

Frost was a student at Croydon School of Art. He shows with different groups.

FROST, George
British, 18th - 19th century.
Born c. 1754, in Barrow (Suffolk); died 28 June 1821, in Ipswich.
Painter. Landscapes.

George Frost was an amateur artist who imitated Gainsborough and was a close friend of Constable.

MUSEUMS AND GALLERIES:
GLASGOW (Gal.): sketch.

AUCTION RECORDS:
NEW YORK, 1 May 1930, *Near Ipswich,* USD 225. LONDON, 29 June 1972, *Working in the Fields,* Gns 420.

FROST, George Albert
American, 19th century.
Born 27 December 1843, in Boston; died 1907, in Cambridge.
Painter. Landscapes.

George Albert Frost was a pupil of R. de Keyser at the Royal Academy of Belgium.

AUCTION RECORDS:
NEW YORK, 25 Jan 1980, *View of Novgorod* (oil on canvas, 20 x 30 ins / 51 x 76 cm) USD 2,200. LONDON, 16 Oct 1987, *View of the Cornhill, Ipswich* (oil on canvas, 17 x 24 ins / 43.2 x 61 cm) GBP 2,600. MIAMI, 22 April 2001, *Mountain Landscape* (oil on canvas, 26 x 40 ins / 66 x 102 cm) USD 4,000. BOSTON, 22 March 2002, *Lovell, Maine* (1893, oil on canvas) USD 1,500. BOSTON, 16 May 2003, *Home Stretch, a Dog Sledding Scene* (1896, watercolour and graphite, 13 x 17 ins / 32 x 44 cm) USD 2,000. EAST DENNIS, 5 Aug 2004, *Fall Landscape* (oil on canvas, 15 x 27 ins / 38 x 69 cm) USD 3,900.

FROST, H.
British, 20th century.
Active in London.
Painter.

AUCTION RECORDS:
LONDON, 21 Nov 1930, *The 'Speedwell' Pursuing the 'Aquila',* GBP 5.

FROST, James
British, 18th century.
Painter. Landscapes.

James Frost exhibited on 37 occasions at London's Free Society between 1766 and 1783.

FRÖST, Johann
German, 18th century.
Sculptor.

Fröst decorated the church at Uderwangen in Prussia (now Chekhovo, Poland).

FROST, John
American, 20th century.
Born 14 May 1890, in Philadelphia; died 1937.
Painter. Landscapes.

John Frost was awarded several distinctions by artists' associations in California.

John Frost

AUCTION RECORDS:
NEW YORK, 11 March 1981, *Wester Summer* (1919, oil on canvas, 23 3/4 x 28 ins / 60.5 x 71 cm) USD 1,100. LOS ANGELES-SAN FRANCISCO, 7 Feb 1990, *Desert in Bloom* (1922, oil on canvas, 27 x 32 ins / 68.5 x 81 cm) USD 44,000. LOS ANGELES, 29 April 1999, *Meadow in Sierras* (1929, oil on canvas, 30 x 36 ins / 76 x 91 cm) USD 15,000. PASADENA, 19 Oct 1999, *Wooded Landscape with Flower Field in the Foreground* (1913, oil on canvasboard, 16 x 12 ins / 41 x 30 cm) USD 3,250. PASADENA, 14 Nov 2000, *Indian Shack with Figure in a Landscape* (1921, oil on canvas, 27 x 32 ins / 69 x 81 cm) USD 47,500. PASADENA, 19 June 2001, *Atmospheric Landscape* (1920, oil on canvas, 13 x 16 ins / 33 x 41 cm) USD 10,000. NEW YORK, 28 Nov 2001, *Palm Springs* (1913, oil on canvas, 28 x 24 ins / 71 x 61 cm) USD 80,000. SAN FRANCISCO, 9 June 2002, *Indian Shack* (oil on canvas, 27 x 32 ins / 69 x 81 cm) USD 110,000. BOSTON, 22 Nov 2002, *Sunlight Study, California Scene* (1923, oil on canvas, 24 x 28 ins / 61 x 71 cm) USD 70,000. PASADENA, 18 Feb 2003, *Desert Landscape* (1921, oil on canvasboard, 18 x 20 ins / 46 x 51 cm) USD 22,500. EAST DENNIS, 21 Nov 2003, *Buckboard and Two Horses under Trees against Lavender Mountains and Sunset* (oil on canvas, 24 x 28 ins / 61 x 71 cm) USD 80,610. MILFORD, 6 May 2004, *Tranquil Reflections* (1935, oil on board, 19 x 23 ins / 48 x 58 cm) USD 17,000. HAYDEN, 24 July 2004, *Live Oaks* (1921, oil on canvas, 32 x 40 ins / 81 x 102 cm) USD 300,000.

FROST, Joseph
Australian, 20th century.
Painter (gouache). Landscapes with figures.

AUCTION RECORDS:
SYDNEY, 2 Dec 1991, *Circular Quay* (gouache, 6 3/4 x 9 ins / 17 x 22 cm) AUD 1,400; *Balmoral Beach* (gouache, 6 1/4 x 9 ins / 16 x 22 cm) AUD 1,400. SYDNEY, 29-30 March 1992, *River Crossing* (gouache, 7 x 7 ins / 18 x 18 cm) AUD 1,500. SYDNEY, 15 Nov 1999, *Endeavour at Dusk* (oil on board, 14 x 18 ins / 35 x 45 cm) AUD 3,500. SYDNEY, 15 Nov 1999, *Anthill Park Country Club* (oil on board, 24 x 33 ins / 61 x 84 cm) AUD 4,250. SYDNEY, 27 March 2000, *Entrance to Port Jackson* (oil on canvas, 14 x 16 ins / 35 x 40 cm) AUD 3,500. MELBOURNE, 2 May 2002, *In the Mist* (oil on canvas, 17 x 22 ins / 44 x 55 cm) AUD 2,800.

FROST, Julius. H.
American, 19th century.
Born 11 July 1867, in New Jersey; died 1934.
Painter, sculptor.

Julius H. Frost, a self-taught artist, was a member of the Society of Independent Artists and the American Federation of Arts.

FROST, Terry, or Terence Ernest Manitou Frost
British, 20th century.
Born 1915, in Leamington Spa; died 2003.
Painter.

Terry Frost originally worked in radio. He was taken prisoner during World War II and found himself in the same camp as Adrian Heath who introduced him to painting in 1943. Liberated and demobbed in 1945, Frost continued his artistic training with the St Ives group where he met Ben Nicholson and Barbara Hepworth. He became their assistant. He also met Victor Pasmore who was to have an important influence on his work. The friends Frost made and the influences he received led him in the direction of abstraction. However, he almost never abandoned a final link with the appearance of reality, which is suggested by angular and curved forms, landscapes and human, animal and horse forms. He painted in touches of thick pigment or washes, giving the painted surface an uneven, rough appearance and using basic colours (the six colours of the light spectrum) and browns and neutral greys, exploiting the sensations associated with the perception of colour: spatial and synesthetic sensations that can be associative and tactile. Although often close to abstraction, Frost's work still retains a spontaneous freshness.

He exhibited in group exhibitions in 1958 at the Guggenheim Museum, New York, in 1955 and 1958 at the Carnegie Foundation, Pittsburgh, and in 2003 in the *Painting Not Painting* exhibition at Tate St Ives. He exhibited solo in London from 1952 and in New York from 1960. In 2000, he had a retrospective, *Terry Frost, Six Decades*, at the Royal Academy in London.

BIBLIOGRAPHY:

Knowles, Elizabeth/Lewis, David, *Terry Frost: a personal narrative*, Scolar P., Aldershot, 1994. Stephens, Chris, *Terry Frost*, Tate Pub., London, 2000. *Terry Frost, Six Decades*, exhibition catalogue, Royal Academy of Arts, London, 2000.

MUSEUMS AND GALLERIES:

LEEDS (City AG): *Brown Verticals* (1958-1959, oil on canvas) - LONDON (National Portrait Gal.): *Sir Terence ('Terry') Frost* (1947, oil/panel, self-portrait) - LONDON (Tate Collection): *Brown and Yellow* (c. 1951-1952, oil/panel); *Black and White Movement* (1952, oil/panel); *Khaki and Lemon* (1956, oil on canvas); *Winter 1956, Yorkshire* (1956, oil/panel); *Yellow Triptych* (1957-1959, oil/panel); *May 1962 (Stays)* (1962, oil and collaged canvas/canvas); *R. B. and W. Spiral for A.* (1991, oil and acrylic/canvas); around 50 works/paper.

AUCTION RECORDS:

LONDON, 14 June 1971, *Painting* (1964) GBP 150. LONDON, 5 March 1980, *Orange and Yellow* (1960, watercolour heightened with gouache, 15 1/2 x 21 ins / 39.5 x 53.5 cm) GBP 230. LONDON, 30 Nov 1982, *December* (1968, acrylic/canvas, 59 3/4 x 40 ins / 152 x 101.5 cm) GBP 300. LONDON, 5 Dec 1985, *Ochre and Grey* (1962, oil on canvas, 60 1/2 x 60 ins / 153.5 x 152.5 cm) GBP 5,000. LONDON, 25 Feb 1988, *Composition* (1961, watercolour/paper, 22 3/4 x 15 1/4 ins / 58 x 39 cm) GBP 418. LONDON, 9 June 1988, *Verticals* (1959, oil on canvas, 35 1/2 x 23 1/2 ins / 90 x 60 cm) GBP 1,540. LONDON, 29 July 1988, *Seated Woman* (1975, pencil and wash, 26 1/2 x 10 1/4 ins / 67.5 x 26.3 cm) GBP 858. LONDON, 9 June 1989, *Mars Yellow* (1959, oil on canvas, 25 x 30 ins / 63.5 x 76.3 cm) GBP 4,950. LONDON, 9 March 1990, *Whirlwind* (1958, oil on card, 18 x 33 ins / 45.5 x 83.9 cm) GBP 6,600. LONDON, 24 May 1990, *The Three Graces* (1960, oil on canvas, 76 x 48 3/4 ins / 193 x 124 cm) GBP 15,400. LONDON, 9 Nov 1990, *Black and White Painting* (1959, oil on canvas, 59 3/4 x 40 1/4 ins / 152 x 102 cm) GBP 13,200. LONDON, 25 Jan 1991, *Cyclists Crossing on Albert Bridge Road* (1948, oil on panel, 9 1/2 x 7 ins / 24 x 18 cm) GBP 1,430. LONDON, 8 March 1991, *Black Form with Blue and Red* (oil on card, 49 x 49 ins / 124.5 x 124.5 cm) GBP 9,020. LONDON, 7 June 1991, *Umber and Ochre* (1961, oil on canvas, 24 1/2 x 30 ins / 62 x 76 cm) GBP 3,300. LONDON, 8 Nov 1991, *Umber and Grey Form* (1957, oil on card, 34 3/4 x 17 ins / 88.5 x 43 cm) GBP 2,750. LONDON, 11 June 1992, *Blue, Black and White, May 59* (oil on canvas, 60 x 36 ins / 152.5 x 91.5 cm) GBP 6,050. LONDON, 26 March 1993, *Heart Collage* (1987, oil and collage/paper, 41 x 47 1/4 ins / 104 x 120 cm) GBP 2,530. LONDON, 25 Nov 1993, *Red and Yellow* (1973, acrylic/canvas, 84 x 60 ins / 213.6 x 152.6 cm) GBP 6,325. LONDON, 25 Oct 1995, *Figure* (1957, oil on card, 34 3/4 x 17 1/4 ins / 88.4 x 43.8 cm) GBP 2,645. LONDON, 23 Oct 1996, *Blue and Black Verticals* (1957, oil on card, 84 x 63 ins / 213.5 x 160 cm) GBP 6,325. LONDON, 11 Dec 1997, *Spiral for Blue* (1994, oil on canvas, 17 x 17 ins / 43.2 x 43.2 cm) GBP 920. LONDON, 5 March 1999, *Yellow and Purple* (oil on canvas, 48 x 48 ins / 122 x 122 cm) GBP 6,500. LONDON, 5 Nov 1999, *Brown and Orange* (1960, oil on canvas, 24 x 48 ins / 61 x 122 cm) GBP 6,500. LONDON, 9 June 2000, *Big Blue* (oil on board, 48 x 48 ins / 122 x 122 cm) GBP 14,500. LONDON, 9 June 2000, *Earth Figure* (1959, oil on canvas, 36 x 60 ins / 91 x 152 cm) GBP 15,000. PENZANCE, 24 April 2001, *Composition - in Blue and Grey* (oil on canvas, 30 x 30 ins / 76 x 76 cm) GBP 11,500. LONDON, 8 June 2001, *Black and White, 1959* (oil and collage on canvas, 25 x 30 ins / 63 x 76 cm) GBP 9,500. LONDON, 4 July 2002, *July Red* (oil on canvas, 20 x 25 ins / 51 x 63 cm) GBP 7,500. LONDON, 4 June 2003, *Yellow Chevron for Blue* (1956, oil on canvas, 48 x 29 ins / 122 x 74 cm) GBP 17,000. LONDON, 21 Nov 2003, *Blue and Red - Harbour* (oil on canvasboard, 24 x 30 ins / 61 x 76 cm) GBP 12,500. LONDON, 15 June 2004, *Blue and White Figure* (1959, oil and charcoal on canvas, 42 x 29 ins / 106 x 73 cm) GBP 25,000. LONDON, 17 Nov 2004, *Yellow Quay* (1952, oil on board, 19 x 10 ins / 48 x 25 cm) GBP 38,000.

FROST, William Edward

British, 19th century.

Born 1810, in Wandsworth; died 4 June 1877, in London.

Painter. History painting, figures.

William Edward Frost worked at the Sass Academy and the Royal Academy. He enrolled at the latter institution in 1829 and was awarded a gold medal for his *Prometheus Bound* of 1829. He was greatly influenced by the works of William Etty and, after working as a portrait painter for 14 years, abandoned the genre to follow in Etty's footsteps. He was awarded a prize of 100 GBP at the Westminster Hall competition of 1843 for his *Nymph Surprised by Fauns*. He was elected to associate membership of the Royal Academy in 1846, but it was not until 1871 that he was admitted to full membership following the submission of a work entitled *Nymph and Cherub*. His best work is generally held to include *Sabrina* (1843), *Wood Nymphs* (1847), *Dance* (1861) and *Puck* (1869).

MUSEUMS AND GALLERIES:

DUBLIN: *Nymphs Dancing* - LONDON (Victoria and Albert Mus.): *Male Study*; *Female Study*; *Contemplation* (female head).

AUCTION RECORDS:

PARIS, 1859, *Diana and Acteon*, FRF 17,550. LONDON, March 1861, *Wood Nymphs Surprised while Bathing*, FRF 9,415. LONDON, April 1863, *Euphrosyne*, FRF 20,510; *Sirens*, FRF 7,350. LONDON, March 1875, *Aurora and Zephyr*, FRF 9,970. LONDON, 11 April 1908, *Bacchanale*, GBP 14. LONDON, 4 April 1910, *Seascape*, GBP 23. LONDON, 10 June 1910, *Panope* (1862) GBP 48. LONDON, 1 June 1923, *Cupid Disarmed*, GBP 15. LONDON, 17 Dec 1928, *Sirens*, GBP 8. LONDON, 13 June 1929, *Cupid's Games*, GBP 21. LONDON, 12 May 1932, *Cupid Disarmed*, GBP 15. LONDON, 21-24 Feb 1936, *Scene from Milton's Comus*, GBP 5. LONDON, 30-31 July 1936, *Diana and her Suitors*, GBP 13. LONDON, 17 Dec 1937, *Chastity*, GBP 5. LONDON, 20 Dec 1940, *Bathers*, GBP 25. LONDON, 23 Dec 1943, *Bather*, GBP 31. LONDON, 20 July 1945, *Nude*, GBP 63. LONDON, 12 Dec 1972, *Sirens*, GBP 520. LONDON, 27 March 1973, *Sirens* (1849) GBP 2,400. LONDON, 13 Oct 1978, *Sabrina* (1845, oil on canvas, 44 x 71 1/2 ins / 112 x 181.6 cm) GBP 10,000. LONDON, 26 Nov 1982, *Chastity* (oil on canvas, 48 x 72 ins / 122 x 182.8 cm) GBP 4,500. LONDON, 15 March 1983, *Panope* (1862, oil on canvas, 28 x 36 ins / 71 x 91.5 cm) GBP 2,800. LONDON, 12 April 1985, *Panope* (1862, oil on canvas, 27 1/2 x 35 1/2 ins / 70 x 90 cm) GBP 5,000. LONDON, 15 June 1988, *Nymph Bathing* (oil on panel, 16 x 11 1/2 ins / 40.5 x 29 cm) GBP 2,420. LONDON, 26 May 1989, *Portrait of a Young Boy in a Green Coat and White Trousers, Seated and Reading a Book* (1840, oil on canvas, 28 1/4 x 22 1/2 ins / 71.8 x 57.2 cm) GBP 4,400. LONDON, 26 Sept 1990, *Grape Harvest* (oil on card, 7 3/4 x 6 ins / 20 x 15 cm) GBP 1,540. NEW YORK, 26 May 1992, *Sirens* (oil on panel, 5 x 7 1/2 ins / 12.8 x 19 cm) USD 1,760. LONDON, 5 Sept 1996, *Water-Nymph* (oil on canvas, 34 x 21 ins / 86.4 x 53.3 cm) GBP 6,900. LONDON, 7 Nov 1996, *Rape of Hylas* (oil on canvas, 13 x 10 1/4 ins / 33 x 26 cm) GBP 2,875. NEW YORK, 26 Feb 1997, *Nude in a Wooded Landscape* (1853, oil on panel, 16 1/2 x 11 3/4 ins / 41.8 x 29.8 cm) USD 5,750. LONDON, 13 March 1997, *Nymph* (oil on paper/panel, oval, 5 3/4 x 4 3/4 ins / 14.8 x 12 cm) GBP 5,500. PORTSMOUTH, 20 March 1999, *Venus Disarming Cupid* (1852, oil on canvas, 35 x 28 ins / 89 x 71 cm) USD 8,500. LONDON, 27 March 2001, *Country Feast* (oil on canvas, 22 x 30 ins / 57 x 77 cm) GBP 1,200. LONDON, 22 Nov 2001, *Two Gentlemen in a Gig* (1835, oil on canvas, 18 x 24 ins / 46 x 62 cm) GBP 10,000. LONDON, 20 Feb 2003, *Venus and Cupid* (oil on canvas, 13 x 18 ins / 32 x 46 cm) GBP 8,500. LONDON, 20 Feb 2003, *Venus Disarming Cupid* (1852, oil on canvas, arched top, 35 x 31 ins / 90 x 78 cm) GBP 32,000. LONDON, 27 May 2004, *Sea Nymph* (oil on canvas, arched top, 36 x 22 ins / 91 x 56 cm) GBP 6,000. LONDON, 23 Nov 2004, *Andromeda* (1849, oil on canvas) GBP 2,200.

FROSTÉ, Nicolas-Sébastien
French, 19th century.
Born 21 August 1790, in Paris; died 1856, in Odessa, Ukraine.
Painter.

He enrolled at the École des Beaux-Arts on 17 August 1810 and studied under Regnault; he was a medal winner in 1824. Frosté exhibited portraits and some other compositions at the Salon from 1812 to 1831. In addition to examples of his work housed in museums, mention should be made of *Deathwatch near Atala, St Stephen, the First Martyr* (housed in the Interior Ministry), *Jesus Curing an Epileptic* (church of Notre-Dame-des-Blancs-Manteaux, Paris), *St Carlo Borromeo* (church of St-Louis, Versailles), and a *View of the Piazzetta, Venice*.

MUSEUMS AND GALLERIES:
ORLÉANS: *Good Samaritan* - TROYES: *Smoking Odalisque; Slumber* - VERSAILLES (Petit Trianon): *Duke of Angoulême Visiting the Military Hospital in Chiclana, Spain*.

FROSTERUS-SALTIN, Alexandra Theodora
Finnish, 19th century.
Born 6 December 1837.
Painter.

Several of the works of Alexandra Theodora Frosterus-Saltin are in the museum of Helsinki: *Blind Musician, Boat Voyage to the Cemetery, A Mother by the Side of her Sick Child, Small Sorrows* and *Councillor H. Rosenberg*.

FROSTERUS-SEGERSTRALE, Johanna Wilhelmina
Finnish, 19th - 20th century.
Born 23 October 1867, in Helsinki.
Active in Vaasa.
Painter. Portraits.

Johanna Wilhelmina Frosterus-Segerstrale received an honourable mention in 1900. Her pastel, *Head of a Young Girl*, is in the museum of Helsinki.

FROTHINGHAM, James
American, 19th century.
Born 1786, in Charlestown; died 1864, in New York.
Painter. Portraits.

James Frothingham was a member of the National Academy and painted mainly portraits.

AUCTION RECORDS:
NEW YORK, 18 and 19 April 1934, *George Washington* (after Gilbert Stuart) USD 150. NEW YORK, 28 Sept 1983, *Portrait of a Gentleman* (oil on panel, 9 1/4 x 7 ins / 23.5 x 17.8 cm) USD 750.

FROUART, Jean
French, 17th century.
Painter.

Jean Frouart was an abbot at Ethival in 1627.

FROUCHAUD, Auguste
French, 19th century.
Active c. 1836.
Sculptor. Figures.

MUSEUMS AND GALLERIES:
AIX: *Young Girl Wearing a Crown of Plants*.

FROUIN, Jean-Michel
French, 20th - 21st century.
Born 1960.
Painter.

Jean-Michel Frouin studied at the École Nationale Supérieure des Beaux-Arts. His paintings appear abstract, but have conceptual connotations. From 1979 to 1991, he took part in the Salon de la Jeune Peinture de Paris. He has also staged a number of solo exhibitions in the Centre Georges Pompidou and in various private galleries, among other venues.

AUCTION RECORDS:
PARIS, 5 March 1990, *Uncertainty* (oil on canvas, 47 1/4 x 51 1/4 ins / 120 x 130 cm) FRF 4,000. PARIS, 14 April 1991, *Untitled* (1991, acrylic/paper/canvas, diptych, 31 1/2 x 31 1/2 ins / 80 x 80 cm) FRF 5,000.

FROUIN, Micheline
French, 20th century.
Born 7 September 1919, in Paris.
Painter, potter. Landscapes, flowers, fruit.

Micheline Frouin worked in her hometown of Neuilly-sur-Seine. She became a member of the Salon des Artistes Français in Paris in 1961 and also of the Salon des Indépendants in the same year. In Paris she also exhibited at the Salon Comparaisons. She was awarded the Ville de Bourges first prize in 1977.

FROUIN, Nicolas Alexis
French, 18th century.
Active in Paris in 1768.
Painter, sculptor.

FROULLE, Auguste-Adolphe, called Varnier
French, 19th century.
Born 15 July 1821, in Paris.
Engraver. Mythological subjects. Cameos.

He exhibited at the Paris Salon from 1848 to 1878; examples of his work include *Diogenes, Mars and Venus, Death of Hyrnétho, Apollo at Tethys*, and *Alcides Overcoming Jealousy*.

FROUMENTIN, Michel
French.
Glass painter.

Froumentin was the son of Pierre Froumentin. There is reference to a stained-glass window, *Sacrifice of Abraham*, in the church of Notre-Dame, Alençon.

FROWD, Thomas T. J.
British, 19th century.
Painter. Landscapes.

Thomas T. J. Frowd was active in Windsor and a frequent exhibitor in London from 1847 to 1864.

AUCTION RECORDS:
LONDON, 23 Sept 1980, *Eton College; Windsor Castle* (1849, oil on canvas, a pair, 12 x 15 ins / 30.5 x 38 cm) GBP 480.

FROWIN
German, 12th century.
Died 23 March 1178.
Illuminator.

This artist was abbot of the monastery of Englebert, where he founded a school of painting. He decorated the books in the monastery's library.

FROWIS, Martin
German.
Born in Rheinfelden.
Stucco artist, sculptor.
He created ornaments for the church of Beromünster.

FROY, Martin
British, 20th century.
Born 1926, in London.
Painter.
Martin Froy studied at the Slade in London until 1951. He held his first solo exhibition in 1952.

FROYMONS, Jan
Dutch, 17th century.
Died before 1616, perhaps in Amsterdam.
Painter.

FRUCHARD, Amélie (Mme)
Maiden name: Four
French, 19th century.
Painter, pastellist, watercolourist. Figures, flowers.
MUSEUMS AND GALLERIES:
TULLE: *Head* (pastel); *Flowers* (watercolour).

FRUCTUOSO, or Frictosus
Spanish, 11th century.
Miniaturist.
This artist wrote and illustrated a book of prayers at the library of the University of St James of Compostela.

FRUCTUS, Joseph
French, 18th - 19th century.
Painter, draughtsman.
Joseph Fructus, who appears to have been an amateur, produced drawings and lithographs in Lyons, from the last few years of the 18th century until 1825. His work shows views of Lyons and the surrounding area as well as monuments and contemporary events. In 1827, he exhibited a picture: *Sunset* in Lyons. One of his lithographs depicts the *Château of St Chamond, Drawn from Nature, in 1787*. He engraved an etching entitled *View of Pierre Encize*, signed with the monogram: *JFR*.

FRUCTUS, Joseph Benezet
French, 18th - 19th century.
Born c. 1743, in Avignon; died 14 May 1831, in Lyons.
Painter (?).

FRUEAUF, Rueland, the Elder
Austrian, 15th century.
Born c. 1440; died 1507, in Passau (Bavaria).
Painter, fresco artist. Religious subjects, portraits.
Salzburg School.
At the beginning of his career, Rueland Frueauf the Elder executed a considerable number of paintings in Salzburg, particularly for the Benedictine monks of the town. He appears to have been an assistant to Konrad Laib. He became a burgher of Salzburg in 1478 and of Passau in 1480. He travelled in the Netherlands.

Frueauf's first work is thought to have been an altarpiece showing twelve scenes from the *Passion*, painted for Regensburg in about 1475. During his time in Passau, in 1480, he completed the frescoes in the town hall. While in Nuremberg in 1487, he painted some scenes on the retable of the high altar in the Augustinian church. Four important paintings dating from 1491 and thought to be by Frueauf, now in the museum in Vienna, show scenes from the Passion: *The Garden of Gethsemane, Flagellation, Christ Carrying the Cross* and *Calvary*. These panels come from a retable made for Salzburg. On their reverse sides were scenes from the *Life of the Virgin*. Frueauf also painted a *Portrait of a Young Man*, dated around 1500.

The dramatic power of these works is achieved through the very extreme expressions of some of the figures in the compositions. The faces of the bystanders, particularly, in the *Crucifixion, The Death of the Virgin* and *St John the Baptist Preaching* are reminiscent of the work of Pieter Bruegel. He makes use of rich, deep colours against a background or of more sober colours against a background of sky or sometimes a mixture of deep colours giving an impression of an abstract background, as in *The Man of Sorrows* (Munich).
MUSEUMS AND GALLERIES:
BUDAPEST: *Annunciation* - CAMBRIDGE, MA (Fogg AM, Harvard University): *Visitation* - HERZOGENBURG: *Presentation of the Virgin in the Temple* - MUNICH: *The Man of Sorrows* - ST FLORIAN: *Death of the Virgin* - VENICE (Mus. Correr): *Nativity; Presentation in the Temple* - VIENNA (Österreichische Gal. Belvedere): *Mount of Olives; Flagellation; Christ Carrying the Cross; Calvary* (1491); *Portrait of a Young Man*.
AUCTION RECORDS:
BERLIN, 20 Sept 1930, *St Jerome*, DEM 10,500. LONDON, 28 June 1935, *Portrait of a Cardinal*, GBP 18.

FRUEAUF, Rueland, the Younger
Austrian, 15th - 16th century.
Born in Passau (Bavaria), Germany.
Painter. Religious subjects.
Danube School (or style of).
This artist was the son of Rueland Frueauf the Elder. It is not easy to distinguish his work from that of his father. However, a number of panels from retables in the abbey of Klosterneuburg, near Vienna, have been fairly confidently attributed to Rueland the Younger: *Mount of Olives, Arrest of Christ, Crown of Thorns* and *Calvary*. Also, dating from 1505, is the work *The Legend of St Leopold*, which is made up of panels showing: *Departure of St Leonard, Boar Hunt, Apparition of the Veil* and *The Building of Klosterneuburg*.

Rueland Frueauf the Younger's art is perhaps more narrative than that of his father, as can be seen in his *St John the Baptist* and the *Foundation of the Abbey by Leopold the Glorious*. Landscape and architecture are given a prominent role. Some of the figures in his *Beheading of St John the Baptist* recall the small figures of gondoliers painted by Gentile Bellini and Carpaccio in their Venetian scenes.
BIBLIOGRAPHY:
Buschbeck, Ernst H., *Primitifs autrichiens*, Éd. d'Histoire de l'Art, Paris, 1937. Baldass, L., *Conrad Laib und die beiden Rueland Frueauf*, Vienna, 1946.
MUSEUMS AND GALLERIES:
NUREMBERG: *Crucifixion* - VIENNA (Kunstmus.): *St Anne, the Virgin and Child with a Donor Presented by Patron Saints*.

FRUEHAUF, Johann
German, 19th century.
Born 26 February 1791, in Bamberg; died c. 1843.
Lithographer.
Fruehauf is credited with, among other works, some *Views of Bamberg*.

FRUGERY, Niccolo
German, 18th century.
Active in Rome.
Engraver.
Frugery is noted for a *St Theresa*, after Mancini.

FRUGIER, Françoise
French, 20th - 21st century.
Born 1950, in Paris.
Sculptor.
Françoise Frugier obtained a higher diploma in the visual arts, specialising in sculpture, in 1977. She founded the Académie du Viaduc des Arts in Paris in 1995, and served as its director. She won the Sculpture Prize in Ballancourt in 1990, and the Grand Prix de Sculpture at the Salon de Brecey in

1995 and 2001. She sculpts figurines of women, or of sumo wrestlers engaged in battle, in which she tries to find the 'point of equilibrium'.

She has taken part in numerous group exhibitions in Paris since 1974, including: the Salon de Mai, the Salon de la Jeune Peinture and the Salon d'Automne (of which she was made an associate in 1989); and the ADAC Galerie Atelier in 2002. She has also staged a number of solo exhibitions, including the following: at the Galerie Pierre Robin in Paris in 1977; at the Galerie de l'ADAC in Paris, every other year since 1984; at the Centre Culturel de la Ville de Gagny from 1987 to 1990; and at the Galerie Racine in Paris from 1999 to 2000.

Bibliography:

Alain Coutret, Barbara Debard, Françoise Frugier, Jacques Vernière, exhibition catalogue, ADAC-Gal.- Atelier, Paris, 1984.

FRÜH, Eugen

Swiss, 20th century.
Born 1914, in St Gall; died 1975, in Zurich.
Painter. Landscapes.

Auction records:

Zurich, 30 May 1981, *Seashore* (1967, mixed media, 18 1/4 x 25 1/4 ins / 46.5 x 64 cm) CHF 1,300. Zurich, 14 May 1982, *Branson under a Green Sky* (1970, oil on canvas, 15 3/4 x 17 3/4 ins / 40 x 45 cm) CHF 4,000. Zurich, 9 Nov 1984, *View of Venice at Dusk* (1963, oil on canvas, 15 3/4 x 23 1/2 ins / 40 x 60 cm) CHF 2,800. Zurich, 7 June 1985, *Joshida* (1940, oil on card, 24 3/4 x 18 1/2 ins / 63 x 47 cm) CHF 3,000. Zurich, 24 Nov 1993, *Near La Sage* (oil on canvas, 18 1/2 x 28 3/4 ins / 47 x 73 cm) CHF 4,600.

FRUH, Oscar

Swiss, 20th century.
Born 25 May 1891, in Teufen (Appenzell).
Painter. Animals.

Oscar Fruh exhibited regularly in Paris at the Salon des Artistes Indépendants and the Salon d'Automne. He painted mainly horses.

FRÜHBECK, Franz

American, 19th century.
Active at the beginning of the 19th century.
Draughtsman, painter.

Franz Frühbeck is known for his drawn and painted journal of the journey he made in 1817 and 1818 through Brazil. This is now in the possession of the Hispanic Society of America in Philadelphia, and was reproduced, edited by R.C. Smith and G. Ferrez, in 1960.

FRUHMANN, Johan

Austrian, 20th century.
Born 1928, in Weissenstein an der Drau (Carinthia) Austria.
Painter, engraver.

Johan Fruhmann studied in Graz and Vienna. He has taken part in many group exhibitions, including the 1954 Venice Biennale. He has held solo exhibitions since 1952, mainly in Vienna, and has also exhibited monotypes and small-format paintings. His work is abstract and makes use of signs and symbols, sometimes resembling graffiti or doodles.

Auction records:

Vienna, 7 April 1987, *Untitled* (1962, oil on panel, 14 1/4 x 17 1/4 ins / 36 x 44 cm) ATS 12,000. Vienna, 19 May 1999, *Untitled Composition* (1955, tempera on jute, 38 x 45 ins / 97 x 114 cm) ATS 70,000. Vienna, 13 Oct 1999, *Untitled* (1984, oil on canvas, 51 x 47 ins / 130 x 120 cm) ATS 75,000. Vienna, 28 April 2004, *Untitled* (oil on canvas, 59 x 51 ins / 150 x 130 cm) EUR 14,000.

FRÜHOLZ, Jacob

German, 18th - 19th century.
Born 2 March 1769, in Geislingen (Baden-Württemberg); died 1846, in Geislingen.
Painter.

A draughtsman and miniaturist, Früholz also executed an altarpiece representing the *Last Supper* for the church at Amstetten.

FRÜHSORG, Heinrich

Swiss, 16th century.
Active in Freiburg im Brisgau (Baden-Württemberg) at the beginning of the 16th century.
Painter, glass painter.

FRUHTRUNK, Günther

German, 20th century.
Born 1923, in Munich; died 1982, in Munich.
From 1954 also active in France.
Painter.

After studying architecture from 1940 to 1941, Günther Fruhtrunk served in the army for the remainder of the war. In 1945, he joined Wilhelm Straube's private art school where he continued until 1950. In 1952, he was advised by Fernand Léger at his school in Paris and a bursary enabled him to return there in 1954. From then on he divided his time between France and Germany. In 1955, he also received advice from Jean (Hans) Arp. At that time he met the painters of the Galerie Denise René.

His first abstract paintings were composed of geometric figures, especially squares, rectangles and circles, arranged on the support without any effect of depth. From 1906 he reduced the figures to lines of different colours and widths arranged horizontally, vertically or obliquely, using optical effects of contrast and watering to create rhythms and dynamism. However, he was aiming more for the purity of Constructivism than the instability of Op Art. In his strict compositions often based on diagonals, which became something of a trademark for him, he strongly affirms his association with the aesthetics of Geometric Abstraction.

He took part in a very large number of group exhibitions, especially those devoted to neo-Constructivist trends, notably in Paris between 1955 and 1961, at the Salon des Réalités Nouvelles, Salon de Mai and Salon Comparaisons. He exhibited at the Venice Biennale in 1968. He also showed his works in many solo exhibitions, the first of which was in 1947 in Freiburg im Breisgau. Others followed, notably Paris 1960, Milan 1962, 1964 and 1966, Marseilles 1963 and 1965, Düsseldorf 1964, Munich 1964, 1965 and 1966, Cologne 1965, Vienna and Frankfurt am Main 1968 and others. He received commissions for a concrete relief for the town of Leverkusen in 1965 and a large mosaic for the exterior of the auditorium of the School of Engineering in Düsseldorf in 1966. In 1967, he was appointed professor at the Munich academy of fine arts.

Museums and Galleries:

Grenoble (Mus. de Grenoble): *Critical Point* - Marseilles (Mus. Cantini): *Violet Intervals* (1965) - Münster (Westfälisches Landesmus.): *Cantus Firmus III* (1964-1965) - Paris (MNAM-CCI).

Auction records:

Rome, 18 May 1976, *Monastery Garden* (1962, tempera/canvas, 48 x 50 3/4 ins / 121 x 129 cm) ITL 1,900,000. Zurich, 17 Nov 1976, *Red on Black and Yellow* (1970, oil on canvas, 31 1/2 x 31 ins / 80 x 79 cm) CHF 6,000. Munich, 26 May 1978, *Composition* (1963-1968, oil on canvas, 39 1/4 x 39 1/4 ins / 100 x 100 cm) DEM 9,000. Milan, 15 March 1983, *Monastery Garden* (1962, tempera/wood, 48 x 50 3/4 ins / 121 x 129 cm) ITL 1,700,000. Cologne, 6 Dec 1983, *Composition* (1962, vinyl./panel, 30 3/4 x 35 ins / 78 x 88 cm) DEM 12,000. COLOGNE, 9 Dec 1986, *Composition with a White Circle* (1955, oil/jute, 51 1/4 x 63 3/4 ins / 130 x 162 cm) DEM 34,000. LOKEREN, 28 May 1988, *Dynamic Fields* (1962, oil on panel, 15 1/2 x 16 1/4 ins / 39.5 x 41 cm) BEF 110,000. LONDON, 29 June 1989, *Untitled* (1966, acrylic/panel, 30 x 31 ins / 76.5 x 78.8 cm) GBP 15,400. LONDON, 17 Oct 1991, *Fluctuatuion between Red and Blue* (oil on card, 28 1/4 x 28 ins / 71.5 x 71 cm) GBP 9,350. MUNICH, 26 May 1992, *Epitaph for Arp* (1974, silk screen print in colour, 27 1/4 x 28 ins / 69.5 x 71 cm) DEM 1,265. PARIS, 19 March 1993, *Blue Circles* (paint/panel, 29 1/4 x 32 1/4 ins / 74 x 82 cm) FRF 55,000. LONDON, 1 Dec 1994, *Yellow Constants* (1968, acrylic/canvas, 15 3/4 x 23 ins / 40 x 57.5 cm) GBP 5,520. PARIS, 16 March 1997, *Untitled* (1954, oil on canvas, 32 x 39 1/4 ins / 81 x 100 cm) FRF 57,000. PARIS, 15 Dec 1997, *Cantus Firmus* (c. 1970, oil on panel, 20 1/2 x 23 1/2 ins / 52 x 60 cm) FRF 40,000. LONDON, 26 March 1999, *Power House* (1964, oil and acrylic, 46 x 44 ins / 118 x 113 cm) GBP 8,000. COLOGNE, 12 Nov 1999, *Red Lines II* (1959, acrylic and kasein, 31 x 31 ins / 79 x 80 cm) DEM 35,000. HAMBURG, 8 June 2000, *Center of Energy* (1964, acrylic, 46 x 44 ins / 118 x 113 cm) DEM 36,000. COLOGNE, 10 Nov 2000, *Narrow - Hight - Depth - Width* (1980, acrylic, 77 x 102 ins / 195 x 258 cm) DEM 85,000. MUNICH, 19 May 2001, *Open Green 11* (1969, acrylic and kasein, 31 x 28 ins / 80 x 70 cm) DEM 22,000. HAMBURG, 28 Sept 2002, *Falling Diagonals in Black, Red and Blue - Paris* (1965-1966, oil and kasein on panel, 17 x 14 ins / 42 x 35 cm) EUR 4,800. LONDON, 3 Feb 2003, *Radiation/Example* (1959, oil on board, 50 x 52 ins / 126 x 131 cm) GBP 13,000. LONDON, 3 Feb 2003, *Unbedingtes und blau-violetter widerhall* (*Confidence and Blue/Violet Echo*) (1959, oil on board, 49 x 64 ins / 125 x 162 cm) GBP 14,000. MILAN, 25 May 2004, *Red and Green Energy* (1971, acrylic, 31 x 31 ins / 80 x 80 cm) EUR 11,000.

FRUHTRUNK, Wolf
German, 20th century.
Born 1935, in Hamburg.
Engraver.

Wolf Fruhtrunk took part in the Tokyo Engraving Biennale in 1970.

FRÜHWIRTH, Johann
Austrian, 17th century.
Born 1640, in Vienna; died 13 November 1701, in Vienna.
Sculptor.

Johann Frühwirth was court sculptor, interior decorator and architect to the Austrian court. He executed several monuments in Hofburg and Klosterneuburg in the Baroque style.

FRÜHWIRTH, Johann Gabriel
German, 17th - 18th century.
Born 23 March 1668; died after 1734.
Sculptor.

Johann Gabriel was the son of Johann Frühwirth and worked in particular for the Emperor Joseph I.

FRÜHWIRTH, Karl Josef
Austrian, 18th century.
Born 2 June 1675, in Vienna; died 17 February 1714, in Vienna.
Sculptor.

Karl Josef was the son of Johann and the brother of Johann Gabriel Frühwirth, with whom he collaborated.

FRUIT, Paul
French, 15th century.
Illuminator.

Fruit illuminated the manuscript of the *Roman de Guérin* for the Duke of Burgundy.

FRUITIER, Maurice
French, 20th century.
Born 23 February 1911, in Paris.
Painter. Figures, landscapes.

Maurice Fruitier studied at the École des Beaux-Arts in Paris. He also studied under the direction of Othon Friesz, André Lhote and Fernand Léger and spent long periods with Maurice de Vlaminck. His painting stands at the crossroads between stylised Post-Cubism and Expressionism; it is characterised by the use of clear colours and an evident concern for construction.

He took part in group exhibitions, including: the Salon d'Hiver in 1936-1939 and 1944-1945; the Salon d'Automne in Paris in 1944; the Salon des Surindépendants in Paris in 1945 and 1946; regularly at the Salon des Indépendants in Paris from 1949; regularly at the Salon Populiste in Paris from 1954. He was selected for the Prix de la Critique in Paris in 1958 and the Salon de Bourges in 1987, where he was awarded the Grand Prix de Peinture and a gold medal.

Fruitier also exhibited his work in solo exhibitions, including: in Paris in 1942; at the Galerie Cimaise in Paris in 1947; and regularly at the Galerie Artère, Maisons-Lafitte. He was awarded first prize for portraiture by the Ville de Paris in 1936.

FRULLI, Gioacchino
Italian, 18th century.
Active in Bologna.
Sculptor.

Gioacchino Frulli was a pupil of Scandellari.

FRULLI, Giovanni Battista
Italian, 19th century.
Died c. 1826.
Active in Bologna.
Painter, engraver.

A pupil of Toselli and Gandolfi, Frulli imitated the style of the Carracci. He was a teacher at the Accademia di Belle Arti in Bologna for many years.

FRULLINI, Luigi
Italian, 19th century.
Born 25 March 1839, in Florence; died July 1897, in Florence.
Sculptor.

Frullini's first show was in Florence in 1861; he then went on to exhibit in Paris, London and Vienna. He left behind a large number of sculpted portraits: *Garibaldi* and *Mazzini* were just two of his subjects.

FRULLINI, Nicotera
Italian, 19th - 20th century.
Born in Rome.
Painter.

In 1900 Frullini entered the Alinari competition, with a painting entitled *Surprise*.

FRÜMANN. See **FRÜHMANN**

FRUMENTI, Niccolo
Italian, 15th century.
Active c. 1460.
Painter.

Frumenti painted a tryptych (dated 1461) depicting the Raising of Lazarus, which is now in Florence.

FRUMERIE, Agnes de
Maiden name: Kjellberg
Swedish, 19th - 20th century.
Born 20 November 1869, in Skövde; died 1937, in Stockholm.
Sculptor.

Agnes de Frumerie studied in Stockholm and travelled widely in Germany and Italy. From 1903, she exhibited in Paris at the Société Nationale des Beaux-Arts, of which she became an associate. See also Agnes Kjellberg.

FRUNZ, Kaspar
Swiss, 17th century.
Active in Samen in 1614.
Sculptor.

FRUOSINO, Bartolommeo de.
See **BARTOLOMMEO DI FRUOSINO**

FRUSSOTTE, C.
French, 18th century.
Active at the end of the 18th century.
Engraver.

C. Frussotte's works include *Four Seasons*, after Quéverdo.

FRUSTIER, François
French, 17th century.
Active in Paris in 1614.
Painter, sculptor.

FRUTET, Frans
Dutch, 16th century.
Active in Seville c. 1548.
Painter. History painting.
School of Seville.

The date and place of birth of this artist are not known, nor are we certain when he died. His work show the influence of Raphael and Michelangelo, although his palette is Flemish.

MUSEUMS AND GALLERIES:
SEVILLE: *Christ Falls on the Road to Calvary; Deposition; Christ Between the Two Thieves; The Last Supper* (triptych) - TROYES: *Ball at the Flemish Court.*

FRUTIER, Jean-Jacques
French, 19th century.
Born in Paris.
Painter.

He studied under Ary Scheffer and exhibited at the Paris Salon from 1835 to 1844. Examples of his work include *Gilbert at the Hôtel-Dieu Hospice Some Days before his Death* and *André Chénier at St-Lazare.*

FRUTOS, Diego
Spanish, 18th century.
Born c. 1700, near Segovia; died 30 December 1754, in Valladolid.
Painter.

Diego Frutos, a monk at the Franciscan monastery in Valladolid, produced decorative paintings for the monastery. Most of these are now in the Valladolid museum.

FRUWIRTH, Carl
Austrian, 19th century.
Born 24 January 1810, in Vienna; died 17 January 1878, in Vienna.
Painter. Genre scenes, landscapes, still-lifes.

Carl Fruwirth was a pupil at the academy in Vienna. He travelled to Italy, staying notably in Venice and Naples.

AUCTION RECORDS:
MUNICH, 30 June 1983, *Seaside Scene, Capri* (oil on panel, 16 x 26 1/2 ins / 40.5 x 67.5 cm) DEM 6,000.

FRUYTIERS, Lodewyk Joseph
Flemish School, 18th century.
Born 21 February 1713, in Mechelen; died 22 February 1782, in Antwerp.
Engraver.

He executed engravings after Jouffroy, as illustrations for a work by Siré.

FRUYTIERS, Philip
Flemish School, 17th century.
Born 10 January 1610, in Antwerp; died 19 June 1666, in Antwerp.
Painter, miniaturist. History painting, portraits.

Biographers gave widely differing dates for Fruytiers' birth (between 1607 and 1625) and death (between 1660 and 1665). He became a master in the Guild of St Luke in Antwerp around 1631. His works include a number of highly regarded portraits in watercolour and gouache.

PF.

MUSEUMS AND GALLERIES:
ANTWERP: *A Family.*

AUCTION RECORDS:
PARIS, 1857, *A Lady with her Children* (miniature) FRF 570.
BRUSSELS, 24 March 1976, *Children Playing with a Dog* (oil on canvas, 65 x 56in/165 x 142cm) BEF 550,000.

FRY, Adam. See **FREY**

FRY, Anthony
British, 20th century.
Born 1927, in Theydon Bois (Essex).
Painter. Figures.

Anthony Fry studied art in Edinburgh and London. From 1950 to 1952, he studied in Rome after receiving a bursary. When he returned to Britain he taught at the Fine Arts Academy in Bath before receiving another bursary, this time to study in the USA. After this he taught at Chelsea College of Art until 1993. Fry is principally known for a series of major compositions on the theme of dancers. He specialised in painting figures, giving strong outlines to his forms and often conferring on them a sense of tragedy.

FRY, Arthur Malcolm
British, 20th century.
Born 20 May 1909.
Painter, watercolourist.

Arthur Fry was a member of the Royal Scottish Academy. He exhibited regularly in London and was director of the Central Institute of Art and Design.

FRY, Edwin Maxwell
British, 20th century.
Born 2 August 1899, in Wallasey (Cheshire); died 3 September 1987, in London.
Architect, painter. Architecture, urban planning.

Maxwell Fry studied at the Liverpool University school of architecture, graduating in 1923. During this period, he worked briefly for Carrère and Hastings in New York. He worked as an architect for Adams & Thompson, as Chief Assistant in the architects' department of Southern Railways (1927-1930), and then became a partner in Adams & Thompson until 1934, when he went into partnership with Walter Gropius. From 1937 he continued his practice alone.

He married the architect Jane Drew in 1942. They worked abroad advising in town planning in West Africa in 1943, and formed Fry, Drew & Partners in 1946, which included the architects Lindsay Drake, Denys Lasdun, Frank Knight and Norman Creamer at various times. Fry and Drew were appointed senior architects from 1951 on the project to build Chandigarh, the new capital city of the Punjab in India. He was elected a fellow of the Royal Institute of British Architects in 1930, and won the Institute's Gold Medal in 1964. Elected to the Royal Academy in 1972, he became its professor of architecture.

Fry's architectural work was strongly influenced by the Modernist movement, especially by Wells Coates, and he strove to combine Modernist design with architecture promoting social reform, by creating well-planned and economic living spaces. In 1931 he was one of the founders of the highly influential Modern Architectural Research group (MARS), which staged the *New Architecture* exhibition in 1938 and put forth their Plan of London proposal in 1942. The group used reinforced concrete as a revolutionary material that allowed them to design buildings with proportions which were no longer dependent on mass. Fry described his philosophy of architecture as direct collaboration with industry, subject to scrutiny which revealed the human and mechanical needs inherent in the structures, and which are in contact with their surrounding settings.

Fry and Drew continued their commitment to African architecture by designing many large projects adapted to African tropical conditions and using local materials, such as Aburi School and College, Adisadel College and Accra Community College in Ghana (1946); Ashanti Secondary School for Boys in Kumasi (1950); Amedzoffe College in Togoland, now Togo (1946); colleges in Wudil and Kano in Nigeria (1958); University College in Ibadan (1959); and schools in Lagos (1960).

During his long career, Fry designed a vast number of important and innovative buildings and urban plans, which include Sun House in Hampstead (1936), in the International Style; the women's hostel Cecil House in Gower Street, London (1940); Riverside Restaurant at the South Bank Exhibition in London (1951); the Legislative Assembly at Port Louis, Mauritius (1966); and the redevelopment of Hatfield Old Town (1972). As well as being an architect, Fry painted, showing his paintings at Drian and Fieldborne Galleries, and was a collector of works by young artists.

Bibliography:

Fry, Maxwell/Drew, J. B., *Tropical Architecture in the Humid Zones*, Batsford, London, 1956. Fry, Maxwell/Drew, J. B., *Tropical Architecture in the Dry and Humid Zones*, Batsford, London, 1964. *Jane Drew/Maxwell Fry Collection*, Exhibition catalogue, Fermoy Art Gallery, King's Lynn, 1965. Fry, Maxwell, *Art in a Machine Age*, Methuen, London, 1969. Fry, Maxwell, *Autobiographical Sketches*, Illustrated book, Elek, London, 1975. Hitchins, S. (ed.), *Fry, Drew, Knight, Creamer: Architecture*, Lund Humphries, London, 1978. Joshi, Kiran, *Documenting Chandigarh: The Indian Architecture of Pierre Jeanneret, Edwin Maxwell Fry, Jane Beverly Drew*, Illustrated book, Mapin Publishers, Ahmadabad, 1999.

FRY, George

British.

Painter. Architectural views.

Museums and Galleries:

Cardiff: *Marble Hall Twickenham.*

FRY, Georgia

Maiden name: Timken

American, 19th century.

Born 3 February 1864, in St Louis; died 1921, in Beijing, China.

Active in New York.

Painter. Landscapes, animals.

Georgia Fry, the wife of the artist John H. Fry, was a pupil of Sebnenek, A. Morot and Cazin in Paris. She painted mainly landscapes with sheep.

FRY, Gladys Windsor

British, 20th century.

Painter, watercolourist.

Gladys Fry studied at London Art School and exhibited at a number of English venues.

FRY, Hans

Swiss, 17th century.

Glass painter.

Fry worked in Aarau in about 1606.

FRY, John Hemming

American, 19th century.

Born c. 1860, in Indiana; died 1946.

Painter.

John Hemming Fry, the husband of the artist Georgia Fry, completed his studies under Boulanger and Cormon in Paris. Among his works are *Autumn* and *Paolo and Francesca.*

FRY, Laura

British, 19th century.

Born c. 1835, in Eltham.

Painter (porcelain).

Laura Fry exhibited in London from 1855.

FRY, Marshal

American, 20th century.

Born 9 August 1878, in Syracuse (New York).

Painter, ceramicist.

Marshal Fry studied under William Chase, (Arthur?) Dow and (Henry?) Snell in New York, and then under Whistler in England.

FRY, Roger Eliot

British, 19th - 20th century.

Born 1866, in London; died 1934, in London.

Painter. Portraits, landscapes, still-lifes, flowers.

Bloomsbury Group, Omega Workshops.

Roger Fry originally studied science at Cambridge before studying art and art history in Paris and Italy. In 1899, he published an essay on Giovanni Bellini, then a work on *Giotto* in 1900-1901, *Vision and Design* in 1920 and in 1926 a work on *Seurat*. In 1903, he became editor of the *Burlington Magazine*, and from 1905 to 1910 he was curator of the Metropolitan Museum. In 1933, he was appointed to teach at Oxford. Fry was a member of the Bloomsbury Group led by Virginia Woolf. In 1910 and again in 1912, with the participation of the New English Art Club, he organised two international exhibitions on *Manet and the Post-Impressionists* which were instrumental in introducing modern and particularly French modern art to England. Fry was also behind the creation in 1913-1919 of the Omega Workshops, research workshops specialising in decorative furnishings for everyday living. From 1913, Wyndham Lewis, the theoretician of Vorticism, openly opposed Fry's ideas. As a practising painter from 1888, Fry painted a variety of subjects and landscapes captured during his trips to Italy and Provence. He was influenced by Cézanne through the period of Othon Friesz's return to form.

The art collection he bequeathed to the Courtauld Institute in London includes works by Seurat, Bonnard, Rouault and Derain. In 1999, the exhibition *Art Made Modern: Roger Fry's Vision of Art* at the Courtauld Institute in London presented a broad panorama of his ideas.

Bibliography:

Woolf, Virginia, *Roger Fry. A biography*, Macmillan Company, Toronto, 1940. Bell, Quentin/Troutman, Philip, *Vision and design, The life, work and influence of Roger Fry, 1866-1934*, exhibition catalogue, Arts Council, London, 1966. Falkenheim, Jacqueline V., *Roger Fry and the beginnings of formalist art criticism*, UMI Research Press, Ann Arbor, 1980. Spalding, Frances, *Roger Fry. Art and life*, Elek, London, 1980. Green, Christopher (ed.), *Art Made Modern: Roger Fry's Vision of Art*, exhibition catalogue, Courtauld Institute, London, 1999. Elam, Caroline, *'Roger Fry and the Burlington Magazine'* in *The Burlington Magazine*, periodical, London, March 2003.

Museums and Galleries:

London (National Portrait Gal.): several portraits including a self-portrait - London (Tate Collection): *The Zoo, Two Fragments* (1911, tempera/canvas, fragments of decoration from the Borough Polytechnic dining room); *Still-life: Flowers* (c. 1912, oil on canvas); *River with Poplars* (c. 1912, oil/wood, Poitou landscape); *Essay in Abstract Design* (1914 or 1915, oil and collage/wood); *Bridge over the Allier* (c. 1933, oil/wood); lithographs, prints.

Auction records:

London, 12 Dec 1927, *Flowers in a Vase*, GBP 17. London, 25 July 1928, *Cassis*, GBP 20. London, 23 July 1931, *Still-life*, GBP 5; *André Gide*, GBP 10. London, 3 May 1939, *Gladioli*, GBP 14. London, 12 Oct 1973, *Farmyard*, Gns 360. London, 22 June 1977, *The Bridge, Pontigny* (c. 1925, oil on canvas,

20½ x 25 ins / 52 x 63.5 cm) GBP 500. LONDON, 10 June 1981, *Still-life with Fruit* (1919, oil on canvas, 13½ x 17¼ ins / 34 x 44 cm) GBP 1,100. LONDON, 27 June 1984, *The Forum of Constantine, Rome* (oil on card, 12 x 16 ins / 30.5 x 40.5 cm) GBP 2,400. LONDON, 13 March 1987, *Portrait of Zoum Vanden Eeckhout* (1915, oil on canvas, 28 x 36 ins / 71 x 91.5 cm) GBP 9,500. LONDON, 3-4 March 1988, *Mountain River in France* (1926, oil on canvas, 19¾ x 28½ ins / 50 x 72.50 cm) GBP 2,640. LONDON, 9 June 1988, *Valley of the Seine* (oil on canvas, 30½ x 42¼ ins / 77.5 x 107.5 cm) GBP 2,640. LONDON, 9 June 1989, *Lytton Strachey Writing in the Garden* (1917, pastel and pencil, 12 x 18½ ins / 30.5 x 46.8 cm) GBP 4,400. LONDON, 5 March 1999, *Provence* (c. 1925, oil on canvas, 18 x 24 ins / 46 x 61 cm) GBP 6,000. LONDON, 4 June 1999, *The Barn at Charleston* (1917, oil on canvas, 18 x 24 ins / 46 x 61 cm) GBP 3,500. LONDON, 24 Nov 2000, *In the Barn* (1926, oil on canvas, 29 x 24 ins / 73 x 60 cm) GBP 4,500. LONDON, 20 March 2001, *Venice, 1913* (oil on board, 10 x 13 ins / 25 x 33 cm) GBP 3,800. LONDON, 4 July 2001, *Winifred Gill at the Pool at Durbins* (oil on board, 28 x 22 ins / 72 x 55 cm) GBP 5,200. SALISBURY, 18 March 2002, *Still-life with Flowers in a Vase on a Ledge* (1930, oil on canvas, 16 x 13 ins / 41 x 33 cm) GBP 5,000. CREWKERNE, 24 July 2003, *Still-life of Bottle, Cup and Bowl of Fruit on a Tray* (oil on canvas, 16 x 12 ins / 41 x 31 cm) GBP 6,600. LONDON, 19 Nov 2004, *Summer Flowers* (c. 1919, oil on board, 13 x 16 ins / 32 x 40 cm) GBP 12,000. LONDON, 19 Nov 2004, *September in Sussex* (1933, oil on board, 16 x 22 ins / 40 x 55 cm) GBP 12,000.

FRY, Samuel
British, 19th century.
Active in London.
Painter, sculptor.

Samuel Fry exhibited at London's Royal Academy on 18 occasions between 1877 and 1890.

FRY, Sherry Edmondson
American, 20th century.
Born 29 September 1879; died 1966.
Sculptor. Figures, animals.

Sherry Fry studied at the Chicago Art Institute and in Paris. He was a member of the National Sculpture Society. He was awarded many distinctions, including some at the Paris Salon.

AUCTION RECORDS:
NEW YORK, 3 May 1972, *Spartan Mother* (patinated bronze) USD 1,500. NEW YORK, 12 April 1991, *Dolphin* (bronze, group for a fountain, h. 34 ins / 86.3 cm) USD 13,750. NEW YORK, 3 Dec 1996, *Young Girl Sitting on a Basin* (bronze, h. 17½ ins / 44.5 cm) USD 5,750.

FRY, Thomas
British, 18th century.
Active 1704-1710.
Painter.

Thomas Fry worked in Somerset, painting in churches in Wells (1704) and Dunster (1708). He also painted the drapery of an unfinished portrait (1710).

FRY, William Thomas
British, 19th century.
Born 1789; died 1843.
Active in London.
Engraver.

William Thomas Fry exhibited at the Suffolk Street Gallery in London from 1824 to 1830.

FRYCZ, Karol
Polish, 20th century.
Born 1877, in Cieszków.
Painter.

Karol Frycz trained in Vienna, Paris and London. He was then active in Warsaw and Cracow.

FRYDAG, Bernhard
German, 20th century.
Born 18 June 1879, in Münster; died April 1916.
Sculptor. Monuments.

Bernhard Frydag carved the war memorial in Münster.

FRYDMAN, Maurice
French, 20th century.
Born 24 September 1928, in Paris.
From 1955 active in Belgium.
Sculptor, painter, draughtsman, designer.

Maurice Frydman studied at the Académie de la Grande-Chaumière in Paris.

He exhibited his work in solo exhibitions in Ferrara in 1969 and at the Veranneman Foundation in Kruishoutem in 1978. In 1995 a collection of his work was shown at the Théâtre du Vieux-Colombier gallery in Paris and in 2001 at the Centre Wallonie-Bruxelles in Paris.

During the 1950s, Frydman took as the subjects of his paintings the death camps and also the couple and the child. In 1967 he began to produce sensually-formed sculptures based on anthropomorphic relationships. His work is incorporated architecturally as polyester high-reliefs in the form of doors, balustrades and ceilings. He works with transparency and opacity using clingfilm and plexiglas as a medium for paintings previously executed on cloth.

BIBLIOGRAPHY:
Maurice Frydman, Skira, Éd. du Seuil, Paris, 2001 (text in English, French and Dutch).

FRYDMAN, Monique
French, 20th century.
Born 1943, in Nages (Tarn).
Painter (including mixed media), pastellist, engraver.

Monique Frydman studied at the École des Beaux-Arts de Toulouse, and later (in 1964) at the École des Beaux-Arts de Paris. Once she had completed the initial stages of her artistic development, Frydman felt the need to stop painting altogether. When she started painting again, she depicted forms inspired by the human body, using herself as a model. Later, she freed herself from the constraints of this approach, and aspired to convey a sense of absolute reality in her paintings.

She placed her canvases on the ground while working on them. Her emphasis was, and always has been, on light, especially the tactile qualities and 'tastes' of different colours. She combined different techniques, using powdered pigments and pastels, mixing them in solution and rubbing them on damp canvas, trying, for example, to attain a Titian yellow. In the late 1980s, Frydman added another dimension to her paintings: she scratched or smoothed their surface, as if to add thin veils, impulsive markings or cryptic inscriptions to her work. Around 1990, however, after she had produced her *Shadow of Red* series, Frydman almost dropped these sporadic 'scribbles' altogether, in favour of a new strategy. Obviously as a tribute to Rothko, she would prepare an almost monochrome background, and place a traced quadrilateral of a very different colour upon it, which took up most of the centre of the painting.

Throughout these phases, Monique Frydman's style has been significantly influenced by American painting, especially Minimalism. Yet her work is not confined to primary forms and apsychic sensations. She is also very much a Lyricist, an Action Painter, an Informal Materialist and an Expressionist.

She has taken part in the following exhibitions: at the Musée de l'Abbaye Sainte Croix in Sables-d'Olonne, 1981; Galerie Baudoin-Lebon in Paris, 1981, 1983, 1985, 1988 and 1991; *La Voie Abstraite* (*The Abstract Way*), in the Salle St-Jean in Paris City Hall, in 1985; Nice in 1986; Toulouse, Melbourne and Bordeaux in 1987; Centre Régional d'Art Contemporain de Toulouse, Centre d'Art de Flaine and the Galerie Gill Favre de Lyon in 1989; Lausanne in 1990; Musée des Beaux-Arts in Caen in 1995; *L'Absinthe 1989*, at the Galerie Jacques Elbaz in Paris, in 1996; *Les Dames de Nage 1992-1995* (*The Swimming Ladies 1992-1995*), Galerie Laage-Salomon in Paris, in 1996; Musée de Beaux-Arts de Caen, also in 1996; FIAC (Foire Internationale d'Art Contemporain), staged by the Galerie Jacques Elbaz in Paris, in 1997; Galerie Laage-Salomon in Paris, 2001; Musée de Brou in Bourg-en-Bresse, 2002; at the Musée d'Art Moderne in Céret in 2003; and, also in 2003, *L'Oeuvre sur Papier* (*Works on Paper*), at the Musée des Beaux-Arts in Tourcoing.

BIBLIOGRAPHY:

Davvetas, D./Francblin, C./Frydman, M., *Monique Frydman*, exhibition catalogue, Gal. Baudoin Lebon, Paris, 1988. Bataillon, Françoise, '*Monique Frydman*' in *Beaux-Arts Magazine*, periodical, Paris, October 1988. Francblin, Catherine, '*Interview: Monique Frydman, cette perfection-là*' in *Art Press* n° 169, periodical, Paris, May 1992. '*Dossier Monique Frydman*' in *Verso Arts et Lettres* n° 3, periodical, Paris, July 1996.

AUCTION RECORDS:

PARIS, 6 April 1994, *Yellow Major I* (1988, mixed media/canvas, 77 1/4 x 76 ins / 196 x 193 cm) FRF 34,000.

FRYDRYCHOWICZ, Tomasz
Polish, 17th century.
Active in Cracow.
Painter.

FRYE, Johann George Christian
German, 18th - 19th century.
Born c. 1750, in Osnabrück (Lower Saxony); died 24 November 1824, in Tivoli (Italy).
Painter. Landscapes.

The last years of Frye's life were spent in Italy, in the company of the painter Karl Gottlieb Lenz.

FRYE, Thomas, or Fry
Irish, 18th century.
Born c. 1710, in Dublin; died 2 or 3 April 1762, in London.
Active in England from 1735.
Painter, pastellist, miniaturist, engraver. Portraits.

Born into a poor family in Ireland, Thomas Frye received very little education. His early works, dating from 1734 when he was still in Ireland, are crayon portraits like *Portrait of a Young Boy* and suggest an influence from Rosalba Carrera. In 1735 he went to London with Herbert Stoppelaer. There he studied under John Brooks of the Battersea Enamel Factory. He made his name as a painter, miniaturist and engraver of portraits for the London society and for royalty. While his early works show Jean Baptiste van Loo's influence, his later portraits suggests knowledge of Hogarth. They include: *Frederick, Prince of Wales in Garter Robes* (1741); *Self-portrait* (1759); *Jeremy Bentham* (1760); *Simon Lloyd, Plas Power, Wrexham* (1749); *Sarah Lloyd of Plas Power, Wrexham* (1749); *Sir Charles Townley, (1713-1774); Garter King of Arms*; *Henry Crispe of the Custom House* (1746). He was also a noted engraver and painted miniatures throughout his life.

While pursuing a career as a portrait painter and engraver, Frye became involved in porcelain production and in 1744 took out a patent for the manufacture of artificial soft-paste porcelain with his partner Edward Heylen. By 1749, with the backing of the powerful Peers family, the Bow Porcelain Factory was in production. The operation, variously described as a success or a failure, was certainly detrimental to Frye's health. By 1759 the prolonged exposure to the environment of the factory furnaces had taken its toll and Frye relinquished his position as manager. He went to Wales to regain his health and after one year he returned to London and resumed his occupation as an engraver, publishing a series of life-size portraits in mezzotint. He exhibited portraits in crayons, oil and miniature at the Society of Artists of Great Britain (1760 and 1761). He died of consumption in 1762. His epitaph described him 'the inventor and first manufacturer of porcelain in England', but he will be best remembered as an original portrait painter and engraver.

The mezzotints for which Frye is chiefly remembered are 17 life-size heads, which he published in two series between 1760 and 1762. Although probably drawn from real life, the engravings of the first series were issued without titles and, with the exception of Frye's self-portrait, were not presented as portraits but as a series of 'fanciful heads' arranged in various poses. The second series *Ladies, Very Elegantly Attired in the Fashion, and in the Most Agreeable Attitudes* (1761-1762) demonstrates his interest in fine costume and elegant jewellery.

Frye often made engravings of his own paintings, and his works have also been engraved by R. Houston, W. Bromley, D. Dodd, John Faber Jr, Macarol, Nusbiegel, B. Reading, J. Watson and William Pether, who was his pupil. His work was included in the exhibition *Irish Portraits 1660-1860* in Dublin, London and Belfast.

BIBLIOGRAPHY:

Wills, G., '*A Forgotten Artist*' in *Country Life*, periodical, January 1955. Wynne, Michael, '*Thomas Frye*' in *Burlington Magazine*, vol 114, periodical, February 1972. Wynne, Michael, '*Thomas Frye (1710-62) Reviewed*' in *Burlington Magazine*, vol 124, periodical, October 1982.

MUSEUMS AND GALLERIES:

CANBERRA (National Library): *Her Most Excellent Majesty Charlotte Queen of Great Britain* (1762, hand-coloured mezzotint, signed 'Thos. Frye ad vivam delineavit et sculpsit') - CARDIFF (National Museums and Galleries): *Portrait of a Lady* (oil on canvas) - DUBLIN (NG): *John Allen of Bridgewater* (1739) - LONDON (Collection of HM the Queen) - LONDON (College of Arms): *Sir Charles Townley (1713-1774), Garter King of Arms* (1740, oil on canvas) - LONDON (Courtauld Institute of Art): *Bust Portrait of a Lady* (1761, black chalk, watercolour on paper) - LONDON (National Portrait Gal.): *Jeremy Bentham* (1760, oil on canvas); *Fashionable Woman in an Ermine-lined Cloak* (1762, mezzotint) - LONDON (Royal College of Physicians): *John Allen of Bridgewater* (originally full length, now reduced) - LONDON (Science Mus., Science and Society Library): *Thomas Wright* (mezzotint) - LONDON (Tate Collection): *Henry Crispe of the Custom House* (1746, oil on canvas) - LONDON (Victoria and Albert Mus.): *Portrait of an Unknown Man* (1761, miniature, watercolour on ivory, signed 'TF' and dated) - NEW YORK (Metropolitan Mus. of Art): *Head of a Man in a Turban* (mezzotint) - SAN FRANCISCO (FAM): *Portrait of a Lady* (1761); *Portrait of Mrs Frye* (1760); *Self-portrait* (1760) - WARWICK (Court House): *Portrait of Richard Leveridge* - WREXHAM (Country Borough Mus.): *Simon Lloyd, Plas Power, Wrexham* (1749); *Sarah Lloyd of Plas Power, Wrexham* (oil on canvas).

AUCTION RECORDS:

LONDON, 26 March 1928, *Robert Webb*, GBP 25. LONDON, 18 July 1928, *Gentleman*, GBP 16. LONDON, 2 Dec 1929, *Portrait of Suzanne Walker*, GBP 25. LONDON, 5 June 1930, *Portrait of Thomas Wharton*, GBP 105. LONDON, 4 July 1930, *Portrait of the Duchess of Bedford*, GBP 21. LONDON, 19 May 1939, *Sir Charles Towneley*, GBP 35. LONDON, 27 Oct 1943, *Female Portrait* (pastel) GBP 10. LONDON, 17 March 1967, *Portrait of Richard Leveridge*, Gns 400. LONDON, 19 Nov 1982, *Portrait of a Gentleman of the Crispe Family* (1746, oil on canvas, 49 x 40 ins / 124.3 x 101.6 cm) GBP 15,000. LONDON, 15 March 1983, *Self-portrait* (mezzotint, 19 3/4 x 13 3/4 ins / 50.3 x 35.2 cm) GBP 850. LONDON, 11 July 1984, *Portrait of Mrs. Wardle* (oil on canvas, 48 1/2 x 39 ins / 123 x 99 cm) GBP 11,000. LONDON, 15 March 1985, *View of Montrésor* (oil on panel, 13 1/4 x 13 3/4 ins / 33.6 x 35 cm) GBP 1,600. LONDON, 12 March 1986, *Portrait of Two Young Girls* (oil on canvas, 59 3/4 x 46 ins / 152 x 117 cm) GBP 17,000. LONDON, 14 July 1993, *Bust Portrait of Edward Goldney wearing a Brown Velvet Coat* (1739, oil on canvas, 29 1/4 x 24 1/2 ins / 74 x 62 cm) GBP 4,600. LONDON, 10 July 1996, *Portrait of a Gentleman of the Lloyd Family wearing a Brown Coat with Lace Cuffs and Jabot* (oil on canvas, 36 x 28 ins / 91.5 x 71 cm) GBP 4,600. NEW YORK, 4 Oct 1996, *Bust Portrait of James Hanson wearing a Blue Coat* (oil on canvas, 36 x 28 ins / 91.3 x 71.1 cm) USD 4,600. MALMÖ, 13 Nov 1999, *Dionysus* (1753, oil on canvas, 31 x 26 ins / 78 x 66 cm) SEK 18,000. LONDON, 17 May 2001, *Portrait of Two Young Children, Elder Girl Building a House of Cards, Younger Playing* (oil on canvas, 61 x 48 ins / 156 x 121 cm) GBP 25,000. OXFORD, 27 June 2001, *Portrait of a Gentleman with White Stock and Brown Top Coat* (oil on canvas, 29 x 24 ins / 74 x 61 cm) GBP 2,500. LONDON, 27 May 2004, *Portrait of Henry Hansons* (oil on canvas, 36 x 28 ins / 91 x 71 cm) GBP 5,800. LONDON, 28 June 2004, *Self-portrait* (mezzotint, 20 x 14 ins / 50 x 35 cm) GBP 3,400.

FRYER, Edward H.
British, 19th century.
Painter. Landscapes.

Edward H. Fryer was a frequent exhibitor in London between 1834 and 1843.

FRYER, Gaetano
Italian, 18th century.
Born 1746, in Verona; died 1776, in Verona.
Active in Verona and Parma.
Painter.

Gaetano Fryer was a painter of English extraction who studied under Cignaroli.

FRYER, Leonard
British, 17th century.
Active in London c. 1600.
Painter.

Leonard Fryer was retained as a 'sergeant painter' by Queen Elisabeth I.

FRYG, Ludwig. See **FRIG**

FRYON, Georges
French, 16th century.
Born in Cambrai.
Sculptor (wood).

Fryon worked on the wood carvings in Valenciennes Cathedral in 1550.

FRYS, F.
Flemish School, 19th century.
Painter. History painting.

He is mentioned by Siret. A pupil of Jos Paelinck in Ghent, he was active in Brussels in 1830.

FRYSOU, Pieter Frans
Flemish School, 18th century.
Active in Bruges (West Flanders), in the middle of the 18th century.
Painter.

FRYTOM, Frederik van, or Frutom, Freytom
Dutch, 17th century.
Born in Delft; died 1658.
Painter (porcelain). Landscapes.

Frytom was best known as a painter on porcelain.

F:V:FRYTOM

FRYTOM, Joanna van
Dutch, 17th century.
Painter.

Joanna van Frytom was a relative of Frederik van Frytom, possibly his daughter.

FU BAOSHI, or Fu Pao-Shih
Chinese, 20th century.
Born 1904, in Jiangxi; died 1965, in Nanjing.
Painter, calligrapher, print artist. Landscapes with figures, figures, figure compositions. Seals.

Fu Baoshi served as an apprentice in a ceramic shop. In 1921 he graduated from Jiangxi College of Education. In 1933-1935 he studied at the Imperial School of Fine Arts in Tokyo, and on his return was appointed professor in the fine arts department of National Central University, Nanjing. He served on various arts committees for the Ministry of Education. He spent the war in Sichuan, in 1946 taking up teaching again in Nanjing. In 1949, he was appointed head of the Jiangsu Academy, and in 1960 vice-president of the Chinese Artists Association and president of its Nanjing branch. In about 1950, Fu Baoshi travelled across China with a group of artists. In 1957, he visited Czechoslovakia (now the Czech Republic) and Romania. After his death, his Nanjing residence was turned into a museum, the Fu Baoshi Museum. In 1982, his work was included in the exhibition *Cinq grands peintres chinois - la tradition au XXème siècle* (*Five Great Chinese Painters: Tradition in the 20th century*) held at the Musée d'Art Moderne, Paris.

Fu Baoshi's experience of Japan as a student allowed him to distance himself from Chinese pictorial tradition, to absorb and adapt it in his own way. He painted mostly landscapes and figures. Where the latter are concerned, he considered himself the heir to the masters of the Tang dynasty (618-906) as well as Chan Buddhist masters such as Liang Kai (active mid-13th century), the painter of figures 'in broken ink'. He was also deeply influenced by the subtle eccentricity of Chan Hongshou (1598-1652). As for his landscapes, he refers directly to the teachings of Shitao (Daoji, 1641-1720).

In addition to his work as a painter, Fu Baoshi was also a seal carver and wrote several works on the theory and history of painting, including a study on dating Shitao, which remains a standard work. Although he worked in a traditional style, albeit with an occasional trace of western artistic influence, his work is very personal. This comes from his delicate brushstrokes, even though his style is loose, and his colour sense, which despite being slightly decorative, is a subtle harmony of greys and greens, pale blues and warm browns. With a fan-shaped paintbrush, he paints dense foliage over panoramic horizons, often watery expanses. He likes to cover large areas of his pictorial space with very fine brush strokes, and to insert a group of figures, glimpsed through the clouds or bathed in hazy sunlight, into a critical part of the composition. If his technique remains traditional, he adds a modern touch to his pictures by adding high-voltage power lines, factory chimneys, or steamships. Fu Baoshi's work is considered to be occasionally uneven, but his successful works are among some of the most distinctive of the first half of the 20th century.

BIBLIOGRAPHY:

Ryckmans, P., '*Fu Baoshi*' in *Encyclopædia Universalis* vol. IV et XVI, Paris, 1972. Boissier, Jean-Louis, *Cinq grands peintres chinois - la tradition au XXème siècle*, exhibition catalogue, Musée d'Art moderne de la Ville de Paris, Paris, 1982. Andrews, Julia F., *Painters and Politics in the People's Republic of China: 1949-1979*, University of California Press, Berkeley, 1994. Vainker, Shelagh, '*A Landscape by Fu Baoshi: traditional painting in modern China*' in *Apollo*, vol 143, no. 409, March 1996. Yang Xin and others, *Three Thousand Years of Chinese Painting*, Yale University Press, 1997. Clunas, Craig, *Art in China*, Oxford University Press, Oxford and New York, 1997. Fahr-Becker, Gabriele, *The Art of East Asia: Volume 1*, Konemann, Cologne, 1998.

Museums and Galleries:

Beijing (Nat. Assembly Nat.): *Zhongshan's Tomb (Sun Yat-sen's Tomb, near Canton)* (in collaboration with the painter Guan Shanyue) - Gatineau (Musée Canadien des Civilisations): *Landscape* (1964, scroll) - Nanjing (Fu Baoshi Commemorative Mus.): large collection of work; *Shitao's Studio* (1945, scroll) - New York (Metropolitan Mus. of Art): *Playing Weiqi at Water Pavilion* (hanging scroll) - Paris (Mus. Cernuschi): *Dreamer*.

Auction records:

Hong Kong, 11 May 1983, *Scholar Playing Qin* (ink and colour, 35 ins / 88 cm x 23 1/4 ins/59 cm) HKD 110,000. Hong Kong, 12 Jan 1986, *Listening to Waterfall on Bridge* (1945, ink and colour on paper, hanging scroll, 46 x 15 1/2 ins / 117 x 39.5 cm) HKD 200,000. Hong Kong, 12 Jan 1987, *Boating on Autumn River* (ink and colour on paper, hanging scroll, 52 x 15 ins / 132 x 38 cm) HKD 140,000. Hong Kong, 17 Nov 1988, *Waterfalls* (1964, ink and colour on paper, hanging scroll, 27 x 17 3/4 ins / 68.5 x 45.4 cm) HKD 176,000; *Pavilion on Hill* (1945, ink and colour on paper, hanging scroll, 33 1/2 x 20 ins / 85 x 51 cm) HKD 209,000. Hong Kong, 16 Jan 1989, *Game of Go under Pavilion* (ink and colour on paper, hanging scroll, 50 x 12 3/4 ins / 127 x 32.5 cm) HKD 154,000; *Album of Nine Weavers* (ink and colour on paper, 11 leaves, each 10 1/2 x 12 1/2 ins / 26.5 x 32 cm) HKD 3,410,000. Hong Kong, 18 May 1989, *From a Poem by Shitao* (diluted ink and colour on paper, hanging scroll, 34 1/4 x 22 3/4 ins / 86.8 x 57.8 cm) HKD 715,000; *Landscape with Waterfall* (1944, ink and colour on paper, hanging scroll, 36 x 24 ins / 91.4 x 61 cm) HKD 1,320,000. New York, 31 May 1989, *Figure in Landscape* (ink and colour on paper, hanging scroll, 40 3/4 x 24 ins / 103.5 x 61 cm) USD 8,800. Hong Kong, 15 Nov 1989, *Two Young Women with Musical Instrument* (1945, ink and colour on paper, hanging scroll, 27 x 18 ins / 68.5 x 45.8 cm) HKD 1,100,000. New York, 4 Dec 1989, *Contemplating Waterfall* (ink and colour on paper, hanging scroll, 28 3/4 x 15 3/4 ins / 73 x 40 cm) USD 17,600. New York, 31 May 1990, *Landscape* (ink and colour on paper, hanging scroll, 38 x 21 1/4 ins / 96.5 x 54 cm) USD 14,300. Hong Kong, 15 Nov 1990, *Snowy Landscape* (1945, ink and light colour on paper, hanging scroll, 35 x 22 ins / 89 x 56 cm) HKD 484,000. New York, 26 Nov 1990, *Landscape with Figures* (ink and colour on paper, hanging scroll, 54 x 15 3/4 ins / 137.3 x 40 cm) USD 30,800. Hong Kong, 31 Oct 1991, *Songs of Autumn* (1946, ink and light colour on paper, hanging scroll, 25 1/4 x 16 ins / 64.2 x 39.7 cm) HKD 308,000. New York, 25 Nov 1991, *Watching Waterfall* (ink and colour on paper, hanging scroll, 27 x 18 1/4 ins / 68.3 x 46.3 cm) USD 17,600. Hong Kong, 30 March 1992, *Paintings on themes of the Ancient Poets* (ink and colour on paper, album of twelve leaves, each 9 3/4 x 12 ins / 25 x 30.4 cm) HKD 1,320,000; *Landscape that Inspired the Poem by Du Mu* (ink and colour on paper, hanging scroll, 80 x 49 1/2 ins / 203 x 125.5 cm) HKD 2,090,000. Hong Kong, 28 Sept 1992, *Seven Wise Men in Bamboo Plantation* (ink and colour on paper, 13 1/2 x 85 ins / 34.2 x 215.8 cm) HKD 825,000. Hong Kong, 22 March 1993, *Meeting in Orchid House* (ink and colour on paper, hanging scroll, 85 3/4 x 24 1/2 ins / 218.1 x 62.3 cm) HKD 570,000. Hong Kong, 29 April 1993, *Young Woman in Garden* (ink and colour on paper, hanging scroll, 54 1/4 x 13 1/2 ins / 138.1 x 34.3 cm) HKD 680,000. New York, 16 June 1993, *Game of Go in Pavilion on Piles by Pond* (ink and colour on paper, hanging scroll, 53 ins / 134.500 cm) USD 134,500. Hong Kong, 5 May 1994, *Snowy Landscape* (ink and colour on paper, 43 x 13 1/2 ins / 109.5 x 34 cm) HKD 526,000. Hong Kong, 3 Nov 1994, *Portrait of Tao Yunming* (1957, ink and colour on paper, hanging scroll, 28 1/4 x 19 1/2 ins / 72 x 49.5 cm) HKD 548,000. Hong Kong, 28 April 1997, *Snowy Mountain Stream* (1944, ink and colour on paper, hanging scroll, 53 1/4 x 19 ins / 135.5 x 48.5 cm) HKD 345,000. Hong Kong, 26 April 1999, *Scholar Standing in Lakeside Pavilion* (ink colour, 13 x 16 ins / 34 x 40 cm) HKD 200,000. Hong Kong, 26 April 1999, *Historical Figures* (ink colour, a pair, 12 x 9 ins / 30 x 23 cm) HKD 350,000. Hong Kong, 28 Oct 2001, *Farewell to Yangkwan* (1944, ink and colour, scroll, 24 x 39 ins / 62 x 100 cm) HKD 2,600,000. Hong Kong, 6 May 2002, *Journey at Sunset* (ink and colour, 13 x 20 ins / 32 x 50 cm) HKD 200,000. Hong Kong, 6 May 2002, *Landscape Inspired by Mao Zedong's Poem* (1964, ink and colour, 17 x 23 ins / 44 x 58 cm) HKD 250,000. Hong Kong, 28 April 2003, *Two Ladies* (1950, ink and colour, hanging scroll, 35 x 24 ins / 90 x 61 cm) HKD 1,200,000. Hong Kong, 27 Oct 2003, *Bidding Farewell to Shitao* (1942, ink and colour, hanging scroll, 33 x 23 ins / 84 x 58 cm) HKD 5,200,000. Hong Kong, 26 April 2004, *Strolling in Spring* (1945, ink and colour, 52 x 16 ins / 133 x 41 cm) HKD 1,800,000. Hong Kong, 26 April 2004, *Seven Sages* (1946, ink and colour, hanging scroll, 44 x 26 ins / 113 x 67 cm) HKD 5,400,000.

FU DAOKUN, or Fu Tao-k'un
Chinese, 17th century.
Born in Kuaiji (Zhejiang).
Active during the first half of the 17th century.
Painter.

Fu Daokun was the wife of a scholar named Fan. She painted landscapes in the style of the masters of the Tang and Song dynasties (7th-13th centuries).

Museums and Galleries:

Beijing (Palace Mus.): *Two Dead Trees and Bamboo near Rock* (signed and dated 1621).

FU HI. See **MA YUAN-YU**

FU JUANFU
Chinese, 20th century.
Born 1910, in Zhejiang.
Painter.

Fu Juanfu's father taught him calligraphy and seal carving from an early age. At the age of 17, he went to the Hangzhou Academy. His work was shown in exhibitions in Japan, Korea and the USA.

Auction records:

Taipei, 18 Oct 1992, *Scholars Contemplating Waterfall* (ink and colour on paper, hanging scroll, 36 1/2 x 21 1/4 ins / 93 x 54 cm) TWD 198,000.

FU MEI, style names: Shoumao, Xunan, sobriquets: Zhuling, Mi daoren
Chinese, 17th century.
Born 1628; died 1682.
Painter.

Fu Mei was the son of the painter Fu Shan (1605-1684). Like his father, he was a poet, calligrapher and seal carver, but above all a landscape artist, known for the atmosphere evoked in his paintings.

Museums and Galleries:

Tianjin: *Landscape* (album leaf in colour on silk).

FU PAO-SHIH. See **FU BAOSHI**

FU SHAN, style names: Dingchen, Qingzhu, sobriquets: Zhenshan, Selu, Gongzhita, Renzhong, Liuchi, Suili, Silu, Zhuyi, Shi daoren
Chinese, 17th century.
Born 1602, 1605 or 1606, in Yangquan or Taiyuan (Shanxi); died 1683 or 1684, 1690 according to some sources.
Painter.

Fu Shan was a physician, painter, and a great calligrapher, but is known above all for his brilliant career as a high-ranking official, which he cut short at the fall of the Ming dynasty in 1644, retiring to the country to look after his mother. Even after peace was restored, he continued to live alone as a peasant farmer, and although in 1678, during the reign the Qing Emperor Kangxi, he was named 'Scholar of Vast Knowledge' and appointed secretary to the Grand Secretariat, he resolutely declined to accept this prestigious position and returned to his place of birth near Taiyun. After his death, a commemorative temple, the Fugongci, was erected in his honour. The legendary stories of his great talent as a calligrapher and painter are still current among the peasant farmers of northwestern China. Many of his writings were collated and published, first in 1747, then in 1853 and 1911, under the title *Shuanghongkan ji*, then *Selu zazhu*. Fu worked in the painterly tradition of Dong Qichang (1555-1636) and of the eccentrics of the early Qing dynasty, painting landscapes and bamboo. His landscapes are freely executed, with a curious way of arranging space in sequences of simplified geometric shapes and other sequences that are almost pointillist. His mountains lack detailed texture but have a great sense of internal structure, while his bamboo paintings have been praised for the qiyun shengdong, or spirit resonance, that brings them to life.

BIBLIOGRAPHY:

Bai, Qianshen, *Fu Shan's World: The Transformation of Chinese Calligraphy in the Seventeenth century*, Harvard University Press, 2003.

MUSEUMS AND GALLERIES:

BEIJING (Palace Mus.): *Bridges and Pavilion on Piles over Stream at Foot of Mountain* (inscription dated 1666) - HONG KONG (Ho Kuan-Wu): *Monk Sitting with Ghost before Begging Bowl* (long signed inscription) - OSAKA (Municipal Mus. of Art): *Cliff* (ink on silk) - TIANJIN: *Landscape* (colour on silk, leaf from an album).

AUCTION RECORDS:

NEW YORK, 4 Dec 1989, *Landscape* (ink on gilded paper, hanging scroll, 76 3/4 x 21 3/4 ins / 195 x 55.5 cm) USD 9,900. NEW YORK, 31 May 1990, *Fishing* (ink on gilded paper, painted fan, 6 x 17 1/4 ins / 15.3 x 43.8 cm) USD 3,575. NEW YORK, 26 Nov 1990, *Calligraphy in running script* (hanging scroll, 76 x 22 1/4 ins / 193 x 56.2 cm) USD 11,000. TAIPEI, 10 April 1994, *Album of Letters* (ink on paper, 36 leaves of different sizes) TWD 977,500. NEW YORK, 31 May 1994, *Calligraphy in grass script* (ink on paper, hanging scroll, 66 1/2 x 21 1/2 ins / 168.9 x 54.3 cm) USD 5,750. NEW YORK, 21 March 1995, *Poem by Du Mu* (ink on satin, hanging scroll, 75 x 17 ins / 190.5 x 43.2 cm) USD 18,400.

FU SIDA, or Fu Ssu-ta
Chinese, 20th century.
Died 1960.
Painter, draughtsman, illustrator.

At first, Fu Sida studied traditional Chinese painting in Beijing. In 1937, he left for the USA, then India and Malaya. During World War II, he taught at the Guilin Institute, and then in Shanghai. During the 1950s he was imprisoned and persecuted. Fu was one of a generation of artists who had come into contact with western painting during the war. His drawing is sober and effective. He made a series of studies of the traditional Chinese theatre, which stand comparison with the work of Guan Ling and Lin Fengmian, more in terms of his aims than his style.

BIBLIOGRAPHY:

Sullivan, Michael, *Chinese Art in the Twentieth century*, University of California Press, Berkeley, 1959.

FU SSU-TA. See **FU SIDA**

FU TAO-K'UN. See **FU DAOKUN**

FU WEN, or Fu Wên, style name: Zilai, sobriquet: Kaiting
Chinese, 18th century.
Born in Guanging (Manchuria).
Painter.

Fu Wen was a finger painter who worked in the style of Gao Qipei (c.1672 to c.1734).

MUSEUMS AND GALLERIES:

COLOGNE (Mus. für ostasiatische Kunst): *Old Man Contemplating Waterfall* (finger painting, signed) - PARIS (Mus. National des Arts asiatiques-Guimet): *Old Man before Musical Stone* (finger painting, signed).

FUAREZ, Anne. See **FAURE**

FUCCIO
Italian, 13th century.
Sculptor, architect.

In Assisi this artist sculpted the *Tomb of the Queen of Cyprus*. He also worked in Rome and Naples.

FUCCIO, Cola di. See **COLA DI FUCCIO**

FUCHÉ, G.
French, 19th century.
Lithographer.

MUSEUMS AND GALLERIES:

ROCHEFORT: *Gleaners* (after Millet).

FUCHS
German, 19th century.
Active in France.
Painter, decorative artist.

This artist worked for the Paris opera.

FUCHS, Adam
German, 16th century.
Born c. 1540, in Nuremberg; died 1606.
Active from 1542 to 1580.
Engraver (copper/wood).

Fuchs made portrait engravings and engravings of landscapes.

FUCHS, Alois
Austrian, 19th century.
Born 1838, in Berwang.
Sculptor.

Alois Fuchs was a pupil of Renner.

FUCHS, Anton
Austrian, 19th century.
Born 27 June 1807, in Innichen; died 10 February 1886, in Innichen.
Painter.

FUCHS, Auguste
German, 19th century.
Born c. 1800, in Heilbronn (Baden-Württemberg).
Painter.

Auguste Fuchs spent some time in Rome before settling in Stuttgart.

FUCHS, C. C.
Dutch, 19th century.
Died c. 1850, in Amsterdam.
Engraver.

Fuchs produced copies of old master paintings.

FUCHS, Carl
Austrian, 19th century.
Born 26 November 1842, in Innichen; died 27 June 1883, in Innichen.
Sculptor.

The museum in Merano (Trentino-Alto Adige, Italy) has statues by this artist.

FUCHS, Caspar
German, 18th century.

Died 14 February 1741.
Painter.
Caspar Fuchs executed paintings for the church in Bad Saulgau (Baden-Württemberg).

FUCHS, Charles
German, 19th century.
Born 28 October 1803, in Prague; died 5 March 1874, in Hamburg.
Lithographer.
Charles Fuchs studied art in Strasbourg (Alsace) and mainly executed portraits and landscapes.

FUCHS, Danièle
French, 20th century.
Born 16 May 1931.
Painter, watercolourist, engraver, illustrator, designer. Landscapes with figures, waterscapes, urban landscapes, flowers.
Danièle Fuchs studied under Édouard Goerg and Robert Cami at the École des Beaux-Arts in Paris and lives and works in Paris. She comes from a family of horticultural specialists and has continued in the family tradition with her paintings of flowers. She has also painted views of Normandy and Venice and landscapes of Colorado. She has illustrated various books and produced engraved copper and stone stations of the cross for Notre-Dame-du-Chêne at Viroflay.

She has exhibited at numerous group exhibitions, including: in Paris, at the Salon d'Automne, the Salon des Artistes Indépendants, the Salon of the Société Nationale des Beaux-Arts and also at the Galerie Charpentier, the Musée Galliéra and the Bibliothèque Nationale. She has shown her work in solo exhibitions: regularly in Paris since 1961, in Versailles, in 1966 at the Institut Français in Hamburg; in 1968 in Nassau and also in Chambéry and Strasbourg and in 2002 at the Galerie St-Hubert in Lyons. She has received various awards at exhibitions on the outskirts of Paris. She is a member of the École de Versailles created in 1974.

MUSEUMS AND GALLERIES:
AMIENS - ANGERS - BAYEUX - DIJON - STRASBOURG - TOURS.

AUCTION RECORDS:
NEW YORK, 13 May 1981, *The Trance* (1973, oil on card, 34 1/2 x 26 3/4 ins / 87.5 x 68 cm) USD 2,000. LE TOUQUET, 12 Nov 1989, *Harvest in Touraine* (1969, oil on canvas, 25 1/2 x 32 ins / 65 x 81 cm) FRF 12,500. CALAIS, 4 March 1990, *Banks of the Loire* (oil on canvas, 32 x 39 1/4 ins / 81 x 100 cm) FRF 11,000. LE TOUQUET, 11 Nov 1990, *The Lefebvres' Rock Partridge at Chantemerle les Grignans* (1975, oil on canvas, 25 1/2 x 39 1/4 ins / 65 x 100 cm) FRF 8,000.

FUCHS, Emil
Austrian, 19th - 20th century.
Born 9 August 1866, in Vienna.
Sculptor. Busts.
Émile Fuchs studied with Victor Tegner in Vienna and Ernst Herter in Berlin. He exhibited in Paris, receiving an honourable mention at the Salon des Artistes Français in 1907.

FUCHS, Ernst
Austrian, 20th century.
Born 1930, in Vienna.
Painter, draughtsman, engraver, illustrator, sculptor, collage artist, decorative designer. Scenes with figures, figures. Stage sets.
Groups: Hundsgruppe (Dog's group), Phantastischer Realismus group.
Ernst Fuchs enrolled at the Akademie der Bildenden Künste in Vienna in 1945. From 1946 to 1950, he was a pupil of Gütersloh, whom Salvador Dalí considered the most important painter of his time (after himself). In around 1950, he was one of the founders of the Viennese Hundsgruppe (Dog's Group), which represented Fantastic Realism, along with Ernst Bauer, Hausner, Hutter, Anton Lehrnden and Arnulf Rainer. He travelled in the USA from 1954 to 1956 and he often stayed in France between 1950 and 1959. He was closely associated with Dali and also knew Magritte, Max Ernst, Victor Brauner, Félix Labisse and Léonor Fini.

He converted to Catholicism in 1956, after which religious themes were much to the fore in his very diverse body of work. He only began exhibiting in 1958. He was opposed to Functionalism and the Bauhaus; his tastes led him towards the poetry of the Symbolists and Surrealists and, looking back to the past, towards William Blake, Gustave Moreau and Odilon Redon. As far as Expressionism is concerned, he started by admiring Klimt and Schiele, Camperdonk and Munch. Later, after 1946, and especially after 1961, he studied what he called the 'vanished style', the meticulous technique of Grünewald, Altdorfer, Schongauer and Dürer, as well as such Mannerists as Jacques Belange and Antoine Caron. He found echoes both of these ancient techniques and of the strength of expression of 16th century German painters in the works of Otto Dix and Georg Grosz, which also influenced him at one time. His engravings and illustrations are reminiscent of the ornamental affectations of Aubrey Beardsley and Gustav Klimt. It must be said that not only does his work take on many different forms, it is also difficult to follow logically and chronologically the succession of artists he admired and whom he allowed to influence him according to what he thought he needed, especially as he was also interested in Babylonian, Hittite, Assyrian and native American art.

Fuchs' subsidiary activities were so important that they must have taken up as much of his working life as his work as a painter and leader of the Fantastic Realists. He was extremely versatile, among other things a composer of music, a television producer, a furniture designer and a sculptor. He designed the sets and costumes for *Lohengrin, Parsifal, the Magic Flute, the Tales of Hoffmann, the Golem* and *the Legend of Joseph*. He produced important series of engravings, such as *Samson*, 1960-1964, *Esther*, 1964-1967 and *Sphinx*, 1966-1967. In 1961, he finally managed to acquire the country house of the architect Otto Wagner, which he completely refurbished for his own use.

As a young man, he showed great skill and control in his imaginary pictures of biblical cities. Mention can be made of *Christ before Pilate* of 1955-1956, which shows the influence of the New Objectivity of Dix and Grosz. In 1956-1957, he painted *Moses and the Burning Bush* and between 1958 and 1961, he painted the three great *Rosaries* for the Church of the Rosary in Hetzendorf-Meidling, works which are characteristic of these years. He is among the modern descendants of the Fantastic Art movement, which was regenerated by the Surrealists. He draws on the areas of esotericism, alchemy and Wagnerian mythology for his subject matter, but most of all on the Bible. In 1977-1978, he painted the great mural of the *Sign of Moses*. Later, using a more colourful palette, he added mythical figures to his landscapes, for instance in *Arcadia* of 1982-1984, which revisits the subject used by Poussin.

In his ideas, beliefs and practices, Ernst Fuchs invested the artist with a mystical duty, a prophetic mission. The sheer abundance of his work defies comprehension and definition. Influences are interwoven, themes superimposed. Through the biblical subjects, which are not necessarily religious, he also expresses the contemporary world of man on earth today. From the point of view of his use of symbols and of his style in general, his work appears to be an extension into a later age of the transitional period of Symbolism, the Secession and the Nouveau Style, which probably caused his traditional themes and his original spirituality to become somewhat corrupted when they came into contact with the heretical world of the Surrealists.

BIBLIOGRAPHY:

Brion, Marcel, *La peinture allemande*, Éd. Pierre Tisné, Paris, 1959. Brion, Marcel, *Ernst Fuchs*, exhibition catalogue, Paris, 1974.

MUSEUMS AND GALLERIES:

VIENNA (Österreichische Gal. Belvedere): *Moses and the Burning Bush* (1956-1957).

AUCTION RECORDS:

MUNICH, 26 Nov 1973, *Head of a Cherub*, DEM 20,000. MUNICH, 25 Nov 1974, *The Two Friends (recto)* (pastel); *Nude (verso)* (charcoal) DEM 12,500. VIENNA, 25 June 1976, *The Queen Mother* (1961, etching) ATS 5,000. VIENNA, 25 June 1976, *The Sign of Moses* (1964, pencil and pen/paper, 12 x 18¾ ins / 30.5 x 47.5 cm) ATS 40,000. VIENNA, 18 March 1977, *Standing nude* (1970, pastel/blue paper, 25½ x 19¾ ins / 65 x 50 cm) ATS 25,000. LONDON, 7 Dec 1977, *Medusa* (1968, acrylic and coloured chalk, 21 x 16½ ins / 53.5 x 42 cm) GBP 1,500. LONDON, 3 April 1979, *Woman and Wild Animal* (watercolour, 19½ x 12¼ ins / 49.5 x 31 cm) GBP 4,800. PARIS, 23 Oct 1981, *Seated Nude* (charcoal/paper, 24¾ x 18¾ ins / 63 x 47.5 cm) FRF 5,000. VIENNA, 11 Oct 1983, *The Kiss of Pan* (etching in silver, with a gold-leaf border, 9¼ x 7 ins / 23.5 x 17.5 cm) ATS 12,000. HEIDELBERG, 14 April 1984, *Flowers in a Red Vase* (1983, pastel and tempera, 28½ x 18 ins / 72.5 x 45.5 cm) DEM 13,000. VIENNA, 15 May 1984, *The Town* (1946, pencil, 35½ x 24¾ ins / 90 x 63 cm) ATS 180,000. ZURICH, 7 June 1985, *Die beiden Erdteile* (*The Two Continents*) (1967-1969, tempera, 22½ x 30 ins / 57.4 x 76 cm) CHF 90,000. ZURICH, 7 June 1985, *Das Licht des Thora* (*Thora's Light*) (1961, charcoal and colouring pencil, 42¼ x 59½ ins / 107 x 151 cm) CHF 38,000. VIENNA, 17 March 1987, *Portrait of Hannelore Elsner* (1977-1978, lead pencil and coloured chalk, 13½ x 10 ins / 34 x 24.5 cm) ATS 45,000. PARIS, 24 Nov 1987, *Portrait with a Bird* (1962, drawing and collage/paper, 10¼ x 8¾ ins / 26 x 22.5 cm) FRF 18,000. ZURICH, 4 Dec 1987, *Sphinx* (1977, bronze, h. 7¾ ins / 19.5 cm, Long. 14¼ ins/36 cm) CHF 6,000. PARIS, 21 March 1988, *Daphne* (patinated bronze sculpture, h. 14½ ins / 37 cm) FRF 6,000. LONDON, 22 Feb 1989, *Janus* (1954, oil/parchment, 14 x 8¾ ins / 34.7 x 22.1 cm) GBP 10,450. PARIS, 4 April 1989, *History of the World* (1949, etching, 35½ x 16½ ins / 90 x 42 cm) FRF 6,000. PARIS, 27 Oct 1990, *Composition* (ink and watercolour/paper, 18 x 13¼ ins / 46 x 33.5 cm) FRF 39,000. HEIDELBERG, 12 Oct 1991, *In the Kingdom of the Dead* (1950, etching, 8½ x 3¾ ins / 21.5 x 9.7 cm) DEM 3,000. PARIS, 15 April 1992, *The Stone Staircases* (1991, charcoal/paper, 10¼ x 13¾ ins / 26 x 35 cm) FRF 4,000. HEIDELBERG, 3 April 1993, *Masks* (soft-ground etching, 20¾ x 16¼ ins / 53 x 41.5 cm) DEM 1,450. PARIS, 23 April 1993, *Apparition in the Crypt* (charcoal/paper, 10¼ x 13¾ ins / 26 x 35 cm) FRF 4,500. HEIDELBERG, 5-13 April 1994, *Barcarolle* (1977, etching with watercolour, 10 x 11½ ins / 25.5 x 29.2 cm) DEM 1,350. ZURICH, 13 Oct 1994, *Salome* (1970, metal sculpture) CHF 1,100. VIENNA, 21 April 1999, *Cherubim Like Made of Turquoise* (oil on board, 36 x 28 ins / 91 x 72 cm) ATS 220,000. VIENNA, 13 Oct 1999, *Golgotha* (1948, pencil, 18 x 16 ins / 46 x 41 cm) ATS 650,000. VIENNA, 29 Nov 2000, *By the Water at Night* (1946, linocut, 13 x 9 ins / 32 x 24 cm) ATS 100,000. VIENNA, 29 Nov 2000, *Still-life of Flowers* (mixed media on paper, 30 x 22 ins / 75 x 56 cm) ATS 120,000. BREMEN, 12 Oct 2001, *Harvest Flowers* (1986, pastel, 28 x 18 ins / 72 x 45 cm) DEM 10,000. VIENNA, 27 Nov 2001, *Flowers in Vence* (1985, pastel, 24 x 19 ins / 62 x 47 cm) ATS 120,000. VIENNA, 14 May 2002, *Portrait of Adlmuller* (1957, oil on board, 19 x 24 ins / 49 x 60 cm) EUR 13,000. VIENNA, 27 Nov 2002, *In Spring* (1989, mixed media, 20 x 15 ins / 50 x 37 cm) EUR 9,500. VIENNA, 20 May 2003, *Sphynx in Eva* (1965, gouache, colour pen and charcoal, 21 x 15 ins / 53 x 38 cm) EUR 10,000. VIENNA, 26 Nov 2003, *White Negro Woman* (1968, oil and tempera, 31 x 22 ins / 78 x 55 cm) EUR 17,000. VIENNA, 27 Jan 2004, *Fantasy Flowers* (1992, oil on canvas, 24 x 31 ins / 60 x 80 cm) EUR 15,000. VIENNA, 23 Nov 2004, *Mallow Flowers* (1984, pastel, 25 x 19 ins / 63 x 47 cm) EUR 11,000.

FUCHS, Félix Cajetan Christoph

Swiss, 18th - 19th century.

Born 1749, in Rapperswil; died 14 March 1814, in St Gall.

Painter, sculptor, draughtsman.

Félix Fuchs began his studies in Augsburg and completed them in Rome. He is noted for his illustrations for Shakespeare's *Hamlet* and *Macbeth*.

FUCHS, Georg

German, 19th century.

Born c. 1835; died 30 January 1885.

Active in Cologne (North Rhine-Westphalia).

Painter, copyist.

Georg Fuchs was first and foremost a copyist.

FUCHS, Georg Friedrich

German, 18th century.

Active in Abtsbessingen (Thuringia).

Potter.

FUCHS, Georg Mathias

Austrian, 18th century.

Born c. 1719, in Vienna; died 5 April 1797, in Copenhagen, Denmark.

Painter, engraver, decorative artist. Genre scenes, portraits, landscapes, landscapes with figures.

Georg Mathias Fuchs was a pupil of Amigoni in Italy. He later lived in Copenhagen, where he executed some notable decorative pieces.

AUCTION RECORDS:

COPENHAGEN, 23 April 1987, *Landscape with a Bridge and Peasants with Dogs at the River's Edge* (1758, oil on canvas, 21¼ x 27¼ ins / 54 x 69 cm) DKK 28,000. LONDON, 9 Dec 1992, *Bird Trap; Rural Love* (1766, oil on canvas/card, a pair, each 35½ x 50½ ins / 90 x 128 cm) GBP 7,700. COPENHAGEN, 6 Sept 1993, *Portrait of the Teacher Ove Malling* (oil on canvas, 31½ x 24½ ins / 80 x 62 cm) DKK 18,000. COPENHAGEN, 15 Nov 1993, *Portrait of a Lady wearing a Red Cape with a Fur Collar and a Pearl Necklace and Earrings* (oil on canvas, 30¼ x 23½ ins / 77 x 60 cm) DKK 6,000. COPENHAGEN, 7 June 2004, *Portrait of Baron Reinhard Iselin* (1766, oil on canvas, 31 x 24 ins / 78 x 62 cm) DKK 40,000.

FUCHS, Gustave

19th century.

Died 10 November 1905, in New York, committed suicide.

Painter, sculptor.

FUCHS, Hans

Swiss, 15th century.

Born c. 1404, in Lucerne; died 5 December 1458, in Lucerne.

Glass painter.

Lucerne School.

Most of this artist's work, in Lucerne, dates from the period 1424-1445.

FUCHS, Hans

German, 16th century.

Died 1561, in Nordlingen (Bavaria).

Sculptor (wood).

Hans was the father of Michael Fuchs.

FUCHS, Hans
Austrian (?), 16th century.
Active in Prösel in 1541.
Sculptor (wood).
This is probably the same artist as the Hans Fuchs who died in 1561.

FUCHS, Hermann
German, 19th - 20th century.
Born 1871, in Hochdahl (North Rhine Westphalia).
Sculptor.
Hermann Fuchs was active in Berlin.

FUCHS, Hieronymus Franz
German, 17th century.
Active in Nuremberg (Bavaria).
Painter.
Hieronymus Fuchs is almost certainly the same artist as Hans Franz Fuchs.
MUSEUMS AND GALLERIES:
MUNICH (Mus.): a miniature.

FUCHS, J. G.
German, 18th century.
Active in Augsburg (Bavaria) during the second half of the 18th century.
Painter.
Nilson engraved this artist's *Portrait of Princess Sophie Frederika of Hohenlohe-Waldenburg.*

FUCHS, J. G. H.
German, 18th century.
Painter. Portraits.
The museum in Gotha has a work by this artist. He may well be the same artist as the one above.

FUCHS, Jacques
Swiss, 20th century.
Born 27 August 1922, in Lausanne; died 25 November 1980, in Cully.
Painter, sculptor. Figures, landscapes, animals.
Jacques Fuchs learned the rudiments of the trades of blacksmith and locksmith from his father. He studied at the school of fine arts in Lausanne, winning several prizes, and a federal bursary in 1959. He joined groups in Lausanne and many cities in Switzerland. His first exhibition was in 1944 in Lausanne and he organised another in 1959. He travelled in North and Sub-Saharan Africa and produced a lot of work in the USA and Mexico. He painted on the coasts of Brittany, Normandy and the Cotentin Peninsula, in the English and Irish countryside and in Holland, Belgium, Spain and Portugal. He also travelled to Martinique and Guadeloupe. He went to Paris in 1946 and joined the studio of André Lhote. His landscapes are slightly reminiscent of Derain's classical period.
AUCTION RECORDS:
ZURICH, 12 Nov 1976, *Landscape in Provence* (oil on canvas, 12 3/4 x 18 ins / 32.5 x 46 cm) CHF 2,400. ZURICH, 16 Dec 1981, *New York Docks* (1973, oil on canvas, 11 x 19 3/4 ins / 27 x 50 cm) CHF 4,200. ZURICH, 25 Jan 1984, *Algerian Women* (oil on canvas, 51 1/4 x 63 3/4 ins / 130 x 162 cm) CHF 13,000. ZURICH, 28 Oct 1987, *Priscott* (1973, oil on canvas, 24 x 28 1/4 ins / 61 x 72 cm) CHF 7,000.

FUCHS, Johann
Austrian, 19th century.
Born 7 October 1812, in Hopfgarten; died 1895.
Sculptor.
Johann Fuchs studied in Munich. He is noted for his *Mary at the Foot of the Cross* (in the church at Hopfgarten).

FUCHS, Joseph
French, 19th century.
Born in Bräunlingen (Baden-Württemberg).
Painter. History painting.
He studied under Dulfer and exhibited pen-and-ink drawings at the Paris Salon from 1865 to 1877, including *Ruth and Naomi* (1839). Joseph Fuchs also painted some major frescoes for the church of Sulzen.
BIBLIOGRAPHY:
Braignac, Véronique de, *'Le paysage exotique dans le papier peint panoramique français au 19e siècle'* in *Échanges et influences culturelles dans l'Océan Indien occidental: organisation de l'éspace et construction du paysage: actes du colloque organisé par la Maison française du meuble créole*, symposium proceedings, St-Gilles, 1994.

FUCHS, Karl
German, 19th century.
Born 6 December 1836, in Meiningen (Thuringia); died 10 March 1886, in Bern, Switzerland.
Painter. Landscapes.
Karl Fuchs studied in Thun under the guidance of Bühlmann.
AUCTION RECORDS:
BERN, 6 May 1981, *Alpine Landscape* (oil on canvas, 18 1/2 x 24 ins / 47 x 61 cm) CHF 1,200. BERN, 11 May 1984, *View of Lake Thun* (1864, oil on card, 9 x 11 3/4 ins / 22 x 30 cm) CHF 1,200.

FUCHS, Konrad
German, 17th century.
Active in Kulmbach (Bavaria).
Painter.
Konrad Fuchs painted an altarpiece for the church at Gesees.

FUCHS, Lodewijk Juliaan or Louis Julien
French, 19th century.
Born 1814, in Lille; died 23 April 1873, in Antwerp.
Active in Belgium from 1846.
Painter, engraver, lithographer. Landscapes.
Flemish-born artist who, like many of his fellow-countrymen, served in the French navy. He lived mainly in Antwerp and settled there permanently in 1846 when he entered the academy of fine arts. Fuchs painted beauty spots in the Scheldt valley, the countryside of the Kempen region and views of towns.

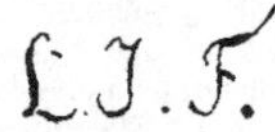

MUSEUMS AND GALLERIES:
ANTWERP: *Landscape*.
AUCTION RECORDS:
PORTLAND, 5 Nov 1983, *View of Bruges* (1863, oil on panel, 6 1/4 x 9in/16 x 22cm) USD 1,300.

FUCHS, Lorenz
Austrian, 19th century.
Died 1863, in Vienna.
Painter (porcelain).

FUCHS, Louis-Joseph-Gustave
French, 19th century.
Born in Paris.
Engraver, lithographer.
A pupil of E. Aucourt, he was awarded a bronze medal in 1890, a silver in 1892, and a further bronze at the Exposition Universelle of 1900.

FUCHS, Martin
Austrian, 18th century.
Active in Innsbruck.
Painter.

Martin Fuchs was a pupil of Martin Knoller. He is mainly credited with interiors and genre scenes inspired by the Dutch School.

FUCHS, Martin
German, 18th century.
Painter.
The church of St Peter in Cologne, Germany, has an *Adoration of the Shepherds* by this artist, painted in 1726.

FUCHS, Matthaeus
German, 17th century.
Born c. 1670; died 1699, in Breslau (now Wroclaw, Poland).
Painter (?).

FUCHS, Maurus Christoph
German, 19th century.
Active in Griesbach in 1801.
Painter.
Maurus was the son of Vitus Fuchs, and was still working in 1843 in Staab, Bohemia.

FUCHS, Maximilian Heinrich
German, 18th - 19th century.
Born c. 1767, in Cologne; died 17 May 1846, in Cologne.
Painter, draughtsman.
Maximilian Fuchs produced drawings for the cathedral in Cologne, Germany, and for various other churches in the city.

FUCHS, Michael
German, 16th century.
Sculptor (wood).
Nuremberg School.
Michael Fuchs became a burgher of Nuremberg in 1544.

FUCHS, Peter
German, 19th century.
Born 27 September 1829, in Mülheim (North Rhine-Westphalia); died 31 July 1898.
Sculptor.
Peter Fuchs worked mainly in Cologne, Hamburg and Frankfurt and specialised in religious sculpture.

FUCHS, Richard
German, 19th century.
Born 7 March 1852, in Berlin.
Painter. Local scenes.
Orientalism.
Richard Fuchs lived for a long time in Italy and North Africa.
AUCTION RECORDS:
NEW YORK, 24 Nov 1987, *Arabs in a Landscape in Southern Tunisia* (1906-1907, oil on canvas, 15 3/4 x 11 ins / 40.2 x 27.8 cm) USD 2,100. AHLDEN, 3 May 2002, *Mounted Bedouins* (oil on canvas, 11 x 19 ins / 27 x 48 cm) EUR 2,060. LONDON, 26 March 2003, *Birds on a Lake by Sunset* (oil on canvas, 31 x 21 ins / 79 x 54 cm) GBP 2,500. LONDON, 26 March 2003, *Arab Camp at Sunset* (oil on canvas, 24 x 39 ins / 60 x 100 cm) GBP 3,500.

FUCHS, Robert
German, 20th century.
Born 20 February 1874, in Saarbrücken.
Painter.
Robert Fuchs studied and later exhibited regularly in Frankfurt an Main.

FUCHS, Vitus
German, 18th century.
Active in Tischenreuth (Bavaria).
Painter.
Vitus Fuchs worked for the churches in Münchenreuth and Schwarzenbach, among others.

FÜCHSEL, Hermann, or Fuechsel, Fueschel
German, 19th - 20th century.
Born 8 August 1833, in Brunswick; died 30 September 1915, in New York.
Active in the USA.
Painter. Landscapes.
After studying with Brandes and Lessing in Düsseldorf, Hermann Füchsel settled in New York in 1858 or 1868.

H. Fuechsel

AUCTION RECORDS:
COLOGNE, 22 Nov 1973, *Church in a Landscape* (1878) DEM 4,600. NEW YORK, 24 April 1981, *Mountain Road* (1874, oil on canvas, 12 x 20 ins / 30.7 x 50.8 cm) USD 5,500. NEW YORK, 23 March 1984, *Farmyard on the Upper Hudson* (oil on canvas, 16 1/4 x 30 1/4 ins / 41 x 76.9 cm) USD 4,200. NEW YORK, 20 June 1985, *Waterfall* (1861, oil on canvas, rounded at the top, 52 x 25 ins / 132.1 x 63.5 cm) USD 10,500. NEW YORK, 24 June 1988, *River Landscape* (1869, oil on canvas, 11 3/4 x 19 3/4 ins / 30 x 50 cm) USD 14,850. NEW YORK, 24 May 1989, *Dream of New England* (oil on canvas, 35 x 46 1/4 ins / 88.9 x 117.4 cm) USD 40,700. NEW YORK, 30 May 1990, *Church on the Island* (1866, oil on canvas, 18 x 30 ins / 45.5 x 76.3 cm) USD 2,750. NEW YORK, 25 Sept 1991, *The White Mountains* (oil on canvas, 24 x 40 ins / 61 x 101.6 cm) USD 8,800. NEW YORK, 2 Dec 1992, *On the Lake* (oil on canvas, 11 x 20 ins / 27.9 x 50.8 cm) USD 1,870. NEW YORK, 11 March 1993, *Fishing in the lake* (oil on canvas, 15 x 30 ins / 38.2 x 76.4 cm) USD 8,050.

FUCHSHUBER, Hans
German, 17th century.
Active in Stettin, Prussia (now Szczecin, Poland) from the beginning of 1616.
Sculptor (wood).

FUCHSLI, Jakob, or Fuchssli
Swiss, 16th century.
Died 1559.
Active in Bremgarten.
Glass painter.

FÜCHSLI, Karl
Swiss, 18th century.
Active c. 1700.
Engraver.
Füchsli is credited with illustrations and vignettes.

FUCHSLIN, Johann Friedrich
Swiss, 19th century.
Born 22 November 1801, in Brugg; died 2 February 1857, in Hofstetten.
Portrait artist.
Fuchslin was mainly active in Bern.

FUCHSLOCH, Johann
German, 17th century.
Active in Obermachtat in 1698.
Sculptor.

FUCHSTHALLER, Alajos
Hungarian, 19th century.
Born c. 1815, in Budapest; died 1863.
Engraver.
Alajos Fuchsthaller studied under Kohlmann, and worked for various periodicals.

FUCIGNA
Italian, 17th century.
Born in Carrara.
Active also in Pisa.
Sculptor.

FUCIGNA, Ceccardo
Italian, 19th century.
Born in Carrara.
Sculptor.
Fucigna exhibited ten times at the Royal Academy in London between 1863 and 1879.

FUCINI, Giovanni Battista
Italian, 17th century.
Died 1630.
Active in Bologna.
Painter.
Giovanni Battista Fucini was a pupil of Garbieri.

FUCIUS
British.
Engraver.
Mentioned in *Art Prices Current.*

FUCKER, András
Hungarian, 18th century.
Active in Eperjes (now Prešov, Slovakia) at the end of the 18th century.
Engraver.

FÜCKER, Florian
Czech, 18th century.
Born c. 1676; died 3 March 1758.
Active in Glatz (now Kladsko, Poland).
Painter.
Florian Fücker appears in records in relation to his wife's death. He carried out a lot of work for the church at Wambierzyce in Poland.

FUCKERAD, Bernard
German, 17th century.
Born 1601, in Thuringia; died 21 April 1662, in Cologne (North Rhine-Westphalia).
Painter.
A monk with the Society of Jesus, Fuckerad executed various paintings for the church of the Jesuits and for the church of St Andreas in Cologne.

FUDGE, J.
British, 19th century.
Painter. Urban landscapes, architectural views, landscapes.
J. Fudge exhibited 25 works at the Royal Academy in London between 1815 and 1846.

FÜDRER, Rupprecht
German, 15th century.
Active in Passau and in Wasserburg (Bavaria) in the middle of the 15th century.
Glass painter.

FUECHSEL. See **FÜCHSEL**

FUEG, Ursus, or Fieg
Swiss, 18th century.
Born c. 1680; died 12 November 1750.
Active in Pruntrut.
Sculptor.
Fueg worked for the churches of Rheinau and St Urban.

FUENTES, Francisco Antonio
Italian, 19th century.
Born 1827, in Santa Marina del Obre.
Sculptor.
Fuentes lived and worked in the Noya region of Italy.

FUENTES, Giorgio
Italian, 18th - 19th century.
Born 1756, in Milan; died 1821, in Milan.
Painter.
Giorgio Fuentes was a pupil of Gonzagua. He painted decorative compositions for Milan's La Scala, the Frankfurt Theatre (1796-1805) and the Paris Opéra.

FUERRAS, Dionisio
Spanish, 19th century.
Born in the 19th century, in Ballota (Asturias).
Painter. History painting, portraits, genre scenes.
Dionisio Fuerras studied under F. de Madrazo at the Academia de San Fernando and experimented with all the different genres of painting. Between 1860 and 1866 he exhibited in Madrid, Paris and London. His best works include *Fiesta in Santiago; Artist's Studio;* and *Leaving after Mass in Galicia.*

FUERTES, Louis Agassiz
American, 20th century.
Born 7 February 1874, in Ithaca; died 1927.
Painter (gouache), watercolourist. Animals.
Louis Fuertes studied art in Boston. He painted almost exclusively birds.

BIBLIOGRAPHY:
Norelli, Martina R., *American Wildlife Painting,* Watson-Guptill (New York, 1975), Phaidon (London, 1976).

AUCTION RECORDS:
NEW YORK, 17 Nov 1978, *Birds of Massachusetts* (gouache, 19 1/2 x 14 1/2 ins / 49.5 x 37 cm) USD 1,900. NEW YORK, 6 Dec 1984, *Eagle on Catalina Island* (1921, watercolour, 29 x 19 1/2 ins / 73.6 x 49.5 cm) USD 14,000. NEW YORK, 20 June 1985, *Bird's Head* (watercolour and ink, 7 1/2 x 9 1/4 ins / 19 x 23.5 cm) USD 4,000. NEW YORK, 24 Jan 1989, *Pink Flamingos* (gouache/card, 14 x 23 1/2 ins / 35.6 x 59.7 cm) USD 17,600. NEW YORK, 24 May 1989, *Return of the Wild Ducks* (1919, watercolour and gouache/paper, 21 1/2 x 28 1/2 ins / 54.5 x 72.3 cm) USD 14,300. NEW YORK, 24 May 1990, *White-tufted Tamarin* (watercolour and gouache/paper, 13 x 9 1/4 ins / 33 x 23.5 cm) USD 18,700. NEW YORK, 15 May 1991, *Three Eagles* (watercolour/paper, 19 1/4 x 15 1/2 ins / 48.9 x 39.4 cm) USD 5,500. NEW YORK, 30 Oct 1996, *Saker Falcon* (gouache/paper, 18 1/4 x 13 1/4 ins / 46.4 x 33.7 cm) USD 4,312. BOSTON, 12 March 1999, *Old Squaw: Portrait of a Bird* (1909, watercolour, 9 x 12 ins / 23 x 30 cm) USD 6,000. NEW YORK, 7 Dec 1999, *Duck Pond* (watercolour, 19 x 24 ins / 48 x 61 cm) USD 2,000. BOSTON, 10 March 2000, *Prairie Falcon, Pyramid Lake, Nevada* (1926, gouache on paper on board, 30 x 22 ins / 76 x 55 cm) USD 16,000. BOSTON, 22 Sept 2000, *Sparrowhawk* (1896, watercolour and gouache en grisaille, 10 x 8 ins / 26 x 21 cm) USD 7,500. BOSTON, 9 March 2001, *Sparrows* (watercolour on paper laid down, 14 x 11 ins / 35 x 28 cm) USD 2,000. HAYDEN, 28 July 2001, *Heron Study* (gouache, 15 x 10 ins / 38 x 25 cm) USD 16,000. NEW YORK, 3 April 2003, *Two Pintails Flying over a Marsh* (watercolour and gouache on board, 11 x 8 ins / 29 x 20 cm) USD 5,000. BOSTON, 12 Sept 2003, *Kestrels in Flight* (watercolour on paper on board, 15 x 20 ins / 38 x 50 cm) USD 6,000.

FUES, Christian Friedrich
German, 18th - 19th century.
Born 1772; died 19 September 1836, in Nuremberg.
Painter, engraver. Portraits, genre scenes, landscapes with figures.
Active in Tübingen (Baden-Württemberg), Fues was a pupil of Harper and Hetsch in Stuttgart and taught at the academy in Nuremberg. He engraved landscapes and portraits and is also credited with some lithographs.

AUCTION RECORDS:
NEW YORK, 17 Jan 1990, *Landscape with People and Animals* (oil on canvas, 35 1/4 x 45 3/4 ins / 89.6 x 116.2 cm) USD 2,200.

FUESCHEL, Hermann. See **FÜCHSEL Hermann**

FUETER, Andreas
Swiss, 17th - 18th century.
Born 1660, in Bern; died 16 March 1742, in Bern.
Glass painter.
Andreas Fueter worked for the churches of Gryon, Murten, Muri, and others.

FUETER, Charlotte, or Madame Rytz Fueter
Swiss, 19th century.
Born 23 August 1804, in Bern; died 4 November 1880, in Bern.
Painter.
Charlotte Fueter took part in art exhibitions in 1824 and 1835.

FUETSCH, Karl
Austrian, 19th century.
Born 3 November 1823, in Mitteldorf; died 23 November 1902, in Patriasdorf.
Sculptor.
Fuetsch was a pupil of B. Gasser, and subsequently of his son, Joseph. He worked mainly for a large number of churches in the Austrian Tyrol, such as those at Dölsach and Nikolsdorf. The museum at Linz has a work by him entitled *Joseph and the Child*.

FUETSCHER, Christian Johann
German, 18th - 19th century.
Painter. Religious subjects.
Christian Fuetscher was active in Ludesch (Vorarlberg, Austria). He was the brother of Michael Anton and worked with his other brother, Johannes, for the church at Nüziders.

FUETSCHER, Johannes
German, 18th - 19th century.
Sculptor. Religious subjects.
Johannes Fuetscher was active in Ludesch. He was the brother of Michael Anton and Christian Johann, and worked with the latter for the church at Nüziders.

FUETSCHER, Michael Anton
German, 18th - 19th century.
Born 21 July 1774, in Ludesch; died 11 November 1827, in Frankfurt am Main.
Painter, engraver. Landscapes.
Michael Fuetscher was an outstanding pupil at the academy in Vienna and settled in Frankfurt in about 1807.

FUGAI, real name: Taira, monk's name: Entsu-ji Fugai, artist names: Fugai, Kojaku-ji, Fugai, Koyü, Shun'en
Japanese, 19th century.
Born 1779; died 1847.
Painter.
Nanga (literati) school.
Fugai was a Zen monk at the Kojaku-in temple, Mikawa (Aichi).

FUGE, James
British, 19th century.
Died 1838, in London.
Watercolourist.
James Fuge exhibited from 1832.

FUGE, W.H.
British, 19th century.
Active in Bocking (Essex).
Painter.
W.H. Fuge exhibited portraits and genre compositions at the Royal Academy between 1849 and 1866.

FUGEL, Gebhard
German, 19th century.
Born 14 August 1863, in Oberklöcken, near Ravensburg (Baden-Württemberg).
Painter. History painting.
Fugel was a pupil of Grunenwald at the art school in Stuttgart, and later studied under Clemens Schraudolph. He settled in Stuttgart and made his salon début in about 1885.

FUGELSCHAUG, Elias
Norwegian, 17th century.
Active in Bergen.
Painter.
Elias Fugelschaug painted mostly religious works but also some portraits. Some of his works are in the museum of Bergen.

FÜGER, Friedrich Heinrich
Austrian, 18th - 19th century.
Born 5 November 1751, in Heilbronn (Baden-Württemberg), Germany; died 8 December 1818, in Vienna.
Painter, miniaturist, fresco artist, draughtsman, engraver. Religious subjects, allegorical subjects, mythological subjects, portraits.
Friedrich Füger's first master was Nicolas Guibal in Stuttgart. He then worked in the legal profession in Halle in 1768, before taking up his paint brush again in 1770 and working under the guidance of Adam Friedrich Oeser in Leipzig. He later travelled to Dresden, where he executed several portraits. Queen Maria Theresa, in whose service he travelled to Vienna in 1774, was a great patron of his, providing him with the means to go to Rome in 1776, where he studied works of classical antiquity and the grand masters. In 1782 Füger completed several frescoes representing *Allegories on the Origins of Science* at the palace of Caserta in Naples. In 1783 he was appointed deputy director of the Austrian imperial gallery.

In his early years Füger concentrated mainly on miniature portraits, including that of *Maria Theresa Surrounded by her Family*, and history paintings. He was famous for having illustrated the *Messiah* by the poet Klopstock with twenty drawings that were engraved by Lexbold. As his sight gradually deteriorated, he abandoned miniature painting and once more devoted himself to portraiture.

MUSEUMS AND GALLERIES:
BERLIN: *Princess Varvara Vassiliewna Galitzin* - BUDAPEST: *Bathsheba* - GRAZ (Landesmus. Joanneum, Alte Gal.): *Mythological Scene; Portrait of the Count of Sauram* - LONDON (National Portrait Gal.): *Horatio Nelson, Viscount Nelson* (1800, oil on canvas) - LONDON (Wallace Collection): *Portrait* (study); *Two Sisters* (miniature) - MUNICH: *Mary Magdalene Repenting* - STUTTGART: *Death of Virginia* - VIENNA (Albertina Mus.): *Maria Theresa Surrounded by her Family* (miniature) - VIENNA (Czernin'sche Gemäldegal.): *Coriolanus Takes Leave of his Mother Veturia; Mary Magdalene Resting* - VIENNA (Österreichische Gal. Belvedere): *Allegory on Peace; Hector Bids Andromache Farewell; St John the Baptist; Mary Magdalene; Adam and Eve Weep over the Death of Abel; Miss Theresa Saal; Portrait of Baroness Dupont; Self-portrait.*
AUCTION RECORDS:
PARIS, 1864, *Antigone*, FRF 210. PARIS, 27 May 1932, *Elisabeth of Württemberg*, FRF 42,000. LONDON, 23 March 1934, *Wedding Night*, GBP 31. NEW YORK, 5 Feb 1942, *Portrait of the Countess of Bellegarde*, USD 225. PARIS, 8 April 1954, *Portrait of a Young Woman Wearing a White Dress and an Orange Shawl*, FRF 42,000. COLOGNE, 15 April 1964, *Portrait of Duke Friedrich von Erthal, Archbishop of Mainz*, DEM 9,500. LONDON, 27 Nov 1970, *Portrait of a Noblewoman*, Gns 850. VIENNA, 21 March 1972, *Portrait of the Pianist Gottlieb*

Christian Füger, the Artist's Brother, ATS 120,000. MUNICH, 1 June 1973, *Portrait of Countess Maria Caroline,* DEM 4,500. VIENNA, 11 Nov 1980, *The Three Graces Taking Cupid to his Parents* (1816, oil on canvas, 18 3/4 x 23 1/4 ins / 47.5 x 59 cm) ATS 160,000. MONTE CARLO, 14 Feb 1983, *Portrait of a Young Woman* (1796, oil on canvas, 30 x 25 1/4 ins / 76 x 64 cm) FRF 34,000. LONDON, 17 June 1986, *Mythological Scene* (oil on canvas, 55 1/2 x 80 1/4 ins / 141 x 204 cm) GBP 7,500. NEW YORK, 11 Jan 1989, *Poseidon* (oil on canvas, 58 x 39 1/2 ins / 147.3 x 100.5 cm) USD 22,000. MUNICH, 10 Dec 1992, *Thetis Asking Zeus for Achilles' Arms* (oil on canvas, 73 1/4 x 61 ins / 186 x 155 cm) DEM 20,340. LONDON, 11 March 1993, *Adam and Eve Crying over the Death of Abel* (oil on canvas, 28 1/2 x 36 ins / 72.5 x 91.5 cm) GBP 2,070. NEW YORK, 19 May 1994, *St John the Baptist in the Desert* (1809, oil on canvas, 21 1/4 x 26 3/4 ins / 54 x 67.9 cm) USD 4,600. MUNICH, 21 June 1994, *Frescoes on the Cupola of St Paul of Parma* (coloured etching, 17 1/2 x 21 3/4 ins / 44.5 x 55.5 cm) DEM 1,725. NEW YORK, 19 Jan 1995, *St Catherine* (charcoal and ink wash/blue-grey paper, 28 1/2 x 20 1/2 ins / 72.4 x 52.1 cm) USD 5,175. LONDON, 1 Nov 1996, *Penitent Mary Magdalene* (oil on canvas, 21 x 27 ins / 53.4 x 68.6 cm) GBP 5,980. PARIS, 16 Dec 1997, *Young Mother and her Child* (oil on canvas, 14 1/4 x 11 1/2 ins / 36 x 29 cm) FRF 22,000. LONDON, 16 April 1999, *Portraits of Prince and Princess Galitzin* (1795, pastel, oval, a pair, 21 x 17 ins / 54 x 44 cm) GBP 3,500. LONDON, 13 July 1999, *Field Marshall Gideon Ernst, Freiherr von Loudon* (c. 1787, miniature, h. 3ins / 8cm) GBP 1,800. DÜSSELDORF, 31 Jan 2000, *Portrait of Three Ladies with Child* (oil on canvas, 28 x 30 ins / 72 x 77 cm) DEM 38,000. LONDON, 24 May 2000, *Young Officer in Hungarian Uniform* (miniature) GBP 7,500. VIENNA, 22 March 2001, *Portrait of Maria Carolina Barbara Claudia von Tschoffen, in a Landscape* (oil on canvas, 43 x 33 ins / 109 x 85 cm) ATS 1,150,000. LONDON, 6 Nov 2001, *Young Gentleman in Brown Doublet with Wide Collar* (miniatures, oval, h. 4ins / 10cm) GBP 22,000. VIENNA, 21 March 2002, *Emperor Joseph II in Armour* (oil on canvas, 17 x 12 ins / 43 x 31 cm) EUR 6,500. LONDON, 10 July 2002, *Two Portraits of a King* (pen with grey ink wash heightened with pink over black chalk, a pair, 17 x 8 ins / 42 x 21 cm) GBP 3,000. LONDON, 9 Dec 2003, *Young Lady* (miniature, oval, h. 3ins / 7cm) GBP 19,000.

FUGER, Wolfgang
German, 17th century.
Painter.

Wolfgang Fuger was a painter in the Episcopal court of Bamberg (Bavaria) at the beginning of the 17th century.

FUGÈRE, Claudia. See **DAVID-FUGÈRE**

FUGÈRE, Henry
French, 19th - 20th century.
Born 7 September 1872, in St-Mandé; died 1944.
Sculptor.

Henry Fugère studied under Pierre Jules Cavelier. He exhibited in Paris at the Salon des Artistes Français, of which he was a member, and received a commendation in 1927.

AUCTION RECORDS:
LONDON, 8 March 1976, *Dancer* (bronze and ivory, h. 17 ins / 43 cm) GBP 480. LONDON, 29 Nov 1978, *It's Burning Hot; La botte à papa* (two bronzes, h. 8 1/2 ins / 21.5 cm) GBP 550. NEW YORK, 29 Sept 1983, *Salome* (gilded bronze, h. 16 ins / 40.5 cm) USD 1,800. LONDON, 5 Nov 1987, *Young Woman Standing* (c. 1900, reddish-brown patinated bronze, h. 28 3/4 ins / 73 cm) GBP 1,500. PADDINGTON, 3 June 2001, *Semi-naked Dancer* (bronze and ivory, h. 17 ins / 42 cm) AUD 9,500. LONDON, 13 May 2004, *Salome* (gilt cold patinated bronze and ivory, 15 x ?x? ins / 38 x ?x? cm) GBP 2,400.

FUGÈRE, Jean-Marie, called Joanny
French, 19th century.
Born 28 April 1818, in Lyons; died 1 January 1882, in Lyons.
Draughtsman, engraver.

He was the son of an engraver whose family ran a printing works in Lyons until around the end of the 19th century. He studied under Vibert at the École des Beaux-Arts in Lyons from 1833 to 1839. Fugère spent some time in Paris but returned to Lyons in 1845 and worked for the next thirty years as an engraver for Louis Perrin, contributing to the *Généalogie de la maison de Savoie* (*Genealogy of the House of Savoy*) and numerous other publications. His own engravings include portraits of *Louis Perrin, A.-J.-B. d'Aigueperse, A. de Terrehasse, J. Spon* and *Ropin Thoyras*, together with two series of 50 etchings and 25burin engravings showing, respectively, actors from the Théâtre du Vaudeville and the Comédie-Française, of which arguably the outstanding examples depict *Fréd. Lemaître, Beauvallet, Rachel* and *Mademoiselle Georges.* He signed his work *J. M. Fugère.*

FUGG, Max von
German, 19th century.
Active in Munich.
Draughtsman, lithographer.

FUGLEM, Karilee
Canadian, 20th century.
Installation artist.

Karilee Fuglem lives and is active in Montreal. She created the installation *Nothing Between,* a plaster wall dotted with round bumps gently heated by light bulbs from behind, evoking the human body. She had previously embarked on this theme of associating buildings with the body when she created a latex wall which appeared to breathe. She shows her works in solo exhibitions, including one in Montreal in 1996.

BIBLIOGRAPHY:
Couëlle, Jennifer, *'Jayce Salloum - Karilee Fuglem - Karin Trenkel'* in *Art Press* n° 222, periodical, Paris, March 1997. Liss, David, *'Luminous Life'* in *Canadian Art,* vol. 17, no. 3, pp. 50-52, periodical, 2000.

FÜGLISTER, Wilhelm
Austrian, 19th century.
Born 27 May 1861, in Vienna.
Sculptor.

Füglister was responsible for the interior decoration of the Grand Duke's palace in Karlsruhe (Baden-Württemberg).

FUGO, Johann Georg
Austrian, 17th century.
Born 1 June 1618, in Vienna.
Painter.

This artist was the son of Martin Fugo, and was married in 1653.

FUGO, Martin
Austrian, 17th century.
Born c. 1580.
Active in Vienna.
Painter.

Martin was the father of Johann Georg Fugo.

FUHR, Charles Jérémie
French, 19th century.
Born 1832, in Bayonne.
Lithographer.

He studied under Feillet-Fuhr and went on to work for the *Panthéon des illustrations françaises* (*Pantheon of French Illustrations*); examples of his work were exhibited at the Paris Salon from 1861 to 1874.

FUHR, Franz Xaver
German, 20th century.

Born 1898, in Neckarau, near Mannheim; died 1973, in Regensburg.

Painter. Urban landscapes, harbour scenes.

Franz Xaver Fuchs was self-taught. He more or less adopted the aesthetic principles of the Neue Sachlichkeit (New Objectivity) group, formed in 1918 around Otto Dix and Georg Grosz, and intended as a reaction against the distortions of Expressionism, though not merely adhering to the strict reproduction of reality. After the Nazis came to power in 1933, Fuhr was one of those categorised as a 'degenerate artist', forbidden to paint or exhibit. After the war, he was offered a post at the Munich academy and exhibited regularly in Munich from 1945 on. He took part in the Venice Biennale in 1953, Documenta in Kassel in 1955 and in other exhibitions.

However, after World War I, the New Objectivity artists remained closer to the accusatory Expressionist movement than to a merely critical Realism. As Marcel Brion said: 'Even when the Neue Sachlichkeit artists go in search of the banal, they almost always encounter the fantastic'. Fuhr himself was closer to naive art. Brion also said: 'His draughtsmanship is precise, his colours vivid and contrasting, with the chalky tones of the Sunday Painters. He has the same sympathy as they do for the sad, poor areas of the big city'. His urban motifs, often of harbours, with precise details of cranes, bridges and boats, frequently have vague foregrounds with a subjective attitude to perspective. Sometimes he also painted imaginary Far-Eastern street scenes.

AUCTION RECORDS:

BERN, 20 June 1973, *House in the Suburbs* (c. 1930) CHF 1,800. MUNICH, 26 May 1977, *Market Scene* (39 1/4 x 29 1/2 ins / 100 x 75 cm) DEM 5,500. COLOGNE, 6 May 1978, *Trees in Autumn* (watercolour, 11 3/4 x 24 ins / 30 x 61 cm) DEM 2,200. COLOGNE, 2 Dec 1978, *The Red Boat* (oil on canvas, 30 x 40 1/2 ins / 76 x 103 cm) DEM 14,000. MUNICH, 5 June 1981, *Ruins in a Mountain Landscape* (watercolour, 21 1/4 x 27 1/4 ins / 54 x 69.5 cm) DEM 3,700. MUNICH, 28 May 1984, *Schoolgirls* (watercolour heightened with white, 24 1/2 x 16 1/2 ins / 62 x 42 cm) DEM 4,800. MUNICH, 6 June 1986, *Autumn* (c. 1946, oil on canvas, 22 3/4 x 27 1/2 ins / 58 x 70 cm) DEM 3,000. COLOGNE, 9 Dec 1986, *Reflections in the Water* (1970, watercolour, 22 1/2 x 15 1/4 ins / 57 x 38.5 cm) DEM 6,000. HEIDELBERG, 5-13 April 1994, *Bunch of Flowers in front of Red Curtains* (oil on card, 23 1/2 x 23 1/2 ins / 59.5 x 59.5 cm) DEM 12,500. NEW YORK, 14 June 1995, *Boats in Harbour* (oil on canvas, 43 3/4 x 30 1/4 ins / 111.1 x 76.8 cm) USD 9,200. STUTTGART, 23 Oct 1999, *Mosque* (1960-1961, gouache, 8 x 23 ins / 21 x 58 cm) DEM 35,000. COLOGNE, 10 Nov 1999, *Capricious Woman* (oil on panel, 24 x 28 ins / 60 x 70 cm) DEM 26,000. STUTTGART, 14 April 2000, *Church of St Kulian in Heilbronn* (oil on canvas, 56 x 42 ins / 141 x 107 cm) DEM 45,000. BERLIN, 25 Nov 2000, *Dome of Regensburg* (c. 1929-1930, oil on canvas, 40 x 26 ins / 102 x 65 cm) DEM 43,000. STUTTGART, 10 May 2001, *French Coast* (c. 1964-1970, oil on board, 24 x 31 ins / 60 x 80 cm) DEM 22,500. MUNICH, 1 Dec 2001, *Skiers* (c. 1964-1970, oil on canvas, 40 x 22 ins / 101 x 55 cm) DEM 30,000. BERLIN, 8 June 2002, *Yellow Snake* (oil on canvas, 30 x 59 ins / 75 x 150 cm) EUR 7,000. HAMBURG, 7 Dec 2002, *Bay* (oil on canvas, 28 x 43 ins / 70 x 110 cm) EUR 18,000. COLOGNE, 13 Dec 2003, *Village Street* (oil on canvas, 12 x 16 ins / 30 x 41 cm) EUR 2,000. ERLANGEN, 23 Oct 2004, *Fishing Boats on Beach* (oil on canvas, 24 x 37 ins / 60 x 94 cm) EUR 4,200.

FUHR, Karl Friedrich von der

German, 18th - 19th century.

Born in Saxony.

Engraver.

Fuhr settled in Russia in about 1809, where he engraved portraits and book illustrations.

FÜHRER, Johann Jakob

German, 18th century.

Died 30 April 1745.

Active in Heidelberg.

Sculptor.

Führer was a pupil of Van den Branden.

FUHRER, Maurice

French, 20th century.

Born 27 February 1892, in Déville-lès-Rouen.

Painter.

Maurice Fuhrer exhibited in Paris from 1923 at the Salon des Artistes Français and was awarded a silver medal in 1927.

FÜHRER, Richard

Hungarian, 19th - 20th century.

Born 18 July 1873, in Budapest.

Sculptor.

Richard Führer was Antal Loranfi's student. He travelled a great deal in Italy and France where he exhibited at the Paris Exposition Universelle in 1900, winning a bronze medal.

FÜHRICH, Josef von

Austrian, 19th century.

Born 9 February 1800, in Kratzau (now Chrastava); died 13 March 1876, in Vienna.

Painter, fresco artist, engraver, draughtsman, illustrator. Religious subjects.

Having worked in Prague under Bergler, Führich studied in Vienna in 1827 and drew and painted several romantic scenes.

Führich travelled to Rome in 1827, where he executed three frescoes representing scenes from the epic poem *Gerusalemme Liberata* by Torquato Tasso. From this period on, he became an imitator of Fritz Overbeck and, in 1865, started his great works in the church of Altlenchenfelder in Vienna, representing *The Raising of Lazarus* and the *Last Judgement*. Works for which Führich is noted include illustrations for the *King of the Alders*, by Goethe, *Jesus Entering the Garden of Gethsemane, The Virgin Going up to Calvary* (Vienna gallery), *Eight Scenes from the Life of the Prodigal Child, Fifteen Scenes from the Resurrection.*

MUSEUMS AND GALLERIES:

VIENNA (Gal.): *The Virgin Going Up to Calvary.*

AUCTION RECORDS:

LONDON, 9 Dec 1980, *King David with Virgil and Horace* (pencil and black ink/paper, 10 x 11 1/2 ins / 25.5 x 29.4 cm) GBP 650. VIENNA, 5 Dec 1984, *Biblical Scene* (c. 1839, oil on canvas, 12 1/2 x 15 3/4 ins / 31.5 x 40 cm) ATS 50,000. HEIDELBERG, 14 Oct 1988, *Archangel Michael Casting Lucifer and his Throne into the Abyss* (1860, pencil, 11 3/4 x 9 3/4 ins / 29.8 x 24.8 cm) DEM 1,800. MUNICH, 6 Dec 1994, *Birth of the Legend of Klosterneuburg, near Vienna* (black ink/paper, 11 3/4 x 9 1/4 ins / 30 x 23.5 cm) DEM 7,130. MUNICH, 23 June 1997, *Christ's Entry into Jerusalem* (1849, pencil/paper, 13 1/2 x 17 1/2 ins / 34.5 x 44.5 cm) DEM 6,240. DÜSSELDORF, 31 Jan 2000, *St Christopher* (oil on canvas, 41 x 30 ins / 103 x 75 cm) DEM 14,000. BERLIN, 1 Dec 2000, *Portrait of Marquess Massimi* (pencil, 9 x 7 ins / 23 x 17 cm) DEM 33,000. COLOGNE, 19 May 2001, *Genoveva's Murderers Have Pity* (pen, 9 x 12 ins / 23 x 30 cm) DEM 11,000. LONDON, 9 April 2002, *The Triumph of Christ* (oil on panel, 23 x 31 ins / 58 x 78 cm) GBP 10,000.

FUHRLAGH, or Fuhrlogh
British, 18th century.
Sculptor.

Fuhrlagh was a Society of Artists exhibitor in 1733 and 1774.

FUHRMAN, Ludwig
German, 19th century.
Born 12 March 1783, in Breslau (now Wroclaw, Poland); died 13 January 1829, in Posen (now Poznan, Poland).
Painter. Religious subjects, portraits.

Fuhrman studied at the art academy in Prague, after which he worked in Rome, where he produced some valuable paintings. Following his return to Posen, he made a long trip to Turkey with Count Antoine Raczynski. In 1821 he exhibited in Warsaw *St Marcellus, Family of Count Raczynski, Ignatius, Count Raczynski, Former Bishop of Posen, Archbishop of Danzig, Holy Family.*

FUHRMANN
German, 18th century.
Active c. 1729.
Painter. Portraits.

Fuhrmann almost certainly worked in Lichtenberg.

FUHRMANN, C. G.
German, 19th century.
Active in Hamburg c. 1850.
Lithographer.

This artist specialised in views of ruins and fires.

FUHRMANN, Max
German, 19th century.
Born 1860, in Munich; died 31 May 1908.
Painter. Landscapes with figures, still-lifes.

Max Fuhrmann lived mainly in Pasing and produced glass models, together with other artefacts.

AUCTION RECORDS:
NEW YORK, 29 May 1980, *Still-life with Flowers* (oil on canvas, 27 3/4 x 23 3/4 ins / 70.5 x 60.5 cm) USD 3,500. HEIDELBERG, 12 April 1986, *Flock in a Landscape* (oil on canvas, 19 3/4 x 27 1/2 ins / 50 x 70 cm) DEM 3,000.

FUHRMANN, Petr Romanovich
Russian, 19th century.
Born 8 October 1816, in Livlan; died 8 January 1856, in St Petersburg.
Painter, writer.

Fuhrmann was a pupil of Vorob'ev at the St Petersburg academy of fine arts. After having lived for a long time in Prussia, he made a name for himself on his return to Russia, above all as an art critic.

FUJIHATA, Masaki
Japanese, 20th century.
Installation artist.

Fujihata Masaki exhibited *Global Interior Project n°2* in the 1996 Linz Ars Electronica Festival. It was made up of virtual 'rooms', each connected to an object and a concept, with an installation of boxes containing sculptures corresponding to these objects.

FUJIKAWA, Yuzo
Japanese, 20th century.
Born 1883, in Takamatsu (Shikoku); died c. 1935.
Sculptor.

Fujikawa Yuzo graduated from the Tokyo School of Fine Arts in 1908. Having obtained a scholarship from the Japanese Ministry of Trade and Agriculture, he left for France. He studied drawing at the Académie Julian and was noticed by Rodin, who engaged him as an assistant. He returned to Japan in 1916, and in 1919 took part in creating the sculpture department of the Nika-kai, of which he became a member. He was also a member of the Imperial Art Academy. He played an important role in guiding young artists. With regard to his own style, he described it as calm and serious, and in harmony with his feelings.

MUSEUMS AND GALLERIES:
TOKYO (National MMA).

FUJIMAKI, Yoshio
Japanese, 20th century.
Born 1909, in Gumma Prefecture; died 1935.
Painter, print artist, illustrator.

Fujimaki Yoshio's work was published in 1931in the print artists' magazine *Kitsutsuki.* In 1931 and 1932, he took part in events at the Japan Print Association. In 1935, he began a series of illustrations for a book on the Sumidagawa, the river that crosses Tokyo, but he died before completing them. His early style swung between expressionism and cubism and later evolved into a form of abstraction.

MUSEUMS AND GALLERIES:
TOKYO (National MMA).

FUJINO, Shuzaku Paul
Japanese, 20th century.
Born 5 September 1925, in Japan; died 1 March 1982, in Paris.
Active in France from 1953.
Painter, decorative artist.

Paul Fujino first studied in Japan. Arriving in France in 1935, he attended the Académie Julian and the École Nationale des Beaux-Arts, where he worked under Souverbie, between 1955 and 1956. He also worked in Lacasse's studio from 1935 to 1956. He exhibited in Japan from 1948 and took part in numerous group exhibitions in France and abroad. His first solo exhibition was held in 1960 in Paris at the Galerie Jacques Massol. He exhibited in London in 1961, in Columbus, Ohio, in 1963, in Brussels in 1964, in Berlin in 1965, and in Paris in 1972. He was awarded the Prix Julian in 1955.

In 1965 he worked with the architects P. Chemetovet and J. Deroche on a home for the elderly in Romainville (painted concrete and tiles), in 1966 on the central building in Vigneux (painting), in 1969 for the stadium in Villejuif (concrete relief), and in 1971 for the Vigneux social security department (enamel tiles). In 1972 he worked on the Chatillon-Malakoff stadium (concrete, pebbles and tiles). Fujino carried out other large-scale works in Osaka, Paris, Avignon and Vitry. His paintings are abstract, representing on the surface smooth shapes, which appear to be assembled according to a distant geometric order.

FUJIOKA, Hajime
Japanese, 20th century.
Born in Japan.
Painter.

Fujioka Hajime exhibited two paintings at the Salon des Tuileries in 1930.

FUJIOKA, Noboru
Japanese, 20th century.
Born 10 January 1896, in Hiroshima.
Painter.

Fujioka Noboru exhibited at the Salon d'Automne in 1930 and 1931.

FUJISHIMA, Takeji
Japanese, 19th - 20th century.
Born 1867, in Kagoshima, Kyushu; died 1943.
Painter.

Fujishima Takeji came from a family of painters. He studied from an early age with the painter Hirayama Togaku of the Shijo school in his home town. He then became a pupil of Kawabata Gyokusho in Tokyo. At the age of 20 he received first prize for Japanese painting in an official exhibition. He decided nevertheless to study western painting, which he did under Soyama Yukihiko and Yamamoto Hosei. In 1906, he left for Europe with a grant from the Japanese Ministry for Cultural Affairs, and spent two years in Paris followed by two years in Rome, perfecting his oil painting technique. Returning to Japan in 1910, he was appointed teacher at the Tokyo School of Fine Arts, and also sat on the panel of judges for the Bunten, the annual exhibition organised by the Ministry of Education. In 1937, he was awarded the Order of Culural Merit.

His works are colourful and sensual. Highly influenced by Odilon Redon, he was considered in the years 1910-1920 to be imitating a style still tainted with Romanticism.

Museums and Galleries:

Tokyo (National MMA): *Reverie* (1913).

Auction records:

New York, 30 April 1996, *Female Profile* (oil on panel, 18 x 15 ins / 45.5 x 38 cm) USD 684,500. New York, 14 Nov 1996, *New Year's Day in Taipei Port* (1935, oil on canvas, 18 x 23 3/4 ins / 45.7 x 60.6 cm) USD 90,500.

FUJITA, Kenji

Japanese, 20th - 21st century.
Born 1955.
Active in the USA.
Assemblage sculptor.

Kenji Fujita constructs monumental assemblages out of various objects, which, while remaining abstract, still refer to reality.

Auction records:

New York, 2 May 1991, *Elephant's Ear* (1988, mural sculpture, acrylic on wood, galvanised tin, moulded plastic and rubber piping, 20 x 32 x 22 1/2 ins / 50.8 x 81.2 x 57.2 cm) USD 6,600. New York, 17 Nov 1992, *Untitled* (1988, acrylic on wood with galvanised objects and cables, 18 x 17 x 21 1/2 ins / 45.7 x 43.1 x 54.6 cm) USD 2,200. New York, 7 May 1993, *The Walls of Jericho* (1988, acrylic on wood, moulded plastic, gum, wire and screws, hanging sculpture, 34 x 33 x 18 ins / 86.5 x 84 x 46 cm) USD 1,150. New York, 10 Oct 1996, *The Wrong Doctor* (1987, wood and metal, 24 x 21 x 19 ins / 61 x 53.3 x 48.3 cm) USD 690.

FUJITA, Tsuguharu, later Léonard

Japanese, 20th century.
Born 27 November 1886, in Edogama, near Tokyo, baptised in 1959; died 29 January 1968, in Zurich.
Active in Paris from 1913, naturalised in 1955.
Painter (including gouache), watercolourist, draughtsman (including ink/wash), fresco artist, print artist (including lithography/etching/aquatint), illustrator, decorative artist. Religious subjects, figures, nudes, portraits, scenes with figures, urban landscapes, urban views, still-lifes, animals, cats. Wall decorations, stage sets, designs for stained glass.

Léonard Fujita was the son of a samurai. He lost his mother at the age of five and was brought up by his elder sister. He studied at the Tokyo School of Fine Arts from 1915. Rewarded by his Japanese exhibitions, and helped by the purchase of one of his works by the Emperor and a commission to paint the portrait of the Emperor of Korea (*Portrait of the Emperor of Korea*, 1911), he seemed set for a brilliant career in Japan. However, after having studied European painting, particularly the work of the avant-garde French painters, he went to Paris in 1913. The following year he spent a short time in London, where he took up various occupations. On his return to Paris in 1915, he settled in the Cité Falguière, and soon became one of the colourful figures of Montparnasse, becoming friends with Picasso (preferring his paintings by Henri Rousseau to his own cubist works, which tempted him only very briefly) and Soutine. In 1926, the French state bought his painting *Friendship*. In 1928, he produced the stage set for a Japanese play produced at the Théâtre de l'Odeon. From 1930 to 1950, he spent his time travelling in England, Belgium, Holland, Switzerland, Italy, Germany and the USA, building his reputation. He built a studio in Paris in 1934, and a house in 1938. The Japanese government then sent him to Manchuria as artistic attaché to the army, where, according to some, he campaigned in favour of the country's militarism. In 1949, Fujita went to the USA, having been invited to teach at the Brooklyn School of Fine Arts. In 1950, he returned to Paris, and the following year donated four paintings to the Musée National d'Art Moderne. In 1955, he took up French citizenship and converted from Buddhism to Catholicism, being baptised at the age of 73 in Reims cathedral with the name Léonard, as a tribute to Leonardo da Vinci. From 1965, he worked on frescoes and stained glass windows for the chapel of Notre-Dame de la Paix in Reims, where he is buried. In 1924, he was elected a member of the Tokyo Academy of Fine Arts and was made a Chevalier de la Légion d'Honneur in France. The Japanese government awarded him the posthumous title of the Order of the Sacred Treasure.

His first exhibition in Paris was at the Galerie Chéron in 1917. He came to the fore with his submissions to the Salon d'Automne, especially in 1921, and also exhibited at the Salon des Tuileries. He took part in various exhibitions in Japan between 1930 and 1950. He decorated the Japanese Hall at the Cité Universitaire in Paris, worked on the decoration of the Cercle interallié, and decorated the bar of the Palais de Chaillot with Duffy in 1931. In Japan, he produced several murals, including several for the Sogo department stores in Osaka (1935), the Maison franco-japonaise in Kyoto (1936), and the house of the collector Masakichini Hirano in Atika (1937), which later became the Fujita Museum.

He published two albums, *Nudes* and *Children, Cats* and illustrated numerous other books: *Songs of Geishas, The Honourable Country Outing*, by T. Raucat (Paris 1927); *The Black Bird in the Rising Sun*, by P. Claudel; *Comments of an Intoxicated Man*, by J. Boissière; *Madam Prune's Third Youth* and *Madam Chrysanthemum*, by P. Loti (Paris 1926); *Eros's Enjoyments*, by Brindejonc-Offenbach; *Poems of Jealousy* by C. and L. Goll; *The Eight Renowned*, by Kikou Yamata (Paris, 1927); *Parallel Bars*, by M. Vaucaire; *Amal and the King's Letter*, by R. Tagore; and *The Dragon of the Seas*, by Jean Cocteau (Paris, 1925).

Fujita's early watercolours demonstrate the influence of artists such as Marie Laurencien and Modigliani. A graceful painter and a draughtsman of rare versatility, he uses processes close to those traditionally used by Japanese painters, barely covering the canvas and using a dabber as much as a paintbrush. However, the whole of his work is marked by distinct periods subjected to different western influences: Naïve (Bauchant, among others), Expressionist (Dix) and purely historical, some works revealing a great knowledge of painting of past centuries. Nevertheless, Fujita always leaves room for the decorative delicacy of traditional Japanese art. He painted numerous self-portraits, and also executed portraits of women. His many nudes were to be greatly appreciated for the eroticism of their shapely figures. He drew young girls with slightly slanting eyes, flowers, stripey cats, a few still-lifes (glasses, calligraphy ink, pendulums), then after his conversion to Catholicism, a number of religious subjects. In summary, Fujita was the creator of a western modernism based on Japanese tradition. The Fondazione Prada in Milan gave him a posthumous tribute with the exhibition *Fujita. A Japanese Artist.*

Foujita

BIBLIOGRAPHY:

Bauer, G./Rey, R./Recio, G.C., *'Fujita'* in *coll. Cahiers de la Peinture*, Presses Artistiques, Paris, 1958. Selz, Jean, *Fujita*, Flammarion, Paris, 1980. Buisson, , Dominique, *'La Vie et l'œuvre de Léonard-Tsuguharu Fujita'* in vol. I, catalogue raisonné, ACR Édition, Paris, 1987. Bougault, V., *Paris Montparnasse*, in English, Terrail, Paris, 1997. Buisson, Sylvie, *'La Vie et l'œuvre de Léonard-Tsuguharu Fujita'* in vol. II, catalogue raisonné, ACR Édition, Paris, 2001.

MUSEUMS AND GALLERIES:

GENEVA (Petit Palais): *Salon in Montparnasse* (1930); *Female Lion Tamer with Lion* (1930) - LONDON (British Mus.) - NEW YORK (Metropolitan Mus. of Art) - PARIS (former Mus. du Jeu de Paume) - PARIS (MAMVP): *Nude with Toile de Jouy* (1922) - PARIS (MNAM-CCI): *My Studio* (1921); *My Studio* (1922); *My Paris Interior* (1922); *Self-portrait* (1928); *At the Café* (1949); *Quai aux Fleurs, Notre Dame de Paris* (1950).

AUCTION RECORDS:

PARIS, 6 Nov 1924, *Les Invalides, place Vauban* FRF 1,200. PARIS, 4 June 1925, *Snow* (watercolour) FRF 510. PARIS, 12 Feb 1926, *Study of Sleeping Woman with Bare Breasts* (pen and pencil) FRF 350. PARIS, 20 May 1926, *View of Cagnes*, FRF 11,150. PARIS, 4 June 1926, *View of Cagnes*, FRF 950. PARIS, 3 May 1929, *Reclining Woman*, FRF 3,300. NEW YORK, 25 and 26 Nov 1929, *Nude*, USD 100. NEW YORK, 25 and 26 March 1931, *Landscape*, USD 160. PARIS, 30 April 1931, *Nude with Blond Hair* (drawing) FRF 1,600. PARIS, 19 Feb 1932, *Still-life*, FRF 600. PARIS, 24 Nov 1932, *Sleeping Cat*, FRF 1,300. PARIS, 29 April 1933, *Studies of Athletes* (drawing) FRF 270. PARIS, 6 April 1936, *Reclining Nude*, FRF 3,700. PARIS, 8 Dec 1941, *Cats* (1924, painting on silk) FRF 1,050. PARIS, 15 April 1942, *Cats* (watercolour) FRF 320. PARIS, 19 June 1942, *Children Playing* (1924) FRF 2,400. PARIS, 27 Nov 1942, *The Pont des Invalides*, FRF 4,000. PARIS, 7 April 1943, *The Two Friends* (graphite) FRF 2,600. PARIS, 1 July 1943, *Portrait of a Woman* (1927, pen and stump) FRF 900. PARIS, 10 Nov 1943, *Allegory* (1917, watercolour) FRF 900. NEW YORK, 18-20 Nov 1943, *Sleeping Cat*, USD 80. PARIS, 23 Feb 1945, *Seated Nude* (pencil) FRF 2,900. NEW YORK, 12 April 1945, *Portrait of the Artist* (drawing) USD 50. PARIS, 29 June 1945, *Bust of Stretching Woman* (1928) FRF 5,200; *La Fontaine's Fables* (1922) FRF 5,200. PARIS, July 1946, *Bust of Woman Facing Right* (pencil heightened with watercolour); *Head of Dark-haired Woman in Profile* (pen and highlights, both) FRF 6,000. PARIS, 12 Nov 1946, *Woman's Head* (watercolour) FRF 5,800. PARIS, 23 April 1947, *Two Standing Nudes* (drawing) FRF 580. PARIS, 13 June 1947, *Praying Shepherdess* (watercolour) FRF 10,000. PARIS, 25 April 1955, *Little Girl*, FRF 53,000. PARIS, 4 June 1958, *Cat*, FRF 210,000. NEW YORK, 18 May 1960, *Woman with Cherries* (watercolour) USD 600. PARIS, 16 June 1961, *Studies of Nudes* (chalk) FRF 1,700. PARIS, 10 Dec 1966, *Young Woman with Little Dog*, FRF 52,000. PARIS, 24 June 1968, *Temptation of Buddha* (watercolour and gouache on gold background) FRF 16,500. PARIS, 1 Dec 1969, *Nude with Cat*, FRF 330,000. LONDON, 28 Nov 1972, *Reclining Nude*, Gns 17,000. ORLÉANS, 17 June 1973, *Children of Ghardaya*, FRF 85,000. GENEVA, 7 Dec 1973, *Still-life*, CHF 65,000. PARIS, 21 March 1974, *Breakfast*, FRF 170,000. PARIS, 5 June 1974, *Two Sisters*, FRF 200,000. PARIS, 1 March 1976, *Bust of Woman Facing Right* (etching) FRF 3,500. NEW YORK, 28 May 1976, *Nun* (1959, oil on canvas, 13¼ x 7¾ ins / 33.5 x 19.5 cm) USD 11,500. LONDON, 30 Nov 1976, *Dancers* (c. 1917, gouache on gold leaf, 14½ x 20¾ ins / 37 x 53 cm) GBP 9,500. LONDON, 29 June 1977, *Estuary at Sunset* (watercolour heightened with white, 5 x 7 ins / 12.5 x 17.8 cm) GBP 550. PARIS, 14 Oct 1977, *Self-portrait with Cat* (lithograph on Japanese paper) FRF 3,600. NEW YORK, 16 Dec 1977, *Cat* (1949, oil on canvas, 8 x 10 ins / 20.5 x 25.5 cm) USD 22,000. LONDON, 27 June 1978, *Reclining Nude* (1929, oil on canvas, 11¾ x 18 ins / 30 x 46 cm) GBP 15,000. LOS ANGELES, 18 Sept 1978, *Standing Nude* (etching and roulette in colour, 22 x 14¾ ins / 56 x 37.3 cm) USD 5,000. LONDON, 4 April 1979, *Lovers* (watercolour and ink, 14 x 14¾ ins / 35.5 x 37.5 cm) GBP 2,600. NEW YORK, 9 May 1979, *Reclining Nude* (etching, 16 x 23 ins / 40.5 x 58.5 cm) USD 5,000. PARIS, 24 June 1981, *Woman with Folded Hands* (1917, watercolour, 9 x 4½ ins / 23 x 11.5 cm) FRF 52,000. PARIS, 17 Feb 1984, *In the Studio: Self-portrait with Cat* (1929, oil on canvas, 32 x 25½ ins / 81 x 65 cm) FRF 1,600,000. NEW YORK, 2 May 1984, *Children: Young Girl Holding Bird* (1929, etching, 14 x 10½ ins / 34.7 x 26.7 cm) USD 7,000. NEW YORK, 17 May 1984, *Young Girl and Cat* (1958, pen and wash, 12¾ x 10 ins / 32.5 x 25 cm) USD 32,000. NEW YORK, 14 Nov 1984, *Christ on the Cross* (gouache, watercolour, gold-leaf and pen on paper, 18 x 11 ins / 45.5 x 27 cm) USD 12,000. NEW YORK, 15 May 1985, *Large Reclining Nude* (1928, pencil and wash, 25½ x 39¼ ins / 65 x 100 cm) USD 47,500. NEW YORK, 20 Nov 1986, *Young Girl with Green Shirt* (watercolour and ink heightened with white gouache on paper mounted on card, 10¾ x 8½ ins / 27.3 x 21.9 cm) USD 80,000. LONDON, 30 June 1987, *Puppet* (1949, oil on canvas, 30 x 24¾ ins / 76 x 63 cm) GBP 570,000. PARIS, 25 Nov 1987, *Young Seated Nude* (aquatint) FRF 75,000. PARIS, 7 Dec 1987, *Drawing* (black pencil, heightened in coloured pencil and wash, 13½ x 7¾ ins / 34 x 19.5 cm) FRF 29,000. NEW YORK, 18 Feb 1988, *Woman's Head* (1926, ink on paper, 12¾ x 10 ins / 32.4 x 25.4 cm) USD 12,100; *Portrait of a Girl* (oil on canvas, 13¼ x 8¾ ins / 33.6 x 22.2 cm) USD 220,000. MONACO, 20 Feb 1988, *Kitten* (1949, ball-point, 4½ x 6 ins / 11.5 x 15 cm) FRF 17,760. PARIS, 22 Feb 1988, *Sacred Cow and Animals* (pen drawing, 14¼ x 19¾ ins / 36 x 50 cm) FRF 30,000. PARIS, 15 March 1988, *Nativity* (watercolour on gold background, 13 x 15¾ ins / 33 x 40 cm) FRF 580,000. LONDON, 29 March 1988, *Two Girls* (oil on canvas, 16¼ x 13¼ ins / 41.4 x 33.4 cm) GBP 264,000. PARIS, 15 April 1988, *Portrait of a Woman* (1928, oil on canvas, 9½ x 7½ ins / 24 x 19 cm) FRF 540,000. BERN, 30 April 1988, *Woman Playing Xylophone* (oil on canvas, 28¼ x 39 ins / 72 x 99 cm) CHF 10,000. NEW YORK, 12 May 1988, *Her Peeling Potatoes* (oil on canvas, 13¼ x 9¾ ins / 33.8 x 24.9 cm) USD 462,000. LONDON, 18 May 1988, *Woman's Portrait* (Indian ink, 14¾ x 10¾ ins / 37.3 x 27.3 cm) GBP 5,500. PARIS, 8 June 1988, *Young Girl with Cat* (1951, oil on canvas, 13 x 9½ ins / 33 x 24 cm) FRF 2,250,000. L'ISLE-ADAM, 11 June 1988, *Paris: La Porte de Chatillon* (1921, watercolour, 9¾ x 13½ ins / 25 x 34 cm) FRF 100,500; *Young Girl with Blue Eyes* (1932, Indian ink used as watercolour and gouache, 15¾ x 11¾ ins / 40 x 30 cm) FRF 350,000. PARIS, 12 June 1988, *Woman's Profile* (1929, watercolour, 9¾ x 8¼ ins / 25 x 21 cm) FRF 200,000. PARIS, 22 June 1988, *Standing Nude* (1923, oil on canvas, 32 x 17¾ ins / 81 x 45 cm) FRF 1,920,000. LONDON, 28 June 1988, *Cherry Branches in Blossom in Stoneware Vase* (oil on canvas, 21½ x 14¼ ins / 54.6 x 36.2 cm) GBP 77,000. LONDON, 29 June 1988, *Cat* (1947, oil on canvas, 10¾ x 8¾ ins / 27.5 x 22.2 cm) GBP 73,700. CALAIS, 3 July 1988, *Young Child* (red and black ink, 19¾ x 14½ ins / 50 x 37 cm) FRF 55,000. NEW YORK, 6 Oct 1988, *Head of Girl* (1930, ink and watercolour on paper, 11 x 8¾ ins / 28 x 22.3 cm) USD 14,300. LONDON, 21 Oct 1988, *La Porte de Vanves* (1927, oil on canvas, 15 x 18¼ ins / 38 x 46.5 cm) GBP 49,500. PARIS, 26 Oct 1988, *Head of Black Child in Profile* (etching) FRF 44,000. NEW YORK, 12 Nov 1988, *Reclining Nude* (1931, ink and watercolour on paper, 20 1/2 x 28 1/4 ins / 51.8 x 72 cm) USD 286,000. PARIS, 20 Nov 1988, *Mother and Child* (1932, watercolour, 13 3/4 x 11 1/2 ins / 35 x 29 cm) FRF 310,000; *Young Woman and Child* (1950, ink and watercolour, 10 3/4 x 8 1/4 ins / 27.6 x 20.9 cm) FRF 420,000; *Sleeping Nymph* (1951, oil on canvas, 9 1/2 x 13 ins / 24 x 33 cm) FRF 2,100,000. PARIS, 23 Nov 1988, *Reclining Nude* (1930, colour etching) FRF 85,000. PARIS, 24 Nov 1988, *Woman's Portrait* (graphite, 9 1/4 x 6 1/2 ins / 23.5 x 16.5 cm) FRF 75,000; *The Swing* (c. 1918, watercolour heightened with gold, 14 1/4 x 17 ins / 36 x 43 cm) FRF 940,000. PARIS, 12 Dec 1988, *Young Woman in Half Profile facing Left* (1924, pen, pencil and stump, 8 x 6 1/4 ins / 20.3 x 16 cm) FRF 95,000. NEW YORK, 11 May 1989, *Cat* (1940, oil on canvas, 13 x 16 1/4 ins / 33 x 41 cm) USD 187,000. PARIS, 18 May 1989, *Young Woman with Glass* (1917, watercolour and gouache, 10 x 7 1/2 ins / 25.5 x 19 cm) FRF 323,000; *Sleeping Blonde* (oil on canvas, 7 3/4 x 11 ins / 20 x 27 cm) FRF 610,000. PARIS, 17 June 1989, *Two Children Carrying Bread and Milk* (oil on canvas, 13 3/4 x 11 ins / 35 x 27 cm) FRF 1,800,000. PARIS, 20 June 1989, *Mother and Child* (oil on paper, 8 1/4 x 6 3/4 ins / 21 x 17 cm) FRF 1,600,000. LONDON, 27 June 1989, *Girl with Violet* (1953, oil on canvas, 9 x 6 1/4 ins / 22 x 16 cm) GBP 126,500. VERSAILLES, 25 Sept 1989, *Self-portrait for Kimiyo* (etching, 14 3/4 x 11 ins / 37.5 x 28 cm) FRF 8,500. NEW YORK, 5 Oct 1989, *Two Male Nudes* (pencil drawing on coloured paper, 30 x 39 ins / 75.9 x 98.8 cm) USD 22,000. NEW YORK, 6 Oct 1989, *View of Hailar in Manchuria* (oil on canvas, 19 1/2 x 23 3/4 ins / 49.8 x 60.6 cm) USD 93,500. ZURICH, 25 Oct 1989, *Cat* (1953, ink, 7 3/4 x 10 ins / 19.5 x 24.5 cm) CHF 8,500. NEW YORK, 14 Nov 1989, *Children with Doll* (oil on canvas, 21 3/4 x 18 1/4 ins / 55.3 x 46.3 cm) USD 3,740,000. PARIS, 19 Nov 1989, *Virgin and Child* (1959, oil on canvas, 10 3/4 x 8 3/4 ins / 27.5 x 22.5 cm) FRF 1,900,000. LONDON, 28 Nov 1989, *Nude with Raised Arms* (1926, oil on canvas, 16 x 13 1/4 ins / 40.6 x 33.6 cm) GBP 154,000. PARIS, 7 Dec 1989, *Little Rider* (1955, oil on canvas, 29 1/4 x 20 ins / 74 x 51 cm) FRF 8,840,000. PARIS, 11 Dec 1989, *Woman with Cat* (1926, oil on canvas, 22 x 18 ins / 55 x 46 cm) FRF 1,530,000. AVRANCHES, 17 Dec 1989, *Paris Street* (oil on canvas, 11 3/4 x 9 1/2 ins / 30 x 24 cm) FRF 1,120,000. NEW YORK, 26 Feb 1990, *Girl with Potatoes* (oil on canvas, 19 1/2 x 13 ins / 49.5 x 33 cm) USD 451,000. PARIS, 21 March 1990, *Little Girl Asleep with Doll* (1950, pen drawing and wash, 8 1/2 x 12 1/4 ins / 21.5 x 31 cm) FRF 455,000. BRUSSELS, 27 March 1990, *Girl with Cat* (print, 37 3/4 x 39 1/4 ins / 96 x 100 cm) BEF 85,000. PARIS, 1 April 1990, *Reclining Model* (1928, graphite and stump on mounted paper, 12 1/2 x 19 ins / 32 x 48 cm) FRF 2,000,000. LONDON, 4 April 1990, *Children on Wall at Meudon* (oil on canvas, 9 3/4 x 16 1/2 ins / 25 x 42 cm) GBP 319,000. NEW YORK, 16 May 1990, *Girl in Park* (1957, oil on canvas, 20 x 25 3/4 ins / 50.8 x 65.4 cm) USD 6,050,000. PARIS, 15 June 1990, *Reclining Nude* (Indian ink, 18 1/2 x 32 3/4 ins / 47 x 83 cm) FRF 450,000. CALAIS, 8 July 1990, *Little Girl with Cat* (1950, sepia, 11 x 8 1/4 ins / 27 x 21 cm) FRF 500,000. NEW YORK, 14 Nov 1990, *Lost Child* (oil on canvas, 22 1/2 x 17 1/4 ins / 57.3 x 43.7 cm) USD 1,365,000. CHARTRES, 25 Nov 1990, *The Concierge's Daughter* (oil on canvas, 11 x 9 ins / 27 x 22 cm) FRF 2,000,000. PARIS, 25 Nov 1990, *Family Portrait* (1954, oil on canvas on panel, 7 x 5 ins / 18 x 13 cm) FRF 2,200,000. LONDON, 5 Dec 1990, *Still-life* (oil on canvas, 24 3/4 x 18 1/4 ins / 62.8 x 46.4 cm) GBP 159,500. NEW YORK, 8 May 1991, *Trompe-l'œil* (1956, oil on canvas, 9 x 10 3/4 ins / 22 x 27.5 cm) USD 137,500. PARIS, 25 May 1991, *Virgin and Child or Mother and Children* (oil on canvas and applied gold leaf in the background, 16 1/4 x 13 1/4 ins / 41.3 x 33.5 cm) FRF 4,700,000. LONDON, 26 June 1991, *At School* (1957, oil on canvas, 9 1/2 x 7 1/2 ins / 24.2 x 19 cm) GBP 121,000. BELFORT, 15 Dec 1991, *Little Girl in front of Church* (1957, oil on canvas, 16 1/2 x 9 3/4 ins / 42 x 25 cm) FRF 690,000. NEW YORK, 12 May 1992, *Girl with Cat* (1952, oil on canvas, 13 x 9 1/2 ins / 33 x 24.1 cm) USD 165,000. NEW YORK, 11 Nov 1992, *Lady of the Manor and her Little Daughter* (1962, oil on canvas, 16 1/4 x 9 1/2 ins / 41.3 x 24.4 cm) USD 181,500. LONDON, 24-25 March 1993, *Cat* (ink and watercolour on card, 9 1/4 x 10 1/4 ins / 23.8 x 26.2 cm) GBP 14,950. ZURICH, 21 April 1993, *Dream (nude)* (coloured lithograph, 22 x 24 3/4 ins / 55 x 63 cm) CHF 2,400. AMSTERDAM, 26 May 1993, *Portrait of Little Girl* (oil on canvas, 10 3/4 x 7 1/2 ins / 27.5 x 19 cm) NLG 161,000. LYONS, 6 June 1993, *Bunch of Roses* (oil on canvas, 16 1/4 x 13 ins / 41 x 33 cm) FRF 250,000. LOKEREN, 12 March 1994, *Nude* (lithograph on Japanese paper, 15 3/4 x 12 ins / 40.3 x 30.5 cm) BEF 60,000. PARIS, 18 April 1994, *Bust of Japanese Man* (graphite on tracing paper, 16 1/4 x 14 1/2 ins / 41 x 37 cm) FRF 15,500. NEW YORK, 11 May 1994, *Two Girls* (oil on canvas on synthetic resin, 5 1/2 x 7 ins / 14.2 x 17.8 cm) USD 85,000. PARIS, 25 Nov 1994, *Life* (1917, oil on canvas, 22 x 18 ins / 55 x 46 cm) FRF 455,000. PARIS, 21 June 1995, *Cat and Kitten* (1930, etching and aquatint) FRF 19,500. LONDON, 28 June 1995, *My studio, Paris Landscape* (1939, oil on canvas, 22 x 18 ins / 55 x 46 cm) GBP 47,700. PARIS, 18 March 1996, *Cupid* (1924, oil on canvas, 18 x 15 ins / 46 x 38 cm) FRF 180,000. AMSTERDAM, 4-5 June 1996, *Little Girl with Doll* (1939, oil on canvas, 18 x 15 ins / 46 x 38.4 cm) NLG 118,000; *Gathering of Cyclists* (1939, oil on canvas, 5 1/2 x 7 ins / 14 x 18 cm) NLG 59,800. LONDON, 25 June 1996, *Girl with Cap* (watercolour, 11 x 7 1/2 ins / 27.9 x 19.1 cm) GBP 27,600. PARIS, 26 June 1996, *Portrait of a Woman* (1929, stump and Indian ink on card, 14 x 12 3/4 ins / 35.5 x 32.7 cm) FRF 40,000. NEW YORK, 9 Oct 1996, *Portrait of a Woman* (1930, gouache, watercolour and pencil/paper, 21 3/4 x 15 ins / 55.3 x 38.4 cm) USD 19,550. LONDON, 23 Oct 1996, *In Concarneau* (1919, oil on canvas, 15 x 18 ins / 38 x 46 cm) GBP 25,300. NEW YORK, 13 Nov 1996, *Motherhood and Cat* (1957, oil on canvas, 21 1/2 x 13 ins / 54.9 x 33 cm) USD 189,500. PARIS, 18 Nov 1996, *Two Nuns* (c. 1917-1918, watercolour, gouache and Indian ink, 12 1/2 x 11 1/2 ins / 31.5 x 28.9 cm) FRF 38,000. PARIS, 9 Dec 1996, *Little Girl with Plaits* (c. 1950, Indian ink and ink wash on paper on card, 12 1/2 x 8 3/4 ins / 31.5 x 22.5 cm) FRF 98,000. PARIS, 10 Dec 1996, *Woman with Cat* (coloured lithograph, 40 1/2 x 15 ins / 103 x 38 cm) FRF 4,000. PARIS, 18 Dec 1996, *Kitten and Mother* (1929, etching and colour aquatint, 12 1/2 x 15 1/4 ins / 32 x 38.5 cm) FRF 48,000. PARIS, 16 March 1997, *Portrait of a Woman* (1930, Indian ink and stump on paper, 15 1/4 x 11 1/2 ins / 38.5 x 29.5 cm) FRF 54,000. PARIS, 16 June 1997, *Mother and Child* (1951, oil on canvas, 13 x 9 3/4 ins / 33 x 25 cm) FRF 580,000; *Young Woman with Ribbon* (1951, ink and ink wash, 10 1/4 x 7 ins / 26 x 18 cm) FRF 80,000; *Love Riding a Dolphin* (red and black gouache, line-drawing, 19 3/4 x 14 1/4 ins / 50 x 36 cm) FRF 38,000. LONDON, 25 June 1997, *Portrait of Young Boy* (c. 1928, pen and ink and grey wash on paper, 11 x 11 ins / 28 x 27.8 cm) GBP 10,925. AMSTERDAM, 1 Dec 1997, *Little Girl with Bottle; Young Boy with Book; Little Girl with Saucepan* (pen, ink and watercolour on paper, three works, each 6 1/4 x 4 1/2 ins / 15.7 x 11.6 cm) NLG 11,800. PARIS, 5 Feb 1998, *Bust of a Girl, Head Leaning on Left Hand* (1930, colour etching, probably one of the five illustrations to The Flower with a Thousand Gold Petals) FRF 2,200. PARIS, 31 March 1998, *Girl with Cat* (1956, oil on canvas, 18 1/4 x 13 1/4 ins / 46.5 x 33.5 cm) FRF 1,170,000. PARIS, 1 April 1998, *Profile of Woman with Blue Veil*. L'ISLE-ADAM, 26 April 1998, *Girl with Blue Dress* (1950, watercolour, 9 x 6 3/4 ins / 23 x 17 cm) FRF 141,500.

FUJIU. See **YI HAI**

FUJIWARA, Goshin

Japanese, 14th century.

Active during the second half of the 14th century.

Monk-painter. Historical portraits.

Fujiwara Goshin was the son of the courtier Fujiwara Tamenobu and a fourth-generation descendant of the painter Fujiwara no Nobuzane. He served as a painter at the imperial court, specialising in figure paintings and portraits. He later became a monk.

BIBLIOGRAPHY:

Tazawa, Yutaka, *Biographical Dictionary of Japanese Art*, Kodansha International Ltd, Tokyo, 1981.

MUSEUMS AND GALLERIES:

KYOTO (Chofuku-Ji): *Portrait of Emperor Hanazono (1308-1318).*

FUJIWARA, Kazumichi
Japanese, 20th century.
Born 1943, in Kurashiki.
Sculptor.

Fujiwara Kazumichi began his career in 1963 as a composer. In 1966, he decided to retreat to the mountain of Oku-yoshino. It was here that he experimented with curious and enormous music machines, which he exhibited some years later, particularly at the 1975 Paris Biennale. Made from enormous tree trunks, pieces of timber, lengths of cable, rocks and concrete, these machines require, in addition to audience participation, a real physical effort to make them work.

FUJIWARA, Nagataka, monk's name: Kaishin (Kaikan)
Japanese, 13th century.
Active in Kyoto during the second half of the 13th century.
Painter.
Yamato-e school (painting in the Japanese style).

FUJIWARA NO KORENOBU. See **KORENOBU**

FUJIWARA NO NOBUZANE. See **NOBUZANE**

FUJIWARA NO TAKACHIKA. See **TAKACHIKA**

FUJIWARA NO TAKANOBU. See **TAKANOBU**

FUJIWARA NO TAKASUKE. See **TAKASUKE**

FUJIWARA NO TAKAYOSHI. See **TAKAYOSHI**

FUJIWARA NO TAMETSUGU. See **TAMETSUGU**

FUJIWARA NO YUKIMITSU. See **YUKIMITSU**

FUJIWARA NO YUKINAGA. See **YUKINAGA**

FUJIWARA TSUNETAKA. See **TSUNETAKA**

FUKITA, Fumiaki
Japanese, 20th century.
Born 1926, in Tokushima (Shikoku).
Print artist.

Fukita Fumiaki is a woodblock artist who trained as a teacher before going to the Tokyo College of Art. He has regularly taken part in the Tokyo International Print Triennale since 1960. He is a member of the Japan Modern Art Association and has taken part in its events since 1955, and a member of the Japan Print Association, winning the Onchi prize in 1958. In 1960 he won the prize at the First International Colour Print Triennale at Grenchen, Switzerland; in 1965, at the International Northwest Print Exhibition in the USA and in 1967, the São Paulo Biennale. His work fluctuates between a sort of naivety and a tendency towards abstraction.

FUKIYA, Koji
Japanese, 20th century.
Born 1898, in Shin Hotta (Niigata); died 1979.
Painter, print artist, illustrator.

Acting on the recommendation of the mayor of Niigata, Fukiya Koji went to study under the painter Otake in Tokyo at the age of 14. Between 1916 and 1919, he was a roaming painter in the Karafuto area, then a poster artist in Tokyo. Following an encounter with the draughtsman Takehisa, he worked as an illustrator for the Kodansha publishing house, producing successful covers for books and magazines for young girls and women. In 1925, still wishing to become a painter, he left for Paris, where he met Fujita. The following year, one of his paintings, *Child of Mixed Race and its Parents* was selected at the Salon d'Automne. He exhibited there again in 1927 and 1928. In 1929, the book *Selected Drawings by Koji Fukiya* was published in Shanghai. In 1929, he exhibited at the Galerie René Zivy in Paris. In the same year, having to return to Japan to meet the needs of his two brothers, he resumed his profession of illustrator.

Fukiya was involved in the creation of the first Japanese cartoons in 1954, published an autobiography *Bride's Doll* in 1967, and was co-author with Daigaku Horiguchi, the well-known translator of French literature, of *The Rainbow's Poem*. He began a series of regular exhibitions at the Odakyu Gallery in Tokyo in 1968 and had an exhibition of illustrated books at Mitsukoshi in 1975.

Fukiya's graphic work is characterised by its finesse, precision and elegant drawing. From Japanese tradition he draws a feeling for composition, choice of colours and decorative references that is quite original. His favourite subjects were figures, children's heads and portraits. Occasionally, we can sense how contact with western art influenced his work: some of his ink drawings are reminiscent of Beardsley or Vallotton.

BIBLIOGRAPHY:

Tazawa, Yutaka, *Biographical Dictionary of Japanese Art*, Kodansha International Ltd, Tokyo, 1981.

MUSEUMS AND GALLERIES:

SHIN NOTTA (Koji Fukiya Mus.).

FUKS, Aleksandr
Russian, 19th century.
Born 7 June 1863, in Nikolayev.
Painter.

Fuchs was he a pupil of Raupp and of Raab in Munich and painted mostly portraits as he travelled through the Germanic countries.

FUKUDA, Heihachiro
Japanese, 20th century.
Born 1892, in Oita, Kyushu; died 1972.
Painter. Landscapes.

Fukuda Heihachiro graduated from the Kyoto Municipal College of Painting in 1918. He exhibited at the Teiten and from 1924 was a member of its jury. In 1930, he founded the Rokucho (Sixth Tide) group. In 1949, he received the first *Mainichi* Fine Arts Grand Prize and in 1961 was awarded the Order of Cultural Merit. He was a member of the Japan Art Academy. As a student, Fukuda worked in figurative style. He then evolved to a more personal form of expression, paying particular attention to nature, leading to a rationalised simplification, sometimes symbolic, bordering on constructed abstraction. However, his work remains lively and somewhat decorative.

BIBLIOGRAPHY:

Posthumous Exhibition of Heihachiro Fukuda, National Museum of Modern Art, Tokyo, 1975 (in Japanese and English).

MUSEUMS AND GALLERIES:

TOKYO (National MMA): *Rain.*

FUKUDA, Kitsu. See **HANKO**

FUKUDA, Shigeo
Japanese, 20th century.
Draughtsman, poster artist, graphic designer, sculptor.
Op Art.

Fukuda Shigeo is an international figure. He exhibits frequently, receiving numerous awards. He first exhibited in France in 1992, at the Quimper Contemporary Art Centre, and later at the Echirolles Mois du graphisme exhibition. Working in the tradition of Escher, he has become a master of illusionism. Drawings and objects can immediately be seen in two ways, familiar and disturbing, even absurd or impossible. His outlines, his even style of drawing, his flat colours all contribute to this visual tension.

BIBLIOGRAPHY:

Barré, François/Ueki, Hiroshi/Le Quernec, Alain, *Fukuda c'est fou*, Centre d'Art contemporain Le Quartier, Quimper (text in French, Japanese and English).

FUKUDA, Toyoshiro

Japanese, 20th century.
Born 1904, in Akita Prefecture.
Painter.

Fukuda Toyoshiro studied under Kawabata Ryuko and Tsuchida Hosen, and graduated from the Kyoto Municipal College of Painting in 1928. He soon exhibited at the imperial exhibition (Teiten). In 1934, he co-founded the Shin Nihonga Kenkyu-kai (New Japanese Painting Research Society) and after World War II he helped to found Sozo Bijutsu (Creative Art). What distinguishes Fukuda from other traditional painters is the way in which he has managed to preserve a certain regional use of colour in what is a very closely-defined discipline.

FUKUI, Ryonosuke

Japanese, 20th century.
Born 1922, in Tokyo.
Painter, print artist. Figures, nudes, still-lifes.

Fukui Ryonosuke graduated from the applied arts department of Tokyo School of Fine Arts in 1944. From 1962, he took part in the Tokyo Print Biennale, and in 1963 and 1965 in the Ljubljana Biennale. He had a solo exhibition in Tokyo every year since 1959. His work is essentially figurative, but very stylised, particularly his still-lifes.

AUCTION RECORDS:

NEW YORK, 29 Nov 1984, *Two Nudes* (oil on canvas, 51¼ x 63½ ins / 130 x 161.5 cm) USD 9,500. NEW YORK, 12 Feb 1987, *Sitting Girl* (oil on canvas, 36 x 25¾ ins / 91.5 x 65.7 cm) USD 8,000. NEW YORK, 8 March 2001, *Blue Flower with Two Leaves. Blue Flower with Three Leaves* (c. 1950, gouache, pencil and casein, a pair, 36 x 26 ins / 91 x 66 cm) USD 3,200. SHAKER HEIGHTS, 10 March 2001, *Untitled* (mixed media, a pair, 11 x 16 ins / 28 x 41 cm) USD 2,000. NEW YORK, 3 Dec 2003, *Profile of Woman* (oil on canvas, 21 x 13 ins / 53 x 33 cm) USD 3,250.

FUKUOKA, Takatsugu

Japanese, 20th century.
Born in Tokyo.
Painter.

Fukuoka Takatsugu exhibited at the 1926 Salon d'Automne.

FUKUSHIMA, Kin'ichiro

Japanese, 20th century.
Born in Okayama.
Painter.

Fukushima Kin'ichiro exhibited at the 1929 Salon d'Automne.

FUKUZAWA, Ichiro

Japanese, 20th century.
Born 1898, in Tomioka (Gumma).
Painter, collage artist, sculptor.

Fukuzawa Ichiro went to Tokyo University in 1918 to study literature, aesthetics and art history. Between 1918 and 1919, he studied sculpture under Asukura Fumio. In 1922, he took part in the Teiten imperial exhibition. He then left for Europe, and lived in Paris from 1924 to 1931. After exhibiting a watercolour at the 1928 Salon d'Automne, he abandoned sculpture for painting and went travelling in Europe. In 1929, at the beginning of his Surrealist phase, when he was strongly influenced by de Chirico and Max Ernst, ten of his works were selected for the *Nika* salon, of which he became a member in 1930. He returned to Japan in 1931, and continued to produce works in the Surrealist spirit, giving them a satirical, or simply controversial content. In 1939 he was instrumental in founding the Bijutsu Bunka Kyokai (Art Culture Association), a forum for Japanese artists linked to Surrealism. It held a group exhibition in 1940, and helped to make Surrealism accepted in Japan.

In 1941, at the time of the Berlin-Rome-Tokyo axis, the Surrealists were likened to Communists and Fuzukawa was sent to prison. He was not released until after the war. When he resumed painting, he favoured social criticism in his works, metaphorically attacking the different states of disorder that followed the defeat of a caste society and the emerging middle-class desire for democratisation and modernisation.

In 1951, he was the first Japanese painter since the war to take part in the São Paulo Biennale. From 1952 to 1954, he returned to Paris, passed through Spain and stayed in Brazil and in Mexico, with the aim of widening his pictorial repertoire. In 1952 and 1955 he exhibited at the Venice Biennale and from 1955 at the Tokyo International Art Exhibition. In 1957, he was awarded the grand prize at the Tokyo Biennale. In 1958, he travelled to India. In 1964, on the occasion of the Olympic Games, he took part in the exhibition organised by the Tokyo National Museum of Modern Art. In 1965, he went to the USA. From 1971, he worked on the theme of hell, basing his work on both Dante's Divine Comedy and Japanese mythology.

Fukuzawa's work is the most representative of avant-garde Japanese painting of the first half of the century. In the 1930s, he was the key player in introducing Surrealism to Japan. He knew how to reconcile, in his own way, a part of the Surrealist spirit with his wish to play a role in freeing the Japanese soul, stating that 'my desire to paint comes from wanting to create something from nothing. The way I approach my themes is related to current social and political conditions.'

BIBLIOGRAPHY:

Tazawa, Yutaka, *Biographical Dictionary of Japanese Art*, Kodansha International Ltd, Tokyo, 1981.

FUKUZAWA, Shiro

Japanese, 20th century.
Born 1907, in Tochigi Prefecture.
Print artist.

Fukuzawa Shiro trained at the Kawabata School of Painting. In 1966 and 1968, he took part in the Tokyo International Print Biennale, in 1968 and 1969 in the eighth and ninth Contemporary Japanese Art Exhibition, and in 1969, in the International Print Biennale in Ljubljana.

FUKUZAWA, Yukio

Japanese, 20th century.
Born 1924, in Yamagata Prefecture.
Print artist.

Fukuzawa Yukio graduated from the art metalwork department of the Tokyo National University of Fine Arts in 1957. Since then he has taken part in the exhibitions of the Japan Print Association and the Tokyo International Print Biennale, winning the grand prize in 1957. In 1959 he was awarded the Shell prize, and in 1962 the prize for excellence at the Contemporary Japanese Art Exhibition. He also took part several times in the Lugano International Print Biennale and the São Paulo Biennale. He likes to use several processes simultaneously. He often goes in for the subtle exploration of different textures. His style can be qualified as Surrealist in its subject matter.

FULCARO, Sebastiano
Italian, 16th - 17th century.
Active in Rome.
Engraver.

Fulcaro is referred to as having produced a *Last Judgement*, based on the work of Michelangelo. He is undoubtedly the same person as Sebastian Fulcarus.

FULCARUS, Sebastian, or Furch
German, 17th century.
Born 1589, in Goslar or in Alterkülz (Lower Saxony); died 1666, in Frankfurt.
Draughtsman, engraver (burin).

Fulcarus engraved views, portraits and emblems. He began by working in Rome before returning to Germany, where he settled in Frankfurt am Main in 1620.

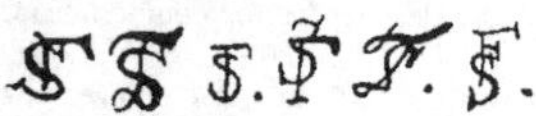

FULCHIRON (Mme)
French, 19th century.
Painter. Figures, portraits, landscapes with figures.

Museums and Galleries:
Le Havre: *Portrait of Jean-Baptiste Eyries.*

Auction records:
Paris, 27 June 1991, *Antique Shepherds near an Aqueduct* (oil on canvas, 21 1/2 x 18in/54.5 x 45.5cm) FRF 20,000.

FÜLCK, Johann David
German, 18th century.
Active in Wiesentheid (Bavaria).
Draughtsman.

Fülck drew up plans for garden designs and ornaments for the pleasure grounds at Wiesentheid, which were published.

FULCO, Giovanni, or Fulcho
Italian, 17th century.
Born 1605, in Messina; died c. 1680.
Painter.

Giovanni Fulco started studying drawing and composition in his native Messina before travelling to Naples where he studied under Massimo Stanzione. Fulco's work was almost entirely lost during a series of earthquakes, but in his *Memorie de Pittore Messinese* (*Recollections of Painters from Messina*), Habert describes Fulco as an accomplished draughtsman who excelled in the portrayal of children. The crucifixion chapel in Messina's Nunziata de Teatine has preserved his oil painting *Birth of the Virgin*.

Auction records:
Paris, 19 March 1982, *St Francis and the Stigmata* (pen, brown ink and brown wash, 10 3/4 x 7 1/2 ins / 27.6 x 19 cm) FRF 2,700.

FULCONIS, Louis Guillaume
French, 19th century.
Born 15 February 1818, in Avignon; died 11 May 1873, in Paris.
Sculptor. Religious subjects. Religious furnishings (altars), funerary monuments, busts.

Louis Guillaume Fulconis was trained at the École des Beaux-Arts, Avignon, and featured at the Salon de Paris from 1857 to 1870. He spent a period in Algeria and then settled in Paris in 1855.

He produced numerous sculptures for the churches of Rouen, especially noteworthy being the stone statues of *St Bartholomew* and *St James the Less* at the door of the church of St Laurent and *The Tomb of the Prince of Croy* at Rouen Cathedral, the 'high altar' of the church of Bonsecours near Rouen, and the sculptures for the church of La Délivrande near Caen. He also produced work for the churches of Paris. Other works worthy of note are: *Acteon* (1861) at the Château de Fontainebleau, *La Coupo Santo* (1867), *Princess Clémence* (1868), *Doctor Camille Raspail*, a bronze bust, *Count Guyot*, a marble bust, *Ouled-Naïl, Bayadere* (Musée de Gray), *Abraham Lincoln* (Fondation Raspail, Cachan).

Bibliography:
Daum, Patrick, *Vie et œuvre des sculpteurs Guillaume Fulconis, 1818 - 1873 et Victor Fulconis, 1851 - 1913*, dissertation, Université de Provence, Aix-Marseilles, 1986.

Museums and Galleries:
Gray: *Ouled Naïl, Bayadere.*

FULCONIS, Victor Louis Pierre
French, 19th - 20th century.
Born 18 January 1851, in Algiers; died 3 September 1913, in Oran, Algeria.
Sculptor, painter. Figures, religious subjects. Busts.

Victor Fulconis was the son of Louis Guillaume Fulconis. He studied first with his father and then attended the studios of Jouffroy, Cavalier and Bonassieux. He taught drawing and art and often worked with the architect Eugène Barthélemy.

From 1872 to 1912 he exhibited at the Paris Salon. He became a member of the Société des Artistes Français in 1888 and received a commendation the same year.

Fulconis produced a statue of *St Mark* for the church of St-Ouen in Rouen and a statue of *St John* for the church of Caudebec-lès-Elbeuf. It is not known whether *Entrance to the Equebonille District at Roche-sur-Yon* (in the Musée de la Roche-sur-Yon) is the work of the father or the son. Fulconis's other works include; *Glorification of St Denis* (a high-relief in the parish church of St-Denis at Ste-Adresse, 1880); *The Bird Nester* (1894); *The Nativity* (1895); *Fire at the Bazar de la Charité* (1899); and *Princess Clémence* (1902).

Bibliography:
Daum, Patrick, *Vie et œuvre des sculpteurs Guillaume Fulconis, 1818 - 1873 et Victor Fulconis, 1851 - 1913*, dissertation, Université de Provence, Aix-Marseilles, 1986.

Museums and Galleries:
Avignon (Mus. Calvet): *Ultima optima* (1904) - La Roche-sur-Yon: *Glory; Entrace to the Equebonille District at Roche-sur-Yon* (attributed to the father or the son) - Rouen: *Bust of Jouvenet.*

FULCRAND, Pierre
French, 20th century.
Born 10 December 1914, in Montpellier.
Painter. Figures, nudes, still-lifes.

Pierre Fulcrand studied at the École des Beaux-Arts (in either Montpellier or Paris). During the 1950s he exhibited mainly in Paris at group exhibitions alongside Post-Cubist painters and at the Salon d'Automne, of which he was a member, Salon de Mai, Salon Comparaisons, Salon des Réalités Nouvelles and Salon des Indépendants. He took part in the *Five Young French Painters* exhibition in Nuremberg in 1957; the *Exhibition of French Painting from Gauguin to the Present Day* in Warsaw in 1959; and the São Paulo Biennale in 1961.

He also showed his work in solo exhibitions, including: 1946 at the Galerie Visconti in Paris; 1947 at the Galerie Génégaud in Paris; 1951 at the Galerie St-Placide in Paris; and 1967, 1969 and 1988 at the Galerie Michel d'Auberville in Paris.

Until around 1960, Fulcrand painted figures, nudes and still-lifes carefully constructed in accordance with the precepts elaborated during the years of Cubism. After this his style became more supple and the resemblance to the model more simplified, limited to just a few strong lines before disappearing entirely. He went on to paint in a radical abstract style characterised by violent action and aggressive colours.

MUSEUMS AND GALLERIES:
MONTPELLIER (Mus. Fabre) - PARIS (MAMVP) - PARIS (MNAM-CCI) - TOURCOING (MBA).

FULDA, Albert
German, 19th century.
Born c. 1820, in Halle (Saxony-Anhalt).
Miniaturist, draughtsman, lithographer.
Fulda, who was primarily a portrait painter, also worked in Leipzig.

FULDE, Edward B.
American, 19th - 20th century.
Born in St Louis.
Painter. Genre scenes, landscapes.
Edward Fulde studied under Joseph and Franck Bail in Paris. He stayed there for a significant period, exhibiting his work at the Salon des Artistes Français from 1896 until 1912.
AUCTION RECORDS:
PARIS, 4 Dec 1944, *Yport, Le Chicard* FRF 280. PARIS, 30 Oct 1987, *Sitting in the Artist's Studio* (1906, oil on canvas, 28¾ x 36¼ ins / 73 x 92 cm) FRF 40,000. PARIS, 13 June 1990, *Young Woman in a Landscape* (oil on canvas, 28¾ x 35¾ ins / 73 x 91 cm) FRF 15,000. PARIS, 31 March 2000, *Quai St Pierre at Cannes* (1892, oil on canvas, 21 x 30 ins / 53 x 77 cm) FRF 38,000.

FULFORD, Patricia
Canadian, 20th century.
Born 1935, in Toronto.
Sculptor.
Patricia Fulford studied at Ontario College of Art from 1954 until 1957 and returned as a teacher in 1960, staying until 1963.
In her youth she was influenced by Gothic and Roman art. At that time her work was figurative and greatly inspired by these forms of architecture. After 1966 she experimented with new, more expressive forms. Then, conversely, her sculptures evolved into a very structured abstraction, incorporating painted geometric elements.

FULGHUM, Caroline Mercer
American, 20th century.
Born 1875, in Goldsborough.
Painter, illustrator.
Caroline Fulghum was active in her home town. She studied under Phoebe Bunker, Albert Wenzell and Elliot Daingerfield in New York.

FULIGNATE, Nicolas
Italian, 14th century.
Active in Milan.
Painter. History painting.
Fulignate signed his work *Nicolaus Fulginas*.

FULIGNY-DAMAS. See **GROLLIER, Marchioness of**

FULINCKX, Louis
Flemish School.
Painter. Landscapes.
MUSEUMS AND GALLERIES:
LIVERPOOL: *The Path in the Forest; The Outskirts of Anvers.*

FULLA, Ludovit
Slovak, 20th century.
Born 27 February 1902, in Ruzomberok; died 21 April 1980.
Painter. Scenes with figures, landscapes with figures. Designs for mosaics, tapestries.
Ludovit Fulla was a student at the school of arts and crafts in Prague between 1922 and 1927 and taught from 1929 at the school of arts in Bratislava where he stayed until 1939. From 1940 almost up to 1960 he lived in Slovakia, in Martin and Zilina. Between 1949 and 1952 he taught at the college of fine arts in Bratislava.
Between 1930 and 1932 he published books of *Private Letters* in collaboration with his friend Mikuláš Galanda, which then defined what modern Slovak art should be. Fulla worked across the disciplines: graphic arts, illustrations, set design, tapestry where the weaving was generally done in Jindrichuv Hradec's workshops, and mosaics including one at the International Exhibition in Montreal in 1967. His paintings are often reminiscent of mosaic or collage because of a sort of systematic breaking-up of the surfaces. The same harmonious sequence can be noted throughout his work. He is regarded as one of the most important representatives of Czechoslovak painting between the brilliant generation of Kupka, Sima and Filla and the more recent artists such as Medek, Vozniak, Sklenar and Kolar. He was still expressing himself in a formal language resulting from the Expressionism of 1910 onwards, influenced to some extent, through Cézanne, by Cubism, which was very much in favour in Czechoslovakia after World War I. Anxious to allow some modernity while preserving Slovak popular tradition, he divided his work between painting villages in the Slovakian countryside and their inhabitants and a less realistic line of work, where the heroes are mythical figures from popular legend, whom he also developed beyond any law of gravity. This is also often true of Chagall's figures, who have no trouble flying above the steeples. His method of communicating a permanent poetic message through the formal language of the time can also be compared to the work of Paul Klee.
Fulla took part in many national and international collective exhibitions, including: Venice Biennale (1934, 1942, 1956, 1962 and 1966); São Paulo Biennale (1957); Lausanne Biennale (1965); Expositions Interntionales, Brussels (1935 and 1958 winning a gold medal); Exposition Internationale, Paris (1937); *Fifty years of Czechoslovak Painting from the Collections of the Galleries, 1918-1958* touring the Czechoslovak museums in for the Republic's 50th anniversary (1968); *Exposition d'Art Slovaque*, Musée d'Art Moderne de la Ville de Paris (1974). In 1963 he was appointed national artist; in 1966 won the Czechoslovak State Prize; and in 1972 he was awarded the Order of the Republic.
BIBLIOGRAPHY:
Fifty years of Czechoslovak Painting from the Collections of the Galleries, 1918-1958, exhibition catalogue, Slovenska Narodna Gal., Bratislava, 1968 (in commemoration of the 50th anniversary of the Republic of Czechoslovakia).
MUSEUMS AND GALLERIES:
PRAGUE (Národní Gal.) - RUZOMBEROK (Liptovské Múzeum): a large proportion of his works.

FULLARD, George
British, 20th century.
Born 1924, in Sheffield; died 1973.
Sculptor of assemblages.
George Fullard exhibited in London from 1958. Using a variety of objects he creates diabolical machines not dissimilar to those of Tinguely. These mini war machines appear intended to inspire a sense of horror.

FULLBROOK, Samuel Sydney, called Sam
Australian, 20th century.
Born 1922.
Painter.
Samuel Fullbrook's work is entirely inspired by European painting. Rich in pale colours and allusive figures, it takes its inspiration from the Blaue Reiter movement of 1910.
AUCTION RECORDS:
SYDNEY, 6 Oct 1976, *Young Girl* (oil on card, 18 x 20 ins / 45.8 x 50.5 cm) AUD 1,500. SYDNEY, 2 March 1981, *The Miner* (oil on canvas, 13¾ x 10 ins / 35 x 25.5 cm) AUD 1,600. SYDNEY, 24 Nov 1986, *Storm Coming* (oil on canvas, 15¼ x 16¼ ins /

39 x 41 cm) AUD 4,500. LONDON, 1 Dec 1988, *Still-life with a Cod on a Tray* (oil on canvas, 15 1/2 x 22 ins / 39.4 x 55.8 cm) GBP 5,280. MELBOURNE, 26 April 1999, *Sunday Bonnet* (oil on canvas, 30 x 24 ins / 75 x 62 cm) AUD 22,000. MELBOURNE, 28 June 2000, *Kimberley Sketch* (oil on canvas laid on board, 8 x 11 ins / 21 x 28 cm) AUD 24,000. MELBOURNE, 9 May 2001, *My Filly* (oil on canvas, 22 x 16 ins / 55 x 40 cm) AUD 34,000. MELBOURNE, 26 Nov 2001, *Pat Murray, Horse Trainer* (oil on canvas, 33 x 30 ins / 85 x 75 cm) AUD 27,000. PADDINGTON, 25 Aug 2002, *Tulips* (oil on canvas, 28 x 28 ins / 72 x 72 cm) AUD 26,000. MELBOURNE, 6 May 2003, *Visitation* (1981, oil on canvas, 33 x 29 ins / 83 x 74 cm) AUD 35,000. MELBOURNE, 2 Sept 2003, *Flower Piece No 1* (oil on canvas, 42 x 38 ins / 106 x 96 cm) AUD 48,000. MELBOURNE, 16 June 2004, *Flowers* (oil on canvas, 18 x 20 ins / 46 x 51 cm) AUD 28,000.

FULLER, Augustus
American, 19th century.
Miniaturist.

Augustus Fuller was the half-brother and first teacher of George Fuller.

FULLER, Charles Francis
British, 19th century.
Born 1830; died 10 March 1875, in Florence, Italy.
Sculptor.

Charles Francis Fuller exhibited in London at the Royal Academy on 28 occasions between 1859 and 1875. He was particularly noted for his busts.

FULLER, Cynthia
British, 20th century.
Active c. 1940-1970.
Painter. Figures, landscapes.
Symbolism.

Cynthia Fuller was a self-taught artist. Her paintings reveal a poetic inspiration more or less in the tradition of the Pre-Raphaelites but moving towards Modernism in its bold use of colour. She is known for *The Dreaming Giantess, Dream Landscape* and from 1940, *Shelter.*

FULLER, Denise
French, 20th century.
Born in Paris.
Painter.

Denise Fuller studied under Jules Adler and Joseph Bergès. She exhibited in Paris at the Salon des Artistes Français from 1927.

FULLER, Edmund G.
British, 19th - 20th century.
Died after 1930.
Painter. Genre scenes, landscapes.

Edmund Fuller worked in St Ives, Cornwall, in the late 19th century.

AUCTION RECORDS:

NEW YORK, 31 Jan-2 Feb 1900, *Bringing Home the Cow,* USD 1,550; *Lorette,* USD 3,600. NEW YORK, 8-9 Jan 1903, *The Quadroon,* USD 5,500. NEW YORK, 9-10 Feb 1905, *The Baudet Road,* USD 480. LONDON, 28-29 July 1927, *Rocky Coast; Silence* (both) GBP 23. CHESTER, 24 June 1981, *Fish on Sale, St Ives* (1894, oil on canvas, 42 1/4 x 31 ins / 107 x 79 cm) GBP 850. LONDON, 12 June 1987, *Saturday Afternoon* (oil on panel, 15 1/4 x 12 ins / 38.6 x 30.5 cm) GBP 1,000.

FULLER, George
American, 19th century.
Born 1822, in Deerfield; died 21 March 1884, in Boston.
Painter. Portraits, genre scenes, landscapes.

George Fuller painted portraits and landscapes inspired by Millet and was one of the first artists to make the French 19th-century painters known in America.

AUCTION RECORDS:

NEW YORK, 14 Nov 1934, *Portrait of a Young Girl,* USD 25. NEW YORK, 15 Jan 1937, *Freshly Ploughed Field,* USD 145. NEW YORK, 11-13 Jan 1945, *Girl with a Doll,* USD 150. NEW YORK, 4 May 1945, *Letter,* USD 120. BOLTON, 20 May 1980, *Reverie* (oil on canvas, 24 x 18 ins / 61 x 46 cm) USD 800. NEW YORK, 21 Oct 1983, *Young Woman on the Edge of a Wood* (oil on canvas, 24 x 18 ins / 61 x 45.7 cm) USD 900. NEW YORK, 24 June 1988, *Portrait of Miss Wynne* (oil on canvas, 24 1/2 x 20 1/4 ins / 62.5 x 51.4 cm) USD 990. NEW YORK, 14 Nov 1991, *Portrait of John Quincy Adams Ward* (1868, oil on canvas, 16 x 14 ins / 40.6 x 35.5 cm) USD 1,760. MAINE, 1 May 1999, *Figures in a Wooded Landscape* (oil on canvas, 21 x 27 ins / 53 x 69 cm) USD 2,000. NORTH BETHESDA, 21 May 1999, *Landscape with Figures* (oil on board, 9 x 13 ins / 23 x 33 cm) USD 1,800. NEW YORK, 4 Oct 2000, *Study for the Quadroon* (oil on canvas, 30 x 25 ins / 76 x 64 cm) USD 6,000. NEW YORK, 16 Jan 2001, *Woman in a Landscape* (oil on canvas, 20 x 16 ins / 51 x 41 cm) USD 4,000. MAINE, 3 Jan 2004, *Connecticut Valley* (oil on canvas, 15 x 27 ins / 38 x 69 cm) USD 4,600. LOS ANGELES, 28 April 2004, *The Sprite* (c. 1880, oil on canvas, 20 x 16 ins / 50 x 41 cm) USD 3,000.

FULLER, Henry Brown
American, 19th - 20th century.
Born 3 October 1867, in Deerfield; died 1934.
Painter.

Henry Fuller studied at Cowles Art School in Boston and under Collin in Paris. He lived in Windsor (USA). He received a bronze medal in Buffalo in 1901. He is known for his figures.

AUCTION RECORDS:

NEW YORK, 1 April 1981, *The Maenad* (oil on canvas, 24 x 20 ins / 61 x 50.8 cm) USD 2,000.

FULLER, Horace
British, 19th century.
Painter. Waterscapes, landscapes.

Horace Fuller was an exhibitor at London's Royal Academy in 1874, 1876 and 1884.

FULLER, Isaac
British, 17th century.
Born 1606; died 17 July 1672, in London.
Painter, engraver, draughtsman. Religious subjects, portraits.

Isaac Fuller worked with François Perrier in Paris between 1645 and 1650 and later painted murals for the chapels of Wadham College (*Children of Israel Collecting Manna*) and Magdalen College (an altarpiece), Oxford. He also produced five compositions depicting the *Flight of Charles II after the Battle of Worcester,* subsequently preserved in the Irish Parliament. He settled in London and was a portraitist of some distinction. He also engraved a number of plates for the *Libro da Disegnare,* an Italian treatise on drawing.

MUSEUMS AND GALLERIES:

LONDON (National Portrait Gal.): *King Charles II at Whiteladies, King Charles II in Boscobel Wood, King Charles II and Colonel William Carlos in the Royal Oak, King Charles II on Humphrey Penderel's Mill Horse, King Charles II and Jane Lane riding to Bristol* (1660s?, oil on canvas, series of paintings showing Charles II's 'Escape from the Battle of Worcester'); *Isaac Fuller* (c. 1670, oil on canvas) - LONDON (Tate Collection): *Portrait of an Unknown Man* (c. 1660, oil on canvas).

AUCTION RECORDS:

LONDON, 20 June 1947, *Sir Thomas Baines,* GBP 42. LONDON, 13 April 1994, *Portrait of the Artist in a Brown Coat and Red Hat, his Arms Resting on Statuettes and with his Son on his Right* (oil on canvas, 45 x 41 1/2 ins / 114 x 105.5 cm) GBP 25,300. LONDON, 9 April 1997, *Portrait of the Artist and his Son* (c. 1670, oil on canvas, 52 1/4 x 42 1/4 ins / 133 x 107.5 cm)

GBP 52,100. NEW YORK, 28 Jan 1999, *Portrait of Woman* (pen and brown ink, 6 x 5 ins / 14 x 12 cm) USD 7,000.

FULLER, Leonard John
British, 20th century.
Born 1891, in London; died 1973.
Painter.

Leonard Fuller studied at the Royal Academy in London. He exhibited in Paris from 1927 at the Salon des Artistes Français, where he received a silver medal.

AUCTION RECORDS:
LONDON, 16 Sept 1981, *Shops Across the Way* (oil on canvas, 23 1/2 x 19 1/2 ins / 59.5 x 49.5 cm) GBP 360. LONDON, 9 Nov 1984, *The Interior of Woolworths: Threepence, Sixpence* (oil on canvas, 40 x 50 ins / 101.6 x 127 cm) GBP 2,000. LONDON, 24 July 1985, *Reclining Nude* (1939, oil on canvas, 22 x 40 ins / 56 x 101.5 cm) GBP 500. LONDON, 5 March 1987, *The People's Store, the Interior of Woolworth's* (oil on canvas, 40 x 50 ins / 101.5 x 127 cm) GBP 7,500. PENZANCE, 15 June 2004, *At his Studio, St Ives* (oil on canvas, 24 x 28 ins / 61 x 71 cm) GBP 1,000.

FULLER, Lucia, Mrs Henry B. Fuller
Maiden name: Fairchild
American, 19th - 20th century.
Born 6 December 1872, in Boston; died 1924.
Painter.

Lucia Fuller lived and was active in New York. She studied under Dennis M. Bunker in Boston, and Henry Siddons Mowbray and William Chase at the Art Students' League in New York. She took part in the Paris Salon at the Exposition Universelle of 1900, where she was awarded a bronze medal, and the Buffalo Exhibition in 1901, where she received a silver medal.

BIBLIOGRAPHY:
Miller, Lucia, *'John Singer Sargent in the diaries of Lucia Fairchild, 1890 and 1891'* in *Archives of American Art Journal XXVI/4*, 1986 (pp. 2-16). Garfinkle, Charlene G., *'Lucia Fairchild Fuller's 'lost' Woman's Building Mural'* in *American Art*, vol. 7, no. 1, 1993 (pp. 2-7).

FULLER, Meta Vaux Warrick
Maiden name: Warrick
American, 19th - 20th century.
Born 9 June 1877, in Philadelphia; died 13 March 1968.
Sculptor (plaster, bronze), illustrator.
Harlem Renaissance.

Meta Vaux Warrick Fuller studied at the Pennsylvania Museum School for Industrial Arts (today Philadelphia College of Art) from 1894 to 1899 and the Pennsylvania Academy of the Fine Arts from 1903 to 1907. She lived in Paris from 1899 to 1903, studying sculpture at the Académie Colarossi from 1899 to 1902 and drawing at the École des Beaux-Arts. She was also a pupil of Rodin. While in Paris she met W.E.B. DuBois, the African-American sociologist who founded the National Association for the Advancement of Colored People (NAACP). In 1909 she married the physician Solomon Fuller, who was born in Liberia. She lived in Boston and Framingham. Much of her early work was destroyed when her studio burned down in 1910. In 1962, she was awarded an honorary doctorate by Livingstone College, Salisbury, North Carolina.

Her early work from the 1880s had something of the grotesque about it. She became known as the 'sculptor of horror', as her figures treated death, despair and anguish in starkly realist terms. Then she created black figures such as *Ethiopia Awakening* (1914), which represents a mummy whose bands above the waist have come undone, revealing the head and body of an African woman wearing the headdress of an ancient Egyptian queen. Here, Ethiopia symbolises a mythical Africa, one that includes Egypt as the cradle of black African culture. Meta Fuller's work was consistently pan-African and anti-colonial; this places her among the forerunners of the Harlem Renaissance, for which she was a model although she never lived in Harlem. She interpreted African legends and created works of religious and mythological inspiration. Her style recalls the romantic realism of 19th century French sculpture, albeit with expressionist accents. Her papers are preserved in the Schomburg Center, for Research in Black Culture, New York Public Library.

Meta Vaux Warrick Fuller took part in various group exhibitions, such as the 1898, 1899 and 1903 Paris Salons; 1902, Galerie l'Art Nouveau, Paris; 1931, 1933, Harmon Foundation, New York; 1906, 1908, 1920, 1923, Pennsylvania Academy of Fine Arts, Philadelphia; 1927, Art Institute, Chicago; 1940, *American Negro Exposition*; 1961, Howard University, Washington DC; 1967, City College, New York. After she died her work was also included in a number of thematic exhibitions, such as in 1996, *Three Generations of African-American Women Sculptors: A Study in Paradox*, Afro-American Historical and Cultural Museum, Philadelphia, and in 1984 a retrospective *An Independent Woman: The Life and Art of Meta Warrick Fuller* was held at the Danforth Museum of Art, Framingham, Massachusetts.

BIBLIOGRAPHY:
Fonvielle-Bontemps, Jacqueline (ed.), *Forever Free: Art by African-American Women*, group exhibition catalogue, Illinois State University, Normal (USA,IL, Stephenson Inc., Alexandria, VA, 1980. *An Independent Woman: The Life and Art of Meta Warrick Fuller*, exhibition catalogue, Danforth Museum of Art, Framingham (MA), 1984. Driskell, David/Levering Lewis, David/Willis Ryan, Deborah, *Harlem Renaissance. Art of Black America*, group exhibition catalogue, The Studio Museum in Harlem, Harry N. Abrams, New York, 1987.

MUSEUMS AND GALLERIES:
BOSTON (Mus. of Afro-American History): *Mary Turner (A Silent Protest against Mob Violence)* (1919); *Talking Skull* (1937, bronze) - CLEVELAND (MA) - FRAMINGHAM, MA (Danforth Mus. of Art): *Mother and Child* (1914-1920) - NEW YORK (Public Library): *Ethiopia Awakening* (1914, bronze) - SAN FRANCISCO (FAM).

FULLER, Ralph Briggs
American, 20th century.
Born 1890, in Michigan; died 1963.
Painter, draughtsman, illustrator.

Ralph Fuller was a member of the Salmagundi Club. He was known for his humorous drawings.

FULLER, Richard Henry
American, 19th century.
Born 1822, in Bradford; died 1871, in Chelsea, near Boston.
Painter. Landscapes.

From 1852 to 1866 Richard Henry Fuller spent all his spare time cultivating the arts. Between 1867 and his death he devoted himself to painting, bringing great poetic feeling to the various types of American landscapes he depicted. He is deemed one of the best American landscape painters. He bequeathed 90 of his works to the Boston Art Club.

AUCTION RECORDS:
NEW YORK, 30 April 1969, *Fishing Boat in an Estuary*, USD 1,300. NEW YORK, 25 Sept 1992, *Cottage in a Landscape* (oil on panel, 8 x 12 ins / 20.3 x 30.5 cm) USD 1,540. NEW YORK, 7 Dec 1999, *Man and Dog along a Country Road* (oil on canvas, 18 x 26 ins / 46 x 66 cm) USD 3,000. WASHINGTON, 16 Sept 2000, *Along the Path* (oil on canvas, 18 x 26 ins / 46 x 66 cm) USD 1,600. LONDON, 13 Oct 2004, *Extensive River Landscape* (oil on canvas, 30 x 48 ins / 76 x 122 cm) GBP 1,700.

FULLER, S. and H.
French, 19th century.
Painters.

They worked together on an altarpiece of *St Vincent de Paul*, dated 1847, for the church of St-Médard, Paris.

FULLER, S. E. W. (Mrs)
American, 19th century.
Born in America; died 6 July 1907.
Draughtswoman, engraver (wood), lithographer.

S.E.W. Fuller studied wood engraving and lithography in New York and gained a considerable reputation. After the War of Secession she settled in Washington, where she devoted herself to teaching.

FULLER, Sarah E.
American, 19th century.
Born 1829; died 14 December 1901, in Lynbrook (New York).
Engraver (wood/steel).

Sarah E. Fuller was one of the first artists in America to engrave on wood and steel. For a long time she collaborated with the Harper company. She worked for the most important New York publishers.

FULLER, Spencer
American, 19th - 20th century.
Born 25 February 1863, in Deerfield; died 9 May 1911, in Deerfield.
Painter. Landscapes.

Spencer Fuller was the son of George Fuller and the brother of Henry Brown Fuller.

FULLERTON, C. A.
British, 19th century.
Painter, watercolourist. Landscapes.

MUSEUMS AND GALLERIES:
LONDON (Victoria and Albert Mus.): *View of Edinburgh*.

FULLEYLOVE, John
British, 19th century.
Born 18 August 1845, in Leicester; died 22 May 1908, in London.
Painter, watercolourist. Landscapes.

John Fulleylove was a Member of the Royal Institute of Painters in Watercolours and a frequent exhibitor in London between 1871 and 1893. He was awarded a bronze at the Exposition Universelle in Paris in 1889 and an honourable mention at the 1900 Exposition Universelle.

MUSEUMS AND GALLERIES:
CARDIFF: *Versailles; Cottages; Villefranche* - LEICESTER: *Acropolis, Athens; Hampton Court* - LIVERPOOL: *Temple of Jupiter at the Acropolis, Athens* - LONDON (Victoria and Albert Mus.): *Magdalen College, Oxford; Entrance to Queen's College, Oxford; Arena Ruins, Arles; St-Germain-l'Auxerrois, Paris*.

AUCTION RECORDS:
LONDON, 1908, *Hampton Court* (1885, watercolour) GBP 11. LONDON, 1 Feb 1908, *Ludgate Hill* (1885, watercolour) GBP 7. LONDON, 20 Dec 1922, *Wooded Landscape* (drawing) GBP 33. LONDON, 27 April 1923, *Tenby*, GBP 6. LONDON, 26 Nov 1923, *Parthenon* (drawing) GBP 4; *Gulf of Spezia* (drawing) GBP 6; *Port of Genoa* (drawing) GBP 6; *Port of Genoa* (drawing) GBP 3; *Medici Gardens; Sea of Galilee* (drawing, both) GBP 8; *Facade of the British Museum* (drawing) GBP 4; *Jerusalem at Sunset* (drawing) GBP 6; *Interior of St Paul's Cathedral* (drawing) GBP 6; *Clumber* (drawing) GBP 6; *Versailles Gardens* (drawing) GBP 5; *Papal Palace, Avignon* (drawing) GBP 3; *Parc Monceau, Paris* (drawing) GBP 3; *Nice* (drawing) GBP 8; *Place des Vosges; Château St-Germain* (drawing, both) GBP 5. LONDON, 26 Nov 1923, *Interior of the Omar Mosque*, GBP 4; *Jerusalem at Dawn*, GBP 3. LONDON, 8 May 1925, *Brussels*, GBP 5; *Torcello; On the Rialto Bridge; Emmanuel College; Ingarsby Priory* (four drawings) GBP 15. LONDON, 25 Feb 1929, *Honeymoon's End* (drawing) GBP 5. LONDON, 19 April 1929, *Columns of the Temple of Zeus, Athens* (drawing) GBP 11; *Magdalen College* (drawing) GBP 5; *Florence* (drawing) GBP 9. LONDON, 2 July 1971, *Versailles Gardens* (1883) Gns 180. LONDON, 24 July 1973, *Hampton Court*, GBP 220. LONDON, 14 May 1976, *Piazzeta, Venice* (oil on panel, 11 1/2 x 9 1/2 ins / 29 x 24 cm) GBP 320. LONDON, 12 Oct 1977, *Jerusalem at Sunset* (1903, oil on canvas, 32 x 54 ins / 81 x 137 cm) GBP 5,000. LONDON, 23 July 1981, *Jerusalem* (watercolour, 9 3/4 x 6 3/4 ins / 25 x 17 cm) GBP 300. LONDON, 17 Nov 1983, *Barges on the Canal at Leicester* (1868, watercolour outlined in pencil heightened with gouache, 7 x 10 1/2 ins / 18 x 26.5 cm) GBP 850. PARIS, 12 March 1984, *Garden in Spring* (oil on canvas, 12 1/2 x 18 ins / 31.5 x 45.5 cm) FRF 16,500. LONDON, 28 Nov 1986, *Garden of Love* (oil on canvas, 12 1/2 x 18 ins / 31.5 x 46 cm) GBP 2,600. LONDON, 27 Oct 1987, *Hampton Court Palace* (1885-1886, watercolour and pencil, 23 1/4 x 35 ins / 59 x 88.7 cm) GBP 3,000. LONDON, 19 Dec 1991, *Isola Tiberina, Rome; Belvedere Michelangelo* (oil on panel, pair, 5 x 14 3/4 ins / 12.7 x 37.5 cm and 5 x 14 ins/12.7 x 35.5 cm) GBP 1,540. LONDON, 20 Jan 1993, *Naval Battle off Spezia* (1888, watercolour, 8 x 14 ins / 20.5 x 35.5 cm) GBP 517. LONDON, 13 July 1993, *Scraptoft, Leicestershire* (pencil and watercolour, 7 x 10 ins / 17.5 x 25.1 cm) GBP 460. LONDON, 17 Nov 1994, *Interior of the Dome of the Chain, Jerusalem* (pencil and watercolour/paper, 10 x 15 ins / 25.7 x 37.8 cm) GBP 7,475. LONDON, 29 March 1996, *St Paul's Churchyard* (1884, pencil and watercolour with touches of white, 5 x 7 ins / 12.7 x 17.8 cm) GBP 977. LONDON, 30 June 1999, *Theatre Royal, Haymarket, Leicester. Corn Exchange, Leicester* (watercolour, a pair, 9 x 8 ins / 24 x 20 cm) GBP 1,900. BILLINGSHURST, 20 July 1999, *Tenby* (1884, oil on panel, 9 x 13 ins / 24 x 34 cm) GBP 2,500. LONDON, 8 June 2000, *View of Genoa Harbour from the Villa Doria* (pencil, watercolour and gum arabic, 11 x 15 ins / 28 x 39 cm) GBP 2,200. LONDON, 27 June 2001, *Taormina, Sicily* (watercolour, 11 x 15 ins / 27 x 37 cm) GBP 1,000. LONDON, 5 Sept 2002, *University Church of St Mary's, Oxford* (oil on panel, 9 x 6 ins / 24 x 14 cm) GBP 1,300. LONDON, 22 Oct 2002, *Acropolis from the Temple of Jupiter, Olympus, Athens* (1895, watercolour, 10 x 15 ins / 26 x 38 cm) GBP 3,000. LEWES, 28 Jan 2003, *Paris Viewed from the Seine* (watercolour, a pair, 5 x 7 ins / 13 x 18 cm) GBP 1,200. LONDON, 26 March 2003, *Jerusalem from the Mount of Olives* (watercolour, 23 x 39 ins / 59 x 100 cm) GBP 3,500. LONDON, 3 June 2004, *Virgin's Fountain, Nazareth* (1901, pencil and watercolour heightened with gouache, 10 x 14 ins / 26 x 36 cm) GBP 2,400. LONDON, 1 July 2004, *Hampton Court Palace from the Long Water* (1885, pencil and watercolour, 13 x 19 ins / 32 x 49 cm) GBP 1,600.

FÜLLMAURER, Heinrich
Swiss, 16th century.
Active in Basel c. 1542.
Draughtsman, painter.

Some of the works of this artist were engraved by Specklin.

FÜLLMAURER, Josias
German, 16th century.
Active in Württemberg c. 1562.
Painter.

Josias Füllmaurer worked for Duke Christoph of Württemberg.

FULLSCHENK, Detloff
German, 17th century.
Active c. 1600.
Sculptor (wood).

The museum in Kiel (Schleswig-Holstein) has a work by this artist.

FULLWOOD, Albert Henry
British, 19th - 20th century.
Born 1863 or 1864, in Birmingham; died 1930.
Painter, watercolourist. Landscapes.

Albert Fullwood studied at Birmingham School of Art. He then lived in Australia until 1900 and painted landscapes. He also travelled in America before returning to London where he participated in various group exhibitions, including those of the Royal Academy.

H Fullwood

BIBLIOGRAPHY:

'Albert Henry Fullwood' in *The Art Bulletin of Tasmania*, periodical, Anne Gray, Tasmanian Museum of Art Gall., Hobart, 1983. Kolenberg, Hendrik/Kolenberg, Juliana, *Tasmanian Vision, the Art of 19th century Tasmania*, Tasmanian Museum and Art Gall., Hobart, 1988.

MUSEUMS AND GALLERIES:

SYDNEY: *The Frontier; Jervis Bay; Shoalhaven River; The Cathedral Rocks near Kiama; Kangaroo Valley.*

AUCTION RECORDS:

ROSEBERY, 29 June 1976, *Peel Valley* (1922, oil on canvas, 26 3/4 x 33 1/2 ins / 68 x 85 cm) AUD 2,000. SYDNEY, 4 Oct 1977, *Landscape* (1930, oil on canvas, 23 3/4 x 35 3/4 ins / 60.5 x 91 cm) AUD 750. SYDNEY, 10 Sept 1979, *Portland* (gouache, 11 1/2 x 22 1/2 ins / 29 x 57 cm) AUD 1,400. SYDNEY, 20 Oct 1980, *View of a Port* (oil on card, 5 1/4 x 7 ins / 13.5 x 17.5 cm) AUD 900. SYDNEY, 29 June 1981, *The Conversation* (1897, watercolour, 19 3/4 x 13 ins / 50 x 33 cm) AUD 2,200. SYDNEY, 17 Oct 1984, *The Store and Bridge, Mosman Bay* (1890, oil/cigar box lid, 5 3/4 x 8 3/4 ins / 14.5 x 22.3 cm) AUD 13,500; *Sydney from Mosman* (1880, watercolour, 11 x 16 1/4 ins / 27 x 41 cm) AUD 8,000. SYDNEY, 23 Sept 1985, *The Conversation of Young Woman and Parrot* (1897, watercolour, 19 3/4 x 12 1/2 ins / 50 x 32 cm) AUD 7,500. MELBOURNE, 30 July 1986, *The Hawkesbury* (oil on card, 12 1/4 x 23 3/4 ins / 31 x 60.5 cm) AUD 80,000. SYDNEY, 4 July 1988, *Coastal Landscape* (watercolour, 23 1/4 x 33 3/4 ins / 59 x 86 cm) AUD 2,500. SYDNEY, 3 July 1989, *Lake Wakatipiu* (watercolour, 6 x 11 ins / 15 x 27 cm) AUD 1,800. HOBART, 26 Aug 1996, *The Hobart Ferry* (oil on panel, 6 x 10 ins / 15.2 x 25.4 cm) AUD 27,600. MELBOURNE, 26 April 1999, *Cattle Crossing River* (oil on board, 10 x 16 ins / 25 x 41 cm) AUD 16,000. SYDNEY, 27 July 1999, *View of the Village* (1913, oil on canvas laid on board, 38 x 48 ins / 97 x 123 cm) AUD 15,000. MELBOURNE, 2 May 2000, *Mosman Bay* (1921, oil on board, 5 x 7 ins / 13 x 18 cm) AUD 8,500. MELBOURNE, 3 May 2000, *European Valley* (1913, oil on canvasboard, 40 x 51 ins / 102 x 129 cm) AUD 18,000. SYDNEY, 10 Dec 2001, *Untitled - Panning for Gold* (watercolour, 8 x 14 ins / 20 x 35 cm) AUD 4,500. MELBOURNE, 5 March 2002, *Argyle Cut, Sydney* (1885, watercolour and gouache, 7 x 10 ins / 18 x 26 cm) AUD 5,500. MELBOURNE, 2 April 2003, *Sirius Cove* (c. 1894, oil on panel, 8 x 9 ins / 20 x 24 cm) AUD 25,000. PADDINGTON, 25 Aug 2003, *View from Balmoral* (oil on wood panel, 10 x 13 ins / 25 x 33 cm) AUD 24,000. PADDINGTON, 24 Aug 2004, *Store and Bridge, Mosman Bay* (1890, oil on wood panel, 5 x 8 ins / 13 x 21 cm) AUD 19,000.

FULLWOOD, John

British, 19th - 20th century.
Born 1854, in Buckingham; died 1931.
Painter, engraver. Landscapes.

John Fullwood lived in Twickenham and was a member of the Royal Society of British Artists and the Royal Institute of Painters in Watercolours. He exhibited frequently in London from 1881 to 1890.

AUCTION RECORDS:

LONDON, 7 July 1981, *The Village Church* (watercolour, 10 x 14 1/4 ins / 25.5 x 36 cm) GBP 240.

FULPIUS, Élisabeth Caroline

Swiss, 20th century.
Born 16 January 1878, in Geneva.
Sculptor, engraver. Figures. Busts.

Élisabeth Fulpius studied at the school of fine arts in Geneva. She completed her training in Paris where she exhibited at the Salon des Artistes Français, receiving an honourable mention in 1906.

MUSEUMS AND GALLERIES:

GENEVA (MAH): *Bust of a Woman.*

FULPIUS, Mireille

Swiss, 20th - 21st century.
Born 2 February 1951, in Geneva.
Sculptor.

Fulpius attended the École Supérieure d'Art Visuel in Geneva. She lives and works in Geneva, and in Marchissy in the canton of Vaud. Fulpius uses prefabricated metal elements, which she assembles in a very free, geometric style. She has exhibited since 1977, mainly in Switzerland, but also in Paris at the Salon Grands et Jeunes d'Aujourd'hui since 1985 and at the Salon des Femmes Peintres et Sculpteurs since 1986. Fulpius is represented by the Galerie Galise Petersen in Thonon-les-Bains. She has held solo shows in Geneva in 1981, 1983 1986, 1995, 1997 and 1999, and in Thonon-les Bains in 1987.

FULTON, David

British, 19th - 20th century.
Born 1848, in Scotland; died 1930.
Painter, watercolourist. Figures, genre scenes, landscapes, animals.

David Fulton exhibited in London, Berlin, Munich and Venice. He lived mainly in Glasgow.

D FULTON

DAVID FULTON

AUCTION RECORDS:

SCOTLAND, 25 Aug 1972, *Young Girl*, GBP 320. SCOTLAND, 1 Sept 1981, *Young Girl Picking Flowers* (oil on canvas, 20 x 15 1/4 ins / 51 x 39 cm) GBP 1,600. EDINBURGH, 12 April 1983, *On the River Ayr, Catrine* (oil on canvas, 20 x 24 ins / 51 x 61 cm) GBP 1,350. LONDON, 13 Nov 1986, *The Poppy Picker* (oil on canvas, 21 x 14 ins / 53.5 x 35.5 cm) GBP 13,000. LONDON, 26 April 1988, *Queen of the Meadow* (oil on canvas, 16 1/4 x 14 1/4 ins / 41 x 36 cm) GBP 1,540. LONDON, 3 June 1988, *Woman Gathering Flotsam Wood* (1883, oil on canvas, 20 x 30 ins / 50.8 x 76.2 cm) GBP 2,860. GLASGOW, 7 Feb 1989, *Young Girls by the River* (oil on canvas, 10 x 18 ins / 25.5 x 46 cm) GBP 2,090. PERTH, 29 Aug 1989, *The Saddell Ferry, Morning* (oil on canvas, 28 x 36 ins / 71 x 91.5 cm) GBP 4,620. GLASGOW, 6 Feb 1990, *Off Arran* (oil on canvas, 14 1/4 x 21 1/4 ins / 36 x 54 cm) GBP 1,760. PERTH, 27 Aug 1990, *Lying in the Cornfield* (1882, oil on canvas, 12 x 20 ins / 30.5 x 51 cm) GBP 2,860. SOUTH QUEENSFERRY, 23 April 1991, *Autumn in Kintyre* (watercolour, 15 1/4 x 19 1/2 ins / 39 x 49.5 cm) GBP 1,320. EDINBURGH, 2 May 1991, *The Seamstress* (oil on canvas, 14 x 12 ins / 35.6 x 30.5 cm) GBP 528. NEW YORK, 21 May 1991, *Feeding Poultry* (oil on canvas, 14 x 16 ins / 35.5 x 40.6 cm) USD 1,760. PERTH, 26 Aug 1991, *Reverie* (oil on canvas, 20 x 30 ins / 51 x 76 cm) GBP 10,450. EDINBURGH, 23 March 1993, *Spaniel* (oil on canvas, 20 1/2 x 15 1/4 ins / 52 x 39 cm) GBP 3,450. PERTH, 31 Aug 1993, *Dream Day* (1889, oil on canvas, 24 x 36 ins / 61 x 91.5 cm) GBP 5,290. GLASGOW, 14 Feb 1995, *The Ayr Mountains* (oil on canvas, 18 x 24 ins / 46 x 61 cm) GBP 1,035. PERTH, 29 Aug 1995, *In the Fields in a Fine Autumn* (1926, oil on canvas, 30 x 25 ins / 76 x 63.5 cm) GBP 8,625. GLASGOW, 16 April 1996, *The Wait* (1883, oil on canvas, 10 x 18 ins / 25.5 x 46 cm) GBP 977. AUCHTERARDER, 26 Aug 1997, *Reverie* (1889, oil on canvas, 24 x 36 ins / 61 x 91.5 cm) GBP 9,660.

FULTON, Dorothy

American, 20th century.
Born 1897, in Pennsylvania.
Painter.

Dorothy Fulton studied under Garber, Hale, Breckenridge and MacCarter at Pennsylvania Fine Arts Academy. She exhibited at Tampa Art Institute in 1928, where she won first prize. She exhibited regularly until 1946.

FULTON, Hamish

British, 20th - 21st century.
Born 1946, in London.
Painter (mixed media), sculptor, photographer. Artists' books.
Conceptual Art, Land Art.

After studying in London at St Martin's from 1966 to 1968, Hamish Fulton went on to study photography in 1969. Fulton is interested in landscape and has much in common with Land Art, although his approach is quite different. Unlike Richard Long - with whom he travelled in South America - Fulton does not intervene on site. He builds his work around the physical impression that a space leaves on the body when walking, first in timeless photographs with brief captions and then, from 1981, in painting. At the same time, he began to comment more fully on his photographs, creating a poetic presence and choosing with care an attractive typography. In a series inspired by a long walk across France in 1991-1992, and accompanied by descriptive titles - *Comptant 5000 Premiers Points pour les 5000 Premiers Pas* (*Counting 5000 First Points for the First 5000 Steps*), *Comptant 5040 points, nulle pensée* (*Counting 5040 Points, Nothing in Mind*) - he paints long, grey rectangles dotted with small, coloured circles. Fulton's work belongs to conceptual art, which requires an analysis of the work and its component parts. Fulton exploits the ambiguity of the image, its psychological and emotional impact, its lack of objectivity. Working with photos of landscapes, he describes what could be the memory of places or environments, without any obvious attempt at narrative.

He has taken part in many group exhibitions in Britain and abroad, including Documenta V in Kassel in 1972, which featured conceptual art; in 2001, *Imago Mundi*, an exhibition on the geography of nature, at the Capc-Musée d'Art Contemporain, Bordeaux; in 2002, *Les Années 70: l'Art en Cause* (*The 1970s: Art in Question*), at the Capc-Musée d'Art Contemporain, Bordeaux; in 2002, *Sans Commune Mesure. Image et Texte dans l'Art Actuel* (*Without Common Measure: Image and Text in Contemporary Art*), at the Musée d'Art Moderne Lille Métropole, Villeneuve d'Ascq; in 2003, *Paysages* (*Landscapes*), an exhibition exploring man's new experience of landscape as seen through contemporary art, organised as part of *Trésors Publics, 20 Ans de Création dans les Fonds Régionaux d'Art Contemporain (FRAC)* (*Public Treasury, 20 Years of Creation in the Regional Collection of Contemporary Art (FRAC)*) at the Centre Européen d'Actions Artistiques Contemporaines, Strasbourg. He has also shown his work in solo exhibitions in London and abroad: in 1981 at the Musée National d'Art Moderne, Paris; in 1983 at the Capc-Musée d'Art Contemporain, Bordeaux; in 1985 at the Van Abbe Museum, Eindhoven; in 1990 at the Albright-Knox Art Gallery, Buffalo, New York; in 1992 at the Réfectoire de l'Abbaye de St-Savin; in 1995 at the Kunstbau Lenbachhaus, Munich; in 1999 at the Crawford Arts Centre, St Andrews; and in 2002 at Tate Britain, London.

BIBLIOGRAPHY:

Reason, D./Auping, M., *Hamish Fulton, Camp Fire*, Le Nouveau Musée, Villeurbanne, 1985. *Hamish Fulton: selected walks, 1969-1989*, exhibition catalogue, Albright-Knox Art Gall., Buffalo (NY), 1990. Ardenne, Paul, '*Hamish Fulton*' in *Art Press* n° 173, periodical, Paris, October 1992. Boudou, Dominique, '*Fulton: l'invitation au voyage*' in *Beaux-Arts Magazine* n° 119, periodical, Paris, January 1994. *Thirty one horizons: Hamish Fulton*, exhibition catalogue, Kunstbau Lenbachhaus, Munich, 1995. Fulton, Hamish, *Walking artist: the separation of subject and medium*, exhibition catalogue, Crawford Arts Centre, St. Andrews, Morning Star, Edinburgh, 1999. Fulton, Hamish, *Wild Life. Walks in the Cairngorms*, Pocketbooks, Edinburgh, 2000. Vettese, Angela/Longhi, Antje/Kalthoff, Brigitte, *Walking artist. Hamish Fulton*, Richter, Düsseldorf, 2001 (text in English and German). Zahm, Olivier (preface), et al., *Trésors publics, 20 ans de création dans les Fonds régionaux d'art contemporain*, Flammarion, Paris, 2003 (text in French and English).

MUSEUMS AND GALLERIES:

AMSTERDAM (Stedelijk Mus.) - BORDEAUX (CAPC-MAC): *Lizard* (1980); *Counting 10182 Dots* (1982) - BUFFALO (Albright-Knox AG): *Touching By Hand One Hundred Rocks (Fifty Three, Fifty Four, Sixty)* (1989, photograph) - CARQUEFOU (FRAC Pays de la Loire): *The Heron Stands and Waits* (1989) - CHÂTEAUGIRON (FRAC Bretagne): *Bird Song* (1987); *A View from the West Coast of Arran across...* (1978) - EINDHOVEN (Van Abbe Mus.) - LONDON (Arts Council Collection, Hayward Gal.): installation (sausages); *Heap 4* (1967, jute sacking and sand); *Soprano 1981 Bronze No. 7* (1981, bronze) - PARIS (MNAM-CCI) - ROCHECHOUART (Mus. Départemental d'Art Contemporain): *Untitled* (1986).

AUCTION RECORDS:

LONDON, 22 Feb 1990, *Rigdom Gompa* (1978, montage of a black and white photograph/card, 18 x 22 3/4 ins / 46 x 58 cm) GBP 4,400. PARIS, 20 Jan 1991, *The Yark, River Maine* (1972, photos and text, 19 3/4 x 23 1/2 ins / 50 x 60 cm) FRF 28,000. NEW YORK, 19 Nov 1992, *To Reach the Summit* (1985, montage of three black and white photos/card in a frame by the artist, 36 x 95 1/4 ins / 91.5 x 242 cm) USD 24,200. NEW YORK, 24 Feb 1993, *Sunrise* (1982, montage by the artist of four black and white photos in a frame, 30 1/2 x 95 1/2 ins / 77.5 x 242.6 cm) USD 11,000. LONDON, 25 March 1993, *Bird Rock* (1987, photograph and printed text/card, 52 x 40 3/4 ins / 132 x 103.4 cm) GBP 3,680. NEW YORK, 10 Nov 1993, *Lake by Moonlight* (1985, black and white photograph framed by the artist, 55 3/4 x 43 3/4 ins / 141.8 x 111 cm) USD 14,950. LONDON, 30 Nov 1995, *Untitled* (black and white and coloured photos/card, 28 3/4 x 23 3/4 ins / 73 x 60.5 cm) GBP 6,900. NEW YORK, 21 Nov 1996, *Silent Horizons...* (1987, black and white photograph and graphite/paper, 30 x 88 1/2 ins / 76 x 225 cm) USD 20,700. NEW YORK, 23 Feb 2000, *Drum-two Connecting Walks in Tarahumara Sierra, Mexico* (silkscreen, black and white photograph on board, 45 x 43 ins / 114 x 108 cm) USD 4,000. NEW YORK, 23 Feb 2000, *Day 11, No Eyes-in the Direction of Listening* (1987, black and white photograph, triptych, 37 x 96 ins / 95 x 244 cm) USD 14,000. LONDON, 28 March 2001, *Bird Rock* (black and white photograph, 20 x 20 ins / 51 x 51 cm) GBP 3,600. PARIS, 23 June 2001, *Bird Rock* (1984, text and black and white photograph, 54 x 7 ins / 138 x 19 cm) FRF 33,000. NEW YORK, 13 Nov 2002, *Black Smoke Caves* (1987, black and white photograph, 37 x 96 ins / 95 x 245 cm) USD 8,000. PARIS, 9 Dec 2003, *Juniper* (1986, black and white photograph, 57 x 46 ins / 144 x 118 cm) EUR 4,800. MILAN, 16 Dec 2003, *Untitled* (photograph, a pair, 11 x 7 ins / 28 x 18 cm) EUR 5,700. LONDON, 4 Feb 2004, *Counting 48/49 Dots* (1993, acrylic on board, pencil and acrylic on paper, two parts) GBP 3,500. LONDON, 24 June 2004, *Sunrise, Places Seen and Visited* (black white photograph on board, 30 x 95 ins / 77 x 242 cm) GBP 3,800.

FULTON, Robert

American, 18th - 19th century.
Born 1765, in Little Britain (now Fulton); died 23 February 1815, in New York.
Painter.

Robert Fulton, an engineer of genius who developed the steamboat, was initially a painter of portraits and historical scenes.

FULTON, Samuel
British, 19th century.
Born 1855; died 1941.
Painter. Animals.

Samuel Fulton specialised in painting dogs, both as recognisable portraits of individual animals and as unspecified general dogs.

SAM FULTON
SAM-FULTON

AUCTION RECORDS:
GLASGOW, 15 June 1932, *Fox*, GBP 7. PERTH, 27 Aug 1985, *King Charles Spaniel* (oil on canvas, 19 3/4 x 23 1/2 ins / 50 x 60 cm) GBP 3,600. EDINBURGH, 30 Aug 1988, *Spaniel* (oil on canvas, 16 x 20 ins / 40.5 x 50.5 cm) GBP 825. GLASGOW, 7 Feb 1989, *Highland Terrier* (oil on card, 16 1/4 x 12 ins / 41 x 30.5 cm) GBP 660. PERTH, 29 Aug 1989, *Jack Russell Terrier* (oil on canvas, 15 x 11 ins / 38 x 28 cm) GBP 3,740. EDINBURGH, 23 March 1993, *Terrier* (oil on canvas, 18 x 14 ins / 45.5 x 35.5 cm) GBP 1,495. LONDON, 25 March 1994, *Guard Dog on the Alert* (oil on canvas, 24 x 20 ins / 61 x 50.8 cm) GBP 8,970. PERTH, 29 Aug 1995, *Great Friends* (oil on canvas, 24 1/4 x 20 ins / 61.5 x 51 cm) GBP 3,450. PERTH, 26 Aug 1996, *Highland Terrier* (oil on canvas, 20 x 16 1/4 ins / 51 x 41 cm) GBP 5,980. LONDON, 15 June 2000, *Best of Friends* (oil on canvas, 24 x 20 ins / 61 x 51 cm) GBP 4,000. LONDON, 30 Nov 2000, *West Highland Terrier* (oil on canvas, 18 x 14 ins / 46 x 36 cm) GBP 3,600. NEW YORK, 13 Feb 2001, *At Home* (oil on canvas, 24 x 20 ins / 61 x 51 cm) USD 13,000. LONDON, 5 Sept 2001, *Guards* (oil on canvas, 20 x 24 ins / 51 x 61 cm) GBP 8,000. NEW YORK, 12 Feb 2002, *Prize Spaniel with a Terrier in a Kennel* (oil on canvas, 24 x 20 ins / 61 x 51 cm) USD 15,000. LONDON, 7 March 2002, *Artist's Models, Spaniel and Cairn Terrier* (oil on canvas, 25 x 20 ins / 63 x 51 cm) GBP 5,500. LONDON, 27 Aug 2003, *Best Friends* (oil on canvas, 20 x 24 ins / 51 x 61 cm) GBP 6,500. NEW YORK, 5 Dec 2003, *West Highland Terrier* (oil on canvas on board, 14 x 10 ins / 36 x 25 cm) USD 14,000. NEW YORK, 10 Feb 2004, *Two Cairn Terriers* (oil on canvas, 17 x 20 ins / 43 x 51 cm) USD 8,000. LONDON, 26 May 2004, *Fox Terrier in a Kennel* (oil on canvas, 18 x 14 ins / 45 x 35 cm) GBP 2,900.

FULUTTI, Leonardo
Italian, 15th - 16th century.
Born in Tolmezzo.
Painter.

In 1550, Fulutti worked for the church in Tolmezzo (N.E. Italy).

FULUTTI, Pietro
Italian, 16th century.
Born in Tolmezzo.
Painter.

Pietro Falutti was working in Udine (N.E. Italy) around 1515.

FUMADELLES, Augustin
French, 19th century.
Born 1844, in Agen.
Sculptor.

He received an honourable mention in 1884.

FUMAGALLI, Alvise
Italian, 16th century.
Active in Legnano (Lombardy) in 1517.
Painter.

FUMAGALLI, Ambrogio
Italian, 19th century.
Active in Milan.
Watercolourist.

Ambrogio Fumagalli exhibited a watercolour in 1830.

FUMAGALLI, Christian
French, 20th - 21st century.
Born 8 December 1946, in Gray (Haute-Saône).
Active in Besançon.
Painter. Figures, portraits, still-lifes, animals.
Symbolism.

Christian Fumagalli trained at the École des Beaux-Arts in Besançon under Jean Ricardon. He departed from his Abstract beginnings to produce works with a balance of metaphysical and Symbolist ideas, presenting reality as if it were in a whirlwind; an original vision of the world surrounding him. His work was shown on various occasions in Paris, including at the *Tendances de la Peinture Figurative Contemporaine* (*Trends in Contemporary Figurative Painting*) exhibitions held in 1981-1982, at the Salon Mac 2000 in 1983, and at the Salon de Mai in 1985. He exhibited at the Seoul Museum of Modern Art in 1986. He also held solo exhibitions, notably at the Centre Culturel Pierre Bayle in Besançon in 1982 and at the Gabrielle Fliegans Gallery in Strasbourg in 1991.

BIBLIOGRAPHY:
Christian Fumagalli, exhibition catalogue, Centre culturel Pierre-Bayle, Besançon, 1982. Xuriguera, Gérard, *Regards sur la peinture contemporaine*, Arted, Paris, 1983. Xuriguera, Gérard, *Les Figurations de 1960 à nos jours*, Éd. Mayer, Paris, 1985.

MUSEUMS AND GALLERIES:
BESANÇON (MBA et d'Archéologie): *People Surprised by a Storm* (1972); *Hand* (1971) - PARIS (FNAC): *Indifference* (1981) - PARIS (MAMVP) - TAIPEI (MCA).

FUMAGALLI, Ignazio
Italian, 19th century.
Born 1778, in Milan; died 1842.
Painter, engraver. History painting.

In 1810 Ignazio Fumagalli produced designs for a *St Bartholomew*, sculpted by Denelli, for Milan Cathedral.

FUMÉE, Jean and Jesson
French, 15th century.
Active in Rheims (Marne).
Glass painters.

These two artists may have worked at the church of St-Pierre-le-Vieil.

FUMERAN
French, 19th century.
Painter.

He exhibited at the Paris Salon from 1831 to 1833. Examples of Fumeran's work include *View of the Station Bookshop*, *View of the Outskirts of Royat* and *Gate in Royat*.

FUMERON, René
French, 20th century.
Born 1921, in Peyroux.
Painter, poster artist, designer. Wall decorations, designs for tapestries, designs (wallpapers/fabrics).

René Fumeron studied at the École des Arts Appliqués and then at the École Nationale Supérieure des Beaux-Arts in Paris. He originally produced mural decorations and designs for wallpaper, fabrics and posters and from 1949 produced numerous tapestry cartoons. He worked for the State and for private companies.

AUCTION RECORDS:
VERSAILLES, 29 Oct 1989, *Red Sea* (tapestry, 42 1/2 x 91 1/4 ins / 108 x 232 cm) FRF 10,000. PARIS, 14 Dec 1992, *Bank of Gold* (tapestry, 35 1/2 x 65 1/4 ins / 90 x 166 cm) FRF 12,000.

FUMIANI, Giacomo
Italian, 17th - 18th century.
Born 1680; died 1709.
Active in Parma.
Painter.
Giacomo Fumiani is cited by Zani.

FUMIANI, Giovanni Antonio
Italian, 17th - 18th century.
Born 1643, in Venice; died 8 April 1710, in Venice.
Painter. Figure compositions. Murals.
Giovanni Antonio Fumiani worked mostly in Venice but also in Bologna. The church of La Canta in Bologna houses his *Christ Debating with the Doctors*, considered by Lanzi to be Fumiani's best work. Between 1680 and 1704 Fumiani painted the immense ceiling and vault decorations in the church of S Pantaleone in Venice, a remarkable accomplishment distinguished by a subtle use of perspective applied over complex architectural surfaces. It was reputed to be the largest painting of its kind in the world. Fumiani also painted a *Christ Driving the Merchants from the Temple* for the Venice church of S Rocco.
AUCTION RECORDS:
NEW YORK, 25 March 1983, *Landscapes with Allegorical Figures* (two oils on panel, 26 1/4 x 22 1/2 ins / 66.5 x 57 cm) USD 8,000. PARIS, 17 March 1987, *King Solomon and the Queen of Sheba* (oil on canvas, 34 1/2 x 48 ins / 87.5 x 121 cm) FRF 55,000. LONDON, 26 Oct 1994, *Christ and the Widow of Nain* (oil on canvas, 31 x 38 1/4 ins / 79 x 97 cm) GBP 6,325. MILAN, 24 Nov 1999, *The Doge Receives Caterina Cornaro* (oil on canvas, 25 x 20 ins / 63 x 50 cm) ITL 7,000,000. LONDON, 26 April 2001, *Abraham and the Three Angels* (oil on canvas, 51 x 72 ins / 129 x 183 cm) GBP 13,000.

FUMICELLI, Lodovico
Italian, 16th century.
Born in Treviso.
Painter.
Venetian School.
Active in the Veneto, Fumicelli may have been a pupil of Titian. Lanzi regards him as one of Titian's most skilled imitators. In 1536, he produced the main altar painting for the church of the Padri Eremitani in Padua, representing *The Virgin and Child Seated in Clouds with St Augustine, St James and St Maurice*. According to Rodolfi, this work is worthy of the greatest masters. In the church of the Servite Fathers in Treviso, he did a painting of *St Liberatus and St Catherine* with two accompanying paintings of *St Sebastian and St Philip*.

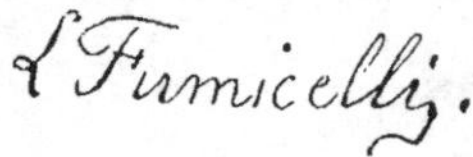

FUMIERE, Adolphe
Belgian, 19th century.
Active in Tournai.
Sculptor.
Fumiere received an honourable mention from the Salon jury of 1859.
AUCTION RECORDS:
PARIS, 28 Oct 1985, *Segond-Weber* (bronze, h. 29 1/2in/75cm) FRF 12,500.

FUMO, Antonio
Italian, 18th century.
Active in Naples.
Painter.
Antonio Fumo painted an *Ascension of St Benedict*.

FUMO, Basilio
Italian, 18th century.
Born probably in Naples; died 20 June 1797, in Madrid.
Sculptor, potter.

FUMO, Matteo
Italian, 17th century.
Sculptor (wood).
Matteo Fumo is on record as having worked in the church of S Giuseppe Maggiore in Naples in 1696.

FUMO, Niccolo
Italian, 18th century.
Died 2 July 1725, in Naples.
Sculptor.
Niccolo Fumo executed a very large number of religious sculptures in marble, wood and plaster.

FUNAJOLI, L.A.
British, 19th century.
Sculptor.
L.A. Funajoli exhibited at the Royal Academy in London in 1860.

FUNAKI, Ichiro
Japanese, 20th century.
Born in Osaka.
Painter.
Funaki Ichiro exhibited at the 1926 Salon d'Automne.

FUNAKOSHI, Yasutake
Japanese, 20th century.
Born 1912, in Ninohe, Iwate; died 5 February 2002, in Tokyo.
Sculptor.
Funakoshi Yasutake he entered the sculpture course at Tokyo School of Fine Arts in 1934. In 1939 on graduating he co-founded the sculpture division of the Shin Seisaku Kyokai and started to carve in marble. In 1941 he opened a joint exhibit with Matsumoto Shunsuke in Morioka. He also entered works in Kokuga-kai exhibitions, receiving honourable mentions. In 1950 he converted to Roman Catholicism and in 1962 won the fifth Takamura Kotaro Prize for his work, The 26 Martyrs of Nagasaki. In 1972 he won the Nakahara Teijiro Prize for Hara-no-Jo (a Christian samurai). In 1967 he became professor at Tokyo National University of Fine Arts and Music, retiring in 1980 but being appointed honorary professor until 1986. In 1999 he was awarded the Order of Cultural Merit.
AUCTION RECORDS:
PARIS, 14 May 1982, *Head of Girl* (white marble, h. 16 1/2 ins / 42 cm) FRF 7,200.

FUNARO, Giuseppe
Italian, 18th century.
Painter.
Giuseppe Funaro worked on the decoration of the Naples church of S Croce di Lucca in 1763.

FUNASAKA, Yoshisuke
Japanese, 20th century.
Born 1 January 1939, in Gifu.
Painter, print artist (woodcuts).
Funasaka Yoshisuke studied at the University of Tokyo. He took part in the 5th and 7th Tokyo Print Biennale and the Ljubljana Print Biennale. His work was also shown at the 4th Ile-de-France Print Biennale held in Versailles in 2003.

FUNCH, Edgar
Danish, 20th century.
Born 1915, on Bornholm.
Sculptor.
Edgar Funch was a self-taught artist. He was a member of the Decembrist group from 1957 to 1966 and the Grönningen group from 1966. He exhibited at the official Danish exhibitions, such as the Easter exhibition in Aarhus from 1951 to 1957 and the autumn exhibition in Copenhagen. He also exhibited in Stockholm, at the Riverside Museum, New York, in 1958, in Amsterdam, Oslo and others. In Paris, he featured

in an exhibition at the Musée Rodin in 1966 and in *Danish Art 1945-1973* at the Grand Palais in 1973.

He produced a large number of decorative sculptures for public institutions such as schools. His sculptures are abstract, often in granite or bronze. His forms recall the Viking civilisation and makes use of the motifs found on the coats of arms and ships of his ancestors. He also drew inspiration from organic forms whose cycles he observed in nature.

MUSEUMS AND GALLERIES:
AALBORG (Nordjyllands Kunstmus.) - AARHUS - COPENHAGEN (Statens Mus. for Kunst) - ODENSE.

FUNCH, Hermann Frederik
Danish, 19th century.
Born 4 November 1841, in Rendsburg.
Painter, sculptor.

Hermann Frederik Funch was a pupil of Bisser in Copenhagen. He had a predilection for sculpture and the painting of animals, but also painted portraits and landscapes.

FUNCK, Adam
German, 19th century.
Died c. 1852, in Marburg (Hesse).
Painter, lithographer.

Adam Funck is noted for his *Views of Marburg*.

FUNCK, Joseph Charles
French, 20th century.
Born in Luxembourg.
Painter.

Joseph Funck studied under J.-P. Laurens and exhibited at the Salon des Artistes Français from 1928.

FUNCK, Theodor
German, 19th - 20th century.
Born 10 March 1867, in Elberfeld.
Painter. Genre scenes.

Theodor Funck took part in group exhibitions in Düsseldorf where he won a medal in 1902.

MUSEUMS AND GALLERIES:
DÜSSELDORF: *At the House of the Widow Prins.*

FUNCK-HELLET, Madeleine Lucie
French, 20th century.
Born in Clichy.
Painter, pastellist.

Madeleine Funck-Hellet exhibited at the Salon of the Société Nationale from 1926 and at the Salon des Indépendants.

FUNCKE, Johann Heinrich
German, 19th century.
Active in Berlin at the beginning of the 19th century.
Engraver.

Funcke exhibited a series of sepias after the masters of the Italian Renaissance in 1818.

FUNCKEN, Armand
Belgian, 20th century.
Born 1875, in Verviers; died 1940, in La Louvière.
Painter, designer of ornamental architectural features.

Armand Funcken was the son of François Funcken, a travelling painter who worked for circuses and fairs. He painted everyday items such as signs and ice cream carts.

FUNDI, John
Mozambican, 20th century.
Born 1939, in Mueda, Mozambique.
Sculptor. Figures. Groups.

The political situation and economic conditions prevailing in Mozambique led John Fundi to leave the highlands where he was a farmer and move to the Tanzanian bushland where he was better able to work as a sculptor.

Fundi describes how while he is sleeping his spirit leaves his body and attends magic ceremonies. When he awakes he transcribes what he has seen, first in drawings and then in the form of carvings in ebony. His subjects derive from the traditions of oral history which he combines with his own fantasies. The result is a strange world of monstrous beings tortured by sexual obsessions.

FUNDULLI, Giovanni Paolo. See **FONDULO**

FUNEL, Vincent
French, 17th century.
Born c. 1648; died 15 April 1694.
Active in St-Maximin.
Sculptor (wood).

Vincent Funel belonged to the Dominican order.

FUNES, Juan
Flemish School, 16th century.
Born 1508; died 1572, in Seville.
Painter.

Funes is believed to have established himself as an artist in Spain at an early age.

FUNGAI, Bernardino, real name: Bernardino Cristofano da Fungaia
Italian, 15th - 16th century.
Born c. 1460, in Siena; died 1516.
Painter. Religious subjects.

Bernardino Fungai was a pupil of Benvenuto del Guasta. There is something rather dry and stiff about his style, which was also characteristic of his predecessors. Of his works, often produced with the assistance of Pachiarotti, it is worth mentioning a *Nativity of Christ*, in the cathedral at Chiusi, and, in the Accademia in Siena, an *Ascension*, *Christ between St Francis and St Jerome*, and a *Madonna*.

MUSEUMS AND GALLERIES:
CHAMBÉRY (MBA): *Virgin and Child* - CORAL GABLES (Lowe AM, University of Miami): *Madonna and Child with Saints and Angels* (c. 1510-1515, tempera/wood) - LONDON (NG): *The Virgin and Child with Cherubim* (1495-1510, tempera and oil/wood) - SIENA (Pinacoteca Nazionale): *Coronation of the Virgin with Saints and Angels*.

AUCTION RECORDS:
LONDON, 1886, *Virgin and Child with Cherubs; Landscape*, FRF 10,765. LONDON, 4 and 7 May 1923, *Madonna and Child*, GBP 68. LONDON, 4 July 1924, *Nativity*, GBP 50. LONDON, 2 July 1928, *Nativity*, GBP 33. LONDON, 17 July 1929, *The Dead Christ*, GBP 65. LONDON, 12 June 1931, *Madonna and Child*, GBP 567. NEW YORK, 17 and 18 May 1934, *Madonna and Child*, USD 2,100. LONDON, 6 March 1936, *Angel of the Annunciation*, GBP 11. LONDON, 18 May 1938, *Adoration of the Infant Jesus*, GBP 500. LONDON, 30 July 1947, *Pietà*, GBP 120. LONDON, 14 Dec 1962, *Virgin and Child with St John in a Wooded Landscape*, Gns 1,200. LONDON, 4 Dec 1964, *Charity*, Gns 1,000. NEW YORK, 29 April 1965, *A Sibyl*, USD 2,250. NEW YORK, 22 Oct 1970, *The Virgin Kneeling before the Infant Jesus*, USD 7,000. LONDON, 8 Dec 1971, *Holy Family*, GBP 3,400. NEW YORK, 20 Jan 1983, *The Virgin Adoring the Infant Jesus, with Two Angels* (tempera/gold background, 23 1/2 x 16 1/2 ins / 59.4 x 41.9 cm) USD 24,000. MILAN, 17 Dec 1987, *St Anthony of Padua* (oil on panel, 24 3/4 x 20 3/4 ins / 63 x 53 cm) ITL 30,000,000. LONDON, 14 Dec 1990, *Virgin and Child* (tempera/panel with gilt ground, 16 3/4 x 11 1/2 ins / 42.8 x 29 cm) GBP 132,000. NEW YORK, 11 Jan 1991, *Christ Supported by Two Angels* (predella, oil on panel, 17 1/4 x 25 1/2 ins / 43.5 x 65 cm) USD 77,000. PARIS, 28 June 1993, *Virgin and Child between Two Saints* (oil on poplar panel with gold background, 24 3/4 x 20 ins / 63 x 50.5 cm) FRF 950,000. NEW YORK, Jan 1998, *Madonna and Child with Landscape Background* (tempera/panel, 28 1/2 x 20 3/4 ins / 72.4 x 52.7 cm) USD 68,500. LONDON, 10 July 2003, *Scipio Proclaims his Candidature for Command of the Roman Forces in Spain* (oil on panel, 24 x 42 ins / 61 x 106 cm) GBP 50,000.

FUNHOF, Hinrich or Hinrik
German, 15th century.
Died c. 1485, in Hamburg.
Painter. Religious subjects.
Hamburg School.

Funhof worked at several churches in Hamburg, and his name appears several times in documents in the town archives. His work is so similar to that of Dirck Bouts that he must have been his pupil and may have completed some of his master's paintings. When he moved to Hamburg he took over from the painter Hans Bornemann whose widow he married. He also worked in Lüneburg.

Like Dirck Bouts, Funhof portrays the different characters in the Scriptures in contemporary dress and in an everyday setting.

Museums and Galleries:
Hamburg (Kunsthalle): *The Virgin in the Temple.*

Auction records:
London, 29 May 1959, *The Feeding of the Five Thousand,* GBP 3,360. New York, 24 Oct 1962, *The Feeding of the Five Thousand,* USD 22,000.

FUNI, Virgile, called Achille
Italian, 20th century.
Born 1890, in Ferrara; died 1972, in Appiano Gentile.
Painter, draughtsman, watercolourist, illustrator.
Mythological subjects, historical subjects, figures, portraits, nudes, landscapes, urban landscapes, architectural views. Murals, designs for mosaics, frescoes, church decoration.
Futurism, Novecento Italiano.
School of Milan.

Virgile Funi (known as Achille) studied at the Dosso Dossi Institute in Ferrara, then at the Brera Accademia di Belle Arti, in Milan, from 1906 to 1910, where he was a student of Tallone. In 1912, he founded the 'perifuturist' group Nuove Tendenze (New Tendencies), with Dudreville, Sant Elia and Nizzoli, among others. He was in the army from 1915 till 1918, then in 1919 he volunteered for the batalion of *Volontari ciclisti* (*Volunteer Cyclists*), and joined the main Futurist movement of Carra and Boccioni, presenting his paintings at the Great Futurist Exhibition. In 1920, he was a co-signatory, with Leonardo Dudreville, Luisi Russol and Mario Sironi, of the manifesto *Contra tutti ritorni in pittura. Manifesto del futurismo* (*Against All Turning Back in Painting. Futurist Manifesto*) (Futurist Movement Management, Milan, 1920). From 1922, he was one of the founders of the Group of Seven of the Novecento Italiano and was a member of the management committee from 1926. He joined forces with Sironi until 1930 in militant campaigning for the 'Novecento' movement, their targets being the 19th century and academism. In 1933, he co-authored the *Manifesto della pittura murale* (*Manifesto of Mural Painting*) with Sironi. From 1954, he held the chair of fresco painting at the Accademia Carrara, Bergamo, an institution of which he was director until 1953, the year in which he became director of the Accademia di Belle Arti in Milan.

From the 1930s, encouraged by contemporary interest in the monumental, he created chiefly mural compositions and church decoration in Milan and Rome, as well as Tripoli. In 1933, with Campigli, Carra, Chirico, Severini and Sironi, he did decorative work for the 5th Milan Triennale. From 1934 until the war, the Fascist Party commissioned numerous works from him. From 1934 to 1937, he decorated the Ferrara Palazzo Communale, in 1946 the Manzoni Theatre in Rome, and in 1951 the Bank of Rome; in 1955 and 1962, he created mosaics for St Peter's in Rome. After a brief Futurist period: *Rhythmic and Chromatic Sensation of a Dance, The Motorcyclist,* he modified his style to one of a traditional figuration, while learning from Cézanne how to simplify volumes, as may be seen from his *Venus in Love,* which he painted in 1928, a period that could be likened to Derain's reversion to classicism. From the end of the 1920s, he demonstrated his attraction to the Renaissance, the careful attention to perspective, the draughtsmanship, the colours and the studio lighting, but this was a Renaissance to which he added the weight of a certain grandiloquence. In 1934, he completed the mural fresco for the Church of Christ the King in Rome. On this date he began, in collaboration with Orei, the cycle of the *Myth of Ferrara,* the various parts of which were inspired by Tasso, Ariosto and local myths. From 1936, his style regained its simplicity, coming closer to the poetic quality of 15th-century Ferrara painting. Towards the end of his life, he returned for his subject matter to landscape and seascapes.

Group exhibitions at which his work was shown have included: 1922 and 1924, Venice Biennale; 1999, *Scoperta del Mare. Pittori lombardi in Liguria tra 1800 e 1900* (*Discovering the Sea: Lombard Painters in Liguria between 1800 and 1900*), Palazzo Ducale, Genoa; 2003, *De Chirico and Italian Painting Between the Two Wars,* Musée de Lodève.

His solo shows have included: 1973, Palazzo della Permanente, Milan; 1987, Palazzo dell'Arsenale, Chiesa di San Giovanni and Chiesa dei Disciplini, Iseo 1996, Stellini Foundation, Milan; 2001, Centre St-Bénin, Aoste.

A Funi

Bibliography:
Sarfatti-Grassini, Margherita, *Achille Funi,* Ulrico Hoepli, Milan, 1925. Clair, Jean/Schmied, Wieland/Birolli, Zeno, *Les Réalismes,* group exhibition catalogue, Éd. du Centre Georges-Pompidou, Paris, 1980. Weber, Susanna, *Achille Funi e la pittura murale fra le due guerre,* SPES, Florence, 1987. De Grada, Raffaele, *Achille Funi: dal futurismo alla maniera grande,* exhibition catalogue, Palazzo dell'arsenale, Iseo, Mazzotta, Milan, 1987. Scardino, L., *Achille Funi - Itinerari di un affrescatore,* Ferrara, 1988. De Grada, Raffaele, et al., *Achille Funi: dipinti, cartoni, disegni,* exhibition catalogue, Palazzo Bagatti Valsecchi, Vangelista, Milan, 1992. Colombo, Nicoletta (ed.), *Achile Funi. 1.Catalogo ragionato dei cartoni,* catalogue raisonné, Leonardo arte, Milan, 1996. Colombo, Nicoletta (ed.), *Achille Funi. 2. Catalogo ragionato dei dipinti,* catalogue raisonné, Leonardo arte, Milan, 1996. Ginex, Giovanna/Rebora, Sergio, *Scoperta del Mare. Pittori lombardi in Liguria tra 1800 e 1900,* group exhibition catalogue, Palazzo Ducale, Genoa, Mazzetta, Milan, 1999. Pontiggia, Elena/Colombo, Nicoletta (ed.), *Achille Funi 1890-1972. L'artista e Milano,* exhibition catalogue, Spazio Oberdan, Mazzetta, Milan, 2001. Bonito Oliva, Achille/Iovane, Giovanni/Lista, Giovanni, et al., *De Chirico et la peinture italienne de l'entre-deux guerres,* group exhibition catalogue, Musée de Lodève, 2003.

Museums and Galleries:
Ferrara (Mus. d'Arte Moderna e Contemporanea Filippo de Pisis): *Ritratto della sorella* (*Portrait of my Sister*) (1921) - Milan (Castello Sforzesco): watercolours - Milan (Civico Mus. d'Arte Contemporanea): *Ritratto di bambina* (*Portrait of Young Girl*) (1920) - Milan (Gal. d'Arte Moderna): *Man Stepping off a Tram* (1914); *Venus in Love* (1928) - Rome (Gal. Comunale d'Arte Moderna e Contemporanea).

Auction records:
Milan, 4 June 1974, *Seated Nude,* ITL 2,800,000. Milan, 9 Nov 1976, *Venus Awakening* (1928, oil on canvas, 47 1/4 x 59 ins / 120 x 150 cm) ITL 5,500,000. Milan, 13 Dec 1979, *Nude, Mid-length* (oil/hardboard, 39 1/4 x 31 1/2 ins / 100 x 80 cm) ITL 1,900,000. Milan, 26 Feb 1981, *Soldiers in the Trench* (1917, watercolour, 13 1/2 x 20 ins / 34.3 x 50.8 cm) ITL 5,700,000. Milan, 15 March 1983, *Sleeping Nude* (1930, mixed me-

dia/mounted card, 53 1/2 x 42 1/4 ins / 136 x 107 cm) ITL 5,000,000. MILAN, 4-5 April 1984, *Portrait of a Young Girl* (pencil, 20 3/4 x 17 ins / 53 x 43 cm) ITL 2,000,000; *Temptation* (oil on canvas, 70 3/4 x 47 1/4 ins / 180 x 120 cm) ITL 7,500,000. MILAN, 10 April 1986, *Portrait* (mixed media/mounted paper/hardboard, 41 1/4 x 27 1/2 ins / 105 x 70 cm) ITL 6,500,000. MILAN, 9 Dec 1986, *La Bersagliera* (1920, oil on canvas, 23 1/2 x 15 3/4 ins / 60 x 40 cm) ITL 19,000,000. ROME, 7 April 1988, *Architect* (oil on panel, 20 1/2 x 17 3/4 ins / 52 x 45 cm) ITL 14,000,000. MILAN, 14 May 1988, *Recumbent Woman* (pencil and ink watercolour, 16 x 21 ins / 40.5 x 53.5 cm) ITL 1,000,000. MILAN, 8 June 1988, *Studio* (mixed media, 15 3/4 x 22 ins / 40 x 56 cm) ITL 3,800,000; *Woman Seated in front of an Architectural Background* (1922, distemper/paper, 19 3/4 x 14 1/4 ins / 50 x 36 cm) ITL 15,000,000. MILAN, 14 Dec 1988, *Roman Senator* (wax crayon and charcoal/paper, 65 x 31 1/2 ins / 165 x 80 cm) ITL 5,000,000. ROME, 17 April 1989, *St Anthony of Padua* (1936, sketch for a mixed media fresco/canvas, 94 x 46 1/2 ins / 239 x 118 cm) ITL 6,200,000. MILAN, 7 June 1989, *Bust of a Woman* (1937, oil on panel, 25 1/4 x 22 3/4 ins / 64 x 58 cm) ITL 16,500,000. MILAN, 27 March 1990, *Villa Borghese* (1929, oil on panel, 25 1/2 x 24 1/4 ins / 65 x 61.5 cm) ITL 21,000,000. MILAN, 12 June 1990, *Allegory of Zeus and Juno* (pastel, chalk and charcoal/mounted paper, 67 x 60 ins / 170 x 151.5 cm) ITL 26,500,000. ROME, 9 Dec 1991, *Susanna Bathing* (1960, oil on canvas, 57 x 41 1/4 ins / 145 x 105 cm) ITL 25,300,000. MILAN, 23 June 1992, *Tuscan Landscape* (mixed media/card, 27 1/2 x 19 3/4 ins / 70 x 50 cm) ITL 5,000,000. MILAN, 9 Nov 1992, *Woman Seated* (1930, oil on canvas, 47 1/4 x 42 1/2 ins / 120 x 108 cm) ITL 24,000,000. ROME, 27 May 1993, *Still-life* (1930, oil on canvas/card). MILAN, 16 Nov 1993, *Proserpine* (1965, tempera/synthetic resin, 28 1/4 x 20 1/2 ins / 71.5 x 52 cm) ITL 5,175,000. MILAN, 22 Nov 1993, *Nude Figures* (oil on canvas, 30 3/4 x 38 1/4 ins / 78 x 97 cm) ITL 9,428,000. MILAN, 5 Dec 1994, *Adolescent* (1930, oil on canvas, 63 x 63 1/2 ins / 160 x 161 cm) ITL 40,250,000. MILAN, 22 June 1995, *Study for Bust and Head* (mixed media/mounted paper, 70 3/4 x 47 1/4 ins / 180 x 120 cm) ITL 13,800,000. MILAN, 10 Dec 1996, *Portrait* (pencil/paper, 21 x 16 1/2 ins / 52.5 x 42 cm) ITL 2,097,000. MILAN, 24 Nov 1997, *Still-life* (1923, oil on canvas, 22 3/4 x 30 1/4 ins / 58 x 77 cm) ITL 24,150,000. MILAN, 15 April 1999, *Sister* (1923, tempera on canvas, 35 x 30 ins / 90 x 75 cm) ITL 160,000,000. VENICE, 13 Nov 1999, *Lady Playing the Violin* (mixed media on paper/canvas, 207 x 89 ins / 525 x 225 cm) ITL 21,000,000. VERCELLI, 17 June 2000, *Still-life* (oil on masonite, 14 x 19 ins / 35 x 48 cm) ITL 8,000,000. MILAN, 28 Nov 2000, *Woman in Profile* (mixed media on cardboard, 22 x 16 ins / 55 x 40 cm) ITL 3,500,000. MILAN, 27 March 2001, *Seated Nude* (red chalk, charcoal and watercolour, 27 x 20 ins / 68 x 51 cm) ITL 5,500,000. MILAN, 27 March 2001, *Robed Woman* (1960-1965, oil on board, 24 x 20 ins / 60 x 50 cm) ITL 19,000,000. ROME, 21 Nov 2002, *Comic Muse* (c. 1946, paint on cardboard, 87 x 53 ins / 220 x 135 cm) EUR 6,000. MILAN, 4 Dec 2002, *Allegorical Figure* (c. 1935, pastel on paper/canvas, 82 x 30 ins / 209 x 75 cm) EUR 7,500. TURIN, 17 Nov 2003, *Young Shepherd* (1937, 64 x 50 ins / 162 x 126 cm) EUR 19,000. MILAN, 16 Dec 2003, *Nude Study* (1928, oil on canvas, 34 x 28 ins / 86 x 71 cm) EUR 33,000.

FUNK, Adolf
Swiss, 20th century.
Born 1903, in Nidau (Bern); died 1996, in Zurich.
Painter.

AUCTION RECORDS:
ZURICH, 5 June 1996, *Green Red* (1977, oil on canvas, 16 1/4 x 13 ins / 41 x 33 cm) CHF 2,070.

FUNK, Emil
German, 19th century.
Active in Königsberg, East Prussia (now Kaliningrad, Russia).
Painter. Genre scenes.

Emil Funk exhibited in Berlin between 1854 and 1864.

FUNK, Friedrich
German, 19th century.
Born 11 August 1804, in Leipzig; died 15 December 1882, in Leipzig.
Sculptor.

Friedrich Funk was a pupil of Franz Pettrichs in Dresden. He executed a large number of monuments in Leipzig, such as that of J.A. Hiller or of the singer Thekla Podleska.

FUNK, Hans, the Elder
Swiss, 15th - 16th century.
Born c. 1470, in Zurich; died 1539, in Bern.
Glass painter.

Hans Funk the Elder made painted-glass windows for a church and the town halls in Bern, Fribourg and Aarau. He was one of the most important artists of the early 16th century in his field.

MUSEUMS AND GALLERIES:
BASEL: *Portrait of a Young Man*.

FUNK, Hans, the Younger
Swiss, 16th century.
Died 1562.
Active in Zurich.
Glass painter.

FUNK, Heinrich
German, 19th century.
Born 12 December 1807, in Herford (North Rhine-Westphalia); died 22 November 1877, in Stuttgart.
Painter. Landscapes.

Heinrich Funk made his début in 1829 at the academy in Düsseldorf, where he was a pupil of J.-W. Schirmer. After this he worked with Lazinsky, Pose, Rethel, Rustige, Teicho and Zwecker. He began exhibiting in Düsseldorf in 1833. In 1854 he was appointed professor at the art school in Stuttgart.

MUSEUMS AND GALLERIES:
COLOGNE: *Landscape* - FRANKFURT AM MAIN: *Landscape* - MAINZ: *Mill in Schwarbach* - STUTTGART: two landscapes.

AUCTION RECORDS:
LONDON, 14 Nov 1973, *Mountain Tarn at Twilight* (1843) GBP 4,900. NEW YORK, 13 Oct 1978, *Mountain Tarn* (1851, oil on canvas, 16 x 22 ins / 40.5 x 56 cm) USD 2,500. COLOGNE, 19 Nov 1987, *Italian Landscape* (oil on panel, 12 1/2 x 11 ins / 32 x 28 cm) DEM 3,600. MUNICH, 29 Nov 1989, *Chiemsee with the Island of Herrenchiemsee* (1846, oil on canvas, 31 x 44 3/4 ins / 78.5 x 113.5 cm) DEM 35,200. MUNICH, 10 Dec 1991, *View of Isartal* (oil on canvas, 28 1/4 x 46 3/4 ins / 72 x 119 cm) DEM 12,650. MUNICH, 21 March 2001, *Gothic Monastery Ruins on Mountain Lake Shore* (1860, oil on canvas, 37 x 60 ins / 94 x 153 cm) DEM 6,500. VIENNA, 29 Nov 2001, *Gothic Monastery Ruins on Mountain Lake Shore* (1860, oil on canvas, 37 x 60 ins / 94 x 153 cm) ATS 80,000.

FUNK, Jakob, the Elder
Swiss, 16th century.
Glass painter.

Jakob Funk the Elder worked at St-Urbain.

FUNK, Jakob, the Younger
Swiss, 16th century.
Died 1564, in Zurich.
Glass painter.

This artist was the brother of Hans the Elder.

FUNK, Johann Friedrich, the Elder
Swiss, 18th century.
Born 1706, in Marten; died 1 April 1775, in Bern.
Sculptor.

Johann Friedrich Funk was the father of Johann Friedrich Funk the Younger.

FUNK, Johann Friedrich, the Younger
Swiss, 18th - 19th century.
Born 26 October 1745, in Bern; died 4 December 1811, in Bern.
Sculptor.
Johann Friedrich Funk studied in Paris under the guidance of Vallé. He came to prominence through his sculpting a mortuary monument to King Stanislas in Nancy (Meurthe-et-Moselle, France).

FUNK, Jonas Paulus
German, 18th century.
Active in Nuremberg (Bavaria).
Draughtsman, engraver.
Jonas Funk was responsible for a portrait of *J.J. Kuhn*.

FUNK, Josef Anton
German, 18th century.
Died c. 1740, in Wilten.
Painter.
Josef Funk was a pupil of Waldmann.

FUNK, Karl
Bohemian School, 18th - 19th century.
Active in Prague.
Draughtsman, engraver.
Karl Funk is known for a portrait, drawn and engraved, of the architect W. Chelm Florentin.

FUNK, Ludwig
Swiss, 15th - 16th century.
Born before 1470, in Zurich; died before 1532.
Glass painter.
Ludwig Funk was responsible for producing the windows for the church of St Martin in Zurich.

FUNK, Philipp
Austrian, 18th century.
Born 1750, in Vienna.
Painter.
Philipp Funk specialised in painting on boxes.

FUNK, Sigmund Emmanuel
Swiss, 18th century.
Died 1781.
Sculptor.

FUNK, Ulrich, the Elder
Swiss, 16th century.
Died c. 1512, in Zurich.
Glass painter.
He was the brother of Ludwig.

FUNK, Ulrich, the Younger
Swiss, 16th century.
Active in Zurich.
Glass painter.
Ulrich Funk the Younger was the brother of Hans the Elder and Jacob the Younger, and son of Ulrich the Elder.

FUNK, Valerian
German, 18th century.
Born in Nymphenburg (Bavaria).
Engraver, architect.
Valerian Funk was active in Munich.

FUNK, Wilhelm Heinrich
German, 20th century.
Born 14 January 1886, in Hanover.
Also active in the USA.
Painter.
Wilhelm Funk studied in Munich then settled in New York. He exhibited in New York, Munich and Paris.

FUNKE, Bernhard Dietrich
German, 19th century.
Born 1799, in Varel (Lower Saxony); died 29 December 1837, in Bremen.
Painter, lithographer.
Bernhard Funke executed portraits of several prominent personalities in the court of Oldenburg.

FUNKE, Carl
German, 19th century.
Active in Berlin.
Engraver, lithographer.
Carl Funke exhibited between 1826 and 1832.

FUNKE, Wilhelm
German, 19th century.
Active in Berlin.
Painter.
Wilhelm Funke exhibited between 1839 and 1860.

FUNKE-KÜPPER, Bernhard Anton
Dutch, 20th century.
Born 1869; died 1955.
Painter.
AUCTION RECORDS:
AMSTERDAM, 5-6 Nov 1991, *Woman Knitting in an Interior* (1921, oil on canvas, 22 x 17 1/4 ins / 55 x 44 cm) NLG 2,760. AMSTERDAM, 24 Sept 1992, *Still-life with Marguerites in an Earthenware Jug, Apples and a Shell* (oil on canvas/card, 15 3/4 x 20 ins / 40 x 50.5 cm) NLG 1,150. AMSTERDAM, 20 April 1993, *Still-life with Fruits* (oil on canvas, 17 1/4 x 25 1/4 ins / 44 x 64 cm) NLG 5,520. AMSTERDAM, 19 April 1994, *Still-life with Flowers and Apples* (oil on canvas/panel, 15 1/4 x 19 1/2 ins / 38.5 x 49.5 cm) NLG 4,370. ROTTERDAM, 5 Nov 2002, *Hunting Still-life* (oil on canvas, 47 x 37 ins / 119 x 95 cm) EUR 3,000.

FUNNO, Michele
Italian, 19th century.
Born before 1837; died after 1851.
Painter (gouache), watercolourist. Seascapes.
Funno was one of the many artists who painted 'ship portraits' rather than seascapes.
AUCTION RECORDS:
LONDON, 6 June 1984, *The Brig 'Racer'* (watercolour and gouache, 19 x 28 ins / 48 x 71 cm) GBP 600. LONDON, 30 March 1990, *The Bay of Naples* (gouache, 19 1/4 x 29 1/2 ins / 49 x 75 cm) GBP 2,090. LONDON, 16 July 1993, *The 'Pembrokeshire Lass' Coming into and Going out of Naples* (1842, gouache, a pair, 17 1/2 x 25 ins / 44.5 x 63.5 cm and 18 3/4 x 25 1/2 ins/47.5 x 65 cm) GBP 2,530. LONDON, 11 May 1994, *The Two-Master 'Catherine Boland' in the Bay of Naples* (1851, gouache, 19 3/4 x 28 1/2 ins / 50 x 72.5 cm) GBP 977.

FUNRUP VON
Austrian, 19th century.
Born 1800; died 1876.
Active in Vienna.
Painter. History painting.
This artist was curator of the museum of Vienna and one of the founders of the Neo-Christian School in Austria.

FUNTUSOV, Condratu
Russian, 19th century.
Painter.
This artist worked at the Ostankino Palace, near Moscow, in about 1800.

FURBY, Charles Jean
French, 20th century.
Born in Aix-en-Provence.
Painter. Landscapes.
Charles Furby exhibited in Paris at the Salon des Indépendants from 1927 onwards.

FURCH, Sebastian. See **FULCARUS**

FÜRCHTER, Johann Georg
German, 18th century.
Painter.
Johann Fürchter executed a *Way of the Cross* with the collaboration of his sons, Franz Caspar Johann and Michall, for the church at Aussee in 1727.

FURCK, Heinrich
German, 17th century.
Died 3 October 1685, in Frankfurt am Main.
Painter.
The son of Sebastian Furck, Heinrich Furck worked in 1680 for the church of St Catherine.

FURCK, Sebastian
German, 17th century.
Born in Alterkülz; died 1655, in Frankfurt am Main.
Painter, engraver.
Sebastian Furck was the father of Heinrich. He engraved in particular a large number of portraits.
AUCTION RECORDS:
PARIS, 11 April 1992, *Portrait of a Gentleman with a Dog* (oil on panel, 5 1/2 x 4 1/4 ins / 14 x 10.5 cm) FRF 18,000.

FURCY DE LAVAULT, Albert Tibule
French, 19th century.
Born 1847, in St-Genis-d'Hiersac (Charente); died 1915.
Painter. Harbour scenes, still-lifes (flowers/fruit).
He received an honourable mention in 1888 and was curator of the museum at La Rochelle.

MUSEUMS AND GALLERIES:
CAMBRAI: *Flowers and Fruit* - LA ROCHELLE: *Flowers* (two works); *Corner of the Garden* - ROCHEFORT: *Path in the Woods; Still-life* - SAINTES: *Hollyhocks; Chrysanthemums.*
AUCTION RECORDS:
PARIS, 23 Dec 1918, *Port of La Rochelle,* FRF 95. LINDAU, 6 May 1981, *Vase of Flowers* (oil on canvas, 32 1/4 x 17in/82 x 43cm) DEM 4,200. PARIS, 27 Nov 1987, *Vase and Basket of Peonies and Roses* (oil on canvas, 40 1/4 x 28 3/4in/102 x 73cm) FRF 32,000. RHEIMS, 22 Oct 1989, *Landscape with Mill* (oil on canvas, 9 x 13 3/4in/23 x 35cm) FRF 4,000. CALAIS, 5 July 1992, *Basket of Dahlias* (1892, oil on canvas, 21 1/4 x 28 3/4in/54 x 73cm) FRF 18,000. PARIS, 4 April 1997, *Still-life with Flowers and Fruit* (1881, oil on canvas, 36 x 59 1/4in/90.5 x 150.5cm) FRF 57,000. NEW YORK, 23 Oct 1997, *Roses; Dahlias* (oil on canvas, a pair, each 32 x 23 3/4in/81.3 x 60.3cm) USD 16,100. NEW YORK, 18 March 1998, *Still-life with Flowers and Jewel Box* (1877, oil on canvas, 32 1/4 x 43in/81.9 x 109.2cm) USD 8,050.

FÜRENSCHILT, Hännslein
German, 16th century.
Born in Regensburg (Bavaria).
Painter.
Fürenschilt was a pupil of Peter Seyger in Nuremberg.

FURET
French, 19th century.
Painter, watercolourist.
He exhibited paintings of church interiors at the Paris Salon from 1822 to 1824.

FURET, Claude, called Le Maçon
French, 17th century.
Active in Provence.
Sculptor.
Claude Furet sculpted coats-of-arms on a gate at Villeneuve-lès-Arles in 1600, and in 1612 he decorated the Marcat-Nou gate in Arles, with the arms of France and Poland.

FURET, François
Swiss, 19th - 20th century.
Born 24 January 1842, in Geneva; died 1919, in Geneva.
Painter, draughtsman. History painting, genre scenes, landscapes, landscapes with figures.
François Furet studied at the school of fine arts in Geneva. His landscapes are distinguished by their pale, delicate coloration. He is best known for *The Count of Gruyère Preaching about the Crusades, Landscape with Figures* and *Fire Scene.* He won a bronze medal at the 1889 Exposition Universelle.
MUSEUMS AND GALLERIES:
GENEVA (MAH): *Herons; Haystacks* - GENEVA (Mus. Ariana): *View over Lake Thun.*
AUCTION RECORDS:
BERN, 7 May 1976, *Lake Lucerne* (oil on canvas, 11 3/4 x 18 ins / 30 x 46 cm) CHF 900. GENEVA, 12 June 1981, *Landscape* (oil on canvas, 13 1/2 x 11 ins / 34 x 28 cm) CHF 3,700. BERN, 11 May 1984, *View of the Dent de Morgon in Spring* (oil on canvas, 22 x 25 1/2 ins / 55 x 65 cm) CHF 2,400. BERN, 2 May 1986, *Landscape in the Valais seen from the Dent-Blanche* (oil on canvas, 21 1/4 x 25 1/2 ins / 54 x 65 cm) CHF 2,800. BERN, 26 Oct 1988, *Landscape in the Valais near Saas Fee* (oil on canvas, 24 x 17 ins / 61 x 43 cm) CHF 1,900. ZURICH, 8 Dec 1994, *Lake Biel with St Peter's Island* (charcoal and watercolour/paper, 11 3/4 x 18 ins / 30 x 46 cm) CHF 1,265.

FURET, Jan
Dutch, 18th century.
Born in The Hague.
Painter.
Furet studied at the academy in The Hague.

FUREZ DE MUÑIZ, Jerónimo (Don)
Spanish, 17th century.
Painter. History painting, genre scenes.
Don Jerónimo Furez de Muñiz was a knight of the order of St James and a gentleman in the service of Philip IV. Siret mentions him as an art enthusiast and amateur painter.

FURIA, Eugenio
Italian, 19th century.
Born 1855, in Parma.
Painter.
Furia is known for his views of monuments.

FURICH, Johann Philipp
German, 17th - 18th century.
Born 1655, in Strasbourg; died after 1735.
Painter, engraver.
Johann Furich was a pupil of Johann-Heinrich Roes in Frankfurt. He imitated rather slavishly the style of his master.

FURICH, Remigius
German, 18th century.
Born 1688, in Frankfurt am Main; died 8 February 1724, in Frankfurt.
Painter.
Remigius may have been the brother of Johann Philipp Furich.

FURINACCIO
Italian, 18th century.
Painter. Genre scenes.
Furinaccio imitated Watteau. His *Figures from the Commedia dell'Arte* is housed in the museum of Nancy.

FURINI, Filippo, called Pippo Sciamerone
Italian, 16th - 17th century.
Active in Florence.
Painter. History painting, portraits.
Filippo was the father and teacher of Francesco Furini.

FURINI, Francesco
Italian, 17th century.

Born 1604, in Florence; died 19 August 1646, in Florence.

Painter. Religious subjects, portraits.

Francesco Furini was the son and pupil of Filippo Furini (himself an accomplished portraitist). He studied subsequently under Passignano and Roselli. He travelled to Rome and Venice where he developed a new appreciation of colour. In 1644 he was named *curé* of Mugello, near Borgo San Lorenzo, and it was there that he produced some of his finest work, including *The Three Graces* for the Palazzo Stozze and *Nymphs Abducted by Satyrs* for the Casa Galli.

Furini painted with elegance and finesse, never more so than when portraying women and children, when he cleverly juxtaposed luminous features and penumbra. He clearly admired Albani and did not hesitate to imitate his style, which he did with conspicuous success.

furini.

MUSEUMS AND GALLERIES:
BUDAPEST: *Liberality; Venus and Adonis; Tancredi and Herminia* - CHAMBÉRY (MBA): *Head of a Young Man* - CHERBOURG: *Judith Seizing the Sword of Holofernes* - COPENHAGEN (Statens Mus. for Kunst): *Penitent Magdalene* - DARMSTADT: *Female Saint* - DRESDEN: *Martyr with a Wound on his Neck* - DUBLIN: *Charity* - EDINBURGH (Nat. Gal. of Scotland): *Poetry* (oil/paper/panel, allegoric figure); *St Sebastian* (oil on canvas) - FLORENCE (NG): *Portrait of the Artist* - FLORENCE (Palazzo Pitti): *Adam and Eve in the Garden of Eden* - MADRID (Prado): *Lot and his Daughters* - MUNICH: *Rinaldo in the Enchanted Forest* - NANCY: *Persephone Surprised by Pluto* - VIENNA: *Penitent Mary Magdalene; Penitent Magdalene.*

AUCTION RECORDS:
PARIS, 1843, *Mary Magdalene*, FRF 305. PARIS, 1870, *St Sebastian, Martyr*, FRF 1,750; *St Agatha, Martyr*, FRF 4,800. PARIS, 1881, *St Sebastian and St Irene*, FRF 800. LONDON, 25 Feb 1924, *Mary Magdalene*, GBP 6. LONDON, 16 Dec 1927, *Three Sibyls*, GBP 13. LONDON, 21 Dec 1928, *Justice*, GBP 9. LONDON, 22 Nov 1929, *Judith with the Head of Holofernes*, GBP 23. LONDON, 2 July 1937, *Andromeda*, GBP 6. LONDON, 11 Feb 1938, *Churchman*, GBP 13. LONDON, 16 June 1938, *Mary Magdalene at Prayer*, GBP 5. LONDON, 31 March 1939, *Sigismund*, GBP 23. PARIS, 23 March 1942, *St Sebastian* (attributed) FRF 25,000. LONDON, 2 Oct 1942, *Artist's Portrait*, GBP 63. LONDON, 7 July 1978, *Sophonisbe and the Poisoned Chalice* (oil on canvas, 27 1/2 x 22 1/2 ins / 70 x 57.3 cm) GBP 4,200. LONDON, 23 June 1982, *Generosity* (oil on canvas, 47 1/4 x 35 1/2 ins / 120 x 90 cm) GBP 9,000. NEW YORK, 10 June 1983, *Sirens* (oil on canvas, 47 x 40 ins / 119.5 x 101.5 cm) USD 10,000. LONDON, 10 April 1987, *St Irene Tending St Sebastian* (oil on canvas, octagonal, 40 x 40 1/4 ins / 101.5 x 102.2 cm) GBP 30,000. STOCKHOLM, 19 April 1989, *St Sebastian* (oil on canvas, 30 x 24 1/2 ins / 76 x 62 cm) SEK 7,700. NEW YORK, 12 Jan 1995, *St Sebastian Holding an Arrow* (oil on canvas, 46 1/4 x 35 1/2 ins / 117.5 x 90.2 cm) USD 46,000. PARIS, 20 Jan 1998, *Head of a Woman* (black chalk/brown paper, 9 x 6 ins / 22 x 15.3 cm) FRF 26,000. VENICE, 9 Feb 2002, *Nereids* (oil on canvas, 47 x 46 ins / 120 x 118 cm) EUR 50,000. FLORENCE, 17 March 2003, *Allegory of Temperance* (oil on canvas, 25 x 20 ins / 64 x 52 cm) EUR 5,000. MILAN, 4 June 2003, *Allegory of Vanity* (oil on canvas, 27 x 22 ins / 68 x 55 cm) EUR 15,000.

FURINI, Niccolo

Italian, 18th century.

Painter.

Niccolo Furini worked around 1700 for the church of S Maria Alberighi in Florence.

FURLANELLI, Francesco

Italian, 17th century.

Born 1615, in Tesero; died 1685, in Cavalsee.

Painter.

Francesco Furlanelli painted a series of major frescoes for the church in his adopted Cavalsee.

FURLANETTO, Matteo

Italian, 18th century.

Painter.

Matteo Furlanetto painted an *Ascension of the Virgin* for L'Aquila Cathedral in 1793.

FURLANI, Andrea

Italian, 16th century.

Active in Milan.

Sculptor, designer of ornamental architectural features.

Andrea was no doubt the son of Gaspare Furlani. He may well be the Andrea da Lucca who collaborated with Luca Cambiaso.

FURLANI, Bonaventura

Italian, 18th century.

Active in Bologna.

Sculptor, designer of ornamental architectural features.

Bonaventura Furlani was a pupil of Scandellari.

FURLANI, Gaspare

Italian, 16th century.

Born in Lucca; died March 1602, in Genoa.

Sculptor (wood).

The brother of Giuseppe Furlani, Gaspare is known mainly for his work in Genoa cathedral.

FURLANI, Giuseppe

Italian, 16th century.

Born in Lucca; died April 1593, in Genoa.

Sculptor, designer of ornamental architectural features.

Giuseppe was the brother of Gaspare Furlani.

FURLANI, Paolo

Italian, 16th century.

Born in Verona.

Engraver.

Paolo Furlani is known for his landscape engravings.

FÜRLER, Mathias

German, 18th century.

Born 30 December 1702, in Meran (now Merano, Italy).

Painter.

The museum in Merano has two paintings by this artist.

FURLIGIN, J. P.

Russian, 19th century.

Born 1858.

Painter.

The Rumiantsev Museum in Moscow has a painting by him entitled *At Work*.

FURLONG, Charles Wellington

American, 19th - 20th century.

Born 13 December 1874, in Cambridge; died 1967, in Hanover (New Hampshire).

Painter. Figures, animals.

Charles Furlong began his education in Boston, before attending the École des Beaux-Arts in Paris, where he studied under Jean-Paul Laurens, William Bouguereau and Alphonse Mucha. He specialised in North African subjects.

AUCTION RECORDS:
NEW YORK, 22 Oct 1982, *Among the Litters* (1910, oil on canvas, 24 1/4 x 16 1/4 ins / 61.5 x 41.2 cm) USD 6,000.

FURLONG, Thomas
American, 20th century.
Born in St Louis.
Painter, illustrator. Church decoration.
Thomas Furlong studied at the Art Students' League in New York, of which he later became a member. He produced church decorations.
BIBLIOGRAPHY:
Kettlewell, James K., *Artists of Lake George, 1776-1976*, exhibition catalogue, 1976.

FURLONGER, Stephen
New Zealander, 20th century.
Born 1939.
Sculptor.
In 1962, Stephen Furlonger received the New Zealand Arts Council Prize.

FURLONI, Pietro
Italian, 18th century.
Died 16 November 1740, in Rome.
Painter.
Pietro Furloni painted portraits of the king and queen of Poland and their son.

FURMENT, Pedro
Spanish, 16th century.
Born c. 1488; died 1540, in Barcelona.
Sculptor.
For Barcelona Cathedral, Pedro Furment carved four marble low reliefs of the *Martyrdom of St Eulalie*.

FURNASS, John Mason
American, 18th century.
Active in Boston in 1785.
Painter, engraver.
John Mason Furnass painted mainly portraits.

FURNELL, C. (Miss)
British, 19th century.
Active in Norwood.
Miniaturist.
C. Furnell exhibited at the Royal Academy in London in 1860.

FURNERIUS, Abraham, or Farnerius
Dutch, 17th century.
Born c. 1628.
Painter, draughtsman. Landscapes.
Furnerius was a pupil of Rembrandt. His work remains obscure, but he is thought to have been the son of a doctor named Johannes Furnerius, who married the sister of the painter Philips de Koninck in 1641.

AUCTION RECORDS:
LONDON, 11 April 1935, *Landscape* (drawing) GBP 15. LONDON, 10-14 July 1936, *Landscape,* GBP 99.

FURNESS, William H.
American, 19th century.
Born 1827, in Philadelphia; died 1867.
Painter, draughtsman. Portraits.
William H. Furness studied in Dresden and Paris.

FURNIO
Italian, 16th century.
Active in Friuli.
Painter.

FURNISS, Harry
British, 19th - 20th century.
Born 26 March 1854, in Wexford; died 1925.
Caricaturist, illustrator.
Harry Furniss was Irish by birth. He worked for several London newspapers.

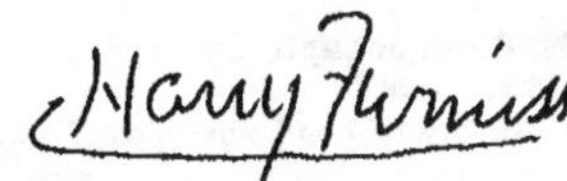

AUCTION RECORDS:
LONDON, 23 July 1985, *Our Famous Pictures: The Cry is Still They Go!* (pen and wash, 11 x 8 ins / 27 x 20.6 cm) GBP 1,300.

FURNIUS, B.C.
British, 19th century.
Active in London.
Sculptor.
B.C. Furnius exhibited at the Royal Academy in London from 1829 to 1833.

FURNIUS, Pieter Jalhea, or Pieter de Four or Foere, called de Salzes
Flemish School, 16th - 17th century.
Born c. 1545, in Liège; died 1626.
Draughtsman, engraver.
A pupil of Lambertus Lombard, Pieter Furnius worked between 1578 and 1610 at the church of St Bartholomew in Liège. One of his most important works is the tomb of Bishop Gerard of Groesbeck in Liège. At the time of his death, Furnius was a doorkeeper at the hospital of St James in Liège. Giambologna was his pupil.

FURNIVAL, John
British, 20th century.
Painter.
Visual Poetry.
John Furnival's work forms part of the movement known as visual poetry or concrete poetry. He uses typography to create a form of writing intended to be seen before being read and reconstructs real or imaginary monuments described in the text itself.
AUCTION RECORDS:
NEW YORK, 24 Nov 1981, *Thomas Meyer, Blind Date* (11 etchings and embossings, 13 x 12¼ ins / 32.8 x 31.1 cm) USD 1,200.

FURNO, Jean de
French, 14th century.
Sculptor.
Jean de Furno was one of the sculptors involved in the construction of Sens Cathedral (Yonne).

FURNO, Stefano. See **DUFOUR Étienne**

FURNO, Stefano del, called Gallo, or Francese ('the Frenchman')
French, 16th century.
Born to a family originally from Besançon (Doubs).
Painter, mosaicist.
Stefano del Furno worked in Italy and particularly at Orvieto Cathedral. It is thought likely that he was the same person as the artist Étienne Dufour.

FURNO Y ABAD, Joaquín
Spanish, 19th century.
Born in Barcelona.
Engraver.
Joaquín Furno y Abad illustrated Balaguer's *History of Catalonia*.

FÜRNSCHILT, Endres
German, 16th century.

Died 1531.
Active in Regensburg (Bavaria).
Painter.

FURON, Aimé Joseph, called Furoni
French, 18th century.
Born 10 February 1687, in Épinal; died 17 May 1729, in Épinal.
Painter.

Aimé Furon lived in Rome for 12 years, where he worked in the Italian style.

FURSE, Charles Wellington
British, 19th century.
Born 13 January 1868, in Staines; died 16 October 1904, in London.
Painter. History painting, portraits.

Charles Wellington Furse was a frequent exhibitor in London between 1885 and 1892. He was an Associate of the Royal Academy from 1904.

AUCTION RECORDS:
LONDON, 8-18 July 1940, *Field Marshal Earl Roberts,* GBP 273. LONDON, 15 Feb 1973, *Battle Scene from the Boer War* (1896) Gns 700. LONDON, 30 July 1981, *Moroccan Beauty* (oil on canvas, 72 x 48 ins / 183 x 122 cm) GBP 420. LONDON, 14 Nov 1984, *Female Portrait* (1889, oil on canvas, 32 1/4 x 22 ins / 82 x 56 cm) GBP 3,800. LONDON, 24 April 1985, *Portrait of a Lady* (oil on canvas, 28 1/4 x 24 ins / 72 x 61 cm) GBP 1,200. LONDON, 8-9 June 1993, *Portrait of Mary Cane* (oil on canvas, 61 x 32 ins / 155 x 81.5 cm) GBP 8,280. NEW YORK, 14 Oct 1993, *Moroccan Woman in Red* (oil on panel, 13 1/2 x 10 ins / 34.3 x 25.4 cm) USD 1,725. LONDON, 7 Sept 2000, *Study for the Equestrian Portrait of Field Marshal Earl Roberts* (oil on canvas, 30 x 25 ins / 76 x 63 cm) GBP 1,800. DUBLIN, 28 Feb 2001, *Wagoneers Hauling Logs* (oil on canvas, 18 x 31 ins / 46 x 78 cm) IEP 1,700. LONDON, 11 June 2004, *Portrait of the Artist's Wife, the Late Dame Katherine Furse* (oil on canvas, 26 x 20 ins / 66 x 51 cm) GBP 10,000.

FURSE, John Henry Mensell or Monsell
British, 19th century.
Born 6 March 1860, in London.
Sculptor. Animals.

John Henry Mensell Furse was educated at Trinity College, Oxford and exhibited examples of his work in London from 1891.

AUCTION RECORDS:
LONDON, 7 June 1984, *Recumbent Greyhound* (bronze, l. 16 1/2 ins / 42 cm) GBP 800.

FURSE, W.H.
British, 19th century.
Active in Rome.
Painter. Figures.

W.H. Furse exhibited in London between 1831 and 1850.

FURSINICUS DE LACU LUGANI
Italian, 16th century.
Active in Bellinzona, Switzerland.
Painter. Religious subjects.

He painted a picture of the *Virgin Enthroned between St Jerome and St Blaise,* kept in one of the churches of Bellinzona, dated 1520.

FURSMAN, Frederick
American, 19th - 20th century.
Born 1874, in Illinois; died 12 June 1943.
Painter.

Frederick Fursman went to Paris to complete his education at the Académie Julian. He was awarded many distinctions.

BIBLIOGRAPHY:
Barter, Judith A., *Currents of Expansion: Painting in the Midwest, 1820-1940,* St Louis Art Museum, 1977.

FÜRST, Albert
German, 20th century.
Born 20 April 1920, in Hamburg.
Sculptor.

Albert Fürst trained in Düsseldorf, then in Cologne. He took part in group exhibitions and held solo shows in Düsseldorf in 1954 and Paris in 1956. A retrospective was organised in 2000 by the Forum d'Art Franco-Allemand at the Château de Vaudréamont near Colombey-les-Deux-Églises. Fürst's sculpture became abstract around 1954, suggesting lyrical forms.

FÜRST, Edmund
German, 19th - 20th century.
Born 1874, in Berlin.
Painter, engraver, illustrator. Landscapes.

Edmund Fürst began exhibiting in 1904 in Munich and Berlin.

AUCTION RECORDS:
LONDON, 20 Oct 1989, *The Bridge* (oil on canvas, 14 x 19 ins / 35.5 x 48.2 cm) GBP 770.

FÜRST, Else
German, 19th - 20th century.
Born 25 June 1873, in Leipzig.
Sculptor.

Else Fürst studied in Berlin and Paris, in the studio of Denys Puech.

AUCTION RECORDS:
LONDON, 18 April 1986, *The Airman's Dream* (c. 1925, bronze, h. 24 1/2 ins / 62 cm) GBP 1,700.

FÜRST, Florence Wilkins
American, 20th century.
Born 27 April 1885, in Wisconsin; died 1955.
Active in France.
Painter.

Florence Fürst was active in Paris. She was a member of several artists' associations.

FÜRST, Gustav
German, 19th century.
Born 2 October 1840, in Berlin.
Painter. Figures.

AUCTION RECORDS:
COPENHAGEN, 25-26 April 1990, *Young Girl after Bathing* (1890, oil on canvas, 27 1/2 x 19 ins / 70 x 48 cm) DKK 9,000.

FÜRST, J.
German, 19th century.
Active c. 1835.
Miniaturist.

This artist is known for a signed portrait of a young girl.

FÜRST, Johann Heinrich
German, 17th century.
Active c. 1635.
Engraver.

Johann Fürst was responsible for a series of plates after J.H. Nicolaï.

FÜRST, Josef
German, 18th century.
Active in Albrechtsberg in 1798.
Painter.

Josef Fürst worked for the church in Albrechtsberg.

FÜRST, Julius
Danish, 19th century.
Born 4 April 1861, in Dänischenhagen.
Painter, illustrator.

Julius Fürst was a pupil of Pfeiffer in Hamburg, and then of Seidtz in Munich.

FÜRST, Magdalena
German, 17th - 18th century.

Born 1652, in Nuremberg; died 1717, in Vienna.
Painter. Flowers, fruit.
Magdalena was the sister of Rosina Helena Fürst.

FÜRST, Max
German, 19th century.
Born 15 October 1846, in Traunstein (Bavaria).
Painter. History painting.
Max Fürst exhibited in Munich and Vienna. He was a pupil of Schraudolph.

FÜRST, Paul
German, 17th century.
Born c. 1605, in Nuremberg; died 1666, in Nuremberg.
Engraver.
Paul was the father of Magdalena and Rosina Helena Fürst.

FÜRST, Rosina Helena
German, 17th century.
Active in Nuremberg (Bavaria).
Engraver.
Rosina Helena Fürst was the daughter of Paul Fürst.

FÜRST, Thomas
Austrian, 18th century.
Painter.
Thomas Fürst worked on the sculpture for the high altar of the church in Marbach in 1747.

FÜRSTE
German, 19th century.
Active in Magdeburg (Saxony-Anhalt) at the beginning of the 19th century.
Painter, draughtsman.

FÜRSTENBERG, Caspar von
German, 16th century.
Active probably in the middle of the 16th century.
Engraver (wood).

FURSTENBERG, Michel
Polish, 20th century.
Born in Warsaw.
Sculptor.
Michel Furstenberg exhibited in Paris at the Salon des Artistes Français from 1913 onwards.

FÜRSTENBERG, Solly
German, 19th century.
Born 1810, in Berlin.
Painter. Genre scenes, portraits.
Solly Fürstenberg was a pupil of Wach in Berlin. After having completed his studies in Düsseldorf, he became a drawing teacher in Trier (Rhineland-Palatinate).

FÜRSTENBERG, Theodor Caspar von (Baron)
German, 17th century.
Died 21 September 1675, in Mainz (Rhineland-Palatinate).
Engraver, painter.
Theodor von Fürstenberg was a pupil of Ludwig von Siegen. He engraved portraits and historical subjects.

FURSTENBERGER, Isaak
Swiss, 19th century.
Born 1799, in Basel; died 1828, in Gsteig.
Painter.
Furstenberger studied under the tutelage of Peter Birmann.

FÜRSTIN, Madeleine
German, 17th - 18th century.
Born 1652; died 1717.
Active in Nuremberg (Bavaria).
Miniaturist. Flowers.
Madeleine Fürstin was a pupil of Jean Fischer and Marie Sibylle Merian; she worked in Vienna.

FURT, Henri
French, 19th century.
Born in Bordeaux.
Painter.
He submitted three landscapes to the 1878 Salon.

FURT, Pierre Léonce or Léon
French, 19th - 20th century.
Born in Bordeaux.
Painter, watercolourist. Genre scenes, landscapes.
Pierre Furt exhibited in Paris at the Salon des Artistes Français. He received a commendation in 1904 and became a member of the Salon in 1905.
AUCTION RECORDS:
PARIS, 1899, *View in the South of France,* FRF 36. PARIS, 23 May 1986, *People Walking in a Fairground* (oil on canvas, 18 1/2 x 25 1/2 ins / 47 x 65 cm) FRF 25,000. CALAIS, 3 July 1988, *The Port of Rouen* (1920, oil on canvas, 15 x 18 1/2 ins / 38 x 47 cm) FRF 7,300. PARIS, 24 March 1996, *Banks of the Seine, Paris* (1905, oil on canvas, 12 1/2 x 15 3/4 ins / 32 x 40 cm) FRF 7,000. DEAUVILLE, 16 Aug 2002, *Port of Cherbourg* (oil on panel, 6 x 9 ins / 16 x 24 cm) EUR 3,000.

FURTCHTEGOTT, Thessel
German, 19th century.
Born 1830; died 1873, in Dresden.
Landscapist.
This artist is referred to by Siret.

FURTENAGEL, Jorg, the Elder
German, 15th - 16th century.
Active in Augsburg (Bavaria).
Painter.
Jorg was the father of Lucas Furtenagel.

FURTENAGEL, Jorg, the Younger
German, 16th century.
Active in Augsburg (Bavaria).
Painter.
Jorg was the brother of Lucas Furtenagel.

FURTENAGEL, Lucas
German, 16th century.
Born 1505, in Augsburg.
Painter.
Among the main works by this artist is an illustration in Martin Luther's version of the Bible and a *Portrait of Luther.* A strange picture in the museum in Vienna, long attributed to Burgkmair himself, has been reattributed since restoration to one of the Furtenagels, who painted it in 1529. The artist was probably Lucas Furtenagel, but he must have painted it according to very specific instructions from Burgkmair, since it shows the sitter and his wife, Anna Allerlahn, looking into a convex mirror that reflects back not their own image but two skulls. The inscription on this *memento mori* portrait reads 'This is what we both once were, but the mirror shows something very different'.

FURTER, Brandolf Wolf
Swiss, 16th century.
Glass painter.

FURTER, Hans
Swiss, 16th century.
Active in Bern.
Painter.

FURTER, Wolfgang
Swiss, 16th century.
Active in Bern.
Glass painter.

FURTH, Johann van der
Flemish School, 17th century.
Born in Ypres (West Flanders).
Sculptor.

Van der Furth executed work for the chapel of the town hall in Ypres.

FURTH, Michael van
Dutch, 18th century.
Sculptor.

Furth is known to have been active in Frankfurt am Main, Mainz and other cities.

FURTHNER, Balthasar
German, 16th - 17th century.
Active in Frauenchiemsee (Bavaria).
Painter.

Balthasar Furthner was painter to Duke William V of Bavaria.

FURTMAYER, Berthold, or Furtmayr
German, 15th century.
Active in Regensburg (Bavaria) at the end of the 15th century.
Miniaturist.

Furtmayer painted the illuminations illustrating the two volumes of *Weldchronik* ('History of the World') in the library of the Prince of Wellerstein in Meiringen.

FURTMEIR, Wilhelm
German, 15th century.
Active in Nuremberg (Bavaria) at the end of the 15th century.
Illuminator.

FURTNAGEL. See **FURTENAGEL**

FURTO, pseudonym of Nils Björklund
Swedish, 20th century.
Born 22 October 1912, in Roltogsjo.
Painter, engraver.

Furto lived in France from 1947. He exhibited in France and Sweden.

FURTTENBACH, Josef
German, 17th century.
Born 7 November 1632, in Ulm (Baden-Württemberg); died 1655, in Ulm.
Painter, engraver, architect.

Furttenbach was the pupil of Jonas Arnold, but is better known as an architect and writer on art.

FURUDOI, Koji
Japanese, 20th - 21st century.
Born 1947, in Kobe.
Active in France since 1974.
Painter, draughtsman.

Koji Furudoi had his first solo exhibition in Tokyo in 1972. Since then he has taken part in exhibitions in Europe and the USA. He had a solo exhibition, *Paintings and Drawings 1970-1990*, at the Galerie d'Art International in Paris in 1990.

He develops the theme of sculptural anthromorphic volumes, painted in monochrome in a very precise and smooth manner. He also seems to have practised cloudy splatter painting drawing its inspiration from the 1950s.

AUCTION RECORDS:
PARIS, 7 Oct 1991, *G. 1-2* (1980, acrylic on canvas, 46 x 32 ins / 116 x 81 cm) FRF 3,500.

FURUHASHI, Teiji
Japanese, 20th century.
Born 1960; died 29 October 1995, in Kyoto, of AIDS.
Installation artist, video artist. Multimedia.
Dumb Type Collective.

Teiji Furuhashi was the founder of the performance group Dumb Type, an internationally-recognized, Kyoto-based arts collective whose members started to work together in 1982 at Kyoto University of the Arts. Dumb Type created technically-charged performances and installations that cast an irreverent, critical eye on Japanese society and humanity's relationship with technology. At the 1995 Lyons Biennale, Furuhashi exhibited his first solo work, *Lovers*, a video installation in which nude images were played in slow motion and projected on to the four walls of the environment, where they rotated and floated in the air before fading out.

FURUHJELM, Dagmar
Finnish, 19th - 20th century.
Born 1868, in Kirkkonummi; died 1918.
Painter. Genre scenes.

MUSEUMS AND GALLERIES:
HELSINKI: *A Mother's Affliction*.

AUCTION RECORDS:
BRUSSELS, 13 Dec 1984, *The Weaving Workshop* (oil on card, 59 x 85 1/2 ins / 150 x 217 cm) BEF 180,000. LONDON, 18 June 1986, *Women Weaving* (oil on canvas, 59 3/4 x 86 1/2 ins / 152 x 220 cm) GBP 4,000. STOCKHOLM, 10 Dec 1986, *The Weaving Workshop* (oil on canvas, 59 x 86 1/2 ins / 150 x 220 cm) SEK 62,000.

FURUKAWA, Ryusei
Japanese, 20th century.
Born 1894, in Tochigi.
Print artist.

Furukawa Ryusei graduated from the traditional painting department of the Tokyo School of Fine Arts in 1924 and at once started to take part in events organised by the Japan Print Association. In 1927 he was selected for the Shunyokai exhibition. He then converted to Christianity and became a priest. During the war he abandoned his work as an print artist but took it up again afterwards. Furukawa Ryusei carved his own woodblocks with a rounded chisel, without making preliminary drawings. This gave his work great spontaneity and a certain evocative power.

FURUTA, An
Japanese, 20th century.
Born 1915, in Oita (Kyushu).
Painter.
Tekkei-Kai group.

Furuta An studied traditional Japanese painting in Kyoto with different masters from 1937 to 1943, including Sakakibara Shiho. He then served with the Japanese army in China until the war ended, returning to Japan in 1947. From 1954 to 1957, he played an active role in post-war art in Kyoto and Osaka. In 1962 and 1964, he took part in the Contemporary Japanese Art Exhibition organised by the *Mainichi* newspaper. In 1966, he took part in the 8th Tokyo Biennale and had a solo exhibition in Mexico. In 1958, Furuta founded the Tekkei-kai group, to promote an independent spirit in the area of painting. However, he reacted against the internationalism prevalent in Japanese art in the 1950s and against the lack of knowledge that the Japanese painters had of their own pictorial world. His own style has a Surrealist touch, but attempts to take into account traditional technical means.

FURUTRÄD, Carl Christian
Swedish, 18th century.
Born 1766; died 8 June 1808.
Miniaturist.

Carl Christian Furuträd studied at the academy in Stockholm.

FURY, Dominique
French, 20th - 21st century.
Born 20 June 1953, in Paris.
Painter (mixed media), screen printer.
Pop Art.

Dominique Fury points to the influence of Pop Art in her work, with its techniques, silk-screen transfers to canvas and images borrowed from the media, which she has freely put to her own use.

She has taken part in group exhibitions, including at the following: the Salon de Montrouge (1984, 1986); *10 Jeunes pour Demain* (*10 Young Artists for Tomorrow*) in Amiens (1985); *An Aspect of the Artistic Situation in France* in Berlin (1985); the Grand Palais (1987); and the Galérie du Jour Agnès B. in Paris (1988). She held a solo exhibition at the latter gallery in 1985, and in 1994 and 1995 the Thorigny Patricia Heuilleit Gallery in Paris held exhibitions of her work, the latter entitled *Fury dans ses Éléments* (*Fury in her Elements*).

AUCTION RECORDS:

PARIS, 13 April 1988, *Imus Nocte* (mixed media/canvas, 39 1/4 x 32 ins / 100 x 81 cm) FRF 3,000; *Ché, Ché, Ché* (ink, silkscreen printing and mixed media/canvas, 53 1/4 x 63 3/4 ins / 135 x 162 cm) FRF 5,000. PARIS, 12 Feb 1989, *Module* (1989, ink and acrylic/canvas, 59 x 59 ins / 150 x 150 cm) FRF 10,000. PARIS, 11 Oct 1989, *Composition No. 9* (1989, mixed media, 59 x 59 ins / 150 x 150 cm) FRF 13,500.

FUS
German, 19th century.
Painter. History painting.
This artist is referred to by Siret.

FUSARO, Jean
French, 20th century.
Born 19 May 1925, in Marseilles.
Painter, watercolourist. Figures, landscapes with figures, waterscapes.

Based in Lyons, Jean Fusaro studied at the École des Beaux-Arts there for three years and later became a teacher there around 1970. He exhibited at numerous group exhibitions, notably in Paris at the Salon d'Automne and the Salon des Peintres Témoins de leur Temps. He took part in the Menton Biennale in 1951, was awarded the Fénéon prize in 1953 and the Ville de Marseille prize in 1957. His first solo exhibition took place in Lyons in 1947 and was followed by many others, particularly in Lyons and Paris, including a retrospective in 1977 at the Musée Paul Valéry, Sète, an exhibition at the Musée de Melun in 1978 and at Artfrance in Paris in 1984.

Fusaro was an important figure in the Lyons School, together with Cottavoz, Couty and others. His lively and sometimes deliberately naive draughtsmanship is reminiscent of Dufy. He depicts a wide range of scenes in heavily painted landscapes in a very fresh range of colours. His use of pigment is characteristic of the contemporary painters of the Lyons School to which Fusaro brings a joyous interpretation.

MUSEUMS AND GALLERIES:

LYONS (MBA) - PARIS (MAM).

AUCTION RECORDS:

PARIS, 23 May 1981, *Beach on the Coast Road* (oil on canvas, 35 x 46 ins / 89 x 116 cm) FRF 4,500. VERSAILLES, 18 March 1984, *Still-life with Pheasant* (oil on canvas, 28 3/4 x 49 1/4 ins / 73 x 125 cm) FRF 15,000. LYONS, 23 Oct 1985, *Sunday Crowd* (oil on canvas, 37 3/4 x 57 ins / 96 x 145 cm) FRF 30,000. CANNES, 28 Jan 1986, *The Canal du Midi* (oil on canvas, 20 x 13 ins / 51 x 33 cm) FRF 5,500. PARIS, 23 June 1988, *Portrait of Madame Fusaro* (oil on canvas, 45 1/4 x 32 1/4 ins / 115 x 82 cm) FRF 10,000. PARIS, 27 Oct 1988, *Canal at Dementer* (1966, oil on canvas, 26 x 32 1/4 ins / 66 x 82 cm) FRF 16,000. VERSAILLES, 6 Nov 1988, *Port Scene with Figures* (watercolour, 15 x 21 3/4 ins / 38 x 55.5 cm) FRF 5,000. PARIS, 14 Dec 1988, *Man from Marseilles* (oil on canvas, 11 x 16 1/4 ins / 27 x 41 cm) FRF 9,200. PARIS, 18 June 1989, *The White Table* (1957, oil on canvas, 13 1/2 x 17 ins / 34 x 43 cm) FRF 12,000. PARIS, 8 Nov 1989, *Circus* (oil on canvas, 13 x 20 ins / 33 x 51 cm) FRF 28,000. CALAIS, 10 Dec 1989, *View of Venice* (oil on canvas, 15 x 22 ins / 38 x 55 cm) FRF 32,000. PARIS, 26 April 1990, *Autumn Vines* (1962, oil on canvas, 21 1/4 x 32 ins / 54 x 81 cm) FRF 76,000. PARIS, 6 Feb 1991, *Water Festival* (oil on card, 7 x 10 ins / 18 x 24.5 cm) FRF 17,000. PARIS, 17 March 1991, *The Lagoon, Venice* (oil on canvas, 25 1/2 x 39 1/4 ins / 65 x 100 cm) FRF 112,000. LE TOUQUET, 19 May 1991, *Rainbow at St-Paul-de-Léon* (1976, oil on canvas, 19 3/4 x 28 1/4 ins / 50 x 72 cm) FRF 70,500. PARIS, 23 March 1992, *Countryside in Portugal* (oil on canvas, 32 x 39 1/4 ins / 81 x 100 cm) FRF 75,000. NEW YORK, 9 May 1992, *Regatta with Flag* (oil on canvas, 15 x 18 ins / 38.1 x 45.7 cm) USD 2,860. LE TOUQUET, 30 May 1993, *Seaside with Figures* (1953, oil on canvas, 11 3/4 x 19 ins / 30 x 48 cm) FRF 16,000. NEW YORK, 2 Nov 1993, *Still-life with Blue Sky* (oil on canvas, 21 1/4 x 28 3/4 ins / 54 x 73 cm) USD 4,025. PARIS, 25 March 1994, *Sète* (1963, oil on canvas, 25 1/2 x 32 ins / 65 x 81 cm) FRF 94,000. NEW YORK, 8 Nov 1994, *Sail Boats* (1955, oil on canvas, 28 3/4 x 46 ins / 73 x 116 cm) USD 4,370. NEW YORK, 7 Nov 1995, *White Flowers* (1955, oil on canvas, 39 x 29 3/4 ins / 99.3 x 75.5 cm) USD 5,175. CALAIS, 24 March 1996, *Landscape* (watercolour, 16 1/4 x 21 1/4 ins / 41 x 54 cm) FRF 4,000. CALAIS, 7 July 1996, *Town Canal* (1958, oil on canvas, 25 1/2 x 32 ins / 65 x 81 cm) FRF 28,200. PARIS, 20 March 1997, *Boats on the Rhône* (oil on canvas, 13 x 19 3/4 ins / 33 x 50 cm) FRF 17,000. PARIS, 4 Nov 1997, *Harvests* (oil on canvas, 28 3/4 x 39 1/4 ins / 73 x 100 cm) FRF 30,000. PARIS, 5 June 1999, *Sooty Sky over Lyons* (oil on canvas, 9 x 13 ins / 22 x 33 cm) FRF 13,800. PARIS, 5 June 1999, *Dredgers on the Rhone* (oil on canvas, 9 x 14 ins / 24 x 35 cm) FRF 20,000. LONDON, 27 June 2000, *Danieli, Venice* (1981-1982, oil on canvas, 26 x 36 ins / 65 x 92 cm) GBP 1,800. LYONS, 8 Oct 2000, *The Harbour* (oil on canvas, 13 x 18 ins / 32 x 45 cm) FRF 28,000. PARIS, 22 June 2001, *Play of Light on the Seine* (oil on canvas, 18 x 24 ins / 46 x 61 cm) FRF 43,000. CALAIS, 9 Dec 2001, *Beach with Figures* (oil on canvas, 22 x 30 ins / 56 x 76 cm) FRF 21,000. PARIS, 16 April 2002, *Onlookers by the Water* (1967, oil on canvas, 15 x 18 ins / 38 x 46 cm) EUR 2,410. CALAIS, 19 May 2002, *Family Scene* (oil on canvas, 15 x 22 ins / 38 x 56 cm) EUR 2,500. LYONS, 9 Feb 2003, *Canal in Sète* (1951, oil on canvas, 23 x 28 ins / 59 x 72 cm) EUR 9,000. PARIS, 29 April 2003, *Embarkation of St Pauline at Ostia* (1957, oil on canvas, after Claude Lorraine, 18 x 22 ins / 46 x 55 cm) EUR 6,000. ORLEANS, 20 March 2004, *The Harbour* (oil on canvas, 13 x 19 ins / 34 x 48 cm) EUR 4,100. BERN, 12 May 2004, *Parisian Street in Winter* (oil on canvas, 11 x 16 ins / 27 x 41 cm) CHF 4,000.

FUSCH, Hans
German, 19th century.
Died 1813.
Portrait artist.
Hans Fusch is referred to by Siret.

FUSCO, Cristofaro. See **FASTO Cristofaro**

FUSCO, Giovanni Tommaso di
Italian, 16th century.
Active in Naples at the end of the 16th century.
Painter.

FUSELI, Henry, or Füssli, Hans Heinrich or Johann Heinrich or Henri
Swiss, 18th - 19th century.
Born 1741, in Zurich; died 16 April 1825, in Putney Heath, Surrey, England.
Painter, illustrator. Figure compositions, mythological subjects, religious subjects, figures, portraits.

Henry Fuseli was the second son of Johann Caspar Füssli, portrait painter and writer on art. His father guided him towards a career in the church and, despite feeling drawn towards art, he submitted to the will of his father, studying theology at the University of Zurich. Alongside his theological studies, he read English and it was through this that he became acquainted with the philosopher Johann Kaspar Lavater (1741-1801). Fuseli and Lavater read Shakespeare together and discussed poetry, physiology and art. Drawn together by their shared interests, as well as their different aptitudes and studies, they developed a friendship that was to last throughout their lifetimes. Having learnt that a magistrate in Zurich, the bailiff Grebel, was constantly committing acts of injustice, the two men wrote to him, demanding that he make amends for his misdeeds or else they would make them public. When the magistrate ignored their letter, they published a work entitled *The Unjust Judge, or Complaints of a Patriot*. The public supported them, but they were advised to leave the country and went first to Venice and then to Berlin, where they studied with Sulzer, author of a dictionary of art. Under the patronage of Sulzer, Fuseli began to draw subjects taken from English books. Two of these works, *Macbeth* and *King Lear and Cordelia*, were bought by Sir Robert Smith, British Ambassador to Prussia. It was he who advised Fuseli to visit England and gave him letters of recommendation. Once there, he initially devoted himself to literature before taking up the post of tutor to an aristocratic family. Fuseli accompanied his pupil to Paris and this new situation was to mark the start of his rising fortunes. Having a good deal of time on his hands and being free from any financial concerns, he was able to concentrate on studying painting. He met Joshua Reynolds who, having examined several of his drawings, advised him to go to Italy. He set off for Rome with his friend Armstrong, where he zealously studied the classical masterpieces and formed a friendship with Mengs and Winckelmann. He also visited Genoa, Florence, Venice and Naples. He had a strong preference for the works of Michelangelo and it was this artist that he studied most assiduously may well have contributed to the development of Fuseli's steadfast, natural and elevated style. He returned to London in 1779.

Fuseli became an associate member of the Royal Academy in London in 1788 and a full member in 1790. In 1799 he was appointed professor of painting, a chair he occupied until 1804, when hostile forces compelled him to resign from his position. However, in 1810 he was re-elected professor and continued teaching until the end of his life. He was extremely popular with his students and exerted a considerable influence over them. In 1817 he was awarded membership of the Academy of St Luke in Rome. Fuseli died while visiting the Countess of Guildford on Putney Heath. He is buried in St Paul's Cathedral in London.

Fuseli first exhibited his most famous painting *The Nightmare* at the Royal Academy in London; due to its highly imaginative nature, it attracted public attention and his talents were immediately recognised. An erotically draped young woman lies on a bed, with a deathly pale complexion and overcome by unimaginable convulsions. Crouching on her stomach is a hairy gnome that looks out from the painting. Around the figures, the shadowy light of dark curtains provides a backdrop for a horse's head with glowing eyes, reflecting the play on words contained in the title. This painting marked the point of departure for a series of works displaying the obsessions and fantasies of Fuseli, whose subconscious tendencies constitute a rich vein for psychoanalytical study. This work is also fascinating for the way in which it combines a Neo-Classical technique with Pre-Romantic inspiration and, beyond this, surrealist hallucinations. Fuseli was two men - the painter and the teacher. As a painter he enjoyed a great reputation, while as a writer his views were often at variance with the characteristics and concerns of his own art. If his colours occasionally left something to be desired, his drawing almost always displayed a boldness, a truth and a variety that left a profound impression on the spirit. However, it was the idea that lay behind the composition that was Fuseli's real forte. His imagination was lively and unfailingly fertile, and the originality of his conception sometimes approached the fantastic. He also applied himself to rendering physical pain accurately; he could express nuances of emotion admirably, but for him this was simply a means of conveying moral affliction. Among the masterpieces of this genre, mention should be made of his lunatic figures. Yet he also excelled in painting joy, love, and other positive emotions.

Fuseli was greatly influenced by his friend Lavater's ideas, and vice versa. The painter's intense interest in the animated qualities of the human face, and his belief that it gave an insight into a person's soul, came directly from Lavater's studies of physiognomy. Fuseli's great understanding of how the inner life of people could be reflected externally explains his exquisite rendition of expression, which was subtle, lifelike and acknowledged all the pecularities of the state of the soul. Like Lavater, Fuseli came to regard hallucinations and dreams as almost a saintly state. However, where he departed from Lavater was in his ability to blend the fantastic with the real and observable.

The works that made Fuseli's reputation are two series of paintings and illustrations, on Shakespeare and on Milton's *Paradise Lost* respectively. In these works, he was able to give full rein to his genius, expressing all his eccentricities, and his grandiose and phantasmagorical ideas. It was during a dinner attended by Fuseli at Boydell's that five or six high-minded individuals (Well, Hoole, Romney, Hayley, Nicol, Paul Sandby) came up with the idea of the Shakespearian gallery. Fuseli produced eight magnificent paintings for the series, on the following subjects: *The Tempest, A Midsummer Night's Dream, Macbeth, Henry IV Part II, Henry V, King Lear, and Hamlet*. The Milton collection is composed of 47 pictures; Fuseli's imaginative powers are in full cry in this cycle, and timorous critics wasted no time in labelling his exuberant expression as self-indulgent extravagance. The centrepiece of this collection is *The Hospital*. Fuseli also gained inspiration from the Old Testament (especially the Flood), Greek mythology, and German mythology and Romantic literature - in particular, the legend of the Nibelungen, Wieland's *Oberon*, Friedrich de la Motte-Fouqué's *Undine*, and other classics.

As a professor of painting, Fuseli's courses were renowned for the acuity of his criticism, the elegance of his style and the profundity of his scientific insight. He translated Winkelmann's *Reflections on the Painting and Sculpture of the Greeks* into English, and was the author of an edition of Pilkington's *Dictionary of Painters*, with additions and corrections. He started but failed to complete a history of modern art.

Opinion is sharply divided about Fuseli's work. The critic Maurice Raynal, who was not drawn towards the fantastic, said of his work: 'It is the interpretation of nightmares. But his art is not genuine, to the extent that his visions appear to be less inspired than premeditated. He is an apriorist who retains the indelible mark of academic training. His painting is not as terrifying as he would like, it remains rather juvenile; it tells stories, it describes, the style remains cold and stiff.' Marcel Brion shows greater understanding in this respect in his work *German Painting* (1959): 'His best works are those where, in a fawn and russet chiaroscuro, he brings about the appearance of mysterious figures, the horse in *The Nightmare* at the museum in Zurich, the *Little Fairy* in Basel, the colossal heroes of Ariosto and Milton. He allows the supernatural to rush into the surface of real figures, with an ingenious candour that makes him move effortlessly into the unreal, which was his actual reality.' Marcel Brion goes on to insist on the influence he exerted on those who created German Romantic painting: 'Josef Anton Koch and Peter von Cornelius knew him well. The *Witches of Macbeth* in the first case, the *Death of Kriemhild* in the second, would never have been what they were without Fuseli and Carstens, in the same way as the *Entombment* of Eberhard Wächter, or the *Macbeth with the Witches* of Franz Pforr'. The principal charge levelled against Fuseli and his followers - indeed against all Romantic painters - is that they produced 'literary' painting. However, this is unfair criticism of what is unashamedly literary art, which saw no contradiction between this aspiration and the quality of its pictorial expression.

There are five portraits of Fuseli, the best of which is by his friend Sir Thomas Lawrence. A marble bust of Fuseli was executed by E.H. Baily.

Several of Fuseli's caricatures were shown in the exhibition *Karikaturen von Hogarth bis Daumier* (*Caricatures from Hogarth to Daumier*) at the Zurich Kunsthaus in 2001.

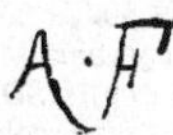

BIBLIOGRAPHY:

Pointon, M., *Milton and English Art*, Manchester, 1970. Powell, N., *Fuseli: The Nightmare*, London, 1972. Tomory, P., *The Life and Art of Henry Fuseli*, London, 1972. *Füssli*, exhibition catalogue, Musée du Petit Palais, Paris, 1975. Becker, Christoph/Hattendorff, Claudia, *Johann Heinrich Füssli. Das verlorene Paradies*, Hatje Cantz, Ostfildern, 1997.

MUSEUMS AND GALLERIES:

BASEL: *Treasure Hunter; Little Fairy* - DALLAS (MA): *Satan and the Birth of Sin* (Illustration of Paradise Lost by John Milton, Book II, 746-758) - LIVERPOOL: *Oedipus and his Daughters* - LONDON (Royal Academy of Arts): *Thor Battering the Midgard Serpent* (*Thor Battering the Midgard Serpent*) (1790, oil on canvas) - LONDON (Victoria and Albert Mus.): *Female Head; Part of the picture 'Dream of Queen Catherine'; Sketch of a Lady in 17th century Dress; Spirit in the Shape of a Young Girl Rising up in front of an Old Couple* - NOTTINGHAM: *Study of Figures; Study of Three Female Figures* (study) - ZURICH (Kunsthaus): *Falstaff in the Laundry Basket* (1792); *Silence* (1799-1902); *The Nightmare*.

AUCTION RECORDS:

LONDON, Sept 1848, *A Midsummer Night's Dream*, FRF 1,700. NEW YORK, 29 Jan 1902, *Portrait of Miss Johnson*, USD 300. LONDON, 8 April 1910, *Portrait of a Lady*, GBP 10. LONDON, 6 July 1925, *Scenes from Much Ado About Nothing*, GBP 54. LONDON, 25 March 1927, *Illustrations for Milton*, GBP 162. LONDON, 27 June 1927, *The Merry Wives of Windsor*, GBP 168. LONDON, 26 March 1928, *Theseus Receiving the Son of Ariadne*, GBP 36. LONDON, 5 Dec 1928, *Milton Child*, GBP 34. LONDON, 13 Nov 1934, *Birth of Shakespeare*, GBP 26. LONDON, 26 June 1936, *Mrs Pritchard*, GBP 22. LONDON, 12 March 1937, *Scene at the Tomb* (drawing) GBP 26; *Woman* (drawing) GBP 29. PARIS, 29 and 30 March 1943, *An Archer* (pen) FRF 3,200. PARIS, 30 June 1943, *Scene from Roman History* (pen, attributed) FRF 1,250. LONDON, 10 and 12 Feb 1947, *Female Nude on a Throne; Female Nude Sitting* (two drawings) GBP 37. PARIS, 17 March 1947, *Head of Erinnyes* (black chalk, heightened with white, attributed) FRF 550. LONDON, 9 May 1947, *Richard Nevill*, GBP 31. LONDON, 18 Nov 1960, *Cupid and Psyche*, GBP 336. LONDON, 10 March 1965, *Mrs Siddons and Lady Macbeth*, GBP 3,800. ZURICH, 21 Oct 1969, *The Couple*, CHF 30,000. LONDON, 18 March 1970, *Beatrice in Much Ado about Nothing*, GBP 6,500. LONDON, 13 Dec 1972, *Scene from the Illiad*, GBP 9,000. LONDON, 4 April 1973, *Lady Constance, Arthur and Slisbury*, GBP 5,800. BERN, 11 June 1976, *Young Girl Standing* (1797, drawing, 8 1/2 x 6 1/4 ins / 21.8 x 15.6 cm) CHF 6,400. ZURICH, 12 Nov 1976, *Silence* (c. 1799-1801, oil on canvas, 25 x 20 1/4 ins / 63.5 x 51.5 cm) CHF 80,000. ZURICH, 25 Nov 1977, *Euphrosyne...* (c. 1820, oil on canvas, 36 x 27 3/4 ins / 91.5 x 70.5 cm) CHF 44,000. LONDON, 30 Nov 1978, *Dr James Paying a Bill* (watercolour and pen, 11 1/2 x 8 1/4 ins / 29 x 21 cm) GBP 3,400. LONDON, 19 March 1981, *Themistocles at the Court of Admetus* (c. 1805, pen and wash/paper, 11 3/4 x 15 3/4 ins / 30 x 40 cm) GBP 7,500. LONDON, 23 Nov 1984, *Head of Caractacus* (oil on card, 9 x 7 ins / 22.9 x 17.8 cm) GBP 5,000. LONDON, 9 July 1985, *Study of a Female Portrait, probably Mrs Fuseli (front); Studies of Legs in Crayon (back)* (c. 1790-1800, black chalk heightened with white, 12 1/2 x 12 1/4 ins / 32 x 30.8 cm) GBP 105,000. AMSTERDAM, 12 Sept 1985, *Views around Lake Zurich* (c. 1795, coloured etching, 16 3/4 x 24 1/2 ins / 42.8 x 62.1 cm) NLG 28,000. LONDON, 22 Nov 1985, *The Creation of Eve* (oil on canvas, 50 x 40 ins / 126.9 x 101.6 cm) GBP 70,000. LONDON, 16 July 1987, *A Woman in Chains (front); A Figure (back)* (pen, brown ink and pencil, 18 3/4 x 11 ins / 47.5 x 28 cm) GBP 11,000. LONDON, 14 March 1990, *Lysander with Helena and Hermia in A Midsummer Night's Dream* (oil on canvas, 36 x 27 1/4 ins / 90.5 x 69.5 cm) GBP 41,800. LONDON, 12 April 1991, *The Three Witches Appear to Macbeth and Banquo* (oil on canvas, 34 1/4 x 44 ins / 87 x 112 cm) GBP 71,500. LONDON, 2 July 1991, *King David Put on Guard by the Prophet Nathan (front); Nude Standing (back)* (black chalk and grey wash, 24 1/4 x 36 1/4 ins / 61.6 x 91.8 cm) GBP 30,800. MONACO, 5-6 Dec 1991, *Vision of the Flood* (oil on canvas, 97 1/4 x 81 ins / 247 x 206 cm) FRF 777,000. NEW YORK, 13 Jan 1993, *Fallen Cavalry Soldier Attacked by an Enormous Serpent (front); Temptation of Job and his Wife by Satan (back)* (chalk, ink and wash) USD 22,000. LONDON, 13 July 1993, *Stoning of St Stephen* (1777, ink and wash, 7 3/4 x 12 1/2 ins / 19.9 x 31.8 cm) GBP 2,990. PARIS, 8 June 1994, *Perseus Holding Medusa's Head* (1816, pen, 8 3/4 x 7 1/4 ins / 22.5 x 18.4 cm) FRF 52,000. LONDON, 9 Nov 1994, *Head and Shoulder Portrait of the Artist's Wife* (oil on paper, oval, 9 x 7 1/4 ins / 22 x 18.5 cm) GBP 7,820. LONDON, 12 April 1995, *Romeo and Juliet* (oil on canvas, 55 1/2 x 43 3/4 ins / 141 x 111 cm) GBP 41,100. ZURICH, 12 Nov 1996, *Shakespeare Child between Tragedy and Comedy* (1805-1810, oil on canvas, 72 x 60 1/4 ins / 183 x 153 cm) CHF 110, 000. LONDON, 12 Nov 1997, *Seven-Branch Candlestick seen by St Joan* (1796, oil on canvas, 52 x 39 3/4 ins / 132 x 101 cm) GBP 137,900. NEW YORK, 28 Jan 1999, *Seated Nude* (pen and brown ink, double-sided, 9 x 7 ins / 22 x 17 cm) USD 16,000. LONDON, 6 July 1999, *Conversion of St Paul* (1778, pen with ink wash heightened with white, 7 x 12 ins / 19 x 30 cm) GBP 9,000. NEW YORK, 23 May 2000, *Vision of the Deluge* (oil on canvas, 97 x 81 ins / 247 x 206 cm) USD 130,000. ZURICH, 29 May 2000, *At the Theatre* (1770, pencil and ink, triptych, 7 x 20 ins / 19 x 50 cm) CHF 230,000. LONDON, 14 June 2001, *Themistocles at the Court of Admetus* (pen with ink wash over pencil, 12 x 15 ins / 31 x 39 cm) GBP 35,000. ZURICH, 19 June 2001, *Euphrosyne Visiting the Country Dance* (oil on canvas, 36 x 28 ins / 91 x 70 cm) CHF 100,000. NEW YORK, 23 Jan 2002, *Flora Surrounded by the Four Elements* (pencil, 9 x 7 ins / 24 x 18 cm) USD 24,000. LONDON, 21 March 2002, *Romeo and Juliet* (oil on canvas, 56 x 44 ins / 141 x 111 cm) GBP 30,000. NEW YORK, 24 Jan 2003, *Three Witches, or the Weird Sisters* (oil on canvas, 25 x 30 ins / 63 x 77 cm) USD 320,000. LONDON, 20 Feb 2003, *Vision of the Deluge* (oil on canvas, 100 x 83 ins / 254 x 210 cm) GBP 85,000. LONDON, 3 June 2004, *Callipyga - Mrs Fuseli with her Skirts Lifted to her Waist* (brown ink, 6 x 4 ins / 16 x 9 cm) GBP 8,500. LONDON, 8 July 2004, *Female Nude Lying Backwards on a Bed - Study for The Nightmare* (black chalk, 3 x 5 ins / 7 x 12 cm) GBP 26,000.

FUSELLA, Giovanni

Italian, 19th century.
Active in Florence.
Engraver.

Fusella is known for an engraving after Raphael.

FUSI, Francesco

Italian, 18th century.
Active in Milan.
Painter.

Francesco Fusi worked, among other things, on Modena Cathedral.

FUSILIER

French, 19th century.
Active in Amiens.
Painter. Portraits, genre scenes, landscapes.

His works includes a *Portrait of Abbé Bertin*.

FUSINA, Andrea da, the Elder
Italian, 16th century.
Born in Fusina; died 1526, in Milan.
Sculptor, architect.

Fusina is mentioned as having sculpted a *Mary Magdalene* for the façade of Milan Cathedral.

FUSINA, Andrea da, the Younger
Italian, 18th century.
Sculptor.

Andrea da Fusina the Younger lived and worked in Rome during the papacy of Clement XI.

FUSINATI, Giuseppe
Italian, 19th century.
Born 1803, in Arsié.
Engraver.

Fusinati was active in Italy. He engraved a *Magdalene* after Titian.

FUSS, Heinrich
Austrian, 19th - 20th century.
Born 6 July 1845, in Guntramsdorf, Lower Austria; died 10 December 1913, in Innsbruck.
Sculptor.

Heinrich Fuss was the son of an architect of the same name. He studied at the Akademie der Bildenden Künste in Vienna. He always showed a predilection for mythological and historical subjects, and also left a large number of portraits.

FUSS-AMORE, Élisabeth
French, 20th century.
Born in Paris.
Painter. Portraits, genre scenes, landscapes.

Élisabeth Fuss-Amore painted circus scenes and was particularly known for her portraits of children.

She exhibited in Paris at the Salon d'Automne from 1921, Salon des Artistes Indépendants, Salon de la Société Nationale des Beaux-Arts and Salon des Tuileries.

AUCTION RECORDS:
PARIS, 27 Dec 1926, *Dog,* FRF 350; *Child with Rose,* FRF 350. PARIS, 7 Feb 1927, *Landscape,* FRF 1,500. PARIS, 10 Nov 1943, *Landscape,* FRF 190. PARIS, 15 June 1994, *Popular Accordion Dance* (1920, oil on canvas, 31 1/2 x 31 1/2 ins / 80 x 80 cm) FRF 4,000.

FUSSBENDER, Joseph
German, 20th century.
Born 1903.
Painter.

Joseph Fussbender is mentioned by Herbert Read.

BIBLIOGRAPHY:
Read, Herbert, *A Concise History of Modern Painting,* Frederick A. Praeger, New York.

FÜSSEL, Carl Christian August
Danish, 19th century.
Born 4 May 1811, in Copenhagen; died 1 May 1849, in Middelfort.
Painter.

Carl Füssel was a pupil at the Kunstakademi in Copenhagen. He produced mostly genre paintings.

FUSSEL, Michael. See **FUSSELL**

FUSSELL, Alexander
British, 19th century.
Active in London.
Painter. History painting.

Alexander Fussel was a frequent exhibitor between 1838 and 1881.

FUSSELL, Charles Lewis
American, 19th - 20th century.
Born 25 October 1840, in Philadelphia; died 1909.
Active in St Media.
Painter, watercolourist. Portraits, genre scenes, landscapes, seascapes.

Charles Lewis Fussell was a pupil of Rothermel.

AUCTION RECORDS:
NEW YORK, 18 and 19 April 1934, *Abraham Lincoln,* USD 1,600. NEW YORK, 20 March 1980, *Pennsylvania Memorabilia* (1900, oil on card, 22 x 29 3/4 ins / 56 x 75.8 cm) USD 800. NEW YORK, 26 Oct 1984, *Quarry Workers* (1903, gouache and watercolour, 20 x 31 1/2 ins / 50.8 x 80.3 cm) USD 11,000. RALEIGH, 5 Nov 1985, *Pennsylvania Memorabilia* (1900, oil on card, 22 x 30 ins / 56 x 76.2 cm) USD 3,200. NEW YORK, 3 Dec 1987, *Stone Quarry* (1903, watercolour, 19 x 23 ins / 48.2 x 58.2 cm) USD 10,000. NEW YORK, 24 Jan 1989, *Our Old Colonial House* (1901, oil on canvas/card, 8 1/4 x 11 1/2 ins / 21 x 29.5 cm) USD 2,200. NEW YORK, 27 May 1993, *Spring Blossoms* (1902, watercolour and gouache/paper, 20 x 24 ins / 50.8 x 61 cm) USD 11,500. NEW YORK, 20 March 1996, *Children Wading in a Stream* (1905, watercolour and gouache/paper, 23 1/2 x 20 ins / 59.7 x 50.8 cm) USD 2,530. NEW YORK, 11 March 1999, *Summer Afternoon* (watercolour and gouache, 20 x 13 ins / 51 x 34 cm) USD 1,900. NEW YORK, 11 March 1999, *Backyard* (1902, watercolour and gouache, 24 x 20 ins / 60 x 50 cm) USD 9,500. DOWNINGTON, 21 April 2000, *Pennsylvania Memorabilia, Trompe l'oeil* (1900, tempera on board, 22 x 30 ins / 56 x 76 cm) USD 1,700.

FUSSELL, Joseph
British, 19th - 20th century.
Born 1818, in Birmingham; died 6 May 1912, in Point Loma (California).
Painter, engraver. Religious subjects, genre scenes, landscapes with figures, landscapes, seascapes, harbour scenes.

Joseph Fussell studied at the Royal Academy Schools. He worked as an engraver and is known for illustrating the *Kittos Encyclopedia* and similar works. He became a teacher at Nottingham School of Art. Fussell exhibited frequently in London from 1821 to 1845, particularly at the Royal Academy.

MUSEUMS AND GALLERIES:
NOTTINGHAM (Castle Mus. & AG): *Spring, Noon.*

FUSSELL, Michael, or Fussel
British, 20th century.
Born 1927, in Southampton; died 1974.
Painter. Landscapes, still-lifes.

Michael Fussell studied at St Martin's School of Art and the Royal College of Art in London. He began by painting landscapes and still-lifes in a very sombre range of tones. In 1961, he started to produce a kind of white or silver low relief, using a combination of 'froissé' paper and medium, which evokes the effect of light on seascapes or shores. He took part in many group exhibitions, including the Carnegie International in Pittsburgh in 1961. He held solo exhibitions in London in 1956, 1958 and 1962.

MUSEUMS AND GALLERIES:
LONDON (Tate Collection): *Skywards* (1961, oil and mixed media/canvas).

FUSSIN, Nicolas Henri Joseph de
French, 20th century.
Painter. Landscapes with figures.

AUCTION RECORDS:
PARIS, 12 June 1929, *Italian Landscape with Peasant Family and their Animals; Animals Grazing in a Mountain Landscape* (collection) FRF 4,000.

FÜSSLI, Anna
Swiss, 18th century.
Born 16 September 1749, in Zurich; died 24 February 1772, in Zurich.

Painter. Flowers, insects.
Anna was the daughter of Johann Caspar Füssli.

FÜSSLI, Elisabeth
Swiss, 18th century.
Born 15 April 1744, in Zurich; died 1780, in Zurich.
Painter. Flowers, insects.
Elisabeth was the daughter of Johann Caspar Füssli, and is mentioned in the annals of the Swiss Museum.

FÜSSLI, Friedrich Salomon
Swiss, 19th century.
Born 31 December 1802, in Zurich; died 1847, in Zurich.
Draughtsman.
Salomon Füssli was the son of Rudolf Hendrich.

FÜSSLI, Hans Caspar
Swiss, 18th century.
Born 1743, in Zurich; died 4 May 1786, in Winterthur.
Painter. Flowers, insects.
Hans Caspar was the son of Johann Caspar Füssli.

FÜSSLI, Hans Rudolf, the Elder
Swiss, 17th - 18th century.
Born 1645, in Zurich; died 1711, in Zurich.
Painter.
Hans Rudolf Füssli the Elder's father was David Füssli.

FÜSSLI, Hans Rudolf, the Younger
Swiss, 18th century.
Born 12 February 1680, in Zurich; died 1761, in Horgen.
Painter.
This artist was the father of Johann Caspar Füssli.

FÜSSLI, Heinrich, the Elder
Swiss, 18th century.
Born 17 March 1720, in Horgen; died 10 January 1802, in Horgen.
Painter, draughtsman.
Heinrich Füssli the Elder was the son of Rudolf Füssli the Elder, and painted mainly landscapes.

FÜSSLI, Heinrich, the Younger
Swiss, 18th - 19th century.
Born 14 April 1755, in Horgen; died 1 May 1829, in Zurich.
Draughtsman, engraver. Landscapes.
Heinrich Füssli the Younger travelled to Switzerland and produced drawings that were published under the title *Wonderful Places in Switzerland*. He was a pupil of his uncle Johann Caspar Füssli.

FÜSSLI, Johann
Swiss, 19th century.
Born 1784, in Zurich; died 1844, in Paris.
Draughtsman.
Johann Füssli settled in Paris in 1812.

FÜSSLI, Johann or Hans Heinrich.
See **FUSELI, Henry**

FÜSSLI, Johann Caspar
Swiss, 18th century.
Born 1707, in Zurich; died 6 May 1782, in Zurich.
Painter, draughtsman. Mythological subjects, portraits.
Johann Caspar Füssli was a pupil of Gran and Meyens in Vienna. Having traveled widely in France, Italy and Germany, he lived in Nuremberg and Ludwigsburg, among other places. He was also a writer on art.

BIBLIOGRAPHY:
Boerlin-Brodbeck, Yvonne, *Johann Caspar Füssli und sein Briefwechsel mit Jean-Georges Wille: Marginalien zu Kunstliteratur und Kunstpolitik un der zweiten Hälfte des 18. Jahrhunderts*, Schweizerisches Institut für Kunstwissenschaft, Zurich, 1978.

AUCTION RECORDS:
LONDON, 7 July 1983, *Medea (recto); Flight of a Murderer (verso)* (1771 and 1774, brush and wash/pencil outlines, 17 1/2 x 25 1/4 ins / 44.5 x 64 cm) GBP 38,000. ZURICH, 12 June 1995, *Portraits of the Historian and Counsellor Johann Heinrich Fussli and his Wife Maria Barbara Fussli-Schulthess* (oil on wood, a pair, each 6 3/4 x 5 ins / 17 x 12.5 cm) CHF 4,600. AMSTERDAM, 4 May 1999, *Flowers and Fruit in Baskets with Peaches and Roses on Ledges* (oil on canvas, octagonal, a pair, 15 x 11 ins / 37 x 27 cm) NLG 20,000.

FÜSSLI, Johann Melchior
Swiss, 18th century.
Born 1677, in Zurich; died 1736, in Zurich.
Painter, engraver.
Some of this artist's engravings are to be found in the collection of the art society in Zurich. He was a pupil of Joh. Meyer in Zurich and of C.-F. Blesendorf in Berlin.

FÜSSLI, Johann Rudolf, the Elder
Swiss, 18th century.
Born 5 September 1709, in Zurich; died 12 September 1793, in Zurich.
Painter.
Johann Rudolf Füssli the Elder studied in Zurich under the guidance of the painter and engraver Johann Melchior Füssli. In Paris he executed miniatures under the guidance of Loutherbourg.

FÜSSLI, Johann Rudolf, the Younger
Swiss, 18th century.
Born 1737, in Zurich; died April 1806, in Vienna.
Painter.
Johann Rudolf Füssli the Younger began his studies under the guidance of his father, Johann Caspar Füssli, and completed them in Vienna.

FÜSSLI, Konrad
Swiss, 18th century.
Born 1675, in Zurich; died 1743, in Zurich.
Miniaturist.
Konrad Füssli was the son of Mathias Füssli III.

FÜSSLI, Mathias I
Swiss, 17th century.
Born 1598, in Zurich; died 20 October 1665, in Zurich.
Painter, engraver.
Mathias Füssli began his studies under the guidance of Gotthard Ringgli and completed them during trips to Italy. He produced landscapes, war scenes and frescoes.

FÜSSLI, Mathias II
Swiss, 17th century.
Born 1639, in Zurich; died 27 October 1708.
Painter. Portraits.

FÜSSLI, Mathias III
Swiss, 17th - 18th century.
Born 3 March 1671, in Zurich; died 11 September 1739, in Zurich.
Painter. Portraits.
This artist, the son of the painter Mathias Füssli II, studied in Italy under B. Luti.

FÜSSLI, Rudolf Heinrich
Swiss, 19th century.
Born 1791, in Zurich; died 1828, in Zurich.
Draughtsman.
Rudolf Heinrich Füssli produced illustrations for the work *The Most Original Swiss Costumes*.

FÜSSLI, Wilhelm Heinrich
Swiss, 19th - 20th century.
Born 16 January 1830, in Zurich; died 11 January 1916, in Baden-Baden, Germany.
Painter. Figures, portraits.
Wilhelm Füssli studied in Munich and Venice, where he became disenchanted with modern painting. In Paris, the influence of Couture and the art treasures of the Louvre confirmed him in his ideas. He exhibited in Zurich.
AUCTION RECORDS:
LUCERNE, 21 May 1980, *Portrait of a Young Woman* (1871, oil on canvas, 56 x 40 1/2 ins / 142 x 103 cm) CHF 2,200. HANOVER, 25 Sept 1982, *Portrait of a Child* (1860, oil on canvas, 19 3/4 x 15 1/2 ins / 50 x 39.5 cm) DEM 4,000. ZURICH, 5 June 1996, *The Student* (1887, oil on canvas, 22 x 18 1/4 ins / 56 x 46.5 cm) CHF 1,725. ZURICH, 10 Dec 1996, *The Family of Julius Meyer* (1867, oil on canvas, 78 3/4 x 98 1/2 ins / 200 x 250 cm) CHF 10,925.

FUSSMANN, Klaus
German, 20th century.
Born 1938.
Painter (gouache), watercolourist, draughtsman.
Portraits, interiors with figures, still-lifes, landscapes.
Klaus Fussmann featured in *New Subjectivity* in 1976, an exhibition within the framework of the Paris autumn festival, the idea of Jean Clair, and again in 1979 in *New Subjectivity Nouvelle Subjectivité*, an exhibition arranged by Jean Clair on the return of figurative expression and the genre scene in painting at the end of the 20th century, at the Palais des Beaux-Arts in Brussels.
AUCTION RECORDS:
MUNICH, 2 June 1980, *View of the Studio* (watercolour, 28 1/4 x 28 ins / 71.5 x 71 cm) DEM 2,100. MUNICH, 1 June 1981, *Interior* (1977, pen/paper, 28 x 28 1/4 ins / 71 x 72 cm) DEM 2,100. MUNICH, 30 May 1983, *Winter Landscape* (1977, gouache, 26 1/4 x 28 1/4 ins / 66.5 x 71.5 cm) DEM 3,200. HAMBURG, 9 June 1983, *Barbara F. and Gregor F. outside Beveroe* (1978, oil on canvas, 63 x 67 ins / 160 x 170 cm) DEM 18,000. COLOGNE, 4 June 1985, *Pink Bed in front of a Mirror* (1979, oil on canvas, 61 x 67 1/4 ins / 155 x 171 cm) DEM 11,000. AMSTERDAM, 31 May 1994, *Still-life* (1978, oil on canvas, 12 x 14 1/4 ins / 30.5 x 36.5 cm) NLG 3,220. AMSTERDAM, 4 June 1996, *Studio* (1978, watercolour/paper, 28 1/4 x 28 1/4 ins / 71.5 x 72 cm) NLG 7,080. AMSTERDAM, 2-3 June 1997, *Protrait of Georg Fussmann* (1981, watercolour/paper, 25 1/2 x 29 1/2 ins / 65 x 75 cm) NLG 4,956.

FUST, Willi
Swiss, 20th century.
Born 1926, in Winterthur; died 2003.
Painter.
Op Art.
Willi Fust was brought up in Basel. He trained as a locksmith for two years, then as an architectural draughtsman. Since 1953, he worked as an architect in Olten. He had a parallel career as a painter, taking part in many group exhibitions in Switzerland and abroad. He has held solo exhibitions in major Swiss cities since 1963, at the Galerie Suzanne Bollag in Zurich, in Olten and other cities.

His paintings are made up of broad horizontal bands or of squares divided by the two medians or by the two diagonals or by the square inscribed between the centres of the four sides, and are either in monochrome, or have colours allocated as a function of a dominant tone that gives each painting its name. This kind of painting derives more from Op Art than from Minimalism.

FUSTER, Alberto
Mexican, 19th century.
Born in Tlacotulpan.
Painter.
Alberto Fuster received a commendation at the Exposition Universelle of 1900.

FUSTERO, Elvira
Spanish, 20th - 21st century.
Born 1949, in Saragossa.
Painter (mixed media).
Elvira Fustero lives and works in Barcelona. She has taken part in numerous group exhibitions since 1986, in Madrid and in several other Spanish towns and cities, as well as abroad. She has also shown her work in solo exhibitions since 1976, mainly in Barcelona.
BIBLIOGRAPHY:
Catálogo nacionál de arte contemporaneo 1990-1991, Ibérico 2Mil, Barcelona, 1990-1991.

FUSTINI, Giuseppe
Italian, 18th - 19th century.
Born 1766, in Fidenza; died 1816, in Parma.
Miniaturist.

FÜSTLER, Heinrich
Austrian, 19th century.
Active in Vienna c. 1832.
Miniaturist.

FÜTERER, Ulrich
German, 15th century.
Born in Landshut (Bavaria); died c. 1498, in Munich.
Painter, poet.
Ulrich Füterer worked in Landshut and Munich His main works are some large frescoes that he painted in the Munich town hall. He also made stained glass.

FUTTERER, Josef
German, 19th - 20th century.
Born 1871; died 1930.
Painter (gouache). Scenes with figures, figures, portraits, genre scenes, flowers.
AUCTION RECORDS:
MUNICH, 26 May 1978, *Couple with a Dog in a Garden* (c. 1905, oil on card, 10 1/4 x 7 ins / 26 x 17.5 cm) DEM 4,800; *Young Woman peeling an Apple* (gouache, 9 1/2 x 7 1/4 ins / 24 x 18.5 cm) DEM 2,400. MUNICH, 30 May 1980, *Rustic Scene* (c. 1905, oil on card, 31 x 22 ins / 79 x 56 cm) DEM 3,800. MUNICH, 13 Sept 1984, *Bunch of Flowers in a Vase* (oil on card, 31 1/2 x 25 1/2 ins / 80 x 65 cm) DEM 3,800. LUCERNE, 15 May 1986, *Portrait of Max Pallenberg as Zawadil* (1914, oil on canvas, 39 3/4 x 33 1/2 ins / 101 x 85 cm) CHF 3,600.

FUX, Demenik
Austrian, 18th century.
Born c. 1752; died 21 January 1788.
Active in Vienna.
Painter.
Demenik Fux was the brother of Franz Fux.

FUX, Franz
Austrian, 18th century.
Born 1745, in Vienna.
Painter. Portraits.
There are two known signed portraits by this artist, who was a pupil at the academy in Vienna.

FUX, Franz Xaver
German, 18th century.
Active c. 1745.
Draughtsman.
There is a single known work by this artist called *View*, engraved by Gleich.

FUX, J.-G.
German, 18th century.
Painter.
There are records of a signed work by an artist of this name in the chapel of Schallenkamp near Ambach.

FUX, Johann Adam
German, 18th century.
Active in Griesstetten c. 1750.
Painter.
There is a fresco signed by Johann Adam Fux in the church of the small town of Griesstetten in Bavaria.

FUX, Johann Georg
Austrian, 18th century.
Born 1755, in Vienna.
Painter.
Johann Georg was the brother of Franz Fux.

FUX, Josef
Austrian, 19th century.
Born 2 December 1841, in Steinhof; died 30 March 1904, in Vienna.
Painter. History painting, genre scenes, portraits.
Josef Fux was a pupil at the art academy in Vienna under Christian Rubens. He completed his studies in contact with Makart and Matejko, and subsequently worked in Vienna.
MUSEUMS AND GALLERIES:
VIENNA: *Going Hunting*.

FUX, Wilhelm
Austrian, 19th century.
Born c. 1808.
Miniaturist.
Wilhelm Fux was a pupil at the academy in Vienna in c. 1820.

FUXA Y LEAL, Manuel
Spanish, 19th century.
Born c. 1850, in Barcelona.
Painter.
Manuel Fuxa y Leal studied at the school of fine arts in Barcelona. He was awarded a bronze medal in Madrid in 1871 and a silver medal in 1881, and also received a silver medal at the Exposition Universelle in Paris in 1900.

FUXEDER, Adam Josef
Austrian, 18th century.
Born 5 November 1763, in Vienna.
Painter.

FUXEDER, Franz, the Elder
Austrian, 18th century.
Born 17 January 1725, in Vienna; died 1797.
Painter.
Fuxeder was painter to the Imperial court and mainly executed genre paintings.

FUXEDER, Franz, the Younger
Austrian, 18th century.
Born 16 May 1752, in Vienna.
Painter.

FUXEDER, Jacob
Austrian, 19th century.
Active in Vienna.
Painter. Landscapes.

FUXEDER, Johann, the Elder
Austrian, 18th century.
Born c. 1691; died 17 May 1743.
Active in Vienna.
Painter.
Johann Fuxeder the Elder was the father of Josef the Elder, Johann the Younger and Karl.

FUXEDER, Johann, the Younger
Austrian, 18th century.
Born 6 March 1716, in Vienna.
Painter.
This artist was the son of Johann the Elder.

FUXEDER, Josef, the Elder
Austrian, 18th century.
Born 1710, in Vienna.
Painter.

FUXEDER, Josef, the Younger
Austrian, 18th century.
Born c. 1734; died 6 January 1789.
Active in Vienna.
Miniaturist.

FUXEDER, Josef Andreas
Austrian, 18th century.
Born 16 July 1747, in Vienna.
Painter.
Josef was the son of Josef Fuxeder the Elder.

FUXEDER, Karl
Austrian, 18th century.
Born 19 February 1721, in Vienna.
Painter.
Karl was the son of Johann Fuxeder the Elder.

FUXEDER, Martin
Austrian, 18th century.
Active in Vienna.
Painter.
Martin Fuxeder was the father of Josef the Younger and Franz the Elder.

FUXEDER, Michael
Austrian, 18th century.
Born 6 September 1744, in Vienna.
Painter.
Michael was the son of Josef Fuxeder the Elder.

FUXHOFFER, Josef
Austrian, 18th century.
Born 1709, in Vienna; died 5 July 1785, in Vienna.
Painter.
Josef Fuxhoffer was a pupil of Vasal, and may also have lived in Mariahilf.

FUXHOFFER, Matthias
Austrian, 18th century.
Active in Vienna in 1768.
Engraver.
Matthias was almost certainly the son of Josef Fuxhoffer.

FUYANG. See **ZHANG FU**

FUYO, real name: Oshima Mohyu, familiar names: Ikki, Kondo Itsuki, artist names: Fuyo, Chugakugashi, Hyogaku sanjin, Kantan no kyo, Ko Fuyo
Japanese, 18th century.
Born 1722; died 1784, in Tokyo.
Painter.
Nanga (literati) school.
Fuyo was a Nanga style landscape painter who is also known as a seal carver. He lived in Kyoto and was a friend of the Ike family of painters.

FUYO, real name: Suzuki Yo, popular name: Shimbei, artist names: Fuyo, Roren
Japanese, 18th - 19th century.
Born 1749; died 1816.
Painter.
Nanga school.
Fuyo was a gifted writer of prose and poetry and a Nanga style painter of landscapes and portraits. He studied under Buncho (1725-1794) in Edo (now Tokyo) and later was in the service of Lord Awa.

FUYTER, Jacob de
Dutch, 17th century.
Born 1618; died 1686, in Amsterdam.
Painter.
He was the brother of Louis and Leon de Fuyter.

FUYTER, Louis de
Dutch, 17th century.
Born 1613, in The Hague; died c. 1669, in Amsterdam.
Painter.

FUYTER, OR FUIJTER, Leonard de, or Leon de, Lyon de
Dutch, 17th century.
Died 1658, in Amsterdam.
Painter.

FUZER, P.
French, 19th century.
Engraver. Historical figures.
MUSEUMS AND GALLERIES:
LE PUY-EN-VELAY: *General Lafayette* (coloured engraving, after Adam).

FUZIER, François
French, 8th century.
Active in Grenoble.
Sculptor.

FYFE, William Baxter Collier
British, 19th century.
Born c. 1836, in Dundee; died 15 September 1882, in London.
Painter. History painting, portraits, genre scenes, landscapes.

William Baxter Collier Fyfe was educated at the Royal Academy of Scotland. He exhibited his first major work at the 1861 Exhibition (*The Abdication of Queen Mary at Lochleven Castle*). He settled in London in 1863 and went on to paint portraits, and the occasional landscape or genre composition.
AUCTION RECORDS:
LONDON, 10 Dec 1923, *Day of Rest*, GBP 23. LONDON, 23 March 1927, *Grandfather's Watch*, GBP 9. PERTH, 7 April 1980, *Young Girl Hanging Out Washing* (1875, oil on canvas, 32 x 22 ins / 81 x 56 cm) GBP 520. LONDON, 23 Nov 1982, *Young Woman at Work in a Kitchen* (1870, oil on canvas, 40 x 32 ins / 101.5 x 81 cm) GBP 1,200. AUCHTERARDER, 1 Sept 1987, *Back from Market* (1864, oil on canvas, 24 3/4 x 30 ins / 63 x 76 cm) GBP 10,500. NEW YORK, 10 Feb 1998, *Little Princess* (oil on canvas, 33 x 24 3/4 ins / 83.8 x 63 cm) USD 6,900. LONDON, 5 June 2001, *Brotherly Love* (oil on canvas) GBP 2,000. COLOGNE, 24 Nov 2001, *Peasant Boy Admonishing a Begging Dog* (1873, oil on canvas, 32 x 30 ins / 82 x 76 cm) DEM 6,500. LONDON, 15 April 2002, *Abdication of Mary Queen of Scots at Lochleven Castle* (1860, oil on canvas, 57 x 80 ins / 146 x 204 cm) GBP 15,000. LONDON, 5 Sept 2002, *Bide a See* (1873, oil on canvas, 36 x 26 ins / 91 x 66 cm) GBP 6,000. LONDON, 6 March 2003, *Orange Girl* (1879, oil on canvas, 15 x 10 ins / 39 x 26 cm) GBP 2,800. LEYBURN, 17 July 2003, *Young Flower Seller* (oil on canvas, 13 x 9 ins / 33 x 24 cm) GBP 1,100.

FYHN, Jens Jørgen
Danish, 19th century.
Born 9 February 1788, in Kolding; died 25 February 1866, in Copenhagen.
Painter.

Jens Jørgen Fyhn was self-taught and executed an altarpiece for a church in Copenhagen.

FYLL, Robert
British, 16th century.
Active in London in 1502.
Painter.

FYNIAN
German, 14th century.
Active in Brunswick (Lower Saxony).
Sculptor.

FYNSON, Jacques and Louis. See **FINSON**

FYODOROV, Vyacheslav Andreyevitch
20th century.
Born 1918, in Ivanovo-Voznessenski (near Moscow), Russia; died 1985.
Painter. Landscapes.

Fyodorov began his studies at the Ivanovo School of Art, then went to the Repin Institute of Art in St Petersburg, where he obtained a degree in 1951. He was an eminent member of the Artists' Union. Many of his works can be found in Russian museums and private collections.
AUCTION RECORDS:
LONDON, 2 May 1996, *The Jetty* (1947, oil on canvas/card, 13 1/2 x 22 3/4 ins / 34 x 58 cm) GBP 632. LONDON, 11 April 1997, GBP -.

FYOL, Hans
German, 15th - 16th century.
Born c. 1450; died 1530.
Active in Frankfurt am Main.
Painter.

Hans was the son of Konrad Fyol.

FYOL, Konrad
German, 15th century.
Died c. 1500.
Active in Frankfurt am Main.
Painter.

Konrad was the son of Sebald Fyol and father of Hans Fyol. He did some work at the church of Rödelheim and at the monastery of Seebold.
MUSEUMS AND GALLERIES:
ANTWERP: *Adoration of the Magi; Nativity; Circumcision* (triptych).

FYOL, Sebald
German, 15th century.
Died 1463, in Frankfurt am Main.
Painter.

Sebald Fyol may have been born in Nuremberg, Bavaria. A painting in the museum in Frankfurt depicting *The Virgin in the Gardens of Paradise* has been attributed to him.

FYSSEL, Gottlieb
Czech, 18th century.
Painter.

Gottlieb Fyssel produced a painting of *St Candida* for the town of Tepl (now Tepla Mesto) in 1766.

FYT, Jacob, or Vyt
Flemish School, 17th century.
Painter.

He was a pupil of Hans van den Berch in Antwerp in 1619. He was made a master of the Guild of St Luke in Antwerp in 1644.
AUCTION RECORDS:
PARIS, 4 May 1943, *Flowers and Still-life* (attributed) FRF 9,100.

FYT, Jan
Flemish School, 17th century.
Born 1611, in Antwerp; died 11 September 1661, in Antwerp.
Painter, draughtsman, engraver. Hunting scenes, animals, dogs, still-lifes.

Fyt entered the studio of Jan van Berch in 1621, at the age of 12, and later became a pupil of the Flemish painter Frans Snyders. In 1629, at the age of 20, he was incorporated as a master of the Guild of St Luke in Antwerp. He is known to have left for Italy shortly afterwards, although the date and duration of the trip are uncertain; in 1650 he became a member of the Guild of Romanists, composed exclusively of artists who had travelled to Italy. His first collection of etchings features a title-page and dedication in Italian, dated 1640, beneath an emblem comprising two greyhounds; the other works in the collection are dated 1642. Fyt had clearly returned from Italy by 1645, the date of a painting incorporating figures by Jordaens, executed for the fraternity of archers. The animals in the picture have sometimes been attributed to Rubens, although the latter died in 1640, when Fyt was almost certainly in Italy. Fyt's collaborators were, however, pupils of Rubens, including Jordaens and, most notably, Thomas Willeboirts Bosschaert, with whom he painted *Diana at Rest*, now in Vienna. In 1652 he was Dean of the Guild of Romanists. He married in 1654. Highly prolific, Fyt seems to have painted mostly animal subjects, particularly dogs and game, although a number of still-lifes and flower paintings also survive. Fyt experimented boldly with composition, lighting and texture in his work and was at the forefront of a revival in Baroque still-life painting. His rendering of the fur of a recently killed animal conveys an extraordinarily tactile sense of warmth and softness.

J. Fijt. f. Johnus. Fyt. f. J.Fy

BIBLIOGRAPHY:

Bernt, W., *Netherlandish Painters of the Seventeenth century*, Oxford, 1969. Keys, G., '*Still-life Drawings by Fyt and Snyders*' in *Burlington Magazine*, Cxix, 1977. Sullivan, S. A., *The Dutch Gamepiece*, Totowa and Montclair (NJ), 1984.

MUSEUMS AND GALLERIES:

AMIENS: *Game on a Stone Slab; Game and Hunting Equipment* - ANTWERP: *Eagles; Two Hares* - BAYONNE: *Cat Waiting to Pounce on a Dead Pheasant* - BERLIN: three still-lifes; *Diana Hunting* - BÉZIERS: *Wild Cat on the Scent of Game* - BORDEAUX: *Still-life* - BREMEN: *Kitchen Scene* - BRUSSELS: *Cart Loaded with Game Pulled by Dogs; Flowers and Fruit in a Landscape; Still-life* - BUDAPEST: *Hunting Dog; Still-life* - CHERBOURG: *Arms and Game Guarded by Dogs* - DUBLIN: *Study of a Boar* - DUNKIRK: two still-lifes - EDINBURGH (Nat. Gal. of Scotland): *A Wolf* (oil on canvas); *A Dead Wolf* (oil on canvas) - FLORENCE (NG): *Poultry Alarmed by the Approach of a Falcon* - FRANKFURT AM MAIN: *Still-life* - GENEVA (Mus. Ariana): *Boar Hunt* - GRAZ: *Ducks Seized by Hunting Dogs; Still-life* - HAMBURG: *Still-life* - KASSEL: *Dead Game; Game Guarded by a Dog; Dogs beside a Kill* - LA FÈRE: three still-lifes - LIÈGE: *Fruit* - LILLE: *Animals* - LONDON (NG): *A Still-life with Fruit, Dead Game and a Parrot* (1645-1650, oil on canvas, attributed); *Dead Birds in a Landscape* (1640s, oil on canvas) - LONDON (Wallace Collection): *Still-life with a Page* (1644, oil on canvas) - MADRID (Prado): *Poultry-seller; Dead Game; Inn; Hare Chased by Dogs; Dog Attacking a Bird of Prey; Concert of Birds* - MAINZ: *Animals* - METZ: *Head of a Dog and Dead Partridges* - MILAN (Pinacoteca di Brera): *Dead Game* - MUNICH: *Roe Deer Chased by Dogs; Bear Hunt; Boar Hunt; Dead Swan on a Table with Fruit; Two Dogs Fighting over a Calf's Head in a Basket* - NANTES (MBA): *Hunting Dog Chasing a Hare; Cat Eyeing Game* - NARBONNE: *Woman Cooking* - OPORTO: *Dead Game* - OSLO: *Dogs and Wolves Fighting* - PARIS (Louvre): *Game and Fruit; Game under a Cloche; Dog Devouring Game; Game* - ROHRAU (Schlossmuseum, Graf Harrach'sche Familiensammlung): *Guard Dog; Garland of Fruit* - ROTTERDAM: *Dead Peacock* - ST PETERSBURG (Hermitage): *Still-life; Fruit* - STOCKHOLM: *Dead Game; Dead Woodcock; Dead Quails and a Partridge; Still-life* - VENICE (Gal. dell'Accademia): *Still-life* - VIENNA: *Animals and Fruit; Hunting Spoils; Fruit and Poultry; Diana Hunting.*

AUCTION RECORDS:

PARIS, 1838, *Fish Market*, FRF 370; *Basket of Fruit with Game; Cat and Dog*, FRF 470. PARIS, 1852, *Game Guarded by Dogs*, FRF 2,050. PARIS, 1864, *Game, Fruit and Flowers*, FRF 2,550. PARIS, 1869, *Birds Envious of the Peacock*, FRF 16,100. PARIS, 1870, *Fruit and Game*, FRF 18,000. PARIS, 1882, *Game and Fruit*, FRF 22,500. PARIS, 1890, *Fruit and Game*, FRF 4,200; *Fruit*, FRF 2,700. PARIS, 1894, *Dogs at Rest*, FRF 3,200. PARIS, 4 March 1895, *Lion Hunt*, FRF 3,400. PARIS, 1898, *Birds*, FRF 920; *Game*, FRF 740. PARIS, 1898, *Still-life*, FRF 3,950. PARIS, 1899, *Dead Birds*, FRF 500. PARIS, 1899, *Hunting the Hare*, FRF 2,875. MUNICH, 5 June 1899, *Still-life*, FRF 350. PARIS, 31 March 1900, *Game*, FRF 600. PARIS, 22 May 1919, *Hunting the Hare*, FRF 3,500. PARIS, 18 Dec 1920, *Hunting Dogs*, FRF 15,500. PARIS, 11-12 Feb 1921, *Still-life*, FRF 1,550. PARIS, 21 April 1921, *Still-life*, FRF 7,500. PARIS, 13 Jan 1923, *Still-life*, FRF 5,100. PARIS, 15 Feb 1923, *Return from the Hunt*, FRF 580. PARIS, 26-27 March 1923, *Dog near a Basket with Dead Game, a Hen and a Chick*, FRF 980. LONDON, 8 June 1923, *Landscape with a Dog and Game; Landscape* (together) GBP 21. LONDON, 1 Feb 1924, *Landscape with Dogs and Game*, GBP 94; *Dead Birds*, GBP 10. PARIS, 5 June 1924, *Dog Guarding Game*, FRF 5,800. PARIS, 17-18 June 1924, *Birds Squabbling*, FRF 20,000; *Game and a Basket of Fruit*, FRF 8,600. LONDON, 27 June 1924, *Flowers in a Glass Vase*, GBP 151. LONDON, 12 Feb 1925, *Parrot, Dog and Dead Hare* (drawing) GBP 252. LONDON, 1 May 1925, *Dead Game and Dogs*, GBP 120. PARIS, 8 May 1925, *Game and a Stoneware Pitcher on a Stone Table*, FRF 4,000. LONDON, 11 May 1925, *Cockfight*, GBP 168. LONDON, 17 July 1925, *Dogs and Dead Game*, GBP 294. LONDON, 6 Dec 1926, *Dead Game on a Table*, GBP 63. LONDON, 6 May 1927, *Basket ofFruit and Dead Game*, GBP 33. LONDON, 18 July 1928, *Still-life*, GBP 52. PARIS, 8 Nov 1928, *Dead Birds*, FRF 1,000. LONDON, 7 Dec 1928, *Dead Hare*, GBP 283. PARIS, 24 April 1929, *Still-life*, FRF 3,700. LONDON, 27 June 1930, *Dog and Dead Game*, GBP 44. LONDON, 18 July 1930, *Fruit and Dead Game*, GBP 120. PARIS, 26 Feb 1931, *Hunting Trophy* (attributed) FRF 2,950. LONDON, 8 July 1932, *Dog and Dead Game*, GBP 15. PARIS, 8 Dec 1933, *Dead Birds*, FRF 2,100. LONDON, 2 March 1934, *Landscape*, GBP 16. LONDON, 26 June 1934, *Still-life*, GBP 28. PARIS, 23 Oct 1935, *Dead Hare*, FRF 380. PARIS, 5 March 1936, *Hunting Trophy* (attributed) FRF 2,320. LONDON, 24 July 1936, *Dog and Dead Game*, GBP 31. PARIS, 29 Oct 1936, *Still-life* (attributed) FRF 5,450. LONDON, 24 Feb 1937, *Dogs and Dead Game*, GBP 145. LONDON, 12 March 1937, *Dog and Dead Game* (drawing) GBP 39. LONDON, 22 Dec 1938, *Parrots and Fruit*, GBP 26. LONDON, 23 June 1939, *Dead Game* (drawing) GBP 23. LONDON, 16 Feb 1940, *Dead Birds*, GBP 78. LONDON, 12 Sept 1941, *Dead Game*, GBP 25. PARIS, 15 June 1942, *Dead Birds* (attributed) FRF 11,000. GLASGOW, 20 Oct 1942, *Birds*, GBP 16. PARIS, 23 Nov 1942, *Still-life*, FRF 95,000. LONDON, 24 Sept 1943, *Dead Game*, GBP 42. LONDON, 18 Feb 1944, *Poultry*, GBP 73. PARIS, 6-7 Dec 1944, *Dogs Guarding Game* (attributed) FRF 1,600. NEW YORK, 15 March 1945, *Still-life*, USD 300. PARIS, 18 April 1945, *Wildfowl* (attributed) FRF 15,300. LONDON, 17 Oct 1945, *Fruit and Dead Game*, GBP 320. PARIS, July 1946, *Cat, Dog, Wildfowl and Fish*, FRF 15,500. PARIS, 21 Oct 1946, *Hunting the Lynx* (attributed) FRF 6,000. LONDON, 31 Jan 1947, *Dead Game*, GBP 47. PARIS, 17 Feb 1947, *Falcons*, FRF 26,000. LONDON, 25 June 1947, *Fruit and Game*, GBP 50. PARIS, 5 Dec 1951, *Vase of Flowers*, FRF 520,000. LUCERNE, 3 Dec 1955, *Still-life with a Vase of Flowers*, CHF 7,100. VIENNA, 10 June 1958, *Nine Hares*, ATS 18,000. BERN, 16 June 1960, *Hunting Trophies and a Hare*, CHF 1,350. LONDON, 28 Nov 1962, *Still-life*, GBP 1,300. LONDON, 20 March 1964, *Gentleman Hunting with a Falcon*, Gns 950. LONDON, 3 March 1965, *Still-life with Game*, GBP 2,500. NEW YORK, 3 Nov 1967, *Poultry and Rabbits in a Park; Interior with Dead Game* (together) USD 7,000. COLOGNE, 27 Nov 1969, *Still-life*, DEM 26,000. LONDON, 24 March 1971, *Vase of Flowers*, GBP 7,400. NEW YORK, 17 May 1972, *Still-life*, USD 10,500. VERSAILLES, 20 June 1974, *Still-life*, FRF 110,000. AMSTERDAM, 3 May 1976, *Growling Dog* (drawing, 6 1/2 x 8in/16.5 x 19.4cm) NLG 1,500.

LONDON, 1 July 1980, *Dogs* (series of eight etchings, 6 1/2 x 8 1/2in/16.8 x 21.7cm) GBP 280. LONDON, 15 April 1983, *Still-life with Game* (1645, oil on canvas, 28 3/4 x 37in/73 x 94cm) GBP 18,000. AMSTERDAM, 25 April 1983, *Dogs in a Landscape* (red chalk, 6 3/4 x 9 1/2in/17 x 24.4cm) NLG 3,800. LONDON, 4 July 1986, *Basket of Fruit and Dead Poultry on a Draped Entablature* (oil on panel, 22 x 28in/56 x 71cm) GBP 75,000. NEW YORK, 3 June 1988, *Landscape with a Still-life of Dogs Guarding the Kill* (1649, oil on canvas, 54 x 78 3/4in/137 x 200cm) USD 132,000. MONACO, 19 June 1988, *Hare and other Game with a Gun, Hunting Dogs and Dead Birds, with a Basket* (1655, oil on canvas, a pair, each 24 1/4 x 37 3/4in/61.5 x 96cm) FRF 444,000. AMSTERDAM, 14 Nov 1988, *Still-life with a Hare and Game Placed on top of Hunting Accessories* (oil on canvas, 31 1/2 x 39 1/4in/80 x 100cm) NLG 17,250. ROME, 13 Dec 1988, *Still-life with a Hare and Fruit in a Dish on a Pedestal, Still-life of Fruit with a Hare and a Dog* (oil on canvas, a pair, each 33 1/4 x 47 1/4in/84.5 x 120cm) ITL 140,000,000. ROME, 23 May 1989, *Concert of Birds* (oil on canvas, 45 x 64 1/4in/114 x 163cm) ITL 28,000,000. ROME, 27 Nov 1989, *Still-life with Fruit, Game and a Copper Utensil* (oil on canvas, 30 1/4 x 35 1/2in/77 x 90cm) ITL 27,600,000. PARIS, 8 Dec 1989, *Hunting Trophy incorporating a Hare* (oil on canvas, 23 x 28 1/2in/57.5 x 72.5cm) FRF 89,000. NEW YORK, 11 Jan 1990, *Rocky Landscape with Three Hares Eating Blackberries* (oil on canvas, 38 1/2 x 48 1/2in/98 x 123cm) USD 60,500. LONDON, 11 April 1990, *Still-life of Fruit and Vegetables in a Landscape with a Yellow-crested Cockatoo, a Weasel and a Guinea-pig* (oil on canvas, 53 x 78 1/2in/134.5 x 199.5cm) GBP 253,000. NEW YORK, 16 Jan 1992, *Hunting Scene with a Hare, Partridge and Birds beside a Gamebag* (oil on canvas, 22 3/4 x 29in/57.8 x 73.7cm) USD 24,200. LONDON, 9 Dec 1992, *Still-life with Wildfowl* (oil on panel, 21 1/4 x 34in/53.7 x 86.2cm) NLG 22,000. NEW YORK, 11 Jan 1995, *Fish, Oysters and Shellfish, with Cats, a Tub and a Copper Platter at the Foot of a Column on a Quayside, with a Castle on the Seashore in the Background* (oil on canvas, 60 1/4 x 106in/153 x 269 cm) USD 134,500. NEW YORK, 12 Jan 1996, *White and Pink Roses in a Glass Vase* (oil on canvas, 18 1/2 x 14 1/4in/47.3 x 36.2cm) USD 365,500. NEW YORK, 15 May 1996, *Chained Dog Eating from a Dish* (oil on canvas, 22 1/4 x 25 1/2in/56.5 x 65cm) USD 9,775. AMSTERDAM, 12 Nov 1996, *Two Dogs before a Still-life, a Hunter in the Background* (black chalk and brown wash heightened with white, 11 1/2 x 17in/29.2 x 42.3cm) NLG 9,440. LONDON, 9 July 1999, *Dead Songbirds, Jay and Snipe in Landscape* (oil on canvas, 15 x 22 ins / 38 x 57 cm) GBP 11,000. LONDON, 9 July 1999, *Studies of Head of Wild Boar* (oil on canvas, 21 x 41 ins / 53 x 105 cm) GBP 40,000. LONDON, 5 July 2000, *Dead Songbirds, Jay and Snipe on a Bank* (oil on canvas, 15 x 22 ins / 38 x 57 cm) GBP 15,500. PARIS, 6 Dec 2000, *Hunting Trophy Guarded by a Dog* (oil on canvas) FRF 250,000. NEW YORK, 23 Jan 2001, *Study of a Mastiff with a Leather Collar* (black chalk, 7 x 9 ins / 19 x 24 cm) USD 8,500. PARIS, 19 Dec 2001, *Two Dogs Watching Dead Game* (oil on canvas, 44 x 59 ins / 111 x 149 cm) FRF 950,000. VENICE, 9 Feb 2002, *Still-life with Dead Game. Still-life with Birds and Cage* (oil on canvas, a pair, 22 x 27 ins / 56 x 69 cm) EUR 12,000. LONDON, 11 July 2002, *Two Hounds Crossing a River and Surprising a Cormorant, with a Landscape Beyond* (1651, oil on canvas, 46 x 41 ins / 118 x 105 cm) GBP 20,000. MADRID, 30 Sept 2003, *Dead Game and Cat* (oil on canvas, 37 x 30 ins / 93 x 75 cm) EUR 14,000. BERLIN, 27 Nov 2003, *Greyhound* (brush wash, 4 x 7 ins / 11 x 18 cm) EUR 1,900. NEW YORK, 22 Jan 2004, *Peacock in a Landscape with Roosters, Turkeys, Ducks and a Heron* (oil on canvas, 47 x 68 ins / 119 x 173 cm) USD 85,000. BRUSSELS, 25 May 2004, *Two Dogs Guarding Game* (oil on canvas, 31 x 48 ins / 80 x 121 cm) EUR 18,000.

G.
Monogram of an engraver (copper).

G. A. F.
Italian, 16th century.
Monogram of an engraver (copper).
The engraver who used this monogram worked from drawings produced by Giorgio Vasari, at the end of the 16th century.

G. B. A.
Monogram of an engraver (copper).

G. D.
17th century.
Monogram of a sculptor (ivory).

G. D. B.
German, 16th century.
Monogram of an engraver (etching).
Active around the year 1569, he is known for a work depicting a *Lute Player*.

G. E., MASTER OF THE INITIALS
17th century.
Painter. Portraits.

AUCTION RECORDS:
COPENHAGEN, 18 Nov 1992, *Portrait of the Chamberlain Christian Friis of Kragerup Clothed in Black, Carrying the Order of the Elephant; Portrait of His Wife Barbara in a Black Dress Trimmed with Lace and Red Ribbons* (oil on canvas, 45 1/4 x 32 3/4 ins / 115 x 83 cm and 39 1/4 x 32 1/4 ins/100 x 82 cm) DKK 140,000.

G. F.
German, 16th century.
Monogram of an engraver.
This engraver was working between 1534 and 1537.

G. F.
17th century.
Monogram of a sculptor (ivory).
G.F. was probably Dutch or else lived in Holland, as a stork forms part of the armorial bearings of The Hague.

G. G.
German.
Monogram of an engraver.
Work by G.G. includes *Female Saint with a Child* and *Condemned Man*.

G. H.
16th century.
Monogram of an engraver (wood).
This engraver was working in about 1580; he is identified from the drawings of Jost Amman.

G. H. I. B.
17th century.
Monogram of an engraver (burin).
G.H.I.B. was active in Germany in 1640. His work included an engraved landscape called *Das Kalte Bad in Sommer* (1640).

G. H., MASTER OF THE INITIALS
Hungarian, 15th century.
Painter.

This artist was active during the second half of the 15th century. He produced three panels for the altarpiece of the Trinity of Mosoc. The central panel bears his initials and is dated 1471.

G. J.
School of Champagne.
Monogram of a glass painter.
G. J. worked in Troyes, where his monogram appears on a window of the church of St John.

G. L.
German.
Monogram of an engraver (wood).
His work included a *St Luke Writing his Recollections*.

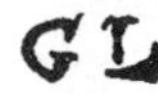

G. M. B.
Flemish School, 15th century.
Monogram of a painter.
This artist was working towards the end of the 15th century.

G. S.
German.
Monogram of an engraver (wood).
G.S. is known to have produced 12 engravings representing *The Labours of Hercules*.

G. Z., MASTER OF THE INITIALS
16th century.
Draughtsman.
The Master of the Initials G.Z. was active in Germany from 1516 to 1522.
BIBLIOGRAPHY:
Rowlands, John, *The Age of Dürer and Holbein: German Drawings 1400-1500*, Cambridge University Press, Cambridge, 1988.
AUCTION RECORDS:
LONDON, 2 July 1991, *Christ on the Cross in a Mountainous Landscape* (ink heightened with white/blue paper, 6 1/4 x 3 1/2 ins / 15.7 x 8.6 cm) GBP 15,400.

GAAB
British, 18th century.
Active in London.
Sculptor.
Gaab exhibited three works at the Free Society in 1783.

GAADI, Donald da
American, 20th century.
Active in Los Angeles.
Painter.
Donald da Gaadi took part in the International Exhibition of Watercolours at the Chicago Art Institute in 1937 and 1938.

GAAG, Lotti van der
Dutch, 20th century.
Born 1923; died 1999.
Also active in France.
Painter, draughtsman, sculptor (including bronze).
Figures, interiors with figures.
CoBrA group (related to).
Lotti van der Gaag first worked alongside Appel, Corneille with one or two other Dutch artists. She then shared her time between The Hague and Paris. The Dutch Institute in Paris showed a collection of her work in 1992.

She produced mainly drawings in the 1950s and sculptures in the 1960s, which caused people to look on her as the sculptor of the CoBrA group. After that, she produced mainly paintings on paper, often on autobiographical themes. She portrayed characters, often her friends, jazz musicians, and glimpses of her studios in The Hague and Paris. Her figures are extremely distorted in a savage, primitive way, the pictures jerkily drawn, full of thorns and spines, their brutality exacerbated by her use of colour.
BIBLIOGRAPHY:
Schierbeek, Bert, *Lotti Van der Gaag*, Institut néerlandais, Paris, 1992.
MUSEUMS AND GALLERIES:
ROTTERDAM (Mus. Boijmans Van Beuningen): large donation of drawings.
AUCTION RECORDS:
AMSTERDAM, 24 May 1989, *Abstract Composition* (1961, oil on canvas, 15 3/4 x 19 3/4 ins / 40.3 x 50.3 cm) NLG 2,070. PARIS, 11 March 1990, *Journey to the East* (mixed media, 25 1/2 x 19 3/4 ins / 65 x 50 cm) FRF 15,000. AMSTERDAM, 11 Dec 1991, *Couple* (1952, lead pencil and water/paper, 25 1/4 x 19 ins / 64 x 48 cm) NLG 2,875. AMSTERDAM, 19 May 1992, *Figures with a Bird* (1953, bronze relief, 17 3/4 x 12 ins / 45 x 30.5 cm) NLG 2,530. AMSTERDAM, 8 Dec 1994, *Composition* (1961, oil on canvas, 15 3/4 x 19 3/4 ins / 40 x 50 cm) NLG 4,600. AMSTERDAM, 25 June 2002, *Two Women* (1948, bronze, h. 81 ins / 205 cm) EUR 2,600. AMSTERDAM, 9 June 2004, *Gatepaan* (1958, grey patinated bronze, h. 17 ins / 44 cm) EUR 5,500.

GAAL, Abraham
Dutch, 17th - 18th century.
Active in Delft.
Delftware-maker.
He was the brother of Johannes Gal.

GAAL, Adriaen, the Elder, or Gael
Dutch, 17th century.
Born c. 1590, in Haarlem; died 8 March 1660.
Painter. Landscapes.
He was a pupil of Barend Gaal and Jacob de Wet. He was made a master of the Guild of St Luke in Haarlem in 1642.
MUSEUMS AND GALLERIES:
MAINZ: *Forest Landscape*.

GAAL, Adriaen, the Younger, or Gael
Dutch, 17th century.
Born in Haarlem; died May 1665, in Haarlem.
Painter.
He was the son of Adriaen Gaal the Elder, and probably his pupil. He was enrolled as a member of the Guild of St Luke in Haarlem in 1660.

GAAL, Barend, or Gael
Dutch, 17th century.
Born c. 1620 or 1635, in Haarlem; died c. 1687 or 1703; probably in Amsterdam (North Holand).
Painter. Genre scenes, village scenes, landscapes with figures, landscapes.

He was a pupil of Wouwerman, and was active in Haarlem in 1660, where he taught Cornelis Adriaensz. Gaal. He later moved to Amsterdam. He painted mostly village scenes, in the style of Adriaen and Isack van Ostade.

B.GAAL.

BIBLIOGRAPHY:

Bernt, W., *Netherlandish Painters of the Seventeenth Century*, Oxford, 1969.

MUSEUMS AND GALLERIES:

GLASGOW: *Rustic Group* - LA FÈRE: *Livestock Market* - LEIDEN: *Poultry Market with Numerous Figures; In Front of the Village Inn* - MAINZ: *Rider at the Inn; Rider in Front of a Farm* - ORLÉANS: *Cavalry Alarum* - ROTTERDAM: *The Pastry-cook; Village Inn* - ST PETERSBURG: *An Inn.*

AUCTION RECORDS:

PARIS, 9 Dec 1811, *Landscape with an Inn and Riders*, FRF 260. PARIS, 1838, *Huntsmen on Horseback*, FRF 779. PARIS, 1840, *Rider Passing through a Village*, FRF 680. PARIS, 1843, *Landscape*, FRF 230. PARIS, 1847, *Cart at the Door of an Inn*, FRF 315. PARIS, 1865, *Two Horses in a Stable* (a pair) FRF 290; *Riders at Rest*, FRF 250. PARIS, 1897, *Landscape with Riders*, FRF 111. PARIS, 27 June 1900, *Halt in Front of an Inn*, FRF 115. LONDON, 17 Feb 1908, *Convoy under Attack*, GBP 4. LONDON, 28 Feb 1910, *Falconers Resting*, GBP 6. LONDON, 10 Dec 1910, *Riders at an Inn*, GBP 5. LONDON, 25 Feb 1911, *Trumpeter on Horseback*, GBP 5. LONDON, 11 March 1911, *Horse Fair in a Dutch Village*, GBP 8. LONDON, 16 June 1911, *Gathering in a Dutch Village*, GBP 24. LONDON, 2 March 1921, *Halt at an Inn*, FRF 350. LONDON, 11 April 1924, *Halt at an Inn*, FRF 950. LONDON, 11 April 1924, *Riders and Figures before a Tavern*, GBP 12; *Village Scene*, GBP 52. LONDON, 24 Nov 1924, *Horses and Figures before a Tavern*, GBP 13. PARIS, 17-18 June 1925, *Hay Wagon*, FRF 6,900. LONDON, 12 March 1926, *Landscape*, GBP 8. PARIS, 2-3 June 1926, *The Encampment*, FRF 2,000. LONDON, 18 Feb 1927, *Village Celebration*, GBP 9. LONDON, 9 May 1927, *Riders and other Figures before a Tavern*, GBP 23. LONDON, 28-29 July 1927, *Rider Drinking before a Tavern*, GBP 37. LONDON, 1 Feb 1928, *Woman, Dog and Horse in Front of an Inn*, GBP 9. LONDON, 20 Feb 1930, *Exterior of an Inn; Exterior of an Inn* (together) GBP 15. LONDON, 17 April 1931, *Riders Resting*, GBP 10. LONDON, 2 March 1934, *Village scene*, GBP 8. LONDON, 19 Dec 1934, *Two Inn Scenes*, GBP 22. LONDON, 22 Nov 1935, *Village Street*, GBP 7. LONDON, 4 Dec 1936, *Town beside a River*, GBP 18. LONDON, 9 Dec 1938, *Village*, GBP 5. LONDON, 24 Sept 1943, *Riders*, GBP 29. PARIS, 14 June 1945, *Landscape*, FRF 9,800. PARIS, Oct 1945-July 1946, *Hay Wagon*, FRF 34,000. LONDON, 26 June 1946, *Peasants on their Way to Market*, GBP 42. PARIS, 29 June 1951, *The Blacksmith*, FRF 46,000. PARIS, 14 June 1954, *Dancing in Front of an Inn; Poultry Market*, FRF 120,000. LONDON, 24 Oct 1958, *Village Scene*, GBP 504. LONDON, 25 July 1969, *Market Scene*, Gns 1,400. LINDAU, 14 May 1971, *Peasants in Front of an Inn*, DEM 12,000. LONDON, 24 March 1976, *Horse Fair* (oil on panel, 19 x 25 1/4in/48 x 64cm) GBP 4,800. VIENNA, 20 Sept 1977, *Hunting with a Falcon* (oil on card, 3 1/2 x 6in/9 x 15cm) ATS 90,000. COPENHAGEN, 9 Nov 1977, *Travellers' Rest* (oil on canvas, 8 3/4 x 11in/22.5 x 27cm) DKK 17,000. BERN, 20 June 1980, *Travellers and Peasants in Front of an Inn* (c. 1660-70, black chalk heightened with pen on paper, 7 3/4 x 12 1/4in/19.5 x 31cm) CHF 3,200. VIENNA, 19 May 1981, *Village Scene* (oil on canvas, 26 1/2 x 32 3/4in/67 x 83.5cm) ATS 220,000. NICE, 26 May 1982, *In Front of an Inn* (oil on canvas, 19 1/4 x 22 1/2in/49 x 57cm) FRF 19,000. VIENNA, 23 March 1983, *Riders and Horses in Front of a Forge* (oil on canvas, 10 1/4 x 13 1/2in/26 x 34cm) ATS 250,000. PARIS, 5 March 1986, *Riders at the Edge of a Village* (oil on panel, 9 1/2 x 11 1/2in/24 x 29.5cm) FRF 30,000. MONACO, 17 June 1988, *Shepherds and their Flock* (oil on panel, 15 3/4 x 20 3/4in/40 x 53cm) FRF 16,650. AMSTERDAM, 14 Nov 1988, *Figures on an Italian Shore* (chalk and wash, 7 3/4 x 12 1/2in/19.6 x 31.7cm) NLG 3,910. TORONTO, 30 Nov 1988, *Departure of the Hunt* (oil on panel, diam. 6in/15cm) CAD 3, 800. PARIS, 9 Dec 1988, *The Old Louvre Seen from the Pont Neuf* (painting on canvas, 28 x 49 1/2in/71 x 125.5cm) FRF 172,000. NEW YORK, 12 Jan 1989, *Peasants in the Yard of an Inn* (oil on canvas, 15 x 18in/38 x 46cm) USD 13,200. MILAN, 4 April 1989, *Village in Flanders, with Figures* (oil on canvas, 10 1/4 x 18in/26 x 46cm) ITL 28,000,000. AMSTERDAM, 20 June 1989, *Hunting Scenes* (oil on canvas/panel, a pair, each 7 1/4 x 9 1/2in/18.3 x 24.2cm) NLG 32,200. LONDON, 27 Oct 1989, *Travellers Preparing for Departure beneath the Town Ramparts* (oil on panel, 8 3/4 x 11in/22.2 x 28.2cm) GBP 3,740. AMSTERDAM, 28 Nov 1989, *Peasants Feeding their Horses in a Village Street* (oil on canvas, 22 x 20 1/4in/56 x 51.2cm) NLG 39,100. LONDON, 15 Dec 1989, *Travellers and Dogs in Front of an Inn* (oil on panel, 15 3/4 x 21 3/4in/40 x 55.3cm) GBP 4,400. MILAN, 27 March 1990, *Landscape with Figures near a Fountain* (oil on panel, 9 x 11 1/2in/23 x 29cm) ITL 11,500,000. NEW YORK, 4 April 1990, *Hunting Party* (oil on panel, diam. 5 3/4in/14.8cm) USD 7,700. LONDON, 30 Oct 1991, *Sheep Market; Poultry Market* (oil on canvas, 9 1/2 x 9in/24 x 23cm) GBP 14,300. LONDON, 15 April 1992, *Village Celebration with Peasants Drinking and Watching Games on Horseback in Front of an Inn* (oil on canvas, 25 1/2 x 32 1/4in/64.8 x 82cm) GBP 10,500. LONDON, 23 April 1993, *Travellers Halted in Front of an Inn* (oil on canvas, 24 1/2 x 34 3/4in/62.2 x 88.5cm) GBP 6,670. STOCKHOLM, 30 Nov 1993, *Village Scene with Peasants and Horses* (oil on panel, 22 1/2 x 28 1/4in/57 x 72cm) SEK 26,000. AMSTERDAM, 10 May 1994, *Travellers and Horses beside a Water Trough in Front of an Inn* (ink and wash over black chalk, 7 1/4 x 11 1/4in/18.3 x 28.4cm) NLG 7,820. NEW YORK, 6 Oct 1994, *Travellers on a Track in a Wooded Landscape* (oil on panel, 16 1/4 x 21 1/2in/41.2 x 54.6cm) USD 3,450. PARIS, 28 Oct 1994, *Village Market Scene* (black chalk and grey wash, 5 1/4 x 10 1/2in/13.5 x 26.5cm) FRF 25,000. AMSTERDAM, 15 Nov 1995, *Travellers in Front of a Village Inn* (black chalk and wash, 7 3/4 x 12 1/4in/19.6 x 31cm) NLG 4,248. LONDON, 16 April 1997, *Horse and Cart with Figures Resting at an Inn* (oil on panel, 14 1/4 x 11 3/4in/36.1 x 29.8cm) GBP 5,980. NEW YORK, 16 Oct 1997, *Peasants Selling Pigs at the Edge of a Village, with a Distant Mountain Landscape* (oil on panel, 10 x 13 1/2in/25.4 x 34cm) USD 14,950. LONDON, 3 Dec 1997, *Travellers outside a Blacksmith's Forge; Peasants Merry-making in Front of an Inn* (oil on panel, a pair, 10 1/4 x 12 3/4in/26 x 32.7cm and 10 1/4 x 12 1/2in/26 x 32cm) GBP 16,675.

GAAL, Cornelis Adriaensz., the Elder, or Gael
Dutch, 17th century.
Active in Haarlem.
Painter.

He was the brother of Adriaen Gaal the Elder, and was also active in Amsterdam.

GAAL, Cornelis Adriaensz., the Younger, or Gael
Dutch, 17th century.
Born c. 1620, in Haarlem.
Painter.

He was the son of Adriaen Gaal the Elder.

MUSEUMS AND GALLERIES:

MAINZ: attributed (painting).

GAAL, Cornelis Jacob, or Gael
Dutch, 17th century.
Died before 1635.
Active in Haarlem.
Painter.

GAAL, Gustav
Austrian, 19th century.
Active in Vienna.
Painter.
Gustav Gaal was mainly responsible for landscapes.

GAAL, Ignacz
Austrian, 19th century.
Born c. 1820, in Szatmar.
Painter.
Ignacz Gall mainly painted still-lifes. He worked in Vienna and Budapest.

GAAL, István
Hungarian, 20th century.
Born 6 June 1883, in Korosladany.
Painter, medallist.
István Gaal studied in Budapest, Munich and with Jean-Paul Laurens in Paris.

GAAL, Jacobus Cornelis
Dutch, 19th century.
Born 5 September 1796, in Oost Souburg (Zeeland); died c. 1858.
Miniaturist, engraver.
He was the son of Pieter Gaal and a pupil of J.-P. Bourjès. He was director of the academy at Middelburg.

GAAL, Johannes
Dutch, 17th - 18th century.
Died 1725.
Active in Delft.
Delftware-maker.
A number of works exist signed with this name.

GAAL, Miklos
Hungarian, 19th century.
Born 1799, in Szegvár; died 30 November 1854, in Budapest.
Painter, engineer.
Miklos Gaal worked for the military and painted battle scenes. Some of his works are in the museum in Arad.

GAAL, Nandor
Hungarian, 20th century.
Born c. 1885; died 2 November 1915.
Sculptor.
Nandor Gaal is known for his statue of *Kossuth*, the maker of an independent Hungary.

GAAL, Pieter
Dutch, 19th century.
Born c. 1785, in Middelburg (Zeeland); died 12 January 1819, in Middelburg.
Painter. History painting, portraits, genre scenes, landscapes, still-lifes.
He was a pupil of Schweickhardt in The Hague, as well as of J. Perkais and of his father Thomas Gaal. He lived in Paris, London, Switzerland and Germany, and visited certain regions of Italy, before settling in his home town.

GAAL, Thomas
Dutch, 18th - 19th century.
Born 9 July 1739, in Dendermonde (East Flanders); died 16 July 1817, in Middelburg (Zeeland).
Painter. Portraits, animals, flowers.
He was admitted to the painters' guild in Middelburg in 1764. He later founded the town's academy of fine arts and became its director in 1778. His pupils included J. Perkais, Karem Maertens, J.-H. Koekkoek and S. de Koster.

GAAL, Willem
Dutch, 17th - 18th century.
Active in Delft.
Delftware-maker.
Son of Johannes Gaal.

GAALON, Jacques de
French, 19th - 20th century.
Born in Les Moutiers-en-Cinglais.
Active in Caen.
Sculptor.
Jacques de Gaalon studied at the École des Beaux-Arts in Caen. He first exhibited at the Salon of 1876 and became a member of the Société des Artistes Français in 1883.

GAART, Josephus van
Dutch, 18th century.
Active in Middelburg (Zeeland), in 1713.
Painter.

GABAIN, Éthel Léontine
French, 20th century.
Born 1883, in Le Havre; died 1950.
Painter, engraver. Still-lifes.
Éthel Gabain exhibited in Paris at the Salon of the Société Nationale des Beaux-Arts from 1925.

AUCTION RECORDS:
LONDON, 8 March 1990, *Feathers and Green Gloves* (oil on canvas, 19 1/2 x 23 1/4 ins / 49.4 x 59 cm) GBP 4,620.

GABANI, Giuseppe
Italian, 19th century.
Born 1846, in Senigallia (Marche); died 1899 or 1900, in Rome.
Painter, watercolourist, draughtsman. Genre scenes, animals.
Orientalism.
Gabani's most notable exhibitions were in Rome, Venice and Melbourne.

G. Gabani

AUCTION RECORDS:
PARIS, 16-17 July 1892, *Cavaliers,* FRF 180; *In Winter,* FRF 240; *Drinking Trough,* FRF 180. NEW YORK, 27 Feb 1982, *Farm Animals* (watercolour, 20 3/4 x 30 ins / 53 x 76.5 cm) USD 1,100. LONDON, 26 Jan 1984, *Arab Cavalier in the Desert* (watercolour/pencil outlines, 21 x 14 ins / 53.5 x 35.5 cm) GBP 850. NEW YORK, 29 Feb 1984, *Elegant Cavaliers and Coach Drawn by Four Horses* (oil on canvas, 33 x 61 ins / 83.8 x 155 cm) USD 8,000. CHESTER, 4 Oct 1985, *Snake Charmer* (oil on card, 11 1/2 x 19 1/4 ins / 29.5 x 49 cm) GBP 5,800. NEW YORK, 25 Feb 1988, *Arab Cavaliers* (watercolour, 21 x 29 1/4 ins / 53.3 x 74.3 cm) USD 6,050. NEW YORK, 16 Feb 1993, *Fantazia* (watercolour and gouache/paper, 21 x 30 ins / 53.3 x 76.2 cm) USD 1,760. ROME, 27 April 1993, *Horses and Stablemen in the Roman Countryside* (watercolour/paper, 14 x 20 ins / 35.3 x 50.5 cm) ITL 4,504,200. LONDON, 17 Nov 1994, *Arab Warriors* (pencil and watercolour/paper, 35 x 48 ins / 88 x 121 cm) GBP 16,100. LONDON, 15 March 1996, *Snake Charmer* (oil on panel, 11 1/4 x 18 ins / 28.5 x 45.5 cm) GBP 8,280. PARIS, 17 Nov 1997, *Cavaliers outside the Curiosity Shop* (oil on panel, 12 1/2 x 19 1/2 ins / 32 x 49.5 cm) FRF 31,000. LONDON, 13 Oct 1999, *Lion Hunt* (oil on canvas, 60 x 113 ins / 153 x 287 cm) GBP 58,000. PARIS, 29 Nov 1999, *Arab Horsemen* (watercolour, 29 x 20 ins / 74 x 51 cm) FRF 36,500. PARIS, 5 April 2001, *Arab Horsemen* (watercolour, 18 x 13 ins / 46 x 32 cm) FRF 28,000. ROME, 6 June 2001, *Tuscan Cowboys Riding* (watercolour, 15 x 20 ins / 38 x 52 cm) ITL 4,500,000. LONDON, 5 March 2002, *Buffalo Grazing in the Campagna* (watercolour, 14 x 23 ins / 36 x 59 cm) GBP 1,400. NEW YORK, 23 April 2002, *Lion Attack* (1886, oil on canvas, 38 x 66 ins / 96 x 168 cm) USD 17,000. NEW YORK, 22 April 2004, *Snake Charmer* (oil on panel, 11 x 19 ins / 29 x 47 cm) USD 15,000. LONDON, 23 Sept 2004, *Cart on an Estuary Track* (1868, oil on canvas, 26 x 47 ins / 67 x 119 cm) GBP 3,500.

GABANO, Jacopo
Italian, 18th century.
Active in Padua.
Sculptor.
Jacopo Gabano worked on various projects in Padua Cathedral.

GABARDI, Giacomo
Italian, 18th - 19th century.
Born 1774, in Venice; died 6 August 1850, in Venice.
Sculptor.
Giacomo Gabardi was a pupil of Giovanni Ferrari. He worked mostly on projects for Modena Cathedral.

GABARRON, Cristóbal
Spanish, 20th century.
Born 1945, in Murcia.
Painter, sculptor.
In 1986, the World Federation of United Nations Associations published a reproduction of one of Cristóbal Gabarron's works to celebrate the International Year of Peace. In 1990, he was awarded the national prize for fine arts. In 1991, a 325 feet (100-metre)-long wall depicting the *History of the Olympic Games* that he had designed for the 1992 Olympic Games in Barcelona was inaugurated. A private exhibition of the preparatory work for this piece toured Leningrad, Moscow, Atlanta and Vienna, and a selection of the work was shown in Belgium.

GABAY, Esperanza
American, 20th century.
Born in New York.
Painter.

GABBIANI, Antonio Domenico
Italian, 17th - 18th century.
Born 13 February 1652, in Florence; died 22 November 1726, in Florence.
Painter, engraver, draughtsman. History painting, religious subjects, mythological subjects, portraits, genre scenes.
Antonio Domenico Gabbiani studied initially under Justus Sustermans and Vincenzo Dandini, then enjoyed the protection and patronage of Grand Duke Cosmo III, which enabled him to attend the Florentine Academy in Rome, where he was a pupil of Ciro Ferri. He spent some time at the court in Vienna, where he painted a portrait of the emperor, together with some historical compositions for the imperial collection. On his return to Italy he painted several altarpieces, notably an *Assumption, Rest on the Flight into Egypt* and his celebrated *St Philip.* Gabbiani died in Florence as the result of a fall from a scaffold.

MUSEUMS AND GALLERIES:
CHAMBÉRY (MBA): *Diana the Huntress* - CHERBOURG: *Virgin Appearing to St Urbido and St Bernard* - DRESDEN: *Meal at the House of Simon* - FLORENCE (NG): *Virgin; Self-portrait; Ganymede Abducted by Jupiter* - LILLE: drawings - MONTPELLIER: *Driving the Traders from the Temple* (drawing) - OBERSCHLEISSHEIM: *St Peter of Alcantara; St Francis of Assisi with Stigmata; Holy Family.*
AUCTION RECORDS:
LONDON, 20 March 1964, *Painting,* Gns 1,200. MILAN, 20 May 1982, *Portrait of a Gentleman* (oil on canvas, 29 1/2 x 26 3/4 ins / 75 x 68 cm) ITL 2,800,000. ROME, 15 March 1983, *Tarquin and Lucretia* (oil on canvas, 51 1/4 x 66 1/2 ins / 130 x 169 cm) ITL 5,000,000. PARIS, 4 March 1988, *Ninety Detailed Studies* (lead pencil and red chalk) FRF 5,000. LONDON, 5 July 1993, *Prisoners Appearing before a Roman Magistrate (recto); Studies for 'Prisoners Appearing before a Roman Magistrate' (verso)* (ink, wash and red chalk, 13 1/4 x 18 ins / 33.8 x 46 cm) GBP 2,530. LONDON, 3 July 1995, *Page of Studies of a Figure Kneeling, a Head and Hands* (black chalk and red chalk, 10 1/4 x 15 1/2 ins / 26.1 x 39.4 cm) GBP 920. LONDON, 16-17 April 1997, *Head in Profile* (red chalk, two studies, 7 1/4 x 7 ins / 18.5 x 16.9 cm and 8 1/4 x 6 3/4 ins/21 x 17 cm) GBP 517; *Hands and Draperies* (red chalk/beige paper, study, 9 1/4 x 16 1/4 ins / 23.7 x 41.4 cm) GBP 575. NEW YORK, 14 Oct 1999, *Portrait of Two Boys Dressed as Hunters* (oil on canvas, 56 x 79 ins / 142 x 200 cm) USD 35,000. VIENNA, 30 March 2000, *Portrait, Possibly of a Young Medici Prince* (oil on canvas, 19 x 13 ins / 48 x 33 cm) ATS 150,000. NEW YORK, 18 Oct 2000, *Group of Musicians Playing a Viola da Gamba, Two Violins and a Clavichord* (oil on canvas, 43 x 54 ins / 110 x 136 cm) USD 18,000. PARIS, 25 June 2002, *Portrait of Ferdinando de Medici with his Brother Gian Gastone* (oil on canvas, 59 x 79 ins / 150 x 200 cm) EUR 95,000. LONDON, 11 Dec 2002, *Rape of the Sabines* (pen/ink wash over black chalk, 3 x 9 ins / 7 x 24 cm) GBP 1,100. NEW YORK, 21 Jan 2003, *Invention of the Cross* (pen/ink wash, 13 x 18 ins / 33 x 45 cm) USD 6,000.

GABBIANI, Gaetano
Italian, 18th century.
Born in Florence; died c. 1750.
Painter, pastellist.
Gaetano Gabbiani was the nephew and pupil of Antonio Gabbiani.

GABBIANI, Giacomo
Italian, 20th century.
Born 18 September 1900, in Milan.
Painter. Religious subjects, figure compositions, nudes, portraits, genre scenes, landscapes, still-lifes.
Giacomo Gabbiani studied under Riccardo Brambilla and Giuseppe Amisani. He first exhibited in 1925 in Milan, where he lived his whole life. He took part in some group exhibitions, but mostly showed his paintings in solo exhibitions - almost all of them in Milan. He was awarded a number of distinctions. In 1948 Gabbiani set up a free academy, with himself as director.

His pictorial technique was traditional, and he chose a wide variety of subjects. He sometimes tackled major themes - most notably, a *Way of the Cross.*
BIBLIOGRAPHY:
Nicodemi, Giorgio, *Giacomo Gabbiani,* Officina Grafika Gioia, Cantù, 1966.
MUSEUMS AND GALLERIES:
MILAN (Gal. d'Arte Moderna).

GABBIANI, Giuseppe
Italian, 19th century.
Born 6 January 1862, in Barletta (Puglia).
Painter.
Giuseppe Gabbiani was a pupil of Calo. He exhibited in Turin, Rome, London and St Louis in the USA. He spent most of his life in Naples.

GABBRIELLI, Cammillo
Italian, 17th century.
Born c. 1660, in Pisa.
Painter.
Cammillo Gabbrielli studied in Rome under Ciro Ferri. Examples of his work are to be found in the Pisa church of S Maria del Carmine.

GABBUGIANI, Baldassare
Italian, 18th century.
Engraver.
Baldassare Gabbugiani engraved a number of plates for *Museo Fiorentino* published in Florence between 1747 and 1766.

GABÉ, Nicolas-Edward
French, 19th century.
Born 1814, in Paris; died 4 January 1865, in Paris.

Painter, miniaturist. Portraits, genre scenes, landscapes, seascapes, still-lifes.

He exhibited at the Paris Salon from 1835 to 1864. Gabé initially executed portrait miniatures before going on to paint genre compositions, hunting and animal scenes, still-lifes, landscapes and seascapes. His body of work includes *Boar Hunt, Snared Fox, Wolf's Head, Rustic Meal, Boarding, Building the Wooden Fort at Boulogne-sur-Mer, 1803, The Parasites.*

BIBLIOGRAPHY:

Les Années romantiques, la peinture française de 1815 à 1850, exhibition catalogue, Musée des Beaux-Arts, Nantes; Gal. Nationales du Grand Palais, Paris, 1996.

MUSEUMS AND GALLERIES:

DIJON (Mus. Magnin): *Landscape with Water Mill and Angler* - LAVAL: *Salmon Fishing* - LONDON (Wallace Collection): *Young Woman in State of Undress* (miniature) - MULHOUSE: *Seascape; Fishing Boat; Ploughing.*

AUCTION RECORDS:

LONDON, 4 Feb 1911, *Children's Offering,* GBP 6. PARIS, 21 Feb 1924, *Eastern Seascape,* FRF 300. PARIS, 1 July 1942, *Scene from 'The Barber of Seville',* FRF 4,400. PARIS, 13 July 1942, *Fortified City Gate* (1844) FRF 550. PARIS, 19 March 1945, *Bay of Naples* (1847) FRF 24,000. BERN, 26 Aug 1978, *The Mousetrap* (oil on canvas, 12 1/2 x 15 1/4 ins / 32 x 39 cm) CHF 2,400. LOS ANGELES, 5 Oct 1981, *Figures beside the Bay of Naples* (1847, oil on canvas, 32 x 47in/81 x 119.5cm) USD 5,750. VERSAILLES, 25 Nov 1990, *Seascape* (1854, oil on canvas, 22 1/2 x 38 ins / 57 x 96.5 cm) FRF 10,000. LONDON, 28 Oct 1992, *Children at Play* (1858, oil on panel, 12 1/4 x 16 1/4 ins / 31 x 41 cm) GBP 1,430. RHEIMS, 13 March 1994, *Neapolitan Scene* (oil on panel, 13 x 9 1/2 ins / 33 x 24 cm) FRF 4,000. NEUILLY, 22 June 1999, *Sailing Ships Beached in Port and Transporter Bridge* (1855, oil on canvas, 19 x 26 ins / 49 x 65 cm) FRF 14,500. PARIS, 7 April 2000, *Gentle Word* (oil on panel, 21 x 17 ins / 53 x 44 cm) FRF 11,500. LONDON, 5 April 2001, *Proposal. An Approach* (oil on canvas, a pair, 26 x 21 ins / 65 x 54 cm) GBP 3,000. LONDON, 23 May 2001, *Figures on the Waterfront with Bay of Naples and Vesuvius Beyond* (1847, oil on canvas, 32 x 47 ins / 81 x 119 cm) GBP 3,600. NEW ORLEANS, 26 Jan 2002, *Cargo Ship at Dockside* (oil on panel, 10 x 7 ins / 25 x 18 cm) USD 1,750. PARIS, 16 Dec 2002, *Fishing Boats on the Shore* (oil on canvas, 15 x 24 ins / 39 x 61 cm) EUR 5,000. SAN FRANCISCO, 14 May 2003, *Ships Beached by a Jetty with Numerous Figures* (oil on canvas, 18 x 24 ins / 45 x 60 cm) USD 3,750. CHERBOURG, 11 Aug 2003, *Sailing Ships Returning to Port* (oil on canvas, 16 x 22 ins / 41 x 57 cm) EUR 3,200. PARIS, 25 June 2004, *Diligence launched to a Gallop* (1840, oil on canvas, 19 x 23 ins / 48 x 59 cm) EUR 2,500. CHERBOURG, 9 Aug 2004, *Fishing on the Open Sea* (oil on panel, 15 x 20 ins / 37 x 50 cm) EUR 3,700.

GABEL, Johann Georg

German, 18th - 19th century.

Born in Hildburghausen (Thuringia).

Painter.

Gabel was responsible for paintings on porcelain, and also created works in other media.

GABEL, P. E.

German, 20th century.

Active in Elbing (now Elblag, Poland).

Painter.

P. E. Gabel exhibited *Woman making Nets* in Berlin in 1909.

GABELLA, Giuseppe

Italian, 18th century.

Active in Milan in 1732.

Painter.

Giuseppe Gabella painted a *St Juliana* for the church of S Maria della Consolazione.

GABELLE, Giovanni dalle

Italian, 15th century.

Active in Ferrara.

Painter.

Gabelle was in the service of Duchess Parisina Malatesta.

GABEO, Luis

Spanish, 16th - 17th century.

Sculptor, architect.

A Castilian artist, Luis Gabeo almost always worked with Domingo de Albitiz, another sculptor and architect, with the result that it is difficult to distinguish between their works. They lived for many years in Burgos, where they were commissioned by the cathedral chapter, in 1592, to restore the choir and complete some parts of the building. In performing this delicate task, they proved themselves to be skilled and conscientious artists.

GABER, Aimée

Maiden name: Richter

German, 19th century.

Born 27 May 1834, in Dresden; died 12 October 1863, in Dresden.

Engraver.

Aimée Gaber was the daughter of Ludwig Richter and the wife and pupil of August Gaber.

GABER, August

German, 19th century.

Born 14 November 1823, in Köppernig; died September 1894, in Berlin.

Engraver, illustrator.

August Gaber was responsible for illustrations after Ludwig Richter, among other things.

GABER, Ibrahim

Egyptian, 20th century.

Born in Alexandria.

Sculptor.

Ibrahim Gaber was a pupil of Paul Landowski. He exhibited his work regularly at the Salon des Artistes Français.

GABEREL, Abraham

Swiss, 17th - 18th century.

Born 28 February 1641, in Ligerz; died 1719.

Sculptor (wood).

The museum in Bern has works by this artist.

GABET, Charles Henry Joseph

French, 19th century.

Born 31 March 1793, in Courbevoie (Hauts-de-Seine); died 27 December 1860, in Paris.

Miniaturist, watercolourist, writer. Portraits.

A committed liberal, he was obliged to relinquish his post as the chief editor at the Ministry of the Interior. In 1830 Gabet was appointed commissioner to the city of Paris. He was a talented miniaturist, whose body of work includes portraits of *M. Desfeuchère, Prince Narischkin, Princess Galitzin, Lieutenant-Colonel Bobillier,* and *M. Barbosa,* the Portuguese chargé d'affaires. He also wrote a *Dictionnaire des Artistes de l'École Française au XIXe siècle* (*Dictionary of Artist's of the French School up to the 19th Century*), an extremely fastidious and most useful reference work published in 1831.

GABET, Franz

Austrian, 18th - 19th century.

Born 20 January 1765, in Vienna; died 1847, in Vienna.

Draughtsman, engraver (etching).

Gabet engraved landscapes.

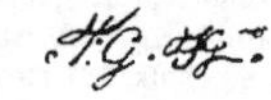

GABILLOT, François-Amédée, called Francisque
French, 19th century.
Born 23 September 1818, in Lyons; died 4 November 1876, in Belley (Ain).
Painter, watercolourist, draughtsman, engraver.
Landscapes, urban landscapes.

He lived variously in Paris, Lyons, the region of Le Bugey in the southern Jura and in the Ain region before finally settling in Lyons. He exhibited at the Salon from 1839 until 1870, when he gave up painting. Gabillot painted detailed, not to say documentary views of Lyons and its surroundings, typically in charcoal, pen-and-ink and Indian ink, at times heightened with watercolours. He also produced about twenty etchings.

GABILLOT VAN PARYS, Louise (Mrs).
See **PARYS**

GABIN, Jean
French, 18th century.
Active in Paris in 1760.
Painter.

GABINI, Romolo
Italian, 15th century.
Born 1429, in Parma; died 1476, in Parma.
Painter.

GABINO, Amadeo
Spanish, 20th century.
Born 1922, in Valencia.
Sculptor.
Neo-Constructivism.

Amadeo Gabino studied at the Valencia school of fine arts until 1944. He then travelled in Europe, spending time in Rome in 1949-1950 and living in Hamburg from 1957 to 1959. He took part in international sculpture exhibitions, including the São Paulo Biennale in 1959 and an exhibition at the Musée Rodin in Paris in 1961. His sculpture is Constructivist and Abstract in style.

MUSEUMS AND GALLERIES:
GENEVA (MAH) - HAMBURG - MADRID (Mus. Nacional Centro de Arte Reina Sofía) - MANNHEIM - NEW YORK (Brooklyn Mus.).

GABION, Andrée
French, 20th century.
Born in Paris.
Painter.

Andrée Gabion exhibited at the Salon d'Automne from 1928.

GABIROUX, Robert
French, 20th century.
Painter.

In 1950, Robert Gabiroux exhibited at the Salon des Indépendants. His painting was interestingly constructed in flat areas of strident tones.

GABL, Alods
Swiss, 19th century.
Born 24 September 1845, in Wies; died 27 February 1893, in Munich.
Painter. Genre scenes.

Gabl studied at the art academy in Munich, where he worked with Schraudolph, Ramberg and Karl von Piloty. He later came under the influence of Defregger. In 1874 he was awarded a gold medal in Berlin and a second-class medal in Munich in 1879.

MUSEUMS AND GALLERIES:
MUNICH: *Vaccine* - STUTTGART: *Savoyard in a Tyrolean Family*.

AUCTION RECORDS:
NEW YORK, 3 Feb 1904, *Before the Bath*, USD 400. MUNICH, 17 Nov 1971, *Tyroleans Dancing*, DEM 6,600. NEW YORK, 24 Feb 1983, *Scene in a Tavern* (1876, oil on canvas, 25¼ x 19 ins / 64 x 48 cm) USD 1,300. LONDON, 12 Feb 1986, *The Blessing* (oil on canvas, 30¾ x 41¾ ins / 78 x 106 cm) GBP 5,500. AMSTERDAM, 24 April 1991, *Peasant Feeding Her Child in a Kitchen* (oil on canvas, 18¾ x 14¾ ins / 47.5 x 37.5 cm) NLG 32,200. AHLDEN, 24 Nov 2000, *Puppet Seller* (oil on panel, 26 x 21 ins / 65 x 54 cm) DEM 30,000. MUNICH, 26 Sept 2001, *Peasant Woman by Baby's Crib* (oil on canvas, 19 x 15 ins / 48 x 37 cm) DEM 4,500.

GABLE, Master of the. See **MASTERS**

GABLER, Ambrosius
German, 18th - 19th century.
Born 13 December 1762, in Nuremberg; died 20 March 1834, in Nuremberg.
Painter, miniaturist, engraver.

This artist is referred to by Siret.

AUCTION RECORDS:
AMSTERDAM, 1886, *Interior of a Sheep-Fold*, FRF 2,467.

GABLER, Johann Jakob
German, 17th century.
Born in Augsburg.
Engraver.

GABLER, Nikolaus
German, 18th century.
Painter, engraver.

Nikolaus was the father of Ambrosius Gabler.

GABO, Naum (Sir), pseudonym of Pevsner Nathanael Neemia
Russian, 20th century.
Born 5 August 1890, in Bryansk; died 23 August 1977, in Waterbury (Connecticut), USA.
Active in Germany from 1922 to 1932, in France from 1933 to 1935, in England from 1936 to 1946, active from 1946 and naturalised in the USA.
Sculptor, painter, engraver.
Constructivism, Kinetic Art.
Abstraction-Création group.

While Antoine Pevsner, a few years older than his brother Naum, was destined from the outset for a career in art and had pursued the appropriate studies, the future Gabo studied medicine, which took him in 1909 to the University of Munich and then to the Polytechnic, where he studied physics and civil engineering. However, he was also interested in the arts, attended Heinrich Wölfflin's courses, read W. Worringer, went to view the Cubist exhibition in 1910 and became acquainted with Kandinsky, whose *The Spiritual in Art* published in 1910, he read. He had contacts with Der Blaue Reiter. His brother Antoine's vocation took him to Paris and Naum joined him in 1913, after touring Florence and Venice on foot, and they met their compatriot Archipenko in 1914. In Paris he took an interest in the works and writings of Gleizes, Metzinger and the entire group of the Section d'Or. Returning to Munich, he tried his hand at his first sculpture, a figurative *Head of a Black Man*.

At the outbreak of World War I, Naum withdrew to Copenhagen and then Christiania (now Oslo) with his other brother Aleskei. There he laid the foundations of what would become *Constructivism*. Antoine Pevsner's works from this period are not known, whereas Naum, who took the pseudonym Gabo to distinguish himself from him, executed a *Bust* and a *Woman's Head* in 1916. The 1917 Revolution drew the three brothers to Moscow. Lunatcharski, who was then in charge of cultural affairs, appointed Naum Gabo and Antoine Pevsner at the school of fine art where Kandinsky and Malevich were already teaching. They met Vladimir

Tatlin. Gabo's rare works from this period are inspired by Cubism and influenced by Archipenko, such as the *Constructed Torso* of 1917, executed in wood, metal and sheets of celluloid. In 1920, the two brothers wrote the *Realist Manifesto*, demonstrating Constructivism, published on 5 August by putting up posters on the streets of Moscow. Antoine contributed his knowledge of artistic practice and Naum his scientific knowledge, notably on the three-dimensional representation of mathematical formulae. In it they asserted that they were moving away from Cubism and Futurism. However, where the futurists stated: 'Transparent planes in glass or celluloid, sheets of metal, wires, internal or external electric lights, shall show the planes, trends, tones and semi-tones of a new reality', their manifesto announced: 'We renounce volume as a plastic form of space... Consider our real space: what is it, if not a continuous depth? We declare depth to be a unique plastic form of space. In sculpture, we renounce mass as a sculptural element... In so doing, we restore line as direction to the sculpture'. In both instances, this involves isolating the full volume in favour of the transparent space, the 'active vacuum'. It should again be noted that the term 'kinetic' can be found for the first time in this manifesto, as used in the expression 'kinetic rhythms', but it should also be noted that their 'kinetic' was not very different from the Futurists' 'dynamic'.

Between 1917 and 1922, aesthetic discussions on the fine arts had essentially crystallised around four groups: Malevich's Suprematism, the principles of which he had been formulating since 1913; the radically non-figurative Sensualism, which was leading to solutions not far removed from those that Mondrian would later develop; the Functionalism or Productivism of Tatlin, who challenged any aesthetic point of view resulting from dated, bourgeois culture, and became fully involved in the concept of everyday utilitarian objects, a point of view that would be one of the concerns of the Bauhaus; and Constructivism, defined by the two Pevsner brothers in their 1920 Manifesto. In 1922, Gabo went to the Van Diemen gallery in Berlin to organise an exhibition of Russian art, again under government supervision. Like several others, he took advantage of this trip to leave the USSR for good. The following year his brother joined him while Kandinsky left and met up with Gropius again at the Bauhaus in Weimar. Of the many others who stayed behind, the majority sank into oblivion or worse. Tatlin had to become a draughtsman and almost nothing more was heard of Malevich despite the definitive position he had acquired in the history of creative plastic thought.

In 1922, Gabo settled in Berlin, where he stayed for ten years spreading the principles of Constructivism with Lissitzky and Moholy-Nagy, but dividing his time between Berlin and Paris, contributing to the avant-garde movements of both cities and joining the management of the Novembergruppe in 1925 in Berlin. The same year an exhibition of his designs was also organised at the Percier gallery in Paris. It did not elicit any great response except that Diaghilev commissioned stage sets and costumes for his company's ballet *La chatte*, which Gabo designed in 1927 together with Antoine Pevsner in metal and transparent materials. Innovative expatriot Russian artists converged on Diaghilev's Ballets russes (Russian Ballets) . Between 1925 and 1930, Gabo gave lectures at the Bauhaus and published articles in the magazine. A new exhibition of his works took place at the Kestnergesellschaft, Hanover (1930). In 1931, he took part in the competition to design the Palace of the Soviets in Moscow and in 1933 he went to Paris where he stayed for three years, joining or at any rate taking part in the activities of Abstraction-Création, a group resulting from the Cercle et Carré group set up by Michel Seuphor. Then in 1935, he went to England where he stayed throughout World War II, writing an article that caused repercussions in *Circle* in 1937, contributing to the Abstract movement and in 1944 becoming a member of the Design Research Unit until his departure in 1946 for the USA, where he became an influential teacher at Harvard.

Between 1920 and 1922 Gabo in sculpture and Antoine Pevsner in painting based their work on radical abstraction, with the exception of the mathematical and geometric realities, partly under Malevich's influence. Gabo executed his first abstract constructions in wood, metal and plastic, in particular a *Kinetic Construction* formed by a metal stick set vibrated by a motor. He did not continue further with his research into moving sculptures since he was not satisfied with the actual running, noise and size of the motors available at the time. In 1923 in Berlin Gabo executed *Column*, a purely geometric construction in glass, metal and plastic and *Monument for an Aerodrome* in 1924. In 1925 he designed a plan for *Monument for an Institute of Physics and Mathematics* in glass and bronze, which again included kinetic elements where the movement defined virtual volumes in space. Generally speaking, the transparent materials he used also meant that the space could be increased. After 1932, in England, he executed works where the curves supplanted the previous planes and angles, marking them with thin tubes or plastic threads, creating frameworks which interfere with each other according to the angle at which the spectator views them while moving. Soto's kinetic images are a mere repetition of that. He then executed spatial constructions with aluminium, bronze, steel and gold threads generally calculated on the basis of the dihedral plane, kinds of endless ribbon related to the Mœbius strip, twisting and twisting over itself again, enclosed in the space of a transparent cube. In the USA, he was able from 1946 onwards to execute monumental works, including a monument in plastics and wires for the Rockefeller Center in New York, made up of spirals winding round a luminous column. Between 1954 and 1957 he designed the large steel monument of the De Bijenkorf shops in Rotterdam. In his subsequent executions, by remaining faithful to the principles of the 1920 manifesto, he increasingly used the viewer's movement around the work to generate, or rather suggest, a kineticism inherent in the form in space, thus extending it in the dimension of time. It seems very clear subsequently that Gabo, whose work is inseparable from Pevsner's, is the source of the sudden flourishing in the art world in the 1960s of these developments before they became optical curiosities with an amusing physical appearance: interference in Soto's frameworks, optical effects around Vasarely, kineticism around Nicolas Schoeffer, simulations of space with Kowalski among others.

Two retrospectives of his work were held at the Kunsthaus in Zurich and at the Tate Gallery in London in 1965. After his death, the Museum of Art in Dallas organised the exhibition *Sixty Years of Constructivism* (1985). The Museum of Modern Art in Oxford organised *Naum Gabo, the Constructivist Idea* (1987-88); the Galerie de France, Paris displayed a set of works (1989-90); Tate St Ives put on *Naum Gabo in Space and Time* (2002); finally the exhibition *Immaterial: Brancusi, Gabo and Moholy-Nagy* was held at Kettle's Yard, Cambridge (2004).

Gabo was knighted by the British government in 1971.

BIBLIOGRAPHY:

Herbert Read, Leslie Martin, *Gabo, Constructions, Sculptures, Paintings, Drawings, Engravings*, Harvard University Press, Cambridge (MA). Pevsner, Alexei, *A Biographical Sketch of my Brothers: Naum Gabo and Antoine Pevsner*, Amsterdam, 1964. Pevsner, Antoine, *Naum Gabo et Antoine Pevsner*, Zwanendurg, 1968. Pevsner, Antoine, *'Naum Gabo'* in *Abstraction, création, art non-figuratif*, periodical, Arno Press, New York, 1968. *Naum Gabo*, exhibition catalogue, Kunstverein, Hanover, 1971. *Naum Gabo, Skulpturen,*

Gemälde, Zeichnungen, exhibition catalogue, Nationalgalerie Stiftung Preußischer Kulturbesitz, Berlin, 1971. Newman, T., *Naum Gabo, the Constructive Process*, Tate Gall. Publications, London, 1976. Lodder, C., *Russian Constructivism*, New Haven, 1983. Nash, Steven A./Merkert, Jörn, *Naum Gabo: Sixty Years of Constructivism: including Catalogue Raisonné of the Constructions and Sculptures*, exhibition catalogue, Dallas Museum of Art, Dallas, Prestel, Munich, 1985. Gibson, B., *Naum Gabo au Musée Guggenheim*, The New Criterion, New York, 1986. Nash, S. A./ Merkert, J./ Lodder, C.(ed.), *Naum Gabo: Sixty Years of Constructivism*, exhibition catalogue, Art Museum, Dallas, 1986 (includes catalogue raisonné of constructions and sculptures and extgensive bibliography compiled by C.C. Sanderson). Hale, Nathan Cabot, *'Théorie et pensée artistique de Gabo'* in *World of Art*, periodical, London, April, 1986. Williams, G. (ed.), *Naum Gabo: Monoprints*, exhibition catalogue, Cambridge, Kettle's Yard, 1987. *Naum Gabo, 1890-1977*, exhibition catalogue, Annely Juda Fine Art, London, 1990. Merkert, Jörn/Hammer, Martin/Lodder, Christina, *Naum Gabo y el concurso para le Palacio de los Soviets, Moscú 1931-1933*, exhibition catalogue, Berlinische Gal., Berlin, Institut Valencia d'Art Modern, Centre Julio González, Valencia, 1993. Hammer, Martin/Lodder, Christina, *Constructing Modernity, the art and Career of Naum Gabo*, Yale University Press, New Haven and London, 2000. *Naum Gabo in Space and Time.*, exhibition catalogue, Tate St Ives, St Ives, 2002. Barassi, Sebastiano/Lodder, Christina, et al., *Immaterial: Brancusi, Gabo, Moholy-Nagy*, exhibition catalogue, Kettle's Yard, Cambridge, 2004.

Museums and Galleries:

Berlin (Berlinische Gal.): *Figure Kneeling* (c. 1915); *Constructed Torso* (1917-1918); *Draft for the Palace of the Soviets Competition* (1931) - Cambridge (Kettle's Yard, University of Cambridge): *Linear Construction* (c. 1942, Plexiglas and nylon) - Grenoble (Mus. de Grenoble): *Linear Construction in Space No. 2* - New Haven (AG, Yale University): *Construction* (1924) - New York (MoMA): *Head of a Woman in a Recess* (1916-1917); *Column* (1923) - New York (Solomon R. Guggenheim Mus.): *Linear Construction* (1942); *Transparent Variation on the Sphere Theme* (1951) - Paris (MNAM-CCI).

Auction records:

New York, 2 May 1974, *Vertical Construction No. 1* (phosphorus and stainless steel wire, bronze) USD 95,000. New York, 6 Nov 1981, *Suspended* (c. 1957-1964, metal, transparent plastic, nylon, l. 11½ ins / 29.2 cm) USD 71,000. London, 26 March 1984, *Linear Construction No. 1* (1942-1943, plastic and nylon cord, 8¼ x 8¼ x 2¼ ins / 21 x 21 x 5.5 cm) GBP 16,000. Rome, 20 Nov 1984, *La Chatte, Costume Drawing* (pencil/squared paper, 10¾ x 8¾ ins / 27.2 x 22.2 cm) GBP 9,500. London, 25 June 1985, *Model for a Sculpture in Rotterdam* (painted in black in parts, bronze, h. 60½ ins / 153.5 cm) GBP 100,000. London, 30 March 1987, *Linear Construction in Space No. 2* (1957/1958, perpex with nylon cord on a wooden base, h. 15 ins / 38 cm) GBP 130,000. New York, 16 May 1990, *Linear Construction in Space No. 2* (1950, Plexiglas and nylon cord, total h. 17 ins / 43.2 cm) USD 473,000. London, 25 March 1992, *Sketch* (1940, charcoal and colouring pencil, 16¼ x 18¾ ins / 41 x 47.8 cm) GBP 3,300. Amsterdam, 26 May 1993, *Model for the Construction of Bijenkorf* (wood and Plexiglas construction, 9½ x 2½ ins / 24 x 6.5 cm) NLG 20,700. New York, 4 Nov 1993, *Linear Construction in Space No. 2* (1961, Plexiglas with nylon cord on a Plexiglas base, h. 32¼ ins / 81.9 cm) USD 134,500. New York, 28 Sept 1994, *Structure Suspended in Space* (nylon cord in a bronze semi-circle on an aluminium base, l. 12¼ ins / 31.1 cm) USD 25,300. London, 28 June 1999, *Vertical Construction No.1* (c. 1962-1967, phosphor, bronze wire) GBP 290,000. London, 29 June 1999, *Construction in Space - Suspended* (c. 1957-1964, nylon, perspex, bronze and metal, 9 x 11 x 11 ins / 24 x 29 x 27 cm) GBP 16,000. London, 7 Feb 2001, *Monument for an Airport* (c. 1937, perspex and wooden base, 4 x 11 x 6 ins / 9 x 27 x 14 cm) GBP 25,000. New York, 5 Nov 2001, *Vertical Construction No.1* (1964-1965, stainless steel, spring, wire and bronze on wooden base) USD 210,000. Cologne, 4 Dec 2002, *Study for a Construction* (1934, pencil, 9 x 8 ins / 24 x 21 cm) EUR 4,000. Hamburg, 10 June 2004, *Construction with Alabaster Carving* (bronze, 8 x 6 x 2 ins / 21 x 16 x 4 cm) EUR 12,000.

GABOR, Aron

Hungarian, 20th - 21st century.
Born 1954, in Budapest.
Painter (including mixed media). Scenes with figures.

Aron Gabor won a Derkovits study scholarship and graduated from the school of fine arts in Budapest. Figurative, if not narrative, in style, he also expresses himself in gestural techniques inspired by Lyrical Abstraction. He uses various media, including installations, videos and films.

Since 1983 he has exhibited overseas, including at the following: Helsinki (1983); Rome (1984); the University of California (1985); Documenta in Kassel (1987); and *New Art in Hungary* with Geza Samu, Imre Bukta and Janos Szirtes in San Francisco (1989). His work is represented in the Ludwig Collections in Germany.

Auction records:

Paris, 14 Oct 1991, *Noah* (mixed media, 49¼ x 41¼ ins / 125 x 105 cm) FRF 13,000.

GABOR, Jeno

Hungarian, 20th century.
Born 1893, in Pécs; died 1968.
Painter. Scenes with figures.

Jeno Gabor was a student at the academy of fine art in Budapest between 1911 and 1915. In Pécs in 1919 he was in touch with artists close to the abstract avant-garde: Forbat, Molnar and others. He himself was a figurative painter, dealing with idyllic subjects.

A commemorative exhibition of all his work was organised in Pécs in 1971.

Bibliography:

Passuth, Krisztina/Szabó, Júlia, *L'Art en Hongrie 1905-1930. Art et révolution*, exhibition catalogue, Musée d'Art et d'Industrie, Saint-Étienne, musée d'Art moderne de la Ville de Paris, Paris, 1980.

GABOR, Marianne, later Mme Ronay Andras Mihaly

Hungarian, 20th century.
Born 26 April 1917.
Painter. Portraits, landscapes.

Marianne Gabor was a student at István Szönyi's school of art between 1931 and 1933, then at the school of fine art in Budapest between 1935 and 1940. She started exhibiting in 1938. In 1941 she was awarded the Hatvany prize. She frequently exhibited in Hungary and Italy: Rome and Palermo (1964), Venice, Grosseto and again in Rome (1966), Grosseto (1967) and France (1974).

Museums and Galleries:

Budapest (Magyar Nemzeti Gal.).

GABORIAUD, Josué

French, 20th century.
Born 1883; died 1955.
Painter, illustrator. Figures, nudes, landscapes, still-lifes, flowers.

Josué Gaboriaud was one of the many painters who formed part of the inter-war Paris School and who were followers of the detached, realist approach of the major contemporary movements. Between 1900 and 1906 he adopted a pointillist technique.

AUCTION RECORDS:
PARIS, 16 Dec 1920, *Apples and Flowers,* FRF 240. PARIS, 14 May 1925, *The Bridge and Esturgeon Restaurant at Poissy,* FRF 550. PARIS, 11 June 1927, *Landscape,* FRF 700. PARIS, 19 Feb 1943, *Still-life,* FRF 5,800. PARIS, 12 Nov 1946, *Nude,* FRF 1,200; *Flowers,* FRF 3,200. PARIS, 18 April 1947, *Dancer in her Dressing Room* (1931, pastel) FRF 3,300. VERSAILLES, 9 Dec 1973, *Woman in a Swimsuit,* FRF 1,800. VERSAILLES, 24 Oct 1976, *Young Woman Reading with Green Couch* (oil on canvas, 43 1/4 x 35 1/2 ins / 110 x 90 cm) FRF 8,500. DOUARNENEZ, 12 Aug 1983, *Washerwoman at Pont-Aven* (oil on panel, 9 x 11 ins / 22 x 27 cm) FRF 9,500. ZURICH, 18 May 1984, *Still-life with a Vase of Flowers and Teapot* (oil on canvas, 62 1/2 x 35 1/2 ins / 159 x 90 cm) CHF 4,800. ZURICH, 8 Nov 1985, *Seascape, Marseilles* (oil on paper remounted/canvas, 39 1/2 x 32 ins / 100.5 x 81.4 cm) CHF 6,500. VERSAILLES, 17 April 1988, *Still-life with Vase of Flowers* (1918, oil on canvas, 32 x 39 1/4 ins / 81 x 100 cm) FRF 5,000. VERSAILLES, 18 Dec 1988, *Barges and Boat Moored by a Bridge* (1924, oil on canvas, 23 1/2 x 32 ins / 60 x 81 cm) FRF 18,500. RHEIMS, 23 April 1989, *Still-life with Oysters* (oil on panel, 17 1/4 x 27 1/4 ins / 44 x 69 cm) FRF 5,000. VERSAILLES, 9 Dec 1990, *Still-life with Oysters* (oil/hardboard, 17 1/4 x 27 1/4 ins / 43.5 x 69 cm) FRF 5,000. PARIS, 7 June 1991, *Still-life with Vase of Tulips* (gouache/card, 12 x 10 ins / 30.5 x 25.5 cm) FRF 3,500. BOULOGNE-SUR-SEINE, 12 March 1995, *Vase of Tulips* (oil on canvas, 18 x 22 ins / 46 x 55 cm) FRF 5,000. PARIS, 8 Feb 2002, *Woman before a House* (oil on canvas, 32 x 39 ins / 81 x 100 cm) EUR 1,700.

GABORIT, Jean Hugues Léon Hippolyte
French, 19th - 20th century.
Born 16 July 1874, in Lyons.
Painter. Figures, portraits, landscapes.

Jean Gaborit studied under Nicolas Sicard at the École des Beaux-Arts in Lyons and then under Fernand Cormon in Paris. He exhibited in Lyons from 1903 and was awarded a bronze medal in 1910. He gained first prize in a competition to decorate the Salle Rameau in Lyons.

GABOURD, Irma
French, 19th century.
Painter.

She exhibited a number of portraits at the Paris Salon between 1843 and 1849.

GABOVICH, Josif
Russian, 19th century.
Born 19th century, in Colno (now Kolno, Poland).
Sculptor.

Gabovich was a pupil of Thomas. His work appeared at the Salon des Artistes Français of 1898 for which he received an honourable mention and at the Exposition Universelle in Paris in 1900, where he received a bronze award.

AUCTION RECORDS:
NEW YORK, 9 Jan 1997, *Mother and Child* (marble, h. 29 1/2 ins / 74.9 cm) uSD 7,475.

GABRIÉ, Marie, pseudonym of Marie Maurel
French, 19th century.
Born 1867, in Rouen.
Engraver (wood).

She regularly exhibited examples of her work at the Paris Salon.

GABRIEL
French, 15th century.
Active in Cambrai in 1482.
Painter.

GABRIEL
German, 15th - 16th century.
Born at the end of the 15th century, in Wasserburg (Bavaria).
Painter.

GABRIEL (Vicomte)
French, 19th century.
Born in Limoges.
Painter, pastellist.

He studied under A. Loyer and exhibited at the Paris Salon in 1868 with *Voltigeurs of the Guard in Combat,* followed in 1869 with a composition entitled *Alone!*.

GABRIEL
German, 19th century.
Born in Neuss (North Rhine-Westphalia).
Active c. 1838.
Painter.

Gabriel was a pupil of Hildebrandt, and is referred to by Siret.

GABRIEL, A.
Painter. Landscapes.

The Museum of Liège has two landscapes signed *A. Gabriel.*

MUSEUMS AND GALLERIES:
LIÈGE: *View of Amiens; The Sea at Etaples.*

GABRIEL, C.
French, 18th century.
Active c. 1760.
Engraver.

C. Gabriel engraved five small plates after H.-C. Gravelot.

GABRIEL, Claus
German, 17th century.
Born in Flensburg (Schleswig-Holstein).
Sculptor.

Claus Gabriel was the son of the painter Hans Petersen and studied in Copenhagen. He died between 1651 and 1655.

GABRIEL, E.
French, 19th century.
Active in Paris c. 1840.
Lithographer.

He provided illustrations for Eugène Sue's *Les Enfants trouvés* (*The Foundlings*) .

GABRIEL, Edith Mabel
British, 20th century.
Born 1882, in London; died 1972.
Sculptor.

Edith Gabriel exhibited in Paris from 1925, including regularly at the Salon des Artistes Français.

GABRIEL, Else
German, 20th - 21st century.
Born 1962, in Halberstadt, near Harzrand.
Installation artist.

Originally from East Germany, Gabriel works in Berlin and Los Angeles. Since 1990, she has worked with Ute Wrede. She uses computing and its capacity for infinite combinations to establish links between languages, signs and objects, but also to emphasize the limitations of human beings and their perceptions.

She participates in many group exhibitions in Germany, in Berlin and Nuremberg, in addition to abroad: Boston, Rome, New York, Washington and in Paris in 1992, in *Qui, Quoi, Où?* (*Who, What, Where?*) at the Musée d'Art moderne de la Ville de Paris. She holds solo shows in Germany.

GABRIEL, F.
French (?), 19th - 20th (?) century.
Painter. Landscapes.

F. Gabriel is mentioned by Miss Florence Levy and may be the same as the painter A. Gabriel, two of whose landscapes are in the Musée de Liège.

AUCTION RECORDS:
NEW YORK, 15 and 16 Feb 1906, *Landscape,* USD 50.

GABRIEL, François
American (?), 20th century.

Born 1893; died 1993.
Painter. Still-lifes (flowers/fruit).

François Gabriel's works have only recently appeared in public auctions and then only in New York. He followed in the great tradition of still-lifes of flowers and fruit which has remained fashionable since the 18th century, particularly in The Netherlands. His paintings, although decorative, nevertheless required a skilful technique.

AUCTION RECORDS:

NEW YORK, 17 Jan 1990, *Still-life with Flowers and Butterflies* (oil on panel, 16 x 11½ ins / 39.7 x 29.5 cm) USD 2,750. NEW YORK, 16 July 1992, *Still-life of Flowers in a Vase* (oil on panel, 19½ x 15½ ins / 49.5 x 39.4 cm) USD 2,750. NEW YORK, 20 Jan 1993, *Still-life of Grapes, Peaches and Plums near a Glass of Wine on an Entablature* (oil on panel, 20 x 16 ins / 50.8 x 40.6 cm) USD 5,175. NEW YORK, 16 Feb 1993, *Floral Composition on a Marble Entablature* (oil on panel, 20 x 16 ins / 50.5 x 40.6 cm) USD 2,420. NEW YORK, 22-23 July 1993, *Still-life of Flowers in a Glass Bowl* (oil on panel, 20 x 16 ins / 50.8 x 40.6 cm) USD 7,763. NEW YORK, 19 Jan 1994, *Still-life with Fruit* (oil on panel, 20 x 16 ins / 50.8 x 40.6 cm) USD 5,175. NEW YORK, 19 Jan 1995, *Still-life of Flowers* (oil on canvas, 50 x 40 ins / 127 x 101.6 cm) USD 5,750. NEW YORK, 20 July 1995, *Still-life of Flowers* (oil on canvas, 48 x 35¾ ins / 121.9 x 91.1 cm) USD 6,670. NEW YORK, 18-19 July 1996, *Still-life of Flowers in a Vase* (oil on canvas, 48 x 36 ins / 121.9 x 91.4 cm) USD 3,737. NEW YORK, 9 Jan 1997, *Still-life of Flowers and Fruit on an Entablature* (oil on canvas, 48 x 36 ins / 121.9 x 91.4 cm) USD 7,475; *Still-life of Flowers in an Urn on an Entablature* (oil on canvas, 40 x 30 ins / 101.6 x 76.2 cm) USD 6,612.

GABRIEL, Gabrielle
American, 20th century.
Born 1904, in Pennsylvania.
Painter.

GABRIEL, Georges François Marie
French, 18th - 19th century.
Born 1775, in Paris.
Painter, miniaturist, watercolourist, draughtsman, lithographer. Portraits.

Georges Gabriel was a student of Naigeon and Regnault. He produced his drawings for a major work at the Egyptian Institute.

GABRIEL, Henri, pseudonym of Henri Jean Brouwers
Belgian, 20th century.
Born 1918, in Anderlecht.
Sculptor, painter, graphic designer.
Lumino-Kinetic Art.

Henri Gabriel exhibited in Brussels, Antwerp, Ghent, Paris and elsewhere from 1959. From 1960, relatively early for this trend, he produced paintings, then swiftly turned to suspended mobiles in a succession of different materials including paper, Plexiglas, aluminium and foil. From 1976, he created 'poly-sculptures' composed of a number of interchangeable elements, and then 'mobilo-sculptures', which had some weight-bearing parts that were fixed and other suspended parts that were mobile.

GABRIEL, Jacques Ange
French, 18th century.
Born at the beginning of the 18th century, in Paris; died 1782.
Draughtsman, architect. Architectural views.

AUCTION RECORDS:

PARIS, 31 May 1920, *King's Library at Versailles* (pen) FRF 5,600; *Sketch of the Façade for the Petit Trianon Château* (pen) FRF 180. PARIS, le 12 June 1953, *Sketch for a Festival in a Park* (drawing) FRF 32,000.

GABRIEL, Jean
French, 17th - 18th century.
Born 28 July 1669, in Mulhouse; died 26 July 1718, in Mulhouse.
Painter.

Jean Gabriel worked for the town hall and the church of St Étienne in Mulhouse.

GABRIEL, Jean
Belgian, 20th century.
Born 1919, in Ligneuville.
Painter.

Jean Gabriel was a stonemason who learned to paint using a realist technique that tended towards photographic reproduction.

GABRIEL, Justin J.
French, 19th century.
Born 1838, in Brignoles (Var).
Painter, engraver. Landscapes, mountainscapes, waterscapes, flowers.

He studied under Ziem and Gleyre and exhibited at the Paris Salon from 1865, then at the Salon des Artistes Français; he received an honourable mention at the Exposition Universelle of 1900. Justin Gabriel travelled extensively throughout France, painting a broad variety of compositions ranging from pasture land in Normandy to the impressive solitude of the French Alps.

MUSEUMS AND GALLERIES:

FÉCAMP (Mus. des Arts et de l'Enfance): *Flower Market, Rouen.*

AUCTION RECORDS:

PARIS, 12 Feb 1920, *Windmill in Holland*, FRF 300. PARIS, 26 Oct 1922, *Narrow Street in Venice*, FRF 320. PARIS, 16 Dec 1926, *Grand Canal, Venice*, FRF 1,000. PARIS, 11-12 June 1928, *Lake Zurich*, FRF 500. VERSAILLES, 27 Jan 1980, *Bouquet of Roses* (oil on panel, 18¼ x 13in/46.5 x 33cm) FRF 2,100. AMSTERDAM, 16 Nov 1988, *Gondoliers on the Grand Canal in Venice with S Maria della Salute in the Background* (1898, oil on canvas, 18¼ x 21¾in/46.5 x 55.5cm) NLG 2,760.

GABRIEL, Louis
French, 19th century.
Born in Paris.
Engraver (line-engraving/stippling).

His works include a series of engravings after the *Life of Maria de' Medici* after Rubens.

GABRIEL, Matthäus Joseph
Austrian, 18th century.
Born 1692, in Planonowitz; died 1745.
Painter (porcelain).

Matthäus Gabriel worked especially in Vienna.

GABRIEL, Paul Joseph Constantin
Dutch, 19th century.
Born 5 July 1828, in Amsterdam; died 23 August 1903, in Scheveningen.
Active in Belgium from 1860 to 1884.
Painter. Genre scenes, landscapes, landscapes with figures, waterscapes, flowers.
Member of the artists' colony at Oosterbeek, The Hague School.

Gabriel worked as an apprentice carpenter before taking up painting. He studied at the school of fine arts in Amsterdam and later went to study with Barend Cornelis Koekkoek at Cleves, near Düsseldorf. He subsequently settled in Haarlem, where he met Anton Mauve, who greatly advanced his career. Gabriel worked for three years in Oosterbeek before moving to Brussels, where he lived from 1860 to 1884, at the request of a noted art lover. He returned to his native Holland in 1884, settling in Scheveningen. He painted numerous landscapes evoking the Dutch landscape and climate, such as marshlands and canals under lowering skies. His works are characterised by their subtle colour and delicate touch. Piet Mondrian was struck by their rigorous composition and structure: in 1895 he made a copy of Gabriel's painting *In July* (1888). Gabriel's work has featured in a number of themed exhibitions, including *Stad & Land. 19de-eeuwse meesterwerken uit het Stedelijk Museum* (*Town and country: 19th-century Masterpieces from the Stedelijk Museum*), held at the Nieuwe Kerk, Amsterdam, in 2003.

BIBLIOGRAPHY:

Berko, P./Berko, V., *Dictionary of Belgian Painters Born between 1750 and 1875*, Brussels, 1981. Flippo, W. C., et al., *Lexicon of the Belgian Romantic Painters*, Antwerp, 1981. *The Hague School: Dutch Masters of the 19th Century*, exhibition catalogue, Gemeentemuseum, The Hague; Royal Academy, London, London and The Hague, 1983. Bionda, R., C. Blotkamp, et al. (ed.), *The Age of Van Gogh: Dutch Painting 1880-1895*, Glasgow and Amsterdam, 1991. Peters, Moniek, et al., *Paul Joseph Constantin Gabriel, 1828-1903: Colorist van de Haagse School*, exhibition catalogue, Dordrecht Museum, Dordrecht, 1999.

MUSEUMS AND GALLERIES:

AMSTERDAM (Rijksmus.): *In July; Village View; Windmill; View Painted from Abcoude in July* - AMSTERDAM (Stedelijk Mus.): *Landscape; Shop Interior in Abcoude* - ANTWERP: watercolour - GRONINGEN: four landscapes - LIÈGE: *Farmyard Scene* - ROTTERDAM: *Landscape* - THE HAGUE: *In the Peat Bog at Kampen; Flowers.*

AUCTION RECORDS:

AMSTERDAM, 1898, *In Broad Daylight,* FRF 1,410. PARIS, 1899, *After Rain,* FRF 1,880. NEW YORK, 25 Oct 1904, *The Farm,* USD 250. NEW YORK, 15 March 1907, *In the Wheatfield,* USD 500. LONDON, 16 July 1909, *Landscape with Windmill,* GBP 110. LONDON, 11 July 1924, *Boat under Full Sail,* GBP 86. NEW YORK, 7 Nov 1935, *Autumn in Holland,* USD 140. THE HAGUE, 5-7 Nov 1946, *Landscape,* NLG 2,600; *Twilight in the Polders,* NLG 3,600. AMSTERDAM, 8 Feb 1966, *The Farm,* NLG 12,800. AMSTERDAM, 22 Oct 1974, *Landscape,* NLG 15,000. AMSTERDAM, 15 Nov 1976, *Landscape with a River* (oil on canvas, 15 x 21 1/4in/38 x 54cm) BEF 4,000. AMSTERDAM, 26 April 1977, *Riverscape with Boat* (1879, oil on canvas, 7 3/4 x 13 3/4in/19.5 x 35cm) NLG 7,800. AMSTERDAM, 12 Feb 1980, *Thatched Cottages beside a River* (oil on canvas, 17 1/2 x 23 1/4in/44.5 x 59cm) NLG 4,800. AMSTERDAM, 1 Oct 1981, *Landscape around Abcoude* (watercolour, 15 x 18 1/2in/38 x 47cm) NLG 7,000. VIENNA, 17 Nov 1982, *Landscape in the Polders* (oil on canvas, 15 3/4 x 24 3/4in/40 x 63 cm) ATS 70,000. AMSTERDAM, 15 March 1983, *Peasant Woman in the Fields near a Farm* (oil on canvas, 17 1/4 x 29 1/4in/44 x 74.5cm) NLG 8,200. AMSTERDAM, 28 May 1986, *Riverscape with a Windmill* (oil on canvas, 27 3/4 x 39 3/4in/70.5 x 101cm) NLG 36,000. AMSTERDAM, 3 May 1988, *Landscape with a Fisherman on a Riverbank, a Peasant Woman and a Windmill in the Background* (1850, oil on canvas, 10 1/2 x 14 1/2in/26.5 x 37cm) NLG 19,550. AMSTERDAM, 16 Nov 1988, *Farm in a Wooded Landscape with a Pond in the Foreground* (oil on canvas, remounted on panel, 12 1/4 x 18 1/2in/31 x 47cm) NLG 5,175; *Poppies and Roses in a Vase Placed on the Ground* (oil on canvas, 18 x 14 1/4in/45.5 x 36cm) NLG 6,900. AMSTERDAM, 28 Feb 1989, *The Zandweg: an Avenue in a Park along a Dyke* (oil on canvas/panel, 12 1/2 x 16 1/2in/31.5 x 42cm) NLG 4,370; *View of the Dutch Polders* (oil on canvas, 11 1/2 x 18 1/4in/29.5 x 46.5cm) NLG 23,000. AMSTERDAM, 5 June 1990, *Windmill in the Polders* (oil on canvas, 11 1/2 x 18 1/2in/29.5 x 47cm) NLG 21,850. AMSTERDAM, 11 Sept 1990, *Wooded Riverscape* (oil on canvas/panel, 8 x 11 3/4 ins / 20.5 x 30 cm) NLG 1,725. AMSTERDAM, 6 Nov 1990, *Sunny Farmyard* (1886, oil on canvas, remounted on panel, 13 x 17 1/4in/33 x 44cm) NLG 4,600. AMSTERDAM, 30 Oct 1991, *Vast Landscape in the Polders with a Distant Bell-tower* (oil on canvas, 14 1/4 x 23 1/2in/36 x 59.5cm) NLG 15,525. AMSTERDAM, 5-6 Nov 1991, *Village in the Dunes* (1872, oil on canvas, 10 1/4 x 16 1/4in/26 x 41.5cm) NLG 10,120. AMSTERDAM, 18 Feb 1992, *Small Red Windmill* (1866, oil on canvas, remounted on panel, 7 1/2 x 14 1/2in/19 x 37cm) NLG 5,520. AMSTERDAM, 14-15 April 1992, *Landscape in the Polders with Windmills* (watercolour, 13 1/2 x 22in/34 x 56cm) NLG 21,275. AMSTERDAM, 22 April 1992, *Sailboat Navigating along a Canal* (oil on canvas, 15 1/4 x 9 1/2in/39 x 24cm) NLG 18,400. AMSTERDAM, 21 April 1993, *Polder Landscape with a Cottage near a Windmill* (oil on paper, remounted on card, 7 3/4 x 11in/19.5 x 28cm) NLG 1,610. AMSTERDAM, 19 Oct 1993, *Riverscape with a Fisherman near a Small Wooden Bridge* (oil on canvas, 15 1/2 x 22in/39.5 x 56cm) NLG 16,100. AMSTERDAM, 21 April 1994, *Summer Landscape with a Peasant Unloading his Boat* (1875, oil on panel, 7 x 12 1/2in/18 x 32 cm) NLG 25,300. AMSTERDAM, 16 April 1996, *Afternoon* (oil on canvas, remounted on panel, 8 x 13 1/2in/20.5 x 34 cm) NLG 9,204. AMSTERDAM, 19-20 Feb 1997, *Polder Landscape with a Farm* (oil on canvas, remounted on wood, 6 1/4 x 9 3/4in/16 x 25cm) NLG 2,306. AMSTERDAM, 22 April 1997, *Skaters on a Frozen River near a Windmill* (oil on panel, 9 3/4 x 13 1/4in/25 x 33.5 cm) NLG 10,856. AMSTERDAM, 22 April 1997, *De Winkel, a Windmill near Abcoude* (oil on canvas, 25 1/2 x 40 1/4in/65 x 102cm) NLG 76,700. AMSTERDAM, 27 Oct 1997, *Village and Church* (watercolour, 12 1/2 x 19 3/4in/31.5 x 50cm) NLG 7,080. AMSTERDAM, 27 April 1999, *Countryside near Amsterdam at Daybreak* (1878, oil on canvas, 26 x 40 ins / 65 x 101 cm) NLG 60,000. AMSTERDAM, 26 Oct 1999, *Summer - Polder near Kortenhoef* (oil on canvas, 36 x 59 ins / 91 x 150 cm) NLG 260,000. BRUSSELS, 15 Feb 2000, *Morning at Veenendaal* (1870, oil on canvas, 16 x 24 ins / 40 x 62 cm) BEF 600,000. AMSTERDAM, 18 April 2000, *Watermill* (oil on panel, 10 x 16 ins / 25 x 40 cm) NLG 130,000. AMSTERDAM, 23 April 2001, *Farmhouse by a Canal* (oil on canvas mounted on panel, 17 x 21 ins / 43 x 53 cm) NLG 38,000. AMSTERDAM, 23 Oct 2001, *Painter, possibly W B Tholen, at Work in Punter on a Sunny Day* (oil on canvas, 13 x 21 ins / 33 x 53 cm) EUR 60,000. AMSTERDAM, 23 April 2002, *Windmills in a Polder Landscape* (c. 1868-1870, oil on canvas, 15 x 24 ins / 37 x 60 cm) EUR 32,000. AMSTERDAM, 22 Oct 2002, *Windmills in a Landscape near Abcoude* (oil on canvas, 11 x 18 ins / 29 x 46 cm) EUR 26,000. LONDON, 29 Jan 2003, *Landscape with Windmill* (oil on canvas, 11 x 18 ins / 28 x 45 cm) GBP 11,500. AMSTERDAM, 21 Oct 2003, *Windmills in a Polder Landscape* (oil on canvas, 12 x 18 ins / 30 x 46 cm) EUR 25,000. AMSTERDAM, 20 April 2004, *Windmill near Abcoude* (watercolour, 14 x 24 ins / 35 x 62 cm) EUR 6,000. AMSTERDAM, 21 April 2004, *Landscape with a White Bridge* (oil on canvas mounted on panel, 7 x 11 ins / 19 x 29 cm) EUR 4,200.

GABRIEL, Paulus Joseph

Dutch, 19th century.

Born 1785, in Amsterdam; died 31 December 1833, in Amsterdam.

Painter, miniaturist, sculptor.

Gabriel studied under his father, a sculptor, and later in Paris and Rome under P. Cartelier and Canova. He was a protégé of Lucien Bonaparte. In 1820 he was appointed director of the Amsterdam academy. Kramm gives the date of his death, incorrectly, as 2 July 1853.

GABRIEL, Pierre

French, 17th century.

Painter.

Pierre Gabriel was a master craftsman for the painters in Lyons in 1680.

GABRIEL, R.

French, 18th century.

Draughtsman. Portraits.

AUCTION RECORDS:
PARIS, 1 July 1992, *Portrait of the Princess de Lamballe* (lead pencil, 5 1/4 x 4 ins / 13.5 x 10 cm) FRF 15,000.

GABRIEL BORBA FILHO, José
Brazilian, 20th century.
Born 1942, in São Paulo.
Painter.
José Gabriel Borba Filho lived in Europe from 1962 to 1963, mainly in Florence where he studied at the drawing academy. In 1964 he returned to Brazil where he joined the architecture faculty at São Paulo. In 1965 he began studying mosaics at the school of fine arts in Lima. He has taught at the São Paulo fine arts faculty since 1971 and has held numerous solo exhibitions in Brazil.

Much of Borba Filho's work is politically inspired and is expressed using figurative and narrative techniques close to Pop Art. As his work developed, he became more open to experimentation.

GABRIEL-BELOT. See **BELOT Gabriel**

GABRIEL-FOURNIER. See **FOURNIER Gabriel**

GABRIEL-ROUSSEAU
French, 20th century.
Painter. Urban landscapes.
Gabriel-Rousseau exhibited in Paris at the Salon of the Société Nationale des Beaux-Arts and at the Salon des Artistes Indépendants which, in 1943, held an exhibition of his collected work.

GABRIELE DA PIACENZA
Italian, 14th century.
Active in Treviso c. 1373.
Sculptor (wood).
Gabriele da Piacenza did work for Treviso Cathedral.

GABRIELE DA RHO
Italian, 15th century.
Active in Milan c. 1470.
Sculptor.
Gabriele da Rho sculpted a *St Joseph* for Milan Cathedral.

GABRIELE DAGLI OCCHIALI.
See **FERRANTINI Gabriele**

GABRIELE DE CIPELLI. See **CIPELLI Gabriele di**

GABRIELE DELLA SELLA. See **SELLA Gabriele de**

GABRIELE DI BATTISTA
Italian, 15th century.
Died 13 March 1505, in Palermo.
Sculptor.
Gabriele di Battista worked with Andrea Mancino.

GABRIELE DI ROMA
Italian, 15th - 16th century.
Active at the end of the 15th and at the beginning of the 16th centuries.
Sculptor.
Gabriele di Roma worked on the façade and arcades of the church of the Annunziata in Palermo.

GABRIELI, Antonio
Italian, 18th century.
Born 29 July 1694, in Belluno.
Painter.

GABRIELI, Francesco
Italian, 18th century.
Died 24 January 1730, in Belluno.
Active in Bassano.
Painter.

GABRIELLE, pseudonym of Vignesoult, Gabrielle
French, 20th century.
Born 10 July 1925, in Tarbes (Hautes-Pyrenées).
Painter, sculptor. Religious subjects, figures, portraits.
Gabrielle exhibited in Paris from 1976 at the Salon des Artistes Français, where she received a commendation, and at the Salon d'Automne. She also showed her work in solo exhibitions in Abidjan, Dakar, Algiers and Paris.

She fashioned her portraits with a eloquence reminiscent of the mischievousness of Van Dongen and sculpted figures in a stylised manner.

MUSEUMS AND GALLERIES:
LOURDES (Biblitohèque Municipale): a bronze - TARBES (Conservatoire Henri-Duparc): *The Bandstand*; *Flute Players*.

GABRIELLE-DUMONTET. See **DUMONTET Gabriel, Mrs**

GABRIELLI, Amedeo
Italian, 19th century.
Died 1817, in Bassano (Veneto).
Engraver.
Amedeo Gabrielli engraved a large number of portraits and made reproductions of famous paintings.

GABRIELLI, Antonio
Italian, 17th century.
Born c. 1625, in Città di Castello.
Architect. Theatre decoration.
Antonio Gabrielli painted theatre décor and sets.

GABRIELLI, Camillo
Italian, 18th century.
Born in Pisa; died 1730.
Painter. History painting.
Camillo Gabrielli was a pupil of Ciro Ferri. He was reputed for his fresco work, notably for the grand hall in the Palazzo Allicata. He also painted some oils for the Carmelite order.

AUCTION RECORDS:
LONDON, 16 Nov 1960, *Communion of Mary Magdalene*, GBP 780.

GABRIELLI, Francesco dei.
See **FRANCESCO DEI GABRIELLI**

GABRIELLI, Gaspare
Italian, 19th century.
Born 1770, in Rome; died 1828.
Active in Dublin at the beginning of the 19th century.
Painter. Landscapes, urban landscapes, gardens, ruins, architectural views, architectural interiors.
Gaspare Gabrielli appears to have studied in Rome. He arrived in Dublin prior to 1811 and remained there until 1819. He exhibited twice at the Royal Academy in London, in 1811 and 1819. He returned to Rome some time after 1819. His *View of the Roman Forum* in the Glasgow Art Gallery and Museum bears the inscription 'Rome, 1824'.

MUSEUMS AND GALLERIES:
GLASGOW: *View of the Forum* (1824) - ST-OMER: *Italian Landscape* (two canvases).

AUCTION RECORDS:
LONDON, 10 April 1930, *Interior of the National Gallery*, GBP 7. LONDON, 13 July 1939, *In a Park*, GBP 9. VIENNA, 20 Sept 1977, *Forum Romanum* (oil on canvas, 19 1/4 x 34 ins / 49 x 86.5 cm) ATS 25,000. BERN, 17 May 1999, *View of Roman Forum* (1818, oil on canvas, a pair, 18 x 23 ins / 46 x 58 cm) CHF 67,000.

GABRIELLI, Gioseffo
Italian, 18th century.
Born 1686; died 1767.
Active in Bologna.
Painter.

GABRIELLI, Giuseppe
Italian, 19th century.
Active in London.
Sculptor.

Giuseppe Gabrielli played an active part in the exhibitions held at the Royal Academy in London, from 1863 to 1880.

GABRIELLI, Ignazio
Italian, 19th century.
Born at the beginning of the 19th century, in Camaiore (Tuscany).
Painter.

Ignazio Gabrielli worked for the church of Viareggio.

GABRIELLI, Louis
French, 20th century.
Born 1901, in Corte, Corsica.
Painter.

Louis Gabrielli studied law in Aix-en-Provence. He went to Paris in 1928 and began to paint and model in 1930. However, he did not begin exhibiting until after World War II. In 1950 he exhibited at the Salon des Réalités Nouvelles. He also showed collections of his work in solo exhibitions in Paris in 1949, 1952 and 1955.

He was part of the Informal Abstraction movement which uses only colour and materials to the exclusion of any defined form.

GABRIELLO, Onofrio, also known as Onofrio da Messina
Italian, 17th century.
Born 1611, in Messina; died 1706.
Painter. History painting, portraits.

Onofrio Gabriello studied initially under Antonio Ricci, then in Rome under Pietro da Cortona. He spent time in Venice before returning to Messina, where he worked extensively for churches and private collectors, producing numerous portraits. The 1672 revolution obliged him to leave his native town and move to Padua. His best work is housed in the church of S Francesco di Paola in Messina.

GABRINI, Pietro
Italian, 19th - 20th century.
Born 1856, in Rome; died 1926.
Painter, watercolourist. Genre scenes, landscapes.

Pietro Gabrini exhibited in Paris, Quebec and Chicago. Given the number of his works on the English market, it is reasonable to assume that he spent some time in Britain.

He painted a few religious and historical compositions, including *St Catherine and St Elizabeth*. However, the majority of his paintings were either familiar genre scenes, such as *Boat Trip*, or landscapes and views of towns (particularly Venice).

AUCTION RECORDS:
LONDON, 29 June 1908, *Dandy* (watercolour) GBP 56. LONDON, 6 March 1936, *St Catherine and St Elizabeth,* GBP 60. LONDON, 8 Nov 1946, *Lagoons (Venice),* GBP 33. LONDON, 15 March 1974, *The Bay of Naples,* Gns 1,500. VIENNA, 20 Sept 1977, *Return of the Fishing Boats* (oil on canvas, 27 x 48 ins / 68.5 x 122 cm) ATS 30,000. NEW YORK, 9 June 1981, *Harem* (watercolour and pencil, 23 x 17 1/2 ins / 58.5 x 44.5 cm) USD 1,600. NEW YORK, 25 Feb 1983, *Recital* (oil on canvas, 28 1/2 x 51 ins / 72.5 x 129.5 cm) USD 2,000. NEW YORK, 31 Oct 1985, *Game of Cards* (watercolour, 21 x 29 1/2 ins / 53.3 x 75 cm) USD 3,300. LONDON, 9 Oct 1987, *Return of the Harvesters in the Roman Countryside* (oil on canvas, 26 x 51 1/2 ins / 66 x 131 cm) GBP 5,000. NEW YORK, 25 Feb 1988, *Piazza Barbarini and the Temple of Vesta* (oil on canvas, 31 x 49 ins / 78.7 x 124.5 cm) USD 16,500. LONDON, 17 March 1989, *Boat Trip* (1913, watercolour, 25 1/2 x 38 1/2 ins / 65 x 98 cm) GBP 4,400. NEW YORK, 24 May 1989, *The Grand Canal* (oil on canvas/card, 25 3/4 x 40 1/2 ins / 65.4 x 102.8 cm) USD 17,600. LONDON, 6 June 1990, *Declaration* (oil on canvas, 20 1/4 x 14 1/4 ins / 51.5 x 36 cm) GBP 1,100. LONDON, 15 Feb 1991, *Returning Home: Tivoli* (watercolour/paper, 38 1/2 x 24 1/2 ins / 97.8 x 62.2 cm) GBP 3,300. PARIS, 24 May 1991, *Conversation at the Water's Edge* (oil on canvas, 21 1/4 x 33 ins / 54 x 84 cm) FRF 24,000. LONDON, 4 Oct 1991, *Return to Naples after a Trip at Sea* (1907, oil on canvas, 25 1/4 x 43 3/4 ins / 64.1 x 111.1 cm) GBP 7,920. ROME, 24 March 1992, *Lover's on a Boat* (watercolour, 21 1/4 x 29 1/4 ins / 54 x 74 cm) ITL 3,680,000. BOLOGNA, 8-9 June 1992, *Auction in Ancient Rome* (oil on canvas, 25 1/2 x 43 1/4 ins / 65 x 110 cm) ITL 4,600,000. LONDON, 2 Oct 1992, *Goatherd* (pencil and watercolour/paper, 28 1/2 x 21 1/4 ins / 72.5 x 54 cm) GBP 1,540. NEW YORK, 29 Oct 1992, *Fishermen at Dawn* (oil on canvas/synthetic resin, 40 1/4 x 26 ins / 102.4 x 66 cm) USD 5,500. MILAN, 17 Dec 1992, *Chapel near the Lagoon* (oil on canvas, 40 x 25 1/2 ins / 101.5 x 65 cm) ITL 5,000,000. ROME, 16 Dec 1993, *On Board a Boat at Sunset* (oil on canvas, 28 1/4 x 52 ins / 72 x 132 cm) ITL 11,500,000. AMSTERDAM, 19 April 1994, *Suitor* (1878, watercolour, 18 1/4 x 15 1/2 ins / 46.5 x 39.5 cm) NLG 3,450. ROME, 31 May 1994, *Country Fair* (oil on canvas, 28 x 51 1/2 ins / 71 x 131 cm) ITL 44,783,000. LONDON, 18 Nov 1994, *Grape Harvester* (oil on canvas, 63 x 44 1/2 ins / 160.3 x 113 cm) GBP 9,200. LONDON, 10 Feb 1995, *Arrival* (1882, oil on canvas, 59 1/4 x 33 ins / 150.4 x 84 cm) GBP 12,075. MILAN, 31 May 1999, *Threatening Weather* (watercolour, 21 x 15 ins / 54 x 38 cm) ITL 4,000,000. TORONTO, 2 Dec 1999, *Festival of Spring* (1907, oil on canvas, 54 x 39 ins / 136 x 100 cm) CAD 9,000. NEW YORK, 25 Oct 2000, *Grape Picker* (watercolour, 38 x 24 ins / 97 x 62 cm) USD 3,000. COLOGNE, 25 Nov 2000, *Fishing Boat off Rocky Coast* (oil on canvas, 23 x 17 ins / 58 x 44 cm) DEM 9,000. NEW YORK, 3 Oct 2001, *Outing on the Bay* (oil on canvas/board, 29 x 53 ins / 74 x 135 cm) USD 9,500. LONDON, 29 Nov 2001, *Young Maidens Feeding a Swan* (watercolour, 13 x 28 ins / 34 x 71 cm) GBP 1,400. PHILADELPHIA, 22 June 2003, *Day's Catch* (watercolour, 25 x 39 ins / 64 x 98 cm) USD 2,500. FLORENCE, 9 Dec 2003, *Auction in Rome* (oil on canvas, 25 x 43 ins / 64 x 108 cm) EUR 24,000. NEW YORK, 30 March 2004, *Exotic Beauty* (watercolour, a pair, 24 x 18 ins / 61 x 46 cm) USD 13,000. NEW YORK, 23 April 2004, *Royal Visit* (1882, oil on canvas, 33 x 59 ins / 84 x 149 cm) USD 19,000.

GABRINO DA PARMA
Italian, 15th century.
Born 1419, in Parma; died c. 1470, in Reggio.
Painter.

Gabrino was a monk.

GABRIO DA CREMONA
Italian, 13th century.
Active c. 1288.
Painter.

This artist painted a *Christ on the Cross* for the church of S Eustorgio in Milan.

GABRISCHEVSKY, Eugen
Russian, 20th century.
Born 1893, in Moscow.
Painter, watercolourist.

Eugen Gabrischevsky was actually a doctor, a well-known geneticist. During an illness that kept him isolated from the world, he started to express himself in images. He portrayed his bright dreams in watercolours that were sometimes soft and sometimes harsh. Once he had recovered, he stopped all his painting. In 2002, he was represented at the exhibition *The Crowd*, a collection of Art Brut (Outsider Art) in Lausanne.

AUCTION RECORDS:
PARIS, 27 May 1991, *Figures Against a Pink Background* (watercolour, 11 x 11 ins / 27 x 27 cm) FRF 4,200.

GABRON, Antoon
Flemish School, 17th century.
Born 1 January 1622, in Antwerp.
Painter.

He was the brother of Guilliam Gabron. He became a master of the Guild of St Luke in Antwerp in 1641.

GABRON, Guilliam or William or Willem
Flemish School, 17th century.
Born 28 October 1619, in Antwerp; died 2 August 1678, in Antwerp.
Painter. Still-lifes (including game), animals.

He was a member of the Antwerp Guild of St Luke from 1640-1641, and was active in Italy as well as in Antwerp. He was related to the family of the painter Cassiers, and his sister married the sculptor Arthur Quellinus.

MUSEUMS AND GALLERIES:
HANOVER: *Still-life* - MUNICH: *Still-life*.
AUCTION RECORDS:
NEW YORK, 27 Nov 1968, *Still-life*, USD 2,600. LONDON, 29 Nov 1974, *Still-life*, Gns 7,000. LONDON, 18 July 1986, *Still-life with Game* (oil on canvas, 36 1/2 x 48 3/4in/93 x 123.9cm) GBP 4,000. PARIS, 18 April 1991, *Still-life: Hunting Trophies* (oil on canvas, 23 1/4 x 28 3/4in/59 x 73cm) FRF 70,000. PARIS, 17 Nov 1995, *Still-life in Candlelight with Pewter Utensils* (oil on canvas, 17 1/4 x 22in/43.5 x 55cm) FRF 98,000. NEW YORK, 11 Jan 1996, *Still-life with a Pewter Pitcher, a Peeled Lemon and a Spilt Glass on a Table Covered with a Green Cloth* (oil on canvas, 20 1/2 x 27in/52.1 x 68.6cm) USD 54,625. NEW YORK, 16 May 1996, *Still-life with Fruit, Gold and Silver Plates and a Squirrel on a Table Covered with an Oriental Rug* (oil on canvas, 61 1/4 x 47 1/2in/155.6 x 120.7cm) USD 85,000. NEW YORK, 31 Jan 1997, *Dead Game at the Foot of a Tree with a Falcon, a Hound and Hunting Equipment* (oil on canvas, 34 x 44 1/2in/85.5 x 113cm) USD 19,550. LONDON, 17 Dec 1999, *Silver Salt-cellar, Tazza, Pewter Flagon, Roemer, Peeled Lemon on Table* (1644, oil on panel, 33 x 38 ins / 84 x 97 cm) GBP 90,000. PARIS, 23 March 2000, *Seven Peregrine Falcons Perched on Rocks* (oil on canvas, 45 x 56 ins / 115 x 143 cm) FRF 360,000. VIENNA, 1 Oct 2003, *Still-life with Ham and Bread on Pewter Plate* (oil on panel, 19 x 16 ins / 49 x 40 cm) EUR 12,000.

GABRUS, Zakarias
Hungarian, 19th century.
Born 18 August 1794, in Gherla; died 27 April 1870, in Gherla.
Painter.

Zakarias Gabrus worked on Gherla cathedral.

GABUGGIANI, Baldassare.
See **GABBUGIANI**

GABUTI, Lorenzo
Italian, 17th - 18th century.
Active in Pisa c. 1705.
Engraver.

Lorenzo Gabuti engraved illustrations on religious themes.

GABY, Charlot
French, 16th century.
Active in Tours.
Sculptor.

Gaby participated in the preparations for the festivities staged in honour of the entry into Tours of Queen Anne of Brittany.

GACAUD, J.
Dutch, 18th century.
Active c. 1793.
Miniaturist.

Only one portrait by this artist is known. He may have lived in Breda.

GACH, George
Hungarian, 20th century.
Born 27 January 1909.
Active from 1952 in the USA.
Sculptor (including bronze), painter. Figures, sporting subjects, animals, horses, portraits, landscapes, still-lifes. Sculpted groups.

The son of István Gach, George Gach studied at the academy of fine art in Budapest. In 1942 he was awarded a grant to study for a year in Rome. He taught sculpture at the academy of fine art in Beirut between 1947 and 1952 and travelled and worked a great deal across Europe, the Americas and Australia before settling in New York.

He works in wood, terracotta and plastic, but his favourite technique is to obtain unique pieces in bronze with lost wax. His main theme is the horse, usually mounted, though he also sculpted other animals including birds. He has often treated dance and all kinds of sport. One of the characteristics of his work is the frequency of groups: several horses jumping over a fence, several polo players scoring, American football players in full, violent action, a parade of clerics with pomp and ceremony, a group of dancers, the sculptor and his model. His statuettes and groups are unpretentious, all the more readily taking on a touch of humour and skilfully expressing particularly dynamic, vivacious attitudes.

George Gach has featured in collective and solo exhibitions in the main cities of the USA. A member of the Allied Artists of America, the National Sculpture Society and other associations, he has won many awards in Lebanon and in the USA.

GACH, István or Stephen
Hungarian, 20th century.
Born 31 March 1880.
Sculptor.

István Gach was Gyorgy Zala's student in Budapest. He completed his training in Paris. Like his master, Zala, he sculpted monuments. These included the *Monument to the Battle for Hungary's Independence*. He was George Gach's father.

GACHET, Étienne
French, 17th century.
Sculptor.

GACHET, Jules
Swiss, 19th century.
Born 18 March 1859, in Echallens.
Painter.

Gachet studied painting in Geneva. He is noted for his landscapes of the shores of Lake Geneva and Ticino.

GACHET, Paul (Dr), pseudonym: Paul Van Ryssel
French, 19th century.
Born 30 July 1828, in Lille; died 9 January 1909, in Auvers-sur-Oise.
Painter, engraver.

Gachet studied medicine in Paris and was a regular customer at the Brasserie des Martyrs, where he mingled with Charles Baudelaire, Gustave Courbet, Théodore de Banville and the author Jules Champfleury. An occasional painter, he exhibited at the 1872 Salon; as a collector of engravings, he assembled works by Bresdin and Meyron. He signed his work *Paul Van Ryssel* (from 'Rijsel', the Flemish name for Lille).

Gachet formed close ties with Claude Monet and Edgar Degas and was perhaps the first to purchase canvases by Paul Cézanne. He also befriended Edouard Manet and Auguste Renoir and, not least, Vincent van Gogh. In short, Gachet took it upon himself to befriend what were in essence the least understood artists of the day and to take them under his wing, even providing them with accommodation at his house in Auvers-sur-Oise. He can also take at least some credit for introducing these and other artists, notably Cézanne, to the discipline of engraving. Cézanne lived at Auvers for two whole years, between 1872 and 1874, and it was during that time, when he painted *The Suicide's House* (*House of the Hanged Man*), that he abandoned his dark and brooding baroque manner and embarked on his quest to develop a 'modern classicism'. It was Gachet to whom Auguste Renoir entrusted the care of his young friend and model Marie in a bid to cure her tuberculosis. In late May 1890, when Van Gogh came out of his 'exile' at the asylum at St-Rémy, he was counselled by Camille Pissarro to seek out Gachet who, despite doing his best for his patient, was unable to prevent Van Gogh committing suicide on July 27 of that year. That said, Van Gogh somehow found time to dash off no fewer than about fifty canvases during his two months in Gachet's care, including *Mademoiselle Gachet at the Piano* and the *Portrait of Dr Gachet in a White Bonnet*, not to mention such masterpieces as *Church at Auvers* and *Crows in a Wheat-field*. In 1952 Paul Gachet's son donated to the Louvre most of what had meanwhile become one of the most celebrated private collections in the world; it is now in the Musée d'Orsay.

BIBLIOGRAPHY:

Gachet, P. (ed.), *Lettres impressionistes: Pissarro, Cézanne, Guillaumin, Renoir, Monet, Sisley, Vignon, Van Gogh et autres*, Paris, 1957. Saltzman, Cynthia, *Portrait of Dr Gachet, the Story of a Van Gogh Masterpiece: Modernism, Money, Politics, Collectors, Dealers, Taste, Greed, and Loss*, Viking, New York, 1998. Distel, Anne/Stein, Susan-Alyson, et al., *Cézanne to Van Gogh: the Collection of Doctor Gachet*, exhibition catalogue, Metropolitan Museum of Art, New York, 1999. Solomon Kiefer, Carol, *The Hanged Man: Cézanne and the Art of the Print*, Mead Art Museum, Amherst (MA), 1999.

GACHNANG, Johannes

Swiss, 20th century.
Born 1939, in Zurich.
Engraver.

Johannes Gachnang studied architecture in Zurich, then in Paris and Berlin. He has exhibited as an engraver since 1966. The affinity with architecture can be sensed in his engravings, in which thousands of tiny mosaic facets interfere with and are superimposed on one another in strange arabesques. This technique hints at an anguished, obsessive Realism with its roots in Byzantine art.

GACHON, Pol

French, 20th century.
Born 1943, in Aubusson (Creuse).
Painter.
Nouvelle Figuration.

Pol Gachon's painting has evolved in an unadorned, Minimalist manner. It revolves around the world of machines and automation. His pictorial elements include tippers, screws, springs and other mechanical paraphernalia and tools which he paints in an industrial style and places on what appears to be a smooth, tense film floating in abstract space.

He has exhibited his work in Paris since 1967, notably at the Salon Grands et Jeunes d'Aujourd'hui. He has participated in numerous other group exhibitions, including those in the following: Basel (1972); Lille (1973); Nantes (1979); Düsseldorf (1985); Antwerp (1986); Paris (1988-1990, 1992-1993); Grenoble (1991); Pau (1993); Montargis (1993); Strasbourg (1996); and Portugal (1997). Solo exhibitions have been held mainly in Paris, but also in Lisbon, Nantes, St-Tropez and Oporto, among other cities.

GACI, Lodovico

Italian, 15th century.
Active in Cremona c. 1489.
Miniaturist.

The library in Wernigerode (Germany) owns a manuscript written and illuminated by Lodovico Gaci.

GACI, Rutilio

Italian, 17th century.
Born in Castiglione; died c. 1635, in Madrid.
Sculptor, medallist.

By 1600 Rutilio Gaci was already living and working in Spain. He produced some wax busts and sculpted some funerary monuments, but the bulk of his work comprises a large number of medals.

GACON, Anne

French, 20th century.
Born 15 September 1913, in Ecrouves (Meurthe-et-Moselle).
Painter.

Anne Gacon studied at the École des Beaux-Arts in Nancy. She exhibited in Paris at the Salon des Artistes Indépendants, of which she was a member.

Her painting is figurative with some Modernist touches.

GACON, J.

French, 17th century.
Active in Paris.
Engraver.

J. Gachon produced a *Portrait of C. P. Richelet*.

GACS, Gabor

Hungarian, 20th century.
Born 1930.
Engraver, illustrator.

Between 1951 and 1955, Gabor Gach was a student at the school of fine art and then at the faculty of graphic arts in Budapest. His works were exhibited in 1956 and 1965 at the Ernst Museum and won him awards in Vienna and Lugano.

BIBLIOGRAPHY:

Hongrie 68, exhibition catalogue, Pannonia, Budapest, 1968.

GAD, Hans

Swedish, 16th century.
Active c. 1530.
Painter.

Gad painted frescoes in the churches at Delsbo, Forssa, Järfsö and Hassela.

GADALA, Paul C.

French, 19th century.
Active in Paris.
Painter.

He was a member of the Société des Artistes Français from 1897 and a participant in its exhibitions.

GADAN, Antoine

French, 19th - 20th century.
Born 1854, in Seurre; died 1934, in Bône (now Annaba), Algeria.
Painter. Local scenes, figures, landscapes with figures, still-lifes.
Orientalism.

Antoine Gadan's family was originally from Burgundy. He left his native Seurre in 1881 for Algeria accompanied by his father and brother. He produced almost all his work in Algeria, where he was joined by another artist from Seurre, Louis Carbonnel. He painted picturesque scenes and local characters. His small number of still-lifes also contain exotic items. Gadan's work was slow to appear in public auctions in Paris and later New York.

In 2003 his work was shown at a group exhibition entitled *Lumineuse Algérie, sous le Regard des Peintres de Marines (1830-1960)* (*Luminous Algeria, Through the Eyes of Seascape Painters (1830-1960)*) at the Musée National de la Marine in Toulon.

BIBLIOGRAPHY:

Mourot, Marjolaine/Vidal-Bué, Marion/Cazenave, Elisabeth, et al., *Lumineuse Algérie, sous le regard des peintres de marines (1830-1960)*, exhibition catalogue, Musée national de la Marine, Toulon, 2003.

AUCTION RECORDS:

PARIS, 2 Dec 1985, *The Golden Stream* (oil on canvas, 23 1/2 x 39 1/4 ins / 60 x 100 cm) FRF 28,000. PARIS, 6 April 1990, *The Young Shepherdess* (oil on canvas, 21 1/4 x 39 1/4 ins / 54 x 100 cm) FRF 19,000. PARIS, 8 April 1991, *Fruit Picking in Algeria* (oil on canvas, 23 1/2 x 38 1/2 ins / 60 x 98 cm) FRF 14,000. PARIS, 13 April 1992, *The Young Shepherdess* (oil on canvas, 21 1/4 x 39 1/4 ins / 54 x 100 cm) FRF 22,000. PARIS, 22 June 1992, *Wadi in Southern Algeria* (oil on canvas, 28 1/2 x 51 1/4 ins / 72.5 x 130 cm) FRF 78,000. PARIS, 5 April 1993, *The Little Shepherds* (oil on canvas, 22 x 39 3/4 ins / 56 x 101 cm) FRF 16,000. PARIS, 22 April 1994, *Shepherdess by the Sea outside Bône* (oil on canvas, 22 1/2 x 39 1/4 ins / 57 x 100 cm) FRF 23,000. PARIS, 7 Nov 1994, *Water Carriers by a Wadi* (oil on canvas, 70 3/4 x 51 1/4 ins / 180 x 130 cm) FRF 40,000. PARIS, 12 June 1995, *Caravan Crossing a Wadi* (oil on canvas, 16 1/4 x 28 1/2 ins / 41 x 72.5 cm) FRF 10,000. PARIS, 21 April 1996, *Water Carrier* (1883, oil on canvas, 24 x 37 1/2 ins / 61 x 95 cm) FRF 24,000. PARIS, 9 Dec 1996, *Shepherd in the Countryside near Bône* (oil on canvas, 19 3/4 x 32 ins / 50 x 81 cm) FRF 16,000. NEW YORK, 9 Jan 1997, *Still-life with a Bottle of Champagne, Pomegranate and Orange Quarters* (oil on canvas, 26 x 32 3/4 ins / 65.1 x 83.2 cm) USD 13,800. PARIS, 17 Nov 1997, *Encampment at Biskra* (1889, oil on canvas, 27 3/4 x 43 1/2 ins / 70.5 x 110.5 cm) FRF 12,000. PARIS, 26 March 1998, *Pastoral Scene outside Bône* (oil on canvas, 18 x 32 ins / 46 x 81 cm) FRF 15,000.

GADANYI, Jenö

Hungarian, 20th century.
Born 1896; died 1960.
Painter (mixed media/gouache), pastellist.
European School group.

Jenö Gadanyi was part of the important Hungarian art group called the European School, which took over from the Nagybánya School, so deeply rooted in the national background. The European School, as its name indicates, was firmly directed towards the art movements shaking Europe from Munich and Berlin, where most Russians were working, as far as Holland and Paris.

Gadanyi's crucial period was between 1945 and his death in 1960. Like a number of contemporary Russian artists, he did not clearly differentiate between Fauvism, Expressionism, Cubism, Abstraction and Surrealism and while he maintained a distinctive approach in his drawing and in his palette, Gadanyi easily switched styles though constantly striving to remain faithful to his country's popular traditions.

BIBLIOGRAPHY:

Németh, Lajos, *Moderne ungarische Kunst*, Corvina Kiadó, Budapest, 1969.

AUCTION RECORDS:

PARIS, 12 May 1993, *Stormy Sky* (1927, gouache and pastel/paper, 23 1/4 x 33 1/2 ins / 59 x 85 cm) FRF 50,000. BUDAPEST, 16 May 2003, *Hilly Landscape with Sundisc* (oil on card, 12 x 17 ins / 31 x 43 cm) HUF 1,000,000. BUDAPEST, 12 Dec 2003, *Woman with a Cockerel* (1951, oil on canvas, 39 x 29 ins / 98 x 73 cm) HUF 1,600,000.

GADBOIS, Louis

French, 18th - 19th century.
Died 1826.
Painter (including gouache), watercolourist. Genre scenes, landscapes, landscapes with figures.

Louis Gadbois was active in Paris. His work appeared in exhibitions at the Louvre from 1791 to 1812.

AUCTION RECORDS:

PARIS, 26-27 Jan 1923, *L'Étang et le troupeau* (gouache) FRF 750; *Leaving for the Hunt* (watercolour) FRF 1,000. PARIS, 19 April 1929, *Wooded Landscape with Sacrifice to a Deity; Wooded Hilly Landscape, with River and Cascade* (two drawings) FRF 3,300. PARIS, 29 Jan 1943, *Park, Ornamental Lake and Figures; Farm, Peasants and Animals* (two gouache and watercolours) FRF 75,000. PARIS, 24 and 25 Feb 1943, *Meeting at the Edge of the Lake* (1794) FRF 3,600. PARIS, 4 June 1947, *Walk in the Park* (gouache) FRF 5,500. PARIS, 9 Dec 1952, *Park*, FRF 100,000. PARIS, 21 Nov 1966, *Figures by a Staircase in a Château Park; Returning from the Hunt* (two gouaches) FRF 11,500. NEW YORK, 13 Jan 1993, *Two Ladies Walking along the Paths in a Park* (watercolour heightened with white, oval, 10 x 13 1/2 ins / 25.5 x 34.4 cm) USD 1,320. PARIS, 30 Oct 1996, *View of the Château in Dieppe; Couple of Figures by a Kiosk in a Park* (ink, wash and red chalk, a pair, each 17 x 22 ins / 43 x 56 cm) FRF 77,000. PARIS, 22 Oct 1997, *Landscape with Young Musicians, Shepherd and His Flock* (gouache, 14 1/2 x 19 3/4 ins / 37 x 50 cm) FRF 9,000. PARIS, 5 Feb 1998, *Forest Landscape with Couple and Mule Crossing a Bridge* (gouache, 17 1/2 x 20 3/4 ins / 44.5 x 53 cm) FRF 8,000.

GADBURY, Harry Lee

American, 20th century.
Born 1890, in Greenfield.
Painter, illustrator.

GADDI, Angelo di Taddeo or Agnolo

Italian, 14th century.
Born c. 1345, in Florence; died 1396, in Florence.
Active in Florence between 1369 and 1396.
Painter, fresco artist. Religious subjects. Murals.
Florentine School.

Angelo was the son and pupil of Taddeo Gaddi. He ran his own workshop in Florence from 1369 to 1396, and it is said that he lived for a time in Venice. He is buried in the church of S Croce in Florence.

One of his earliest works was a *Raising of Lazarus*, painted for the church of S Jacopo in Florence. Between 1380 and 1390, he was commissioned to decorate the Florentine church of S Croce, painting eight frescoes of the *Legend of the Cross* in the choir and a *Christ with St Francis* for the ceiling. For S Croce, he is also said to have painted the *Evangelists*, a *Beheading of Cosroe and the Entry of Heraclius into Jerusalem*, and some *Saints*. He also supplied the drawing of the *Virtues* for the Loggia dei Priori. In Prato, between 1394 and 1396, he decorated the Cintola Chapel, illustrating the life of the Virgin Mary and the legend of St Thomas' belt. He also painted the altarpiece for the church of S Miniato al Monte, which dates from 1394-1396.

Although he had learned from the example of Giotto, he was more drawn to Sienese painting, which is why his style is described as 'late Gothic'.

MUSEUMS AND GALLERIES:

BERLIN: *Virgin and Child* - FLORENCE (Gal. dell'Accademia): *Evangelists, the Church Doctors and the Church; Scene from the Life of St John the Evangelist; St John the Baptist; St Nicholas and St Anthony* - FLORENCE (Uffizi): *Annunciation* - MUNICH: *St Nicholas of Bari; St Julian* - PARIS (Louvre): *Annunciation* - PARMA (Gal. Nazionale): *Virgin and Sts.*

AUCTION RECORDS:

LONDON, 8 July 1925, *Virgin and Child*, GBP 94. LONDON, 20 Nov 1936, *Madonna and Child*, GBP 220. LONDON, 19 June 1942, *St Elizabeth of Hungary and St Catherine of Alexandria*, GBP 47. LONDON, 26 June 1970, *Virgin and Child*, Gns 4,500.

LONDON, 23 March 1973, *Virgin and Child Surrounded by Four Sts*, Gns 7,500. LONDON, 6 April 1977, *St Dominic* (oil on panel, 9 x 6 ins / 22 x 15 cm) GBP 3,500. NEW YORK, 9 June 1978, *Discovery of the True Cross* (oil on panel, gold background, 12 x 26 1/2 ins / 30.5 x 67 cm) USD 50,000. LONDON, 21 April 1982, *The Virgin Adored by St Anthony, St John the Baptist and St Francis* (39 1/4 x 22 3/4 ins / 100 x 58 cm) GBP 18,000. LONDON, 5 July 1989, *Virgin and Child in Majesty Surrounded by Angels Playing Instruments and Receiving the Prayers of Sts Anthony, John the Baptist, Catherine and Lucy* (oil and tempera/panel with gilt ground, 23 1/4 x 15 3/4 ins / 59 x 40 cm) GBP 660,000. LONDON, 6 July 1990, *Virgin of Humility with the Annunciation Depicted in Two Circles in the Corners* (tempera/panel with gilt ground, 12 1/2 x 9 ins / 32 x 22 cm) GBP 99,000. LONDON, 6 July 1994, *Virgin and Child Surrounded by Angels Playing Instruments with St Anthony, St John the Baptist, St Catherine and St Lucy in Worship* (oil and tempera/panel with gilt ground, 23 1/4 x 15 3/4 ins / 59 x 40 cm) GBP 177,500. LONDON, 11 Dec 1996, *Madonna and Child* (tempera/panel, 22 x 11 3/4 ins / 55 x 30 cm) GBP 51,000. LONDON, 8 July 1999, *Martyrdom of St Andrew* (tempera on panel, 11 x 15 ins / 27 x 37 cm) GBP 220,000. PARIS, 28 June 2000, *Madonna Enthroned Suckling the Infant Jesus* (tempera on panel, 35 x 20 ins / 90 x 52 cm) FRF 350,000. NEW YORK, 24 Jan 2002, *Madonna of Humility* (tempera on panel, 10 x 9 ins / 26 x 23 cm) USD 190,000. LONDON, 10 July 2002, *St Bartholomew and Angel* (tempera on board, 57 x 22 ins / 146 x 55 cm) GBP 140,000. NEW YORK, 24 Jan 2003, *Madonna and Child with St Catherine of Alexandria and St John the Baptist* (tempera on panel, 35 x 21 ins / 90 x 53 cm) USD 320,000.

GADDI, Gaddo di Zanobi

Italian, 13th - 14th century.

Born c. 1260, in Florence; died probably in 1333.

Painter, mosaicist. Religious subjects, portraits.

Gaddi was a friend of Cimabue and Giotto, and is buried in the cloister of the church of S Croce in Florence.

He is referred to as having produced a mosaic, below the windows of the Baptistery in Florence, depicting scenes from the lives of Jesus and St John, as well as a *Coronation of the Virgin* for the cathedral. He is also believed to have produced mosaics for the church of S Maria Maggiore and the choir of St Peter's in Rome. Surviving paintings by Gaddo Gaddi can be seen in the church of S Francesco in Arezzo, and mosaics in the old cathedral of that town. A portrait of him, painted by his son, is included in a fresco (a *Marriage of the Virgin*) in the Baroncelli Chapel, S Croce, Florence. He may also have visited Rome.

GADDI, Giovanni di Taddeo

Italian, 14th century.

Died 1383, in Florence.

Painter.

Giovanni di Taddeo was the son of Taddeo Gaddi and a pupil of his brother Angelo. He painted a *Christ in the Temple* and other similar works for the Florentine church of S Spirito, which were destroyed when the church was rebuilt.

GADDI, Niccolo

Italian, 14th century.

Active in Florence.

Painter.

Niccolo was the son of Taddeo Gaddi.

GADDI, Taddeo di Gaddo

Italian, 14th century.

Born c. 1300, in Florence; died 1366, in Florence.

Painter, fresco artist. Religious subjects. Murals.

Florentine School.

Taddeo Gaddi first studied under his father, Gaddo di Zanobi Gaddi, then for 24 years (from 1313 to 1337) was assistant to Giotto. His own pupils included Giovanni da Milano and Jacopo del Casentino. In 1989, he was the subject of an exhibition, held at Poppi.

As a member of Giotto's workshop, he was involved in the creation of the *Stefaneschi Polyptych* in the Vatican. Youthful works attributed to him include the S Francesco *Madonna* in Pisa and frescoes for the castle chapel in Poppi, depicting scenes from the *Life of the Holy Virgin, St John the Baptist* and *St John the Evangelist*. He produced a number of mural paintings for the church of S Croce in Florence (chapels, sacristy and former refectory). Of particular interest are portraits of his father and *Andrea Tafi*, in the Baroncelli Chapel, and a *Deposition*, in the Bardi di Vernio Chapel.

Taddeo Gaddi was a prolific artist but, sadly, few of his works have survived. His frescoes for S Spirito and the Servite church, altar paintings for S Stefano del Ponte Vecchio, and allegories for the Mercanzia court house have all been lost. However, some of his work for the Camposanto in Pisa is still extant. There, between 1340 and 1342, he painted six vast *Episodes from the Life of Job*. In *Satan's Pact with God*, the influence of Fiorentino Stefano (another of Giotto's disciples) is undeniable, particularly in the six angels ranged around the majestic figure of Christ. Other works ascribed to him include an altar painting in the sacristy of S Pietro at Megognano, and a reredos bearing the inscription: *Anno Dni MCCCXXXIIII mensis septembris Tadues me fecit.* He was also famous as an architect and sat on the committee charged with the construction of Florence Cathedral from 1359 to 1366.

Taddeo Gaddi's originality is expressed in his unusually lively range of colours and the shimmering effects he imparts to the garments worn by the figures in his paintings. He developed the spatial and lighting innovations introduced by Giotto, with special emphasis on nocturnal lighting effects, but his painting is more anecdotal and lacks the breadth of Giotto's work.

BIBLIOGRAPHY:

Jewett Mather, Frank, *The Isaac Master, a Reconstruction of the Work of Gaddo Gaddi*, Princeton University Press, Princeton (USA, NJ), H. Milford, Oxford University Press, London, 1932. Caleca, A., *Pisa. Museo delle Sinopie del Camposanto Monumentale*, Pisa, 1979. *Gli affreschi di Taddeo Gaddi nel castello dei conti Guidi di Poppi: le storie della Vergine, di San Giovanni Evangelista e di San Giovanni Battista*, exhibition catalogue, Edizioni della Bibliotheca comunale Rilliana, Poppi, 1991. *Pittura murale in Italia. Del tardo Duecento ai primi del Quattrocento*, Bolis, Bergamo, 1995.

MUSEUMS AND GALLERIES:

BAGNÈRES-DE-BIGORRE: *St Eloi* - BERLIN: *Descent of the Holy Spirit; Virgin and Child with Two Donors; Anno Dni MCCCXXXIIII mensis septembris Tadeus me fecit* (retable) - BERN: *Tryptych with Gold Background* - FIESOLE (Mus. Bandini): *Annunciation* - FLORENCE (Gal. dell'Accademia) - FLORENCE (Uffizi): *Madonna with Angels* - GENEVA: *Adoration of the Virgin Surrounded by Saints* - MUNICH (Alte Pinakothek) - PARIS (Louvre): *Beheading of St John; Calvary; Martyrdom of a Saint.*

AUCTION RECORDS:

PARIS, 1845, *Saints*, FRF 770. PARIS, 1897, *Nativity*, FRF 1,520; *St Anne and St Zachariah*, FRF 1,400. PARIS, 1900, *Annunciation*, FRF 2,100; *Calvary*, FRF 470. LONDON, 25-26 May 1911, *Virgin and Child Enthroned*, GBP 1. LONDON, 16 Jan 1925, *Christ Rising from the Tomb*, GBP 78. LONDON, 6 Feb 1931, *Crucifixion*, GBP 28. LONDON, 24 Feb 1939, *Agony in the Garden; Pilate Washing his Hands* (both) GBP 75. LONDON, 6 March 1942, *Madonna and Child with Saints* (tryptych) GBP 27. LONDON, 14 Dec 1945, *Coronation of the Virgin*, GBP 325.

LONDON, 9 Dec 1959, *Crucifixion*, GBP 4,000. LONDON, 24 May 1991, *High Altar of Bromley Davenport, the Suffering Christ flanked by Saints Peter, Francis, Paul and Andrew, with Prophets in the Upper Part of the Panels* (tempera/panel with gilt background, polyptych, consisting of five panels, Christ 42 1/2 x 23 ins / 107.8 x 58.5 cm, St Peter 36 x 18 1/4 ins/90.5 x 46.5 cm, St Francis and Paul 36 x 19 1/2 ins/90.5 x 49.5 cm, St André 36 x 19 ins/90.5 x 48.3 cm) GBP 1,980,000. PARIS, 26 June 1992, *St Leonard with Donor* (tempera/poplar panel with gold background, 22 3/4 x 8 ins / 58 x 20.5 cm) FRF 400,000. NEW YORK, 28 Jan 2000, *Crucifixion with Madonna and St John the Evangelist* (tempera on panel, 24 x 13 ins / 60 x 32 cm) USD 625,000. NEW YORK, 26 Jan 2001, *St John the Evangelist* (tempera on panel, 22 x 14 ins / 55 x 35 cm) USD 130,000. VENICE, 15 Dec 2001, *Imago Pietatis* (tempera on board, 15 x 11 ins / 37 x 27 cm) ITL 170,000,000. NEW YORK, 23 Jan 2003, *St Matthew Pinnacle to the S Giovanni Fuorcivitas Polyptych* (tempera on panel, 24 x 9 ins / 61 x 24 cm) USD 720,000.

GADE, Hari Ambadas
Indian, 20th century.
Born 15 August 1917, in Amaravati (Maharashtra); died 2001.
Painter. Figures, landscapes.

Hari Gade received a degree in science from Nagpur university and was a casual art student there, obtaining a master's degree in art from Nagpur school of art in 1950. His figures and landscapes fall into the post-Cubist tradition and are painted in a sensitive range of colours. He has taken part in many joint exhibitions featuring contemporary Indian art in India and abroad. In 1956 he was part of a delegation of Indian artists that visited the former USSR and eastern Europe.

GADEGAARD, Poul or Paul
Danish, 20th century.
Born 1920.
Painter.
Neo-Constructivism.

Poul Gadegaard was included in the Salon des Réalités Nouvelles in Paris in 1950. He was associated with Neo-Constructivism, strongly represented in Denmark by the painter Richard Mortensen and the sculptor Robert Jacobsen.

AUCTION RECORDS:
COPENHAGEN, 4 March 1992, *Composition* (1949, oil on canvas, 15 x 22 ins / 38 x 55 cm) DKK 10,000. COPENHAGEN, 2-3 Dec 1992, *Composition* (1952, oil on canvas, 51 1/4 x 76 3/4 ins / 130 x 195 cm) DKK 22,000. COPENHAGEN, 3 June 1993, *Composition* (1952, oil on canvas, 18 x 25 1/2 ins / 46 x 65 cm) DKK 7,000. COPENHAGEN, 8-9 March 1995, *Composition* (1955, oil on canvas, 23 1/2 x 28 3/4 ins / 60 x 73 cm) DKK 7,800. COPENHAGEN, 12 March 1996, *Composition* (1952, oil on canvas, 18 x 22 ins / 46 x 55 cm) DKK 4,000. COPENHAGEN, 29 Jan 1997, *Composition* (1954, oil on canvas, 22 x 18 ins / 55 x 46 cm) DKK 6,000. COPENHAGEN, 17 Nov 1999, *Composition* (1952, oil on canvas, 18 x 22 ins / 46 x 55 cm) DKK 12,000. COPENHAGEN, 9 Feb 2000, *Composition* (1955, oil on canvas, 24 x 29 ins / 60 x 73 cm) DKK 62,000. COPENHAGEN, 3 Oct 2000, *Constructive Composition* (1953, oil on canvas, 29 x 24 ins / 73 x 60 cm) DKK 55,000. COPENHAGEN, 2 April 2001, *Composition* (1963, oil on canvas, 24 x 29 ins / 60 x 73 cm) DKK 32,000. COPENHAGEN, 19 Sept 2001, *Composition* (1955, oil on canvas, 29 x 24 ins / 73 x 60 cm) DKK 24,000. COPENHAGEN, 29 May 2002, *Composition* (1954, oil on canvas, 15 x 22 ins / 38 x 55 cm) DKK 15,000. COPENHAGEN, 29 May 2002, *Composition* (1953, oil on canvas, 18 x 22 ins / 46 x 55 cm) DKK 20,000. COPENHAGEN, 26 Feb 2003, *Composition* (1953, oil on canvas, 36 x 29 ins / 92 x 73 cm) DKK 15,000. COPENHAGEN, 17 Sept 2003, *Composition* (1955, oil on canvas, 24 x 29 ins / 60 x 73 cm) DKK 22,000. HAVNEN, 24 April 2004, *Concrete Composition* (oil on canvas, 53 x 60 ins / 135 x 153 cm) DKK 30,000. COPENHAGEN, 5 Oct 2004, *Concrete Composition* (1952, oil on canvas, 29 x 36 ins / 73 x 92 cm) DKK 50,000.

GADENNE, Bertrand
French, 20th - 21st century.
Born 1951, in Proverville (Aube).
Active in Paris.
Installation artist.

Bertrand Gadenne's light installations are similar in some ways to those by Michel Verjux, where only certain parts of the installation are lit, the rest remaining in complete darkness.

He has taken part in group exhibitions, including at the following: the Paris Biennale (1980); *Itinéraires* (*Itineraries*) at the Direction Régionale des Affaires Culturelles in Metz (1983); the Maision des Expositions in Genas (1984, 1992); the Musée d'Art et d'Histoire in Metz (1988); *Feuilles* (*Leaves*) at the Musée National d'Art Moderne in Paris (1988); and *Le Portrait s'Envisage* (*The Portrait Face to Face*) at the Château de Tanlay in Yonne (2002). He has held solo exhibitions since 1982, notably at the French Institute in Tel Aviv in 1991, the Galerie Aline Vidal in Paris in 1994 and 1996, and the Alsace Fonds Régional d'Art Contemporain (FRAC) in Epfig in 2003.

BIBLIOGRAPHY:
Thomas, Mona, '*Gadenne, le faiseur de rêves*' in *Beaux-Arts Magazine*, no. 130, periodical, Paris, January 1995. Huitorel, Jean-Marc, '*Bertrand Gadenne. Le petit prince des ténèbre*' in *Art Press*, no. 279, periodical, Paris, May 2002.

MUSEUMS AND GALLERIES:
DUNKIRK (FRAC Nord-Pas de Calais): *Rat* (2001, video) - METZ (FRAC Lorraine) - SÉLESTAT (FRAC Alsace).

GADENNE, Charles
French, 20th century.
Born 30 July 1925, in Roubaix.
Sculptor.

Charles Gadenne studied under Marcel Gimond at the École des Beaux-Arts in Paris until 1952. He exhibited in Paris at the Salon of the Société Nationale des Beaux-Arts and the Salon d'Automne, of which he was a member.

BIBLIOGRAPHY:
Charles Gadenne: une vie de sculpteur, exhibition catalogue, Médiathèque municipale, Condé-sur-Noireau, 1999.

GADI, Camillo
Italian, 18th century.
Active in Bologna at the end of the 18th century.
Painter.

Camillo Gadi was the son of Francesco Gadi.

GADI, Francesco
Italian, 18th century.
Died 1784, in Bologna.
Painter.

Francesco Gadi was a pupil of V. M. Bigari.

GADIO, Giovanni
Italian, 15th century.
Active in Cremona.
Miniaturist.

Giovanni Gadio transcribed and illuminated manuscripts in collaboration with his brother Giovanni Pietro Gadio.

GADIO, Giovanni Gazzo
Italian, 15th century.
Active in Genoa in 1461.
Painter.

GADIO, Giovanni Pietro
Italian, 15th century.
Active in Cremona at the end of the 15th century.
Miniaturist.

He worked with his brother Giovanni.

GADOR, István
Hungarian, 20th century.
Born 1891.
Sculptor, ceramicist.

István Gador exhibited from 1914 onwards. His main exhibitions were held at the Belvedere Museum (1921) and the Ernst Museum (1922, 1961 and 1966); he featured in the Venice Biennale (1962). Between 1945 and 1957 he taught at the school of decorative art in Budapest. An officially recognised artist, he was awarded the title of Artist Emeritus and the Kossuth Prize.

BIBLIOGRAPHY:
Hongrie 68, exhibition catalogue, Pannonia, Budapest, 1968.

GADOU-ROYER, Jeanne Élise
French, 19th century.
Born 1820, in Bordeaux; died 1907.
Painter, miniaturist.

She studied under Alaux and A. Gilbert and submitted examples of her work to the Paris Salons of 1874 and 1875. Her better-known works include a *Portrait of M. Lalanne, Slumber*, and a composition entitled *Last Moments of P. Lacordaire*.

GADOWSKY, Valery
Polish, 19th century.
Born 1833, in Cracow.
Sculptor.

Valery Gadowsky studied draughtsmanship under Stisler in Cracow, and sculpture under Kossovsky. He then spent two years studying at the Akademie der Bildenden Künste in Vienna. In 1877 he started teaching sculpture at the fine arts academy in Cracow.

MUSEUMS AND GALLERIES:
CRACOW: *Portrait of Countess Potocki; Herodias.*

GADSBY, William Hippon
British, 19th - 20th century.
Born 1844, in Derby; died 1924, in London.
Active in London.
Painter. Genre scenes.

William Gadsby was a member of the Royal Society of British Artists and exhibited regularly at the Suffolk Street Gallery from 1869. He also exhibited at the Royal Academy.

AUCTION RECORDS:
LONDON, 30 Nov 1907, *Tired*, GBP 3; *A Fairy Tale*, GBP 1. PARIS, 23 Feb 1945, *Tired*, FRF 3,300. LONDON, 21 July 1978, *Two Young Girls Arranging Flowers* (oil on canvas, 35 x 27 1/4 ins / 89 x 69 cm) GBP 1,200. LONDON, 30 March 1982, *House of Cards* (oil on canvas, 28 x 36 ins / 71 x 91.5 cm) GBP 850. LONDON, 23 Sept 1988, *Forms in the Flames* (oil on canvas, 20 x 30 ins / 50.5 x 76.5 cm) GBP 3,520. LONDON, 3 Feb 1993, *Sunday Evening* (oil on canvas, 27 x 22 ins / 68.5 x 55 cm) GBP 747.

GAEBERT, Johann Gottlieb
German, 18th century.
Died 27 December 1799, in Wildenfels (Saxony).
Sculptor.

Johann Gaebert, the brother of Karl Heinrich Gaebert, worked for the convent of Altzelle near Wessen.

GAEBERT, Karl Heinrich
German, 18th century.
Active in Wildenfels (Saxony).
Sculptor.

Karl Heinrich was the brother of Johann Gottlieb Gaebert.

GAECKLE, Albert, or Gackle
German, 19th century.
Born 25 August 1853, in Stuttgart.
Sculptor.

Gaeckle studied in Vienna, Munich and Paris before returning to settle in Stuttgart. He worked for different churches in that city and the surrounding area.

GAEDE, Heinrich, or Gade
German, 19th century.
Active in Berlin at the beginning of the 19th century.
Painter.

Heinrich Gaede exhibited at the academy in Berlin between 1814 and 1816.

GAEDE, Lilla Pauline Emilie, or Gade
German, 19th century.
Born 8 September 1852, near Kiel (Schleswig-Holstein).
Painter.

Lilla Gaede studied in Karlsruhe, then lived in Hamburg and Kiel. She is particularly noted for her flower paintings.

GAEDE, Philip Friedrich, or Gade
German, 19th century.
Born c. 1782, in Berlin; died 2 May 1840, in Berlin.
Sculptor (wood).

Philip Gaede exhibited at the academy in Berlin in 1800 and 1832.

GAEL. See also **GAAL**

GAËL, Anna, pseudonym of Rouanet, Yvonne
French, 20th century.
Born 13 April 1936, in Mazamet (Tarn).
Painter. Figures, genre scenes, flowers.

Anna Gaël first studied painting at a private studio in Toulouse. She tackles a variety of subjects including figures, genre scenes, animals and landscapes and is particularly known for her detailed and accurate flower paintings.

Since 1977 she has taken part in group exhibitions in many towns in the provinces and in Paris at the Salon d'Automne from 1990, Salon de la Société Nationale des Beaux-Arts and Salon des Artistes Français since 1991. She also showed her work in solo exhibitions at the Galerie Ror Volmar in Paris in 1984, 1985, 1986, 1989 and 1991.

GAEL, Barend. See **GAAL Barend**

GAEL, Jacob Frans
Dutch, 18th century.
Engraver.

Gael was noted for his caricatures.

GAELEN, Alexander van, or Goelen
Dutch, 17th - 18th century.
Born 28 April 1670, in Amsterdam; died 1728.
Painter. Battles, hunting scenes, portraits.

Van Gaelen was a pupil of Johann van Huchtenburgh. He travelled to Germany in 1694, where he became court painter in Cologne. He was later active in England, where he painted a portrait of *Queen Anne* and a number of battle scenes.

AUCTION RECORDS:
LONDON, 1 July 1931, *Hunting Scene*, GBP 8. LONDON, 17 Feb 1936, *Landscape*, GBP 6. PARIS, 21 Oct 1946, *Cavalry Alarum* (attributed) FRF 4,400. MILAN, 2 Dec 1999, *Battles* (oil on canvas, a pair, 15 x 20 ins / 39 x 52 cm) ITL 6,000,000.

GAELMAN, Arnould
Flemish School, 14th century.
Active in Louvain.
Painter (glass).

Known to have been working between 1311 and 1324, Gaelman is the earliest recorded painter in Louvain. He may be the same person as Armand Gaelmann.

GAELMANN, Armand
14th century.
Died c. 1323.
Miniaturist.

GAENSSLEIN, Otto Robert, or Gaensslen
American, 20th century.
Born 6 June 1876, in Chicago; died 1915.
Also active in France.
Painter.
Otto Gaensslein studied under Karl von Marr at the art academy in Munich. He then went to Paris, where he studied under Jean-Paul Laurens, and where he then settled. He exhibited at the Salon des Artistes Français, receiving an honourable mention in 1906. He was also a member of the Chicago Society of Artists.
AUCTION RECORDS:
SAN FRANCISCO, 21 Jan 1981, *Twilight* (oil on canvas, 16 x 20 ins / 40.5 x 51 cm) USD 475.

GAER-FAY
British, 20th century.
Born 7 April 1899, in London.
Sculptor.

GAEREMYN, Jan Anton. See **GAREMYN**

GAERTNER, Alfred, or Gärtner
German, 19th century.
Born 4 March 1868, in Stuttgart.
Painter, lithographer.
Alfred Gaertner was a pupil of Grünenwald in Stuttgart and of Robert Fleury in Paris. He was mainly responsible for landscapes and genre scenes.

GAERTNER, Carl Frederick
American, 20th century.
Born 18 April 1898, in Cleveland; died 1952.
Painter, illustrator.
Carl Gaertner spent his entire career in Cleveland, where he was also a teacher.
AUCTION RECORDS:
NEW YORK, 9 Sept 1993, *Road to the End of the World* (1948, oil/synthetic resin, 28 x 48 ins / 71.1 x 121.9 cm) USD 690. CLEVELAND, 14 Sept 2000, *Building a Dam* (1930, oil on canvas, 35 x 41 ins / 89 x 104 cm) USD 4,000. CLEVELAND, 22 Feb 2001, *Barn* (c. 1930, oil on canvas, 30 x 35 ins / 76 x 89 cm) USD 2,400. SAN FRANCISCO, 12 Dec 2001, *Night in Pittsburgh* (1938, oil on canvas, 36 x 49 ins / 91 x 124 cm) USD 8,000. NEW YORK, 7 Oct 2003, *Covert's Old Pasture* (1947, tempera on masonite, 22 x 30 ins / 55 x 75 cm) USD 3,500. BETHESDA, 7 May 2004, *Lewis Hollow* (1945, oil on panel, 22 x 29 ins / 56 x 74 cm) USD 3,100.

GAERTNER, Christian, or Gärtner
German, 18th century.
Died 27 February 1712, in Freiberg (Saxony).
Painter.
Christian Gaertner was active in Freiberg, as well as in Bilberstein.

GAERTNER, Christian Salomon, or Gärtner
German, 17th - 18th century.
Born 18 November 1672, in Freiberg (Saxony).
Painter.
Christian Salomon was the son of Christian Gaertner.

GAERTNER, Christoph
German, 17th century.
Born in Arnstadt (Thuringia).
Painter, sculptor (wood).
Christoph Gaertner worked in Arnstadt, then in Brunswick for the princes regent. A work by him still survives in the church at Wobeck, near Schöningen.

GAERTNER, Eduard. See **GAERTNER Johann Philipp Eduard**

GAERTNER, Friedrich, or Gärtner
German, 19th century.
Born 11 January 1824, in Munich; died 9 October 1905, in Munich.
Painter. Architectural views.
Friedrich was the son of the architect Friedrich von Gärtner. He was a pupil at the academy in Munich and studied under the painter of seascapes, Simonsen. He continued his studies in Paris in the studio of the genre painter Cl. Jacquand. In 1870 he went to Algeria. He exhibited in Munich and Vienna between 1858 and 1873. Gaertner is noted for his *Convent Kitchen*.
MUSEUMS AND GALLERIES:
MUNICH: *Interior of a Moorish House*; *Cloister Courtyard in Moonlight*.
AUCTION RECORDS:
MUNICH, 5 Nov 1986, *Church Interior* (oil on canvas, 26 x 22 ins / 66 x 56 cm) DEM 5,000.

GAERTNER, Fritz. See **GÄRTNER**

GAERTNER, Georg, the Elder, or Gärtner
German, 17th century.
Died 1640.
Active in Nuremberg (Bavaria).
Miniaturist, watercolourist. Portraits.
This artist was the father of Georg the Younger.

GAERTNER, Georg, the Younger, or Gärtner
German, 17th century.
Died 1654.
Active in Nuremberg (Bavaria).
Painter.
Georg Gaertner the Younger copied and imitated Dürer.

GAERTNER, Georg Paulus, or Gärtner
German, 18th century.
Active in Nuremberg (Bavaria) c. 1700.
Painter.

GAERTNER, Heinrich, or Gärtner
German, 19th century.
Born 22 February 1828, in Neustrelitz (Neubrandenburg); died 19 February 1909, in Dresden.
Draughtsman, painter. Landscapes with figures, landscapes.
Heinrich Gaertner worked on drawings with Ruscheweyh. In 1845 he studied landscape painting with F.W. Schirmer in Berlin and in 1847 was under the tutelage of Ludwig Richter in Dresden. He continued his studies in Rome, before taking part in an exhibition in Leipzig, where he was awarded second prize. In 1889 he executed two large pictures for the high school in Elbing (now Elblag, Poland). He became an honorary member of the academy of Dresden. Gaertner is noted for his *Summer's Evening*. He exhibited in Munich and Dresden between 1854 and 1888.
MUSEUMS AND GALLERIES:
LEIPZIG: *Italian Landscape*; *Lake Nemi*.
AUCTION RECORDS:
MUNICH, 28 Nov 1979, *Procession in a Woodland Landscape* (1847, pen, 13½ x 11¾ ins / 34 x 30 cm) DEM 9,400.

GAERTNER, Johann, or Gärtner
German, 17th century.
Active in Nuremberg (Bavaria) c. 1600.
Painter.
There is a known landscape and portrait engraved after this artist.

GAERTNER, Johann Christoph, or Gärtner
German, 17th century.
Active in Mainz.
Painter.

GAERTNER, Johann Jacob, or Gärtner
German, 18th century.

Born 10 October 1697, in Hanau (Hesse); died December 1750, in Frankfurt am Main.
Painter.
Johann Gaertner worked mainly in Frankfurt.

GAERTNER, Johann Philipp Eduard, or Gärtner
German, 19th century.
Born 2 June 1801, in Berlin; died 22 February 1877, in Berlin.
Painter. Architectural views.
Johann Philipp Gaertner was a pupil of Karl Gropius in Berlin. He continued his studies in Paris. Between 1837 and 1839 he worked for Tsar Nicolas in St Petersburg and Moscow. In 1833 he became a member of the academy of Berlin. He exhibited in Berlin from 1822 to 1872. He was renowned for his well-observed skies with interesting light effects. He most famously executed a six-part *Panorama of Berlin.*
MUSEUMS AND GALLERIES:
BERLIN: *Old Streets of Brittany; Royal Bridge in Berlin* - BERLIN (Alte Nationalgal.): *View of the Backs of Houses on the Castle Precinct* (1855) - BERLIN (Schloss Charlottenburg, Gal. der Romantik): *Neue Wache (New Guard)* (1833).
AUCTION RECORDS:
MUNICH, 18 May 1988, *Berlin: Opernplatz and Unter den Linden at Dusk* (1845, oil on canvas, 16 1/2 x 30 3/4 ins / 42 x 78 cm) DEM 1,012,000. LONDON, 18 June 1993, *The Castle Precinct: View of the Castle Bridge in Berlin* (1855, oil on canvas, 22 x 37 3/4 ins / 56 x 96 cm) GBP 936,500. MUNICH, 21 June 1994, *Rear Courtyard in Colmar (Alsace)* (watercolour/paper, 11 x 9 ins / 28 x 22 cm) DEM 20,700. LONDON, 13 Oct 1994, *Unter den Linden in Berlin* (1836, oil on canvas, 8 1/2 x 16 ins / 21.5 x 40.5 cm) GBP 243,500. MUNICH, 5 July 2000, *Berlin Interior* (1851, watercolour over pencil heightened with white, 8 x 11 ins / 21 x 28 cm) DEM 6,000. BERLIN, 30 Nov 2001, *Portrait of Balduin Wilhelm Beck* (oil on canvas, 7 x 6 ins / 18 x 15 cm) DEM 16,000. LONDON, 19 June 2003, *Thorn Seen from the Bazer-Kampe* (1849, oil on canvas, 13 x 20 ins / 33 x 52 cm) GBP 40,000.

GAERTNER, Melchior, or Gärtner
German, 17th century.
Born in Eichstätt (Bavaria).
Painter.
Melchior Gaertner worked mainly in Vienna, where he collaborated with Frans Luycx.

GAESBEECK, Adriaen van
Dutch, 17th century.
Born 1621, in Leiden; died at the beginning of 1650, in Leiden.
Painter. Religious subjects, portraits, genre scenes.
He is generally thought to have been a pupil of Gerrit Dou. He was a member of the Leiden artists' guild in 1649. It is probable that he may be identified as the artist A. van Gaebseeck, mentioned in *Bryan's Dictionary,* but with a twenty-year disparity in their dates.

A. van Gaesbeeck fecit

MUSEUMS AND GALLERIES:
AMSTERDAM: *Young Man in a Study* - DOUAI: *Studio Interior* - LEIDEN (Stedelijk Mus. De Lakenhal): *Holy Family; Portrait of a Man.*
AUCTION RECORDS:
PARIS, 5 Oct 1892, *Holy Family at Rest,* FRF 380. LONDON, 10-11 March 1911, *Philosopher,* GBP 7. AMSTERDAM, 13 Nov 1995, *Serving-woman at Work in a Kitchen with a Small Boy Offering her an Apple, and a Dead Duck and Vegetables on a Table* (1648, oil on panel, 27 3/4 x 22 3/4in/70.8 x 57.8cm) NLG 92,000.

GAETA, Enrico
Italian, 19th century.
Born November 1840, in Castellammare di Stabia; died July 1887, in Castellammare.
Painter. Genre scenes, landscapes, architectural views.
Gaeta was a student at the academy of fine arts in Naples. He began painting around 1873, and exhibited in Vienna, Naples, Turin, Milan and Venice.
AUCTION RECORDS:
ROME, 14 Dec 1989, *Coastal Landscape in Sorrento with Vesuvius in the Background* (oil on canvas, 15 x 23 1/4 ins / 38 x 59 cm) ITL 3,450,000. ROME, 21 Nov 2000, *Interior of Church* (oil on canvas, 41 x 32 ins / 105 x 82 cm) ITL 8,500,000. COPENHAGEN, 5 March 2001, *House in Pompeii* (oil on canvas, 20 x 25 ins / 51 x 64 cm) DKK 62,000.

GAETA, Francesco
Italian, 17th century.
Active in Pisa.
Sculptor, engraver.
Francesco Gaeta worked on Pisa Cathedral. He also engraved landscapes.

GAETAN, Pedro
Spanish, 17th - 18th century.
Active in Seville at the end of the 17th century and at the beginning of the 18th century.
Sculptor.
Pedro Gaetan worked in a number of different genres. He is known to have produced a Baroque-style shield for use as the emblem of one of the guilds of the Holy Sacrament (it includes a monstrance at the centre); under the same signature he produced various statues of shepherds at the birth of Christ.

GAETANO, Antonio
Italian, 17th century.
Born c. 1630, in Messina; died c. 1700, in Messina.
Painter, engraver.
Antonio Gaetano was a pupil of Barbalonga. He worked on projects in Messina Cathedral.

GAETANO, Carlo
Italian, 17th century.
Active in Naples in 1683.
Painter.

GAETANO, Francesco
Italian, 17th century.
Active in Naples.
Painter.
Francesco Gaetano studied under Massino Stanzione and worked principally on the church of St Nicholas in Naples.

GAETANO, Giovanni Battista
Italian, 17th century.
Active during the second half of the 17th century.
Draughtsman.
It is almost certain that Giovanni Battista Gaetano was retained by the Spanish Queen Marie-Louise de Bourbon and that he was both a painter and engraver. According to Nagler, Gaetano is identical with Urbinas Caejetanus.

GAETANO MARIA DA MANTOVA (Fra)
Italian, 16th century.
Active in Ascoli Piceno.
Painter.

GAETKE, Heinrich
German, 19th century.
Born c. 1814; died c. 1879.
Painter. Landscapes, seascapes.
Gaetke exhibited in Berlin, Dresden and Vienna between 1842 and 1878. He is noted for his *Landscape* and *Storm.*

GAFA, Melchior
Italian, 17th century.
Born 1635, in Malta; died 1680.
Painter. History painting.
Melchior Gafa is cited by Siret.

GAFFER, Bernardo
Spanish, 15th century.
Painter.
Bernardo Gaffer, who may have been of German origin, painted altarpieces for the church of S Maria del Mon in Barcelona in the second half of the 15th century.

GAFFURI, Giuseppe
Italian, 16th century.
Active in Como.
Sculptor (wood).
Giuseppe Gaffuri produced a number of items for Como Cathedral. He may also have worked in Florence and Milan.

GÄFGEN, Wolfgang
German, 20th century.
Born 12 September 1936, in Hamburg.
Active in France since 1961.
Painter, watercolourist, draughtsman, engraver.
Wolfgang Gäfgen studied in Hamburg and then from 1957 to 1961 at the art school and the academy in Stuttgart. He went on a study trip to gain experience with Otto Dix, the Neue Sachlichkeit (New Objectivity) painter, in 1961, and settled in Paris immediately afterwards.

His first success with the public came at the exhibition *72/72* at the Grand Palais in Paris in 1972. The sudden rapid success encountered in the 1970s and at the beginning of the 1980s, after he had abandoned painting in favour of drawing in 1967, was linked to the success of the Hyperrealist movement at the time, as he was one of its international stars and the one most visible in Europe. The success of Hyperrealism was itself linked to a widespread renewal of Realism in general. Moreover, thanks to a lack of a clear definition, the fact that Hyperrealism was in vogue gave rise to much confusion, most often concerning the Trompe-l'œil painters who were only too pleased to find themselves suddenly considered modern and avant-garde after the Salon des Artistes Français. It was possible to find an abundantly illustrated magazine article on Hyperrealism with no Hyperrealist pictures at all, only Trompe-l'œils, because the distinction between the two was so blurred. With the true Hyperrealists and Gäfgen in particular, the Realism is only apparent and only concerns the perfection of the reproduction. Regarding the distinction between Hyperrealism and Trompe l'œil and traditional Realism, Gäfgen's case is quite illuminating: his extreme Realism is never more than a concept of Realism because the object being imitated is not the object and no Trompe-l'œil ever fooled anyone for long. His Realism is even further from reality because, in his Hyperrealist period, he only used black pencil and black engraving.

In 1972 he produced a series of manière noire prints, for which he isolated the objects depicted from any plausible context, placing them on sheets of white paper, as if in a void. It was not the nature of these objects that interested him, but their texture (ropes, wood), their position (torn sheets, pieces of fabric placed on the corners of cubes) and their materials (leather, stones, chains, twigs). However, the illusion works. In the pleats and folds you can feel the satin, touch the sleek, polished leather, be captivated by the reflections. Despite his assertion that 'to draw is to capture, that is all I do', his Realism allows him to project his visions or fantasies into the reality of the drawing. He does not look coldly at reality, though he gives it an icy glance. The human element is only present in traces left behind in objects that have since been abandoned, very obviously in his early drawings of pillows or clothes that have retained the imprint of a head or a body, if less so later on, when he drew places marked by an event, or a gash on an object, or on nothing at all, a ditch dug into the land or into emptiness.

Hyperrealism, at least in Gäfgen's case, stands in a confrontational relationship with reality, not with its image (simple Realism) but with the fantasies that pervade it. One might wonder whether Gäfgen intended this interpretation at all, working only for the simple pleasure of drawing or capturing a moment of reality; in this case his Hyperrealism would be no more than Realism in another guise, as Claude Rossignol decrees in Hazan's Dictionary: 'Though Gäfgen's work has benefited from the craze for Hyperrealism, his work seems to belong more to the long tradition of Germanic draughtsmen and engravers'. Yet what is most striking about his work is that, by the very excess of detail of the object, isolated like an exhibit connected with some crime on the immaculate page, never quite seen in reality, it feels unreal and, as such, brings us back to the spiral of anguish, part of which was its baselessness.

Latterly, Gäfgen radically changed his style, a bold move for such a successful artist. In an exhibition at the Galerie Baudoin-Lebon in Paris in 1990 (represented at the FIAC (Foire Internationale d'Art Contemporain) in 1992) he exhibited paintings with nothing in common with his prior Hyperrealist work. At the Galerie Baudoin-Lebon in 1995, the works on show were of three kinds: wood engravings, découpages and outline drawings. The wood engravings, more than 6 feet (2 metres) high, represent his most finished work. The forms he used had an organic, vegetal character, a world filled with garlands and ribbons, in which black was ever-present alongside brilliant colours. In contrast were small découpages like Chinese shadow puppets, silhouettes cut from black paper standing out against a white background. 'Engravings and découpages,' he declared, 'are done in game mode'. In the engravings, the game consists of repeating and recycling the same forms from one work to the next. In the découpages, the pieces of paper are no more than scraps, fallen papers salvaged from those that have accumulated on the studio floor. The outline drawings, inspired by antique decorated vases, demand much greater concentration because, according to the artist, 'there is nothing there at the start, there is everything to do'.

Before this change in style, he took part in group exhibitions including: 1963, an exhibition of the work of the pupils of the engraver Friedlaender at the La Hune gallery and bookshop in Paris, and Young Artists' Biennale in Paris; 1966, Grand Salon and Salon des Jeunes d'Aujourd'hui; 1968, Salon de Mai and *Living Art 1965-1968* at the Maeght Foundation in St-Paul-de-Vence; 1970, *Images-drawings* at the Musée d'Art Moderne de la Ville de Paris; 1971, 7th Paris Biennale; 1972, *72/72* at the Grand Palais, and Cracow Biennale as an engraver; 1977, Dokucumenta VI in Kassel.

He also showed his creations, which were few and far between because it took him so long to produce them, in solo exhibitions. The first of these was in Paris in 1966 at the Galerie Jacob. The next was in 1968 in Lübeck, followed by 1970, Goethe Institute in Marseilles, 1971, Kunsthalle in Bielefeld, 1972, Galerie AAA in Paris, 1973, his first at the Galerie Karl Flinker in Paris, followed by others in 1976, 1979 and 1984. He exhibited in 1976 in the State Graphics collection in Munich and the Hamburg Kunsthalle, in 1977 in Lübeck and Munich, in 1982 at the Hamburg Kunsthalle and Nuremberg Kunsthalle, then several times at the Galerie Baudoin-Lebon in Paris.

BIBLIOGRAPHY:
Hyperréalistes américains, réalistes européens, exhibition catalogue, Centre national d'Art contemporain, Paris, 1974. Léonard, Pierre, *Zeichnungen-Dessins 1970-1976*, Éd. du Chêne, Paris, 1978. Wismann, Heinz (preface), *Gäfgen*, exhibition catalogue, Gal. Karl Flinker, Paris, 1979. Pernoud, Em-

manuel, '*Wolfgang Gäfgen, les loques du merveilleux*' in *Art Press* n° 210, periodical, Paris, February 1996.
Museums and Galleries:
Marseilles (Mus. Cantini): *Large Nest no. II* (1982, wash).
Auction records:
Paris, 13 Oct 1989, *Composition* (graphite, 22 x 30 ins / 56 x 76 cm) FRF 6,000. London, 21 March 1991, *Charlie's Sofa* (1972, pencil/paper, 39 1/4 x 51 1/4 ins / 100 x 130 cm) GBP 825.

GAFIERO, Salvador
Spanish, 19th century.
Active at the beginning of the 19th century.
Painter. History painting.

GAFORI, Damiano
Italian, 16th century.
Born in Novara; died 1538.
Miniaturist.
Gafori transcribed and illuminated a number of liturgical works for Carpi Cathedral.

GAGA. See **KOVENTCHUK Guerorguy**

GAGARIN, Grigori or Grigorevich (Prince)
Russian, 19th century.
Born 29 April 1810, in St Petersburg; died 18 January 1893, in Châtellerault.
Painter (gouache), watercolourist. History painting, genre scenes, landscapes, battles.
Gagarin's work depicts numerous events from Russian military history; he was also a remarkable draughtsman as his *Portrait of Cholokaeva* now at the Russiam Museum in St Petersburg, shows.
Museums and Galleries:
Moscow (Alexander III Mus.): *Scene of the securing of the Caucasus; Battle between Russian Troups and the Circassians; Passing Troup* - Moscow (State Tretyakov Gal.): *The Meeting between General Klukketon-Kluquenau and Schamyl.*
Auction records:
London, 15 June 1995, *Lake Gokchk or Sevang in Armenia* (gouache and pencil/buff-coloured paper, 11 x 14 1/4 ins / 28 x 36 cm) GBP 1,150. London, 14 Dec 1995, *Still-life with Plums* (watercolour, 8 1/4 x 6 ins / 20.7 x 15.3 cm) GBP 2,530. London, 19 Dec 1996, *Still-life with Plums* (watercolour, 8 1/4 x 6 ins / 20.7 x 15.3 cm) GBP 1,725. London, 10 May 2000, *Young Greek Warrior* (watercolour and gouache over pencil, 17 x 11 ins / 42 x 28 cm) GBP 2,900.

GAGARIN-STURDZA, Carmina (Princess)
Ukrainian, 19th - 20th century.
Born 19th century, in Odessa.
Painter.
A student of Saintpierre, Henner and Paul Chabs, Carmina Gagarin-Sturdza exhibited in Paris at the Salon des Artistes Français, of which she became a member in 1909. She received an honourable mention in 1909 and a bronze medal in 1910.

GAGE, Joachim
German, 18th century.
Active in Würzburg (Bavaria) c. 1702.
Sculptor.
Gage worked for the church at the university in Würzburg.

GAGE, Louis-Léon
French, 19th century.
Died 1902.
Painter.
He was a member of the Société des Artistes Français and a regular participant in its exhibitions.

GAGE, Paul
French, 20th century.
Born 10 November 1902, in Paris; died 6 December 1983, in Paris.
Painter, draughtsman, watercolourist. Urban landscapes, landscapes.
Paul Gage was a self-taught painter. He studied architecture at the École Nationale des Arts Décoratifs, leaving in 1922 after being awarded first prize. He painted landscapes of Brittany, Allier, central France, the south of France, Italy, Spain, the Hoggar region of north Africa and numerous views of Paris.

From 1932 to 1979 he took part in numerous exhibitions, including in Paris: the Salon des Artistes Français (commendation in 1949); the Salon de la Société des Beaux-Arts d'Outre-Mer; the Salon d'Hiver; and the Salon des Paysagistes Français. He also showed his work in solo exhibitions in Paris and the provinces.
Museums and Galleries:
Hérisson.
Auction records:
Paris, 1 Dec 1989, *The Halles Food Market* (oil on paper, 16 1/4 x 13 ins / 41 x 33 cm) FRF 6,200. Paris, 28 May 1990, *Flower Market* (oil on canvas, 14 1/4 x 17 1/4 ins / 36 x 44 cm) FRF 9,000. Paris, 7 Dec 1992, *Street in Algiers with Figures* (oil on canvas, 22 x 18 ins / 55 x 46 cm) FRF 3,500. Paris, 22 April 1994, *Visit to El Kettar* (oil on canvas, 18 x 22 ins / 46 x 55 cm) FRF 4,000.

GAGE, Robert Merrell
American, 20th century.
Born 1892, in Kansas; died 1981.
Painter.
Robert Merrell Gage studied at the Art Students' League in New York and was a member of the California Art Club. He was awarded a gold medal by the Kansas City Institute in 1921. He was also a teacher.

GAGEL, Karl August
German, 19th - 20th century.
Born 9 February 1861, in Heidelberg; died 21 April 1916, in Karlsruhe.
Painter.
Karl August Gagel was mainly interested in woven fabrics.

GAGELIN, François
French, 18th century.
Active in Pontarlier c. 1750.
Sculptor (wood).
François Gagelin worked for the church of St Bénigne.

GAGEN, Robert Ford
British, 19th - 20th century.
Born 1847 or 1848, in London; died 1926.
Active in Canada from c. 1880.
Painter, watercolourist. Landscapes, mountainscapes, waterscapes, seascapes.
Robert Gagen lived and worked in Toronto. He took part in many exhibitions, particularly in Ottawa.
Auction records:
Toronto, 17 May 1976, *Steep Landscape, Canada* (1904, watercolour, 19 x 12 1/2 ins / 48 x 32 cm) CAD 1,000. Toronto, 19 Oct 1976, *Mountain Landscape with River* (1910, oil on canvas, 15 x 20 ins / 38 x 51 cm) CAD 1,000. Toronto, 26 May 1981, *Rocky Mountain Stream* (1900, watercolour, 13 1/4 x 9 1/4 ins / 33.8 x 23.8 cm) CAD 2,300. Toronto, 18 Nov 1986, *Maritime Scene* (oil on canvas, 28 x 39 ins / 71.3 x 98.8 cm) CAD 7,000.

GAGET, Paul
French, 16th century.
Born 1500, in Bar-le-Duc (Meuse).
Sculptor.
A pupil of Ligier Richier, in around 1555 Gaget painted two altarpieces, one for the chapel of St Anne at the abbey of Ste-

Vanne in Verdun, and the other, showing both a *Nativity* and an *Adoration of the Shepherds* in the Chapel of the Princes at Bar-le-Duc

GAGEY, Adolphe
French, 19th century.
Born 26 March 1809, in Paris.
Painter. Portraits, landscapes.
He studied under Monvoisin and exhibited at the Paris Salon from 1842 to 1857.

GAGEY, André
French, 20th century.
Born in Chalon-sur-Saône.
Painter. Landscapes.
André Gagey exhibited in Paris at the Salon des Artistes Français from 1921. He was awarded a gold medal in 1930.
AUCTION RECORDS:
PARIS, 16 Feb 1983, *The Pardon Religious Festival in Brittany* (oil on canvas, 51 1/2 x 78 3/4 ins / 131 x 200 cm) FRF 11,000. LONDON, 10 April 2000, *Working in the Garden. House with Red Roof. French Village* (1927-1928, oil on canvas, three, 24 x 29 ins / 61 x 73 cm) GBP 4,500. LONDON, 10 April 2000, *Anemones* (1928, oil on canvas, 24 x 28 ins / 61 x 71 cm) GBP 8,000.

GAGEY, Auguste
French, 19th century.
Born in Paris.
Painter. Landscapes.
He submitted watercolours entitled *Undergrowth in Vincennes* and *Château de Lubersac* to the 1877 Salon, followed in 1880 by a watercolour of *Evening in the Tuilerie Woods near Ferrières*.

GAGG, Gebhard
Swiss, 19th century.
Born 1838, in Lucerne.
Painter.
Gagg made study trips to Germany and Switzerland and in 1869 he became drawing teacher at the high school in Konstanz, Germany.

GAGG-LÖWENBERG, Friedrich von
German, 19th century.
Born 1799, in Wertheim-am-Main; died 14 June 1874, in Karlsruhe (Baden-Württemberg).
Painter. Landscapes.
Gagg-Löwenberg lived primarily in Freiburg-im-Breisgau and in Karlsruhe (Baden-Württemberg).

GAGGIA, Leonardo
Italian, 19th century.
Born 1821, in Cusiano.
Sculptor (wood).
Gaggia is remembered for his works in the churches of Cles, Predazzo, Ligoretto and Nomi, near Milan.

GAGGINI, Antonello, called Antonio da Carrara
Italian, 16th century.
Born 1478, in Palermo; died 1536, in Palermo.
Sculptor.
Antonello Gaggini was the son of a sculptor and the father of Antonio, Fazio and Vincenzo Gaggini, as well as of Carlo Filippo and Giacomo da Bissone. He lived mainly in Sicily, in Messina, Palermo and Nicosia. For 15 years, he was engaged on the choir of Palermo Cathedral. He used a polychrome technique. Vasari speaks highly of his work, which includes six marble statues (in the cathedral of Montelione di Casa Pignatelli, Calabria), representing the *Madonna, St John the Evangelist, Mary Magdalene, the Virgin and Child, St Luke* and *Our Lady of the Snows*. Three other sculptures of the Madonna, carved by Antonello, were transferred from Palermo to Montelione Cathedral.

GAGGINI, Antonio I
Italian, 16th century.
Active in Palermo.
Sculptor.
Antonio I was one of the sons of Antonello Gaggini.

GAGGINI, Antonio II
Italian, 16th century.
Died c. 1530, in Carrara.
Active in Genoa.
Sculptor.
Antonio II was the brother of Giovanni Gaggini I and Pace Gaggini. He can be identified with the Antonio da Bissone who was working in Venice in the early 16th century and in Genoa in 1526.

GAGGINI, Antonuzzo
Italian, 16th - 17th century.
Died 21 July 1627, in Caltagirone.
Sculptor.
Antonuzzo Gaggini was the son of Giovanni Domenico Gaggini I and the father of Giovanni Domenico Gaggini II. He is believed to have worked in Ferrara in 1589 under the name of Antonio Gazini.

GAGGINI, Bernardino
Italian, 16th century.
Active in Spain.
Sculptor.
The son of Antonio Gaggini II, Bernardino Gaggini worked mainly in Seville and Toledo.

GAGGINI, Bernardo I
Italian, 18th - 19th century.
Active in Genoa.
Sculptor.
Bernardo Gaggini I was the father of Giuseppe Gaggini III.

GAGGINI, Bernardo II
Italian, 19th century.
Active in Genoa.
Sculptor.
Bernardo Gaggini II was the nephew and pupil of Giuseppe Gaggini III.

GAGGINI, Domenico
Italian, 15th century.
Died September 1492, in Palermo.
Sculptor (marble). Religious subjects. Ornaments.
Domenico Gaggini is recorded as having sculpted the ornamentation for the façade of the chapel of St John the Baptist in Genoa Cathedral.
AUCTION RECORDS:
MILAN, 25 Oct 1988, *Virgin and Child* (marble, h. 35 1/2 ins / 90 cm) ITL 30,000,000.

GAGGINI, Elia
Italian, 16th - 17th century.
Died before 1611, in Genoa.
Sculptor.
Elia Gaggini produced a number of sculptures for the chapel of St John the Baptist in Genoa Cathedral.

GAGGINI, Fazio
Italian, 16th century.
Born 1520, in Palermo; died 27 May 1567, in Palermo.
Sculptor.
One of the sons of Antonello Gaggini, Fazio worked mainly in Palermo Cathedral.

GAGGINI, Francesco
Italian, 17th century.
Born June 1610, in Caltagirone, Sicily; died 3 December 1643, in Caltagirone.
Sculptor.

Francesco Gaggini was the son of Giovanni Domenico Gaggini II.

GAGGINI, Giacomo I. See **GIACOMO DA BISSONE**

GAGGINI, Giacomo II
Italian, 18th century.
Born c. 1699, in Genoa; died 1763.
Sculptor.
Giacomo Gaggini II was an imitator of Bernini.

GAGGINI, Giovanni Domenico I
Italian, 16th century.
Born c. 1503; died before 1567.
Sculptor.
The son of Antonello Gaggini, Giovanni Domenico I worked with his father on Marsala Cathedral. He spent most of his life in Messina and Palermo.

GAGGINI, Giovanni Domenico II
Italian, 16th - 17th century.
Active in Caltagirone.
Sculptor.
Giovanni Domenico II worked in Palermo and Caltagirone.

GAGGINI, Giovanni Francesco
Italian, 18th century.
Born in Bissone.
Active primarily in Brescia in the latter half of the 18th century.
Painter.

GAGGINI, Giovanni I
Italian, 16th century.
Born in Bissone; died 1517, in Mendrisio.
Sculptor.
Most of Giovanni I's work was done in Genoa.

GAGGINI, Giovanni II
Italian, 15th century.
Born c. 1470, in Palermo.
Sculptor.
Giovanni II is recorded as having sculpted the *Tomb of Gaspare di Marino* in Girgenti Cathedral.

GAGGINI, Giuseppe I
Italian, 16th century.
Died 13 September 1579.
Active in Palermo.
Sculptor.
Giuseppe I is recorded as having sculpted a *Virgin Mary* for the church in Mirto. He was no doubt the son of Giacomo I Gaggini.

GAGGINI, Giuseppe II
Italian, 18th century.
Active in Genoa.
Sculptor.
Giuseppe Gaggini II was an imitator of Bernini and the brother of Giacomo Gaggini II. He worked on the Palazzo Doria in Sestri Levante.

GAGGINI, Giuseppe III
Italian, 19th century.
Born 25 April 1791, in Genoa; died 2 May 1867, in Genoa.
Sculptor.
Giuseppe Gaggini III was a pupil of Canova. After spending some time in Milan and Rome, he settled in Turin, where he built a large number of monuments for the kings of Piedmont.

GAGGINI, Pace
Italian, 16th century.
Born in Bissone.
Sculptor.
Pace Gaggini worked for a number of churches, mainly in Genoa and Pavia.

GAGGINI, Stefano
Italian, 15th century.
Active in Palermo.
Sculptor.
Stefano Gaggini worked alongside Domenico Gaggini.

GAGGINI, Vincenzo
Italian, 16th century.
Born 8 August 1527, in Palermo; died 15 March 1595, in Palermo.
Sculptor.
A son of Antonello Gaggini, Vincenzo worked mainly for Palermo Cathedral.

GAGGIOTTI-RICHARDS, Emma
Italian, 19th - 20th century.
Born 1825, in Rome; died June 1912, in Velletri (Lazio).
Painter. History painting, portraits.
Emma Gaggiotti-Richards lived in Italy, and is known for the works *Alexander von Humboldt* (1854) and *Portrait of the Artist*.

GAGINI, Antonello. See **GAGGINI**

GAGLIARDELLI, Giovan Francesco
Italian, 16th century.
Born in Città San Angelo.
Painter, sculptor.
Giovan Francesco Gagliardelli is known for his work at Ripatransone.

GAGLIARDELLI, Girolamo
Italian, 16th century.
Born in Macerata.
Painter.
Most of Girolamo Gagliardelli's work was done for Osimo Cathedral.

GAGLIARDELLO
Italian, 16th century.
Active at the end of the 16th century.
Miniaturist.

GAGLIARDI, Bartolommeo, or Gagliardo, called Lo Spagnoletto
Italian, 16th - 17th century.
Born 1555, in Genoa; died c. 1620.
Painter, fresco artist, engraver. History painting.
Bartolommeo Gagliardi lived for a long time in Spain and the West Indies, hence his nickname of 'lo Spagnoletto'. Towards the end of his life, he was paralysed by a fall from the scaffolding on which he was working.

He decorated the façade of a residence near to the cathedral in Genoa, with allegorical depictions of the four elements. In his style of painting, he could fairly be described as an imitator of Michelangelo. His style as an engraver is akin to that of Cherubino Alberti. A number of his plates have survived, including the magnificent title page to Gaspero Oliva's *Conclusioni Filisofiche*.

B Gagliardo.

BIBLIOGRAPHY:
Allgemeines Künstler-Lexikon, E.A. Seemann, Leipzig, 1953-1962.

AUCTION RECORDS:
NEW YORK, 13 Jan 1993, *St Francis in Prayer before a Crucifix (recto); Evangelist Writing at a Desk (verso)* (ink and wash, 7 x 6 1/2 ins / 18 x 16.6 cm) USD 2,200.

GAGLIARDI, Bernardino
Italian, 17th century.

Born 1609, in Città di Castello; died 18 February 1660, in Perugia.

Painter. History painting.

Bernardino Gagliardi was a pupil of Avanzino Nucci. He painted a *Martyrdom of St Crescentius* for the cathedral of his native Città di Castello, and a masterful *St Pellegrino* for the Rome church of S Marcello.

GAGLIARDI, Filippo

Italian, 17th century.

Born in Rome; died 1659.

Painter, architect. Church interiors.

Filippo Gagliardi is known only as a painter of architectural subjects working around 1610.

Museums and Galleries:

Madrid (Prado): *Church Interior.*

GAGLIARDI, Giovanni

Italian, 19th century.

Painter. Portraits.

Giovanni Gagliardi was a Roman artist who was active in the 19th century. The Musée d'Avignon in southern France has two of his portraits, depicting 17th-century Jesuits from that town, which were commissioned by the museum administration in 1865.

Museums and Galleries:

Avignon: *17th-Century Jesuit of Avignon* (two portraits).

GAGLIARDI, Pietro

Italian, 16th century.

Active in Rome in 1564.

Sculptor.

GAGLIARDI, Pietro

Italian, 19th century.

Born 1809, in Rome; died 1890, in Frascati (Lazio).

Painter.

Pietro Gagliardi decorated a large number of churches in Rome.

GAGLIARDINI, Bernardino

Italian, 18th century.

Born c. 1760.

Sculptor.

Bernardino Gagliardini was active in Turin before moving to settle in Lisbon.

GAGLIARDINI, Julien Gustave

French, 19th - 20th century.

Born 1 March 1846 or 1848, in Mulhouse; died 1927, in Paris.

Painter, engraver. History painting, portraits, genre scenes, landscapes, landscapes with figures, waterscapes, seascapes.

Julien Gagliardini studied under Soulary and L. Cogniet. From 1869 to 1880 he sent portraits and some genre scenes to the Paris Salon. He received the following awards: a commendation in 1883; a bronze medal in 1884; a silver medal in 1886; and a silver medal in 1889 at the Exposition Universelle. He was made a Chevalier of the Légion D'Honneur in 1893 and received a gold medal in 1900 at the Exposition Universelle. He became a member of the Société des Artistes Français in 1883.

He is known for *The Archbishop's Palace, Salzburg, The Seaside at Grandchamp* and *Shrimp Fishers at Grandchamp.*

He abandoned historical painting to concentrate on landscapes and specialised in painting picturesque locations in the south of France.

Gagliardini

Museums and Galleries:

Amiens: *Seascape* - Arras: *Road at Gordes* - Cambrai: *Street in Gordes* - Montpellier: *Midday in Auvergne* - Mulhouse: *The Hamlet of Serret* - Paris (Louvre): *Sunny Landscape* - Rheims: *Hidden Village in the Basses-Alpes* - Rochefort: *The Port of Cassis* - Tourcoing: *On the Stroke of Midday, Old Provence; Sails Drying, Italy.*

Auction records:

Paris, 27 March 1897, *Les Martigues,* FRF 375; *Road outside Toulon,* FRF 225; *Fishermen,* FRF 210. Paris, 2 Jan 1898, *Village Street,* FRF 330. Paris, 8 May 1900, *On the Shores of the Mediterranean,* FRF 280. Paris, 11 April 1910, *Laguepie,* FRF 350; *Village in Sunlight,* FRF 245. Paris, 13 Nov 1918, *Public Holiday in Provence,* FRF 340. Paris, 13 April 1921, *Martigues Canal,* FRF 905; *Road at Salernes,* FRF 1,210. Paris, 28 June 1923, *Village Street in Sunlight,* FRF 505. Paris, 21 Feb 1924, *Sails Drying,* FRF 1,000; *Quay in Venice,* FRF 2,000. Paris, 30 Nov 1925, *Recollection of the South of France,* FRF 1,800. Paris, 15 Feb 1926, *Les Martigues,* FRF 1,320. Paris, 10 May 1926, *Boats and Fishermen on the Beach at Low Tide,* FRF 1,400. Paris, 23 June 1928, *Sunlit Street, Provence,* FRF 3,000. Paris, 24-26 April 1929, *Shores of the Mediterranean,* FRF 580. Paris, 28 April 1937, *At the Port,* FRF 250. Paris, 16-17 May 1939, *Les Martigues,* FRF 1,000; *Coast Road,* FRF 900; *Cassis-sur-Mer,* FRF 1,880; *Fishing Port in the Morning,* FRF 620. Paris, 29 June 1939, *Les Martigues,* FRF 500. Paris, 12 March 1941, *Boats Laid Up,* FRF 880. Paris, 23 May 1941, *Road in Provence,* FRF 1,000; *Lake Lugano,* FRF 1,700. Paris, 20 Feb 1942, *Sorting Fish,* FRF 7,000. Paris, 11 May 1942, *Fishing Port - Morning,* FRF 4,800. Paris, 22 June 1942, *Wash Day,* FRF 4,200. Paris, 29 June 1942, *Death of Tarquin* (pencil) FRF 900. Paris, 12 April 1943, *The Promenade des Anglais, Nice,* FRF 8,200. Paris, 23 June 1943, *Farmyard,* FRF 5,000. Paris, 2 July 1943, *Port in the South of France* (1892) FRF 1,800. Paris, 13 Oct 1943, *Sunny Street in Provence,* FRF 5,100. Paris, 3 May 1944, *The Steamship Departs,* FRF 2,500. Paris, 10 May 1944, *Port in the South of France,* FRF 6,100. Paris, 15 May 1944, *Grape Picking,* FRF 4,350. Paris, 23 Feb 1945, *Sorting the Fish,* FRF 6,000. Paris, Oct 1945 - July 1946, *Quay in a Port,* FRF 1,600; *Road in a Village in Provence,* FRF 7,900; *Seascape,* FRF 15,000; *Sunlit Street,* FRF 15,000. Paris, 18 Nov 1946, *Young Peasant Girl on a Path,* FRF 3,000; *The Procession,* FRF 2,700; *Cottages,* FRF 8,000; *Peasant Woman,* FRF 10,100; *Sailboats,* FRF 8,100. Lille, 16-20 Dec 1946, *Les Martigues,* FRF 9,100. Paris, 24 March 1947, *Grape Picking in Provence,* FRF 14,500; *Flock of Sheep and Shepherdess near a Village* (1883) FRF 4,600. Paris, 13 June 1947, *Port in the South of France,* FRF 15,000. Versailles, 27 June 1976, *Sunlit Shore* (oil on canvas, 18¼ x 24¼ ins / 46.5 x 61.5 cm) FRF 2,500. Paris, 13 Feb 1978, *By the Sea* (oil on panel, 9 x 12½ ins / 22 x 32 cm) FRF 5,000. Milan, 6 Nov 1980, *The Port of Cassis* (oil on canvas, 20¾ x 15 ins / 53 x 38 cm) ITL 900,000. Paris, 28 June 1982, *Sunlit Village Street* (oil on panel, 11 x 16¼ ins / 27 x 41 cm) FRF 3,000. Lille, 11 Dec 1983, *Lake Como* (oil on panel, 9½ x 12¾ ins / 24 x 32.5 cm) FRF 12,000. Versailles, 25 May 1986, *Old Bridge over a River in a Village* (oil on canvas, 31 x 39¼ ins / 78.5 x 100 cm) FRF 15,000. Paris, 30 Nov 1987, *Washerwomen* (6½ x 10 ins / 16.5 x 24.5 cm) FRF 5,200. Paris, 7 March 1988, *Seascape* (oil on panel, 14¾ x 22 ins / 37.5 x 55 cm) FRF 4,300. Paris, 27 April 1988, *Village of Roussillon* (oil on canvas, 15¼ x 22 ins / 38.5 x 55.8 cm) FRF 30,000. Versailles, 23 Oct 1988, *Port in the South of France* (oil on panel, 15 x 21½ ins / 38 x 54.5 cm) FRF 6,100. Amsterdam, 19 Sept 1989, *Young Boy Slicing Bread* (1887, oil on canvas, 13¾ ins / 35 cm, 2 x 11¼ ins/5 x 28.5 cm) NLG 1,840. Paris, 24 Jan 1990, *Village by the Sea* (oil on canvas, 13½ x 6¼ ins / 34 x 16 cm) FRF 15,000. Paris, 29 Nov 1990, *The Shore* (oil on panel, 14¼ x 21¼ ins / 36.5 x 54 cm) FRF 39,000. Paris, 17 Nov 1991, *Fishermen* (oil on panel, 15¾ x 13½ ins / 40 x

34 cm) FRF 14,000. NEW YORK, 16 July 1992, *Women Mending Fishing Nets* (oil on panel, 9½ x 14 ins / 24.1 x 35.6 cm) USD 1,650. PARIS, 25 Nov 1992, *People Gathering Wrack* (oil on panel, 17¾ x 22 ins / 45 x 55 cm) FRF 10,500. LONDON, 7 April 1993, *Washerwomen on a Beach* (oil on panel, 9½ x 13¾ ins / 24 x 35 cm) GBP 805. AMSTERDAM, 31 May 1994, *The Château of Galifet in Salernes in the Var* (oil on canvas, 18 x 25½ ins / 46 x 65 cm) NLG 8,050. PARIS, 17 June 1994, *Landscape* (oil on canvas, 15 x 22 ins / 38 x 55 cm) FRF 11,000. CALAIS, 3 July 1994, *Young Woman in Crinoline on a Beach* (oil on panel, 16¼ x 12½ ins / 41 x 32 cm) FRF 13,000. CALAIS, 10 March 1997, *River Bank* (oil on canvas, 11 x 15¾ ins / 27 x 40 cm) FRF 4,200.

GAGLIARDO DI RICCARDO DA NAPOLI
Italian, 14th century.
Died 1348, in Naples.
Sculptor, architect.

Gagliardo built and decorated a number of churches in the Naples area.

GAGNAIRE, Aline
French, 20th century.
Born 11 September 1911, in Paris; died 11 February 1997, in Paris.
Painter (mixed media), illustrator. Figures.
Lettrism.
Oupeinpo Group.

Aline Gagnaire painted from childhood but for many years remained outside artistic circles. In 1938 she participated in the activities of the Réverbères group, who were close to the Surrealists, and during the German Occupation was part of La Main à Plume, illustrating many books including the poetry of Noël Arnaud. Little concerned with self-promotion and difficult to categorise because of the disparate nature of her interests and production, Gagnaire exhibited little. In 1974 she showed a sculpture at the Salon de Mai; the piece was very stark and almost sign-like. In 1993 a mini retrospective of her work was held at the Elga Wimmer Gallery in New York.

Gagnaire was initially influenced by Surrealism and frequented Surrealist circles in Paris during the 1930s and 1940s, spending time with Breton and Picabia. She later became interested in Art Brut and met Dubuffet, and then in art relating to Zen Buddhism, which she studied. She went on to create relief pieces using a variety of materials such as pieces of rag in her 'tableaux-chiffons' - sometimes in the manner of Enrico Baj, and also 'tableaux-matières' and 'tableaux-clous'. She worked with Maurice Lemaître and produced pictograms in accordance with Lettrist principles. Almost always taking the human figure as her subject, she treated it with both tenderness and condemnation and evoked it almost remotely in strange, white plaster reliefs.

Gagnaire's work is varied, full of humour and in a state of constant renewal thanks to her exploration of diverse techniques and materials and above all of creative techniques. Like Baj, she was a member of Oupeinpo (Ouvroir de Peinture Potentielle or Potential Painting Workshop). Like Raymond Queneau's Oulipo (Ouvroir de Littérature Potentielle or Potential Literature Workshop), which attracted Georges Pérec, Italo Calvino and Günter Grass, the Oupeinpo artists devoted themselves to the study of and experimentation with a possible methodology of artistic creation. The activities of Oulipo, like those of Oupeinpo, were crowned by the superior authority of the 'Collège de Pataphysique', whose reference to Jarry also relates back to Dada. As part of this tradition Gagnaire produced a series of Père Ubu heads. In 1986 she participated in the Venice Biennale by invitation of Arturo Schwarz.

BIBLIOGRAPHY:
Aline Gagnaire. Un parcours, Jean-Yves Barczyk, Paris.
Breerette, Geneviève, '*Aline Gagnaire, une artiste pataphysicienne*' in *Le Monde*, periodical, Paris, 18 February 1997.

AUCTION RECORDS:
PARIS, 3 June 1996, *The Solar Man or Silence* (1980, lead/panel, relief painting, 63 x 31½ ins / 160 x 80 cm) FRF 5,500.

GAGNAIRE, Charles Joseph
French, 20th century.
Born in Callas (Var).
Painter. Portraits.

Charles Gagnaire exhibited at the Paris Salon from 1930.

GAGNANT, Jean Nicolas Victor
French, 18th century.
Born 1767, in Paris; died 10 October 1796.
Painter.

Jean Gagnant played a part in the political events of the Revolution. On 31 August 1793, he was made a police deputy in the Commune but several months later was stripped of his responsibilities. The Committee of public health ordered his arrest and the seizure of his documents on 29 March 1794. However, he managed to regain his freedom. He became secretary to Drouot in 1796 and helped him escape from the Abbey. On the night of 9 September, he went to the encampment at Grenelle to incite the soldiers to rise up against the Directoire. He was then arrested, incarcerated in the Temple and condemned to death. Although he escaped while being led to the scaffold, he was stabbed to death by a mounted policeman.

GAGNE, Alphonse
French, 19th century.
Painter. Landscapes.

AUCTION RECORDS:
PARIS, 12-15 April 1899, *Quai des Orfèvres and the Branch of the Seine*, FRF 50.

GAGNÉ, Jacques, pseudonym Jules Gagniet
French, 19th century.
Born 31 August 1820, in St-Priest-la-Feuille (Creuse); died 1864, in Paris.
Pastellist, watercolourist, lithographer, engraver.

He enrolled at the École des Beaux-Arts on 31 March 1836 and studied under Naudet and Pauquet.

GAGNÉ, Paul-Auguste
French, 19th century.
Born in Paris.
Painter, sculptor.

He was the son and pupil of Jacques Gagné. He went on to study under Roger and submitted a watercolour to the 1861 Salon and a plaster low relief entitled *Titans Transfixed* to the 1865 Salon.

GAGNEAU, Paul Léon
French, 19th - 20th century.
Born in Paris; died 1910, in Harcourt.
Painter. Genre scenes.

Paul Gagneau was trained by Pils, Lehmann and Laugée. He exhibited at the Paris Salon from 1879 and then at the Salon des Artistes Français, of which he became a member in 1884. He received a commendation in 1890, a bronze medal in 1892, a silver medal in 1898 and a bronze medal in 1900 at the Exposition Universelle.

L. Gagneau

AUCTION RECORDS:
PARIS, 28 Jan 1924, *Shepherdess Sitting by a Stream*, FRF 155. PARIS, 14 March 1947, *The Pond* (1899) FRF 1,300;

Marshland (1900) FRF 3,600; *The Boatman*, FRF 3,100; *Washerwomen*, FRF 3,000; *Forest Interior*, FRF 300; *Young Poultry Seller*, FRF 3,000. PARIS, 8 Dec 1980, *Farm by a Pond with Figures* (1899, oil on canvas, 59 x 89 ins / 150 x 226 cm) FRF 15,000. PARIS, 18 March 1985, *The Turkey Girl* (1907, oil on canvas, 15 1/4 x 21 3/4 ins / 38.5 x 55.5 cm) FRF 10,500.

GAGNÉE, Pierre Eustache
French, 18th century.
Active in Paris in 1787.
Painter (?), sculptor (?).

GAGNEREAUX, Baptiste
French, 18th - 19th century.
Born 1 June 1765, in Dijon; died 9 October 1846, in Dijon.
Painter, engraver.

Baptiste Gagnereaux was a student of Devosges in Dijon and brother of Bénigne Gagnereaux. He established a reputation mainly as a portrait artist but he never attained his brother's level of fame.

GAGNEREAUX, Bénigne, or Gagneraux
French, 18th century.
Born 24 September 1756, in Dijon; died 18 August 1795, in Florence.
Also active in Italy.
Painter, draughtsman. Mythological subjects, allegorical subjects, genre scenes, portraits, animals, landscapes.

A student of François Devosges III in Dijon, Bénigne Gagnereaux was sent to Rome in 1776 at the expense of the province of Bourgogne. He became an historical painter to King Gustav III of Sweden, and professor at the academy of fine arts in Florence in 1793.In 1784, he produced four great bacchanalian subjects, in charcoal and chalk, on the cloister walls of the Carthusian monastery in Rome, This attracted some attention. His pictures *Oedipus Blinded*, and *King of Sweden's Audience with Pope Pius VI at the Vatican*, were bought by the King of Sweden. For the King he also produced in 1787 *Education of Achilles* and, for the Princess of Sweden, *Blessed by Diomedes*, *Venus Is Transported to Olympus by Iris and the Spirit of Peace*.For the Baron Taube, King Gustav III's prime minister, he produced *Ariadne and Bacchus*, *Love Overcoming Power*, and *Hebe Giving Drink to the Eagle of Jupiter*. During his stay in Rome, he painted on the vaulting of the third room in the Borgia Villa *Jupiter and Antiope* and, at the Altieri Palace, *Psyche Awakened by Love*.He travelled to Florence in 1793 and painted there for the Duke Regent, Charles of Sweden, *Psyche Carried by Zephyrs to the Palace of Love*, which earned him his title of painter to the King of Sweden. The drawing style of his works evokes the paintings on the vases of Greek antiquity.

His work was represented in 2000 at the Louvre in *D'après l'antique* (*After Antiquity*), an exhibition which looked at the interface between antique masterpieces and the works that they inspired. There was also a presentation of his work in 1983 at the museum in Dijon.

B Gagneraux

BIBLIOGRAPHY:
Sandström, Birgitta, *Bénigne Gagneraux: éducation, inspiration, œuvre*, Stockholms universitet, Stockholm, 1981 (French edition). Laveissière, Sylvain, *Bénigne Gagneraux: un peintre bourguignon dans la Rome néo-classique*, Musée des Beaux-Arts, Dijon, 1983. Cuzin, Jean-Pierre (ed.), *D'après l'antique*, group exhibition catalogue, Musée du Louvre, Réunion des musées nationaux, Paris, 2000.

MUSEUMS AND GALLERIES:
DIJON (MBA): *Soranus and Servilia*; *Battle of Senef*; *Crossing the Rhine*; *Bacchanalian Dance*; *Triumph of Neptune* - FLORENCE (Uffizi): *Knights in Combat*; *Self-portrait*; *Lion Hunt* - GENEVA: *Spirit of Peace Stopping the Horses of Mars* (1794) - MILAN: *Magician* - MONTPELLIER (Mus. Fabre): *Shock Troops from the Cavalry*; *Landscape* - PARIS (Louvre): *Prométhée attaché au Caucase* - STOCKHOLM: *Blind Oedipus*; *Pope Pius VI Shows Gustav III the Sculpture Gallery in the Vatican* (1785).

AUCTION RECORDS:
DIJON, 12 Feb 1900, *Frightened Horse*, FRF 206. PARIS, 26 Jan 1911, *Portrait of Coffinet* (drawing) FRF 11. DIJON, 21 Feb 1919, *Coffinet* (pencil) FRF 30. LONDON, 20 Oct 1982, *Lion Hunt* (1775, oil on canvas, 36 x 44 ins / 91.5 x 111.5 cm) GBP 1,500. STOCKHOLM, 11 April 1984, *Faun and Cupid Sleeping* (oil on canvas, oval, 8 1/4 x 12 1/2 ins / 21 x 32 cm) SEK 22,000. PARIS, 28 Jan 1985, *Portrait of a Man with a White Poodle* (1789, oil on canvas, 24 1/2 x 29 1/2 ins / 62 x 75 cm) FRF 180,000. MONTE CARLO, 20 June 1987, *Portrait of M. Caze* (1789, oil on canvas, 29 1/4 x 24 ins / 74 x 61 cm) FRF 300,000. DIJON, 5 June 1994, *Spirit of the Arts* (1789, oil on canvas, 42 1/2 x 32 1/4 ins / 108 x 82 cm) FRF 200,000. PARIS, 25 June 1996, *Education of Achilles* (1785, oil on canvas, 37 3/4 x 49 1/2 ins / 96 x 125.5 cm) FRF 450,000. LONDON, 7 July 1999, *Lion Hunt* (oil on canvas, 31 x 38 ins / 80 x 96 cm) GBP 7,500. ZURICH, 8 Sept 1999, *Youth Reading Book* (1786, oil on canvas, 18 x 15 ins / 46 x 38 cm) CHF 28,000. LONDON, 14 Dec 2000, *Education of Achilles* (1785, oil on canvas, 38 x 49 ins / 97 x 125 cm) GBP 100,000. PARIS, 23 March 2001, *Venus Transported to Olympus by Iris* (black ink, study, 13 x 19 ins / 32 x 47 cm) FRF 12,000. PARIS, 27 Nov 2002, *Blind Oedipus Commends his Family to the Gods* (1783, oil on paper/canvas, 23 x 32 ins / 59 x 82 cm) EUR 11,000. SAN FRANCISCO, 19 Nov 2003, *Classical Figures at an Anvil* (pen/ink, sepia wash, a pair, 13 x 19 ins / 33 x 47 cm) USD 2,000.

GAGNERY, Jean-Auguste
French, 19th century.
Born 21 May 1778, in Paris.
Painter. Religious subjects, portraits, genre scenes, landscapes, seascapes, animals.

He studied from 1817 in François-Joseph Heim's workshop at the École des Beaux-Arts in Paris. He exhibited at the Paris Salon from 1822 to 1845. Gagnery painted predominantly historical subjects, genre compositions and landscapes. Examples of his work include *Bathsheba*, *Duke of Angoulême Entering Madrid*, *View near Honfleur*, *Arrival of the Stagecoach*, *Seascape*, *A Cow*, *View of the Villette Basin*, *Back from Market*, *Returning to the Village* and *View of Edinburgh Castle from the Haymarket*.

BIBLIOGRAPHY:
Les Années romantiques, la peinture française de 1815 à 1850, exhibition catalogue, Musée des Beaux-Arts, Nantes; Gal. Nationales du Grand Palais, Paris, 1996.

MUSEUMS AND GALLERIES:
DOUAI: *Post Stage Arriving in Honfleur* - VERSAILLES: *View of Paris*.

GAGNEUR, Étienne
French, 17th century.
Active in Paris in 1668.
Engraver.

GAGNEUR DE PATORNAY, Ange-Marie-Maurice
French, 19th century.
Born in Paris.
Sculptor.

He was a pupil of Peynot. From 1892 he was a member of the Société des Artistes Français and took part in its exhibitions.

GAGNEUX, Paul
French, 19th century.
Died 1892.
Painter. Still-lifes.

He was a member of the Société des Artistes Français and took part in its exhibitions.

Auction records:

London, 7 April 1993, *Peonies and Copper Pot on a Table* (oil on canvas, 31 x 37 3/4 ins / 79 x 96 cm) GBP 4,830. New Orleans, 17 Nov 2000, *Lock on the Sichon Canal* (1884, oil on canvas, 39 x 59 ins / 99 x 150 cm) USD 11,000. Neuilly, 28 March 2003, *Fisherman* (oil on canvas, 26 x 19 ins / 65 x 48 cm) EUR 1,500. Neuilly, 27 June 2003, *Seashore at Royan* (oil on panel, 7 x 9 ins / 18 x 24 cm) EUR 7,500.

GAGNEY, Pierre Étienne

French, 18th century.
Active in Paris in 1787.
Painter (?), sculptor (?).

GAGNIER, John (Mrs)

British, 18th century.
Active 1720-1725.
Painter. Portraits.

Mrs John Gagnier, wife of a professor of Arabic at Oxford, and professional artist, has been described as a 'second class portrait painter'.

GAGNIÈRE, Jean. See **GANIÈRE**

GAGNIET, Jules. See **GAGNÉ Jacques**

GAGNON, Charles

Canadian, 20th century.
Born 1934, in Montreal.
Painter.

Charles Gagnon trained during a stay in New York from 1956 until 1960, when Abstract Expressionism was at its height. It is therefore natural that Expressionism should have had a very strong influence on him in his early career, and at his first exhibition in Montreal his paintings were considered unrestrained and frenzied. His use of vivid colours with a total disregard for unity, violent brush strokes and areas simply spattered with paint resulted in work that was expressive rather than decorative. However, he developed from the spontaneity of Abstract Expressionism to a form of reflection on the act of painting itself. He divided the painting into superimposed squares, and when he wanted to break up the surface to catch the colour modulations, he incorporated steel plates into his pictures. His painting developed a certain refinement in 1966 and *Stamp* is presented as the simple juxtaposition of a polished square and a brown rectangle.

In addition to his painting he works as a photographer and has also created boxes, collecting together diverse objects.

Bibliography:

James, Geoffrey, *Contemporary Canadian Painters: Peintres Canadiens Contemporains*, exhibition catalogue, 1977 (exhibition of works from the Canada council art bank). Fry, Philip, *Charles Gagnon*, exhibition catalogue, Musée des Beaux-Arts, Montreal, 1978. Cambell, James D., *Parminedian Puzzles: Paradox and Discovery in the Paintings of Charles Gagnon*, exhibition catalogue, Parachute, Montreal, 1989. Nasgaard, Roald, '*A Visit with Charles Gagnon*' in *Canadian Art*, vol. 18, no. 1, pp. 60-66, 2001.

Museums and Galleries:

Montreal (MAC): *Cassation of a New Day; Coast* (1958-1959); *Field* (1961); *Screen-Grey Space* (1966, stainless steel and oil-based enamel/wood); *Inquiry No2* (1968) - Montreal (MBA): *Untitled* (1965); *Steps* (Dec 1968-69) - Toronto (AG of Ontario): *Cassation/Dark/Sombre* (1976).

GAGNON, Clarence Alphonse

Canadian, 20th century.
Born 1881 or 1882, in Montreal; died 1942.
Painter, engraver. Landscapes.

Clarence Gagnon studied under the direction of William Brymner at the Montreal Art Association from 1897 until 1900. He then made the ritual journey to France and Italy, studying at the Académie Julian. He returned to Montreal in 1909, but went back to Paris several times - from 1912 to 1914, then 1917 to 1919; he then lived there from 1924 until 1936.

He began by painting rural scenes around Baie-St-Paul, such as *Oxen Ploughing* of 1903. When he returned to Montreal in 1909 after travelling in Europe he showed the influence of the Barbizon School, then endeavoured to capture the atmosphere of villages in the mist, for example with *Wayside Cross, Autumn* of about 1915. In France he was known particularly for his illustrations, notably for *Le Grand Silence Blanc* by L.F. Rouquette and *Maria Chapdelaine* by L. Hémon. In around 1926 he abandoned the atmospheric aspect of his early landscapes in favour of painting views in bright colours, in which anecdotal details are very clearly shown. His paintings in this style include *Village in the Laurentians*, of around 1926.

He received an honourable mention at the Salon des Artistes Français in Paris in 1906.

Bibliography:

Ostiguy, Jean René, *Modernism in Quebec Art, 1916-1946*, exhibition catalogue, National Gallery of Canada, Ottawa, 1983. Mac Hardy, C.W., '*Clarence Gagnon's etchings, 1905-1909*' in *Racar. Revue d'Art Canadienne*, vol. 11, no. 1-2, pp. 117-123, 1984. Reid, Dennis, *A Concise History of Canadian Painting*, Oxford University Press, Toronto, 1988.

Museums and Galleries:

Fredericton (Beaverbrook AG): *Two Beaches: Paramé and St-Malo* (c. 1908) - Montreal (MBA): *Oxen Ploughing* (1903); *Autumn, Baie-St-Paul* (1909) - Ottawa (NG. of Canada): *Wayside Cross, Autumn* (c. 1915); *Village in the Laurentians* (c. 1926).

Auction records:

Montreal, 3 May 1974, *Beach Scene*, CAD 7,500. Toronto, 19 Oct 1976, *Half-finished Study, Charlevoix* (oil on card, 4 1/2 x 6 1/2 ins / 11.3 x 16.3 cm) CAD 1,900. Toronto, 5 Nov 1979, *Hunter's Cabin* (colouring pencil, 7 3/4 x 11 1/2 ins / 19.5 x 29.5 cm) CAD 1,400. Toronto, 2 Nov 1982, *Winter in the Laurentians* (oil on canvas, 21 x 28 ins / 53.1 x 71.3 cm) CAD 75,000. Toronto, 14 May 1984, *Snowy Landscape, Charlevoix* (oil on panel, 6 1/2 x 9 ins / 16.3 x 23.1 cm) CAD 18,000. Toronto, 27 Nov 1986, *Kiki from Montparnasse* (gouache, 5 1/4 x 4 3/4 ins / 13.4 x 12 cm) CAD 2,200. Montreal, 20 Oct 1987, *Winter in Charlevoix* (1909, oil on panel, 11 x 15 1/4 ins / 28 x 39 cm) CAD 39,000. Montreal, 25 April 1988, *Village in Winter* (oil on canvas, 23 1/2 x 32 ins / 60 x 81 cm) CAD 75,000. Montreal, 30 Oct 1989, *Ship* (gouache, 4 x 5 ins / 10 x 13 cm) CAD 2,860. Montreal, 19 Nov 1991, *Indian Summer in Baie-St-Paul* (oil on panel, 6 1/2 x 9 1/4 ins / 16.5 x 23.5 cm) CAD 5,250. Montreal, 21 June 1994, *Clock Tower in Dinan* (etching, 8 1/2 x 5 1/2 ins / 21.5 x 14 cm) CAD 1,700. Montreal, 3 Dec 1996, *San Pietro Canal, Venice* (1906, etching, 6 x 8 1/2 ins / 15.2 x 21.5 cm) CAD 1,900. Toronto, 1 June 1999, *Study for Maria Chapdelaine* (mixed media, 6 x 9 ins / 16 x 22 cm) CAD 10,000. Montreal, 13 Dec 1999, *Old Elm, Baie St-Paul* (1909, oil on canvas, 6 x 9 ins / 16 x 23 cm) CAD 15,000. Toronto, 23 May 2000, *Winter Moonlight, Baie St Paul, Quebec* (1909, oil on canvas, 20 x 24 ins / 50 x 62 cm) CAD 270,000. Vancouver, 9 Nov 2000, *Project to Illustrate the Great White Silence* (gouache, 7 x 6 ins / 17 x 16 cm) CAD 5,000. Toronto, 29 May 2001, *Rue des Cordiliers, Dinan* (1908, etching, 7 x 9 ins / 19 x 24 cm) CAD 5,000. Boston, 7 Sept 2001, *Road to Town, Winter Landscape with Horsedrawn Sleigh* (oil on canvasboard, 10 x 7 ins / 25 x 18 cm) USD 39,000. Toronto, 14 May 2002, *Quebec Village in Winter* (oil on canvas, 21 x 28 ins / 53 x 71 cm) CAD 250,000. Toronto, 3 June 2002, *Sunset in the Hills* (1921, colour pastel, 19 x 25 ins / 48 x 63 cm) CAD 36,000. Toronto, 3 June 2003, *Baie St Paul* (oil on panel, 6 x 9 ins / 16 x 23 cm) CAD 20,000. Toronto, 2 Dec 2003, *Sunday Mass* (gouache, 7 x 5 ins / 17 x 12 cm) CAD 26,000. TORONTO, 31 May 2004, *Landscape at Baie St Paul* (oil on canvas, 20 x 26 ins / 51 x 66 cm) CAD 600,000. TORONTO, 1 June 2004, *Lake at St Sulpice's Seminary, Montreal* (1909-1917, etching, 7 x 9 ins / 19 x 24 cm) CAD 22,000.

GAGOINE
French, 16th century.
Sculptor (wood).
Fontainebleau School.
Gagoine worked at Fontainebleau between 1568 and 1570, during the same period as Noël Biard, Noël Millon and Gilles Bauge.

GAGONE, Anton
Austrian, 18th - 19th century.
Born 23 March 1743, in Marburg (Hesse); died 11 February 1811, in Graz.
Sculptor.
Gagone worked for Graz town hall. Some of his works are held in the Graz museum.

GAHAGAN, C.
British, 19th century.
Active in London.
Sculptor.
C. Gahagan was an occasional exhibitor at the Royal Academy in London and the Suffolk Street Gallery between 1824 and 1836.

GAHAGAN, Edwin
British, 19th century.
Active in London.
Sculptor.
Edwin Gahagan took part in various exhibitions in London between 1830 and 1857, notably at the Royal Academy, the British Institution and the Suffolk Street Gallery.

GAHAGAN, L. (Jr.)
British, 19th century.
Active in London.
Sculptor.
L. Gahagan was the son of Laurence Gahagan the Younger. He showed at the 1817 Royal Academy exhibition in London.

GAHAGAN, Laurence, the Elder
18th - 19th century.
Active in London.
Sculptor.
Gahagan appears to have been the head of a family of sculptors by this name. From 1798 to 1817, he exhibited frequently at the Royal Academy and once at the British Institution.

GAHAGAN, Laurence, the Younger
British, 19th century.
Active in London.
Sculptor.
Laurence Gahagen was noted for his busts of *Prince William, Son of King George III* and *Queen Charlotte Sophie*.
AUCTION RECORDS:
LONDON, 1 Feb 1972, *George III* (bronze) Gns 400. PORTSMOUTH, 3 Aug 2003, *George III* (bronze, h. 11 ins / 28 cm) USD 2,200.

GAHAGAN, Sally
British, 18th - 19th century.
Active in London.
Sculptor.
Sally Gahagen exhibited at the Royal Academy in London from 1802 to 1835.

GAHAGAN, Sebastian
British, 19th century.
Active in London.
Sculptor.
Sebastian Gahagan exhibited in London from 1817 to 1853, notably at the Royal Academy and the British Institution.

GAHAGAN, V.
British, 18th - 19th century.
Active in London.
Sculptor.
V. Gahagan exhibited at the Royal Academy in London from 1804 to 1823.

GAHÉRY-ULRIC, Angèle (Mme)
French, 19th century.
Born in Paris.
Painter.
Studied under Mlle Thévenin and exhibited work at the 1878 and 1882 Salons. Examples of her output include *Mirror with Cupids, Glory, At Prayer* and *Young Chorister*.

GAHRLIEB VON DER MÜHLEN, Gustaf Casimir
Swedish, 17th - 18th century.
Born 24 December 1630, in Gripsholm, near Stockholm; died 1717, in Alt Lansberg, near Berlin.
Miniaturist, poet.
Gustaf Casimir Gahrlieb von der Mühlen was physician to Prince William in Berlin. He painted several miniature portraits.

GAI, Antonio
Italian, 18th century.
Born 3 May 1686, in Venice; died 4 June 1769, in Venice.
Sculptor.
Antonio Gai is remembered chiefly for his *Monument to Doge N. Sagredo and the Patriarch A. Sagredo* at S Francesco della Vigna, together with his allegorical statues of *Faith and Power* for the church of S Vitale, and a *St Mark* for the church of S Maria della Pietà in Venice. Gai also worked on Rovigo Cathedral.
AUCTION RECORDS:
LONDON, 22 April 1986, *Meleager* (1735, white marble, h. 56 1/4 ins / 143 cm) GBP 65,000.

GAI, Domenico
Italian, 18th century.
Active in Venice.
Sculptor.
Domenico Gai was the son of Giovanni Maria Gai. He continued his father's work.

GAI, Francesco
Italian, 17th - 18th century.
Active in Venice.
Sculptor (wood).
Francesco Gai was the father of Antonio Gai.

GAI, Giovanni Maria
Italian, 18th century.
Active in Venice.
Sculptor.
Giovanni Maria Gai was probably the son of Antonio Gai. He is known to have worked on a marble sculpture of *St John the Baptist*.

GAÏ, Stano
Polish, 20th century.
Painter.
Stano Gaï exhibited in Paris at the Salon de la Société Nationale des Beaux-Arts from 1924 onwards and at the Salon des Indépendants from 1932.

GAI, Zuane
Italian, 18th century.
Active in Venice.
Sculptor.

Zuane Gai was the son of Giovanni Maria Gai and the brother of Domenico Gai, with whom he collaborated.

GAI QI, or Kai Ch'i, style name: Boyun, sobriquets: Xiangbai, Qixiang, Yuhu waishi, Yuhu Shanren
Chinese, 18th - 19th century.
Born 1774, in Songjiang (Jiangxi); died 1829.
Painter, draughtsman. Figure compositions, portraits, landscapes, flowers.

Gai Qi's ancestors came from Xinjiang but settled in Songjiang. He is known as a poet and painter of figures, landscapes, flowers and bamboo who worked in the styles of Li Longmian, Zhao Mengfu (1254-1322), Tang Yin (1470-1523) and Chen Hongshou (1599-1652). He is known for several signed works.

AUCTION RECORDS:

NEW YORK, 2 June 1988, *Immortals* (ink on paper, hanging scroll, 47 3/4 x 28 3/4 ins / 121.5 x 73 cm) USD 3,080. NEW YORK, 4 Dec 1989, *Beauty* (ink and colour on paper, hanging scroll, 38 1/2 x 13 ins / 98 x 33 cm) USD 2,200. NEW YORK, 6 Dec 1989, *Portrait of Lu Zhu* (ink and colour on paper, 50 1/2 x 17 1/4 ins / 128.3 x 43.8 cm) USD 16,500. NEW YORK, 29 May 1991, *Figures after Chen Hongshou* (ink and colour on silk, hanging scroll, 35 1/4 x 18 ins / 89.5 x 45.8 cm) USD 11,000. NEW YORK, 1 June 1993, *Lotus* (ink and colour on paper, fan, 7 1/4 x 20 1/4 ins / 18.1 x 51.4 cm) USD 1,840. NEW YORK, 29 Nov 1993, *Flowers* (ink on silk, album of eight leaves, each 9 1/4 x 12 ins / 23.5 x 30.5 cm) USD 2,300. NEW YORK, 21 March 1995, *Scholar and Attendant in Garden* (ink and colour on silk, hanging scroll, 82 1/4 x 20 ins / 209.2 x 50.8 cm) USD 2,300. HONG KONG, 4 May 1995, *Immortals* (ink on silk and ink and colour on silk, set of four hanging scrolls, each 15 1/2 x 7 1/2 ins / 39.4 x 19.1 cm) HKD 80,500. HONG KONG, 28 April 1997, *Floral Burial* (1817, ink and colour on paper, hanging scroll, 45 1/4 x 11 1/4 ins / 115 x 28.5 cm) HKD 57,500. HONG KONG, 26 April 1999, *Resting in Studio* (ink and colour on silk, 9 x 11 ins / 22 x 29 cm) HKD 22,000. HONG KONG, 25 April 2004, *Flowers* (ink and colour, album of six leaves, 8 x 10 ins / 20 x 26 cm) HKD 30,000. HONG KONG, 25 April 2004, *Flowers* (1823, ink and colour on silk, scroll, 12 x 41 ins / 31 x 105 cm) HKD 32,000.

GAIA, Giovanni Antonio della
Italian, 16th century.
Active in Ascona.
Painter.

In 1519, Gaia painted a retable for the church of S Maria in Ascona.

GAIA, Pietro
Italian, 16th century.
Active in Perugia and Ascoli.
Painter.

Pietro Gaia was an imitator of Giac. Bassano.

GAIANI
Italian, 19th century.
Born in the 19th century, in Ancona (Marche).
Painter.

Around 1825, this artist was working on a commission for the Rosenstein palace near Stuttgart.

GAIANI, Antonio
Italian, 19th century.
Born in Bologna; died 1821.
Engraver, illustrator.

Antonio Gaiani was a pupil of Longhi. He engraved portraits, made reproductions of old paintings and illustrated a large number of books.

GAIANI, Egisto
Italian, 19th century.
Born 16 August 1832, in Florence; died c. 1890.
Sculptor.

Egisto Gaiani studied under Barbetti and Morini.

GAIANI, Gaspare
Italian, 18th - 19th century.
Active in Bologna and Modena.
Engraver. Portraits.

Gaspare Gaiani is known principally for his body of portrait work.

GAIARINI, Francesco
Italian, 19th century.
Born in Contea.
Sculptor.

Gaiarini was a pupil of Ulisse Cambi and Lorenzo Bartolini; he worked mostly in Florence.

GAIASSI, Vincenzo
Italian, 19th century.
Born 1801, in Rome; died 1861, in Rome.
Sculptor, engraver.

Gaiassi is best remembered for his *Statue of Palladio* in the Piazza Maggiore in Vicenza.

GAIBANO, Giovanni
Italian, 13th century.
Miniaturist.

This artist was a priest in Trisigola, near Ferrara.

GAIBAZZI, Giovanni
Italian, 19th century.
Born 15 November 1808, in Parma; died 24 May 1888.
Painter. Religious subjects.

Gaibazzi was a pupil of Giovanni Tebaldi; most of his paintings were on religious subjects.

GAIBLER, Alois
German, 18th century.
Active in Bavaria.
Painter.

Gaibler worked in about 1790 for the churches of Gutenberg and Jachenau.

GAIDAN, Louis
French, 19th - 20th century.
Born 1847, in Nîmes; died 1925.
Painter. Landscapes.

Louis Gaidan studied under Charles François Jalabert and Paulin André Bertrand. He painted mainly the shores and inlets of the Mediterranean coast. He adopted the technique of Cézanne, with whom he became friends.

From 1887 to 1903 he exhibited at the Salon des Artistes Français, of which he became a member in 1889, and at the Salon de Nîmes, the Salon de Toulon, the Salon d'Hyères and the Salon de Monaco.

MUSEUMS AND GALLERIES:

SÈTE: *View of Carqueiranne* - TOULON: *Evening among the Pines*.

AUCTION RECORDS:

LONDON, 29 June 1977, *Ancient Chapel of Bormes-les-Mimosas, Var* (oil on canvas, 19 1/4 x 28 1/4 ins / 49 x 71.5 cm) GBP 1,100. LONDON, 3 March 1982, *Sunset in the Mediterranean* (oil on canvas, 19 1/2 x 28 1/4 ins / 49.5 x 72 cm) GBP 600. VOUGEOT, 24 Nov 1984, *Under the Pines at Carqueiranne* (oil on canvas, 43 1/4 x 67 ins / 110 x 170 cm) FRF 82,000. PARIS, 17 Feb 1988, *Cap Brun* (oil on canvas, 21 1/4 x 28 3/4 ins / 54 x 73 cm) FRF 140,000. LONDON, 21 Oct 1988, *Under the Pines at Carqueiranne* (oil on canvas, 43 1/2 x 59 1/4 ins / 110.5 x 150.8 cm) GBP 18,700. PARIS, 20 Nov 1988, *Start of the Jetty at Les Salettes* (oil on canvas, 21 1/4 x 28 3/4 ins / 54 x 73 cm) FRF 90,000. VERSAILLES, 5 March 1989, *Village on a Hill* (oil on canvas, 15 x 22 ins / 38 x 55 cm) FRF 11,100. NEUILLY, 5 Dec 1989, *Shore at Toulon* (oil on wood, 11 x 16 1/2 ins / 27 x 42 cm) FRF 17,500. PARIS, 6 July 1993, *Village by a River* (oil on panel, 19 3/4 x 28 3/4 ins / 50 x 73 cm) FRF 20,000. PARIS, 27 June 1997, *Provence Landscape* (oil on canvas, 19 3/4 x 27 1/2 ins / 50 x 70 cm) FRF 38,000. LONDON, 22 Oct 1997, *House in

Provence (oil on canvas, 20 x $27\frac{1}{4}$ ins / 50.5 x 69.5 cm) GBP 10,120.

GAIDANO, Paolo
Italian, 19th - 20th century.
Born 28 December 1861, in Poirino (Piedmont); died 1917, in Turin.
Painter. Genre scenes, portraits.
Gaidano studied in Turin, where he began his career, around 1884. He also exhibited in Venice.

GAIDON, Antonio
Italian, 18th - 19th century.
Born 1738, in Castiglione di Brentonico; died 2 November 1829, in Bassano.
Active in Bassano.
Sculptor, architect.

GAIGH, Joseph
Austrian, 18th - 19th century.
Active in Vienna.
Painter.
The municipal museum in Vienna has a drawing by Gaigh representing *Area Surrounding the Church of St Charles in Vienna*.

GAIGHER, Horazio
Austrian, 20th century.
Born 20 April 1870, in Levico.
Painter, engraver.
Horazio Gaigher worked mainly in Salzburg and Innsbruck. During a stay in Paris, he studied with Jules Lefebvre and Tony Robert-Fleury.
AUCTION RECORDS:
NEW YORK, 20 July 1995, *Reverie* (oil on card, $18\frac{1}{2}$ x $26\frac{1}{4}$ ins / 47 x 66.7 cm) USD 1,725.

GAIGNERON, Jean de
French, 20th century.
Born 22 February 1890, in Paris; died 1976.
Painter, engraver. Figures, portraits, local scenes. Orientalism.
Jean de Gaigneron had moved to Taza by 1922. He exhibited in Paris at the Salon des Indépendants, the Salon d'Automne and the Salon des Tuileries.

Jean Gaigneron

BIBLIOGRAPHY:
Thornton, Lynne, '*Palettes exotiques*' in *Muséart*, periodical, Paris, 1993.
AUCTION RECORDS:
ENGHIEN-LES-BAINS, 17 April 1983, *Arabs outside a Kasbah* (oil on canvas, $25\frac{1}{2}$ x 32 ins / 65 x 81 cm) FRF 12,500. PARIS, 25 March 1993, *Arabs outside a Kasbah* (oil on canvas, $25\frac{1}{2}$ x 32 ins / 65 x 81 cm) FRF 25,000. PARIS, 13 March 1995, *Halt outside the Kasbah* (oil on canvas, $25\frac{1}{2}$ x 32 ins / 65 x 81 cm) FRF 80,000. PARIS, 22 April 1996, *Encampment in Southern Morocco* (oil on card, 11 x $13\frac{3}{4}$ ins / 27 x 35 cm) FRF 6,000. PARIS, 9 Dec 1996, *Old Moroccan Man* (oil on card, $13\frac{3}{4}$ x 11 ins / 35 x 27 cm) FRF 3,500.

GAIGNON, Paule
French, 20th century.
Born 1916, in Caen.
Painter. Scenes with figures.
Paule Gaignon was a self-taught artist. She exhibited in Paris at the Salon International d'Art Naïf during the 1980s. Her paintings are of scenes of everyday life and domestic celebrations.

GAIL, Françoise de
French, 20th - 21st century.
Born 1951, in Hennebont (Morbihan).
Painter. Scenes with figures.
Françoise de Gail's subjects include figures drawn from La Belle Époque and jumping and cantering horses. Her style is reminiscent of Henri Rousseau. She has been exhibiting her work since 1979, in particular at the Salon International d'Art Naïf in Paris.

GAIL, Mathias Joseph
Austrian, 19th century.
Born 1796, in Vienna; died 15 January 1866, in Vienna.
Painter.

GAIL, Wilhelm
German, 19th century.
Born 7 March 1804, in Munich; died 26 February 1890, in Munich.
Painter, engraver, draughtsman, lithographer. Landscapes, architectural views, animals.
Wilhelm Gail was a pupil at the art academy in Munich and studied under Peter Hess. In 1825 he accompanied Baron Malsen to Turin, where he drew thirteen subjects for *Roman Monuments in the Sardinian States*. He travelled to Italy and in 1829 published his impressions in thirty lithographs. In 1830 Gail went to Paris, then visited Normandy. In Venice he painted the *Corridor of the Doge's Palace* in 1831. After a trip to Spain, where his studies focused on monuments of the Moorish period, he published a series of sketches with his impressions of Spain. Gail exhibited in Munich and Dresden between 1829 and 1854.
MUSEUMS AND GALLERIES:
MUNICH (Pinakothek): *Interior of the Cathedral at Córdoba; Doges' Palace in Venice; San Lazaro degli Armeni in Venice*.
AUCTION RECORDS:
COLOGNE, 21 Nov 1985, *Horses at Water* (oil on panel, $14\frac{1}{4}$ x $18\frac{3}{4}$ ins / 36.5 x 47.5 cm) DEM 6,000. MUNICH, 21 March 2001, *Italian Castle Courtyard* (oil on canvas, 17 x 21 ins / 44 x 54 cm) DEM 6,000. MUNICH, 5 Dec 2001, *Ruins of the Temple of Minerva* (1826, watercolour over pencil, 17 x 13 ins / 42 x 33 cm) DEM 3,300. RUDOLSTADT, 28 Nov 2003, *Bullfighters Waiting for the Bullfight* (1870, oil on canvas, 20 x 24 ins / 51 x 61 cm) EUR 1,800. FONTAINEBLEAU, 6 June 2004, *Harvest* (oil on panel, a pair, 13 x 16 ins / 33 x 41 cm) EUR 5,100.

GAILDE, Jean, or Gaide, Gualde, Gailda, Guailda, called Grand-Jean
French, 15th - 16th century.
Died 1519, in Troyes.
Active in Troyes.
Sculptor, architect.
Gailde was appointed master of the works at the church of St Mary Magdalene in Troyes in 1495 and it was here that he made his most important work, the rood screen. Starting the screen in 1508 and completing it in 1517, he was assisted by his pupils François Matray, Hugues Bailly, Martin de Vaux, Nicolas Mauvoisin and Jean Brisset. In 1506, he rebuilt the choir, apse and ambulatory of the church. He was buried beneath his rood screen.

GAILDRAU, Charles-Valentin
French, 19th century.
Born in Paris.
Painter.
He studied under Léon Cogniet and contributed drawings and pastel portraits to the Paris Salon between 1849 and 1859.

GAILDRAU, Jules
French, 19th century.
Born 18 September 1816, in Paris; died January 1898.
Painter.
He exhibited at the Salon between 1848 and 1857, chiefly drawings and a watercolour entitled *Pilgrims returning from*

Mecca Encamped in the Custom House Courtyard in Algiers. His work for the periodical *Illustration* was widely appreciated.

GAILHARD, Pedro
French, 19th - 20th century.
Painter.

Pedro Gailhard was a very Parisian figure. Originally a singer, he dabbled in all the arts and for many years was director of the Opéra in Paris.

AUCTION RECORDS:
PARIS, 15 June 1924, *Village Entrance in the Snow* (wash) FRF 40.

GAILIS, Werner
German, 20th century.
Born 1925, in Berlin.
Sculptor. Religious subjects, figures. Busts, statues.

Werner Gailis studied at the free university in Berlin, then in the art teaching department of the Berlin art school, where he studied fine arts with Professor Schrieber. From 1955 he was head of the metal workshop in the art teaching department of the Berlin art school and undertook a number of study tours.

Far from being preoccupied with Modernism, he preferred to model natural lines, for instance structuring the inner and outer space of the lifesize female figures he created. Usually naked, standing, lying, crouching, with their arms in their hair or round their waists, they seem to live in time with the reflections of their smooth, polished surfaces. Gailis also produced busts, portraits and religious figures to order, (such as the *Pietà* for St Bernard's church in Berlin-Tegel of 1977) an area in which he receives many commissions.

He took part in group exhibitions and held solo shows, including his first in France at Sèvres; in the Orangerie in the Luxembourg Gardens in 1977 and at the National Museum in Warsaw in 1981 and 1982.

BIBLIOGRAPHY:
Werner Gailis, exhibition catalogue, Orangerie du Luxembourg, Paris, 1977.

GAILL, Franz von Paula
German, 18th - 19th century.
Born 7 August 1754, in Aibling (Bavaria); died 1810, in Munich.
Painter.

Franz was the son and pupil of Johann Georg Gaill. He worked at the church of St Sebastian in Aibling, among other places.

GAILL, Johann Georg
German, 18th century.
Active in Aibling (Bavaria).
Painter, fresco artist.

Johann Georg Gaill worked for the church of St Leonard at Reichersdorf.

GAILLAN, Eugénie
French, 19th century.
Painter. Genre scenes.

MUSEUMS AND GALLERIES:
TOULOUSE: *Spanish Beggars*.

GAILLARD (Mrs). See **GAILLARD Louise**

GAILLARD
French, 13th century.
Active in Grenoble in 1251.
Painter.

GAILLARD
French, 17th century.
Active in Grasse in 1643.
Painter.

Gaillard may be the artist also known as Gaspard, who was living in Rome in 1645.

GAILLARD
French, 18th century.
Active in Paris in 1723.
Sculptor.

Gaillard worked for the church of the Petits-Augustins.

GAILLARD, Antoine
French, 16th century.
Painter.

Antoine Gaillard was living in Lyons in 1516, working on preparations for a royal entry into the town.

GAILLARD, Arthur
French, 19th century.
Born in Chaumont (Haute-Marne).
Painter.

He studied under Gérome and Becker and exhibited at the Paris Salon from 1878 to 1882. In 1880 he submitted a painting entitled *Clearing Snow from the Pont au Change*

GAILLARD, Bernardino. See **GAGLIARDI**

GAILLARD, Claude-Ferdinand
French, 19th century.
Born 7 January 1834, in Paris; died 20 January 1887, in Paris.
Painter, engraver. History painting, portraits.

He studied both painting and engraving at the École des Beaux-Arts in Paris, mainly under Léon Cogniet. He won second prize in the engraving category of the Prix de Rome in 1852 and the Grand Prix de Rome itself in 1856. He duly travelled to Rome, but found that his personal approach was at variance with that promulgated by the Villa Medici: he was effectively starved of commissions and, in addition, his engraved portrait of *Jean Bellin* was rejected by the 1863 Salon. That said, the quality of his work was later recognized by several awards from the Salon: engraving medals in 1867 and 1869, a gold medal in 1872 and a gold at the 1878 Exposition Universelle, together with awards of gold medals for painting in 1872 and at the 1878 Exposition Universelle, following a silver medal in 1872. Gaillard was subsequently made a Chevalier of the Légion d'Honneur.

From early in his career Gaillard engraved in the manner made fashionable by James Hopwood and Le Couturier. He worked as an engraver for the *Gazette des Beaux-Arts*. The French state commissioned him to engrave Leonardo da Vinci's *Last Supper* and *La Gioconda* (*Mona Lisa*), but he was unable to take the project on due to ill-health. Arguably the best examples of his work remain engravings of a *Man with Carnation* (after Van Eyck), *Oedipus* (after Ingres), *Twilight* (after Michelangelo), the *Orléans Madonna* (after Raphael), a *Wax Head in Lille Museum*, and portraits of *Pius IX*, *Leo XIII*, *Dom Gueranger* and *Sister Rosalie*.

MUSEUMS AND GALLERIES:
PARIS (Mus. d'Orsay): *St Sebastian*; *Man with a Carnation*.

AUCTION RECORDS:
PARIS, 1896, *Male Portrait*, FRF 30. PARIS, 1897, *Half-length Portrait of a Woman (after David)* (lead pencil on paper) FRF 104. PARIS, 1 May 1900, *Portrait of Susse Gérard*, FRF 400. PARIS, 2-4 June 1920, *Pilgrims at Emmaus* (watercolour) FRF 2,160. PARIS, 30 Nov-2 Dec 1920, *Sleeping Child* (graphite) FRF 115. PARIS, 13 Feb 1924, *Self-portrait*, FRF 580. PARIS, 31 May 1928, *Head of a Prelate*; *Hand Study* (pencil on paper) FRF 350. COLOGNE, 18 March 1989, *The Nymph* (oil on card, 13 3/4 x 11in/35 x 27cm) DEM 1,200.

GAILLARD, Corneille
Flemish School, 17th century.

Active in Bruges (West Flanders).
Sculptor.
He executed the marble funerary monument to *Maximilien van Praet* in the church (now cathedral) of St-Salvator in Bruges.

GAILLARD, Denis
French, 17th - 18th century.
Active in Paris.
Sculptor.
Denis Gaillard worked at the château at Versailles and the abbey at Cluny.

GAILLARD, François
French, 18th century.
Active in Paris in 1766.
Painter, sculptor.

GAILLARD, François. See also **GAILLIARD Franz**

GAILLARD, Gabriel
French, 17th century.
Painter.
Gabriel Gaillard was master craftsman for the painters in Lyons in 1650 and 1658.

GAILLARD, Georges
French, 20th century.
Born 1924, in La Roche-Vineuse (Saône-et-Loire).
Painter, lithographer, potter.
Georges Gaillard studied at the École des Beaux-Arts in Mâcon and then at the École des Beaux-Arts in Paris until 1945. He exhibited regularly from 1948 both in the provinces and in Paris. He executed a composition in enamelled lava for the Lycée de Tournus in 1970-1971.
Gaillard's paintings convey a strong sense of atmosphere sustained through a harmony of colour and light.

GAILLARD, Jean Marie
French, 20th century.
Born 19 January 1929, in St-Hilaire-les-Places.
Draughtsman, painter, potter.
From 1943 to 1946, Jean Gaillard studied at the École des Arts Décoratifs in Limoges. In 1950 he began studying under Vikke van der Bergh and Marie Floirat-Bourbon.
Since 1969 he has exhibited regularly in Paris at the Salon des Artistes Français and the Salon des Indépendants. He was rated as 'one of the best workers of France' as an architectural model maker in 1958 and was made a Chevalier du Mérite Meilleur Ouvrier de France (1960). He was awarded the silver medal of Arts, Sciences et Lettres for his enamels and a bronze medal by the Académie Européenne des Arts in 1970.

GAILLARD, Jeannin
French, 16th century.
Died 1538.
Active in Salins (Cantal).
Glass painter.

GAILLARD, Léon Jacques
French, 20th century.
Born in Preignac (Gironde); died during World War I (1914-1918), on the battlefield.
Sculptor.
Léon Gaillard studied under Falguière and exhibited at the Salon des Artistes Français.

GAILLARD, Louis
French, 20th century.
Born in Modane (Savoy).
Painter.
Louis Gaillard exhibited in Paris at the Salon des Indépendants from 1940.

GAILLARD, Louise
Maiden name: Chaceré de Beaurepaire
French, 18th century.
Born 18th century.
Painter, miniaturist, engraver (burin). Portraits.
A student of Augustin, Louise Gaillard exhibited miniature portraits under her maiden name, from 1798 to 1827, and in 1823 under the name of Mme Gaillard. She was the wife of René Gaillard.
AUCTION RECORDS:
PARIS, 1900, *Portrait of an Attendant of the Pope* (miniature) FRF 149.

GAILLARD, Marcel, or Marcel-Gaillard
French, 20th century.
Born 17 June 1886, in Abbeville; died 8 July 1947, in Liesville-sur-Douve (Manche).
Painter. Landscapes.
Marcel Gaillard exhibited at the major Paris Salons. He was awarded the Prix de l'Afrique Équatoriale.
AUCTION RECORDS:
PARIS, 11 April 1927, *Landscape,* FRF 115. PARIS, 24 Nov 1928, *Landscape,* FRF 650. PARIS, 2 March 1934, *On the Shore of the Bay at Concarneau,* FRF 100.

GAILLARD, Marie Marguerite Héloïse
French, 19th century.
Born in Montagne-St-Émilion (Gironde).
Engraver (wood).
She participated in the Salon des Artistes Français, and received an honourable mention in 1900 and a bronze medal in 1901.

GAILLARD, Marthe
Maiden name: Mary
French, 19th century.
Born in Paris.
Painter.
She exhibited watercolour portraits and genre compositions at the Salons of 1879 and 1880: *Happy Occasion, The Pearl* and *Laughing Woman.*

GAILLARD, Nicolas
French, 16th century.
Active in Salins (Cantal).
Glass painter.
Nicolas was the son and pupil of Jeannin Gaillard.

GAILLARD, Nicolas
French, 17th century.
Active in Paris in 1674.
Painter, sculptor, engraver, illuminator.

GAILLARD, Paul Benoît
French, 20th century.
Born in Langres.
Painter.
Paul Gaillard exhibited regularly in Paris at the Salon des Indépendants from 1925.

GAILLARD, Pierre
French, 18th century.
Active in Paris in 1740.
Painter.

GAILLARD, René
French, 18th century.
Born c. 1719; died 11 April 1790, in Paris.
Engraver.
René Gaillard engraved in the styles of Greuze (*Paternal Curse*), F. Boucher and H. Rigaud.

GAILLARD, Robert
French, 18th century.
Born 1722, in Paris; died 1785.
Engraver (burin).

Robert Gaillard produced engravings with religious, genre and historical themes. He may be the artist also known as René Gaillard.

GAILLARD DE LONJUMEAU, Pierre Joseph, Laurent (Baron)
French, 18th century.
Active in the middle of the 18th century.
Draughtsman, engraver.

Pierre Gaillard de Lonjumeau produced some engravings with genre subjects.

GAILLARD-DESCHAMPS, Alexandre
French, 20th century.
Born c. 1903, in St-Saturnin (Mayenne); died September 1984.
Painter. Landscapes, seascapes.

Alexandre Gaillard-Deschamps exhibited in Paris at the Salon of the Société Nationale des Beaux-Arts from 1930 and at the Salon des Indépendants from 1935.

GAILLARDIN, Jean, or Gallardon
French, 16th century.
Sculptor.
Fontainebleau School.

Gaillardin was one of several artists working on the decoration of the Château at Fontainebleau between 1537 and 1550.

GAILLARDOT, Pierre
French, 20th century.
Born 2 August 1910, in St-Florent (Yonne); died 2002.
Painter, watercolourist.

Pierre Gaillardot exhibited at many of the annual Paris Salons, of which he was also a member, including the Salon d'Automne, the Salon des Indépendants, the Salon of the Société Nationale des Beaux-Arts, the Salon des Terres Latines, the Salon Comparaisons and the Salon des Peintres Témoins de leur Temps. He was chief curator of the Salon du Dessin et de la Peinture à l'Eau. He held solo exhibitions in Paris and in the provinces in Cannes, Antibes, Nantes, Dijon, Nice and other towns. He received a number of awards, prizes and gold medals.

Self-taught, he painted a variety of subjects including boats, cycling races and polo players in bright colours with cursorily executed brushwork.

AUCTION RECORDS:
LOS ANGELES, 21 Sept 1976, *The Weighing Room* (oil on canvas, 31½ x 42½ ins / 80 x 108 cm) USD 550. PARIS, 25 May 1988, *The Dock at Deauville* (1959, oil on canvas, 18 x 24 ins / 46 x 61 cm) FRF 4,500. CALAIS, 13 Nov 1988, *The Polo Match* (oil on canvas, 23½ x 28¾ ins / 60 x 73 cm) FRF 10,000. PARIS, 22 Nov 1988, *Game of Tennis* (watercolour, 17¾ x 23¼ ins / 45 x 59 cm) FRF 4,500. PARIS, 30 Oct 1990, *Course de Haies* (oil on canvas, 11 x 13¾ ins / 27 x 35 cm) FRF 7,800. LE TOUQUET, 30 May 1993, *Ste-Maxime Port and Beach* (1958, oil on canvas, 18 x 22 ins / 46 x 55 cm) FRF 9,000. PARIS, 22 March 1994, *Paddock* (oil on canvas, 23½ x 28¾ ins / 60 x 73 cm) FRF 12,000. DEAUVILLE, 19 Aug 1994, *The Weigh In at Deauville* (watercolour, 19¾ x 25½ ins / 50 x 65 cm) FRF 15,500. PARIS, 16 Oct 1996, *Showjumping* (oil on canvas, 23½ x 32 ins / 60 x 81 cm) FRF 10,000. DEAUVILLE, 25 Aug 2000, *Polo Match* (c. 1980, oil on canvas, 22 x 18 ins / 55 x 46 cm) FRF 11,000. DEAUVILLE, 25 Aug 2000, *Rond de Présentation* (watercolour, 18 x 26 ins / 46 x 65 cm) FRF 14,000. DEAUVILLE, 17 Aug 2001, *Polo in Deauville* (oil on canvas, 26 x 21 ins / 65 x 54 cm) FRF 15,000. DEAUVILLE, 24 Aug 2001, *Deauville Before the Race* (c. 1965, watercolour, 17 x 21 ins / 43 x 53 cm) FRF 14,000. DEAUVILLE, 23 Aug 2002, *Sulky Route* (1989, oil on canvas, 21 x 25 ins / 53 x 63 cm) EUR 2,200. DEAUVILLE, 20 April 2003, *Clairefontaine* (1971, oil on canvas, 11 x 16 ins / 27 x 41 cm) EUR 1,600. DEAUVILLE, 13 July 2003, *Port of Deauville* (watercolour, 22 x 28 ins / 57 x 70 cm) EUR 1,500. RENNES, 21 Feb 2004, *Sulky Race* (watercolour, 19 x 25 ins / 47 x 64 cm) EUR 1,900.

GAILLET, Lily
Swiss, 19th century.
Born 1867, in Biel.
Painter. Flowers.

Gaillet studied at the art school in Geneva.

GAILLIARD, Franz, for François Désiré Antoine, known in error as Bernard
Belgian, 19th - 20th century.
Born 30 November 1861, in Brussels; died 17 February 1932, in Forêt (Brussels).
Painter, pastellist, engraver, draughtsman, illustrator. Portraits, genre scenes, landscapes, landscapes with figures, urban landscapes.

Franz Gaillard studied at the Brussels academy of fine art. He travelled in Italy, Algeria and Greece. According to some sources, he was associated with Émile Claus and James Ensor. He was the director of the Académie St-Gilles. He exhibited at the Salon de Bruxelles from 1882, the Salon des Artistes Français in Paris from 1882 to 1891 and also in Venice and Düsseldorf. He was the father of Jean-Jacques Gaillard.

He produced drawings of current events for French, English and Belgian weeklies, including *Le Patriote Illustré*, *Le Petit Bleu* and the *Illustrated London News*. He painted a few large genre scenes, portraits and landscapes. After starting off as a traditional realist, he came under the influence of the French Impressionist school, then in his last period, he turned to the Luminist-Divisionist technique.

AUCTION RECORDS:
ANTWERP, 29 April 1981, *To the Sea* (oil on canvas, 15 x 18 ins / 38 x 46 cm) BEF 40,000. LONDON, 23 March 1984, *Rue Fossé-aux-Loups, Brussels* (1884, oil on canvas, 35½ x 26 ins / 90 x 66 cm) GBP 7,000. BRUSSELS, 30 Sept 1987, *Under the Plane Trees* (oil on canvas, 67 x 48¾ ins / 170 x 124 cm) BEF 2,000,000. LOKEREN, 28 May 1988, *New Acquisition* (oil on canvas, 45 x 42½ ins / 114 x 108 cm) BEF 1,600,000. LONDON, 29 June 1988, *Under the Plane Trees of the Royal Park in Brussles* (oil on canvas, 67¼ x 49¼ ins / 170.5 x 125 cm) GBP 5,500. LONDON, 19 Oct 1988, *Walk* (oil on panel, 14½ x 18 ins / 36.6 x 45.8 cm) GBP 12,650. LONDON, 19 Oct 1989, *Fair* (pastel/paper/canvas, 15 x 18 ins / 38.1 x 45.7 cm) GBP 4,400. LONDON, 16 Feb 1990, *Boulevards in Brussels* (oil on canvas, 49½ x 67 ins / 125.7 x 170.3 cm) GBP 4,950. LIÈGE, 11 Dec 1991, *Lively Scene in the Parc du Cinquantenaire* (watercolour wash/paper, 10¾ x 16¼ ins / 27.5 x 41.5 cm) BEF 100,000. LOKEREN, 23 May 1992, *Touches of White on the Sea* (oil on canvas, 49¼ x 67¾ ins / 125 x 172 cm) BEF 2,400,000. LOKEREN, 10 Oct 1992, *Children's Games on a Beach* (oil and gouache/card, 39¼ x 31½ ins / 100 x 80 cm) BEF 1,500,000. AMSTERDAM, 26 May 1993, *Four Teddy Bears* (oil on card, 17¼ x 23½ ins / 44 x 59.5 cm) NLG 6,900. LOKEREN, 12 March 1994, *Lilacs* (oil on canvas, 27½ x 22 ins / 70 x 55 cm) BEF 190,000. LOKEREN, 11 March 1995, *Lady Looking at Her-*

self in a Mirror (oil on card, 26½ x 20¾ ins / 67.5 x 53 cm) BEF 900,000. Calais, 25 June 1995, *Busy Street in Paris* (oil on panel, 13 x 9½ ins / 33 x 24 cm) FRF 20,000. London, 28 June 1995, *Under the Plane Trees of the Royal Park in Brussels* (oil on canvas, 67¼ x 49¼ ins / 170.5 x 125 cm) GBP 36,700. Antwerp, 28 April 1999, *Workmen Resting* (oil on canvas, 51 x 67 ins / 130 x 170 cm) BEF 800,000. Brussels, 19 June 2000, *Morrocan Nomad* (1998, oil on canvas, 14 x 18 ins / 36 x 46 cm) BEF 95,000. Brussels, 21 Nov 2000, *Procession* (oil on canvas, 50 x 67 ins / 126 x 171 cm) BEF 660,000. London, 27 June 2001, *In the Sun* (oil on canvas, 51 x 67 ins / 129 x 170 cm) GBP 60,000. Brussels, 28 Aug 2001, *Roses* (oil on canvas, 28 x 22 ins / 70 x 55 cm) BEF 110,000. Brussels, 28 May 2002, *Woman in the Dunes* (oil on canvas, 15 x 22 ins / 38 x 56 cm) EUR 6,500. Brussels, 26 Nov 2002, *Street of Athens* (oil on panel, 27 x 22 ins / 68 x 55 cm) EUR 2,000. Brussels, 20 Jan 2003, *Parc de Bruxelles with Figures* (mixed media on card, 35 x 27 ins / 88 x 68 cm) EUR 7,500. Amsterdam, 27 May 2003, *Beach* (oil on canvas/board, 15 x 22 ins / 38 x 57 cm) EUR 11,000. Brussels, 17 Feb 2004, *Acropolis* (oil on canvas, 67 x 49 ins / 170 x 125 cm) EUR 20,500. New York, 22 April 2004, *Sidewalk Cafe* (1884, oil on canvas, 26 x 20 ins / 65 x 51 cm) USD 42,000.

GAILLIARD, Jean, called Jean-Jacques
Belgian, 20th century.
Born 22 November 1890, in Brussels; died 17 April 1976, in St-Gilles-lez-Bruxelles.
Painter, draughtsman, engraver, lithographer, fresco artist. Portraits, landscapes, still-lifes.

Jean Gaillard studied at the Brussels conservatory until 1914, then with his father, Franz Gaillard, and Jean Delville at the Brussels academy, where he discovered the works of Swedenborg. He was a friend of James Ensor, whom he probably met through his father, and Michel de Ghelderode. He was a member of the Belgian royal academy.

In Paris, between 1920 and 1924, and later in Belgium, he produced a series of abstract canvases in a style freer than Constructivism, a kind of Tachisme in which the dabs of colour create impressions of nature or from the imagination. He called it Surimpressionism. He then distanced himself from the abstract to investigate a world of dreams and fantasies. He wanted to create an art of fantasy and magnificence in order to explore the areas neglected by the Surrealists so, along with Serge Hutin, he became one of the founders of the Fantasmagie movement. Without being radically different from Surrealism, it preferred to find its sources in the long tradition of Flemish fantasy painting that stretches from Bosch to Ensor. He was passionately interested in Swedenborg, and tried to include in his paintings the continuation of a transcendental reality.

Jean Jacques
Gailliard

Museums and Galleries:
Brussels: *Familiarity of Objects; The Rue des Trois Têtes* - Brussels (Conservatoire royal de musique).

Auction records:
Antwerp, 25 Oct 1977, *The Promenade Albert I* (oil on panel, 15 x 24 ins / 38 x 61 cm) BEF 50,000. London, 4 July 1980, *Castle at Ballybrack* (oil on canvas, 14 x 20 ins / 35.5 x 50.7 cm) GBP 380. Brussels, 16 Dec 1982, *Courtyard in the Rue de Thy in St-Gilles* (oil on canvas, 36½ x 29¼ ins / 93 x 74 cm) BEF 80,000. Antwerp, 26 April 1983, *'Dead Houses', Ostend* (oil on panel, 18½ x 24¾ ins / 47 x 63 cm) BEF 65,000. Brussels, 22 April 1985, *The Piazza della Signoria, Florence* (1918, watercolour, 23½ x 16½ ins / 60 x 42 cm) BEF 40,000. Brussels, 16 Sept 1985, *The Apse of St-Gudule in Brussels* (oil on canvas, 51¼ x 41¼ ins / 130 x 105 cm) BEF 260,000. Amsterdam, 24 May 1989, *Still-life with Summer Flowers in Vase and Red Currants in Bowl on a Table* (oil on canvas/card, 14½ x 11½ ins / 37 x 29.5 cm) NLG 10,950. Lokeren, 9 Oct 1993, *The Atlantic, seen from Connemara* (oil on panel, 13¼ x 17¼ ins / 33.5 x 44 cm) BEF 38,000; *The Starfish at Home* (1961, oil on panel, 15¼ x 22½ ins / 38.5 x 57 cm) BEF 180,000. Lokeren, 12 March 1994, *The Chapelle St-Hubert* (oil on panel, 22 x 15 ins / 55 x 38 cm) BEF 100,000. Lokeren, 9 Dec 2000, *The Wellington, Ostend* (1950, oil on canvas, 18 x 22 ins / 45 x 55 cm) BEF 170,000. Brussels, 8 May 2001, *Ensor from Ostend* (oil on canvas, 33 x 38 ins / 83 x 96 cm) BEF 950,000. Brussels, 5 Nov 2001, *Asia Minor* (oil on canvas, 34 x 24 ins / 86 x 61 cm) BEF 320,000. Brussels, 28 May 2002, *Corner of St Gudule* (1947, oil on panel, 21 x 13 ins / 54 x 33 cm) EUR 3,000. Brussels, 28 May 2002, *Solitude* (oil on panel, 27 x 20 ins / 69 x 50 cm) EUR 3,400. Brussels, 15 Sept 2003, *Ensor at Tervuren* (oil on panel, 15 x 19 ins / 37 x 47 cm) EUR 7,500. Brussels, 10 Nov 2003, *Casino at Ixelles* (oil on panel, 18 x 26 ins / 46 x 65 cm) EUR 5,600. Brussels, 15 March 2004, *Entry to Paradise* (c. 1945, oil on canvas, 24 x 16 ins / 60 x 40 cm) EUR 4,200. Brussels, 6 Dec 2004, *Summer Day in the Garden* (oil on card, 14 x 20 ins / 35 x 51 cm) EUR 4,000.

GAILLIOT, Geneviève Élisabeth
French, 20th century.
Born 1896, in Paris.
Sculptor.

After working at the École des Beaux-Arts, Geneviève Gailliot exhibited at the Paris Salon from 1924. She was also a member of the Salon.

GAILLOIS, Marie Anne
French, 18th century.
Active in Paris in 1764.
Painter.

GAILLON, Jean Baptiste
French, 18th century.
Active in Paris in 1738.
Painter.

GAILLOT, Bernard
French, 19th century.
Born 17 February 1780, in Versailles; died 17 June 1847, in Paris.
Painter. Religious subjects, portraits.

He studied under David and exhibited at the Paris Salon between 1817 and 1831, securing a silver medal in 1817. He died suddenly following a stroke. Notable examples of his work include *Cornelia, the Mother of the Gracchi, 'Suffer the Little Children to Come unto Me'* and, for Sens Cathedral, *St Louis Carrying the Crown of Thorns*. Among the commissions he executed for churches in Paris were the *Conversion of St Augustine* and *Vision of St Monica*, both for the church of Notre-Dame-des-Victoires, *Joseph's Dream* for the church of St-Vincent-de-Paul, and a *St Francis of Assisi Appearing before Pope Innocent III* for the church of St-François-d'Assise.

Bibliography:
Breon, Emmanuel, *'A Report' on the Coronation of Charles X'* in *Bulletin de la Société de l'Histoire de l'Art Français*, 1981.

Museums and Galleries:
Versailles: *Portrait of Lieutenant-Colonel Crillon; Charles, Constable of Bourbon.*

Auction records:
Paris, 29 Nov 1976, *Male Portrait* (oil on canvas, oval, 11 x 8in/27 x 20.5cm) FRF 2,200.

GAILLOT, Édouard
French, 20th century.

Born 17 October 1877, in Objat (Corrèze).
Engraver.

Édouard Gaillot studied under Baschet and Royer. He exhibited in Paris from 1912 at the Salon des Artistes Français.

GAINCA, Martín
Spanish, 16th century.
Active in Seville c. 1527.
Sculptor.

Martín Gainca is believed to have taken over from Maestro Rano, who had been directing the building of Seville Cathedral, on the latter's death.

GAINDRAND, Antoine. See **GUINDRAND**

GAINEAU, Jean Louis, the Elder
French, 18th century.
Died 7 February 1766, in Paris.
Painter.

GAINEAU, Jean Louis, the Younger
French, 18th century.
Active in Paris.
Painter.

Jean Gaineau was the son of Jean Louis the Elder.

GAINEAU, Louis Claude
French, 18th century.
Died 9 June 1772, in Paris.
Painter.

Louis Gaineau was the son of Jean-Louis the Elder.

GAINER, J.
Irish, 18th century.
Active in Dublin.
Engraver.

J. Gainer studied in London under J. Dixon.

GAINES, Charles
American, 20th century.
Born 1944, in Charleston (South Carolina).
Painter. Landscapes.

Gaines lived and worked in Fresno (California). He was a student at the MFA Rochester Institute of Technology. He was first thought of as a conceptual artist, due to his remoteness from painting. Opposed to a romantic artistic vision, he nonetheless returned to painting, with 'scientifically' conceived works. His series *Numbers and Trees 111*, painted in the 1980s, is worked out axiomatically: 'in each painting there are between one and eleven trees, which are superimposed mathematically' (Gaines). On a grid drawn on a sheet of Plexiglas, he paints a tree, sketched on the cross-ruling, with numbers and colours, which stand out from a background on masonite, where the whole enlarged tree is represented. In the second painting, he uses the elements of the same tree again, over which he superimposes the second one, the 'system of sketching and superimposing continues up to the eleventh painting, which is composed of eleven superimposed trees' (Gaines).

He has taken part in group exhibitions including those at the Oakland Museum (1973, 1975), the Biennial of the Whitney Museum of American Art, New York (1975), Yale University (1978-1979), the Santa Barbara Museum of Art (1980), the Aldrich Museum of Contemporary Art, Ridgefield (1981), the Basel art fair (1982) and the Chicago Museum of Contemporary Art. He has had solo exhibitions since 1969 at the University of Southern California, Los Angeles (1972, 1975), the Leo Castelli Gallery, New York (from 1980), the Los Angeles Institute of Contemporary Art (1984) and the California State University, Los Angeles (2002).

BIBLIOGRAPHY:

Charles Gaines, exhibition catalogue, Gal. Lavignes-Bastille, Paris, 1988. Zellen, Jody, '*Charles Gaines*' in *Art Press* n° 280 p. 69, periodical, Paris, June 2002.

GAINES, G.
British, 18th century.
Active in London.
Painter. Landscapes.

G. Gaines exhibited from 1770 to 1787 at the Royal Academy and the Free Society in London.

GAINSBOROUGH, Thomas
British, 18th century.
Born 1727, in Sudbury (Suffolk), where he was baptised 14 May; died 2 August 1788, in London.
Painter, watercolourist, engraver, draughtsman. Genre scenes, portraits, landscapes with figures, animals, landscapes, waterscapes.

Thomas Gainsborough was the youngest son of John Gainsborough, a tailor and clothier. As a child, he demonstrated his artistic leanings by drawing familiar sites of natural beauty in the Suffolk region. He was sent to study under one of his uncles, but quickly showed a greater interest in drawing than in formal studies. He moved to London around 1742 and was introduced to the French painter and engraver Hubert Gravelot, who took him on as his assistant, subsequently enrolling him at St Martin's League Academy. Gainsborough also worked with Frank Hayman, then at Hatton Garden in London, where he produced models and a number of early landscapes.

Having learned the rudiments of technique, Gainsborough opted to return to his native Sudbury, where he set himself up as a portraitist and landscape painter. At the age of nineteen, he married Margaret Burr, the illegitimate daughter of the Duke of Beaufort and a young lady of some means; this enabled him to pursue an artistic career. Around 1746 he moved to Ipswich, and several years later (around 1758) he settled in Bath. He had a considerable following by this point and, almost inevitably, moved to London in 1774. From this date his fame spread rapidly.

Gainsborough was elected to the Society of Artists in 1766 and began to exhibit in London. In 1769 he emerged as one of the founder members of the Royal Academy of Arts. At the 1783 Royal Academy exhibition, Gainsborough and Reynolds clashed; Gainsborough had submitted 18 compositions comprising portraits of the King, Queen and other members of the royal family, but a row ensued over how and where one of the portraits - a group of three princesses, now in Windsor Castle - was to be displayed. Gainsborough failed to get his way and promptly withdrew the works from the exhibition. He subsequently refused to have any further dealings with the Academy. The hostility between Gainsborough and Sir Joshua Reynolds, has been much commented upon. However when Reynolds visited him on his deathbed and Gainsborough was at pains to dispel any vestige of enmity between Reynolds and himself. He faced death with commendable equanimity and is reported to have said to Reynolds that the two of them would 'meet again in Heaven, with Van Dyck for company'.

By 1750, Gainsborough was painting three-quarter-length portraits for 5 guineas. He quickly increased his price to 8 guineas and asked 100 guineas for a full-length portrait. By this time, Gainsborough was producing landscapes which rank alongside those of the Flemish Masters at their best, but the public at large only had eyes for his portraiture. He was the favourite painter of King George III, who posed for him on no fewer than eight occasions. He was also in great demand from the Queen, the nobility and the leading personalities of the day. In his benchmark study of Gainsborough, Fulcher lists 300 paintings, some 200 of which are portraits. As an engraver, Gainsborough was less prolific, but he is noted for 18 landscape and genre etchings and 3 aquatints. Overall, his work is said to exhibit more character than that of Sir Joshua Reynolds; in particular, he is noted for his female portraits, which exhibit a lyrical, sentimental grace and charm that is typically English.

Gainsborough's work has featured in a number of major exhibitions, notably at the Tate Britain in London (1980); in Paris, at the Galeries Nationales du Grand Palais (1981); at *The Young Gainsborough* (National Gallery, London, 1997); and, in 2002, at London's Tate Gallery, at the National Gallery of Art in Washington, DC, and at the Museum of Fine Arts in Boston.

BIBLIOGRAPHY:

Bell, Arthur, *Gainsborough, a Record of his Life and Works*, Bell, London, 1897. Amstrong, Walter, *Gainsborough et sa place dans l'école anglaise*, Hachette, Paris, 1899. Waterhouse, Ellis, *Gainsborough*, E. Hulton, London, 1958. Hayes, John, *Gainsborough as Print Maker*, A. Zwemmer, London, 1971. *Gainsborough*, exhibition catalogue, Gal. nationales du Grand Palais, Réunion des musées nationaux, Paris, 1981. Lindsay, Jack, *Thomas Gainsborough: His Life and Art*, Granada, London, 1981. Hayes, John, *The Landscape Paintings of Thomas Gainsborough: A Critical Text and Catalogue Raisonné*, Sotherby Publications, London, 1982. Cormack, Malcolm, *The Paintings of Thomas Gainsborough*, Cambridge University Press, Cambridge, 1991. *Gainsborough and Reynolds: Constrasts in Royal Patronage*, exhibition catalogue, Queen's Gallery, Buckingham Palace, London, 1994. Rosenthal, Michael, *The Art of Thomas Gainsborough*, Yale University Press, London, 1999. Vaughan, William, *Gainsborough*, Thames & Hudson, London, 2002. Belsey, Hugh, *Thomas Gainsborough: A Country Life*, Prestel, Munich, 2002. *Gainsborough*, exhibition catalogue, Tate Gall., London, 2003.

MUSEUMS AND GALLERIES:

BATH (Holburne Mus. of Art): *Portrait of Dr. Rice Charleton* (1764, oil on canvas) - BERLIN: *J. Wilkinson* - BERLIN (Gemäldegal.): *Joshua Grigby* (c. 1765) - BIRMINGHAM (Barber Institute of Fine Arts): *Harvest Wagon* (c. 1767) - BIRMINGHAM (Mus. and AG): *Sir Charles Holte* (1770-1774, oil on canvas); *Lewis Bagot, Bishop of Bristol* (1770-1774, oil on canvas); *Prodigal Son* (oil on canvas); *Miss Isabelle Bell Franks* (oil on canvas); *Portrait of Matthew Hale* (oil on canvas); *Thomas Coward* (oil on canvas); *Wooded Landscape: Autumn Evening* (oil on canvas); *Landscape with a Cottage and Cart* (oil on canvas) - BOLOGNA (Civico Museo Bibliografico Musicale): *Johann Christian Bach* (1776) - BUDAPEST: *Charles Hotchkiss* - CORAL GABLES (Lowe AM, University of Miami): *Portrait of Mrs Collins* (c. 1770-1775, oil on canvas) - DUBLIN: *View of Suffolk; Hugh, Duke of Northumberland; James Quinan* - EDINBURGH: *Middleton, Surgeon* - EDINBURGH (Nat. Gal. of Scotland): *The Hon. Mrs. Graham* (oil on canvas) - FORT WORTH (Kimbell AM): *Suffolk Landscape* (mid-1750s, oil on canvas); *Miss Lloyd* (c. 1750, oil on canvas) - IPSWICH (Ipswich Mus.): *William Wollaston* (1758-1759) - LEEDS (City AG): *Shepherd and his Flock* (c. 1775, drawing, watercolour and gouache) - LEICESTER: *Miss Adney* - LONDON (Dulwich Picture Gal.): *Thomas Linley the Elder* (late 1760s, oil on canvas); *The Linley Sisters (Mrs Sheridan and Mrs Tickell)* (1772?, oil on canvas); *Philippe Jacques de Loutherbourg* (c. 1777-1778, oil on canvas); *Mrs Elizabeth Moody and her two Sons* (c. 1778-1782, oil on canvas) - LONDON (Iveagh Bequest, Kenwood): *Evening Landscape* (c. 1768-1771) - LONDON (National Portrait Gal.): *Sarah Kirby (née Bull); John Joshua Kirby* (c. 1751-1752, oil on canvas); *Edward Vernon* (c. 1753, oil on canvas); *Thomas Gainsborough* (c. 1758-1759, oil on canvas); *John Russell, 4th Duke of Bedford* (c. 1770, oil on canvas); *Stringer Lawrence* (c. 1774-1775, oil on canvas); *John Henderson* (c. 1777, oil on canvas); *George Colman the Elder* (c. 1778, oil on canvas); *Charles Cornwallis, 1st Marquess Cornwallis* (1783, oil on canvas) - LONDON (Royal Academy of Arts): *Romantic Landscape* (c. 1783, oil on canvas); *Self-portrait of Thomas Gainsborough* (c. 1787, oil on canvas) - LONDON (Tate Collection): *Wooded Landscape with a Peasant Resting* (c. 1747, oil on canvas); *The Rev. John Chafy Playing the Violoncello in a Landscape* (c. 1750-1752, oil on canvas); *Peter Darnell Muilman, Charles Crokatt and William Keable in a Landscape* (c. 1750, oil on canvas); *Sunset: Carthorses Drinking at a Stream* (c. 1760, oil on canvas); *Abel Moysey* (c. 1764, oil on canvas); *Gainsborough Dupont* (c. 1770-1775, oil on canvas); *The Artist's Daughter Margaret* (c. 1772, oil on canvas); *Tristram and Fox* (c. 1775-1785, oil on canvas); *Pomeranian Bitch and Puppy* (c. 1777, oil on canvas); *Gypsy Encampment, Sunset* (c. 1778-1780, oil on canvas); *The Rev. Sir Henry Bate-Dudley, Bart* (c. 1780, oil on canvas); *Musidora* (c. 1780-1788, oil on canvas); *The Housemaid* (c. 1782-1786, oil on canvas); *Giovanna Baccelli* (exhibited in 1782, oil on canvas); *The Baillie Family* (c. 1784, oil on canvas); *Boy Driving Cows near a Pool* (c. 1786, oil on canvas); *The Bridge* (c. 1786, oil on canvas); *The Watering Place* (chalk/paper); *Study of a Cow* (pencil/paper); *Upland Landscape with River and Horsemen Crossing a Bridge* (c. 1785-1788, chalk and stump/paper) - LONDON (Victoria and Albert Mus.): *Portrait of John Joshua Kirby* (c. 1754-1756, oil on canvas); *Portrait of John Purling* (c. 1770-1780, oil on canvas); *The Painter's Two Daughters* (c. 1758, oil on canvas); landscapes, studies - LONDON (Wallace Collection): *Mrs. Mary Robinson ('Perdita')* (c. 1781, oil on canvas); *Miss Elizabeth Haverfield* (early 1780s, oil on canvas) - LOS ANGELES (Getty Mus.): *James Christie* (1778, oil on canvas); *Lady Walking in a Garden with a Child* (c. 1783-1785) - MANCHESTER: watercolour - MELBOURNE (Nat. Gal. of Victoria): *Mouth of the Thames* (1783); *The Hon. Wolfran Cornwall* (c. 1785-1786); *Officer* (1770) - MONTREAL (Learmont) - MONTREAL (MBA): *Mrs George Drummond* - NEW HAVEN (Yale Center For British Art): *John and Ann Gravenor with their Daughters* (c. 1754, oil on canvas); *Major John Dade of Tannington, Suffolk* (c. 1755, oil on canvas); *William Johnstone-Pulteney, later 5th Baronet* (c. 1772, oil on canvas); *Landscape with Cattle* (c. 1773, oil on canvas); *Landscape with Flock of Sheep* (c. 1773-1777, oil on canvas) - NEW YORK (Metropolitan Mus. of Art): *Charles Rousseau Burney* (1770); *Nathaniel Burrough; Queen Charlotte* (1782); *Mount Hamleth* (1783); *Farm Children* (1787) - PARIS (Louvre): *Lady Alston; Landscape; Reaper; Richard Owen Cambridge; Landscape with Man and Woman* (1746); *Conversation in a Park* - READING: *Storm* - SAN MARINO, CA (Huntington Library, Art Collections and Botanical Gardens): *Penelope, Viscountess Ligonier* (1771); *Carl Friedrich Abel* (1777); *Lord and Lady Ligonier* - SOUTHAMPTON (City AG): *George Venables Vernon, 2nd Lord* (1767) - STUTTGART: *Queen Charlotte of England; Octavius of England* - WASHINGTON DC (NGA): *Master John Heathcote* (c. 1771- 1772, oil on canvas); *Mountain Landscape with Bridge* (c. 1783-1784, oil on canvas); *Mrs Richard Brinsley Sheridan* (1785-1787, oil on canvas) - WORCESTER, MA (AM): *Portrait of the Artist's Daughters* (c. 1763-1764, oil on canvas).

AUCTION RECORDS:

LONDON, May 1829, *Market Cart*, FRF 27,550. LONDON, April 1863, *Rest*, FRF 20,510; *Landscape with Sheep*, FRF 9,970. PARIS, 1872, *Richard Brinsley Sheridan* (full-length) FRF 80,000. LONDON, May 1878, *Portraits of the Artist's Daughters*, FRF 18,237. LONDON, 1887, *Sisters*, FRF 272,630. LONDON, 1890, *Portrait of Lord Hamilton dressed in Blue*, FRF 110,240; *Portrait of Alexander, Duke of Hamilton, dressed in Black*, FRF 39,370. LONDON, June 1893, *Lady Rodney*, FRF 60,360; *Mrs Drummond of Stanmore*, FRF 175,040. LONDON, 23 March 1895, *View of Surrey*, FRF 15,780. LONDON, 1896, *Mr and Mrs Dehanrey and Daughters*, FRF 55,125; *Dorothea, Lady Eden*, FRF 131,200; *Landscape at Schochervireck*, FRF 81,320; *Portrait of Lady Rowley*, FRF 38,000. PARIS, 1897, *Portrait of Ch. Fred. Abel*, FRF 31,500; *Portrait of Madame Puget, née Hawkins*, FRF 126,000; *Anne Elisabeth, Lady Mulgrave*,

FRF 26,750. PARIS, 1898, *Lady Clarges*, FRF 48,550. LONDON, 1898, *Mr Hamilton in Purple and White*, FRF 19,675. NEW YORK, 25 Feb 1898, *Edge of The Landes*, USD 2,700; *Going to Market*, USD 3,800; *Countess of Buckinghamshire*, USD 5,000. LONDON, Nov 1898, *Three Small Landscapes*, FRF 17,850. PARIS, 17 Dec 1900, *Bust Portrait of an English Admiral* (drawing) FRF 450. NEW YORK, 20 March 1902, *Portrait of Mrs Owen*, USD 5,400. NEW YORK, 22 and 23 Feb 1907, *Portrait of William Pettin*, USD 2,600. LONDON, 14 March 1908, *Portrait of William Jones*, GBP 52. LONDON, 16 March 1908, *Wooded Landscape with River*, GBP 126. LONDON, 28 March 1908, *Portrait of the Earl of Shaftesbury* (pastel) GBP 52; *Portrait of Countess Spencer*, GBP 73. LONDON, May 1908, *Portrait of The Hon. Campbell Skenner*, GBP 294. LONDON, 22 May 1908, *View of Suffolk*, GBP 861. LONDON, 29 May 1908, *Portrait of the Artist's Daughter Mary, latterly Mrs Fischer*, GBP 4,777; *Portrait of the Artist's Wife*, GBP 2,782. LONDON, 25 June 1908, *Harvest Wagon*, GBP 735. LONDON, 3 July 1908, *Portrait of General Wolfe*, GBP 1,890; *Horses Drinking at a Trough*, GBP 420. LONDON, 5 April 1909, *Child Portrait of Miss Valander*, GBP 37. LONDON, 7 May 1909, *Landscape with Young Girl, Seated*, GBP 409. LONDON, 21 May 1909, *Wood with Figures*, GBP 52. LONDON, 16 July 1909, *Artist's Daughter as a Gleaner*, GBP 357. LONDON, 26 Feb 1910, *Head of Young Woman*, GBP 75. LONDON, 6 May 1910, *Landscape with Animals*, GBP 4,200; *Pomeranian and Young Dog*, GBP 945. LONDON, 3 June 1910, *Portrait of J. Tompion*, GBP 840. LONDON, 19 May 1911, *Portrait of Mrs Bell*, GBP 3,054; *Portrait of Mr Bell*, GBP 1,608; *Cottage Door*, GBP 1,050. LONDON, 1 June 1911, *Portrait of a Gentleman and a Lady* (two pendants) GBP 199; *Portrait of Garrick*, GBP 110; *Portrait of Mrs Woodward*, GBP 273. LONDON, 16 June 1911, *Portrait of Lady Ines*, GBP 3,780; *Portrait of Thomas Meolycott*, GBP 4,410. LONDON, 19 June 1911, *Portrait of a Gentleman*, GBP 945. LONDON, 14 July 1911, *Portrait of Viscount Derby*, GBP 262; *Portrait of R. Hurd, Bishop of Worcester*, GBP 357; *Portrait of Anne Ponsonby*, GBP 8,715. PARIS, 22 May 1919, *Self-portrait*, FRF 9,500. LONDON, 19 May 1920, *Portrait of Mr and Mrs William Carter of Ballington House, Bulmer, Essex* (oil on canvas, 35 1/2 x 27 1/4 ins / 90.1 x 69.2 cm) GBP 105. PARIS, 8-10 June 1920, *Cart* (drawing) FRF 8,100. PARIS, 21-22 June 1920, *Portrait of a Young Man* (red chalk) FRF 3,100. PARIS, 6-8 Dec 1920, *Man Reading*, FRF 24,000. PARIS, 21-22 Nov 1922, *Portrait of a Young Man* (red chalk) FRF 3,500. LONDON, 1 Dec 1922, *Marquis Townshend*, GBP 25; *Forest Path*, GBP 21. LONDON, 23 March 1923, *Portrait of Mark Beaufroy*, GBP 9; *Portrait of Mrs Damer*, GBP 16. LONDON, 11 May 1923, *Forest Path* (black chalk heightened with white) GBP 33; *Shepherd and Flock* (Indian ink heightened with white) GBP 54; *Margaret and Mary Gainsborough as Young Girls*, GBP 3,045; *Artist, Wife and Child*, GBP 3,150; *Duc d'Arenberg*, GBP 903; *Miss Susan Gardiner as a Child*, GBP 1,785. LONDON, 13 July 1923, *Returning from Market*, GBP 5,040. LONDON, 1 May 1925, *Miss Theodosia Magill*, GBP 3,045; *Mrs William Monck*, GBP 5,040; *Lord John and Lord Bernard Stuart in the manner of Van Dyck*, GBP 3,255. PARIS, 23 Nov 1927, *Portrait of Mr Hammond*, FRF 195,000. LONDON, 16 Dec 1927, *Wooded Landscape*, GBP 231. LONDON, 1 June 1928, *Portrait of a Woman (black and white)*, GBP 9; *Landscape*, GBP 47. LONDON, 8 June 1928, *Small Street* (charcoal drawing) GBP 23; *Portrait of a Woman* (pencil) GBP 199; *J. Henderson, Actor*, GBP 54. LONDON, 8 June 1928, *Portrait of a Woman*, GBP 6,090. LONDON, 28 June 1929, *General Meyrick*, GBP 4,620. LONDON, 24 July 1929, *Lady Napter*, GBP 390. LONDON, 13 Dec 1929, *Dr Hill*, GBP 273. NEW YORK, 20 Feb 1930, *Captain Bragge*, USD 4,550. LONDON, 7 March 1930, *David Middleton*, GBP 1,365. LONDON, 23 May 1930, *Hilly Landscape* (drawing) GBP 12; *Wooded Landscape* (drawing) GBP 42; *Mrs Bond* (drawing) GBP 29; *Landscape* (drawing) GBP 78; *Horseman* (drawing) GBP 52; *Rest* (drawing) GBP 173. LONDON, 20 June 1930, *Charles Rousseau Burney*, GBP 4,620. LONDON, 18 July 1930, *Lady Impey*, GBP 4,200. NEW YORK, 26 May 1932, *Landscape*, USD 6,700. LONDON, 24 June 1932, *Samuel Campbell*, GBP 336. LONDON, 24 Nov 1933, *Col. Thomas Fletcher*, GBP 420. PARIS, 2 April 1936, *Portrait of Mrs Charles Tudway, née Hannah Moore, Wife of Charles Tudway, Esq., M.P., The Cedars, Wells, Somerset*, FRF 40,000. LONDON, 9 July 1937, *Morning*, GBP 2,100. NEW YORK, 4-5 Dec 1941, *William Pitt*, USD 26,000; *William Gelverton Davenport*, USD 16,000; *Jack Hill*, USD 16,500. LONDON, 15 May 1942, *Cowgirl* (drawing) GBP 11. LONDON, 16 and 17 July 1942, *Wooded Landscape with Plough* (two drawings) GBP 57. LONDON, 7 Aug 1942, *Paul Pechell*, GBP 157. LONDON, 18 Sept 1942, *Three Peasants on a Mule* (drawing) GBP 32. NEW YORK, 2 April 1943, *Country Road* (watercolour) USD 175. LONDON, 5 May 1943, *Landscape* (drawing) GBP 125; *Landscape* (drawing) GBP 320; *Landscape* (drawing) GBP 270; *Going to Market* (drawing) GBP 280. LONDON, 22 Oct 1943, *David Garrick*, GBP 47. NEW YORK, 18-20 Nov 1943, *Two Young Women in a Garden* (drawing) USD 800. NEW YORK, 5 April 1944, *After the Storm*, USD 325; *Karl Friedrich Abel*, USD 800. NEW YORK, 24 May 1944, *John Coltman*, USD 300. LONDON, 9 June 1944, *William Pitt*, GBP 2,940. LONDON, 1 Dec 1944, *By the Lake* (drawing) GBP 78. PARIS, 25 May 1945, *Valley* (black chalk, lightly heightened with white, school of Thomas Gainsborough) FRF 18,500. LONDON, 1 June 1945, *By the Sea*, GBP 5, 040. LONDON, 13 July 1945, *Peasant Driving Cattle* (drawing) GBP 115; *Peasant Family* (drawing) GBP 199. NEW YORK, 15 Nov 1945, *John Gisborne*, USD 800. LONDON, 19-20 March 1946, *Returning from Church* (drawing) GBP 32; *Shaded Stream* (drawing) GBP 24; *Landscape* (drawing) GBP 135; *Storm Cloud*, GBP 280; *Landscape*, GBP 30; *Landscape*, GBP 34. NEW YORK, 28 March 1946, *John Shrimpton*, USD 1,500. LONDON, 3 May 1946, *Lady Draper*, GBP 483. LONDON, 12 July 1946, *William McCall*, GBP 115; *Miss Edgar*, GBP 525. NEW YORK, 18-19 Oct 1946, *Landscape* (drawing) USD 275. LONDON, 6 Dec 1946, *Portrait of a Woman*, GBP 252. LONDON, 10-12 Feb 1947, *Hilly Landscape* (drawing) GBP 32. LONDON, 19 March 1947, *Cattle*, GBP 520; *Evening Landscape*, GBP 380; *At the Cottage Door*, GBP 900. LONDON, 11 June 1947, *Mouth of the Thames*, GBP 4,000. LONDON, 25 June 1947, *Descent from the Cross (after Rubens)*, GBP 160. NEW YORK, 17 Oct 1956, *Wooded Landscape*, USD 20,500. NEW YORK, 16 June 1957, *Miss Tryon*, USD 11,000. LONDON, 25 Oct 1957, *Portrait of John Nigh, Esq.*, GBP 1,470. LONDON, 27 June 1958, *Portrait of Miss Kildebee*, GBP 3,675; *Portrait of William Henry, Duke of Gloucester*, GBP 22,050. LONDON, 18 Nov 1959, *Portrait of Anne, Countess Chesterfield*, GBP 34,000. LONDON, 23 March 1960, *Portrait of Mr and Mrs Robert Andrews*, GBP 130,000. LONDON, 30 Nov 1960, *Portrait of Dr William Blake Marsh*, GBP 3,000. NEW YORK, 8 April 1961, *Suffolk Landscape*, USD 13,500. LONDON, 14 June 1961, *Portrait of Mrs George Scott Chad*, GBP 4,000. NEW YORK, 15 Nov 1961, *Dorothea, Lady Eden (c. 1770-1775)*, USD 35,000. LONDON, 3 July 1963, *Portrait of Maria, Lady Gedeon*, GBP 54,000. LONDON, 7 July 1965, *Hagar and Ishmael in a Wooded Landscape*, GBP 10,000. LONDON, 18 Nov 1966, *Landscape with Travellers and Cattle*, Gns 19,000. LONDON, 7 July 1967, *Two Little Beggars*, Gns 13,000. LONDON, 26 June 1968, *Mountain Landscape with Shepherd on the Banks of a River*, GBP 36,000. NEW YORK, 20 May 1971, *Portrait of Mary and Henrietta Maria, the Viscountesses Dillon*, USD 100,000. LONDON, 19 July 1972, *Portrait of Mr and Mrs John Gravenor and their Two Daughters*, GBP 280,000. LONDON, 27 June 1973, *The Sisters Elisabeth and Sarah Cruttenden*, GBP 110,000; *Portrait of Theodosia Magill, Countess Clanwilliam* (1765) GBP 24,000. LONDON, 21 June 1974, *Romantic Landscape*, Gns 10,000. LONDON, 31 March 1976, *Wooded Landscape with Cart* (oil on canvas, 24 x 29 ins / 61 x 73.5 cm) GBP 17,000. LONDON, 9 Nov 1976, *Rocky Wooded Landscape* (ink and wash, 11 1/4 x 14 1/2 ins / 28.5 x 37 cm) GBP 3,200. LONDON, 24 Nov 1977, *Wooded Landscape with Village*

Scene (watercolour, black ink and oil on reddish-brown paper, 16¼ x 20¾ ins / 41 x 53 cm) GBP 17,000. LONDON, 25 Nov 1977, *Wooded Landscape with Shepherds and Flock by a Pond* (oil on canvas, 46½ x 58½ ins / 118.1 x 148.6 cm) GBP 180,000. LONDON, 22 March 1979, *Peasants and Cart in a Wooded Landscape* (watercolour, pencil and black chalk, 9¼ x 12¼ ins / 23.5 x 31 cm) GBP 13,000. LONDON, 28 June 1979, *Wooded Landscape with Figures and Two Carts* (etching, 12¾ x 15½ ins / 32.4 x 39.2 cm) GBP 700. LONDON, 19 July 1979, *Village Street (study)* (pencil, black and white chalks, 6 x 8¼ ins / 15 x 21 cm) GBP 900. LONDON, 17 Nov 1981, *Carriage Passing Through Park Gates* (pen and wash/paper, 10 x 14½ ins / 25.5 x 37 cm) GBP 5,500. LONDON, 22 April 1983, *Portrait of Mr and Mrs William Carter of Ballington House* (oil on canvas, 35½ x 27¼ ins / 90.1 x 69.2 cm) GBP 130,000. LONDON, 15 March 1984, *Wooded Upland Landscape with Herdsman, Cow and Dog* (1780, black chalk, gouache and grey wash, 11 x 14½ ins / 28 x 37 cm) GBP 25,000. LONDON, 5 March 1985, *Wooded Landscape with Two Country Carts and Figures* (1779, etching/paper, 11¾ x 15¼ ins / 29.7 x 39 cm) GBP 10,500. NEW YORK, 9 May 1985, *Portrait of Miss Theodosia Magill, Countess Clanwilliam* (1765, oil on canvas, 50 x 40 ins / 127 x 101.6 cm) USD 300,000. LONDON, 21 Nov 1985, *Wooded Landscape with Travellers and Sheep* (black and white chalks and stump, 9½ x 12¼ ins / 24 x 31 cm) GBP 38,000. LONDON, 30 June 1986, *Seated Lady wearing a Straw Hat (study recto)* (black chalk and stump heightened with white/blue paper); *Young Girl Seated (verso)* (black chalk, 12½ x 9¼ ins / 31.7 x 23.8 cm) GBP 200,000. LONDON, 24 April 1987, *Portrait of Lt.-Col. Jonathan Bullock of Faulkbourn Hall* (oil on canvas, 89½ x 60 ins / 227.3 x 152.4 cm) GBP 1,000,000. LONDON, 16 July 1987, *Wooded Landscape with Farm and Manor House* (watercolour and black chalk heightened with white with grey and white paint, 8½ x 11½ ins / 21.5 x 29.5 cm) GBP 75,000. LONDON, 25 Jan 1988, *Herdsman and Cow on Path in Mountainous Landscape* (ink/panel, 8 x 10¼ ins / 20.5 x 26 cm) GBP 935. NEW YORK, 3 June 1988, *Portrait of a Gentleman in Red* (oil on canvas, 29½ x 24½ ins / 75 x 62 cm) USD 34,100. LONDON, 18 Nov 1988, *Bust Portrait of Anna, Lady Mendip, in a Black Gown and with her Hair covered by a White Mantle* (oil on canvas, 29 x 24 ins / 73.6 x 60.9 cm) GBP 99,000. NEW YORK, 12 Jan 1989, *Portrait of J. Banks, Esq.* (oil on canvas, 50 x 40 ins / 127 x 101.5 cm) USD 33,000. LONDON, 12 July 1989, *Bust Portrait of Louis-Edmond Quentin de Richebourg, Chevalier de Champcenetz, wearing a Dark Coat* (oil on canvas, 26¾ x 22 ins / 68 x 55 cm) GBP 77,000. LONDON, 15 Nov 1989, *Two Horses and a Dog Drinking at a Waterfall in a Rocky Landscape with a Village in the Distance* (oil on canvas, 48½ x 39 ins / 123 x 99 cm) GBP 715,000. LONDON, 6 Dec 1989, *Young Page in Blue* (oil on canvas, 65 ins / 165 cm, 2 x 44½ ins/5 x 113 cm) GBP 1,100,000. NEW YORK, 10 Jan 1990, *Open Landscape* (oil on canvas, 21½ x 29½ ins / 54.6 x 74.9 cm) USD 176,000. LONDON, 11 July 1990, *Portrait of Dr Richard Warren Wearing a Green Frock Coat and Leaning on a Table* (oil on canvas, 50 x 40 ins / 127 x 101.5 cm) GBP 159,500. NEW YORK, 11 Oct 1990, *Portrait of Anne Furye* (oil on canvas, 29½ x 24½ ins / 75 x 62 cm) USD 18,700. LONDON, 14 Nov 1990, *Bust Portrait of Constantine John, 2nd Baron Mulgrave in Naval Officer's Uniform, sitting by a Window* (oil on canvas, 49½ x 59 ins / 126 x 150 cm) GBP 50,600; *The Suffolk Plough* (oil on canvas, 19¾ x 23¾ ins / 50 x 60.5 cm) GBP 55,000. LONDON, 10 April 1991, *Bust Portrait of Lady Margaret Fordyce in a Dark Gown trimmed with Lace and Pearls* (oil on canvas, 30 x 24½ ins / 76 x 62 cm) GBP 85,800. LONDON, 10 July 1991, *Wooded Landscape with Figures, Mules, a Bridge, a Village and a Mountain in the Distance* (oil on canvas, 14 x 17½ ins / 35.5 x 44.5 cm) GBP 231,000. LONDON, 13 Dec 1991, *Wooded Landscape with Two Lovers and a Shepherd and Flock by a Pond* (oil on canvas, 46½ x 58½ ins / 118 x 148.6 cm) GBP 836,000. LONDON, 20 Nov 1992, *Portrait of a Gentleman (presumed to be General Thomas Meyrick)* (oil on canvas, oval, 30 x 25¼ ins / 76.5 x 64 cm) GBP 55,000. LONDON, 13 July 1993, *Wooded Landscape with Figures Resting by the Roadside near a Building* (chalks and watercolour, 8¾ x 12½ ins / 22.1 x 31.8 cm) GBP 36,700. LONDON, 14 July 1993, *Wooded Landscape with Portraits of Peter Darnal Muilman, Charles Crockatt and William Keeble* (oil on canvas, 29½ x 24½ ins / 75 x 62 cm) GBP 1,079,500. LONDON, 12 April 1995, *Portrait of Master John Truman-Villebois and his Brother Henry, dressed in Brown and sitting on a Column Pedestal* (oil on canvas, 61 x 51 ins / 155 x 129.5 cm) GBP 661,500. LONDON, 3 April 1996, *Bust Portrait of Elizabeth Cochrane in a Blue Gown with a White Shawl* (oil on canvas, 29¼ x 24½ ins / 74.5 x 62 cm) GBP 54,300. NEW YORK, 30 Jan 1997, *Portrait of Francis, Wife of Alexander Champion* (oil on canvas, 29½ x 24¾ ins / 74.9 x 62.9 cm) USD 305,000. NEW YORK, 31 Jan 1997, *River Landscape with Travellers Resting in a Forest Glade* (oil on canvas, 30½ x 50½ ins / 77.5 x 128.3 cm) USD 442,500. LONDON, 9 April 1997, *Landscape with Lamps, a Fence and a Slope* (c. 1741-1745, oil on canvas, 8½ x 9¾ ins / 21.5 x 25 cm) GBP 60,900. LONDON, 12 Nov 1997, *Portrait of Philip Dupont* (c. 1775, oil on canvas, oval, 27½ x 24 ins / 70 x 61 cm) GBP 47,700. NEW YORK, 29 Jan 1999, *Wooded Landscape with Herdsmen, Cows and Sheep near a Pool* (oil on canvas, 24 x 29 ins / 61 x 74 cm) USD 1,900,000. LONDON, 11 Nov 1999, *Wooded Landscape with Sheep Grazing by a Winding Track* (black chalk and watercolour heightened with white, 11 x 15 ins / 28 x 38 cm) GBP 100,000. LONDON, 22 March 2000, *Portrait of Admiral Vernon in a Red Coat, Holding a Sword* (oil on canvas, 49 x 39 ins / 124 x 99 cm) GBP 155,000. LONDON, 6 Nov 2000, *Study of a King Charles Spaniel* (coloured chalk, 9 x 12 ins / 23 x 31 cm) GBP 195,000. LONDON, 7 June 2001, *Wooded Landscape with Shepherd and Sheep* (pencil, black ochre, chalk, stump and wash, 9 x 12 ins / 23 x 31 cm) GBP 58,000. LONDON, 30 Nov 2001, *Portrait of Miss Elizabeth Edgar* (oil on canvas, 30 x 25 ins / 76 x 63 cm) GBP 70,000. LONDON, 13 June 2002, *Dancers with Musicians in a Woodland Glade* (black chalk and wash heightened with white, 11 x 14 ins / 27 x 35 cm) GBP 80,000. LONDON, 13 June 2002, *Portrait of Colonel John Bullock* (oil on canvas, 89 x 60 ins / 227 x 152 cm) GBP 2,400,000. LONDON, 19 March 2003, *Portrait of Lady Alston* (oil on canvas, 29 x 24 ins / 74 x 61 cm) GBP 50,000. LONDON, 27 Nov 2003, *Portrait of Richard Tickell in a Brown Coat* (oil on canvas, 29 x 24 ins / 74 x 62 cm) GBP 1,650,000. LONDON, 3 June 2004, *Wooded Landscape with Sheep Grazing by a Winding Track* (black chalk, stump and watercolour heightened with white, 11 x 15 ins / 28 x 38 cm) GBP 35,000. BURY ST EDMUNDS, 6 Oct 2004, *Extensive Wooded Upland Landscape* (c. 1786, oil on canvas, 10 x 13 ins / 25 x 33 cm) GBP 25,000.

GAINSBOROUGH-DUPONT. See **DUPONT Gainsborough**

GAINSFORD, F.F.G.
British, 18th - 19th century.
Active in London.
Painter. Portraits.

F.F.G. Gainsford exhibited at the Royal Academy in London from 1805 to 1816.

MUSEUMS AND GALLERIES:
LONDON (National Portrait Gal.): *John William Polidori* (c. 1816, oil on canvas).

GAINU, Pierre, or Gainy, or Gaing
French, 16th century.
Died c. 1602.
Active in Grenoble.
Engraver.

GAINZA, Juan
Spanish, 16th century.

Active in Seville.
Sculptor.

Juan Gainza sculpted some of the ribs of the vault of Seville Cathedral.

GAIR, Gilles

British, 19th century.
Active in London.
Painter. Portraits.

Gilles Gair exhibited from 1872 to 1874 at London's Royal Academy and Suffolk Street Gallery.

GAIRAD, Paul

19th century.
Active in Spain.
Sculptor. Figures. Groups.

MUSEUMS AND GALLERIES:
MADRID (Prado): *Group of Children.*

GAIRAL DE SEREZIN, Eugène

French, 19th - 20th century.
Born 1873, in Lyons.
Sculptor, medallist.

Eugène Gairal de Serezin studied under Verlet. He exhibited in Paris at the Salon des Artistes Français from 1905.

GAIRINT, Jean

French, 19th century.
Painter.

He exhibited views of the Forest of Fontainebleau at Paris Salons between 1845 and 1848.

GAIROARD, Eugenio

Italian, 19th century.
Born in Sicily.
Painter. Genre scenes.

Gairoard began his artistic career around 1883, and exhibited in Turin, Milan and Venice.

MUSEUMS AND GALLERIES:
MAINZ: *Cavalier; Maid.*

AUCTION RECORDS:
MILAN, 22 April 1982, *The Tabarin Ball, Paris* (1860, oil on panel, 6 3/4 x 11 ins / 17 x 27 cm) ITL 3,000,000. MILAN, 1 June 1988, *Tabarin* (1860, oil on panel, 7 1/2 x 11 ins / 19 x 27 cm) ITL 8,500,000.

GAIROUARD, Barthélémy

French, 17th - 18th century.
Active in Toulon.
Painter.

In 1715 Barthélemy Gairouard was working for the cathedral.

GAISSER, Jakob Emmanuel

German, 19th century.
Born 21 November 1825, in Augsburg; died 21 January 1899, in Munich.
Painter. Genre scenes.

Gaisser attended the art academy in Munich with Gaertner, Zimmermann and Julius Schnorr. After studying as the pupil of Joh. Geyer in Augsburg, he returned to Munich and settled there. He exhibited in Munich, Vienna, Bremen and London between 1867 and 1890. He is noted for his *Romantic Farce.*

AUCTION RECORDS:
COLOGNE, 27 May 1971, *Card Players,* DEM 7,000. LONDON, 26 July 1973, *Monks and Cavalry Soldiers,* Gns 20,300. LONDON, 12 June 1974, *Concert at the Public-House - Concert in the Cardinal's Apartments* (forming a pair) GBP 1,900. VIENNA, 30 Nov 1976, *Game of Cards* (oil on panel, 15 3/4 x 12 1/4 ins / 40 x 31 cm) ATS 130,000. LONDON, 20 July 1977, *Game of Cards* (oil on panel, 15 1/2 x 11 1/2 ins / 39.5 x 29.5 cm) GBP 1,000. MUNICH, 21 Sept 1978, *Music Time* (1869, oil on panel, 14 1/2 x 11 1/2 ins / 37 x 29 cm) DEM 12,000. COLOGNE, 12 June 1980, *Gossips* (oil on panel, 10 3/4 x 7 3/4 ins / 27.5 x 20 cm) DEM 5,000. NEW YORK, 26 Feb 1982, *Game of Chess* (oil on panel, 11 x 15 1/4 ins / 28 x 39 cm) USD 1,800. COLOGNE, 21 May 1984, *Game of Cards* (1873, oil on panel, 15 x 12 1/4 ins / 38 x 31 cm) DEM 6,500. VIENNA, 4 Dec 1986, *Merry Gathering in an Interior* (oil on panel, 16 1/4 x 20 1/2 ins / 41 x 52 cm) ATS 120,000. BERN, 30 April 1988, *Fabric Seller* (oil on panel, 8 1/4 x 7 3/4 ins / 21 x 20 cm) CHF 3,500. LONDON, 4 Oct 1989, *Grace before Lunch* (oil on canvas, 37 x 46 1/2 ins / 94 x 118 cm) GBP 13,200. NEW YORK, 23 Oct 1990, *A Good Joke; Letter* (oil on canvas, a pair, 25 1/2 x 30 ins / 64.8 x 76.2 cm) USD 9,900. PARIS, 24 May 1991, *Game of Cards* (oil on panel, 13 1/4 x 17 1/4 ins / 33.5 x 44 cm) FRF 25,000. LONDON, 19 June 1991, *Game of Cards* (oil on panel, 12 1/4 x 15 ins / 31 x 38 cm) GBP 4,950. LONDON, 7 April 1993, *A Bit of Banter* (oil on panel, 13 3/4 x 17 3/4 ins / 35 x 45 cm) GBP 2,990. NEW YORK, 12 Oct 1993, *Elegant Reception around a Table* (oil on panel, a pair, each 12 x 15 1/2 ins / 30.2 x 39.3 cm) USD 8,625. NEW YORK, 16 Feb 1994, *An Unexpected Guest; The Pretender* (oil on panel, a pair, each 11 3/4 x 15 3/4 ins / 29.8 x 40 cm) USD 10,350. NEW YORK, 20 July 1995, *Concert in the Cardinal's Apartments* (oil on panel, 16 1/2 x 21 ins / 41.9 x 53.3 cm) USD 3,105. LONDON, 17 Nov 1995, *Apologies* (oil on canvas, 37 x 46 1/4 ins / 94 x 117.5 cm) GBP 17,250. NEW YORK, 15 June 1999, *Storyteller* (1891, oil on canvas, 40 x 34 ins / 102 x 86 cm) USD 20,000. LONDON, 16 Sept 1999, *Musical Evening* (oil on canvas, 12 x 18 ins / 30 x 46 cm) GBP 3,000. MUNICH, 5 July 2000, *Happy Party Round a Table* (oil on panel, 13 x 16 ins / 33 x 41 cm) DEM 6,500. STOCKHOLM, 5 Dec 2000, *The Small Circus* (oil on canvas, 25 x 19 ins / 63 x 48 cm) SEK 42,000. COLOGNE, 28 June 2001, *Interior Scene with Children* (oil on panel, 17 x 21 ins / 44 x 53 cm) DEM 8,000. COLOGNE, 17 Nov 2001, *Family Scene in Interior of the Van Dyck Epoch* (oil on panel, 15 x 12 ins / 39 x 30 cm) DEM 7,100. AMSTERDAM, 24 April 2002, *Light Entertainment* (oil on panel, 13 x 16 ins / 33 x 41 cm) EUR 7,000. STUTTGART, 5 Dec 2002, *Figures in Historical Costume* (oil on canvas, 44 x 34 ins / 113 x 86 cm) EUR 5,500. AMSTERDAM, 29 April 2003, *Revellers in Monastery Cellar* (oil on panel, 12 x 16 ins / 30 x 40 cm) EUR 4,500. BREMEN, 5 Dec 2003, *Celebration in Castle Room* (oil on panel, 24 x 31 ins / 60 x 79 cm) EUR 7,500. LONDON, 9 March 2004, *Toasting a New Song* (oil on panel, 15 x 11 ins / 38 x 28 cm) GBP 1,800. HAMBURG, 28 April 2004, *Surprise Homecoming* (1876, oil on canvas, 26 x 35 ins / 65 x 90 cm) EUR 3,600.

GAISSER, Max

German, 19th - 20th century.
Born 22 June 1857, in Munich; died 1922.
Painter. Genre scenes.

Max Gaisser was the son of Jakob Emmanuel Gaisser. He studied at the Munich academy. He exhibited in Munich, Bremen and Dresden from 1883, as well as at the Salon des Artistes Français in Paris, where he won a third class medal in 1910.

MUSEUMS AND GALLERIES:
BREMEN: *The Trumpet's Tale; Lunch* - BUCHAREST (Muz. National de Arta al României): *Words of Love* - MUNICH: *At the Lawyer's Office.*

AUCTION RECORDS:
NEW YORK, 1899, *Village Politicians,* FRF 1,800. NEW YORK, 19 and 20 March 1903, *War Stories,* USD 625. NEW YORK, 12

March 1908, *Horsemen Singing a New Song,* USD 200. LONDON, 29 May 1929, *Politicians,* GBP 11. NEW YORK, 17 and 18 May 1934, *The Cup that Cheers,* USD 80; *Difficult Problem,* USD 300. PARIS, 15 June 1934, *The Scribe,* FRF 800. LONDON, 6 Nov 1936, *Voyage of Discovery,* GBP 189. NEW YORK, 21 Oct 1937, *At the Window,* USD 80. NEW YORK, 16 Jan 1942, *Dutch Interior,* USD 75. NEW YORK, 21 Feb 1945, *Triptych,* USD 600. NEW YORK, 26 and 27 Feb 1947, *Connoisseur,* USD 260; *Interiors with figures,* USD 225. COLOGNE, 25 Oct 1968, *Cabaret Scene,* DEM 15,000. COLOGNE, 24 Nov 1971, *At the Antiquary's,* DEM 17,000. LUCERNE, 22 June 1974, *Horseman in an Interior,* CHF 23,000. ZURICH, 28 May 1976, *The Proposal* (1886, oil on canvas, 30 x 43 1/4 ins / 76 x 110 cm) CHF 24,000. NEW YORK, 7 Oct 1977, *Interesting Reading* (oil on canvas, 22 x 27 3/4 ins / 55 x 70.5 cm) USD 4,000. VIENNA, 17 Nov 1981, *The Proposal* (1886, oil on canvas, 30 x 43 1/4 ins / 76 x 110 cm) ATS 250,000. LONDON, 22 June 1984, *The Antiquaries* (oil on canvas, 38 1/2 x 45 1/4 ins / 97.8 x 115 cm) GBP 4,000. VIENNA, 11 Dec 1985, *Discussion in the Library* (oil on panel, 19 3/4 x 24 ins / 50 x 61 cm) ATS 130,000. NEW YORK, 19 July 1990, *Shipowners* (oil on panel, 19 1/4 x 24 ins / 48.7 x 61 cm) USD 8,800. NEW YORK, 16 Feb 1994, *Conversation over Dinner* (oil on panel, 23 3/4 x 19 1/2 ins / 60.6 x 49.5 cm) USD 17,250. AMSTERDAM, 19 April 1994, *The New Pipe* (oil on panel, 14 1/2 x 19 ins / 37 x 48 cm) NLG 10,350. NEW YORK, 23 May 1997, *The Proposition* (oil on panel, 24 x 19 1/2 ins / 61 x 49.5 cm) USD 39,100.

GAITAN, Pedro
Spanish, 18th century.
Active in Seville c. 1700.
Sculptor.

Pedro Gaitan is known for some terracotta pieces.

GAITET, Louis Alphonse
French, 19th - 20th century.
Born 26 March 1836, in Marsannay-la-Côte (Côte-d'Or); died 13 December 1919, in Marsannay-la-Côte.
Painter, engraver. Portraits, genre scenes, landscapes with figures.

On 9 October 1856, Louis Gaitet joined the École des Beaux-Arts in Paris and studied under Picot. He exhibited at the Paris Salon from 1859 to 1879.

Gaitet is known for his portraits and some genre pieces, including: *Satyr Enchained by Nymphs*; *The Old Fiddler*; *The Childhood of Prud'hon*; *The Angelus*; and *Sleeping Child*.

AUCTION RECORDS:
LONDON, 11 Oct 1995, *Goddess Unmasked in a Garden* (1882, oil on canvas, 82 x 45 ins / 208 x 114 cm) GBP 3,450.

GAITIS, Yannis
Greek, 20th century.
Born 4 March 1923, in Athens; died 22 July 1984, in Athens.
Active in France from 1954.
Painter, sculptor, lithographer.
Nouvelle Figuration, Figuration Narrative.

Yannis Gaitis was a student at the school of fine art in Athens during World War II and was active in the Resistance. He settled in Paris in 1954. He uses a style reducing figures to a simple expression, recalling the beginnings of animated drawing. The title of his sculptures: *In Camera, Shells and Chrysalises* and *Mandel's Laws* denote an overcast world, an inevitable heritage, a fate instead of a destiny. In his human-robot alignments, in the same checked jackets and similar hats, symbols of their alienation, the soft, humorous smile is still present. To begin with he executed abstract, action paintings. He quickly moved on to a progressively figurative Expressionism influenced early on by the strong narrative trend that resulted from the appearance of pop art in the 1960s.

Yannis Gaitis exhibited a lot, in Athens to begin with, then in Brussels, Florence, Naples and London; he featured at the Salon des Réalités Nouvelles in Paris (1956). He took part in collective exhibitions organised by G. Gassiot-Talabot: *Mythologies Quotidiennes* (*Everyday Mythologies*), Musée d'Art Moderne de la Ville in Paris (1964); *Figuration Narrative* (1965).

BIBLIOGRAPHY:
Gassiot Talabot, Gérald (preface), *Mythologies quotidiennes*, exhibition catalogue, Musée d'Art moderne de la Ville de Paris, Paris, 1964. Gassiot Talabot, Gérald, *La Figuration narrative dans l'art contemporain*, Imprimerie Mazarine, Paris, 1965. *Yannis Gaitis*, exhibition catalogue, Pinacothèque nationale, Athens, 1984. Serafini, Giuliano, *Yannis Gaitis*, Medusa, Athens, 1988.

MUSEUMS AND GALLERIES:
ANDROS (Mouseío Synchronis Technis - Idruma Goulandri): *Oh! Ye Gods* - ATHENS (Gal.): *Red and Black Collective Transport*; *Heads* - CYPRUS (MMA): *Quadriple* - GLYFADA (Pinakothíki Dimitri Pieridi/Pierides Gallery): *Warriors* - PARIS (BNF) - SKOPJE (Muzej na Sovremena Umetnost): *Stowaways*.

AUCTION RECORDS:
PARIS, 16 May 1990, *Figure* (oil on canvas, 39 1/4 x 25 1/2 ins / 100 x 65 cm) FRF 24,000. PARIS, 28 Oct 1991, *Three Profiles and their Shadow* (1971, assemblage in cut wood, 16 1/2 x 21 3/4 x 5 1/2 ins / 42 x 55.5 x 14 cm) FRF 6,500. PARIS, 29 Nov 1991, *Sunrise* (1958, oil on canvas, 23 1/2 x 31 1/2 ins / 60 x 80 cm) FRF 4,000. PARIS, 8 July 1993, *Composition* (oil on canvas, 39 1/4 x 28 1/2 ins / 100 x 72.5 cm) FRF 4,000. PARIS, 16 Nov 1995, *Composition* (oil on canvas, 18 x 22 ins / 46 x 55 cm) FRF 4,800. NEW YORK, 19 Nov 1996, *Blue* (acrylic/canvas, 21 1/4 x 25 1/2 ins / 54 x 64.8 cm) USD 4,370. PARIS, 23 Nov 1997, *Untitled* (oil on canvas, 46 x 32 ins / 116 x 81 cm) FRF 11,000.

GAITONDE, V. S.
Indian, 20th century.
Born 1924, in Nagpur.
Painter.

Gaitonde was a student at the art school in Bombay (now Mumbai), where he subsequently taught. He was inspired by traditional Indian art and European surrealist painters such as Klee and Miró. His work featured in several collective exhibitions in India and abroad. In 1951 he was awarded a prize at the exhibition of young Asian painters in Tokyo.

MUSEUMS AND GALLERIES:
NEW DELHI (NGMA).

GAITTE, Antoine Joseph
French, 18th - 19th century.
Born 1753, in Paris.
Engraver. Urban landscapes. Monuments.

Antoine Gaitte's work appeared in the Salon in Paris in 1835. He produced some interesting views of Paris.

GAIUS OF LYSTRA
1st - 2nd (?) century.
Sculptor.
Ancient Roman.

Gaius, a sculptor like his brother, has left no known surviving works.

GAJARINI, Francesco
Italian, 19th century.
Born in Contea (Tuscany).
Sculptor.

He was a pupil of Ulisse Cambi in Florence, and later of Lorenzo Bartolini. He began his professional career in 1864.

GAJDOS, Janos
Hungarian, 20th century.
Born 1912.

Active in the Szabolcs region.
Painter.
A gifted, instinctive painter appreciated in his regional context, Janos Gajdos attended the Budapest school of fine art at the age of 38 after World War II. There he lost his initial freshness and gained nothing in return.

GAJEWSKI
Polish, 18th century.
Active c. 1790.
Painter.
The museum in Cracow owns several portraits by this artist. He could be the same artist as Michael Cajewski.

GAJEWSKI, Anton
Polish, 18th century.
Active in Korzec at the end of the 18th century.
Painter (porcelain).

GAJEWSKI, Louise
Polish, 18th - 19th century.
Painter.
The museum in Lviv owns a miniature signed by this artist, and dated 1812.

GAJEWSKI, Michael
Polish, 19th century.
Engraver, draughtsman.
Michael Gajewski produced several portraits.

GAJONI, Antonio Luigi
Italian, 20th century.
Born 4 May 1889, in Milan.
Painter.
Gajoni was a student at the school of applied arts in Milan, and also took a life-drawing class at the Accademia di Belle Arti di Brera. He lived in Paris from 1928 to 1940, where he mostly exhibited at the Salon des Artistes Indépendants and the Salon des Surindépendants. He won a gold medal at the International Exhibition of 1937 (Papal pavilion). Gajoni also took part in numerous exhibitions in Italy, most notably the Brera national exhibition, from 1918 to 1959. He decorated many churches in Italy.
MUSEUMS AND GALLERIES:
FLORENCE (Gal. d'Arte Moderna) - MILAN (Gal. d'Arte Moderna).

GAKOKEN. See **TOREI**

GAKUO, artist name: Gakuo, posthumous name: Zokyu
Japanese, 15th century.
Born 1504; died 1520.
Active during the late 15th and early 16th century.
Painter.
Gakuo was a Zen monk painter at the time when ink painting in Japan was developing in Zen Buddhist circles before it spread to the laity. Inspired by the work of his master Shubun (active 1425-1450), he remained faithful to the traditional style, but took to washes: a number of his signed landscapes atest to his distinct personality.
BIBLIOGRAPHY:
Akiyama, Terukazu, *La Peinture japonaise*, Skira, Geneva, 1961.

GAKUSO. See **GEIAMI**

GAKUTEI, real name: Yashima Harunobu, original name: Sugawara, artist names: Gogaku, Ichiro, Nanzan, Yotei, Koen, Shinkado, Shingakudo, Horikawa Taro, Ryosa, Yosai, Yotei, Gakutei, Gakurado
Japanese, 19th century.
Born c. 1786; died 1868.
Active c. 1815-1830.
Painter, print artist. Landscapes, animals.
Gakutei was an Edo painter who lived in Osaka from the late 1820s to the mid-1830s, designing landscapes, numerous actor prints and some surimono (de-luxe prints produced as greetings cards, New Year's greetings, and the like, in very small print runs), all of which were printed in Osaka. He took his inspiration from Hokusai.
AUCTION RECORDS:
LONDON, 9 Nov 1988, *Carp in Water Plants* (print, 8 1/4 x 7 3/4 ins / 21.2 x 19.7 cm) GBP 2,090. NEW YORK, 21 March 1989, *Carp Swimming among Water Plants* (kakuban woodblock print, 8 1/2 x 7 1/2 ins / 21.6 x 18.9 cm) USD 7,700. PARIS, 3 June 1992, *View of Storm in Tempozan, Osaka* (1838, oban woodblock print, 9 3/4 x 14 1/2 ins / 24.6 x 36.7 cm) FRF 35,000.

GAL
Hungarian, 19th century.
Active in Tata in 1825.
Painter.
Gal painted a portrait of Prince G. Rakoczy.

GALACHOV, L.
Russian, 18th century.
Active in 1783.
Engraver.
The only known work by Galachov is a signed illustration plate.

GALACHOVSKY, Daniel
Russian, 17th - 18th century.
Active in Kiev.
Engraver.
Daniel Galachovsky produced illustrations of religious subjects.

GALAIZE
French, 18th century.
Active in La Rochelle in 1787.
Painter. Genre scenes, seascapes, landscapes.

GALAKHOV, Nikolai
Russian, 20th century.
Born 1928.
Painter. Landscapes.
A student of Ilya Repin in Leningrad (now St Petersburg), Nikolai Galakhov was a painter of exuberance and of calm waters. He featured in collective exhibitions, showcases for official art, including: Autumn Salon, Leningrad (1952); *40 Years of Communist Youth*, Moscow (1958); *L'Art soviétique contemporain*, Paris (1966); *60 Years of the USSR*, Leningrad winning the first prize (1983); *Painters for the People*, Moscow (1985); Spring Salon, Leningrad (1990). He was a member of the Association of Painters of Leningrad.
BIBLIOGRAPHY:
L'École de Leningrad, auction catalogue, Drouot, Paris, 19 November 1990.
MUSEUMS AND GALLERIES:
BRYANSK (Mus. of Russian Art) - IRKUTSK (MFA) - KIEV (Mus. of Russian Art) - MOSCOW (Mus. of the Revolution) - ST PETERSBURG (Academy) - ST PETERSBURG (Gosudarstvennyj Russkij Muz.) - TOKYO (Guekosso Art Gal.).
AUCTION RECORDS:
PARIS, 13 April 1992, *Edge of the Wood* (oil on card, 12 1/2 x 15 3/4 ins / 32 x 40 cm) FRF 5,800. PARIS, 20 May 1992, *Summer's Day* (oil/hardboard, 24 1/2 x 28 1/4 ins / 62 x 72 cm) FRF 5,200. PARIS, 17 June 1992, *Wharf on the Neva* (oil on canvas, 46 3/4 x 33 ins / 119 x 84 cm) FRF 11,000. PARIS, 12 Oct 1992, *Waterlilies* (oil/hardboard, 32 1/4 x 26 1/2 ins / 82 x 67 cm) FRF 5,000.

GALAKTINOV, Afanassii
Russian, 17th century.
Born in Kostrova.
Icon painter.
Worked in Moscow in 1670.

GALAKTIONOV, Stepan Filippovich
Russian, 19th century.
Born c. 1779, in St Petersburg; died 1854, in St Petersburg.
Painter, engraver. Portraits, landscapes.

Galaktionov was a pupil of M.M. Ivanov at the St Petersburg academy of fine arts. He painted and above all engraved a great number of landscapes. We also owe him portraits of the Russian Royal Family.

AUCTION RECORDS:
LONDON, 5 March 1981, *A Monastery near Moscow* (watercolour, 6 ins / 15 cm 10 ins/25.5 cm) GBP 230.

GALAN, Julio
Mexican, 20th - 21st century.
Born 1958 or 1959, in Muzquiz (Coahuila).
Also active in the USA.
Painter.

As a young man, Julio Galan moved to Monterrey in northern Mexico. From 1978 to 1982 he studied architecture.

Galan was an admirer of Frida Kahlo and his painting shows similarities with her work. He uses themes of popular and Mexican Catholic imagery but always with a Surrealist irony, combining these with other images, intimate evocations, children's illustrations and Pre-Columbian icons. It is often difficult to find a common meaning in his work as the temptation to see it as simply narrative is thwarted by the clear interplay of mysterious associations.

Julio Galan has taken part in group exhibitions, the most recent being: *Art in Intercultural Limbo*, Rooseum, Malmö; *Myth and Magic in America - the 1980s*, New Museum of Contemporary Art, Monterrey and *Magiciens de la Terre* (*Magicians of the Earth*), Musée Nationale d'Art Moderne, Centre Georges Pompidou and Grande Halle de la Vilette, Paris (1991); *Artistes Latino-Américains* (*Latin American Artists*), Galerie Daniel Templon, Paris (1997); *Phantom der Lust. Visionen des Machochismus in der Kunst* (*Phantom of Desire. Visions of Masochism in Art*), an exhibition devoted to Sacher-Masoch, the creator of masochism, Neue Galerie am Landesmuseum, Graz (2003). Galan has also shown his work in solo exhibitions: Gallery of Contemporary Mexican Art, Monterrey, (1980, 1982 and 1983); Clave Gallery, Guadalajara (1984); Mexican Consulate, New York (1985); Barbara Farber Gallery, Amsterdam (1986); Monterrey Museum (1987); Sperone Gallery, Rome (1990); Witte de With Centre for Contemporary Art, Rotterdam (1990); Thaddeus Ropac Gallery, Paris (1999).

BIBLIOGRAPHY:
Martin, Jean-Hubert/Mark, Francis/Magnin, André/Marcadé, Bernard, *Les Magiciens de la terre*, exhibition catalogue, Éd. du Centre Georges-Pompidou, Paris, 1989. Pellizi, Francesco, *Julio Galan*, exhibition catalogue, Annina Nosei Gall., New York, 1990. Poot, Jurrie, *Julio Galan: pastels*, Stedelijk Museum, Amsterdam, 1992. *Julio Galan*, exhibition catalogue, Timothy Taylor Gallery, 1998. Weibel, Peter (ed.), '*Phantom der Lust. Visionen des Masochismus in der Kunst*' in *2 vol.*, exhibition catalogue, Neue Galerie am Landesmuseum, Graz, Belleville Verlag, Munich, 2003.

AUCTION RECORDS:
NEW YORK, 18 Nov 1987, *The Accomplices* (1987, oil on canvas, 74 3/4 x 90 1/2 ins / 190 x 230 cm) USD 7,500. NEW YORK, 19-20 Nov 1990, *Clown* (1980, oil on canvas, 63 3/4 x 47 ins / 162 x 119.2 cm) USD 19,800. NEW YORK, 25 Nov 1992, *The Plaything* (1984, oil and collage/canvas, 20 x 26 ins / 51 x 66 cm) USD 7,150. NEW YORK, 18 May 1994, *The Ball of the 9* (oil and pastel with collage of mica/canvas, 31 1/2 x 23 1/2 ins / 80 x 60 cm) USD 10,925. NEW YORK, 29-30 May 1997, *Niño Elefante Tomando Elerat 7 (From the Medication Series)* (1985, oil and acrylic/canvas, 46 x 74 ins / 117 x 188 cm) USD 43,125. NEW YORK, 2 June 1999, *El Lobo sí se comió de verdad a Caperucita* (*The Wolf Really Did Eat Little Red Riding Hood*) (pastel and collage on paper, 39 x 28 ins / 100 x 70 cm) USD 13,000. LONDON, 29 June 1999, *Tiziana* (pastel and collage on card, 26 x 20 ins / 65 x 50 cm) GBP 2,800. NEW YORK, 20 Nov 2000, *Así fue* (*It was like that*) (1993, oil, acrylic and collage on canvas, 24 x 20 ins / 60 x 51 cm) USD 8,000. NEW YORK, 20 Nov 2000, *Untitled* (1997, oil and collage on canvas, 75 x 52 ins / 190 x 131 cm) USD 35,000. NEW YORK, 30 May 2001, *Double Life* (1991, mixed media assemblage on canvas, 71 x 90 ins / 180 x 229 cm) USD 18,000. NEW YORK, 31 May 2001, *Aladdin and Queen Victoria* (1990, oil, acrylic and collage elements on canvas, 91 x 59 ins / 230 x 149 cm) USD 21,000. NEW YORK, 19 Nov 2002, *Argentina* (1980, oil, mixed media and collage on canvas, 39 x 39 ins / 99 x 100 cm) USD 12,000. NEW YORK, 20 Nov 2002, *Like a Garden* (1990, oil and collage on paper, 83 x 63 ins / 210 x 160 cm) USD 48,000. NEW YORK, 26 May 2004, *Collage* (1998, oil, collage and mixed media on canvas, 75 x 51 ins / 190 x 130 cm) USD 24,000.

GALAN, N.
Spanish, 19th century.
Born 19th century.
Engraver.

N. Galan worked for a number of journals and magazines.

GALAN Y SANCHEZ, Rafael
Spanish, 19th century.
Born in Madrid.
Sculptor. Groups.

MUSEUMS AND GALLERIES:
MADRID (Prado): *At School* (plaster group).

GALAND, Jules
French, 19th - 20th century.
Born 1869; died 1924, in Saigon, Indochina (now Ho Chi Minh City, Vietnam).
Painter, pastellist.

Jules Galand was a second lieutenant in Indochina and travelled in Japan where he discovered Japanese engravings and lacquerware. After returning to France he worked under the direction of the painter and engraver Henri Paillard. He was promoted to colonel and at the end of World War I was posted to Marrakech and then to Rabat. He went to Saigon in 1923. A retrospective of his work was held at the Galerie Charpentier in Paris in 1927.

His powerfully coloured, balanced work displays a fine, lively touch.

BIBLIOGRAPHY:
André-Pallois, Nadine/Ménonville, Corinne de, *Paris-Hanoï-Saigon, l'aventure de l'art moderne au Viêt Nam*, exhibition catalogue, Pavillon des Arts, Paris, 1998.

GALAND, Léon Laurent
French, 20th century.
Born 18 April 1872, in Montpellier; died 14 November 1960, in Clichy-la-Garenne.
Painter, illustrator. Figure compositions, figures, nudes, portraits.

Léon Galand was awarded a bursary by the town of Montpellier and studied under E. Michel, Delauney, G. Moreau, Cormon and Blanc. He exhibited regularly in Paris at the Salon des Artistes Français, of which he became a member in 1904. He received numerous awards, including: second prize in the Prix de Rome; a commendation in 1903 at the Salon des Artistes Français; a bronze medal in 1909; and a gold medal. He was decorated by the Légion d'Honneur.

Galand is known for his portraits and nudes. He also illustrated *Aline, Reine de Golconde*.

L. GALAND

Museums and Galleries:
Montpellier: *The Flaying of Marsyas; Vulcan, Assisted by Strength and Violence, Enchains Prometheus.*
Auction records:
Paris, 24-26 April 1929, *The Bar at the Folies-Bergères*, FRF 270. Paris, 24 Sept 1946, *Young Female Nude Seated by a Hearth*, FRF 700. Lucerne, 20 May 1980, *Reclining Nude, Seen from the Back* (1929, oil on canvas, 28 3/4 x 39 3/4 ins / 73 x 101 cm) CHF 1,500. Lyons, 18 March 1987, *Pastorale; Country Dance* (1910, oil on canvas, a pair, 108 1/4 x 128 ins / 275 x 325 cm) FRF 275,000. Rheims, 24 Oct 1987, *Reclining Female Nude* (oil on canvas, 18 x 22 ins / 46 x 55 cm) FRF 2,800. Paris, 19 June 1989, *Young Female Nude Reclining* (oil on canvas, 9 1/2 x 16 1/4 ins / 24 x 41 cm) FRF 6,000. Paris, 26 Jan 1990, *The Bois de Boulogne* (oil on canvas, 18 1/2 x 20 3/4 ins / 47 x 53 cm) FRF 4,800. Stockholm, 24 Nov 1999, *Scene of Parisian Life* (1904, oil on canvas, 20 x 24 ins / 51 x 62 cm) SEK 68,000. Paris, 26 Jan 2000, *Boats on the Quay* (oil on canvas, 20 x 24 ins / 50 x 60 cm) FRF 15,500. New Orleans, 29 July 2000, *Still-life with Oranges and Brioche* (oil on canvas, 10 x 14 ins / 25 x 36 cm) USD 3,400. London, 8 Feb 2001, *Ladies in the Midst of a Walk with Mountains Beyond* (oil on canvas, 15 x 18 ins / 38 x 46 cm) GBP 1,600. Paris, 24 April 2002, *Narcissus* (1896, oil on canvas, 38 x 57 ins / 97 x 146 cm) EUR 5,800. Brussels, 1 Oct 2002, *Young Woman Reading in the Garden* (oil on canvas, 20 x 24 ins / 50 x 61 cm) EUR 4,600.

GALAND, Madeleine
French, 20th century.
Born in Laval (Mayenne).
Painter.

Madeleine Galand exhibited in Paris at the Salon des Indépendants from 1935.

GALANDA, Mikulas
Slovak, 20th century.
Born 4 May 1895, in Turcianske Teplice; died 5 June 1938, in Bratislava.
Painter.

Mikuláš Galanda studied at the academy of fine art in Budapest between 1914 and 1916 and in 1922 at the school of arts and crafts in Prague with V.H. Brunner. From then until 1927 he attended Brömse's and Thiele's workshops at the academy of fine art in Prague and was involved at this time, between 1924 and 1926, in putting together the magazine *Dav*, mouthpiece of the left-wing intelligentsia. In 1930, he travelled to Paris and on his return, he taught at the school of arts and crafts in Bratislava from 1930 until he died. Between 1930 and 1932, he wrote and published with Fulla the *Private Letters*, the first manifesto of modern art in Slovakia. He also worked in theatrical art and graphic art. Galanda's painting bears the mark of its human content at every stage. Its form, which is the result of bold simplifications and distortions, preserves its lyrical, melancholic accent, a melancholia in which Galanda saw the reflection of the Slovak soul he was trying to convey in painting, aiming at reaching beyond simple folklore.

In the 1930s Mikuláš Galanda took part in exhibitions of Slovak art and in the Exposition Universelle in Paris in 1937, receiving a silver medal for graphic art. In 1939 was held a posthumous exhibition of his work.

GALANINI, Il. See **ALOISI Baldassare**

GALANIS, Demetrios Emmanuel
Greek, 20th century.
Born 23 May 1882, in Athens; died 20 March 1966.
Active and naturalised in France in 1916.
Painter, watercolourist, draughtsman (ink/wash/red chalk/charcoal), newspaper cartoonist, engraver (etching), illustrator. Nudes, portraits, scenes with figures, landscapes, still-lifes, animals.

Demetrios Emmanuel Galanis attended the Cormon workshop of the École des Beaux-Arts in Paris in 1900. He enrolled at the outbreak of war in 1914, and while serving in Corfu he acquired French nationality. A member of the Institute, he taught at the École Nationale des Beaux-Arts.

To begin with, Galanis became known particularly as a landscape painter. He made a living by collaborating with comic magazines of the time: *L'Assiette au Beurre, Gil Blas, Le Rire*. In no way a cartoonist, Galanis has left thumbnail sketches, all of which make up a true panorama of the brothels at the beginning of the 20th century. Galanis who mixed with the best painters and writers of his time like Jean Moréas, was determined to move on and become an eminent engraver sought after by publishers of luxury books.

He illustrated a hundred or so works with his engravings, including: *Le Deuil des Primevères* (*The Mourning of the Primroses*) by F. Jammes; *Voyage musical au pays du passé* (*Musical Journey to the Country of the Past*) by R. Rolland; *La Gageure* (*The Challenge*) by Brébeuf; *Les Nuits d'octobre* (*October Nights*) by G. de Nerval; *Bouclier du Zodiaque* (*Shield of the Zodiac*) by A. Suarès; *Coeurs à prendre* (*Coeurs à prendre*) by G. Gabory; *La Nuit de Saint Barnabé* (*St Barnabas Night*) by A. Arnoux; *Female Lover* by G. de Porto-Riche; *Laurette ou le cachet rouge* (*Laurette or the Red Seal*) by Alfred de Vigny; *La Célestine* (*Celestine*) by F. de Rojas; *La Bohême de mon coeur* (*The Bohemian girl of my heart*) by F. Carco; *Poésies pour dames seules* (*Poems for Single Ladies*) by G. Gabory; *Inscriptions pour les sept péchés capitaux* (*Inscriptions for the Seven Capital Sins*) by R. Allard; *Terres étrangères* (*Foreign Lands*) by M. Arland; *entations d'Alec Souffi, Akrivie Phrangopoulo* (*Temptations of Alec Souffi, Akrivie Phrangopoulo*) by Count Gobineau; *Les grandes orgues* (*The Great Organ*) by H. Bachelin; *Rien que la terre* (*The Land Alone*) by P. Morand; *La Mort d'Hippolyte* (*Death of Hippolytus*) by J. de Lacretelle; *Polyphème* (*Polyphemus*) by A. Samain; *Le Grand Meaulnes* (*Le Grand Meaulnes*) by A. Fournier; *Monique* by M. Arland; *Odes* by P. Valéry; *Nourritures terrestres* by André Gide; *Deux dialogues* (*Two Dialogues*) by Crébillion fils; *Paradise Lost and Paradise Regained* by Milton.

Galanis' landscapes of the South of France are particularly prized as is the *Child on a Mechanical Horse*, a fine portrait of the artist's son who died in the war. G. Gabory and A. Malraux devoted monographs to Galanis' work. André Malraux was particularly attached to the painter, of whom he wrote: 'Galanis can be compared with many of the old masters; he cannot be subjected to any one. He always differs in some essential aspect because his art is part of the art world of today, its style profoundly modern'. He exhibited for the first time in Paris in 1904 at the Salon of the Société Nationale des Beaux-Arts and also featured at the Salon d'Automne and at the Salon des Humoristes. A posthumous exhibition was organised in 1976.

D. Galanis.

D. G

Bibliography:
Gabory, G., *Galanis*, La Nouvelle Revue Française, Paris, 1926. Beucler, A., *Portrait de D. Galanis*, Manuel Bruker, 1954 (decorated with original etchings).
Auction records:
Paris, 25 March 1921, *Still-life*, FRF 300. Paris, 18 June 1925, *Woman with a basket*, FRF 385. Paris, 12 and 13 Oct 1942, *Still-life with Fruit*, FRF 520. Paris, 20 June 1944, *Still-life with Pheasants*, FRF 9,500. Paris, Oct 1945-July 1946, *Liber-*

ation (monochrome painting) FRF 1,500. PARIS, 9 July 1980, *Nude Standing, Arms Raised* (etching heightened with colouring pencil) FRF 1,100. PARIS, 8 Dec 1980, *Oriental Woman* (watercolour, 9 x 5½ ins / 23 x 14 cm) FRF 2,000. VERSAILLES, 1 March 1981, *Rotten Luck* (watercolour, 10¾ x 9¾ ins / 27.5 x 25 cm) FRF 5,100. LONDON, 8 May 1985, *Still-life with Figs* (oil on card, 7¼ x 14¾ ins / 18.5 x 37.7 cm) GBP 1,400. PARIS, 8 Dec 1987, *Rue Cortot* (oil on canvas, 16¼ x 13 ins / 41 x 33 cm) FRF 7,000. PARIS, 17 Feb 1988, *Provençal Landscape* (oil on canvas, 23½ x 30 ins / 60 x 76 cm) FRF 70,000. LONDON, 24 Feb 1988, *Two Nudes on the Beach* (pastel, 19½ x 16¼ ins / 49.5 x 41 cm) GBP 2,640. PARIS, 6 May 1988, *Rocky Landscape* (1918, oil on canvas, 36¼ x 28¾ ins / 92 x 73 cm) FRF 40,000. PARIS, 5 July 1988, *Beloved Animals* (c. 1905, lead pencil, Indian ink, white gouache heightenings, 13 x 9¾ ins / 33 x 25 cm) FRF 6,000. PARIS, 12 Oct 1988, *What Dirty Fingers you Have! (intimate scene)* (charcoal, Indian ink wash and blue pencil, 13½ x 10¾ ins / 34.5 x 27.5 cm) FRF 2,500. PARIS, 30 March 1995, *Portrait of a Woman* (graphite, 24¾ x 19 ins / 63 x 48 cm) FRF 3,500. PARIS, 5 Dec 1997, *Nude with Tambourine* (red chalk, 25½ x 19¾ ins / 65 x 50 cm) FRF 3,000. PARIS, 5 Feb 1998, *Landscape* (1957, red chalk, 12¼ x 18½ ins / 31 x 47 cm) FRF 1,800.

GALANO, Orazio
Italian, 19th century.
Active in Naples (Campania) in 1858.
Painter.

GALANT, René
French, 20th century.
Born 1914, in the Dordogne; died 26 January 1997.
Painter. Designs for tapestries.

After travelling, René Galant attended the Académie Julian and the Académie de la Grande-Chaumière in Paris. He held solo exhibitions of his work in Paris, St-Tropez, Geneva and Brussels.

galant

AUCTION RECORDS:
ZURICH, 8 Nov 1985, *At the Café* (oil on canvas, 23½ x 28¾ ins / 59.5 x 73 cm) CHF 3,800. LA VARENNE-ST-HILAIRE, 16 June 1990, *At the Café* (1974, oil on canvas, 21¼ x 25¼ ins / 54 x 64 cm) FRF 7,000. PARIS, 14 Dec 1992, *Dance* (tapestry, 70¾ x 94½ ins / 180 x 240 cm) FRF 40,000.

GALANTE, Francesco
Italian, 20th century.
Born 1884; died 1972, in Naples.
Painter. Genre scenes, landscapes.

AUCTION RECORDS:
MILAN, 10 June 1981, *Paris Streets* (two oils on panel, 10¼ x 15 ins / 26 x 38 cm) ITL 2,000,000. ROME, 1 June 1983, *The Dancing Lesson* (oil on panel, 11¾ x 19¾ ins / 30 x 50 cm) ITL 1,400,000. ROME, 19 Nov 1992, *Towards the Bay* (oil/plywood, 11½ x 18¾ ins / 29 x 47.5 cm) ITL 4,600,000. MILAN, 22 March 1994, *Posillipo seen from Villa Cappella* (oil on panel, 6 x 7¾ ins / 15 x 20 cm) ITL 1,380,000. ROME, 13 Dec 1994, *The Mender of Earthenware* (oil on canvas, 15¼ x 14¼ ins / 39 x 36 cm) ITL 4,025,000. ROME, 23 May 1996, *Motherhood* (oil on canvas, 15¾ x 19¾ ins / 40 x 50 cm) ITL 2,760,000. NAPLES, 9 Nov 1999, *Morning at Mergellina* (oil on canvas, 16x20ins / 40x50 cm) ITL 3,800,000. NAPLES, 9 Nov 1999, *Woman with Blonde Hair* (oil on canvas, 32x28 ins / 82x70 cm) ITL 9,000,000. ROME, 14 Nov 2000, *Posillipo* (1930-1940, oil on cardboard, 10x14 ins / 25x35 cm) ITL 2,200,000. ROME, 14 Nov 2000, *Bourgeois Interior* (oil on board, 18x22 ins / 45x55 cm) ITL 5,500,000. VIENNA, 16 April 2002, *Piazze Dante in Naples* (oil on panel, 6x9 ins / 16x22 cm) EUR 1,000. ROME, 11 June 2003, *Coastal View with Bathers* (oil on canvas/board, 10x14 ins / 25x35 cm) EUR 1,200. NAPLES, 19 May 2004, *Reading* (oil on canvas, 26x21 ins / 67x53 cm) EUR 6,500. NAPLES, 11 Dec 2004, *Pine Trees Overlooking Naples* (oil on canvas, 22x26 ins / 55x65 cm) EUR 9,000.

GALANTE, Severino
Italian, 18th - 19th century.
Born c. 1750, in Civitella Casanova; died 1827.
Painter.

Severino Galante studied under Mengs and Batoni. He worked in Naples with Bonito.

GALANTE DA BOLOGNA
Italian, 14th century.
Born 14th century, in Bologna.
Painter. History painting, portraits.

A pupil of Lippo di Dalmasio, Galante is said to have surpassed his teacher in the art of drawing.

GALANTINI, Ippolito, called Il Cappucino, also known as Il Prete Genevese
Italian, 17th century.
Born 1627, in Florence; died 1706, in the monastery of Montughie.
Painter. History painting.

Ippolito Galantini studied under Padre Stefaneschi, who influenced his decision to take holy orders and become a Capuchin monk, which lead to his two soubriquets: Il Cappucino and Il Prete Genevese. Galantini was sent as a missionary to the Indies, where he spent a number of years. On his return to Europe he painted several compositions for churches of the Capuchin order. His self-portrait is in the Uffizi in Florence.

GALARD
French, 19th century.
Born 1846, in Marseilles.
Sculptor.

He was possibly a member of the Galard family, and is known to have sculpted several busts.

GALARD, Georges de
French, 19th century.
Born in Bordeaux; died 1834, in Bordeaux.
Painter.

H was the son of Count Gustave de Galard. He exhibited female portraits at the Paris Salon, but died young.

MUSEUMS AND GALLERIES:
BORDEAUX: *Chimney Sweep (study)*.

GALARD, Gustave de (Comte)
French, 19th century.
Born 1779, in the château at Lille; died 1841, in Bordeaux.
Painter, draughtsman, caricaturist. Portraits, landscapes, landscapes with figures, flowers.

He exhibited at the 1838 Paris Salon. Comte Gustave de Galard spent several months in prison for drawing caricatures that found disfavour with Louis-Philippe. He is also remembered for a painting entitled *View of the Landes near Bordeaux*.

BIBLIOGRAPHY:
Coustet, Robert, '*The Landes in the Painting of Bordeaux*' in *Bulletin de la Société de Borda*, 1977.

MUSEUMS AND GALLERIES:
BORDEAUX (MBA): *Portrait of Jean Armand de Mareilhac; Portrait of Joseph Desforges; View of the Teste; Portraits of M. and Mme Marandon de Montyel* - MONTPELLIER: *Portrait of a Young Woman* - QUIMPER (MBA): *Shepherds in the Landes; Landscape with Livestock*.

AUCTION RECORDS:
PARIS, 25 June 1990, *Bouquet of Flowers* (oil on canvas, 13½ x 11 ins / 34.5 x 27 cm) FRF 25,000. MONACO, 7 Dec 1990, *Bouquet of Flowers* (oil on canvas, 13 x 10in/33 x 24.5cm) FRF 33,300. RENNES, 7 Oct 2001, *Portrait of Madame Tronquoy de la Lande* (1826, oil on canvas, 30 x 24 ins / 77 x 62 cm) FRF 14,000.

GALASSI, G.
Italian, 18th - 19th century.
Active in Sardinia.
Sculptor.
G. Galassi is credited with having sculpted the tomb of the wife of Louis XVIII, Queen Josepha Marie-Louise, who died in 1810 and was entombed in Cagliari Cathedral.

GALASSI, Luigi
Italian, 18th century.
Active in Bologna and Sardinia.
Painter, musician.

GALASSI, Vincenzo
Italian, 19th century.
Active in Rome.
Sculptor, engraver.
Vincenzo Galassi illustrated a book on St Benedict by A. M. Ricci.

GALASSI-GALASSO, also known as Galasso di Matteo Piva
Italian, 15th century.
Born c. 1423, in Ferrara; died c. 1473.
Painter. History painting, portraits.
Galassi-Galasso's earliest works can be seen in the Ferrara Museum. In Ferrara, it is also possible to see a *Trinity* (at the Castabili Gallery), an *Entombment* and a *Virgin and Child*. From the accounting records of the Este court, we know that he was employed in decorating the Palazzo di Belreguardo from 1450 to 1453. In 1455, he painted an *Annunciation* and completed a *Portrait of Cardinal Bessarton*, which can be seen at S Maria in Monte, Bologna. The Marchese Strozzi owns a *Crucifixion* by him, and Professor Saroli a *Christ on the Mount of Olives*

GALASSINI, Giovanni Angelo
Swiss, 17th century.
Born in Lugano (Ticino).
Sculptor.
Galassini worked at the church of St Peter in Rome.

GALATA, José
Spanish, 19th century.
Born in the 19th century, in Valencia.
Painter. Portraits.
José Galata is known for his portrait of King Alfonso XIII.

GALATERI, Filiberto, also known as Carle di Genola
Italian, 19th century.
Born 1846, in Cheprasco.
Painter. Landscapes.
Galateri studied initially under Perotti, and then under Calame. He mostly painted landscapes of the Piedmont region, exhibiting in Turin, Milan and Venice.

GALATERI DI GENOLA, Annibale (Count)
Italian, 19th century.
Born 1864, in Savigliano (Piedmont).
Sculptor.
Aninibale Galateri di Genola studied in Rome and Turin, and is remembered for his *Monument to General Arimondi*.

GALATIN, Hans
Swiss, 16th century.
Active c. 1550.
Draughtsman, sculptor (wood).
This artist may be identical to H.C. Gallati, a maker of stained glass.

GALATON
2nd century BC.
Painter.
Ancient Greek.
Galaton is thought to have worked in Alexandria in Egypt.

GALAUT, or Galaud
French, 18th century.
Sculptor.
A member of the Académie de St-Luc, Galaut featured in the 1753 exhibition with a low relief: *Apollo after the Defeat of Python the Serpent, Encountering Love and Contempt*.

GALAY, J.
Dutch, 17th century.
Painter. Genre scenes.
Galay is mentioned by Siret.

GALBATI, Giovanni
Italian, 16th century.
Active in Sicily.
Sculptor.
Galbati worked for Troina Cathedral.

GALBERG, Samuel Friedrich Ivanovich.
See **HALLBERG**

GALBESIO, Giuseppe
Italian, 17th century.
Active in Milan and Brescia during the first half of the 17th century.
Painter.

GALBICH, J.
19th century.
Born 1814, in Russia; died 1882.
Sculptor.
MUSEUMS AND GALLERIES:
ST PETERSBURG (Gosudarstvennyj Russkij Muz.): *Bust of the Grand Duchess Helena Powlowna.*

GALBIENI Y MERSEGUER, Antonio
Spanish, 19th century.
Born 19th century, in Valencia.
Painter. History painting, portraits.
Antonio Galbieni y Merseguer studied at the Academia de San Fernando in Valencia. He first exhibited around 1864 and went on to exhibit in Valencia, Madrid and Malaga. In 1876 he was appointed as a teacher at the school of fine arts in Malaga.

GALBRAITH, Thomas
British, 16th century.
Active in Scotland c. 1500.
Painter.
Galbraith worked with Charlmer on the royal palaces of Stirling and Falkland (Fife).

GALBRAITH, W.C.
British, 19th century.
Active in Whilley.
Painter. Landscapes.
W.C. Galbraith was a frequent exhibitor in London, notably at the Suffolk Street Gallery from 1866 to 1870.

GALBRIS
French.
Painter. Landscapes.
MUSEUMS AND GALLERIES:
ROUEN: a landscape.

GALBRUND, Alphonse-Louis
French, 19th century.

Born 30 June 1810, in Paris; died 3 June 1885, in Neuilly (Hauts-de-Seine).
Painter, pastellist, draughtsman. Allegorical subjects, portraits, animals.

He enrolled at the École des Beaux-Arts on 2 April 1828, where he studied under Regnault and Gros. He exhibited at the Paris Salon between 1839 and 1880, and was awarded a silver medal in 1865. In 1842 he travelled to Naples, where he painted portraits of *Princess Gagarine* and *Prince Stroganoff's Son*. Galbrund was appointed curator of Le Havre Museum in 1870. Most of his work comprises pastel portraits.

Museums and Galleries:
Le Havre: *The Schoolgirl*; *Portrait of the Curé of St-Eustache-la-Forêt*; *Woman Collecting in the Street at the Time of the First Empire*; *Maidservant at the time of Louis XV* - Louviers (Mus. municipal): *Peasant Woman of the 18th Century*; *Allegorical Figure* - Paris (Louvre): *Young Housekeeper* - Rouen: *Grandmother*.

Auction records:
Paris, 17 March 1910, *Portrait of a Young Man* (1843, lead pencil, heightened with pastels) FRF 62. Monte Carlo, 23 June 1985, *Child with Dog* (1870, pastel, 36 x 28 1/4 ins / 91 x 72 cm) FRF 15,500. London, 9 March 2004, *Portrait of a Young Lady* (1876, pastel, 21 x 12 ins / 53 x 31 cm) GBP 1,000.

GALBRUND, Marie-Laurence

French, 19th century.
Painter, pastellist. Still-lifes.

She exhibited a pastel entitled *Apples on a Plate* at the 1897 Salon.

Museums and Galleries:
Pontoise: *Apples on a Plate* (pastel).

GALBRUNNER, Louise C.

French, 19th century.
Painter.

She was a member of the Société des Artistes Français from 1887 and participated in its exhibitions.

GALBRUNNER, Norbert Louis

French, 19th century.
Sculptor.

He was a member of the Société des Artistes Français from 1894 and participated in various of its exhibitions.

GALBRUNNER, P. Charles

French, 19th century.
Died 1905.
Engraver.

He was a member of the Société des Artistes Français.

GALBUSERA, Gioachimo or Giovacchino

Italian, 19th - 20th century.
Born 2 April 1870 or 1871, in Milan; died 1944, in Lugano (Ticino canton), Switzerland.
Painter. Landscapes, mountainscapes, still-lifes (flowers/fruit).

Galbusera worked mostly in Lugano.

Auction records:
Bern, 22 Oct 1982, *View of the Bernese Oberland* (1912, oil on panel, 17 1/4 x 13 1/2 ins / 43.5 x 34 cm) CHF 1,800. Lucerne, 3 June 1987, *Bosco* (oil on panel, octagonal, 25 1/2 x 25 1/2 ins / 64.5 x 64.5 cm) CHF 7,000. Monaco, 21 April 1990, *Still-life with Peaches and Grapes* (oil on canvas, 34 x 21 ins / 85.5 x 53.5 cm) FRF 88,800. London, 20 Nov 1996, *Alpine Landscape* (oil on canvas, 35 1/2 x 43 3/4 ins / 90 x 111 cm) GBP 10,925. Zurich, 10 Dec 1996, *Still-life with Roses* (oil/Pavatex, 20 1/2 x 24 1/2 ins / 52 x 62 cm) CHF 4,600. Bern, 7 May 1999, *Figures and Boats on Shore of Lake Lugano* (oil on canvas, 12 x 19 ins / 30 x 47 cm) CHF 4,000. Bern, 12 May 2000, *Mountain Lake* (oil on panel, 18 x 20 ins / 45 x 51 cm) CHF 4,800. Bern, 3 Nov 2000, *Still-life with Flowers* (oil on canvas, 33 x 23 ins / 84 x 59 cm) CHF 7,000. Bern, 9 Nov 2001, *Rocky Hill with Birch Trees* (oil on masonite, 14 x 10 ins / 35 x 26 cm) CHF 3,000. Bern, 9 Nov 2001, *San Bernardino with View of Lake Moesola* (oil on panel, 25 x 33 ins / 64 x 84 cm) CHF 17,000. Bern, 8 Nov 2002, *Piz Uccello, San Bernardino* (oil on masonite, 18 x 21 ins / 46 x 54 cm) CHF 4,200. Bern, 8 Nov 2002, *Chapel in Ticino* (oil on canvas, 25 x 33 ins / 63 x 84 cm) CHF 4,600. Bern, 9 May 2003, *San Bernardino with View of the Moesolasee* (oil on masonite, 14 x 19 ins / 35 x 49 cm) CHF 6,000. Bern, 7 Nov 2003, *Flower Children* (oil on canvas, 59 x 38 ins / 151 x 96 cm) CHF 13,000. Bern, 14 May 2004, *Still-life with Pears and Black Grapes* (oil on canvas, 11 x 22 ins / 28 x 57 cm) CHF 4,200. Bern, 14 May 2004, *Woman Walking in Ticino Alps* (oil on canvas, 12 x 20 ins / 31 x 52 cm) CHF 4,500.

GALCEPTIANOV, S. F.

Russian, 19th century.
Born 1809; died 1854.
Painter. Military subjects.

The Tretyakov Gallery has a work by this artist entitled: *Military manoeuvres in 1804*.

GALCERAN, Antonio

Spanish, 16th century.
Painter. Genre scenes.

A pupil of Esquarte, Antonio Galceran moved from Italy to Saragossa in 1580. He painted in the bishop's palace and in the cathedral at Barbastro.

GALCERAN, Balthasar

Spanish, 16th century.
Active in Valencia in 1513.
Painter.

GALCERAN, Vicente

Spanish, 18th century.
Born 1726, in Valencia; died 9 July 1788, in Valencia.
Engraver. Portraits, natural history.

Vicente Galceran was a pupil of Ravanals and Rovira. At the age of 12 he made an engraving of *St Vincent Ferrer*. In 1750 he went to Madrid and shortly after was employed by the chapter of Toledo to touch up various plates sent from Rome by Cardinal Portocarrero. He also worked for natural history publications, made portrait engravings of the kings of Spain for Berni's *Titulos de la Castilla* (*Castilian Nobility*) (printed in Valencia in 1769), and produced a portrait engraving of Bishop Cervera of Cádiz among others. It is said that he left no fewer than 700 plates when he died.

GALDIKAS, Adas

Lithuanian, 20th century.
Born 1893, in Lithuania; died 1969.
Painter.

Adas Galdikas initially painted landscapes and traditional subjects. Inspired by French examples, he then moved more towards plasticity, freeing himself from his initial literary intentions. He was a colourist with a sense of movement.

GALDOU, Jean

French, 20th century.
Born 28 February 1901, in Paris.
Painter, engraver.

Jean Galdou exhibited in Paris at the Salon d'Automne and the Salon des Indépendants. He illustrated *St Dominic* by Bernanos.

GALE, André

Italian, 16th century.
Active in Rome at the end of the 16th century.
Engraver (wood).

Gale is mentioned by Nagler.

GALE, Ann

American, 20th century.

Born in the USA.
Painter.
Ann Gale's paintings depict a universe of dereliction, where suspended time can no longer satisfy the existential turpitude of the characters. She uses the Impressionist technique to give a hazy image of them, creating a pictorial blur, but actually giving a view of the other side and in many aspects the harsh reality of the mirror image. She showed her works in a solo exhibition at the Dean Jensen gallery in Milwaukee in 1995.

BIBLIOGRAPHY:
Scarborough, James, '*Ann Gale*' in *Art Press* n° 206, periodical, Paris, October 1995.

GALE, George
British, 20th century.
Born 16 November 1893, in Bristol; died 1951.
Active in the USA.
Painter, illustrator, etcher. Marine life, nautical scenes.
George Gale was born in Bristol but soon moved to the USA. He worked in the whaling industry and was best known as one of Rhode Islands most accomplished nautical painters. He was also a member of many artists' associations.

GALE, R.L.
British, 19th century.
Active in Liverpool.
Painter. Landscapes.
R.L. Gale was a member of the Society of British Artists. He exhibited in London from 1832 to 1841, notably at the Royal Academy and the Suffolk Street Gallery.

GALE, Walter R.
American, 20th century.
Born 17 January 1878, in Maryland.
Painter, illustrator.
Walter Gale produced very elaborate studies. He was a member of the American Federation of Art.

GALE, William
British, 19th - 20th century.
Born 1823, in London; died 1909.
Painter, watercolourist. History painting, religious subjects, portraits, genre scenes, local scenes.
William Gale was a prolific artist who played a very active part in exhibitions in London from 1844, particularly those of the Royal Academy, the British Institution and the Suffolk Street Gallery. His name appears frequently in English sales catalogues.

MUSEUMS AND GALLERIES:
GLASGOW: *Dance of the Nymphs* (1855).

AUCTION RECORDS:
LONDON, 1861, *The Eyes of the Blindman* (watercolour) FRF 2,750. LONDON, 1870, *M. F.'s Aunt*, FRF 1,575. LONDON, 1875, *Jew's Place of Wailing*, FRF 7,700. LONDON, 1 Feb 1908, *Peasants and Priest*, GBP 3; *Head of a Child*, GBP 4. LONDON, 6 Feb 1909, *M. F's Aunt*, GBP 24. LONDON, 4 Feb 1911, *Young Girl*, GBP 9. LONDON, 7 Feb 1930, *The Song of the Prophetess Myriam*, GBP 5. LONDON, 28 March 1930, *A Little Cardinal*, GBP 11. LONDON, 11 July 1934, *The Wailing Wall, Jerusalem*, GBP 14. LONDON, 28 Jan 1972, *Invasion of the Danes*, Gns 600. LONDON, 31 March 1978, *Algerian Water Carriers* (oil on canvas, 26 x 34 ins / 66 x 86.5 cm) GBP 800. NEW YORK, 5 March 1981, *Isabella and the Pot of Basil* (oil on panel, 11 1/4 x 16 1/4 ins / 28.5 x 41 cm) USD 550. CHESTER, 17 Jan 1986, *Two Lovers* (oil on card, 10 x 6 1/2 ins / 24.5 x 16.5 cm) GBP 3,500. LONDON, 21 March 1990, *Rosalind* (oil on panel, 7 x 5 ins / 18 x 12.5 cm) GBP 770. LONDON, 13 Nov 1992, *In a Near Eastern Garden* (oil on canvas, 50 1/2 x 40 ins / 128.3 x 101.6 cm) GBP 9,020. LONDON, 6 June 1996, *Young Beauty, Head and Shoulders* (1866, oil on panel, diam. 8 1/2 ins / 21.5 cm) GBP 1,150. NEW YORK, 18-19 July 1996, *Apprentice in a Studio* (oil on canvas, 39 1/2 x 50 ins / 100.3 x 127 cm) USD 4,312. LONDON, 14 March 1997, *Fig Seller, Nazareth* (oil on canvas, 25 1/4 x 12 1/2 ins / 64 x 32 cm) GBP 2,760.

GALEA, Luigi Maria
Maltese, 19th - 20th century.
Born 1847; died 1917.
Painter. Landscapes, seascapes.
Works by Luigi Galea were late to appear at public auction. Although his name suggests he was of Italian origin, his work suggests that he lived in Malta. Galea specialised in painting town views and particularly the port of Valletta in Malta.

AUCTION RECORDS:
LONDON, 5 Oct 1990, *The Port of Valletta; The Medina, Malta* (1904, oil on card, 11 1/4 x 30 1/4 ins / 28.8 x 77 cm) GBP 4,180. LONDON, 18 Oct 1990, *The 'Furious' Leaving the Port of Valletta* (1904, oil on canvas, 11 x 20 3/4 ins / 28 x 53 cm) GBP 1,100. LONDON, 17 May 1991, *Valletta at Sunrise; Valletta at Sunset* (oil/card, a pair, each 6 x 13 1/4 ins / 15 x 33.5 cm) GBP 2,090. LONDON, 20 May 1992, *The Cruiser 'Caesar' off Valletta* (1902, oil on card, 11 x 17 ins / 28 x 43 cm) GBP 1,430. LONDON, 17 July 1992, *The Port of Valletta, Malta* (oil on card, 5 1/2 x 13 ins / 14 x 33 cm) GBP 1,705. LONDON, 18 June 1993, *The Port of Valletta* (1912, oil on panel, 19 x 32 1/4 ins / 48.5 x 82 cm) GBP 7,820. NEW YORK, 17 Feb 1994, *Port* (oil on card, 9 x 21 1/2 ins / 22.9 x 54.6 cm) USD 4,830. LONDON, 22 Nov 1996, *The Ruins of the Sun Temple at Baalbec* (1929, oil on panel, 16 x 26 ins / 40.6 x 66 cm) GBP 2,760. LONDON, 26 March 1997, *Entrance to the Port of Valletta, Malta* (oil on panel, 7 3/4 x 20 1/2 ins / 20 x 52 cm) GBP 2,760. EDINBURGH, 15 May 1997, *Port of Valletta, Morning; Port of Valletta, Evening* (oil on panel, a pair, 6 1/4 x 14 ins / 16 x 35.5 cm) GBP 2,990.

GALEANI, Giovanni Battista
Italian, 16th - 17th century.
Active in Lodi.
Painter.
In 1611, Galeani was working in Piacenza Cathedral.

GALEANI, Jean
French, 20th century.
Born in Montpellier.
Painter. Genre scenes.
Jean Galeani exhibited regularly in Paris at the Salon des Indépendants from 1926.

GALEAS, Francisco (Father)
Spanish, 16th - 17th century.
Born c. 1567, in Seville; died 1614.
Miniaturist.
Francisco Galeas first qualified as a doctor in law, then in 1590 entered the monastery of S Maria de las Cuevas. The monastery reliquary has two miniatures by him representing *Death* and the *Resurrection of Christ*.

GALEAZZA
Italian, 16th century.
Born possibly in Urbino.
Painter. History painting.
Galeazza was a pupil of Leonardo da Vinci. His family name is not known.

GALEAZZI, Agostino
Italian, 16th century.
Born 1523, in Brescia.
Painter.
Agostino Galeazza was a pupil of Moretto and worked mainly in Brescia and Vicenza.

GALEAZZI, Domenico
Italian, 17th - 18th century.

Born 20 May 1647, in Bologna; died 9 April 1731, in Bologna.
Painter.
Domenico Galeazzi was a pupil of Cignani.

GALEAZZI, Giovanni Battista
Italian, 16th century.
Active in Brescia.
Painter.
Giovanni Battista was the son and pupil of Agostino Galeazzi.

GALEFFI, Ernesto
Italian, 20th century.
Born 1917; died 1986.
Painter, sculptor, draughtsman, graphic designer.
Ernesto Galeffi took part in collective exhibitions such as the one at the Galleria Numero in Florence (1956). The Ernesto Galeffi museum of modern art was created under the auspices of the Accademia del Poggio in his villa in Montevarchi, Tuscany.
BIBLIOGRAPHY:
Grassi, Luigi, *50 Disegni di Ernesto Galeffi: Meditazione intorna a una scultura*, G. Spinelli & C., Florence, 1964. Bettochi, C./Carli, E. (preface), *Scultura di Ernesto Galeffi*, Ed. Arnaud, Florence, 1965. Panzetta, Alfonso, *Ernesto Galeffi, scultore 1917-1986*, catalogue raisonné, Umberto Allemandi, Turin, 2001.

GALEK, Stanislav
Polish, 20th century.
Born 1876, in Mokrzyska.
Painter. Landscapes.
Stanislav Galek worked in particular in Cracow.

GALEMBERT, Louis-Charles-Marie de
(Comte)
French, 19th century.
Born in Vendôme (Loir-et-Cher).
Painter.
He studied under Steuben and exhibited religious compositions at the Paris Salon in 1841, 1848 and 1861.
BIBLIOGRAPHY:
Davy, Christian, '*Saint-Martin-de-Limet et le comte de Galembert*' in *303*, No.37, 1993. Caffort, Michel, '*Le Christ, source de vie ou notes sur les peintures murales du comte de Galembert*' in *La tradizione classica nella medaglia d'arte dal Rinascimento al neoclassico: atti del convegno internazionale, Castello di Udine*, Maurizio Buora, Editreg, Trieste, 1999.

GALEN, Nicolaes van
Dutch, 17th century.
Born c. 1620.
Painter.
He seems to have lived mostly in Kampen, but was also active in Amsterdam and Hasselt, where he executed decorations for the town hall.

GALEN, Thyman van
Dutch, 17th century.
Born 1590, in Utrecht.
Painter, decorative artist. Architectural views, perspectives.
After visiting Italy, he returned, via Switzerland, to his native city in 1615, and was admitted as a master of the Guild of St Luke. He presented a painting of a temple to the hospital of St-Job.

GALEOTA, Leopoldo, or Galeota-Russo
Italian, 19th - 20th century.
Born 13 March 1868, in Naples; died 1938.
Painter. Genre scenes, landscapes.
Galeota was taught by Gioacchino Toma and Rubens Santoro.
AUCTION RECORDS:
MILAN, 25 May 1978, *The Amalfi Coast* (oil on canvas, 21 x 34 ins / 53.5 x 86.5 cm) ITL 1,600,000. MILAN, 24 March 1982, *Posillipo* (oil on canvas, 21 1/4 x 40 3/4 ins / 54 x 103.5 cm) ITL 3,600,000. MILAN, 27 March 1984, *Rocky Landscape, Quinto* (oil on canvas, 19 3/4 x 37 ins / 50 x 94 cm) ITL 2,200,000. ROME, 16 April 1991, *Study of a Landscape* (oil on canvas, 14 x 20 ins / 35.5 x 51 cm) ITL 2,185,000. MUNICH, 8 Nov 2000, *Houses at Capri* (oil on canvas, 14 x 19 ins / 35 x 48 cm) DEM 9,000. LUCERNE, 11 Nov 2000, *Country Road with Peasants* (oil on canvas, 14 x 20 ins / 35 x 51 cm) CHF 3,400. ROME, 11 Dec 2003, *Market in the Square* (oil on panel, 12 x 16 ins / 30 x 40 cm) EUR 1,600.

GALEOTTI, Giovanni Battista
Italian, 18th century.
Painter.
Giovanni Battista Galeotti was the son of Sebastiano Galeotti and the brother of Giuseppe Galeotti. He worked in collaboration with the latter.

GALEOTTI, Giuseppe
Italian, 18th century.
Born 1708, in Florence; died 11 March 1778, in Genoa.
Painter.
Giuseppe Galeotti was the son of Sebastiano Galeotti. He painted predominantly religious and mythological subjects. Examples of his work are to be found in Chiavari Cathedral.

GALEOTTI, Sebastiano
Italian, 18th century.
Born 1676, in Florence; died 1746, in Vico, near Mondovi.
Painter, fresco artist, draughtsman. Religious subjects, mythological subjects.
Sebastiano Galeotti was initially a pupil of Alessandro Gherardini. He studied subsequently in Bologna under Giovanni Gioseffo dal Sole. There are few examples of his work in his native Florence. His work is mainly preserved in Piacenza, Parma and, above all, Turin, where he served as principal of the fine arts academy. His two sons, Giuseppe and Giovanni Battista Galeotti, were also painters. According to Ratti, Galeotti was entrusted with major projects for the church of the Maddalena in Genoa. He was known to be an accomplished fresco painter.
AUCTION RECORDS:
PARIS, 1775, *Old Man Welcomed to Olympus* (pen); *Samaritan Woman* (Indian ink, two drawings) FRF 48. LONDON, 29 and 30 March 1911, *Justine* (sold with three other drawings by different artists) GBP 4. LONDON, 24 April 1981, *Glorification of St Cecilia* (oil on canvas, 27 1/2 x 18 1/2 ins / 69.8 x 47 cm) GBP 2,800. PARIS, 7 April 1995, *Rape of Persephone* (ink and black chalk, 7 1/2 x 5 3/4 ins / 19 x 14.5 cm) FRF 5,000. PARIS, 9 April 1999, *Design for Decoration with Angels* (colour ink/colour wash/black crayon, 16 x 13 ins / 41 x 32 cm) FRF 13,000. PARIS, 27 March 2003, *Seated Faun* (pencil/ink wash, 9 x 9 ins / 23 x 23 cm) EUR 2,800. MILAN, 12 May 2003, *Decoration for Part of a Ceiling with Satyr and Female Figures* (pen/black ink/grey watercolour, 18 x 15 ins / 46 x 39 cm) EUR 2,200.

GALEPPINI, Giuseppe Maria
Italian, 17th century.
Born c. 1625.
Painter.
Giuseppe Maria Galeppini worked predominantly in Bologna, where he was responsible for decorative work in several churches.

GALER, Thomas
German, 16th century.
Active in Marburg (Hesse).
Sculptor.

Galer is known for *Tomb of Anna of Mecklenburg* in the church of St Elizabeth in Marburg.

GALERA
Brazilian, 20th century.
Born 1926, in São Paulo.
Active in Japan from 1968.
Painter.

Galera has worked as a painter since 1964 and his numerous visits abroad have enabled him to exhibit in a wide range of countries. In 1974 the State Museum of São Paulo devoted an exhibition to his work. Galera's work is abstract showing a tendency towards lyrical and gestural abstraction.

GALERNE, Prosper
French, 19th century.
Born 28 April 1836, in Patay (Loiret).
Active in La Ferté-Alais (Essonne).
Painter. Landscapes.

He studied under Eugène Le Poittevin and Jean-Baptiste Henri Durand-Brager. Galerne exhibited at the Paris Salon from 1870 then, as a member of the Société des Artistes Français from 1889, at the latter Salon. He received an honourable mention in 1883 and was awarded a bronze medal in 1887, together with an honourable mention at the 1889 Exposition Universelle. Most of Galerne's work comprises views of the Île-de-France and the Loire River.

MUSEUMS AND GALLERIES:
CHÂTEAUDUN - COUTANCES: *St Martin's Cove* - ORLÉANS - POITIERS.

AUCTION RECORDS:
PARIS, 22 Feb 1900, *Banks of the Seine*, FRF 105. BERN, 26 Oct 1978, *Banks of the Seine* (1872, oil on canvas, 11 x 15 3/4 ins / 27 x 40 cm) CHF 3,600. LONDON, 17 June 1999, *Beside the Loire* (oil on canvas, 16 x 20 ins / 40 x 50 cm) GBP 1,800. LONDON, 18 June 2003, *On the Banks of the Seine at Meudon* (1881, oil on canvas, 16 x 24 ins / 40 x 60 cm) GBP 1,700.

GALERY, Charles
French, 16th century.
Painter.

Galery's *Portrait of Pierre Faber, President of the Parliament in Toulouse* was engraved by Filleul.

GALESTRUZZI, Giovanni Battista
Italian, 17th century.
Born 1615, in Florence; died c. 1669.
Painter, engraver.

Giovanni Battista Galestruzzi studied initially under Francesco Furini and then moved to Rome where, in 1652, he was admitted into the Accademia di San Luca. Giacomo Rossi has catalogued his extensive engravings. Galestruzzi was a friend of Stefano della Bella, whose style he imitated and who, according to Huber, later completed several engravings left unfinished by Galestruzzi on his death.

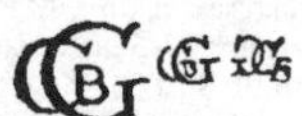

GALESTRUZZI, Lorenzo
Italian, 17th century.
Active in Florence.
Painter, engraver.

GALETTI, Carlo Andrea
Swiss, 18th century.
Born in San Fedele d'Intelvi (Lombardy), Italy; died 7 June 1806, in Altdorf.
Sculptor (marble).

Galetti worked with his sons, Carlo Giuseppe and Antonio, for the church at Altdorf.

GALEY, Gaston Pierre
French, 20th century.
Born 19 May 1880, in Toulouse; died 10 August 1959, in Collonge-sous-Salève (Haute-Savoie).
Painter, watercolourist, draughtsman, designer. Figure compositions, figures, genre scenes, landscapes with figures, urban landscapes. Murals.

Gaston Galey was the brother of Jean Fabien Galey. He moved to Paris in 1901 to study architecture but abandoned this in favour of painting. He attended the École des Beaux-Arts where he studied under Léon Bonnat and later under Luc-Olivier Merson and Octave Guillonet. In 1907 he made an extended trip to Venice. He was called up for service in 1914 and returned from the Front with drawings and watercolours. In 1918 he went back to Paris after several months of rest in the Basque Country. In 1936 he moved to Collonge-sous-Salève in Haute-Savoie.

He produced many figure compositions, portraits, urban landscapes and genre scenes. His works include: *Portrait of Madame Galey*, 1906; *Venice*, 1907; *The Concert*, 1915; *Pierrot, Harlequin and Colombine*, 1916; *The Red Steps*, 1923; *Pierrot with Moon*, 1927; *Ornamental Pond*, 1933; and *Horsemen and Nymphs*. He also decorated the Capuchin chapel at Challes-les-Eaux in Savoy. He pursued his art in a solitary manner, remaining aloof from the great artistic movements of the period such as Fauvism, Cubism and Surrealism. However, his work does display a certain colourful Symbolism.

He first exhibited at the Salon d'Automne in Paris in 1911 and went on to exhibit at the Salon des Artistes Français on 19 occasions between 1911 and 1939. He also exhibited at the Exposition des Artistes Toulousains at the Musée Galliera in 1932 in Paris. There have been retrospectives of his work in London in private galleries in 1972, 1973, 1978 and 1980.

BIBLIOGRAPHY:
Luthi, Jean-Jacques, *Gaston Pierre Galey*, Geneva, 1972.

MUSEUMS AND GALLERIES:
ALBI - BAYONNE - BIARRITZ - TOULOUSE (Mus. Toulouse-Lautrec): *Fantasy*.

AUCTION RECORDS:
LUCERNE, 26 June 1976, *Mother and Children in a Garden* (oil on card, 13 1/2 x 13 3/4 ins / 34 x 35 cm) CHF 4,300. ZURICH, 17 Nov 1976, *Woman with Hat* (gouache, 11 3/4 x 7 ins / 30 x 17.5 cm) CHF 2,100. ZURICH, 23 Nov 1978, *Corner of the Gardens* (1933, gouache, 11 1/2 x 16 1/2 ins / 29 x 42 cm) CHF 3,200. ZURICH, 7 Nov 1981, *Resting under the Trees* (watercolour, 14 1/2 x 10 1/2 ins / 37 x 26.5 cm) CHF 750. LONDON, 26 June 1984, *Basket of Flowers* (watercolour, 4 x 5 1/2 ins / 10 x 14 cm) GBP 1,000. LONDON, 26 June 1984, *Harlequin on a Terrace, Leaning against a Column, Venice* (1907, oil on canvas, 31 3/4 x 23 1/2 ins / 80.6 x 59.7 cm) GBP 8,000. LONDON, 19 June 1985, *Table in a Sunny Garden* (oil on canvas, 28 x 36 ins / 71 x 90.5 cm) GBP 3,200. LONDON, 29 Nov 1999, *Harlequin* (watercolour, 17 x 12 ins / 43 x 30 cm) GBP 2,000. LONDON, 21 Nov 2000, *Young Arabesque* (watercolour and gouache, 13 x 9 ins / 33 x 24 cm) GBP 1,550. LONDON, 3 April 2003, *Figure under a Tree* (pencil and watercolour, 14 x 10 ins / 36 x 26 cm) GBP 1,100. LONDON, 3 April 2003, *Venetian Fruit Seller* (oil on board, 21 x 17 ins / 54 x 44 cm) GBP 5,800.

GALEY, Jean Fabien
French, 20th century.
Born 6 July 1877, in Toulouse; died 11 March 1966, in Biarritz.
Painter. Religious subjects, scenes with figures.

Jean Galey studied under J.P. Laurens. He was a member of the Salon des Artistes Français in Paris and began exhibiting there in 1911. He later taught at the École des Beaux-Arts in Toulouse. He executed decorative work for the town hall of Muret in Haute-Garonne. His works include *The Way of the Cross* in the church of Chartrons, Bordeaux, and *Life of St Mary Magdalene* at the church of Lalande, Toulouse.
BIBLIOGRAPHY:
Dictionnaire biographique français, Paris, 1980.

GALEZOWSKA, Marie Iza
French, 20th century.
Born 1880, in Paris.
Painter, pastellist. Landscapes.
Marie Galezowska studied under Baschet and Royer. She was a member of the Salon des Artistes Français and regularly showed landscapes at their exhibitions.

GALGAN, C.
French, 15th century.
Active in St-Gal (near Muret, Haute Garonne).
Sculptor.
Galgan worked at the church of St-Gal.

GALGANO DI DUCCIO
Italian, 14th century.
Painter.
Sienese School.
Galgano di Duccio was the son of Duccio di Buoninsegna.

GALGANO DI GIOVANNI SENESE
Italian, 14th century.
Active in Siena.
Architect, sculptor.
Galgano di Giovanni Senese worked mainly for the cathedral and various churches in Siena, and also for the Palazzo Comunale in Perugia.

GALGANO DI MINUCCIO
Italian, 14th century.
Died 9 March 1387, in Siena.
Painter. History painting.
There is no doubt that Galgano di Minuccio was the son of Minuccio. He worked with Paolo di Neri, particularly for Siena Cathedral.

GALGARIO (Fra). See **GHISLANDI Vittore** or **Giuseppe**

GALGON, Yves
German, 20th - 21st century.
Born 1948, in Dessau, near Halle.
Also active in Spain.
Painter.
Galgon attended the art school in Hanover, then studied under Professor Almir Mavignier at the art academy in Hamburg. Since 1977, he has been a member of the 'Bund Bildender Künstler' (artists' association). His painting is made up of signs, an interpretation of the abstract. Since 1973, Galgon has held solo shows mainly in Germany (the Leopold Hoesch Museum, Düren), but also in Spain.

GALI, István
Hungarian, 18th - 19th century.
Painter.
István Gali spent many years in Italy.

GALI-KEL, pseudonym of Keltchewsky Gali
Russian, 20th century.
Born 6 March 1921, in Petrograd (now St Petersburg).
Painter. Nudes, landscapes, still-lifes, flowers.
Gali-Kel was a student at the École des Arts Appliqués Duperré in Paris. A fashion and theatrical costume designer for the Paris Casino to begin with, she was a classical dancer for ten years, then a trilingual translator in a ministerial department. In 1971 she left Paris and settled in Agde in southern France and devoted herself entirely to painting. Gali-Kel's nudes have been praised by critics, her still-lifes and flowers are the result of true observation and she reveals the most personal sensitivity in her landscapes, seascapes and harbour scenes in which a technique inherited from Impressionism allows her to express the eddies in the water and the racing clouds, the changes in the light according to the time, season and weather.

She featured in numerous collective exhibitions in Paris at the Salon d'Automne from 1980 onwards, and with various groups in Cap d'Agde, Deauville, Monte Carlo, Béziers, Marseilles and in New York and Geneva. Solo exhibitions include: Marceau gallery, Paris (1994), Agde, Béziers, Marseilles and Nice winning several regional awards.

GALIACHOVSKY, Damian
Russian, 18th century.
Active in Kiev.
Draughtsman.
This artist was possibly the son of Daniel Galachovsky.

GALIANI
Spanish, 19th century.
Active in Madrid.
Painter. Local figures, landscapes.
The Prado in Madrid has works by Galiani after David.
MUSEUMS AND GALLERIES:
LOUVIERS (Mus. municipal): *View of Lorient in the Morning; Lorient at Sunset* - MADRID (Prado).
AUCTION RECORDS:
PARIS, 1883, *Moorish Merchant*, FRF 340.

GALIANO
Italian, 17th century.
Painter. Church interiors.
Siret refers to an interior painted by Galiano for a church in Rome.

GALIANY, Eugène. See **GALIEN-LALOUE Eugène**

GALIBERT, Pierre
French, 19th century.
Born in Marseilles.
Painter.
He studied under A. Aubert and exhibited still-lifes at the Salon between 1870 and 1876.

GALICE, Louis
French, 19th century.
Draughtsman.
He contributed illustrations to a publication entitled *Fleurs du Persil* (*Parsley Flowers*).

GALICHANIN, Grigori
Russian, 17th century.
Active in Moscow.
Painter.

GALICHANIN, Kosma
Russian, 17th century.
Active in Moscow c. 1675.
Painter.

GALICHANIN, Semjon
Russian, 17th century.
Active in Moscow.
Painter.

GALIE
19th century.
Painter. Seascapes.

AUCTION RECORDS:
PARIS, 28 June 1897, *Naval Parade*, FRF 60. PARIS, 19 Dec 1997, *Small Boats and Sailing Boats in the Bay* (canvas, 20 x 30 1/4 ins / 51 x 77 cm) FRF 23,500.

GALIE, Gaston
French, 20th century.
Died November 1911.
Sculptor.

GALIEN-LALOUE, Eugène, or Gallien-Laloue, pseudonyms: Liévin, J. Liévin, Eugène Dupuy, L. Dupuy, Galiany, M. Lenoir
French, 19th - 20th century.
Born December 1854, in Paris; died 18 April 1941, in Chérence (Val-d'Oise).
Painter (gouache), watercolourist. Military subjects, genre scenes, landscapes with figures, urban landscapes.

Eugène Galien-Laloue was a skilled and productive artist, particularly when working in gouache and producing small-scale works. He painted almost exclusively the most picturesque spots of Paris, notably the Grands-Boulevards. He enjoyed a considerable reputation in the early years of the 20th Century and painted the happy pre-war period when the city was filled with omnibuses and carriages. His work evokes the atmosphere of turn-of-the-century Paris and retains a documentary value. He also painted landscapes of Normandy, Seine-et-Marne, Marseilles, Italy and Venice and, in 1914, began painting military scenes.

Galien-Laloue is known to have used various pseudonyms, among which were J. Liévin and Liévin. This raises the question of whether the painter Jacques Liévin, to whom paintings on the same themes as those of Eugène Galien-Laloue have been attributed, was also merely a pseudonym of the latter. Jacques Liévin is said to have studied under Léon Germain Pelouse in the early years of the 20th century, while Galien-Laloue is believed to have studied under one Charles Laloue; however no evidence of the existence of Charles Laloue has been found. To add to the mystery, while Galien-Laloue was mainly a watercolourist and gouache painter, Jacques Liévin worked mainly in oil; it is therefore possible that Galien-Laloue used this false identity specifically for his oil paintings.

Whether or not Jacques Liévin was real, the museums of La Rochelle, Mulhouse and Louviers attribute the following paintings - very reminiscent of Galien-Laloue's style - to him: *Place de la République, Paris; Banks of the Seine; Quai Voltaire, Paris; Pont-Royal; Evening, Place de la Concorde; Oats at Angerville; Corn in Beauce.*

Meanwhile, Galien-Laloue exhibited under his own name from 1877 at the Salon des Artistes Français in Paris.

E. Galien-Laloue

E Galiany

Lievin

BIBLIOGRAPHY:
Klein, David, *Édouard Cortès et Eugène Galien-Laloue*, Klein Art Gall., Los Angeles, 1993. Willer, Noö, '*Eugène Galien Laloue. Le Triomphe de Paris*' in vol. 1, catalogue raisonné, Kahan Fine Arts, New York, 1999.

MUSEUMS AND GALLERIES:
LA ROCHELLE (MBA): *Place de la République, Paris* (gouache signed Liévin); *Banks of the Seine - Quai Voltaire, Paris* (gouache signed Liévin) - LOUVIERS (Mus. municipal) - MULHOUSE.

AUCTION RECORDS:
PARIS, 8 Feb 1898, *The Quai du Louvre*, FRF 80. PARIS, 11 Feb 1919, *Celebration in Place de la Nation* (gouache) FRF 205. PARIS, 29 June 1927, *Porte St-Martin in Winter at Twilight* (watercolour and gouache) FRF 850. PARIS, 12 May 1941, *The Louvre, seen from the Quays*, FRF 1,750; *Flea Market*, FRF 2,100. PARIS, 15 March 1943, *Quai Malaquais* (watercolour and gouache) FRF 7,800. PARIS, 11 Dec 1944, *Place de la Concorde* (gouache) FRF 5,500. PARIS, 24 April 1947, *Place St-Denis*, FRF 18,000. PARIS, 5 Feb 1951, *Place Clichy; Avenue de la Grande-Armée* (gouaches, a pair) FRF 24,500. PARIS, 26 Feb 1951, *The Trois Quartiers; Place de la République* (watercolour and gouache, collection) FRF 52,000. PARIS, 23 June 1954, *Flower Market in Place de la Madeleine*, FRF 115,000. PARIS, 20 Jan 1969, *Place de la Madeleine and Rue Royale under Snow* (watercolour and gouache) FRF 9,000. LONDON, 1 Dec 1970, *Porte St-Martin*, Gns 1,250. VERSAILLES, 31 May 1972, *Port of Marseilles*, FRF 19,300. PARIS, 11 June 1974, *Porte St-Denis* (gouache) FRF 15,000. ROUEN, 3 March 1975, *Washerwomen* (oil on canvas, 17 3/4 x 14 1/2 ins / 45 x 37 cm) FRF 7,000. PARIS, 8 Dec 1976, *Porte St-Martin in Winter* (gouache, 12 1/2 x 7 1/2 ins / 32 x 19 cm) FRF 9,500. ENGHIEN-LES-BAINS, 11 Dec 1977, *Port of Marseilles* (oil on canvas, 17 1/4 x 24 1/2 ins / 44 x 62 cm) FRF 10,000. ENGHIEN-LES-BAINS, 9 Dec 1979, *Fun Fair on the Grands Boulevards* (gouache and watercolour, 7 1/2 x 12 1/4 ins / 19 x 31 cm) FRF 24,000. VERSAILLES, 25 Oct 1981, *Place Clichy, Paris* (watercolour, 7 1/2 x 12 1/2 ins / 19 x 31.5 cm) FRF 38,200. VERSAILLES, 27 May 1984, *Market Scene on the Boulevards* (oil on canvas, 11 x 14 1/4 ins / 28 x 36 cm) FRF 34,500. LONDON, 21 June 1984, *Place Clichy* (gouache and pen/pencil outlines, 24 x 36 3/4 ins / 61 x 93.5 cm) GBP 16,000. NEW YORK, 23 May 1985, *Boulevard St-Denis and Porte St-Denis in Winter* (gouache/paper, 20 3/4 x 30 1/4 ins / 53 x 77 cm. LONDON, 26 June 1987, *Place du Théâtre-Français* (1902, oil on canvas, 35 x 54 ins / 89 x 137 cm) GBP 30,000. PARIS, 25 Nov 1987, *The Grands Boulevards under Snow near La République* (gouache, 7 1/2 x 12 1/2 ins / 19 x 31.5 cm) FRF 52,000. PARIS, 11 Dec 1987, *The Boulevards, Paris* (gouache, 7 1/2 x 12 1/2 ins / 19 x 32 cm) FRF 41,000. NEW YORK, 25 Feb 1988, *Figures in a Paris Street* (gouache and ink, 7 3/4 x 12 1/4 ins / 19.7 x 31.4 cm) USD 14,300. LONDON, 24 March 1988, *Flower Market under Snow at the Madeleine* (oil on canvas, 25 1/4 x 35 3/4 ins / 64 x 91 cm) GBP 24,200. PARIS, 21 April 1988, *Village by a River* (oil on canvas, 13 x 18 ins / 33 x 46 cm) FRF 10,000. VERSAILLES, 15 May 1988, *Paris, Place de la Bastille with Figures under Snow* (gouache, 7 x 11 1/2 ins / 18 x 29 cm) FRF 47,000. PARIS, 15 June 1988, *Flower Market, Paris* (oil on canvas, 18 1/4 x 13 1/2 ins / 46.5 x 34.5 cm) FRF 105,000. CALAIS, 3 July 1988, *Place du Châtelet under Snow* (oil on canvas, 15 x 22 ins / 38 x 55 cm) FRF 42,000. PARIS, 7 Oct 1988, *Flower Market at the Madeleine* (watercolour, 7 1/2 x 12 1/4 ins / 19 x 31 cm) FRF 64,000; *Walking along the Quays of the Seine* (watercolour, 11 x 18 ins / 28 x 45.5 cm) FRF 80,000. VERSAILLES, 6 Nov 1988, *Peasant Women near a Village* (gouache, 11 3/4 x 15 ins / 30 x 38 cm) FRF 16,000. PARIS, 22 Nov 1988, *The Grands Boulevards under Snow* (watercolour, 9 x 13 ins / 23 x 33 cm) FRF 61,000. VERSAILLES, 18 Dec 1988, *Boats Moored and San Giorgio, Venice* (1881, oil on canvas, 25 1/2 x 36 1/4 ins / 65 x 92 cm) FRF 46,000. PARIS, 12 Feb 1989, *Notre-Dame under Snow* (watercolour, 10 1/4 x 13 1/2 ins / 26 x 34 cm) FRF 140,000. LONDON, 17 March 1989, *Boulevard Haussmann, Paris* (watercolour, 7 x 12 ins / 17.8 x 30.5 cm) GBP 9,350. PARIS, 22 March 1989, *The Seine at Bercy looking towards Notre-Dame* (lead pencil and white gouache/buff-coloured

paper, 13 1/2 x 22 1/2 ins / 34.5 x 57 cm) FRF 28,500. NEW YORK, 3 May 1989, *The Grands Boulevards* (gouache/paper, 6 x 9 1/4 ins / 15 x 23.5 cm) USD 38,850. LONDON, 21 June 1989, *Street Scene near Place de la République, Paris* (oil on panel, 12 1/2 x 18 ins / 32 x 46 cm) GBP 6,050. LONDON, 6 Oct 1989, *The Quays of the Seine, Paris*. PARIS, 23 Nov 1989, *The Quays under Snow* (watercolour, 15 3/4 x 23 1/2 ins / 40 x 60 cm) FRF 152,000. PARIS, 24 Jan 1990, *House by a Pond* (1891, oil on canvas, 25 3/4 x 39 1/4 ins / 65.5 x 100 cm) FRF 33,000. NEW YORK, 1 March 1990, *Eating on a Terrace Overlooking the Bay of Naples* (oil on canvas, 18 1/2 x 25 3/4 ins / 47 x 65.4 cm) USD 9,900. PARIS, 21 March 1990, *Village by the Water* (oil on panel, 13 x 9 1/2 ins / 33 x 24 cm) FRF 30,000. BRUSSELS, 27 March 1990, *Boulevard Bonne Nouvelle, Paris* (gouache, 9 x 12 1/4 ins / 23 x 31 cm) BEF 280,000. LONDON, 30 March 1990, *Porte St-Denis, Paris* (gouache, 74 3/4 x 122 ins / 190 x 310 cm) GBP 11,550. AMSTERDAM, 10 April 1990, *Mediterranean Village* (pencil, watercolour and gouache/paper, 19 1/2 x 27 1/4 ins / 49.5 x 69 cm) NLG 5,175. MONACO, 15 June 1990, *The Quays of the Seine and Notre-Dame* (gouache, 14 1/2 x 21 1/4 ins / 37 x 54 cm) FRF 183,150. PARIS, 19 June 1990, *The Arc de Triomphe, Paris* (gouache, 8 1/4 x 12 ins / 21 x 30.6 cm) FRF 41,000. PARIS, 12 Oct 1990, *Auction at Twilight in Dieppe* (oil on canvas, 18 1/2 x 25 3/4 ins / 47 x 65.5 cm) FRF 60,000. NEW YORK, 23 Oct 1990, *The Madeleine in Winter* (watercolour/paper, 13 x 8 1/4 ins / 33 x 21 cm) USD 12,100. MONTREAL, 5 Nov 1990, *Street Scene in Paris* (gouache, 7 1/2 x 12 1/4 ins / 19 x 31 cm) CAD 15,400. STOCKHOLM, 14 Nov 1990, *Place du Châtelet* (watercolour, 7 1/2 x 12 1/4 ins / 19 x 31 cm) SEK 36,000. PARIS, 7 Dec 1990, *Houses by a Pond* (1891, oil on canvas, 25 3/4 x 39 1/4 ins / 65.5 x 100 cm) FRF 18,000. LONDON, 19 June 1991, *Figures by a Flower Stall in a Paris Street* (ink and gouache, 15 1/4 x 22 3/4 ins / 39 x 58 cm) GBP 13,750. NEW YORK, 16 Oct 1991, *Boulevard Montmartre in Winter* (gouache/paper, 12 3/4 x 19 1/2 ins / 32.4 x 49.8 cm) USD 18,700. PARIS, 5 April 1992, *Landscape with Pond* (1891, oil on canvas, 25 1/2 x 39 1/4 ins / 65 x 100 cm) FRF 56,000. PARIS, 22 June 1992, *Place Clichy, Paris* (gouache, 7 1/4 x 12 ins / 18.5 x 30.5 cm) FRF 20,000. PARIS, 22 March 1993, *The Flower Market in Place de la Madeleine, Paris* (gouache, 7 1/4 x 12 1/4 ins / 18.5 x 31 cm) FRF 58,000. AMSTERDAM, 9 Nov 1993, *Porte St-Denis, Paris* (gouache, 7 1/2 x 12 1/4 ins / 19 x 31 cm) NLG 23,000. LE TOUQUET, 14 Nov 1993, *The Quays and Pont des Arts, Paris* (gouache, 7 x 11 3/4 ins / 18 x 30 cm) FRF 50,000. NEW YORK, 15 Feb 1994, *Street Scene, Paris* (gouache and charcoal/paper, 10 1/2 x 16 ins / 26.8 x 40.6 cm) USD 20,700. PARIS, 22 June 1994, *Place de la Bastille under Snow, Paris* (watercolour and gouache, 15 1/2 x 21 ins / 39.5 x 52.5 cm) FRF 75,000. CALAIS, 3 July 1994, *River Bank* (oil on canvas, 18 x 25 1/2 ins / 46 x 65 cm) FRF 17,000. LONDON, 18 Nov 1994, *Morning at the Moulin Rouge, Paris* (pencil, gouache and black chalk/paper, 14 1/2 x 21 1/4 ins / 36.9 x 54 cm) GBP 21,275. PARIS, 24 March 1995, *The Flower Market on the Quai de l'Horloge, Paris* (gouache, 11 1/2 x 12 1/2 ins / 29 x 32 cm) FRF 52,000. LOKEREN, 20 May 1995, *Paris Boulevard under Snow* (gouache, 11 x 10 1/2 ins / 27 x 26.5 cm) BEF 240,000. NEW YORK, 1 Nov 1995, *Place de la République, Paris* (gouache, 14 1/2 x 21 1/4 ins / 36.8 x 54 cm) USD 21,850. LYONS, 4 Dec 1995, *The Bazar de l'Est* (gouache, 12 1/2 x 15 1/2 ins / 31.5 x 39.5 cm) FRF 49,000. LONDON, 13 March 1996, *Place du Châtelet under Snow* (oil on canvas, 25 1/4 x 36 1/4 ins / 64 x 92 cm) GBP 54,300. NEW YORK, 23 May 1996, *Corner of the Boulevard St-Michel; Place de la République* (gouache/canvas, a pair, each 12 x 7 1/2 ins / 30.5 x 19.1 cm) USD 20,700. CALAIS, 7 July 1996, *Horses Harnessed to a Hearse* (oil on panel, 9 x 16 1/4 ins / 22 x 41 cm) FRF 7,500. LONDON, 31 Oct 1996, *The Quays, Notre-Dame* (gouache, 7 x 12 1/4 ins / 18 x 31 cm) GBP 7,475. PARIS, 22 Nov 1996, *Secondhand Booksellers on the Quai de la Tournelle, Paris* (watercolour, 22 x 38 1/2 ins / 55 x 98 cm) FRF 295,000. CALAIS, 15 Dec 1996, *Secondhand Booksellers and the Théâtre du Châtelet* (gouache, 7 1/2 x 12 1/4 ins / 19 x 31 cm) FRF 36,000. NEW YORK, 12 Feb 1997, *The Grand Boulevards of Paris at Twilight* (oil on canvas, 25 x 45 ins / 63.5 x 114.3 cm) USD 65,750. NEW YORK, 26 Feb 1997, *The Arc de Triomphe* (gouache and traces of pencil/paper, 7 3/4 x 12 1/2 ins / 19.6 x 31.7 cm) USD 14,950. LONDON, 13 March 1997, *The Old Trocadero at the 1900 Exposition Universelle, Paris* (gouache, 17 1/2 x 12 1/2 ins / 44.5 x 31.7 cm) GBP 4,025. CALAIS, 23 March 1997, *Paris at Nightfall* (gouache and watercolour, 9 1/2 x 6 ins / 24 x 15 cm) FRF 23,000. LONDON, 26 March 1997, *The Flower Market at the Madeleine, Paris* (gouache heightened with charcoal, 10 1/4 x 9 ins / 26 x 23 cm) GBP 9,200. NEW YORK, 23 May 1997, *The Boulevards of Paris* (watercolour/traces of pencil/card, set of four, each 7 1/2 x 12 1/4 ins / 19.1 x 31.1 cm) USD 57,500. LONDON, 11 June 1997, *The Théâtre du Gymnase* (gouache, 12 1/2 x 17 3/4 ins / 32 x 45 cm) GBP 17,825. PARIS, 16 June 1997, *Figures outside the Gare de l'Est* (gouache, 7 3/4 x 12 ins / 19.5 x 30.5 cm) FRF 51,000. PARIS, 18 June 1997, *The Théâtre du Gymnase, Paris* (gouache/mounted paper/canvas, 15 x 22 ins / 38 x 55 cm) FRF 142,000. PARIS, 19 Oct 1997, *The Secondhand Booksellers of Notre-Dame* (gouache, 7 1/2 x 12 1/2 ins / 19 x 31.5 cm) FRF 56,000. NEW YORK, 22 Oct 1997, *Place de la Madeleine, Paris* (gouache/paper, 7 3/4 x 12 1/2 ins / 19.7 x 31.8 cm) USD 17,250. SENLIS, 8 Feb 1998, *Place de la République; The Palais de Justice* (two gouaches, 10 1/4 x 13 1/2 ins / 26 x 34 cm) FRF 104,000. NEW YORK, 10 Feb 1998, *In the Garden* (oil on canvas, 29 x 36 1/4 ins / 73.6 x 92 cm) USD 9,200. PARIS, 9 March 1998, *The Sacré-Cœur seen from the Square d'Anvers* (gouache, 11 3/4 x 7 3/4 ins / 30 x 20 cm) FRF 72,000. NEW YORK, 18 March 1998, *The Quays of the Seine with the Trocadero and the Eiffel Tower* (oil on canvas, 18 x 25 1/2 ins / 46 x 64.8 cm) USD 9,775. NEW YORK, 5 May 1998, *View of Paris* (gouache/paper, 16 x 22 ins / 41 x 56 cm) USD 30,000. NEW YORK, 6 May 1999, *The Porte St-Denis in the Snow* (gouache, 18 x 30 ins / 46 x 77 cm) USD 50,000. NEUILLY, 23 Oct 1999, *View of Paris, Quai de l'Hôtel de Ville in the Snow* (gouache, 20 x 33 ins / 50 x 83 cm) FRF 410,000. PARIS, 7 June 2000, *The Flower Market at the Madeleine, Snow Effect* (gouache, 24 x 37 ins / 61 x 93 cm) FRF 590,000. LONDON, 23 Nov 2000, *Boulevard Bonne-Nouvelle* (gouache, 15 x 22 ins / 38 x 55 cm) GBP 20,000. PARIS, 20 June 2001, *Porte de Chatillon* (oil on canvas, 26 x 36 ins / 66 x 92 cm) FRF 280,000. NEW YORK, 23 April 2002, *Book Sellers on the Quai de Tournelle, Paris* (gouache, 22 x 39 ins / 55 x 98 cm) USD 75,000. LONDON, 20 June 2002, *Parisian Street Scene* (pencil and gouache, 13 x 18 ins / 33 x 46 cm) GBP 22,000. LONDON, 3 June 2003, *Busy Street Scene Near the Porte St Denis at Night* (oil on canvas, 18 x 26 ins / 46 x 65 cm) GBP 51,000. PARIS, 20 June 2003, *The Porte St-Denis in the Snow, The Flower Market* (watercolour, pair, 15 x 17 ins / 37 x 44 cm) EUR 72,000. LYONS, 17 Oct 2004, *Paris, Winter, Snow, Boulevard Bonne Nouvelle, at the Theatre du Gymnase* (gouache, 21 x 37 ins / 54 x 94 cm) EUR 140,000. ZURICH, 26 March 2004, *Paris, Street Scene* (gouache, 17 x 28 ins / 42 x 72 cm) CHF 65,000.

GALIETTO, Giuseppe

Italian, 17th century.

Active in Naples.

Sculptor (wood).

GALIMARD, Claude Olivier, or Gallimard

French, 18th century.

Born 1719, in Paris; died 2 March 1774, in Paris.

Engraver, draughtsman.

Some biographers say that Claude Galimard was born in Troyes. He was made an associate of the academy in 1752 but never became an academician. His engraved work is substantial and encompasses genre and religious subjects and allegories. Galimard worked in Rome.

AUCTION RECORDS:
PARIS, 5 and 6 May 1898, *Perspectival View of the Garden of M. de St-James,* FRF 200.

GALIMARD, Nicolas-Auguste
French, 19th century.
Born 25 March 1813, in Paris; died 16 January 1880, in Montigny-lès-Cormeilles (Val d'Oise).
Painter, pastellist, draughtsman, lithographer, art critic. Religious subjects, allegorical subjects, still-lifes. Designs for stained glass.

He studied initially under his uncle Auguste Hesse before going on to complete his artistic education in the studios of Jean Auguste Dominique Ingres and Denis Foyatier. He exhibited at the Paris Salon from 1835 to 1880, and was awarded a bronze medal in 1835 and a silver in 1846. Galimard was principally a draughtsman and lithographer. He also produced cartoons for stained glass for the choir of the church of Celle-St-Cloud and for chapels in the Paris churches of St-Laurent, St-Germain-l'Auxerrois and St-Philippe-du-Roule. Galimard's canvas of *Leda and the Swan* (subsequently repeated in pastel) was rejected by the 1855 Salon committee on the grounds of its 'indecency', but was promptly acquired by Napoleon III for his private collection. Galimard's draughtsmanship clearly betrays the influence of his mentors, notably Ingres (a caricature produced by Nada for the periodical *Les Artistes* shows two people admiring a painting. 'An Ingres?', says one; 'No', replies the other, 'for once, a decent Galimard!') Galimard himself was also an art critic whose books included a treatise on stained glass. Not least, writing under various bynames, he wrote articles and reviews of Salons for the *Revue des Beaux-Arts, La Patrie* and *L'Artiste*.

BIBLIOGRAPHY:
Les Années romantiques, la peinture française de 1815 à 1850, exhibition catalogue, Musée des Beaux-Arts, Nantes; Gal. Nationales du Grand Palais, Paris, 1996.

MUSEUMS AND GALLERIES:
CHOLET: *Three Marys at the Tomb* - NARBONNE: *Jealous Juno.*

AUCTION RECORDS:
PARIS, 20 Nov 1922, *Statue* (graphite drawing) FRF 110.
MONTE CARLO, 29 Nov 1986, *Leda and the Swan* (1863, pastel, 19 3/4 x 29 1/2in/50 x 75cm) FRF 30,000.

GALIMBERTI, Francesco
Italian, 18th century.
Born 1755, in Venice; died 1803, in Vienna.
Painter, engraver.

Francesco Galimberti engraved copies of numerous works by Carpaccio and Veronese.

MUSEUMS AND GALLERIES:
GRENOBLE (Mus. de Grenoble): drawing.

GALIMBERTI, Giuseppe
Italian, 18th century.
Active in Verona.
Painter.

One of Giuseppe Galimberti's drawings is preserved in the Uffizi in Florence.

GALIMBERTI, Sándor
Hungarian, 20th century.
Born 1883, in Kaposvár; died 20 July 1915, in Budapest.
Painter.

Of Italian origin, Sándor Galimberti began his studies with Jozsef Rippl-Ronai and continued in Nagybánya and Munich where he was a student of Hollósy. He completed his studies at the Académie Julian in Paris. In 1914 he spent a few months in Holland then went back to Hungary at the outbreak of war. He committed suicide just after the death of his wife. He was one of the important representatives of Cubism in Hungary.

From 1908 onwards he exhibited in Paris at the Salon d'Automne and at the Salon des Indépendants. In 1914 he exhibited with his wife Valeria Dénes at the National Exhibition in Budapest. A retrospective of his works was organised in 1918. He featured in *L'art en Hongrie 1905-1930. Art et Révolution* (*Art in Hungary 1905-1930. Art and Revolution*), Musée d'Art Moderne de la Ville de Paris.

GALIMBERTI, Silvio
Italian, 19th - 20th century.
Active in Rome.
Painter.

Galimberti is mostly remembered for his landscapes and frescoes.

GALIMBERTI, Valéria or Valy. See **DÉNES**

GALIMSKY, Vladislav Mikhailovich
Ukrainian, 19th century.
Born 1860, in Kiev.
Painter.

The Russian Museum has a work by Galimsky. He was a student at the St Petersburg academy.

GALINDEZ, Martín
Spanish, 16th - 17th century.
Born 1547, in Haro; died 1627, at the Charterhouse in El Paular.
Painter, sculptor (wood).

In 1548, Galindez entered the charterhouse at Paular, where he devoted his leisure time to research in mechanics. He painted a large number of religious pictures and also produced some wood carvings.

GALINDO, Benito
Spanish, 16th century.
Born in Extremadura.
Painter.

Galindo worked mainly in Barcelona.

GALINIER, Nicolas
French, 19th century.
Born c. 1790, in Marseilles.
Sculptor.

He studied under Bosio. His works include a bust of Louis XIV for the façade of the Hôtel de Ville in Marseilles.

GALIOT, Désirée-Charlotte, Mme Sauvageot
French, 19th century.
Painter. Portraits.

She studied under Bouchet and exhibited examples of her work at the 1819 Salon.

MUSEUMS AND GALLERIES:
SOISSONS: *Portrait of a Child.*

GALIPOT, Guy, also known as Lacroix
French, 18th century.
Active in Paris in 1770.
Painter, sculptor.

GALITSKY, Rostislav Nikolaevich
Russian, 20th century.
Born 1920, in Rostov.
Painter.

Rostislav Nikolaevich Galitsky graduated from the Surikov Institute in Moscow in 1956.

MUSEUMS AND GALLERIES:
ST PETERSBURG (Gosudarstvennyj Russkij Muz.).

AUCTION RECORDS:
VERSAILLES, 9 Dec 1990, *Relaxing in the Palm Grove* (1945, oil on canvas/card, 49 1/4 x 36 1/4 ins / 125 x 92 cm) FRF 3,500.

GALITSYN, Leo
Russian, 19th century.
Active in Moscow.
Sculptor.

Galitsyn was a pupil of Ramasanov.

GALITZINE, Marc Augustin
French, 20th century.
Born in Paris.
Painter. Landscapes.
Marc Galitzine exhibited at the Salon of the Société Nationale from 1923.

GALIZIA, Annunzio
Italian, 16th century.
Born in Trento.
Miniaturist.
Galizia is undoubtedly the same person as Annunzio Fede. He was the father of Fede Galizia, and he worked mainly in Milan.

GALIZIA, Fede, or Gallizi
Italian, 16th - 17th century.
Born c. 1578, in Milan; died after 1630.
Painter. Mythological subjects, religious subjects, portraits, landscapes, still-lifes (flowers/fruit).
Fede Galizia studied under her father Annunzio Galizia, a miniaturist living and working in Milan. She proved particularly adept in the genre of portrait miniatures. An example of her work is a *Portrait of the Chronicler Paolo Morigia*, painted when she was just 18 years old.
MUSEUMS AND GALLERIES:
MILAN (Ambrosiana): *Portrait of the Chronicler Paolo Morigia* - MILAN (Pinacoteca di Brera): *Christ Appearing to Mary Magdalene*.
AUCTION RECORDS:
MILAN, 20 Nov 1963, *Still-life with Fruit*, ITL 1,500,000. LONDON, 20 March 1964, *Still-life with Flowers and Fruit*, Gns 1,000. AMSTERDAM, 17 May 1983, *Still-life* (oil on panel, 14 1/2 x 18 ins / 37 x 45.5 cm) NLG 19,000. MILAN, 24 April 1988, *Judith and Holofernes* (oil on canvas, 47 1/4 x 35 1/2 ins / 120 x 90 cm) ITL 35,000,000. ROME, 13 Dec 1988, *Still-life with Peaches on a Pewter Dish and Two Pears* (oil on canvas, 14 1/4 x 19 ins / 36.5 x 48.5 cm) ITL 22,000,000. PARIS, 9 April 1990, *Still-life with Peaches* (oil on oak panel, total surface, 12 x 15 1/2 ins / 30.5 x 39.5 cm) FRF 600,000. NEW YORK, 28 Jan 1999, *Dish of Fruit Resting on Table* (oil on panel, 11 x 15 ins / 29 x 39 cm) USD 60,000. ZURICH, 18 March 1999, *Quince in Woven Basket* (oil on panel, 16 x 21 ins / 41 x 54 cm) CHF 120,000. MILAN, 15 Nov 2003, *Fruit Bowl with Grapes, Plums and Pears* (oil on board, 9 x 14 ins / 22 x 35 cm) EUR 141,000. MILAN, 26 May 2004, *Metal Bowl with Peaches and Flowers* (oil on board, 12 x 17 ins / 31 x 43 cm) EUR 100,000.

GALIZZI. See also **SANTACROCE**

GALIZZI, Battista
Italian, 19th century.
Born 1824, in Bergamo.
Painter. Religious subjects.
MUSEUMS AND GALLERIES:
BERGAMO (Accademia Carrara): *St George*.

GALIZZI, Giovan Battista
Italian, 20th century.
Born 1882, in Bergamo; died 1963.
Painter. Genre scenes.
AUCTION RECORDS:
MILAN, 10 June 1981, *Forge* (oil on canvas, 35 x 43 1/4 ins / 89 x 110 cm) ITL 700,000. ROME, 21 March 1985, *Dogs on the Beach* (oil on canvas, 89 x 64 1/4 ins / 226 x 163 cm) ITL 1,700,000. MILAN, 21 Dec 1993, *Procession of Wedding Presents through a Village* (oil on card, 25 x 20 ins / 63.5 x 50.5 cm) ITL 2,070,000.

GALKIN, Volodja
Russian, 20th century.
Born in the second half of the 20th century.
Sculptor.
Op Art, Kinetic Art.
Dvizhenie Group.
Galkin was part of the Dvizhenie (Movement) group with Francisco Infante and Stepanov in which Lev Nusberg brought together technicians of various disciplines, with whom he executed important kinetic and luminist works.
BIBLIOGRAPHY:
Popper, Frank, *Naissance de l'art cinétique*, Gauthier-Villars, Paris, 1967.

GALKINE, Ilia Savich or Ilya Savvich, or Galkin
Russian, 19th - 20th century.
Born 1860, in Russia; died 1915.
Painter. Figure compositions, genre scenes.
Ilia Savich Galkine worked in St Petersburg in particular.
MUSEUMS AND GALLERIES:
ST PETERSBURG (Gosudarstvennyj Russkij Muz.): *The Lecture*.
AUCTION RECORDS:
LONDON, 11-12 June 1997, *Little Girl with Flowers* (oil on canvas, 36 1/2 x 25 1/4 ins / 92.5 x 64 cm) GBP 5,175.

GALL
Austrian, 15th century.
Sculptor (wood).
Gall was active in Innsbruck in around 1472. He worked for the church of Seefeld.

GALL, Biserka
Croat, 20th century.
Born 23 July 1942, in Zagreb.
Active in France from 1965.
Painter, engraver, pastellist. Designs for tapestries.
Biserka Gall studied at the school of fine arts in Zagreb from 1960 to 1965. Her paintings and engravings are influenced by Constructivism and she uses dark tones and Lyrical Figuration. Shapes, cubes, rectangles, parallelograms and projected planes glide over the heart of the canvas, somewhere between sky and earth. Magical architecture and inter-stellar cities seem to reach up towards infinity.

Group exhibitions include those at the following: the Salon de Mai in Paris (1965, 1966); the second International Engraving Biennale in Seoul (1972); the Bibliothèque Nationale in Paris (1973); the Banja Luka Salon in Yugoslavia (1973); the Salon des Réalités Nouvelles in Paris (1974); the Bibliothèque Nationale in Lausanne (1974); the Musée d'Art Moderne de la Ville de Paris (1975); and the first International Engraving Biennale in Givet. Solo exhibitions since 1965 include those in Zagreb (1966, 1978), Paris (1965-1967, 1971, 1975-1977, 1980, 1981, 1983), Brussels (1968, 1973) and Belgrade (1975, 1979).
BIBLIOGRAPHY:
Gall et Kemal, exhibition catalogue, Gal. d'Art contemporain, Chamalières, 1986.

GALL, François or Ferenc
Hungarian, 20th century.
Born 22 March 1912, in Kolozsvár (now Cluj-Napoca, Romania), to Hungarian parents; died 9 December 1987, in Paris.
Active from 1936, naturalised in France in 1945.
Painter, watercolourist. Figure compositions, figures, portraits, interiors with figures, landscapes with figures, urban landscapes, architectural views, gardens, seascapes.
François Gall studied in Rome at the Accademia de Belle Arti while performing manual jobs. In 1930 he obtained a grant from the Hungarian government and settled in Paris in 1936 where he trained with Devambez at the École Nationale des Beaux-Arts.

He was influenced by the French Impressionists and specialised in painting young, pretty Parisian girls, whom he observed in every situation of their busy day, from their private life, across typical Parisian scenes, in the bustle of the cafes or in the world of theatre and dance, as far as at the beaches and at the fashionable horse races.

Alongside his painting, François Gall had important administrative roles in the arts. He was Vice-President of the national retirement fund for the arts (IRCEC), administrator of the Society of Independent Artists (Vice-President from 1976 to 1981), administrator of the Taylor Foundation and administrator of the ADAGP. Gal became Officier des Arts et des Lettres and was awarded the gold medal for distinguished services by the French government.

Since 1936 Gall featured in numerous collective exhibitions in Paris including: Salons des Artistes Français (winning awards and medals); Salon des Indépendants; Salon d'Automne, Salon des Peintres Témoins de leur Temps; Salon du Dessin; Salon de Peinture à l'eau; Salon Comparaisons. He also participated in many exhibitions outside Paris and abroad. Solo exhibitions include: Durand-Ruel gallery, Paris (1949); Marlborough Gallery, London; Touraine Art Gallery, New York (1953). François Gall won the Francis Smith prize in 1963.

Bibliography:

Flament, André, *F. Gall*, Vision sur les arts, Paris (extensive documentation). Fleury, Jean, *Oeuvres de François Gall*, Paris, 1980.

Auction records:

New York, 8 Nov 1957, *Landscape in the Fauve style,* USD 1,500. New York, 22 Jan 1960, *Tuileries Garden* (Paris) USD 350. Zurich, 5 May 1972, *Pont-Neuf,* CHF 3,700. Paris, 27 Feb 1976, *Beach at Trouville* (oil on canvas, 11 x 18 ins / 27 x 46 cm) FRF 3,200. Versailles, 8 June 1977, *Young Girl in a Red Dress with Daisies or Young Girl from the Quercy region* (oil on canvas, 23 1/2 x 28 3/4 ins / 60 x 73 cm) FRF 10,800. Versailles, 30 Nov 1980, *In Front of the Mirror* (oil on canvas, 32 x 25 1/2 ins / 81 x 65 cm) FRF 22,000. Versailles, 6 March 1983, *Getting Ready* (oil and gouache, 20 3/4 x 14 1/4 ins / 53 x 36 cm) FRF 6,000. Versailles, 17 Nov 1985, *On the Cafe Terrace* (oil on canvas, 23 1/2 x 28 3/4 ins / 60 x 73 cm) FRF 48,000. Paris, 27 Nov 1987, *Young Woman in a Blue Dress in Paris* (oil on canvas, 28 x 23 1/2 ins / 71 x 60 cm) FRF 24,000. Versailles, 13 Dec 1987, *Young Girl at a Cafe Table* (oil on canvas, 24 x 18 ins / 61 x 46 cm) FRF 29,500. La Varenne-St-Hilaire, 6 March 1988, *The Lecture* (oil on canvas, 11 x 9 ins / 27 x 22 cm) FRF 24,000. Paris, 11 April 1988, *The Grenelle Bridge and the Eiffel Tower* (oil on card, 8 1/4 x 8 1/2 ins / 21 x 21.5 cm) FRF 12,500. Versailles, 15 June 1988, *Young Woman in Luxembourg Gardens* (1947, oil on canvas, 21 1/4 x 25 1/2 ins / 54 x 65 cm) FRF 60,000. Paris, 12 July 1988, *Landscape* (oil on canvas, 24 x 31 1/2 ins / 61 x 80 cm) FRF 10,100. Versailles, 25 Sept 1988, *Paris, a Cafe Terrace* (oil on canvas, 18 x 24 ins / 46 x 61 cm) FRF 30,000. Montreal, 17 Oct 1988, *Young Girl at the Piano* (oil on canvas, 14 1/4 x 11 ins / 36 x 27 cm) CAD 3,800. Paris, 27 Oct 1988, *Sunday Afternoon in the Park* (oil on canvas, 9 x 11 ins / 22 x 27 cm) FRF 30,000. Toronto, 30 Nov 1988, *At the Cafe* (oil on canvas, 15 1/2 x 11 1/2 ins / 39.5 x 29 cm) CAD 4,000. Paris, 16 Dec 1988, *Landing Stage* (oil on paper, 7 3/4 x 11 ins / 20 x 28 cm) FRF 11,000. London, 21 Feb 1989, *Young Woman on the Beach* (oil on card, 8 3/4 x 11 ins / 22.3 x 27 cm) GBP 3,080. Paris, 27 April 1989, *Place du Tertre in Montmartre* (oil on panel, 12 1/2 x 16 1/4 ins / 32 x 41 cm) FRF 23,000. Montreal, 1 May 1989, *Piano Study* (oil on canvas, 18 x 15 ins / 46 x 38 cm) CAD 7,500. New York, 9 May 1989, *Lunch on the Grass* (oil on canvas, 19 1/4 x 23 1/2 ins / 49.2 x 60 cm) USD 7,150. Stockholm, 22 May 1989, *Passers-by on the Pont-Neuf in Paris* (oil on panel, 28 1/4 x 35 3/4 ins / 72 x 91 cm) SEK 62,000. Paris, 22 Oct 1989, *Walk along the Banks of the Seine in Paris* (oil on canvas, 29 1/4 x 23 1/2 ins / 74 x 60 cm) FRF 58,000. Paris, 23 Nov 1989, *Female Dancers* (oil on canvas, 10 3/4 x 8 3/4 ins / 27.5 x 22.5 cm) FRF 35,000. La Varenne-St-Hilaire, 3 Dec 1989, *Riders in the Forest* (1943, oil on canvas, 23 1/2 x 32 ins / 60 x 81 cm) FRF 72,000. St-Dié, 11 Feb 1990, *Place du Tertre* (oil on panel, 12 1/2 x 16 1/4 ins / 32 x 41 cm) FRF 28,000. New York, 21 Feb 1990, *On the Pier at Trouville* (oil on canvas, 25 1/2 x 31 3/4 ins / 65 x 80.6 cm) USD 22,000. Bern, 12 May 1990, *Lunch Break* (oil on canvas, 23 1/2 x 19 3/4 ins / 60 x 50 cm) CHF 22,000. Stockholm, 14 June 1990, *View of Paris* (1946, oil on canvas, 13 x 16 1/4 ins / 33 x 41 cm) SEK 30,000. Calais, 8 July 1990, *Beach at Trouville* (oil on canvas, 11 x 18 ins / 27 x 46 cm) FRF 75,000. Le Touquet, 11 Nov 1990, *Wooden Merry-go-round in Martel-en-Quercy* (watercolour, 6 3/4 x 7 3/4 ins / 17 x 20 cm) FRF 5,800. Calais, 9 Dec 1990, *Young Girl in a Boater* (oil on canvas, 24 x 19 3/4 ins / 61 x 50 cm) FRF 58,500. New York, 13 Feb 1991, *Young Girl in Pink* (oil on canvas, 24 x 20 ins / 61.2 x 50.7 cm) USD 8,800. Amsterdam, 23 April 1991, *Feeding the Baby* (oil on panel, 11 x 13 3/4 ins / 27 x 35 cm) NLG 13,800. New York, 12 June 1991, *Deauville* (oil on canvas, 10 3/4 x 18 ins / 27.3 x 45.7 cm) USD 7,700. Honfleur, 18 Aug 1991, *Lunch in the Garden* (oil on canvas, 13 3/4 x 11 ins / 35 x 27 cm) FRF 70,000. New York, 5 Nov 1991, *In the Wings* (oil on canvas, 18 1/4 x 15 ins / 46.3 x 38.4 cm) USD 10,450. Montreal, 19 Nov 1991, *In the Wing* (oil on canvas, 10 1/2 x 8 1/2 ins / 26.6 x 21.5 cm) CAD 3,000. Munich, 26-27 Nov 1991, *Summer Landscape with a Flowering Shrub* (oil on canvas, 12 1/2 x 17 ins / 31.5 x 43 cm) DEM 1,265. New York, 9 May 1992, *On the Beach* (oil on canvas, 10 3/4 x 18 ins / 27.3 x 45.7 cm) USD 7,700. Stockholm, 21 May 1992, *Paris Scene* (oil on panel, 27 1/2 x 35 1/2 ins / 70 x 90 cm) SEK 18,000. New York, 10 Nov 1992, *At the Deux Magots* (oil on canvas, 11 x 9 ins / 27 x 22 cm) USD 6,600. Sceaux, 13 Dec 1992, *Beach in Dieppe* (oil on canvas, 10 1/4 x 18 ins / 26 x 45.5 cm) FRF 13,000. Paris, 18 Dec 1992, *Pier in Trouville* (oil on canvas, 24 x 19 3/4 ins / 61 x 50 cm) FRF 24,100. New York, 29 Sept 1993, *Marie-Lise in the Cafe* (oil on canvas, 23 1/2 x 29 ins / 59.7 x 73.7 cm) USD 12,075. Paris, 14 March 1994, *Young Girl from the Quercy Region* (oil on canvas, 23 1/2 x 29 1/4 ins / 60 x 74 cm) FRF 60,000. London, 15 June 1994, *Street Scene in Rome* (oil on card, 19 x 13 ins / 48 x 33 cm) GBP 2,185. Paris, 26 March 1995, *Young Woman in the Fields* (oil on canvas, 10 3/4 x 9 ins / 27.2 x 22 cm) FRF 15,000. Amsterdam, 6 Dec 1995, *View of Notre Dame in Paris* (oil on canvas, 23 1/2 x 19 3/4 ins / 60 x 50 cm) NLG 4,025. New York, 30 April 1996, *Pont-Neuf* (oil on canvas, 19 3/4 x 24 ins / 50 x 61 cm) USD 2,875. New York, 10 Oct 1996, *Eugenie in a Red Dress* (oil on panel, 18 1/4 x 13 ins / 46.4 x 32.1 cm) USD 2,415. New York, 12 Nov 1996, *Woman in the Mirror* (c. 1970, oil on canvas, 24 x 18 ins / 61 x 46 cm) USD 5,750. Paris, 5 June 1997, *Arcachon, Figure on the Beach* (oil on canvas, 9 x 11 ins / 22 x 27 cm) FRF 11,000. Paris, 23 June 1997, *Montmartre, Sacré-Coeur* (oil on canvas, 15 x 18 ins / 38 x 46 cm) FRF 8,000. Paris, 22 March 1998, *Portrait of Babette* (oil on canvas, 11 x 9 ins / 27 x 22 cm) FRF 13,500. New York, 27 Feb 1998, *Ballerina Tying her Slipper* (oil on canvas, 11 x 9 ins / 27 x 22 cm) USD 17,000. Bern, 21 Oct 1998, *Portrait of Woman in Red Dress* (oil on canvas, 20 x 24 ins / 50 x 61 cm) CHF 16,000. London, 26 March 1999, *At the Beach* (oil on canvas, 18 x 26 ins / 46 x 65 cm) GBP 13,000. Bern, 5 May 1999, *Girl in a Red Dress in a Garden* (oil on canvas, 22 x 18 ins / 55 x 46 cm) CHF 27,000. New York, 8 May

2000, *Dance Lesson in Paris* (oil on canvas, 18 x 22 ins / 46 x 55 cm) USD 10,000. NEW YORK, 7 Nov 2000, *At the Café in Paris* (oil on canvas) USD 9,500. NEW YORK, 22 May 2001, *Paris - Boulevard de Montparnasse* (oil on canvas) USD 10,000. BERN, 1 May 2002, *A Woman Outside the Hairdressers* (oil on canvas, 29 x 24 ins / 73 x 60 cm) CHF 20,000. LONDON, 3 April 2003, *The Beach at Trouville* (oil on canvas, 25 x 30 ins / 64 x 76 cm) GBP 8,000. NEW YORK, 25 Sept 2003, *Jardin des Tuileries, Paris* (c. 1939-1940, oil on canvas, 19 x 29 ins / 49 x 73 cm) USD 7,500. NEW YORK, 25 Feb 2004, *Eugenie on the River Bank* (oil on canvas, 9 x 11 ins / 22 x 27 cm) USD 18,000. NEW YORK, 29 Sept 2004, *Marie-Lize in a Red Hat* (oil on canvas, 24 x 20 ins / 61 x 50 cm) USD 13,000.

GALL, G.
French, 19th century.
Painter. Landscapes.

MUSEUMS AND GALLERIES:
ST-LÔ: *Fog on the Mountain at Aubrac.*

GALL, Joseph
French, 19th century.
Born 1807, in Nevers (Nièvre).
Painter. Landscapes.

He exhibited at the Paris Salon from 1842 to 1876, typically showing landscapes, some rustic scenes and a few religious paintings. Examples include: *Stone Cross, Christ Installing St Peter as Primate, Benedictine Monk Meditating, Woodsmen, Massacre of the Protestants in the Cévennes* and *Pastures.*

AUCTION RECORDS:
NEW YORK, 28 Oct 1987, *Figures in a Church* (oil on canvas, 19 x 14 1/2in/48.2 x 36.8cm) USD 16,000.

GALL FABRA, Francisco de Asís or Francesc
Spanish, 20th century.
Born 1880, in Barcelona; died 23 September 1965, in Barcelona.
Painter, decorative designer.

Francisco Galí began studying architecture but soon abandoned this in favour of painting and engraving which he studied at the La Lonja school of fine art. He later taught drawing and drew up a teaching method that was put into practice in schools in Catalonia. He lived in England for a time.

In addition to his paintings, he also decorated many ceilings and domes in public and private buildings.

BIBLIOGRAPHY:
Arnáiz, José Manuel/López Jiménez, Javier/Merchán Díaz, Manuel (ed.), *'Cien años de pintura en Espana y Portugal (1830-1930)'* in vol. III, Antiqvaria, Madrid, 1989 (One Hundred Years of Painting in Spain and Portugal (1830-1930)).

MUSEUMS AND GALLERIES:
BARCELONA (MAC) - MADRID (Mus. Nacional Centro de Arte Reina Sofía).

GALLACCIO, Anya
British, 20th - 21st century.
Born 1963, in Paisley, near Glasgow.
Active in London.
Sculptor, installation artist.

Anya Gallaccio studied at the Kingston Polytechnic (1984-1985) and at Goldsmith's College in London (1985-1988). In 1998 she was awarded the Sargent Fellowship by the British School in Rome. She was shortlisted for the Turner Prize in 2003.

Gallaccio was discovered in the 1980s along with other Young British Artists in the exhibition *Freeze*. She is known for her predilection for working with organic materials such as flowers, fruit, ice and grass which naturally decay in time. Her choice of materials and the materials themselves embody Gallaccio's interest in the themes of transformation, change, the passing of time and the nature of impermanence. Her resistance to any documentation of her work emphasises their ephemeral nature and site-specificity, and further underlines her interest in the nature of time and impermanence. In 1996 she positioned a 32-tonne block of ice with a ball of rock salt at its heart over an old pumping station in Wapping, leaving it to melt. In 2002 she was invited to create a new installation for the Tate's Duveen Galleries. Here she created *Preserve 'Beauty'*, a wall of gerbera daisies behind a sheet of glass. She has also worked in bronze, making casts of living things, although she combines these pieces with organic materials.

Solo exhibitions of her work include *Keep off the Grass* at the Serpentine Gallery in London (1997), *Glaschu* at the Tramway in Glasgow (1999), and other exhibitions at Sadler's Wells in London (1999), the Kunsthalle in Bern (2000) and the Lehman Maupin Gallery in New York (2001).

BIBLIOGRAPHY:
Anya Gallaccio, exhibition catalogue, Galerie Krinzinger, Vienna, 1993. *Chasing Rainbows: Anya Gallaccio*, exhibition catalogue, Tramway, Glasgow, 1999. Horlock, Mary/Reitmaier, Heidi/Schama, Simon, *Beat*, exhibition catalogue, Tate Galleries, London, 2002.

MUSEUMS AND GALLERIES:
LONDON (Tate Collection): *Spider's Leg at 400x* (silver gelatin print).

GALLACINI, Giuseppe
Italian, 18th century.
Active in Leiden in 1778.
Painter.

GALLAGHER, Ella Sheppard. See **SHEPPARD**

GALLAGHER, Ellen
American, 20th - 21st century.
Born 1965, in Providence (Rhode Island).
Painter, draughtswoman.

Ellen Gallagher studied at Oberlin College in Ohio and the School of the Museum of Fine Arts in Boston. Her work explores racial issues, questions of identity and transformation. She uses a variety of materials to create collages such as ink, Plasticene, tape, vintage advertisements, and paint. She has also worked with 16mm film, creating five film projections for *Murmur* in 2003. From a distance Gallagher's works appear abstract, but looking closer at works such as

Falls and Flips (2001) the small squares, up to several hundred, are made up of stereotypical images of black culture. Gallagher modified the images by painting blonde wigs on top of the portraits. In this way her work reaches back into the past while engaging with contemporary issues of race and identity.

Gallagher's work became widely known after she was included in the Whitney Biennial and the exhibition *Inside Visible* at the Institute of Contemporary Art in Boston, both in 1995. In 1996 she exhibited work in two solo shows, one at the Mary Boone gallery in New York and another at the Anthony d'Offay gallery in London. These were followed by shows at the Gagosian Gallery (1998), the Galerie Max Hetzler (1999), and the Mario Diacono Gallery (1999). In 2001, Gallagher had several shows including *Blubber* at the Gagosian Gallery and *Preserve* at the Drawing Center. *Murmur* took place at the Galerie Max Hetzler (2003) and was followed by *The Pinocchio Theory* at the Henry Art Gallery (2004) and *Ellen Gallagher: Murmur and Deluxe* (2005) at MOCA.

BIBLIOGRAPHY:
Grosenick, Uta, *Women Artists in the 20th and 21st Century*, Taschen, Cologne, 2001. Gallagher, Ellen, *Preserve*, Des Moines Art Center, 2001. Morgan, Jessica, *Ellen Gallagher*, Zzdap Publishing, 2001. Gallagher, Ellen, *Blubber*, Gagosian Gallery, 2001. *Vitamin P - New Perspectives in Painting*, Phai-

don Press, London, 2002. Grosenick, Uta, *Art Now*, Tachen, Cologne, 2002. Goodeve, Thyrza Nichols, *Ellen Gallagher*, Anthony d'Offay, 2002.

MUSEUMS AND GALLERIES:

BERLIN (Mus. für Gegenwart) - NEW YORK (MoMA) - NEW YORK (Solomon R. Guggenheim Mus.) - SAN FRANCISCO (MoMA).

AUCTION RECORDS:

NEW YORK, 20 May 1999, *Untitled* (1992, graphite and collage on panel, 60 x 15 ins / 152 x 38 cm) USD 40,000. NEW YORK, 15 May 2001, *Soma* (1998, oil and pencil on paper laid on canvas, 96 x 84 ins / 244 x 213 cm) USD 100,000. NEW YORK, 14 May 2002, *Wild Kingdom* (1995, oil and graphite on paper laid on canvas, 84 x 72 ins / 213 x 183 cm) USD 95,000. NEW YORK, 13 Nov 2002, *Untitled* (1999, oil and ink on paper laid on canvas, 120 x 96 ins / 305 x 244 cm) USD 85,000. NEW YORK, 15 May 2003, *Untitled* (1996, ink, 28 x 27 ins / 71 x 69 cm) USD 4,200. NEW YORK, 23 Sept 2003, *Shiner* (1993, oil, pencil and collage on canvas, 24 x 24 ins / 61 x 61 cm) USD 26,000.

GALLAGHER, Genevieve

American, 20th century.
Born 19 January 1899, in Baltimore.
Painter.

Genevieve Gallagher won the Baltimore Art Society prize in 1921. She was also a teacher.

GALLAGHER, John

British, 19th century.
Born in Dublin.
Sculptor.

John Gallagher was an exhibitor at London's Royal Academy from 1832 to 1844.

GALLAGHER, Sears

American, 20th century.
Born 30 April 1869, in Boston; died 1955.
Painter, engraver.

Sears Gallagher studied under Jean-Paul Laurens and Benjamin-Constant in Paris. He was a member of many American artists' associations. He received awards and distinctions, particularly for his talent as an engraver, including silver medals for etching in California in 1929 and Boston in 1930.

AUCTION RECORDS:

SAN FRANCISCO, 27 Feb 1986, *Children Playing on the Beach* (watercolour, 13 x 19½ ins / 33 x 49.5 cm) USD 2,500. WILTON, 6 March 2000, *Sand Dunes* (oil on canvas, 20 x 23 ins / 51 x 58 cm) USD 7,500. BOLTON, 20 July 2000, *Rose Garden* (watercolour, 15 x 20 ins / 38 x 51 cm) USD 2,600. FAIRFIELD, 22 Aug 2001, *Maine Mariner with Sextant* (watercolour, 17 x 13 ins / 43 x 33 cm) USD 5,250. BOSTON, 2 Dec 2001, *SS Cephalonia - Captain Seccombe* (1895, watercolour, ink and pencil, 14 x 10 ins / 36 x 25 cm) USD 3,000. FAIRFIELD, 8 Jan 2004, *Summer Clouds, Gloucester* (watercolour, 13 x 19 ins / 33 x 48 cm) USD 2,200.

GALLAIT, Louis

Belgian, 19th century.
Born 10 March 1810, in Tournai (Hainaut); died 20 November 1887, in Schaerbeek (Brussels).
Painter, draughtsman. History painting, religious subjects, mythological subjects, genre scenes, portraits.

Gallait studied first at the academy of fine arts in Tournai, under Philippe Auguste Hennequin, and later in Antwerp and Paris, where he entered the studio of Ary Scheffer in 1834. Paul Delaroche was a fellow student and close associate. He subsequently settled in Brussels, and exhibited in France, Germany and Austria. He also exhibited regularly in London from 1836 to 1872, and was the subject of a major one-man retrospective in 1862. Gallait became a member of the academies of Belgium and Berlin in 1843, Dresden and Munich in 1844, and Vienna in 1853. In Brussels, in 1844, he was made a member of the Légion d'Honneur and a Commander of the Order of Leopold. Gallait's favoured subject-matter was Flanders during the time of the Spanish occupation. He treated this quintessentially Romantic theme in the classical style, and with great concern for historical accuracy. He was well regarded in France and received commissions for paintings to be hung at Versailles, including the *Coronation of Baldwin I, Count of Flanders*. Other noted works include the *Fall of Antioch, Christopher Columbus in Prison* and *Final Homage to the Counts of Egmond and Hoorn*, of which he produced several versions. Several of his drawings and sketches were exhibited in Tournai in 1971. Fourteen of his studies featured in the exhibition *Le Clair et l'Obscur* (*The Light and the Dark*) in Brussels in 1970, which gathered together the drawings of some 200 Belgian artists.

BIBLIOGRAPHY:

Le Bailly de Tilleghem, S., '*La Formation néo-classique d'un maître romantique: Louis Gallait à l'Académie de Tournai, analyse de dessins inédits*' in *Rev. Archéologues & Historiens A. Louvain*, Ix, 1976. Berko, P./Berko, V., *Dictionary of Belgian Painters Born between 1750 and 1875*, Brussels, 1981. Flippo, W. C., et al., *Lexicon of the Belgian Romantic Painters*, Antwerp, 1981.

MUSEUMS AND GALLERIES:

AMSTERDAM (Stedelijk Mus.): *Evening; A Neglected Woman* - ANTWERP: *Final Homage to Counts of Egmond and Hoorn* - BERLIN: *Last Hours of Egmond* - BRUSSELS (MBA): *Abdication of Charles V; Plague in Tournai; Capture of Antioch by the Crusaders; Joanna the Mad; Leopold II; Art and Liberty; Champion of Villeneuve; Queen Marie-Henrietta; M. Barthélémy de Mortier; Mme Dick, the Painter's Mother-in-law; Mme Louis Gallait and her Daughter; Souvenir of Blankenberghe; Gypsy Woman and her Children; Falling Leaves; The Wedding Dress* - COLOGNE: *Portrait of a Woman* - FRANKFURT AM MAIN: *Abdication of Charles V* - GHENT: *Jewish Family Accused of Harbouring Stolen Religious Artefacts; Render unto Caesar* - HAMBURG: *Consolation* - LIÈGE: *Old Beggar* - LILLE: *Job; Ch. Cousin in Arab Dress* - LONDON (Wallace Collection): *The Duke of Alva in the Netherlands* (1835, oil on canvas) - MUNICH: *A Monk Giving Food to the Poor* - TOURNAI: *Lepez; Louis Haghé; The Severed Heads; Colonel Hallart; The Artist's Mother and Sister; Luis and Charles Hague; H. Campan de Nice* - VERSAILLES: *Fall of Antioch; Louis Brancas; Charles de Gontaut-Biron; Battle of Kassel* - YPRES: *The Broken Bow*.

AUCTION RECORDS:

PARIS, 1850, *Abdication of Charles V*, FRF 8,190. PARIS, 1870, *Art and Liberty*, FRF 25,500. NEW YORK, 8-9 Jan 1903, *Young Mother*, USD 550. LONDON, 30 Jan 1909, *The Fracas; Card Players*, GBP 7. NEW YORK, 18 April 1945, *The Prisoner*, USD 300; *Coronation of Baldwin I, Count of Flanders* (watercolour) USD 150. BRUSSELS, 5 Oct 1976, *Historic Meeting with the Prince de Condé* (oil on canvas, 46½ x 67¾in/118 x 172cm) BEF 120,000. NEW YORK, 12 May 1978, *The Prisoner of Rome* (1862, oil on panel, 20¾ x 16¾in/53 x 42.5cm) USD 3,750. VIENNA, 17 March 1981, *Art and Liberty* (watercolour, 28 x 21¼in/71 x 54cm) ATS 11,000. NEW YORK, 25 Oct 1984, *Young Minstrel* (1885, oil on canvas, 52 x 41in/132.1 x 104.2cm) USD 6,500. PARIS, 21 Dec 1987, *Fall of Antioch* (oil on canvas, 9½ x 13in/24 x 33cm) FRF 3,500. AMSTERDAM, 14 Sept 1993, *Christ* (1845, oil on canvas, 39½ x 32½in/100.5 x

82.5cm) NLG 3,450. AMSTERDAM, 19 April 1994, *Death of the King* (oil on panel, 10 1/2 x 8 1/4in/26.5 x 21cm) NLG 5,060. NEW YORK, 19 Jan 1995, *Delilah* (oil on panel, 21 x 16 1/4in/53.3 x 41.3cm) USD 2,875. LONDON, 9 Oct 1997, *Escape Plot* (1868, watercolour on paper, 15 1/4 x 11 1/2in/38.6 x 29.2cm) GBP 1,150. LOKEREN, 9 Oct 1999, *Violin Player, Art and Freedom* (1847, watercolour, 28 x 21 ins / 71 x 53 cm) BEF 160,000. ANTWERP, 19 March 2001, *Portrait of a Lady* (oil on canvas, 26 x 21 ins / 65 x 54 cm) BEF 90,000. ZURICH, 22 March 2004, *Young Woman from Rome* (oil on canvas, 45 x 30 ins / 115 x 76 cm) CHF 4,600. PARIS, 30 March 2004, *The Assumption, Church of S Maria Gloriosa dei Frari, Venice* (oil on canvas, after Titian, 35 x 20 ins / 88 x 50 cm) EUR 1,900.

GALLAIX, Louis de. See **DEGALLAIX**

GALLAND, André

French, 20th century.

Born 27 July 1886, in Sedan; died 12 September 1965, in Paris.

Draughtsman, illustrator, poster artist.

André Galland studied in Paris under Paul Renouard at the École des Arts Décoratifs and under Gabriel Ferrié at the École des Beaux-Arts. He exhibited in Paris at the Salon des Humoristes and the Salon des Artistes Français and was awarded a medal in 1946. He was made an Officier of the Légion d'Honneur.

A draughtsman and illustrator, Galland worked for many newspapers, tackling such subjects as current affairs, politics, trials, theatre and sport. He succeeded Paul Renouard on *L'Illustration* and worked for the publication for 20 years. He also illustrated children's books.

GALLAND, François

French, 17th century.

Born c. 1670; died 9 August 1694, in Paris.

Engraver.

GALLAND, Gilbert

French, 19th - 20th century.

Born 1870, in Lyons; died 1956, in Algiers.

Painter, watercolourist, designer. Genre scenes, local scenes, landscapes, landscapes with figures, seascapes. Murals.

Gilbert Galland studied under Hippolyte Dubois. He produced numerous watercolours of Marseilles and its old port and views of Brittany, Algeria and the Far East. He was commissioned by transatlantic liner companies to decorate their lounges, dining rooms and cabins. His works include: *Algiers, Admiralty Harbour Basin; The German Liner Fürst-Bismarck Leaving the Port of Algiers*.He exhibited at the Salon des Artistes Français in Paris. In 2003 his work was shown as part of the group exhibition *Lumineuse Algérie, sous le Regard des Peintres de Marines (1830-1960)* (*Luminous Algeria, Through the Eyes of Seascape Painters (1830-1960)*) at the Musée National de la Marine in Toulon.

BIBLIOGRAPHY:

Mourot, Marjolaine/Vidal-Bué, Marion/Cazenave, Elisabeth, et al., *Lumineuse Algérie, sous le regard des peintres de marines (1830-1960)*, exhibition catalogue, Musée national de la Marine, Toulon, 2003.

AUCTION RECORDS:

PARIS, 11 Feb 1919, *The Brittany Coastline* (watercolour) FRF 40. PARIS, 14 and 15 Dec 1927, *Fishing Boats in Port* (watercolour) FRF 250. PARIS, 27 Jan 1943, *The Bay, Sanary*, FRF 1,100. PARIS, 23 April 1945, *The Shore* (watercolour) FRF 260. PARIS, 18 April 1988, *Southern Landscape* (oil on canvas, 12 1/4 x 25 1/2 ins / 31 x 65 cm) FRF 4,500. BERN, 26 Oct 1988, *Landscape of Bou-Saada* (oil on canvas, a pair, each 15 3/4 x 26 3/4 ins / 40 x 68 cm) CHF 1,700. PARIS, 19 Nov 1991, *Ports of Algiers* (three watercolours, two of 19 x 12 1/4 ins / 48 x 31 cm and one of 10 1/4 x 14 1/4 ins/26 x 36 cm) FRF 8,000. PARIS, 13 April 1992, *Fishermen on the Bosphorus* (oil on canvas, 31 x 65 ins / 79 x 165 cm) FRF 57,000. ST-BRIEUC, 25 June 1995, *View of Jerusalem, the Temple Esplanade and the Dome of the Rock* (oil on canvas, 32 x 51 1/4 ins / 81 x 130 cm) FRF 35,000. PARIS, 3 April 1996, *Sailing Boat and Fishermen in Boats in the Port of Algiers* (watercolour, 17 1/4 x 22 1/4 ins / 43.5 x 56.5 cm) FRF 4,200. PARIS, 5-7 Nov 1996, *The Sand Collectors* (oil on canvas, 17 1/4 x 39 1/4 ins / 44 x 100 cm) FRF 8,000. PARIS, 9 Dec 1996, *Boats by the Golden Horn* (oil on canvas, 39 1/4 x 24 1/4 ins / 100 x 61.5 cm) FRF 25,000. PARIS, 26 March 1998, *Spinner in a Red Dress* (oil on canvas, 24 x 18 ins / 61 x 46 cm) FRF 10,000. LYONS, 31 Jan 1999, *Three-master in Marseilles Harbour. Arrival in Marseilles Harbour* (watercolour, two, 5 x 14 ins / 13 x 35 cm) FRF 10,000. LYONS, 31 Jan 1999, *Entrance to Marseilles Harbour* (watercolour, 22 x 28 ins / 56 x 70 cm) FRF 15,000. PARIS, 14 Nov 2000, *Washerwomen at the Golden Rock, Bou Saada* (oil on canvas, 26 x 39 ins / 65 x 100 cm) FRF 50,000.

GALLAND, J. R.

French, 19th century.

Active in London at the beginning of the 19th century.

Miniaturist.

He exhibited at the Royal Academy in London in 1818.

GALLAND, Jacques

French, 19th - 20th century.

Active in Paris.

Stained glass painter.

Jacques Galland was the son of Pierre Victor Galland. He decorated several churches.

GALLAND, Jean

French, 20th century.

Born 1880, in Vienne (Isère).

Painter.

Jean Galland studied under Lespinasse. He was a member of the Société des Artistes Français and regularly exhibited landscapes at their Salons.

GALLAND, Jean Pierre

French, 18th century.

Active in Le Puy-en-Velay (Haute-Loire) in 1726-1759.

Painter.

GALLAND, John

American, 19th century.

Active in Philadelphia c. 1800.

Engraver.

John Galland collaborated on the illustration of James Stewart's *History of France*.

GALLAND, Joséphine (Mme)

French, 19th - 20th century.

Born in Lyons.

Painter.

Joséphine Galland exhibited in Lyons from 1892, showing still-lifes, flowers and landscapes.

GALLAND, Laurent

French, 20th - 21st century.

Born 1959.

Installation artist.

Laurent Galland has exhibited in group exhibitions in Paris, Caen, Marseilles and Hamburg since 1982. He has had solo exhibitions in Montpellier and St-Étienne.

GALLAND, Marie

French, 20th century.

Born 20th century, in Paris.

Sculptor.

Marie Galland exhibited in Paris at the Salon des Artistes Français. She was also a writer.

GALLAND, Pierre-Victor
French, 19th century.
Born 15 July 1822, in Geneva, of French parents; died 30 November 1892, in Paris.
Painter, decorative designer. Figures. Murals.

He studied under Michel-Martin Drolling at the École des Beaux-Arts in Paris, then under Henri Labrouste and Pierre-Luc Charles Cicéry. Galland taught a special course on the decorative arts at the École des Beaux-Arts from 1873 and was retained as artistic director of the Gobelins factory from 1877. Early in his career he produced figures for the leading decorative painters. He later received numerous commissions to decorate public buildings such as the Panthéon, the Hôtel de Ville and the church of St-Eustache (all in Paris), together with other commissions, notably for the Continental Hotel in Paris and the palace of an Armenian prince in Constantinople (1851). He also decorated numerous ceilings in private houses of the nobility, both in France and abroad. His compositions frequently show women and children 'floating' on clouds against a backdrop of ornamental figures and motifs reminiscent of 18th-century architectural decoration. He drew his inspiration from flowers and shrubs, which he stored in containers in his studio; in 1980 the Musée des Arts Décoratifs exhibited a selection of plant and vegetable drawings acquired from Galland in 1884. His body of work was not without influence on subsequent decorative artists, notably on ornamentalists of the Art Nouveau movement, and a posthumous retrospective of his work featured at the Palais de l'Industrie, Paris, in March 1894.

Stamp of sale

Bibliography:
Findlay, Mimi, '*Pierre-Victor Galland, 1822-1892, and 19th century decorative painting, part II*' in *Nineteenth-Century*, Xvii/1, 1997. Wood, Ghislaine, '*Henri Bellery-Desfontaines, 1867-1909: a Forgotten Modern*' in *Apollo*, Cli, no.459, 2000.

Museums and Galleries:
Paris (Mus. des Arts décoratifs): *Small Columns in the shape of Lilac Tree Branches*; numerous drawings.

Auction records:
Paris, 27 Feb 1896, *Pastures*, FRF 125. Paris, 30 June 1900, *Springtime*, FRF 200. Paris, 4 June 1923, *Autumn*, FRF 120. Paris, 13 June 1923, *Ceiling Ornamentation (study)*, FRF 100. Paris, 19-20 May 1926, *Portrait of Arago*, FRF 220. Paris, 2 June 1980, *The Market* (oil on canvas, 32 x 25 1/2 ins / 81 x 65 cm) FRF 2,400. Aix-en-Provence, 21 July 1980, *Near Ste-Victoire* (gouache) FRF 1,000. Paris, 11 Dec 1987, *Timbre de l'atelier* (oil on canvas, 45 1/4 x 36 1/4 ins / 115 x 92 cm) FRF 7,000. New York, 26 Oct 1990, *Nymph for a Ceiling in The Louvre (sketch)* (oil on canvas, 18 1/2 x 23 ins / 47 x 58.4 cm) USD 4,400. Paris, 28 Oct 1990, *Trophies* (oil on canvas, 122 x 76 3/4 ins / 310 x 195 cm) FRF 145,000. Paris, 15 Dec 1993, *Cupid Playing Pan's Pipes against an Architectural Background of Ornamental Fruit and Musical Instruments* (oil on canvas, 67 1/4 x 65 ins / 171 x 165 cm) FRF 83,000. Paris, 12 May 1995, *Diana* (oil on card, 26 x 30 3/4 ins / 66 x 78 cm) FRF 10,000. Cleveland, 31 May 2000, *Putti in Clouds* (oil on canvas, oval, 41 x 37 ins / 104 x 94 cm) USD 1,700. Paris, 16 June 2003, *Study for a Violin Placed on a Shelf* (oil on canvas, 14 x 17 ins / 35 x 44 cm) EUR 1,600. Paris, 16 June 2003, *Design for Pediment of the Gate at Fontainebleau* (oil on cardboard, 15 x 15 ins / 39 x 39 cm) EUR 1,800.

GALLANT, François
French, 16th century.
Active in Paris.
Sculptor.

Between 1568 and 1570, François Gallant worked under Primaticcio on the decoration of the tomb of Henri II.

GALLANT, Marcial
French, 16th century.
Active in Paris in 1556.
Illuminator.

Marcial Gallant worked for the French court.

GALLARATI, Francesco Maria
Italian, 18th century.
Born in Milan.
Active in Rome in 1786.
Painter.

GALLARD, Gabriel
Spanish, 18th century.
Died 6 July 1749, in Palma, Majorca.
Sculptor.

GALLARD, Michel de
French, 20th century.
Born 22 April 1921, in Villefrance-d'Allier.
Painter (mixed media). Landscapes, urban landscapes, flowers, animals.
Groupe l'Homme Témoin.

After studying medicine, Michel de Gallard attended the Académies Libres in Paris while working in a number of different occupations. He was one of the generation of artists, including Soutine and Modigliani, who frequented the *La Ruche* studio, formerly a machine pavilion at the 1889 Exposition Universelle, which was moved to Vaugirard.

Resolutely realist with a tendency to concentrate on the more sordid aspects of life, De Gallard's meticulous painting also shows certain naive qualities in the manner of Jean Eve. He enjoys translating the bittersweet poetry of city suburbs and the humble countryside. He moved to the village of La Borde near the Yonne and paints the area as it changes with the seasons. The film maker Paul Paviot mentions his 'use of white as a dominant value, the organisation of the lines, volumes and colours on the surface of the canvas, with its trees, solitary or in clumps, but always bare of leaves... like black, very personal scratch marks, heightened with browns, greens, blues and discreet touches of red'.

His official debut as an artist coincided with the exhibition that accompanied the publication of the *L'Homme Témoin* manifesto in 1948, along with Lorjou and Rebeyrolle. He went on to exhibit at the annual Paris Salons, notably at the Salon de la Jeune Peinture for a number of years after becoming a founding member, then at the Salon of the Société Nationale des Beaux-Arts, the Salon des Peintres Témoins de leur Temps, the Salon Comparaisons and the Salon d'Automne. He became a member of the Salon d'Automne in 1949 and was guest of honour at the Salon in 1987, when tribute was paid to his work.

He also showed his work in solo exhibitions, including: in 1956 and 1958 at the Galerie Framond, Paris; in 1961 at the Galerie St-Georges, Lyons; in 1964 at the Galerie Musson, Orléans; 1967 at the modern gallery, Caracas; in 1968, 1970, 1975, 1977, 1978 and 1985 at the Zantman Gallery, Carmel, California; in 1974 at the Martal Gallery, Montreal; in 1978 and 1986 at the Galerie de la Présidence, Paris; in 1983 in Johannesburg; in 1984 in Osaka, Tokyo and Nagoya; and in 1988 in Nagoya.

He was the recipient of many prizes and awards: in 1949 the Ville de Paris national bursary; in 1951 a prize at the Salon de la Société Nationale des Beaux-Arts; in 1952 the Prix Antral; in 1952 and 1953 prizes at the Menton Biennale; and in 1960 a prize at the Salon Comparaisons.

De Gallard has also illustrated books, including: *Beaux Desperados* by Juliette Darle published by Librairie des Lettres, 1956; *Léonard et la Machine Volante*, La Farandole,

1957; *Routes et Chemins*, prefaced by Jean Giono, published by Éditions des Peintres Témoins de leur Temps, 1961; *Histoire de la France*, published by Éditions du Club du Livre, 1962; *L'Événement*, published by Éditions des Peintres Témoins de leur Temps, 1963; *L'Amour*, published by Éditions des Peintres Témoins de leur Temps, 1964; *Le Piéton de Paris* by Léon-Paul Fargue, Éditions Robert Léger, 1969; and *Ville de la Fumée Humaine* by Chowki Abdelamir, Éditions G.P. Maisonneuve et Larose, 1979.

M DE GALLARD

BIBLIOGRAPHY:
Pietri, Rolan/Gaudibert, Pierre, '*Michel de Gaillard*' in *coll. La Nouvelle École de Paris*, Éd. Pierre Cailler, Geneva, 1962. *Recent Paintings by Michel de Gallard*, The Lefevre Gall., London, 1971. *Michel de Gallard*, exhibition catalogue, Gal. de la Présidence, Paris, 1978. *Michel de Gallard*, exhibition catalogue, Gal. Quatre Pièces, 1989.
MUSEUMS AND GALLERIES:
PARIS (MAMVP) - YAMAGATA (MA).
AUCTION RECORDS:
PARIS, 2 June 1961, *Landscape*, FRF 1,700. PARIS, 19 Nov 1976, *The Village* (1958, oil on canvas, 28 3/4 x 36 1/4 ins / 73 x 92 cm) FRF 3,200. BREST, 21 May 1978, *La Cave* (oil on canvas, 51 1/2 x 76 3/4 ins / 131 x 195 cm) FRF 9,000. VERSAILLES, 27 Jan 1980, *The Goose* (1957, oil on canvas, 28 3/4 x 23 1/2 ins / 73 x 60 cm) FRF 4,000. VERSAILLES, 28 Feb 1982, *The Village* (oil on canvas, 32 x 39 1/4 ins / 81 x 100 cm) FRF 12,500. VERSAILLES, 18 March 1984, *The Painter's Studio* (oil on canvas, 38 1/4 x 57 1/4 ins / 97 x 145.5 cm) FRF 21,000. PARIS, 7 Dec 1987, *Flowers in a Vase* (oil on canvas, 28 3/4 x 23 1/2 ins / 73 x 60 cm) FRF 25,500. VERSAILLES, 17 April 1988, *The Farmer's Wife* (1957, oil on canvas, 22 x 15 ins / 55 x 38 cm) FRF 4,000. CALAIS, 3 July 1988, *At the Roadside* (1942, oil on canvas, 28 3/4 x 39 1/4 ins / 73 x 100 cm) FRF 13,000. VERSAILLES, 25 Sept 1988, *Thistles* (oil on canvas, 39 1/4 x 19 3/4 ins / 100 x 50 cm) FRF 14,500. VERSAILLES, 23 Oct 1988, *Road at the Entrance to a Village* (1962, oil on canvas, 28 3/4 x 39 1/4 ins / 73 x 100 cm) FRF 13,500. PARIS, 7 Dec 1988, *Flowers in a Vase* (oil on canvas, 28 3/4 x 23 1/2 ins / 73 x 60 cm) FRF 25,500. PARIS, 26 Jan 1990, *Composition* (1988, mixed media, 17 1/4 x 14 1/4 ins / 44 x 36.5 cm) FRF 6,000. PARIS, 25 June 1990, *Landscape* (1963, oil on canvas, 28 3/4 x 36 1/4 ins / 73 x 92 cm) FRF 18,000. PARIS, 21 Nov 1990, *Study for a Cock Fight* (1957, oil on canvas, 25 1/4 x 39 1/4 ins / 64 x 100 cm) FRF 31,000. PARIS, 7 Dec 1990, *Village in the Country* (oil on canvas, 15 3/4 x 31 1/2 ins / 40 x 80 cm) FRF 32,000. PARIS, 20 Nov 1991, *The Suburbs* (1955, oil on panel, 23 1/2 x 32 ins / 60 x 81 cm) FRF 21,000. PARIS, 11 March 1992, *Barges* (oil on canvas, 38 1/4 x 51 1/4 ins / 97 x 130 cm) FRF 32,000. PARIS, 16 June 1993, *Roofs* (oil on canvas, 46 x 35 ins / 116 x 89 cm) FRF 33,000. LE TOUQUET, 22 May 1994, *Village in the Snow through the Trees* (oil on canvas, 38 1/4 x 51 1/2 ins / 97 x 131 cm) FRF 49,000. PARIS, 18 Nov 1994, *Woman Washing Clothes* (1958, oil on canvas, 38 1/4 x 51 1/4 ins / 97 x 130 cm) FRF 22,000. CALAIS, 24 March 1996, *The Painter's Studio* (oil on canvas, 38 1/4 x 51 1/2 ins / 97 x 131 cm) FRF 26,000. PARIS, 16 Sept 1996, *Young Girl with Chaise Longue* (oil on canvas, 35 x 46 ins / 89 x 116 cm) FRF 36,000. PARIS, 23 Feb 1997, *Peasant Woman at Market* (1953, oil on canvas, 22 x 13 ins / 55 x 33 cm) FRF 7,000. CALAIS, 23 March 1997, *The Banks of the Seine, Paris* (oil on canvas, 4 x 19 3/4 ins / 10 x 50 cm) FRF 18,000. PARIS, 12 Dec 1997, *Jetée de Fleurs* (1961, oil on canvas, 46 x 28 3/4 ins / 116 x 73 cm) FRF 8,200. MONTREAL, 13 Dec 1999, *Village Street* (oil on canvas, 32 x 39 ins / 81 x 100 cm) CAD 2,900. PARIS, 17 Nov 2000, *Young Woman on Cane Sofa* (1961, oil on canvas, 29 x 24 ins / 73 x 60 cm) FRF 25,500. PARIS, 17 Nov 2000, *The Village* (oil on canvas, 51 x 38 ins / 130 x 97 cm) FRF 39,500. PARIS, 22 Jan 2001, *Houses through the Trees* (1958, oil on canvas, 28 x 39 ins / 72 x 100 cm) FRF 13,000. PARIS, 22 Jan 2001, *Paris, Ile Saint Louis* (1963, oil on canvas, 31 x 39 ins / 80 x 100 cm) FRF 15,000. PARIS, 5 March 2003, *Pears and Bottles* (oil on canvas, 36 x 29 ins / 92 x 73 cm) EUR 3,650. PARIS, 13 Oct 2003, *Vase of Sunflowers* (oil on canvas, 46 x 35 ins / 116 x 89 cm) EUR 2,500. PARIS, 27 May 2004, *Passage Dantzig, Paris* (1956, oil on masonite, 26 x 32 ins / 65 x 81 cm) EUR 2,600. NEW YORK, 13 July 2004, *Rooftops* (oil on canvas, 35 x 46 ins / 89 x 116 cm) USD 3,200.

GALLARD-LEPINAY, Paul-Charles-Emmanuel

French, 19th century.
Born 23 May 1842, in Aulnay (Charente-Maritime); died March 1885, in Paris.
Painter. History painting, genre scenes, landscapes, landscapes with figures, seascapes.

He studied under Claude Jacquand and exhibited at the Paris Salon from 1864 (the year of his appointment as official artist to the naval ministry). Gallard-Lepinay specialized in marine subjects; his numerous views of Venice, shipwrecks, and landscapes in Normandy and around La Rochelle demonstrate a keen awareness for changing light effects.
MUSEUMS AND GALLERIES:
AMSTERDAM: *View of Venice* - CHERBOURG: *Grévy, Say and Gambetta Visiting the French Squadron at Cherbourg.*
AUCTION RECORDS:
PARIS, 1883, *Seascape: Venice*, FRF 355; *Morning Landscape*, FRF 100. PARIS, 15 Nov 1900, *View of Venice*, FRF 220. PARIS, 18 March 1920, *Schooner and Fishing Boats at their Moorings*, FRF 400. PARIS, 15 June 1931, *View of Venice*, FRF 400. PARIS, 11 June 1942, *Boaters*, FRF 600. PARIS, 5 March 1943, *View of Venice*, FRF 1,450. PARIS, 1 Dec 1943, *Frigate and Gondolas on the Grand Canal near the Ducal Palace, Venice*, FRF 4,100. NEW YORK, 23-24 May 1945, *Venice*, USD 400. PARIS, 16 Oct 1946, *Vessels Crippled by the Storm*, FRF 5,200. VERSAILLES, 23 March 1980, *Gondolas on the Grand Canal, Venice* (oil on canvas, 18 x 28 3/4 ins / 46 x 73 cm) FRF 12,000. HONFLEUR, 1 Jan 1982, *Leaving the Port of Honfleur* (oil on canvas, 18 x 25 1/2 ins / 46 x 65 cm) FRF 15,000. PARIS, 14 Oct 1983, *Yachts in Venice* (oil on canvas, a pair, 18 x 28 3/4 ins / 46 x 73 cm) FRF 18,000. BERN, 2 May 1986, *View of the Bosphorus* (oil on canvas, 15 x 22in/38 x 56cm) CHF 7,500. CALAIS, 8 Nov 1987, *View of Venice* (oil on canvas, 26 1/2 x 39 3/4 ins / 67 x 101 cm) FRF 51,000. NEW YORK, 26 May 1992, *Grand Canal, Venice* (oil on canvas, 21 x 36in/53.3 x 91.4cm) USD 4,400. LONDON, 11 May 1994, *Le Havre* (1876, oil on canvas, 32 x 52in/81 x 132cm) GBP 3,910. LYONS, 18 May 1994, *Seascape* (oil on canvas, 13 1/2 x 22 1/2 ins / 34 x 57 cm) FRF 11,500. PARIS, 12 Dec 1996, *Rescue at Sea* (oil on canvas, 15 3/4 x 23 1/2 ins / 40 x 60 cm) FRF 11,000. PARIS, 20 Oct 1997, *Yacht Entering the Grand Canal, Venice* (oil on canvas, 18 1/4 x 29 ins / 46.5 x 73.5 cm) FRF 43,000. AMSTERDAM, 20 April 1999, *Le Havre* (1877, oil on canvas, 22 x 35 ins / 57 x 88 cm) NLG 6,000. PARIS, 8 Nov 1999, *Return of Fishermen at Dusk* (oil on canvas, 13 x 22 ins / 32 x 55 cm) FRF 11,000. PARIS, 30 June 2000, *Seascape* (oil on canvas, 14 x 24 ins / 36 x 61 cm) FRF 20,500. ZURICH, 5 Oct 2001, *Sailing Ship at Dusk* (1882, oil on canvas, 50 x 33 ins / 128 x 84 cm) CHF 5,500. PARIS, 16 Nov 2001, *Boats Setting out Along the Coast* (oil on canvas, 20 x 30 ins / 50 x 75 cm) FRF 28,000. LILLE, 10 March 2002, *Three-masters in Rear Wind Returning to Port* (oil on canvas, 18 x 31 ins / 45 x 80 cm) EUR 8,000. LILLE, 23 June 2002, *Three-masters Leaving Port with Sails Unfurled* (1883, oil on canvas, 18 x 31 ins / 46 x 80 cm) EUR 6,000. SAN FRANCISCO, 14 May 2003, *View of Istanbul with Ships in the Foreground* (oil on canvas, 22 x 38 ins / 55 x 96 cm) USD 6,000. GRANVILLE, 1 Feb 2004, *Seascape* (oil on canvas, 18 x 29 ins / 46 x 74 cm) EUR 8,000. RENNES, 21 Feb 2004, *Three-master at Entrance to Port* (oil on canvas, 18 x 29 ins / 46 x 74 cm) EUR 6,000.

GALLARDO, Antonio

Spanish, 18th century.
Active in Cádiz in 1720.

Painter.
There is a painting of *Christ on the Mount of Olives* signed and dated by Antonio Gallardo in the church of S Antonio in Cádiz.

GALLARDO, Mario
Cuban, 20th century.
Born 1937, in Havana.
Painter.
Mario Gallardo studied at the Academia San Alejandro from 1966. He was awarded a gold medal for painting at the 2nd International Contemporary Art Triennale of the West Indies in 1971 and first prize for painting and graphical illustration with commendation at the first Salon des Jeunes in 1971.
BIBLIOGRAPHY:
Carpentier, Alejo, *Cuba, peintres daujourd'hui*, exhibition catalogue, Musée d'Art moderne de la Ville de Paris, Paris, 1977-1978.

GALLARDO, Mateo
Spanish, 17th century.
Active in Madrid in 1657.
Painter.
A painting of the head of Christ and several of the head of the Virgin by Mateo Gallardo survive.

GALLARDO RUIZ, Gustavo
Spanish, 20th century.
Born 3 June 1891, in Seville; died 1971.
Painter. Portraits, genre scenes, landscapes.
Gustavo Gallardo Ruiz studied at the school of fine arts in Seville and was taught by Virgilo Mattoni and Gonzalo Bilbao. In 1913 he travelled to Morocco and Portugal and in 1917 was awarded a bursary to study in Rome and Paris. In 1919 he received a bursary from his native city of Seville. He later became a teacher at the Seville school of fine arts, where he taught for three years, and then at the school of arts and crafts. In 1910 he exhibited in Madrid at the exhibition of the national fine arts society. In 1924 he was awarded a bronze medal.
BIBLIOGRAPHY:
Arnáiz, José Manuel/López Jiménez, Javier/Merchán Díaz, Manuel (ed.), '*Cien años de pintura en Espana y Portugal (1830-1930)*' in vol. III, Antiqvaria, Madrid, 1989 (One Hundred Years of Painting in Spain and Portugal (1830-1930)).

GALLARDON, Jean. See **GAILLARDIN**

GALLARZA, Marcos
Spanish, 17th century.
Active in Barbastro (Aragon) in 1622.
Sculptor.
Marcos Gallarza worked for the cathedral.

GALLAS, Josef
German, 18th century.
Active in Weisskirchen (now Bela Crkva, Serbia) c. 1770.
Sculptor.
This artist was also active in Blansko Jedowitz, Liebau and Rosenau.

GALLATI, Hans Caspar
Swiss, 17th century.
Active in Will during the second half of the 17th century.
Glass painter.

GALLATIN, Albert Eugene
American, 20th century.
Born 1882, in Villanova (Pennsylvania); died 1952, in New York.
Painter.
Neo-Constructivism.
American Abstract Artists (AAA).
Albert Gallatin studied law at the New York Law School. He made frequent visits to Paris from 1921 until 1938, where he was acquainted with the avant-garde of the art world, and built up a famous collection which he called the *Gallery of Living Art*. Today this is an integral part of the Philadelphia Museum and includes works by the Cubists Picasso, Braque, Gris and Delaunay, as well as Miró, Arp, Mondrian, Vantongerloo, Hélion, Klee, Lissitzky, Schwitters and Domela, and American artists such as Demuth, Sheeler and Hartley. In 1936 he was a founder member of the American Abstract Artists (AAA). From 1937 to 1938 he helped on the publication of the journal *Plastique*, which was founded in Paris by Sophie Taeuber-Arp and César Domela. He was a self-taught painter, beginning his career in 1926 under the influence of Cubism, when his works were similar in style to those of Fernand Léger. He then evolved towards Abstract Constructivism.

He was often invited to take part in group exhibitions in cities in the USA and Europe, including the Salon des Réalités Nouvelles in Paris. He exhibited in the group exhibitions of the AAA until 1952. He also held many solo exhibitions in New York from 1938.
BIBLIOGRAPHY:
Balken, Debra Bricker, *Albert Eugene Gallatin and His Circle*, exhibition catalogue, University of Miami Art Museum, Coral Gables (FL), 1986. Stavitsky, Gail, *The A.E. Gallatin Collection: An Early Adventure in Modern Art*, exhibition catalogue, Philadelphia Museum of Modern Art, 1994.
MUSEUMS AND GALLERIES:
PHILADELPHIA (MA): entire collection.
AUCTION RECORDS:
LOS ANGELES, 6 Nov 1978, *Abstract Composition* (1937, oil on canvas, 16¼ x 12¼ ins / 41 x 30.8 cm) USD 2,100. NEW YORK, 16 Feb 1982, *Abstraction* (oil on canvas, 12 x 9 ins / 30.5 x 22.9 cm) USD 1,300. NEW YORK, 1 June 1984, *Abstraction* (1943, oil on canvas, 16 x 20 ins / 40.6 x 51.1 cm) USD 7,500. NEW YORK, 4 Dec 1987, *Abstraction* (1939, oil on canvas, 24¼ x 17¼ ins / 61.6 x 43.8 cm) USD 19,000. NEW YORK, 25 May 1989, *Triangles Linked Together* (1951, oil on canvas, 24 x 20 ins / 60.9 x 50.8 cm) USD 16,500. NEW YORK, 28 May 1992, *Classical Abstraction* (1940, oil on canvas, 14 x 12 ins / 35.7 x 30.5 cm) USD 5,500. NEW YORK, 23 Sept 1992, *Composition* (1938, oil on canvas, 16¼ x 12 ins / 41 x 30.5 cm) USD 7,700. MILFORD, 25 April 2002, *Composition* (1940, oil on canvas, 12 x 9 ins / 30 x 23 cm) USD 12,000. MILFORD, 24 Oct 2002, *Abstraction* (1939, oil on panel, 16 x 12 ins / 41 x 30 cm) USD 5,000. CHICAGO, 9 Nov 2003, *Abstract Composition* (1940, oil on board, 16 x 12 ins / 41 x 30 cm) USD 20,000.

GALLAUD, Édouard Charles
French, 20th century.
Born 1873, in Paris.
Painter, engraver.
Édouard Gallaud was a member of the Salon des Artistes in Paris. He was awarded a bronze medal in 1928.

GALLAUD, Marie
French, 20th century.
Born 1867, in Paris.
Sculptor, medallist.
Marie Gallaud exhibited in Paris at the Salon des Artistes Français.

GALLAUDET, Edward
American, 18th - 19th century.
Active in New York.
Engraver. Ex-libris plates.
Edward Gallaudet was probably related to Elisha Gallaudet.

GALLAUDET, Elisha
American, 18th century.
Born c. 1730; died 1805, in New York.
Active in New York.
Engraver.

Among Elisha Gallaudet's works is a *Portrait of the Reverend George Whitefield.*

GALLAWAY, Mary Louise
American, 20th century.
Born 1942, in Houston.
Active in France.
Sculptor, ceramicist, pastellist, jeweller. Monuments.

Mary Louise Gallaway has lived and worked in France since 1971. She received a master's degree in art from the University of Paris in 1988. She studied ceramics in Japan, under Matsatsugu Hitomi, and engraving at the Pratt Graphic Art School, New York. She runs the École d'Arts Plastiques in Suresnes near Paris. In 1975, she was awarded a gold medal at the Biennale Internationale de la Céramique in Vallauris. In 2003, She showed her works in a solo exhibition in Le Mans. She has obtained several commissions for monuments in the town of Suresnes.

BIBLIOGRAPHY:
Gallaway, Mary Louise/Waechter, Roger, *Technique du plâtre: éléments de modelage et de moulage*, Le Temps Apprivoisé, Paris, 1999.

GALLAY-CHARBONNEL, Nina (Mme)
French, 19th century.
Born in Paris.
Painter. Landscapes.

She participated in the Salon de la Nationale des Beaux-Arts from 1899.

GALLAYS, Pierre
French, 18th century.
Active in Paris in 1713.
Engraver.

Pierre Gallays' works include portraits of *Louis XV* and *Jean Bart.*

GALLAZZI, Beltramo
Italian, 15th century.
Active in Milan.
Sculptor (wood).

GALLE
French, 19th century.
Lithographer.

He exhibited at the 1834 Salon.

GALLE, Ambroise
Flemish School, 18th century.
Died 27 January 1755, in Antwerp, in the hospital of the St Elisabeth Gasthuis.
Active in Antwerp.
Sculptor.

He was a master of the Guild of St Luke in Antwerp in 1714.

GALLE, Anthoine
French, 17th century.
Born c. 1622; died 8 August 1667, in Paris.
Sculptor.

Anthoine Galle was sculptor-in-ordinary to the king.

GALLÉ, Antonius
Flemish School, 18th century.
Sculptor.

He was a master of the Guild of St Luke in Antwerp in 1710.

GALLE, Cornelis, the Younger
Flemish School, 17th century.
Born 1615, in Antwerp; died 18 October 1678, in Antwerp.
Engraver. Religious subjects, allegorical subjects, portraits.

He was the son of Cornelis Galle the Elder. He was accepted as a master of the Guild of St Luke in Antwerp in 1638, and was married in the same city in 1641.

GALLE, Cornelis III
Flemish School, 17th century.
Baptised on 12 November 1642 in Antwerp.
Died in Antwerp.
Engraver.

He was the son of Cornelis Galle the Younger. He was accepted as a master of the Guild of St Luke in Antwerp in 1663, and was married in the city in 1670.

GALLE, Cornelis or Cornelius, the Elder
Flemish School, 17th century.
Born 1576, in Antwerp; died 29 March 1650, in Antwerp.
Painter, engraver, draughtsman. Religious subjects.

He was the pupil of his father Philippe Galle, and was a member of the Guild of St Luke in Antwerp in 1610. The best-known member of the Galle family of artists, he spent many years in Rome. His output includes a number of engravings.

AUCTION RECORDS:
MADRID, 28 Jan 1992, *Descent from the Cross* (oil on copper, 19 x 14 1/4in/48.5 x 36cm) ESP 448,000.

GALLÉ, Émile
French, 19th century.
Born 1846, in Nancy; died 1904, in Nancy.
Painter, ceramicist, decorative designer, glassmaker.
Figures, still-lifes.
Art Nouveau.
Nancy School.

He studied art in Weimar. Emile Gallé was passionately interested in painting on glass and opened a glassware factory in Nancy in 1874. He was one of the founders of the celebrated Nancy School, a precursor of the Art Nouveau movement. Gallé enjoyed worldwide renown for the quality of his glassware, typically in the form of flower vases, which are invariably inventive, elegant and technically perfect. He also designed and manufactured furniture with complex marquetry decoration. His paintings are principally still-lifes that attest to his love of botany and which anticipate the floral style of Art Nouveau.

BIBLIOGRAPHY:
Tiffany to Ben Tre: a Century of Glass, exhibition catalogue, Milwaukee Art Museum, 1993. Ertberg, Marianne, '*Poetry in Glass: Emile Gallé and the Danish Museum of Decorative Art*' in *Scandinavian Journal of Design History*, V, 1995. Debize, Christian, *Emile Gallé and the École de Nancy*, Serpenoise, Metz, 1999. Le Tacon, François, *Emile Gallé: maître de l'Art nouveau*, Nuée Bleue, Heillecourt, 2004.

MUSEUMS AND GALLERIES:
NANCY (Mus. de L'École de Nancy): table for the shop 'L'Escalier de Cristal' (c. 1885-1889).

AUCTION RECORDS:
PARIS, 24 March 1982, *Engineer's Dessert* (1894, oil on canvas, 23 1/2 x 35 1/2 ins / 60 x 90 cm) FRF 5,200. LONDON, 19 June 1991, *Young Model Dressing* (1892, oil on canvas, 21 1/4 x 13 3/4 ins / 54 x 35 cm) GBP 2,860. PARIS, 5 Dec 1997, *Vosges Landscape with Butterfly* (acid-etched cameo, decoration for a table lamp, h. 13 3/4 ins / 35 cm) FRF 84,000. PARIS, 22 April 2001, *Sleeping Fawn* (glazed coloured gilt ceramic, 5 x 9 ins / 13 x 22 cm) FRF 23,000. PONTOISE, 13 Oct 2001, *Animal and Natural Scenes* (oil on panel, set of four, 13 x 21 ins / 34 x 54 cm) FRF 29,500.

GALLE, Françoise
French, 20th century.
Born 4 October 1940, in Paris.
Painter, textile artist.

Françoise Galle's study of art was largely theoretical and she wrote her master's dissertation on the sculptor Charles Malfray in 1972. Her training as a practising artist came from her various trips and visits to museums. These included: London in 1954; Portugal in 1959; Greece and Italy in 1961; India and Japan in 1963; Mexico in 1967; Rome, Sicily and Greece in 1968; Tassili in 1969; Peru and Bolivia in 1973; Chad and Cameroon in 1974; New York in 1975; Brazil in 1979, 1980 and 1984, where she founded the first textile research centre at the school of visual arts in Rio de Janeiro and created a course in art experimentation in São Paulo; Spain and Canada in 1985; and Martinique in 1986. She has been a member of the Taylor Foundation since 1995.

Galle began painting from nature in 1954 in the Dauphiné and later in Provence during her travels. In 1973 she developed towards abstraction and in 1976 began studying textile fabrics and textures. In 1977 she produced her first three-dimensional tapestries using a variety of materials. After her return to France in 1985 her work began to focus on the transparency of colour and material. In 1987 to 1988 she returned to figurative painting in Paris and the Dauphiné region, where she set up a studio in 1990 and returned once again to abstraction. In 1991 to 1992 she produced action paintings and since 1993 she has explored the dynamics of light.

Galle has taken part in group exhibitions, including: from 1978 the Salon Comparaisons in Paris; 1978, the Salon d'Automne, Paris; from 1992 the Salon des Artistes Français, Paris; and in numerous exhibitions at museums of modern art and galleries in Brazil. She has also shown collections of her work in solo exhibitions, including: São Paulo in 1979 and 1981; Rio de Janeiro in 1983 and 1985; the Galerie Autre Regard, Paris in 1987; with Jean Lehmans at the Cité Internationale des Arts, Paris in 1989, 1991, 1995 and 2003; and at the Agence Société Générale, Denfert-Rochereau, Paris in 2002.

GALLE, Hieronymus, the Elder
Flemish School, 17th century.
Born 1625, in Antwerp; died after 1679.
Active in Antwerp.
Painter. Still-lifes (flowers), insects.

He was a pupil of Abraham Sack.

MUSEUMS AND GALLERIES:

FLORENCE (Uffizi): *Garland of Flowers* (1655) - TOURCOING: two flower paintings.

AUCTION RECORDS:

LONDON, 27 June 1930, *Flowers in a Vase*, GBP 31. PARIS, 28 May 1954, *Vase of Flowers with Game*, FRF 150,000. COPENHAGEN, 27 April 1971, *Still-life*, DKK 25,000. LONDON, 12 July 1972, *Still-life with Flowers and Fruit*, GBP 4,500. LONDON, 12 Dec 1986, *Still-life with Fruit* (oil on canvas, 39 1/2 x 44 1/2in/100.3 x 113cm) GBP 38,000. ROME, 10 April 1988, *Vase of Flowers* (oil on canvas, 23 1/4 x 16 1/2in/59 x 42cm) ITL 12,000,000. EDINBURGH, 22 Nov 1988, *Still-life with Summer Flowers and Insects* (oil on canvas, a pair, 20 3/4 x 15 1/2in/52.7 x 39.4cm) GBP 75,000. LONDON, 27 Oct 1993, *Still-life with Flowers, Fruit and Copper Utensils* (oil on canvas, 35 x 52 3/4in/89 x 134cm) GBP 14,950. LONDON, 9 Dec 1994, *Flowers in an Urn on a Pedestal* (oil on canvas, 24 3/4 x 19in/62.8 x 48.3cm) GBP 4,370. LONDON, 18 Oct 1995, *Still-life with a Large Floral Composition* (1667, oil on canvas, 26 3/4 x 18in/68 x 46cm) GBP 16,100. AMSTERDAM, 7 May 1996, *Still-life with Flowers: Guelder-roses, Anemones, Peonies, Poppies and Carnations* (oil on canvas, 24 1/2 x 31 ins / 62.5 x 77.8 cm) NLG 86,250. MONACO, 14 June 1996, *Flowers in a Vase Placed on a Balustrade* (oil on canvas, 16 1/4 x 12 1/2 ins / 41 x 32 cm) FRF 58,500. MILAN, 2 Dec 1999, *Still-life with Various Birds. Still-life with Game* (1660, oil on canvas, a pair, 60 x 74 ins / 152 x 187 cm) ITL 85,000,000.

GALLE, Hieronymus, the Younger
Flemish School, 17th - 18th century.
Born 13 September 1656, in Antwerp; died 1713.
Painter.

He was the nephew of Hieronymus Galle the Elder, and a pupil of Jan Erasmus Quellinus in 1674. Galle was the father of 13 children.

GALLE, Hubert
Flemish School, 17th century.
Painter.

He was a pupil of Obr. Sack in 1637.

GALLE, Jean Joseph
French, 20th century.
Born 1884, in Rennes.
Sculptor, medallist, engraver. Monuments.

Jean Galle studied under Coutan. He exhibited at the Salon des Artistes Français in Paris. Galle produced various monuments, including the monument to the fallen in Dinard.

GALLE, Jérôme
French, 19th century.
Painter. Still-lifes (including game).

Gieronimo Galle f

MUSEUMS AND GALLERIES:

ORLÉANS: *Fowl, Game and Vegetables on a Stone Slab.*

AUCTION RECORDS:

PARIS, 29 Nov 1900, *Birds and Flowers*, FRF 100.

GALLE, Joan
Flemish School, 17th century.
Baptised on 27 September 1600, in Antwerp; died 20 September 1676, in Antwerp.
Engraver.

He was the elder son of Theodor Galle. He became a master of the Guild of St Luke in Antwerp in 1627.

JG exc.

GALLE, Louis-Octave
French, 19th century.
Active in Paris.
Painter. History painting, genre scenes, landscapes.

He first exhibited at the Paris Salon in 1841.

AUCTION RECORDS:

PARIS, 3 Dec 1937, *Landscape*, FRF 130.

GALLE, Marcel
French, 20th century.
Born in Paris.
Painter. Landscapes.

Marcel Galle exhibited landscapes of the Pyrenées at the Salon des Indépendants.

GALLE, Norbert
Flemish School, 17th century.
Born 1648, in Antwerp; died c. 1694.
Painter.

He was the son of Joan Galle. He became a master of the Guild of St Luke in Antwerp in 1667.

GALLE, Oswald
German, 19th century.
Born 26 April 1868, in Dresden.
Painter, sculptor.

Having initially trained in wood sculpture, Oswald Galle's interests turned to painting. He travelled to Italy, then lived mainly in Dresden and Berlin. He is noted for his important decorations for the Realgymnasium in Blasewitz, near Dresden.

GALLE, Philipp
Dutch, 16th - 17th century.

Born 1537; died 12 or 29 March 1612, in Haarlem.
Active in Haarlem.
Draughtsman, engraver (burin).
Antwerp School.

Philipp Galle engraved a number of works including *Historical Scenes, Portraits* and *Genre scenes* and, particularly, works of Brueghel. In 1570, he was made a member of the guild in Antwerp and in 1571 he became a citizen of the town. He had Barbe and Hendrick Goltzius as pupils.

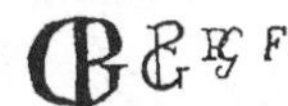

AUCTION RECORDS:
LONDON, 29 June 1987, *Rhinoceros* (1586, engraving/copper, 8 x 10 3/4 ins / 20.5 x 27.5 cm) GBP 4,200.

GALLE, Pierre Vincent
French, 20th century.
Born 8 February 1883, in Rennes; died 11 November 1960, in Rennes.
Painter. Genre scenes.

Pierre Galle may have been the brother of Jean Joseph Galle. He exhibited in Paris at the Salon des Artistes Français after studying under Cormon and Luc-Olivier Merson.

GALLE, Theodor
Flemish School, 16th - 17th century.
Born 1571, in Antwerp; died 18 December 1633.
Draughtsman, engraver (burin).

Theodor was the pupil of his father, Philippe Galle. He made engravings of *Historical Subjects, Portraits and Genre Subjects*.

GALLEAN, E.
German, 19th century.
Active in 1815.
Sculptor.

A signed work by this artist is still in existence.

GALLEANO, Francesco
Italian, 17th - 18th century.
Born 1636, in Genoa; died 1735, in Cádiz.
Active in Spain.
Sculptor (wood).

Francesco Galleano was the brother of Pietro Galleano.

GALLEANO, Pietro
Italian, 18th century.
Born 1687, in Genoa; died April 1761, in Genoa.
Active in Genoa and Turin.
Sculptor (wood).

Pietro Galleano was a pupil of Maragliano.

GALLEE, Cornelis, or Galle
Flemish School, 18th century.
Active in Bruges (West Flanders).
Painter.

Gallee is first recorded in 1695 and seems to have died in 1720.

GALLEGO
Spanish, 16th century.
Painter.

Gallego was active in Valladolid around 1523. His name appears in a list, compiled in 1531, of artists who worked on the cathedral of S Benito de la Calzada.

GALLEGO, A.
Spanish, 16th century.
Active c. 1544.
Painter, sculptor.

Gallego produced a number of paintings for the monastery of S Maria de Nascera.

GALLEGO, Antonio
French, 20th - 21st century.
Born 1956, in Villennes-sur-Seine (Yvelines).
Painter (including mixed media), intervention artist.
Nouvelle Figuration.
Banlieue-Banlieue Group, Ne Pas Plier (Don't Bend) Group.

Antonio Gallego was one of the founders and leaders of the Banlieu-Banlieu Group between 1982 and 1987. In 1985 he executed the sets for the film *I Love You* by Marco Ferreri. In 1986 he exhibited *Le Grand Paris* in Italy and at the Centre Georges Pompidou in Paris and in 1987 he produced a setting for a Paris theatre.

As a reaction against the war in the former Yugoslavia, from 1992 onwards he took action covering road signs with the word 'Sarajevo' in the same original typography in order to emphasise the proximity of the conflict.

AUCTION RECORDS:
PARIS, 13 April 1988, *Look at Oedipus* (mixed media, 28 3/4 x 36 1/4 ins / 73 x 92 cm) FRF 4,000. PARIS, 8 Oct 1989, *Untitled* (mixed media, 76 3/4 x 51 1/4 ins / 195 x 130 cm) FRF 10,500.

GALLEGO, Cristóbal
Spanish, 16th century.
Active in Seville c. 1530.
Painter.

Cristóbal Gallego worked for the Alcazar.

GALLEGO, Fernando. See **GALLEGOS**

GALLEGO, Francisco
Spanish, 17th century.
Active in Salamanca in 1627.
Sculptor.

Francisco Gallego worked for various churches and monasteries.

GALLEGO, Pedro
Spanish, 16th century.
Active in Seville in 1539.
Painter.

Pedro Gallego worked for the Alcazar. There is no doubt that he is the same artist who produced ornamental sculpture in Seville between 1536 and 1539.

GALLEGO Y ALVÁREZ, Domingo
Spanish, 19th century.
Born 1817, in Tembleque.
Painter. History painting, genre scenes.

Domingo Gallego y Alvárez was a pupil of Antonio Bejarano. He first exhibited in Madrid in 1840 with *The Death of Charles V*. He also exhibited in Paris and Bordeaux. He is known for his *Enactment of a Naval Battle*; *Armourer from the 17th-Century*; and some views of seaports.

GALLEGOS, Fernando, or Gallego
Spanish, 15th - 16th century.
Born c. 1440, in Salamanca; died after 1507.
Painter. Religious subjects, landscapes.

In Spain, as in Italy, Flemish painting was an important influence in the 15th century. Queen Isabella owned a tryptych by Rogier ven der Weyden and a work by Dieric Bouts. By Gallegos' time, Spanish artists had more or less assimilated the Flemish manner and were often able to interpret it in a personal way. From this point of view, Gallegos represents the full flowering of the Hispano-Flemish style. His reputation was such that he had to employ assistants to fulfil his commissions, many of which have since been lost.

Before 1467, he painted the *St Ildefonse* altarpiece for Zamora Cathedral. His angular, rigid treatment of the draperies is reminiscent of D. Bouts. In 1475, he was commissioned to paint six altarpieces for Coria Cathedral, but all have been lost. In 1507, with Pedro de Tolosa, he decorated the gallery of the chapel at Salamanca University, where he also produced paintings for the library. For the new cathedral at Salamanca, he painted a tryptych of the *Virgin and*

Child, influenced by the engravings of Schongauer and the work of Conrad Witz. He also painted a *Pietà* in a style similar to that of Rogier van der Weyden. However, despite these influences, Gallegos' work is interesting in its own right. His style is austere and rigid. His figures wear agonised expressions, with distorted features, bulging eyes and mouths twisted with pain. His desolate, desert-like landscapes evoke the tablelands of Castille. Having thoroughly assimilated the Flemish style, Gallegos is authentically Spanish in the way he dramatises his subjects.

Gallegos has featured in a number of thematic exhibitions: 2002, *The Age of Jan Van Eyck: the Mediterranean world of early Netherlandish painting, 1430-1530*, Groeningemuseum, Briges; 2003, *Hispano-Flemish Gothic Painting. Bartolomé Bermejo and his Time*, Museu Nacional d'Art de Catalunya, Barcelona.

Bibliography:

Gaya Nuño, Juan Antonio, *Fernando Gallego*, Instituto Diego Velázquez, Madrid, 1958. Felipe Ferrero, Felipe, *Visicitudes de el mayor retablo español del siglo XV: las treinta y cinco tablas de Arcenillas (pintor, Fernando Gallego)*, Gráficas Andres Martín, Valladolid, 1975. García Sebastián, José Luis, *Fernando Gallego y su taller en Salamanca*, Caja de Ahorros y Monte de Piedad, Salamanca, 1979. *Le Siècle de Jan Van Eyck. Le monde méditerranéen et les Primitifs flamands, 1430-1530*, exhibition catalogue, Groeningemuseum, Bruges, Flammarion, Paris, 2002. *Hispano-Flemish Gothic Painting. Bartolomé Bermejo and his time*, group exhibition catalogue, Museu Nacional d'Art de Catalunya, Barcelona, 2003 (pub. in Spanish, Catalan and English).

Museums and Galleries:

Dallas (Meadows Mus.): *Acacio y los 10.000 mártires del Monte Ararat* (*Acacius and the 10,000 Martyrs on Mount Ararat*) (tempera and oil on wood, attributed to Fernando or Francisco; fragment of retable) - Madrid (Prado): *Pietà*.

Auction records:

New York, 14 Nov 1934, *Crucifixion*, USD 160. London, 30 July 1943, *Christ on the Cross*, GBP 47. Geneva, 21 June 1976, *Apostle* (panel of retable, 23 1/2 x 20 1/2 ins / 60 x 52 cm) CHF 180,000. London, 8 Dec 1989, *Pentecost* (oil on panel, 53 1/4 x 41 1/4 ins / 135.2 x 105 cm) GBP 154,000.

GALLEGOS, Francisco, or Gallego

Spanish, 15th - 16th century.

Painter. Religious subjects.

Francisco Gallegos was undoubtedly the son of Fernando Gallegos, with whom he collaborated, and he is often confused with his father. He worked in Salamanca.

The *St Catherine* altarpiece, painted in 1500 in Salamanca, is attributed to him.

Auction records:

London, 25 March 1977, *Deposition* (oil on panel, 33 x 22 ins / 84 x 56 cm) GBP 9,000.

GALLEGOS MARQUINA, Jesús

Spanish, 20th century.

Born 5 February 1900, in Zamora (Castilla y León).

Painter, draughtsman. Portraits, genre scenes.

Jesús Gallegos Marquina studied at the Real Academia de Bellas Artes de San Fernando in Madrid. He travelled in Europe and was awarded a bursary by the Paular academy in 1926. He taught drawing and took part in collective exhibitions as well as holding solo exhibitions in Madrid and Zamora. He was awarded first prize at the Academia de San Fernando and received the Madrigal medal.

Bibliography:

Arnáiz, José Manuel/López Jiménez, Javier/Merchán Díaz, Manuel (ed.), '*Cien años de pintura en Espana y Portugal (1830-1930)*' in vol. III, Antiqvaria, Madrid, 1989 (One Hundred Years of Painting in Spain and Portugal (1830-1930)).

Museums and Galleries:

Madrid (Mus. Nacional Centro de Arte Reina Sofía).

GALLEGOS Y ARNOSA, José

Spanish, 19th - 20th century.

Born 3 May 1859, in Jerez de la Frontera (Andalusia); died 1917, in Anzio, Italy.

Painter. Genre scenes, local scenes, scenes with figures, church interiors, group portraits, local figures, religious subjects, architectural views, urban landscapes. Church decoration.

Orientalism.

José Gallegos y Arnosa studied in Madrid under Federico de Madrazo. In 1881 he left for Rome where he frequented the Accademia Chigi and the international fine arts circle. He then visited Morocco.

From 1881 he took part in the exhibition of the national fine arts society and in exhibitions organised by the Círculo de Bellas Artes in 1880-1881 and 1882, in the *Esposizione Artistica Internazionale* in Rome in 1883. He also exhibited in Berlin where he was awarded a gold medal in 1891, and in Munich. He is known for his painting *A Slave* and *Neapolitan*. He decorated the altar of the church of Santiago in Jerez between 1900 and 1906. His paintings of cardinals brought him great success. He also painted oriental subjects in very detailed settings such as *Guard Smoking a Narghile* of 1884. His work is characterised by a profusion and richness of detail and by consummate skill in execution.

Bibliography:

González López y Montse Martí, Carlos, *Pintores españoles en Roma (1850-1900)*, Tusquets Editores, Barcelona, 1987 (Spanish Painters in Rome (1850-1900). Juler, Caroline, *Les Orientalistes de l'école italienne*, ACR Édition, Paris, 1994 (Orientalists of the Italian School).

Museums and Galleries:

Bautzen (Stadtmus.) - Boston (MFA) - Madrid (Mus. Nacional Centro de Arte Reina Sofía): *Moroccan Wedding*.

Auction records:

Paris, 23 April 1897, *Choir Boy*, FRF 800. New York, 3 Feb 1905, *Wedding*, USD 1,300. London, 12 Feb 1910, *Feast of the Madonna, Seville Cathedral*, GBP 304. London, 18 June 1928, *Reading the Will*, GBP 65. New York, 14-16 Jan 1943, *Picador in the Bullring*, USD 95. London, 22 Nov 1961, *Baptism, Rome* (1888) GBP 1,850. Munich, 29-30 Sept 1965, *Spanish Communion*, DEM 14,000. London, 17 Feb 1971, *The First Communion*, GBP 3,200. Munich, 27 June 1973, *At the Pharmacist's* (1898) DEM 62,000. London, 12 June 1974, *Harlequin at the Ball*, GBP 3,600. London, 11 Feb 1976, *Matadors Entering a Church* (1910, oil on canvas, 13 x 24 ins / 33 x 61 cm) GBP 4,800. London, 22 July 1977, *Bullfighter and his Girl* (1909, oil on panel, 9 1/2 x 16 ins / 24 x 40.5 cm) GBP 2,000. London, 20 June 1980, *A Canal in Venice* (oil on panel, 23 3/4 x 14 1/2 ins / 60.3 x 36.8 cm) GBP 3,200. London, 27 Nov 1985, *The First Communion* (1897, oil on panel, 18 x 28 ins / 45.5 x 71 cm) GBP 32,000. London, 23 Nov 1988, *Celebration on a Terrace in Seville* (1891, oil on panel, 15 3/4 x 22 3/4 ins / 40 x 58 cm) GBP 37,400. London, 17 Feb 1989, *The Serenade* (oil on panel, 9 3/4 x 5 3/4 ins / 24.7 x 14.6 cm) GBP 14,300. New York, 24 May 1989, *The Geographers* (1902, oil on panel, 9 x 12 ins / 22.9 x 30.5 cm) USD 66,000. London, 15 Feb 1990, *Church Choir* (1886, oil on panel, 14 1/2 x 21 ins / 36.7 x 53.4 cm) GBP 132,000. New York, 23 May 1991, *Carnival in Venice* (oil on panel, 12 1/4 x 20 ins / 31.4 x 51.1 cm) USD 66,000. New York, 20 Feb 1992, *The Pharmacy* (oil on panel, 13 1/2 x 21 ins / 34.3 x 53.3 cm) USD 198,000. New York, 26 May 1993, *Flower Market* (1893, oil on panel, 15 x 24 ins / 38.1 x 61 cm) USD

107,000. LONDON, 19 Nov 1993, *Interior of Seville Cathedral* (oil on panel, 11 1/2 x 9 ins / 29.5 x 22 cm) GBP 18,400. LONDON, 16 March 1994, *St Mark's Square, Venice* (1882, oil on panel, 16 x 10 ins / 40.5 x 25.5 cm) GBP 21,850. LONDON, 15 Nov 1995, *Cardinals in a Library* (oil on panel, 13 1/2 x 20 ins / 34 x 51 cm) GBP 16,100. NEW YORK, 23-24 May 1996, *Boys' Choir* (oil on canvas, 36 x 24 1/2 ins / 91.4 x 62.2 cm) USD 57,500. LONDON, 21 Nov 1996, *Visit to the Cardinal* (1903, oil on panel, 17 1/4 x 24 ins / 43.8 x 61 cm) GBP 41,100. LONDON, 13 June 1997, *La Fiesta* (oil on panel, 15 1/2 x 23 1/2 ins / 39.5 x 59.7 cm) GBP 63,100. LONDON, 19 Nov 1997, *The Church of SS Giovanni e Paolo and the Colleoni Equestrian Monument, Venice* (oil on panel, 15 1/4 x 9 3/4 ins / 39 x 25 cm) GBP 33,350.

GALLEI, Franz Nestor
German, 17th century.
Died 19 January 1694, in Munich.
Painter.

GALLEL Y BELTRAN, José
Spanish, 19th century.
Born 4 November 1825, in Valencia.
Painter. History painting, landscapes.

José Gallel y Beltran first exhibited around 1855 in Valencia, and also in Saragossa in 1867.

GALLEL Y PRIZENETA, Fernando
Spanish, 19th century.
Born in the 19th century, in Valencia.
Painter. Genre scenes.

Fernando Gallel y Prizeneta first exhibited in Valencia in 1875.

GALLELLI, Massimiliano
Italian, 19th century.
Born 17 December 1863, in Cremona.
Painter. Religious subjects, genre scenes.

Gallelli lived in Rome. In 1900 he took part in the Alinari competition with a painting entitled *Mater Christi*.

AUCTION RECORDS:

NEW YORK, 13 Nov 1909, *Scene in Pompeii*, USD 228. NEW YORK, 17 and 18 May 1934, *Love Song*, USD 100. NEW YORK, 28 May 1981, *Terrace* (oil on canvas, 31 1/2 x 18 1/4 ins / 80 x 46.5 cm) USD 4,500. NEW YORK, 19 Jan 1994, *Terrace* (oil on canvas, 31 1/2 x 18 ins / 80 x 45.7 cm) USD 4,600. NEW YORK, 17 Jan 1996, *Concert* (oil on canvas, 25 x 40 1/2 ins / 63.5 x 102.9 cm) USD 8,050. NEW YORK, 25 Oct 2000, *Lyrist's Serenade* (oil on canvas, 24 x 40 ins / 62 x 102 cm) USD 12,000. VERSAILLES, 7 April 2002, *Gondolas in Venice* (oil on canvas, 16 x 26 ins / 40 x 65 cm) EUR 3,600. ROME, 26 Nov 2002, *Lady with a Pearl Necklace* (oil on canvas, 31 x 23 ins / 78 x 58 cm) EUR 2,000.

GALLEN, Harald. See **HARALD-GALLEN Arthur**

GALLEN-KALLELA, Akseli Valdemar
Finnish, 19th - 20th century.
Born 26 or 29 May 1865, in Pori, 26 April according to some sources; died 7 March 1931, in Stockholm.
Painter, pastellist, fresco artist, engraver, illustrator. Genre scenes, portraits, landscapes.
Symbolism.

Akseli Gallen-Kallela began his studies at the Finnish fine arts school in Helsinki in 1881 and continued at Adolf von Becker's private academy. From 1884 he studied with William Bouguereau and Tony Robert-Fleury at the school of fine arts in Paris and with Bastien-Lepage and Fernand Cormon at the Académie Julian, all of whom influenced him greatly. He was friendly with the Scandinavian artists Edelfelt and Zorn, and saw a lot of August Strindberg in Paris. Under the influence of some of the ideas of John Ruskin, he decided in favour of a Finnish Nationalist ideology and returned to Finland in 1890. He made further stays in Paris, London and Berlin in 1895 and Italy in 1897-1898. In 1907 he changed his name officially from Gallén to Gallen-Kallela. He travelled to Kenya in 1909-1910 and New Mexico in 1920-1924. He was made a Chevalier of the Légion d'Honneur.

From 1890 he developed pre-Expressionist tendencies and painted large frescoes inspired by the Finnish legends of the *Kalevala* with great freedom of design and a very vivid range of colours. When the Munich artists gathered around Kirchner, Schmidt-Rottluff and others founded the group Die Brücke, they showed the high esteem in which they held him by inviting him to take part in their exhibitions. He was an imposing interpreter of folk poetry, but is also known for boldly realistic portraits, scenes of working-class life, typical snowy Finnish landscapes and forest fires inspired by his visit to Africa. In 1901 and 1904, he painted frescoes for the Juselius Mausoleum in Pori, which were destroyed by fire in 1931. He also had a great deal of influence on modern Finnish architecture.

He exhibited works inspired by his teachers at the Paris Salon in 1888 and 1889. He continued to be associated with the Société Nationale des Beaux Arts after 1891, winning a silver medal at the time of the 1889 Exposition Universelle. He won another at the 1900 Exposition Universelle for a painting celebrating *the Conquest of the Pole* and also decorated the Finnish pavilion at this event. His paintings formed part of the *Lumières du Nord: La Peinture Scandinave 1885-1905* (*Northern Lights: Scandinavian Painting 1885-1905*) exhibition at the Petit Palais in Paris in 1987.

He showed his works in solo exhibitions, the first of which was in 1889 at the Ateneum Art Gallery in Helsinki. There have been regular celebrations of his work for some years, for instance in 1992 at the Finnish Cultural Centre in Paris, a sizeable collection within the framework of the exhibition *Visions du Nord* (*Visions of the North*) at the Musée d'Art Moderne in Paris in 1998, and *Les Mondes intérieurs. Le Symbolisme finlandais* (*Inner Worlds: Finnish Symbolism*) at the Musée d'Ixelles in Brussels in 2002.

BIBLIOGRAPHY:

Martin, T./Sivén, D., *Akseli Gallen-Kallela*, Watti-Kustannus, Helsinki, 1985. Kämäräinen, E., *Aksei Gallen-Kallela: Artist and Visionary*, Söderströms Förlag, Helsinki, 1994. *Visions du Nord*, group exhibition catalogue, Musée d'Art moderne de la Ville de Paris, Paris, 1998.

MUSEUMS AND GALLERIES:

ESPOO (Gallen-Kallela Mus.): *The Hills of Hwandoni* (1909-1910) - HELSINKI: *Midsummer; The Imp; Aino; Portrait of Doctor Autell; Smatra in Winter Dress; Head of a Girl; The Conquest of the Pole* (sketches of the fresco for the 1900 Exposition Universelle); *Subject from Scandinavian Mythology* - HELSINKI (Ateneumin Taidemus.): *On the River* (1903); *Spring 1903* (study for the Juselius Mausoleum frescoes); *The River in the Valley* (1909); *Mount Kenya* (1909); *Mount Donia Sabuk* (1909); *Dwarf Tree on the Steppes* (1909-1910) - HELSINKI (Didrichsenin Taidemus.): *Columns of Cloud* - HELSINKI (Sigrid Juséliuksen säätiö): *Autumn Five Crosses* (1902, study for the Juselius Syksy Mausoleum frescoes); *Winter Landscape in Kalela 1903* - HELSINKI (Suomen Kansallismus.): *The Myth of Aino* - MÄNTTÄ (Gösta Serlachiuksen taidemuseo): *Autumn* (1903, distemper and oil on canvas, study); *Felled Pine Tree* (1904); *Lynx's Lair* (1906).

AUCTION RECORDS:

COPENHAGEN, 28 Sept 1976, *Landscape with a Lake* (oil on canvas, 14 1/2 x 13 3/4 ins / 37 x 35 cm) DKK 20,000. COPENHAGEN, 8 June 1977, *Picture of Aino* (triptych, central panel 37 3/4 x 37 1/2 ins / 96 x 95 cm; lateral panels 37 3/4 x 19 1/4 ins/96 x 49 cm) DKK 14,000. LOS ANGELES, 16 March 1981, *The Last Spot of Fig Wine* (1924, colouring pencil/paper, 10 1/4 x 12 1/2 ins / 26 x 32 cm) USD 900. LONDON, 29 Nov 1984, *The Studio of Count Deheaulme de Vallonbreuse, 36 Rue Jouffroy, Paris* (1888, pastel, 23 x 16 3/4 ins / 58.4 x 42.5 cm) GBP 6,500. STOCKHOLM, 28

Oct 1985, *Interior* (pastel, 23 1/4 x 17 ins / 59 x 43 cm) SEK 95,000. LONDON, 29 Nov 1985, *Autumn Landscape, The Five Crosses* (1902, oil on canvas, 30 x 57 ins / 76 x 145 cm) GBP 70,000. LONDON, 24 March 1988, *Italian Beauty* (oil on canvas, 17 x 13 3/4 ins / 43 x 35 cm) GBP 24,200. LONDON, 19 June 1990, *Reflections of Lights on a Lake* (1908, oil on canvas, 19 x 16 3/4 ins / 48 x 42.5 cm) GBP 16,500. LONDON, 28 June 1999, *Lake Keitele* (1905, oil on canvas, 21 x 26 ins / 53 x 66 cm) GBP 220,000. HELSINKI, 11 Dec 1999, *View across the Sea* (1917, oil on canvas, 40 x 32 ins / 102 x 82 cm) FIM 830,000. LONDON, 7 April 2000, *White Roses* (1906, oil on canvas, 24 x 23 ins / 62 x 58 cm) GBP 223,500. HELSINKI, 9 Dec 2000, *Lynx in the Old Dry Pine Tree* (1906, oil on canvas, 22 x 13 ins / 56 x 32 cm) FIM 400,000. HELSINKI, 12 May 2001, *Girl by the Fireplace* (1891, oil canvas/board, 15 x 13 ins / 39 x 33 cm) FIM 270,000. LONDON, 6 June 2001, *Beside the Lake* (c. 1907, oil on canvas, 18 x 18 ins / 45 x 45 cm) GBP 28,000. HELSINKI, 30 Nov 2002, *Lady Dressed in White Party Dress* (1887, oil on panel, 8 x 6 ins / 20 x 15 cm) EUR 50,000. HELSINKI, 1 Dec 2002, *Summer Morning at Ruovesi* (1889, oil on card, 14 x 10 ins / 35 x 25 cm) EUR 39,000. HELSINKI, 17 May 2003, *Late Winter Landscape, Konginkangas* (1906, oil on canvas, 9 x 22 ins / 22 x 57 cm) EUR 38,000. HELSINKI, 29 Nov 2003, *Woodland Tarn* (1883, oil on card, 9 x 14 ins / 23 x 36 cm) EUR 46,000. HELSINKI, 8 May 2004, *Sunlit Pine Tree* (1898, oil on card, 7 x 5 ins / 19 x 13 cm) EUR 41,000. HELSINKI, 8 May 2004, *Female Nude Rowing* (1909, pastel, 28 x 28 ins / 72 x 71 cm) EUR 42,000.

GALLENCAMP, B.
Danish, 17th century.
Active c. 1660.
Painter. Portraits.
Two portraits by B. Gallencamp are in a church in Sæby.

GALLENIUS, Lars
Finnish, 17th - 18th century.
Born c. 1665; died c. 1750.
Painter.
Lars Gallenius worked in a number of churches, including that of Hailuoto.

GALLENSTEIN. See **KURZ August**

GALLER, Bernard de
German, 17th century.
Painter. Landscapes.
A catalogue of works at the gallery in Warsaw mentions Bernard de Galler as being the Bishop of Münster. There is a known work by him representing a flood in Holland.

GALLES, Bastien
French, 16th century.
Sculptor.
Galles worked under the direction of Pierre Bontemps and alongside Pierre Bigoigne and Jean de Bourges on the ornamentation of the tomb of Francis I in 1555.

GALLET
French, 17th century.
Active in Paris in 1699.
Sculptor.

GALLET, Alphonse
French, 19th century.
Died 1831.
Painter. Genre scenes, landscapes.
MUSEUMS AND GALLERIES:
ROUEN: *Greeks Leaving Parga for Corfu.*

GALLET, Antoine
French, 17th century.
Active in Voroy.
Sculptor.

GALLET, Hélène
French, 20th century.
Born 16 February 1905, in Le Havre.
Painter. Landscapes.
Hélène Gallet exhibited at various group exhibitions, mainly the Paris Salons.

GALLET, Jean Charles
Belgian, 19th - 20th century.
Born 1872, in Brussels.
Painter. Seascapes.
Jean Gallet studied with Portaels at the Brussels academy.

GALLET, Jean-Baptiste
French, 19th century.
Born 22 May 1820, in La Guillotière, Lyons; died 15 December 1848, in St-Génis-Laval (Rhône).
Painter.
He studied from 1834 to 1840 under Thierriat at the École des Beaux-Arts in Lyons, where he enrolled using the name 'Gallay'. He exhibited still-lifes of flowers and fruit in Lyons from 1842-43 and in Paris in 1847 and 1848.
MUSEUMS AND GALLERIES:
LYONS: *Bouquet of Mixed Flowers* (1848).
AUCTION RECORDS:
MONTE CARLO, 7 Dec 1987, *Still-life with Flowers in a Sculpted Urn and Peaches, Grapes and Blackcurrants on a Ledge* (oil on canvas, 39 1/2 x 32in/100.5 x 81.5 cm) FRF 150,000.

GALLET, Laurent
French, 17th century.
Active in Cambrai.
Sculptor, architect. Religious subjects.
Cambrai School, Arras School.
In 1617, Laurent Gallet took over responsibility for continuing the work on the rood-screen at the church at the abbey of St Waast in Arras; he also made a calvary showing four figures for this church. In 1631, he produced a statue of the Virgin Mary for the gate at Le Malle in Cambrai and in 1633 he was nominated as grand master of his guild.

GALLET, Louis
French, 18th century.
Active in Paris in 1786.
Painter, sculptor.

GALLET, Louis
French, 20th century.
Born 16 November 1873, in La Chaux-de-Fonds (Neuchâtel), Switzerland.
Painter, sculptor.
Louis Gallet joined the Salon of the Société Nationale des Beaux-Arts in 1904 and exhibited at the Society's Salons.
MUSEUMS AND GALLERIES:
LAUSANNE (Cantonal MFA): *Cock Crowing* (c. 1904).

GALLET-LEVADE, Louise Émilie, Mme Louisa
French, 19th - 20th century.
Born 11 March 1865, in Versailles; died 21 August 1937, in Le Havre.
Painter, miniaturist. Portraits.
Louise Gallet-Levade studied under Jules Lefebvre, Tony Robert-Fleury and Henry Royer. She specialised in portrait miniatures. She exhibited in Paris at the Salon des Artistes Français and later became a member of the Salon. She was awarded a bronze medal in 1900 at the Exposition Universelle, a commendation in 1903 and a silver medal in 1922. She was also made an Officier de l'Instruction Publique.

GALLETTA, Peter Paul
German, 17th century.
Died 8 July 1708, in Neisse (now Nysa, Poland).
Painter.

GALLETTE, C.
Painter. Landscapes.
Mentioned by Florence Levy.

AUCTION RECORDS:
NEW YORK, 9-10 Feb 1905, *Path in a Wood*, USD 110.

GALLETTI, Carlo Andrea
Italian, 15th - 16th century.
Active in Siena.
Sculptor.
Carlo Andrea was the father of Giovanni Andrea and Giulio Galletti.

GALLETTI, Filippo Maria (Fra)
Italian, 17th - 18th century.
Born 1636, in Florence; died 23 February 1714.
Painter.
Filippo Maria Galletti was a pupil of Vincenzo Dandini. A portrait of Galletti hangs in the Uffizi.

GALLETTI, Francesco
Italian, 19th century.
Born 14 July 1833, in Cento.
Sculptor.
Francesco Galletti was a pupil of Baruzzi in Bologna, and embarked on his artistic career around 1870. He is known for a *Statue of St Laurence* in the Campo Verano cemetery in Rome.

GALLETTI, Giacomo
Italian, 17th century.
Active in Treviso in 1696.
Painter.

GALLETTI, Giovanni Andrea
Italian, 16th century.
Born 2 June 1500, in Siena; died c. 1539, in Siena.
Sculptor.
The son of Carlo Andrea Galletti, Giovanni Andrea Galletti studied under G. Cozzarelli. With his father, he performed significant work for Siena Cathedral.

GALLETTI, Giulio
Italian, 16th century.
Active in Siena.
Sculptor.
Giulio Galletti was the brother of Giovanni Andrea Galletti.

GALLETTI, Lia
Cuban, 20th century.
Born 1943, in Havana.
Active in the USA.
Painter, engraver, draughtswoman. Figures.
Lia Galletti was born in Havana and studied at Queens College, New York and the Coral Gables Metropolitan Museum and Art Center, Florida. She paints figures using an Expressionist technique with Goyaesque accents but she is best known for her drawings and engravings. She has taken part in numerous collective and solo exhibitions in the USA, Canada, Spain and Israel.
AUCTION RECORDS:
NEW YORK, 16 Nov 1994, *Babalawo Wow* (1992, acrylic/canvas, 71 x 50 ins / 180.3 x 127 cm) USD 6,900. NEW YORK, 27 May 1998, *La razón del corazón* (*The Heart's Reason*) (1992, oil on canvas, 68 x 50 ins / 173 x 127 cm) USD 4,000.

GALLETTI, Niccolo
Italian, 17th century.
Active in Treviso in 1696.
Painter.

GALLETTI, Stefano
Italian, 19th century.
Born 14 June 1833, in Cento; died 1905, in Rome.
Sculptor.
Early on in his career, Stefano Galletti worked in Cento and Ferrara. His most famous work in Rome is the *Monument to Cavour*, which was erected in 1895.

GALLEY, Jean-Baptiste
French, 19th century.
Born in St-Étienne.
Painter.
He exhibited landscapes in Paris in 1879, 1880 and 1881.

GALLEZOT, Jean Joseph
French, 18th century.
Died 1753.
Active in Besançon.
Sculptor.

GALLHOF, Wilhelm
German, 20th century.
Born 24 July 1878, in Iserlohn; died June 1918.
Painter, sculptor, engraver. Equestrian portraits.
Wilhelm Gallhof studied with Herterich the Elder in Munich. He exhibited in Berlin, Munich, Bremen and Mannheim.
MUSEUMS AND GALLERIES:
ELBERFELD - WEIMAR.
AUCTION RECORDS:
MUNICH, 10 May 1989, *Horsewoman* (1910, oil on canvas, 38 3/4 x 26 3/4 ins / 98.5 x 68 cm) DEM 6,600.

GALLI. See also **BIBIENA**

GALLI, Alberto
Italian, 19th century.
Born 1843, in Rome.
Sculptor.
Alberto Galli was in charge of the Vatican sculpture collection.

GALLI, Aldo
Italian, 20th century.
Born 1906, in Como; died 1981, in Lugano (Ticino canton), Switzerland.
Painter, draughtsman, sculptor, engraver.
In 1919 and 1920 Aldo Galli studied painting, drawing and engraving on his own, before taking lessons in Como and Milan. He returned to Como in 1932, renewing his friendships with the painters Rho, Radice and Badiali. He exhibited at the Salon des Réalités Nouvelles in Paris from 1947 to 1950.

Galli's compositions fall strictly within the abstract tradition, with a bias towards geometric forms, and subtle gradations of light. In 1934 he produced his first abstract drawings and sculptures, before returning to painting in 1940. He also produced engravings.
BIBLIOGRAPHY:
Aldo Galli: oli, acquerelli, disegni, incisioni, rilievi, exhibition catalogue, Vismara arte contemporanea, Vismara, Milan.
Bortone, A., *Aldo Galli*, Como, 1964.
AUCTION RECORDS:
MILAN, 10 March 1986, *Composition* (1941, mounted card, 14 1/2 x 19 ins / 37 x 48.5 cm) ITL 15,000,000. MILAN, 16 Oct 1986, *Composition* (1956, tempera/card, 18 x 13 1/2 ins / 45.5 x 34 cm) ITL 9,000,000. MILAN, 6 June 1989, *Composition* (1972, oil on panel, 13 3/4 x 22 1/4 ins / 35 x 56.5 cm) ITL 25,000,000.

GALLI, Angelo
Italian, 17th century.
Active in Milan.
Painter.
Angelo Galli was a pupil of Ladriani (Duchino).

GALLI, Antonio
Italian, 19th century.
Died 1862, in Milan.
Sculptor.
Antonio Galli was taught by Somaini and Thorvaldsen. He left behind a large number of mythological and allegorical sculptures, as well as some busts.

GALLI, Cristofano Paolo
Italian, 17th century.
Active c. 1600.
Engraver.
Cristofano Paolo Galli is known only from his signature on two landscapes.

GALLI, Eduardo
Italian, 19th century.
Born 20 November 1854, in Naples.
Painter. Portraits, genre scenes.
Eduardo Galli exhibited in Rome, in 1883, and in Venice, in 1887.
AUCTION RECORDS:
MILAN, 18 Oct 1990, *Young Peasant Girl and Her Goat on a Forest Path* (oil on canvas, 42 1/4 x 67 ins / 107 x 170 cm) ITL 16,000,000. PARIS, 30 April 1999, *Adolescent with Bouquet of Pansies* (1883, oil on panel, 29 x 12 ins / 74 x 31 cm) FRF 70,000.

GALLI, Elias, the Elder
German, 17th century.
Painter. History painting, portraits, still-lifes.
Galli worked for different churches, such as the church of St George in Hamburg or the church of Horsen in Jutland. His *Still-life* at the museum in Leipzig is signed and dated.
MUSEUMS AND GALLERIES:
LEIPZIG: *Still-life*.

GALLI, Elias, the Younger
German, 18th century.
Active at the beginning of the 18th century.
Painter.
Elias Galli was almost certainly the son of Elias the Elder. He spent all his life in the service of the Dukes of Holstein-Gottorff. He is noted for his works for the castles of Gottorff and Husum (Schleswig-Holstein).

GALLI, Emira
Italian, 19th century.
Born in the 19th century.
Painter. Genre scenes, portraits.
Emira Galli exhibited in Turin and Milan around 1880.

GALLI, Ferdinando
Italian, 19th century.
Born 18 June 1814, in Milan.
Painter. Genre scenes.
Ferdinando Galli was the brother of Luigi Galli.

GALLI, Fortunato
Italian, 20th century.
Born in Livorno; died 19 April 1918, in Florence.
Sculptor. Figures, historical figures. Statues.
Fortunato Galli sculpted a statue of *Gregory VII* for Florence Cathedral.
AUCTION RECORDS:
LONDON, 20 March 1986, *Young Musician* (c. 1880, marble, h. 44 ins / 112 cm) GBP 10,500.

GALLI, Giacomo
Italian, 18th century.
Active in Ferrara.
Painter. Religious subjects, genre scenes.
Giacomo Galli is believed to have painted an altarpiece for the church of S Maria della Roga.
AUCTION RECORDS:
LONDON, 13 July 1977, *St Francesca Romana with an Angel* (oil on canvas, 18 1/2 x 27 1/4 ins / 47 x 69 cm) GBP 3,600. NEW YORK, 9 Oct 1980, *Discussion* (oil on canvas, 37 3/4 x 53 1/4 ins / 96 x 135.5 cm) USD 52,500.

GALLI, Gino
Italian, 20th century.
Born 1893, in Rome; died 1954, in Florence.
Painter.
Gino Galli was the pupil and close friend of Giacomo Balla, and participated in the activities of the Futurist group in 1919 and 1920, although little evidence of this remains.
AUCTION RECORDS:
MILAN, 18 Dec 1984, *Nocturne* (gouache, 12 3/4 x 8 3/4 ins / 32.5 x 22.5 cm) ITL 2,800,000.

GALLI, Giovanni
Italian, 16th century.
Born in Bergamo.
Painter.
Giovanni Galli studied under Tintoretto in Venice. A *Head of an Old Man*, kept in the Budapest Museum and traditionally regarded as a work by Tintoretto, was attributed to him by Berenson.

GALLI, Giovanni Antonio, called Lo Spadarino
Italian, 17th century.
Born 1585, in Rome; died 1653, in Rome.
Active in Rome.
Painter. Historical subjects, religious subjects, figures, portraits, genre scenes, animals, still-lifes. Ornaments.
.
Giovanni Antonio Galli was little more than a Caravaggio plagiarist.

BIBLIOGRAPHY:
Spinosa, Nicolà, et al., *Les Mystères de Naples. Sublime et triviale: la peinture napolitaine*, collective exhibition catalogue, Musée Fesch, Ajaccio, 2003.
MUSEUMS AND GALLERIES:
ROME (Palazzo Doria Pamphili): *Young Man Playing the Lute*.
AUCTION RECORDS:
PARIS, 10 June 1988, *Still-life with Watermelon* (oil on canvas, 18 1/2 x 24 1/2 ins / 47 x 62 cm) FRF 70,000. ROME, 14 Nov 1995, *St John the Baptist* (oil on canvas, 26 1/4 x 20 1/4 ins / 66.5 x 51.5 cm) ITL 3,450,000.

GALLI, Giovanni Battista
Italian, 17th century.
Active in Naples and Venice.
Sculptor.
Giovanni Battista Galli collaborated with Giannandrea Lazzari to contribute sculptures to the main altar of the Venice church of S Niccolo.

GALLI, Giovanni Battista
Italian, 18th century.
Active in Florence and Ferrara at the end of the 18th century.
Engraver (burin).
Giovanni Battista Galli engraved illustrations for the publication *Raccolta delle Piu Belle Vedute*, a collection of 'the most beautiful views'.

GALLI, Louis-Octave
French, 19th century.
Painter.
He exhibited genre compositions at the Paris Salon from 1841 to 1850. Examples of his work include *Heron Hunt*, *Grandmother's Blessing*, *Love under the Chestnut Trees*, *Ground Ivy* and *Cellier's Brother*.

GALLI, Luigi Mauro
Italian, 19th century.
Born 1820, in Milan; died 1900 or 1906.
Painter. Religious subjects, figures, nudes.
Luigi Galli studied under Sabatelli, Hayez and Brulot. In 1900 he entered his painting of the *Madonna and Child* into the Alinari competition.

AUCTION RECORDS:
MONTE CARLO, 9 Feb 1981, *Recumbent Nude* (oil on card, 12½ x 7½ ins / 32 x 19 cm) FRF 2,000. MILAN, 21 April 1983, *Bacchic Scene* (oil on canvas, 52 x 72¾ ins / 132 x 185 cm) ITL 13,000,000. ZURICH, 4 Nov 2000, *Arcadian Landscape with Figures* (1870, watercolour, 13 x 20 ins / 34 x 50 cm) CHF 2,800. MILAN, 14 Oct 2003, *Diana Bathing* (oil on board, 22 x 12 ins / 56 x 30 cm) EUR 2,800.

GALLI, Pietro
Italian, 17th century.
Active in Piacenza.
Painter.
Pietro Galli worked in 1656 at the church of S Fiorenzo at Firenzuola d'Arda.

GALLI, Pietro
Italian, 19th century.
Born 1804, in Rome; died 1877, in Rome.
Sculptor.
Pietro Galli studied under Thorvaldsen, and subsequently assisted him in his work. After his master's death, Galli finished several monuments that Thorvaldsen had been unable to complete.

GALLI, Riccardo
Italian, 19th century.
Born 1839, in Nice, France.
Sculptor, painter.
Riccardo Galli began working in Naples around 1877, and was also active in Milan. He exhibited in Rome and Turin as well.
MUSEUMS AND GALLERIES:
AMSTERDAM (Stedelijk Mus.): *Head of a Woman.*

GALLI, Riccardo
Italian, 19th - 20th century.
Born 1869, in Milan; died 1944, in Barzio (Lombardy).
Painter, pastellist. Figures, portraits, genre scenes, landscapes with figures, urban landscapes.
AUCTION RECORDS:
MILAN, 14 Dec 1976, *The Red Kimono* (oil on card, 26 x 23½ ins / 66 x 60 cm) ITL 600,000. MILAN, 15 March 1977, *Little Girl Getting Dressed* (pastel/card, 33½ x 27½ ins / 85 x 70 cm) ITL 750,000. MILAN, 10 Dec 1980, *Frankfurt Cathedral* (19¾ x 23½ ins / 50 x 60 cm) ITL 750,000. ROME, 1 June 1983, *Portrait of a Woman* (1909, pastel/canvas, 30¼ x 22½ ins / 77 x 57 cm) ITL 850,000. LONDON, 27 March 1987, *Lake Lecco: Washerwomen* (oil on panel, 6½ x 11½ ins / 16.5 x 29.5 cm) GBP 1,700. ROME, 14 Dec 1988, *Bust of a Woman* (pastel/paper, 13½ x 10¼ ins / 34.5 x 25.8 cm) ITL 1,500,000; *Reading* (oil on canvas, 9 x 7 ins / 23 x 17.5 cm) ITL 1,700,000. MILAN, 14 June 1989, *Bust of a Woman* (pastel/paper, 13¾ x 9¾ ins / 35 x 25 cm) ITL 1,900,000. MILAN, 6 June 1991, *Carriers on the Road to the Mine* (oil on panel, 13½ x 19½ ins / 34.5 x 49.5 cm) ITL 3,000,000. ROME, 10 Dec 1991, *Portrait of a Woman* (pastel/paper/canvas, 30¼ x 22½ ins / 77 x 57 cm) ITL 1,000,000. MILAN, 12 Dec 1991, *Mountainscape* (oil on canvas/card, 15¾ x 19¾ ins / 40 x 50 cm) ITL 1,500,000. LUGANO, 1 Dec 1992, *Washerwoman* (oil on canvas, 22 x 30 ins / 55 x 76 cm) CHF 9,500. MILAN, 17 Dec 1992, *Return from the Fields* (oil on canvas, 19¾ x 27½ ins / 50 x 70 cm) ITL 2,400,000. MILAN, 9 Nov 1993, *The Seine in Paris* (oil on panel, 15¾ x 19¾ ins / 40 x 50 cm) ITL 5,405,000. MILAN, 29 March 1999, *Narrow Street in Macugnaga* (oil on panel, 20 x 24 ins / 50 x 60 cm) ITL 3,600,000. BERN, 5 May 1999, *Woman and Children outside Their Home* (1918, oil on canvas, 21 x 29 ins / 54 x 74 cm) CHF 3,200. MILAN, 10 Dec 2003, *Strolling with Geese* (oil on cardboard/canvas, 19 x 13 ins / 47 x 32 cm) EUR 3,200. MILAN, 19 May 2004, *Nude at Stream* (oil on canvas, 24 x 20 ins / 60 x 50 cm) EUR 2,800. MILAN, 19 May 2004, *View of Alagna* (oil on canvas, 24 x 30 ins / 61 x 77 cm) EUR 4,600.

GALLI DELLA LOGGIA, Ettore (Count)
Italian, 19th century.
Born in the 19th century, in Turin.
Painter. Landscapes.
Galli della Loggia exhibited in Turin around 1880. He is remembered for landscapes of France and Italy.

GALLIAC, Louis
French, 19th - 20th century.
Born 25 August 1849, in Dijon; died 1934, in Paris.
Painter. Genre scenes.
Louis Galliac studied under Adolphe Yvon, Alexandre Cabanel and Léon Bonnat. He exhibited at the Paris Salon from 1879 to 1923 and then at the Salon des Artistes Français, of which he was a member, from 1889. He received a commendation in 1889, a bronze medal in 1892, a silver medal in 1894 and a bronze medal in 1900. He was made a Chevalier of the Légion d'Honneur in 1902.
AUCTION RECORDS:
LONDON, 2 April 1910, *Contemplation,* GBP 2. ZURICH, 29 Nov 1978, *Woman Ironing* (oil on panel, 13¾ x 10½ ins / 35 x 26.5 cm) CHF 3,500. BERN, 23 Oct 1980, *Young Peasant Girl Resting* (oil on canvas, 25½ x 21¼ ins / 65 x 54 cm) CHF 3,200. NEW YORK, 15 Feb 1985, *The Model Has a Snack* (oil on canvas, 28¾ x 25¼ ins / 73 x 64 cm) USD 4,500. GIEN, 26 June 1988, *Woman Reading* (oil on canvas, 25½ x 20¾ ins / 65 x 53 cm) FRF 25,000.

GALLIADI, Giambattista
Italian, 18th - 19th century.
Born 1749, in San Archangelo; died 1811.
Painter. Genre scenes, portraits.
Giambattista Galliadi was a pupil of Lazzarini.

GALLIAN, Octave Lazare George Victor
French, 19th - 20th century.
Born 21 July 1855, in Toulon.
Painter. Portraits, genre scenes, landscapes, seascapes. Murals.
Octave Gallian studied at the École des Beaux-Arts in Paris under Jules Lefebvre, Gustave Boulanger and Charles Ginoux. He exhibited at the Paris Salon and then at the Salon des Artistes Français from 1878 to 1904, receiving a commendation in 1884.

He painted seascapes, fishing scenes, landscapes of Provence and views of Toulon. However, he is best known for his portraits, in which his subjects are treated with great litheness. He also produced mural paintings to decorate the Musée de Toulon.
MUSEUMS AND GALLERIES:
TOULON: *Fishing; Harvesting; Portrait of a Woman Leaning on a Bench on a Terrace Overlooking the Sea.*
AUCTION RECORDS:
PARIS, 7 May 1945, *Outside Toulon,* FRF 2,900. VERSAILLES, 14 Oct 1979, *Rocky Coast* (oil on canvas, 10¼ x 13¾ ins / 26 x 35 cm) FRF 2,300; *Young Woman by a Stream* (oil on canvas, 10¼ x 13¾ ins / 26 x 35 cm) FRF 2,600. VERSAILLES, 17 May 1981, *La Calanque* (oil on canvas, 18 x 24 ins / 46 x 61 cm) FRF 3,500. PARIS, 2 July 1987, *Portrait of a Boy in a Dark Outfit and a Little Girl in a Blue Dress* (1881, oil on canvas, 56 x 42½ ins / 142 x 108 cm) FRF 36,000.

GALLIANI, Omar
Italian, 20th - 21st century.
Born 1954, in Montecchio (Emilia).
Painter (mixed media), illustrator. Mythological subjects.
Citazionismo.
Galliani's heavily drawing-oriented painting draws on the repertory of traditional mythological Classicism. He fills his spaces with running objects and figures which he presents as apparitions, whose presence calls their representation

into question, inviting us to look beyond appearances. He began to exhibit towards the end of the 1960s. In 1987, he participated in the International Exhibition of Art against World Hunger at the Minnesota Museum. His solo shows include the Galerie Barbaro & Cie in Paris (1990).

BIBLIOGRAPHY:

Omar Galliani, Gall. d'Arte Moderna, Bologna, 1995.

AUCTION RECORDS:

ROME, 3 Dec 1985, *Perseus and the Chimera* (mixed media and collage/canvas, 78 3/4 x 94 1/2 ins / 200 x 240 cm) ITL 3,200,000; *The Sound of the Unicorn* (1983, oil on canvas, 7 3/4 x 59 ins / 20 x 150 cm) ITL 9,000,000. MILAN, 25 May 1987, *Cleaving* (oil on canvas, 31 1/2 x 39 1/4 ins / 80 x 100 cm) ITL 4,200,000. MILAN, 13 Dec 1990, *Untitled* (1980, collage and mixed media/paper, 38 1/2 x 50 1/2 ins / 98 x 128.5 cm) ITL 4,200,000. NEW YORK, 12 June 1991, *By Transparency* (1985, oil on canvas, 16 x 16 ins / 40.6 x 40.6 cm) USD 2,750. MILAN, 23 June 1992, *Tiger* (1982, oil on canvas, 23 1/4 x 31 1/2 ins / 59 x 80 cm) ITL 1,300,000. VENICE, 13 Nov 1999, *Alessandro Primo* (1988, oil on canvas, 47 x 47 ins / 120 x 120 cm) ITL 5,800,000. ROME, 25 Nov 1999, *Modern Mona Lisa* (1991, mixed media on panel, 12 x 12 ins / 30 x 30 cm) ITL 4,000,000. PRATO, 24 Nov 2000, *Pearls* (oil on canvas, 33 x 33 ins / 85 x 85 cm) ITL 6,000,000. PRATO, 24 Nov 2000, *Pearls* (oil on canvas, 34 x 34 ins / 86 x 86 cm) ITL 6,000,000. PRATO, 25 May 2001, *Atanor* (1988, oil on canvas, 47 x 47 ins / 120 x 120 cm) ITL 8,500,000. PRATO, 25 May 2001, *Sidereal Virgin* (1987, oil on canvas, 79 x 79 ins / 200 x 200 cm) ITL 15,000,000. FLORENCE, 16 May 2002, *Maybe Icarus* (1983, oil on canvas, 20 x 30 ins / 50 x 75 cm) EUR 3,000. MILAN, 4 Dec 2002, *Shipwreck* (1982, oil on canvas, 81 x 94 ins / 205 x 238 cm) EUR 7,000. VERCELLI, 1 March 2003, *Traces* (graphite on board, 39 x 39 ins / 100 x 100 cm) EUR 6,500. VERCELLI, 6 Sept 2003, *If You Do Not Open Your Eyes* (graphite and pastel board, 24 x 24 ins / 60 x 60 cm) EUR 4,200. VERCELLI, 13 March 2004, *Miriam's House* (1998, graphite on board, 22 x 74 ins / 57 x 187 cm) EUR 6,000. PRATO, 2 April 2004, *In Your Heart* (1990, oil on canvas, 35 x 31 ins / 88 x 78 cm) EUR 4,000.

GALLIARD, Sansonetti

French, 19th century.
Born 1865, in Nancy.
Sculptor.

He studied under Raphaël Collin and Geoffroy. Examples of his work include *Bulldog Bitch* (plaster, 1894); *Death of Brunehaut* (plaster group, 1895); *Bulldog Bitch* (bronze, 1896); *Orpheus* (plaster, 1894); *Hero and Leander* (marble low relief, gold medal winner 1896, acquired by the French state); *Medea* (marble group, 1896, acquired by the state); and two marble busts (1897).

MUSEUMS AND GALLERIES:

PAU: *Greyhounds* (1897, plaster group).

GALLIARDI, Antonio

Austrian, 17th century.
Fresco artist.

Antonio Galliardi decorated several churches, including those at Garsten and at Kremsmünster.

GALLIARDI, Gottlieb Antonio

Austrian, 18th century.
Fresco artist, decorative artist.

Gottlieb Galliardi decorated the cathedral of Neutra in Hungary, among others.

GALLIARI, Bernardino

Italian, 18th century.
Born 3 November 1707, in Andorno; died 31 March 1794, in Andorno.
Painter, draughtsman, decorative artist. Religious subjects, figures, landscapes, architectural views. Stage sets.

Bernardino Galliari was one of the three sons of Giovanni Galliari the Elder. He started out working under Giorgio Clerici. He and his two brothers were in great demand all over Europe.

Examples of his work featured in *I Galliari: Premi Scenegrafi della Scala* (*The Galliaris: first stage designers of the Scala*), an exhibition held at the Museo Teatrale alla Scala in Milan in 1983.

BIBLIOGRAPHY:

Avogadro di Valdengo dell'Abate, Gustavo, *Sulla vita e sulle opere di Bernardino Galliari*, Stamperia Reale, Turin, 1847. Bossaglia, Rossana, *I Fratelli Galliari pittori*, Ceschina, Milan, 1962. Angrisani, Simonetta, *I Galliari: primi scenografi della Scala*, exhibition catalogue, Alinari, Florence, 1983.

MUSEUMS AND GALLERIES:

MILAN (Pinacoteca di Brera): *Adoration of the Shepherds*.

AUCTION RECORDS:

LONDON, 11 June 1981, *Stage Set Study* (pen and wash/paper, 14 1/4 x 10 1/2 ins / 36.3 x 26.8 cm) GBP 1,150. NEW YORK, 12 Jan 1994, *Architectural Drawing* (ink and wash/paper, 14 1/4 x 17 3/4 ins / 36 x 45.2 cm) USD 1,150. VIENNA, 6 Oct 1999, *Allegory of Painting* (oil on canvas, one of four, 38 x 42 ins / 97 x 107 cm) ATS 180,000. VIENNA, 6 Oct 1999, *Allegory of Poetry* (oil on canvas, one of four, 38 x 42 ins / 97 x 107 cm) ATS 200,000.

GALLIARI, Fabrizio

Italian, 18th century.
Born 1709, in Andorno; died 1790, in Treviglio.
Painter, decorative artist. Perspectives. Stage sets.

Fabrizio Galliari was the son of Giovanni Galliari the Elder and the brother of Bernardino and Giovanni Antonio Galliari. He studied under the architect Mariani and began his career under Giorgio Clerici. His principal work is his decoration of the cupola of Bergamo Cathedral. Additionally, he collaborated with his brother Bernardino to design theatre stage sets and décors. He and his two brothers were very much in demand across Europe.

Galliari's work was featured at the exhibition held in the Museo Teatrale alla Scala in Milan in 1883, *I Galliari: Premi Scenegrafi della Scala* (*The Galliaris: first stage designers of the Scala*).

BIBLIOGRAPHY:

Bossaglia, Rossana, *I Fratelli Galliari pittori*, Ceschina, Milan, 1962. Angrisani, Simonetta, *I Galliari: primi scenografi della Scala*, exhibition catalogue, Alinari, Florence, 1983.

GALLIARI, Gasparo

Italian, 18th - 19th century.
Born c. 1760, in Treviglio; died 1823, in Milan.
Painter, decorative artist, draughtsman. Waterscapes, urban landscapes, landscapes. Stage sets.

Gasparo Galliari was the son of Giovanni Antonio Galliari. He worked in the family tradition, painting theatre stage sets and décors.

MUSEUMS AND GALLERIES:

MILAN (Pinacoteca di Brera): *View of Venice*.

AUCTION RECORDS:

NEW YORK, 15 Jan 1992, *Harbour View from the Arcades of an Italian Town* (chalk, ink and wash, 8 1/4 x 12 ins / 21 x 30.2 cm) USD 3,520. PARIS, 15 April 1996, *Garden Summerhouses (Studies)* (watercolour and brown ink on pencil sketch, a pair, each 10 1/2 x 12 1/4 ins / 26.5 x 31 cm) FRF 12,500. MILAN, 7 May 2002, *By a Stable. Outside an Inn* (1812, gouache, a pair, 11 x 9 ins / 28 x 22 cm) EUR 2,130.

GALLIARI, Giovanni, the Elder

Italian, 18th century.
Born c. 1680; died 1722, in Andorno.
Painter, fresco artist, decorative artist. Religious subjects, perspectives.

Giovanni Galliari the Elder was the father of Fabrizio, Giovanni Antonio and Bernardino Galliari. He painted interior frescoes for the chapel of Maria al Tempio at the Oropa sanctuary in Piedmont. He also painted scenes in the royal palace in Turin and in the ducal palace in Milan.

GALLIARI, Giovanni, the Younger, called Giovannino
Italian, 18th - 19th century.
Born 1746; died 1818.
Painter, decorative artist. Stage sets.
Giovanni Galliari the Younger was the son of Fabrizio Galliari. He worked in Berlin with his uncle Bernardino Galliari. He also painted decorations for the principal congress hall in the royal academy of sciences in Turin.

GALLIARI, Giovanni Antonio
Italian, 18th century.
Born 1718, in Andorno; died 1783, in Milan.
Painter. Flowers. Stage sets.
Giovanni Antonio Galliari worked in Milan alongside his brothers Bernardino and Fabrizio Galliari. He was appointed director of the college of theatre design at Milan's La Scala. He and his two brothers were in great demand throughout Europe.

The work of the three brothers featured in the 1983 exhibition at the Museo Teatrale alla Scala in Milan, *I Galliari: Premi Scenegrafi della Scala* (*The Galliaris: first stage designers of the Scala*).

Bibliography:
Bossaglia, Rossana, *I Fratelli Galliari pittori*, Ceschina, Milan, 1962. Angrisani, Simonetta, *I Galliari: primi scenografi della Scala*, exhibition catalogue, Alinari, Florence, 1983.

GALLIARI, Giuseppe
Italian, 19th century.
Born 1748; died 1817, in Milan.
Painter, decorative artist, architect. Stage sets.
Giuseppe Galliari was one of Fabrizio Galliari's three sons. He worked in Turin and elsewhere.

Auction records:
London, 16-17 April 1997, *Design for a Stage Set* (pen and brown ink, brown and grey wash, 7 3/4 x 11 1/2 ins / 19.9 x 29.3 cm) GBP 460.

GALLIBERT, Geneviève Marie
French, 20th century.
Born 9 February 1888, in Paris.
Painter, engraver, illustrator, watercolourist.
Geneviève Gallibert exhibited regularly in Paris at the Salon d'Automne, of which she became a member in 1922; she also exhibited at the Salon des Tuileries. She was appointed official painter to the French Air Ministry.

Her work provides a direct and often seductive record of Paris during the 1920s and 1930s.

She took part in numerous official exhibitions in France and abroad, including: *Artistes de ce Temps* (*Artists of our Age*) at the Petit Palais, Paris in 1938; the Exposition d'Art Français Contemporain at the Musée de l'Orangerie in 1940; and in New York in 1936. She was made a Chevalier of the Légion d'Honneur. She also illustrated *Les Provinciales* by Giraudoux, *Demi-Dieu* by J. de Lacretelle and *Vent de Sable* by J. Kessel.

Museums and Galleries:
Antibes (Mus. Picasso) - Nice (MBA Jules-Chéret) - Paris (MAMVP) - Paris (MNAM-CCI).

Auction records:
Paris, 4 June 1925, *The Carrousel Triumphal Arch* (watercolour) FRF 1,350. Paris, 14 Nov 1927, *Window*, FRF 300. Paris, 3 May 1928, *The Beach, Cannes* (watercolour) FRF 125. Paris, 29 April 1933, *Panoramic View of Meknes* (watercolour) FRF 1,000. Paris, 6 Nov 1942, *The Pont-Neuf* (watercolour) FRF 50. London, 4 June 1947, *Landscape*, GBP 24. Calais, 5 April 1992, *View of the Massif de l'Estérel* (oil on canvas, 23 1/2 x 28 1/4 ins / 60 x 72 cm) FRF 5,500.

GALLICE, André
French, 17th century.
Sculptor.
In 1640, André Gallice made a small shrine for the collegiate church in Avallon.

GALLICE, Odette
French, 20th century.
Born 18 December 1916, in Paris.
Painter, pastellist, watercolourist. Portraits, landscapes, still-lifes, flowers.
Odette Gallice studied at the École des Arts Décoratifs in Strasbourg. She also attended the Académie de la Grande-Chaumière. She was a painter of flowers and still-lifes; she also executed pastel portraits and watercolour and pastel landscapes inspired by her many travels abroad.

She took part in various Salons in the provinces and in Paris, including the Salon d'Automne, the Salon des Artistes Français and the Salon des Indépendants.

Auction records:
Calais, 10 March 1991, *Bunch of White Dahlias* (oil on canvas, 22 x 26 ins / 55 x 66 cm) FRF 4,000.

GALLICUS. See first name

GALLIEN, Louise
French, 20th century.
Born 25 June 1870, in Paris.
Miniaturist.
Louise Gallien studied under Lefebvre. She exhibited in Paris at the Salon des Artistes Français from 1892 and was awarded a silver medal in 1931.

GALLIEN, Pierre Antoine
French, 20th century.
Born 14 December 1896; died 3 May 1963.
Painter (gouache), engraver. Portraits, urban landscapes.
Pierre Gallien studied at the École des Beaux-Arts, the École des Arts Décoratifs and the École du Louvre in Paris. He was a teacher and inspector of art education. He is believed to have known Kandinsky, Villon and Kupka. He exhibited at various group exhibitions, notably at the Salon des Indépendants in Paris.

He engraved many plates of the Montparnasse district and also produced portraits of well-known artistic and literary figures such as S. Valadon, Utrillo, Le Fauconnier, Chabanian, A. Nakache, Raymond Queneau and Pierre Mac Orlan.

Bibliography:
Imbard, Patrick, *Catalogue raisonné de l'œuvre de Pierre-Antoine Gallien*, dissertation, École des Hautes Études en sciences sociales, Paris, 1984 (thesis).

Auction records:
London, 6 Dec 1973, *Painting with Black Line*, GBP 800. Enghien-les-Bains, 8 June 1980, *Vertical Lines* (oil on canvas, 29 1/2 x 29 1/2 ins / 75 x 75 cm) FRF 101,000. Saumur, 29 June 1986, *Untitled* (1923, oil on canvas, 28 3/4 x 46 ins / 73 x 116 cm) FRF 790,000. Saumur, 26 April 1987, *Woman Reading in Red* (1919, gouache/paper, 14 x 15 ins / 35.5 x 38 cm) FRF 18,000. Milan, 26 March 2003, *Synthesis of the Dance Hall* (tempera on card, 9 x 7 ins / 24 x 17 cm) EUR 1,600.

GALLIEN, Raymonde. See **BOUQUET-GALLIEN**

GALLIEN-BERTHON, Marie Clotilde
French, 20th century.
Born 25 September 1870, in Constantine, Algeria.
Painter, watercolourist. Local figures.

Marie Gallien-Berthon studied under Jules Lefebvre and Baschet. She was a member of the Salon des Artistes Français in Paris and regularly exhibited watercolours and paintings of an Orientalist inspiration.

AUCTION RECORDS:

PARIS, 20 Nov 1990, *Algerian Woman* (1921, watercolour, 48 x 37 3/4 ins / 121 x 96 cm) FRF 15,000. PARIS, 8 April 1991, *Washerwomen* (oil on canvas, 25 1/2 x 32 ins / 65 x 81 cm) FRF 13,500.

GALLIEN-LALOUE. See **GALIEN-LALOUE**

GALLIER, Achille Gratien

French, 19th century.

Born 6 June 1814, in Bayonne; died 26 September 1871, in Paris.

Painter.

He studied under Gros and d'Aligny and exhibited at the Paris Salon from 1834 to 1870, principally rustic scenes. Examples of his work include *Smallholding on the Outskirts of Bayonne* and *Labourer's Cottage near Bayonne*.

MUSEUMS AND GALLERIES:

MOULINS: *Landscape*.

AUCTION RECORDS:

PARIS, 2 Dec 1946, *River Tiber in the Roman Countryside* (1850, watercolour, lightly heightened with gouache) FRF 500. BERN, 8 May 1987, *Farmyard* (oil on canvas, 17 1/4 x 27 1/2in/44 x 70cm) CHF 4,300. PARIS, 25 Nov 1997, *Viva Pio Nino* (1854, lead pencil, sepia wash and pastel heightened with white, 10 1/2 x 17in/26.5 x 43cm) FRF 2,600.

GALLIER, Claude

French, 18th century.

Active in Paris during the beginning of the 18th century.

Sculptor.

GALLIER, Jean Claude

French, 18th century.

Active in Paris in 1751.

Painter, sculptor.

Jean Claude Gallier may be Claude Gallier.

GALLIÉRO, Sauveur

French, 20th century.

Born 1914, in Algiers; died 1963, in Paris.

Painter. Scenes with figures.

School of Algiers.

Born in Algeria, Galliéro had a studio in the Kasbah. His aesthetic borrows from Primitivism. He featured in *L'École d'Alger* (*The School of Algiers*), Musée des Beaux-Arts, Bordeaux (2003).

BIBLIOGRAPHY:

Dubergey, Marie-Josèphe, *Quatre ou cinq vérités sur une figue de barbarie*, film, RTF, Algiers, 1960. Cazenave, Elisabeth/Dalia, Mahammed-Orfali/Vidal-Bué, Marion, *L'École d'Alger*, exhibition catalogue, Musée des Beaux-Arts, Bordeaux, 2003.

MUSEUMS AND GALLERIES:

ALGIERS (Mus. National des Beaux-Arts): *Bathers at the Pier*.

GALLIMARD, Catherine

French, 20th - 21st century.

Born 30 June 1971.

Painter, illustrator.

Catherine Gallimard illustrates and contributes to various magazines. She began her painting career in 1993. Since then, she has frequently exhibited in both France and abroad, including at the following: the Salon de la Figuration Critique in Paris (1994); the Salon Itinéraires in Levallois (1966); the International Contemporary Art Fair in Beirut (1999); DDB Advertising in Paris (1999); the Carrie Haddad Gallery in New York (2000); and the Fondation Taylor in Paris (2002). Her work is on permanent exhibition at the Galerie Peinture Fraîche and the Galerie Kallisté, both in Paris. She was awarded the Bornhauser Molinari Prize in 1995 and the Prix Victor Choquet in 1996.

GALLIMARD, Claude Olivier. See **GALIMARD**

GALLIMORE, Samuel

British, 19th century.

Active in Huddersfield.

Painter. Genre scenes.

Samuel Gallimore was the brother of the ceramicist William Wood. He exhibited in London from 1861, notably at the Royal Academy.

GALLINA, Eugène

French, 20th century.

Born 15 January 1879, in Paris; died 17 February 1955, in St-Michel-sur-Orge.

Painter, lithographer. Landscapes.

Eugène Gallina trained at the Montparnasse academies. He painted many views of Brittany. He exhibited in Paris, showing lithographs at the Salon des Indépendants from 1922 and also at the Salon des Artistes Français, receiving a number of awards.

MUSEUMS AND GALLERIES:

ST-DIÉ-DES-VOSGES.

GALLINA, Gallo

Italian, 19th century.

Born 15 October 1796, in Cremona; died 14 December 1874, in Milan.

Painter, engraver, lithographer.

Gallo Gallina studied with Beltrami, and at the academy of Milan. Active principally in Milan, Cremona and Brescia, his best-known work is the *Baptism of Christ* in Brescia Cathedral.

AUCTION RECORDS:

MILAN, 17 Dec 1987, *Meleager on the Hunt* (black and white chalk, 22 1/2 x 25 1/2 ins / 57 x 65 cm) ITL 1,600,000.

GALLINA, Giovanni

Italian, 17th century.

Sculptor.

Giovanni Gallina worked on the church of Castrogiovanni (now Enna) in Sicily.

GALLINA, Lodovico

Italian, 18th century.

Born 25 August 1752, in Brescia; died 4 January 1787, in Venice.

Painter.

Lodovico Gallina studied under Zucchi, Dusi and Maggiotto. He worked on churches in Artogone and Bedizzole, as well as on the Venice church of S Lio.

GALLINA, Luigi

Italian, 19th century.

Born 1865, in Castrogiovanni (now Enna, Sicily).

Painter. Portraits.

Luigi Gallina studied under Morelli and Prosperi.

GALLINA, Pio

Italian, 17th century.

Active in Tortona (Piedmont) in 1639.

Painter.

GALLINARI, Giacomo

Italian, 17th century.

Born probably in Bologna.

Active in Bologna in 1676 and in Padua in 1685.

Engraver.

Giacomo Gallinari produced the two engravings *Lady* and *Venus and Cupid*.

GALLINARI, Giovanni Battista

Italian, 16th - 17th century.

Died 1608, in Bologna.

Painter.
Gallinari is recorded as living in Ferrara in 1593.

GALLINARI, Pietro, called Pietro del Signor Guido
Italian, 17th century.
Born in Bologna; died 1664, in Modena.
Painter. History painting.
Pietro Gallinari painted a small number of historical subjects which are believed to have been retouched by Guido Reni, of whom Gallinari was a favourite pupil.

GALLINER, Edith
British, 20th century.
Born 1914, in London.
Painter, collage artist.
Edith Galliner trained in London and Paris from 1933 to 1939 and continued her studies while teaching in London. From 1961 to 1965 she spent an extended period in Berlin before returning to London. Her work is abstract and very free and lyrical in style with a great richness of colour range, particularly deep blues. Much of her work evokes a submarine world and landscape. Galliner took part in numerous group exhibitions in Germany and England, notably at the Hampstead Artists' Council, London, in 1967. She also showed her work in solo exhibitions in 1963 in Berlin; in 1964 in Munich, in 1965 in Cologne and in 1967 in London.
MUSEUMS AND GALLERIES:
BERLIN: a collage.

GALLINGER, Martin
German, 16th century.
Active in Munich.
Painter.
Gallinger was working in Rome in 1542.

GALLINI, Antonio
Italian, 16th century.
Born in Padua.
Sculptor.
Antonio Gallini was working on the Doge's Palace in Venice in 1566.

GALLINO, Gaetano
Italian, 19th century.
Active in Genoa.
Painter. Portraits.
Gaetano Gallino was a pupil of Tagliafichi, and for many years lived in Montevideo, Uruguay.

GALLINONE, Orazio
Italian, 16th century.
Born in Treviglio d'Adda.
Painter.
Gallinone painted a number of surviving frescoes.

GALLIOT, Antoine Louis
French, 18th century.
Active in Paris in 1759.
Painter.

GALLIOT, Jacques
French, 17th century.
Born c. 1640, in Péronne.
Painter, sculptor.
Jacques Galliot was working in Paris in 1672, but he also seems to have lived and worked in Amiens.

GALLIOT, Jean
Belgian, 15th century.
Born in Brussels.
Painter.
Jean Galliot was appointed 'Painter to the Prince of Orange', but seems also to have worked at the court of the princes of Savoy.

GALLIOT, Pierre
French, 15th century.
Painter, decorative artist.
Pierre was the son of Jean Galliot.

GALLIS, Pieter
Dutch, 17th century.
Born 1633; died 1697, in Hoorn, or Le Havre.
Painter. Landscapes, still-lifes (flowers/fruit/sea shells).
According to Nagler, Gallis died at Le Havre. He was active in Enkhuizen and Hoorn from 1661 to 1683.

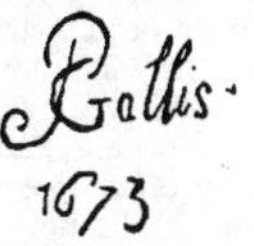

MUSEUMS AND GALLERIES:
AMSTERDAM: *Still-life; Fruit* - GLASGOW: *Still-life.*
AUCTION RECORDS:
LONDON, 11-12 May 1911, *Oysters and Still-life,* GBP 23. LONDON, 22 March 1929, *Still-life,* GBP 194. LONDON, 1 Nov 1972, *Still-life with Fruit,* GBP 3,200. AMSTERDAM, 18 May 1976, *Still-life with Flowers* (oil on canvas, 14 1/4 x 11in/36 x 28cm) NLG 32,000. LONDON, 17 Nov 1982, *Still-life with Sea-shells* (oil on canvas, 13 3/4 x 21 1/4in/35 x 54cm) GBP 5,800. LONDON, 22 July 1983, *Still-life with Flowers in a Vase on an Entablature* (oil on canvas, 18 x 15in/45.7 x 38.1cm) GBP 7,000. NEW YORK, 17 Jan 1985, *Still-life with Fruit* (1668, oil on canvas, 20 3/4 x 18 1/2in/53 x 47cm) USD 17,000. NEW YORK, 9 Oct 1991, *Compositions with Fruit, a Vine Branch, Peaches, Plums, a Melon, Medlars, etc.* (oil on canvas, 25 1/2 x 21 1/2in/64.8 x 54.3cm) USD 18,700. LONDON, 22 April 1994, *Still-life with Fruit, a Carnation, a Walnut and a Butterfly on an Entablature* (oil on canvas, 15 x 13in/37.8 x 33cm) GBP 21,850. LONDON, 13 Dec 1996, *Oysters on a Silver Dish, an Orange and Lemon in a Porcelain Bowl, and a Venetian Glass Goblet on a Table* (oil on canvas, 26 x 23 1/2in/65.2 x 59.8cm) GBP 8,625. BOSTON, 12 May 2000, *Still-life with Lobster, Platter, Lemon and Jug* (oil on canvas, 29 x 26 ins / 74 x 66 cm) USD 10,000. NEW YORK, 29 May 2001, *Roses, Carnations, Poppies and Other Flowers by a Tree Trunk and Basket of Fruit, in a Garden* (oil on canvas, 42 x 33 ins / 106 x 83 cm) USD 15,000. AMSTERDAM, 14 May 2003, *Swag of Mixed Flowers in a Niche* (oil on panel, 14 x 17 ins / 36 x 44 cm) EUR 26,000.

GALLISON, Henry Hammond
American, 19th - 20th century.
Born 20 May 1850, in Boston; died 12 October 1910, in Boston.
Painter. Landscapes.
Henry Gallison studied under Bonnefoy in Paris. He received a special mention in Turin in 1897, an honourable mention at the Salon des Artistes Français in Paris in 1900, for the Exposition Universelle in that year, and a bronze medal in St Louis in 1904.
AUCTION RECORDS:
NEW YORK, 1 July 1982, *Verdant Landscape* (oil on canvas, 40 x 53 3/4 ins / 101.5 x 136.5 cm) USD 400. NEW YORK, 31 March 1994, *Grey Day* (oil on canvas, 35 x 45 ins / 88.9 x 114.3 cm) USD 3,738.

GALLIZI, Fede. See **GALIZIA**

GALLIZIO, Giuseppe, known as Pinot, Pinot-Gallizio
Italian, 20th century.
Born 12 February 1902, in Alba (Piedmont); died 13 November 1964, in Alba.
Painter, monotype artist, mixed media.
Lettrism.

Groups: International Movement for an Imaginist Bauhaus, Situationist International.

Originally a pharmacist, Gallizio was passionate about archaeology, ethnology and geology, and was a local councillor in his home town of Alba. He did not begin to paint until he was 53 years old. His friendship with Asger Jorn and the painter Piero Simondo inspired him to turn his pastille factory in Alba into the first 'Experimental Laboratory' of the International Movement for an Imaginist Bauhaus, in September 1955. Other members of this movement included Constant and Enrico Baj. In 1956 Gallizio organised the Primo Congresso Mondiale degli Artisti Liberi (First World Congress of Free Artists) in Alba, along with Jorn, Simondo, Baj, Ettore Sottsass Jr and Elena Verrone. In 1957 he was among the champions of the Situationist International movement, a forerunner of the global backlash against the industrial and consumer civilisations. The group split up in 1960. Then, for a time, Gallizio was involved with the Lettrist International movement.

In 1959, in his laboratory, Gallizio created what he called 'industrial painting', and exhibited it at the Galerie Drouin in Paris under the title *The Cavern of Antimatter.* The gallery walls were covered with 145 metres of rolls of 'industrial painting', impregnated with scent, and concealing a machine emitting ultrasonic waves. This polysensorial work contributed to the 'permanent revolution in everyday life' advocated by the Situationist movement. That same year he wrote his *Manifesto of Industrial Painting,* and also created his 'collusion paintings', which involved covering his own paintings with works by other artists. Industrial painting was designed to be sold by the metre: the intention was to challenge the traditional status of artworks and their value on the market. The technique he used combined oil paints with resins. His works were essentially experimental, and in the spirit of the Cobra group. The wide culture of the artist is reflected in his work, most notably taking shape in 'ribbons of signs and colours (initially sewn by hand by his aunt), produced at high speed, sometimes with his eyes closed' (Rafael Pic). His painting is a form of Expressionism that attempts to communicate 'words in colour'. In 1962 he created the *Notti di Cristallo (Crystal Nights)* cycle and the series *Oggetti e Spazi per un Mondo Peggiore e Fabbriche del Vento (Objects and Spaces for a Worse World and Factories of the Wind).* Between 1963 and 1964 he produced a series of black paintings and covered his previous works, and a section of his studio, in black paint as well. The Gallizio archives are kept by the municipality of Alba.

Gallizio took part in a number of group exhibitions, including the 'Experimental Laboratory' exhibition of 1956 at the Corino theatre and cinema in Alba; *L'informale in Italia fino al 1957* (*Art Informel in Italy up to 1957*) in Livorno, in 1963; and *Galeries Pilotes du Monde* (*Pilot Galleries of the World*), at the Musée Cantonal in Lausanne, Switzerland (also in 1963). He also showed his work in solo exhibitions, including the *Prima Mostra di Pittura Industriale (First Exhibition of Industrial Painting),* at the Galleria Notizie, Turin, in 1958; and exhibitions in 1959 at the Galerie René Drouin, Paris; in 1960, at the Stedelijk Museum, Amsterdam; in 1959 and 1962, at the Van de Loo gallery, Munich; in 1961, at the Birch gallery, Copenhagen; and at the 1964 Venice Biennale. His work has also featured posthumously in several thematic exhibitions, such as *Situacionistas* at the museum of contemporary art in Barcelona, in 1996. There have been a number of retrospective exhibitions of his work: in 1974 at the Galleria Civica d'Arte Moderna, Turin; in 1975 and 1988 at the Galleria Martini e Ronchetti, Genoa; in 1989 at the Galerie 1900-2000, Paris; in 1992, *Pinot Gallizio nell'Europea dei Dissimetrici (Pinot Gallizio in Dissymetric Europe)* at the Promotrice delle Belle Arti, Turin; in 2001, *Pinot Gallizio et l'Internationale Situationniste* (*Pinot Gallizio and the International Situationist*) at the French cultural centre in Turin; in 2002, an exhibition marking the centenary of his birth at the Museo di Arte Contemporanea di Villa Croce, Genoa; *Pinot Gallizio: Oggetti e Spazi per un Mondo Peggiore (Objects and Spaces for a Worse World)* at the Galleria Martini e Ronchetti, Genoa; and *Pinot Gallizio: Trenta Opere per il Centenario (Thirty Works for His Centenary)* at the Galleria Martano, Turin.

BIBLIOGRAPHY:

Gallizio, Pinot, *'Manifesto della pittura industriale: per un arte unitaria applicabile'* in *Notizie Arti Figurative* n° 9 (French edition: Revue ' Internationale Situationniste' No 3, 1959). Pic, Rafael, *'Giuseppe Pinot-Gallizio'* in *Art Press* n° 178, periodical, Paris, 1960. *Pinot Gallizio e il Laboratorio sperimentale d'Alba del Movimento internazionale per una Bauhaus immaginista (1955-1957) e dell'Internazionale situazionista (1957-1960),* exhibition catalogue, Galleria Civica d'Arte Moderna, Turin, 1974. Simondo, Piero, *'Testimonianza su Pinot Gallizio'* in *Pinot Gallizio e il Laboratorio Sperimentale d'Alba,* exhibition catalogue, Galleria Civica d'Arte Moderna, Turin, 1974. *Pinot Gallizio,* exhibition catalogue, Gal. 1900-2000, Paris, 1989. Poli, F./Corgnati, M., *Pinot Gallizio nell'Europea dei dissimetrici,* exhibition catalogue, Promotrice delle Belle Arti, Turin, 1992. Buccolo, Arturo, et al., *'Pinot Gallizio. L'uomo, l'artista e la città. 1902-1964'* in *Momenti* n° 4, periodical, Alba, 2000 (exhibition catalogue at the Fondazione Ferrero, Alba). Roberto, Maria Teresa, et al., *Pinot Gallizio, catalogo generale delle opere 1953-1964,* catalogue raisonné, Mazzotta, Milan, 2001.

MUSEUMS AND GALLERIES:

ALBA (Archivio Gallizio) - PARIS (MNAM-CCI): *Blind Night* (1962).

AUCTION RECORDS:

MILAN, 8 June 1988, *Untitled* (1963, oil on card, 27 1/2 x 19 3/4 ins / 70 x 50 cm) ITL 1,800,000. COPENHAGEN, 30 May 1990, *Composition* (1961, oil on canvas, 36 1/4 x 28 3/4 ins / 92 x 73 cm) DKK 35,000. MILAN, 14 April 1992, *Composition* (gouache/paper, 19 3/4 x 27 1/2 ins / 50 x 70 cm) ITL 3,000,000. COPENHAGEN, 2-3 Dec 1992, *Composition* (1961, oil on canvas, 55 x 31 1/2 ins / 140 x 80 cm) DKK 10,500. AMSTERDAM, 1 Dec 1997, *Archetype* (1962, oil on canvas, 51 1/4 x 41 1/4 ins / 130 x 104.5 cm) NLG 23,600. COPENHAGEN, 26 May 1999, *Town Comes into View* (1961, oil on canvas, 32 x 26 ins / 81 x 65 cm) DKK 15,000. COPENHAGEN, 17 May 2000, *Composition* (1961, oil on canvas, 29 x 24 ins / 73 x 60 cm) DKK 15,500. PARIS, 8 Feb 2001, *Untitled* (oil on canvas, 24 x 29 ins / 60 x 73 cm) FRF 18,000. PARIS, 15 May 2001, *Untitled* (oil on canvas, 31 x 55 ins / 80 x 140 cm) FRF 25,000. AMSTERDAM, 3 Dec 2002, *Untitled* (1961, oil on canvas, 32 x 26 ins / 81 x 65 cm) EUR 5,500. VEJLE, 10 March 2003, *Composition* (1961, oil on canvas, 28 x 24 ins / 72 x 60 cm) DKK 24,000. TURIN, 17 Nov 2003, *Untitled* (1959, oil on canvas, 39 x 59 ins / 100 x 150 cm) EUR 15,500. COPENHAGEN, 5 Oct 2004, *Too Late* (1961, oil, metal, paint, 18 x 22 ins / 46 x 55 cm) DKK 33,000.

GALLIZIOLI, Giuseppe

Italian, 20th century.

Born 18 January 1935, in Brescia.

Painter, draughtsman, watercolourist, engraver (etchings/aquatints), pastellist, illustrator. Mythological subjects, seascapes, animals. Murals.

Phases group.

Giuseppe Gallizioli trained with Migliorizzi, Rosetti and Cattini. In 1969, he won a scholarship to study in Wolfsburg in Germany. In 1970, he settled in Paris, where he joined the Phases group. He subsequently visited Poland, Belgium, Holland and Czechoslovakia. He lives and works in Brescia.

Giuseppe Gallizioli paints landscapes as well as animals and mythological figures. During summer visits to the island of Cres (Croatia) from 1975 on, he was inspired by the sea. In 1973, he painted *Angel of Auschwitz* following a visit to the former concentration camp. He also illustrated Carlo Dossi's

Incendio di Legna Vecchia (Fire of Old Wood), published by Editrice Il Melangolo.

Giuseppe Gallizioli has participated in collective exhibitions, including the Milan Biennale (1973); *Attraverso l'Immagine (Through the Image)* at the Centro culturale in Cremona (1995); and *Le Mouvement Phases de 1952 à l'horizon 2001 (The Phases Movement from 1952 to the New Millennium)* at the Kiosque Centre Culturel in Mayenne and the Centre Noroit in Arras (2000). He has also shown work in solo shows at the Galleria Alberti, Brescia (1960), in Poland (1974) and at the Galleria dell'Incisione, Brescia (1999).

BIBLIOGRAPHY:

Jaguer, Édouard/Cassa Salvi, Elvira, *Genèse et mutation d'un périscope: La peinture de Gallizioli comme tobogan reversible du passé vers l'avenir*, Grafo, Brescia, 1976 (text in Italian and French). *Attraverso l'Immagine*, group exhibition catalogue, Centro culturale Santa Maria della Pietà, Cremona, 1995. Montalto, Domenico, *Giuseppe Gallizioli: opere 1996-1998*, Antologia Galleria d'Arte, Monza, 1998.

GALLMANN, Rita

Swiss, 20th century.
Born 2 September 1924, in Madrid.
Draughtsman, watercolourist, pastellist, painter (gouache). Nudes, portraits, still-lifes, landscapes. Murals, designs for mosaics.

Rita Gallmann's parents came originally from Switzerland, and returned there from Spain in 1931. She studied at the school of fine arts in Geneva from 1939 to 1944, where she was taught by Alexandre Blanchet and Herbert Theurillat. She made many study visits to different parts of Europe from 1949 and settled in Zurich in 1954. She won several bursaries and prizes, including the Holzer scholarship, the first prize at the Geneva Art School in 1943, and the Lissignol-Chevalier and Charles-Galland awards in Geneva in 1946, 1948 and 1949.

She shows equal mastery of oils, watercolours, gouache and pastels, producing works executed with broad strokes using a range of warm colours, generally yellow ochre and browns. Her bright colours, elaborate compositions and simple motifs forming landscapes, genre scenes and still-lifes all make a spirited contibution to the sensitive realism she expresses. In her portraits, such as *Portrait of my Father*, the facial expression, and indeed the whole person, show an acute sense of observation put at the disposal of emotion.

She took part in group exhibitions such as at the National Art Exhibition at the museum of Art and History in Geneva in 1946, the Society of Women Painters at the Musée Rath, Geneva, in 1947 and 1951, *Self-portrait* at the Musée Rath in 1978, the Paris Salon d'Automne in 1990, 1992 and 1993, the First International Fair for 19th and 20th Century Art, Chicago, in 1990, and Europ'Art, Geneva, in 1995. She has had solo exhibitions in various galleries and institutions in Switzerland since 1977, notably *40 Years of Painting*, CERN, Geneva in 1984, *60 Years of Painting*, Espace NogaHilton, Geneva, in 2000, and *Homage to the Carouge of Yesteryear*, in Carouge in 2001.

BIBLIOGRAPHY:

R., G., '*Rita Gallmann*' in *coll. Petite monographie du Monde des Arts*, Arti Grafiche Il Torchio, Florence, 1976. '*Rita Gallmann*' in *Répertoire des artistes suisses*, Institut suisse pour l'étude de l'art, Zurich, 1980-1990. Barrer, Patrick-F., *Quand l'art du XXe siècle était conçu par des inconnus..., L'Histoire du Salon d'Automne de 1903 à nos jours*, Les Éditions Arts et Images du Monde, Paris, 1992. '*Rita Gallmann*' in *Dictionnaire biographique de l'art suisse*, Institut suisse pour l'étude de l'art, Zurich, Lausanne, 1998.

MUSEUMS AND GALLERIES:

CAROUGE (Town Collection) - DUBENDORF (Town Coll.): several works - GENEVA (City Collection) - GENEVA (State Collection).

GALLMETZER, Valentin

Austrian, 19th century.
Born 9 February 1870, in Hintereggenthal.
Sculptor.

Gallmetzer worked for the churches of Klausen (now Chiusa, Italy), Troppau (now Opava, Czech Republic) and Kaltern (now Caldaro, Italy) in the Austrian Tyrol.

GALLNER, Bonifacius

Austrian, 18th century.
Died 1727.
Active in Melk.
Painter.

Gallner was a pupil of Andrea Pozzo and also worked in Dürnstein.

GALLO. See FURNO Stefano del

GALLO, Francesco, called Ciccio

Italian, 18th century.
Active in Naples.
Sculptor.

Francesco Gallo worked for porcelain manufacturers, among other things.

GALLO, Frank

American, 20th century.
Born 1933.
Sculptor. Figures, nudes.

Frank Gallo often uses synthetic resins in his work, and very often creates his figures on a human scale.

BIBLIOGRAPHY:

Weisberg, Gabriel P., *Materials and Techniques of 20th-Century Artists*, exhibition catalogue, Cleveland Museum of Art, 1976. *Paintings and Sculpture by Midwest Faculty-artists: An Exhibition*, exhibition catalogue, Indiana University Museum of Art, 1976.

AUCTION RECORDS:

NEW YORK, 16 May 1980, *Trophy Figure* (1971, plastic, h. 22 ins / 56 cm) USD 3,200. NEW YORK, 9 Nov 1983, *Chair* (c. 1970, wood and fibreglass, 62 x 28 3/4 x 29 ins / 157.5 x 73 x 73.5 cm) USD 6,500. NEW YORK, 10 Oct 1990, *Seated Nude* (epoxy resin, h. 33 ins / 83.9 cm) USD 4,125. NEW YORK, 6 Nov 1990, *Young Girl Standing* (1966, polyester resin/wooden base, h. 66 ins / 167.7 cm) USD 16,500. NEW YORK, 7 May 1991, *Bather* (1970, polyester resin/wooden base, 60 x 34 1/4 ins / 151.5 x 87 cm) USD 7,700. NEW YORK, 12 Nov 1991, *Winged Figure* (polished bronze/Plexiglas base, h. 76 1/2 ins / 194.3 cm) USD 6,600. CHICAGO, 18 March 2000, *Reclining Nude* (resin and polychrome decoration, h. 6 ins / 14 cm, w. 7 ins/17 cm) USD 1,700. CHICAGO, 9 Nov 2003, *Quiet Nude* (1966, epoxy resin and mahogany, h. 31 ins / 79 cm, w. 27 ins/69 cm) USD 2,000. NEW YORK, 29 June 2004, *Quiet Nude* (1966, polychromed epoxy resin on revolving wooden base, h. 32 ins / 81 cm) USD 4,500.

GALLO, Giovanni

Italian, 16th century.
Active in Lombardy.
Sculptor (wood).

Some commentators identify Giovanni Gallo, probably wrongly, with Jean Salomon of Lyons.

GALLO, Giovanni Battista

Italian, 19th century.
Born in the 19th century, in Osimo (Marche).
Painter. Genre scenes, portraits.

Giovanni Gallo exhibited in Turin, Milan and Rome.

GALLO, Giuseppe

Italian, 17th century.
Sculptor.

Giuseppe Gallo worked at Naples Cathedral and for various churches in that city, as well as for a church in Gaeta.

GALLO, Giuseppe
Italian, 20th - 21st century.
Born 1954.
Painter, sculptor.

Gallo endeavours to show the relationships between objects as affected by the problem of the metaphysical duality of being and substance, idea and form, in an arrangement that recalls the 'metaphysical psychology' of De Chirico. In his works on paper exhibited in Paris in 1991, he showed a discreet presence of figures, elements and silhouettes, cabalistic signs travelling through space, waiting, looking for a referent that could emerge from the pictorial representations of the past or unconscious psychic manifestations. He has participated in collective exhibitions including the Galerie Yvon Lambert, Paris (1979); the Nouvelle Biennale de Paris (1985); Galerie Claudine Bréguet (1986); and the 1990 Venice Biennale. He has also had solo exhibitions in Italy and France, including: Galerie Claudine Bréguet (1985); Galerie Gutharc-Ballin, Paris (1991); *Croisements Amoureux* (Amorous Crossings) at the Galerie Vidal-Saint Phalle (1998), and again at the Galerie Vidal-Saint Phalle in 2001.

BIBLIOGRAPHY:

Braun, Emily, *Giuseppe Gallo, oh vocazione*, exhibition catalogue, Gian Enzo Sperone, Rome, 1990 (text in Italian and English). Tío Bellido, Ramón, *Giuseppe Gallo*, exhibition catalogue, Gal. Di Meo, Paris, 1992.

AUCTION RECORDS:

PARIS, 26 Oct 1988, *Bullfighting* (1983, charcoal and chalks, 17 1/4 x 13 3/4 ins / 43.5 x 35 cm) FRF 8,000; *Without End* (1984, oil on canvas, 110 1/4 x 74 3/4 ins / 280 x 190 cm) FRF 35,000. NEW YORK, 27 Feb 1990, *Untitled* (1986, encaustic/panel, 43 x 12 3/4 ins / 109.3 x 32.5 cm) USD 6,325. PARIS, 15 Oct 1990, *Agora* (1984, oil on canvas, 59 x 78 3/4 ins / 150 x 200 cm) FRF 56,000. NEW YORK, 12 June 1992, *Narcissus* (oil and pencil/wood in two panels, in all 3 1/2 x 19 ins / 8.9 x 48.3 cm) USD 1,210. NEW YORK, 23 Feb 1994, *Untitled* (oil on canvas, 12 x 12 ins / 30.5 x 30.2 cm) USD 1,035. LONDON, 6 Dec 1996, *Untitled* (1990, oil on canvas, 24 3/4 x 19 3/4 ins / 63 x 50 cm) GBP 2,530. NEW YORK, 20 May 1999, *Untitled* (oil on wood, 35 x 51 ins / 88 x 129 cm) USD 3,200. PRATO, 24 Nov 2000, *I Raised My Eyes* (mixed media on board, 19 x 44 ins / 47 x 111 cm) ITL 9,000,000. PRATO, 25 May 2001, *Composition* (1999, oil on canvas, 18 x 16 ins / 45 x 40 cm) ITL 3,600,000. PRATO, 25 May 2001, *Dance Steps* (1990, oil on canvas, 68 x 44 ins / 173 x 113 cm) ITL 9,500,000. FLORENCE, 20 Nov 2002, *Untitled* (oil on paper, 19 x 30 ins / 47 x 75 cm) EUR 1,600. VERCELLI, 23 Nov 2002, *Hyena* (2000, oil on canvas, 38 x 20 ins / 97 x 52 cm) EUR 3,000. MILAN, 16 Dec 2003, *Unity* (1987, oil on paper, 19 x 14 ins / 47 x 36 cm) EUR 2,000. LONDON, 4 Feb 2004, *Meta-Meta* (1987, oil on wood, 61 x 60 ins / 156 x 152 cm) GBP 10,000.

GALLO, Ignacio
Spanish, 20th century.
Born in Valladolid.
Sculptor.

Ignacio Gallo exhibited in Paris at the Salon des Indépendants, showing bronzes of women bathing, of dancers and pagan goddesses notable for their sense of movement.

GALLO, Jacopo
Italian, 17th century.
Active in Naples.
Sculptor.

Jacopo Gallo is known to have worked at the church of the Annunziata around 1660.

GALLO, Marco
Italian, 15th century.
Active in Naples.
Painter.

In 1465, Marco Gallo was working on the church of the Annunziata in Marcianisi.

GALLO, Salvatore, called Salvatore
Italian, 20th century.
Born 1928, in Vittoria (Sicily).
Active in France since 1964.
Sculptor. Figures.

Salvatore Gallo initially studied under Carlo Carrà in Turin, and later under Siqueiros in Mexico. He settled in Paris in 1964. Since 1972 he has been working at the artists' colony in Nogent-sur-Marne.

Gallo has executed a number of public commissions - particularly for fountains and funerary monuments. After Neo-Cubist, Baroque and Surrealist beginnings, his sculptures took on a more simplified form during the mid-1970s. He works mostly with marble, highlighting the sobriety of the material, the dynamic of line and the sensuality of form through slender figures, monumental faces and representations of motherhood.

Gallo's work has featured in several group exhibitions, including: in 1972 and 1973 at the museum in Toulon; and in 1974 at the Salon de Mai, the Salon de la Jeune Sculpture and the Salon des Réalités Nouvelles in Paris. He has also shown his works in solo exhibitions in 1965 at the Académie Dufaux, Paris; and in 1976 at Aurillac, Clermont-Ferrand.

GALLO, Vincent
American, 20th - 21st century.
Born 1961.
Painter (mixed media).

Also known as a film actor and director, Vincent Gallo works in an unusual range of materials, often on metallic surfaces.

BIBLIOGRAPHY:

Gallo, Vincent, *Vincent Gallo: Paintings and Drawings 1982-1988*, Kyoto Shoin, Kyoto, 1989.

AUCTION RECORDS:

PARIS, 15 June 1988, *Listening* (1987, painting/metal, 20 3/4 x 41 1/4 ins / 53 x 105 cm) FRF 16,000. NEW YORK, 4 Oct 1989, *The First Last Supper* (1986, oil, cement and graphite/steel, 48 x 57 ins / 122 x 145 cm) USD 11,000. NEW YORK, 23 Feb 1990, *Some Things Don't Come in a Bottle* (1986, oil, pencil, cement and sand/sheet of aluminium/plywood, 38 x 43 1/2 ins / 96.5 x 110.8 cm) USD 9,900. NEW YORK, 12 Nov 1991, *Yes, I'm Lonely* (1985, oil and graphite/steel, 48 x 30 x 1 1/2 ins / 122 x 76.2 x 3.9 cm) USD 2,200.

GALLOC, François
French, 18th century.
Active in Paris in 1753.
Painter, sculptor.

GALLOCHE, Louis
French, 17th - 18th century.
Born 24 August 1670, in Paris; died 21 July 1761, in Paris.
Painter. Religious subjects, mythological subjects, landscapes.

Louis Galloche entered the studio of Louis de Boulogne and showed a strong aptitude for painting. In 1695, he won the first Grand Prix de Rome with *Joseph's Brothers Bringing Jacob, Their Father, His Son's Bloodied Robes*. However, he was not awarded an allowance. Undeterred, he went to Rome at his own expense and stayed two years. On his return to Paris, he opened a studio.

On 3 March 1703, Galloche was made an associate of the academy. After receiving the appreciation that he deserved, he received an allowance from the king and lodgings at the Louvre. He became an academician on 30 January 1711, a rector on 26 March 1746 and a chancellor on 6 July 1754.

Galloche took part in the Louvre's exhibitions from 1737 to 1751.

His masterpiece, *Translation of the Relics of St Augustine,* was produced for the church of the Petits-Pères. In 1705, for the fraternity of silversmiths and goldsmiths he painted the picture in Notre-Dame Cathedral of *St Paul Receiving the Farewells of the Ephesian Priests on His Departure from the Town of Miletus.* He also executed *Raising of Lazarus* for the chapel of Charity; *Institution for Foundlings* for the ancient church of St Lazare; and *The Samaritan* and *Cure of One Possessed* for the church of St Martin-des-Champs. He was also a musician.

Galloche.

Museums and Galleries:
Caen: *Roland Learning of the Loves of Angelica and Medoro* - Compiègne: *Aeneas Landing at Carthage; Meal of Aeneas and Dido* - Fontainebleau: *Venus and Adonis* - Nancy: *St Martin Resuscitating a Child* - Orléans: *Coriolanus in the Camp of the Volsci, Begged by His Family to Resume Command of the Roman Army* - Paris (Louvre): *Hercules Returning Alcestis to Admetus* - Rennes: *St Peter Taken Captive* - Rheims: *Penitent Magdalene* - Versailles (Trianon): two landscapes.

Auction records:
Paris, 1777, *Diana Discovering Callisto's Pregnancy,* FRF 1,401. Paris, 27 May 1988, *St Scholasticus Imploring the Heavens for a Storm to Detain St Benedict* (black chalk heightened with white/blue paper, 8 1/2 x 18 ins / 21.7 x 45.5 cm) FRF 15,000. London, 5 July 1989, *Aeneas Received by Dido* (oil on canvas, 39 x 57 ins / 99 x 145 cm) GBP 19,250. Paris, 10 April 1992, *Diana and Acteon* (oil on canvas, 38 1/2 x 51 1/2 ins / 98 x 130.5 cm) FRF 280,000. Paris, 23 Feb 1998, *Diana and Callisto* (oil on canvas, 20 x 26 1/2 ins / 51 x 67 cm) FRF 45,000.

GALLOIS, or Galoys, Gallays

French, 16th century.
Painters.

These two painters, Denis and Louis, were living in Lyons in 1521 and 1523.

GALLOIS

French, 19th century.
Active in Paris c. 1850.
Sculptor.

He sculpted several statuettes for the church of St-Gervais-St-Protais, Paris.

GALLOIS, Émile

French, 20th century.
Born 16 October 1882, in Ligny-en-Barrois (Meuse); died 28 February 1965, in Clichy-la-Garenne.
Painter, illustrator.

Émile Gallois regularly exhibited landscapes and views of cathedrals in Paris at the Salon des Indépendants as well as abroad.

Auction records:
Paris, 13 April 1988, *Washerwomen on the Banks of the Loing* (oil on canvas, 24 x 18 ins / 61 x 46 cm) FRF 2,000. Amsterdam, 13 Dec 1989, *View of Villeneuve-les-Avignon* (oil on canvas, 23 1/2 x 15 3/4 ins / 60 x 40 cm) NLG 4,600.

GALLOIS, François

French, 17th century.
Active in Avignon.
Sculptor (wood).

François Gallois worked for the church of St Pierre.

GALLOIS, Marcelle, later (Mère) Geneviève Gallois

French, 20th century.
Born 22 September 1888, in Montbéliard; died 19 October 1962.
Painter, engraver. Designs for stained glass.

Marcelle Gallois moved to Paris, where she studied under Cormon at the École Nationale des Beaux-Arts. In 1917 she entered the Benedictine convent in the Rue Monsieur in Paris. It was at an exhibition of decorations and drawings held at the convent in 1936 that her work was spotted by an art enthusiast who supplied her with the materials needed for engraving. After the war she exhibited and showed her work at sacred art events and a solo exhibition of her work in Paris in 1953 attracted considerable attention.

Before she became a nun, Gallois's work was directly influenced by her native Jura region and included rugged peasants' heads, market scenes and public dances. In Paris she depicted the congestion, cyclists, buses, weddings and burials with great satirical verve; the humour of her art stayed with her after she joined the convent. She went on to depict convent life in swirling, broken lines. With the war came hospital scenes and around 1953 she began to produce brightly-coloured stained glass windows in an Expressionist style for the small church of Petit-Appeville near Dieppe and in 1955 for the abbey of Limon and the abbey of Joques from 1956 until her death. Around 200 of her drawings, dating from 1914 to 1917 and totally unknown, were sold in February 1975.

Bibliography:
'*Les Dessins de la Mère Geneviève*' in *L'Œil,* periodical, Paris, April 1975. *Vitraux de l'église abbatiale de Limon composés, peints et commentés par Mère Geneviève Gallois,* SAEP, Ingersheim, 1976.

Museums and Galleries:
Jouques (Abbaye Notre-Dame-de-Fidélité): entire museum devoted to the works of Mère Geneviève Gallois.

GALLOIS, N.

French, 16th century.
Active in Burgundy.
Painter.

This artist painted a retable for the church of St-Trivier in Courtes (Saône-et-Loire).

GALLON, Robert

British, 19th - 20th century.
Born 1845; died 1925.
Active in London.
Painter, watercolourist, draughtsman. Portraits, landscapes, landscapes with figures, waterscapes.

Robert Gallon specialised in painting picturesque sites in Great Britain and was highly regarded by the British public. He was a regular exhibitor at the Royal Academy in London and at the Suffolk Street Gallery from 1868.

Museums and Galleries:
Sunderland.

Auction records:
London, 9 Dec 1907, *God's Acre,* GBP 6; *Evening Lights,* GBP 7. London, 25 April 1908, *The Old Mill,* GBP 11. London, 4 Dec 1909, *Welsh Landscape,* GBP 9; *Deepdale, near Barnard Castle* (1883) GBP 11; *Welsh River* (1884) GBP 12. London, 22 April 1911, *Church in the County of Essex,* GBP 6. London, 28 April 1924, *Splashes* (drawing) GBP 4. London, 5 June 1924, *Sheep Grazing; Fishing Village* (both) GBP 8. London, 23 Dec 1925, *River* (drawing) GBP 8. London, 5 March 1926, *Evening Calm,* GBP 10. London, 17 Dec 1928, *The Llugwy,* GBP 5. London, 1 July 1932, *Strensham Church,* GBP 6. London, 22 Oct 1971, *River Landscape,* Gns 380. London, 28 Nov 1972, *Summer Landscape,* GBP 500. London, 16 March 1973, *Landscape,* Gns 1,200. London, 9 March 1976, *Sunset* (oil on canvas, 24 x 40 1/4 ins / 61 x 102 cm) GBP 950. London, 6 Dec 1977, *Knaresborough Castle* (1879, oil on canvas, 23 1/2 x 39 1/2 ins / 60 x 100.5 cm) GBP 1,200. London, 18

March 1980, *A Welsh River Scene* (oil on canvas, 23 1/4 x 39 ins / 59 x 99 cm) GBP 3,200. LONDON, 27 April 1982, *A Canal Barge* (watercolour, 19 1/2 x 27 ins / 49.5 x 68.5 cm) GBP 650. LONDON, 27 July 1984, *Woman and Child on a Wooden Bridge* (oil on canvas, 44 x 59 3/4 ins / 111.7 x 151.7 cm) GBP 2,800. CHESTER, 9 April 1987, *The Church Pool, Bettwys-Y-Cœd* (oil on canvas, 23 x 39 ins / 58.5 x 99 cm) GBP 7,200. LONDON, 15 June 1988, *Near Goring on Thames* (oil on canvas, 24 x 36 ins / 61 x 91.5 cm) GBP 6,050. TORONTO, 30 Nov 1988, *The Ford* (oil on canvas, 27 1/2 x 21 1/4 ins / 70 x 54 cm) CAD 3,600. LONDON, 2 June 1989, *On the Landing Stage* (oil on card, 7 3/4 x 12 1/2 ins / 20 x 31.5 cm) GBP 825. CHESTER, 20 July 1989, *Estuary at Low Tide with a Mountain Landscape in the Background* (1879, oil on canvas, 30 x 50 ins / 76 x 127 cm) GBP 2,200. LONDON, 9 Feb 1990, *Landscape with Cottage* (oil on canvas, 24 x 40 ins / 61 x 101.6 cm) GBP 14,850. LONDON, 25-26 April 1990, *Windsor Castle* (watercolour, 7 3/4 x 14 1/4 ins / 20 x 36 cm) GBP 1,210. LONDON, 1 Nov 1990, *River Landscape with Harvesters* (1894, oil on canvas, 24 x 40 1/4 ins / 61 x 102 cm) GBP 6,050. LONDON, 14 June 1991, *Children Playing by a River* (1882, oil on canvas, 24 x 40 ins / 61 x 101.5 cm) GBP 6,050. LONDON, 13 March 1992, *A Lake in the Highlands* (oil on canvas, 36 x 28 ins / 91.4 x 71.2 cm) GBP 2,640. LONDON, 3 March 1993, *Evening* (oil on canvas, 20 x 30 ins / 51 x 76 cm) GBP 2,760. NEW YORK, 13 Oct 1993, *Cottage by a River* (oil on canvas, 24 x 40 ins / 61 x 101.6 cm) USD 10,350. LONDON, 25 March 1994, *Richmond Castle in Yorkshire* (oil on canvas, 24 x 40 ins / 61 x 101.6 cm) GBP 3,220. LONDON, 2 Nov 1994, *Loading Reeds by a River* (oil on canvas, 18 1/4 x 32 ins / 46.5 x 81.5 cm) GBP 5,980. LONDON, 10 March 1995, *Self-portrait* (1913, oil on canvas, 20 x 16 ins / 50.8 x 40.6 cm) GBP 690. LONDON, 29 March 1996, *Hambledon Weir* (1879, oil on canvas, 14 x 21 1/4 ins / 35.6 x 54 cm) GBP 5,060. LONDON, 8 Nov 1996, *Moel Siabod from the Lledr Valley, North Wales; Snowdon* (oil on canvas, a pair, 20 x 30 1/4 ins / 50.8 x 76.7 cm) GBP 12,500. NEW YORK, 26 Feb 1997, *On the River Yare* (oil on canvas, 24 x 40 1/4 ins / 61 x 102 cm) USD 8,050. LONDON, 13 March 1997, *Water Hole on the Lledr, North Wales* (oil on canvas, 20 x 30 ins / 50.8 x 76.4 cm) GBP 3,000. LONDON, 14 March 1997, *Little Chart Mill, Kent* (oil on canvas, 20 x 30 ins / 50.8 x 76.2 cm) GBP 4,379. LONDON, 5 June 1997, *Summer, Surrey* (oil on canvas, 24 x 40 ins / 60.9 x 101.8 cm) GBP 11,270.

GALLON, Robert Samuel Ennis
British, 19th century.
Active in Greenwich.
Painter, lithographer. Figures.

Robert Samuel Ennis Gallon exhibited in London between 1830 and 1868, notably at the Royal Academy, the British Institution and the Suffolk Street Gallery. He was the father of Robert Gallon.

GALLOPIE, Maurice
French, 16th century.
Active in Tours in 1551.
Painter.

GALLORI, Emilio
Italian, 19th century.
Born 3 April 1846, in Florence.
Sculptor.

This remarkable artist was a student at the academy of fine arts in Florence, and worked in Florence and Naples. He exhibited in Turin, Milan and Rome, and at the Royal Academy in London from 1875 to 1878. He won a gold medal at the Exposition Universelle in Paris in 1900.

GALLOS, Carlos François
French, 20th century.
Born in the North.
Painter.

Carlos Gallos exhibited landscapes at the Salon des Artistes Français in Paris from 1930.

GALLOT. See **GALOT**

GALLOT-PERRELET, Samuel Ferdinand
Swiss, 18th - 19th century.
Born 1774, in Neuchâtel; died 1854, in Basel.
Engraver, lithographer.

This artist produced lithographs of numerous views of Switzerland, notably of the waterfalls at St Beat and the surrounding area of Chaux-de-Fonds. He was responsible for inventing a lithographic technique.

GALLOTTI, Alessandro
Italian, 20th century.
Born 1879, in Pavia; died 1961, in Milan.
Active in Milan.
Painter. Genre scenes, landscapes, mountainscapes.

Alessandro Gallotti painted views of the Alps and scenes of Alpine life.

AUCTION RECORDS:

MILAN, 17 June 1981, *Mountainous Landscape* (oil on canvas, 16 x 23 3/4 ins / 40.7 x 60.4 cm) ITL 600,000. MILAN, 22 March 1994, *Portrait of the Painter Vincenzo Irolli with His Palette* (oil on card, 13 1/2 x 8 3/4 ins / 34 x 22.5 cm) ITL 1,725,000. MILAN, 14 June 1995, *Serina Landscape; Rustic House in Serina* (oil on card, a pair, each 6 3/4 x 11 1/2 ins / 17 x 29 cm) ITL 2,070,000.

GALLOWAY, A.
British, 19th century.
Active at the beginning of the 19th century.
Miniaturist.

GALLOWAY, S. (Jr.)
British, 19th century.
Active in London c. 1832.
Painter. Portraits.

An artist by this name, probably related to Samuel Galloway, exhibited at the Society of British Artists.

GALLOWAY, Samuel
British, 19th century.
Active in London.
Painter. Flowers.

Samuel Galloway exhibited from 1827 to 1855 at London's Royal Academy and Suffolk Street Gallery.

GALLOWAY, Vincent
British, 20th century.
Born 30 January 1894; died 1977.
Painter. Portraits.

Vincent Galloway studied at the Hull College of Art and exhibited at the Royal Society of Portrait Painters.

GALLUCCI, Giovanni
Italian, 19th century.
Born 1 December 1815, in Ancona (Marche).
Painter.

Giovanni Gallucci was a pupil of T. Minardi in Rome, and went on to work in Florence, Venice, Imola and Castel Nuovo.

GALLUCCI, Niccolo. See **NICCOLO DA GUARDIAGRELE**

GALLUCCI, Paolo
Italian, 17th century.
Active in Pisa c. 1650.
Painter.

Paolo Gallucci painted a retable for the church of S Michele.

GALLUCCI, Sandro
Italian, 20th century.
Painter.

The gallery of modern art in Florence has a painting entitled *Il Fratellino* by Sandro Gallucci.

GALLUCCIO, Giovan Antonio
Italian, 17th century.
Active in Naples at the beginning of the 17th century.
Sculptor.
Giovan Antonio Galluccio was the brother of Scipione. He sculpted several tombs.

GALLUCCIO, Pasquale
Italian, 18th century.
Active in Naples at the end of the 18th century.
Painter.
Pasquale Galluccio was employed by the royal porcelain manufacturing works in Naples.

GALLUCCIO, Scipione
Italian, 16th - 17th century.
Active in Naples.
Sculptor.
A pupil of Federico Vetorale, Scipione Galluccio worked mainly with his brother Giovan Antonio.

GALLUS. See **BELLY Jacques**

GALLUS
Bohemian School, 16th - 17th century.
Active in Prague in 1587 and 1612.
Painter.
Gallus produced several highly accomplished historical portraits.

GALLUZZI, Andrea
Italian, 18th century.
Born c. 1700, in Piacenza.
Active in Piacenza and Modena.
Painter, architect.
In Modena, Andrea Galluzzi was entrusted with decorations for the celebration of the wedding of Francesco d'Este to Charlotte Aglaé of Orléans.

GALLUZZI, Giovanni Battista
Italian, 18th century.
Born in Piacenza.
Active in Madrid.
Painter, architect.

GALLUZZI, Pietro
Italian, 17th century.
Born in Urbino.
Active in Modena.
Painter.
Pietro Galluzzi was a pupil of Jean Boulanger.

GALLWEY, Antoinette-Célestine
French, 19th century.
Born in Le Havre.
Sculptor.
She studied under Barye and exhibited examples of her work (typically, animal groups in wax) at the Paris Salon between 1867 and 1870.

GALLWEY, Emmeline-Henriette
French, 19th century.
Born in Paris.
Sculptor.
She exhibited animal groups in wax at the Paris Salon from 1864 to 1877, together with a bronze statue of a goat (1877).

GALLY, Félix C.
French, 19th century.
Active in Argenteuil (Val-d'Oise).
Engraver.
He was a member of the Société des Artistes Français and took part in its exhibitions from 1894.

GALLY, Gilles
French, 20th - 21st century.
Born 12 January 1961, in Semur-en-Auxois (Côte d'Or).
Sculptor of assemblages.
Gilles Gally trained at the École des Beaux-Arts in Dijon. He completed the five-year course successfully in 1986, maintaining that while his interest lay with sculpture, he owed much to the painter Busse. He has strong emotional and civic ties to Auxois, his birthplace. To his father, a blacksmith, he owes his penchant for natural materials such as wood and iron.

Using traditional tools such as the hammer, clamp, anvil, blow-lamp and drill, Gally precision-cuts pieces of wood into perfect rectangles, or metal into arcs and circles, and assembles them into sculptures. These are either symmetrical and inward-looking or seemingly erratic, open spiral shapes. Used to the open countryside, he works on a large scale, fully in the round. His works are playful. Some, although well-balanced and safely anchored, quiver or shake at any given moment, giving the impression of not being totally under control. Others, although supplied with wheels, remain ironically and immovably in place. While Gally celebrates the whimsical child in his nature, the titles of his creations reflect solidly on the materials he uses: *Oak and Iron*, for example, tells of the fine feel of wood and the malleability of iron. His work seems to be less a matter of the sculptor at work than of a midwife in the process of revealing the hidden identity of these natural materials.

His work was included in group exhibitions at the following: the museum of La Charité-sur-Loire (1987, 1995); Stuttgart (1987); Dijon (1987); the Salon des Réalités Nouvelles in Paris (1987); Cluny and Joigny (1988); the Espace des Arts in Chalon-sur-Saône (1989); Joigny and Poilly in Oise (1990); the Dijon Fonds Régional d'Art Contemporain (FRAC) (1991); *L'Oeuvre et le Sacré* (*Artwork and the Sacred*) in Annemasse and Clamecy (1991); and the museum of Clamecy (1994). In 1993 Gally held a joint exhibition with Claude Viallat entitled *Question de Forme* (*A Question of Form*) at the Atelier Cantoisel in Joigny. A solo exhibition entitled *Deux Poids, Deux Mesures* (*Two Weights, Two Measures*) was held at the Théâtre Granit in Belfort in 1993.

BIBLIOGRAPHY:
Vô-Thi-Anh Cheylus, Marie-France, '*Gilles Gally, Pierre-Yves Magerand, Pierre Mathey*' in *Art Press*, no. 118, periodical, Paris, 1987. *FRAC Bourgogne*, catalogue, Fonds régional d'Art contemporain de Bourgogne, Dijon, 1989. Bonnefoi, Christian, *La Mesure de la distance*, Atelier Cantoisel, Joigny, 1990. Dobbels, Daniel, *Question de forme: Viallat, Gally*, exhibition catalogue, Musée de La Charité-sur-Loire, La Charité-sur-Loire, Musée de Clamecy, Clamecy, 1993-1994. Le Panse, Jérôme, '*Exposition Claude Viallat, Gilles Gally*' in *L'Yonne Républicaine*, periodical, Auxerre, 3 July 1993.

MUSEUMS AND GALLERIES:
DIJON (FRAC Bourgogne): *Bridge*.

GALLYS
French, 20th century.
Painter. Genre scenes.
AUCTION RECORDS:
LE TOUQUET, 8 Nov 1992, *At the Violon Bleu Bar* (oil on canvas, 18 x 15 ins / 46 x 38 cm) FRF 5,000.

GALMACHE, José
Belgian, 20th century.
Born 1914, in Mons.
Painter, draughtsman.

GALMES, Guillermo
Spanish, 19th century.
Active in Palma, Majorca.
Sculptor.
Guillermo Galmes worked for Palma Cathedral.

GALMES Y BLANQUER, Manuel

Spanish, 19th century.
Born c. 1852, in Valencia; died 3 March 1873, in Valencia.
Painter.

Manuel Galmes y Blanquer worked mainly in Madrid and Valencia. He painted landscapes and religious subjects.

GALMIER-BLAY

French, 19th century.
Painter.

He exhibited portraits at the Paris Salon from 1833 to 1845.

GALMUZZI

Italian, 19th century.
Active in Italy.
Sculptor.

Galmuzzi received an honourable mention in Paris at the Exposition Universelle of 1889.

GALOFRE Y COMA, José

Spanish, 19th century.
Born 1819, in Barcelona; died 10 January 1877, in Barcelona.
Painter.

José Galofre y Coma studied in Italy and only returned to Spain around 1850. He exhibited in Madrid, and in Paris in 1855. He is known for his *Coronation of Alfonso V of Aragon*, *Zobaida Bathing*, *Episode in the Granada War* and numerous portraits. He also established a reputation as an art critic.

MUSEUMS AND GALLERIES:

VERSAILLES (Château): *Portrait of Pope Pius IX.*

AUCTION RECORDS:

PARIS, 18 May 1897, *Bullfight in Andalusia,* FRF 3,000. NEW YORK, 13 and 14 Feb 1900, *The Bird Charmer,* USD 425. NEW YORK, 12 and 13 March 1903, *On the Lagoon* (watercolour) USD 310. NEW YORK, 27 Jan 1905, *Bay of Naples,* USD 200. LONDON, 11 April 1908, *The Wandering Musician* (1872) GBP 14. LONDON, 2 April 1910, *The King is Entertained,* GBP 65. LONDON, 6 March 1911, *Pottery Market in Naples,* GBP 22.

GALOFRE Y GIMÉNEZ, Baldomero

Spanish, 19th century.
Born 24 May 1849, in Reus near Tarragona (Catalonia); died 26 July 1902, in Barcelona.
Painter (gouache), watercolourist, pastellist, draughtsman. Genre scenes, landscapes, waterscapes, seascapes.

After training as an artist, Baldomero Galofre y Giménez travelled to Italy where he developed a strong individual style. When he returned to Spain he scoured the country for picturesque subjects, gathering a large number of studies and sketches for a monumental work he planned to publish under the title *España (Spain)* . He enjoyed painting processions, popular gatherings and other types of scenes to which he could bring movement, gaiety and life. Some of his watercolours and gouaches survive.

MUSEUMS AND GALLERIES:

NANCY: *Fishing Boats at Cività-Vecchia.*

AUCTION RECORDS:

PARIS, 5 Dec 1923, *Spanish Scene,* FRF 780. PARIS, 21 Jan 1924, *Shrimp Fishing* (watercolour) FRF 680. PARIS, 26 and 27 May 1924, *Boats on the Shore* (pastel) FRF 180. LONDON, 13 May 1927, *Return from the Fair,* GBP 28; *Holiday,* GBP 35. PARIS, 21 April 1943, *Fishing by Moonlight* (charcoal) FRF 50. PARIS, 9 Feb 1944, *Boat Run Aground* (watercolour) FRF 600. COLOGNE, 27 Nov 1969, *Market in Andalusia,* DEM 7,000. MILAN, 10 Nov 1970, *Sunday in the Countryside,* ITL 2,600,000. BUENOS AIRES, 14 Nov 1973, *Andalusian Scene,* ARS 14,000. MADRID, 17 May 1976, *Seascape* (oil on canvas, 9½ x 16¼ ins / 24 x 41.5 cm) ESP 270,000. MADRID, 11 Nov 1976, *Boats on the Shore* (watercolour, 18¼ x 25 ins / 46.5 x 63.5 cm) ESP 75,000. NEW YORK, 14 Jan 1977, *Market Scene in Andalusia* (oil on panel, 7¾ x 12½ ins / 20 x 32 cm) USD 2,300. NEW YORK, 29 May 1980, *Ox Cart* (oil on canvas, 30¼ x 50½ ins / 77 x 128 cm) USD 9,500. BARCELONA, 21 Dec 1982, *Fisherman* (watercolour, 25¼ x 38¼ ins / 64 x 97 cm) ESP 370,000. MILAN, 29 May 1984, *Landscape with Gypsies on Horseback* (oil on panel, 13½ x 19¾ ins / 34 x 50 cm) ITL 6,700,000. BARCELONA, 29 Oct 1985, *Peasant Woman* (pencil, 23½ x 17¾ ins / 60 x 45 cm) ESP 230,000. MADRID, 20 Oct 1987, *Caravans at a Celebration* (1889, oil on panel, 16¾ x 26¼ ins / 42.5 x 66.5 cm) ESP 4,750,000. NEW YORK, 24 Nov 1987, *Gypsy Celebration* (1890, gouache and pen, 9 x 10¾ ins / 22 x 27.5 cm) USD 4,600. LONDON, 23 Nov 1988, *Village Market* (oil on panel, 8¼ x 14¼ ins / 21 x 36 cm) GBP 9,900. LONDON, 17 Feb 1989, *Horse-Breakers* (1893, oil on panel, 26½ x 17 ins / 67 x 43 cm) GBP 49,500. LONDON, 22 Nov 1989, *Repairing Nets on the Beach* (watercolour, 26 x 39¼ ins / 66 x 100 cm) GBP 13,200. ROME, 12 Dec 1989, *On the Way to Market* (chalk, watercolour and lead-white/beige paper, 10 x 13½ ins / 25.5 x 34.5 cm) ITL 1,300,000. LONDON, 14 Feb 1990, *Market Day* (oil on panel, 7½ x 13 ins / 19 x 33 cm) GBP 18,700. NEW YORK, 23 May 1990, *Ox Carts Leaving the Village* (oil on panel, 9 x 15¼ ins / 22.9 x 38.7 cm) USD 8,250. NEW YORK, 28 Feb 1991, *Gypsy Camp* (oil on panel, 9¼ x 15¼ ins / 23.5 x 38.7 cm) USD 35,200. NEW YORK, 26 May 1992, *Boats Run Aground* (watercolour/paper/card, 18 x 27¼ ins / 45.5 x 69.2 cm) USD 1,430. LONDON, 29 May 1992, *Gypsy Camp outside the Town Walls* (oil on panel, 13 x 18¾ ins / 33 x 47.5 cm) GBP 12,100. MADRID, 25 May 1993, *Gypsy Woman and Donkey* (oil on card, 9½ x 6¾ ins / 24 x 17 cm) ESP 80,500. NEW YORK, 9 March 1996, *Fishermen on the Shore* (watercolour/paper, 17½ x 23½ ins / 44.5 x 59.7 cm) USD 2,300. LONDON, 31 Oct 1996, *View of the Bay of Naples* (watercolour, 20½ x 27¼ ins / 52 x 69 cm) GBP 2,760. MADRID, 28 Sept 1999, *Romeria* (1889, watercolour, 10x13 ins / 26x34 cm) ESP 260,000. NEW YORK, 8 March 2000, *Country Farm* (oil on panel, 9x15 ins / 23x39 cm) USD 16,000. AHLDEN, 5 May 2001, *Vine Harvest* (oil on canvas, 18x22 ins / 46x56 cm) DEM 19,000. MADRID, 17 Dec 2002, *Seascape* (1887, watercolour, 20x14 ins / 52x36 cm) EUR 2,100. NEW YORK, 5 Feb 2003, *Fishing Boats on the Shore* (oil on canvas, 10x17 ins / 25x43 cm) USD 30,000. MADRID, 24 Feb 2004, *Encampment* (oil on board, 8 x 12 ins / 20x31 cm) EUR 12,000.

GALOFRE Y OLLER, Francisco

Spanish, 19th - 20th century.
Born 1865, in Valls (Tarragona); died 8 January 1942, in Barcelona.
Painter. History painting, religious subjects, portraits, genre scenes.

Francisco Galofre y Oller trained at the academy in Barcelona where he studied under Antonio Caba and at the Real Academia de Bellas Artes de San Fernando in Madrid.

He took part in all the major national painting exhibitions in Madrid and Barcelona. He received a commendation at the Universal Exhibition of 1888. Galofre y Oller executed paintings for churches including a chapel in the church at Valls and a *Coronation of the Virgin* for a basilica in Barcelona.

He painted in a naturalist style and was influenced by the work of Dionisio Baixeras and Joaquin Sorolla. His best-known work is *Boria Avall,* dated 1892, showing punishment by whipping in a town in the mid-17th century.

BIBLIOGRAPHY:

Arnáiz, José Manuel/López Jiménez, Javier/Merchán Díaz, Manuel (ed.), *'Cien años de pintura en Espana y Portugal (1830-1930)'* in vol. III, Antiqvaria, Madrid, 1989 (One Hundred Years of Painting in Spain and Portugal (1830-1930)).

MUSEUMS AND GALLERIES:

BARCELONA (MAM del Mus. Nacional d'Art de Catalunya).

Auction records:
Madrid, 11 Nov 1976, *Boria Avall* (1894, oil on canvas, 37 x 59 ins / 94 x 150 cm) ESP 500,000. Madrid, 24 Oct 1983, *Boria Avall* (1894, oil on canvas, 37 x 59 ins / 94 x 150 cm) ESP 1,100,000.

GALÓN, José
Spanish, 19th century.
Born in the 19th century.
Painter.
José Galón studied at the Academia de San Fernando.

GALONI, Melchiorre de
Italian, 16th century.
Active in 1550.
Painter.

GALOPIN, Ancelot
French, 15th century.
Painter.
Galopin worked on decorations for a banquet in Lille (Nord) in 1453.

GALOPINI, Giacomo
Italian, 15th century.
Active in Mantua.
Miniaturist.
Giacomo Galopini was a priest. Most of his work was done between 1416 and 1437.

GALOS, Victor
French, 19th century.
Born 1828, in Pau; died 1879.
Painter. Mountainscapes, landscapes, portraits.
He studied under Eugène Devéria. Except for a few months spent in Paris, he never left the region of his birthplace, but he appears to have become acquainted with painters of the Barbizon School when they visited the Béarn region, notably Narcisse Diaz de la Peña. Galos drew his inspiration principally from the Pyrenées, which he painted time and again. His early style was essentially classical to the extent that he looked to achieve harmony and balance. Subsequently, however, the influence of nascent Impressionism became apparent: his basic theme remained unchanged, yet his treatment of it showed considerable variation depending on the time of the year and the hours of the day. A retrospective exhibition on Galos was mounted in Pau in 1967, effectively resuscitating an artist who had been largely ignored for almost a full century, and the same museum held another exhibition in 2002.
Bibliography:
Amboise, Guillaume (foreword), *Victor Galos, 1828-1879: du gave aux Pyrénées, la vision d'un peintre*, Pin à crochets, Pau, 2002.
Auction records:
Paris, 16 Feb 1983, *Landscape in the Pyrenees* (oil on canvas, 36¼ x 24in/92 x 61cm) FRF 16,000.

GALOT, or Gallot
French, 18th - 19th century.
Miniaturist.
Galot was a professor of drawing at the École Centrale in Chartres and father of Théodore Alphonse Galot.
Museums and Galleries:
Chartres: *Joan of Arc.*

GALOT, Jean-Joseph, or Gallot or Galot-Blot
French, 19th century.
Active in Chartres, at the beginning of the 19th century.
Watercolourist.
He was related to Théodore-Alphonse Gallot.
Museums and Galleries:
Chartres: *Views of Chartres and the Surrounding District* (numerous drawings and watercolours).

GALOT, Théodore-Alphonse, or Gallot
French, 19th century.
Born 16 April 1806, in Chartres; died in Rio de Janeiro, Brazil.
Painter.
He exhibited at the Paris Salon from 1833 to 1842, showing various views of the countryside around Puy-de-Dôme, Chartres and the Seine. He was later Director of Museu Nacional in Rio de Janeiro.
Museums and Galleries:
Chartres: *View of Chartres from the Filles-Dieu Hills.*

GALOTOLON, or Galotelon
French, 14th century.
Illuminator.
Galotolon is mentioned in records in Lyons in 1346 and 1352 as a *illuminator librorum* ('illuminator of books').

GALOUKHINA, Elena
Russian, 20th - 21st century.
Born 1957.
Painter. Urban landscapes, still-lifes.
Elena Galoukhina studied at the school of fine arts in Leningrad (now St Petersburg) and also attended the Repin Institute there. She became a member of the former Association of Young Leningrad Painters. Her paintings follow the traditions of Maclet and Marquet.

GALOYER, François
French, 20th century.
Born 1944.
Sculptor. Animals, birds.
François Galoyer attended the École des Arts Appliqués and the Académie de Montparnasse in Paris. He studied with Volti. His animal sculptures, mainly of birds, are highly stylised.

GALOYER, Raymond
French, 20th century.
Born 28 June 1896, in Paris.
Painter, lithographer. Landscapes.
Raymond Galoyer studied under Desvergnes. He exhibited regularly, showing lithographic landscapes in Paris at the Salon des Artistes Français. He also showed three landscapes at the Salon des Tuileries in 1930.

GALRAPP, Michael
German, 18th century.
Active in Munich.
Painter.
Galrapp is especially noted for his frescoes. In 1754 he worked in Donauwörth.

GALSTER, Henrik Ludvig
Danish, 19th century.
Born 22 January 1826, in Norre Sundby, near Aalborg; died 24 June 1901, in Copenhagen.
Painter. Portraits, waterscapes.
Henrik Ludvig Galster was a pupil of Moller and Hansen. He studied in Copenhagen and then in London. He is noted for his *Portrait of the Queen Mother of Denmark, Caroline Amalie.*
Auction records:
Copenhagen, 2 March 1983, *Port of Copenhagen* (1879, oil on canvas, 37¾ x 74¾ ins / 96 x 190 cm) DKK 23,000.

GALSWORTHY, Gordon C.
British, 19th century.
Active in London.
Painter. Genre scenes.
Gordon C. Galsworthy exhibited at the Royal Academy in London from 1893.

GALSWORTHY, W.H.
British, 19th century.

Active in London.
Painter. Landscapes.

W.H. Galsworthy exhibited in London between 1847 and 1856, notably at the Royal Academy, the British Institution and the Suffolk Street Gallery.

AUCTION RECORDS:
LONDON, 3 June 1988, *Path Through a Thicket* (oil on canvas, 25 1/2 x 30 ins / 65 x 76 cm) GBP 1,100.

GALT, Alexander
American, 19th century.
Born 1827, in Norfolk (Virginia); died March 1863, in Richmond.
Sculptor.

Among Alexander Galt's works is a *Portrait of Thomas Jefferson*.

GALT, Cameron
British, 20th - 21st century.
Born 1949.
Painter. Figure compositions, figures.

Cameron Galt works in a realist style reminiscent of the German Neue Sachlickhkeit (New Functionalism). He casts a cold and gloomy look over a shady world of bars where people come together and separate.

AUCTION RECORDS:
LONDON, 22 Oct 1997, *Old Haunt* (oil on canvas, 61 x 68 1/2 ins / 154.9 x 174 cm) GBP 3,450. LONDON, 4 June 1999, *Study for Couple and Tortoise* (1991, charcoal and pastel, 39 x 24 ins / 100 x 60 cm) GBP 1,500. LONDON, 4 June 1999, *Study for The Old Haunt* (1989-1990, charcoal, pastel and wash, 48 x 60 ins / 122 x 153 cm) GBP 4,200.

GALT, Charles Franklin
American, 20th century.
Born 1884, in St Louis.
Painter.

Charles Galt studied under R.E. Miller and exhibited his work at the Salon de la Société Nationale des Beaux-Arts in Paris.

GALTEAUX, P.
French.
Painter. Fruit.

MUSEUMS AND GALLERIES:
ROCHEFORT: a work.

GALTER, Pietro
Italian, 19th century.
Born in the 19th century, in Venice.
Painter. Landscapes.

Galter was a pupil at the school of fine arts in Venice. He exhibited landscapes and seascapes in Milan, Rome and Venice.

GALTIÉ, André Léon
French, 20th century.
Born in Toulouse; died 4 August 1983, in Briançon.
Medallist.

André Galtié was awarded a silver medal in Paris in 1944 at the Salon des Artistes Français.

GALTIER-BOISSIÈRE, Élisabeth Marie Victorine Zoé, later Mme Renaud
French, 19th century.
Born in Paris.
Engraver.

She studied under Bléry and exhibited at the Paris Salon from 1869 to 1880. She also exhibited at the Société Nationale and at the Autumn Salon.

GALTIER-BOISSIÈRE, Jean
French, 20th century.
Born January 1891; died 1966.
Painter, draughtsman, illustrator. Still-lifes, flowers.

Jean Galtier-Boissière exhibited in galleries in Paris in 1917 and 1919. His career as an artist was brief. Often his drawings were accompanied by texts on the life of pleasure and later on the war, which he depicted harshly with various sketches made on the Front. He continued painting flowers for his own pleasure and then began a career as a writer. In 1916 he founded the *Crapouillot*, a journal of the trenches which reappeared after World War II. Galtier-Boissière brought together many talented artists to work on the journal.

AUCTION RECORDS:
PARIS, 1 April 1920, *End of the Review* (watercolour) FRF 410. PARIS, 24 Nov 1928, *Local Theatre*, FRF 200. PARIS, 1 July 1943, *Hydrangeas; Still-life* (two oils on canvas) FRF 550.

GALTIER-BOISSIÈRE, Louise
French, 20th century.
Born 19th century, in Paris.
Painter. Genre scenes, still-lifes.

Louise Galtier-Boissière was the mother of the draughtsman and lampoonist Jean Galtier-Boissière and sister of the painter René Ménard. She joined the Salon of the Société Nationale des Beaux-Arts in Paris in 1906. She also painted decorative flower panels.

GALVAGNI, Giovanni
Italian, 18th century.
Born in Isera.
Active in Rovereto.
Engraver.

GALVAN, Antonio
Spanish, 17th century.
Active in Saragossa.
Painter.

Antonio Galvan is known for his painting of *St Bartholomew*.

GALVAN, José
Spanish, 18th century.
Born 19 June 1705, in Castile; died 21 February 1766, in Calatayud (Aragon).
Sculptor, architect.

José Galvan was a pupil of Juan Ron in Madrid and also worked in Huesca, Teruel and Manresa.

GALVAN, Juan Pérez
Spanish, 17th century.
Born c. 1586, in Lucena (Cordova); died 1658, in Saragossa.
Painter.

According to Palomino, Juan Pérez Galvan lived for a time in Rome. When he returned to Spain he often lived in Saragossa, where he was a member of the guild and painted works for the cathedral including *Nativity*, *St Just*, *St Rufin* and other works for which Cean Bermudez provided the colouring. His master work is *Birth of the Virgin*. He also painted the dome of S Justa y Ruffina and a picture of the *Holy Trinity* for the Discalced Carmelites.

DJ Galvan.

BIBLIOGRAPHY:
Ponz, Antonio, in *Viaje de España, 4*, Aguilar, Madrid, 1988.

AUCTION RECORDS:
LONDON, 19 April 1909, *Pilgrim* (wash); *Study of a Beggar; St John in the Wilderness*, GBP 13.

GALVAN Y CANDELA, José Maria
Spanish, 19th century.
Born 1837, in Madrid; died 1899.
Painter, engraver.

José Maria Galvan y Candela studied under Luis Fagundiez and at the Academia de San Fernando. He first exhibited at the exhibition of the national fine arts society of Madrid in 1864 as an engraver and is known primarily for his work in this discipline. He engraved from works by Velázquez, Goya, Murillo and Zurbaran.

BIBLIOGRAPHY:

Rada y Delgado, Juan de Dios de la, *Frescos de Goya en la ermita de San Antonio de la Florida grabados al aguafuerte por José M. Galván y Candela*, Ayuntamiento, Madrid, 1994.

GALVANI, Carlo
Italian, 19th century.
Active in Venice c. 1830.
Miniaturist, lithographer.

MUSEUMS AND GALLERIES:

TRIESTE (Civico Mus. Revoltella): *Portrait of Canova*.

GALVANO. See also **CALVANO**

GALVANO, Albino
Italian, 20th century.
Born 1917, in Turin.
Painter.

From 1928 to 1931 Albino Galvano was a student at the Felice Casorati school. In 1953 he signed the *Urban* manifesto, along with Biglione, Parisot and Scroppo. He was an art critic and also taught history and philosophy.

Until the 1950s, Galvano's paintings were figurative. He then became an advocate of the Concrete Art movement, which held that the truly concrete aspect of art was the combination of form and colour, emancipated from its function of representing a reality outside the nature of the work itself.

Galvano's work appeared in the numerous exhibitions held by this group, most notably at the Venice Biennale in 1930, 1936, 1948, 1950, 1952, 1954 and 1956; and at the Rome Quadriennale, in 1931, 1935 and 1948.

GALVANO, Alessandro
Italian, 18th century.
Active in Padua.
Painter.

Alessandro Galvano worked on Padua Cathedral.

GALVANO, Sebastiano
Italian, 16th century.
Active in Padua at the end of the 16th century.
Painter.

Sebastiano Galvano is recorded as having worked for the church of S Benedetto Novello.

GALVEZ, Alejandro Miguel de. See **MIGUEL Y GALVEZ Alejandro**

GALVEZ, Bernabé
Spanish, 19th century.
Active in Toledo in 1807.
Painter.

Bernabé Galvez produced paintings for the church of Sta Maria Magdalena in Toledo.

GALVEZ, Juan
Spanish, 18th - 19th century.
Born 1774, in Mora; died 1847, in Madrid.
Painter, decorative designer. Genre scenes.

Juan Galvez studied at the Academia de San Fernando. Among other decorative works he painted the frescoes in the Palacio de los Infantes at the Escorial and those of a stairway at the Prado. He is known for his religious paintings and genre pieces.

BIBLIOGRAPHY:

Album de los Sitios de Zaragoza: Láminas dibujadas y grabadas por D. Juan Gálvez y D. Fernando Brambila, Cecilio Gasca, Saragossa, 1905. Contento Márquez, Rafael, *Juan Gálvez, pintor de cámara de Fernando VII y director general de la Real Academia de San Fernando de Madrid*, Editorial de la Universidad Complutense, Madrid, 1993.

GALVEZ, Marina de
Spanish, 18th century.
Painter.

The museum in Saragossa has a painting by Marina de Galvez entitled *Pyramus and Thisbe*.

GALVEZ Y PARDO, Ramón
Spanish, 19th century.
Born in the 19th century, in Saragossa.
Painter. Architectural views.

Ramón Galvez y Pardo studied at the school of fine arts in Saragossa. He first exhibited in 1876.

GALWEY Y GARCIA, Enrique
Spanish, 19th - 20th century.
Born 1864, in Barcelona; died 10 February 1931, in Barcelona.
Painter. Landscapes.

Enrique Galwey y García studied at the school of fine arts in Barcelona. Around 1885 he was a pupil of Joaquin Vayreda; he also spent time in Paris. Galwey y García was a landscape painter. His work incorporates the aesthetic values of the Barbizon School and also some of the dramatic resonance of English landscape artists and seeks to convey man's feelings and sense of concern when confronted with nature.

Enrique Galwey y García took part in various group exhibitions: Barcelona (1885 and 1890); Madrid school of fine arts (1895); Berlin (1896). He also showed work in Düsseldorf, Paris, London, Buenos Aires and Venice and at the exhibitions of the national fine arts society of Madrid. He held a solo exhibition in Barcelona in 1922 and retrospectives of his work were also held in Barcelona in 1943 and 1970. He received a silver medal in 1897 for his painting *Preludio de la Noche* (*Prelude to Night*) and another in 1906. He was awarded a gold medal at the Barcelona international arts exhibition of 1907 and a silver medal at the Brussels international exhibition of 1909.

BIBLIOGRAPHY:

Arnáiz, José Manuel/López Jiménez, Javier/Merchán Díaz, Manuel (ed.), *'Cien años de pintura en Espana y Portugal (1830-1930)'* in vol. III, Antiqvaria, Madrid, 1989 (One Hundred Years of Painting in Spain and Portugal (1830-1930)).

AUCTION RECORDS:

BARCELONA, 19 June 1980, *The Farmhouse* (1885, oil on canvas, 26 3/4 x 45 1/4 ins / 68 x 115 cm) ESP 125,000. BARCELONA, 24 March 1983, *Landscape* (oil on panel, 19 x 27 1/2 ins / 48 x 70 cm) ESP 97,000. MADRID, 27 March 1985, *Landscape* (oil on canvas, 29 1/4 x 48 ins / 74 x 122 cm) ESP 440,000. MADRID, 20 Dec 1999, *Landscape* (oil on canvas, 11 x 16 ins / 27 x 41 cm) ESP 400,000. MADRID, 21 Jan 2003, *Landscape* (oil on canvas, 47 x 31 ins / 120 x 80 cm) EUR 2,500.

GALY, Hippolyte-Marius
French, 19th century.
Born 19th century, in Algiers.
Sculptor.

He studied under Dumont and Cormon. As a member of the Société des Artistes Français from 1898, he participated in its exhibitions and received an honourable mention in 1898. He was made a Chevalier of the Légion d'Honneur in 1900.

GALY, Suzanne. See **COURBET Suzanne**

GAMACHES, Pierre
French, 15th century.
Active in Rouen.
Sculptor (wood).

Pierre Gamaches worked under Philippot Viart on the carving of the choir stalls in Rouen Cathedral in 1467.

GAMAIN, Louis-Honoré-Frédéric
French, 19th century.
Born 22 April 1803, in Le Crotoy (Somme); died 1 March 1871, in Le Havre.
Painter. Seascapes.

He studied under Gudin and exhibited at the Paris Salon from 1833 to 1843.

MUSEUMS AND GALLERIES:
LE HAVRE: *The Humboldt at Anchor in the Gulf of Florida*.

AUCTION RECORDS:
PARIS, 24 Jan 1927, *Two Yachts* (a pair) FRF 1,680. FÉCAMP, 7 Nov 1982, *Three-Master: The Elizabeth* (oil on canvas, 23 1/2 x 28 1/4 ins / 60 x 72 cm) FRF 16,500. MONTE CARLO, 26 June 1983, *View of St-Pierre, Martinique* (oil on canvas, 16 1/2 x 23 ins / 42 x 58.5 cm) FRF 30,000. PARIS, 28 Oct 1990, *Seascape* (oil on canvas, 17 x 23 1/2 ins / 43 x 60 cm) FRF 15,000. PARIS, 28 Nov 1999, *'Clipper Francais', 'Pigeon du Cap'* (1868, oil on canvas, 20 x 25 ins / 50 x 64 cm) FRF 18,000. PARIS, 24 Sept 2000, *Free Schooner* (1860, oil on canvas, 20 x 28 ins / 52 x 71 cm) FRF 28,000. PARIS, 24 April 2002, *Le Havre under Snow* (1871, oil on canvas, 20 x 29 ins / 51 x 73 cm) EUR 2,800. PARIS, 24 April 2002, *Visit of Queen Victoria to the Port of St-Malo* (oil on canvas, 22 x 32 ins / 56 x 82 cm) EUR 4,200.

GAMALIEL DE HERDE, R. J.
French, 17th century.
Active in Paris in 1600.
Painter.

GAMARD, Jean
French, 18th century.
Active in Paris in 1744.
Painter, sculptor.

GAMARRA, José
Uruguayan, 20th century.
Born 1934, in Tacuarembo.
Active in France from 1963 or 1965.
Painter, lithographer. Landscapes with figures.

José Gamarra studied at the school of fine arts in Montevideo. In 1959 he left Uruguay for southern Brazil and in 1963 moved to Paris.

Gamarra originally worked in the area of Latin-American abstract art. He then became heavily influenced by Pop Art, but by the style rather than the deeper aesthetic and sociological motivations. In a naive, brightly coloured and apparently charming imagery, he recounts stories of flying, motorised, striped and multi-coloured crayfish and lobsters launching attacks on amusement park fortresses. His work has sometimes been compared with that of Jan Voss which poses the question of whether Pop artists can really be naive. Beyond their appealing exteriors, Gamarra's paintings raise questions about the current situation of Latin America. The jungle, which is omnipresent in his work, symbolises the lost paradise for which both animals and primitive man still yearn but which poses a threat to the emblematic representations of the supposed civilisation brought by the Conquest.

Gamarra has exhibited at many group exhibitions including the Venice Biennale in 1964. He also took part in the travelling exhibition *Art of the Fantastic, Latin America 1920-1970* organised by the Indianapolis museum in 1987. He has also held several solo exhibitions in various South American countries and in France.

BIBLIOGRAPHY:
Vision 24 Pittori et Scultori America Latina, Istituto Italo-Latino Americano, Rome, 1970. Day, H. T./Sturges, H. (eds.), *Art of the Fantastic: Latin America, 1920-1987*, exhibition catalogue, Museum of Art, Indianapolis, 1987. *José Gamarra*, exhibition catalogue, Galerie Albert Loeb, Paris, 1992. Pérez Oramas, L., *'José Gamarra: Después del Edén'* in *Art Nexus*, vol 8, 1993.

AUCTION RECORDS:
NEW YORK, 25 Nov 1986, *Mystic Hunt* (1984, oil on canvas, 54 3/4 x 54 3/4 ins / 139 x 139 cm) USD 6,000. NEW YORK, 17 April 1988, *Painting P 64105* (1964, 51 x 63 3/4 ins / 129.3 x 162 cm) USD 4,400. LONDON, 6 April 1989, *The Revenge of the Green Dragon* (acrylic/canvas, 32 x 39 1/2 ins / 81.3 x 100.3 cm) GBP 3,080. NEW YORK, 17 May 1989, *Ancestors* (1980, oil on canvas, 46 x 35 ins / 116 x 89 cm) USD 17,600. NEW YORK, 19-20 May 1992, *La Risa del Chaja* (1986, oil on canvas, 59 x 78 3/4 ins / 149.9 x 200 cm) USD 29,700. NEW YORK, 18-19 May 1993, *The Missionaries of the Impossible* (1962, oil on canvas, 35 x 46 ins / 89.2 x 116 cm) USD 11,500. NEW YORK, 18 May 1994, *Painting P 64114* (1964, oil on canvas, 79 1/2 x 79 1/4 ins / 201.8 x 201.2 cm) USD 13,800.

GAMBA, Antonio
Italian, 18th century.
Active in Naples.
Painter.

Antonio Gamba was a pupil of Solimena.

GAMBA, Crescenzo. See **LA GAMBA**

GAMBA, Enrico
Italian, 19th century.
Born 3 January 1831, in Turin; died 19 October 1883, in Turin.
Painter, watercolourist, draughtsman. History painting, portraits, genre scenes, landscapes.

In 1850 Enrico Gamba arrived in Frankfurt am Main, where he studied with Theodor Steinlen. He lived in Italy, and exhibited in Vienna and Frankfurt between 1873 and 1881.

He is known for *Landscape* and *The Kiss*.

AUCTION RECORDS:
LONDON, 25 April 1924, *Return to the Town*, GBP 24. ROME, 6 June 1984, *Figures in front of a Castle* (1871, oil on canvas, 75 1/2 x 59 1/2 ins / 192 x 151 cm) ITL 8,000,000. MILAN, 7 Nov 1985, *Fishing Boat on Rough Seas* (1855, oil on canvas, 35 3/4 x 52 ins / 91 x 132 cm) ITL 9,500,000. MADRID, 21 Oct 1986, *Gallant Conversation* (watercolour, 22 3/4 x 13 3/4 ins / 58 x 35 cm) ESP 350,000. LONDON, 15 Dec 1988, *Beautiful Young Girl* (pencil and watercolour, 20 x 15 ins / 50.6 x 37.9 cm) GBP 462. MILAN, 8 March 1990, *At the Fountain* (oil on canvas, 16 1/4 x 23 1/2 ins / 41 x 60 cm) ITL 11,000,000. VERCELLI, 18 Nov 2000, *Savoia Visit to the Soldiers* (oil on canvas, 15 x 29 ins / 39 x 73 cm) ITL 15,000,000. ROME, 21 Nov 2000, *St Matthew* (oil on canvas, 20 x 11 ins / 51 x 29 cm) ITL 6,500,000. ROME, 4 June 2001, *On the Tago, Belem* (1873, oil on canvas, 14 x 24 ins / 35 x 62 cm) ITL 22,000,000. VERCELLI, 18 Nov 2001, *Roman Shepherd* (oil on canvas, 18 x 13 ins / 46 x 32 cm) ITL 4,800,000.

GAMBA, Francesco
Italian, 19th century.
Born 1818, in Turin; died 10 May 1887, in Turin.
Painter. Genre scenes, waterscapes, seascapes.

Francesco was the brother of Enrico Gamba. He exhibited mostly in Milan and Turin.

MUSEUMS AND GALLERIES:
GENOA: *Seascape* - TRIESTE: *Rouen Motif*.

AUCTION RECORDS:
MILAN, 17 Dec 1992, *A Good Catch* (1850, oil on canvas, 37 1/2 x 39 1/4 ins / 95.5 x 100 cm) ITL 4,800,000. BOSTON, 10 March 2000, *Village Market Place* (1875, oil on canvas, 35 x 52 ins / 88 x 133 cm) USD 26,000.

GAMBA, Giovanni Battista
Italian, 19th century.
Born 1846, in Binago, near Varese (Lombardy).
Sculptor.

Giovanni Battista Gamba studied at the Accademia di Belle Arti di Brera in Milan, and with the sculptor Vincenzo Vela. He decorated several palaces in Bergamo, Rome and Nice, and exhibited in Naples, Milan and Rome. He was one of the most highly-regarded Italian sculptors of the 19th century.

GAMBA, Paolo
Italian, 18th century.
Born 30 October 1712, in Ripabottoni; died 26 December 1782, in Ripabottoni.
Painter.
Paolo Gamba was a pupil of Solimena. He worked in various towns in the Abruzzi region.

GAMBA DE PREYDOUR, Jules-Alexandre
French, 19th century.
Born 1846, in Paris.
Painter. Figures, genre scenes, landscapes, still-lifes.
He was a pupil of Gérôme. He exhibited at the Paris Salon from 1869, showing portraits, still-lifes and the occasional genre composition. Gamba de Preydour was a member of the Société des Artistes Français from 1886.
MUSEUMS AND GALLERIES:
CHARTRES: *Parnassus* (after Raphael).
AUCTION RECORDS:
PARIS, 2-3 July 1929, *Peira-Fourniga, near Nice,* FRF 1,800. PARIS, 12 Dec 1996, *Elegant Lady with an Umbrella* (oil on canvas, 13¾ x 8½ ins / 35 x 21.5 cm) FRF 4,800. NEW YORK, 29 Nov 1999, *Training the Turtle* (oil on canvas, 22 x 17 ins / 56 x 42 cm) USD 19,000. LONDON, 22 Sept 2000, *Roses. Marguerites* (oil on canvas, a pair, 9 x 6 ins / 22 x 16 cm) GBP 2,800. LONDON, 26 Sept 2001, *Still-life with Peaches* (oil on canvas, 15 x 22 ins / 38 x 55 cm) GBP 2,200.

GAMBACCIANI, Francesco, or Ganbaccini
Italian, 18th century.
Born 1701, in Florence.
Painter. History painting, portraits.
Florentine School.
Francesco Gambacciani's works are found mainly in Siena and Florence. A portrait of him hangs in the national gallery in Florence.

GAMBAGUOLA, Bartolommeo
Illuminator.
He illuminated several books in the style of Mantegna and Antonio da Monza, which are of great value.

GAMBALINI
Italian, 18th century.
Painter (?), draughtsman (?).
Brookshaw engraved a portrait of Gambalini.

GAMBARA, Lattanzio, or Lattanzio Cremonese
Italian, 16th century.
Born c. 1530, in Brescia; died 1574, in Brescia.
Active in Cremona and in Brescia.
Painter, draughtsman. Religious subjects, figures.
According to Lanzi, Lattanzio Cremonese worked in the Milan School in Venice. In *Le Miniere della Pittura (The Mines of Painting)*, Boschini refers to him as being among the contemporaries of Galleazzo Campi in Cremona at the beginning of the 16th century. After studying with Giulio Campi in Cremona, he went on to work in Gerolamo Romanino's studio. He created frescoes for palace façades and interiors and painted altarpieces.
MUSEUMS AND GALLERIES:
LOS ANGELES (Getty Mus.): *Study for a Ceiling* (c. 1565, drawing) - MILAN (Pinacoteca Ambrosiana): several drawings.

GAMBARATO, Girolamo
Italian, 17th century.
Died 1628.
Active in Venice.
Painter. History painting.
Girolamo Gambarato's *Peace Treaty Concluded by the Doge, Frederick Barbarossa and the Pope* hangs in the great council chamber of the ducal palace in Venice.

GAMBARD, Henri-Auguste
French, 19th century.
Born 30 October 1819, in Sceaux (Hauts-de-Seine); died 1882.
Painter. History painting, mythological subjects.
He enrolled at the École des Beaux-Arts in Paris in 1839 and studied initially under Emile Signol, then under Paul Delaroche. He exhibited at the Paris Salon from 1845 to 1869. Throughout his life, Henri-Auguste Gambard adhered to the conventions and canons of historical painting: he reached the final stage of the Prix de Rome competition on no fewer than six occasions. Examples of his work include *Oedipus at Colonna, Oedipus Banished from Thebes* and the *Death of Alexander.* A contemporary critic, writing in the *Journal des Artistes,* remarked that Gambard's work was 'directly in line with that of Girodet; he does not have the crispness of the latter, but he has good qualities. He is not an instinctive painter, but he knows how to handle a brush and how to achieve results that are elegant, pure and true-to-life'.
AUCTION RECORDS:
NEW YORK, 21 May 1987, *Alexander's Illness* (1846, oil on canvas, 45 x 58in/114.2 x 147.3cm) USD 25,000.

GAMBARDELLA, Michele
Italian, 17th century.
Active in Naples.
Painter.
Michele Gambardella studied under Vaccaro.

GAMBARDELLA, Spiridone, or Gambardella
British, 19th century.
Born c. 1815; died 1886.
Active in England.
Painter. Portraits, mythological subjects.
It seems likely that a *Portrait of the Lawyer Ledru* signed 'Gambandella' and now in the Arras Museum, as well as several portraits in the Liverpool Museum are the work of this artist, who exhibited in London between 1842 and 1852 at the Royal Academy and the British Institution and was also known as Gambadella.
MUSEUMS AND GALLERIES:
ARRAS: *Portrait of the Lawyer Ledru* - LIVERPOOL: *Portrait of James Pownall; Portrait of Charles Sylvestre; Portrait of Joseph Sanders; Portrait of George Stephenson* - LONDON (Apsley House, Wellington Mus.): *The Rt. Hon. Charles Arbuthnot* (1849, oil on canvas, oval portrait).

GAMBARELLI, Crescenzio
Italian, 16th century.
Born 16th century, in Siena.
Painter. History painting.
Gambarelli was a pupil of Nasini. He is undoubtedly the artist who painted an altarpiece for the church of S Maria del Carmine in Pisa.

GAMBARINI, Giuseppe
Italian, 18th century.
Born 1680, in Bologna; died 11 September 1725, in Bologna.
Painter. Religious subjects, mythological subjects, portraits, genre scenes, landscapes.
Giuseppe Gambarini studied under Pasinelli until the latter's death. He then became a pupil of Cesare Gennari, whose style he adopted and some of whose work he later copied. Persuaded he had insufficient talent to tackle historical themes, Gambarini started painting scenes from everyday life. They proved popular and may even have been instrumental in persuading Pietro Longhi to follow suit, forsaking

major compositions in favour of more down-to-earth subjects drawn from daily life. Gambarini's work is found chiefly in churches in Bologna, most notably a portrait of *St Maria Egiziaca* in the church of that name and a *St Catherine Vigri Entering Bologna* in the church of the Osservanti.

AUCTION RECORDS:

PARIS, 1816, *Works of Charity* (two pendants) FRF 271. LONDON, 19 April 1909, *Monks Distributing Food to Beggars*, GBP 4. NEW YORK, 23-25 Jan 1947, *Portrait of the Artist*, USD 160. MILAN, 9 Nov 1971, *Interior Scenes* (two pendants) ITL 3,800,000. LONDON, 12 Dec 1973, *Landscape with Figures*, GBP 4,000. LONDON, 10 April 1981, *Embroideress on a Terrace* (oil on canvas, 23 3/4 x 29 1/4 ins / 60.2 x 74.2 cm) GBP 16,000. NEW YORK, 18 Jan 1984, *Peasant Family; Washerwomen* (oil on canvas, a pair, 25 1/4 x 20 ins / 64 x 51 cm) USD 26,000. LONDON, 2 July 1986, *Wine Merchant; Fruit Seller* (oil on canvas, a pair, 38 1/4 x 29 1/4 ins / 97 x 74 cm and 38 1/4 x 26 1/4 ins/97 x 66.5 cm) GBP 115,000. LONDON, 6 July 1987, *Figure Studies* (blue wash heightened with white/grey paper, 12 3/4 x 16 ins / 32.6 x 40.6 cm) GBP 1,450. MILAN, 10 June 1988, *Landscape with Quarrelling Peasant Women; Landscape with Hunters and Peasants* (oil on canvas, a pair, each 27 1/2 x 35 3/4 ins / 70 x 91 cm) ITL 30,000,000. PARIS, 27 June 1989, *Bacchus and Ariadne on Naxos* (canvas in the shape of a half moon, 65 3/4 x 72 1/2 ins / 167 x 184 cm) FRF 160,000. PARIS, 30 Nov 1990, *Peasant Celebrations* (oil on canvas, a pair, each 54 x 48 3/4 ins / 137 x 124 cm) FRF 265,000. MONACO, 7 Dec 1990, *Landscape with Musicians* (oil on canvas, 18 1/2 x 25 1/2 ins / 47 x 65 cm) FRF 255,300. MONACO, 5-6 Dec 1991, *Rebecca at the Well* (oil on canvas, oval, 37 1/2 x 28 1/4 ins / 95 x 71.5 cm) FRF 77,700. LONDON, 6 July 1999, *Maenad Beating Tambourine with Infant and Goat in Formal Garden* (oil on canvas, 29 x 24 ins / 74 x 62 cm) GBP 6,800.

GAMBARO, Lattanzio, or Gambara
Italian, 16th century.
Born c. 1530, in Brescia; died c. 1574.
Painter. History painting, portraits.

Lattanzio Gambaro's father wanted him to become a tailor and punished him severely when he spent his leisure time in drawing. Having examined the youth's drawings, however, Antonio Campi discerned a remarkable talent and persuaded his father to let Lattanzio join his school. The boy studied there for 10 years, then, at the age of 18, was placed with Girolamo Romanino, who later gave him his daughter in marriage.

In Brescia, the street named after him (Strada del Gambero) is decorated with a number of attractive fresco paintings by Lattanzio depicting mythological and classical subjects. The works he did for the cloister of the Benedictine fathers of S Euphremia in Brescia are often referred to. He also painted frescoes for the town's castle, including a *Triumph of Bacchus*. In the cathedral in Parma, there are 12 frescoes by him depicting episodes from the life of Christ. His most admired oil paintings are a *Birth of the Virgin Mary*, in the church of S Faustino Maggiore, Brescia, and a *Pietà*, in the church of S Pietro, Cremona. He met his death falling from a ladder.

MUSEUMS AND GALLERIES:

BRESCIA (Castello): *Triumph of Bacchus* (fresco) - BRESCIA (Church of SS Faustino e Giovita): *Birth of the Virgin Mary* - BRESCIA (Pinacoteca Tosio-Martinengo) - CREMONA (Church of S. Pietro al Po): *Pietà* - PARMA (Cathedral): *Scenes of Christ's Life* (12 frescoes).

AUCTION RECORDS:

PARIS, 1858, *Study of Draped Woman* (bistre drawing) FRF 10. LONDON, 27-29 May 1935, *Ceiling Decoration* (drawing) GBP 6; *Madonna and Child* (drawing) GBP 9. LYONS, 21 May 1987, *Study of Draped Woman* (pen and brown wash, 11 x 6 1/4 ins / 27 x 16 cm) FRF 48,000. LONDON, 2 July 1990, *Sketch for a Hexagonal Ceiling Representing Jupiter Crowning Justice and Putti Bringing her Attributes* (ink heightened with white/grey-green paper, 11 1/4 x 12 3/4 ins / 28.7 x 32.5 cm) GBP 2,860. NEW YORK, 21 Jan 2003, *Design for the Decoration of a Spandrel* (red chalk, 17 x 10 ins / 43 x 26 cm) USD 11,000. VENICE, 14 Dec 2003, *Deposition* (oil on board, 40 x 32 ins / 102 x 82 cm) EUR 96,000.

GAMBART, Jean-Hector-Henri
French, 19th century.
Born 1854, in Péronne (Somme); died 1891.
Painter.

He exhibited at the Paris Salon in 1881 with a composition entitled *Little Beggar Girl*, followed in 1882 with *Pauper Family* and *Souvenir of Menton*.

MUSEUMS AND GALLERIES:

AMIENS: *Pilgrimage to the Tomb of St Valerius; Pauper Family at Bagnères-de-Luchon*.

GAMBARTES, Leonidas
Argentinian, 20th century.
Born 1909, in Rosario (Santa Fé); died 1963, in Rosario.
Painter, illustrator. Figures, landscapes.

Leonidas Gambartes studied in Rosario. He founded the *Litoral Group* and took part in exhibitions held by the group in many towns in Argentina. He also exhibited at the Venice Biennale in 1956, the San Pablo Biennale in 1957, the Brussels exhibition in 1958, the Mexico Biennale and the *150 Years of Argentinian Art* exhibition. He held his first solo exhibition in Buenos Aires in 1947 and was awarded prizes at exhibitions in Paraná, Córdoba and Tucumán.

BIBLIOGRAPHY:

Elliott, D., et al., *Art from Argentina, 1920-1994*, exhibition catalogue, MoMA, Oxford, 1994. Pachecho, M., '*Argentina*' in *Latin American Art in the Twentieth Century*, London, 1996 (ed. E. Sullivan). López Anaya, J., *Historia del arte argentino*, Buenos Aires, 1997.

AUCTION RECORDS:

NEW YORK, 17 May 1989, *Yuyera* (gesso/card, 31 1/2 x 23 1/2 ins / 80 x 60 cm) USD 9,350. NEW YORK, 20-21 Nov 1990, *Paye* (gesso/panel, 22 x 14 1/2 ins / 55 x 37 cm) USD 5,500. NEW YORK, 18-19 May 1992, *Coast* (chromogesso/card treated with gesso, 15 3/4 x 23 3/4 ins / 40 x 60.4 cm) USD 8,800. NEW YORK, 18 May 1994, *The Healers* (1951, gouache/card treated with gesso, 17 3/4 x 12 1/2 ins / 45 x 32 cm) USD 3,680. NEW YORK, 28 May 1997, *Ámbito y Figuras* (c. 1959, plaster and chrome/canvas, 24 x 34 1/4 ins / 61 x 87 cm) USD 19,550. BUENOS AIRES, 7 Sept 2004, *Figures* (print on card, 18 x 13 ins / 45 x 32 cm) USD 5,500.

GAMBASSI, Giovanni. See **GONNELLI**

GAMBAU, Antonio
Spanish, 15th century.
Born in Barcelona.
Sculptor.

Gambau is recorded, in 1426, as working on Palermo Cathedral.

GAMBEL
British, 18th century.
Active in England.
Miniaturist.

Gambel was an exhibitor at the Free Society in London in 1773.

GAMBELLO, Vittore
Italian, 15th - 16th century.
Born c. 1460, in Venice; died 1537, in Venice.
Sculptor, medallist.
Venetian School.

A pupil of Giovanni Bellini, in his drawings Vittore Gambello imitated his master's technique. He also lived in Rome and was best known as a maker of medals.

GAMBERAI, Felica
Italian, 17th century.
Active in Florence and c. 1620 in Mantua.
Sculptor (wood).

GAMBERATI, Jerome
Italian, 17th century.
Died 1628.
Painter. History painting.
Jerome Gamberati studied under J. Porta and Palma the Younger.

GAMBERINI, Giovacchino
Italian, 19th century.
Born 1859, in Ravenna.
Painter. Genre scenes.
Gamberini was a pupil of Lanfredini at the academy of fine arts in Pisa. He made his debut in Florence around 1886, and in Turin in 1889.
AUCTION RECORDS:
ROME, 22 March 1988, *Indiscretion* (oil on canvas, 7 3/4 x 6 ins / 20 x 15 cm) ITL 600,000. AMSTERDAM, 30 Oct 1991, *Juggler and Acrobat Performing Their Act before an Elegant Assembly in a Street* (oil on canvas, 21 1/2 x 25 3/4 ins / 54.5 x 65.5 cm) NLG 9,200. NEW YORK, 19 Jan 1995, *Chit-chat around a Well* (oil on canvas, 31 1/2 x 41 1/2 ins / 80 x 105.4 cm) USD 2,875. LONDON, 20 Nov 1996, *S Maria Novella, Florence* (oil on canvas, 29 1/2 x 22 3/4 ins / 75 x 58 cm) GBP 4,025.

GAMBERRUCI, Cosimo
Italian, 17th century.
Born in Florence.
Active at the beginning of the 17th century.
Painter. History painting.
Cosimo Gamberruci was a pupil of Battista Naldini. Although Gamberruci proved to be a somewhat less than successful artist, some of his work is not without redeeming qualities, such as his *St Peter Healing the Paralytic* painted for the church of S Pietro Maggiore in Florence. Gamberruci's canvases found their way into several private collections in Florence.

GAMBETELLO, Girolamo
Italian, 16th century.
Born in Fano.
Painter.
Gambetello lived in Rome and produced a number of paintings for the Vatican Palace.

GAMBEY, André
French, 19th century.
Born in Louhans (Saône-et-Loire).
Painter.
He studied at the Dijon Académie and submitted a *View of the Town and Buildings of Creusot* to the 1874 Paris Salon, followed in 1879 by a canvas entitled *Game*.

GAMBEY, Léon
French, 20th century.
Born 1883, in Chalon-sur-Saône; died 1 December 1914, in Bois d'Ailly, on the battlefield.
Painter. Military subjects.
Most of Léon Gambey's work is inspired by the Napoleonic Wars.

GAMBIER, Léon
French, 20th century.
Born 25 November 1917, in Dieppe.
Painter, illustrator, designer. Landscapes, seascapes.
Léon Gambier studied at the École des Beaux-Arts in Rouen and at the École des Arts Décoratifs in Paris, in the fresco studio in particular. He was one of the creators of the Atelier de Ville d'Avray. He exhibited at the Salon des Artistes Français in Paris, where his work was well received. He was awarded a silver medal in 1939 and the Cyrille Besset prize in 1943. He received various awards including the Salon de Boulogne prize in 1981. In 1959 Gambier was appointed official painter to the French navy. He exhibited in group exhibitions in France and abroad, including in 2003 the *Peintres Officiels de la Marine* (*Official Naval Painters*) exhibition at the Galerie St-Hubert in Paris.
MUSEUMS AND GALLERIES:
BELFAST (Ulster Mus.): *Port de Dieppe* (*Port of Dieppe*) (1948, oil on canvas).
AUCTION RECORDS:
NICE, 29 June 1977, *Young Woman with her Child* (oil on canvas, 28 1/4 x 21 1/4 ins / 72 x 54 cm) FRF 11,800.

GAMBIER, Louis
Belgian.
Painter. History painting.
MUSEUMS AND GALLERIES:
LIÈGE (musée): *The Holy Sepulchre in Jerusalem*.

GAMBIER D'HURIGNY, Maurice
French, 20th century.
Born 20th century, in Paris.
Sculptor.
Maurice Gambier d'Hurigny studied under Henri Bouchard. He exhibited in Paris at the Salon des Artistes Français, receiving various awards and distinctions.

GAMBINO, José
Spanish, 18th century.
Born at the beginning of the 18th century, in Galicia; died 24 August 1775, in Santiago de Compostela.
Sculptor.
José Gambino's father was from Genoa. He first worked in Portugal, before returning to Galicia, and is known for his statues in Orense and Santiago.
BIBLIOGRAPHY:
Álvaro, Milagros, *Gambino, 1719-1772*, Galaxia, Vigo, 1997.

GAMBINO, Manuel
Spanish, 18th century.
Active in Santiago.
Sculptor.
Manuel Gambino was the son of José Gambino.

GAMBINO, Tomás
Spanish, 18th century.
Active in Santiago.
Sculptor.
Tomás Gambino was the son of José Gambino.

GAMBLE
French, 19th century.
Active in Paris.
Engravers.
Engravers by this name are cited in *Current Art Prices*.

GAMBLE, Edwin
American, 20th century.
Born 1 October 1876, in Chicago.
Also active in France.
Painter.
Edwin Gamble was active in Paris and Evanston (USA).

GAMBLE, James
British, 19th century.
Active in London at the end of the 19th century.
Sculptor.
James Gamble exhibited at the Royal Academy in London.

GAMBLE, John Marshall
American, 19th - 20th century.

Born 25 November 1863, in New Jersey; died 7 April 1957.
Painter. Landscapes.

John Marshall Gamble studied at the San Francisco School of Design under Virgil Williams and Emil Carlsen; he then trained at the Académie Julian in Paris under Jean Paul Laurens and Benjamin-Constant, before returning to San Francisco in 1893, where he opened a studio. When the studio burned down in the fire following the earthquake of 1906, Gamble moved to Santa Barbara, where he remained for the rest of his life. He was a member of the American Federation of Art. He exhibited in several American cities including St Louis, Seattle and Los Angeles.

Auction records:

Los Angeles, 23 June 1981, *California Coastline* (oil on canvas, 20 x 30 ins / 51 x 76 cm) USD 2,600. Bolton, 17 Nov 1983, *Wooded Landscape* (oil on canvas, 18 x 24 ins / 45.7 x 61 cm) USD 1,600. Los Angeles-San Francisco, 12 July 1990, *Lupins and Poppies on the Californian Coast* (oil on canvas, 14 x 10 ins / 35.5 x 25.5 cm) USD 7,700. Los Angeles-San Francisco, 10 Oct 1990, *Wild Flowers of California* (oil on canvas, 30 x 40¼ ins / 76 x 102 cm) USD 22,000. New York, 12 April 1991, *Joyous Spring* (oil on canvas, 26 x 20 ins / 66 x 50.8 cm) USD 16,500. New York, 14 Sept 1995, *Moon Rising* (oil on canvas, 30 x 40 ins / 76.2 x 101.6 cm) USD 28,750. New York, 26 Sept 1996, *Wild Heliotrope* (oil on canvas, 25 x 30 ins / 63.5 x 76.2 cm) USD 40,250. Los Angeles, 29 April 1999, *Poppies and Lupine* (oil on canvas, 30 x 40 ins / 76 x 102 cm) USD 155,000. Los Angeles, 28 Oct 1999, *Wild Buckwheat near Ortega Hill, Santa Barbara* (c. 1915, oil on canvas, 20 x 30 ins / 51 x 76 cm) USD 130,000. Los Angeles, 3 May 2000, *Field of Wildflowers* (watercolour and gouache on board, 7 x 9 ins / 19 x 24 cm) USD 7,500. Los Angeles, 3 May 2000, *Wild Lilac and Mist* (1918, oil on canvas, 30 x 44 ins / 76 x 112 cm) USD 170,000. Pasadena, 19 June 2001, *Stream in a Landscape, Field of Yellow* (watercolour, 6 x 10 ins / 15 x 25 cm) USD 3,500. Los Angeles, 7 Nov 2001, *Spring Afternoon near Santa Barbara, Wild Mustard and Radish* (oil on canvas, 18 x 24 ins / 46 x 61 cm) USD 140,000. San Francisco, 9 June 2002, *Landscape with Poppies and Lupin* (oil on canvas, 16 x 24 ins / 41 x 62 cm) USD 140,000. Los Angeles, 20 Nov 2002, *Rising Moon* (oil on board, 30 x 25 ins / 76 x 63 cm) USD 90,000. Pasadena, 18 Feb 2003, *Poppies and Lupin in Rolling California Landscape* (oil on canvas, 14 x 20 ins / 36 x 51 cm) USD 55,000. Los Angeles, 18 June 2003, *Blooming Fields* (1903, oil on canvas, 12 x 16 ins / 30 x 41 cm) USD 60,000. Los Angeles, 28 April 2004, *Poppy Field* (oil on canvas, 30 x 40 ins / 76 x 101 cm) USD 65,000. Los Angeles, 28 April 2004, *Wild Buckwheat* (oil on canvas, 20 x 30 ins / 50 x 76 cm) USD 65,000.

GAMBLE, Roy C.

American, 20th century.
Born 1887; died 1872.
Painter.

Roy C. Gamble studied in Detroit, New York and Paris. He was a member of the Scarab Club, where he received various awards. His works are mainly found in Pennsylvania.

GAMBOA, Martin de

Spanish, 16th century.
Born 1525, in the Basque Country; died 22 February 1587, near Madrid.
Sculptor.

Martin de Gamboa was appointed by Philip II to decorate the choir stalls of the Escorial. He died before completing the task, which was continued by his son Juan Gamboa.

GAMBOGI, Émile

French, 19th century.
Born in Naples, Italy, of French parents.
Painter. Portraits.

He exhibited at the Paris Salons of 1868, 1870 and 1878.

Museums and Galleries:

Toulouse (MBA, Mus. des Augustins): *Portrait of Cardinal D'Astros; Portrait of Cardinal Desprez.*

Auction records:

London, 24 June 1981, *Young Woman at her Piano* (1861, oil on canvas, 30¼ x 24½ ins / 77 x 62 cm) GBP 800. Paris, 30 April 1999, *Woman with Cockatoos* (oil on canvas, 24 x 31 ins / 61 x 78 cm) FRF 30,000. Toulouse, 12 Nov 2003, *Portrait of Young Girl* (oil on canvas, 51 x 38 ins / 129 x 96 cm) EUR 2,700. Toulouse, 12 Nov 2003, *Portrait of Two Young Women* (oil on canvas, 61 x 49 ins / 155 x 124 cm) EUR 3,400.

GAMBOGI, Fanny

Maiden name: Taillefer
French, 19th century.
Born in Toulouse.
Painter.

She exhibited at the Paris Salon from 1850 to 1879. Examples of her work include *Charity, Before School, Branches* and *Serenade.*

Auction records:

Paris, 15 May 1931, *Empress Eugénie at St-Cloud,* FRF 150. London, 20 March 2003, *Rest on the Journey* (1882, oil on canvas, 19 x 26 ins / 49 x 65 cm) GBP 1,200.

GAMBOGI, Raffaello

Italian, 20th century.
Born 1874, in Livorno; died 1943.
Painter. Genre scenes.

Museums and Galleries:

Helsinki: *Tired.*

Auction records:

Milan, 30 Oct 1984, *Peasant Woman on a Sunlit Road* (oil on panel, 14½ x 14½ ins / 37 x 37 cm) ITL 2,600,000. Milan, 30 May 1990, *Piazza Nibbiaia in Livorno* (oil on canvas/card, 10½ x 13¾ ins / 26.5 x 35 cm) ITL 2,200,000. London, 20 Nov 1996, *Rest during the Harvest* (1896, oil on canvas, 47¼ x 94½ ins / 120 x 240 cm) GBP 47,700. Helsinki, 10 May 2001, *Girl in an Alley* (oil on panel, 11 x 6 ins / 27 x 14 cm) FIM 20,000. Helsinki, 10 May 2001, *Picking Berries* (oil on canvas, 28 x 16 ins / 71 x 41 cm) FIM 20,000.

GAMBOMÉ

French, 19th century.
Active in Marseilles, during the second half of the 19th century.
Painter. Portraits.

Auction records:

Paris, 1894, *Neapolitan Woman,* FRF 67; *A Philosopher,* FRF 58.

GAMBONE, Bruno

Italian, 20th century.
Born 1936, in Viehisul-Mare.
Painter.

Bruno Gambone lived in New York from 1963 to 1968, which is where he held his first exhibition. He then returned to Italy, where he began showing his work.

Gambone's painting is primarily a study of space. His canvases are monochrome reliefs. He plays with perceived space, superimposing canvases of different formats, or playing with angles in relief.

GAMBORG, Knud Frederik

Danish, 19th century.
Born 30 June 1828, in Tikøb; died 3 January 1900, in Copenhagen.
Painter, illustrator.

Knud Frederik Gamborg travelled in Italy and was particularly interested in caricature.

AUCTION RECORDS:
COPENHAGEN, 21 May 1997, *Infantrymen at the Colosseum* ($38^{1/2}$ x $61^{3/4}$ ins / 98 x 157 cm) DKK 22,000.

GAMBORINO, Miguel
Spanish, 18th - 19th century.
Born 1760, in Valencia; died c. 1828, in Madrid.
Painter, engraver.

Miguel Gamborino studied at the Academia de San Carlos in Valencia, and is known mainly as an engraver.

BIBLIOGRAPHY:
Calvo Torija, José Antonio, *Los gritos de Madrid: colección de setenta y dos grabados de Miguel Gamborino*, Guillermo Blázquez, Madrid, 1997.

GAMBS, J.
German, 18th century.
Born in Freiburg im Brisgau (Baden-Württemberg); died 1751.
Painter.

Gambs worked for the castle of Ebnet and for the churches in Sölden and Riegel.

GAMBS, Philippe Charles
French, 18th century.
Active in Paris in 1774.
Painter.

A member of the Académie de St-Luc, Philippe Gambs featured in the exhibition of this society in 1774 with several miniature portraits.

GAMBUS
French, 20th century.
Painter, draughtsman. Urban landscapes, still-lifes, flowers.

Gambus took part in group exhibitions, including the Salon d'Automne in Paris. He has also shown his work in solo exhibitions, in 1980 at the Musée des Beaux-Arts in Valence. Gambus depicts the everyday in a warm palette of tones using broad brushwork and heavily applied pigment.

BIBLIOGRAPHY:
Gambus, exhibition leaflet, Musée des Beaux-Arts, Valence, 1980.

GAMBUT, P.
French, 20th century.
Born 1871, in Tournus; died 1937, in Paris.
Painter. Landscapes.

P. Gambut exhibited in Paris at the Salon des Indépendants.

GAMEIRO, Roque. See **ROQUE GAMEIRO**

GAMEL, Adèle
French, 19th century.
Died 1889.
Painter. Portraits, landscapes.

Adèle Gamel was one of eight children and was the cousin of the painter Blanc-Fontaine. With her sisters Hélène and Annette she belonged to the small cultural circle of 'La Plaine' in St-Martin d'Hères, near Grenoble, active from 1830 to 1840. Their father, a confectionery wholesaler, had in fact restored and turned into a factory the old premises of the convent of Minims of la Plaine, and several other artists liked to join this bucolic group. The painter Diodore Rahoult who often visited with Blanc-Fontaine depicted them in his painting: *Three Young Ladies in Spring Costume*. With her sister Annette she frequented the studio of Fantin the Elder, one of the numerous visitors to La Plaine. Subsequently she entered the Orders, joining the Daughters of Charity at the Military Hospital of the Valley of Grace using the name of her sister Julie.

She did not show her work in any public exhibition but was represented in the retrospective of the Amis des Arts (Friends of the Arts) in Grenoble in 1932. In 2003 her work appeared in the thematic collective *Femmes peintres en Dauphiné XIXe et XXe siècles* (*Women Painters in the Dauphiné in the 19th and 20th Centuries*) in the Musée de Mainssieux in Voiron.

Adèle Gamel executed portraits of their family circle, painting oils on paper which she did not sign, and it has been possible to record very few of her paintings. She and her sister Annette worked in symbiosis on the same subjects (often painting portraits of the same person) making it difficult to attribute the works to either one or the other. She executed copies of paintings, notably a copy of an Assumption by Murillo for the old church of St-Martin d'Hères. The painting was returned to the family when the church became disaffected. It is probable that Adèle is the author of *Christ in the Garden of Gethsemane* and of *Child Pressing Against its Guardian Angel Before the Menacing Serpent*, preserved in Corenc, as also *Allée du réservoir* depicting her sister Hélène.

BIBLIOGRAPHY:
Femmes peintres en Dauphiné XIXe et XXe siècles, group exhibition catalogue, Musée de Mainssieux, Voiron, 2003.

GAMEL, Annette
French, 19th century.
Painter. Portraits.

Annette, with her sisters Adèle and Hélène were cousins of the painter Jules Flandrin and formed the hub of the little cultural group 'La Plaine', in St-Martin d'Hères near Grenoble around 1830 to 1840. Their father, who was a confectionery wholesaler, had restored the ancient ruins of the Convent of Minims of La Plaine in St-Martin d'Hères for use as a factory. The painter Diodore Rahoult who frequented la Plaine with their cousin the artist Blanc-Fontaine portrayed them in his painting *Three Young Ladies in Spring Costume*. Annette frequented the studio of Frantin the Elder with her sister Adèle. She married a confectioner from Grenoble, Monsieur Ravin. She did not take part in any public exhibition but her work was represented, along with that of her sister, in the retrospective of the Amis des Arts (Friends of the Arts) of Grenoble in 1932, then in 2003 in the thematic collective exhibition *Femmes peintres en Dauphiné XIXe et XXe siècles* (*Women Painters in the Dauphiné 19th and 20th Centuries*) in the Musée de Mainssieux in Voiron.

With her sister Adèle she executed copies of works and portraits of people in their circle. Her painting *Adèle Painting* (1840) is a captivating study of a young woman at work, her face hidden by curls flowing onto her cheeks. The sisters painted the same models and used the same props so it is difficult to distinguish their works from each other inasmuch as they were unsigned. Annette worked in the family workshop with the workers painting 'on sugar'.

BIBLIOGRAPHY:
Femmes peintres en Dauphiné XIXe et XXe siècles, group exhibition catalogue, Musée de Mainssieux, Voiron, 2003.

GAMEL, François
French, 18th century.
Active in Paris in 1738.
Painter, sculptor.

GAMEL, Hélène
French, 19th century.
Painter.

Hélène and her sisters Adèle and Annette were cousins of the painter Jules Flandrin and were the driving force behind the small cultural circle 'La Plaine' in St-Martin d'Hères near Grenoble which was active around 1830-1840. The painter Diodore Rahoult portrayed the sisters in his painting *Three Young Ladies in Spring Costume*. Hélène died at the age of twenty. She also worked with her sisters painting 'on sugar' in the family workshop. She was painted by her sister Adèle in the painting *L'Allée du réservoir*. None of her works have yet been recorded.

BIBLIOGRAPHY:
Femmes peintres en Dauphiné XIXe et XXe siècles, group exhibition catalogue, Musée de Mainssieux, Voiron, 2003.

GAMELIN, Jacques

French, 18th century.

Born 3 October 1738, in Carcassonne; died 12 October 1803, in Carcassonne.

Painter, watercolourist, draughtsman. History painting, religious subjects, mythological subjects, portraits, military portraits, battles, genre scenes.

Under the patronage of the Marquis of Puymaurin, Jacques Gamelin first studied at Toulouse with the Chevalier Rivalz, then came to Paris, where at the studio of Deshays he won first prize for painting. He finally went on to Rome, where he completed his artistic training with David and Vien. Gamelin got married in Rome. He was accepted into the Accademia di San Luca in 1771, and was appointed painter to the Pope Clement XIV, then professor at the Accademia di San Luca. The members of the academy offered Pope Pius VI Gamelin's acceptance picture, for which he had expressed his admiration on a visit to the academy. In 1774, he was called to Toulouse to be made professor at the academy, and two years later was made director of the École de Montpellier. As it was favourably disposed towards the ideas of the Revolution, this institution provided Gamelin with the opportunity of becoming an army painter. When he died, he was teaching at the École Central de l'Aude.

In 2003, the Musée des Beaux-Arts of Carcassonne presented the exhibition *Gamelin, peintre de batailles* (*Gamelin, Painter of Battles*) on the occasion of the bicentenary of his death.

At Perpignan, from 1784 to 1785, Gamelin did some paintings for the cathedral and for the Chapelle de la Conception. When under the command of General Dugommier in the army of the Pyrénées-Orientales with the rank and pay of a captain of the engineers, he produced, among others, four canvases (now held by the Préfecture of the Pyrénées-Orientales), which, quite apart from their artistic value, are of great local interest: *The Union Camp, The Battle of Peyrestortes*, and the portraits of Generals *Dagobert* and *Dugommier*. The 2003 Carcassonne exhibition showed examples of ancient battles inspired by Greek and Roman history based on the author Rollin, fantasy battles in which the uniforms of the horsemen are difficult to identify, and finally, pictures of the Roussillon military campaign referred to above. With his rich and varied output, imbued with powerful coloration, Jacques Gamelin is rightly regarded as one of the finest artists of the Midi.

Gamelin an 7 R

BIBLIOGRAPHY:
Michel, Olivier/Cadé, Michel, *Gamelin, peintre de batailles*, exhibition catalogue, Musée des Beaux-Arts, Carcassonne, 2003.

MUSEUMS AND GALLERIES:
AMIENS (Mus. de Picardie): *Le Grand Condé à Rocroy* (*The Great Condé at Rocroy*) (gouache) - BÉZIERS (MBA): *Titus Granting Freedom to Prisoners; Head of Child; Épisode de l'armée des Pyrénées en 1794 (Le Boulou)* (*Episode from the Army of the Pyrenees in 1794 (Le Boulou)*) (oil on canvas); *Two Seated Women* - BORDEAUX (MBA): *Socrates Drinking Hemlock; Départ d'Abradate pour le combat* (*Abradates Departing for Battle*) (oil on canvas); *Mort d'Abradate* (*Death of Abradates*) (oil on canvas) - BOURGES (Mus. du Berry): *Déroute des Perses* (*Rout of the Persians*) (drawing/paper) - CARCASSONNE (MBA): 31 further oils and 36 works on paper; *Scène de corps de garde* (*Guardroom Scene*) (oil on canvas) - MONTAUBAN (Mus. Ingres): *Combat de cavaliers* (*Cavalry in Battle*) (pen and wash/paper) - MONTPELLIER: *Drinker and his Family* - MONTPELLIER (Mus. Fabre): *Ajax défendant le corps de Patrocle contre les efforts des Troyens* (*Ajax Defending the Body of Patrocles against theTrojans.*) (drawing); *L'Ombre de Patrocle apparaît à Achille endormi* (*The Shade of Patrocles Appears to Achilles as he Sleeps*) (oil on canvas) - MUNICH (Schloss Nymphenburg): *Crossing the Bridge at Lodi* (1800, oil on canvas) - NARBONNE: three battle paintings, *Portraits by J. Gamelin* - NARBONNE (MAH): *Le Siège de Damiette* (*Siege of Damiette*) (pen and wash); *Bataille de Boulou* (*Battle of Boulou*) (drawing); *Choc de cavalerie, deux hussards dans la nuit* (*Cavalry Attack. Two Hussars in the Darkness*) (oil on canvas); *Choc de cavalerie, le passage du pont* (*Cavalry Attack. Crossing the Bridge*) (oil on canvas) - PARIS (Louvre): *Choc de cavaliers* (*Cavalry Attack*) (oil on canvas) - PERPIGNAN: *St Yves, Patron Saint of Lawyers; The Dying Christ; Birth of Jesus; Head of the Magdalene; The Dying Christ; Full-length Portrait of Frion* - PEZENSK (musée Vulliod St-Germain): *Scène de bataille* (*Battle Scene*) - ROUEN (MBA): *Bataille de cavalerie* (*Cavalry Battle*) (oil on canvas) - TOULOUSE: *Ulysses Slaughtering his Wife's Suitors* (sepias), *Death of Priam; Return of Idomeneus; Orgy* - TOULOUSE (MBA, Mus. des Augustins): *Achille traînant le corps d'Hector autour des remparts de Troie* (*Achilles Dragging the Body of Hector round the Walls of Troy*) (wash heightened with white/blue paper) - TOULOUSE (Mus. du Vieux Toulouse): *Scène de bataille antique* (*Ancient Battle Scene*) (oil on wood); *Choc de Cavalerie à l'armée des Pyrénées-Orientales* (*Cavalry Attack of the Army of the Pyrénées-Orientales*) (wash).

AUCTION RECORDS:
PARIS, 1881, *Reading the Newspaper*, FRF 200; *Spanish Brigands Attacking Travellers*, FRF 180. PARIS, 1899, *Il Berdomire* (study) FRF 125; *Feast of Bacchus* (drawing) FRF 82; *Wise Dog* (Indian ink and watercolour) FRF 130. PARIS, 8-10 June 1920, *Ancient Combat* (drawing) FRF 430. PARIS, 13 Nov 1922, *Itinerant Musicians*, FRF 2,500; *Cavalry in Combat*, FRF 1,700. PARIS, 8 Nov 1924, *Offering to the Goddess Juno* (pen and wash, heightened with gouache) FRF 1,350. PARIS, 17-18 March 1927, *Wise Dog* (watercolour) FRF 2,000. PARIS, 24 April 1929, *Peasants Dancing* (two canvases) FRF 1,250. PARIS, 20 and 21 April 1932, *Agesistrata and Archidamus Pleading with Amphares for Agis* (pen and watercolour wash) FRF 260; *Episode from the Spartan Wars* (pen and watercolour wash) FRF 220. PARIS, 30 March 1942, *Sophonisba Receiving the Poison; Biton Trailing the Chariot of Cydippe* (two watercolours/pen outlines) FRF 2,000; *The Continence of Scipio; Adoration of the Magi* (two watercolours/pen outlines) FRF 2,000. PARIS, 25 May 1945, *Bacchanalian Dance* (pen and Indian ink wash) FRF 4,600. PARIS, 27 March 1953, *Itinerant Musicians*, FRF 150,000. PARIS, 24 Nov 1972, *Cavalry in Combat; Cavalry Officer Giving Orders* (two pendants) FRF 12,000. VERSAILLES, 8 March 1981, *Portrait of a Young Revolutionary* (oil on canvas, 14 1/4 x 12 1/4 ins / 36 x 31 cm) FRF 17,000. TOULOUSE, 1 March 1983, *Adoration of the Shepherds* (1788, oil on canvas, 23 1/4 x 38 1/2 ins / 59 x 98 cm) FRF 26,000. BERN, 22 June 1984, *Battle Scene* (1793, watercolour, gouache and Indian ink, 21 x 27 3/4 ins / 53.4 x 70.5 cm) CHF 4,400. LONDON, 3 April 1985, *Horatio Killing His Sister Camilla* (oil on canvas, 12 3/4 x 16 1/4 ins / 32.5 x 41 cm) GBP 2,400. PARIS, 18 Dec 1987, *Offering to the Goddess Juno* (pen, bistre wash heightened with white gouache, 15 x 19 1/4 ins / 38 x 49 cm) FRF 28,000. PARIS, 18 Dec 1987, *Offering to the Goddess Juno* (pen, bistre wash heightened with white gouache, 15 x 19 1/2 ins / 38 x 49.5 cm) FRF 28,000. PARIS, 11 March 1988, *Scylla Walking towards the Enemy* (1792, pencil, pen and watercolour, diam. 6 ins / 15.5 cm) FRF 9,000. MONACO, 15 June 1990, *Marcus Curius Refuses Presents from the Samnites* (brown ink on black chalk, 9 3/4 x 13 ins / 24.7 x 32.8 cm) FRF 11,100. PARIS, 18 April 1991, *Death of Darius* (oil on canvas, monochrome blue paint, 25 x 38 1/4 ins / 63.5 x 97 cm) FRF

48,000. LONDON, 23 April 1993, *Defeat of Sennacherib* (oil on card, in grisaille, 10 x 12 3/4 ins / 25.3 x 32.5 cm) GBP 2,530. MONACO, 2 July 1993, *Combat at the Gates of a Town under Siege* (black chalk and wash, 18 1/2 x 23 3/4 ins / 47 x 60.5 cm) FRF 53,280. LONDON, 9 Dec 1994, *Cavaliers Attacked at Night in a Wood* (1783, oil on canvas, 23 1/2 x 38 1/2 ins / 59.6 x 97.5 cm) GBP 5,175. PARIS, 6 Nov 1995, *Scene from Ancient History* (oil on canvas, 12 1/2 x 19 ins / 32 x 48 cm) FRF 7,000. PARIS, 13 March 1995, *Battle Scene* (Indian ink and white gouache, 13 1/2 x 26 3/4 ins / 34.3 x 67.8 cm) FRF 9,000. PARIS, 1 April 1996, *Theophanes Foretelling the Future of Idomeneus* (gouache and black ink, 9 3/4 x 18 ins / 25 x 45.5 cm) FRF 15,000. PARIS, 28 June 1996, *Cavalry in Combat by a Bridge* (oil on canvas, 38 1/2 x 53 1/4 ins / 97.5 x 135 cm) FRF 48,000. PARIS, 27 June 1997, *Battle Scene* (1792, pen, watercolour, round, diam. 6 ins / 15.5 cm) FRF 7,100. LONDON, 5 July 1999, *Death of Voltaire* (oil on canvas, grisaille, 18 x 22 ins / 45 x 55 cm) GBP 1,400. PARIS, 8 Dec 1999, *Death of Pantheus* (oil on canvas, 13 x 19 ins / 32 x 49 cm) FRF 23,000. PARIS, 21 March 2002, *Cleobis and Biton Taking their Mother to Juno's Temple* (chalk, pen, ink wash, 5 x 17 ins / 13 x 42 cm) EUR 4,800. PARIS, 18 Oct 2002, *Martyrdom of Vitellius* (Indian ink wash/pen heightened with white, 16 x 21 ins / 40 x 54 cm) EUR 6,200. BERLIN, 27 Nov 2003, *'Orate ne intretis in tentationem'* (etching, 14 x 9 ins / 35 x 24 cm) EUR 3,000.

GAMEN-DUPASQUIER, Auguste-Claude-François
French, 19th century.
Born 16 July 1811, in Chambéry; died 16 May 1858, in Paris.
Painter. History painting.

He enrolled at the École des Beaux-Arts in Paris on 6 October 1832. Between 1840 and 1849 he exhibited portraits at the Paris Salon, including one of *Madame Gamen-Dupasquier, née St-Yon*. He took out French citizenship on 6 May 1848. He is remembered for a *Portrait of Prince Lucien Murat*, later engraved by Al. Fr. Girard.

GAMET, Pierre
French, 20th century.
Painter.

From 1949 to 1955, Pierre Gamet exhibited regularly at the Salon des Réalités Nouvelles in Paris, showing carefully executed abstract compositions with clear arabesque forms, painted in subtle gradations of tones.

GAMIZ, Pedro de. See **LÓPEZ DE GAMIZ**

GAML, Vital
Austrian, 19th - 20th century.
Born 18 August 1759, in Salzburg; died May 1911, in Salzburg.
Painter.

Vital Gaml studied at the Akademie der Bildenden Künste in Vienna. He is best known for flower painting.

MUSEUMS AND GALLERIES:
SALZBURG (Carolino Augusteum Mus.): several drawings.

GAMLEY, Henry Snell
British, 19th century.
Born 1865, in Logie Pert (Forfarshire), Scotland.
Sculptor.

Henry Snell Gamley was a pupil of W.D. Stevenson. He worked predominantly in Edinburgh.

GAMMA, Francesco
Italian, 18th century.
Died 1767.
Painter.

Francesco Gamma was the son of Gaspare Gamma. He was first and foremost a portraitist.

GAMMA, Gaspare
Italian, 17th - 18th century.
Born 1670, in Switzerland; died 1753, in Bologna.
Painter.

Gaspare Gamma was a pupil of Cignani.

GAMMA, Sebastiano
Italian, 18th century.
Born 1711; died 1768.
Active in Bologna.
Painter.

Sebastiano Gamma was the son of Gaspare Gamma. He worked principally for churches in Bologna.

GAMMAGE, Emma (Miss)
British, 19th century.
Active in Liverpool.
Painter. Figures.

Emma Gammage exhibited between 1865 and 1868 at the British Institution and the Suffolk Street Gallery in London.

GAMMELGAARD, Albert
Danish, 20th century.
Born 27 June 1897, in Vester Hassing; died 18 March 1963, in Copenhagen.
Painter.

GAMMELL, Robert Hale Ives
American, 20th century.
Born 1893; died 1981.
Painter.

Robert Gammell was a member of the American Federation of Art and other artists' associations.

AUCTION RECORDS:
NEW YORK, 22 Sept 1993, *End of an Era* (1967, oil/synthetic resin, 18 1/4 x 12 1/2 ins / 46.5 x 31.8 cm) USD 6,900. BOSTON, 22 Sept 2000, *Wellfleet Bay* (1962, oil on canvas, 22 x 32 ins / 56 x 81 cm) USD 5,000.

GAMMIUS, Hélène
German, 19th century.
Born 1854, in Hamburg.
Painter. Portraits, landscapes.

Gammius lived mainly in Dresden.

GAMMON, James
British, 17th century.
Active in London c. 1660.
Engraver. Portraits.

James Gammon was noted for a number of portraits. He is thought to be the same person as James Gamniou.

GAMMON, Reginald Adolphus
American, 20th century.
Born 31 March 1921, in Philadelphia.
Painter, photographer. Figure compositions, figures, portraits.
Spiral Group.

Reginald Gammon studied at the Philadelphia Museum College of Art and the Tyler School of Fine Arts, Philadelphia. He was a member of the Spiral Group and the Black Emergency Cultural Coalition (BECC), two groups of African-American artists created during the 1960s. While the Spiral Group (founded in 1963) sought to define an aesthetic theory specific to African-American culture, BECC (founded in 1969) staged protests against the exclusion of African-American artists from the institutional art world. In 1983, he took up a teaching post at Western Michigan University, Kalamazoo. He settled in Albuquerque.

Gammon's work depicts great figures in African-American history, such as *The Young Jack Johnson*, the boxing champion (1967) and *The Scottsboro Mothers* (1970), a reference to the Scottsboro trials, where a number of young blacks had been falsely accused of rape. His most famous work, however, is *Freedom Now* (1965), which was inspired by a photograph by Moneta Sleet taken during the 1963 March on Washington, at the height of the civil rights movement. Here, in a figurative work full of dramatic tension, where the use of flat colour accentuates the contrasts of the volumes, Gammon treats his figures in his customary stylised geometric manner, yet giving their faces distorting traces of expressionism. In common with many other African-American artists of the 1960s and 1970s, who were involved in the civil rights movement and the development of new cultural models, Gammon has an approach close to that of social realism.

Gammon has taken part in various group exhibitions, including in 1965, *Black and White*, a Spiral Group exhibition held in the Christopher Street Gallery, New York; 2003, *In Memory of Martin: The Living Legacy of Dr. Martin Luther King, Jr.*, Smithsonian International Gallery, Washington DC and 2003, Albuquerque Museum, Albuquerque, New Mexico. He has also had a number of solo exhibitions, including 1974, Acts of Art Gallery, New York; 1997, Impost Artspace, Albuquerque and 2003, Magnifico Gallery, Alburquerque.

Bibliography:

Baranik, Rudolf/Andrews, Benny (ed.), *Black Emergency Cultural Coalition Artists and Writers Protest Against the Vietnam War*, Attica Book, South Hackensack, 1972. *Reginald Gammon: paintings in oil and acrylics with mixed media*, exhibition catalogue, Acts of Art Gall., New York, 1974. '*Reginald Gammon: The Carnal Art of the Tattoo*' in *Black Arts Quaterly* vol. VII n° 1, periodical, Hampton University Museum, Hampton, 1982.

Museums and Galleries:

Wilberforce, OH (National Afro-American Mus. and Cultural Center): *Freedom Now* (1965).

GAMNIOU, James

British, 17th century.
Active in London c. 1660.
Engraver.

James Gamniou produced a number of portraits painted in a rather stiff and conventional style, among them likenesses of Queen Catherine of Braganza, Henry, Duke of Gloucester, Richard Cromwell and Edward Mascall. He and James Gammon are thought to be one and the same.

GAMOND, Elisa de

Flemish School, 19th century.
Active in Brussels, c. 1837.
Painter. Genre scenes.

She was a pupil of Jos Paelinck.

GAMOT

French, 18th - 19th century.
Born 1771.
Painter. History painting.

Gamot was a student at the school of drawing in Lille. He exhibited at its Salon as early as 1784.

GAMOT, Joseph

French, 18th century.
Active in Lille at the beginning of the 18th century.
Draughtsman. Portraits.

Joseph Gamot is certainly the same artist as the medallist who worked under this name.

GAMOT Y LLURIA, José

Spanish, 19th century.
Born in Barcelona; died 1890, in Barcelona.
Sculptor.

José Gamot y Lluria studied under Novas and at the school of fine arts in Barcelona. He first exhibited in 1876 in Madrid.

GAMP, Ludwig

German, 19th - 20th century.
Born 1855, in Germany; died 23 May 1910, in Munich.
Sculptor.

Ludwig Gamp was a pupil of Widnmann.

GAMPENRIEDER, Karl

German, 19th century.
Born 1 February 1860, in Munich.
Painter. History painting, portraits, genre scenes.

Gampenrieder was a pupil at the academy in Munich, studying under J. Benczur, Alex Wagner and W. Lindenschmit. He continued his studies in Paris with Bouguereau and Robert-Fleury. He is noted for his *Princess Elvira of Bavaria*.

Auction records:

Retford, 30-31 May 1946, *The Introduction*, GBP 44. London, 24 June 1987, *Well-Dressed Woman in front of a Mirror* (1883, oil on canvas, 43 1/4 x 28 ins / 110 x 71 cm) GBP 3,400. London, 23 March 1988, *Tea Time* (oil on canvas, 56 3/4 x 38 1/2 ins / 144 x 98 cm) GBP 8,250.

GAMPER, Gustav Adolf

Swiss, 20th century.
Born 10 September 1873, in Troyen; died 1948, in Zurich.
Painter, draughtsman, engraver.

Gustav Gamper studied at the academies in Karlsruhe and Stuttgart. He began exhibiting in 1897.

GAMPER, Johann

Swiss, 17th - 18th century.
Born c. 1655; died 1 January 1738.
Active in Jauer (now Jawor, Poland).
Painter.

GAMPERT, Jean-Louis

Swiss, 20th century.
Born 1884, in Geneva; died 1943.
Active in France.
Painter, decorative designer. Landscapes, still-lifes. Designs for tapestries.

Jean-Louis Gampert studied at the Munich academy, then with Paul Sérusier in Paris. He exhibited at various Paris Salons.

He painted light, calm compositions, especially landscapes, and was clearly influenced by the work of his friend Roger de la Fresnay, who in turn was influenced by Synthetic Cubism. A lot of his work was in the field of decoration, including designs for seats and other furniture, and cartoons for tapestries.

GAMPERT, Otto

Swiss, 19th - 20th century.
Born 27 October 1842, in Ottenbach (Zurich); died 1924, in Zurich.
Painter, engraver. Landscapes, landscapes with figures, mountainscapes, waterscapes.

Otto Gampert exhibited in Munich, notably in 1888 and 1889.

Museums and Galleries:

Munich (Pinakothek): *The Inn at Mühldorf*.

Auction records:

Lucerne, 25 June 1976, *Landscape with Pond* (oil on canvas, 35 1/2 x 55 ins / 90 x 140 cm) CHF 2,200. Zurich, 7 Nov 1981, *View of Gothard* (oil on canvas, 16 1/4 x 13 1/2 ins / 41.5 x 34.5 cm) CHF 750. Bern, 6 May 1983, *Stormy Landscape, Munich* (oil on canvas, 23 1/4 x 28 3/4 ins / 59 x 73 cm) CHF 4,000. Bern, 28 May 1985, *Still-life in a Kitchen* (oil on canvas, 18 1/2 x 26 3/4 ins / 47 x 68 cm) CHF 2,200. Bern, 26 Oct 1988, *The Stilserjoch* (oil on canvas, 17 3/4 x 13 1/2 ins / 45 x 34.5 cm) CHF 700. Cologne, 18 March 1989, *Sheep near a Stream* (oil on canvas, 22 3/4 x 35 1/2 ins / 58 x 90 cm) DEM 5,500. Zurich, 3 April 1996, *Spring* (oil on canvas, 12 3/4 x 18 3/4 ins / 32.5 x 47.7 cm) CHF 1,200.

GAMROTH, Johannes
German, 18th century.
Died 1733, in Oppeln, Silesia (now Opole, Poland).
Painter.

GAMSARAGAN, Daria
Egyptian, 20th century.
Born 24 April 1907, in Alexandria; died 1 March 1986.
Active from 1925 in France.
Sculptor, medallist.

Daria Gamsaragan went to France to study sculpture, settling there in 1925. She entered the academy of La Grande Chaumière and became a pupil of Bourdelle. She also worked with Csaky and Constant. From 1927 to 1939 she exhibited her work in Paris at the Tuileries Salon and the Salon d'Automne. Gamsaragan took part in the Venice Biennale and in the Paris Exposition Universelle. After the war, she presented her work at the Salon Comparaisons and the Salon d'Automne in Paris, as well as at exhibitions of sculpture organised by the Rodin and Bourdelle museums.

Gamsaragan specialised in sculpture in miniature, and in this capacity worked for jewellers and fashion houses. She was also a portrait artist and was awarded many medals. Under the pseudonym of Anna Sarag she published *Journey with a Shadow* and *Ring of Fire*.

MUSEUMS AND GALLERIES:
ALEXANDRIA (MMA) - CAEN (MBA) - CAIRO (Egyptian MMA) - PARIS (MAMVP).

GAMSER, Joseph
Swiss, 18th century.
Glass painter.

GAN, Gösta. See **ADRIAN-NILSSON**

GANA, Antonio
Chilean, 19th century.
Born 1822; died 1847.
Painter.

Antonio Gana worked in Santiago and travelled in Europe.

GANAHL, Rainer
Austrian, 20th - 21st century.
Born 1961, in Bindenz.
Active in the USA.
Assemblage artist, installation artist.
Conceptual Art.

Ganahl lives and works in New York. He presents his work in the form of series, as an informative exercise with no frills. His work includes objects such as doormats and disks, slide projections and murals reproducing enlarged computer language onto the various walls of the exhibition venue. He has participated in various exhibitions and has held solo shows: 1989, the Museum Folkwang, Essen; 1991, New York; 1992, the Galerie Roger Pailhas, Paris; 1992, the Dallas Museum of Art, Dallas; 1993, the Galerie Roger Pailhas, Marseilles; 2000, Toronto; 2001 Milan, New York, Vienna and Brussels; 2005, Vienna, New York, Hong Kong and Brussels.

BIBLIOGRAPHY:
Schwabsky, Barry, '*À propos de l'art de Rainer Ganahl*' in *Art Press* no. 179, periodical, Paris, April 1993.

GANAL
French, 18th century.
Active in Paris in 1770.
Painter, sculptor.

Ganal is possibly to be identified with Ferdinand Ganal.

GANAL, Ferdinand
German, 18th century.
Active in Saarlouis (Saarland).
Sculptor.

Ganal also worked in Saarbrücken.

GANASSINI, Marzio
Italian, 17th century.
Active in Rome.
Painter. History painting.

Marzio Ganassini worked for various churches.

GANAY, Isabelle de
French, 20th - 21st century.
Born 1960.
Painter. Landscapes.

Isabelle de Ganay trained at the École de Beaux-Arts of Rouen and at the Académie Julian and the École des Beaux-Arts in Paris. She has exhibited at the Salon des Artistes Français in Paris, of which she is a member. Her work has also been shown in solo exhibitions, notably at the Galerie Katia Granoff in Paris in 1993. She has received several awards.

I de Ganay

I de Ganay

AUCTION RECORDS:
PARIS, 20 Nov 1991, *Snow along the Banks of the Seine* (oil on canvas, 28 3/4 x 23 1/2 ins / 73 x 60 cm) FRF 10,000. PARIS, 2 June 1993, *Monet's House* (oil on canvas, 15 x 18 ins / 38 x 46 cm) FRF 16,000. CALAIS, 4 July 1993, *Orchard in Blossom* (oil on canvas, 32 x 39 1/4 ins / 81 x 100 cm) FRF 12,000. WASHINGTON, 14 Dec 2002, *Figures Resting on a Hillside along the Coast of Menton* (1932, oil on canvas, 54 x 77 ins / 137 x 195 cm) USD 8,500.

GANAY, Sébastien de
French, 20th century.
Painter.

Sébastien de Ganay first exhibited in Paris in a solo exhibition at the Galerie Jacqueline Moussion.

His work is suggestive of Abstract Expressionism but is based on an original process. He covers the stretcher with sheets of plastic film containing paint and waits for several weeks for the colour to set.

BIBLIOGRAPHY:
Davila, Thierry, '*Sébastien de Ganay*' in *Art Press* n° 198, periodical, Paris, January 1995.

GANBARDELLA, Spiridone.
See **GAMBARDELLA**

GANCHON, Pierre, or Gauchon
French, 16th - 17th century.
Painter.

Adopted by the *Aumône Générale* (a charitable almsgiving body) in Lyons, Ganchon asked permission to serve his apprenticeship in Mâcon with a stained glass maker. He was established in Toulouse by the early years of the 17th century.

GAND, de. See first name

GAND, Henri. See **GOUDT Hendrick**

GANDARA, de La. See **LA GANDARA**

GANDARIAS, Justo de
Spanish, 19th century.
Born in the 19th century, in Barcelona.
Sculptor.

Justo de Gandarias first exhibited in Madrid in 1881 and later exhibited frequently at Salons in Paris. He received a commendation in 1878 at the Universal Exhibition.

MUSEUMS AND GALLERIES:
MADRID: *Child and Duck*; *Love and Interest*.

GANDAT
French, 18th century.
Died 1797, in Ermenonville, near Paris.
Painter.
Gandat exhibited at the Salon de la Jeunesse in 1779 and painted a landscape depicting Rousseau's tomb.

GANDI, Bonaventura
Italian, 17th - 18th century.
Active in Florence.
Painter.

GANDI, Giacomo
Italian, 19th century.
Born 1846 or 1850, in Savigliano (Piedmont).
Painter. Genre scenes.
Initially a pupil of Castaldi in Turin, Gandi went to Rome to finish his studies. He exhibited in Turin, Milan and Rome, and was decorated with the title of Knight of the Order of the Crown.
AUCTION RECORDS:
MILAN, 12 Dec 1985, *The Little Cobbler* (oil on canvas, 17 3/4 x 17 1/4 ins / 45 x 44 cm) ITL 7,000,000.

GANDIA, Juan Fernandez de
Spanish, 18th century.
Active c. 1720.
Painter. Landscapes, architectural views, perspectives.
AUCTION RECORDS:
PARIS, 1822, *Landscape, Workshops, Turret, Pond,* FRF 190.

GANDIER, Pierre Antoine
French, 18th century.
Active in Paris in 1765.
Painter, sculptor.

GANDINI, Antonio
Italian, 17th century.
Born in Brescia; died 17 July 1630, in Ronchi.
Painter. History painting, portraits.
Antonio Gandini was a pupil of Paolo Veronese. His principal work is a *Crucifixion* for the former cathedral of Brescia.

GANDINI, Bernardino
Italian, 17th century.
Born 1587; died 1651.
Active in Brescia.
Painter.
Bernardino Gandini was the son of Antonio Gandini. He painted predominantly religious themes.

GANDINI, Carlo Antonio
Italian, 17th century.
Active in Brescia.
Painter.
Carlo Antonio Gandini was the son of Bernardino Gandini.

GANDINI, Domenico
Italian, 19th century.
Active in Milan.
Engraver.
Domenico Gandini is remembered for his engravings of works by Bassano and Perugino.

GANDINI, Francesco
Italian, 18th century.
Born 4 October 1723, in Cremona; died c. 1778, in St Petersburg.
Painter, engraver.
Francesco Gandini was a pupil of Subleyras, on whose death Gandini toured the principal courts of Europe, painting and engraving portraits.

GANDINI, Giorgio, also known as Gandini del Grano
Italian, 16th century.
Born c. 1489, in Parma; died 1538, in Parma.
Painter. History painting.
It has been suggested that Gandini was a pupil of Correggio, who often put the finishing touches to his works. It has also been suggested that he is the author of the large S Michele altar painting, wrongly attributed by Ruta to Lelio Orsi. It is possible to see two paintings by Gandini - *Penitent Magdalene* and *Holy Family* - in the Oldenbourg Gallery, while his *Picture with Entire Figures* is displayed in the Constance Museum.
AUCTION RECORDS:
LONDON, 16-17 April 1997, *Madonna and Child with St John the Baptist and Canonised Bishops* (red chalk heightened with white, 6 x 6 ins / 15.2 x 14.3 cm) GBP 1,610.

GANDINI, Marcolini
Italian, 20th century.
Born 1937, in Turin.
Painter.
AUCTION RECORDS:
ROME, 3 Dec 1985, *Dipinto No 1* (1965, oil on moulded canvas, 47 1/4 x 51 1/4 ins / 120 x 130 cm) ITL 1,200,000.

GANDINI, Mardino
Italian, 20th century.
Born 6 March 1937, in Turin.
Painter.
Mardino Gandini's paintings are abstract, with geometric segments cut out and arranged like giant jigsaw puzzles.

GANDINI, Saverio
Italian, 18th century.
Born c. 1729, in Cremona; died 9 March 1796, in Brescia.
Painter. Architectural views.
Saverio Gandini studied under Bibiena.

GANDOLFI, Antonio
Italian, 19th century.
Born 1821, in Bologna.
Painter.
Antonio Gandolfi worked for Forlì Cathedral.

GANDOLFI, Camilla
Maiden name: Guiscardi
Italian, 19th century.
Born in Genoa.
Painter, lithographer.
Camilla Gandolfi is remembered for her *Portrait of Queen Marie Adelaide of Piedmont with Her Daughter Clotilda*.

GANDOLFI, Democrito
Italian, 19th century.
Born 1797, in Bologna; died 1874, in Bologna.
Sculptor.
Democrito Gandolfi was the son of Mauro Gandolfi. He studied sculpture in Milan, and sculpted several major monuments.
MUSEUMS AND GALLERIES:
AMIENS: *Beggar Woman; Woman Crying.*
AUCTION RECORDS:
MONTE CARLO, 14 June 1982, *Bust of a Woman* (1825, white marble, h. 22 ins / 56 cm) FRF 12,000.

GANDOLFI, Francesco
Italian, 19th century.
Born 1824, in Chiavari (Liguria); died 1873, in Chiavari.
Painter.
Francesco Gandolfi studied under Baratta and Bezzuoli.

GANDOLFI, Gaetano
Italian, 18th century.
Born 30 August 1734, in San Matteo della Decima; died 30 June 1802, in Bologna.

Painter, sculptor, engraver, draughtsman. Religious subjects, allegorical subjects, mythological subjects, nudes, portraits.

Gaetano Gandolfi was taught initially by his older brother Ubaldo. He went on to study at the fine arts academy in Bologna under Stefano Torelli, Ercole Graziani the Younger and Ercole Lelli. He spent a study year in Venice before settling definitively in Bologna, where he was elected to membership of the Clementina Academy in 1760.

During his time in Bologna, Gandolfi painted an *Assumption* for the ceiling of the church of S Maria della Vita and a *Wedding Feast in Cana* for the church of Santissimo Salvatore. In Naples he painted a *Martyrdom of St Pantaleon* and a self-portrait for the church of S Girolimini. As an engraver he is perhaps best remembered for an *Adoration of the Shepherds* from an original by Niccolo dell'Abate in the Palazzo Leoni in Bologna, and versions of Guido Reni's *St Peter* and *St Paul*.

A number of retrospectives have focused on the work of the Gandolfi artist dynasty, including *I Gandolfi: Ubaldo, Gaetana, Mauro. Disegni Dipinti* (*The Gandolifis: Ubaldo, Gaetana, Mauro. Drawings and Paintings*) held at the Isola de S Giorgio Maggiore in Venice in 1987 and subsequently at the Palazzo Pepoli Campogrande in Bologna; *Bella Pittura: The Art of the Gandolfi* mounted in 1993 at the National Gallery of Canada in Ottawa and at the Arkansas Art Centre in Little Rock; and *Gaetano e Ubaldo Gandolfi: Opere Scelte* (*Gaetano and Ubaldo Gandolfi: Selected Works*), an exhibition of selected works by the two artists at the San Lorenzo Auditorium in Cento in 2002.

BIBLIOGRAPHY:

Bettagno, Alessandro (ed.), *I Gandolfi: Ubaldo, Gaetano, Mauro. Disegni e dipinti*, travelling exhibition catalogue, Isola di San Giorgio maggiore, Venezia, Palazzo Pepoli Campogrande, Bologna, Neri Pozza, Vicenza, 1987. Cazort, Mimi/Perini, Giovanna, *Bella pittura: the art of the Gandolfi*, travelling exhibition catalogue, Arkansas Arts Center, Little Rock (USA, AR), National Gall. of Canada, Ottawa, 1993 (text in English and French). Biagi Maino, Donatella, *Gaetano Gandolfi*, monograph, Umberto Allemandi, Turin, 1995.

MUSEUMS AND GALLERIES:

BALTIMORE (Walters AM): *Wedding Feast at Cana* (sketch) - BOLOGNA (Mus. Civico) - BOLOGNA (Pinacoteca Nazionale): *Wedding Feast at Cana* - NAPLES (Pinacoteca): *Self-portrait* - PARIS (Louvre): *Allegoria della Giustizia* (*Allegory of Justice*) - PISA (Mus. Civico): *Foundation for Foundling Children*.

AUCTION RECORDS:

LONDON, 7-8 Nov 1910, *Adoration of the Shepherds* (sepia) GBP 6; *Charity* (drawing) GBP 6. PARIS, 29 Oct 1937, *Venus Asking Vulcan to Forge Arms for Aeneas*, FRF 1,850. LONDON, 14 June 1961, *Christ and the Woman Taken in Adultery*, GBP 1,800. LONDON, 10 April 1970, *Head of a Young Girl*, Gns 4,200. LONDON, 30 March 1976, *Portrait of a Young Boy* (drawing, 13 x 9 3/4 ins / 33 x 24.7 cm) GBP 1,700. VIENNA, 13 June 1978, *Liberation of St Peter* (oil on canvas, 37 1/2 x 27 1/2 ins / 95.5 x 70 cm) ATS 280,000. LONDON, 22 June 1978, *Young Man Sleeping* (1762, terracotta, 11 1/2 x 19 3/4 ins / 29 x 50 cm) GBP 4,000. NEW YORK, 5 June 1979, *St Roch before Kneeling Figures* (pen and wash/traces of black chalk, 11 x 7 1/2 ins / 28 x 19 cm) USD 2,600. LONDON, 9 Dec 1980, *Reclining Nude Seen from Behind* (red chalk/paper, 10 1/2 x 17 1/4 ins / 26.5 x 44 cm) GBP 2,200. MILAN, 24 Nov 1983, *Children Reading* (charcoal and pastel, 13 1/4 x 9 ins / 33.5 x 23 cm) ITL 16,000,000. NEW YORK, 19 Jan 1984, *Jesus and the Adulteress* (oil on canvas, 37 x 44 ins / 94 x 112 cm) USD 23,000. PARIS, 20 March 1985, *Study of Female Legs and Torso* (lead pencil and stump, 16 1/2 x 11 3/4 ins / 42 x 30 cm) FRF 80,000. LONDON, 13 Dec 1985, *Allegory: Young Cavalier Firing a Pistol at the Statue of an Old Man* (oil on canvas, 30 1/4 x 23 ins / 76.9 x 57.5 cm) GBP 15,000. PARIS, 4 March 1988, *Study of a Seated Male Nude* (red chalk, 16 1/4 x 11 3/4 ins / 41 x 30 cm) FRF 21,000. MONACO, 16 June 1989, *Holy Family* (oil on canvas, 34 1/4 x 27 1/4 ins / 87 x 69 cm) FRF 488,400. NEW YORK, 11 Jan 1990, *Holy Family* (oil on canvas, 25 1/2 x 29 1/2 ins / 65 x 75 cm) USD 45,100. ROME, 8 March 1990, *Portrait of an Adolescent* (1767, oil on canvas, 19 x 15 ins / 48 x 38 cm) ITL 50,000,000. NEW YORK, 5 April 1990, *Holy Family with God the Father and the Holy Ghost* (oil on canvas, 17 x 13 ins / 43 x 33 cm) USD 49,500. LONDON, 2 July 1990, *Samson and Delilah* (ink and wash heightened with white, a pair, each 6 x 6 3/4 ins / 15 x 17.2 cm) GBP 12,100. LONDON, 6 July 1990, *Head in Profile: Bearded Old Man* (oil on canvas, 17 1/4 x 13 1/4 ins / 43.6 x 33.7 cm) GBP 71,500. NEW YORK, 8 Jan 1991, *Martyrdom of St Eusebius* (ink and wash, 11 3/4 x 8 1/4 ins / 30 x 20.9 cm) USD 17,600. NEW YORK, 11 Jan 1991, *Assumption of the Virgin* (oil on canvas, 37 1/4 x 53 1/2 ins / 94.6 x 135.8 cm) USD 495,000. NEW YORK, 14 Jan 1992, *Triumphal Procession Entering a City* (ink/black chalk, 15 1/4 x 20 ins / 39 x 51 cm) USD 27,500. LONDON, 6 July 1992, *Head Studies* (ink, 11 1/4 x 8 ins / 28.7 x 20.6 cm) GBP 3,410. SCEAUX, 13 Dec 1992, *The Four Seasons* (set of four oils on canvas, each 17 1/4 x 13 3/4 ins / 44 x 35 cm) FRF 1,800,000. NEW YORK, 13 Jan 1993, *Pluto and Persephone on the Styx with Charon* (1798, black chalk, 13 x 15 1/2 ins / 33.3 x 39.2 cm) USD 26,400. NEW YORK, 15 Jan 1993, *Isaac Receiving Jacob's Blessing* (oil on canvas, 63 x 47 1/4 ins / 160 x 120 cm) USD 145,500. NEW YORK, 12 Jan 1995, *Head of a Young Man Looking Up to the Left* (red and white chalk/buff-coloured paper, 12 1/2 x 8 1/2 ins / 31.5 x 21.5 cm) USD 21,850. LONDON, 3 July 1995, *Page of Head Studies with Various Hairstyles* (ink, 11 1/2 x 8 ins / 29 x 20.3 cm) GBP 24,150. AVIGNON, 1 Oct 1995, *Portrait of a Bearded Man with a Turban* (oil on canvas, 25 1/2 x 21 1/4 ins / 65 x 54 cm) FRF 150,000. LONDON, 3 July 1996, *Plan for a Ceiling Decoration: Virgin in Glory with the Prophets* (ink and wash, 8 3/4 x 11 3/4 ins / 22.1 x 29.9 cm) GBP 5,750. NEW YORK, 29 Jan 1997, *Portrait of a Young Boy* (red and black chalk, 6 1/4 x 5 ins / 15.6 x 11.8 cm) USD 14,950. NEW YORK, 30 Jan 1997, *San Giacomo della Marca with St Marguerite and San Diego Caring for an Invalid* (oil on canvas, 19 3/4 x 12 1/2 ins / 50.2 x 31.8 cm) USD 63,000. LONDON, 18 April 1997, *Profile Bust oif Young Girl with a Rose in her Hair* (oil on canvas, 17 1/4 x 13 1/4 ins / 44 x 33.6 cm) GBP 43,300. LONDON, 2 July 1997, *Five Young Women with Elaborate Hairstyles* (pen and brown ink, study, 7 3/4 x 10 3/4 ins / 20 x 27.3 cm) GBP 17,250. NEW YORK, 30 Jan 1998, *Portrait of a Woman with an Earring* (c. 1768, oil on canvas) USD 40,250. NEW YORK, 29 Jan 1999, *St Cecilia* (1791, oil on canvas, 16 x 12 ins / 41 x 31 cm) USD 660,000. LONDON, 17 Dec 1999, *Allegory of Prudence. Allegory of Temperance* (oil on canvas, pair, 13 x 17 ins / 34 x 44 cm) GBP 55,000. NEW YORK, 27 Jan 2000, *Studies of Head of a Young Man and Girl* (oil on canvas, 20 x 14 ins / 51 x 36 cm) USD 92,000. LONDON, 4 July 2000, *Pentecost* (black chalk/pen/brown ink/grey wash, 7 x 6 ins / 18 x 15 cm) GBP 3,200. NEW YORK, 23 May 2001, *Christ and the Woman Taken in Adultery* (oil on canvas, 37 x 44 ins / 94 x 112 cm) USD 60,000. LONDON, 10 July 2001, *An Allegory of Justice* (black and white chalk, 17 x 12 ins / 43 x 31 cm) GBP 32,000. PARIS, 21 March 2002, *Studies of Heads* (pen/ink, 8 x 6 ins / 21 x 15 cm) EUR 8,000. MILAN, 7 May 2002, *Massacre of the Lambs* (pen/ink/watercolour, 8 x 6 ins / 21 x 14 cm) EUR 8,240. PARIS, 27 March 2003, *Studies of Heads* (pen/ink, 6 x 7 ins / 14 x 19 cm) EUR 15,000. ST. LOUIS, 21 June 2003, *Sleeping Endymion* (oil on canvas, 13 x 15 ins / 33 x 38 cm) USD 17,000. NEW YORK, 21 Jan 2004, *Study of Five Heads* (pen/brown ink, 9 x 7 ins / 23 x 17 cm) USD 10,000. NEW YORK, 22 Jan 2004, *Judith and Esther, with Other*

Figures on a Cloud (black and white chalk, 17 x 13 ins / 42 x 32 cm) USD 6,500.

GANDOLFI, Luigi

Italian, 19th century.

Born 1810, in Turin; died 12 November 1869, in Turin.

Miniaturist.

Luigi Gandolfi was a student of Biscarra at the academy in Turin.

GANDOLFI, Mauro

Italian, 18th - 19th century.

Born 18 September 1764, in Bologna; died 4 January 1834, in Bologna.

Painter, watercolourist, engraver, draughtsman.

Religious subjects, mythological subjects, portraits.

Mauro Gandolfi studied initially under his father Gaetano Gandolfi. At an early age he joined the army and was stationed with his regiment in Paris. He later visited England, where he worked under Sharp and Bartolozzi. This was followed by some time in Rome. When his work was criticised, Gandolfi promptly left Europe, travelling first to North America, then to Africa. By 1821 he was back working in Bologna.

Gandolfi started out painting in oils but during his stay in Paris he began to concentrate on engraving. His first major engraving was a version of his father's *Diogenes and Alexander*. During his productive period in Bologna, he engraved works by Corregio. Typical examples of his work include *Jesus as a Child Asleep on the Cross* and *Judith Holding the Head of Holofernes*.

A number of retrospectives have been held to celebrate the work of the Gandolfi family. Among the more recent are *I Gandolfi: Ubaldo, Gaetano, Mauro. Disegni e Dpinti* (*The Gandolifis: Ubaldo, Gaetana, Mauro. Drawings and Paintings*) held at the Isola S Giorgio Maggiore in Venice in 1987 and subsequently at the Palazzi Pepoli Campogrande in Bologna; and *Bella Pittura: The Art of the Gandolfi* held at the National Gallery of Canada in Ottowa and at the Arkansas Art Center in Little Rock in 1993.

BIBLIOGRAPHY:

Bettagno, Alessandro (ed.), *I Gandolfi: Ubaldo, Gaetano, Mauro. Disegni e dipinti*, travelling exhibition catalogue, Isola di San Giorgio maggiore, Venezia, Palazzo Pepoli Campogrande, Bologna, Neri Pozza, Vicenza, 1987. Cazort, Mimi/Perini, Giovanna, *Bella pittura: the art of the Gandolfi*, travelling exhibition catalogue, Arkansas Arts Center, Little Rock (USA, AR), National Gall. of Canada, Ottawa, 1993 (text in English and French). Cazort, Mimi, *Mauro in America. An Italian Artist Visists the New World*, Yale University Press, London, 2003.

MUSEUMS AND GALLERIES:

BOLOGNA (Pinacoteca Nazionale).

AUCTION RECORDS:

MILAN, 29 May 1979, *Holy Family* (pen and colour wash, oval, 9¾ x 7½ ins / 25 x 19 cm) ITL 1,700,000. MILAN, 18 June 1981, *Mythological Scene* (pen and bistre wash/paper, 16¼ x 11½ ins / 41 x 29 cm) ITL 2,000,000. LONDON, 1 Dec 1983, *Dream of the Artist* (watercolour/parchment, 27¾ x 20½ ins / 70.5 x 52.3 cm) GBP 14,000. MILAN, 27 Nov 1984, *Head Studies* (pen and wash, 8¼ x 11½ ins / 20.8 x 29 cm) ITL 7,500,000. MILAN, 4 Nov 1986, *Child Portrait* (oil on canvas, 17¼ x 13¼ ins / 43.5 x 33.5 cm) ITL 10,500,000. LONDON, 6 July 1987, *Three Young Women* (red and black chalk, 7¼ x 9¼ ins / 18.5 x 23.5 cm) GBP 6,800. MILAN, 10 June 1988, *Virgin* (oil on canvas, 17½ x 13½ ins / 44.5 x 34 cm) ITL 6,500,000. NEW YORK, 11 Jan 1989, *Nine Head Studies, Including One of St Francis* (ink, 7¾ x 10¼ ins / 19.7 x 26 cm) USD 4,620. MONACO, 16 June 1989, *Portrait of a Young Girl* (oil on canvas, 16½ x 13 ins / 42 x 33 cm) FRF 310,800. LONDON, 2 July 1990, *Head Studies* (ink, 6¼ x 9¾ ins / 15.7 x 25 cm) GBP 10,450. NEW YORK, 8 Jan 1991, *Portrait of a Young Girl Reading while Resting her Chin on her Hand* (red and black chalk, 17¾ x 13½ ins / 45 x 34 cm) USD 6,600. NEW YORK, 13 Jan 1993, *Busts of Three Young Girls* (red and black chalk, 7¼ x 9¼ ins / 18.4 x 23.3 cm) USD 39,600. NEW YORK, 27 Jan 1999, *Studies of Heads* (pen/brown ink, 8 x 6 ins / 20 x 15 cm) USD 12,000. MILAN, 24 Nov 1999, *St Peter and St Paul* (tempera on vellum, 8 x 6 ins / 21 x 16 cm) ITL 17,000,000. PARIS, 27 Oct 2000, *St Anne, St Joachim and the Baby Jesus* (oil on canvas, 12 x 9 ins / 30 x 23 cm) FRF 33,000. MILAN, 8 May 2001, *Portrait of Young Woman* (brush/watercolour/vellum, 4 x 5 ins / 11 x 13 cm) ITL 13,000,000. LONDON, 11 July 2001, *Portrait of a Man, an Allegorical Female in the Background* (oil on paper/canvas, 21 x 16 ins / 53 x 40 cm) GBP 20,000.

GANDOLFI, Ubaldo

Italian, 18th century.

Born 1728, in San Matteo della Decima; died 25 July 1781, in Ravenna.

Painter, sculptor, engraver, draughtsman. Religious subjects, mythological subjects, figures, portraits.

Ubaldo Gandolfi, the older brother of Gaetano Gandolfi, studied under Stefano Torelli, Ercole Graziani the Younger and Ercole Lelli at the fine arts academy in Bologna. He decorated *palazzi* and churches in and around Bologna. Major examples from his body of work include two statues of *Prophets* for the Bologna church of S Giuliano and a series of drawings entitled *Life of Christ*. He also produced a number of anatomical studies. As Gandolfi's reputation grew, he received commissions not only from all over Italy but from as far afield as Vienna and Moscow.

A number of retrospectives have been held to celebrate the work of the Gandolfi family. Among the more recent are *I Gandolfi: Ubaldo, Gaetano, Mauro. Disegni e Dpinti* (*The Gandolifis: Ubaldo, Gaetana, Mauro. Drawings and Paintings*) held at the Isola S Giorgio Maggiore in Venice in 1987 and subsequently at the Palazzo Pepoli Campogrande in Bologna; *Bella Pittura: The Art of the Gandolfi* held at the National Gallery of Canada in Ottowa and at the Arkansas Art Center in Little Rock in 1993; and *Gaetano e Ubaldo Gandolfi: Opere Scelte* (*Gaetano and Ubaldo Gandolfi: Selected Works*), a selection of works by the two artists exhibited at the San Lorenzo Auditorium in Cento in 2002.

BIBLIOGRAPHY:

Bettagno, Alessandro (ed.), *I Gandolfi: Ubaldo, Gaetano, Mauro. Disegni e dipinti*, travelling exhibition catalogue, Isola di San Giorgio Maggiore, Venezia, Palazzo Pepoli Campogrande, Bologna, Neri Pozza, Vicenza, 1987. Biagi Maino, Donatella, *Ubaldo Gandolfi*, monograph, Umberto Allemandi, Turin, 1990. Cazort, Mimi/Perini, Giovanna, *Bella pittura: the art of the Gandolfi*, travelling exhibition catalogue, Arkansas Arts Center, Little Rock USA, AR), National Gall. of Canada, Ottawa, 1993 (text in English and French).

MUSEUMS AND GALLERIES:

BOLOGNA (Pinacoteca Nazionale): *Head of a Little Girl*; *Resurrection of Christ*; *Bishop Saint*; *Ritratto del Marchese Casali* - CENTO (Pinacoteca Civica): *Madonna con Bambino e San Gaetano da Thiene* (*Madonna with Child and St Cajetan of Thiene*); *Annunciazione* (*Annunciation*) - FLORENCE (Uffizi): *Busto di Vecchio con Turbante* (*Bust of an Old Man with a Turban*) - OXFORD (Ashmolean Mus.): *Busto di Donna* (*Bust of a Lady*); *Portrait of a Young Woman, Thought to be the Artist's Wife* (oil on canvas) - PARIS (Louvre): *Studio di Testa di Donna* (*Study of a Female Head*) - STOCKHOLM (Nationalmus.): *Deposition* (drawing from the 'Life of Christ' series) - VIENNA (Albertina Mus.): *Lamentation* (drawing from the 'Life of Christ' series).

AUCTION RECORDS:

LONDON, 2 Oct 1942, *Christ and the Woman Taken in Adultery*, GBP 63. MILAN, 16 Dec 1971, *Female Portrait*, ITL

1,900,000. LONDON, 14 April 1978, *Discovery of the True Cross* (oil on canvas, rounded pediment, sketch, 29 3/4 x 16 1/2 ins / 75.5 x 42 cm) GBP 2,400. LONDON, 28 June 1979, *Study of a Child's Head* (black and red chalks/graphite, 11 1/2 x 8 ins / 29.1 x 20.1 cm) GBP 3,200. NEW YORK, 21 Nov 1980, *A Man and Woman* (pen and wash/paper, 6 1/2 x 5 ins / 16.5 x 12.5 cm) USD 1,600. NEW YORK, 11 June 1981, *Study of Old Men* (oil on canvas, 13 x 16 ins / 33 x 40.5 cm) USD 18,000. MILAN, 18 March 1982, *Head Studies* (pen, 9 1/4 x 7 ins / 23.6 x 17.5 cm) ITL 4,200,000. LONDON, 12 April 1983, *Head of a Young Girl Looking to the Right* (red and white chalk, 13 1/4 x 10 3/4 ins / 33.6 x 27.3 cm) GBP 7,000. LONDON, 2 July 1986, *Portrait of an Old Woman* (oil on canvas, 19 x 15 ins / 48.5 x 38 cm) GBP 10,000. MILAN, 4 Dec 1986, *Hercules* (red chalk, 17 x 10 3/4 ins / 43.3 x 27.6 cm) ITL 15,500,000. LONDON, 1 April 1987, *God the Father Appearing to the Holy Family* (pen and wash, 7 3/4 x 5 3/4 ins / 19.8 x 14.7 cm) GBP 3,500. MONACO, 17 June 1988, *Holy Family* (oil on canvas, 12 1/2 x 15 1/4 ins / 31.5 x 38.5 cm) FRF 277,500. HEIDELBERG, 14 Oct 1988, *Joseph Explaining Pharaoh's Dream* (brown ink, 7 3/4 x 11 3/4 ins / 19.7 x 29.7 cm) DEM 2,600. PARIS, 27 Feb 1989, *Diana and Endymion* (pen and watercolour, 5 3/4 x 8 ins / 14.5 x 20.5 cm) FRF 13,000. MILAN, 4 April 1989, *Mars and Venus; Venus and Cupid* (oil on canvas, two pendants, each 21 x 15 ins / 52.5 x 38 cm) ITL 130,000,000. NEW YORK, 12 Jan 1990, *Plan for a Monument with a Cartouche Framed by a Male and a Female Figure and Surmounted by Three Putti Holding a Garland* (ink and wash/red chalk, 11 3/4 x 8 1/4 ins / 30 x 21 cm) USD 15,400. ROME, 8 March 1990, *Portrait of a Young Girl* (oil on canvas, 19 x 15 ins / 48 x 38 cm) ITL 64,000,000. MONACO, 15 June 1990, *St Helen Discovering the True Cross (Invention of the Cross)* (ink and wash, 11 1/2 x 6 3/4 ins / 29 x 17 cm) FRF 57,720. LONDON, 2 July 1990, *Flagellation of Christ* (ink and wash/black chalk, 10 1/2 x 7 1/2 ins / 26.7 x 19.3 cm) GBP 4,950. PARIS, 9 April 1991, *Hercules and the Hound Cerberus* (oil on canvas, 86 x 46 1/2 ins / 217.5 x 118 cm) FRF 700,000. ROME, 23 April 1991, *St Camilla of Lellis* (oil on canvas, 41 3/4 x 29 1/4 ins / 106 x 74 cm) ITL 27,000,000. SENLIS, 23 June 1991, *Child Portrait* (oil on canvas, 19 x 15 1/4 ins / 48 x 39 cm) FRF 500,000. LONDON, 15 April 1992, *Repentance of St Peter* (oil on canvas, 17 3/4 x 14 3/4 ins / 45 x 37.3 cm) GBP 38,000. PARIS, 31 March 1993, *St Paul* (ink and wash, 10 3/4 x 7 1/4 ins / 27.5 x 18.5 cm) FRF 12,000. PARIS, 11 March 1994, *Annunciation* (pen and brown wash, 11 x 7 1/2 ins / 27 x 19 cm) FRF 29,000. MONACO, 20 June 1994, *Christ and the Woman from Cana* (black chalk, ink and wash, 8 1/4 x 11 1/2 ins / 21.2 x 29.5 cm) FRF 277,500. PARIS, 7 June 1995, *Studies of Putti* (brown ink and wash, 11 1/4 x 7 3/4 ins / 28.7 x 19.7 cm) FRF 14,000. NEW YORK, 10 Jan 1996, *Head of a Young Man in Left Profile* (red and white chalks, 13 1/4 x 10 1/4 ins / 33.5 x 26 cm) USD 11,500. NEW YORK, 29 Jan 1997, *Plan for a Fountain with Two Satyrs, Nymphs and Putti Playing with Dolphins* (pen, brown ink and wash, 11 1/2 x 8 1/4 ins / 29.5 x 20.9 cm) USD 25,300. NEW YORK, 28 Jan 1998, *Flagellation of Christ* (pen, brown ink and wash/black chalk, 9 3/4 x 8 ins / 24.6 x 20.1 cm) USD 9,775. MILAN, 22 March 1999, *The Deposition* (ink, 8 x 6 ins / 21 x 15 cm) ITL 4,000,000. NEW YORK, 25 May 1999, *Holy Family in the Carpenter's Shop* (oil on canvas, 17 x 13 ins / 43 x 33 cm) USD 100,000. LONDON, 4 July 2000, *The Baptist Preaching in the Wilderness* (black chalk/pen/brown ink/brown wash, 11 x 7 ins / 27 x 19 cm) GBP 4,800. LONDON, 4 July 2000, *The Annunciation* (chalk/pen/ink wash, 11 x 7 ins / 27 x 19 cm) GBP 8,000. NEW YORK, 23 Jan 2001, *Andromeda Rescued by Perseus* (colour ink/colour wash, 7 x 9 ins / 19 x 24 cm) USD 90,000. PARIS, 27 March 2001, *Study of Figures for St Helen Discovering the True Cross* (colour ink/black crayon/colour wash, 12 x 9 ins / 30 x 22 cm) FRF 22,000. NEW YORK, 23 Jan 2002, *Madonna and Child with St Gaetano of Thiene* (chalk/ink/wash, 11 x 8 ins / 27 x 21 cm) USD 45,000. ROME, 19 March 2002, *Portrait of Lady in Pink Dress* (oil on canvas, 43 x 33 ins / 108 x 84 cm) EUR 91,000. PARIS, 27 March 2003, *Allegory of Wealth* (chalk/pen/ink wash, oval, 8 x 7 ins / 21 x 17 cm) EUR 17,000. LONDON, 10 Dec 2003, *Sibyl* (oil on canvas, 33 x 25 ins / 85 x 63 cm) GBP 80,000. NEW YORK, 22 Jan 2004, *Christ on the Way to Calvary* (black chalk/pen/brown ink/grey wash, 11 x 7 ins / 28 x 19 cm) USD 22,000. MILAN, 25 Feb 2004, *Holy Family* (oil on canvas, 35 x 28 ins / 89 x 70 cm) EUR 78,000.

GANDOLFINO D'ASTI

Italian, 15th century.

Active in Piedmont c. 1493.

Painter. History painting.

Gandolfino is referred to by Siret. He may possibly be identified with the painter Giovanni de Roreto.

MUSEUMS AND GALLERIES:

TURIN: one work.

AUCTION RECORDS:

LONDON, 14 Dec 1923, *Virgin and Child*, GBP 39.

GANDOLFO, Antonino

Italian, 20th century.

Died 21 March 1910, in Catana (Sicily).

Painter.

Antonino Gandolfo was a pupil of Stefano Ussi in Florence.

GANDOLFO, Francesco

Italian, 19th century.

Painter.

Francesco Gandolfo lived and worked in Genoa.

MUSEUMS AND GALLERIES:

GENOA: sketch.

GANDON, Adolphe

French, 19th century.

Born 28 July 1828, in Nîmes; died 27 March 1889, in Courgenay (Yonne).

Painter. History painting, battles, genre scenes.

Studied in Geneva under Diday and spent the rest of his life in Switzerland, where he was acknowledged as a major artist. Examples of his work include *Trench outside Sebastopol*, *Hunting Rats* and *Swiss Dragoons*.

MUSEUMS AND GALLERIES:

BERN: *Cuirassier Charge at Waterloo* - GENEVA: *Battle Scene; Closed Ranks; Country Forge; Convoy of Vagrants Escorted by Mounted Police; Ambush; Scout Company at Rest; Ford; Lying in Wait; Reconnaissance Patrol Doing the Rounds; Souvenir of Ditches in Geneva; Sentry at Arms; Password; Artillery Post; Sentry Box; Deployment of Artillery; Dragoon Advance-Guard; Battle of Morat; Battle in the Crimea.*

AUCTION RECORDS:

TORONTO, 30 Nov 1988, *Before the Mirror* (oil on canvas, 48 x 30 3/4 ins / 122 x 78 cm) CAD 4,000. NEW ORLEANS, 17 Nov 2000, *Boulogne 1805* (oil on canvas, 21 x 25 ins / 53 x 64 cm) USD 3,400. SION, 7 Dec 2002, *Campaign Artillery* (oil on canvas, 13 x 19 ins / 32 x 48 cm) CHF 2,500.

GANDON, André

French, 20th century.

Painter.

Neo-Constructivism.

From 1949 to 1956, André Gandon exhibited at the Salon des Réalités Nouvelles in Paris, showing abstract compositions which soon developed towards Neo-Constructivism in a style very similar to the work of Auguste Herbin.

GANDON, Pierre

French, 20th century.

Born 20 July 1899, in L'Hay-les-Roses.

Painter, engraver, illustrator. Postage stamps.

Pierre Gandon studied under Cormon. He exhibited in Paris at the Salon des Artistes Français, where he received various awards. He executed a major composition for the Tourism Pavilion at the International Exhibition of 1937. In 1922 he was awarded a travel bursary and the Prix de la Ville de Paris in 1935. Gandon was made a Chevalier of the Légion D'Honneur. Among the many literary works he illustrated are *De Goupil à Margot* by L. Pergaud and Alain Fournier's *Le Grand Meaulnes*.

Gandon also specialised in postage stamp design and created many for France, the French colonies and other foreign countries.

GANDON, Yves
French, 20th century.
Illustrator.

Yves Gandon illustrated Stendhal's *Mémoires d'un Touriste* (*Memoirs of a Tourist*) in 1927.

GANDOZ, Benoît
French, 16th century.
Active in Grenoble.
Painter.

GANDRI, Simon-François
French, 19th century.
Born in St-Jean-les-Deux-Jumeaux (Seine-et-Marne).
Sculptor.

Simon-François Gandri studied under Hardouin and Perrault and exhibited a medallion and a bust at the Salons of 1875 and 1879 respectively.

GANDTNER, Christoph
Austrian, 16th century.
Active in Innsbruck.
Sculptor.
Tyrolean School.

Gandtner worked for Archduke Ferdinand of Tyrol.

GANDTNER, Johann Georg
Austrian, 18th century.
Active in Innsbruck c. 1700.
Painter.

GANDULFINUS
Italian, 11th century.
Active in Bologna c. 1090.
Painter.

GANDULFO
Spanish, 19th century.
Active in Cádiz c. 1800.
Sculptor.

Gandulfo is known for his religious sculptures.

GANDY
British, 18th century.
Active in Liverpool.
Painter. Seascapes.

Gandy exhibited two seascapes at the Free Society in London in 1778.

GANDY, Celia, later Mrs Spencer
British, 19th century.
Active in London at the beginning of the 19th century.
Painter. Flowers, fruit.

Celia Gandy was the sister of Hannah Gandy.

GANDY, F.
British, 19th century.
Active in London.
Painter. Portraits.

F. Gandy exhibited at the Royal Academy in London from 1848 to 1859.

GANDY, Hannah (Miss)
British, 19th century.
Active in London.
Painter. Flowers.

Hannah Gandy was an exhibitor at London's Royal Academy in 1829 and again in 1853.

GANDY, Herbert
British, 19th - 20th century.
Active in London.
Painter (gouache), watercolourist. History painting, religious subjects, genre scenes, landscapes.

Herbert Gandy first exhibited in London in 1879 and continued to submit work for exhibition, notably to the Royal Academy. He specialised in landscape painting.

AUCTION RECORDS:

LONDON, 29 Jan 1910, *Pro Patria* (1904) GBP 31. LONDON, 17 Dec 1910, *Pro Patria* (1904) GBP 18. NEW YORK, 25 Feb 1983, *The Love Letter* (1895, oil on canvas, 25 x 45 ins / 63.5 x 114.4 cm) USD 6,000. LONDON, 20 June 1986, *The Sword of Damocles* (oil on canvas, 65 x 65 ins / 165 x 165 cm) GBP 12,000. LONDON, 26 Sept 1990, *The Daughter of Jephta* (1931, oil on canvas, 48 x 84 ins / 122 x 213.5 cm) GBP 17,600. LONDON, 9 May 1996, *The Footbridge* (1875, watercolour and gouache, 9 x 17 3/4 ins / 23 x 45 cm) GBP 598. CRANBROOK, 25 Jan 1999, *Arthurian Princess Cleodolinda Clothed in Robes in Misty Landscape* (1877, oil on canvas, 19 x 7 ins / 48 x 18 cm) GBP 1,000.

GANDY, James
British, 17th century.
Born 1619, in Exeter; died 1689, in Ireland.
Portrait artist.

James Gandy was allegedly a pupil of Van Dyck. He enjoyed the patronage of the Duke of Ormond and made a career for himself as a portraitist working in Ireland.

GANDY, Joseph Michael
British, 18th - 19th century.
Born 1771, in London; died 1843.
Painter, draughtsman. Religious subjects, landscapes, architectural views.

Joseph Michael Gandy was elected to associate membership of the Royal Academy in London in 1803. He also worked as an architect.

MUSEUMS AND GALLERIES:

LONDON (British Architectural Library): *New Senate House, London* (1835, watercolour, unfinished).

AUCTION RECORDS:

LONDON, 24 April 1925, *Merlin's Tomb*, GBP 11. LONDON, 14 March 1978, *Fall of Babylon* (watercolour, gouache and pen, 28 1/4 x 48 3/4 ins / 71.5 x 124 cm) GBP 6,500. LONDON, 19 June 1979, *View of an Imaginary Harbour* (watercolour and pen heightened with white, 21 x 26 1/2 ins / 52.5 x 67.5 cm) GBP 700. LONDON, 24 March 1981, *Atina in Abruzzo, Italy* (c. 1794, watercolour and pencil, 13 3/4 x 19 3/4 ins / 35 x 50 cm) GBP 900. LONDON, 17 May 1984, *Interior with a Tomb* (watercolour and pen/pencil outlines, 27 1/2 x 42 1/4 ins / 70 x 107 cm) GBP 14,000. LONDON, 13 July 1993, *Capriccio: Roman Port during a Storm* (pencil and watercolour, 14 1/2 x 21 ins / 36.8 x 53.2 cm) GBP 3,220. LONDON, 31 March 1999, *Jason before the Temple of Amphitrite* (watercolour over pencil heightened with gouache, 18 x 25 ins / 45 x 63 cm) GBP 2,600. LONDON, 20 Nov 2003, *Album of Landscapes and Studies from Nature including Views of Dorking* (1820-1826, pencil and watercolour, 5 x 8 ins / 12 x 21 cm) GBP 18,000.

GANDY, Peter, pseudonym: Deering
British, 19th century.
Born 1787; died 2 March 1850, in Lee.
Architect, illustrator.

Peter Gandy produced occasional illustrations, notably for Sir William Gell.

GANDY, Walton
British, 19th - 20th century.
Active in London.
Painter. Landscapes.

Walton Gandy first exhibited at the Suffolk Street Gallery in 1893.

GANDY, William
Irish, 17th - 18th century.
Born c. 1660, in Kilkenny; died 1729, in Exeter.
Painter. Portraits.

William Gandy was the son of James Gandy. He is believed to have worked with Gaspar Smitz. He lived and worked principally in Exeter and most of his work is found in Devon and Cornwall.

AUCTION RECORDS:
LONDON, 16 April 1923, *William Yonge*, GBP 3. LONDON, 22 July 1925, *McIvie*, GBP 10. LONDON, 14 Dec 1928, *Master Willcocks*, GBP 241. LONDON, 20 Dec 1929, *Master Willcocks*, GBP 50. LONDON, 18 Oct 1985, *Portrait of Sir Francis Warre; Portrait of the Artist's Second Wife, Margaret* (oil on canvas, two ovals, 13½ x 11½ ins / 34.3 x 29.2 cm) GBP 1,400. LONDON, 30 Nov 2000, *Portrait of Sir Richard Pyne, Lord Chief Justice of the Common Pleas in Ireland* (oil on canvas, 29 x 24 ins / 74 x 62 cm) GBP 3,500. LONDON, 11 June 2004, *Portrait of a Young Boy in a Blue Coat with a Red Cloak, Holding a Parakeet* (oil on canvas, 30 x 25 ins / 76 x 63 cm) GBP 8,000.

GANEN-GANGULY
Indian, 20th century.
Born on the Indian subcontinent.
Draughtsman.

GANERE, Theodore van
Flemish School, 15th century.
Illuminator.
Bruges School.

Theodore van Ganere entered the guild in Bruges in 1470.

GANESCO, Alexandre
Belgian, 20th century.
Born in Brussels; died after 1944.
Active in France.
Painter.

Son of the sculptor and painter Constantin Ganesco, who was his teacher, Alexandre Ganesco painted landscapes of the Bourbon region, pictures of rural life and scenes of the Maquis (the French resistance) between 1940 and 1944. He exhibited at the Salon d'Automne and was invited to the Salon des Tuileries in Paris.

AUCTION RECORDS:
PARIS, 7 March 1988, *Patinage général* (1933, oil on canvas, 38¼ x 51¼ ins / 97 x 130 cm) FRF 5,000.

GANESCO, Constantin
Romanian, 19th - 20th century.
Born 1864, in Bucharest.
Active in France.
Sculptor, painter. Religious subjects.

Constantin Ganesco lived in France for many years; G. Cohen stated that as early as 1896 he was in Nice where he met Ziem who advised him. Ganesco started as a sculptor producing many works in wax, before tackling painting around 1914. He dealt with romantic subjects in a fantastical, sometimes grotesque, style. He started exhibiting in 1922.

AUCTION RECORDS:
LOKEREN, 19 April 1986, *Temptation of St Anthony* (brown patinated bronze, h. 9½ ins / 24 cm) BEF 44,000.

GANGA-MIRO, José
Spanish, 18th century.
Active in Murcia c. 1750 and in the province of Granada.
Sculptor.

GANGAIEV, Pancrat Stepanovich
Russian, 18th century.
Active in Nijni-Novgorod c. 1750.
Icon painter.

GANGAND, Arthur
French, 19th - 20th century.
Active in Paris.
Sculptor.

Arthur Gangand became a member of the Société des Artistes Français in 1901 and exhibited at the Society's Salons.

GANGERI, Lio
Italian, 19th - 20th century.
Born 1844, in Messina (Sicily); died 4 February 1913, in Salerno (Campania).
Sculptor.

From 1880 onwards Lio Gangeri exhibited in Rome, Turin and Milan. He sculpted numerous busts of late 19th-century kings and queens of Italy. Gangeri was awarded an honourable mention at the Paris Exposition Universelle of 1889.

GANGLOFF, Carl Wilhelm
German, 19th century.
Born 17 May 1790, in Leutkirch-im-Allgäu (Bavaria); died 16 May 1814, in Merklingen.
Draughtsman. Religious subjects.

This self-taught artist mainly illustrated biblical subjects.

GANGLOFF, Georges
French, 19th century.
Born in Phalsbourg (Moselle).
Painter.

He exhibited portraits at the Paris Salon between 1866 and 1870, together with two genre compositions, *Dressing for the Ball* and *Preparing to Go for a Walk*.

MUSEUMS AND GALLERIES:
LA ROCHE-SUR-YON: *Portrait of Chevreul*.

GANGLOFF, Maria
French, 20th century.
Born 11 August 1877, in Lyons.
Painter.

Maria Gangloff studied under J.P. Laurens. She exhibited in Paris at the Salon des Artistes Français.

GANGOITI, Juan de
Spanish, 19th century.
Born 12 July 1816, in Madrid; died 8 February 1878, in Madrid.
Engraver.

GANGOITI, Nicolás de
Spanish, 19th century.
Born 30 September 1804, in Madrid; died 6 January 1857, in Madrid.
Painter.

Nicolás de Gangoiti was a pupil of Vicente Lopéz, and the brother of Juan de Gangoiti.

BIBLIOGRAPHY:
Gangoiti, N., *Carta esférica de una parte de la costa occidental de Francia desde el Plantío Flamand hasta el Vidasoa y de la Setentrional de España desde ese río*, Dirección Hidrográfica, Madrid, 1840. Gangoiti, N., *Plano de la Bahía de Fuenterrabía*, Dirección de Hidrografía, Madrid, 1846. Gangoiti, N., *Carta Esférica de la Costa Cantábrica*, Dirección de Hidrografía, Madrid, 1860.

GANGOITI, Pedro Manuel de
Spanish, 19th century.
Born 16 February 1779, in Bilbao; died 15 August 1830, in Madrid.
Painter. History painting.

Pedro Manuel Gangoiti was the father of Juan and Nicolás Gangoiti.

GANGOLF, Paul
French, 20th century.
Painter, engraver. Genre scenes.

Paul Gangolf exhibited in Paris at the Salon des Tuileries from 1927, showing many genre paintings.
AUCTION RECORDS:
COLOGNE, 1 June 1984, *Cathedral* (watercoloured lithograph, 9 x 10 1/2 ins / 23 x 26.7 cm) DEM 2,000.

GANGOLF, Serge
Belgian, 20th century.
Born 1943, in Wegnez (Verviers).
Sculptor.
Gangolf attended the Institut de St Luc in Liège. In 1969 he won the Louis Schmidt prize, and the Prix de Rome in 1974. In 1968 Gangolf produced the war memorial for Visé and several other monumental sculptures for administrative buildings. Serge Gangolf produces very solid aluminium or bronze sculptures. He has participated in group exhibitions in Belgium and abroad. He has held solo shows in Verviers, Düren, Liège and Brussels.
MUSEUMS AND GALLERIES:
LIÈGE (Mus. of Modern and Contemporary Art) - LIÈGE (Prov.).

GANGYNER, Georg Anton
Swiss, 19th century.
Born 1807, in Lachem; died 17 December 1876, in Lachem.
Portrait artist.
Gangyner was a pupil at the academy in Munich.

GANIER, Jacques Denis
French, 18th century.
Active in Paris in 1772.
Painter, sculptor.

GANIÈRE, Étienne
French, 17th - 18th century.
Active in Paris.
Engraver, printer.
Étienne Ganière was the son of Jean and the father of Pierre.

GANIÈRE, George Etienne
American, 19th century.
Born 26 April 1865, in Chicago; died 1935, in Hendersonville (North Carolina).
Sculptor.
George Etienne Ganière was a pupil at the Art Institute of Chicago and a member of the Chicago Art Society.

GANIÈRE, Jean, or Gagnière
French, 17th century.
Died June 1666, in Paris, buried in the parish of Saint-Séverin.
Active in Paris.
Engraver (burin).
Jean Ganière produced engravings with religious, historical and genre themes. He was probably the son of an engraver who was a dealer in line-engravings. He was also an editor.

GANIÈRE, Pierre
French, 17th - 18th century.
Born c. 1663; died 15 June 1721.
Active in Paris.
Engraver, geographer.
Pierre Ganière was the grandson of Jean. He is also known as a geographer.

GANIS, Anselmo de
Italian, 16th century.
Active in Mantua.
Painter.

GANIUCHKIN, Ivan
Russian, 18th century.
Born 1742.
Painter, engraver.
Ganiuchkin studied at the St Petersburg academy of fine arts.

GANKEVICH, Aleksandr
Russian, 20th century.
Painter. Still-lifes, flowers.
Aleksandr Gankevich was a student at the academy of fine art in St Petersburg and worked under Isaak Brodsky's direction. His highly meticulous technique is reminiscent of the major period of the painting of still-lifes with flowers. He was nominated People's Artist and was a member of the Artists' Association of the USSR.
MUSEUMS AND GALLERIES:
MOSCOW (Pushkin MFA) - MOSCOW (State Tretyakov Gal.) - ST PETERSBURG (Academy) - ST PETERSBURG (Gosudarstvennyj Russkij Muz.).
AUCTION RECORDS:
PARIS, 18 March 1991, *Still-life with Flowers* (1931, oil on canvas, 9 3/4 x 7 1/2 ins / 25 x 19 cm) FRF 5,000.

GANKU, family name: Kishi, personal name: Koma, given name: Masaaki Saeki, alternate name: Funzen, popular name: Utanosure, artist names: Kayo, Dokokan, Kakando, Kotokan, Tenkaikutsu, Tansai
Japanese, 18th - 19th century.
Born 1756, in Kanazawa (Ichikawa); died 1838.
Painter. Animals.
Ganku was a late Edo period animal painter in whose style can be seen a mixture of the precepts of the Kano school and the teachings of Maruyama Okyo (1733-1795). It is known that as a boy he was apprenticed to a dyer and at the same time may have taken painting lessons from a Kano school painter. Then, after having travelled widely in Japan, he settled in Kyoto, where he was in the service first of Prince Arisugawa, and afterwards of the court. In 1836 he was given the honorary title Lord of Echizen. He had many disciples, who went on to form the Kishi school. He is renowned for his paintings of tigers.
BIBLIOGRAPHY:
Tazawa, Yutaka, *Biographical Dictionary of Japanese Art*, Kodansha International Ltd, Tokyo, 1981.

GANNA, Aquiline von Aquila
Italian, 19th century.
Born 1800, in L'Aquila (Abruzzi); died 1845, in L'Aquila.
Painter.
Ganna studied art in Milan. His best-known work is *The Martyrdom of St Agatha*.

GANNE, Pierre Christian
French, 20th century.
Born in Algeria.
Painter. Genre scenes, portraits.
Pierre Ganne studied under Rochegrosse and exhibited in Paris at the Salon des Tuileries. He was awarded the James Bertrand prize in 1931.

GANNE, Yves
French, 20th century.
Born 1931.
Painter. Landscapes with figures, still-lifes.
In 1994, the Galerie F. Barlier showed a collection of Yves Ganne's beach landscapes. His reserved style of painting displays an harmonious sense of composition.
AUCTION RECORDS:
PARIS, 5 Feb 1992, *Earthenware Jar* (1954, oil on canvas, 32 x 23 1/2 ins / 81 x 60 cm) FRF 4,000. NEW YORK, 10 Nov 1992, *Still-life* (1967, oil on canvas, 21 1/2 x 25 3/4 ins / 54.5 x 65.4 cm) USD 1,430. CALAIS, 14 March 1993, *Still-life with Pitcher* (1961, oil on canvas, 22 x 25 1/2 ins / 55 x 65 cm) FRF 5,000.

GANNET, Jehan
French, 15th century.
Active in Lille.

Painter.

In 1468, Jehan Gannet was working in Bruges.

GANNET, Piérard, or Gaunet
Flemish School, 15th century.
Painter.

Piérard Gannet worked with Jehan in Lille (Nord) in 1453 and in Bruges in 1468.

GANS, Carl
German, 17th century.
Active in Bayreuth (Bavaria) c. 1672.
Painter.

GANS, Johann
German, 17th century.
Active in Mainz in 1661.
Painter.

GANSAUGE, Hans
German, 16th century.
Active in Breslau (now Wroclaw, Poland) in 1548.
Painter.

Gansauge may have been the brother of Johannes Ganssog.

GANSEL, Jean
French, 15th century.
Active in Paris.
Sculptor, architect.

The reconstructed portal of the church of St-Germain-l'Auxerrois, as we see it today, was the work of Gansel. He carved six statues: St Vincent, St Marcel, an angel, St Genevieve, King Childebert and Queen Ultrogoth.

GANSER, Anton
German, 19th century.
Born 1811, in Munich.
Sculptor.

Ganser was a pupil of Schwanthaler.

MUSEUMS AND GALLERIES:
MUNICH (Mus.): a work.

GANSES, Paul
Dutch, 18th century.
Active in Naples in 1700.
Painter. Seascapes.

Despite the reference in *Bryan's Dictionary*, Paul Ganses was not a Neapolitan.

GANSKY, Piotr
Russian, 19th - 20th century.
Active in Paris.
Painter.

Piotr Gansky exhibited at the Salon Artistes Français and Indépendants in Paris.

GANSO, Emil
American, 20th century.
Born 1895, in Germany; died 1941.
Painter, engraver.

Emil Ganso was a member of the American Society of Painters.

BIBLIOGRAPHY:
Den Broeder, Frederick, *Emil Ganso (1895-1941)*, exhibition catalogue, University of Connecticut, William Benton Museum of Art, 1976. Smith, Donald E., *The Prints of Emil Ganso*, Fairleigh Dickinson Press, Madison, N.J./Associated University Press, London, 1997.

AUCTION RECORDS:
NEW YORK, 20 and 21 Oct 1943, *French Port*, USD 90. NEW YORK, 6 Feb 1947, *Two Nudes*, USD 210. NEW YORK, 20 May 1981, *Sleeping Female Nude* (gouache, 16 1/4 x 22 ins / 41 x 56 cm) USD 650. NEW YORK, 23 Jan 1985, *Sunbathing* (oil on canvas, 16 x 25 ins / 40.6 x 63.5 cm) USD 1,000. NEW YORK, 26 Sept 1986, *Cubist Landscape* (1925, gouache, 12 1/4 x 17 1/4 ins / 30.8 x 43.5 cm) USD 1,200. NEW YORK, 7 April 1988, *Two Women* (wash/paper, 12 3/4 x 17 3/4 ins / 32.5 x 45 cm) USD 827. NEW YORK, 24 Jan 1990, *Sleeping Nude* (charcoal and red chalk/paper, 16 x 20 3/4 ins / 40.8 x 52.8 cm) USD 1,320. NEW YORK, 14 Feb 1990, *Seated Nude* (oil/synthetic resin, 22 x 17 3/4 ins / 56 x 45 cm) USD 1,650. NEW YORK, 15 April 1992, *Port Scene* (oil on canvas, 26 x 40 ins / 66 x 101.6 cm) USD 1,760. NEW YORK, 23 Sept 1992, *Reclining Nude* (1929, charcoal and pastel/unbleached paper, 19 x 13 ins / 48.5 x 33 cm) USD 1,045. NEW YORK, 25 Sept 1992, *Sleeping Nude with Stockings* (oil on canvas, 14 x 21 ins / 35.6 x 53.3 cm) USD 5,225. PARIS, 8 June 1994, *Reclining Nude* (lead pencil and stump, 18 1/4 x 14 ins / 46.3 x 35.3 cm) FRF 5,000. NEW YORK, 17 May 2001, *Recling Female Nude* (oil on board, 14 x 21 ins / 36 x 53 cm) USD 1,500. NEW YORK, 17 May 2001, *Winter Landscape, Woodstock* (oil on paper on card, 16 x 20 ins / 41 x 51 cm) USD 2,000. NEW YORK, 23 May 2002, *Reclining Female Nude with Green Dress. Woman in Pink Dress Reading* (1930, watercolour, a pair, 16 x 22 ins / 40 x 57 cm) USD 1,700. WASHINGTON, 14 Dec 2002, *Still-life with Peaches* (oil on masonite, 12 x 16 ins / 31 x 41 cm) USD 13,000. NEW YORK, 18 May 2004, *Bather* (oil on board, 21 x 14 ins / 54 x 36 cm) USD 12,000.

GANSS, Asmus
German, 16th century.
Active in Leipzig (Saxony) in 1535.
Glass painter.

GANSS, Egbert. See **JANSZ**

GANSSER, Matthaüs
Swiss, 16th century.
Painter.

GANSSOG, Johannes
German, 16th century.
Born c. 1555, in Breslau (now Wroclaw, Poland).
Sculptor.
Breslau School.

Johannes Ganssog may have been the brother of Hans Gansauge. He worked mainly in Breslau but also in Lund in Sweden and at the castle of Kronborg.

GANSWEIG, Wilhelm von
Austrian, 17th century.
Born c. 1615; died 1665, in Vienna.
Painter.

GANT, James Y.
British, 19th century.
Active in London.
Painter. Landscapes with figures, landscapes.

James Y. Gant exhibited landscapes between 1827 and 1841.

AUCTION RECORDS:
LONDON, 12 March 1980, *Gathering Firewood; Landscape with Shepherds and Flock* (oil on canvas, a pair, 10 1/4 x 13 3/4 ins / 26 x 35 cm) GBP 1,500.

GANTAI, real name: Kishi Tai, original name: Saeki, popular name: Chikuzen-nosuke, artist names: Takudo, Dokokan, Shisui
Japanese, 19th century.
Died 1865.
Active in Kyoto.
Painter.

Gantai was a pupil of his father Ganku.

GANTE, de. See first name

GANTER, Dionys
Austrian, 19th century.
Active in Vienna.
Painter. Portraits.

Ganter exhibited a miniature at the academy in Vienna in 1824.

GANTER, Hans
German, 16th century.
Glass painter.

GANTHOIS, Jean
French, 17th century.
Active near Valenciennes in 1613.
Sculptor (wood).

Jean Ganthois worked for the church in Sebourg.

GANTNER, Albert Henri
Swiss, 19th - 20th century.
Born 1866, in Geneva.
Painter.

GANTNER, Bernard
French, 20th century.
Born 16 August 1928, in Belfort.
Painter (including gouache), watercolourist, engraver, illustrator. Landscapes, harbour scenes, still-lifes.

Bernard Gantner began exhibiting in Paris in 1950; he also exhibited in Zurich, Geneva and Tokyo. In 1960 he was awarded the Prix de la Critique. Gantner illustrated Maupassant's short stories and E. Verhaeren's poetry.

He was principally a landscape artist of a strongly classical nature. He painted mainly the Vosges region in dominant tones of black and white, constructed in broad areas of colour.

AUCTION RECORDS:
PARIS, 28 June 1976, *The Muddy Road* (oil on canvas, 57 1/2 x 45 ins / 146 x 114 cm) FRF 3,000. ENGHIEN-LES-BAINS, 27 May 1979, *Village at a Crossroads* (1971, gouache, 12 1/4 x 11 ins / 31 x 27 cm) FRF 4,000. PARIS, 23 June 1981, *Village in the Plain* (1964, gouache, 11 1/2 x 7 3/4 ins / 29 x 20 cm) FRF 2,200. VERSAILLES, 16 Oct 1983, *Houses in the East* (oil on canvas, 28 1/2 x 23 1/2 ins / 72.5 x 60 cm) FRF 8,200. VERSAILLES, 15 June 1988, *Farm at Twilight* (1978, oil on canvas, 32 x 46 ins / 81 x 117 cm) FRF 60,500. PARIS, 23 June 1988, *The Frosted Torrent* (1972, 24 x 18 ins / 61 x 46 cm) FRF 26,000. CALAIS, 3 July 1988, *Village* (oil on canvas, 28 3/4 x 39 1/4 ins / 73 x 100 cm) FRF 45,000. VERSAILLES, 23 Oct 1988, *Le cirque du Fer à Cheval* (1978, oil on canvas, 29 x 36 1/4 ins / 73.5 x 92 cm) FRF 36,500. VERSAILLES, 6 Nov 1988, *Venice* (oil on canvas, 23 1/2 x 32 ins / 60 x 81 cm) FRF 31,000. ST-DIÉ, 23 July 1989, *Still-life with Winter Landscape* (40 1/4 x 17 1/2 ins / 102 x 44.5 cm) FRF 19,000. PARIS, 23 Oct 1989, *Garden in the Snow* (1961, oil on canvas, 9 1/2 x 13 ins / 24 x 32.8 cm) FRF 5,500. CALAIS, 10 Dec 1989, *Landscape with Snow* (1961, oil on canvas, 9 1/2 x 13 ins / 24 x 33 cm) FRF 13,000. PARIS, 26 Jan 1990, *Village Street* (oil on canvas, 28 3/4 x 23 1/2 ins / 73 x 60 cm) FRF 13,500. CALAIS, 4 March 1990, *Half-timbered Houses* (oil on canvas, 28 3/4 x 23 1/2 ins / 73 x 60 cm) FRF 48,000. VERSAILLES, 8 July 1990, *Pond at Twilight* (gouache, 10 x 9 1/4 ins / 25.5 x 23.25 cm) FRF 17,000. NEW YORK, 10 Oct 1990, *Forest Edge under Snow* (1978, oil on canvas, 29 x 36 ins / 73.7 x 91.6 cm) USD 12,100. FONTAINEBLEAU, 18 Nov 1990, *Boats in Port* (oil on canvas, 23 1/2 x 32 ins / 60 x 81 cm) FRF 35,000. CALAIS, 9 Dec 1990, *View of Paris in the Snow* (gouache, 8 1/4 x 7 3/4 ins / 21 x 20 cm) FRF 10,000. PARIS, 20 March 1991, *Forest in Autumn* (1969, oil on canvas, 25 1/2 x 32 ins / 65 x 81 cm) FRF 21,000. LE TOUQUET, 8 June 1992, *Farm in Autumn* (1965, gouache and watercolour, 7 3/4 x 9 3/4 ins / 20 x 25 cm) FRF 6,000. NEW YORK, 12 June 1992, *Sky at Dusk* (gouache and ink/paper, 9 x 9 1/2 ins / 22.9 x 24.1 cm) USD 1,650. NEW YORK, 10 Nov 1992, *House in Haute Saône* (1972, oil on canvas, 32 x 39 1/2 ins / 81 x 100.5 cm) USD 6,600. PARIS, 4 Dec 1992, *Normandy Landscape* (1969, oil on canvas, 38 1/4 x 51 1/4 ins / 97 x 130 cm) FRF 12,500. PARIS, 22 Dec 1993, *House in Haute-Loire* (oil on canvas, 32 x 39 1/4 ins / 81 x 100 cm) FRF 22,000. NEW YORK, 24 Feb 1995, *The Port of Basel in Switzerland* (1965, oil on canvas, 32 x 39 ins / 81.3 x 99.1 cm) USD 2,875. PARIS, 21 March 1995, *Snow Falling* (1970, oil on canvas, 51 1/2 x 38 1/2 ins / 131 x 98 cm) FRF 16,000. PARIS, 18 Nov 1996, *Red Roofs* (1962, oil on canvas, 28 3/4 x 39 1/4 ins / 73 x 100 cm) FRF 10,000. PARIS, 24 Nov 1996, *Fir Tree in Ballon d'Alsace* (1974, gouache/paper, 13 1/4 x 10 1/4 ins / 33.5 x 26 cm) FRF 4,000. PARIS, 16 March 1997, *Snowy Landscape* (oil on canvas, 21 1/4 x 28 1/2 ins / 54 x 72.5 cm) FRF 7,000. NEW ORLEANS, 9 April 1999, *The Vosges in Winter* (1971, oil on canvas, 39 x 57 ins / 99 x 145 cm) USD 4,000. PARIS, 11 June 1999, *Winter Light* (oil on canvas, 24 x 32 ins / 60 x 81 cm) FRF 21,000. PARIS, 17 May 2000, *Valley under Frost* (oil on canvas, 36 x 26 ins / 92 x 65 cm) FRF 12,000. CALAIS, 2 July 2000, *Barges on the Rhine* (1965, oil on canvas, 20 x 26 ins / 50 x 65 cm) FRF 19,000. PARIS, 7 Dec 2001, *Landscape with Tall Trees* (oil on canvas, 21 x 29 ins / 54 x 73 cm) FRF 11,000. CALAIS, 19 May 2002, *Marshalling Yard* (1961, oil on canvas, 32 x 26 ins / 81 x 65 cm) EUR 2,400. CALAIS, 19 May 2002, *Village in the Snow* (1965, oil on canvas, 35 x 46 ins / 89 x 116 cm) EUR 4,000. NEW YORK, 4 Aug 2004, *Sun on a Canal in Venice* (1975, oil on canvas, 39 x 51 ins / 99 x 130 cm) USD 2,200.

GANTNER, Hans
Austrian, 19th - 20th century.
Born 1853, in Feldkirchen; died 4 May 1914, in Steinhof.
Painter.

Hans Gantner worked mainly in Vienna and Munich and exhibited in Prague.

GANTNER, Josef
Swiss, 18th century.
Active c. 1700.
Sculptor (wood).

GANTNER, Simon
18th century.
Active in Kleinkinzighofen in the middle of the 18th century.
Sculptor (wood).

GANTOKU, real name: Aoki Toku, popular name: Shido, artist names: Gantoku, Shishin, Renzan
Japanese, 19th century.
Born 1805; died 1859.
Active in Kyoto.
Painter.

Gantoku was the disciple and adopted son of Ganku. He later developed into a realistic painter in the style of Goshun's Shijo school.

GANTON, Camille Marie
Belgian, 20th century.
Born 1872, in Verviers; died 1946, in Ghent.
Painter (including glass), potter.

Camille Ganton studied at the St-luc academy of Fine art in Ghent. She worked almost exclusively for churches, in Belgium, the Netherlands, England, Switzerland and China.

GANTREL, Estienne
French, 17th century.
Born 1646, in Metz; died 1 November 1706.
Active in Paris.
Engraver.

Estienne Gantrel was an ordinary engraver to the king. He produced engravings on religious, historical and genre themes.

GANTREL, Marius
French, 20th century.
Born in Pantin.
Painter.
Marius Gantrel exhibited in Paris at the Salon d'Automne, the Salon of the Société Nationale des Beaux-Arts and the Salon des Indépendants.

GANTZ, John
British, 18th - 19th century.
Painter, watercolourist.
MUSEUMS AND GALLERIES:
LONDON (British Mus.): four landscapes.

GANUCHAUD, Paul
French, 20th century.
Born 1881, in Paris.
Sculptor.
Paul Ganuchaud exhibited at the major Paris Salons.

GANUCHEV, Nikolai
Bulgarian, 20th century.
Born in Rozgrad.
Painter.
Nikolai Ganuchev is known for his nudes. He exhibited in Paris at the Salon des Artistes Français and at the Salon des Tuileries.

GANZ, Andreas
German, 17th century.
Died 1656, in Berlin.
Painter. Portraits.

GANZ, Edwin
Swiss, 19th - 20th century.
Born 1871, in Zurich; died 1957, in Brussels.
Active in Belgium.
Painter, draughtsman. Figures, landscapes, animals.
Edwin Ganz studied with Blanc-Garin and Portaels in Brussels, and with the painter Édouard Detaille in Paris. He exhibited at the Brussels Triennial in 1893. He is known for his pictures of horses, one of which is entitled *The Grenadiers Attacking the Plateau of Montaigu.*
AUCTION RECORDS:
ANTWERP, 29 Oct 1980, *Horses* (oil on canvas, 28 1/4 x 40 1/2 ins / 72 x 103 cm) BEF 24,000. BRUSSELS, 19 Dec 1989, *Horse and Man* (oil on canvas, 9 3/4 x 12 1/2 ins / 25 x 32 cm) BEF 38,000. BRUSSELS, 11 May 1999, *Peasant and Two Horses Crossing the Forest* (oil on canvas, 40 x 28 ins / 102 x 72 cm) BEF 85,000. BRUSSELS, 17 Sept 2001, *Farmer on his Brabandt* (oil on canvas, 40 x 28 ins / 102 x 72 cm) BEF 90,000. BRUSSELS, 20 Jan 2004, *Draft Horses* (1907, oil on canvas, 22 x 28 ins / 55 x 70 cm) EUR 2,200.

GANZ, Hans
Swiss, 20th century.
Born 1890, in Zurich; died 1957, in Bern.
Painter. Landscapes.
AUCTION RECORDS:
BERN, 26 Oct 1988, *Landscape of the Avignon Region* (1929, oil on card, 13 x 16 1/4 ins / 33 x 41 cm) CHF 750.

GANZ, Henry F. W.
British, 19th - 20th century.
Active in London.
Painter, engraver.
Henry Ganz studied under Legros. He exhibited in Venice, Dresden, Paris and London.

GANZ, Johann Philipp
German, 18th century.
Born 1746, in Eisenach (Thuringia).
Engraver.
Johann Ganz studied in Vienna and worked mainly in Hanover and Göttingen.

GANZ, Johannes
Swiss, 19th century.
Born 26 February 1821, in Bülach; died 16 April 1886, in Zurich.
Painter. Seascapes.
Johannes Ganz studied in Zurich and Munich and was a pupil of Ulrich.

GANZ, Joseph
German, 19th century.
Active in Schönthal in 1824.
Sculptor.

GANZ, Julian Johann
Swiss, 19th century.
Born 9 January 1844, in Zurich; died 31 January 1892, in Brussels.
Painter. Portraits, landscapes.
He was the son of Johannes.

GANZAGA, or Gansago
Russian, 18th - 19th century.
Active at the end of the 18th and the beginning of the 19th century.
Painter. Landscapes.
Ganzaga worked initially for the Italian theatres, then in St Petersburg from 1794 to 1804. He was still alive in 1821.

GANZAUGE, Georg Paul
German, 18th century.
Active in Leipzig (Saxony).
Painter.

GANZER
French, 18th century.
Active in Besançon in 1785.
Sculptor.
Ganzer worked on the decoration of the château at Étupes.

GANZEVOORT, Wybrand
Belgian, 20th century.
Born 1930, in Ghent.
Painter, sculptor.
Op Art, Kinetic Art.
Wybrand Ganzevoort studied at the college in Antwerp and then at the Académie de la Grande Chaumière in Paris. He lives in Antwerp. His art is kinetic and makes play with optical reflections.

GAO BIN, or Kao Pin
Chinese, 18th century.
Active during the first half of the 18th century.
Painter.
Although Gao Bin is not mentioned in the biographies of the painters, he was probably a relation of the painter Gao Qipei. He left a finger painting, *Five Fish in Water*, dated 1739.

GAO BING, or Kao Ping
Chinese, 18th century.
Active during the first half of the 18th century.
Painter.
Gao Bing learned the technique of finger painting from his great-uncle, Gao Qipei. He was also a great theoretician and the author of the *Zhitou Huashuo* (c. 1705), in which he collected Qipei's theoretical and practical lessons on finger painting. Even though finger painting is a very specific tech-

nique, Gao Qipei's ideas cover a much wider area and apply to painting in general. Consequently, Gao Bing's treatise is of great interest.

Bibliography:

Ryckmans, Pierre, *Les Propos sur la peinture' de Shitao. Traduction et commentaires pour servir de contribution à l'étude terminologique et esthétique des théories chinoises de la peinture*, Institut belge des hautes études chinoises, Brussels, 1970.

GAO CEN, or Kao Ts'en, style name: Weishang, sobriquet: Shanchang
Chinese, 17th century.
Born in Hangzhou (Zhejiang).
Active 1643-1679.
Painter, draughtsman. Landscapes, flowers.

Gao Cen was one of the Eight Masters of Nanjing. He was a skilful painter of flowers and landscapes.

Bibliography:

Yang Xin/and others, *Three Thousand Years of Chinese Painting*, Yale University Press, 1997.

Museums and Galleries:

Berlin: *Landscapes* (dated 1672, ink and colour on paper, twelve leaves from an album after the Song and Yuan masters, with an inscription by the artist on the last leaf).

Auction records:

New York, 31 May 1990, *Landscape after Wu Zhen* (ink on silk, hanging scroll, 63 3/4 x 33 3/4 ins / 162 x 85.7 cm) USD 27,500.

GAO CENGYUN, or Kao Ts'eng-yun, style name: Erbao, sobriquet: Suyuan
Chinese, 17th century.
Born 1634, in Huating (Jiangsu); died 1690.
Painter.

Gao Cengyun was a scholar, art connoisseur and calligrapher. He painted landscapes in the style of Dong Qichang (1555-1636).

GAO CHAO
Chinese, 20th century.
Born 1927, in Heibei.
Painter. Figures, genre scenes, landscapes, flowers.

Gao Chao was a member of the Chinese Artists Association. He taught at the Beijing Academy of Art. His painting was academic and realist and demonstrates a knowledge of Western art. He had a solo exhibition at the Cité internationale des Arts in Paris.

GAO CHENGMO, or Kao Ch'eng-mo
Chinese, 18th century.
Active at the end of the 18th century.
Painter.

Gao Chengmo is not mentioned in the biographies of the painters.

Museums and Galleries:

Boston (MFA): *Cat Watching Butterfly* (signed and dated, probably 1770).

GAO ERYI
Chinese, 20th - 21st century.
Born 1946, in Shanghai.
Painter, watercolourist.

Gao Eryi graduated in 1969 from Zhejiang Academy, later becoming an associate professor and its president.

Auction records:

Hong Kong, 30 Oct 1995, *Town of Wine* (1994, watercolour on paper, 29 1/2 x 22 ins / 74.9 x 55.9 cm) HKD 18,400.

GAO FENGHAN, or Kao Feng-han, style name: Xiyuan, sobriquets: Nancun, Nanfu laoren, Guiyun laoren
Chinese, 18th century.
Born 1683, in Jiaozhou (Shandong); died c. 1748 or 1749.
Painter, draughtsman. Landscapes, flowers.

Gao Fenghan painted landscapes and flowers. He tended to avoid traditional techniques and his flower paintings are sometimes very beautiful. He is most famous for his free, improvised style, which dates from the time when rheumatism prevented him from using his right arm and he began to write and paint with his left (hence calling himself Houshang-zuosheng). Some of his compositions are lively, with quick, fluid lines and pale ink washes and fresh colours which give a certain volume to his rocks. He is sometimes thought to have been one of the Eight Eccentrics of Yangzhou, but he was not native of the city, nor did he ever live there.

Bibliography:

Cahill, James, *Chinese Painting*, Skira, Geneva, 1960.

Museums and Galleries:

Beijing (Palace Mus.): *Group of Rocks in Mountain River with Man Sitting on Bank* (dated 1727, ink on silk); *Lotus and Mudan Flowers in Vases* (dated 1741, ink); *Studies of Rocks, Old Trees and Bamboo* (ink and colour on paper, six album leaves) - Berlin: *Album of Six Landscapes* (1736, signed and dated) - London (British Mus.): *Studies of Landscapes, Rocks, Pines and Flowers* (twelve fan paintings, dated between 1722 and 1725, some with inscriptions by the artist), *Flowers, Fruit and Vegetables* (ink and colour on silk, large, ten-leaf landscape-format album); *Roses and Jasmine* (after Yun Shouping, signed) - Osaka (Municipal Mus. of Art): *Chrysanthemum near Cottage* (ink and light colour on paper); *Peonies and Rocks* (dated 1734, ink and light colour on paper, album leaf) - Shanghai: album of landscapes painted with the left hand, with inscriptions by Zheng Xie (colour on paper) - Stockholm (Nationalmus.): *Crows in Bare Trees* (signed).

Auction records:

New York, 31 May 1989, *Calligraphy in running script* (ink on paper, hanging scroll, 59 1/4 x 21 1/4 ins / 150.5 x 54 cm) USD 9,350.

GAO JIAN, or Kao Chien, style name: Danyu, sobriquet: Luyun shanren
Chinese, 17th century.
Born 1634, in Suzhou (Jiangsu); died 1708.
Painter. Landscapes.

Gao Jian is known as a landscape artist.

Museums and Galleries:

Beijing (Palace Mus.): *River Landscape with Wooded Hills* (colour) - London (British Mus.): *Landscape in Autumn Rain* (signed and dated 1694).

GAO JIANFU, or Kao Chien-fu, Gao Lun (Kao Lun)
Chinese, 19th - 20th century.
Born 1879 or 1881, in Canton; died 1951, in Canton.
Painter.
Lingnan school.

When he was still very young, Gao Jianfu left for Tokyo, where he was among the first members of the political party founded by Sun Yat-sen, the Tong menghui, which later became the Guomindang. He studied western painting in Tokyo (probably at the Japan Fine Art Institute) and returned to China in 1908. After the 1911 revolution in China, he abandoned politics and, convinced that traditional Chinese painting should adapt to the demands of modern life, founded the Qunxue art school in Canton in 1912 to teach his revolutionary aesthetic principles. Gao's aim was to create a new art of Chinese painting, retaining all the essential qualities of the ancient masters but assimilating the best aspects of Western painting. This resulted in the formation of the Xin Guohua (new national painting) movement, and in the 1920s the formation of movements such as the Xin Song

Yuan Pai (new Song and Yuan school) and Xin Wenren Hua (new literati painting), as well as the magazine *Zhenxiang Huabao* (*Artistic Magazine of Reality*) . He travelled widely in India and South-East Asia and taught in several schools, including that of Sun Yat-sen and National Central University, Nanjing. He also published works on Chinese and Indian art and the reform of Buddhism.

The name of Gao Jianfu and that of his brother Gao Qifeng remained linked to the Lingnan school, which represented precisely their attempt to synthesize Chinese and Western techniques.

The characteristics of Gao Jianfu's works are realistic perspective, light and shade, and the modelling of shapes, with Chinese brushwork and a concession to Japanese decorative effects of the time (such as a soft and oily texture). The wish to be modern at all costs, particularly in his choice of subject matter (trains, aircraft, bridges, ruined towns), does not give Gao Jianfu the status of a true contemporary artist. His mental attitude, which was purely technical and theoretical, seems to leave all his works devoid of feeling. It is not surprising that this new national art lasted for a long time, since the revival of Chinese art depended not on new methods, but on a new vision.

BIBLIOGRAPHY:

Sullivan, Michael, *Chinese Art in the Twentieth Century*, University of California Press, Berkeley, 1959. Clunas, Craig, *Art in China*, Oxford University Press, Oxford and New York, 1997. Yang Xin/and others, *Three Thousand Years of Chinese Painting*, Yale University Press, 1997.

AUCTION RECORDS:

HONG KONG, 12 Jan 1986, *Eagle in Snowstorm* (1948, ink and colour on paper, hanging scroll, 67 3/4 x 37 ins / 172 x 94 cm) HKD 370,000. HONG KONG, 19 May 1988, *Eagle* (black ink and colour on paper, hanging scroll, 57 1/2 x 29 ins / 146.2 x 73.5 cm) HKD 253,000. HONG KONG, 17 Nov 1988, *Weeping Willows in Spring Breeze* (inks, hanging scroll, 51 1/4 ins / 130 cm, 3 1/2 x 23 3/4 ins/9 x 60.4 cm) HKD 220,000; *Bird Perched on Branch* (inks/paper, hanging scroll, 51 1/4 x 24 3/4 ins / 130 x 63 cm) HKD 115,000. HONG KONG, 16 Jan 1989, *Egret on Pine Branch* (1923, ink and colour on paper, 46 3/4 x 23 1/2 ins / 118.7 x 59.7 cm) HKD 39,600. HONG KONG, 18 May 1989, *Branches of Banana Tree* (1930, ink and colour on paper, hanging scroll, 37 3/4 x 14 1/2 ins / 96 x 37 cm) HKD 55,000. HONG KONG, 15 Nov 1989, *Owl* (ink and colour on paper, hanging scroll, 51 3/4 x 14 1/2 ins / 131.5 x 37 cm) HKD 110,000. NEW YORK, 31 May 1990, *Chrysanthemums* (ink on paper, 41 x 13 1/2 ins / 104 x 34.3 cm) USD 2,200. HONG KONG, 15 Nov 1990, *Lady in White* (ink and colour on paper, hanging scroll, 46 3/4 x 18 1/2 ins / 119 x 47.2 cm) HKD 154,000. HONG KONG, 2 May 1991, *Pine Trunk and Branch* (1923, ink on paper, hanging scroll, 51 1/4 x 25 ins / 130 x 63.2 cm) HKD 88,000. HONG KONG, 28 Sept 1992, *Hydrangea Blossom and Rock* (ink and colour on paper, hanging scroll, 50 1/2 x 22 ins / 128 x 56 cm) HKD 143,000. HONG KONG, 22 March 1993, *Himalayas* (ink and colour on paper, 37 3/4 x 17 1/4 ins / 96 x 43.5 cm) HKD 133,000. HONG KONG, 29 April 1993, *Mouse in Basket of Grapes* (1946, ink and colour on paper, hanging scroll, 34 1/4 x 17 ins / 86.8 x 43.2 cm) HKD 218,500. NEW YORK, 16 June 1993, *Nine Carp* (ink and colour on paper, hanging scroll, 53 x 26 1/2 ins / 134.6 x 67.3 cm) USD 11,500. HONG KONG, 4 May 1995, *Storm at Night* (ink and light colour on paper, hanging scroll, 51 1/4 x 24 1/2 ins / 130.2 x 62.5 cm) HKD 69,000. NEW YORK, 18 March 1997, *Fish* (1935, ink and colour on paper, hanging scroll, 46 1/2 x 25 ins / 118.1 x 63.5 cm) USD 13,800; *Lily* (ink and colour on paper, hanging scroll, 20 x 21 ins / 50.8 x 53.3 cm) USD 6,325. HONG KONG, 28 April 1997, *Ink Orchid* (ink on paper, hanging scroll, 54 x 12 3/4 ins / 136.3 x 32.7 cm) HKD 97,750. HONG KONG, 26 April 1999, *Crows by Straw Pile* (1917 and 1930, ink and colour, hanging scroll, 57 x 28 ins / 146 x 71 cm) HKD 210,000. HONG KONG, 6 May 2002, *Building Sites in Mountains* (ink and colour, scroll, 44 x 20 ins / 111 x 51 cm) HKD 80,000. HONG KONG, 27 Oct 2003, *Pine Branches* (1928, ink and colour, hanging scroll, 44 x 20 ins / 112 x 50 cm) HKD 190,000. HONG KONG, 26 April 2004, *Night Journey* (1908, ink and colour, hanging scroll, 53 x 23 ins / 134 x 58 cm) HKD 180,000. LONDON, 9 June 2004, *Monkey on Hilltop* (ink and colour, 11 x 7 ins / 27 x 17 cm) GBP 8,000.

GAO JIANSHENG, or Gao Jianseng
Chinese, 20th century.
Born 1894; died 1916.
Painter. Landscapes with figures.

AUCTION RECORDS:

HONG KONG, 19 May 1988, *Woman in Winter Landscape* (1910, black ink and colour on silk, hanging scroll, 37 x 15 1/4 ins / 94 x 38.5 cm) HKD 82,500. HONG KONG, 16 Jan 1989, *Figure on Bridge over Mountain Stream* (ink and colour on paper, hanging scroll, 33 1/2 x 16 ins / 85.1 x 40.6 cm) HKD 55,000. HONG KONG, 28 Sept 1992, *Three White Egrets* (ink and colour on paper, hanging scroll, 52 3/4 x 25 1/2 ins / 134 x 65 cm) HKD 98,000. HONG KONG, 29 April 1993, *Fox Carrying off Prey by Moonlight* (1914, ink and colour on paper, 52 1/4 x 24 3/4 ins / 133 x 63 cm) HKD 241,500. HONG KONG, 5 May 1994, *Eagle on Pine Branch* (1910, ink and colour on paper, hanging scroll, 45 x 19 1/4 ins / 114.5 x 48.8 cm) HKD 23,000.

GAO KEGONG, or Kao K'o-kung, original name: Shian, style name: Yanjing, sobriquet: Fangshan laoren
Chinese, 13th - 14th century.
Born 1248, in Datong (Shanxi); died probably after 1310.
Painter.

Gao Kekong's family were Muslim Uighurs from eastern Turkestan who had assimilated to Han culture. His father was a scholar from Datong, but he himself went to live in Wulin. Gao Kekong began his official career in 1275 as a mninister of justice and governor of two provinces. An amateur painter and part of the Yuan administration in Beijing, he was greatly respected by his contemporaries and even more so by the following generation as the eldest of the great landscape painters of this period. He painted with difficulty, most often when he was 'just right' after having been drinking. He excelled in bamboo and landscape painting, which he executed in lightly coloured ink. Unfortunately, almost all of his landscapes have been lost. His first works were in the style of Mi Fu (1051-1107) and Mi Youren (1086-1165). Later he turned to Dong Yuan (died 962) and Juran (active 960-980). He tried to achieve a synthesis of old styles and his own originality to satisfy the antiquated tastes of the time and his personal need for expression. He and several of his contemporaries tried to revive the great Northern Song landscape tradition and disregard the knowledge acquired over the two preceding centuries; they mark the beginning of a new era in the history of Chinese painting. Even if they did not find immediate solutions, they were brilliant innovators.

BIBLIOGRAPHY:

Cahill, James, *Chinese Painting*, Skira, Geneva, 1960. Yang Xin/and others, *Three Thousand Years of Chinese Painting*, Yale University Press, 1997.

MUSEUMS AND GALLERIES:

BEIJING (Palace Mus.): *Mountains in Clouds* (colophon by Wang Jian, attributed) - SHANGHAI: *Mountain before Rain* (colour on silk) - TAIPEI (National Palace Mus.): *Hills in Rain*; *Hills and Waterfall in Clouds*; *Green Hills and White Clouds* (1245-1320, ink and colour on silk, handscroll, attributed); *Verdant Peaks Emerging from Clouds* (ink and colour on silk, hanging scroll, unsigned, with two contemporary inscriptions, one dated 1309 by the painter Li Kan).

GAO KEMING, or Kao K'o-ming
Chinese, 11th century.
Born in Jiangzhou (Shaanxi).
Painter. Figures, landscapes.

Gao Keming was a friend of Yen Wengui. He was a member of the Imperial Painting Academy from about 1008 until 1053. Like other contemporary members of the academy, he was undoubtedly influenced by Guo Xi (c. 1020-1100) and imbued with the a new, more personal spirit in landscape painting. One of his scrolls, *First Snow on River*, signed and dated 1035, is an imaginary journey along a river, with pine woods and bamboo, scholars in their retreats, and fishermen in their boats. The eroded riverbank is drawn in large strokes of diluted ink.

GAO LUN. See **GAO JIANFU**

GAO QIFENG, or Kao Ch'i-feng
Chinese, 20th century.
Born 1889, in Canton; died 1933.
Painter.

Gao Qifeng was the younger brother of Gao Jianfu. He also helped to form the Lingnan school.

AUCTION RECORDS:

HONG KONG, 12 Jan 1986, *Tiger Roaring at Moon* (ink and colour on paper, hanging scroll, 67 3/4 x 37 ins / 172 x 94 cm) HKD 320,000. HONG KONG, 17 Nov 1988, *Bird Perched on Branch with Bamboo Shoot* (ink on paper, hanging scroll, 48 3/4 x 15 3/4 ins / 124 x 40 cm) HKD 74,800; *Crows in Willows* (ink on paper, 16 x 19 ins / 40.8 x 48.2 cm) HKD 187,000. HONG KONG, 16 Jan 1989, *Falcon Taking Flight* (1909, ink and colour on paper, hanging scroll, 69 3/4 x 37 ins / 177 x 94 cm) HKD 286,000. HONG KONG, 15 Nov 1989, *Flowering Cherry in Moonlight* (1924, ink and colour on paper, hanging scroll, 52 1/4 x 18 1/2 ins / 132.5 x 47.3 cm) HKD 704,000. HONG KONG, 15 Nov 1990, *Cicada* (ink and colour on silk, 8 3/4 x 12 3/4 ins / 22.5 x 32.6 cm) HKD 26,400. HONG KONG, 2 May 1991, *Cock and Hen in Landscape* (ink and colour on paper, hanging scroll, 52 1/4 x 18 1/2 ins / 133 x 47 cm) HKD 148,500. HONG KONG, 28 Sept 1992, *Bodhidharma* (ink and colour on paper, hanging scroll, 33 3/4 x 12 1/4 ins / 86 x 31 cm) HKD 440,000. HONG KONG, 29 Oct 1992, *Birds and Flowers* (ink and colour on paper, album of twelve leaves, each 10 1/4 x 14 ins / 26 x 35.5 cm) HKD 1,650,000. HONG KONG, 29 April 1993, *Spring has come* (ink and colour on paper, 51 3/4 x 18 1/2 ins / 131.5 x 46.8 cm) HKD 548,000. NEW YORK, 16 June 1993, *Brick Oven in Canton* (ink and colour on paper, hanging scroll, 46 x 15 3/4 ins / 116.8 x 40 cm) USD 18,400. HONG KONG, 5 May 1994, *Bird in Woods in Winter* (ink on paper, hanging scroll, 51 1/4 x 11 1/2 ins / 130.2 x 29.2 cm) HKD 80,500. HONG KONG, 4 May 1995, *Green Woodpeckers* (ink and colour on paper, hanging scroll, 52 1/4 x 18 1/4 ins / 133 x 46.3 cm) HKD 264,500. HONG KONG, 29 April 1996, *Peonies* (1928, ink and colour on paper, hanging scroll, 31 1/2 x 13 1/2 ins / 80 x 34 cm) HKD 368,000. HONG KONG, 4 Nov 1996, *Landscapes* (ink, set of eight, each 10 1/4 x 14 ins / 25.8 x 35.5 cm) HKD 900,000. HONG KONG, 28 April 1997, *Frozen Village* (ink and colour on paper, hanging scroll, 30 1/4 x 14 1/4 ins / 76.8 x 36.2 cm) HKD 210,000. HONG KONG, 28 Oct 2001, *Mandarin Ducks* (1922, ink and colour, scroll, 46 x 16 ins / 118 x 40 cm) HKD 230,000. HONG KONG, 28 Oct 2001, *Pomegranate and Bird* (ink and colour, scroll, 37 x 17 ins / 94 x 44 cm) HKD 240,000. HONG KONG, 27 Oct 2003, *Sketches of Monkeys* (ink, album of 76, 7 x 5 ins / 19 x 13 cm) HKD 400,000. HONG KONG, 27 Oct 2003, *Return of Spring* (ink and colour, hanging scroll, 61 x 19 ins / 156 x 49 cm) HKD 700,000. HONG KONG, 26 April 2004, *Ape, Carp* (1915, ink on silk, hanging scrolls, a pair) HKD 800,000. HONG KONG, 26 April 2004, *Landscape* (1967, ink and colour, eight, 10 x 14 ins / 25 x 35 cm) HKD 3,500,000.

GAO QIPEI, or Kao Ch'i-p'ei, style name: Weizhi, sobriquets: Qieyuan, Nancun, Changbai shanren
Chinese, 17th - 18th century.
Born 1660, in Liaoyang (now Liaoning), Manchuria; died c. 1734.
Painter, draughtsman. Portraits, landscapes, animals.

At the time of the great individualist painters of the end of the 17th century and beginning of the 18th centuries, such as Shitao or Bada Shanren, some Chinese artists felt that they had to create a new style to mark their originality. Gao Qipei is a typical example of this forced originality. Already a very good painter at the age of eight, he was appreciated at court, where he held an important position. But at the age of 20 he was already concerned about not having formed his own style and the traditional brush was no longer enough for him. He invented a finger-painting technique, making the washes and large strokes by applying ink and colours with the tips of his fingers and sides of his hands, and drawing lines with a long fingernail which he had carefully cut at the end. This method, which was not entirely new, gave his work a novel appearance, which explains his great popularity. Many of his works are, however, more vigorous than refined, sometimes shocking in the crudeness of their execution. Gao is even believed to have engaged other artists to spread the colours on his paintings. He was best suited to the album, where themes and motifs abound unrestrained and the rough drawing merges with the loose washes, into which touches of light colour blend peacefully. But despite his lack of inhibition, Gao's fingers convey little ardent expression. Gao Qipei's theoretical ideas were collated by his great-nephew, Gao Bing, in a treatise entitled *Zhitou Huashuo*. These teachings go beyond pure finger painting and are of great interest.

BIBLIOGRAPHY:

Cahill, James, *Fantastics and Eccentrics in Chinese Painting*, Asia Society, New York, 1972. Clunas, Craig, *Art in China*, Oxford University Press, Oxford and New York, 1997. Fahr-Becker, Gabriele (ed.), *The Art of East Asia: Volume 1*, Könemann, Cologne, 1998.

MUSEUMS AND GALLERIES:

AMSTERDAM (Rijksmus.): *Album of Twelve Landscape Studies* (ink and light colour on paper, each inscribed and signed) - BERLIN: *Zhong Kui with Bat* (signed) - BOSTON (MFA): *Album of Ten Finger Paintings* (dated 1698, ink and colour on paper) - COLOGNE (Mus. für Ostasiatische Kunst): *Young Girls with Flowers* (ink and light colour on paper, signed); *Li Taipo in Lushan* (ink and light colour on paper, signed) - LONDON (British Mus.): *Man with Parasol* (signed) - SEATTLE (AM): *Man with Horse near Tree* (poem by the artist) - SHANGHAI: *Album of Finger Drawings* (ink on paper).

AUCTION RECORDS:

NEW YORK, 2 June 1988, *Fish* (ink, hanging scroll, 54 x 29 1/2 ins / 137 x 75 cm) USD 4,400. NEW YORK, 31 May 1989, *Guan Gong* (1714, ink and colour on paper, hanging scroll, 78 x 33 ins / 198.1 x 83.9 cm) USD 8,800. NEW YORK, 4 Dec 1989, *Album of Various Birds* (ink and colour on silk, eight leaves, each 5 3/4 x 6 3/4 ins / 14.5 x 17 cm) USD 60,500. NEW YORK, 29 May 1991, *Colony of Fish* (ink on paper, hanging scroll, 24 x 12 1/2 ins / 61 x 32 cm) USD 8,800. NEW YORK, 25 Nov 1991, *Frog* (ink and light colour on paper, hanging scroll, 29 3/4 x 15 ins / 75.6 x 38.3 cm) USD 3,190. NEW YORK, 2 Dec 1992, *Tigers* (ink and colour on paper, hanging scroll) USD 5,500. NEW YORK, 21 March 1995, *Six-Leaf Album of Various Subjects* (ink and colour on paper, each 9 1/4 x 12 3/4 ins / 23.5 x 32.7 cm) USD 4,025. NEW YORK, 22 Sept 1997, *Landscapes* (ink and pigments, album of twelve leaves, 11 x 18 1/4 ins / 27.9 x 46.4 cm) USD 87,750. HONG KONG, 6 July 2003, *Fish* (ink, hanging scroll, 44 x 21 ins / 111 x 53 cm) HKD 65,000. HONG KONG, 26 Oct 2003, *Winter Landscape* (ink on silk, 78 x 21 ins / 197 x 53 cm) HKD 70,000. HONG KONG, 25 April 2004, *Gazing at Waterfall* (ink and colour, hanging scroll, 69 x 30 ins / 174 x 77 cm) HKD 170,000.

GAO RANHUI, or Kao Jan-hui
Chinese, 13th - 14th century.
Painter.
Yuan dynasty.
Gao Ranhui is mentioned not in the Chinese biographies of the painters but in a Japanese catalogue, the *Kundaikan Sayuchoki*, number 71. He is sometimes confused with Gao Kekong and may have been Korean. He is known to have produced several landscapes.

GAO SHIQI, or Kao Shih-ch'i, style name: Danren, sobriquet: Jiangcun
Chinese, 17th century.
Born 1645; died 1704.
Active in Qiantang (Zhejiang).
Painter.
Gao Shiqi was an art connoisseur and collector, and was vice-president of the Bureau of Rites. He wrote two treatises: *Jiangcun Xiaoxia Lu* and *Kangzi Xiaoxia Lu*.

GAO SHUCHENG, or Kao Shu-ch'eng, style name: Jinyu, sobriquet: Maian
Chinese, 18th century.
Born in Qiantang (Zhejiang).
Active during the second half of the 18th century.
Painter.
Gao Shucheng sat the triennial *juren* (provincial) examinations in 1770. He painted landscapes in the style of the Yuan masters.

GAO TINGLI, or Kao T'ing-li, real name: Bing, style name: Yanhui, sobriquet: Manshi
Chinese, 14th - 15th century.
Born 1350, in Jiangluo; died 1423.
Painter.
Ming dynasty.
Gao Tingli was a member of the Hanlin academy during the reign of Emperor Yongle (1403-1425). He painted landscapes in the style of Mi Fu (1051-1107).

GAO XIANG, or Kao Hsiang, style name: Fenggang, sobriquets: Xitang, Shanlin waichen
Chinese, 18th century.
Born 1688, in Yangzhou (Jiangsu); died 1754.
Active c. 1700-1730.
Painter. Landscapes, flowers.
Gao Xiang was one of the Eight Eccentrics of Yangzhou. He painted plum blossom. The clarity and softness of his brushwork, with a few large strokes, make his work pleasing to the eye.

MUSEUMS AND GALLERIES:
BEIJING (Palace Mus.): *Gentle Hills Rising above River in Mist* (dated 1724, after a Yuan master) - SHANGHAI: *Small Album of Landscape Studies* (ink on paper, signed poem).

AUCTION RECORDS:
NEW YORK, 29 Nov 1993, *Flowering Cherry* (ink and colour on paper, hanging scroll, 32 x 14 1/4 ins / 81.3 x 36.2 cm) USD 4,600.

GAO XIAOHUA
Chinese, 20th - 21st century.
Born 1955, in Nanjing.
Painter. Figures, scenes with figures.
Gao Xiaohua began his studies at Sichuan Academy of Art, graduating in 1982. Immediately afterwards he re-enrolled, this time to study oil painting. A year later he was admitted into the Central Academy of Fine Arts. He won the silver award at the 30th anniversary celebration of the National Art Exhibition. He emigrated to the USA in 1985 and in 1999 returned to Sichuan, where he became vice dean of the School of Arts and Humanities at Chongqing University.

AUCTION RECORDS:
HONG KONG, 4 May 1995, *Yi Woman Playing Harmonica* (oil on canvas, 24 x 20 ins / 61 x 51 cm) HKD 46,000.

GAO XINGJIAN
Chinese, 20th century.
Born 4 January 1940, in Ganzhou (Jiangxi Province).
Active in France.
Painter, draughtsman, writer, illustrator. Stage sets.
The Nobel-prizewinning writer Gao Xingjian was a painter even before becoming a novelist, essayist, dramatist and director. He studied painting at Nanjing under the painter Yu Yungzhong. Then, in 1962, he took a degree in French at the department of foreign languages in Beijing, translating various French writers such as Ionesco, Prévert, Michaux, Ponge and Pérec into Chinese. During the cultural revolution, he was sent to a re-education camp where he taught for six years, at the same time practising black-and-white photography. In 1978 he visited France and Italy as an interpreter and he returned there in 1987, this time being granted political asylum. He became a French citizen in 1997. In 2000, Gao was awarded Italy's Premio Letterario Feronia and the Nobel prize for literature for *Soul Mountain*. In France, he was named Chevalier des Arts et des Lettres in 1992 and Chevalier of the Légion d'Honneur in 2000. In 2001, the Chinese University of Hong Kong made him an honorary doctor of literature. He was also made doctor honoris causa by Sun Yat-Sen University, Taipei, in 2001 and the University of Provence in Aix-en-Provence in 2002.

Photography permits Gao to incorporate light into his work in ink on rice paper. He has distanced himself from traditional Chinese techniques in order to paint completely spontaneously and not to create from models or in self-affirmation but to reveal a world of feeling, of which he offers us 'glimpses which change from moment to moment as time passes'. Music plays a key role in his creative process as an artist, for, as he sees it, music, like painting, is free of concepts and sense and allows one to express pure sensation and spiritual states. When painting, he listens to western music, from Bach to contemporary composers. In this scheme of things, where everything is directed towards capturing an inner feeling, where nature looms up in an enigmatic form, stealing away from its appearance at the very moment in which it yields itself up, the very notions of abstract and figurative are no longer meaningful. And in this, Gao Xingjian is very much in the mainstream of Chinese painting and part of his own story as a writer. In the dark masses of ink, interspersed with streams of light, he confronts the reality both of being an exile, a witness to and victim of the atrocities of the Communist regime, and a creator standing outside time and history. Gao makes a distinction between his painting and his writing: his painting inhabits a physical, spiritual, internal, non-verbal space, while in his writing he explores thought and lends an ear to the world. 'In literature,' he has said, 'I chase words like sounds. In painting, the gesture comes from the body.' For him, painting is simply the act of transposing an interior state that has been stripped of all desire to exhibit intimacy. The tumultuous washes of his work, the infinite variety of his grays as they sink towards the deep black through which light passes stubbornly, bear eloquent witness to his dictum.

Gao also designed the sets for his opera *Snow in August*, which was staged in Taipei in 2002, and designs cover illustrations for his own books. He took part in the 1989, 1990 and 1991 Figuration Critique exhibitions at the Grand Palais in Paris. He had solo exhibitions in 1985 at the Berliner Kunsterhaus Bethanien in Berlin; in 1996 at the Espace d'Art Contemporain Le Cercle Bleu in Metz; in 2001 (a retrospective) at the Grande Chapelle du Palais des Papes in Avignon; in 2002 at the Museo Nacional Centro de Arte Reina Sofia, Madrid; in 2002 at the Musée des Beaux-Arts in Mons; in

2003 at the Musée des Tapisseries in Aix-en-Provence and at the Chapelle de la Vieille Charité in Marseilles; in 2003 *Gao Xingjian: inchiostri su carta 1983-1993* (*Gao Xingjian: Paintings in Ink on Paper 1983-1993*) at the Galleria Torbandena and Teatro Miela in Trieste; in 2004 at the Galerie Claude Bernard in Paris; and in 2004 at the Museu d'Art Modern in Barcelona.

BIBLIOGRAPHY:
Ink Paintings by Gao Xingjian, Taipei Fine Arts Museum, Taipei, 1995. Xingjian, Gao, *Pour une autre esthétique*, Flammarion, Paris, 2001. *Gao Xingjian*, exhibition catalogue, Palais des Papes, Avignon, 2001. *Gao Xingjian, le goût de l'encre*, exhibition catalogue, Musée des Beaux-Arts, Mons, Hazan, Paris, 2002. Xingjian, Gao, *Ink Paintings by Gao Xingjian*, Homa & Sekey Books, Dumont (NJ), 2002. Xingjian, Gao, *Return to Painting*, Perennial, 2002. Mondzain, Marie-Josée (introduction), *Gao Xingjian. Ni mots, ni signes*, exhibition catalogue, Musée des Tapisseries, Aix-en-Provence, 2003.

MUSEUMS AND GALLERIES:
FREIBURG (Morat-Institut für Kunst und Kunstwissenschaft) - MALMÖ (Krapperrus Konsthall) - STOCKHOLM (Moderna Mus.) - STOCKHOLM (Ostasiatiska Museet) - TAIPEI (Taipei Fine Arts Mus.) - TAIPEI (Taiwan National History Mus.).

GAO YAN, or Kao Yen, style name: Wanggong
Chinese, 17th century.
Born 1616, in Xinhui (Guangdong); died c. 1687.
Active during the second half of the 17th century.
Painter, calligrapher. Landscapes.

Gao Yan was a poet, calligrapher and painter, working particularly as a painter towards the end of his life. He liked to paint in the moonlight. There is a signed landscape by him, probably dated 1666.

AUCTION RECORDS:
NEW YORK, 2 June 1988, *Landscape at Beginning of Spring* (ink on paper, hanging scroll, 16 x 10 1/2 ins / 40.7 x 26.5 cm) USD 9,350.

GAO YANG, or Kao Yang, style name: Qiufu
Chinese, 17th century.
Born in Siming (Zhejiang).
Active c. 1623-1631.
Painter, draughtsman. Landscapes, architectural views, gardens, birds, flowers.

Gao Yang was the son-in-law of Zhao Bei. He painted mostly flowers, birds and rocks, but towards the end of his career also produced landscapes.

MUSEUMS AND GALLERIES:
COLOGNE (Mus. für Ostasiatische Kunst): *Temple in Mountain Gorge* (signed and dated 1623, ink and light colours on gold-flecked paper fan) - STOCKHOLM (Nationalmus.): *Rock Garden* (ink and colour on paper, large album leaf, signed, two seals of the artist).

GAO YU, or Kao Yu, style name: Yuji
Chinese, 17th century.
Active at the end of the 17th century.
Painter.

Gao Yu was the nephew of the painter Gao Cen. He painted landscapes in the manner of his uncle, but is not one of the Eight Masters of Nanjing.

GAO ZIMING. See **HUXIAN, peasant painters of**

GAO ZIMING, or Kao Tse-ming
Chinese, 20th century.
Painter. Scenes with figures.

Gao Ziming was trained classically. His involvement with the Huxian peasant painting movement enabled him in his own work to preserve the freshness of his own vision.

GAONA, Gabriel Vicente
Mexican, 19th century.
Born 1828, in Mérida (Yucatan); died 1899, in Mérida.
Painter, engraver, illustrator.

GAONA DE LOS REYES, José
Spanish, 19th century.
Born in the 19th century.
Painter. Flowers, fruit.

José Gaona de los Reyes exhibited in Cádiz between 185[illegible] and 1862.

GAOZONG. See **QIANLONG**

GAOZONG, or Kao-tsung
Chinese, 12th century.
Born 1107; died 1187.
Painter. Figures, landscapes, flowers.

Gaozong (1127-1162) was the son of Emperor Huizong and the first of the Southern Song emperors. He was also a painter and connoisseur.

MUSEUMS AND GALLERIES:
BEIJING (Palace Mus.): *River Landscape with Fishing Boa[t]* (leaf from an album, poem by the emperor).

GAPP, Alois
Austrian, 19th century.
Born 21 June 1838, in Telfs (Tyrol); died 10 April 1906, in Graz.
Sculptor.

Gapp was the pupil of Renn before completing his studies in Munich, where he later settled.

GAPPNIG, Valentin
German, 18th century.
Active in Oberwölz, Austria c. 1700.
Painter.

Gappnig is noted for his view of Oberwölz and Rottenfels.

GARA, Arnold
Hungarian, 20th century.
Born 25 February 1882, in Budapest.
Painter.

Arnold Gara painted landscapes and portraits.

GARABETIAN, Cricor
Romanian, 20th century.
Born 7 November 1908, in Bucharest.
Painter. Religious subjects, landscapes.

Cricor Garabetian studied at the school of fine art in Bucharest before settling in France in 1930. He painted in a figurative style essentially inspired by religion and also executed landscapes. In France he lived in Lyons since 1947 where he exhibited, and also took part in a number of Paris Salons.

MUSEUMS AND GALLERIES:
ANNECY - BUCHAREST - LYONS.

GARABITO
Spanish, 16th century.
Active in Seville.
Sculptor.

GARACCI, Carlo
French, 19th century.
Born 1818, in Nice; died 1895.
Painter. Portraits, genre scenes.

He was a much-respected principal of the College of Design in Nice. He painted a large number of interiors and scenes of monastic life.

MUSEUMS AND GALLERIES:
NICE: *Portrait of the Princesse de Solms*.

GARACHE, Claude
French, 20th century.
Born 1930, in Paris.
Painter, engraver, illustrator. Nudes.

Claude Garache began producing his first paintings and sculptures in 1950. Between 1950 and 1959 he travelled all over the world. His first success was as an engraver and led to an invitation to join the Salon de Mai, which he did, resigning from it in 1970. Garache showed his engravings and paintings at the Salon's exhibitions. In 2001 his work was featured in the *Corps à Corps* (*Body to Body*) exhibition at the Centre Wallonie-Bruxelles in Paris which brought together some sixty engravings and artists' books from the second half of the 20th century relating to the theme of the representation of the human body, clothed and nude, alone or in groups, entire or in part. Since 1965 he has also held numerous solo exhibitions of his paintings at the Galerie Maeght and then the Galerie Lelong and further exhibitions in Europe and the USA and in 1983 at the Musée Grobet-Labadié in Marseilles.

Garache's work - engravings and paintings - often takes as its theme the evocation of the female form, but reduced to a very cursory indication of the general form and specific shape and devoid of faces. The fineness of his use of light, often translated in discreet pink tones, and his delicate suggestion of flesh tints characterise a very personal vision and manner of evoking not so much woman as a person but the flavour of the female body in its potential to awake desire. This obsessional painting and the permanence of desire in the gustative suggestion of its undescribed object have enticed many writers and Garache has provided illustrations for several collections of poetry, including Yves Bonnefoy's *L'Ordalie*.

BIBLIOGRAPHY:

Starobinski, Jean/Jacottet, Philippe, '*Garache*' in *coll. Repères-Cahiers d'art contemporain*, Gal. Lelong, Paris, 1984. Fumaroli, Marc, *Garache*, Gal. Lelong, Paris, 1988. Starobinski, Jean, *Garache*, Flammarion, Gal. Lelong, Paris, 1988.

MUSEUMS AND GALLERIES:

MARSEILLES (Mus. Cantini): *Avocet* (1973).

AUCTION RECORDS:

PARIS, 24 March 1984, *Epiaire* (1974, oil on canvas, 45 x 57 1/2 ins / 114 x 146 cm) FRF 34,500. PARIS, 3 Dec 1987, *Vaucienne* (oil on canvas, 45 x 57 1/2 ins / 114 x 146 cm) FRF 11,000. PARIS, 26 Oct 1988, *La Verte* (c. 1966, oil on canvas, 30 1/4 x 22 1/2 ins / 77 x 57 cm) FRF 11,000. PARIS, 28 Oct 1988, *Vaumoise* (1975, oil on canvas, 45 x 57 1/2 ins / 114 x 146 cm) FRF 6,000. PARIS, 26 Nov 1989, *Composition in Pink* (oil on canvas, 57 1/2 x 45 ins / 146 x 114 cm) FRF 25,000. PARIS, 10 June 1990, *Red Woman Crouching* (1971, oil on canvas, 45 x 57 1/2 ins / 114 x 146 cm) FRF 30,000. PARIS, 29-30 June 1995, *Bapaume* (1972, oil on canvas, 45 1/4 x 57 1/4 ins / 115 x 145.5 cm) FRF 26,000. PARIS, 10 Dec 1995, *Gesse* (1974, oil on canvas, 57 1/2 x 45 ins / 146 x 114 cm) FRF 10,000.

GARAFULIC, Lily

Chilean, 20th century.
Born 1914, in Siantago.
Sculptor. Religious subjects, figures.

In 1934, Lily Garafulic enrolled at the school of fine arts in Santiago. She studied under Lorenzo Dominguez who, together with Julio Antonio Vásquez and Samuel Román, brought about a unique blossoming in Chilean statuary. In 1944 she was awarded a Guggenheim bursary that enabled her to work in the USA. In 1951 she was appointed to teach at the school of fine arts in Santiago. Up to 1957 her sculpture remained within the confines of Expressionist representation but with some roots in primitive Chilean art. After this date her style became less ornamented, showing a tendency towards the abstract.

Garafulic exhibited in various group exhibitions. She also held solo exhibitions in Santiago in 1944, 1947 and 1949 which led to important commissions from the public authorities, notably for 16 grandiose figures of the prophets, capitals and mosaics for the Chilean basilica of Lourdes and important reliefs in the city of Valparaíso, among other works.

BIBLIOGRAPHY:

Ivelic, M., *La escultura chilena*, Santiago, 1979. Nelly, R., *Margins and Institutions*, Melbourne, 1986. *Recovering Histories: Aspects of Contemporary Art in Chile since 1982/Historias recuperadas: Aspectos del arte contemporáneo en Chile desde 1982*, exhibition catalogue, Rutgers University, Zimmerli A. Mus., New Brunswick, 1993. Cruz de Amenabar, I., *Arte: Lo mejor en la historia de la pintura y escultura en Chile*, Santiago, 1995. Ivelic, M., '*Chile*' in *Latin American Art in the Twentieth Century*, London, 1996 (ed. E. Sullivan).

GARAICAO, Carlos

Congolese, 20th century.
Installation artist.

In 1995, Carlos Garaicao took part in the *Africus* Biennale in Johannesburg.

GARAL, Marcos

Spanish, 17th century.
Sculptor.

GARAMENDI, Bernabé de

Spanish, 19th century.
Born c. 1840, in Bilbao; died 1898.
Sculptor.

Bernabé de Garamendi exhibited at the exhibition of the national fine arts society of Madrid from 1865. He was awarded a gold medal in Bilbao in 1882.

BIBLIOGRAPHY:

Paliza, Maite, *Bernabé de Garamendi: un escultor bilbaíno: 1833-1898*, Bilbao Bizkaia Kutxa, Bilbao, 1999.

GARAND, Edme

French, 18th century.
Active in Paris in 1752.
Painter, sculptor.

GARAND, Jean Baptiste, or Garant

French, 18th century.
Died c. 1780, in Paris.
Painter, miniaturist, engraver, draughtsman. Portraits.

Jean Garand was a member of the Académie de St-Luc. He took part in the exhibitions at this society from 1762 to 1774. He is known for his miniature portraits and etchings.

AUCTION RECORDS:

PARIS, 12 and 13 March 1926, *Portrait of Jean-Pierre de Joly* (pen and wash) FRF 250. PARIS, 10 Dec 1990, *Woman Selling Flowers* (black chalk and coloured chalks, 10 3/4 x 8 3/4 ins / 27.2 x 22.2 cm) FRF 4,500.

GARANJOUD, Claude

French, 20th century.
Born 18 March 1926, in La Tronche, near Grenoble.
Painter (including gouache), collage artist, engraver, draughtsman, illustrator.

Claude Garanjoud studied at the École des Arts Décoratifs in Grenoble and from 1949 continued his studies in Paris. He lives and works in Paris and Villeneuve-lès-Avignon.

From 1955 to 1965 he was immersed in the great abstract movement and painted in a manner that could be called Abstract Landscapism, coming under the influence of artists such as Zao Wou-ki and Nicolas de Staël. From 1966 to 1970 he developed towards a more lyrical form of abstraction in which the element of action was more openly and amply expressed in large horizontal and vertical planes. From 1971 his work moved towards a stripping down of form and a reduced palette of colour - from black to white via greys and blues with touches of red. He is the heir of Kandinsky's historical lyricism and is also interested in the Far East, particularly in calligraphy and the religious philosophy from which it derives and in the relationship between the individual and the world. He seeks to dematerialise his painting, in both the figurative and literal sense (reducing the use of impasto) and to see it as a transcription of signs, of ideograms, to read it as a form of writing, to experience it as an internal, spiritual event.

He has taken part in group exhibitions, including: the Salon de la Jeune Peinture in Paris, of which he was a member; the Salon d'Automne, Paris; the Paris Biennale; in 1963 the *20 Jeunes Peintres de l'École de Paris* (*20 Young Painters of the Paris School*) exhibition at the Musée National d'Art Moderne; in 1968 at the Musée de Tous-les-Saints, Schaffhouse; in 1973 at the Maison de la Culture, Grenoble; in 1983, the *10 Années d'Acquisitions* (*A Decade of Acquisitions*) exhibition at the Musée de Grenoble; in 1983, the *150 Livres d'Artistes* (*150 Artists' Books*) exhibition at the Palais Synodal, Sens; in 1987, the *Carte Blanche à Kenneth White* (*Carte Blanche to Kenneth White*) exhibition at the Maison de la Poésie, Paris; in 1988, the *l'Atelier Lacourière Frélaut, Trois Générations de Graveurs et d'Éditeurs* (*The Lacourière Frélaut Studio - Three Generations of Engravers and Publishers*) exhibition at the Centre d'Art le Grand Huit, Rennes; and in 1991, SAGA (Salon of Graphical Art), Paris, presented by the Lacourière Frélaut studio.

He has also held numerous solo exhibitions, including: in 1954 at the Galerie Repellin-Perriot, Grenoble; in 1957, 1958, 1960, 1961 and 1970 at the Galerie Guilmin, Grenoble; in 1982 and 1984 at the Foire Internationale d'Art Contemporain, Paris, presented by the Galerie Cupillard from Grenoble; in 1989 at the Musée Hébert (Hébert-d'Uckermann Foundation), La Troche - an exhibition of his paintings; in 1989 at the Bibliothèque Municipale d'Étude, Grenoble - an exhibition of his books; in 1991 at the Galerie Lacourière Frélaut in Paris; in 1994 at the Galerie Askeo, Paris; in 1995 at the Libraire Lettres et Images, Paris; in 2001 *Livres avec les Poètes* (*Books with Poets*) at the Bibliothèque Municipale d'Étude et d'Information, Grenoble; and in 2003 at the Musée Calvet, Avignon. He was awarded the Prix de la Jeune Peinture in 1958 and the Menton Biennale prize in 1964.

Since 1968 he has illustrated a large number of books, including the writing of St-John Perse (*Snows*, 1975); René Char's *Le Nu Perdu*, 1974, *La Truite*, 1984, *Toute Vie*, 1986, *L'Alouette*, 1986, *La Fauvette des Roseaux*, 1987 and *Le Martinet*, 1989; and Kenneth White's *The White Mistral*, 1980, *Les Portes de l'Ouest*, 1981 and *Signes du Mont Blanc*, 1984.

Bibliography:

Garanjoud, catalogue, La Tronche, Bibliothèque nationale d'étude, musée Hébert, Grenoble, 1989. *Garanjoud*, 1997.

Museums and Galleries:

Grenoble (Bibliothèque municipale) - Grenoble (Maison de la Culture) - Paris (BNF).

GARANTA, Nicolo

Italian, 16th century.
Active in Ferrara.
Painter, miniaturist.

Garanta worked for Cardinal Luigi d'Este.

GARAT, Francis, pseudonym of Jean-Jacques Francisque Garat

French, 19th - 20th century.
Born 16 July 1853; died probably c. 1914.
Active in Paris.
Painter, watercolourist, draughtsman. Genre scenes, figures, landscapes, urban landscapes.

Francis Garat was the son of Jules Garat who under the pseudonym Ridendo published short stories, poems and tales. He joined the Salon des Artistes Français in Paris in 1898. Garat painted numerous views of Paris in a broad, solid style.

FRANCIS GARAT

Auction records:

Paris, 15 Nov 1898, *The Place des Victoires* (watercolour) FRF 72; *Place de la République* (watercolour) FRF 42. Paris, 21 Nov 1899, *Panoramic View of the Trocadéro* (watercolour) FRF 220; *Place Clichy and Boulevard des Batignolles* (watercolour) FRF 220. Paris, 8 Nov 1918, *The Luxembourg and the Panthéon* (watercolour) FRF 95. Paris, 26-28 Dec 1922, *Scaffolding at the Madeleine* (watercolour) FRF 140. Paris, 30 Nov 1925, *Snow* (watercolour) FRF 100; *Boulevard* (watercolour) FRF 210; *The Sea* (watercolour) FRF 130. Paris, 10 May 1926, *The Ham Fair* (watercolour) FRF 150; *Posters* (drawing heightened) FRF 210; *View of Paris - the Omnibus* (watercolour) FRF 250. Paris, 14 and 15 Dec 1927, *Winter Sunday on the Fortifications* (watercolour) FRF 140. Paris, 31 Jan 1929, *Porte Pouchet* (watercolour) FRF 210. Paris, 24-26 April 1929, *Pont St-Michel with Snow* (watercolour) FRF 270. Paris, 7 Dec 1931, *Boulevard*, FRF 125. Paris, 5-7 Nov 1941, *The Quays and the Pont des Arts* (watercolour) FRF 480. Paris, 13 March 1942, *The Pont des Arts* (watercolour) FRF 600. Paris, 25 Sept 1942, *Place de la Concorde* (1890, watercolour) FRF 850. Paris, 2 June 1943, *The Seine in Winter* (watercolour) FRF 220. Paris, 16 and 17 May 1945, *The Carrousel* (watercolour) FRF 700; *The Cité* (watercolour) FRF 1,800; *The Madeleine; View of Paris* (two watercolours) FRF 4,200. Paris, Oct 1945-July 1946, *The Place des Victoires* (watercolour) FRF 1,700; *The Seine in Paris* (watercolour) FRF 800. Paris, 20 Nov 1946, *Place de la Concorde* (watercolour) FRF 2,000. Paris, 26 Feb 1947, *Pont Alexandre in the Rain* (watercolour) FRF 1,950. Paris, 20 Dec 1976, *Place de la Concorde* (watercolour, 17¼ x 13½ ins / 44 x 34.5 cm) FRF 3,000. Lille, 24 April 1983, *Nude in the Painter's Studio* (1883, oil on canvas, 19¾ x 24 ins / 50 x 61 cm) FRF 23,000. Neuilly, 13 Dec 1983, *Society Ladies on the Place de la Concorde* (watercolour, 11 x 13¾ ins / 27 x 35 cm) FRF 8,100. New York, 25 April 1988, *Crossing the Square* (1890, oil on canvas, 13 x 9¼ ins / 33 x 23.5 cm) USD 3,300. Versailles, 5 March 1989, *Society Ladies and Barouche on the Grand Boulevard* (watercolour, 10¾ x 19 ins / 27.5 x 48 cm) FRF 7,800. Paris, 19 June 1989, *Place du Châtelet* (watercolour, 11½ x 13¾ ins / 29 x 35 cm) FRF 35,000. Versailles, 18 March 1990, *Worksite on the Banks of the Seine* (watercolour, 18 x 29¼ ins / 45.5 x 74.5 cm) FRF 5,200. Paris, 12 July 1990, *View of Paris* (watercolour, 7 x 10¾ ins / 17.5 x 27.5 cm) FRF 13,000. Paris, 2 Dec 1991, *Place de la République with Figures, Paris* (watercolour, 28 x 39 ins / 71 x 99 cm) FRF 16,000. Paris, 2 Dec 1992, *Place de l'Hôtel de Ville in the Rain* (watercolour, 9¾ x 7¼ ins / 25 x 18.5 cm) FRF 3,200. Paris, 22 March 1994, *Harem Guard* (1872, watercolour, 14½ x 11 ins / 37 x 28 cm) FRF 3,500. Calais, 3 July 1994, *Omnibus and Carriages at Auteuil* (1895, watercolour, 13 x 9¾ ins / 33 x 25 cm) FRF 4,000. Paris, 27 Feb 1996, *The Flower Market at Christmas* (watercolour, 12½ x 8½ ins / 32 x 21.5 cm) FRF 4,000. Paris, 16 March 1998, *A Paris Square* (mixed media, 5 x 8¼ ins / 12.5 x 21 cm) FRF 2,000.

GARATE Y CLAVERO, Juan José

Spanish, 20th century.
Born 12 July 1870, in Arbalete del Arzobispo (Teruel); died 1939, in Madrid.
Painter. Figure compositions, portraits, genre scenes.

Juan José Garate y Clavero studied at the Aragon school of fine arts before receiving a bursary to study in Madrid and later Rome. He taught at the Saragossa school of fine arts from 1897 to 1911, when he moved to Madrid.

Garate y Clavero's work is in a traditional style and reveals a high degree of technical mastery of both draughtsmanship and colour. His work often records intimate moments of everyday life.

He took part in the exhibition of the national fine arts society of Madrid in 1895 (and was awarded a bronze medal), in the Paris exhibition of 1899 (bronze medal), the national exhibition in Madrid in 1904 (silver medal), the Saragossa regional exhibition in 1905 (gold medal), the exhibition of decorative arts in Madrid in 1911 (silver medal) and the Panama international exhibition of 1916 (gold medal). He also exhibited at collective exhibitions in 1924 and 1925 in Saragossa, in 1924 in Madrid and held solo exhibitions of his work.

BIBLIOGRAPHY:

Arnáiz, José Manuel/López Jiménez, Javier/Merchán Díaz, Manuel (ed.), *Cien años de pintura en Espana y Portugal (1830-1930)*, Antiqvaria, Madrid, 1989 (One Hundred Years of Painting in Spain and Portugal (1830-1930)).

MUSEUMS AND GALLERIES:

SARAGOSSA (Mus. de Zaragoza).

AUCTION RECORDS:

NEW YORK, April 1903, *The Lovers' Repose*, USD 360; *The Water Carrier*, USD 400. MADRID, 24 March 1981, *Al Fondo Zaragoza* (oil on canvas, 15 3/4 x 25 1/2 ins / 40 x 65 cm) ESP 100,000. NEW YORK, 16 Dec 1987, *Village Scene* (oil on canvas, 13 3/4 x 20 ins / 35 x 51 cm) ESP 1,100,000. LONDON, 14 Feb 1990, *The Interrupted Banquet* (oil on canvas, 19 1/4 x 30 3/4 ins / 49 x 78 cm) GBP 19,800. PARIS, 1 July 1992, *Bride and Groom in the Living Room* (1908, oil on card, 11 x 13 3/4 ins / 27 x 35 cm) FRF 3,500. NEW YORK, 16 Feb 1995, *View of Venice* (oil on panel, 11 x 21 ins / 27 x 52.4 cm) USD 17,825. MADRID, 22 Feb 1999, *La tertulia del torero* (oil on panel, 11 x 6 ins / 27 x 16 cm) ESP 1,300,000. MADRID, 23 March 1999, *Bathers* (oil on canvas, 43 x 63 ins / 108 x 160 cm) ESP 600,000. MADRID, 24 Jan 2000, *Landscape Reflected in Lake* (oil on board, 12 x 16 ins / 30 x 40 cm) ESP 300,000. BUENOS AIRES, 22 May 2001, *Venetian Canal* (oil on canvas, 26 x 39 ins / 66 x 99 cm) USD 12,900. MADRID, 17 Sept 2002, *Venice* (oil on canvas, 28 x 39 ins / 70 x 100 cm) EUR 2,500. MADRID, 17 Dec 2002, *Party* (oil on board, 6 x 8 ins / 14 x 21 cm) EUR 4,000. MADRID, 25 March 2003, *Village* (oil on canvas, 26 x 39 ins / 67 x 100 cm) EUR 6,000. LONDON, 18 Sept 2003, *Enel Souk* (oil on canvas, 23 x 31 ins / 58 x 79 cm) GBP 4,500. MADRID, 22 March 2004, *Bay* (oil on canvas, 28 x 39 ins / 70 x 100 cm) EUR 1,900. NEW YORK, 27 Oct 2004, *Flamenco Serenade* (1895, oil on canvas, 20 x 14 ins / 50 x 36 cm) USD 10,000.

GARATOLI, Gherardo de

Italian, 19th century.
Active in Piacenza.
Painter.

GARAU, Juan

Spanish, 17th century.
Active in Barcelona in 1696.
Painter.

GARAUD, Gustave Césaire

French, 19th - 20th century.
Born 25 July 1844, in Toulon; died 23 June 1914, in Nice.
Painter, designer. Landscapes, landscapes with figures, waterscapes. Murals.

Gustave Garaud studied under François Louis Français. He worked in Provence and Paris and had a studio in the Rue Notre-Dame des Champs. He travelled in Indochina and painted numerous landscapes inspired by Provence, Corsica, the Ile-de-France and Brittany. He also worked as a decorative artist, receiving commissions to paint murals in private houses.

He exhibited at the Paris Salon and then at the Salon des Artistes Français from 1878 to 1914. He received a commendation in 1881, a bronze medal in 1889, a silver medal in 1893 and a bronze medal at the Exposition Universelle of 1900.

MUSEUMS AND GALLERIES:

AJACCIO: *Banks of the Gapeau* - DRAGUIGNAN: *Douarnenez* - LA ROCHE-SUR-YON: *The Old Bridge over the Rance* - LE PUY-EN-VELAY: *Banks of the Viosne; Morning in Valmondor* - NICE: *The Beach at Nice* - TOULON: *Pines at Notre-Dame below Fenouillet.*

AUCTION RECORDS:

PARIS, 10 April 1894, *The Footbridge to Guenrod*, FRF 1,680; *Autumn Morning outside Dampierre*, FRF 780. PARIS, 5 May 1928, *Path in a Clearing*, FRF 280. PARIS, 11 June 1942, *Harvest*, FRF 1,050. RHEIMS, 11 June 1989, *Autumn Landscape with Figures* (oil on canvas, 35 3/4 x 26 ins / 91 x 66 cm) FRF 20,000. ROME, 24 March 1992, *Returning from the Fields* (oil on canvas, 11 x 15 1/4 ins / 27 x 39 cm) ITL 2,070,000. NEW YORK, 27 May 1993, *Reading by a River* (oil on panel, 9 1/2 x 13 ins / 24 x 33 cm) NLG 6,900.

GARAUDEAUX, Suzanne

French, 20th century.
Born in St-Morel (Ardennes).
Painter, watercolourist.

Suzanne Garaudeaux exhibited at the Paris Salon from 1933.

GARAVAGLIA, Giovita

Italian, 19th century.
Born 18 March 1790, in Pavia; died 27 April 1835, in Florence.
Engraver.

Initially a pupil of Anderloni, Garavaglia entered the academy of Milan in 1803. In 1813 he won a prize for his engraving of *Herod*, after Luini; then in 1817 he won another prize for his *Holy Family in a Landscape*, after Raphael. In 1833 he was appointed to teach engraving in Florence.

AUCTION RECORDS:

PARIS, 28 Feb 1945, *Vo Victis!* (pen and wash, heightened with white) FRF 300.

GARAVENTA, Giambattista

Italian, 19th century.
Born 1777, in Marassi; died 1840, in Genoa.
Sculptor.

Garaventa was a pupil of Niccolo Traverso, and mostly painted religious subjects.

GARAY, Akos

Hungarian, 19th century.
Born 1866, in Apáthi.
Painter.

Akos Garay studied in Budapest and Munich.

GARAY, Camilla

Hungarian, 19th century.
Active in Budapest.
Painter.

Camilla Garay painted mainly landscapes.

GARAY, Marie

French, 19th century.
Born 11 April 1861, in St-Pierre-d'Irube; died 3 December 1953, in Biarritz.
Painter. Figure compositions, local scenes, landscapes.

She studied drawing and composition under Achille Zo at the municipal college of art in Bayonne, then in Paris under Pierre-Auguste Cot, Paul Robert, Henner, Carolus-Duran and Bonnat. She was a member of the Société des Artistes Français from 1898 and exhibited her *Corpus Christi Procession at Bidaray* at its 1889 Salon and, later, at the 1900 Exposition Universelle in Paris.

In 2001 the Musée Bonnat in Bayonne mounted an exhibition built around a newly restored painting by Zo entitled *Léon Bonnat et ses élèves basques et béarnais* (*Léon Bonnat and his Basque and Béarnais Pupils*) (1914), designed to feature work by some of the artists who feature in the painting. Among these was Marie Garay who, as one of Bonnat's pupils, was a member of what Parisian critics of the day referred to as the 'Bayonne School'.

Museums and Galleries:
Bayonne (Mus. Basque): *Corpus Christi Procession at Bidaray* (1889, oil on canvas, from the Pau municipal collection) - Bayonne (Mus. Bonnat): *Léon Bonnat et ses élèves* (*Léon Bonnat and his Pupils*) (1914, oil on canvas).
Auction records:
Paris, 1 March 1936, *Pretty Cake-seller* (watercolour) FRF 150.

GARAY, Pedro de
Spanish, 17th century.
Active in Toledo.
Sculptor.

GARAY MACUA, Eloy
Spanish, 20th century.
Born 1879, in Labastida (Álava, Basque Country); died 1974, in Bilbao.
Painter. Landscapes. Murals.
Eloy Garay Macua mainly painted landscapes of the area in which he was born.

GARAY Y AREVALO, Manuel
Spanish, 19th century.
Born in the 19th century, in Madrid.
Painter. Genre scenes.
Manuel Garay y Arevalo studied under Carlos Luis de Rivera, at the fine arts academy in Madrid and at the École des Beaux-Arts in Paris.
Museums and Galleries:
Sheffield: *The Mouse; Preparations for the Ball.*
Auction records:
New York, 13 Dec 1985, *A Helping Hand* (oil on panel, 17 x 20½ ins / 43 x 52.3 cm) USD 3,500. New York, 23 May 1990, *Winding Up the Skein* (oil on card, 17 x 20¾ ins / 43.2 x 52.7 cm) USD 22,000. Madrid, 27 April 1999, *Game of Cards* (oil on canvas, 14x17 ins / 36x43 cm) ESP 170,000. London, 3 April 2001, *Flirtation; Proposal* (oil on panel, a pair, 14x11 ins / 35x27 cm) GBP 6,500. Madrid, 12 March 2002, *Flirting* (oil on board, 14x11 ins / 35x27 cm) EUR 3,000. Madrid, 18 Feb 2003, *Unravelling the Plot* (oil on board, 17x21 ins / 43x53 cm) EUR 6,500. Madrid, 24 Feb 2004, *Flirting* (oil on board, 14x11 ins / 35x27 cm) EUR 3,000.

GARAY Y LORENZO, Octavio
Spanish, 19th century.
Born in the 19th century, in Madrid.
Painter. Genre scenes.
Octavio Garay y Lorenzo was a pupil of Manuel García Martínez.

GARBAN, André
French, 20th century.
Born in St-Amand.
Painter. Landscapes.
André Garban exhibited at the Salon des Indépendants in Paris from 1921.
Auction records:
Paris, 20 Nov 1985, *Landscape with Red Tree* (oil on canvas, 18 x 22 ins / 46 x 55 cm) FRF 5,800.

GARBANELLI, Alberto
Italian, 16th century.
Active in Ferrara at the end of the 16th century.
Painter.
Alberto Garbanelli was the son of Ilaria Garbanelli.

GARBANELLI, Antonio
Italian, 15th century.
Active in Ferrara during the first half of the 15th century.
Painter.

GARBANELLI, Ilario
Italian, 15th century.
Active in Ferrara.
Painter.
Ilario Garbanelli was the son of Antonio Garbanelli.

GARBANELLI, Isopo
Italian, 16th century.
Active in Ferrara at the end of the 16th century.
Painter.
Isopo Garbanelli was the son of Ilario Garbanelli.

GARBARI, Tullio
Italian, 20th century.
Born 1892, in Pergine near Trento (Trentino-Alto Adige); died 1931, in Paris.
Painter.
In 1908 Tullio Garbari enrolled as a student at the academy of fine arts in Venice, where he exhibited over 30 works at Ca' Pesaro. He exhibited there again in 1909, alongside Umberto Boccioni. During this time he was working for several newspapers. After World War I, he exhibited with Carlo Carrà in Milan. He then gave up painting to study philosophy and literature. He did not exhibit again until 1927, in Milan, then in Amsterdam and Hamburg after that. In 1931 he exhibited at the Galerie del Milione in Milan, and became friends with Gino Severini, whom he had met on one of his numerous visits to Paris. The Galerie del Milione held a major retrospective exhibition of his work after his premature death in 1931.

It is perhaps surprising that Garbari should have associated with so many former Futurists, since he painted pastoral and popular scenes, sometimes with a religious slant. He was inspired by the narrative talent he saw in the works of primitive artists, and had a particularly constructive and robust feel for the composition of a painting, and for detail when shaping the contours of his forms.
Auction records:
Milan, 25 Nov 1965, *La Corte delle Colombe* ITL 1,400 000. Milan, 21 Dec 1982, *Shepherd* (1930, oil on card, 19¾ x 13½ ins / 50 x 34.5 cm) ITL 7,800,000. Milan, 15 Nov 1983, *Shepherdess* (pencil, 11½ x 8¾ ins / 29.5 x 22.5 cm) ITL 3,000,000. Milan, 8 Nov 1984, *Landscapes* (1912-1913, oil on card, three items, 6 x 5½ ins / 15 x 14 cm and 9 x 2¾ ins/22 x 7 cm) ITL 7,000,000. Milan, 19 June 1986, *Houses* (oil on panel, 12 x 15¾ ins / 30.5 x 40 cm) ITL 11,000,000. Milan, 27 Nov 1986, *Landscape* (watercolour, 4¼ x 5¾ ins / 11 x 14.5 cm) ITL 2,200,000. Milan, 14 Nov 1991, *Rustic Muse* (1928, oil on mounted card, 19½ x 15½ ins / 49.5 x 39.5 cm) ITL 42,000,000.

GARBAYE, Georges Louis
French, 20th century.
Born 1892, in Paris.
Painter.
Georges Garbaye exhibited at the Salon of the Société Nationale des Beaux-Arts.

GARBE, Herbert
German, 19th - 20th century.
Sculptor.
Herbert Garbe was the husband of Emy Roeder-Garbe.

GARBELL, Alexandr
Latvian, 20th century.
Born May 1903, in Riga; died 31 December 1970.
Active in France from 1923.
Painter. Figures, landscapes with figures, landscapes, urban landscapes.
Having trained with Bissière at the Académie Ranson, Alexandr Garbell was very soon painting on his own, maintaining independence from his very early years. His painting moved towards abstraction where he continued to use the resources of a particularly bright palette. Nevertheless, some regretted this non-figurative expression including

Pierre Courthion who wrote: 'Pieces of meat (as seen at the butcher's), with their fine tonality between the golden yellow and the reds, have an unforgettable brilliance in which the painter manages to bring their real nature to life in an enchanting display of colours'. Some of his favourite subjects were the Normandy beaches and the narrow streets of Naples.

Alexandr Garbell took part in various Salons in Paris very early on including: Salon des Surindépendants, Salon des Tuileries, d'Automne, Salon de Mai, Salon des Réalités Nouvelles and Salon des Grands et Jeunes d'Aujourd'hui. He also had numerous solo exhibitions in Paris between 1928 and 1970 as well as abroad including: Copenhagen (1950-1951), Milan, Lausanne, Turin and London (1955), New York (1956-1961-1965), Basel and Amsterdam (1967). The museums in Zurich and Lausanne also devoted a special exhibition to him in 1952. After his death, many tributes were paid to him, including a show at the Salon des Réalités Nouvelles (1972).

Museums and Galleries:

Grenoble - Haifa - Jerusalem - Luxembourg - Milwaukee - Paris (MAMVP) - Rio de Janeiro - Tel Aviv - Tokyo.

Auction records:

Paris, 12 Dec 1946, *Landscape*, FRF 6,500. Paris, 21 Dec 1972, *On the Pier*, FRF 5,100. Versailles, 18 June 1974, *Young Girl, Child and Dog Near the Village*, FRF 9,100. Paris, 15 Dec 1976, *In Brittany* (1969, oil on canvas, 19 x 26 3/4 ins / 48 x 68 cm) FRF 3,500. Paris, 2 Dec 1980, *Market Day* (oil on panel, 13 1/2 x 11 3/4 ins / 34 x 30 cm) FRF 2,700. Paris, 5 July 1982, *Woman in an Interior* (1967, oil on canvas, 63 x 70 ins / 160 x 178 cm) FRF 5,000. Paris, 24 April 1983, *The Elk* (1956, oil on canvas, 40 1/4 x 32 ins / 102 x 81 cm) FRF 9,000. Paris, 15 Feb 1985, *Street in Naples* (1965, oil on canvas, 76 3/4 x 38 1/4 ins / 195 x 97 cm) FRF 12,000. Paris, 6 June 1988, *Bathers* (oil on canvas, 9 1/2 x 13 ins / 24 x 33 cm) FRF 3,800. Paris, 16 April 1989, *Harbour* (oil on canvas, 25 1/2 x 39 1/4 ins / 65 x 100 cm) FRF 50,000. Paris, 19 Jan 1990, *Park in Winter* (oil on canvas, 24 x 25 1/2 ins / 61 x 65 cm) FRF 6,200. Paris, 14 March 1990, *Fish Market* (oil on canvas, 22 x 21 1/4 ins / 55 x 54 cm) FRF 13,000. Paris, 27 March 1990, *Calves* (oil on canvas, 315 x 39 1/4 ins / 800 x 100 cm) FRF 35,000. Paris, 8 April 1990, *Fishing Harbour* (oil on canvas, 18 x 24 ins / 46 x 61 cm) FRF 38,000. Paris, 6 Oct 1990, *Beach at Low Tide* (1964, oil on canvas, 31 1/2 x 63 ins / 80 x 160 cm) FRF 40,000. Paris, 5 Dec 1990, *On the Table* (1946, oil on canvas, 9 1/2 x 16 1/4 ins / 24 x 41 cm) FRF 12,000. New York, 13 Feb 1991, *In the Cafe* (1954, oil on canvas, 28 3/4 x 26 ins / 73 x 66 cm) USD 2,750. Paris, 14 April 1991, *Harbour* (oil on canvas, 25 1/2 x 39 1/4 ins / 65 x 100 cm) FRF 35,500. New York, 7 May 1991, *View of London* (1962, oil on canvas, 35 x 46 ins / 89 x 117 cm) USD 4,400. Paris, 13 April 1992, *Workshop* (1957, oil on canvas, 57 1/2 x 45 ins / 146 x 114 cm) FRF 18,000. Paris, 10 Feb 1993, *Motherhood* (oil on canvas, 39 1/4 x 35 1/4 ins / 100 x 89.5 cm) FRF 25,000. Paris, 6 Dec 1993, *Motherhood* (oil on canvas, 39 1/4 x 35 1/4 ins / 100 x 89.5 cm) FRF 10,500. Paris, 16 Oct 1994, *River Banks in Paris* (oil on canvas, 28 3/4 x 39 1/4 ins / 73 x 100 cm) FRF 7,500. Paris, 6 Nov 1995, *Landscape* (1966, oil on canvas, 59 x 59 ins / 150 x 150 cm) FRF 40,000. Paris, 24 March 1996, *Walls of Ischia* (oil on canvas, 47 1/4 x 47 1/4 ins / 120 x 120 cm) FRF 16,000. Paris, 19 June 1996, *Market Scene* (1953, oil on canvas, 21 1/4 x 25 1/2 ins / 54 x 65 cm) FRF 6,000. Paris, 28 April 1997, *Composition* (1960, oil on canvas, 31 1/2 x 31 1/2 ins / 80 x 80 cm) FRF 7,000; *Composition* (1956, oil on canvas, 31 1/2 x 39 1/4 ins / 80 x 100 cm) FRF 5,000. Paris, 25 May 1997, *Street in Naples* (1960, oil on card, 25 1/2 x 13 3/4 ins / 65 x 35 cm) FRF 7,000. London, 11 Dec 1997, *At the Abattoir at La Villette* (1959, oil on canvas, 13 x 16 ins / 33 x 40.6 cm) GBP 552. Paris, 9 March 1998, *Composition* (1958, oil on canvas, 7 3/4 x 16 3/4 ins / 20 x 42.5 cm) FRF 6,000. Paris, 1 April 1998, *On the Shore in the Environs of Etretat* (oil on canvas, 31 1/2 x 45 ins / 80 x 114 cm) FRF 6,500. Paris, 3 Dec 2001, *Woman in Red* (c. 1947, oil on canvas, 29 x 21 ins / 73 x 54 cm) FRF 12,500. London, 3 Feb 2003, *Composition* (1955, oil on canvas, 25 x 21 ins / 64 x 54 cm) GBP 1,000.

GARBELL, Camille

French, 20th century.
Born 15 July 1945.
Sculptor.

Camille Garbell works in a Surrealist vein using a wide variety of materials such as metals, synthetic resins and plastics. He has also worked in the field of electro-acoustic sculpture. He has shown his work at several exhibitions in Paris, including the Salon d'Automne, the Salon de la Jeune Sculpture and the Salon des Réalités Nouvelles. He held solo exhibitions in Paris in 1973 and 1975 and in London.

Auction records:

Paris, 4 Feb 1991, *Genesis I* (1990, bronze, 13 x 9 ins / 33 x 23 cm) FRF 15,000. Paris, 3 June 1991, *Osiris* (1988, bronze, 13 3/4 x 6 3/4 ins / 35 x 17 cm) FRF 8,000. Paris, 15 Dec 1997, *Couple* (bronze, h. 7 3/4 ins / 19.5 cm) FRF 1,500.

GARBER, Daniel

American, 19th - 20th century.
Born 11 April 1880, in North Manchester (Indiana); died 5 July 1958, in Cuttalossa, Lumberville (Pennsylvania).
Painter, printmaker. Landscapes, portraits.

Daniel Garber studied at the Art Academy of Cincinnati with V. Nowottny and Frank Duveneck, and at the Pennsylvania Academy of Fine Arts with Thomas Anschutz and J. Alden Weir. In 1905 he won a fellowship from the Pennsylvania Academy to study abroad, and went to England until 1907. Upon returning to the USA, Garber established a studio in Lumberville, Bucks County, Pennsylvania, where he became a central figure in the New Hope art community. Garber taught at the Pennsylvania Academy from 1919 to 1949. He received the first Hallgarten Prize, National Academy of Design, New York (1909); the Lippincott Prize, Pennsylvania Academy (1911); a Gold Medal, Panama-Pacific Exposition, San Francisco (1915); the Altman Prize, National Academy of Design (1915); and the W.A. Clark Prize and Gold Medal, Corcoran Gallery of Art, Washington DC (1921).

Garber had two modes of painting, the first being lightly painted works in conventional style, with care in shape and detail; while the second was more decorative and poetic with luminous light, such as the oil *Tohickon* (1920). His works were noted for their precise draughtsmanship, vibrant shimmering colours, and the landscapes for their tapestry-like quality. Garber often used the woods and quarries of Bucks County as subject matter.

Garber exhibited at the Panama-Pacific Exposition in San Francisco in 1915, and held a solo exhibition at the Woodmere Art Gallery, Philadelphia, 1942. Since his death his work has featured in a retrospective at the Pennsylvania Academy of the Fine Arts (1980); in group exhibitions at the Terra Museum of American Art in Chicago on numerous occasions since 1985; *Masterworks of American Impressionism: Edward Redfield and the New Hope Group*, James A. Michener Art Museum, Doylestown, Pennsylvania (1994); *An American Tradition: The Pennsylvania Impressionists*, Westmoreland Museum of American Art, Greensburg, Pennsylvania (1997); and *Visions of Home: American Impressionist Images of Suburban Leisure and Country Comfort*, Indianapolis Museum of Art (1999).

Bibliography:

Daniel Garber, 1880-1958, exhibition catalogue, Pennsylvania Academy of the Fine Arts, Philadelphia, 1980. Hélène Ahrweiler, Roger Mandle, D. Scott Atkinson, William H. Gerdts, Carole L. Shelby, Jochen Wierich, *Lasting Impressions: American Painters in France 1865-1915*, exhibition catalogue, Musée d'Art américain, Giverny, Terra Foundation for the Arts, Evanston (IL), 1992.

MUSEUMS AND GALLERIES:

CHICAGO (AI): *The Hills of Byram; Towering Trees* - CHICAGO (Terra Foundation for American Art): *Fisherman's Hut* (c. 1940, oil on canvas) - CINCINNATI (AM): *Winter - Richmont* - DETROIT (Institute of Arts): *Vineclad Trees* (1916, oil on canvas) - DOYLESTOWN (James A. Michener AM): *November Day* (1918); *Lambertville Beach* (oil on canvas); *Day in June* (oil on canvas) - LOS ANGELES (Mus. of Art and Science): *Down the River, Winter* - NEW YORK (Metropolitan Mus. of Art) - PHILADELPHIA (Pennsylvania Academy of the Fine Arts): *Portrait of Walter H. Gardner* (1922-1923, charcoal); *Winter Evening* (1929-1930, charcoal); *The Quarry* (c. 1917, charcoal); *Self-portrait* (dry-point and etching); *Quarry* (1917, oil on canvas); *Students of Painting* (1923, oil on canvas) - PHILADELPHIA (Woodmere Art Mus.): *Spring Valley Inn* (oil on canvas) - PITTSBURGH (Carnegie Institute): *March* - READING, PA (Reading Public Mus.): *Goat Hill* (oil on canvas) - ST LOUIS (AM): *September Fields* - SWARTHMORE (Gal.) - WASHINGTON DC (Corcoran Gal. of Art): *April Landscape; South Room - Green Street* - WASHINGTON DC (Phillips Collection) - WASHINGTON DC (Smithsonian American AM): *Tohickon* (1920, oil on canvas).

AUCTION RECORDS:

NEW YORK, 21 Nov 1945, *Old Apple Tree*, USD 300. NEW YORK, 27 Oct 1978, *Tanis* (oil on canvas, 60 x 46¼ ins / 152.4 x 117.5 cm) USD 55,000. NEW YORK, 30 April 1980, *Pear Tree* (oil on canvas, 17½ x 21½ ins / 44.5 x 54.6 cm) USD 7,000. NEW YORK, 4 June 1982, *Summer Fantasy* (oil on canvas, 30 x 30 ins / 76.2 x 76.2 cm) USD 25,000. NEW YORK, 23 March 1984, *The Jersey Shore* (oil on canvas, 25½ x 30½ ins / 64.5 x 77.5 cm) USD 22,000. WASHINGTON DC, 6 Dec 1985, *Summer Fantasy* (1916, oil on canvas, 30¼ x 30 ins / 77 x 76.4 cm) USD 45,000. NEW YORK, 1 Dec 1988, *End of Autumn* (oil on canvas, 30 x 28 ins / 76.5 x 71.1 cm) USD 23,100. NEW YORK, 24 May 1989, *Green Mansions* (1934, oil on canvas, 52½ x 56½ ins / 133.4 x 143.5 cm) USD 154,000. NEW YORK, 28 Sept 1989, *Tohickon Bridge* (1923, oil on card, 18 x 20 ins / 46 x 51 cm) USD 23,100. NEW YORK, 30 Nov 1989, *Old Stover's Mill* (oil on canvas, 18 x 21½ ins / 45.7 x 54.5 cm) USD 20,900. NEW YORK, 6 Dec 1991, *Grey Day, April* (oil on panel, 18 x 22 ins / 46 x 56 cm) USD 39,600. NEW YORK, 4 Dec 1992, *Along the Delaware* (oil on canvas, 28¼ x 30 ins / 71.8 x 76.5 cm) USD 71,500. NEW YORK, 23 Sept 1993, *30 April* (1952, oil on card, 18 x 24 ins / 45.7 x 61 cm) USD 25,300. NEW YORK, 25 May 1994, *Mending* (1918, oil on canvas, 46 x 42 ins / 116.8 x 106.7 cm) USD 398,500. NEW YORK, 25 May 1995, *June* (oil on canvas, 36¼ x 44¼ ins / 92.1 x 112.4 cm) USD 162,000. NEW YORK, 22 May 1996, *Stockton Church* (oil on canvas, 40 x 36 ins / 101.6 x 91.4 cm) USD 151,000. NEW YORK, 6 June 1997, *Saturday Afternoon, Cold Spring Harbor* (c. 1922, oil on panel, 18 x 20 ins / 45.7 x 50.8 cm) USD 54,625. NEW YORK, 26 May 1999, *River Bend* (oil on canvas, 50 x 60 ins / 127 x 152 cm) USD 150,000. NEW YORK, 27 May 1999, *Corn* (oil on canvas, 42 x 50 ins / 107 x 128 cm) USD 250,000. NEW YORK, 30 Nov 2000, *Late Afternoon - September* (1915, oil on canvas, 42 x 46 ins / 107 x 117 cm) USD 500,000. NEW YORK, 28 Nov 2001, *Mary Maxwell House* (oil on canvas, 30 x 25 ins / 76 x 63 cm) USD 210,000. HATFIELD, 6 March 2002, *Rodgers Meadow, with Barn, and Woman Feeding Chickens* (oil on canvas, 30 x 30 ins / 76 x 76 cm) USD 220,000. NEW YORK, 22 May 2002, *June* (oil on canvas, 36 x 44 ins / 92 x 112 cm) USD 380,000. BOSTON, 21 Nov 2003, *Milford Road* (oil on board, 14 x 16 ins / 35 x 41 cm) USD 71,000. NEW YORK, 3 Dec 2003, *Byram Hills, Springtime* (1937, oil on canvas, 42 x 50 ins / 107 x 127 cm) USD 1,000,000. HATFIELD, 29 Sept 2004, *Portrait of a Woman* (pencil, 9 x 7 ins / 23 x 18 cm) USD 2,250.

GARBERS, Karl

German, 19th century.
Born 11 May 1864, in Hamburg.
Sculptor.

Garbers was a pupil of Häknel at the academy in Dresden He lived and worked in Hamburg, among other places.

GARBET, Félix-Émile

French, 19th century.
Died c. 1846.
Active in Paris.
Painter. Genre scenes.

He exhibited at the Paris Salon from 1831 to 1846. Examples of his work include *Going Fishing* and *Children Building a Play House*.

AUCTION RECORDS:

PARIS, 23 Dec 1861, *Music Lesson*, FRF 615. LOKEREN, 10 March 2001, *Bustle by the Tuilleries, Paris* (oil on panel, 19 x 28 ins / 48 x 72 cm) BEF 170,000.

GARBI, Anton Maria

Italian, 18th century.
Born 1718, in Tuoro; died 21 May 1797, in Perugia.
Active in Perugia.
Painter.

Anton Garbi studied in Rome under Placido Constanzi and painted decorative compositions for churches in and around Perugia.

GARBI, Domenico

Italian, 18th - 19th century.
Active in Perugia.
Painter, miniaturist.

Domenico was the son and pupil of Anton Maria Garbi.

GARBIERI, Carlo

Italian, 17th century.
Painter. History painting.

Carlo was the son and pupil of Lorenzo Garbieri. His *Death of St Mary of Egypt* is in the Bologna church of S Giovanni in Monte.

GARBIERI, Lorenzo, called Il Nepote

Italian, 17th century.
Born 1580, in Bologna; died 8 April 1654, in Bologna.
Painter, draughtsman. Religious subjects, mythological subjects.

Lorenzo Garbieri studied under Ludovico Carracci and was one of the latter's most accomplished imitators. The church of S Antonio in Milan boasts several paintings by Lorenzo that Sant'Agostino wrongly attributed to Carracci. Garbieri's body of work includes: *Plague in Milan* and *Procession of Penitents*, both in the Bologna church of S Paolo de Barnabiti; *St Paul Resuscitating Eutychianus* in the Chiesa Filipina in Fano; a *Martyrdom of St Felicity and Seven Other Virgins*, for the church of S Maurizio in Mantua; a *Death of St Joseph* for the church of S Ludovico in Bologna; a *Crucifixion* for the Capuchin church; *Episodes from the Lives of Saints Benedict and Cecilia* for the church of S Michele de Bosco, and a *Circe* for the Pinacoteca.

L. Garbieri.

MUSEUMS AND GALLERIES:

BOLOGNA (Church of S Giuseppe dei Cappuccini): *Crucifixion* - BOLOGNA (Church of S Ludovico): *Death of St Joseph* - BOLOGNA (Church of S Michele in Bosco): *Scene from the Life of St Benedict; Scenes from the Life of St Cecilia* - BOLOGNA (Church of S Paolo Maggiore): *Plague in Milan; Procession of Penitents* - BOLOGNA (Pinacoteca Nazionale): *Circe* - FANO (Church of S Pietro in Valle): *St Paul Resuscitating Eutychianus* - MANTUA (Chiesa di S Maurizio): *Martyrdom of St Felicity and Seven Other Virgins* - MILAN (Church of S Antonio): several paintings.

AUCTION RECORDS:
PARIS, 1775, *Four Elements, The* (bistre drawing heightened with white) FRF 41; *Two Drawings* (pen) FRF 23. PARIS, 9 and 10 March 1927, *Flight into Egypt* (pen and wash) FRF 150. LONDON, 9 Dec 1980, *Goddess Assailing the Winds* (pen and wash and oil on ochre paper, oval, 20 1/4 x 15 ins / 51.3 x 37.8 cm) GBP 1,000. NEW YORK, 12 Jan 1995, *Virgin Grieving over the Body of Christ in the Company of Three Angels* (oil/copper, 23 x 17 ins / 58.4 x 43.2 cm) USD 10,350. LONDON, 3 July 1995, *Study of a Reclining Man* (black chalk on grey paper, 5 1/4 x 6 3/4 ins / 13.6 x 17.1 cm) GBP 1,380. NEW YORK, 28 Jan 1999, *Juno Unloosing the Winds, with Neptune and Vessel Below* (black chalk/colour ink/colour wash heightened with white, oval, 20 x 15 ins / 52 x 38 cm) USD 16,000. VIENNA, 30 March 2000, *The Lamentation of Christ* (oil on panel, diptych, 57 x 51 ins / 146 x 129 cm) ATS 200,000. LONDON, 11 July 2002, *Madonna and Child Adored by Santa Felicita and her Son* (oil on copper, 17 x 11 ins / 42 x 28 cm) GBP 19,000. VIENNA, 1 Oct 2003, *Jacob in Rock Cave* (oil on canvas, 28 x 24 ins / 72 x 60 cm) EUR 2,400.

GARBINI, R.
19th century.
Painter. Genre scenes.
Mentioned by Florence Levy.
AUCTION RECORDS:
NEW YORK, 30 Jan 1902, *In the Cellar,* USD 375.

GARBINO, Domenico
Italian, 15th century.
Active in Venice in 1490.
Painter.

GARBO, Raffaelo or Raffaellino del.
See **CAPPONI**

GARBOSSETTI, Denis
French, 15th century.
Active in Avignon in 1495.
Painter.

GARBRAND, Caleb J.
British, 18th century.
Active in London.
Painter. Portraits.
Caleb J. Garbrand exhibited in London from 1773 to 1780, notably at the Society of Artists, the Free Society and the Royal Academy.
AUCTION RECORDS:
LONDON, 2 July 1928, *Woman in Blue,* GBP 44. LONDON, 1 Feb 1929, *Lt. Kecling Radford,* GBP 126. LONDON, 20 Nov 1931, *Thomas Master,* GBP 3. LONDON, 17 April 1936, *Boy in Green,* GBP 18.

GARBRANTZ, Jan
Dutch, 17th century.
Active c. 1610.
Painter.
Garbrantz was a leading member of the Guild of St Luke in Delft in 1610.

GARBUZ, Yair
Israeli, 20th century.
Born 1945.
Painter (mixed media).
Garbuz was born in Givatayim, near Tel Aviv, and from 1962 to 1969 was taught by Raffi Lavie. Between 1965 and 1970, he took part in the exhibitions of 'Group 10+'. In 1972 he also took part in *Image and Figure,* at the Artists' Centre in Tel Aviv. In 1973, he had his first solo exhibition at the Museum of Tel Aviv.

He paints in a free and expressionist figurative style, which he associates with inserted collages, thus creating narrative ensembles or juxtapositions.

AUCTION RECORDS:
TEL AVIV, 3 May 1980, *Figures* (1968, mixed media, 21 x 32 ins / 53.5 x 81 cm) ILS 12,000. TEL AVIV, 17 June 1985, *Figures* (1972, mixed media/card, 31 1/2 x 47 1/4 ins / 80 x 120 cm) ILS 9,000,000. TEL AVIV, 2 Jan 1989, *Repetition of Lines* (1971, mixed media, 31 1/2 x 47 1/4 ins / 80 x 120 cm) USD 990. TEL AVIV, 1 Jan 1991, *Figures* (1972, mixed media/card, 55 x 47 1/4 ins / 140 x 120 cm) USD 1,760. TEL AVIV, 6 Jan 1992, *Figures* (1972, mixed media/card, 31 1/4 x 47 1/4 ins / 79.5 x 120 cm) USD 1,320. TEL AVIV, 27 Sept 1994, *Untitled* (1972, oil/collage of paper and mixed media/panel, 31 1/4 x 47 1/4 ins / 79.5 x 120 cm) USD 3,450. TEL AVIV, 5 Jan 1999, *Figures in a Landscape* (1992, oil and mixed media on board, 16x23 ins / 40x59 cm) USD 1,000. TEL AVIV, 4 July 1999, *Figures* (1992, oil and mixed media on wood, 23x23 ins / 59x59 cm) USD 1,100. TEL AVIV, 29 June 2000, *Objects in a Landscape* (1992, mixed media on plywood, 16x23 ins / 40x59 cm) USD 1,700. TEL AVIV, 29 June 2000, *Jars* (1992, mixed media and collage on plywood, 16x24 ins / 40x60 cm) USD 1,200. TEL AVIV, 15 Jan 2001, *Figures* (1973, mixed media, 19x28 ins / 49x70 cm) USD 650. TEL AVIV, 16 April 2001, *Untitled* (1970, oil and mixed media on canvas, 51x51 ins / 130x130 cm) USD 5,000. TEL AVIV, 7 April 2002, *Untitled* (mixed media and collage on board, 46x46 ins / 116x117 cm) USD 5,000. TEL AVIV, 27 April 2003, *Untitled* (1971-1972, mixed media, 51x35 ins / 130x88 cm) USD 4,000.

GARCELON, Adrien Jacques
French, 20th century.
Painter.
Adrien Garcelon studied at the École des Beaux-Arts. He exhibited at the Salon des Artistes Français from 1934.

GARCEMENT, Alfred
French, 19th century.
Born in Varzy (Nièvre).
Painter. Genre scenes, landscapes with figures, landscapes.
He studied under Pils and Hanoteau. He first exhibited at the Paris Salon in 1868, before becoming a member of the Salon des Artistes Français in 1883 and receiving an honourable mention in 1896. Examples of his work include *Orchard in the Nièvre, Geese Returning, Geese Nesting* and *Old Shepherd.*
MUSEUMS AND GALLERIES:
CLAMECY: *Narrow Path in the Woods; Landscapes.*
AUCTION RECORDS:
PARIS, 24 Sept 1946, *Cattle in a Shaded Meadow,* FRF 2,500. BERN, 6 Nov 1981, *In the Fields* (oil on canvas, 13 x 18in/33 x 46cm) CHF 2,500. COLOGNE, 18 March 1989, *Sunset on a Flower Meadow* (oil on canvas, 18 1/4 x 13 ins / 46.5 x 33 cm) DEM 1,600. NEW YORK, 1 Nov 1995, *Village in Winter* (oil on canvas, 34 x 48in/86.4 x 121.9cm) USD 9,200. SWITZERLAND, 1 Dec 2000, *River Landscape with Cows and a Fisherman* (oil on canvas, 14 x 19 ins / 36 x 47 cm) CHF 2,500.

GARCES, Francisco
Spanish, 20th century.
Born in the Balearic Islands.
Painter.
Francisco Garces exhibited at the Salon of the national fine arts society of Madrid. He is known for his paintings *Market in Nice* and *Casa d'Azul in Majorca.*

GARCES, José
Spanish, 18th century.
Died 1802.
Painter. Flowers.
José Garces was made a member of the Academia de San Fernando on 5 May 1772.

GARCÈS, Pedro
Spanish, 15th century.

Active in Saragossa in 1445.
Sculptor.

GARCES, Salvador Domingo
Spanish, 19th century.
Born in Cádiz; died 1857.
Sculptor.

Salvador Domingo Garces was a teacher of modelling at the fine arts academy in La Coruña.

GARCÍA, Alfonso
Spanish, 15th century.
Active in Seville.
Painter.

Alfonso García was commissioned by the city authorities to paint the candles for the Corpus Christi festival in 1430.

GARCÍA, Andrés
Spanish, 16th century.
Active in Seville.
Painter.

Andrés García may be the same person as the sculptor of the same name.

GARCÍA, Andrés
Spanish, 16th century.
Active in Seville.
Sculptor.

Andrés García produced decorative sculpture for public buildings.

GARCÍA, Ángel
Spanish, 19th - 20th century.
Born in Madrid.
Sculptor.

Ángel García studied under Francisco Bellver.

GARCÍA, Antonio
Spanish, 19th century.
Painter.

Antonio García was a pupil of Matias Lavina and an outstanding exponent of the Modern Spanish School. He first exhibited in Madrid in 1858.

AUCTION RECORDS:
LONDON, 30 Nov 1907, *Florinda and her Nymphs; Country Fair* (two pendants) GBP 36.

GARCÍA, Baltasar
Spanish, 16th century.
Active in Seville.
Painter.

On 3 May 1552, in Seville, Burgos Joan acted as godfather to García's daughter.

GARCÍA, Bernabé
Spanish, 18th century.
Born 1679, in Madrid; died 1731, in Madrid.
Painter. History painting.

Bernabé García was a pupil of Juan Delgado. He worked for a church in Alcala de Henares.

GARCÍA, Bernardo
Spanish, 19th century.
Active in Saragossa.
Painter.

The provincial museum in Saragossa has a painting of *Cain and Abel* by Bernardo García.

GARCIA, Carlos
Cuban, 20th - 21st century.
Born 1959, in Cuba.
Active in France.
Painter (mixed media).

Carlos García studied in Havana at the Academia de Artes Plásticas de San Alejandro and the Academia de Bellas Artes and then at the Massachusetts art university. He works in Paris. García's painting blends abstraction with figuration through association on canvases in a palette of muted, even cold colours.

García has taken part in collective exhibitions including: Museo de Bellas Artes, Havana (1980); *Cuban Painting* exhibition, Bogotá and Casa de las Américas, Havana (1983); Festival International de la Peinture at Cagnes-sur-Mer (1984); São Paulo Biennale (1987); Mocha Gallery, New York (1988). Solo exhibitions include: Havana (1983); Buenos Aires (1987); Museo de Bellas Artes, Havana and Galerie Artuel, Paris. (1989).

BIBLIOGRAPHY:
Carlos Garcia, catalogue, Gal. Artuel, Paris.

AUCTION RECORDS:
PARIS, 9 April 1989, *Untitled* (acrylic/paper, 20½ x 29 ins / 52 x 73.5 cm) FRF 6,800.

GARCÍA, Carolina
Spanish, 19th century.
Born 1846, in Bilbao; died 1864.
Painter. Portraits, landscapes.

Carolina García was a pupil of Juan Conrate y García. She exhibited in Madrid in 1856 and 1864, and also in Bayonne.

GARCÍA, Diego
Spanish, 17th century.
Active in Seville in 1650.
Painter.

The painter Francisco Polanco acted as a guarantor for Diego García in 1650.

GARCÍA, Elias
Spanish, 19th century.
Born in the 19th century, in Alcoy.
Painter.

Elias García first exhibited in 1878 and was awarded a medal at the Alicante exhibition.

GARCÍA, Elizena
Brazilian, 20th century.
Born 20th century.
Painter.

Elizena García exhibited psychedelically inspired paintings in São Paulo.

GARCÍA, Federico
Spanish, 19th century.
Born in the 19th century, in Madrid.
Painter.

Federico García studied at the college of painting, sculpture and engraving.

GARCÍA, Feliciano
Spanish, 20th century.
Born 19th century.
Active in France.
Painter, sculptor.

Feliciano García exhibited at the first Salon d'Automne in Paris in 1905. He is known primarily for his portraits and busts.

GARCIA, Fernandes
Portuguese, 16th century.
Active between 1514 and 1565.
Painter. Religious subjects.

In 1514, Fernandes Garcia was active in the workshop of Jorge Afonso. In 1518, he married a daughter of the painter Francesco Henriquez, who died of the plague in Lisbon in 1519, when he was working on the decoration of the court of justice. Garcia was engaged to complete the work. It is certain that he painted the transept of S Francisco d'Évora, in the years 1531-1533. He is also believed to be the author of a tryptych depicting *Christ Appearing to the Virgin Mary*

(1531); the *Passion* tryptych at the Vila Viçosa; and a *Presentation in the Temple*.

There is a Mannerist tendency about his work.

MUSEUMS AND GALLERIES:
LISBON: *Presentation in the Temple* (1538).

GARCÍA, Fernando
Spanish, 15th century.
Active in Toledo.
Sculptor.
In 1459, Fernando García was working for Toledo Cathedral.

GARCÍA, Fernando
Spanish, 19th century.
Born in Gerona; died 1877.
Painter.
Fernando García mainly painted portraits.

GARCÍA, Francisco
Spanish, 16th century.
Active in Seville.
Sculptor.

GARCÍA, Gabino
Spanish, 19th century.
Born in the 19th century, in Bilbao.
Painter. Genre scenes.
Gabino García studied under Juan José Martínez Espinosa and at the École des Beaux-Arts in Paris. He exhibited in 1862 at the national fine arts society of Madrid.

GARCIA, Gaetano
Italian, 18th century.
Born in Palermo.
Painter.
Garcia studied in Naples under Solimena.

GARCÍA, Geronimo
Spanish, 16th - 17th century.
Born in Zasmora.
Sculptor.
Geronimo García was the twin brother of Miguel García. He studied in Madrid under Morales, and became a canon of the church of S Salvador in Granada. He was influenced by the style of Alonso Cano and may have benefited from his teaching.

GARCÍA, Gilbert
French, 20th century.
Born 1926, in Messanges (Landes).
Painter.
Gilbert García exhibited at the Salons des Arts du Languedoc (Narbonne 1949 and 1950), at the Salon de la Jeune Peinture Méditerranéenne (Nice 1959) and the Salon de l'Éducation Nationale. He took part in the *Vingt-Cinq Ans d'Acquisitions (1959-1984)* (*25 Years of Acquisitions 1959-1984*) exhibition at the Musée d'Art et d'Histoire in Narbonne in 1984. He was co-founder of the Atelier Narbonnais in 1960.

MUSEUMS AND GALLERIES:
NARBONNE (MAH): *Street*.

GARCÍA, Gregorio
Spanish, 17th century.
Active in Santiago de Compostela.
Sculptor (wood).

GARCÍA, Gregorio
Spanish, 17th century.
Active in Cueca near Toledo c. 1690.
Painter. History painting.

GARCÍA, Hernan
Spanish, 16th century.
Born c. 1501.
Active in Valladolid.
Painter.
Hernan García featured as an expert witness in legal proceedings brought by Berruguete in 1523.

GARCIA, Honorio. See **CONDOY Honorio**

GARCÍA, Ignacio
Spanish, 18th - 19th century.
Born at the end of the 18th century, in Valencia.
Sculptor.
In 1817, Ignacio García was made a member of the Academia de San Carlos. He was considered a remarkable artist.

GARCÍA, José
Spanish, 19th century.
Born in the 19th century, in Madrid.
Sculptor.
José García studied at the Madrid school of fine arts. He first exhibited in Madrid in 1881.

GARCÍA, Josefa
Spanish, 19th century.
Born 1846, in Bilbao; died 1864.
Painter.
Josefa García was a pupil of Juan Conrotte. She exhibited portraits and historical paintings in Madrid from 1856 to 1864.

GARCÍA, Juan
Spanish, 17th century.
Active in Seville c. 1650.
Sculptor (wood).
Juan García was a pupil of Juan Martínez el Montanes.

GARCÍA, Juan
Spanish, 19th century.
Born in the 19th century.
Painter. History painting.
Juan García exhibited from 1849 to 1850 at the Academia de San Fernando.

GARCÍA, Juan
Spanish, 19th century.
Painter. Genre scenes.
From 1879 to 1882, Juan García took part in exhibitions in Seville and Cádiz.

GARCÍA, Juan Gil
Spanish, 20th century.
Born 1879, in Madrid.
Active in Cuba from 1899.
Painter, lithographer. Landscapes, still-lifes.
Juan Gil García was born in Madrid and went to Cuba in 1899. As a lithographer he produced limited print runs and his work has now become very rare. His paintings describe everyday life during the early days of the Cuban republic. He painted still-lifes and landscapes which can be found in reproduction in many Cuban homes.

AUCTION RECORDS:
NEW YORK, 22-23 Nov 1993, *Pineapple, Soursop and Passion Fruits* (1918, oil on canvas, 13¼ x 27½ ins / 33.7 x 69.9 cm) USD 3,450.

GARCÍA, Juana
Spanish, 19th century.
Born 1845, in Bilbao; died 1864.
Painter. Genre scenes.
Juana García was the sister of Carolina and Josefa García and, like them, studied under Juan Conrotte. She exhibited in Madrid from 1860.

GARCÍA, Justo
Spanish, 19th century.
Sculptor.
Justo García was a pupil of Baratta.

GARCÍA, Lino
Spanish, 19th century.
Born in the 19th century, in Madrid.
Painter. History painting.
Lino García studied at the Academia de San Fernando and under Vicente Lopéz. He first exhibited in Madrid in 1856.

GARCÍA, Marcos
Spanish, 17th century.
Active in Valladolid.
Sculptor.
On 9 September 1613, Marcos García was commissioned, together with Francisco Ruez, to execute a retable for the church of S Pedro de Olmos in Esgueve.

GARCÍA, Miguel
Spanish, 17th century.
Active in Granada.
Sculptor.
Miguel García was the brother of Gerónimo García.

GARCIA, Milo
20th century.
Installation artist, sculptor.
A solo exhibition of his work was held in 1996 in London, where he showed *The Door, the Toilet and a Man*, constructed in birch.

GARCÍA, Nuno
Spanish, 16th century.
Active in Seville c. 1500.
Miniaturist.

GARCÍA, Pedro
Spanish, 15th century.
Active between 1456 and 1496.
Painter. Religious subjects.
Catalan School.
On the death of Bernardo Martorell, Pedro García took over the latter's Barcelona workshop and remained there from 1455 to 1461. He then worked in Lerida, before settling in Barbastro, where he resided from 1481 to 1496. Other sources say that he worked in Benabarre (Aragon) during the last quarter of the 15th century, to the point of being referred to as Padro García of Benabarre. One of his collaborators was Pedro Espalargues.

His works include the *St Clare and St Catherine Altarpiece*, in Barcelona Cathedral, a *Virgin and Child*, now in the Barcelona Museum, and the *St John the Baptist Altarpiece*, originally in the church of S Juan del Mercado, Lerida. His altarpieces manifest a love of the picturesque and are characterised by intense colours in harmony with gold backgrounds. His style is somewhat archaic compared with that of his contemporary Jaime Huguet.

Pedro García featured in the exhibition entitled *La pintura gótica hispano flamenca: Bartolomé Bermejo y su época* (*Hispano-Flemish Gothic Painting. Bartolomé Bermejo and his Time*), held at the Museu Nacional d'Art de Catalunya, Barcelona, in 2003.

BIBLIOGRAPHY:
Hispano-Flemish Gothic Painting. Bartolomé Bermejo and his time, group exhibition catalogue, Museu Nacional d'Art de Catalunya, Barcelona, 2003 (pub. in Spanish, Catalan and English).

MUSEUMS AND GALLERIES:
BARCELONA (Diocesan Mus.): *St Quirce and St Julita* - BARCELONA (Mus. Nacional d'Art de Catalunya): *Virgin and Child; St John the Baptist Altarpiece* - CASTRES: *Adoration of the Kings* - PARIS (Mus. des Arts décoratifs): *Virgin and St Vincent Ferrier*.

AUCTION RECORDS:
NEW YORK, 12 Jan 1996, *Annunciation to St Joachim* (oil on panel, 42 1/2 x 23 1/2 ins / 108 x 60 cm) USD 43,700.

GARCÍA, Pedro
Spanish, 16th century.
Sculptor.
Pedro García was active in Seville.

GARCÍA, Pedro
Spanish, 16th - 17th century.
Sculptor.
Pedro García was working in Valencia around 1600. He may be the same person as the artist of the same name active in Seville.

GARCIA, Rafael
Spanish.
Painter. History painting.
The Museum of Seville has the following works by this artist, about whom we can find no details: *St Sebastian, Holy Bishop, St Laurent* and *Holy Pontiff*.

GARCIA, Rupert
American, 20th century.
Born 1941, in California.
Painter, pastellist, screen printer.
Rupert Garcia is a 'Chicano' artist and became the spokesman for this minority group of Mexicans who have emigrated to the USA. In the 1960s he led a campaign against 'Yankee' values and culture, using public notices, posters and screen prints. He became less radical in later years and began to create intimist works.

He has taken part in collective and solo exhibitions in the USA and Europe, including at the San Francisco Museum of Modern Arts in 1978 and 1984; the Mexican Museum, San Francisco, in 1978, 1980, 1981 and 1986; the Museum of Modern Art, New York, in 1988 and the Fine Art Museum of San Francisco in 1990. He held solo exhibitions at the Galerie Claude Samuel in Paris in 1987, 1989 and 1990.

BIBLIOGRAPHY:
Castellon, Rolando, *Rupert Garcia, Pastel Drawings*, exhibition catalogue, Museum of Modern Art, San Francisco, 1978. Lippard, Lucy R., *Rupert Garcia: Prints and Posters, 1967-1990*, exhibition catalogue, San Francisco Fine Arts Museums, Northeastern University Press, 1990. Nochlin, Linda, *Rupert Garcia*, exhibition catalogue, Rena Branston Gallery, San Francisco, 1997.

GARCÍA, Santos
Spanish, 16th century.
Active in Valladolid.
Sculptor.

GARCÍA, Stephanus
Spanish, 11th century.
Illuminator.
This artist painted miniatures and decorations for a commentary by Beatus on the Apocalypse, and illustrated the Apocalypse of St-Sever.

GARCIA, Torres. See **TORRES GARCÍA**

GARCÍA ANGUERA, Saturnino.
See **GARCIANGUERA**

GARCÍA ASARTA, Inocencio
Spanish, 19th - 20th century.
Born 1862, in Gastiáin (Navarre); died 1921, in Bilbao.
Painter.
Inocencio García Asarta began his art training in Vittoria in Sicily. He was awarded a bursary by the province of Navarre and studied in Rome.

He received a commendation at the exhibition of the national fine arts society of Madrid in 1897 and in 1900 became official artist to the city of Bilbao.

GARCÍA BENITO, Eduardo
Spanish, 20th century.
Born 1891, in Valladolid; died 1981, in Valladolid.

Painter, engraver, illustrator, poster artist. Figure compositions, portraits, urban landscapes.

Eduardo García Benito studied at the Real Academia de Bellas Artes de San Fernando in Madrid. He was awarded a bursary by his native town of Valladolid and went to study in Paris in 1911, remaining there for about ten years. He was an associate member of the national fine arts society and continued to exhibit at their Salons up to 1934 and also took part in the Salon des Tuileries in 1923. He is believed to have been secretary to the Salon d'Automne and the national fine arts society in 1919. In 1921 he went to the USA, remaining there until 1958, when he returned to Valladolid.

In France he painted many portraits including one of *M and Mme Paul Poiret*. He also produced illustrations for works such as *Le Testament* by P. Bourget and *24 Sonnets* by Góngora; he produced colour engravings for *The Great War, 1914-1918*. His talents were wide-ranging: in *Woman Playing the Guitar* of 1920-1923, for example, there is a clear reference to Cubism which is successfully assimilated in his double portrait of the Poirets, while in other works such as *My Beautiful Parisian Ladies* of 1927 the influence of Van Dongen is apparent. He also painted landscape views of Paris. In the USA he collaborated on society publications of the period such as *Vogue* and *Vanity Fair*, often providing the cover illustrations. These pieces recall his Cubist influences and link him with the stylisation characteristic of the 1930s Art Deco movement. As a decorative artist he was commissioned to decorate Gloria Swanson's residence. Now almost forgotten, García Benito technically and stylistically tried his hand at almost everything, often belatedly and in a rather uninspired manner, but with a genuine talent that deserves greater recognition.

BIBLIOGRAPHY:

Arnáiz, José Manuel/López Jiménez, Javier/Merchán Díaz, Manuel (ed.), *Cien años de pintura en Espana y Portugal (1830-1930)*, Antiqvaria, Madrid, 1989 (One Hundred Years of Painting in Spain and Portugal (1830-1930)).

AUCTION RECORDS:

PARIS, 18 Nov 1925, *Conversation*, FRF 300. PARIS, 9 May 1955, *Place de la Concorde*, FRF 11,000. NEW YORK, 13 June 1980, *Homage to Beardsley* (1919, watercolour and Indian ink, 11 1/4 x 7 1/2 ins / 28.8 x 19.3 cm) USD 500. MONTE CARLO, 17 March 1985, *Woman with Blue Fan* (c. 1925, gouache, Indian ink and watercolour, 10 1/4 x 15 1/4 ins / 26 x 38.5 cm) FRF 4,500. VERSAILLES, 25 March 1990, *At the Races* (oil on card, 25 1/2 x 19 3/4 ins / 65 x 50 cm) FRF 16,500. PARIS, 24 March 1995, *Man with Book* (1945, oil on canvas, 39 1/4 x 32 1/4 ins / 100 x 82 cm) FRF 5,000.

GARCÍA BUSTO, Arturo

Mexican, 20th century.
Born 1926, in Mexico City.
Painter, engraver.

GARCÍA CADMIO, Pedro

Spanish, 20th century.
Born 17 July 1897, in Madrid; died 1 April 1963.
Painter. Portraits.

Pedro García Cadmio studied at the Real Academia de Bellas Artes de San Fernando in Madrid. He was awarded a bursary and continued his studies in London and in 1927 in Belgium, Holland and Italy. He was secretary of the Painters' and Sculptors' Association and director of the *Gazette des Beaux Arts* (*Fine Arts Review*). He held several exhibitions in Madrid, Barcelona and Bilbao. He was an honorary member of the Salon d'Automne receiving a gold medal in 1933, a bronze medal in 1924, a silver medal in 1926 and a first prize in 1956. He also took part in the exhibitions of the national fine arts society in Madrid.

BIBLIOGRAPHY:

Arnáiz, José Manuel/López Jiménez, Javier/Merchán Díaz, Manuel (ed.), *Cien años de pintura en Espana y Portugal (1830-1930)*, Antiqvaria, Madrid, 1989 (One Hundred Years of Painting in Spain and Portugal (1830-1930)).

GARCÍA CEBALLOS, Miguel

Mexican, 20th century.
Born 15 July 1945, in Guadalajara.
Painter. Scenes with figures, urban landscapes.

Miguel García Ceballos studied architecture. He paints scenes from life in a simple, picturesque style in fresh colours

He has held solo exhibitions of his work in Mexico City, notably in 1975 at the city museum and also in the USA.

GARCÍA CONDOY, Julio

Spanish, 20th century.
Born 1889, in Saragossa; died 1977, in Aranjuez (Castile-La Mancha).
Painter, decorative designer.

The brother of Honorio García, Julio García Condoy began training under his father at the Saragossa school for arts and industry. He continued his studies in Paris in 1908 and in Rome in 1913. He was appointed curator of the naval museum in 1930.

He took part in national fine arts exhibitions in Madrid in 1915, 1917 (bronze medal) and 1920. He also exhibited at the Franco-Spanish exhibition in Saragossa in 1919. He was awarded first prize at the exhibition of artists of Aragon in 1943.

BIBLIOGRAPHY:

Arnáiz, José Manuel/López Jiménez, Javier/Merchán Díaz, Manuel (ed.), '*Cien años de pintura en Espana y Portugal (1830-1930)*' in vol. III, Antiqvaria, Madrid, 1989 (One Hundred Years of Painting in Spain and Portugal (1830-1930)).

GARCÍA CORREA, Fernando

Mexican, 20th century.
Active in France.
Sculptor.

Fernando García Correa studied at the Escuela Nacional de Pintura y Escultura La Esmeralda in Mexico City and from 1980 to 1983 at the École des Beaux-Arts in Paris. He lives and works in Paris. He favours simplicity in volume and form and his work displays a very refined figurative style.

Garcia Correa has exhibited in 1982-1983 at the ARC at the Musée d'Art Moderne in Paris, at the Museo del Chopo in Mexico City and at the Salon de Montrouge. In 1988 he exhibited at the Korean cultural centre in Paris. He has also had solo exhibitions including one in 1986 at the Mexican cultural centre in Paris.

GARCÍA DE CANEDO, Miguel

Spanish, 18th century.
Born 1728, in Santiago de Compostela.
Active in Galicia.
Sculptor (wood).

GARCÍA DE CORDOBA, José

Spanish, 19th century.
Born in Écija, near Cordova; died c. 1875.
Active in Cordova.
Painter.

GARCÍA DE LA CAL, Francisco

Spanish, 19th century.
Born in the 19th century, in Avila.
Painter. Genre scenes.

Francisco García de la Cal studied at the school of fine arts in Madrid, and received funding from his native town of Avila to study in Rome. He first exhibited in Madrid in 1881.

GARCÍA DE LA ROSA, Teofilo
Spanish, 19th century.
Active in Valencia.
Painter. Genre scenes.
Teofilo García de la Rosa first exhibited in Valencia around 1879.

GARCÍA DE LOS ALAMOS, Bartolomé
Spanish, 16th century.
Active in Seville in 1545.
Painter.
The painter Alonso de Maldonado is recorded as having rented a house to García de los Alamos on 26 April 1542.

GARCÍA DE MIRANDA, Juan, the Elder
Spanish, 17th - 18th century.
Born 12 September 1677, in Madrid; died 8 May 1749, in Madrid.
Painter. History painting.
The parents of Juan García de Miranda the Elder were Asturian. He learned to paint under Juan Delgado and produced mainly religious subjects, including a number of examples of the *Immaculate Conception* as private commissions. Born without a right hand, he used the end of his arm to hold his brushes. In 1735 he was appointed painter to Philip V. His son Juan showed promise as an artist but died at the age of 21. García ably restored paintings damaged by the fire at the Alcazar in 1734.
BIBLIOGRAPHY:
Jiménez Priego, María Teresa, *Juan García de Miranda, pintor de Cámara del Rey Felipe V, en Guadalupe*, Diputación Provincial Institución de Servicios Culturales, Badajoz, 1976.
MUSEUMS AND GALLERIES:
MADRID (Prado): *Birth and Marriage of the Virgin.*

GARCÍA DE MIRANDA, Juan, the Younger
Spanish, 17th - 18th century.
Active in Valladolid.
Painter.
Juan García de Miranda the Younger produced paintings showing scenes from the life of the Virgin for the church of S Lorenzo. He died at the age of 21.

GARCÍA DE MIRANDA, Nicolás
Spanish, 18th century.
Born 1698; died 1738.
Painter. Landscapes.
Nicolás García de Miranda painted landscapes in which he placed religious figures. He was the brother and pupil of Juan García de Miranda.

GARCÍA DE PADILLA, Pedro
Spanish, 16th century.
Active in Seville.
Painter.
Various documents enable us to follow the career of Pedro García de Padilla from 1540 to 1573. He may be the same person as the Padilla who worked in Seville as an illuminator.

GARCÍA DE PRADAS, Juan
Spanish, 16th century.
Active in Granada c. 1525.
Sculptor, architect.
There are references to work done by Juan García de Pradas in Granada Cathedral.

GARCÍA DE SANTIAGO, Bartolomé
Spanish, 18th century.
Born c. 1680, in Seville; died 1740.
Sculptor.
A record shows that Bartolomé García de Santiago was involved in a lawsuit, which he lost. The sale of his furniture by the court indicates that he was of modest means and from a declaration dated 1727 we know that he was 30 years old at that time.

GARCÍA DE SANTIAGO, Manuel
Spanish, 18th century.
Born 1711, in Seville.
Sculptor.
Manuel García de Santiago was the son and pupil of Bartolomé de Santiago.

GARCIA DEL BARCO. See **BARCO García del**

GARCÍA DEL CORRAL, Federico
Spanish, 19th century.
Active in Seville.
Painter. Genre scenes.
Federico García del Corral exhibited in Seville in 1878, and in Vienna in 1882, and is known for his *Garden of the Alcazar.*
AUCTION RECORDS:
NEW YORK, 23 Oct 1997, *Preparing for the Fiesta* (oil on canvas, 32 1/4 x 21 1/2 ins / 81.9 x 54.6 cm) USD 32,200. MADRID, 21 Feb 2000, *Lady of Seville* (watercolour, 13x7 ins / 32x19 cm) ESP 75,000.

GARCÍA EL HIDALGO, Josef
Spanish, 17th - 18th century.
Born c. 1650, probably in Muriedro; died 28 June 1717, in Madrid.
Painter, engraver (etching). History painting.
Josef García El Hidalgo studied under Mateo Gilarte, Nicolas de Villacis in Murcia and Giacinto Brandi in Rome; Pietro da Cortona, Salvator Rosa and Carlo Maratti also gave him their advice. He was unable to cope with the Italian climate and had to return to Spain, where he joined Carreño. From 1674 to 1711 he worked in Madrid in the service of Charles II and Philip V. For Charles II he executed various works including a series of 24 paintings of scenes from the life of St Augustine for the cloister of S Felipe El Real. Philip V made him his chief painter in 1703. He published several studies on art. There are examples of his work in Madrid, Valencia, Siguenza, Santiago and Guadalajara.

GARCIA FERNANDES. See **GARCIA Fernandes**

GARCÍA FERNÁNDEZ, Joaquín, signed himself Joaquín
Spanish, 20th century.
Born 1892, in Murcia; died 1956, in Barcelona.
Painter.
Symbolism.
Joaquín García Fernández participated in numerous exhibitions. He produced relatively few works in small formats, which contain references to Goya and Velázquez.
BIBLIOGRAPHY:
Arnáiz, José Manuel/López Jiménez, Javier/Merchán Díaz, Manuel (ed.), *'Cien años de pintura en Espana y Portugal (1830-1930)'* in vol. IV, Antiqvaria, Madrid, 1990.

GARCÍA FLOREZ, Juan
Spanish, 19th century.
Painter. Genre scenes, landscapes.
Juan García Florez first exhibited in Madrid in 1882. He mainly painted watercolours.

GARCIA FONS, Pierre
Spanish, 20th century.
Born 29 July 1928, in Badalona near Barcelona.
Active in France from 1938.
Painter, watercolourist, lithographer, illustrator.
Nudes, portraits, landscapes, still-lifes.
Pierre García Fons was born to Spanish parents. His mother and family, and later his father, took refuge in Perpignan before the end of the Spanish Civil War in 1938. In 1946 he

joined the Perpignan school of fine arts and in 1950 the Grande Chaumière academy in Paris. He was awarded a French state travel bursary in 1956 which enabled him to work all over France. In 1960 he travelled to Holland and then Italy, returning in 1964. The same year he began to produce lithographs at Mourlot's studio. In 1968 he travelled in Spain. He illustrated *Marguerite de la Nuit* and *Le Bal du Pont du Nord* by Pierre Mac Orlan (1969); *The Maltese Falcon* by Dashiell Hammet (1969); *Midi-Minuit* by Jean Cayrol (1972); *L'Envers du Music-Hall, L'Entrave* and *Mistsou* by Colette (1974); and Albert Camus' *Theatrical Adaptations* (1979). In 1956 he was awarded the Antral prize, in 1958 the Fénéon prize, in 1962 the Ville de Chartres prize and in 1967 the Onze prize.

García Fons took part in collective exhibitions in France (including Paris, Besançon, Cahors, Chartres and Lille) and abroad (including Berlin, Brussels, Chicago, Jakarta and Montreal). On the recommendation of André Dunoyer de Segonzac he took part in an exhibition devoted to this artist at the Galerie du Chêne in Lausanne in 2001. In Paris he also exhibited at the Salon de la Jeune Peinture (in 1950 with *The Flayed Ox*), at the Salon de Mai, the Salon d'Automne, the Salon des Grands et Jeunes d'Aujourd'hui, the Salon du Dessin et de la Peinture à l'Eau, the Salon Comparaisons and the Salon des Peintres Témoins de leur Temps. He also held solo exhibitions of his work: Perpignan (1949); St-Placide gallery, Paris (1957); Musée de Chartres (1963); Galerie de la Main de Fer, Perpignan (1965 and 1981); Galerie Boissière, Paris (1968); Tamenaga Gallery, Tokyo (1971); Galerie Guiot, Paris (1970, 1977, 1980 and 1983); Palacio de los Reyes, Majorca (1980), the Musée Hyacinthe Rigaud, Perpignan (1980); Galerie Guiot and Galerie Bernheim, Paris (1983).

Clearly a figurative artist, García Fons' leading lights are Soutine and Bonnard. In 1960 he said: 'I paint jubilation according to Bonnard'. However, over the years his concept of painting varied. In 1980 he stated: 'I only paint from life, but in accordance with accumulated desires, sensations, ideas and fragments of culture'. At his Paris exhibition of 1983, his paintings with their flat tints emphasised the transparency and reflection of the subject (fruit, statues) within structured spaces, drawing attention to reflections of reflections.

Bibliography:

Cabanne, Pierre, '*Entretien avec cinq peintres*' in *Arts*, periodical, Paris, 1965 (In Conversation with Five Painters). Rey, Marius (preface), *Pierre Garcia-Fons*, exhibition catalogue, Gal. de la Main de Fer, Perpignan, 1968. Olbadia, R. de (preface), *Pierre Garcia-Fons*, exhibition catalogue, Gal. Guiot, Paris, 1977. Valaison, Marie Claude (preface), *Pierre Garcia-Fons*, exhibition catalogue, Palais des Rois, Majorque, Musée Hyacinthe Rigaud, Perpignan, 1980. Ferrier, Jean-Louis (preface), *Pierre Garcia-Fons*, exhibition catalogue, Gal. Guiot, Paris, 1983.

Museums and Galleries:

Paris (MNAM-CCI).

Auction records:

Paris, 26 April 1982, *Landscape* (oil on canvas, 18 x 22 ins / 46 x 55 cm) FRF 2,700. Paris, 21 Nov 1989, *Bunch of Daisies* (oil on canvas, 19¾ x 24 ins / 50 x 61 cm) FRF 5,500. Paris, 23 Feb 1990, *Landscape* (oil on canvas, 28¾ x 23½ ins / 73 x 60 cm) FRF 4,800. Paris, 10 Oct 1990, *The Wild Coast at Croisic* (oil on canvas, 23½ x 28¾ ins / 60 x 73 cm) FRF 4,500. Paris, 25 March 1991, *Three Hens* (1960, oil on canvas, 36¼ x 25½ ins / 92 x 65 cm) FRF 7,100. Paris, 15 June 1994, *Farmyard* (1960, oil on canvas, 36½ x 25½ ins / 93 x 65 cm) FRF 4,000.

GARCÍA JUNCEDA SUPERVIA, Juan

Spanish, 20th century.
Born 1881, in Barcelona; died 1948, in Blanes (Catalonia).
Painter, draughtsman, illustrator.

Juan García Junceda Supervia took part in many collective exhibitions. He produced a large number of humorous drawings showing local customs and manners as well as political and satirical works. He illustrated several literary publications including *Don Quixote* by Cervantes, *Gulliver's Travels* by Swift and *Treasure Island* by Robert Louis Stevenson.

Bibliography:

Arnáiz, José Manuel/López Jiménez, Javier/Merchán Díaz, Manuel (ed.), '*Cien años de pintura en Espana y Portugal (1830-1930)*' in vol. III, Antiqvaria, Madrid, 1989 (One Hundred Years of Painting in Spain and Portugal (1830-1930)).

GARCÍA LABRADOR, Juan

Spanish, 16th century.
Died before 1548.
Active in Seville.
Painter.

Francisco Morales (the painter), Pedro de Villegas and Gutierre de Alcaraz are recorded as taking legal proceedings with García Labrador on 5 April 1541. He was probably the father of Juan Labrador.

GARCÍA LESME, Aurelio

Spanish, 20th century.
Born 1884, in Valladolid; died 12 March 1942, in Mexico City.
Painter, draughtsman. Portraits, landscapes.

Aurelio García Lesme trained at the school of arts and crafts in Valladolid and studied under the painter Luciano Sanchez Santaren. In 1903 he was awarded a bursary to study at the school of painting in Madrid where he was taught by Muñóz Degrain. He later became a drawing teacher. In 1939, at the end of the Spanish Civil War, he fled to Mexico City. García Lesme took part in exhibitions of the national fine arts society in Madrid in 1906, 1907, 1910, 1912 and 1914 and was awarded a bursary. In 1915 he exhibited at the modern art exhibition in Madrid. In 1916 he showed his work at the fine arts circle in Madrid, in 1919 at Valladolid town hall and in 1920 and 1921 in London. In 1926 a tribute to him was held and a major exhibition was organised at the museum of modern art in Madrid in 1931. He received a number of awards: in 1917 a bronze medal, in 1922 a silver medal and in 1926 a gold medal.

García Lesme painted the countryside of Castile with full colour and strong light.

Bibliography:

Arnáiz, José Manuel/López Jiménez, Javier/Merchán Díaz, Manuel (ed.), '*Cien años de pintura en Espana y Portugal (1830-1930)*' in vol. III, Antiqvaria, Madrid, 1989 (One Hundred Years of Painting in Spain and Portugal (1830-1930)).

Museums and Galleries:

Salamanca (Mus. de Salamanca): *Fields at Zaratan* - Valladolid (Casa Mus. de Cervantes).

GARCÍA LORCA, Federico

Spanish, 20th century.
Born 1898, in Fuente Vaqueros (Granada); died 1936, in Fuente Vaqueros (Granada).
Painter, draughtsman.

Federico García Lorca, the great poet and dramatist of the early 20th century Spain, was also an artist. He made sketches of theatrical sets and was a member of the theatre group *La Barraca*. The group was formed with an educational intent and also included Benjamin Palencia and José Caballero. Lorca was a friend of Dalí and they exchanged a prolific correspondence.

He was influenced by Picasso and Juan Gris. His drawings show naivety and grace.

Auction records:

London, 4 April 1974, *Boats on a Beach*, GBP 900. Paris, 28 April 1981, *Composition* (ink/paper, 8 x 5¼ ins / 20 x 13.5

cm) FRF 5,200. MADRID, 26 Sept 2000, *Bowl of Fish* (1927, ink drawing, 13 x 9 ins / 32 x 22 cm) ESP 400,000. MADRID, 26 Sept 2000, *Lady on Balcony* (1927, ink drawing, 13 x 10 ins / 32 x 25 cm) ESP 650,000. SEVILLE, 14 Nov 2002, *Drawing for Altar* (ink drawing, 8 x 6 ins / 21 x 15 cm) EUR 6,000.

GARCÍA MARTINEZ, Emilio
Spanish, 20th century.
Born 15 September 1875; died 1950.
Painter. Landscapes.

Emilio García Martínez spent time at the Accademia Spagnola in Rome. From 1895 to 1901 he took part in the exhibitions of the Madrid fine arts school and from 1904 exhibited regularly at events organised by the fine arts school and was awarded several medals. In 1924 he was made an honorary member of the Autumn Exhibition in Madrid. In 1933 a retrospective of his work was held in Madrid.

BIBLIOGRAPHY:
Arnáiz, José Manuel/López Jiménez, Javier/Merchán Díaz, Manuel (ed.), '*Cien años de pintura en Espana y Portugal (1830-1930)*' in vol. III, Antiqvaria, Madrid, 1989 (One Hundred Years of Painting in Spain and Portugal (1830-1930)).

GARCÍA MESA
Bolivian, 20th century.
Painter.

GARCÍA MULET, Antonio
Spanish, 20th century.
Born 1932, in Barcelona.
Active in France.
Painter.

Antonio García Mulet took part in collective exhibitions in France, Italy and Spain and also held solo exhibitions: in 1970, 1972 and 1974 at the Le Soleil dans la Tête gallery in Paris; in 1973, 1975, 1977, 1985 and 1988 at the Ynguanzo gallery in Madrid; and in 1985 at St Savin Abbey, Vienne (France).

García Mulet describes his work as follows: 'My approach may be disconcerting because of the diversity of subjects I address on my canvases, but there is a common denominator always present: a kind of texture which is the inspiration behind a vision that cannot ignore graffiti, torn posters, scribblings and deletions'.

MUSEUMS AND GALLERIES:
CUAUHTÉMOC - PARIS (CNAC) - TURIN (Centro Internazionale di Ricerche Estetiche).

GARCIA NUNEZ, Armando. See **NUNEZ Armando Garcia**

GARCÍA SEVERO, J. L.
Spanish, 20th century.
Born 7 November 1936, in Barcelona.
Active in France.
Painter.
Symbolism.

J.L. García Severo took part in the 30th Venice Biennale in 1960; in the 2nd Young Artists Biennale in Paris in 1961; in a group exhibition in Seattle in 1963; in the 33rd Venice Biennale in 1966; in the 5th Paris Biennale in 1967; and in the 5th Nice-Antibes Festival of the Fine Arts in 1968.

His work consists of cold forms executed in an impersonal manner and is symbolic and esoteric.

GARCIA SEVILLA, Ferran
Spanish, 20th - 21st century.
Born 22 October 1949, in Palma (Majorca).
Installation artist, painter (mixed media). Multimedia.
Conceptual Art, Figuration Libre.

Ferran Garcia Sevilla studied literature, philosophy and history in Barcelona. Since 1981, he has taught painting at the faculty of fine arts. He lives in Barcelona.

Originally a conceptual artist Garcia Sevilla, like many artists, favoured idea over material and object over execution. In 1974, he took part in a group exhibition entitled *What to do?* at the Sala Vinçon; the preface to the exhibition states the artists' collective desire to 'destroy an idealist conception of the work of the artist'. Skilfully handling the concepts of semiology and analytical philosophy, he created installations and launched actions. In one of his first installations, he placed a piece of cloth just above the ground, held by a thread. He also wrote a pamphlet for this event, entitled *To All Revolutionary Artists.*

Later, his work became more elaborate and theoretical. In 1973, steeped in phenomenology, he formulated 131 proposals designed to 'embrace the entire world through a point of view - not without many - artistic - doubts'. In a Spain marked by Francoist culture, his work also incorporated much psychoanalytical material and critical reflections of a political nature. In his various installations, also designed to provoke, Garcia Sevilla does not hesitate to attack the taboo of sexuality (*El Far/Lo del Poder*, a wordplay on the Catalan words 'far' (lighthouse) and 'falo' (phallus), at the Mataró museum, 1976) and socio-political repression. While his work of this period may reveal the legacy of Kosuth and Vito Acconci, it also has its own particularities - his paintings capture the power of representation, highlight the role of the iconic object and emphasise the permanence of the human body.

In 1977, with the end of the vogue for conceptual art, Garcia Sevilla made the transition to painting. Around 1980, he adopted a style that has been described as 'primitivist' - a content of tension, even stiffness in the meaning itself (with his series of excessive sexual penetrations) deployed in a kind of disorganised, un-channelled violence. It is a painting that seeks to achieve 'automatism', combining the impetus of the popular images of Art Brut with those of European Expressionist Figuration Libre. His compositions, with their simple, unrefined strokes, bring together disparate elements such as trees, insects, spiders' webs, heads with pointed ears, hand prints, linguistic signs. Among his works are: *Hard Surprise or I may be exaggerating or I'm going to stay with you all night; I am the Beast's Entertainment; Look at me, Buy and Forget.* These include esoteric and religious symbols (such as crosses), or simply figures of men and women. They are sources of energy that the artist brings together like a kaleidoscope in the painted space, where it is up to the viewer to interpret possible relationships within their fabric.

Garcia Sevilla took part in the *First Exhibition of Young Art* at Granollers in 1971, which was the first public manifestation of conceptual art in Catalonia. In 1978, his piece entitled *Pintura* (*Painting*) was awarded 2nd prize at the 2nd Biennale of contemporary painting in Barcelona. He has exhibited at numerous other group exhibitions, notably at the Venice Biennale in 1986, and has also exhibited his work in solo exhibitions, starting in 1970 at the Casa de la Cultura in Majorca. This was followed by further exhibitions: in 1972, 1973 and 1976, at the Fundació la Caixa, Barcelona; in 1974, at the German institute in Barcelona; in 1978, at the Temps gallery in Valencia; in 1981, at the Central gallery, Madrid, and at the Maeght gallery in Barcelona; in 1982, at the Ciento gallery in Barcelona; in 1984, at the Brinkman gallery in Amsterdam; in 1985, at the Galerie Yvon Lambert in Paris; in 1987, *Paintings 1980-1986* at the Musée d'Art Contemporain, Nîmes; in 1988, at the Galerie Lelong in Paris; and, in 1989, a double exhibition at the Casa de la Caridad and Santa Monica art centre in Barcelona.

BIBLIOGRAPHY:
'*Garcia-Sevilla*' in *coll. Repères-Cahiers d'art contemporain*, periodical, Gal. Lelong, Paris, 1988. Victoria Combalia, '*L'Outrage et l'Exorcisme: Garcia Sevilla*' in *Artstudio* n° 14, periodical, Gal. Templon, Paris, autumn 1989.

MUSEUMS AND GALLERIES:
BARCELONA (Fundació La Caixa): *Tot I* (1987).
AUCTION RECORDS:
PARIS, 15 June 1988, *Halt* (1983, oil on canvas, 76 3/4 x 94 1/2 ins / 195 x 240 cm) FRF 62,000. NEW YORK, 6 Nov 1990, *Untitled* (1985, acrylic/canvas, 63 1/2 x 51 ins / 161.2 x 129.5 cm) USD 5,500. STOCKHOLM, 5-6 Dec 1990, *Composition* (oil on canvas, 64 1/4 x 51 1/4 ins / 163 x 130 cm) SEK 62,000. PARIS, 24 April 1992, *Black Series = 17* (1990, painting/card, 19 3/4 x 27 1/2 ins / 50 x 70 cm) FRF 14,000. NEW YORK, 9 May 1992, *Pariso 22* (oil on canvas, 76 3/4 x 67 ins / 195 x 170.2 cm) USD 7,150. PARIS, 24 June 1994, *Untitled* (1984, gouache/paper, 28 3/4 x 36 ins / 73 x 90.5 cm) FRF 4,500. PARIS, 12 Oct 1994, *Nude with Matches* (acrylic/canvas, 51 1/4 x 64 ins / 130 x 162.5 cm) FRF 30,000. PARIS, 24 Nov 1995, *Untitled* (oil on paper, 28 3/4 x 32 ins / 73 x 81 cm) FRF 8,000. PARIS, 19 June 1996, *Polygon 35* (1988, mixed media/canvas, 98 1/2 x 98 1/2 ins / 250 x 250 cm) FRF 35,000.

GARCIA TELLA. See **TELLA José García**

GARCÍA Y AGUIRRE, Pedro
Spanish, 17th century.
Active in Valencia c. 1600.
Sculptor (wood).
Pedro García y Aguirre worked on the construction of a church in Valencia.

GARCÍA Y ALCAZAR, Lino
Spanish, 19th century.
Born 19th century, in Madrid.
Painter. Genre scenes.
Lino García y Alcazar studied at the Academia de San Fernando. He first exhibited in Madrid in 1887.

GARCÍA Y ALONSO, Celestino
Spanish, 19th century.
Born in the 19th century, in Sigüenza.
Sculptor.
Celestino García y Alonso studied at the school of fine arts in Madrid. He first exhibited at the Madrid exhibition of 1871.

GARCÍA Y BARCELÓ, Joaquín
Spanish, 19th century.
Born in Valencia; died 30 March 1879, in Valencia.
Painter. History painting.
Joaquín García y Barceló first exhibited in 1845 in Madrid and was appointed to teach at the Madrid conservatory of arts. He is known for his religious paintings, including a very large canvas entitled *Virgin of Mount Carmel Delivering Souls from Purgatory*; he is also known for his portraits, which include some of Queen Isabel II.

GARCÍA Y BARCIA, Manuel
Spanish, 19th century.
Born in the 19th century.
Painter, draughtsman. History painting, genre scenes.
Manuel García y Barcia first exhibited in Cádiz in 1858. In 1877 he was appointed as a teacher at the fine arts academy in Cádiz. He mainly painted historical subjects, with great authority.
AUCTION RECORDS:
LONDON, 20 Feb 1976, *Fiesta* (1859; *Country Dance* (1859, two oils on canvas, 24 x 32 ins / 61 x 81.5 cm) GBP 1,400. PARIS, 27 May 1987, *Couple* (pen and Indian ink wash, 10 x 6 ins / 25.5 x 15 cm) FRF 2,000.

GARCÍA Y BAS, Mariano
Spanish, 19th century.
Born in the 19th century, in Valencia.
Sculptor.
In 1822, Mariano García y Bas received funding from the provincial government of Valencia to study in Rome. He is known for his *Bust of Pope Calixtus III*.

GARCÍA Y CHICANO, José
Spanish, 19th century.
Died 1858, in Cádiz.
Painter. History painting.
José García y Chicano studied at the fine arts academy in Cádiz. He taught drawing at the fine arts academy in Cádiz and in Malaga.

GARCÍA Y ESCUCHA, Ignacio
Spanish, 17th century.
Born 1580, near Gijon (Asturias); died 10 October 1628, in Santa Fe de Bogotá, Columbia.
Sculptor.
Ignacio García y Escucha was a pupil of Alonso Sánchez Cotán in Toledo. He collaborated with Sánchez Cotán and married his sister in 1612. He left his wife to go to South America and settled in Santa Fe where he worked at the Franciscan monastery.

GARCÍA Y FERRER, Mosen
Spanish, 17th century.
Active in Valencia.
Painter.
MUSEUMS AND GALLERIES:
VALENCIA: a work.

GARCÍA Y FERRER, Pedro, called El Licenciado
Spanish, 17th century.
Died 1659, in Toledo.
Painter, sculptor.
Although a priest, Pedro García y Ferrer worked as a painter in Valencia and Madrid. He painted several *Crucifixions* (one dated 1632) and other religious subjects. He established an outstanding reputation as an artist.

GARCÍA Y GARCÍA, Rafael
Spanish, 19th century.
Born in the 19th century.
Painter. History painting, genre scenes.
Rafael García y García studied at the school of fine arts in Cádiz. He exhibited in Seville in 1876. There is a study of a nude by García y García in the provincial museum in Cádiz.

GARCÍA Y GONZÁLEZ, Luis
Spanish, 19th century.
Born c. 1839, in Murcia; died 1885, in Madrid.
Painter. Genre scenes, portraits.
Luis García y González studied under Pascual Ventosa and at the school of fine arts in Madrid. He first exhibited around 1870, and is known for his *Portrait of King Alfonso XII*. He was a knight of the order of Charles III.

GARCÍA Y GUERRA, Antonio
Spanish, 19th century.
Born in the 19th century, in Madrid.
Painter. Genre scenes.
Antonio García y Guerra was a pupil of Vicente Palmoroli. He exhibited in Madrid and Paris.

GARCÍA Y GUERRA, Eduardo
Spanish, 19th century.
Born 1827, in Granada.
Painter. History painting.
Eduardo García y Guerra studied at the Academia de San Fernando in Madrid and the Gleyre academy in Paris. He first exhibited in Madrid in 1856.

GARCÍA Y HISPALETO, Manuel
Spanish, 19th century.
Born 22 November 1836, in Seville; died 26 December 1898, in Madrid.
Painter. Religious subjects, portraits, genre scenes.
Manuel García y Hispaleto was the brother of Rafael García y Hispaleto and trained in Seville. Struck by his early promise, Ignacio Muñoz de Baena funded him to go to Rome.

Manuel García y Hispaleto later returned to Spain and, from 1862, exhibited regularly at the exhibition of the national fine arts society of Madrid.

His works from this period include *Grief of the Orphaned Girl* and the *Apparition of St Ines*. He is also known for his *Milliners' Studio, Dancer* and various portraits. Manuel García was one of the outstanding painters of the Spanish Impressionist School.

AUCTION RECORDS:

LONDON, 24 Nov 1976, *At the Dressmaker's* (oil on canvas, 26 x 35 ins / 66 x 89 cm) GBP 3,300. MADRID, 22 Dec 1999, *Children with Shell* (oil on canvas, after Murillo, 24x30 ins / 62x75 cm) ESP 100,000. MADRID, 5 June 2000, *Gypsy Girl with Jug* (watercolour, 19 x 13 ins / 49x34 cm) ESP 180,000. MADRID, 20 March 2001, *Harvesting in the Old Days* (oil on canvas, 40 x 59 ins / 101x151 cm) ESP 600,000. MADRID, 23 Sept 2002, *Monk* (oil on canvas, 15 x 10 ins / 39x26 cm) EUR 1,600. COPENHAGEN, 9 Dec 2003, *Toreador Entrance to Town* (1864, oil on canvas, 31 x 35 ins / 78x90 cm) DKK 230,000.

GARCÍA Y HISPALETO, Rafael

Spanish, 19th century.

Born 1833, in Seville; died 1854, in Paris.

Painter. History painting, genre scenes.

Rafael García y Hispaleto was a remarkable artist who could have become a great painter had he not died at the age of 21. Most of his work was exhibited after his death and was much admired by critics. He is known for the paintings *Harvester* and *Beggar*.

GARCÍA Y IBAÑEZ, Francisco

Spanish, 19th century.

Born 8 November 1825, in Madrid.

Painter. History painting.

Francisco García y Ibañez studied under Juan Ribera. He was commissioned to restore damaged paintings at the Prado and later at the Academia de San Fernando.

GARCÍA Y MARCO, Francisco

Spanish, 19th century.

Born in the 19th century, in Valencia.

Painter. History painting.

Francisco García y Marco first exhibited in Valencia around 1875.

GARCÍA Y MARTÍNEZ, Juan

Spanish, 19th century.

Born 1829, in Calatayud; died 1890, in Madrid.

Painter. Genre and history painting.

Juan García y Martínez was a pupil of Federico de Madraro and Léon Cogniet. He first exhibited around 1856 at the exhibition of the national fine arts society of Madrid. He was a remarkable artist who used bright colours and showed great talent for composition.

MUSEUMS AND GALLERIES:

BARCELONA: *Death of Macias* - MADRID: *Raising of Lazarus; Lovers of Teruel; Death of Don Sancho at Zamora; Water Seller* - MURCIA: *Francis I at the Bidassoa* - SARAGOSSA: *The Rout of Fraga*.

GARCÍA Y MENCIA, Antonio

Spanish, 19th - 20th century.

Born c. 1853, in Madrid; died 1915.

Painter, watercolourist. Allegorical subjects, genre scenes.

Antonio García y Mencia studied at the fine arts academy in Madrid. He first exhibited at the national fine arts society in Madrid in 1871. He also exhibited in Paris from 1876.

AUCTION RECORDS:

PARIS, 1899, *El Pelele* (*The Rag Doll*) (1871) FRF 1,700. PARIS, 14 and 15 Dec 1925, *The Gallant Bullfighter*, FRF 1,000. PARIS, 8 Dec 1941, *The Picnic Lunch*; *The Boating Party* (two pendants) FRF 8,000. NEW YORK, 12 May 1978, *Young Woman with Binoculars* (oil on canvas, 16 x 13 ins / 40.5 x 33 cm) USD 5,250. NEW YORK, 24 Feb 1983, *The Picnic* (1874, oil on canvas, 15 x 18 ins / 38 x 46 cm) USD 14,000. LONDON, 27 Nov 1987, *Elegant Lady Looking into the Distance with Binoculars* (oil on canvas, 16 x 13 ins / 40.5 x 33 cm) GBP 5,000. LONDON, 23 Nov 1988, *The Violinist* (watercolour, 26 x 39 ins / 66 x 99 cm) GBP 3,850. NEW YORK, 24 May 1989, *The Favourite* (watercolour/pencil, 27 x 19 1/4 ins / 68.4 x 48.7 cm) USD 6,050. LONDON, 14 Feb 1990, *Allegory of Time* (watercolour, 22 x 31 ins / 56 x 79 cm) GBP 5,280. NEW YORK, 17 Feb 1993, *The Musical Gathering* (1874, oil on canvas, 29 x 23 1/4 ins / 73.7 x 59.1 cm) USD 29,900. NEW YORK, 26 May 1994, *The Orange Seller* (1880, oil on canvas, 49 1/4 x 35 1/2 ins / 125.1 x 90.2 cm) USD 28,750.

GARCÍA Y PÁRAMO, Ventura

Spanish, 19th century.

Born in Madrid; died January 1881, in Madrid.

Painter. History painting, genre scenes, portraits.

Ventura García y Páramo studied at the Academia de San Fernando. He first exhibited around 1860 with *Episode from the African War*. He produced numerous portraits and many illustrations for magazines.

GARCÍA Y PARRENO, Joaquín

Spanish, 19th century.

Born in Barcelona; died 1 August 1876, in Barcelona.

Painter.

GARCÍA Y PELAYO, José

Spanish, 18th - 19th century.

Painter. History painting.

GARCÍA Y PERATE, Carlos

Spanish, 19th century.

Born in the 19th century, in Madrid.

Painter. Genre scenes.

Carlos García y Perate was a pupil of Antonio Pérez Rubio. He first exhibited around 1871.

GARCÍA Y PRIETO, Andrés

Spanish, 19th century.

Born in Peral de Arlanza, near Burgos.

Painter. Portraits, genre scenes.

Andrés García y Prieto trained as an artist in Madrid.

GARCÍA Y RAMOS, Dolores

Spanish, 19th century.

Born in Madrid; died 5 November 1871, in Madrid.

Painter.

Dolores García y Ramos was a pupil of Federico de Madrazo.

AUCTION RECORDS:

NEW YORK, 12 and 13 March 1903, *Guitar Player*, USD 100. ST LOUIS, 7 Dec 2002, *Portrait of a Woman Seated in a Landscape* (oil on canvas, 29x21 ins / 74x53 cm) USD 1,200.

GARCÍA Y RAMOS, José

Spanish, 19th - 20th century.

Born 1852, in Seville; died 1912, in Seville.

Painter. Portraits, genre scenes.

José García y Ramos studied under José Jimenez Aranda. In 1872 he went to Rome to complete his studies and then to Paris, returning to Rome and remaining there until 1881. In 1882, when he returned to Spain, he was appointed director of the free school of fine arts. He exhibited at the Salon des Artistes Français in Paris and was awarded a bronze medal in 1900 Exposition Universelle.

He is known for *Italian Musician* and *Dawn*.

Garcia y Ramos

BIBLIOGRAPHY:
Pintura española del siglo XIX obras para una colección, Gal. Concha Barrios, Madrid, 1990.
MUSEUMS AND GALLERIES:
MADRID (Prado): *Oh My Christ.*
AUCTION RECORDS:
MADRID, 8 Dec 1973, *The Seville Feria*, ESP 90,000. NEW YORK, 15 Oct 1976, *Wedding in Seville* (oil on canvas, 27 x 43 1/4 ins / 68.5 x 110 cm) USD 11,000. LONDON, 5 July 1978, *Wedding, Seville* (oil on canvas, 27 1/4 x 43 3/4 ins / 69 x 111 cm) GBP 14,000. NEW YORK, 28 May 1980, *An Hidalgo and his Lady* (oil on panel, 11 1/2 x 6 3/4 ins / 29.2 x 17.2 cm) USD 1,600. NEW YORK, 26 Feb 1982, *The Conversation* (oil on canvas, 17 1/4 x 13 1/2 ins / 44 x 34.5 cm) USD 9,000. MONTE CARLO, 9 Dec 1984, *The Studio* (oil on canvas, 23 1/2 x 15 ins / 60 x 38 cm) FRF 36,000. MADRID, 24 Feb 1987, *The Studio* (oil on canvas, 23 1/2 x 15 ins / 60 x 38 cm) ESP 950,000. LONDON, 22 June 1988, *Patio in Seville* (oil on canvas, 28 3/4 x 33 1/2 ins / 73 x 85 cm) GBP 35,200. LONDON, 23 Nov 1988, *Musical Interlude* (oil on canvas, 27 1/4 x 17 1/4 ins / 69 x 44 cm) GBP 30,800. LONDON, 17 Feb 1989, *Intimate Conversation* (oil on canvas, 18 1/4 x 11 1/4 ins / 46.3 x 28.3 cm) GBP 6,600. NEW YORK, 24 May 1989, *Spanish Tavern* (oil on panel, 10 3/4 x 6 1/2 ins / 27.3 x 16.5 cm) USD 28,600. LONDON, 15 Feb 1990, *Holy Week in Seville* (oil on canvas, 57 x 32 3/4 ins / 145 x 83 cm) GBP 35,200. LONDON, 16 June 1993, *Young Girl with Cat* (oil on canvas, 23 1/2 x 15 3/4 ins / 60 x 40 cm) GBP 5,520. LONDON, 1 Oct 1993, *Arab Seated* (oil on canvas, 17 x 13 ins / 43.2 x 33 cm) GBP 3,220. NEW YORK, 23 May 1997, *Leaving the Theatre* (1905, oil on canvas, 27 3/4 x 41 ins / 70.5 x 104.1 cm) USD 211,500.

GARCÍA Y REYNOSO, Antonio

Spanish, 17th century.
Born c. 1623, in Cabra; died 12 July 1677, in Cordova.
Painter. History painting, landscapes.

Antonio García y Reynoso worked in Jaén with Sebastián Martínez. A number of his works are in churches and private collections in Cordova. Palomino mentions an altarpiece of *Holy Trinity and Various Saints* in the Capuchin church in Andújar.

GARCÍA Y RODRIGUEZ, Manuel

Spanish, 19th - 20th century.
Born 1863, in Seville; died 6 May 1925, in Seville.
Painter. Local scenes, genre scenes, landscapes, landscapes with figures.

Manuel García y Rodriguez studied at the school of fine arts in Seville and painted mainly picturesque scenes of the area where he was born. He took part in various exhibitions at the school and received a number of awards. He also took part in collective exhibitions, notably in 1888 at the Barcelona Universal Exhibition where he was awarded a bronze medal.

BIBLIOGRAPHY:
Arnáiz, José Manuel/López Jiménez, Javier/Merchán Díaz, Manuel (ed.), *Cien años de pintura en Espana y Portugal (1830-1930)*, Antiqvaria, Madrid, 1989. *Pintura española del siglo XIX obras para una colección*, Gal. Concha Barrios, Madrid, 1990.
AUCTION RECORDS:
LONDON, 29 Oct 1976, *View of Sanlucar* (1905, oil on panel, 14 x 23 ins / 35.5 x 58.5 cm) GBP 2,200. LONDON, 20 July 1977, *Patio* (1913, oil on canvas, 24 1/4 x 17 1/2 ins / 61.5 x 44.5 cm) GBP 1,500. MADRID, 14 March 1978, *The Gardens of Seville* (1921, oil on canvas, 26 3/4 x 48 1/2 ins / 68 x 123 cm) ESP 420,000. MADRID, 20 May 1981, *Gardens of Seville* (1906, watercolour, 7 1/2 x 11 3/4 ins / 19 x 30 cm) ESP 50,000. NEW YORK, 25 Feb 1983, *Landscape with Stream and Figures* (1911, oil on canvas, 13 3/4 x 23 1/2 ins / 35.1 x 59.6 cm) USD 1,600. MADRID, 22 Oct 1984, *Patio of a House in Alcalá* (oil on canvas, 21 3/4 x 10 1/2 ins / 55.5 x 26.5 cm) ESP 375,000. LONDON, 21 March 1986, *Excursion by Boat* (1904, gouache, 11 3/4 x 16 ins / 29.7 x 40.6 cm) GBP 5,500. LONDON, 21 March 1986, *Seville* (oil on canvas, 28 x 49 1/4 ins / 71.1 x 125.1 cm) GBP 16,000. LONDON, 23 March 1988, *On the Banks of the Guadalquivir* (oil on canvas, 21 1/4 x 31 1/2 ins / 54 x 80 cm) GBP 11,550. NEW YORK, 25 May 1988, *Figures around a Fountain in Seville* (oil on canvas, 29 1/2 x 35 1/4 ins / 75 x 89.5 cm) USD 6,600. LONDON, 22 June 1988, *On the Banks of the Guadalquivir* (1897, oil on canvas, 21 3/4 x 48 ins / 55.5 x 121 cm) GBP 20,900. LONDON, 23 Nov 1988, *Three Young Women on a Terrace Overlooking the Guadalquivir* (1910, watercolour and gouache, 22 1/4 x 15 1/4 ins / 565 x 39 cm) GBP 16,500; *Figure on a Mule* (oil on canvas, 18 x 10 1/4 ins / 46 x 26 cm) GBP 4,400. LONDON, 17 Feb 1989, *Road to the House* (1904, oil on canvas, 13 1/2 x 10 ins / 34.3 x 25.3 cm) GBP 7,700. NEW YORK, 23 Feb 1989, *Figures in a Patio* (1919, oil on card, 10 1/2 x 13 3/4 ins / 26.6 x 34.8 cm) USD 8,800. LONDON, 21 June 1989, *Figures on the Bank of the Guadalquivir in Seville* (1921, oil on canvas, 37 x 26 ins / 94 x 66 cm) GBP 61,600. NEW YORK, 17 Jan 1990, *View of a Village* (oil on panel, 7 3/4 x 12 3/4 ins / 19.7 x 32.4 cm) USD 3,410. LONDON, 15 Feb 1990, *In the Patio* (1888, oil on canvas, 16 x 23 1/2 ins / 39.8 x 59.7 cm) GBP 19,800. NEW YORK, 28 Feb 1990, *Romantic Words from the Garden* (1896, oil on canvas, 9 1/2 x 15 ins / 24.1 x 38.1 cm) USD 19,800. NEW YORK, 23 Oct 1990, *In the Patio* (1906, oil on panel, 11 1/2 x 18 ins / 29.2 x 45.7 cm) USD 22,000. NEW YORK, 24 Oct 1990, *Mother and Daughter Sewing in the Patio*. NEW YORK, 22 May 1991, *The Well* (1920, oil on canvas, 20 x 28 ins / 50.5 x 70.2 cm) USD 20,900. LONDON, 19 June 1991, *A Garden in Seville* (1919, oil on canvas, 19 1/4 x 28 ins / 49 x 71 cm) GBP 19,800. LONDON, 29 May 1992, *The Marchena Gate in the Alcazar Gardens in Seville* (1924, oil on canvas, 28 x 43 1/2 ins / 71 x 110.5 cm) GBP 17,600. NEW YORK, 29 Oct 1992, *Market Place with the Giralda Tower in the Background* (1919, oil on card, 10 3/4 x 14 ins / 27.3 x 356 cm) USD 13,750. NEW YORK, 13 Oct 1993, *In the Patio* (1907, oil on canvas, 23 1/2 x 32 1/2 ins / 59.7 x 82.6 cm) USD 23,000. NEW YORK, 24 May 1995, *Sunlit Garden in Seville* (oil on canvas, 29 x 38 1/2 ins / 73.7 x 97.8 cm) USD 34,500. LONDON, 13 March 1996, *Enclosed Garden in Seville* (1905, oil on panel, 11 x 17 ins / 28 x 43 cm) GBP 24,150. NEW YORK, 23-24 May 1996, *Two Men Travelling on Donkeys along a Path* (1902, oil on panel, 16 3/4 x 9 1/4 ins / 42.5 x 23.5 cm) USD 9,200. LONDON, 12 June 1996, *Morning Walk along the Canal* (1904, oil on canvas, 10 1/4 x 14 1/2 ins / 26 x 37 cm) GBP 1,725. LONDON, 26 March 1999, *At the Well* (1911, oil on canvas, 41 x 52 ins / 105 x 133 cm) GBP 15,000. MADRID, 26 Oct 1999, *Landscape* (1910, oil on panel, 6 x 10 ins / 16 x 25 cm) ESP 40,000,000. NEW YORK, 1 May 2000, *Courtyard in Seville* (1922, oil on canvas, 21 x 31 ins / 54 x 79 cm) USD 28,000. LONDON, 22 June 2000, *Flowered Patio* (oil on canvas, 23 x 28 ins / 58 x 70 cm) GBP 15,000. LONDON, 19 Nov 2001, *Andalusian Courtyard* (1919, oil on canvas, 26 x 37 ins / 65 x 95 cm) GBP 50,000. COLOGNE, 24 Nov 2001, *Landscape near Alcalá de Guadaira - Seville* (1899, oil on canvas, 50 x 79 ins / 126 x 200 cm) DEM 44,000. LONDON, 19 Nov 2002, *Sevillian Courtyard* (1925, oil on canvas, 22 x 28 ins / 56 x 70 cm) GBP 15,000. LONDON, 19 Nov 2002, *Gardens in Seville* (1905, oil on board, 15 x 12 ins / 39 x 31 cm) GBP 28,000. MADRID, 24 June 2003, *Ladies with Mantillas in the Alcázar Gardens* (oil on canvas, 23 x 28 ins / 59 x 70 cm) EUR 70,000. LONDON, 18 Nov 2003, *Sevillian Courtyard* (1922, oil on canvas, 17 x 22 ins / 43 x 55 cm) GBP 29,000. NEW YORK, 22 April 2004, *Spanish Courtyard* (1919, oil on canvas, 20 x 28 ins / 50 x 72 cm) USD 18,000. LONDON, 14 July 2004, *Garden in Seville* (1896, oil on canvas, 18 x 10 ins / 46 x 26 cm) GBP 10,000.

GARCÍA Y SALMERON, Cristóbal

Spanish, 17th century.
Born c. 1603, in Cuenca; died 1666, in Madrid.
Painter. History painting, animals.

Cristóbal García y Salmeron was a pupil of Pedro Orrente. The church of S Francisco in Cuenca has one of his best works, a *Nativity*. He executed a number of works for the cathedral in his native town of Cuenca and for the monastery of the Discalced Carmelites. Philip IV commissioned him to paint a *Bullfight* for the birthday of Charles II of Spain.

GARCÍA Y SALMERON, Francisco
Spanish, 17th century.
Active in Murcia.
Painter.

Francisco García y Salmeron was the brother of Cristobal García y Salmeron.

GARCÍA Y TORREBESANO, Petronila
Spanish, 19th century.
Born in Cordova.
Sculptor.

Petronila García y Torrebesano first exhibited around 1839.

GARCÍA Y VALDEAVELLANO, Agapito
Spanish, 19th century.
Born in the 19th century, in Montenegro de Cameros (Soria).
Painter. History painting, genre scenes.

Agapito García y Valdeavellano was a pupil of Antonio Mariá Esquivel. He first exhibited in Madrid in 1860.

GARCÍA Y VALDEMORO, Juan
Spanish, 19th century.
Born in the 19th century, in Castillo, near Burgos.
Painter. Landscapes.

Juan García y Valdemoro studied at the Academia de San Fernando. He first exhibited around 1860 at the exhibition of the national fine arts society of Madrid. He was made a knight of the order of Charles III.

J. Garcia

GARCÍA Y VILLAMALA, Justo
Spanish, 19th century.
Born in the 19th century, in Barcelona.
Painter. History painting.

Justo García y Villamala studied at the school of fine arts in Barcelona and under José Serra. He first exhibited at the exhibition of the national fine arts society around 1864, and later in Madrid and Barcelona.

GARCÍA YORK, Roberto
Cuban, 20th century.
Born 10 January 1929, in Havana.
Active in France.
Painter.

Roberto García York has exhibited in Havana, Madrid, Mexico and Paris, where he has lived since 1964.

GARCÍA-CORDERO, José
Dominican, 20th - 21st century.
Born 1951.
Painter.

José García Cordero began studying in Santo Domingo and continued his studies at the University of Paris VIII, eventually working in the studio of the painter Hernández Ortega. He lived in Paris until 1977 and made frequent visits to his native Dominican Republic. His work is permeated by a sense of fantasy and humour. He has taken part in numerous exhibitions in the USA, France and Central America and is also a philosopher, critic and architect.

GARCÍA-LLORT, Josep Maria
Spanish, 20th century.
Born 8 November 1921, in Barcelona.
Painter. Figures, figure compositions, animals, still-lifes.

Josep García Llort's studies in Barcelona were interrupted by the Spanish Civil War and by the tuberculosis he contracted in 1940. He studied draughtsmanship, though he was largely self taught, and held his first solo exhibition in his native city in 1948. In 1950 he was awarded a French state bursary and went to Paris. Following his marriage to Martha Crockett in 1953 he went to the USA before finally settling in Barcelona in 1960. He continued to travel and exhibit in many galleries, in Barcelona mainly, but also in Madrid, Paris, Bordeaux and the USA.

García Llort has been reluctant to talk about his art, arguing that if it fails to speak for itself words will not improve matters. His only aim is to look at the world and to transcribe it, without intellectual analysis, which is perhaps why his paintings sometimes have a raw, primitive look. In his early years he was mainly influenced by Chagall and Rouault; his work shows a marked affinity with the latter in its flamboyant use of deep colours outlined in black and his way of filling the entire space of the canvas without leaving any 'neutral' area so that each detail is a work in its own right. This meticulous execution and the repetition of iconographic and symbolic motifs (the bird, for example) also recall the spirit of Mozarabic miniatures, although, according to García Llort, this is coincidental. The majority of his compositions convey a certain irony emphasised by their titles.

BIBLIOGRAPHY:

Benet, Jordi, *Garcia-Llort*, catalogue, Sala Dalmau, Barcelona, 1993.

GARCÍA-ROSSI, Horacio
Argentinian, 20th century.
Born 1929, in Buenos Aires.
Active in France.
Painter (including gouache), sculptor, decorative designer.
Kinetic Art.
GRAV (Groupe de Recherche d'Art Visuel).

Horacio García-Rossi studied at the national fine arts school in Buenos Aires between 1950 and 1957. In 1960 he was one of the co-founders of the Groupe de Recherche d'Art Visuel (GRAV) in Paris. He creates objects by using networks, screens and, first and foremost, light sources that are coloured and variable, playing on the confusion created between real space and suggested space which he defines by the term 'immaterial realism'. Since 1959, he has been researching form, light and movement.

He took part in all the group's events until it disbanded in 1968, as well as in many other group exhibitions including: in 1959 the Paris Biennale at the Musée d'Art Moderne; in 1964 *Mouvement II* (*Movement II*) at the Denise René Gallery in Paris; Documenta III, Kassel; in 1965 *The Responsive Eye* at the Museum of Modern Art in New York; in 1967 *Dix Ans d'Art Vivant* (*Ten Years of Living Art*) at the Maeght Foundation in St-Paul de Vence; *Lumière et Mouvement* (*Light and Movement*) at the Musée d'Art Moderne in Paris; *De Mondrian au Cinétisme* (*From Mondrian to Kinetic Art*) at the Denise René Gallery in Paris; in 1984 the 1st Havana Biennale in Cuba; in 1986 the Venice Biennale. He has also held solo exhibitions: in 1967 at the Rubbers Gallery in Buenos Aires; in 1973 at the Zen Gallery in Milan, then in Parma, Neuchâtel, Zurich, Padua, Rome and Paris, and again in Buenos Aires. In 1991, he exhibited at the Espace Latino-Américain in Paris. In 1992 he was given his own exhibition at the *Salon Découvertes 92* (*Discoveries 92 Exhibition*) by the Alexandre de la Salle Gallery. In 1993, he exhibited again in Paris, at the St-Charles de Rose Gallery, and in 1994 and 1996 at the Lélia Mordoch Gallery. Garcia Rossi has been awarded prizes on many occasions and notably received a prize at the 1st Havana Biennale in 1984.

BIBLIOGRAPHY:

Aupetitallot, Yves/Popper, Frank/Hohfeldt, Marion, *GRAV. Groupe de recherche d'art visuel*, Centre d'Art contemporain, Grenoble, 1998.

Museums and Galleries:
Buenos Aires (MFA) - Cholet (MAH) - Havana (Casa de Las Americas) - Paris (FNAC) - Paris (MAMVP) - Washington DC (Hirshhorn Mus. and Sculpture Garden).

GARCIANGUERA, pseudonym of García Anguera Saturnino
Spanish, 20th century.
Born 2 October 1912, in Girona; died 8 September 1963, in Tarragona.
Painter, draughtsman. Figures, landscapes.

Garcianguera painted compositions in a realist style in the tradition of the great Spanish classical artists. He later developed a new and more informal style of painting.

He took part in many exhibitions in Spain, France, Germany, England, Italy and the USA including: Casino de l'Amirauté gallery, Cherbourg (1962); and, as a guest of honour, Cherbourg Biennale (1960 and 1962). He taught at the school of fine arts in Tarragona.

GARCIN, Antoine
French, 17th century.
Born in Marseilles.
Sculptor.

Antoine Garcin was commissioned in 1628 for the decoration of a royal gallery that was built in Toulon.

GARCIN, B.
French, 18th century.
Active in St-Maximin.
Painter.

GARCIN, Germaine Marie
French, 20th century.
Born in Marseilles.
Painter. Landscapes.

Germaine Garcin exhibited in Paris at the Salon des Artistes Français.

GARCIN, Jeanne, Mme Boudènes-Garcin since 1907
French, 19th - 20th century.
Born in Lyons.
Painter.

Jeanne Garcin studied under L. Guy and at the Académie de Peinture. She exhibited in Lyons from 1887, showing oil and pastel portraits, and was awarded a gold medal in 1894.

GARCIN, Jenny Laure
French, 20th century.
Born 20 June 1896, in Paris; died 19 September 1978, in Paris.
Painter.
Abstraction-Création group.

Jenny Garcin briefly interrupted her work as an artist to write a thesis on the influence of dreams in fine arts. Since 1948 she has produced numerous short films which, accompanied by the words of poems by Rimbaud, Apollinaire, St-John Perse and others, give concrete form to a synthesis of the movement and expression of painting and three-dimensional art. From 1950 to 1960 she worked as a lecturer at French national museums. In 1970 she produced a major work entitled *Grandville*.

From 1937 to 1939 she began exploring dreams through her art, a direction that would determine the development of her later work and thought. From 1948 her art made use of the allusive resources of automatic and 'informel' art, seeking to capture the secret movements of unconscious imagination.

From 1927 to 1929 she exhibited at the Salon d'Automne in Paris and was a committee member of the Association des Surindépendants from its inception. She later exhibited with the Abstraction-Création group from 1935 to 1937. She held a first solo exhibition of her work in Paris in 1933 at the Galerie Vignon and later the same year at the Galerie Jeanne Bucher. She held further solo exhibitions in Paris, notably an exhibition prefaced by Gaston Bachelard in 1957 and another in 1963.

Bibliography:
Bachelard, Gaston, *Cosmos et matière*, Gal. 93, Paris, 1957. *Laure Garcin*, exhibition catalogue, Gal. Coard, Paris, 1963. *Laure Garcin: peintures récentes*, exhibition catalogue, L. Garcin, Paris, 1972. Fabre, Gladys C., *Abstraction-Création 1931-1936*, exhibition catalogue, Westfälisches Landesmuseum für Kunst und Kulturgeschichte, Münster, Musée d'Art moderne de la ville de Paris, Paris, 1978.

GARCIN, Louis or Gilles
French, 18th century.
Active in Aix-en-Provence c. 1700.
Painter.

Louis Garcin was a student of Pierre Mignard. He painted some religious pictures in Mignard's style in Provence.

GARCIN, Louis-Marius
French, 19th century.
Born 25 August 1821, in Hyères (Var); died 20 February 1898, in Hyères.
Painter. Historical subjects, figure compositions, portraits, genre scenes, landscapes with figures, waterscapes, animals.

While he was still young he moved to Paris to study under Michel Drolling and, later, Ary Scheffer. He then visited Italy. He exhibited at the Paris Salon from 1848 to 1864. Although he painted some portraits and historical subjects, most of Garcin's output comprises landscapes, nearly always crowded with figures, featuring the region where he was born and views of Italy painted from memory. Typical works by Garcin include: *Departure of the Society of the Decameron from the Piazza S Maria Novella in Florence during the Plague of 1348, Giotto and Cimabue in the Valley of Vespignano, View of the Îles d'Hyères, Tuscan Peasants Crossing the Sieve River, Souvenir of Venice, Recalcitrant Goat, Women Working the Salt Marshes of Hyères, Women Winnowing the Crop* and *Cattle Herd*.

Museums and Galleries:
Hyères: *Panning in the Vieux-Salins Salt Marshes of Hyères; Banks of the Roubeau at Hyères; La Gondole; Chicken Feed; Rabbits; Portrait of Alexis Riodet; Self-portrait* - Toulon: *The Decameron; Portrait of the Artist Vincent Courdouan.*

Auction records:
Copenhagen, 7 Nov 1984, *Gondola Ride* (1852, oil on canvas, 32 x 49 1/4in/81 x 125cm) DKK 19,000.

GARCIN, Philippe
French, 16th century.
Active in Avignon in 1512.
Painter.

He worked at the church of St-Pierre in Avignon.

GARD, Léon
French, 20th century.
Born 12 July 1901, in Tulle (Corrèze); died 12 November 1979, in Paris.
Painter. Figures, landscapes, still-lifes, flowers.

Léon Gard studied under Ernest Laurent at the École des Beaux-Arts in Paris. In 1918 he exhibited for the first time at the Salon d'Automne in Paris. He also exhibited at the Salon of the Société Nationale des Beaux-Arts, of which he became a member.

As well as portraits - notably of Sacha Guitry, Lucien Daudet and Georges Renand - he painted large, simple, stark compositions on the customary themes of nature and the seasons, often represented metaphorically as elements of his numerous still-lifes. He was also a restorer of paintings and after the war founded the art journal *Apollo*.

Bibliography:
Gard, Léon, *Révolution, procès de l'Art moderne*, Île du Levant, 1985.
Auction records:
Paris, 2 March 1934, *Still-life*, FRF 180. Paris, 2 July 1936, *Still-life - Peppers* (tomatoes and glassware) FRF 400. Nice, 11 March 1943, *Still-life with Glassware, Ceramics and Tomatoes*, FRF 3,300. Paris, Oct 1945, *Vase of Flowers*, FRF 10,000. Paris, July 1946, *Sailing Boats at Sea*, FRF 4,500. Paris, 24 Jan 1990, *The Parc des Bonshomme, Barbizon* (oil on card, 15 x 18 ins / 38 x 46 cm) FRF 10,000. Paris, 11 March 1991, *Jeannine Andrade with Violin* (oil on canvas, 21 1/4 x 25 1/2 ins / 54 x 65 cm) FRF 22,000.

GARDAIR, Christian
French, 20th century.
Born 1938, in Brest.
Painter.

Christian Gardair spent his childhood in Morocco and began painting from nature at the age of 15. In 1962 he worked at the studio of Madame Calcagni, a close friend of Bissière, who introduced him to the work of Vieira da Silva, Tal Coat, Bazaine and other artists.

In his early work, the geometric motifs and emblematic signs juxtaposed in linear bands suggest coloured weaving, no doubt recalling the North African carpets of his childhood. He soon abandoned this structure and explored surface, creating a network of light lines and rapid, skilfully executed brushstrokes. Taking inspiration from both town and country he brings life to the canvas through the subtle interplay of intertwining straight lines, geometric forms and colours, creating intimate landscapes that express emotion. He seeks, through tirelessly repeated motifs, to open up a new space in which air and energy can circulate freely.

Gardair took part in numerous group exhibitions, notably: from 1971 to 1976 at the Salon des Réalités Nouvelles in Paris; from 1977 to 1978 at the Galerie Jacob, Paris; in 1982 at the Salon des Artistes Français, Paris; in 1986 at FIAC (Foire Internationale d'Art Contemporain) in Paris; in 1986 at the Galerie Olivier Nouvellet, Paris; and in 2002 the *Histoires d'Eaux* (*Water Stories*) exhibition at the Galerie le Troisième Oeil, Paris. He has shown his work in solo exhibitions since 1965, including: in 1980, 1992, 1993 and 2003 at the Galerie le Troisième Œil, Bordeaux; in 1981 at the Musée Léon Bonnat, Bayonne; in 1988 at the Musée des Beaux-Arts, Libourne; in 1989, 1994 and 1998 at the Galerie Protée, Paris; in 2000 at the Gallery K, Washington DC; and in 2003 at the Galerie le Troisième Oeil, Paris.

Christian GARDAIR

Bibliography:
Maulpoix, Jean-Michel, '*Christian Gardair - La Naissance des souffles*' in *Cimaise* n° 198, periodical, Paris, Jan-Feb 1989.
Museums and Galleries:
Paris (FNAC) - Paris (MAMVP) - Perpignan (Mus. Hyacinthe-Rigaud).

GARDAIRE, Claude Damien
French, 18th century.
Active in Besançon 1740-1747.
Sculptor.

GARDANNE, Auguste
French, 19th century.
Born in Ancona, Italy, to French parents.
Painter.

He studied under Cogniet and Yvon and exhibited military subjects at the Paris Salon from 1864 to 1879.
Museums and Galleries:
Compiègne (Mus. Antoine Vivenel): *Portrait of M. Delorme* - Pontoise: *Military Operations* - Rochefort: *Marine Infantryman*.
Auction records:
Paris, 27 and 28 Dec 1927, *Cuirassier Passing through a Village*, FRF 130; *Haystacks*, FRF 375. Lucerne, 8 Nov 2000, *Soldiers in Encampment* (oil on canvas, 11 x 9 ins / 27 x 22 cm) CHF 9,000.

GARDAVSKA, Marie
Czech, 19th - 20th century.
Born 14 March 1871.
Painter. Landscapes.

Marie Gardavska worked above all in Prague and Munich.

GARDE, Ferdinand
French, 20th century.
Born in St-Étienne.
Painter.

Ferdinand Garde studied under Désiré Lucas and exhibited at the Salon des Artistes Français.

GARDEL, Jean-Baptiste
French, 19th century.
Born 5 May 1818, in Limoges; died 1874.
Painter. Portraits, landscapes.

He enrolled at the École des Beaux-Arts on 5 April 1843 and exhibited landscapes at the Paris Salon from 1836 to 1857. Gardel was awarded a medal at the Limoges Exhibition of 1858.
Museums and Galleries:
Limoges: *Cincinnatus; Portrait of Dr Chastaing; Portrait of General Lugnot.*

GARDEL, Louis
French, 19th century.
Sculptor.

He exhibited at the Paris Salon in 1837 and 1849, notably with a number of medallions.
Museums and Galleries:
Troyes: *Portrait of A. J. Hervey.*

GARDEL-LEISER, Emma
French, 20th century.
Born 11 October 1911, in Saverne (Bas-Rhin); died 4 August 1964, in Garches.
Painter.

Emma Gardel-Leiser studied at the École des Beaux-Arts in Paris. She exhibited at the Salon des Artistes Français.

GARDELL-ERICSON, Anna Maria
Maiden name: Gardell
Swedish, 19th - 20th century.
Born 10 October 1853, in Visby; died 1939.
Painter, watercolourist. Landscapes with figures, waterscapes, landscapes.

Anna Maria Gardell-Ericson was the wife of Johan Erik Ericson. She studied in Stockholm and Paris. She is known for her watercolours of Swedish landscapes and she also painted in Brittany.
Museums and Galleries:
Stockholm: *Skåne.*
Auction records:
Göteborg, 24 March 1976, *Seashore* (1895, watercolour, 12 1/4 x 17 1/4 ins / 31 x 44 cm) SEK 4,600. Stockholm, 13 April 1981, *Fishermen in a Boat* (watercolour, 13 1/2 x 19 1/4 ins / 34 x 49 cm) SEK 7,100. Stockholm, 20 April 1983, *Sailing Boats off the Coast* (watercolour, 13 x 19 1/4 ins / 33 x 49 cm) SEK 8,000. Stockholm, 4 Nov 1986, *Young Woman and her Daughter angling by a Lake* (1912, watercolour and gouache, 15 x 22 ins / 38 x 55 cm) SEK 43,500. Stockholm, 14 Nov 1990, *Girl on a Forest Path in Spring near Concarneau* (watercolour, 10 1/4 x 15 ins / 26 x 38 cm) SEK 27,000. Stockholm, 29 May 1991, *Coastal Village and Moored Boats by Moonlight* (watercolour,

5 1/2 x 20 ins / 14 x 51 cm) SEK 13,500. Stockholm, 13 April 1992, *Girl in a Yard* (1894, oil on canvas, 23 1/4 x 29 1/2 ins / 59 x 75 cm) SEK 11,000. Stockholm, 19 May 1992, *Girl on a Forest Path Walking past a Pond at Nightfall* (watercolour, 10 x 13 1/2 ins / 24.5 x 34.5 cm) SEK 12,500. Stockholm, 5 Sept 1992, *Summer Landscape* (watercolour, 9 1/2 x 12 3/4 ins / 24 x 32.5 cm) SEK 10,500. Stockholm, 10-12 May 1993, *Young Woman Contemplating an Inscription Engraved on a Tree Trunk* (1882, watercolour, 15 1/4 x 11 ins / 39 x 28 cm) SEK 20,000. Stockholm, 30 Nov 1993, *The Waterfall at Ronneby* (watercolour, 25 1/2 x 19 ins / 65 x 48 cm) SEK 33,000.

GARDELLA, Luigi
Italian, 19th century.
Active in Genoa (Liguria) c. 1800.
Painter.

GARDELLE, Charlotte
French, 20th century.
Born 31 January 1879, in Galati, Romania.
Painter, watercolourist. Portraits, landscapes.

Charlotte Gardelle studied at the Académie Julian in Paris. She exhibited at the Salon d'Automne from its foundation in 1903 and at the Salon des Tuileries. She also exhibited abroad, notably at the Wiesbaden museum. She worked in the south of France.

She was an incisive and sensitive artist and alongside her portraits (including one of the painter Hermine David) she painted views of St-Tropez and Vence.

GARDELLE, Daniel
Swiss, 18th century.
Born 2 October 1679, in Geneva; died 9 October 1753.
Painter.

Daniel Gardelle was born into a Genevan family that originally hailed from Lyons, Rhône (France). Two albums of his work are in existence, one of which contains miniatures, portraits of well-known individuals. In the style of Fuseli, he had a genuine talent as a miniaturist.

GARDELLE, Elie
Swiss, 18th century.
Born 1688, in Geneva; died 1748.
Enameller.

Elie Gardelle created a portrait on enamel of an aristocrat from Geneva.

GARDELLE, Jacques André
Swiss, 18th century.
Born 11 August 1725, in Geneva.
Miniaturist.

Jacques was the nephew of Elie Gardelle.

GARDELLE, Robert
Swiss, 18th century.
Born 6 April 1682, in Geneva; died 7 March 1766.
Painter, engraver. Portraits.

Robert Gardelle's biography was written by Füssli. He studied art in Germany and was the pupil of Largillicre. He worked in Geneva, Bern and Neuchâtel in the Swiss canton of Vaud.

R·G· R G

Museums and Galleries:
Geneva (MAH): *Portrait of J.A. Chanet; Male Portrait* - Geneva (Mus. Ariana): *Portrait of a Man.*

Auction records:
London, 21 Dec 1928, *Portrait of a Nobleman,* GBP 18. Bern, 21 Oct 1977, *Portrait of Albrecht von Haller* (oil on canvas, 32 x 25 3/4 ins / 81.5 x 65.5 cm) CHF 7,500. Lucerne, 19 Nov 2003, *Portrait of Maria Catharina Effinger von Wildegg-von Diessbach* (oil on canvas, 36 x 29 ins / 92 x 73 cm) CHF 3,000.

GARDELLE, Théodore
Swiss, 18th century.
Born 30 November 1722, in Geneva; died 4 April 1761, in London, executed.
Miniaturist.

Théodore, the son of Elie Gardelle, worked in Brussels, Paris and London. He was condemned to death for murder.

GARDEN, Francis
British, 18th century.
Born in London.
Engraver.

Francis Garden lived and worked mainly in Boston (USA).

GARDEN, Joseph
French, 19th - 20th century.
Born 26 December 1857, in Grenoble; died 14 October 1937, in Grenoble.
Painter, watercolourist, draughtsman. Landscapes.

Joseph Garden studied under Ravanat and Apvril. Alongside his activities as an artist he worked for a bank. Some of his drawings were published in the magazine *Actualité Dauphiné.* His work conveys the atmosphere and light of his native region of Grenoble.

Bibliography:
Wantellet, Maurice, *Deux siècles et plus de peinture dauphinoise,* M. Wantellet, Grenoble, 1987.

GARDEN, William Fraser
British, 19th - 20th century.
Born 1856, in Bedford; died 1921.
Painter, watercolourist. Landscapes.

William Garden exhibited at the Royal Academy and the New Water-Colour Society in London from 1882 to 1890.

Auction records:
New York, 19 May 1981, *Hunters in a Snowy Landscape* (1888, watercolour, 7 1/4 x 14 1/2 ins / 18.5 x 37 cm) GBP 1,700. London, 20 Oct 1981, *Buildings by the Ouse in Winter* (1913, watercolour, 14 3/4 x 11 ins / 37.5 x 27 cm) GBP 280. London, 15 Dec 1983, *The Ouse at St Ives* (1890, watercolour, 7 1/4 x 11 ins / 18.5 x 27 cm) GBP 700. London, 5 June 1984, *A Fen Village* (1886, watercolour heightened with white, 11 x 15 1/2 ins / 28 x 39.5 cm) GBP 2,600. London, 16 Oct 1986, *River Banks* (1890, watercolour heightened with gouache, 11 x 15 ins / 27 x 38 cm) GBP 3,600. London, 25 Jan 1989, *The Avon near Stratford in Warwickshire* (1886, watercolour, 7 3/4 x 11 ins / 19.5 x 28 cm) GBP 1,760. London, 31 Jan 1990, *Houses beside a Sound* (1904, watercolour, 11 x 7 ins / 27 x 18 cm) GBP 1,045. London, 25-26 April 1990, *By the River* (1902, watercolour, 11 x 15 1/4 ins / 28 x 39 cm) GBP 3,080. London, 29 Oct 1991, *In the Woods; The Forest at Dawn* (watercolour, a pair, 10 3/4 x 15 ins / 27.3 x 38.2 cm) GBP 11,000. London, 13 Nov 1992, *Recollection of Stevington in Bedfordshire* (1882, watercolour, 7 1/4 x 10 1/4 ins / 18.4 x 26 cm) GBP 990. London, 3 March 1993, *St Neot Bridge, St Ives* (1895, watercolour, 18 1/4 x 23 ins / 46.5 x 57.5 cm) GBP 8,280. London, 25 March 1994, *St John's Church, St Ives* (1903, pencil and watercolour, 7 3/4 x 11 ins / 19.7 x 28.2 cm) GBP 2,185. London, 10 March 1995, *The Village Ford* (1893, pencil and watercolour, 8 x 11 1/2 ins / 20.3 x 29.2 cm) GBP 2,415. New York, 8 Nov 1995, *By the River* (1888, watercolour, 11 x 15 ins / 27 x 38 cm) USD 2,990. London, 6 Nov 1996, *Twilight Scene in Finland; Dawn in Finland* (1894, watercolour, a pair, 6 x 10 1/2 ins / 15 x 26.5 cm and 5 1/2 x 11 ins/14 x 28 cm) GBP 1,207.

GARDENIER, Jean Jacques
Dutch, 20th century.
Born 7 September 1930, in Delft.
Painter, engraver. Landscapes.

Jean Jacques Gardenier exhibited in Paris at the Salon d'Automne and Salon Grands et Jeunes d'Aujourd'hui. Inspired by urban scenes and landscapes, especially Les Halles in Paris before they were demolished, he has created a unique world of allusions, sometimes close to the abstract. He is more intent on showing an interior reality than on describing the world as it appears, so he leaves aside the classical rules of perspective and naturalist analysis. He decomposes and metamorphoses his subjects in order to redefine the space within the painting.

GARDENS OF LOVE, Master of the.
See **MASTERS**

GARDENTY, Georges A.
French, 19th century.
Active in Paris.
Painter.

He was a member of the Société des Artistes Français from 1887 and took part in its exhibitions.

GARDERA, Francis
19th century.
Painter. Architectural views, landscapes.

AUCTION RECORDS:
PARIS, 19 April 1943, *The Monastery; The Bridge over the Torrent* (two canvases, one dated 1847) FRF 800.

GARDET
French, 19th century.
Painter. Landscapes.

He may be the artist by the same name whose *Infant Jesus Sleeping* is housed in the museum at Châlons-sur-Marne.

MUSEUMS AND GALLERIES:
MONTAUBAN: *Ruined Castle on the Catalan Coast.*

GARDET, Georges
French, 19th - 20th century.
Born 11 October 1863, in Paris; died 16 February 1939, in Paris.
Sculptor. Animals.

Georges Gardet studied under Aimé Millet and Frémiet. A powerful creator of animal sculptures, he showed himself to be a master artist from the outset. The handsome group *Panther and Lion* in the Parc Montsouris in Paris, which was shown at the Salon des Artistes Français in Paris in 1887, revealed him to be a worthy successor to Barye and Mêne. He is also known for two large pieces, *Tiger* and *Bison*, which decorate the entrance of the Musée de Laval. The Exposition Universelle of 1900 provided him with an opportunity to demonstrate his skill as a monumental sculptor.

He received various awards: a commendation in 1886; a bronze medal in 1887; a silver medal in 1889; a medal at the Exposition Universelle in Paris in 1889; a travel bursary in 1889; he was made a Chevalier of the Légion d'Honneur in 1896; received a medal of honour in 1898; was made an Officier of the Légion d'Honneur in 1900; received the Grand Prix of the Exposition Universelle in Paris in 1900 for a group of lions and a group of tigers executed for the Château de Vaux-le-Vicomte. He exhibited in Paris at the Salon des Artistes Français, of which he became a member. In 1918 he was made a member of the Académie des Beaux-Arts.

MUSEUMS AND GALLERIES:
BUCHAREST (Muz. National de Arta al României): *Two Panthers* - HAMBURG: *The Precursor* - LIMOGES: *Lion and Lioness; The Dogs of Chantilly* - PARIS (MAM): *Panthers; Budgerigars* - PARIS (Mus. d'Orsay): *Panthers Fighting* - PARIS (Mus. du Petit Palais): *Great Dane* - ROANNE: *Mézenc after the Fire.*

AUCTION RECORDS:
ENGHIEN-LES-BAINS, 2 March 1980, *Panther Fight* (brown-patinated bronze, h. 18 ins / 46 cm) FRF 8,000. NEW YORK, 16 Oct 1984, *Great Danes* (bronze, l. 58 ins / 147.5 cm) USD 20,000. ENGHIEN-LES-BAINS, 6 Oct 1985, *Large Stag* (bronze, h. 43 1/4 ins / 110 cm) FRF 60,500. NEW YORK, 9 June 1988, *Great Dane Reclining* (bronze, h. 18 1/2 ins / 47 cm) USD 2,090. NEW YORK, 23 Feb 1989, *Setter* (bronze, h. 11 1/2 ins / 29.2 cm) USD 2,860. PARIS, 20 March 1991, *Tiger and Dog from Fô* (bronze, h. 12 3/4 ins / 32.5 cm, l. 25 1/4 ins/64 cm, w. 7 3/4 ins/20 cm) FRF 14,000. NEW YORK, 5 June 1992, *Panther* (green-patinated bronze, h. 13 ins / 33 cm, l. 17 1/2 ins/44.5 cm) USD 1,925. PARIS, 16 March 1994, *Tiger and Dog from Fô* (bronze, h. 11 ins / 28 cm) FRF 6,000. LOKEREN, 28 May 1994, *Lion and Lioness* (bronze, h. 14 1/4 ins / 36 cm, w. 19 3/4 ins/50 cm) BEF 60,000. LOKEREN, 11 March 1995, *Irish Wolfhound* (bronze, h. 11 ins / 28 cm, w. 22 3/4 ins/58 cm) BEF 44,000. LEICESTER, 1 July 1999, *Pointer Seeking Scent* (bronze, h. 19 ins / 48 cm) GBP 2,000. PARIS, 3 Dec 1999, *Group of Budgerigars* (green stone, h. 9 ins / 24 cm) FRF 19,000. LONDON, 5 July 2000, *Sleeping Lion* (polychrome marble, 11 x 27 ins / 28 x 68 cm) GBP 7,000. LONDON, 13 Dec 2000, *Two Panthers Fighting* (cream yellow marble, h. 29 ins / 49 cm) GBP 16,000. NEW YORK, 6 June 2001, *Two Lions* (dark brown patinated bronze, w. 28 ins / 71 cm) USD 8,500. LONDON, 2 Nov 2001, *Recumbent Great Dane* (dark brown patinated bronze, 10 x 17 ins / 26 x 44 cm) GBP 2,200. LONDON, 16 April 2002, *Tiger Playing with a Tortoise* (brown-green patinated bronze, 7 x 17 ins / 19 x 42 cm) GBP 1,800. LONDON, 16 April 2002, *Lion and Lioness Grooming* (red-brown patinated bronze, 15 x 19 ins / 37 x 49 cm) GBP 2,800. LONDON, 9 April 2003, *Standing Lamb* (brown patinated bronze, 19 x 13 ins / 47 x 33 cm) GBP 2,000. LONDON, 14 Oct 2003, *Pointer* (mid-brown patinated bronze, 11 x 22 ins / 28 x 55 cm) GBP 2,800. NEUILLY, 11 June 2004, *Tigress and her Young* (marble, onyx, bronze and molten glass, h. 20 ins / 50 cm) EUR 18,000. LONDON, 9 July 2004, *Standing Antelope* (patinated bronze, 36 x 28 ins / 91 x 70 cm) GBP 7,500.

GARDET, Joseph
French, 19th - 20th century.
Born c. 1830; died April 1914, in Paris.
Sculptor.

Joseph Gardet was the father of Antoine and Georges Gardet.

GARDET, Joseph Antoine
French, 19th century.
Born 22 February 1861, in Paris; died 24 February 1891, in Paris.
Sculptor.

He was the son of Joseph Gardet and brother of Georges Gardet.

MUSEUMS AND GALLERIES:
PARIS (ENSBA): *Mother Holding the Body of a Spartan Soldier Killed in Combat* - PARIS (Mus. d'Orsay): *Portrait Bust of Etienne Dollfus* - ROANNE (MBA).

GARDETH, Johann Kaspar
German, 18th century.
Born in Buchloe (Bavaria); died 1795.
Painter, sculptor.

Gardeth worked for the church at Unterostendorf.

GARDETTE, de La. See **LAGARDETTE de**

GARDETTE, Louis
French, 19th century.
Born in Paris.
Painter. Genre scenes.

He studied under Pils and Lehmann and exhibited at the Salon des Artistes Français, where he obtained an honourable mention in 1886 and a bronze medal and travel scholarship in 1899. Gardette also received an honourable mention at the Exposition Universelle of 1889.

MUSEUMS AND GALLERIES:
GRAY: *Death of General Marguerite; Imperial Dragoon.*

AUCTION RECORDS:
PARIS, 10 Nov 1944, *Dragoon*, FRF 250. VERSAILLES, 15 Nov 1987, *Nubian Woman* (1888, oil on canvas, 37 1/2 x 37 1/2in/95 x 95cm) FRF 30,000.

GARDEUR, Jean Nicolas
French, 18th century.
Active in Paris in 1778.
Painter (?), sculptor (?).

GARDEY, Germaine
French, 20th century.
Born 21 August 1904, in St-Androny (Gironde); died 2 May 1995, in Paris.
Painter. Figures, landscapes, seascapes, waterscapes, flowers.

From 1922 to 1923, Germaine Gardey studied at the École des Beaux-Arts in Bordeaux and from 1924 to 1927 under Lucien Simon at the École des Beaux-Arts in Paris. From 1938 to 1951 she took part in various Paris Salons, including the Salon d'Automne, the Salon de l'École Française and the Salon de la Marine. From 1922 she also exhibited at many regional group exhibitions where she sold various works and received a number of awards. From 1932 to 1983 she showed her paintings in solo exhibitions in Paris and the French provinces.

Her approach varied according to the period and subject, from Post-Impressionism to a certain degree of Expressionism in her use of pigment and gesture. The 1950s and 1960s were dominated by seascapes, the 1960s to 1980s by allusive landscapes and paintings of marshes; she also painted people at work and engaged in physical labour.

GARDI, Domenico
Italian, 17th century.
Active in Modena in 1694.
Draughtsman.

GARDIE (Mrs)
British, 19th century.
Miniaturist.

Gardie made her Royal Academy début in 1828. She moved to Paris and is reputed to have enjoyed considerable success there. She painted miniatures of Madame Malibran, of her second violinist husband, and of Bériot. She exhibited porcelain miniatures at the Paris Salon from 1831 to 1837.

GARDIE, A. N.
British, 19th century.
Active in London.
Painter.

GARDIE, S.L.
British, 19th century.
Active in London.
Sculptor.

S.L. Gardie exhibited at London's Royal Academy from 1850 to 1854.

GARDIES, Michel
French, 18th century.
Active in Paris.
Sculptor (wood).

Michel Gardies also worked in Sweden.

GARDIMIE, Simon
19th century.
Painter. Flowers.

Mentioned by Florence Levy.

AUCTION RECORDS:
NEW YORK, 16 and 17 Feb 1911, *Flowers,* USD 80.

GARDIN
French, 18th century.
Active in Rouen in 1757.
Painter, designer of ornamental architectural features.

GARDINER, Anna
British, 20th century.
Born 1866, in London; died 1959.
Painter.

Anna Gardiner exhibited in Paris at the Salon of the Société Nationale des Beaux-Arts from 1923 and at the Salon des Artistes Indépendants.

GARDINER, Clive
American, 20th century.
Born 1891; died May 1960.
Painter, engraver.

Clive Gardiner was greatly influenced by Fauvism and a certain method of structuring the canvas in the 1920s. He then returned to figuration.

GARDINER, Eliza (Miss)
British, 18th century.
Active in England.
Painter. Figures.

Eliza Gardiner was a Society of Artists exhibitor from 1762 to 1770.

AUCTION RECORDS:
LONDON, 3 Dec 1926, *Woman,* GBP 81. LONDON, 31 July-1 Aug 1930, *Self-portrait,* GBP 33.

GARDINER, Eliza
American, 19th - 20th century.
Born 1871, in Providence; died 1955.
Painter, engraver.

Eliza Gardiner's coloured woodcuts usually represent compositions of children with great and touching simplicity.

BIBLIOGRAPHY:
Falk, P.H. (ed.), *Eliza Draper Gardiner: Master of the Color Woodblock,* Sound View Press, Madison (CT), 1987.

MUSEUMS AND GALLERIES:
CHICAGO (Terra Foundation for American Art Collection): *Boy and Goose* (c. 1920, coloured woodcut); *On his Back* (1920, colour linocut) - KANSAS CITY (Nelson-Atkins MA).

GARDINER, Gerald
British, 20th century.
Born 17 January 1902; died 1959.
Painter.

Gerald Gardiner studied at the Royal College of Art in London. He exhibited in London at the Royal Academy and at various other English exhibitions.

GARDINER, William Nelson
Irish, 18th - 19th century.
Born 11 June 1766, in Dublin; died 8 May 1814, in London, committed suicide.
Engraver.

William Nelson Gardiner was educated at Dublin Academy, then moved to London where he was hired as an assistant to Bartolozzi, helping him prepare engravings for Harding's *Shakespeare,* De Grammont's *Mémoires* and Lady Diana Beauclercle's illustrations for Dryden's *Fables.* Gardiner also copied portraits. He was an exhibitor at the Royal Academy in London from 1781 to 1793. Towards the end of his life he worked as a librarian.

MUSEUMS AND GALLERIES:
LONDON (National Portrait Gal.): *Sarah Wilson as Harriet in Holcroft's 'Seduction'* (published in 1787, stipple engraving, after Sylvester Harding); *Philip Yorke, 1st Earl of Hardwicke* (c. 1800, watercolour, after William Hoare) - NOTTINGHAM: two drawings.

GARDINIER, Frédéric
French, 20th - 21st century.
Born 4 August 1955, in Paris.
Painter.

AUCTION RECORDS:
PARIS, 13 April 1988, *Green Series: The Charioteer of Delphi* (acrylic, 79 1/2 x 76 3/4 ins / 202 x 195 cm) FRF 19,000. PARIS, 18 July 1990, *Composition* (acrylic/canvas, 52 x 53 1/4 ins / 132 x 135 cm) FRF 4,000.

GARDNER, Charles Reed
American, 20th century.
Born 17 August 1901; died 1974.
Painter, illustrator.

Charles Gardner was a member of the American Artists Professional League.

GARDNER, Daniel
British, 18th - 19th century.
Born 1750, in Kendal; died 8 July 1805, in London.
Painter (gouache), pastellist, draughtsman. Portraits.
Daniel Gardener travelled to London at an early age and enrolled at the Royal Academy. He came to the attention of Joshua Reynolds, who offered him help and encouragement. He soon started producing accomplished small portraits in oils, pastels and chalks and quickly made a reputation for himself. He is on record as having taken part in only one formal exhibition, namely at the Royal Academy in 1771. Gardner earned himself a small fortune before distancing himself from the arts and living the life of a recluse. His particular talent lay in portraying typically 'English' beauties. Lord Carlington amassed an impressive collection of Gardner's work in the form of 63 drawings which subsequently sold at auction at Christie's on 11 July 1911.

AUCTION RECORDS:
LONDON, 29 May 1908, *Portrait of Mrs Minchin, née Mary Willett Miller; Portrait of Captain Willett Miller* (two pastels) GBP 157. LONDON, 16 July 1909, *Portrait of Elizabeth Hall* (pastel) GBP 136. LONDON, 28 Jan 1911, *Portrait of Mrs Adelaide Preston* (pastel) GBP 189. LONDON, 11 Feb 1911, *Major Andrew* (pastel) GBP 52. LONDON, 19 May 1911, *Mrs Robinson in the Role of Perdita* (pastel) GBP 1,155. LONDON, 6-8 Dec 1920, *Portrait of a Young Woman* (pastel) FRF 9,800. LONDON, 1 Dec 1922, *Charles Theobald,* GBP 37. LONDON, 23 Feb 1923, *Women in Mauve* (pastel) GBP 4. LONDON, 29 June 1923, *Woman in White* (pastel) GBP 44; *Miss Burgoyne* (pastel) GBP 33. LONDON, 21 Dec 1923, *Miss Blunt,* GBP 34; *Woman in Black,* GBP 21. LONDON, 18 July 1924, *Naval Officer; Woman* (two gouaches) GBP 89. LONDON, 13 Feb 1925, *Young Girl in White* (pastel) GBP 73. LONDON, 1 May 1925, *Theodosia, Wife of J.G. Shaw* (gouache) GBP 189. LONDON, 3 Dec 1925, *Woman (Thought to be Mrs Forster)* (pastel) GBP 105. LONDON, 12 Feb 1926, *Music; Painting* (two) GBP 378. LONDON, 1 July 1927, *Drake Family* (gouache) GBP 110; *Mrs Charlotte Gwatkin* (pastel) GBP 126. LONDON, 28 Nov 1927, *Mrs Siddons,* GBP 220. LONDON, 27 Jan 1928, *Woman as Saint Cecilia* (pastel) GBP 60. LONDON, 8 Feb 1929, *Head of Boy,* GBP 73. LONDON, 5 April 1929, *Joe Pennington,* GBP 94. LONDON, 19 Feb 1930, *Lady Aylesford* (pastel) GBP 10; *Mrs Pournall* (pastel) GBP 10. LONDON, 21 Feb 1930, *William Rowley,* GBP 105. LONDON, 23 May 1930, *Self-portrait with Two Members of the Pennington Family,* GBP 99. NEW YORK, 4 and 5 Feb 1931, *Madame Labille-Guiard,* USD 150. NEW YORK, 22 June 1931, *Lady Mexborough* (gouache) GBP 178; *John Saville* (gouache) GBP 178. NEW YORK, 26 June 1931, *Female Portrait* (drawing) GBP 16. PARIS, 8 Feb 1934, *Portrait of a Dignitary,* FRF 180. LONDON, 27 April 1934, *Miss Draper,* GBP 22. NEW YORK, 17 and 18 May 1934, *Portrait of a Boy,* USD 70. LONDON, 14 Dec 1934, *Woman Member of the Cholmondeley Family,* GBP 52. LONDON, 4 Dec 1936, *Two Young Girls,* GBP 84. LONDON, 25 Feb 1938, *Commander Andrew* (drawing) GBP 16. LONDON, 27 May 1938, *Reverend W. Heathcote, Commander Vincent H. Gilbert and W. Heathcote,* GBP 325. PARIS, 15 June 1938, *Portrait (Thought to be that of Mrs Clarke)* (gouache) FRF 7,100. PARIS, 9 Dec 1938, *Margaret Stanley; John Thomas Stanley* (two drawings) GBP 162. PARIS, 28 July 1939, *Anthony, 3rd Earl Shaftesbury* (drawing) GBP 27. PARIS, 25 April 1940, *Miss Marston* (drawing) GBP 42. PARIS, 28 June 1940, *Gentleman in Blue,* GBP 6. PARIS, 25 June 1941, *Mrs Hippisley,* GBP 9. PARIS, 25 Sept 1941, *Admiral Sheriff* (pastel) GBP 25. PARIS, 29 July 1942, *Mrs S. Eliot and Daughters* (pastel) GBP 17. PARIS, 19 July 1944, *Elisabeth Templeton* (pastel) GBP 29. PARIS, 15 Nov 1944, *Bridget Pennington,* GBP 160; *Three Children,* GBP 62; *Child with Faun,* GBP 32; *Self-portrait with a Member of the Pennington Family,* GBP 52. PARIS, 18 Jan 1946, *Woman* (gouache) GBP 25. PARIS, 1 Feb 1946, *Young Man,* GBP 52. NEW YORK, 28 March 1946, *Wife of W. Milburn,* USD 300. LONDON, 13 Dec 1946, *Viscount Castlereagh* (gouache) GBP 42. PARIS, 13 June 1952, *Interrupted Reading,* FRF 250,000. NEW YORK, 7 April 1961, *Margaret, Lady Walsh* (gouache) USD 500. NEW YORK, 16 March 1967, *Massacre at Mount Meadows,* USD 2,500. LONDON, 12 July 1967, *Marquis of Shaftesbury and his Sister* (pastel) GBP 800. LONDON, 19 March 1968, *Portrait of Sir John Thomas* (pastel and gouache) Gns 3,800. LONDON, 19 March 1968, *Portrait of Frances, Daughter of Sir Thomas Rumod* (1783, pastel and gouache, 38 1/4 x 27 1/2 ins / 97 x 70 cm) Gns 120. LONDON, 2 March 1976, *Portrait of a Music Lover* (pastel, diam. 19 3/4 x 15 1/2 ins / 50 x 39.5 cm) GBP 350. LONDON, 14 June 1977, *Portrait of Sir John Taylor* (pastel, watercolour and gouache, 34 x 23 1/2 ins / 86.5 x 59.5 cm) GBP 3,500. LONDON, 17 Nov 1981, *Portrait of Frances, Daughter of Sir Thomas Rumod* (1783, pastel and gouache, 38 1/4 x 27 1/2 ins / 97 x 70 cm) GBP 3,800. LONDON, 15 June 1982, *Portrait of Miss Reay and her Mother* (pastel, 18 x 23 ins / 45.7 x 58.5 cm) GBP 500. LONDON, 20 Nov 1984, *Portrait of Margaret, Lady Walsh* (1775, pastel, 18 x 14 1/2 ins / 45.7 x 37 cm) GBP 4,800. LONDON, 13 March 1985, *Portraits of Lewis Thomas, Baron Sondes and his Wife Mary* (two oils on canvas, oval, 24 x 22 ins / 61 x 56 cm) GBP 5,500. LONDON, 19 Nov 1987, *Portraits of a Lady of Quality Seated at a Table* (1779, gouache/pencil outlines, pair, oval; each 33 x 24 3/4 ins / 84 x 63 cm) GBP 8,500. LONDON, 5 June 1997, *Portrait of Lewis, Baron Sondes; Portrait of Mary, Wife of Baron Sondes* (oil on canvas, pair, oval; 25 x 21 ins / 63.5 x 53.4 cm) GBP 7,475. LONDON, 15 July 1999, *Portrait of Margaret, Lady Stanley* (mixed media, 24 x 20 ins / 62 x 51 cm) GBP 3,000. LONDON, 24 Nov 1999, *Portrait of Angelica Kauffman, Wearing Dark Blue Headdress Holding a Pencil* (oil on canvas, 25 x 19 ins / 63 x 48 cm) GBP 25,000. LONDON, 28 Nov 2000, *Portrait of Lady Watkin Williams-Wynn, in a White Dress* (pencil and pastel heightened with gouache, 11 x 9 ins / 27 x 22 cm) GBP 9,000. LONDON, 28 Nov 2000, *Portrait of Charles, 1st Marquis of Cornwall, in Uniform, Holding a Cane* (pencil and gouache, 30 x 24 ins / 75 x 62 cm) GBP 17,000. DUBLIN, 28 May 2001, *Portrait of Boy, with Long Hair, Wearing Stock and in Buttoned Brown Coat* (pastel, 9 x 8 ins / 24 x 20 cm) IEP 4,500. LONDON, 13 June 2001, *Group Portrait of Sir John Taylor and his Wife Elizabeth, Brother Simon and Children* (pencil, pastel and gouache, 41 x 32 ins / 104 x 81 cm) GBP 55,000. LONDON, 21 March 2002, *Portrait of a Lady and Child, Seated in a Landscape* (pastel, oval, 23 x 18 ins / 58 x 45 cm) GBP 4,200. LONDON, 6 June 2002, *Portrait of Charles, 1st Marquis Cornwallis* (1782, pencil, pastel and gouache, oval, 35 x 26 ins / 90 x 66 cm) GBP 9,000. LONDON, 10 June 2003, *Portrait of a Gentleman in a Brown Coat, Holding a Hat, in a Wooded Landscape* (oil on canvas, 21 x 18 ins / 53 x 46 cm) GBP 4,500. LONDON, 16 Oct 2003, *Portrait of Philadelphia de Lancy* (gouache, 39 x 28 ins / 98 x 70 cm) GBP 1,000. LONDON, 26 March 2004, *Portrait of Elizabeth Farren, Later Countess of Derby, Seated at an Organ* (gouache, 33 x 22 ins / 84 x 55 cm) GBP 3,800. LONDON, 26 May 2004, *Portrait of Admiral Sir William Sidney Smith KCB and Vice Admiral Thomas Pringle* (watercolour and gouache, a pair, oval, 9 x 9 ins / 24 x 22 cm) GBP 2,200.

GARDNER, Derek George Montague
British, 20th century.
Born 1914.
Painter. Historical subjects, naval battles, boats.

AUCTION RECORDS:
LONDON, 11 June 1976, *Naval Action between French and English Men-o-War* (1961, oil on canvas, 18 x 24 ins / 46 x 61 cm) GBP 680. LONDON, 18 Jan 1984, *The Three-Master 'Spindthrift'* (oil on canvas, 28 x 42 1/4 ins / 71 x 107 cm) GBP 1,500. BRUSSELS, 15 Sept 1986, *Seascape* (oil on canvas, 32 1/4 x 48 ins / 82 x 122 cm) BEF 440,000. LONDON, 22 Sept 1988, *High Tide at Greenwich* (oil on canvas, 23 1/2 x 35 1/2 ins / 59.7 x 90.2 cm)

GBP 1,980. LONDON, 20 Jan 1993, *The Tea Clipper 'Spindthrift'* (oil on canvas, 28 x 42 ins / 71 x 106.5 cm) GBP 6,900. LONDON, 16 July 1993, *Driving Hard, Tea Clipper 'Sir Lancelot'* (oil on canvas, 13 3/4 x 18 ins / 35 x 46 cm) GBP 1,265. NEW YORK, 3 June 1994, *Nelson's Ships off Toulon, 30 July 1803* (oil on canvas, 20 x 36 ins / 50.8 x 91.4 cm) USD 10,925. LONDON, 13 May 1999, *Northern Waters: Loch Venachar. Clearing the Land: Waimate* (oil on canvas, a pair, 14 x 18 ins / 35 x 46 cm) GBP 4,000. CHICHESTER, 23 April 2002, *Racing Home from China 1866* (oil on canvas, 30 x 36 ins / 76 x 91 cm) GBP 6,600. JERSEY, 19 June 2002, *I Will Escort You* (1987, oil on canvas, 29 x 39 ins / 74 x 100 cm) GBP 4,000. LONDON, 17 Feb 2004, *Emigrant Ship, Morayshire* (oil on board, 10 x 16 ins / 25 x 41 cm) GBP 3,200. LONDON, 14 Sept 2004, *Clan Mackenzie Running Under Full Sail* (oil on canvas, 24 x 36 ins / 61 x 91 cm) GBP 7,000.

GARDNER, E. M. (Mrs)
American, 20th century.
Born in Colchester (Connecticut); died 1916, in Pitman, near New York.
Painter.

E.M. Gardner also lived in Philadelphia.

GARDNER, Edwin C.
British, 19th century.
Active in London.
Painter. Genre scenes.

Edwin C. Gardner exhibited in London between 1867 and 1888, notably at the Royal Academy.

GARDNER, Elisabeth Jeanne.
See **BOUGUEREAU W.-A., Mrs**

GARDNER, Gertrude
American, 20th century.
Born in Iowa.
Painter.

Gertrude Gardner was a member of the American Federation of Arts.

GARDNER, J. L.
British, 19th century.
Active in London.
Painter. Genre scenes.

J. L. Gardner exhibited in London from 1880 to 1888 at the Royal Academy and the Suffolk Street Gallery.

GARDNER, Lisa
American, 20th - 21st century.
Born 1956, in New York.
Painter (mixed media), collage artist.

Lisa Gardner studied art at the University of British Columbia, the University of Guelph and the Ottawa School of Art, from 1994-1996. In 1987, she won a two-year bursary to study in Paris, at the Cité Internationale des Arts, where she also exhibited. Her abstract paintings are characterised by their delicate drawing and tonalities.

Her work has featured in a number of group exhibitions in the USA.

AUCTION RECORDS:
PARIS, 14 Oct 1991, *Untitled* (1991, acrylic and collage/canvas, 31 1/2 x 31 1/2 ins / 80 x 80 cm) FRF 4,000.

GARDNER, Mabel
American, 20th century.
Born 2 March 1892, in Providence.
Active from 1922 in France.
Sculptor.

Mabel Gardner exhibited her work in the principal French salons.

GARDNER, Thomas
British, 18th century.
Engraver.

Thomas Gardner engraved a series of plates for James Harris' *Collected Paraphrastic Prayers* (1735).

GARDNER, William Biscombe
British, 19th - 20th century.
Born c. 1847; died 1919.
Painter, watercolourist, engraver, draughtsman. Genre scenes, landscapes.

William Gardner lived and worked in London and became a highly regarded exhibitor at the Royal Academy from 1874. He exhibited at the Salon des Artistes Français in Paris and received a silver medal in 1900 at the Exposition Universelle. He is also known for his etchings.

AUCTION RECORDS:
LONDON, 25 Jan 1924, *At the Blacksmith's*, GBP 2. LONDON, 24 May 1984, *Children Feeding Cats outside a Cottage* (watercolour heightened with white, 7 x 10 ins / 17.5 x 25.5 cm) GBP 800. LONDON, 14 June 1991, *Sheep by a Stile in a Wooded Landscape* (1868, pencil and watercolour heightened with white, 6 x 9 1/4 ins / 15.5 x 23.8 cm) GBP 715. LONDON, 3 June 1992, *Ferreting* (oil on canvas, 34 x 44 ins / 86.5 x 112 cm) GBP 880. LONDON, 6 Nov 1996, *Sunset on the Creek* (watercolour, 7 3/4 x 14 ins / 19.5 x 35.5 cm) GBP 690.

GARDNER ANNUNCIATION, Master of the.
See **MASTERS**

GARDNER-SOPER, James Hamlin
American, 20th century.
Born 17 July 1877, in Flint (Michigan); died 1939.
Painter, illustrator.

James Gardner-Soper lived and was active in New York. He was awarded a gold medal at the Exposition Universelle in Paris in 1900 and a bronze medal in St Louis in 1904.

AUCTION RECORDS:
NEW YORK, 3 Dec 1996, *Gala Evening* (oil on canvas, 28 1/2 x 19 1/2 ins / 72.5 x 49.5 cm) USD 4,370.

GARDNOR, John (Revd.)
British, 18th century.
Born 1729; died 6 January 1808, in Battersea.
Painter. Landscapes.

John Gardnor was a clergyman honoured by the Society of Arts in 1767, whose work was exhibited at the Royal Academy in London between 1782 and 1786. He illustrated Williams' *History of Monmouthshire* and, in 1788, published a collection entitled *Rhine Views*.

GARDNOR, Richard
British, 18th century.
Painter.

Richard Gardnor exhibited from 1786 to 1793 at the Free Society and the Royal Academy in London.

GARDOM, Barbara
British, 19th century.
Born in Longford.
Active in Paris.
Miniaturist.

Barbara Gardom was a pupil of Adolphe William Bouguereau.

GARDON, Félix J.
French, 19th - 20th century.
Born in Choisy-le-Roi.
Active in Écouen.
Painter. Landscapes.

Félix Gardon studied under Bellet and Lequien. He became a member of the Société des Artistes Français in 1892 and exhibited at the Society's Salons.

AUCTION RECORDS:
PARIS, 20 Feb 1931, *Spray of Flowers* (watercolour) FRF 75.

GARDON, Gaspard
French, 17th - 18th century.

Painter.

Gaspard Gardon worked in Lyons, where he was master craftsman three times from 1701-1715.

GARDON, Marius Jean

French, 20th century.

Born 27 June 1914, in Lyons; died 14 July 1990, in Cannes.

Painter. Genre scenes, landscapes, urban landscapes, still-lifes, flowers.

Marius Gardon was the son of a family from Marseilles and lived in the city until the age of eight, when he moved to Cannes. He was a self-taught painter but was not able to devote himself entirely to art until 1952. Some of his work was purchased by the Ville de Paris and the French State.

He started out by applying pigment with a knife and then went through a period which he described as Tachist-Expressionist. These works depict a feeling of virtual reality which draws the viewer into an imaginary world. He went on to paint urban Parisian landscapes in a more classical style using dull greys. In the early 1960s he extended his palette and began, unexpectedly, to paint still-lifes with accurately coloured fruit and adopting a freer form of brushwork. He also produced numerous monotypes.

He took part in group exhibitions, including: in 1956 the Salon de l'Art Libre; in 1963, the Salon des Terres Latines; in 1968 and 1971, the Salon des Indépendants; and in 1968, 1971 and 1974, the Salon des Surindépendants.

He also showed his work in solo exhibitions: first in 1954 at the Galerie Martin-Cruson in Paris; in 1954 at the Galerie Henri Tronche in Paris; in 1959 at the Galerie Bernheim Jeune in Paris; in 1963 at the Galerie Espace, Paris; in 1964 and 1967 at the Galerie 7 Mlle Henry, Paris; in 1977 and 1980 at the Galerie Berri-St-Honoré, Paris; in 1982 at the Galerie des Peintres Européennes, Paris; and in 1987, monotypes at the Galerie H. Bénézit, Paris.

BIBLIOGRAPHY:

Parrot, Jacques/Imbourg, Pierre (preface), *Gardon*, Éd. Mazarine, Paris, 1961.

MUSEUMS AND GALLERIES:

CANNES (Town Hall) - PARIS (Mairie) - PARIS (MAMVP).

AUCTION RECORDS:

PARIS, 25 May 1956, *Harlequin and Dancer,* FRF 28,000; *Snow* (gouache) FRF 18,000.

GARDONA, Battista

Italian, 16th century.

Sculptor.

Battista Gardona worked with Francesco Casella on the cathedral of S Maria delle Consolazioni at Fodi.

GARDOS, Aladar

Hungarian, 20th century.

Born 12 April 1878, in Budapest.

Sculptor.

After lengthy studies in Munich and Paris, Aladar Gardov finally settled in Budapest.

GARDOT, Jules

French, 19th century.

Born in Toulouse.

Painter.

He studied at the École des Beaux-Arts in Toulouse and in Paris. Between 1861 and 1880 he exhibited portraits and still-lifes at the Paris Salon.

GARDOT, René

French, 20th century.

Born 1908, in the Charente-Maritime.

Painter, watercolourist. Figures, landscapes, still-lifes.

René Gardot did not become a full-time artist until 1972. He exhibited in Paris at the Salon des Artistes Français, of which he was a member. He received numerous prizes an awards for his work.

Gardot painted mainly landscapes of Le Marais Poitevi and the Ile d'Oléron and Ile de Ré.

AUCTION RECORDS:

PARIS, 21 Sept 1988, *Les Tourettes, Ile de Ré* (1972, oil on pane 15 x 22 ins / 38 x 55 cm) FRF 2,500; *At Tuna Boat Time* (1972, oi on panel, 25 1/2 x 32 ins / 65 x 81 cm) FRF 4,500; *Locks at La Sotterie* (1968, oil on panel, 15 x 18 ins / 38 x 46 cm) FRF 3,400.

GARDY, Eugène Benoist

French, 19th century.

Born 23 April 1856, in Paris.

Painter. Stage sets.

He was a pupil of Lequien and Robecchi, and worked extensively in America.

GARDY, Gauderic

French, 19th century.

Active in Bagnères-de-Bigorre (Hautes-Pyrénées).

Sculptor.

He was a member of the Société des Artistes Français from 1899 and exhibited at its Salons.

GARDY, Michel

French, 18th century.

Active in Paris in 1738.

Painter, sculptor.

GARDY-ARTIGAS, Joan

French, 20th century.

Born 1938, in Boulogne-Billancourt.

Also active in Spain.

Sculptor, draughtsman, illustrator.

Until the age of 20, Joan Gardy-Artigas lived in Spain. After studying at the École du Louvre in Paris he set up a ceramics studio in the city and worked there with Georges Braque and Marc Chagall. He lives and works in Paris and Gallifa in Spain.

In 1960 he produced his first sculptures and met Alberto Giacometti. In 1962 he executed some large sculptures in epoxy resin. In 1965 he began producing lithographs and in 1970 he illustrated *Les Bœufs Meurent Aussi* for Éditions Maeght. In 1970-1972 he created a fountain for Vitry-sur-Seine and in 1976 a sculpture for the Barcelona-Paris motorway. Taking a synedochical approach, he creates shapes that the viewer has to reconstruct in the same way as a palaeontologist. However, his work finds its fullest expression in its fragmentation which allows it to be read as the story of a gestation or a cataclysm that are far more meaningful than any reconstruction.

He took part in numerous group exhibitions from 1976 onwards and regularly in Paris at the Salon de Mai and the Salon de la Jeune Peinture. He has shown his work in solo exhibitions in Spain and France, notably at the Galerie Maeght in Paris and also in Japan.

BIBLIOGRAPHY:

L'Univers d'Aimé et Marguerite Maeght, Fondation Maeght, St-Paul-de-Vence, 1992.

AUCTION RECORDS:

PARIS, 7 Oct 1995, *Untitled* (graphite/paper, 58 1/4 x 70 3/4 ins / 148 x 180 cm) FRF 7,500.

GARDYN DU. See **DUJARDIN**

GARE, Domenico, called Franzosino

Italian, 16th century.

Active in Carrara.

Sculptor.

Gare was originally from Lorraine.

GARE, G.
British, 18th - 19th century.
Active in London.
Miniaturist.

G. Gare exhibited at the Royal Academy in London from 1802 to 1818.

GAREIS, Anton, the Elder
German, 19th century.
Born 29 March 1793, in Klosterfreiheit; died 23 July 1863, in Prague.
Painter, lithographer, engraver.

Anton Gareis studied in Dresden, Berlin and Breslau (now Wroclaw, Poland). He produced mainly copies of works by the masters, genre scenes and caricatures.

GAREIS, Anton, the Younger
Bohemian School, 19th century.
Born 20 November 1837, in Prague.
Painter. Genre scenes, portraits.

Anton Gareis the Younger studied at the art academy in Prague, under Engerth. He exhibited in Dresden in 1870 and 1871. His works include a *Christmas Eve*. He was the son of Anton Gareis the Elder.

GAREIS, Johann Franz Peter Paul
German, 18th century.
Born 28 June 1775, in Klosterfreiheit; died 31 May 1803, in Rome.
Painter, draughtsman.

Johann Gareis studied under Casanova at the academy in Dresden. He travelled to Paris and Rome, and exhibited in Dresden in 1803. He is noted for his *Orpheus*.

GAREIS, Josef Hieronymus Ferdinand
German, 18th - 19th century.
Born 30 September 1773, in Klosterfreiheit.
Sculptor.

Josef was the brother of Franz Gareis.

GAREIS, Pius
German, 19th century.
Born 1804, in Sulzbach (Saarland).
Painter. History painting, portraits.

Pius Gareis was a pupil of Cornelius.

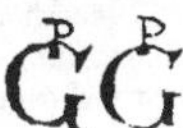

GAREL, Alex
French.
Born in Rennes.
Painter. Still-lifes.

Self-taught, Garel has taken part in salons in Paris and in the provinces. He had a solo exhibition of his work in 1982 at the Guigné gallery, Paris. He paints antique objects, fruit and game, books and musical instruments in a classically elegant style.

GAREL, Philippe
French, 20th century.
Born 1945, in Trébeurden (Côte-d'Armor).
Active in Paris.
Painter, sculptor, draughtsman. Figure compositions, figures, still-lifes. Statues, busts.

Philippe Garel trained from 1961 to 1969 at the École des Beaux-Arts in Quimper, Rennes and finally Paris. He took up a teaching post at the École des Beaux-Arts in Rouen in 1977.

Of Garel's early, brightly coloured, Abstract paintings, he later retained only the flat, single-coloured backgrounds. He moved quickly towards Figurative painting, influenced by historical or contemporary painters of that genre. His oil paintings describe a disquiet world set with still-lifes and figures which are usually posed standing. Imaginary items featuring in different works are detailed so painstakingly that they seem to be real. Alongside hackneyed items such as pale bouquets of wild flowers, lemons, bottles, enamelled plates full of dried cereals and vegetables, Garel places uncompromisingly contemporary items such as canned fruit, plastic buckets and surgical kidney bowls containing what appear to be dried kidney beans. In 1982 he painted a coat hanger in *Hidden Object* and rubber gloves in *Gloves*, apparently his final word on the matter of still-lifes. He paints flat, shadowy backgrounds which flatten the perspective and enhance the interplay of light and shadow. Geometric compositions lend floating, structural forms to the whole.

Garel's portraits are akin to his still-lifes; lacking specific identity and adrift in time and space, they emerge out of the shadowy background. The 1984 series of black men and women is a case in point. Dressed up in all their Garel-invented finery, the subjects are caught in pose against a neutral background as if behind glass, with pots of flowers in their laps or with their arms crossed. Items borrowed from the still-lifes, such as birds, plates, buckets and so on, are set around them. In the 1991 series *Offerings to Rembrandt* executed on large format canvases and little, pre-cut cards, Garel pays homage to the master of light and shadow. However, in this series, completed with bronze-coloured backgrounds and a plethora of relief and detail, Garel interprets composition and scale liberally, thus reinventing Rembrandt's world.

In tandem with his paintings, Garel produces sculptures in bronze, stone, clay or polystyrene foam. They consititute a form of homage to artists of the past who have influenced and inspired him: Dürer, Géricault, Velázquez and, particularly, Rembrandt. Garel writes the name, date and place of birth and titles of works of the artists on the necks, foreheads and cheeks of his sculptures, and signs them with their signatures in relief or carved out. He leaves the imprints of his fingers on these works in recognition of the close, almost intimate relationship he shares with the masters. He also makes three-dimensional still-lifes and, especially, standing figurines, incorporating mirrors and chains, among other elements, into the works. Here again, he incises words along fingers, writing the name of the artist and the nature of the work, as in *Self-portrait: Light-dark*.

In his paintings, Garel acknowledges the power of obscurity, the place of the taboo and the unsayable and, by contrast, of light, which is given the same importance as the elements it permits him to portray. By turning tradition on its head, manipulating still-lifes and portraiture into disquieting forms, he creates a new Baroque-style dream.

Garel has been showing his work at group and solo exhibitions since his public début at the Maison de la Culture in Rennes in 1974. Exhibitions include those at the following: Brussels and Paris (1977); the FIAC (Foire Internationale d'Art Contemporain) in Paris, presented by the Brussels Lauzenberg Gallery (1980, 1985, 1993); the Salon d'Art Graphique in Paris, presented by the Galerie Flora J. (1990); Bologna (1990); and *Portraits d'Afrique* (*Portraits of Africa*) at the Galerie Trigano in Paris (1999).

BIBLIOGRAPHY:

Philippe Garel, exhibition catalogue, Gal. Loeb, Paris, 1984. Masini, Celide, *Philippe Garel*, exhibition catalogue, Gall. Forni Tendenze, Bologna, 1990. *Offrandes à Rembrandt, Philippe Garel*, exhibition catalogue, Gal. Patrice Trigano, Paris, 1992.

MUSEUMS AND GALLERIES:

CAEN (FRAC Basse-Normandie) - CHÂTEAUGIRON (FRAC Bretagne) - PARIS (MNAM-CCI).

AUCTION RECORDS:

PARIS, 4 June 1987, *Portrait à la Coiffe Rouge* (1984, oil on canvas, 78 1/4 x 48 ins / 199 x 122 cm) FRF 30,000. PARIS, 29

Jan 1988, *Portrait* (1984, oil on panel, 35 3/4 x 25 1/2 ins / 91 x 65 cm) FRF 4,000. PARIS, 18 May 1992, *Mirror* (1989, bronze, 34 3/4 x 11 ins / 88.5 x 27 cm) FRF 6,000; *Paint Box* (1988, bronze, 16 1/4 x 21 1/4 ins / 41 x 54 cm) FRF 7,000. PARIS, 23 Nov 1999, *Portrait of a Man* (1998, pastel, 46 x 31 ins / 118 x 79 cm) FRF 20,000. PARIS, 2 Aug 2001, *Portrait of an African Woman in a Red Dress with a Long Necklace* (1998, pastel, 47 x 31 ins / 120 x 80 cm) FRF 18,000. VERSAILLES, 15 Dec 2002, *Homage to Rembrandt* (1989, green patinated bronze, 24 x 11x7 ins / 62 x 28x17 cm) EUR 1,600. PARIS, 4 Aug 2004, *Portrait of an African Woman in a Red Dress with a Long Necklace* (1998, pastel, 47 x 31 ins / 120 x 80 cm) EUR 1,800.

GARELLA, Antonio
Italian, 19th - 20th century.
Born in Bologna.
Sculptor.

Garella worked mainly in Florence.

GARELLI
German, 18th century.
Active in Frain c. 1727.
Painter.

GARELLI, Franco
Italian, 20th century.
Born 1909, in Diano d'Alba (Piedmont).
Sculptor.

After initially studying medicine, Garelli devoted himself entirely to sculpture. He participated in many group exhibitions: the Venice Biennale, from 1948 onward; the Rome Quadriennale; and the Osaka festival of 1958. He staged his first solo exhibition in 1936 in Turin; then from 1957 to 1958 in Paris; and in 1963 in Milan. In 1958 he won the Carnegie Prize in Pittsburgh.

Garelli was particularly interested in the problem of how sculpture could be truly integrated into the surrounding space, skilfully playing on the relationship between the negative space inside his sculptures and the external space. He worked mostly with metal, and built some major monumental sculptures, one of which has been incorporated into a modern monument in Turin.

AUCTION RECORDS:

ROME, 22 May 1984, *L'Amica* (1960, bronze, h. 11 3/4 ins / 30 cm) ITL 3,000,000. ROME, 20 May 1986, *Figure in the Mirror* (1962, iron, relief, 17 3/4 x 19 1/4 ins / 45 x 49 cm) ITL 3,000,000. MILAN, 20 May 1996, *Untitled* (1957, iron sculpture, 34 1/2 x 13 1/2 x 5 3/4 ins / 87.5 x 34 x 14.5 cm) ITL 5,750,000. MILAN, 20 Nov 2001, *Untitled* (iron, 11 x 29x11 ins / 29 x 73x27 cm) ITL 4,000,000. MILAN, 14 May 2002, *Geisha* (1959, bronze, h. 14 ins / 35 cm) EUR 2,600.

GARELLI, Sonia
French, 20th - 21st century.
Born 29 February 1956, in Paris.
Sculptor.

Sonia Garelli was a student of Jacques Delahaye at the École de Beaux-Arts in Paris. She later received guidance from Stanislas Lélio.

To suit her needs, Garelli has developed and refined specific work methods and materials. She initially works on very small pieces (12 to 20 in/30 to 50 cm), which she considers works in their own right but which she may also investigate in terms of their potential as larger versions (around 5 feet/1.5 metre). These are then constructed in a special stucco made of thin leaves of wood which she cuts, braids and weaves together, allowing her concept to develop in layers until she achieves a desirable result. The whole is then brought together with a final unifying layer on which she applies a patina, the finishing touch to her light, hollow and extremely amenable sculptures. The elegant, Abstract sculptures are evocative of previously seen forms, moments of the past, metaphors of what has been, and are often created in series such as the six-piece *Colocynths* (1988-1989) and the 13-piece *Girame* (1990-1991).

Since 1980, Garelli has shown her work yearly at the Salon des Réalités Nouvelles in Paris.

GARELLI, Tommaso d'Alberto, also known as Masacodo
Italian, 15th century.
Active in Bologna.
Painter.

GAREMYN, Jan Anton, or Gaeremyn
Flemish School, 18th century.
Baptised on 15 April 1712 in Bruges (West Flanders); died 23 June 1799.
Painter, engraver, draughtsman. Religious subjects, allegorical subjects, genre scenes, rustic scenes, landscapes, decorative motifs (chinoiseries).

Garemyn studied under R. Aerts, L. Roons, J. Beernaert, Ypres and Mathias de Visch. In 1756 he was appointed professor at the academy of fine arts in Bruges. He is probably identifiable as the painter Jean-Baptiste Garemyn, who exhibited a seascape and a landscape (both with figures) at the Lille Salon in 1779 and 1786. He executed a number of church paintings, notably an altarpiece for St-Maartenskerk in Courtrai. His works show a marked 18th-century taste for chinoiserie and Orientalist subjects, as well as for rustic scenes painted with a bold, quick touch in fresh, brilliant colours.

BIBLIOGRAPHY:

Gerson, H./Ter Kuile, E.H., *Art and Architecture in Belgium 1600-1800*, Penguin Books, Harmondsworth, 1960. De Vos, D., *Groeningemuseum, Bruges: the Complete Collection*, Bruges, 1984.

MUSEUMS AND GALLERIES:

BRUGES: two landscapes - LILLE: two landscapes; *Portrait of a Cleric*.

AUCTION RECORDS:

PARIS, 5 Dec 1891, *Promenade at the Château*, FRF 775. PARIS, 20 March 1924, *Lute Player* (red chalk, studies) FRF 3,900; *Hurdy-gurdy Player* (red chalk, studies) FRF 4,800. PARIS, 23 Nov 1927, *Bagpipe Player; Viol Player* (two drawings in red chalk) FRF 4,300. PARIS, 15 March 1935, *Allegorical Figures (Children)* (series of five compositions) FRF 5,100. PARIS, 6 Dec 1935, *Children in Flowery Landscapes* (series of five decorative compositions) FRF 2,500. PARIS, Oct 1945-July 1946, *Sabbath Scene* (1750) FRF 9,600. BRUGES, 5 Nov 1966, *Group of Cupids Playing beside a Fountain*, BEF 80,000. GARGRAVE, 26 Oct 1982, *Village Fête* (oil on panel, 11 x 14 1/4in/27 x 36cm) GBP 5,500. PARIS, 25 Nov 1985, *The Cake-seller* (oil on canvas, 37 x 46in/94 x 117cm) FRF 60,000. LONDON, 5 July 1989, *Landscape with Putti Playing with Garlands of Flowers* (oil on canvas, 22 3/4 x 54 1/4in/58 x 138cm) GBP 4,620. LONDON, 12 Dec 1990, *Village Celebration in Dudzele near Bruges, with a Castle in the Background* (1773, oil on canvas, 98 1/2 x 189in/250 x 480cm) GBP 49,500. PARIS, 26 April 1991, *Allegory of Taste* (oil on canvas, 29 1/4 x 71 1/2in/74 x 181.5cm) FRF 26,000. PARIS, 19 Nov 1992, *Three Hand Studies* (red chalk, 7 x 11 1/2in/18 x 29cm) FRF 5,200. PARIS, 27 March 1996, *Villagers Conversing beside a Lake* (oil on canvas, 18 1/4 x 21 3/4in/46.5 x 55.5cm) FRF 17,500. AMSTERDAM, 6 May 1996, *Fishermen Selling their Catch in Front of a House near the Beach* (oil on canvas, 38 1/4 x 53 1/4in/97 x 135cm) NLG 20,060. AMSTERDAM, 12 Nov 1996, *Lion with Raised Paw* (1742, black and white chalk on blue paper, study, 10 3/4 x 7 1/2in/27.3 x 19cm) NLG 1,298. PARIS, 21 June 1999, *Sheep Shearing. Working in the Fields* (wash heightened with white, a pair, 9 x 11 ins / 22 x 29 cm) FRF 68,000.

GAREN, Georges-Félix
French, 19th century.
Born 24 February 1854, in Paris.
Engraver.

He studied under Boussard, E. Yon and Guignolet. Garen was a member of the Société des Artistes Français from 1891; he received an honourable mention in 1883, a bronze medal in 1902 and a silver medal in 1906.

GARET, Jedd
American, 20th - 21st century.
Born 1955, in Los Angeles.
Painter. Portraits, still-lifes.

Jedd Garet studied at the Rhode Island School of Design (1975(1976) and at the School of Visual Arts, New York, where he obtained a BFA in 1977. Part of the 1980s Neo-Expressionist movement, Garet typically combines figuration and abstraction in paintings of raw discordant colours. In the 1980s, he painted a series of work of which he says that there were no natural elements, as the figures were statues rather than people, and notes that the sense of artifice in his painting reflects his homosexuality. He has sometimes used two canvases for his work in order to paint on a larger scale, and to skew the image by misaligning the two sections.

Exhibitions include: 1983, *American Still-life 1945-1983*, Houston Contemporary Arts Museum; 1984, *An International Survey of Recent Painting and Sculpture*, Museum of Modern Art, New York; 1984, *The Human Condition*, San Francisco Museum of Modern Art; 1985 and 1981, Whitney Biennials; 1985, *Correspondence: New York Art Now*, Laforet Museum, Tokyo; 1987, *A View of Nature*, Aldrich Museum of Contemporary Art, Ridgefield, CT; 1988, solo show at Origrafico, Malmö, Sweden; 1988, *Figure as Subject*, Whitney Museum of American Art, New York; 1989, *Painting Beyond the Death of Painting*, Kuznetsky Most Exhibition Hall, Moscow; 1991 *de-Persona*, Oakland Museum.

BIBLIOGRAPHY:
Jedd Garet, Exhibition catalogue, Robert Miller Gallery, New York, 1981. Pincus-Witten, Robert, *Jedd Garet*, Illustrated book, Twelvetrees Press, Pasadena, 1984. *Jedd Garet*, Exhibition catalogue, Robert Miller Gallery, New York, 1989.

MUSEUMS AND GALLERIES:
BRUNSWICK, ME (MA, Bowdoin College) - CAMBRIDGE, MA (Harvard University) - HONOLULU (Academy of Arts) - LONDON (Tate Collection): *To Rule the World* (1985, acrylic painting) - MINNESOTA (University) - NEW YORK (Brooklyn Mus.) - NEW YORK (MoMA) - NEW YORK (Whitney Mus. of American Art) - NIAGARA FALLS, NY (Castellani AM, Niagara University): *Curtain of Protection* (1980, acrylic painting) - SAN FRANCISCO (FAM): *Behind Your Back* (1983, colour lithograph); *Orange Rocks* (1983, colour lithograph); *Night Boy* (1983, colour lithographs).

AUCTION RECORDS:
NEW YORK, 1 Nov 1984, *Untitled* (1979, acrylic/canvas, 72 x 54 ins / 182.8 x 137 cm) USD 17,000. NEW YORK, 1 May 1985, *White Vase* (1983, acrylic/canvas, 105 x 84 ins / 266.5 x 213.5 cm) USD 15,000. NEW YORK, 3 May 1985, *Another Party* (1980, pencil, 29 x 23 ins / 73.6 x 58.5 cm) USD 1,500. NEW YORK, 13 Nov 1986, *Fire Toga* (1981, acrylic/bronze, 46 1/4 x 31 1/2 x 7 ins / 117.5 x 80 x 17.8 cm) USD 10,000. NEW YORK, 5 May 1987, *Portrait No. II* (1979, mixed media/paper, 50 x 38 ins / 127 x 96.5 cm) USD 3,500. NEW YORK, 5 Oct 1989, *'Mom and Dad'* (1983, acrylic/canvas, 73 x 57 ins / 185.5 x 144.7 cm) USD 3,850. NEW YORK, 21 Feb 1990, *Growing Vegetation* (1981, acrylic/canvas, 45 1/2 x 17 1/4 ins / 115.6 x 43.9 cm) USD 1,100. LONDON, 22 Feb 1990, *Poisoned Gems* (1985, oil on canvas, 72 3/4 x 57 ins / 185 x 145 cm) GBP 4,400. NEW YORK, 6 Nov 1990, *Modern Sculpture* (1979, acrylic/synthetic resin, 54 x 42 x 3 1/2 ins / 137.1 x 106.7 x 8.9 cm) USD 2,640. NEW YORK, 27 Feb 1992, *The Next Room* (1980, oil on canvas, diam. 42 ins / 106.7 cm) USD 825. NEW YORK, 9 May 1992, *The Black Vase* (1985, acrylic/cut canvas, 72 3/4 x 57 ins / 185.1 x 144.5 cm) USD 1,980. NEW YORK, 30 June 1993, *She* (1987, acrylic/canvas, 73 x 56 3/4 ins / 185.4 x 144.1 cm) USD 4,600. NEW YORK, 24 Feb 1994, *Sliding* (1981, acrylic/canvas, 73 x 57 ins / 185.7 x 144.8 cm) USD 5,750. NEW YORK, 10 Oct 2001, *Hotel* (1980, acrylic on canvas) USD 5,500.

GARF, Salomon
Dutch, 20th century.
Born 6 December 1879, in Amsterdam; died 1943.
Painter. Genre scenes, still-lifes.

MUSEUMS AND GALLERIES:
BUCHAREST (Muz. National de Arta al României): *Peasant Woman from Laren.*

AUCTION RECORDS:
AMSTERDAM, 30 Oct 1991, *Still-life with Books, Sunflowers in a Terracotta Vase, a Candle and a Statuette on a Table* (oil on canvas, 19 x 25 ins / 48 x 63.5 cm) NLG 1,495. AMSTERDAM, 28 Oct 1992, *Peasant Woman by the Hearth in a Farmhouse* (1925, oil on canvas, 23 1/4 x 19 1/4 ins / 59 x 49 cm) NLG 1,725. AMSTERDAM, 9 Nov 1993, *Baby Listening to its Mother Playing the Piano* (oil on canvas, 22 1/2 x 19 1/4 ins / 57 x 49 cm) NLG 5,520. PARIS, 25 April 1996, *Still-life with Pipe* (oil on panel, 13 1/2 x 17 1/4 ins / 34 x 44 cm) FRF 4,000. AMSTERDAM, 5 Nov 1996, *Still-life with Grapes, Peaches and a Small Jug on a Table* (oil on canvas, 12 1/2 x 18 ins / 31.5 x 46 cm) NLG 3,540. AMSTERDAM, 7 July 1999, *Playing with Doll* (1909, oil on canvas, 21 x 18 ins / 54 x 45 cm) NLG 7,000. THE HAGUE, 9 May 2000, *Still-life with White Gloves, Small Vase and Fan* (oil on canvas, 13 x 20 ins / 33 x 51 cm) NLG 6,500. AMSTERDAM, 5 Sept 2000, *Summer Day at Zandvoort Beach* (1910, pencil and watercolour, 5 x 6 ins / 12 x 14 cm) NLG 6,500. AMSTERDAM, 22 Jan 2002, *Still-life with Apples* (oil on canvas, 15 x 17 ins / 37 x 44 cm) EUR 4,200. AMSTERDAM, 20 Oct 2003, *At the Dressing Table* (pastel, 28 x 21 ins / 70 x 53 cm) EUR 17,000.

GARFBEECK, A. van
Dutch, 19th century.
Painter. Genre scenes.

MUSEUMS AND GALLERIES:
CAPE TOWN: *Dutch Family.*

GARFINKIEL, David
Polish, 20th century.
Born 31 July 1902, in Radom; died 1970, in Paris.
Active and naturalised in 1932 in France.
Painter, engraver, draughtsman. Genre scenes, figures, portraits, still-lifes.

David Garfinkiel studied at the school of fine art in Warsaw before settling in Paris in 1932, where he studied at the Académie Julian and the Académie de la Grande Chaumière. His figurative paintings depict a poeticised reality tinged with Expressionism influenced by his Jewish origins, particularly in the traditional marriage scenes

David Garfinkiel featured in collective exhibitions including: Salon d'Automne and Salon des Indépendants, Paris; Salon de Taverny (1960); Salon de Versailles (1966); International Art Exhibition, Tel Aviv (1970). Solo exhibitions include: Lyons (1942); Galerie Zak, Paris (1958); Tel Aviv and Bat Yam (1961). After his death there was a tribute to him at the Salon des Indépendants (1972); at the Galerie Aleph, Paris (1979); and at the Galerie Colette Dubois, Paris (1989).

BIBLIOGRAPHY:
Garfinkel (1902-1970), exhibition leaflet, Gal. Colette Dubois, Paris, 1989. Nieszawer, Nadine/Boyé, Marie/Lanzmann, Claude (preface), *Peintres juifs de l'école de Paris 1905-1939*, Denoël, Paris, 2001.

AUCTION RECORDS:
VERSAILLES, 8 Feb 1981, *Rabbi and his Goat* (oil on canvas, 22 x 18 ins / 55 x 46 cm) FRF 2,500. PARIS, 20 March 1988, *Jewish Orchestra* (oil on canvas, 22 x 18 ins / 55 x 46 cm) FRF 5,500. PARIS, 8 April 1990, *Still-life with Flowers and Fruit* (oil on

canvas, 23 1/2 x 28 3/4 ins / 60 x 73 cm) FRF 10,500. PARIS, 27 March 1994, *14 July at the Sacré-Coeur* (oil on canvas, 32 x 25 1/2 ins / 81 x 65 cm) FRF 5,800. PARIS, 16 Oct 1996, *Young Girls with a Red Bird* (oil on canvas, 23 1/2 x 28 3/4 ins / 60 x 73 cm) FRF 13,800. PARIS, 24 Nov 1996, *Bunch of Flowers* (oil on canvas, 22 x 18 ins / 55 x 46 cm) FRF 4,100. PARIS, 10 March 1997, *Landscape* (oil on panel, 17 3/4 x 20 3/4 ins / 45 x 53 cm) FRF 7,600.

GARGALLI, Filippo
Italian, 18th century.
Active in Bologna.
Painter.

Gargalli studied under Pedretti and Crescimbeni.

GARGALLO, Luis
Spanish, 19th century.
Born in the 19th century, in Valencia.
Sculptor.

GARGALLO, Pablo
Spanish, 20th century.
Born 5 January 1881, in Maella (Aragon); died 28 December 1934, in Reus near Tarragona.
From 1925 active in France.
Sculptor, draughtsman. Figures.

In 1898, Pablo Gargallo became a student at the school of fine arts in Barcelona. He also frequented the Quatre Gats café, the meeting place of Bohemian intellectuals, and met Picasso there. In 1902 he was awarded a travel bursary and, fascinated by the artistic life of the city, he went to Paris. He returned to Spain and lived mainly in Madrid until 1915 studying the masterpieces in the Prado Museum, except for a stay in Paris in 1911 where he discovered Picasso's early Cubist works and discovered African carvings. He also painted Picasso's portrait. In 1917 he became a teacher of fine arts and in 1925 settled permanently in Paris.

Gargallo's very personal art was influenced by the transcendental investigations of his French and Spanish companions who had moved to Paris before him and formed the avant-garde of the period. However, no matter how intellectually intrigued he was, Gargallo never broke faith with reality, or at least not sufficiently to become a forerunner of the abstract art that flourished after his death. In his early years he produced many religious and allegorical sculptures for public buildings in Barcelona in a traditional 1900s style. A passion for humanity persists in his somewhat irrational figures, as in *Study for a Prophet*, which has often been reproduced. Gargallo enjoyed working with the hardest materials; his work in stone is moving. Although Gargallo remained firmly naturalist in his works in stone, close to Maillol but less solid and more sinuous, in his metal sculptures he showed a great inventiveness that places him among the great creators of modern art. Around 1911-1913, using thin strips of metal, lead and copper, he began to produce masks closely inspired by the African art he had seen in Paris. He first produced cardboard models of each piece and then transferred the forms on to metal sheets which he then cut and welded. These early pieces display an elegant virtuosity in the cutting technique but lack in depth; they now appear somewhat dated.

His second period in Paris, beginning in 1923, produced more accomplished works along the same style: *Christ on the Cross* (1923); *Dancer* (1924); *Harlequin with Flute* (1927-1932); *Bacchante and Antinous* (1932); and *The Prophet* (1933). Gargallo was unable or unwilling to distance himself from an essentially classical conception of form. As a result, the technical skills he employed when not working in stone or marble but in metal produced additions and decorations. However, he developed metalworking techniques which later opened the way to Julio Gonzales and other modern metal sculptors. In Joseph-Émile Muller's words: 'He replaces volume with a hollow or a flat surface, or with a void defined by a line; he deliberately transforms the convex into the concave, closed form into open form and the palpable into the simply suggested...'.

Gargallo exhibited in Paris (Salon d'Automne, of which he was a member and Salon des Tuileries) and abroad (Brussels, Darmstadt, Stockholm and Venice). Solo exhibitions of his work include: Musée d'Art Moderne, Paris and Madrid (1981); Saragossa (1986); Galerie Marwam Hoss, Paris (1989 1993 and 1999); Palacio de Cristal, Madrid (1981); Centre Culturel de l'Isle-sur-la-Sorgue (1995); Musée de la Monnaie, Paris (2001); Centro Julio Gonzalez at the Valencia Modern Art Centre, Valencia (2004).

P. Gargallo

BIBLIOGRAPHY:

Courthion, Pierre, *Gargallo*, Skira, Geneva, 1937. *Pablo Gargallo*, exhibition catalogue, Palacio de Cristal, Madrid, 1981. Gargallo, Pierrette/Dagen, Philippe (preface), *Pablo Gargallo - Catalogue raisonné de l'œuvre*, Éd. de l'Amateur, Paris, 1999. Courbet-Viron, Lionelle, *Gargallo*, exhibition catalogue, Monnaie de Paris, Paris, 2001.

MUSEUMS AND GALLERIES:

ALGIERS (Mus. National des Beaux-Arts) - ALICANTE (Mus. de La Asegurada) - ANTWERP (Openluchtmus. Middelheim) - BALTIMORE (MA) - BARCELONA (MAM del Mus. Nacional d'Art de Catalunya): *Bacchante* (1932) - BILBAO (MBA) - BRUSSELS (Mus. royaux des Beaux-Arts de Belgique) - BUFFALO (Albright-Knox AG) - CALAIS (MBA et de la Dentelle) - CÉRET (Mus. municipal d'Art moderne) - DIJON (MBA) - DUISBURG (Wilhelm Lehmbruck Mus.) - LISBON (Centro de Arte Moderna José de Azeredo Perdigão, Fundação Calouste Gulbenkian) - MADRID (Mus. Nacional Centro de Arte Reina Sofía) - MILAN (Gal. d'Arte Moderna) - MONT-DE-MARSAN (Mus. Despiau-Wlérick) - NEW YORK (Metropolitan Mus. of Art) - NEW YORK (MoMA) - NORWICH (Sainsbury Centre For Visual Arts) - PARIS (MAM): *Harlequin with Flute* (1927-1932); *Prophet* (1933) - PARIS (MAMVP) - SARAGOSSA (Mus. Pablo Gargallo) - SÈTE (Mus. Paul Valéry) - SITGES (Mus. Cau Ferrat) - ST-CYPRIEN (Mus. Desnoyer) - ST-RÉMY-LÈS-CHEVREUSE (Fondation de Coubertin) - TEL AVIV (MMA) - TOKYO (Bridgestone MA) - WASHINGTON DC (Smithsonian American AM).

AUCTION RECORDS:

PARIS, 24 Feb 1934, *Mask* (bronze) FRF 700. PARIS, 24 Nov 1967, *Mask with Hair*, FRF 9,000. NEW YORK, 4 April 1968, *Head of a Young Girl*, USD 4,250. LONDON, 4 April 1974, *Picador* (copper) GBP 4,800. LONDON, 1 July 1980, *Nude Standing* (1908, bronze, h. 9 1/2 ins / 24.3 cm) GBP 2,200. NEW YORK, 4 Nov 1982, *Mask of Kiki de Montparnasse* (1928, gilt-patinated carved bronze, h. 8 ins / 20.5 cm) USD 13,000. LONDON, 6 Dec 1983, *Man with Flower* (1907, bronze, total height 24 1/2 ins / 62 cm) GBP 5,000. PARIS, 19 March 1985, *Spanish Woman with Mantilla* (1930, copper, black patina, h. 18 ins / 46 cm) FRF 460,000. PARIS, 22 Nov 1988, *Motherhood* (1922, brown-patinated bronze with shades of green, h. 12 1/2 ins / 32 cm) FRF 510,000. LONDON, 29 Nov 1988, *Head of a Man* (1927, welded iron, h. 10 ins / 25.1 cm) GBP 93,500. PARIS, 1 Feb 1989, *Mother and Child* (1924, ink, 9 3/4 x 8 1/4 ins / 25 x 21 cm) FRF 19,000. LONDON, 26 June 1989, *Dancer* (1934, welded copper, h. 30 3/4 ins / 78 cm) GBP 264,000. LONDON, 26 June 1990, *Homage to Marc Chagall* (bronze, h. 15 ins / 38 cm) GBP 55,000. NEW YORK, 14 Nov 1990, *Mask of Greta Garbo with Eyelashes* (1930, iron, 10 3/4 ins / 27.4 cm) USD 297,000. LONDON, 2 Dec 1991, *The Tragedy* (1915, sheet of iron, h. 13 3/4 ins / 35 cm) GBP 77,000. NEW YORK, 11 Nov 1992, *Picador* (wrought iron, h. 9 1/2 ins / 24.1 cm) USD 154,000. NEW YORK, 10 May 1993, *The Eter-*

nal Mediterranean (ink/paper/card, 5 1/4 x 8 1/2 ins / 13.4 x 21.3 cm) USD 1,380. NEW YORK, 4 Nov 1993, *Small Dancer* (1925, welded iron, h. 13 3/4 ins / 34.9 cm) USD 233,500. PARIS, 24 Nov 1993, *Mask of a Man* (cut copper, h. 4 1/2 ins / 11.4 cm, w. 3 1/4 ins/8.2 cm) FRF 230,000. NEW YORK, 12 May 1994, *Man with Flower* (bronze, h. 24 1/2 ins / 62.2 cm) USD 31,050. PARIS, 13 June 1994, *Sleeper* (1924, stone, unique piece, h. 11 3/4 ins / 30 cm, l. 23 1/4 ins/59 cm, depth 16 1/2 ins/42 cm) FRF 220,000. NEW YORK, 8 May 1995, *David Playing the Lyre* (bronze, h. 20 1/2 ins / 52.1 cm) USD 68,500. LONDON, 29 Nov 1995, *David* (bronze, h. 20 3/4 ins / 52.7 cm) GBP 32,000. PARIS, 7 Dec 1995, *Spanish Woman with Mantilla* (1930, dark-green-patinated copper, 18 x 16 1/2 x 7 3/4 ins / 46 x 42 x 19.5 cm) FRF 790,000. NEW YORK, 14 Nov 1996, *Small Dancer* (c. 1925, welded copper, h. 14 1/4 ins / 36.2 cm) USD 178,500. PARIS, 23 Nov 1997, *The Little Fauness* (1908, patinated bronze, h. 9 3/4 ins / 25 cm) FRF 112,000. PARIS, 12 Dec 1997, *Front View of Fauness* (1925, green-patinated bronze, h. 9 ins / 23 cm) FRF 83,000. PARIS, 22 March 1998, *The Slave* (bronze, 13 x 9 1/2 x 9 ins / 33 x 24 x 22 cm) FRF 180,000. LONDON, 1 July 1999, *Young Man with Daisy* (1927, brown-patinated bronze, h. 27 ins / 69 cm) GBP 24,000. PARIS, 27 Oct 1999, *Kiki de Montparnasse* (brown-black patinated bronze, 15 x 8x4 ins / 37 x 20x11 cm) FRF 700,000. NEW YORK, 10 May 2000, *Petite Star* (oil on copper, 5 x 6x2 ins / 13 x 14x6 cm) USD 140,000. PARIS, 19 Dec 2000, *Mask of Picasso* (brown-patinated bronze, h. 9 ins / 23 cm) FRF 600,000. NEW YORK, 5 Nov 2001, *Mask of Kiki de Montparnasse* (c. 1928, gilded bronze, h. 10 ins / 26 cm) USD 120,000. PARIS, 19 Dec 2001, *Kiki de Montparnasse* (gilt patinated bronze, h. 8 ins / 1 cm) FRF 680,000. LONDON, 25 June 2002, *Dormeuse or Moissonneuse* (1924, bronze, w. 10 ins / 26 cm) GBP 28,000. PARIS, 27 Nov 2002, *Young Spanish Girl* (black patinated bronze, 15 x 12x10 ins / 37 x 30x25 cm) EUR 44,000. LOS ANGELES, 9 Nov 2003, *Woman Carrying Water* (1925, brown-patinated bronze, h. 17 ins / 44 cm) USD 27,500. MADRID, 6 Oct 2004, *Boy with Daisy* (bronze, 25 x 9x7 ins / 63 x 23x18 cm) EUR 50,000.

GARGAULT, Antoine, or Garnault
French, 17th century.
Active in Bourges.
Sculptor.

Antoine Gargault's works include: the coats-of-arms at Bourges and those of the town hall on the ramparts (1610), the portal of the church of the Pères Minimes (1619), the king's coat-of-arms and those of M. le Prince. He also did coats-of-arms of the town, the town hall and the aldermen on the rebuilt portal of St Privé (1622) and a gallery in the former town hall (now a small secondary school) with his colleague Lejuge (1622-1623). He also did the construction of the tower of this monument, a set of stone steps and a wooden church tower at the Carmelite convent. Other works include a stone figure at the town hall (1625) and, a *Virgin Mary* and two coats-of-arms at the portal of Auron (1630-1631).

GARGAULT, François, or Garnault
French, 16th - 17th century.
Sculptor.

This architect was commissioned by the town of Bourges (Cher) in 1599 to create a stone cross with a crucifix and the coat of arms of Bourges. The monument was erected at Moult-Joye, on the spot where the inhabitants of Bourges had defeated the English in the 15th century. In 1613, Gargault repaired the fountain of St-Firmin in the suburb of St-Privé. In 1620, working alongside Antoine Gargault (probably his brother), he made a cross erected on the site of the amphitheatre.

GARGIOLI, Clemente
Italian, 17th century.
Active in Rome.
Sculptor.

Gargioli sculpted the tomb of Cardinal Sfondrato in 1623.

GARGIOLI, Francesco
Italian, 16th century.
Born in Settignano.
Sculptor.

Francesco Gargioli worked mainly in Florence.

GARGIOLI, Giovanni
Italian, 16th century.
Active in Florence.
Sculptor (wood).

Giovanni Gargioli worked in several Florentine convents and churches. A wood-carver of the same name was working in Pisa in 1592, and was probably the same person.

GARGIULIO, Domenico, also known as Micco Spadaro
Italian, 17th century.
Born between 1609 and 1612, in Naples; died 1675 or 1679.
Painter. Religious subjects, figures, landscapes.

Domenico Gargiulio lived and worked exclusively in Naples apart from a short period spent in Rome around 1630. He studied in Aniello Falcone's workshop where he met Salvador Rosa, who was to prove an influence on Gargiulio's landscapes and figures. Subsequently, Filippo Napoletana and Johann Heinrich Schöldfeld were also to play an important role in the development of his style, as would the engravings of Jacques Callot, notably those illustrating Christ's Passion. Gargiulio also embellished architectural views by his friend Viviani Codagora and inserted small figures after the manner of Della Bella. In 2002, the Museo di San Martino in Naples exhibited 100 works by Gargiulio currently in collections across the globe.

MUSEUMS AND GALLERIES:
GENEVA (MAH): *Port of Ostia* - NAPLES: *Moses Striking Water from the Rock; Adoration of the Shepherds; Martyrdom of St Sebastian; Death of Absalom; St Onofrius in the Desert; Saints Paul and Anthony; Battle between the Jews and the Amalekites* - PARIS (Louvre): *Combat* - ROME (Mus. e Gal. Borghese): *Neapolitan Imbibing* - VIENNA: *Two Roman Combats.*

AUCTION RECORDS:
MILAN, 23 Nov 1972, *Horseman*, ITL 7,500,000. LONDON, 29 June 1974, *Wooded Landscape*, Gns 2,500. MILAN, 25 Nov 1976, *Martyrdom of St Bartholomew* (oil on canvas, 49 1/2 x 70 1/2 ins / 126 x 179 cm) ITL 8,000,000. LONDON, 27 May 1977, *Hagar and Ishmael* (oil on canvas, 21 1/2 x 28 ins / 54.6 x 71 cm) GBP 1,400. ROME, 27 March 1980, *St Paul on Malta* (oil on canvas, 19 x 29 1/4 ins / 48 x 74 cm) ITL 2,800,000. LONDON, 10 Dec 1986, *Immaculate Conception* (oil/amethyst/slate, octagonal, 6 x 5 ins / 15.5 x 12.5 cm) GBP 11,500. MONTE CARLO, 3 April 1987, *Conversion of St Paul; Calling of St Peter and St Andrew* (oil on canvas, a pair, 34 1/2 x 47 ins / 87.5 x 118.5 cm) FRF 380,000. MILAN, 4 April 1989, *Martyrdom of St Lawrence* (oil on canvas, 19 3/4 x 28 1/4 ins / 50 x 72 cm) ITL 9,500,000. LONDON, 5 July 1989, *Elijah Sacrificing on Mount Carmel* (oil on canvas, 51 1/2 x 72 ins / 131 x 183 cm) GBP 63,800. ROME, 8 March 1990, *The Flood* (oil on canvas, 19 3/4 x 30 ins / 50 x 76 cm) ITL 16,000,000. LONDON, 11 April 1990, *Collecting Manna* (oil on canvas, 41 x 49 1/4 ins / 104 x 125 cm) GBP 143,000. MILAN, 5 June 1990, *Capriccio of Imaginary Harbour with Ruins and Figures* (oil on canvas, 30 x 43 3/4 ins / 76.5 x 111 cm) ITL 110,000,000. NEW YORK, 30 May 1991, *Way of the Cross* (oil on canvas, 49 x 70 ins / 124.5 x 178 cm) USD 23,000. LONDON, 8 July 1992, *David with the Head of Goliath (portrait of Salvator Rosa)* (oil on canvas, 43 1/2 x 31 ins / 110.5 x 78.7 cm) GBP 22,000. NEW YORK, 14 Jan 1993, *Abraham and Three Angels* (oil on canvas, 25 1/4 x 19 3/4 ins / 64.4 x 50.4 cm) USD 18,700. MILAN, 19 Oct 1993, *Palace Courtyard and Gardens*

with Figures (oil on canvas, 29¼ x 24¾ ins / 74 x 63 cm) ITL 52,900,000. MILAN, 31 May 1994, *Landscape with Harbour and Ruins* (oil on canvas, 29½ x 49½ ins / 75 x 126 cm) ITL 63,250,000. ROME, 22 Nov 1994, *Abraham and the Three Angels* (oil on canvas, 49¼ x 81½ ins / 125 x 207 cm) ITL 92,000,000. LONDON, 19 April 1996, *Noah's Sacrifice* (oil on canvas, 41½ x 54¼ ins / 105.4 x 137.5 cm) GBP 14,950. LONDON, 18 April 1997, *Martyrdom of St Lawrence* (oil on canvas, 41 x 51¾ ins / 104 x 131.7 cm) GBP 41,100. NEW YORK, 29 Jan 1998, *Adoration of the Shepherds* (oil on canvas, 52 x 61½ ins / 132 x 156 cm) USD 51,750. MILAN, 19 May 1999, *Seascape* (oil on canvas, 19 x 26 ins / 47 x 65 cm) ITL 10,000,000. PARIS, 20 Oct 2000, *Warrior's Helmet* (pen/brown ink, 6 x 8 ins / 14 x 20 cm) FRF 17,000. MILAN, 8 May 2001, *Don Giovanni d'Austria enters Naples. Study of Man* (brush/ink/watercolour over pencil, double-sided, 10 x 15 ins / 25 x 38 cm) ITL 18,000,000. ROME, 12 Dec 2001, *Reclining Bacchus* (pen/ink, 4 x 7 ins / 10 x 18 cm) ITL 5,000,000.

GARGIULLO, Antonio
Italian, 19th century.
Painter, watercolourist. Genre scenes.
Orientalism.

Antonio Gargiullo took advantage of the fascination with Islamic culture that was fashionable during the late 19th century, and painted local Orientalist scenes, often in watercolours.

BIBLIOGRAPHY:

Juler, Caroline, *Les Orientalistes de l'école italienne*, ACR Édition, Paris, 1994.

GARGIULO, Francesco
Italian, 17th century.
Born 1601, in Nocera.
Painter.

GARGIULO, Oronzio
Italian, 19th - 20th century.
Born 1869, in Lecce (Puglia); died 1906.
Active in Naples (Campania).
Sculptor. Portraits.

Gargiulo exhibited in Paris, Brussels, Berlin and Barcelona.

AUCTION RECORDS:

MILAN, 14 June 1995, *Head of a Young Boy* (bronze, h. 11¾ ins / 30 cm) ITL 2,530,000.

GARGOT, Jean
French, 17th century.
Active in Poitiers.
Sculptor (wood).

MUSEUMS AND GALLERIES:

POITIERS: one work.

GARGOUROMIN-VERONA, Arthur
Romanian, 19th century.
Born 1868; died 1946.
Painter. Portraits, genre scenes.

Arthur Gargouromin was awarded a bronze medal at the 1900 Exposition Universelle in Paris.

GARGURICH-OHMULEVICH, Pietro.
See **OHMUCEVIC-GRGURIC Peter**

GARIAZZO, Pier Antonio
Italian, 20th century.
Born 1879, in Turin; died 1935.
Painter, engraver.

Gariazzo studied under Bruschi and Vitalini at the academy of fine arts in Rome.

AUCTION RECORDS:

AMSTERDAM, 5 June 1990, *Monica the Dancer* (1935, oil on card, 25¼ x 23¼ ins / 64 x 59 cm) NLG 1,092. LOKEREN, 9 Dec 1995, *Two Nudes* (1935, oil on panel, 35 x 43¼ ins / 89 x 110 cm) BEF 30,000. PARIS, 25 June 1996, *Balinese Dancers* (oil on panel, 19¼ x 29½ ins / 49 x 75 cm) FRF 35,000. SINGAPORE, 4 April 2004, *Three Balinese Maidens* (1959, oil on panel, 25 x 24 ins / 64 x 60 cm) SGD 3,200.

GARIBALDI, Domenico
Italian, 18th century.
Born 1676, in Genoa; died 10 September 1756.
Sculptor.

Garibaldi was a pupil of Parodi.

GARIBALDI, Guilliam
Flemish School, 17th century.
Active in Antwerp at the beginning of the 17th century.
Painter.

GARIBALDI, Joseph
French, 19th - 20th century.
Born 12 May 1863, in Marseilles; died 1941.
Painter. Landscapes, landscapes with figures, waterscapes, seascapes.

Joseph Garibaldi studied under Jacques Antoine Vollon in his studio in Paris before moving back to his native city of Marseilles. He exhibited at the Salon des Artistes Français from 1884 and received a commendation in 1887 and a silver medal in 1897, the year in which he became a member.

Garibaldi was essentially a painter of the south, executing picturesque views of towns and ports in Provence, the rural landscape above Cassis and Bandol and also seascapes. His works include: *Entrance to the Port of Marseilles, Old Parish Church at Cassis, Village in Provence* and *By the Sea.*

MUSEUMS AND GALLERIES:

AIX-EN-PROVENCE (Mus. Granet): *Port of Aude* - ARRAS: *Albi Cathedral* - AVIGNON: *Two Views of Marseilles* - BÉZIERS: *Old House at Brest* - COMPIÈGNE: *View of Cassis* - TOURCOING: *View of Bandol; Old Parish Church at Cassis.*

AUCTION RECORDS:

PARIS, 23 May 1900, *The Old Port of Marseilles*, FRF 340. PARIS, 2 July 1980, *The Old Port of Marseilles* (oil on canvas, 32 x 23¼ ins / 81 x 59 cm) FRF 14,100. VERSAILLES, 7 Nov 1982, *Church and Village* (1890, oil on canvas, 43¼ x 29½ ins / 110 x 75 cm) FRF 8,000. PARIS, 23 March 1988, *Fishing Port in the South of France* (oil on canvas, 51¼ x 76½ ins / 130 x 194 cm) FRF 90,000. NEW YORK, 24 Oct 1989, *Village in Provence* (oil on canvas, 41 x 27½ ins / 104 x 70 cm) USD 6,050. VERSAILLES, 19 Nov 1989, *Village* (1891, oil on canvas, 15 x 18 ins / 38 x 46 cm) FRF 9,000. LONDON, 28 March 1990, *View of Marseilles* (oil on canvas, 22 x 25½ ins / 55 x 65 cm) GBP 9,900. PARIS, 25 Nov 1990, *People Walking near a Village* (oil on canvas, 18 x 22 ins / 46 x 55 cm) FRF 8,200. NEUILLY, 11 June 1991, *By the Sea* (oil on canvas, 8¼ x 12½ ins / 21 x 32 cm) FRF 10,600. PARIS, 22 June 1992, *Entrance to the Port of Marseilles* (oil on canvas, 18 x 24 ins / 46 x 61 cm) FRF 25,000. PARIS, 10 Feb 1993, *Mediterranean Landscape* (oil on canvas) FRF 50,000. NEW YORK, 12 Oct 1994, *View of Auxerre Cathedral* (oil on canvas, 47¼ x 63½ ins / 120 x 161.4 cm) USD 26,450. PARIS, 6 April 1998, *Harvesting* (1890, oil on canvas, 18 x 22 ins / 46 x 55 cm) FRF 6,000. MUNICH, 27 Sept 2000, *Coastal Landscape, Possibly Southern France* (1895, oil on canvas, 29 x 45 ins / 73 x 115 cm) DEM 7,000. NEW YORK, 30 Oct 2001, *Outside the Village* (1885, oil on panel, 11 x 14 ins / 27 x 35 cm) USD 1,500. LUCERNE, 14 Nov 2001, *Mediterranean Beach Landscape* (1895, oil on canvas, 29 x 45 ins / 73 x 115 cm) CHF 14,000. LONDON, 20 March 2003, *Port of Marseilles* (oil on canvas, 21 x 26 ins / 54 x 65 cm) GBP 8,500. NEW YORK, 28 Oct 2003, *View of Auxerre Cathedral* (oil on canvas, 46 x 63 ins / 118 x 161 cm) USD 24,000. THOMASTON, 28 Aug 2004, *View of Capri, Italy* (1896, oil on canvas, 21 x 26 ins / 53 x 66 cm) USD 4,500.

GARIBALDO, Marco Antonio
Flemish School, 17th century.
Born 21 June 1620, in Antwerp; died before 19 October 1678.

Painter. History painting.
Garibaldo's family were of Italian origin but settled in Antwerp in the late 16th century. He became a master of the Guild of St Luke in 1652, and was also active in Italy.

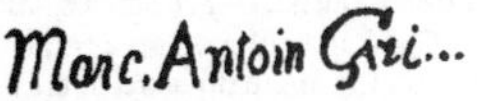

Museums and Galleries:
ANTWERP: *Flight into Egypt.*

GARIBBO, Luigi
Italian, 19th century.
Born 1784, in Genoa; died January 1869, in Florence.
Painter.
In 1859 Garibbo was appointed an honorary member of the academy of Genoa.

GARIBOLDI, Gaetano
Italian, 19th century.
Born 8 November 1815, in Milan; died 11 July 1857, in Milan.
Painter. Landscapes.
Gariboldi studied under Bisi and Sabatelli.

GARIGUE
French, 17th century.
Portrait artist.
Museums and Galleries:
AVIGNON: *Portrait of Charles de Siffredy de Mirnas.*

GARIN
French, 14th century.
Active in Troyes in 1367.
Miniaturist.

GARIN, Aleksei
Russian, 20th - 21st century.
Born 1961, in Nizhniy Novgorod.
Painter. Scenes with figures.
Aleksei Garin attended the Surikov Institute of art in Moscow where he worked under the direction of Perednin.
Museums and Galleries:
KRASNODAR (MCA) - MOSCOW (Ministry of Culture) - PSKOV (MFA).
Auction records:
PARIS, 26 April 1991, *Bear Hunt* (oil on canvas, 28 x 39 1/4 ins / 71.2 x 100 cm) FRF 6,900. PARIS, 27 Jan 1992, *Scene from Village Life* (oil on canvas, 23 1/2 x 31 1/2 ins / 60 x 80 cm) FRF 5,100.

GARIN, Jean-Baptiste Joseph Léon
French, 19th century.
Born 2 March 1822, in Paris.
Painter. History painting, genre scenes.
He enrolled at the École des Beaux-Arts on 6 October 1847, where he studied under Picot and Yvon. He exhibited at the Salon between 1849 and 1859.
Museums and Galleries:
NICE: *Lake Garda; Harbour Entrance, Nice* - VIRE: *Assassination of Thomas à Becket.*

GARIN, Louis
French, 20th century.
Born 23 June 1888, in Rennes; died 13 October 1959, in Val d'Iré.
Painter, illustrator. Landscapes, local scenes.
Louis Garin exhibited at the Société Nationale des Beaux-Arts in Paris. A painter and illustrator of folk tales, he specialised in depicting Brittany and Breton life.
Auction records:
ST-BRIEUC, 7 April 1980, *La Ronde devant la Mer* (oil on canvas, 32 x 46 ins / 81 x 116 cm) FRF 2,800. BREST, 15 May 1983, *Mending Nets in the Golfe du Morbihan* (oil on canvas, 30 1/4 x 80 3/4 ins / 77 x 205 cm) FRF 5,800. PARIS, 19 June 1989, *Rural Life in Brittany* (oil on canvas, 35 1/2 x 74 3/4 ins / 90 x 190 cm) FRF 15,000. PARIS, 26 Jan 2000, *Allegories* (1954, oil on canvas, set of four, 56 x 215 ins / 142 x 545 cm) FRF 50,000. BREST, 10 Dec 2000, *Day of Pardon in Brittany, Blessing of Horses and Riders* (oil on canvas, 29 x 39 ins / 73 x 100 cm) FRF 48,000. BREST, 11 May 2003, *Tuna Boats at Anchor* (oil on canvas, 47 x 24 ins / 120 x 60 cm) EUR 4,200. PONTIVY, 16 May 2004, *Procession in Houat* (1920, oil on canvas, 29 x 36 ins / 73 x 92 cm) EUR 3,000.

GARIN, Paul
French, 20th century.
Born 1898, in Nice; died 1963.
Painter, watercolourist. Figures, landscapes, urban landscapes, seascapes, still-lifes.
After studying law, Paul Garin became interested in painting and taught himself to paint in museums. He painted on the Côte d'Azur and in Nice and later in Normandy for the light; he was strongly influenced by Cézanne.
Auction records:
PARIS, 18 Feb 1998, *Women Bathing* (oil on canvas, 33 x 40 1/4 ins / 84 x 102 cm) FRF 6,500; *Still-life with Cauliflower* (oil on canvas, 23 1/2 x 28 3/4 ins / 60 x 73 cm) FRF 3,800.

GARINE, Viacheslav
Ukrainian, 20th century.
Born in Nikolayev.
Active in France.
Sculptor.

GARINEI, Giovanni
Italian, 19th century.
Born 1846, in Florence.
Painter. Genre scenes.
Garinei's first teacher was Henri Andreotti; he later enrolled in the academy of fine arts in Florence. In 1900 he took part in the Alinari competition, showing a painting entitled *Beatam Me Dicent Omnes Generationes.*
Auction records:
CHESTER, 22 July 1983, *Dancing to the Tambourine* (oil on canvas, 23 1/2 x 35 1/2 ins / 59.5 x 90 cm) GBP 820. LONDON, 21 Nov 1997, *In Raphael's Studio* (oil on canvas, 30 3/4 x 52 1/4 ins / 78 x 133 cm) GBP 4,600.

GARINO, Angelo
Italian, 19th century.
Born 27 August 1860, in Turin; died 1945, in Nice, France.
Active in France.
Painter, pastellist. Religious subjects, portraits, genre scenes, landscapes, flowers.
Angelo Garino was a pupil at the Accademia Albertina in Turin. He made his debut around 1884.

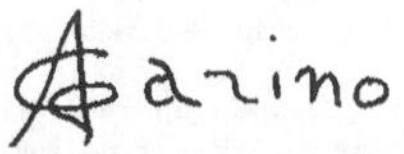

Museums and Galleries:
FÉCAMP (Musées): *Portrait of Jean Lorrain.*
Auction records:
LONDON, 29 Nov 1984, *Little Girl with Her Dog* (pastel, 55 x 37 ins / 140 x 94 cm) GBP 5,000. LONDON, 25 March 1987, *Portrait of a Young Girl* (1898, pastel, 53 1/4 x 35 3/4 ins / 135 x 91 cm) GBP 5,000. NEW YORK, 19 May 1987, *Swans in a Landscape with a Lake* (oil on canvas, 36 1/2 x 45 1/2 ins / 93 x 115.5 cm) USD 6,500. MONACO, 17 June 1988, *Hortensias* (1914, oil on canvas, 25 1/2 x 32 ins / 65 x 81 cm) FRF 19,980; *View of the Countryside Inland from Nice* (1900, watercolour, 25 x 35 3/4 ins / 63.5 x 91 cm) FRF 9,990. MILAN, 19 Oct 1989, *Portrait of a Young Oriental Woman with a Fan* (1883, oil on canvas, 46 3/4 x 27 1/4 ins / 119 x 69 cm) ITL 17,500,000. LONDON, 30 Nov 1990, *Picking Flowers in Nice* (1905, oil on canvas, 25 1/2

x 32 ins / 64.8 x 81 cm) GBP 11,550. MONACO, 21 June 1991, *View of the Alps* (oil on canvas, 23 1/2 x 32 ins / 60 x 81 cm) FRF 49,950. LONDON, 17 March 1993, *Mediterranean Port* (1908, oil on panel, 19 x 25 1/2 ins / 48.5 x 64.5 cm) GBP 3,450. MILAN, 29 March 1995, *The Most Holy Virgin* (1902, oil on canvas, 57 3/4 x 35 1/4 ins / 146.5 x 89.5 cm) ITL 10,350,000. MILAN, 14 June 1995, *Fishing Port in Liguria* (1908, oil on canvas, 19 3/4 x 26 1/4 ins / 50 x 66.5 cm) ITL 14,950,000. FRANKFURT, 9 June 2001, *Mountain Landscape* (1908, oil on canvas, 1 x 36 ins / 3 x 92 cm) DEM 11,000. HAVNEN, 27 Sept 2003, *Coastal Landscape from St Jean a Bautien* (1899, oil on canvas, 29 x 36 ins / 73 x 92 cm) DKK 17,000.

GARINO, Carlo
Italian, 19th century.
Born 1864, in Turin; died in Nice, France.
Painter. Portraits, landscapes.

Carlo Garino was a student at the Accademia Albertina in Turin. He spent time in Naples, where he was influenced by the work of Domenico Morelli, then moved to Nice at the end of the 19th century. He began exhibiting in Turin and Venice in 1884.

Garino mostly painted portraits, and displayed a particular fondness for drama and theatrical composition. His reduced colour palette, consisting of black, grey and dark red, gives his subjects an austere character, as *Mephisto* and his *Self-portrait* demonstrate.

MUSEUMS AND GALLERIES:
TURIN: *Mephisto*.

GARION, Charles Louis, also known as Dumont
French, 18th century.
Active in Paris in 1784.
Painter (?), sculptor (?).

GARIOT, Paul-Césaire
French, 19th century.
Born 1811, in Toulouse.
Painter. Portraits, landscapes.

He studied at the Real Academia de Bellas Artes de S Fernando in Madrid. After he returned to France, he exhibited at the Paris Salon from 1843 to 1880, showing principally religious compositions. He was awarded a bronze medal in 1843.

AUCTION RECORDS:
LONDON, 14 Jan 1981, *Peasant with Basket of Flowers* (1870, oil on canvas) GBP 550. NEW YORK, 23 Oct 1990, *Pandora's Box* (1877, oil on panel, 32 x 22 1/4in/81.3 x 56.5cm) USD 15,400. PARIS, 27 Nov 1992, *Landscape at Sunset* (oil on panel, 7 1/4 x 11in/19 x 27cm) FRF 10,000.

GARIPUY, Jules
French, 19th century.
Born 1817, in Toulouse; died 24 January 1893, in Toulouse.
Painter. History painting, portraits, genre scenes.

He exhibited a variety of works at the Paris Salon from 1855 to 1869. He was director of Toulouse Museum.

MUSEUMS AND GALLERIES:
TOULOUSE: *Attila Departing after the Sack of Aquileia; Invasion of the Cimbri; Death of Ariana; Child and Puppet; Italian Peasants at Rest.*

AUCTION RECORDS:
NICE, 18 Feb 1981, *Portrait of a Child* (1861, oil on canvas, 57 x 40 1/4in/145 x 102cm) FRF 13,800.

GARISON, François
French, 16th century.
Born in Rennes.
Active c. 1565.
Glass painter.

This artist is mentioned by Siret.

GARLAND, Charles Trevor
British, 19th century.
Born 1855; died 1906.
Active in London.
Painter, watercolourist. Genre scenes, landscapes.

Charles Trevor Garland exhibited on a regular basis in London from 1874, notably at the Royal Academy and at the Suffolk Street Gallery. He also showed examples of his work at New Water-Colour Society exhibitions.

AUCTION RECORDS:
LONDON, 17 June 1987, *Drink to Me Only with Thine Eyes* (1885, oil on canvas, 22 x 16 1/4 ins / 56 x 41 cm) GBP 4,800. LONDON, 15 June 1990, *Doddy and the Family Dogs* (1885, oil on canvas, 16 1/4 x 11 1/2 ins / 41.5 x 29.5 cm) GBP 8,250. LONDON, 19 Feb 2004, *Mending Nets* (oil on canvas, 24 x 20 ins / 61 x 51 cm) GBP 1,100.

GARLAND, H.
British, 19th century.
Active in London.
Sculptor.

H. Garland exhibited at the Royal Academy in London from 1867 to 1878.

GARLAND, Henry
British, 19th century.
Born in Winchester.
Painter. Genre scenes, landscapes, animals.

Henry Garland exhibited in London from 1854 to 1890, notably at the Royal Academy, the Suffolk Street Gallery and the British Institution.

MUSEUMS AND GALLERIES:
LEICESTER: *Cool Shelter* - SUNDERLAND: *Crossing the Ford*.

AUCTION RECORDS:
PARIS, 21 Nov 1900, *Off to Market*, FRF 1,500. LONDON, 25 Jan 1908, *Animal Race* (1871) GBP 25. NEW YORK, 1 April 1909, *Scottish Animals*, USD 280. LONDON, 21 July 1911, *Scottish Landscape* (1877) GBP 24. LONDON, 6 April 1923, *Qualified Welcome*, GBP 6. LONDON, 21 March 1924, *Highland Cattle*, GBP 14. LONDON, 22 July 1927, *Highland Landscape*, GBP 18. LONDON, 31 Aug 1973, *Fishermen on the Shore*, GBP 450. LONDON, 15 Oct 1976, *Returning Flock* (1877, oil on canvas, 19 1/4 x 29 1/4 ins / 49 x 74 cm) GBP 380. LONDON, 25 Oct 1977, *String Quartet* (oil on canvas, 19 1/4 x 15 1/4 ins / 49 x 38.5 cm) GBP 750. LONDON, 30 March 1981, *Rabbit's Feast* (oil on canvas, 10 1/2 x 14 1/2 ins / 26.5 x 37 cm) GBP 850. LONDON, 27 Jan 1986, *Best of Friends* (1892, oil on canvas, 19 3/4 x 29 1/4 ins / 50 x 74 cm) GBP 3,200. TORONTO, 30 Nov 1988, *Souvenirs* (oil on canvas, 18 1/2 x 15 1/4 ins / 47 x 39 cm) CAD 2,200. SOUTH QUEENSFERRY, 1 May 1990, *Misty Mountain Landscape with Highland Cattle* (oil on canvas, 24 x 36 ins / 61 x 91.5 cm) GBP 4,180. LONDON, 8 Feb 1991, *Glencoe* (1902, oil on canvas, 49 1/2 x 39 ins / 125.5 x 99.1 cm) GBP 3,520. EDINBURGH, 28 April 1992, *Herd at Rest* (1895, oil on canvas, 20 x 30 ins / 51 x 76 cm) GBP 2,750. NEW YORK, 22-23 July 1993, *Herd at Glen Dochart* (1900, oil on canvas, 24 1/4 x 36 ins / 61.6 x 91.4 cm) USD 3,450. LONDON, 4 Nov 1994, *Watch the Pincers, Jack!* (oil on canvas, 30 x 50 1/4 ins / 76.2 x 127.9 cm) GBP 3,450. GLASGOW, 16 April 1996, *Highlanders by the Roadside* (1895, oil on canvas, 29 1/2 x 50 ins / 75 x 127 cm) GBP 2,070. NEW YORK, 26 Feb 1997, *Herd of Cattle in the Highlands* (1899, oil on canvas, 24 x 36 ins / 61 x 91.4 cm) USD 4,370. AYLSHAM, 25 June 1999, *In the Highlands, Figures, Cattle and Dog* (oil on canvas, 19 x 29 ins / 48 x 74 cm) GBP 5,200. SYDNEY, 10 Aug 1999, *Highland Drive, Argyllshire* (c. 1885, oil on canvas, 23 x 35 ins / 59 x 90 cm) AUD 15,000. BILLINGSHURST, 25 May 2000, *Highland Drove, near Inveroran, Argyleshire* (1899, oil on canvas, 24 x 35 ins / 60 x 90 cm) GBP 5,000. LONDON, 17 Aug 2000, *Highland Cattle in an Extensive Landscape* (oil on canvas, 36 x 28 ins / 91 x 71 cm) GBP 4,000. BURY ST EDMUNDS, 9 May 2001, *Ninepence an Hour* (1892, oil on canvas, 15 x 28 ins / 38 x 71 cm) GBP 2,900.

EDINBURGH, 20 Oct 2001, *Turning the Drove* (oil on canvas, 30 x 50 ins / 76 x 128 cm) GBP 8,000. LEICESTER, 11 July 2002, *Pet Rabbits* (oil on canvas, 10 x 8 ins / 25 x 20 cm) GBP 1,700. BRISTOL, 23 July 2002, *Highland Drove* (1902, oil on canvas, 29 x 49 ins / 74 x 124 cm) GBP 10,400. LEEDS, 10 June 2003, *Driving the Cattle Home* (1895, oil on canvas, 36 x 28 ins / 91 x 71 cm) GBP 3,900. LONDON, 30 Oct 2003, *Highlanders Resting* (1898, oil on canvas, 14 x 21 ins / 36 x 53 cm) GBP 3,500. LONDON, 21 April 2004, *Keeping the Herd at Bay* (1881, oil on canvas, 14 x 27 ins / 36 x 68 cm) GBP 7,500. JOHANNESBURG, 26 Oct 2004, *Reading the Letter* (oil on canvas, 23 x 19 ins / 59 x 49 cm) ZAR 38,000.

GARLAND, Ida
French, 20th century.
Painter.
Ida Garland exhibited at the Salon des Indépendants from 1919.

GARLAND, Mollie
British, 20th century.
Born 23 July 1920.
Painter.
Mollie Garland studied art in England. She exhibited at the Royal Academy in London and at exhibitions of other art societies.

GARLAND, R.
British, 19th century.
Active in London.
Draughtsman. Urban landscapes, urban views.
R. Garland was noted for views of London and the surrounding area.

GARLAND, Valentine Thomas
British, 19th - 20th century.
Active in Winchester between 1884 and 1903.
Painter, watercolourist. Genre scenes, hunting scenes, animals.
Valentine Garland was an artist much sought after at English auctions. He exhibited frequently at the Royal Academy and the Suffolk Street Gallery from 1884.

Valentine T Garland

AUCTION RECORDS:
LONDON, 9 Dec 1907, *The Best Meat is Near the Bone*, GBP 7. LONDON, 4 Dec 1909, *Highland Cattle*, GBP 2; *Scottish Landscape*, GBP 24. LONDON, 21 March 1910, *Fjord in the Highlands*, GBP 15. LONDON, 15 July 1910, *Scottish Cattle* (1899) GBP 17. LONDON, 22 April 1911, *Young Dogs*, GBP 8. NEW YORK, 8 June 1984, *Three Puppies* (oil on canvas, 20 x 16 ins / 50.8 x 40.6 cm) USD 2,500. GLASGOW, 30 April 1986, *Six Couple of Basset Hounds in a Kennels* (1894, oil on canvas, 16 x 22 ins / 40.6 x 55.8 cm) GBP 7,500. LONDON, 28 Sept 1988, *A Terrier* (oil on panel, 10 x 13 ins / 25.5 x 33 cm) GBP 3,960. LONDON, 14 Feb 1990, *Out of Reach* (oil on canvas, 12 1/4 x 9 1/2 ins / 31.2 x 24.2 cm) GBP 1,430. LONDON, 21 March 1990, *Dog Tired* (oil on canvas, 13 x 11 ins / 33 x 28 cm) GBP 3,300. LONDON, 5 June 1991, *Sharing* (1899, oil on panel, 12 x 16 1/4 ins / 30.5 x 41 cm) GBP 1,760. LONDON, 11 Oct 1991, *Fox Terrier Puppy with a Ball* (1895, oil on panel, 9 1/2 x 13 ins / 24.2 x 33 cm) GBP 1,100. LONDON, 12 Nov 1992, *Hound Puppies* (oil on canvas, 16 1/4 x 12 ins / 41 x 30.5 cm) GBP 2,750. LONDON, 30 Aug 1993, *Stranger in their Midst* (1893, watercolour, 10 x 13 1/2 ins / 24.5 x 34 cm) GBP 2,070. NEW YORK, 12 April 1996, *Four Jack Russell Terriers in a Barn* (watercolour/paper, 10 x 7 1/2 ins / 25.4 x 19.1 cm) USD 4,312. LONDON, 7 June 1996, *The New Puppies* (oil on panel, 10 x 8 ins / 25.3 x 20.2 cm) GBP 5,800.

GARLAND, William
British, 19th century.
Died 30 August 1882.
Active in Winchester.
Painter. Landscapes with figures, animals.
William Garland exhibited in London from 1857 to 1874, notably at the Royal Academy and the Suffolk Street Gallery.
AUCTION RECORDS:
LONDON, 20 July 1990, *Landscape with Pack of Dogs* (1865, oil on canvas, 20 x 23 3/4 ins / 50.5 x 60.3 cm) GBP 4,620. NEWBURY, 10 Oct 2001, *Study of Boxer the Dog before His Kennel* (1867, oil on canvas, 15 x 19 ins / 37 x 47 cm) GBP 1,150.

GARLANDI
Italian.
Watercolourist. Ruins.
MUSEUMS AND GALLERIES:
SYDNEY: *Ruins at Isola Farnese*.

GARLENDE, Raoul de
French, 16th century.
Active in Rouen.
Illuminator.

GARLICK, Harry G.
Australian, 19th - 20th century.
Painter, watercolourist. Figures, animals.
Harry Garlick belonged to a school of young painters born in Australia, or living there, who sought to translate life in Australia into art. He exhibited regularly at the Royal Art Society of New South Wales.
MUSEUMS AND GALLERIES:
SYDNEY: *Darby and Joan*; *Shiels Filly* (watercolour).
AUCTION RECORDS:
SYDNEY, 14 March 1983, *Goldie at Shiels Farm* (1904, watercolour, 9 x 11 ins / 22 x 28 cm) AUD 650.

GARLING, Henry Bayly
British, 19th century.
Died 4 December 1909, in Folkestone.
Active in London.
Painter. Landscapes.
Henry Bayly Garland was better known as an architect.

GARLONN
French, 20th century.
Born in Brittany.
Painter. Local scenes, landscapes.
Garlonn paints Brittany and the region's folklore, depicting them with a strong hint of Surrealism.

GARLUZZO
19th century.
Active at the beginning of the 19th century.
Painter, draughtsman.
AUCTION RECORDS:
PARIS, 13 and 14 Dec 1897, *Different Views of Paris* (drawing) FRF 27. PARIS, 6 Dec 1946, *View of the Galleries in the Palais-Royal* (gouache) FRF 60,000.

GARMEAU, Simon
French, 14th century.
Active in Poitiers.
Sculptor.
Garmeau was engaged by Duke Jean de Berry in 1383 to assist in the decoration of the castle at Poitiers.

GARMEIN
Danish, 19th century.
Active in Copenhagen c. 1820.
Painter (porcelain).

GARMINANTI, Bartolomeo
Italian, 16th century.
Active in Faenza.
Painter.

GARMONT, Antoine
French, 17th century.
Born 1657; died 12 December 1687, in Paris.
Sculptor.

GARNAAS, Jørgen Christensen
Norwegian, 18th century.
Born 1723, in Nes; died c. 1803, in Bergen.
Sculptor (wood).
In the museum of Bergen are several wood or ivory statues representing Norwegian peasants by Jørgen Christensen Garnaas.

GARNAIZ
French, 15th - 16th century.
Active in Paris.
Sculptor.
This master mason was summoned to Troyes (Aube), where he carried out various works in 1503 and 1504.

GARNAUD, Achille-Charles
French, 19th century.
Born 26 January 1830, in Paris.
Sculptor.
He studied under A. Toussaint and exhibited at the Salon from 1861 to 1873. His body of work includes *Awakening* (marble statuette), *Child and Bacchante* (bronze group) and *Child in a Boat* (bronze statue).

GARNAUD, Antoine-Martin
French, 19th century.
Born 30 November 1796, in Paris; died 19 December 1861, in Paris.
Architect, lithographer.
He first exhibited at the Salon in 1831.

GARNAULT, Antoine and François.
See **GARGAULT**

GARNELO Y ALDA, José Ramón
Spanish, 19th - 20th century.
Born 25 July 1867, in Enguera (Valencia).
Painter. History painting.
José Ramón Garnelo y Alda received a commendation in 1896 at the Salon des Artistes Français in Paris. At the Royal Academy in London in 1909 he exhibited *Romans Making Sacrifices in an Iberian Shrine*.
MUSEUMS AND GALLERIES:
MADRID (Prado): *Death of Lucan*.
AUCTION RECORDS:
MADRID, 13 Dec 1973, *The Watering Place* (1897) ESP 120,000. MADRID, 20 April 1999, *Woman in the Temple of Paestum* (1930, oil on canvas, 42 x 33 ins / 107 x 84 cm) ESP 600,000. MADRID, 28 Sept 1999, *Meeting in Drawing Room* (1896, oil on canvas, 11 x 18 ins / 29 x 46 cm) ESP 600,000. MADRID, 20 March 2000, *Veturia in Front of the Shop of Marcus Coriolanus* (oil on panel, 26 x 34 ins / 66 x 87 cm) ESP 3,750,000. MADRID, 20 March 2000, *The Teacher* (oil on panel, 27 x 35 ins / 68 x 89 cm) ESP 3,750,000. MADRID, 14 Nov 2001, *Reclining Female Nude* (oil on canvas, 49 x 71 ins / 125 x 180 cm) ESP 11,000,000. MADRID, 19 Nov 2001, *Landscape* (oil on card, 12 x 15 ins / 30 x 38 cm) ESP 325,000. MADRID, 23 Jan 2002, *To War!* (1865, oil on canvas) EUR 18,000. MADRID, 25 Feb 2002, *Neapolitan Woman with Rosary and Roses* (oil on canvas, 39 x 26 ins / 98 x 66 cm) EUR 8,500.

GARNELO Y ALDA, José Santiago
Spanish, 19th - 20th century.
Born 25 July 1866, in Valencia; died 28 October 1944, in Montilla (Cordova).
Painter.
José Santiago Garnelo y Alda was the son of the painter José Ramón Garnelo y Gonzalvez. After studying philosophy and letters he attended the school of fine arts in Seville where he was taught by Eduardo Cano de la Peña and Manuel Ussel de Guimbarda. He then studied at the Academia de San Fernando in Madrid. In 1888 he was a resident student in the history painting department at the Academy of Rome. He taught in various fine arts schools, notably in Saragossa and Seville. He took part in many exhibitions in Europe and exhibited his work in solo exhibitions in Barcelona, Madrid, Paris, London, Rome and Brussels, receiving many prizes and awards.
He painted landscapes, genre scenes, portraits and historical subjects.
BIBLIOGRAPHY:
Arnáiz, José Manuel/López Jiménez, Javier/Merchán Díaz, Manuel (ed.), '*Cien años de pintura en Espana y Portugal (1830-1930)*' in vol. III, Antiqvaria, Madrid, 1989.

GARNELO Y ALDA, Manuel
Spanish, 19th - 20th century.
Born 1 January 1878, in Montilla (Cordova); died 4 May 1941.
Sculptor.
Manuel Garnelo y Alda was born in the Cordova region but lived mainly in Madrid. He exhibited in Madrid and Rome.

GARNELO Y FILLOL, Jaime
Spanish, 19th century.
Painter. Genre scenes.
MUSEUMS AND GALLERIES:
MADRID (Prado): *Inseparable Friends; If You Don't Mind*.

GARNER, Thomas
British, 19th century.
Born 1789, in Birmingham; died 14 July 1868, in Birmingham.
Engraver.
Thomas Garner was a pupil of Lines. He contributed at the start of the 19th century to a large number of contemporary periodicals. Notable among his engravings for the *Art Journal* is an *Allegro* from an original by W.E. Frost. Garner spent most of his life in his native Birmingham, where he produced a large number of portraits of local dignitaries.

GARNERAY, Auguste, or Garnerey
French, 19th century.
Born 1785, in Paris; died March 1824, in Paris.
Painter, watercolourist, miniaturist, draughtsman.
History painting, mythological subjects, portraits, genre scenes, landscapes, flowers.
He was the second son of Jean-François Garneray. He studied under his father and under the painter Jean-Baptiste Isabey. From 1808 to 1824 he exhibited at the Paris Salon, being awarded a silver medal in 1812. Auguste Garneray was retained as personal artist to Queen Hortense and, later, as the Duchesse de Berri's drawing and composition tutor. His own work comprises portraits and various historical subjects which ensured him imperial and royal recognition (his name crops up repeatedly in the memoirs of Queen Hortense and of Madame Cochelet). He also designed costumes for the Paris Opéra. His body of work includes *Family Group in a Gothic Interior, Napoleon at the Head of his General Staff Passing Boulevard St-Martin and St-Denis, Empress Josephine Standing near a Large Urn of Flowers, in Front of a Lake in the Grounds of a Château*.
BIBLIOGRAPHY:
Hubert, Gérard, *Garneray: vues de la Malmaison*, Société des Amis de Malmaison, Paris, 1992.
MUSEUMS AND GALLERIES:
RUEIL-MALMAISON (Mus. national des châteaux de Malmaison et Bois-Préau): *The Hothouse* (1814, watercolour).
AUCTION RECORDS:
PARIS, 27-29 May 1880, *Eleven Portraits of Actresses* (watercolour) FRF 145. PARIS, 30 March 1925, *Mythological Sub-*

jects (twelve compositions for vignettes in sepia wash) FRF 1,100. PARIS, 2 Dec 1925, *Male Portrait* (miniature) FRF 3,700. PARIS, 7 July 1927, *Napoleon at the Head of his General Staff Passing Boulevard St-Martin and St-Denis,* FRF 1,650. PARIS, 31 May-1 June 1929, *Design for a Clock* (watercolour) FRF 1,100. PARIS, 21 Oct 1936, *Empress Josephine Standing near an Urn of Flowers in Front of a Lake in the Grounds of a Château* (watercolour) FRF 16,500. LONDON, 26 March 1981, *Louis XIV Appointing Françoise d'Aubigné to the Marquisate of Maintenon in 1674* (1811, watercolour and pencil, 16 x 22 1/2in/40.5 x 57cm) GBP 600. PARIS, 30 Sept 1985, *Gothic Interior* (1821, watercolour, 6 x 7 3/4in/15 x 20cm) FRF 19,000. LONDON, 19 June 1991, *Lady next to a Balustrade; Couple at Abelard's Tomb* (watercolour, a pair, 7 1/2 x 6 1/4in/19 x 16cm and 7 x 6 3/4in/18 x 17cm) GBP 2,750. PARIS, 20 Dec 1996, *Empress Josephine Standing near an Urn of Flowers in Front of a Lake in the Grounds of a Château* (1813, watercolour on vellum, 10 3/4 x 9 1/2in/27.5 x 24cm) FRF 370,000.

GARNERAY, Hippolyte Jean-Baptiste

French, 19th century.
Born 23 February 1787, in Paris; died 7 January 1858, in Paris.
Painter, watercolourist, engraver, draughtsman.
History painting, landscapes, architectural views.

He was the third son of Jean-François Garneray and studied exclusively under his father. Hippolyte Garneray exhibited at the Paris Salon from 1831 to 1858. Most of his output comprises landscapes. He was awarded a medal in 1819 and was decorated with the Légion d'Honneur on 27 January 1852.

BIBLIOGRAPHY:

Les Années romantiques, la peinture française de 1815 à 1850, exhibition catalogue, Musée des Beaux-Arts, Nantes; Gal. Nationales du Grand Palais, Paris, 1996.

MUSEUMS AND GALLERIES:

BESANÇON: a watercolour - DOUAI: *Portal of the Church of St-Jacques, Rouen* - LA ROCHELLE: *View of Château-Giron* - LISIEUX: *Auxerre: Gate and Tower of Charles the Bold* - VIRE: *Landscape.*

AUCTION RECORDS:

PARIS, 21 Feb 1919, *View of Old Honfleur,* FRF 800. PARIS, 2-4 June 1920, *Gothic Church, Normandy* (watercolour) FRF 340. PARIS, 19 March 1924, *Louis XVIII Landing at Boulogne on 25 April 1814* (Indian ink and sepia) FRF 2,800. PARIS, 11 June 1924, *Town in Normandy* (watercolour) FRF 900. PARIS, 27-28 Nov 1924, *Arrival of the Stagecoach,* FRF 3,200. PARIS, 23 June 1925, *Promenading around the Pond at Fontainebleau during the Reign of Louis XIII,* FRF 5,500. PARIS, 10 March 1926, *Chance Meeting in the Castle Grounds,* FRF 3,950. PARIS, 30 Nov 1927, *Banks of the Seine with the Pont Royal and the Louvre,* FRF 1,900. PARIS, 13 Dec 1935, *Seascape,* FRF 250. PARIS, 17 Nov 1948, *Arrival of the Stagecoach,* FRF 72,000. LONDON, 15 March 1974, *Washerwomen on the River Bank,* Gns 1,100. PARIS, 29 April 1981, *St. Valéry-en-Caux; Fécamp* (two watercolours, a pair, 7 x 11 1/4 ins / 17.5 x 28.5 cm) FRF 6,500. LONDON, 1 March 1983, *Harbour View* (watercolour heightened with white, 4 3/4 x 7 1/4 ins / 12 x 18.5 cm) GBP 400. BORDEAUX, 14 Feb 1985, *Street Scenes* (two gouaches, 4 1/4 x 5 1/2 ins / 10.5 x 13.8 cm) FRF 10,000. NEUILLY, 3 Feb 1991, *Gothic Church Porch; Old Houses* (watercolour, a pair, each 4 x 3in/10.2 x 7.8cm) FRF 6,200. PARIS, 21 March 1994, *Port in Normandy* (watercolour, a pair, each 4 3/4 x 7 ins / 12 x 18 cm) FRF 5,000. PARIS, 13 June 1994, *Old Town, Rouen* (oil on canvas, 11 x 8 1/2 ins / 27 x 21.5 cm) FRF 20,000. PARIS, 12 Dec 1997, *Town in Normandy* (oil on canvas, 16 x 12 3/4 ins / 40.5 x 32.5 cm) FRF 41,000. NICE, 20 Dec 2000, *Old Rouen* (oil on canvas, 9 x 7 ins / 24 x 18 cm) FRF 16,000. PARIS, 16 Nov 2001, *Busy Street in Town of Laon* (oil on canvas, 18 x 15 ins / 46 x 38 cm) FRF 48,000.

GARNERAY, Jean Simon

French, 18th century.
Active in Paris.
Painter.

Jean Garneray was the son of François Jean.

GARNERAY, Jean-François

French, 18th - 19th century.
Born 1755, in Paris; died 11 June 1837, in Paris.
Painter, engraver, draughtsman. History painting, mythological subjects, portraits, genre scenes, waterscapes, landscapes, church interiors.

Jean-François Garneray was a student of Jacques-Louis David. He exhibited work at the Salon in Paris from 1791 to 1835. He painted mainly church interiors, intimist scenes and episodes recording the martyrdom of Louis XVI.

His works include: *Mme de Maintenon in Her Oratory, Louis XVI at the Temple, Diane de Poitiers Asking François I to Pardon Her Father; Duc de Montausier Leading the Grand Dauphin into a Peasant's Cottage; Mary Stuart, Queen of Scotland; Portrait of a Woman Tuning Her Harp; Portrait of Citizen Piersse; Little Gourmande; House of Queen Blanche* and *Prisoner Returning to His Family.* His small-scale portraits after Jean-Baptiste Isabey include: *Charlotte Corday, under Cross-Examination* and *Bailly, Mayor of Paris, under the Revolution.* Jean-François Garneray also engraved many compositions illustrating customs and festivals in ancient Greece.

BIBLIOGRAPHY:

Les Années romantiques, la peinture française de 1815 à 1850, exhibition catalogue, Musée des Beaux-Arts, Nantes, Galeries nationales du Grand Palais, Paris, 1996.

MUSEUMS AND GALLERIES:

ANTWERP: *Portrait of J.-E. Houssement* - AURILLAC: *Roger Ducos* - AZAY-LE-FERRON: *Flowers in a Vase and Bird* - PARIS (Mus. Carnavalet): *Bailly* - PONTOISE (Mus. Tavet-Delacour): *Portrait of M. Rombour.*

AUCTION RECORDS:

PARIS, 1852, *Lady at the Court of Louis XIII,* FRF 400. PARIS, 1899, *Portrait of Mme de St-Aubin* (drawing) FRF 400; *Concert* (drawing) FRF 1,250. PARIS, 28 June 1926, *Napoleon Leading His Army along the Grand Boulevards,* FRF 2,000. LONDON, 24 April 1931, *Portrait of a Gentleman,* GBP 12. PARIS, 13 Feb 1941, *Reading Abandoned,* FRF 66,000. PARIS, 16 April 1943, *Morning Toilette,* FRF 23,000. PARIS, 10 June 1971, *Louis XVI at the Temple,* FRF 7,500. PARIS, 26 May 1972, *View of the Port of Marseilles,* FRF 26,000. PARIS, 5 Dec 2001, *Scolding a Servant* (oil on canvas, 16 x 10 ins / 41 x 25 cm) FRF 40,000. VIENNA, 24 Nov 2003, *Visit of the Grand Dauphin, Son of Louis XIV* (oil on canvas, 44 x 58 ins / 113 x 147 cm) EUR 22,000.

GARNERAY, Louis-Ambroise

French, 19th century.
Born 19 February 1783, in Paris; died 11 September 1857, in Paris.
Painter (gouache), watercolourist, engraver. History painting, landscapes, waterscapes, seascapes, architectural views.

He was the oldest son of Jean-François Garneray. He studied painting under his father and engraving under Debucourt. From 1817 to 1857 he exhibited at the Paris Salon, and was awarded a silver medal in 1819. Louis-Ambroise Garneray led an adventurous life, including a period as a prisoner of war in England from 1806 to 1814, and was generally regarded as something of a privateer (not to say an out-and-out pirate). He was retained as a court painter by the Duc d'Angoulême and was curator of Rouen Museum from 1832 to 1837. He was made a Chevalier of the Légion d'Honneur in 1852.

Garneray was a prolific and expressive painter whose artistic output included a number of major works: *Duchesse d'Angoulême aboard the 'Royal Sovereign', Whaling, Fishing for Sturgeon, Salmon Fishing, Trout Fishing, Chinese Junk Attacked by Malay Pirates in the Sunda Strait, Fishing for Eel, Fishing for Dogfish, Fishing for Devilfish off the Cape of Good Hope, Cliffs at Fécamp* and *Demasted Dutch Galliot Wrecked off the Norwegian Coast.*

L. Garneray.

BIBLIOGRAPHY:
Louis Garneray, peintre écrivain, aventurier, exhibition catalogue, Musée Eugène-Boudin, Honfleur; Musée Portuaire, Dunkirk, Anthèse, Arcueil, 1997.

MUSEUMS AND GALLERIES:
ARRAS: *Bombardment of Mogador* - AVIGNON: *Naval Battle* (signed L. Garneray) - CAMBRAI: *Beach* - DOUAI: *View of the Scheldt* - LA ROCHELLE: *View near Amsterdam; Bay of Bengal: Taking of the 'Kent' by the Privateer 'La Confiance'* - LE HAVRE: *English Vessels at Anchor* - NANTES (MBA): *Battle of Navarino* - NARBONNE: *Battle of Navarino* - NICE: *Dardanelles* - PONTOISE: *Group Study* - ROCHEFORT: *Frigate 'La Virginie' in Action on 17 July 1795* - ROUEN: *Fishing for Cod* - VERSAILLES: *Historical Scenes* (three works).

AUCTION RECORDS:
PARIS, 1862, *Wreck of the 'Superbe'*, FRF 94. PARIS, 1869, *Seascape* (drawing) FRF 42. PARIS, 18 March 1920, *Naval Battle*, FRF 230. PARIS, 26 Feb 1923, *Mouth of the Adour River, Bayonne*, FRF 300. LONDON, 25 Nov 1929, *Town on a River*, GBP 8. PARIS, 4 March 1943, *La Pêche au brulot*, FRF 1,500. PARIS, 13-14 Dec 1943, *Sailing Ships in the Harbour* (1831, watercolour, no forename given) FRF 700. PARIS, 16-17 May 1945, *River Mouth* (watercolour) FRF 4,800; *Harbour* (watercolour) FRF 4,600. PARIS, 18 Oct 1946, *St-Germain-l'Auxerrois* (watercolour) FRF 700. PARIS, 2 Dec 1946, *Vessel at Anchor in a Mediterranean Bay* (heightened watercolour) FRF 4,700; *Fortified Castle on the Coast* (heightened watercolour) FRF 1,600. PARIS, 27 March 1947, *Port of Antwerp* (no forename given) FRF 32,000. LONDON, 24 May 1968, *Port of Amsterdam*, Gns 720. VERSAILLES, 14 May 1977, *Fishermen in Rough Waters* (1840, oil on canvas, 13 1/2 x 17 3/4 ins / 34.5 x 45 cm) FRF 7,200. PARIS, 5 April 1978, *Naval Battle off a Fortified Town* (watercolour and gouache, 9 x 16 1/2 ins / 23 x 42 cm) FRF 7,200. ZURICH, 16 May 1980, *Fishermen Home from the Sea* (1838, oil on canvas, 18 x 21 1/2 ins / 46 x 54.5 cm) CHF 3,800. PARIS, 30 June 1982, *Net-Fishing* (oil on canvas, 14 3/4 x 18 ins / 37.5 x 46 cm) FRF 6,200. NEW YORK, 1 Feb 1986, *The Hornet and the Peacock* (1813, oil on panel, 14 3/4 x 20 ins / 37.5 x 50.8 cm) USD 7,000. PARIS, 11 Dec 1987, *Shipwreck* (oil on canvas, 32 x 39 1/4 ins / 81 x 100 cm) FRF 7,500. PARIS, 20 April 1988, *Seascape* (oil on card, 13 x 16 1/2 ins / 33 x 42 cm) FRF 27,000. LONDON, 14 July 1989, *Galleys in Portsmouth Harbour* (oil on canvas, 21 x 41 1/2 ins / 53.4 x 105.5 cm) GBP 14,300. FONTAINEBLEAU, 27 May 1990, *Naval Battle Scene* (oil on canvas, remounted on card, 13 1/2 x 20 1/4 ins / 34 x 51.5 cm) FRF 25,000. PARIS, 8 April 1991, *Bayonne Harbour* (watercolour and black chalk, 6 x 9in/15 x 23cm) FRF 32,000. MONACO, 4 Dec 1992, *Fishing for Shad* (oil on canvas, 50 1/4 x 69 ins / 127.5 x 175 cm) FRF 122,100. PARIS, 10 Dec 1992, *Bay View (presumed to be in Brazil); Landscape by the Sea* (gouache, a pair, each 7 x 11in/18 x 28cm) FRF 28,000. PARIS, 12 June 1995, *Street Scenes in Constantinople and Smyrna* (oil on panel, a pair, 10 x 5 ins / 25 x 13 cm) FRF 30,000. LONDON, 3 April 1996, *Floating Prison in Portsmouth Harbour* (oil on canvas, 21 x 40 1/2 ins / 52.5 x 103 cm) GBP 9,775. PARIS, 10 March 1999, *Naval Battle* (oil on canvas, 19 x 24 ins / 49 x 60 cm) FRF 52,000. LILLE, 28 March 1999, *Boat Entering English Port in a Storm* (oil on canvas, 15 x 19 ins / 38 x 47 cm) FRF 42,000. PARIS, 25 Feb 2000, *View of Oriental Port* (watercolour, 5 x 8 ins / 13 x 21 cm) FRF 18,000. PARIS, 2[illegible] March 2000, *Boat Put Out to Sea* (oil on canvas, 15 x 18 ins / 3[illegible] x 46 cm) FRF 38,000. BILLINGSHURST, 6 March 2001, *Naval Engagement* (oil on canvas, 12 x 15 ins / 30 x 38 cm) GBP 5,400. PARIS, 7 Dec 2001, *Storm* (oil on canvas, 15 x 18 ins / 38 x 4[illegible] cm) FRF 45,000. LONDON, 15 Nov 2002, *Figures Pulling a Boat to Sea Whilst under Attack* (oil on canvas, 15 x 19 ins / 38 x 4[illegible] cm) GBP 6,000. PARIS, 18 Dec 2002, *View of Batavia* (1817, oil on panel, 9 x 11 ins / 24 x 29 cm) EUR 10,000. LONDON, 22 Jan 2003, *Capture of H.M.S Macedonian by the American Frigate United States, 25th October 1812* (oil on panel, 9 x 14 ins / 23 x 35 cm) GBP 7,000. NEW YORK, 29 May 2003, *View of a Tropical Port* (1817, oil on panel, 19 x 11 ins / 49 x 29 cm) USD 21,000.

GARNERAY, Pauline. See **CABANNE**

GARNEREY. See **GARNERAY**

GARNERY, P.
British, 18th century.
Active in London.
Painter. Portraits.

P. Garnery exhibited at the Royal Academy in London in 1785.

GARNESSON, Jean
French, 17th century.
Active in Paris in 1691.
Painter, sculptor, engraver, illuminator.

GARNET, Christoffel
Dutch, 17th century.
Active in The Hague, c. 1647.
Portrait artist.

Garnet worked for the Prince of Orange at the Dutch royal court.

GARNET, Colard or Nicolas
Dutch, 14th century.
Sculptor.

Colard Garnet worked for the counts of Brabant between 1363 and 1367.

GARNETT (Miss)
British, 20th century.
Painter.

Miss Garnett was a member of the Ridley Art Club.

GARNI, Juan
Spanish, 16th century.
Sculptor.

Juan Garni features as a witness in a public document in Valladolid, in 1518.

GARNIE, J. B.
Dutch, 17th century.
Active in The Hague, c. 1658.
Miniaturist.

GARNIER
French, 13th - 14th century.
Painter.

Garnier ' *lo peinturer* ' (the painter) was living in Lyons in 1306.

GARNIER, André
French, 19th century.
Painter.

He exhibited at the Paris Salon from 1831 to 1848, chiefly with views of woodlands and forests.

AUCTION RECORDS:
PARIS, 17 Dec 1927, *View of Paris from Montmartre*, FRF 500. PARIS, 12 May 1937, *Bowl of Milk* (charcoal, red chalk and gouache) FRF 450. PARIS, 17-18 Dec 1941, *The Fruit-seller* (watercolour) FRF 50. PARIS, 29 Dec 1941, *Guitar Player*, FRF 240.

GARNIER, Anne
Belgian, 20th century.
Born 1939, in Liège.
Painter, sculptor, engraver.
Anne Garnier studied at the academies of art in Liège, Brussels, Wantermael-Boitsfort and La Cambre. As well as working as an artist, she was the director of the art school in Wavre.

GARNIER, Antoine
French, 17th century.
Active in Paris between 1625 and 1646.
Engraver.
Antoine Garnier produced engravings in the styles of Primaticcio, Poussin and Caravaggio, as well as some on religious themes.

GARNIER, Antoine, called Tony
French, 19th - 20th century.
Born 13 August 1869, in Lyons; died 19 January 1948, in La Bédoule.
Painter, watercolourist, draughtsman, architect. Landscapes.
Antoine Garnier studied at the École des Beaux-Arts in Lyons and in Paris and later became director of the École des Beaux-Arts de Lyons. He exhibited paintings and drawings from 1887 in his native city of Lyons and then in Paris from 1896. He was awarded the Grand Prix de Rome for architecture in 1899.

Alongside his activities as a painter, Garnier was also one of the first town planners. He is responsible for the États-Unis district in Lyons, the La Mouche abattoirs and the municipal stadium.

In 2002 his monumental watercolour drawings of Tusculum were shown as part of the *Italia Antiqua* exhibition at the École Nationale Supérieure des Beaux-Arts in Paris. The exhibition was shown at the Villa Medici in Rome later the same year.

BIBLIOGRAPHY:
Guiheux, Alain, et al., *Tony Garnier: l'œuvre complète*, exhibition catalogue, catalogue raisonné, Éd. du Centre Georges-Pompidou, Paris, 1989. *Italia Antiqua*, exhibition catalogue, École nationale supérieure des beaux-arts, Paris, 2002.

GARNIER, Auguste-François
French, 19th century.
Active in Paris.
Engraver.
He is known principally as a book illustrator.

GARNIER, Auguste-Léopold
French, 19th century.
Died 1867, in Paris.
Painter.
He exhibited landscapes and still-lifes at the Paris Salon from 1834 to 1850.

GARNIER, Augustin
French, 17th century.
Born 1579.
Painter.
Augustin Garnier worked in the studios of the château at Fontainebleau.

GARNIER, Benoît-Joseph-Gustave, pseudonym: Girrane
French, 19th century.
Born 13 May 1865, in Lyons.
Draughtsman, illustrator.
He enrolled at the École des Beaux-Arts in Lyons in 1886. His many drawings showing views of Lyons, its monuments and street scenes, may be found in *Le Croquis Lyonnais* (*Lyons Sketchbook*) , which he illustrated and published in 1890, *Le Progrès illustré* (*Progress Illustrated*) and in Grand-Carteret's *L'Enseigne, son histoire, sa philosophie* (*History and Meaning of Shop Signs*) (1902).

GARNIER, Charles François
French, 18th century.
Active in Paris in 1782.
Painter, sculptor.

GARNIER, Christophe
French, 20th - 21st century.
Born 1960, in Amiens.
Active in Nantes.
Painter.
Christophe Garnier's works reveal the influence of Francis Bacon. He exhibited at the Salon de Mai in Paris in 1989.

AUCTION RECORDS:
PARIS, 23 April 1990, *L'Encapé* (1989, acrylic/canvas, 46 x 32 ins / 116 x 81 cm) FRF 7,500.

GARNIER, Claude
French, 19th century.
Born in Aunez-le-Grand.
Sculptor.
He studied under Barre. Between 1857 and 1870 he exhibited at the Paris Salon, chiefly plaster sculptures of genre themes such as *The Moral of the Sticks* and *Urn of Universal Suffrage*.

GARNIER, Claude Charles
French, 18th century.
Born 1707, in Salins; died 4 September 1752, in Besançon.
Sculptor.

GARNIER, Clément Firmin
French, 19th century.
Born 27 April 1800, in Paris.
Painter.
He enrolled at the École des Beaux-Arts, Paris, on 10 November 1823 and studied under Guillon-Lethière. He exhibited at the Paris Salon from 1831 to 1879.

GARNIER, Émilie
French, 20th century.
Miniaturist.
Émilie Garnier exhibited at the Paris Salon of 1901.

GARNIER, Étienne Barthélémy
French, 18th - 19th century.
Born 24 August 1759, in Paris; died 16 November 1849, in Paris.
Painter, draughtsman. History painting, mythological subjects, portraits, genre scenes, still-lifes.
Étienne Garner's masters were Durameau, Doyen and Vien. In 1787, he obtained the second Grand Prix de Rome with: *Nebuchadnezzar Has Sedecius' Children Killed in Their Father's Presence*, and won the first Grand Prix de Rome in 1788 with *Death of Tatius*. He became a member of L'Institut de France in 1816. His work, which generally portrayed historical subjects, appeared at the Salon in Paris from 1793 to 1846.

Garnier.

MUSEUMS AND GALLERIES:
ANGERS (MBA): *Eponina and Sabinus* (1810) - ANGOULÊME: *Consternation of Priam's Family* - CHARTRES: *Meeting of the Duke and Duchess of Angoulême in Chartres in 1823* - HAARLEM: *Portrait of M. Andriaan Cornelis Fabricius; Portrait of Haasje Van Notten* - MONTAUBAN: *Phaedra and Hippolytus* - PARIS (Louvre): *Hercules with the Golden-Horned Deer* - TROYES: *Ajax Assailed by the Storm* - VERSAILLES: *Henri IV Building the Louvre Galleries.*

AUCTION RECORDS:

PARIS, 1859, *Officer's Departure*, FRF 840. PARIS, 1891, *Portrait of Napoleon I*, FRF 590. PARIS, 4 Oct 1994, *Academy for Men* (1791, black chalk heightened with white, 23 1/4 x 17 3/4 ins / 59 x 45 cm) FRF 7,500. LONDON, 5 Dec 1997, *Carnations, 'Parrot' Tulips, Morning Glories and Other Flowers in a Bowl with Apples, Plums, Grapes and Porcelain Vases on a Table Partly Covered with a Cloth* (oil on canvas, 32 3/4 x 51 1/4 ins / 83.2 x 130.2 cm) GBP 3,680. NEW YORK, 21 May 1998, *Sophocles before the Magistrate of Athens. Cornelia, Mother of the Gracchi* (oil on canvas, a pair, 13 x 16 ins / 32 x 41 cm) USD 9,000. NEUILLY, 16 June 2003, *Portrait of Cardinal Jean Sifrein Maury* (1836, oil on canvas, 52 x 39 ins / 133 x 98 cm) EUR 4,000.

GARNIER, Étienne Claude
French, 18th century.
Active in Paris in 1783.
Painter, sculptor.

GARNIER, Étienne-Marie Alfred
French, 19th century.
Born 1848, in Puiseaux (Loiret); died 1908 (?), in Bazoches.
Painter, enameller. Historical subjects, portraits.

He studied under Cabanel at the École des Beaux-Arts in Paris and exhibited portraits at the Paris Salon from 1874 to 1878. Garnier joined forces with the enamellist Paul Grandhomme to reproduce portraits and works by Gustave Moreau (*The Voices*), Botticelli (*Primavera (Spring)*), Crivelli (*Virgin and Child*) and Mantegna (*Minerva*). Working on his own, Garnier painted an *Assassination of Henry III* and *Solange, Souvenir of Berry*. The work of Garnier and Grandhomme was featured in an exhibition held in the Louvre in 1993 entitled *Copier Créer. De Turner à Picasso: 300 œuvres inspirées par les maîtres du Louvre* (*To Copy: From Turner to Picasso - 300 Works Inspired by the Masters of the Louvre*) .

BIBLIOGRAPHY:

Cuzin, Jean-Pierre, *Copier Créer. De Turner à Picasso: 300 œuvres inspirées par les maîtres du Louvre*, exhibition catalogue, Musée du Louvre, Paris, 1993.

GARNIER, Félix-Louis
French, 19th century.
Painter.

He exhibited miniatures at the Paris Salon in 1822 and 1824.

GARNIER, François
French, 17th century.
Born c. 1600, in Paris; died 17 April 1672, in Paris.
Painter. Still-lifes (including fruit).

François Garnier worked at the courts of Louis XIII and Louis XIV. There are traces of his activity between 1627 and 1658. He was also a dealer in paintings.

One of his paintings *Gooseberries and Cherries* from 1644, is kept at the Louvre.

Though he showed less intellectual depth than Baugin and less brilliance than Jacques Linard, Garnier can be counted among the French artists who perpetuated the Flemish still-life tradition and imbued it with a gravity of vision inherited from Caravaggio.

Louise Moillon was his daughter-in-law. It seems likely that he would have given her advice and, though she did not venture beyond the genre of still-lifes with flowers and fruit, she displayed an extremely rich talent.

MUSEUMS AND GALLERIES:

PARIS (Louvre): *Gooseberries and Cherries* (1644).

AUCTION RECORDS:

MONTE CARLO, 8 Dec 1984, *Still-life with Fruit on a Stone Console* (oil on canvas, 28 1/4 x 45 ins / 71.5 x 114.5 cm) FRF 65,000. ENGHIEN-LES-BAINS, 29 March 1987, *Basket of Cherries and Bowl of Gooseberries; Basket of Plums* (oil on panel, a pair, 19 1/4 x 25 1/4 ins / 49 x 64 cm) FRF 466,000. PARIS, 11 Dec 1992, *Still-life with Cherries, Wild Strawberries, Artichokes and Two Bullfinches* (oil on canvas, 27 3/4 x 36 1/4 ins / 70.5 x 92 cm) FRF 135,000. LONDON, 11 Dec 1996, *Dish of Strawberries* (oil on panel, 7 1/4 x 11 3/4 ins / 18.6 x 30 cm) GBP 20,700. PARIS, 31 March 1998, *Bowl of Wild Strawberries on a Console* (oil on oak panel, 10 1/4 x 13 1/4 ins / 26 x 33.5 cm) FRF 640,000. PARIS, 27 June 2003, *Still-life with Basket of Cherries and Bowl of Strawberries* (oil on panel, 12 x 17 ins / 31 x 43 cm) EUR 55,000. PARIS, 27 June 2003, *Still-life with Dish of Cherries* (oil on panel, 12 x 17 ins / 31 x 43 cm) EUR 115,000.

GARNIER, François
French, 19th century.
Born 1 September 1812, in Gouesnou, near Brest (Finistère).
Painter, engraver.

He was a pupil of Guérin and Bervic. From 1824 to 1850 he exhibited at the Paris Salon, and was awarded a silver medal for engraving in 1824 and a gold in 1831.

GARNIER, François-Auguste
French, 19th century.
Engraver.

He exhibited at the Paris Salon from 1836 to 1848.

GARNIER, Gaston
French, 19th century.
Active in Paris.
Painter.

He was a member of the Société des Artistes Français from 1886 and exhibited at its Salons.

GARNIER, Guillaume
French, 17th century.
Painter.

Guillaume Garnier was the son of Augustin. He worked at the château in Fontainebleau.

GARNIER, Gustave-Alexandre
French, 19th century.
Born 15 August 1834, in the Sarthe region.
Sculptor. Figures, portraits.

He enrolled at the École des Beaux-Arts on 6 April 1854 and studied under Duret and Yvon. He exhibited at the Paris Salon from 1859. Examples of his work include *Prisoner of Love, Early Education* (group), *David Defeating Goliath, Marble Bust of Léon Foucault* and *Allegory of Spring* (bronze statue). The Grenoble Préfecture commissioned him to sculpt a stone bust of *General Marchand*.

MUSEUMS AND GALLERIES:

DIEPPE: *Sleeping Fisherman*.

AUCTION RECORDS:

PARIS, 20 Nov 1990, *Bust of Sultan Abdul-Aziz* (white marble, 30 x 22 3/4in/76 x 58cm) FRF 130,000.

GARNIER, Hélène Henriette
French, 19th - 20th century.
Born in Paris.
Miniaturist.

Hélène Garnier exhibited regularly at the Paris Salon.

GARNIER, Henri-Adolphe
French, 19th century.
Born 1803, in Paris.
Sculptor.

He exhibited from 1831 to 1835 at the Paris Salon, where he showed busts, medallions and some genre pieces. His works include *Ajax Struck by Lightning, Gaius Mucius Scaevola Appearing before the Tribunal of Porsena, Bust of Elizabeth Taylor, Charondas* (statue) and *Echo* (monumental statue).

GARNIER, Hippolyte-Louis
French, 19th century.
Born 12 July 1802, in Paris; died 12 June 1855, in Paris.
Painter, miniaturist, lithographer, engraver.

He enrolled at the École des Beaux-Arts, Paris, on 6 September 1819 and studied under Hersent. From 1822 to 1853 he exhibited engravings, paintings and lithographs at the Paris Salon. Among his canvases are *View of a Gothic Castle* and *Argyll's Shade Appearing to Fergus*.

GARNIER, Jacques
Italian, 13th - 14th century.
Born in Piedmont.
Painter.
Jacques Garnier is recorded as working in Lyons in 1306.

GARNIER, Jacques
French, 18th century.
Died 1748, in Paris.
Painter.
Jacques Garnier was the father of Jean Baptiste.

GARNIER, Jean
French, 12th century.
Enameller.
This artist was active in Limoges.

GARNIER, Jean
French, 15th century.
Active in Troyes.
Sculptor.
Working in Troyes, this artist produced a large number of works between 1417 and 1445. He was commissioned to provide the sculptural decoration for the church of St-Jean.

GARNIER, Jean
French, 17th century.
Born 1632, in Meaux; died 23 October 1705, in Paris.
Painter. Portraits, still-lifes.
On 30 January 1672 Jean Garnier was accepted as an academician. His work featured at the Salon in Paris from 1693 to 1704.
MUSEUMS AND GALLERIES:
VERSAILLES: *Portrait of Louis XIV*.
AUCTION RECORDS:
PARIS, 10 June 1980, *Still-life in the Realm of the Zodiac* (oil on canvas, 50 3/4 x 74 ins / 129 x 188 cm) FRF 40,000.

GARNIER, Jean Baptiste
French, 18th century.
Died 1759, in Paris.
Painter.
Jean Garnier specialised in chinoiserie.

GARNIER, Jean Gabriel
French, 18th century.
Active in Paris in 1743.
Painter, sculptor.

GARNIER, Jean Nicolas
French, 17th century.
Painter.
Jean Garnier was accepted as an academician on 28 June 1680.

GARNIER, Jean-François-Marie
French, 19th century.
Born 1820, in Lyons; died 1895, in Paris.
Sculptor. Allegorical subjects.
He exhibited at the Salon des Artistes Français, where he gained an honourable mention in 1892.
MUSEUMS AND GALLERIES:
LYONS (MBA): *Dante's 'Inferno': Those Who Live in Luxury*.
AUCTION RECORDS:
PARIS, 25 May 1984, *Dante's 'Inferno': Those Who Live in Luxury* (bronze dish, decorated in semi-relief, diam. 23in/58.5cm) FRF 5,500.

GARNIER, Jules-Arsène
French, 19th century.
Born 22 January 1847, in Paris; died 25 December 1889, in Paris.
Painter, watercolourist. Scenes with figures, genre scenes, landscapes.
He studied at the École des Beaux-Arts in Toulouse, and then under Gérôme at the École des Beaux-Arts in Paris. He exhibited at the Paris Salon from 1869 to 1889, and then at the Salon des Artistes Français. Garnier painted numerous landscapes based on his travels to Belgium, the Netherlands and Spain, but it was his corpus of anecdotal paintings (frequently inspired by the work of Rabelais) that brought him broad popular success, notably with a composition entitled *Liberator*. His other works include *Cup of Chivalry*, *Bacchanale*, *Don't Wake Baby!*, *Enjoy Life to the Full*, *Tattle-Tale*, *Kingly Pleasure* and *Pantagruel*. Some of his work featured in an exhibition entitled *Équivoques* (*Equivocations*) held at the Musée des Arts Décoratifs in Paris in 1973.

JULES GARNIER · 87
JULES GARNIER
JULES GARNIER

BIBLIOGRAPHY:
Hirshler, Eric, '*A French Salon Painting Reconsidered*' in *Apollo*, Cxxi, no. 280, 1985.
MUSEUMS AND GALLERIES:
ANGERS: *Landscape* - DIJON (MBA): *Flotsam and Jetsam*.
AUCTION RECORDS:
PARIS, 18 Feb 1895, *Kingly Pleasure*, FRF 2,100. PARIS, 1899, *Crossing the Stream*, FRF 7,500. PARIS, 21 June 1900, *Cup of Chivalry*, FRF 310. PARIS, 12 June 1920, *Enjoy Life to the Full*, FRF 3,350. PARIS, 26-27 May 1941, *Mandolin Player* (watercolour) FRF 70. PARIS, 28 March 1945, *Two Peasants in the Countryside*, FRF 2,200. PARIS, 25 May 1945, *Pantagruel*, FRF 1,300. LONDON, 14 June 1974, *Don't Wake Baby!*, Gns 1,400. PARIS, 4 Nov 1980, *Droit du Seigneur* (1872, oil on canvas, 27 1/2 x 49 1/2 ins / 70 x 126 cm) FRF 20,000. MILAN, 24 March 1982, *Interior* (oil on canvas, 24 1/2 x 15 1/4 ins / 62 x 39 cm) ITL 1,000,000. BARBIZON, 27 Feb 1983, *Gallant Musketeer* (1872, oil on panel, 16 1/4 x 12 3/4 ins / 41 x 32.5 cm) FRF 18,000. LONDON, 19 March 1986, *Awakening* (1882, oil on canvas, 47 1/4 x 78 3/4 ins / 120 x 200 cm) GBP 16,000. NEW YORK, 25 May 1988, *Couple Sporting under a Tree* (1880, oil on canvas, 31 x 18 1/2 ins / 78.7 x 47 cm) USD 7,700. NEW YORK, 24 Oct 1989, *Droit du Seigneur* (1872, oil on canvas, 27 1/4 x 49 1/4 ins / 69.5 x 125 cm) USD 19,800. NEW YORK, 17 Jan 1990, *In Flagrante Delicto* (oil on panel, 11 x 14 1/2 ins / 27 x 36.6 cm) USD 5,775. LONDON, 28 March 1990, *Report of Adultery* (oil on canvas, 105 1/2 x 141 ins / 268 x 358 cm) GBP 24,200. LONDON, 17 May 1991, *Romeo and Juliet* (oil on canvas, 16 1/4 x 10 3/4 ins / 41.2 x 27.2 cm) GBP 2,750. NEW YORK, 23 May 1991, *Courtly Gestures* (1880, oil on canvas, 31 x 18 1/2 ins / 78.7 x 47.3 cm) USD 9,900. CALAIS, 14 March 1993, *Bottoms Up!* (oil on panel, 10 x 6 ins / 25 x 15 cm) FRF 10,000. NEW YORK, 17 Feb 1994, *French Town by a River* (oil on card, 11 1/2 x 21 ins / 29.2 x 53.4 cm) USD 2,300. NEW YORK, 16 Feb 1995, *Relaxing in a Hammock* (oil on panel, 11 x 8 1/2 ins / 27.9 x 21.9 cm) USD 11,500. VENDÔME, 28 Jan 2002, *St Victor Library* (oil on canvas, 13 x 16 ins / 33 x 41 cm) EUR 3,900. MELUN, 1 Dec 2002, *Chatting by the Water* (oil on canvas, 19 x 13 ins / 47 x 32 cm) EUR 4,700. STOCKHOLM, 4 June 2003, *Trio* (oil on panel, 8 x 13 ins / 20 x 32 cm) SEK 20,000. HELSINKI, 15 May 2004, *Girl Chatting to Two Travelling Monks* (oil on panel, 8 x

13 ins / 21 x 33 cm) EUR 4,000. FONTAINEBLEAU, 6 June 2004, *Encounter* (oil on canvas, 16 x 11 ins / 41 x 28 cm) EUR 3,800.

GARNIER, Julien J.
French, 19th century.
Active in Paris.
Painter.
He was a member of the Société des Artistes Français from 1900 and participated in its exhibitions.

GARNIER, Louis
French, 17th - 18th century.
Born c. 1639, in Paris; died 21 September 1728.
Sculptor.
Louis Garnier worked mainly for Versailles and Invalides.

GARNIER, Louis-Joseph
French, 19th century.
Born 1822, in Valenciennes.
Painter. History painting.
He was a pupil of Picot and is cited by Siret.

GARNIER, Marie (Mme)
French, 19th century.
Active in Paris.
Miniaturist.

GARNIER, Maurice
French, 20th century.
Died 1945, in Vaux-sur-Mer (Charente-Maritime).
Painter, sculptor, designer.
Maurice Garnier produced some curious decorative pieces. He was one of the organisers of the Musée des Arts et Tradition Populaires in Paris.

GARNIER, Michel
French, 18th century.
Born 1753, in St-Cloud; died 1819.
Painter. Portraits, genre scenes.
Between 1793 and 1814, Michel Garnier exhibited several works in the style of the day at the Salon in Paris.
AUCTION RECORDS:
PARIS, 17 and 18 Dec 1918, *Treasured Portrait*, FRF 6,500. PARIS, 8-9 Dec 1919, *Young Girl Playing the Guitar*, FRF 430. PARIS, 22 Nov 1923, *Mother Placing a Crown on Her Child's Head*, FRF 6,000. PARIS, 4 May 1927, *Portrait of the Comte de H.*, FRF 4,600. PARIS, 14 Dec 1936, *Lady with Muff, Fashionable Figure* (watercolour) FRF 600. PARIS, 22 Jan 1941, *Gentle Resistance* (1793) FRF 48,000; *Young Musician*, FRF 23,600. PARIS, 9 March 1951, *Endangered Rose*; *Letter* (two pendants) FRF 1,000,000. PARIS, 29 March 1960, *Young Artist*, FRF 2,000. PARIS, 9 Dec 1967, *Musical Party*, FRF 11,500. MONTE CARLO, 20 June 1987, *Belle under the Arches of the Palais Royal* (1787, oil on canvas, 17 3/4 x 14 1/2 ins / 45 x 37 cm) FRF 1,900,000. MONACO, 16 June 1989, *Young Girl Punished* (1794, oil on canvas, 17 1/2 x 21 1/4 ins / 44.5 x 54 cm) FRF 1,554,000. PARIS, 22 June 1992, *They Agree* (1786, oil on canvas, 18 1/2 x 15 ins / 47 x 38 cm) FRF 660,000. PARIS, 22 March 1995, *Young Woman in a Park* (gouache, 7 x 5 3/4 ins / 18 x 14.5 cm) FRF 15,500. LONDON, 5 April 1995, *Young Girl Listening to Two Lovers Talking* (1789, oil on canvas, 18 1/2 x 153 ins / 46.7 x 388.5 cm) GBP 76,300. PARIS, 12 Dec 1995, *Young Woman Completing her Toilette* (1796, oil on canvas, 18 1/4 x 15 ins / 46.5 x 38 cm) FRF 280,000. PARIS, 27 May 1997, *Portrait of a Figure of Note from the Empire* (1805, oil on canvas, 23 1/2 x 19 3/4 ins / 60 x 50 cm) FRF 15,500. NEW YORK, 21 Oct 1997, *Music Lesson*; *Hide-and-Seek* (1789 and 1788, oil on panel, a pair, 5 3/4 x 4 1/2 ins / 14.6 x 11.4 cm and 5 1/2 x 4 1/4 ins/14 x 11.1 cm) USD 92,700. LONDON, 6 July 2000, *Interior with Lady Seated, Playing a Harp, Young Man Standing Behind Playing a Violin* (oil on canvas, 22 x 19 ins / 56 x 47 cm) GBP 24,000. NEW YORK, 25 Jan 2001, *Fashionably Dressed Young Woman in the Arcade of the Palais Royal, Paris* (1787, oil on canvas, 18 x 15 ins / 46 x 37 cm) USD 560,000. PARIS, 5 Dec 2001, *Young Lady Giving a Letter to her Servant* (oil on canvas, 17 x 21 ins / 44 x 54 cm) FRF 320,000. PARIS, 26 June 2002, *Departure of Monsieur de St-Marc for the Battle of Fontenoy* (1788, oil on canvas, 23 x 29 ins / 59 x 73 cm) EUR 265,000. PARIS, 2 Dec 2003, *Tearful Young Lady Reading a Letter, or The Wait* (1793, oil on canvas, 18 x 22 ins / 46 x 55 cm) EUR 85,000.

GARNIER, Narcisse
French, 19th century.
Painter.
He studied under David and exhibited portraits at the Paris Salon in 1822 and 1831.
BIBLIOGRAPHY:
Les Années romantiques, la peinture française de 1815 à 1850, exhibition catalogue, Musée des Beaux-Arts, Nantes; Gal. Nationales du Grand Palais, Paris, 1996.
MUSEUMS AND GALLERIES:
AUXERRE: *Male Portrait* - CAMBRAI: *Portrait of Cardinal d'Ailly; Portrait of Enguerrand de Monstrelet.*

GARNIER, Noël
French, 15th century.
Active in Paris at the end of the 15th century.
Engraver.
Noël Garnier was one of the earliest French engravers of ornamental work.

GARNIER, Pierre, also known as Préfichault
French, 15th century.
Painter, illuminator.
This artist worked at the court of King René of Anjou.

GARNIER, Pierre
French, 17th century.
Active in Paris in 1686.
Sculptor.

GARNIER, Pierre
French, 19th century.
Born 10 May 1847, in Lyons.
Painter.
He enrolled at the École des Beaux-Arts in Lyons in 1862 and studied under Reignier. He exhibited in Lyons from 1872 and in Paris from 1896, chiefly still-life compositions of fruit and flowers. His work is signed *P. Garnier*.

GARNIER, Thérèse
French, 20th century.
Engraver.
Thérèse Garnier exhibited at the Salon des Artistes Français from 1932.

GARNIER, Thérèse. See also **LAUDIER**

GARNIER, Tony. See **GARNIER Antoine**

GARNIER, Victor-Alexandre-Humbert
French, 19th century.
Born in Nancy.
Painter. Landscapes.
He was a pupil of J. Adler.
MUSEUMS AND GALLERIES:
LANGRES: *Season's End in the Vosges.*
AUCTION RECORDS:
PARIS, 28 May 1945, *Library of St-Victor*, FRF 1,750.

GARNIER. See also **GRANIER**

GARNIER-GEOFFROY, Daniel
French, 20th century.
Born 1923.
Draughtsman, watercolourist, painter (gouache).
Nudes, landscapes, seascapes.
Daniel Garnier-Geoffroy used the red chalk drawing technique of the Italian Renaissance and 17th-century French painters to convey the charm of the young female nudes he painted with such delicacy. For his landscapes and sea-

scapes he preferred to use ink, gouache or watercolour, which allowed him to capture fleeting moments of inspiration from nature.

GARNIER-RAFAT, Émilie
French, 19th - 20th century.
Born in Paris.
Miniaturist.
Émilie Garnier-Rafat exhibited in Paris at the Salon des Artistes Français and became a member of the Society in 1908.

GARNIER-SALBREUX, Pierre Henri
French, 20th century.
Born 1880, in Neuilly-sur-Seine.
Painter. Portraits.
Pierre Garnier-Salbreux studied under Humbert. He exhibited in Paris at the Salon des Artistes Français from 1910.

GARNJOBST, Hans
Swiss, 19th century.
Born 7 July 1863, in Basel.
Painter. Landscapes.
Garnjobst was a pupil of Gérome at art school. He travelled to Italy. He is noted for his *Autumn* and *Evening*. He won an honourable mention at the Exposition Universelle in Paris in 1900.

GARNON, François
French, 18th century.
Born 1738, in Paris; died 1769, in Paris.
Painter.
François Garnon worked for the Sèvres porcelain works.

GARNOT, André Saint Fare
French, 20th century.
Born in Paris.
Painter, draughtsman. Landscapes.
As well as his interesting landscapes, André Garnot produced humorous drawings. He took part in the major Paris Salons, notably the Salon des Tuileries.

GARNOT, Lucie
French, 19th - 20th century.
Born in Lyons.
Engraver.
Lucie Garnot studied under Lucien Gautier. She exhibited at the Salon des Artistes Français in Paris and received a commendation in 1910.

GARNOT-BEAUPÈRE, Marguerite
French, 19th - 20th century.
Born 19th century, in Nevers.
Painter. Genre scenes.
Marguerite Garnot-Beaupère became a member of the Société des Artistes Français in 1907. She exhibited at the Society's Salons and received a commendation in 1895.

GARNSEY, Elmer Ellsworth
American, 19th century.
Born 24 January 1862, in Holmdel; died 1946, in Atlantic City.
Active in White Plains.
Painter.
Elmer Ellsworth Garnsey was a pupil of George Maynard and Francis Lathrop in New York. He was awarded a bronze medal in Chicago in 1893 and an honourable mention at the Exposition Universelle in Paris in 1900. He painted mainly mural decorations.

GARNSEY, Julian Ellsworth
American, 20th century.
Born 1887, in New York; died 1969.
Painter, decorative designer.
Julian Ellsworth Garnsey was taught by Jean-Paul Laurens in Paris. He very soon became interested in the problems associated with large-scale mural decoration. He was a member of a number of American artists' associations, from which he received several awards.

GAROFALINI, Giacinto
Italian, 17th - 18th century.
Born 1665 or 1666, in Bologna; died 7 September 1723.
Painter. Religious subjects.
Garofalini was taught by a relative (M.A. Garofalini); he painted compositions for churches in Bologna, Brescia, Modena and Rimini.
AUCTION RECORDS:
ROME, 21 Nov 1989, *The Adoration of the Shepherds* (oil on canvas, oval 42 1/4 x 32 1/4 ins / 107 x 82 cm) ITL 5,500,000.

GAROFALO, Giuseppe
Italian, 18th century.
Active in Rome at the beginning of the 18th century.
Engraver.

GAROFALO, Tisio. See **TISIO BENVENUTO DA GAROFALO**

GAROFOLI, Lorenzo
Italian, 18th century.
Born at the beginning of the 18th century, in Arcieva.
Painter.
Garofoli studied under Conca.

GAROFOLI, Tommaso
Italian, 16th century.
Born in Pesaro.
Miniaturist.
Tommaso Garofoli transcribed and illuminated the statutes of the comune of Sigillo in Umbria.

GAROFOLO, Carlo
Italian, 17th century.
Painter (glass), designer of ornamental architectural features. Genre scenes.
Garofolo was a pupil of Luca Giordano.

GAROLI, Pietro Francesco, or Garola
Italian, 17th - 18th century.
Born 1638, in Turin; died 5 January 1716, in Rome.
Painter. Mythological subjects, portraits, interiors with figures, landscapes with figures, architectural views.
Garoli worked initially as a painter and restorer at the court of Savoia, then went to Venice where he was appointed professor of perspective at the Accademia di San Luca.
MUSEUMS AND GALLERIES:
ROME (Gal. dell'Accademia Nazionale di S Luca): *Portrait*.
AUCTION RECORDS:
PARIS, 1862, *Colosseum Interior, Rome*, FRF 38. LONDON, 26 Nov 1976, *Adonis Looking at a Painting of the Abduction of Europa* (oil on canvas, 37 1/2 x 52 ins / 95.3 x 132 cm) GBP 4,000. MILAN, 26 Nov 1985, *Landscape with Ruins and Figures* (oil on canvas, 13 x 16 1/4 ins / 33 x 41 cm) ITL 5,000,000. PARIS, 10 Dec 1993, *Dido and Aeneas in a Renaissance Architecture Setting; Temple Interior with Cleobis and Biton* (oil on canvas, a pair, each 26 1/2 x 35 ins / 67 x 89 cm) FRF 240,000. LONDON, 11 Dec 1996, *Capriccio of the Colosseum in Rome with Figures Inspecting the Ruins* (oil on canvas, 32 3/4 x 41 1/4 ins / 83 x 104.6 cm) GBP 6,900.

GARON, P.
French, 18th century.
Active in Paris.
Engraver (burin).
P. Garon engraved a series of 11 plates with animal subjects after J.-B. Oudry.

GARONNAIRE, Jean
French, 20th century.
Born 13 March 1945, in St-Étienne.
Active in Picardy from 1972.

Painter. Landscapes with figures.
Symbolism.

Jean Garonnaire's paintings have dreamy titles, such as *Isle of Daydreams* and *What Young Girls Dream Of*. They describe a mysterious, poetical world peopled by pale, enigmatic figures set against sad, dark, crumbling backgrounds.

Garonnaire began showing his work in group exhibitions in France in 1972, notably in Paris at the Salon d'Automne and the Société Nationale des Beaux-Arts. He also exhibited in Belgium, Japan, Morocco and the USA, among other countries. Solo exhibitions include those at the Galerie Bernheim in Paris in 1976 and the Centre Culturel Français in Casablanca in 1983. He received much recognition and numerous prizes.

GARONOT, Jacques
French, 16th century.
Active in Troyes at the beginning of the 16th century.
Painter.

GAROPESANI, Ferrucio
Italian, 20th century.
Born 1914, in Milan.
Painter. Fish.

Garopesani studied at the Accademia di Belle Arti di Brera in Milan and at the Grande Chaumière in Paris. He took part in the Venice Biennale of 1946 and the Rome Quadriennale of 1947. He subsequently exhibited at the Salon of the Société des Artistes Français in Paris.

AUCTION RECORDS:
BERN, 12 May 1990, *Shoal of Fish* (oil on canvas, 29 3/4 x 45 3/4 ins / 75.5 x 116.3 cm) CHF 2,500.

GAROUSTE, Gérard
French, 20th - 21st century.
Born 10 March 1946, in Paris.
Active in Marcilly-sur-Eure from 1984.
Painter (including gouache), installation artist, sculptor, engraver, draughtsman, illustrator. Mythological subjects, religious subjects, figure compositions, genre scenes, portraits, nudes, landscapes, still-lifes. Wall decorations, stage sets.
Nouvelle Figuration.

Gérard Garouste was mostly self-taught. He went to the École des Beaux-Arts in Paris for a brief period in 1970 during which he attended the studio of Gustave Singier. After seeing an exhibition of Dubuffet's work at the Musée des Arts Décoratifs in Paris, Garouste gave up his chosen career in humorous drawings, turning to painting and to his work in the theatre. Success came almost immediately. As Georges Durozoi commented: 'He quickly became the leader of a Post-Modern current; after having assimilated the essence of the different Avant-Garde groups, he returned to the tradition of "great painting".' State commissions included: a ceiling for the private apartments of the Élysée and the painting *St Theresa of Avila*, commissioned by the national committee of sacred art (1983); *Challenge of the Sun*, sculptures for the Palais-Royal gardens in Paris (1988); and the stage curtains for the Théâtre du Châtelet in Paris (1990).

Garouste began his long and extremely prolific career in theatrical scenery and décor in the mid-1960s. In 1965 he worked on *Chez l'Illustre Écrivain* (*At the Illustrious Writer's*) by Mirabeau in 1969, on *Le Lai de Barabas* by Arrabal at the Champs-Élysées studio and, in 1970, on *Les Fraises Musclées* (*The Brawny Strawberries*) by Jean-Michel Ribes at the Théatre La Bruyère. In 1977 Garouste presented *The Classical and the Indian* at Le Palace in Paris. The piece was a mixture of happening, performance art, and conceptual action based partly on Italian theatre, and Garouste was the author, producer, designer and actor.

Garouste then returned to painting, producing the *Police Comedy* series which made fun of the rigid rules of classical French theatre, while the 1979 work entitled *La Règle du Je* (*The Rule of I*) , a pun on *la règle du jeu* or 'the rule of the game', involved a series organised according to a mathematical code. From this, Garouste moved on to Greek and Roman mythology in works including *Canis Major* and *Lucretia*.

From 1984 Garouste turned his attention to literary texts, and in 1986 produced drawings for *Débat du Cœur et du Corps* (*Struggle of Heart and Body*) by François Villon. His 1987 *Away from the Calm*, based on Dante's *Divine Comedy*, was composed of drawings, engravings and paintings. With *Hell* Garouste began to develop his own, dream-like, vividly coloured, less figurative style. Later works draw their inspiration, at least indirectly, from the Bayeux Tapestry, 15th-century paintings, and the Old Testament, in particular the books of Isaiah and Ecclesiastes. From stage scenery painted in acrylic colours, Garouste also developed through gouache and engraving. His work also includes small reliefs in terracotta as well as full-sized statues where he takes his cue from the figures in his paintings. Garouste has drawn his inspiration from many sources; however, instead of allowing himself to be trapped into sterile repetition, he has used the opportunities to develop his own sardonic style and to create a world of his own.

Garouste has exhibited extensively, including at the following: the Musée d'Art et d'Industrie in St-Étienne (1980); the XIIth Paris Biennale (1980); the Musée National d'Art Moderne in Paris (1980, 1984); the Venice Biennale (1980, 1984); *Statement 1* in New York (1982); *Sainte Thérèse d'Avila dans l'Art Contemporain* (*St Theresa of Avila in Contemporary Art*) at the Musée du Luxembourg in Paris and the Tokyo Museum of Modern Art (1983); the São Paulo Biennale (1987); the Sydney Biennial (1988); and *Esprit des Lieux* (*The Spirit of Places*) , an exhibition of contemporary art and its presentation space, organised in the context of *Trésors Publics: 20 Ans de Création dans les Fonds Régionaux d'Art Contemporain* (*Public Treasury, 20 Years of Creation in the Regional Collection of Contemporary Art (FRAC)*) at the Papal Palace in Avignon (2003).

Solo exhibitions include the following: *Dessins Monumentaux* (*Monumental Drawings*) at the Galerie Zunini in Paris (1969) repeated 10 years later at the Galerie Travers in Paris and the Cannaviello Gallery in Milan; regular exhibitions at the Galerie Durand-Dessert in Paris (from 1980); regular exhibitions at the Castelli Gallery in New York; at the Musée National d'Art Moderne in Paris (1988); at the Stedelijk Museum in Amsterdam (1988); at the Kunsthalle in Düsseldorf (1988); *Rétrospective 1979-1991* (*Retrospective 1979-1991*) at the Galerie Durand-Dessert in Paris (2001); *Peintures et Indiennes* (*Paintings and Indians*) at the Musée des Beaux-Arts in Évreux (2001); *Ellipse*, an attempt at combining paintings and installations, at the Fondation Cartier in Paris (2001); *Les Saintes Ellipses de Gérard Garouste* (*Holy Ellipses by Gérard Garouste*) at the Chapelle St-Louis de la Salpêtre in Paris (2003); and an exhibition at the Galerie Daniel Templon in Paris (2004).

BIBLIOGRAPHY:
Joppolo, Giovanni, '*L'Épos de Gérard Garouste*' in *Opus International*, no. 95, periodical, Paris, autumn 1984. *Nouvelle Biennale de Paris*, exhibition catalogue, Electa, Le Moniteur, Paris, 1985. Lemaire, Gérard-Georges, '*Le Triomphe de la peinture*' in *Opus International*, no. 99, periodical, Paris, winter 1986. Millet, Catherine, *L'Art contemporain en France*, Flammarion, Paris, 1987. Martin, Jean-Hubert/Blistène, Bernard/Guidieri, Remo/Lageira, Jacinto, *Gérard Garouste*, exhibition catalogue, Musée national d'Art moderne, Éd. du Centre Georges-Pompidou, Paris, 1988. Millet, Catherine, '*L'Aventure personnelle de Gérard Garouste commence*' in *Art Press*, no. 121, periodical, Paris, January 1988. '*Dossier Gérard Garouste*' in *Opus International*, no. 108, periodical, Paris, May June 1988. Pacquement, Alfred, '*Indienne - Gérard Garouste*' in *Acquisitions 1989*, Fonds national d'Art contemporain, Par-

is, 1989. Dagbert, Anne, *'Gérard Garouste'* in *Art Press,* no. 165, periodical, Paris, 1992. Dagbert, Anne, *Gérard Garouste,* Georges Fall, Paris, 1996. *'Dossier Gérard Garouste'* in *Verso Arts et Lettres,* no. 14, periodical, Paris, April 1999. Cabanne, Pierre, *Gérard Garouste,* Expressions contemporaines, Angers, 2000. Zahm, Olivier (preface), et al., *Trésors publics, 20 ans de création dans les Fonds régionaux d'art contemporain,* Flammarion, Paris, 2003 (text in French and English).

MUSEUMS AND GALLERIES:

BORDEAUX (FRAC Aquitaine): *Banks of the Eunoe* (1986) - LYONS (FRAC Rhône-Alpes): *Dark Companion* (1982) - MARSEILLES (Mus. Cantini): *Orion and Cedalion* - MEXICO CITY (MMA) - MONTREAL (MAM) - PARIS (FNAC): *Untitled* (terracotta) - PARIS (MNAM-CCI): *Classical Orion, Indian Orion* (oil on canvas); *Orthos and the Classical* (drawing) - RHEIMS (FRAC Champagne-Ardenne): *Indian* (1987) - ROCHECHOUART (Mus. Départemental d'Art Contemporain): *Still-life* (1984) - SYDNEY (MMA) - TOKYO (MMA).

AUCTION RECORDS:

VERSAILLES, 28 June 1987, *Cerebus and the Mask* (1980, oil on canvas, 32 x 25 1/2 ins / 81 x 65 cm) FRF 59,000. PARIS, 14 Oct 1987, *Untitled* (1972, pastel, 21 1/2 x 39 1/4 ins / 54.5 x 99.5 cm) FRF 42,000. PARIS, 3 Dec 1987, *Reflection* (oil on canvas, 29 x 23 1/2 ins / 73.5 x 60 cm) FRF 28,000. PARIS, 13 Oct 1989, *Dog Lying Down* (oil on canvas, 25 1/2 x 21 1/4 ins / 65 x 54 cm) FRF 80,000. PARIS, 18 Feb 1990, *Untitled* (Indian ink, 9 3/4 x 9 ins / 25 x 22 cm) FRF 15,000. PARIS, 28 March 1990, *Police Comedy: The Three Objects, Masked Figures, Child Seen from Behind* (1979, oil on canvas, 28 3/4 x 39 3/4 ins / 73 x 101 cm) FRF 160,000. LONDON, 21 March 1991, *Goupil the Fox* (1982, charcoal and pencil/paper, 48 x 56 1/4 ins / 121 x 143 cm) GBP 4,950. PARIS, 5 Dec 1991, *To Whom Does the Dog Belong? Police Comedy Series* (oil on canvas, 50 1/2 x 66 1/4 ins / 128 x 168 cm) FRF 160,000. PARIS, 21 May 1992, *Two Figures* (1971, oil on canvas, 28 3/4 x 23 1/2 ins / 73 x 60 cm) FRF 38,000. PARIS, 29 Nov 1993, *Untitled* (1985, pastel/wallpaper, 48 x 32 ins / 121 x 81 cm) FRF 25,000. PARIS, 24 June 1994, *Police Comedy* (drawing, 31 x 23 ins / 78.5 x 57.5 cm) FRF 9,800. PARIS, 15 Dec 1994, *Indian* (1988, acrylic/canvas, 77 1/2 x 82 3/4 ins / 197 x 210 cm) FRF 120,000. PARIS, 13 Dec 1995, *Untitled* (oil on canvas, 78 3/4 x 70 3/4 ins / 200 x 180 cm) FRF 150,000. PARIS, 10 June 1996, *Untitled* (1987, drawing in Indian ink/paper, 13 x 16 1/4 ins / 33 x 41 cm) FRF 5,000. PARIS, 19 June 1996, *Constellation of the Dog* (1982, oil on canvas, 98 1/2 x 116 1/4 ins / 250 x 295 cm) FRF 180,000. PARIS, 28 April 1997, *Red Nude* (1982, oil on canvas, 51 1/4 x 63 1/2 ins / 130 x 161.5 cm) FRF 174,000. LONDON, 27 June 1997, *The Classical, the Mirror and the Dog* (1982, oil on canvas, 51 1/4 x 63 3/4 ins / 130 x 162 cm) GBP 13,800. PARIS, 21 March 1999, *Adhara, Study* (1981, oil on canvas, 51 x 67 ins / 130 x 170 cm) FRF 210,000. PARIS, 13 Oct 1999, *Untitled* (gouache, 26 x 20 ins / 65 x 50 cm) FRF 25,000. VERSAILLES, 2 April 2000, *Undergrowth* (oil on canvas, 51 x 77 ins / 130 x 195 cm) FRF 185,000. PARIS, 16 Dec 2000, *Untitled* (oil on canvas, 93 x 79 ins / 235 x 200 cm) FRF 235,000. PARIS, 21 Dec 2001, *Three Objects* (mixed media, 29 x 39 ins / 73 x 100 cm) FRF 70,000. PARIS, 16 April 2002, *Untitled* (c. 1984, pastel, red chalk and crayon, 22 x 39 ins / 55 x 100 cm) EUR 7,750. PARIS, 19 June 2002, *Allegorical Composition* (charcoal and graphite heightened with pastel, 31 x 22 ins / 78 x 57 cm) EUR 2,400. PARIS, 11 Oct 2003, *Man in a Green Jacket, Self-portrait* (1984, oil on canvas, 91 x 79 ins / 230 x 200 cm) EUR 59,000. PARIS, 21 Oct 2003, *Minemosye* (bronze, 22 x 8x6 ins / 55 x 21x14 cm) EUR 6,000. PARIS, 2 July 2004, *Untitled* (gouache, diptych, 26 x 20 ins / 65 x 50 cm) EUR 5,000.

GAROVI, Paolo, or Garvi
Italian, 16th century.
Active in Bissone.
Sculptor.

Paolo Garovi carved the sculptures of the baptismal fonts at Atril (Abruzzi).

GARP, Bo Mattson
Swedish, 16th century.
Active in Sweden c. 1500.
Painter.

Garp painted the frescoes in the church at Skelleftea.

GARP, Elon
Swedish, 20th century.
Born 1930, in Dalarna.
Painter.

Elon Garp studied at an art school in Stockholm from 1950 to 1952. He travelled in France, Spain, Greece, Turkey, Italy and Albania. He exhibited his works in a number of solo shows in Stockholm and various cities in Sweden, as well as in Paris in 1969. After some youthful works influenced by Post-Cubism, which might be called the Academicism of the mid 20th century, he found his way in a violent form of Expressionism, often bordering on the abstract in its indifference to the subject. His technique is similar to that of the CoBrA group.

GARRAND, Marc or Marcus. See **GERARDS Marcus, the Younger**

GARRARD, Charles
British, 19th century.
Active in London.
Sculptor.

Charles Garrard exhibited in London from 1816 to 1829, notably at the Suffolk Street Gallery, at the British Institution and, above all, at the Royal Academy.

GARRARD, E.
British, 18th century.
Active in London.
Painter. Landscapes.

E. Garrard exhibited at the Royal Academy in London in 1793.

GARRARD, George
British, 18th - 19th century.
Born 31 May 1760; died 8 October 1826, in Brompton.
Painter, sculptor. Portraits, genre scenes, landscapes, animals.

George Garrard worked for Sawray Gilpin before going on to study at the Royal Academy School. He made his Academy début in 1781 and was elected to associated membership in 1800. Examples of his work include *Peasant Attacked by Wolves* and *Woburn Abbey.*

AUCTION RECORDS:

LONDON, 17 June 1966, *Thoroughbred and Stable Lad,* Gns 2,400. LONDON, 24 Nov 1972, *Self-portrait,* Gns 2,400. LONDON, 31 March 1976, *Portrait of the Holderness Heifer* (oil on canvas, 40 1/4 x 52 ins / 102 x 132 cm) GBP 5,500. LONDON, 18 May 1977, *Thomas Crib, Pugilist* (1825, bronze, h. 10 1/2 ins / 26.5 cm) GBP 600. MENTMORE, 25 May 1977, *Landscape with Gentleman and a Bay Horse* (oil on canvas, 26 3/4 x 35 ins / 68 x 89 cm) GBP 5,800. LOS ANGELES, 9 Nov 1977, *Kneeling Nude* (1921, bronze, h. 36 1/2 ins / 92.7 cm) USD 1,900. LONDON, 27 March 1981, *Landscape with Thoroughbred and Groom* (oil on canvas, 37 x 49 1/4 ins / 94 x 125 cm) GBP 19,000. LONDON, 18 Oct 1985, *Forge* (oil/copper, 7 1/4 x 9 3/4 ins / 18.4 x 24.8 cm) GBP 1,600. LONDON, 20 April 1990, *Courtyard of the Whitbread Brewery, Chiswell Street, London* (1783, oil on canvas, 28 x 36 ins / 71 x 91.5 cm) GBP 35,200. LONDON, 13 Nov 1996, *Landscape with Young Stallion and Owner* (oil on canvas, 37 x 50 1/2 ins / 94 x 128.5 cm) GBP 12,650. NEW YORK, 26 Feb 1997, *Various Portraits* (oil on canvas/panel, series of six, 17 1/2 x 14 1/4 ins / 44.5 x 36.2 cm) USD 18,400.

GARRARD, H.
British.

Painter.
Mentioned in *Art Prices Current.*
AUCTION RECORDS:
LONDON, 24 March 1911, *Fox-hunting,* GBP 11.

GARRATT, Arthur Paine
British, 19th century.
Born 19th century, in London.
Painter.
Arthur Paine Garratt was awarded a silver medal at the 1903 Salon des Artistes Français.

GARRATT, William
British, 19th century.
Active in London.
Painter. Landscapes.
William Garratt exhibited in London from 1827 to 1831, notably at the Royal Academy, the British Institution and the Suffolk Street Gallery.

GARRAUD, Gabriel-Joseph
French, 19th century.
Born 23 March 1807, in Dijon; died 5 June 1880, in Dijon.
Sculptor.
He studied initially in Dijon, then under Rude in Paris. He exhibited at the Salon from 1838 to 1875, showing group compositions, and was awarded a bronze medal in 1838 and a silver in 1844. Garraud was appointed to a directorship of the École des Beaux-Arts in Paris in 1848 and then as an inspector (an appointment that was subsequently rescinded). He is remembered for his marble statue of the *Marquis de Laplace* in the Paris Observatory.
MUSEUMS AND GALLERIES:
DIJON: *Orpheus; Secret of Love; James de Montry;* four low reliefs - VERSAILLES: *Christophe de Thou, First President of the Paris Parliament; Field Marshal Jean Werestanz.*

GARRAUD, Léon
French, 20th century.
Born 19 January 1877, in St-Moreil (Creuse); died 27 August 1961, in Lyons.
Painter. Figures, portraits, genre scenes, landscapes, urban landscapes, still-lifes.
Léon Garraud spent his childhood in Oullins in the Rhône region and later moved to Lyons where he studied at the École des Beaux-Arts in the studio of Pierre Bonnaud and Tony Tollet. He made a trip to Italy and returned with numerous studies of Florence and Venice. He exhibited at the Salon de Lyons from 1902, receiving a bronze medal in 1905 and again in 1907, and at the Salon des Artistes Français in Paris from 1920 to 1938.

He mainly painted landscapes of the suburbs of Lyons and portraits and genre scenes. In 1912, Henry Béraud described him as 'A talent made of strength and serenity... After those of Jacques Martin, his portraits are the most solid and most alive seen in any Lyons Salon of the last ten years. As a landscapist he wanders among the grey and sorry suburbs of our city and returns with large landscapes barricaded with crooked trees, morning and twilight scenes which are heartrending apotheoses of desolation'. He was a prolific artist and his works include *Bridge on the Saône at St-Georges; The Saône at Pont du Change, Lyons; Still-life with Fruit.*
AUCTION RECORDS:
LYONS, 9 June 1982, *Bridge on the Saône at St-Georges* (oil on panel) FRF 2,400; *Still-life with Fruit,* FRF 5,600. LYONS, 24 Oct 1984, *Still-life with Grapes,* FRF 3,000. LYONS, 4 March 2001, *Still-life with Grapes* (oil on canvas, 14 x 18 ins / 35 x 46 cm) FRF 11,000. LYONS, 4 March 2001, *Still-life with Peaches* (oil on canvas, 12 x 16 ins / 30 x 40 cm) FRF 11,500.

GARRAUD, Sylvie
20th century.
Sculptor.
She took part in the exhibition *Colour and Construction* at the Museum of Grenoble in 1996.
BIBLIOGRAPHY:
Suchère, Éric, '*Couleur et construction*' in *Art Press* n° 212 periodical, Paris, April 1996.

GARRAUX, Florentin
Swiss, 19th century.
Born 2 October 1859, near Solothurn.
Painter.
Garraux worked and exhibited in Bern, Basel and Zurich.

GARRAWAY, Edward
British, 19th century.
Active in London.
Painter. Genre scenes.
Edward Garraway exhibited in London from 1875 to 1878, chiefly at the Suffolk Street Gallery.

GARRAWAY, George Hervey
British, 19th century.
Active in Liverpool.
Painter. History painting, genre scenes.
George Hervey Garraway exhibited in London from 1870, mainly at the Royal Academy and the Suffolk Street Academy.
MUSEUMS AND GALLERIES:
LIVERPOOL: *Florentine Poet.*
AUCTION RECORDS:
LONDON, 7 July 1987, *Whitby* (1878, oil on canvas, 39¼ x 60 ins / 100 x 152.5 cm) GBP 1,100.

GARREAU, Alphonse
French, 19th century.
Born 17 April 1792, in Versailles.
Painter. Religious subjects, portraits, landscapes.
He enrolled at the École des Beaux-Arts, Paris, on 4 March 1816, where he studied under Gros. He exhibited at the Paris Salon from 1819 to 1827. Garreau produced portraits and other diverse compositions, among them *Othryades, Spartan Leader, Martyred St Sebastian* and *Young Nymph.*
AUCTION RECORDS:
PARIS, 3 Dec 1987, *View of the gardens at Versailles* (oil on canvas, 29¼ x 39¼in/74 x 100cm) FRF 9,500.

GARREAU, Georges Raoul
French, 20th century.
Born 6 February 1885, in Paris.
Watercolourist, sculptor.
Georges Garreau exhibited at the Salon des Artistes Français in Paris.
AUCTION RECORDS:
LOKEREN, 8 Oct 1994, *Spanish Dancers* (bronze, h. 17½ ins / 44.5 cm, w. 10½ ins/26.5 cm) BEF 55,000.

GARREAU, Louis
French, 18th century.
Active in Paris.
Draughtsman, engraver (burin).
Louis Garreau produced some engravings with genre themes.
AUCTION RECORDS:
PARIS, 4 and 5 June 1928, *Figures and a Boat near a Cave* (watercolour) FRF 1,100.

GARREAU, Marguerite
French, 20th century.
Born in Paris.
Watercolourist, pastellist.
Marguerite Garreau exhibited in Paris at the Salon des Artistes Français.

GARRELS, Frédéric
Belgian, 20th century.
Born 1919, in Antwerp.
Painter, illustrator, decorative designer.

Frédéric Garrels studied with Professor Opsomer at the Antwerp academy.

GARRET, Françoise
French, 20th century.
Born 3 July 1945, in Paris.
Painter. Portraits, scenes with figures, animals.

Françoise Garret is a painter but also explores the potential of the computer and does graphic art. Her work is Abstract, tending to the decorative. She uses dynamic forms and bright colours, introducing Figurative motifs such as the horse. She has exhibited at different Salons in Paris, including the Salon d'Automne, the Salon Comparaisons and the Salon du Dessin et de la Peinture à l'Eau. Solo exhibitions include those at the museum of Draguignan in 1985 and the Musée des Jacobins in Toulouse in 1988. She was awarded the Prix Othon Freisz in 1971.

BIBLIOGRAPHY:
Au triple galop. Peintures à l'huile et peintures sur ordinateur de Françoise Garret, exhibition catalogue, Banque Bred, Paris, 1990 (office of the Paris-Opéra).

GARRET, G.
British.
Painter. Landscapes, animals.

Mentioned in *Art Prices Current*.

AUCTION RECORDS:
LONDON, 20 March 1911, *Two Landscapes, Livestock* (three items) GBP 3.

GARRET, H.
British, 17th century.
Active in London c. 1650.
Painter.

GARRET, Jedd. See **GARET**

GARRET, William
British, 18th century.
Active in Newcastle at the end of the 18th century.
Engraver (wood).

William Garret published a series of 13 small drawings, the last of which represents *Death Leading a Woman to the Tomb*.

GARRET, Xavier
French, 19th century.
Born in Vesoul (Haute-Saône).
Painter. Still-lifes.

He first exhibited at the Salon in 1880.

GARRETSON, Della
American, 19th century.
Born 19th century, in Logan (Ohio).
Painter.

Della Garretson exhibited at the Salon des Artistes Français in 1902.

GARRETT, Clara Maria, or Mrs Edmund A. Pfeifer
American, 20th century.
Born 2 March 1882, in St Louis.
Sculptor.

Clara Garrett studied in her home town, then went to work in Paris at the École des Beaux-Arts and with Bourdelle and Marqueste. She was awarded a bronze medal in St Louis in 1904.

GARRETT, Edmund Henry
American, 19th - 20th century.
Born 19 October 1853, in Albany; died 1929.
Active in Boston.
Painter, engraver, illustrator. Landscapes.

Edmund Garrett studied in Paris with Jean-Paul Laurens, Boulanger, Lefebvre and Leroux. He was awarded a silver medal in Boston.

AUCTION RECORDS:
NEW YORK, 19 June 1981, *Twelfth Night* (1914, oil on canvas, 29 x 18 3/4 ins / 73.6 x 47.6 cm) USD 1,000. NEW YORK, 31 Jan 1985, *Landscape at Sunset* (oil on canvas, 25 1/4 x 14 1/2 ins / 64.1 x 36.8 cm) USD 1,600.

GARRETT, Thomas Balfour
Australian, 20th century.
Born 1879; died 1952.
Painter, watercolourist, monotype artist. Genre scenes, scenes with figures, landscapes, landscapes with figures.

AUCTION RECORDS:
MELBOURNE, 11 March 1977, *Green Door with White Cat* (mixed media/mounted paper/card, 13 1/4 x 12 1/2 ins / 33.5 x 31.5 cm) AUD 900. MELBOURNE, 20 March 1978, *Tired* (monotype, 12 3/4 x 11 ins / 32.5 x 27 cm) AUD 800. SYDNEY, 20 Oct 1980, *The Blue Door* (monotype, 9 3/4 x 8 3/4 ins / 25 x 22.5 cm) AUD 3,200. SYDNEY, 29 June 1981, *Evening* (watercolour, 5 x 7 ins / 12.5 x 17.5 cm) AUD 700. SYDNEY, 28 June 1982, *The Country Road* (monotype, 11 x 15 ins / 27 x 38 cm) AUD 2,800. ARMADALE, 11 April 1984, *Street Scene* (watercolour, 9 1/2 x 7 1/2 ins / 24 x 19 cm) AUD 900. MELBOURNE, 7 Nov 1984, *Middle Harbour* (monotype, 10 1/4 x 10 ins / 26 x 25.5 cm) AUD 2,600. MELBOURNE, 6 April 1987, *Lepkins Castle* (watercolour, 16 1/2 x 14 1/2 ins / 42 x 37 cm) AUD 9,500. SYDNEY, 17 April 1988, *The Red Orchard Parramatta* (watercolour, 23 1/4 x 11 3/4 ins / 59 x 30 cm) AUD 3,000. SYDNEY, 4 July 1988, *Pastoral Morning* (watercolour, 9 x 17 ins / 23 x 43 cm) AUD 3,750. SYDNEY, 2 July 1990, *The Isolated Cove* (watercolour, 9 3/4 x 14 1/4 ins / 25 x 36 cm) AUD 3,000. MELBOURNE, 26 April 1999, *Cityscape* (watercolour, 15 x 12 ins / 37 x 31 cm) AUD 3,600. VICTORIA, 9 Nov 1999, *Green Door* (watercolour, 9 x 11 ins / 24 x 27 cm) AUD 3,200. VICTORIA, 8 Aug 2000, *Convent* (monotype and gouache, 15 x 13 ins / 37 x 34 cm) AUD 4,600. PADDINGTON, 3 June 2001, *Gums and Old Dray by a Pool* (oil on canvas, 19 x 23 ins / 48 x 58 cm) AUD 7,000. MELBOURNE, 2 April 2003, *Figure Approaching a House* (watercolour, 9 x 12 ins / 23 x 30 cm) AUD 2,800. VICTORIA, 10 May 2004, *Stone Bridge* (mixed media on paper, 9 x 12 ins / 24 x 30 cm) AUD 3,200.

GARREZ, René-Joseph
French, 19th century.
Born 1802, in Paris; died 1852, in Paris.
Painter, architect. Urban landscapes.

MUSEUMS AND GALLERIES:
AVIGNON: *View of the Town*.

AUCTION RECORDS:
PARIS, 31 March-1 April 1924, *Upper Chapel of S Francesco at Assisi* (watercolour) FRF 115. PARIS, 27 March 1926, *View of Venice* (watercolour) FRF 250.

GARRI, Colomba
Italian, 18th century.
Active in Naples.
Painter. Still-lifes, flowers.

Colomba Garri was the wife of the ornamental artist Tommaso Castellano. Her four daughters were all artists: Francisca and Bibiena were landscape painters, Ruffina painted flowers and Apollonia painted figures and scenes.

GARRI, Giorgio
Italian, 18th century.
Died c. 1731, in Naples.
Painter.

Georgio Garri was a pupil of Casissa; he painted landscapes and seascapes.

AUCTION RECORDS:
LONDON, 28 Nov 1962, *Two women bring flowers to a fountain; Woman by fountain decorating a bust*, GBP 2,200.

GARRICQ, François
French, 17th century.

Active in Paris in 1675.
Painter, sculptor, engraver, illuminator.

GARRIDO, Eduardo Leon
Spanish, 19th - 20th century.
Born 20 February 1856, in Madrid; died 24 February 1949, in Caen.
Also active in France.
Painter. History painting, genre scenes, figures, portraits.

Eduardo Garrido studied under the painter Vicente Palmaroli y Gonzalez and spent a brief period in Paris. He taught at the school of arts and crafts in Varennes. He exhibited in Spain, Munich, London and at various Paris Salons.

After his visit to Paris he became interested in society painting. He painted scenes from the life of the aristocracy, balls and receptions in Rococo interiors, each being a pretext for the celebration of the youthful beauty of women. His paintings include: *Lady Playing a Lute, The Masked Ball, Dancing Scene, Portrait of a Man, Portrait of a Woman, The Letter, Repose, The Great Boulevards of Paris, The Road* and *Return from the Walk.*

E L Garrido

Bibliography:

Arnáiz, José Manuel/López Jiménez, Javier/Merchán Díaz, Manuel (ed.), '*Cien años de pintura en Espana y Portugal (1830-1930)*' in vol. III, Antiqvaria, Madrid, 1989. *Pintura española del siglo XIX obras para una colección*, Gal. Concha Barrios, Madrid, 1990.

Auction records:

London, 24 Nov 1976, *Colombine* (oil on panel, 18 x 14 1/2 ins / 46 x 37 cm) GBP 1,100. New York, 12 May 1978, *Stroll in the Park* (oil on panel, 16 x 12 1/4 ins / 40.5 x 31 cm) USD 2,700. London, 20 June 1980, *The Letter* (oil on panel, 18 x 14 1/2 ins / 46 x 37 cm) GBP 2,500. Barcelona, 25 May 1982, *Portrait of a Woman* (oil on canvas, 29 1/2 x 46 ins / 75 x 116 cm) ESP 310,000. Madrid, 22 Oct 1984, *Artist and Model* (oil on panel, 19 1/2 x 24 ins / 49.5 x 61 cm) ESP 900,000. New York, 27 Feb 1986, *The Minuet* (oil on panel, 21 1/4 x 25 3/4 ins / 54 x 65.5 cm) USD 10,000. Paris, 9 April 1987, *Young Woman with a Letter* (oil on canvas, 39 1/4 x 32 ins / 100 x 81 cm) FRF 210,000. Paris, 30 Nov 1987, *Young Woman* (oil on panel, 9 1/2 x 7 1/2 ins / 24 x 19 cm) FRF 215,000. Paris, 16 Oct 1988, *Elegant Young Woman* (oil on panel, 13 3/4 x 11 ins / 35 x 27 cm) FRF 26,000. London, 17 Feb 1989, *A Good Book* (oil on panel, 8 x 9 3/4 ins / 20.5 x 25 cm) GBP 6,820. New York, 24 May 1989, *Elegant Woman with her Dog* (oil on panel, 16 x 12 1/4 ins / 40.6 x 31.1 cm) USD 28,600. Monaco, 17 June 1989, *Elegant Women at a Café* (1884, oil on panel, 22 x 18 ins / 55 x 45.5 cm) FRF 488,400. New York, 24 Oct 1989, *The Serenade* (oil on panel, 20 3/4 x 25 1/2 ins / 53 x 65 cm) USD 39,600. New York, 25 Oct 1989, *Elegant Young Woman in a Red Dress* (oil on canvas, 33 3/4 x 45 1/2 ins / 85.6 x 115.6 cm) USD 77,000. London, 22 Nov 1989, *Woman with Fan* (oil on panel, 21 3/4 x 15 ins / 55.5 x 38 cm) GBP 9,350. London, 15 Feb 1990, *The Beautiful Musician* (oil on panel, 9 1/4 x 12 1/2 ins / 23.5 x 32 cm) GBP 4,400. New York, 28 Feb 1990, *Stroll in the Village* (oil on panel, 10 1/4 x 13 3/4 ins / 26 x 34.9 cm) USD 30,800. New York, 23 May 1990, *Young Women on a Terrace* (oil on panel, 28 1/2 x 22 3/4 ins / 72.7 x 57.8 cm) USD 38,500. London, 22 Nov 1990, *Young Woman Dressing in Front of her Mirror* (oil on card, 13 x 9 1/2 ins / 33 x 24 cm) GBP 2,860. London, 28 Nov 1990, *Lady with a Basket of Flowers* (oil on canvas, 45 x 32 3/4 ins / 114 x 83 cm) GBP 19,800. New York, 22 May 1991, *Woman with Mandolin* (oil on panel, 24 x 19 3/4 ins / 61 x 50.2 cm) USD 29,700. New York, 17 Oct 1991, *The Minuet* (oil on panel, 28 1/4 x 36 1/4 ins / 72 x 92 cm) USD 47,300. New York, 20 Feb 1992, *The Farandole* (oil on panel, 31 1/2 x 39 3/4 ins / 80 x 101 cm) USD 71,500. New York, 28 May 1992, *The Secret* (oil on panel). Paris, 1 July 1992, *The Minuet* (oil on panel, 25 1/4 x 31 3/4 ins / 64 x 80.5 cm) FRF 160,000. New York, 30 Oct 1992, *Young Woman Reading in a Drawing Room* (oil on panel, 8 x 10 3/4 ins / 20.6 x 27.2 cm) USD 12,100. New York, 17 Feb 1993, *The Sketch Book* (oil on panel, 21 1/2 x 15 3/4 ins / 54.9 x 40.3 cm) USD 24,150. Milan, 16 March 1993, *The Collector* (oil on canvas, 13 x 9 1/2 ins / 33 x 24 cm) ITL 6,500,000. London, 18 June 1993, *Young Woman Admiring a Picture* (oil on panel, 13 x 9 1/2 ins / 33 x 24 cm) GBP 4,830. Calais, 4 July 1993, *Portrait of a Man Sitting Smoking a Pipe* (oil on panel, 11 x 13 3/4 ins / 27 x 35 cm) FRF 9,000. Paris, 19 Nov 1993, *The Concert* (oil on panel, 24 x 28 3/4 ins / 61 x 73 cm) FRF 150,000. New York, 15 Feb 1994, *Elegant Young Woman Holding a Fan* (oil on panel, 16 x 12 1/4 ins / 40.6 x 31.4 cm) USD 9,775. Paris, 22 March 1994, *Preparations for the Ball* (oil on panel, 19 3/4 x 24 ins / 50 x 61 cm) FRF 80,000. New York, 16 Feb 1995, *Gathering Wild Flowers* (1891, oil on panel, 30 x 23 ins / 76.2 x 58.4 cm) USD 28,750. London, 17 March 1995, *On the Beach* (oil on panel, 13 x 9 1/2 ins / 33 x 24 cm) GBP 10,120. New York, 24 May 1995, *The Beautiful Guitar Player* (oil on panel, 21 1/2 x 18 ins / 54.9 x 45.7 cm) USD 9,200. London, 15 Nov 1995, *The Mandolin Player* (oil on panel, 21 1/4 x 17 3/4 ins / 54 x 45 cm) GBP 7,475. Carpentras, 28 Jan 1996, *Elegant Woman Playing the Violin; Elegant Woman en Deshabillé* (oil on panel, a pair, 24 x 19 ins / 61 x 48 cm and 24 x 17 1/4 ins/61 x 44 cm) FRF 205,000. New York, 23-24 May 1996, *The Courtsey* (oil on panel, 30 x 21 3/4 ins / 76.2 x 55.2 cm) USD 17,250. New York, 23 Oct 1997, *Garden Flowers* (oil on panel, 21 1/2 x 18 ins / 54.6 x 45.7 cm) USD 17,250.

GARRIDO, Juan
Spanish, 17th century.
Active in Valladolid.
Sculptor.

Juan Garrido is referred to as a sculptor in the inventory of goods relinquished by Juana Martínez, widow of Isaac de Juni, in 1602.

GARRIDO, Leandro Rámon
Spanish, 19th - 20th century.
Born 27 September 1868, in Bayonne, France; died 1909, in Bayonne.
Active in France from 1890.
Painter. Portraits, genre scenes, landscapes with figures.

Leandro Garrido had an English mother and spent his youth in Paris and then Great Britain. By 1890 he had returned to Paris to study at the school of fine arts. He exhibited at the Salon des Artistes Français in Paris from 1893 to 1898.

Garrido painted genre scenes, landscapes with figures and portraits with a romantic atmosphere, including: *Midnight Swim, En Conseil de Famille (Board of Guardians), Young Girl Taking Tea* and *Lady with Gloves.* His work is reminiscent of Zuloaga in its choice of subject, rejecting the anecdotal and in its simplified approach.

Bibliography:

Arnáiz, José Manuel/López Jiménez, Javier/Merchán Díaz, Manuel (ed.), '*Cien años de pintura en Espana y Portugal (1830-1930)*' in vol. III, Antiqvaria, Madrid, 1989.

Museums and Galleries:

Glasgow: *Lady with Gloves* - Liverpool: *En Conseil de Famille (Board of Guardians).*

Auction records:

Paris, 24 Feb 1928, *The Comparison,* FRF 2,900. Paris, 4 April 1928, *At the Entrance to the Alcove,* FRF 720. London, 5 Feb 1982, *Reverie* (oil on canvas, 26 1/2 x 19 1/2 ins / 67.2 x 49.5 cm) GBP 1,100. London, 21 March 1984, *Reverie* (1890, oil on canvas, 25 1/2 x 19 1/4 ins / 65 x 49 cm) GBP 1,500. Lokeren, 28 May 1988, *Reverie* (1904, oil on canvas, 25 1/2 x 19 1/4 ins / 65 x 49 cm) BEF 200,000. Los Angeles, 9 June 1988, *Dancing Reflections* (1891, oil on canvas, 26 x 17 1/2 ins / 66 x 44.5 cm) USD

1,870. LONDON, 15 Feb 1990, *The Doll* (1902, oil on canvas, 32 1/4 x 25 1/2 ins / 82 x 65 cm) GBP 6,600. LOKEREN, 15 May 1993, *The Flute Player* (1899, oil on canvas, 35 1/2 x 51 1/4 ins / 90 x 130 cm) BEF 240,000. PARIS, 27 May 1994, *Elegant Lady at a Masked Ball* (oil on panel, 16 1/4 x 13 ins / 41 x 33 cm) FRF 29,000. NEW YORK, 12 Feb 1998, *Woman Dressed in a Kimono* (1899, oil on canvas, 31 3/4 x 23 ins / 80.7 x 58.5 cm) USD 18,400.

GARRIDO, Louis Édouard
French, 20th century.
Born 1 July 1893, in La Varenne-St-Maur; died 13 May 1982, in Caen.
Painter, engraver. Landscapes, seascapes.

Louis Garrido was the son of a Spanish immigrant. He moved to Caen in 1921 and became involved in various social and cultural activities. In 1950 he moved to St-Vaast-La-Hougue. Sometimes referred to as an animal engraver, he was principally a painter of the typical landscapes of Normandy and of seascapes of the Normandy coast.

From 1926 onwards he took part in many regional group exhibitions, including regularly at the Salon des Artistes Bas-Normands. In 1972 he exhibited a collection of his paintings at the Hôtel d'Escoville in Caen. In 1982 his work was celebrated with an event at the Grenier à Sel in Honfleur.

GARRIDO, Louis-Édouard
French (?), 19th century.
Born 1856; died 1906.
Painter. Figures.

Perhaps confused with an artist of the same name or possibly even his own father, also a painter.

BIBLIOGRAPHY:
Vatin, J. L., *Louis-Édouard Garrido: le peintre de la Normandie*, C. Corlet, Condé-sur-Noireau, 1983.

AUCTION RECORDS:
PARIS, 23 May 1990, *Self-portrait with Palette* (oil on panel) FRF 5,000.

GARRIDO DE HERRERA, Juan
Spanish, 19th century.
Born in the 19th century.
Painter, watercolourist. Genre scenes.

From 1881, Juan Garrido de Herrera took part in the exhibitions of the society of watercolourists in Madrid.

GARRIDO Y AGUDO, María de la Soledad
Spanish, 19th century.
Born in the 19th century, in Salamanca.
Painter. Portraits, genre scenes.

María Garrido y Agudo was a pupil of Juan Peyro. She first exhibited in Madrid in 1876 and in the same year in Philadelphia.

AUCTION RECORDS:
PARIS, 16 and 17 May 1892, *Sudden Gale*, FRF 360. PARIS, 6 March 1893, *Model Resting*, FRF 400. PARIS, 27 April 1897, *Rest*, FRF 115. PARIS, 21 March 1898, *At the Ball*, FRF 320. NEW YORK, 18 and 19 Feb 1904, *Fortune Teller*, USD 225; *Pavane*, USD 810. LONDON, 11 April 1908, *Contemplation*, GBP 2. PARIS, 30 and 31 March 1910, *Minuet*, FRF 780. PARIS, 30 Oct 1925, *Pavane*, FRF 2,300.

GARRIGA, Joseph Grau. See **GRAU GARRIGA Joseph**

GARRIGUE, François
French, 17th century.
Painter.

François Garrigue was a member of the Académie St-Luc and was reportedly in Paris on 19 April 1675.

GARRIGUE, Honoré
French, 17th century.
Active in Marseilles.
Sculptor (wood).

GARRIGUES, Arnaud
French, 17th century.
Painter.

Arnaud Garrigues worked for the cathedral in Rodez in 1614.

GARRIGUES, Bernard
French, 16th century.
Born in Pézenas (Hérault).
Painter.

Bernard Garrigues was living in Lyons in 1508 and 1511. He is known to have painted pennants and banners.

GARRIOT
French, 18th century.
Born in Toulouse.
Miniaturist.

GARRISON, Eve
American, 20th century.
Born in Boston.
Painter.

Eve Garrison studied at the Chicago Art Institute. She superimposes classical figuration on backgrounds created using abstract geometric techniques, allowing the background to show through the subject. She has exhibited her work several times in the USA.

GARRO, José
Spanish, 17th century.
Sculptor.

José Garro worked for Huesca Cathedral in 1610.

GARROD, Violet
British, 20th century.
Born 1898.
Painter, watercolourist.

Violet Garrod was a member of many art societies. She exhibited at the Royal Academy in London and various other exhibitions.

GARRON, Jules-Paul de
French, 19th century.
Born in Paris.
Engraver.

He studied under Bury and Pfnor. Between 1861 and 1879 he exhibited at the Paris Salon.

GARRONE, Joséphine
French, 19th century.
Died 1888 or 1889, in Lyons.
Painter.

She lived and worked in Lyons and exhibited oil and pastel portraits and figure studies at the Lyons Salon from 1868 to 1885.

GARROTE Y RAMOS, Damaso
Spanish, 19th century.
Born in the 19th century, in Madrid.
Painter. Genre scenes.

Damaso Garrote y Ramos was a pupil of Luis Ferrant. He first exhibited in Madrid around 1871.

GARROUSTE, Henri
French, 20th century.
Born 1890, in Paris.
Painter, designer. Figures, portraits.

Henri Garrouste exhibited *Balinese Woman with Bare Breasts* at the Salon des Artistes Indépendants in Paris in 1926. He went on to exhibit at other Salons, including the Salon des Artistes Français, the Salon d'Hiver and the Salon de Mai in 1958.

He also produced a mural decoration for the Maison des Combattants Républicains in Paris.

MUSEUMS AND GALLERIES:
ORADOUR-SUR-GLANE: *Pietà*.
AUCTION RECORDS:
CALAIS, 9 Dec 1990, *Bathing by Moonlight* (oil on canvas, 23 1/2 x 19 3/4 ins / 60 x 50 cm) FRF 11,000.

GARRY, Augustin Marie Joseph
French, 19th - 20th century.
Sculptor.
Augustin Garry worked at Maisons-Lafitte. He exhibited in Paris at the Salon des Artistes Français, becoming a member of the Salon in 1896.

GARRY, Charley
French, 20th century.
Born 1891, in Paris.
Painter. Nudes, landscapes.
Charley Garry studied under Jules Adler and Gabriel Ferrier. From 1912 onwards he exhibited regularly at the Salon des Artistes Français in Paris. He also exhibited at the Salon de la Société Nationale des Beaux-Arts and the Salon des Indépendants in Paris.

Garry's light-hearted scenes enjoyed a certain degree of success.
AUCTION RECORDS:
PARIS, 17 July 1942, *Landscapes* (two pendants) FRF 60. PARIS, 21 Feb 1947, *Landscape,* FRF 5,500. BRUSSELS, 15 June 1999, *Jazy* (1941, oil on canvas, 36 x 26 ins / 92 x 65 cm) BEF 115,000.

GARSIA, Stephanus. See **GARCIA**

GARSIDE, Oswald
British, 19th - 20th century.
Born 1879; died 1942.
Painter, watercolourist. Landscapes.

Oswald Garside

MUSEUMS AND GALLERIES:
WARRINGTON: *Bewsey Lock in Winter* (watercolour); *Old Staithes, near Whitby* (watercolour).
AUCTION RECORDS:
LONDON, 25 Jan 1989, *Calm Evening* (watercolour, 11 1/2 x 17 ins / 29 x 43 cm) GBP 660. LONDON, 12 May 1993, *Ackers Lane in Stockton Heath* (1925, watercolour and pastel, 11 1/2 x 10 1/2 ins / 29.5 x 26.5 cm) GBP 575.

GARSIDE, Thomas Hilton
Canadian, 20th century.
Born 1906; died 1980.
Painter. Landscapes.
Thomas Garside painted a wide variety of landscapes in the province of Quebec.
AUCTION RECORDS:
TORONTO, 9 May 1977, *Red River* (oil on card, 19 3/4 x 23 1/2 ins / 50 x 60 cm) CAD 1,300. NEW YORK, 26 June 1985, *Curling, Newfoundland* (oil on canvas, 15 x 20 ins / 38.3 x 50.8 cm) USD 1,900. MONTREAL, 1 May 1989, *Mountain River Landscape in Autumn* (oil on canvas, 12 1/4 x 16 1/4 ins / 31 x 41 cm) CAD 1,100. MONTREAL, 30 Oct 1989, *Northern River in Winter* (pastel, 21 1/4 x 29 1/2 ins / 54 x 75 cm) CAD 2,640. MONTREAL, 30 April 1990, *Summer Landscape* (oil on canvas, 8 1/4 x 11 ins / 21 x 28 cm) CAD 2,640. MONTREAL, 5 Nov 1990, *Levis Ferry Crossing in Winter* (pastel, 19 x 25 1/4 ins / 48 x 64 cm) CAD 2,200. MONTREAL, 23-24 Nov 1993, *Baie-St-Paul* (oil on canvas, 8 1/4 x 11 ins / 21 x 28 cm) CAD 750. MONTREAL, 3 Dec 1996, *Northern River in Winter* (pastel, 21 1/2 x 29 1/2 ins / 54.5 x 75 cm) CAD 2,000. MONTREAL, 17 June 1997, *Roadside Gossip, Rawdon, Quebec* (oil on canvas, 16 x 20 ins / 40.6 x 50.8 cm) CAD 3,000. TORONTO, 4 Dec 2001, *Laurentian Autumn: Lievre River* (c. 1951, oil on canvas, 24 x 31 ins / 60 x 80 cm) CAD 2,400.

GARSOIAN, Inna
Armenian, 20th century.
Painter.
Inna Garsoian exhibited in the 1930s in the main Paris Salons.

GARSON, Victor-René
French, 19th century.
Born 8 December 1796, in Ploërmel (Morbihan).
Painter.
He enrolled at the École des Beaux-Arts, Paris, on 19 February 1814 and studied under Marsey and Abel de Pujol. He exhibited at the Paris Salon from 1817 to 1833.

GARSTIN, Elisabeth
American, 20th century.
Born 1897.
Sculptor.
Elisabeth Garstin was a member of the American Federation of Art.

GARSTIN, Norman
British, 19th - 20th century.
Born 1847; died 1926.
Also active in France.
Painter, watercolourist. Genre scenes.
School of Newlyn.
Although Norman Garstin lived in Paris at the start of his career, he frequently exhibited in London, particularly at the Royal Academy and the Grosvenor Gallery after 1882. He later settled in London.

NORMAN GARSTIN

AUCTION RECORDS:
PARIS, 9 Feb 1927, *Household Chores,* FRF 300. LONDON, 11 Nov 1981, *Cottage in Normandy* (watercolour, 11 1/4 x 9 ins / 28.5 x 22 cm) GBP 320. LONDON, 25 May 1983, *The Morning Lesson* (1882, oil on canvas, 16 1/2 x 19 ins / 42 x 48 cm) GBP 8,500. LONDON, 12 June 1987, *The Butt and Oyster Inn, Pin Mill, Suffolk* (watercolour, 14 3/4 x 18 ins / 37.7 x 46 cm) GBP 1,500. LONDON, 3-4 March 1988, *Circus performers with torches* (oil on canvas, 21 1/2 x 18 ins / 54.3 x 45.6 cm) GBP 3,520. BELFAST, 28 Oct 1988, *Breton Woman Seated* (oil on canvas, 20 x 16 ins / 51 x 40.7 cm) GBP 990. LONDON, 30 Jan 1991, *On the Way to School at Petit Andely* (watercolour, 6 3/4 x 4 3/4 ins / 17 x 12 cm) GBP 1,320. LONDON, 2 June 1995, *The Chalk Pit* (oil on canvas, 36 x 28 ins / 91.5 x 71 cm) GBP 4,370. LONDON, 9 May 1996, *The Morning Round* (oil on canvas, 22 x 16 ins / 55.8 x 40.6 cm) GBP 4,600.

GARTENSCHMIDT, Wolf
German, 18th century.
Born in the 18th century, in Munich.
Painter.
Gartenschmidt was the pupil of Beintner and illustrated religious subjects.

GARTH, B.
British, 19th century.
Active in London.
Painter. Landscapes.
B. Garth exhibited at the Royal Academy in London from 1796 to 1800.

GARTHMANN, Albert
German, 20th century.
Born 1 May 1876, in Gransee (Brandenburg).
Painter, decorative designer.
Albert Garthmann studied with Peter Jansen at the Düsseldorf academy.

GARTHWAITE, Josette
French.

Born in Paris.
Sculptor.
She regularly exhibited at the Salon de Paris.

GARTIER, Pierre
French, 20th century.
Born 1930, in Valence.
Painter, watercolourist, engraver. Figures, landscapes, still-lifes.

Pierre Gartier studied at the École des Beaux-Arts in Lyons and then in Paris at the École du Louvre and the École Estienne. He was taught by Bissière, Swoboda and Pierre Dubreuil. During 1961-1962 he spent time in Algiers as the final resident artist at the Villa Abd-El-Tif. In Paris he was awarded the Prix de la Critique in 1961 and the Prix Antral in 1964. He was awarded a residency In 1967 by the Fondation de Lourmarin and in 1968 by the Fondation Desnoyer. He lives and works in the Montpellier-Sommières region.

He paints in a free and very sensual style, tackling a variety of themes - often rather unusual kinds of still-life, for example a jumble of clothes in a wardrobe. His rhythmic and colourful approach displays a tendency towards the abstract.

From 1958, Gartier has taken part in numerous group exhibitions and Salons, notably in Paris at the Salon d'Automne, Salon des Artistes Indépendants, Salon Comparaisons, Salon des Artistes Français, Salon du Dessin et de la Peinture à l'Eau and the Panorama de la Jeune Peinture. He also often exhibited in the regions of Montpellier, Sommières, Toulouse, Béziers and Nîmes and has received many prizes and awards.

From 1960 he held solo exhibitions at various institutions and galleries in Paris and the French regions, including: Galerie Romanet in Algiers in 1961; Galerie Vendôme in Paris in 1965 and 1973; Musée Fabre in Montpellier in 1977; Galerie Kuentz in Montpellier in 1978 and 1982; Centre Laurence Durell in Sommières in 1990; and Maison des Arts in Bédarieux in 1996.

MUSEUMS AND GALLERIES:
MONTPELLIER (Artothèque) - MONTPELLIER (FRAC Languedoc-Roussillon) - PARIS (MAMVP).

GARTNER
Belgian, 20th century.
Born in Antwerp.
Painter.

Gartner took part in many group exhibitions in Belgium and the USA. He also showed in solo exhibitions in New Jersey in 1991 and Brussels in 1992. His paintings are pictures within pictures, monochrome on monochrome, in many variations. Repeating the shape and colour of the background, the surface that has been strongly marked by the brush, he paints one or more rectangles superimposed. Often he traces a fine black character with many curves or a white circle recalling a knotted string. His motifs seem to dance in space. His compositions, whether luminous or darker, are full of subtlety and describe an interior world rich in emotions.

GÄRTNER. See also **GAERTNER**

GARTNER, Franz
Austrian, 19th century.
Active in Vienna.
Painter.

Franz Gartner worked for porcelain factories.

GÄRTNER, Fritz, or Geartner
German, 20th century.
Born 1882, in Aussig; died 1958, in Munich.
Painter, engraver, sculptor.

Fritz Gärtner studied art in Munich.

MUSEUMS AND GALLERIES:
LEIPZIG - PRAGUE.

AUCTION RECORDS:
COLOGNE, 5 June 1982, *Earth and Iron* (oil on panel, 24 x 32 ins / 61 x 81 cm) DEM 1,000. COLOGNE, 22 March 1985, *Poppy Field* (1910, oil on canvas, 45 1/4 x 63 ins / 115 x 160 cm) DEM 5,500. COLOGNE, 18 March 1989, *Industry* (1912, oil on canvas, 57 1/2 x 56 1/4 ins / 146 x 143 cm) DEM 3,300.

GARTNER, Hermine
Italian, 19th century.
Born c. 1850; died 24 April 1905, near Genoa.
Painter.

Hermine Gartner was a pupil of Josef Hoffmann in Vienna.

GARTNER, Jorg
German, 16th century.
Active in Passau (Bavaria) c. 1505.
Sculptor.

Jorg Gartner worked particularly on marble tombs and monuments.

GÄRTNER, Klaus
20th century.
Creator of environments.

Gärtner shows his work in solo exhibitions, notably in 1993 at the Kunstverein in Freiburg. He transforms the gallery space after having made a model of it, installs his sculptures and then photographs the whole arrangement.

GARTNER, Paul
Austrian, 16th century.
Active in Innsbruck.
Painter. Portraits.
Tyrolean School.

The brother of Simon, Paul Gartner worked for Archduke Ferdinand II.

AUCTION RECORDS:
LONDON, 10-14 July 1936, *Portrait of an Ecclesiastic* (drawing) GBP 65.

GARTNER, Simon
Austrian, 17th century.
Died 1611, in Innsbruck.
Painter.

Simon Gartner was court painter first to Ferdinand II, and then to Maximilian of Austria.

GÄRTNER DE LA PEÑA, José, or Gaertner
Spanish, 19th - 20th century.
Born 1866, in Malaga; died January 1918, in Madrid.
Painter. Seascapes, landscapes.

José Gärtner de la Peña studied under Emilio Ocon Rivas. He took part in many group exhibitions in Spain, notably in the exhibitions of the national fine arts society, and also in Boston (1883), Hamburg (1886), Berlin (1887), Washington (1890), Chicago (1893) and Brussels (1899). He received many prizes and awards.

His work is atmospheric in its depiction of light, mists, water and reflections. He is known for *The Mediterranean Shore at Málaga*.

BIBLIOGRAPHY:
Arnáiz, José Manuel/López Jiménez, Javier/Merchán Díaz, Manuel (ed.), '*Cien años de pintura en Espana y Portugal (1830-1930)*' in vol. III, Antiqvaria, Madrid, 1989.

MUSEUMS AND GALLERIES:
MADRID (Prado): *The Invincible*.

GARTZEN, Peter
German, 19th century.
Active in Cologne (North Rhine-Westphalia) at the end of the 19th century.
Sculptor.

Gartzen is credited with the sculptures on the main façade of Cologne town hall.

GARVENS, Oskar
German, 20th century.
Born 20 November 1874, in Hanover.
Sculptor.
Oskar Garvens exhibited in Berlin in 1909.

GARVEY, Edmund
British, 19th century.
Died 1813.
Painter, watercolourist. Landscapes.
Edmund Garvey lived in Bath from 1769 to 1777. He was elected to associate membership of the Royal Academy in 1770 and to full membership in 1783. He exhibited on a regular basis until 1809 at London's Royal Academy and also participated in Free Society and British Institution exhibitions. He painted in both oils and watercolours.
AUCTION RECORDS:
LONDON, 13 July 1984, *Wooded Landscape with a View of Rome in the Distance* (oil on canvas, 27 1/2 x 37 1/2 ins / 69.9 x 95.2 cm) GBP 1,000. LONDON, 27 Sept 1994, *Landscape with View of Rome in the Distance* (oil on canvas, 27 1/4 x 37 1/2 ins / 69.5 x 95 cm) GBP 2,070. DUBLIN, 29 May 2002, *View of Hastings from the North* (oil on canvas, 22 x 37 ins / 56 x 93 cm) EUR 2,700. LONDON, 13 Nov 2003, *Figures in the Grounds of Hestercombe, Somerset* (oil on canvas, 31 x 47 ins / 79 x 119 cm) GBP 4,000.

GARVEY DE SAN JUAN, Mariá
Spanish, 19th century.
Active in Cádiz c. 1862.
Painter.
Mariá Garvey de San Juan exhibited in Cádiz and Seville.

GARVI, Paolo. See **GAROVI**

GARVIE, Thomas Bowman
British, 19th - 20th century.
Born 1859; died 1944.
Painter. Portraits, landscapes.
Thomas Bowman Garvie worked in Rothbury (Northumberland), and exhibited at the Royal Academy in London.
AUCTION RECORDS:
TORONTO, 22 Oct 1981, *The Lily Maid of Astolat* (oil on canvas, 19 1/2 x 15 1/2 ins / 49.5 x 39.4 cm) CAD 800.

GARVILLE, de (Mme)
French, 18th century.
Active in Paris in 1761.
Draughtswoman, engraver.
Mme de Garville produced some engravings with genre themes.

GARWOOD, Eileen Lucy or Tirzah
British, 20th century.
Born 1908; died 1951.
Painter, engraver. Local scenes, landscapes.
Eileen Lucy Garwood studied at the Eastbourne School of Art and married the English watercolourist Eric Ravilious, who was a teacher there. After his death in 1942, she married Henry Swanzy. She painted Essex landscapes, street and market scenes, and was known for her book illustrations. She took part in the 10th and 11th annual exhibitions of the Society of Wood Engraveers at the Redfern Gallery, London, in 1929 and 1930; in the *Pictures for Schools* exhibitions at the Tate Gallery in 1948 and at the Whitechapel Art Gallery in 1949; in the Tirzah Garwood memorial exhibition at the Towner Art Gallery in 1952; and in the Arts Council Gallery exhibition in 1952.
BIBLIOGRAPHY:
Tirzah Garwood Memorial Exhibition, Arts Council Gallery, London, 1952.

GARY, Lucien
French, 19th - 20th century.
Painter. Landscapes.
Lucien Gary exhibited at the Salon d'Automne and the Salon de la Société Nationale in Paris.

GARZA, Alexandro P.
Italian, 20th century.
Painter. Genre scenes.
AUCTION RECORDS:
NEW YORK, 13 Jan 1911, *Launch of a Boat*, USD 150.

GARZA Y BANUELOS, Ciriaco de La. See **LA GARZA Y BANUELOS**

GARZATORI, Sebastiano del
Italian, 15th - 16th century.
Born in Schio, near Vicenza.
Painter.
Sebastiano del Garzatori worked mainly in Venice, where he decorated several churches.

GARZI, Luigi
Italian, 17th - 18th century.
Born 1638, in Pistoia; died 2 April 1721, in Rome.
Painter, draughtsman. Religious subjects, mythological subjects, portraits, landscapes.
Luigi Garzi studied in his native Pistoia under S. Boccali and then in Rome under Andrea Sacchi; he was a contemporary (and rival) of Carlo Maratti. His principal paintings in Rome include decorative compositions for the cupola of the Cibo chapel in the church of S Maria del Popolo, *Marys at Christ's Tomb* for the church of S Marta and *The Prophet Joel* for the church of S Giovanni in Laterano. He also worked on the royal palace in Naples and in the church of S Caterina in Formelo. His enormous *Assumption*, painted for the cathedral in Pescia, is considered his most outstanding work.
MUSEUMS AND GALLERIES:
AJACCIO: *Infant Jesus Contemplating the Instruments of His Passion; Exaltation of the Cross; Prophet Joel* - NEW HAVEN (Knights of Columbus Mus.): *St Paul Received into Heaven.*
AUCTION RECORDS:
LONDON, 8 Dec 1981, *Holy Family* (black and white chalk/grey-blue paper, 14 1/4 x 9 3/4 ins / 36 x 24.6 cm) GBP 450. NEW YORK, 7 Nov 1984, *Apotheosis of St Clare and St Francis of Assisi* (oil on canvas, 54 x 20 1/2 ins / 137 x 52 cm) USD 7,000. LONDON, 9 April 1986, *Allegory of Abundance* (oil on canvas, oval, 23 1/2 x 18 1/2 ins / 59.5 x 47 cm) GBP 19,000. MILAN, 12 June 1989, *Bacchus* (oil on canvas, 40 1/4 x 51 1/4 ins / 102 x 130 cm) ITL 8,500,000. NEW YORK, 17 July 1991, *Glorification of St Francis* (red and black chalk/paper, study for the Church of St Francis of the Stigmata in Rome, 9 3/4 x 6 1/2 ins / 25 x 16.5 cm) USD 1,300. NEW YORK, 11 Jan 1996, *Rebecca near the Well* (oil on canvas, 29 x 39 3/4 ins / 73.7 x 101 cm) USD 21,850. NEW YORK, 27 Jan 2000, *St John the Baptist Preaching to the Multitude* (oil on canvas, 38 x 28 ins / 97 x 71 cm) USD 23,000. LONDON, 19 April 2000, *Finding of Moses* (oil on canvas, 11 x 10 ins / 28 x 25 cm) GBP 9,500. LONDON, 25 April 2001, *Diana and Callisto* (oil on canvas, 39 x 59 ins / 100 x 151 cm) GBP 28,000. ROME, 23 Oct 2001, *The Resurrection of Lazarus* (oil on canvas, 30 x 39 ins / 75 x 99 cm) ITL 33,000,000. PARIS, 14 Dec 2002, *Holy Family with other Saints* (oil on canvas, 59 x 47 ins / 150 x 120 cm) EUR 18,000.

GARZI, Mario
Italian, 18th century.
Active in Rome c. 1700.
Painter.
Mario was the son and pupil of Luigi Garzi. Pascoli's *Guida di Roma* (*Guide to Rome*) mentions two of his paintings.

GARZO, Berthold
Hungarian, 20th century.
Born 11 January 1882, in Ungvár (now Uzhhorod, Ukraine).
Painter, engraver, watercolourist.

GARZOLI, Francesco
Italian, 19th century.
Active in Italy.
Engraver (burin).

GARZÓN, Alfredo
Argentinian, 20th century.
Born 23 August 1940, in Salta.
Active in France from 1976, naturalised French.
Painter, sculptor, engraver, draughtsman.

Alfredo Garzón taught at the school of fine arts in Salta and then at the national university of Córdoba where, in 1966, he was awarded the school of fine arts gold medal. He has lived and worked in Villeneuve-St-Georges since 1983. Inspired by freedom, Garzón gives free rein to his imagination, creating jewellery, Baroque sculptures, relief engravings and masks of paper mounted on canvas. Using the most diverse materials - marble, stone, wood, metals etc - which he paints in a wide range of colours, he plays, composes, assembles and dismantles, always pursuing the same goal: to achieve equilibrium. From 1965 Garzón has taken part in group exhibitions in Argentina, Canada, the USA, France, Greece and Mexico. He has exhibited his work at various solo exhibitions both in France - at the Galerie La Petite in Paris - and abroad. An award winner at some 20 competitions, he has received five first prizes.

BIBLIOGRAPHY:
Alfredo Garzon, exhibition catalogue, Gal. La Petite, Paris, 1990.

AUCTION RECORDS:
PARIS, 26 May 1979, *Sculpture* (1988, painted ebony and bronze, h. 15 1/2 ins / 39.5 cm) FRF 4,500. PARIS, 15 April 1991, *Figure* (1983, white marble and patinated bronze, 17 1/4 x 5 1/2 ins / 44 x 14 cm) FRF 6,500. PARIS, 23 Nov 1997, *Power* (welded painted brass, 26 x 17 3/4 x 12 3/4 ins / 66 x 45 x 32.5 cm) FRF 10,000.

GARZON, Juan
Spanish, 18th century.
Died 1729, in Madrid.
Active mainly in Seville.
Painter.

For some time Juan Garzon was a pupil of Murillo. He assisted Osorio with most of his works but there are no details of any works executed solely by Garzon.

J Garzon.

AUCTION RECORDS:
PARIS, 1843, *Virgin and Infant Jesus,* FRF 150.

GARZONI, Angelo
Italian, 17th century.
Born in Padua.
Active in Venice and Verona.
Painter.

GARZONI, Giovanna
Italian, 17th century.
Born 1600, in Ascoli (Marche); died 1670, in Rome.
Painter (gouache), miniaturist. Portraits, still-lifes, flowers.

Giovanna Garzoni lived and studied intermittently in Rome, where her talent was gradually recognised. From 1642 to 1651, she worked in Florence in the service of Ferdinando II de' Medici and his brothers, and Cardinals Giovan Carlo and Leopoldo, painting portraits of the Medicis and other leading figures of the nobility. She also produced numerous paintings of plants and flowers, often together with fruit, insects and reptiles, which are both decorative and scientifically accurate. On her death, she bequeathed her considerable art collection to the Accademia di San Luca in Rome, which duly erected a monument to her.

In 2002, some of her work featured in *The Flowering of Florence: Botanical Art for the Medici,* an exhibition held at the National Gallery of Art in Washington, D.C.

BIBLIOGRAPHY:
Casale, Gerardo/Lanzara, Paola, *Giovanna Garzoni, 1600-1670: Insigne miniatrice,* Jandi Sapi, Milan, 1991. De Medici, Lorenza, *Florentines: a Tuscan feast. Giovanna Garzoni 1600-1670,* Pavilion, London, 1992, 1994. Casale, Gerardo, *Gli Incanti dell'iride: Giovanna Garzoni pittrice nel Seicento,* Silvana, Cinisello Balsamo, 1996. Tongiorgi Tomasi, Lucia/Hirschauer, Gretchen A., *The Flowering of Florence: Botanical Art for the Medici,* exhibition catalogue, National Gall. of Art, Washington DC, 2002.

MUSEUMS AND GALLERIES:
LOS ANGELES (Getty Mus.): *Still-life with Bowl of Citrons* (1645-1650, tempera/vellum).

AUCTION RECORDS:
LONDON, 2 July 1985, *Vase of Carnations and an Apple; Vase of Carnations and a Pear* (two watercolours and gouaches/blue paper, 15 x 18 1/4 ins / 38.2 x 46.2 cm) GBP 7,000. MONACO, 18-19 June 1992, *Still-life with a Basket of Fruit, Shells and a Vase of Carnations* (gouache/vellum, 13 x 17 1/4 ins / 33 x 44 cm) FRF 555,000. NEW YORK, 12 Jan 1994, *Still-life with Flowers in a Painted Bowl* (tempera/vellum, 9 1/2 x 12 1/4 ins / 24.3 x 31.3 cm) USD 25,300. NEW YORK, 24 Jan 2002, *Still-life with a Basket of Fruit, Vase of Carnations and Shells All Resting on a Table* (gouache on vellum, 13 x 17 ins / 33 x 44 cm) USD 130,000. VENICE, 19 Oct 2002, *Birds* (tempera/watercolour/vellum, set of 6, 13 x 11 ins / 34 x 27 cm) EUR 62,000.

GARZOTTI, Francesco
Italian, 16th century.
Active in Venice in 1549.
Sculptor.

GARZOTTI, Girolamo
Italian, 16th century.
Active in Venice.
Sculptor.

Girolamo Garzotti is mentioned as having worked in St Mark's and at the churches of S Clemente and S Maria.

GASBARRA, Giuseppe
Italian, 19th century.
Born 1849, in Rome.
Sculptor.

Gasbarra made his debut around 1877. He exhibited in Naples, Turin, Rome and Venice.

GASC, Anna Rosina de. See **LISZEWSKA Anna Rosina**

GASC, Charles-Jean
French, 19th century.
Born 31 January 1822, in Paris.
Painter.

He was a pupil of H. Garneray, and exhibited fan paintings at the Salon from 1864 to 1870.

GASCARD, Alexander
German, 19th century.
Born 14 September 1807, in Hamburg; died 22 September 1837.
Architect, lithographer.

Gascard engraved views of church interiors.

GASCARD, Henri, or Gascar, Gascars
French, 17th century.
Born c. 1635, in Paris; died 18 January 1701, in Rome.
Painter, engraver. Portraits.

Henri Gascard worked in Italy, then in London, in particular for the Duchess of Portsmouth. In 1679, he was in Holland for a while before returning to France. He was accepted as an academician on 26 October 1680.

He produced many portraits of the British aristocracy. He introduced into both paintings and engravings a 'French' style, especially in the contours of drapes and in the horizontal oval format that was often used (*Louise Kéroualle, Duchess of Portsmouth, and Her Son Charles Lennox, First Duke of Richmond and Lennox*).

In 2001, his work was represented in the exhibition *Painted Ladies. Women at the Court of Charles II* at the National Portrait Gallery in London.

BIBLIOGRAPHY:

MacLeod, Catharine/Marciari Alexander, Julia/Sharpe, Kevin/Dethloff, Diana/Wynne, Sonya, *Painted Ladies. Women at the Court of Charles II*, exhibition catalogue, National Portrait Gall., London, 2001.

MUSEUMS AND GALLERIES:

LONDON (British Mus.): *Barbara Villiers, Duchess of Cleveland, with Her Daughter, Lady Barbara Fitzroy* (c. 1675, engraving, after his own painting); *Louise Kéroualle, Duchess of Portsmouth* (c. 1675, engraving, attributed to the artist, probably copied after one of his paintings now lost) - PARIS (Louvre): *Portrait of the Painter Louis Elle; Ferdinand the Elder; Pierre de Sève the Younger.*

AUCTION RECORDS:

NEW YORK, 9-10 March 1900, *Portrait of Mme d'Orville*, USD 325. LONDON, 21 Dec 1907, *Portrait of a Woman*, GBP 19. LONDON, 29 Feb 1908, *Portrait of a Young Prince*, GBP 11. LONDON, 17 July 1908, *Portrait of Nell Gwynne*, GBP 42. LONDON, 27 May 1909, *Portrait of a Young Girl*, GBP 32. LONDON, 13 Dec 1910, *Lady with Pearls*, GBP 2. LONDON, 16 March 1923, *Duchess of Grafton*, GBP 31. LONDON, 27 July 1923, *Young Girls*, GBP 14. LONDON, 27 June 1924, *Woman in White*, GBP 21. LONDON, 15 May 1925, *Woman Awakening*, GBP 27. LONDON, 13 April 1927, *Woman*, GBP 54. LONDON, 17-18 May 1928, *Woman*, GBP 157. LONDON, 18 July 1929, *Countess of Shrewsbury*, GBP 50. LONDON, 29 Nov 1929, *Portrait of Edith, Wife of Edward Phelips*, GBP 31. LONDON, 25 Nov 1938, *Elisabeth Pierrepont*, GBP 8. LONDON, 3 May 1940, *Henry Goodrick*, GBP 7. LONDON, 17 Dec 1982, *Portrait Presumed To Be of Madame de Sévigné* (oil on canvas, 44 x 24 3/4 ins / 111.7 x 63 cm) GBP 3,800. NEW YORK, 4 April 1990, *Portrait of a Young Lady in an Embroidered White and Yellow Dress Seated near a Table in a Landscape* (1725, oil on canvas, 42 x 32 ins / 106.7 x 81.3 cm) GBP 5,500. NEW YORK, 10 Oct 1990, *Three-Quarter Length Portrait of a Lady in a Brocade Dress, Seated near a Pedestal Table; Portrait of a Gentleman in Armour Holding a Baton* (oil on canvas, a pair, each 24 3/4 x 19 3/4 ins / 62.8 x 50.2 cm) USD 9,900. NEW YORK, 30 May 1991, *Portrait of a Lady* (oil on canvas, 45 x 35 1/2 ins / 114.5 x 90 cm) USD 22,000. LONDON, 13 July 1994, *Portrait of James II; Portrait of His Wife Mary of Modena* (oil on canvas, a pair, each 24 1/2 x 19 1/2 ins / 62 x 49.5 cm) GBP 15,870. LONDON, 12 July 1995, *Portrait of Barbara, Duchess of Cleveland, and Her Daughter Charlotte Fitzroy, Countess of Lichfield* (oil on canvas, oval, 38 3/4 x 46 3/4 ins / 98.5 x 119 cm) GBP 7,475. NEW YORK, 31 Jan 1997, *Three-Quarter Length Portrait of a Lady, Seated, with her Dog, in front of an Open Window, an Italian Landscape in the Background* (oil on canvas, 34 1/2 x 45 ins / 87.6 x 114.3 cm) USD 12,650. LONDON, 9 July 1997, *Portrait of Frances Jennings* (oil on canvas, oval, 24 x 20 ins / 61 x 51 cm) GBP 11,500. LONDON, 15 July 1998, *Portrait of Louise of Kerouaile, Duchess of Portsmouth* (oil on canvas, 49 x 39 ins / 124 x 99 cm) GBP 9,000. NEW YORK, 23 May 2001, *Portrait of a Lady* (oil on canvas, 46 x 36 ins / 117 x 91 cm) USD 18,000. MUNICH, 21 June 2002, *Kurfurst Max Emanuel von Bayern* (oil on canvas, 45 x 36 ins / 115 x 91 cm) EUR 9,000. LONDON, 4 March 2004, *Portrait of Hortense Mancini, Duchess of Mazarin, Seated in a Landscape* (1680, oil on canvas, 38 x 48 ins / 96 x 121 cm) GBP 5,000. LONDON, 1 July 2004, *Portrait of Barbara Villiers, Countess of Castlemaine and her Daughte* (oil on canvas, oval, 38 x 49 ins / 97 x 125 cm) GBP 26,000.

GASCARD, Léon
French, 19th century.
Born 1861, in the Somme département.
Painter.

He exhibited at the Salon for many years.

GASCARD, Pierre, or Gascar, Gasquart
French, 17th century.
Died 17 April 1665.
Sculptor, painter.

Pierre Gascard was undoubtedly the father of Henri.

GASCH, Agustín
Spanish, 18th century.
Active in Alcora near Valencia in the first half of the 18th century.
Painter.

GASCH, Antonio
Spanish, 19th century.
Active in Valencia at the end of the 19th century.
Sculptor.

GASCH, Christoph
Spanish, 18th century.
Active in Alcora near Valencia between 1730 and 1750.
Painter.

GASCH, Joseph
Spanish, 18th century.
Active in Alcora near Valencia.
Painter.

GASCH, Luis
Spanish, 19th century.
Born in the 19th century, in Valencia.
Painter. Genre scenes.

AUCTION RECORDS:

RAMBOUILLET, 30 Oct 1985, *Spanish Fiesta* (1892, oil on panel, 11 x 15 ins / 27 x 38 cm) FRF 22,500.

GASCHEN, Christoph
German, 18th century.
Sculptor.

Gaschen worked for the cathedral of Treves in about 1725.

GASCO, Joan
Spanish, 16th century.
Active in Navarre at the beginning of the 16th century.
Painter. Religious subjects.

The father of Pere Gasco, Joan Gasco worked in Barcelona.

AUCTION RECORDS:

BARCELONA, 19 Dec 1984, *St Sigismond; St Severus* (oil on panel, a pair, 43 1/4 x 9 1/2 ins / 110 x 24 cm) ESP 2,600,000.

GASCO, Pere
Spanish, 16th century.
Active in Barcelona.
Painter. Religious subjects.

Pere Gasco was the son of Joan Gasco, who taught him his craft.

GASCOIGNE, de. See first name

GASCOIGNE, Ethel G., or Gascoyne
British, 19th - 20th century.
Active in London.
Painter. Genre scenes.

Ethel Gascoigne was the wife of George Gascoigne. She exhibited at the Royal Academy in 1871. She was a member of the Ridley Art Club in 1909.

GASCOIGNE, George, or Gascoyne
British, 19th - 20th century.
Painter, engraver. Genre scenes.

George Gascoigne lived and worked in London. He exhibited at the Royal Academy from 1882. He was a member of the English Society of Painter-Etchers.

Museums and Galleries:

London (Victoria and Albert Mus.): *Returning from Work* (etching).

Auction Records:

London, 23 Sept 1988, *The Harrow* (1887, oil on canvas, 39 3/4 x 59 3/4 ins / 101 x 152 cm) GBP 8,800.

GASCOIGNE, Rosalie

Australian, 20th century.

Born 1917.

Installation artist.

Bibliography:

Creating Australia: 200 Years of Art 1788-1988, exhibition catalogue, Art Gall. Board of South Australia, Adelaide, 1988.

GASCON, Antonio

Spanish, 19th century.

Active in Saragossa c. 1860.

Painter, miniaturist.

GASCÓN DE GOTOR, Anselmo

Spanish, 19th - 20th century.

Born 1865, in Saragossa; died 1927, in Huesca.

Painter, draughtsman. Local scenes.

Anselmo Gascón de Gotor studied at the school of fine arts in Saragossa. He took part in various exhibitions including the national fine arts exhibitions in 1885 and 1890. He received many prizes and awards. His painting is realist and shows scenes of everyday life with a certain naivety but great rigour of execution.

Bibliography:

Arnáiz, José Manuel/López Jiménez, Javier/Merchán Díaz, Manuel (ed.), *'Cien años de pintura en Espana y Portugal (1830-1930)'* in vol. III, Antiqvaria, Madrid, 1989.

Museums and Galleries:

Saragossa (Mus. de Zaragoza): *The Wait* (1904).

GASIER, Claude

French, 16th century.

Painter, enameller.

In 1582 and 1592 Gasier was living in Lyons. A son was born to him there in 1591.

GASINSKY, Bolenaw

Polish, 20th century.

Painter, engraver.

Bolenaw Gasinsky was a student of S. Szczepanski, E. Eibisch and S. Gierowski and received a painting and engraving diplomas from the school of fine art in Warsaw with an award for excellence in 1966. He has taken part in many exhibitions both in Poland and abroad.

GASIOROWSKI, Gérard

French, 20th century.

Born 30 March 1930, in Paris; died 19 August 1986, in Lyons.

Painter.

Neo-Conceptual Art.

Gérard Gasiorowski began painting in 1951, after studying applied arts. However, from 1953 to 1964 he abandoned painting - a fact he always insisted was mentioned in any biography. Although unrecognized as an artist for many years, curiously enough attention was drawn to his work by the success of Hyperrealism, although in fact the relationship between this essentially American movement and Gasiorowski's painting was extremely tenuous if not non-existent. However, it is true to say that it was the arrival of Pop Art in France that prompted Gasiorowksi to begin painting again, rediscovering a new stimulus after a gap of ten years in the obviousness of the Pop Art image. Using only non-colours, that is to say black and white, he painted scenes, stiff portraits, images that gradually shade away in a gradation produced by the trickling effect of his so-called Barbizon period. At the end of the 1960s he produced, as if by accident, four 'croûtes' using impasto and colours in the style of Montmartre; in these the sense of derision found in his later work is already apparent.

Scared by the spontaneous direction his painting was taking, no doubt taken together with the graduated images he had already produced, Gasiorowski returned to a more measured painting style, which soon enjoyed success in the *Albertine* series. This Proustian reference is an indicator of the meaning of his painting, which is an embroidery of memory, a 'remembrance of things past', an evocation of memories of a lost universe, reconstituted through scraps and fragments. Working from photographs 'rendered in paint' on to canvas (hence the association with Hyperrealism), he retranscribes memories of childhood or perhaps the arbitrarily reconstructed 'possible moments' of any childhood. The atmosphere of his black and white paintings and the titles chosen, which reinforce this atmosphere, give the work an undeniable literary aftertaste, a cultural label from which Gasiorowski soon stands aloof. Despite the success he enjoyed, or no doubt because of it, the images he produces begin again to 'degrade', occupying only a tiny area of the canvas which is otherwise untouched, like the illustrations found in old dictionaries, from which he also borrows his subjects and titles. This *Impuissances* series was quickly followed by another series entitled *Régressions*; these were paintings of flowers in the style of studies executed when training.

In a reaction against painting, Gasiorowski's work led quite naturally to the *War* and *Catastrophes* series - paintings of tanks, planes, soldiers and the tools of war - and then to the manufacture of the same equipment in cardboard copiously coated in vinyl paint. He also used children's toys, splattering them, burning them and breaking them and then presenting them in boxes, simulating rail accidents, a vast hotchpotch of painted boxes, damaged, disembowelled toys, secret toolbags, hidden drawings thrown randomly about, piled up as if in some settling of scores, which cannot fail to produce a sense of unease. Maintaining the same derisory approach, perhaps driven further still by a kind of masochism of failure, Gasiorowski executed and exhibited a series of *Self-portraits*, the technique of which recalls his earlier impasto 'croûtes', but which, nonetheless, continue to reveal his ability as a painter. In an exacerbation of this, the following year he embarked on a similar approach but one even better suited to translating a sense of neurotic energy, in which the image of his face is replaced by that of his sexual organs.

Between 1973 and 1975 he began work on the two series *Amalgames* and *Les Fleurs*, both of which he finished ten years later. In the first series, in the unusual format of A4 typing paper, he sets out his history of art, his artistic references, 'copying' side by side works by Matisse, Picasso, Klee, Malevitch and others. In the second series he appends to the lightness of flowers aerial signs dancing on the paper, the heavy surfaces of pots in a simple expression of the pure joy of painting. Not long after, taking a completely new direction, he felt the need to disappear, erasing his own name and creating a fiction whose main character is his double, Worosis Kiga (an anagram heteronym), director of an academy of the same name - the A.W.K. - who is responsible for seeing that his pupils Beuys, Serra, Kosuth, Bertrand, Ben, Tapiès, etc, sit their exams. He decided to paint a hat in the style of each artist, reducing the painting in this series of 'quotations' to a mark, a mere signature. Through often humorous captions Gasiorowski endeavoured to place himself as a human being. Having disappeared as Gasiorowski, he had recourse to his body and to his bodily functions to express himself: using liquid excrement he drew objects and primitive figures in the series *Les Jus*; he also exhibited excrement mixed with earth and straw in the series *Kiga, les Tourtes*, in which in subtitles he again specifies his references including Cézanne and Manet. Through this experience, this successful attempt to exorcise his anguish - the anguish of being reduced to a name, a label - he picked up the baton of the action painting tradition.

There are further series in which he continued to affirm the act of painting: a series of pictures with a line running through expressing the continuity of art from Lascaux to the dawn of the 21st century. In his final works, *Stance, Ex-Voto* and *Fertility*, he pursued his ambition to move towards the distant light, to leave a trace that merges with the very act of painting. Haunted by the history of art, from which his name is struck out, Gasiorowski bears witness to the singularity of his position through his complexity: often derisory, he showed himself able to construct a body of work in perpetual upheaval, always grating and aggressive yet in spite of itself a work of quality, of a quality inherent in the artist and against which he appeared to battle, to rid himself of it like as one would a cumbersome label. Far from seeking to produce a representation of appearance, he tirelessly pursued the same quest: to rediscover the adventure of painting, to disappear in order to take part in the oeuvre to come.

He took part in numerous group exhibitions: in 1965, *Indicateurs* at the Mathias Fels gallery in Paris; in 1972 *72/72, 12 Ans d'Art Contemporain* (*72/72, 12 Years of Contemporary Art*) at the Grand Palais national galleries in Paris; in 1973 at the CNAC (the national contemporary art centre) in Paris; in 1975, *Le Désespoir du Peintre* (*The Painter's Despair*) at the old market hall in Jouy-en-Josas, an exhibition conceived and mounted by Jean Clair and which was later shown at the Maison de la Culture in Grenoble in 1976; in 1982, *Qu'est-ce que l'Art Français?* (*What is French Art?*) at the Musée Ste-Croix in Poitiers; in 1983 at the Musée National d'Art Moderne in Paris; and in 1986 the *Les Années-Mémoires* (*Memory Years*) exhibition at Meymac, Bar-le-Duc, Nice.

He exhibited solo first in 1970 in Cologne and then in Essen at the Galerie Thelen. He quickly became known and went on to hold numerous solo exhibitions, notably in Paris since 1982, regularly at the Adrien Maeght gallery and in 1983 at the Musée d'Art Moderne. Since his death there have been various retrospectives, including: in 1988 a retrospective at the Musée d'Art Moderne of Villeneuve-d'Ascq; in 1991 at the Maeght gallery, the Musée St-Pierre in Lyons and the Centre de Création Contemporaine in Tours; in 1994 the *L'A.W.K. Les Fleurs* exhibition at the Adrien Maeght gallery in Paris; in 1995 a major collection of his work at the Pompidou Centre, Musée National d'Art Moderne, Paris; and in 2002 at the Maeght gallery, Paris.

BIBLIOGRAPHY:

Gasiorowski - Peinture, exhibition catalogue, Musée d'Art moderne de la Ville de Paris, Paris, 1983. Enrici, Michel, *Gasiorowski*, Maeght, Paris, 1984. '*Écritures dans la peinture*' in *2 vol.*, exhibition catalogue, Villa Arson-Centre national des Arts plastiques, Nice, 1984. *Entretiens*, La Différence, Paris, 1986. Dagen, Philippe, '*Gasiorowski - Un Hymne à l'invention*' in *Art Press* n° 107, periodical, Paris, October 1986. Kaeppelin, Olivier, '*Gasiorowski: la peinture contre le nom*' in *Artstudio*, periodical, Gal. Templon, Paris, summer 1987. Kaeppelin, Olivier/Bordaz, Jean-Pierre, '*Gasiorowski - Les Amalgames*' in *coll. Carnets de voyage*, Maeght, Paris, 1993. Kaeppelin, Olivier/Enrici, Michel, '*Gasiorowski - Les Fleurs*' in *coll. Carnets de voyage*, Maeght, Paris, 1993. '*Gasiorowski*' in *coll. Contemporaines/Monographies*, exhibition catalogue, Éd. du Centre Georges-Pompidou, Paris, 1995. Maeght, Yoyo, '*Catalogue raisonné*' in vol. I, Maeght, Paris, winter 1995 (5 vol.).

MUSEUMS AND GALLERIES:

NANTES (MBA) - PARIS (FNAC) - PARIS (MNAM-CCI).

AUCTION RECORDS:

PARIS, 26 Nov 1984, *Limits of my Thinking* (1969, acrylic/canvas, 76 3/4 x 51 1/4 ins / 195 x 130 cm) FRF 10,000. PARIS, 27 Nov 1987, *You know, it's about cows* (1978, oil on paper, 27 1/2 x 11 3/4 ins / 70 x 30 cm) FRF 20,000. VERSAILLES, 20 Dec 1987, *God Exists, or Portrait of a Quite Extraordinary Man* (oil on canvas, 36 1/4 x 28 3/4 ins / 92 x 73 cm) FRF 32,000. PARIS, 2[illegible] March 1988, *The Madwoman* (1971, acrylic/canvas, 51 1/4 x 3[illegible] ins / 130 x 81 cm) FRF 31,000. PARIS, 8 Oct 1989, *Pots of Flowers* (1980, acrylic/paper, 30 x 24 1/2 ins / 76 x 62.5 cm) FRF 82,000. PARIS, 3 May 1990, *And Sometimes Like Wanting to Cry* (oil on panel, 14 1/4 x 10 1/2 ins / 36 x 26.5 cm) FRF 40,000. PARIS, 3 July 1991, *Free Exercise* (1980, acrylic/paper, 14 1/4 x 62 1/4 ins / 36 x 158 cm) FRF 50,000. PARIS, 16 April 1992, *Votive Offering* (1986, acrylic/paper/canvas, 19 3/4 x 19 3/4 ins / 50 x 50 cm) FRF 22,000. PARIS, 17 Oct 1994, *Rash Fool in the Bath* (1972, acrylic/canvas, 22 x 15 ins / 55 x 38 cm) FRF 31,500. PARIS, 29-30 June 1995, *Flowers* (acrylic/paper, four framed sheets, 29 1/4 x 24 ins / 74 x 61 cm) FRF 27,000. PARIS, 16 Nov 1995, *Pots of Flowers* (oil on paper, four sheets, 29 1/4 x 23 1/2 ins / 74 x 60 cm) FRF 23,000. PARIS, 22 March 1998, *Six Bowler Hats* (1973, acrylic/paper, 15 3/4 x 12 1/2 ins / 40 x 32 cm) FRF 10,000. PARIS, 28 June 1999, *Tank's Progress* (acrylic on paper, 16 x 19 ins / 40 x 47 cm) FRF 11,000. PARIS, 28 June 1999, *Tank* (acrylic on paper, 16 x 19 ins / 40 x 47 cm) FRF 13,000. PARIS, 7 June 2000, *Grande Frise des Chevaux* (1972, acrylic and pencil, 39 x 39 ins / 100 x 100 cm) FRF 30,000. PARIS, 19 Dec 2001, *Tank* (mixed media on panel, 31 x 22 ins / 78 x 56 cm) FRF 16,460. PARIS, 4 June 2002, *Three Flower Pots* (1973, acrylic on paper, three in one frame, 14 x 11 ins / 36 x 29 cm) EUR 5,410. PARIS, 19 June 2002, *Picasso Museum Poster* (acrylic on poster, a pair, 24 x 16 ins / 60 x 40 cm) EUR 5,000. PARIS, 29 April 2003, *The Big Tomb* (1971, acrylic on canvas, 21 x 32 ins / 54 x 81 cm) EUR 2,700. PARIS, 9 Dec 2003, *Four Pots* (1973, acrylic on canvas, 31 x 25 ins / 78 x 63 cm) EUR 4,500.

GASKELL, Anna

American, 20th - 21st century.

Born 1969, in Des Moines.

Photographer, draughtswoman.

Anna Gaskell studied at Bennington College in Vermont, graduating in 1990, and the Art Institute of Chicago, obtaining a BFA in 1992. In 1995 she graduated from Yale University School of Arts with a MFA. In 2000 she won the Citigroup Private Bank Photography Prize.

Gaskell presented *Wonder*, a collection of colour photographs showing a pair of twins dressed as Lewis Carroll's Alice in Wonderland in blue apron dresses, white tights and black Mary Janes. The two Alices are photographed playing in the woods and on the grass, posing to re-create moments from the story of Alice. Gaskell created dramatic images using stark contrasts, chiaroscuro lighting and sharp cropping of the photographs. The overarching theme is identity but also issues such as gender, ethnicity, and growing up. In 1999 the series *Hide* was shown at the Musée d'Art Moderne de la Ville de Paris. This work was based on a Grimm tale *The Magic Donkey* in which an adolescent girl creates a costume from animal hides which enables her to escape her father's sexual advances. The theme of prepubescent sexuality, also making reference to Nabolov's *Lolita*, is recurrent throughout Gaskell's work. She continued to pursue these themes in *Anna Gaskell* (2001), her first monograph, and *Resemblance* (2002), her first artist's book. Both of these series appear to depict innocent child's play but also reveal violent and sadistic behaviour such as pulling of hair, girls in groups turning their backs to the spectator, girls seemingly at play but looking frightened. Gaskell reveals an ambiguous world of childish innocence but suggestive of violent behaviour, abuse and emerging sexuality.

Gaskell's work has been the subject of several solo exhibitions including shows at Galerie Yvon Lambert (2004), at the

Menil Collection (2002), *Future's Eve* at New Langton Arts (2001), *Resemblance* at Castello di Rivoli Mueso d'Arte Comtemporanea (2001) and *Remarkable Places* at the Kölnischer Kunstverein (2001), Casey Kaplan (2001), Hide at White Cube (1999) and MOMA (1999).

BIBLIOGRAPHY:

Gaskell, Anna, *Anna Gaskell*, Powerhouse Books, 2001. Gaskell, Anna, *Resemblance: Photographs by Anna Gaskell*, Addison gallery of American Art, 2002. Tuchman, Phyllis, *Variety Photoplays*' in *Art in America*, no. 6, New York, June 2002. Lavrador, Judicaël, '*Virgin Suicide*' in *Beaux Arts Magazine* no. 238, Paris, March 2004.

MUSEUMS AND GALLERIES:

AMSTERDAM (Mus. van Loon) - ATHENS, GA (Deste Foundation Centre for Contemporary Art) - COLOGNE (Mus. Ludwig) - JERUSALEM (Israel Mus.) - LONDON (Tate Collection) - LOS ANGELES (MCA) - MIAMI (MCA) - MINNEAPOLIS (Walker Art Center) - NEW YORK (Solomon R. Guggenheim Mus.) - OSLO (Astrup Fearnley Mus. for Moderne Kunst) - SAN FRANCISCO (MoMA) - TURIN (Fondazione Sandretto Re Rebaudengo per l'Arte).

AUCTION RECORDS:

NEW YORK, 17 May 2000, *Untitled - Num. 21* (cibachrome print mounted on Plexiglas, 57 x 69 ins / 144 x 174 cm) USD 16,000. NEW YORK, 15 May 2003, *Untitled no. 5* (1996, colour coupler print mounted on cintra, 50 x 40 ins / 127 x 102 cm) USD 28,000. NEW YORK, 12 Nov 2003, *Untitled no. 56* (1999, colour coupler print on Plexiglas, 50 x 60 ins / 127 x 152 cm) USD 14,000. NEW YORK, 12 May 2004, *Untitled, Wonder Series* (1997, colour coupler print on Plexiglas, 29 x 35 ins / 74 x 89 cm) USD 38,000. NEW YORK, 14 May 2004, *Untitled Num. 50* (1999, cibachrome print, 50 x 60 ins / 127 x 152 cm) USD 5,500.

GASKELL, George Arthur

British, 19th century.
Active in London.
Painter. Figures, portraits, landscapes.

George Arthur Gaskell exhibited in London from 1871 to 1879, notably at the Royal Academy and the Suffolk Street Gallery.

AUCTION RECORDS:

LONDON, 20 Oct 1981, *Lady Godiva* (1875, watercolour and pencil, 18 1/2 x 12 1/2 ins / 47 x 32 cm) GBP 320. NEW YORK, 28 May 1992, *Advent of Spring* (1897, oil on canvas, 50 1/2 x 34 ins / 128.3 x 86.4 cm) USD 11,000. LONDON, 19 April 1999, *Cat Cradle* (1900, watercolour and gouache, 27 x 20 ins / 68 x 51 cm) GBP 1,650. LONDON, 14 March 2001, *Time for Tea* (1901, watercolour, 29 x 22 ins / 73 x 55 cm) GBP 1,300. LONDON, 25 Oct 2001, *Teatime* (1901, pencil and watercolour, 28 x 21 ins / 72 x 53 cm) GBP 1,100.

GASKELL, George Percival

British, 19th - 20th century.
Born 1 January 1868, in Shipley.
Painter, engraver.

George Percival Gaskell was a member of the Royal Society of British Artists and the Society of Engravers. He exhibited at the Royal Academy in 1909.

GASKELL, John

British, 18th century.
Active in London.
Miniaturist.

John Gaskell was an exhibitor between 1774 and 1778 at the Society of Artists and the Royal Academy in London.

GASKIN, Arthur Joseph

British, 19th - 20th century.
Born 1862, in Birmingham; died 4 June 1928.
Painter, watercolourist, draughtsman, illustrator, worker in precious metals, designer. Religious subjects, allegorical subjects, portraits. Jewellery.
Arts and Crafts.

Arthur Joseph Gaskin studied at the Birmingham School of Art, where he later taught. He was a member of the Arts and Crafts movement founded by William Morris, whose aim was to revitalise the decorative arts. From 1899, together with his wife Georgina Cave France, he created gold and silver jewellery, sometimes decorated with enamel. In 1902, he replaced R. Catterson Smith as director of the Birmingham School of Jewellery. He exhibited paintings at the Royal Academy in London in 1889 and 1890 and jewellery at the 1900 Paris Exposition Universelle.

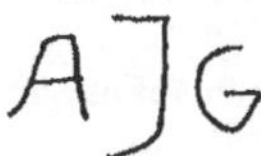

MUSEUMS AND GALLERIES:

BIRMINGHAM (Mus. and AG): portrait of Georgie, the artist's wife, as a character from Boccacio's 'Decameron'*Fiammetta* (1898, tempera on panel); *Kilhwych, the King's Son* (1901, tempera on panel); from a poem by Tennyson*The Lady of Shalott* (1888, drawing).

AUCTION RECORDS:

LONDON, 12 Nov 1982, *Portrait of Margaret Cary Gaskin* (1926, tempera, 18 x 11 3/4 ins / 45.7 x 30 cm) GBP 300. LONDON, 7 Nov 1985, *The Nativity* (1925, tempera, pencil and coloured chalk/canvas, 15 1/2 x 18 1/2 ins / 39.5 x 47 cm) GBP 3,200. LONDON, 29 July 1988, *Portrait of Margaret Cary Gaskin (the artist's daughter)* (1926, 19 1/4 x 13 ins / 48.8 x 33.2 cm) GBP 550. LONDON, 1 Dec 1989, *The Three Kings* (watercolour, 13 1/2 x 27 1/4 ins / 34.2 x 69.2 cm) GBP 2,420. LONDON, 30 March 1990, *Psyche* (1900, tempera/panel, 21 x 15 1/4 ins / 52.4 x 38.5 cm) GBP 17,600. LONDON, 11 March 2003, *Head Study of a Youth* (1891, red chalk and pencil, 9 x 12 ins / 23 x 30 cm) GBP 5,500. LONDON, 4 Nov 2003, *Blue Feather* (watercolour, sold with 16 drawings by same hand, 8 x 5 ins / 21 x 13 cm) GBP 4,800.

GASNIER, Charles-François

French, 19th century.
Born 1789, in Paris; died c. 1835, in Mannheim (Baden-Württemberg).
Painter. Flowers.

He was the son of Pierre-Guillaume Gasnier.

GASNIER, Pierre-Guillaume

French, 19th century.
Painter, decorative designer.

He emigrated to Germany at the beginning of the 19th century, settling in Mannheim with his son Charles-François.

GASONBERG, Cornilles van, or Gassenberg

15th century.
Painter.

He worked in 1467 at the feast of the Order of the Golden Fleece, Bruges.

GASPAR, Jean-Marie

Belgian, 19th century.
Born 1864, in Arlon (Luxembourg).
Sculptor. Animals.

MUSEUMS AND GALLERIES:

BRUSSELS: *Walking Elephant*.

GASPAR, Miklos

Hungarian, 20th century.

Born 1885.
Active in the USA.
Painter, decorative artist, watercolourist.

Miklos Gaspar began his art studies in Hungary before finally settling in the USA where he joined several American art societies. In 1920 he obtained a prize in Budapest for his watercolours.

GASPARD
Flemish School, 16th century.
Active in Ghent.
Sculptor.

GASPARD. See also **JASPARD**

GASPARD, Abraham
French, 17th century.
Sculptor.

Abraham Gaspard sculpted a tabernacle for the church of St Jacques in Lunéville in 1611.

GASPARD, Leon Schulman
Russian, 20th century.
Born 1882, in Vitebsk (near Moscow); died 1964, in Taos (New Mexico).
Active in New Mexico from 1919.
Painter (gouache). Figures, portraits, local scenes (kermesses), still-lifes, flowers, landscapes.

As a child Leon Schulman Gaspard accompanied his father, a retired Russian officer, on fur trading expeditions into Asia where he was exposed to exotic and colourful cultures which remained themes throughout his life's work. His early studies took place in his home town of Vitebsk, in Odessa, and at the academy in Moscow. He then moved to Paris and studied alongside Marc Chagall and under Adolphe Bouguereau and Edouard Toudouze at the Académie Julian where he was heavily influenced by French Impressionism and the Abstract. He was especially drawn to the painting of Modigliani and Matisse, and the sculpture of Rodin.

During World War I Gaspard's successful Parisian painting career was interrupted by his service to the French Air Corps. When his plane was shot down and he was badly injured he went to recuperate with the family of his American wife, Evelyn Adell, in New York. Seeking a better climate, in 1919 the couple moved to Taos, New Mexico, where he became intrigued by the native culture which reminded him of the colourful cultures he had encountered as a child on his trips into Siberia.

Although they settled in Taos for the rest of their lives, Leon Gaspard and his wife also travelled to China, Mongolia, Tibet, Morocco and other parts of Northern Africa. Gaspard drew extensively on these trips, reaching isolated cultures via wagon, pony, camel, automobile, riverboat and airplane.

Gaspard's style combined French Impressionism and Realism, and he remained staunchly resistant to Modernism until his death. His paintings of the homes, costumes and rituals of the Taos region are noted for their brilliant coloration and intricate patterning.

Exhibitions of Gaspards work have included *Leon Gaspard: A Retrospective Exhibition,* Maxwell Galleries, San Francisco in 1967 and *Leon Gaspard: Paintings of Many Worlds,* Kennedy Galleries, New York in 1974.

BIBLIOGRAPHY:
Waters, Frank, *The Sketches of Leon Gaspard,* Southwest Museum, Los Angeles, c. 1962. Waters, Frank, *Leon Gaspard,* Northland Press, Santa Fe (NM), c. 1981 (forward by Forrest Fenn). *Leon Gaspard,* Berry-Hill Galleries, New York, c. 1986.

MUSEUMS AND GALLERIES:
ANN ARBOR (University of Michigan Mus. of Art) - CHICAGO (AI) - PHOENIX (AM) - SANTA FE (Museum of New Mexico) TAOS (The Harwood Museum of Art).

AUCTION RECORDS:
NEW YORK, 14 May 1976, *Soldiers' Farewell* (1914, oil on canvas remounted on board, 10¼ x 17¾ ins / 26 x 45 cm) USD 7,500. LONDON, 9 June 1976, *King Solomon* (1940, gouache and gold-leaf, 30 x 24 ins / 76.2 x 61 cm) USD 11,000. LOS ANGELES, 9 March 1977, *Horse in a Landscape* (1919, oil/silk, 8 x 22 ins / 20.3 x 56 cm) USD 4,750. NEW YORK, 8 Nov 1979, *Russian Market* (1922, gouache/canvas remounted on board, 9¼ x 16¾ ins / 23.5 x 42.8 cm) USD 12,000. NEW YORK, 2 June 1982, *Still-life with Flowers* (1945, oil/hardboard, 23 x 17½ ins / 58.5 x 44.7 cm) USD 10,000. NEW YORK, 22 Oct 1982, *Festival of the Eagles* (mixed media, 51 x 48 ins / 129.5 x 122 cm) USD 38,000. NEW YORK, 9 Dec 1983, *Russian Christmas* (1914, oil on canvas remounted on board, 32 x 47½ ins / 81.3 x 120.6 cm) USD 95,000. NEW YORK, 29 May 1986, *Russian Peasant Parade* (1911, oil on canvas, 24 x 28¾ ins / 61 x 73 cm) USD 50,000. NEW YORK, 5 Dec 1986, *Moscow* (1959, pastel/paper, 12½ x 9¼ ins / 31.9 x 23.2 cm) USD 2,200. NEW YORK, 26 May 1988, *Souks, Tunis* (1931, oil on canvas, 12¼ x 13½ ins / 30.8 x 34.1 cm) USD 15,400. NEW YORK, 30 Nov 1989, *Autumn Festivals* (oil on card, 23¼ x 22¼ ins / 59.1 x 56.5 cm) USD 52,250. NEW YORK, 24 May 1990, *End of the Kermesse* (1918, oil on card, 37 x 47 ins / 94 x 119.4 cm) USD 275,000. NEW YORK, 30 May 1990, *Portrait of a Small Girl* (1918, oil on canvas, 6 x 5¼ ins / 15.2 x 13.3 cm) USD 3,080. NEW YORK, 26 Sept 1990, *In the Siberian Desert* (1926, oil on card, 34 x 30 ins / 86.3 x 76.2 cm) USD 55,000. NEW YORK, 17 Dec 1990, *Barges and Tugboat on Divina* (oil on panel, 9 x 11 ins / 22.9 x 28 cm) USD 5,500. NEW YORK, 12 April 1991, *Early Winter* (oil on card, sketch, 10½ x 8½ ins / 26.7 x 21.6 cm) USD 6,600. NEW YORK, 6 Dec 1991, *Russian Peasants' Parade* (1911, crayon and oil on canvas, 23¾ x 28½ ins / 60.3 x 72.3 cm) USD 115,500. NEW YORK, 15 April 1992, *Village Street* (oil on card, 8½ x 13 ins / 21.6 x 33 cm) USD 5,170. NEW YORK, 27 May 1992, *Wedding Chair, Peking* (1921, oil on canvas, 21 x 29¾ ins / 53.3 x 75.6 cm) USD 41,250. NEW YORK, 4 Dec 1992, *Twining Canyon* (1954, oil on card, 48½ x 32½ ins / 123.2 x 82.6 cm) USD 231,000. NEW YORK, 2 Dec 1993, *Russian Snow Scene* (1914, oil on canvas, 26½ x 24 ins / 67.3 x 61 cm) USD 255,500. NEW YORK, 25 May 1995, *Siberian Winter Festival, La Kermesse* (1921, oil on card, 20 x 22 ins / 50.8 x 55.9 cm) USD 79,500. NEW YORK, 29 Nov 1995, *Old Moscow* (oil on canvas, 37¾ x 36 ins / 95.9 x 91.4 cm) USD 189,500. NEW YORK, 26 Sept 1996, *Urga Horses* (1921, oil on canvas, 8½ x 10 ins / 21.6 x 25.4 cm) USD 2,415.

GASPARD-MAILLOL. See **MAILLOL Gaspard**

GASPARE, Romano
Italian, 16th century.
Active in Naples c. 1500.
Miniaturist, architect.

GASPARE D'AGOSTINO
Italian, 15th century.
Painter.
Sienese School.

Gaspare worked for Siena Cathedral.

GASPARE DA CARONA
Swiss, 15th century.
Born in Carona.
Active in Carona.
Sculptor.

Gaspare is known for the sculptures around the portals of the palace of the Genoese and particularly for that of the Sauli family dating from 1494. Some fragments of sculpture by him survive in Carona, including a statuette of the Madonna.

GASPARE DA COLLE
Italian, 15th century.
Active in Tuscany, c. 1434.
Sculptor (wood).

GASPARE DA VERONA
Italian, 16th century.
Painter.
An altarpiece in the church at Riva, painted in 1524, is attributed to Gaspare da Verona.

GASPARE DI BENEDETTO DA PESARO
Italian, 15th century.
Painter.
The father of Benedetto, Gaspare was active in Pesaro and also worked in Palermo and Monreale.

GASPARE DI GIOVANNI DA VOLTERRA
Italian, 15th century.
Died 1474, in Siena.
Glass painter.
Sienese School.
Gaspare worked mainly for Siena Cathedral.

GASPARE DI JACOPO
Italian.
Active in Foligno.
Sculptor (wood).

GASPARI, Angelo de, or Gasparini
Italian, 19th century.
Died 21 October 1855, in Padua.
Painter, decorative artist.
Angelo de Gaspari decorated palaces and churches in Padua.

GASPARI, Antonio
Italian, 17th - 18th century.
Born c. 1670, in Venice; died c. 1730, in Venice.
Painter, draughtsman. Architectural views. Statues.
An architect by profession, Antonio Gaspari painted mostly views of ruins.
AUCTION RECORDS:
PARIS, 31 March and 1 April 1924, *Architectural Composition* (pencil and bistre) FRF 400. NEW YORK, 13 Oct 1989, *Capriccio: Port with Figures and Ancient Ruins* (oil on canvas, 49 x 69 3/4 ins / 124.5 x 177 cm) USD 29,700.

GASPARI, Antonio
Italian, 19th century.
Born 3 April 1793, in Cremona.
Painter, decorative artist.
Antonio Gaspari was a pupil of Francesco Motta.

GASPARI, Carlo
Italian, 18th century.
Died c. 1800.
Active in Venice.
Painter. Architectural views. Decorative schemes.
Carlo Gaspari worked on the church of the Apostle Saints in Venice.
AUCTION RECORDS:
PARIS, 31 March 1924, *Architectural Composition* (pencil and bistre) FRF 400. PARIS, 27 Oct 1926, *Architectural Composition* (pen and wash) FRF 155.

GASPARI, Giovanni Paolo
Italian, 18th century.
Born 1714, in Venice; died 1775, in Munich.
Painter, designer. Architectural views.

GASPARI, Pietro Giovanni
Italian, 18th century.
Born c. 1720, in Venice; died c. 1785, in Venice.
Painter, architect.
Pietro Gaspari provided decorative compositions for the Theatre Royal in Munich and engraved several architectural illustrations. In 1775, he was involved in decorating the doors and staircases of the Royal Gallery in Venice.

GASPARINI, Andrea
Italian, 19th century.
Active in Rome in 1844.
Draughtsman, engraver. Urban views, architectural views.
MUSEUMS AND GALLERIES:
FLORENCE (Uffizi): *View* (two versions).

GASPARINI, Gaspare
Italian, 16th century.
Born in Macerata; died c. 1570, in Macerata.
Painter. History painting.
Gaspare Gasparini was a pupil of Girolamo da Sermoneta. For the church of S Venanzio in Fabriano, he painted a *Baptism of Christ*, a *Last Supper* and *St Peter and St John Healing the Paralytic*. He also painted a very fine *St Francis Receiving the Stigmata*, which can be seen at the conventual church in Macerata.

GASPARINI, Luigi
Italian, 19th century.
Born 1765 or 1779, in Zenson di Piave or Bologna; died in Venice.
Painter. Landscapes, waterscapes.
Luigi Gasparini was a pupil of Vincenzo Martinelli.
AUCTION RECORDS:
ROME, 26 May 1993, *The Gondolier (A Kiss for Daddy)* (oil on canvas, 42 1/2 x 57 ins / 108 x 145 cm) ITL 25,000,000. NEW YORK, 2 Nov 1999, *Suitor Arriving in Salon Observed by Elegant Ladies* (oil on canvas, 28 x 37 ins / 70 x 95 cm) USD 6,000. NEWCASTLE, 14 March 2000, *Venice in the 18th Century* (oil on canvas, 27 x 37 ins / 68 x 94 cm) GBP 4,000.

GASPARINI, Sebastiano
Italian, 16th century.
Painter.
Sebastiano Gasparini is believed to have worked in the church of S Biagio at Acoli.

GASPARO
Italian, 16th century.
Miniaturist.
Around 1520, Gasparo illuminated a codex of Pliny.

GASPARO
Italian, 16th century.
Active in Venice c. 1565.
Engraver (burin).
Gasparo produced engravings of genre scenes.

GASPARO DE LUCA, or Lucca
Italian, 16th century.
Sculptor.
Gasparo de Luca was active in Lucca. In 1583, he was summoned to Spain by Philip II and contributed to the decoration of the church at the Escorial.

GASPARO DI FIORI. See **LÓPEZ Gasparo**

GASPAROLI
Austrian, 19th century.
Miniaturist.
Gasparoli was active in Vienna at the beginning of the 19th century.

GASPART, Alfred
Argentinian, 20th century.
Born 3 August 1900, in St Nicolas de los Arroyos, to an Argentinian mother and a French father.
Active in France from 1903.
Painter, draughtsman. Figures, landscapes, still-lifes.

Alfred Gaspart studied at the Germain Pilon School before spending a short period in Cormon's studio at the school of fine arts in Paris. He was a painter of reality, addressing the humblest of subjects with a magnificent and striking lack of ornamentation. Gaspart served as a soldier and spent time as a prisoner between 1940 and 1945, managing to escape on two occasions. The sketches he brought back from this period are among his most moving work. He exhibited in Paris at the Salon d'Automne and the Salon des Indépendants and received the Prix de Captivité awarded in Geneva.

GASPARY, Eugène de
French, 20th century.
Active in Paris.
Sculptor.

Eugène de Gaspary received a commendation in 1894.

GASPARY, Robert Fernand
French, 19th - 20th century.
Born in Tripoli.
Painter. Genre scenes.

Robert Gaspary studied under Baschet, Gervais and Gourdault. He exhibited at the Salon des Artistes Français and received a commendation in 1909.

GASPE, Eugène. See **GASPERINI**

GASPER, Amandus
Austrian, 17th century.
Died 19 February 1643, in Vienna.
Painter.

It would appear that this artist worked in Antwerp in 1624.

GASPERI, Cristofano
Italian, 18th century.
Born 1716, in Maggiore; died 13 February 1804, in Perugia.
Painter.

Gasperi studied first under Giacento Boccanera, then under Agostino Masucci. He was highly successful in his day and was commissioned to decorate most of the churches in Perugia.

GASPERI, Raphaël
French, 19th century.
Active in Brives (Corrèze).
Painter. Landscapes.

MUSEUMS AND GALLERIES:
PÉRIGUEUX: *Winter Evening* - TULLE: *Stormy Evening in Corrèze*.

GASPERINI, Eduard
German, 19th century.
Painter. Portraits, genre scenes.

Gasperini was a pupil at the academy in Berlin.

AUCTION RECORDS:
PARIS, 19 March 1945, *Neapolitan Scenes* (forming a pair) FRF 5,000.

GASPERINI, Eugène, pseudonym: Gaspe
French, 19th - 20th century.
Born 1873, in Parma, to French parents.
Engraver.

Eugène Gasperini studied under Charles Brabant. He exhibited in Paris at the Salon des Artistes Français, where he received a commendation in 1906 and a bronze medal in 1908.

GASPERINI-LILLAZ, Germaine
French, 20th century.
Engraver (wood).

Germaine Gasperini-Lillaz exhibited in Paris at the Salon des Artistes Français from 1920.

GASPERO D'IMOLA
Italian, 16th century.
Born in Imola.
Painter. History painting.

GASPERS, Jan Baptist, or Jaspers
Flemish School, 17th century.
Born in Antwerp; died 1691, in London.
Painter. Portraits.

Gaspers studied under Thomas Willeborts and, possibly, Th van Bossaert. He travelled to London during Cromwell's Protectorate (1653-1659) as the protégé of the leading English parliamentarian General John Lambert. Following the restoration of Charles II, he was employed by the portraitists Sir Peter Lely and Sir Godfrey Kneller. He is known for a number of portraits of Charles II, notably one in the Great Hall of St Bartholomew's Hospital in London. Gaspers was also an accomplished draughtsman, and produced designs for a number of tapestries.

GASPIRINI, Luigi
Italian, 19th century.
Born in Zenson di Pavia (Lombardy).
Sculptor.

Luigi Gaspirini exhibited in Turin and Venice from 1880 onward.

GASQ, Paul Jean-Baptiste
French, 19th - 20th century.
Born 31 May 1860, in Dijon; died 28 October 1944, in Paris.
Sculptor. Figures. Monuments, statues.

Paul Gasq studied at the École des Beaux-Arts in Dijon and then at the École des Beaux-Arts in Paris with Jouffroy and Hiolle. He was awarded the Premier Prix de Rome in 1890, a medal of honour in 1911 for his group *Aux Volontaires de la Révolution* (*To the Volunteers of the Revolution*) (1792) and a Grand Prix in 1900. He was made a member of the Institut in 1935 and is known for his *Low-relief* of 1893.

MUSEUMS AND GALLERIES:
DIJON: sculptures - PARIS (Louvre): *Monument to Houdon; Medea* - PARIS (MAM): *Hero and Leander.*

AUCTION RECORDS:
LONDON, 17 March 1983, *Allegory of Peace* (c. 1890, green-patinated bronze, h. 35 ins / 88 cm) GBP 750. PARIS, 18 Nov 1985, *The Nymph Flora* (bronze, patina medal, h. 37 1/2 ins / 95 cm) FRF 14,000. BILLINGSHURST, 29 Jan 2001, *Diana the Huntress* (golden brown patinated bronze, h. 30 ins / 76 cm) GBP 1,400. PARIS, 10 July 2002, *Thought* (patinated bronze, h. 35 ins / 88 cm) EUR 2,850. PARIS, 10 July 2002, *Diana and the Eagle Struck by Lightning* (patinated bronze, h. 35 ins / 89 cm) EUR 4,000. PARIS, 25 June 2003, *Shepherd and Sheep* (brown patinated bronze, h. 28 ins / 70 cm) EUR 2,000.

GASQUET, Jean-Michel
French, 20th century.
Born 1929, in Nîmes.
Painter, pastellist, sculptor.

Initially producing works rich in colour and energy, Jean-Michel Gasquet went on to create wooden mural sculptures in which colour is refined down to an exploration of black and its relationship with light. He took a radical approach to geometric abstraction, confirmed by the interest Aurélie Nemours took in his work.

He exhibited in Paris at the Salon des Grands et Jeunes d'Aujourd'hui. He also showed his work in solo exhibitions: in 1990 at the Galerie Michèle Heyraud in Paris and in 1998 in a major exhibition of his work at the Galerie Lahumière in Paris.

BIBLIOGRAPHY:
Nemours, Aurélie, *Gasquet*, exhibition catalogue, Gal. Lahumière, Paris, 1998.

GASQUET, Maurice Vasco
French, 20th century.
Born 14 February 1931, in Paris.
Painter, engraver (including etching), screen printer, illustrator.

Maurice Vasco Gasquet studied lithography at the École Supérieure Estienne des Arts et des Industries Graphiques in Paris in 1946. He illustrated books by Vercors such as *Drôme*. He has signed his works as *Vasco Gasquet* since 1968.

Collective exhibitions include: Salon de la Jeune Peinture, Paris (1956 to 1963, 1977, 1978); *Art Junction International*, Nice (1991); *Critique et utopie. Livres d'artistes et autres publications d'artistes, en France, des années 60 à nos jour* (*Critique and Utopia: Artists' Books and Other Publications by Artists, in France, from the 1960s to the Present Day*) , Limoges (2001). Solo exhibitions include: Galerie Weiller, Paris (1956); Galerie Ventadour, Paris (1963); Médiathèque, Palaiseau (1998).

BIBLIOGRAPHY:
Gasquet, Vasco, *Les 500 Affiches de mai 1968*, Balland, Paris, 1978.

GASSEL, Lucas Van. See **HELMONT**

GASSEL, Mariette. See **SALBETH**

GASSELIN, Noël
French, 17th century.
Active in Paris in 1667.
Painter.

AUCTION RECORDS:
PARIS, 3 Dec 1959, *Scene from the commedia dell'arte* (signed N. Gasselin) FRF 3,000,000.

GASSELIN, Pierre
French, 17th century.
Born 1623, in Le Mans.
Painter.

Pierre Gasselin worked in Angers from 1647.

GASSELIN, Pierre Jacques
French, 18th century.
Active in Paris in 1760.
Painter.

GASSEN, Francisco
Spanish, 17th century.
Born 1598, in Barcelona; died 1658, in Barcelona.
Painter. History painting.

Francisco Gassen collaborated with Pedro Cuquet on paintings of scenes from the life of St Francis of Paola for the Minim convent in Barcelona.

J Gassen.

GASSEN, Gottlieb
German, 19th century.
Born 2 August 1805, in Ehrenbreitstein (Rhineland-Palatinate); died 3 June 1878, in Koblenz (Rhineland-Palatinate).
Painter. History painting.

Gottlieb Gassen was a pupil of Cornelius. In 1827 he settled in Munich, where his frescoes can still be seen. He is also noted for his *Assault on Godesberg by the Bavarians in 1583*.

GASSER, Anton
German, 17th century.
Active in Augsburg (Bavaria) at the beginning of the 17th century.
Painter.

Anton Gasser also worked in Dresden.

GASSER, Franz
Austrian, 19th century.
Born in Eisentratten; died 1838.
Painter. Portraits.

Franz was the brother of Hanns Gasser. He lived in Vienna.

GASSER, Georg
German, 19th century.
Born 23 May 1857, in Rentsch.
Painter.

Georg Gasser was a pupil of Johann Hintner. He worked in Munich and in Bozen (now Bolzano, Italy).

GASSER, Hanns
Austrian, 19th century.
Born 2 October 1817, in Eisentratten; died 24 April 1868, in Budapest.
Painter, sculptor. Figures, nudes, portraits.

Hanns Gasser was a pupil of Klieber and Kahssmann at the art academy in Vienna and of Leitung von Schwanthaler in Munich. He worked mainly in Vienna and spent some time as a teacher at the academy. Some of his colossal statues, executed with excessive haste, have been destroyed.

MUSEUMS AND GALLERIES:
VIENNA: *Portrait of the Artist* (oil painting).

AUCTION RECORDS:
VIENNA, 4 Dec 1984, *Nude Standing* (1866, bronze, h. 11 ins / 28 cm) ATS 35,000.

GASSER, Henry Martin
American, 20th century.
Born 1909; died 1981.
Painter (gouache). Genre scenes, interiors with figures, local scenes, urban landscapes.

AUCTION RECORDS:
NEW YORK, 24 June 1987, *Gloucester* (oil on canvas, 30 x 36 ins / 76.2 x 91.5 cm) USD 3,500. NEW YORK, 22 Sept 1987, *Mining Town* (watercolour, 21½ x 29 ins / 54.5 x 73.5 cm) USD 2,250. NEW YORK, 17 March 1988, *Harlem Palladium* (oil on paper, 11¾ x 16¼ ins / 30 x 41 cm) USD 7,150. NEW YORK, 17 Dec 1990, *Teacher in Love with a Dancer* (gouache/paper, 8 x 9¾ ins / 20.3 x 24.8 cm) USD 5,775. NEW YORK, 15 May 1991, *Returning from the Mine* (oil on canvas, 30 x 36 ins / 76.2 x 91.4 cm) USD 3,300. NEW YORK, 21 May 1991, *Chinese Restaurant* (oil on card, 15¼ x 12 ins / 38.8 x 30.5 cm) USD 3,300. NEW YORK, 14 Nov 1991, *Hoboken, New Jersey* (oil on canvas/synthetic resin, 23 x 36½ ins / 58.5 x 92.8 cm) USD 2,750. NEW YORK, 10 June 1992, *Harlem Palladium* (oil on reinforced canvas, 12 x 17 ins / 30.5 x 43.1 cm) USD 1,980; *Turner's Grocery Store* (watercolour/paper, 19¾ x 25 ins / 50.2 x 63.4 cm) USD 3,080. NEW YORK, 31 March 1993, *House of Hoffman* (watercolour/paper, 15½ x 22½ ins / 39.4 x 57.2 cm) USD 2,530. NEW YORK, 31 March 1994, *Engelhorn's Bar and Grill, Newark Tavern* (watercolour/card, 22 x 30 ins / 55.9 x 76.2 cm) USD 2,875. LOS ANGELES, 9 Dec 1999, *Laundry Day* (watercolour, 19 x 22 ins / 48 x 57 cm) USD 6,000. BOSTON, 22 Sept 2000, *December Snow* (watercolour and gouache on board, 7 x 9 ins / 19 x 24 cm) USD 1,500. NORTH BETHESDA, 22 May 2001, *Noon in Montparnasse* (watercolour on paper on cardboard, 22 x 16 ins / 56 x 41 cm) USD 1,700. PASADENA, 12 Feb 2002, *Underpass* (watercolour, 21 x 30 ins / 53 x 76 cm) USD 4,000. NEW YORK, 4 Sept 2002, *Parisian Street Scenes* (watercolour and gouache, three, 9 x 7 ins / 22 x 19 cm) USD 2,400. PASADENA, 18 Nov 2003, *Underpass* (watercolour, 8 x 11 ins / 20 x 29 cm) USD 5,000. NEW YORK, 3 Dec 2003, *Backyard in Newark* (watercolour on paper on board, 19 x 24 ins / 48 x 61 cm) USD 6,000. PHILADELPHIA, 2 April 2004, *Harbour Vista* (oil on board, 16 x 20 ins / 41 x 51 cm) USD 3,750. NEW YORK, 26 May 2004, *Main Street, Winter* (watercolour, 19 x 24 ins / 48 x 61 cm) USD 3,500.

GASSER, Johann
Austrian, 19th century.
Died 1868.
Active in Graz in 1803.

Sculptor.
The museum at Klagenfurt (Carinthia) has works by this artist.

GASSER, Leonardo
Italian, 19th century.
Born 1831, in Florence.
Painter. Portraits, genre scenes.
Gasser was a pupil of Gordigiani.
AUCTION RECORDS:
TORONTO, 22 Oct 1982, *Musical Interlude* (oil on canvas, 15 1/4 x 11 1/4 ins / 38.8 x 28.6 cm) CAD 1,600. COLOGNE, 18 March 1983, *Chamber Music* (oil on remounted canvas/panel, 15 1/2 x 12 ins / 39.5 x 30.5 cm) DEM 3,000. LONDON, 15 Nov 1995, *Portrait of a Young Girl* (oil on canvas, 25 x 19 ins / 63.5 x 48 cm) GBP 8,050. LONDON, 21 Nov 1996, *The Knight's Wife* (oil on canvas, 37 3/4 x 28 1/2 ins / 96 x 72.5 cm) GBP 12,075. PARIS, 5 Feb 1998, *Elegant Lady with a Fan* (1878, oil on canvas, 51 1/4 x 30 1/2 ins / 130 x 77.5 cm) FRF 30,000. LONDON, 18 June 2003, *Thoughtful Moment* (1871, oil on canvas, 22 x 18 ins / 56 x 46 cm) GBP 3,500.

GASSER DE VALHORN, Josef
Austrian, 19th century.
Born 22 November 1816, in Praegratten; died 28 October 1900, in Praegratten.
Sculptor.
Gasser de Valhorn sculpted four large figures for the portal of the cathedral at Spire and the *Seven Liberal Arts* for the new opera house in Vienna.

GASSER-JACOB, Jenny (Mme)
French, 19th century.
Born in Paris.
Miniaturist.
She was a member of the Société des Artistes Français from 1890 and showed examples of her work at its exhibitions.

GASSET-HOUSSET, Hélène
French, 20th century.
Born 1889, in the Hautes-Pyrenées; died 28 January 1966, in Toulouse.
Painter, designer. Animals. Designs for carpets, designs (fabrics/ceramics/furniture).
Hélène Gasset-Housset exhibited in Paris at the Salon des Artistes Indépendants, the Salon d'Automne, the Salon des Artistes Décorateurs and the Salon des Femmes Peintres et Sculpteurs. She designed jewellery, carpets, fabrics, lacquer ware, ceramics, furniture and bindings. All her work is characterised by the richness of the materials used. Her major decorative pieces, often lacquer ware, are almost always based on animal themes.

GASSETTE, Grace
American, 20th century.
Born in Chicago.
Active in France.
Painter, sculptor.
Grace Gassette studied under Mary Cassatt.

GASSIER, Henri Paul
French, 20th century.
Born 1883, in Marseilles; died 1951.
Draughtsman, illustrator.
Henri Gassier lived in both Notre-Dame-de-la-Garde in the Bouches-du-Rhône region and in Montmartre in Paris. A caricaturist, prior to World War I Gassier built up a strong reputation through his collaboration on satirical magazines and papers such as: *La Guerre Sociale* and *L'Humanité* in 1909-1922; *L'Internationale* in 1921-1922; *Ce Soir* in 1927; as well as on *Le Canard Enchaîné* and *Le Merle Blanc*. Gassier took a sardonic view of political life, creating a kind of comic parliament. André Salmon describes him thus: 'A polemicist, he was not savage in a partisan way - he preferred to poke fun at hypocrisy, false eloquence and false dignity'.

BIBLIOGRAPHY:
Halturin, Aleksandr/Hulten, Pontus/Gunar, Karl (ed.), *Paris Moscou*, group exhibition catalogue, Éd. du Centre Georges-Pompidou, Paris, 1979.

GASSIES, Jean-Baptiste Georges
French, 19th - 20th century.
Born 1829, in Paris; died 1919, in Montluçon (Allier).
Painter, watercolourist. Genre scenes, landscapes with figures, landscapes.
Barbizon School.
Jean-Baptiste Gassies studied under Michel Drolling in Paris. In 1852 he left his studio in Chailly-en-Bière in Seine-et-Marne to join the painters of the Barbizon School at th Ganne inn near Barbizon. In 1863 he moved into the las house in the village of Barbizon, on the very edge of the forest. He became one of the central figures of the Barbizor group and exhibited at the Paris Salon from 1857 to 1881, receiving a commendation in 1859.

Gassies painted mainly genre scenes and landscapes in oi or watercolour. His works include: *Forge Interior; Forest a the Start of Summer; The First Meetings; The Rocky Pond* Unlike most of his companions of the Barbizon School, he enjoyed painting figures and animals in his forest interiors.
MUSEUMS AND GALLERIES:
AUTUN (Mus. Rolin): *Scottish Landscape* - SEMUR-EN-AUXOIS: *Regulus Returning to Carthage Bids Farewell to his Family.*
AUCTION RECORDS:
PARIS, 12-15 April 1899, *Harvest*, FRF 40. PARIS, 27-28 Jan 1928, *Young Women under a Tree* (watercolour) FRF 45. PARIS, 22 July 1942, *Forest Interior* (watercolour) FRF 290. PARIS, 17 Feb 1947, *Landscape*, FRF 550.

GASSIES, Jean-Bruno
French, 19th century.
Born 25 October 1786, in Bordeaux; died 12 October 1832, in Paris.
Painter, engraver. Mythological subjects, genre scenes, waterscapes, seascapes.
He enrolled at the École des Beaux-Arts in Paris on 2 March 1804 and studied under Vincent and Lacour. He served in the French navy, was captured by the English and remained a prisoner-of-war for some time. Between 1810 and 1833 he exhibited at the Paris Salon. Gassies was awarded the Légion d'Honneur on 21 August 1822.

MUSEUMS AND GALLERIES:
DOUAI: *Labourer Uncovering a Skeleton; Seated Man* - PARIS (Louvre): *Diana and Endymion; Interior of the Church of St-Prix, Val de Montmorency* - SEMUR-EN-AUXOIS: *Regulus Bidding Farewell to his Family before Returning to Carthage.*
AUCTION RECORDS:
PARIS, 1861, *During the Storm*, FRF 108; *After the Storm*, FRF 115. PARIS, 21 Oct 1992, *Rowing Boat in Rough Seas* (1825, oil on canvas, 16 1/2 x 25 1/2 ins / 42 x 65 cm) FRF 3,200. PARIS, 1 Dec 1997, *Portrait of a Young Architect Working on a Blueprint* (1831, oil on canvas, 29 1/2 x 23 1/2 ins / 75 x 60 cm) FRF 10,000. PARIS, 15 March 2002, *View of Loch Lomond in Scotland* (1824, oil on canvas, 9 x 13 ins / 24 x 32 cm) EUR 10,000. FRANKFURT, 1 June 2002, *Steep Coast with Figures* (1825, oil on panel, 28 x 48 ins / 71 x 122 cm) EUR 4,600. NEW YORK, 1 April 2003, *Boy in an Interior with a Top Hat* (oil on canvas, 18 x 15 ins / 46 x 37 cm) USD 3,000.

GASSIOT DE CAZES. See **CAZES Gassiot de**

GASSL, Gottfried
Czech, 18th century.
Born c. 1708.

Sculptor (wood).
Gottfried Gassl was a monk in Frauenzell, near Regensburg.

GASSLER, Franz
Austrian, 18th century.
Born in Telf (Tyrol).
Sculptor.
Franz Gassler was a pupil of J.A. Renns and worked in Vienna.

GASSMANN, Beat Jakob
Swiss, 17th century.
Painter.
Beat Gassmann worked at the convent of St Urbain in Lucerne.

GASSMANN, Christoffel
German, 17th century.
Active in Düsseldorf (North Rhine-Westphalia).
Sculptor.
Christoffel Gassmann worked for the church of Idstein.

GASSNER, Franz Anton
German, 17th century.
Born in Altdorf.
Painter.
Franz Gassner was active in Berg, near Ravensburg (Bavaria).

GASSNER, Nicolaus
German, 17th century.
Born in the 17th century, in Frankfurt am Main.
Painter. Landscapes.
Nicolaus Gassner worked in Dresden, Kassel and Copenhagen.

GASSNER, Simon
Austrian, 18th - 19th century.
Born 10 February 1755, in Steinberg; died 1830.
Painter, engraver. History painting, landscapes.
Simon Gassner was the pupil of Gallrap and of Deniel in Munich. The Marquis of Baden commissioned him to decorate a room in Karlsruhe. Gassner later re-emerged in Munich in 1790, living there until 1825. He used etching and the mezzotint method of engraving. There is in existence a plate by him representing *A Temple in the English Gardens in Munich.*

GASSO Y VIDAL, Leopolda
Spanish, 19th century.
Born in the 19th century, in Quintanar de la Orden.
Painter. Landscapes.
Leopolda Gasso y Vidal was a pupil of Manuel Martínez Ferrer and Isidoro Lozano. She first exhibited around 1875 in Madrid.

GASSON, Jules
French, 19th century.
Active in Paris.
Painter.
He exhibited at the Paris Salon from 1836 to 1881. He is remembered for compositions entitled *Young Roman Peasants* and *Breton Peasants at Rest.*
AUCTION RECORDS:
LONDON, 12 Feb 1910, *Street in Algiers,* GBP 8. LONDON, 11 Oct 1996, *Pasha's Favourite* (oil on canvas, 11 x 14in/27 x 35.5cm) GBP 2,990.

GASSOWSKI, Alexandre de
French, 19th century.
Born 10 February 1835, in Dôle; died c. 1900, in Grand-Fontaine (Doubs).
Painter, draughtsman. Portraits, genre scenes, still-lifes, flowers.
He was a pupil of Tabar and exhibited at the Paris Salon in 1868 and 1869.
AUCTION RECORDS:
LONDON, 2 Dec 1907, *Thoughts,* GBP 1. BERN, 16 May 1981, *Woman Collecting Firewood* (oil on panel, 10½ x 16¼ ins / 26.5 x 41 cm) CHF 1,500. PARIS, 21 June 1990, *Hungarian Dance at the Closerie des Lilas* (lead pencil and watercolour, 6½ x 7½ ins / 16.5 x 19 cm) FRF 6,500. PARIS, 19 April 2002, *Model in Painter's Studio* (oil on canvas, 22 x 18 ins / 57 x 46 cm) EUR 4,000.

GAST, Bertram
British, 19th century.
Active in London.
Painter. Landscapes.
Bertram Gast exhibited in London from 1888 at the Royal Academy and at the Suffolk Street Gallery.

GAST, Frank
British, 19th century.
Active in London.
Painter. Rustic scenes.
Frank Gast exhibited in London in 1891 and 1892 at the Royal Academy and the Suffolk Street Gallery.

GAST, Michiel de
Flemish School, 16th century.
Also active in Italy.
Painter. Landscapes.
Antwerp School.
In 1558, Michiel de Gast was a member of the Antwerp guild. He worked for many years in Rome, where he painted landscapes with figures and ruins that he signed with a monogram. No works have been attributed to him with any certainty.

GASTAGER, Joseph
Yugoslav, 18th century.
Painter.
Produced paintings for the church of St Mark of Zagreb, done in about 1755.

GASTAL (Mme)
French, 19th century.
Miniaturist.
She exhibited at the Paris Salon of 1849.

GASTALDI, Andrea
Italian, 19th century.
Born 16 April 1810, in Turin; died 9 January 1889, in Turin.
Painter. History painting, portraits.
Gastaldi studied in Paris, where he became an extremely popular artist. In the final years of his life, right up to his death, he occupied the post of director of the Turin school of art. One of his finest paintings depicts *Frederick Barbarossa Fleeing on the Road to Legnano.*

A. Gastaldi

MUSEUMS AND GALLERIES:
ALENÇON: *Ophelia.*
AUCTION RECORDS:
MILAN, 20 March 1980, *Portrait of a Woman* (oil on canvas, 30 x 31½ ins / 76 x 80 cm) ITL 750,000. TURIN, 4 Dec 2000, *Stream by Mount Cervino* (1856, oil on canvas, 32 x 26 ins / 81 x 65 cm) ITL 7,800,000. NEW YORK, 29 Oct 2002, *Duke d'Este Mourning Death* (oil on canvas, 78 x 94 ins / 199 x 240 cm) USD 9,500.

GASTALDI, Lorenzo
Italian, 17th century.
Active in Liguria.
Painter.

GASTALDI Y BO, José
Spanish, 19th century.
Born 11 July 1842, in Valencia.
Painter. Genre scenes.

José Gastaldi y Bo studied at the Academia de San Carlos in Valencia, then at the Academia de San Fernando in Madrid and under the painter Plácido Frances. He also worked at the studio of Pablo Gonzalvo. He first exhibited around 1864, and is known for his *Viaticum* and *The Lost Capital*.

GASTALDI-LESCUYER, Léonie
French, 19th century.
Born in Paris.
Miniaturist.

A pupil of Andrea, she is known to have worked in Turin from 1860.

GASTALDY, François
French, 18th century.
Born 1706; died 1773.
Active in Nancy.
Painter, decorative designer.

François Gastaldy was the father of Joseph.

GASTALDY, Joseph, called Pinseau
French, 18th century.
Active in Nancy.
Painter.

Joseph Gastaldy was the son of François.

GASTAUD, Pierre
French, 20th century.
Born 1920, in Nice.
Painter (including gouache), sculptor.

Pierre Gastaud was a self-taught painter. He decided to devote himself exclusively to art in 1950 and won the Prix de la Jeune Peinture in Nice that year and the Menton Biennale prize in 1951.

After a relatively figurative period, he moved towards Abstract Landscapism. Jean-Louis Ferrier describes his work as 'germinations, suckings, to the point of becoming a troubling work of roots, arising from the sap of canals... sedimentary deposits at the bottom of certain lakes which, over the course of the centuries, have built up layer upon layer'.

He took part in numerous group exhibitions including the Salon de Mai, notably in 1962 when he was chosen for the selection for exhibition in Japan; the Venice Triennale in 1968; and the Salon des Réalités Nouvelles in 1969. He also showed his work in various solo exhibitions including in 1954 at the Musée Antibes; in 1955 in Turin; in 1957 in Milan; in 1959 in La-Chaux-de-Fonds; in 1960 and 1961 in Paris; in 1963 at Auvernier-Neuchâtel; in 1968 at the Musée d'Art Moderne de la Ville de Paris with Longobardi under the generic title *Structurations*; in 1969 in Cannes; and in 2003 a retrospective of his work at the Centre International d'Art Contemporain at Carros in the Alpes-Maritimes.

BIBLIOGRAPHY:

Ferrier, Jean-Louis, '*Gastaud à la recherche des espaces perdus*' in *Temps Modernes* n° 230, periodical, Paris, July 1965. Ferrier, Jean-Louis, *Gastaud. Le Papier dans tous les états 1960-1990*, exhibition catalogue, Laurent de Puybaudet, Gal. Laurent Teillet, Paris, 1990. Altmann, Frédéric, et al., *Pierre Gastaud, rétrospective*, L'Ormaie, Vence, 2003 (exhibition catalogue, Carros).

AUCTION RECORDS:

PARIS, 17 Dec 1985, *Composition* (oil on canvas, 45 x 77¼ ins / 114 x 196 cm) FRF 13,000. NEUILLY, 20 June 1988, *Composition* (1963-1964, oil on canvas, 25½ x 32 ins / 65 x 81 cm) FRF 5,500. PARIS, 21 Sept 1989, *Composition* (1959, oil on canvas, 32 x 39¼ ins / 81 x 100 cm) FRF 5,000. LE TOUQUET, 12 Nov 1989, *Composition* (oil on canvas, 25½ x 21¼ ins / 65 x 54 cm) FRF 8,000. PARIS, 14 March 1990, *Composition* (oil on canvas, 39¼ x 32 ins / 100 x 81 cm) FRF 15,000. PARIS, 2 July 1990, *Varia* (mixed media, 38¼ x 27½ ins / 97 x 70 cm) FRF 28,000. CALAIS, 7 July 1991, *Composition* (1961, watercolour and gouache, 22 x 20 ins / 56 x 51 cm) FRF 5,000. PARIS, 1[illegible] March 1993, *Tropics* (1988, oil on canvas, 39¼ x 32 ins / 100 x 81 cm) FRF 5,000. LE TOUQUET, 14 Nov 1993, *Composition* (oil on canvas, 25¼ x 31½ ins / 64 x 80 cm) FRF 7,000. PARIS, 18 Dec 1997, *Untitled* (c. 1960, oil on paper, 19¾ x 49¼ ins / 50 x 125 cm) FRF 3,500.

GASTAUER, Anton
German, 18th - 19th century.
Active in Boppard (Rhineland-Palatinate).
Draughtsman, lithographer.

Gastauer worked in Koblenz, among other places.

GASTÉ, Constant Georges
French, 19th - 20th century.
Born 30 August 1869, in Paris; died 1 October 1910, in Madurai (Tamil Nadu), India.
Painter. Portraits, genre scenes, local scenes, landscapes with figures.
Orientalism.

Constant Gasté studied under Alexandre Cabanel and Raphaël Collin. Keen to explore the world, he began by visiting Morocco in 1892 and this became the starting point for many more journeys. He spent a long time in Algeria; he also explored Tunisia in 1898 as well as Egypt, Palestine, India and the holy sites of Christianity. He exhibited at the Salon des Artistes Français in Paris and received a commendation in 1896 and a bronze medal in 1897. Three years after his death, in 1913, the Société des Peintres Orientalistes Français held a retrospective of his work.

Georges Gasté paintings were exclusively Orientalist: portraits, interiors and scenes of daily life inspired by his travels. He is remembered for the paintings: *Young Hindu in a Turban, God's Servant* and *Portrait of a Young Girl from Bou-Saada*.

MUSEUMS AND GALLERIES:

ALGIERS: *Famine in India* - VILLENEUVE-SUR-LOT (Mus. Rapin): *Deva Dassy, Servant of the Gods*.

AUCTION RECORDS:

PARIS, 18 March 1927, *Old Egyptian Man*, FRF 410. PARIS, 17-18 Dec 1941, *Islet Sacred to Madura*, FRF 110; *Young Hindu in a Turban*, FRF 800; *Part of the Madura Temple*, FRF 75; *Siesta*, FRF 600. VERSAILLES, 13 Nov 1983, *Young Berber Girl* (1896, oil on panel, 15¾ x 11¾ ins / 40 x 30 cm) FRF 17,100. LONDON, 20 June 1985, *Egyptian Beauty* (1902, oil on canvas, 23½ x 18½ ins / 60 x 47 cm) GBP 1,600. PARIS, 8 Nov 1993, *Three Portraits of Young Girls from Bou-Saada* (1896, oil on panel, each 16 x 12½ ins / 40.5 x 32 cm) FRF 23,000. PARIS, 23 March 1994, *Portrait of a Young Girl from Bou-Saada* (1896, oil on panel, 15¾ x 12½ ins / 40 x 32 cm) FRF 23,000. PARIS, 7 Nov 1994, *Young Algerian Girl with Green Waistcoat* (1896, oil on panel, 16¼ x 13 ins / 41 x 33 cm) FRF 16,000. PARIS, 21 April 1996, *The Perfume Souk, Tunis* (1903, oil on canvas, 25½ x 21¼ ins / 65 x 54 cm) FRF 13,000. PARIS, 25 June 1996, *Portrait of a Man* (oil on panel, 11 x 8 ins / 27 x 20.5 cm) FRF 18,000. PARIS, 9 Dec 1996, *Woman Spinning* (1896, oil on panel, 16½ x 10 ins / 42 x 25.5 cm) FRF 10,500.

GASTE, Pierre
French, 20th century.
Born 30 October 1938, in Bouchemaine (Maine-et-Loire).
Painter, draughtsman, engraver.

From 1959 to 1962, Pierre Gaste studied at the École des Beaux-Arts in Angers. Since 1984 he has taught at the École des Beaux-Arts in Angoulême. A highly skilled draughtsman and engraver, he did not turn to painting until 1988. His drawings and engravings, which show great manual dexterity, combine real mineral, plant and animal forms in a static, solitary context. He has been described as having a mythological imagination. From engraving he moved on to monotypes in which he incorporates objects that have been pressed. His paintings, a blend of figuration and abstraction, make use of a variety of papers such as tracing paper and photographic paper and various techniques, combining pencil and acrylics to create effects of transparency. In his works of 1991-1992 he establishes a relationship between earth and the cosmos by gluing earth to polycarbonate paper, one of his preferred media.

Since 1964 he has taken part in numerous Salons and group exhibitions, including: in 1965 and 1975 at the Salon de la Nouvelle Figuration and the Salon de Mai in Paris; in 1969 and 1971 at the Paris Biennale; in 1977, 1979 and 1989 at the Salon de Montrouge, where he was awarded first prize for drawing in 1989; in 1982 at the Musée de la Seita in Paris and the Knoxville Museum in Tennessee in the USA; and in 1990 at FIAC (Foire Internationale d'Art Contemporain) in Paris. His first solo exhibition was in 1962. Since then Gaste has exhibited regularly both in France - at the Galerie Alain Oudin from 1989 in particular - as well as abroad.

GASTEIGER, Anna Sophie
German, 20th century.
Born 26 February 1878; died 1954, in Munich.
Painter. Flowers.

Anna Sophie Gasteiger studied with Dasio. She was active in Munich and Dresden.

AUCTION RECORDS:
AMSTERDAM, 18 June 1996, *Still-life with Flowers* (oil on canvas, 25 1/2 x 30 ins / 64.5 x 76 cm) NLG 2,760. MUNICH, 20 May 1999, *Summer Bouquet in Vase on Table* (oil on panel, 28 x 23 ins / 72 x 58 cm) DEM 8,000. MUNICH, 11 Nov 1999, *Still-life of Flowers in Two Bowls on Table* (1915, oil on card, 19 x 22 ins / 49 x 55 cm) DEM 6,500. MUNICH, 18 May 2000, *Still-life of Flowers* (oil on canvas, 30 x 38 ins / 77 x 96 cm) DEM 8,500. MUNICH, 16 Nov 2000, *Garden with Stream* (oil on card, 28 x 19 ins / 70 x 49 cm) DEM 10,000. MUNICH, 17 May 2001, *American Poppies* (oil on panel, 27 x 21 ins / 69 x 54 cm) DEM 7,000. MUNICH, 15 Nov 2001, *Still-life of Flowers* (oil on board, 40 x 29 ins / 102 x 74 cm) DEM 6,500. COLOGNE, 4 July 2002, *Bunch of Sunflowers in Vase and Plums in Dish with River Landscape behind* (oil on canvas/board, 33 x 29 ins / 85 x 74 cm) EUR 3,500. KEMPTEN, 11 July 2002, *Still-life of Corn Poppies in a Vase* (oil on canvas, 24 x 18 ins / 60 x 46 cm) EUR 2,500. MUNICH, 13 May 2004, *Autumn Flowers with Fruit Basket* (oil on card, 28 x 20 ins / 71 x 52 cm) EUR 3,500. AHLDEN, 17 Sept 2004, *Still-life with Coral Coloured Flowers* (oil on board, 26 x 31 ins / 65 x 80 cm) EUR 3,000.

GASTEIGER, Jakob
Austrian, 20th - 21st century.
Born 1953, in Salzburg.
Painter.

Gasteiger builds up heavy layers of thick paint on the monochrome canvas, which he arranges in parallel lines. Thus, he endeavours to make the canvas impersonal. Since 1984, Gasteiger has participated in many group exhibitions in Vienna, Salzburg, Luxembourg, Belgium and France, notably: 1992, at the Salon des Découvertes in Paris; 2002, *Diskursive Malerei* (*Discursive Painting*) , the MUMOK (Museum Moderner Kunst Stiftung Ludwig), Vienna. He has held solo shows in Austria and the Netherlands.

GASTEIGER, Matthias
German, 19th - 20th century.
Born 24 June 1871.
Sculptor. Religious subjects, allegorical subjects.

Matthias Gasteiger studied with Eberle in Munich and worked in Dachau.

MUSEUMS AND GALLERIES:
LEIPZIG: *Judith*; *Adam and Eve*; *Spring*.

GASTEL, Frans van
Flemish School, 19th century.
Active c. 1843.
Painter, watercolourist. Flowers, fruit.

Van Gastel exhibited at Antwerp and Brussels.

GASTEL, P. H.
German, 18th century.
Painter (porcelain).

GASTELL, Franz
German, 19th century.
Born 21 February 1840, near Frankfurt am Main.
Sculptor.

Gastell was a pupil at the academy in Vienna.

GASTELLIER, Emma
French, 19th century.
Painter. Landscapes.

She exhibited at the Paris Salon.

GASTELLIER, Zoé Jeanne
French, 19th century.
Born 1824, in Versailles.
Painter, watercolourist.

She exhibited views of the Berry region from 1857 to 1879.

GASTEMANS, Émile
Belgian, 20th century.
Born 1883, in Borgerhout near Antwerp; died 1956.
Painter, lithographer. Portraits, genre scenes, landscapes.

Émile Gastemans studied at the Antwerp academy, but learned mainly from books and museums. He started the group Als ik kan (As I Can) . He brought back many exotic scenes from his travels. His works, though in 'shot' colours, have a muted harmony and are monumental in design.

MUSEUMS AND GALLERIES:
ANTWERP - BRUSSELS - GHENT.

AUCTION RECORDS:
ANTWERP, 23 April 1985, *At Table* (oil on canvas, 31 1/2 x 36 1/2 ins / 80 x 93 cm) BEF 55,000. LOKEREN, 21 March 1992, *Summer Landscape with a Country Lane* (oil on canvas, 30 x 47 1/4 ins / 76 x 120 cm) BEF 90,000. LOKEREN, 8 Oct 1994, *Seated Woman* (oil on canvas, 16 1/4 x 12 1/2 ins / 41.5 x 32 cm) BEF 26,000. LOKEREN, 7 Oct 1995, *Marriage Proposal* (oil on canvas, 31 1/2 x 36 1/2 ins / 80 x 93 cm) BEF 26,000. LOKEREN, 9 Oct 1999, *Fair, Antwerp* (1917, pastel and colour crayon, 23 x 26 ins / 58 x 65 cm) BEF 85,000. ANTWERP, 24 March 2003, *Women at Work in Docks* (1926, oil on canvas, 24 x 31 ins / 60 x 80 cm) EUR 3,200. ANTWERP, 20 Oct 2003, *Interior in Sevilla with Figures* (oil on canvas, 4 x 41 ins / 10 x 103 cm) EUR 4,000. ANTWERP, 27 April 2004, *Three Spaniards and their Child* (oil on canvas, 32 x 39 ins / 81 x 100 cm) EUR 1,700. ANTWERP, 27 April 2004, *Figures infront of a Door in a Spanish Landscape* (oil on canvas, 28 x 31 ins / 70 x 80 cm) EUR 2,600.

GASTET, Lambert, or Gatet
French, 17th century.
Painter.

Lambert Gastet was living in Lyons in 1660; he was master craftsman for the painters four times from 1661 to 1678.

GASTETON, Joseph
Austrian, 19th century.
Born 1865, in Vienna.
Painter. Landscapes.

Gasteton was a pupil of Lichtenfels in Vienna. He was awarded a medal in Madrid for a painting entitled *Landscape of Alcalá*.

Museums and Galleries:
Madrid (Prado): *Landscape* (charcoal).

GASTINE, Camille-Auguste
French, 19th century.
Born 30 January 1819, in Paris; died 3 April 1867, in Paris.
Painter.

He studied under Delaroche, Hesse and Picot. Between 1844 and 1867 he exhibited portraits and some religious compositions at the Paris Salon.

Museums and Galleries:
Orléans: *St Catherine of Alexandria, Virgin and Martyr.*

GASTINE, Charles A.
French, 19th century.
Active in Paris.
Painter.

He was a member of the Société des Artistes Français from 1899 and exhibited at its salons.

GASTINEAU, Henry
British, 19th century.
Born 1791; died 17 January 1876, in Camberwell.
Painter, watercolourist, engraver, draughtsman. Genre scenes, landscapes, waterscapes, architectural views.

Henry Gastineau studied at the Royal Academy in London. He began his career as an engraver, then turned to oils and ultimately - in 1824 - became a member of the Society of Painters in Watercolours, where he was on close terms with Turner, David Cox, Copley Fielding and others. From 1812 to 1875, he exhibited in London - at the Royal Academy, at the British Institution and at the Society of Painters in Watercolours, to which he submitted 300 compositions.

Museums and Galleries:
Bath (Holburne Mus. of Art): *Lake Scene with Castle* (watercolour); *Coast Scene* (watercolour) - London (Victoria and Albert Mus.): *Penrhyn Castle* (watercolour); *Five Views of England and Italy* (watercolour).

Auction records:
London, 14 March 1909, *Near Linton,* GBP 5. London, 26 Nov 1910, *View of Wales* (drawing) GBP 12. London, 22 April 1911, *Dunluce Castle, Ireland* (drawing) GBP 39. London, 27 Nov 1922, *Landscape* (drawing) GBP 6. London, 16 Feb 1923, *Waterfall* (drawing) GBP 13. London, 25 Jan 1924, *Lecco* (drawing) GBP 12. London, 20 June 1924, *Hospital* (drawing) GBP 86. London, 23 Feb 1925, *Aberystwyth* (drawing) GBP 9. London, 4 May 1925, *Off the Hebridean Coast* (drawing) GBP 8. London, 18 July 1927, *Cowdray Park,* GBP 8. London, 22 June 1928, *Isola di San Giulio* (drawing) GBP 22; *Lake Windermere* (drawing) GBP 25. London, 1 March 1929, *Folkestone,* GBP 8. London, 16 May 1930, *Derry,* GBP 15. London, 27 March 1931, *Meridian; Coming Home,* GBP 12. London, 10 Nov 1933, *Llandovery Castle* (drawing) GBP 13. London, 16 Jan 1936, *Salzburg* (watercolour) GBP 10. London, 28 June 1937, *Worcester Cathedral* (drawing) GBP 18. Manchester, 12 and 13 May 1939, *Harbour,* GBP 5. London, 24 March 1977, *River Dochart* (1860, watercolour, 35 x 52¼ ins / 89 x 133 cm) GBP 500. County Meath, 12 May 1981, *Carlingford Abbey, Co. Louth, Ireland* (1865, watercolour, 24½ x 36½ ins / 62 x 92.5 cm) GBP 760. New York, 25 May 1984, *Customs House, Dublin* (watercolour heightened with white and pen/pencil outlines, 23½ x 35½ ins / 59.6 x 90.2 cm) USD 3,000. London, 25 Jan 1988, *Lucerne, Switzerland* (watercolour, 16¼ x 25 ins / 41 x 63.5 cm) GBP 440. Paris, 20 Dec 1988, *Customs House, Dublin* (1853, watercolour, 23¾ x 35½ ins / 60.5 x 90 cm) FRF 82,000. Edinburgh, 26 April 1990, *Busy Estuary Scene with Fishing Boats before Castles and Ruins* (watercolour and gouache, 31 x 52¼ ins / 78.7 x 132.8 cm) GBP 3,080. London, 13 July 1993, *Salzburg* (pencil and watercolour, 30 x 52 ins / 76.2 x 132.1 cm) GBP 6,325. Shrewsbury, 10 Nov 1999, *Near Rhayader, North Wales* (watercolour, 11 x 15 ins / 28 x 38 cm) GBP 1,000. London, 29 Nov 2000, *Lake Como* (1861, pencil and watercolour heightened with gum arabic and scratching out, 11 x 15 ins / 27 x 37 cm) GBP 1,600. London, 10 April 2001, *Richmond Hill* (watercolour over pencil heightened with scratching out, 15 x 20 ins / 38 x 52 cm) GBP 2,700. Newbury, 16 May 2001, *Figures and Cattle before a North Italian or Swiss Lake* (pencil and colour wash heightened with white, 19 x 25 ins / 48 x 63 cm) GBP 1,500. Leominster, 17 April 2002, *Panoramic View of Lake Maggiore with Figures near a Campanile* (1861, watercolour, 4 x 6 ins / 11 x 15 cm) GBP 1,250. Leeds, 4 Feb 2003, *Park near Middleham Castle, Yorkshire, Henry VI pt III, Act IV Scene V* (1840, watercolour, 10 x 15 ins / 26 x 37 cm) GBP 1,800. Leeds, 4 Feb 2003, *Grange, Cumberland* (1855, pencil and watercolour, 24 x 36 ins / 61 x 91 cm) GBP 2,600.

GASTINEAU, J.C.
British, 19th century.
Active in London.
Painter. Landscapes.

J.C. Gastineau exhibited at the Royal Academy in London in 1826.

GASTINEAU, Jean Baptiste
French, 18th century.
Active in Paris c. 1740.
Painter (?), sculptor (?).

GASTINEAU, Maria
British, 19th century.
Active in London.
Painter. Landscapes.

Maria Gastineau was a member of the Society of Lady Artists. She exhibited in London from 1865 to 1867, notably at the Suffolk Street Gallery.

GASTINEAU, Nicolas Claude
French, 18th century.
Active in Paris in 1740.
Sculptor.

GASTINEL, Jean Claude
French, 18th century.
Painter.

Jean Gastinel won the second prize of the Académie Royale in Paris in 1758.

GASTINI, Marco
Italian, 20th century.
Born 1938, in Turin.
Painter.
Arte Povera.

Marco Gastini first exhibited in Turin in 1963, and again in 1965. Since then, he has taken part in many group exhibitions - both in Italy, alongside other avant-garde artists, and abroad, in cities such as Paris, Chicago and Bonn. He has also held solo exhibitions in Italy, and in galleries overseas, most notably: in 1993, at the Galerie Appel und Fertsch in Frankfurt; at the Kunstverein (a retrospective); and in 1996 at the Galerie Krief in Paris. In 2001 the Städtische Galerie im Lenbachhaus und Kunsthaus in Munich held a retrospective exhibition of Gastini's work, under the title *Malräume - Arbeiten 1969-2001* (*Painterly Spaces - Works 1969-2001*) .

Gastini's work tends to translate art into an attitude and a mode of behaviour. Reducing creative expression to a minimum of violent energy, he was involved with the Arte Povera movement, which was at the forefront of the Italian avant-garde in 1968. At that time, he often used neon in his works, juxtaposing it with other raw materials. He then returned to painting, reducing it to just a few symbols scattered across a virgin canvas or grid: always extremely sparing, and in a spirit of minimalism, his aim is to reveal the continuity of space. He paints on large-scale formats, and sometimes uses round canvases. Some of his works are like a painting within a painting - comprising, for example, a piece of paper stuck to the centre of the canvas, with scraps of paper then glued all over the surface. As his style has evolved, so has the range of materials used: these include plaster, wood, wire, stone and canvas sheeting. Gastini has also harnessed the translucent properties of polycarbonate and the iridescence of mother-of-pearl powder to make beautiful variations on the low relief.

BIBLIOGRAPHY:

Marco Gastini, exhibition catalogue, Gal. Appel und Fertsch, Frankfurt am Main, 1981. *Marco Gastini. Malräume - Arbeiten 1969-2001*, exhibition catalogue, Städtische Gal. im Lenbachhaus und Kunstbaus, Munich, 2001.

GASTMAYR
Austrian, 18th century.
Active in Vienna.
Painter.

Gastmayr also worked in Salzburg.

GASTO, Francisco del
Spanish, 16th century.
Active in Valladolid.
Sculptor.

In 1597, Francisco del Gasto is recorded as receiving payment for bronze frames and mouldings he had made for the Escorial monastery.

GASTO, János
Hungarian, 19th century.
Engraver.

János Gasto produced a portrait of Archduke Ferdinand Carl Joseph.

GASTO VILANOVA, Pedro
Spanish, 20th century.
Born 1908, in Barcelona.
Painter.

Pedro Gasto Vilanova studied at the school of fine arts in Barcelona. He won the Barcelona City Council Prize in 1944 and 1951. He began painting in 1932 but he truly found his style only in 1943; this derived from Picasso's blue and pink periods gradually developing towards a disintegration of form but always within the boundaries of representational art.

MUSEUMS AND GALLERIES:

BARCELONA.

AUCTION RECORDS:

MADRID, 20 Dec 1976, *Pietà* (1974, oil on canvas, 28 3/4 x 36 1/4 ins / 73 x 92 cm) ESP 80,000. MADRID, 24 Feb 1977, *Three Young Girls against a Pink Background* (1972, oil on canvas, 25 1/2 x 32 ins / 65 x 81 cm) ESP 105,000. BARCELONA, 7 Oct 1980, *Portrait of a Woman* (1965, pen/paper, 25 1/2 x 24 1/2 ins / 64.5 x 62 cm) ESP 85,000. MADRID, 27 Oct 1983, *Three Figures* (1971, oil on canvas, 15 x 22 ins / 38 x 55 cm) ESP 90,000. MADRID, 9 March 1999, *Portrait of Woman in Blue* (1974, oil on canvas, 29 x 24 ins / 73 x 60 cm) ESP 425,000. MADRID, 18 Feb 2000, *Female Figure* (1974, oil on canvas, 29 x 24 ins / 73 x 60 cm) ESP 690,000. MADRID, 18 Dec 2000, *Actors* (oil on canvas, 29 x 36 ins / 73 x 92 cm) ESP 600,000. MADRID, 3 April 2001, *Fish* (oil on canvas, 29 x 36 ins / 73 x 92 cm) ESP 800,000. MADRID, 2 Oct 2001, *Woman* (1974, oil on canvas, 29 x 24 ins / 73 x 60 cm) ESP 675,000. MADRID, 4 Nov 2003, *Actor* (oil on canvas, 19 x 15 ins / 47 x 39 cm) EUR 2,400.

GASTON, also known as (le) Zoologue
French, 20th century.
Born 1920, in the Pas-de-Calais.
Draughtsman.

Gaston is mentioned by José Pierre in *Le Surréalisme* (published by Rencontre, Lausanne, 1966). He was institutionalised on his 20th birthday. In 1946 he began producing dreamlike drawings.

GASTON, Pedro
Spanish, 16th century.
Painter.

On 19 March 1548, Pedro Gaston was called to give his opinion in a law suit between Giralte and Juni, at Valladolid, regarding a work of art. In 1555, he received payment for panels he had painted for the church of the Antigua in Valladolid. He also worked with Alejo de Encina on the high altar of the chapel of the monastery of S Pablo.

GASTON, Pierre-Marc Bassompierre
French, 19th century.
Born 1786, in Paris.
Painter.

He studied under David. Between 1812 and 1838 he exhibited at the Paris Salon and was awarded a medal in 1824. He was appointed professor of drawing and composition at the La Flèche military academy in 1816.

GASTON-BROQUET. See **BROQUET Gaston**

GASTON-GÉRARD. See **GÉRARD Gaston**

GASTON-GUITTON, Victor Édouard Gustave. See **GUITTON Gaston**

GASTYNE, Marco de
French, 20th century.
Born 14 July 1889, in Paris.
Painter. Portraits, genre scenes.

Marco de Gastyne joined the École Nationale des Beaux-Arts in Paris at a young age and studied there under Cormon. He exhibited in Paris at the Salon des Artistes Français, where he was awarded a bronze medal in 1910. In 1911 he was awarded the Grand Prix de Rome. De Gastyne was also interested in cinematography.

GASULL, Agustín
Spanish, 18th century.
Born in Valencia.
Active c. 1700.
Painter.

Agustín Gasull studied under Carlo Maratta in Rome. The church of S Juan del Mercado in Valencia has four important works of his: *St Andrew*; *St Stephen*; *The Virgin of Hope*; and *St Joseph*.

GASVRE, Pacquet de
French, 15th century.
Sculptor (wood).

Pacquet de Gasvre carved the choir stalls of the church of St-Pierre in Saumur (Maine-et-Loire) in 1475.

GASZYNSKI, Mathias
Polish, 19th century.
Born c. 1805; died c. 1868.
Painter, draughtsman.

Mathias Gaszynski lived in France for a long time.

GAT, Eliahu
Israeli, 20th century.
Born 1919; died 1987.
Painter. Landscapes with figures, landscapes.

AUCTION RECORDS:

TEL AVIV, 16 May 1983, *Landscape* (oil on card mounted/canvas, 26 3/4 x 38 ins / 68 x 96.5 cm) ILS 36,000. TEL AVIV, 3 Jan 1990, *Landscape* (oil on canvas, 19 3/4 x 27 1/2 ins / 50 x 70 cm) USD 2,200. TEL AVIV, 19 June 1990, *Mountain Landscape* (1978, oil on canvas, 23 3/4 x 31 3/4 ins / 60.5 x 80.5 cm) USD 2,200. TEL AVIV, 1 Jan 1991, *Landscape* (oil on canvas, 31 1/2 x 39 1/4 ins / 80 x 100 cm) USD 2,200. TEL AVIV, 12 June 1991, *Landscape* (oil on canvas, 19 1/2 x 27 1/4 ins / 49.5 x 69.5 cm) USD 2,420. TEL AVIV, 6 Jan 1992, *Landscape* (oil on canvas,

39 1/4 x 39 1/4 ins / 100 x 100 cm) USD 3,080. TEL AVIV, 14 Jan 1996, *Bathers by the Galilean Sea* (oil on panel, 27 1/2 x 39 1/4 ins / 70 x 100 cm) USD 3,450. TEL AVIV, 8 April 1999, *Landscape* (oil on canvas, 31x39 ins / 80x100 cm) USD 6,000. TEL AVIV, 4 July 1999, *Still-life with Jugs and Fruit* (oil on canvas, 19x27 ins / 49x68 cm) USD 1,400. TEL AVIV, 29 June 2000, *Landscape* (oil on canvas, 19x27 ins / 48x68 cm) USD 2,600. LONDON, 26 Oct 2000, *Landscape* (oil on canvas, 24x31 ins / 61x78 cm) USD 3,000. TEL AVIV, 15 Jan 2001, *Mountain Landscape* (ink, 13x18 ins / 32x46 cm) USD 500. TEL AVIV, 12 June 2001, *Landscape* (oil on paper/board, 13x19 ins / 32x47 cm) USD 800. TEL AVIV, 1 March 2004, *Reclining Female Nude* (oil on canvas, 20x29 ins / 51x73 cm) USD 1,100. TEL AVIV, 1 Oct 2004, *Houses in a Landscape* (oil on canvas, 24x31 ins / 60x80 cm) USD 1,800.

GATA, José
Portuguese, 19th century.
Born 1778, in Viseu; died 1831, in Viseu.
Painter.

José Gata was a pupil of Barros and worked in Spain and Portugal.

GATARD, Denise
French, 20th century.
Born 1921; died 1992.
Potter.

Denise Gatard executed works, notably an earthenware jug, in a Cubist style.

GATARD, Jeanne
French, 20th century.
Born 1937.
Painter (mixed media), draughtswoman. Figures, landscapes.

Jeanne Gatard lives and works in Paris. From 1977 to 1983, Gatard produced *La Grande Sieste* (*The Long Siesta*) (3 x 164 feet or 1 x 50 metres), a book of hours on silk comprising paintings sewn and sometimes over-embroidered and incorporating text; the aim of the piece was to see 'all world events' experienced through poetry. She depicts a universe of affection populated by temples, animals, palm trees, volcanoes, chairs and figures but also by real objects such as books, games and cassettes slipped inside half-open pockets - a vast epic of a forgotten time, captioned by handwritten or typed texts. The first part, which consists of a dozen chapters, is accompanied by a book highlighting the inflections of the plastic language. The second part is a variation around a portrait of a seated man who 'rame sa vie' (rows his life) - and these words are written on the canvas. She continued this exploration in the series *Anges et Rameurs* (*Angels and Oarsmen*) and *Les Barques* (*The Boats*) . Again, the slender silhouettes of beings and objects exist momentarily side by side, images of a life 'which runs its course between the marvellous and the disastrous'. After this she returned to drawings on paper in the series *Armchairs - Angels - Boats without Return - Pyramids - Paced Words* and from 1986, used texts and drawings in various books including *Vers l'Oiseau* (*Towards the Bird*) (1986), *Les Anges du Vide* (*Angels of the Void*) (1988), *Le Fragile* (*Fragile One*) (1991) and *L'Homme de la Ligne* (*Man with Line*) (1993).

She has taken part in various group exhibitions: between 1960 and 1970 in the Salon de la Jeune Peinture in Paris and the Paris Biennale; in 1981 at the École des Beaux-Arts in Limoges and the *Le Point à la Ligne* exhibition at the Musée Nationale d'Art Moderne in Paris; in 1984 the *L'Écriture dans la Peinture* exhibition at the CNAC (Centre National d'Art Contemporain) in Nice; in 1987 at the Salon de Mai in Paris; and in 1988 at the Isetan Museum in Tokyo. She has shown her paintings regularly in solo exhibitions in Paris notably from 1986 at the Galerie Charles Sablon but also in 1976 at the Centre Culturel d'Aix-en-Provence, in 1978 at the Maison de la Culture in Amiens, in 1979 at the Bellomo museum in Syracuse, in 1989 and 1991 at the Galerie des Beaux-Arts in Bordeaux and in 1999 at the Galerie Claude Samuel in Paris.

BIBLIOGRAPHY:
'Écritures dans la peinture' in *2 vol.*, exhibition catalogue, Villa Arson-Centre national des Arts plastiques, Nice, 1984. *Cinq artistes en 89*, exhibition catalogue, Gal. des Beaux-Arts, Bordeaux, 1989.

GATCH, Lee
American, 20th century.
Born 1902; died 1968.
Painter (mixed media). Landscapes, landscapes with figures.

Lee Gatch sometimes used mixed media, for example charcoal and oil, and produced collages among other things.

BIBLIOGRAPHY:
Loughery, John, *'The Lyrical Abstractions of Lee Gatch'* in *Arts Magazine LXII/8* (pp. 78-80). Callicott, Burton H., *The Art Today Collection*, Memphis, 1977.

AUCTION RECORDS:
NEW YORK, 29 April 1976, *Tundra Tapestry* (1961, oil and collage/canvas, 21 x 40 ins / 53.5 x 101.5 cm) USD 2,300. NEW YORK, 4 June 1982, *Cyclists* (1958, oil on canvas, 32 3/4 x 38 ins / 83.2 x 96.5 cm) USD 3,500. NEW YORK, 18 March 1983, *Chicken Thief* (oil on canvas, 33 x 26 1/2 ins / 84 x 67 cm) USD 5,500. NEW YORK, 30 May 1985, *Chicken Thief* (oil on canvas, 33 x 24 ins / 83.8 x 61 cm) USD 10,500. NEW YORK, 24 June 1988, *Morning in the East* (1943, oil on canvas, 21 1/2 x 39 1/4 ins / 54.5 x 100 cm) USD 6,600. NEW YORK, 25 May 1989, *New York* (1955, oil on canvas, 14 x 26 1/2 ins / 35.5 x 67 cm) USD 6,600. NEW YORK, 28 Sept 1989, *Holy Mountain* (oil on canvas, 22 3/4 x 30 ins / 58 x 76 cm) USD 4,620. NEW YORK, 16 March 1990, *Recalcitrant Farmer* (1952, oil on canvas, 22 x 38 ins / 56 x 96.5 cm) USD 3,300. NEW YORK, 30 May 1990, *Racing Team* (1956, oil on canvas, 21 x 40 ins / 53.3 x 101.6 cm) USD 3,300. NEW YORK, 31 May 1990, *Carbon Stove* (oil on canvas, 24 x 10 1/4 ins / 60.9 x 26 cm) USD 880. NEW YORK, 15 May 1991, *Untitled Composition* (1960, mixed media and collage/card, 30 x 24 ins / 76.2 x 61 cm) USD 1,320. NEW YORK, 12 March 1992, *Easter Morning* (oil and charcoal/canvas, 22 x 40 1/4 ins / 56 x 102 cm) USD 5,500. NEW YORK, 31 March 1993, *Corridor* (1960, oil and collage/canvas, 38 3/4 x 25 ins / 98.4 x 63.8 cm) USD 1,955. NEW YORK, 31 March 1994, *Farm in Pennsylvania* (oil on canvas, 14 x 45 ins / 35.6 x 114.3 cm) USD 3,450. NEW YORK, 21 May 1996, *Night Court* (oil on canvas, 38 x 22 ins / 96.7 x 55.9 cm) USD 4,025. NEW YORK, 30 Sept 1997, *Jura* (1961, mixed media/panel, 24 x 48 ins / 61 x 121.9 cm) USD 10,350. SAN FRANCISCO, 26 Oct 1999, *Pacific Rhythm* (1967, mixed media and collage on board, 24 x 35 ins / 61 x 89 cm) USD 3,000. NEW YORK, 30 Oct 2003, *Under the Street Lamp* (oil on canvas, 16 x 20 ins / 40 x 51 cm) USD 6,000. PHILADELPHIA, 7 Dec 2003, *Amphora* (1962, oil, collage and mixed media on board, 34 x 26 ins / 86 x 66 cm) USD 9,000. NEW YORK, 31 March 2004, *Untitled* (collage and oil on canvas, 36 x 50 ins / 92 x 127 cm) USD 8,500. PHILADELPHIA, 27 June 2004, *Study in White* (1926, oil on canvas, 20 x 14 ins / 51 x 36 cm) USD 27,000.

GATCHEV, Vassil
Bulgarian, 20th century.
Born in Bulgaria.
Sculptor.

GATE, Camille
French, 19th century.
Born 1856, in Nogent-le-Rotrou (Eure-et-Loir); died 21 August 1900.
Sculptor, writer.

He exhibited at the Salon des Artistes Français, receiving an honourable mention in 1887. He was awarded a bronze medal at the Exposition Universelle of 1889.

GATENBY, John William
American, 20th century.
Born 1903, in Illinois.
Painter, writer.
John Gatenby studied with Buck, Elliot, Forsberg, Lyford, Tomaso and Larson. He painted *Blue Parrot "Go Way"* a water-colour on paper.

GATES, Alice
British, 20th century.
Painter.

GATET, André
French, 17th - 18th century.
Engraver (line-engraving), medallist. Seals.
André Gatet was living in Lyons in 1698 and 1713 and was employed at the Mint there. As well as engravings for tokens, medals and seals, he produced line-engravings.

GATET, Lambert. See **GASTET**

GATHY, Jan Hendrik
Flemish School, 18th - 19th century.
Born 1752, in Liège; died 12 August 1811, in Liège.
Sculptor.
MUSEUMS AND GALLERIES:
LIÈGE: *Rape of Proserpina.*

GATIER, Pierre Louis
French, 20th century.
Born 12 January 1878, in Toulon; died 15 October 1944, in Joigny (Yonne).
Painter, watercolourist, engraver, draughtsman, designer. Portraits, genre scenes, waterscapes, mountainscapes, seascapes. Murals.
Pierre Gatier attended the École des Beaux-Arts in Toulon and then in Paris, where he studied at the studio of Fernand Cormon. Lionel Aristide Lecouteux introduced him to the art of engraving and to aquatint in particular. In 1907 he was appointed as an official painter to the French navy. From 1930 to 1937 he abandoned painting almost completely and moved to Haute-Savoie.

He soon became known as a watercolourist and draughtsman and then an engraver, producing line and drypoint engravings first in colour and then in black and white. He painted various scenes of life in Paris, nightclub scenes and society portraits. He also painted mountain landscapes and views of ports, particularly Toulon and its harbour. In 1913 he discovered the Channel coast and the area of Isle-Adam, and the skies of Normandy became a revelation that influenced the rest of his work. He also produced several decorative panels for the French admiralty and some murals for the church of St-Georges in Toulon.

He took part in group exhibitions at the Paris Salons: in 1901, 1907 and 1908 at the Salon des Artistes Français; in 1907, 1911, 1924, 1926 and 1930 at the Salon des Indépendants; in 1922, 1923 and 1930 at the Salon d'Automne; in 1928 and 1931 at the Salon of the Société Nationale des Beaux-Arts, of which he was a member; in 1937 at the Exposition Internationale des Arts et Techniques; in 1942 at the Salon de la Marine; and in 1955 in a retrospective at the Salon de la Société Nationale des Beaux-Arts. His work was also shown in solo exhibitions: in 1917 at the Musée de Rochefort; in 1957 at the Musée Galliera in Paris; in 1974 at a retrospective at the Salon de la Marine in Paris; in 1975 in a tribute exhibition at the Musée Eugène Boudin in Honfleur; in 1976 at the Musée des Beaux-Arts in Boulogne-sur-Mer and the Musée Louis Senlecq in Isle-Adam; and in 1988 at the Musée Carnavalet in Paris. In 1935 he was made a Chevalier of the Légion d'Honneur for his work for the navy.
BIBLIOGRAPHY:
Pierre Gatier 1878-1944, la vie parisienne, exhibition catalogue, Musée Carnavalet, Paris, 1988.
MUSEUMS AND GALLERIES:
BERCK-SUR-MER (Mus. d'Histoire et d'Archéologie) - BOULOGNE-SUR-MER (MBA) - CHICAGO (Field Mus. of Natural History) - HONFLEUR (Mus. Eugène Boudin) - L'ISLE-ADAM (MAH Louis-Senlecq) - LE BOURGET (Mus. de l'Air et de l'Espace) - PARIS (Bibliothèque d'Art et d'Archéologie, Fondation Jacques-Doucet): *Portrait of Lina* (1907, aquatint); *Portrait of a Woman in Blue* (1907); *The Champs-Elysées* (1910, aquatint) - PARIS (BNF, Prints Collection): *The Petite Rue Royale* (burin) - PARIS (Mus. Carnavalet) - PARIS (Mus. d'Orsay): *Milliner* (1907, aquatint) - PARIS (Mus. de la Marine) - TOULON (MA).
AUCTION RECORDS:
PARIS, 28 Oct 1990, *Rocks at Low Tide at Les Sables d'Olonne* (1928, oil on canvas, 21 1/4 x 25 1/2 ins / 54 x 65 cm) FRF 8,000.
PARIS, 25 Nov 1990, *Floodtide at Les Sables d'Olonne* (1928, watercolour, 7 3/4 x 11 1/2 ins / 20 x 29.5 cm) FRF 3,700.

GATINE, Georges Jacques or Jean
French, 18th - 19th century.
Born c. 1773, in Caen; died after 1824.
Engraver (burin), illustrator, reproductions engraver.
Genre scenes, costume studies.
George Gatine belongs to the category of minor artists whose efforts focused on the role of the 'painter of manners' and the absurdities of their era. Gatine drew or engraved costumes and genre scenes. He was one of the iconographers of the dandies and the whims of fashion. He is interesting from a documentary viewpoint and his works are highly sought after.

GATINEAU, Antoine Louis
French, 18th century.
Active in Paris in 1738.
Painter, sculptor.

GATINES, René-Charles-Félix de
French, 19th century.
Born 1853, in Paris; died 1902.
Painter. Landscapes.
He first exhibited at the Paris Salon in 1879.

GATING, J. van
Dutch, 17th century.
Active c. 1675.
Painter.
MUSEUMS AND GALLERIES:
AMSTERDAM: *Self-portrait.*

GATLEY, Alfred
British, 19th century.
Born 1816, in Bollington; died 28 June 1863, in Rome.
Sculptor.
Alfred Gatley was a frequent exhibitor at London's Royal Academy between 1841 and 1852.
MUSEUMS AND GALLERIES:
SALFORD (Museum and AG): *Greek Hero Leading a Bull to be Sacrified; Euripides* (sculpture).

GATO DELERNA, Nicolás
Spanish, 19th century.
Born 1820, in Madrid; died 4 February 1883, in Madrid.
Painter. Landscapes.
Nicolás Gato Delerna was a pupil of Vicente Lopéz. He exhibited in Madrid and Paris, notably at the Exposition Universelle of 1855. In 1859 he was made a member of the Academia de San Fernando.

GATOR, Nicolas
French, 16th century.
Painter.
This painter was a Franciscan monk.

GATORI, Damiano
Italian, 16th century.
Miniaturist.
Damiano Gatori worked for the cathedral in Carpi around 1520.

GATSCHET, John Rudolf von
Swiss, 19th century.
Died 1856, in Bern.
Painter.

GATSCHET, Niklaus
Swiss, 18th - 19th century.
Born 9 August 1736, in Bern; died 11 March 1817, in Rennes.
Painter, engraver.
Niklaus Gatschet exhibited in Bern and Zurich.

GATT, Ferdinand
Austrian, 19th century.
Born 10 December 1847, in Innsbruck; died 16 September 1909, in Brixen, South Tyrol (now Bressanone, Italy).
Painter, watercolourist. Mountainscapes, landscapes.
AUCTION RECORDS:
HAMBURG, 5 June 1985, *High Mountain Landscape with Glacier* (watercolour, 11 3/4 x 10 ins / 30 x 24.5 cm) DEM 2,800. PARIS, 25 Oct 1994, *Getting a Bargain, rue de Sèvres in 1871, Distribution of English Gifts* (watercolour, 4 1/4 x 12 1/2 ins / 10.5 x 32 cm) FRF 5,000. VIENNA, 19 March 2002, *Spring Landscape* (watercolour, 12 x 16 ins / 30 x 40 cm) EUR 2,200. VIENNA, 26 March 2004, *Brenner Mountain Valley* (watercolour, 19 x 27 ins / 48 x 69 cm) EUR 2,600.

GATTA, Bartolommeo della. See **PIETRO DI ANTONIO DI GIOVANNI DI DEO DEI**

GATTA, José d'Ameida or d'Almeida
Portuguese, 19th century.
Born in Viseu; died 1832.
Painter.

GATTA, Saverio Xavier della
Italian, 18th century.
Died 1829.
Painter (gouache), watercolourist, draughtsman. Genre scenes, hunting scenes, landscapes.
Gatta was a pupil of Cestaro; he worked in Naples in 1777.
AUCTION RECORDS:
LONDON, 21 March 1974, *Bay of Naples* (gouache) GBP 1,100. LONDON, 19 Aug 1978, *Hunt Scene* (1783, gouache, 12 1/4 x 21 ins / 31 x 53.5 cm) GBP 2,150. LONDON, 26 March 1981, *Encounter* (1791, watercolour and gouache, 14 1/2 x 21 ins / 37 x 53.5 cm) GBP 1,500. LONDON, 13 Dec 1984, *View of Paestum* (1783-1784, gouache, 10 3/4 x 16 1/2 ins / 27.2 x 41.7 cm) GBP 2,700. LONDON, 9 Dec 1986, *View of Naples* (gouache, 20 3/4 x 30 1/4 ins / 52.6 x 76.9 cm) GBP 18,000. PARIS, 9 Dec 1987, *Fisherman with a Pipe* (oil on canvas, 10 1/2 x 8 1/4 ins / 26.5 x 21 cm) FRF 5,200. LONDON, 24 June 1988, *Woman from Caieta* (1828, pencil and watercolour, 9 x 6 ins / 22 x 15 cm) GBP 1,700. LONDON, 30 March 1990, *Dance* (1815, watercolour, 7 1/2 x 11 1/2 ins / 19 x 29 cm) GBP 2,310. LONDON, 19 June 1991, *Strolling Musicians, Naples* (1814, watercolour, 6 x 9 ins / 15 x 23 cm) GBP 3,520. NEW YORK, 27 May 1992, *Neapolitan Air* (1822, watercolour and ink, 7 3/4 x 10 1/4 ins / 19.7 x 25.8 cm) USD 6,050. LONDON, 17 June 1992, *Group of Nuns* (1803, watercolour, 9 3/4 x 14 1/2 ins / 25 x 37 cm) GBP 770. NEW YORK, 13 Jan 1993, *View from Palazzo Donn'Anna with Posillipo in the Distance and Fishermen in the Foreground* (1780, tempera, 12 1/2 x 22 ins / 31.5 x 56 cm) USD 29,900. LONDON, 5 July 1993, *Xapuana Gate, Naples* (1780, gouache, 11 1/2 x 15 1/2 ins / 29 x 39.2 cm) GBP 33,350. MILAN, 2 Dec 1993, *Wine Merchant* (1829, watercolour/paper, 8 1/4 x 11 1/4 ins / 21 x 28.5 cm) ITL 4,025,000. PARIS, 1 June 1994, *Ruins of an Ancient Temple* (1800, gouache, a pair, each 12 1/2 x 17 1/4 ins / 32 x 43.5 cm) FRF 23,500. MONACO, 20 June 1994, *Italian Costumes* (1809, watercolour, a pair each 12 x 17 1/4 ins / 30.2 x 43.6 cm) FRF 99,900. PARIS, 22 March 1995, *Creek, Italy* (1813, gouache and ink, 12 x 18 1/4 ins / 30.6 x 46.5 cm) FRF 29,500. NEW YORK, 20 July 1995, *The Sorbet Seller* (1820, gouache/paper, 8 3/4 x 10 1/4 ins / 22.2 x 26 cm) USD 4,025. PARIS, 27 Feb 1996, *Eating Pasta* (1811, black chalk and watercolour, 10 1/4 x 14 1/2 ins / 26 x 37 cm) FRF 12,500. MILAN, 3 April 1996, *Il Cavallo di Puglia; Playing Mora* (1799, gouache/ paper, a pair, 8 x 5 3/4 ins / 20.5 x 14.5 cm) ITL 9,775,000. PARIS, 17 Oct 1997, *View from Lake Fusaro towards Ischia, near Naples* (1813, gouache, 13 3/4 x 21 1/4 ins / 35 x 54 cm) FRF 38,000.

GATTEAUX, Jacques-Édouard
French, 19th century.
Born 4 November 1788, in Paris; died 8 February 1881, in Paris.
Sculptor, medallist.
He studied under Moitte, won the Prix de Rome for medal-engraving in 1809, and exhibited sculpture at the Paris Salon from 1814 to 1855. He was an officer of the Légion d'Honneur and a member of the Institut de France. Examples of his work include *Woman Bathing* (marble low relief), *Minerva after the Judgement of Paris* (bronze statue), *Pomone* (marble statue), *Sedaine* (marble bust) and *Chevalier d'Assas* (bronze statuette).
BIBLIOGRAPHY:
Ternois, Daniel, '*Ingres et Albert Magimel: lettres et documents*' in *Bulletin du Musée Ingres*, 1988. Vigne, Georges, '*Le carton des académies*' in *Bulletin du Musée Ingres* no. 71, 1998.
MUSEUMS AND GALLERIES:
PARIS (Louvre): *Michelangelo* (bronze bust) - VERSAILLES: *François Rabelais* (marble bust).

GATTEAUX, Nicolas Marie
French, 18th - 19th century.
Born 2 August 1751, in Paris; died 21 June 1832, in Paris.
Sculptor, medallist.
Nicolas Gatteaux was the inventor of a machine used by sculptors for honing. He produced engravings for lottery tickets, banknotes and government stamps. He was the father of Jacques Édouard Gatteaux. The Louvre museum holds a bronze by him: *The Spirit of History*.

GATTEGNO-WEIL, A. M.
French, 19th - 20th century.
Painter.
A. M. Gattegno-Weil worked in Marseilles and exhibited at the Salon of the Société des Artistes Français, of which she became a member in 1903.

GATTERER, Andreas
Austrian, 19th century.
Born 1810, in Linz.
Miniaturist, lithographer.
Gatterer is mainly credited with portraits.

GATTERI, Giuseppe Lorenzo
German, 19th century.
Born 1830, in Trieste; died 1884, in Trieste.
Painter. Genre scenes.
Gatteri exhibited in Dresden in 1883. He is noted for his *Start of the Carnival*. The Revoltella museum in Trieste has works by him entitled *Female Costume, 16th Century* and *Lucretia Borgia*.
AUCTION RECORDS:
VENICE, 1894, *Catherine Cornaro delivering the Royal Insignia to the Doge Mocenigo*, FRF 206.

GATTERSLEBEN, G. J.
German, 18th century.

Active in Marienthal in 1746.
Sculptor.

GATTERSTEDT, Clara von
German, 14th century.
Painter. Portraits.
A nun in Kreuzburg, Upper Silesia (now Kluczbork, Poland) in 1306, Clara von Gatterstedt painted a portrait of the abbot of Fulda.

GATTESCHI, G.
Italian.
Engraver.
There is reference to an engraving by this artist of a reconstruction of Rome in about AD 300.

GATTI
Italian, 18th century.
Active in Genoa.
Painter. Portraits.
Gatti may be the same artist as a 'Gatti', on record as having worked in Rovigo.

GATTI
French, 19th century.
Active in 1826.
Sculptor.
Gatti's bust of *Bailly* is housed in the municipal library in Grenoble.

GATTI, Angelo
Italian, 20th century.
Born 27 July 1939, in Novara (Piedmont).
Painter, watercolourist. Landscapes.
Angelo Gatti exhibits regularly in Italy, and has been involved in a range of group exhibitions. He has been awarded numerous prizes and distinctions.

Driven by a desire to understand and penetrate the world around him, Gatti paints the natural world in rhythm with the seasons and the sea.

GATTI, Annibale
Italian, 19th century.
Born September 1828, in Forlì; died 13 August 1909, in Florence.
Painter, fresco artist. History painting, mythological subjects, genre scenes.
Annibale Gatti is regarded as one of the most remarkable Italian painters of the 19th century. He won a gold medal in Florence in 1872. He exhibited *Lafayette and Washington* in Boston. He taught at the academy of fine arts in Florence, and was made a knight of the Order of the Crown. Gatti painted a large number of frescoes. His best-known work is *Rinaldo and Armida*, in the Villa Favard in Florence.

AUCTION RECORDS:
LONDON, 8 Nov 1972, *Galileo Receiving John Milton*, GBP 450. MILAN, 12 Dec 1983, *Concert at the Russian Court* (oil on canvas, 19 x 29 3/4 ins / 48.5 x 75.5 cm) ITL 3,600,000. LONDON, 9 Oct 1987, *Leonardo Receiving Visitors in His Studio* (oil on canvas, 52 x 75 ins / 132 x 190.5 cm) GBP 4,000. LONDON, 7 June 1989, *John Milton with Galileo in His Observatory* (oil on canvas, 31 1/2 x 46 ins / 80 x 117 cm) GBP 4,180. LONDON, 18 March 1992, *John Milton with Galileo in His Observatory* (oil on canvas, 31 1/2 x 45 3/4 ins / 80 x 116.5 cm) GBP 4,180. MILAN, 18 March 2003, *Allegory of Drama* (oil on canvas, 47 x 67 ins / 120 x 170 cm) EUR 35,000. ROME, 10 June 2004, *Beach on the Sorrento Coast. Gallant Scene on the Beach* (gouache, oval, a pair, 11 x 13 ins / 27 x 33 cm) EUR 2,200.

GATTI, Antoine
French, 19th century.
Born in Marseilles.
Painter. Landscapes, flowers.
He studied under Motel and first exhibited at the Paris Salon in 1880.

GATTI, Antonio
Italian, 17th century.
Active in Bologna c. 1600, and in Modena.
Painter.

GATTI, Bernardino, called Il Sojaro
Italian, 16th century.
Born c. 1495, in Pavia; died 1575 or 1576, in Cremona.
Painter, draughtsman. Religious subjects, portraits.
Bernardino Gatti was one of Correggio's most talented pupils. In the refectory of the church of S Pietro in Cremona can be seen his large *Feeding of the Five Thousand*, dated 1552. In 1560, he painted one of his most significant works, an *Assumption*, in the cupola of the Madonna della Steccata in Parma. A large number of his works are housed in Parma, Racenzo and Cremona. There is a *Nativity* by him in the church of S Pietro in Cremona and a *Pietà* in the church of St Mary Magdalene in Parma. Gatti also completed the decoration of the gallery of S Maria di Campagna in Piacenza, which Bordone had left unfinished at the time of his death.

MUSEUMS AND GALLERIES:
BERGAMO (Accademia Carrara): *Virgin and Child with Two Saints* - FLORENCE (Uffizi): *Self-portrait* - NAPLES: *Ecce Homo; Christ Crucified* - TURIN: *Adoration of the Shepherds*.

AUCTION RECORDS:
NEW YORK, 24 March 1905, *Adoration of the Shepherds*, USD 500. LONDON, 3 July 1984, *Study of an Apostle Looking Up to the Left* (red and black chalk for the head; grey-black ink applied with a brush with grey wash and white highlights, 16 x 8 1/2 ins / 39.8 x 21.7 cm) GBP 85,000. MILAN, 13 May 1993, *Study of Man's Head* (red and white chalk, 4 1/4 x 3 3/4 ins / 10.7 x 9.8 cm) ITL 1,100,000. NEW YORK, 12 Jan 1994, *Man's Head Looking Upwards* (red chalk, heightened with white, 4 1/4 x 3 3/4 ins / 10.5 x 9.6 cm) USD 4,313. MONACO, 20 June 1994, *Drapery Study of a Kneeling Monk* (red chalk and pink wash, heightened with white, 9 1/4 x 6 1/4 ins / 23.6 x 16 cm) USD 288,600. MILAN, 13 June 2001, *St Dominic* (oil on canvas, 42 x 32 ins / 106 x 81 cm) ITL 16,949,150. OXFORD, 3 Oct 2003, *Study of the Virgin Mother and Child* (sepia chalk, 11 x 8 ins / 28 x 20 cm) GBP 22,000. NEW YORK, 22 Jan 2004, *Madonna and Child with the Infant John the Baptist, with Subsidiary Studies* (red chalk, 11 x 8 ins / 29 x 21 cm) USD 48,000.

GATTI, Filippo
Italian, 19th century.
Active in Rome.
Sculptor.
From 1877 onwards Filippo Gatti exhibited in Naples, Rome and Turin.

GATTI, Fortunato
Italian, 17th century.
Born 1597, in Parma; died 1651.
Painter. History painting.

MUSEUMS AND GALLERIES:
PARMA: *Holy Virgin between St Basil and St Bernard*.

GATTI, Geraldo
French, 19th century.
Active in Paris at the end of the 19th century.
Sculptor.
He exhibited at the Paris Salon from 1881 to 1887.

GATTI, Gervasio, called Il Sojaro
Italian, 16th - 17th century.
Born 1549; died 1631.
Active in Cremona.
Painter. History painting, portraits.
Gervasio Gatti was the nephew and pupil of Bernardino Gatti, who taught him to imitate the style of Correggio, as is

clear from his early paintings. Later in his career, he adopted the manner of the Carracci. He was also an excellent portrait painter. In his native town, his *Death of St Cecilia* can be seen in the church of S Pietro.

GATTI, Gesualdo
Italian, 19th century.
Born 11 February 1855, in Naples; died c. 1893.
Sculptor. Portraits, animals.

Gesualdo Gatti worked in Paris, and exhibited at the Salon between 1881 and 1887. He also exhibited in Munich and Vienna. He mostly sculpted dogs, but also made some busts.

AUCTION RECORDS:
PERTH, 29 Aug 1995, *Dogs Resting: One Asleep, the Other on the Lookout* (bronze, a pair, 4 x 7 3/4 ins / 10 x 20 cm and 5 1/2 x 7 3/4 ins/14 x 20 cm) GBP 1,380.

GATTI, Giacomo
Italian, 19th century.
Died c. 1817.
Active in Mantua.
Painter.

Giacomo Gatti was a pupil of Cadioli.

GATTI, Giovanni Battista
Italian, 19th century.
Active in Italy.
Draughtsman, engraver (burin).

GATTI, Girolamo
Italian, 17th - 18th century.
Born 1662, in Bologna; died 11 May 1726.
Painter. History painting, portraits.

Girolamo Gatti was a pupil of Marc-Antonio Franceschini. He generally opted for small paintings, but also produced some large-scale compositions for churches and palazzi in Bologna, including a *St Augustine, St Petronius and St Gregory Interceding on behalf of Souls in Purgatory* for the church of S Maria Incoronata, a *Presentation to the Temple* for the Church of the Nativity, and *Charles V Receiving the Crown from Pope Clement VII*.

GATTI, Giuseppe
Italian, 19th century.
Born 15 August 1807, in Milan; died 16 June 1880, in Urbino (Marche).
Painter.

Giuseppe Gatti was a pupil of Durelli at the academy of Milan.

GATTI, Jacques
French, 20th century.
Born 1927, in Algiers.
Painter, watercolourist. Landscapes.

Jacques Gatti began painting at an early age, working in watercolours and from life. Until Algeria gained its independence he exhibited regularly in Oran and Algiers. He returned to mainland France in 1965 and worked in advertising while continuing to paint. He has exhibited in Paris and in the south of France and has received numerous prizes and awards.

Gatti enjoys painting picturesque views of Provence and Brittany - a village street, a small chapel, a twisted olive tree; but also electric posts, road signs and old cans. He captures the light and warmth of earth and sky with great passion.

BIBLIOGRAPHY:
Les Peintres de Saint-Tropez, Ste-Maxime, 1990.

GATTI, Oliviero
Italian, 17th century.
Born in Piacenza; died after 1648.
Painter, engraver.

Although formally a pupil of Giovanni Ludovico Valesio, Oliviero Gatti must also have received instruction in engraving from Agostino Carracci, as their styles are strikingly similar. As a painter, Oliviero is relatively unknown, but as an engraver, his output was prolific.

Gatti was admitted to membership of the Bologna academy in 1626 and continued to work in Bologna until 1648. Examples of his engraved work include *St Francis Xavier Retrieving a Crucifix Floating on the Water* (from his own drawing), a *St Jerome* from 1602 (after Agostino Carracci), a *St Roch* from 1605 and an album of engravings taken from drawings by Guercino.

GATTI, Pietro
Italian, 19th century.
Active in Italy.
Engraver (burin).

GATTI, Saturnino de
Italian, 15th - 16th century.
Born 1463, in San Vittorino; died c. 1521.
Painter, sculptor.

Saturnino de Gatti worked mainly in the region of L'Aquila.

GATTI, Tommaso
Italian, 17th century.
Born 1642, in Pavia.
Painter. History painting.

Tommaso Gatti trained under Carlo Sacchi before travelling to Venice to study the work of the old masters. He then returned to his native Pavia and painted compositions for various churches in the city.

GATTI, Uriele, called Il Sojaro
Italian, 16th - 17th century.
Born c. 1560; died 1629.
Active in Cremona.
Painter. History painting.

Lanzi believes Uriele Gatti to be the brother of Gervasio Gatti. There is a *Crucifixion* by him, dated 1601, in the church of S Sepolcro, Piacenza.

GATTIKER, Hermann
Swiss, 19th - 20th century.
Born 12 March 1865, in Enge, (Zurich); died 1950.
Painter, engraver. Landscapes.

Hermann Gattiker studied in Dresden. From 1886 to 1892, he was entrusted with the education of Prince George of Saxony. His best known works are the painting *Evening Walk* and the engravings *Summer* and *The Mysterious House*.

AUCTION RECORDS:
ZURICH, 11 Nov 1981, *Einsiedeli* (1889, oil on canvas, 15 1/4 x 23 1/2 ins / 38.5 x 60 cm) CHF 9,000.

GATTIN, Ivo
Croat, 20th century.
Born 1926, in Split; died 1978, in Zagreb.
Painter.

During his studies at the school of fine art in Zagreb in 1953, Ivo Gattin was influenced by Surrealism, from which he soon broke loose to tackle abstraction, closely related to 'Art Informel'. Unconcerned about defining forms, he explored new media including sand, wax, tar.

GATTINGER, Wilhelm
German, 19th century.
Born 16 July 1861, in Frankfurt am Main.
Painter.

Gattinger is mainly credited with landscapes.

GATTO, Carmelo
Italian, 19th century.
Died 1895, in Reggio di Calabria.
Sculptor.

GATTO, Saverio
Italian, 20th century.

Born 15 August 1877, in Reggio di Calabria.
Sculptor.
Saverio Gatto studied under Achille d'Orsi. He exhibited at the Salon of the Société des Artistes Français in Paris.

GATTON, Franciszek
Polish, 19th century.
Died in Lemberg (now Lviv, Ukraine).
Painter.
Franciszek Gatton painted miniatures and landscapes and taught at the academy of fine arts from 1834.

GATTONI, Battista
Italian, 16th century.
Active in Pavia c. 1500.
Sculptor.

GATTONI, Pierre
Swiss, 20th - 21st century.
Born 1958, in La Chaux-de-Fonds (Neuchâtel).
Painter, designer.
Alongside his painting, Gattoni has produced many cinema sets. Some of his works flirt with figuration; for example, a square canvas of 1990, with a reduced colour range from black to white, is reminiscent of a target more than a network of circles. There may be a direct reference to American painter and sculptor Jasper Johns in the work.

Since 1981, Gattoni has participated in group exhibitions in Switzerland and France, including 1987, the Biennale Cantonale des Beaux Arts, La-Chaux-de-Fonds, where he won the Prize for the best submission; 1992, the FIAC (Foire Internationale d'Art Contemporain), and Paris. He has held solo shows, including Lausanne in 1984 and Geneva in 1988.

GATTOZUNI, Paolo
Russian, 19th century.
Active in St Petersburg at the beginning of the 19th century.
Sculptor.
Worked in 1826.

GATTY, Margaret
Maiden name: Scott
British, 19th century.
Born 1809, in Burnham; died 1873, in Ecclesfield.
Engraver.
Margaret Gatty was the daughter of Lord Nelson's chaplain, Dr Scott. She was known principally as an author of children's books, but also engraved several landscapes between 1837 and 1843.

GAUBAULT, Alfred-Émile
French, 19th century.
Born in Paris; died 1895.
Painter. History painting, battles, genre scenes.
He first exhibited at the Paris Salon in 1880.

A. Gaubault

AUCTION RECORDS:
NEW YORK, 19 Jan 1906, *Studying the Map,* USD 575. NEW YORK, 12-14 March 1907, *Intelligence,* USD 125. PARIS, 3-4 May 1923, *On the Lookout,* FRF 50. LONDON, 13 April 1928, *Incident from the Franco-Prussian War,* GBP 9. PARIS, 26 April 1942, *Four Military Scenes,* FRF 840. NEW YORK, 14 May 1976, *Trumpet and Drum* (oil on canvas, a pair, 13 3/4 x 11in/35 x 27cm) USD 700. LONDON, 24 May 1978, *Scene from the War of 1870* (oil on canvas, 25 1/2 x 31 1/2in/65 x 80cm) GBP 1,000. VIENNA, 26 May 1982, *Scene from the War of 1870* (oil on canvas, 25 1/2 x 31 1/2in/65 x 80cm) ATS 50,000. NEW YORK, 18-19 July 1996, *Pathfinders* (oil on canvas, 29 1/2 x 32in/74.9 x 81.3cm) USD 4,025.

GAUBERT, Albin
French, 19th century.
Born in Saverdun (Ariège); died October 1895.
Painter, watercolourist, sculptor. Scenes with figures.
He was a pupil of Falguière. He exhibited at the Salon des Artistes Français until his death in 1895.
AUCTION RECORDS:
LONDON, 12 June 1996, *Hôtel des Princes* (1880, watercolour, 15 1/2 x 15in/39.5 x 38cm) GBP 920.

GAUBERT, George Frederick
British, 19th century.
Active in London.
Painter. Seascapes.
George Frederick Gaubert exhibited in London from 1829 to 1861 at the Royal Academy and the Suffolk Street Gallery.

GAUBERT, Pierre
French, 17th - 18th century.
Born 1659, in Fontainebleau; died 1741, in Paris.
Portrait artist.
Pierre Gaubert was a member of the Académie royale in Paris. The museum in Dresden had a portrait of a woman by him.

GAUBERT, Roland
French, 20th century.
Born 5 January 1914, in Dôle.
Painter, watercolourist. Portraits, figures, local scenes, landscapes, still-lifes.
Roland Gaubert attended the schools of fine arts in Tours, Dijon and Algiers, where he did his military service, and in 1937 the École des Beaux-Arts in Paris where he studied in the studio of Charles Guérin. He also worked at the Grande Chaumière academy. In his own particular manner and approach, he brings a Cubist interpretation to the world around him, showing the road leading to his house, a widow, an orphan or a couple. He captures instants, moments of life, in fragmented form.

From 1937 he took part in group exhibitions: in 1937 the Exposition Internationale in Paris; in 1946 the Salon des Artistes Indépendants in Paris; in 1955 the Menton Biennale; and in 1962 the *Confrontation* exhibition with B. Buffet, Manessier, Picasso, Singier and Couty in Dijon. In 1938 he held his first solo exhibition in Paris at the Galerie L'Équipe, where he later exhibited with Le Moal, Estève, Tal Coat and Gischia. In 1986 the Musée de Dole held a retrospective of his work. Gaubert received numerous prizes and awards and in 1983 was made a Chevalier des Arts et des Lettres.
BIBLIOGRAPHY:
Roland Gaubert, exhibition catalogue, Musée de Dole, Dole, 1986.

GAUCHARD, Félix-Jean
French, 19th century.
Born 12 March 1825, in Paris; died 1872, in Paris.
Engraver.
He studied under Porret and exhibited at the Paris Salon from 1851 to 1872.

GAUCHAT, Jeannette
Swiss, 19th - 20th century.
Born 1871, in Bern; died 27 May 1915, in Leysin.
Painter. Landscapes.
MUSEUMS AND GALLERIES:
BERN: *Forest Interior.*

GAUCHER, Charles Étienne
French, 18th century.
Born 1741, in Paris; died 18 November 1804, in Paris.
Engraver.
Charles Gaucher produced engravings with religious themes and portraits. He was a student of Bazan and Lebas.

AUCTION RECORDS:
PARIS, 1883, *Portrait of J. Herivaux* (drawing in lead pencil) FRF 26; *Portrait of Denise Savari* (drawing in lead pencil, heightened with watercolour) FRF 100. PARIS, 12 and 13 March 1926, *Portrait of Hubert Gravelot* (graphite) FRF 450; *Portrait of Prince Henry of Prussia* (graphite) FRF 300; *Portrait of Pascal* (red chalk) FRF 310. PARIS, 14 May 1936, *Denise the Beauty* (medallion in graphite) FRF 1,200.

GAUCHER, Émile
French, 19th century.
Born 1860, in Blois; died 1909, in Challans (Vendée).
Sculptor.

He exhibited at the Salon des Artistes Français and received an honourable mention in 1894.

GAUCHER, Jacques
French, 16th century.
Active in Orléans.
Painter. Portraits.

GAUCHER, Jacques
French, 17th century.
Active in Orléans.
Painter.

GAUCHER, Jean
French, 16th century.
Active in Orléans.
Painter. History painting.

GAUCHER, Louis Thomas
French, 18th century.
Active in Paris in 1757.
Painter, sculptor.

GAUCHER, Luc Gabriel
French, 18th century.
Died 1759, in Langres.
Painter.

Luc Gabriel produced some landscapes.

GAUCHER, Mathieu
French, 15th century.
Active in Orléans.
Painter.

GAUCHER, Mathieu
French, 16th century.
Active in Orléans.
Painter.

GAUCHER, Yves
Canadian, 20th century.
Born 1934, in Montreal; died September 2000.
Painter, engraver.
Minimal Art.

Yves Gaucher gave up painting between 1960 and 1964 in order to concentrate solely on engraving, after training for four years in an engraving studio at the École des Beaux-Arts in Montreal. He used new techniques in relief engraving and achieved textural effects in informal realism. He progressively introduced line as a simple element. Stimulated by reading Albers' *Irradiation of Color* and by Webern's music, he adopted a formal language of experimentation with visual rhythms. He was also influenced by the American trend in Minimal Art. In 1969 he exhibited a collection of large canvases painted in the full range of grey tones, using a single monochrome for each work, in which the feeling of calm was highlighted by the discreet intervention of a few broken lines. In spite of, or perhaps because of their minimal nature, his works have a meditative, calm and intimist feel to them.

He took part in many exhibitions, including in London in 1969 and the retrospective *Yves Gaucher 1963-1978* at the Art Gallery of Ontario in Toronto in 1979.

BIBLIOGRAPHY:
Rombout, Luke, *Yves Gaucher and Christopher Pratt: A Touring Exhibition of Prints organized in Collaboration with Mira Godard Gallery*, exhibition catalogue, 1978. Nasgaard, Robert, *Yves Gaucher: A Fifteen-year Perspective, 1963-1978*, exhibition catalogue, Art Gallery of Ontario, Toronto, 1979. *Les 20 ans du musée à travers sa collection*, exhibition catalogue, Musée d'Art contemporain, Montreal, 1985.

MUSEUMS AND GALLERIES:
MONTREAL: *Brown, Blue, Grey* (1972) - MONTREAL (MAC): *Foreign Space* (1965); *Brown, Red, Orange, Yellow and Green* (1974); *Yellow and Ochres* (1975); *Jericho: A Variation* (1978).

GAUCHER DE REIMS
French, 13th century.
Active between 1244 and 1252.
Architect, sculptor.

This artist's name is one of four (with those of Jean d'Orbais, Bernard de Soissons and Jean le Loup, whom he succeeded) that appear on the plan of Rheims Cathedral in a 16th-century copy. It is known that he was also a sculptor and 'opened the arches and porches ' of the west façade. He was, therefore, one of those to whom we owe the magnificent and famous statuary of this cathedral.

GAUCHER-DUNOIS, Jeanne
French, 20th century.
Born 1891, in Paris.
Painter. Landscapes.

Jeanne Gaucher-Dunois studied under Jules Adler. She exhibited in Paris at the Salon des Artistes Français and specialised in painting gardens and scenes with flowers.

GAUCHEREL, Émile-Lambert
French, 19th century.
Born 13 February 1813, in Paris; died 11 January 1885, in Stes (Charente-Maritime).
Draughtsman.

He was the brother of Léon Gaucherel.

GAUCHEREL, Lambert
French, 18th century.
Painter. Landscapes.

MUSEUMS AND GALLERIES:
DIJON: *View of Rome*.

GAUCHEREL, Léon
French, 19th century.
Born 21 May 1816, in Paris; died 7 January 1886.
Engraver, painter.

He exhibited at the Paris Salon from 1847 to 1879 and awarded medals on several occasions (1855, 1859, 1861 and 1863). He was awarded the Légion d'Honneur on 9 August 1864. Gaucherel is particularly noted for his etchings for A. Lance's *Excursion en Italie* (*Travels in Italy*) , published in 1873.

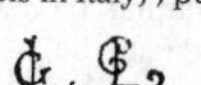

MUSEUMS AND GALLERIES:
LONDON (Victoria and Albert Mus.).

AUCTION RECORDS:
PARIS, 26 Feb 1943, *Port Navalo, Gulf of Morbihan*; *The Angler* (charcoal drawing) FRF 450. LONDON, 24 June 1987, *Still-life with Roses and Bird's Nest* (oil on canvas, 15 x 18in/38 x 46cm) GBP 1,300.

GAUCHETTE, Armand
French, 18th century.
Active in Paris in 1748.
Painter, sculptor.

GAUCHON, Pierre. See **GANCHON**

GAUCI, G.
British, 19th century.
Active in London.

Lithographer.

G. Gauci exhibited in London at the Royal Academy and Suffolk Street Gallery between 1810 and 1827.

GAUCI, M.

British, 19th century.

Active in London at the beginning of the 19th century.

Lithographer.

M. Gauci was the father of W. and Paul Gauci.

GAUCI, Paul

British, 19th century.

Active in London.

Painter. Landscapes.

Paul Gauci exhibited in London on several occasions between 1834 and 1863 at the Royal Academy, the British Institution and the Suffolk Street Gallery.

GAUCI, W.

British, 19th century.

Active in London.

Lithographer.

W. Gauci was the son of M. Gauci and brother of Paul Gauci.

GAUD, Émile

French, 20th century.

Born 7 May 1920, in St-Tropez.

Painter. Landscapes, still-lifes, scenes with figures.

Émile Gaud was a self-taught painter. He exhibited at the Salon d'Automne and also in both solo and group exhibitions in St-Tropez and towns on the south coast of France.

He takes a realist approach, using precise draughtsmanship and creating the illusion of three dimensions, working in smooth, enamelled pigment to produce fantastical subjects, dreamlike views of St-Tropez, unusual fruits and vegetables and the roots of hanging trees mutating into human beings. He is fond of compositions in which the elements or figures depicted float in the air, often above the sea in a bay that is recognisably that of St-Tropez.

GAUD, Jules

Swiss, 19th - 20th century.

Born 8 August 1848, in Geneva; died 7 March 1912, in Geneva.

Painter. Landscapes.

Jules Gaud was the brother of Léon Gaud and a pupil of Barthélemy Menn. His works figured in the Expositions Universelles of 1889 and 1900, where he won a bronze medal and a silver respectively. Inspired by the shores of Lake Geneva, he painted many aquatic landscapes with a characteristic use of broad areas of light, among them *Villeneuve, Lake Geneva* and *Lake Shore near Villeneuve*.

MUSEUMS AND GALLERIES:

GENEVA (MAH).

AUCTION RECORDS:

BERN, 22 Oct 1982, *Willows* (1900, oil on canvas, 13 3/4 x 10 3/4 ins / 35 x 27.5 cm) CHF 1,800. BERN, 3 May 1985, *The Square in Auvernier, Neuenburgersee* (oil on card, 12 x 18 1/2 ins / 30.5 x 47 cm) CHF 2,300.

GAUD, Léon

Swiss, 19th century.

Born 1844, in Geneva; died 1908, in Geneva.

Painter. Genre scenes, landscapes.

Gaud was the pupil of Barthélemy Menn.

MUSEUMS AND GALLERIES:

GENEVA (MAH): *Beating; Conquest of Bread; Artist; In Lugardon; Last Cartload of the Harvest* - NEUCHÂTEL: *Burning Grass*.

AUCTION RECORDS:

BERN, 22 Oct 1982, *View of Lake Geneva at Night* (oil on canvas, 11 x 16 1/4 ins / 27 x 41 cm) CHF 2,500. ZURICH, 12 June 1995, *Village House* (oil on card, 9 1/2 x 12 1/2 ins / 24 x 32 cm) CHF 1,150. ZURICH, 9 June 1999, *Fisherfolk beside Lake at Sunset* (1883, oil on canvas, 28 x 43 ins / 70 x 110 cm) CHF 15,000. SION, 8 June 2001, *By Lake Leman, Young Woman and Children* (oil on canvas, 12 x 22 ins / 30 x 55 cm) CHF 13,500. SION, 7 Dec 2002, *Fishing Trip on Lake Leman* (oil on canvas, 13 x 19 ins / 33 x 49 cm) CHF 7,400.

GAUD, Michel

French, 20th century.

Born in St-Tropez.

Painter.

Michel Gaud was the son of his namesake but took a different approach and was not influenced by his father. He exhibits in solo and group exhibitions in St-Tropez and in towns on the south coast of France. He paints primitive compositions without backgrounds in flat tints showing humans and animals side by side.

BIBLIOGRAPHY:

Les Peintres de Saint-Tropez, Ste-Maxime, 1990.

GAUDAEN, Gérard

Belgian, 20th century.

Born 1927, in St-Niklaas (Waes).

Engraver. Allegorical subjects.

Gérard Gaudaen studied at the Academies of St-Niklaas (Waes) and Ghent, where he later taught. He was awarded many prizes and distinctions. His works, generally in black and white, show his great mastery of engraving techniques.

MUSEUMS AND GALLERIES:

BRUSSELS (Bibliothèque royale Albert Ier).

GAUDAIRE-THOR, Jean

French, 20th - 21st century.

Born 16 October 1947, in Sens.

Painter.

Jean Gaudaire-Thor is a prolific painter. In 1962 he was a prize-winner at the Salon des Artistes Français in Paris. From 1973 to 1976 he participated in the Salon des Réalités Nouvelles in Paris, and in 1994 and 1995 in the Salon Grands et Jeunes d'Aujourd'hui in Paris. His numerous travels to Greece, Turkey, Egypt, Spain and Sicily have greatly influenced his work.

BIBLIOGRAPHY:

Persin, Patrick-Gilles, *Jean Gaudaire-Thor*, Il Patio, Ravenna, Éd. de l'Orme, Paris, 1995 (extensive documentation).

GAUDAR DE LA VERDINE, Auguste Alphonse

French, 18th century.

Born 1780, in Bourges; died 16 September 1804, in Siena.

Painter. History painting.

In 1799, Auguste Gaudar de La Verdine won the first Grand Prix de Peinture for *Manlius Torquatus Condemning His Son to Death*.

GAUDARD DE THAVANNES, Charles Philippe

Swiss, 18th century.

Born 1753, in Lausanne.

Draughtsman.

GAUDE-ROZA-BONNARDEL

French, 20th century.

Born 23 September 1903, in Tiemcem, Algeria.

Painter, illustrator.

Gaude-Roza-Bonnardel exhibited at the various Paris Salons. He is principally known for his illustrations, notably for *Manon Lescaut, Gulliver's Travels and The Tales of Perrault.*

GAUDEAUX, Léon
French, 20th century.
Born 1893; died 1947.
Painter. Portraits, landscapes, still-lifes.

Léon Gaudeaux exhibited a series of landscapes, mainly of the Ile-de-France at a Paris gallery in 1948.

GAUDEFROY, Alphonse
French, 19th - 20th century.
Born 25 March 1845, in Gentilly; died 1936, in Bréhat (Côtes-d'Armor).
Painter. Mythological subjects, hunting scenes, genre scenes, landscapes with figures, animals. Murals, designs for tapestries.

Alphonse Gaudefroy was the son of the painter Pierre Julien Gaudefroy and studied under Léon Cogniet and Alexandre Cabanel at the École des Beaux-Arts in Paris. In 1870 he was seriously wounded, along with his friend Henri Regnault who in fact died.

He specialised in hunting scenes and landscapes with animals or young washerwomen and shepherdesses. He had great talent as a decorative artist and his figures are placed in a majestic vision of nature. He received commissions for large mural compositions for various châteaux and private residences and from 1870 to 1873 decorated a large proportion of M. Menier's private residence at Parc Monceau. He painted a major piece showing a view of the studio of his friend the sculptor Aimé Jules Dalou working on *Triumph of the Republic*. He also designed tapestry cartoons including one of *Neptune and Amphitrite*.

He was awarded the second Grand Prix de Rome in 1874. He exhibited at the Paris Salon, receiving a commendation in 1884. He was appointed as a restorer at the Manufacture de Beauvais where he was responsible for preserving tapestry cartoons.

AUCTION RECORDS:
PARIS, 1890, *New Wine*, FRF 28. NEW YORK, 1 Feb 1906, *Nymph in the Woods*, USD 340. NEW YORK, 18-19-20 April 1906, *Bear Hunt*, USD 260. PARIS, 16 Feb 1927, *Child with Magpie*, FRF 210. NEW YORK, 12 May 1978, *Huntsman and Washerwoman* (oil on canvas, 23 1/4 x 28 ins / 59 x 71 cm) USD 2,800. LONDON, 27 Nov 1985, *Studio of the Sculptor Dalou* (1889, oil on canvas, 24 x 19 3/4 ins / 61 x 50 cm) GBP 12,000. LONDON, 22 June 1990, *In the Studio of the Sculptor Dalou* (1889, oil on canvas, 24 x 19 3/4 ins / 61 x 50 cm) GBP 12,650. NEW YORK, 19 Jan 1995, *Flirtation* (1899, oil on canvas, 24 3/4 x 30 1/4 ins / 62.9 x 76.8 cm) USD 2,300.

GAUDEFROY, Louise
Maiden name: Martin
French, 19th - 20th century.
Born 1856, in Amiens.
Painter, sculptor.

Louise Gaudefroy became a member of the Société des Artistes Français in 1900. She exhibited at the Society's Salons.

GAUDEFROY, Maurice Henri
French, 20th century.
Painter.

In 1928, Maurice Gaudefroy exhibited at the Salon des Tuileries in Paris.

GAUDEFROY, Pierre-Julien
French, 19th century.
Born 1 February 1804, in Paris.
Painter.

He enrolled at the École des Beaux-Arts on 24 March 1820 and studied under Gros. He exhibited a portrait at the 1824 Salon, followed by *Leicester* in 1831 and *Child's Play* in 1845. Gaudefroy was responsible for the decoration of the municipal theatre in Versailles and the Salle Ventadour (1841) for the Théâtre Italien.

AUCTION RECORDS:
PARIS, 6-7 Dec 1944, *Portrait of a Young Woman* (1833) FRF 1,100.

GAUDEMARIS, Anatole Henry Pierre Théodore de (Marquis)
French, 19th century.
Born c. 1853, in Paris; died 4 September 1908, in Massillan, near Orange (Vaucluse).
Painter.

He initially pursued a military career before going to Lyons to study under Dumas and Scohy. He exhibited in Paris from 1886 and in Lyons from 1890, chiefly historical subjects and genre compositions. Gaudemaris painted decorative compositions for various churches, including those of Les Stes-Maries-de-la-Mer (*The Three Marys Escorted by Angels*, 1886), Ste-Croix (Ain, 1891), Fontaines-sur-Saône (1892 and 1895), Beauregard (Ain, 1892) and Denicé (Rhône, 1893).

GAUDENFUCHS, Jakob
Austrian, 15th century.
Active in the Tyrol in 1473.
Painter.

Jakob Gaudenfuchs worked at the castle of Stenico.

GAUDENZI, Alfredo or Alf
Italian, 20th century.
Born 1908, in Genoa; died 1980.
Illustrator, potter.
Futurism.

Alfredo Gaudenzi owes his nickname 'Alf' to Marinetti, who he met in Milan. He turned to painting after qualifying as an accountant but failing to establish himself in a career. He was also a journalist and a commercial artist. He joined the Futurist Group in Turin, then, in 1929, went to live in Rome, where he worked as an illustrator. He shared the management of both the periodical and the Theatre *2000* and designed theatrical sets. He took part in Futurist exhibitions and in 1930 founded the Sintesi (Synthesis) Group. He also organised exhibitions for the group. During the 1930s, he broke off his creative activity and did not resume it until after World War II. In 1967, he opened the Il Vicolo gallery in Genoa, where he presented Futurist works.

He illustrated publications such as *Giro di ronda* (*Strolling Around*) , by Constanzo Carbone (1937) and created ceramics, often with Tullio Mazzotti. His work was shown in the 1973 group exhibition: *Futurisme 1909-1916* (*Futurism 1909-1916*) , Musée National d'Art Moderne.

BIBLIOGRAPHY:
Ballo, Guido/Cachin, Françoise/Leymarie, Jean/Russoli, Franco, *Futurisme 1909-1916*, group exhibition catalogue, Musée national d'Art Moderne, Réunion des Musées Nationaux, Paris, 1973. Bottaro, Silvia, '*Alf Gaudenzi il futurista*' in *Liguria* n° 10/11, periodical, 1998.

GAUDENZI, Pietro
Italian, 20th century.
Born 1880, in Genoa; died 1955, in Anticoli Corrado (Lazio).
Painter. Figure compositions, landscapes with figures, still-lifes, flowers.

AUCTION RECORDS:
MILAN, 26 May 1977, *Il Fiore della Vita* (oil on card, 15 1/2 x 13 ins / 39.5 x 33 cm) ITL 1,300,000. PARIS, 12 June 1981, *Vase of Flowers* (oil on canvas, 30 3/4 x 26 ins / 78 x 66 cm) ITL 650,000. ROME, 15 Nov 1988, *Threshing the Grain* (1940, mixed media, first study, 22 3/4 x 17 ins / 58 x 43 cm) ITL 1,500,000. MILAN, 6 Dec 1989, *Holy Motherhood* (oil on canvas, diam. 41 ins / 104 cm) ITL 15,000,000. STOCKHOLM, 14 Nov 1990, *Landscape with a Shepherd and His Sheep* (oil on panel, 24 1/2 x 39 1/4 ins / 62 x 100 cm) SEK 20,000. ROME, 4 Dec 1990, *Vase of Flowers on an Entablature* (oil on canvas, 29 x 23 1/2 ins / 73.5 x 60 cm) ITL

3,000,000. STOCKHOLM, 29 May 1991, *Landscape with a Shepherd and His Sheep* (1903, oil on panel, 24 1/2 x 39 1/4 ins / 62 x 100 cm) SEK 10,000. BOLOGNA, 8-9 June 1992, *Shepherd and His Flock near a Landing Stage* (1903, oil on panel, 23 1/2 x 38 1/4 ins / 60 x 97 cm) ITL 5,175,000. MILAN, 20 Dec 1994, *Vase of Flowers* (oil on panel, 19 1/2 x 15 1/4 ins / 49.5 x 39 cm) ITL 3,105,000. ROME, 25 Nov 1999, *Family* (1911, oil on canvas, 43 x 33 ins / 110 x 84 cm) ITL 18,000,000. TURIN, 21 March 2000, *History of Planning* (mixed media) ITL 30,000,000. ROME, 21 May 2001, *Maternity* (oil on board, 24 x 19 ins / 60 x 47 cm) ITL 4,200,000. MILAN, 24 March 2004, *Three Graces* (oil on board, 24 x 12 ins / 60 x 30 cm) EUR 2,500.

GAUDENZIO, Milanese. See **FERRARI Gaudenzio**

GAUDET, Étienne

French, 20th century.

Engraver (wood).

Étienne Gaudet exhibited at the Salon des Artistes Français in Paris.

GAUDET, Gabriel

French, 20th century.

Born 1886.

Sculptor.

Gabriel Gaudet exhibited at the Paris Salon.

GAUDET, Raymond

French, 20th century.

Born in Grenoble.

Painter. Landscapes.

Raymond Gaudet exhibited in Paris in 1925 at the Salon d'Automne and in 1927 and 1928 at the Salon des Tuileries.

GAUDEZ, Adrien-Étienne

French, 19th century.

Born 9 February 1845, in Lyons; died 23 January 1902, in Neuilly (Hauts-de-Seine).

Sculptor. Busts, groups, monuments.

He studied under Jouffroy. He first exhibited at the Paris Salon in 1864, when he was awarded a bronze medal, followed by a gold in 1881. Gaudez sculpted the *Florian* monument in Alès and the war memorial in Remiremont commemorating *Citizens of the Vosges Who Gave Their Lives for France*.

BIBLIOGRAPHY:

Wiesinger, Véronique, '*Quelques précisions sur la restauration de la porte Saint-Denis après la Commune de Paris (1885-1887)*' in *Bulletin de la Société de l'Histoire de l'Art Français*, 1988.

AUCTION RECORDS:

LONDON, 7 June 1972, *Portrait Bust of a Young Girl* (patinated bronze) GBP 460. PARIS, 22 Nov 1977, *Rustic Couple* (patinated bronze medal, h. 25 1/2in/65cm) FRF 9,200. PARIS, 23 April 1980, *Morning Star* (patinated bronze medal, h. 36 1/4in/92cm) FRF 8,650. LONDON, 7 June 1984, *Molière as a Young Man* (c. 1870, bronze, h. 28in/71cm) GBP 3,400. LOKEREN, 22 Feb 1986, *David* (1870, brown-patinated bronze, h. 29 1/4in/74cm) BEF 190,000. NEW YORK, 25 May 1988, *David* (bronze, h. 31 3/4in/80.7cm) USD 2,420. PARIS, 6 July 1989, *Morning Star* (bronze, h. 27 1/2in/70cm) FRF 5,000. PARIS, 5 July 1991, *Mozart* (bronze, h. 13 1/2in/34cm) FRF 4,100. PARIS, 13 Dec 1992, *Hope of France* (bronze, h. 19in/48cm) FRF 3,800. NEW YORK, 16 Feb 1994, *Bust of an Eastern Beauty* (bronze, h. 29 3/4in/75.6cm) USD 21,850. PARIS, 24 June 1994, *The Sower* (bronze, h. 32 1/4in/82cm) FRF 5,700. LOKEREN, 9 March 1996, *Marguerite* (bronze and ivory, h. 16in/40.5cm) BEF 36,000.

GAUDEZ, Cécile Delphine

French, 19th century.

Born 21 December 1851, in St-Étienne.

Painter.

She was a pupil of Henner and Carolus-Duran, and exhibited miniatures at the Paris Salon from 1869 to 1880.

GAUDEZ, Jean-Marie

French, 19th century.

Born 1808, in Tournus (Saône-et-Loire).

Painter. Genre scenes.

He studied at the École des Beaux-Arts in Lyons.

MUSEUMS AND GALLERIES:

TOURNUS: *Old Lady Seated*.

GAUDFROY, Fernand

Belgian, 20th century.

Born 1885, in Tournai; died 1964.

Painter. Figures, nudes, portraits, still-lifes, flowers.

Fernand Gaudfroy studied with Isodore Verheyden and Hermann Richir.

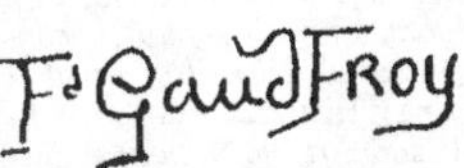

AUCTION RECORDS:

NEW YORK, 15 Nov 1984, *Little Girl with her Dog* (1911, oil on canvas, 35 1/2 x 39 1/4 ins / 90 x 100 cm) USD 3,000. NEW YORK, 13 Feb 1985, *Best Friends* (1911, oil on canvas, 35 3/4 x 39 1/2 ins / 90.9 x 100.5 cm) USD 6,000. PARIS, 9 Dec 1988, *Young Boy* (oil on canvas, 35 3/4 x 20 ins / 91 x 50.5 cm) FRF 14,000. BRUSSELS, 16 Jan 2001, *Tinker* (1924, oil on canvas, 36 x 28 ins / 91 x 71 cm) BEF 110,000. NEW YORK, 27 Feb 2002, *Two Cats* (1912, oil on canvas, 42 x 66 ins / 107 x 168 cm) USD 5,500.

GAUDÍ Y CORNET, Antoni

Spanish, 19th - 20th century.

Born 25 June 1852, in Reus (Catalonia); died 10 June 1926, in Barcelona.

Architect, sculptor, decorative designer.

Art Nouveau.

Antoni Gaudí y Cornet was descended from a branch of the Gaudin family of Clermont-Ferrand. His father was a coppersmith and then an inspector of weights and measures. The family lived in the town of Reus in the province of Tarragona. Gaudí was very influenced by his environment and a keen observer of nature, the sea, the mountains and the organic structure of things around him. He became an architect in 1878 and soon enjoyed considerable success. However, a number of deaths in the family appear to have caused him to sink into a depression from which he would never recover and he spent the final years of his life as a recluse, living on charity. He died in an accident.

Originally inspired by Viollet-le-Duc and by Oriental styles, Gaudí later became the leader of the Modernist movement, advocating the use of natural forms. He was interested in the possibilities of geometric language to express a sense of continuity with the elements of nature. Gaudí, the inspired architect of Barcelona's unfinished temple of the Sagrada Familia, of the Casa Calvet, the church of the Colonia Güell (1898-1915), the Parc Güell (1900-1914) and of the Casa Vicens (1883-1888), designed his prodigious and unique creations down to the very last detail. His work as a sculptor was as important as his architectural production. He was a devout man, yet he did not hesitate to make moulds from the bodies of dead infants to ensure that his sculptures of the Holy Innocents were cruelly realistic; he crucified skeletons and asked living models to become temporary re-enactors of Christ's Passion.

In the hands of this visionary, this scrupulous realism gave rise to a fantastical and sometimes disquieting world of stone, closer to the Baroque religious sculptures and buildings of South America than to the Spanish Gothic with which the artist was so familiar. His role as a decorative artist (religious and civic buildings, stained glass window designs) is also important: here too Gaudí was careful to ensure that even the smallest detail conformed to his overall concept. A contemporary of Victor Horta and Hector Guimard, Gaudí belonged to the European Art Nouveau Movement and was the only genuine representative of it that Catalonia produced. He remains the demiurge of a universe of plants and minerals at times deeply malevolent, recalling Hieronymus Bosch in the polychrome façade of the Nativity at the Sagrada Familia and Max Ernst in the decorated bars and gates of certain houses and parks in Barcelona. Gaudí is buried, in accordance with his wish, in the crypt of the Sagrada Familia.

In 2002, the year of the 150th anniversary of his birth, a retrospective of Gaudí's work was held in Barcelona. The exhibition entitled *Gaudí's Universe* was held at the centre of contemporary culture in Barcelona and then at the Museo Reina Sofia in Madrid. Other events were also held to celebrate the anniversary, including: *Gaudí. La recerca de la forma: espai, egometria, estructura i construcció* (*Gaudí Exploring Form: Space, Geometry, Structure and Construction*) at the Museu d'Historia de la Ciutat, Barcelona; *Gaudí. Art y Disseny* (*Gaudí Art and Design*) at the Caixa Catalunya cultural centre, Barcelona; *Eusebi Güell and Antoni Gaudí, Dos homes i un projecte* (*Eusebi Güell and Antoni Gaudí, Two Men, One Project*) at the Palau Güell, Barcelona; *Gaudí and the Parc Güell. Arquitectura i natura* (*Gaudí and the Parc Güell. Architecture and Nature*) at the interpretation centre of the Parc Güell, Barcelona; *Gaudí i el seu Taller* (*Gaudí and his Studio*) at the museum of the Temple of the Sagrada Familia, Barcelona, 2002. Many buildings either created or renovated by Gaudí were also opened to the public: the Casa Batlló (1904-1906), the Casa Milà known as La Pedrera (1905-1910) and the Palau Güell (1886-1889).

Gaudí created many other buildings in Barcelona, such as the Casa Calvet (1898-1904), now the headquarters of the Caixa Catalunya foundation, the Col·legi Santa Teresa (1888-1894), the Casa Bellesguard (1900-1902) and the Gate to the Finca Miralles (1901-1902). He also designed the Bodegas Güell (1895-1898) at Garraf on the Mediterranean coast and a number of projects that were never carried out such as the Tangier project and the American Hotel.

Bibliography:

Gaudí, pionnier du XXe siècle, exhibition catalogue, Musée des Arts décoratifs, Paris, 1971. Martinelli, César, *Gaudí: his life, his theories, his work*, MIT Press, Cambridge (MA), 1975. Zerbst, Rainer, *Antoni Gaudi*, Taschen, Paris, 1993. Güell, Xavier, *Gaudí*, Guías de Arquitectura Electa España, Madrid, 1996. Gómez Serrano, Josep, *L'Obrador de Gaudí*, Edicions UPC, Sant Cugat, 1996. Carandell, Josep M./Vivas, Pere, *El Templo de la Sagrada Familía*, Triangle Postals, S.L., Sant Lluís (Menorca), 1997. Permanyer, Lluis, *Gaudí of Barcelona*, Rizzoli, New York, 1997. Carandell, Josep M./Vivas, Pere, *Park Güell, Utopia de Gaudí*, Triangle Postals, S.L., Sant Lluís (Menorca), 1998. Lahuerta, Juan José, *Antoni Gaudí*, Sociedad Editorial Electa España, Madrid, 1999. Tarragona, Josep, *Gaudí*, Proa Biografia, Barcelona, 1999. Bergós Massó, Juan, *Gaudí: The Man and his Work*, Little, Brown, Boston, 1999 (trans. from the Catalan by Gerardo Denis). Tate, Cabré, *Guida de la Ruta del modernisme*, Mediterrania, Barcelona, 2000. Lahuerta, Juan José/Rusiñol, Santiago/Güell Viscount, et al., *Univers Gaudí*, exhibition catalogue, Centre de cultura contemporània de Barcelona, Barcelona, 2002. *Antoni Gaudí, la nature et les formes*, Musée des Arts et Métiers, Paris, 2002. Lahuerta, Juan José, *Antoni Gaudí*, Phaidon Press, London, 2003.

GAUDIBERT, Jean Raphaël Auguste

French, 20th century.
Born in Orange (Vaucluse).
Engraver, lithographer.

Jean Gaudibert exhibited in Paris at the Salon des Artistes Français and received a commendation there in 1907.

GAUDICHAUD-BEAUPRÉ, Charles

French, 19th century.
Born 4 September 1780, in Angoulême; died 16 January 1854.
Draughtsman, illustrator.

A botanist by profession, Gaudichaud-Beaupré made meticulous drawings of flora he had observed in the course of his extensive sea voyages all over the world; he also contributed illustrations to numerous scientific publications.

GAUDICHIER, Henriette

Maiden name: Jardin
French, 19th century.
Active in Paris.
Painter.

A member of the Société des Artistes from 1883, she participated regularly in its exhibitions.

GAUDIER-BRZESKA, Henri, pseudonym of Gaudier, Henri

French, 20th century.
Born 4 October 1891, in St-Jean-de-Braye (Loiret); died 5 June 1915, in Neuville-St-Vaast (Pas-de-Calais), at the front.
From 1911 active in England.
Sculptor, painter, pastellist, draughtsman. Figures, animals.
Vorticism.
London Group.

Henri Gaudier-Brzeska came from a humble background: his father followed in the family tradition of stonecutting, although according to some sources he was a carpenter. Gaudier-Brzeska was a self-taught artist; after studying in Orléans he became a regular visitor to libraries, particularly the Ste-Geneviève library in Paris. During educational visits to England and also to Holland, Belgium and Germany, he accumulated thousands of drawings from nature, copied from works in museums and showed an early interest in primitive art, admiring 'the art of blacks, reds and yellows' at the British Museum. At the age of 19 he began a relationship with Sophie Brzeska, a Polish woman 20 years his senior; he added her surname to his own and passed her off as his sister. In 1910 he decided to concentrate entirely on sculpture. As a supporter of utopian revolutionary ideas and an anti-militarist, he refused to do his national service in the North African Rif war, which was one of the reasons for his move to England. He returned to France later, but only after learning of the bombardment of Rheims Catherdral; there he joined the French forces and was killed at the age of 24, leaving behind a legacy that went far beyond mere potential. The story and romanticism surrounding his short life gave Gaudier-Brzeska an almost legendary quality.

In 1913 he became one of the founder members of the London Group; he is considered an important contributor to English Modernism. His early work was taken up by the critic MacCall, the writer Katherine Mansfield and her entourage and Paul Morand, who at the time was attached to the French embassy. Gaudier-Brzeska joined the Vorticist movement which, under some broad and ill-defined precepts, united the English literary and artistic avant-garde around the figures of the writer Wyndham Lewis and the American poet Ezra Pound. Other artists who joined the movement include the painters Edward Wadsworth, William P. Roberts and Frederick Etchells and the sculptor Jacob Epstein. With Epstein, Gaudier-Brzeska was responsible for the revival of direct carving in sculpture, the practice then being enthusiastically adopted by Henry Moore (known to be directly influenced by Gaudier-Brzska) and Barbara Hepworth. The aim of the Vorticists was to attain the ultimate in strength and energy of expression by assimilating the potential of all forms of representation - whatever they were and wherever they came from - to the dynamism of the machine and thus to achieve an expression as devoid as possible of insignificant detail. The activities of the Vorticist group, despite its rejection of its obvious relationship with Italian Futurism, made it the starting point of modern art in Britain. Gaudier-Brzeska played an active part in this, notably through his articles in the journal *Blast* and through the works he produced with their obvious relationship with industrial form. His contribution was recognised after his death and the Musée d'Orléans devoted a permanent exhibition room to his work. In 1933 the Musée d'Orléans held a retrospective of his work which was shown later that autumn at the Musée d'Art Moderne in Toulouse.

Gaudier-Brzeska's numerous early drawings, nearly always executed with a purity of line developing into arabesques, seem to offer a synthesis between the elegance of Matisse and the Expressionism of Picasso. However, when he found that drawing alone was no longer sufficient to translate the plenitude of form towards which he was moving, he turned to sculpture which allowed him to achieve a 'more palpable form'. He produced his first sculptures under the influence of Rodin's work, as can be seen in *Dancer* of 1913; he was also influenced by Maillol as in *Motherhood* of 1913. After moving to London in 1911, in 1912 and 1913 he received several commissions for busts. Although his sculptural output was limited to the period 1912 to 1914, he left an important body of work: around a hundred bronze, stone and marble sculptures, paintings, and an enormous quantity of drawings. The interplay of voids balanced by solids in some of his final pieces, notably *Motherhood No. 2*, suggests that Henry Moore was familiar with his work.

Key pieces of Gaudier-Brzeska's work include: *Monkeys* of 1912; *Hieratic Head of Ezra Pound; Motherhood No. 1; Female Torso* of 1913; *Motherhood No. 2; Men Carrying a Basin; Garden Ornament; The Little Imp; Dog; Door Knocker; Bird Swallowing a Fish* of 1914. Works such as *Portrait of Horace Brosky; Mademoiselle B.* preceded the Neo-classical heads of Picasso and sculptures such as *Birds Standing; Stags; Red Dancer* can perhaps be considered abstract pieces. His membership of the Vorticist group brought him close to Italian Futurism and hence to the French artist Raymond Duchamp-Villon, to whose career war also put an early end. Gaudier-Brzeska's talent as a sculptor was beyond question and he played a determining role in the early years of 19th-century sculptural development. Although his sculptures continued to display a process of stylisation, it would appear that intellectually he was moving towards genuine abstraction and would almost certainly have become one of the earliest exponents of this genre. Roger Fry made a posthumous tribute to him in which he wrote that it was 'only natural that the experiments of Cubism, and its offshoot Vorticism, should attract him'. Fundamentally, he was 'seeking to create a classic art, one of purely formal expression' and his 'talent was sufficiently formed, his future sufficiently outlined, to make us feel how terrible a waste the loss of such a life is'.

BIBLIOGRAPHY:

Ouverture de la salle Gaudier-Brzeska, catalogue, Musée national d'Art moderne, Paris, 1965. Pound, Ezra, *Gaudier-Brzeska: a Memoir*, memoir, W.W. Norton and Co., 1970. Ede, H.S., *Savage Messiah: Biography of the Sculptor Henri Gaudier-Brzska*, biography, Gordon Fraser, 1971. *Sixty Drawings by Henri Gaudier-Brzeska, 1891-1915*, catalogue, Mercury Gallery, London, 1975. Cole, R., *Burning to Speak, the Life and Art of Henri Gaudier-Brzeska*, monograph, Phaidon, Oxford, 1978. Secrétain, Roger, *Un sculpteur maudit, Gaudier-Brzeska*, monograph, Éd. du temps, Paris, 1980. Baude, Laurent/Fauquembergue, Bernard, *Henri Gaudier-Brzeska, vu et raconté par les élèves du Lycée Professionnel de Saint-Jean-de-Braye*, memoir, Orléans, 1986 (good bibliography). Harrison, Charles, *English Art and Modernism 1900-1939*, study, Yale University Press, New Haven and London, 1994. Silber, Evelyn, *Gaudier-Brzska: Life and Art, with a Catalogue Raisonne of the Sculpture*, monograph, Thames and Hudson, 1996. O'Keefe, Paul, *Gaudier-Brzeka: An Absolute Case of Genius*, monograph, Allan Lane, 2004.

MUSEUMS AND GALLERIES:

CAMBRIDGE (Kettle's Yard, University of Cambridge): *Self-portrait* (c. 1912, pencil, pen and ink on paper, three); *The Dancer* (1913, bronze); *Bird Swallowing a Fish* (1914, plaster); *Portrait of Ezra Pound* (pencil and ink on paper); *Wrestlers Relief* (1914, major collection, approx. 150 works) - LONDON (Tate Collection): *The Dancer* (1913, bronze); *Red Stone Dancer* (c. 1913, red Mansfield stone); *Torso of a Woman* (1913, bronze, cast 1930); *Maternity* (1913, bronze, cast c. 1965); *Sleeping Fawn* (1913, painted plaster, posthumous cast); *Horace Brodzky* (1913, bronze, bust, cast 1956); *Bird Swallowing a Fish* (c. 1913-1914, bronze, cast 1964); *The Imp* (c. 1914, alabaster); *Wrestlers* (1914, plaster, cast c. 1965, relief); *Garden Ornament* (1914, plaster, several versions in bronze (later castings)); *Doorknocker* (1914, bronze, cast 1965); *Monkeys* (1914, cast stone, cast c. 1965); *Dog* (1914, bronze, cast 1964); *Ornament* (1914, bronze); *Torso* (1914, marble, from the Victoria and Albert Museum); around 30 sculptures; *Sophie Brzeska* (1913, pastel/paper); around 30 drawings - LONDON (Victoria and Albert Mus.): *The Wrestlers* (1913, marquetry in wood, plate for Omega Workshop) - NEW HAVEN (AG, Yale University): *Totem; Portrait of Ezra Pound* - NEW YORK (MoMA): *Birds Standing* - ORLÉANS (MBA): a room of sculptures, paintings and drawings - PARIS (MNAM-CCI): *Seated Woman* (drawings).

AUCTION RECORDS:

LONDON, 12 June 1940, *Seated Female Nude* (drawing) GBP 5. LONDON, 15 April 1964, *Bohm and Karsavina in The Firebird* (bronze) GBP 820. LONDON, 14 July 1967, *Still-life* (pastel) Gns 620. LONDON, 26 Nov 1969, *Bird and Fish* (bronze) Gns 3,200. LONDON, 18 July 1972, *Still-life with Lemons* (pastel) Gns 2,200. NEW YORK, 6 June 1974, *Adolf Bohm and Karsavina in The Firebird* (bronze) USD 2,400. PARIS, 28 June 1976, *Portrait of Lord Fraser* (1911-1912, bronze, h. 27 1/2 ins / 70 cm, w. 26 1/2 ins/67 cm) FRF 16,500. LONDON, 22 June 1977, *Sleeping Faun* (bronze, l. 10 ins / 25.5 cm) GBP 1,800. LONDON, 8 March 1978, *Wrestlers* (c. 1913, marquetry, round, diam. 23 1/2 ins / 60 cm) GBP 3,600. LONDON, 29 June 1978, *Wrestlers* (1912, linocut, 9 x 11 ins / 22.8 x 28.1 cm) GBP 380. LONDON, 5 March 1980, *Siren* (bronze, long. 10 3/4 ins / 27.5 cm) GBP 900. LONDON, 10 June 1981, *Male Nude Standing* (pencil/paper, 20 x 15 1/4 ins / 51 x 38.5 cm) GBP 900. LONDON, 3 Nov 1982, *Sleeping Faun* (bronze, l. 10 ins / 25.5 cm) GBP 2,800. LONDON, 9 March 1984, *Ornamental Mask* (bronze, h. 28 1/2 ins / 72.5 cm) GBP 6,000. LONDON, 23 May 1984, *Study of a Male Nude* (watercolour and black chalk, 20 3/4 x 16 ins / 53 x 40.5 cm) GBP 5,200. LONDON, 6 Feb 1985, *Standing Nudes* (1913, pen, 15 x 19 ins / 38 x 48 cm) GBP 1,600. LONDON, 8 Nov 1985, *Cupid* (c. 1912-1913, alabaster, h. 18 ins / 45.7 cm) GBP 19,000. LONDON, 2 Dec 1986, *Maria Carmi as the Madonna in The Miracle* (1912, pastel, charcoal and gold paint, 29 x 21 1/2 ins / 73.8 x 54.7 cm) GBP 10,000. LONDON, 29 July 1988, *Woman in Uniform* (1914, ink, 12 1/4 x 7 ins / 31.3 x 17.5 cm) GBP 3,300. LONDON, 9 June 1989, *Self-portrait* (pencil, 14 x 10 ins / 35.6 x 25.4 cm) GBP 5,500. LONDON, 10 Nov 1989, *Sleeping Faun* (1913, dark-green-patinated, h. 9 1/2 ins / 24.4 cm) GBP 20,900. LONDON, 9 March 1990, *Sleeping Faun* (1913, brown-patinated bronze, h. 4 1/2 ins / 11.4 cm) GBP 20,900. LONDON, 3 May 1990, *Reclining Nude* (ink, 9 3/4 x 14 1/2 ins / 25 x 37 cm) GBP 880. LONDON, 8 June 1990, *Garden Ornament* (lead, h. 14 1/2 ins / 37 cm) GBP 8,580. LONDON, 9 Nov 1990, *Motherhood* (green-patinated bronze, h. 11 ins / 28 cm) GBP 17,600. LONDON, 7 March 1991, *Pastiche of Day and Night by Michelangelo* (ink, 27 1/2 x 21 1/2 ins / 70 x 54.5 cm) GBP 4,620. LONDON, 14 May 1992, *Male Nude Standing, Back View towards the Right* (ink, 14 1/2 x 9 ins / 37 x 23 cm) GBP 1,430. CALAIS, 14 March 1993, *Son of Volmar* (graphite, 11 x 8 1/4 ins / 27 x 21 cm) FRF 4,500; *Crouching Nude* (charcoal, 12 1/4 x 9 3/4 ins / 31 x 25 cm) FRF 10,000. PARIS, 20 May 1994,

Figure (1913, bronze) FRF 20,000. NEW YORK, 16 Sept 1999, *Duck. Lion* (c. 1910, pen, two, 7 x 10 ins / 19 x 25 cm) USD 3,000. PARIS, 2 Dec 1999, *The Doorknocker* (ink and watercolour, 8 x 6 ins / 21 x 15 cm) FRF 29,000. LONDON, 28 April 2000, *Study of Sophie* (pencil, 6 x 4 ins / 15 x 9 cm) GBP 1,400. LONDON, 6 Dec 2000, *Walking Man* (pen and ink, 10 x 7 ins / 25 x 19 cm) GBP 1,500. CAMBRIDGE, 21 Feb 2001, *Pike* (watercolour, 11 x 16 ins / 27 x 40 cm) GBP 5,600. LONDON, 14 June 2001, *Study of a Male Nude* (black chalk, watercolour and gouache, 21 x 16 ins / 53 x 40 cm) GBP 9,000. LONDON, 4 July 2002, *Wrestlers* (linocut, 9 x 11 ins / 22 x 28 cm) GBP 7,500. LONDON, 22 Nov 2002, *Duck* (1914, bronze, w. 5 ins / 12 cm) GBP 8,000. LONDON, 6 June 2003, *Ornamental Mask* (1969-1970, green patinated bronze, h. 30 ins / 76 cm) GBP 9,500. LONDON, 10 Sept 2003, *Portrait of Ossip Zadkine* (pastel and watercolour, 25 x 20 ins / 64 x 51 cm) GBP 3,600. LONDON, 8 April 2004, *Ezra Pound* (brush and ink, 15 x 10 ins / 38 x 26 cm) GBP 36,000. LONDON, 2 June 2004, *Motherhood* (patinated bronze, h. 11 ins / 27 cm) GBP 41,000.

GAUDIN, Adrien
Swiss, 19th century.
Born 1842, in Geneva.
Sculptor (wood).
Adrien Gaudin was in Paris in 1882.

GAUDIN, Auguste Jean
French, 20th century.
Born 29 July 1914, in Argentré-du-Plessis.
Painter, engraver.
Auguste Gaudin studied under Pierre Galle at evening classes at the École des Beaux-Arts in Rennes. He produced etchings, dry-point and line engravings as well as lithographs. At the *Peintres et Graveurs Français* (*French Painters and Engravers*) exhibition of 1947 and the Cercle de la Librairie exhibition, also in 1947, he showed *Le Livre Que Je Voudrais Illustrer* (*The Book I Would Like to Illustrate*) and popular scenes, Paris landscapes, theatrical figures and literary illustrations.

GAUDIN, Charles Théophile
Swiss, 19th century.
Born 1822, in Le Petit-Château; died 1866, in Lausanne.
Draughtsman, painter.

GAUDIN, Claude-Hubert
French, 19th century.
Born c. 1800, in Champagnole (Jura); died 2 February 1860, in Dôle.
Sculptor.

GAUDIN, Hélène
French, 19th century.
Born in Paris.
Painter.
She was a pupil of Mme Thoret, and sent examples of her painted fans to the Salons of 1870 and 1880.

GAUDIN, Léonard
Swiss, 18th century.
Born 1762, in Geneva.
Enameller.

GAUDIN, Léonce Maurice
French, 20th century.
Painter.
Although relatively unknown, Léonce Gaudin exhibited at the Salon des Réalités Nouvelles in Paris between 1952 and 1955.

His solid, abstract compositions are based on an elaborate balance between simple forms in blacks, greys and whites.

GAUDIN, Luis Pascual
Spanish, 16th - 17th century.
Born 1556, in Villa Franca; died 1621, in the Scala Dei monastery.
Painter. History painting.
Gaudin was a monk at the Scala Dei charterhouse, which he entered in 1595. He painted a large number of religious subjects for the monastery. He then travelled throughout Spain, acquiring such a reputation that Pope Gregory XV summoned him to Rome to work in St Peter's. However, having fallen ill, Gaudin could not obey the papal command and died soon afterwards.

L P Gaudin

GAUDIN, Pierre
French, 18th century.
Active in Paris in 1745.
Painter, sculptor.

GAUDIN, Simone
French, 20th century.
Born 5 May 1902, in Houilles.
Painter. Portraits, landscapes.
Simone Gaudin exhibited in Paris at the Salon des Artistes Français and became a member of the Salon in 1935.

GAUDINET, Pierre
French, 18th century.
Active in Paris in 1751.
Painter, sculptor.
Pierre Gaudinet may possibly be a diminutive form of 'Pierre Gaudin', or alternatively may be his son.

GAUDION, A.
French, 17th century.
Active in Aix-en-Provence in 1612.
Painter.
At the church of St Jean there is a painting signed by A. Gaudion.

GAUDION, Georges
French, 20th century.
Illustrator, watercolourist.
Georges Gaudion produced watercolour illustrations for a collection of *Poems* by Paul Morand (Toulouse 1926) and *À la manière de...* (*In the Style of...*) by Paul Reboux (Toulouse 1927).

GAUDIOSO, Michele
Italian, 17th century.
Active in Naples.
Sculptor.

GAUDIOSO, Paolo, the Elder
Italian, 17th - 18th century.
Active in Naples.
Painter.

GAUDIOSO, Paolo, the Younger
Italian, 17th - 18th century.
Active in Naples.
Painter.

GAUDIOSO, Pietro
Italian, 17th century.
Active in Naples.
Painter.

GAUDISSARD, Émile, or Gaudissart
French, 19th - 20th century.
Born 1872, in Algiers.
Painter, sculptor, designer. Figures, nudes, portraits, local scenes, flowers.
Orientalism.
Émile Gaudissard produced a series of Orientalist paintings from 1892 to 1900 including scenes of nomads, oases and Kabyle shepherds. He also carved busts and figures and dec-

rated the Théâtre de la Danse in Algiers with sculptures, paintings and fabrics.

He exhibited at the Salon des Artistes Français in Paris from 1892 and received a commendation in 1896. He also took part in the Exposition Universelle of 1900. He was awarded a bronze medal and a travel bursary in 1904 and a silver medal in 1906, becoming a member of the Salon the same year.

MUSEUMS AND GALLERIES:

ALGIERS: *Kindness; Édouard Cat; Major Lamy; The Unfortunate Job on the Dunghill.*

AUCTION RECORDS:

PARIS, 7 June 1923, *Small Bunch of Flowers in a Stemmed Glass,* FRF 85. PARIS, 2 March 1929, *Bunch of White Flowers in a Vase,* FRF 650. PARIS, 24 Feb 1934, *Flowers,* FRF 370. PARIS, 30 June 1941, *Seated Odalisque,* FRF 400. PARIS, 23 Feb 1945, *Moorish Baths,* FRF 1,000. LINDAU, 7 Oct 1980, *Floral Composition* (oil on canvas, 78 3/4 x 101 1/4 ins / 200 x 257 cm) FRF 4,700. PARIS, 17 March 1989, *Nude with Turban* (oil on card, 41 3/4 x 30 ins / 106 x 76 cm) FRF 58,000. PARIS, 19 Nov 1991, *Nude with Turban* (oil on card, 41 3/4 x 30 ins / 106 x 76 cm) FRF 55,000. PARIS, 8 March 1999, *Harem Scenes* (1897, oil on canvas, a pair, 24 x 29 ins / 60 x 73 cm) FRF 15,000. PARIS, 16 Nov 1999, *Stroll by the Sea* (oil on canvas, 18 x 24 ins / 46 x 61 cm) FRF 25,000. PARIS, 14 Nov 2000, *View of the Heights of Algiers* (oil on canvas, 31 x 42 ins / 78 x 107 cm) FRF 18,000. PARIS, 14 June 2004, *Cap Cavallo, Bougie* (1908, oil on canvas, 21 x 26 ins / 54 x 65 cm) EUR 3,400.

GAUDISSART

French, 19th century.
Active in Paris.
Caricaturist.

GAUDISSART, Pierre Joseph

French, 18th century.
Active in Paris in 1767.
Painter.

GAUDRAN, Louis-Gustave

French, 19th century.
Born 1829, in Paris.
Sculptor, painter.

He was a pupil of A. Toussaint. He first exhibited at the Paris Salon in 1870 and received an honourable mention in 1887. Gaudran is remembered for his stone statue of *John II the Good, Count of Anjou,* sculpted for Angoulême Cathedral.

BIBLIOGRAPHY:

Thibièrge, M. T., *'Les sculpteurs de Viollet-le-Duc pour la restauration du château de Pierrefonds, 1858-1885'* in *Bulletin de la Société de l'Histoire de l'Art Français,* 1985.

GAUDRAT, Marie Laurence

French, 20th - 21st century.
Born January 1952, in Paris.
Painter. Figures, interiors with figures, landscapes, still-lifes.

Marie Laurence Gaudrat did not receive formal training in art, but she was guided by Maurice Mazo who followed the teachings of Othon Friesz at the Académie de la Grande-Chaumière. Her experience with the restoration team at the Assemblée Nationale in 1974, 1983 and 1985 would also prove valuable. In 1994 she worked on the set of the James Ivory film, *Jefferson in Paris.*

Gaudrat paints nature and living beings: young women resting in gardens, playing the piano in the shadows of a room, nature dormant under a coat of snow, trees awakening in the spring. Her mastery of a deceptively simple style is adapted by her use of the brush or the palette knife as she reorchestrates according to a pleasing Bonnard or a nostalgic Balthus.

She has shown her work in group exhibitions at the Salon d'Angers in 1987 and 1994 and in Paris at the Salon d'Automne, of which she is both a member and active on the board of administration. Solo exhibitions include those in Paris in 1983 and 1985, and those at the Galerie Frégnac in 1989, 1991, 1994 and 1996. She has received various prizes, including the Prix Paul Louis Weiller in 1984.

BIBLIOGRAPHY:

Perrault, Gilles/Mougenot, Jacques/Comte-Sponville, André, *à Marie-Laurence Gaudrat,* Somogy, Paris, 2001.

GAUDREAUS, Antoine-Robert

French, 18th century.
Born 1682; died 6 May 1746.
Cabinet maker.

Gaudreaus was one of the main suppliers to the furniture depository of the French Crown.

GAUDRIER, Joseph-Émile

French, 19th century.
Active in Paris.
Painter.

He was a member of the Société des Artistes Français from 1883 and an exhibitor at its salons.

GAUDRILLET

French, 16th century.
Sculptor, architect.

Gaudrillet was the son-in-law of Hugues Sambin, and collaborated with him on work on the portal of the church of St-Michel in Dijon (Côte-d'Or).

GAUDRION, Francine

French, 20th century.
Born 1885, in Montrouge; died 1942.
Painter, watercolourist.

Francine Gaudrion exhibited regularly in Paris at the Salon des Artistes Français.

GAUDRION, Thérèse Marie

French, 20th century.
Born 1883, in Paris; died February 1954, in Paris.
Miniaturist.

Thérèse Gaudrion exhibited regularly at the Salon des Artistes Français in Paris.

GAUDRY, Louis Alexandre

French, 18th - 19th century.
Born 1749; died 1815.
Painter (porcelain).

Louis Gaudry was a student of Louis Watteau. He worked at the St-Amand factory.

GAUDRY-ALLARD, Julie

French, 20th century.
Born in Argenteuil.
Miniaturist.

Julie Gaudry-Allard studied under Barrias, Bellay and Pelez. She lived and worked in Nevers and received a commendation in 1906.

GAUDRY-CHARONAT, Lucie

French, 19th - 20th century.
Active in Paris.
Painter.

Lucie Gaudry-Charonat became a member of the Société des Artistes Français in 1905 and exhibited at the Society's Salons.

GAUDUBOIS-FEUILLAS, Andrée

French, 20th century.
Born 1891.
Painter, engraver.

Andrée Gaudubois-Feuillas studied under J.-P. Laurens. She exhibited regularly in Paris at the Salon des Artistes Français.

GAUDY, Georges

Belgian, 19th - 20th century.

Born 6 October 1872, in St Joost-ten-Node.

Painter, draughtsman, watercolourist, pastellist, illustrator, poster artist. Figures, sporting subjects, landscapes, animals.

Georges Gaudy began as an illustrator, poster artist and decorator. He was active in Brussels and exhibited coloured drawings at the 1913 Salon National des Aquarellistes.

MUSEUMS AND GALLERIES:

BERLIN: *Tyrolean Well; Forge near Salxburg* - GRAZ: *Wolves; Returning through the Storm*; six paintings of animals - LEIPZIG: *Landscape with Flock* - VIENNA: *The Forge; Resting in the Fields; The Ploughman; The Watering Place; Vulture and Dying Stag* - VIENNA (Czernin'sche Gemäldegal.): *Horse*.

AUCTION RECORDS:

NEW YORK, 18 May 1897, *Landscape with Flock,* FRF 1,149. NEW YORK, 15 and 16 April 1909, *Veteran,* USD 50. PARIS, 20 June 1984, *Jenatzy Tyres* (1912-1913, poster in colour, 33 x 46 ins / 84 x 117 cm) FRF 6,500.

GAUERMANN, Carl

Austrian, 19th century.

Born 1804; died 1829, in Vienna.

Painter.

Carl, the son of Jacob Gauermann, was a pupil at the academy in Vienna.

GAUERMANN, Friedrich

Austrian, 19th century.

Born 20 September 1807, in Miesenbach; died 7 July 1862, in Vienna.

Painter, watercolourist, draughtsman. Genre scenes, landscapes, animals.

Friedrich was a pupil of his father, Jakob Gauermann, and studied at the art academy in Vienna. A Viennese Biedermeier painter, Gauermann's work is characterised by an adaptable, picturesque style. In 1836 he became a member of the same academy. He exhibited in Vienna, Berlin and Dresden. Some of his works appeared in the *Masterpieces from the Belvedere in Vienna* exhibition in 1994 at the Marmottan museum in Paris.

Stamp of sale

MUSEUMS AND GALLERIES:

VIENNA (Österreichische Gal. Belvedere).

AUCTION RECORDS:

VIENNA, 1878, *Village Fountain in the Alps,* FRF 7,500; *Storm over the Lake at Zell,* FRF 7,750. PARIS, 1896, *Study of a Dead Fox* (watercolour) FRF 70; *Study of a Dying Stag* (drawing) FRF 65; *Study of a Bay Horse* (drawing) FRF 80; *Study of a Rabbit* (drawing) FRF 40. LONDON, 23 June 1939, *Peasants and Animals on the Way to Market,* GBP 31. LONDON, 12 Feb 1942, *Landscape,* GBP 50. VIENNA, 1 Sept 1961, *Village Well in Mittenwald,* ATS 130,000. VIENNA, 14 June 1966, *Landscape with Woodcutters,* ATS 180,000. VIENNA, 19 March 1968, *Attack on the Mailcoach,* ATS 450,000. VIENNA, 16 March 1971, *Flock Quenching its Thirst in a Mountain Landscape,* ATS 180,000. VIENNA, 21 March 1972, *Flock Quenching its Thirst,* ATS 250,000. VIENNA, 20 March 1973, *Hunting,* ATS 140,000. VIENNA, 3 Dec 1974, *Shepherd and Flock Sheltering beneath a Tree* ATS 320,000. VIENNA, 22 June 1976, *Old Sawmill* (1826, oil on canvas, 22 3/4 x 31 ins / 58 x 79 cm) ATS 200,000. VIENNA, 1[?] March 1977, *Eagles in an Alpine Landscape* (oil on paper, 8 x 5 1/2 ins / 20.5 x 14 cm) ATS 80,000. VIENNA, 12 Dec 1978, *Peasants and Animals Taking Shelter from the Storm beneath a Tree* (oil on canvas, 27 1/2 x 36 1/4 ins / 70 x 92 cm) ATS 1,200,000. VIENNA, 15 Sept 1981, *Resting at the Foot of the Tree* (pen and wash/paper, 9 1/2 x 14 1/4 ins / 24 x 36 cm) ATS 22,000. NEW YORK, 24 Feb 1983, *Stag in Undergrowth* (1832, oil on panel, 11 x 15 ins / 28 x 38 cm) USD 19,000. VIENNA, 23 March 1983, *Peasant and Flock in an Alpine Landscape* (pen, watercolour/pencil outlines, 6 1/4 x 8 1/2 ins / 15.9 x 21.7 cm) ATS 25,000. VIENNA, 20 May 1987, *Rural Scene* (1849, oil on panel, 6 x 8 1/4 ins / 15.3 x 21 cm) ATS 1,000,000. VIENNA, 23 Feb 1989, *Roe-Deer, Doe and Buck in a Mountainous Landscape* (oil on canvas, 17 3/4 x 14 ins / 45 x 35.8 cm) ATS 451,000. NEW YORK, 23 Feb 1989, *Hunter on the Way Home* (oil on canvas, 12 1/2 ins / 32 cm, 1 1/2 x 15 ins/4 x 38 cm, 2 3/4 ins/7 cm) USD 14,300. NEW YORK, 24 Oct 1989, *Village Fountain* (1836, oil on panel, 29 1/4 x 37 3/4 ins / 74.3 x 95.9 cm) USD 308,000. PARIS, 5 April 1990, *Collier's Family* (oil on canvas, 19 x 24 3/4 ins / 48 x 63 cm) FRF 70,000. MUNICH, 12 June 1991, *Cattle Quenching their Thirst* (ink and wash, 8 1/4 x 11 1/4 ins / 21 x 28.5 cm) DEM 2,750. NEW YORK, 20 Feb 1992, *Shepherdess with her Flock* (oil on panel, 17 1/2 x 22 ins / 44.5 x 55.9 cm) USD 104,500. MUNICH, 10 Dec 1992, *Boar Hunting in an Oak Forest* (crayon and wash/paper, 6 1/2 x 8 1/2 ins / 16.7 x 21.3 cm) DEM 2,938. MUNICH, 7 Dec 1993, *Two Urchins with their Horses in a Meadow* (1824, oil on panel, 7 x 10 3/4 ins / 18 x 27.5 cm) DEM 18,400. LONDON, 11 Oct 1995, *Fox Taking a Chicken to her Young* (oil on panel, 17 1/2 x 14 ins / 44.5 x 35.5 cm) GBP 12,650. PARIS, 24 June 1996, *Bridge over the Waterfall* (oil on canvas, 25 1/2 x 31 1/4 ins / 65 x 79.5 cm) FRF 12,000. NEW YORK, 24 Oct 1996, *Wolves attacking a Stag in a Rugged Landscape* (1830, oil on canvas, 29 x 22 ins / 73.7 x 55.9 cm) USD 46,000. VIENNA, 20 May 1999, *Sheltering Tree - Family Group and Animals Sheltering from a Storm* (oil on panel, 27 x 36 ins / 68 x 92 cm) ATS 2,500,000. VIENNA, 27 May 1999, *Cow Licking Calf* (1826, oil on panel, 15 x 18 ins / 37 x 46 cm) ATS 800,000. VIENNA, 3 Oct 2000, *Cow with Calf before Landscape* (colour ink wash over pencil, 7 x 11 ins / 19 x 27 cm) ATS 35,000. NURNBERG, 23 Nov 2000, *Mill by the Stream* (oil on canvas, 13 x 17 ins / 32 x 42 cm) DEM 14,000. LONDON, 29 March 2001, *Hunt on the Shores of the Chiemsee* (oil on panel, 33 x 29 ins / 84 x 73 cm) GBP 95,000. VIENNA, 27 Nov 2001, *Large Boulder in Forest Clearing* (1841, oil on paper/board, 14 x 18 ins / 36 x 45 cm) ATS 350,000. VIENNA, 25 Nov 2002, *Hohensalzburg Castle* (oil on paper/canvas, 12 x 17 ins / 30 x 42 cm) EUR 70,000. VIENNA, 28 Nov 2002, *Drover at Zellersee* (1862, oil on canvas, 40 x 58 ins / 102 x 147 cm) EUR 140,000. LONDON, 3 June 2003, *Two Bears by a Spring* (oil on panel, 12 x 15 ins / 31 x 39 cm) GBP 22,000. VIENNA, 24 Nov 2003, *Boy with Two Horses* (1832, oil on canvas, 28 x 37 ins / 71 x 95 cm) EUR 150,000. FURTH, 14 May 2004, *Mountain Thunderstorm* (oil on canvas, 14 x 17 ins / 36 x 44 cm) EUR 17,000. VIENNA, 27 May 2004, *Hunting Party in a Rocky Ravine with Gutenstein Mountain in the Background* (1831, oil on panel, 29 x 21 ins / 73 x 54 cm) EUR 40,000.

GAUERMANN, Jakob

German, 18th - 19th century.

Born 3 September 1773, in Oeffingen; died 27 March 1843, in Miesenbach.

Painter, watercolourist, draughtsman, engraver. Genre scenes, landscapes.

Jakob Gauermann was a pupil at the Karlsakademie in Stuttgart, after which he moved on to the art academy in Vienna in 1798. In 1818 he became painter to the court of the Grand Duke. He travelled and worked in the Austrian Tyrol.

AUCTION RECORDS:
VIENNA, 17 Nov 1981, *Landscape at the Waterfalls* (watercolour, 3$^{3/4}$ x 5$^{1/2}$ ins / 9.5 x 14 cm) ATS 15,000. VIENNA, 20 March 1986, *Alpine Landscape* (watercolour, 8$^{1/4}$ x 11 ins / 21 x 27 cm) ATS 65,000. VIENNA, 15 May 2001, *Market at Aussee* (pen and pencil, 14 x 20 ins / 35 x 51 cm) ATS 25,000. VIENNA, 11 June 2002, *Herders Walking along River Path* (oil on canvas, 25 x 33 ins / 63 x 84 cm) EUR 14,000. STUTTGART, 3 July 2003, *Extensive Landscape with Illtal* (oil on canvas, 18 x 26 ins / 46 x 66 cm) EUR 16,000. STUTTGART, 3 July 2003, *Extensive Landscape with Altaussee* (oil on canvas, 18 x 26 ins / 46 x 66 cm) EUR 16,000.

GAUFF, Johannes

German, 19th century.
Born 26 December 1804, in Frankfurt am Main; died 29 March 1858, in Frankfurt am Main.
Painter, lithographer.

Gauff is credited with portraits and battle scenes.

GAUFFIER, Louis

French, 18th century.
Born 1761, in Poitiers or in La Rochelle; died 20 October 1801, in Livorno, Italy.
Painter (gouache), draughtsman. History painting, religious subjects, portraits, genre scenes, landscapes.

Louis Gauffier was a student of Taraval. In 1784, he won the first Grand Prix de Peinture for: *Samaritan Woman at Jesus' Feet*. He took part in the Salons in Paris from 1789 and was made an associate of the academy on 24 August in the same year. He adopted the style of Poussin.

In 2001, several of his Tuscan landscapes were displayed at the exhibition *Un Paese incantato. Italia dipinta da Thomas Jones a Corot* (*An Enchanted Country. Italy Depicted by Artists from Thomas Jones to Corot*) at the international centre of art and culture at the Tè Palace in Mantua.

L Gauffier F.t L-Gauffier

BIBLIOGRAPHY:
Marmottan, Paul, *'Le Peintre Louis Gauffier'* in *Gazette des Beaux-Arts*, Paris, 1926. Ottani Cavina, Anna (ed.), *Un Paese incantato. Italia dipinta da Thomas Jones a Corot*, exhibition catalogue, Electa, Milan, 2001.

MUSEUMS AND GALLERIES:
KARLSRUHE (Staatliche Kunsthalle): *Prince Augustus Frederick, then Duke of Sussex* (1793, oil on canvas) - LONDON (National Portrait Gal.): *Unknown man* (1796, oil on canvas, formerly known as 'Henry Richard Vassall Fox, 3rd Baron Holland') - MONTPELLIER (Mus. Fabre): *Study of a Tree on the Edge of the Tiber; Group of Trees around a Large Pond at Vallombrosa; Herminie; Holy Family; Painter; View of the Convent at Vallombrosa, in Tuscany; View of the Arno Valley and the Convent at Vallombrosa, near Paradisino; View of the Abbey at Vallombrosa* (pencil); *View of the Arno Valley from the Little Paradise of Vallombrosa* (oil on paper mounted on panel); *View of the Convent at Vallombrosa* (oil on canvas); *View of the Arno Valley from the Little Paradise of Vallombrosa* (pencil drawing) - PARIS (Mus. Marmottan-Monet): *Salnée Family; View of Vallombrosa; Vallombrosa: Monks Talking to a Traveller* (oil on canvas) - PHILADELPHIA (MA): *View of the Arno Valley from the Little Paradise of Vallombrosa* (oil on canvas) - ROCHEFORT: *Return of the Prodigal Son* - VERSAILLES: *General Dessole and Two Figures; Three Groups of Strangers; Miot Family.*

AUCTION RECORDS:
PARIS, 1844, *Roman Ladies Making a Gift of Their Jewellery to the Nation*, FRF 321. PARIS, 1869, *Portraits of the Artist, His Wife and His Stepmother*, FRF 290. PARIS, 6 Feb 1925, *Portrait Presumed To Be of the Painter and His Wife* (gouache) FRF 400. LONDON, 15 Feb 1929, *Vanity*, GBP 9. LONDON, 19 Feb 1931, *Vanity*, GBP 3. LONDON, 4 Dec 1936, *Russian Empress*, GBP 12. PARIS, 25 June 1943, *Generosity of the Roman Ladies* (1790) FRF 12,000. STOCKHOLM, 30 Oct to 1 Nov 1946, *General Michaud*, SEK 1,060. LONDON, 16 Nov 1960, *Portrait of the Duke of Sussex*, GBP 1,150. LONDON, 4 April 1962, *Dr Penrose*, GBP 1,200. PARIS, 1 April 1965, *Marquis of Aylesbury*, FRF 16,500. LONDON, 16 March 1966, *View of Florence*, GBP 1,200. COLOGNE, 26 Nov 1970, *View of the Arno Valley*, DEM 13,000. LONDON, 13 Dec 1974, *Views of Vallombrosa* (four canvases in pairs) Gns 19,000. LONDON, 2 Dec 1977, *Mother Teaching Her Son about the Virtues of His Ancestors* (1794, oil on canvas) GBP 2,000. NEW YORK, 3 June 1980, *Academy for Men* (red chalk/paper, 17 x 20$^{1/2}$ ins / 42.3 x 52 cm) USD 2,700. MILAN, 8 May 1984, *Craggy Landscape with Figures* (oil on canvas, 17$^{3/4}$ x 22 ins / 45 x 56 cm) ITL 4,500,000. LONDON, 11 July 1986, *Portrait of Prince Augustus Frederick, Later the Duke of Sussex, Lying on a Roman Tomb, with Ruins of an Aqueduct and the Vatican in the Distance* (1793, oil on canvas, 27 x 19$^{3/4}$ ins / 68.5 x 50 cm) GBP 190,000. PARIS, 15 April 1988, *Achilles Recognised by Ulysses; Venus Offering Adonis and Love to Diana* (two drawings, 9$^{1/4}$ x 12$^{3/4}$ ins / 23.5 x 32.5 cm) FRF 48,500. NEW YORK, 13 Oct 1989, *Angel Liberating St Peter from His Prison* (1788, oil on paper/canvas, 7$^{1/2}$ x 5 ins / 19 x 12.5 cm) USD 52,250. MONACO, 18-19 June 1992, *Portrait of a man with Vesuvius in the Background* (oil on canvas/panel, 3$^{3/4}$ x 2$^{3/4}$ ins / 9.5 x 7 cm) FRF 53,280. LONDON, 13 Dec 1996, *Portrait of Elizabeth, Lady Webster, Later Lady Holland* (1795, oil on canvas, 20 x 26$^{1/2}$ ins / 51 x 67.6 cm) GBP 100,500. NEW YORK, 23 May 2000, *Portrait of a Young Man with Mount Vesuvius Beyond* (oil on canvas, 4 x 3 ins / 9 x 7 cm) USD 28,000. NEW YORK, 25 Jan 2001, *Abraham Accepting Hagar* (oil on canvas, 21 x 26 ins / 54 x 65 cm) USD 20,000. PARIS, 27 June 2002, *Literary Subject* (1789, oil on canvas, 9 x 12 ins / 24 x 30 cm) EUR 21,000. NEW YORK, 22 Jan 2003, *Cornelia Presenting her Two Young Sons* (chalk/pen/ink wash heightened with white, 13 x 20 ins / 34 x 52 cm) USD 8,500.

GAUFFIER, Pauline

Maiden name: Chatillon
French, 18th century.
Died 1801, in Florence.
Painter. Portraits, genre scenes.

Pauline Gauffier was a student of her husband and of Drouais; Bartolozzi engraved several of her paintings. She featured at the Salon in Paris in 1798.

AUCTION RECORDS:
PARIS, 20 and 21 April 1932, *Oath*, FRF 500. LONDON, 6 April 1973, *Portrait of the First Marquis of Allesbury*, Gns 400. LONDON, 21 April 1989, *Family Scene in the Courtyard of a Villa with a Woman Encouraging a Spaniel to Dance* (oil on canvas, 24 x 29$^{1/2}$ ins / 61 x 75 cm) GBP 24,200.

GAUFFRIDI, Jean

French, 15th century.
Active in Avignon.
Painter, glass painter.

GAUGAIN, Anne

British, 19th century.
Active in London c. 1840.
Painter.

Anne Gaugain exhibited in London from 1838 to 1847, showing at both the Royal Academy and the Suffolk Street Gallery.

GAUGAIN, Henri

French, 19th century.
Active in Paris.
Print publisher, lithographer.

He is best known for his portraits.

GAUGAIN, Philip A.
British, 18th - 19th century.
Active in London.
Painter. Genre scenes, portraits.

Philip A. Gaugain exhibited in London from 1783 to 1847, notably at the Free Society, the Royal Academy and the British Institution.

GAUGAIN, Thomas
French, 18th century.
Born 1748, in Abbeville; died c. 1805, in London.
Painter, engraver.

Thomas Gaugain went to England at an early age and was a pupil of Houston. He engraved after Reynolds, Morland, Cosway and Northcote. His output is considerable and is now highly sought after by art lovers. Gaugain also tried his hand at genre painting and exhibited at the Royal Academy in London from 1778 to 1782. This venture must have had little impact, for none of his biographers mentions it. He mainly engraved with burin and stipple.

AUCTION RECORDS:
LONDON, 13 Nov 1997, *Walk in Hyde Park; Figures at the Royal Exchange; View of Large Camp on Cox Heath; View of London; Principal Buildings in London* (1796, 1778 and 1792, dry-point engraving, etching, aquatint, eight items) GBP 3,450.

GAUGÉ, Élisa
French, 19th century.
Painter.

She exhibited examples of her watercolours at the Paris Salons of 1838 and 1839.

GAUGENGIGL, Ignaz Marcel
German, 19th - 20th century.
Born 29 July 1855, in Passau (Bavaria); died 1932.
Also active in the USA.
Painter. Genre scenes.

Ignaz Gaugengigl studied at the Munich academy then went to live in Boston. He won a medal in New Orleans and was appointed an associate of the National Academy in 1906.

AUCTION RECORDS:
NEW YORK, 10-11 April 1902, *The Smoker,* USD 250. NEW YORK, 29 Oct 1931, *Cantabile,* USD 45; *The Unbelievable,* USD 40. NEW YORK, 10 and 11 Jan 1946, *His Hobby-horse,* USD 120. BERN, 7 May 1976, *The Violininst* (oil on panel, 8 1/4 x 7 ins / 21 x 18 cm) CHF 90,000. NEW YORK, 20 March 1982, *The Hat* (oil on panel, 10 x 7 ins / 25.5 x 18 cm) USD 2,800. NEW YORK, 28 May 1987, *Portrait of a Man with a Dog* (c. 1905, oil on panel, 24 x 17 1/4 ins / 61 x 43.7 cm) USD 70,000. NEW YORK, 26 May 1988, *the Hat* (oil on panel, 10 x 7 ins / 25.1 x 17.5 cm) USD 13,200. NEW YORK, 21 May 1991, *The Right Direction* (1876, oil on panel, 7 1/4 x 9 1/2 ins / 18.4 x 24.2 cm) USD 1,210. NEW YORK, 28 May 1992, *The Painter* (oil on panel, 8 1/4 x 6 ins / 21 x 14.3 cm) USD 14,300. NEW YORK, 14 March 1996, *On the Way to the Ball* (1880, oil on panel, 12 x 7 3/4 ins / 30.5 x 19.7 cm) USD 4,600. NEW YORK, 3 Dec 1996, *Breezy Day on the Shoal Islands* (oil on panel, 17 1/4 x 23 1/4 ins / 44 x 59 cm) USD 3,680.

GAUGER, Emilia Karlovna
Russian, 19th century.
Born 1836, in St Petersburg.
Painter.

Emilia Gauger was a pupil of Beidemann. We owe her genre scenes and portraits.

GAUGNEUR, Guillaume le. See **LE GAUGNEUR**

GAUGSBURGER, Conrad
Austrian, 15th century.
Born in Schönau (Tyrol).
Glass painter.
Tyrolean School.

Gaugsburger worked particularly in Meran, South Tyrc (now Merano, Italy).

GAUGUET, Eugène
French, 19th - 20th century.
Born 6 February 1872, in Quimper.
Engraver.

Eugène Gauguet studied under Cormon. He exhibited regularly in Paris at the Salon des Artistes Français, receiving a silver medal in 1922 and a gold medal in 1926. He was made a Chevalier of the Légion d'Honneur in 1931.

GAUGUET-LAROUCHE, Jean
Canadian, 20th century.
Born 1935, in La Malbaie (Quebec).
Sculptor.

Jean Gauguet-Larouche is a writer and poet. He pursued his research into fine arts with 'musical sculptures', using linear forms in particular in order to express a rhythm. He took part in an exhibition of sculpture at the Musée Rodin in Paris in 1966.

GAUGUIN, Jean René
French, 20th century.
Born 12 April 1881, in Paris; died 1961.
From 1884 active and from 1909 naturalised in Denmark.
Sculptor, potter. Figures.

Jean Gauguin was the son of Paul Gauguin.

AUCTION RECORDS:
COPENHAGEN, 1 June 1983, *The Potter* (1937, Roche ceramic, h. 54 ins / 137 cm) DKK 9,000. LOKEREN, 8 Oct 1988, *Spirit of the Lake* (1941, ceramic, h. 26 3/4 ins / 68 cm) BEF 75,000. PARIS, 30 June 1989, *The Rape of Europa* (sculpture in stanniferous polychrome earthenware, h. 27 1/2 ins / 70 cm) FRF 21,500. COPENHAGEN, 22 Nov 1989, *Harmonica Player* (bronze, h. 12 1/4 ins / 31 cm) DKK 8,800. COPENHAGEN, 1 April 1992, *Bust of Einer Hollbol* (bronze, h. 14 1/4 ins / 36 cm) DKK 3,200. COPENHAGEN, 26 April 1995, *Seated Accordion Player* (1917, bronze, H.12 1/2 ins / 32 cm) DKK 5,000. PARIS, 22 March 1998, *Portrait of Paul Gauguin* (enamelled terracotta, 5 3/4 x 4 3/4 x 2 3/4 ins / 14.5 x 12 x 7 cm) FRF 6,800.

GAUGUIN, Paul
French, 19th century.
Born 7 June 1848, in Paris; died 8 May 1903, in Fatu Iva in the Marquesas Islands.
Painter (including gouache), watercolourist, pastellist, draughtsman, sculptor (wood/bronze), potter, engraver (wood), monotype artist, illustrator. Religious subjects, figure compositions, local figures, nudes, portraits, interiors, rustic scenes, landscapes, landscapes with figures, still-lifes, animals. Low reliefs.
Symbolism, Japonisme.
Pont-Aven School.

Although born in distinctly humdrum surroundings at 56 Rue Notre-Dame-de-Lorette, Eugène-Henri-Paul Gauguin's family background was such that he appears, albeit with hindsight, to have been predestined for an exotic life and career. Gauguin's father was a radical journalist from Orléans, his mother a militant socialist, the natural child of a liaison between a Frenchwoman and a colonel in the Peruvian dragoons serving in France. In 1849, when Gauguin was barely two years old, his parents made plans to move to Peru; the family sailed for Lima, but Gauguin's father died during the voyage. As a result, Gauguin spent his early years as a ward of his mother's uncle, Don Pio de Tristan Moscoso. The impressionable youngster must surely have been marked by this early experience. Some four years later, Gauguin and his mother returned to France and settled with his father's family in Orléans, where he proved to be a decidedly unruly pupil at primary school, before he was sent to boarding school in Paris. He opted to go to sea at the age of seventeen and signed on as a pilot for a voyage to Rio de Janeiro. He spent the next six years at sea, from 1865 to 1871, ending up serving on a French warship during the Franco-Prussian War.

Gauguin's mother died in 1867, entrusting her children to the care of the financier Gustave Arosa, who found a position for him in 1871 as a stockbroker with Bertin's bank in Paris. He rapidly showed a talent for business and in 1873 he married Mette-Sophie Gad, a Danish girl from a 'good' family, who bore him five children between 1874 and 1883. Meanwhile his early interest in art was encouraged by Arosa who, although he specialised in photographing ancient Greek and Roman monuments, was also a lover of modern art. Through Arosa, Gauguin was introduced to a friend of Charles Baudelaire, the photographer Gaspard-Félix Nadar, who had hosted the First Impressionist Exhibition in April 1874 in his former studio on the Boulevard des Capucines. Gauguin came to know the early Impressionists and started to invest in their work, using his profits from the stock market to purchase canvases by Jongkind, Cézanne, Guillaumin and Pissarro (who described Gauguin as a 'remarkably astute' collector and dealer).

In 1874 Gauguin had begun to paint and sculpt, taking instruction in the latter discipline from a rather obscure sculptor called Jules Ernest Bouillot. Emile Schuffenecker, a fellow stockbroker and painter, was instrumental in encouraging him to take courses at the Académie Colarossi, while Camille Pissarro began to coach him in the use of expressive colour and brushwork. Gauguin rapidly came to know the other Impressionists and was eventually invited to exhibit alongside them at the fifth Impressionist Exhibition in 1880. With the crash of the Parisian stock market in 1882 Gauguin found himself without a job. He was convinced he could earn a living as a full-time painter, but his hopes quickly proved illusory and he was obliged to move with his wife and five children to Rouen, where the cost of living was less onerous than in the French capital. Mette found their change in living standards unacceptable and returned to Copenhagen to live with her family. In 1884 Gauguin accepted a poorly paid salesman's job in order to join her in Denmark, but Mette's family were far from sympathetic to his precarious financial situation, and he and his wife soon separated for good.

A saddened Gauguin returned to Paris in June 1885, but his continuing near-penury decided him to 'flee this poor man's wilderness' and pursue his artistic goals elsewhere. It is debatable whether Gauguin's romantic aspirations at this time were wholly genuine or whether they merely masked an inability to live up to his responsibilities. What is certain, however, was that the Impressionists had by this time drifted apart as the initial sense of community that underpinned the 'movement' was progressively diluted. Individuals went their own way, seeking out their own artistic direction. It was a time when, as the art critic Félix Fénéon pointed out in an observation that can be applied equally to Seurat, Van Gogh, Cézanne and Gauguin himself, 'anecdote had been sacrificed to arabesque, nomenclature to synthesis, and permanence to transience'. Impressionism, as such, had reached a turning-point: the Impressionist Exhibition held in 1886 was the last of its kind. Brittany appealed to Gauguin as a region of France that had retained much of its 'primitive purity' and he spent the second half of 1886 there, getting to know the region and its people and trying his hand at ceramics. Soon, however, his roving spirit was to take him much farther afield, and the following year he sailed to Panama and Martinique, where his stay was cut short when he contracted malaria. His appetite for the exotic (and not least for the lithe grace of beautiful young women) was by this time well and truly whetted.

Gauguin returned to France in 1887 and met up again with Van Gogh, who was in his Parisian Impressionist phase at the time. By February 1888 he was again in Pont-Aven, Britanny, and later in the year he was working alongside Emile Bernard in developing concepts of 'cloisonnism' ('partitionism') and 'synthetism'. Gauguin was now increasingly sure of his own vision and talent. In October he famously 'instructed' Paul Sérusier in the art of painting, supervising the completion of the latter's small canvas entitled *Talisman*. After Sérusier returned to Paris he showed it to friends such as Maurice Denis, Jean-Edouard Vuillard and Pierre Bonnard, and the painting became the genuine talisman of what became the Nabi movement.

In late October 1888 Gauguin finally went to Arles following persistent requests from Van Gogh. The two months they spent there together has passed into legend owing to the dramatic confrontations between two volatile artists. Gauguin left for Paris at the first opportunity, lodging with Schuffenecker, painting a group portrait of the family, producing several pieces of pottery and trying his hand at zinc engraving. He made friends with Daniel de Monfreid, of whom Gauguin's daughter Pola would later write that 'he took particular pleasure in meddling in other people's affairs'. To be fair, de Monfreid provided Gauguin with somewhere to stay for the next few months, setting him up in a studio complex he maintained at the Cité des Artistes on Boulevard Arago; the link between Gauguin and de Monfreid (and thence to the Parisian art world), sustained over many years, is evident from the regular correspondence between the two when Gauguin was in Tahiti.

Gauguin travelled back to Brittany in early 1889, residing initially in Pont-Aven (where an exhibition had been scheduled at the Café Volpini) and later - when Pont-Aven became 'too crowded' for his taste - in Le Pouldu, where he spent the whole of 1890. Gauguin's search for spiritual meaning was underpinned by his obsession with the exotic, fuelled by his childhood in Peru, his years at sea and his exposure to the 'primitive purity' of Brittany. At Van Gogh's prompting, he had read the exotic and beautifully crafted novels of the popular author Pierre Loti and was clearly attracted to the island paradise of Tahiti; that said, there were other - mercantile - reasons which prompted Gauguin to consider exiling himself in Martinique, Madagascar or Tongking, venues where French colonialism had spawned a market for exotica. Gauguin admitted as much: 'I tend to agree with Vincent that the future of painting lies in the tropics. Little has been painted there and new motifs should appeal to a gullible buying public.' This is not to say that Gauguin was motivated solely by the prospect of financial rewards; on the contrary, he saw exotic 'myth' as a fertile area in terms of uncovering 'new artistic resources such as physiognomies, religious practices, mysticism and symbolism'.

In the months that followed his return to Paris, Gauguin frequented literary circles, in particular seeking out the company of the Symbolists around Stéphane Mallarmé, who had accepted him as a kindred spirit on the strength of his work in Pont-Aven and Le Pouldu. In a sense, Gauguin's 'imminent' departure for Tahiti became something of a Symbolist event in itself. Alphonse Daudet remarked on this: 'And then we have our friend Gauguin, perpetually bound for Tahiti but apparently in no great hurry to leave Paris - to the point where even his best friends keep telling him: Go! Just go!' This perhaps begs the question of whether Gauguin was happy in Symbolist company and, indeed, of whether he himself was a Symbolist. Possibly, possibly not: despite producing a lithograph entitled *You Shall be a Symbolist*, following a banquet in his honour hosted by Mallarmé at the Café Voltaire to celebrate Gauguin's departure, the guest of honour was heard to remark: 'And what about the waiters? I suppose they're Symbolists as well?'

Before finally leaving Paris, Gauguin held an exhibition at the Hôtel Drouot and sold 31 canvases. Ary Renan, son of the historian and philosopher Ernest Renan, secured Gauguin a posting to Papeete in French Polynesia, where he arrived in June 1891 and immediately set about making useful contacts. He settled in a village in the south, far from the 'despicably Westernised capital', and spent two years there, painting, sculpting and developing new subject matter, gradually integrating into the local culture and 'returning to a state of noble savagery'. Nevertheless, by 1892 he was already considering a return to France, which he did at the end of August 1893. An inheritance from his guardian and mentor enabled him to set himself up in an exotic studio in the Rue Vercingétorix and pose as an eccentric artist, perennially accompanied by his mistress, the striking 'Annah from Java'. A solo exhibition at the Galerie Durand-Ruel, however, was greeted with blank incomprehension. He painted little in Paris, being more preoccupied with monotypes and woodcuts, and with preparing the text and illustrations for *Noa Noa*, which was not published until 1901. He also spent an unproductive time in Brittany, notable only for an altercation in Concarneau with his Javanese companion, which left him nursing wounds that contributed to a steady deterioration in his health. Things were going so badly that he mounted another unsuccessful exhibition in a bid to underwrite his return to Papeete.

In 1895 Gauguin again left for Tahiti. He had next to no money and practically no fixed abode; in addition, he was frequently hospitalised for his 'condition' (syphilis). Nevertheless, he contrived to keep his head above water by working at various jobs, including journalism, writing articles critical of the local administration, which did not endear him to the authorities. In 1897 news reached him that Aline, his favourite daughter, had died. From that point on, Gauguin ceased to correspond with his wife. Arguably, all these elements combined to inspire his major 1897

composition entitled *Where Do We Come From? What Are We? Where Are We Going?*. In January 1898 he attempted suicide. Completely without means, he finally secured a post in the local administration as a surveyor. Then, in September 1901, he again took flight, sailing to Hiva Oa, an island 'untouched by Western civilization' in the outer fringes of the Marquesas Islands. There he built himself a 'pleasure palace', the *Maison de Jouir*, the entrance of which was flanked by low relief effigies of his two principal obsessions - the bishop and the gendarme. There he entertained a succession of *vahinés* (Tahitian Maori for 'wife' or 'woman'), mixed with the local population and defended their perceived interests at the level of the colonial administration, an activity which saw him condemned to a five-month prison sentence he was not destined to serve. He died on 8 May 1903 at Fatu Iva.

Gauguin only exhibited once at the official Paris Salon (subsequently the Salon des Artistes Français), showing a painting entitled *Undergrowth*) in 1876. He exhibited at the Fifth Impressionist Exhibition in 1880, followed by the sixth in 1881, the seventh in 1882 (where he showed twelve paintings and pastels and a sculpture), and the eighth and final Impressionist Exhibition of 1886. He also participated in the 1889 Exposition Universelle, albeit within the framework of an impromptu protest exhibit entitled *Impressionist and Synthetist Group* mounted on the walls of the Café Volpini, just outside the Beaux-Arts, and involving Schuffenecker, Emile Bernard, Anquetin, Daniel de Monfreid and himself. Gauguin was involved in several group exhibitions, including those at the Durand-Ruel and Ambroise Vollard galleries in Paris in 1895 and 1898 respectively. The retrospective of his work held at the Autumn Salon in 1906 was the first of many, including that held in Paris in 1949 to commemorate the centenary of his birth, and those at London's Tate Gallery in 1966 and the Museum of Modern Art, New York, in 1984. Later exhibitions of note include *Gauguin and Van Gogh in Copenhagen in 1893* (1984) at the Ordrupgaardsamlingen in Charlottenlund, Copenhagen, and those at the Galeries Nationales du Grand Palais in Paris (1989), the Musée d'Art Modern et d'Art Contemporain in Liège (1994), the Fondation Pierre Gianadda in Martigny (1998), and *Paul Gauguin. Paradise Lost* (1998) at the Nationalgalerie in Berlin and the Folkwang Museum in Essen. An exhibition in 2002 at the Van Gogh Museum in Amsterdam (*Van Gogh et Gauguin: L'Atelier du Midi*) focused on works created from October to December 1888 during their time together at the Yellow House in Arles. Several exhibitions were held in 2003 in celebration of the centenary of his death, including *Gauguin et l'école de Pont-Aven* (*Gauguin and the Pont-Aven School*) at the Musée du Luxembourg in Paris, the Musée des Beaux-Arts in Quimper and the Museo Capodimonte in Naples; *Gauguin et ses amis* (*Gauguin and his Friends*) at the Maison Marie-Henry in Clohars-Carnoët in Le Pouldu, Finistère (together with the inauguration of a street in their honour called Chemin des Peintres); *Gauguin: Tahiti* at the Galeries Nationales du Grand Palais in Paris; *Sur les traces de Gauguin et de Flora Tristan au Pérou* (*In the Footsteps of Gauguin and Flora Tristan in Peru*) at the *mairie* of the 16th arrondissement in Paris; and a special exhibition at Pont-Aven Museum.

Paul Gauguin's first forays into art were tentative, gradually learning how to paint, sculpt, engrave and, from 1895, how to produce woodcuts. His sculpture was at best sporadic during his period in Brittany but emerged as a essential element of his body of work during his time in Polynesia. He produced only one etching, his *Portrait of Mallarmé*, and very few lithographs, including *Manao Tupapau*, together with some zincographs of Brittany and Martinique. His output of woodcut engravings - a 'crude' medium eminently suited to his quest for the primitive - increased during his times in Brittany and, more especially, in Polynesia. A number of publications by Gauguin or by others were illustrated with his woodcuts, including *Noa Noa* (1901, 1926, 1927); *Marehurehu, entre le jour et la nuit* (*Marehurehu at Dusk*) (Marc Chadourne and Maurice Guierre, 1925); and *Ancien culte mahori* (*Ancient Maori Cult*) (eventually published in 1951). To the extent that painting was Gauguin's predominant medium throughout his life, however, it is appropriate to review his body of work period by period.

The earliest surviving paintings, from about 1875, show the work of a talented and passionate amateur. These were chiefly landscapes in the style of the Barbizon School and Corot, together with some still-lifes painted in sombre and rather thickly applied colours. His evident admiration for the work of the Impressionists in general is corroborated by not only by his decision to start collecting their work but also his commitment to imitating their style. In other words, Gauguin's early period was clearly impressionist in the broad sense of the term. Camille Pissarro introduced him to expressive *plein-air* painting, the application of shaded colour and the overall technique of spontaneity. Gauguin considered himself a pupil of Pissarro to the point where he imitated the latter's orthogonal approach to landscape composition and his use of oblique comma-like brushstrokes. From 1880 to around 1885 Gauguin continued to paint themes favoured by his Impressionist contemporaries, such as landscapes, still-lifes and flowers. He also painted views outside his lodge at Vaugirard and interior scenes featuring his children, in which his use of diagonal composition and rejection of marginal figures betray his increasing interest in the work of Degas. Comparatively early on, however, Gauguin was conscious of his own increasing disenchantment with both the aims espoused by the Impressionists and their execution, as well as what, to him, appeared to be a lack of ambition and audacity. When they met at Pissarro's house in Pontoise in 1881, Cézanne drew Gauguin's attention to the importance of spatial relationships and the need to move from sensation to construction. In his works up to those submitted to the last Impressionist Exhibition in 1886, Gauguin's colours remain muted, not to say strangled, but he was already developing a unique perspective on the symbolic potency of form and colour. Undoubtedly this was partly caused by the personal crisis provoked by the radical change in his and his family's circumstances, as well as by the influence of Charles Baudelaire's benchmark essay on Delacroix, and he was becoming more and more conscious of the need to infuse his work with genuine meaning.

Gauguin's first stay in Pont-Aven represented a sea change, as did his second visit early in 1888, following his voyage to Panama and Martinique. A break with formal Impressionism was imminent although, in terms of technique, the change was gradual rather than abrupt. He continued to paint using the short brushstrokes of the Impressionists, but increasingly deployed the angled comma-like touches favoured by Pissarro or the flatter strokes of Cézanne; what is more, he began to paint with more clearly delineated swathes of colour and more pronounced contours. The influence of Degas and Japanese art is revealed in flat, two-dimensional figures that are set into his shallow landscapes composed of points of colour applied on the diagonal, with scarcely a vestige of sky. Little of consequence came from Gauguin's first meeting with Emile Bernard, but when they met again in 1888 he profited not only from their long theoretical discussions but also from a practical demonstration of Bernard's approach as the latter painted his *Breton Women in the Meadow* directly for Gauguin's benefit. Nor should it be forgotten that Gauguin was then close to the Breton impressionist Ernest de Chamillard, an artist who introduced him to indigenous Breton folklore and culture and together with whom Gauguin started producing wood-carvings. Certain paintings from the Pont-Aven years, among them *Vision after the Sermon: Jacob Wrestling with the Angel* (1888) or the *Yellow Christ* (1889), clearly demonstrate Gauguin's determination to restore to painting a sense of meaning. To do so, he chose not to rely on conventional illustrative techniques or academic allegory. Instead he elected to convey meaning via the sum of the elements that go into a painting, not merely by reference to narrative content *per se* but also by reference to the formal elements and colours that comprise the painting as a whole and impart a holistic meaning to it. Gauguin expressed himself unequivocally on this point when he spoke of 'clothing the idea in forms and colours' and praising the 'beautiful thoughts that can be evoked by form and colour'. In praising 'synthetism' of form and colour, however, Gauguin was not restating the Impressionist credo. Far from it: the limited synthetism of Emile Bernard's *Breton Women in the Meadow* contrives a simplification of line and a partitioning of colour ('cloisonnism'), whereas Gauguin's synthetism is one of explicit form and implicit meaning, as he explained by reference to his *Vision after the Sermon*, when he expressed the belief that his figures had successfully combined to express both 'great rustic and superstitious simplicity' or, as the critic Octave Mirabeau observed, 'heightened conceptual complexity through radical formal simplification'.

Gauguin's work from the Pont-Aven period resulted in his emergence and recognition as a prime exponent of Symbolism in painting. By this time, and not without certain misgivings, Gauguin had come to the point of endorsing the hallucinatory world of Van Gogh in preference to the hedonistic naturalism of the Impressionists. At Van Gogh's urging, Gauguin spent the final two months or so of 1888 in Arles, where tensions and tempers ran high. While his short stay there can scarcely be deemed sufficient to qualify it as an 'Arles' period, he produced some significant paintings during those turbulent weeks, including those of the hospice gardens, Alyscamps, vineyards and, by no means least, his *Portrait of Van Gogh Painting Sunflowers*.

After returning to Paris in some haste, Gauguin again travelled to Brittany, spending 1889 and 1890 in Pont-Aven and, later, in Le Pouldu. His work from this period shows no major departure from his earlier efforts in Brittany and does not merit the designation 'Second Breton Period'. It is, however, distinguished by its thematic content, typically by the introduction of quasi-biblical elements into everyday Breton life, where Gauguin even identifies with Christ's betrayal (*Agony in the Garden*) by imposing his own features on those of his subject. In *Self-portrait as the Yellow Christ*, Gauguin portrays himself between one of his own grotesque ceramic pots and the 'yellow' Christ, highlighting the conceptual contrast between his own primitive side and the spiritual transcendence of Christ. This introspection also extends to his rendering of the arduous life of Breton peasants: 'I am looking to invest these desolate figures with the savage beast that I see there and in myself'.

In effect, Gauguin's 'Breton' period as a whole revolves around attempts to give expression to this dichotomy between unfettered paganism and quasi-mystical aspiration. Mirabeau, writing in 1891, described this as a 'disturbing yet tantalising blend of barbaric splendour, Catholic liturgy, Hindu reflection, Gothic imagery and subtle and obscure symbolism'. Also in 1891, the poet Albert Aurier, the spokesman-apologist of the Symbolist movement, went on to derive from Gauguin's Breton paintings the five core attributes to which a work should ideally conform: 'idea, symbol, synthesis, subjectivity and decoration'.

Gauguin's later ('Tahiti') period, which may be considered as extending from his first stay in Tahiti until his death, comprises Tahitian themes and images compounded by his musings on desire, death and syncretist spiritual aspiration. As such it represents a radical extension and affirmation of synthetist principles. His first visit to Tahiti saw him produce drawings, painting and sculpture with extremely clear ('synthetised') lines that trace the particular morphology of Tahitian women: their ponderous yet somehow majestic figures, their matt skin tones, their frank yet strangely mongoloid features, each with an enigmatic expression of apparent indifference to the outside world, each with a faraway look, a latent sensuality, an aura of mystery, which he described in a letter to his wife, 'Now that I have come to know this place, its people, its landscapes and smells, I find my most enigmatic Tahitians are Maoris rather than orientals from Batignolles...' He portrays a land many thousands of kilometres distant, far removed from familiar customs and surroundings, where each painting resolves (much as in a painting by Gustav Klimt) into a swirl of curved lines, arabesques and blocks of colour that convey a myriad of sensory expressions representing both symbol and synthesis. Moreover, he was able to express this congruity not only on canvas but also in words: 'Overall harmony, sombre, sad, frightening, resonating on the eye like a death knell. Violet, dark blue and orange-tinged yellow. I paint the yellow cloth with a greenish hue, first because the cloth is of beaten bark and unlike ours, second because it suggests the cast of light (the women here never sleep in the dark yet I do not seek the effect of artificial lamplight), and third, because the relationships between this yellow and the orange-yellow and blue complete the full musical chord...'.

After the trials and tribulations of Paris, and despite his deteriorating health, Gauguin's years on Tahiti and in the Marquesas were highly productive: when physical pain precluded painting, he would write at length, exploring themes such as local customs and religion, ethical values, art and his own inner self. The many sketches and studies he had collected during his first stay in Tahiti were sufficiently detailed and comprehensive to enable them to be built into more complex and ambitious compositions, mostly group paintings on a large scale, featuring typical landscapes and interiors and reflecting aspects of Maori culture and beliefs often epitomised in the wood-carvings that appear in some of his work. In 1900 Gauguin had committed to supplying Vollard with a specified number of paintings each year; accordingly (yet without prejudice to his major canvases), he repainted some of his earlier still-lifes and flower canvases. His final paintings evidence a cleaner, more classical composition and carry echoes of earlier models, notably Poussin or Puvis de Chavannes. These paintings, among them perhaps his most extraordinary and celebrated work, *Where Do We Come From? What Are We? Where Are We Going?*, are to a large extent motivated by his preoccupation with philosophical issues. It was no doubt for this reason that Gauguin discarded the beautifully sonorous Maori titles in favour of French-language texts - almost as if expressing his disenchantment with the charm of exotic climes and his nostalgia for his native culture.

In 1902, when on the point of death, Gauguin's dream was to return to Europe. Daniel de Montfreid, a loyal friend to the end, made every effort to dissuade him, however cruel that might at first appear, arguing that his physical return to France would tarnish the aura and dilute his reputation: 'You are a living legend - a great and definitive artist lost to the world, living far away in remotest Oceania, an artist who sends these magnificent and disconcerting paintings back to the world at large.' Even for de Monfreid, who knew and admired his work, Gauguin was a hostage to the myth that had been created around him.

Gauguin was not the first painter - and certainly far from the only one - to use lines, forms and colours to attempt a coherent and congruous narrative of the human condition but, in his day, he was the one who did so in the most consistent and practical way. His body of work marks him as a successor to Puvis de Chavannes as a modern symbolist and exponent of synthetism: he points the way forward to the major innovative movements of the late 19th century and the early 20th - the graceful arabesques of the Nabis, the dynamic Fauves, the primeval savagery of line, form and colour of Die Brücke and the Expressionists, and the clinically analytical approach of the Cubists.

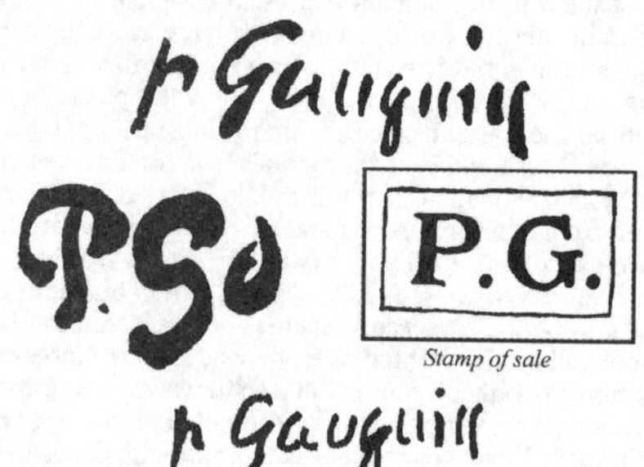

Stamp of sale

BIBLIOGRAPHY:
Gauguin, Paul/Morice, Charles, *Noa Noa*, Paris, 1901. Guérin, Marcel, *L'Œuvre gravé de Paul Gauguin*, H. Floury, Paris, 1927. Alexandre, Arsène, *Paul Gauguin, sa vie et le sens de son œuvre*, Bernheim, Paris, 1930. Chassé, Charles, *Gauguin et son temps*, La Bibliothèque des Arts, Paris, 1955. *Gauguin, sa vie, son œuvre*, Wildenstein, Paris, 1958. Gray, Christopher, *Sculpture and Ceramics of Paul Gauguin*, Johns Hopkins Press, Baltimore, 1963. Bodelsen, Merete, *Gauguin's Ceramics: a Study in the Development of his Art*, Faber and Faber, London, 1964. Wildenstein, Georges, *Gauguin*, Les Beaux-Arts, Paris, 1964. Chassé, Charles, *Gauguin sans légende*, Éd. du temps, Paris, 1965. *Gauguin and the Pont-Aven Group*, exhibition catalogue, Tate Gall., London, Arts Council, London, 1966. Russell, John, *Gauguin*, UNESCO, Bibliothèque d'Art, Paris, 1968. Cachin, Françoise, *Gauguin*, Livre de poche illustré, Paris, 1969. Roskill, Mark, *Van Gogh, Gauguin and the Impressionist Circle*, Thames and Hudson, London, 1970. Gauguin, Paul, *Oviri, écrits d'un sauvage*, Gallimard, Paris, 1974. Danielsson, Bengt, *Gauguin à Tahiti et aux îles Marquises*, Éd. du Pacifique, Papeete (Tahiti), 1975. Leprohon, Pierre, *Paul Gauguin*, Diffusion Gründ, Paris, 1975. Cucchi, Roger (ed.), *Gauguin à la Martinique*, Calivran Anstalt, Vaduz, 197[illegible] (an imaginary museum including his paintings, drawings, sculptures, ceramics, forgeries, his letters and exhibition catalogues). Fezzi, Elda (ed.), *Gauguin, the Complete Paintings*, Granada, London, 1980. Merlhès, Victor (ed.), *Correspondance de Paul Gauguin*, Fondation Singer-Polignac, Paris, 1984. Boyle-Turner, Caroline, *Gauguin and the School of Pont-Aven: Prints and Paintings*, Royal Academy, London, Thames and Hudson, London, 1986. Moffett, C.S., *The New Painting, Impressionism, 1874-1886*, exhibition catalogue, Fine Arts Museums of San Francisco, San Francisco; National Gall. of Art, Washington, DC; R. Burton, Seattle, 1986. Brettell, Richard, et al., *The Art of Paul Gauguin*, National Gall. of Art, Washington, DC, 1988. Cachin, Françoise, *Gauguin, Ce malgré moi de sauvage*', Gallimard, Paris, 1989. *Gauguin*, exhibition catalogue, Gal. Nationales du Grand Palais, Paris, 1989. *Gauguin: actes du Colloque Gauguin, Musée d'Orsay et École du Louvre, Paris, 11-13 janvier 1989*, La Documentation française, Paris, 1991. Monod, Luc, *Manuel de l'amateur de livres illustrés modernes 1875-1975*, Ides et Calendes, Neuchâtel, 1992. Monfreid, Georges Daniel de, *Gauguin's Letters from the South Seas*, Constable, London, 1992. Cusinberche, Jean-Marie, *Gauguin e i suoi amici pittori in Bretagna: Pont-Aven et Le Pouldu*, exhibition catalogue, Museo Archeologico Regionale, Aosta; Fabbri ed., Milan, 1993 (text in Italian, English, French). Sweetman, David Paul, *Gauguin, a Complete Life*, Hodder & Stoughton, London, 1995. Busse, Jacques, *L'Impressionnisme: une dialectique du regard*, Ides et Calendes, Neuchâtel, 1996. Pickvance, Ronald, *Gauguin and the School of Pont-Aven*, exhibition catalogue, Museum Würth, Sigmaringen, 1997. Prouté, Paul, *Gauguin: dessins, estampes*, exhibition catalogue, Gal. Paul Prouté, Paris, 1998. Pickvance, Ronald, *Paul Gauguin*, exhibition catalogue, Fondation Pierre Gianadda, Martigny, 1998 (texts in French and English). Wildenstein, Daniel, *Paul Gauguin: Premier itinéraire d'un sauvage (1873-1888)*, catalogue raisonné, Skira, Éd. du Seuil, Paris, 2001. Druick, Douglas W./Zegers, Peter Kort, *Van Gogh et Gauguin: l'atelier du Midi*, exhibition catalogue, Van Gogh Museum, Amsterdam; Gallimard, Paris, 2002. Leduc, Alain, *Les Céramiques de Gauguin*, catalogue raisonné, Éd. de l'Amateur, Paris, 2002. Madeline, Laurence, *Gauguin sculpteur*, Adam Biro, Paris, 2002. Rookmaaker, Hendrik Roelof, *Art, Artists and Gauguin*, Piquant, Carlisle, 2002. Wildenstein, Daniel, *Gauguin, a Savage in the Making: Catalogue Raisonné of the Paintings (1873-1888)*, Wildenstein Institute, Skira Editore, 2002. Saquet, Jean-Louis, *Koké*, Le Motu, Maharepa-Moorea, 2003. Gauguin, Paul, *Racontars de rapin*, Mercure de France, Paris, 2003 (reprinted). Brettell, Richard R./Fonsmark, Anne-Birgitte, *Gauguin and Impressionism*, exhibition catalogue, Ortdrupgaard, Copenhague, Yale University Press, New Haven, 2005.

MUSEUMS AND GALLERIES:
AMSTERDAM (Van Gogh Mus.): *Van Gogh Painting Sunflowers* (1888) - BALTIMORE (MA): *Woman with Mango* (1892) - BASEL (Kunstmus.): *Breton Landscape; Self-portrait; Tahitian Woman* (pastel); *Ta Matete* (1892); *Nafea Faa Ipoipo* (*When Shall We Be Married?*) (1892) - BOSTON (MFA): *Women and a White Horse; Love and Be Happy* (1890, polychrome wood low relief); *Where Do We Come From? What Are We? Where Are We Going?* (1897) - BROOKLYN, NY: *Tahitian Woman* - BRUSSELS (Mus. royaux): *Calvary; Miss Brambridge* - BUDAPEST (Szépmuvészeti Múz.): *Black Pigs* (1891) - BUENOS AIRES (Mus. Nacional de Bellas Artes): *Vahine no te miti* (*The Spectre Watches over her*) (1892) - BUFFALO (Albright-Knox AG): *Yellow Christ* (1889);

Manao Tupapau (Spirits of the Dead Watch Over You) (1892) - CAMBRIDGE (Fitzwilliam Mus.): *Landscape* (1873, oil on canvas) - CHICAGO (AI): *Women of Arles* (1888); *Tahitian Woman; Tahitian Child; Tahitian Drinking; Portrait of Marie Lagadu* (1890); *Aerahi metua no tehamana (Ancestors of Tehamana)* (1893, oil on canvas); *Mistral* - CINCINNATI (AM): *Mahana Ma'a (Mahana Ma'a)* (painting); *Buddha* (woodcut) - CLEVELAND (MA): *Call* (1902) - COPENHAGEN (Kunstindustrimus.): *Vase Decorated with a Female Dancer* (1886-87, ceramic); *Pot in the Form of a Head* (1889, flame-decorated earthenware) - COPENHAGEN (Ny Carlsberg Glyptotek): *Woman Singing* (1880, polychrome medallion, sculpted in wood); *Garden in the Snow* (1883); *Study for a Nude (Suzanne Sewing)* (1880) - DALLAS (MA): *Portrait of a Man* (c. 1880, oil on canvas); *I Raro Te Oviri (Under the Pandanus)* (1891, oil on canvas); *Bretonne à la barrière (Breton Woman Standing by a Gate)* (1889, lithograph); *Portrait Vase of Madame Schuffenecker* (1889, earthenware) - EDINBURGH (Nat. Gal. of Scotland): *The Vision after the Sermon (Jacob wrestling with the Angel)* (1888, oil on canvas) - ESSEN (Folkwang Mus.): *Barbarian Tales* (1902) - FORT WORTH (Kimbell AM): *Self-portrait* (1885, oil on canvas) - GIFU (MFA): *Tahitian Landscape* (c. 1894, monotype) - GRENOBLE (Mus. de Grenoble): *Portrait of Madeleine Bernard* - HARTFORD (Wadsworth Atheneum): *Nirvana: Portrait of Meyer de Haan* (gouache/cotton); a drawing, several prints - HELSINKI (Ateneumin Taidemus.): *Mahana Maa* (1892) - KANSAS CITY (Nelson-Atkins MA): *Faaturuma (Melancholic)* (1891, oil on canvas) - LIÈGE: *Tahiti* - LONDON (British Mus.): *Two Men from the Marquesas* (c. 1902, monotype) - LONDON (Courtauld Institute of Art): *Haymaking* (1889, oil on canvas); *Te Rerioa* (1897, oil on canvas); *Nevermore* (1897, oil on canvas); engravings and drawings - LONDON (Tate Collection): *Faa Iheihe (Tahitian Pastoral)* (1898, oil on canvas); *Harvest: Le Pouldu* (1890, oil on canvas); two studies on paper - LYONS (MBA): *Nave Nave Mahana (Holiday)* - MERION (Barnes Foundation): *Loulou (Loulou)* (1890, oil on canvas) - MINNEAPOLIS (IA): *I Raro te oviri (Under the Pandanus)* (1891, oil on canvas) - MOSCOW (Pushkin MFA): *Still-life with Fruit* (1888); *Matamoe (Peacock Country)*; *Landscape* (1889); *What! Are You Jealous?* (1892); *Te arii vahine (The King's Wife)* (1896); *The Ford* (1901); *Great Buddha* - NEW YORK (Metropolitan Mus. of Art): *Ia orana Maria (Hail Mary)* (1891-92); *Breasts with Red Flowers* - NEW YORK (MoMA): *Moon and Earth* - NORFOLK (Chrysler MA): *Loss of Virginity* (1890-91) - OSLO: *Portrait of a Lady; Still-life with Exotic Fruits* - OTTERLO (Kröller-Müller Mus.): *Portrait of Young Prince Afiti* - PARIS (Mus. d'Orsay): *River Seine at the Pont d'Iéna; Alyscamps* (1888); *La Belle Angèle* (1889); *Self-portrait* (1889, earthenware sculpture); *Self-portrait as the Yellow Christ* (1889-91); *Women of Tahiti* (1891); *Mask of Tehura* (1891-93, polychrome wood sculpture); *Pearl Idol* (1891-93, polychrome wood sculpture); *Shell Idol* (1893, sculpture); *Oviri (Savage)* (1894, enamelled earthenware sculpture); *Gate of the Maison du Jouir: Love and Be Mysterious* (1890, collection of sculpted polychrome wood panels); *White Horse* (1898, oil on canvas); *And the Gold of their Bodies* (1901); *Madame Death* (drawing) - PARIS (Mus. de l'Orangerie): *Landscape* (1901) - PARIS (Mus. du Petit Palais): *Man with Cane* - PONT-AVEN (Mus. de Pont-Aven): *Two Heads of Bretons Women* (1894, pastel) - PRAGUE (Národní Gal.): *Bonjour Monsieur Gauguin!* (1889); *Flight* (1902) - QUIMPER (MBA): *Goose* - RENNES (MBA): *Still-life* - RHEIMS (MBA): *Still-life* - ROTTERDAM (Mus. Boijmans Van Beuningen): *Landscape* (1885) - ST PETERSBURG (Hermitage): *Te Avae No Marie (Month of Mary)* (1899, oil on canvas); *Parau Parau* (1891); *Tahitian Countryside* (1892); *Idol* (1898); *Sunflowers* (1901) - TOLEDO: *Tahiti Street Scene* - TORONTO (AG of Ontario): *Hina Tefatou* (1892-93, wooden sculpture) - WASHINGTON DC (NGA): *Breton Girls Dancing, Pont-Aven* (1888, oil on canvas); *Self-portrait* (1889, oil/wood); others paintings, sculptures, numerous drawings and engravings - WEST PALM BEACH (Norton MA): *Agony in the Garden (Christ in the Garden of Olives)* (1889, oil on canvas) - WORCESTER, MA (AM): *Portrait of Mademoiselle Manthey* (1884, pastel on paper); *Te Faaturuma (Brooding Woman)* (1891, oil on canvas).

AUCTION RECORDS:

PARIS, 1895, *Te fare Maorie* (*Maori House*, FRF 420; *Vahine no te vi* (*Woman with a Mango*, FRF 450; *Manaotupapau* (*Guardian Spirit*, FRF 900; *Matamua* (*Once Upon a Time*, FRF 500; *Arearea* (*Joy*, FRF 420; *I raro te Oviri* (*Under the Pandanus*, FRF 380; *Nave nave demua* (*Delightful Land*, FRF 500; *Vahine no te miti* (*Women of the Sea*, FRF 400; *Noa Noa* (*Fragrance*, FRF 360; *Faturuma* (*Sullen Woman*, FRF 400; *Salt Marshes*, FRF 460; *Te Fare* (*The House*, FRF 180; *Bonjour Monsieur Gauguin!*, FRF 410; *Landscape*, FRF 120; *Les Batteuses* (*Women Threshing*, FRF 100; *Copy of Olympia*, FRF 230; *Eve* (drawing) FRF 60; *Woman Bathing* (drawing) FRF 28; *Women in the Fields* (two drawings) FRF 32; *Female Magician* (pastel) FRF 80; *Fishing* (drawing) FRF 16; *Virgin and Child* (drawing) FRF 25. PARIS, 10 April 1897, *Tahiti*, FRF 160; *Bonsoir, Gauguin!*, FRF 152; *Donkey Resting*, FRF 80. PARIS, Dec 1898, *Path in the Woods*, FRF 170. PARIS, 2 Dec 1899, *Calvary*, FRF 100. PARIS, 10 June 1900, *Cattle by a River*, FRF 580; *Boats*, FRF 480. PARIS, 30 June 1900, *Landscape*, FRF 180. PARIS, 24 Feb 1919, *Girl with Dog* (charcoal) FRF 280. PARIS, 27 Feb 1919, *Aubé, the Sculptor, with his Son* (pastel, diptych) FRF 3,100. PARIS, 13-14 March 1919, *Ia orana Maria* (*Hail Mary*, FRF 58,000. PARIS, 28 March 1919, *Woman with Mangoes* (heightened drawing) FRF 1,550. PARIS, 8-9 April 1919, *Sunflowers (Helianthus)*, FRF 3,400. PARIS, 22 May 1919, *Window Box with Flowers*, FRF 850. PARIS, 21 June 1919, *Mandolin*, FRF 340. PARIS, 1-3 Dec 1919, *The Willow*, FRF 7,200. PARIS, 16-17 Dec 1919, *Pink House near a Paddock*, FRF 1,050. PARIS, 2-4 June 1920, *Seated Female Nude* (pastel) FRF 2,750. PARIS, 19 June 1920, *Portrait of the Painter Stewinski*, FRF 2,900; *Two Small Peasant Girls* (pastel) FRF 1,305. PARIS, 21 June 1920, *Two Breton Women* (watercolour) FRF 430. PARIS, 16 March 1921, *Women Gathering Flowers*, FRF 11,650. PARIS, 20 Nov 1922, *Road Winding by the Woods*, FRF 2,100. PARIS, 24 Nov 1922, *Sketch and Note Book*, FRF 1,000. PARIS, 20 March 1923, *Washerwomen at Pont-Aven*, FRF 4,300; *Souvenir of Tahiti*, FRF 4,300; *Two Heads*, FRF 1,250; *Breton Man*, FRF 1,000. PARIS, 14 April 1923, *Portrait of the Painter Roy* (charcoal) FRF 55; *Still-life*, FRF 6,600; *Still-life*, FRF 14,000; *Shepherdess*, FRF 2,250; *Head of Young Oriental*, FRF 1,050; *Houses in the Snow*, FRF 1,300; *Still-life with Peaches*, FRF 2,600. PARIS, 5 June 1923, *Cow Drinking at Dusk*, FRF 1,880; *Garden Scene at Dusk*, FRF 900. LONDON, 6 Feb 1924, *Portrait of the Artist*, GBP 95. PARIS, 7 April 1924, *Cattle at Pasture*, FRF 15,300. PARIS, 23 April 1925, *Tahitian Man* (pastel) FRF 2,100. PARIS, 23 June 1925, *Village in Martinique*, FRF 15,500. PARIS, 2 June 1926, *Tahiti* (five watercolour sketches) FRF 5,000; *Portrait of Madame Kohler*, FRF 15,000; *Farmyard*, FRF 15,200; *Houses in Vaugirard*, FRF 26,000. PARIS, 20 Oct 1926, *Pont Saveur, Martinique*, FRF 5,100. PARIS, 20-21 Dec 1926, *Snow Scene*, FRF 6,600. PARIS, 14 Feb 1927, *Cellist (portrait of Monsieur Sch.)*, FRF 60,200. PARIS, 30-31 May 1927, *Breton Landscape with Willow Tree by a River*, FRF 25,100; *Hilly Landscape in Brittany*, FRF 6,100. PARIS, 29 Oct 1927, *Tahitian Man* (pastel) FRF 5,100. PARIS, 12 Dec 1927, *Undine*, FRF 14,100. PARIS, 15 Dec 1927, *Tahitian Woman with Both Hands Clasped to her Head*, FRF 3,200. PARIS, 29 Dec 1927, *Landscape near Arles*, FRF 2,400. PARIS, 27 Feb 1928, *Cattle at the Trough*, FRF 1,900. PARIS, 24-29 Feb 1928, *Portrait of Moréas* (highlighted charcoal) FRF 2,500; *Madame Death* (charcoal) FRF 690. PARIS, 23 June 1928, *Breton Village*, FRF 62,000. LONDON, 8 Feb 1929, *Young Girl with Cherries*, GBP 14. LONDON, 9 May 1929, *Woodland in Tahiti* (watercolour) GBP 17; *Two Tahitian Women*, GBP 6. NEW YORK, 27-28 March 1930, *River in Brittany*, USD 2,000. PARIS, 12 April 1930, *Martiniquaise Crouching on the Grass*, FRF 14,500. PARIS, 21 May 1930, *Women of Tahiti* (lead pencil) FRF

4,100; *Fruit Harvest in Tahiti* (red chalk) FRF 1,420. PARIS, 14 June 1930, *Tahitian Doing her Hair*, FRF 5,000. PARIS, 22 Nov 1930, *Still-life with Oranges*, FRF 14,000. PARIS, 11 March 1931, *Goose Warden* (fan in gouache) FRF 5,300. PARIS, 21 May 1931, *Breton Dance*, FRF 10,000; *Breton Woman at the Foot of a Cliff*, FRF 3,600; *Tahitian Men and a Woman* (watercolour and lead pencil, sketchbook) FRF 4,500; *Fisherman's Wife on the Beach* (pen) FRF 480; *Male Portrait* (pen) FRF 400. PARIS, 27 June 1931, *Tahitian Study* (drawing) FRF 370; *Album page from Tahiti* (drawing) FRF 800. PARIS, 4 March 1932, *Landscape at Radepont* (gouache) FRF 1,450. LONDON, 18 March 1932, *Breton Landscape*, GBP 220. PARIS, 15 Dec 1932, *Figures in Tahiti*, FRF 50,100. PARIS, 5 May 1933, *Drinking Trough*, FRF 7,300. PARIS, 24 May 1933, *Antilles Landscape with Martiniquaises* (watercolour); *Apse of a Gothic Church* (drawing) FRF 520. PARIS, 1 June 1933, *Fruit-Picking in Tahiti* (red chalk) FRF 460. PARIS, 21 March 1934, *Water Mill in Brittany* (watercolour) FRF 380. PARIS, 26 June 1934, *Tahiti*, FRF 95,500. NEW YORK, 14 Nov 1934, *Flowers*, USD 170; *Frederiksberg Gardens*, USD 120. PARIS, 20 June 1935, *Flowers and Fruit* (watercolour on silk) FRF 610. PARIS, 24 Feb 1936, *Blast Furnaces at Night* (pastel) FRF 870. PARIS, 5 June 1936, *Grazing Land in Martinique; View of Martinique* (gouaches, fan-shaped pair) FRF 16,000. LONDON, 10 June 1936, *Portrait of a Child* (pastel) GBP 15. LONDON, 9 July 1936, *Blue Boat*, GBP 42. PARIS, 28 April 1937, *Study of Cattle and a Chicken* (black chalk) FRF 45. NEW YORK, 29 April 1937, *Tahiti*, USD 1,700. PARIS, 5 May 1937, *Landscape by the Sea*, FRF 4,600. LONDON, 13 Dec 1937, *Baby (study)*, GBP 5. PARIS, 31 Jan 1938, *Tahiti* (drawing) FRF 430. PARIS, 23 March 1938, *Landscape by the Sea*, FRF 4,200. PARIS, 6 March 1940, *Page from a Sketchbook* (recto-verso) FRF 350. LONDON, 12 June 1940, *Still-life*, GBP 170. PARIS, 8 Nov 1940, *Tahitian Women by the Sea* (watercolour) FRF 5,000; *Exotic Landscape* (watercolour) FRF 3,000. PARIS, 20 June 1941, *Figure and Profile Studies* (drawing) FRF 260; *Young Bretons* (pastel) FRF 300; *Study (page)* (pastel) FRF 3,000; *Breton Woman* (watercolour) FRF 8,000; *Creole Hut* (watercolour) FRF 2,000; *Among the Maoris* (watercolour) FRF 2,000; *Young Creole* (1891) FRF 31,000. PARIS, 24 Nov 1941, *Brittany*, FRF 14,100; *Gathering Wrack*, FRF 60,000. NEW YORK, 8-9 Jan 1942, *Tahitian Woman*. PARIS, 19 March 1942, *Tahitian Woman Reclining Nude* (pencil and pastel) FRF 9,000. PARIS, 1-2 June 1942, *Mysterious Water* (polychrome carved wood) FRF 99,000; *Tahitian Men and Women*, FRF 20,000. PARIS, 20 Nov 1942, *Cattle (study)* (pencil, double-sided) FRF 2,000. PARIS, 30 Nov 1942, *Diverse Studies* (drawing) FRF 1,800. PARIS, 11 Dec 1942, *Two Figures on a Cliff in Brittany*, FRF 1,100,000. PARIS, 24 Dec 1942, *Landscape* (pencil, monotype transfer printed on the back) FRF 830; *Head of Young Girl; Hand Study (verso)* (pencil, sketch) FRF 1,000; *Seated Woman* (graphite) FRF 2,000; *Ducks; Pigs (study; verso)* (graphite) FRF 550; *Head of Dog* (graphite) FRF 300; *Pig* (graphite) FRF 380. PARIS, 12 March 1943, *Seated Breton Woman* (monotype) FRF 51,500. PARIS, 12 April 1943, *Landscape* (1884) FRF 166,000. PARIS, 21 May 1943, *Flowers* (1881) FRF 122,000. PARIS, 2 June 1943, *Portfolio pages (recto/verso)* (graphite) FRF 2,600. PARIS, 22 Oct 1943, *Wash House at Plormagel* (watercolour) FRF 27,000. LONDON, 10 Dec 1943, *Portrait of Jean Gauguin* (pastel) GBP 126. PARIS, 10 Dec 1943, *Maori Landscape* (woodcut) FRF 2,400; *Young Tahitian Woman*, FRF 215,000. PARIS, 3 Feb 1944, *Cattle Lying under a Tree*, FRF 100,000. NEW YORK, 2 March 1944, *Incantation*, USD 9,100. PARIS, 10 March 1944, *Breton Man and Woman in an Orchard*, FRF 105,000. NEW YORK, 20 April 1944, *Tahiti*, USD 3,800. NEW YORK, 4 May 1944, *Landscape*, USD 1,700. PARIS, 8 May 1944, *Party Wall* (1881) FRF 290,000. PARIS, 10 May 1944, *Geese* (graphite, sketch) FRF 600. PARIS, 14 June 1944, *Portrait of a Pont-Aven Woman (Marie Louarn?)*, FRF 12,000. NEW YORK, 17-18 Jan 1945, *French Mas (Farmhouse)* (drawing) USD 5, 000. NEW YORK, 12 April 1945, *Venus*, USD 700; *Village in the Snow*, USD 4,500. COPENHAGEN, 1 March 1956, *Wood[e] Landscape*, DKK 8,600. PARIS, 14 June 1957, *Still-life with Ap[ples]* (1901) FRF 120,000,000. PARIS, 14 June 1957, *Landscap[e] with Pink Blossoms, Pont-Aven*, FRF 14,000,000; *Still-life wi[th] Apples* (1901) FRF 104,000,000. NEW YORK, 7 Nov 1957, *Ma Taporo (Gathering Limes*, USD 180,000. NEW YORK, 15 Ja[n] 1958, *Fishermen's Wives and Young Girls beside a Lake* (char[]coal and watercolour) USD 1,200. NEW YORK, 19 March 195[] *Basket of Flowers*, USD 54,000. PARIS, 15 Dec 1958, *Sma[ll] Stream in Brittany* (1883) FRF 6,500,000. PARIS, 16 March 195[] *Place Mat Decoration* (watercolour) FRF 1,700,000; *Chapel o[f] St Mandé in Le Pouldu* (watercolour) FRF 3,600,000; *Mimi an[d] her Cat* (watercolour) FRF 3,011,000. PARIS, 16 March 195[] *Chapel of St Mandé in Le Pouldu* (1890, gouache on card) FR[F] 3,600,000. NEW YORK, 15 April 1959, *River Seine, Paris*, US[D] 9,000. PARIS, 16 June 1959, *Houses at Vaugirard* (1880) FR[F] 16,200,000. LONDON, 25 Nov 1959, *Te Tiai Na Ve Ite Rata* [] *Await the Letter*, GBP 130,000. NEW YORK, 9 Dec 1959, *Head o[f] Tahitian Woman* (charcoal) USD 11,000. NEW YORK, 16 Marc[h] 1960, *Young Breton Woman*, USD 22,000. PARIS, 21 June 196[0] *Landscape in Brittany* (gouache on silk) FRF 20,000. LONDON, [] July 1960, *Breton Coast*, GBP 9,000. LONDON, 23 Nov 196[0] *Women Sitting in the Shade under the Palm Trees*, GBP 38,00[0] HAMBURG, 26 Nov 1960, *View of Martinique Harbour*, DEM 9[0] 000. PARIS, 21 June 1961, *Exotic Eve* (oil on card) FRF 140,00[0] LONDON, 28 June 1961, *Still-life with Apples and Grapes*, GB[P] 45,000. LONDON, 29 June 1962, *Breton Childhood* (waterco[]lour) FRF 88,000. NEW YORK, 31 Oct 1962, *Landscape nea[r] Rouen*, USD 47,500. LONDON, 11 June 1963, *Dance of Thre[e] Breton Women*, GBP 75,000. LONDON, 19 June 1964, *Oviri (Th[e] Savage)* (bronze, low relief) Gns 7,500. LONDON, 24 Nov 1964 *Tahitian Woman and a Boy*, GBP 90,000. NEW YORK, 14 Oc[t] 1965, *Hina Maruru (Festival of the Moon*, USD 275,000. NEW YORK, 8 Dec 1965, *Head of Tahitian Woman* (gilt bronze) USD 9,500. LONDON, 29 Nov 1967, *Aline and Pola* (pastel) GBP 25,000. GENEVA, 6 Nov 1969, *Bonjour Monsieur Gauguin!*, CHF 1,350,000. NEW YORK, 5 May 1971, *Self-portrait with Palette*, USD 420,000. GENEVA, 2 July 1971, *Lust* (bronze) CHF 34,000. LONDON, 28 June 1972, *Head of Tahitian Woman* (pastel) GBP 23,000. PARIS, 19 March 1973, *Near Rouen*, FRF 500,000. LONDON, 29 March 1973, *Study of the Painter Roy* (1889) Gns 48,000. GENEVA, 29 June 1973, *Place d'Elseneur*, CHF 202,000. LONDON, 2 April 1974, *Young Nude Girl Sitting on the Edge of a Bed* (pastel) GBP 55,000. LONDON, 4 April 1974, *Breton Vase* (1886, coloured earthenware) GBP 5,500 PARIS, 13 June 1974, *Exotic Fruits and Peppers on a Platter*, FRF 1,250,000. LONDON, 5 Dec 1974, *Oviri* (bronze) GBP 11,000. NEW YORK, 17 March 1976, *Still-life with Japanese Print* (1889, oil on canvas, 28 1/2 x 37in/72.4 x 93.7cm) USD 1,400,000. BERN, 9 June 1976, *Te Ateu (The Gods)* (woodcut) CHF 60,000. LONDON, 29 June 1976, *Oviri* (lost-wax bronze, h. 29 1/4in/74cm) FRF 25,000. LONDON, 30 Nov 1976, *Landscape* (1880, watercolour and gouache, 9 x 13 3/4in/23 x 35cm) GBP 4,800. BREST, 15 May 1977, *Hina and Fatou* (bronze, h. 12 1/2in/32cm) FRF 24,000. BERN, 8 June 1977, *Te Atua (The Gods)* (1893-94, coloured woodcut) CHF 27,000. LONDON, 27 June 1977, *Garden in Winter, Rue Carcel* (1883, oil on canvas, 46 x 35 1/2in/117 x 90cm) GBP 98,000. NEW YORK, 20 Oct 1977, *Head of Tahitian Woman* (c. 1895-1903, watercolour, 12 1/4 x 7 1/2in/31 x 18.8cm) USD 6,250. NEW YORK, 17 May 1978, *Sunny Landscape near Pontoise* (1879, oil on panel, 6 x 9 3/4in/15.2 x 25cm) USD 27,500. BERN, 7 June 1978, *Te Faruru (Here We Make Love)* (1893-94, woodcut in three colours) CHF 25,000. PARIS, 8 Dec 1978, *Eve* (bronze, h. 23 1/4in/59cm) FRF 27,000. NEW YORK, 9 June 1979, *Male Head in Profile; Head of Mimi* (c. 1888-89, Indian ink wash and lead pencil, 6 1/2 x 7 3/4in/16.2 x 19.8cm) USD 7,500. LONDON, 26 Nov 1979, *Manao Tupapau* (1894, coloured woodcut on Japanese paper, 15 x 9in/37.8 x 22.6cm) GBP 27,000. BERN, 18 June 1980, *Thérèse* (1901, partially gilded wood, h. 26in/66cm) CHF 255,000; *Head of Young*

Tahitian Woman (c. 1892, charcoal on paper, 17 3/4 x 12 1/4in/45 x 31.4cm) CHF 126,000. NEW YORK, 19 May 1983, *Undine III (recto); Joys of Brittany (verso)* (gouache and watercolour, fan-shaped, 4 3/4 x 14 3/4in/12 x 37.6cm) USD 75,000. LONDON, 7 Dec 1983, *Tahiti* (1892-93, brush, Indian ink and wash, 7 3/4 x 6 1/2in/19.5 x 16.5cm) GBP 9,000. LYONS, 18 Dec 1983, *Double Pot* (glazed terracotta with painted decoration, h. 6in/15.5cm) FRF 86,000. NEW YORK, 15 May 1984, *Trees Flowering in a Garden in Rouen* (1884, oil on canvas, 28 1/2 x 23 1/2in/72.5 x 59.7cm) USD 400,000. PARIS, 21 June 1984, *Amphora-shaped Vase with Three Low Reliefs: Veiled Dancer, Lamb in Dazzling Sunlight, and a Woman with a Deer* (polychrome terracotta) FRF 190,000. LONDON, 6 Dec 1984, *Noa Noa* (1894-1895, coloured woodcut, 14 x 8in/35.7 x 20.5cm) GBP 28,000. NEW YORK, 15 May 1985, *Conversation with Women of the Tropics or Negresses* (1887, oil on canvas, 24 1/4 x 30in/61.5 x 76cm) USD 1,700,000. ENGHIEN-LES-BAINS, 13 April 1986, *Children Fighting, Pont-Aven* (1888, pastel, 22 1/2 x 15in/57 x 38cm) FRF 2,450,000. BERN, 18 June 1986, *Woman Singing* (painted mahogany, round and in relief, 21 1/4 x 20in/54 x 51cm) CHF 370,000. PARIS, 26 June 1986, *Duck Pond* (1881, oil on canvas, 12 1/2 x 19 3/4in/32 x 50cm) FRF 2,250,000. NEW YORK, 17 Nov 1986, *Young Girl with Fox* (c. 1890-91, charcoal heightened with white chalk on yellow paper, 12 1/2 x 13in/31.6 x 33.2cm) USD 310,000. PARIS, 8 Dec 1986, *Fishermen and Bathers on the River Aven* (1888, oil on canvas, 28 3/4 x 23 1/2in/73 x 60 cm) FRF 5,800,000. LONDON, 30 Nov 1987, *Three Huts, Tahiti* (1891-92, oil on canvas, 16 1/4 x 26 1/4in/41 x 66.8cm) GBP 2,200,000. NEW YORK, 18 Feb 1988, *Man in Tall Hat (recto); Woman (study; verso)* (coloured chalks on paper, 9 x 11in/22 x 28cm) USD 8,800. VERSAILLES, 21 Feb 1988, *Abduction of Europa* (woodcut) FRF 18,000. PARIS, 15 March 1988, *Two Studies of Goats (recto); People and Cats (studies; verso)* (pencil, sheet of sketches, 6 x 4 1/4in/15 x 11cm) FRF 36,000. PARIS, 3 Oct 1988, *Tahitian Woman* (ink drawing, 6 x 3 1/4in/15 x 8.5cm) FRF 91,000. NEW YORK, 12 Nov 1988, *Oviri* (ink and watercolour on paper, 11 1/2 x 8 1/4in/29.3 x 21cm) USD 220,000; *Nativity (recto); Head of a Marquesas Woman (verso)* (gouache, 12 1/2 x 10 3/4in/31.5 x 27.4cm) USD 77,000. NEW YORK, 13 Dec 1988, *Woman Seen from Behind* (watercolour, 6 1/4 x 4in/16 x 10cm) FRF 40,000. ROME, 21 March 1989, *Auti Te Pape (Women by the River)* (1895, coloured lithograph, 8 x 14in/20.5 x 35.5cm) ITL 45,000,000. LONDON, 4 April 1989, *Female Torso* (bronze, h. 11 1/2in/29 cm) GBP 22,000. PARIS, 8 April 1989, *Toilette* (1882, sculpted pearwood, 13 1/2 x 22in/34 x 55cm) FRF 2,850,000. PARIS, 9 April 1989, *Studio Interior with Tahitian Women and Angels* (1902, monotype, 20 3/4 x 19in/53 x 48cm) FRF 1,100,000. NEW YORK, 9 May 1989, *Mata Mua (Once Upon a Time)* (1892, oil on canvas, 34 1/2 x 25 3/4in/87.5 x 65.5cm) USD 24,200,000. NEW YORK, 10 May 1989, *Farm in Britanny II* (1894, oil on canvas, 36 1/2 x 29in/92.8 x 73.7cm) USD 6,820,000. PARIS, 22 May 1989, *Afternoon of a Faun* (light-brown-patinated bronze, 13 1/2 x 4 x 5in/34 x 10 x 13cm) FRF 300,000. LONDON, 27 June 1989, *Exotic and Red Fruits* (1887, oil on canvas, 12 3/4 x 18 1/2in/32.4 x 46.8cm) GBP 2,310,000. NEW YORK, 18 Oct 1989, *Cattle by the Sea* (1886, oil on canvas, 29 1/2 x 44in/75 x 112cm) USD 3,960,000. NEW YORK, 15 Nov 1989, *Lilies* (1889, oil on canvas, 36 1/4 x 28 3/4in/92 x 73cm) USD 11,000,000. LONDON, 28 Nov 1989, *Young Breton with a Goose* (1889, oil on canvas, 36 1/4 x 28 3/4in/92 x 73cm) GBP 4,400,000. TEL-AVIV, 3 Jan 1990, *Woman with Figs* (1895, print, 10 1/2 x 17 1/2in/26.8 x 44.5cm) USD 1,650. PARIS, 3 April 1990, *Fiancée (Woman by an Open Windown)* (1888, oil on canvas, 13 x 16 1/4in/33 x 41cm) FRF 4,260,000. LONDON, 3 April 1990, *Ia Orana Ritou* (watercolour and pencil on paper, 12 1/2 x 8 1/2in/31.7 x 21.4cm) GBP 264,000; *Young Breton Girl beside the Sea II* (1889, pastel, 29 1/4 x 20in/74.5 x 51cm) GBP 616,000. PARIS, 3 April 1990, *Fiancée (Woman by an Open Window)* (1888, oil on canvas, 13 x 16 1/4in/33 x 41cm) FRF 4,260,000. NEW YORK, 17 May 1990, *Women Sacrificing to the Moon Goddess Hina* (wood, double-sided statuette, h. 15 1/4in/38.7cm) USD 1,485,000. LONDON, 17 Oct 1990, *Near the Farm* (1874, oil on canvas, 13 3/4 x 11in/35 x 27cm) GBP 99,000. PARIS, 7 Nov 1990, *The Orchard or the Party Wall* (1881, oil on canvas, 12 1/4 x 18 1/2in/31 x 47cm) FRF 950,000. NEW YORK, 14 Nov 1990, *Winter Landscape, Copenhagen* (1885, oil on canvas, 18 1/4 x 12 1/2in/46.5 x 32cm) USD 605,000. LONDON, 19 March 1991, *Portrait of Emile Gauguin at the Age of Five Months* (1875, watercolour on paper, mounted on card, 2 x 1 1/2in/5.2 x 4cm) GBP 15,400. NEW YORK, 8 May 1991, *The Orchard (Party Wall)* (1881, oil on canvas, 12 x 18 1/2in/30.5 x 47cm) USD 352,000. PARIS, 15 June 1991, *Tahitian Woman Crouching* (monotype, drawing, 12 x 20in/30.5 x 51cm) FRF 3,200,000. LONDON, 26 June 1991, *Flower Vase* (hand-painted earthenware, h. 9in/23cm, l. 11 1/2in/29cm) GBP 104,500. HEIDELBERG, 12 Oct 1991, *Mahno no varua ino* (woodcut, 8 x 14in/20.2 x 35.4cm) DEM 3, 800. PARIS, 21 Oct 1991, *Madame Death* (1891, charcoal, 13 1/4 x 9in/33.5 x 23cm) FRF 380,000. PARIS, 7 Nov 1991, *Te Faré (The House)* (1892, oil on canvas, 28 3/4 x 36 1/4in/73 x 92cm) FRF 52,000,000. LONDON, 2 Dec 1991, *Tahitian Women* (charcoal, 17 1/4 x 12 1/4in/44 x 31cm) GBP 473,000. NEW YORK, 14 May 1992, *Head of Breton Woman* (1888, oil on canvas, 13 x 9 1/4in/33 x 23.5cm) USD 198,000. PARIS, 12 June 1992, *Flageolet Player on a Cliff* (1889, oil on canvas, 28 3/4 x 36 1/4in/73 x 92cm) FRF 16,500,000; *Self-portrait* (graphite, 6 x 4in/15 x 10cm) FRF 325,000. LONDON, 30 June 1992, *Afternoon of a Faun* (lost-wax bronze, h. 13 3/4in/35cm) GBP 6,600; *Children in the Fields* (1884, oil on canvas, 25 3/4 x 18in/65.5 x 46cm) GBP 440,000. LONDON, 2 Dec 1992, *Full-length Female Nude* (lost-wax bronze, h. 26 3/4in/68cm) GBP 28,600. NEW YORK, 13 May 1993, *Young Parisienne II* (bronze, h. 10 3/4in/27.3cm) USD 36,800. LONDON, 22 June 1993, *Peasants Huddling by the Fire near a River* (1886, oil on canvas, 45 3/4 x 35in/116.3 x 89.2cm) GBP 1,651,500. PARIS, 17 Nov 1993, *Young Parisienne* (bronze, h. 11in/27.1cm) FRF 50,000. PARIS, 22 Nov 1993, *Woman of Tahiti* (1892, gouache on paper, fan-shaped, 4 3/4 x 17 1/4in/12 x 44 cm) FRF 2,000,000. NEW YORK, 9 May 1994, *River Aven at Pont-Aven* (1888, oil on canvas, 28 1/4 x 36 1/2in/72 x 93cm) USD 4,182,500. NEW YORK, 10 May 1994, *Rue Carcel in the Snow* (1883, oil on canvas, 46 x 35 1/2in/117 x 90cm) USD 2,532,500. COPENHAGEN, 16 May 1994, *Male and Female Heads, Tahiti (studies)* (ink, 12 1/4 x 7 3/4in/31 x 20cm) DKK 80,000. LONDON, 28 June 1994, *Ave Maria* (ink and pencil, 25 x 20 1/4in/63.5 x 51.2cm) GBP 386,500. NEW YORK, 8 May 1995, *Bouquet of Flowers* (1882, oil on panel, 5 x 7 1/4in/12.7 x 18.4cm) USD 156,500. PARIS, 20 June 1995, *Te Atua (The Gods)* (1902, sculpted and painted, sequoia wood, 7 3/4 x 22 3/4in/20 x 58cm) FRF 300,000. LONDON, 27 June 1995, *Tahitian Women by a Stream* (oil on canvas, 28 3/4 x 36 1/4in/73 x 92cm) GBP 5,501,500. NEW YORK, 9 Nov 1995, *Lilacs in a Vase* (1885, oil on canvas, 13 3/4 x 11in/34.9 x 27cm) USD 310,500. PARIS, 19 March 1996, *Dog Racing in the Meadow* (1888, oil on canvas, 36 1/4 x 28 1/2in/92 x 72.5cm) FRF 2,280,000. NEW YORK, 1 May 1996, *Still-life* (1889, oil on canvas, 12 1/4 x 16in/31.4 x 39.7cm) USD 398,500. BERN, 21 June 1996, *Woman by the River* (1893-94, coloured woodcut, 8 x 14in/20.6 x 35.6cm) CHF 42,000. NEW YORK, 12 Nov 1996, *Tahitian Women* (c. 1891-93, charcoal on paper, 16 1/4 x 12 1/4in/41 x 31.1cm) USD 992,000. PARIS, 9 Dec 1996, *Chirst on the Cross with Polynesian Motifs* (c. 1894, pale brown-patinated bronze, h. 20in/50.5cm) FRF 80,000. NEW YORK, 12 May 1997, *Still-life with Bitter Apples* (1889, oil on canvas, 16 x 20 1/2in/40.6 x 52cm) USD 3,412,500. NEW YORK, 14 May 1997, *Gauguin at his Easel* (c. 1884-85, oil on canvas, 26 x 21 1/2in/65.2 x 54.3cm) USD 3,852,500. PARIS, 10 June 1997, *Seated Male Nude (recto)* (monotype); *Study of a Leg (verso)* (c. 1901-02, graphite, 13 3/4 x 11in/35.1 x 28cm) FRF 340,000. LONDON, 23 June 1997, *Cow on All Fours* (1888, oil on canvas, 19 x 13 1/2in/47.4 x 34cm) GBP 221,500. PARIS, 27 Nov 1997, *Woman with Figs* (1963, etching on zinc, 10 1/2 x 16 1/2in/26.8 x 42cm) FRF 3,200. NEW YORK, 5 May 1998, *Les Dindons - Pont*

Aven Landscape (1888, oil on canvas, 36 x 28 ins / 91 x 72 cm) USD 2,600,000. London, 24 June 1998, *Rider in front of the Cabin* (1902, oil on canvas, 23 x 13 ins / 58 x 34 cm) GBP 880,000. London, 29 June 1999, *To Make a Bouquet* (1880, oil on canvas, 21 x 26 ins / 54 x 65 cm) GBP 1,550,000. New York, 8 May 2000, *The Blue Roof (Farmyard in Pouldou)* (1890, oil on canvas, 28 x 35 ins / 71 x 90 cm) USD 4,800,000. New York, 10 May 2000, *Fisherman and Swimmers on the Aven* (1888, oil on canvas, 29 x 24 ins / 73 x 60 cm) USD 2,600,000. London, 6 Feb 2001, *Arles Landscape with Bushes* (1888, oil on canvas, 29 x 36 ins / 74 x 92 cm) GBP 1,800,000. New York, 9 May 2001, *Women on the River Bank* (1892, oil on canvas, 13 x 16 ins / 32 x 40 cm) USD 6,000,000. London, 4 Feb 2002, *Lollichon Field and Pont-Aven Church* (1886, oil on canvas, 28 x 36 ins / 71 x 92 cm) GBP 600,000. New York, 6 Nov 2002, *Hut under the trees* (1892, oil on canvas, 28 x 17 ins / 72 x 43 cm) USD 4,200,000. New York, 7 May 2003, *Still-life with Japanese Print* (1888, oil on canvas, 13 x 22 ins / 32 x 55 cm) USD 2,800,000. London, 23 June 2003, *Tha Apparition* (1902, oil on canvas, 26 x 30 ins / 66 x 76 cm) GBP 6,800,000. London, 4 Feb 2004, *View of the Beach at Bellangenay* (1889, pastel on board, 12 x 17 ins / 31 x 43 cm) GBP 150,000. New York, 3 Nov 2004, *Cows by the Sea* (1886, oil on canvas, 30 x 44 ins / 75 x 112 cm) USD 1,800,000.

GAUGUIN, Paul René
Norwegian, 20th century.
Born 1911, in Copenhagen, to a Norwegian mother; died February 1976, in Málaga, Spain.
Active in Norway.
Painter, sculptor, engraver. Stage sets.

Paul René Gauguin was the grandson of Paul Gauguin and son of Pola Gauguin. He took his mother's nationality. He was handicapped all his life by his famous name. He went to secondary school in France. He was a fisherman, a journalist and a stage designer. He fought in the ranks of the International Brigades in the Spanish Civil War. He showed his works in a solo exhibition in Paris in 1975.

Auction records:
Copenhagen, 21 Oct 1992, *Tiger* (stone sculpture, h. 9½ ins / 24 cm, l. 22 ins/55 cm) DKK 4,200.

GAUGUIN, Pola
French, 20th century.
Born 6 December 1883, in Paris; died 1961.
From 1884 active in Denmark.
Painter. Local scenes, landscapes.

Pola Gauguin was the son of Paul Gauguin.

Museums and Galleries:
Oslo.

Auction records:
Montreal, 19 Nov 1991, *View of a Market in a Town* (oil on canvas, 22¾ x 30 ins / 57.8 x 76.2 cm) CAD 2,000.

GAUJARD, Louis François
French, 18th century.
Active in Paris in 1767.
Painter.

GAUJEAN, Eugène
French, 19th century.
Born 1850, in Pau; died 8 January 1900, in Andrésy.
Engraver.

Studied under Pils and Martinet and exhibited at the Salon de Paris from 1877. Eugène Gaujean owes his place among modern engravers to his significant contributions to the *Gazette des Beaux-Arts*. A gold medal awarded him at the 1899 Exposition Universelle helped consolidate his reputation.

GAUJON, Jean
French, 16th century.
Born in Rouen; died 1572, in Paris.
Miniaturist.

GAUKEL, Hans
German, 19th - 20th century.
Born 23 September 1872, near Göppingen; died 30 Ma 1914, in Stuttgart.
Painter, lithographer.

Hans Gaukel started out as a lithographer. He was active i Munich and Stuttgart.

GAUL, August
German, 19th - 20th century.
Born 22 October 1869, in Gross-Anheim, near Hanau; died 1921.
Sculptor. Animals.

August Gaul was the son of a stonemason. From 1886 t 1888, he was apprenticed to a goldsmith while taking draw ing lessons at the academy in Hanau. He then studied in Ber lin, first at the school of applied arts and then at the academy of fine arts. From 1894 to 1899 he worked as a sculptor's as sistant in the studio of Reinhold Begas, where he was re sponsible for modelling the lions for the *Monument t William I*. During this time he won the Prix de Rome at th Berlin academy in 1897 and spent a year in Rome, where he met Tuaillon and the pupils of Hans von Marées. In 1899 he showed the lions he had modelled at the exhibition of the Berlin Secession. In 1902, he was accepted as a member o the Secession and from then on he was considered the bes animal sculptor of that time.

Although he was a Realist, he stood out among the artists of his age because of the care he took in combining the characteristic size and posture of the animal or animals, which he usually portrayed at rest, helping him to give permanence to this size, after the manner of Hildebrand in Germany and Pompon in France. He created a *Swan Fountain* in Krefeld, a *Bison Fountain* in Königsberg (now Kaliningrad, Russia) and a *Penguin Fountain* for the grounds of a private property by the Wannsee, near Berlin.

Museums and Galleries:
Berlin: *Two Pelicans; Lion; Sheep at Rest* - Bremen: *Bears Playing; Ostrich; Geese* - Hamburg: *Animals* (eleven bronzes).

Auction records:
Cologne, 30 Nov 1971, *Seated Bear* (bronze) DEM 3,800. Cologne, 25 Nov 1972, *Two Lion Cubs* (bronze) DEM 3,600. London, 9 April 1976, *Running Bear* (green-patinated bronze, h. 2¼ ins / 5.5 cm) DEM 800. Cologne, 21 May 1977, *Three Penguins* (1912, bronze, 6¾ x 8¼ ins / 17.2 x 21 cm) DEM 6,500. Cologne, 6 May 1978, *Three Penguins* (1912, bronze, 6¾ x 8¼ ins / 17.2 x 21 cm) DEM 5,500. Berlin, 24 April 1980, *Two Goats* (1898, patinated bronze, h. 10¼ ins / 26 cm and long. 16½ ins/42 cm) DEM 7,000. Cologne, 5 June 1982, *Boy Riding a Donkey* (1912, bronze, h. 6½ ins / 16.5 cm) DEM 24,000. Cologne, 6 Dec 1983, *Two Penguins* (bronze, h. 6½ ins / 16.4 cm) DEM 9,000. Cologne, 3 Dec 1985, *Ostrich Walking* (1902, patinated bronze, h. 13½ ins / 34 cm) DEM 14,000. Berlin, 27 Nov 1992, *Seated Tapir* (silver, h. 2¼ ins / 5.5 cm) DEM 4,746. Zurich, 2 Dec 1994, *Duck* (bronze, h. 11½ ins / 29.5 cm) CHF 4,200. Munich, 27 Feb 1999, *Penguin at Penguin Fountain, Hamburg* (brown patinated bronze, h, 14 ins / 35 cm) DEM 16,000. Cologne, 13 Nov 1999, *Penguin* (dark gold patinated bronze, 9 x 6x6 ins / 24 x 15x16 cm) DEM 19,000. Amsterdam, 8 June 2000, *Penguin* (c. 1914, bronze, h. 9 ins / 22 cm) NLG 18,000. Amsterdam, 8 June 2000, *Two Young Swans* (1906, bronze, h. 9 ins / 22 cm) NLG 20,000. Ahlden, 5 May 2001, *Donkey Walking* (brown patinated bronze, h. 4 ins / 10 cm) DEM 10,500. Hamburg, 8 Dec 2001, *Two Penguins* (gilded bronze, 6 x 7x4 ins / 16 x 17x10 cm) DEM 16,000. Berlin, 8 June 2002, *Three Pheasants* (1909, brown patinated bronze, h. 6 ins / 15 cm) EUR 5,500. Cologne, 4 Dec 2002, *Seated Lion Cub* (1898, bronze marble, 9 x 5x1 ins / 24 x 12x2 cm) EUR 4,800. Ahlden, 9 May 2003, *Lion Cub* (1893, dark brown patinated bronze, h. 7 ins / 19 cm) EUR 3,400. Cologne, 29 May 2003,

Girl Riding Donkey (dark brown patinated bronze, h. 6 ins / 15 cm) EUR 10,000. COLOGNE, 4 Dec 2004, *Drake* (bronze, h. 20 ins / 51 cm) EUR 6,200. COLOGNE, 4 Dec 2004, *Duck Standing on One Leg* (bronze, h. 15 ins / 37 cm) EUR 8,000.

GAUL, Franz

Austrian, 19th century.

Born 29 July 1837, in Vienna; died 3 July 1906, in Vienna.

Painter.

Franz was the brother of Gustav Gaul. He mainly devoted himself to theatre decoration.

GAUL, Gustav

Austrian, 19th century.

Born 6 February 1836, in Vienna; died 7 September 1888, in Hinterbrühl.

Painter. History painting, portraits, genre scenes.

Gustav Gaul studied at the academy in Vienna and was a pupil of Karl Rahl. He made study trips to Germany, Holland, France and Italy. Gaul exhibited in Munich, Vienna and Dresden between 1858 and 1888.

MUSEUMS AND GALLERIES:

COLOGNE: *Francesca and Paolo* - VIENNA: portrait (watercolour).

GAUL, William Gilbert

American, 19th - 20th century.

Born 31 March 1855, in Jersey City; died 1919.

Painter, watercolourist, illustrator. Military subjects, genre scenes, landscapes with figures.

William Gaul was born in New Jersey and studied at the Claverack Military Academy, then at the National Academy of Design in New York and under J.G. Brown. He lived in Ridgefield Park in the USA. He received many awards, including the gold medal from the American Art Association in 1881 for *Hold the Line at All Hazards*; a bronze medal at the Exposition Universelle in Paris of 1889 for *Charging the Battery*; a medal in Chicago in 1893 and another in Buffalo in 1901. He became a member of the National Academy of New York in 1882.

He was inspired by episodes in the American Civil War and his works were often published in the 1880s.

AUCTION RECORDS:

NEW YORK, 8 Feb 1903, *Wounded in the Rearguard*, USD 170. NEW YORK, 3 April 1903, *Battery Attack*, USD 200. NEW YORK, 6 Feb 1907, *Critics*, USD 100. NEW YORK, 18 Feb 1909, *On the Line*, USD 425. NEW YORK, 27 Oct 1971, *Cavalryman and his Horse at the River*, USD 1,250. NEW YORK, 20 April 1972, *Seated Indian*, USD 5,500. NEW YORK, 11 April 1973, *Indian Camp*, USD 13,000. NEW YORK, 30 Jan 1980, *Scene from the Civil War* (gouache, 23 x 19 1/2 ins / 58.4 x 49.5 cm) USD 2,800. NEW YORK, 22 Oct 1982, *Wounded Cavalryman* (oil on canvas, 25 x 30 ins / 63.5 x 76.2 cm) USD 20,000. NEW YORK, 2 June 1983, *Tending the Fire* (oil on canvas, 28 x 22 ins / 71.1 x 56 cm) USD 9,000. NEW YORK, 23 March 1984, *Jersey at Dusk* (watercolour and black ink, 12 1/4 x 18 1/2 ins / 31 x 47 cm) USD 950. NEW YORK, 7 Dec 1984, *Union Soldier* (oil on canvas, 20 1/4 x 16 1/4 ins / 51.3 x 41.2 cm) USD 28,000. NEW YORK, 15 March 1985, *Woman Sitting beside the Sea* (1877, oil on canvas, 20 1/4 x 30 1/4 ins / 51.3 x 76.8 cm) USD 13,000. NEW YORK, 24 May 1989, *'Molly Pitcher' at the Battle of Monmouth in 1778* (oil on card, 34 x 40 ins / 86.3 x 101.7 cm) USD 9,900. NEW YORK, 24 Jan 1990, *Battle of Lake Monaco* (watercolour/card, 13 x 19 1/2 ins / 33.3 x 49.5 cm) USD 2,200. NEW YORK, 15 May 1991, *Young Woman Filling a Bucket at the Spring* (1885, oil on canvas, 18 x 14 ins / 45.7 x 35.6 cm) USD 4,675. NEW YORK, 27 May 1992, *Mohawk Indian Camp* (oil on canvas, 20 x 25 ins / 50.8 x 63.5 cm) USD 16,500. NEW YORK, 2 Dec 1992, *Wounded Man at an Outpost* (oil on canvas, 25 x 30 1/4 ins / 63.5 x 76.7 cm) USD 27,500. NEW YORK, 26 May 1993, *Gathering of the Elders* (oil on canvas, 18 x 24 ins / 46 x 61 cm) USD 13,800. NEW YORK, 3 Dec 1993, *Young Hunter* (oil on canvas, 25 x 30 ins / 63.5 x 76.5 cm) USD 16,100. NEW YORK, 21 Sept 1994, *Deserter* (oil on card in grisaille, 18 1/2 x 24 1/2 ins / 47 x 62.2 cm) USD 1,725. NEW YORK, 14 March 1996, *Village in the South* (oil on card, 9 3/4 x 13 1/2 ins / 24.8 x 34.3 cm) USD 4,600. NEW YORK, 23 April 1997, *Seated Indian Woman* (oil on canvas, 10 x 8 ins / 25.5 x 20.4 cm) USD 2,990.

GAUL, Winfred

German, 20th century.

Born 1928, in Düsseldorf.

Painter.

Gruppe 53.

Winfred Gaul studied German literature, ethnology and art history and from 1950 to 1953 at the Munich academy, where the painter Willi Baumeister was one of his teachers. In 1961 he made a long stay in Rome, where he became aware of the problems of large urban agglomerations. In 1965-1966 he spent time as an assistant in various educational establishments in England. He started exhibiting in 1953.

The early part of his work is the product of a kind of discreet, contemplative Tachisme, which he himself called 'landscape of the imagination'. Around 1960, he became extremely economical in his use of colour and form, before producing, in 1962, a few completely white paintings, enlivened by the occasional shadow. It was at this time that he began thinking about road signs, inventing some that were purely imaginary and exhibiting them in the open air. Since then, he has increasingly favoured a form of art that is totally integrated into the framework of life, consisting of very simple geometric shapes in bright colours, which take over all the different planes making up the surrounding space.

He took part in numerous group exhibitions: 1958, Carnegie International in Pittsburgh; 1959, Documenta in Kassel; 1960, *Antagonismes* (*Antagonisms*) at the Musée d'Arts Décoratifs in Paris; 1965, *Pop Art and New Realism* at the Palais des Beaux-Arts in Brussels; 1967, Kunstverein in Stuttgart and the Kunsthalle in Bern. He has also had solo exhibitions in Amsterdam, Bremen, Berlin, Düsseldorf, Brussels, Cologne, Milan, New York (from 1962), London, Paris, Rome, Rotterdam, Stuttgart and Vienna.

BIBLIOGRAPHY:

Freitag, Eberhard, *Winfred Gaul, Werkverzeichnis der Druckgraphiken und Objekte*, catalogue raisonné, Kunsthalle, Kiel, 1978. Weichardt, J., *Winfred Gaul: Malerei in 2.3.N Phasen*, exhibition catalogue, Gal. Schüppenhauer, Cologne, 1988.

MUSEUMS AND GALLERIES:

BELGRADE (Muz. savremene umetnotsi) - BOCHUM (Mus. Bochum) - BREMEN (Kunsthalle) - DÜSSELDORF (Kunstmus.) - HEIDELBERG (Kurpfälzisches Mus.) - KAISERSLAUTERN (Pfalzgal.) - KREFELD (Kaiser Wilhelm Mus.) - NEW YORK (MoMA) - PITTSBURGH (Carnegie MA): *No. 1, 1958* (1958) - STUTTGART (Gal. der Stadt) - WIESBADEN (Wiesbaden Mus.) - WOLFSBURG (Städtische Gal.).

AUCTION RECORDS:

COLOGNE, 5 Dec 1981, *Composition* (1956, pen/paper, 11 1/4 x 16 1/2 ins / 28.8 x 41.7 cm) DEM 2,200. COLOGNE, 31 May 1986, *Composition* (1956, oil/hardboard, 26 x 38 1/4 ins / 66 x 97 cm) DEM 9,500. BERLIN, 25 Nov 2000, *Untitled* (1959, oil on canvas, 55 x 39 ins / 140 x 100 cm) DEM 23,000. COLOGNE, 29 May 2002, *Untitled* (1957, gouache, 19 x 24 ins / 48 x 62 cm) EUR 2,000. MUNICH, 6 Dec 2002, *O T* (1957, oil on canvas, 26 x 37 ins / 65 x 95 cm) EUR 6,000. COLOGNE, 27 Nov 2003, *Arguing with Mr Pythagoras* (1985, acrylic, 71 x 71 ins / 180 x 180 cm) EUR 10,000. COLOGNE, 15 May 2004, *Composition* (1957, oil on panel, 70 x 51 ins / 179 x 130 cm) EUR 12,000. COLOGNE, 4 June 2004, *Untitled* (1955-1956, oil, collage and newspaper on masonite, 25 x 38 ins / 64 x 96 cm) EUR 5,000.

GAULA Y CORNEJO, Antonio

Spanish, 19th century.

Active in Spain.
Painter. Seascapes.

MUSEUMS AND GALLERIES:
MADRID (Prado): two seascapes.

GAULARD, Lucien

French, 20th century.
Active in Marseilles.
Sculptor.

Lucien Gaulard became a member of the Société des Artistes Français in 1902.

GAULCHER, Jean

French, 16th century.
Died 1607.
Active in Orléans.
Painter. History painting.

GAULD, David

British, 19th - 20th century.
Born 1865; died 1936.
Painter. Animals, landscapes.

David Gauld lived and worked in Glasgow. He was a member of the International Society of Painters, Sculptors and Engravers. He exhibited at the Royal Institute of Fine Arts in 1909.

Gauld was one of the brilliant group of powerful realists who made up the Glasgow School. In addition to his landscapes of the British countryside, he painted a number of pictures during a stay in France.

MUSEUMS AND GALLERIES:
GLASGOW: *Contentment.*

AUCTION RECORDS:
LONDON, 21 Dec 1923, *Two Cows in a Meadow,* GBP 9. LONDON, 10 June 1927, *Cows by a Stream,* GBP 11. EDINBURGH, 2 March 1929, *Old Mill,* GBP 15. GLASGOW, 27 March 1931, *Calves,* GBP 30. EDINBURGH, 11 Nov 1933, *Old Mill,* GBP 21. GLASGOW, 7 Oct 1937, *Calves,* GBP 19. GLASGOW, 14 June 1938, *French Pastoral Scene,* GBP 31. GLASGOW, 26 March 1941, *Calves,* GBP 26. GLASGOW, 9 Oct 1942, *Winter in Montreuil,* GBP 17; *Ayrshire Landscape with Cows,* GBP 10. GLASGOW, 7 April 1943, *Three Calves,* GBP 26. GLASGOW, 21 Jan 1944, *Mill in Galloway,* GBP 21. GLASGOW, 25 April 1945, *Frenchwoman,* GBP 40. GLASGOW, 2 July 1947, *Calves,* GBP 16. GLASGOW, 16 Jan 1973, *Calves in the Byre,* GBP 220. SCOTLAND, 24 Aug 1976, *Herd in a Landscape* (oil on canvas, 23 1/2 x 35 1/2 ins / 59.5 x 90 cm) GBP 420. SCOTLAND, 29 Aug 1978, *Two Calves in a Landscape* (oil on canvas, 19 1/4 x 22 1/2 ins / 49 x 57 cm) GBP 1,000. SCOTLAND, 26 Aug 1980, *Calves in a Byre* (oil on canvas, 24 x 36 ins / 61 x 91.5 cm) GBP 1,500. GLASGOW, 1 Dec 1982, *Herd in a Sunlit Field* (oil on canvas, 28 x 36 ins / 71 x 91.5 cm) GBP 1,350. PERTH, 27 Aug 1985, *Herd by the Waterside* (oil on canvas, 27 1/2 x 35 1/2 ins / 70 x 90 cm) GBP 3,800. EDINBURGH, 29 July 1988, *Portrait of a Woman in a Yellow Shawl* (oil on canvas, 19 3/4 x 15 3/4 ins / 50 x 40 cm) GBP 352. EDINBURGH, 30 Aug 1988, *Calves in a Byre* (oil on canvas, 24 x 36 ins / 61 x 91.5 cm) GBP 4,400. EDINBURGH, 22 Nov 1988, *The Old Mill* (oil on canvas, 24 x 30 ins / 61 x 76.2 cm) GBP 3,800. GLASGOW, 7 Feb 1989, *Calves by the River* (oil on canvas, 20 x 30 ins / 51 x 76 cm) GBP 4,620. PERTH, 29 Aug 1989, *Ayrshire Calves* (oil on canvas, 40 1/4 x 50 1/2 ins / 102 x 128 cm) GBP 8,250. EDINBURGH, 26 April 1990, *Three Ayrshire Calves* (oil on canvas, 24 x 36 ins / 61 x 91.5 cm) GBP 6,600. GLASGOW, 5 Feb 1991, *Calves* (oil on canvas, 22 x 30 ins / 56 x 76 cm) GBP 1,980. PERTH, 26 Aug 1991, *Kirkcudbrightshire Landscape* (oil on canvas, 28 1/4 x 36 ins / 71.5 x 91.5 cm) GBP 3,080. PERTH, 1 Sept 1992, *Ayrshire Calves* (oil on canvas, 24 x 36 ins / 61 x 91.5 cm) GBP 3,080. PERTH, 30 Aug 1994, *Calves in the Shade of the Trees* (oil on canvas, 20 x 24 ins / 50.5 x 61 cm) GBP 3,450. GLASGOW, 14 Feb 1995, *Calves around a Water Trough* (oil on canvas, 24 x 35 3/4 ins / 61 x 91 cm) GBP 7,475. PERTH, 26 Aug 1996, *Summer Afternoon in Britanny* (oil on canvas, 19 x 32 1/2 ins / 48 x 82.5 cm) GBP 6,900. LONDON, 15 April 1997, *Tw Heifers* (oil on canvas, 20 x 30 ins / 51 x 76 cm) GBP 7,36 GLASGOW, 25 Aug 1997, *Three-quarter Portrait of a Man in Grey Suit, Holding a Pair of Opera Glasses in his Right Han* (oil on canvas, 54 x 37 ins / 137.2 x 94 cm) GBP 345. AUCHTERARDER, 26 Aug 1997, *Calves by a River* (oil on canvas, 28 1/4 x 3 ins / 72 x 91.5 cm) GBP 7,360. PAISLEY, 19 March 1999, *Tw Calves with Tree and Fence in Background* (oil on canvas, 20 24 ins / 50 x 60 cm) GBP 4,800. TORONTO, 17 May 1999, *Wate Mill, Normandy* (oil on canvas, 24 x 30 ins / 61 x 76 cm) CAI 4,400. BURY ST EDMUNDS, 29 June 2000, *Three Calves in a Paddock* (oil on canvas, 28 x 36 ins / 71 x 91 cm) GBP 8,500. EDINBURGH, 8 Dec 2000, *Calves in Byre* (oil on canvas, 28 x 35 ins 70 x 90 cm) GBP 6,000. EDINBURGH, 24 Aug 2001, *Cattle on th Ayrshire Coast in Summer* (oil on canvas, 24 x 33 ins / 61 x 8 cm) GBP 5,400. LONDON, 5 Sept 2001, *Calves* (oil on canvas, 2 x 30 ins / 51 x 76 cm) GBP 5,200. LONDON, 31 Oct 2002, *Wate Mill* (oil on canvas, 24 x 30 ins / 62 x 77 cm) GBP 8,000. EDINBURGH, 6 Dec 2002, *New Bonnet* (oil on board, 14 x 10 ins / 3 x 25 cm) GBP 19,000. EDINBURGH, 21 Aug 2003, *Normand Farm* (oil on canvas, 28 x 36 ins / 70 x 91 cm) GBP 6,500. LONDON, 27 Aug 2003, *Young Trio* (oil on canvas, 28 x 36 ins / 71 91 cm) GBP 6,500. EDINBURGH, 28 May 2004, *Calves by a Wate Butt* (oil on canvas, 25 x 30 ins / 63 x 75 cm) GBP 8,500. LONDON, 1 Sept 2004, *Broken Free* (oil on canvas, 20 x 26 ins / 51 66 cm) GBP 7,500.

GAULET, Henry

French, 19th century.
Born 4 December 1863, in Paris.
Painter.

Exhibited on a regular basis at all the principal Paris salons up to and including 1936. Gaulet's body of work has an apparent facility that should not be allowed to disguise the fact that he had a solid grounding in draughtsmanship and composition.

GAULEY, Robert David

Irish, 20th century.
Born 12 March 1875, in Carnaveigh; died 1943.
Active in the USA.
Painter.

Robert David Gauley studied with W. Ross in Cambridge, F.W. Benson and Edmond C. Tarbell in Boston, and with Bouguereau and Ferrier in Paris. He was awarded a bronze medal at the Paris Exposition Universelle in 1900, an honourable mention in Buffalo in 1901, a bronze medal in St-Louis and the Prix Isidor of the Salmagundi Club in 1907 and the Clarke Prize from the National Academy in 1908. He became a member of the Academy in the same year.

AUCTION RECORDS:
NEW YORK, 29 May 1987, *Intervale, New Hampshire* (1894, oil on canvas, 18 x 24 ins / 46 x 61 cm) USD 3,200.

GAULIER, Nicole

French, 20th century.
Born 1939.
Painter, collage artist, pastellist.

Between 1970 and 1989 Nicole Gaulier's embroidered pieces were based on pastels and then collages. Her approach then developed and she began painting canvases that she then cuts up and recombines to create a new space. Having broken the original structure she explores the surface, creating tension between form and colour. The way she organises forms bears a similarity with the work of Kandinsky.

She exhibited at various group exhibitions, including: in 1980 at the Musée de la Poste in Paris; in 1986 at the Musée Nationale d'Art Moderne in Paris; in 1988-1989 at the Musée Isetam, Japan; in 1991 at the *Rencontres - Cinquante Ans de Collages* (*Encounters - Fifty Years of Collage*) exhibition organised by Françoise Monin at the Galerie Claudine Lustman, Paris; and in 1995 with St-Cricq and Kichinevski at the *Assemblages-Collages* exhibition at the Galerie Claudine ıstman, Paris. She has also shown her work in solo exhibi- ons, including: 2003, *Nicole Gaulier: Mystères et Décou- ertes de la Matière (Nicole Gaulier - Mysteries and iscoveries of Materials)*, her first monographic exhibition t the Musée Lambinet, Versailles.

IBLIOGRAPHY:

Ionnin, Françoise, *Rencontres - Cinquante ans de collages*, xhibition catalogue, Gal. Claudine Lustman, Paris, 1991.

GAULIS, Fernand

Swiss, 19th - 20th century.
Born 1860, in La Chablière near Lausanne; died 1924.
Painter, watercolourist, pastellist. Landscapes, landscapes with figures.

'ernand Gaulis moved to Paris to study at the Académie ulian with Jules Lefebvre and Gustave Boulanger. He then tudied with the famous Norwegian landscape painter Hans 'rederik Gude at the Karlsruhe academy in Germany. In 894, he stayed in Venice and on the French and Italian Riv- era. When he was about 30 his health deteriorated and he uffered occasionally from problems with his sight, which ffected the quality of his painting. He exhibited at the Paris alon in 1900. He painted almost exclusively landscapes in ils, watercolours or pastels. He very soon moved away rom the academic rules imposed by his first two teachers nd introduced Impressionist features into his work.

AUCTION RECORDS:

COLOGNE, 18 March 1989, *Lakeside Landscape in Summer* oil on canvas, 21 1/4 x 40 1/4 ins / 54 x 102 cm) DEM 5,500.

GAULIS, Louis Daniel Edouard

Swiss, 19th - 20th century.
Born 1835, in Cossonay; died 10 February 1911, in Lausanne.
Painter.

Louis Gaulis took part in the exhibitions of the Swiss Society of Fine Arts in Geneva.

GAULLE, Edmé

French, 18th - 19th century.
Born 4 January 1762, in Langres; died January 1841, in Paris.
Sculptor.

Edmé Gaulle was a student of Dévosges in Dijon. In 1799, he won the second Grand Prix de Rome and in 1803 won the first prize with *Ulysses Recognised by His Nurse Euryclea* His work appeared in the Salon from 1808 to 1827.

His works include: *Nature Study*, a low relief at the fountain in the place de la Bastille, *Claude Perrault* (marble bust), *Louis XVI* (marble statue, at the Ministry of the Interior). Gaulle worked on the shaft of the Vendôme column and on the dec- orations for various festivals of the Empire. He was given the post of curator of the government's marble statuary.

MUSEUMS AND GALLERIES:

LANGRES: *Napoleon I* (marble bust).

GAULLI, Alessandro

Italian, 18th century.
Died 7 May 1728, in Rome.
Painter, architect.

Alessandro Gaulli was the son of Giovanni Battista.

GAULLI, Giovanni Battista, also known as Baciccia or Baciccio

Italian, 17th century.
Born 8 May 1639, in Genoa; died 2 April 1709, in Rome.
Painter, fresco artist, draughtsman, copyist. Religious subjects, portraits.

Giovanni Battista Gaulli was born into a family of Venetian extraction. His first teacher was Luciano Borzone, one of the most accomplished teachers living in Genoa at the time. Gaulli lost his parents and nine siblings during the plague year of 1657. To eke out a living, he was obliged to turn to manual labour, but this in no way diluted his ambitions as a painter and in his spare time he made copies of frescoes painted in the Palazzo Doria by Pierino del Vaga. However, the young 'Baciccia' (a diminutive of his Christian name) was determined to move to Rome and did so by smuggling him- self aboard the Genoese ambassador's galley. He was dis- covered but, to his relief, the ambassador took no punitive action, instead taking the young Gaulli under his wing.

In Rome, Gaulli hired on as a copyist in the studio of a French painter and, as part of his training, copied works by Raphael. In time, he came to the notice of Bernini, who liked what he saw, encouraged the young artist and procured him some modest commissions. Gaulli's *Virgin and Child with St Anne* was incorporated into Bernini's overall architectural designs for the Altieri Chapel in the church of S Francesco in Ripa. Then, barely 20, Gaulli made his mark with a *St Roch Imploring the Virgin on behalf of Those Afflicted by the Plague*, painted for the church of S Rocco in Ripetta, fol- lowed by a *Cardinal Virtues* for the cupola of the church of S Agnese in Agone (1668-1672). The young Gaulli was then presented to Pope Alexander VII, who commissioned Gaulli to paint his portrait.

The stage was now set for a brilliant career. In quick succes- sion, Gaulli painted a *Holy Trinity* for the church of S Maria sopra Minerva, together with a *St Louis Bertrand Meditating on a Pistol Transformed into a Crucifix*, followed by a *St Paul Preaching* for the church of S Nicolas de Tolentino, and three episodes from the life of St Martha for the convent of that name. At that juncture, P. Oliva - the then commanding gen- eral of the Jesuit Order - followed Bernini's counsel and ac- corded Gaulli full responsibility for the decoration of the church of Gesù, a monumental task that was to occupy Bacic- cia for the next 13 years of his life (from 1672 to around 1685). It would emerge as his most important work.

The principal element in the Gesù is Gaulli's *Triumph of the Name of Jesus*, a vast composition that fills the entire span of the main vault. It depicts hierarchies of angels and saints in humble yet graceful adoration of Christ's name; devils and de- mons are portrayed falling into the abyss, detaching them- selves, as it were, from the vault. Lanzi is not alone in his praise for the overall mastery of perspective and the skilful permutation of the various elements. The author Henri Stendhal would later express particular admiration for the 'warm and beautiful disorder' that characterises the group portraying the Vices thrown into disarray by the beam of light radiating from Christ's name. This, said Stendhal, was a truly astonishing effect achieved by an artist whom he did not con- sider to be 'of the first rank'. The Gesù is distinguished by oth- er sets of motifs - the Coronation of the Virgin (cupola), the Apostles (pendentives), the Lamb of God (gallery) and an Apotheosis (chapel of S Ignazio). Gaulli is reported to have re- ceived 12,000 écus as an honorarium for the Gesù project and, it is said, would have received more, had his irascible (even vi- olent) nature not alienated the Jesuit fathers.

Irascible or not, Gaulli continued to enjoy one success af- ter another. In 1693, he returned to Genoa, where he had been invited to paint the large vault of the ducal palace. The Genoa Senate finally withdrew the commission in the face of what it regarded as 'unreasonable' financial demands made by the artist. He returned to Rome some time later, where he was commissioned to produce a *Triumph of the Franciscan Order* for the vault of the church of SS Apostoli. The agreed fee was 2,000 écus, but Gaulli accepted a down-payment of 500 écus and generously waived the balance. This was a ma- jor commission, but one that Gaulli completed in a mere 55 days. It is generally conceded that the fresco shows signs of having been painted quickly and with a certain lack of atten- tion to detail, which is not evidenced in his earlier work. At the time, Gaulli was already 67 and the tragic loss of his son had devastated him to the point where he even contemplated suicide and had to be 'locked away' for the better part of a year for his own protection. Gaulli eventually died on 2 April 1709 following a severe cold contracted during the erection of statues commissioned for the dome of St Peter's by Pope Clement XI.

It is often maintained that Gaulli was greatly influenced throughout his career by Bernini and that, when the latter passed away, Gaulli's own body of work suffered a falling-off in terms of quality. However, Bernini died in 1680, when Gaulli was only 41 and still working on the Gesù frescoes. Gaulli admitted his indebtedness to Bernini, particularly in the manner in which he approached portraiture of which he was an accomplished exponent. Typically, Gaulli would first determine and paint in the principal facial features, then allow his subject to move freely, speaking and laughing as he did so. He applied this technique to the portraits of the seven popes under whose papacy he had lived and worked, and also to the various dignitaries he portrayed.

Gaulli was, to all intents and purposes, both an official court painter and a monumentalist. His work mainly comprises frescoes for a number of churches in Rome and for various palazzi, as well as his portrait work, which contributed significantly to his reputation and renown. The Louvre boasts some 30 drawings by Gaulli, several of which are from the Crozat and Mariette collections.

Gaulli's work has featured in a number of group retrospectives, most notably in *Cieux en gloire* (*Celestial Glories*), a 2002 exhibition at the Musée Fesch in Ajaccio, which celebrated major examples of Roman decorative art of the Baroque in the form of sketches and models (bozzetti and modelli). Single-artist showings of Gaulli's work have included an exhibition at Düsseldorf's Kunstmuseum in 1976, a retrospective featuring 75 oils and 40 drawings at the Palazzo Chigi in Ariccia in 1999, and an exhibition at the Museo Diocesana in Ascoli Piceno in 2001.

BIBLIOGRAPHY:

Enggass, Robert, *The Religious Paintings of Giovanni Battista Gaulli*, dissertation, catalogue raisonné, University of Michigan, Ann Arbor, 1954. Enggass, Robert, *The Painting of Baciccio, Giovanni Battista Gaulli, 1639-1709*, catalogue raisonné, Pennsylvania State University Press, University Park (PA), 1964. *Die Handzeichnungen von Guglielmo Cortese und Giovanni Battista Gaulli*, exhibition catalogue, Kunstmuseum, Düsseldorf, 1976. Czére, Andrea, *I Cartoni di Giovanni Battista Gaulli, detto il Baciccio, nel Museo di Budapest*, 1996. Fagiolo dell'Arco, Maurizio (ed.), *Giovan Battista Gaulli, Il Baciccio*, Skira, Milan, 1999 (catalogue of exhibition held at the Palazzo Chigi, Ariccia, 1999). Olivesi, Jean-Marc (ed.), *Cieux en gloire*, exhibition catalogue, Musée Fesch, Ajaccio, 2002.

MUSEUMS AND GALLERIES:

AJACCIO (Mus. Fesch): *Apotheosis of St Peter* - AUSTIN (Jack S. Blanton MA, University of Texas): *Mercury Guiding the Spirit of Geography* (c. 1690) - FERMO (S Maria del Carmine): *Adoration of the Shepherds* (1687, oil on canvas) - FIASTRA (SS Paolo e Lorenzo): *Conversion of St Paul* (c. 1700, oil on canvas) - GENOA: *Jesus the Infant Saviour* - PARIS (Louvre): drawings - ROME (Palazzo Corsini): *Portrait of Pope Clement IX; Halt during the Flight into Egypt* - ROUEN: *Assumption of the Virgin* - VERSAILLES: *Portrait of Cardinal Bouillon* - VIENNA (Czernin): *Holy Family in a Landscape* - WORCESTER, MA (AM): *Vision of St Ignatius at La Storta* (c. 1684-1685, oil on canvas, model of the altar for the Church of Gesù).

AUCTION RECORDS:

PARIS, 1857, *First Thoughts; Angels Study* (two drawings for a ceiling) FRF 99. PARIS, 1895, *Fresco Study: St Michael Slaying the Dragon* (drawing with bistre wash) FRF 62. PARIS, 24 Nov 1924, *St Michael Slaying the Dragon* (pen and watercolour, heightened with white) FRF 310. PARIS, 4 July 1929, *Nativity* (drawing) FRF 160. MILAN, 23 Nov 1972, *Noah Giving Thanks to the Heavens; Adoration of the Golden Calf* (two canvases) ITL 110,000,000. LONDON, 23 March 1973, *Three Marys at Christ's Tomb*, Gns 6,500. LONDON, 5 Dec 1977, *Cherubim* (pen and wash, 11 1/4 x 17 ins / 28.4 x 43 cm) GBP 850. NEW YORK, June 1981, *St Elizabeth and the infant St John* (black chalk, pen and wash, 14 1/2 x 10 3/4 ins / 36.6 x 27.3 cm) GBP 2,200. LONDON, 6 April 1984, *St Agnes with the Holy Virgin, St John the Baptist and the Holy Trinity* (oil on canvas, 18 1/4 x 21 3/4 ins / 46.5 x 55.2 cm) GBP 4,600. MILAN, 27 Nov 1984, *Adoration of the Infant Jesus* (pen and wash, 8 x 9 3/4 ins / 20.4 x 24.8 cm) ITL 7,000,000. LONDON, 2 July 1985, *Adoration of the Shepherds* (black chalk, pen and wash heightened with white, 11 x 8 1/4 ins / 27.1 x 21.3 cm) GBP 24,000. LONDON, 10 Dec 1986, *Three Marys at the Sepulchre* (oil on canvas, 33 x 44 ins / 84 x 111.5 cm) GBP 46,000. MONTE CARLO, 20 June 1987, *Allegory of Truth and Other Figures (Study for a Decorative Ceiling)* (pen, brown ink and grey wash/black chalk, 10 3/4 x 16 ins / 27.5 x 40.9 cm) FRF 200,000. NEW YORK, 15 Jan 1988, *Portrait of a Young Priest* (oil on canvas, 28 x 22 1/2 ins / 71.1 x 57.2 cm) USD 8,800. ROME, 10 May 1988, *Rinaldo and Armida* (oil on canvas, 50 1/2 x 39 1/2 ins / 128.5 x 100.5 cm) ITL 24,000,000. MILAN, 1? June 1988, *Portrait of a Cardinal* (oil on canvas, 28 1/4 x 22 3/4 ins / 72 x 58 cm) ITL 5,000,000. NEW YORK, 8 Jan 1991, *Naked Slave with Hands Tied behind his Back and Head and Shoulders of an Old Man with Beard (Study)* (red chalk heightened with white, 11 x 14 1/2 ins / 28.2 x 37.1 cm) USD 16,500. LONDON, 2 July 1991, *Sacrifice of Isaac* (black chalk, ink and grey and brown wash, 12 1/2 x 9 1/4 ins / 31.7 x 23.2 cm) GBP 110,000. MONACO, 5-6 Dec 1991, *Male Portrait* (oil on canvas, 27 1/4 x 21 3/4 ins / 69.5 x 55.5 cm) FRF 111,000. NEW YORK, 13 Jan 1993, *Martyrdom of a Saintly King before a Church Entrance (St Edmund?)* (black chalk, ink and brown wash heightened with white, 10 1/4 x 7 3/4 ins / 26.2 x 20 cm) USD 30,800. PARIS, 11 March 1994, *Allegory* (pen and brown wash, 7 x 9 ins / 18 x 23 cm) FRF 10,000. MONACO, 20 June 1994, *Virgin and Child near a Bowl* (black chalk, ink and wash/cream paper, 15 x 10 1/4 ins / 37.2 x 26 cm) FRF 188,700. PARIS, 9 June 1995, *Apotheosis of Christ* (oil on canvas, oval, 25 1/2 x 19 ins / 64.5 x 48 cm) FRF 92,000. LONDON, 3 July 1995, *Virgin in Gloria Blessing a Crowd of Penitents* (ink/traces of black chalk, 9 x 65 3/4 ins / 22.8 x 167 cm) GBP 5,520. NEW YORK, 10 Jan 1996, *Bearded Man and Hands (Study); Female Head, Torso and Hand (Study; verso)* (red chalk/brown paper, 11 x 16 1/4 ins / 28 x 41 cm) USD 3,795. LONDON, 3 July 1996, *Moses Discovered* (ink and wash/traces of black chalk, 8 1/2 x 12 1/4 ins / 21.5 x 31 cm) GBP 12,650. PARIS, 20 Nov 1996, *Triumph of the Name of Jesus* (pen and brown ink, 16 1/2 x 11 ins / 42 x 27 cm) FRF 72,000. NEW YORK, 28 Jan 1999, *Adam and Eve Expelled from Paradise* (black chalk/pen/brown ink wash, 8 x 11 ins / 21 x 29 cm) USD 25,000. NEW YORK, 28 May 1999, *God the Father with the Body of Christ Surrounded by Angels* (oil on canvas, 21 x 29 ins / 53 x 74 cm) USD 85,000. NEW YORK, 28 Jan 2000, *Designs for Obverse of Medals* (black chalk/pen/brown ink/brown wash heightened with white, pair, 7 x 7 ins / 18 x 18 cm) USD 15,000. NEW YORK, 29 May 2001, *Bearded Nude Seated on a Rock in Profile* (red chalk heightened with white, 16 x 22 ins / 41 x 55 cm) USD 3,200. LONDON, 10 July 2002, *Study of a Kneeling Female Nude* (pen/ink/grey wash over black chalk, 13 x 9 ins / 33 x 24 cm) GBP 5,800. ROME, 30 March 2004, *Strength and Charity* (oil on canvas, 26 x 24 ins / 65 x 60 cm) EUR 80,000. LONDON, 7 July 2004, *Continence of Scipio* (oil on canvas/panel, 13 x 17 ins / 33 x 44 cm) GBP 60,000.

GAULLIER, Henri

French, 19th century.

Sculptor.

Together with the architect Lemesle, Henri Gaullier produced a Neo-Gothic altarpiece (1866) for the church of St-Martin in Tassillé, to which was added a terracotta low relief of unknown origin representing the *Adoration of the Shepherds*.

GAULME, Jacques
French, 20th century.
Born 9 July 1915, in Bizeneville (Allier).
Painter.
Jacques Gaulme exhibited in Paris at the Salon d'Automne and the Salon des Artistes Indépendants.

GAULOIS, Jules
French, 19th century.
Born 19th century, in Sablé.
Painter.
Pupil of Victor Bertin; exhibited views of Brittany and the Dauphiné at Paris Salons between 1848 and 1853.

GAULRAP, Erhard
Bohemian School, 16th century.
Born c. 1550; died c. 1580, in Prague.
Painter. Portraits.
Prague School.
Erhard Gaulrap worked mainly for Rudolph II and Maximilian II.

GAULT, Henri
French, 20th century.
Born 1920, in Anjou.
Painter. Military subjects, portraits, still-lifes, flowers.
Henri Gault studied at the École des Beaux-Arts and exhibited regularly in Paris at the Salon des Artistes Français and Salon des Artistes Indépendants, of which he is a member. He also exhibits at the Salon of the Société Nationale des Beaux-Arts.

GAULT DE SAINT-GERMAIN, Anna. See **RAJECKA Anna**

GAULT DE SAINT-GERMAIN, Pierre Marie
French, 18th - 19th century.
Born 9 February 1754, in Paris; died 11 November 1842, in Paris.
Painter.
Pierre Gault de Saint-Germain was a student of Durameau. From 1791 to 1801, he exhibited some good landscapes at the Salon: *Shepherds Guided by the Angel, St Jerome* (at the general hospital in Paris), *Assumption of the Virgin Mary* (in the church of St Julien in Domfront) and *Satyr and Passer-By* (produced for the king of Poland).
MUSEUMS AND GALLERIES:
CHARTRES: *Cascade of the River Dore.*

GAULTHIER. See also **GAULTIER, GAUTHIER, GAUTIER**

GAULTHIER, Germain, or Gautier
French, 16th - 17th century.
Born 1571, in Paris.
Painter, sculptor.
Germain Gaulthier was the son of Michel Gaultier and nephew of Germain Pilon. He journeyed to Tours (Indre-et-Loire) and while there, between 1594 and 1596, decorated the great hall of the town hall with the coats of arms of the first *échevin* (municipal magistrate), the lord of Lavallière, the mayor of Tours, and the lord of Candé Victor Brodeau. Moving to Orléans (Loiret), he was commissioned in 1599 to make a life-size statue of Henri IV that was placed above the large portal of the church of St-Salomon at Pithiviers.

GAULTIER. See also **GAULTHIER, GAUTHIER, GAUTIER**

GAULTIER, Antoine Charles
French, 18th century.
Active in Paris in 1784.
Painter, sculptor.

GAULTIER, Augustin
French, 18th century.
Active in Angers c. 1760.
Painter.
Augustin Gaultier worked for the church in Erigné.

GAULTIER, B. or Jean Baptiste, or Gautier
French, 17th century.
Active in the middle of the 17th century.
Engraver (burin), printer.
B. Gaultier produced engravings on religious themes. He was the brother of François Gaultier.

GAULTIER, Daniel. See **CRANE de, family of artists**

GAULTIER, François
French, 18th century.
Active in Paris.
Engraver.

GAULTIER, Gérard, or Gauthier
French, 16th century.
Born in St-Nicolas-de Port.
Active at the end of the 16th century.
Painter. History painting.
Gérard Gaultier was working at the ducal palace in Nancy (Meurthe-et-Moselle) in around 1593.

GAULTIER, J.
French, 17th century.
Engraver.
J. Gaultier may be related to Léonard Gaultier.

GAULTIER, Jacques
French, 16th century.
Active in Bordeaux in 1579.
Painter.
Jacques Gaultier was the official painter to the town of Bordeaux.

GAULTIER, Jean
French, 16th - 17th century.
Active in Bordeaux.
Painter.
The son of Jacques Gaultier, Jean succeeded his father as town painter.

GAULTIER, Leonard, or Golter
German, 16th - 17th century.
Born 1561, in Mainz; died 1641, in Paris.
Active in France.
Draughtsman, engraver (burin).
Although born in Germany, Léonard Gaultier is generally considered to be part of the French School. He came to Paris - probably when quite a young man - and seems to have become successful very rapidly. His style is reminiscent of that of Wierix, but more supple. He worked exclusively on burin engravings and produced a large number of works. The abbot of Marolles possessed more than 800 proofs by him, although some may have been duplicates. Gaultier was engraver to Henri III, Henri IV, Marie de' Medici and Louis III, all of whose portraits he engraved. He has also left images of many of the notable lords of the period. His engraving were generally made from his own drawings or after works by French and Italian artists.

GAULTIER, Michel
French, 16th century.
Active in Paris between 1585 and 1590.
Painter.

GAULTIER, Michel
French, 16th century.
Born c. 1537.

Active in Paris.
Sculptor.

In 1564 and 1565, Michel Gaultier was involved in carving the tomb of Henri II. He is thought to have worked in around 1558 for Catherine de' Medici on the decoration of her chateau at Montceaux-en-Brie. Gaultier married Noémie Piulon, sister of Germain Pilon.

GAULTIER, Nicolas
French, 16th - 17th century.
Born 1575, in Paris.
Engraver (burin).

Nicolas Gaultier engraved a series of plates illustrating episodes from the life of Henri IV. He may be the same person as Léonard Gaultier.

GAULTIER, Pierre Jacques
French, 18th century.
Born in Paris; died in Parma.
Active in Naples.
Engraver (burin).

A student of G. Galimard. He produced engravings on historical themes.

GAULTRON, Hippolyte Charles
French, 19th century.
Born 19th century, in St-Denis.
Painter.

Studied under Eugène Delacroix; exhibited landscapes and still-lifes at Paris Salons between 1848 and 1861.

GAUMAIN, Louis
French, 18th century.
Born 1676; died 14 April 1720.
Active in Marseilles.
Sculptor (wood).

Louis Gaumain worked for the church of St Maximin.

GAUME, Henri René
French, 19th century.
Born 17 May 1834, in Clamart (Seine).
Painter.

Submitted genre compositions to Paris Salons between 1866 and 1870.

AUCTION RECORDS:
PARIS, 7 and 8 March 1891, *Young Man*, FRF 70.

GAUME, Marie Madeleine
French, 19th century.
Born 19th century, in Versailles.
Painter.

Studied under Collin and Foulogne; exhibited still-lifes at the Salons of 1879 and 1880.

GAUME, Mélanie
French, 19th century.
Active in Besançon in 1832.
Enameller.

GAUMEL, Jean Alexandre
French, 19th century.
Born 19th century, in Paris.
Painter.

Studied under Flers and Brémond and exhibited watercolours at the Salon between 1875 and 1882.

MUSEUMS AND GALLERIES:
PONTOISE: *View of Follenville; Cam Sea off Honfleur* - RHEIMS: *View of Rheims.*

GAUMONT, Marcel
French, 20th century.
Born 27 January 1880, in Tours.
Sculptor. Religious subjects. Monuments.

Marcel Gaumont studied under Sicard and Coutan. In 1908 he was awarded the Prix de Rome, in 1935 a gold medal and in 1937 a Grand Prix at the International Exhibition in Paris. He was also awarded the Croix de Guerre. In 1925 he was made a Chevalier and in 1938 an Officier of the Légion d'Honneur.

He produced several monuments to the fallen, notably at the Lycée St-Louis in Paris, in Tours and in Laon. He also decorated numerous buildings including the Cambrai chamber of commerce, the Messageries Maritimes, châteaux and churches.

GAUMONT, Maria. See **GOMON**

GAUNES, Barthélemy de
French, 16th century.
Painter.

Barthélemy de Gaunes was involved in the preparations for the entry of Queen Eleonor into Lyons in 1533.

GAUNET, Pierart. See **GANNET**

GAUNT, Thomas Edward
British, 19th century.
Active in Tottenham (London).
Painter. Figures.

Thomas Edward Gaunt exhibited in London from 1876 to 1883, chiefly at the Suffolk Street Gallery but occasionally at the Royal Academy.

GAUNT, William
British, 20th century.
Born 5 July 1900; died 1980.
Painter.

William Gaunt studied at the Westminster School of Art. He was an art critic and writer as well as a painter. He exhibited in London at the Royal Academy, the Redfern Gallery and the Lefevre Gallery.

GAUNTLETT, Gertrude E. (Miss)
British, 19th century.
Active in London.
Painter. Genre scenes.

Gertrude E. Gauntlett was a regular exhibitor in London at the Suffolk Street Gallery from 1866 to 1880, and also exhibited on one occasion at the Royal Academy.

GAUPILLAT, Henry
French, 19th century.
Painter.

Member of the Société des Artistes Français from 1883.

GAUPILLAT, Jeanne
Maiden name: Boure
French, 19th century.
Active in Paris.
Painter, engraver.

Member of the Société des Artistes Français from 1887.

GAUPILLAT, Jenny
Maiden name: Cheilley
French, 19th century.
Died 1892.
Sculptor.

Exhibited at the Salon from 1884 to 1891.

GAUPMANN, Rudolf
Austrian, 19th century.
Born 20 March 1815, in Vienna; died 1 November 1877, in Graz.
Painter, lithographer. Portraits.

Gaupmann was a pupil at the academy in Vienna and mainly painted watercolours and miniatures.

GAUPP, Gustav Adolf
German, 19th century.
Born 19 September 1844, in Markgröningen.
Painter, engraver. History painting, portraits, genre scenes.

Gaupp studied at the art school in Stuttgart under Gnauth. In 1870 he went to the art academy in Munich. In 1873 he became a pupil of Karl von Piloty, and settled in Stuttgart from 1876 onwards. He exhibited in Berlin, Munich and Bremen from 1876 until 1890.

MUSEUMS AND GALLERIES:

STRASBOURG: *Scene in a Cloister* - STUTTGART: *Cardinal Playing Chess; Hans Richter.*

AUCTION RECORDS:

ZURICH, 9 Nov 1983, *Elegant Scene* (1893, oil on canvas, 39 1/4 x 28 1/4 ins / 100 x 72 cm) CHF 15,000. STUTTGART, 4 Dec 1998, *Studio* (oil on canvas, 39 x 28 ins / 99 x 70 cm) DEM 9,000. ZURICH, 21 March 2001, *Standing Woman with Bowl of Fruit* (1879, oil on canvas, 43 x 30 ins / 109 x 77 cm) CHF 7,500. STUTTGART, 26 April 2004, *Girl by Fence* (1905, oil on canvas, 48 x 33 ins / 121 x 84 cm) EUR 6,500.

GAUQUIÉ, Henri Désiré

French, 19th - 20th century.

Born 16 January 1858, in Flers-les-Lille; died 1927, in Paris.

Sculptor, medallist. Busts, monuments.

Henri Gauquié studied under Cavelier. In 1881 he exhibited in Paris at the Salon des Artistes Français, showing a bust and, in 1882, a medallion. In 1895 he was awarded the Salon's grand medal. He received a bronze medal and a travel bursary in 1886, a bronze medal at the Exposition Universelle of 1889 in Paris, a silver medal in 1890 and silver medal in 1900. In 1900 he was made a Chevalier of the Légion d'Honneur and produced a bronze statue of Alexander the Great for the Benedictine monastery of Fécamp.

AUCTION RECORDS:

COLOGNE, 18 March 1983, *The Struggle for Life* (bronze, h. 25 1/2 ins / 65 cm) DEM 3,500. LOKEREN, 18 Oct 1986, *Nilvertuti Invium* (1900, grey-green patinated bronze, h. 35 ins / 88 cm) BEF 380,000. NEW YORK, 18-19 July 1996, *Vae Victis* (bronze, h. 15 ins / 38 cm) USD 3,450.

GAURET, Adolphe

French, 20th century.

Active in Toulouse.

Painter.

Adolphe Gauret became a member of the Société des Artistes Français in 1902.

GAUSACHS ARMENGOL, José, or Josep

Spanish, 20th century.

Born 1891, in Barcelona.

Painter. Landscapes, seascapes.

José Gausachs Armengol studied at the Barcelona academy where he was taught decorative composition by Felix Mestres. He travelled in France and the USA and was a teacher of fine arts in Santo Domingo. He took part in many group exhibitions including those organised by the Barcelona school of fine arts.

BIBLIOGRAPHY:

Arnáiz, José Manuel/López Jiménez, Javier/Merchán Díaz, Manuel (ed.), *'Cien años de pintura en Espana y Portugal (1830-1930)'* in vol. III, Antiqvaria, Madrid, 1989.

MUSEUMS AND GALLERIES:

BARCELONA (MAM del Mus. Nacional d'Art de Catalunya).

AUCTION RECORDS:

TORQUAY, 16 June 1980, *Seascape* (oil on canvas, 20 x 16 1/4 ins / 51 x 41 cm) ESP 38,000.

GAUSE, Wilhelm

German, 19th - 20th century.

Born 27 March 1853, in Krefeld; died 1916, in Stein an der Donau, Lower Austria.

Painter, draughtsman. Genre scenes.

Wilhelm Gause studied at the Düsseldorf academy. He exhibited in Vienna in 1888. He is best known for *Race at Friedenau.*

AUCTION RECORDS:

VIENNA, 22 June 1976, *Ball at Court* (oil on canvas in grisaille, 14 1/2 x 19 1/4 ins / 37 x 49 cm) ATS 18,000. MUNICH, 22 June 1993, *Emperor Franz Joseph I Hunting* (1910, oil on canvas, a pair, each 24 3/4 x 35 ins / 63 x 89 cm) DEM 11,500. NEW YORK, 23 May 1997, *At the 1881 Salon* (oil on paper/canvas, in grisaille, 8 1/4 x 12 1/4 ins / 21 x 31.1 cm) USD 28,750.

GAUSSEL

French, 18th century.

Active in Montpellier in 1779.

Painter, draughtsman.

Gaussel was a professor at the Société des Beaux-Arts in Montpellier.

GAUSSEN, Adolphe Louis

French, 19th - 20th century.

Born 12 May 1871, in Marseilles; died 1954.

Painter. Urban landscapes, landscapes, waterscapes, seascapes.

Adolphe Gaussen studied painting at the École des Beaux-Arts in Marseilles and later at the studio of Jean-Baptiste Olive. He spent some time in Paris and exhibited in the city from 1893 at the Salon des Artistes Français, of which he became a member, and at the Salon de la Société Coloniale at the École des Beaux-Arts. He also held numerous solo exhibitions. He was appointed official painter to the naval department and curator of the Musée Cantini in Marseilles. He was made an Officier of the Légion d'Honneur.

He produced only landscapes and found his inspiration in the ports of the Mediterranean, the sea shores and various picturesque spots in the region of Provence; his work was strongly inspired by a love of nature on both land and sea. His numerous works include: *Porquerolles, The Mont-Rose Cliff near Marseilles, Entrance to the Port of La Joliette, Marseilles* and *L'Argade, Bay of St-Tropez.*

AL. Gaussen

MUSEUMS AND GALLERIES:

AIX-EN-PROVENCE (Mus. Granet) - AMSTERDAM - ARLES - BEAUNE - DIGNE-LES-BAINS - MARSEILLES - NEW YORK - NÎMES - PARIS (Mus. du Petit Palais) - TOULON - TROYES.

AUCTION RECORDS:

PARIS, 11 Feb 1921, *Entrance to the Port of La Joliette, Marseilles,* FRF 250. PARIS, 29 Oct 1921, *The Cathedral, Les Martigues,* FRF 950. PARIS, 24 Nov 1922, *L'Argade, Bay of St-Tropez,* FRF 580. PARIS, 30 Dec 1925, *The Mont-Rose Cliff, near Marseilles,* FRF 430. PARIS, 13 March 1926, *Shores of the Mediterranean,* FRF 200. PARIS, 24 March 1930, *Iles d'Hyères, Porquerolles,* FRF 410. PARIS, 26 Feb 1934, *View of La Corniche,* FRF 210. PARIS, 9 Oct 1942, *Côte d'Azur Landscape,* FRF 920. PARIS, 28 Jan 1943, *Sea Shore,* FRF 1,900. PARIS, 4 Dec 1944, *Porquerolles,* FRF 4,100. VERSAILLES, 13 Dec 1987, *Rocks Overlooking the Sea* (oil on canvas, 19 3/4 x 25 1/2 ins / 50 x 65 cm) FRF 17,500. PARIS, 27 Nov 1989, *Fishermen on the Shore* (oil on panel, 12 1/2 x 16 1/4 ins / 32 x 41 cm) FRF 9,000. BRUSSELS, 19 Dec 1989, *View of the Bosphorus* (oil on canvas, 14 1/2 x 18 1/2 ins / 37 x 47 cm) BEF 75,000. MONTREAL, 30 April 1990, *The Coast Road, Marseilles* (oil on panel, 15 x 18 ins / 38 x 46 cm) CAD 2,860. PARIS, 6 Feb 1991, *Port of La Joliette, Marseilles* (oil on canvas, 19 3/4 x 25 1/2 ins / 50 x 65 cm) FRF 15,500. PARIS, 24 May 1991, *Equinoctial Storm in Provence* (oil on canvas, 19 3/4 x 25 1/2 ins / 50 x 65 cm) FRF 10,000. PARIS, 26 June 1995, *Landscape of the South of France* (oil on canvas, 32 x 39 1/4 ins / 81 x 100 cm) FRF 27,500. PARIS, 29 Nov 1996, *Port of Marseilles* (oil on canvas, 19 3/4 x 25 1/2 ins / 50 x 65 cm) FRF

13,000. ZURICH, 7 Dec 1999, *Marseilles Harbour* (oil on canvas, 13 x 16 ins / 33 x 41 cm) CHF 2,600. CALAIS, 12 March 2000, *View of Marseilles Harbour* (oil on panel, 13 x 16 ins / 33 x 41 cm) FRF 26,000. LYONS, 10 June 2001, *Still-life with Fruit. Still-life with Faience* (oil on canvas, a pair, 15 x 22 ins / 38 x 55 cm) FRF 22,000. PARIS, 27 Oct 2001, *Seaside* (oil on canvas, 24 x 32 ins / 60 x 81 cm) FRF 56,000. BERN, 16 May 2002, *Marseilles Harbour* (oil on panel, 15 x 18 ins / 38 x 46 cm) CHF 3,800. PARIS, 26 March 2003, *Quays in Marseilles* (oil on panel, 13 x 16 ins / 32 x 40 cm) EUR 4,200. NEUILLY, 27 June 2003, *La Ciotat* (oil on canvas, 24 x 32 ins / 60 x 81 cm) EUR 6,000. LONDON, 8 April 2004, *The Quays* (oil on canvas, 18 x 22 ins / 46 x 55 cm) GBP 3,800.

GAUSSEN, Louis
Swiss, 19th century.
Born c. 1829.
Painter.

Gaussen was a pupil of Louis Mesmet. He exhibited in Geneva in 1861.

GAUSSEN-SALMON, Jacqueline
French, 20th century.
Died September 1948; as the result of an accident.
Painter. Scenes with figures, landscapes with figures, village views.

Jacqueline Gaussen-Salmon studied in Paris at the École Nationale des Beaux-Arts and exhibited there at the Salon des Artistes Français, Salon d'Hiver and Salon des Indépendants. An exhibition of her paintings was held in 2003 at the Espace Lawrence Durrel in Sommières, the town where she lived and worked.

In an article on Sommières, Jacky Vilacèque writes: 'There is a grace in her early paintings, gravity in the portraits of women she often produced, and a heaviness in the elaborate canvases of her final period' (Le Monde, 21 June 2003).

BIBLIOGRAPHY:

Gaussen, Frédéric (ed.), *Jacqueline Gaussen Salmon. Catalogue raisonné de l' œuvre peint*, Les Editions du Cardinal, Paris, 1998. Gaussen, Frédéric (preface), *Les visages de la réalité: Jacqueline Gaussen Salmon, Jacques Bollo*, exhibition catalogue, Espace Lawrence Durrell, Sommières, 2003.

AUCTION RECORDS:

PARIS, 9 June 1988, *Sea Shore* (oil on panel, 12 3/4 x 16 1/4 ins / 32.5 x 41 cm) FRF 3,600.

GAUSSER, Max
American, 19th century.
Born 1857.
Painter.

AUCTION RECORDS:

NEW YORK, 25 Oct 1834, *Ship Plans*, USD 350. NEW YORK, 25 Jan 1935, *The Cup that Comforts*, USD 35.

GAUSSON, Léo Marie
French, 19th - 20th century.
Born 14 February 1860, in Lagny-sur-Marne; died 27 October 1944, in Lagny-sur-Marne.
Painter, watercolourist, draughtsman, engraver, sculptor, medallist. Landscapes.

Léo Gausson began studying wood sculpture and then trained in engraving under Chauvel. He became a member of the Neo-Impressionists along with Signac, Maximilien Luce and Pissarro. At this period he received advice from Luce and Pissarro, who influenced his work. Around 1890 he moved in literary circles and associated particularly with Gustave Kahn and Adolphe Retté, whose poems he illustrated. He also played an active part in organising the first Lagny Salons. Later, in 1901, perhaps disheartened, he joined the civil service and was posted to Guinea. He painted in Brittany from 1910 to 1914.

A genuinely talented colourist, he produced fine, picturesque engravings of reproductions copied after Millet's *The Gleaners* and *First Steps*. He also executed a medallion portrait of Millet. Around 1890 his style developed towards that of the Synthetists.

From 1887 to 1895 he exhibited at the Salon des Indépendants in Paris; in 1892 he was invited with Luce, Pissarro and Toulouse-Lautrec to exhibit at the *Groupe des Vingt* exhibition in Brussels. His work has often been shown at exhibitions on the Neo-Impressionists: in 1968, *Neo-impressionism* at the Guggenheim Museum in New York; in 1978 at the Musée Maximilien-Luce, Mantes-la-Jolie; in 1985 at the Musée Camille-Pissarro, Pontoise; and in 1987-1988 at the Fondation Septentrion, Marcq-en-Barœul. During his life he showed his work in solo exhibitions: in 1896 at the Galerie Lafitte in Paris; in 1899 a retrospective at the Théâtre Antoine in Paris; and in 1988 at the Musée Municipal Gatien-Bonnet in Lagny-sur-Marne.

BIBLIOGRAPHY:

Léo Gausson, exhibition catalogue, Musée municipal Gatien-Bonnet, Lagny-sur-Marne, 1988. Hanotelle, Micheline, *'Le Néo-Impressionnisme dans l'œuvre de Léo Gausson'* in *Gazette des Beaux-Arts* n° 63, periodical, Paris, 1989. Hanotelle, Micheline, *'Léo Gausson et Zola'* in *Les Cahiers naturalistes* n° 63, periodical, 1989. Thornton, Lynne, *Les Africanistes, peintres voyageurs*, ACR, Paris, 1990. Coret, Noël, *Les Peintres de la vallée de la Marne*, Casterman, Paris, 1996. Hanotelle, Micheline, *Léo Gausson, 1860-1944: un peintre méconnu du Post-impressionisme*, Presses universitaires du Septentrion, Villeneuve d'Ascq, 2001.

MUSEUMS AND GALLERIES:

AMSTERDAM (Van Gogh Mus.): *Le Clocher de Bussy-St-Georges (Bussy-St-Georges Bell Tower)* (1886) - GENEVA (Petit Palais): *Les Voiliers (Sailing Ships)* (1887); *Des maisons, soleil de juillet (Houses, July Sunshine)* (1886) - INDIANAPOLIS (MA): *Barges on the Marne at Lagny* (c. 1888) - LAGNY-SUR-MARNE (Mus. Gatien-Bonnet) - PARIS (Mus. d'Orsay): *Chemin bordé d'un mur (Road with a Wall running alongside)* (1886).

AUCTION RECORDS:

PARIS, 7-8 Dec 1928, *Farm Buildings Standing on the Edge of a Meadow*, FRF 450. PARIS, 21 April 1943, *Road*, FRF 150. PARIS, 12 July 1961, *Red Structure*, FRF 4,100. VERSAILLES, 26 June 1968, *Triel-sur-Seine* FRF 13,000. PARIS, 21 March 1974, *Trees in a Landscape*, FRF 7,000. LONDON, 8 Dec 1977, *Eragny Bell Tower* (1891, oil on canvas, 13 3/4 x 11 ins / 35 x 27 cm) GBP 1,200. PARIS, 3 Dec 1979, *Sad House* (1893, watercolour, gouache and charcoal, 9 3/4 x 12 1/2 ins / 25 x 32 cm) FRF 6,500. MUNICH, 30 May 1980, *Path in a Park* (1897, watercolour, 12 1/2 x 9 1/2 ins / 32 x 24 cm) DEM 1,370. LONDON, 30 March 1982, *On the Edge of the Wood* (oil on canvas, 18 x 15 ins / 46 x 38 cm) GBP 400. LONDON, 7 Dec 1983, *Estuary in Brittany* (c. 1890, oil on canvas, 29 1/2 x 29 1/4 ins / 75 x 74 cm) GBP 13,000. ENGHIEN-LES-BAINS, 25 June 1987, *Brittany Landscape* (1891, oil on canvas, 22 x 18 ins / 55 x 46 cm) FRF 155,000. PARIS, 10 Feb 1988, *On the Brittany Coast at Perros-Guirec* (watercolour, 9 1/4 x 12 1/2 ins / 23.5 x 31.5 cm) FRF 2,600. PARIS, 20 Nov 1988, *The Mill* (1899, oil on canvas, 15 x 18 ins / 38 x 46 cm) FRF 45,000. PARIS, 11 March 1990, *Country Road* (oil on canvas/card, 17 3/4 x 12 1/2 ins / 45 x 32 cm) FRF 18,000. PARIS, 22 Nov 1990, *Village by a River* (oil on canvas, 11 x 15 3/4 ins / 28 x 40 cm) FRF 100,000. PARIS, 6 April 1993, *Village* (1889, oil on canvas, 9 1/2 x 13 ins / 24 x 33 cm) FRF 28,000. LONDON, 28 June 1994, *House by a River* (oil on canvas, 23 1/2 x 39 1/4 ins / 60 x 100 cm) GBP 17,250. PARIS, 7 Dec 1994, *Trees in a Landscape* (oil on panel, 10 1/2 x 13 3/4 ins / 26.5 x 35 cm) FRF 5,000. PARIS, 28 Nov 1995, *Landscape with Millstones* (1895, oil on card, 10 1/2 x 13 3/4 ins / 26.5 x 35 cm) FRF 7,100. PARIS, 25 May 1997, *Landscape outside Lagny* (c. 1887-1889, oil on canvas, 9 x 11 1/2 ins / 23 x 29 cm) FRF 77,000. PARIS, 20 March 1998, *Trees* (1891, coloured pencil and charcoal, 9 1/2 x 12 ins / 24 x 30.5 cm) FRF 4,200.

LONDON, 20 Oct 1999, *Peasant Woman in the Street* (oil on canvas, 22 x 15 ins / 55 x 38 cm) GBP 2,600. TOULOUSE, 3 Oct 2000, *Pont des Arts* (oil on canvas, 13 x 18 ins / 33 x 46 cm) FRF 71,000. CALAIS, 10 Dec 2000, *Harvest* (oil on canvas, 15 x 24 ins / 39 x 60 cm) FRF 27,000. LONDON, 6 Feb 2001, *Pont des Arts* (c. 1890-1891, oil on canvas, 13 x 18 ins / 33 x 46 cm) GBP 15,000. PONTOISE, 19 May 2001, *Path in the Park* (oil on canvas, 18 x 26 ins / 46 x 65 cm) FRF 18,000. PARIS, 11 Oct 2002, *Landscape* (c. 1890, oil on card, 6 x 9 ins / 16 x 23 cm) EUR 2,000. PARIS, 11 Oct 2002, *Winding Path* (oil on panel, 11 x 14 ins / 27 x 35 cm) EUR 2,800. LONDON, 22 Oct 2003, *Haystacks* (oil on canvas, 13 x 18 ins / 33 x 46 cm) GBP 6,500. LONDON, 24 March 2004, *Road Through the Village of Thorigny, near Lagny* (1888, oil on canvas, 15 x 18 ins / 38 x 46 cm) GBP 5,000. PARIS, 7 April 2004, *Country Path* (1889, coloured crayons and pastel, 8 x 13 ins / 21 x 34 cm) EUR 2,700.

GAUSSOT, Geneviève Marie
French, 20th century.
Born in Belfort.
Sculptor.

Geneviève Gaussot exhibited at the Paris Salon from 1929.

GAUT, Justinien or Justin
French, 19th century.
Born 1817, in Aix-en-Provence; died 1880, in Aix-en-Provence.
Painter. Scenes with figures.

Justinien Gaut showed some of his paintings at the group exhibition *Au fil de l'eau. École Provençale* (*Going with the Flow: The Provencal School*) at the Musée des Tapisseries in Aix-en-Provence, 2000.

MUSEUMS AND GALLERIES:
AIX-EN-PROVENCE: *Scene with Troubadours* - AIX-EN-PROVENCE (Mus. Granet): *Scène de troubadours dans un parc* (*Scene with Troubadours in a Park*) (oil on canvas).

GAUTADOTTIR, Nina
Icelandic, 20th century.
Active in France.
Sculptor.

Nina Gautadottir studied painting and sculpture at the school of fine arts in Paris until 1977. She then began working with textiles. She has taken part in group exhibitions including in 1974 at the Centre Culturel in Pontoise, the 1975 Salon d'Automne in Paris, 1976 and 1977 at the Salon des Artistes Français in Paris, 1977 at the American Cultural Centre in Paris and 1980 at the Salon Comparaisons in Paris. She has also had solo shows including 1980 at the Museum of Contemporary Art in Reykjavik, 1983 at the Franco-Nigerian Cultural Centre in Niamey, 1983 at Listmunahusid in Reykjavik and 1984 at La Grande Masse des Beaux-Arts in Paris. From 1981 to 1983, she lived in Nigeria and discovered the possibilities of working with leather.

Her works highlight the properties of the materials she uses. Dyed skins in natural shapes, strongly three-dimensional, with hollows and reliefs, make play with light and shade. These are suspended and stretched out in space by a collection of thin strings. These works, which can almost be described as installations, give an impression of baroque archaism.

GAUTERI, Pierre, real name: St-Paulet, Marquis of
French, 19th - 20th century.
Born in Carpentras (Vaucluse).
Painter. Genre scenes.

Pierre Gauteri studied under Kuwasseg.

MUSEUMS AND GALLERIES:
AVIGNON: *The Fisherman's House, Beaulieu.*

GAUTHERET, Henri
French, 20th - 21st century.
Born 1953.
Active in Dijon.
Sculptor.

Henri Gautheret exhibited his stone and granite sculptures, simple forms aspiring to the monumental, at the Salon des Nouvelles Réalités in Paris in the 1980s and 1990s.

GAUTHERIN, Georgette
French, 20th century.
Born 10 April 1886, in Chablis; died October 1973, in Annay-sur-Serein.
Painter. Landscapes, still-lifes.

Georgette Gautherin studied under René His and Louis Willaume. She exhibited in Paris from 1921 to 1930 at the Salon des Artistes Français and the Salon de l'École Française.

She was a friend of Michel Kikoine and spent time with Morgan Russell in the village of Annay-sur-Serein, where he lived from 1923 to 1946.

GAUTHERIN, Jacques
French, 20th century.
Born 1929.
Painter (gouache). Genre scenes, figures, landscapes, seascapes.

AUCTION RECORDS:
VERSAILLES, 18 Dec 1982, *The Petunia Border* (oil on canvas, 28¾ x 23½ ins / 73 x 60 cm) FRF 3,700. RAMBOUILLET, 16 Feb 1986, *The Pleasures of Sailing at Vermouillet* (oil on canvas, 28¾ x 36¼ ins / 73 x 92 cm) FRF 19,500. VERSAILLES, 15 May 1988, *The Gondolier* (1960, oil on canvas, 18 x 24 ins / 46 x 61 cm) FRF 8,500. VERSAILLES, 6 Nov 1988, *Field of Corn with Poppies* (1958, gouache and diluted oil paint/mounted paper/canvas, 18 x 24 ins / 46 x 61 cm) FRF 8,000. VERSAILLES, 20 June 1989, *Antibes* (1959, oil on card, 18 x 22 ins / 46 x 55 cm) FRF 11,000. VERSAILLES, 25 March 1990, *Jockeys Mounting* (1958, oil/hardboard, 23½ x 28¾ ins / 60 x 73 cm) FRF 22,500. PARIS, 26 March 1990, *Dinghies and Sailing Boats, L'Esclade* (1959, oil on canvas, 21¼ x 25½ ins / 54 x 65 cm) FRF 27,000. CALAIS, 8 July 1990, *Village View* (oil on canvas, 18 x 23¼ ins / 46 x 59 cm) FRF 19,500. PARIS, 16 Oct 1994, *Antibes from the Cape* (1959, oil on canvas, 18 x 22 ins / 46 x 55 cm) FRF 18,000. PARIS, 5 Feb 1998, *The Port of Nice* (oil/card, 13 x 16¼ ins / 33 x 41 cm) FRF 2,200. BRUSSELS, 14 Feb 2000, *Clotilde* (brown patinated bronze, h. 27 ins / 68 cm) BEF 120,000.

GAUTHERIN, Jean
French, 19th century.
Born 28 December 1840, in Ouroux (Rhône); died 21 July 1890, in Paris.
Sculptor. Busts, statues, monuments.

Enrolled at the École des Beaux-Arts in Paris and studied there under Gumery and A. Dumont; exhibited at the Paris Salon from 1865 and was a medal winner in 1868, 1870 and 1873. Gautherin was made a Chevalier of the Légion d'Honneur in 1878. He is remembered for his *Statue of Diderot* for the Place St-Germain-des-Prés in Paris.

MUSEUMS AND GALLERIES:
BORDEAUX: *Awakening* - LYONS: *Bust of Paul Chenevard* - NANCY: *Project for a Monument to Claude Gellée* - PARIS (MAM): *Bust of a Woman* - PARIS (Mus. d'Orsay): *Bust of Mme Gumery, née Emilia de Madeiros* - PARIS (Mus. du Petit Palais): *Paradise Lost* - TOULON: *French Republic.*

AUCTION RECORDS:
NEW YORK, 15 June 1985, *Young Peasant Woman* (brownish green patinated bronze, h. 34½ ins / 87.6 cm) USD 1,100. ANTWERP, 19 Feb 2001, *The Blandan Soldier* (sculpture, brown patinated bronze, h. 31 ins / 80 cm) BEF 75,000. BETHESDA, 7 Feb 2004, *Head of Jesus* (sculpture, red brown-patinated bronze, h. 13 ins / 32 cm) USD 2,500.

GAUTHERON, Émile Xavier
French, 19th - 20th century.
Born 29 October 1871, in Frangy (Saône-et-Loire).

Painter, watercolourist. Landscapes.

Émile Gautheron studied in Lyons under André Perrachon and in Le Puy. He exhibited in Lyons from 1895, showing some oil paintings but mainly watercolours.

GAUTHEROT, Claude

French, 18th century.

Born 1729, in Paris; died 1802, in Paris.

Sculptor, potter.

Claude Gautherot started in sculpture and achieved some success with figure modelling. As quartermaster to the Duchesse de Lauraguais, he was posted to the military office during the Revolution. From 1770-1780, the same era as Jean-Baptiste Nini, he worked at the earthenware factory established at Chaumont-sur-Loire by Le Ray. He was the father of Pierre Gautherot. The attribution of busts or medallions of *Voltaire, Jean-Jacques Rousseau, Turgot, Bailly* and *Gluck* to him is likely to stem from a confusion with the works of Nini, unless there were copies made by him.

GAUTHEROT, Pierre, erroneously known as Claude

French, 18th - 19th century.

Born 1765 or 1769, in Paris; died July 1825, in Paris.

Painter. History painting, mythological subjects, portraits.

Pierre was the son of Claude Gautherot, with whom he has often been confused. He entered David's studio in 1787 and, under the patronage of the master, who had become his friend, opened a school, which turned out excellent pupils.

In 1820, he was the editor and one of the contributors to *Galerie française - ou Collection des portraits des hommes et des femmes qui ont illustré la France dans les XVIe, XVIIe et XVIIIe siècles* (*The French Gallery - or A Collection of Portraits of Men and Women Who Have Illustrated France in the 16th, 17th and 18th Centuries*). His daughter, Uranie, married one of his students, Pierre Roch Vigneron.

He took part in the Louvre exhibitions from 1793 to 1824. By 1793, he had already obtained his first medal. His subjects were mainly drawn from mythology, episodes from the Napoleonic era and numerous portraits of figures of the day, many of which are preserved in French museums.

Museums and Galleries:

Angers: *Venus Vaccinated by Aesculapius* (1824) - Auxerre: *Baron Fourrier* - Bagnères-de-Bigorre: *Constantine Exhorting His Son to Clemency* (1804); *Heroism of Mlle Cazotte Rescuing Her Father* (1817); *Naked Woman* - Chambéry (MBA): *Study for Apollo; Study for Orpheus* - Melun: *Pyramus and Thisbe* (1799) - Versailles: *Napoleon Haranguing His Troops at Lech, 12 October 1805* (1808); *Portrait of Count Étienne Portalis; Napoleon Wounded before Regensburg* (1810); *Portrait of Maréchal Davout.*

Auction Records:

London, 26 March 1928, *Woman*, GBP 94. London, 3 July 1980, *Maréchal Davout with a Landscape Background* (oil on canvas, 80 3/4 x 51 1/4 ins / 205 x 130 cm) FRF 17,000.

GAUTHIER

French, 18th century.

Painter.

Gauthier painted porcelain for the Manufacture Nationale de Sèvres around 1790.

GAUTHIER. See also **GAUTIER, GAULTIER, GAULTHIER**

GAUTHIER, A.

French, 17th - 18th century.

From the Périgord region.

Painter.

Gauthier worked in Bordeaux, and later in Paris.

GAUTHIER, Albert Jacques Edmond

French, 20th century.

Born 1903, in Saumur.

Painter.

Albert Gauthier exhibited regularly at the Salon of the Société Nationale des Beaux-Arts in Paris.

GAUTHIER, Antoine

French, 19th century.

Born in Louhans (Saône-et-Loire).

Sculptor.

Honourable mention in 1896.

GAUTHIER, Charles

French, 19th century.

Born 7 December 1831, in Chauvirey-le-Châtel; died 5 January 1891, in Paris.

Sculptor.

Enrolled at the École des Beaux-Arts on 6 April 1854 and studied under Jouffroy. Charles Gauthier was awarded silver at the 1861 Prix de Rome and received further medal awards in 1865, 1866 and 1869. He was made a Chevalier of the Légion d'Honneur in 1872. Gauthier exhibited at the Salon from 1859 to 1882. He is remembered for a bronze *Charlemagne* for the main altar of the collegiate church of St-Quentin; a plaster statue of *Our Lady of Humility* for the church at Argenteuil; a stone statue of *St Matthew* for the Church of the Trinity; and an allegorical statue entitled *Moderation* for the foyer of the Paris Opera House.

Museums and Galleries:

Besançon: *Claude de Jouffroy* - Limoges: *Poacher; Angel Sounding a Trumpet* - Saumur: *Shipwreck Scene* - Vire: *St Sebastian.*

GAUTHIER, Charles Gabriel

French, 19th century.

Born 29 April 1802, in Tonnerre; died 1858, in Paris.

Painter. Genre scenes, animals.

Enrolled at the École des Beaux-Arts on 7 March 1818, where he studied under Callot and Abel de Pujol; exhibited landscapes with figures, animal paintings and genre compositions at the Paris Salon between 1827 and 1848.

GAUTHIER, Charles Michel

French, 18th century.

Active in Paris in 1772.

Painter, sculptor.

GAUTHIER, Claude

Monegasque, 20th century.

Born 19 July 1939, in Neuilly-sur-Seine.

Painter. Local scenes, landscapes.

Claude Gauthier worked as a police officer and has lived in Monaco from 1964. As a painter he is self-taught. His work is characterised by two main aspects: a draughtsmanship which he himself describes as stylised in its depiction of buildings, plants and figures; and a palette of striking and varied colours which he lavishly applies in the boldest juxtapositions. With rare exceptions he paints views of the Côte d'Azur, the town and monuments of Monaco, traditional celebrations and, in particular, the annual Festival du Cirque.

He has taken part in group exhibitions, notably those presented by the Comité National Monégasque des Arts Plastiques in Belgrade in 1977, in New Orleans in 1984, in Andorra in 1985, Ostend in 1986 and Crespano, Italy in 1988. Since 1975 he has exhibited at the annual Salon of the Comité National Monegasque d'Arts Plastiques. From 1970 to 1984 he took part in the Grand Prix International d'Art Contemporain de la Principauté. He has taken part in the exhibitions of the Musée International d'Art Naif in Nice since 1982. Since 1970 he has held many solo exhibitions, mainly in Monaco and in towns on the Côte d'Azur and also at the town hall of the 13th district of Paris in 1994 where he was guest of honour of the Salon Interministériel.

Museums and Galleries:

Holstebro: *View of Monaco* - Nice (Mus. International d'Art Naïf Anatole-Jakovsky): *The Festival du Cirque, Monaco* (1977) - Vicq (Mus. International d'Art Naïf): *View of the Rocher de Monaco*.

GAUTHIER, Didier

French, 16th century.
Active in Dôle (Jura) c. 1550.
Glass painter.

GAUTHIER, Dominique

French, 20th - 21st century.
Born 1 August 1953, in Paris.
Active in Assas (Hérault).
Painter.

Dominique Gauthier trained at the École des Beaux-Arts in Paris before going to the École des Beaux-Arts in Marseilles where he met the painters of the Supports-Surfaces group. He taught at the École des Beaux-Arts in Montpellier (1979-1993), the École des Beaux-Arts in Cergy (1993-2000) and the École des Beaux-Arts in Paris (from 2000).

Initially attracted by Abstract art, Gauthier developed Stella-like, highly coloured compositions out of fragmented shapes which, in the 1980s, would form the background in his *Operas* series, where he introduced dramatic scenes involving fighters, shipwrecks, citations, nude men, friezes, vegetation and skulls. In a later phase, he returned to Abstraction and dispensed with figures, but the Baroque aspect of his work still remains. Gauthier lets the paint run and develop into relief and geometric shapes, and also includes pieces of wood and metal which appear to be escaping from the canvas.

He participated in many group exhibitions, including the following: the Salon de Mai in Paris (1976); *Impact III* at the Musée d'Art et d'Industrie in St-Étienne (1978); the Venice Biennale (1980); at the CAPC Musée d'Art Contemporain in Bordeaux (1980); the New Delhi Biennale (1982); at the Fundació Joan Miró in Barcelona (1982); *France, une Nouvelle Génération* (*France, a New Generation*) at the town hall in Paris (1984); and at the Fondation Cartier in Jouy-en-Josas (1987).

Solo exhibitions include those at the following: the ADDA gallery association in Marseilles (1978); the CAPC Musée d'Art Contemporain in Bordeaux (1979); the Musée National d'Art Moderne in Paris (1982); the Galerie Daniel Templon in Paris (1984); the Galerie Interface in Nîmes (1990); Crédac, the Centre d'Art in Ivry-sur Seine, the Musée d'Art Moderne in Céret (also in 2001) and the Musée Bossuet in Meaux (1993); the Musée d'Art Moderne in Collioure (1996); and *Aller au Plus Court, Longuement, C'est-à-dire Partout* (*The Longest Way to the Short Cut*), five solo exhibitions presenting Gauthier's work at the Centre Regional d'Art Contemporain (CRAC) in Altkirch (2000).

Bibliography:

Michaud, Yves, *Dominique Gauthier*, exhibition catalogue, Abbaye de Sénanque, Gordes, 1981. Stoulig, Claire/Fourcade, Dominique, *Dominique Gauthier*, exhibition catalogue, Musée national d'Art moderne, Éd. du Centre Georges-Pompidou, Paris, 1982. Van Doren, Madeleine/Arnaudies, Jacques/Collins, George R./Partouche, Marc, *Dominique Gauthier, peinture et dessins*, exhibition catalogue, Crédac centre d'Art contemporain, Ivry-sur-Seine, 1992. Ardenne, Paul, *Art. L'Âge contemporain. Une histoire des arts plastiques à la fin du XXe siècle*, Éd. du Regard, Paris, 1997. Michaud, Yves/Valabrèghe, Frédéric, *Dominique Gauthier*, monograph, Éd. du Regard, Paris, 2001. Goumarre, Laurent, '*Dominique Gauthier. La Mécanique du reflet. Interview*' in *Art Press*, no. 270, p 39, periodical, Paris, July-August 2001.

Museums and Galleries:

Bordeaux (FRAC Aquitaine) - Carquefou (FRAC Pays de la Loire) - Marseilles (FRAC Provence-Alpes-Côte d'Azur) - Marseilles (Mus. Cantini): *Opera, Word and Soul* (1985) - Montpellier (FRAC Languedoc-Roussillon) - Paris (FNAC): *Gardens after Auschwitz No. VI* (1988) - Paris (MNAM-CCI) - Toulouse (FRAC Midi-Pyrénées).

Auction records:

Paris, 8 Oct 1989, *Opus I* (1987, oil on canvas, 36 1/4 x 27 1/2 ins / 92 x 70 cm) FRF 4,000.

GAUTHIER, Étienne

French, 16th century.
Born to a family originally from Besançon (Doubs).
Sculptor (wood).

Working with Mathieu Vigneron in 1585, Étienne Gauthier completed a monumental altarpiece for the church of St-Pierre in Dôle, where it can still be seen. This work, set within twined pillars, consists of a central panel with a carved crucifixion and four niches containing the statues of Saints Peter, Paul, Sebastian and Jerome. The cornice, supported by four columns, included a carving of God the Father surrounded by angels and foliage.

GAUTHIER, François Henri

French, 19th century.
Born 4 January 1868, in Paris.
Painter, architect.

Remembered for his *Portraits of Women* and *Views of Belle-Isle*.

Museums and Galleries:

Toulouse (MBA, Mus. des Augustins): *Landscape at Leguivy*.

GAUTHIER, Frédéric

French, 19th century.
Born 14 January 1860, in Cherbourg; died in Valognes.
Painter (porcelain), miniaturist. Portraits.

Museums and Galleries:

Cherbourg: *Portrait of J.-F. Millet* (miniature/porcelain); *Portrait of Marie Rapenel* (miniature/ivory).

GAUTHIER, Jean

Flemish School, 15th century.
Active in Lille in 1452.
Painter.

GAUTHIER, Jean

French, 16th century.
Sculptor.

Jean Gauthier was commissioned, along with another sculptor, Jacques Desfloques, to make a crucifix for a church near Pontoise (Val-d'Oise).

GAUTHIER, Jean

French, 17th century.
Active in Ornans c. 1657.
Sculptor.

GAUTHIER, Jean

French, 18th century.
Active in Dôle c. 1718.
Sculptor (wood).

Jean Gauthier sculpted an altarpiece for the church of Notre-Dame in Parisot.

GAUTHIER, Jean-Marc

French, 20th - 21st century.
Born 28 July 1963, in Paris.
Painter. Figures.
Figuration Libre.

Jean-Marc Gauthier began training as a painter in 1976. In 1983 he worked with M. Journiac on body art and studied sculpture with A Garzon. He paints in the primitive, loosely Figurative style typical of the 1980s. His brightly coloured, ramshackle figures get into all sorts of misadventures. *Cheap Wine Charmer, A Foot in the Grave* and *In-laws* are good examples.

In 1984, 1985 and 1989 he exhibited at the Salon de la Jeune Peinture in Paris. Since then, he has shown his work regularly in group exhibitions in France and elsewhere, notably at the International Fair of Contemporary Art in Barcelona (1990) and at the Salon d'Art Contemporain in Rouen (1991). He has also exhibited solo since 1988, notably at the Galerie L'Œil du Boeuf in Paris.

Auction records:

Paris, 20 Nov 1988, *Family* (mixed media/wood, 47 x 48 1/4 ins / 119.5 x 122.5 cm) FRF 6,500. Paris, 9 April 1989, *Skaters* (1988, mixed media/panel, 47 1/4 x 35 1/2 ins / 120 x 90 cm) FRF 5,000. Paris, 18 June 1989, *Café Waiters' Race, or Curriculum Vitae* (1989, mixed media/panel, 39 1/4 x 59 ins / 100 x 150 cm) FRF 7,000. Les Andelys, 19 Nov 1989, *Couple* (oil on wood, 32 3/4 x 48 ins / 83.5 x 122 cm) FRF 5,000. Paris, 26 April 1990, *The Unsustainable Lightness of Being* (oil on panel, 39 3/4 x 30 ins / 101 x 76 cm) FRF 5,500. Paris, 10 June 1990, *Cramps* (oil on panel, 39 3/4 x 30 ins / 101 x 76 cm) FRF 5,000.

GAUTHIER, Joseph

French, 20th century.
Born in Carcassonne.
Painter, sculptor.

Joseph Gauthier began exhibiting at the Salon des Artistes Français in Paris in 1925.

GAUTHIER, Léon Ambroise

French, 19th century.
Born 8 November 1822, in Paris; died 1901.
Painter. Portraits, genre scenes, landscapes.

Enrolled at the École des Beaux-Arts on 8 April 1841 and studied under Picot; exhibited at the Paris Salon from 1844 to 1879 and received an honourable mention in 1863.

Bibliography:

Wilson-Bareau, Juliet, '*The Portrait of Ambroise Adam by Edouard Manet*' in *Burlington-Magazine,* vol 126, no. 981, 1984.

Auction records:

Versailles, 4 Oct 1982, *Rustic Scene* (oil on canvas, 12 1/2 x 13 1/2 ins / 32 x 34.5 cm) FRF 11,000.

GAUTHIER, Louis Joseph

French, 18th century.
Active in Paris in 1772.
Painter, sculptor.

GAUTHIER, Marie

French, 19th - 20th century.
Born in Lyons.
Painter.

Marie Gauthier studied with Toller. In 1889 she began to exhibit portraits, figures, genre and flower paintings in oils, watercolours and pastels in Lyons.

GAUTHIER, Oscar

French, 20th century.
Born 7 September 1921, in Fours.
Painter (including gouache).
Nouvelle Figuration.

Oscar Gauthier studied at the École des Beaux-Arts in Paris 1941-1947 and at the same time attended the studio of Othon Friesz at the Académie de la Grande Chaumière. In 1948, after a period in the USA, he made the acquaintance of Sonia Delaunay, Albert Gleizes, Francis Picabia, and Hans Hartung and of younger artists like Jean Atlan and Corneille.

Gauthier was one of the first young post-war painters to discover the possibilities of abstraction. He produced abstract structured action paintings, in which facets of bright colour are laid on, often with a knife, and hang suspended in the links of a chequerboard composition. Around 1960 he painted a series of canvases where the lavishly coloured abstract action painting makes no attempt at concealing the humour of a floral composition. Then came a questioning period when he adopted the narrative style of the strip cartoons introduced into Europe by American Pop Art. From *The Class Dolly* of 1962 to the 1965 *Let's Go to the Moon,* Gauthier gently mocked pop artists' passion for strip cartoons while laughing at his own work as well. From 1965 to 1969, he took his themes from the music hall, from theatres and the circus, representing their movements by an interpenetrating dance of points and circles. He then returned in *Botanographies* to a style of action painting enhanced by subtle techniques: the imprints of real leaves or their negative outlines airbrushed in, so as to stress the pleasant plant motifs. Around 1985, when fashion and the market had discovered the appeal of 1950s abstract art, two developments occurred: a large number of his abstract paintings reappeared, and he returned to this style, producing a long series of paintings consisting of bands of brilliant and contrasting colour brushed on in parallel and obliquely from top to bottom of the canvas and from left to right.

Oscar Gauthier began exhibiting in 1944, 1945 and 1946 at the Salon des Moins de Trente Ans in Paris, and later showed work in many salons in Paris, and in collective exhibitions including: Salon d'Octobre (1952-1953); *Jeune Peinture en France,* a travelling exhibition in Germany (1955); the Salon des Réalités Nouvelles, of which he was a committee member until the late 1970s (regularly from 1955); *Cinquante ans de peinture abstraite* organised in Paris by Michel Seuphor (1957); *Nouvelle École de Paris* organised by Roger van Gindertael in Mannheim (1958); 1961 São Paulo Biennale; Salon d'Automne, where he was a member of the committee (regularly from 1962); *L'art français contemporain* Belgrade and Zagreb (1963); *La figuration narrative* organised in Paris by G. Gassiot-Talabot (1965); *L'âge du jazz* Musée Galliera, Paris (1967); *Une aventure de l'art abstrait* an itinerant exhibition staged by Michel Ragon touring in several museums in France (1967-1968); Salon de Mars, Paris (1989, 1990, 1991); FIAC (Foire Internationale d'Art Contemporain), Paris (1989). Solo exhibitions include: Galerie Arnaud, then Galerie R. Cazenave, Paris (1952-1958); Galerie Arnoux, Paris (from 1987); Palace of Fine Art, Brussels (1956); Frankfort (1961); Athenaeum Museum, Geneva (1966); centre for art and leisure, Sochaux (1986). He also painted open-air works: *Dragonfly Paradise,* mural for the technical Lycée, St-Quentin (1962); mosaic, classical Lycée, Maubeuge (1964-1968); mosaic, technical Lycée, Vitry-le-François (1970). Oscar Gauthier was awarded the Lissone prize in Milan (1957).

OSCAR GAUTHIER

Bibliography:

Van Gindertael, Roger, *Oscar Gauthier,* Cazenave, Paris, 1960. Grenier, Jean, *Entretiens avec dix-sept peintres non-figuratifs,* Calmann-Lévy, Paris, 1963. Harambourg, Lydia, *Oscar Gauthier,* Gal. Arnoux, La Différence, Paris, 1987. Persin, Patrick-Gilles, '*Oscar Gauthier*' in *Cimaise* n° 200, periodical, Paris, summer 1989. *Oscar Gauthier,* exhibition catalogue, Pérouges, 1991.

Museums and Galleries:

Paris (MAMVP) - Paris (MNAM-CCI).

Auction records:

Paris, 24 April 1983, *Composition* (1953, gouache, 12 1/2 x 19 3/4 ins / 32 x 50 cm) FRF 5,000. Paris, 14 Oct 1984, *Grouse* (1957, oil on canvas, 19 3/4 x 59 ins / 50 x 150 cm) FRF 13,000. Paris, 9 April 1987, *Composition* (1954, oil on canvas, 46 x 28 1/4 ins / 116 x 72 cm) FRF 70,100. Paris, 22 April 1988, *Composition* (1958, oil on canvas, 46 x 35 ins / 116 x 89 cm) FRF 19,000. Paris, 1 June 1988, *Composition* (1954, gouache, 17 3/4 x 12 1/2 ins / 45 x 32 cm) FRF 5,600. Paris, 15 June 1988, *Com-*

position (1952, watercolour and gouache, 13 1/2 x 18 3/4 ins / 34.5 x 47.5 cm) FRF 7,000. NEUILLY, 20 June 1988, *Untitled* (1948, crumpled paper, 27 1/2 x 22 ins / 70 x 55 cm) FRF 8,000. PARIS, 20-21 June 1988, *Composition* (oil on canvas, 32 x 51 1/4 ins / 81 x 130 cm) FRF 38,000. PARIS, 16 Oct 1988, *Abstract Composition* (1948, oil on kraft paper, 19 x 12 1/4 ins / 48 x 31 cm) FRF 12,000. NEUILLY, 22 Nov 1988, *Composition* (1958, oil on canvas, 46 x 35 ins / 116 x 89 cm) FRF 47,000. PARIS, 4 June 1989, *Coloured Composition* (1958) FRF 122,000. NEUILLY, 6 June 1989, *Composition* (1953, oil on canvas, 24 x 19 3/4 ins / 61 x 50 cm) FRF 71,000. PARIS, 23 June 1989, *Composition* (1948, gouache, 19 3/4 x 12 1/2 ins / 50 x 32 cm) FRF 16,000. PARIS, 29 Sept 1989, *Composition* (gouache, 12 1/2 x 19 3/4 ins / 32 x 50 cm) FRF 14,000. PARIS, 8 Oct 1989, *Abstraction* (oil on canvas, 32 x 25 1/2 ins / 81 x 65 cm) FRF 120,000. PARIS, 9 Oct 1989, *Composition* (1948, oil on canvas, 28 3/4 x 36 1/4 ins / 73 x 92 cm) FRF 100,000. PARIS, 12 Feb 1990, *Untitled* (gouache/paper, 19 1/4 x 12 1/4 ins / 49 x 31 cm) FRF 10,000. PARIS, 25 April 1990, *Composition* (1948, oil on canvas, 18 x 23 1/2 ins / 46 x 60 cm) FRF 70,000. PARIS, 2 July 1990, *Untitled* (oil on canvas, 36 1/4 x 28 1/4 ins / 92 x 72 cm) FRF 64,000. LONDON, 18 Oct 1990, *Untitled* (1953, oil on canvas, 28 3/4 x 36 1/4 ins / 73 x 92 cm) GBP 3,850. PARIS, 12 Dec 1990, *Composition* (1958, oil on canvas, 45 1/2 x 35 ins / 115.5 x 89 cm) FRF 58,000. PARIS, 9 July 1992, *Composition* (gouache, 19 1/4 x 12 1/4 ins / 49 x 31 cm) FRF 7,500. PARIS, 24 Oct 1993, *Composition* (1950, oil on canvas, 28 3/4 x 36 1/4 ins / 73 x 92 cm) FRF 16,000. PARIS, 10 Feb 1994, *Composition* (1948, oil on canvas, 36 1/2 x 25 1/2 ins / 93 x 65 cm) FRF 40,000. LOKEREN, 10 Dec 1994, *Composition* (1961, oil on panel, 28 3/4 x 21 1/4 ins / 73 x 54 cm) BEF 28,000. PARIS, 7 Oct 1995, *Composition 34* (1954, oil on canvas, 28 1/4 x 21 1/4 ins / 72 x 54 cm) FRF 11,000. PARIS, 24 March 1996, *Composition* (oil on canvas, 25 1/2 x 21 1/4 ins / 65 x 54 cm) FRF 8,000. PARIS, 29 April 1997, *Composition* (oil on canvas, 23 1/2 x 36 1/4 ins / 60 x 92 cm) FRF 10,500. PARIS, 27 Oct 1997, *Composition* (1948, gouache, 12 1/2 x 19 ins / 32 x 48 cm) FRF 5,000. PARIS, 22 March 1998, *Painting* (1921, oil on canvas, 34 1/4 x 46 ins / 87 x 116 cm) FRF 10,000. PARIS, 26 April 2001, *Untitled, Blue Background* (oil on canvas, 36 x 29 ins / 92 x 73 cm) FRF 36,000. PARIS, 26 April 2001, *Untitled* (oil on canvas, 24 x 47 ins / 60 x 120 cm) FRF 37,000. PARIS, 29 March 2002, *Composition* (1953, oil on canvas, 46 x 29 ins / 116 x 73 cm) EUR 4,500. PARIS, 19 June 2002, *Composition* (1959, oil on canvas, 46 x 35 ins / 116 x 89 cm) EUR 3,000. VERSAILLES, 14 Dec 2003, *Composition* (oil on canvas, 36 x 29 ins / 92 x 73 cm) EUR 2,200. VERSAILLES, 14 Dec 2003, *Composition* (oil on canvas, 46 x 35 ins / 116 x 89 cm) EUR 3,400. PARIS, 29 June 2004, *Composition* (oil on canvas, 36 x 24 ins / 92 x 60 cm) EUR 6,600. NEUILLY, 23 Sept 2004, *Composition* (oil on canvas, 32 x 26 ins / 81 x 65 cm) EUR 3,400.

GAUTHIER, Philippe Eugène
French, 18th century.
Active in Paris in 1761.
Painter, sculptor.

Probably the same as Philippe Gautier.

GAUTHIER, Pierre. See **GAUTHIER-DUBÉDAT**

GAUTHIER, Zina
Russian, 20th century.
Born in Kazan; died 1930, in Paris.
Active and naturalised in France.
Painter, engraver. Urban landscapes. Designs for tapestries.

Zina Gauthier studied at the academy in Moscow. She executed a tapestry cartoon for the Manufacture Nationale de Beauvais and also painted the picturesque quality of the outskirts of Paris with emotion on small canvases. She exhibited regularly from 1923 in Paris at the Salon des Artistes Indépendants, the Salon d'Automne and, by invitation, at the Salon des Tuileries.

GAUTHIER DE CAMPE. See **CAMPE Gauthier de**

GAUTHIER-CHARTRETTE, Agnès
French, 20th - 21st century.
Born 11 July 1955, in Paris.
Engraver, lithographer.

Agnès Gauthier-Chartrette was a student at the École des Beaux-Arts in Paris. She received her diploma in engraving in 1980. She took up a teaching post in engraving at the Ateliers Beaux-Arts de la Ville de Paris (municipal fine arts studios) in 1988.

Gauthier-Chartrette makes exclusively black and white etchings on copper, a practice which Jean Signovert maintains reflects the true essence of engraving and to which Gauthier-Chartrette appears to be adhering. Her range of tones runs from the very pale to the white and from the very dark to the black; the range of middle grey tones is absent. The core of her work is the result of a trip made to Egypt in 1988 and consists of 30 engravings produced over a period of four years. The series meanders between Figurative depictions of deserts, water and architectural elements, such as columns, and Abstraction. Following the series, Gauthier-Chartrette moved more towards Abstraction as she increasingly focused on the actual malleable properties of her medium. Figurative elements are faint reminders of something that can be seen or perhaps sensed and serve to humanise her otherwise rigorously Abstract compositions.

She started showing work in group exhibitions in 1982 at the École des Beaux-Arts in Paris, and then at the following: the Salon d'Automne in Paris, of which she became a member in 1987 (1986); the Salon de la Jeune Gravure Contemporaine in Paris (1987-1991); *Le Mois de l'Estampe* (*Month of the Print*) in Créteil (1990); Poland and Nîmes (1992); the Fondation Laurent-Vibert in Lourmarin, from which she received grants in 1993 and 1994 (1993); the Salon des Arts Graphiques (SAGA) in Paris (1993); Prague and the Salon Le Trait in Paris (1994); the Salon de l'Estampe in Rueil (1995); *Ateliers d'Artistes du VIe* (*Artists' Studios of the Sixth Arrondissement*) in Paris (1995); the Salon Le Trait in Paris and the Salon d'Automne in Nancy (1996); *Journées Portes Ouvertes du XIVe* (*Open Days at the XIVth Arrondissement*) in Paris (1996, 1997); the second Egyptian International Print Triennale in Cairo (1997); and *Portes* (*Doors*) at the Galerie Michèle Broutta in Paris (1997).

Gauthier-Chartrette has also had solo exhibitions of her print work, including at the Centre Culturel of Ville-d'Avray in 1987, *30 Eaux-fortes Égyptiennes* (*30 Egyptian Etchings*) at the Centre Culturel Égyptien in Paris in 1994, and *Eaux-Fortes: Égypte, Rome et de Natura* (*Etchings: Egypt, Rome and Nature*) at the Centre Culturel Égyptien in Paris in 1998. In 1999 she was awarded the Prix Jeune Gravure (Young Engravers' Prize) at the Salon d'Automne in Paris.

GAUTHIER-DUBÉDAT, Pierre, or Gauthier
French, 20th century.
Born 21 January 1938, in Bordeaux.
Painter, engraver, draughtsman, watercolourist, illustrator. Landscapes.

From 1938 to 1952, Pierre Gauthier-Dubédat lived in Bayonne, where he studied painting and drawing with Louis-Frédéric Dupuis at the École des Beaux-Arts from 1950 to 1952. He went on to train at the École des Beaux-Arts de Versailles from 1952 to 1955 and from 1955 to 1964 studied at the École Nationale Supérieure des Beaux-Arts in Paris, with Maurice Brianchon for painting and Pierre-Eugène Clairin for lithography. He then worked at Friedlaender's studio from 1966 to 1967. He taught engraving and lithography at the fine arts faculty of the university of Damascus from 1968 to 1974. He then lived in Madrid from 1974 to 1981 where, alongside his activities as an artist, he was artistic director of the Almodóvar Bibliophile publishing house. He returned to France in 1981, living in Burgundy until 1995 and then in the Basque Country. He was awarded the Lions Club prize in 1955, the École des Beaux-Arts de Lyons Prix Chenavard and the gold medal of the Salon d'Hiver.

In his early period in the 1950s and 1960s, Gauthier-Dubédat's work came quite close to Expressionism, with its violent action and sombre palette. From the 1970s landscape began to dominate in a style that could be described as lyrical abstraction were it not for the fact that the elements of nature depicted always remain recognisable. His compositions are firmly structured and sustained by the interplay of colour, line, shade and light. Marina Gauthier-Dudébat describes his work thus: 'Always and above all else lyrical, though Pierre Gauthier-Dudébat's art may sometimes recall that of Nicolas de Staël, Soulages or Vieira da Silva, it is only a remote resemblance as it is too strongly marked by its own definite and unique character to be subject to any determining influence. At times it may bear a strong and surprising similarity to Expressionist Futurism with its unstable rocky and geometric structures that appear to collapse upon us'. Gauthier-Dudébat also produced six engravings to illustrate *El Rayo de Luna* by G. A. Bécquer (published by Almodóvar).

He has taken part in group exhibitions since 1962, notably: in 1967 at Camden Arts Centre, London; in 1986 at the Salon de Mai, Paris; 1988, the first world Triennale of small format engraving in Chamalières; 1989 at the Franco-Norwegian Centre in Stavinger; and in 1997 at the Musée de Guéthary. He has also shown his work in solo exhibitions in France and other countries (particularly Spain): in 1962 at the Maison des Beaux-Arts in Paris; in 1971 at the Alliance Française in Lima; in 1971 at the Hispanic cultural centre, Damascus; in 1973 at the Arab cultural centre, Damascus; in 1976 at the Caja de Ahorros de Madrid; in 1982 at the Musée des Ursulines, Mâcon; in 1985 at the Galería Tórcilo, Madrid; in 1989 at the Atelier du Puits de l'Orme, Paris; in 1992 at the Galerie Martine Namy-Caulier, Paris; and in 2000 at the Musée Saraguilenea, Guéthary.

MUSEUMS AND GALLERIES:
BAYONNE (Bibliothèque municipale) - CHAMALIÈRES (MAC) - DAMASCUS (National Mus.) - MÂCON (Bibliothèque Municipale) - MÂCON (Mus. des Ursulines) - MADRID (Biblioteca Nacional) - MADRID (Instituto Cervantes) - PARIS (BNF, Prints Collection) - PARIS (FNAC) - VILLAFAMÉS (Mus. Popular de Arte Contemporáneo).

GAUTHON, Pierre or Peyre
French, 14th century.
Active in Montpellier c. 1380.
Painter. Historical subjects. Ornaments.

Pierre Gauthon was nominated six times as consul.

GAUTIER
French, 14th century.
Painter.

Gautier worked at Troyes Cathedral (Aube) in around 1384.

GAUTIER, or Gaultier
French, 15th century.
Born in Paris.
Sculptor.

This artist went to Troyes (Aube), where he worked between 1419 and 1435.

GAUTIER
French, 16th century.
Painter. Portraits.

Siret says that the name of this painter is mentioned in the lines written beneath an old portrait dating from around 1499. The reference may be to one of the Gauthiers discussed above.

GAUTIER
French, 17th century.
Sculptor (wood).

Gautier sculpted two decorative figures for the Trianon apartments in 1688 and 1689.

GAUTIER
French, 18th century.
Active in London.
Painter. Landscapes.

Exhibited at the Royal Academy in 1792.

GAUTIER. See also **GAUTHIER, GAULTIER, GAULTHIER**

GAUTIER, Albert Clément Valéry
French, 19th - 20th century.
Died 1938.
Painter. Portraits, genre scenes, local scenes.

A.C.V. Gautier lived in Lille. He began exhibiting his oriental paintings at the Paris Salon in 1878.

AUCTION RECORDS:
PARIS, 8 Dec 1976, *The Tribe Departs* (oil on panel, 10 1/4 x 13 3/4 ins / 26 x 35 cm) FRF 4,300. RUMBEKE, 20-23 May 1997, *View of a Town in Normandy* (oil on panel, 9 1/4 x 12 3/4 ins / 23.5 x 32.6 cm) BEF 41,950. BRUSSELS, 19 April 2004, *View of Constantinople* (oil on canvas, diptych, 9 x 13 ins / 23 x 33 cm) EUR 2,000.

GAUTIER, Armand Désiré, sometimes Aman, called (le) peintre des Sœurs de charité
French, 19th century.
Born 19 June 1825, in Lille; died 29 January 1894, in Paris.
Painter, watercolourist, pastellist, lithographer. History painting, religious subjects, portraits, genre scenes, landscapes, still-lifes.

Enrolled at the École des Beaux-Arts in Paris on 8 April 1852, where he studied under Léon Cogniet; exhibited at the Paris Salon from 1853, receiving an honourable mention in 1887. To the extent that Armand Gautier was a friend of Eugène Boudin and that several of his canvases featured in the sale of Camille Pissarro's private collection, one may assume that he belonged to the Impressionist group. He is remembered above all as the painter of the Sisters of Charity, whom he portrayed in pale, almost black-and-white colours and against an austere background.

MUSEUMS AND GALLERIES:
CAEN: *Still-life; Ironing* - LILLE: *National Guard Upholding the Constitution; Sisters of Charity; Self-portrait; In the Bath; Musotte; Cast-net Fishing; Portrait du Docteur Gachet* - NIORT: *Poor Mother!* - NIORT (Petit Palais): *Madwoman* - PARIS (MAM): *Portrait of a Young Diva* - PARIS (Mus. d'Orsay): *Mother and Daughter* - RHEIMS: *Sister of Charity Watering Flowers* - ROCHEFORT: *Skate* - ST-DENIS (MAH): *Henri Rochefort in his Cell at Mazas Prison* - TOULOUSE (MBA, Mus. des Augustins): *Portrait du Poete Armand Silvestre* - TOURCOING: *Far from the City*.

AUCTION RECORDS:
PARIS, 1883, *Sister of Charity Cooking*, FRF 920. PARIS, 1890, *Morning Walk* (watercolour) FRF 25. PARIS, 1899, *Still-life*

with Pears and Apples, FRF 150; Dessert, FRF 175. Paris, 16 and 17 Dec 1919, *Mother Hen at Ecouen*, FRF 160. Paris, 28 Nov 1928, *Landscape with River in a Storm* (pastel) FRF 1,600. Paris, 7 and 8 Dec 1928, *Background Study for 'Poor Mother' (cliff by the sea)* (pastel) FRF 400; *Peasant Dwelling in a Winter Landscape* (pastel) FRF 650. London, 8 June 1983, *Still-life with Fish and Vegetables* (oil on canvas, 17 x 28 1/4 ins / 43 x 72 cm) GBP 400. Göteborg, 18 May 1989, *Garden* (1884, oil on canvas, 22 x 15 1/4 ins / 55 x 39 cm) SEK 6,500. London, 26 Sept 2001, *Still-life* (oil on canvas, 20 x 28 ins / 51 x 70 cm) GBP 1,700. New York, 7 Oct 2003, *Nuns* (oil on panel, 13 x 9 ins / 33 x 23 cm) USD 1,900.

GAUTIER, Charles Albert
French, 19th century.
Born 20 May 1846, in Paris.
Painter, architect.

Painted landscapes and watercolour views.

GAUTIER, Élisabeth
French, 17th - 18th century.
Painter. Portraits.

GAUTIER, Émile
French, 20th century.
Born 27 September 1920, in St-Nazaire.
Painter.

Émile Gautier, a figurative painter influenced by impressionism, exhibited at the Salon des Artistes Français in Paris.

GAUTIER, Étienne
French, 18th century.
Born c. 1732; died 25 December 1789.
Engraver.

GAUTIER, Étienne
French, 19th century.
Born March 1842, in Marseilles; died 6 February 1903, in Paris.
Painter.

Studied in Lyons under J. Chatigny before settling in Paris around 1860. Travelled to study classical painting in Italy, Germany and the Low Countries. He made his Paris Salon début in 1867 with *The Money Changer* (Rouen Museum) and *Study*, and went on to exhibit at subsequent Salons with *St Sebastian* (1869), *St George* (1873; silver medal; Lyons Museum), *Portrait of a Man* (1875), and *St Cecilia* (1878, gold medal; Musée du Luxembourg). He stopped painting after 1878 and devoted his time to architecture and charitable works. He was decorated in 1871 for distinguished services during the 1870 war. His output was sporadic: a *Virgin of the Baldachin* painted in 1873 is to be found in Lyons Museum, while other canvases and sketches have remained in his family, including a *St Jerome*, two versions of a *Rose Crucifixion*, *Japonaises*, *St Hubert* and *Little Girl with a Parrot* and *Young Tobias*. He signed his work either *E. Gautier* or *Et. Gautier*.

Museums and Galleries:

Lyons: *St George; Virgin of the Baldachin* (1873) - Paris (former Mus. du Luxembourg): *St Cecilia* - Roanne (MBA): *The Money Changer*.

GAUTIER, Eugénie
French, 19th century.
Born 19th century, in Paris.
Painter.

Pupil of Belloc; exhibited examples of her portrait work at the Paris Salon from 1834 to 1869, receiving a bronze medal in 1839 and a silver in 1845.

GAUTIER, Firmin
French, 19th century.
Born 1838, in Grenoble; died 1877.
Painter. Religious subjects, portraits, genre scenes.

Studied under Hébert and Cabanel and exhibited at the Paris Salon from 1866 to 1877.

Museums and Galleries:

Chambéry (MBA): *Head of Woman* - Grenoble: *Holy Family; Studio Interior; Open-Air Concert*.

GAUTIER, François
French, 19th century.
Born 19th century, in Marseilles.
Painter.

Exhibited views of Marseilles and genre compositions at the Paris Salon between 1866 and 1870.

GAUTIER, Gabriel
French, 18th century.
Active in Paris c. 1740.
Sculptor.

GAUTIER, Gérard
French, 18th century.
Born 14 January 1723, in Château-Porcien; died 9 September 1795, in Château-Porcien.
Sculptor. Figures, portraits.

Sent to Rome in 1746 as a stone lathe operator, he was noticed by the Abbot Hachette-Desportes, Bishop of Sidon and Grand Archdeacon of Rheims. Through his influence, Gérard Gautier entered Falconet's studio to study sculpture.

Museums and Galleries:

Troyes: *Pallas; The Abbot of Chauvelin*.

Auction records:

London, 9 April 1979, *Marie-Antoinette and the Dauphin* (1773, terracotta, h. 13 ins / 33 cm) GBP 1,400.

GAUTIER, J. B.
French, 19th century.
Active in Paris at the beginning of the 19th century.
Engraver (burin).

GAUTIER, Jacques
French, 19th century.
Born 13 December 1831, in Paris.
Sculptor.

Pupil of Rude; exhibited at the Paris Salon from 1855 to 1868.

GAUTIER, Jacques
French, 19th century.
Born 19th century, in Châtelet.
Sculptor.

Salon exhibitor from 1870 to 1874.

GAUTIER, Jacques Joseph
French, 18th century.
Active in Paris in 1785.
Painter (?), sculptor (?).

GAUTIER, Jean Fabien, the Elder, or Gauthier
French, 18th century.
Born 1747, in Paris.
Painter, engraver. Portraits.

The eldest son and pupil of Jacques Gautier d'Agoty, Jean Fabien, probably assisted his father as his brothers did. His personality is discernable only in a few portraits - most notably those of Louis XV and Cardinal Fleury - and in some engravings of anatomy and natural history.

GAUTIER, Jean François
French, 18th century.
Active in Paris in 1751.
Painter, sculptor.

GAUTIER, Jean Rodolphe
Swiss, 18th - 19th century.
Born 20 January 1764, in Geneva; died 1820, in Paris.
Painter, enameller.

Jean Gautier was first apprenticed to the painter and enameller J.-F. Favre in 1784, but quickly gained an interest in

painting and left for Italy. After 1789 Gautier sent three Italian landscapes from Rome to the Geneva exhibition. Gautier settled in Paris in around 1793 and lived there until his death. He exhibited landscapes at the Salon from 1793 and his works were still referred to in the 1817 Salon. He is also credited with a number of paintings of military scenes, numerous pencil drawings, sepias and watercolours.
MUSEUMS AND GALLERIES:
NANTES (MBA): *Seascape (View of the Port of Genoa)* - VERSAILLES: *Coastal Army Reunited close to Boulogne; Battle for the Bridge of Chiusella; Passage of French Artillery under the Fort of Bard.*
AUCTION RECORDS:
PARIS, 15 May 1950, *Portrait of a Young Boy* (enamel) FRF 51,000. PARIS, 8 March 2000, *View of the Port in Marseille* (watercolour, 14 x 21 ins / 35 x 54 cm) FRF 25,000. LONDON, 25 May 2004, *Girl in White Dress with Brown Plaited Hair* (enamel on copper, miniature, h. 2ins / 6cm) GBP 3,800.

GAUTIER, Jules Claude
French, 19th - 20th century.
Painter. Portraits, genre scenes.
Jules Claude Gautier showed work at the Société des Artistes Français in Paris, and became a member in 1885.
AUCTION RECORDS:
LONDON, 1 May 1908, *The Marriage Contract,* GBP 23. PARIS, 10 Nov 1920, *At the Artist's,* FRF 125. BERN, 12 May 1990, *Portrait of a Young Woman* (oil on canvas, 20 x 11 1/2 ins / 50.5 x 29.5 cm) CHF 2,200.

GAUTIER, Léon
French, 18th century.
Painter, sculptor.
Worked in Paris in 1738.

GAUTIER, Léon
French, 19th century.
Painter. Nudes, portraits, genre scenes.
AUCTION RECORDS:
PARIS, 4 Dec 1991, *Nude Dancer* (oil on canvas, 25 1/2 x 21 1/4 ins / 65 x 54 cm) FRF 5,500. NEW YORK, 16 Feb 1993, *Elegant Young Woman Seated* (oil on canvas, 31 1/2 x 25 1/4 ins / 80 x 64.1 cm) USD 2,420.

GAUTIER, Louis
French, 18th century.
Active in Paris in 1785.
Painter, sculptor.

GAUTIER, Louis Adolphe
French, 19th century.
Born 19th century, in Paris.
Engraver.
Pupil of Jazet; exhibited at the Salon from 1847 to 1876.

GAUTIER, Louis François Léon
French, 19th - 20th century.
Born 10 October 1855, in Aix-en-Provence; died 1947, in Aix-en-Provence.
Painter, designer. Portraits, landscapes. Murals.
Funded by a grant from the municipality of Aix-en-Provence, Louis Gautier studied in Paris under Alexandre Cabanel from 1880 to 1884. He painted a number of portraits, including one of *Corot,* but specialised in views of the Vaucluse region, Languedoc and Lubéron. His precise and detailed landscapes, painted in a delicate range of colours, earned him the nickname of 'the landscape Meissonier' He also painted murals for the town hall and theatre in Aix-en-Provence.

Louis Gautier showed work at the Salon des Artistes Français in Paris, and also at the Marseilles Salon and in various collective exhibitions in Montpellier, Avignon and Aix-en-Provence. His work featured in themed collective exhibitions, including *Au fil de l'eau. École Provençale (Flowing Water, Provençale School)* at the tapestry museum in Aix-en-Provence (2000).

MUSEUMS AND GALLERIES:
AIX-EN-PROVENCE (Mus. du Vieil Aix): *Winter 1902, Aix-en-Provence* (oil/panel) - AIX-EN-PROVENCE (Mus. Granet): *Ingres; Landscape* - AIX-EN-PROVENCE (Pavillon de Vendôme): *Landscape in Snow* (1890, oil/paper) - MONTPELLIER (Mus. Fabre): *Landscapes* (three).

GAUTIER, Louis Joseph Antoine Désiré
French, 19th century.
Born February 1789; died after 1824.
Draughtsman, engraver (burin).
Engraved views and genre compositions.

GAUTIER, Lucien Marcelin
French, 19th century.
Born 8 January 1850, in Aix-en-Provence; died 1925.
Draughtsman, engraver (etching).
Studied in Aix under Marius Reynaud and in Paris under Gaucherel. Lucien Gautier must rank among the better engravers of the day on the strength of several plates engraved from Corot originals, but his reputation rests on engravings of street scenes, at which he excelled. He produced views of Paris, Marseilles, Venice and Scotland, together with familiar views of Rome, London and cities in France. Gautier received an honourable mention in 1884, a bronze in 1894, and a silver in 1900.
BIBLIOGRAPHY:
Baille, Frank/Guth, Paul, *Les Petits Maitres d'Aix a la Belle Epoque, 1870/1914,* P. Roubaud, Aix-en-Provence, 1981.
AUCTION RECORDS:
PARIS, 12 Dec 1997, *Notre-Dame de Paris* (1914, engraving, triptych in the same frame, 40 1/4 x 6 1/4 ins / 102 x 16 cm) FRF 7,500.

GAUTIER, Marie, wife of Antoni
French, 19th - 20th century.
Born 1870, in Paris; died 1960, in Paris.
Painter, watercolourist. Flowers.
School of Algiers.
Marie Gautier exhibited in Paris, Berlin, Dresden and Vienna. Some of her work was included in the 2003 collective exhibition *L'École d'Alger (The School of Algiers)* in Bordeaux art museum.
AUCTION RECORDS:
PARIS, 15 Dec 1927, *Rose Branch; Branch of Hydrangea* (two watercolours) FRF 160.

GAUTIER, Paul Albert
French, 20th century.
Born 19 September 1884, in Guyana.
Sculptor. Busts.
Paul Albert Gautier, a pupil of Coutant, exhibited regularly at the Salon des Artistes Français in Paris. He won numerous distinctions for his busts of children, including a silver medal in 1921 and a gold in 1926.

GAUTIER, Philippe
French, 18th century.
Active in Paris in 1749.
Painter, sculptor.
Probably identical to Philippe Eugène Gauthier.

GAUTIER, Philippe
French, 20th century.
Born 24 December 1928, in Fresnay-sur-Sarthe.
Painter. Figures, nudes, portraits, scenes with figures, landscapes, still-lifes, flowers.

Philippe Gautier trained at the École des Beaux-Arts in Paris, with Jean Dupas from 1948 and in 1952 with Leguelt, the same year he entered the Prix de Rome. His admiration for Corot is clear in his early landscapes of his native Sarthe region. He then began to study Cézanne, and this naturally led in 1957 to an evident postcubist construction in his various compositions, scenes with figures, figures, landscapes and still-lifes. This postcubist discipline continued to shape his whole output, although less strongly after the 1970s. After 1970 he more or less gave up painting landscapes, although until 1980 he continued to produce still-lifes. From then onwards he concentrated almost exclusively on figures, alone or in scenes. These were female figures, nude or almost nude, shown in a glittering array of light and colour, painted as it were an echo, a vision made real, of the elegant painting of the 18th century.

Philippe Gautier's work has been shown in collective exhibitions, including the Salon Comparaisons and the Salon de la Société des Beaux-Arts, Paris (from 1956); Salon des Peintres Témoins de leur Temps, Paris (from 1959 and regularly until 1971); Salon du Doyenné, St-Émilion (from 1973); Galerie Vendôme, Paris (from 1975). He also exhibited abroad, especially in Germany. His solo exhibitions include: Galerie Carlier, Paris (1961); the Musée de Tessé, Le Mans (1973); Galerie Vendôme, Paris (regular shows since 1976 and especially in 1998); city museum, Solingen, Germany (1980); Michels gallery, Hilden, Germany and Maïté Aubert gallery, Le Havre(from 1981). In 1954 and 1955 he participated in the young painters' prize in Paris.

BIBLIOGRAPHY:

Philippe Gautier, Presse d'Argraphie, Paris, 1978. *30 ans de recherche*, Éd. Mémoire vivante, Paris, 1981. Le Capitaine, René, *Philippe Gautier*, Presse d'Argraphie, Paris, 1986 (good documentation). Gautier, Philippe, *Philippe Gautier*, Léopard d'or, Paris, 1997.

GAUTIER, Pierre Gabriel
Swiss, 18th century.
Born 1755, in Geneva; died in Paris.
Enameller.

Pierre was the son of the goldsmith Jean Gautier, and a pupil of Roux. He had a successful career painting commercial enamels.

GAUTIER, Pierre Jules Théophile
French, 19th century.
Born 30 August 1811, in Tarbes (Hautes-Pyrenées); died 23 October 1872, in Neuilly-sur-Seine.
Painter, watercolourist, pastellist, engraver, draughtsman, illustrator, poet, writer, art critic.
Figures, portraits, genre scenes, local scenes.
Orientalism.

Had moved to Paris by 1828 in order to study painting. In 1830, he took life classes under Louis Edouard Rioult. Pierre Gautier travelled to Algeria in 1830, anxious to follow a dual career as both a painter and an author. Around that time, while still young, he abandoned painting in favour of writing. That said, his work was considered of a sufficiently high standard to be included in an exhibition entitled Drawings by 19th Century French Authors mounted at the Maison de Balzac in Paris in 1983-1984.

Gautier's paintings and sketches run the gamut of various genres - from caricature to portraiture by way of oriental subjects and genre compositions - and different media: oil, watercolour, pastel, pen-and-ink and (occasionally) lithograph engraving. He painted numerous studies of women, including his daughter Estelle. His style is delicate and perceptive, and his sketches evidence the influence of Ingres and Delacroix, two artists he is on record as having greatly admired. As an author and poet, his work has a pronounced pictorial quality. Pierre Gautier also worked as a Salon critic, penning reviews for *L'Artiste, La Presse and Le Moniteur.*

BIBLIOGRAPHY:

Gould, Cecil Hilton Monk, *Delaroche and Gautier: Gautier's Views on the Execution of Lady Jane Grey and on other Compositions by Delaroche*, National Gallery, London, 1975. Brown, Marilyn, *'Ingres, Gautier, and the Ideology of the Cameo Style of the Second Empire'* in *Arts-Magazine*, vol 56, no. 4, 1981. Snell, Robert, *Theophile Gautier; a Romantic Critic of the Visual Arts*, Clarendon Press, Oxford, 1982. Allen, Virginia, *The Femme Fatale: Erotic Icon*, Whitston, Troy, 1983.

GAUTIER, Pierre Louis Joseph
French, 19th century.
Born 1796, in Arras; died 1871, in Paris.
Painter. Genre scenes, portraits.

Studied under Leroy and Liancourt and exhibited at the Paris Salon in 1834 and 1835. He taught in the École de Beaux-Arts in Arras.

MUSEUMS AND GALLERIES:

ARRAS: *Grieving Mother; Portrait of Mr Lambert.*

GAUTIER, René Georges
French, 20th century.
Born 20 January 1887, in Paris.
Painter. Military subjects.

René Georges Gautier exhibited in Paris at the Salon des Artistes Français. He won many distinctions, including a silver medal in 1924 and a gold in 1927.

GAUTIER, Saint Elme
French, 19th century.
Born 16 January 1849, in La Rochelle.
Painter, engraver. Genre scenes.

Pupil of Gérome; exhibited at the Paris Salon from 1870 to 1876.

GAUTIER, Valérie
French, 19th century.
Born 19th century, in Lille.
Sculptor.

Made her Paris Salon début in 1870.

GAUTIER AND GEORGE
Flemish School, 16th century.
Painters (glass).

These two artists lived in Italy and worked for Giorgio Vasari.

GAUTIER D'AGOTY, Arnauld, or Arnault Éloi, or Gauthier
French, 18th century.
Died 1771, in Florence, Italy, or 1783 according to some sources.
Painter, engraver, illustrator. Portraits.

Arnauld was both son and pupil of Jacques Gautier d'Agoty. He assisted with his father's work and would later carry on the family business. He is noted for his *Observations périodiques sur l'histoire naturelle, la physique et les arts* (*Periodic Observations on Natural History, Physics and the Arts*) , which included colour plates. Published in 1771, this work was produced by Abbé Rosier. Arnauld Gautier d'Agoty also illustrated Jadelot's complete course on anatomy (1773).

AUCTION RECORDS:

PARIS, 22-23 Feb 1905, *Portrait of a Man; Portrait of a Woman*, FRF 400. PARIS, 1 June 1931, *Portrait Presumed to be of Maupéou at his Work Table*, FRF 620.

GAUTIER D'AGOTY, Édouard, or Gauthier
French, 18th century.
Died 1784, in Milan.
Painter, engraver. Portraits.

Son and pupil of Jacques Gautier d'Agoty, Édouard was the family member who seemed to be the most devoted to art. He contributed significantly to the development of colour engraving. His work included 12 large engravings. Several of these were copies of paintings from the Gallery of the Duc d'Orléans, including reproductions of Allegri, Titian Vecelli, Guido Reni, Turchi and Raphael (*The Sidon Madonna*, 1786). He also executed portraits, the most notable of these being *Mme Du Barry, Gilbert des Voisins, The Duke of Richelieu, President Maupéou* and *Charles Emmanuel of Savoy*.

GAUTIER D'AGOTY, Honoré Louis, or Gauthier
French, 18th century.
Born 1746, in Paris.
Painter, engraver. Landscapes.

He was the fourth son of Jacques Gautier d'Agoty. Like his brother Édouard, he engraved scenes of Italy.

GAUTIER D'AGOTY, Jacques Fabien, the Elder, or Gauthier
French, 18th century.
Born 1710, in Marseilles; died 1781, in Paris.
Painter (gouache), pastellist, engraver. Historical scenes, figures, portraits, genre scenes, anatomical subjects.

He came to Paris in 1737, and was assistant to J.-C. Leblond, the inventor of colour engraving. Upon Leblond's death, Gautier inherited his privileges. Jacques Fabien Gautier participated in the 1779 exhibition of the Salon de la Correspondance. There he showed his *Portrait of Marie-Antoinette*. He was a member of the Académie de Dijon before being ousted.

His writings include: *Essais d'anatomie* (*Essays on Anatomy*) (1745); *Lettre concernant le nouvel art d'imprimer les tableaux avec quatre couleurs* (*Letter Concerning the New Art of Printing Paintings in Four Colours*) (1749); *Nouveau système de l'Univers* (*New System of the Universe*) (1750); *Chromogénèse ou génération des couleurs, contre le système de Newton* (*Chromogenesis or the Generating of Colour, Against Newton's System*) ; *Observations sur les tableaux anciens et modernes et observations sur la physique, l'histoire naturelle et la peinture* (*Observations on Old and Modern Paintings and Observations on Physics, Natural History and Painting*) (1752-1755). Following publication of the latter, the artist founded the *Journal de Physique* (*Journal of Physics*).

MUSEUMS AND GALLERIES:
BERLIN: *Louis XV Presenting the Portrait of Marie-Antoinette to the Heir Apparent.*

AUCTION RECORDS:
PARIS, 28 Feb 1920, *Portrait of a Man in Red; Portrait of a Woman in Headdress* (two) FRF 500. PARIS, 17 Dec 1920, *Figures in the Room of a Palace,* FRF 15,500. PARIS, 8 June 1928, *Portrait of a Magistrate Sitting at his Work Table,* FRF 1,000. PARIS, 24 May 1929, *The Dance at the Dovecote; The Dance of the Staff* (two gouaches, attributed) FRF 10,300. PARIS, 28 May 1931, *Portrait Presumed to be of Monsieur de Montillet, Commander of the King's Hunting Police* (pastel) FRF 920. PARIS, 30 Nov - 1 Dec 1936, *The Apartment of Marie-Antoinette at the Château of Versailles* (gouache) FRF 10,100. PARIS, 26 June 1951, *Portrait of Maria-Josephe de Savoie; Portrait of Marie-Therese de Savoie,* FRF 620,000. VERSAILLES, 21 March 1971, *Portrait of Marie-Antoinette,* FRF 7,500. ROUEN, 3 March 1976, *Portrait of a Woman* (1777, oil on canvas, oval, 31 1/2 x 25 1/4 ins / 80 x 64 cm) FRF 2,500. MONTE CARLO, 5 March 1984, *Interior* (oil on canvas, 17 1/2 x 23 3/4 ins / 44.5 x 60.5 cm) FRF 36,000. PARIS, 16 March 1993, *Lacerated Face (from 'Anatomie de la tête en tableaux imprimés')* (1748, coloured mezzotint, 16 1/4 x 12 1/2 ins / 41.5 x 32 cm) FRF 3,100.

GAUTIER D'AGOTY, Jean-Baptiste André, or Gauthier
French, 18th century.
Born 1740; died 1786.
Painter, engraver. Portraits, genre scenes.

He was the only one of the five sons of Jacques Fabien Gautier to devote himself to painting; his brothers were engravers. He made his career in Paris. He completed several portraits of Marie-Antoinette, whose protection he enjoyed. Only his unfinished works are cited, notably: *Gallery of Famous French Men and Women,* and *The French Monarchy* both appearing in 1770.

AUCTION RECORDS:
PARIS, 7-8 Dec 1954, *Portrait in Full of Marie-Antoinette,* FRF 2,160,000. PARIS, 3 Feb 1978, *The Countess of Barry and her Slave Zamore* (coloured mezzotint, after Drouais) FRF 4,000. MONACO, 3 July 1993, *The Marriage Contract or The Nervous Wait* (oil on canvas, 41 x 53 1/2 ins / 104 x 136 cm) FRF 355,200.

GAUTIER D'AGOTY, Pierre Edouard, or Gauthier
French, 19th century.
Born 12 September 1775, in Florence, Italy; died 29 January 1871, in Bordeaux.
Painter, miniaturist. Portraits.

Son of Edouard Gautier d'Agoty; a portrait by him was in the private collection of Madame Arman de Caillavet.

AUCTION RECORDS:
NEW YORK, 21 Oct 1988, *Portrait of a Little Girl Playing with Flowers in an Urn* (1802, oil on canvas, 11 3/4 x 8 1/4 ins / 30 x 21 cm) USD 3,850. NEW YORK, 31 Jan 1997, *Portrait Bust of a Young Girl wearing a Feathered Hat and Holding a Riding Crop* (oil on canvas, 17 x 21 ins / 43 x 53.5 cm) USD 8,050. LONDON, 22 Nov 1999, *Boy in Striped Coat and Trousers* (miniatures, gold mount) GBP 2,400. LONDON, 22 Nov 1999, *Boy in Striped Short-sleeved Jacket* (miniatures, gold mount) GBP 5,800. LONDON, 24 May 2000, *Two Young Ladies in White Dresses* (1837, miniatures, gilt bronze frame) GBP 2,800. LONDON, 21 Nov 2000, *Young Lady in Fur-bordered Blue Silk Dress* (1824, miniatures, gilt metal mount) GBP 2,500. LONDON, 5 Nov 2002, *British Officer, possibly of Commissiariat, Wearing Dark Blue Uniform* (miniatures, gold frame, oval, 2 x ? ins / 6 x ? cm) GBP 2,300.

GAUTIER D'ANVERS
French, 16th century.
Active in Lyons c. 1548.
Painter.

GAUTIER DORE, Gisèle
French, 20th century.
Born 20 June 1927, in Villecresnes.
Painter, watercolourist, draughtsman, ceramicist. Figures, scenes with figures, landscapes, still-lifes (flowers/fruit).

Gisèle Gautier Dore trained at the Grande Chaumière and at the Julian Académies, and lived and worked in Brunoy. Her early work was figurative, inspired by every day events and depicted with a firm and precise touch. She was interested in emotions, and she recreated an interior world, moving towards abstraction and employing a range of pastel tones. Gisèle Gautier Dore featured in several collective exhibitions, including the Salon d'Automne (regularly from 1972), the Salon des Artistes Français (1973, 1976, 1977), the Salon de la Société Nationale des Beaux-Arts (from 1973), and the Salon des Indépendants (from 1977). Her solo shows include Loches (1979) and the Brunoy museum (1982).

GAUTIER-GALLET, Gustave
French, 20th century.
Born c. 1880; died 1950.
Painter. Urban landscapes, still-lifes.

Gustave Gautier-Gallet was an actor as well as a painter. From 1913 onwards he exhibited at the Salon des Artistes Français in Paris. He painted numerous views in Paris.

Auction records:
Versailles, 18 March 1990, *Still-life with Apples* (watercolour, 24 3/4 x 22 ins / 63 x 56 cm) FRF 3,800.

GAUTIEZ, Pierre
French, 20th century.
Born 2 February 1923, in Joigny.
Painter. Landscapes, seascapes.
Pierre Gautiez studied at the Rouen art college. From 1959 he exhibited at the Salon d'Automne, the Salon des Artistes Français, where he won a gold medal and the hors concours, and the Salon de la Société Nationale des Beaux-Arts, where he was awarded a prize. His solo exhibitions include: the Musée des Beaux-Arts, Rouen (1962); the museum of modern art, Moscow (1986); and Chicago (1987).
Museums and Galleries:
Hamburg - Los Angeles - Paris - Philadelphia - Rouen.

GAUTRONNEAU, André
French, 20th century.
Born 1920.
Painter.
In the 1980s and 1990s André Gautronneau exhibited regularly in Paris at the Salon des Réalités Nouvelles.

GAUTROT
French, 18th century.
Active in Paris.
Engraver (burin), printer.
He engraved portraits.

GAUTZKE, Briccius
German, 15th century.
Active in Görlitz, Saxony c. 1470.
Painter.
Gautzke was a pupil of Stephan Aldenberg.

GAUVAIN, Jean
French, 16th century.
Born to a family originally from Nancy.
Sculptor.
The son of Mansuy Gauvin, Jean collaborated with his father, in 1531, on the new fountain constructed in the garden of the ducal palace. He also carved a marble *Crucifixion* (1542-1543) for the chapel of the convent of Ste-Claire in Pont-à-Mousson.

GAUVAIN, Louise de. See **GOUSSAINCOURT DE GAUVAIN**

GAUVAIN, Mansuy
French, 16th century.
Born to a family originally from Nancy.
Sculptor.
Lorraine School.
Sculptor to Duke Antoine of Lorraine, Gauvain made a series of works for the ducal palace: an equestrian statue of the duke (1512); sculptural decorations for the fountain in the garden (1528); a marble fireplace for the duchess's private room (1530); a new fountain for the garden, made with the assistance of his son Jean (1531); a low relief of *The Vision* for the duchess's oratory (1538). He also made portraits of the duke's children for the church of the Cordeliers in Nancy, provided sculptural decorations for the chapel of the convent of Ste-Claire in Pont-à-Mousson and executed the tombs of Dukes Jean and Nicolas.

GAUVAIN-BARILLOT, Jeanne
French, 20th century.
Born 1887, in the Calvados region.
Watercolourist.
Jeanne Gauvain-Barillot showed her work in Paris at the Salon des Artistes Français.

GAUVIGNARD, Jean
French, 18th century.
Active in Paris in 1752.
Painter, sculptor.

GAUVIN, Alain
French, 20th century.
Born 1936, in Paris.
Painter.
Until 1982 Alain Gauvin painted scenery at the Opéra in Paris. From 1983 onwards he taught at the art college in Tours. He lives and works in Paris and in the Charente-Maritime region. Alain Gauvin marks out huge signs on his canvas, adds layer upon layer, scrapes down to the base, scrapes the colours, sticks on bits of paper and fragments of cloth, covers them, scrapes, dashes on more material, breaks it all down again. Each fragment reveals the origin of the painting in its constant state of becoming. Since 1974 his work has featured in numerous collective exhibitions, including *Trois Peintres français contemporains autour de l'œuvre graphique de Bram Van Velde* (*Three Contemporary French Painters and the Drawings of Bram van Velde*) (1978); *SAGA*, Paris (1988); and the Frankfurt art fair (1989). He exhibited regularly in the main Paris Salons, including the Salons des Comparaisons, Grands et Jeunes d'Aujourd'hui, Jeune Peinture, Réalités Nouvelles and Mai. He has held solo shows since 1973.
Bibliography:
Daniel, Émilie, *Alain Gauvin*, exhibition catalogue, Gal. Charles Sablon, Paris, 1988.
Museums and Galleries:
Paris (FNAC).
Auction records:
Copenhagen, 14 June 1994, *I'm Waiting* (1977, oil on canvas, 32 x 39 1/4 ins / 81 x 100 cm) DKK 5,500.

GAUVIN, Albert
French, 19th century.
Sculptor. Medallions.
Museums and Galleries:
Rouen: three bronze medallions.

GAUVIN, Alfred
French, 19th century.
Born 5 May 1830, in Héricourt-en-Caux (Seine-Maritime); died 27 December 1892, in Paris.
Sculptor.
Museums and Galleries:
Paris (Mus. Galliera).

GAUVREAU, Pierre
Canadian, 20th century.
Born 23 August 1922, in Montreal.
Painter, draughtsman.
Groupe des Automatistes.
Pierre Gauvreau studied at the École des Beaux-Arts in Montreal. He was noticed in 1941 by the artist Paul Émile Borduas, who was a teacher at the school of furniture at the time. After that he regularly visited the latter's studio. He gave up painting around 1950 in favour of the cinema and television. In the 1960s he made some short-lived attempts at Tachism.

After a period when he was influenced by Fauvism around 1941, he took part in the Automatistes adventure from its outset, creating paintings free of any kind of restraint in a fairly sombre register. He places one mass next to another, creating tensions between them without preconceived ideas. Organic images are generated from this spontaneity, giving a new interpretation of the artist's state of mind, allowing a unique form of written expression with its own individuality to appear. His work is meant to be a biographical gesture.

He has taken part in many collective exhibitions, including at the Gesu school in Montreal in 1941, where he presented works of a Fauvist nature; the principal exhibitions of the Refus Global (Total Refusal) group from 1948, whose manifesto he co-signed; the International Exhibition at the Musée d'Art

Contemporain in Montreal in 1967; *Borduas et les Automatistes* at the Galeries Nationales du Grand Palais in Paris and the Musée d'Art Contemporain in Montreal, 1971-1972; Edmonton Art Gallery in Alberta, 1978; Winnipeg Art Gallery in Manitoba, 1979; Bibliothèque Nationale du Québec in Montreal, 1988; and a travelling exhibition organised by the Canadian Museum of Fine Arts in Ottawa, 1994-1996. He held his first solo exhibition in Montreal in 1947, followed by many others in 1979 at the Musée d'Art Contemporain in Montreal; in Toronto in 1979, 1981 and 1984; at the Musée du Québec in Quebec in 1981; at the Maison des Arts in Laval, 1994; and at Domaine Cataraqui in Quebec, 1996-1997.

BIBLIOGRAPHY:
Wilkin, Karen, *Pierre Gauvreau: The First Decade*, exhibition catalogue, 1981. Paikowsky, Sandra, *Montreal Painting: A Second Look*, exhibition catalogue, 1985. *Les 20 ans du musée à travers sa collection*, exhibition catalogue, Musée d'Art moderne contemporain, Montreal, 1985. Gagnon, François-Marc, *Refus global (1948), le manifeste du mouvement automatiste*, group exhibition catalogue, Centre culturel canadien, Paris, 1998.

MUSEUMS AND GALLERIES:
MONTREAL (MAC): *L'Oblongue 'étalène'* (1947).

AUCTION RECORDS:
MONTREAL, 30 Oct 1989, *Abstract Composition* (1947, ink, 10¼ x 16½ ins / 26 x 42 cm) CAD 3,960. MONTREAL, 16 Oct 2000, *Composition* (1947, oil on panel, 17 x 13 ins / 42 x 33 cm) CAD 9,000.

GAUW, Gerrit Adriensz
Dutch, 17th century.
Died 1638, in Haarlem.
Engraver (burin).
He produced a portrait of Persyn.

GAUZEFRED
French, 12th century.
Active in Le Puy-en-Velay c. 1180.
Sculptor.
This artist made the former doors of Puy Cathedral.

GAUZI, François, or Gauzy
French, 19th - 20th century.
Born 1862, in Fronton; died 1933, in Toulouse.
Painter, illustrator, engraver. Figures, portraits, genre scenes, landscapes with figures.
François Gauzi received advice from Puvis de Chavannes and Alfred Roll. He trained at the Toulouse art college and then in 1885 in the studio of Fernand Cormon. Here he became a close friend of Toulouse-Lautrec, who painted his portrait several times and included him in several of his compositions. His works consist mainly of family portraits, of landscapes in the Frontonnais region and around Toulouse, and of some allegories. He also published four illustrated books, including *Images et boniments en Pays d'Oc* (*Pictures and Patter in the Pays d'Oc*) (1925), and recorded his memories of Toulouse-Lautrec in *Lautrec and his Times*, which appeared posthumously in 1954. François Gauzi exhibited in Paris in 1892 and 1893 at the Salon des Indépendants. Having returned to Toulouse, in 1905 he helped found the Société des Artistes Méridionaux, of which he was president from 1912 to 1919 and where he regularly showed his work. Towards the end of his life he became interested in engraving on wood and on copper, and illustrated various publications.

BIBLIOGRAPHY:
Gauzi, François, *Lautrec et son temps*, David Perret, Paris, c. 1954.

MUSEUMS AND GALLERIES:
TOULOUSE (MBA, Mus. des Augustins): *Young Woman at the Piano* (1907); *Shepherd Girl among her Sheep* - TOULOUSE (Mus. du Vieux Toulouse): *Quai de la Daurade; Rue du Taur.*

GAUZY, Jeanne L.
French, 20th century.
Born 1886, in Paris; died 30 September 1968, in Aix-en-Provence.
Painter, fresco artist. Portraits.
Jeanne L. Gauzy exhibited in Paris at the Salon des Artistes Français, where she won a gold medal. She painted portraits, and also decorated a Syrian church in Paris.

GAVAGNIN, Leonardo
Italian, 19th century.
Born March 1809; died 1887, in Venice.
Painter. History painting.
Leonardo Gavagnin was a pupil of Politi.

GAVAGNIN, Napoleone
Italian, 19th century.
Born 1840, in Venice.
Painter. History painting.
Napoleone Gavagnin was a pupil at the academy of fine arts in Venice. Besides historical works, he also painted a few portraits.

GAVAGNIN, Natale
Italian, 19th century.
Born 1851, in Venice.
Painter. History painting, genre scenes, landscapes.
A student at the academy of fine arts in Venice, Natale Gavagnin's career began around 1871. He exhibited mostly in Venice and Milan.

AUCTION RECORDS:
LONDON, 17 April 1909, *On the Lagoon in Venice* (watercolour sold with 'The Grand Canal', a watercolour by G. Peruzzi) GBP 5. VENICE, 12 Dec 1999, *View of the Lagoon* (oil on canvas, 8 x 20 ins / 20 x 50 cm) ITL 4,000,000. LONDON, 23 Sept 2004, *Valletta Harbour, Malta* (oil on board, 9 x 21 ins / 22 x 53 cm) GBP 3,500.

GAVARD, C.
French, 19th century.
Painter.
Exhibited at the Salon in 1833 and 1834. Gavard is remembered principally as the inventor of the 'diagraph', an instrument for mechanically drawing projections or making copies (consisting of a pen governed by cords and pulleys which, in turn, are controlled by a pointer).

GAVARDIE, Jean de
French, 20th century.
Born 10 May 1909, in La Roche-sur-Yon; died August 1961, in Dax.
Painter, watercolourist. Landscapes, still-lifes.
Jean de Gavardie, a self-taught artist, did not take up painting until after a military career. He also won the 24 hour Le Mans motor race in 1933. In 1937 he began exhibiting in Paris at the Salon des Artistes Indépendants. In 1938 he exhibited at the Salon d'Automne and the Tuileries, and in 1951 jointly with Raoul Dufy in Madrid. In 1944 he met Braque, whose influence is clear in all his later work. His work is characterised by elegance and restraint.

AUCTION RECORDS:
PARIS, 27 Oct 1988, *The Dressing Table* (oil on canvas, 36½ x 23½ ins / 93 x 60 cm) FRF 20,000. LE HAVRE, 7 April 1991, *Boats and Nets* (oil on canvas, 19¾ x 24 ins / 50 x 61 cm) FRF 36,000. COPENHAGEN, 30 May 1991, *Violin* (gouache, 4¼ x 9½ ins / 11 x 24 cm) DKK 3,500. COPENHAGEN, 4 Dec 1991, *Composition* (oil on canvas, 18 x 22 ins / 46 x 55 cm) DKK 6,000. PARIS, 25 March 1994, *The Arbour* (gouache/paper, 20 x 14¾ ins / 50.5 x 37.5 cm) FRF 4,500. COPENHAGEN, 19 June 2001, *Still-life of Guitar and Palette with Brushes* (oil on canvas, 18 x 22 ins / 46 x 55 cm) DKK 14,000.

GAVARDINI, Carlo
Italian, 19th century.

Active in Rome c. 1850.
Painter.
A pupil of Consoni, Gavardini painted frescoes in several churches in Rome.

GAVARDINI, Cesare
Italian, 18th century.
Born 1755, in Pesaro; died 1782, in Pesaro.
Painter.
Gavardini worked on the decoration of several churches in Pesaro.

GAVARDINO DA BOLOGNA
Italian, 15th - 16th century.
Active in Bologna c. 1500.
Engraver (wood), sculptor.

GAVARNI, Paul, pseudonym of Chevalier Sulpice Guillaume
French, 19th century.
Born 13 January 1804, in Paris; died 24 November 1866, in Paris.
Painter (gouache), watercolourist, engraver, draughtsman, illustrator, caricaturist. Genre scenes.

By his own admission, Paul Gavarni started life as a 'pen-pusher', a civil servant seconded to the town surveyor's office in Tarbes, where he had ample time to make various sketches and studies of the nearby Pyrenées region. He submitted a number of these to the 1829 Salon, where his name was misprinted in the Salon catalogue as 'Gavarnie', the editor having mistaken the title of the work for the name of the author: it was thus that Sulpice Guillaume Chevalier came to be known as Paul Gavarni. Of more significance, however, was the fact that his entry - while by no means up to the standard of his later work - evidenced a grace and sensitivity that was immediately acknowledged. Despite this early success, however, Gavarni was still a virtual pauper and actually served a sentence in the debtor's prison in Clichy. In 1844, Gavarni met and married Jeanne Bonabry, a musician very much in vogue at the time. The marriage did not last, and Gavarni left for England three years later - in 1847. His name is in the catalogue of the Royal Academy Exhibition of 1850.

Around this time, Emile de Girardin was in the process of setting up the fashion journal *La Mode*; Gavarni's contribution to the success of that publication proved considerable. He also worked for *L'Artiste* and, in 1832, for *La Silhouette*, before he made a major career move, going on to work at *Charivari* from 1832. There, he produced caricatures and, in 1837, his *Fickleness of Women in Matters of the Heart*. His time spent in debtors' prison had provided him with a wealth of material for his strikingly witty caricatures. During his stay in England, Gavarni produced numerous drawings. On his return to Paris, he demonstrated that he had not lost his 'Parisian' touch, however: *'Sharing', History of Politics, Ramblings of Thomas Tonguetwister, Enfants Terribles* and a goodly number of other series all date from this period in his life.

Paul Gavarni produced a large body of work satirising the full spectrum of Parisian society. He may have lacked the acerbic power of Daumier but, on the other hand, he was particularly adept at capturing and rendering feminine charms.

Gavarni

Gavarni

Bibliography:
Armelhault, J./Bocher, E., *L'Œuvre de Gavarni, catalogue raisonné*, Librairie des bibliophiles, Paris, 1873. Goncourt, Edmond de/Goncourt, J. de, *Gavarni, l'homme et l'œuvre*, Plon, Paris, 1873. Lemoisne, P.-A., *'Gavarni, peintre et lithographe'* in *2 vol.*, H. Floury, Paris, 1924-1928. Olson, Nancy, *Gavarni; the Carnival Lithographs*, exhibition brochure, Yale University Art Gallery, 1979. Stamm, Therese Dolan, *Gavarni, Caricature, and the Critics*, UMI Research, Ann Arbor, 1981. Wechsler, Judith/Sennett, Richard, *A Human Comedy; Physiognomy and Caricature in 19th Century Paris*, University of Chicago Press, Chicago, 1982. Hall, Melissa, *'Manet's Ball at the Opera: A Matter of Response'* in *Rutgers Art Review*, vol. 5, 1984. Sheon, Aaron, *'Parisian Social Statistics: Gavarni, Le Diable a Paris, and Early Realism'* in *Art Journal*, vol. 44, no. 2, 1984. Dolan, Therese, *'Upsetting the Hierarchy: Gavarni's Les Enfants Terribles and Family Life During the Monarchie de Juillet'* in *Gazette-des-Beaux-Arts*, vol. 111, 1987. Beaulieu, Brooks, *'Gavarni at Yale'* in *Yale University Art Gallery Bulletin*, vol. 40, no. 2, 1988. Kinsman, Jane, *'Developing Character: Gavarni's Lithographs for Paris: 1852-1853'* in *Gazette-des-Beaux-Arts*, vol. 115, no. 1452, 1990. Sutton, Denys, *'Gavarni and the Goncourts'* in *Gazette-des-Beaux-Arts*, vol. 109, no. 1466, 1991. Mahérault, Marie-Joseph-François/Bocher, E., *L'Œuvre de Gavarni: lithographies originales et essais d'eau-forte et de procédés nouveaux*, catalogue raisonné, L'Échelle de Jacob, Paris, 2002.

Auction records:
Paris, 27-28 May 1880, *Grasshopper Pays a Visit to the Ant* (watercolour) FRF 870; *I'm Leaving Paul for Jules* (drawing) FRF 860; *Water-Carrier's Wife* (drawing) FRF 1,000; *Colic is Good for Your Health* (drawing) FRF 1,700; *Young Stevedore* (watercolour) FRF 1,020; *Stevedore and Pierrot after the Ball* (watercolour) FRF 630. Paris, 1888, *Taking the Road in the Icy Cold*, FRF 240. Paris, 6 May 1891, *Lorettes*, FRF 415; *Roadsweeper* (watercolour) FRF 700. Paris, 1897, *Thomas Tonguetwister* (watercolour) FRF 700; *Dressing-Up* (pencil drawing) FRF 175; *Portfolio of Seventy-Five Drawings of Gowns, Coiffures, Furnishings, etc.* (watercolour, Indian ink wash, sepia, pencil) FRF 1,900. Paris, 27 Jan 1897, *Hercules* (watercolour) FRF 400. Paris, 1898, *No, no Faisandet! Women! Nonsense!* (watercolour) FRF 1,000; *Innocence* (watercolour) FRF 680; *Small Trade* (watercolour) FRF 400. New York, 3-4 Feb 1898, *Badinguet Tribe Conversing* (watercolour) FRF 1,000. Paris, 1900, *Carnival Time* (watercolour and gouache) FRF 325; *Idyll* (watercolour) FRF 100; *Big Wedding at La Madeleine* (drawing) FRF 48. Paris, 26 Feb 1900, *Only the Nose is Missing* (drawing) FRF 305. Paris, 13 Nov 1918, *Fanfan from Hiroux* (watercolour) FRF 410. Paris, 7-8 March 1919, *How's Business?* (watercolour) FRF 900. Paris, 16-19 June 1919, *Lobster for the Gentleman, Preferably...* (watercolour) FRF 3,100. Paris, 20-22 May 1920, *Meadow Flowers* (watercolour) FRF 600; *Aragon* (watercolour) FRF 480. Paris, 2-4 June 1920, *Latter-Day Chorister* (watercolour) FRF 450; *Erstwhile Ballet Dancer* (watercolour) FRF 1,000; *Newly-Weds out for a Stroll* (watercolour) FRF 1,250. Paris, 1-2 Dec 1920, *King of Comedy* (watercolour) FRF 2,750; *What'll They Think of Me?* (watercolour) FRF 1,850. Paris, 7 Feb 1921, *Home with Framboisy* (watercolour) FRF 1,250. Paris, 26 Oct 1922, *St Sebastian and Yours Truly - What a Pair!* (watercolour) FRF 4,120. Paris, 7 Dec 1922, *Lieutenant in the Grand Chicard* (watercolour) FRF 3,900. Paris, 11-13 June 1923, *Women with Shawl* (pen, heightened with gouache) FRF 1,300. Paris, 19 March 1924, *Duchess of Choiseul-Praslin, Daughter of Marshal Sebastiani and Mademoiselle de Coigny* (watercolour) FRF 1,700. Paris, 17-18 June 1925, *Chambermaid* (watercolour) FRF 4,300. Paris, 22 June 1925, *Woman Sleeping* (pencil drawing and wash) FRF 2,020. Paris, 3 Dec 1925, *Impresario* (pen, wash and watercolour) FRF 1,450;

Raise your Hat when you Address the Concierge (watercolour) FRF 3,100. PARIS, 30 Dec 1925, *Small Trade* (watercolour) FRF 1,320. PARIS, 16 June 1926, *Curious Dancer* (watercolour) FRF 10,200; *Egalité, Fraternité,* FRF 20,000; *House of Gold at Eight in the Morning,* FRF 15,500. PARIS, 2 July 1926, *Never Discuss Jupiter with the Middle Classes* (pen and watercolour) FRF 1,450; *Mr. X. of Framboisy* (watercolour) FRF 13,600; *Square on the Hypotenuse?* (watercolour) FRF 5,200; *Egg-Seller* (watercolour) FRF 7,100; *Dressing for the Costume Ball* (drawing and gouache) FRF 4,600; *Propriety* (watercolour) FRF 4,100; *The Gentleman is Unwell?* (watercolour) FRF 5,500; *Allié aux Framboisy par les femmes* (watercolour) FRF 6,000; *A Small Glass Won't Do a Girl Any Harm* (watercolour) FRF 4,500; *Manners, Gentlemen, Manners!* (watercolour) FRF 4,200; *Keeping One's Eyes Peeled* (watercolour) FRF 17,800; *Captive Balloon* (watercolour) FRF 28,000; *What I Like about Dancing is the Food* (watercolour) FRF 5,600; *The Hussies aren't Funny this Year...,* FRF 4,600; *Le Pêcheur* (watercolour) FRF 20,500; *Charity* (watercolour) FRF 10,000; *Pipe* (watercolour) FRF 34,000; *Kashmiri* (watercolour) FRF 20,000; *I'm Leaving Paul for Jules* (watercolour) FRF 20,150; *Flirtatious* (watercolour) FRF 35,000; *Ten Degrees on the Réaumur Scale* (watercolour) FRF 10,000; *Taxus Baccata* (watercolour) FRF 29,000; *Lady of the Camelias* (20 watercolours) FRF 87,400. PARIS, 2-3 Dec 1926, *Ever Seen a Gentleman Pick his Nose without Shooting his Cuffs?* (watercolour and gouache) FRF 13,700. PARIS, 13 June 1927, *Waiting for his Sweetheart* (red chalk and watercolour) FRF 5,250. PARIS, 9 Feb 1928, *18th Century Scene* (watercolour) FRF 2,250. PARIS, 15 Nov 1928, *Apothecary's Accounts* (watercolour) FRF 6,000. LONDON, 12 Dec 1928, *Woman; Group of Figures* (two watercolours) GBP 36. PARIS, 25 Jan 1929, *Degenerate* (drawing) FRF 4,850; *Lorette* (drawing) FRF 4,950; *Daydream* (drawing) FRF 5,000. PARIS, 26 Jan 1929, *Marshal Castellane,* FRF 1,200. PARIS, 27 Feb 1929, *Member of the Orchestra,* FRF 3,100. PARIS, 24 May 1929, *My Word, Aren't Women Astonishing?* (watercolour) FRF 11,500; *A Time to Work and a Time to Play* (watercolour) FRF 10,200; *Where's My Handkerchief?* (watercolour) FRF 9,200. PARIS, 17 May 1930, *Eight Years since the Last Time* (watercolour) FRF 4,800. PARIS, 21 May 1930, *That'll do, Mark Anthony,You're Making Me Feel Naughty...* (watercolour) FRF 4,800. PARIS, 14 Dec 1931, *Englishman* (watercolour) FRF 900. PARIS, 25 May 1932, *Carnival Colourist* (watercolour and gouache) FRF 1,250. PARIS, 10 March 1933, *Rag-and-Bone Men* (watercolour and gouache) FRF 1,280. PARIS, 10 May 1933, *Pierrot* (watercolour and gouache) FRF 610. PARIS, 9 June 1933, *Frenchmen as They See Themselves* (20 drawings in Indian ink, of which 11 are watercolours and 9 are heightened with white gouache) FRF 4,600. PARIS, 7 Dec 1934, *Sponsor Wanted* (watercolour) FRF 3,000; *Never Mind the Flattery, I'd Prefer the Lamb...* (watercolour and gouache) FRF 5,100; *What I like about Dancing is the Food* (watercolour and gouache) FRF 5,100. LONDON, 3 Nov 1937, *Three Figures,* GBP 6. PARIS, 9 March 1939, *Secondhand Mexican* (watercolour) FRF 1,900; *Women Notice Me* (watercolour) FRF 1,820. PARIS, 24 March 1939, *Masks* (fan decoration in gouache) FRF 4,150. PARIS, 16 and 17 May 1939, *In Need of Support* (pencil drawing) FRF 220. PARIS, 2 April 1941, *Watercolour,* FRF 1,800. PARIS, 30 April 1941, *Bust of Peasant* (pen drawing) FRF 1,000. PARIS, 27 June 1941, *Puppets* (watercolour) FRF 1,200. PARIS, 30 June 1941, *Smuggler* (drawing in gouache) FRF 600. PARIS, 5-7 Nov 1941, *She Detests Fresh Water,* FRF 6,800; *Putting Jalouret in his Place* (two drawings with watercolour) FRF 7,200. PARIS, 8 Dec 1941, *Gowns (study)* (drawing with watercolour) FRF 1,320. PARIS, 17-18 Dec 1941, *Male Portrait* (Indian ink) FRF 500. PARIS, 13 March 1942, *Un Pêcheur* (heightened drawing) FRF 2,600. PARIS, 24 June 1942, *Flower-Merchant* (watercolour and gouache) FRF 8,800. PARIS, 28 Dec 1942, *To Eat or Not to Eat, That is the Question!* (watercolour) FRF 6,500. PARIS, 1 March 1943, *Local Policeman* (pen drawing, heightened wit white gouache) FRF 2,500. PARIS, 12 April 1943, *Two Italia Peasant Women* (watercolour) FRF 2,100. PARIS, 14 Apr 1943, *Philosophy of an Idea* (watercolour) FRF 4,000. PARIS 23 June 1943, *En Route for Toulon* (watercolour) FRF 5,70 PARIS, 15 April 1944, *I was once a Great Dancer!,* FRF 1,50 PARIS, 24 Jan 1945, *Shareholder Collecting his Dividend* (watercolour and gouache) FRF 12,800; *Pierrot* (gouache) FR 2,800; *Spanish Beggar* (sepia wash heightened wit gouache) FRF 3,800. PARIS, 23 March 1945, *Illustrations* (watercolour and gouache) FRF 6,000. PARIS, 14 May 1945, *Episode from 'Robinson Crusoe'* (watercolour and gouache FRF 2,600. PARIS, 29 June 1945, *Pierrot* (charcoal and wash heightened with gouache) FRF 2,700. PARIS, 18 Oct 1945 *Pierrot and Domino* (watercolour and gouache/pen outline FRF 3,600. PARIS, July 1946, *Man in Pyrenean Costume* (watercolour) FRF 3,700; *Young Woman in a Blue Gown; Young Woman* (two gouaches) FRF 5,800; *Male Portraits* (two gouaches) FRF 3,600. PARIS, 7 Nov 1946, *Costume Folio* (watercolour) FRF 580. PARIS, 18 Dec 1946, *Pierrot Drinking* (pen, heightened with watercolour and gouache) FRF 2,690. PARIS, 17 Feb 1947, *Figure from the Commedia dell'Arte* (drawing) FRF 600. PARIS, 17 March 1947, *Happy Homecoming,* FRF 2,600. PARIS, 10 May 1950, *Fashion Designer* (watercolour and gouache) FRF 41,600. PARIS, 25 May 1955 *Mister Biblot* (watercolour and gouache) FRF 25,500. BERN, 28 May 1964, *Scholar with his Right Hand on a Manuscript* (watercolour) CHF 1,000. PARIS, 23 Nov 1965, *Little Red Riding Hood* (watercolour) FRF 1,400. PARIS, 4 May 1966, *Little Red Riding Hood; Baker's Wife with Money to Burn* (two watercolours) FRF 3,000. PARIS, 5 Oct 1970, *Burglar* (watercolour) FRF 1,500. PARIS, 3 Dec 1971, *Escapism* (watercolour and gouache) FRF 2,000. PARIS, 31 May 1972, *Not at all Bad!* (watercolour and gouache) FRF 1,500. LONDON, 4 July 1973, *Bourgeois Couple* (watercolour) GBP 140. NEW YORK, 7 June 1979, *Thalia* (watercolour heightened with white, 11 x 8 ins / 28 x 20.2 cm) USD 2,000. LONDON, 26 March 1981, *Attentive Young Man* (watercolour and pencil, 9 1/2 x 7 ins / 24 x 18 cm) GBP 2,300; *Two Pierrots* (pencil and red chalk heightened with white gouache) GBP 2,200. PARIS, 16 Feb 1983, *Party* (oil on canvas, 28 1/4 x 23 1/4 ins / 72 x 59 cm) FRF 16,000. NEW YORK, 23 Feb 1983, *Portrait of the Sub-Prefect* (watercolour, pencil and gouache, 11 3/4 x 8 1/4 ins / 29.8 x 21 cm) USD 1,600. PARIS, 27 May 1987, *Small Trade* (watercolour, 10 1/2 x 7 ins / 26.5 x 18 cm) FRF 20,500. PARIS, 10 Dec 1987, *Partygoer* (watercolour, 10 1/2 x 7 3/4 ins / 26.5 x 19.5 cm) FRF 12,500. PARIS, 10 Feb 1988, *Pierrot* (drawing, 11 x 7 3/4 ins / 27 x 20 cm) FRF 16,000. MONACO, 20 Feb 1988, *Conversation* (watercolour and pencil, 8 1/2 x 7 ins / 21.5 x 17.8 cm) FRF 4,440. NEW YORK, 17 Jan 1990, *Laundress* (watercolour/paper, 10 x 6 3/4 ins / 24.5 x 17.4 cm) USD 2,750. MONACO, 8 Dec 1990, *Turk* (ink heightened with white/brown paper, 8 x 5 1/2 ins / 20.3 x 14 cm) FRF 5,328. PARIS, 12 Dec 1990, *Self-portrait* (1835, lead pencil and brown wash, 6 1/2 x 4 1/2 ins / 16.5 x 11.5 cm) FRF 105,000. NEW YORK, 9 Jan 1991, *Back from the Front after Seven-and-a-Half Years...* (watercolour, gouache and ink/lightly tinted paper, 13 x 18 1/4 ins / 33.3 x 46.4 cm) USD 4,400. PARIS, 28 June 1991, *Two Children* (watercolour, 6 1/4 x 4 3/4 ins / 16 x 12 cm) FRF 5,500. PARIS, 22 Nov 1991, *Hussars' Wives* (watercolour and gouache, 6 x 7 3/4 ins / 15 x 20 cm) FRF 19,000. HEIDELBERG, 9 Oct 1992, *Flower-Seller and Couple in a Park* (pencil, 8 x 6 1/2 ins / 20.5 x 16.4 cm) DEM 1,100. NEW YORK, 29 Oct 1992, *Charlatan* (pencil/cream paper, 10 x 8 1/2 ins / 25.4 x 21.9 cm) USD 550. PARIS, 22 March 1995, *From Paris to Canton* (Indian ink and watercolour, 7 3/4 x 13 1/2 ins / 19.5 x 34.5 cm) FRF 9,000. PARIS, 20 June 1995, *Indian* (watercolour and gouache, 12 1/4 x 7 3/4 ins / 31 x 20 cm) FRF 20,000. PARIS, 13 Oct 1995, *Gypsy Prisoner* (gouache, 7 x 10 3/4 ins / 18 x 27.5

:m) FRF 21,500. PARIS, 14 May 1997, *Beggar* (pen and watercolour, 11 1/4 x 8 1/4 ins / 28.5 x 21 cm) FRF 3,500. LONDON, 9 July 2001, *Portrait of Minouminard, Leaning on a Stick. Man in an Overcoat, Holding a Top Hat* (pen/ink/watercolour/heightened white, 13 x 8 ins / 32 x 20 cm) GBP 1,500. PARIS, 22 March 2002, *Fouchtra* (watercolour/pen/ink, 11 x 8 ins / 27 x 20 cm) EUR 2,000. NEW YORK, 29 Oct 2002, *On the Road to Toulon. One Spoke to Her* (pencil/watercolour/gouache/heightened white, two, 13 x 8 ins / 33 x 21 cm) USD 1,700. PARIS, 24 March 2003, *Man with Opera Hat* (watercolour/pen/ink/heightened/gouache, 12 x 8 ins / 31 x 20 cm) EUR 1,500. PARIS, 24 March 2003, *Loup rose et loup bleu* (watercolour over crayon, 6 x 8 ins / 15 x 20 cm) EUR 2,200.

GAVARNI, Pierre
French, 19th - 20th century.
Born 1846, in Paris; died 1932.
Painter. Genre scenes, landscapes with figures.

Pierre Gavarni was a son of Paul Gavarni and a pupil of Fromentin. His work includes *Reclining Woman, Marriage at the Madeleine, A Game of Croquet, Rendezvous, Diplomatic Dinner* and *Rostrum in a Riding School.* Pierre Gavarni showed work at the Salon de Paris from 1870, winning a third-class medal in 1874, and in 1883 he became a member of the Société des Artistes Français.

AUCTION RECORDS:
PARIS, 24 Nov 1950, *By the Shore,* FRF 50,000. LONDON, 27 Nov 1986, *A Busy Scene on the Steps of the Madeleine Church* (1874, watercolour, pen and pencil, 19 x 25 3/4 ins / 48 x 65.5 cm) GBP 3,600. BAYEUX, 10 March 1991, *Woodland Walk with Figures* (c. 1880, oil on canvas, 47 1/4 x 76 3/4 ins / 120 x 195 cm) FRF 770,000. BAYEUX, 3-4 April 1994, *Un cours de haute école de dames, la demi-volte* (1892, oil on canvas, 45 1/4 x 69 1/4 ins / 115 x 176 cm) FRF 1,750,000. NEW YORK, 19 Jan 1995, *Study of Parisian Women in the Country* (oil on canvas, a pair, 20 1/4 x 26 ins / 51.4 x 65.1 cm and 19 1/2 x 26 ins/49.5 x 65.1 cm) USD 9,775.

GAVAROTTI, Giovanni Battista
Italian, 17th century.
Born in Rimini.
Active in Venice.
Painter. Flowers.

GAVARRET, Eudoxie
French, 19th century.
Born 19th century, in Paris.
Watercolourist.

Exhibited examples of her work at the Salon from 1870.

GAVASETTI, Camillo
Italian, 17th century.
Born in Modena; died 1628, in Parma, young.
Painter. Religious subjects, allegorical subjects. Frescoes.

Camillo Gavasetti was the son and pupil of the miniaturist Stefane Gavasetti, but was clearly influenced by the manner of the Carracci. He was commissioned, alongside Piarini, to paint subjects from the holy scriptures. A fresco by Gavasetti of an apocalyptic scene is in the presbytery of the church of S Antonio in Piacenza; Guercino believed it to be the most beautiful work of art in Piacenza. In any event, Camillo Gavasetti's work appears to have been more appreciated in Piacenza than in Modena and Parma, where he also lived and worked.

AUCTION RECORDS:
MILAN, 29 Nov 1990, *Allegory of Geometry* (oil on canvas, 22 x 18 3/4 ins / 56 x 47.5 cm) ITL 2,000,000.

GAVAZZENI, Giovanni
Italian, 19th century.
Born 1841, in Talamone, near Grosseto (Tuscany).
Painter.

Gavazzeni studied at the Accademia Carrara di Belle Arti in Bergamo under Scuri. When he returned to his native region, he carried out some major works for Count Paolo Paravicini di Morbegno. He painted a number of frescoes in Sondrio Cathedral, which were commissioned by the archpriest, who went on to become Bishop of Parma. In 1900 Gavazzeni entered the paintings *Ecce Redemptor Mundi* and *Maria Mater Gratiæ* for the Alinari competition.

GAVAZZI, Agostino
Italian, 16th century.
Painter.

Agostino Gavazzi was probably the son of Giovanni Giacomo Gavazzi. Works known to be by this artist include the wooden *All Saints* altarpiece in the church at Membro, near Bergamo; *St Augustine between St Stephen and St Lawrence,* in the church of S Niccolo; a *Virgin and Child,* in the church of S Sebastiano; and a fresco of the *Virgin and Child with Saints,* in the courtyard of Casa Longhi. Tassi refers to a painting by Gavazzi, dated 1527, of the *Virgin and Child with Saints,* as being in the parish church of S Giacomo at Piazzatore.

GAVAZZI, Giovanni Giacomo
Italian, 16th century.
Born in Pescante; died c. 1512.
Painter. History painting.

There are paintings by Giovanni Giacomo Gavazzi in the Carrara Gallery in Bergamo, and a *Virgin Mary Surrounded by Angels* (1512) can be seen at Colonna (near Sant'Alessandro). He worked mainly in Bergamo.

MUSEUMS AND GALLERIES:
BERGAMO (Accademia Carrara): *Two Saints* (three works); *Apostle* (three works); *Saint; Ex-voto; Adoration of the Magi.*

GAVAZZO-BUCHARDO, Jean
Argentinian, 20th century.
Born 1888.
Painter.

GAVEL, Charlotte von
German, 19th century.
Born 16 February 1833, in Livonia (now part of Latvia/Estonia).
Painter. Genre scenes, still-lifes.

Charlotte von Gavel exhibited in Munich, Bremen and Dresden between 1879 and 1890. She is noted for her works *A Scholar* and *Still-life.*

GAVELIN, Margareta
Maiden name: Capius
Finnish, 18th century.
Painter.

One of Margareta Gavelin's religious paintings is in the museum in Helsinki.

GAVELLA, Bartolomeo
Italian, 15th century.
Active in Modena in 1490.
Painter.

Bartolomeo Gavella also worked in Ferrara.

GAVELLA, Bartolomeo
Italian, 16th century.
Active in Modena c. 1540.
Sculptor.

Bartolomeo Gavella produced terracotta sculptures.

GAVEN, George
British, 18th century.
Painter, draughtsman. Portraits.

George Gaven was a pupil of Robert West. He was active in Dublin around 1756.

AUCTION RECORDS:
LONDON, 2 June 1995, *Portrait of the Speaker John Ponsonby, Dressed in Red and Standing by his Desk* (oil on canvas, 58 1/4 x 46 ins / 148 x 117 cm) GBP 10,350.

GAVENCKY, Frank J
American, 20th century.
Born 1888, in Chicago; died 1966.
Painter.
Frank Gavencky was awarded many prizes in the regional artistic circles he frequented.

GAVERE, Cornelis de
Dutch, 20th century.
Born 25 January 1877, in Batavia, now Jakarta.
Active in the USA.
Painter.
Cornelis de Gavere was taught by Janssen and Guérin. He was active in Santa Cruz, California.

GAVERE, Theodore van
Flemish School, 15th century.
Active in Bruges.
Illuminator.

GAVET, Charles
French, 19th century.
Born 19th century, in Paris.
Painter.
Exhibited landscapes, seascapes, portraits and genre compositions at Salons between 1836 and 1852.
MUSEUMS AND GALLERIES:
LISIEUX: *Landscape*; *Fisherman's Family*.

GAVEY, R.E.
British, 19th century.
Active in London.
Painter. Figures.
R.E. Gavey exhibited in London from 1828 to 1839, mainly at the British Institution and at the Suffolk Street Gallery.

GAVIGNANI, Giovanni
Italian, 17th century.
Born 23 June 1615; died 1680.
Active in Carpi.
Painter, mosaicist (?).
Giovanni Gavignani was a pupil of Fassi.

GAVIGNANI, Pietro
Italian, 17th century.
Active in Carpi c. 1660.
Painter.
Pietro was the brother and collaborator of Giovanni Gavignani.

GAVIN, Hector
British, 19th century.
Active in Edinburgh c. 1800.
Engraver.
Hector Gavin was noted for a large number of ex libris.

GAVIN, Robert
British, 19th century.
Born 1827, in Leith (Edinburgh); died 5 October 1883, in Newhaven.
Painter. Religious subjects, portraits, genre scenes, local scenes, landscapes.
Orientalism.
Robert Gavin studied at art college in Edinburgh and then travelled extensively, spending some time in Tangier, where he painted a number of Moorish themes. He also spent time in the USA. He exhibited on a regular basis from 1855 and became a member of the Royal Scottish Academy in 1879. He painted Negro subjects but is best remembered as an accomplished orientalist.
MUSEUMS AND GALLERIES:
EDINBURGH (Royal Scottish Academy): *Moorish Maiden' First Love* (1879, oil on canvas) - LIVERPOOL (Walker AG): *Rebecca at the Well* (1879).
AUCTION RECORDS:
LONDON, 4 July 1910, *Young Girl*, GBP 5. LONDON, 25 Ja[n] 1924, *Gleaner*, GBP 12. LONDON, 7 Feb 1930, *Babes in th[e] Wood*, GBP 24. EDINBURGH, 8 March 1930, *Young Mooris[h] Girl*, GBP 5. EDINBURGH, 3 April 1937, *Oriental Landscape* GBP 5. GLASGOW, 3 July 1980, *Tangier* (oil on canvas, 32 1/2 x 42 1/2 ins / 82.5 x 108 cm) GBP 2,300. LONDON, 27 Oct 1982 *Three Negro Heads* (oil on canvas, 17 x 13 3/4 ins / 43 x 35 cm) GBP 1,600. AUCHTERARDER, 1 Sept 1987, *Sleeping Harves[t] Girl* (oil on card, 9 x 12 ins / 23 x 30.5 cm) GBP 2,600. GLASGOW, 7 Feb 1989, *Trough* (oil on canvas, 36 1/2 x 23 1/2 ins / 93 x 59.5 cm) GBP 3,850. PERTH, 27 Aug 1990, *Lamb* (oil on canvas, 27 1/4 x 18 ins / 69 x 46 cm) GBP 4,950. LONDON, 7 June 1995, *Flowers for the Poorly* (oil on canvas, 28 1/4 x 41 1/4 ins / 72 x 104.5 cm) GBP 4,600. LONDON, 3 June 1999, *Bathing Poo[l]* (oil on canvas, 30 x 25 ins / 76 x 64 cm) GBP 6,000. LONDON, 28 Oct 1999, *Spanish Girl with Fan* (oil on canvas, 24 x 17 ins / 60 x 44 cm) GBP 2,800. CHESTER, 1 Nov 2000, *Musical Reverie* (oil on canvas, 13 x 17 ins / 32 x 42 cm) GBP 1,150. LONDON, 5 Sept 2001, *Fooling Around* (oil on canvas, 25 x 30 ins / 63 x 76 cm) GBP 8,500. EDINBURGH, 25 March 2004, *Gir[l] from New Orleans* (oil on canvas, 26 x 19 ins / 67 x 47 cm) GBP 2,800. LONDON, 1 Sept 2004, *Italian Shepherdess* (oil on canvas, 27 x 18 ins / 69 x 46 cm) GBP 4,500.

GAVIRATI, Antonio
Italian, 18th century.
Born in Cesena.
Active mainly in Ferrara.
Painter.

GAVIRIA, Bernarbé de
Spanish, 17th century.
Active in Granada c. 1600.
Sculptor (wood).
Bernabé de Gaviria carved statues for churches in Granada.

GAVONI, Tommaso
Italian, 18th century.
Active mainly in Ludwigsburg, Germany.
Sculptor.

GAVOTY, Joseph
French, 17th century.
Active in Toulon at the end of the 17th century.
Painter.
He worked in the decoration of warships. He is probably the same artist as that cited under the name of Jean Joseph.

GAVREL, Geneviève
French, 20th century.
Born 1909, in Tunisia; died 25 January 1999.
Painter. Interiors, landscapes, still-lifes, flowers.
Geneviève Gavrel studied at the art college in Tunis, where she lived probably until 1956. Her painting is figurative, to some extent expressionist, and is reminiscent of the Paris School. Her strongly coloured canvases are particularly noticeable because of their balanced composition and the perfect distribution of the planes. In 1957 she began to exhibit in Paris at the Salon d'Automne, at the Salon des Artistes Indépendants, the Salon Comparaisons and at the Salon of the Société Nationale des Beaux-Arts. She also held solo exhibitions in France and abroad.

GAVREL, Pierre
French, 16th century.
Active in Roye (Somme) c. 1585.
Glass painter.

GAVRIIL
Russian, 18th century.
Active c. 1727.
Engraver.
Was a monk.

GAVRILIATCHENKO, Serguei
Russian, 20th - 21st century.
Born 1956.
Painter, draughtsman. Historical subjects.
Serguei Gavriliatchenko studied at the Surikov Institute of Art in Moscow. Most of his works take the history of the Russian Cossacks as their theme.
AUCTION RECORDS:
PARIS, 4 May 1994, *Family Pride* (oil/hardboard, 35 1/2 x 35 1/2 ins / 90 x 90 cm) FRF 8,000.

GAVRILOV, Aleksandr Aleksandrovich
Russian, 19th century.
Born 1839, in St Petersburg.
Sculptor.
Gavrilov worked in his home town and in Moscow.

GAVRILOV, Aleksei
Russian, 17th century.
Active in Moscow in 1676.
Painter.
We owe Aleksei Gavrilov a great number of icons.

GAVRILOV, Fedor
Russian, 17th century.
Active in Moscow.
Painter.
We owe Fedor Gavrilov frescoes and icons.

GAVRILOV, Vasili
Russian, 17th century.
Active in Moscow.
Painter.
Vasili Gavrilov worked on the decoration of the Kremlin.

GAVRILOVIC, Ivan
Yugoslav, 19th century.
Active in Carlovitz c. 1800.
Painter, engraver. Religious subjects.

GAW, R. M.
American, 19th century.
Active c. 1825.
Engraver.

GAWDIE, John Bart (Sir)
British, 17th century.
Born 4 October 1639, in West Harling; died 1699.
Painter. Portraits.
John Bart Gawdie was a deaf mute who studied under Lely and dabbled in the arts. Evelyn described him as a noteworthy painter.

GAWEN, Joseph
British, 19th century.
Active in London.
Sculptor.
Joseph Gawen exhibited at the Royal Academy in London from 1850 to 1882.

GAY, Abel
French, 20th century.
Born 1877, in Pollien; died c. 1938.
Painter, designer. Landscapes, still-lifes. Murals.
Abel Gay studied with Louis Jourdan. He produced charcoal and oil views of the scenery of the Dombes region in the south-east of France, such as *Moonrise over the Heath at Les Bruyères - October Morning - Before the Storm.* He also painted a mural for the *La Taverne* café in Lyons, calling it *Mist on the Rhône*. He lived in Lyons and in 1903 began to exhibit in the Salon there, winning a second-class medal in 1909.
AUCTION RECORDS:
PARIS, 20 Jan 1988, *Still-life with Cherries* (oil on card, 17 3/4 x 24 3/4 ins / 45 x 63 cm) FRF 12,000.

GAY, Antoine
French, 17th century.
Born 1668, in Le Puy-en-Velay; died 2 March 1709.
Painter.
Antoine was the son of François Gay.

GAY, Berthe
French, 19th century.
Born 14 June 1852, in Paris.
Painter. Landscapes.
Exhibited in Geneva in 1885.

GAY, Edward B.
American, 19th - 20th century.
Born 27 April 1837, in Dublin, Ireland; died 1928.
Active in the USA.
Painter, watercolourist. Landscapes with figures, waterscapes, landscapes.
Edward Gay began his education in New York with J.-H. Hart and then went to work in Karlsruhe with J. Schirmer and Lessing. He was a member of the National Academy in 1907, and the New York Watercolor Club. He was active in Mount Vernon. In 1887 he won a prize of $2000 for his landscape *Broad Acres*, which was offered to the Metropolitan Museum in New York in 1887. He was also awarded medals in San Francisco, New Orleans and Buffalo in 1901.
BIBLIOGRAPHY:
Craft, John Richard, *A Love For Landscape: A Retrospective Exhibition. Oils, Watercolours, Drawings by Edward Gay, N.A. 1837-1928*, 1974.
MUSEUMS AND GALLERIES:
NEW YORK (Metropolitan Mus. of Art).
AUCTION RECORDS:
NEW YORK, 23-24 Jan 1901, *Stream in a Wood*, USD 115. NEW YORK, 8 Feb 1901, *In the Month of May*, USD 205. NEW YORK, 20 Feb 1903, *Summer*, USD 130. NEW YORK, 8 Dec 1904, *Birches*, USD 250. NEW YORK, 9 Dec 1904, *Evening on the Riverbank*, USD 225. NEW YORK, 7 March 1906, *In the Shade of a Willow*, USD 105. NEW YORK, 12 Nov 1909, *On the River*, USD 85. NEW YORK, 27 April 1911, *Evening*, USD 55. NEW YORK, 25 and 26 March 1931, *Twilight Glow*, USD 100. NEW YORK, 15-18 June 1943, *River and Fishermen*, USD 120. LOS ANGELES, 22 May 1973, *Summer Afternoon* (1886) USD 1,250. NEW YORK, 10 June 1976, *Landscape* (1916, oil on canvas, 24 x 36 ins / 61 x 91.5 cm) USD 500. NEW YORK, 1 July 1982, *Rural Landscape* (oil on canvas, 20 x 36 ins / 51 x 91.5 cm) USD 2,300. NEW YORK, 5 Oct 1983, *Misty Morning* (1903, oil on canvas, 26 1/4 x 31 3/4 ins / 66.5 x 80.5 cm) USD 2,800. NEW YORK, 28 May 1987, *Cragsmoor* (oil on canvas, 27 x 37 1/2 ins / 68.6 x 95.2 cm) USD 17,000. NEW YORK, 17 March 1988, *Boats in the Marshes* (1910, oil on canvas, 32 1/2 x 42 1/4 ins / 82.5 x 107.5 cm) USD 2,200. NEW YORK, 24 June 1988, *Country Road* (oil on card, 15 3/4 x 11 3/4 ins / 40 x 30 cm) USD 2,640. NEW YORK, 24 Jan 1989, *Fishermen on the Shoreline* (1885, oil on canvas, 46 3/4 x 71 ins / 118.8 x 179.5 cm) USD 18,700. NEW YORK, 14 Feb 1990, *Harvesters in a Field in Autumn* (1897, watercolour and pencil/paper/card, 9 1/4 x 13 ins / 23.2 x 33 cm) USD 3,080. NEW YORK, 17 Dec 1990, *Crossing the River on the Ferry* (oil on canvas, 20 x 36 ins / 50.8 x 91.6 cm) USD 3,300. NEW YORK, 21 May 1991, *Half-light at East Chester Creek* (oil on panel, 7 3/4 x 13 ins / 19.7 x 33 cm) USD 2,420. NEW YORK, 12 March 1992, *Camp on the Lakeside* (1875, oil on canvas, 18 x 36 ins / 46 x 91.5 cm) USD 11,000. NEW YORK, 2 Dec 1992, *Pond* (1906, oil on reinforced canvas, 10 x 13 3/4 ins / 25.4 x 35.2 cm) USD 1,430. NEW YORK, 31 March 1993, *Winter Scene* (1879, oil on canvas, 20 x 16 ins / 50.8 x 40.6 cm)

USD 2,990. NEW YORK, 15 Nov 1993, *Fitting the Fish Hooks* (oil on canvas, 20 x 36 ins / 51 x 91.5 cm) USD 10,350. NEW YORK, 28 Nov 1995, *Sheep Grazing under the Apple Trees* (oil on canvas/synthetic resin, 17 x 27 ins / 43.1 x 68.5 cm) USD 2,875. NEW YORK, 21 May 1996, *Far Far Away in the Hills* (oil on panel, 17 x 27 ins / 43 x 68.6 cm) USD 6,325.

GAY, Elisabeth
French, 20th century.
Painter.

Elisabeth Gay became a member of the Société des Artistes Français in 1907.

GAY, François
French, 17th century.
Born in Le Puy-en-Velay.
Active between 1642-1682.
Painter.

GAY, George Howell
American, 19th - 20th century.
Born 1858, in Milwaukee; died 1931.
Painter. Landscapes, seascapes.

George Gay studied seascape painting with Paul Brown and landscapes with Henry Arthur Elkins at the Academy of Design in Chicago. He left for New York in 1889. He took part in the exhibition at the National Academy of Design in 1890.

He painted meticulous coastal landscapes of New England and New York State.

AUCTION RECORDS:
NEW YORK, 18 Nov 1977, *Seaside* (two watercolours on paper, 13¼ x 28¼ ins / 33.5 x 72 cm and 16¼ x 25 ins/41 x 63.5 cm) USD 1,700. NEW YORK, 11 April 1981, *The Geese Fly Home* (watercolour, 17 x 27¼ ins / 43 x 69 cm) USD 650. NEW YORK, 21 Sept 1984, *Stormy Landscape* (watercolour and gouache, 13¾ x 30¾ ins / 35 x 78 cm) USD 750. NEW YORK, 3 Dec 1992, *Rollers at Northampton, Long Island* (watercolour on paper, 16 x 39¼ ins / 40.6 x 99.7 cm) USD 3,850. NEW YORK, 28 Nov 1995, *Coast of New Jersey* (watercolour on paper, 14¼ x 27 ins / 36.4 x 68.6 cm) USD 1,380.

GAY, Girard, also known as Girard de Han
French, 14th century.
Active in Troyes during the 14th century.
Sculptor.

Between 1383 and 1385, he carved two statues of *St Paul* for Troyes Cathedral, one of which was placed at the opening through the rood screen.

GAY, Guillaume
French, 17th century.
Born 1667, in Toulon.
Sculptor.

He worked in the decoration of ships.

GAY, Jacques
Swiss, 16th century.
Born c. 1511, in Geneva.
Painter.

GAY, Jacques Louis
French, 19th - 20th century.
Born 22 February 1851, in Voreppe; died 6 May 1925, in Grenoble.
Painter, draughtsman, designer. Portraits, genre scenes, landscapes. Murals.

Jacques Louis Gay came from an modest background, and began his working life as a printer and proof-reader. In 1878 he joined the studio of Léon Gérôme in the École des Beaux-Arts in Paris. He later settled in Grenoble. He depicted the tools of craftsmen with accuracy and used them to good effect to highlight his canvases. Under the direction of Anto ine Auguste Hébert, Gay also worked on the decoration o the cupola of the Pantheon in Paris. From 1878 to 1902 he ex hibited in Paris at the Salon and then at the Salon des Ar tistes Français, where he won a medal in 1881 for hi *Meditation.* He also showed work from time to time at th Salon in Grenoble and, in 1981, featured at the exhibition *L portrait en Dauphiné au XIXe siècle* (*The Portrait in the Dau phiné Region in the 19th Century*) at the Fondation Héber d'Uckermann in La Tronche.

BIBLIOGRAPHY:
Wantellet, Maurice, *Deux siècles et plus de peinture dauph noise*, M. Wantellet, Grenoble, 1987.

MUSEUMS AND GALLERIES:
GRENOBLE (Mus. de Grenoble): *Portrait of M. Debelle Former Curator* (1881); *Portrait of M. Henri Second.*

AUCTION RECORDS:
PARIS, 21-22 March 1927, *Portrait of a Woman* (drawing) FRI 1,020. VERSAILLES, 17 Oct 1982, *Elegant Girl Seated by a Lak* (oil on canvas, 21½ x 17¼ ins / 54.5 x 43.5 cm) FRF 2,600.

GAY, Jean Joseph Pascal
French, 19th century.
Born 14 April 1775, in Lyons; died 10 May 1832, in Lyons.
Architect, watercolourist.

Studied under Grognard at the art college in Lyons, then under the architect Donat Cochet; remained in Lyons as professor of architecture at the École des Beaux-Arts and worked as the official city architect. Gay left drawings and watercolours, including scenes from the French Revolution, designs for medals, and decorations for the ceiling of Lyons's Grand Théâtre, etc.

GAY, Jean Maurice
French, 20th century.
Painter.

Jean Maurice Gay's abstract compositions are minutely detailed; they are often plans for complicated and apparently useless machinery which probably would have produced excellent spatial kinetic objects if realised in three dimensions. Jean Maurice Gay exhibited in Paris at the Salon des Réalités Nouvelles from its foundation in 1947 until 1957. He lived in Bordeaux.

GAY, Le. See also **LE GAY**

GAY, Lydia, later Mrs Gay-Guillet
French, 19th century.
Active in Paris.
Sculptor.

Pupil of Legros.

GAY, Mathieu
French, 17th century.
Active in Toulouse in 1655.
Sculptor.

GAY, Michel
French, 16th century.
Active in Pontarlier c. 1594.
Sculptor.

He made several statues in 1594 for the chapel of St-Roch in Pontarlier.

GAY, Nikolai Nikolaevich, or Ge, Gue
Russian, 19th century.
Born 15 February 1831, in Voronezh, of French descent; died 1 June 1894, in Moscow.
Painter, sculptor. Religious subjects, portraits.
Founder member of the Peredvizhniki (Wanderers) group.

Studied mathematics before becoming a pupil of P. Bassin at the academy of fine arts from 1850 to 1857. He won a scholrship to Italy where he became a teacher in 1864. Gay returned to Russia in 1870 and left St Petersburg for the Ukraine. After having been influenced by Ivanov, he became interested in the German Nazarenes, then became the exponent of Tolstoy's ideas, painting *The Last Supper* (1863) and *The Crucifixion*. He was famous for his historical painting: *Peter the Great Questioning the Tsarevich Alexis at Peterhof* (1871).

MUSEUMS AND GALLERIES:

MOSCOW (Chekhov Mus.): *Pushkin Reading* - MOSCOW (Rumiantsev Mus.): *The Last Supper; Christ in the Garden of Gethsemane; Bielinsky* (bronze bust) - MOSCOW (State Tretyakov Gal.): *The Resurection; Christ Walking towards Gethsemane; Christ in Gethsemane; Christ and the Sister of Lazarus; The Last Supper; The Head of Christ; Christ at the House of St John; Jesus with his Disciples; Jesus and Nicodemus; Judas; Golgotha; Sanhedrin; What is the Truth?; Peter the Great and the Tsarevich; Catherine the Great and Elizabeth Petrovna; Tolstoy at his Desk; N. Ikonisky; A.N. Pypin; Kostomarov; Aleksandr Hertzen* - PARIS (MAM): *Golgotha* - ST PETERSBURG (Academy): *Saul and the Witch of Endor* - ST PETERSBURG (Gosudarstvennyj Russkij Muz.): *The Last Supper; Merkulov; N.A. Nekrassov; M.I. Saltyov; Peter the Great and the Tsarevich*.

GAY, P.

18th century.
Active in 1792.
Miniaturist.

Gay may have been English and might have worked in London in about 1810.

GAY, Rita Marguerite

French, 19th century.
Born 27 March 1865, in Aigle.
Painter. Landscapes, flowers.

Awarded a medal at the City of Rouen Exhibition in 1889.

MUSEUMS AND GALLERIES:

ROUEN: *Village Street in Britanny; Stream at La Roque*.

GAY, Rosalie

Swiss, 19th century.
Born 26 July 1852, in Lausanne.
Painter. Flowers.

Gay made her début at the 1878 Salon.

GAY, Walter

American, 19th - 20th century.
Born 22 January 1856, in Boston; died 1937, at the Château de Bréau.
Active in France.
Painter (including gouache), pastellist, watercolourist, draughtsman, decorative designer. Portraits, genre scenes, interiors with figures, landscapes with figures, architectural interiors.
Groupe de la Bande Noire.

Walter Gay was a flower painter in Boston until 1876. That year he went to Paris and studied with Léon Bonnat until 1879. He travelled to Spain, where he discovered Velázquez. The following year he shared a studio on the Boulevard de Clichy with three American artists. Under the aegis of Jacques-Émile Blanche he joined the group of 33, which brought together good mainstream artists in opposition to the revolutionaries of the time. As was the American custom he joined many artists' associations, both in the USA and in Belgium and France, including the Bande Noire (Black Group), a group of Post-Impressionist artists whose members included Charles Cottet, René Ménard and Lucien Simon. He was made a Chevalier, then Officier and finally Commandeur of the Légion d'Honneur in 1927. He collected works of art and decorative objets d'art, which were bequeathed to the Louvre by his widow in 1938.

After visiting Brittany in 1884 he painted genre scenes in a naturalist style in the manner of Bastien-Lepage. He was fond of richly decorated interiors, provincial sitting rooms and dining rooms adorned with hallmarked chests of drawers, paintings by masters and pieces of porcelain mounted on bronze. He drew his inspiration from the great rooms in the Château de Versailles, the Musée Carnavalet and his own rooms in the Château de Bréau. Although his interiors showed a tranquillity worthy of Chardin in their precision and subtlety of arrangement, this opulence lost favour with the public. Around 1935 he began painting less sumptuous interiors once again, portraying private apartments, as can be seen, for example, in the work entitled *White Room*.

He exhibited in many Salons, bringing back gold medals from Vienna in 1893, and exhibiting in Antwerp in 1894, Munich in 1895 and Paris in 1900. In 2002 he was represented in the exhibition *L'Impressionisme américain 1880-1915* (*American Impressionism 1880-1915*) at the Fondation de l'Hermitage in Lausanne.

BIBLIOGRAPHY:

Reynolds, Gary A., *Walter Gay: A Retrospective*, exhibition catalogue, New York University, Grey Art Gallery, 1980. Rieder, William, *A Charmed Couple: The Art and Life of Walter and Matilda Gay*, H.N. Abrams, New York, 2000. Cikovski, Nicolai/Hauptman, William, *L'Impressionnisme américain 1880-1915*, exhibition catalogue, Fondation de l'Hermitage, Lausanne, 2002.

AUCTION RECORDS:

NEW YORK, 1895, *In Holland*, FRF 700. PARIS, 1899, *Interior* (pastel) FRF 120. NEW YORK, 27 Jan 1905, *Provincial Home*, USD 850. PARIS, 6 June 1906, *Dining Room*, FRF 1,000. PARIS, 3 Feb 1919, *Fireplace*, FRF 1,350. PARIS, 20-22 May 1920, *Louis XV Alcove* (watercolour) FRF 2,190. PARIS, 13 March 1924, *Interior*, FRF 2,000. PARIS, 15 Dec 1927, *Drawing Office*, FRF 7,100. PARIS, 26 June 1929, *Interior*, FRF 1,000. LONDON, 28 Nov 1930, *Sitting Room*, GBP 11. PARIS, 10 Feb 1932, *Interior* (pastel) FRF 820. NEW YORK, 28 Oct 1936, *Wise Pigeons*, USD 650. PARIS, 24 June 1938, *Hall and Staircase*, FRF 550. PARIS, 17-18 Dec 1941, *Interior at Carnavalet*, FRF 5,000. NEW YORK, 7-9 Oct 1943, *Apothecary*, USD 350. NEW YORK, 19-20 Jan 1945, *Batchelor's Problems*, USD 300. NEW YORK, 11-13 April 1946, *Interior at the Palace of Fontainebleau*, USD 475. NEW YORK, 26-27 Feb 1947, *Provincial Home*, USD 175. NEW YORK, 6 Dec 1958, *Sitting Room in Château Fortroiseau*, USD 1,200. NEW YORK, 19 April 1968, *Boudoir, Château de Chalis*, USD 2,200. LOS ANGELES, 22 May 1973, *Interior*, USD 2,000. NEW YORK, 28 Oct 1976, *Picture Framer* (oil on panel, 15 1/4 x 11 1/4 ins / 38.5 x 28.5 cm) USD 3,200. NEW YORK, 18 Nov 1977, *Interior* (oil on canvas, 21 3/4 x 18 ins / 55.5 x 45.7 cm) USD 2,100. NEW YORK, 19 Jan 1978, *Interior with Chinese Vase; Snowy Landscape* (double-sided gouache and watercolour, 14 x 11 ins / 35.5 x 27 cm) USD 650. NEW YORK, 27 March 1981, *Interior* (1914, watercolour and pencil, 30 3/4 x 21 3/4 ins / 78.1 x 55.2 cm) USD 1,700. NEW YORK, 3 June 1983, *'Japonisme'* (oil on panel, 16 1/4 x 13 ins / 41.3 x 33 cm) USD 5,500; *Library in Château Bréau* (watercolour, 15 1/4 x 11 ins / 38.5 x 28.1 cm) USD 2,400. NEW YORK, 14 March 1986, *Vase (Ante-Room in the Château de Bréau)* (watercolour/mounted paper/card, 21 1/4 x 17 1/2 ins / 54 x 44.3 cm) USD 3,800. NEW YORK, 3 Dec 1987, *Embroideresses* (1895, oil on canvas, 27 1/2 x 36 ins / 69.9 x 91.4 cm) USD 64,000. NEW YORK, May 1989, *In the Garden* (1878, oil on canvas, 18 x 15 1/4 ins / 46 x 38.5 cm) USD 13,200. NEW YORK, 28 Sept 1989, *Fencing Lesson in the Park* (oil on canvas, 27 x 42 3/4 ins / 68.6 x 108.5 cm) USD 8,800. NEW YORK, 24 Jan 1990, *Entrance Hall and Staircase in the artist's house in Fontainebleau* (watercolour/card, 19 3/4 x 15 ins / 50.2 x 37.8 cm) USD 2,860. NEW YORK, 30 May 1990, *Sitting Room in the Château de Bréau* (gouache and ink/paper, 10 3/4 x 14 ins / 27.3 x 35.6 cm) USD 2,200. NEW YORK, 31 May 1990, *Napoleon's Throne Room in Fontainebleau* (oil on canvas, 24 x 28¾ ins / 61 x 73 cm) USD 3,850. PARIS, 13 June 1990, *Embroideress at the Window* (1987, drawing in lead pencil, 17¾ x 10¼ ins / 45 x 26 cm) FRF 4,500. NEW YORK, 21 May 1991, *Yellow Curtains in the Château de Bréau* (oil on canvas, 22 x 18¼ ins / 55.9 x 46.3 cm) USD 5,280. NEW YORK, 22 May 1991, *Frame Carver* (oil on panel, 15¼ x 11¼ ins / 39 x 28.5 cm) USD 16,500. NEW YORK, 6 Dec 1991, *Sitting Room* (oil on canvas, 18 x 22¼ ins / 46 x 56.5 cm) USD 16,500. NEW YORK, 25 Sept 1992, *Coat* (watercolour and gouache/paper, 14½ x 11 ins / 36.8 x 27.9 cm) USD 7,975. PARIS, 1 Dec 1992, *Young Girl with Geranium* (1890, drawing, 14¼ x 11½ ins / 36 x 29 cm) FRF 10,000. NEW YORK, 27 May 1993, *Charity* (1889, oil on canvas, 96 x 87 ins / 243.8 x 221 cm) USD 27,600. LONDON, 17 Nov 1994, *Artist's Studio* (oil on canvas, 15½ x 12½ ins / 39.4 x 31.7 cm) GBP 5,175. NEW YORK, 28 Sept 1995, *Walkers Admiring a Sculpture in a Park* (1879, oil on canvas, 25¾ x 20 ins / 65.4 x 50.8 cm) USD 4,312. NEW YORK, 9 March 1996, *Young Woman with her Harp* (oil on panel, 9 x 6¼ ins / 22.8 x 15.9 cm) USD 8,625. NEW YORK, 3 Dec 1996, *Bust at Hellen's Place* (oil on card, 21¾ x 18 ins / 55.2 x 45.7 cm) USD 23,000. NEW YORK, 3 Dec 1997, *Palazzo Quirini Stampaglio* (oil on canvas, 21½ x 26 ins / 54.6 x 66 cm) USD 16,100. NEW YORK, 1 Dec 1998, *Interior* (oil on canvas, 22 x 18 ins / 55 x 46 cm) USD 30,000. BOSTON, 6 Dec 1998, *Pavillon Petit Colombe* (oil on canvas, 22 x 18 ins / 56 x 46 cm) USD 45,000. LOS ANGELES, 15 Sept 1999, *The New York Salon of Miss Elsie de Wolfe* (c. 1900, oil on canvas, 22 x 18 ins / 56 x 46 cm) USD 34,000. NEW YORK, 15 March 2000, *Lavender Poppies* (oil on panel, 17 x 11 ins / 42 x 28 cm) USD 60,000. JOHANNESBURG, 17 Oct 2000, *The New Sword* (oil on canvas, 29 x 24 ins / 73 x 60 cm) ZAR 130,000. NEW YORK, 14 March 2001, *Study of Hollyhocks* (oil on canvas, 24 x 15 ins / 61 x 38 cm) USD 30,000. NEW YORK, 23 May 2001, *Library Interior* (oil on canvas, 21 x 26 ins / 54 x 65 cm) USD 27,500. NEW YORK, 25 April 2002, *Salon des Aigles, Hotel Crillon, Paris* (oil on canvas, 26 x 21 ins / 65 x 54 cm) USD 38,000. NEW YORK, 4 Dec 2002, *Council Chamber Fontainebleau* (oil on canvas, 24 x 29 ins / 60 x 73 cm) USD 27,500. PARIS, 20 June 2003, *Salon of the Chateau de Reveillon* (oil on board, 21 x 26 ins / 54 x 66 cm) EUR 31,000. NEW YORK, 18 Oct 2003, *Drawing room, Paris* (oil on canvas, 32 x 39 ins / 81 x 99 cm) USD 50,000. NEW YORK, 27 Sept 2004, *New Sword* (1884, oil on canvas, 29 x 25 ins / 73 x 64 cm) USD 12,000.

GAY, Winkworth Allen or Alban
American, 19th - 20th century.
Born 18 August 1821, in Hingham (Massachusetts); died 23 February 1910, in Hingham.
Painter. Landscapes with figures, landscapes.

Winkworth Gay studied under Troyon in Paris.

AUCTION RECORDS:
LONDON, 28 May 1981, *Chinese Fishermen on a Lake* (1879, oil on canvas, 16 x 30 ins / 40.5 x 76 cm) GBP 460. NEW YORK, 21 Sept 1984, *Homoko, Japan* (oil on canvas, 16¼ x 22¼ ins / 41.4 x 56.5 cm) USD 1,500. NEW YORK, 21 May 1991, *Tokyo with Mount Fujiyama in the Distance* (1884, oil on canvas, 29 x 23½ ins / 73.7 x 59.8 cm) USD 6,050. LONDON, 7 April 1993, *Shepherd and his Sheep near a Farm* (oil on panel, 7 x 9 ins / 17.5 x 22 cm) GBP 632. NEW YORK, 9 Sept 1993, *Landscape near Inoshino* (oil on reinforced canvas, 11 x 17 ins / 27.9 x 43.2 cm) USD 2,760.

GAY-GUILLET (Mrs). See **GAY Lydia**

GAY-VULLIEN, Georges Jean Baptiste
French, 19th century.
Born 19th century, in Paris.
Painter. Portraits.

Studied under Yvon and Henner; exhibited at the Salon from 1876 to 1880.

GAYARD, Michel
French, 20th - 21st century.
Born 10 May 1948, in St-Étienne.
Painter, draughtsman.

Michel Gayard trained at the École des Beaux-Arts in Mâco and Marseilles before completing his studies at the Écol Nationale Supérieure des Arts Décoratifs in Paris. He bega teaching in 1977. He draws jagged, rising forms. His colour give shape to silent landscapes dominated by rock formations such as cliffs, mountains and faultlines. Between fu and empty areas, his line comes into force, stretching breaking and disappearing in a quasi-Abstract world wher cold and warm colours play off each other and transparenc comes into play.

He began taking part in group exhibitions in 1976, in particular in Paris at the Salon des Surindépendants (1976), th Salon du Dessin et de la Peinture à l'Eau (1980), and the Salon Révélations (1984). His first solo exhibition was held ir 1977.

GAYE, Joseph
French, 19th century.
Born 10 May 1803, in Tarbes; died 1862, in Paris.
Miniaturist.

Studied under Aubry and exhibited at the Salon from 1831 tc 1861, receiving a medal in 1837. Examples of Gaye's miniatures are preserved in the Wallace Collection in London namely a *Portrait of Napoleon III* and another of the *Empress Eugénie*.

GAYET, Antoine Juste Ernest
French, 19th century.
Painter.

Studied under Fonville in Lyons and exhibited in that city from 1845-1846 to 1851-1852, chiefly with landscapes of the Savoie, Switzerland and around Bugey.

GAYET, Claude
French, 18th century.
Active in Paris in 1740.
Painter, sculptor.

GAYET-TANCRÈDE, Paul. See **SAMIVEL**

GAYEZ, Jean Baptiste Julien
French, 18th century.
Active in Paris in 1759.
Painter, sculptor.

GAYFERE, Thomas
British, 18th - 19th century.
Died 1828.
Active in England.
Architect, painter.

Thomas Gayfere exhibited at the Society of Artists and Royal Academy in London from 1777 to 1780.

GAYLE, Marsha
American, 20th century.
Painter. Landscapes, portraits.

Marsha Gayle's figurative paintings are brightly coloured, constructed with light touches broken up by solid areas of colour. She held her first exhibition in France in 1960, and the following year she took part in the Salon des Artistes Indépendants. She then exhibited in Italy, Spain and the USA.

GAYLEARD, Sophia (Miss)
British, 19th century.
Active in London.
Painter. Portraits.

Sophia Gayleard exhibited in London at the Royal Academy and at the Suffolk Street Gallery.

GAYON, Pierre
French, 15th - 16th century.
Painter.

He is known to have been living in Lyons in 1485 and 1515. In 1499 he made escutcheons with arms and devices, for which J. Perréal had provided a template, for a gateway.

GAYOR, Tibor
Hungarian, 20th century.
Born 1929, in Budapest.
Performance artist.

Tibor Gayor's work, based on photographic reports and actions which in the West in the 1960s were rather commonplace, was undoubtedly fairly exceptional due to its avant-garde nature in Hungary. His symbolically loaded actions and attitudes tend to define the human condition in relation to the environment.

GAYOT, René
French, 20th century.
Born 3 July 1925, in Rouen.
Painter, engraver, draughtsman. Landscapes.

René Gayot moved to Cabries in the Aix region of Provence at a young age. He made quick sketches from nature and reworked them in his studio, a method that had enabled Jongkind and Signac to produce remarkable watercolours. Gayot was able to avoid arbitrary simplifications and focus on the essential in his work.

GAYOU, Bastien
French, 17th century.
Born in Paris.
Sculptor.

In 1603, in association with Pierre de France, another sculptor, he created the coat of arms for the newly erected pillar of justice in the town square of Albi.

GAYRAL, Jean Philippe
French, 19th - 20th century.
Born 1872, in Donnazac.
Painter. Interiors with figures, landscapes.

Jean Philippe Gayral specialised in painting landscapes, and also depicted the interiors of artists' studios and art schools. He exhibited in Paris at the Salon des Artistes Français, where he won a silver medal in 1932.

GAYRARD, Paul Joseph Raymond
French, 19th century.
Born 3 September 1807, in Clermont; died 22 July 1855, in Enghien-les-Bains.
Sculptor. Figures, animals. Busts.

Studied under his father Raymond Gayrard and exhibited at the Paris Salon from 1831 to 1855, obtaining a silver medal in 1834 and a gold medal in 1846. Paul Gayrard was very much a favourite of the high society of his day. He sculpted numerous busts of leading figures, together with statues of the four apostles now to be found in the church of St-Clotilde.

MUSEUMS AND GALLERIES:
CAEN: *Daphnis and Chloe* - LE HAVRE: *Penitent Magdalene*; *Ancelot* - PARIS (Mus. de la Comédie-Française): *Monrose Sr.*; *Casimir Bonjour* - RODEZ: *Fisherman with Trident* - TOURS: *Dr. Bretonneau* (marble bust); *Dr. Trousseau* (marble bust).

AUCTION RECORDS:
LONDON, 8 Nov 1984, *Horse Race with Monkey Jockeys* (bronze, h. 9 ins / 23 cm) GBP 1,450. LONDON, 21 March 1985, *Hunting Dog* (c. 1850, patinated bronze, h. 5 ins / 12.5 cm) GBP 1,100. NEW YORK, 9 June 1988, *Monkey Steeplechase* (1846, bronze, h. 9 ins / 22.6 cm) USD 5,280. NEW YORK, 23 Feb 1989, *Scottish Hound Reclining* (1848, bronze, h. 12½ ins / 31.8 cm) USD 2,420. PARIS, 8 Nov 1995, *Dray Wearing Harness and Bridle* (bronze, h. 13 ins / 33 cm) FRF 40,000. LONDON, 19 April 2000, *Recumbent Chihuahua* (sculpture, brown patinated bronze, 4 x 6x? ins / 10 x 16x? cm) GBP 1,200. LONDON, 5 July 2000, *Allegorical Figure of the Arts* (sculpture, white marble, h. 37 ins / 95 cm) GBP 5,000. NEW YORK, 12 Feb 2002, *Irish Wolfhound* (1848, sculpture, brown patinated bronze, 5 x 12x? ins / 12 x 30x? cm) USD 1,700. LONDON, 6 Nov 2002, *Monkey Steeplechase* (sculpture, brown patinated bronze, 9 x 9x? ins / 23 x 23x? cm) GBP 1,700. FONTAINEBLEAU, 31 Jan 2004, *Cheval de l'Empereur Napoleon III enharnachement de parade* (sculpture, dark patinated bronze, 23 x 27x? ins / 58 x 68x? cm) EUR 7,000.

GAYRARD, Raymond
French, 19th century.
Born 25 October 1777, in Rodez; died 4 May 1858, in Paris.
Sculptor.

Son of Paul Gayrard; studied under Boizot, Taunay and Geoffroy and exhibited at the Salon from 1814 to 1871, showing medallions and busts of celebrities of the day, together with groups and individual statues. He was made a Chevalier of the Légion d'Honneur.

MUSEUMS AND GALLERIES:
DIJON: *Michelangelo* - MONTPELLIER: *Child Playing with a Greyhound Bitch* - RODEZ: *Bishop St Germain Predicting the Fate of St Genevieve* (low relief); *Baptism of Christ*; *Sleeping Lioness*; *Viscount Francois de Gissac*; *Abbot Raynal*; *Monseigneur Frayssinous*; *Allegory of Goodness*; *General Bételle*; *Louis-Philippe*; *Napoleon III*; *Count de Chambord and Henry IV*; *Eugène de Barreau*; *Woman Bather*; *Cupid Testing his Arrows*; *Monument to Monseigneur Affre at Aveyron (project)*; *Justice Protecting Innocence and Punishing Crime* - ROUEN: *Bust of General Le Breton* - VERSAILLES: *King Charles IV of Frances*; marble bust; *Jeanne d'Evreux*.

GAYRIN, Louis Albert
French, 20th century.
Born 29 September 1911, in Bordeaux; died 22 May 1971, in Paris.
Active in the USA from 1945.
Painter. Landscapes, still-lifes.

Before settling in Hollywood in the USA, where he is thought to have led a very fashionable life, Louis Albert Gayrin travelled widely before World War II.

His work is clearly influenced by Braque; his painting is postcubist, brilliantly coloured, slightly abstract, and adorned with large arabesques.

AUCTION RECORDS:
PARIS, 6 Dec 1973, *St-Tropez*, FRF 4,900. PARIS, 10 Oct 1974, *Cubist Composition with Guitar*, FRF 10,000. PARIS, 12 Dec 1977, *Exotic Composition* (oil on canvas, 51¼ x 63½ ins / 130 x 161 cm) FRF 10,000; *Santa Barbara* (1963, watercolour and gouache, 59 x 84¼ ins / 150 x 214 cm) FRF 8,000.

GAYS, Eugenio
Italian, 19th - 20th century.
Born 1861, in Rivara Canavese; died 1938.
Painter. Landscapes, still-lifes.

Eugenio Gays began his artistic career in Turin around 1884. He also exhibited in Milan and Venice.

AUCTION RECORDS:
BERN, 23 Oct 1980, *Still-life with Fruit* (1934, watercolour, 22½ x 30¾ ins / 57 x 78 cm) CHF 1,000.

GAYWOOD, Robert
British, 17th - 18th century.
Born c. 1650; died c. 1711.
Engraver. Figures, historical figures.

Robert Gaywood was a pupil and imitator of Hollar. Examples of his work include *Mary Queen of Scots Holding a Crucifix*, *Queen Maria Henrietta*, *Oliver Cromwell*, *Countess of Portland*, *Hans Holbein*, *Sir Anthony van Dyck*, and the *Countess of Carlisle*.

AUCTION RECORDS:
LONDON, 11 July 1928, *Young Flautist* (drawing) GBP 6.

GAZA, N.
19th century.
Painter. Animals.
Mentioned by Florence Levy.
AUCTION RECORDS:
NEW YORK, 7 Feb 1907, *Lioness and her Cubs,* USD 225.

GAZAGNE, Marguerite Marie
French, 20th century.
Born in Montreuil-sous-Bois.
Painter.
Marguerite Marie Gazagne first exhibited at the Salon des Artistes Français in Paris in 1928.

GAZALIS, Bartolommeo
Italian, 18th century.
Born in Genoa.
Active mainly in Milan.
Draughtsman, engraver.

GAZAN, Francisco
Spanish, 17th century.
Born 1684; died 1732.
Engraver.
Francisco Gazan engraved a portrait of the Spanish poet and writer Quevedo, after Salva Jordan.

GAZAN, Henry
French, 20th century.
Born 1887, in Paris.
Draughtsman, illustrator.
Henry Gazan worked on several satirical journals and illustrated a number of works. He also produced some landscapes.

GAZARD, François Valentin
French, 18th - 19th century.
Born in Toulouse; died 1817, in Versailles.
Painter. Figures, genre scenes, seascapes.
He exhibited at the Salon from 1796 to 1814. In 1802, he became curator of the museum in Versailles.
MUSEUMS AND GALLERIES:
ARRAS: *The Calm after the Storm* - TOULOUSE: *Attack of the Bandits; The Storm.*
AUCTION RECORDS:
PARIS, 11 April 1909, *Fisherman at the Mouth of a Port,* FRF 125. PARIS, 14-15 June 1923, *Bust of a Man with a Scarf Tied Around the Neck,* FRF 220. PARIS, 17 June 1927, *Fisherman with Net,* FRF 2,600.

GAZE, Harold
New Zealander, 20th century.
Born 1885, in New Zealand; died 1962.
Active in the USA from 1927.
Watercolourist, draughtsman, illustrator.
Harold Gaze studied in London. In 1927, he settled in Pasadena, California. His illustrations for children's books are characterised by their opalescent colours and his joyous sense of the grotesque. He often gave human form to rocks, waves or trees.
AUCTION RECORDS:
NEW YORK, 22 June 1983, *A Romance of Two Worlds* (1920, watercolour, Indian ink and pencil, 12 1/4 x 9 ins / 31 x 22.8 cm) USD 1,000. NEW YORK, 25 June 1986, *The Baby Stealer* (1931, watercolour, ink and pencil/mounted paper/card, 14 x 10 1/4 ins / 35.5 x 26 cm) USD 1,500. NEW YORK, 25 Feb 1988, *Fairytale Garden* (watercolour and ink, 13 x 10 ins / 33 x 25.3 cm) USD 3,850. NEW YORK, 20 March 1996, *Lonely* (1926, watercolour and ink/paper, 13 x 9 1/4 ins / 33 x 23.5 cm) USD 4,025. NEW YORK, 25 March 1997, *Making Acquaintance* (1952, coloured ink, gouache and traces of pencil/paper, 4 1/4 x 11 1/2 ins / 11.1 x 28.9 cm) USD 3,737.

GAZEAU, Antoine Xavier Gabriel de (Comte de La Bouère), called Tancrède de la Bouère
French, 19th century.
Born 1801, in Jallais (Maine-et-Loire); died 1881.
Painter. Landscapes.
Orientalism.
Participated in the Algerian expedition of 1830 as a captai on the general staff; painted landscapes of Algeria, Egyp and Spain.
BIBLIOGRAPHY:
Les années romantiques, la peinture française de 1815 à 185(exhibition catalogue, Musée des Beaux-Arts, Nantes, Ga nationales du Grand Palais, Paris, 1996.
MUSEUMS AND GALLERIES:
ANGERS (MBA): *Algerian Countryside; Desert beyond Sue Poussin's Factory* - TROYES (MBA): *Countryside near Rome a Harvest Time.*

GAZET, Louis Bernard
French, 18th century.
Active in Paris in 1761.
Painter, sculptor.

GAZET-CHANABAS
French, 20th century.
Painter. Nudes, landscapes, seascapes, still-lifes.
At the age of 16, Gazet-Chabanas was a pupil at the art col lege in Marseilles. He also trained under Louis Cloquet Chevreul and Édouard Fer. He learned painting and indus trial drawing, and produced brochures and catalogues. He also wrote short stories, some of which inspired his paintings.

Gazet-Chabanas normally painted from life, aiming to seize every aspect of the light. In all his light-filled canvases he tried to create the illusion of a third dimension, probably influenced by his photographic work.

GAZI, Dragan
Croat, 20th century.
Born 1930, in Hlebine; died 1983, in Hlebine.
Painter. Portraits, local scenes, landscapes.
School of Hlebine.
Dragan Gazi was born in the same village as Ivan Generalic, whose example and glory motivated him greatly. A genuine peasant farmer, he only painted in his leisure time. He began drawing in his childhood and Generalic showed him the rudiments of painting glass pictures.

He painted landscapes of his region with flat colours and the peasants from his village, to whom he gave a great deal of expression in the manner of the German Primitives as well as groups at celebrations, festivals and weddings.

He exhibited with painters in Hlebine, at exhibitions in Zagreb and Koprivnica. Dragan Gazi showed his works in a solo exhibition in Belgrade in 1957 and featured in the exhibition *Die Naïven, aufbruch ins verlorene Paradies* (*The Naïve Painters, Journey to a Lost Paradise*) , Kunsthaus, Vienna, which brought under one roof around 200 works by naive artists from the Charlotte Zander Museum collection in Bönnigheim (2001).
BIBLIOGRAPHY:
Bihalji-Merin, Oto, *Les Peintres naïfs,* Delpire, Paris, 1960. *Die Naive, aufbruch ins verlorene paradies,* exhibition catalogue, Kunsthaus, Vienna, 2001 (text in German and English).
MUSEUMS AND GALLERIES:
BÖNNIGHEIM (Mus. Charlotte Zander).
AUCTION RECORDS:
ZURICH, 20 May 1980, *Grandfather and Grandson on a Road covered in Snow* (1964, oil on panel, 18 1/4 x 21 3/4 ins / 46.5 x 55.5 cm) GBP 380. GRENOBLE, 15 Dec 1980, *Sunset in Winter* (oil on canvas, 22 x 18 ins / 56 x 46 cm) FRF 3,800.

GAZIER, Jean
French, 20th century.
Active in Paris.
Painter.
Jean Gazier exhibited abstract compositions at the Salon des Réalités Nouvelles from 1947 to 1954.

GAZOUKIN, Valery
Russian, 20th - 21st century.
Born 1951, in Orenburg.
Painter. Figures, portraits.
Valery Gazoukin studied at the Guertsen Institute of education and at the faculty of graphic art, both in Leningrad (now St Petersburg), graduating in 1974. He became a member of the Union of Soviet Artists in 1980. His work has featured in several national and international exhibitions. The cities of Orenburg and Tallinn have both held retrospectives of his work.
AUCTION RECORDS:
PARIS, 11 Dec 1991, *Portrait in April* (1988, oil on card, 32 x 30 1/4 ins / 81 x 77 cm) FRF 4,500. PARIS, 16 Feb 1992, *In the Village* (oil on canvas, 35 1/2 x 35 1/2 ins / 90 x 90 cm) FRF 5,800; *The Apostle Paul* (oil on canvas, 59 x 78 3/4 ins / 150 x 200 cm) FRF 10,000.

GAZOUX, pseudonym of Gilles Rouxel
French, 20th - 21st century.
Born 1951, in Tours.
Painter, draughtsman, writer.
Gazoux started out producing humorous drawings for newspapers. He then trained between 1973 and 1975 at the École des Arts Appliqués et Métiers d'Art in Paris. From 1975 to 1981 he gradually embarked on what would become a full-time career as a painter and graphic artist. He has travelled widely in France as well as to Martinique and Brazil.
During his stay in Brazil, Gazoux focused his attention on colour in Figurative paintings. He then turned to line and subsequently to movement, as in his *Waves*, before experimenting with material elements. His work ranges from Abstraction to Hyperrealism, sometimes in the same work. He is the author of a book entitled *À mes regrettés voisins* (*To My Lamented Neighbours*) , which he also illustrated.
He began exhibiting in São Paulo in 1983 and then went on to show work in Paris, Cassis, Martinique, Tours, Lyons, Villeneuve-lès-Avignon, Blois, Aubagne and Sens, among other places.

GAZYMALA, Maria
French, 20th century.
Painter.
Maria Gazymala assembled small items in her pictures with a clear feeling of nostalgia.

GAZZANIGA, Silvio
Italian, 20th century.
Sculptor.
Silvio Gazzaniga is most famous for designing the FIFA World Cup trophy, which is in the form of a globe held aloft by two athletes.

GAZZARINI, Tommaso
Italian, 19th century.
Born 16 February 1790, in Livorno; died 7 February 1853, in Florence.
Painter. History painting, religious subjects.
Gazzarini was a pupil of Benvenuti. After spending some time in Rome, he settled in Florence. He chiefly painted religious pictures.

GAZZERA, Romano
Italian, 20th century.
Born 18 August 1906, in Ciriè (Piedmont); died 24 May 1985, in Turin.
Painter. Portraits, landscapes, still-lifes, flowers.
Romano Gazzera took up painting when he was very young, although his father insisted that he take a degree in arts and law. After working as a lawyer for a few years, he gave it up to devote himself to painting.
Gazzera staged his first exhibition in 1941, in Milan, and took part in numerous art events after that. He also showed his works in solo exhibitions, both in Italy and abroad: in France (most notably at the Hôtel de Ville in Paris), Germany, Switzerland, Canada, the USA and other countries. His paintings earned him many prizes and distinctions.
From 1950 onwards, Gazzera's work became luminous and brightly coloured. This was the year that he created the giant flower motif, which later went on to be used in advertising and fashion. His canvases always depict either small figures in landscapes with vast skies full of giant flowers, or figures with flowers for heads. His works also often make reference to well-known painters, such as Raphael, Da Vinci and Goya.
BIBLIOGRAPHY:
Gazzera, Fabbri, Milan, 1987. Gazzera, Romano, *La Rosa di Clarissa*, Mediolanum Ed. Associati, Milan, 1990. *Romano Gazzera*, exhibition catalogue, Musée de la Chasse et de la Nature, mairie du VIe arrondissement, Paris, 1997.
AUCTION RECORDS:
MILAN, 6 May 1984, *Le Cavallette e la Strelitzia* (1965, oil on card, 35 1/2 x 27 1/4 ins / 90 x 69 cm) ITL 6,500,000. VIENNA, 9 April 1987, *Dalie della Valdinievole* (1965, oil on canvas, 35 1/2 x 27 1/2 ins / 90 x 70 cm) ITL 7,200,000. MILAN, 7 June 1989, *Tulips and Narcissi* (1975, oil on canvas, 25 1/2 x 20 ins / 65 x 51 cm) ITL 6,000,000. ROME, 14 Nov 1995, *Gentleman* (oil on panel, 9 1/2 x 7 3/4 ins / 24 x 20 cm) ITL 1,150,000. MILAN, 12 Dec 1995, *Scarecrow* (oil on canvas, 35 1/2 x 27 1/2 ins / 90 x 70 cm) ITL 7,245,000. MILAN, 10 Dec 1996, *Flowers* (oil on canvas, 35 1/2 x 27 1/2 ins / 90 x 70 cm) ITL 7,572,000. VERCELLI, 23 Nov 2002, *Peugeot Heading East* (1965, oil on cardboard/canvas, 5 x 20 ins / 13 x 50 cm) EUR 2,000. TURIN, 26 June 2003, *Confidences under the Geraniums* (1984, oil on masonite, 16 x 12 ins / 40 x 30 cm) EUR 3,000. MILAN, 28 Oct 2003, *Mythological Landscape* (oil on canvas, 35 x 28 ins / 90 x 70 cm) EUR 3,000. TURIN, 22 March 2004, *Red Anemones* (oil on board, 15 x 22 ins / 37 x 56 cm) EUR 3,200. TURIN, 22 March 2004, *Tropical Plant* (oil on canvas, 35 x 28 ins / 90 x 70 cm) EUR 6,700.

GAZZETTA, Francesco
Italian, 18th century.
Born c. 1735, in Este.
Active in Rovigo.
Sculptor.

GAZZOTTI, Elvezia. See **PAÏNI Lotus de**

GAZZOTTO, Vincenzo
Italian, 19th century.
Born 10 August 1807, in Padua.
Painter. History painting.
Gazzotto was a pupil of J. Demin. The Uffizi in Florence and the Museo Civico in Padua both have drawings by this artist.

GE YILONG, or Ko I-lung, style name: Zhenfu
Chinese, 16th - 17th century.
Born 1567; died 1640, in Suzhou (Jiangsu).
Painter.
Ge Yilong worked in the style of Chen Shun (1483-1544).

GE ZHENGQI, or Ko Cheng-ch'i, style name: Wuqi, sobriquet: Jiekan
Chinese, 17th century.
Born in Haining (Zhejiang).
Active during the first half of the 17th century.
Painter. Landscapes.

Ge Zhengqi passed the national *jinshi* (accomplished scholar) examinations in 1628 and went on to make a career as an official.

GEA, Juan de
Spanish, 18th century.
Active in Murcia.
Sculptor, architect.
Juan de Gea worked for Murcia Cathedral.

GÉA-PANTER, pseudonym of Dellove, Geneviève
French, 20th century.
Born October 1909, in Caudry.
Painter.
Géa-Panter was self-taught, except for a period of some months when she trained with Léger in 1950. Her painting is abstract, strongly coloured, lively and lyrical. She began exhibiting, mostly in Holland, in 1955. She also showed work in Paris at the Salon de Mai and the Salon des Indépendants.
MUSEUMS AND GALLERIES:
AMSTERDAM - JERUSALEM.

GEANTEAU, Charles Antoine
French, 18th century.
Active in Paris in 1774.
Painter.

GEAR, Joseph
British, 18th - 19th century.
Born 1769, in Gosport; died 1853, in Cambridge, Massachusetts.
Painter, watercolourist.

GEAR, Joseph William
British, 19th century.
Active in London.
Painter, engraver. Portraits.
Joseph William Gear exhibited in London at the Royal Academy and Suffolk Street Gallery from 1821 to 1852.

GEAR, Mabel
British, 20th century.
Born 1900.
Watercolourist, painter (gouache). Animals.
Mabel Gear specialised in portraying pedigree dogs.
AUCTION RECORDS:
LONDON, 14 Feb 1990, *Tricolour Cavalier King Charles Puppy* (pencil, watercolour and gouache, 12 x 9 3/4 ins / 30.4 x 24.6 cm) GBP 440. LONDON, 20 Sept 1990, *Vanity of Vanities* (oil on canvas, 24 1/2 x 29 1/2 ins / 62 x 75 cm) GBP 1,100. LONDON, 15 Jan 1991, *A West Highland Terrier and Two Scotties* (watercolour and gouache heightened with white, 12 x 18 ins / 30.4 x 45.7 cm) GBP 1,100. LONDON, 28 March 1996, *Cocker Spaniels on a Staircase* (watercolour heightened with white, 8 1/2 x 11 ins / 21.6 x 27.8 cm) GBP 1,092. LEYBURN, 16 July 1999, *Great Danes* (oil on board, 15 x 18 ins / 39 x 46 cm) GBP 2,100. NEW YORK, 15 Feb 2000, *Wire Fox Terrier and Puppies. Wire Fox Terrier and Puppy by Basket* (watercolour and gouache, a pair, 9 x 13 ins / 24 x 34 cm) USD 2,800. BILLINGSHURST, 5 Dec 2000, *By the Fireside* (oil on panel, 7 x 11 ins / 19 x 28 cm) GBP 3,000. DRIFFIELD, 6 April 2001, *Vanity of the Vanities* (oil on canvas, 24 x 29 ins / 61 x 74 cm) GBP 1,000. NEW YORK, 12 Feb 2002, *Highlanders* (watercolour heightened with white, 12 x 7 ins / 30 x 19 cm) USD 3,500. DRIFFIELD, 20 Sept 2002, *Bathtime* (pencil heightened with white, 4 x 6 ins / 9 x 15 cm) GBP 1,700. LONDON, 12 Feb 2003, *Best Friends* (pastel and chalk, 15 x 13 ins / 39 x 34 cm) GBP 1,000. NEW YORK, 10 Feb 2004, *Portrait of a Bulldog* (watercolour heightened with white on paper laid on board, 10 x 6 ins / 25 x 15 cm) USD 1,900.

GEAR, William
British, 20th century.
Born 1915, in Fife, Scotland; died 1997.
Painter.
William Gear studied Fine Art at Edinburgh College of A[rt] from 1932 to 1936 and Art History at Edinburgh Universi[ty] in 1937, then won a travel scholarship to study with Léger i[n] Paris in 1937-1938. After serving in the army during Worl[d] War II, he returned to live in Paris from 1947 to 1950. Fro[m] 1958 to 1964, he was Curator of the Towner Art Gallery i[n] Eastbourne and from 1964 to 1975, he was head of fine art [at] Birmingham College of Art.

In his earliest works, he paid great attention to the play [of] light. Between 1948 and 1951, he followed the activities [of] the CoBrA group with great interest. In his more radical ab[-]stract period, he turned to thick black graphics on a whit[e] ground, or vice versa, filling the space on the canvas with [a] kind of tracery composed either of very sharp, highly con[-]structed, angular lines or of more random curves. Afte[r] 1951, his style became calmer. He structured the space mor[e] rigorously by means of geometrical shapes and patches [of] bright or earthy colours in order to reproduce the rhythm o[f] nature. The eye is led through a maze of moving forms. O[n] the subject of his abstract painting, he wrote: 'I do not re[-]gard my work as a denial of nature, but rather as an exten[-]sion of it.'

From 1940 on, he took part in group exhibitions at the Tat[e] Gallery and Royal Academy in London, but also abroad, no[-]tably in Paris, where he featured alongside Bryen[,] Boumeester and Sauer in the exhibition *La Rose des Vent[s]* (*The Windrose*), which helped to establish the Lyrical Ab[-]straction movement, and at the Salon des Réalités Nouvelle[s] from 1948 to 1950 and the 1948 Salon des Indépendants[,] where he met Asger Jorn. He began holding solo exhibition[s] in 1944 in Siena and Florence, then showed in 1948 at th[e] Galerie Arc-en-Ciel in Paris, at Gimpel Fils in London and a[t] the Betty Parsons Gallery in New York, and later also i[n] Hamburg and Florence. In 1988, a collection of his works was shown at the Galerie 1900-2000 in Paris.

BIBLIOGRAPHY:
William Gear, exhibition catalogue, Gal. 1900-2000, Paris, 1983. Jaguer, Éd./Lambert, Jean-Cl., *William Gear: Cobrabstractions 1946-1949*, exhibition catalogue, Gal. 1900-2000, Paris, 1988.
MUSEUMS AND GALLERIES:
BIRMINGHAM (Mus. and AG): *Mau-Mau* (1953, oil on canvas); *Cold Spring* (oil on canvas); *Landscape Image No 1. 1961* (oil on canvas) - CANBERRA (Nat. Gal. of Australia) - LIMA (MCA) - LONDON (Tate Collection): *Landscape Structure* (1948, gouache/panel); *Interior* (1949, oil on canvas); *Composition* (1949, oil on canvas); *The Sculptor* (1953, oil on canvas); *Feature in Landscape* (1960, oil on canvas) - LONDON (Victoria and Albert Mus.) - MANCHESTER (City AG) - NEW YORK (MoMA) - OTTAWA (NG. of Canada) - SOUTHAMPTON (City AG): *Winter Landscape* (1960) - SYDNEY (AG of New South Wales) - TEL AVIV (MA).
AUCTION RECORDS:
LONDON, 20 May 1987, *Interior* (1949, oil on canvas, 23 3/4 x 32 ins / 60.4 x 81.3 cm) GBP 3,200. LONDON, 30 Nov 1987, *Composition, Two Figures* (1947, gouache, pen and pencil, 18 1/2 x 11 1/4 ins / 47 x 28.5 cm) GBP 1,200. LONDON, 9 June 1988, *Paris 1948* (gouache and watercolour, 18 1/4 x 24 1/4 ins / 46.3 x 61.5 cm) GBP 1,045. COPENHAGEN, 8 Nov 1988, *Landscape* (1947, gouache, 11 3/4 x 19 3/4 ins / 30 x 50 cm) DKK 30,000. LONDON, 25 May 1989, *Structure* (1949, gouache and oil on card, 19 3/4 x

4 ins / 50 x 61 cm) GBP 2,420. AMSTERDAM, 22 May 1990, *The White Tree* (1950, oil on canvas, 25 1/2 x 25 1/2 ins / 65 x 65 cm) NLG 23,000. LONDON, 8 June 1990, *Landscape with two Tree-trunks* (1962, oil on canvas, 32 1/4 x 22 ins / 82 x 56 cm) GBP 080. PARIS, 31 Oct 1990, *Composition* (1952, watercolour and ink, 13 3/4 x 9 3/4 ins / 35 x 25 cm) FRF 4,500. LONDON, 8 March 1991, *Grey Landscape* (1951, oil on canvas, 15 x 24 ins / 38 x 61 cm) GBP 1,980. LONDON, 21 March 1991, *Landscape with Blue* (1959, oil on canvas, 38 3/4 x 27 1/2 ins / 98.5 x 70 cm) GBP 4,620. NEW YORK, 5 Nov 1991, *Garden* (1963, coloured inks/paper, 21 3/4 x 30 3/4 ins / 55.3 x 78.4 cm) USD 1,100. AMSTERDAM, 12 Dec 1991, *Summer Landscape* (1948, watercolour and gouache/paper, 19 1/4 x 24 3/4 ins / 49 x 63 cm) NLG 4,025. PARIS, 20 May 1992, *Composition* (1949, oil on paper/canvas, 20 3/4 x 30 ins / 53 x 76 cm) FRF 4,300. AMSTERDAM, 21 May 1992, *Untitled* (1948, gouache/paper, 18 1/2 x 22 1/4 ins / 47 x 56.5 cm) NLG 3,795. LONDON, 11 June 1992, *Landscape in April* (1951, oil on canvas, 36 x 24 ins / 91.5 x 61 cm) GBP 2,420. LONDON, 3 Dec 1993, *October Landscape* (1960, oil on canvas, 48 x 32 ins / 122 x 81 cm) GBP 3,450. PARIS, 26 March 1995, *Winter, Hedgrow* (1951, oil on canvas, 39 1/4 x 32 ins / 100 x 81 cm) FRF 4,500. LONDON, 5 March 1999, *Composition* (1949, oil and gouache on card on board, 16 x 22 ins / 41 x 56 cm) GBP 3,400. LONDON, 2 Nov 1999, *November '63* (1963, oil on canvas, 48 x 32 ins / 122 x 81 cm) GBP 3,600. LONDON, 5 April 2000, *Peinture* (1950, oil on canvas, 26 x 21 ins / 65 x 54 cm) GBP 5,500. LONDON, 24 Nov 2000, *Paysage* (1948, oil on canvas, 22 x 32 ins / 57 x 81 cm) GBP 6,500. LONDON, 1 March 2001, *Abstract* (1962, oil on canvas, 46 x 35 ins / 117 x 89 cm) GBP 4,000. EDINBURGH, 7 Dec 2001, *Process of a Thought* (oil on canvas, 24 x 15 ins / 60 x 38 cm) GBP 4,000. COPENHAGEN, 20 March 2002, *White Tree, Paris* (1949-1950, oil on canvas, 26 x 26 ins / 65 x 65 cm) DKK 60,000. LONDON, 3 July 2002, *Winter Study* (1955, oil on canvas, 24 x 27 ins / 61 x 68 cm) GBP 9,000. LONDON, 3 June 2003, *Composition, Blue Centre* (1949, oil on canvas, 19 x 24 ins / 47 x 62 cm) GBP 3,200. LONDON, 4 June 2003, *Summer Landscape* (1951, oil on canvas, 30 x 25 ins / 76 x 63 cm) GBP 3,600. LONDON, 19 April 2004, *Sculpture Project* (oil on canvas, 32 x 48 ins / 81 x 121 cm) GBP 10,000. LONDON, 17 Nov 2004, *Spring Study* (1951, oil on canvas, 36 x 24 ins / 91 x 61 cm) GBP 7,500.

GEARHART, Frances

Maiden name: Hammel
American, 19th - 20th century.
Born 1869, in Henderson County (Illinois); died 1958, in Los Angeles.
Painter, print artist (woodcuts), watercolourist. Mountainscapes.
Japonisme.

Frances Gearhart was a high school art teacher in Los Angeles. She studied with Arthur Wesley Dow but was otherwise self-taught. Her sisters May and Edna were also artists; sometimes the three sisters exhibited together.

Influenced by Japanese woodcuts, Gearhart specialised in colour woodblock prints of the Western landscape, pictures full of contrasting relief, the contours of the rocks in her mountainscapes accentuated by thick black lines. She could capture a feeling of intense cold in brilliant fashion.

Frances Gearhart exhibited her work in solo exhibitions in Los Angeles from 1911. After she died, her work was also included in group exhibitions, for example, 2002, *Collects California*, Fisher Gallery, University of Southern California, Los Angeles; as part of the exhibition *Made in California: Art, Image and Identity, 1900-2000*, Los Angeles County Museum of Art, Los Angeles and 2002, *Le Japonisme en Amérique: œuvres sur papier, 1880-1930 (Japonism in America: works on paper 1880-1930)*, Musée d'art américain/Terra Foundation for the Arts, Giverny.

BIBLIOGRAPHY:

Petteys, Chris (ed.), *Dictionary of Women Artists: an International Dictionary of Women Artists Born Before 1900*, G.K. Hall, Boston, 1985. Hughes, Edan Milton, *Artists in California, 1786-1940*, Hughes Pub. Co., San Francisco, 1986. Heller, Jules/Heller, Nancy G., *North American Women Artists of the Twentieth Century: a biographical dictionary*, Garland, New York, 1995. Leard, Lindsay, '*Prints, Arts and Crafts Tradition*' in *Magazine Antiques*, September, 1996. '*Arthur Wesley Dow: American Arts/Crafts*' in *American Art Review*, periodical, December, 1999. *Le Japonisme en Amérique: œuvres sur papier, 1880-1930*, exhibition catalogue, Musée d'art américain, Giverny, Terra Foundation for the Arts, Evanston, 2002.

MUSEUMS AND GALLERIES:

CHICAGO (Terra Foundation for American Art Collection): *Chill December* (1936, woodcut) - ST LOUIS (AM).

AUCTION RECORDS:

PASADENA, 29 Oct 2002, *October Splendour* (colour block, 10 x 8 ins / 25 x 20 cm) USD 2,750. BOSTON, 6 Dec 2003, *Incoming Fog* (woodcut, 10 x 11 ins / 25 x 28 cm) USD 3,300.

GEBAUER, Christian David

German, 19th century.
Born 15 October 1777, in Neusalz (now Nowa Sól, Poland); died 15 September 1831, in Aarhus, Denmark.
Painter, engraver. Hunting scenes, landscapes, animals.

Christian Gebauer was a pupil of Lorentzen at the Kunstakademi in Copenhagen. He settled in Dresden in 1813 and was admitted to the academy there in 1815. He later went on to establish a school of drawing in Aarhus.

MUSEUMS AND GALLERIES:

COPENHAGEN: *Bull and Cow*; *Sleigh Run*; *Hunters on Horseback*.

AUCTION RECORDS:

COPENHAGEN, 4 Oct 1972, *Hunting Scene*, DKK 6,600. COPENHAGEN, 10 Feb 1976, *Landscape* (oil on canvas, 12 1/2 x 13 3/4 ins / 31.5 x 35 cm) DKK 4,200. COPENHAGEN, 7 Oct 1981, *Cossacks on the Outskirts of Dresden* (1813, oil on canvas, 14 1/4 x 16 1/2 ins / 36 x 42 cm) DKK 11,800. COPENHAGEN, 13 June 1984, *Three Horses in a Landscape* (oil on canvas, 27 1/4 x 34 1/4 ins / 69 x 87 cm) DKK 22,000. COPENHAGEN, 27 Feb 1985, *Flock in a Landscape* (1816, oil on canvas, 15 1/4 x 18 ins / 39 x 46 cm) DKK 20,000. COPENHAGEN, 5 May 1993, *Horse Fair* (1809, oil on canvas, 13 x 17 1/4 ins / 33 x 44 cm) DKK 14,000. LONDON, 11 Feb 1994, *Lining the Streets*; *Rest after the Hunt* (oil on canvas, a pair, each 7 1/4 x 9 1/4 ins / 18.4 x 23.5 cm) GBP 4,600. COPENHAGEN, 2 March 1999, *Horses and Cattle Watering in Summer* (oil on canvas, 11 x 15 ins / 28 x 38 cm) DKK 23,500. COPENHAGEN, 27 Nov 2001, *Pastoral Scene with Young Man Giving Garland of Flowers to Girl* (oil on canvas, 21 x 26 ins / 54 x 66 cm) DKK 15,000.

GEBAUER, Paul Ernst

German, 19th century.
Born 23 May 1782, in Lietzen; died 7 July 1865, in Berlin.
Portrait painter.

Paul Gebauer exhibited in Berlin from 1812 until 1826. He is noted for his *Portrait of Prince Charles* (third son of Frederick William III).

GEBB

French, 20th century.
Born 14 April 1908, in Paris.
Painter.

Gebb began by studying drawing and decoration. She belonged to the Société des Artistes Français and the Salon des Indépendants, and exhibited at the Salon des Femmes Peintres and the Salon of the artists of lower Normandy. She was awarded a painting prize in Amsterdam in 1973.

GEBEL, Gérard

French, 20th century.
Born 1937, in Lauw.

Painter. Nudes, landscapes, flowers.
Gérard Gebel exhibited mainly in Paris, at the Salon des Artistes Français and at the Salon des Indépendants. He has held solo shows in Lauw, Mulhouse, Basel and Brussels.

GEBEL, Johannes
Hungarian, 18th century.
Active in Brassó (now Brasov, Romania) c. 1760.
Sculptor.
Johannes Gebel sculpted statues of *St Stephen* and *St Lawrence*.

GEBEL, Mathes
German, 16th century.
Active in Nuremberg.
Sculptor, medallist.
A large number of medals can be attributed to this artist.

GEBENS, Adolf
Russian, 19th century.
Of Swedish origin.
Active in St Petersburg in 1861.
Painter.
We owe him mostly genre paintings.

GEBHARD, Albert
German, 19th century.
Active in Berlin c. 1830.
Painter.
Albert Gebhard exhibited landscapes at the academy in Berlin.

GEBHARD, Albert
Finnish, 19th century.
Born 29 April 1869, in Toholampi.
Active in Helsinki.
Painter. Genre scenes.
Albert Gebhard's *Abandoned* is in the museum of Helsinki. He received a silver medal at the 1900 Exposition Universelle in Paris.

GEBHARD, Andreas
German, 18th century.
Active in Prüfening (Bavaria).
Painter.
Andreas Gebhard also worked in Reichenbach.

GEBHARD, August
German, 20th century.
Born 15 December 1880, in Gueberschwihr.
Painter, lithographer.
August Gebhard studied at the Karlsruhe academy.

GEBHARD, Benedikt Albert
German, 18th century.
Active in Prüfening (Bavaria).
Painter.
Benedikt Gebhard is credited with church decorations in the Regensburg area. He died at a very early age.

GEBHARD, Franz Xaver
German, 19th century.
Born 1775, in Munich.
Engraver (burin/stippling).
Franz Xaver Gebhard was a pupil of Kress. He engraved portraits and mythological subjects.

GEBHARD, Johann
German, 18th century.
Born c. 1675; died 13 February 1756.
Active in Prüfening (Bavaria).
Painter.

GEBHARD, Johann Andreas
German, 17th - 18th century.
Born 1 February 1656; died 23 August 1725.
Active in Nuremberg (Bavaria).
Painter. History painting.
Johann Gebhard was a pupil of Johann Muncken.

GEBHARD, Johann Nepomuk
Austrian, 19th century.
Born in Brno.
Painter. Portraits.
Johann Gebhard studied in Vienna.
MUSEUMS AND GALLERIES:
BRNO: portraits.

GEBHARD, Julius
German, 19th century.
Died 1844, in Berlin.
Sculptor.
Julius Gebhard was a pupil of Wichmann and exhibited a the academy in Berlin from 1830 until 1844.

GEBHARDT, Friedrich Wilhelm
German, 19th century.
Born 30 November 1827, in Meissen (Saxony); died 16 May 1893, in Dresden.
Painter. Genre scenes, landscapes.
Friedrich Gebhardt studied at the academy in Dresden an was a pupil of Ludwig Richter. In 1874 he became a drawin teacher at the high school in Neustadt-Dresden. He exhibited in Dresden from 1874 to 1877.

GEBHARDT, Jacob C. W.
German, 18th century.
Active in Bamberg in 1711.
Fresco artist.

GEBHARDT, Karl
German, 19th - 20th century.
Born 23 March 1860, in Munich; died May 1917.
Painter. History painting, genre scenes.
Karl Gebhardt exhibited in Munich, Dresden and Berlin between 1880 and 1883. He is best known for *Hero and Leande* and *The Fratricide*.
AUCTION RECORDS:
NEW YORK, 20 May 1987, *The Monk's Visit* (oil on canvas 23 1/2 x 29 1/4 ins / 60 x 74.3 cm) USD 4,000.

GEBHARDT, Karl Franz Eduard von
Estonian, 19th - 20th century.
Born 13 June 1838, in St Johannis, Estonia; died 1925.
Painter. History painting, religious subjects, genre scenes.
Karl Franz Eduard von Gebhardt studied at the academy in St Petersburg between 1855 and 1858, then at the art school in Strasbourg and, in 1860, he attended Wilhelm Sohn's workshop in Düsseldorf. He is known for his *Crucifixion* in Tallin cathedral. A professor and a member of the academies in Berlin, Munich and Vienna from 1875, he won medals in Berlin (1872), Vienna (1873), Munich (1879) and a gold medal in Paris at the 1900 Exposition Universelle.
MUSEUMS AND GALLERIES:
BERLIN: *The Last Supper*; *Ascension of Christ* - BUCHAREST: *Peasant*; *Lady* - DÜSSELDORF: *Doubting Thomas*; *Christ before Pilate*; *Nichodemus, the Rich Disciple, with Christ* - HAMBURG: *The Crucifixion*; *Schoolboys at the Convent School* - LEIPZIG: *At the Time of the Reformation* - MUNICH: *Christ on the Cross* - WROCLAW: *Healing of the Paralytic*.
AUCTION RECORDS:
COLOGNE, 12 Nov 1976, *Jesus Preaching* (1911, oil on panel, 29 1/2 x 24 ins / 75 x 61 cm) DEM 4,400. MUNICH, 4 June 1981, *The Angry Man* (oil on panel, 20 3/4 x 13 3/4 ins / 53 x 35 cm) DEM 1,000. LONDON, 14 June 1996, *Suspicious Customer* (oil on canvas, 29 x 38 3/4 ins / 73.5 x 98.5 cm) GBP 10,350.

GEBHARDT, Konrad
German, 19th century.

Born 17 June 1868, in Dresden.
Painter, draughtsman.

.onrad was the son of Friedrich Wilhelm Gebhardt. He was pupil at the academy in Dresden.

GEBHARDT, Ludwig
German, 19th century.
Born 20 July 1830, in Munich; died 6 October 1908, in Munich.
Painter. Landscapes with figures, landscapes.

.udwig Gebhardt was a pupil at the academy in Munich. He xhibited in Munich, Bremen, Vienna and Dresden from 866 until 1888.

\UCTION RECORDS:

'IENNA, 5 Dec 1984, *Konigsee* (1869, oil on canvas, 34 3/4 x 61 1/4 ins / 88.5 x 117.5 cm) ATS 60,000. VIENNA, 29-30 Oct 996, *Harvest Time* (oil on canvas, 33 1/2 x 46 1/4 ins / 85 x 17.5 cm) ATS 63,250. MUNICH, 10 March 1999, *Moon above ake* (oil on canvas, 17 x 22 ins / 43 x 57 cm) DEM 4,500. 3ATH, 23 July 2001, *Echo Sounding in a Fjord* (oil on canvas, 4 x 51 ins / 86 x 129 cm) GBP 1,450. MUNICH, 17 March 2004, *Harlaching near Munich. Lakeside garden in Lindau* (oil on panel, a pair, 6 x 11 ins / 16 x 28 cm) EUR 1,700.

GEBHARDT, Max
German, 19th century.
Born 13 September 1864, in Meisen.
Painter. Genre scenes, landscapes.

Max Gebhardt was a pupil at the academy in Dresden, in the Mohn studio. He settled in Dresden and exhibited there from 1887 until 1890.

GEBHARDT, Otto
German, 18th century.
Born c. 1700; died 8 March 1773.
Active in Regensburg (Bavaria).
Painter.

As Painter to the Episcopal court, Otto Gebhardt was commissioned with church decoration.

GEBHARDT, Vilhelmina Fedorovna, or Guebhardt
Russian, 19th century.
Born 1809; died 1888.
Painter. Portraits.

MUSEUMS AND GALLERIES:

MOSCOW (State Tretyakov Gal.): *Portrait of Prince P.A. Meshchersky.*

GEBHARDT, Wolfgang Magnus, or Gebhard
German, 18th century.
Active in Nuremberg (Bavaria) between 1730 and 1750.
Engraver. Genre scenes, landscapes.

AUCTION RECORDS:

NEW YORK, 10 Oct 1990, *Figures next to a Fountain with a Statue of Poseidon above it in a Landscape of Classical Ruins* (oil on canvas, 31 x 39 ins / 78.8 x 99.1 cm) USD 8,250.

GEBLER, Josef
Austrian, 18th century.
Active in Graz.
Painter.

Gebler also worked in Marburg (Hessen).

GEBLER, Otto Friedrich
German, 19th - 20th century.
Born 18 September 1838, in Dresden; died February 1917, in Munich.
Painter. Animals.

Otto Gebler studied at the Dresden academy, then at the Munich academy under Karl von Piloty. He won medals in Munich in 1874 and 1883 and in London in 1878. He is best known for *The Shepherd's Rest* and *The Sad End of the Fox.*

O. Gebler

MUSEUMS AND GALLERIES:

KALININGRAD: *Flock of Sheep* - LEIPZIG: *Pastoral Life* - MAINZ: *Animals* - MUNICH: *The Death of the Fox.*

AUCTION RECORDS:

NEW YORK, 8-10 April 1908, *In the Dutch Art Gallery*, GBP 370. MUNICH, 24 and 26 June 1964, *Young Shepherd Resting*, DEM 18,000. MUNICH, 19-20 March 1969, *Cowshed*, DEM 28,000. BERLIN, 15 April 1977, *Flock in a Landscape* (oil on canvas, 30 1/2 x 46 3/4 ins / 77.5 x 119 cm) DEM 34,000. COLOGNE, 20 March 1981, *Calf and Fowls in a Wooded Landscape* (oil on canvas, 15 1/4 x 19 1/4 ins / 39 x 49 cm) DEM 38,000. WASHINGTON DC, 9 Dec 1984, *Young Shepherd with a Flock of Sheep* (oil on panel, 9 1/4 x 15 1/4 ins / 23.5 x 38.6 cm) USD 17,000. COLOGNE, 20 May 1985, *Flock of Sheep by the Cowshed Door* (1870, oil on canvas, 31 x 46 3/4 ins / 79 x 119 cm) DEM 46,000. AMSTERDAM, 30 Oct 1991, *Sheep and Chickens in a Barn* (oil on panel, 14 1/4 x 19 1/4 ins / 36.5 x 49 cm) NLG 50,600. LONDON, 29 Nov 1991, *Shepherdess and her Flock near a Pond* (1882, oil on panel, 22 x 26 3/4 ins / 55 x 68 cm) GBP 16,500. MUNICH, 7 Dec 1993, *Shepherd and his Sheep near Two Horses Harnessed to a Plough* (oil on panel, 7 1/2 x 12 1/2 ins / 19 x 32 cm) DEM 18,400. MUNICH, 21 June 1994, *Oxen in front of a Cowshed* (oil on canvas, 10 3/4 x 13 1/2 ins / 27.5 x 34.5 cm) DEM 17,250. LONDON, 13 Oct 1994, *The Hunter Caught in a Trap* (oil on canvas, 29 3/4 x 41 ins / 75.6 x 103.3 cm) GBP 28,750. LONDON, 11 June 1997, *A Good Rest* (1868, oil on canvas, 30 x 40 ins / 76.5 x 101.5 cm) GBP 23,000. LONDON, 9 Oct 1997, *Sheep in the Fold* (oil on panel, 20 1/4 x 24 1/4 ins / 51.5 x 61.5 cm) GBP 9,200.

GEBOERS, Jos
Belgian, 20th century.
Born 1913, in Lommel; died 1983.
Painter.

Jos Geboers was awarded the Kaiser Lothar prize by the town of Prum in Germany in 1970. In his canvases he recreates cosmic life with the help of colour and gesture.

GECELLI, Johannes, or Geccelli
German, 20th century.
Born 1925, in Königsberg (now Kaliningrad, Russia).
Painter.

After the war, Johannes Gecelli studied at the Düsseldorf academy and in 1952 he became a secondary school teacher. He was a member of the Deutscher Künstlerbund (Association of German Artists) from 1961. In 1965 he taught at the Berlin academy. Since 1957 he has taken part in various group exhibitions in Germany and elsewhere, notably Paris, Brussels, Florence and Tokyo. In 1957 he had his first solo exhibition in Düsseldorf, which was followed by many others, notably in Wuppertal in 1960, Berlin 1961, Ulm 1961 and Stuttgart 1962. He was awarded the North Rhine Westphalia State Prize in 1958, the Young Artists' prize in 1959 and the Villa Romana Prize in 1960. He competed for the Prix Marzotto in 1960-1961.

Starting from a Cézannian construction of space, he finished by producing almost entirely white works with a virtually abstract construction of space. In the 1960s he reintroduced colour - reds, blues and yellows - that was almost fluorescent. In his luminous works he meticulously put together a series of bands made up of small lines of richly contrasting colours, creating effects close to Kinetic art.

BIBLIOGRAPHY:

Johannes Gecelli, exhibition catalogue, Gal. Appel und Fertsch, Frankfurt am Main, 1975.

AUCTION RECORDS:
LONDON, 30 June 1988, *The Oval Table* (1960, oil on canvas, 23 3/4 x 31 1/2 ins / 60.4 x 80.3 cm) GBP 4,620. HEIDELBERG, 15 April 1994, *Hurrying Through the Light II* (1970, acrylic/paper, 39 1/4 x 27 1/2 ins / 100 x 70 cm) DEM 5,200. COLOGNE, 6 June 2000, *Warm Circle* (1980, acrylic, 39 x 35 ins / 100 x 89 cm) DEM 10,000. HEIDELBERG, 6 April 2001, *Green Walk* (1968, watercolour, 26 x 20 ins / 67 x 51 cm) DEM 3,200. HAMBURG, 14 June 2002, *Fast in Light II* (acrylic, 39 x 28 ins / 100 x 70 cm) EUR 3,900. BERLIN, 26 Oct 2002, *Female Figure* (1962, oil on canvas, 55 x 39 ins / 139 x 99 cm) EUR 3,000. BERLIN, 26 April 2003, *Composition in Maroon* (1985-1986, acrylic, 71 x 79 ins / 180 x 200 cm) EUR 3,000. BERLIN, 31 May 2003, *Kore* (1964, oil on hessian, 51 x 39 ins / 130 x 100 cm) EUR 4,000.

GECHTER, Jean François Théodore
French, 19th century.
Born 1796, in Paris; died 11 December 1844, in Paris.
Sculptor. Statues, groups, monuments.

Studied under Bosio and Gros; exhibited at the Salon from 1827 to 1844, obtaining a silver medal in 1839. He was made a Chevalier of the Légion d'Honneur in 1837. Gechter's body of work includes a *Battle of Abu Qir* (low relief for the Arc de Triomphe de l'Étoile, Paris), *Rhine and Rhône* (statues for the Place de la Concorde, Paris), and a *St Jean Chrysostom, Archbishop of Constantinople* (marble statue for the chamber of the Council of State).

MUSEUMS AND GALLERIES:
BORDEAUX: *Statuette* - PARIS (Louvre): *The Death of Trancred* - VERSAILLES: *Bust of Marshal de St André.*

AUCTION RECORDS:
LONDON, 6 May 1971, *Arab Horseman* (bronze) GBP 150. PARIS, 17 March 1976, *Greyhound Bitch and Hare* (1843, patinated bronze, h. 16 1/4 ins / 41 cm) FRF 2,950. LONDON, 19 Dec 1977, *Arab Warrior on Horse* (bronze, w. 13 1/2 ins / 34 cm) GBP 900. PARIS, 14 Dec 1984, *Horse Combat* (bronze, 19 x 17 x 9 1/2 ins / 48 x 43 x 24 cm) FRF 15,000. PARIS, 1 July 1986, *Horse Combat* (1838, brown-patinated bronze, h. 29 1/2 ins / 75 cm) FRF 42,000. NEW YORK, 9 June 1988, *Ploughhorse* (bronze, h. 15 3/4 ins / 40 cm) USD 1,870. NEW YORK, 23 May 1991, *Charles Martel in Battle with the Saracen King Abderame* (1839, bronze with black-green patina, h. 23 3/4 ins / 60.4 cm) USD 7,700. NEW YORK, 30 Oct 1992, *Ploughhorse* (bronze, h. 16 1/2 ins / 41.9 cm, l. 17 1/4 ins/43.7 cm) USD 1,540. NEW YORK, 27 May 1993, *Francis I Hunting Boar* (bronze, h. 18 1/2 ins / 47 cm) USD 5,750. NEW YORK, 14 Oct 1993, *Arab Hunter Shooting Tiger* (bronze horse group, h. 13 1/2 ins / 34.3 cm) USD 2,185. PARIS, 8 Nov 1995, *Horse at Pasture* (bronze, h. 13 1/2 ins / 34.5 cm) FRF 19,000. LOKEREN, 8 March 1997, *Francis I Hunting Boar* (1843, bronze, 22 3/4 x 22 ins / 58 x 55 cm) BEF 170,000. PARIS, 14 April 1999, *Draught Horse* (sculpture, green patinated bronze, h. 15 ins / 39 cm) FRF 27,500. LOKEREN, 11 Dec 1999, *François I Hunting the Boar* (1843, sculpture, brown patinated bronze, green marble base, 23 x 22x? ins / 58 x 55x? cm) BEF 200,000. LOKEREN, 13 May 2000, *The Wounded Amazon* (1841, sculpture, light brown patinated bronze, 11 x 15x? ins / 28 x 39x? cm) BEF 145,000. LONDON, 5 Oct 2000, *Harnessed Draught Horse* (sculpture, brown patinated bronze, 16 x 18x? ins / 41 x 45x? cm) GBP 5,200. BILLINGSHURST, 23 April 2001, *Dray Horse in Traces* (sculpture, bronze, ebonised wood plinth, h. 22 ins / 55 cm) GBP 1,350. LONDON, 14 Dec 2001, *Charles Martel Fighting the Saracen King, Abderan* (sculpture, dark brown patinated bronze, 19 x 17x? ins / 47 x 43x? cm) GBP 2,700. LONDON, 9 July 2002, *Joan of Arc Overcoming the English* (sculpture, dark brown patinated bronze, 27 x 19x? ins / 68 x 47x? cm) GBP 17,000. LONDON, 5 Nov 2002, *Death of Charles the Bold* (sculpture, brown patinated bronze, 22 x 19x? ins / 56 x 47x? cm) GBP 10,000. LONDON, 8 July 2003, *St George and the Dragon* (1842, sculpture, brown patinated bronze, 15 x 13x? ins / 37 x 34x? cm) GBP 5,500. PARIS, 28 Nov 200 *Combat* (sculpture, patinated bronze, 14 x 15x8 ins / 35 39x21 cm) EUR 5,800. LONDON, 21 April 2004, *Joan of A Defeating the English* (sculpture, brown patinated bronze, 2 x 19x? ins / 69 x 48x? cm) GBP 4,000.

GECIN
Canadian, 20th century.
Born 1907, in Montreal.
Painter, draughtsman.

Gecin was a primary school teacher for 35 years and did nc begin to paint until he was 47 years old. He was self-taugh and his drawings are very imaginative and detailed, with th lines developing into gossamer-like curls. Sometimes ab stract, sometimes figurative, the shapes intermingle with certain refinement. He exhibited in Paris in 1973.

GECIN, Matthaeus
German, 17th century.
Active in Bautzen (Saxony) in 1641.
Painter.

There is a signed painting by this artist in the cathedral a Bautzen.

GEDAM
17th century.
Painter. Religious subjects.

MUSEUMS AND GALLERIES:
BORDEAUX: *St Jerome* (1613, signed).

GEDDES, Andrew
British, 19th century.
Born 5 April 1783, in Edinburgh; died 5 May 1844, in London.
Painter, engraver. Religious subjects, portraits.

Andrew Geddes studied at Edinburgh University. He en rolled at the Royal Academy School in 1807 and studiec alongside Haydon, Jackson and Willkie. He travelled exten sively in Europe, visiting Holland, France and Germany, and then went on to divide his time between Edinburgh and London. He became a member of the Royal Scottish Academy and exhibited in London from 1806 to 1844.

In 1821, he painted portraits of Sir David Wilkie, Henry Mackenzie, Dr Chalmers and other leading lights of the day In that same year, he also painted a large composition depicting a number of famous Scots, including Sir Walter Scott.

Geddes will justifiably be remembered primarily as a portraitist, but he also painted a number of more ambitious compositions, notably an altarpiece for the church of St James Garlickhythe in London. He was also an accomplished engraver: the 40 or so etchings attributable to him are today considered collector's items.

MUSEUMS AND GALLERIES:
EDINBURGH (Nat. Gal. of Scotland): *Andrew Plimer* (oil/panel); *The Artist's Mother* (oil on canvas); *George Sanders* (oil/panel); *Mrs Douglas Dickson* (oil on canvas); *Hagar* (oil on canvas) - EDINBURGH (Nat. Gal. of Scotland, Print Room): *Miss Charlotte Nasmyth (study for 'Summer')* (pastel, two) - EDINBURGH (Scottish National Portrait Gallery): several portraits.

AUCTION RECORDS:
LONDON, 5 Dec 1908, *Portrait of Lady Belhaven* (1817) GBP 22. LONDON, 10 June 1909, *Female Portrait*, GBP 136. LONDON, 19 March 1910, *River Scene*, GBP 3. LONDON, 20 Feb 1911, *Portrait of James Wardrop*, GBP 7. LONDON, 27 July 1923, *Camuccini*, GBP 10. LONDON, 15 May 1929, *Margaret Wardrop*, GBP 24. EDINBURGH, 8 Feb 1930, *Portrait of a Little Girl*, GBP 35. LONDON, 28 March 1934, *The Artist's Mother*,

GBP 8. LONDON, 5 April 1935, *Young Falconer,* GBP 230. LONDON, 6 March 1936, *Portrait of an Old Woman,* GBP 22. GLASGOW, 7 Oct 1937, *Still Life,* GBP 5. LONDON, 31 July 1939, *James Wardrop,* GBP 21. LONDON, 14 May 1976, *Portrait of George Cumming* (oil on panel, 25 x 20¾ ins / 63.5 x 53 cm) GBP 600. GLASGOW, 10 Dec 1981, *Miss Amelia Penrose Cumming of Altyre* (oil on panel, 28 x 19¾ ins / 71 x 50 cm) GBP 1,200. LONDON, 22 Nov 1985, *Portrait of the Six Daughters of George Arbuthnot of Elderslie* (1839, oil on canvas, 72 x 94 ins / 182 x 239 cm) GBP 14,000. LONDON, 12 July 1991, *Bust Portrait of a Gentleman (presumed to be David Wilkie) in Black with a Watch Chain at his Waistcoat* (1834, oil on canvas, 30 x 25 ins / 76 x 63.5 cm) GBP 3,300. EDINBURGH, 23 March 1993, *Young Girl with a Red Shawl* (1840, oil on canvas, 30 x 25¼ ins / 76.5 x 64 cm) GBP 2,070. LONDON, 4 July 2002, *Portrait of Sir John Marjoribanks* (oil on canvas, 56 x 43 ins / 141 x 110 cm) GBP 6,000. EDINBURGH, 10 April 2003, *Portrait of William Hay Leight at His Desk. Portrait of His Wife* (1839, oil on canvas, a pair, 19 x 15 ins / 49 x 39 cm) GBP 1,900.

GEDDES, Ewan

British, 19th century.
Born 1866, in Blairgowie (Perthshire); died 1935, in Blairgowie.
Active in Edinburgh.
Painter. Landscapes.

Ewan Geddes exhibited at London's Royal Academy from 1891. He was generally accepted as numbering among the leading British landscape artists. He was a member of the Royal Scottish Watercolour Society.

AUCTION RECORDS:

NEW YORK, 29 and 30 March 1905, *Landscape with Child,* USD 750. NEW YORK, 12 au 14 March 1906, *In the Woods,* USD 726. EDINBURGH, 25 April 1931, *Jock Howieson's House; On the Almond* (two watercolours) GBP 6.

GEDDES, Margaret

British, 20th century.
Born 7 November 1914; died 1998.
Painter. Landscapes.

Margaret Geddes studied at the Westminster School of Art, where she was taught by Mark Gertler. She showed at the major British exhibitions. In 1998, a retrospective of her work was mounted at the Woodlands Art Gallery in London. She was influenced by the British Neo-Romantics, Estève and Gottlieb.

BIBLIOGRAPHY:

Wilcox, Denys J., *Margaret Geddes*, St. Ives Printing and Publishing Co., St. Ives, Woodlands Art Gall., London, 1998.

GEDELER, Elias

German, 17th century.
Born 27 September 1620, in Elgenberg Castle; died 30 July 1693, in Hildburghausen (Thuringia).
Architect, painter. History painting, portraits.

After his studies Gedeler travelled to Italy, and thereafter spent a long time in Nuremberg.

GEDEN, Denis

Canadian, 20th century.
Born 1944, in North Bay (Ontario).
Also active in France and England.
Painter, lithographer. Figures, portraits, still-lifes, animals.

Denis Geden graduated from the Sir George Williams School of Art in Montreal, in 1966. He produced lithographs at the Desjorbert studio in Paris in 1972-1973, and at the Curwen Studio in London in 1975-1976. His work is drawn largely from his own imagination, but also features mythological characters, such as *Iphigenia,* transposed into new environments and contexts. His often timeless scenes are Intimist in character, and somewhat Primitivist in execution.

Geden's work has featured in a number of group exhibitions, including: 1974, touring exhibition, Society of Painter-Engravers, Canada; 1975, Burnaby Biennale; 1976, International Triennale of Original Graphic Prints, Grenchen (Switzerland); 1981, American Biennale of Graphic Arts, Cali (Colombia). His work has also featured in a number of individual shows, including: 1973, La Cimaise Gallery, Toronto; 1977, 1979, 1981, 1983, White Water Gallery, Haileybury (Ontario); 1980, Peterborough Gallery, Peterborough (Ontario); 1984, Redfern Gallery, London; 1986, Centre Culturel Canadien, Paris.

GEDÉON, Baril

French, 19th century.
Born 1832, in Amiens.
Caricaturist.

Contributor to satirical periodicals published in Paris at the close of the 19th century.

Gédéon

AUCTION RECORDS:

PARIS, 27 March 1926, *La coiffure du chien; Portrait* (two watercolours) FRF 270.

GEDLEK, Ludwig

Austrian, 19th century.
Born 30 June 1847, in Cracow, Poland.
Painter. Animals.

Gedlek exhibited in Dresden from 1882 until 1890.

AUCTION RECORDS:

PARIS, 4 Feb 1925, *Tatar Horsemen,* FRF 315. LONDON, 17 July 1930, *Attack,* GBP 5. LONDON, 4 Feb 1972, *Battle Scene,* Gns 340. PERTH, 13 April 1976, *Still-life with Salmon* (oil on canvas, 15¼ x 25¼ ins / 39 x 64 cm) GBP 220. LONDON, 9 June 1981, *Blacksmith* (1878, oil on canvas, 10 x 14¼ ins / 25.5 x 36 cm) GBP 240. VIENNA, 14 Sept 1983, *Hunt Meeting* (1882, oil on canvas, 26¾ x 48 ins / 68 x 121 cm) ATS 180,000. VIENNA, 4 Dec 1986, *Wedding Procession in Galicia* (oil on panel, 6¼ x 8¼ ins / 16 x 21 cm) ATS 80,000. EDINBURGH, 22 Nov 1988, *The Pedlar and his Customers* (1869, oil on canvas, 18 x 24½ ins / 45.7 x 62.3 cm) GBP 4,800. LONDON, 21 March 1990, *In Sunday Best* (1871, oil on canvas, 24 x 34 ins / 61 x 86.5 cm) GBP 990. PERTH, 1 Sept 1992, *First Prize in the Island's Fishing Competition* (1879, oil on canvas, 20 x 30 ins / 51 x 76.5 cm) GBP 7,150. PERTH, 31 Aug 1993, *Salmon on the River Bank* (oil on canvas, 28 x 43 ins / 71 x 109 cm) GBP 7,820. PLAINVILLE, 22 March 1999, *Winter Sleigh Ride Scene* (oil on canvas, 14 x 22 ins / 36 x 56 cm) USD 6,500. PARIS, 1 Dec 1999, *Cavaliers on the Plain* (1881, oil on panel, 12 x 25 ins / 31 x 63 cm) FRF 19,500. LUCERNE, 11 Nov 2000, *Farmer with Horse and Cart* (oil on canvas, 26 x 33 ins / 65 x 85 cm) CHF 12,000. ST LOUIS, 2 Dec 2000, *Travellers in Horse-drawn Cart* (oil on canvas, 17 x 27 ins / 43 x 69 cm) USD 12,500. MONTREAL, 19 June 2001, *Cossacks Arriving for the Hunt* (oil on board, 14 x 23 ins / 35 x 58 cm) CAD 8,500. GRAVENHAGE, 7 Nov 2001, *Landscape with Cossack on Horse* (oil on canvas, 14 x 22 ins / 35 x 56 cm) NLG 14,000. WARSAW, 10 March 2002, *Figures with Horse-drawn Cart outside Farmstead* (oil on canvas, 14 x 23 ins / 36 x 58 cm) PLN 55,000. WARSAW, 16 June 2002, *Hunting Scene with Riders and their Dogs* (1882, oil on canvas, 22 x 47 ins / 57 x 120 cm) PLN 76,000. WARSAW, 30 March 2003, *Departure of the Hunt* (c. 1890, oil on panel, 14 x 23 ins / 36 x 58 cm) PLN 50,000. WARSAW, 19 Oct 2003, *Taking a Break* (c. 1890, oil on canvas, 31 x 25 ins / 78 x 63 cm) PLN 30,000. LONDON, 10 March 2004, *Cossacks* (oil on canvas, 23 x 39 ins / 58 x 100 cm) GBP 4,500. SAN FRANCISCO, 18 May 2004, *Cossack Figures Gathered by a Wall* (oil on panel, 8 x 13 ins / 21 x 32 cm) USD 5,000.

GEDON, Friedrich
Austrian, 18th century.
Active in Vienna.
Painter.
In 1732 Friedrich Gedon was awarded first prize by the academy in Vienna.

GEDON, Lorenz
German, 19th century.
Born 12 November 1843, in Munich; died 27 December 1883.
Sculptor, architect.
Lorenz Gedon worked mainly for Duke Ludwig II of Bavaria.

GEDON, Thomas
Austrian, 18th century.
Died 1734, in Vienna.
Painter. Portraits.
Thomas was the father of Friedrich Gedon.

GEDROITS, Romuald (Prince)
Russian, 19th century.
Also active in France.
Sculptor.
Romuald Gedroits worked in Paris with Jules Jouant.

GEDROITS, V. (Prince)
Russian, 19th century.
Active in Paris.
Painter.
V. Gedroits exhibited seascapes (the Black Sea and the Sea at Biarritz) at the Salon in Paris from 1888 to 1890.

GEEDTS, Josse Pieter
Belgian, 18th - 19th century.
Born 5 January 1770, in Louvain; died 17 December 1834, in Louvain.
Painter. History painting.
Geedts was a pupil of Herreyns at the academy in Antwerp. He was appointed professor at the academy in Louvain in 1800 but was dismissed (unjustly, it is thought) towards the end of his life.

GEEDTS, Pieter Pauwels
Belgian, 19th century.
Born 1 April 1793, in Louvain; died 6 March 1856, in Louvain.
Painter. History painting, portraits.
He was the son and pupil of Josse Pieter Geedts. He also studied at the academy in Louvain, where he won several prizes, and was later appointed professor at the same institution; he resigned in protest at his father's dismissal. Geedts executed paintings for St Jacobskerk, Louvain, in 1824.

GEEFS, Alexander
Flemish School, 19th century.
Born 1 January 1829, in Antwerp; died 27 August 1866, in Schaerbeek, Brussels.
Sculptor.
He was a pupil of Braent, and the brother of Willem Geefs.

GEEFS, Aloysius, or Geeffs
Belgian, 19th century.
Born 1817, in Antwerp; died 31 August 1841, in Auteuil, Paris.
Sculptor, painter. History painting.
He was the brother and pupil of Willem Geefs.
AUCTION RECORDS:
PARIS, 1850, *Geneviève de Brabant, Stripped of her Clothes, Holds her Child to her Breast* (drawing) FRF 4,620; *Naked Child Playing with a Dog* (drawing) FRF 5,092; *The Angel of Evil Holding a Broken Sceptre* (drawing) FRF 7,560; *Fisherman's Daughter Reclining with Flowers* (drawing) FRF 7,650.

GEEFS, Charles
Belgian, 19th century.
Active in Brussels.
Sculptor.
He exhibited at the Royal Academy in London in 1858.

GEEFS, Fanny
Maiden name: Corr
Belgian, 19th century.
Born 1807, in Brussels; died 23 January 1883, in Schaerbeek, Brussels.
Painter. Genre scenes.
She was a pupil of Navez and the wife of Willem Geefs.
AUCTION RECORDS:
GHENT, 1856, *Young Girl Fording a River*, FRF 40. COPENHAGEN, 7 Dec 1976, *Drawing* (oil on canvas, 42½ x 35in/108 x 88cm) DKK 9,500. NEW YORK, 22-23 July 1993, *The Lovers Tree* (1859, oil on canvas, 42 x 34¾in/106.7 x 88.3cm) USD 1,725. BRUSSELS, 12 May 1998, *Pity, Love and Pain* (oil on canvas, triptych, 41 x 57 ins / 105 x 145 cm) BEF 180,000.

GEEFS, Jan
Belgian, 19th century.
Born 25 April 1825, in Antwerp; died 4 May 1860, in Brussels.
Sculptor.
He was the brother of Willem Geefs. In his work he favoured mythological and allegorical subjects.

GEEFS, Joris, or Georges
Belgian, 19th - 20th century.
Born 1850, in Antwerp; died 1933.
Sculptor. Busts, groups, monuments.
Joris Geefs was the son of Josef Geefs and the nephew of Willem Geefs, and collaborated with them. He studied at the Antwerp academy and became a teacher there. He was an active member of the academic council from August 1892. He was awarded medals in Antwerp in 1876, Brussels in 1878 and Paris in 1879. He created the monument *The French Fury* in Antwerp.
MUSEUMS AND GALLERIES:
ANTWERP: *Bust of his Father; Leander Cast Dying onto the Shores of the Hellespont.*
AUCTION RECORDS:
LONDON, 20 June 1985, *Woman and Lion* (brown-patinated bronze, h. 17 ins / 43 cm) GBP 1,400.

GEEFS, Josef
Belgian, 19th century.
Born 23 December 1808, in Antwerp; died 19 October 1885, in Brussels.
Sculptor.
He was the brother and pupil of Willem Geefs. He won the Prix de Rome in 1836, and was appointed professor at the academy in Antwerp in 1841. He received many honours, becoming a member of the Belgian royal academy in 1842, and was made a knight, officer and commander of the Order of Leopold. He was also an executive member of the Belgian Conseil Académique in 1852.
BIBLIOGRAPHY:
Van Lennep, Jacques, *The Monuments and Statues of Brussels*, Pandora, Brussels, 2000.
MUSEUMS AND GALLERIES:
ANTWERP: *Floris van Erthorn; Nicaise de Keyser; Frans Josef Stoof; Young Fisherman Drawn to the Call of the Siren.*

GEEFS, Théodore
Belgian, 19th century.
Born 15 February 1827, in Antwerp; died 1 January 1867, in London.
Sculptor.
He was the brother of Willem Geefs. He produced a wide range of religious works.

GEEFS, Willem, or Guillaume
Belgian, 19th century.
Born 10 September 1805, in Antwerp; died 24 January 1883, in Brussels.
Sculptor.

After Joseph, Willem was the most famous of the four Geefs brothers (all sculptors). He studied at the Antwerp academy, winning the school's Grand Prix in 1828. He subsequently studied under Ramey, in Paris, and taught at the Antwerp academy for a time on his return. In 1852 he was an executive member of the Belgian Conseil Académique. With his brother Joseph and the sculptors Fraikin and Simonis, he collaborated on the decorative sculpture for the Congress Column in the Place du Congrès, Brussels. His unexceptional, rather mawkish work is typical of the Belgian School at the time; as such, he was highly regarded by his bourgeois contemporaries, whose custom and tastes he courted and flattered, and became sculptor to the King. He was nonetheless capable of producing work of simplicity and quality, as evidenced by his tomb for Comte Frédéric de Mérode in the cathedral of Sts-Michel-et-Gudule, Brussels.

BIBLIOGRAPHY:
Van Lennep, Jacques, *The Monuments and Statues of Brussels*, Pandora, Brussels, 2000.

MUSEUMS AND GALLERIES:
ANTWERP: *Self-portrait*; *Geneviève de Brabant* - DOUAI: *Louis-Philippe* - LIÈGE: *Geneviève de Brabant*; *Hygieia*.

AUCTION RECORDS:
STOCKHOLM, 22 April 1986, *Love's Awakening* (white marble, h. 83 3/4in/213cm) SEK 105,000. BRUSSELS, 7 Nov 2000, *General Augustin Daniel Belliard* (patinated bronze, h. 35 ins / 89 cm) BEF 140,000.

GEEL, Daniel van
Dutch, 17th century.
Active c. 1660.
Landscape painter.

MUSEUMS AND GALLERIES:
ROTTERDAM: *Landscape*.

GEEL, Jacob Jacobsz. van
Dutch, 17th century.
Born c. 1585, in Middelburg (Zeeland); died after 1638, in Dordrecht.
Painter. Religious subjects, landscapes, landscapes with figures, mountainscapes.

He was active in Middelburg, Delft and Dordrecht from 1615 to 1633.

iacob v geel 1635

BIBLIOGRAPHY:
Bernt, W., *Netherlandish Painters of the Seventeenth Century*, Oxford, 1969.

MUSEUMS AND GALLERIES:
AMSTERDAM (Rijksmus.): *Group of Trees* - DETROIT (IA): *Landscape*.

AUCTION RECORDS:
PARIS, 23 March 1968, *Temptation of Christ*, FRF 16,000. LONDON, 5 Dec 1969, *Wooded Landscape*, Gns 3,500. VERSAILLES, 13 Nov 1977, *Landscape with Cascade* (oil on panel, 14 3/4 x 20in/37.5 x 50.5cm) FRF 12,500. AMSTERDAM, 29 May 1986, *Travellers in a Wooded Landscape with a River* (oil on panel, 6 x 8in/14.3 x 20.6cm) NLG 26,000. LONDON, 27 Oct 1993, *Vast Landscape with Figures Crossing a Bridge* (oil on panel, 25 1/2 x 43in/65 x 109cm) GBP 10,350. AMSTERDAM, 16 Nov 1993, *Rocky Landscape* (oil on panel, 6 1/4 x 7 1/2in/16 x 20cm) NLG 17,250. PARIS, 13 Dec 1996, *Traveller Attacked by Brigands*; *Figures Walking beside a Stretch of Water* (oil on panel, a pair, 19 1/4 x 25 1/2in/49 x 64.5cm) FRF 210,000. NEW YORK, 23 May 1997, *Vast Landscape with a Castle Surrounded by Ditches and Figures on a Track* (1637, oil on canvas, 13 1/4 x 20 1/2in/33.7 x 52.2cm) USD 27,600. AMSTERDAM, 11 Nov 1997, *Travellers and Peasants on a Sandy Footpath at the Edge of a Wood, with a Distant Valley* (oil on panel, 7 1/4 x 12 1/2in/18.4 x 31.9cm) NLG 14,991. STOCKHOLM, 28 May 2002, *Mountain Landscape with Figures* (1638, oil on panel, 13 x 22 ins / 33 x 55 cm) SEK 120,000.

GEEL, Jan Frans van. See **GEEL Johannes Franciscus van**

GEEL, Johannes Franciscus van, known as Jan Frans van
Belgian, 18th - 19th century.
Born 17 September 1756, in Mechelen; died 20 January 1830, in Antwerp.
Sculptor.

He was a pupil of Pieter Valckx. He became a professor at the academy in Mechelen and also taught at Antwerp in 1817.

GEEL, Johannes Ludovicus van, or Jan Lodewijk
Belgian, 19th century.
Born 28 September 1787, in Mechelen; died 10 April 1852, in Brussels.
Sculptor.

He was the son and pupil of the sculptor Johannes Franciscus van Geel. He travelled to Paris in 1809, where he became a pupil of David and Roland. He was awarded first prize for sculpture at the Paris Salon in 1811. Upon his return to Brussels, van Geel was appointed sculptor to the Prince of Orange. In the early 1820s he produced the colossal cast iron lion for the monument on the battlefield of Waterloo.

GEEL, Joost van, also known as Jan van
Dutch, 17th century.
Born 20 October 1631, in Rotterdam; died 31 December 1698, in Rotterdam.
Painter. Portraits, genre scenes, seascapes.

He was probably a pupil of Gabriel Metsu. He travelled to Germany, France and England, and painted genre scenes and seascapes. He was also an art dealer.

JVGEEL

MUSEUMS AND GALLERIES:
AMSTERDAM: *Self-portraits* - LYONS: *Seascape* - ROTTERDAM: *Mother, Wetnurse and Child* - ST PETERSBURG (Hermitage): *A Concert*.

AUCTION RECORDS:
PARIS, 1808, *Self-portrait*, FRF 556. LONDON, 24 May 1937, *Fishing Boats*, GBP 12. LONDON, 14 Feb 1938, *Wooded Landscape*, GBP 24. NEW YORK, 12 Jan 1995, *Fishing Boat Lowering its Sails while the Fishermen Unload their Catch* (oil on canvas, 19 3/4 x 25in/50.2 x 63.5cm) USD 11,500.

GEELEN, Christian van, the Elder
Dutch, 18th - 19th century.
Born 19 August 1755, in Utrecht; died 1826.
Painter. Portraits, genre scenes.

He was a pupil of Jacob Maurer, and was appointed director of the college at Utrecht in 1794. His pupils included J. J. van Straater and A. J. W. van Deeler.

GEELEN, Christian van, the Younger
Dutch, 19th century.
Born 16 September 1794, in Utrecht; died 13 May 1826, in Utrecht.
Painter, watercolourist. Portraits, genre scenes, landscapes.

He was the son and pupil of Christian van Geelen the Elder.

Museums and Galleries:
Utrecht: *Self-portrait; City View; Organ Player.*
Auction records:
Paris, 16 Nov 1993, *Casoar (Casuarius novae Hollandiae)* (watercolour, pen and lead pencil, 8½ x 10in/22 x 25.5cm) FRF 4,000. London, 24 Feb 1995, *Portrait Bust of Baron van Tuyll in Armour* (1802, oil on canvas, oval, 27 x 22in/68.9 x 56cm) USD 805.

GEENE, Hendrik Gysbert
Dutch, 19th century.
Born 1865, in Roermond (Limburg).
Active in St Gall.
Sculptor.
Geene studied in Düsseldorf before settling in Switzerland.

GEENEN, Pauline Van
French, 19th century.
Born in Strasbourg.
Miniaturist.
Known primarily as a portraitist.

GEENENS, Robert Hector
Belgian, 20th century.
Born 1896, in Ghent; died 1976, in Antwerp.
Painter.
Magical Realism.
Robert Geenens studied at the academies in Rotterdam and Ghent. In 1928, he gave up his career as a naval lieutenant in order to devote himself to painting. He was a member of the group Fantasmagie, centred around Aubin Pasque, which brought together artists who drew inspiration from Flemish fantastic art rather than surrealism. His work, which was close to Magic Realism, developed in the direction of Lyrical and Magical Abstraction, without ever quite abandoning the figurative.
Bibliography:
Horemans, Karel, *Robert Geenens*, Standaard, Antwerp, 1943.
Museums and Galleries:
Antwerp - Ostend.
Auction records:
Lokeren, 16 Feb 1985, *Sunny Landscape* (1942, oil on canvas, 23½ x 31½ ins / 60 x 80 cm) BEF 40,000.

GEENS, H. J.
Flemish School, 18th century.
Active in Bruges (West Flanders).
Painter.
Geens was decorated by the Antwerp academy in 1773.

GEENS, Jean Joseph
Flemish School, 19th century.
Active in Ghent (East Flanders).
Painter. History painting.
He was a pupil of Paelinck.

GEENS, Louis
Belgian, 19th century.
Active in Ghent (East Flanders).
Painter.

GEER, Cyrill
17th century.
Draughtsman.
There is known to be an engraving of *The Siege of Prague by the Swedes* made after a drawing by Geer.

GEER, Franz Ferdinand von
Austrian, 17th - 18th century.
Born 1673; died 11 July 1722, in Vienna.
Painter.
Geer is noted for his painting *Death of St Joseph.*

GEER, Grace Woodbridge
American, 19th century.
Born 1854, in Boston; died 1938.
Active in Boston.
Painter, miniaturist. Portraits.
Grace Woodbridge Geer was a pupil of F.H. Tomkins, Trescott and Tarbell in Boston.

GEER, M. J.
19th century.
Active c. 1800.
Painter.
There is known to be a miniature portrait signed with this name.

GEER-BERGENSTRAHLE, Marie-Louise Ekman de
Swedish, 20th century.
Born 1944, in Stockholm.
Painter, draughtswoman.
Since 1967, De Geer-Bergenstrahle has participated in many group exhibitions and has held numerous solo shows.
Museums and Galleries:
Helsinki (Ateneumin Taidemus.) - Stockholm (Moderna Mus.) - Stockholm (Nationalmus.).
Auction records:
Stockholm, 5-6 Dec 1990, *Woman Crying* (watercolour/silk, 9 x 6¾ ins / 23 x 17 cm) SEK 31,000. Copenhagen, 4 Dec 1991, *Composition* (1973, oil on canvas, 23½ x 28¾ ins / 60 x 73 cm) DKK 19,000.

GEERAERTS, Jan
Flemish School, 19th century.
Born 1818; died 1890.
Active in Antwerp.
Painter. Church interiors.
Museums and Galleries:
Antwerp: *Interior of the Dominican Church at Antwerp.*
Auction records:
New York, 17 Feb 1994, *Church Interior with the Tomb of William the Silent in Holland [Nieuwe Kerk, Delft]* (oil on panel, 32½ x 26½in/82.5 x 67.5cm) USD 5,175.

GEERAERTS, Marten
Flemish School, 16th century.
Active in Bruges in 1546.
Painter.

GEERAERTS, Marten Jozef
Flemish School, 18th century.
Born 1707, baptised 7 April 1707, in Antwerp; died 16 February 1791, in Antwerp.
Painter. History painting, religious subjects, allegorical subjects, mythological subjects, portraits.
Geeraerts was a pupil of Abraham Godyn. He became a master of the Guild of St Luke in Antwerp in 1731. He painted grisailles. In 1741 he was appointed director and professor of the Antwerp academy, and later that year he was among a group of six professors teaching pupils free of charge when the school was forced to close, due to lack of funds.
Museums and Galleries:
Antwerp: *Mus. of Fine Arts* - Brussels: *Seven Scenes from the Old and New Testaments* - Lille: *Children's Games* (grisailles) - The Hague: *Allegory* - Vienna: *Imitation of a Low-relief.*
Auction records:
London, 7 May 1909, *Portrait of a Gentleman*, GBP 31. London, 28 Nov 1969, *Portrait of Lady Tanfield*, Gns 1,900. London, 11 April 1990, *The Infant Hercules Surrounded by Putti Bringing him Musical Instruments, a Quiver and Crown of Laurels; The Infant Hercules Surrounded by Putti Bringing him a Helmet, a Club, an Antique Mask and Arrows* (oil on canvas in grisaille, pair, each 53¼ x 61½in/135 x 156cm) GBP 66,000. New York, 8 Oct 1993, *Putti Playing* (oil on can-

vas in grisaille, 35 1/4 x 60in/89.5 x 152.4cm) USD 5,750. NEW YORK, 7 Oct 1994, *Putti Playing with Soap Bubbles* (oil on canvas, 35 1/4 x 60in/89.5 x 152.4cm) USD 12,075.

GEERARDS, Jasper, or Geeraerts
Dutch, 17th century.
Born c. 1620; died 1649 or 1654.
Painter. Still-lifes.

AUCTION RECORDS:
NEW YORK, 17 Jan 1986, *Still-life with Fruit and a Langoustine* (oil on canvas, 29 1/2 x 38 1/4in/75 x 97cm) USD 33,000. LONDON, 8 Dec 1995, *Bowl of Peaches and Grapes with a Roemer and Lemons in a Pewter Platter on a Table Covered with a Cloth* (1648, oil on panel, 29 1/4 x 22 3/4in/74 x 57.8cm) GBP 36,700. LONDON, 4 July 1997, *Nautilus and a Lemon on a Pewter Platter, a Ham on a Silver Tazza, a Roemer, a Bunch of Grapes and a Peeled Lemon on a Table Partly Covered with a Cloth* (oil on panel, 29 1/4 x 23in/74.3 x 58.7cm) GBP 34,500. AMSTERDAM, 11 Nov 1997, *Grapes, a Nautilus, a Flute, a Silver Goblet on a Platter, a Peeled Lemon and a Lobster on a Table Covered with a Cloth* (oil on panel, 25 1/2 x 19 3/4in/65 x 50.4cm) NLG 98,022. AMSTERDAM, 14 May 2003, *Pronk Still-life of a Roemer, Partly Peeled Lemon, and Lobster on a Pewter Plate* (oil on canvas, 29 x 38 ins / 74 x 97 cm) EUR 90,000.

GEERARDS, Marcus. See **GERARDS**

GEERE, J.
British, 19th century.
Active in London.
Painter. Landscapes.

J. Geere was an exhibitor at the British Institution in London from 1858 to 1888.

GEERNAERT, Jan Hermansz.
Flemish School, 18th century.
Born 1714; died 1777.
Sculptor.

Originally from Ghent, he travelled to Italy and lived mainly in Piacenza.

GEERS, Kendell
South African, 20th - 21st century.
Born May 1968, in Johannesburg.
Installation artist, performance artist, video artist.

In his work, Kevin Geers questions the relationship of ethics and aesthetics. His work reflects his political engagement. In 1994, he took part in the *Un Art Contemporain d'Afrique du Sud* (*Contemporary Art of South Africa*) at the Galerie de l'Esplanade in La Défense, Paris. In 2002, he showed his work at a solo exhibition at the contemporary arts centre at the Tokyo palace.

BIBLIOGRAPHY:
Hanru, Hou, '*Kendell Geers*' in *Cream*, Phaidon, London, 1998. Macel, Christine, '*Kendell Geers. L'Œuvre Phénix. Interview*' in *Art Press* n° 257 p. 28, periodical, Paris, May 2000. *Kendell Geers. My tongue in your cheek*, exhibition catalogue, Centre d'art palais de Tokyo, Paris, 2002.

GEERTGEN TOT SINT JANS (LITTLE GERARD OF THE BRETHREN OF ST JOHN), or Geert tot Sint Jans, or Geeraert Van Haarlem, or Gerrit
Dutch, 15th century.
Born perhaps in 1465, probably in Leiden; died c. 1495.
Painter.
Haarlem School.

There are few details about the life of this interesting Dutch painter, who was a pupil of Albert Van Outwater. Some scholars believe that he travelled in the southern part of the Netherlands, an area that had attracted many Dutch artists, including Dieric Bouts. If this journey did indeed take place, it was of brief duration and must have been when Geertgen was still young. It is possible that it was in 1475 or 1476, the time when a new member of the guild of illuminators in Bruges was recorded by the name of Gheerkin ('little Gerard') de Hollandere. It is tempting to identify this Gheerkin with Geertgen tot Sint Jans, particularly after the discovery of one of his earliest works, a *Madonna and Child* (Milan, Biblioteca Ambrosiana), a miniature on velum reminiscent in style of the work of Van Eyck, already glowing with a mysterious light. Apart from this possible journey, Geertgen remained all his life in Holland. His very diverse output has made it difficult to create a chronology for his paintings, although it seems likely from its excessively intricate complexity that a painting of the *Family of the Virgin* (Amsterdam) may be an early work. A painting of the *Raising of Lazarus* still shows the influence of Van Ouwater. He lived for several years in the commandery (house) of the knights of St John in Haarlem, and while there painted several important works. One of these was a triptych for the high altar of the chapel, depicting scenes from the life of Christ: *Calvary*, *The Deposition* and *The Resurrection*. The outer sides of the wings showed scenes from the life of St John the Baptist. One of the wings, depicting the Deposition and four scenes from the life of St John, is in Vienna, now split in two to show the two sides together. The powerful pyramidal composition of the Deposition scene is formed by the figures of the mourning Virgins and Apostles that create a strong diagonal line on one side. The folds of the fabrics have a sculptural quality, while the pathos of the whole scene is emphasised by the incongruous presence of a dog regarding the events taking place on a hillside. The only gesture that seems out of place is that of Mary Magdalene, a less extreme version of the Magdalene painted by Rogier Van der Weyden in his *Deposition*. His approach to *Scenes from the Life of St John*, a subject less easy to approach since it allows less freedom, is highly successful in its composition, using different levels, and its rhythmical use of colours, particularly blacks. He painted three versions of the *Adoration of the Kings*, the best of which is that in Prague, masterly in the technical and iconographic refinement both of the details and the whole. The composition is arranged over three grounds. The main scene, which takes place under a roof and is therefore static and characterised by a gentle chiaroscuro, is placed in the foreground. Further back, outside the building, the sun shines on villagers going about their daily lives. Finally, an almost ghostly town painted in shades of blue can be made out on the distant horizon. Geertgen frequently uses the device seen here of contrasting the pathos or contained emotion of a religious scene with the indifference or banality of the daily activities going on around it. In his *Adoration of the Magi* we see all the technical virtuosity of the Flemish School, in the glass ball held by one of the kings, the pewter vase on the ground and, particularly, in the rendering of St Adrian's armour and helmet that reflect the events taking place before him. A *Nativity* in the National Gallery in London has now been firmly attributed to Geertgen. The picture is a remarkable 'nocturne', the scene being lit by three different sources of artificial light: the body of the Christ Child is haloed in a divine glow that lights up the people and animals present in the stable of the Nativity, while above the stable, the light of the star that guided the shepherds gleams here and there from the roof and stones of the ruined stable building; in the fields, the shepherds have lit a fire that picks out details of the countryside and the people warming themselves around it. In the Rotterdam *Virgin in Glory* the Virgin's robe, of a bright carmine red, seems to exude a pink and gold light that gradually fades at the edges of the picture where diaphanous angels appear transparent against the darkness of the night. The *St John the Baptist* in Berlin, by contrast, shows the saint meditating in a landscape lit by natural daylight, that of the dawn, and by the delicate glowing relationship between the blues and greens of the landscape and the saint's cloak. The vigorous expressions of the figures in the *Crucifixion* in Vienna or the bloodied body of *Christ* in Utrecht show the diversity of his talent. Given the unusual quality of the work of this still relatively little-known artist - who, according to Van Mander, died at only 28 - Geertgen should be seen as one of the precursors of painters as diverse as J. Joest Van Calcar, Quentin Metsys, Lucas Van Leyden and Hieronymus Bosch. While Dutch painters until this period were entirely influenced by Flemish art, from the time of Van Ouwater and, particularly, Geertgen tot Sint Jans, Dutch painters began to leave their mark on Flemish art. As one of earliest *tenebrosi* (painters of night scenes), Geertgen played an important role in the discovery of lighting effects from artificial sources of light. Before long, this motif was taken up by Flemish painters, culminating in the work of Honthorst, subsequently spreading throughout Europe and into Italy. Here Caravaggio was to apply the device to his dramatic scenes, leading to the style called, in both Spain and France, 'Caravaggesque'.

BIBLIOGRAPHY:

Balet, Leo, *Der Frühholländer Geertgen tot Sint Jans*, M. Nijhoff, The Hague, 1910. Kessler, J.J., *Gérard de Saint Jean*, Utrecht, 1930. Vogelsang, W., *Gérard de Saint Jean*, Amsterdam, 1942. Genaille, Robert, *La Peinture dans les anciens Pays-Bas. De Van Eyck à Bruegel*, Éd. Pierre Tisné, Paris, 1954. Leymarie, Jean, *La Peinture hollandaise*, Skira, Geneva, 1956. Sip, Jaromir, *Geertgen tot Sint Jans, l'Adoration des rois Mages*, Artia, Prague, 1963. Châtelet, Albert, *Gérard de Saint-Jean et la peinture dans les Pays-Bas du Nord au XVe*, dissertation, Université de Lille III, Lille, 1979.

MUSEUMS AND GALLERIES:

AMSTERDAM: *Tree of Jesse*; *Adoration of the Magi*; *Martyrdom of St Lucy*; *Nativity*; *Virgin and Child* - BERLIN: *Madonna* - BERLIN (Gemäldegal.): *St John the Baptist* - BRUNSWICK: *Diptych* - BRUSSELS: *Life of Christ* - LEIPZIG: *Legend of the Rosary of St Dominic* - LONDON (NG): *The Nativity at Night* (late 15th century, oil/wood) - MILAN (Ambrosiana): *Virgin and Child* - PARIS (Louvre): *Raising of Lazarus* - PRAGUE (Národní Gal. V Praze): *Adoration of the Magi* (triptych) - ROTTERDAM: *Virgin in Glory* - ST PETERSBURG: *Anne of Cleves* - THE HAGUE: *St James* - UTRECHT (Mus. Catharijneconvent): *The Man of Sorrows* - VIENNA: *Julian the Apostate Orders the Burning of the Bones of St John the Bapist*; *Deposition*.

AUCTION RECORDS:

LONDON, 20 Nov 1925, *Nativity*, GBP 94. LONDON, 14 May 1926, *Nativity*, GBP 39.

GEERTS, Edouard

Belgian, 19th century.

Born 10 January 1846, in Brussels; died 24 November 1889, in Ixelles (Brussels).

Sculptor.

Geerts was highly commended by the jury of the 1889 Exposition Universelle in Paris.

GEERTS, Frans

Belgian, 19th century.

Active in Antwerp c. 1850.

Painter. Genre scenes.

AUCTION RECORDS:

BRUSSELS, 23 March 1977, *Rustic Interior with Card Players* (1854, oil on canvas, 15 x 19¼in/38 x 49cm) BEF 65,000.

GEERTS, Joseph de

Flemish School, 18th century.

Active in Temse (East Flanders).

Painter.

He was a pupil at the Antwerp academy in 1797.

GEERTS, Karel Hendrik

Belgian, 19th century.

Born 10 August 1807, in Antwerp; died 16 June 1885, in Louvain.

Sculptor, wood carver, engraver.

Geerts was a pupil of J. B. van Hool and J.-A. van der Ven and was a professor at the academy in Louvain. His works include a number of the statues decorating the choir-stalls of Antwerp cathedral.

GEERTS, Wilfried

Belgian, 20th - 21st century.

Born 1952.

Painter, engraver.

Geerts attended the Koninklijke Academie voor Beeldende Kunsten in Mechelen and the Nationaal Hoger Instituut voor Schone Kunsten in Antwerp.

GEERTSEN, Ib

Danish, 20th century.

Born 1919, in Copenhagen.

Painter, sculptor.

Ib Geertsen was self-taught. He took part in many group exhibitions in Denmark, especially the autumn exhibitions in Copenhagen in 1940, 1942-1948 and 1956-1957, as well as abroad in Milan and Bucharest in 1953 and New York in 1965. He has also shown his work in solo exhibitions since 1940.

His paintings and sculptures are rigorously constructed, with geometrical forms prevailing, especially combinations of circles and squares, which he is particularly fond of. He also pays great attention to the tensions between hot and cold colours (green-blue-orange, yellow-blue-orange, yellow-green-orange). His compositions swirl in the air to form colour 'spaces'. For some years he has pursued his investigations by creating colourist spaces in hospitals.

BIBLIOGRAPHY:

Galy-Carles, Henry, *Art danois, 1945-1973*, exhibition catalogue, Gal. nationales du Grand Palais, Paris, 1973.

AUCTION RECORDS:

COPENHAGEN, 22 Nov 1989, *Composition* (1960, oil on canvas, 25½ x 19¾ ins / 65 x 50 cm) DKK 5,000. COPENHAGEN, 30 May 1990, *Composition* (1955, oil on canvas, 51¼ x 31½ ins / 130 x 80 cm) DKK 10,000. COPENHAGEN, 14-15 Nov 1990, *Composition* (1952, oil on canvas, 38¼ x 51¼ ins / 97 x 130 cm) DKK 4,500. COPENHAGEN, 30 May 1991, *Composition* (1946, oil on canvas, 49½ x 35¾ ins / 126 x 91 cm) DKK 12,000. COPENHAGEN, 4 Dec 1991, *Composition* (1955, oil on canvas, 51¼ x 31½ ins / 130 x 80 cm) DKK 13,000. COPENHAGEN, 2-3 Dec 1992, *Composition* (1960, oil on canvas, 25½ x 21¼ ins / 65 x 54 cm) DKK 6,000; *Blue Spiral* (1953, painted iron/stone plinth, h. 29½ ins / 75 cm, l. 102¼ ins/260 cm) DKK 32,000. COPENHAGEN, 10 March 1993, *Series of Orange Rooms* (1968, oil on canvas, 25½ x 19¾ ins / 65 x 50 cm) DKK 3,800. COPENHAGEN, 22-24 Oct 1997, *Composition* (1958, oil on canvas, 36½ x 29¼ ins / 93 x 74 cm) DKK 4,000. COPENHAGEN, 29 Nov 2000, *Composition in Violet and Ochre* (1958, oil on canvas, 19 x 13 ins / 47 x 33 cm) DKK 14,000. AARHUS, 6 May 2002, *Folding II- Composition* (1966, oil on canvas, 36 x 29 ins / 92 x 73 cm) DKK 13,000. COPENHAGEN, 29 May 2002, *Composition* (1958, oil on canvas, 26 x 20 ins / 65 x 50 cm) DKK 14,000.

GEERTZ, Henry Ludwig

German, 19th - 20th century.

Born 19 July 1872, in Düsseldorf.

Painter.

Geertz was the son of the genre painter Julius Geertz.

GEERTZ, Julius

German, 19th century.

Born 21 April 1837, in Hamburg; died 21 October 1902, in Brunswick (Lower Saxony).

Painter. Portraits, genre scenes.

Geertz was a pupil of the brothers Martin and Gunther Gendler in Hamburg, of Descoudre in Karlsruhe and of Jordan in Düsseldorf. In 1873 he was awarded a medal in Vienna.

AUCTION RECORDS:
LONDON, 19 June 1981, *The Last Adornment* (oil on canvas, 57 1/2 x 52 ins / 146 x 132 cm) GBP 1,400. AMSTERDAM, 2 May 1990, *Young Beggar with his Guinea-Pig* (oil on panel, 13 3/4 x 10 1/4 ins / 35 x 26 cm) NLG 7,475. NEW YORK, 20 Jan 1993, *Young Girl with her Doll* (1884, oil on canvas, 10 x 8 ins / 25.4 x 20.3 cm) USD 6,325. LONDON, 11 April 1995, *Punishment in Class* (1880, oil on canvas, 28 x 25 ins / 71 x 63.5 cm) GBP 4,140. MUNICH, 3 Dec 1996, *Obligatory Breaks in Class* (oil on wood, 37 1/2 x 27 1/2 ins / 95 x 70 cm) DEM 10,200.

GEEST, Arthur
Belgian, 20th century.
Born 1894, in Lokeren.
Painter. Figures, landscapes.
AUCTION RECORDS:
LOKEREN, 28 May 1988, *Houses beside a Canal in Ghent* (oil on canvas, 17 3/4 x 14 1/2 ins / 45 x 37 cm) BEF 36,000.

GEEST, Cornelis van der
Flemish School, 17th century.
Born 1577, in Antwerp; died 10 March 1638, in Antwerp.
Engraver.
He produced engraved portraits.

GEEST, Gillis de
Dutch, 17th century.
Painter (glass).
He was possibly the brother of Wybrand Simonsz. de Geest. He became a burgher of Utrecht in 1604 or 1605.

GEEST, Jacobus De, or Ghest
Flemish School, 16th - 17th century.
Born 1570, in Antwerp; died 1612, in Antwerp.
Painter. History painting.
Pilkington mentions a De Gheest who painted historical subjects in Antwerp and who died in 1672. According to Siret, he may be the same artist as Jacobus De Geest.

GEEST, Juliaan Franciscus de, or Julius Felix de
Flemish School, 17th century.
Died 25 May 1699, in Antwerp.
Painter. Portraits, still-lifes, vanitas.
He was the son of Wybrand Simonsz. de Geest. He was a pupil of Erasmus Quellinus and, in 1657, of Mytens.
AUCTION RECORDS:
NEW YORK, 13 Oct 1989, *Vanitas: Portrait of a Gentleman Holding a Skull* (1662, oil on panel, 17 x 14in/43 x 35.5cm) USD 5,500.

GEEST, Wybrand de, the Younger
Flemish School, 17th century.
Died before 1716.
Active in Antwerp c. 1690.
Painter. History painting.
He was the son and pupil of Juliaan de Geest. He also studied with Jan Michiel Coxcie, to whom he dedicated his study of antique statuary (1702).

GEEST, Wybrand Simonsz. de, the Elder, known as 'the Frisian eagle'
Dutch, 17th century.
Born 16 August 1592, in Leeuwarden (Friesland); died 1659, in Leeuwarden, in 1643 according to Bryan's Dictionary.
Painter. Portraits.
He was the son and pupil of the Louvain painter Symon de Geest, who also lived in Antwerp. In 1613 Wybrand Simonsz. de Geest was working with Bloemaert in Utrecht. He later travelled to Belgium and France, and spent four years in Rome. Upon his return to Utrecht, he married Hendrickje Uylenborch, the sister of Rembrandt's wife Saskia. He was subsequently active in Amsterdam and Louvain, and his pupils included Jacobus Potma. His son, Juliaan, was also a painter.

BIBLIOGRAPHY:
Bernt, W., *Netherlandish Painters of the Seventeenth Century*, Oxford, 1969. Slive, S., *Dutch Painting, 1600-1800*, London, 1995.
MUSEUMS AND GALLERIES:
AMSTERDAM: *Self-portrait; The Artist's Wife; Ernest Casimir of Nassau* (two versions); *Henry Casimir I of Nassau* (two versions); *William Frederick of Nassau; Johann-Conrad Wilder Ryngranf; Sophia Hedwig of Brunswick, Countess of Nassau; A Lady of Quality; High-ranking Officer; The Brothers of William the Silent: John, Henry, Louis and Adolphe* - HAARLEM (Frans Halsmus.): *Alef van Beyma; His van Popma; Johan Bœsms; Geerbruyt van der Dussen* - LILLE: *A Prince of Orange; Dutch Family* - STUTTGART: *Family Portrait.*
AUCTION RECORDS:
PARIS, 1850, *Girl with a Butterfly* (drawing) FRF 4,252. PARIS, 16 Feb 1923, *Portrait of a Man with a Ruff*, FRF 2,000. LONDON, 23 March 1923, *Portrait of a Man*, GBP 294; *Madame de Wint*, GBP 430. LONDON, 17-18 May 1928, *Spanish Gentleman*, GBP 220. PARIS, 30 Oct 1946, *Portrait of a Man*, FRF 19,100. PARIS, 20 March 1953, *Woman Wearing a Ring; Man with a Glove*, FRF 75,000. NEW YORK, 17 May 1972, *Portrait of a Young Girl*, USD 3,000. LONDON, 28 Oct 1987, *Portrait of a Young Boy* (oil on canvas, 69 x 43 1/4in/175 x 110cm) GBP 13,800. PARIS, 14 Dec 1989, *Full-length Portrait of a Child Holding a Flower and an Apple* (oil on canvas, 35 1/2 x 27 1/2in/90 x 70cm) FRF 80,000. AMSTERDAM, 6 May 1993, *Portrait of a Young Woman in a Black Dress with a Ruff of White Lace, a Six-stringed Necklace and a Red Belt* (oil on panel, 27 3/4 x 23 1/2in/70.8 x 59.8cm) NLG 59,800. NEW YORK, 12 Jan 1995, *Portrait of Henry West, 4th Baron De La Warr* (1627, oil on panel, 17 1/4 x 12 3/4in/43.8 x 32.4cm) USD 11,500. LONDON, 6 July 1999, *Portrait of Gentleman, Wearing Armour, Lace Ruff and Embroidered Red Cloak* (oil on panel, 25 x 20 ins / 63 x 51 cm) GBP 2,500. NEW YORK, 26 Jan 2001, *Family Portrait of Two Brothers aged Eleven and Seven and Two Sisters aged Four and Nine, the Younger Stroking a Dog* (1627, oil on panel, 31 x 45 ins / 79 x 115 cm) USD 32,000.

GEETERE, Frans de
Belgian (?), 20th century.
Watercolourist, draughtsman, illustrator.
De Geetere illustrated *Lettres d'un Satyre* (*A Satyr's Letters*) and *La Toison d'Or* (*The Golden Fleece*) by Rémy de Gourmont.
AUCTION RECORDS:
PARIS, 20 Nov 1984, *Suzy Solidor Reclining* (watercolour, 24 x 33 ins / 61 x 84 cm) FRF 4,500. PARIS, 4 March 1991, *Carnival* (1917, Indian ink and gouache/card, 27 1/2 x 21 1/4 ins / 70 x 54 cm) FRF 7,800.

GEETERE, Georg Frans van
Belgian, 19th century.
Active in Namur, c. 1890.
Painter. Portraits, local scenes.
He was a pupil of Portaels.

AUCTION RECORDS:

PARIS, 25 Nov 1985, *Portrait of a Woman* (oil on canvas, 23 1/2 x 31 1/2in/60 x 80cm) FRF 48,000. NEW YORK, 25 May 1988, *Harem Guard* (1885, oil on canvas, 80 x 47in/203.2 x 119.4cm) USD 17,600. NEW YORK, 14 Oct 1993, *Harem Guard* (oil on canvas, 80 x 47in/203.2 x 119.4cm) USD 16,100.

GEETS, Willem

Belgian, 19th - 20th century.

Born 20 January 1838, in Mechelen; died 1919.

Painter, watercolourist, pastellist. Religious subjects, portraits, genre scenes.

Geets attended the art academies in Mechelen and Antwerp. He continued his studies notably with Nicasie de Keyser. He was appointed director of the art academy in Mechelen and in 1877, he won a medal in Ghent; in 1893, he received an honourable mention in Paris.

Willem Geets

MUSEUMS AND GALLERIES:

ANTWERP: *Exorcism of Jeanne de Castille, Known as the Madwoman* - BIRMINGHAM (Mus. and AG): *A Martyr in the 16th Century: Johanna van Santhoven, a Protestant Led out to be Buried Alive* (oil) - LIVERPOOL (Walker AG): *Awaiting an Audience* (1886, oil on canvas).

AUCTION RECORDS:

NEW YORK, 13-14 Feb 1900, *Empty Cradle*, USD 170. LONDON, 19 Dec 1908, *Portrait of a Young Girl*, GBP 10. NEWCASTLE, 18 April 1932, *Lovers' Kiss*, GBP 26. LONDON, 8 March 1937, *Baptism*, GBP 13. BRUSSELS, 11 Dec 1937, *Christmas Song*, BEF 10,000. BRUSSELS, 27 Oct 1976, *Figures in a Renaissance Interior* (oil on canvas, 44 1/2 x 67 3/4 ins / 113 x 172 cm) BEF 200,000. CHESTER, 31 July 1981, *Woman Writing a Letter* (oil on panel, 18 1/2 x 15 1/2 ins / 47 x 39.5 cm) GBP 850. BRUSSELS, 18 Feb 1982, *Maid Dreaming of her Native Country* (watercolour, 13 3/4 x 9 1/2 ins / 35 x 24 cm) BEF 24,000. BRUSSELS, 27 Feb 1985, *Little Girl in the Snow* (1891, pastel, 35 1/2 x 22 ins / 90 x 55 cm) BEF 40,000. NEW YORK, 24 May 1989, *Polishing Brass and Copper* (oil on canvas, 36 x 54 ins / 91.5 x 137.2 cm) USD 13,200. LONDON, 17 April 1996, *Jewellry Dowry* (1907, oil on canvas, 44 x 67 3/4 ins / 112 x 172 cm) GBP 12,650. LONDON, 13 June 1997, *Soldiers Looting a House* (1915, oil on canvas, 59 1/2 x 89 ins / 151 x 226 cm) GBP 31,050. PARIS, 12 Dec 1997, *Seated Young Woman* (1903, oil on canvas, 41 x 41 ins / 104 x 104 cm) FRF 35,000.

GEFFCKEN, Walter

German, 19th - 20th century.

Born 4 April 1872, in Hamburg; died 1950.

Painter. Local scenes.

Geffcken was active in Munich and then studied under Jean-Paul Laurens and Benjamin Constant in Paris.

AUCTION RECORDS:

PARIS, 5 March 1942, *Breakfast*, FRF 300. COLOGNE, 17 March 1978, *The Hearing* (1919, oil on card, 26 x 33 1/2 ins / 66 x 85 cm) DEM 3,000. COLOGNE, 21 March 1980, *Interior* (19 3/4 x 24 3/4 ins / 50 x 63 cm) DEM 2,600. BOSTON, 12 May 2000, *Figures by a Fountain in a Park* (oil on board, 19 x 15 ins / 47 x 37 cm) USD 4,250. STOCKHOLM, 24 Oct 2001, *Rococo Interior with Elegant Figures* (oil on canvas, 23 x 31 ins / 59 x 80 cm) SEK 16,500. MUNICH, 24 Sept 2003, *Figures round a Table in a Rococo Salon* (oil on board, 23 x 30 ins / 58 x 76 cm) EUR 1,600.

GEFFELS, Frans de

Flemish School, 17th century.

Painter, engraver (etching), architect. Architectural views, scenes with figures.

De Geffels was active at the court of Mantua from 1666 to 1671. He is best known for his series of seven plates in portrait format, *Architecturen, Ruinen, mit landschaftlichen Hintergrunden und Figuren* (*Architecture, Ruins, with Landscape Backgrounds and Figures*), and for the highly sought after plate showing the *Catafalque of Carlo II Gonzaga, Duke of Mantua, in the church of S Barbara* (1666).

£ geffels.

AUCTION RECORDS:

CANNES, 7 Aug 1997, *Chivalrous banquet* (canvas, 22 x 33 1/2in/55 x 85cm) FRF 60,000.

GEFFROY, Edmond Aimé Florentin

French, 19th century.

Born 29 July 1804, in Maignelay-Montigny (Oise); died 8 February 1895, in St-Pierre-les-Nemours (Seine-et-Marne).

Painter. Religious subjects, portraits.

Edmond Geffroy divided his time between painting and the theatre, where he was a well-known actor and a member of the Théâtre de la Comédie-Française until 1865. As a painter, he studied under Amaury Duval and exhibited at the Paris Salon from 1829 to 1868, obtaining bronze and silver medals (1841). The great majority of his work comprises individual or group portraits: between 1851 and 1863, he portrayed his fellow actors either in or out of costume (in the latter case, in their favourite role), including *Augustine Brohan, Bonval, Madeleine Brohan, Régner, Provost, Leroux, Favart, Coquelin, Delaunay, Maillart, Victoria Lafontaine*, and *Jouassin*. Additionally, Geffroy painted historical and religious subjects (among them a *Virgin and Child*), which evidence not only his indebtedness to Raphael but also his own well-developed compositional sense.

BIBLIOGRAPHY:

Les Années romantiques, la peinture française de 1815 à 1850, exhibition catalogue, Musée des Beaux-Arts, Nantes, Gal. nationales du Grand Palais, Paris, 1996.

MUSEUMS AND GALLERIES:

BOURG-EN-BRESSE: *Virgin and Child* - ROUEN (MBA): *Virgin with Child*.

GEFLOWSKI, E. Edward

British, 19th century.

Active in London.

Sculptor.

E. Edward Geflowski was a frequent exhibitor in London at the Royal Academy and the Suffolk Street Gallery from 1867.

MUSEUMS AND GALLERIES:

LIVERPOOL: *Busts of Garibaldi; Bust of Edwing Wangh.*

GEGAN, J.J.

British, 19th century.

Active in Maidstone.

Painter. Landscapes.

J.J. Gegan exhibited in London from 1844 to 1860, mainly at the Royal Academy and the Suffolk Street Gallery.

GEGENBAUER, Joseph Anton von

German, 19th century.

Born 6 March 1800, in Wangen; died 31 January 1876, in Rome.

Painter. History painting, architectural views.

Gegenbauer was a pupil of R. von Langer. He made several trips to Rome, before travelling to Stuttgart, where he was summoned by the King of Württemberg to decorate his castle with pictures depicting the history of his realm. These works took him eighteen years to complete. In 1836 he was appointed court painter.

MUSEUMS AND GALLERIES:

KONSTANZ: *Madonna* - STUTTGART: *The Artist's Father; The Artist's Mother; Hercules and Omphale*; same subject; sketches.

GEGER, Christoph Daniel
Hungarian, 17th century.
Active in Jeszenova in 1661.
Painter.

GEGERFELT, Charlotta von
Swedish, 19th - 20th century.
Born 14 June 1834; died 22 May 1915, in Göteborg.
Painter.

GEGERFELT, Wilhelm von
Swedish, 19th - 20th century.
Born 1844, in Göteborg; died 1920.
Active in France between 1872 and 1888.
Painter, watercolourist. Genre scenes, harbour views, fishing scenes, interiors, landscapes, landscapes with figures, waterscapes, urban landscapes, seascapes, harbour scenes, architectural views.

Von Gegerfelt studied at the art academy in Stockholm, then from 1867 to 1872 at the art academy in Düsseldorf. From 1872 to 1888, he lived in Paris. Then he returned to Göteborg before settling in Vadero for good. He visited Venice on several occasions. He painted numerous landscapes depicting a wide variety of scenes of nature. In France, he was inspired by Normandy and the Côte de Grâce; in Italy, by the lagoon: he produced numerous seaside landscapes at high or low tide, harbours, canals, quays, seascapes, at sunset or under the effects of moonlight. He also produced landscapes of his own region - woods, hamlets in sunny conditions or under snow.

He exhibited at the Paris Salon, then at the Salon des Artistes Français from 1876 to 1888; he exhibited in Vienna from 1888, when he won a silver medal; he also exhibited in Munich.

W. Gegerfelt 73

MUSEUMS AND GALLERIES:

FÉCAMP (Mus. des Arts et de l'Enfance): *Winter Landscape* (oil on canvas) - LEIPZIG: *Canal, Sunset* - LIMOGES: *Swedish Landscape* - RHEIMS: *Winter in Holland* - STOCKHOLM: *Coast at Vadero* (a watercolour).

AUCTION RECORDS:

PARIS, 1882, *Skaters*, FRF 1,000; *Jetty in Venice*, FRF 1,510. NEW YORK, 20 March 1909, *Dutch Scene*, USD 200. PARIS, 20 Nov 1925, *The Thaw, Sun Effect*, FRF 3,000. PARIS, 23 June 1943, *Mill*, FRF 8,100. PARIS, Oct 1945-July 1946, *Harbour at Sunset*, FRF 35,000; *Winter Landscape* (watercolour) FRF 7,000. PARIS, 25 March 1949, *Harbour Scene*, FRF 91,000. GÖTEBORG, 8 Nov 1973, *Seaside*, SEK 13,000. VERSAILLES, 8 Feb 1976, *Farmyard* (oil on wood, 17 x 11 ins / 43 x 28 cm) FRF 3,500. GÖTEBORG, 31 March 1977, *Fishing Boats* (oil on canvas, 25 1/2 x 36 1/4 ins / 65 x 92 cm) SEK 19,000. STOCKHOLM, 26 April 1982, *Italian Landscape* (watercolour and gouache, 18 1/2 x 9 3/4 ins / 47 x 25 cm) SEK 6,000. STOCKHOLM, 30 Oct 1984, *Seaside* (watercolour, 16 1/4 x 25 1/4 ins / 41 x 64 cm) SEK 11,500. GÖTEBORG, 7 Nov 1984, *Italian Village* (oil on canvas, 46 x 32 ins / 116 x 81 cm) SEK 42,000. STOCKHOLM, 4 Nov 1986, *View of Venice* (1882, oil on canvas, 30 x 17 3/4 ins / 76 x 45 cm) SEK 190,000. STOCKHOLM, 20 Oct 1987, *View of Venice* (watercolour and gouache, 18 x 20 1/2 ins / 46 x 52 cm) SEK 28,000. STOCKHOLM, 20 Oct 1987, *Canal Scene, Venice* (oil on canvas, 39 1/4 x 30 ins / 100 x 76 cm) SEK 210,000. STOCKHOLM, 27 April 1988, *Road at the Entrance to the Village under Snow* (1874, oil on canvas, 17 3/4 x 28 3/4 ins / 45 x 73 cm) SEK 26,000. STOCKHOLM, 15 Nov 1988, *Coast with Cliffs and Figures* (oil, 13 3/4 x 17 3/4 ins / 35 x 45 cm) SEK 30,000. LONDON, 16 March 1989, *Boats Run aground* (oil on canvas, 13 3/4 x 18 1/4 ins / 35 x 46.2 cm) GBP 11,000. STOCKHOLM, 19 April 1989, *Landscape with a Boat-House near a Torrent* (oil on canvas, 15 x 20 ins / 38 x 51 cm) SEK 50,000. GÖTEBORG, 18 May 1989, *Venetian Quays and Warehouses, Evening* (oil on canvas, 30 x 48 ins / 76 x 121 cm) SEK 280,000. STOCKHOLM, 15 Nov 1989, *Activities on the Canal Banks in Venice at Sunrise* (oil, 25 1/4 x 35 3/4 ins / 64 x 91 cm) SEK 150,000. PARIS, 21 Nov 1989, *Sailing Boats at Low Tide; Winter Undergrowth* (two oils on panel, matching pair, each 16 1/4 x 12 1/2 ins / 41 x 32 cm) FRF 80, 000. CALAIS, 4 March 1990, *Bois de Boulogne under Snow* (1873, oil on panel, 16 1/4 x 12 1/2 ins / 41 x 32 cm) FRF 42,000. NEW YORK, 23 Oct 1990, *A Venetian Canal* (oil on canvas, 65 x 39 1/2 ins / 165.1 x 100.3 cm) USD 44,000. STOCKHOLM, 14 Nov 1990, *Venetians Watching out for the Return of Boats in Foggy Conditions* (oil on canvas, 29 1/4 x 39 1/4 ins / 74 x 100 cm) SEK 65,000. STOCKHOLM, 29 May 1991, *Harbour Activities and Ship-Yards* (oil on panel, 23 1/2 x 38 1/4 ins / 60 x 97 cm) SEK 42,000. STOCKHOLM, 13 April 1992, *Rustic House near a Stream in Winter* (oil on canvas, 23 1/4 x 37 ins / 59 x 94 cm) SEK 13,500. STOCKHOLM, 19 May 1992, *Beach with Child Playing in Puddles in Brittany* (oil on canvas, 24 x 35 3/4 ins / 61 x 91 cm) SEK 45,000. STOCKHOLM, 5 Sept 1992, *Canal Scene in Venice* (oil on canvas, 37 x 26 ins / 94 x 66 cm) SEK 60,000. NEW YORK, 30 Oct 1992, *Fishing in the Lagoon* (1883, oil on canvas, 26 1/2 x 37 1/2 ins / 67.3 x 95.2 cm) USD 12,100. LONDON, 16 June 1993, *View of Venice* (oil on canvas, 29 1/4 x 49 1/2 ins / 74 x 126 cm) GBP 10,925. STOCKHOLM, 30 Nov 1993, *Ponte Longo Canal in Venice* (oil on canvas, 11 1/2 x 17 ins / 29 x 43 cm) SEK 17,500.

GEH, Peter
German, 19th century.
Born 25 June 1865, in Offenbach (Hesse).
Engraver, illustrator.

Geh was active in Berlin.

GEHART, Johann
German, 14th century.
Active in Erfurt c. 1370.
Sculptor.

GEHBE, Eduard
German, 19th century.
Born 30 March 1845, in Meiningen (Thuringia).
Painter.

Gehbe was a pupil of Preller in Weimar.

GÉHIN, Thierry
French, 20th century.
Video artist, photographer. Multimedia.

Thierry Géhin studied at the Lyons art college. He practices video art and in 1994 he was involved in the 9th Vidéoformes Festival.

GEHLER
German, 18th century.
Active in Leipzig (Saxony).
Painter.

Gehler executed portraits in miniature.

GEHR, Andreas
Swiss, 20th century.
Born 1942, in Appenzell.
Sculptor, environmental artist.

Gehr attended the École des Arts Appliqués in Lucerne. He has participated in a few group exhibitions in Switzerland, notably at the Musée de Lucerne in 1975; and he exhibited at the 9th Biennale de Paris in 1975. Gehr has also held a solo show in Lucerne and in Olten, in 1973 and 1974, respectively.

BIBLIOGRAPHY:
IXe Biennale de Paris, exhibition catalogue, Idea Books, Musée d'Art moderne de la Ville de Paris, Paris, 1975.
MUSEUMS AND GALLERIES:
LUCERNE.

GEHR, Johann Ferdinand
Swiss, 20th century.
Born 1896, in Niederglatt (Zurich); died 1996.
Painter, draughtsman. Designs for stained glass, murals.

AUCTION RECORDS:
LUCERNE, 21 Nov 1992, *Composition with Flowers* (1970, wax crayon/paper, 10 1/2 x 7 1/2 ins / 26.5 x 19 cm) CHF 1,200. ZURICH, 19 Nov 1997, *Men and Stars* (1967, coloured woodcut, 8 1/2 x 4 1/4 ins / 21.5 x 11 cm) CHF 1,100. ST GALL, 21 April 1999, *Evening Landscape in Rhine Valley* (1956, tempera on canvas, 35 x 49 ins / 90 x 125 cm) CHF 53,000. ST GALL, 10 Dec 1999, *Apples I* (1971, watercolour, 26 x 20 ins / 65 x 50 cm) CHF 17,000. ST GALL, 10 May 2000, *Roses* (1986, watercolour and gouache, 20 x 25 ins / 50 x 63 cm) CHF 23,000. ST GALL, 10 May 2000, *Landscape near Altstatten* (1942, tempera on canvas, 24 x 35 ins / 60 x 90 cm) CHF 36,000. ST GALL, 8 May 2001, *Still-life with Flowers* (1959, watercolour, 21 x 17 ins / 53 x 42 cm) CHF 25,000. ST GALL, 21 Nov 2001, *Zinnia* (1983, tempera on canvas, 28 x 24 ins / 70 x 60 cm) CHF 23,000. ST GALL, 22 May 2002, *Three Substances* (1974, oil on canvas, 21 x 23 ins / 53 x 59 cm) CHF 16,000. ST GALL, 22 May 2002, *Zinnia and Rudbeckia* (1984, watercolour over charcoal, 16 x 16 ins / 40 x 41 cm) CHF 24,000. ST GALL, 24 Oct 2003, *Peonies and Roses* (1986, watercolour over charcoal, 26 x 20 ins / 66 x 51 cm) CHF 28,000. ST GALL, 24 Oct 2003, *Yarrow and Phlox* (1950, tempera on canvas, 24 x 30 ins / 60 x 75 cm) CHF 76,000. ST GALL, 1 Oct 2004, *Garden with Poppies* (1978, watercolour, 26 x 20 ins / 65 x 50 cm) CHF 26,000. ST GALL, 1 Oct 2004, *Madonna and Child* (1926, tempera on canvas, 24 x 20 ins / 61 x 50 cm) CHF 29,000.

GEHREN, Cord von
German, 16th century.
Active in Lübeck in 1594.
Painter.

GEHREN, Gregor von
German, 16th century.
Died 1590.
Active in Lübeck.
Painter.

GEHREN, Moritz
German, 16th century.
Active in Lübeck c. 1595.
Painter.

He was the son of Gregor.

GEHRI, Christian Schnitzler
Swiss, 19th century.
Born August 1808, in Riggis; died 1882.
Engraver (wood).

GEHRI, Franz
Swiss, 20th century.
Born 15 April 1882, in Seedorf.
Painter, engraver.

Gehri was the son of Karl Gehri. He produced portraits, landscapes and genre scenes.

GEHRI, Karl
German, 19th - 20th century.
Born 25 June 1850, in Seedorf; died after 1913.
Painter. Genre scenes, landscapes.

Gehri studied under Drether and Valech in Bern, and under Franz von Defregger and Grob in Munich.
MUSEUMS AND GALLERIES:
BERN: *Young Roman Woman (Painted in Two Hours); Golden Wedding; Stone Gun; Landscape.*
AUCTION RECORDS:
BERN, 6 May 1981, *Wandering Minstrel* (oil on card, 21 1/2 x 16 1/4 ins / 54.5 x 41 cm) CHF 2,500. ZURICH, 13 June 1986, *Peasant Woman Playing the Guitar* (1896, oil on canvas, 27 1/4 x 22 3/4 ins / 69 x 58 cm) CHF 5,000.

GEHRI, Max
Austrian, 19th century.
Born 11 November 1847, in Innsbruck; died 1909, in Mühlau.
Painter. Church decoration.

Max Gehri was a pupil of Plattner.

GEHRIG, Charles
Swiss, 20th century.
Born 1932.
Painter.

AUCTION RECORDS:
LUCERNE, 24 Nov 1990, *Untitled* (1969, oil on wood relief, 63 x 23 1/2 ins / 160 x 60 cm) CHF 2,000.

GEHRIG, Jacob
German, 19th century.
Born 1846, in Flawil.
Active in Munich.
Painter. Landscapes.

Gehrig is credited with views of Venice.

GEHRKE, Fritz
German, 19th - 20th century.
Born 16 July 1855, in Woisenthin; died 1916, in Berlin.
Painter, illustrator.

Gehrke studied under Guslow.

GEHRKEN, Karl
Russian, 19th century.
Active in St Petersburg at the beginning of the 19th century.
Painter.

GEHRMANN, Franz Octavio
German, 18th century.
Born 9 June 1728, in Hamburg; died 10 May 1787, in Hamburg.
Painter.

Franz was the son and pupil of Johann Michael Gehrmann.

GEHRMANN, Johann Michael
German, 18th century.
Died 27 July 1770, in Hamburg.
Painter.

Johann Michael Gehrmann was the pupil of Johann Rundt.

GEHRTS, Anna
Maiden name: Kottgen
German, 19th century.
Died 8 June 1901, in Düsseldorf.
Painter. Landscapes.

Anna was the wife of Karl Gehrts.

GEHRTS, Franz
German, 19th century.
Born 18 May 1860, in Hamburg; died 5 October 1894, in Halle (Saxony-Anhalt).
Painter.

Franz was the brother of Johannes and Karl Gehrts.

GEHRTS, Johannes
German, 19th century.
Born 26 February 1855, in Hamburg.

Painter, draughtsman. Historical subjects, genre scenes. ohannes was the younger brother of Karl Gehrts. He studed in Weimar and Düsseldorf. In 1873 he worked with his rother on the decoration of the Villa Meyer, near Altona Hamburg). He exhibited in Berlin, Munich and Dresden beween 1878 and 1887. He is noted for his work *Chief of Germanic Tribe with Attendants.*

GEHRTS, Karl
German, 19th century.
Born 11 May 1853, in St Pauli (Hamburg); died 17 July 1898, in Endenich.
Painter, draughtsman. Allegorical subjects, genre scenes.

n 1871 Karl Gehrts studied at the art school in Weimar with Gussow and Alb. Baur. He obtained an honourable mention n Berlin in 1886 and in Dresden in 1887, as well as a gold medal in 1890. He is noted for his *Empress Gisela before the Body of her Son* and *Demetrius.*

AUCTION RECORDS:
HEIDELBERG, 18 Oct 1980, *Allegory on the Arts* (1873, pen and wash/paper, 12 3/4 x 19 3/4 ins / 32.5 x 50 cm) DEM 3,000. LUCERNE, 15 May 1986, *Hermit Reading Aloud to Dwarfs* (painting, 18 1/4 x 23 3/4 ins / 46.5 x 60.5 cm) CHF 26,000.

GEHRY, Frank
Canadian, 20th century.
Born 1929, in Toronto.
Sculptor and architect.

Frank Gehry is known both as an architect and as a sculptor. Among his most celebrated work is his design of the Guggenheim Museum in Bilbao, opened in 1997. He studied at UCLA in 1954 and at the Graduate School of Design, Harvard, from 1956 to 1957. He is known to be influenced by fine art and post-modernism and sees architecture as art. '[Gehry] is an architect of immense gifts who dances on the line separating architecture from art but who manages never to let himself fall,' wrote Paul Goldberger, architecture critic of the New York Times.

Fish are a recurring motif in his work and he designed a 175 feet (54 metre) steel fish sculpture for the portal of the Olympic stadium in Barcelona. His other major commissions and buildings include the Law School Building for Loyola University, Los Angeles, the California Aerospace Museum (1982), the Walt Disney Concert Hall in Los Angeles (1989-2004), University of Minnesota Art Museum at Minneapolis (1990) and the Kobe Fish restaurant in Japan.

BIBLIOGRAPHY:
Arnell, P./Beckford, T., *Frank Gehry: Buildings and Projects*, New York, 1985. Haag Bletter, R., *The Architecture of Frank Gehry*, New York, 1986. Richardson, S., *Frank O. Gehry: A Bibliography*, Monticello (IL), 1987. Lacy, B./de Menil, S. (ed.), *Angels and Franciscans: Innovative Architecture from Los Angeles and San Francisco*, New York, 1992 (pp. 78-102). Bruggen, Coosje van, *Frank O Gehry: Guggenheim Museum Bilbao*, Guggenheim Museum Publications, distributed by H.N. Abrams, 1997.

AUCTION RECORDS:
NEW YORK, 8 Nov 1989, *Lamp-Fish* (1984, formica and electric montage, 79 x 36 x 24 ins / 200.6 x 91.5 x 61 cm) USD 53,900. SAN FRANCISCO, 26 Oct 1999, *Pair of Wiggle Side Chairs* (corrugated cardboard, 34 x 16x22 ins / 86 x 40x55 cm) USD 7,000. NEW YORK, 13 Nov 2002, *Snake Lamp* (c. 1982, colorcore, wood, wire and incandescent light, 24 x 43x28 ins / 60 x 109x71 cm) USD 32,500. NEW YORK, 13 Nov 2002, *Fish Lamp, Boathouse* (glass electrical fixture, 43 x 19x14 ins / 109 x 48x36 cm) USD 85,000. NEW YORK, 14 May 2003, *Snake Lamp* (gouache, papier mâché, modeled paper and electrical unit, 67 x 13x3 ins / 170 x 33x8 cm) USD 20,000.

GEIAMI, real name: Nakao Shingei, artist names: Gakuso, Geiami
Japanese, 15th century.
Born 1431; died 1485.
Painter.

Geiami was the son of Noami (1397-1471) and the father of Saomi (?-1525), all of whom were hereditary artistic advisors to the Ashikaga shoguns. The Ami family, which came from Kyoto (the suffix 'Ami' indicates that they were devotees of Amida Buddha), was pre-eminent in the art of monochrome wash painting and is often regarded as a school. During this time, the second half of the 15th century, monochrome painting, which until then had developed in Zen Buddhist circles, extended its sphere of influence to lay society. The Ami family style, characterised by its wash technique, gradually freed itself from Chinese influence. Although devotees of Amida, they also worked for the Zen monasteries.

To their talent as art connoisseurs we owe the *Kundai-kan Socho-ki* (Notebook of the Shogun's Art Secretary), which lists the names of illustrious Chinese painters whose works appear in the shogun's collections, as well as listing works of calligraphy and other items, classified according to the taste at the time.

BIBLIOGRAPHY:
Akiyama, Terukazu, *La Peinture japonaise*, Skira, Geneva, 1961. Tanaka, Ichimatsu, *Japanese Ink Painting: Shûbun to Sesshû*, Weatherhill, New York, 1972. Tazawa, Yutaka, *Biographical Dictionary of Japanese Art*, Kodansha International Ltd, Tokyo, 1981.

MUSEUMS AND GALLERIES:
TOKYO (Nezu Institute of Fine Arts): *Spectacle of a Waterfall* (dated 1480, ink and colour on paper, hanging scroll, inscriptions by Osen Keisan and two other priests).

GEIBEL, Carl
German, 18th - 19th century.
Born in Halle.
Painter, lithographer.

Carl Geibel is noted for his miniatures and watercolours.

GEIBEL, Casimir
German, 19th century.
Born 12 January 1839, in Bad Kreuznach (Rhineland-Palatinate); died 22 May 1896, in Weimar (Thuringia).
Painter. History painting, portraits, genre scenes.

Casimir Geibel was a pupil of Pauwel. He exhibited mainly in Berlin, Dresden and Vienna between 1866 and 1887. He is credited with portraits and historical paintings. He is noted for his *Wrong Road* and *Summer Landscape.*

AUCTION RECORDS:
BERLIN, 30 Oct 1969, *Grape Harvest*, DEM 7,300. NEW YORK, 17 Jan 1990, *Card Game* (oil on canvas, 24 1/4 x 20 1/4 ins / 61.6 x 51.4 cm) USD 4,675. NEW YORK, 29 Oct 1992, *Ploughing* (oil on canvas, 26 1/4 x 39 1/2 ins / 66.7 x 100.4 cm) USD 6,050. MUNICH, 23 June 1999, *Forest Workers in Winter* (oil on canvas, 20 x 28 ins / 52 x 70 cm) DEM 5,500. COPENHAGEN, 2 Dec 2002, *Farmers and Horses in Field* (oil on canvas, 26 x 40 ins / 67 x 101 cm) DKK 36,000.

GEIBEL, Hermann
German, 20th century.
Born 14 May 1889, in Freiburg im Breisgau.
Sculptor.

Geibel studied in Dresden and then settled in Munich.

GEIBEL, Margarete
German, 20th century.
Born 5 June 1876, in Weimar.
Engraver.
Margarete Geibel was the daughter of Casimir Geibel.

GEIBEL, Stephan
German, 18th century.
Born in Bamberg.
Painter.
Stephan Geibel executed several religious pictures in Frankfurt am Main.

GEIGENBERGER, August
German, 20th century.
Born 16 June 1875, in Wasserburg; died 5 March 1909, in Munich.
Painter, illustrator.
Geigenberger produced illustrations and caricatures.

GEIGER, Adam
German, 17th century.
Active in Landshut (Bavaria).
Painter.

GEIGER, Andreas
Austrian, 18th - 19th century.
Born 27 July 1765, in Vienna; died 31 October 1856, in Vienna.
Engraver (mezzotint).
Andreas Geiger's best works include *Death of Cato*, after Caravaggio, and *The Entombment of Christ*, after Van der Werff.

GEIGER, Andreas, the Younger
Austrian, 19th century.
Active in Vienna.
Engraver.
This artist was the son of Andreas Geiger the Elder.

GEIGER, Carl Joseph
Austrian, 19th century.
Born 14 December 1822, in Vienna; died 19 October 1905, in Vienna.
Painter, illustrator.
Carl Joseph was the grandson of Andreas Geiger. He was the pupil of Fuhrich at the academy in Vienna and worked with him on the decoration of the church of St Joan in Vienna. He also painted numerous decorations for various palaces in Vienna and theatre décor. Carl Geiger exhibited in Vienna from 1869.
MUSEUMS AND GALLERIES:
VIENNA: *Romeo and Juliet*.

GEIGER, Carl van
German, 19th century.
Born 1806, in Munich.
Painter.
Carl van Geiger is credited with landscapes and genre paintings.

GEIGER, Christoph
Austrian, 16th century.
Active in Innsbruck at the beginning of the 16th century.
Sculptor.
He executed a considerable number of funerary monuments.

GEIGER, Conrad
German, 18th century.
Born 18 February 1751, in Erlangen; died 4 September 1808, in Schweinfurt (Bavaria).
Painter. Genre scenes.
Conrad Geiger worked in Bamberg, Nuremberg and Munich.
AUCTION RECORDS:
NEW YORK, 24 March 1983, *Unexpected Observation* (1790, oil on canvas, 25 1/2 x 31 3/4 ins / 65 x 80.5 cm) USD 2,600. MUNICH, 27 Feb 1999, *Portrait of Young Man* (oil on canvas, 28 x 25 ins / 72 x 64 cm) DEM 6,500.

GEIGER, Ernst Samuel
German, 20th century.
Born 1 February 1876, in Turgi; died 1965, in Neuenstadt.
Painter. Landscapes.
Geiger studied in Zurich and Munich and Paris.
MUSEUMS AND GALLERIES:
BERN: *Moonlight*.
AUCTION RECORDS:
BERN, 11 May 1984, *Bielersee and Jolimont* (1916, oil on mounted card, 13 x 19 3/4 ins / 33 x 50 cm) CHF 3,800. BERN, 3 May 1985, *View of Bielersee* (oil on canvas, 18 x 15 ins / 46 x 38 cm) CHF 5,000. BERN, 30 April 1988, *View across Bielersee and St-Peter's Island, Summer Morning* (oil on canvas, 22 x 26 ins / 56 x 66 cm) CHF 3,600. BERN, 26 Oct 1988, *Summer on Bielersee* (1926, oil on canvas, 31 1/2 x 43 1/4 ins / 80 x 110 cm) CHF 5,200. ZOFINGEN, 28 May 1999, *Over the Bay of Auvernier* (oil on hessian, 22 x 26 ins / 56 x 65 cm) CHF 8,500. BERN, 5 Nov 1999, *View of a Church in Ligerz* (1922, oil on canvas, 15 x 18 ins / 38 x 46 cm) CHF 5,000. BERN, 12 May 2000, *Lake Landscape in Spring near Kapf* (1918, oil on canvas, 31 x 43 ins / 80 x 108 cm) CHF 45,000. BERN, 3 Nov 2000, *Lake Landscape* (1924, oil on canvas, 28 x 39 ins / 70 x 100 cm) CHF 45,000. BERN, 11 May 2001, *Extensive Landscape* (1913, oil on canvas, 18 x 24 ins / 45 x 60 cm) CHF 45,000. ZURICH, 31 May 2001, *Lake Landscape in Autumn* (1915, oil on canvas, 27 x 35 ins / 69 x 90 cm) CHF 30,000. BERN, 8 Nov 2002, *Bieler Lake Landscape in the Evening* (oil on canvas, 18 x 22 ins / 46 x 55 cm) CHF 12,000. BERN, 8 Nov 2002, *Autumn Afternoon* (1918, oil on canvas, 20 x 26 ins / 51 x 66 cm) CHF 18,000. LUCERNE, 4 June 2003, *Autumn Reeds* (oil on canvas, 26 x 22 ins / 65 x 56 cm) CHF 3,500. BERN, 14 May 2004, *Bielersee* (oil on canvas, 18 x 22 ins / 45 x 55 cm) CHF 65,000.

GEIGER, Franz Josef
German, 18th century.
Born in Landshut (Bavaria); died c. 1716, in Landshut.
Painter, engraver. History painting.
Franz Josef Geiger worked at the court of the kings of Bavaria.

GEIGER, Georg, or Giger, Cyger
Swiss, 17th century.
Died 1639.
Glass painter.
Georg Geiger was a pupil of Nuscheler. He was active in Zurich.

GEIGER, Hans Konrad
Swiss, 17th century.
Born 27 July 1599, in Zurich; died 25 September 1674, in Zurich.
Glass painter.
Hans Konrad was the son of Georg Geiger.

GEIGER, Henny, or Spiegel
German, 19th century.
Active in Berlin.
Sculptor.
Henny was the wife of Nicolaus Geiger. She exhibited in Paris, Munich and Berlin.

GEIGER, Jakob
German, 17th century.

Active in Ulm (Baden-Württemberg).
Draughtsman.

GEIGER, Johann
Austrian, 19th century.
Died 1870.
Active in Vienna.
Engraver.
Johann was the son of Andreas Geiger.

GEIGER, Johann Conrad. See **GEIGER Hans Konrad**

GEIGER, Jorg
Austrian, 17th century.
Active in Admont in 1637.
Painter.

GEIGER, Joseph
Austrian, 19th century.
Born 1781, in Vienna; died 1814, in Vienna.
Sculptor.
Joseph was the father of Peter Johann Geiger.

GEIGER, Karl
German, 19th century.
Born 1823, in Schwabmünchen.
Engraver.

GEIGER, Kaspar Augustin
German, 19th - 20th century.
Born 28 August 1847, in Laningen; died 1924.
Painter. Historical subjects, figures, portraits, genre scenes, interiors with figures.
Geiger attended the art academy in Munich and studied under Stahuber, then under Raab and Diez. He stayed in Venice for a long time. In 1889, he settled in Munich. From 1881, he exhibited in Vienna and Munich.

AUCTION RECORDS:
MUNICH, 27 May 1977, *Interiors with figures* (1882, oil on panel, 13¼ x 10½ ins / 33.5 x 26.5 cm) DEM 7,200. STUTTGART, 9 May 1981, *Violinist* (1876, oil on panel, 15¼ x 12½ ins / 39 x 31.5 cm) DEM 8,000. LONDON, 18 Nov 1994, *The Fashion Trader's Visit* (1878, oil on canvas/card, 23 x 13¾ ins / 57.5 x 35 cm) GBP 11,500.

GEIGER, Margarete
German, 18th century.
Born 24 May 1783, in Schweinfurt (Bavaria); died 4 September 1809, in Vienna.
Painter, watercolourist.
Margarete was the daughter of Conrad Geiger. She was the pupil of Ch. Fesel.
AUCTION RECORDS:
MUNICH, 3 Nov 1983, *Schweinfurt Costume* (watercolour and gouache, 13¼ x 9¾ ins / 33.9 x 25 cm) DEM 2,400.

GEIGER, Maurice Raphaël
French, 20th century.
Born in Nantes.
Sculptor.
Maurice Raphaël Geiger exhibited at the Société Nationale des Beaux-Arts until 1931.

GEIGER, Nicolaus
German, 19th century.
Born 6 December 1849, in Laningen; died 27 November 1897, in Berlin.
Sculptor, painter.
Nicolaus Geiger was pupil at the academy in Munich before studying under Knabl. He settled in Berlin, and exhibited both there and in Munich between 1884 and 1888. His is noted for his *Agreement*. Geiger's best works are his vast decorations of public buildings and churches.
MUSEUMS AND GALLERIES:
BERLIN: *After the Fall; Heads of a Young Girl and a Woman; Centaur and Nymph*.

GEIGER, Paul
German, 17th century.
Active in Landshut (Bavaria) in 1699.
Painter.

GEIGER, Peter Johann Nepomuk
Austrian, 19th century.
Born 11 January 1805, in Vienna; died 29 October 1880, in Vienna.
Painter, watercolourist, engraver. Religious subjects, allegorical subjects, genre scenes, local scenes.
Peter Johann Geiger was a pupil at the academy in Vienna, where he became a drawing teacher in 1844. In 1850 he accompanied the Grand Duke Ferdinand Max on his trips to the Far East.
In 1850 Geiger decorated the ceiling of the citadel of Ofen with three paintings. He is noted for his *Slave Market in Smyrna* and *The Old and the New Testaments*.

Stamp of sale

MUSEUMS AND GALLERIES:
VIENNA: *Idyll*.
AUCTION RECORDS:
NEW YORK, 13 Dec 1985, *Painting - Music* (two watercolours with Indian ink, oval, 12½ x 14¾ ins / 31.5 x 37.5 cm) USD 2,600. COLOGNE, 28 June 2001, *Interior with Woman and Men* (oil on board, 15 x 18 ins / 37 x 45 cm) DEM 9,500.

GEIGER, Richard
Austrian, 19th - 20th century.
Born 29 June 1870 or 1872, in Vienna; died 1945.
Painter. Figures, nudes, portraits, genre scenes.
Geiger's favourite subjects were scenes of merry-making and carnivals in fancy-dress, in addition to oriental theatrical productions.
AUCTION RECORDS:
VIENNA, 17 March 1981, *Harlequin and Colombine* (oil on canvas, 39½ x 29¼ ins / 100.5 x 74.5 cm) ATS 10,000. VIENNA, 12 Sept 1984, *Reverie* (1935, oil on canvas, 19¾ x 23½ ins / 50 x 60 cm) ATS 60,000. VIENNA, 11 Sept 1985, *Young Beauty* (oil on canvas, 18½ x 17¼ ins / 47 x 44 cm) ATS 20,000. STOCKHOLM, 15 Nov 1988, *Portrait of a Young Girl in Oriental Costume* (oil on canvas, 33¾ x 29½ ins / 86 x 75 cm) SEK 11,000. AMSTERDAM, 23 April 1991, *Carnival* (oil on canvas, 22¾ x 30¾ ins / 58 x 78 cm) NLG 2,875. NEW YORK, 15 Oct 1991, *Slave Market* (oil on canvas, 23 x 30¼ ins / 58.4 x 76.8 cm) USD 2,860. AMSTERDAM, 5-6 Nov 1991, *Standing Nude* (oil on canvas, 31 x 22¾ ins / 78.5 x 58 cm) NLG 3,450. AMSTERDAM, 14-15 April 1992, *Venus and the Satyrs* (oil on canvas, 23¼ x 30¾ ins / 59 x 78 cm) NLG 2,300. AMSTERDAM, 20 April 1993, *Flirtation* (oil on canvas, 23¼ x 31½ ins / 59 x 80 cm) NLG 1,380. NEW YORK, 22-23 July 1993, *Portait of a Lady Dressed as Pierrette* (1917, oil on panel, 31¼ x 12 ins / 79.4 x 30.5 cm) USD 1,150. LONDON, 27 Oct 1993, *Presentation of a Slave to the Pasha* (oil on canvas, 23 x 31 ins / 58.5 x 78.5 cm) GBP 7,130. AMSTERDAM, 9 Nov 1994, *Centre of Interest* (oil on canvas, 23½ x 31½ ins / 60 x 80 cm) NLG

2,530. LONDON, 9 Oct 1997, *Meeting with Colombine* (oil on canvas, 29 1/2 x 39 1/4 ins / 75 x 100 cm) GBP 632. LONDON, 28 Nov 2001, *Flirtatious Harlequin* (oil on canvas, 31 x 23 ins / 79 x 59 cm) GBP 1,000. SALZBURG, 28 Nov 2001, *Girl and Parrot* (oil on canvas, 30 x 40 ins / 75 x 101 cm) ATS 28,000. LONDON, 13 Feb 2003, *Reclining Female Nude* (oil on canvas, 33 x 48 ins / 84 x 121 cm) GBP 1,300. VIENNA, 8 April 2004, *Nymph and Satyr* (oil on canvas on panel, 26 x 34 ins / 67 x 87 cm) EUR 1,800. MUNICH, 25 June 2004, *Piero and Columbine at Fasching Party* (oil on canvas, 29 x 39 ins / 73 x 98 cm) EUR 1,800.

GEIGER, Robert

German, 19th century.

Born 25 December 1859; died 4 December 1903.

Painter. Genre scenes.

Robert Geiger exhibited in Munich, Dresden, Berlin and Bremen from 1886 to 1890.

GEIGER, Rupprecht

German, 20th century.

Born 26 January 1908, in Munich.

Painter.

After completing his studies in architecture, Rupprecht Geiger taught himself painting. During this period, he travelled to Spain and Greece. He began by working as an architect, only coming to painting in 1945. In 1949, he was one of the founder members of the Zen group, together with Willi Baumeister and Julius Bissier. From 1965, he taught at the art academy in Düsseldorf. His large canvases emerge from architectural integration and Far-Eastern philosophies. Large dark surfaces, or by contrast light surfaces against a dark background, almost monochromatic, but are which enhanced by a subtle modulation painted in monochrome or by a streak of red or blue light.

He started to exhibit in 1950 and contributed works to many group exhibitions, in particular: 1955, the Documenta II Gallery in Kassel; 2003, *Berlin-Moscow/Moscow-Berlin 1950-2000*, held at the Martin-Gropius-Bau Gallery in Berlin and the Tretyakov Gallery in Moscow; following the exhibition covering the period 1900-1950, it threw open to debate 50 years of German(Russian artistic and cultural relations, marked by political change. In 1953, he exhibited his works for the first time in solo shows in Munich and Cologne.

BIBLIOGRAPHY:

Tío Bellido, Ramón/Beurard, Patrick/Raffenschied-Wiegel, Beate, *Rupprecht Geiger. La couleur est élément: oeuvres depuis 1945*, exhibition catalogue, Hôtel des arts, Paris, 1992. '*Berlin-Moskau/Moskau-Berlin 1950-2000*' in *2 vol*, exhibition catalogue, Martin-Gropius-Bau, Berlin, 2003 (text in German).

AUCTION RECORDS:

COLOGNE, 28 April 1971, *Composition*, DEM 5,000. COLOGNE, 21 May 1977, *Composition* (pencil, 20 x 28 1/2 ins / 51 x 72.5 cm) DEM 900. MUNICH, 30 May 1983, *Composition* (1960, gouache, 21 3/4 x 15 1/2 ins / 55.2 x 39.5 cm) DEM 2,400. COLOGNE, 9 Dec 1986, *Abstract Composition* (acrylic/panel, 26 x 29 1/2 ins / 66 x 75 cm) DEM 9,000. AMSTERDAM, 21 May 1992, *366/62* (oil on canvas, 39 1/4 x 47 1/4 ins / 100 x 120 cm) NLG 41,400. MUNICH, 20 Nov 1999, *Composition* (1959, oil on canvas, 59 x 57 ins / 151 x 146 cm) DEM 83,000. HAMBURG, 3 Dec 1999, *642/72* (acrylic on canvas, 31 x 35 ins / 80 x 90 cm) DEM 38,000. BERLIN, 29 Sept 2000, *Object no. 0* (wood, 43 x 47x8 ins / 110 x 120x21 cm) DEM 75,000. HAMBURG, 18 May 2001, *Composition* (1961, pencil, 20 x 28 ins / 51 x 70 cm) DEM 3,900. MUNICH, 19 May 2001, *Composition* (1957, oil on canvas, 34 x 36 ins / 86 x 91 cm) DEM 83,000. COLOGNE, 5 June 2002, *644/72* (acrylic on canvas, 31 x 35 ins / 80 x 90 cm) EUR 24,000. BERLIN, 30 Nov 2002, *311/60* (1960, oil on canvas, 42 x 46 ins / 106 x 116 cm) EUR 36,950. MUNICH, 5 Dec 2003, *E 14* (1950, egg tempera on canvas, 20 x 33 ins / 50 x 84 cm) EUR 22,000. MUNICH, 5 Dec 2003, *Picture 1* (1959, egg tempera on canvas, 45 x 47 ins / 115 x 120 cm) EUR 46,000. COLOGNE, 1 May 2004, *372/62* (oil on canvas, 20 x 37 ins / 50 x 95 cm) EUR 30,000. HAMBURG, 11 June 2004, *469/67* (oil on canvas on panel, 35 x 31 ins / 90 x 80 cm) EUR 25,000.

GEIGER, Willy

German, 20th century.

Born 17 August 1878, in Schönnbrunn; died 1971, in Munich.

Painter, watercolourist, engraver.

Willy Geiger attended the art academy in Munich. He produced some ex-libris. In 1929, his work was featured at the important exhibition *Peintres et Graveurs Allemands* (*German Painters and Engravers*) in Paris. In 2003, his work was shown at the group exhibition *Phantom der Lust. Visionen des Machochismus in der Kunst* (*Phantom of Desire. Visions of Masochism in Art*) which was held at the Neue Galerie am Landesmuseum in Graz, Austria.

Geiger

BIBLIOGRAPHY:

Weibel, Peter (ed.), '*Phantom der Lust. Visionen des Masochismus in der Kunst*' in *2 vol*, exhibition catalogue, Neue Galerie am Landesmuseum, Graz, Belleville Verlag, Munich, 2003.

AUCTION RECORDS:

MUNICH, 26 Nov 1976, *St Sebastian* (1914, oil on canvas, 48 x 39 1/4 ins / 121 x 100 cm) DEM 1,500. MUNICH, 28 Nov 1980, *View of Chiemsee* (1945, watercolour, 19 3/4 x 27 1/2 ins / 50 x 70 cm) DEM 2,800. MUNICH, 6 Dec 1982, *View of Chiemsee* (1938, watercolour, 19 3/4 x 27 1/2 ins / 50 x 70 cm) DEM 1,550. MUNICH, 30 Nov 1984, *Chiemgau Landscape* (1934, watercolour, 19 3/4 x 27 3/4 ins / 50 x 70.5 cm) DEM 5,000. NEW YORK, 26 June 1985, *Chiemsee at Dawn* (1940, watercolour, 14 x 20 ins / 35.5 x 51 cm) DEM 2,500. MUNICH, 3 June 1987, *St Sebastian* (1914, oil on canvas, 75 1/2 x 43 1/4 ins / 192 x 110 cm) DEM 15,000. HEIDELBERG, 9 Oct 1992, *Bull Fight* (1907, ink, 10 1/4 x 17 1/2 ins / 26 x 44.3 cm) DEM 1,000. LONDON, 25 Oct 1995, *The End of All Things* (1902, ink and wash, 7 x 7 ins / 17.8 x 17.8 cm) GBP 862. MUNICH, 28 March 2001, *Sunflower* (1933, oil on canvas, 28 x 25 ins / 72 x 63 cm) DEM 7,000. MUNICH, 18 April 2002, *Still-life with Flowers* (1967, oil on canvas, 22 x 16 ins / 55 x 40 cm) EUR 3,500.

GEIGER-THURING, August

German, 19th century.

Born 1861; died 28 December 1896, in Munich.

Painter. Landscapes.

August Geiger-Thuring exhibited regularly at the academy in Berlin.

GEIGER-WEISHAUPT, Fanny von

German, 19th - 20th century.

Active in Munich.

Painter.

Von Geiger-Weishaupt was the wife of Victor Weishaupt. She painted primarily animals and landscapes.

GEIGES, Fritz

German, 19th century.

Born 2 December 1853, in Offenburg (Baden-Württemberg).

Glass painter.

Geiges was a pupil of Neher in Stuttgart, and worked in Freiburg-im-Brisgau, Berlin, Mainz and Magdeburg, among other places.

GEIJP, Adriaan Marinus. See **GEYP**

GEIKIE, Walter
British, 19th century.
Born 9 November 1795, in Edinburgh; died 1 August 1837, in Edinburgh.
Painter, draughtsman, engraver. Genre scenes.

Walter Geikie was a deaf-mute artist who studied under Patrick Gibson and at the Academy. His first works started appearing from 1815. He was elected to membership of the Royal Scottish Academy in 1837. Despite his infirmity - or perhaps because of it - Geikie depicted aspects of everyday life with considerable humour.

MUSEUMS AND GALLERIES:
EDINBURGH (Royal Scottish Academy): *Cottage Scene* (oil/panel).

GEILER, Hans, or Jean de Fribourg
German, 16th century.
Active in Fribourg.
Sculptor.

His most important work, made in collaboration with Manuel of Bern, was a carved altar. In 1523, he made a statue for the bridge in Bern. He also made a number of monumental fountains in Fribourg. Between 1544 and 1546, he made one of his most attractive works, a table that can still be seen in the Hall of the Grand Council.

GEILING, Christian Friedrich Julius
German, 19th century.
Born 31 October 1831, in Dresden.
Engraver (wood).

Geiling was a pupil of Burkner.

GEILINGER, Johann Hans Jacob, the Elder, or Gerliger
Swiss, 17th century.
Glass painter.

GEILINGER, Johann Jacob, the Younger
Swiss, 17th century.
Born 10 September 1642, in Lucerne; died c. 1702.
Glass painter.

GEILLE, Amédée Félix Barthélémy
French, 19th century.
Born 1802, in La Ciotat; died 1843, in Paris.
Engraver.

Engraved from Raphael and from 17th and 18th century French masters.

GEILLE DE SAINT-LÉGER, Léon
French, 19th century.
Born 6 December 1864, in Algiers.
Painter, illustrator. Portraits, seascapes, landscapes. Orientalism.

Geille de St-Léger was awarded a scholarship from the city of Algiers to study at the École des Beaux-Arts in Paris, where his mentors were Hébert, L.O. Merson, J. Lefebvre and A. Dumont. His body of work includes, notably, *Fishing Boat at Honfleur* (1893); *Summer Day in Brittany* and *Vessels* (1895); *Town in the Sahara* (1896); and *Old Boats among the Dunes* (1897). He also provided illustrations for various periodicals.

MUSEUMS AND GALLERIES:
ALGIERS: *Portrait of a Young Woman* (1883) - ALGIERS (Salle du Conseil Général): *Birth of Samson* - ALGIERS (Town Hall): *Head of Christ*.

AUCTION RECORDS:
PARIS, 25 June 1996, *El Kantara Gorge* (oil on canvas, 19 1/4 x 25 1/2 ins / 49 x 64.5 cm) FRF 5,600. PARIS, 5 Dec 1997, *Casbah in Algiers* (oil on canvas, 25 1/4 x 17 1/4 ins / 64 x 44 cm) FRF 5,000. PARIS, 14 May 2001, *Conversation at the Entrance to a House* (oil on canvas, 17 x 25 ins / 43 x 63 cm) FRF 18,000. PARIS, 23 Oct 2002, *Camel Drivers* (oil on canvas, 15 x 24 ins / 38 x 61 cm) EUR 1,900. PARIS, 19 Oct 2003, *Caravan* (oil on canvas, 15 x 24 ins / 38 x 61 cm) EUR 1,800. PARIS, 19 Oct 2003, *Halt of the Caravan* (oil on canvas, 13 x 18 ins / 33 x 46 cm) EUR 2,200.

GEILSDORF, Joachim Friedrich
German, 18th century.
Born c. 1695; died 25 December 1759, in Freiberg (Saar).
Sculptor.

GEINING, Gérard
Painter. History painting, portraits.

Mentioned by Hoet the Younger.

GEIRNAERT, Jozef Theodore Lodewyk
Belgian, 19th century.
Born 27 August 1791, in Eeklo (East Flanders); died 20 March 1859.
Painter. Historical subjects, portraits, scenes with figures, genre scenes, interiors with figures.

He was a pupil of Herreyns and Paelinck.

AUCTION RECORDS:
PARIS, 1856, *Maria-Theresa, Accompanied by Two Ladies-in-waiting, Visiting an Elderly Invalid Woman,* FRF 11,500; *Game Market,* FRF 300. PARIS, 1898, *Hungarian Doctor,* FRF 1,350. PARIS, 20 May 1925, *Visit to the Curate,* FRF 720. LONDON, 11 Dec 1942, *At the Notary's Office,* GBP 115. AMSTERDAM, 19 May 1981, *The Doctor's Visit* (1840, oil on panel, 28 3/4 x 20 3/4in/73 x 53cm) NLG 8,000. LONDON, 3 June 1983, *Young Woman at her Toilette* (1825, oil on panel, 19 3/4 x 15in/50 x 38cm) GBP 1,500. VERSAILLES, 19 Nov 1989, *Boy Thieves* (1825, oil on panel, 14 1/2 x 12 1/2in/37 x 32 cm) FRF 30,000. AMSTERDAM, 25 Oct 2000, *Confidences* (1855, oil on panel, 18 x 13 ins / 45 x 32 cm) NLG 6,500. BRUSSELS, 11 Dec 2000, *Suitors and Card Players* (1825, oil on panel, 16 x 13 ins / 41 x 33 cm) BEF 340,000. BRUSSELS, 15 Oct 2001, *Les Boniments (Sales Talk)* (1835, oil on panel, 18 x 13 ins / 46 x 32 cm) BEF 170,000. ANTWERP, 22 April 2002, *After the Hunt* (1830, oil on panel, 14 x 11 ins / 36 x 29 cm) EUR 2,200. BRUSSELS, 13 May 2003, *Strolling Musicians* (oil on canvas, 55 x 44 ins / 140 x 112 cm) EUR 7,000. AMSTERDAM, 20 April 2004, *Blowing Bubbles* (1842, oil on panel, 17 x 14 ins / 44 x 36 cm) EUR 3,500.

GEIRNAERT, W.
Belgian, 19th century.
Painter. Genre scenes.

Mentioned in *Current Art Prices.*

AUCTION RECORDS:
LONDON, 19 July 1909, *The Date Agreed,* GBP 16. LONDON, 14 April 1924, *Rent Day,* GBP 21.

GEISELER, Peter
German, 19th century.
Born 15 May 1782, in Sackstadt.
Sculptor.

Peter Geiseler studied in Frankfurt and also worked in Vienna.

GEISENHOFER, Chrisostomus
German, 18th century.
Active in Wasserburg (Bavaria) in 1785.
Sculptor.

GEISENHOFER, Thomas
German, 18th century.
Active in Roding (Bavaria) at the end of the 18th century.
Painter.

GEISER, Jakob
German, 19th century.

Active in Munich.
Miniaturist.

This may be the same Jakob Geiser who was also a lithographer.

GEISER, Karl
Swiss, 20th century.
Born 1898, in Bern; died 1957, in Zurich.
Sculptor, engraver. Figures, nudes.

Geiser taught himself sculpture. He stayed in Berlin, then settled in Zurich in 1922. In 1926, he won the city of Bern competition with his two monumental groups intended for the Lycée. It took him about ten years to produce these two groups. In his final years, he received many commissions, including a *David* for the town of Soleure (Switzerland) in 1944, as well as a *Monument to the Glory of Work*, a sculpture which kept him occupied from 1952 to 1957; these last two monuments were unfinished. At first, he became known for his figures of young boys, which were either busts or full-size sculptures and sometimes multi-coloured, in particular with regard to the eyes, which gave them a disturbing living presence and made his works reminiscent of the masks of Fayoum. His series on *Figures of Women* seemed more sensual and were produced from 1943 until his death, from the same single model; the fullness of the feminine forms in this series evokes the work of Aristide Maillol. In 1941, a group exhibition of his work was organised in Winterthur, Switzerland. After his death, a retrospective exhibition was held in Basel in 1958.

BIBLIOGRAPHY:
George, Waldemar, *Karl Geiser*, Quatre Chemins, Paris, 1932.

AUCTION RECORDS:
ZURICH, 23 Nov 1977, *David* (1945-1946, bronze, h. 30 1/4 ins / 77 cm) CHF 5,500. BERN, 10 June 1978, *Bust of Nelly Bär* (1944, bronze, h. 18 1/4 ins / 46.5 cm) CHF 6,000. ZURICH, 24 Oct 1979, *Doris* (1943, bronze, h. 69 ins / 175 cm) CHF 17,000. BERN, 19 June 1985, *Seated Nude* (c. 1925, bronze, h. 15 3/4 ins / 40 cm) CHF 8,400. ZURICH, 9 June 1993, *Mother and Children* (lost-wax bronze, h. 9 1/2 ins / 24 cm) CHF 6,900. ZURICH, 13 Oct 1993, *Adolescent Standing* (bronze, h. 20 1/2 ins / 52 cm) CHF 15,000. ZURICH, 24 Nov 1993, *Head of Hermann Burte* (lost-wax bronze, h. 12 1/4 ins / 31 cm) CHF 4,600. ZURICH, 23 March 1999, *Head* (bronze, h. 14 ins / 35 cm) CHF 8,500. ZURICH, 8 Dec 1999, *Study of David* (bronze, h. 30 ins / 77 cm) CHF 14,000. ZURICH, 21 March 2000, *Standing Female Nude* (bronze, h. 24 ins / 60 cm) CHF 9,000. ZURICH, 19 June 2001, *David* (bronze, h. 30 ins / 77 cm) CHF 8,000. ZURICH, 29 Sept 2003, *Study for 'David'* (patinated bronze, h. 33 ins / 85 cm) CHF 8,000. ZURICH, 26 May 2004, *Woman with Scarf* (1933, bronze, h. 22 ins / 55 cm) CHF 8,500.

GEISER, Leonhard
German, 19th century.
Born 8 February 1776, in Nuremberg; died 12 April 1830.
Painter (porcelain).

GEISIUS, Johann
German, 17th century.
Died 10 November 1676.
Painter.

Signed paintings by this artist are still to be found in Görlitz (Saxony).

GEISS, Caspar
German, 17th century.
Died 1640.
Draughtsman.

Caspar Geiss was active in Saxony and also in Darmstadt (Hessen).

GEISSBUHLER, Arnold
Swiss, 20th century.
Sculptor. Busts.

Geissbuhler exhibited regularly at the Salon des Tuileries in Paris. He produced many busts.

GEISSELBRUNN, Jeremias
German, 17th century.
Active in Cologne (North Rhine-Westphalia) in 1624.
Sculptor.

Geisselbrunn is credited with religious sculptures in wood and stone.

GEISSER, Balthasar
Swiss, 16th century.
Active in Schwyz.
Engraver (wood).

GEISSER, Johann Joseph
Swiss, 19th century.
Born 29 March 1824, in Altstätten; died 10 October 1894, in Lausanne.
Painter. Genre scenes, landscapes.

Between 1842 and 1886 Johann Geisser participated in exhibitions by the Société des Beaux-Arts. He founded the Vaudois section of the Society of Swiss Painters and Sculptors in 1866.

AUCTION RECORDS:
ZURICH, 5 May 1976, *Alpine Landscape* (oil on canvas, 27 1/2 x 46 ins / 70 x 116 cm) CHF 2,200. NEW YORK, 30 May 1980, *Alpine Lake with Figures* (oil on canvas, 20 3/4 x 32 3/4 ins / 52.7 x 83.3 cm) USD 2,500. ZURICH, 7 Nov 1981, *Old Woman and Child in the Kitchen* (oil on card, 13 3/4 x 17 3/4 ins / 35 x 45 cm) CHF 3,200. ZURICH, 9 Nov 1984, *Cows on the Edge of a Stream in an Alpine Landscape* (1885, oil on canvas, 22 x 25 1/2 ins / 55 x 65 cm) CHF 4,000. LUCERNE, 15 May 1986, *Mountain Lake* (oil on canvas, 20 3/4 x 32 3/4 ins / 53 x 83 cm) CHF 7,500. BERN, 26 Oct 1988, *Village in Southern Italy Built on a Hillside* (oil on canvas, 18 x 13 3/4 ins / 46 x 35 cm) CHF 1,500. NEW YORK, 19 Jan 1994, *Mountain Landscape* (oil on canvas, 18 1/2 x 25 3/4 ins / 47 x 65.4 cm) USD 1,150. LONDON, 18 March 1994, *Mont Blanc* (oil on canvas, 33 x 24 1/4 ins / 83.8 x 61.6 cm) GBP 4,600. LONDON, 30 Nov 1999, *Figures in Alpine Lake Landscape* (oil on canvas, 13 x 18 ins / 34 x 46 cm) GBP 1,300. ZURICH, 2 May 2001, *Peasant Woman* (oil on canvas, 33 x 25 ins / 83 x 64 cm) CHF 3,000. LUCERNE, 15 May 2002, *Landscape* (oil on canvas, 19 x 14 ins / 47 x 35 cm) CHF 2,400. BERN, 15 May 2003, *Portrait of a Boy* (1853, oil on canvas/pavatex, 53 x 37 ins / 135 x 94 cm) CHF 3,000. GENEVA, 16 Nov 2003, *Rimpfischorn, Strahlhorn, Adlerhorn, Zermatt* (oil on canvas, 31 x 47 ins / 80 x 120 cm) CHF 5,500. BERN, 14 May 2004, *Alpine Pasture* (oil on panel, 11 x 16 ins / 28 x 41 cm) CHF 3,800.

GEISSHUSLER, Johann
Swiss, 19th century.
Born 1828, in Romersivil.
Painter, draughtsman. Religious subjects.

GEISSLEHNER, Johann Peter
German, 17th - 18th century.
Born in Amberg (Bavaria).
Sculptor.

Geisslehner was active in Freystadt.

GEISSLER, Alois
German, 19th century.
Born 20 July 1777, in Iglau (now Jihlava, Czech Republic); died 11 June 1832, in Iglau.
Painter.

Alois Geissler was a pupil of J.N. Steiner. He decorated churches in Iglau with portraits and religious paintings.

GEISSLER, Christian
German, 19th century.

Active in Nuremberg (Bavaria).
Engraver.
This artist was the brother of Friedrich Geissler.

GEISSLER, Christian Gottfried Heinrich
German, 18th - 19th century.
Born 26 June 1770, in Leipzig; died 27 April 1844, in Leipzig.
Draughtsman, engraver (burin).
Christian Geissler engraved costumes and landscapes with figures and worked in Russia.

GEISSLER, Christian Gottlieb
German, 18th - 19th century.
Born 1729, in Augsburg; died 2 November 1814, in Geneva.
Painter, miniaturist, engraver (burin).
Chruistian Gottlieb Geissler was a pupil of Baumeister. Primarily a painter of miniatures, he devoted himself to this genre of painting and particularly to natural history. Geissler also painted religious pictures and engraved views.

GEISSLER, Heinrich Christian
German, 19th century.
Born 1782, in Leipzig; died 1839.
Painter, illustrator.
Heinrich Geissler is noted for his numerous watercolour illustration models.

GEISSLER, J. G.
German, 18th century.
Active in Breslau (now Wroclaw, Poland) at the end of the 18th century.
Painter.
This artist is credited with portraits.

GEISSLER, Joh. Martin Friedrich
German, 19th century.
Born 31 March 1778, in Nuremberg; died 9 January 1853, in Nuremberg.
Painter, engraver.
This artist began his studies under the guidance of Henrich Guttemberg, then continued them in Paris. He mainly engraved landscapes and architectural subjects after Berchem, Ruysdael, Wynants, and others.

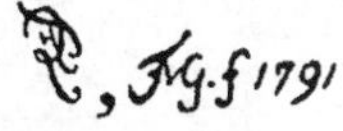

GEISSLER, Johann Ulrich
Swiss, 17th century.
Active in Lucerne.
Engraver.

GEISSLER, Julius
German, 19th century.
Born 30 April 1822, in Göttingen (Lower Saxony); died 10 October 1904; committed suicide.
Painter, lithographer.
Julius Geissler was a pupil of Grape and Erhard in Dresden. He later settled in Hamburg, where he became renowned as a portrait painter.

GEISSLER, Klaus
German, 20th century.
Born 1933, in Leipzig; died c. 1980.
Active in France.
Sculptor.
Nouvelle Figuration.
Geissler studied painting at the École des Beaux-Arts in Geneva, then continued his training in Karlsruhe and Berlin. Having decided to dedicate himself to sculpture, he settled in Paris. He taught at the École Nationale des Beaux-Arts in Bourges. At first he produced metal constructions, and soon added transparent or translucent resins. Generally his works appear in some form of large ball with portholes, sometimes provided with lenses, magnifying or reducing the size. In the entrails of these eggs are strange dolls, disturbing creatures, indeterminate organs, inaccessible testimonies of dark celebrations. This interaction of hidden forces, possibly magnetic fields, and funereal lighting, give the semblance of spasmodic life to these succubi. The modern chemistry of laminated polyester enabled Geissler to produce his complicated machinations to a high degree of expertise. In the 1970s, he took up painting again, producing dream-like architectural views, and was clearly reviving Surrealist imagery.

He contributed works to many group exhibitions in Paris, notably the Biennale des Jeunes Artistes, the Salon de Mai, and the groups organised by the writer Gérald Gassiot-Talabot including: 1964, *Mythologies Quotidiennes* (*Everyday Mythologies*) ; 1965, *La Figuration Narrative* (*Narrative Figuration*) . He displayed his work in solo shows in Paris, London and Amsterdam.

AUCTION RECORDS:
PARIS, 26 June 1995, *Ball* (1965, light installation in Plexiglas with an electric motor, h. 35 1/2 ins / 90 cm) FRF 8,000.

GEISSLER, Ludwig
German, 18th century.
Active in Zwittau (now Svitavy, Czech Republic) in 1742.
Painter.

GEISSLER, Michael
German, 18th century.
Painter.
Michael Geissler taught portrait painting at the academy in Berlin at the start of the 18th century.

GEISSLER, Niklaus
German, 17th century.
Born in the 17th century, in Schweinfurt (Bavaria).
Sculptor, draughtsman.
Niklaus Geissler settled in Lucerne at an early age, where his religious sculptures brought him great success.

GEISSLER, Paul
German, 20th century.
Born 25 June 1881, in Erfurt.
Painter, engraver, illustrator. Landscapes.
Geissler studied under Marc Thedy, probably in Weimar. He produced a large number of illustrations.

GEISSLER, Peter Carl
German, 19th century.
Born 2 January 1802, in Leipzig; died 27 February 1872, in Leipzig.
Watercolourist, engraver.
Peter Carl Geissler was the son of Christian Gottfried Heinrich Geissler, and the father of Rudolf.

GEISSLER, Robert
German, 19th century.
Born 7 February 1819, in Göttingen (Lower Saxony); died 7 October 1893, near Göttingen.
Painter, engraver, lithographer, writer.
A pupil of Wedemeyer, Robert Geissler made a name for himself primarily as a lithographer.

GEISSLER, Rudolf Carl Gottfried
German, 19th century.
Born 15 January 1834, in Nuremberg; died 15 September 1906, in Nuremberg.
Painter, draughtsman, engraver. Genre scenes.

Rudolf Carl Geissler was a pupil of Reindel and of Kreling, and continued his studies in Leipzig and Dresden. In 1861 he returned to Nuremberg. He exhibited in Düsseldorf and Dresden between 1880 and 1881. Geissler is noted for his *Fairy of the Alps*.

GEISSLER, Wilhelm
German, 19th century.
Born c. 1803, in Berlin.
Painter.
Wilhelm Geissler is credited with portraits and flower pictures.

GEISSLER, Wilhelm
German, 19th century.
Born 1848, in Hanover.
Painter, lithographer. Genre scenes.
Wilhelm Geissler, the son of Robert Geissler, was a medal-winner in Berlin in 1879. He is noted for his *Return from the Holiday Camp*.

GEISSMANN, François
French, 20th - 21st century.
Born 1948, in Paris.
Sculptor of assemblages (ceramics).
François Geissmann spent his childhood in Argentina. During his first stay in Japan between 1971 and 1973, he stayed at a Zen monastery before studying pottery. From 1975 to 1979, with the help of a French government grant, he studied ceramic art at the fine arts school in Kyoto. In 1980 he settled in Barbuise in the Aube region of France. He took up a teaching post at the École des Beaux-Arts in Dijon in 1981.

Geissmann's early sculptures show hands coming out of the pages of a book and pages of writing piled up and exploding. In a later phase, he worked with manufactured pipes which he would break, mend and assemble into sculptures.

He showed work in group exhibitions, including: in Kyoto (1975); in Tokyo (1977, 1978); at the Salon Grands et Jeunes d'Aujourd'hui in Paris (1981); at the Centre Culturel in Troyes (1982); in *Terre* (*Earth*) at the Centre Georges Pompidou in Paris (1982); and at the Salon de Montrouge (1982, 1983).

GEIST, Andreas
German, 19th century.
Died 1860.
Painter, watercolourist. Portraits, landscapes, seascapes.
Andreas was the father of August Geist.

GEIST, August Christian
German, 19th century.
Born 15 October 1835, in Würzburg (Bavaria); died 15 December 1868, in Munich.
Watercolourist, engraver. Landscapes.
August was the son and pupil of Andreas Geist. In 1853 he studied under Fr. Bamberger in Munich, and in 1856 founded a studio there. He travelled to Switzerland and along the Rhine. In 1865 he went to Italy and lived in Rome until 1867. He painted landscapes inspired by his travels. Geist exhibited in Munich, Bremen, Hamburg, Cologne and Augsburg.

GEIST, Karl Friedrich Wilhelm
German, 19th - 20th century.
Born 9 December 1870, in Reichelsheim.
Painter. Landscapes.
Geist studied in Karlsruhe, and was then active in Stuttgart.
AUCTION RECORDS:
VIENNA, 18 Jan 1980, *Autumn Landscape* (oil on canvas, 37 1/2 x 48 ins / 95 x 122 cm) ATS 8,000.

GEIST, Wilhelm
German, 17th century.
Active in Nuremberg on 14 November 1635.
Painter.

GEIT, F. van
Flemish School, 19th century.
Active c. 1842.
Painter. Flowers, fruit.
He is mentioned by Siret.
AUCTION RECORDS:
PARIS, 10-11 June 1929, *Vase of Flowers*, FRF 8,200. LONDON, 5 April 2001, *Peonies, Tulips and Other Summer Flowers in a Glass Vase* (oil on canvas, 22 x 18 ins / 56 x 45 cm) GBP 2,200. HAMBURG, 8 Dec 2001, *Still-life of Roses, Lily-of-the-Valley, Pair of Butterflies and Bird's Nest* (oil on panel, 18 x 14 ins / 45 x 35 cm) DEM 4,800.

GEITEL, Ignatius
German, 20th century.
Born in Bochum.
Painter.
In 1954 and 1957, Geitel's work was featured at the Salon des Réalités Nouvelles in Paris.

GEITEL, Johann Georg
German, 18th century.
Born 1683, in Brunswick; died 1771, in Åbo (now Turku), Finland.
Painter.
Geitel ended his career as a drawing teacher in Finland.

GEITLINGER, Ernst
German, 20th century.
Born 13 February 1895, in Frankfurt am Main; died 28 March 1972, in Seeshaupt, on Starnberg Lake.
Painter (including gouache).
Neo-Constructivism.
From 1913 to 1929, Geitlinger lived with his parents in New York, where he attended the art academy, then he worked as a set designer. In 1922, he enrolled at the art academy in Munich, where he worked until 1931, in spite of interruptions when he made visits to New York. In 1932, he settled in Munich, where he exhibited with the Association of German Artists and the Neue Sezession. In 1936, the Nazis forbade him to exhibit.

In 1942, he settled in Seeshaupt. In 1946, after World War II, he was one of the co-founders of the Neue Gruppe (New Group) in Munich. From 1951 to 1965 he taught at the art academy in Munich. In 1965, still in Munich, he established the Ernst Geitlinger School of Painting. Amongst his pupils were Gerhard von Graevenitz, Dieter Hacker, Uli Pohl and Jan Voss. In the 1940s, he was influenced by Paul Klee and Marc Chagall. He found his own way with Abstraction, progressively developing a more rigorous approach. In the 1960s, he made a few montages based on objects he had found, and mainly produced monochrome or bichrome paintings. His key work was produced in his final years and developed into Neo-Constructive Abstraction, yet without losing contact with the concrete, except in a few of his last paintings which verged on international Minimalism. In 1974, the Municipal Gallery of the Lenbachhaus in Munich presented a group exhibition of their work. In 1989, the Ludwigshafen Wilhelm-Hack-Museum in Rhein-Palatinate dedicated a retrospective exhibition to him.
BIBLIOGRAPHY:
Ernst Geitlinger 1895-1972, exhibition catalogue, Lenbachhaus, Munich, 1974. '*Lexicon des Kunst: Malerei, Architektur, Bildhauerkunst*' in *12 vol*, Herder, Freiburg, 1987-1990.
MUSEUMS AND GALLERIES:
MUNICH (Bayerisches Nationalmus.): *Two Opposite Blues* - NEU-ULM: a significant donation of works.
AUCTION RECORDS:
MUNICH, 27 Nov 1981, *Still-life with Flowers* (1946, gouache, 19 3/4 x 12 1/2 ins / 50 x 32 cm) DEM 3,500. MUNICH, 25 Nov 1985, *Canal in Munich* (1936, oil on canvas, 25 1/4 x 35 1/2 ins / 64.3 x 90 cm) DEM 3,200. MUNICH, 14 May 2004, *New York*

oil on canvas, 31 x 24 ins / 80 x 60 cm) EUR 19,000. MUNICH, 14 May 2004, *Variety Show* (oil on canvas, 24 x 31 ins / 61 x 80 cm) EUR 25,000.

GEITLINGER, Johann Jacob
German, 18th century.
Active in Baden in 1746.
Painter.

GEITNER, Joseph
German.
Sculptor.
He carried out the exterior decoration of a church in the area of Osnabrück.

GEKKO, real name: Tai Masanosuke, artist name: Ogata Gekko
Japanese, 19th - 20th century.
Born 1859; died 1920.
Painter.
Gekko was a self-taught painter from Tokyo who is known as a genre painter and illustrator. He also taught himself the art of woodblock printing.

GELANDIA, Bernaldino. See **BERNALDINO DE GELANDIA**

GELANZE, Giuseppe
Italian, 19th century.
Born 19 January 1867, in Naples.
Painter. Genre scenes.
Gelanze was a pupil of Domenico Morelli; he worked in Naples, Palermo and Monaco.

GELASIO DI NICCOLO
Italian, 13th century.
Born in Ferrara.
Painter.
A pupil of Theophanes in either Venice or Constantinople.

GELATI, Girolamo
Italian, 19th century.
Born 1796, in Parma; died 1862.
Painter.
Girolamo Gelati painted frescoes in several churches.

GELATI, Lorenzo
Italian, 19th century.
Born January 1824, in Florence; died 1893, in Florence.
Painter. Interiors, landscapes with figures, urban landscapes, urban views.
Lorenzo Gelati studied under Marko. He exhibited in Rome, Florence and Bologna.
MUSEUMS AND GALLERIES:
PRATO (Mus. Civico): *Landscape with Figures.*
AUCTION RECORDS:
NEW YORK, 30 June 1981, *Landscape in Italy* (oil on canvas, 15 x 30 ins / 38 x 76 cm) USD 2,750. ROME, 31 May 1994, *View of Rome from the Pincio* (oil on canvas, 17 3/4 x 29 1/4 ins / 45 x 74 cm) ITL 11,785,000. ROME, 23 May 1996, *Vicolo Fiorentino con Frate* (oil on canvas, 17 1/4 x 15 ins / 44 x 38 cm) ITL 5,750,000.

GELBERT, Adolphos
Greek, 19th - 20th century.
Born 1866, in Athens.
Painter, architect.
Adolphos Gelbert settled in Paris in 1900 and trained at the École des Beaux-Arts.

GELBERT, Peter
German, 19th - 20th century.
Born c. 1860; died 18 July 1915, in Ludwigshafen am Rhein.
Sculptor.
Gelbert specialised in portrait medallions.

GELBKE, Georg Hermann
German, 20th century.
Born 12 September 1882, in Rochlitz.
Painter, engraver. Landscapes.
Gelbke attended the art academy in Dresden.

GELD, Emile de
Belgian, 20th century.
Born 1909, in Brussels; died 1972, in London.
Painter. Landscapes.
De Geld was self-taught and produced forest landscapes of Soignes and the Ardennes, but also picturesque districts of Brussels and London.
MUSEUMS AND GALLERIES:
BRUSSELS.

GELDER, Aart, Aert or Arent, Johansz. de
Dutch, 17th - 18th century.
Born 26 October 1645, in Dordrecht; died c. 28 August 1727, in Dordrecht.
Painter. History painting, religious subjects, mythological subjects, portraits, genre scenes, local scenes.
He was a pupil of Samuel van Hoogstraten and later (around 1660) of Rembrandt, in Amsterdam. He then returned to Dordrecht, where he settled. De Gelder painted religious scenes and Orientalist subjects in the style of Rembrandt. Between 1680 and 1687 he executed a series of canvases based on the Old Testament Book of Esther. He was an artist of considerable power, and one of Rembrandt's few exceptionally talented pupils. During the later 17th century his anecdotal subjects (like those of Flinck) proved more popular than the weightier, more profound paintings of his illustrious master. He was the subject of a retrospective at the Wallraf-Richartz museum in Cologne in 1999.

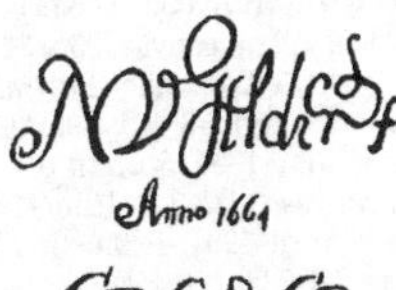

BIBLIOGRAPHY:
Sumowski, W., *Drawings of the Rembrandt School*, New York, 1981. Blankert, A., et al., *The Impact of a Genius: Rembrandt, his Pupils and Followers in the 17th Century*, exhibition catalogue, Amsterdam and Groningen, 1983. Slive, S., *Dutch Painting, 1600-1800*, London, 1995.
MUSEUMS AND GALLERIES:
AMIENS: *Artemis* - AMSTERDAM: *Johan van der Burch and Ch. Elisabeth van Blyenburgh, his Wife; E. van Beveren; Peter the Great; Captive Jesus; Jesus before the Sanhedrin* - BERLIN: *Landscape with Ruth and Boaz* - BRIGHTON (Mus. and AG): *The Marriage Contract* (oil on canvas) - BRUSSELS: *The Gift* - BUDAPEST: *Esther and Mordecai* - COPENHAGEN: *An Oriental Prince; Mordecai Honoured by Ahasuerus* - DRESDEN: *Ecce homo* (1671); *A Halberdier; The Charter* - FRANKFURT AM MAIN: *Self-portrait* - HANOVER: *Portrait* - LONDON (Dulwich Picture Gal.): *Jacob's Dream* (1710-1715, oil on canvas) - MOSCOW (Rumiantsev Mus.): *Lot and his Daughters* - MUNICH: *The Jewish Bride; Study; The Ascent to Golgotha* - MUNICH (Alte Pinakothek): *Esther* - POTSDAM (Schloss Sanssouci): *Esther* - ST PETERSBURG (Hermitage): *Young Soldier; Self-portrait* - THE HAGUE: *Judah and Thamar; Herman Boerhave* - VIENNA (Schönborn-Buckheim): *Virgin and Child.*
AUCTION RECORDS:
PARIS, 1868, *David and Bathsheba*, FRF 870. PARIS, 1897, *Tancred's Farewell to Armida*, FRF 500. PARIS, 1898, *The Gift Rewarded*, FRF 9,750. NEW YORK, 23-24 Feb 1906, *Mandolin Lesson*, USD 310. LONDON, 12 Dec 1908, *Studio Interior*, GBP

8. LONDON, 19 Feb 1910, *Old Man Seated at a Table, Writing,* GBP 157. LONDON, 24 July 1911, *Old Man,* GBP 40. LONDON, 6 July 1923, *Pontius Pilate,* GBP 441. LONDON, 10 April 1929, *The Philosophers,* GBP 160. GENEVA, 28 Aug 1934, *Bust of a Woman at Prayer,* CHF 1,150. LONDON, 10-14 July 1936, *David and Jonathan* (watercolour and Indian ink) GBP 94. LONDON, 16 April 1937, *David and the Prophet Nathan* (signed 1683) GBP 462. LONDON, 15 Dec 1937, *Joseph Holding the Cup,* GBP 210. NEW YORK, 4 March 1938, *Woman Blowing Soap Bubbles,* USD 425. LONDON, 13 June 1942, *Abimelech Presenting the Sword of Goliath to David,* GBP 577. LONDON, 8-9 April 1943, *Angel Appearing to Manoah,* GBP 105. LONDON, 9 July 1943, *Woman,* GBP 30. PARIS, 1 Dec 1943, *The Good Samaritan* (attributed) FRF 8,800. PARIS, 20 Dec 1943, *Head of an Old Woman* (attributed) FRF 11,000. NEW YORK, 28 Feb 1945, *Portrait of a Woman Dressed as a Sibyl,* USD 425. LONDON, 15 Feb 1946, *David Playing the Harp before Saul,* GBP 735. LONDON, 12 July 1946, *Officer,* GBP 357. STOCKHOLM, 3 Nov 1955, *Rembrandt Drawing in his Studio,* SEK 7,300. LONDON, 9 Dec 1959, *Presentation in the Temple,* GBP 320. PARIS, 16 June 1960, *Portrait of a Young Boy,* FRF 30,000. LONDON, 22 June 1960, *Family Group,* GBP 15,000. COLOGNE, 11 Nov 1961, *Hagar and Ishmael,* DEM 10,000. LONDON, 13 July 1962, *Christ Preaching in the Wilderness,* Gns 750. LONDON, 2 July 1965, *Esther and Ahasuerus,* Gns 3,800. LONDON, 25 Nov 1966, *Agony in the Garden,* Gns 4,800. LONDON, 10 April 1970, *Joseph and the Cup of Gold,* Gns 3,500. PARIS, 22 Nov 1972, *The Gallant Writer,* FRF 12,000. LONDON, 29 June 1973, *Portrait of a Gentleman and a Lady of Quality,* Gns 15,000. AMSTERDAM, 26 April 1976, *Judah and Thamar* (oil on canvas, 25 1/4 x 33 3/4in/64 x 86cm) NLG 21,000. AMSTERDAM, 31 Oct 1977, *King David with the Prophet Nathan* (oil on canvas, 39 1/2 x 49 1/2in/100.5 x 126cm) NLG 38,000. COLOGNE, 19 Nov 1987, *Judah before Joseph* (oil on canvas, 39 x 44 1/2in/99 x 113cm) DEM 76,000. LONDON, 22 April 1988, *Grace before the Meal* (oil on canvas, 36 x 31in/90.5 x 78.5cm) GBP 93,500. NEW YORK, 5 April 1990, *Portrait of a Gentleman* (oil on canvas, rounded top, 36 1/4 x 29in/92 x 73.5cm) USD 6,600. NEW YORK, 31 May 1990, *Portrait of a Young Man in a Brown Hat* (oil on canvas, 16 1/2 x 14 1/2in/41.9 x 36.8cm) USD 28,600. LONDON, 22 April 1994, *Esther* (oil on canvas, 32 x 24 1/2in/81.2 x 62 cm) GBP 20,700. NEW YORK, 29 Jan 1998, *Esther at her Toilette* (oil on canvas, 43 1/4 x 48 1/2in/110 x 123 cm) USD 772,500. NEW YORK, 29 Jan 1999, *Archangel Raphael* (oil on canvas, 21 x 17 ins / 53 x 43 cm) USD 72,000. LONDON, 14 Dec 1999, *Banishment of Hagar and Ishmael* (1646, oil on canvas, 31 x 39 ins / 80 x 98 cm) GBP 30,000. BUDAPEST, 12 Dec 2003, *Kisfiu Porteja* (oil on canvas, 22 x 19 ins / 57 x 47 cm) HUF 9,500,000.

GELDER, Eugène Joseph Adolphe van
Belgian, 19th century.
Born 24 June 1856.
Painter, draughtsman. Genre scenes.

He was a pupil of Portaels and exhibited in Berlin in 1886. His works include *Playing Truant.*

E van Gelder

AUCTION RECORDS:
PARIS, 6 Dec 1993, *Rehearsal of the Union Instrumentale in Brussels* (1883, pencil, 17 x 23 1/4in/43 x 59cm) FRF 7,500.

GELDER, J. V. van
Dutch, 19th century.
Sculptor.

MUSEUMS AND GALLERIES:
ROTTERDAM (Boymans Mus.): *Bust of Koekkoek.*

GELDER, Jan van, or Vingeldri, Giovanni
Flemish School, 17th century.
Born in Antwerp.
Painter.

He was active in Italy, especially Modena, where he was known as Giovanni Vingeldri.

GELDER, Lucia Mathilde von
German, 19th century.
Born 15 November 1865, in Wiesbaden (Hesse); died 18 April 1899, in Munich.
Painter. Genre scenes.

Lucia Gelder exhibited in Munich in 1883 and is noted for her work *In Church.*

AUCTION RECORDS:
NEW YORK, 14 Jan 1977, *Threesome in the Tavern* (oil on canvas, 29 1/2 x 25 ins / 75 x 63.5 cm) USD 2,000. LONDON, 14 June 1996, *Grandfather's Tales* (oil on canvas, 27 x 34 3/4 ins / 68.6 x 88.2 cm) GBP 8,625.

GELDER, Nicolaes van
Flemish School, 17th century.
Born 1620 or 1625, in Leiden; died c. 1677.
Painter. Still-lifes.

Nicolaes van Gelder was active in Stockholm in 1661, and later resident in Amsterdam.

MUSEUMS AND GALLERIES:
AMSTERDAM: still-lifes - BERLIN: still-lifes - COPENHAGEN: still-lifes - LEIDEN: still-lifes - ROTTERDAM: *Still-life with Birds* - VIENNA: *Still-life with Wild Ducks.*

AUCTION RECORDS:
LONDON, 11 April 1930, *Still-life with Fruit,* GBP 44. AMSTERDAM, 23 Nov 1971, *Still-life,* NLG 11,500. COPENHAGEN, 29 April 1980, *Still-life* (oil on canvas, 43 1/4 x 34 1/4in/110 x 87cm) DKK 320,000. NEW YORK, 12 Jan 1995, *Still-lifes with Fruit in a Ming Bowl, one with a Nautilus Set on a Foot of Goldsmiths' Work, the other with a Glass and a Carafe* (oil on canvas, a pair, 23 1/2 x 19 1/2in/59.7 x 49.5cm and 23 1/2 x 19 1/4in/59.7 x 48.9cm) USD 167,500. LONDON, 4 July 1997, *Grapes, Peaches, Plums and Cherries with a Snail Hanging in a Stone Niche, with Apricots and a Bee on an Entablature* (1666, oil on canvas, 24 x 19in/60.7 x 48cm) GBP 23,000. LONDON, 9 July 2003, *Strawberries in a Blue and White Chinese Porcelain Bowl. Lobster and Partly Peeled Lemon on a Stone Ledge* (1662, oil on canvas, 22 x 17 ins / 57 x 43 cm) GBP 110,000.

GELDER, P.M. van
British, 18th century.
Active in London.
Sculptor.

P.M. Van Gelder studied at the Royal Academy in London.

GELDER, Pieter
Dutch, 17th century.
Active c. 1655.
Painter.

He was probably a pupil of Rembrandt, and a relative of Aart de Gelder.

GELDERBLOM, Laurens
Dutch, 18th century.
Born 1748, in Dordrecht; died c. 1778.
Painter. Flowers.

He was a pupil of Joris Ponsen.

GELDERSMANN, Vincentius. See **SELLAER Vincent**

GELDMACHER
German, 18th century.
Born in Kassel; died 1780, in Verona (Veneto, Italy).

Painter.
Geldmacher was the pupil of Tischbein.

GELDORP, Georg
Flemish School, 16th - 17th century.
Born c. 1610, in Cologne or in Antwerp; died c. 1658, in London.
Active in England.
Painter. Religious subjects, portraits.
Antwerp School.

He studied in Antwerp and was received there as a master in 1610. In 1613, he married the daughter of Willem de Vos. In 1630, he went to England where he was appointed to the position of keeper of King Charles I's pictures. Among his acquaintances were Rubens, Van Dyck and Peter Lely. He was also a picture dealer.

MUSEUMS AND GALLERIES:
LONDON (National Portrait Gal.): *Portrait of the Earl of Totnes* - VIENNA: *Portrait of a Man.*

AUCTION RECORDS:
LONDON, 16 July 1909, *Portrait of a Woman,* GBP 25. LONDON, 7 July 1911, *Two Wings of an Altarpiece with Portraits of Four Donors,* GBP 33. LONDON, 12 Dec 1924, *Woman,* GBP 14. LONDON, 19 Nov 1986, *Portrait of a Young Boy with his Dog* (oil on canvas, 56 3/4 x 45 ins / 144 x 114 cm) GBP 26,000.

GELDORP, Gortzius, or Gelsdorp or Gualdorp
Flemish School, 16th - 17th century.
Born 1553, in Louvain; died c. 1618, in Cologne.
Painter. Religious subjects, mythological subjects, portraits.

A pupil of Frans Franck in Antwerp and then of Frans Pourbus, he became painter to Duke Carlos of Aragon and travelled with him to Cologne in 1579. An artist of the Miereveldt School, he was best known for his portraits.

MUSEUMS AND GALLERIES:
AMSTERDAM: *Gualtero del Prado and His Wife Lucretia Pellicorne; Hortensia del Prado* (two works); *Jean Fourmenois; Jeremias Bourdinos and His Wife Lucretia del Prado; Catherine Fourmenois and Child; A Sister of Catherine Fourmenois* - BUDAPEST: *Bruyn Van Blankevort; Portrait of a Woman* - COLOGNE: *Elizabeth von Steinrodt; Hermann von Wedich;* three portraits of men and one of a woman; *A Burgomeister; A Benefactor; Two Female Benefactors* - HANOVER: *Elizabeth von Kreps; Female Patrician; Old Man* - LONDON (National Portrait Gal.): *G. Carew, Earl of Totnes* - MAINZ: *Young Man; Two Members of the Schick Family* - MILAN (Pinacoteca di Brera): *Portrait of a Woman* - ROHRAU (Schlossmuseum, Graf Harrach'sche Familiensammlung): *Portrait of a Man* - ST PETERSBURG: *Lucretia; Portrait of a Man; Godefroy Hautappel and His Wife Cornelia Boot* - THE HAGUE: *Saint in Ecstasy* - VIENNA (Schönborn-Buckheim): *Portrait of a Man; Eberhard von Geilen* - WEIMAR: *Portrait of a Man.*

AUCTION RECORDS:
COLOGNE, 1862, *Portrait of a Woman,* FRF 183; *Portrait of a Richly Dressed Lady,* FRF 112; *Portrait of a Richly Dressed Girl,* FRF 525; *Portrait of a Seated Man,* FRF 206. BERLIN, 24 Jan 1899, *Portrait,* FRF 340. BERLIN, 20 Sept 1930, *Portrait of a Child,* DEM 800. LONDON, 12 Feb 1932, *Portrait of a Dutch Woman,* GBP 7. NEW YORK, 11 Jan 1989, *Portrait of a Gentleman* (1612, oil on panel, 31 3/4 x 25 ins / 80.8 x 63.6 cm) USD 30,800. LONDON, 31 March 1989, *Portrait of an Eleven-Year-Old Girl in a Black Dress with Embroidered Sleeves, a Ruff and a Gold Chain* (1601, oil on canvas, 21 1/2 x 17 3/4 ins / 54.6 x 45.1 cm) GBP 7,920. COLOGNE, 29 June 1990, *Penitent Magdalene* (oil on canvas, 30 1/4 x 22 ins / 77 x 55 cm) DEM 1,100. STOCKHOLM, 14 Nov 1990, *Head and Shoulders Portrait of a Man with a Lace Collar* (oil on canvas, 30 1/4 x 24 3/4 ins / 77 x 63 cm) SEK 27,000. STOCKHOLM, 29 May 1991, *Elegant Couple with Their Servants at the Fish Market* (oil on canvas, 53 1/2 x 87 1/2 ins / 136 x 222 cm) SEK 200,000. LONDON, 13 Sept 1991, *Head and Shoulders of Diana the Huntress* (oil on canvas, oval 24 1/4 x 22 ins / 61.5 x 55.9 cm) GBP 2,200. PARIS, 26 June 1992, *Venus* (oil on panel, 25 x 19 ins / 63.5 x 48 cm) FRF 60,000. PENRITH (CUMBRIA), 13 Sept 1994, *Portrait of Susan Hoste* (1617, oil on canvas, 45 x 32 3/4 ins / 114 x 83.5 cm) GBP 17,250. LONDON, 5 July 1996, *Half Portrait of a Girl in a Black Dress with a White Lace Ruff holding a White Rose* (oil on panel, 23 x 19 ins / 58.2 x 48.2 cm) GBP 53,000. AMSTERDAM, 7 May 1997, *Half Portrait of a woman* (1602, oil on panel, 27 x 21 ins / 68.6 x 52.5 cm) NLG 8,072. LONDON, 3 Dec 1997, *Penitent Magdalene* (oil on panel, 26 1/2 x 20 3/4 ins / 67.6 x 52.8 cm) GBP 17,250. COLOGNE, 15 May 1999, *Portrait of Anna Selbdritt* (1604, oil on panel, 51 x 48 ins / 129 x 123 cm) DEM 25,000. COLOGNE, 20 May 2000, *Allegory of Love* (1610, oil on panel, 26 x 20 ins / 67 x 50 cm) DEM 15,000. PARIS, 30 June 2000, *Penitant Mary Magdalene* (oil on canvas, 26 x 22 ins / 65 x 55 cm) FRF 21,000. LONDON, 11 Dec 2001, *Portrait of a Lady Wearing a Black Dress* (oil on panel, 26 x 22 ins / 66 x 56 cm) GBP 8,000. AMSTERDAM, 5 Nov 2002, *Portrait of a Man Wearing a Black Costume* (1619, oil on canvas, 23 x 15 ins / 58 x 39 cm) EUR 4,000. AMSTERDAM, 18 May 2004, *Portrait of a Lady aged 28, Wearing a Black and White Dress* (1597, oil on canvas, 20 x 17 ins / 52 x 43 cm) EUR 20,000.

GELDORP, Melchior
Flemish School, 17th century.
Active in Cologne (North Rhine-Westphalia) from 1615 to 1637.
Portrait artist.

He was a son or nephew of Gortzius Geldorp.

GELDTER, Johann Maximilien
Austrian, 18th century.
Active in Vienna at the beginning of the 18th century.
Painter.

GELÉE, Antoine François, or Gellée
French, 19th century.
Born 13 May 1796, in Paris; died 27 February 1860, in Paris.
Engraver, lithographer.

Studied under Girodet and Pauquet and was awarded the Grand Prix de Rome silver in 1829 and the gold in 1824. He exhibited at the Salon from 1822 to 1853. Gelée engraved genre subjects, receiving a gold medal in 1842 for his version of Prudhon's *Justice Pursuing Crime.*

BIBLIOGRAPHY:
Janson, H.W., '*Daphnis and Chloe in the American Wilderness*' in *Auro Prior: Studia Toanni Bialostocki Sexagenario Dicata,* Juliusz A. Chroscicki, Panstwowe Wydawnictwo Naukowe, Warsaw, 1981.

GELENG, Angelo
German, 19th - 20th century.
Born in Italy.
Painter.

The son of Otto Geleng, Angelo also exhibited landscapes.

GELENG, Otto
German, 19th century.
Born in Berlin.
Painter. Landscapes.

Geleng exhibited views of Italy in Berlin.

GELENIUS, Sigismund
Bohemian School, 16th century.
Born 1497, in Prague; died 1554, in Basel.
Engraver.

Sigismund Gelenius probably produced 12 accomplished engravings of *The Labours of Hercules.*

GELERT, Johannes Sophus
Danish, 19th century.
Born 19 December 1852, in Nybel.
Active in the USA.
Sculptor.

Johannes Sophus Gelert was a pupil at the Kunstakademi in Copenhagen and received a travel grant from the Danish government to study in Italy. He later settled in New York and become an American citizen. He received many awards: a gold medal in Nashville (1897); a gold medal (1899); an honourable mention at the Exposition Universelle in Paris (1900); and Buffalo (1901).

GELEYN
Belgian, 19th century.
Active in Paris c. 1870.
Draughtsman.

He painted a series of portraits of the leading French marshals.

GELEYN, Gaston
Belgian, 20th century.
Born 1892, in Brussels; died 1946, in Grimbergen.
Painter. Figures, portraits, landscapes, seascapes, flowers, fruit.

Geleyn attended the Académie Royale des Beaux Arts in Brussels. He produced a considerable amount of work; his landscapes are said by some to have a strange quality about them.

MUSEUMS AND GALLERIES:
BRUSSELS.

GELEYN, Joseph Louis
Belgian, 19th - 20th century.
Born 1863, in Bruges; died 1934, in Ukkel.
Sculptor.

Geleyn studied under Thomas de Vinçotte. He contributed works to the 1897 Exposition Universelle. Some of his works can be seen in Brussels Botanical Garden and in Moscow.

MUSEUMS AND GALLERIES:
TERVUREN.

GELHAAR, Emil
Swedish, 19th century.
Born 1862, in Gefle (now Gävle).
Painter.

Emil Gelhaar established himself early in the USA, where he participated in numerous exhibitions.

GELHAAR, Theodor
Russian, 19th century.
Born 1805, in Lemsal; died 1871, in Lemsal.
Lithographer.

We owe him views of Reval (now Tallinn).

GELHAY, Édouard
French, 19th - 20th century.
Born 1856, in the Aisne region.
Painter, pastellist. Portraits, genre scenes, landscapes, waterscapes.

Édouard Gelhay trained with Alexandre Cabanel, William Bougureau and Tony Robert-Fleury. He painted genre scenes, portraits and landscapes in oils or in pastel, using an impressionist style. His works include *Abandoning a Child to State Care, Morning Walk, Village Street, Country Wedding.* He exhibited from 1878 at the Salon des Artistes Français in Paris, winning many distinctions. He was made Chevalier of the Légion d'Honneur in 1908.

MUSEUMS AND GALLERIES:
ARRAS: *Before the Examining Magistrate; Rest* - LA ROCHELLE: *Solitude* - LILLE: *A Book-Lover* - TOURCOING: *Morning Walk.*

AUCTION RECORDS:
PARIS, 16 May 1924, *The Poppy* (pastel) FRF 320; *The Loing Canal* (pastel) FRF 550. PARIS, 24 May 1945, *Woman with a Rose,* FRF 650. PARIS, 21 March 1977, *Country Wedding* (oil on canvas, 25 1/2 x 32 ins / 65 x 81 cm) FRF 3,400. VERSAILLES, 26 June 1977, *Washerwomen* (pastel, 20 1/2 x 25 1/2 ins / 52 x 6[illegible] cm) FRF 3,200. VERSAILLES, 12 Oct 1980, *Walk under the Trees* (oil on panel, 13 x 16 1/4 ins / 33 x 41 cm) FRF 4,200. NEW YORK, 24 Feb 1987, *Waiting* (oil on canvas, 21 1/2 x 26 ins / 54.6 x 6[illegible] cm) USD 8,500. NEW YORK, 24 May 1989, *Reflection in a Mirror* (oil on canvas, 25 1/2 x 21 1/4 ins / 64.8 x 54 cm) USD 9,350. PARIS, 9 Nov 1990, *Farm Girl in the Yard* (oil on canvas, 15 x 22 ins / 38 x 56 cm) FRF 14,100. PARIS, 7 Dec 1994, *Banks of the Loing at Nemours* (pastel, 19 1/2 x 25 1/4 ins / 49.5 x 64 cm) FRF 15,500. NEW YORK, 18 March 1998, *An Attractive Reading* (oil on canvas, 24 x 17 1/4 ins / 61 x 43.8 cm) USD 8,625.

GÉLIBERT, Gaston
French, 19th century.
Born 1850, in the Pyrenées; died 1931.
Painter. Animals.

Studied under his father Paul Gélibert; awarded the Prix Rosa Bonheur in 1921 and a silver medal in 1925. He continued to exhibit at the Salon until 1931.

AUCTION RECORDS:
PARIS, 28 Feb 1984, *Setter and Mallards* (1887, oil on canvas, 57 1/2 x 38 1/2 ins / 146 x 98 cm) FRF 6,000. PARIS, 16 March 1998, *Fox Lying in Wait* (1888, watercolour, 15 x 19 ins / 38 x 48 cm) FRF 3,800. LIBOURNE, 5 May 1998, *Duck Shoot* (oil on canvas, 70 x 39 1/4 ins / 178 x 100 cm) FRF 67,000. PARIS, 1 Dec 2000, *Le piqueux et les chiens* (watercolour, 19 x 15 ins / 47 x 37 cm) FRF 23,500. MELUN, 1 Dec 2002, *The Flight of the Duck* (oil on canvas, 26 x 31 ins / 65 x 80 cm) EUR 4,700.

GÉLIBERT, Jules Bertrand
French, 19th - 20th century.
Born 27 November 1834, in Bagnères-de-Bigorre; died 1916.
Painter, watercolourist, draughtsman. Religious subjects, hunting scenes, animals. Murals.

Jules Bertrand Gélibert was a pupil of his father Paul Gélibert. He specialised in hunting and animal scenes, in watercolours or pencil drawings, such as *Death of a Roebuck - Hanged Fox - Spaniel Retrieving a Rabbit - Druid, Prince Napoleon's Hound.* He concentrated on the hounds and their prey, merely sketching in the landscape. He also produced a large mural, *The Miracle of St Hubert,* for the church of Cap-Breton in the Landes region in south-west France. He exhibited at the Paris Salon and at the Salon des Artistes Français, winning a medal (1869) and a second-class medal (1883). He also was awarded bronze medals at the 1889 and 1900 Expositions Universelles. He held exhibitions abroad in Brussels and Berlin and was made a Chevalier of the Légion d'Honneur.

Jules Bt Gelibert

MUSEUMS AND GALLERIES:
BAGNÈRES-DE-BIGORRE: *Study of Hounds* - CAMBRAI: *Another One Caught* - GIEN: *Hare-Coursing* - NANTES (MBA): *Hounds* - ST-ÉTIENNE (Mus. d'Art et d'Industrie): *Pyrenean Sheep.*

AUCTION RECORDS:
NEW YORK, 12 April 1911, *Hounds at the Meet* (watercolour) USD 300. PARIS, 4 March 1925, *Death of a Roebuck,* FRF 850. PARIS, 14 June 1944, *Spaniel with a Partridge* (drawing heightened) FRF 1,250. PARIS, July 1946, *Hounds* (two pendants) FRF 5,000. NEW YORK, 15 Oct 1976, *Huntsman and his Hounds* (1880, oil on canvas, 20 x 32 ins / 50.5 x 81 cm) GBP 2,300. PARIS, 2 June 1978, *Griffon Retrieving a Hare* (1888, watercolour, 16 1/2 x 13 1/2 ins / 42 x 34 cm) FRF 2,600. PARIS, 17 Oct 1978, *Boar Hunt* (oil on canvas, 69 x 119 ins / 175 x 302 cm) FRF 16,500. PARIS, 18 May 1982, *Hounds beside the Fireplace* (watercolour and gouache) FRF 6,500. NEW YORK, 26 Feb 1986, *The Kennels* (1880, watercolour/pencil outlines,

51/4 x 181/2 ins / 38.6 x 47.2 cm) USD 2,600. NEW YORK, 24 Feb 1987, *Huntsman and Pack in Woodland* (1885, oil on canvas, 193/4 x 24 ins / 50.2 x 61 cm) USD 5,750. PAU, 26 Jan 1991, *Hounds* (1906, oil on canvas, 26 x 193/4 ins / 66 x 50 cm) FRF 26,000. NEW YORK, 5 June 1992, *Hounds Catching a Hare* (oil on canvas, 25 x 203/4 ins / 63.5 x 52.7 cm) USD 6,325. LIBOURNE, 27 Oct 1992, *Pack of Hounds* (oil on canvas, 20 x 253/4 ins / 50.5 x 65.7 cm) FRF 30,500. NEW YORK, 4 June 1993, *Druide, Prince Napoleon's Hound* (bronze, h. 131/2 ins / 34.3 cm, l. 11 ins/27.9 cm) USD 6,038. NEW YORK, 15 Oct 1993, *On the Scent* (watercolour/paper, 14 x 191/2 ins / 35.5 x 49.5 cm) USD 1,093. PARIS, 9 Dec 1994, *Hounds Resting after the Hunt* (oil on canvas, 231/2 x 311/2 ins / 60 x 80 cm) FRF 14,500. PARIS, 16 Oct 1996, *Spaniels and Mallards* (oil on canvas, 193/4 x 26 ins / 50 x 66 cm) FRF 21,000.

GÉLIBERT, Paul Jean Pierre

French, 19th century.

Born 29 April 1802, in Laforce; died 24 September 1882, in Barte-de-Nesle.

Painter, watercolourist. Genre scenes, landscapes with figures, mountainscapes, animals.

Exhibited at the Paris Salon from 1835 to 1880, securing a bronze medal in 1843. Gélibert painted predominantly Pyrenean landscapes with herdsmen and their animals.

BIBLIOGRAPHY:

Les Années romantiques, la peinture française de 1815 à 1850, exhibition catalogue, Musée des Beaux-Arts, Nantes, Gal. nationales du Grand Palais, Paris, 1996.

MUSEUMS AND GALLERIES:

BAGNÈRES-DE-BIGORRE: *Wolf's Head* - LA FÈRE: *Landscape with Animals; Sheep* - NARBONNE: *Landscape with Figures and Animals* - ST-ÉTIENNE (Mus. d'Art et d'Industrie): *Bull (study)* - TOULOUSE: *Herds Descending the Mountain*.

AUCTION RECORDS:

PARIS, 20 April 1945, *Horse in a Meadow*, FRF 150. PARIS, 29 June 1945, *Grazing Herd*, FRF 2,500. VERSAILLES, 5 March 1989, *Herdsman* (oil on canvas, 17 x 241/4 ins / 43 x 61.5 cm) FRF 9,800. PARIS, 25 Nov 1991, *Farmer's Wife Herding Cattle* (oil on canvas, 171/4 x 24 ins / 44 x 61 cm) FRF 15,000. RHEIMS, 21 April 1996, *Sheep-Shearing* (1837, oil on canvas, 203/4 x 173/4 ins / 53 x 45 cm) FRF 9,000. STOCKHOLM, 28 Nov 2000, *Mountain Landscape with Bull Fighting with Bear* (1845, oil on canvas, 47 x 64 ins / 120 x 162 cm) SEK 40,000. PARIS, 20 Dec 2000, *Herdswoman* (oil on canvas, 17 x 24 ins / 44 x 61 cm) FRF 15,000.

GELINECK, Ferencz

Hungarian, 18th century.

Painter.

Ferencz Gelineck taught draughtsmanship in Budapest at the end of the 18th century.

GÉLINET, Marcel

French, 20th century.

Born in Marseilles.

Painter. Nudes, urban landscapes.

Marcel Gélinet exhibited in Paris from 1927 to 1931 at the Salon.

AUCTION RECORDS:

ENGHIEN-LES-BAINS, 20 April 1980, *The Quai des Orfèvres in Paris* (oil on canvas, 211/4 x 253/4 ins / 54 x 65.5 cm) FRF 2,000. PARIS, 15 Feb 1988, *Nude Seated in an Armchair* (oil on canvas, 361/2 x 303/4 ins / 93 x 78 cm) FRF 5,200.

GÉLIS, Daniel

French, 20th century.

Born 14 March 1942, in Orléans.

Painter, draughtsman. Figures, nudes, scenes with figures, interiors with figures, landscapes with figures, landscapes, boats.

Daniel Gélis is believed to have trained at the École des Beaux-Arts in Orléans for three years. He subsequently taught drawing until 1971. In his misty style and bringing out their most appealing aspects, Gélis paints conventional themes such as languid nudes, party scenes, Mediterranean landscapes, crowded beaches and sailing yachts with big triangular sails.

He exhibited in regional group exhibitions and in Paris at the Salon des Artistes Français, winning a gold medal in 1982, the Salon d'Automne and the Salon du Dessin et de la Peinture à l'Eau, being a member of all three Salons. He also exhibited at the Salon Comparaisons. He held solo exhibitions in various cities in France as well as in other countries.

BIBLIOGRAPHY:

Fédorkow, A.A., *Gélis*, Imprimerie Copie 45, Chécy, 1989.

AUCTION RECORDS:

LE TOUQUET, 12 Nov 1989, *Profile of a Young Girl* (oil on canvas, 32 x 251/2 ins / 81 x 65 cm) FRF 10,000. VERSAILLES, 8 July 1990, *Wind and Water* (oil on canvas, 271/2 x 271/2 ins / 70 x 70 cm) FRF 4,000.

GÉLIS, Martine

French, 20th - 21st century.

Born 1959, in Toulouse.

Painter (including gouache).

Martine Gélis exhibited at the Galerie Édouard Manet in Gennevilliers in 1998. In 2003, her work featured in the exhibition *Autour de Mark Tobey* (*Around Mark Tobey*) at the Galerie Darthea Speyer in Paris, where she showed abstract works composed of interlaced designs in different colours based on the superimposition of forms.

GELIS, Meinert

Dutch, 17th century.

Active c. 1620.

Engraver.

Known for his decorative and grotesque ornamental designs.

GELISSEN, Maximilien Lambert

Belgian, 19th century.

Born 27 February 1786, in Brussels; died 19 March 1867, in Brussels.

Painter. Genre scenes, landscapes with figures.

He was a pupil of H. van Asche, Crété and Mortelèque.

AUCTION RECORDS:

LONDON, 6 May 1977, *Wooded Landscape with a River and Figures* (oil on canvas, 171/2 x 211/2in/44.6 x 54.5cm) GBP 1,150. VIENNA, 6 Nov 1985, *Meeting at the Edge of a Wood* (oil on panel, 141/2 x 181/2in/37 x 47cm) ATS 40,000. AMSTERDAM, 5-6 Nov 1991, *Street Entertainer with a Monkey* (oil on canvas, 141/2 x 19in/37 x 48cm) NLG 4,600. AMSTERDAM, 20 April 1993, *Figures on a Track in a Wooded Landscape* (oil on canvas, 271/2 x 373/4in/70 x 96cm) NLG 9,430. LONDON, 13 March 1996, *Figures on a Track in a Wooded Landscape* (1823, oil on panel, 251/4 x 32in/64 x 81cm) USD 3,450. BRUSSELS, 6 Dec 1999, *Encounter by the River* (oil on canvas, 22 x 21 ins / 57 x 54 cm) BEF 85,000. BRUSSELS, 21 Nov 2000, *Rutted Lane with Figures* (oil on canvas, 15 x 20 ins / 38 x 51 cm) BEF 108,000. AMSTERDAM, 15 March 2004, *Extensive Wooded Landscape with Horseman, Maid and Other Travellers on a Path* (1823, oil on panel, 26 x 33 ins / 65 x 84 cm) EUR 2,400.

GELL, Freenman (Mrs)

Maiden name: Ada Eversbed

British, 19th century.

Active in Brighton.

Sculptor.

Mrs Freenman Gell exhibited in London from 1887, notably at the Royal Academy and the Suffolk Street Gallery.

GELL, William (Sir)

British, 18th - 19th century.

Born 1774, in Hopton; died 4 February 1836, in Naples.

Painter, draughtsman, illustrator, architect.
Topographical views.
William Gell was educated at the Academy School. He was an architect by profession, but was better known as a publisher of illustrated volumes on Greek and Italian antiquity. Examples of his topographical studies include *Geography and Antiquities of Ithaca* (1807), *Peloponnese Journey* (1818) and *Topography of Rome* (1820).

GELLE, André
French, 17th century.
Born in Arras.
Painter.

GELLE, Johann
Flemish School, 17th century.
Died before March 1625.
Active in Cologne (North Rhine-Westphalia).
Engraver.
Gelle died shortly after his marriage in 1624. Some sources date the publication in Antwerp of his work *L'Académie de l'Espée* to 1628, after his death.

GELLE, Jules
French, 19th century.
Born 19th century, in Anzin.
Painter, sculptor.
Studied at the École des Beaux-Arts in Valenciennes and exhibited at the Paris Salon from 1868 to 1880.

GELLE, Paul
French, 19th century.
Died 1814, in Niort.
Painter, engraver. Genre scenes.
Painted scenes of everyday life in and around Niort.
MUSEUMS AND GALLERIES:
NIORT: drawing.

GELLÉE, A.
French, 17th century.
Sculptor.
He sculpted a triptych in 1627 which is now located at the church of St Maurice in Épinal.

GELLÉE, Claude. See **LORRAINE Claude**

GELLÉE, Didier
French, 16th century.
Born in Blamont.
Painter.
He was married in Nancy in 1600.

GELLÉE, Jean
French, 17th century.
Active in Freiburg im Brisgau.
Engraver (wood).
According to Baldinucci, Jean Gellée was the brother of Claude, also known as Lorrain.

GELLEM, B.
18th century.
Painter. Portraits.
Mentioned in *Art Prices Current*.
AUCTION RECORDS:
LONDON, 29 Feb 1908, *Portrait of a Young Boy* (1736) GBP 13.

GELLENBECK, Ann P.
American, 20th century.
Born in Minneapolis.
Painter.
Ann Gellenbeck was a member of the American Federation of Arts.

GELLENTIN, Gottfried
Danish, 18th century.
Active in Copenhagen c. 1756.
Miniaturist.

GELLEQUIN DE BRUXELLES
Flemish School, 14th century.
Painter.
He was working for the Duke of Burgundy in 1345.

GELLER
Enameller.
MUSEUMS AND GALLERIES:
ROCHEFORT: *Beatrix*.

GELLER, Emil Oswald
German, 19th century.
Born 3 November 1821, in Neusalz (now Nowa Sól, Poland).
Engraver (wood).
Emil Geller studied in Dresden.

GELLER, Johann Nepomuk
Austrian, 19th - 20th century.
Born 21 March 1860, in Vienna; died 1954.
Painter. Genre scenes, urban landscapes, market scenes.
Geller attended the Akademie der Bildenden Künste in Vienna and won a bronze medal at the 1900 Exposition Universelle. He also exhibited in Berlin, Munich, Düsseldorf and Paris.

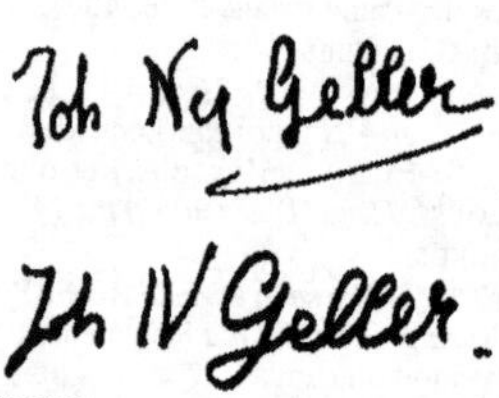

AUCTION RECORDS:
VIENNA, 22 Sept 1971, *View of Nuremberg*, ATS 30,000. VIENNA, 22 March 1972, *Grand Square in Nuremberg*, ATS 25,000. VIENNA, 29 Nov 1977, *Market Scene in Budweiss* (oil on canvas, 37 1/2 x 55 ins / 95 x 140 cm) ATS 60,000. VIENNA, 12 Dec 1978, *Cracow Market* (oil on canvas, 27 1/2 x 39 1/4 ins / 70 x 100 cm) ATS 40,000. VIENNA, 17 March 1982, *Christmas Market* (mixed media, 14 3/4 x 19 3/4 ins / 37.5 x 50 cm) ATS 60,000. VIENNA, 16 Nov 1983, *Market Scene, Budweiss* (oil on canvas, 37 1/2 x 55 ins / 95 x 140 cm) ATS 150,000. VIENNA, 6 Dec 1984, *Market Scene* (mixed media/canvas remounted on board, 3 1/2 x 6 ins / 9 x 15 cm) ATS 20,000. VIENNA, 16 Jan 1985, *Procession* (oil on paper remounted on board, 11 x 15 ins / 27 x 38 cm) ATS 55,000. VIENNA, 15 Oct 1987, *View of Weissenkirchen* (1936, watercolour, 15 3/4 x 22 3/4 ins / 40 x 58 cm) ATS 25,000. NEW YORK, 18 Feb 1993, *Marketplace in Misfrau* (oil on canvas/card, 22 1/2 x 30 ins / 57 x 76 cm) USD 19,800. VIENNA, 29 April 1999, *View of Klosterneuburg* (watercolour, 13 x 20 ins / 32 x 50 cm) ATS 75,000. VIENNA, 20 May 1999, *Figures Resting in Meadows in Vienna Prater* (oil on board, 17 x 14 ins / 42 x 36 cm) ATS 130,000. VIENNA, 23 May 2000, *Woman Sitting on Steps, Stein an der Donau* (oil on board, 13 x 8 ins / 32 x 20 cm) ATS 35,000. VIENNA, 21 Nov 2001, *Village Square with Ox Cart before Monument* (charcoal and watercolour heightened with white on board, 13 x 9 ins / 32 x 23 cm) ATS 45,000. VIENNA, 21 Nov 2001, *Entrance to Farmstead in Weissenkirchen* (oil on board, 14 x 13 ins / 35 x 33 cm) ATS 50,000. MELBOURNE, 25 Nov 2002, *Market Scene* (oil and ink on card, 13 x 15 ins / 32 x 38 cm) AUD 5,000. VIENNA, 22 May 2003, *Marketplace* (oil on board, 11 x 16 ins / 27 x 40 cm) EUR 4,500. VIENNA, 28 Oct 2003, *Inner Courtyard in Wachau* (oil on canvas on board, 12 x 8 ins / 30

20 cm) EUR 1,500. VIENNA, 27 May 2004, *Sunday in the 'rater* (oil on canvas, 22 x 35 ins / 57 x 88 cm) EUR 10,000. VI-NNA, 12 Oct 2004, *Bremen Marketplace* (oil on canvas, 44 x 5 ins / 112 x 140 cm) EUR 25,000.

GELLER, Peter Isaakovich
Russian, 19th - 20th century.
Born 1862, in Kertch; died 1963.
Painter. Military subjects.

'eter Isaakovich Geller painted also military paintings for he Academy in St Petersburg.

AUCTION RECORDS:
SAN FRANCISCO, 4 May 1980, *Ivan the Terrible and the Hermit* oil on canvas, 59 x 81 ins / 150 x 206 cm) USD 3,000. LONDON, 15 Feb 1984, *After the Wedding* (1897, oil on canvas, 37 x 51 1/4 ins / 94 x 130 cm) GBP 3,800. HELSINKI, 8 May 2004, *In he Garden* (oil on canvas, 15 x 18 ins / 38 x 46 cm) EUR 5,200.

GELLER, William Overend
British, 19th century.
Active in London.
Painter, engraver.

William Overend Geller was a British Institution exhibitor from 1834 to 1846.

GELLERSTEDT, Albert Theodor
Swedish, 19th - 20th century.
Born 6 October 1836, in Sweden; died 7 April 1914.
Painter, watercolourist. Landscapes, seascapes.

Gellerstedt was also an architect.

MUSEUMS AND GALLERIES:
STOCKHOLM: five watercolours.

AUCTION RECORDS:
STOCKHOLM, 21 Nov 1988, *Archipelago in Summer* (watercolour, 6 3/4 x 4 3/4 ins / 17 x 12 cm) SEK 4,200.

GELLERT, Émery
Hungarian, 20th century.
Born 1889.
Active in the USA.
Painter.

In 1925 Émery Gellert won the Cleveland Museum Prize.

GELLERT, Hugo
Hungarian, 20th century.
Born 1892.
Active in the USA.
Painter. Murals.

Hugo Gellert painted a mural at the Workers' Center in New York.

GELLERT, Johann
Bohemian School, 19th century.
Born 23 December 1821, in Prague; died 1846.
Painter. Landscapes.

Johann Gellert exhibited in 1844.

AUCTION RECORDS:
VIENNA, 16 Jan 1985, *Steep Landscape* (1843, oil on canvas, 27 1/2 x 21 1/4 ins / 70 x 54 cm) ATS 22,000.

GELLES, Karl
Austrian, 20th century.
Born in Vienna.
Sculptor.

Gelles exhibited widely, notably in Spain, and in 1913 at the Salon des Artistes Français in Paris.

GELLI, Odoardo or Edoardo
Italian, 19th - 20th century.
Born 5 September 1852, in Savona; died 1933, in Florence.
Painter, watercolourist. History painting, portraits, genre scenes.

Odoardo Gelli studied at the Accademia di Belle Arti, the Accademia di S Luca and the Ciseri academy in Florence. He started working around 1873, and staged successful exhibitions in Munich in 1888 and 1890.

In 1886 Gelli was commissioned to paint a portrait of the Emperor of Austria. Soon after that, he was appointed president of the artistic society of Florence. He was a highly talented, technically adept painter, whose work is characterised by the use of bold colours.

AUCTION RECORDS:
BERLIN, 1894, *In the Summertime: Monk on a Journey*, FRF 387; *Cloister Scene*, FRF 912; *Singer*, FRF 2,000; *Altar Painting*, FRF 631. NEW YORK, 5 April 1907, *Guard*, USD 100. PARIS, 18 June 1930, *Concert*, FRF 2,550. LONDON, 8 July 1966, *Dancing to the Tambourine*, Gns 1,600. LONDON, 7 Oct 1987, *The Skin of the Ferocious Lion* (oil on canvas, 15 1/4 x 23 3/4 ins / 38.5 x 60.5 cm) GBP 4,000. BERN, 26 Oct 1988, *Return from the Hunt* (watercolour, 20 3/4 x 16 1/2 ins / 53 x 42 cm) CHF 1,000. AMSTERDAM, 2 May 1990, *Drunken Old Man* (oil on panel, 17 1/2 x 12 1/4 ins / 44.5 x 31 cm) NLG 17,250. LONDON, 13 March 1997, *Toast* (oil on panel, 12 x 8 1/2 ins / 30.5 x 21.6 cm) GBP 3,220. LONDON, 1 Dec 1999, *Celebration in a Tavern* (1882, oil on canvas, 38 x 79 ins / 96 x 200 cm) GBP 30,000. LONDON, 21 March 2002, *Elegant Woman* (1887, oil on canvas, 62 x 35 ins / 157 x 90 cm) GBP 5,000. ZURICH, 17 June 2002, *Interior with Young Woman* (oil on panel, 12 x 8 ins / 31 x 20 cm) CHF 5,000. LONDON, 29 Jan 2003, *Woman in a Wine Cellar* (oil on board, 12 x 8 ins / 31 x 21 cm) GBP 1,700.

GELLIG. See **GILLIG**

GELLY, Victor
French, 19th century.
Died 1899, in Chennevières-sur-Marne.
Painter.

Member of the Société des Artistes Français; exhibited between 1892 and 1894.

AUCTION RECORDS:
PARIS, 1898, *In Flagrante Delicto*, FRF 1,500.

GELON, Joseph
French, 19th century.
Painter. Allegorical subjects, portraits.

MUSEUMS AND GALLERIES:
BOURGES: *Portrait of Cardinal du Pont, Archbishop of Bourges*.

AUCTION RECORDS:
PARIS, 19 June 1994, *Allegory of the Dance* (1894, oil on canvas, 15 x 18 ins / 38 x 46 cm) FRF 17,500.

GELOT, Raymonde
French, 20th century.
Born in Paris.
Painter, pastellist. Landscapes.

Raymonde Gelot began to show work at the Salon des Indépendants in 1924.

AUCTION RECORDS:
PARIS, 23 June 1943, *The Pool* (pastel) FRF 110.

GELOT-MERCIER, Germaine
French, 20th century.
Born in Algiers.
Painter. Genre scenes, local scenes.

Germaine Gelot-Mercier began to show her Algerian paintings at the Salon des Artistes Français in Paris in 1930.

GELPI, Antonio, the Elder
Italian, 18th century.
Born 1740, in Como; died 1804, in Bergamo.
Sculptor.

Gelpi was a pupil of Perovani; he worked principally on Bergamo Cathedral.

GELPI, Antonio, the Younger
Italian, 19th century.
Died c. 1825.

Sculptor.
Antonio Gelpi the Younger was the nephew of Antonio Gelpi the Elder, and assisted him on his works in Bergamo Cathedral.

GELTON, Toussaint
Dutch, 17th century.
Born c. 1630; died 1680, probably in Copenhagen.
Painter. History painting, allegorical subjects, mythological subjects, portraits, genre scenes.

He was a member of the painters' guild at The Hague in 1659. He lived in Amsterdam from 1655 to 1661, and was active in Stockholm between 1666 and 1668. In 1673 he was appointed court painter to Christian V of Denmark. In 1674 and 1675 he worked in Saxony and Heidelberg. He was an imitator of Gerrit Dou and Poelenburch.

T. gelton fecit
A°. 1680

MUSEUMS AND GALLERIES:
COPENHAGEN: *Death and the Wise Man* - STOCKHOLM: *Young Man Writing; Portraits of Charles X of Sweden and his Sister Marie-Euphrasine, George, Brother of Christian V, and Queen Charlotte-Amelia.*

AUCTION RECORDS:
COLOGNE, 24 May. 1982, *Moses Rescued from the Waters* (oil on copper, 12¾ x 10¼in/32.5 x 26cm) DEM 7,500. COPENHAGEN, 12 Nov 1985, *Diana and Actaeon* (oil on canvas, 11 x 13½in/27 x 34cm) DKK 25,000. COPENHAGEN, 5 April 1989, *Venus and Cupid* (oil on canvas, oval, 6 x 4¾in/15 x 12cm) DKK 20,000. LONDON, 6 July 1994, *Diana Sleeping* (oil on panel, 5¼ x 6¾in/13.5 x 17cm) GBP 1,610. COPENHAGEN, 8 Feb 1995, *Diana and her Nymphs* (oil on panel, 11 x 13½in/27 x 34cm) DKK 18,000.

GELUWE, Ludovic van
Belgian, 19th century.
Active in Paris in 1850.
Painter, miniaturist. Genre scenes, portraits.

He exhibited genre paintings in Brussels in 1851.

GELVEZON-TÉQUI, Ofélia
Filipino, 20th century.
Born 4 June 1942, in Guimbal (Iloilo), Philippines.
Active in France from c. 1972.
Engraver, collage artist. Figure compositions, religious subjects.

Ofélia Gelvezon-Téqui graduated in art from the University of the Philippines in 1964, and again in 1966, in English. In 1967 she graduated from the Accademia di Belle Arti in Rome, and in 1968 undertook specialist study in graphic art at the Pratt Institute in New York.

Her prints, representing a variety of sacred and secular subjects and produced with a sophisticated polychrome technique, are very engaging with a subtle charm that is difficult to define. They could perhaps be classed as naive, or belonging to a populist vein, though they often reveal a practical familiarity with pop art technique. She has worked as a teacher and administrator in various Filipino institutions.

Ofélia Gelvezon-Téqui has featured in many collective exhibitions including: Manila (1968); Salon de la Figuration Critique, Paris; Salon de l'Union des Femmes Peintres et Sculpteurs, Paris; Salon des Réalités Nouvelles (1987); print Biennales, Tokyo and São Paulo; *The Philippines: the Country, its Art and its People* exhibition, UNESCO's Salle des Pas Perdus, Paris (1974). Solo exhibitions include: Makati (1970, 1971, 1980, 1982 and 1983); Manila (1972); Hallway Museum, Manila (1989); Museum of Filipino Art, Manila (1989); and Paris (1987). She received several awards including the Filipino Engravers' Association prize and a gold medal, Manila (1982).

GELZER, Gilgian
20th century.
Painter.

Gelzer has had in solo exhibitions at the Maison d'art contemporain, Chaillou de Fresnes (1994), the Bernard Jordan gallery, Paris (1994 and 1999), the ESAD, Reims (1997) and the Jordan-Devarrieux gallery, Paris.

From interlocked or superimposed geometric or organic shapes, he builds solid compositions, in harsh, strongly contrasting colours. For him, 'Painting allows one to slip between appearances and categories, to develop signs which are not part of an established code'.

BIBLIOGRAPHY:
Jover, Manuel, '*Gelzer: géométries organiques*' in *Beaux Arts Magazine* n° 126, periodical, Paris, September 1994.

GELZER, Wilhelm
Swiss, 19th century.
Born 19 September 1842; died 20 December 1875, in Paris.
Active in Schaffhausen.
Lithographer, draughtsman.

Gelzer also worked in Geneva, Perpignan and Paris.

GEMAYEL, César
Lebanese, 20th century.
Born 1898, in Aïn el Touffaha, near Bikfaya; died 1958.
Painter. Figures, portraits, scenes with figures.

Gemayel began by studying pharmacy, but on the advice of Khalil Saleeby he turned to painting. In 1927, he left for Paris and enrolled himself at the Académie Julian, where he studied under Jean-Pierre Laurens and E. R. Pougheon for three years. In 1930, he was awarded a prize at the Exposition Coloniale in Paris, following which he returned to Lebanon. He taught at the Lebanese academy of fine arts from its foundation in 1937. He regularly exhibited at the UNESCO Salons in Beirut, as well as in exhibitions organized in the Lebanese parliament building between 1936 and 1942. In 1965, the Sursock Museum paid him tribute during the fifth Autumn Salon. He received the National Order of the Cedar.

His work is very colourful and he often painted young women in positions of repose. He is considered to be one of the founders of modern Lebanese painting.

BIBLIOGRAPHY:
Liban. Le Regard des peintres. 200 ans de peinture libanaise, exhibition catalogue, Institut du Monde Arabe, Paris, 1989.

MUSEUMS AND GALLERIES:
AIN EL TOUFFAHA (Maison Natale): a considerable part of his work.

GEMBARZEVSKI
Polish, 19th century.
Active at the beginning of the 19th century.
Painter, watercolourist. Figures.

The museum in Rapperswil near Zurich owns some watercolours by Gembarzevski.

AUCTION RECORDS:
PARIS, 11 April 1919, *Two Horsemen* (watercolour) FRF 70.

GEMBEI. See **KATSUSHIGE**

GEMBERLING, Grace Thorp
American, 20th century.
Born 1903, in Philadelphia.
Painter.

Grace Thorp Gemberling was awarded a gold medal by the Philadelphia Academy of Fine Arts in 1931.

GEMEINERT, G. G.
German, 19th century.

Born in Sorau, Brandenburg (now Zary, Poland).
Painter. Landscapes.
Gemeinert was a pupil of Schirmer in Berlin.

GEMELICH, Andreas
German, 17th century.
Born 1602, in Frankfurt am Main.
Sculptor.
Andreas Gemelich also worked in Mainz.

GEMELICH, Anton
German, 17th century.
Active in Landsberg (Bavaria) in 1614.
Sculptor.

GEMELICH, Georg
German, 17th century.
Died 24 August 1640, in Frankfurt am Main.
Sculptor.

GEMELICH, Hans Leonhard
German, 16th century.
Active in Augsburg c. 1574.
Sculptor.
He was a pupil of Christoph Murmann the Elder.

GEMELIN, Johann
Bohemian School, 17th century.
Born in Aichstadt.
Active in Prague.
Sculptor.

GEMELLI, Bonaventura
German (?), 19th century.
Born 1798; died 1863.
Painter.
Nazarenes group (associated).
The sole mention of this artist is in a work by Marcel Brion, who likens him to Jacob Asmus Carstens in his romantic treatment of classical subjects. Gemelli was associated with the Nazarenes, a group of artists assembled by Johann Friedrich Overbeck at the disused monastery of San Isodoro in Rome, and who shared a deep attachment to the values of the Italian Renaissance. He lived with the Nazarenes for some time, and painted mainly mythological or fabulous subjects, but also touched on medieval themes, such as the life of a witch, or the passion of the artist figure. Gemelli's work evokes the romanticism of nature treated in the classical style of painters of the School of Fontainebleau.

GEMERT, Joos Lambrecht van
Flemish School, 18th century.
Born 23 January 1720; died 8 December 1782.
Painter, goldsmith. Church interiors.
He was dean of the Guild of St Luke in Antwerp from 1758 to 1775.

GEMES-GINDERT, Peter
Hungarian, 20th century.
Born 23 March 1876, in Tinnye.
Sculptor.
Gemes-Gindert studied under Lajos Gyorgy Matrai and completed his studies in Munich. He worked in Tinnye in particular.

GEMIARI, Giovanni Battista
Italian, 17th century.
Born in Cento.
Active c. 1606.
Painter. History painting.
A member of the Bologna Guild, Gemiari is identified by Lanzi as one of Guercino's teachers. He produced a work for the church of the Trinity: a *Madonna Surrounded by Saints* dated 1606.

GEMIGNANI, Ludovico. See **GIMIGNANI**

GÉMIGNANI, Michel
French, 20th century.
Born 27 August 1941, in Méricourt (Yvelines).
Painter, sculptor.
Michel Gémignani is the son of the sculptor Ulysse Gémignani and the composer Yvonne Desportes-Gémignani, both of whom won the Prix de Rome. After completing secondary school in Paris, Gémignani trained at the École des Arts Appliqués in Paris from 1956 to 1959, and at the École des Beaux-Arts from 1960 to 1967. He was awarded the Grand Prix de Rome in 1966. He returned to the École des Beaux-Arts as an assistant to Chapelain-Midy from 1971 to 1974 and as assistant to Louis Nallard in 1975. In 1978 he created the experimental studio Couleurs et Formes (Colours and Shapes).

Since 1966 he has made a great number of monumental works using a variety of materials and techniques such as glass and mosaic. These works include: a mural for the royal palace in Casablanca (1968); a 130 long x 6 feet high (40 x 2 metres) polychrome wall relief in copper and stratified resin at Neauphle-le-Vieux (1970); a 3800 sq feet (350-square metre) wall painting for the Lycée Albert Camus in Bois-Colombes (1974); a 33 long x 6 feet high (10 x 1.8 metres) polychrome wall relief in stratified resin for the Collège d'Enseignement Secondaire at Conflans-Ste-Honorine (1978); a 164 long x 16 feet high (50 x 5 metres) wall painting entitled *Fields* for the Collège d'Enseignement Technique in Mézières-Charleville (1978); and two tapestries for the royal palace in Marrakesh (1978). In 1988 he decorated 41 sheep to make fun of the nuclear power station in Cattenom.

From 1980 Gémignani initially worked more as a sculptor than as a painter. In wood he produced full, elongated forms which, at first glance, seem to share the spirituality of Brancusi or Arp; however, phallic connotations would appear more apt. The series paintings of the same period are less ambiguous. His cows, for example, appear as a ground covering of their hides. After 1985, painting made such heavy demands on his time that he appeared to have abandoned sculpture permanently. Distancing himself from the purist lines of his sculpture, Gémignani sees himself as a De Kooning type of Expressionist, painting less the real appearance of things than what he feels they should look like and concentrating more on the paint than his subject matter.

Beginning in 1967, Gémignani has participated in group exhibitions in Paris such as the Salon des Artistes Français from 1966 to 1975, the Salon d'Automne in 1970, the Salon Comparaisons in 1973, and the Salon de Mai in 1988. He began exhibiting at the Salon des Réalités Nouvelles in 1976, later being nominated a member of the committee and, in 1992, vice president.

Solo exhibitions of his works include the following: at the Académie Internationale in Nice (1970); at the Musée de la Chasse in Paris (1973); at La Galerie in Paris (1982); at the Maison des Arts in Évreux (1984); at the Galerie Ariel in Paris (from 1987); at the Galerie Ariel Rive Gauche in Paris (1991); at the church of la Madeleine and the castle in Châteaudun (1996); *Rétrospective: Peintures, Dessins 1985-1995* (*Retrospective: Paintings, Drawings, 1985-1995*) at the Galerie Vie Privée in Chambéry (1996); and *Défilé* (*Procession*) at the same gallery (1998).

BIBLIOGRAPHY:
Planet, Robert, et al., *Michel Gémignani*, exhibition catalogue, La Galerie, Paris, 1982. Delpierre, Jean-Christophe, *Michel Gémignani*, exhibition catalogue, Gal. Ariel, Paris, 1989. Michaud, Yves, et al., *Michel Gémignani*, exhibition catalogue, Gal. Ariel Rive-gauche, Paris, 1991.

MUSEUMS AND GALLERIES:
PARIS (FNAC): *Fountain* (1979, wooden sculpture) - PARIS (Mus. de la Chasse): seven paintings.

Printed and bound in Italy
by G. Canale & C. S.p.A. - Borgaro T. se (Torino)
February 2006